P9-DSZ-513

BUSINESS

THE ULTIMATE RESOURCE™

BUSINESS

THE ULTIMATE RESOURCE™

PERSEUS
PUBLISHING
A Member of the Perseus Books Group

Cataloging-in-Publication Data is available from the Library of Congress

ISBN 0-7382-0242-8
Perseus Publishing is a member of the Perseus Books Group
Find us on the World Wide Web at http://www.perseuspublishing.com

Perseus Publishing books are available at special discounts for bulk purchases in the U.S. by corporations, institutions, and other organizations. For more information, please contact the Special Markets Department at the Perseus Books Group, 11 Cambridge Center, Cambridge, MA 02142, or call (800) 255-1514 or (617) 252-5298, or e-mail j.mccrary@perseusbooks.com.

Text design by Fiona Pike, Pike Design, Winchester, U.K.
Typeset by RefineCatch Limited, Bungay, Suffolk, U.K.

First printing, August 2002
1 2 3 4 5 6 7 8 9 10–

Advisory Board

Publishing, Editorial, and Production Staff

Perseus Publishing

President and C.E.O., The Perseus Books Group
Jack McKeown

Vice President and Publisher
David Goehring

Vice President, Associate Publisher, and Marketing Director
Elizabeth Carduff

Vice President Sales and Marketing, The Perseus Books Group
Matthew Goldberg

Vice President and Director of Manufacturing
Tari Warwick

Executive Editor and U.S. Project Manager
Nick Philipson

Managing Editor
Christina Coffin

Bloomsbury Publishing

Publisher
Nigel Newton

Publishing Director
Kathy Rooney

Product Director
Jonathan Glasspool

Production Director
Penny Edwards

Database Manager
Edmund Wright

Marketing Manager
Gordon Kerr

Production Editor
Nicky Thompson

Managing Editor
Lisa Carden

Project Manager
Katy McAdam

Editorial Project Coordinator
Helen Szirtes

Design Director
William Webb

Contributors

Vendoline von Bredow • Larry Brotzge • Timothy J. Buckley • David Buchan • Alan Burkitt-Gray • Tim Burt • Gregory L. Busick • William Chislett • Stuart Crainer • Scheherazade Daneshkhu • Martin Daniel • Charles R. Day, Jr. • Des Dearlove • Kevin Done • Gordon Edge • Steve Fitzgerald • Richard Green • Wendy Grossman • Rita Herron Brown • Colin Holland • Ira Kalish • Tammy Keely • Jeremy Kourdi • Diane Cameron Lawrence • David Lawson • Ian Linton • Amy Kathleen Lorson • Laura Lorson • Alan Mackie • Jon Marks • Peter Marsh • Melissa Master • Gerry McGovern • Rich McLaughlin • Dena Michelli • Kenneth Quandt • Ann Milnes Roberts • Judi Neal • Alexander Nicoll • Gillian O'Connor • David Pilling • Simon Pirani • Rod Prince • David Shirref • Jim Smith • Russ Swan • Richard Synge • Harold "Mac" Thornton • Susan Traill • Nancy Vinsel • John Wheaton • Bill White • Mick Whitworth • Mark Wilson • Hilary Wortley

Editors/Proofreaders
Sandra Anderson • Carol Baker • David Barnett • Steve Curtis • Barbara Docherty • Kate Gaylor • Gloria George • Peter Gibbs • Catherine Gough • Sarah Hall • David Hallworth • Stephen Handorff • Kate Hardcastle • Ruth Hillmore • Stan Kurzban • Irene Lakhani • Laura Lawrie • Alan Levy • Adele Linderholm • Mark Miller • Mike Munro • James Randall • Karen Stern • Sarah Waldram • Pamela White • Jill Williams • Sarah Williamson

Table of Contents

Management Checklists

PEOPLE MANAGEMENT

PERSONAL EFFECTIVENESS

HR/TRAINING

MARKETING

MANUFACTURING/OPERATIONS

SMALL BUSINESS

BUSINESS PLANNING

ACTIONLISTS

E-COMMERCE

MARKETING

PERSONAL DEVELOPMENT

BUSINESS THINKERS

MANAGEMENT GIANTS

Contributors

Karl Albrecht is a management consultant, futurist, speaker, and author. He has written more than 25 books on business performance, including the best-selling *Service America!: Doing Business in the New Economy* (with Ron Zemke; McGraw-Hill, 2001) which is widely credited with launching the worldwide service revolution. As Chairman of Karl Albrecht International, he oversees the practical application of his ideas through a consulting group, a seminar firm, and publishing company.

Keith Alexander is Director of the Centre for Facilities Management (CFM) at Salford University, England, and has a Chair in facilities management. He is Associate Head of Academic Enterprise and a member of the school executive. He is a member of the Research Institute for Business and Informatics, and of Salford University's five star-rated Research Centre for Built and Human Environment. Alexander has been at the forefront of developments in education, research, and practice in facilities management for over 20 years.

David Allen, founder and President of the management consulting and training company David Allen & Co., was labeled by *Fast Company* as "one of the world's leading thinkers" in personal productivity. He wrote the bestseller *Getting Things Done: The Art of Stress-free Productivity* (Viking Penguin, 2001), and his e-newsletter, *David Allen's Productivity Principles*, has thousands of subscribers worldwide.

Christopher Bartlett is Thomas D. Casserly, Jr. Professor of Business Administration and Chair of the Program for Global Leadership at Harvard Business School. Before joining the HBS faculty, he was a marketing manager with Alcoa in Australia, a management consultant in McKinsey and Company's London office, and General Manager of Baxter Laboratories' subsidiary company in France. He has published eight books, including (coauthored with Sumantra Ghoshal): *Managing Across Borders: The Transnational Solution* (Harvard Business School Press, 1988; reissue 1998)—named by the *Financial Times* as one of the 50 most influential business books of the century; and *The Individualized Corporation* (HarperBusiness, 1997), winner of the Igor Ansoff Award for the best new work in strategic management and named one of the best business books of the millennium by *Strategy + Business* magazine. He has also authored or coauthored over 50 chapters or articles which have appeared in leading journals such as the *Harvard Business Review*, *Sloan Management Review*, and *The Academy of Management Review*.

Peter Bebb leads the Cedar Business Alignment practice, initiating sustainable success through enterprise performance management. He has worked as a director, consultant, and project manager in various industries and companies across the world, including Sema Group Consulting, Proudfoot Europe, Kleinwort Benson Investment Management, and James Martin Associates.

Meredith Belbin is Consultant to the European Commission, the U.S. Department of Labor and the OECD, and is Senior Associate Professor at Cambridge University. He is a partner in Belbin Associates, a company known principally as the producer of Interplace—a company-based, team-role advice system, used internationally. Belbin has written several successful business books, including the European bestseller *Management Teams* (reissue, Butterworth-Heinemann, 1996) and, most recently, *Managing without Power* (Butterworth-Heinemann, 2001).

Chip R. Bell manages the Dallas, Texas, office of Performance Research Associates, Inc., a firm that provides consulting for large and medium-sized corporations and nonprofit enterprises on service quality, customer loyalty, and creating a customer-driven culture. A renowned keynote speaker, he is the author or coauthor of 14 books, including *Customers As Partners* (Berrett-Koehler, 1994), *Managers As Mentors* (Berret-Koehler, 1998), and *Dance Lessons: Six Steps to Great Partnerships in Business and Life* (with Heather Shea; Berrett-Koehler, 1998).

Warren Bennis is Distinguished Professor of Business Administration at the University of Southern California and a consultant to multinational companies and governments throughout the world. He is the author of over 25 books and dozens of articles on leadership, including the best-selling *On Becoming a Leader* (2nd ed., Perseus, 1994) and *Organizing Genius* (Perseus, 1997).

Peter L. Bernstein is President of Peter L. Bernstein, Inc., established in 1973 as an economic consulting firm to institutional investors. He writes and publishes *Economics and Portfolio Strategy*, a semi-monthly analysis of the capital markets and the real economy. His recent books include *The Power of Gold: The History of an Obsession* (John Wiley, 2001), *Against the Gods: The Remarkable Story of Risk* (John Wiley, 1998), and *Capital Ideas: The Improbable Origins of Modern Wall Street* (reprint, Free Press, 1993).

General Sir Peter de la Billiere was born in 1934 and was educated at Harrow in England. In 1956, after tours with the British army in Korea and Egypt, he joined the Special Air Service (SAS) and went to Oman as part of a force assisting the Sultan against the rebels. He was awarded the Military Cross for his work there, and received another award for a tour of duty in Borneo. In 1972 he became an SAS Commanding Officer. In 1978 he was made an SAS Director and dealt with important military challenges such as Northern Ireland, the Iranian Embassy Siege, and the Falklands War. He was made a CBE in 1983. In 1990, as he was preparing to retire, Iraq invaded Kuwait, precipitating the Gulf War, and he was appointed Commander in Chief of British forces in the Middle East, where he led Operations Desert Shield and Desert Storm. After the war, he was promoted to General, became a military advisor to the government, and received a KBE. He finally retired in 1992. He is the author of *Storm Command* and *Looking for Trouble*, both published by HarperCollins.

Drayton Bird is founder of the Drayton Bird Partnership, a consulting firm specializing in marketing. For seven years he was a partner of Trenear-Harvey, Bird & Watson, a firm which was sold to Ogilvy and Mather in 1984. As Vice Chairman and Creative Director, he helped O & M Direct become the world's largest direct marketing agency network, and was elected to the worldwide Ogilvy Group board. As well as being a consultant, he is a celebrated speaker and regularly contributes articles to international journals. He is the author of the bestseller *Commonsense Direct Marketing* (4th ed., Kogan Page, 2000), *Marketing Insights and Outrages* (Kogan Page, 2000), and *How to Write Sales Letters That Sell* (new ed.; Kogan Page, 2002).

Don Blohowiak is Executive Director of Lead Well, a leadership development firm based in Princeton, New Jersey, which consults worldwide. He is the author of six management books, including *Your People Are Your Product* (Chandler House, 1998) and *The Complete Idiot's Guide to Great Customer Service* (Simon & Schuster, 1997). He is also the founder and editor of *The Productive Leader*, a newsletter published by The Economics Press.

Steve Bone is the Managing Director for Applied Value in the United Kingdom (Applied Value is a global professional services firm with six offices around the world). Prior to joining, he was the practice leader for Arthur D. Little in European technology and innovation management practice. He has been a technology and innovation management consultant for over 15 years, during which time he has specialized in: technology strategy and planning; intellectual property evaluation and exploitation; R&D management; and assisting organizations to be more innovative. He is a well-known speaker on the strategic and operational aspects of technology and innovation management.

Edward de Bono is the originator of "lateral thinking," and "parallel thinking." He qualified as a doctor, going on to study psychology, and from this basis developed his work in the practical aspect of human thinking. His work in the area of perception provided the basis for the DATT program in business and the CoRT program in schools. His many publications include *Six Thinking Hats* (rev. ed., Penguin, 2000), and *New Thinking for the New Millennium* (Penguin, 2000).

George Boulden is currently Chairman and Managing Director of Action Learning Associates International Ltd., which he founded in 1980 with Professor Reg Revans and Alan Lawlor to promote the use of Action Learning in solving business problems. He works with clients such as Motorola, ICL, ACE Insurance, Nacco Materials Handing Group, and TRW Lucas to help them to design and deliver people development programs. His international work takes him to Japan (where he advises a major Japanese consulting organization), the United States, and Central and Eastern Europe. He works with many international agencies including the International Labour Organization, EC-PHARE, UNDP, WHO, and the Know How Fund. George Boulden is a member of the International Foundation for Action Learning and a Fellow of the Institute of Management Consultants. He has written a number of papers and articles on action learning and organizational productivity.

R. Brayton Bowen is author of *Recognizing and Rewarding Employees* (McGraw-Hill, 2000). As well as being a former senior executive with five major corporations, an author, speaker, and columnist, Bowen is President and Senior Consultant of The Howland Group, a management consulting firm based in Louisville, Kentucky, which specializes in organizational strategy, structure, and systematic change initiatives.

William Bridges is a consultant and lecturer based in Mill Valley, California. Past President of the Association for Humanistic Psychology, he was rated by the *Wall Street Journal* as one of the ten most popular executive development consultants in the United States. His numerous books include *Managing Transitions: Making the Most of Change* (Perseus, 1991) and *JobShift: How to Prosper in a Workplace without Jobs* (Perseus, 1994).

Mark Brown is Visiting Professor of Innovation at Henley Management College and Managing Director of Innovation Centre Europe. His life is divided between consulting for a variety of *Fortune* 500 companies, writing management books and articles, and continuing research at Henley about why some individuals and organizations are more creative and innovative than others. His last major publication was *The Dinosaur Strain* (Element, 1988). "Ideas into Action," a video released by Melrose in 1993, has now won 16 international awards. Since then, Melrose has released three more award-winning videos by Brown.

Peter Brown founded The Top Pay Research Group in 1991 to provide an independent source of information on all aspects of main board remuneration. The group now has 127 clients, ranging from FTSE 100 companies to government organizations and charities, and its annual *Independent Chairman and Non-executive Director Survey* has established itself as the primary source of information on independent directors' pay, responsibilities, and attitudes in the United Kingdom. The Top Pay Research Group is a well-respected and actively-managed niche consulting group, creating effective and relevant remuneration structures for both public and private bodies.

Thomas L. Brown, one of *Business*'s Best Practice editors, authored the first online book on leadership: *The Anatomy of Fire*. It is now a required textbook at numerous universities and has received five-star reviews. He has also written more than 400 articles for management journals such as *Across the Board* and the *Wall Street Journal*; been the keynote speaker at major meetings, including the International Association of Management; presented his ideas to many corporations; and lectured at several universities. He recently helped to establish BrownHerron LLC, a company providing information worldwide about leading-edge management and leadership thinking via electronic documents (e-docs) that are universally and quickly available.

Matthew Budman has worked in journalism for 15 years, the last several as managing editor of a Manhattan-based bimonthly business magazine, The Conference Board's *Across the Board*. The Conference Board is a global, independent membership organization that conducts research, convenes conferences, makes forecasts, assesses trends, publishes information and analysis, and brings executives together to learn from one another.

Peter Bunce is a program director at the CAM-I European office in the United Kingdom. He is currently managing the Beyond Budgeting Round Table—a major international research project—and coordinating a European program on manufacturing systems. His experience also encompasses computer-aided process planning, factory management and sculptured surfaces.

Robert Buttrick is widely known for his refreshing and practical insight into business-led project management. His bestselling book, *The Project Workout* (Prentice Hall/Financial Times, 2000), is widely adopted by major corporations and business schools alike, both in the United Kingdom and around the world. He is also a key speaker at conferences as well as in-company events. Buttrick has lived and worked in countries as diverse as the United States, Yemen, Sudan, Senegal, Mauritius, Bahrain, and Japan.

Sir Adrian Cadbury joined the Cadbury business in 1952, becoming Chairman of Cadbury Limited in 1965, and retiring as Chairman of Cadbury Schweppes in 1989. He is a European expert on corporate governance, and was Chairman of the U.K. Committee on Corporate Governance from

1991 to June 1995 and member of the OECD Corporate Governance Business Advisory Group. He has also served as Director of the Bank of England, Director of IBM (U.K.), Chancellor of Aston University, and was a member of the Panel of Conciliators for the International Center for Settlement of Investment Disputes.

After a 20-year career in financial and public services, **Terry Carroll** "reinvented" himself as a motivational speaker and performance coach. Working at the leading edge of personal growth technologies, he integrates NLP, emotional intelligence, accelerated learning, and other proven techniques into the "best of the best" for personal and group change. An established author, his books range from personal growth to finance, risk, and the psychology of markets.

Susan Cartwright is senior lecturer in organizational psychology at the Manchester School of Management, UMIST, England. Her research interests and publications are in the area of occupational stress and organizational culture and change, particularly in the context of mergers, acquisitions, and joint ventures. She has worked extensively with public and private organizations on a variety of projects related to stress management and human merger integration. Cartwright is currently coeditor of the *Leadership and Organization Development Journal* and book review editor for *Stress Medicine*. She is coauthor of *Managing Workplace Stress* (with Cary L. Cooper; Sage, 1997).

John Case is a veteran observer and analyst of the business world and an internationally-known expert on the subject of open-book management. He is the author of five books, including *The Open Book Experience: Lessons from over 100 Companies Who Successfully Transformed Themselves* (Perseus, 1999), collaborator on three others, and has written for a wide variety of periodicals. At present he is contributing editor for *Inc.* magazine, writing a monthly column on growth markets.

James Champy is Chairman and Head of Strategy of Perot Systems consulting practice, providing strategic direction to the company's team of business and management consultants. He is an authority on management issues surrounding organizational change and corporate renewal. He wrote the bestsellers *Reengineering the Corporation* (with Michael Hammer; HarperBusiness, 2001) and *Reengineering Management* (HarperBusiness, 1996). His newest book is *The Arc of Ambition* (with Nitin Nohria; Perseus, 2001). He moderates programs for the PBS Business Channel and has also been a guest on Wall Street Week. Champy provides regular columns for magazines such as *Forbes* and *Computer World*.

Debashis Chatterjee is a Professor of Business at the Indian Institute of Management in Lucknow. He is the author of the internationally acclaimed book, *Leading Consciously* (Butterworth-Heinemann, 1998). A Fulbright Scholar and Harvard Business School's thought leader, Chatterjee has taken his revolutionary leadership insights into four continents of the world. He has been a trainer in several *Fortune* 100 Companies and has taught at the Center for Public Leadership at Harvard University.

Cary Cherniss is Professor of Applied Psychology at Rutgers University. He specializes in the areas of emotional intelligence, work stress, management training and development, planned organizational change, and career development. He has published over 50 scholarly articles and book chapters on these topics, as well as six books, including *Promoting Emotional Intelligence in the Workplace* (with Mitchel Adler; American Society for Training and Development, 2000) and *Beyond Burnout*, (Routledge, 1995). In addition to his research and writing, Cherniss has consulted with many organizations in both the public and private sectors.

Subir Chowdhury is Executive Vice-President at the international consulting firm ASI (American Supplier Institute). As well as being a renowned consultant in the field of quality management and leadership. Chowdhury has written several books on these subjects, some of them award-winning. His most recent books include *The Power of Six Sigma* (Financial Times/ Prentice Hall/Dearborn Trade, 2001) and *The Talent Era* (Financial Times/Prentice Hall, 2001).

Stewart Clegg received the George R. Terry Book Award of the American Academy of Management (1998) for outstanding contributions to management. He directs the Organizational Researchers on Collaboration and Alliances (ORCA) at the University of Technology, Sydney.

Peter S. Cohan is President of Peter S. Cohan & Associates, a management consulting and venture capital firm. He is also a frequent speaker and TV commentator on high technology, and author of four books, including *Net Profit: How to Invest and Compete in the Real World of Internet Business* (rev. ed., Jossey-Bass, 2001) and *e-Stocks: Finding the Hidden Blue Chips Among the Internet Impostors* (HarperBusiness, 2001).

Jim Collins started his research and teaching career at the Stanford Graduate School of Business, where he received the Distinguished Teaching Award multiple times. Since 1995 he has operated a management laboratory in Boulder, Colorado, where he conducts multi-year research and works with senior executives. He is the coauthor of *Built to Last* (HarperBusiness, 1994) and author of *Good to Great* (HarperBusiness, 2002).

Cary L. Cooper is currently BUPA Professor of Organizational Psychology and Health in the Manchester School of Management, and Deputy Vice Chancellor of the University of Manchester Institute of Science and Technology, England. He is a European guru on stress management, regularly contributing to national newspapers, academic journals, TV, and radio. He has authored, coauthored, and edited over 80 titles related to occupational stress, women at work, and industrial and organizational psychology, including *Organizational Stress* (with Philip J. Dewe and Michael P. O. Driscoll; Sage, 2001) and *The Blackwell Encyclopedic Dictionary of Management* (with Chris Argyris; Blackwell, 1997).

Robert G. Cooper is President of the Product Development Institute, Inc.; Professor of Marketing at the Michael G. DeGroote School of Business, McMaster University, Ontario, Canada; and on the faculty of the Institute for the Study of Business Administration. Creator of the widely employed Stage-Gate™ product development process, he was made a Fellow of the Product Development and Management Association in 1999 and is the author of several books on product development, including *Product Leadership* (Perseus, 1998) and the bestselling *Winning at New Products* (3rd ed., Perseus, 2001).

Anne Covey is the owner of Covey & Associates, P.C., and Adjunct Professor at Monmouth University. She practices exclusively in Labor and Employment Law, providing representation of clients in all aspects of the employment relationship from prehiring considerations through to post-termination concerns. She is the author of *The Workplace Law Advisor* (Perseus, 2000), and her articles have been published in several magazines. She is also regularly interviewed by newspapers, television, and radio stations regarding employment laws and developments. As a frequent lecturer at business seminars, she continues to educate clients on the laws and regulations affecting the workplace and employee relations.

Michael J. Cunningham is President and C.E.O. of the Harvard Computing Group, an international strategy and technology consulting firm geared to creating innovative strategies and to developing powerful Web-enabled solutions. He speaks and consults to clients and industry groups internationally and regularly writes articles on Web business and e-commerce for publications such as *E-Business Advisor*. Cunningham has authored three books on the topic of e-commerce: *Partners.com: How to Profit from the New DNA of Business* (Perseus, 2001), *B2B: How to Build a Profitable e-Commerce Strategy* (Perseus, 2000), and *Smart Things to Know About e-Commerce* (John Wiley, 2001).

Thomas H. Davenport is Director of the Accenture Institute for Strategic Change, a research center in Cambridge, Massachusetts, and also distinguished scholar in residence at Babson College. He is a widely-published author and acclaimed speaker on the topics of information and knowledge management, reengineering, enterprise systems, and the use of information technology in business. His books include *Mission Critical: Realizing the Promise of Enterprise Systems* (Harvard Business School Press, 2000), and he is coauthor of *The Attention Economy* (with John Beck; Harvard Business School Press, 2001) and *Working Knowledge* (with Laurence Prusak; Harvard Business School Press, 2000).

Stan Davis is an independent author, speaker, and consultant, best known for linking fundamentals of science and technology to likely futures in business and management. Along with Christopher Meyer, he is coauthor of two books, *Blur: The Speed of Change in the Connected Economy* (Perseus, 1998) and *Future Wealth* (Harvard Business School Press, 2000), and many articles.

Charles R. Day, Jr. is the former Editor-in-Chief of *IndustryWeek*. A journalist and writer, his career spans more than 32 years including some 25 years covering and commenting on business and management. He has spoken to many audiences, and appeared on radio and television. He now heads his own firm on Ponte Vedra Beach, Florida, and is researching and writing two books, one on business management and another on the history of the Super Bowl and the professional football merger in the United States. He is also an adjunct professor at the University of North Florida.

Dinna Louise C. Dayao is the author *of Asian Business Wisdom: Lessons from the Region's Best and Brightest Business Leaders* and its revised edition, *Asian Business Wisdom: From Deals to Dot.Coms*, published by John Wiley & Sons Asia Pte. Ltd. in 2000 and 2001, respectively. Both books feature insightful and informative articles from visionary Asian C.E.O.s. As a freelance writer and editor, she has contributed articles on management, executive lifestyle, and telecommunications to publications such as *Chief Executive China* and *World-room.com*. She is based in Makati City, the Philippines.

Donryn Dewar is currently the Manager of the Outsourcing and Support Centre Business for Plaut U.K. and Ireland, managing clients systems both from a technical, application support, and development perspective. Her focus is on ongoing client partnerships and managing these relationships.

Alan Downs is a management psychologist and consultant who specializes in strategic human resources planning and helping business executives reach their maximum potential. He has authored several books, including AMACOM's *Corporate Executions* (1995), the much-acclaimed exposé on downsizing, *The Seven Miracles of Management* (Prentice Hall, 1998), and *The Fearless Executive* (AMACOM, 2000). Downs is widely sought for interviews by newspaper, TV, and radio broadcasts. He has also written on management topics for numerous national newspapers and trade publications, including *Management Review* and *Across the Board*.

Scott J. Edgett is an internationally recognized expert in the field of new product development and portfolio management. He is C.E.O. and cofounder of the Product Development Institute and an Associate Professor of Marketing at the Michael G. DeGroote School of Business, McMaster University, Ontario, Canada. He is also on the Board of Directors for the Product Development Management Association and Vice-President of Publications. He is coauthor of *Portfolio Management for New Products* (Perseus, 2000) and *Product Development for the Service Sector* (Perseus, 1999).

Leif Edvinsson is a leading expert on Intellectual Capital (IC). As former Vice-President and the world's first Corporate Director of Intellectual Capital at Skandia of Stockholm, Sweden, he has been a key contributor to the theory of IC and oversaw the creation of the world's first corporate Intellectual Capital Annual Report. Formerly, Edvinsson was senior Vice-President for training and development of S-E Bank, and President and Chairman of Consultus AB, a Stockholm-based consulting company. As a result of his work in these areas, he has been a special advisor to the Swedish Ministry of Foreign Affairs, the Swedish Cabinet, and the United Nations International Trade Center. As well as an international speaker, he is author of *Intellectual Capital* (with Michael S. Malone; HarperBusiness, 1997) and numerous articles on the service industry and on IC.

John Elkington is founder and Chairman of SustainAbility, one of Europe's leading think-tank and consulting firms focusing on business strategies for sustainable development. He has written or coauthored over 30 books and published reports, including best-sellers *The Green Consumer Guide* (Gollancz, 1988) and *Cannibals With Forks* (Capstone, 1997), which introduces the triple bottom line. His most recent book, *The Chrysalis Economy* (Capstone, 2001), explores the challenge of integrating societal values and corporate value creation.

Melanie Ellis is a senior project manager for Plaut U.K. and Ireland, where her primary focus is on delivery on projects and leading the development of Plaut's Fast Track Templated implementation methodology.

Marc J. Epstein is presently Distinguished Research Professor of Management at Jones Graduate School of Management at Rice University in Houston, Texas. He has completed extensive academic research and has great practical experience in the implementation of corporate strategies and the development of performance metrics for use in these implementations. He is author of a dozen books and over 100 professional papers. He also provides seminars, executive courses, and lectures to senior managerial audiences throughout the world.

Liam Fahey is Adjunct Professor of Strategic Management at Babson College, Massachusetts, and Visiting Professor of Strategic Management at the Cranfield School of Management in the United Kingdom. His research, teaching, and consulting center on competitive strategy, macroenvironmental and competitor analysis, with special emphasis on linking strategy, scenarios, and knowledge. He is the author or editor of eight books and over 40 articles or book chapters. His most recent books, published by John Wiley, include *Learning from the Future* (1998), *Competitors: Outwitting, Outmaneuvering and Outperforming* (1999), and *The Portable MBA in Strategy* (2nd ed., 2001).

Martha I. Finney is the author of *Find Your Calling, Love Your Life* (with Deborah Dasch; Simon & Schuster, 1998) and producer of "Working from the HeartLand," a Web site exploring joy in the U.S. workplace. A veteran human resources reporter, she is internationally recognized as a leading authority in self-actualization through work.

After a languages degree at Oxford, **John G. Fisher** started his business career in direct marketing and the insurance industry before establishing one of the United Kingdom's leading performance improvement and incentive agencies. In 1998 he sold the business to the management team to concentrate on consulting. He now specializes in employee incentives, staff communication, and conference/event planning. He is a regular seminar speaker and has written four business books on the subjects of incentives, conferences, benchmarking, and e-commerce, including most recently *E-business for the Small Business* (Kogan Page/Sunday Times, 2001).

Patrick Forsyth runs Touchstone Training & Consultancy, an independent firm based in the United Kingdom specializing in marketing, sales, and communications skills. He conducts courses for individual clients, public seminars for a number of management institutes, and has worked in a variety of industries in many parts of the world. He writes extensively on matters of marketing and management in articles for management journals and is the author of a number of successful books, including *Communicating with Your Staff* (Texere, Orion Toolkit Series, 1999).

Robin Fraser, formerly a management consulting partner at PriceWaterhouseCoopers, led the development of PriceWaterhouseCoopers' Priority Base Budgeting and ABM practices and CAM-I's Advanced Budgeting study. He has 30 years experience in business planning, performance improvement and cost reduction. He is a regular presenter of the "Beyond Budgeting" Mastercourse run by the U.K.'s Chartered Institute of Management Accountants (CIMA).

Business strategy and marketing consultant, **John Frazer-Robinson** pioneered the movement towards Customer Relationship Management and is acknowledged internationally as an authority on marketing, sales, advertising, and customer service. He is the author of several books, including most recently *It's All About Customers!* (Kogan Page & Institute of Directors, 2000), and he has worked all over the world as a speaker, trainer, and lecturer. In 1995, he was elected as one of the first honorary Fellows of the British Institute of Direct Marketing.

Mike Freedman is partner and Executive Vice-President of Kepner Tregoe Inc., a global consulting firm. He is responsible for the Worldwide Strategy Practice. Previously, he ran practices in Europe, North America, and Japan. He joined Kepner Tregoe in 1982, after ten years as a senior line manager in Xerox. He also spent three years from 1994–97 as Personal Advisor to Tom (now Lord) Sawyer, who was General Secretary of the Labour Party at the time. He has stood for Parliament himself, and held various community roles.

Robert Fritz is the author of *The Path of Least Resistance* (rev. ed., Fawcett, 1989), *Creating* (reprint, Fawcett, 1993), and *The Path of Least Resistance for Managers* (Berrett-Koehler, 1999). He codesigned (with Peter Senge and Charles Kiefer) the original "Leadership and Mastery" course on which *The Fifth Discipline* is partly based. His firm, RobertFritzInc. provides leading edge consulting, training, and products which are based on the creative process and Structural Dynamics.

Sumantra Ghoshal is Robert P. Bauman Professor of Strategic Leadership at the London Business School and is the founding dean of the Indian School of Business. Previously he taught at INSEAD, France, and at MIT's Sloan School of Management. With Christopher Bartlett he has coauthored a number of highly influential books, including *Managing Across Borders* (Harvard Business School Press, reissue, 1998), *Transnational Management* (McGraw-Hill, 1990), *Organization Theory and the Multinational Corporation* (Palgrave, 1993), and *The Individualized Corporation* (HarperBusiness, 1997). He has also authored or coauthored more than 60 academic articles, including a series in the *Harvard Business Review* on "The Changing Role of Top Management" that looked at how leaders can unleash the human spirit.

Jerry W. Gilley is Professor in Human Resource Development at Colorado State University, and was a principal at William M. Mercer, Inc. He has authored and coauthored 13 books and over 60 articles, book chapters, and monographs. His books include *Principles of HRD* (2nd ed., Perseus, 2002) and *Organizational Learning, Performance, and Change: An Introduction to Strategic HRD* (Perseus, 2000), which he coauthored with Ann Maycunich Gilley and which won the Academy of Human Resource Development Book of the Year Award for 2000.

Jules Goddard is an independent teacher, writer, and consultant in the areas of creativity, strategic innovation, and business transformation. He currently holds the position of Visiting Fellow at London Business School and Guest Lecturer at INSEAD, but previous appointments include Gresham Professor of Commerce and Mercers School Memorial Professor at the City University and Visiting Professor of Marketing at the Ecole Nationale des Ponts et Chaussées in Paris. Goddard has published various articles on corporate strategy in leading European strategy and consulting magazines, including "The Architecture of Core Competence" (*Business Strategy Review*, 1997, Spring 8:1, pp. 43–52).

Beverly Goldberg is a management consultant and Vice-President of The Century Foundation, an 80-year-old nonprofit think tank in New York City that examines America's economic, political and social policies. Before coming to the foundation some 20 years ago, Goldberg had worked in publishing and administration. She also is the cofounder and principal of Siberg Associates, a management consulting firm. She has authored four books, which include *Age Works: What Corporate America Must Do to Survive the Graying of the Workforce* (The Free Press, 2000), and *Overcoming High-tech Anxiety* (Jossey-Bass, 1999).

Daniel Goleman is the author or coauthor of several bestsellers, including *Emotional Intelligence* (Bantam, 1997) and *Primal Lead-*

ership (Harvard Business School Press, 2002). A psychologist, he worked for many years for the *New York Times* covering the brain and behavioral sciences. He has also been a visiting faculty member at Harvard University and serves as Co-Chair of the Consortium for Research on Emotional Intelligence in the Graduate School of Professional and Applied Psychology at Rutgers University. He is a founder of the Collaborative for Social and Emotional Learning at the University of Illinois at Chicago. He speaks on emotional intelligence and leadership worldwide.

Edward E. Gordon is a consultant, writer, speaker, academician, and President of Imperial Consulting, a firm specializing in human capital development. He has taught at three Chicago-based universities, appeared on television and radio, and is the author or coauthor of 10 books, including bestsellers such as *Skill Wars: Winning the Battle for Productivity and Profit* (Butterworth/Heinemann, 2000) and *FutureWork: The Revolution Reshaping American Business* (Praeger, 1994).

Michael Griggs is an IT professional of some 36 years standing. For the last 12 years he has provided consulting services to senior business management on IT Strategy. He joined Sopra Group (previously CS Rand) in 1993, and currently manages the data services practice. Operational achievements include direction of major projects in financial services, utilities, and retail. He is a champion for the reconciliation of business information needs and IT objectives, delivery, and value.

Jim "Gus" Gustafson is Vice-President and General Manager of ELECTRICjob.com, one of the three internet recruitment sites belonging to MECHdata, Inc. He has operational and marketing responsibility for the overall performance of the electrical business unit. He was formerly with Square D/ Schneider Electric and was recently named Leader of Organizational Learning, Development, and Customer Education. He has also held various positions in Engineering, Sales, and Marketing at Honeywell, Inc. Gustafson is currently writing his doctoral dissertation entitled "Socially Responsible Leadership: Organizing to Positively Change the World."

Cliff Hakim is the author of *We Are All Self-employed* (Berrett-Koehler, 1994) and the President of Rethinking Work®, a Boston, Massachusetts-based consulting firm focused in the areas of Executive Development and Career consulting.

Katherine Hammer is the cofounder, President, C.E.O., and Chairman of the board of Evolutionary Technologies International (ETI), a recognized leader in the field of enterprise data integration management software. She joined the Microelectronics and Computer Technology Corporation (MCC) in the mid-80s, where her research led to the development of technology that automates the exchange of data between incompatible systems. In 1991 she cofounded ETI, and began marketing this new technology, becoming a pioneer in technology commercialization. She is the author of *Workplace Warrior* (AMACOM, 2000) and a regular columnist for *Fast Company*.

Michael Hammer is the originator of both the concept of "reengineering" and of "the process enterprise." Through his teaching and research, he works with the management teams of leading companies to bring about fundamental change in their organizations. He is the coauthor of *Reengineering the Corporation* (HarperBusiness, 1993; reissue 2001) and author of *Beyond Reengineering* (HarperBusiness, 1996) and *The Agenda* (Crown, 2001).

Richard S. Handscombe is an international business consultant and author, who has worked in some 30 countries and 40 industries. His publications include: *The Product Management Handbook* (McGraw-Hill, 1988) and *Strategic Leadership–Managing the Missing Links* (McGraw-Hill, 1993).

After working as an executive at Shell International, **Charles Handy** became a professor at the then fledgling London Business School. Today he is an independent writer and broadcaster, and describes himself as a social philosopher. Handy's enduring concern is the implications for society, and for individuals, of the dramatic changes which technology and economics are bringing to the workplace and their wider lives. His most influential books are: *The Age of Unreason* (Harvard Business School Press, 1989); *Gods of Management* (reprint, Oxford University Press, 1996); *The Age of Paradox* (Harvard Business School Press, 1994); and *The Hungry Spirit* (reprint, Broadway Books, 1999). His latest book, *The Elephant and the Flea*, was published in 2001 by Harvard Business School Press. Handy now limits his speaking appearances, and with his wife Elizabeth has come to exemplify the new world of work he so successfully and humanely commentates on. At a personal level, he appears to have the answers. Whether these can be translated into answers for others remains the question and the challenge.

Sir John Harvey-Jones joined ICI as a work-study officer in 1956, after serving in the navy for 19 years. He rose to be Chairman in 1982, and was largely responsible for reshaping the company, doubling the price of ICI shares and turning a loss into a one billion pound profit after only 30 months in the job. Since his knighthood in 1985, he has written several books, including the bestsellers *Making It Happen* (HarperCollins, new ed., 1994) and *Getting It Together* (Ulverscroft, 1992). He also took part in the making of a TV series entitled *Troubleshooter* where he was invited to visit and advise businesses.

Oren Harari is a consultant, speaker, author, and Professor of Management at the University of San Francisco. For nine years he was a monthly columnist for *Management Review* (American Management Association), and is now a senior weekly columnist for *MWorld*, the AMA's online management information portal. His books include *Leapfrogging the Competition* (2nd ed., Prima Publishing, 1999), *Beep! Beep! Competing in the Age of the Roadrunner* (with Chip R. Bell; Warner, 2000), and *The Leadership Secrets of Colin Powell* (McGraw-Hill, 2002).

Robert Heller was the founding editor of *Management Today* and editorially responsible for the launch of highly successful business magazines such as *Campaign*, *Computing*, *Accountancy Age*, and *Marketing*. The many books he has written since the best-selling *The Naked Manager* (Sidgwick & Jackson, 1971) have confirmed his position as the United Kingdom's best-known author on business management. His latest books include the highly popular Dorling Kindersley series, *Essential Managers* and *Business Masterminds*. Heller speaks frequently to management audiences on many subjects. He has worked all over the world with many of its leading companies.

Antoine Hermens leads research on strategic alliances and joint ventures at the University of Technology, Sydney, Australia.

Christopher Hoenig is founder, Chairman, and C.E.O. of Exolve, Inc., a company providing strategic knowledge about problem-solving concepts, techniques, and tools. He is an experienced entrepreneur, corporate consultant, and government executive. As

Director of Information Technology issues at the General Accounting Office—the investigative arm of Congress—Hoenig designed and implemented a historic reform of technology and information management for the U.S. government, saving several billion dollars to date. He is frequently in the national media and speaks regularly to audiences of corporate and government executives on information and technology management and how they apply to vital public and private sector issues. He recently authored *The Problem Solving Journey* (Perseus, 2000).

Jeremy Hope, a chartered accountant, spent 10 years in business management before becoming an independent consultant. As well as lecturing and speaking regularly at international conferences, he has written many articles and three books. His "Beyond Budgeting" article (coauthored with Robin Fraser) won the prestigious IFAC award for the best international accounting article of 1998. Since 1998, he has also been Research Director for the Beyond Budgeting Round Table—a major international research project involving many global companies that are seeking solutions to their planning and budgeting problems. His most recent book is *Beyond Budgeting* (Harvard Business School Press, 2002).

Maria-Therese Hoppe is a member of the international think tank "The Global Future Forum." Here teams of prominent international futurists cooperate in order to offer challenging and constructive perspectives of the future to businesses and organizations worldwide. She is much in demand as an international keynote speaker, as well as frequently commentating on television and radio, and being interviewed by newspapers and magazines. In the magazine *Børsens Nyhedsmagasin* she writes her own column. She also regularly contributes articles to the futurist magazine, *Fremtidsorientering*. Hoppe was part of the team developing the concepts behind the international bestseller *The Dream Society* by Rolf Jensen (McGraw-Hill, 1999).

Masaaki Imai is one of the most widely acknowledged theorists on incremental change. As well as a lecturer and consultant, he is founder and Chairman of the international Kaizen Institute, an organization that helps Western companies introduce kaizen concepts, systems, and tools. As one of the leaders of the quality movement and a champion of the kaizen philosophy, he has authored several best-selling books on the subject, including *Kaizen: The Key to Japan's Competitive Success* (McGraw-Hill, 1986) and *Gemba Kaizen: A Common-sense, Low-cost Approach to Management* (McGraw-Hill, 1997).

Bill Jensen is an information architect with more than 20 years experience in communication and change consulting. He is C.E.O. of The Jensen Group, a consulting group whose mission is to "help clients succeed simply by changing how they organize and deliver what they know." He has pioneered the design of organizational Mapping, Message Mapping and their work-tools for implementation strategies such as Behavioral Communications and Change Navigation. As well as speaking and teaching in well known organizations, he regularly contributes articles to magazines and journals and has authored two books: *Simplicity* (Perseus, 2001) and *Work 2.0* (Perseus, 2002).

Daniel T. Jones is one of the world's leading experts on supply chain management and coauthor of the bestseller *The Machine That Changed the World* (reprint, HarperCollins, 1991). His main interest has been understanding the differences in industrial performance and the transfer of a set of ideas, called lean thinking, from the auto industry in Japan, to a wide range of industries across the globe. He has led a series of pioneering benchmarking and action research programs, articulating and carrying lean thinking through to pilot implementation. Appointed Professor of Manufacturing Management at Cardiff University Business School, Wales, in 1989, he established the Lean Enterprise Research Centre in 1994. He is currently a member of the STI Automotive Innovation and Growth Team and the grocery industry's Efficient Consumer Response (ECR) European Academic Advisory Panel, and Editor of the *ECR* journal.

Sharon Jordan-Evans is founder and President of the Jordan-Evans Group, a leading organizational development and executive coaching business. With Beverly Kaye, she coauthored the bestseller, *Love 'Em or Lose 'Em: Getting Good People to Stay* (Berrett-Koehler, 1999).

Robert S. Kaplan is the Marvin Bower Professor of Leadership Development at Harvard Business School. His research, teaching, and consulting focus on linking cost and performance measurement systems to strategy implementation and operational excellence. Together with David Norton, he developed the Balanced Scorecard, an aid to achieving strategy by showing how key measures interrelate to track progress towards strategy, and both Kaplan and Norton serve as Directors with the Balanced Scorecard Collaborative—a global network to support organizations implementing the Balanced Scorecard. Their most recent books include *The Strategy Focused Organization* (Harvard Business School Press, 2001) and *The Balanced Scorecard* (Harvard Business School Press, 1996).

Michael de Kare-Silver is a Member of PA's Management Group, and previously Director of E-commerce for Great Universal Stores plc (GUS). He began his consulting career at McKinsey, where he worked for several years on a variety of international assignments, mostly concerning financial services and consumer goods. He subsequently set up his own consulting operation (Kalchas), which became a significant player in the strategy and e-commerce consulting field. When the firm was acquired by Computer Sciences Corporation, he became Vice-President and a member of the CSC European Management Committee, with special emphasis on the growing e-commerce activities in Europe and North America. He has also written widely, most notably with *E-shock*, a leading book on e-commerce development. Most recently his work in e-commerce has been recognized with an appointment as Visiting Professor in the Technology Department of Middlesex University Business School in London.

Beverly Kaye is President and founder of Career Systems International, Inc., a publisher of career development tools. She also works as a consultant, lecturer, and writer, authoring the classic *Up Is Not The Only Way* (Davies Black, 1997). She earned a doctorate at UCLA and did graduate work in organization development at the Sloan School of Management at MIT. With Sharon Jordan-Evans, she coauthored the bestseller, *Love 'Em or Lose 'Em: Getting Good People to Stay* (Berrett-Koehler, 1999).

Lucy Kellaway is Management Editor of the *Financial Times*, and author of *Sense and Nonsense in the Office* (Financial Times/ Prentice Hall, 1999). She joined the *Financial Times* in 1985, and for the last five years has written a column about business and management, and interviewed a wide variety of chief executives for her Business Lunch series. She has also written for the Lex Column, been oil correspondent, Brussels correspondent, and edited the management page.

Allan A. Kennedy is a Boston-based management consultant and writer. He is coauthor with Terrence Deal of *Corporate Cultures* (Perseus, 1982; reissue, 2000) and *The New Corporate Cultures* (Perseus, 1999). He is also the author of *The End of Shareholder Value* (Perseus, 2000) and numerous articles. He is currently working on a new book about the unusual but effective management practices of creative companies.

Debbe Kennedy is President of the Leadership Solutions Companies, a consulting firm which provides custom leadership communications and development products and services. Prior to this, she spent over 15 years in management at IBM, and has served as a strategic business partner in Hewlett-Packard's worldwide diversity initiative since 1995. She is a problem solver, change leader, speaker, group facilitator, and author of several books, including the bestseller *Breakthrough!* (Leadership Solutions, 1998). Her latest contribution is the *Diversity Breakthrough!® Strategic Action Series* seven books and tools published by Berrett-Koehler in 2000.

Maggie Kennedy is a senior consultant in Sopra Group's Oxford data practice. In an IT and financial systems career spanning some 20 years, she has designed and implemented systems for large enterprises and government agencies. Her technical and business skills are key to many major clients' data migration and integration projects, ranging from data architecture through system prototyping and testing to live running.

Peter Killing is Professor of Strategy at the International Institute for Management Development. His areas of particular interest are strategy creation and execution, the management of change, and the design and management of acquisitions and alliances. Much of the work he has done on strategy and change is captured in *Strategic Analysis and Action*, a textbook coauthored with Nick Fry (4th ed., Prentice Hall, 2000). In the alliance area, Killing has written and edited four books and several articles, including one in the *Harvard Business Review*. Through teaching and consulting, Killing has directly impacted the alliance activities of many companies. At IMD he was the founding Director of the Senior Executive Forum and is the Director of the Leading Corporate Renewal program. Prior to joining IMD in 1995, Killing taught at the Ivey School of Business in Canada for 20 years, and was Associate Dean of Executive Education at the time he came to IMD.

Karin Klenke is a Research Professor at the Center for Leadership Studies at Regent University, Virginia, Senior Principal of the Leadership Development Institute (LDI) International, and Chairperson of the Board of Directors of Association of Management/International Association of Management. She has published widely in management and leadership journals, founded and edited several journals including *Journal of Management Systems*, and is author of the award-winning book *Women in Leadership: A Contextual Perspective* (Springer, 1996).

Leslie L. Kossoff is C.E.O. of Menton Productions LLC, a worldwide film and television production company. She is the author of *Executive Thinking* (Davies-Black, 1999) and *Managing for Quality* (Kossoff Management Consulting, 3rd ed., 1998), has served as an associate of W. Edwards Deming, and is a leading speaker at business and educational conferences around the world.

Philip Kotler is S. C. Johnson and Son Distinguished Professor of International Marketing at the J. L. Kellogg Graduate School of Management, Northwestern University. His extensive canon runs to more than 25 books, and includes the classic marketing textbook *Marketing Management: Analysis, Planning, Implementation, and Control* (11th ed., Prentice Hall, 1999), *Kotler on Marketing* (Free Press, 1999), and most recently *Marketing Moves* (Harvard Business School Press, 2002). He has also published more than 100 articles in leading journals such as the *Harvard Business Review* and the *Journal of Marketing and Management Science*.

Thomas M. Koulopoulos is President and founder of Delphi Group, global business and technology advisors, based in Boston, Massachusetts. He lectures at the Boston College Graduate School of Management, frequently contributes to industry publications and nationally broadcast technology reports, and is also the author of six books, including *The X-economy* (Texere, 2001).

Jim Kouzes is the author of numerous books on leadership. He is also the Chairman Emeritus of the Tom Peters Company as well as an executive fellow in the Center for Innovation and Entrepreneurship at the Leavy School of Business, Santa Clara University. He is coauthor of several books, including *The Leadership Challenge* (with Barry Posner; Jossey-Bass, 1995).

Andrew Lambert is cofounder and Director of the Careers Research Forum. This brings together some 50 major employers to fund research and discussion processes concerning the many challenging employment issues that organizations currently face, such as career management, development of talent and leaders, and the psychological contract. He also owns and runs the United Kingdom-based Lambert Consultancy, a firm that specializes in helping companies and their management teams to manage change, chiefly by integrating their business strategy with the way they manage people and relationships. He writes and lectures on various topics, including organizational change, internal communications, organizational identity and branding, and HR strategy.

Formerly a Partner at McKinsey & Company, **Max Landsberg** is now a business author and executive coach. His guide to coaching, *The Tao of Coaching* (HarperCollins, 1996), has become a classic–selling in excess of 100,000 copies and with translations into 12 languages. His other books are *The Tao of Motivation* (HarperCollins, 1999) and *The Tools of Leadership* (HarperCollins, 2000).

Jean-Claude Larréché holds the Alfred H. Heineken Chair at INSEAD and is recognized as one of the most expert authorities in the field of Strategic Marketing. He is a board member of Reckitt Benckiser plc, and Chairman of StratX SA, a company specializing in strategic marketing, consulting, and training. He is also founder and Director of the INSEAD Executive Program "Strategic Management Services." His publications have appeared in numerous international journals and he has authored and coauthored several books, including *Marketing Management* (1997) and *Marketing Strategy* (3rd ed., 1999), both with Harper Boyd and Orville Walker, and published by McGraw-Hill.

Rick Lash is the Hay Group's Leader for Management Development Practices in Canada. He brings over 15 years of experience in the design of competency-based interventions and technologies to change human behavior and accelerate and maximize the learning process and performance of individuals and organizations. He is a frequent keynote speaker at national and international conferences on topics related to organizational effectiveness.

Robert Leaf—consultant, international speaker, and writer of numerous articles—established Robert S. Leaf Consultants in 1997. He specializes in advising corporations and government bodies on establishing a worldwide public relations strategy and how to make the most effective use of their agencies and internal communications departments. For 40 years, Leaf worked for Burson Marsteller, during which he became one of the industry's most knowledgeable counselors on international public relations, winning the Institute of Public Relation's first Alan Campbell-Johnson award for outstanding contributions in this field, in 2000.

Richard J. Leider is founding partner of The Inventure Group, a firm which designs workshops, tools, and processes for organizations in the areas of life planning, leadership, team building, and career coaching. He is also an internationally respected author, speaker, and career coach. He has written five books, including *Whistle While You Work* (with David Shapiro; Berrett-Koehler, 2001) and *The Power of Purpose* (Berrett-Koehler, 1997). He is also a contributing columnist to *Fast Company*'s Web site.

Andrew Leigh's career has spanned marketing, writing business features for the *Observer*, and serving as a senior manager in the public services. He works with a wide range of companies on clarifying and achieving their development needs, and developed the ACE teams computer system for creating team profiles. His books include *The Ultimate Business Presentation Book* (Random House, 1999).

Peter Leyden is knowledge developer at Global Business Network, a futurist think tank and strategic consulting firm specializing in scenario planning. He works with the firm's network of scientists, technologists, and future-oriented thinkers in many different fields. Along with Peter Schwartz and Joel Hyatt, he is coauthor of *The Long Boom* (Perseus, 2000), now published in eight languages.

Bernard Lietaer has had 25 years of professional experience in money systems, from an unusually wide variety of perspectives. For 14 of those years he was a professional management consultant working with multinational corporations, banks, and governments on four continents. While at the Belgian Central Bank, he was one of the codesigners and implementers of the ECU, the convergence mechanism that has now led to the single European currency. He also served as President of the Belgian electronic payment system. He was Professor of International Finance at the University of Louvain, and general manager and currency trader for the Gaia Hedge Funds. He is the author of nine books, written in four languages. The most recent of these are *The Future of Money* (London: Random House, 2001) and *The Mystery of Money* (Munich: Riemann Verlag, 2000).

Christopher Locke is the editor/publisher of the webzine *Entropy Gradient Reversals*, and President of Entropy Web Consulting in Boulder, Colorado. In 2001, he was included in the *Financial Times*' list of top 50 business thinkers worldwide. As well as writing extensively for business journals, he has published several books, including *The Cluetrain Manifesto* (with David Weinberger, Rick Levine, and Doc Searles; Perseus, 2000), *Gonzo Marketing: Winning through Worst Practices* (Perseus, 2001), and *The Bombast Transcripts* (Perseus, 2002).

David H. Maister is a leading authority on the management of professional service firms. For two decades he has advised firms in a broad spectrum of professions all over the world, covering all strategic and managerial issues. He spent six years teaching courses in managing service businesses and production operations at Harvard Business School, during which he published seven books on academic business topics. He has authored and coauthored several books since then, including more recently *The Trusted Advisor* (Free Press, 2000) and *Practice What You Preach* (Free Press, 2001).

Dorothy Marcic is the author of *Managing with the Wisdom of Love: Uncovering Virtue in People and Organizations* (Jossey-Bass, 1997) and *RESPECT: Women and Popular Music* (Texere, 2002). She is an adjunct professor at the Owen Graduate School of Management at Vanderbilt University, a keynote speaker, and performing artist who uses music to create deeper insights and sustained learning. Her audio work includes the production of four CDs in the *A Woman's Voice* series.

John L. Mariotti is a consultant, writer, and speaker, and is President and C.E.O. of The Enterprise Group. He is a former corporate president and serves on the boards of four companies. His three latest books are in the Capstone *Smart Things to Know About* series, on *Brands & Branding* (1999), *Marketing* (2000), and *Partnerships* (2001). He has two forthcoming titles, *Making Partnerships Work* (Capstone/Wiley, 2002) and *Marketing Express* (Capstone/Wiley, 2002).

Steve Markwell is Managing Director of Prime Marketing Publications (PMP), a company which specializes in the consulting and IT marketplace. The PMP Group provides a range of services for those responsible for purchasing, advising on, or marketing IT, and publishes established reports and newsletters.

Ryan Mathews has leveraged his 18 years of experience in retailing to become a top authority on emerging retail channels, electronic commerce, and the future of wholesaling, retailing, and foodservice. He has also pioneered studies in consumerism, including ethnic marketing and non-linear virtual supply chain modeling. He is the coauthor, with Fred Crawford, of *The Myth of Excellence* (Crown, 2001) and, with Watts Wacker, of *The Deviant's Advantage* (Crown, 2002).

Ann Maycunich Gilley is Vice-President of Trilogy Consulting Group, a performance consulting firm, and an adjunct faculty member at Colorado State University where she teaches courses in consulting, communications, and strategic management. Together with Jerry Gilley, she has coauthored five books published by Perseus, including *The Performance Challenge* (2002) and *Beyond the Learning Organization* (1999).

Michael Maynard has led business and management courses across the United Kingdom and in Europe, specializing in creativity, teams, self-expression, and communication skills. He worked as a professional actor and presenter for nearly 20 years. He is regularly invited to speak or run sessions at conferences all over the world, on Teams, Leadership, Creativity and Innovation, Unlocking Potential, Communication, and Sales Motivation. His career has spanned marketing, being a feature writer on the business section of the *Observer*, and a senior manager in the public services. He works regularly with a wide range of companies on clarifying their development needs and identifying the most cost-effective ways of achieving change.

Andrew Mayo is a consultant, speaker, writer, and facilitator in international human resources management, having worked for nearly 30 years in major international organizations. He is the author of four books and numerous articles. He currently runs his own consulting company, MLI (Mayo Learning International Ltd), specializing in organizational strategies for growing human capital. He is also a Fellow and Program Director for in-company programs for the Centre for Management Development at the London Business School and Associate Professor of Human Capital Management at Middlesex Business School.

Malcolm McDonald is Professor of Marketing and Deputy Director at Cranfield School of Management, with special responsibility for e-business. He has extensive industrial experience, including a number of years as Marketing Director of Canada Dry. He is Chairman of six companies and has written or cowritten 30 books, including the best-selling title, *Marketing Plans: How to Prepare Them, How to Use Them* (4th rev. ed., Butterworth-Heinemann, 1999), and many of his papers have been published.

Gerry McGovern is an internationally acclaimed author, journalist, speaker, and consultant on e-business issues. Most recently he has published *Content Critical* (Financial Times/Prentice Hall, 2001) and *The Web Content Style Guide* (Financial Times/Prentice Hall, 2001). He is a regular contributor to *Information World Review* and *Clickz.com*. His main area of expertise is Web content management.

Ronan McIvor is a senior lecturer within the School of International Business at the University of Ulster. He has carried out extensive research in the area of supply chain management and information systems. He is currently researching in the areas of outsourcing and the application of electronic commerce at the buyer–supplier interface.

Regis McKenna is Chairman of The McKenna Group, an international consulting firm specializing in the application of information and telecommunications technologies to business strategies. For the past 30 years, his firm has been advising clients on emerging information technology and telecommunications technologies and markets. He has written and lectured extensively on the social and market effects of technological change. He has also appeared on several television shows, and written four books, including *Relationship Marketing* (reprint, Perseus, 1993) and *Real Time: Preparing for the Age of the Never Satisfied Customer* (Harvard Business School Press, 1997).

Christopher Meyer is an economist and consultant, and a founding Director of Bios, a firm applying complex systems techniques to business. He is also the Director of the Cap Gemini Ernst & Young Center for Business Innovation in Cambridge, Massachusetts. Together with Stan Davis, he is the coauthor of *Blur: The Speed of Change in the Connected Economy* (Perseus, 1998), *Future Wealth* (Harvard Business School Press, 2000), and many articles.

Henry Mintzberg is the John Cleghorn Professor of Management Studies at McGill University in Montreal, and a visiting professor at INSEAD in France. He is the author or coauthor of eight books including *The Nature of Managerial Work* (Prentice Hall, 1973), *Mintzberg on Management* (Free Press, 1989), *The Rise and Fall of Strategic Planning* (Free Press), which won the best book award of the Academy of Management in 1995, and *Strategy Safari* (Simon & Schuster, 1998). Dr. Mintzberg has also contributed to many of the major journals in his field, including the *Harvard Business Review* (for which he has won McKinsey Prizes), the *California Management Review*, the *Sloan Management Review*, and the *Academy of Management Review*. His most recent book, *Why I Hate Flying* (Texere, 2001), takes a sardonic look at management in the airline industry. Next in line is *Developing Managers, Not MBAs*—a book exploring management education, one of Mintzberg's longest held bugbears.

Ian I. Mitroff is the Harold Quinton Distinguished Professor of Business Policy and Founder of the USC Center for Crisis Management which he directed for 10 years at the Graduate School of Business, University of Southern California. He is also the President of Comprehensive Crisis Management, a private consulting firm, and he is generally recognized as one of the founders of the field of crisis management. He has published over 250 articles and 21 books, the most recent being *Managing Crises Before They Happen* (AMACOM, 2001).

Geoffrey A. Moore is a Managing Director with The Chasm Group, a consulting practice based in California that provides market development and business strategy services to many leading high-technology companies. He is also a Venture Partner with Mohr Davidow Ventures, a California-based venture capital firm specializing in specific technology markets, including e-commerce, Internet, enterprise software, networking, and semiconductors. He is a frequent speaker and lecturer at industry conferences and his books are required reading at leading business schools. These books include *Crossing the Chasm* (rev. ed., HarperBusiness, 1999), *The Gorilla Game* (rev. ed., HarperBusiness, 1999), and *Living on the Fault Line* (HarperBusiness, 2002).

Michael S. Morris, a Partner with the New Jersey-based Covey & Associates, P.C., represents organizations in all aspects of the employment relationship—from pre-employment through employment separation—and defends against employment-related actions. Morris is also the author of several law review articles and is a frequent lecturer and trainer.

David J. Morrison is a senior partner of Mercer Management Consulting, a global strategy consulting firm that focuses on the development of strategies for growth in changing markets. With Adrian J. Slywotzky, he is coauthor of several agenda-setting business books, including *How Digital Is Your Business?* (Crown, 2000) and *The Profit Zone* (Times Business/Random House, 1998).

Geoff Mott, C.E.O. of The McKenna Group, joined the firm as Managing Partner in 1998, bringing 20 years experience in management consulting and technology. In addition to leading client engagements, he has expanded the firm's international reach through several strategic partnerships, and has led a strategic initiative to develop the firm's base of emerging technology clients. He has also guided the firm in developing a major market presence in the broadband and Internet communications sectors, as well as the financial services industry. In the last two years, he has spoken at conferences on various topics, including data networking and business strategies on the Internet.

Ken Murrell is Professor of Management at the University of West Florida, President of Empowerment Leadership Systems, and in the process of developing new doctoral programs on the subject of organizational change at Pepperdine University. He has worked around the world helping global organizations improve their effectiveness, and published extensively on the nature of empowerment and the future of work organizations.

Judith A. Neal is the Executive Director of the Association for Spirit at Work, which offers networking, publications, research, courses, and consulting to individuals and organizations seeking a greater integration of spirituality and work. Prior to this, she spent several years as Manager of Organizational Development at Honeywell, after which she ran her own consulting firm, Neal and Associates, and became Management Professor at The University of New Haven. Judi is working on her book *The Four Gateways to Spirit at Work.*

Sue Newell is currently Professor of Management in the School of Management, Royal Holloway, University of London. She is a Chartered Psychologist and has previously worked at Warwick, Aston, and Nottingham Business Schools. Her research interests are varied, covering innovation, human resource management, and business ethics. She has published many journal articles on these topics, as well as a book entitled *Creating the Healthy Organization* (2nd ed, International Thomson Business, 2001).

John Nirenberg is on the faculty of the Management Centre Europe, and has served as Global Best Practice Leader for Strategic Leadership for the American Management Association. He was formerly Dean of Doctoral Studies at the University of Phoenix, and has taught at universities in the United States, Malaysia, Singapore, and Australia. His books include *Power Tools: A Leader's Guide to the Latest Management Thinking* (Prentice Hall, 1997) and *Global Leadership* (Wiley/Capstone, 2002).

David P. Norton is President, C.E.O., and cofounder of Renaissance Solutions, Inc., a management consulting and systems integration firm. Prior to Renaissance, Norton cofounded and spent 17 years as President of Nolan, Norton & Company, which was acquired by Peat Marwick. Together with Robert Kaplan, he developed the Balanced Scorecard, an aid to achieving strategy by showing how key measures inter-relate to track progress towards strategy, and both Kaplan and Norton serve as Directors with the Balanced Scorecard Collaborative—a global network to support organizations implementing the Balanced Scorecard. Their most recent books include *The Strategy Focused Organization* (Harvard Business School Press, 2001) and *The Balanced Scorecard* (Harvard Business School Press, 1996).

Wally Olins is one of the world's most experienced experts on corporate identity and branding. His main interests are the big ideas behind organizations, mergers, and acquisitions, and he has a particular fascination with the branding of regions and nations. His publications include *The New Guide to Identity* (Gower, 1995) and *Trading Identities* (Foreign Policy Centre, 1999).

Hugh Parker is former Managing Partner of McKinsey; he worked with them from 1951 to 1986. For the last 15 of those years he specialized in corporate governance, i.e., effective boardroom management. Parker wrote what was probably the first book on that subject, *Letters to a New Chairman*, published originally (1970) by the Institute of Directors in London. He is generally credited in the United Kingdom with having pioneered that field.

Perry Pascarella, former Vice-President (Editorial) of Penton Publishing Inc. and Editor-in-Chief of *IndustryWeek* magazine, is an award-winning journalist and the author of numerous books on management and leadership, including *Leveraging People and Profit* (with Bernard Nagle; Butterworth-Heinemann, 1997) and *Christ-centered Leadership* (Prima, 1999). He was the recipient of the 1992 American Business Press J. D. Crain award for a distinguished career in journalism.

Louis Patler is President of The B.I.T. Group, an international consulting company, and Near Bridge LLC, a strategic research, trend analysis, and corporate training company. He is the author of numerous articles and three books, *If It Ain't Broke . . . BREAK IT!: Unconventional Wisdom for a Changing Business World* (cowritten with Robert Kriegel; Warner Books, 1991), *TILT!: Irreverent Lessons for Leading Innovation in the New Economy* (Capstone, 2000), and *Rebel without a Pause: The Ironic Truths and Working Contradictions of Lasting Business Excellence* (Prentice Hall, 2002).

Tom Petzinger is the author of three major business books, including his latest, *The New Pioneers* (Simon & Schuster, 1999). His works have been cited by the *New York Times* as "notable books," and he is the winner of the Gerald Loeb Award For Business and Financial Reporting.

Jeffrey Pfeffer is the Thomas D. Dee II Professor of Organizational Behavior in the Graduate School of Business at Stanford University, and author of numerous books, including *The Human Equation: Building Profits by Putting People First* (Harvard Business School Press, 1998) and *The Knowing–Doing Gap* (with Robert I. Sutton; Harvard Business School Press, 2000).

Gifford Pinchot is widely considered the father of the intrapreneuring movement and is the author of *Intrapreneuring: Why You Don't Have to Leave the Corporation to Become an Entrepreneur* (Harper & Row, 1985) and *The Intelligent Organization* (with Elizabeth Pinchot; Berrett-Koehler, 1994). Pinchot & Company, the firm he leads, helps companies to reduce bureaucratic obstacles, and to design and implement more effective and sustainable business practices. He is a worldwide speaker and consultant.

B. Joseph Pine II cofounded Strategic Horizons LLP to explore the frontiers of business and to help executives see the world differently. Prior to that he worked at IBM for 13 years, and is now also a visiting professor at the University of Amsterdam. He is the author of *Mass Customization* (reissue, Harvard Business School Press, 1999) and coauthor, with James Gilmore, of *The Experience Economy* (Harvard Business School Press, 1999).

Salvador Porras leads research on business networks at University of Technology, Sydney, Australia.

Colin Price is a partner of McKinsey & Company, Management Consultants and the coauthor of several books including the bestseller *Straight from the C.E.O.* (Simon & Schuster, 1998) and *Wisdom of the C.E.O.* (John Wiley, 2000). He was formerly global head of the Strategic Change consulting practice at PriceWaterhouseCoopers. He is a regular speaker at international conferences.

Jeffrey F. Rayport is C.E.O. of Marketspace, a consulting and information company that helps executives craft strategies for the networked economy. Before founding Marketspace, a Monitor Group company, Rayport was a professor at Harvard Business School, where he created the first business school course in e-commerce at a top-tier business school. He has also written and cowritten a number of books on e-commerce, including *An Introduction to E-commerce* and *Cases in E-commerce* (both with Bernard Jaworski; McGraw-Hill Higher Education, 2001).

Kathleen Kelley Reardon, Professor of Management and Organization in the University of Southern California Marshall School of Business, has served on the faculty of the MBA, Executive MBA, and International MBA Programs. She is a leading authority on persuasion, politics in the workplace, negotiation, and interpersonal communication. She is the author of five books and numerous articles published in communication and business journals, including the 1994–95 *Harvard Business Review* reprint "Bestseller" case "The Memo Every Woman Keeps in Her Desk" and the book following from that, *They Don't Get It, Do They? Communication in the Workplace—Closing the Gap Between Women and Men*. Her new book for Doubleday, *The Secret Handshake: Mastering the Politics of the Business Inner Circle*, released in early 2001, rapidly became a business bestseller in the United States. The book focuses on strategies for working effectively within organizational political climates.

John Reh is an Internet management consultant, counseling clients on effective use of the Internet. His extensive management experience spans a variety of function areas, including project management, engineering, MIS/IS/IT, product development, marketing, and human resources. He has published more than 100 "best practice" articles.

Dick Richards, Senior Consultant for Ribbongrass Consulting, guides people, teams, and organizations in pursuit of their aspirations. He develops leaders, helps teams find common purpose, and helps organizations improve service, implement strategy, and win the hearts and minds of their people. He is the author of *Artful Work: Awakening Joy, Meaning and Commitment in the Workplace* (Berkley, 1997), which won a Benjamin Franklin Award for Best Business Book, and *Setting Your Genius Free: How to Discover Your Spirit and Calling* (Berkley, 1998).

Jonas Ridderstråle is Assistant Professor at the Centre for Advanced Studies in Leadership at the Stockholm School of Economics. He is the author of *Global Innovation: Managing International Innovation Projects at ABB and Electrolux* (IIB, Stockholm, 1996) and *Funky Business: Talent Makes Capital Dance* (Bookhouse Publishing, 1999). The latter, cowritten with Kjell Nordström, is an international bestseller that has been translated into more than 25 languages.

Al Ries and **Laura Ries** are a father and daughter team. Al is Chairman and Laura is President of Ries & Ries, a marketing strategy firm located in Roswell, Georgia, which they founded in 1994, and which now has affiliates around the world. Their latest books are *The 22 Immutable Laws of Branding* (HarperCollins, 1998) and *The 11 Immutable Laws of Internet Branding* (HarperCollins, 2000).

Gill Ringland graduated as a physicist, spending two years at the University of California at Berkeley and a year as a Fellow at Oxford, before moving into the area of computing. After working for an expanding software house, where she became Chief Technical Consultant, she moved on to work for the Computing Science Committee of the United Kingdom and the Engineering Research Council. In her current post as Group Executive she is responsible for strategy at ICL. She authored *Scenario Planning* (John Wiley, 1997).

Alan M. Rugman is currently L. Leslie Waters Chair of International Business at the Kelley School of Business, Indiana University, where he is also Professor of International Business and Professor of Business Economics and Public Policy. He has served as an advisor and consultant to governmental agencies in Canada and international organizations worldwide. He has also published over 200 articles dealing with the economic, managerial, and strategic aspects of multinational enterprises and with trade investment policy. His 30 books include *The End Of Globalization* (AMACOM, 2001).

Philip Sadler is Vice-President and former Chief Executive of Ashridge Management College, where for many years he led the team that built the College's international reputation as one of the world's leading Business Schools. He now heads Philip Sadler Associates, a U.K.-based consulting firm with core competences in leadership development, organization design, and strategic human resource management. Sadler has also authored several books, including *Designing Organisations* (Kogan Page, 1994), and most recently, *Building Tomorrow's Company* (Kogan Page, 2002).

David R. Sadtler is a Fellow of the Ashridge Strategic Management Centre, and is a teacher and consultant on questions of strategy at both the corporate and business unit levels. He is the author of a number of articles on the issues and challenges of corporate level strategy. He was the cofounder and Executive Vice-President of Medi-Computer Corporation, and served as the first President of Vickers America, Inc. He is a coauthor of *Breakup! When Large Companies Are Worth More Dead Than Alive* (Capstone, 1997) and *Successful Business Acquisition* (Delta Sierra, 2000).

James E. Schrager is a Clinical Professor of Entrepreneurship and Strategy at the University of Chicago, founding editor of *The Journal of Private Equity*, and President of Great Lakes Consulting Group in South Bend, Indiana. He is a board member or advisor to several technology companies and has won numerous teaching awards at Chicago and Notre Dame.

Peter Schwartz is a cofounder and Chairman of Global Business Network, a futurist think tank and strategic consulting firm specializing in scenario planning. He is the coauthor, along with Joel Hyatt and Peter Leyden, of *The Long Boom* (Perseus, 2000) and author of the international bestseller *The Art of the Long View* (Currency/Doubleday, 1996).

John Seely Brown is Chief Scientist for the Xerox Corporation and a renowned author and speaker. His numerous works include the article "Research That Reinvents the Corporation," and the books *Seeing Differently: Insights on Innovation* (Harvard Business School Press, 1997) and *The Social Life of Information* (Harvard Business School Press, 2000).

Jane Galloway Seiling is a consultant, writer, and speaker, and focuses on the concept of achieving a more open and inclusive workplace community. She is the author of *The Membership Organization: Achieving Top Performance through the New Workplace Community* (Davies-Black, 1997) and *The Meaning and Role of Organizational Advocacy: Responsibility and Accountability in the Workplace* (Quorum, 2001).

Patty Seybold is C.E.O. of the Boston-based consulting firm the Patricia Seybold Group, a worldwide strategic (e-)business and technology consulting/research firm, which she founded in 1978. A regular speaker at senior-level executive summits, international conferences, and industry events, she has over 20 years consulting experience in the computer industry, and is known for her insights into designing customer-facing business processes. Seybold has written two books. *Customers.com*

(Times Books, 1998), written with colleague Ronnie Marshak, examined how leading companies design and implement e-business strategies to build customer relationships. In her follow-up book, *The Customer Revolution: How to Thrive When Your Customers Are in Control* (Crown Business, 2001), Seybold argues that successful companies in the future will be those that use customer lifetime value as a strategic management tool, rather than a marketing discipline.

Adrian J. Slywotzky is a senior partner of Mercer Management Consulting, a global strategy consulting firm that focuses on the development of strategies for growth in changing markets. With David J. Morrison, he is coauthor of several agenda-setting business books, including *How Digital Is Your Business?* (Crown, 2000), and *The Profit Zone* (Times Business/Random House, 1998).

John Smythe is founder and Chair of Smythe Dorward Lambert, a leading consulting firm that specializes in employee communication. The company, which is based in London and Boston, is currently concentrating on "putting people at the center of organizational change and renewal," using communication and behavioral techniques. He has led many major communication and change programs. He also lectures internationally and coauthored *Corporate Reputation* (Century, 1992).

Paul Spenley is founder and MD of The Leading Change Partnership, based in the United Kingdom. He is a chartered engineer and an expert in the practical application of best practice benchmarking methods to help organizations achieve and sustain competitive advantage. He has an accomplished career in line management, particularly as a system manager for the ICL operation team that won the prestigious EFQM Quality Award, and he has experienced many years implementing change. He has also authored three business books, including *Riding the Revolution* (with Robert Heller; HarperCollins, 2001), and *Step Change Total Quality* (Kluwer, 1995).

David Stauffer heads Stauffer Bury Inc., a business writing firm that compiles management information and produces business publications for corporate clients. He is the author of several books including *D2D—Dinosaur to Dynamo* (Capstone, 2001), and *Big Shot: Business the Cisco Way* (Capstone, 2001), and numerous articles published in journals such as the *Harvard Management Update* and *The Wall Street Journal*. He also teaches business writing as an adjunct professor at Rocky Mountain College.

Erik Stern is Senior Vice-President and Managing Director of Stern Stewart Europe, a global consulting firm that specializes in helping client companies in the measurement and creation of shareholder wealth through the application of tools based on modern financial theory. He pioneered the development of the EVA® (Economic Value Added) framework and has implemented EVA® programs for companies in several industries in the United States and Europe. He has written articles for a range of publications, including the *Financial Times*, and has appeared frequently on TV, including Sky Business News and Bloomberg.

Thomas A. Stewart is Editorial Director of *Business 2.0* magazine and a member of the board of editors of *Fortune* magazine. He is a Fellow of the World Economic Forum and has received a number of awards and accolades, including being named one of the world's 50 most influential management thinkers by *FT Dynamo*, the online community of the *Financial Times*. He is the author of the best-selling *Intellectual Capital: The New Wealth of Organizations* (Currency/Doubleday, 1997) and the recently published *The Wealth of Knowledge: Intellectual Capital and the Twenty-first Century Organization* (Currency/Doubleday, 2002).

Paul Stobart, a qualified chartered accountant, spent seven years with a London-based merchant bank before moving to Interbrand, an international branding and marketing services consulting firm. During eight years at Interbrand he worked in a number of positions, most recently as Chairman of European Operations. In 1996, he joined Sage, becoming Chief Operating Officer three years later. At Sage, he oversees the continuing development of the Sage brand as a powerful marketing tool. He is the editor of *Brand Power* (New York University Press, 1994), a book examining the branding strategies of leading international brand owners.

Paul Stoltz is President and C.E.O. of PEAK Learning, Inc., an international performance consulting firm that has evolved into the international hub for AQ-related training, consulting, applications, and research. As one of the world's leading experts in human and organizational performance, he is in high demand as a presenter, consultant, and trainer. He and the PEAK team are the authors, lead researchers, and architects of the groundbreaking Adversity Quotient theory, measurement tools, books, and methods. He authored the bestsellers *Adversity Quotient: Turning Obstacles into Opportunities* (John Wiley, 1999) and *Adversity Quotient @ Work* (William Morrow, 2000).

Florence M. Stone has worked with the American Management Association (AMA) for 30 years in numerous management positions, and was most recently promoted to Editorial Director with responsibility for Web, e-newsletters, and print. She has authored nine business books. As Florence Stone, she has written on numerous supervisory and management issues, from coaching and team building, to communications and leadership, and her more recent books include *Coaching, Counseling & Mentoring* (AMACOM, 1998). She has also been published under the pseudonym Rebecca Saunders.

Merlin Stone is the IBM Professor of Relationship Marketing at Bristol Business School and an Executive Consultant with IBM's Business Innovation Services, Financial Services Sector. He is also a director of several companies, including QCi Ltd, an Ogilvy One company specializing in customer management consulting, assessment, and supplies. He is the author of many articles and 20 books, including *Up Close and Personal—CRM @ Work* (with Neil Woodcock and Peter Gamble; Kogan Page, 1999) and, most recently, *Successful Customer Relationship Marketing* (Kogan Page, 2001).

Robert I. Sutton is Professor of Management Science and Engineering at Stanford University and author of *Weird Ideas That Work: 11 and 1/2 Practices For Promoting, Managing, and Sustaining Innovation* (Free Press, 2001). Together with Jeffrey Pfeffer, he wrote *The Knowing–Doing Gap* (Harvard Business School Press, 2000).

Don Tapscott is an internationally sought authority, consultant, and speaker on business strategy and organizational transformation. He is President of New Paradigm Learning Corporation, which he founded in 1992, and Chairman of Maptuit, an application service provider offering location-based and eLogistics services using both wireline and wireless protocols via the Internet. He also cofounded Digital 4Sight, a company that researches and designs new business models for Global 2000 organizations. Tapscott has authored or coauthored seven widely-read books on the application of technology in business. His newest bestseller, coauthored with David Ticoll and Alex Lowy, is *Digital* Capital (Harvard Business School Press, 2000).

Noel M. Tichy is Professor of Organizational Behavior and Human Resource Management at the University of Michigan Business School, where he is the Director of the Global Leadership Program. His numerous books include *The Leadership Engine* (HarperBusiness, 1997) and *Every Business Is a Growth Business* (John Wiley, 1999).

Daniel R. Tobin, based in Framingham, Massachusetts, is a consultant on corporate learning strategies. His work focuses on helping companies best utilize their most important strategic assets: their people, and the knowledge and skills of those people. Tobin is also an adjunct professor in the graduate management program at Emmanuel College in Boston, teaching courses in leadership, effective teamwork, and organizational transformation. He has authored several books, including *All Learning Is Self-directed* (American Society for Training & Development, 2000).

Robert M. Tomasko is a former Arthur D. Little consultant on organization and strategy, who now advises major corporations around the world on the challenges of continued growth. A frequent contributor to business and general news magazines, his articles have appeared in publications such as *Newsweek* and *The Wall Street Journal*. He has also written several books, including *Go for Growth* (John Wiley, 1996) and *Rethinking the Corporation* (AMACOM, 1993), and he has spoken about the ideas in these books to business audiences on six continents.

Fons Trompenaars is founder and Managing Director of THT Consulting, which has offices in Amsterdam, the Netherlands, and Cambridge, Massachusetts. His best-selling books include *Riding the Waves of Culture: Understanding Cultural Diversity in Business* (McGraw-Hill, 1997). He is coauthor of *Building Cross-cultural Competence* (Yale University Press, 2000) and *21 Leaders for the 21st Century* (McGraw-Hill, 2001) with Charles Hampden-Turner. From 1994–2001 he served as a Visiting Professor in Marketing at the City University Business School.

Jim Underwood is Professor of Management at Dallas Baptist University, and a management consultant with The Dallas Strategy Group, Inc. He has won numerous awards for his work in the field of management and complexity-based strategy, receiving the International Competia Award 2001, for his book *Thriving in E-Chaos* (Prima, 2001). He regularly writes articles for business journals and features for radio and television broadcasts in conjunction with his work and publications.

Chris Voss is Deputy Dean of Programmes and Director of the Centre for Operations Management at London Business School. Before moving into academia, he worked for seven years in industry in quality and operations management in both manufacturing and service companies and spent five years consulting. He has taught and researched in a wide range of fields in the areas of operations, service, and technology management. He was coauthor of the first U.K. textbook on service management, and led the U.K. service study which resulted in the "Service in Britain" report. His most recent book, coauthored with Per Lindberg and Kate Blackmon, is *International Manufacturing Strategies* (Kluwer, 1997).

Watts Wacker has written essays for works as diverse as *Architectural Record* and *Scientific American*. He also writes a column for *Entrepreneur Magazine*. With Jim Taylor, he is coauthor of *The 500-Year Delta* (HarperBusiness, 1997), which has been translated into 10 languages. He is also coauthor of *The Deviant's Advantage* (Crown, 2002) with Ryan Mathews.

David Weinberger is coauthor of the best-selling book *The Cluetrain Manifesto* (with Christopher Locke, Rick Levine, and Doc Searls; Perseus, 2000) and author of *Small Pieces Loosely Joined* (Perseus, 2002). He is a frequent commentator on National Public Radio's *All Things Considered* and is a columnist for *Darwin Magazine*, *KMWorld*, and *internet.com*, and writes a highly-regarded e-zine (www.hyperorg.com) about how the Web is changing the way businesses run. He is also the one-person strategic marketing company, Evident Marketing, helping high-tech companies decide what their products can be and how they can talk about them.

John Wells is currently Senior Partner with Netdecisions, a global strategy and technology company. He is responsible for strategy, knowledge management, innovation, and learning. Netdecisions works with major global companies to identify and help them adjust to the strategic impact of technology and to help structure them to be more agile in response to accelerating change. His career started at Unilever in London, where he trained as a Cost and Management Accountant. During his management career, he has worked within numerous companies, including the Boston Consulting Group, PepsiCo, and the Thomson Travel Group. He also cofounded The Monitor Company (with Michael Porter and Mark Fuller), a strategy consulting practice, and Datapaq, a digital data acquisition company serving the automotive and packaging industries that continues to be a leader in its field.

Margaret J. Wheatley earned her liberal arts undergraduate degrees at the University of Rochester (New York) and University College London. After spending time as a Peace Corps volunteer in Korea and working as an educator and administrator for many years, she earned her doctorate from Harvard and worked for two different consulting firms in Cambridge, Massachusetts. Her books include *Leadership and the New Science: A Simpler Way* (coauthored with Myron Kellner-Rogers), and most recently *Turning to One Another: Simple Conversations to Restore Hope to the Future*. Today, she is President of The Berkana Institute (Provo, Utah); she also consults and speaks widely.

Richard C. Whiteley is a successful entrepreneur, writer, and professional speaker. He is the Principal of The Whiteley Group and formerly cofounder of The Forum Corporation. He has written three best-selling, award-winning books: *The Customer Driven Company* (Perseus, 1991), *Customer Centered Growth* (Perseus, 1996), and *Love the Work You're With* (Henry Holt, 2001). A new book, *The Corporate Shaman*, was published in 2002 by HarperCollins.

Priscilla S. Wisner is a Professor of Global Business at Thunderbird, The American Graduate School of International Management, in Arizona. Her research interests are focused on the implementation of corporate strategy to improve social, environmental, and economic performance. She teaches graduate business and executive education classes in managerial accounting, decision analysis, and profit planning and control.

Leslie A. Yerkes is author of *Fun Works: Creating Places Where People Love to Work* (Berrett-Koehler, 2001) and coauthor of *301 Ways to Have Fun at Work* (Berrett-Koehler, 1997). An organizational development/

change management consultant with 20 years of experience, she is the President of Catalyst Consulting Group Inc. based in Cleveland, Ohio. She also writes frequently for the *Plain Dealer* and other publications, travels internationally as a lecturer and keynote speaker, and has taught at John Carroll University, Baldwin-Wallace, and Kent State.

Ron Zemke is President of Performance Research Associates, Inc., a consulting firm specializing in service quality audits, and service management programs. He founded PRA in 1972 to conduct organizational effectiveness and productivity improvement studies for business and industry. He is the author or coauthor of 28 books, including most recently, *E-Service* (AMACOM, 2000) and *Generations at Work* (AMACOM, 1999). In addition to his consulting work, he is a well-known speaker and award-winning business writer. As Senior Editor of Minneapolis-based *Training* magazine and contributing editor for the U.K.-based *Customer Service Management* magazine, he has covered the emergence of the nation's growing service sector as well as other major issues in business and management.

Physicist and philosopher **Danah Zohar** is the author of *The Quantum Self* (reprint, Quill, 1991), *Rewiring the Corporate Brain* (Berrett-Koehler, 1997), and *SQ: Spiritual Intelligence* (Bloomsbury, 2001). She is a Visiting Fellow at the Cranfield School of Management in the United Kingdom.

INTRODUCTION by Daniel Goleman

What special talents allow some people to build a flourishing business from nothing, while others—though given every advantage of background and preparation at the best business schools—run a business into the ground? What abilities allow one person to take a mediocre company and transform it into an industry leader, while others turn great companies into mediocre ones? And what collective qualities let one company flourish year after year while competitors flounder?

The answer must lie not just in luck, breeding or education. Rather there seems to be a certain knack—a preternatural intelligence—at play, one that makes some people naturally talented at the complex demands of business, just as others are naturals at music, math, or soccer. This same ability displays itself at the group level in superlative teams, and at the organizational level in great companies.

This observation leads to the question: could there be a business intelligence—a set of abilities that distinguish those truly outstanding in the world of commerce? Could *business intelligence* be the mark of outstanding individual performers, as well as the building block of the best-performing companies?

I raise the possibility in part to inspire debate and research, as business itself has come into its own as a field of inquiry, theory, and practice. Within the last few decades sophisticated theory and sound quantitative methods have been brought to bear on the study of business. In my own work, I've drawn on this new science to understand the role of emotional intelligence in work performance and leadership. But as I ponder the field of business studies, I wonder whether there might be a case for business intelligence as well.

The question of whether there might be a business intelligence is not far-fetched. Serious thinkers like Howard Gardner at Harvard University look at intelligence not in the traditional, early 20th-century mold of a narrow set of intellectual abilities revolving mainly around verbal agility and alacrity at math. Instead, they think of intelligence as specific to various life domains.

Gardner transformed the way we think about intelligence by challenging its definition in terms of the restricted range of abilities that allow some to excel in the academic world or do well in IQ tests. Instead, he argues convincingly, there are *multiple* intelligences that go far beyond that narrow band, including in the world of movement—as in the football star or gifted dancer—and in the universe of music, as embodied in the genius of a Mozart or Yo Yo Ma.

This expands the term "intelligence" to encompass a range of consequential capacities usually thought of as far beyond its scope. Gardner has even proposed an "intelligence" for understanding the world of nature, as in the great naturalists like John Audobon or Linnaeus—and has speculated on the pros and cons of a spiritual intelligence.

Why not, then, a business intelligence? "Intelligence" in its most basic sense refers to the capacity to solve problems, meet challenges, or create valued products. In this regard, business intelligence describes the essential capacity for success in the marketplace: being able to handle the challenges and crises of the day adeptly, to apply the expertise that offers solutions as needed, and to do all that in ways that add value.

Among the criteria for any candidate, intelligence is an evolutionary plausibility for its role in human survival, a role arrived at via a reverse engineering in which selection pressures in evolution are inferred from the current operation of a faculty. Here, for instance, the case can be made that the modern-day talents for business had antecedents in primitive forms of barter and craftsmanship, primal leadership and negotiation, teamwork and cooperation.

Those who excelled in these proto-business abilities in prehistory would very likely be better able to provide for their progeny, the true mark of evolutionary fitness. Here there is another intriguing bit of data: the evolutionary psychologist David Buss at the University of Michigan has found that in cultures worldwide one of the prime qualities that make a man attractive to women as a potential mate are signs that he can be a good provider. And desirability as a mate makes one that much more likely to pass on one's genes to future generations—the biological meaning of "survival of the fittest."

One mark of any intelligence lies in having a developmental history, a series of landmarks of learning and mastery over the course of life. No intelligence emerges full bloom, but rather is nurtured and developed over the years. When it comes to business, those who emerge as outstanding typically showed signs of a flair for their later talent as far back as their teen years or even childhood. As the biographies of business greats tell us, as they grew they were particularly able learners, refining and honing these natural talents.

The emergence of the human capacity for math speaks to a different criterion for an intelligence: a relevant symbol system. Any intelligence requires a *lingua franca*, a set of symbols that capture the meaningful information needed to operate in that domain—such as musical notation. Historically such symbol systems arose because of a pressing human need. The historical record suggests that the basics of math—counting, adding, subtracting, and the like—emerged to fill the needs of commerce and accounting, keeping track of goods as they were traded and stored. As business has evolved, so too have the symbol systems that serve this intelligence, as they adapt to these dynamic changes.

What might the key elements of business intelligence include? The data trail leads back to the 1970s, when Harvard professor David McClelland first made the argument that what predicted the best performance in business were not traditional academic aptitudes, nor school grades, nor credentials. Instead he focused on the abilities that star performers exhibit, which can differ from job to job, role to role, and company to company—and which have little or nothing to do with academic abilities.

His research showed why academic intelligence matters little as a predictor of success once someone has gotten into a given job—they are largely *threshold* abilities, what anyone needs to enter the field and hold the job. More significant for predicting success are those competencies that *distinguish* the best from the mediocre within a given job, role, or company. If a company wants to cultivate its strengths, it needs to hire, promote, and train people for these distinguishing abilities—just as if we want to succeed in our career, these are the abilities we will need.

Over the last several decades hundreds of studies in organizations of all kinds—from small family-owned retailers to corporate giants, from hospitals to religious orders—have followed McClelland's lead, assessing the capabilities that set the star performers apart from average in jobs within their organization. Those abilities break down into three basic domains: cognitive astuteness, which largely translates into the ability to learn and to think strategically; technical expertise, or the essential crafts we learn to get work done; and emotional intelligence, the ability to manage ourselves and our relationships. Business intelligence, in the sense I propose, subsumes all of these as core sub-abilities—components that, when orchestrated together, create a special business aptitude.

Each of us will inevitably have a profile of strengths and weaknesses across all the varied abilities that make for business intelligence. And each job we hold over the course of a career will have a distinctive set of demands—and so to some extent require a unique recipe of capabilities to excel. As we change jobs and roles, we need to grow our business intelligence through continuous learning—not just to keep up, but also to get and stay ahead.

Of course any intelligence will have its prodigies—those who exhibit the aptitude at its peak. Here the Rothschilds and Rockefellers, the likes of Gates and Branson, make the point. But the simple fact that some have a natural knack for business intelligence, while others have only middling abilities, should not discourage anyone. For one, the abilities that make up business intelligence are all learnable—anyone with motivation can get better. For another, no one need master every element of business intelligence; we can rely on others for much of the expertise we need. And that gets me to my next point: intelligence is distributed.

The Need to Know

An ancient proverb holds, "Best is to know—and know you know. Next best is to know that you don't know. Third best is knowing, but not realizing it. Worst is not to know that you don't know."

That bit of wisdom certainly pertains to business intelligence, which includes an aptitude for grasping the right expertise at just the right time, for the right business purpose. The best business people know what they need to, and use their expertise with confidence. When they don't have a key piece of expertise, they realize their need to know—and know where to find it. And, frankly, given the complexity of business today, any of us can find ourselves in that position—with an urgent need to know—at any moment.

How well we handle that moment speaks to our business intelligence, which can manifest in knowing the critical piece of expertise a pressing need demands—or knowing how to find it. Such access to expertise sets the best business people apart from those who flounder: star performers have a superlative grasp of just the piece of know-how they need to do their jobs well, while mediocre performers don't even know that they don't know. Indeed, in studies of outstanding performers at work, the very best were able to track down an essential bit of expertise four times faster than it took their less able peers. In short, speed of access to key expertise—a distinguishing quality of business intelligence—typifies business stars.

In today's business reality such access is all the more essential because of a fundamental fact: we each know only a part of the information or expertise we need to get our jobs done. For years Robert Kelley of Carnegie-Mellon University has been asking people who work at a wide variety of companies the same question, "What per cent of the knowledge you need to do your job is stored in your own mind?" Back in the mid-1980s the answer was typically around 75 per cent. But by the turn of the millennium, that percentage had slid to as low as 15 per cent.

This dwindling of what we know most certainly reflects the sheer rate of growth of information. More knowledge has been generated in the last century, it is said, then in all history before—and the rate of increase accelerates. Likewise, when it comes to the information and expertise needed to do business, what we need to know seems ever-escalating.

Given that anyone in business inevitably faces a growing dependence on information and expertise that others hold, access to what others know matters as never before. But luckily, none of us need to keep in our heads the ever-multiplying expertise that business today—and tomorrow—will demand. Cognitive scientists tell us that intelligence—what we know, remember, and can put to practical use—is distributed. Instead of studying for years to learn all that we might one day need to know, we may do as well—or better—simply to know how to get the information or skills we'll need at the time we need it. We can access a particular bit of expertise as called for, rather than spending endless years mastering all of it.

Our business intelligence does not stop at our skin—it resides in the tools such as databases, and our networks of associates, office mates, and colleagues whom we can turn to as needed. But there is an inevitable unevenness to the range and depth of expertise that our information tools and personal networks offer. Each of us needs to find ways to make up for the gaps in our personal network of experts and information—to continue to learn—or learn ways to find out what we need to know, when we need to know it.

The implications of business intelligence go beyond each of us to the companies we work for or the people we work with. Within any human group, knowledge and expertise are distributed. In today's complex business reality, no one person can master all the skills or data the organization as a whole will need to run effectively. The financial officer has one set of expertise, the sales people another, those in R&D still another. And the company will only be as "smart" as the timely and appropriate offering up of those diverse bits of expertise allow.

Today's business reality poses a paradox: the challenge of reconciling information overload with lightning-fast decision making. To survive competitively, each of us individually—as well as any company—must gather expertise as needed, and operate or adapt accordingly. This applies to the smallest corner store and the largest corporation alike. It points to the crucial role of information flow throughout an organization in determining its viability. The sum of what everybody in a company knows, and knows how to do—its aggregate business intelligence—gives a company much of its competitive edge—if it can mobilize that expertise well.

Indeed, battle-worn executives like Andrew Grove of Intel argue that the very survival of a company depends on the ability of its top leadership team to be nimble in their response to the surprises and challenges of the marketplace. And systems theory tells us that in an environment of turbulent change and competition, the person—or company—that can take in information most widely, learn from it most thoroughly, and respond most nimbly, creatively, and flexibly, will be the most adaptive. This business imperative was, no doubt, a force in the emergence of the "knowledge management" movement from within the Information Technology enclave to the further reaches of the organization.

In short, at each step of the way, the ability to access needed expertise makes a critical difference. Where are the gaps in our business intelligence? We can ask ourselves if we are completely current in, say, the best ways to get to know our customers and their needs, or how to make a strategic alliance work, or the ins and outs of relationship marketing. Where would we turn in our own personal network to find the answers?

Business Literacy—And Wisdom

Then there's *business literacy*, a working familiarity with the key thinking and writing that business people need to keep up with. Given the thousands of books and articles published each year for business people, it's virtually impossible to keep current with the explosion of new ideas and concepts—not to mention weeding out the quickly fading fads of the moment. The majority of that unwieldy mass of ideas and insights offered up each year will fall away like leaves in autumn. But year after year there are thinkers whose insights prove worthwhile, because they make a practical difference—they add to business intelligence, and prove their worth by ways they matter at work.

Business advantage is gained by harnessing smart ideas—not just amorphous data, the latest technology, or a larger-than-life C.E.O. The editors of the *Harvard Business Review* candidly admit that of all the business ideas that have been proposed in their pages, many are mundane refinements of existing concepts. Only a very few qualify as breakthrough: in 1979, Michael Porter conceived his theory of the forces that shape strategy; in 1990 C. K. Prahalad and Gary Hamel wrote about a company's core competencies; in 1995 Clay Christensen proposed the importance of disruptive technologies. All these ideas are now essentials of business literacy.

Failing at business literacy leaves us behind the curve, or defensive when others bring up important business ideas that we, too, should be familiar with. Worse, it can leave us clueless while others act on powerful new concepts. Business literacy feeds and grows business intelligence. In gauging our own business literacy, we need to ask ourselves, how strong is our working familiarity with the key thinking and writing that anyone in business needs to work well?

Finally, consider what might be called *business wisdom*, which can be seen as the sum total of lessons learned over the course of a career. As each of us goes through the ups and downs, crises and triumphs, of a life in business, the brain automatically extracts lessons for confronting similar situations in the future. Over the years we each build up a set of tacitly learned decision rules—life's lessons—which constitute the sum total of our wisdom on the matter.

But each of us has only a specific, limited set of life experiences—and so a restricted set of lessons—informing our business wisdom. We can each benefit from expanding the pool of lessons learned, given the unpredictable nature of challenges we will face tomorrow. Through human history a traditional way of enlarging our wisdom has been by hearing from the "elders"—those who have gone through what we have yet to face. In the business world such wisdom comes from the most highly seasoned among us—both through what they have to tell us, and what their lives in business reveal to us.

Of course business intelligence, literacy, or wisdom are themselves useless unless we can translate them into action—in short, having an answer to the question of what to do come Monday morning. When all is said and done, it is only in the day-to-day demonstration of wise efforts that business intelligence proves its worth.

Here we can ask ourselves how prepared we've been for the major crisis—or opportunity—of the last week, month, or year. What have we done to gird ourselves for the next such moment? Or we can pause to do an audit of our own business intelligence, looking for the gaps that signal where we might want to build more strengths. Or we can reflect on what we know, what we don't know—and where we would go to find out.

About the Author

Daniel Goleman, Ph.D., is the author or coauthor of several bestsellers, including *Emotional Intelligence* (Bantam, 1997) and *Primal Leadership* (Harvard Business School, 2002). A psychologist, he worked for many years for the *New York Times* covering the brain and behavioral sciences. He has also been a visiting faculty member at Harvard University and serves as Co-Chair of the Consortium for Research on Emotional Intelligence in Organizations, Graduate School of Professional and Applied Psychology, Rutgers University. He is a founder of the Collaborative for Social and Emotional Learning at the University of Illinois at Chicago and speaks on emotional intelligence and leadership worldwide.

See also:
☆ **Emotional Intelligence (pp. 312–13)**

BUSINESS: A USER'S GUIDE

Business has been designed to offer a wide range of insights, information, and practical guidance on every aspect of management.

With over 200 contributors, 2.5 million words of text, 700 illustrations, and 150 maps, *Business* is the most comprehensive single volume ever published on the world of work. Comprised of seven distinct sections, *Business* is extensively cross-referenced throughout and organized to help you navigate both across and within topics.

BEST PRACTICE

Putting the Expertise of the World's Leading Business Writers to Work for You

The Best Practice section presents a powerful array of practical business advice and fresh thinking from some of the world's leading business writers and practitioners.

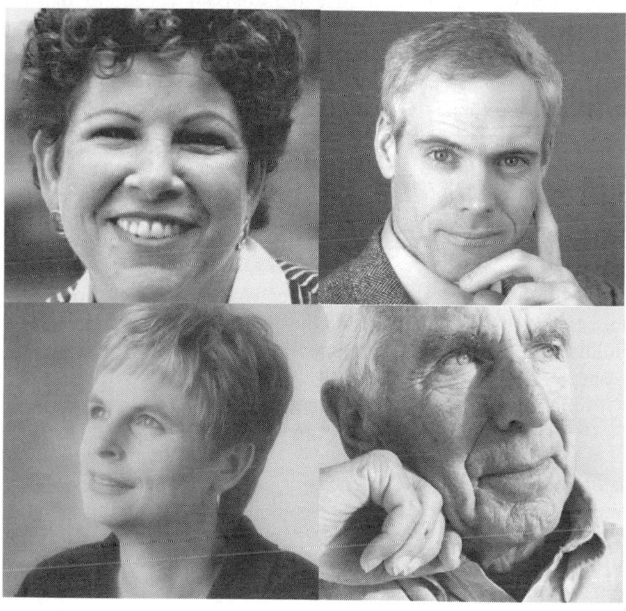

Clockwise from top left: Margaret Wheatley; Jim Collins; Warren Bennis; Patricia Seybold.

These essays reflect the full spectrum of issues that define management today, and serve as concise introductions from experts in each respective topic. Each essay features recommendations of related books and Web sites, and is linked to detailed hands-on advice in the Management Checklists and Actionlists section.

The essays have been organized under eleven broad themes: People and Culture, Marketing, Strategy and Competition, Finance, IT and Information Management, Systems, Structure, Leadership, Renewal and Growth, Productivity, and Personal Effectiveness.

Each essay leads off with an **Executive Summary** for quick reference, outlining the main points in the article. The **Making It Happen** feature shows how you can apply the principles and concepts in practice. Where relevant, authors have provided illustrative case examples and definitions of technical terms.

This section also includes a feature called **Viewpoints**. These pieces are based on a set of exclusive interviews with some of the world's most prominent business authors, as well as forward-looking and agenda-setting articles that explore the future of management in an environment of constant challenge and change.

MANAGEMENT CHECKLISTS AND ACTIONLISTS

Finding Practical Solutions for Everyday Business Problems

The Management Checklists and Actionlists provide you with a comprehensive handbook of practical answers to everyday business challenges. Each list reflects current thinking and best management practice.

The Checklists were developed by experts at the Chartered Management Institute. They provide step-by-step routes to success in a wide variety of practical endeavors, from **Conducting a Performance Appraisal** to **Handling Customer Complaints**. Each Checklist includes a list of dos and don'ts and "thought starters" to stimulate discussion and critical reflection on the topic at hand.

The Actionlists provide essential instruction for tackling specific tasks and solving problems. They address key management tasks in detail, with an emphasis on e-commerce, marketing, accounting and finance, and personal development. They also include a series of "frequently asked questions" (and direct answers), as well as helpful suggestions on how to avoid common mistakes. For additional information, each entry offers resource recommendations and cross-references to the Business Information Sources section.

MANAGEMENT LIBRARY

Summarizing the Most Influential Business Books of All Time

There is a vast literature covering business and the world of work, and thousands more new publications emerge every year. However, only a handful of books become landmarks—forever changing the ways in which management is conceived and practiced.

This section distills the main lessons from the best and most important business books ever published. It includes both influential new titles such as *The Change Masters* and *Blur*, as well as time-honored classics such as Peter Drucker's *The Practice of Management* and Frederick W. Taylor's *The Principles of Scientific Management*.

Frederick W. Taylor and Rosabeth Moss Kanter

Each summary includes a concise overview and analysis of the book's most distinctive contributions to management thinking and practice, along with bibliographic information for the featured title and related works by the author.

Business Thinkers and Management Giants

Profiling the Top Management Thinkers and Pioneers

This section provides over 100 profiles of the most influential or controversial business writers, entrepreneurs, and managers.

Business Thinkers includes summaries of the careers and insights of the most important and influential writers on management, as well as an assessment of their contributions to business theory and practice.

Peter Drucker

Management Giants is a highly selective gallery of the pioneers who have left their indelible stamp on the business landscape—by inventing new technologies, practices, or even industries. These profiles offer insights on the background, defining moments, and legacies of each of these characters—from John Jacob Astor to F. W. Woolworth. Being nice is not one of the main criteria for selection; being effective is.

John Jacob Astor

Dictionary

Defining Business: The Most Up-to-date Global Business English Dictionary

The Dictionary provides jargon-free definitions to more than 5,000 international business terms, abbreviations, and acronyms.

Special features:

- World Business English to reflect the role of the English language in the globalization of the business world; includes business slang
- Abbreviations, acronyms, and their expansions shown in full and cross-referenced
- Mini-essays to explain and illustrate complex concepts
- Expanded biographical entries to detail the lives and careers of key business thinkers and leaders
- Extensive listings of international stock exchanges and trade organizations

management GENERAL MANAGEMENT, HR & PERSONNEL the use of professional skills for identifying and achieving organizational objectives through the deployment of appropriate resources. Management involves identifying what needs to be done, and organizing and supporting others to perform the necessary tasks. A manager has complex and ever-changing responsibilities, the focus of which shifts to reflect the issues, trends, and preoccupations of the time. At the beginning of the 20th century, the emphasis was both on supporting the organization's administration and managing ***productivity*** through increased efficiency. Organizations following ***Henri Fayol***'s and ***Max Weber***'s models built the functional divisions of personnel management, production management, marketing management, operations management, and financial management. At the beginning of the 21st century, those original drivers are still much in evidence, although the emphasis has moved to the key areas of ***competence*** such as people management. Although management is a profession in its own right, its skill-set often applies to professionals of other disciplines.

World Business Almanac

Making Sense of the Wealth of Information about the World's Economy

The World Business Almanac provides you with a one-stop source for statistics, facts, and figures on the global economy and business, pulling together data from thousands of sources into one handy resource.

This section includes up-to-date profiles of over 150 countries, all 50 U.S. states, and 24 industry sectors.

A key feature of the Almanac is the World Economy section, with maps and graphics illustrating a wide variety of business and market statistics as well as demographic and economic information.

Business Information Sources

Providing the Quickest and Easiest Route to the Best Business Information Available

The final section in the work offers 3,000 sources of the best business information from around the world, organized into over 100 subject areas. These include the best management Web sites, the most informative books, magazines and journals, and the most authoritative organizations.

BUSINESS: Monthly Upgrades

Keeping You Up-to-date

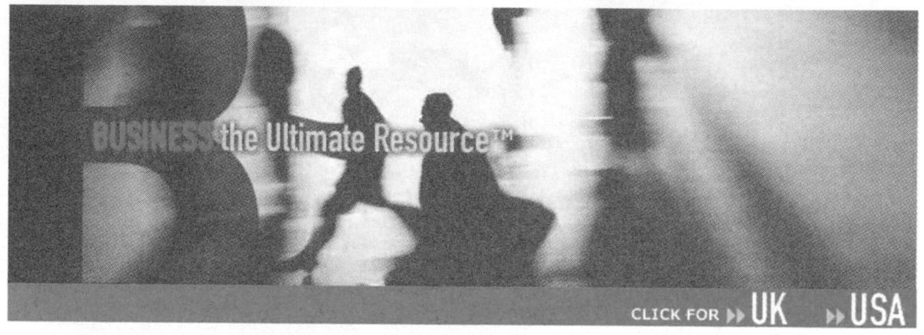

As a user of *Business*, you also are entitled to free monthly upgrades. The upgrades are a powerful new resource available exclusively to *Business* readers.

These will be sent to you in PDF format, in exactly the same design as this book, so you can either read them on screen, or print and store them. Over time, these upgrades will build up to be a substantial reference work in their own right. In addition, these upgrades will be archived on the Web site, so that you can access them online at any time.

Upgrades will include a selection of the following:

- New actionlists and checklists on the latest management topics
- Best Practice Essay of the Month on topical business issues
- Interviews and Viewpoints from leading management thinkers
- Summaries of the latest management bestsellers
- The best new Web sites/information sources for managers

These are available free from our Web site, *www.ultimatebusinessresource.com*

To receive these valuable updates
All you need to do is go to the registration page on our Web site **www.ultimatebusinessresource.com/register**, type in your e-mail address, and add in your password: **mybiz**

Feedback

We welcome any comments you may have about how *Business* might be improved. Let us know, too, if you disagree with any of the points made, or have any correction—we want to hear your views. Write to us at *editorial@ultimatebusinessresource.com* All e-mails to us will receive a reply.

Best Practice

Best Practice

Putting the Expertise of the World's Best Business Thinkers to Work for You
The main objective of the Best Practice Section is to provide you with insights on key problems and business issues you are likely to face at some point in your working life.

With over 160 contributors, this section presents a powerful array of practical business advice and fresh thinking from some of the world's leading business authors and practitioners.

These essays are not designed to be the last word on the subject, but accessible and practical introductions to a wide variety of topics. There are extensive links to "how-to" entries in subsequent sections.

The essays have been organized under eleven broad themes: People and Culture; Marketing; Strategy and Competition; Finance; IT; Systems; Structure; Leadership; Renewal and Growth; Productivity; and Personal Effectiveness.

At the beginning of each essay is an **Executive Summary**, outlining the main points in the article.

The **Making It Happen** section shows how you can apply the principles and concepts in practice. Where relevant, authors have defined specialized terms and/or provided illustrative examples.

Each essay provides you with a list of recommended books and Web sites (**For More Information**).

Lastly, this section includes a number of distinguished **Viewpoints**. These are based on a set of exclusive interviews with some of the world's leading business thinkers such as Charles Handy and Jim Collins, as well as forward-looking articles about the future of business by such authors as Stan Davis and Chris Meyer, Peter Bernstein, and Chris Locke. Our aim here is to stimulate, to provoke, and to inspire.

Contents

  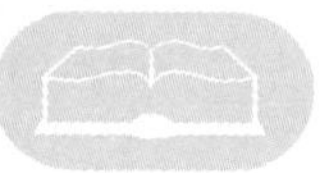    

Marketing

Strategy/Competition

Finance

IT/Information Management

Systems

Structure

LEADERSHIP

RENEWAL/GROWTH

PRODUCTIVITY

PERSONAL EFFECTIVENESS

  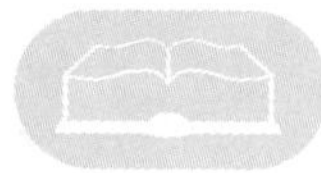    

MANAGEMENT IN THE 21ST CENTURY *by Tom Brown*

From the commencement of my management I viewed the population, with the mechanism and every other part of the establishment, as a system composed of many parts, and which it was my duty and interest so to combine, as that every hand, as well as every spring, lever, and wheel, should effectually cooperate to produce the greatest pecuniary gain to the proprietors.
Robert Owen, "Address: To the Superintendents of Manufactories"

MANAGEMENT: *THEN*

In the beginning—well, it was complex then, too.

To "manage" resources effectively is a concept, says Daniel Wren in *The Evolution of Management Thought*, that can be traced back to the Babylonian King, Hammurabi. That ancient manager, if you will, issued "a code of 282 laws, which governed business dealings, personal behavior, interpersonal relations, wages, punishments, and a host of other societal matters," says Wren. He points out that "Law 104, for example, was the first historical mention of accounting." Consider it very early B2B thinking, which dealt "with the handling of receipts and established an agency relationship between the merchant and the agent." Another law, amazingly, provided very early consumer protection. Hammurabi prescribed a clear-cut consequence for any builder of a house that collapses on the owner and kills him: "[T]hat builder should be put to death."

As Wren expands the evolution of management to more familiar names (Chris Argyris, Henry Ford, John Kotter, Elton Mayo, William Whyte), it's interesting to note that Wren's analyses, in many ways, reveal the same complex skein of critical factors that challenge anyone today who has tried to convert resources into results. The Chinese general, Sun Tzu, really *was* struggling with the principles of managing a 600 B.C. army; and he wasn't planning to start a consultancy or go on a speaking tour. He wanted to get things done. Simply. Effectively. Correctly. *Now.*

In its familiar definition, management is "getting work done through others." Yet anyone who has tried to manage knows that management is never simple, is only sometimes effective, may or may not be done right the first time, and can never happen fast enough. Management may not be rocket science, but it *is* complex. "Management thought did not develop in a cultural vacuum;" says Wren, "managers have always found their jobs affected by the existing culture." Given the elements of any culture (economic variables, social norms, politics, and so on), managers have always had to think first about current norms—*and only then*—move forward.

The *Oxford English Dictionary* starts its derivative history of *management*, the word as it would be used today, with a 1598 citation; *manager*, it says, was actually in use some ten years before. It makes more sense to jump to 1813 and to Robert Owen, the first authority cited in *Classics in Management*, a collection of excerpts from the thinkers who most influenced the profession during its formative years. Owen, a Scottish textile manufacturer, was consciously managing in the Industrial Age. His address to his fellow manufacturing magnates shows that he well understood how "inanimate machines" had altered the workscape permanently. "Many of you have long experienced in your manufacturing operations the advantages of substantial, well-contrived, and well-executed machinery," wrote Owen. He talked excitedly about the wonders of a well-oiled manufacturing machine in the way we might boast of the power and beauty of a pulsing new personal computer. He was also well aware of the potential profits from an investment in new technology, "money expended," he says, "for the chance of increased gain."

His 1813 address was far from a paean to technology and profits alone, however; he spent most of his attention on the numerous advantages of managing *people*. "[W]ill you not afford some of your attention," Owen implores, "to consider whether a portion of your time and capital would not be more advantageously applied to improve your living machines?" He argued that a healthy synergy of workplace conditions (including state-of-the-art technology) and workplace humanism ("care and attention to the living instruments") would yield unheard-of profits. Owen promised his fellow manufacturers that, by following his advice, they too would see returns of "not five, ten, or fifteen per cent, for your capital so expended, but often fifty and in many cases a hundred per cent."

Among the many management gurus who followed, Frederick Winslow Taylor (*The Principles of Scientific Management*), Henri Fayol (*General Principles of Management*), Mary Parker Follett (*Freedom and Co-ordination*), and Elton Mayo (*The Social Problems of an Industrial Civilization*) are forebears to the autograph-signing management stars of today. But Owen, even though he knew that management had always operated in the context of economic variables, social norms, and politics, set *the* essential challenge for all managers thereafter with his elevation of three distinct issues: technology, people, and profits. How do we balance these three elements into the best combination, the most productive combination, the longest sustainable combination: in short, a *winning* combination?

[I]n 1981. . .I said I wanted GE to become "the most competitive enterprise on earth.". . .In the end, I believe we created the greatest people factory in the world, a learning enterprise, with a boundaryless culture.
Jack Welch, Jack: Straight from the Gut

MANAGEMENT: *NOW*

The thousands of management books proffered over the last decade can be easily divided into two stacks. On one side are the numerous bestselling management authors (from thinker Rosabeth Moss Kanter to real-life manager Jack Welch) who often present an overall picture of corporate management doing things exceedingly right. Stellar managers, as presented in some books, have balanced the complexities of technology, people, and profit into distilled and potent commercial certainty. Bookstore racks teem with such tomes; the more cynical readers consider such works "fad books," designed to spawn yet another *program du jour* inside the corporate world. The excel-

lent enterprise may be named General Electric, though it just as well could be called Camelot Inc. Often the same companies and managers are heralded in multiple books by different authors. And those who offer management wisdom gleaned from such paragons seem convinced that managers in *any* company need follow only a few nicely jotted bullet points to guarantee success.

But amid the thunderous accolades accorded those few companies and executives that have earned widespread public adulation, many serious observers talk about working and managing with voices pitched harsh, even doleful. In the July 22, 2001, issue of the *New York Times,* Margo Jefferson, focusing on the drama world, posed an interesting question: "How can the theater make itself matter again?" Her answer, in part, was this: "Theater needs new work. It has to catch something of the way we live here and now: take in the facts and the sensations, show us our minds and bodies as they react and realign themselves. And theater needs to take more risks." Change the word *theater* to *management,* and many would argue that Ms. Jefferson's thoughts apply equally to the complex meshing of technology and people to produce profits.

Throughout *The Working Life,* her eminent study of the history of work, Joanne Ciulla also raises some tough issues; she comments that too many people "can't choose when to go to work and what to do at work. They do not deliberate on management policies or decide how to do the task at hand. Worst of all, many still can't plan for the future because they don't know if they will have a job." Richard Donkin spent six years researching the same subject, work, and reached comparable conclusions in *Blood, Sweat & Tears.* "The more I write," he says about the world of work, "the more I ask myself this recurring question: Why on earth do we do it?" Donkin points out, as do others, that management has become such a prized profession that, with salaries and bonuses, some top executives now easily earn "150 times more than their lowest paid employees." But it's not excessive money making that seems to disturb Donkin the most. His introduction relates how he once sat beside "a FTSE 100 company chief, fishing by the riverbank. . .listening to him giving instructions [to his office] on his mobile phone." Says Donkin: "The craziness is that some of these highly paid individuals are working such long hours they rarely have the opportunity to step outside their jobs and enjoy a moment's leisure."

Christina Maslach and Michael Leiter believe that burnout affects far more than tired top execs. When their book on burnout was published (just a few years ago), they offered this challenging thought: "Burnout is reaching epidemic proportions among North American workers today. It's not so much that something has gone wrong with us but rather that there have been fundamental changes in the workplace and the nature of our jobs. The workplace today is a cold, hostile, demanding environment, both economically and psychologically. . .People are becoming cynical, keeping their distance, trying not to let themselves get too involved." There's perhaps good reason *not* to be too attached to one's job. Citing statistics collected by Challenger, Gray & Christmas, the Associated Press reported at the end of 2001 that job cuts in the United States were the highest in almost a decade. For too many management teams, has strategic planning now been permanently reduced to an exercise in subtraction?

Bill Jensen is actively trying to capture the difference between what the workplace *is* like and what it *should* be like. He speaks and writes about *Work 2.0,* where people (and managers) need to stop thinking about organizational productivity and start thinking about personal productivity. He says we all need to stop focusing on things like operational excellence and tune into "radical simplicity," an awareness of what people really need to get their work done. In a Work 2.0 world, he stresses that people are "business units of one." Another vanguard management thinker on how organizations should be is Thomas Stewart, of *Fortune,* who wrote in *The Wealth of Knowledge:* "The modern corporation, like modern art, is over. The postmodern corporation is different." He argues that one of the chief differences lies in how management defines employment. "It's more accurate—and more useful—to think of employees in a new way: not as assets but as investors. Shareholders invest money in our companies; employees invest time, energy, and intelligence."

Arie de Geus, drawing on his long career at Royal Dutch/Shell, argues in *Business Minds* that management may be suffering a crisis of vocabulary. "[C]ompanies have become trapped in the prison of economic language, which is why so many companies suffer premature deaths. . .[C]ompanies tend to die early because their leaders and executives concentrate on production and profit, and forget that the corporation is an institution. . .a community of human beings." In that same work, Fons Trompenaars argues that, since "culture" today must be defined globally, the basic job of a manager is overdue for a radical redesign. "Just because people speak English does not mean they think alike," he argues. "The international manager needs to go beyond awareness of cultural differences. He or she needs to respect these differences and take advantage of diversity through reconciling cross-cultural dilemmas."

How could modern management, almost 200 years after Robert Owen, be so divided? On the one hand, the biggest best-sellers in management are tied to a daily cartoon strip named "Dilbert" that chronicles the work strife of a high-tech laborer who seemingly debases management for a living. On the other hand, another simple storybook features a cartoon mouse who can't seem to manage a block of cheese. And such contrarian views get even starker. Anita Roddick, founder of The Body Shop chain of stores and a C.E.O. who has also generated considerable controversy, has written two books about both her trade and her views on management. Her latest work acknowledges that, for many, management has made business "a jungle where only the vicious survive." She laments that, for too many, managing a business is about sitting "in front of computer screens, moving millions of dollars from Japan to New York." She yearns for "a new view of business as a community where only the responsible will lead."

Margaret Wheatley is today more a social philosopher than a management guru. Yet by looking at management practices through the lens of modern physics, her early-1990s book, *Leadership and the New Science,* took "scientific management" to a depth that Frederick Winslow Taylor could never have imagined. Today, she says management is *stuck.* "If we don't change the way we manage business in the next ten years," she says bluntly, "we're dead." A chorus of management thinkers, writers, and managers is there to back her up. W. Chan Kim and Renée Mauborgne, talking about the difficulties of managing strategy in a knowledge economy, believe that a quantum leap in management will come only when "fair process" comes to the modern work world, something that involves "major changes in [behavior] and working practices" which "will not be

achieved without people willingly co-operating with the innovation process and making their skills and experience available to a company." It should come as little surprise that Richard Leider these days asks every top exec he meets to answer just one question: *Why would the best people in the world want to work for your company?*

Two Stanford University professors, Jeffrey Pfeffer and Robert Sutton, looking at the corporate world at large, found that, despite all the gleeful chirps by proud executives about their companies being elite learning organizations, there were plenty of organizational examples of the polar opposite. They subsequently wrote *The Knowing-Doing Gap*. Its very first sentence is an indictment of the profession of management today—or, at least, a diagnosis of serious managerial schizophrenia. "We wrote this book because we wanted to understand why so many managers know so much about organizational performance, say so many smart things about how to achieve performance, and work so hard, yet are trapped in firms that do so many things they know will undermine performance." It's as if too few managers (and management thinkers!) had ever read, bothered to think about, act upon, or even recall Douglas McGregor's mournful challenge to the management profession in the closing paragraph of his landmark 1960 work, *The Human Side of Enterprise*. Forty years before Pfeffer and Sutton's research, McGregor had already concluded: "Fads will come and go. The fundamental fact of man's capacity to collaborate with his fellows in the face-to-face group will survive the fads and one day be recognized. Then, and only then, will management discover how seriously it has underestimated the true potential of its human resources."

As we learn more about life. . .Mendel, Darwin, Watson, Crick, Venter. . .will be figures every bit as important as Edison, Einstein, Ford, the Wright brothers. . .What they have taught us and produced is changing each of our lives. . .How we work, live, and think. You can stand on the sidelines and assume fate will guide things. . .(God willing. . .Si Dios Quiere. . .Insha'Allah. . .Shikatta ga nai. . .) Or you can help yourself, your family, your company and country navigate. . .This wondrous and scary adventure.
Juan Enriquez, As the Future Catches You

MANAGEMENT: *TOMORROW*

E-mail and the Internet are two of the technological forces that have altered the job of a manager. Whether the concern be how to manage "virtual employees" who work from home (are they *really* working?) or how to decide who should be able to access the megabytes of intimate corporate data that now course through any modern company, technology is as daunting today as it was for Robert Owen in 1813—with a commensurate impact on people and profits. Yet, for managers, there's an even bigger horizon to glimpse and ponder.

In his role as director of the Life Sciences Project at Harvard Business School, Juan Enriquez has thought deeply about the personal and fiscal import of such society-shaking developments as the recent mapping of the human genome. That may seem like a too-distant subject for someone managing a steel mill, grocery, or factory—or even a software development company. Enriquez thinks otherwise. Referring to the work of Robert Fleishmann and Craig Venter, work that produced "the first genetic map of a living organism," Enriquez reflected that such scientific breakthroughs raise questions that people never even thought they would be *able* to ask. Robert Owen fretted over how best to control the capital assets and human resources of his manufacturing plant; now people are starting to fret over how, as Enriquez says in his book, "To control. . .Directly and deliberately. . .The evolution of our species. . .And that of every other species on the planet." It's a big jump. Can management, as a profession, make it?

We don't know. What we do know is that every manager today has both new *and* old questions to answer. Andrea Gabor probed the lives of ten individuals (whom she called *The Capitalist Philosophers*) who were management heavyweights of the last century, people like Chester Barnard, Abraham Maslow, and W. Edwards Deming. She concluded that management tomorrow has to find an answer to the question that, at heart, also bothered Owen. Says Gabor: "At the root of the conflict between the humanistic and the scientific are two warring images of the business organization and its purpose in. . .society: One sees the corporation as a pivotal institution of democracy with complex responsibilities to a host of constituencies, including its employees, its customer, and the community. The other, much more utilitarian, view recognizes one primary corporate constituent—the shareholder—and a single purpose—profit making."

Technology is now proceeding at a pace that may quickly outstretch management's (and, perhaps, mankind's) ability to decide *what* to do with what we are so rapidly learning *how* to do. The very real prospect arises that many will simply conclude that life and business, both, are irrefutably *unmanageable*. Owen feared that technology would overpower the human being; Deming feared that human myopia about issues like quality would overpower an organization's technological capability to deliver excellent products. Today, some fear that the push for profit could throttle both technology and humanity. Even a sober thinker like Charles Handy (who calls himself "a reluctant capitalist") talks about "elephants" (large companies) and "fleas" (individuals or small groups with innovative ideas), conceding that "[M]any observers think that the big corporations are now both richer and more powerful than many nation states. . .The elephants, people feel, may be out of anyone's control."

AND YET—

And yet one can safely assert that the hundreds of years of management debate have not been without value—that the hundreds of management treatises, the hundreds of management theories, the hundreds of management gurus, the hundreds of management "solutions" (from Theories X and Y to the Managerial Grid to the Eight Principles of Excellence to Business Process Reengineering)—all of this management commotion has not been without a constructive role in society. For the study of management, during the centuries in which it has been active and accepted as a discipline, has always served as the testing ground for how we could and should work, individually and collectively. Management thinking has served as the closest thing to a laboratory where the "genetic code" of human enterprise can be mapped, to see if there *are* new ways to pool the resources tied to every human endeavor into new vistas of human possibilities. As Robert Heller and Tim Hindle note in their illuminating *Essential Manager's Manual*: "A full understanding of what makes people perform well and of the problems that may affect performance in the workplace is therefore

  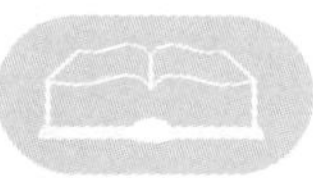    

essential for any manager. He or she will need to employ a wide range of skills, both interpersonal and professional, in order to resolve these problems."

The practice of management, through both its scientific standards and its artistic renderings, remains the best way yet to channel the raw energy of human minds, the brute force of vast capital, and the quixotic capability of new technology to transform people by reshaping their perceptions of what's possible on this planet, and ultimately, even beyond. The marketplace of ideas about management has always been a free market. Accounting, information, logistics, marketing, manufacturing, organizational culture, research and development, sales, social policy—pick *any* discipline within the profession of management, and you'll find intense debate about the questions that matter most to each particular realm of the corporate world. It is as it always was. It is as it should be.

Thus, whenever a large collection of management thinkers are assembled under one roof, one book, or one Web site, the last thing one should expect is congruence. Management, as it has evolved and is evolving, is a battle of ideas and ideals. Management thinkers and practitioners only align with others when they share common views of how technology can be deployed, how humans can best interact with the machines and systems they have created, and how, when combined, these forces can create new wealth. But wealth follows achievement. Businesses do not prosper because of their strategic planning; they succeed because of their strategic execution and because of the extent to which they can attract both investors and customers to share their strategic purpose. And achievement is very much an exercise in managing for the future.

There are still many questions about management that have not been asked or answered. The greatest debates about how to manage ourselves and our companies have yet to be staged. The most salient ideas about how to manage both the workplace (and the world!) have yet to be widely disseminated, considered, and tested. Even the largest collection of management information and ideas is simply a mental cake mix until students and practitioners stir themselves into the blend and begin to practice new forms of management—to become, in essence, new kinds of managers.

Management and human enterprise have brought mankind a long way. We travel fast, communicate easily, shop globally, and learn rapidly. Yet, judging mainly by what management has accomplished in the past (and what it hasn't), we can be quite sure that its study will never become passé. The word will never be pulled from the dictionaries because it has become archaic. We need not quake over the prospect that the study of management will no longer be needed because its best practices have accomplished everything that needs to be done. We need not fear terminal success. Whenever enormous problems involving work, people, and organizations crop up, this question will imminently bubble up too: How do we *manage* this problem? The list is endless but undoubtedly starts with. . .

- Some executives do achieve long-term business success. Yet we really don't know how to replace that executive with one just as capable in order to keep the good corporate times going—nor do we know how to transfer an excellent manager's expertise to another company or another industry. We in management own that problem.
- The power of large corporations rivals many nations; their top managers are often more widely known than presidents or prime ministers. Yet corporations don't really know how to wield that power in ways that do not devastate some communities while disproportionately blessing others. We in management own that problem.
- E-commerce is an increasing force in the buying and selling of goods, both between businesses and between companies/customers. Yet we really don't know how to e-replicate the relationships and loyalty that used to be the greatest asset of any business: customer goodwill. We in management own that problem.
- Corporations no longer have to be *mega* in size to leverage global connections; 24/7 workdays and Internet communications make it probable, not just possible, that for many, the worker "in the next cubicle" will be thousands of miles away. Yet few companies have meshed the unique cultural perspectives of a multinational workforce into a coherent, collaborative team. We in management own that problem.
- Advanced technology has made it possible to fly to outer space and return safely. Yet, all over the globe, people today are struggling with how to fly or drive millions of miles without facing overt terrorism or risking the less obvious terror of enviro-toxic byproducts corrupting the atmosphere permanently. We in management own that problem.
- Even in the most heralded companies boasting a badge of merit that says they are "wonderful" places to work, employees and managers slink to work each day uninspired, even desperate—incapable of connecting the mission of the company with their own mission in life. We in management own that problem.

Management in the 21st century is incomplete, imperfect, and quite often insufficient to meet pressing needs. That makes management tomorrow as exciting as ever, an exhilarating subject to study and a dynamic profession to practice. In almost any corner of your life, your workplace, your community, or your global marketplace, there are problems that simply won't be addressed unless *someone* in management owns them.

Therefore today—right now!—the most important unanswered question in management comes down to four words: *Might that be you?*

  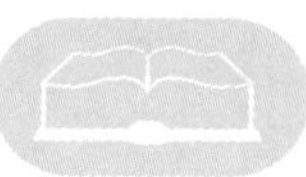    

VIEWPOINT: STAN DAVIS AND CHRISTOPHER MEYER

Create, Connect, Evolve

Stan Davis and Christopher Meyer have coauthored two books, *Blur* and *Future Wealth*, as well as numerous articles. Davis is the author of *Future Perfect* and *Lessons from the Future*, and they are at work on a third book together, describing the economy of the next ten years. Standing on the given—the present—and using the perspective of the past, the two authors in this Viewpoint leap into a future that is challenging, exhilarating, and complex.

Comparing the four phases of the life cycle (of plants, people, industries, or civilizations) to the development of economies, they predict the creation, connection, and evolution of the next economy: a boundary-crossing mix of science and technology. What will the next economy be like? What will be its core products?

Something unprecedented is about to happen: the next economy is already in the wings waiting to come on stage before the information economy is fully mature. The ideas and technologies of these two economies will affect one another during the coming decades, creating a rapidly evolving climate for business and management. This is our take on what's next, what it will be like, what's driving it, and where it is in its life cycle.

In the life cycles of economies, we've seen a succession: from hunting and gathering economies lasting hundreds of thousands of years, to agrarian economies lasting ten thousand years, to the industrial period dominating for slightly less than two hundred years (1760s–1950s), and now the information era. The first half of the information economy was dominated by computers as free-standing boxes, whose importance was measured by their crunching power. The connecting power of networked computers, which began with the explosion of the Internet in the early 1990s, is nowhere near complete and is dominating the second half. We're already five decades into the current information economy, which will likely last only another three—at most.

Everything that has a beginning has an ending, and therefore a life cycle. Plants, planets, and people all have life cycles. So do products, businesses, industries, economies, and civilizations. They all have life cycles, and the cycles seem to follow some basic principles.

Cycles, for example, go through distinct periods or quarters: gestation (Q1), growth (Q2), maturity (Q3), and decline (Q4). The first quarters of economies are dominated by science, the second quarters by technologies that bridge between science and the businesses that mature in Q3s. The fourth quarter focuses on organizational innovation. Thermodynamics led to the steam engine, for example, which led to railroads and the industrial economy, and to top-down rational bureaucratic management models. Solid-state physics led to semiconductors, which led to computers and the information-based businesses of the information economy, whose network-centered organizational form is just beginning to come into focus as we near Q4.

Cycles also overlap, with the next one already gestating while the previous one grows and matures. People may live to their 80s, but most have children in their 20s and 30s. What's new is an economic teenage pregnancy. The next economy has already begun its growth phase before the information economy is mature—two economic generations are increasingly living side by side. The next economy will be marked by three drivers: the creation of value at the molecular level, the connection of infotech and biotech, and an economic environment in which evolution replaces engineering as the dominant source of management and economic ideas. The mindset for the decades ahead is simply this: create, connect, evolve.

CREATE

The clues for the next economy are in the sciences that are becoming technologies, and these increasingly involve the mastery of molecules. This mastery will likely play out in three successive waves: first in organic (bio)technology, then in inorganic composite materials, and ultimately in nanotechnologies.

In the first wave, the appropriate beginning marker is probably Crick and Watson's 1953 discovery of the double helix structure of DNA. Almost five decades later, the completion of the Human Genome Project in 2001 is probably a convenient marker for the start of the second quarter. Q2 will last for at least the next two or three decades, during which we will see the commercialization of many biotech products, and meaningful overlap between biotech and infotech.

Biology operates at distinct nested levels, scaling up through connections among elements at smaller levels: molecules (including DNA)/organisms/species/ecologies. In other words, ecology is derivative of molecules, and not vice versa unless you are a creationist. The design principle of building from the small and scaling up operates in economics as well as in biology. Semiconductors led to computers and then to the Internet, not vice versa. Like biology, economy will also be derivative of molecules—quite literally, not simply as metaphor, which was the case with the social Darwinists a century ago and still is with many management gurus today.

Recombinant DNA, the first biotech ripple (mid-1980s–mid-1990s), used an engineered economic model that was akin to big pharma: big money, big

"There are no such things as applied sciences, only applications of science." (Louis Pasteur)

mixing vats, and big risks because the molecular structure of the targets for these drugs was poorly understood. The management model was still top-down control. Genomics, the current ripple, by contrast, uses techniques akin to molecular biology and genetic engineering. The business model has more in common with infotech startups than with big pharma, and the management model shifts to control from the bottom up.

The second and third waves in the next economy will also involve large-scale commercializing of molecules, but they lie a bit further in the future. There we'll likely see major advances in inorganic composite materials and in nanotechnologies, creating product by programming and self-assembling matter. A new class of ceramics, for example, has heat tolerant properties that could reduce gasoline consumption by a million barrels a day. New structures based on nanotubes are already being exploited to detect environmental toxins. During the next decades we'll also see a smaller and more efficient computing platform emerge. There are currently four candidates: molecular electronics, photonics, quantum computing, and DNA computing.

Whether you're an entrepreneur or an executive, if you've got an eye for the future during the coming decade you should be asking: "How can I deliver value in my business through molecular technologies?"

CONNECT

In 1998 we wrote a book, *Blur*, that said connectivity was changing the rules of business. There, we focused on the information economy. The really big blur, however, is likely to occur as the current and next economies rub up against each other more and more in the decade ahead. That's when economics will borrow more from biology. And that's when we will see the blurring between the organic and inorganic, the natural and artificial, the living and non-living.

Connections between seemingly distinct worlds are clearest at the most basic levels, in their fundamental codes. Codes derived from science create the same world in different ways, just as do codes from religion and from art. They're all different interpretive truths of the same universe. In science, whether we're dealing with material code (based on the 92 elements), genetic code (based on A, C, G, and T) or information code (based on 0 and 1), at the molecular level, code is code. Code crossings, connections, are easier within these worlds than between them, but that's never stopped mankind from seeking connections at all nested levels.

In science we've reached the point where biotech and infotech can literally be translated into each other. The elements in each code scale up through successive layers, branching over micromoments or millennia, until you have enterprises and organisms, industries and species, and ultimately economies and ecosystems. Literally, the world is built on code from the bottom up, and so are the economies that populate it. Still, in its essential and elemental form, code is code. Conceptually, therefore, it can be treated interchangeably, and today's cutting edge technologies are working to make this interchange practical in the world of business. Thus models created by molecular biologists and ecologists are becoming useful for managing business strategies and processes.

Molecules now are regularly moved from one code to another in laboratories, and the results of this R&D are beginning to move into production. Yesterday's science fiction will be tomorrow's over-the-counter home healthcare products. Entire artificial hearts, controlled by microchips, are already a reality. Blending the organic and inorganic at molecular levels will blur the distinction even more. Nerve cells of a leech have been connected to a silicon transistor and an artificial neuron has been implanted in a lobster.

Boundary crossing between different species is also becoming commonplace. Two decades ago, genetic engineering came closer and jumped a code across species, implanting human interferon, for example, into rapidly replicating bacteria and creating pharmaceutical proteins in a factory that is literally alive. And we already grow human elements in mice because they share so much of our genome. More adventurous still, spiders' silk glands and goats' mammary glands share enough similarity that, after isolating the gene that codes for silk protein in spiders, scientists inserted it into the mammary glands of goats. The silk protein comes out in the transgenic goats' milk.

The next step will be to remove it and use it to mass-produce "extreme performance fibers" that might one day result in bio-steel. Yes, manipulating codes predates Mendel and selective breeding is certainly an ancient art, but understanding and connecting the molecular codes and building technologies to manipulate them will produce far more powerful and wide-reaching results. Similarly, the nascent field of bioplastics is at the crossroads of petrochemicals and agriculture, and its intentions are to do things like growing plastics in corn. Plastics come from oil, which is often expensive, unclean, and geopolitically unstable. In the future they may be grown locally, cheaply, and "green." A polystyrene substitute has already been produced by genetically modified corn plants. Biopharming, or molecular farming, is a potential new industry at the boundary between medicine and food. Genetically modified organisms (gmo's) and therapeutic cloning are some controversial results of such code-crossing activities.

Computer software follows the same rules as molecules, "create, connect, evolve." The rapidly growing field of bioinformatics marries infotech and biotech. Evolving systems create simulated, virtual worlds that "self-organize" on the basis of a few simple rules. Digital immune systems work the way mammalian ones do. Genetic algorithms exist only in computers but work by biologics. Silicon retinas may soon be implanted in human eyes. Worlds are connecting, and boundaries are indeed blurring. From the new connections of chemical, biological, and informational codes are emerging new technologies with commercial applications that we have never before con-

"I need to be part of something that is constantly evolving, that's not established." (Judy McGrath)

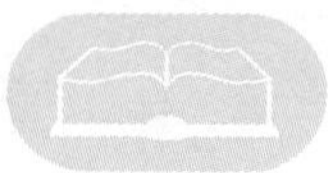

sidered. We are merely at the point of beginning to know what we don't know.

Evolve

When creative elements like molecules or business ideas connect, they begin to evolve. As our economy becomes more connected both within and across codes, the management wisdom of the next decades will come more from evolution than from engineering.

Things are definitely speeding up, so much so that a simple linear extrapolation might lead us to predict that the next era will be a one-minute economy. We think, to the contrary, that it will be much longer lived than the current one. One simple reason is that while generations of new product occur annually, or faster, new generations of living things don't speed up in the same way. Virtual simulations give us a glimpse of what might be, but actual results in people and society will take more time.

Also, every economy has its core product and the molecular era will be no different. But it is still a way off, in what we like to call the adjacent possible. Looking backward, the railroad, using the steam engine, was core to the infrastructure of the industrial economy and, using the combustion engine, the car became the consumerized version of this industrial core. The mainframe computer then the PC, and the Internet then the World Wide Web, held similar importance in the information era.

There's a good chance the next economy's core product will emerge from health care, because it is the economy's largest sector. The reading of the human genome and advances in stem cell research provide a strong platform for commercial products to arise. Alternatively, it may appear in the next largest sector and apply to education, intellectual property, and human capital, but the science here is much less precise.

Whatever it is, and wherever and whenever it emerges, it will not grow from design or from chance. Rather, it will evolve, and it will do so from the bottom up, and quite possibly by using more than one code and connecting across what currently we know as very different worlds. Any environment creating things that connect with each other, whether through microbial soup or through microchips, will evolve. More specifically, we should expect the coevolution of the born and the made—software will breed its own new generations, and new kinds of organisms will be manufactured in mechanical wet labs.

These recombinations are nothing less than directed evolutionary engineering. For this, we have to remove ourselves from the center of things, much as Copernicus had to "stand on the sun" to comprehend the solar system. Then we might marvel at an extraordinary participation in our own evolutionary futures, to say nothing of the artifacts and devices that our imaginations and future factories will create and evolve. Of course, this evolutionary process won't stop with economy.

Above, we said the big blur will be between the organic and inorganic. Many balk at the notion of blurring carbon and non-carbon life. They ask: How can cold code be infused with warm wet life? How can the ineffable qualities of humans be passed on into computers? In return, however, we must ask: How can we accept evolution yet believe that it stops with us?

If it does not stop with us, and we accept the evolution of beings more intelligent than ourselves, where do they come from? Species do not spring into existence *de novo*. They emerge first as mutations and recombinations of codes, creating innovative organisms and differentiated species, ultimately coevolving in even less understood ecologies. And if they evolve from earlier forms, then might not humans evolve into forms more intelligent than themselves? We seem to think the apes did it. Aren't we at least as capable as they were of such creative, connective evolution?

Scientific developments in the past decade offer encouraging support for the line of reasoning we've spelled out above. The further reaches of our argument, by contrast, take us into speculative worlds beyond our current life spans. In the middle distance between molecules and magic, in that adjacent possible, we can see outlines of new products, new businesses, new industries, and the next economy.

For More Information

Web Sites:

Stan Davis's homepage: **www.stanmdavis.com**
Center for Business Innovation: **www.cbi.cgey.com**

"Once a company has adapted to a new environment, it is no longer the organization it used to be; it has evolved. That is the essence of learning." (Arie De Geus)

  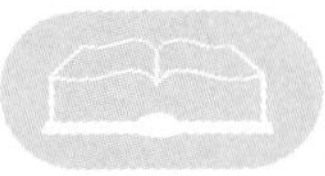    

ACTION LEARNING *by George Boulden*

EXECUTIVE SUMMARY

- Action learning is a proven tool for realizing individual and organizational change.
- It combines knowledge that people have been taught with skills that people have learned, often from experience.
- Action learning requires a supportive environment in which to thrive. Once established, it provides a valuable and powerful stimulus for continuous change, enabling organizations to grow and learn dynamically, rather than remaining static or fixed in one set of circumstances or perspectives.

INTRODUCTION

Action learning (AL) is a powerful tool for individual and organizational change. The term "action learning" was originally used by Professor Reg Revans to identify his philosophy of management development. Revans's approach to management training differed from the conventional approach in that it focused on developing managerial skills rather than just increasing knowledge. Revans had recognized from his work in the mining industry that the major factors affecting a manager's job performance were his or her skills. Revans's idea was to link performance and skills in a practical way by training managers as they worked to solve real problems. The learning and therefore the development of managerial skills are directly linked to the learner's real needs based on actual experience.

Action learning is based on the concept of

L = P + Q

This means that learning [L] is comprised of:

Programmed knowledge [P] (things that people have been taught or that they have learned through experiences) plus

Questioning skills [Q], the ability/willingness to challenge programmed knowledge using the stimulus of real life problems.

In Revans's view, people need the programmed knowledge that they have acquired over the years but in the conditions of rapid change that we live in today, this is not enough for survival. People, and especially managers, must also constructively question both themselves and those around them so that they can adapt successfully to their constantly changing world.

The basic idea of action learning is simple. Individuals are put in a supportive environment with a problem to solve and a facilitator who will encourage them to question their P and to test themselves and each other. The process of questioning and testing produces experiences. Reflection on experience leads to learning. The child learns that the stove is hot, not by touching it (Test), but through the pain that comes from the burn afterwards (reflection). Learning is demonstrated if he or she does not touch the hot stove again.

UNDERSTANDING ACTION LEARNING

KEY APPROACHES AND ROLES

The action learning approach creates learning opportunities through which people develop by:

- working on "life" problems;
- being empowered to question what is happening;
- trying out suggested solutions (doing things differently);
- stepping back and reflecting on what is happening and why;
- sharing the experience with others who are also learning by doing.

There are two main models of action learning: the Revans approach, which focuses on individual development, and the "Inplant" or organizational development model, developed by Action Learning Associates (ALA), which combines individual development with organizational change. Both methods use the same structure:

The problem. This provides the focus for the activity. It is individual in the Revans model and a team problem (project) in the Inplant model.

The client is the person who owns the problem. In Revans's terms this must be someone who knows, cares, and above all can implement its solution if they wish to.

The action learning set. This is the place where participants meet to share their experience. It is the core of the program—the questioning, confrontation, challenging and support which takes place in the set provides the encouragement and stimulus for individuals/groups to carry on. It is the meeting place of "comrades in adversity" as Revans calls them.

The facilitator encourages learning through questioning, mirroring, challenging, and supporting. The facilitator is the grit in the oyster which creates the learning pearl.

The sponsor is the senior manager responsible for the program.

HARNESSING ACTION LEARNING FOR INDIVIDUAL DEVELOPMENT

There are several ways in which action learning is used to develop individuals, including:

- **The Own Job model**
  This aims to enable individuals to maximize their personal effectiveness. Individuals take a problem into the action learning set and they meet at regular intervals over an agreed period of time with an external facilitator. The learning focus is on helping participants to develop the expertise they need to solve their own problems. An example of this approach is Toyota in Japan. Chu-San-Ren, a Japanese management consulting firm based in Nagoya, has been running Own Job action learning programs with Toyota since 1993. Contact Takyuki Furuhashi at **furu@chusanren.or.jp**.
- **The P Development (Academic) model**
  This approach aims to maximize the learning opportunities presented whilst acquiring knowledge (P), and the model combines the personal effectiveness development aspects of the Own Job model with the opportunity to acquire new learning. Sets are formed of people who have the same learning goals and have a dual focus: new knowledge coupled with personal learning. This model is now widely used in more advanced management schools and a number of large corporations. An example of this approach is ACE Insurance, that has adopted this model to train its senior managers. The program provides a three-week development activity for senior people from ACE companies around the world. The core activity is a major business-related project. The approach reflects a balance of "hard inputs" by specialists, live data gathering, and analysis and self-development. The program is designed and facilitated by the OD

"We do not need, and indeed never will have, all the answers before we act. . .It is often through taking action that we can discover some of them."
(Charlotte Bunch)

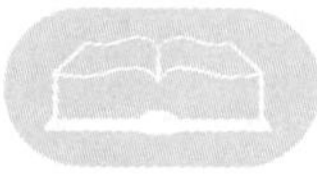

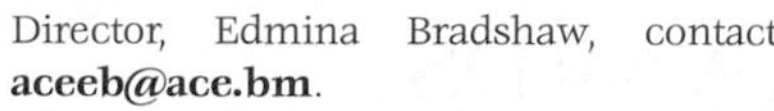

Director, Edmina Bradshaw, contact **aceeb@ace.bm**.

- **The Inplant Action Learning approach**
  Whilst individual action learning programs are very powerful in bringing about individual change, they cannot change organizational culture. One approach to this problem has been to apply the action learning method on an in-plant basis, using problems that exist within the company—real problems it must solve. The approach uses the typical AL structure in which directors and senior managers are cast as "clients," middle managers as "set facilitators," foremen and supervisors working as "fellows" in action learning teams. The whole process is co-ordinated by external "facilitators." Thus all managers and supervisors are involved in a change program at the same time. This structure is classical Revans. The main difference is in the application. The Inplant approach (5) applies action learning to the total management structure of a company in a way which involves everybody.

Making It Happen

- First, consider what you want to achieve: restructure your organization, develop your people, solve specific problems or something else.
- Read the literature, scan the Web sites, talk to someone who has done it.
- Set yourself some output goals. Note these should be both technical, for example, specific problems solved, and behavioral, for example, participants will be able to demonstrate their ability to apply their skills in future projects.
- Design your program. A typical action learning program lasts for about six months and has five main stages:
  1. **Introductory workshop**. This is used to launch the program and can vary in length from one day to three weeks. The aim is to get things started and the more effective this process, the quicker the set starts to function effectively.
  2. **Investigation and Recommendation**. This usually lasts three months and provides the opportunity for participants to analyze the problems to benchmark against best practice and to produce recommendations.
  3. **Presentation and Feedback**. This is usually a two-part stage: the participants present their findings to their clients, and later the clients say what action they would like to sponsor based on the recommendations.
  4. **Implementation**. This usually lasts about three months and involves participants in implementing the recommendations agreed with the client.
  5. **Final review—1 day**. This is an opportunity to review what has or has not been learned or achieved and to agree the way ahead.

Conclusion

Action learning relies on the team working and facilitation process which encourages questioning, empowers participants to try something different, and leads to change. The heart of the action learning process is the group, supported by the facilitator. It provides a safe haven from which individuals can emerge to test themselves and return to share their experience, thereby encouraging and supporting change.

Any team working/problem solving activity can be turned into an action learning program, through the simple addition of a facilitation process. Any personal development programs can be greatly strengthened by forming action learning sets and providing facilitation. Why not do it and maximize the value of your investment?

For More Information

Books:

Boulden, George P. *In-plant Action Learning*. Kingsbridge: ALA International Ltd, April 1993.

Revans, Reg. *ABC of Action Learning*. New edition. London: Lemos and Crane, 1998.

Weinstein, Krystyna. *Action Learning: A Practical Guide*. 2nd ed. Brookfield, VT: Gower, 1998.

Web Sites:

www.ifal.org.uk: the International Foundation for Action Learning (IFAL), formerly The Action Learning Trust, is the best single source of information about action learning.

www.tlainc.com: the International Community of Action Learners (ICAL) is also a useful site. This is a loose federation of action learning practitioners.

www.alaint.demon.co.uk: contact ALA International for information on Organizational Development Applications.

"Learning is a willingness to let one's ability and attitude change in response to new ideas, information, and experiences."

(Peter B. Vaill)

  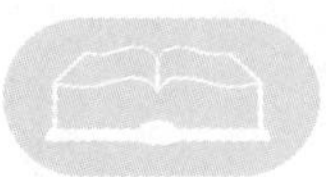    

MAKING RECOGNITION AND REWARDS A "WHOLE-PERSON" EXPERIENCE

by R. Brayton Bowen

EXECUTIVE SUMMARY

- The 21st century requires a holistic approach to recognizing and rewarding employees.
- It's possible to place too much emphasis on pay and other extrinsic rewards.
- The changing nature of the relationship between employers and employees requires a new kind of "currency."

INTRODUCTION

Managing people is increasingly complex. Markets expand globally. Labor forces grow invisible and offices are virtual. People are less committed to organizations emotionally. And running a successful enterprise has become more difficult and competitive. What are the best ways to engage, activate, and motivate employees?

From hourly wages to piece rates, and profit sharing to gain sharing, the number of incentive programs and pay packages is legion. But why do some employees check out—operationally, emotionally, even physically—while others tune in? Why are some organizations confounded by poor returns from reward systems while others rocket ahead? The answer lies in a *whole-person* approach to recognizing and rewarding employees.

Effective systems of recognition and reward engage an individual's entire being. They encourage employees to unleash stores of productive energy while exhibiting regenerative qualities that foster creativity, emotional reserves that translate into passion, and even spiritual attributes that result in the inspired performance needed to achieve a larger vision.

Successful managers respect both people and processes. Abandoning command-and-control management, they emphasize relationships. These managers regard employees as part of their customer base, continuously looking for ways to satisfy and retain employee commitment while ultimately inspiring them to peak performance.

THE NEW MILLENNIUM WORKPLACE

Today's labor force is diverse: Boomers, generation Xers, generation Y, former welfare recipients, the Net generation. Add multicultural and multiracial labor pools and the management challenge becomes enormous. Compensation experts and professional managers have realized that a one-size approach to human resources won't fit all. Different people have different values, needs, wants, and expectations, and unless these conditions can be addressed satisfactorily the outcomes can prove disastrous.

Employees are increasingly knowledge workers. No longer can the workplace house all employees under one roof under the watchful eye of a supervisor; workers often telecommute. Furthermore, individual contributors are joining teams, perhaps with team members scattered around the globe, prompting the need for yet more varied performance management systems and reward programs. Given this diversity, an appropriate blend of recognition and rewards must be available.

THE TRUTH ABOUT CARROTS, STICKS, MOTIVATION, AND REWARDS

Some experts have determined that incentives and alternative pay packages can have a positive influence on employee performance—short-term. Others claim that such packages actually have a negative influence, especially over the long term. Almost all agree it's essential to pay people fairly and competitively. Some experts are wrong, however, in arguing that pay is the chief motivator. For the welfare-to-work employee and minimum-wage earners, money is a basic need, not a motivator. In reality, motivation is an inside job; money may influence behavior, but it's no substitute for motivation. People require a greater sense of achievement and self-actualization.

Enlightened managers use total reward systems that link direct and indirect payments to performance requirements tied to the organization's success. Such an approach is far more effective than simpler, more restrictive, linear systems that function on a quid pro quo basis: produce this widget and you get x. But, even total reward packages fall short of achieving everything that's possible if they fail to engage the whole person. Leading systems are holistic.

MINI-CASES

HOLISTIC SYSTEMS OF REWARD AND RECOGNITION

Toyota encourages employees worldwide to generate new ideas at a rate of some 40,000 *per plant* annually, and each is recognized and rewarded according to its operational impact. Moreover, so imbued is Toyota's culture with concepts of quality, teamwork, and empowerment that a single employee can literally stop production for the good of the ultimate customer, without supervisory approval. Indeed, turning the organizational pyramid upside down is nothing new at Toyota, where managers are viewed as resources for team members and an "office" is simply a desk on the production floor accessible to the team.

Mary Kay Cosmetics may reward outstanding performers with pink Cadillacs, but the organization is focused on enhancing the self-esteem and economic independence of women, especially those who represent the company. Moreover, Mary Kay rewards and recognizes women while having fun. The combination of economic opportunity and psychic income has propelled the organization to phenomenal levels of growth.

Many other organizations, including Federal Express, the Body Shop, Hewlett-Packard, and Disney, have created environments and traditions that have appealed to the emotional, professional, and economic interests of employees. They use holistic systems of reward and recognition via:

- job design
- decision-making processes
- pay equity
- performance planning and management systems
- self-direction
- communication
- organizational culture
- leadership styles
- professional development

"They (employees) have to feel the rewards that go with winning—in the soul as well as in the wallet."

(Jack Welch)

A holistic system is open to incorporating anything that influences employees to unleash their motivation and passion. Holistic systems are especially valuable with free agents.

The Rise of the Free Agent

For some time companies have been downsizing to ensure profitability, even survival, during harsh economic times. Many redundancies have been of middle managers. People that remain, managers and nonmanagers alike, have had to demonstrate their value to their organization to stay employed. Gone is the old-style psychological contract for lifelong employment for performing employees.

The bad news: While companies have been getting meaner and leaner, worker commitment and personal energy to go all out has been lost. The good news: Employees have become more resourceful at finding ways to demonstrate and increase their worth to current and prospective employers. Smart employees see themselves as free agents and are continuously looking for ways to improve their skills, competencies, reputation, and marketability.

In Search of New Currency

Smart managers recognize the needs of free agents by engaging in practices that say: "I'll meet your needs; I expect you to meet mine." Let's work together! Free agents want flexibility to move through organizational systems without being locked in to one department. They want to be recognized and valued for the talents they bring and for results achieved. They prefer teams in which they can realize a more self-directed environment than they can in a single job reporting to a supervisor. While rewards are important, so, too, are responsibility, respect, recognition, and relationships. Moreover, because of their concern for independence and marketability, they have a critical need to protect their reputation; they gravitate to assignments that enhance their standing in the estimation of others.

The new currency that managers must use in today's workplace has respect as its underlying value. Even in situations in which organizations are known to or intend to downsize, smart managers understand the importance of respecting people's intelligence and telling it like it is. They work collaboratively with employees. They make conscious decisions to join forces instead of subordinating or dominating. And as newer systems such as skill-based pay, total-reward programs, pay-for-performance plans, and open-book management become more mainstream, the challenge for management will be to avoid any suggestion that they are manipulative or disrespectful. In fact, placing too much emphasis on pay and pay systems will detract from the intrinsic value of work itself.

Work As Its Own Reward

Recognizing the short-term nature of employment and the need to influence peak performance, organizations have generated elaborate programs to motivate employees, including informal awards (spontaneous shows of appreciation, thank-you gifts for special services) and formal awards (bonuses, prizes, trophies, service awards).

These are all extrinsic awards, providing recognition by means of factors external to the work itself, other examples include:

- base-pay packages
- variable pay plans
- incentives
- cash and cash equivalents
- benefits
- gain-sharing plans
- profit-sharing plans
- commissions
- stock options
- alternative pay programs

Intrinsic rewards, by contrast, are inherent to the nature of the work itself and the context or environment in which it is performed. They are innately energizing and satisfying, either because the work is pleasurable or because it fulfills individuals' desire to support the organization's mission or value system or their own relationships with colleagues. Enlightened managers know the importance of responsibility, respect, recognition, and relationships; these are intrinsically rewarding (and may ultimately result in extrinsic rewards). In the rush to motivate employees, any number of managers have invested heavily in extrinsic rewards, overlooking the enormous value of intrinsic rewards.

Indeed, one intrinsic value of work is that at some level it is a creative expression of self. That's why some people "love" their work. It helps them feel a sense of mission in their life. Consequently, by aligning personal needs, desires, and expectations with the needs of the enterprise, work can be performed, analyzed, and redesigned continuously to create a win-win situation for employer and employee.

The hard reality, however, is that it takes willingness on the part of managers and involvement on the part of employees to construct work assignments and processes that add value for all stakeholders. Indeed, in the new workplace employees will require more respect—and that means more recognition—to feel passionate about their work and motivated to excel. The shared objective for both managers and employees must be to find work that employees can come to love and that they feel valued in doing.

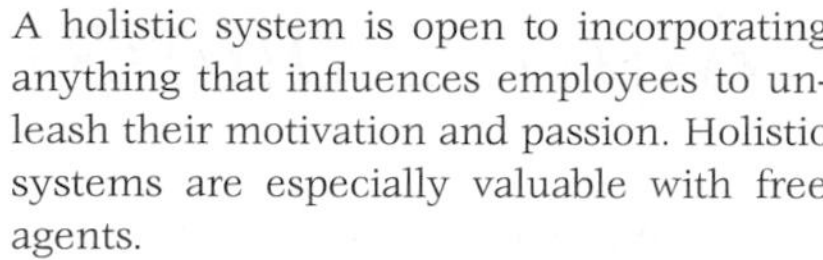

Making It Happen ▸▸

- Begin with a mindset that's passionate about making a difference in people's lives, not just the bottom line.
- Design an environment that encourages people to give their best—because they want to, not because they have to.
- Think big picture! Integrate rewards, benefits, and recognition with the entire work experience.
- Involve employees in the redesign process. Inclusion is the quintessential form of recognition.

Conclusion

True recognition is a whole-person experience. Said one employee, "I appreciate that my manager asks how I *feel* about a situation, then what I *think* about it, and lastly, what I want to *do*." The approach is holistic. It begins with feelings. Smart managers know they may engage the head, but they must also engage the heart of every employee. It's the only way to recognize and reward employees in the workplace of the new millennium.

For More Information

Book:

Hakim, Cliff. *We Are All Self-employed: The New Social Contract for Working in a Changed World.* San Francisco, CA: Berrett-Koehler, 1995.

Web Site:

www.worldatwork.org is a great association site for professionals in compensation, benefits, and total rewards.

See also:

☆ **Matching Pay to Achievement (pp. 297–98)**

"Commitment to objectives is a function of the rewards associated with their achievement."

(Douglas McGregor)

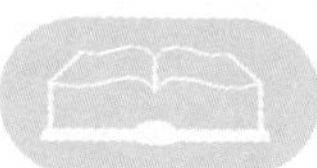

Downsizing with Dignity *by Alan Downs*

Executive Summary

- Downsizing (or redundancy) is a toxic solution. Used sparingly and with planning it can be an organizational lifesaver, but when used repeatedly without a thoughtful strategy it can destroy an organization's effectiveness.
- One outcome of downsizing must be to preserve the organization's intellectual capital.
- How downsized employees are treated directly affects the morale and retention of valued, high-performing employees who are not downsized.
- Downsizing should never be used as a communication to financial centers or investors of the new management's tough-minded, no-nonsense style of management—the cost of downsizing far outweighs any benefits thus gained.

Introduction

Make no mistake: downsizing is extremely difficult. It taxes all of a management team's resources, including both business acumen and humanity. No one looks forward to downsizing. Perhaps this is why so many otherwise first-rate executives downsize so poorly. They ignore all the signs pointing to a layoff until it's too late to plan adequately; then action must be taken immediately to reduce the financial drain of excess staff. The extremely difficult decisions of who must be laid off, how much notice they will be given, the amount of severance pay, and how far the company will go to help the laid-off employee find another job are given less than adequate attention. These are critical decisions that have as much to do with the future of the organization as they do with the future of the laid-off employees.

So what happens? These decisions are handed to the legal department, whose primary objective is to reduce the risk of litigation, not to protect the morale and intellectual capital of the organization. Consequently downsizing is often executed with a brisk, compassionless efficiency that leaves laid-off employees angry and surviving employees feeling helpless and demotivated.

Helplessness is the enemy of high achievement. It produces a work environment of withdrawal, risk-averse decisions, severely impaired morale, and excessive blaming. All of these put a stranglehold upon an organization that now desperately needs to excel.

Avoiding the Pitfalls of Downsizing

Ineffective methods of downsizing abound. Downsizing malpractices such as those that follow are common; they are also inefficient and very dangerous.

Allowing Legal Concerns to Design the Layoff

Most corporate attorneys will advise laying off employees on a last-hired, first-fired basis across all departments. The method for downsizing that is most clearly defensible in a court of law, for example, is to lay off 10% of employees across all departments on a seniority-only basis. This way no employee can claim that he or she was dismissed for discriminatory reasons. Furthermore, attorneys advise against saying anything more than what's absolutely necessary to either the departing employees or the survivors. This caution is designed to protect the company from making any implied or explicit promises that aren't then kept. By strictly scripting what is said about the layoffs, the company is protecting itself from verbal slips by managers who are themselves stressed at having to release valued employees.

This approach may succeed from a legal perspective, but not necessarily from the larger and more important concern of organizational health. First, laying off employees by a flat percentage across different departments is irrational. How can it be that accounting can cope with the same proportion of fewer employees as human resources? Could it be that one department can be externalized and the other left intact? The decision of how many employees to lay off from each department should be based on an analysis of business needs, not an arbitrary statistic.

The concept of laying off employees strictly on the basis of seniority is also irrational. The choice of employees for a layoff should be based on a redistribution of the work, not the date the individual employee was hired. Sometimes an employee of 18 months has a skill far more valuable than one with 18 years' seniority.

Give As Little Notice As Possible

Out of fear and guilt many executives choose to give employees as little forewarning as possible about an upcoming layoff. Managers fear that if employees know their fate ahead of time, they might become demoralized and unproductive—they may even sabotage the business. However, there is no documented evidence that advance notice of a layoff increases the incidence of employee sabotage.

The lack of advance notice, however, does dramatically increase mistrust of management among surviving workers. Trust is based on mutual respect. When employees discover what has been brewing without their knowledge or input (and they will when the first person is let go), they see a blatant disrespect for their integrity, destroying trust. By not giving employees information that could be enormously helpful to them in planning their own lives, management initiates a cycle of mistrust and helplessness that can be very destructive and require years to correct.

Afterward, Act As If Nothing Happened

Many managers believe that after a layoff, the less said about it the better. With luck, everyone will just forget and move on. Why keep the past alive? The reality is, surviving employees will talk about what's happened whether the management team does or doesn't. The more the company tries to suppress these discussions and act as if nothing has happened, the more subversive the discussion becomes. Remaining employees will act as a consequence of what has happened regardless of whether the management does.

Recovery from a layoff is greatly hastened if managers and employees are allowed to speak their minds freely about what's happened. In fact, it can be a great opportunity for the team of surviving employees to pull together and renew ties. When management refuses to acknowledge what has really taken place, it appears emphatically heartless, feeding the employees' sense of helplessness. If management won't talk about it even after the fact, what else is it hiding?

"To downsize effectively you have to have empathy with the people who are losing their jobs."

(Percy Barnevik)

  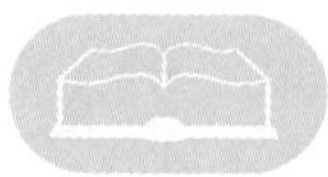    

Downsizing Effectively

When faced with an organization that isn't functioning at optimal efficiency and thinking that a layoff is needed, there are a few key principles to keep in mind. Observing these principles won't completely eliminate the dangers of downsizing, but they will help to avoid the common pitfalls of a poorly planned layoff.

Is the Problem Too Many People or Too Little Profit?

The critical first question to ask before any layoff is: Is the need for this layoff driven by having too many employees or too little profit? If it's too little profit, this is the first warning sign that your company isn't ready for a layoff. Using a layoff solely as a cost-cutting measure is utterly foolish: throwing away valuable talent and organizational learning by dumping employees only makes a bad situation worse. When your business lacks revenue, annihilating intellectual capital and thus reducing the efficiency of remaining resources as well as the potential for future growth is not the solution.

If the answer is too many employees, then you've begun the process of a well-thought-out strategy for change. To legitimately determine if you have too many employees, look at the organization's business plan, not its head count. What product and services will you be offering? Which of these products and services is likely to be profitable? What talent will you need to run the new organization? These questions will help you plan for the post-layoff future. These issues will enable a quick turnaround from the inevitably negative effects of downsizing to positive growth in value and efficiency.

What Will the Post-layoff Company Look Like?

Having a clear, well-defined vision of the new company is imperative *before the layoff is executed*. Management should know what it wants to accomplish, where the emphasis will be in the new organization, and what staff will be needed.

Without being directed according to a clear vision of the future, the new organization is likely to carry forward some of the same problems that initially created the need for the layoff. Unfortunately, many managers underestimate the momentum of the old organization to recreate the same problems anew. Unless there is a clearly defined, shared vision of the new company among the entire management team, the past will be likely to sabotage the future and create a cycle of repeated layoffs with little improvement in organizational efficiency.

Always Respect People's Dignity

The methods employed in many poorly executed layoffs treat employees like children. Information is withheld and doled out. Managers' control over their employees is violated. Human resource representatives scurry around from one hush-hush meeting to another. How management treats laid-off employees is how it vicariously treats remaining employees—everything you do in a layoff is done in the arena, with everyone observing. How laid-off employees are treated is how surviving employees assume they may be treated.

Why does this matter? Because successfully planning for the new organization will keep it going and improve its results. You must keep that exceptional talent, who are also the employees most marketable to other organizations. When they see the company treating laid-off employees poorly, they'll start looking for a better place to work, fearing their heads will be next to roll.

Respect the Law

While it's important not to allow the legal department to design a layoff, it's nevertheless important that you respect the employment laws. In different countries such laws include entitlements tied to civil rights, age discrimination, disabilities, worked adjustment, and retraining. These laws are important and should be respected for what they intend as well as what they prescribe—or proscribe. If you have planned your layoff according to business needs, and not on head count or seniority, you should have no problem upholding the law. You will almost always find yourself in legal trouble when you base your layoff on factors other than business needs.

Mini-cases

Good Examples

During the merger of *BB&T Financial Corporation* and *Southern National Corporation*, redundant positions were eliminated through the strategic use of a hiring freeze.

Hewlett-Packard implemented a so-called fortnight program in which all employees were asked to take one day off without pay every two weeks until business revenue increased.

Bad Example

Scott Paper conducted a layoff of 10,500 employees in the mid-1990s. In the years that followed Scott was unable to introduce any new products and saw a dramatic decrease in profitability, until it was eventually bought out by competitor Kimberly-Clark.

Making It Happen ▸▸

- Downsizing successfully is immensely difficult. The following ideas can help to focus thinking for anyone considering such a move.
- Treat all employees with dignity and respect. Communicate too much rather than withhold information.
- Research applicable laws and follow the spirit of the legislation.
- Afterward, give employees the psychological space to accept, and discuss, what has happened.

Conclusion

There are two important factors to keep in mind when planning a layoff: respecting employee dignity, and business planning. No one, from the mailroom to the boardroom, enjoys downsizing; but when the need for a reduction in staff is unavoidable, a layoff can be accomplished in such a way that the problem is fixed and the organization excels.

For More Information

Books:

Gertz, Dwight, and João P. A. Baptista. *Grow to Be Great: Breaking the Downsizing Cycle*. New York: Free Press, 1995.

Gordon, David M. *Fat and Mean: The Corporate Squeeze of Working Americans and the Myth of Managerial Downsizing*. New York: Free Press, 1996.

Web Sites:

www.amanct.org: the American Management Association site publishes one of the most comprehensive surveys of downsizing available.

www.hrps.org/html: the Human Resource Planning Society offers articles and meetings on effective human resource planning that will eliminate the need for layoffs.

See also:

- ☆ **Finding and Keeping Top Talent (pp. 33–34)**
- ☆ **Power Struggling and Power Sharing (pp. 95–96)**
- ☆ **Response Ability—How Managers Stay Up When Times Are Down (pp. 334–35)**
- ☆ **Viewpoint: Christopher Bartlett (pp. 45–46)**
- ✓ **Leaving with Style: How to Exit with Dignity (pp. 800–01)**

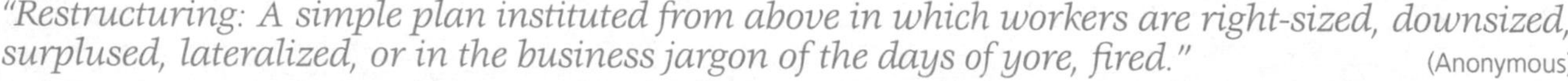

"Restructuring: A simple plan instituted from above in which workers are right-sized, downsized, surplused, lateralized, or in the business jargon of the days of yore, fired." (Anonymous)

MANAGING STRESS
by Cary L. Cooper and Susan Cartwright

EXECUTIVE SUMMARY

- Recognizing the symptoms of stress is an essential measure in taking immediate action to improve the situation.
- Understanding the causes and common sources of workplace stress is vital in preventing it becoming an issue.
- The changing nature of work makes stress in our lives more complex, varied, and quite possibly more common–and dealing with it quickly, early, and effectively is more important now than ever.
- There are a range of techniques and approaches to managing personal stress and these are explored in this section.

INTRODUCTION

The enterprise culture has entailed a substantial personal cost for many individuals. The cost is captured by a single word "stress." Indeed, stress has found as firm a place in our modern lexicon as "fast food," "mobiles," and CDs. "It's a high stress job," someone says, awarding an odd sort of prestige to his or her occupation. But to those whose ability to cope with day-to-day matters is at crisis point, the concept of stress is no longer a casual one; for them, stress can be translated into a four-letter word—*pain*.

BEHAVIORAL AND PHYSICAL SYMPTOMS OF STRESS

Pressure is motivating, stimulating, and energizing, but when pressure exceeds an individual's ability to cope then we are in the stress arena. When a number of the following behavioral and physical symptoms are frequently or nearly always experienced by an individual, it can indicate that he/she has crossed over the dividing line between mere pressure and harmful stress.

Behavioral Symptoms	Physical Symptoms
Constant irritability with people	Lack of appetite
Difficulty in making decisions	Craving for food when under pressure
Loss of sense of humor	Frequent indigestion or heartburn
Suppressed anger	Constipation or diarrhea
Difficulty concentrating	Insomnia
Inability to finish one task before rushing into another	Tendency to sweat for no good reason
Feeling the target of other people's animosity	Nervous twitches, nail biting, etc.
Feeling unable to cope	Headaches
Wanting to cry at the smallest problem	Cramps and muscle spasms
Lack of interest in doing things after returning home from work	Nausea
Waking up in the morning and feeling tired after an early night	Breathlessness without exertion
Constant tiredness	Fainting spells
	Impotency or frigidity
	Eczema

IDENTIFYING THE SOURCES OF WORKPLACE STRESS

Once an individual acknowledges that they are not coping as well with the everyday pressures of work, the next step in the process is to identify the source(s) of the stress at work. Once this is done, then the individual can draw up a plan of action to minimize or eliminate the excess pressure or damaging source of stress. Table 2 identifies some possible daily hassles that trouble people at work. There are of course more significant problem areas as well, such as coping with redundancy or dealing with a bullying boss or trying to cope with a dysfunctional corporate culture (for example, excessive working hours, autocratic management style).

Daily Hassles at Work	
Trouble with client/customer	Travelling associated with the job
Having to work late	Making mistakes
Constant people interruptions	Conflict with organizational goals
Trouble with boss	Job interfering with home/family life
Deadlines and time pressures	Can't cope with inbox
Decision-making	Can't say "No" to work
Dealing with the bureaucracy at work	Not enough stimulating things to do
Technological breakdowns, e.g. computer	Too many meetings
Trouble with work colleagues	Don't know where career going
Tasks associated with job not stimulating	Worried about job security
Too much responsibility	Spouse/partner not supportive about work
Too many jobs to do at once	Family life adversely affecting work
Telephone interruptions	Having to tell subordinates unpleasant things, e.g. redundancy
Traveling to and from work	

PERSONAL STRESS: MANAGING THE DAILY HASSLES

TIME MANAGEMENT

Of all the daily hassles experienced by managers, one of the most stressful is poor time management. Time wasters fall into several categories, requiring different solutions.

The Mañanas. Individuals who fall into this category cause themselves problems because they procrastinate, preferring to "think" about work rather than "do" it. Procrastination often stems from boredom, a lack of confidence, or reluctance to seek clarification. For Mañanas, here are some basic tips to effective time management:

- Break up overwhelming tasks into smaller jobs.
- Draw up a "to do" list of all the tasks you need to complete in the short term (that is, within the next week) and in the long term.

"Brain cells create ideas. Stress kills brain cells. Stress is not a good idea." (Doug Hall)

  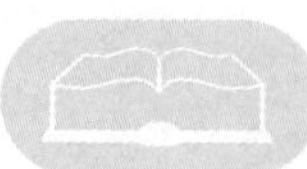    

- When planning your work schedule, attempt to balance routine tasks with the more enjoyable jobs.
- Accept that risks are inevitable, and that no decisions are ever made on the basis of complete information.

The Poor Delegators. Individuals who fall into this category waste a considerable amount of their time doing work that could easily and more effectively have been done by somebody else. They should consider some of the following:

- Delegation does not mean abdication.
- Always take time out to explain exactly what is required; poor delegators are often also poor communicators, which is why they are frequently disappointed with the efforts of others.
- Having delegated a job, leave the person to get on with it.
- Avoid taking on unnecessary work that does not fulfill your objectives or that could be done by others, by learning to say "no" politely and assertively.

The Disorganized. Individuals who fall into this category are instantly recognizable by the mounds of paper that form barricades around their desks. Disorganized individuals frequently miss or are late for appointments. These people frequently think their problems are due to work overload rather than their own poor organizational skills:

They need to:

- Plan effectively before taking action.
- Make a "to do" list regularly at the start of each day and review it each evening.
- Stick to one task and finish it!
- Think before they telephone, drawing up a list of all the information they require from the caller.
- Identify their prime time for working, when their energy levels are high for the complex task, and save the trivial routine tasks for non-prime time.
- When making an appointment in their diary, enter a finish time as well as a start time.

The Mushrooms. Individuals who fall into this category are usually unclear about the purposes, aims, and objectives of what they are required to do. They constantly speculate and inwardly question what they should do rather than do it. They basically lack assertiveness and communication skills. The two most important things for them to do are:

- Learn to say "I don't know," when they don't know something.
- Learn to say "I don't understand" when they don't understand a task, a role or objective.

Managing Interruptions

Another source of personal stress at work for many managers are "constant interruptions," from the telephone, email, drop by colleagues, etc.

New technology

In terms of voice mail, email, mobile phones, and the like, it is important to manage the technology rather than let the technology manage you. There are some general rules that apply to each of the technologies most of us work with and which create unnecessary personal pressure.

For telephone calls: batch phone calls; plan what you are going to say and need to know in advance; and deliberately discipline yourself by placing specific time limits on the length of a call.

For voice mail: use this when you need space to complete complex tasks requiring your full attention, and don't be tempted to access your voice mail messages every ten minutes! Also deal with those messages that are most important first; deal with the others later.

For emails: print off your emails and then prioritize them in order of the most important to deal with in terms of your objectives, then reply to them in this order. All too often, individuals reply to emails in order of their arrival and not in terms of their importance.

For mobiles: don't have it on all the time because it could interrupt some important meeting or activity. Use mobiles on journeys or other periods of downtime to deal with work in your in-tray that you would otherwise have to deal with when back at work.

Drop-by colleagues

Although being interrupted can provide a welcome diversionary break from a boring or tedious task, too many interruptions during the course of the day are a waste of time, distracting, and frequently irritating. There are a range of strategies for controlling these kinds of interruptions.

- Establish quiet hours during which you can work undisturbed. This may mean closing your door and putting a notice outside.
- Establish visiting hours when you are available for drop-in visitors.
- Arrange meetings away from your desk or office; this enables you to take control and leave when you want to.
- Do not hesitate to curb wafflers, in a polite and friendly manner, by asking them to make their main point(s).
- When unexpectedly interrupted, ask the person how much time he or she needs, and if you haven't got the space, then rearrange the meeting.

Interruptions

Interruptions occur for a number of reasons. The person involved may

1. want to exchange information;
2. need reassurance or clarification;
3. lack confidence about a task;
4. want a casual chat because they need a break or are bored, etc.

It is important to attempt to differentiate these, so if it is important to their doing their job properly, you may need to spend some of your time with them, if not, then use some of the above suggestions.

The Changing Nature of Work

Finally, one of the major overriding sources of stress for managers and others today is the fact that jobs are no longer for life—that job security is a vestige of the past. Under the terms of the "new" psychological contract, organizations expect employees to be more flexible, more accountable, and to be hardworking and committed; at the same time, employers offer increasingly limited (or no) assurances or expectations of employment security and career development opportunities. It is not hard to imagine that for significant numbers of future workers, the job is likely to become a freelance activity in the form of a series of temporary or discretely defined tasks or projects undertaken either successively or concurrently for single or multiple employers. For this, the individual receives financial payment, negotiated in advance, either on a fixed-cost basis or dependent on results achieved.

For those individuals currently working in "delayered" organizational structures, coping with changed career expectations requires considerable personal adjustment: one must accept that the onus for career management and training now rests with oneself rather than with the organization. This requires a greater degree of self-initiative and personal planning and control. Although the prospect of pursuing a self-determined career outside the structure of an established organization might seem daunting, research evidence based on experiences of midlife career changes suggests that increased job and life satisfaction is frequently gained from a move to freelancing and self-employment.

Making It Happen ▸▸

To minimize and handle your own stress you should:

- **Understand yourself**—understand what causes *you* stress, when you are likely to become stressed, and how

"I think in every country that there is at least one executive who is scared of going crazy."

(Joseph Heller)

you can avoid these situations. To help, it can be useful to think about previous times that were stressful for you and remember how you felt, how you reacted and behaved, what the result was and whether, with the benefit of hindsight, you handled it in the best way possible.

- **Take responsibility**—too often people either deny their problem, in which case it will almost certainly worsen, or blame someone (or something) else. Even if it is the fault of someone else it is *you* that is being affected and *you* that needs to resolve it. People are often too afraid, ashamed or uncertain to admit that they are suffering from stress, but the longer they delay the worse become the effects of the downward cycle.
- **Consider what is causing stress**—is it resulting from the job, your role, work relationships, change, or something else, perhaps not work related at all? Knowing the symptoms and acknowledging the existence of stress is really only the start: the next key step is to identify the source of the stress. This is often complicated by the fact that stress may often be caused by an accumulation of factors piling onto each other. The solution is to rationally consider how to take down the wall that is encircling you, brick by brick. Stress is rarely removed in one swift leap but often requires action in a range of areas.
- **Anticipate stressful periods (either at work or home) and plan for them**—this may include getting temporary resources or people with specific skills to help during a particular period.
- **Develop strategies for handling stress**—consider what may have worked for you in the past, what you did, and how successful it was. Also consider removing or reducing the cause of stress, or learning to accept it if it cannot be removed.
- **Understand and use management techniques to prevent or reduce stress**—for example, time management and assertiveness are two of the most important skills in reducing and handling stress, as many difficulties are caused either by time pressures or relationship issues that could be prevented by more assertive, controlled behavior. Communication, decision-making and problem-solving also have much to offer once the problem has been acknowledged and the sources of stress are identified.
- **Relax**—easier said than done, but the key is to understand that you need to *work* at relaxing! This may mean planning a holiday or finding a hobby or club that suits you best, and then *absorbing* yourself in it. Time away from the causes of stress can help to put the situation in perspective and lead to a new approach that provides a solution.

If you are responsible for preventing and reducing stress within organizations, you should:

- **Acknowledge stress in others** – as a leader you should not be afraid to comment to someone if you think they are suffering from stress, and then be prepared to help and support them in breaking the downward cycle. Often, just acknowledging the existence of stress and showing understanding can provide enough energy to see the solution, remove the stress, and ultimately overcome the problem.
- **Build a positive team or work environment**—as a leader it is possible to reduce stress for others by developing good communication systems, a supportive team approach, a blame-free environment, and a clear sense of involvement and responsibility. Other factors that can also help include mentoring schemes that prevent, identify, and treat cases of stress; appraisal systems, and simply knowing and understanding the people that work with you. For some senior managers in large organizations this may not be possible, in which case these values need to be passed down the chain of command so that they are supported throughout the organization.

CONCLUSION

In the end, we should begin to truly understand what the English writer and critic John Ruskin said in 1851:

"In order that people may be happy in their work, these three things are needed: they must be fit for it; they must not do too much of it; and they must have a sense of success in it."

For More Information

Books:

Cartwright, Susan, and Cary L. Cooper. *Managing Workplace Stress*. Thousand Oaks, CA: Sage, 1997.

Cooper, Cary L., and S. Palmer. *Conquer Your Stress*. London: Chartered Institute of Personnel and Development Books (CIPD Books), 2000.

Makin, P., Cary L. Cooper, and C. Cox. *Organizations and the Psychological Contract*. Westport, CT: Greenwood Publishing Group, 1996.

"One is more likely. . .to perceive a situation of overload when one has many things demanded. . . than when fewer things are demanded." (Rabi Bhagat)

  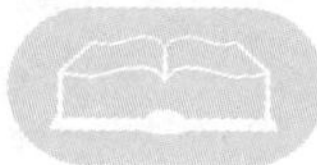    

Fringe Benefits *by John G. Fisher*

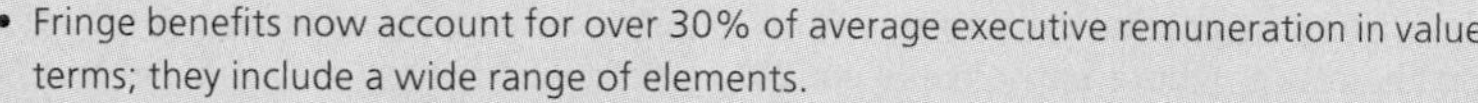

Executive Summary

- Fringe benefits now account for over 30% of average executive remuneration in value terms; they include a wide range of elements.
- Offering nonsalary benefits is seen as crucial in recruiting and retaining staff in a virtually full-employment market.
- Flexible benefits packages offer significant advantages in the management of employee benefits, but administration is still the big issue.
- E-benefits applications are now available to handle administration via the Internet.
- The balance between cash and noncash within the benefits package is changing.
- Personalized remuneration through flexible benefits will become the norm in the 21st century.

Introduction

Employee welfare policies, or benefits, as they are known today, were initiated in the late 19th century as an attempt by Victorian patriarchs to retain staff and to refute the often-made suggestion that industry exploited the working classes without providing any financial or social security. So strong was the pressure on employers to play a paternal as well as an economic role that successive administrations brought in legislation throughout the 20th century to ensure that some fringe benefits were statutory rather than optional.

But the days when employers could get away with offering only paid vacations, severance, sick days, or even pension plans are long gone. Today's employees have much higher expectations, driven by the double-income way of life. Benefits consultants are often asked to research employee attitudes to fringe benefits before implementing new plans. The main drivers of benefits choice in most employee groups are more time off, better health, making ends meet, flexibility should circumstances change, value for money, job security, prospects for advancement, and status (both perceived and actual). These findings are reflected in the wide range of fringe benefits now being offered by employers.

Today's Range of Fringe Benefits

The Reward Group, a remuneration research agency, conducted a survey of 35,000 members of the U.K. Chartered Institute of Personnel Development in 1999 to establish which fringe benefits were the most popular. Measured by employee takeup, the following ranking of preferences emerged in questions about family-friendly benefits:

1. paternity leave
2. parental/domestic leave
3. stress management
4. telecommuting
5. job-sharing

The following rank order was recorded for benefits relating to career and health advice:

1. health screening
2. mentoring
3. stress management
4. career counseling
5. bereavement counseling

These are all life-event concerns and should rightly form the core of any modern benefits program. But less essential elements are also common, for example, dental insurance, legal advice, daycare, elderly parent support, health-club membership, household insurance, automobile insurance, home computer, automobile, parking, continuing education, relocation assistance, gas, to name a few.

But the offer of such benefits has significant cost implications that are often overlooked by employees. In the late 1980s Chrysler calculated that up to $800 per car produced was spent on hidden employee benefits such as life insurance, pensions, and sickness/disability insurance. Often these benefits were underappreciated and misunderstood by employees. Costs were spiraling out of control. In order to reduce costs the company began to present the benefits to employees with specific costs attached in the form of benefit credits. This led to offering employees a choice of how much of each benefit they wanted up to a prescribed limit depending on their personal circumstances. Similar programs sprang up in other parts of the United States, Canada, and Australia as trade journal articles extolled the virtues of benefits transparency. Known as *flex plans*, these programs opened up the debate on the efficiency of employee benefits as a retention and loyalty device.

Flexible Benefits

The principle of flexible fringe benefits is that one size does not fit all; the more personalized your benefits package, the more likely employees are to value it as part of their remuneration. A single person under 30 has a very different way of life from a 45-year-old married main-income earner with children. Senior directors have different priorities from junior data-processors. The solution is to offer a portfolio of benefits up to a set value, the elements of which employees can mix and match according to personal circumstances.

A major U.K. telecommunications company with more than 10,000 staff was spending over $70 million a year on benefits that were largely unappreciated by employees. They included the usual collection of insurance, pensions, and automobile allowances that everyone was given regardless of circumstances. With a new company initiative to treat employees as individuals, the company decided to flex its benefits. Within their specific benefits credit level, employees were allowed to choose varying levels of pension, life insurance, health and dental care, paid vacation, company car, and childcare. Subsequent research showed that employees were genuinely appreciative of being able to choose benefits to suit their own circumstances. No figures were released as to whether the initiative actually improved retention rates, but the likelihood is that it did.

Administration Aided by the Internet

Until quite recently running flex plans was a complex, expensive job involving external benefits consultancies and significant internal systems enhancements. But thanks to the recent accessibility of applications over the Internet, the management of such programs can now be outsourced to online benefits agencies that not only administer the detail, but can liaise directly with staff via an intranet or the Internet itself.

"We listen to what our employees want and it shows up in everything from the layout of our offices to the benefits and amenities."

(Raul Fernandez)

Companies such as Eurobenefits.com, Pensionzone.co.uk and Enviego.com—and in the United States, Probusiness.com and Onlinebenefits.com—all offer a basket of benefits products from which the employer can choose what to offer staff. Such services are of particular interest to companies that operate internationally and wish to manage common cross-border benefits administration.

The Future of Fringe Benefits

Many employees now enjoy fringe benefits never dreamed of by their grandparents. As society becomes more affluent and the economy perhaps more efficient, employers will need to be more open about what fringe benefits they offer within an increasingly competitive job market. We'll see more job ads showing salary-plus-benefits level as the standard format. The ability to deliver benefits glitch-free at the individual level, both domestically and cross-border, will be a basic requirement for every major employer in the 21st century.

Mini-case

Proper Communication Is Vital

When *Saatchi & Saatchi* decided to introduce a flex plan into its North American subsidiary, not everything went as expected. Managers gave themselves only three months to introduce it, and by their own admission did little to consult with staff or think through the communications process. The existing benefits were simply repackaged. The new program had a poor takeup, with most employees perceiving the subject as irrelevant and boring.

A new approach was tried, involving 22 focus groups and a thorough features vs. advantages analysis from the point of view of the potential recipients. Flex choices could be made on-screen, so that participants didn't have to have an appointment with human resources to get things going. Five new benefits were offered, reflecting the lifestyle of different employee groups. Everyone was included in the new program, not just management. Promotions included telephone-booth information points dotted around the office, where participants could put specific questions about their individual situation directly to human resources. Office posters, brief memos, and eye-catching flyers were devised to get the key points across on an ongoing basis. Team briefings were held at crucial times of the financial year.

Making It Happen ⏩

In introducing a flexible benefits plan, it's important to take a few key steps.

- Consult with staff through focus groups before going live.
- Recognize employee needs for time off, healthcare, making ends meet, flexibility if circumstances change, value for money, security, prospects for advancement, and status (both perceived and actual).
- Offer family benefits from the following list (ranked in order of preference): paternity leave, parental/domestic leave, stress management, telecommuting, job-sharing.
- Again in order of preference, choose from these health and career benefits: health screening, mentoring, stress management, career counseling, bereavement counseling.
- Create both formal and informal advice mechanisms.
- Decide how the features can be promoted as advantages.
- Monitor the cost of benefits with great care; use flexible provision, with employee choice, to optimize cost-effectiveness.
- Consider outsourcing management of a flexible plan to an online benefits agency that will administer the detail and liaise directly with staff via the Web.
- Communicate throughout the year, not just at launch, and use research to check that your benefits plan is achieving high employee satisfaction.

For More Information

Book:

Nelson, Bob. *1001 Ways to Reward Employees*. New York: Workman, 1994.

Web Site:

www.eurobenefits.com:
Eurobenefits.com claims to be the first Web-based benefits agency, designed to offer individual advice at any time online with versions in most of the European languages. The system is Internet-based but can be routed through local intranets with relatively modest access fees, charged per employee. Site navigation is clear and the wording is mostly in lay terms so that all levels of employees can understand the advice being given. New software is being developed to enable employees to actually change their choices online, although with some core benefits, they may be referred to an accredited financial adviser before the change can actually be implemented.

See also:

☆ **Making the Workplace Flex, Not Break (pp. 31–32)**
☆ **Retaining Employees (pp. 196–97)**

Making Performance Appraisals a Win-win Experience *by Patrick Forsyth*

EXECUTIVE SUMMARY

Despite the clear necessity for performance evaluation, many managers dislike conducting appraisals. Worse, many people rate their appraisals as worthless—or something even less flattering. In reality appraisals are a major opportunity for both managers and staff.

This checklist will review:

- Why appraisals are necessary and will examine the benefits to managers and staff. Primarily, they ensure and improve future performance.
- How effective appraisals should be planned and undertaken to maximize their positive impact while avoiding negative pitfalls.
- The impact of appraisals on the long-term success of the organization. Appraisals provide considerable opportunity for improving ongoing operations, effective management, and catalyzing change.

Introduction

There are many reasons why appraisals are necessary. Positive reasons include the opportunity to:

- review individuals' past performance;
- plan their future work and role;
- set and agree on specific individual goals for the future;
- identify development needs and set up development activity;
- provide on-the-spot coaching;
- obtain feedback;
- reinforce or extend the reporting relationship;
- act as a catalyst to delegation;
- focus on longer-term career progression;
- underpin or increase motivation.

Often a negative reason is the close relationship between appraisals and employment legislation (for example, lack of appraisal may make it impossible to terminate someone's employment). This is also a factor to keep in mind.

Overall the underlying intention is to improve future performance. The good appraisal presupposes that even the best performance can be improved, and seeks to increase the likelihood of future plans being brought to fruition.

Prepare Carefully

Unsurprisingly, the key to effective appraisals is preparation by both parties.

The *appraiser* must:

- Spend sufficient time with staff during the year.
- Communicate clearly and thoroughly the purpose and form of the appraisal so that people know what to expect. Employees should understand the need for appraisal, its importance, the specific objectives it addresses, and how both parties can get the best from it.
- Prepare throughout the year, keeping clear records. Keeping an appraisal collection file means you don't have to rely on memory. In this, you should note matters that can usefully be raised at appraisals, making notes and filing copies of documents that will assist the process.

The *appraisee* should keep running records and should plan in detail the kind of meeting he or she intends to have.

Successful appraisal is the culmination of a year's worth of thinking. Recalling every detail of a subordinate's working year is difficult, but being seen to be conducting an interview on the basis of incomplete information risks loss of credibility. Managers can only appraise successfully by being informed.

Relevant background information needs checking, for example, the appraisee's job description (which may need amendment after the appraisal), specific past objectives, possible changes to the job, its responsibilities, or circumstances, and the records of any previous appraisals.

Sound preparation gives appraisal meetings structure.

Work the System

It is not the purpose here to specify exactly how formal measurement in appraisal systems should work. But the measurement—rating scale—must ensure consistency, clarity, and fairness.

- Create a good, manageable system or familiarize yourself with what you must use.
- Make its constructive purposes clear.
- Communicate all procedures, documentation, and action clearly to appraisees.
- Use the process objectively.

Details matter; for example, many favor rating scales with the total number even to eliminate the temptation to rate too many criteria as average.

Ultimately you may need to balance what suits you best and what the system you use necessitates. Attention to detail is vital; the following outlines a systematic approach likely to work well.

Before the Appraisal Interview

- *Prepare written notification.* As well as confirming mutually convenient timing, this should recap the purpose of the appraisal and highlight background information. Distribute copies of any documents or forms you intend to use or refer to during the meeting.
- *Study the individual's file.* Make sure you have all the information you need about what was supposed to happen during the year and what actually did happen. Make notes of points needing discussion and see to it that you can navigate the documents easily as the meeting progresses.
- *Check performance factors.* Review agreed-on standards and identify any that are no longer relevant or that need to be changed.
- *Draft a provisional assessment.* Brief notes can provide a starting point, prompt the agenda, and link to the system. Don't prejudge the discussion or make decisions prematurely.
- *Critique your initial thoughts.* Check your rationale, asking yourself a why question about anything noted at this stage. If no clear answer comes, more research may be necessary.
- *Consider specific areas of the appraisal.* It may be clear that some training is necessary, for example. Again without prejudging, it may be useful to check out what might be appropriate and formulate a suggestion before the meeting.
- *Think ahead.* Remember that the most important part of the discussion will be about the future. You may need to plan particular projects and tasks, taking both

"It is much more difficult to measure nonperformance than performance." (Harold S. Geneen)

development and operational considerations into account.

- *Consult with others.* Speak to those who work or deal with the appraisee to get a complete picture.
- *Be clear about the link with pay review.* Many managers feel this should be kept for a separate occasion. Otherwise it can be difficult to stop appraisees from thinking all that matters is the potential raise.

Setting Up the Interview

- *Allow enough time.* You need to do the job and also to reflect the importance of the occasion. Few appraisals will be accomplished properly in less than an hour; some may last two or three hours or more—and will still be time usefully spent.
- *Allow no disturbances.* Pausing to take even one telephone call sends out the wrong signals.
- *Create the right environment.* Appraisals should be held somewhere comfortable, perhaps less formal than across a desk, yet suitably businesslike.
- *Put the individual at ease.* Recognize that even with good communication beforehand, appraisals may be viewed as somewhat traumatic. Anything that can be done to counter this is useful.

During the Meeting

- *Spell out the agenda and how things will be handled.* Ask what priorities the appraisee wants recognized.
- *Act to direct the proceedings.* Do not, however, ride roughshod over the appraisee.
- *Ask questions.* Open questions prompt and focus discussion.
- *Listen.* The meeting is primarily an opportunity for the appraisee to communicate. In a well-conducted appraisal, the appraisee should do most of the talking; the manager's job is to make that happen.
- *Keep primarily to performance factors.* Don't indulge in amateur psychology or attempt to measure personality factors.
- *Use the system.* Use systems and appraisal forms to guide the meeting; working through the form systematically will ensure that most of what needs to happen does.
- *Encourage discussion.* Consider the appraisee's personal strengths and weaknesses, successes and failures, and their implications for the future.
- *Set out action plans.* Describe those that can be decided there and then (who will do what, when); note those needing more deliberation in terms of when and how action will be taken. Deal with each factor separately, for example, by devoting time to develop action.
- *Explain the basis of assessment.* Make the basis and reasons for your assessment clear. Be firm about your decisions.
- *Conclude on a positive note.* Always thank the appraisee for the role he or she has played and for the past year's work. Link this to any subsequent documentation.

After the Meeting

There is one key action here: to complete all documentation and confirmations that are necessary promptly after the meeting. Send copies to the appraisee, flagging any opportunity for further discussion. Also send copies to central departments such as personnel as well as your own file.

Making It Happen ▸▸

- Make sure that everybody understands the need for appraisal, its importance, its objectives, and its mutual benefits.
- Prepare throughout the year, keeping clear records and notes to assist the appraisal process.
- Keep primarily to performance factors, getting the appraisee to do most of the talking—while you listen hard.
- Concentrate the appraisal process on future performance, and don't confuse it with discussion of remuneration.
- Link appraisal deliberately with training and development, and with consultation, counseling, mentoring, and motivation.
- Follow up appraisals promptly, sending all necessary written material to the appraisee and flagging any opportunity for further discussion.

Conclusion

Appraisals are not one-shot deals. No manager can afford to heave a sigh of relief afterward and forget about them for another year. Appraisals achieve most when placed in a long-term context and linked to ongoing operations. Consider

- the ongoing management relationship: an effective appraisal should make all management processes through the year easier
- the link with training and development: consultation, counseling, mentoring, and informal discussions are all just as important extensions of appraisal as formal training
- motivation: appraisals must themselves be motivational, and what stems from them must assist ongoing motivational activity.

For whatever reasons (and there may be many, such as unease with the process, or inflexibility of systems), the considerable opportunity of appraisals is often missed or diluted.

Appraisals are not only a vehicle for change, one that can be precise and powerful, they're also a catalyst for effective management, and thus effective performance. The benefits are considerable and tangible.

For More Information

Books:

McKirchy, Karen. *Powerful Performance Appraisals.* Reprint. Franklin Lakes, NJ: Career Press, 1998.
Sachs, Randi Toler. *Productive Performance Appraisals.* New York: AMACOM, 1992.

See also:

☆ **Matching Pay to Achievement (pp. 297–98)**
☆ **New Yardsticks for Performance and Productivity in an E-world (pp. 285–86)**

"Distinguish between the person and the behavior or performance." (Stephen Covey)

  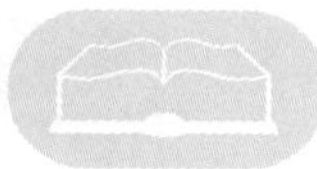    

IMPROVING COMPANY PERFORMANCE WITH AN OLDER WORKFORCE *by Beverly Goldberg*

EXECUTIVE SUMMARY

- The workforce is getting older and this is having a significant impact on the corporate world.
- Those companies that recognize the value of older workers now and create a flexible workplace aimed at attracting and retaining them will have an enormous advantage when the baby boomers begin to reach 65 in 2010.
- Older workers have many clear advantages that prove an invaluable means of using resources effectively and securing competitive advantage. Statistically, older workers have been shown to bring experience, flexibility, loyalty, and reliability, as well as providing a cost-effective means of financing specific projects.
- Despite these advantages, the harsh economic reality facing organizations is that to meet increased and changing future demand, companies will need to address the shortfall in younger employees to meet customer demand. It is essential, therefore, that companies shed their erroneous, stereotypical view of older workers and adopt a strategy of attracting and retaining them. Future success will depend on it.

INTRODUCTION

The months before the collapse of so many dot-coms in 2001 were marked by the influx of senior executives into a once totally youthful culture. These new companies, usually started by twenty-somethings with brilliant, innovative ideas, suddenly brought in older business managers with old-economy experience, to help them weather what seemed like bumps on the fast road to success. For all too many it turned out to be too little, too late.

The lesson of the dot-coms is clear: experience counts. The world's industrial societies remain youth-oriented, even though the so-called baby boomers, the group that brought about this orientation, are now in their mid-fifties.

The aging of the baby boomers, a demographically dominant group born between the end of World War II and 1964, will bring a dramatic change in the age makeup of both the general population of the industrialized countries and the workplace. For example, in 2025, more Italians will be over than under 50 years old. In 2010, in the United Kingdom there will be 25% more workers aged between 45 and 49 than aged 25 to 29. The median age of the U.S. workforce will reach 40 in 2005, and in 2010 50% of all prime-age workers will be over 45.

Moreover, people in the industrialized nations have been retiring well before the usual retirement age. The result: according to the Organization for Economic Cooperation and Development, workforce participation by people over 55 will have to increase by about 25% to maintain a constant employment-to-population ratio from 2005 onward. The message: companies that don't retain and recruit older workers won't be able to meet demand, let alone grow.

Older workers, however, are not just bodies to fill vacancies. Companies need older workers for their experience, institutional memories, work ethic, and, perhaps surprisingly, their ability to accommodate change and to focus—moreover they're likely to remain with an organization longer than younger workers.

A VALUE-ADDED PROPOSITION

Unfortunately, many beliefs about older workers result in companies deciding that younger workers are a better-value proposition when it comes to hiring, training, and retention—these beliefs are patently false.

- **Older workers cost more.** While the actual salaries of new, younger replacements may be lower, there are hidden costs of replacing older workers, for example, severance pay and agency fees for replacements. Corning Glass spends around $40,000 replacing each lost worker. Merck estimates that retraining a successor costs about one-and-a-half times the new person's average salary.
- **Older workers are less creative.** While younger workers may come up with a larger number of ideas in meetings, fewer of those ideas prove to have value. Some have already been tried and have failed, others don't work in the company's culture. Measuring the ultimate value of new ideas is more important than measuring their number.
- **Older workers don't learn as well as younger workers.** Surveys show that the ratings of older workers increased between 1985 and 1994: the percentage of older workers rated excellent for flexibility rose almost 20%; the percentage of older workers who are comfortable with new technology rose almost 15%. One problem may be that the average age of trainers is 33, also people learn differently depending on their age. For example, older workers unfamiliar with a classroom setting may do better learning one-on-one or on the shop floor.
- **Older workers aren't worth retraining, because they won't be around for long.** Today younger workers move from job to job quickly, because they haven't been raised in an environment in which corporate loyalty is a part of their thinking or tradition. Older workers remain longer, partly because they are more concerned about finding a new job if there is an economic slowdown.
- **Older workers have poorer attendance records.** Human resource managers report that older workers are less likely to be late or absent than younger workers. Also, workers over 55 account for 13.6% of the workforce, but only 9.7% of on-the-job injuries, and workers over 50 file far fewer worker compensation claims than younger workers.
- **Older workers are resistant to change.** False. The fastest-growing group of Internet users is people over 50. When training programs are made available to older workers, such as the programs offered by Microsoft Skills 2000, the Green Thumb, Inc., and the federal government, the number of applicants is far greater than the number of openings. More than 350,000 people between the ages of 50 and 64 were full- or part-time students pursuing degrees in the United States in 1998.
- **Older workers have less to contribute.** Not only do older workers contribute, but when organizations are concerned about maintaining their institutional history and values—and maintaining skills and

"Experience. n. The wisdom that enables us to recognize as an undesirable old acquaintance the folly that we have already embraced."

(Ambrose Bierce)

techniques when those remain constant—they turn to older workers. Older workers can train new workers by working side by side with them, passing on the expertise and experience accumulated over long years, often reducing formal training time. Moreover, it takes an institutional memory to answer such questions as, Why were certain decisions about processes made? Why don't we do business with company X? These are things that don't get captured in memos or expert systems; they're the stuff of history, stored in memory, and they're invaluable.

ATTRACTING OLDER WORKERS

No matter how much companies may want to keep older workers, however, they are likely to discover that many such workers don't want to stay—at least, not under the same conditions they had in the past. Many no longer want to devote their lives to work. Even though life expectancy has increased dramatically so that people are no longer afraid they'll never have time to do the things they've always wanted to if they put off retirement, the urge to enjoy life while they're fit and hearty is strong. People want to take that exotic vacation, spend time with grandchildren, take courses, or pursue hobbies now. And often work has become tedious and dull, partly because companies don't offer older workers training opportunities, leaving workers bored and interested in any form of change.

This is where companies need to be imaginative. We've been hearing about the new flexible organization for a decade, and now it's time for flexible companies to apply the concept of flexibility to employment, to wake up to the fact that they can hold on to valuable older workers by being creative. Some companies have adapted, and they're better positioned to take advantage when the baby boomers consider retiring. Flexible arrangements include:

- part-time permanent work, sometimes known as "bridge retirement"—these jobs are scheduled for less than 40 hours a week, whether fewer hours a day or fewer days a week. For those of actual retirement age, it might involve a contract reducing the number of workdays by one day a week for the first three months, two days for the next three, and so on until full retirement is reached.
- full-time and part-time temporary work—an interesting development is the creation of in-house temporary agencies for workers who have retired from the company. Travelers Corporation set up an agency two decades ago and has enjoyed considerable success, encouraging other companies to adopt similar programs.
- Contract work or consulting—this covers temporary assignments on specific projects rather than temporary work for different companies on an as-needed basis. Companies looking for workers for specific assignments often entice retired workers to return for the life of the project because they understand the corporate culture.
- telecommuting—working at home at least part of the time. For older employees, at-home work can make life easier, but it doesn't provide the social interaction that can make work attractive.
- on-call work—this arrangement, found most often in organizations such as hospitals that must be fully staffed at all times, involves a guaranteed minimum number of hours. It usually involves varying shifts, so is ideal for older workers who have few specific demands on their time.
- special assignments—these include temporary assignments, for example, serving on a disaster recovery project, representing the company in a community project, or working abroad. Whirlpool finds it less expensive to hire retired workers for short-term assignments abroad than to relocate full-time workers, while Quaker Oats has used retirees for a project in Shanghai. GTE has also tested this approach and plans to expand it.

MAKING IT HAPPEN ▸▸

Train older workers
Kevin Doran, vice president of human resources and government and public affairs at Philips in Somerset, New Jersey, says that the company has not found it necessary to take age into account when it comes to retraining. For example, when Philips adopted new enterprise software companywide, everyone received "equal training regardless of their demographics.

Take advantage of experience and institutional memory
Texas Refinery Corporation, based in Fort Worth, Texas, hires older workers as independent contractors (as well as full-time employees). In 1995, 500 members of its 3,000-person sales force were past retirement age. The independent contractors who work for the company receive commissions and benefits on the basis of their sales. The company likes these arrangements because it believes that older salespeople have a distinct advantage when it comes to client relationships and that they are inclined to be self-starters.

Be flexible
Neuville Industries of Hildebrand, North Carolina, set up a job-sharing program for employees over the age of 62. The program, which was initiated in the early 1990s, is aimed at employees with at least five years of experience. It provides for job-sharing with younger employees and allows employees to continue working for as long as they want to.

CONCLUSION

Over the next three decades the workforce in general will become older, and the baby boomers will begin to think strongly about retiring. Experience, people skills, a tradition of focus, a strong work ethic, and the desire and ability to learn make these older workers extremely valuable. Attracting and then finding ways to hold onto the best and brightest of these workers is going to be the key to success. Organizations must begin to address misconceptions about older workers and put in place programs to address their needs and aspirations.

For More Information

Books:

Ahlrichs, Nancy S. *Competing for Talent: Key Recruitment and Retention Strategies for Becoming an Employer of Choice*. San Francisco, CA: Davies-Black, 2000.
Zemke, Ron, Claire Raines, and Bob Filipczak. *Generations at Work: Managing the Clash of Veterans, Boomers, Xers, and Nexters in Your Workplace*. New York: AMACOM, 1999.

Web Sites:

www.thirdage.com: this site provides a great deal of information for older workers who want to participate in the world of work.
www.aarp.com: if you want to know what is happening in the world of those over 50, this is the site for you.

See also:

☆ **Generation Veneration (pp. 39–40)**

  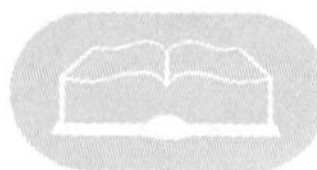  

VIEWPOINT: FONS TROMPENAARS

Redefining What It Means to Manage Globally

In the global business world, how cultures interact in a business setting remains a strangely overlooked area of study. Fons Trompenaars, who works alongside the British academic Charles Hampden-Turner, leads the way in promoting better understanding of the complex dynamics of multiculturalism. Fons has a Ph.D. from Wharton School, University of Pennsylvania, and worked with the Royal Dutch Shell Group in nine countries. He is now director of the Trompenaars Hampden-Turner consulting firm which has offices in the Netherlands and the United States.

Who is the most important person to have influenced your thinking?

Though he is not well known, my honest answer is that Hasan Ozbekhan, my Ph.D. supervisor, most influenced my thinking. Hasan is Turkish and comes from an oral tradition rather than a written one. Though he has written a lot, it has never been published. Russ Ackoff also influenced me, but Hasan's intellect was particularly impressive and he had a more European outlook. Both Russ and Hasan were heads of the social systems department at Wharton, where I spent two years doing the formal part of my degree.

I then did my research at Shell, a period during which many of the roots of my thinking were laid down. In terms of influential books, *The Phenomenology of the Social World* by phenomenologist Alfred Schutz is one I think almost everyone should read. Schutz argued that the big advantage of a natural scientist over a social scientist is that atoms and molecules don't talk back. We social scientists are observing a reality created by human actions, while natural scientists can't ask a molecule what it thinks about something. In social sciences you need to involve people—though consulting firms tend to forget that, even now.

I am more of a talker myself, though I do force myself to write sometimes—I write a column for the Dutch equivalent of the *Financial Times*, for example. But as with most of these things, the combination is important. People have different learning styles. I get my inspiration from talking; writing becomes easier when I have talked about something.

My last big mentor is Charles Hampden-Turner. Charles and I make a wonderful combination. There is no conflict between us, although we are completely different.

I have learned so much from Charles, who I met through Shell. The head of group planning suggested I read an article in a Shell magazine on the effects of culture on marketing. It was called "A tale of two paradigms" by Charles Hampden-Turner—he was a consultant to Shell at the time. It was depressing: I'd worked for five years on my Ph.D., and in one ten-page article it was all summarized and written in much more elegant English!

So I called Charles, and sent him my Ph.D. thesis. He came back and said, "Fons I think we can work together. I reconciled all of your seven dilemmas." That was in 1983; 15 years later I realized the importance of what he'd said.

Completely different again, but highly complementary and synergistic, has been my collaboration with Peter Woolliams, another U.K. university professor. Peter's strengths are his unique analytical skills and insights, which he can translate into software. Together we have built software tools which have enabled me to get closer to our clients through web-based interviews, and to capture thousands of business dilemmas across the globe.

How will business be different in the 21st century?

My Ph.D. was in the typical Anglo-Saxon, Western tradition of dividing culture into sections labeled separately with names such as individualism, communitarianism, and so on. But Charles argued that cultures can combine. If you're an individualist, why can't you also be a communitarian? Look at the success of the semiconductor industry: that takes individualists and forms very creative teams out of them. Reconciling such differences is at the heart of our work and of business in the 21st century.

"We need a readiness to enter a room in the dark and stumble over unfamiliar furniture until the pain in our shins reminds us of where things are."

(Fons Trompenaars)

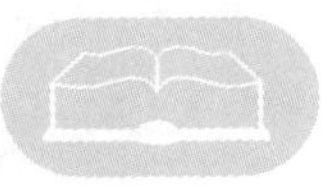

An example Charles uses is that of centralization and decentralization. A company only centralizes when it is decentralized. One value is always connected with its opposite; that's the essence of our work. Typical MBAs and educational systems teach that a person is in one category or another. How many so-called psychological tests or questionnaires place you in one box or another? You might be that one thing, but does that mean you don't also have characteristics from the opposite box?

I'm very hopeful that things will change. Look at the demand for our services. We help managers see the beauty of integration, of reconciliation. Such an outlook means that you do not have to say you are against shareholder value; instead you see that the only way to achieve shareholder value is to integrate it with its opposite. In other words, long-term shareholder value, by definition, is stakeholder value. I've never heard that discussed.

Our consulting firm has some competitors. The worst of them do not take the approach far enough. They say to clients, "Let me tell you what the French are like"; then they leave saying, "Good luck, you now understand them better." In fact it is usually worse, or the client understands the French better and thinks, "Now I know why I hate them!" You see the same thing frequently in the M&A world, where consultants are very good at diagnosing where the problem is. . .but that's where they stop.

The beauty of our work is that once you have explained about reconciliation, you can offer a methodology for achieving it, codifying it step-by-step. So once you identify a dilemma, you can chart it, you can stretch it, you can analyze it, and then come up with action points to resolve it.

We have been saying for a number of years that it would be a mistake to underestimate the counter forces of globalization. You can't live with the belief that there is just one best way of doing things. That kind of attitude is part of what causes upsets like the anti-capitalism protests in Seattle, Geneva, and so on. Becoming international needs to be reconciled with local cultures. Globalization needs to become conciliatory rather than imposing, if it is to be effective.

What new skills will be required?

For a long time, it's been known that an either/or attitude is not enough; and/and was far preferable. However, and/and is now not enough either; the approach should be through/through. So it is not a matter of shareholder value *and* stakeholder value, it is shareholder value *through* stakeholder value. It is not marketing *and* R&D, but marketing *through* R&D. Business should be asking through/through questions rather than and/and questions.

Among the new skills managers will need are the ability to connect and to ask different questions. The trouble is that there aren't too many holistic people—look at statesmen or business leaders—with an overview, a long-term commitment, who think with the heart and with the brain.

Are there new management questions we should be asking?

I wish we were better educated in asking the right questions. This is a good question. MBA education is answer-driven. I annoy MBA students by giving them a test after five or so lectures. I ask "What is the best question you can ask? Please ignore the answer, it doesn't matter." They get upset and say that I should be asking the questions, not them. But our work is about questions rather than answers.

MBA students are often taught to give the most brilliant answers to what are fundamentally the wrong questions. We need to go beyond that. You can, personally, become more demanding of yourself.

There are thousands of consultants who are very intelligent, but their intelligence is often restricted to one value. Companies also need to think more broadly than concentrating on the single issue shareholder value. Or at least they need to realize that, in the long term, shareholder value is only created by social responsibility. It pays back—but you still need to meet the bottom line to meet social goals. It is like a circle. You can argue about where you start the circle and where you end it. In that sense I'm optimistic. We are no longer working for pure physical survival.

How can companies promote enterprises which are profitable and, at the same time, good places for people to work?

Let me give you a simple example. There are conferences entitled things like, "Should we believe in shareholder value?" You shouldn't even ask the question. Obviously the answer is "no," if it is only shareholder value. Everyone who works in business knows that your business is dying if shareholder value is your only value. It leads to short-termism.

I sometimes say that shareholder value is creating value for people who never share. I am not against shareholder value, but it should be considered alongside the value of other stakeholders.

For More Information

Books:

Trompenaars, Fons. *Riding the Waves of Culture: Understanding Cultural Diversity in Business.* 2nd ed. New York: McGraw-Hill, 1997.

Trompenaars, Fons, and Charles Hampden-Turner. *Building Cross-cultural Competence.* New Haven, CT: Yale University Press, 2000.

Trompenaars, Fons, and Charles Hampden-Turner. *21 Leaders for the 21st Century.* New York: McGraw-Hill, 2001.

Web Site:

THT Consulting: **www.thtconsulting.com**

See also:

☆ **Boosting Business Success through Diversity (pp. 29–30)**

"It's a gross distortion of nature to conceive of corporations as if they were Newtonian machines."

(Charles Hampden-Turner)

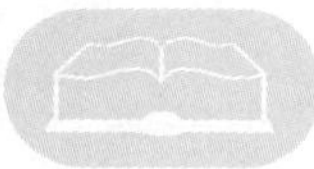

Boosting Business Success Through Diversity *by Debbe Kennedy*

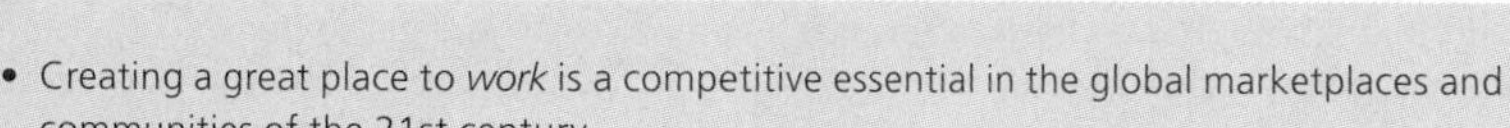

EXECUTIVE SUMMARY

- Creating a great place to *work* is a competitive essential in the global marketplaces and communities of the 21st century.
- Embracing many dimensions of difference and creating a culture of inclusion are key success factors. The business reasons are twofold: attracting and keeping the best people is a must to drive new levels of creativity and innovation; serving the changing needs of an increasingly diverse set of *customers* requires an organization with people that can understand, relate and respond.
- With practice, you can develop three diversity leadership disciplines that can boost business success: create a culture of inclusion, trust and mutual respect; lead by example every day; make diversity and inclusion organizational *habits* in all work.

Introduction

Regardless of your business, organizational goals, or where you live and work in the world, we share two undeniable areas of common ground as leaders. We all have a mission and we all have an increasingly diverse set of "customers" to serve both inside and outside our organizations. Whether your goals are bringing new product and service innovations to the marketplace, serving communities or nations, creating new wealth, or just getting better and better at your brand of excellence in any endeavor, it is clear that our leadership calling across industries, sectors, and geographies is to forge new paths–to lead the way, embracing new faces, cultures, and a broad array of differences in order to fully participate in the opportunities of the 21st century.

Interestingly, we have been talking about such realities all over the world as if they were some new phenomenon. In fact, this leadership calling is not new. Great leaders have always been able to tap into the best in people. You can see examples in the history and success stories of enduring global corporations like Hewlett-Packard, IBM, and General Electric of the United States, Kyocera Corporation of Japan, and Siemens of Germany, just to name a few. Each of them in their own unique way built success upon deeply held beliefs and values about people, striving to create an environment of mutual respect.

Today, leading corporations are expanding their focus on diversity and inclusion worldwide. Their purpose is one that touches every organization today: To attract and retain multicultural, multi-talented workforces. The aim is to enable them to connect and serve a multitude of new *customers* in emerging unexplored *markets,* reaching people, places and potential that will nourish them and ensure their continued business success.

The next generation of bold steps into a more richly diverse world rests with leaders like you. So, what is the link between diversity and business success? What can you learn from what others are doing to make diversity a competitive advantage? What diversity leadership disciplines are essential? These are the important questions we will explore.

The Business Case for Diversity

Don't make the mistake of seeing diversity and inclusion as "nice to do" moral issues, nor quickly dismiss them as North American problems. Not today. It is true that across the world we may need to deal with unique issues of difference in our workplaces, marketplaces, and communities. Additionally, our specific issues about creating an inclusive environment may also be unique, but in principle, a *culture of inclusion* operates in a similar way anywhere. *No one is left out.* More importantly, there is increasing evidence that the business case for diversity and inclusion is one that transcends geographic boundaries.

One of the most compelling presentations of the new business thinking surrounding the topics of diversity and inclusion comes from the research of futurist Joel A. Barker in his landmark film, *Wealth, Innovation, & Diversity.* In his research on innovation and creating new wealth he discovered some startling evidence in history, science, and industry that proves that innovation is driven by diversity and creates new wealth of:

- sustainability
- variety
- innovations
- efficient resource utilization
- new thinking
- lowered risks
- increased predictability
- improved productivity
- economic wealth

Leading companies are recognizing these truths and acting on them to position themselves for success.

Diversity Business Leadership Best Practices

Below are four companies that serve as examples for all of us. Each has a history of leadership in valuing people, reflected in their beliefs, policies and practices. Each is positioning itself for leadership in the 21st century, translating their enduring values into a new level of commitment to diversity and inclusion. Here is a sampling from their efforts:

Mini-cases

Hewlett-Packard (Corporate H.Q. U.S.)

Hewlett-Packard have strengthened their long-held commitment to diversity by establishing diversity and inclusion as key business priorities for HP's reinvention. Their expanded business focus incorporates diversity and inclusion in the marketplace, workplace, and the community, maximizing the opportunity for creativity, invention, profitability and fulfilling their vision of being "a winning e-company with a shining soul."

Our goal is to integrate diversity into the fabric of HP–into all our processes, into day-to-day business practices–creating a mindset within every employee and manager so they think about diversity and inclusion in everything they do.

Emily Duncan, Director, Global Diversity

IBM (Corporate H.Q. U.S.)

As IBM worked to reinforce the link between the marketplace and the workplace, they developed a Global Diversity Council that established six global challenges to guide their actions:

"Staff should reflect the diversity of the company's user base." (Fabiola Arredondo)

- the global marketplace
- multicultural awareness and acceptance
- diversity of the management team
- advancement of women
- work/life balance: dependent care and work flexibility
- integration of people with disabilities within IBM

General managers from the Americas, Asia-Pacific, and EMEA (Europe, Middle East, Africa) and our Global Industry team, come in once a year to present their results and their strategies to address these challenges the next year. Leadership for diversity at the top remains an IBM tradition.

J. T. (Ted) Childs, Jr., Vice President, Global Workforce Diversity

KYOCERA CORPORATION (GLOBAL H.Q. JAPAN)

The "Kyocera philosophy," based on a strong belief in people, led to global expansion, serving a diverse set of customers and a legacy of business success.

Respect the divine and love people. Preserve the spirit to work fairly and honorably, respecting people, our work, our company, and our global community.

As a leader, you must clearly indicate your unselfish stand. You should set a meaningful goal for your group and follow it yourself.

Kazuo Inamori, Founder and Chairman Emeritus, Kyocera Corporation

MAKING IT HAPPEN

"We are what we repeatedly do. Excellence then, is not an act, but a habit." (Aristotle)

To make embracing differences and mastery of creating an inclusive environment a *habit* of your excellence requires developing a conviction to a few leadership disciplines. The rationale is best illustrated with a story.

Some years back, I visited Sue Swenson, president and C.O.O., Leap Wireless International, to discuss her approach to diversity and inclusion. "As a practice, I don't do disconnected programs and separate launches of initiatives", she told me. "I have been on the receiving end of such headquarters-driven programs. As a young manager, I was continuously asked to put energy into new programs. If I had responded to every one, I would have done none of them well. As a leader, I've personally taken responsibility for finding ways to engage the organization—integrating fairness, openness, diversity, and inclusion into our business strategies, measures, recruiting practices, new hire orientation, management training, employee development, recognition programs, and our common protocol of behaviors and expectations for everybody. What has convinced me that this approach works are the results".

So, what can you do take such an integrated approach? Below are three leadership disciplines that when practiced can become *habits of excellence.*

- **Create a culture of inclusion, trust, and mutual respect**. Start by internalizing company values and beliefs that support a culture of inclusion. Learn to express what they mean to you. Set expectations for everyone's behavior by example and through your messages. Guarantee that everyone who does business with you, or who works for you, will experience a culture of inclusion, trust, and mutual respect. Tolerate nothing less.

How to practice: Let your beliefs and values become part of your day-to-day dialog. Develop your own style of integrating them, perhaps subtly, into your messages, conversations, business planning considerations, and interactions to keep beliefs, values, and expectations in the forefront.

- **Lead by example every day**. See every day as an opportunity to set an example for others in building a culture of inclusion. Develop a genuine interest in your employees and customers. Look for the good in others. Appreciate their differences. Model inclusiveness more by your actions than your words. As Gandhi said, "Be the change you want to see in the world."

How to practice: Make a habit of reviewing your behavior and actions at the end of each day. Evaluate your effectiveness as a role model for the culture of inclusion you are working to create.

- **Make diversity and inclusion organizational *habits* in all work.** Integrating diversity and inclusion considerations into your mainstream business procedures, practices, programs, and protocol of behavior starts with thinking and questioning. Keep it simple. Begin by asking questions that cause you to consider diversity and inclusion implications in such practices as hires, job assignments, promotions, development opportunities, meetings, recognition and awards, pay, who you invite into your inner circle, who you talk with, spend time with, and get to know. Your attention will communicate the importance you place on creating a culture of inclusion. It will also help others in the organization develop their own discipline of thinking about considerations of diversity and inclusion in all their work.

How to practice: Help yourself develop your own diversity and inclusion thinking and questioning *habits*. Create a reminder on the back of a business card. Keep it where you can see it as you work through your day. Commit to practicing for two weeks to develop your skill and make it a habit.

CONCLUSION

The great leaders of the 21st century will be those who incorporate considerations of diversity and inclusion into their *habits of excellence* as leaders and into the mainstream of their organizations. It is essential to fully participate in the opportunities of the 21st century.

For More Information

Book:

Inamori, Kazuo. *For People and for Profit: A Business Philosophy for the 21st Century*. Tokyo: Kodansha International Ltd., 1997.

Web Site:

www.DiversityInc.com: a resource for diversity news in the marketplace, workplace and community.

See also:

☆ **Generation Veneration (pp. 39–40)**
☆ **Viewpoint: Christopher Bartlett (pp. 45–46)**
☆ **Viewpoint: Jim Kouzes (pp. 309–11)**
✓ **Implementing a Diversity Management Program (pp. 442–43)**
Diversity (pp. 1955–57)
Equal Opportunities (pp. 1975–77)

"If multicultural management is to become a reality, then skills adequate to the management of diversity must become a central component of management education." (Stewart Clegg)

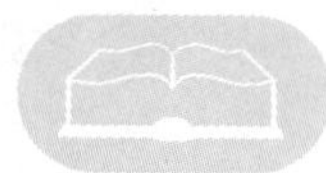

MAKING THE WORKPLACE FLEX, NOT BREAK *by Ken Murrell*

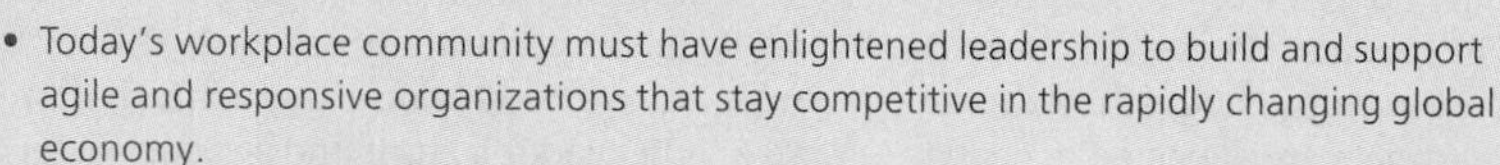

EXECUTIVE SUMMARY

- Today's workplace community must have enlightened leadership to build and support agile and responsive organizations that stay competitive in the rapidly changing global economy.
- Flexibility in the workplace occurs through thoughtful design and an empowered workforce that cares about its work and invests in a spirit of learning, which helps the organization remain competitive.
- Over time success depends on a workplace that has the capacity to change quickly and to create and nurture a workforce that can step up to the challenge of leading change in its own areas of expertise while taking on expanded responsibilities.

INTRODUCTION

Never in history has business played such a central role and been such a globally competitive endeavor. It's also very likely that what we are experiencing today is an easier time for business compared with what is projected to occur in this new century. Dee Hock, founder and C.E.O. Emeritus of Visa International, is correct when he says, "Fasten your seat belts, the turbulence has barely begun."

Staying competitive isn't just about hiring and developing the very best people you can. It's much more than that: it's about building the workplace that allows for these talented individuals to create a sustainable organization that has the capacity to learn and to stay a step ahead.

The roadsides of business growth will be littered with the husks of organizations that once enjoyed success but then couldn't change. Often the failure will have occurred because in the process of building success the organizations broke their people. In the past this breakage was most often a matter of physical breakdown; now more often the breakdown is in the spirit of the work force. Sadly, this also creates a disintegration of the workplace community, often to an irrevocable degree.

How to create flexible and highly competitive workplaces is challenging the best minds in business and the applied behavioral sciences. The Center for Effective Organizations at the University of Southern California, the London School of Economics, the Swedish School of Economics, and countless research universities and consulting firms around the world are grappling with the challenge of creating new forms of organization for the business environment of the 21st century.

WHAT'S NEW? MAYBE OUR WAYS OF RESPONDING

What is the problem? It's the same problem as always! Competitive organizations depend upon people for everything but short-term successes. Market forces and monopolistic positions can generate success for a quarter or even a year, but a healthy workplace is needed for long-term growth. Simple enough to say. Not so easy to do. The challenge is in thinking beyond the current pressures and building the effective workplace as a community in which empowerment occurs naturally. Also needed is a place in which the soul and spirit of the work force are nourished as they produce the excellence that is required of them.

All of this carries with it an obligation to recreate the meaning of work and to base that recreation on the wisdom developed from the knowledge and experimentation among some of the world's most successful organizations. In today's competitive environment, it is essential to transform the workplace. This will necessarily involve a departure from many previous assumptions. Being creative and taking risks produces the learning needed to help drive the change process.

SETTINGS THAT EMPOWER BRING OUT A FLEXIBLE LABOR FORCE

Being competitive requires the full engagement of the workforce. If an organization has to hire and pay management to continually instruct workers, the game is lost: the cost alone would prohibit successful competition with companies in countries in which the wage scale is a fraction of its own. Efficiencies must be found everywhere; managerial overhead costs that do not add value to the product or service must be reduced.

Jim Collins and Jerry Porras have heralded 18 "built-to-last" companies that have done all these things well over the years. One such company is GE, whose "workout" system brings the work force directly into the organizing process. Workouts are offsite sessions at which facilitators help management and workers to look deeply into issues and jointly arrive at new solutions and workable plans of action. Motorola does much the same thing in getting enhanced employee involvement and building ownership for its Six Sigma quality initiatives. Although costly, the investment has a high return.

Companies that become great often have a culture that promotes flexibility. Fad programs are ineffectual: empowerment comes from employees who are able to pursue organizational goals that they're aligned with. In doing this they develop their own work spirit and create a community of others who believe in what everyone—together—is doing. Flexibility comes from people free to do right, with an agreed value base to help guide them. Real settings where this has been created can be found around the world.

The principles in all successful empowerment cases seem to be the same: there must be sincere respect for the people who work for a company, and management must request that people offer their voices as well as their labor. To create such a flexible workplace is possible; and when it is working well the stressfulness of each job is balanced by a shared desire on everyone's part to provide a performance level that guarantees the success of the company overall.

MINI-CASES

The *Toyota* facility in Ontario, Canada (along with its sister sites in many other countries) represents some of the best examples not only of this flexibility but also of the power of *kaizen*, the practice of continuous improvement. Dozens of countries are represented in the plant. The spirit of creating a new way of work and a culture that shows full appreciation for the gifts of each worker has won the facility many awards for learning how to flex and change as each of the company's models requires.

"There's an underutilized work force of well-qualified women who want to work part time."

(Gun Denhart)

The workers understand and adapt without stringent supervision; Toyota has learned to be both flexible and supportive of its workforce.

Similar studies of empowerment success can be found in Asia. Nicholas Kristoff and Sheryl Wu Dunn have reported on a Thai sandwich shop that has succeeded in becoming a major competitor to McDonalds. It achieved this giving its existing employees support and direct help in feeding their families and in creating a new enterprise that would allow them back in the economic game. It's an amazing story of dedication of leadership and a model of how an organization can recreate itself by leveraging maximum flexibility in the workforce.

In Europe, numerous Scandinavian experiments in worker democracy have created the flexible yet empowering work environments that regularly attract study teams from around the world. A work research institute in Norway is also a leading center for such experimentation and change.

Creating More Effective and Efficient Self-Organizing Systems

Creating a workplace and a workforce that have the capacity to change via flexible self-management requires fundamentally new working principles for a new work environment. The following issues need to be addressed:

- Work force environments built on command-and-control assumptions must yield to the higher performance potential of workplace communities. Research indicates there is no one best model; what's needed is a commitment to discover the ideal form that fits the unique culture and work performance.
- Spirit and soul of work are not just interesting phrases but are also necessary conditions for the full investment of the workforce in its work. Work that does not have meaning or cannot give something back to the worker is counter-productive. Work that inspires through meaning and in relationships with others is effective. Inspirational work is a competitive force. Deadening work leads to a broken workforce.
- Work itself is being redefined. As work increasingly depends on knowledge, the place it plays in people's lives is becoming more complex. The whole person must be considered in order to build effective knowledge work. Balance of work and life is the goal.
- The wisdom to know how to lead a new workforce requires careful study and a great deal of self-awareness. Knowing others first requires insight into self.
- The changing global economy demands transformational thinking and outside-the-box ways of creating new work environments. These are best created as partnerships in which both workers and managers are expected to change.

Making It Happen: Six Key Principles

- Align work priorities with a clear vision.
- Involve everyone in deciding those priorities.
- Define and publicly state how people will work with one another.
- Promote the idea of the whole person at work.
- Reward risk-taking to enhance experimentation and discovery.
- Boost performance by boosting learning.

These are not simple or easy principles, but within them lie the answers to the questions that each organization will have to address in the future. Leadership is key to facilitating and guiding the process, but a commitment to creating an empowering workplace is necessary to start the process. Following these key principles will insure success.

Moreover, as a manager you must:

- share information and educate; employees about corporate goals
- develop a guiding structure, not a controlling one;
- lead with others and invite many to join in creating leadership at all levels
- support and encourage involvement;
- be sure the process is adequately resourced in terms of time, money, and team development.

Finally, be sure you have employees who can rise to the occasion. Assume they can meet these challenges; if it appears they can't, address that as the first challenge. Get whatever help you need for the whole system to move forward.

Conclusion

Although the task might appear daunting, there is much help available. The emergent global economy is forcing all organizations to move in this direction. The best are already moving quickly, and they represent potential resources for benchmarking or comparing notes. Since new work structures and cultures are in high demand, the path around the problems created by inflexible and damaging environments is well trodden. Finally, it is essential that workplaces have the capacity to create and recreate themselves. This work will always be important; in essence, this is true job security. It is also the work that creates in the leader a spirit and a potential for finding personally satisfying work. When the only constant in business is change, building a flexible workplace that can adapt to and thrive in the rapidly changing business environment will be the cornerstone of successful companies in the future. To build long-term competitive advantage, the whole company needs to move in the right direction. Successful organizations are characterized by a flexible culture; brittle ones will break and be left by the roadside.

For More Information

Books:

Collins, James C., and Jerry I. Porras. *Built to Last: Successful Habits of Visionary Companies*. New York: HarperBusiness, 1997.

Fisher, Dalmar, David Rooke, and Bill Torbert. *Personal and Organizational Transformations Through Action Inquiry*. Boston, MA: Edge\Work Press, 2000.

Hock, Dee. *Birth of the Chaordic Age*. San Francisco, CA: Berrett-Kohler, 1999.

Kristoff, Nicholas D., and Sheryl WuDunn. *Thunder From the East: Portrait of a Rising Asia*. New York: Vintage, 2001.

Wheatley, Margaret J. *Leadership and the New Science: Discovering Order in a Chaotic World*. 2nd ed. San Francisco, CA: Berrett-Kohler, 2001.

Web Site:

www.Spiritatwork.com

See also:

☆ **Converting Anonymity into Participation in a Membership Organization (pp. 206–07)**
☆ **Fringe Benefits (pp. 25–26)**
☆ **Power Struggling and Power Sharing (pp. 95–96)**
☆ **Tuning into the Harmonics of Management (pp. 253–54)**
☆ **Viewpoint: Sumantra Ghoshal (pp. 190–91)**
✓ **Using Lateral Moves to Further Your Career (pp. 776–77)**

"Flextime is the essence of respect for and trust in people." (David Packard)

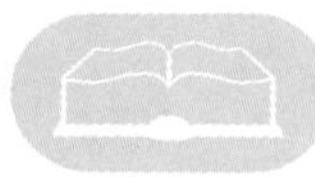

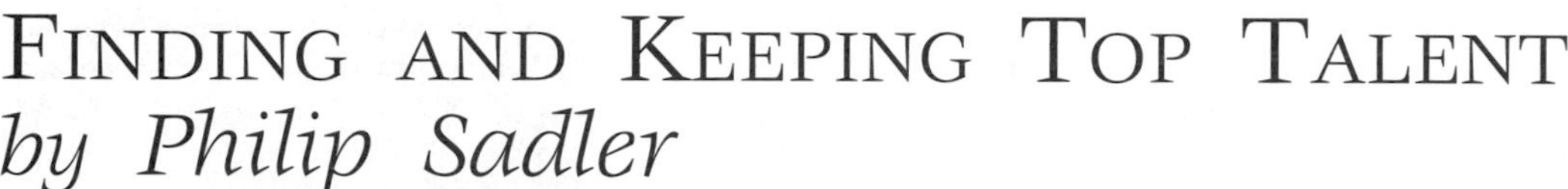

Finding and Keeping Top Talent *by Philip Sadler*

EXECUTIVE SUMMARY

Just as organizations have changed dramatically in nature over the last 20 years, so have people's attitudes to their employers—and the attitudes of the most talented people are no exception.

- Talented employees are increasingly aware of their value and prepared to move to other organizations if they feel they will receive greater respect and reward. Cradle to grave loyalty, if it ever existed at all, is certainly very scarce.
- Knowledge is more important than ever before and a major source of competitive advantage. Attracting, finding, and retaining talented people is therefore vital for success. Not only are people the most decisive and expensive resource, they also determine the success of every activity within the organization.
- Although money remains important, talented people value much more than this alone and an increasingly complex range of factors affects their loyalty, motivation, and effectiveness.
- A disappointingly large number of talented people are already within organizations, their potential largely unfulfilled.

Introduction

Whereas in the past the typical wealth-creating enterprises of the advanced industrial societies were either labor-intensive or capital-intensive, today the businesses of growing economic significance are better described as knowledge-intensive or talent-intensive. The obvious examples are companies in fields such as software, pharmaceuticals, business and professional services, investment banking, music publishing, entertainment, and sports. Many of the new dot-com companies fall into this group. In such organizations, the principal assets consist of the knowledge and skills of talented people rather than the tangible assets of the so-called old economy: financial reserves, capital equipment, buildings, and stocks. The management of knowledge has become a lucrative field for management consultants and academic gurus in recent years, and it is important that a company exploit its knowledge capital to the greatest extent. Sooner or later, however, today's knowledge is obsolete. The competitive edge lies with companies that are focused on seeking out the knowledge and competencies that will be required in the future. The value of a research laboratory to a potential investor lies in the ability of its scientists to make discoveries and develop new products in the future. In a world in which there is no shortage of capital for investment, talent is the only remaining scarce resource.

The kind of talent needed most urgently by many of today's businesses is often not the same as that traditionally involved in building the knowledge base. Fashion designers, international athletes, creative writers, consistently successful investment analysts, entrepreneurs, Web site designers, and others may use some knowledge in their work, but the essential qualities that distinguish them have little to do with their ability to absorb knowledge.

Characteristics of Talent-Intensive Organizations

Talent-intensive organizations share several characteristics:

- their principal assets (that is, their talented people) do not appear on the balance sheet
- these key assets are mobile. They can, despite contracts of service, simply walk away
- talent-intensive organizations rely particularly on creativity and imagination
- the success criteria for talent-intensive organizations stretch far beyond the accountants' bottom line. Winning a Nobel Prize, an Oscar, a fashion design award, or the World Series may weigh far more than profit or cash flow does

Companies increasingly understand that they must frame their human resources policies in the context of a highly competitive international market for talent. There is a constant flow of talented people from countries with lower living standards and rewards or higher levels of personal taxation to countries in which talent enjoys higher reward—the so-called brain drain. The competition consists of not only other companies worldwide, but also the attraction for many talented people of independence and self-employment. The twin challenges for business can be summed up as recruiting and keeping talent.

Recruiting and Finding Talent

The distinction between recruiting talent and finding it is important. Sometimes an organization looks outside for new talent when the potential for outstanding performance already exists unrecognized among existing employees. The recruitment activity itself can be separated into two quite distinct processes. The first is attracting people whose talent has already been established and recognized elsewhere. This can be called the transplanting type of recruiting, equivalent to digging up and repositioning a mature tree or shrub in the quest for an instant garden. In such instances companies often make the mistake of assuming that the cash nexus is the most important factor. An outstanding performer in any field is unlikely to move from one organization to another if it involves a drop in pay, but corporate recruiters seldom give enough weight or consideration to other factors. In the case of highly talented people, for example, a key influence on the decision whether or not to move jobs is the reputation the recruiting organization has in its particular field: Is it at the leading edge? Does it set the pace for its industry? Does the individual feel honored by being approached? Reputation building, therefore, is a key element in recruiting strategy.

The second process can be termed the seedbed or nursery approach, recruiting young people straight from high school or college, nurturing or developing their emerging talents, and bringing them to fruition. This is clearly a longer-term approach and one fraught with obvious risks, for instance, the obstacles to predicting eventual success, including:

- the different maturation rates of individuals' abilities; late developers are often overlooked;

"Surround yourself with the best people you can find, delegate authority, and don't interfere."

(Ronald Reagan)

- the relative weakness of psychometric tests in gauging qualities like creativity and entrepreneurial ability;
- the tendency to give too much weight to academic credentials;
- the failure to value diversity in the work force;
- the fact that motivation and drive may well be more powerful determinants of performance than sheer ability.

Somewhat less risky is the process of finding talent among existing employees. Assuming they've been with the company for some time, a well designed appraisal and development procedure can be effective in selecting promising candidates.

Michael Howe, a specialist in human cognition at Exeter University in England, is one of the world's leading experts on the subject of talent. He points to the danger of seeing talent in a particular field as a gift either you have or you don't: "We are easily convinced that the most striking feats must depend on circumstances which, except for certain rare individuals, are entirely unattainable. Some of the most widespread beliefs about exceptional people revolve around the view that certain individuals are not only remarkable but are inherently so, while the remainder of us are doomed to ordinariness." He challenges such beliefs, producing compelling evidence of the effectiveness of appropriate training and development for exceptional performance.

Here again, the common fault is stereotyping and eliminating some categories of employee from consideration. It is very important for a company to be aware of any cultural bias that may cause it to narrow its search for talent to traditional sources, much as, at one time, corporations essentially restricted management to white males.

RETAINING TALENT

What makes the real difference in keeping talented employees loyal is the extent to which the company provides them with a working environment favorable to creativity, self-expression, and the exercise of initiative. The paradox that faces organizations is that they are hierarchical, bureaucratic, and conformist in order to achieve efficiency and uniformity, yet it is just these characteristics that turn off highly creative people. The term "skunk works" has entered the language of organizations to describe small, informal, tightly knit teams that are shielded from standard company practices and rules in order to foster their creative energies. Warren Bennis gives a graphic description of the very first skunk works, set up by Lockheed to develop the first U.S. jet fighter during World War II. Lockheed's chief designer selected a team of 23 engineers and 30 support staff. They built makeshift quarters from discarded engine boxes roofed with a circus tent. They worked in secrecy, doing their own cleaning and secretarial work. Bennis describes the designer Johnson as "a visionary on at least two fronts: designing airplanes and organizing genius. Johnson seemed to know intuitively what talented people needed to do their best work, how to motivate them, and how to make sure the desired product was created as quickly and cheaply as possible." His unit was characterized by the egalitarian treatment of people, an absence of paperwork, informality of dress, and open debate. The culture of an organization is an important factor in its ability to retain talent. The chief characteristics of a culture that nurtures talent are the following:

- highly cohesive work teams
- authority residing in expertise and competence rather than rank or status
- elites recognized without elitism in that talented people respect and recognize the contribution of those less gifted colleagues who support them
- respected leadership. Talented people are critical people; they know when the emperor has no clothes;
- freedom, autonomy, space, and flexibility
- openness and trust
- encouragement of risk-taking

A dedication to excellence needs to be taken for granted. In other words, the right approach for organizations anxious to retain their most talented people is not so much to create a skunk works inside the company as to make the company as a whole as much like a skunk works as possible.

MAKING IT HAPPEN ▸▸

Finding the best people

It is a mistake to assume that finding top talent will be expensive or lengthy: it need not be, even for the most effective, senior appointments. Consider whether the most talented people in your current team know of someone suitable. Because they understand you, the role, and the organization, they are best placed to find a good candidate. There may be other people in the organization's network that could also suggest a candidate: shareholders, suppliers, customers, professional advisers may all be able to recommend good candidates.

It is also advisable to allow enough time to make the right appointment, and to ensure that others meet with the preferred candidate. Time pressures and isolation are two key factors that can lead managers to make appointments that are flawed.

Keeping the best people

It is important to remember that keeping top talent is as much about the people, the job and the organization, as it is about the specific individual. It is worth asking, at regular intervals, the following key questions:

- Who are your key people?
- What makes them exceptional?
- How are they feeling?
- Are their working environment, terms and conditions of employment competitive?
- Do they know how much you value them?
- What are their aspirations and are they realistic?

Finally, it is worth remembering that whether you are trying to find or to keep someone, remuneration remains important for most people. If not for its own sake, then for the sense of recognition that it brings.

For More Information

Books:

Bennis, Warren, and Patricia Ward Biederman. *Organizing Genius.* Cambridge, MA: Perseus, 1998.

Deems, Richard S. *Hiring: How to Find and Keep the Best People.* Franklin Lakes, NJ: Career Press, 1998.

See also:

- ☆ **Downsizing with Dignity (pp. 16–17)**
- ☆ **The End of Growth: Why Does It Always End? What Can You Do About It? (pp. 269–70)**
- ☆ **How to Walk on the Leading Edge without Falling off the Cliff (pp. 229–30)**
- ☆ **Retaining Employees (pp. 196–97)**
- ☆ **Workers without Borders: Creating Bonds When Workers Have No Loyalty (pp. 204–05)**
- ✔ **Assessing Your Entrepreneurial Profile: Do You Have What It Takes? (pp. 818–19)**
- **Frederick Herzberg (pp. 1002–03)**
- **Employee Benefits/ Compensation (pp. 1959–61)**

"There are two important factors in building a self-motivated team of people—the opportunity to learn through increased effort and trust in the management to give the utmost support." (Tom Farmer)

  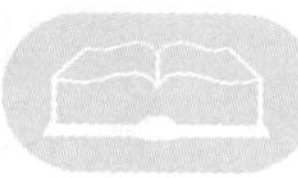    

MANAGING TODAY'S ANGRY WORKFORCE

by Florence M. Stone

EXECUTIVE SUMMARY

- Anger is on the increase in our workplaces, affecting interpersonal relationships at the lowest levels and triggering violent behavior at the highest.
- Organizations are indirectly contributing to the situation by their demands for more work in less time and a throwaway attitude towards members of the workforce.
- Managers need to become sensitive to the levels of stress their employees are under, recognize danger signs, and address issues of stress and anxiety before they become performance issues.
- Companies need to have recognized protocols and processes for managing all levels of anger in the workplace, including a zero-tolerance policy for threats of violence.

INTRODUCTION

Conflict isn't new in the workplace—indeed, disagreements can help select the best among good ideas—but today's offices seem prone to excessive conflict. Studies by Integra Realty Resources of more than 1,000 office workers in the United States and the United Kingdom revealed growing numbers of overworked, overwrought employees. The surveys showed a worldwide pattern of endless complaints, put-downs, angry outbursts, trashed office equipment, and gave a name to the behavioral pattern—"desk rage." The U.S./U.K. findings and subsequent surveys have found anger at work to be pervasive, taking not only the forms of yelling, verbal abuse, and damage to office technology, but of fistfights among office colleagues. One in ten respondents in the Integra survey said they worked in an office where physical violence had occurred.

TICKED OFF. . .AND TICKING

These survey results should not cause surprise. After all, the phrase "going postal," derived from early incidents of employee violence in U.S. post offices, has become part of our vernacular. Although some may see workplace anger as a U.S. phenomenon, it is a worldwide trend.

According to a report from the Geneva-based International Labour Organization in 1997, *Violence at Work* by Duncan Chappell and Vittorio Di Martino, the issue "transcends the boundaries of a particular country, work setting, or occupational group." Because the initial survey on anger was sponsored by a real estate firm considering, among other factors, office working conditions—particularly the "Dilbertization" of the workplace, the accommodation of employees in cubicles barely bigger than their desks—its results were belittled in some quarters. But interviews with security experts have supported the findings. They all point to the same situations in our workplaces: more work, less time, much change in how the work is done, continuous demand for greater productivity.

According to R. Brayton Bowen, anger is often triggered by the threatened loss of something greatly valued. Translate this to the workplace, and I'd rank these three factors as the biggest causes of anger:

- downsizing, or the threat of job loss
- the pressure to do more with less, or the loss of existing resources
- disempowerment, or the loss of control over the work to be done

The high-stress conditions in today's offices make it difficult to achieve teamwork or creativity, but the bigger problem is that they set the stage for unstable people to act out their anger, pushing them over the edge to violent behavior. Circumstances ranging from an unresolved conflict with a coworker or supervisor to a bad performance evaluation or a major change in work procedures can contribute to heightened anxiety and, in turn, to raw anger. If an individual has a predisposition to aggressiveness and perceives the workplace as a hostile environment, experiencing stress can trigger violent behavior, according to Anthony Baron, C.E.O. of Baron Center, California-based organization of trainers specializing in workplace and school violence protection.

The number of homicides is already disturbing: "boss-icide" has doubled in a little more than 10 years. In 1999, 856 homicides were reported in the workplace, more than twice the number reported a dozen years before. On average, workers murder three to four supervisors a month, or double the number a little more than a decade ago. A study by the American Management Association in 1994 found more than half of 500 human resources managers had had to contend with threats of violence in their companies in the previous four years. Multiple occurrences were reported by 30% of respondents.

Security experts contend that most violence-prevention programs are initiated after an incident, not beforehand. As the labor shortage has made it more difficult to find qualified employees, some organizations have forgone reference checks, thereby increasing the potential for negligent hiring. Threats to coworkers or managers are ignored because there is no zero-tolerance policy that covers them. Many supervisors aren't trained to handle on-the-job conflicts, and consequently conflicts are allowed to fester. Employee-assistance programs (EAPs) that exist to help identify and address personal and work-related problems may be not mandatory or not accessible.

DEFUSING AN ANGRY WORKPLACE

On the assumption that intervention by an EAP may come too late, the Purdue Employees Credit Union in West Lafayette, Indiana, also trains its own managers to identify and advise employees on stress-related behaviors that could evolve into threats or violent behavior. Training updates, provided quarterly, keep managers alert to the issue and abreast of the latest need-to-know information.

As we see an increase in desk rage, it's evident that companies should not wait for anger to grow into violent behavior. Yet too often that is exactly what has happened. Employees at U.S. Foodservice in East Allentown, Pennsylvania, have not forgotten the day three years ago when a troubled and angry employee shot three managers, killing one, before fatally shooting himself. Repetition of the incident is unlikely: security has increased since the shootings. U.S. Foodservice has been training managers in its 38 branches about violence in the workplace and how to spot the warning signs of a violent employee, according to Bonna Walker, vice president of marketing and public relations. Managers, in turn, teach their employees. The company also has

"Anger can be an effective negotiating tool, but only as a calculated act, never as a reaction."

(Mark McCormack)

instituted zero-tolerance guidelines on violence in the workplace. A policy on violence existed before the shootings, but has since been rewritten in, says Walker, "plainer language so there is no misunderstanding of what that policy is."

According to Larry Chavez, founder of Critical Incidents Associates, an organization that conducts training seminars on preventing workplace violence, companies should go beyond spelling out policies. Top management should be quick and stern in dealing with violations. Indeed, there should be zero tolerance.

Applied Materials' lawsuit to obtain a restraining order is an example of the way businesses should respond to threats, even when offenders state that they meant nothing by a threatening remark. In the case of Applied Materials, an employee allegedly complained to fellow workers about a potential job reassignment, saying that he would "bring an Uzi and start mowing people down." Concerned not only with the threat but with the coworker's aggressive nature, a colleague reported the remark to a manager. As a consequence, the worker was placed on administrative leave while an investigation was undertaken. The company's response to the verbal threat illustrates the zero-tolerance policy that is spreading across the country.

Steve Kaufer, cofounder of the Workplace Violence Research Institute, compares corporate response to the heightened use of metal detectors in airports. "You can't joke about guns and bombs," he says. "Employees are being trained to understand that those threats aren't appropriate and will be dealt with very seriously." Employees can be placed on unpaid leave or fired if found guilty of making remarks perceived as threatening, since they challenge a company's responsibility to secure the workplace and protect the other employees.

Besides a no-threat policy and supervisory and employee training in violence prevention, a means should be established whereby employees and their family members can anonymously report potential threats. Special consideration should be given to procedures to address involuntary separations and disciplinary actions. These two kinds of incidents trigger almost half of the violent incidents in the workplace.

MINI-CASES

Airlines all have EAPs, but the *Association of Flight Attendants (AFA)* has an additional support system, the Member Assistance Program (MAP). This program provides AFA's 47,000 members, representing 26 airlines, with peer support for work-related or personal problems and referral to professional resources. Volunteer employees receive special training on how to counsel their peers, and to date the AFA has more than 170 peer counselors worldwide. The peer program is considered superior to traditional management-sponsored EAPs in that employees don't have to wait until the problem intrudes on their job performance.

In 1999, *Pfizer* launched its Vista Rx program, which allows salespeople to cut back to a 60% work schedule while retaining 100% of their full-time benefits. The program alleviates a major source of stress—difficulty balancing work and family demands. According to Bruce Fleischmann, national sales director of Vista Rx, the program meets Pfizer's need to have 100+ salespeople calling on physicians, yet also allows the participants to balance work–life issues. For some, Vista Rx is a short-term solution to a family situation; for others, it's a permanent career change. The company limits participation to around 130 employees, and there's currently a waiting list.

MAKING IT HAPPEN ▸▸

Companies need a tandem effort of prevention and protection to defuse and protect against workplace tension.

- Review hiring processes, including background checks, reference verifications, and applicant screening for propensity toward violence.
- Review and implement policies and procedures that ensure that under the worst of circumstances employees are treated with dignity. Many of those who exhibit violent behavior attribute it to actions they say stripped them of their dignity in some way.
- Institute handgun policies covering the carrying of concealed firearms on the premises.
- Institute training programs to educate managers on early-warning signs and emergency procedures.
- Create a safe environment by establishing workplace violence policies, including a zero-tolerance policy on threats of harm. Provide for an employee assistance or counseling program for workers who threaten or harass fellow employees.
- Create a threat management team to detail a specific plan of action to be taken every time a threat is reported, with participants from human resources, security, the EAP, and legal counsel.

CONCLUSION

Companies need to take the issue of growing anger and uncivil behavior among colleagues seriously. Left unchecked, in certain individuals it can trigger violent incidents that can be costly beyond the safety of coworkers and customers. Businesses are facing recent judicial trends that find employers liable for acts of violence due to negligence in hiring, supervision, or retention. Aside from instituting violence prevention/protection programs, companies need to look more closely at surveys that show pervasive anger within their rank and file. Anger in the workplace is a signal that there's something wrong in the system. It's management's responsibility to investigate the corporate climate and culture, identify the causes, and, with its workforce, collaboratively and collectively seek effective solutions.

For More Information

Books:

Denenberg, Richard V., and Mark Braverman. *The Violence-prone Workplace: A New Approach to Dealing with Hostile, Threatening and Uncivil Behavior*. Ithaca, NY: Cornell University Press, 2001.

McClure, Lynne. *Anger and Conflict in the Workplace: Spot the Signs, Avoid the Trauma*. Manassas Park, VA: Impact, 2000.

Potter-Efron, Ronald T. *Working Anger: Preventing and Resolving Conflict on the Job*. Oakland, CA: New Harbinger, 1998.

Web Site:

http://www.angermgmt.com is a site providing information about anger management, and offering a range of services and products including courses, counseling, and a questionnaire measuring your anger level.

See also:

☆ **Driving Fear from the Workplace (pp. 330–31)**
☆ **From Crisis Management to Crisis Leadership (pp. 293–94)**
☆ **Making Cultures Behave (pp. 51–52)**
☆ **Viewpoint: Margaret J. Wheatley (pp. 273–74)**
Stress and Stress Management (pp. 2117–19)

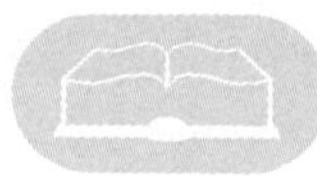

Creating Fun in the Workplace
by Leslie A. Yerkes

EXECUTIVE SUMMARY

- Many bosses feel there's no place for fun at work. Today's employees demand that work be fun. The challenge is to reconcile these two conflicting expectations.
- Fun and work are not incompatible: they can coexist. Work is most productive when it's fused with fun.
- In creating a sustainable organization, fun should be a core essential, not an add-on or a reward for hard work.
- Fun can be an essential element to conducting business, retaining customers, enhancing external perceptions of the business and brand, attracting and retaining talented employees—and helping to build competitive advantage.

Introduction

The perception is still widespread that work should not be fun, that fun is something you earn only after you've worked hard. That position, once the bedrock of workplace behavior, is changing. Companies such as Southwest Airlines, Skandia, Isle of Capri Casinos, and Pike Place Fish have shown that the integration of fun and work not only improves the day-to-day relationships and atmosphere of the workplace, but also it can positively improve the net worth of the company.

Our attitude toward work is not an absolute. Work and our perception of work have changed and evolved. Each of us adopts the attitude towards work that our parents taught us, or assimilate the attitude held by whoever is exerting the strongest current influence, perhaps our peer group or our employer. For many of us, work has become who we are. It's how we define ourselves.

Attitudes Toward Work Are Changeable

When we look at the timeline of work attitudes we can see that work has evolved from Aristotle's "work is for slaves" to Calvin's "work is a commandment," through work is a virtue to work is who I am. Since general attitudes toward work merely reflect the times, people can intentionally alter their individual attitudes. Specifically, it's possible to reintegrate fun into our work.

Historically, fun and work have long coexisted. During the agricultural age, for example, work songs helped turn dreary tasks and repetitive actions into activities that, if not fun, at least contained an element of anticipation and comfort. Barn-raisings changed a task impossible for one or two people into a picnic-style community event. The element of fun turned an impossible task into an eagerly anticipated one, one at which friends, family, and neighbors worked side by side for the common good, caught up on old times, and shared food with one another. Vestiges of this behavior are seen when people get together on a Saturday to clean up a ball diamond, paint a senior citizen's house, or build a playground.

The concept of work is again in the midst of change. We are rediscovering that fun belongs with work, and that when it's isolated, work isn't fun. Fun and work naturally go together: fun works, and work is more productive when it's fun.

Mini-cases

Pike Place Fish is one of three fish markets on the Public Market Dock on Puget Sound in downtown Seattle, Washington. When John Yokoyama bought out the previous owner in 1965 for $3,500, Pike Place Fish was simply a fish market, unremarkable in many ways. "Everyone here hated their jobs. I can remember the owner counting out loud the number of steps it took him to get a dozen clams for a customer and then complaining about it. For a long time, no one working here had fun. I was an angry manager; I was an angry owner. All the tools in my managerial toolkit were fear-based."

When the collective group of owners, managers, and employees decided to become world-famous they began to act the way world-famous fishmongers would act. John transformed himself from a yelling whip-cracker into the Fish King. His job evolved: he checks the mood and makes sure energy is present that allows employees to be themselves—and to have fun!

Pike Place Fish is now valued at 1,000 times more than the original purchase price. During the Christmas season it transacts more business per square foot than any competitive grocery chain in the area. The business has expanded successfully into e-commerce, speaking engagements, training, and consulting. It's served as the setting of numerous films, television commercials, and print ads. Leveraging its image and reputation for fun has generated a strong brand and an enviable position in the market.

Employease is an Atlanta-based application service provider offering proprietary human-resources services. Between its September 1998 startup and June 2000, it enrolled more than 1,000 companies without spending anything on advertising. The secret is twofold: an innovative Web-based product and a company attitude that trusts both people and the process to perform.

Employease is a diverse mix of human-resource and IT experts of all races, ages, backgrounds, sexes, and home states. Employees are trusted to be accountable for their actions and responsible for their results, and to take ownership of their jobs. Employease is an egoless company with low political pressures. Its work ethic says, I'll trust you to do your job, you trust me. In this high-trust environment fun naturally emerges as the social glue that cements the relationships of the diverse staff.

Isle of Capri Casinos has become one of the darlings of Wall Street, going from $2 a share to a projected $19 a share in 2000, and from $800 million in earnings in 1999 to $1 billion in 2000.

Guests who visit an Isle resort aren't looking for a company that exhibits corporate financial security. They're looking for excitement, entertainment, and a good time that includes gambling, shows, and good food. What Isle of Capri Casinos does to make guests return is to ensure that the experience is greater than the anticipation—that it's fun.

The Isle of Capri brand is deeply rooted in a philosophy called Isle Style. When guests arrive at Isle of Biloxi, the door of their car

"If you want creative workers, give them enough time to play." (John Cleese)

is opened by an enthusiastic employee who smiles and welcomes them to Isle of Biloxi. After check-in their bags are carried by a bellhop who asks on the way to the room how they like their coffee. Do they like fluffy towels? Do they prefer a special kind of soap or shampoo? Within minutes the bellhop returns with extra towels and the appropriate cream for the coffee. The goal is to make guests feel that their every need has been attended to. This creates a fun experience that encourages repeat business year after year.

Skandia is the world's largest asset gatherer of nonproprietary market-linked insurance policies. Its goals are to attract the best money managers and financial planners to use Skandia's services and to attract and retain the best employees in order to make that happen. Attracting good people is made easy by success in the marketplace combined with a wide variety of day-to-day amenities—from a world-class gym to upscale coffee bars on each of five floors in their U.S. headquarters. But the method it chooses to retain employees is celebration.

Various awards all celebrate achievement through cash, parties, and plaques. To make each day fun, employees order in food, go to baseball games en masse (covering for each other's work to make it possible), and decorate the offices in anticipation of coming holidays.

"It all comes down to believing and trusting in people," says C.E.O. Wade Dokken. "You have to trust them if you want them to succeed. Then you need to reward them. We celebrate success by giving credit to others. To be successful, you need to share and give power freely. And you need to celebrate their successes."

Making It Happen ▸▸

Successful companies like these have learned that integrating fun and work:

- stimulates creativity and innovation;
- fosters commitment and ownership among all members of the organization;
- creates and secures employee morale;
- increases productivity;
- counters the effects of stress;
- guards against burnout;
- becomes the glue for social relationships;
- mends conflicts;
- stimulates renewal and activity;
- reduces absenteeism;
- creates stronger, deeper, longer-lasting customer relationships.

The successful integration of fun and work comes from the following principles:

- **Give permission to perform**—because of our attitude that fun isn't appropriate in a work environment, fun won't appear unless it's invited. It's essential to give permission to individuals to bring the best of themselves to work each day. This requires a superb leader to create the vision, set the tone for the journey, and believe that only by integrating fun and work can the best results be achieved.
- **Trust the process**—fun takes root in organizations that are high-trust rather than high-fear. The more trust we show, the more fun there is; the more fun there is, the more trust we show. Fun is an energy force that can't be mandated or controlled by rules. If you trust people with your company's most valuable assets, why not trust them to use their judgment in blending fun with work?
- **Be authentic and conscientious**—because we're changing mindsets, this requires initial effort. The integration of work and fun requires a *being* state, not a *doing* state. Attitude isn't a veneer that's applied to a new employee, it's an intrinsic quality that emerges naturally. Search out authentic people who enjoy life and enjoy being around people, and then train them in specific job skills after they've been hired.
- **Celebrate**—what gets recognized gets repeated; what gets celebrated becomes a habit. Individual recognition and group celebration fuel high performance. Make an effort to compliment people doing something right. There's nothing more fun than celebrating a success.

Conclusion

The objective observation of the case companies supports the premise that business works best when fun and work are successfully integrated. It disproves the commonly held perception that there's no place in the work environment for fun. No longer do we believe that the only time we can have fun is when the work is over, or that the only way we can have fun is to earn it through hard work.

Companies that integrate fun and work are best able to attract and retain peak performers in an economy that promotes and rewards the rapid and constant changing of jobs.

For More Information

Books:

Schrage, Michael. *Serious Play: How the World's Best Companies Simulate to Innovate*. Boston, MA: Harvard Business School Press, 1999.

Weinstein, Matt, and Luke Barber. *Work Like Your Dog: Fifty Ways to Work Less, Play More, and Earn More*. New York: Villard, 1999.

See also:

☆ **Breaking the Lead Ceiling (pp. 237–38)**
☆ **Making Cultures Behave (pp. 51–52)**
☆ **Power Struggling and Power Sharing (pp. 95–96)**
☆ **Retaining Employees (pp. 196–97)**
☆ **Self-managed Teams: How They Succeed or Fail (pp. 202–03)**
☆ **Tuning into the Harmonics of Management (pp. 253–54)**
☆ **Urbane Renewal: Trusting Your Own Wisdom—A Competitive (and Satisfying) Advantage (pp. 320–21)**
✔ **Finding Your Calling and Living Your Passion: The Dream Job (pp. 744–45)**
Motivation (pp. 2050–52)

"We are speeding up our lives and working harder in a futile attempt to buy the time to slow down and enjoy it."
(Paul Hawken)

  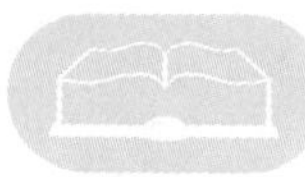    

Generation Veneration *by Ron Zemke*

EXECUTIVE SUMMARY

- At no time in history have so many different generations with such different views, values, and approaches been asked to work together.
- The once-linear nature of power at work, from older to younger, has been dislocated by changes in life expectancy, longevity, and health, as well as changes in lifestyle, technology, and knowledge base.
- Understanding generational differences is critical to managing people effectively.

Introduction

There's a new challenge facing your organization. It doesn't come from downsizing, rightsizing, change, new technology, or competition. It's a problem created by a clash of generational values, ambitions, views, mindsets, and demographics.

The workplace today is awash with the conflicting voices, views, and learning styles of the most diverse workforce the industrialized world has ever known. Look around you. Your customers and your colleagues are a far more age-diverse group than ever before—and more organizationally integrated. Many senior employees are older today than senior employees were in the old days, and these older employees are filling positions once staffed by younger employees—and vice versa. Young employees with mission-critical knowledge and skills are increasingly coming to occupy leadership and management assignments that would have been deemed beyond their years just a few years ago. The new, more horizontal, less segregated-by-function workplace has stirred the generations into a mix of much richer and different proportions than at any time in the past.

According to Walker Smith and Ann Clurman, "New generational differences are causing business upheavals, bringing new categories and ways [of work] into being at warp speed and causing old ones to shrink or disappear." The old way—strict hierarchy, slow promotional tracks, and short life spans—that used to keep one generational cohort together and isolated from others, no longer exists, or exists in a much less rigid, more permeable form. Knowledge, skill, and merit have quickly overcome time as the power factor in today's workplace.

The Players

It isn't uncommon today to find four distinct generations working together on the same project. These four generations—known as *veterans*, *boomers*, *Xers*, and *nexters*—are differentiated not solely by their dates of birth and chronological age, but by the events and experiences that at an early age set their values and views on life. In the words of Canadian demographer David Foote, "We look more like our times and our peers than we do our parents and their views." The 80 years that these four generations span cover an amazingly rich and diverse body of history and social change.

Each generation has a unique perspective, particularly on work. Each has its own views about what makes an attractive work environment and what kind of team is worth joining. Perhaps most confounding for a manager, each generation has unique preferences for acquiring, digesting, organizing, and distilling information and skills; each espouses firm ideas about how a career should develop. Understanding these generational differences is critical for leaders who would enroll the participation of all employees in working for the organization and not against it. These differences are also significant for managers who must meld these different viewpoints with the values, philosophy, and know-how upon which the smooth running of any modern organization is premised.

It is, of course, worth emphasizing that these classifications are generalizations, but they are surprisingly accurate and valid. They are also *perceived* as being accurate and affecting workplace attitudes and behavior.

The Veterans (Born 1922–43)

The veterans were born, and some came of age, before and during the Great Depression and World War II. They're the classic keepers of the grail; they form an irreplaceable repository of lore and wisdom, practical wiliness, and more than a few critical extraorganizational contacts. Their preferred style is formal. From the hiring process to performance reviews, they like things done by the book. They aren't interested in bucking authority, but when asked they'll tell you where the weak spots of a plan are. Though past, at, or nearing retirement, they're nonetheless much interested in continuing to work part-time, on projects or as mentors for younger employees.

The Baby Boomers (Born 1943–60)

Baby boomers were the postwar babies. They're now graying, and they'd really rather not be seen as the problem in the workplace—though they frequently are. They invented "Thank God, it's Monday!" and the 60-hour workweek. Boomers are passionately concerned about participation and spirit in the workplace, about bringing heart and humanity to the office, and about creating a fair and level playing field for all. And they hold way too many meetings for the average Gen-Xer's taste. Gen-Xers frequently report that they see boomers as too wedded to ceremony and ritual and too controlling. Boomers are interested in creating a personal legacy or completing that one last great project before turning their attention toward retirement.

The Xers (Born 1960–80)

The Xers grew up in the post-60s era of Watergate, latchkey kids, and the energy crisis. Their need for feedback and flexibility, coupled with their hatred of close supervision, is but one of the many conundrums they present employers. At the same time they're personally adept and comfortable with change—after all, they've changed cities, homes, and parents all their lives. They are indeed the new change masters. And they're much more inclined to keep their own counsel than are their boomer predecessors.

Xers are very clear about the meaning of balance in their lives. Work is work. And they work to live, they don't live to work. "It's just a job" is a mantra often heard from Xers. Their loyalties revolve around themselves and their friends and families, not their jobs, not your organization. The biggest Xer challenge is retention. The marketplace wants them, almost fights over them, and they have a natural wanderlust fueled by opportunity and fired by the need to add experience and competence to their personal portfolios. A recent study found that 77% of Xers would like to find a company where they could work for a long time, yet 42% described loyalty to one employer as foolish, if not foolhardy.

"The man who views the world at fifty the same as he did at twenty has wasted thirty years of his life."

(Muhammad Ali)

  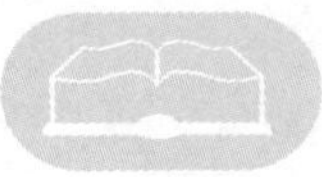    

THE NEXTERS (BORN 1980+)

They may be the smartest, cleverest, most-wanted people to have yet walked the face of the planet. They're an optimistic bunch who express doubt over the wisdom of traditional racial and sexual categorization. They have Internet pen pals in Asia who they can, and do, contact at any hour of the day or night. Those now in the workforce—think fast food, movie theaters, grocery-store carryout, yard work, babysitting, Web-page building, and internships—seem destined to become what Neil Howe and Bill Strauss call "good scouts." They will be a very welcome relief to any organization currently struggling with the boomer–Xer conflicts. But be aware that they come with their own agenda. Members of the class of 2001 clearly see themselves as entrepreneurs-in-training. They expect fantastic training, job counseling, and career planning as part of the job.

Nexters have lived a very organized life, with classes and activities carefully planned out by mom, dad, and school. They expect the same at work. They're eager workers, but not the self-sufficient workers that Xers are. They're very comfortable with collaborative work and are uncomfortable with a competitive atmosphere. They see no reason why everyone can't win.

THE CHALLENGE

These four generations have unique work ethics, different perspectives on work, distinct and preferred ways of managing and being managed, and idiosyncratic styles. They also have unique ways of viewing such work-world issues as quality, service, and, well, just showing up for work. *Managing* this melange of values and views is an increasingly difficult task. For one thing, few of us are able to understand our own generation in context. It's difficult to look at your own life as part of a segment or trend or era—or generation. Each of us feels unique and individual. According to Howe and Strauss, "People of all ages feel a disconnection with history. Many have difficulty placing their own thought and actions, even their own lives, in any larger story." This is diversity management at its most challenging. However, it is this diversity and character that shapes the modern workplace and, when managed effectively, it can be used to enrich organizational effectiveness.

MAKING IT HAPPEN ▸▸

Companies that successfully nurture cross-generational workplaces exhibit common approaches. They are successful at making their environments generationally comfortable and focusing their people's energies on the business: accommodating differences, exhibiting flexibility, emphasizing respectful relations, and focusing on retaining talented employees. A successful approach to harnessing the power of cross-generational workplaces is encapsulated in the acronym ACORN. These potent precepts form the acronym *ACORN*:

Accommodate employee differences.

In order to retain employees, the most generationally friendly companies treat their employees as they would customers—they find out everything they can about them, work to meet their specific needs, and serve them according to their unique preferences. Each generation's icons, language, precepts are acknowledged, and language is used that reflects generations other than those in power.

Create workplace choices.

Generationally friendly companies allow the workplace to shape itself around the work they do, the customers they serve, and the people they employ. Dress policies tend to be casual, bureaucracy is decreased, and the atmosphere is relaxed and informal. This is implemented sensitively, in the least offensive way.

Operate with a sophisticated management style.

Generationally friendly managers have little time for circumlocution. They give those who report to them the big picture, specific goals, and measurements; then they turn their people loose, giving feedback, rewards, and recognition as warranted.

Respect competence and initiative.

Generationally friendly companies assume the best of their people, treating all employees—from the greenest recruit to the most seasoned veteran—as people who have a lot to offer and are motivated to do their best. In the most successful companies this approach becomes a self-fulfilling prophecy.

Nourish retention.

When you consider how difficult it is to find good, conscientious employees in today's job market, you realize why many companies treat employee retention with the same focus as on finding and retaining customers. Generationally friendly companies concern themselves constantly with retention and with making their work environments magnets for excellence. They encourage lateral movement throughout the organization and offer broadened assignments.

CONCLUSION

Generationally savvy organizations value the differences between people and look at differences as strengths. Generationally balanced work groups—balanced not in the arithmetic, but in the human sense—respect and learn from yesterday's experiences; understand today's pressures, dilemmas, and needs; and believe that tomorrow will be different still. The mixed-generation workplace can be thought of as a horror or as a joy of creativity and positive energy. The difference is in how well you embrace and master this important new challenge.

For More Information

Books:

Howe, Neil, and William Strauss. *Millennials Rising: The Next Great Generation*. New York: Vintage, 2000.

Martin, Carolyn, and Bruce Tulgan. *Managing Generation Y: Global Citizens Born in the Late Seventies and Early Eighties*. Amherst, MA: HRD Press, 2001.

Raines, Claire, and Jim Hunt. *The Xers & the Boomers: From Adversaries to Allies—A Diplomat's Guide*. Menlo Park, CA: Crisp, 2000.

Smith, J. Walker, and Ann S. Clurman. *Rocking the Ages: The Yankelovich Report on Generational Marketing*. New York: HarperBusiness, 1998.

Tulgan, Bruce. *Managing Generation X: How to Bring Out the Best in Young Talent*. New York: W.W. Norton, 2000.

Tulgan, Bruce. *Winning the Talent Wars: How to Manage and Compete in the High-Tech, High-Speed, Knowledge-Based, Superfluid Economy*. New York: W.W. Norton, 2001.

See also:

☆ **Boosting Business Success Through Diversity (pp. 29–30)**
☆ **Viewpoint: Christopher Bartlett (pp. 45–46)**
☆ **Who's Guiding Your Corporate Destiny? (pp. 216–17)**
Diversity (pp. 1955–57)

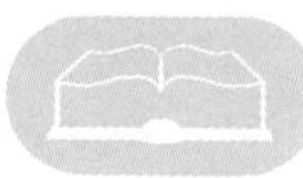

Viewpoint: Christopher Locke

The Case for Business Criticism

What's unique about Chris Locke rapidly comes through when visiting one of the numerous Web site pages dedicated to his work. In a short bio, the first sentence says that he is "Chairman of The Titanic Deck Chair Rearrangement Corporation (NASDAQ: TDCRC)." And, somehow, this is exactly what one might expect from the popular coauthor of *The Cluetrain Manifesto and Gonzo Marketing: Winning Through Worst Practices.*

What is one to make of someone with a point of view that diverges so strongly from standard wisdom? That, Locke would probably point out immediately, is not the most salient question to ask. Here, he puts forth a more fundamental query: Why is it that the business world has not developed its own form of rigorous business criticism? He urges us to establish a new genre of business writing "that recognizes the profound connections between commerce and culture. . ."

Business and society often seem worlds apart, each operating under a separate set of principles that have little to do with the interests of the other. As business becomes more global in scope, and global networks underscore its world-spanning effects, the results of this radical dis-integration are approaching a critical pass. Yet where are the critics to explore, contextualize, and make sense of the changing relations between business and the human societies it both depends upon and shapes?

Any mature field of knowledge has developed a critical community that looks at its history, schools of thought, concepts, categories, language, and practices. Substantial bodies of criticism focus on art, literature, music, and media. Why not business criticism? The counter-intuitive answer seems to be: because we don't take business seriously.

A web search for "business critic[ism]" returns mostly pages denigrating business as a whole. This is not so for other types of criticism. Art critics may deeply dislike particular artists, but few are anti-art. Anthropologists may argue about what "culture" means, but none is anti-culture. Such critics share the basic aims and interests of both practitioners and their audiences. However, most "business critics" are unabashedly anti-business. As a result, they are largely preaching to the choir. Because such criticism is unaligned with the assumptions of business, business tends to ignore it altogether.

The lack of business criticism constitutes a glaring gap in our understanding of today's world. We have data reporting on the financial markets, economic treatises, and business journalism of the who-what-when-where-why variety. However, unlike other forms of criticism, which situate their subjects within an historical context, this sort of business writing typically does not take history into account. It tends to focus almost exclusively on current events, ignoring the larger context that shaped the present business environment. We need to begin thinking critically about business—not to deny its place in the world, but to consider that placement more thoughtfully.

While trade and commerce have long histories, the business we know today is barely 150 years old. When it first emerged in the middle of the 19th century, it had no pedigree whatsoever. The period after Reconstruction saw the establishment of the form of legal incorporation currently recognized in the U.S., and the rise of so-called robber barons such as Andrew Carnegie, John D. Rockefeller, Cornelius Vanderbilt, and Jay Gould. Many of these proto-capitalists were subjected to intense ostracism—not just because they were unschooled, but because they were unlanded. The derogatory label nouveau riche implied that they lacked "culture" and "cultivation"—terms rooted in an earthier sense of culture: agriculture.

Unlike the powerful titans of industry portrayed in high school civics classes, the first capitalists of the modern era were embittered, embattled, defensive, and paranoid. Business was not only rejected by society, it made the rejection mutual. Unhappy with the reception it had received, business began to develop a long-term strategy for revenge.

In short, business realized it could buy the status it had been denied. What conferred the most status in the 19th century was science, which, since the European enlightenment, had overturned ecclesiastical authority and made mankind (women, non-whites, and the "lower classes" excepted) the center of a suddenly knowable universe. The power of science lay in abstraction. Scientific method used hypothesis, observation, and repeatable experiment to establish facts, then employed mathematics and logic to arrive at first principles. Suddenly, the "laws of nature"

"Traditional business defaults to the familiar; it's easy, comfortable, and bonus-building to rely on old business models, outdated templates, yesterday's strategies." (Faith Popcorn)

could be expressed as powerful mathematical abstractions—which also conferred prestige and legitimacy. Even better, the application of such principles enabled companies to survey rail lines, pump oil, smelt ore, charge interest. Business favored this practical approach over the sort of liberal education fostered by the old agrarian elite. Andrew Carnegie wrote: "While the college student has been learning. . .such knowledge as seems adapted for life upon another planet than this as far as business affairs are concerned, the future captain of industry is hotly engaged in the school of experience, obtaining the very knowledge required for his future triumphs. . .College education as it exists is fatal to success in that domain." [Quoted in Laurence R. Veysey, *The Emergence of the American University*, University of Chicago Press, 1965, p. 14.]

Following this sentiment, Carnegie, Cornelius Vanderbilt, Leland Stanford, and others founded their own business schools (the Rockefeller and Ford Foundations later influenced education as a whole). Beginning with Wharton in 1898, business schools grew and prospered through the largesse of wealthy industrialists who wanted to pass along their hard-won knowledge to future generations. The current cachet of the MBA degree, once a humble technical certificate, has made their revenge complete.

In 1911, Frederick W. Taylor claimed to have developed scientific principles. His "scientific management"—with its clipboards, stopwatches, graphs, and charts—reduced complex work to just two abstract dimensions: time and motion. This later became know as "industrial engineering." To leverage the power such abstraction provided, it was necessary to ignore "human factors." Any area of study that involved human beings was folded into an overarching category called social science.

Science introduced a new level of mathematical abstraction, and this kind of abstraction was powerful for business because it supported equations, formulae from which it was possible to construct standard procedures. All the intractable, uncountable stuff about workers and customers—the human factors—get factored out. Business became a paint-by-numbers puzzle-solving exercise; operations experts and bean-counters came into the corporate ascendant, and a mountain of stuff got mass-produced and mass-marketed. This form of applied scientific abstraction worked like a charm.

Ironically, in turning toward such abstraction, business was only following in the footsteps of the society that had previously ostracized it. "High culture"—the cultured and cultivated cadre who delighted in looking down on business—was doing exactly the same thing at the same time. This was called modernism, a reaction against the Enlightenment's goals of rationality and progress filtered through the darker aspects of early industrialism and World War I.

This proscription of social context—often expressed by the slogan "Art for art's sake"—was no less strange than the attitude business adopted toward another kind of abstraction at roughly the same time. "The business of America is business," said president Calvin Coolidge in 1925. In other words: business for business's sake. Through "scientific management," business could ignore those ultimately soft "human factors": people. In the hands of business, abstraction became infinitely more powerful than it did in the world of art. It enabled repeatable procedures, and grounded command and control on powerful principles, equations, formulae, and finally algorithms—the "recipes" underlying computer software.

Like modernist art, business convinced itself it could ignore everything outside the frame—in the case of business: maximize profit. But fixed categories don't work any more. There is no world of art, no world of business—nor of science, politics, religion, music, literature. These "worlds" never existed. They are abstractions. In partial evidence of this, the interdisciplinary field of "economic sociology" is enjoying a remarkable resurgence. Trying to understand human beings as strictly economic, non-social entities doesn't work any better than trying to understand them in strictly social, non-economic terms.

While many fixed categories—sociology, economics, anthropology, business—long ago outlived their usefulness as stand-alone disciplines, much of business continues to depend on their rigid segregation. This "logic" of business as usual has become toxic, a dysfunctional complex of neurotic behaviors and primitive defense mechanisms. In a global economy held together by global networks, it is a fatal mistake for business to isolate itself from society.

Understanding the impact and importance of such errors requires a form of business criticism that is largely lacking today. Half a century ago, we had better examples of what such criticism might look like: *The Lonely Crowd* by David Riesman (1950), *White Collar* by C. Wright Mills (1951), *The Organization Man* by William H. Whyte, Jr. (1956). These works appealed to broad audiences, not just to microscopic specialist readerships. They showed how business and society constitute context to each other. Business is embedded within a deeply social and historical context. The societies in which we live are deeply influenced by corporate actions with respect to physical, psychological, and spiritual environments.

Business depends on both workers and markets, both of which are invisible to abstract algorithms and formulaic procedures. Without a business criticism that recognizes the profound connections between commerce and culture, such blindness will continue, and we will never accomplish the increasingly urgent task of re-integrating business and society.

For More Information

See also:
- ☆ **Viewpoint: Stan Davis and Christopher Meyer (pp. 9–11)**
- ☆ **Viewpoint: Henry Mintzberg (pp. 241–42)**

"In every era, society must strike the right balance between the freedom businesses need to make profits and the preservation of family and community values." (Hilary Clinton)

SQ: Investing in Spiritual Capital
by Danah Zohar

EXECUTIVE SUMMARY

- The central crisis facing capitalism is non-sustainability. Patterns of thought and practice designed for the 18th century will destroy us in the 21st.
- The corporate soul is not about religion. It is about finding and using meaning, deep purpose, and fundamental values in and through our work.
- In the spirited workplace, private corporations will function more as for-profit public service institutions.

Introduction

We've all heard of the Midas touch. Most of us wish we had it. But the original King Midas's ability to turn everything that he touched into gold was a curse placed on him for his greed. When Midas touched his wife or children, they turned to gold. When Midas touched his food, *it* turned to gold, and the cursed king starved to death.

Today, all of us in business or who are *touched* by the ethic of business, are under a Midas curse, put upon us not by the gods but by the dictates of capitalism and business-as-usual. Present-day assumptions of capitalism are (1) that humans are primarily economic beings who thrive in an environment dominated by money and (2) that humans are selfish beings who will always act rationally to improve their own financial best interests. Greed and a justification of greed are built into our capitalistic system. But if everything we have and are is turned to gold, we too, like Midas, will starve to death—emotionally, spiritually, and ultimately even physically.

To lift the curse of contemporary capitalism, we must envision a broader and deeper view of what it means to be human and what motivates human beings. We are not primarily economic beings; we are fundamentally creatures of *meaning*. Our brains are designed to ask deep, existential questions such as *What is the meaning of life? Why was I born? What am I here for? Why must I die?* We are designed to seek an overarching "story" about ourselves that gives meaning, value, and a sense of purpose to our lives.

A Matter of Intelligence

Intelligence is meant to be the tool with which we cultivate our lives and win control over or cooperation with our environment. But IQ alone won't access meaning, value, and purpose: it measures rational, logical, linear intelligence designed to solve practical or abstract problems. EQ (emotional intelligence) enables us to use feelings to boost and complement our IQ. But SQ, spiritual intelligence, allows us to tap into and use our most fundamental needs. To transcend the crisis created by modern capitalism, business has to use its *whole* brain—IQ, EQ, and especially SQ. Spiritual intelligence is the ultimate intelligence needed to elevate the corporate soul.

Why Today's Capitalism Is Unsustainable

Bolstered by Newtonian science and its accompanying technology and by Darwinian "survival of the fittest," capitalism's own "laws of motion" (competition; profit maximization; capital accumulation) have locked business-as-usual into a ruthless pursuit of competitive advantage in a world whose resources its own practices are constantly diminishing. This is not sustainable. Like a monster eating its own flesh, business is destined to consume first its own resources, then itself.

Why Is Business-as-usual Unsustainable?

Six major reasons explain why:

- **Finite resources.** The Western ethic has been that the earth and its resources are there for human use and control. But the earth's resources are finite, while the assumption of business-as-usual is that they are infinite. We arrogantly assume continued and constant growth using our present practices.
- **Environmental damage.** Global warming, floods, holes in the ozone layer, air pollution and its attendant side effects on health, and extreme weather patterns are the result of our reliance on technologies that pollute our own nest.
- **Inequality.** The assumption that human beings are primarily consumers favors the big consumers over the small, those who can pay over those who can't. This deepens inequality between rich and poor nations and between rich and poor groups within nations. Such inequality breeds crime, family breakdown, political instability, and mass, illegal immigration. These things are all bad for business.
- **Leadership crisis.** Making ever more money is not in itself high on the list of what motivates people. The best, most thoughtful, most idealistic people, the best leaders, want to serve something greater than themselves, want their lives to *mean* something—they become doctors, teachers, heads of international aid organizations, go into politics or research. They are seldom found guiding private organizations; there is a critical shortage of great leaders in business today.
- **Short-term thinking.** Concern with maximizing short-term shareholder value deprives business of long-term perspective. It doesn't plan ahead or look at the "big picture." Time comes in quarterly chunks, severely limiting consideration of research needs, long-time viability, and future growth.
- **Human factor.** The mistaken notion that humans are primarily economic creatures increases the stress and exhaustion of the "winners" who serve the existing system. Other values—time with family, time to relax, to nourish inner needs, to enjoy accumulated wealth, to find fulfillment or a sense of fundamental purpose—are all sacrificed to the fast buck. Stressed and exhausted people miss work, suffer disease and premature death. They have reduced creativity and productivity. Stress is bad for business.

Developing Spiritual Capital

If challenged about the prime motive of profit maximization, most business people look dumbfounded, saying, "It has always been that way!" But business as we know it today is only 200 years old. Today's capitalism was conceived by a small handful of 18th century Enlightenment philosophers inspired by Newtonian mechanism. Their idea of capital was solely *material capital*—measured in money.

According to the *Oxford English Dictionary*, capital is "that which confers wealth, profit,

"We need a common ethical framework to inform and to guide the conduct of global business"

(Mark Moody-Stuart)

advantage, or power." This lends itself to broader interpretation. Today we hear a great deal about "social capital." Here, writers mean both the material wealth and social benefit gained by a society that has, for example, low crime, low divorce, and low illiteracy. I want to extend this further by introducing the concept of spiritual capital.

Spiritual capital challenges capitalism's assumption that we are primarily economic creatures and argues instead that human beings are essentially creatures of meaning and purpose. The spiritual qualities of a business or a life are those that show a need for dialogue with meaning, vision, fundamental values, and deep purpose. Spiritual capital takes these as the crucial commodities of exchange. A company or a person who acts in accordance with meaning, vision, purpose, and fundamental values—*while making a profit*—is invested with spiritual capital. Its primary assumption is that companies can make *more* profit by doing more good. We act on this assumption by using our spiritual intelligence.

Criteria for a High SQ

We are all (if healthy) born with a potential for high SQ. It is a basic, innate capacity of our brain; but like all our innate capacities, it needs nurture and development. To encourage the further development of the spiritual intelligence and build the means for companies to commit more deeply to it, we can identify ten criteria for high SQ. The criteria are:

- self-awareness (awareness that we have a "deep" self);
- spontaneity (emergence, self-organization);
- leading from vision and fundamental values;
- holism (seeing the web, the system, the connections);
- compassion (sense of community, sense of belonging to the flow of life);
- celebration of diversity;
- field-independence (standing against the crowd);
- asking fundamental "Why?" questions;
- reframing (seeing the whole, or big picture);
- using, and thriving on, adversity.

Spiritual Leadership in the Future of Business

Does business today need "spiritual" leaders? Definitely yes! Those who managed old-style capitalist systems, with their sterile assumptions about human nature and narrow reliance on mechanistic philosophies, cannot lead us through the human and global challenges facing business today. We need a new kind of leader for a new kind of "servant capitalism."

Taking for granted that global business has the money and the real power to make a significant difference in today's troubled world, elevating the corporate soul envisages business raising its sights above the "bottom line," becoming more service- and value-oriented (largely eliminating the assumed distinction between private enterprise and public institutions), and having a higher proportion of "servant leaders,"—leaders who serve not just colleagues, employees, products, and customers, but the community, the planet, humanity, the future, and life itself.

The bottom-line criterion for business will always be material solvency and a decent profit. Business *is* society's engine of wealth creation. But wealth is broader than *mere* money. Solvency and profit leave room for maximizing meaning, service, quality of life, health, enjoyment of work, for amassing not merely material but also social and spiritual capital, and thereby contributing hugely to the common well-being and self-organizing creativity of life on Earth. That, I believe, is the true purpose of business.

Mini-cases

Here is a small set of companies whose manufacturing or trading behavior elevates the corporate soul.

- *Amul* markets the Indian state of Gujarat's 10,000 milk cooperatives. A peasant with only one bucket of milk to sell per day can earn his vital 20 rupees, competing in his own right, and regardless of caste, with larger dairy farmers. An embodiment of Mahatma Gandhi's social and economic principles, Amul sales are $516 million annually.
- *Van City*, Vancouver's largest credit union, channels lending funds to customers and causes marginalized by mainstream banks—inner city development, risky small business ventures, environmental protection projects, disadvantaged women, and investment funds for the developing world—and has a commitment to corporate social responsibility, with $6.4 billion annual turnover and $39 million profit.
- *Coca-Cola* has put its distribution network in India at the service of the Indian national government to distribute polio vaccine to remote rural areas. It has a similar project in Africa to distribute AIDS medication, providing, at no extra cost, enormous gain in spiritual capital.
- *BP/British Petroleum* has adopted a new motto, "Beyond Petroleum," making it an energy company instead of an oil company. Its heavy investment in developing hydrogen and other alternative energy technologies that both reduce dependence on scarce and damaging hydrocarbon fuels and provide energy for the post-petroleum future, keeps its profits high *by way* of reducing environmental damage.

Making It Happen ▸▸

- Facilitate a corporate conversation that enables habits and a structure for reflection on deep values and fundamental purpose.
- Create corporate infrastructures that respond to a wider environment.
- Learn to negotiate rather than to suppress conflict and difference. Identify and use the "sand in the oyster."
- Cultivate the individual soul—read, reflect, experience.

For More Information

Books:

Fukuyama, Francis. *Trust*. New York: Free Press, 1995.

Gratton, Lynda. *Living Strategy*. Upper Saddle River, NJ: Financial Times Prentice Hall, 2000.

Smith, Simon. *Inner Leadership*. Lanham, MD: National Book Network, 2000.

See also:

☆ **Boosting Business Success Through Diversity (pp. 29–30)**
☆ **Driving Fear from the Workplace (pp. 330–31)**
☆ **Environmental Management (pp. 113–14)**
☆ **Finding and Keeping the Best Talent in the World (pp. 119–20)**
☆ **Finding and Keeping Top Talent (pp. 33–34)**
☆ **Viewpoint: Fons Trompenaars (pp. 27–28)**
☆ **Viewpoint: Sumantra Ghoshal (pp. 190–91)**
☆ **Viewpoint: Tom Petzinger (pp. 163–64)**
☆ **Workers without Borders: Creating Bonds When Workers Have No Loyalty (pp. 204–05)**

"I think that business practices would improve immeasurably if they were guided by 'feminine' principles—qualities like love and care and intuition." (Anita Roddick)

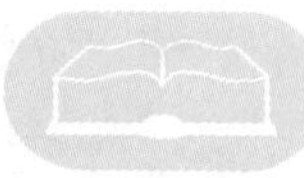

VIEWPOINT: CHRISTOPHER BARTLETT

Helping Managers to Assess the Value of Human Capital

A long-standing faculty member at Harvard Business School, the Australian Christopher Bartlett is best known for his ground-breaking work with Sumantra Ghoshal of the London Business School. Their 20-year writing partnership—a rarity in academe—has produced a steady stream of highly influential articles and books based on in-depth research among practicing managers.

In their most recent work Bartlett and Ghoshal argue that the old corporate model oriented around strategy, structure, and systems is now undergoing a process of rebirth. As human capital usurps financial capital as the key strategic resource, the new model, they say, will be built around purpose, people, and process.

What has had the greatest influence on your thinking on management?

Before I became an academic I used to work for an honest living as a line manager. That evolved into working as a consultant with McKinsey & Company. But the experience as a line manager has had the biggest influence on my thinking. That gave me a frame of reference and a great respect for where the learning really occurs in organizations–in the trenches. It has informed my work. My academic career has been based on clinical field-based research: going into companies, talking to practicing managers. I think sometimes there is an arrogance in business books: the authors imply that they know best. I have the opposite view: that we learn most about management from the people who are making it work on a daily basis.

Who has influenced me most? I'd have to say the hundreds of managers I've interviewed. There is so much I've learned from them. People like Jack Welch, Percy Barnevik, and Bill Gates are the Alfred P. Sloans and Pierre Du Ponts of their generation. I use them as examples because they are icons that people know, but there are many others whose names are less well known from whom I have learned.

How will business be different in the 21st century?

In *The Individualized Corporation*, my last book with Sumantra Ghoshal, we wrote about a management revolution that's in its early stages. Behind the turmoil of restructuring and re-engineering, we argued, is the corporate model that is in rebirth. The fundamental shift is that companies are trying to reorganize themselves around what is now the scarce resource–human capital.

Traditionally, there has been an assumption that financial capital is the scarce resource and that companies should be organized around its effective use. That is reflected in the way that companies have been managed in the past. Return on investment, earnings per share–all the measures we've got are about controlling and managing financial capital. Companies used to create sophisticated systems designed to haul the information to the top of the organization so that senior managers could make decisions about the allocation of financial capital.

It's not that financial capital is no longer important; it's that it is no longer *the* constraining resource. The constraining resources, and therefore the strategic resources, are information, knowledge, and expertise. And unlike financial capital, which you can allocate, measure, and control, the knowledge and expertise reside deep down in the organization, in the minds of individuals and in the relationships between people who are closest to the customers, the competitors, the technology, and the regulatory environment. That is what companies are trying to capture, embed, use, and diffuse through the organization–and that's a very different task.

The company of the 21st century will have to learn how to manage human capital rather than financial capital as a strategic resource. This shifts our whole mindset from one that is about appropriating value to one that is about creating value. Creating value is about generating ideas and innovation, and capturing and leveraging the scarce knowledge, expertise, and best practices that reside inside the organization.

The old strategic models were about the external market. Michael Porter's "Five Forces," which dominated strategic thinking for years, were about industry structure and competitive dynamics. That was the model that was embedded in the 1970s and

"Yesterday's success formula is often today's obsolete dogma. . ." (Christopher Bartlett)

  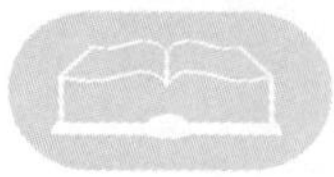    

dominated through the 1980s. But by the time we got into the 1990s we started to think about a very different model of strategy laid on top of that external strategy, and that was looking at organizational capability–core competencies if you like.

That new strategic framework was about looking internally to examine how to build sustainable competitive advantage through hard-to-imitate organizational capabilities, and not just about the external environment. I think it is now becoming clear that these internal processes depend on the ability to attract, motivate, and retain individuals with the requisite knowledge and expertise.

What new skills will be needed to cope with these changes?

The old model of the hierarchical bureaucracy was all about measuring, allocating, and controlling financial capital. The skills required were very much about having accountability for things that were put under your direct control. As we move toward this very different model of organization–and very different sources of competitive advantage–managers will require different skills from those needed for vertical control processes.

There are three core internal processes that they will have to be able to manage. First, they will need to create a process to elicit entrepreneurial initiative. Not just top-down internal directives, although those will remain in terms of the direction and objectives. In the past directives often extinguished the ability for bottom-up initiatives. In the future we will have to create organizations that enable entrepreneurial initiators on the front line.

The second management skill is being able to link and elicit knowledge and expertise in such a way as to diffuse them, and to develop people and relationships as a source of organizational capability. That's very different from the vertical, financially driven control processes.

The third skill is the ability to self-obsolete. Traditionally, what managers have done is to drive their organizations up the learning curve, to get better and better at what they've always done. In future it will be much more about jumping learning curves and being willing to constantly redefine the business, product and processes, and to self-renew.

Are there new management questions that we should be asking?

There's a fundamental question that faces corporations and management. Today the assumption is that corporations are primarily responsible to their shareholders, and legitimately so, because shareholders have historically been the providers of the financial capital that was the scarce strategic resource. Companies had to compete for it and justify their use of it to the shareholders. But as we shift the primary way of gaining competitive advantage from appropriating value to creating value through intellectual capital, the constraining resource becomes people rather than financial capital. Then the question becomes what does this mean for the distribution of the value created?

The assumption at the moment is that the value should be distributed to the owners of the scarce capital resource. But, increasingly, that assumption is starting to fray at the edges. Companies are asking: if the people are so important for the creation of value, then don't we need to find ways to distribute more of the value to them? But we're still measuring, evaluating, and rewarding them by the old rules. Increasingly, companies are using stock options and making their people shareholders. And that's legitimate. But I think the real question is: is the balance moving to the point where we need to think about the distribution of the value to them not as a secondary responsibility but as a primary responsibility–a byproduct of maximizing shareholder returns–and an objective of the organization? I think it is.

That's what sole proprietors do; that's what partnerships do; that's what small start-ups do. It's what the large corporations haven't done. They are stumbling toward it with options. But they are a pretty blunt instrument, with lots of risks attached, as the 2000 "tech wreck" demonstrated.

How can companies best promote enterprises that are a) profitable and b) good places to work?

Companies will *only* be profitable if they are good places to work. Talented people will be attracted to places that engage them and give them meaning and development; that, in turn, will allow those companies to be profitable. How they distribute that financial profit is a question we've already talked about.

For More Information

Web Site:
www.hbs.edu/fac

See also:

- ☆ **Boosting Business Success Through Diversity (pp. 29–30)**
- ☆ **Breaking the Lead Ceiling (pp. 237–38)**
- ☆ **Downsizing with Dignity (pp. 16–17)**
- ☆ **Finding and Keeping the Best Talent in the World (pp. 119–20)**
- ☆ **How Managers Stay Up When Times Are Down (pp. 334–35)**
- ☆ **Human Capital (pp. 115–16)**
- ☆ **Power Struggling and Power Sharing (pp. 95–96)**
- ☆ **Preventing Corporate Systems from Holding You Back (pp. 177–78)**
- ☆ **Retaining Employees (pp. 196–97)**
- ☆ **The Second Coming of Service (pp. 77–78)**
- **Managing Across Borders (p. 922)**
- **Ghoshal and Bartlett (pp. 992–93)**

"Delayering and destaffing do not by themselves provide durable solutions to performance problems. . ."

(Christopher Bartlett)

  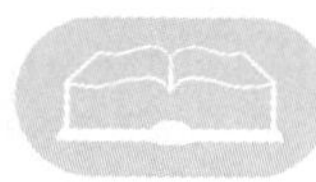    

Tackling Sexual Harassment in the Workplace *by Anne Covey and Michael S. Morris*

EXECUTIVE SUMMARY

- Sexual harassment is conduct that results in a "tangible employment action" such as hiring, firing, promotion or demotion, or is sufficiently frequent or severe to create a hostile work environment.
- A revolution is underway in the United States and other countries where organizations are investing in their employees to provide harassment-free workplaces. There are two types of sexual harassment recognized by the United States Judicial System: Quid Pro Quo and Hostile Work Environment.
- Quid Pro Quo sexual harassment occurs when submission to sexual conduct is made a term or condition of an individual's employment or when sexual conduct by an individual is factored into any employment decisions affecting the individual.
- Hostile Work Environment harassment occurs when unwelcome sexual conduct has the purpose or effect of unreasonably interfering with an individual's work performance, or creates an offensive working environment.
- A recent study determined that a typical sexual harassment case costs a *Fortune* 500 company $6.7 million.

Introduction

Sexual harassment knows no cultural, political, religious, gender, or geographical boundary. The United States Supreme Court has observed: "Everyone knows by now that sexual harassment is a common problem in the American workplace."

However, sexual harassment can take on numerous shades of legal interpretation. Historically, a person had to be the target of sexual harassment to bring a cause of action. Today, courts have expanded the zone of harassment to include those persons beyond the target, for example, those individuals who observe or overhear the sexually harassing conduct. If beauty is in the eye of the beholder, then harassment is within the earshot of the listener. Organizations are legally responsible to all of their employees for making them feel uncomfortable by creating a sexual environment. There is no better incentive for organizations to eradicate such sexual harassment.

Practical and Legal Changes in the Workplace

Sexual harassment, once thought to be the realm of male against female, has been transformed over the years to include any sexual conduct against employees of any gender, fronted by an employee of any gender. Similarly, in the educational arena, the sexual harassment microscope has switched focus from teacher on student sexual harassment to examination of student on student sexual harassment.

The defined parameters of independent contracting are also under siege. In Danco, Inc. v. Wal-Mart Stores, Inc., 178 F. 3d 8 (1st Cir. 1999), the court held that an independent contractor had the right to bring a racial discrimination claim against an employer based on the employer's non-management employees creating a hostile work environment. In the near future, employers may face legal action not only from their employees, but from their independent contractors as well. Accordingly, an outside accountant performing, say, a year-end audit may sue the employer/client, if the accountant is subjected to sexual harassment. Organizations may therefore be responsible to their contractors too, despite not formally employing them.

In a recent legal case, the New Jersey Supreme Court determined that an electronic bulletin board may be so closely related to the workplace environment that sexual harassment on such a forum should also be policed as heavily as in the physical workplace. Inventions are perceived as allowing mankind to advance. Ironically, the Internet is becoming another potential legal liability for organizations as it provides an extended site of workplace sexual harassment.

E-mail, another means of improving communication among diverse employment locations, is now fraught with legal implications. For example, an employer may be liable for an errant electronic mail sent to a co-worker that is opened by another employee who is appalled by the contents of the message or attachments. Lawsuits based on such electronic messages are increasing at an alarming rate. Every employer must now have an electronic mail and Internet policy addressing content which is acceptable, while specifically prohibiting use of its corporate equipment for harassment or other discriminatory purposes.

Technological advances have now become possible legal nightmares for uninformed corporate decision makers. Each such advancement must now undergo legal scrutiny to determine if liability attaches to the latest development.

Establishing the Harassment-free Workplace Environment

The Perils of Ignoring Workplace Harassment

Ida L. Castro, former Commission Chairwoman of the Equal Employment Opportunity Commission, stated: "Employers should realize that they will pay a high price by tolerating, condoning, or ignoring the creation of hostile work place environments." This high price of conducting business can be readily seen in the recent monetary settlements by several *Fortune* 500 companies: Coca-Cola—$192.5 million (racial discrimination); Mitsubishi—$34.0 million (the current EEOC record holder for sexual harassment); and Ford Motor Company—$8.0 million (sexual harassment).

A typical sexual harassment case costs a *Fortune* 500 company $6.7 million dollars. The overt expenses are the awarding of astronomical jury awards and punitive damages. However, the hidden expenses are

"I was extremely lucky that my first two bosses were people who believed in me as a person and felt that gender was totally irrelevant."

(Nicola Horlick)

loss of productive use of employee time and degeneration of employee morale. Some costs can be absorbed while other expenses such as damage to a company's reputation cannot. Management must commit not only to the philosophy of providing a workplace environment free of sexual harassment, but also to take affirmative steps to ensure its existence.

ENSURING A HARASSMENT-FREE WORKPLACE

The goal for employers is to ensure a harassment-free workplace, complete with effective monitoring devices. To do this, corporations must be proactive, not reactive. They must develop appropriate regulatory policies that work to restrict harassment. Policies must be published and clearly state the responsibilities of both the employer and the employee. Just as advertising is used to disseminate information about the product in the marketplace, so too must employers highlight, promote, and distribute their sexual harassment policy. When a problem arises with a defective product redress must be prompt, thorough and confidential. This same approach is applied to sexual harassment complaints.

The key to addressing any sexual harassment complaint is to provide an effective complaint mechanism. All such redress formats must lead to corrective action based upon fairness to all parties. Corporate ombudsmen are replacing the traditional model of redress. Ombuds are third-party entities who process the complaint from intake through investigation to ultimate resolution. The goal is to provide a mechanism that encourages employee complaints to an entity outside of the corporate structure, thereby fostering belief in a system that is beyond corporate manipulation.

THE IMPORTANCE OF EDUCATION, CORPORATE CULTURE, AND EFFECTIVE MONITORING

Companies are implementing proactive management concepts to remedy the lethal virus that is workplace harassment and prejudice. Education lies at the center of reversal and remedial action. Training has become the cornerstone for establishing and maintaining a healthy corporate culture. Some organizations are identifying specific persons within the organization to oversee and monitor the workplace environment while others are hiring outside resources.

Much of mankind's advancement has been through trial and error. However, in times of expensive litigation costs, trials must be avoided and errors pared to a minimum. Organizations seldom realize that the best asset an organization possesses never shows up on any financial statement—the employee. An employee empowered in the workplace, and educated to a sufficient degree, will pay untold dividends in the prevention of potential lawsuits.

MINI-CASES

Coca-Cola is investing approximately $280,000,000 in reforming its corporate culture to provide a harassment-free workplace. Establishment of several watershed initiatives include: partnership with the United Negro College fund; founding of a "Diversity Leadership Academy"; funding for minority businesses; funding of a "Supplier Mentoring Program"; and financial assistance for minority-oriented nonprofit organizations. Coca-Cola seeks to eradicate racial discrimination and harassment from its corporate image and culture through its monetary commitments.

As a result of a complaint, *Mitsubishi* implemented Zero Tolerance Policy and Equality Objectives. Mitsubishi was required to implement a policy to monitor its supervisors' performance based upon the supervisor's handling of harassment issues. This included making it a criterion for qualification as a supervisor that a candidate should make a "commitment to equal employment opportunity." In addition, training was mandated for supervisors on an annual basis, all new employees, and senior management. This resulted in supervisor's advancements within Mitsubishi being based on their sensitivity towards employee multiculturalism as well as their productivity.

MAKING IT HAPPEN ▸▸

To reform your corporate culture into a dynamic, modern and prejudice-free environment that can also deal readily and effectively with incidence of harassment:

- Develop effective and responsive policies and procedures, and enforce them appropriately.
- Educate and train management and non-management employees.
- Review the organization and the way in which it is managed to ensure fairness and equality.
- Immediately investigate sexual harassment complaints.
- Remedy fully and completely any harassing workplace conduct.
- Monitor achievement of goals by independent third parties.
- Make financial commitments to eradicating traditional stereotyping.

CONCLUSION

What is the future for sexual harassment? Achieve tolerance among employees regardless of their race, religion, sex, and national origin or the high costs of the effects of intolerance will continue to be paid. As multi-culturalism takes hold on the workplace, the permutations become greater for lawsuits. Ignorance of the law is no excuse nor is ignorance of common respect and decency. Through the use of proper educational tools and proper monitoring devices organizations can and must provide a working environment with zero tolerance for sexual harassment.

For More Information

Books:

Covey, Anne. *The Workplace Law Advisor: From Harassment and Discrimination Policies to Hiring and Firing Guidelines—What Every Manager and Employee Needs to Know*. Cambridge, MA: Perseus, 2000.

Orlov, Darlene, and Michael T. Roumell. *What Every Manager Needs to Know About Sexual Harassment*. New York: Amacon, 1999.

Webb, Susan L. *Sexual Harassment, Shades of Gray: Guidelines for Managers, Supervisors & Employees*. Las Vegas, NV: Pacific Resource Development Group, 1999.

Web Sites:

www.eeco.gov: The Equal Employment Opportunity Commission issues guidelines for corporations as well as responses to frequently asked questions.

http://overlawyered.com/topics/harass.htm: this site chronicles the high cost of the United States' legal system on a broad range of topics including sexual harassment.

See also:

✓ **Introducing an Equal Opportunities Policy (pp. 440–41)**

Personnel Management and HR Management (pp. 2067–71)

"Women's presence in the office work force challenged the Victorian ideal of separate public and private worlds for men and women."

(Angel Kwolek-Folland)

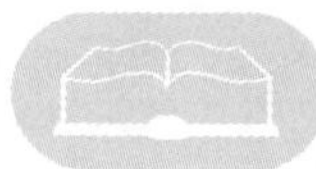

MANAGING INTELLECTUAL CAPITAL *by Leif Edvinsson*

EXECUTIVE SUMMARY

- Intellectual capital is already gaining significantly in recognition and acceptance, as a means of valuing and developing the key intangible assets of a business.
- Surveys indicate that two thirds of all U.S. companies have started to look proactively for new ways to collect and report non-financial data, including intellectual capital.
- At least a third of the current investment decisions by U.S. companies are considered partly on the basis of intangibles. Statistics suggest that greater reliance on non-financial measures results in more accurate earnings forecasts.

INTRODUCTION

Intellectual capital (IC) is an offspring of the knowledge era. It is still in its formative phase, having first been formally recognized in 1991 when the large Swedish corporation Skandia started implementing a comprehensive set of innovative knowledge practices to account for its intangible assets. If the growth of hardware power is an indication, computers will equal the capacity of the human brain by 2011, when we celebrate the 20th anniversary of IC. How will business assets be evaluated then—will they take account of those assets are that are frequently and simultaneously both the most important and the most intangible? It is worth considering:

- Why just a handful of the millions of companies started since 1900 achieved solid growth for two decades, and why most of them failed within less than five years?
- Why managers try to achieve results by imposing financial goals and controls, while knowing next to nothing about their company's products, technologies, and customers?
- How managers succeed without having any idea of the return on investments in network relationships, the costs of seeking information, or the state of their IC-index?

UNDERSTANDING INTELLECTUAL CAPITAL

HOW INTELLECTUAL CAPITAL HAS DEVELOPED

The roots of the IC concept run deep. The economist John Kenneth Galbraith coined the term "Intellectual Capital" in 1969, and Peter Drucker spoke about "knowledge workers" before that. Though systems for recording IC are now proliferating, the concept is still mysterious to most wage-earners.

THE IMPORTANCE OF NON-FINANCIAL MEASURES

The importance of non-financial measures is self-evident. W. Edwards Deming, legendary creator of the quality circles concept, has criticized managers in the United States for spending over 97% of their time analyzing figures, and less than 3% on the intangibles that really matter. In other words, they spend 97% of their time trying to figure out 3% of what is going on.

Every third Nordic company now takes these "soft values" into account. The IC network plays its part in this global value evolution. We work with hundreds of consultants and researchers along two mainstream lines: we assist organizations that are installing IC routines and we cultivate and improve our tools, by developing IC ratings and using intellectual labs like the growing net of Future Centers.

Powerful institutions, like the U.S. Federation of Accounting Standards Board (FASB) and the Securities and Exchange Commission (SEC) in Washington, are now endorsing supplementary accounts. The influential Brookings Institute explores the issue systematically. In Denmark, a government proposal has made it a matter of legislation. When the international magazine *Business Week* ranks business schools, it features indicators of intellectual capital. Since present financial indicators just refer to the past, they create perilous gaps between the bottom line and long-term goals. They offer a frail groundwork for the strategies of leading-edge companies. Clearly, the key to future productivity is to recognize the interplay of psychological, sociological, and political values in entrepreneurship.

To the extent that customers get involved as co-producers, knowledge that used to be external and distant becomes ever more internal and intimate. Obviously, such changes cannot be handled by traditional accounting schemes.

Monetary economies and accounting practices have provided mankind with efficient tools for complex social organization. The present challenge is to make them more multidimensional. Instead of being just black boxes, they could become compasses for charting the course towards tomorrow. The bottom line may be useful when a bank considers lending money to a company. It is not useful for running a company. Cash is only the beginning and the icon of the value-creating process. It is a wonderful enabler, but it can make us forget the reasons for doing something, for creating meaning.

It takes patience, perseverance, and painful re-examinations to make a vision like IC consistently operative. To date, it has been mainly the large and lucrative companies that have taken intangibles into account. Unfortunately, some of them seem to get it all wrong. Instead of using the indicators to advance employee competence, or increase surplus and shareholder value, they often exploit them chiefly as seminar exercises for top management.

This is dangerous, since the emerging talent war has triggered a brain drain from large companies to small and medium-sized enterprises. The future business battles will be about ideas and non-traditional thinking, turned into knowledge innovations.

Certainly, figures cannot be faked as easily as words and symbols. Some people fear that before global standards are established, IC audits will open the gates for arbitrary, even fraudulent practices. Probably, yes. But in the absence of IC, vast areas of corporate reality remain in the dark, just visible to insiders. You might as well argue that IC is just what the doctor ordered to restore public confidence in the stock and securities markets.

A corporate rush to cut the brain's lead times is the name of the competitive game now. One way to win is to start learning before new skills are required. To make qualified guesses, and invest in the supposed future. Buying such intellectual options will be a key strategy in the knowledge economy.

About 7% of humanity is linked in to the World Wide Web. Yet the number of

"Intellectual capital is the sum of everything everybody in a company knows that gives it a competitive edge."

(Thomas Stewart)

connections this small group make up is already staggering. Growing connectivity is to IC what transportation infrastructures are to financial capital.

The Internet now defies the established control of distribution channels and intellectual property. It undermines anyone whose status depends on privileged access to information. It leverages IC by offering extraordinary opportunities to start new businesses and see prompt returns. It is doing all that, and is likely do it much better and faster tomorrow. Maybe it is time to replace Adam Smith's famous metaphor of the market—the invisible hand—and talk about the invisible brain.

Though stock market booms and busts distract attention from what is really happening, the industrial laws of gravity are being supplanted by rules dictated by knowledge. As the costs of copying and distributing products approach zero, old value chains will break or become obsolete.

There is much to be done before IC standards achieve the sophistication and reliability required to earn general respect. Nevertheless, they are already worth their weight in gold. As financial capital becomes ever more questioned and volatile, sustainable earnings capabilities and new wealth will tip the scales in favor of IC.

MAKING IT HAPPEN ▸▸

There is a range of approaches to managing intellectual capital, and as a starting point, it may be helpful to consider the following questions:

- **Can you identify your intangible assets and do you understand what they contribute to your organization?** It is worth considering that shareholders and other stakeholders value them, and they affect market perceptions of the business's value. There is therefore a powerful reason for measuring and actively managing your portfolio of intangible assets.
- **How might you measure and monitor the value of your intangible assets, your intellectual capital?** You can't manage what you can't measure, and given the importance of IC it should be continuously valued and developed.
- **How could you manage and develop the value of your intellectual capital?** At a time of commodity production and information overload, intellectual capital is a major source of competitive advantage, a key differentiator, and this can deliver significant benefits in terms of customer retention, acquisition and innovation.

It is valuable to audit your intellectual capital, understanding its place and significance in the fragmenting value chain, and helping to decide a strategy for managing it. The key to making it happen is to nurture your reputation, people, and other key assets, focusing on how these resources can be fully employed and also developed and grown.

CONCLUSION

How will economic assets be distributed, if the main social distinction is between those who know things and those who do not, rather than between owners of capital and employees? IC may not be a sufficient answer to that question, but it might provide us with instruments to handle it with.

IC is not just any fashionable management fad, like benchmarking, re-engineering, or quality circles. It is not something you can choose to apply or not, as conditions and feelings change. It is more generic.

Classic cost management and accounting was not widely practiced in the business world until the fifties. Let's call these approaches the first generation of knowledge management tools. The costs of failing to change them into second generation IC tools may assume massive proportions. To trade knowledge according to the old financial scorecards is like navigating an airplane just using the fuel meter, and ignoring data about altitude, position, etc. Like accounting for the cost of a check while ignoring the loss of the capital it draws from. Or as awkward as building Lego with boxing gloves.

Jack Welch, the former C.E.O. of General Electric, recently said that we must globalize our intellectual capital, and one way to achieve this is to work towards an international IC system. The key challenge for corporate and political leaders who want to make a difference is not only to develop contexts for future growth. It will take more than communicating intangibles to stakeholders in a repetitive, auditable, and trustworthy way. In the face of coming institutional failures, social entrepreneurship will be a critical concern. The real future space—the IC of nations—will demand significant knowledge innovations.

For More Information

Books:

Cusumano, Michael A., and Constantinos C. Markides, eds. *Strategic Thinking for the Next Economy*. San Francisco, CA: Jossey-Bass, 2001.

Edvinsson, Leif, with Michael S. Malone. *Intellectual Capital*. New York: HarperBusiness, 1997.

Edvinsson, Leif. *Corporate Longitude*. Englewood Cliffs, NJ: Financial Times Prentice Hall, 2002.

Fitz-Enz, Jac. *The E-Aligned Enterprise*. New York: AMACOM, 2001.

Web Site:

www.knowledgeinc.com: the site for Knowledge Inc. has multiple resources, such as articles, interviews, and links to other sites about intellectual capital.

See also:

Intellectual Capital (p. 914)
Chris Argyris (pp. 964–65)
Knowledge Management (pp. 2018–20)

"The only irreplaceable capital an organization possesses is the knowledge and ability of its people."
(Andrew Carnegie)

MAKING CULTURES BEHAVE *by Robert Heller*

EXECUTIVE SUMMARY

- Corporate cultures are the major obstacles to successful change and must themselves change.
- Organizational obstacles can be changed far more easily than human psychology.
- Human resistance can be readily overcome if four preconditions of change are met.
- Cultural change should embody a major shift of emphasis from looking inwards to looking outwards.
- Many cultural change programs are constructed the wrong way around—culture first, behavior second.
- Proactive cultural management bars obstructive behaviors and, instead, supports, reinforces, and rewards constructive ones.
- The leader's personal behavior must be consistent with the demands of cultural change.

OBSTACLES TO CHANGE

Managements wanting to transform their organizations face a fundamental difficulty. Their common problem is that organizational cultures run counter to people's individual inclinations. For example, as customers, everybody wants high standards of quality and service, and knows well what these standards entail. People serving customers are also sensible enough to realize that they cannot expect to receive what they are unwilling to provide themselves. But unless you change the culture, so that it supports rather than obstructs service excellence, the latter will not be achieved.

Conventional wisdom, which portrays culture changes as intrinsically difficult, is therefore mistaken in seeing human resistance and conservatism as the greatest obstacle. Resistance to change is itself cultural, collective as opposed to individual. Above all, it involves the deadening impact of organizational obstacles, such as:

- excessive hierarchy;
- order-and-obey, command-and-control management;
- unresponsiveness to market changes;
- lack of essential skills.

All these can be changed far more easily than human psychology.

BUILDING A NEW CULTURE

Building a new culture is, in this sense, technical. It involves a three-stage process:

1. knowing what to do;
2. knowing how it should be done;
3. actually doing it.

The first two stages are relatively easy: most managers are fully aware of the need to respond faster and more effectively to the market, for example. Most also know what actions will have this effect. Their subordinates are mostly just as well informed. But time and again the organization gets in the way of informed action.

An overall change philosophy which aims to remove the four cardinal faults listed above is therefore easy enough to state, but very hard to execute. It demands dismantling four pillars of the traditional organization. While people as individuals see the drawbacks of this corporate system, as a collective they will close ranks in its defense and resist its overthrow by acting to:

- flatten the hierarchy;
- empower the workers;
- get close to customers;
- train, train, train.

Each part of this quartet of banners is a precondition of a successful cultural program. If you miss out on any of the four, the program will almost certainly fail. The banner headlines are meaningless unless translated into actions that not only impact the culture in real life, but are seen by all to accomplish transformation. Tests include:

1. How close does your new flattened structure come to the ideal minimum?
2. Has all responsibility been delegated to the lowest level at which it can be effectively exercised?
3. Are all activities being designed, monitored, and improved in efficiency in relation to customer needs and satisfaction?
4. Is a high level of continuous training now the clear personal responsibility of everybody in the company and of their leaders?

The four tests sound simple. But their radical nature is extreme. For example, on flattened structures, James Champy (famous for his work on Business Process Reengineering) advises only three levels:

1. "enterprise managers," who are responsible for decisions
2. and are helped in reaching them by "people/process managers"; the latter plan and implement with the aid of
3. the "self-managers" who execute the decisions.

All three levels are backed by supporting "expertise managers," like accountants and technologists.

Radical the answers to the four questions may be. But in the early 21st century, it is hard to envisage a change program that does not embody this major shift of emphasis from looking inwards to looking outwards. The internal program also requires you to shift totally from what Douglas McGregor described as Theory X (which concentrates on order and discipline to achieve results) to the Theory Y approach, which says work and getting results are as natural as play. Theory Y makes change management much easier further down your organization, because it points people in directions in which they want to go.

This does not remove the need for leadership. The role of the leader under Theory Y is even more important than under Theory X. But you need a different kind of leadership to manage change by getting the best out of a true team. Managing in the new way is much harder than command-and-control management, because self-restraint by the leadership is required to enable "coworkers" to contribute to their full potential.

The object is to change behavior, which in turn changes culture. Many cultural change programs are constructed the other way around–culture first, behavior second. Small wonder that they so often fail. To change the behavior of others, the leader must first change his or her own behavior as a key enabling factor, as illustrated in the table below.

This formula is the way to achieve the desired and desirable combination of change with order. As it happens, the

"As international companies begin to compete with each other in the global marketplace, the role of cross-cultural training becomes increasingly important." (Rabi Bhagat)

BEFORE	Play an active part in all the unit's work
AFTER	Concentrate on strategy and overall direction
BEFORE	Intervene in day-to-day decisions and operations
AFTER	Leave details of daily operations to those responsible
BEFORE	Make all decisions personally without consultation
AFTER	Endorse and insist on consensus decisions made by the team
BEFORE	Examine and often countermand team proposals
AFTER	Always approve what the team asks for short-term tasks

cultural developments discussed here are being necessitated by the pressures of the early century. Increasingly, companies need people to form and work in changing teams, drawn from all departments and from all the talents, without any consideration of seniority or status. They want those teams to change from project to project, as do strategies. Companies are even prepared to separate innovative teams completely from the parent organization (which is probably essential for important and radical innovations).

But reactive change is not enough. Proactive cultural management starts with objectives which embody a vision of the future of the organization. Next, it bars obstructive behaviors and, instead, supports, reinforces, and rewards constructive ones. These include:

- the creation of a "learning company" whose members stay in the vanguard of knowledge about the business, its environment, and its management;
- abandoning rigid procedures and principles which are defended as a matter of course and habit;
- substituting an emphasis on creating and sharing new ideas and experimentation;
- recognizing the need for successful behavioral change in the formal or informal assessment and reward of managers, and in planning and budgeting.

It should go without saying that the leader's personal behavior must be consistent with these four foundational attitudes. They must also be reflected in the actions which constitute the cultural change program. How decisions are made and implemented, in particular, will determine its success.

MINI-CASE

In a relatively short corporate life, *Compaq Computer* had developed a very strong "can-do" culture, based on top-end engineering and premium products. When competition from cheaper IBM "clones" undermined this model, and losses followed, a new chief executive, Eckhard Pfeiffer, faced the need to change the culture, using an exceptionally high level of communication as a foundation. He acted swiftly to alter behavior: lower costs and prices became the new targets, with "best-of-breed" engineering supplanted by cost-effectiveness, especially for a new low-priced range of PCs. But the major cultural breakthrough came at the meeting called to inform Texan workers that "Project Ruby" would be made in the Far East. The Texans challenged the management decision, requesting and winning the right to bid for the work. Their successful bid was instrumental in establishing and sustaining a new and immensely successful corporate culture.

MAKING IT HAPPEN

- Reduce the executive hierarchy to two basic levels, with (1) "enterprise managers" in charge of decisions and helped in reaching them by (2)"people/process managers."
- Make the "people/process managers" responsible for planning and implementation with and by (3) the "self-managers" who execute the decisions.
- Insist that leaders exercise self-restraint so that "coworkers" can contribute to their full potential.
- Counter personal fears and insecurities by a genuinely positive program in a culture built on full and free flows of information.
- Promulgate objectives which embody a clear vision of the future of the organization.
- Bar obstructive behaviors and, instead, support, reinforce, and reward constructive ones.

CONCLUSION

The logic of cultural change built on these lines is hard to escape. But powerful, illogical emotions are also active in organizations, including fear. Often, this has no basis in fact. But, whether justified or not, personal fear—say, of job losses or greater insecurity—is both real and serious, and can only be countered by a genuinely positive program. In a culture which is built on full and free flows of information, irrational fear should be far less common, while rational anxieties should be more readily allayed.

There is also the issue of risk. Change always involves risk, ranging from disruption to disastrous error. Staying put sounds and looks much safer. For better or worse, however, organizations no longer have that option. Failure to change involves even greater risk: that of falling fatally behind the competition (and the customer's demands). Fear is the enemy of creativity, innovation, and productive change, without which survival into the second decade of the new century is deeply uncertain. Optimistic realism is the friend of the future, and the foundation of cultural excellence.

For More Information

Books:

Kotter, John P., and James L. Heskett. *Corporate Culture and Performance*. New York: Free Press, 1992.

Schein, Edgar H. *The Corporate Culture Survival Guide*. New York: Jossey-Bass Wiley, 1999.

Senge, Peter M. *The Fifth Discipline: The Art and Practice of The Learning Organization*. New York: Doubleday, 1992.

See also:

☆ **Boosting Business Success Through Diversity (pp. 29–30)**
☆ **Creating Fun in the Workplace (pp. 37–38)**
☆ **Managing Today's Angry Workforce (pp. 35–36)**
Organizational Culture and Leadership (p. 937)
Edgar Schein (pp. 1044–45)
Corporate Culture (pp. 1942–43)

"If a group's survival is threatened. . .it is ultimately the function of leadership to recognize and do something about the situation."
(Edgar H. Schein)

VIEWPOINT: PHILIP KOTLER

Making Marketing Manageable

Philip Kotler (b. 1931) is the world's pre-eminent marketing thinker. A professor at the J. L. Kellogg Graduate School of Management, Northwestern University, his reputation as one of the world's foremost marketing experts is substantially based on the classic marketing textbook *Marketing Management: Analysis, Planning, Implementation, and Control*. Now coming out in an 11th edition, it remains the definitive work on the subject. He has published over 25 other books, covering such topics as the marketing of persons, places, social causes, cultural institutions, professions, higher education, and health care organizations.

Kotler has done more than virtually anyone to cement marketing's reputation as a serious business discipline. He has a flair for neat and useful definitions. "When I am asked to define marketing in the briefest possible way I say marketing is 'meeting needs profitably.' A lot of us meet needs—but businesses are set up to do it profitably," he says.

What is the most important thing and who is the most important person to have influenced your thinking on business and management?

Businesses are finally grasping that winning companies choose target segments and customers and make them central to developing their strategy and operations. Customer focus is critical in a world no longer marked by a shortage of goods but by a shortage of customers.

I am deeply influenced by Peter Drucker, who observed some decades ago that "marketing. . .is the whole business seen from the point of view of its final result, that is, from the customer's point of view." Drucker insisted that a company has only two functions: innovation and marketing.

Compared to the last 50 years, how will business be different in the 21st century?

Technology will have the deepest impact on business. We have already witnessed the impact of lean and flexible manufacturing, computers, the Internet, and wireless. Business success in the future will require knowledge workers who are skilled in specific technologies that might confer a competitive advantage to the firm.

What effect has the advent of the new economy and the Internet had on your thinking and on marketing?

I became fascinated with the potentials of e-commerce and e-business for business success. At first I thought that pure click operators such as Amazon and Yahoo would have a tremendous competitive advantage, as they owned few physical assets. My mind changed when I saw how much they had to spend on marketing to build their brand and attract and keep customers.

At first I thought that pure click operators such as Amazon and Yahoo would have a tremendous competitive advantage, as they owned few physical assets. My mind changed when I saw how much they had to spend on marketing to build their brand and attract and keep customers.

I believe that the Internet will fundamentally change business and marketing practice. The price transparency of the Internet will put great pressure on prices. The growth of business-to-business Web sites and extranets will reduce the number of salespeople involved in routine sales work. Companies will increasingly differentiate their product and service offerings to different tiers of customers according to estimates of customer lifetime value.

In my 11th edition of *Marketing Management*, I show how customers, companies, competitors, and marketplaces are impacted in the information age. The changes will be more profound, with improvements in broadband and m-marketing where cellular phones become our source of e-mail, the Internet, chatting, and even a payment system replacing credit cards.

Are these changes reflected in your current research?

I am doing research on the ability of companies to manage their future through information. I have formulated a concept called "holistic marketing," where companies are able to find, create, and deliver value

"A business's flexibility in adapting to change and market dynamics will mark the winners and losers in this fast-changing Internet Age."

(Michael Dell)

by linking demand management, resource planning, and partner alliances. Central to holistic marketing is the use of the Internet, the company Intranet, and various Extranets to drive the company to profitable growth.

> **Fewer managers will spend their whole career within one company. Managers will be more attached to their knowledge specialty than to their current company. There will be active markets for each knowledge specialty, and managers will be on the lookout for advancement opportunities.**

My research is taking two directions. One is to develop real-time marketing information "dashboards" where managers can continuously monitor sales, prices, and costs in different geographical and segment markets. This will help managers spot growth opportunities as well as problems emerging in the field.

The other research direction is to create "planning dashboards," to be used by brand and product managers to develop stronger marketing plans. They can click to find out how to do any procedure, such as test a marketing concept, develop a sales promotion, test the effectiveness of an ad, or run a test market. The planning dashboard would open a marketing encyclopedia of best marketing practices on the computer screen.

What new skills will be needed to cope with these changes? How can managers best develop these required skills?

Marketers will need skills beyond the four traditional ones of marketing research, sales management, advertising, and sales promotion. Needed are skills in:

- database marketing and data mining;
- customer relationship management (CRM);
- partner relationship management (PRM);
- telemarketing and call center management;
- integrated marketing communications (IMC);
- public relations marketing (including event and sponsorship marketing);
- profitability analysis applied to customers, market segments, channels, geographical area, and order sizes;
- customization of offerings, services and messages;
- experiential marketing (creating a total experience).

Are there new management questions we should be asking? If so, what are they?

Here are a few questions, not necessarily new ones, that management should think through better:

- How much should companies invest in social responsibility programs? How can the payoff be measured?
- Would companies be more profitable if they spent less on advertising and promotion and more on innovation and improving their products?
- How can companies move more of their customers to using less costly channels?
- How can companies speed up the digitalization of their production, marketing, and distribution and service systems?

What will happen to the concept of the career in the future? What career advice would you offer tomorrow's managers?

Fewer managers will spend their whole career within one company. Managers will be more attached to their knowledge specialty than to their current company. There will be active markets for each knowledge specialty, and managers will be on the lookout for advancement opportunities. The key then is for tomorrow's managers to study the various knowledge specialties and choose the one that will yield the most long-run market value and personal satisfaction. Companies will need to develop better inducement packages and conditions for retaining their most valued knowledge workers.

How can companies best promote enterprises that are a) profitable and b) good places for people to work?

Profitability and a good place to work are more compatible than profitability and a bad place to work. In the old days zero sum thinking prevailed, in that a manufacturer thought that he would make the most money by paying the least to his suppliers, employees, and distributors. But this led to poorer inputs and outputs and lots of resource turnover. Smart companies today practice positive sum thinking and make their suppliers, employees, and distributors into partners who are motivated to deliver superior value. "Win-win-win" thinking will prevail over "I win, you lose" thinking.

For More Information

See also:

Marketing Management (p. 924)
Theodore Levitt (pp. 1012–13)
Marketing Management (pp. 2045–48)

"The demands for new knowledge and skills will be constant, no longer a value added element, but the essential factor in determining organizational survival." (Meg Wheatley)

  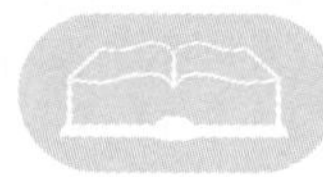    

Managing 1:1 Marketing *by Drayton Bird*

EXECUTIVE SUMMARY

- Direct marketing is a special marketing discipline, not just a medium.
- The object is to increase customer value.
- It focuses on individuals, not masses.
- Direct marketing builds brands; it must be integrated with other disciplines.
- Its principles apply to e-commerce.
- Building and enhancing the database is key.
- Testing and accurate measurement reduce risk and increase return on investment.

Introduction

In late 2000 *Advertising Age* revealed that one in eleven of all new jobs being created in the United States was in direct marketing. Virtually all organizations in advanced economies use it in some way.

Today's direct marketing is essentially a fusion of traditional mail-order selling and direct mail. Yet it's more than a sales process or medium: it's a marketing discipline with special characteristics. It uses all media. It's personal, focusing on individuals, not masses. Every message is coded, so you can gauge return on investment exactly. And it looks to long-term customer value rather than the value of individual sales.

The philosophy of direct marketing is growing in relevance as it applies to e-commerce, which is also conducted directly with individuals; in effect e-commerce is accelerated direct marketing. Increasingly, as businesses face ever-growing competition and products and services can be copied fast, direct marketing makes great sense, because it focuses more on the customer than on what is actually being sold.

Direct marketing is not always a cheaper way of marketing. Nevertheless, when properly managed direct marketing directs your efforts more accurately, giving you more for your marketing money. It does this in three stages.

Three Steps to Success

1. First, you identify those customers, including organizations and the individuals within them, that your offering is most likely to appeal to. You store relevant data about them on a database, which you continually enrich with added information. Thus you can offer what they are most likely to want when they are most likely to want it with growing confidence, eliminating junk messages.
2. Second, by communicating with customers in an increasingly relevant way as you learn more, you strengthen and lengthen your relationship with them. This is important, since retaining customers is far more profitable than attracting them. This fact has helped fuel today's greater focus on the customer.
3. Third, you reduce risk by rigorous measurement, testing on small numbers before spending big money, and comparing different approaches. Seemingly trivial changes can make big differences. Adding—or removing—an element in a mailing may increase return on investment by as much as 90%. Running one TV commercial rather than another, or changing the time it runs, may transform loss into profit. Altering just one word in a headline can have the same effect.

Where and How It Works

Direct marketing is ideal for anything complex that requires detailed explanation that needs to be studied at leisure. It also works where potential customers feel pressured by salespeople. Insurance and investment are good examples—financial services are the biggest direct marketers.

It's a good technique to use when distance is involved. As early as the 15th century Italian printers produced catalogs to sell books directly. It's also good for products people are shy about buying in person—weight-loss and other health-related products, for instance, or exotic lingerie.

Since the database means you can vary messages to suit individuals, direct marketing works well if you sell to businesses, where decision makers have varying motives—value for money matters to financial managers, while executives may care more about efficiency.

Direct marketing complements personal selling. You can use various means—direct-response advertising, the phone, e-mail, or direct mail—to acquire leads, keep in touch with customers between calls, or deal with lower-value customers who don't merit expensive personal visits.

Direct messages are advertising and can build brands fast—Dell computers and Direct Line insurance are good examples of this. Direct marketing must be integrated with other disciplines, which can provide great synergies. The creative work need not slavishly follow your advertising, but it should have the same tone and positioning.

Long copy generally works best, because you're seeking an immediate response, by using and repeating every relevant argument. That's why effective mailings often incorporate many pieces. The letter, being personal, is normally the critical element in a mailing. Response rates vary greatly depending on the proposition: getting someone to buy something costly is far harder than offering them a free chance to win a lottery.

The Database Is Central

At the heart of direct marketing lies the database, incorporating details of each individual or business. You use it to communicate with people by mail, e-mail, fax, or phone. Recording all relevant information is vital. Success turns on how persuasive, relevant, and timely your messages are, and this is determined largely by how well you capture, store, and use the right details.

You develop your database in the same way you develop your knowledge of other people. It starts as just names and addresses; each added scrap of information makes it more valuable. You overlay it with data already in the public domain or gathered by private enterprise.

The electoral roll gives you simple but essential information such as whether the names and address are accurate and how many people live in a particular household. Other valuable data derive from the likely characteristics of different addresses. Some areas are more prosperous than others; generally speaking someone living in a house is wealthier than an apartment-dweller; and a

"The new system takes us a giant step beyond mass production towards increasing customization, beyond mass marketing and distribution towards niches and micromarketing." (Alvin Toffler)

property owner is more prosperous than a tenant.

You enrich your database with relevant facts, such as who buys what, how often and when, how long they remain loyal customers, what else they have bought—thus building a complete picture of their nature and value. This information also helps you to predict behavior; similar individuals behave similarly.

Customer Lifetime Value

In terms of business strategy the most interesting aspect of direct marketing may be its emphasis on customer value. Whereas firms have traditionally measured performance by current sales or profits, direct marketers have always thought in terms of how profitable a customer is over time.

That's because the best early direct marketers were book clubs and catalog companies. They attracted customers, using incentives, which obviously made the first transaction unprofitable—their strategy was to lose money initially in order to make money in the long run. Incentives are important in direct marketing, incentives to buy, or inquire, or simply give information. Thus, an automobile manufacturer may want to know what car a prospect has, what car the person is thinking of buying next and when, and how much money the next car is likely to cost.

The early direct marketers measured loyalty (how long a customer stayed with them—usually between 5 and 7 years) and what they could afford to pay to acquire a customer. In the same way banks, credit-card companies, and insurance firms look to long-term relationships, and automobile manufacturers look to keep customers buying their make repeatedly.

Customer value varies enormously. A small percentage of customers generally buys most of any product or service, and by identifying those individuals you can concentrate your efforts and reap disproportionate rewards. You can eliminate expenditure on less valuable customers and increase it on more valuable ones.

Direct Marketing: A More Precise Tool

Direct marketing is more precise than mass advertising. Mass advertisers concentrate on the most effective media (those more likely to be read or viewed by customers), but this is inevitably imprecise since they're always looking at masses or groups.

Direct marketing, conversely, aims to isolate individuals and place them in groups. The categories will vary according to your purpose. Thus, on a database you could isolate all the individuals over 50 with an annual income above $75,000 within 15 miles of a designated city and offer them the opportunity to buy a car direct from their nearest showroom. The potential of direct marketing is clearly invaluable.

Marketers often spend millions on huge campaigns without knowing in advance what will happen. Intelligent speculation or a hunch can be backed by research predicting likely customer behavior. Very often, though, research fails to predict accurate results. Customers can tell you what they think or believe, but not what they will do when actually asked to part with money, especially with a new product.

The direct marketer tests on a small scale first. Test results tell you pretty exactly what will happen—before you spend. You can discover which creative treatments and media work best and when. (In the case of media, there's often a great discrepancy between those activities research ranks as best and the ones that generate the most responses.)

It is worth noting that different organizations use different names for very similar activities. There's ample room for confusion when managing direct marketing. Some names describe the process, for example, database marketing, dialog marketing, and one-to-one marketing. Others, such as loyalty marketing and relationship marketing (which has metamorphosed into customer relationship management), relate to the objective. All, however, rely on direct-marketing methods.

Making It Happen ▸▸

- Identify the customers and organizations (and individuals within) most likely to want your offering, and store the data on a continually enriched database.
- Use direct marketing to strengthen and lengthen your relationship with profitably retained customers.
- Reduce marketing risk by rigorous measurement, testing on small numbers before spending big money; and comparing different approaches.
- Use direct response advertising, phone, e-mail, or direct mail to complement personal selling by getting leads, keeping in touch, and serving lower-value customers.
- Generally, write long copy and incorporate many pieces of paper—treating the personal letter as the critical element in a mailing.
- Put your emphasis on customer value—how profitable a customer is over time—not on current sales or profits. Customer value is the cornerstone of long-term success.

Conclusion

To be truly effective, one to one marketing involves market segmentation. This involves methods that can accurately analyze groups of current and potential customers. This promotes detailed understanding of the market, targets both current and potential customers, and enables effective marketing plans to succeed. Segmentation is a decisive factor in developing product strategies to optimize profitability and ensuring long-term competitive advantage. Without one to one marketing, organizations will not maximize their potential, especially if their competitors are better positioned through exploiting market segmentation. As markets become increasingly global, diverse, and complex, segmentation and one to one marketing have become increasingly valuable in maintaining the effectiveness of marketing strategies.

For More Information

Books:

Bird, Drayton. *Commonsense Direct Marketing*. 4th ed. Dover, NH: Kogan Page, 2000.

Stone, Bob, and Ron Jacob. *Successful Direct Marketing Methods*. 7th ed. New York: McGraw-Hill Professional, 2001.

See also:

☆ **Avoiding the Mistakes of the Past: Lessons from the Startup World (pp. 129–30)**
☆ **The Business Web (pp. 145–46)**
☆ **Delivering and Delighting—A New Spirit at Work (pp. 71–72)**
✔ **Building One-to-one Relationships (pp. 666–67)**
Direct Marketing (pp. 1953–54)

"It's not just running a restaurant, it's being friends with your customers. It's a personal connection, very personal."

(Mary Kelekis)

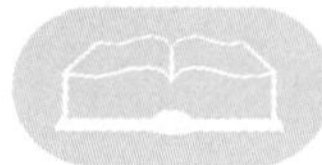

RELATING TO THE PUBLIC *by Robert Leaf*

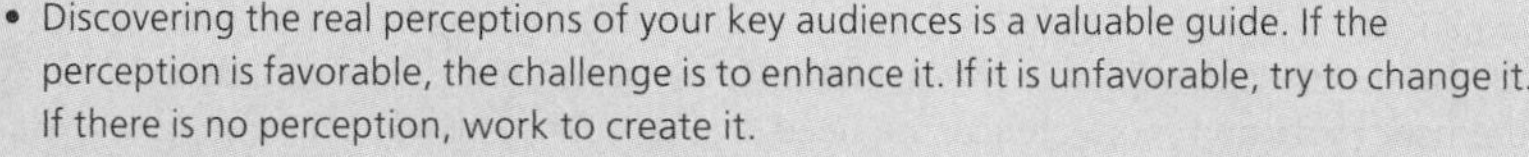

EXECUTIVE SUMMARY

- Discovering the real perceptions of your key audiences is a valuable guide. If the perception is favorable, the challenge is to enhance it. If it is unfavorable, try to change it. If there is no perception, work to create it.
- Write down a clearly defined program that is realistic and achievable with adequate budgets and has measurable, specific objectives. Assign responsibilities clearly, internally and externally; review the program at least quarterly; change it if and when necessary.
- Prepare for crisis management before crisis strikes—don't wait for it to happen.
- Get a thorough grounding in the different media—don't just leave it to the experts.
- Relating to the public is a self-fulfilling prophecy: focus on it and things are likely to improve; ignore it and they will almost certainly worsen.

INTRODUCTION

Business has changed radically in recent decades and is becoming much more sophisticated. The public relations of today has become perception management. Communicators have increasingly come to the conclusion that perception is what really counts. You might run a great company, but if analysts don't feel that way the stock does not go up. And your product might in reality provide great benefits, but if the customer doesn't perceive it that way, it remains on the shelves.

THE INCREASING VALUE OF PR

PR IS PART OF THE TOTAL COMMUNICATIONS MIX

While there are certainly examples where the effective use of public relations by itself was used to solve a problem, public relations, to be most effective, should be part of the total communications mix. Martin Sorrell, C.E.O. of WPP, the world's largest communications organization, says: "Today's sophisticated client demands that every possible form of communications works together to achieve their key objectives." And he is right, because times have changed. Previously ad departments or ad agencies saw PR departments or PR agencies as threats to their egos. Now they appreciate that working together is essential.

THE GROWING NEED FOR COMMUNICATIONS WITH KEY EMPLOYEES

The one public that has grown the most in terms of the need for effective communications are the key employees. The reason is simple. COMPANY LOYALTY IS DEAD. No company will promise lifetime employment. Anyone can be fired, and since they know that, the good employees are nearly always considering other options. So why do they stay with a company if it is not out of loyalty? They stay because they believe in the vision of the company and how they are involved in making that vision happen. So management, whether through the written or spoken word, must continually communicate that vision to the key people and underline their role in making it happen.

MEDIA RELATIONS

Like them or hate them the media are here to stay. I once had the chairman of a British company, upset by what was a somewhat unfair piece of reportage in the *Financial Times*, say to me, "I am not going to deal with the FT anymore." I explained to him, tactfully of course, that he didn't have that option. One of the things he was being paid to do was deal with the *Financial Times*. In dealing with the media there are some key rules. Know the key media and reporters covering your company and decide who within the company should interface with them. Ordinarily this will be a number of people. It is important to understand that everyone in the organization is not equally skilled at media relations, so pick those best qualified. This can vary according to type of media.

Often it is not the chief executive you want for a particular interview, but the C.E.O.'s overall image is very important. A Burson-Marsteller C.E.O. Reputation study showed that 94% of analysts queried said they would recommend a company's stock because of the C.E.O.'s reputation. Only 14% said they had never heard of C.E.O.s from the ten largest U.S. companies while 41% said they had never heard of some of the European C.E.O.s from companies of comparable size and global reach. European managements have always been more reticent than their U.S. counterparts to have programs that include active relations with media but this is beginning to change.

CHECKLIST: PREPARING A PUBLIC RELATIONS PROGRAM

For your public relations campaign to be successful, you must first understand the real perception of your key audiences. There are only three major categories of perceptions but these can vary in degrees. If the perception is favorable, you want to enhance it. If it is unfavorable, you want to change it. If there is no perception, such as with a new product, you want to create it. This underlines the need for intelligent research before any significant program is undertaken.

The key to a successful PR program is: don't wait for a crisis! Too often, public relations is relied upon to help solve a problem. A crisis has occurred. Share price has plummeted. Employees are leaving in droves. New competitors have arisen. But just as you should have checkups when you're healthy, so you should have an active public relations program when times are good. This could ensure times don't become bad. The key is to decide which of your publics need the greatest emphasis and how to reach them effectively. To be successful, your PR activities should take the following issues into consideration:

BALANCING INTERNAL AND EXTERNAL RESOURCES

Years ago the chief internal public relations officers viewed PR consulting firms as a threat to their position. They feared they would have access to top management that they themselves often didn't have. Times have changed. As the understanding of PR has grown dramatically so has the internal function. Internal PR departments are smaller but more effective. The top PR executives are much more qualified and better paid and work closely with the management. They are usually an integral part of the planning process. And it is they who now not only want outside help but have the major say in agency selection. A key rule is: "Don't hire an agency for what can be done in-house."

"Some are born great, some achieve greatness, and some hire public relations officers."

(Daniel Boorstin)

When selecting an agency it is important that you do your homework and use contacts in your industry. In the United Kingdom, the Public Relations Consultancy Association and in the United States the Public Relations Society of America maintain lists you can review. You should also provide a carefully prepared brief. The emphasis should not be on what you want to know about them but on what you feel are your needs and how they would plan to fulfill them. If time allows, it is advisable to call them in for a discussion before they make a presentation. The list should then be narrowed down to three.

You should allow time for questions because it is usually then that you get a better understanding of who really understands your business and its needs. Make sure to find out exactly who will be on your account and the proportion of their time that will be spent working for you. That is far more important than who is making the presentation because you might never see them again. Also ask the hourly rates of those on the account because, in addition to expertise, the only thing a PR firm has to sell is time.

THE INTERNET

The Internet can be used to reach every public of importance including your own staff. New uses are appearing all the time, such as launching a new product or ad campaign, supporting takeovers or IPOS, reporting to the City or Wall Street, fighting elections, and fashion shows. Increasingly journalists are using it for updates on companies and background for articles they are preparing. An international study by *Fortune Magazine* and Burson-Marsteller showed 91% of C.E.O.s log on, spending an average of 6 hours a week online. So the question is not whether to use the Internet but how do it most effectively. Here are some guidelines.

- The use of a company Web site calls for a public relations strategy all its own. Who do you really want to reach and how?
- There is a need for continuous updating, which can be costly.
- It is ideal for monitoring competition.
- It is a major vehicle for advocacy groups, some of whom might be hostile to some aspect of your company, so you must be prepared not only to monitor but to react to claims
- As the number of Web sites grows, giving the user more and more choice, the need for professionalism will continue to increase if your site is to be successful.

CRISIS MANAGEMENT

Burson-Marsteller's Crisis Management Division lists the characteristic of a crisis as: surprise, insufficient information, escalating flow of events, loss of control, intense scrutiny from outside, siege mentality, panic, and short-term focus. The key principles in handling any crisis are:

- Centralize/control information flow.
- Isolate a crisis team from daily business concerns.
- Define the real problem short term and long term.
- Recognize the value of a short-term sacrifice.
- Resist the combative instinct.
- Assume a "worst case" planning position.
- Depend on no one individual fully.
- Understand the media's role and purpose.
- Remember all constituencies, internal and external (e.g. unions, employees, family, local community residents and leaders, local authorities, etc.)
- And remember in the Chinese language there are two characters which together make up the word, "crisis." The first means "problem" and the other means "opportunity."

MAKING IT HAPPEN ▸▸

Certain fundamentals about preparing a public relations program remain:

- Whether handled internally or externally, there should be a clearly defined program in writing. And it should be realistic. What can be accomplished. Not an impossible wish list.
- There should be objectives that are measurable and the objectives should differ according to each public that is to be influenced.
- Responsibilities internally and externally should be clearly assigned.
- There should be time frames for each segment of the program.
- Adequate budgets should be established.
- The program should be reviewed at least quarterly.
- The program should be changed as circumstances warrant.
- Measurement should take place on a continuing basis.

CONCLUSION

The future of public relations/perception management is very exciting. Companies, communities, governments, and government bodies are appreciating a greater need for handling it more professionally. The key now is for those using perception management to use it as effectively as possible.

For More Information

Books:

Cunningham, Michael J. *Partners.com: How to Profit from the New DNA of Business*. Cambridge, MA: Perseus Publishing, 2001.

Stack, Jack, and Bo Burlingham. *A Stake in the Outcome*. New York: Currency/Doubleday, 2002.

Web Site:

www.bls.gov/oco/ocos086.htm: created by the Bureau of Labor Statistics within the U.S. Department of Labor, this is a general outline of a public relations professional's job.

See also:

✔ **Product Public Relations (pp. 728–29)**
✔ **Public Relations Planning (pp. 476–77)**
Public Relations (pp. 2090–92)

"*PR cannot overcome things that shouldn't have been done.*" (Harold Burson)

  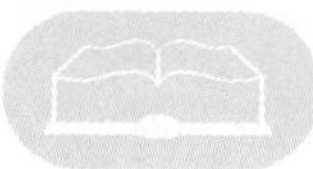    

How to Plan Marketing

by Malcolm McDonald

EXECUTIVE SUMMARY

- Organizations operate in a complex and fast-changing environment and managers need some way of interacting with their environments.
- Marketing planning is merely a managerial process for coping with environmental uncertainty.
- Strategic marketing planning needs to precede tactical marketing planning.
- The output of the process (the plan) spells out how an organization expects to achieve its objectives.
- Academic researchers agree that there is a link between marketing planning and long-term organizational success.
- The planning process is universal, although the formality of its implementation may vary between organizations.
- Organizational culture is the biggest barrier to implementing effective marketing planning.

Introduction

All organizations operate in a complex environment in which hundreds of external and internal factors interact to affect their ability to achieve their objectives. Managers need some understanding, or view, about how all these variables interact. They must try to be rational in making decisions, no matter how important intuition, feel, and experience are as contributory factors. Most managers accept that some kind of procedure for planning the organization's marketing helps to sharpen this rationality, making the complexity of business operations manageable and adding a dimension of realism to the organization's future plans.

This procedure is marketing planning.

The Essence of Marketing Planning

The contribution of marketing planning to the success of an organization, whatever its area of activity, lies in its commitment to detailed analysis of future opportunities to meet customer needs. It offers a wholly professional approach to selling to well-defined market segments those products or services that deliver the desired benefits. Such commitment and activities shouldn't be mistaken for budgets and forecasts, which have always been a commercial necessity. Marketing planning is a more sophisticated approach concerned with identifying what sales are going to be made in the longer term, and to whom, in order to give revenue budgets and sales forecasts a real chance of being achieved.

Marketing Planning Is a Managerial Process

In essence marketing planning is a managerial process, the output of which is a marketing plan. As such it is a logical sequence, a series of activities leading to the setting of marketing objectives and the formulation of plans for achieving them. Conceptually, the process is very simple and is achieved by means of a planning system. The system is little more than a structured way of identifying a range of options for the organization, of making them explicit in writing, of formulating marketing objectives consistent with the company's overall objectives, and of scheduling and costing the specific activities most likely to bring about the achievement of the objectives. It is the systemization of this process that lies at the heart of the theory of marketing planning.

Types of Marketing Plan

There are two principal kinds of marketing plan:

1. **The strategic marketing plan**
   A strategic marketing plan is a plan for three or more years. It is a written document outlining how managers perceive their own position in the market relative to their competitors (with competitive advantage accurately defined), what objectives they want to achieve, how they intend to achieve them (strategies), what resources are required (budget), and what results are expected. Three years is the most common strategic planning period. Strategic marketing-driven plans are not to be confused with scenario planning or the kind of very long-range plans formulated by a number of Japanese companies (which often have planning horizons of between 50 and 200 years!).
2. **The tactical marketing plan**
   A tactical marketing plan is the detailed scheduling and costing of the specific actions necessary for achieving the first year of the strategic marketing plan. The tactical plan is thus usually for one year.

The Correct Sequence of Marketing Plans

Research into the marketing planning practices of organizations shows that successful companies complete the strategic plan before the tactical plan. Unsuccessful organizations often rely largely on sales forecasts and the associated budgets. The problem with this approach is that many managers sell the products and services they find easiest to sell, concentrating on those customers who offer the least resistance. By developing short-term tactical marketing plans first and then extrapolating them, managers merely succeed in extrapolating their own shortcomings. This is just about acceptable when markets are growing rapidly or are regulated in such a way that little effort is required to grow sales. Today, however, few such markets exist. Preoccupation with preparing a detailed short-term marketing plan first is typical of companies that confuse sales forecasting and budgeting with strategic marketing planning.

The Contents of a Strategic Marketing Plan

The contents of a strategic marketing plan are as follows:

- **mission statement,** setting out the raison d'être of the organization and covering its role, business definition, competence, and future indications;

"However numerous your products, the company won't succeed unless each of them is treated with concentrated care."
(Robert Heller)

- **financial summary,** summarizing the financial implications over the full planning period;
- **market overview,** providing a brief but important picture of the market, including market structure, market trends, key market segments, and (sometimes) gap analysis;
- **SWOT analysis,** analyzing the strengths and weaknesses of the organization compared with competitors, and considering opportunities and threats, usually for each key product or segment;
- **issues to be addressed,** derived from the SWOT analysis and usually specific to each product or segment;
- **portfolio summary,** offering a pictorial summary of the SWOT analysis that makes it easy to see at a glance the relative importance of each of the four elements; it is often a two-dimensional matrix in which the horizontal axis measures the organization's comparative strengths and the vertical axis measures its relative attractiveness;
- **assumptions,** listing the underlying assumptions critical to the planned marketing objectives and strategies;
- **marketing objectives,** usually consisting of quantitative statements (in terms of profit, volume, value, and market share) of what the organization wishes to achieve; they are usually given by product, by segment, and overall throughout the organization;
- **marketing strategies,** stating how the objectives are to be achieved; they often involve the four Ps of marketing: product, price, place, and promotion;
- **resource requirements and budget,** showing the full planning- period budget, giving in detail the revenues and associated costs for each year.

The Contents of a Tactical Marketing Plan

The contents of a tactical marketing plan are very similar, except that they often omit the mission statement, the market overview, and SWOT analysis, and the plan goes into much more detailed quantification by product and segment of marketing objectives and associated strategies. An additional feature is more detailed scheduling and costing of the tactics necessary to achieve the first year's planned goals.

Strategic Marketing Planning: A Review of Current Thinking

From an extensive review of the current research into strategic marketing planning, five principal conclusions emerge:

- There is a clear consensus about the desirable outputs of the strategic marketing planning process.
- Strategic marketing planning and the marketing orientation that accompanies it are clearly associated with improved organizational performance across most market situations.
- In unsuccessful companies the prescriptive process of strategic marketing planning is poorly adhered to in practice and is frequently used as a pretext for inadequate budgeting and tactical programs.
- The primary barrier to strategic marketing planning lies in the organizational culture of the company and the values and artifacts that stem from that culture.
- Although the degree of formality of the process can range from a highly creative, entrepreneurial approach to the more structured, rational process described here, there is universal consensus among strategic thinkers and planners that some kind of managerial planning process has to be used to manage the link between an organization and its environment.

Hence, in large, multinational, multiproduct, multicultural organizations it is usual to find a structured process for marketing planning; in smaller organizations the management of the process outlined here tends to be much less formalized and structured. The process and the steps, however, are the same in all consistently successful organizations.

Mini-case

Everyone has an opinion about why the once-mighty *IBM* lost billions of dollars in the 1990s. Indeed, the two books about IBM published at the time both predicted the end of the company. The arrival of Lou Gerstner as chairman and C.E.O., however, heralded a reversal in its fortunes. Like all good managers, he stopped the financial bleeding by introducing operational efficiencies. He came from a consumer-goods background, and it wasn't long before he insisted that his business unit managers introduce the kind of classical market-based planning procedures described here, including the major basis for successful marketing planning—market segmentation. IBM is, due to Lou Gerstner, once again a major global player in the communications market.

Making It Happen

- Identify what sales will be made in the longer term, and to whom in order to turn revenue budgets and sales forecasts into reality.
- Analyze your strengths and weaknesses compared with competitors against key customer success factors, and similarly review opportunities and threats.
- Complete the strategic marketing plan before the tactical plan. Write your strategic marketing plan to cover three or more years, defining competitive advantage, objectives, strategies, and budgets.
- Build marketing strategies around the four Ps of marketing: product, price, place, promotion.
- Write a tactical marketing plan, detailing schedules and costing for the specific actions necessary to achieve the first year of the strategic plan.

Conclusion

Successful marketing planning is the cornerstone of developing strong, durable, and robust organizations. Overcoming an organizational culture that acts as a barrier to effective marketing planning is essential if performance is to be optimized and long-term goals are to be achieved. Given the complexity of the rapidly changing business environment and the high number of variables that influence business performance, it is necessary for managers to have an effective means of making the situation manageable. Thorough and detailed analysis of how to meet future customer needs provides a sophisticated and reliable method for building long-term success. Marketing planning enables the organization's vision to become a reality.

For More Information

Books:

McDonald, Malcolm. *Marketing Plans: How to Prepare Them; How to Use Them.* 4th ed. Woburn, MA: Butterworth-Heinemann, 1999.

Piercy, Nigel F. *Market-led Strategic Change.* 3rd ed. Woburn, MA: Butterworth-Heinemann, 2002.

See also:

☆ **Viewpoint: Philip Kotler (pp. 53–54)**
✓ **Planning a Direct Marketing Campaign (pp. 688–89)**
Marketing Management (p. 924)
Marketing Management (pp. 2045–48)

"Marketing strategy is a series of integrated actions leading to a sustainable competitive advantage."

(John Sculley)

MARKETING: THE IMPORTANCE OF BEING FIRST
by Al Ries and Laura Ries

- Most managers believe the basic issue in marketing is convincing prospects that you have a better product or service. Not true.
- The basic issue in marketing is creating a new category you can be first in.

INTRODUCTION

WHO'S REALLY BEST?

Who has the best rent-a-car service? The best cola? The best ketchup? If you are thinking Hertz, Coca-Cola, and Heinz, you agree with most customers who make these three companies the leaders in their fields. In fact, there is a strong axiom, or belief, in the minds of consumers that "the best product or service wins in the marketplace." After all, this is so logical and so obvious, who could disagree?

We could.

There's a paradox in marketing. While everyone believes that the better product will win in the marketplace, the worst possible strategy for any company is to try to produce a "better product." Why? Because the leader in your field already has the perception of producing the better product. If you try to claim that your product is better, the prospect thinks, "No, it can't be better, otherwise *they* would be the leader." Yet what do most companies try to do? They try to: (a) produce a better product, and (b) communicate that difference to customers and prospects. It's easy to do (a) but it's almost impossible to do (b). Is Royal Crown Cola better tasting than Coca-Cola? Royal Crown thinks so, and their research shows that prospects prefer the taste of Royal Crown to Coca-Cola Classic by 57% to 43%. That's a pretty big difference. Yet Royal Crown Cola has only 2% of the market. What they need to do, you might be thinking, is to communicate that difference. Well, they've tried and it doesn't work; prospects too easily conclude: "If Royal Crown was the better tasting cola, *they* would be the leader, not Coke. There must be something wrong with the research."

WHAT'S IMPORTANT: WHO'S FIRST?

It's our experience that 90+% of all marketing programs are based on communicating the essence of the better product or service. Unless you are already the leader, these programs are bound to fail because the prospect assumes that the leader must have the better product or service. But how did the leader achieve its leadership? Not by introducing a better product or service; invariably the leader in the category got to be the leader by being the first brand in the category. Companies such as Coca Cola, CNN, Dell, Hoover, Pizza Hut, Rolex, and Xerox are all globally recognized as leaders in their respective fields. Some consultants have called this leadership phenomenon, "the first mover advantage," but that is not so. It's an advantage, but it's not the reason that most leader brands were first in their categories. It's the "first minder" advantage. That is, the brand that gets into the mind first is the winner, not the brand that is the first in the category. For examples: Duryea was the first automobile on the road, but never got into the mind. Ford was the first automobile in the mind. MITS Altair 8800 was the first personal computer, but never got into the mind. Apple was the first personal computer to get into the mind. Du Mont made the first television set. Hurley, the first washing machine. But these and many other brands failed to get into the minds of their prospects. You don't win in the marketplace. You win in the mind.

EXAMPLES ABOUND

If you weren't first in your category and you can't win by being better, what can you do?

The answer is obvious: start a new category you can be first in. Marketing is more a battle of categories than it is a battle of products. Winning companies think category first and product second. They try to categorize what they do, not in terms of being better, but in terms of being different.

When Procter & Gamble introduced Tide many years ago, they could have called the product a "new, improved soap." Tide was a soap then, and Tide is a soap today, in the sense that soap is a "cleansing agent." But Tide was made from synthetic materials rather than the fats and lye found in traditional cleaning products like Ivory, Oxydol, and Rinso. Tide could have been called a synthetic soap, but that would have nailed the brand to the soap category. So Procter & Gamble called Tide the "first detergent," a totally new category and even today Tide is the leading brand of detergent.

When Charles Schwab set up Charles Schwab & Co., he could have focused on providing better service to stock buyers. But he didn't. Instead he decided to launch the first discount stock brokerage company, and today Charles Schwab & Co. is one of the leading stock brokerage firms in the country.

When Michael Dell set up Dell Computer, he could have sold his "better" products through conventional computer stores, but he didn't. Instead he launched the first brand of personal computer sold direct by phone. Today Dell Computer is the world's largest seller of personal computers and still doesn't sell any computers through conventional computer stores.

HOW TO START?

Before you launch (or relaunch) a new product or service, ask yourself the following questions:

1. What is the name of the category? Not a name that you might like, but a name the industry gives the category.
2. What is the brand name of the leader in the category? Not necessarily the sales leader, but the brand that customers perceive to be the leader.
3. If there is no dominant brand, or at least not a dominant brand in the mind of most prospects, jump right in with your product or service and try to quickly establish your leadership. Cut prices, cut deals, hire sales people, launch massive publicity campaigns, do everything you can to seize the leadership position before someone else does.
4. Promote your brand as the leading brand. "It's so easy to use," says AOL, "no wonder it's number one." Leave no piece of paper or Web site or TV advertisement or radio commercial without mentioning your leadership. Leadership is the most important aspect of any marketing program. Why? Prospects assume the better product or service will win in the marketplace. Therefore, if you are the leader, you must have the better product.
5. If there is a dominant brand, then move

"In a small company, one person's hunch can be enough to launch a new product. In a big company, the same concept is likely to be buried in committee for months." (Al Ries)

on and set up a new category you can be first in. But make sure you have a new name to match the new category. You can get in serious trouble if you try to use an existing name.

6. You can't dictate the category name. Only the industry and the media can do that. Therefore you have to launch your new brand with publicity and get the media to establish the category name for you.

Making It Happen ▸▸

There's almost always a way to set up a new category. Unfortunately, most companies refuse to even consider the possibility of a new category because "there's no market." Of course, there's no market. If there were, it wouldn't be a new category. This presumed "logic" is the most difficult thing to overcome. You have to have faith that you can succeed in getting acceptance for a new category. What was the market for personal computers sold by phone before Michael Dell launched Dell Computer Company? Zero. What was the market for sports drinks before Gatorade was launched? Zero. What was the market for discount brokerage firms before Charles Schwab was launched? Zero.

Furthermore, a new category doesn't necessarily represent a big, technological advance. Soapsoft, the first liquid soap, was a big commercial success. How difficult is it to take a tub of soap and liquefy it? How difficult is it to take regular beer and add water? Miller Lite, the first light beer, was a big success, but ultimately paid a big penalty for its success. Instead of creating a new brand to match the new category, they used a line extension name which just about killed their regular beer brand (Miller High Life) and caused them lose their light beer leadership to the competition. A new category needs a new name.

The IBM PC was the first 16-bit, serious, office personal computer, but the line extension name caused IBM to ultimately lose their personal computer leadership to first Compaq and then Dell Computer. VisiCalc was the first spreadsheet for personal computers when all personal computers used 8-bit operating systems. Lotus 1-2-3 was the first spreadsheet for 16-bit, IBM-type personal computers, but lost its leadership to Excel, which was the first spreadsheet to use Microsoft Windows.

Listerine was the first mouthwash, but it was a bad-tasting mouthwash, hence the slogan, "the taste you hate, twice a day." Except for Procter & Gamble, all competitors in the category thought that mouthwash had to taste bad. P&G introduced Scope, the first good-tasting mouthwash, which is neck and neck (or mouth and mouth) with Listerine for leadership in the category.

Conclusion

Marketing is not a battle of products. Marketing is a battle of perceptions. And to win the battle of perceptions you have to become the leader in a category. Prospects assume the leader must be better because "everybody knows the better product or service will win in the marketplace." How do you become the leader? You launch a new category you can be first in. It doesn't have to be a big technological advance. Sometimes the simple ideas are the easiest to get into the mind. And where do you win the battle of the marketing battle? You win the battle inside the mind of the prospect.

For More Information

You don't learn to become a marketing expert by reading books, ours or anyone else's. You learn to become a marketing expert by studying case histories and asking yourself: "Why did this company win and why did that company lose?" The best place to find these case histories is in the pages of the general business media. Every serious marketing person should subscribe to some, if not all, of the following publications (and be sure to check their respective Web sites).

- *New York Times*
- *The Economist*
- *Wall Street Journal*
- *USA Today*
- *Investor's Business Daily*
- *Fortune*
- *Forbes*
- *Business Week*

See also:

☆ **Avoiding the Mistakes of the Past: Lessons from the Startup World (pp. 129–30)**
☆ **Creating Powerful Brands (pp. 63–64)**
☆ **Delivering and Delighting—A New Spirit at Work (pp. 71–72)**
☆ **The Power of Identity (pp. 91–92)**
☆ **Viewpoint: Philip Kotler (pp. 53–54)**
☆ **Viewpoint: B. Joseph Pine II (pp. 69–70)**
✓ **Branding a Business Product (pp. 712–13)**
✓ **Introducing a New Product to Market (pp. 720–21)**
✓ **Raising the Awareness of Business Brands (pp. 714–15)**

CREATING POWERFUL BRANDS *by Paul Stobart*

EXECUTIVE SUMMARY

- A brand is defined as the sum of the functional and emotional characteristics that a consumer attributes to a product or service.
- Brands are important both to companies, as a source of competitive advantage, and to consumers, as an aid in making purchase decisions.
- A critical factor in creating powerful brands is a company's ability to differentiate the product and/or service elements of its offerings from those of its competitors.
- Key building blocks in the creation of a brand are brand proposition, brand positioning, and brand identity.
- Brand managers have a number of tools at their disposal, including product design, packaging, and advertising.
- It is important for companies to track their brand equity over time, particularly brand awareness and brand image measures.
- The Internet represents a powerful new medium for creating brands, but it's also encouraging consumers to demand a two-way dialog with brand owners.

WHAT IS A BRAND?

Put simply, a brand is the difference between a bottle of sugared, flavored, carbonated water and a bottle of Coca-Cola. It is the sum of the functional and emotional characteristics, both tangible and intangible, that a consumer attributes to a product or service. These characteristics are embodied in a name, trademark, symbol, or design, or any combination of these.

However, this definition is being increasingly stretched. As the Internet grows ever more pervasive, many online brands have virtually no tangible attributes. It could be argued that brands such as Amazon and Yahoo! exist purely in virtual reality. Moreover, the concept of branding can no longer be restricted to products and services. Movie stars, politicians, and company executives are all realizing that success is dependent on their ability to market themselves as brands.

THE ORGANIZATION AS BRAND

Many companies, and particularly those that have system brands, are realizing that creating a successful brand franchise involves mobilizing the entire organization. Every aspect of the organization, from the premises through the behavior of the employees (particularly those who work in customer-facing roles) to company letterheads and formal marketing communications, should reflect and reinforce the values of the brand.

A good example of the organization as brand is *Sage*, a leading supplier of accounting and payroll software. Unusually for the software industry, where marketing tends to focus on product features, Sage's brand identity communicates a feeling of confident control, leading to peace of mind. Most customers who buy Sage software also purchase an annual telephone support contract. When they phone the hotline the support technician's ability to resolve their problem serves to reinforce the brand promise.

WHY ARE BRANDS IMPORTANT?

For most companies brands are their primary source of competitive advantage and their most valuable strategic asset. Without brands we'd live in a world of commodities—undifferentiated products that are traded solely on price, according to the laws of supply and demand. Branding enables companies to actively influence the demand side of the equation by encouraging consumers to base their purchase decisions on factors other than price.

Brands are also important for consumers. They enable consumers to make informed purchase decisions and help them to navigate their way through the bewildering number of alternatives that exist in any product category. It can also be argued that brands enrich our lives. In a world in which our basic needs have been satisfied, brands give us something to which we can aspire and help in defining our own identities. This, however, is a question of ideology, and many would disagree.

SOURCES OF DIFFERENTIATION

Differentiation is the most important concept in the creation of powerful brands. Essentially brands can be differentiated in terms of product and/or service, leading to four generic brand types.

1. Where an offering is differentiated neither in terms of product nor service, it is a **commodity**. Precious metals and staple food products are still largely traded as commodities (though the increasing demand for organic produce is changing this).
2. Where an offering is differentiated in product, but not in service terms, it is a **product brand**. Product brands can be further differentiated in terms of intrinsic (or functional) benefits and extrinsic (or emotional) benefits. In practice most consumer goods are product brands, and most contain elements of both intrinsic and extrinsic differentiation. Hi-fi manufacturers focus primarily on the functionality of their products, while most mainstream soft-drink brands are differentiated largely in terms of image. The marketing of automobiles, one of the most potent symbols of status and way of life, plays on both function and emotion.
3. An offering based on providing an intangible service is a **service brand**. Financial services are classic examples. Creating service brands can prove difficult, because unlike packaged goods, delivering a service to the consumer relies heavily on humans, and humans are notoriously less reliable than machines.
4. An offering differentiated in both product and service terms is a **system brand**. The McDonalds experience is based on a combination of the quality of the food, the speed of the service, and the cleanliness of the restaurant.

THE BUILDING BLOCKS OF BRAND CREATION

The **brand proposition** is the statement of the functional and emotional benefits that a company believes its product or service offers to the consumer. Coca-Cola's brand proposition is a mixture of functional

"The name Disney is one of the world's most powerful brands." (Michael Eisner)

benefits (taste, refreshment) and emotional benefits (good wholesome fun).

Brand positioning is a description of those at whom the brand is aimed (the target audience) and where it stands relative to the competition.

Brand identity (or **brand image**) is the aggregation of the words, images, and ideas that the consumer associates with a brand. There is an increasing tendency to personify brands, and companies talk about brand personality and brand attitude. This is particularly important in youth markets, in which consumers regard brands as statements of their beliefs and preferences.

THE BRAND-BUILDER'S TOOLBOX

Successful brand creation starts with product design. But it's not just about how the product performs, it's also about how it looks.

In the fast-moving consumer-goods sector, packaging is also a key source of differentiation, both as a powerful tool for creating brand identity and as a means whereby brands can stand out from the crowd on increasingly cluttered supermarket shelves.

Advertising is perhaps the brand manager's most potent tool. Print and broadcast media not only represent a cost-effective mechanism for reaching mass audiences, they also have the power to influence consumer behavior. The press is a particularly effective medium for communicating complex messages, while TV advertising, with its beguiling interplay of sounds and pictures, is ideal for building brand image.

In recent years, however, the brand manager's task has become increasingly complex. Brands have proliferated, media have fragmented, and consumers have become more cynical. Brand owners have had to become more innovative, constantly reinventing their brands to keep one step ahead of their competitors and their consumers. Technology has facilitated increasingly sophisticated consumer segmentation techniques, and many brand owners are moving from a *one-to-many* to a *one-to-one* marketing model.

MEASURING BRAND EQUITY

If brands are a company's most valuable strategic asset, it makes sense to take good care of them. While it is difficult to prove a statistical relationship between advertising and sales because of the sheer number of variables involved, it is possible to prove a relationship between advertising and awareness and between awareness and sales. For this reason most companies track brand awareness levels, together with other measures such as brand loyalty and purchase intention.

It is also important to track brand image, to ensure that the differentiating elements of brand identity a company is attempting to communicate are being received accurately by the consumer. One reason for doing this is to gauge to what extent brand equity can be leveraged into line extensions or new products. Virgin is the classic example of this, with the brand now spanning airlines, trains, soft drinks, and financial services.

In recent years many brand owners have attempted to assign an economic value to their brands on the balance sheet. The brand consultancy Interbrand has been at the forefront of this process, though the accounting profession has yet to fully embrace the concept.

BRANDS IN THE NEW ECONOMY

It took radio 38 years to reach an audience of 50 million, while TV took 13 years. At current growth rates the Internet will reach the same audience in less than 5 years. The Internet is the brand manager's dream: it's instantaneous; it enables one-to-one communication; it's interactive; and it's multimedia, integrating text, sound, and images.

Yet many companies are realizing that creating brands at Internet speed is not as easy as it sounds. Many dot-com startups have been able to create new businesses virtually overnight, unencumbered by the baggage of the old economy, but consumers have been less willing to buy into these new brands. The most successful online brands are arguably those that are rooted in the old economy but have harnessed the Internet to extend their brand franchise.

MAKING IT HAPPEN ⏩

- Seek above all to differentiate the product and/or service elements of your offerings from those of your competitors.
- Build the brand proposition from the functional and emotional benefits you believe your product or service offers to customers.
- Use sophisticated consumer segmentation techniques to move from a one-to-many to a one-to-one marketing model.
- Track brand image to ensure that the differentiating elements of brand identity are being received accurately by the consumer.
- Harness the Internet to extend the customer franchise of your most successful offline brands.
- Work on every aspect of the organization, from employee behavior to premises, so as to reflect and reinforce brand values.

THE FUTURE OF BRANDS

While brands are undoubtedly here to stay, there is growing evidence of a consumer backlash. Ironically it's the Internet that's encouraging consumers, sick of being marketed to by faceless corporations, to demand a dialog with brand owners.

Moreover, disgruntled consumers are using the Internet to undermine the brand equity that has been expensively created by these same faceless corporations. These voices of dissent range from the humorous (***www.ihatemanunited.com***) to the more sinister (***www.aolsucks.org***).

For More Information

Books:

Aaker, David A. *Building Strong Brands.* New York: Free Press, 1995.

Aaker, David A. *Managing Brand Equity: Capitalizing on the Value of a Brand Name.* New York: Free Press, 1991.

See also:

☆ **Marketing: The Importance of Being First (pp. 61–62)**
✔ **Branding a Business Product (pp. 712–13)**
✔ **Raising the Awareness of Business Brands (pp. 714–15)**
💡 **David Ogilvy (pp. 1124–25)**
↻ **Marketing Management (pp. 2045–48)**

"As the retail trade consolidates, it will look more and more at big fresh brands that are constantly innovating."

(Niall Fitzgerald)

  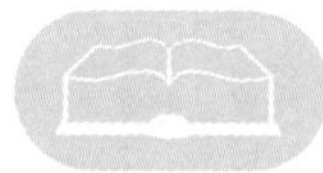    

Managing the Customer *by Merlin Stone*

Executive Summary

- As competition in all its forms intensifies, customer management holds the key to increasing revenues *in a way that also drives profitability.*
- Whether cross-selling or upselling additional products to customers, retaining existing customers, attracting new ones, using customers to help develop new products, or simply providing the same products more efficiently and at less cost—the importance of customer focus and management is without parallel.
- At a time when the number of sales channels are increasing significantly and many other factors are impacting on traditional sales and marketing issues, the need for customer service that is 24/7 and manages the customer is as challenging as ever.

Introduction

There's no ideal way of managing customers. Marketers have been brought up on consumer-goods branding, retail marketing, and sales-force management. Along comes customer-relationship marketing with the claim to replace or substantially supplement these tried-and-true ways of doing business. However, there are many ways of managing customers. The main ways are listed below. In practice many companies combine several.

Models for Managing the Customer

One-on-one

Here most aspects of the marketing mix are actively attuned to the individual, based on information given by the individual before or during contacts, perhaps supplemented by other data (for example, inferred data). Some—but not all—customers are considered receptive to this, that is, customers have different propensities to respond in terms of returning more value. The principles work when applied to large customers whose value justifies the degree of customization implied by this approach.

Transparent Marketing

Many customers would like to manage their relationship with companies rather than the other way around. They try to do this by soliciting information from them and customizing the offer made to them (content, timing, etc.), but they're not usually allowed to do so. Where it is possible (for example, via advanced call centers or the Web) some customers are very responsive. However, most companies do not offer this to their customers, and even waste large amounts of money trying to guess what customers want based on inadequate information.

Customer-relationship Marketing (CRM) through a Few Segmented Offers

This is still the aspiration of most companies. Although most companies make slower progress than they would like, many get solid gains by prioritizing those areas of the relationship in which the offer for target customers (for example, positive- and/or high-value) is most at variance with the need. This model recognizes that the relationship is only one part of the marketing mix, and that there are often situations in which classic elements of the marketing mix are more critical for marketing success.

Personalized Communication and Targeting

Examples of personalized communication and marketing are campaign selection and packaging purposes of a standard offer. The practice grew from good practice in direct mail and telemarketing. It involves good use and management of customer data. It can raise response and conversion rates and save communication costs. In its most advanced form, data given by the customer at the point of contact is used to create or modify the profile and hence the offer made.

Top Vanilla

In this method, leadership is gained by offering excellent customer management (before, during, and after the sale), but to a standard available to everyone in the target market rather than just a few selected customers. In some cases this is combined with one of the other approaches for one or more small segments of highly valuable customers. This approach is characteristic of companies that manage their customers entirely by direct-marketing techniques such as telemarketing, direct mail, and the Internet.

Spot-sell within Managed Roster

For some or all of the products they buy, some customers prefer to get the best deal (value for money, not necessarily lowest price) at the time of purchase, but only from a selected roster of suppliers. This is characteristic of heavy users of fast-moving consumer goods or shopping goods, but also of many industrial purchases in which a roster of suppliers is used to ensure optimal variety, product quality, and service. In such situations attempts to develop behavioral loyalty (so that a customer buys more than the usual proportion from one supplier) usually require some promotional incentive. Branding is usually a critical determinant of inclusion in the roster. For products bought through intermediaries, the supplier's aim is to ensure availability through intermediaries in the customer's roster. Note that the final customer may have a roster of products/brands and a roster of intermediaries. In this model, marketing focuses on getting on the customer's roster and providing best value compared with other companies on the roster. Top vanilla service can add competitive edge. CRM can be used to reinforce the supplier's or intermediary's position in the roster, though it may not help in gaining profit. However, if the supplier's product or the intermediary's offer is good value for money, a fair share of the business can be obtained, so the returns to CRM can be good.

Spot-sell Managed by Agent

In some cases drawing up the roster can be a complex task with which customers feel they need the help of an agent, whether for expert advice, bargaining expertise, or just to delegate some of the transaction management. Some modes of purchase may require the customer to sign on as a registered customer (for example, buying over the telephone or on the Web), but the customer prefers to register with an independent agent rather than the original product or service supplier. So the customer appoints one intermediary to act as an agent, and the agent then draws up the roster. However, CRM techniques can be used very successfully with the intermediaries. This approach can often be combined with top vanilla service for final customers and agents. In an increasing number of cases, the agent may be Web-based.

"To succeed, you have to have confidence in yourself and your product. You have to love what you're doing, and you have to care about your customers." (Mary Kelekis)

Pure Spot-sell

Here the customer rejects all relationships and buys (whether from original supplier or intermediary) purely on the basis of current perceived value. This in turn is strongly influenced by classic marketing-mix variables–brand, perceived product quality, price (including promotional discounts), availability, etc. To avoid being drawn into this situation, suppliers must seek to differentiate their offer such that the customer sees pure spot-buying as being risky.

The Partnership Model

This is a model that seems to have a very good pedigree, but it is quite difficult to implement. It is suggested as a model where both supplier and intermediary have strong visibility of and to the final customer, as in the automotive industry or in financial services.

Classic Marketing Models

There are several classic marketing models in which the nature of customer management is not specified explicitly but there is a very strong implicit model of customer management. These include:

- retailing;
- sales-force management;
- mail order;
- consumer-product and company-brand management;
- business-product management (closely related to technical innovation models).

Adopting the Right Approach

Obviously, these approaches to managing customers overlap, and suppliers may find they need to combine them in different ways for managing different customers and for different products. However, each has characteristic and very different patterns of marketing investment and return.

The choice is affected by factors such as the following:

- **state and rate of change of product technology.** This can lead customers to require uncertainty reduction–available through relationship or agents. But it can also create big differences in spot value;
- **underlying production and distribution techniques and costs,** for example, costs of variety, economies of scale;
- **rate of entry of new-to-category customers,** which affects the role of experience;
- **market structure fundamentals,** for example, patterns of competition or regulation;
- **transfer of learning and expectations of customers between different paradigms of management** that customers know;
- **customer behavior and psychographics** or, more simply, what they think and feel, how they buy, their need to give or take control, and associated way-of-life and life-cycle issues
- **timing issues**–how quickly customers' needs can be identified, and how quickly they can be responded to;
- **customer expertise**–whether customers are good at identifying their own needs (and if so, how long it takes) and associated learning issues;
- **sector**–the strong tendency in some complex business-to-business relationships for customers to prefer a CRM-managed repertoire with spot-buying;
- **state of intermediation**–type of intermediation (for example, by agents, Web-based) and amount and type of value added by intermediaries;
- **relationship between risk and value,** for example, whether customers have high risks (credit, insurance, etc.) attached to them as individuals; what the balance is between good and bad customers and between good and bad customer characteristics;
- **data issues**–quality, legal issues.
- **staffing**–current skill levels, possibilities of recruiting new skill sets, training options, etc.;
- **systems culture of the supplier,** for example, whether managers are able to cope with the latest call-center and Web-based technology.

Making It Happen ▸▸

- Build customer management by combining different approaches in different ways for managing different customers and products.
- Treat one-on-one marketing as an ideal target rather than a practical means of returning more value.
- Don't guess what customers want, but build an accurate picture from well-researched data.
- Recognize that the customer relationship is only one part of the marketing mix, and that other elements may be more critical.
- If possible, offer excellent customer management (before, during, and after the sale) to everyone in the target market, not just a few.
- Review the success of different approaches in your own and parallel markets as part of general corporate strategy reviews.

Conclusion

No one paradigm dominates another. Our research indicates that companies should consider the variety of models of customer management that might work in their market, identifying which might be best for their market as a whole and for particular segments. They should review the extent to which these approaches have really been successful in their own and parallel markets. This review should take place as part of a general corporate strategy review, for each paradigm requires its own operational structure, processes, systems, and policies. There's no point choosing a marketing model that sits badly with other functional strategies. Perhaps most important of all, companies should keep a close watch on the preferred paradigms of their most valued customers–but with a skeptical eye. Often a paradigm only works because customers have been offered nothing better.

For More Information

Book:

Peppers, Don, and Martha Rogers. *Enterprise One-to-one: Tools for Competing in the Interactive Age*. New York: Doubleday, 1999.

See also:

☆ **Managing the Challenge of E-service (pp. 188–89)**
✔ **Increasing Lifetime Customer Value (pp. 676–77)**
Customer Relations/Service (pp. 1948–50)

"You need to bring customers inside your business to create information partnerships. . . relationships become the differentiator, more than products or services." (Michael Dell)

VIEWPOINT: PATTY SEYBOLD

Taking Managers Online for the Customer Revolution

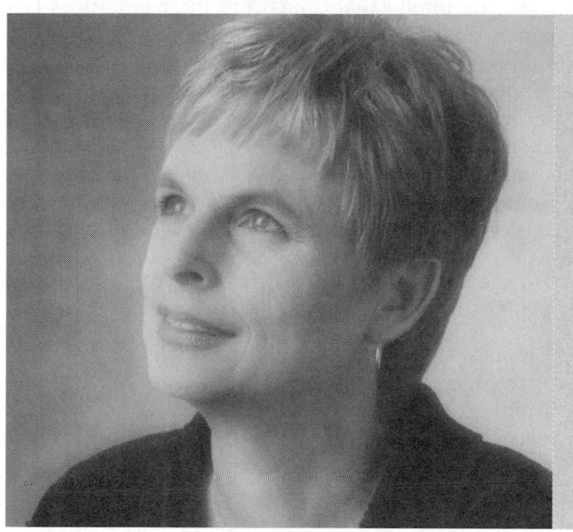

Patty Seybold is best known for her 1998 book *Customers.com*. The book's timing was impeccable. At a time when many companies were wrestling with the strategic and operational implications of the Internet, Seybold argued that customers should come first. "What's the formula for success?" she asked. "Make it easy for customers to do business with you!"

In her most recent book, *The Customer Revolution*, Seybold goes further, arguing that competitive advantage in the future will reside in "customer capital"—the quality of relationships that companies create with their customers. The new economy, she asserts, is a customer economy.

What is the most important thing and who is the most important person to have influenced your thinking on business and management? Why?

My father, John W. Seybold, taught me how to spot and understand emerging technologies, to envision how they would transform businesses and industries, and how to build consensus and shared vision among cross-functional teams to achieve business transformation one step at a time. He also taught me the basic information architecture design principle of keeping form, content, and business rules separate and allowing them to dynamically reformat appropriate offerings based on context.

He developed a tagging system for text, which allowed him to reformat the same text in many different ways and for different purposes. One of the first texts he worked with was the Bible. His seminal work in this area paved the way for the creation of SGML, HTML, and the World Wide Web.

Robert Fritz taught me how the creative process works and how to harness structural tension to achieve business goals. From him I learned the principles of designing a "path of least resistance" that enables people to achieve their shared goals without struggle.

Nancy Post, the founder of Systems Energetics, taught me that the principles of Chinese acupuncture work as well in human systems as they do in human beings. Information, combined with spirit, flows through organizations. This organizational Ch'i can either heal and keep the organization vital, or become blocked and cause dysfunction. I discovered on my own that customer information and interactions are the most cleansing and healing form of organizational information flow. If you truly bathe your organization with customers' input, feedback, priorities, and outcomes, you can keep it vital and thriving.

Fernando Flores, the Chilean-born philosopher and cognitive scientist, taught me that people and information systems use the same commitment management protocols across cultures (request/offer, negotiate conditions of satisfaction, agree, perform, report completion, assess, accept). This understanding of how humans manage their work together, despite cultural differences, has been valuable to me in helping clients design new business processes that combine information, technology, and people.

Doug Engelbart, the father of the ARPAnet (which preceded the Internet) and the inventor of most of the tools and concepts we are still perfecting today, taught me how to use networked technology to augment human intelligence, and how to observe and improve knowledge creation and management.

How will business be different in the 21st century?

Successful companies will be highly adaptive and customer-centric. They will be what I call "sense-and-pro-act" organizations. They will recognize new patterns very quickly—especially in terms of customer behavior. To do so they will require real-time information about that customer behavior.

> **Successful companies will be highly adaptive and customer-centric. They will be what I call "sense-and-pro-act" organizations.**

At Cisco Systems, for example, all senior managers are now required to spend at least 50% of their time talking to customers. It is that sort of continuous interaction, combined with real-time customer metrics,

input, and feedback, that will allow managers to sense emerging patterns.

The way that companies are organized will also change. Federated and networked organizations—extended enterprises—will be the norm. In the past, companies have either been highly centralized, with command and control structures, or highly distributed with autonomous business units, and they have tended to swing from one extreme to the other. They are now beginning to figure out how they can combine the best attributes of these two models to create federal organizations.

In the old economy we were dealing with the allocation of scarce resources. In the customer economy the key resource is knowledge about and relationships with customers.

Another important change will be a more sophisticated approach to measuring profitability. There will be a move toward customer P&Ls (profit and loss information) rather than product line P&Ls. How we understand a brand will also shift from the notion of brand that is evoked through advertising to one that views the brand as a customer experience. So companies will make operational changes based on enhancing the branded customer experience.

This involves a move to what I call Quality of Customer Experience (QCE)™ management. Concepts like total quality management and reengineering became movements as companies recognized that they had to adopt them just to remain competitive. But TQM didn't really translate into service industries. QCE management will take root in service companies, but it is also applicable to manufacturing. It is much more dynamic than TQM. QCE management means being prepared to change processes in response to customer demands. Companies will reorient themselves around two-way relationships with their customers.

This will lead to customer-managed relationships rather than customer relationship or sales management. This will also pave the way for just-in-time customization of most products and services

What new skills set will be needed to cope with these changes?

I've already talked about the ability to sense and respond quickly to new patterns and to customer demands. This has implications all the way up the supply chain. If you look at a Nokia handset, for example, you find there are 200 or so sub-component suppliers. If there is a change in the market, the commitments in the supply chain need to be renegotiated very rapidly. The ability to manage changing commitments across organizational boundaries will be vital.

The ability to identify, codify, package, use, and continuously improve core knowledge, services, and/or capabilities will also be very important. Successful companies will be adept at self-examination to identify what their core competencies are—and then repackaging those core competencies to meet new and emerging customer requirements. In the old economy we were dealing with the allocation of scarce resources. In the customer economy the key resource is knowledge about and relationships with customers. That is infinite. The more you give the more you get.

So the intellectual capital I'm interested in is customer capital. That will be embedded in the minds of employees and in the organization, but it will also be embedded in the company's relationships with its customers. The more customer capital you have, the more successful you are likely to be in meeting customer needs. Leaders will also need the ability to combine vision and strategy and attention to customer-critical detail in day-to-day operations.

How can managers best develop these required skills?

The best way to cultivate these skills is to apprentice with those who already have them. Managers-in-training should be rotated through positions under the people who already embody these skills, rather than being rotated through functional or geographic responsibilities.

Are there new management questions we should be asking? If so, what are they?

What's our customer strategy? Which types of customers do we want to have deeper relationships with? Which types of customers would we like to attract? Do we know what our customers' and prospects' underlying emotional motivations are? Do we know what outcomes our customers need to accomplish? Are we measuring ourselves on our ability to help our customers achieve their outcomes? Do we know which customer scenarios are most important for each group of customers? Are we monitoring the quality of customer experience we're delivering on these customer-critical scenarios? How are we doing on the quality of the branded customer experience we're delivering? How are we doing in increasing our value to customers and the profitability of our customers for our business?

How can companies best promote enterprises that are a) profitable and b) good places for people to work?

Employees will be drawn to enterprises that care about and deliver value to their customers. They will gravitate to customer-centric organizations. Employees will want and value clear customer-focused goals and metrics. Customer-focused companies give employees a sense of mission, purpose, and value, and they are the most profitable companies in the world.

For More Information

See also:

✔ **Running a Customer Loyalty Program (pp. 678–79)**

Customer Relations/Services (pp. 1948–50)

"Trying to get consumers to re-evaluate their behavior is what I enjoy most." (Ric Simcock)

Viewpoint: B. Joseph Pine II

Transforming Business by Making It an Experience

Joe Pine has the unique distinction of having written two books that will be seen as seminal in the 21st century. In *Mass Customization*, he outlined how companies can efficiently provide individually customized goods and services. And, with coauthor James Gilmore, Joe advanced the idea in *The Experience Economy* that goods and services are no longer enough—they're becoming basic commodities. Here, Joe tells not only what these books mean to management, but how they essentially interconnect and project what it will mean to lead in the businesses of tomorrow.

As big a shift as is happening in business today, in 50 years the business world will undergo an even more dramatic shift.

If you think about it, it was almost exactly 50 years ago that the economy shifted from an industrial base to a service base. It was the mass production of goods that made America the number one economic power in the world, but beginning around 1950, more people began to earn their incomes from delivering intangible services than from making physical goods or extracting natural commodities. It took, however, almost 30 years for the trend to be fully recognized, at which time many pundits and professors decried the very notion that an economy could be built on anything other than on the hard and tangible. Remember all the complaints about manufacturing jobs going away, about production moving off-shore, about the very hollowing of America? We don't hear those particular protests any longer, even though the goods and commodities sectors combined have shrunk to less than 20% of employment and GDP. Indeed, it was the very loss of manufacturing jobs that opened the door to all the entrepreneurial talent which has made today's business world such a dynamic place through service innovations.

One of the effects of the burgeoning service economy was that goods became commoditized. Customers–whether consumers or businesses–simply valued the service more than the good. Today, we see the same thing happening to services; they're also being commoditized, where customers care more about price than any other factor.

So now we are in the midst of another economic shift, to an experience economy. The predominant economic activity is rapidly becoming staging experiences–memorable events that engage each customer in an inherently personal way. The prototypical experience is, of course, going to Walt Disney World. Sure, one buys food and parking services, and goods as memorabilia; but the reason one goes is for that shared family experience that lasts for months and even years afterward. Hard Rock Cafés serve food against the backdrop of staging memorable musical moments. And Recreation Equipment Incorporated (REI) places 65-foot climbing mountains and other experiences in its stores to get consumers to experience the goods before they buy them. Those businesses–whatever their product or service line–that miss the shift to experiences will be marginalized.

But now let's look 50 years into the future. Then, experiences will also become commoditized, and businesses will need to shift again to sell a fifth and final economic offering: transformations. The transformation economy will be one in which companies help customers change via life-transforming experiences–where the customer is the product. Many companies are already naturally in the transformation business, including fitness centers, hospitals, schools, and consultants. But today each of these charge for the mere service or experience, not for the transformation. In the future, they'll be paid based on the demonstrated outcome their customers achieve–and there is no more economic value to be gained than by helping someone achieve their aspirations.

But now let's look 50 years into the future. Then, experiences will also become commoditized, and businesses will need to shift again to sell a fifth and final economic offering: transformations.

So what's happening in the business world means that managers need a completely new skill set in

"The professional service firm—with its obsession on clients and projects—must be the new organizational model."

(Tom Peters)

order to prosper in the emerging experience economy and forthcoming transformation economy. They'll need a new skill set even to participate.

First, in terms of the experience economy, managers must realize that work is theater. I'm not using a metaphor here. Whenever workers are in front of guests, they are acting, and need to act in a way that turns the interaction into a memorable event. Managers, therefore, must help their workers take on a role, characterize that role, rehearse it, and then perform it on the bare stage of business.

Then, in terms of the transformation economy, the key skills are caring and empathy. We used to talk about understanding a customer's problems and then providing solutions. This is much more. Managers must care for individuals enough truly to understand their aspirations, and to help them achieve those aspirations. It was, I believe, a Woody Allen character who said "Sincerity–if you can fake that, you've got it made." Well, what I'm suggesting is no joke–you won't be able to fake empathy. The new economic landscape demands authenticity. Why? Educated, demanding customers simply will not deal with businesses that are little more than smoke and mirrors.

Building a physical good that's unique for each and every customer—as IBM learned to do with computers—is part and parcel of providing a special experience that connects in a unique way to each and every guest.

In this regard Jim Gilmore coined the term "world-view segmentation" to describe what's starting to happen in the business world. Customers increasingly will not buy from, nor support, a business that does not share their own world view. In the same way, people will not work for companies that are at odds with their world views. So everything that Jim and I talk about has both external and internal implications. Just as companies must stage experiences and guide transformations to forestall commoditization in their industries, they must stage authentic, life-transforming internal experiences to enable employees to achieve their work aspirations, and become better workers, in all the senses that word implies. And just as companies must mass-customize their economic offerings to attract and keep customers, so must they mass-customize their compensation systems and development plans to attract and keep their workers.

Mass-customization is not at all ancillary to this discussion. My work there led to the discovery of experiences and transformations as distinct economic offerings. I recognized that mass-customizing a product automatically turned it into a service, and applying the same learning process, discovered that mass-customizing services turned them into experiences, and mass-customizing experiences turned them into transformations.

Therefore, I owe a great debt to Stan Davis, who first coined the term "mass-customizing" in his compelling and terrific 1987 book, *Future Perfect*. I first read it when I was a strategic planner at IBM in the late 1980s, and it changed my life.

During the development of the AS/400 computer system, I managed a cross-functional team that brought customers and business partners into the development process. And I learned that every customer was unique. They wanted different characteristics for their systems, they wanted different software, they wanted to integrate the systems in different ways. We had designed the system for a large, homogenous marketplace that simply did not exist!

So when I read Stan Davis's book, it suddenly all made sense. I worked to get his ideas into IBM's plans and strategies, and when the company sent me to the Massachusetts Institute of Technology (MIT) to get my master's degree, spent that entire time investigating the subject further. I eventually turned my thesis into my first book, *Mass Customization.*

As I think back to that time, what's amazing is how it all really connects. Building a physical good that's unique for each and every customer–as IBM learned to do with computers–is part and parcel of providing a special experience that connects in a unique way to each and every guest. As we move to the experience economy and, eventually, through it to the transformational economy, it's crucial to understand that experiences happen inside each person individually–and aspirations belong to each person in unique ways. Goods and services are becoming commodities today; there's nothing special about them. Leaders who want to make their businesses stand out will have to do more. They'll have to stage memorable experiences for their customers, and they'll have to help their customers become the people (and businesses) they've always wanted to be.

For More Information

Books:

Davis, Stan. *Future Perfect*. Cambridge, MA: Perseus, 1997.

Pine, B. Joseph, II. *Mass Customization*. Boston, MA: Harvard Business School Press, 1999.

Pine, B. Joseph, II, and James H. Gilmore. *The Experience Economy*. Boston, MA: Harvard Business School Press, 1999.

Web Site:

Strategic Horizons: **www.strategichorizons.com**

See also:

☆ **Avoiding the Mistakes of the Past: Lessons from the Startup World (pp. 129–30)**
☆ **Delivering and Delighting—A New Spirit at Work (pp. 71–72)**
☆ **Marketing: The Importance of Being First (pp. 61–62)**
☆ **The Second Coming of Service (pp. 77–78)**

"There is far more involved in the relationship with customers than just providing good products and services. It is a question of personal identification." (Mark Moody-Stuart)

Delivering and Delighting—A New Spirit at Work *by Richard C. Whiteley*

Executive Summary

- Although much has been written about customer-centered companies and although many have tried to create them, even today few organizations have broken through to become truly customer centered.
- Often the underlying reason for a corporation's inability to put the customer at its center is what appears to be a standoff between its leaders and employees.
- The key to ending this impasse is to determine what conditions need to exist for employees to embrace the customer-centered way of operating and to teach or encourage corporate leaders to create those conditions.

Introduction

In speeches and company visits over many years, I have often been asked the same questions. Lower level managers, usually in a service function, ask: How can I get senior management to believe in delighting customers as much as I believe in it? With executives, the question flips: How can I get our people to pay attention to our customers? These questions mirror the frustration of many organizations trying to reorient themselves around customers. Too often, neither leaders nor employees seem to be committed; worse, each side seems to be blaming the other. Managers must create four conditions to help employees feel a genuine passion for serving the customer; happily, there are three best practices that leaders can employ to create this most desired attitude.

Create Conditions for Change

The complexity, challenge, and time required for an organization to become truly customer-centric are usually underestimated. It is not just about introducing a new program, training customer contact people to smile over the phone, or conducting a few customer focus groups. Rather, it is about changing the culture of the organization, a challenge that may seem as difficult as, say, rewiring your own DNA. The most successful and dramatic transformation of an organization's culture I have witnessed took place in the 1980s and was led by Sir Colin Marshall at British Airways. When he arrived at the government-owned airline BOAC, it was losing money, abusing customers, and not doing well by its employees. Several years after Sir Colin privatized the company, it was commended for having the most improved service in the industry and for being the most profitable airline in the world. By any standard this remains one of the classic cultural turnarounds.

Study the BOAC success and others like it and patterns emerge of management actions that help create conditions that assist each and every employee to commit to the new direction and engage in the personal change that is required to bring the customer into the equation at all levels of the organization. These actions are to

1. articulate and promote the new direction;
2. make sure each employee knows what is expected;
3. see that each employee has the skills to do what is expected;
4. motivate each employee to do what is expected.

Looking at these four conditions, it is clear that they are deeply based in common sense. But you would be amazed at how difficult it is to implement them. Common sense, it has been said many times, is unfortunately not common at all.

Making It Happen

Articulate and Promote the New Direction

A study by Bain & Company asked C.E.O.s to rate their level of confidence in their ability to perform various aspects of their job. Of those asked, 85% felt they handled strategy development well; strategy execution, conversely, dropped off dramatically to 40%. When asked about aligning their people with their company's strategy, the response was an anemic 10%. Articulating and promoting the new direction speaks directly to this deficit.

- **Create a clear vision and value statement to direct the organization.** This is not a new idea, but many organizations have vision and value statements that seem to have little influence on day-to-day operations. It helps to have a vision and values audit to test the extent to which adopted vision and values are truly guiding the company and having a positive impact.
- **Share the strategy of the organization with all employees.** Ironically, a company's strategy is often deemed so confidential that it is not shared with employees. Sam Walton knew better; his policy was to share each Wal-Mart store's vital performance information with all employees, even part-timers. He reasoned that they were directly responsible for Wal-Mart's success.
- **Actively promote the new direction.** When Sydney Electricity first won Australia's national quality award, I asked C.E.O. John Gillespie what his most difficult challenge was in achieving this honor. He responded that continually selling the vision, repeating it with enthusiasm over and over again at every meeting with one or more of his employees, was the hardest. It simply is not good enough to send an e-mail to all employees stating the new direction.

Make Sure Each Employee Knows What Is Expected

In a multiyear research program that studied 400 organizations, 80,000 managers, and over one million employees, the Gallup Organization found that one of the factors that correlated highly with an organization's success was employees knowing what is expected of them. Sounds obvious, but this is never truer than when a company is changing its strategy.

- **Use the chain of command to discuss and explain what is expected.** When Michael Abrashoff, the commanding officer of the U.S.S. Benfold, took command of the beleaguered, poorly performing destroyer, he first had to establish new standards of behavior. He met in small

"Successful organizations understand the importance of implementation, not just strategy, and, moreover, recognize the crucial role of their people in this process." (Jeffrey Pfeffer)

groups with his 300 officers and enlisted men and women to make sure that they understood the rationale for the changes he was implementing and what their personal impact would be. Under his command the ship went on to establish training, readiness, and retention records and won the coveted Spokane Trophy for operational readiness.

- **Use your hierarchy to communicate new expectations.** Have all managers meet with their people and explain the rationale for the change and what this means for them. The more a picture can be created of appropriate new behavior, the more it is likely to become part of each employee's daily routine.
- **Have employees create a line-of-sight map between them and your customers.** A simple yet powerful exercise: ask employees to start with their location in the organization and create a visual trail direct to customers. While most are not in direct contact with external customers, they all have internal customers within the organization. Employees soon realize that a glitch in the internal customer relationship inevitably leads to a problem for external customers.
- **Put the spotlight on early adopters.** In any organizational change there are fence sitters and early adopters. Fence sitters do little but sit around, complain about another program du jour, and adopt an attitude of "change is good. . .you go first." In contrast the early adopters make a sincere effort at trying on the new behaviors to make the strategy work. Since peer success is a powerful influencer, purposely seek out these early adopters and publicly praise their efforts. Don't wait until all results are in; it's the effort to try things differently that you are actually rewarding. Results will follow.

See That Each Employee Has the Skills to Do What Is Expected
Once people have an idea of what is expected, it is a mistake to assume that they have the necessary skills to accomplish the stated goals. The key to this is employee training. How to start?

- **Conduct internal best practices research.** Identify best performers in each job category and compare them with their marginally performing counterparts. Identify what superior performers do distinctly. Once critical competences are identified, training exercises can be created to develop these skills in every employee.
- **Conduct a strategic training audit.** Create a matrix that lists the critical competencies required for each job in your company on the left vertical axis and each of your training programs along the top horizontal axis. Then, on a scale of 1 to 5, rate each program's contribution to the development of each competency. This will help purge redundant programs and fill gaps in competency development.
- **Make your employees your best trainers.** Rather than assigning all development to your company trainers, make it part of employees' jobs to help. Pret A Manger is a highly successful chain of sandwich shops in the United Kingdom (and now the United States) with legendary service. Many frontline staff (half!) have been promoted to Team Manager Trainer, responsible for training new hires.

Motivate Each Employee to Do What Is Expected
Now comes the hard part: getting people to actually use newly developed skills. Assuming that the compensation and reward system is running smoothly, what are some of the other practices that can create an organization-wide passion for serving the customer?

- **Get everyone in the game.** This means engaging in practices like asking employees to help create the vision and values, seeking their opinions on strategic issues, inviting them to innovate and create new processes, and authorizing them to solve problems now—without having to go through layers of approval. A survey of 551 large employers by Watson Wyatt found that people are more motivated when they believe they have an important place in the organization.
- **Introduce the face of the customer.** While the *voice of the customer* continues to be a critical driver here, consider introducing *the face of the customer*. Find ways to personalize the metrics. For example, videotape focus groups and share the results with every employee. Medical products manufacturer Medtronics keeps employees focused on its real purpose by bringing patients and their families into the company to share their survival stories. Such sessions are both inspiring and moving.
- **Make it fun.** With the seriousness and fear caused by downsizings, mergers, stock price collapses, increased working hours, and a near-maniacal focus on quarterly earnings, all too often the fun has been squeezed out of work. Last year the United States lost $1.5 billion in productivity to stress-related absenteeism. This is more than the total profitability of the *Fortune* 500. It is the unquestioned responsibility of leaders to help put the fun back in to work. In a survey of 1,000 peak performers, Louis Harris and Associates asked what kind of workplace they would be reluctant to leave. Their answer? One that promotes fun.

CONCLUSION

Changing an organization's culture is always a complex, even daunting, task. In order to become customer-centered the leaders of a corporation must first be willing to change themselves. It is their responsibility to create the four conditions cited above that will support each and every employee in understanding the new direction, knowing what is expected, and having the skills and motivation to do what is expected.

For More Information

Books:

Heskett, James L., et al. *The Service Profit Chain: How Leading Companies Link Profit and Growth to Loyalty, Satisfaction, and Value*. New York: Free Press, 1997.

Sobel, Andrew, and Jagdish Sheth. *Clients for Life: How Great Professionals Develop Breakthrough Relationships*. New York: Simon & Schuster, 2000.

Web Site:

www.theRITEstuff.com: an excellent resource that summarizes important research on customer, people, investor, and global best practices.

See also:

☆ **Managing 1:1 Marketing (pp. 55–56)**
Customer Relations/Service (pp. 1948–50)

"The consumer, so it is said, is the king. . .each is a voter who uses his money as votes to get the things done that he wants done."
(Anthony Sampson)

Marketing to the "Real-time" Consumer
by Geoff Mott and Regis McKenna

Executive Summary

- Efforts in the last decade to improve marketing performance via technology have largely been uninspiring.
- The Internet offers a major new vehicle for marketing to reassert its central role in enhancing firm value around core assets such as customers, value propositions, partnerships, and brands.
- Successful marketing companies use technology to build, leverage, and promote a powerful, customer-oriented business infrastructure.

Introduction

Two important questions arise in relation to marketing and the Internet:

1. How does the Internet affect or change the marketing process?
2. How is marketing practiced on the Internet and what room is there for improvement?

According to Peter Drucker in *The Practice of Management* (1982), only two things matter in the corporation: marketing and innovation. This challenging statement suggests that marketing has a key role to play in the enterprise. We would submit that because of the "real-time" connection to the customer and the enterprise value chain, the Internet increases the urgency and criticality of that role. Marketing should embrace activities ranging from managing the product specification process, often with internal and external groups, to operations and logistics, relationships management, and other key business processes that get little mention in the Internet marketing debate.

Enter the Internet

The Internet affects every facet of a firm's value-delivery system, providing critical feedback and insight about the company and its partners/channels; the efficiency and effectiveness of its product/service design and delivery; who the customers are, what they think, and what they value; and how the competition is performing. Companies become great because they build sustainable business infrastructures that are superior to their competitors, and leverage those infrastructures to deliver more value to each customer. The infrastructures that matter most are R&D, operations, logistics, distribution and positioning. Marketing should be critically linked to, if not driving, this infrastructure, because it is visible to the customer and shapes the customer's perspective of the firm.

The Internet is, above all else, a unique vehicle for facilitating and enhancing the performance of this business infrastructure. It helps companies with strong and targeted value propositions develop much richer dialogue with their customers and, as a result, improve innovations in products and services to make the consumer experience even richer and more relevant. An excellent example of this is Lego, which leveraged the Internet to develop and launch blockbuster products like Mindstorms.

Current Internet Marketing Practices: A for Effort, F for Results

The overall track record of marketing in leveraging the Internet has been dismal. Because it is a new landscape, a series of myths have grown up around the Internet as a marketing medium, myths that have proven expensive and frequently disastrous to many of the businesses that bought into them.

Myth 1: The Internet Is a Great Customer Acquisition Vehicle

On average the Internet costs three to ten times the cost of acquiring customers through other retail channels, such as stores or catalogs. The problem is partly hit rate (very low indeed) and partly the initial cost of getting people to a new site. While the cost of acquiring real estate on a Web portal has declined substantially in the recent past, and while there is no doubt that the Internet can serve as a very effective marketing tool, customer acquisition is a very tough process this way.

Myth 2: The Internet Is a Great Messaging and Advertising Medium

A lot of advertising money is spent either to reinforce the presence of brands that have massive distribution advantages or to encourage greater recognition among existing customers. Some money is spent on building awareness for new products, but most of these are line extensions of existing products. Even so, most line extensions fail (upwards of 75%), while more than 90% of truly new products fail.

Internet advertising is supposed to be more targeted since there are many more "channels" than on traditional media. Increasingly, online advertising is concentrated among the few big properties, especially Yahoo and AOL, that offer economies of scale and are likely to survive the current online advertising shake-out. As a result, online advertising is every bit as mass-market and "broadcast" as traditional e-media advertising, notwithstanding personalized home pages and so-called "viral marketing." In an era of superabundance of customer choice in most product categories, the Internet needs to be viewed more as a *listening* than as a *broadcast* medium, a platform more for understanding than for declaiming.

Myth 3: The Internet Makes 1:1 Marketing a Reality

Technologies like collaborative filtering and some new preference-matching programs are supposed to tailor online offerings to the needs of individual consumers. They fall short because they lack context for the suggestions they put forward, the kind of context that only a knowledgeable individual in a store or on the phone could bring to customer interactions. Listening technologies are pervasive, from the ATM to the check-out counter to the remote network management console. Marketing has yet to recognize these listening systems for what they are, contextual windows on the 1:1 customer relationship.

"Marketing takes a day to learn. Unfortunately, it takes a lifetime to master." (Philip Kotler)

Marketing in the Internet Age

The myths described above make most current marketing practices on the Internet marginally valuable and successful, at best. We need to think not about Internet marketing but about marketing in the Internet age—the totality of the marketing challenge in an age where business processes are increasingly mediated by the Internet.

Many organizations have underestimated the extent to which the Internet really does represent a new kind of technology-mediated value proposition. Technology tends to drive rapid commoditization. The Internet supports that trend by virtue of the access it affords to comparison information. As a result, many online companies have rapidly descended to commodity status, resulting in unsustainable business models. A classic example of this is Priceline, which is now facing strong competition not only from new travel industry sites such as Orbitz, but also airline-specific sites such as Southwest.com.

On the other hand, the "new economy" argument has generally failed because it decouples the Internet from the rest of the business system. Three hundred beauty sites opened for business in the 1997–2000 period, almost none of which understood that without availability of top brands such as Lauder and Lancome they would not be interesting to consumers, despite virtual makeover software, digital fragrance generators, and other technology gimmickry. In contrast, one of the very few successful Internet companies (measured in terms of growth and profitability) is eBay, which brilliantly defined its role in the small-items marketplace as the key intermediary and enlisted other players (including a willing customer) to manage key business processes such as payments and logistics.

The challenge for marketers in the Internet age is *marketing at the core*. It requires an understanding of customer pain points (an ability to listen rather than talk), a more-than-passing familiarity with the economics of cost-to-serve and, above all, an approach to customers that is based upon a life-cycle relationship management process.

As an example of the importance of marketing as a repository of customer business process expertise, Citibank has one of the more highly developed Internet-based innovation and marketing strategies in the financial services sector. The company has applied superior marketing insight into the way technology can completely change the value proposition to a key target market—corporate C.F.O.s. These customers have traditionally been served by "stovepiped" product lines, but innovative marketers like Citibank understand that C.F.O.s are really interested in managing their day-to-day activities in a much more integrated fashion. The result has been measurable share gain in corporate financial services. Instead of driving temporary, transient product *differentiation*, they have used Internet platforms to deliver sustainable business value to customers via effective process *integration*.

Making It Happen ▸▸

Answering these questions is an excellent prescription for any executive who wishes to understand what marketing should know about customers and the role of the Internet:

1. How does the Web deliver value to customers, business partners and to my own company?
2. Who am I serving with my Web presence and do the economics deliver enough return to the value network to justify the use of the Web?
3. What is the whole product that I need to bring to my Web business, including, where necessary, non-Web components and partnership components?
4. How do I ensure extraordinary value delivery on the Web, manage that value delivery over time for my customers and build brand value from that total customer experience?
5. How does the Web fit into that total relationship with the customer and why? What roles should it play at different stages of the relationship?
6. Where should the Web fit organizationally such that it leverages and enhances my total marketing strategy and implementation plan?
7. How do I measure success in terms of new customers, repeat customers, loyal customers, total revenue and margin growth, new product success rates, partner business and profitability growth, and so on?

The Web is one of the greatest resources marketers have ever had at their disposal. Successful sites all tend to have the property of expanding consumer choice and control in terms of *how the relationship is managed* without compromising the traditional basis for consumer preference, the choice and control over *what is delivered*. The vast majority of these firms successfully align the rich contextual options of the Internet with a coherent set of content and commerce options that integrate across all relevant touchpoints and distribution channels.

Conclusion

In the short term, all companies can use the Web as a particular part of their marketing approach, reinforcing their ability to understand and deliver value to customers, underscoring their ability to deliver tailored value propositions, facilitating better channel relationships via information sharing and generally extending their presence to become more pervasive and more relevant to customers and business partners.

In the longer run, the Web can help marketing reassert some of the functions that it used to have a large say in but has lost control over in the last decade, such as product definition, control of the value proposition and how it is positioned, a measure of brand control (especially concerning the customer's total brand experience), and even what price is charged and the role of price in the decision process.

For More Information

Books:

Davenport, Thomas. *Process Innovation: Reengineering Work through Information Technology*. Boston, MA: Harvard Business School Press, 1992.

Gerbert, Philipp, and Alex Birch. *Digital Storm: Fresh Business Strategies from the Electronic Marketplace*. Mankato, MN: Capstone, 2001.

Hammer, Michael. *The Agenda: What Every Business Must Do to Dominate the Decade*. New York: Crown, 2001.

Web Site:

www.imtstrategies.com: good information on technology, marketing and business processes.

See also:

☆ **The Business Web (pp. 145–46)**
☆ **Managing the Challenge of E-service (pp. 188–89)**
☆ **X-engineering Success (pp. 245–46)**
✔ **How to Deliver Quality Online Customer Service (pp. 582–83)**

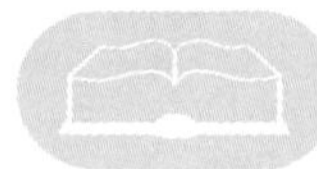

Viewpoint: Charles Handy

Elephants and Fleas

Now approaching 70, Irish-born Charles Handy remains the genteel, civilized voice of management. Handy worked for Shell before pursuing an academic career as a professor at the London Business School. His first book, *Understanding Organizations* (1976), gave little hint of the wide-ranging, social and philosophical nature of what was to come. In his later books Handy coined some of the best known and most useful management concepts of recent years, including "the shamrock organization" and "the portfolio career," and explored federalism in an engagingly accessible way. In his latest book, *The Elephant and the Flea* (2001), he returns to the theme of the changing landscape of working life, focusing on the symbiotic relationship between large companies (elephants) and small businesses (fleas), which include free agents, entrepreneurs inside and outside the organization, and firms with fewer than ten employees. "You will all be fleas one day," he advises, "so enjoy your fleadom."

What is the most important thing and who is the most important person to have influenced your thinking?

I read lots of things and listen to lots of people and absorb them. I take bits and pieces. I like a lot of what Gary Hamel says, for example, but probably because it confirms my own prejudices.

The major influences on my thinking have been my life experiences and my wife Elizabeth. Elizabeth pushed me to step outside organizational life and focus on what I do best—which I think is writing—and to make a business out of that. So I'd say it was the experience of my own life, prodded by my wife, and then influenced by people like Peter Drucker, Gary Hamel, and the American social critic Jeremy Rifkind.

How will business be different in the 21st century?

It will be more shapeless, in the sense that in the past 50 years we had things called companies, and they really were companies—groups of people bound together with roughly the same purpose. Businesses now are much more a collection of globules—partnerships and alliances.

I see business now as much more of a federal creation than it was—a series of autonomous organizations that includes universities, government, and different groupings of people. We are groping toward new ways of thinking about businesses.

What new skills will be needed to cope with these changes?

Key skills will be the ability to win friends and influence people at a personal level, the ability to structure partnerships, and the ability to negotiate and to find compromises. Business will be much more about finding the right people in the right place and negotiating the right deals. So in a funny way the two functions that will be the most important are recruitment and purchasing. It's ironic that neither of these functions has traditionally been seen as the star.

Key skills will be the ability to win friends and influence people at a personal level, the ability to structure partnerships, and the ability to negotiate and to find compromises. Business will be much more about finding the right people in the right place and negotiating the right deals.

Conceptual skills are also becoming much more important. There used to be a big distinction between managerial and technical skills. The ability to analyze numbers was considered most important then. In the last 20 years, the softer, human skills have become more important. But it is conceptual skills that are now coming to the fore. They are what the federal organization is all about.

The new workforce wants to contribute to humankind in some way as well as earning a livelihood. Finding a way to describe a cause is important and useful. The why is as important as the what and the who.

Does this change the role of leadership?

A good C.E.O. spends at least half his or her time on people. The shift now is to the C.E.O. as teacher and missionary, persuading people that his or her priorities are important to them.

Conceptualizing is increasingly important. I think strategy now is much more to do with defining—or

"We were not destined to be empty raincoats, nameless numbers on a payroll. . .If that is to be its price, economic progress is an empty promise." (Charles Handy)

  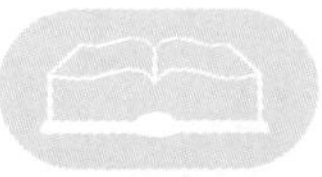    

conceptualizing—what your organization is all about. A lot of the old thinking about strategy is out of date.

Look at Jack Welch. He had great conceptual skills. His strategy in the early days was that he only wanted businesses that were number one or number two in their markets. But he later reversed that. He realized that GE was becoming complacent, so he reframed his message. He said to his people: "Redefine your market so that you only have 10% market share." He forced them numerically to stretch their horizons and broaden their outlook. That sort of conceptualizing is increasingly important. His human skills were also very important.

How do you develop these sorts of skills?

I once said that education is experience understood in tranquillity, and I think that's true. The only way people learn these conceptual skills is by being pushed into roles that are just beyond their grasp, so they are out of their depth and have to stretch themselves. You need to support them, of course, and forgive them when they get it wrong. I don't like the words mentor and coach. Michael Young has a term "educational companion," which I prefer. Organizational companions could be one way to help managers learn these skills.

Are there new management questions we should be asking?

The new management questions aren't really new but they have a new urgency. In my new book I talk about the disappearing middle. The middles of whole industries are disappearing. Take publishing. At present there is a long chain of processes and organizations between me as an author and the reader. Everything in this chain of distribution is now in doubt apart from the beginning and the end—the author and the reader. How the first connects with the second is now open to a wide range of options.

The new workforce wants to contribute to humankind in some way as well as earning a livelihood. Finding a way to describe a cause is important and useful. The why is as important as the what and the who.

We could dispense with the physical bookstore, the option focused on by Amazon.com and its imitators. The publisher too could choose to bypass wholesalers and bookstores and publish electronically. Or, if I was intrepid enough as the author, I could bypass the lot of them and put my words on a Web site for anyone to download for a fee.

This phenomenon of disappearing middles—disintermediation—allows newcomers to insert themselves into the gaps. The question for managers is: how do we redefine ourselves if we're in the middle?

It's quite hard for elephants to do. That's where fleas come in. Elephants are there to connect the talent to the customer, so the fleas need the elephants. But the elephants need the fleas, too, to create new value and to spur innovation.

What will happen to the concept of the career in the future?

It will be a professional career path and not an organizational one. People increasingly define themselves by their profession, and the definition of profession is much wider. It includes everything from beauty technician to chef and even sanitary engineer. We're all professionals now.

Very few jobs in future will be defined as jobs. Those that are—like checkout cashier—will disappear. There will be customer relationship managers or something like that. So people will either be professionals or entrepreneurs—fleas in short.

To promote your career you may work in a large organization—an elephant—for a while to gain skills and expertise. You may go back to elephants periodically to upgrade your skills or credentials. But you will have to take responsibility for your own career and your own life.

It starts as a mental thing. So think customers not jobs. Think skills not grades. What can you sell that is useful to other people? One day you will need to do that. One day you will be a flea.

How can companies best promote enterprises which are a) profitable and b) good places for people to work?

Elephants have to become venture capitalists for the people within their own organizations. If people come up with a good idea that fits with the brand, the organization should back it with money and time.

Look at what Ricardo Semler has done with Semco. We don't have a strategy, he says, it emerges from the initiatives that come up from the front line. For example, the company makes and erects cooling towers. From talking to customers the Semco people heard lots of complaints that the towers kept breaking down because of maintenance problems. So they said to the customers: "If we take on maintenance we want 60 percent of the saving you'll make from preventing breakdowns." Then they went to the Semco board and said: "We want to keep 20% of the 60% ourselves." The board said OK. So Semco is acting like a venture capitalist for its own people.

It's more than just money. It's about persuading people that they can build a business, create something new. People have to believe they can leave a footprint in the sand and all that.

For More Information

See also:

The Age of Unreason (p. 889)
Charles Handy (pp. 1000–01)

"Management by trust, empathy, and forgiveness sounds goods. It also sounds soft. It is in practice tough."

(Charles Handy)

THE SECOND COMING OF SERVICE
by Karl Albrecht

EXECUTIVE SUMMARY

- Executives are discovering that IT is not the magic wand they had been led to believe, and that misapplying it can lead to wasted resources, loss of focus, and even disastrous business results.
- Established, successful firms are making effective use of IT by concentrating on their key strategic priorities and making technology their servant, not their master.
- Strategic customer focus—concentrating on customer value as the primary driving concept—can serve as a powerful organizing principle for reinventing businesses in the age of the Third Wave.

INTRODUCTION

Many firms, particularly in the United States, ran off their rails, strategically speaking, during the Internet craze of the late 1990s. Hypnotized by the e-commerce story, many dot-com businesses made strategic blunders that would be unforgivable on the part of first-year MBA students. Executive teams of many established firms, gripped by the fear of being left behind, threw money at anything that looked as if it might qualify as an Internet strategy.

Apart from the loss of billions of dollars by investors and ill-advised expenditures by established firms, the biggest victim was the customer. Internet operators set back the cause of service quality by a good 10 years in some sectors, and the implosion of dot-mania left an ideological vacuum in the minds of many executives.

A more realistic appraisal of the role of IT in business has forced a return to basic principles: focus on the customer, value creation, culture building, skillful execution of quality practices, and inspired leadership. This return to basic truths may unfold as a second coming of customer focus.

WHAT HAPPENED TO SERVICE?

In 1985 the business world embraced the concept of service management with remarkable enthusiasm. There were books, articles, conferences, seminars, training programs, videos, newsletters, consulting firms, and even professional societies and academic research programs aimed at making customer focus a critical and permanent part of Western management thinking. Even the management gurus, established names on other topics, were moved to declare the primacy of customer value.

The wave didn't last. The service revolution was hijacked somewhere along the road to victory. Like most other management movements before it—management by objectives, participative management, productivity, and quality—customer focus became the object of intense flirtation by many firms, but ultimately the infatuation faded. The same fate befell several other revolutions: TQM, reengineering, and ISO 9000.

The real value and potential impact of the service management model are yet to be realized. We're coming to a stage in business—worldwide—in which we will need its principles more than ever. Western management thinking has lost its way in recent years, particularly with the mindless infatuation with all things digital. There is a deep underlying need, only partly articulated, to return to the most basic and timeless precepts of leadership, management, and enterprise thinking.

THE TECTONIC SHIFT AWAY FROM SERVICE

Around 1995, when TQM, ISO 9000, and service quality movements were fading, U.S. business began to feel the pressure of a more primitive shift in emphasis. American enterprises, and to a lesser extent firms in other countries, moved into a reconstruction phase. An unprecedented period of mergers, acquisitions, and the dramatic growth of retail giants got mixed in with business breakups, spinoffs, delayering, outsourcing, and partnering. A growing economy coupled with low unemployment rates and a remarkably flexible workforce enabled U.S. firms to rearrange themselves to maximize their strengths.

Key phrases such as "core competencies," "strategic partnering," and "supply-chain management" replaced the language of service, quality, and customer value. Thus began an ideological drift in U.S. management thinking toward *resource-based* rather than *value-based* competition. A large banking corporation finds it difficult to win more customers by adding value or reinventing its service package, but it's easy to find profit growth by buying up its smaller competitors. Why have competing banks on opposite sides of the street? Let's just buy out the other bank, close its branches, and add its customers to our inventory.

Why should a large airline try to offer better service when all airlines have conditioned their customers to make their choices solely on the basis of price? Why not buy up, or force out, the smaller airlines and relieve the pricing pressure? Why waste time changing customer service programs that just fizzle out anyway?

This is not to suggest that no companies are interested in service quality as a competitive factor: surely firms like Disney and Federal Express are still in a class by themselves. However, the example set by the giant firms, namely buying their competitors and kidnapping their customers, has drawn more attention in recent years.

THE PENDULUM RETURNS?

Has the so-called new economy lived up to its image? Or is it an intellectual chimera?

Actually, there's no such thing as a new economy (or an old economy) as preached by the Internet hucksters who managed to separate several billion dollars from investors, venture capitalists, and corporate executives. This warped notion of two economies will eventually be seen as one of the most serious conceptual blunders in business thinking of the last 50 years.

There is only one economy: the ever-new, ever-evolving economy of continuous creative destruction, described by theorist Joseph Schumpeter. Information is, and will continue to be, an important resource for economic development, but it is not in itself a—and certainly not *the*—new economy. Nor is the high-tech industry the primary driver of economic growth, as so many business writers have declared. Even Peter Drucker, the *eminence grise* of management theology, has wrongly characterized the U.S. economy as information-based. When the fantasy begins to fade economists, business leaders, journalists, and management theorists will see the information phenomenon

"Let's call this new way of working e-culture—the human side of the global information era, the heart and soul of the new economy."
(Rosabeth Moss Kanter)

in a more realistic perspective: as an inseparable part of the economic structure, but not the magical engine of it.

Information is one of the five key factors of economic growth and development: land, capital infrastructure, energy, labor, and information. Why arbitrarily declare one factor profoundly more important than the others? It is impossible to do anything with information—create it, manipulate it, store it, duplicate it, transmit it, or present it for consumption—without also consuming energy, usually in the form of electricity. Information is not free, and on a macro scale it isn't even cheap.

As business leaders return to the idea of customer value as the ultimate driving force of business success, they will turn a new page in their understanding of the potential of IT, online technology, and abundant information. Instead of trying to turn their businesses into vending machines and building an impersonal digital moat around their companies by replacing people with software, they will begin to see a wholly different set of strategies for using information as a strategic weapon. This understanding will change the meaning of the customer-value focus and reshape our thought processes as they relate to the use of information in business.

MINI-CASES

USAA is the premier provider of insurance services to U.S. military personnel. Founded in 1922 by a group of army officers, the firm has never lost its focus on delivering value to its special population of customers with their special needs. It has stayed at the forefront of applying information technology—with a human face—to the insurance business. With 90% of all military personnel buying their products and a 97% customer retention rate, the firm has proven that customer value counts.

REI (Recreational Equipment, Inc.) is the outfitter of choice for over a million outdoor sports fans and adventure enthusiasts. Successful since 1938, the firm has recently achieved a brilliant convergence of bricks and clicks by marrying online technology and its existing experience of interactive retail stores. Customers can interact seamlessly with its 55 retail outlets in 23 states and its in-depth resources for ordering, advice, and information on its Web site.

Walt Disney's commercial kingdom retains its unchallenged position as a provider of outstanding services in its chosen domain of entertainment. Based in Burbank, California, the Walt Disney Company is the third-largest media and entertainment conglomerate in the world, with operations encompassing movies, broadcasting, the Internet, and theme parks. Its Tokyo Disney Resort draws 16.5 million people a year. Disneyland Paris has emerged as one of the preeminent entertainment destinations in Europe. In all cases the customer experience is the focus of Disney's business operation.

MAKING IT HAPPEN ▸▸

- **Refocus on the customer.** Are you conducting customer research on a regular basis? Do people understand what customer value is in your line of business, and do they know how to deliver it? Do you have a workable system for measuring customer perceptions of value? Do you share findings throughout the organization?
- **Reinvent the service strategy.** What is your core benefit premise, that is, the *customer value proposition* on which you base your business model, the design of your service systems, and the operation of the enterprise? Does it make sense? Does everyone in the organization understand it and take it seriously? Is it time to rethink the business model or realign the priorities?
- **Build organizational intelligence.** Conduct a comprehensive review of your operating systems and an audit of their capacity to deliver on the business strategy. Look for evidence of system craziness, or lack of intelligence. Align the systems, the processes, and the people to the critical success factors of the business.
- **Reenlist the people.** Too many crises, priorities, and brushfires can distract the leaders of the enterprise and put them out of touch with the culture. How well do you understand employees today? What do they want? What do they seek in their jobs and careers? What frustrates them, inhibits them, or demotivates them? Are they switched on, switched off, or just glowing at half-wattage? Get the energy up and get the heads all pointing in the same direction.

CONCLUSION

In the present confusing and rapidly changing business environment, enterprise leaders at all levels must learn to see beyond fads and folklore and concentrate ever more tenaciously on the timeless truths of business:

- Make sure you're selling what the customer wants to buy.
- Concentrate your resources on the strategic advantage.
- Align the systems to meet the mission.
- Mobilize the culture.
- Make technology your servant, not your master.
- Stay on message.

The winning enterprises of the next decade won't be those whose leaders chase fads and fantasies, but those who can integrate new knowledge and new possibilities with their own trusted understanding of the basic truths of business success.

For More Information

Books:

Drucker, Peter F. *Post-capitalist Society*. New York: HarperBusiness, 1994.

Quinn, Feargal. *Crowning the Customer: How to Become Customer Driven*. St. Johnsbury, VT: Raphel Marketing, 2001.

Senge, Peter M. *The Fifth Discipline: The Art and Practice of the Learning Organization*. New York: Doubleday, 1995.

See also:

☆ **Delivering and Delighting—A New Spirit at Work (pp. 71–72)**
☆ **Overcoming the Difficulties Of Managing a Virtual Organization (pp. 208–09)**
☆ **Viewpoint: Christopher Bartlett (pp. 45–46)**
☆ **Viewpoint: B. Joseph Pine II (pp. 69–70)**
☆ **Viewpoint: Patty Seybold (pp. 67–68)**
✓ **Building One-to-one Relationships (pp. 666–67)**
✓ **Communicating Customer Service (pp. 670–71)**
✓ **Extending a Product with Service (pp. 718–19)**
✓ **Getting Promoted: Forget Your Boss, Serve Your Customers (pp. 784–85)**
✓ **How to Implement Customer Relationship Management (pp. 584–85)**
✓ **Offering Customers Self-service (pp. 742–43)**
✓ **Setting Up a Customer Interaction Center (pp. 680–81)**
Customer Relations/Service (pp. 1948–50)

"Adding value has become more than just a sound business principle; it is both the common denominator and the competitive edge."
(Arthur Levitt, Jr.)

Organic Growth versus Acquisition

by Peter Bebb

EXECUTIVE SUMMARY

- Businesses need to change strategy, processes, and roles rapidly, radically, and measurably, if they are to survive and succeed. Individuals need to know precisely what to produce and what reward they'll get for doing so.
- Companies acquiring, merging, and demerging need long-term ways of enhancing shareholder value once the initial and obvious savings have been made.
- Organic growth and growth by acquisition should be complementary strategies. The successful execution of both depends on aligning everyone and everything around a single set of corporate goals, and so achieving these goals faster, better, and cheaper.
- Many organizations suffer from acquisition indigestion, having failed to absorb and make the best of their acquisitions or mergers. All organizations have more scope for organic growth than they realize.

Introduction

Organizations exist in a rapidly changing environment, necessitating responsive and often radical strategic capabilities. To realize potential, organizations can be beset with common difficulties, such as strategic confusion and occupation with day-to-day activities. Despite many attempts to push organizations forward, shareholder value often stagnates or even declines. The solution lies not in focusing on improving the current situation but rather in taking the step-changes necessary to realize the future requirements of the organization.

Understanding the Problems

Dysfunctional Organizations

Most people have difficulty stating their organization's strategy: what the organization wants to become, how it would like its people to behave, and what it will provide, to which customers, in the future. The reality is that the organization's business and operating units march to priorities different from, if not contradictory to, those implied by its strategy. The majority of the people in an organization focus on day-to-day operational matters and their individual aspirations. Consequently the strategy is never realized.

Frustrated by the lack of forward progress, executives launch new communication, reorganization, process redesign, or technology initiatives. Everyone is doing more, and yet performance stagnates or even declines.

Losing the Value of Mergers and Acquisitions

A KPMG report found that, though 82% of respondents believed the deal they had transacted was a success, 83% of the same mergers failed to increase shareholder value. Of these transactions, 30% produced no discernible difference in shareholder value and 53% actually reduced value.

Acquiring, merging, and demerging companies need long-term ways of enhancing shareholder value once the initial and obvious savings have been taken. But they usually focus on tactical integration (for example, of organizational structure, support services, policies) rather than on strategic integration (customers, products, people, systems). However, to succeed, both are needed.

The Performance Management Gap

There is a gap between business performance *management* and individual performance *management* in all businesses, leading to a gap between business performance and individual performance. Business performance management is usually driven through an annual business planning process, which sets financial targets without specifying how they are to be achieved. Individual performance management is conducted through a performance appraisal process that sets mainly nonfinancial personal targets without explaining how they link to financial targets. Both focus on improving the present situation rather than initiating the step-change today's organizations must make if they want to succeed in the future.

The Solution: Translating Strategy into Action

Business Alignment

Business alignment is a unique new approach that:

- defines the issues and resources that are of value, allocating crystal-clear responsibility for them and measuring progress toward their delivery;
- empowers people to set their own objectives in the context of corporate goals ;
- creates a results-oriented performance culture, rewarding the delivery of outcomes rather than the management of resources;
- organizes around results rather than skills;
- challenges and justifies partners' and support units' outcomes, replacing adversarial service-level agreements;
- integrates and automates planning, budgeting, resourcing, measuring, reporting, and rewarding, thus releasing managers and support staff to deliver growth outcomes;
- combines business and individual performance management;
- identifies core processes and prioritizes initiatives;
- continuously reveals duplication, streamlines processes, and optimizes the allocation of resources;
- aligns information technology with the business through the IT alignment matrix;
- integrates people and other resources around common goals after a merger or acquisition.

Business alignment gets everyone to specify what their organization needs to do to produce what it needs to deliver to stakeholders in the future. It defines precisely what needs to be done to extract value from a merger or acquisition once the initial cost savings have been taken, and so enables long-term growth in shareholder value.

By applying business alignment before a merger, the organization goes into the merger negotiation knowing more precisely what it wants out of the merger, and thus is better prepared to extract value from the merger after the event.

Applying the Balanced Scorecard

Translating strategy into business results

"Worldwide, IT companies embarking on the non-organic growth mode have understood the wisdom of mergers and acquisitions on the threshold of the Digital Age." (Narayana Murthy)

with the balanced scorecard is a four-part process:

1. Leaders build and align around an architecture for change.
2. Required outcomes are linked to the activities that will deliver them, and resources are allocated to carry out these activities.
3. Change architecture is cascaded and the organization mobilized for action.
4. A feedback and learning system is built to make strategy development and implementation a continuous adaptive process.

Building and Aligning Leadership

Building an architecture for change involves defining strategy as an integrated set of hypotheses that describe an organization's evolution from the present to the future. The hypotheses are captured in a balanced scorecard, which defines the causal relationships between the things of value to the business, thus enabling value-based and activity-based management. It also defines how these things of value should be measured, thus providing key performance indicators.

Making Strategy Operational

Business process reengineering, activity-based costing, and workflow

The organization's leaders decide on the corporate processes and initiatives required to deliver the outcomes. They use these to assess the relevance of current corporate processes, to prioritize existing initiatives, and to define new initiatives needed for achieving the strategy. Some initiatives and processes are found to be irrelevant to the future of the organization and can be removed. Activity-based costing is used to determine which resources are released by the removal of the activity, and workflow software is applied to the new and remaining processes after their definition or improvement.

Focusing on organizational development

Processes are associated with the outcomes they deliver, and in so doing they suggest an organization that allocates resources to the delivery of strategic outcomes. This is usually radically different from, and more productive than, the functional organization.

IT alignment matrix

The IT alignment matrix (ITAM) defines the knowledge communities of the future and the structure and content of the data warehouses required to inform them. The ITAM reveals the gap between the current databases and systems and those required to deliver the future outcomes defined in the balanced scorecard.

Enterprise resource planning

The types of resource—people and things—needed to deliver the future outcomes are then identified and valued in monetary terms to define a budget. Note that this turns the business planning process on its head, since the traditional process starts with money (and involves too much guesswork). Starting with outcomes enables a rational debate about what should be produced and in what quantity. Information from enterprise resource-planning systems is used to calculate the budget.

Investing in people

Discretionary pay and bonuses are dependent on the delivery of balanced scorecard outcomes and targets. At the executive level the change is the addition of nonfinancial targets. At lower levels the change is more significant, involving specific rewards for deliverables that individuals can influence.

Business alignment integrates individual with business performance management by empowering individuals to say what they can contribute to corporate outcomes. Instead of being told what to do people are invited to say what they can produce. Consequently they have a real opportunity to create their own careers.

Cascading and Mobilization

Now the organization is aligned around the strategic outcomes. There is no formal reorganization in the traditional sense. Instead, individuals are appointed to lead the delivery of the strategic themes, and the rest of the organization is invited to say what it can produce that will assist the delivery of the themes.

Over time, status and rewards are aligned with the delivery of outcomes that help to deliver the themes, and people and other resources gravitate toward the themes. Level by level, organizations achieve strategic focus and alignment.

Feedback and Learning

People at all levels are now aligned to the strategy. What remains is to link them through feedback and learning, using a dynamic enterprise performance-management system. Information about outcomes, activities, and resources is stored electronically, enabling the organization to outpace its peers.

Measures, progress assessments, recommendations, and insights flow from the grassroots to the executive team. Meetings only for reporting results become working sessions to solve problems of which everyone is already aware.

Making It Happen ▸▸

- Work out what customers will buy from the company, and what internal processes are critical to delivering those purchases.
- Decide what the organization must learn, innovate and grow in order to carry out the core processes efficiently and effectively.
- Draw a strategy map to show what outcomes the organization must achieve to deliver its strategy, and which outcome leads to (or causes) another.
- Measure performance against the chosen parameters in the last full reporting period before the development of the balanced scorecard.
- Cascade the corporate outcomes, activities, and resources to the front line so that the people responsible for delivery to customers change their behavior.
- Appoint the C.E.O. as champion of the balanced scorecard development and leader of the workshop activity.

For More Information

Books:

Kaplan, Robert S., and David P. Norton. *The Balanced Scorecard: Translating Strategy into Action*. Boston, MA: Harvard Business School Press, 1996.

Hammer, Michael, and James Champy. *Reengineering the Corporation: A Manifesto for Business Revolution*. Rev. ed. New York: HarperBusiness, 2001.

See also:

☆ **Building Great Internal Partnerships (pp. 281–82)**
☆ **Core Versus Context: Managing Resources in a Downturn (pp. 255–56)**
☆ **Infusing a Company with Cutting-edge Strategy (pp. 83–84)**
Competing for the Future (p. 899)
C. K. Prahalad (pp. 1040–41)
Acquisitions, Takeovers, and Mergers (pp. 1901–03)

"The very best takeovers are thoroughly hostile. I've never seen a really good company taken over. I've only seen bad ones."
(James Goldsmith)

WHY MERGERS FAIL AND HOW TO PREVENT IT

by Susan Cartwright

EXECUTIVE SUMMARY

- Mergers and acquisitions (M & A) are increasing in frequency, yet at least half fail to meet financial expectations.
- The United States and the United Kingdom continue to dominate M & A activity. As the number of cross-border deals increases, however, many other national players are entering the field, further highlighting the issue of cultural compatibility.
- Financial and strategic factors alone are insufficient to explain the high rate of failure; more account needs to be taken of human factors.
- The successful management of integrating people and their organizational cultures is the key to achieving desired M & A outcomes.

INTRODUCTION

The incidence of M & A has continued to increase significantly during the last decade, both domestically and internationally. The sectors most affected by M & A activity have been service- and knowledge-based industries such as banking, insurance, pharmaceuticals, and leisure. Although M & A is a popular means of increasing or protecting market share, the strategy does not always deliver what is expected in terms of increased profitability or economies of scale. While the motives for mergers can variously be described as practical, psychological, or opportunist, the objective of all related M & A is to achieve synergy, or what is commonly referred to as the 2 + 2 = 5 effect. However, as many organizations learn to their cost, the mere recognition of potential synergy is no guarantee that the combination will actually realize that potential.

MERGER FAILURE RATES

The burning question remains—why do so many mergers fail to live up to shareholder expectations? In the short term, many seemingly successful acquisitions look good, but disappointing productivity levels are often masked by onetime cost savings, asset disposals, or astute tax maneuvers that inflate balance-sheet figures during the first few years.

Merger gains are notoriously difficult to assess. There are problems in selecting appropriate indices to make any assessment, as well as difficulties in deciding on a suitable measurement period. Typically the criteria selected by analysts are

- profit-to-earning ratios
- stock-price fluctuations
- managerial assessments

Irrespective of the evaluation method selected, the evidence on M & A performance is consistent in suggesting that a high proportion of M & As are financially unsuccessful. U.S. sources place merger failure rates as high as 80%, with evidence indicating that around half of mergers fail to meet financial expectations. A much-cited McKinsey study presents evidence arguing that most organizations would have received a better return on their investment if they had merely banked their money instead of buying another company. Consequently, many commentators have concluded that the true beneficiaries from M & A activity are those who sell their shares when deals are announced and the marriage brokers—the bankers, lawyers, and accountants who arrange, advise, and execute the deals.

TRADITIONAL REASONS FOR MERGER FAILURE

M & A is still regarded by many decision makers as an exclusively rational, financial, and strategic activity, and not as a human collaboration. Financial and strategic considerations, along with price and availability, therefore dominate target selection, overriding the soft issues such as people and cultural fit. Explanations of merger failure or underperformance tend to focus on reexamining the factors that prompted the initial selection decision, for example:

- payment of an overinflated price for the acquired company
- poor strategic fit
- failure to achieve potential economies of scale because of financial mismanagement or incompetence
- sudden and unpredicted changes in market conditions

This ground has been well trodden, yet the rate of merger, acquisition, and joint-venture success has improved little. Clearly these factors may contribute to disappointing M & A outcomes, but this conventional wisdom only part explains what goes wrong in M & A management.

THE FORGOTTEN FACTOR IN M & A

The false distinction that has developed between hard and soft merger issues has been extremely unhelpful in extending our understanding of merger failure, as it separates the impact of the merger on the individual from its financial impact on the organization. Successful M & A outcomes are linked closely to the extent to which management is able to integrate organizational members and their cultures and sensitively address and minimize individuals' concerns.

By representing sudden and major change, mergers generate considerable uncertainty and feelings of powerlessness. This can lead to reduced morale, job and career dissatisfaction, employee stress, and uncertainty. Rather than increased profitability, mergers have become associated with a range of negative behavioral outcomes such as

- acts of sabotage and petty theft
- increased staff turnover, with rates reported as high as 60%
- increased sickness and absenteeism

Ironically, this occurs at the very time when organizations need and expect greater employee loyalty, flexibility, cooperation, and productivity.

PEOPLE FACTORS ASSOCIATED WITH M & A FAILURE

Studies like the one conducted by the British Institute of Management have identified a range of people factors associated with unsuccessful M & A. These include:

- underestimating the difficulties of merging two cultures;
- underestimating the problem of skills transfer;
- demotivation of employees;
- departure of key people;
- expenditure of too much energy on doing the deal at the expense of postmerger planning;
- lack of clear responsibilities, leading to postmerger conflicts;

"The big danger in mega-mergers is that they are seen as a mating of dinosaurs." (Peter Bonfield)

- too narrow a focus on internal issues to the neglect of the customers and the external environment;
- insufficient research about the merger partner or acquired organization.

Differences between Mergers and Acquisitions

In terms of employee response, whether the transaction is described as a merger or an acquisition, the event will trigger uncertainty and fears of job losses. However, there are important differences. In an acquisition, power is substantially assumed by the new parent. Change is usually swift and often brutal as the acquirer imposes its own control systems and financial restraints. Parties to a merger are likely to be more evenly matched in terms of size, and the power and cultural dynamics of the combination are more ambiguous. Integration is a more drawn-out process.

This has implications for the individual. During an acquisition there is often more overt conflict and resistance and a sense of powerlessness. In mergers, however, because of the prolonged period between the initial announcement and actual integration, uncertainty and anxiety continue for a much longer time as the organization remains in a state of limbo.

Cultural Compatibility

The process of merger is often likened to marriage. In the same way that clashes of personality and misunderstanding lead to difficulties in personal relationships, differences in organizational cultures, communication problems, and mistaken assumptions lead to conflicts in organizational partnerships.

Mergers are rarely a marriage of equals, and it's still the case that most acquirers or dominant merger partners pursue a strategy of cultural absorption; the acquired company or smaller merger partner is expected to assimilate and adopt the culture of the other. Whether the outcome is successful depends upon the willingness of organizational members to surrender their own culture and at the same time perceive that the other culture is attractive and therefore worth adopting.

Cultural similarity may make absorption easier than when the two cultures are very different, yet the process of due diligence rarely extends to evaluating the degree of cultural fit. Furthermore, few organizations bother to try to understand the cultural values and strengths of the acquiring workforce or their merger partners in order to inform and guide the way in which they should go about introducing change.

Making It Happen ▸▸

Making a good organizational marriage currently seems to be a matter of chance and luck. This needs to change so that there is a greater awareness of the people issues involved and consequently a more informed integration strategy. Some basic guidelines for more effective management include:

- extension of the due diligence process to incorporate issues of cultural fit;
- greater involvement of human resource professionals;
- the conducting of culture audits before the introduction of change management initiatives;
- increased communication and involvement of employees at all levels in the integration process;
- the introduction of mechanisms to monitor employee stress levels;
- fair and objective reselection processes;
- providing management with the skills and training to sensitively handle M & A issues such as insecurity and redundancy.

Mini-Case

Paul Hodder was involved as director of human resource management in the formation of *Aon Risk Services*, a merger of four rather different retail-insurance-broking and risk-management companies. A major theme of their integration process was the formation of a series of task groups to review and identify best practice. Another part involved an organization-wide training program to provide individuals with life skills to help them initiate and cope with change, to improve teamwork, and to develop support networks. Enthusiasm for the program has provided several hundred change champions to lead change projects and assume support and mentoring roles. Good communication of early wins and successes has reassured organizational members that the changes are working and are beneficial.

Conclusion

Despite thorough pre-merger procedures, mergers continue to fall far short of financial expectations. The single biggest cause of this failure rate is poor integration following the acquisition. The identification of the target company, the subsequent and often drawn-out negotiations, and attending to the myriad of financial, technical, and legal details are all exhausting activities. Once the target company has been acquired, little energy or motivation is left to plan and implement the integration of the people and cultures following the merger. It seems nonsensical to waste all the resources and energy that has gone into the merger, though inadequate planning of the integration stage of the process, yet all too often organizations do just that. Without a properly planned integration process or its effective implementation, mergers will not be able to achieve the full potential of the acquisition.

For More Information

Books:

Cartwright, Susan, and Cary L. Cooper. *Managing Mergers, Acquisitions, and Strategic Alliances*. 2nd ed. Woburn, MA: Butterworth-Heinemann, 1996.

Cooper, Cary L., and Alan Gregory, eds. *Advances in Mergers and Acquisitions*. Vol. 1. New York: Elsevier Science, 2000.

See also:

- ☆ **Building Great Internal Partnerships (pp. 281–82)**
- ☆ **Workers without Borders: Creating Bonds When Workers Have No Loyalty (pp. 204–05)**
- **Harold S. Geneen (pp. 1084–85)**
- **Aquisitions, Takeovers, and Mergers (pp. 1901–03)**

"When it comes to mergers, hope triumphs over experience." (Irwin Stelzer)

  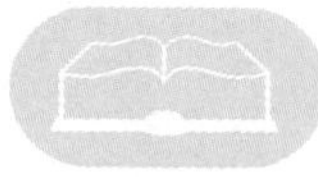  

INFUSING A COMPANY WITH CUTTING-EDGE STRATEGY *by Oren Harari*

EXECUTIVE SUMMARY

- Strategic planning by itself does not guarantee either competitive advantage or business success. Too often companies' strategies simply mimic each other, they are not exciting or inspiring, their execution is poor, or they're built on obsolete premises.
- Strategy is nonetheless relevant. In today's hypercompetitive global economy, infusing a company with a clear, compelling, cutting-edge strategic direction is critical.
- Whether a company is publicly traded or privately held, effective strategy creates value for shareholders and customers. In the New Millennium Economy, value-creation follows new and different paths. Today, one's strategy should generate *unique* value, *breakthrough* value, *startling* value, *personalized* value, *turbo-speed* value, and *employee-driven* value.

INTRODUCTION

We've made strategy far more complicated than necessary. Smart people with advanced degrees and high salaries generate elaborate documents containing complex analysis, algorithms, heuristics, scenarios, and projections which seldom yield competitive advantage. More than 50% of the 1980 *Fortune* 500 companies—each with elegant, complex strategic plans—no longer exist. And literally 60–80% of megamergers—with strategies of impeccable depth, logic, and financial wizardry—have been empirically shown to diminish shareholder value.

WHAT'S WRONG?

First, strategies often wind up looking pretty much the same. It becomes difficult to distinguish oneself in a crowded marketplace. No amount of numbers, graphs, and jargon can stop many strategic plans turning out to be ordinary and mundane, with uninspiring results for customers and investors.

Companies often find that, even if their strategic plan makes sense, their execution fails. Bureaucracy, organizational inertia, and resistance to change subvert or critically delay noble goals, even those which represent genuine competitive opportunity.

It gets worse. Companies often find their strategies have become obsolete "overnight." The long-term growth strategies of the major music recording labels, for example, were based on a known product (the compact disc), a known distribution chain, a known set of competitors, and a known "way of doing things." Then came MP3 formats, P2P file-sharing systems, and other Web-based innovations.

FINDING THE CUTTING EDGE

Strategy is far from irrelevant. Effective strategy creates significant value. But in today's fragmented, nanosecond, hypercompetitive, global economy, value creation follows new and different paths. Singly or combined, these new sources of value creation lead to sustained growth and earnings, shareholder returns, investor enthusiasm, customer fanaticism, and market "buzz." A cutting-edge strategy:

- **Generates *unique* value.** In crowded markets, where competitors are everywhere and customers are overwhelmed with choices, the most important strategic issue is uniqueness. A cutting-edge strategy demonstrates that the company is doing something special and different. It suggests best of-breed and greatness.

  In the 1990s, Dell Computer's built-to-order product customization and direct-to-customer sales channel were so unique that they restructured conventional value propositions and value chains, and in the process catapulted the company to a dominant role in the technology sector. Even today, amidst the rough seas of the post-September 11 environment, Dell maintains a powerful, "best-of-breed" position. Further, it continues its innovative march by using the Web to conduct 75% of its total business, and by applying the company's core skills to new digital niches like servers and storage.

  Where fragmentation, saturation, and constant upheaval exist, *unique* equals value.
- **Provides *breakthrough* value.** What do FedEx, CNN, Siebel Systems and Palm have in common? They created new markets. With so many competitors vying for customers' attention, significant value comes not from incremental improvements, but from marketplace breakthroughs.

  Originally, customers didn't ask for overnight delivery, cable news, customer-relations management software, or Personal Digital Assistants. Smart companies initiated those breakthroughs and profited handsomely. Cutting-edge strategies demonstrate value by leading markets, which includes leading customers, not just by responding to their current desires.
- **Provides *startling* value.** Increasingly, products and services are becoming "me-too" commodities. Companies with cutting-edge strategies create value by providing things that inspire excitement, intrigue, joy, and titillation via exceptional functionality, design, and execution. Think Disney World: need I go on? Sony's PlayStation with its functionality, design, and marketing execution set off a $20 billion computer game industry. Swatch's mission has nothing to do with selling wristwatches; it's about providing "joy in life" through fashionized timepieces and, more recently, through cool-designed, Web-accessible watches that allow you to "save time," not merely tell it.
- **Provides *personalized* value.** Mass (as in mass-production and mass-marketing) is dead as a value-driver. Nowadays, it's all about "markets of one." Cap One has 29 million holders of its credit cards, and no two of them have the same terms. The company's digital capacity allows it to canvass scores of thousands of possible combinations instantaneously, so that a person with a lousy credit history and a fondness for fusion jazz gets a card with an entirely different set of financial and marketing arrangements from someone with a great credit history and a love of the Chicago Bulls.

  GE Power Systems allows a purchaser of its turbine engines to build-to-order and follow the path of the product's construction, all online and while receiving one-to-one—online and face-to-face—consulting help from GE personnel throughout the process. Customized products and personalized services are,

"Challenging the status quo has to be the starting point for anything that goes under the label of strategy."

(Gary Hamel)

increasingly, the primary way that customers conclude that they are receiving true value.

- **Provides *turbo-speed* value.** Whatever winning organizations do, they do *very* fast. They see competitive advantage in how rapidly they can capitalize on changes in technologies, customers, competitors, population demographics, and capital markets. Or how dramatically and exponentially they can shrink decision and cycle times. Or how quickly they can disseminate information and knowledge throughout the organization, put together a team or alliance, implement a change, start an experiment or pilot, and get to market. Winners think about time the way most conventional companies think about costs. They do strategy "on the run."

  Pharmaceutical Novartis launched an extraordinary four new drugs in 2001, including a breakthrough leukemia drug after only 32 months of clinical testing. Medtronics' quick capitalization on new opportunities in the medical products arena has resulted in 70% of its revenues coming from products that didn't exist three years ago. Recognizing that operational speed was critical for competing in the U.S. personal computer market, Fujitsu partnered with FedEx and reduced its order-to-delivery cycle from 30 days to 4.

- **Provides *employee-driven* value.** The traditional scenario of a few high-ranking executives and high-priced consultants determining strategy, then pushing it down for others to execute, is destructively anachronistic. Real value and its corollary, competitive advantage, accrue to organizations that fully invest in and capitalize on the talents of their people. Top management sets broad strategic priorities and directions, as well as clear values and culture. But within those parameters, cutting-edge strategy and accountability, a.k.a. value, bubbles up from anywhere. This is a quantum departure from conventional "empowerment" and "employee participation."

  At PE Biosystems (a billion-dollar division of Perkin Elmer), the 17-year run of 20% annual growth rates is fueled not by a brilliant grand "plan," but by the personal initiatives of engineers, scientists, and marketers. Their efforts result in a large number of projects going on simultaneously, none of which requires any initial approval from top management. As soon as a promising concept emerges from the hubbub, PE Biosystems quickly galvanizes the resources to rush it to market. Copenhagen-based Oticon takes the same approach to leading the hearing-aid market; the self-propelled, cross-disciplinary structure is called a "spaghetti organization."

  Value can be created by all-hands strategic involvement. At GE Capital and Cap One frequent meetings of entrepreneurially minded employees are held to bat around "crazy" business-enhancement ideas and put together project teams to take those ideas to fruition. Intel and Merck take that idea a step further by funding employee-driven startups. Intel has provided over $100 million in seed capital to different employees who have put together viable plans for high-growth businesses that fit into Intel's mission.

  All-hands-driven strategy is not one detailed grand plan, but rather an organizational template. Executives still define the fundamental direction, lead the charge, and take on primary fiduciary responsibility. But employees are viewed as genuine partners, which means that they have: immediate access to any information (including financials); incessant training and development (talent is viewed as an appreciating asset); complete opportunity for self-control (taking full responsibility for initiatives and outcomes); and a healthy dose of outcome- and performance-based compensation (including profit-sharing and equity ownership).

MAKING IT HAPPEN ▸▸

- Have regular and frequent policy-making conversations with colleagues that address the following questions: What are we doing—or what do we need to do—that is unique, special, and different? That generates market breakthroughs? That indicates best-of-breed? That sets us apart from the rest of the pack? And, most important, do customers and investors recognize all that? Build strategy around the answers.
- Concentrate your strategic goals and organizational systems on achieving 100% customized products and 100% personalized services.
- Make speed a strategic priority in goal-setting and execution. Regularly canvass how long it takes to make a decision, launch an investigation or pilot, collect and disseminate relevant information, bring something to market, cut a deal, etc.
- Allow strategic initiatives to emerge from anywhere in the organization. Insist that everyone be responsible for improving the firm's competitive position. Make certain that all hands receive sufficient tools, technology, training, direction, and freedom.

CONCLUSION

A cutting-edge strategy is grounded in constant, relentless innovation and customer-centricity. *What* a cutting-edge strategy does is offer unique, breakthrough, startling, and customized value. *How* it does this is by "collaboration on the run": all hands working together as strategic partners, obsessing on speed, speed, speed. When this process is ignited and fueled by top management, something wonderful happens. Strategy becomes a living, breathing, agile, market-centric collaborative process. It also becomes a lot of fun.

For More Information

Books:

Christensen, Clayton. *The Innovator's Dilemma*. New York: HarperBusiness, 2000.

Foster, Richard, and Sarah Kaplan. *Creative Destruction: Why Companies that Are Built to Last Underperform the Market—And How to Successfully Transform Them*. New York: Doubleday, 2001.

Mintzberg, Henry. *The Rise and Fall of Strategic Planning*. New York: Free Press, 1993.

See also:

☆ **Avoiding the Mistakes of the Past: Lessons from the Startup World (pp. 129–30)**
☆ **Competing on Costs (pp. 111–12)**
☆ **Finding and Keeping the Best Talent in the World (pp. 119–20)**
☆ **The New Frontiers in Old-economy Industries (pp. 99–100)**
☆ **Organic Growth versus Acquisition (pp. 79–80)**
☆ **Switching Strategies (pp. 93–94)**
☆ **Viewpoint: Philip Kotler (pp. 53–54)**
The Rise and Fall of Strategic Planning (p. 949)
Henry Mintzberg (pp. 1024–25)
Corporate Strategy (pp. 1944–46)

"Mold-breaking strategies grow initially like weeds, they are not cultivated like tomatoes in a hothouse."
(Henry Mintzberg)

  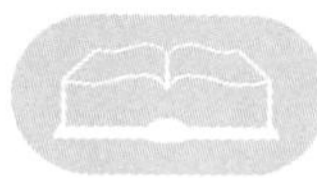    

MAXIMIZING A NEW STRATEGIC ALLIANCE *by Peter Killing*

EXECUTIVE SUMMARY

- Over 60,000 strategic alliances have been formed in the past decade. About half were joint ventures. Only 40% meet or exceed their partners' expectations.
- To be successful with strategic alliances you must be clear about your objectives, get the alliance design right, and manage the alliance effectively after it is formed.
- There is an important difference between shallow and deep alliances, and you should know which type you need and why.
- Alliance success depends in large part on skilled managers who are good with people, have a high tolerance for ambiguity and conflict, and are patient yet persistent.
- The clearest sign of alliance success is growing trust between the partners.

INTRODUCTION

More than 60,000 strategic alliances were formed in the 1990s. About half of these were joint ventures. The other 50% were nonequity arrangements such as technology licensing agreements, joint marketing arrangements, and joint research or development projects. Most of these alliances were international, so it's no surprise to learn that the world's largest multinationals are heavy alliance users: IBM (254 alliances), General Motors (138), Mitsubishi (233), Toshiba (147), Philips (207), and Siemens (200) are just some examples.

Clearly the ability to create and manage strategic alliances is an important skill for most management teams. If you cannot make effective use of alliances in today's world, you will be at a serious competitive disadvantage.

GETTING IT RIGHT

A 1999 study by Andersen Consulting indicates that only 40% of alliances achieve or exceed the initial expectations of their partners, which suggests there's a lot of room for improvement. One of the reasons for the relatively low success rate is that there are many different aspects of the design and management of alliances that you need to get right, from clearly understanding your objectives to managing the alliance after it is formed. They can be grouped into three sequential steps:

1. **Clarify objectives.** What do we need and for how long? Is an alliance the best way to get what we need?
2. **Design the alliance.** What type of alliance should we create? What should our role be?
3. **Manage after the deal is done.** How do we effectively manage the alliance? Can we build trust?

CLARIFY OBJECTIVES

The first challenge is to be clear about what your firm needs to fulfill its strategy, which may be different from what others in your industry need. The second challenge is to decide whether an alliance is the best way to get what you need. Three common reasons for forming alliances are:

- **To enter new markets.** One of the classic purposes of joint ventures is to enter foreign markets. Typically the foreign firm finds the local market attractive, but does not feel confident to enter without local knowledge, and so takes a local partner. In some countries the government insists on such a relationship. In China, for example, joint ventures between foreigners and local firms are prevalent. Often, as foreign firms gain confidence in their ability to operate locally, they end the joint venture by buying out their local partner and creating a wholly owned subsidiary. In this case the alliance is a step on the road to something else.
- **To create new technology and set industry standards.** In technology-intensive industries like computing and telecommunications, companies often use alliances to attempt to create a new technology that will become the industry standard. An example is Symbian, a joint venture formed in 1998 by Psion, Ericsson, Nokia, and Motorola. Symbian's objective is to create an operating system for wireless devices to exchange information efficiently. Its major competitor is Microsoft, which is trying to build its own alliance around its CE operating system with partners including NTT DoCoMo and British Telecom. The competition has shifted from firm versus firm to alliance versus alliance.
- **To shape consolidation.** In consolidating industries such as airlines, telecoms, and the automotive industry, alliances are often formed between firms that fear they are too small to continue independently (and that do not want to be taken over) and those that intend to play a dominant role in the consolidation. The alliance between Fiat and GM was formed for precisely this reason. This deal involves cross-ownership holdings between the two companies, two 50–50 joint ventures, and a variety of smaller cooperative arrangements. Fiat also has an option to sell itself to GM in a few years. The immediate motives behind such alliances are to gain economies of scale and global reach, to eliminate excess capacity, and to keep the smaller firm out of the hands of predators.

WHY USE AN ALLIANCE?

Alliances are often the least-preferred choice of the firms that enter them. Many companies would rather enter a new market themselves, or perhaps make an acquisition. GM, for example, would probably have preferred to buy Fiat, but the company was not for sale. Alliances are often seen as difficult to manage, ambiguous in terms of control and decision making (and as a result slow moving), and requiring an extraordinary amount of management time and attention.

The usual motives, positive and negative, for proceeding with an alliance are:

Positive

- to harness the partner's energy and knowledge;
- to set an industry standard by involving partners;
- to learn something;
- to gain economies of scale or global reach;
- to reduce risk;
- to gain speed.

Negative

- government insists on alliance;
- acquisitions are too expensive or not available;

"We are always willing to be trade partners, but never trade patsies." (Ronald Reagan)

- it's the only financially affordable alternative;
- the company fears being acquired;
- an alliance will prevent a competitor's acquisition of or alliance with the partner;
- closing the business is too expensive; an alliance provides a more graceful exit.

You should be clear on your own motives as well as your partner's. There are no data on this issue, but alliances formed for positive motives may have a higher success rate.

Design the Alliance

There are many types of alliance. The simplest are straightforward license agreements and shared marketing deals; the most complex are multipart arrangements such cross-ownership positions, joint ventures, and cooperative projects between partners. Faced with an abundance of choice, managers entering an alliance need to make a key decision: whether they want a shallow alliance or a deep alliance.

Shallow Alliances–Traveling Light

A shallow alliance might be thought of as a flirtation—a low-commitment alliance that doesn't have a lot of resources devoted to it and that can be broken on short notice. As an example, think of current airline alliances such as the Star and One World alliances, which seem to feature new partners every month. Or consider Cisco and its Internet-related businesses. Cisco often cannot judge if a young company's fledgling technology will prove to be important a year later. The shallow alliance solution is to buy 10% of the firm's stock in a friendly transaction and get a seat on the board and an option to buy the remainder of the equity. The assigned board member can then assess the company's management, its market prospects, and its technology. If it looks good, they buy the rest of the company. If not, they leave. Shallow alliances thus create options for companies in fast-changing industries in which the way ahead is not clear. The alliances are not usually intended to be permanent.

Deep Alliances–Commitment

At the other end of the spectrum are deep alliances involving high levels of financial and managerial commitment by the partners. Deep alliances feature many links between the partners, usually including one or more seats on the board of directors, cross-ownership positions, at least two or three joint ventures, and many less formal but important cooperative projects. Deep alliances are generally slower-moving than shallow alliances, more difficult to manage, and more difficult to end. The benefits of success can be high, but so can the costs of failure. Deep alliances are not for the timid.

Manage After the Deal Is Done

Once you've formed an alliance you'll sooner or later discover that you have brought together partners with different ways of doing things and somewhat different objectives, priorities, and performance standards. These differences make the management of alliances a difficult task. The single most important thing you can do to maximize the probability of success is to assign some of your very best people to work on it. "Best" means managers with excellent people skills, cross-cultural sensitivity, and a tolerance for ambiguity and frustration. Alliance managers need to be patient, yet persistent.

Six months into the life of your alliance you should look closely at the relationship between the partners. Is trust starting to develop? If not, why not? Where are the trouble spots? Many texts advise that when choosing a partner you should choose someone you trust. This is difficult to do unless you have worked together before. The best predictor of the future performance of any alliance is the current level of trust between the partners.

Finally, don't assume that the alliance is done when the deal is signed. This is just the beginning. Be flexible and open to change and learning. There will be plenty of opportunity for both.

Making It Happen

Strategic Alliances are increasingly popular, even necessary, however they are often a high risk strategy. It is worth viewing the alliance in three distinct phases:

- **Before the deal is struck:** the vital period when goals are considered, resources prepared, and partners considered. Internal agreement on the goals, strategy, and resources to be used is important, as is choosing the right partner and evaluating them thoroughly through due diligence.
- **Negotiating the deal:** the terms of the agreement and, significantly, the expectations of each partner and the *spirit* of the agreement, will be decisive in determining the effectiveness of the alliance.
- **Post-agreement management:** successful agreements are those that are consistently and attentively resourced, managed, and valued. If they are not, they are unlikely to survive normal commercial pressures.

Some key questions to consider include:

- Have you formally assessed the aims and benefits of the strategic alliance?
- How does the alliance fit with your overall commercial strategy?
- Who needs to be informed of the alliance–and when?
- Have you sought the advice of professional advisers?
- Have you taken time to understand the target and the commercial implications?
- To what extent should the alliance be integrated into your existing business? Who will lead this?
- Do you have a fully costed and resourced plan for managing the alliance? What are the targets and success criteria for the alliance?

For More Information

Books:

Cauley de la Sierra, M. *Managing Global Alliances: Key Steps for Successful Collaboration*. Reading, MA: Addison-Wesley, 1995.

Doz, Yves L., and Gary Hamel. *Alliance Advantage: The Art of Creating Value Through Partnering*. Boston, MA: Harvard Business School Press, 1998.

Lewis, Jordan D. *Trusted Partners: How Companies Build Mutual Trust and Win Together*. New York: Free Press, 2000.

Web Sites:

www.alliancestrategy.com: this site offers resources and readings on alliance strategy and management. It is maintained by Ben Gomes-Casseres, author of *The Alliance Revolution*.

www.smartalliances.com: this site gives a variety of practical advice and useful information on the fast-growing world of Strategic Alliances, linking users to books, conferences, perspectives and experts.

See also:

☆ **The New Frontiers in Old-economy Industries (pp. 99–100)**
☆ **Organic Growth Versus Acquisition (pp. 79–80)**
☆ **Why Mergers Fail (pp. 81–82)**
Acquisitions, Takeovers, and Mergers (pp. 1901–03)

"We are always willing to be trade partners, but never trade patsies." (Ronald Reagan)

VIEWPOINT: JEAN-CLAUDE LARRÉCHÉ

Beyond Strategy: Market-based Capabilities

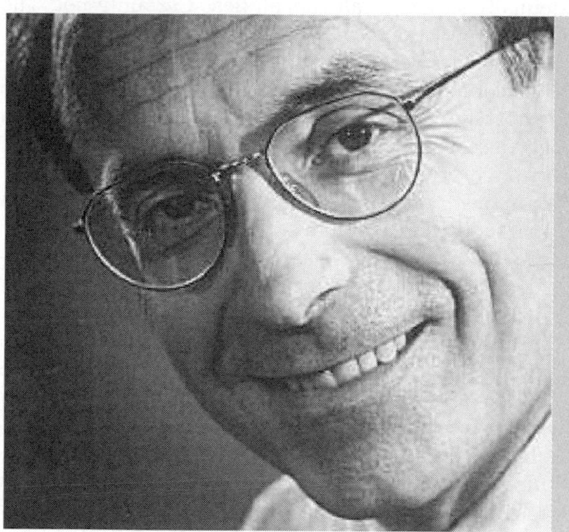

Beyond strategy, great business leadership requires building intangible assets for sustainable long-term success. Market-based capabilities are intangible assets that influence the competitive success of a firm in its markets. In this piece, Jean-Claude Larréché, the Alfred H. Heineken Chaired Professor of Marketing at INSEAD in Fontainebleau, France, sets out his views on four selected key issues concerning market-based capabilities: the concept; measurement; the emergence of capability gaps in specific business sectors; and the development of distinctive superior capability profiles.

Ever since the advent of modern management, the business community–corporations, consulting companies, and business schools alike–have been striving to understand what makes some companies more successful than others. From Peter Drucker's first book in the late 1940s through *In Search of Excellence* and several generations of other best sellers, ample guidance has become available on this most important subject. And "strategy" has now become more of a buzzword in business than in the military.

Jack Welch, as the new chairman of General Electric, came to his first meeting with financial analysts with a "big" message, organized in two parts: "hard" issues–the strategic requirement of being no. 1 or no. 2 in each business unit; and "soft" issues–such as the human element. While the soft issues were essential to General Electric's success for the next decades, the analysts' reaction was cold. In Jack Welch's words: "About halfway through, I had the impression that I would have gotten as much interest if I'd talked about my Ph.D. thesis on drop-wise condensation."

Since that time, the more progressive business leaders and observers have, fortunately, become more enlightened and followed Jack Welch's example. There has been a growing recognition of the importance of intangible assets, or capabilities, such as human resources, customer orientation, corporate culture, or brands. Simultaneously, there has been an increased focus on evaluating these capabilities in terms of their impact on the competitive success of the firm in its markets, not in terms of technically defined criteria. This is emphasized in the expression market-based capabilities.

Some companies have capabilities that are "technically correct" but ineffective when it comes to winning in the marketplace. For example, they may have an impressive well-written mission statement with all the "right" ingredients, which nonetheless causes confusion or cynicism resulting in reduced effectiveness. They may have sophisticated systems based on the latest technologies with wonderful real-time features, but to no avail if these are seen by front-line staff to be more of a competitive handicap than a competitive advantage. On the other hand, companies like Virgin Atlantic, First Direct, or Amazon.com have great competitive fitness capabilities from relatively small investments. There is no need to be a large firm to have great fundamental capabilities. In fact, sometimes the opposite is true; in large firms the muscles can turn to fat so the firm becomes heavier, ineffective, and handicapped in the market place.

The opportunities for improving market-based capabilities for most companies are huge. Opportunities are uncovered by asking a few fundamental questions, not typically asked in the "normal" process of running a business: How fit, in the absolute and relative to my competitors, are these capabilities that are the life blood of the unit I am leading? What progress has been made in the last five years? What is the current trend? What am I going to do about it? At times, responding to these opportunities requires investment, but in other cases it is more a matter of doing less and focusing more. The executive or manager cannot escape responsibility for the competitive fitness of the unit he or she is in charge of. This responsibility is at the core of leadership.

> **A competitive advantage in terms of capabilities is the ultimate form of competitive advantage.**

An important leadership gap is the inability to measure intangible capabilities. In the Competitive Fitness of Global Firms initiative at INSEAD, a framework and an assessment methodology have

"The last remaining source of truly sustainable competitive advantage lies in what we've come to describe as organizational capabilities."

(David Nadler)

been developed to evaluate the fundamental capabilities driving the success of the modern firm. This work has been based on available published research, long-term analyses of about 40 corporations, in-depth case studies, and the cooperation of selected firms.

The Competitive Fitness of Global Firms framework includes 12 fundamental capabilities: Mission and Vision; Customer Orientation; Corporate Culture; Organization and Systems; Planning and Intelligence; Human Resources; Technical Resources; Innovation; Market Strategy; Marketing Operations; International; and Performance. The measurement methodology is based on a diagnostic tool containing 182 indicators to estimate scores on the 12 capabilities, and is available for use by executives at any level in a firm.

Since 1998 a survey has been conducted annually to provide international capability benchmarks on which executives can compare their scores with competitors. This survey covers eight sectors comprising more than 300 of the largest firms from Europe and North America. The *Report on the Competitive Fitness of Global Firms*, based on this survey, is published each year in February.

Beyond short-term results is strategy; beyond strategy are market-based capabilities. By focusing on short-term results, or on a narrow strategy, some businesses are cutting into both fat and muscle.

A competitive advantage in terms of capabilities is the ultimate form of competitive advantage. Products and technologies are visible and well defined and can be imitated by those ready to make the investment. By contrast, capabilities are often intangible and made up of elemental parts–innovation, human resources, corporate culture. Capabilities also tend to endure and provide a competitive edge for a firm in various markets, not just a specific area or segment. A capability advantage is pervasive and sustainable and can therefore be an important engine of value creation for the short and long term.

In the past, "industry practices" prevailed in separate sectors. There was an acceptable way to run a bank, a chemical group, or a consumer goods company. Industry associations, management transfers, and the leadership of large companies contributed to the establishment of these norms. We can now observe a wider gap being created between the capabilities of different firms in the same sector, and recognize that the trend leaders are not always the largest firms.

The *Report on the Competitive Fitness of Global Firms* provides some illustrations of this phenomenon in many sectors. Many financial services firms still believe in an old industry "truth" that innovation advantages are not possible because products are imitated easily. In reality, some firms find ways to go from strength to strength while others lag behind in innovation and other key capabilities. These latter firms are unaware of their sliding competitiveness as they do not have access to a quantified benchmark. They run the risk of realizing it only when their performance suffers, by which time it will be difficult to correct the situation.

Does this mean that all the fittest firms need to be equally strong on all capabilities? Certainly not. The *Report on Corporate Competitive Fitness* shows that the fittest firms very often have a personality, a distinctive competitive fitness profile. There is a unique "capability look" about the fittest companies in a given sector, reminiscent of a specific face, silhouette, or fingerprint.

In addition to a vast array of observations on market-based capabilities, the *Report on the Competitive Fitness of Global Firms* contains the capability profiles of more than 60 firms in 8 sectors. These are the fittest firms among those included in the survey. For instance, the capability profiles of Diageo, Exxon Mobil, and Eli Lilly show that all these firms score highly on overall corporate competitive fitness. They are above their sector's averages on most of the capabilities. In addition, they have a strong atypical profile, the expression of a unique personality that is the result of strong crafting. It may have been achieved over generations or through recent transformations and actions, but such competitive fitness profiles are not developed just through the "normal" way of running a business. It requires strong leadership to invest in what Jack Welch called "soft values." Beyond strategy, the selection of priorities for further capability development is a crucial task of leadership.

Beyond short-term results is strategy; beyond strategy are market-based capabilities. By focusing on short-term results, or on a narrow strategy, some businesses are cutting into both fat and muscle. In the process, they are digging the hole into which they will eventually collapse. The challenge of great leadership is to deliver at all three levels: results, strategy, and market-based capabilities. The latter are the most important for sustainable long-term success. Unfortunately, market-based capabilities are also the most difficult element to comprehend and the easiest to neglect. Effective management of a business's intangible assets requires the three steps described in this article: measuring market-based capabilities, monitoring the emergence of capability gaps in relevant business sectors, and investing in the development of a distinctive superior capability profile.

For More Information

Books:

Larréché, Jean-Claude. *The Competitive Fitness of Global Firms*. Englewood Cliffs, NJ: Financial Times Prentice Hall, 1998.

Welch, Jack. *Jack: Straight from the Gut*. New York:

See also:

☆ **Viewpoint: Warren Bennis (pp. 212–13)**
Warren Bennis (pp. 968–69)

  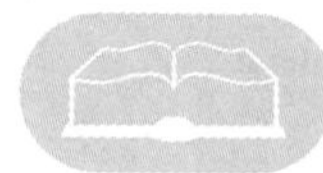    

OUTSOURCING *by Ronan McIvor*

EXECUTIVE SUMMARY

- Outsourcing has become critically important to many organizations due to the strategic implications, but many organizations have not achieved the desired benefits.
- Typical problems include no formal outsourcing process, limited cost analysis, and core business definition.
- Outsourcing should be conducted from a strategic perspective and integrated into the overall strategy of the organization.
- Definitions of the core and noncore activities of the business must be linked with corporate strategy.
- Supply management is a crucial element in ensuring effective management of the outsourcing process.

INTRODUCTION

One of the key issues for many organizations is the growing importance of outsourcing. The potential for outsourcing has moved on from those activities that are normally regarded as peripheral, such as cleaning, catering, and security, to include critical areas such as design, manufacture, marketing, distribution, and information systems, with almost the entire value chain open to the use of outside supply (Jennings 1997). Within organizations the outsourcing decision is being given more consideration because of its strategic implications.

However, there is evidence to suggest that organizations are not achieving the desired benefits from outsourcing. Research conducted by Lonsdale and Cox (1997) has revealed that outsourcing decisions are rarely taken within a thoroughly strategic perspective, with many firms adopting a short-term perspective and being motivated primarily by the search for short-term cost reductions. Also, some commentators have expressed serious concerns over companies that have embarked upon extensive outsourcing without fully understanding the concept (Alexander and Young 1996).

THE DECISION TO OUTSOURCE

The conceptual basis for outsourcing is Williamson's (1975) theory of *transaction cost analysis*. This combines economic theory with management theory to determine the best type of relationship a firm should develop in the marketplace. The central theme of transaction costs theory is that the properties of the transaction determine the governance structure. Asset specificity refers to the nontrivial investment in transaction-specific assets. For example, the level of customized equipment or materials involved in the transaction relates to the degree of asset specificity. When asset specificity and uncertainty are low, and transactions are relatively frequent, transactions will be governed by markets. High asset specificity and uncertainty lead to transactional difficulties, with transaction held internally within the firm—vertical integration. Medium levels of asset specificity lead to bilateral relations in the form of cooperative alliances between the organizations.

A term frequently used in connection with outsourcing is "core competence." The ideas of core competence and its relationship to outsourcing have evolved from the work of Prahalad and Hamel (1990). Prahalad and Hamel argue that the real sources of competitive advantage are to be found in management's ability to consolidate corporate-wide technologies and production skills into competencies that empower individual businesses to adapt rapidly to changing business opportunities. Canon's core competencies in optics, imaging, and microprocessor controls have allowed it to be a significant player in markets as diverse as photocopiers, laser printers, cameras, and image scanners. These core competencies underpin the ability of the organization to outperform the competition and therefore must be defended and nurtured.

KEY PROBLEMS

Many companies have failed to take a strategic view of outsourcing decisions, deciding to outsource for short-term reasons such as cost reduction and capacity constraints. A number of problems encountered by companies in their efforts to formulate an effective outsourcing decision are as follows:

- **No formal outsourcing process.** Many companies have no firm basis for evaluating the outsourcing decision. In many instances, the choice of which parts of the business to outsource is made by ascertaining what will save most on overhead costs, rather than on what makes the most long-term business sense.
- **A fragmented piecemeal approach.** Many companies have failed to integrate outsourcing decisions into their overall strategy. This has led to a fragmented and piecemeal approach with no coherent strategy on how outsourcing should contribute to strategic objectives.
- **Limited cost analysis.** Cost analysis of the outsourcing decision involves comparing the important costs associated with internal work and outsourcing. However, in many cases these calculations tend to focus primarily on manufacturing costs and do not provide a true reflection of the total costs involved. Also, other more qualitative factors, such as the long-term strategic implications and the workforce reaction to outsourcing, may have a greater impact on the decision.
- **Core business definition.** The embedded skills that give rise to the next generation of competitive products cannot be "rented-in" by outsourcing. Too many companies have unknowingly relinquished their core competencies by cutting internal investment in what they mistakenly thought were "cost centers" in favor of outside suppliers. Outsourcing may provide a shortcut to a more competitive product, but it typically contributes little to build the people-embodied skills that are needed to sustain future product leadership.

KEY REQUIREMENTS FOR EFFECTIVE OUTSOURCING

CORE ACTIVITY DEFINITION

Companies must identify their core and noncore activities. A core activity is central to the company successfully serving the needs of potential customers in each market. The activity is perceived by the customers as adding value, and therefore being a major determinant of competitive advantage. Distinguishing between core and noncore activities is a complex task, and care must be taken to ensure the long-term strategic considerations and true benefits are assessed. This process of identifying the core activities should be conducted by

"Thinking must be the hardest job in the world. What people want to do is outsource it to a mantra or a methodology like reengineering."
(Eileen Shapiro)

top management with inputs from teams at lower levels in the organization. Each team should encompass a broad section of members—functionally, divisionally, and hierarchically. Noncore activities for which the company has neither a critical strategic need nor special capabilities should be outsourced. Companies adopting this approach, such as Honda, and Nortel, build their strategies around their core activities and outsource as much of the rest as possible.

Core Activity Capability Analysis

Each core activity must be benchmarked against the capabilities of all potential external providers (both suppliers and competitors) of that activity. This will enable the identification of the relative performance for each core activity along a number of selected measures. Resources should be focused on the activities where pre-eminence can be achieved and unique customer-perceived value can be delivered. For example, Eastman Kodak has world leadership in two of its core activities—chemical and electronic imaging. Thus, these activities are held within the company in order to maintain and build upon this leadership. A key strategic issue in the outsourcing decision is whether a company can achieve a sustainable competitive advantage by performing a core activity internally on an ongoing basis. Many companies assume that because they have always performed the activity internally, then it should remain that way. In many cases, closer analysis may reveal a significant disparity between their capabilities and those of the world's best suppliers. For example, Ford found that many of its internal quality and cost performance indicators were significantly lower than those of suppliers when it conducted a benchmarking exercise across a range of processes for one of its models (Quinn and Hilmer 1994).

Cost Analysis

All the actual and potential costs involved in sourcing the activity, either internally or externally, must be measured. This encompasses all the costs associated with the acquisition of the activity throughout the entire supply chain and not just the purchase price. It is important to consider costs right from idea conception, as in collaborating with a supplier in the design phase of the component, through to any costs (for example, warranty claims) associated with the component once the completed product is being used by the final customer. The data requirements for this stage are quite formidable. Management must break down the company's functional cost accounting data into the costs of performing specific activities. The appropriate degree of disaggregation depends upon the economics of the activities and how valuable it is to develop cross-company comparisons for narrowly defined activities as opposed to broadly defined activities.

Supply Management

As a result of increased outsourcing, companies have become more dependent upon their suppliers, thus making supply management a key success factor. Many companies have been attempting to develop collaborative relationships with suppliers as they seek to reduce the risks associated with outsourcing. Companies may establish a collaborative relationship with a supplier in order to exploit their capabilities. For example, a company may wish to maintain the knowledge (design skills, management skills, manufacturing, etc.) that enables the technology of the activity to be exploited, even when another partner is providing it. Also, it is possible for a company to develop a core competency by learning from partners. For example, NEC top management determined that semiconductors would be the company's most important "core product." Hence, it entered into strategic alliances aimed at building competencies quickly and at low cost. Alternatively, in some circumstances it may be more beneficial to pursue a relationship where the company holds the balance of power rather than pursuing a relationship based upon equality and the mutual sharing of benefits. For example, a company may use its influence to obtain reductions in inventory and cost, which in turn have a positive impact on the achievement of its own competitive position. Also, this may ensure greater flexibility in that the company will not get locked into a long-term relationship with a supplier whose technology or processes may become uncompetitive.

Making It Happen ▸▸

- Take a strategic view of outsourcing decisions—don't act on short-term factors such as cost reduction and capacity constraints.
- Outsource for long-term business sense, not what activities will save most on overhead costs.
- Identify core activities by supporting top management with lower-level teams with broad functional, divisional, and hierarchical membership.
- Benchmark each core activity against the capabilities of all potential external providers (both suppliers and competitors).
- Keep a core activity internally on a continuing basis only if you can achieve a sustainable competitive advantage by doing so.
- Measure all the actual and potential costs involved in outsourcing the activity—not just the purchase price.

For More Information

Books and Journals:

Alexander, M., and D. Young. "Outsourcing: Where's the Value?" *Long Range Planning*, May 29, 1996: 728–30.

Jennings, D. "Strategic Guidelines for Outsourcing Decisions." *Journal of Strategic Change*, April 6, 1997: 85–96.

Lonsdale, C., and A. Cox. "Outsourcing: Risks and Rewards." *Supply Management*, July 3, 1997: 32–4.

McIvor, Ronan. "A Practical Framework for Understanding the Outsourcing Process." *International Journal of Supply Chain Management*, January 5, 2000: 22–36.

Prahalad, C. K., and Gary Hamel. "The Core Competence of the Corporation." *Harvard Business Review*, July–August, 1990: 79–91.

Quinn, J. B., and F. G. Hilmer. "Strategic Outsourcing." *Sloan Management Review*, Summer, 1994: 43–55.

Williamson, Oliver E. *Markets and Hierarchies*. New York: Free Press, 1975.

See also:

☆ **Competing on Costs (pp. 111–12)**
☆ **Core Versus Context: Managing Resources in a Downturn (pp. 255–56)**
☆ **Facilities Management (pp. 179–80)**
✔ **Deciding Whether to Outsource (pp. 490–91)**
Outsourcing (pp. 2061–62)

"Don't subcontract your soul." (Anonymous)

  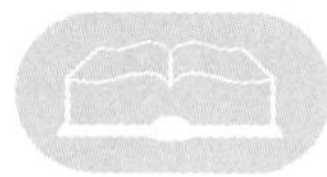    

The Power of Identity *by Wally Olins*

Executive Summary

Corporate identity is the unique identity of a firm that differentiates it from its competitors; it is a complex and valuable asset and influences the organization's strategy, structure, and vision.

- A corporate identity program enables a corporation's individual identity to be managed and projected.
- In order to develop an effective identity program, organizational builders must have a clear idea about what drives the organization—they must have a vision and a sense of strategic direction.
- Organizational builders can consciously construct a structure that enables the organization to project its identity both internally and externally.

Introduction

Organizations have a unique identity that can be employed as a valuable asset. Corporations currently face challenges to their identity from all sides. These challenges are increasingly prompting company boards to regard identity as an important topic. the most common problems regarding identity management are that:

- Products and services are increasingly becoming more similar, making customers purchase products on an emotional basis—a projected sense of corporate personality and rapport with customers boosts business. How can Shell, Texaco, and BP differentiate their products from each other so as to provide competitive advantage?
- Corporate mergers are on the rise, disregarding local boundaries and charging leaders with the problem of how to create a new identity from two old ones. Daimler Chrysler is a good example.
- Organizations are forced through changing technologies, deregulation, and globalization to alter the nature of their business and to manage corporate identity through change and uncertainty. British Telecom is an example of a corporation forced to manage in such a situation.

Corporate identity externally provides a bedrock of valuable, but frequently intangible resources, such as goodwill, loyalty, and respect among customers, while internally providing a strategic direction.

What Is Identity?

Every organization conducts thousands of transactions every day. In each transaction every organization is in some way presenting itself—or part of itself—to the various groups of people it deals with. The totality of the way the organization presents itself can be called its identity. What different audiences perceive is often called its image.

Because the range of its activities is so vast and the manifestations of identity are so diverse, the corporation needs to actively and explicitly manage its identity. Identity management is a corporate resource embracing every part of the organization.

Identity can project four ideas:

- who you are
- what you do
- how you do it
- where you want to go

The Four Vectors

Identity manifests itself primarily through:

- products and services—what you make or sell (think of BMW);
- environments—where you make or sell it (Hilton Hotels);
- communications—how you talk about your product (Coca-Cola);
- behavior—how you behave to your employees and the world outside (Southwest Airlines).

The balance among these four is rarely equal, and an early priority in creating any identity program is to determine which predominates.

The Central Idea/Vision

The fundamental idea behind an identity program is that in everything the organization does, everything it owns, and everything it produces, it should project a clear idea of what it is and what its aims are.

Name/Logo

At the heart of the visual identity is the hierarchy and identification system and the way it is reflected in symbols, logotypes, and marks. The symbol is highly visible. Its prime purpose is to present the idea of the corporation with impact, brevity, and immediacy.

It is sometimes necessary to change the symbol in order to signify a change in direction, as, for example, BP Amoco did. In other cases, for example, Renault or Shell, modification may be more appropriate.

Sometimes it's appropriate to change the name of a corporation for legal reasons or for clarity. Name changes are, however, frequently misunderstood and always excite high levels of emotion, particularly in the media.

Audiences

The audiences of an organization are those people who come into contact with it at any time, in any place, and in any form of relationship. It is often assumed that the most important audience for any corporation is its customers. In a service business, however, employees are by far the most significant audience. They transmit the identity of the organization to customers, so they have to live it.

There are both internal and external audiences. The internal audience comprises staff members and their families. External audiences include shareholders, competitors, suppliers and partners (sometimes these can be identical), the financial world, and opinion-formers of all kinds. These audiences are not always separate and independent; to some extent they do overlap.

Types of Corporate Identity

Monolithic identity. Here the organization uses one name and one visual system throughout all of its interactions. Because everything that the organization does has the same name, style, and character, each part supports the other. Virgin is the most high profile example of this type of identity. The name and identity of Virgin is not associated so much with what it does, but with what it is, how it behaves, and what it seems to stand for.

Endorsed identity. Most corporations grow at least partly by acquisition. The acquiring corporation is often eager to preserve the goodwill (equity) associated with its acquisitions. Under an endorsed identity strategy, the parent endorses its subsidiaries with the corporate name and sometimes its visual style. Nestlé and P&O are examples.

"Our brand awareness went from 65 percent to 81 percent in one year. We weren't advertising so we know exactly what to blame."
(Chris Moore)

Branded identity. Some companies, especially those in the consumer products field, separate their corporate identity from the identities of the brands they own, for example, Unilever, Diageo, and LVMH. The final customer identifies with the brand, other audiences with the corporation. Brands have names, reputations, life cycles, and personalities of their own, and they may even compete with other brands from the same corporation.

STARTING AND MANAGING A PROGRAM

The following points should be considered when implementing a corporate identity program:

- Is it part of a corporate turnaround?
- Does it inspire, invigorate, and create more cohesion internally?
- Is it intended to increase the share price?
- Is it focused on helping to integrate newly acquired companies?
- Is it a response to competitive pressures?

When a corporate identity program is initiated, a senior individual in the organization must be appointed to manage it, and such change should be implemented in a clear and goal-focused manner. Most organizations will need outside assistance from branding, identity, or design consultants. As with every corporate activity, the identity program needs a power base, financial controls, and clear lines of authority. A working party should be formed, which should report to a steering group.

THE STAGES OF WORK

STAGE ONE

Investigation, analysis, and strategic recommendations. The organization has to take a objective look at how it is perceived by its various audiences and how these perceptions compare with its aspirations. If the existing identity is perceived as fragmented, incoherent, unclear, old-fashioned, or otherwise ineffective, senior managers need to agree on the action required to change perceptions. Stage One ends with recommendations for action.

STAGE TWO

Development of the identity. Depending on the results of Stage One, it may be necessary to change the identity of the corporation completely, including name and visual style (Accenture), to keep the same name but change the identity visually (BP Amoco), or simply to make some changes.

Changes of name and visual style are expensive and time-consuming, and they clearly signal to the marketplace that the organization is making a new promise or moving in a new direction. This kind of change makes a promise of changed performance that has to be fulfilled. Never, ever promise more than you can deliver.

On the basis of the recommendations made in Stage One, consultants develop an identity system based on the monolithic, endorsed, or branded model. The identity system usually consists of a name (or names), mark or logo, main and subsidiary typefaces, and colors. These will be applied to a variety of corporate materials such as letterheads, Web sites, and products.

STAGE THREE

Implementation. The new identity has to be codified so that it can be used in the organization and by relevant outside suppliers. Manuals are prepared containing all the identity elements and their precise specifications for a variety of applications. The manual should also demonstrate the spirit that lies behind the organization.

STAGE FOUR

Launch and introduction. If the new corporate identity program is to work, it has to be launched with enthusiasm and commitment. The launch is the first major opportunity for the company's leaders to present the identity as a significant corporate resource and to integrate it into the organizational structure.

Never trivialize your corporate identity. Explain that the new identity is the outward sign of change and explain what that change means. Internal audiences want to know what, why, and particularly how it will affect them as individuals. External audiences only want to know why and how much.

MINI-CASE

The Spanish oil company *Repsol* was formed in the 1980s from Instituto Nacional de Hidrocarburos (INH). INH was a state monopoly with low standards of service, old and badly maintained service stations, and a plethora of names and identities. The central idea/vision emerged naturally from the corporation's new positioning. Spain had just entered the European Union and the corporation had to defend its position. INH had to be revitalized and eventually privatized.

Repsol had the opportunity to become the model for a revitalized Spain. Repsol could become and be seen as the new Spain's industrial and commercial flagship. This was the vision that was presented to and agreed on by the board.

The naming structure and visual identity followed from this brief. The name INH was abandoned in favor of one of the company's brands, Repsol, and a monolithic identity structure was adopted in order to give the organization strength and coherence. A new design was part of the program of change.

MAKING IT HAPPEN ▸▸

- Develop your corporate identity to project the company's approach, values, distinctiveness, and direction.
- Concentrate primarily through three "tangibles": your products and services, the environments where you make or sell them, and communications.
- Also treat the intangibles of behavior—how you behave to your employees and the world outside—as vital.
- As a priority, determine early which of the above four tangible and intangible factors predominates.
- Before starting a corporate identity program, decide what you want it to achieve in the longer term.
- Construct the program in the four stages recommended above.

CONCLUSION

All corporations have an identity, irrespective of whether they control it or effectively manage it. By concentrating on developing a desirable corporate identity and projecting it to customers, as well as employing it as a tool to provide internal direction and orientate strategic development, organizational efficiency can be raised. Remember that a corporate identity program harnesses and manages a valuable corporate asset.

For More Information

Books:

Olins, Wally. *The New Wolff Olins Guide to Identity: How to Create and Maintain Change Through Managing Identity*. Rev. ed. Brookfield, VT: Ashgate, 1995.
Schultz, Majken, Mary Jo Hatch, and Mogens Holten Larsen, eds. *The Expressive Organization*. New York: Oxford University Press, 2000.

See also:

☆ **Core Versus Context: Managing Resources in a Downturn (pp. 255–56)**
☆ **Marketing: The Importance of Being First (pp. 61–62)**
✓ **Producing a Corporate Brochure (pp. 724–25)**

"Corporate identities must not be shortlived." (Clive Chajet)

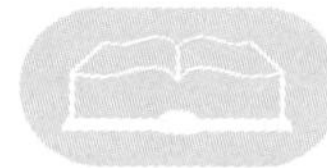

SWITCHING STRATEGIES *by Louis Patler*

EXECUTIVE SUMMARY

- Today good strategy is more important than ever to sustain success in the marketplace.
- The strategic givens and fundamental questions—and their answers—shape good strategy.
- The givens and answers, revisited regularly, also provide early signs whether to stay with or to change strategy.

INTRODUCTION

A five-year-old software company sells for more money than Ford paid to acquire Volvo. Slow-to-change American Express announces the creation of a new senior-level vice president of customer listening. In a matter of a few weeks a loan information company moves from no-com to dot-com to hot-com to no-com.

What do all three of these cases have in common? They all have lessons to teach us about the nature of strategy—the pathways or direction to productivity and profitability. As such, strategy is more macro than micro, more compass than map.

We live in a business world taken over by ironies and oxymorons, a world of walking contradictions in which the line between conventional and unconventional wisdom is drawn with disposable pens filled with invisible ink. The rules that once seemed so useful, even profound, now ebb and flow like a hyperactive harvest moon. With the advent of e-commerce, Internet access, and mobile phones, today's economy evolves and changes before our eyes, and we dare not blink for fear we will miss something.

In the face of such exponential change we have witnessed a commensurate rise in the importance of strategy for the growth and profitability of any enterprise. Sony, for example, took an exponential leap, strategically speaking, when it realized that it was in the miniaturization business as well as the electronics and entertainment business. In fact, the traditional planning process has often been bolstered with a strong commitment to well-conceived strategic planning and research.

This said, the rise of the importance of strategy did not come easily, since conventional wisdom is replete with axioms that lobby for the status quo. If it ain't broke, don't fix it. Never change horses in midstream. The inherent problem with these supposedly tried-and-true concepts is that they have indeed been tried, but they are often no longer true.

Would you want to fly with an airline with the motto, "If it ain't broke, don't fix it?" Would you want to be on an aging horse in a rising stream of rapids and white water?

The real challenge today is to develop strategies that are both viable and flexible, implementable yet nimble. The growing tendency of companies to change their strategic plan, core products, and organizational culture with alacrity typically leaves shareholders bewildered, customers underwhelmed, and employees confused.

Further, the challenge of developing good strategy is exacerbated by the growing tendency of companies worldwide to change direction far too often, thereby confusing flexibility with sloppy thinking and the relative absence of due diligence.

Against this backdrop let's look then at three practical topics affecting strategy formation and change in more detail. First, what are the assumptions that underlie modern strategic thinking? Second, how do you know when it's time to change strategy? And third, what is "good" strategy?

THE STRATEGIC GIVENS: ASSUMPTIONS OF MODERN STRATEGY

It's helpful to overtly identify and understand the broad assumptions that underlie your strategy, to know what the basic cornerstones of your paradigm are. Here are five useful indicative assumptions for the modern business world:

1. **Today the rate of change is exponential, not incremental.** This is a crucial starting point. Things are changing at a fast-forward, willy-nilly pace. This makes it very difficult to use conventional modes of thought, measurement, or planning. Often things don't build up or add up, they just explode to a new level.
2. **Things will never "get back to normal"—this is normal!** The so-called glory days of the bygone past have gone. And they won't be back. So, the new Thoughtware says, "Get over it! Get used to it! THIS is normal from now on!"
3. **Plan as we may, the future has plans of its own.** Because exponential change is here to stay, we have to look down the road with 20/20 vision, focusing on the next 20 minutes and the next 20 years simultaneously. The bad news is that the number of senior executives and key managers who possess 20/20 vision is minimal. The good news is that this is a learnable cognitive skill that a few training programs can teach you.
4. **Organizations that learn how to learn, ask the right questions at the right time, and find out how to find the answers will thrive in a global economy.** Astute organizational strategists know that an organization's verbs will supplant its nouns, that is, diverse methods and responsive processes will be more powerful than tried-and-true facts and off-the-shelf systems. And asking the right questions at the right time will determine the most sustainable and viable answers.
5. **The productive organizations that will excel will be ones that value flexibility, diversity, integrity, cooperation, and innovation.** It's no longer sufficient to add value to products; we have to add values into both the process and the product. Customers, creditors, consumers, and our conscience now require it.

WHEN TO CHANGE GOOD STRATEGY: TO DISMOUNT OR TO RIDE ON?

The seven questions listed below help place parameters around good strategy (good strategy is strategy that is implementable and drives success, growth, and customer loyalty). But remember that these are not seven easy questions, nor are their answers cast in stone. I advise managers to ask these questions—all of them—at least twice a year. Even if the answers haven't changed significantly, at a minimum you'll be thinking on the right level with some regularity. Then, once you have the perspective that this combination of answers offers you, you're ready to act and make hard decisions, because you'll know why you're doing what you're doing, and your decisions will be

"Strategy making is an immensely complex process involving the most sophisticated, subtle, and at times subconscious of human cognitive and social processes." (Henry Mintzberg)

based on sound strategic thinking. Remember, too: strategy is not tactics, it's directionality.

Conversely, by regularly revisiting these seven questions you'll have additional, crucial information to detect the early warning signs of good strategy that has taken a turn for the worse. If, for example, two or more of your strategic givens and/or answers to these seven questions change significantly, it's often an early indicator that fundamental shifts in strategy are appropriate.

MAKING IT HAPPEN

There is strategy and then there is good strategy, and understanding the difference between the two rests on the ability to answer seven fundamental questions:

1. **What business are you in?** Many companies are in more than one business and/or offer a variety of products and/or services without knowing it. Others have a single focus or a few well-conceived products or services. It's important to understand the business you are in, the competition, and the most innovative practices in your industry. Sam Walton started Wal-Mart to bring popular brands to smaller communities at low prices.
2. **What other businesses are you in?** Many companies don't see their business through a wide enough lens. They fail to capitalize on other business opportunities that can accrue from little more than a change in thinking. For example, trucking companies are in the transportation business; banks are in the transaction management business; soccer teams are also in the entertainment business. If Ford and GM make more profit from their automobile financing products than their cars, are they not a financial services company also?
3. **What are your core competencies?** Knowing the core competency of your company will give you an incredible competitive advantage. Competencies are not mere strengths. Every company has its strengths, but only a very few strengths are true competencies that are going to give you an edge over the competition, market differentiators that separate you from others. But core competencies are often very subtle: one billion-dollar computer-connector manufacturing company took much of its skyrocketing growth from an unnoticed core competency—the ability to acquire companies and hold onto their key employees and customers.
4. **What are your core values?** Isolating and identifying core values is crucial. If your core value is short-term profitability, you need to organize your company accordingly. If you value long-term relationships with customers, this requires a different strategy, compensation package, and organizational chart. What you value should inform your strategy through and through. Southwest Airlines has a people-oriented culture, so they hire for hospitality skills and humor.
5. **Which competitor will be your next partner?** Necessity is the mother of odd couplings. It may be to your advantage to form a strategic partnership with a competitor on a specific product, R&D, or other aspects of your business in order to remain a player in your field. The world has changed, and a past competitor can be a future ally. Good strategy is open to new realignments, even with a current competitor. Further, when you research a competitor-as-potential-partner, you will see the company's strengths and weaknesses in a new and strategically important light. When Sun Microsystems looked at some competitors' strategies, it moved to outsource all facilities management functions, realizing that the company wasn't well suited to be in the real estate business.
6. **Are your short-term goals and long-term strategies aligned?** Public companies tend to think from quarter to quarter in order to please financial analysts and shareholders. The pressures of the next quarter too often conflict with the opportunities of the next few years. Companies need to align short-term results with long-term profitability, short-term profits with long-term customer satisfaction. When Barclaycard realized that it had a long-term strategy of individualizing transactions with customers, it altered its credit-card product array significantly.
7. **Do your answers to questions 1–6 complement (or negate) one another?** Too often a company will provide a viable answer to one or two of these questions. The real advantage, however, will go to the company that continuously examines itself in the context of several of these questions. For example, are core competencies, goals, and values working together to meet both long- and short-term goals?

CONCLUSION

Strategy is becoming increasingly important to business success. Good strategy is the result of: knowing the assumptions of your business model; sound investigation; open, curious, and broad thinking; and asking the right questions—often. Though strategy is often changed precipitously, in today's world it is far better to be useful than to be correct. Old ways die hard, so *strategy under constant scrutiny* is best understood as an agent of change.

For More Information

Books:

Collins, James C., and Jerry I. Porras. *Built to Last: Successful Habits of Visionary Companies*. New York: HarperBusiness, 1997.

Hamel, Gary, and C. K. Prahalad. *Competing for the Future*. Boston, MA: Harvard Business School Press, 1996.

Kaplan, Robert S., and David P. Norton. *The Strategy-focused Organization: How Balanced Scorecard Companies Thrive in the New Business Environment*. Boston, MA: Harvard Business School Press, 2000.

See also:

☆ **Avoiding the Mistakes of the Past: Lessons from the Startup World (pp. 129–30)**
☆ **The Balanced Scorecard (pp. 303–04)**
☆ **Infusing a Company with Cutting-edge Strategy (pp. 83–84)**
☆ **Power Struggling and Power Sharing (pp. 95–96)**
Competing for the Future (p. 899)
Corporate Strategy (pp. 1944–46)

"Whatever you shoot is dead for a while before it starts to stink. The same goes for strategies."
(Gary Hamel)

  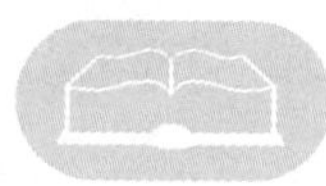    

POWER STRUGGLING AND POWER SHARING *by Jonas Ridderstråle*

EXECUTIVE SUMMARY

- Power has now transferred from producers to consumers and from capitalists to competents, that is, individuals who possess competencies crucial to success.
- Success requires enhancing the value of human, structural, and customer capital.
- E-business may be the future, but *e* must stand also for *emotion*.

INTRODUCTION

Information technology (IT) opens many opportunities for wealth creation, but from a more general economic point of view, IT in general and the Net in particular are best thought of as profit enemy no. 1. The current trends of digitization, deregulation, and globalization are altering the balance of power between those who sell and those who buy, on the one hand, and between capital and competence investors on the other. Combined, these changes make it increasingly difficult for firms to show a profit. Companies must respond by coming up with imaginative strategies to enhance the value of their intellectual capital.

MARKETS MEET MARX

Welcome to the information jungle, where markets flourish because they feed and breed on information. Some 30 years ago only 40% of all individuals lived within a market system. Now around 90% do so. The advent of what we might call global marketification has caused three identifiable trends:

1. *Overcapacity* is often the norm: 40% in automobiles, 100% in bulk chemicals, and 140% in computers.
2. While more products and services are available, they're often incredibly similar: *commoditization* rules.
3. The costs to find the best deal are falling dramatically; thanks to search power, comparison shopping has become a picnic.

In effect we're moving closer to a state of perfect competition. Power is transferred from those who sell to those who buy. The new consumer is a demanding dictator. The stupid, humble, and loyal customer is about to die.

Knowledge is our most critical resource. And just who owns that? We, as individuals, are the owners of our brains. Karl Marx was right: people now control the most critical resources–though individually, not collectively. Modern firms depend heavily on their *core competents*, that is, individuals who make competencies happen. Bill Gates once claimed that if 20 people left Microsoft, the company would risk bankruptcy. Competents are walking monopolies. They stay only as long as the organization can offer something they want. Power is now in the process of being transferred from capital owners to competence owners

Companies will accordingly do business with demanding dictators and negotiate salaries and stock-option plans with the business world's equivalents of Madonna and Tiger Woods. Indeed, one plausible hypothesis is that the more Web-based and knowledge-intensive the business, the less chance that any of the eventual profits will end up in the pockets of the purely financial investors of the company.

Any organization relies on a mix of financial and intellectual capital. Now exchange rates are changing. Financial capital is in the process of being devalued. To prosper, organizations must counter the forces of consumer and competent control by boosting their intellectual capital in three primary ways:

1. attracting human capital
2. transforming it into structural capital, while simultaneously
3. building customer capital

HARNESSING HUMAN CAPITAL

Talented individuals have alternatives every minute, every day. Where competition in the labor market is increasingly generic, we're all players in a great global attraction game. Success is contingent on exploiting the fact that human beings simultaneously want to express their individuality and their need for belonging.

INDIVIDUAL PERSONALIZATION

Attracting talent calls for a more personalized company. Today smart people hire organizations rather than vice versa. Competents have a choice: the organization is disposable, a temporary home. And human beings are not bulk goods. We differ. Firms either manage this differentiation or watch their most precious resources walk away. The consequence is that each and every little system needs to be personalized.

ORGANIZATIONAL TRIBALIZATION

Peter Hagström has helped shaped my thinking on this immeasurably. Not only are people individualistic creatures, we also want to belong. Firms with a future will build organizational tribes in which employees share common traits or interests–rewards, ownership, culture, whatever. Today we see successful companies recruiting people with the right attitude, then training them in skills. Look at Hell's Angels or Greenpeace. Just imagine Hell's Angels hiring for skills! These organizations hire for attitude, because the half-life of knowledge is coming down fast, and it's easier for most of us to change our skills than our values.

SECURING STRUCTURAL CAPITAL

From the outlook of the firm, human capital is best thought of as a liability, while structural capital is definitely an asset on the balance sheet. Companies must therefore transform both the know-how and know-who components of their knowledge bases.

KNOWLEDGE CODIFICATION

The typical company may suffer not from knowing too little, but rather from not knowing what it knows. A critical task is thus to turn core competents into core competencies that are shared throughout the entire organization. Codification means collecting the knowledge of competents or *competeams* and transferring it to the organizational level. This way the firm not only provides others in the organization with an opportunity to learn, but becomes less dependent on a few competents.

CORPORATE SOCIALIZATION

By working in teams and spending time together after work, people in groups soon develop tacit knowledge. Tacit knowledge makes it more difficult for competitors to imitate, and for competents to quit with their skill-sets intact. When knowledge is a combination of know-how and know-who,

"Power is the ability to change things." (Carly Fiorina)

part of it will be nested in a network of relationships with existing colleagues. Anyone threatening to leave can thus only bring the intrapersonal skills along. Socialization = tacit knowledge = knowledge handcuffs.

Creating Customer Capital

In a world of customer control, companies will have to come up with new ways to deal with these demanding dictators. Once again the dual nature of humans, comprising elements of both individualism and collectivism, must be exploited.

Customer Tribalization

We all grew up in a world in which physical proximity ruled. Yesterday's tribes were geographically structured: Russians and Americans. The new tribes are biographically structured: they are global tribes of people who actually believe they have something in common, no matter where they were born. In a geographically structured world companies competed for the local average. Smart firms today go for the global extremes. Consider the case of G & L Internet Bank, the first U.S. bank for homosexuals (G stands for gay and L for lesbian). The basic idea is to target the 21 million or so homosexuals (a group with a combined annual budget of some $800 billion), then to go global.

A second kind of global tribe is more transactional—*buyographical* rather than biographical. While demanding dictators may constitute powerful forces individually, just imagine what happens when they link up. And in a networked world they will. Tribes of customers will interact and create customer unions. So entrepreneurial firms provide platforms on which customers can indeed aggregate their demand. Just look at LetsBuyIt.com, an Internet auction house/coshopper. The company allows you to link with other consumers (anywhere!) who are interested in buying the same product. Whether LetsBuyIt or someone else will eventually dominate the market is beside the point. Coshopping sites will become to global buyographical tribes what traditional cooperatives once were to blue-collar workers in the industrial society.

Total Customization

Within a consumer tribe there must be room for personalization and individual differences. Niches are becoming ever smaller in our fragmenting world. Recent technological developments open up many new opportunities for mass customization. But total customization involves more than the customer offering—it must encompass the entire experience. Innovative organizations help people avoid information overload and aid them in making smart choices. Either companies focus on internally producing this service by employing experts, aggregating information, and comparing prices (the way Pricerunner.com does), or they choose to more actively involve the consumers in the process (as does Amazon.com).

All You Need Is Love

Given today's almost endless choices for customers and competents, only those companies that realize success rests with capturing the emotional human being will stand a chance. Moving from abundance to affection is a question not of applying more reason, but of fusing functionality with ethics and aesthetics. Logic leads to conclusions. Emotions trigger action. Sensibility rather than sense is the road ahead.

Sounds too touchy-feely? Research in neuroscience shows that the brain's limbic system, which governs our feelings, is more powerful than the neocortex that controls intellect. The traffic instructions in our brains are clear: emotions have precedence.

Making It Happen ▸▸

- Define your organizational tribe by asking: Who are we and where do we want to go?
- Hire people for attitude and then train them for skill.
- Replace job descriptions with motivation descriptions.
- Personalize all aspects of all systems and contracts for all competents.
- Get competents to share their competencies—collect, codify, and communicate.
- Promote socialization at and away from work to develop knowledge handcuffs.
- Invite customers to join your tribe—and then constantly reinforce the bond.
- Customize the entire experience for the consumer, not only the customer offering.
- Remember that people differ. Figure out what makes customers and competents mad, sad, and glad. Then ask yourself that question—over and over again.

Conclusion

As digitization, combined with deregulation and globalization, perfects the global market economy, IT is enabling many of the strategies outlined above. Yet for a company to exist just on the Web is a bit like having a toilet back at the office—necessary, but not sufficient for the creation of a sustainable competitive advantage. IT merely provides the means to an end. The road to the future may end up in Silicon Valley, but it must start in Soul and pass through Values on the way to e-(motional) business.

For More Information

Books:

Downes, Larry, and Chunka Mui. *Unleashing the Killer App: Digital Strategies for Market Dominance*. Rev. ed. Boston, MA: Harvard Business School Press, 2000.

Edvinsson, Leif. *Corporate Longitude: Discover Your Position in the Knowledge Economy*. Upper Saddle River, NJ: Financial Times Prentice Hall, 2002.

Seybold, Patricia B. *The Customer Revolution: How to Thrive When Customers Are in Control*. New York: Crown, 2001.

Stewart, Thomas A. *Intellectual Capital: The New Wealth of Organizations*. New York: Bantam, 1998.

See also:

☆ **Creating Fun in the Workplace (pp. 37–38)**
☆ **Downsizing with Dignity (pp. 16–17)**
☆ **Finding and Keeping the Best Talent in the World (pp. 119–20)**
☆ **Making Loyalty Work (pp. 289–90)**
☆ **Making the Workplace Flex, Not Break (pp. 31–32)**
☆ **The New Frontiers in Old-economy Industries (pp. 99–100)**
☆ **Managing in a 24/7 Organization (pp. 200–01)**
☆ **Switching Strategies (pp. 93–94)**
☆ **Viewpoint: Christopher Bartlett (pp. 45–46)**
☆ **Viewpoint: John Seely Brown (pp. 137–38)**
✓ **Conducting Customer Research (pp. 702–03)**
✓ **Handling Customer Incidents (pp. 672–73)**
✓ **Involving Customers in Product Development (pp. 706–07)**
✓ **Setting Up a Customer Interaction Center (pp. 680–81)**

  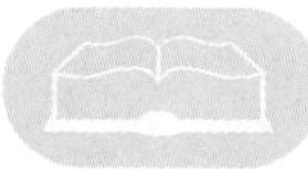    

GLOBALIZATION AND BUSINESS STRATEGY *by Alan M. Rugman*

EXECUTIVE SUMMARY

- Globalization is misunderstood—it does not, and never has, existed in terms of a single world market with free trade.
- Triad-based business is the past, current, and future reality.
- Multinational enterprises operate within triad markets and access other triad markets; they have regional, not global, strategies.
- National governments strongly regulate most service sectors, thereby limiting free-market forces; the extent of regulation is not decreasing.
- Businesses need to think local and act regional; they should forget global.

INTRODUCTION: THE MYTH OF GLOBAL STRATEGY

Recent research suggests that globalization is a myth. Far from taking place in a single global market, most business activity by large firms takes place in regional blocks. There is no uniform spread of U.S. market capitalism, nor are global markets becoming homogenized. Government regulations and cultural differences divide the world into the triad blocks of North America, the European Union, and Japan. Rival multinational enterprises from the triad compete for regional market share and so enhance economic efficiency. As a result, top managers now need to design triad-based regional strategies, not global ones. Only in a few sectors such as consumer electronics is a global strategy of economic integration viable. For most other manufacturing sectors (automobiles, for example) and for all services, strategies of national responsiveness are required, often coupled with integration strategies, as explained in the matrix framework below.

The real drivers of globalization are the network managers of large multinational enterprises. But their business strategies are triadic, or regional, in scope and are responsive to local consumers; they are not global and uniform.

Specialty chemicals and the automotive industry are triad-based, not global. There is no global automobile: more than 90% of all automobiles produced in Europe are sold in Europe, and regional production and predominantly local sales are also the norm in North America and Japan. Successful multinationals now design strategies on a regional basis; unsuccessful ones pursue global strategies.

SOME COMMON GLOBAL MISUNDERSTANDINGS

Globalization has been defined in business schools as the production and distribution of products and services of a homogenous type and quality on a worldwide basis. Simply put, it involves providing the same output to countries everywhere. And in recent years it has become increasingly common to hear business executives, industry analysts, and even university professors talk about the emergence of globalization and the dominance of international business by giant multinational enterprises (MNEs) that are selling uniform products from Cairo, Illinois, to Cairo, Egypt, and from Lima, Ohio, to Lima, Peru.

To back up their claims these individuals often point to the fact that foreign sales account for more than 50% of the annual revenues of companies such as Dow Chemical, Exxon, Hewlett-Packard, IBM, Johnson & Johnson, Mobil, Motorola, Procter & Gamble, and Texaco. (For more on these firms, see the *World Investment Report*.) These are accurate statements, but they fail to explain that most of the sales of so-called global companies are made on a triadic or regional basis. For example, most MNEs that are headquartered in North America earn the bulk of their revenue within their home country or by selling to members of the triad: NAFTA, the European Union (EU), or Japan and a small group of Asian and Oceanian nations. Recent research gives ample supporting data.

1. More than 85% of all automobiles produced in North America are built in North American factories owned by General Motors, Ford, or DaimlerChrysler, or by European or Japanese MNEs. More than 90% of the cars produced in the EU are sold in the EU. More than 93% of all cars registered in Japan are manufactured domestically.
2. In the specialty chemicals sector more than 90% of all paint is made and used regionally by triad-based MNEs. The same is true for steel, heavy electrical equipment, energy, and transportation.
3. In the services sector, which now employs approximately 70% of the workforce in North America, Western Europe, and Japan, business activity is all essentially local or regional.

Another misunderstanding about globalization is the belief that MNEs are globally monolithic and excessively powerful in political terms. Research shows this is not so. MNEs are not monolithic; in fact, the largest 500 multinationals are spread across the triad economies of NAFTA, the EU, and Japan/Asia. Recent research by *Fortune* shows that of these 500 companies, 198 are headquartered in NAFTA countries, 156 in the EU, and 125 in Japan/Asia. Further, these triad-based MNEs compete for global market share and profits across a wide variety of industrial sectors and trade services. And this process of regional competition erodes the possibility of sustainable long-term profits and the possibility of building strong, sustainable political advantage.

A third misunderstanding about globalization is the belief that MNEs develop homogeneous products for the world market and through their efficient production techniques are able to dominate local markets everywhere. In truth, multinationals have to adapt their products for local markets. For example, there is no global automobile. Instead there are regionally based North American, European, and Japanese factories supported by local regional suppliers that provide steel, plastic, paint, and other necessary inputs for producing the automobiles for their respective geographic triad regions. Car designs that are popular in one region of the world are often rejected by customers in other geographic areas. The Toyota Camry that dominates the U.S. market is a poor seller in Japan. The Volkswagen Golf, the largest-selling car in Europe, failed to make an impact in North America. Even pharmaceutical companies, which manufacture medicines that are often regarded as universal products, have

---

"Globalization requires that organizations adopt a cross-cultural perspective to be successful in accomplishing their goals in the context of a global economy." (Rabi Bhagat)

to modify their goods to satisfy national and state regulations, thus making centralized production and worldwide distribution economically difficult.

WORLD TRADE IS HIGHLY REGIONAL

World trade provides a good example of just how regional MNEs are. The amount of trade in terms of exports and imports has grown rapidly over the last decade, but it continues to be dominated by the triad. The latest data show that in 1997 these three regions accounted for 57.3% of world exports and 56.5% of world imports. If these trade data are examined in terms of what might be called the core triad—the United States, the EU, and Japan—the volume of exports that each group sends the others is quite small. For example, the United States exports approximately 20% of its total to the EU and 10% to Japan, while the EU exports only 8% of its total to the United States and less than 1% (0.002, to be exact) to Japan. Meanwhile, Japan exports 28% of its total to the United States and 16% to the EU. An analysis of imports reveals the same general picture. The United States gets 16% of its imports from the EU and 11% from Japan; the EU receives 8% of its imports from the United States and 4% from Japan; and Japan gets 24% of its imports from the United States and 17% from the EU.

Simply put, the core triad members do not rely on each other for most of their exports or imports. On whom do they rely? The answer is: other members of their own triad. For example, as shown in Figure 1, more than 60% of all exports by EU countries goes to other members of that triad. The core triad members can be expanded by adding Canada and Mexico to the United States, which gives us NAFTA, and then constructing a group of countries for Asia. The Asian group consists of Japan, Australia, New Zealand, China, Taiwan, Hong Kong, India, Indonesia, Malaysia, Philippines, Singapore, Thailand, and the smaller Asian Pacific economies. This gives us the broad triad. The results, shown in Figure 1, confirm that the world's trade is controlled by the triad.

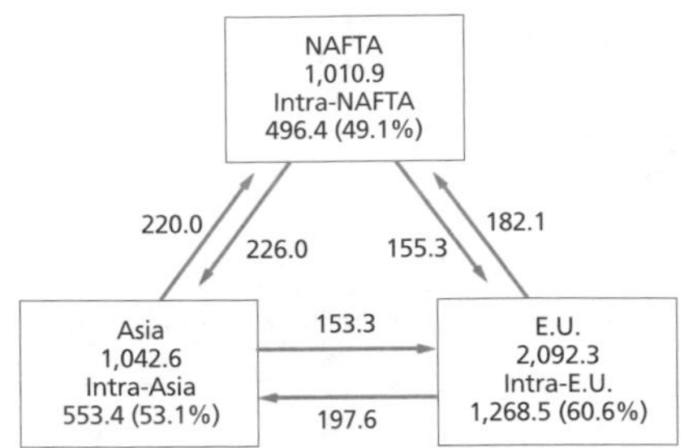

Figure 1: Exports in the broad triad
Note: Data are for 1997, in U.S. $billion.
Source: Rugman (2000)

According to data for 1997 in Figure 1, the triad's export totals U.S. $4,145.8 billion, with 60.6% of the EU exports of U.S. $2,092.3 being internal, at U.S. $1,268.5 billion. The EU exports only 8.7% to NAFTA (U.S. $182.1 billion) and 9.4% to Asia (U.S. $197.6 billion). NAFTA exports 15.4% of its total to the EU (U.S. $155.3 billion) and 22.4% to Asia (U.S. $226.0 billion). Internal NAFTA trade, at 49.1%, is surprisingly high given that Canada is only one-twelfth and Mexico only about one-twentieth the economic size of the United States. Asia exports 21.1% of its total to NAFTA (U.S. $220.0 billion) and 14.7% to the EU (U.S. $153.3 billion). The majority of Asian trade is also intra-regional.

In summary, the extent of intra-EU exports is 60.6%. For NAFTA internal trade is 49.1%, for Asia 53.1%. The majority of world trade in the European and Asian triads is within their internal markets; nearly half of North American trade is intra-regional. Most of the rest of world trade is between triad members. Given the dominance of the triad in world trade (and direct-investment data show the same picture), what strategies are appropriate for individual multinationals?

MAKING IT HAPPEN ▸▸

It is possible to offer some practical strategies for managers who want to increase their company's international revenues and profits. The most useful lessons learned are these:

- Be prepared to design strategies that take into account regional trade and investment agreements such as NAFTA and the single market of the EU.
- Learn to deal with different cultures and become nationally responsive when necessary.
- Develop new thinking and knowledge about regional business networks and triad-based clusters instead of always developing pure global strategies.
- Make alliances and foster cross-cultural awareness in your senior managers.
- Develop analytical methods for assessing regional drivers of success instead of globalization drivers: regional drivers may be more useful in the future in gaining and holding market share.
- Encourage all your managers to think regional, act local—and forget global!

For More Information

Books:

Giddens, Anthony. *Runaway World: How Globalization is Reshaping Our Lives*. New York: Routledge, 2000.
Ohmae, Kenichi. *The Borderless World: Power and Strategy in the Interlinked Economy*. New York: HarperBusiness, 1999.
Ohmae, Kenichi. *The End of the Nation State: The Rise of Regional Economies*. New York: Free Press, 1996.
Rugman, Alan M. *The End of Globalization*. New York: AMACOM, 2001.
Rugman, Alan M., and Joseph R. D'Cruz. *Multinationals as Flagship Firms*. New York: Oxford University Press, 2000.
Yip, George S. *Total Global Strategy: Updated for the Internet and Service Era*. 2nd ed. Englewood Cliffs, NJ: Prentice Hall, 2002.

See also:

The Borderless World (p. 894)
Kenichi Ohmae (pp. 1028–29)
International Management, Cross Cultural Management (pp. 2009–11)

"The United States is just one part of a global marketplace today. There isn't any offshore anymore; it's all onshore."
(Walter Wriston)

THE NEW FRONTIERS IN OLD-ECONOMY INDUSTRIES *by Adrian J. Slywotzky and David J. Morrison*

EXECUTIVE SUMMARY

- Many old-economy companies have hesitated to go digital because they believe that digital business is primarily about technology.
- Digital business is about using digital technology to expand a company's strategic options.
- Digital business design offers even old-economy companies a way to use digital technology to achieve improvements long considered unattainable.

INTRODUCTION

Many old-economy companies are still reluctant to go digital. Over the past two decades the advent of the personal computer, the proliferation of e-mail, the growth of enterprise resource planning systems, and the popularity of the Internet have created a growing awareness of digital technology as both a creative and a disruptive force. Old-economy companies, in the meantime, have tended to be more impressed by the perils than the promise of digital technology. However, there is no reason for them to fear digitization. What digital business can deliver is an expansion of your company's capabilities, its strategic options, greater efficiencies and, above all, improved customer service.

Why are old-economy firms hesitant about going digital? Most people equate digital business with particular technologies or consider it simply the sum total of the high-tech innovations multiplying around us. If they're not themselves involved in high-tech industries, companies may not only be intimidated by digital technology, but may fail to see its relevance to them.

What old-economy companies need to realize is that digital business is not about technology per se. It's not about wiring everybody in the company, providing all your salespeople with laptops, converting your R&D and manufacturing facilities to CAD/CAM, selling products through your Web site, or allowing employees to telecommute from their homes.

Digital business design is about using digital technologies to expand your company's strategic options. It's about serving customers, creating unique value propositions, leveraging talent, achieving massive improvements in productivity, and increasing and protecting profits. These should be the overriding concerns of any business, old- or new-economy.

THE POWER OF DIGITAL BUSINESS DESIGN

A comparison of two companies that most people would classify as new-economy PC manufacturers, Dell and Compaq, shows that being a digital business has nothing to do with being in a high-tech industry. In terms of the way they do business, Dell is a digital business but Compaq is not.

Compaq relies almost exclusively on retail outlets to sell its products. It guesses what demand will be, produces the number of machines it thinks customers might buy, and then tries to sell them to customers through its distributors. By contrast, Dell uses its online configurator (a digital system that allows customers to design their own PCs) to enable the company to build computers to customer specifications quickly and accurately without stockpiling inventory. Since the customer pays in full before the machine is manufactured, Dell uses the customer's money to finance production. Compaq, on the other hand, relies on traditional methods of financing to produce machines that it then ships into its distribution channels, hoping that retailers will eventually pay for them.

The reliance on guesswork can have unfortunate results. A visit to any auto dealer in the fall offers a vivid illustration: rebates, sales, and financing plans that are unprofitable for the producer, all wheeled out in an effort to get rid of unsold inventory to make room for next year's models.

Digital business design uses digital technology to enable companies to know what their customers want and to produce only those products, to do away with the guesswork and the waste of unsold inventory, and to enjoy increases in productivity, profits, and growth. Companies whose feet are planted squarely in the physical world can achieve this just as easily as those that inhabit a purely digital world.

MINI-CASES

DIGITAL PIONEERS FROM THE OLD ECONOMY

In industries from cement to financial services, innovative firms are using digital business design to achieve breakthrough performance.

Consider the cement business, the last place you would expect to find a digitally driven company. The Mexican firm *Cemex* has turned the production and delivery of a basic commodity into one of the world's most sophisticated and innovative businesses. By forging information-intensive links among its customers, production facilities, and truck dispatchers, Cemex has elevated itself to brand-name status, taken significant market share from its competitors in Mexico and elsewhere, and dramatically outpaced the competition in terms of profit margins and revenue growth.

In the office furniture industry *Herman Miller* has similarly made innovative supply-chain thinking the heart of its strategy. Using proprietary software called Z-Axis, Herman Miller created an interactive choiceboard selection system for its customers, introduced greater speed and accuracy into its ordering and manufacturing processes, and leveraged these new efficiencies into faster, more reliable delivery. The operating unit that Herman Miller created to develop these innovations was generating annual sales growth of 25% (more than three times the industry average) and producing a remarkable 40 inventory turns (against an industry average of 20) when it was integrated into the company's larger operation in 1998.

In financial services, the German firm *MLP* used digital technologies to increase revenues and profitability. MLP's growing array of digital tools gives customers opportunities for self-service while adding value to the service its financial consultants

---

"In place of 'industry,' I suggest an alternative, more appropriate term: 'business ecosystem.'"

(James Moore)

provide. By targeting a rapidly growing market of young professionals who are attuned to digital technology, MLP achieved revenue and net income growth at a compounded annual rate of 43% between 1995 and 2000, while its market capitalization increased at a rate of 96%.

Achieving Tangible Benefits from E-business

Companies that exemplify digital business design by integrating a smart business model with business-driven exploitation of digital options produce profit margins that average more than 10 points higher and growth rates almost 20 points higher than their best competition. These are very large differences. And the gap may grow wider over time as the early advantages gained by digital reinventors are consolidated and used as the basis for taking and holding even greater market share.

The pioneers of digital business have achieved such results by taking advantage of eight specific, concrete benefits of digital business design, represented by the following shifts:

- **From guessing to knowing**. With digital business design, the basis of a company's decision making shifts from guessing what customers want to knowing exactly what they want. Using interactive online choiceboards, companies can know what products their customers want before having to manufacture and distribute them, use this knowledge to improve customer satisfaction, and mine real-time customer information to find new opportunities.
- **From mismatch to perfect fit**. A major source of frustration for customers lies in the mismatch between what they actually want and the compromises that they are often forced to accept in choosing from a fixed product line. With digital business design, the value proposition that companies offer their customers shifts to a perfect fit.
- **From lag time to real time**. The need for speed in obtaining information and sharing it within a company is no secret. Digital business design enables the flow of information to shift to real time.
- **From supplier service to customer self-service**. More and more customers actually prefer the convenience of online ordering and customer service to relying on the supplier to perform these tasks. With digital business design, a company's customer service model shifts to customer self-service.
- **From low-value-added work to maximum talent leverage**. Having employees perform routine, repetitive work today is a waste of critical resources. Digital business design shifts employees' time to the most productive, customer-centric tasks.
- **From fixing errors to preventing errors**. Mistakes in order processing, manufacturing, and other processes create frustration for customers and higher costs for suppliers. With digital business design, quality control systems shift to preventing problems and errors.
- **From 10% improvement to 10× productivity**. Incremental improvements in efficiency pale beside order-of-magnitude leaps in productivity. As digitization has taken hold in industry after industry, we've seen productivity growth patterns shift from a norm of 10% improvement to 10× gains.
- **From separate silos to integrated system**. No organization can respond to the challenges and opportunities of a rapidly changing environment without being able to share vital information and act on it with minimal delay. Such rapid organizational response depends in turn on internal integration. With digital business design, organizational structure shifts from a collection of separate silos to an integrated system in which ideas and solutions are shared.

These shifts drive results that go far beyond opening a new sales channel via a Web site or achieving incremental cost reductions by automation. Taken together they offer a means to achieve differentiation, including the ability to become unique.

Making It Happen ▸▸

Ask the following questions:

- What are the most important business issues facing my organization?
- What are the smartest business design choices for responding to those issues?
- Where might digital, particularly online, technology open up new strategic options for my company?
- Which of my current activities involve managing atoms and which involve managing bits? Where can I add bits to atoms or replace atoms with bits?
- Where I must manage bits, how can I develop bit engines that will manage every one of those bits electronically? (Bit engines can include a wide range of technological tools and systems, from internal databases of product and service information to e-commerce switchboards and electronic marketplaces.)

Conclusion

Harnessed to solve your most pressing business issues, digital technologies offer opportunities for any business in any industry. By using digital business design to offer a better deal for customers, create a better system for employees, and generate a better risk-adjusted return for investors, even traditional businesses in unprofitable or slow-growth industries can achieve goals that were long considered unattainable. Digital business design is the wheel with which old-economy companies can spin straw into gold by combining great business design with smart digitization.

For More Information

Books:

Annunzio, Susan. *eLeadership: Proven Techniques for Creating an Environment of Speed and Flexibility in the Digital Economy*. New York: Simon & Schuster, 2001.

Moss Kanter, Rosabeth. *Evolve!: Succeeding in the Digital Culture of Tomorrow*. Boston, MA: Harvard Business School Press, 2001.

Web Sites:

www.mercermc.com deals with overall digital business design.

www.cisco.com; **www.dell.com**; **www.schwab.com** are the sites of three digital pioneers.

See also:

☆ **Avoiding the Mistakes of the Past: Lessons from the Startup World (pp. 129–30)**
☆ **Infusing a Company with Cutting-edge Strategy (pp. 83–84)**
☆ **Investing in Technology (pp. 243–44)**
☆ **Marketspaces (pp. 154–56)**
☆ **Maximizing a New Strategic Alliance (pp. 85–86)**
☆ **Power Struggling and Power Sharing (pp. 95–96)**
☆ **Viewpoint: Philip Kotler (pp. 53–54)**
☆ **Viewpoint: Jeffrey F. Rayport (pp. 147–49)**
✔ **How to Get the Best from E-marketplaces (pp. 634–35)**
Rosabeth Moss Kanter (pp. 1008–09)

"New markets open not only because of novel technologies; shifts in values and culture also are potent sources of innovation."
(Stewart Clegg)

Corporate-level Strategy *by David R. Sadtler*

Executive Summary

- The parent company should add more value than others owners could.
- The skills at the center need to match the improvement opportunities in the businesses.
- Geographic and sectoral diversification are to be avoided; there are other ways to grow.
- Vertical integration is unlikely to succeed.
- When value added no longer seems feasible, demerge or break up completely.
- Good central managers never stop demanding real and substantial value added.

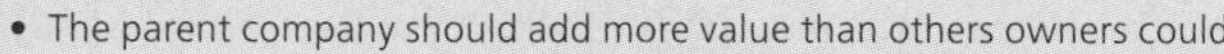

Introduction

Implementing a successful corporate-level strategy has become an urgent priority for all conglomerates. Parent companies must demonstrate that they are creating shareholder value by their own actions and initiatives, and not just reaping the profits of the businesses in their charge. The sanctions for being seen to fail in this challenge can be severe. At the very least, share prices will suffer; at the other extreme, predators will force a breakup.

A Framework

The challenge of corporate-level strategy is to ensure that value is being added to every business in the company's portfolio. That value must, of course, be in excess of its cost. Conglomerates with good corporate strategies do even better: they add more value than other companies in the same businesses.

Ensuring that this value-added process is productive requires several actions by top management:

First, it must identify ways in which each business can be helped. This help must make possible a major improvement in business performance. Without an understanding of where improvement potential exists, the search for value added cannot be real and substantial. These improvement opportunities should be identified and agreed on through managerial dialogue and business-planning systems.

Second, central management must make sure that it possesses the skills to provide the needed help. Different kinds of improvement opportunities require different forms of help. Management must see that it has those capabilities.

Third, it must construct a portfolio of businesses in which this constructive fit—useful skills attuned to the needs of the businesses—exists. How businesses can be helped is bound to change over time. The strength of the fit must be continually reappraised.

Fourth, management must ensure that it is sufficiently familiar with the requirements for success of each business and that it will not damage that business, whether by approving the wrong investment proposals, appointing the wrong general managers, or giving poor strategic guidance.

Questions For Management

The pursuit of added value often presents managers with challenging issues to resolve.

How can we grow if our core business is limited in terms of further expansion? This question arises when management has divested businesses that didn't fit and is left with one core business. If it has a commanding market share, competes in a non-growing market, and has little opportunity for overseas expansion, the dilemma can be a real one. This is especially true in an era in which capital markets reject diversification and demand that companies stick to their knitting.

Capital markets are wary of any form of corporate diversification. They are simply being pragmatic: experience has shown them that diversification doesn't work well. What is the single-business company to do to find growth opportunities? There are four possible answers:

First, seek a way to reinvent the business by looking for new customers, new markets, new ways to present the product, and a better package of customer value to offer. Even commodity products can be differentiated by offering them in a different service context. First, make certain that growth limits really have been reached.

Second, consider moves into related businesses that share existing resources and skills. Such initiatives should possess the same requirements for success. If not, the management skills both at the business-unit level and in the parent company may be inadequate to the challenge.

Third, operate a nursery of new ideas. Business unit managers are always on the lookout for new products and markets. The more promising should be regarded as new-product research and development initiatives. Those that offer promise can then receive modest investment until there is a persuasive reason to make a serious commitment.

Finally, although unconventional in today's environment, it may be smart simply to operate the existing low-growth business for cash flow, eschewing major growth aspirations. Mature industries can often be sustained for a long time without heavy investment and achieve above-average returns.

What's wrong with vertical integration as a way of extending the opportunities for a stagnant business? In other words, why shouldn't we acquire our customer to guarantee an outlet for our products?

Vertical integration has increasingly lost favor among thoughtful managers. While it may seem like a sensible proposition to guarantee a supply of raw materials or markets for your products, vertical integration frequently exhibits three major shortcomings:

First, when one division sells products to another division, disagreement often arises about transfer pricing and product and service quality. The selling division realizes it has a captive customer and often works less hard to retain the business. Much time is wasted resolving such intramural issues.

Second, entry into new upstream or downstream businesses often involves competing with your existing customers. Several corporate breakups have been the result of the realization that this problem was insoluble under the existing ownership arrangements.

Third, entry into new businesses often involves dealing with differing requirements for success; it thus requires a new range of managerial skills and capabilities,

---

"The essence of strategy is not the structure of a company's products and markets, but the dynamics of its behavior."

(Tom Peters)

both at the business-unit level and in the parent company. Mistakes are made, and the business suffers competitively.

Is it wise to limit the number of eggs in our basket? Management teams often seek positions in different industrial sectors simply to spread risk. They reason that when one sector is unattractive owing to a cyclical market turndown, other sectors can take up the slack. While this can give comfort to management teams, it's an unwise strategy in today's markets. Capital markets will say: We can spread our own risk; you do what you know how to do. The management team that focuses its effort and investment on areas in which it has demonstrable skills will be rewarded appropriately in capital pricing.

Demerger and Breakup

When it becomes clear that a failed corporate strategy is in place—when you recognize that substantial and discernible value is not being added—the question of portfolio changes arises. In some cases this may involve simply a trade, sale, or demerger of the business for which there is no fit. Sometimes, when the value-added formula has substantially dissipated, total breakup is indicated: the company ceases to exist in its entirety and breaks into several pieces.

Successful corporate strategists believe in the primacy of value added. They constantly seek out ways to provide the kind of help the businesses in the corporate portfolio need. They continually search for major improvement opportunities among the businesses. They adjust both their portfolio of businesses and the capabilities of the parent company to provide a continuing match between the needs of the business units and what the parent can provide. And when the businesses need no further help of the sort they can offer—and this often happens—they wish them Godspeed and release them into the outside world

Mini-case

The U.K. conglomerate *Hanson Trust* offers a superb example of how to do it right. During the 1970s and 1980s it built a portfolio of low-tech, mature businesses by means of acquisition and disposal. It sought out undermanaged companies with major positions in mature businesses, looking for opportunities to strengthen their competitive position by tight disciplined management. When its acquisitions brought in businesses that didn't fit Hanson's profile, they were disposed of. Hanson was clear about its value-added formula: it found businesses whose fortunes could be dramatically improved through tight financial discipline and strong general management motivation. It worked well and shareholders benefited greatly.

In the 1990s it became apparent that the formula no longer had much to offer shareholders. Major opportunities for the Hanson treatment were waning, especially in the United Kingdom and the United States. All the fat targets had been exploited. At the same time computer-facilitated financial control systems made Hanson's approach an ordinary corporate capability. Finally the businesses in the Hanson stable became so well run that there was little improvement potential left. Realizing that the value-added formula had become obsolete, the company broke itself up into five pieces, each one of which has thrived competitively on its own.

The same caution should be applied to overseas diversification. Some management teams intentionally direct investment to different parts of the world in order to limit exposure in any one area. Unless such geographic expansion is initiated to strengthen one's competitive positioning in a particular global marketplace, the investment community is likely to scorn this form of expansion. There are simply too many downsides to investment abroad to undertake it without a solid competitive business rationale. Currency exposure, entry into alien market environments, and bone-wearying travel all represent significant costs of expanding internationally.

Making It Happen ▸▸

- Make sure that value is being added to every business in the portfolio by identifying ways in which each can be helped to achieve major improvement in performance.
- Restrict the portfolio to activities in which a constructive fit—useful skills attuned to the needs of the businesses—exists at the center.
- If growth prospects appear limited, try reinvention, moves into related businesses, new ideas, or a cash-cow strategy.
- Consider vertical integration as a way of extending strategic opportunities.
- Focus effort and investment on areas in which you have demonstrable skills: don't diversify into unknown areas.
- When substantial and discernible value is not being added, change the portfolio.

For More Information

Books:

Galbraith, Jay R. *Designing Organizations: An Executive Guide to Strategy, Structure, and Process*. San Francisco, CA: Jossey-Bass, 2002.

Goold, Michael, et al. *Corporate-Level Strategy*. New York: John Wiley, 1994.

Kare-Silver, Michael de. *Strategy in Crisis*. New York: New York University Press, 1998.

Kraines, Gerald A. *Accountability Leadership: How to Strengthen Productivity Through Sound Managerial Leadership*. Franklin Lakes, NJ: The Career Press, Inc., 2001.

Mintzberg, Henry. *The Rise and Fall of Strategic Planning*. New York: Prentice Hall, 1994.

Useem, Michael. *Leading Up: How to Lead Your Boss so You Both Win*. New York: Crown Business, 2001.

See also:

☆ **Building Great Internal Partnerships (pp. 281–82)**
☆ **Intrapreneurial Warriors Versus Traditional Managers (pp. 125–26)**
☆ **Turnaround Strategies (pp. 251–52)**
☆ **Viewpoint: Henry Mintzberg (pp. 241–42)**
The Rise and Fall of Strategic Planning (p. 949)
Henry Mintzberg (pp. 1024–25)
Corporate Strategy (pp. 1944–46)

STRATEGIC AGILITY *by John Wells*

EXECUTIVE SUMMARY

- Whenever there's an economic slump, management focus shifts to cutting costs.
- This is only of benefit if at the same time the opportunity is taken to build a more agile business platform.
- There are several different levels of approach to cost management, from talking about it to taking the long-term strategic view.
- Most of these approaches have an impact on systems architecture–or they should.

INTRODUCTION

With the crash of technology stocks turning into a general economic slump, top management focus is shifting from investing in new technology and business ideas to cutting costs. But badly directed cost-cutting delivers no better return on investment than the speculation in e-commerce that was so characteristic of the 2000 boom. When the pressure is on to cut costs, a C.E.O. has a tough choice to make: simply make bold cuts without consideration of future needs, or invest in taking the first steps to building a much more agile business platform that will allow the firm to exploit future opportunities and respond more quickly to change.

How quickly times change. How short are investors' memories. One minute the stock market is booming and companies are being driven to invest in e-commerce at almost any cost to protect their stock rating. The next minute the e-bubble has burst and no C.E.O. who wants to stay on the job is talking about new e-commerce initiatives. It's time for consolidation, focus, cutting costs.

This is unfortunate, because e-commerce, wisely deployed, provides a powerful competitive weapon in a downturn as well as in boom times. But this is not what investors want to hear. They insist that now is the time for bold announcements to cut costs and reduce head count, and there are several approaches to choose from.

MAKING IT HAPPEN ▸▸

Level Zero cost management: talking about it

The simplest and least-disruptive approach to cost cutting is to talk about it but not actually do much. This is common practice in companies that acquire other businesses with the promise of major cost-reduction synergies that then fail to materialize. For instance, Bank of America, which grew from Nations Bank into the number one U.S. consumer bank in a 30-year binge of more than 100 acquisitions, never realized major cost synergies until a new management came in.

Level One cost management: arbitrary cuts

A more dramatic approach to cost management is to cut all discretionary expenses (consultants, bowls of fresh fruit) and demand head count reductions across the board. But cutting costs without tackling the underlying causes is often a short-lived solution. Costs have a nasty habit of growing back. Savings promised by the majority of cost-reduction programs disappear within two years, never delivering the returns required to justify the high price paid for them.

Level One cost management is fast, decisive, and sometimes very necessary in a crisis, but it's seldom optimal. While it may be a short-term palliative for investors, it is seldom in the best long-term interests of the corporation.

Level Two cost management: redesign business processes to meet today's needs

Rather than simply cutting costs, the challenge is to deal with the underlying causes of cost. This takes reengineering business processes to design costs out. Rather than simply reducing the amount of resource allocated to an old process in the hope that it will work harder, the objective is to redesign the process so that it requires less resource in the first place. This is more thoughtful—and more effective–cost-cutting.

Level Three cost management: redesign business processes to meet tomorrow's needs

There is a danger of changing processes to meet today's immediate needs without paying attention to the future, so that when business improves another expensive process redesign is required. Every C.E.O. knows there are a host of actions that must be taken if the firm is to prosper, but some must be deferred until financial conditions improve and shareholders have more of an appetite for investment. The process redesign should take these into account, ensuring that the firm is ready to expand its activities when the time is ripe.

Level Four cost management: meeting unforeseen needs

But how can an organization *really* be future-proof? What about those unforeseen events that demand sudden changes? It's not possible to design a set of business processes to meet every eventuality. And yet an organization can't afford to redesign all of its processes every time it encounters change. The challenge is to shape a process architecture that can be more easily adapted to change.

The way to achieve this is to shape processes in a way that decouples them from each other as much as possible, allowing local changes to be made in a single process without major redesign of the total system. This is component-based process architecture.

Level Five cost management: self-adaptive systems

Decoupling processes also allows the team of people responsible for operating each process to look for improvements continuously. If they are incentivized to behave in this way, then when changes occur the process is quickly modified to meet the new needs. The process and the people who operate it form a component of the organization.
To be really adaptive the component team must have the ability to modify and improve the process themselves. This makes for really rapid response. The component, and the organization as a whole, then become much more agile and adaptive.

"The starting point for next year's strategy is almost always this year's strategy. . .the company sticks to what it knows, even though the real opportunities may be elsewhere." (Gary Hamel)

  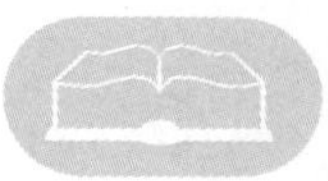    

MINI-CASE

Wells Fargo saw the opportunity to offer loans to small businesses on the Web, collecting credit-check information on each applicant in real time to decide on whether to approve a loan. The company envisaged an automated loan manager and backroom support service that were much more cost-effective than the human variety.

The initial service was very well received. Not only did it cut costs, but it provided much quicker response to the customer, and it began driving up market share.

The next challenge came when Wells Fargo wanted to change its criteria for making loans. This process had traditionally taken up to six months, limiting flexibility and responsiveness to changing market demands. One solution would have been simply to wire in the new loan criteria. However, sufficiently dissatisfied by its past experience, in this phase Wells Fargo sought to componentize the system, isolating the criteria from the rest of the system so that they could be changed more easily. Moreover, rather than simply inserting a new set of criteria into the criteria module, the company built a criteria generator. Instead of requiring expensive IT resource to change the criteria, the department managers could do it themselves, taking days instead of months.

Far from limiting the number of criteria, Wells Fargo made its solution even smarter by making sure that the criteria component allowed the addition of more, as yet unidentified, criteria, providing the system with the agility to react to the unknown. The bank avoided the temptation to implement a Level Two solution and moved directly to a Level Five solution, dealing with known changes and changes as yet unknown while empowering the management team to look continuously for improvements.

THE IMPLICATIONS FOR INFORMATION SYSTEMS: COMPONENTIZED SYSTEMS ARCHITECTURE

Redesigning processes almost always means changing the information systems that support the processes. And the trouble is that old legacy systems get in the way. Hence the frustration with IT departments. Rather than being seen as the driver of change, IT is often seen as the greatest impediment to change in large organizations.

Old legacy platforms are typically hugely complex systems tied together to help run the company. A minor change in one part of the system can have major and unpredictable impact on other parts, rather like the proverbial butterfly that starts a hurricane in the Caribbean by fluttering in South America.

The challenge for legacy IT systems is the same as for organizational processes, to be able to break them down into loosely coupled components so that each component can be changed without affecting the organization as a whole.

The IT components must map 100% onto organizational process components, so that when a department component sees opportunities for improvement it can change without disrupting the whole organization. The IT system can be adapted in parallel to support the change without changing the whole IT system. The capacity for change when this alignment is achieved is obviously very large.

CONCLUSION

Deal with today's challenge with tomorrow in mind.

But when a company is facing major economic challenges how can it find time to worry about componentizing its IT platform? The reality is that a company must be guided by its component architecture whenever it makes change. Take the current plethora of legacy systems and identify the role each will play in a more flexible componentized architecture. In the context of a clear long-term view, legacy systems can be changed in ways that contribute to the long-term agenda.

For More Information

Books:

Fountain, Jane E. *Building the Virtual State: Information Technology and Institutional Change*. Washington, D.C.: Brookings Institution, 2001.

Labovitz, George, and Victor Rosansky. *The Power of Alignment: How Great Companies Stay Centered and Accomplish Extraordinary Things*. New York: John Wiley, 1997.

Moss Kanter, Rosabeth. *Evolve! Succeeding in the Digital Culture of Tomorrow*. Boston, MA: Harvard Business School Press, 2001.

Web Site:

http://cor-ex.com/sites/bestchng/index.htm: with help from Amazon.com, the Best Corporate Change Resources site acts as a gateway to a wide variety of resources—books, journals and Web sites—all on the topic of information technology and change.

See also:

☆ **Integrating Technology into Business (pp. 169–70)**
☆ **The New Frontiers of Old-economy Industries (pp. 99–100)**
Rosabeth Moss Kanter (pp. 1008–09)
Computers, Information Technology, and E-commerce (pp. 1931–33)

VIEWPOINT: WATTS WACKER AND RYAN MATHEWS

The Dance of Authenticity

Watts Wacker and Ryan Mathews are principals in FirstMatter LLC, a company that focuses on the future and its implications for organizations and businesses. While Wacker has roots in both SRI International and Yakelovich Partners, Mathews has an extensive background in retailing. Together, they challenge leaders around the globe to think about change as a primal force, one that must be both understood and managed.

Martin Heidegger, despite his politics perhaps still the greatest metaphysician of the 20th century, argued that the fact that our existence is embodied in cultural context explains our apparently collective predisposition to inauthenticity. Confronted by our fears, he argued, we almost instinctively choose the comfort of anonymity over the burdens of authenticity. As Heidegger saw it, we flee from the core issue of our existence (death) and insulate ourselves in mantles of social convention and conformity, voluntarily abdicating the right and ability to seize control of and define our own lives. In Heidegger's lexicon, authenticity is achieved only when we face what he calls "being-toward-death." Heidegger wasn't alone. In *Hero with a Thousand Faces*, Joseph Campbell echoed the German philosopher when he wrote ". . .the hero would be no hero if death held for him any terror; the first condition is reconciliation with the grave."

To be authentic, Heidegger argued, is to be transformed: to face up clearly and honestly to the responsibility for what one's own life adds up to in its entirety, and to seize onto the possibilities present in our community or shared "heritage" in order to realize a communal "destiny." We agree with Heidegger and Campbell. Authenticity isn't defined by a single act or an isolated moment in time, for either an individual or a corporation. Rather it's a sum total of all the aspects of an individual's or business's being-in-the-world, both their inner being and their public face and presence. Authenticity, then, is about a life, and, by extension, a life's work. In the case of a business, it's about a brand's or company's life and its lifetime relationships with customer or consumers. Authenticity is both life's greatest achievement and, historically, its most daunting challenge. We believe that from this day forward, life, both individual and collective will be characterized by what we call "the abolition of context" or the most complete absence of a unifying and defining social canon. If achieving authenticity has been difficult in the past, it will exponentially be more difficult in the future.

As a society, and as individuals, we're at best ambivalent about authenticity. On the one hand we ostensibly demand the authentic and on the other we live lives slavishly devoted to the heedless and mindless pursuit of the shallow and the banal. We speak of pursuing the eternal truths–love, peace, and freedom–while all the while we're enslaved by style and convention. This ambivalence infects everything we do, from the trivial to the transcendent. We claim to be devoted to the authentic, but we are addicted to the new, no matter how superficial it is. Even our rebellions and statements of personal eccentricity are calculated. We coast through existence as self-styled bohemians in BMWs and as intellectuals pondering the cosmic meaning of MTV. We are publicly virtuous and privately venial.

Our collective obsession with the new deploys cool-hunters, trend pimps, hip social chroniclers, and mass media vampires who are all in search of the next *real* big thing. The irony, of course, is that authenticity is far more often a casualty rather than a characteristic of social acceptance. The faster we drag products, ideas, or individuals from their origins on the fringe toward the center of convention, the faster we kill their authenticity.

Is it possible to balance our insatiable craving for the authentic with our ravenous appetite for the superficial and phoney? Clearly, one of the reasons our search for authenticity yields such barren fruit is that we generally begin it in the wrong places. Really authentic things exist at either end of a continuum that begins beyond the edge we're always told to live on at a place we call "the Fringe," which extends outside the sterile and artificial confines of mainstream social convention. The Fringe is the place where the primordial soup of innovation and creativity resides. Most ideas, people, and products moving out of that part of the continuum lose part of all their authenticity on the journey.

Businesses are as inept in their pursuits of authenticity as people are. Each year global businesses spend billions of dollars prattling on about how their product is genuine, their service personalized, intimate, and engaged, their prices the lowest possible, and about how their companies are devoted to the selfless altruistic principle of the betterment of consumer lives. No wonder we don't trust them! Businesses can't declare themselves to be authentic, that's the customer's job. Brands can't assert they are authentic, they can only be seen as such. And when marketing and advertising tread too close to reality–as in the case of Benetton–they often fall foul of it. Of course, that isn't to say that businesses can't act authentically. Reebok is heavily engaged in the struggle for human rights, values reflected in both its corporate philanthropy and its supply-chain labor policies, but it pub-

"Some of the worst men in the world are sincere and the more sincere they are the worse they are."

(Quintin Hogg)

  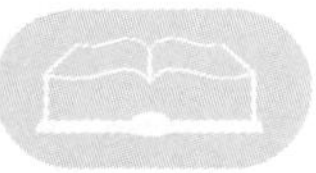    

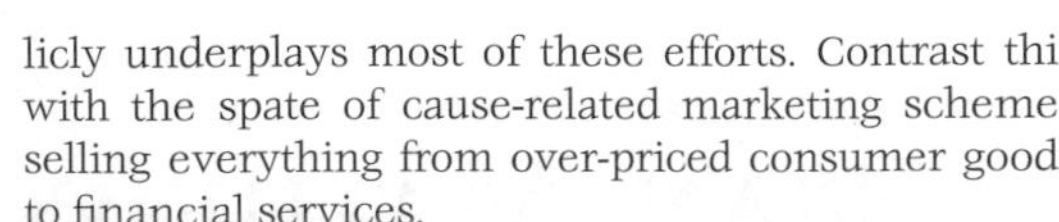

licly underplays most of these efforts. Contrast this with the spate of cause-related marketing schemes selling everything from over-priced consumer goods to financial services.

As the 21st century unfolds, we believe authenticity may be the primary criterion to differentiate products. Technology has simply moved too fast for it to be credible that one can sustain a product innovation on a proprietary basis for any length of time. The best most businesses can hope to enjoy is a six-month innovation advantage before their competitors introduce a similar, and often improved and lower-cost, version of their product. After all, they don't have to recoup all those burdensome research and development costs. Authenticity by its very nature can't be copied, and any attempt to do so makes the clone appear all the more phoney.

Another way to look at this is to say that whatever a company or organization does inherently exists outside the domain of authenticity. Authenticity only comes into play when you stop listening to what a company says and begin examining how it lives and what it believes. The search for authenticity—personal or commercial—isn't easy. If it were, we'd live in a much different world. But no matter how difficult the goal, it's more than worth the effort.

We began this discussion with Martin Heidegger and we'd like to conclude it with the French philosopher, journalist, novelist, and playwright Albert Camus. Camus's work often dealt with antiheroes who acted out of authenticity, which he defined as freedom from any conventional expectations about what "human nature" required in a situation. His characters embrace total personal responsibility and, in their best moments, share an almost painful lucidity that disallows them from living in what Camus called bad faith, or lying to themselves. Obviously, from the point of view of the mainstream, Camus's "heroes" are deviants, oddities, and in fact, often criminals. Given the inauthenticity of the world any genuine act is almost invariably suspect.

Indeed, whenever a business comes dangerously close to acting authentically it is attacked—by prying mediavistas looking for a corporate Achilles heel; by analysts ready to downgrade companies who are honest; and from individuals who have been schooled in the arts of skepticism and negativity. No wonder so many businesses opt for the inauthentic! It generally pays better.

Earlier we said that authenticity night be the only area of sustainable competitive differentiation. In the same way an individual must choose whether to live his or her life authentically or to conform to the inauthentic demands of society or business, commercial entities must choose whether or not they will walk the path of authenticity. Remember, customer rhetoric aside, being authentic isn't always a commercially successful formula. For one thing, authenticity is often expensive. For another, it's rarely socially acceptable. Big Mama Thornton's version of "Hound Dog" is authentic; Elvis Presley's was a commercial success. Somehow white America just wasn't ready for a black woman who dressed in men's clothes growling about illicit sex. Elvis didn't change the words much, but he ratcheted down the menacing attitude enough to not scare the Caucasians. But perhaps authenticity's single largest failing as a market offering is its tendency to remind us of our own inauthenticity. Most of us don't do well by comparison when we find ourselves in the presence of the truly real, the nakedly honest, or something that is undeniably itself.

Things may be a bit different in the 21st century, however. The empty promises of inauthenticity have delivered us into a world of dangerous social inequality, political instability, and a growing consolidation across a broad band of commercial markets. Inauthenticity, it seems, is a scalable offering. The battle, so close to the hearts of 20th century existentialists like Heidegger and Camus, is intensifying in the 21st century. We live in a world in which the inauthentic sells at the same time as the antihero—from the terrorist to the entrepreneurial maverick—routinely triumphs, at least in the short run. We believe both trends. If Camus was correct, are these signs that an authentic world isn't far away?

For More Information

See also:

- ☆ **Corporate Social Responsibility (pp. 291–92)**
- ☆ **Urbane Renewal (pp. 320–21)**
- ☆ **Viewpoint: Charles Handy (pp. 75–76)**
- **Social Responsibility of Management (pp. 2115–17)**

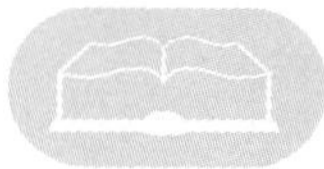

THE HUMAN VALUE OF ENTERPRISE
by Andrew Mayo

EXECUTIVE SUMMARY

- People are often spoken of as assets, but are generally treated as costs, because we have no credible system of valuing them.
- The problem is that in today's knowledge-based organizations value is driven more by people than by any other factor.
- There are five approaches to building a measurement system for people, or human capital.
- One of these, the attempt to value people financially, is known as human resource accounting.
- Current best practice looks at quantifying the value of people in terms of their characteristics and the value they produce in both financial and nonfinancial terms.

INTRODUCTION

Our people are our most important asset. This frequent statement from chief executives is often received with justifiable cynicism. The problem is that people within an organization do not always experience decisions and policies in their everyday work life that support such a belief. They are much more likely to see their organization driven by the search for increased efficiency and minimized costs, in which people are effectively regarded as costs.

There are many reasons for this. One is the illogical domination of management by the bottom line—often resulting in a very short-term mindset. This single-mindedness is illogical because it is out of balance, the drivers and causes of the final outcomes being generally given much less attention. A powerful system of financial processes and targets dominates the life of most managers. Measures of intangibles such as employees' capability or customers' loyalty may exist, but they are excluded from the monitoring and control systems.

Another problem is that people do not fit the strict financial definition of an asset. They cannot be transacted at will, their contribution is individually distinctive and variable (and subject to motivation and environment), and they cannot easily be valued according to traditional financial principles. But perhaps the greatest problem is the lack of pressure for credible measures that relate to people and their contribution. For too long we have been accustomed to think of people solely in terms of costs and head count—the very term *human resources* reflects this.

THE VALUE OF HUMAN RESOURCE ACCOUNTING

IS THERE A PROBLEM TO BE SOLVED?

There is indeed a major problem. The valuation of companies has progressively changed since about 1990, putting a much higher value on intangible assets like knowledge, competence, brands, and systems. These assets are also known as the *intellectual capital* of the organization. The issue is that we have no comparable system of measurement that enables us to give these the same balanced attention we give to financial matters. The result is that decisions about investment and resources are not necessarily in the long-term interest of the shareholders, even though they may appear to be at the time they are made. A classic case is making key people redundant only to hire them back when the value they contributed is suddenly recognized.

"But," says David Norton, coauthor of *The Balanced Scorecard*, believes "the worst grades are reserved for the typical executive team for their understanding of strategies for developing human capital. There is little consensus, little creativity, and no real framework for thinking about the subject. Worse yet, we have seen little improvement in this over the past eight years. The asset that is the most important is the least understood, least prone to measurement, and hence the least susceptible to management."

MEASURING THE PEOPLE DIMENSION

The various ways in which a measurement system has been applied to people can be summarized as follows.

- **Attempting to value people financially as assets: human resource (or asset) accounting**. This will be discussed in more detail below.
- **Creating an index of good HR practices and relating them to business results.** Researchers including Mark Huselid of Rutgers University and consultancies such as Watson Wyatt have shown positive correlation between investment in HR management and shareholder value.
- **Statistically analyzing the composition of the workforce and measures of employees' productivity and output.** The best-known proponent here is Jac Fitz-Enz of the Saratoga Institute, California, who has extensively deployed ratios of all kinds and conducts a worldwide benchmarking practice.
- **Measuring the efficiency of HR functions and processes and the return on investment for people initiatives and programs.** Dave Ulrich of the University of Michigan is the champion of this approach.
- **Integrating people-related measures through a performance management framework.** These are frameworks that look for balance in performance measures between the needs of the different stakeholders, or in relation to the component parts of the total intangible assets. The best known is Robert Kaplan and David Norton's *balanced scorecard*. An alternative approach comes from Karl-Erik Sveiby of Sweden, whose *intellectual capital monitor* chooses a small number of measures for three kinds of intellectual capital—customer, structural, and human.

The most comprehensive approach to the human dimension is found in Mayo's *human capital monitor*. This links three areas of measurement:

- the human capital that people lend to organizations in exchange for the value added to them
- the financial and nonfinancial value for stakeholders that this human capital produces
- the motivation and commitment of the people, which depend primarily on the environment in which they work

"Get to know your people." (Robert Townsend)

VALUING PEOPLE AS ASSETS

There are three criteria for defining any asset.

- It must possess future service potential.
- It is measurable in monetary terms.
- It is subject to the ownership and control of the firm, or it is rented or leased.

Traditional methods of coming to a valuation include

- *cost-based.* This method typically looks at acquisition or replacement cost. The costs of recruiting an employee can be assessed and then depreciated over the expected future service of the person hired. Alternatively the person's gross remuneration can be used as a base.
- *market-based.* The price to be paid in an open market must be a reflection of the value of a person. Value is very difficult to assess, however, and does not take account of the value of service continuity in itself.
- *income-based.* The cash inflows expected by the organization related to the contribution of the human asset, calculated as the present value of the expected net cash flows. This is good for individuals whose efforts are directly related to identifiable income.

Human resource accounting, or human asset accounting, has been primarily developed in the United States under the guidance of Eric Flamholz. Flamholtz sees the value of a person as the product of two interacting variables—their conditional value and the probability that the person will stay with the organization for x years. *Conditional value* is the present worth of the potential services that could be rendered if the individual stayed with the organization, and is a combination of productivity (performance), transferability (flexible skills), and promotability. The latter two elements are heavily influenced by the first. This figure is then multiplied by a *probability* factor: the probability that the person will stay for the x years. This gives the *expected realizable value*, which is a measure of the person's worth. There are a number of difficulties with this approach, not least of which is the estimation of potential future services. It also leads to lower values for older and more experienced people who have less time to render future services. There is a case for looking at them this way if we consider value over a future lifetime, but it fails to take account of the wealth of value in past experience.

MAKING IT HAPPEN ▸▸

Finding a relevant and robust measure of the value of employees has developed as an issue of major importance. Giles and Robinson have developed a factor called the human asset multiplier, which is applied to gross remuneration. This reflects a number of intrinsically valuable attributes of individuals. Mayo came to similar conclusions, namely that whereas it would be really helpful if we could have a realistic, generally accepted, absolute financial formula, this is unlikely to be achieved. But an approach that at least enables people's relative values to be compared against their costs would be a major step forward. He proposed a formula for what he called the human asset worth, where

HAW (human asset worth) = EC (employment cost) × IAM (individual asset multiplier) ÷ 1,000

(The divisor of 1,000 is used so that the resulting number does not look like a financial one.)

The individual asset multiplier is designed to reflect the factors that contribute most of the value that an individual brings. The four identified are

- capability in terms of cumulative skills, knowledge, experience, and useful network
- potential to grow and contribute at a higher level
- contribution to stakeholder value
- alignment with organizational values.

Each of these factors is assessed on a scale of 0.1 to 2.0, weighted for importance, and then added together to give the multiplier.

Such a formula can lead to tools such as a *human asset register*, which can monitor changes and compare teams and units. The process of analyzing the individual components may lead to strategies for change in the organization. It can be argued strongly that such tools are at least as important as those used for cost management.

CONCLUSION

The term *human capital* can be used to describe the asset value of your people. Maximizing human capital through acquisition, retention, and growth should be a major priority of all executives, not an area left to the HR department alone. It is the area in which measurement is least well understood.

It is worth noting that people are the one factor of production that drives all others. The value that a company creates results from the way that people apply their skills, energies, and expertise to the capital and raw materials that customers want. Of all the business levers available to business leaders, the greatest potential to build value is offered by people. It is hardly surprising, therefore, that there should be so much interest and concern about remuneration, designed to attract and retain talented employees. It is also unsurprising that a rigorous approach to valuing this most significant asset should gain in importance.

For More Information

Books:

Davenport, Thomas O. *Human Capital: What It Is and Why People Invest in It.* San Francisco, CA: Jossey-Bass, 1999.
Flamholtz, Eric G. *Human Resource Accounting: Advances in Concepts, Methods, and Applications.* 3rd ed. New York: Kluwer, 1999.
Mayo, Andrew. *The Human Value of the Enterprise: Valuing People as Assets—Monitoring, Measuring, Managing.* Naperville, IL: Nicholas Brealey, 2001.

Web Site:

www.sveiby.se: the very informative site of pioneering thinker Karl Erik Sveiby, who developed the principles of analyzing intellectual capital.

See also:

☆ **Finding and Keeping Top Talent (pp. 33–34)**
☆ **Human Capital (pp. 115–16)**
Accounting (pp. 1899–1901)

"A leader is a man who has the ability to get other people to do what they don't want to do and like it." (Harry Truman)

  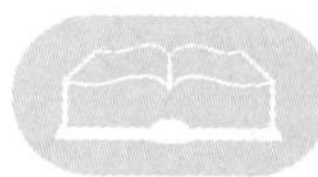    

Return on Talent *by Subir Chowdhury*

Executive Summary

- The performance of an organization is determined by the performance of its employees.
- Organizations must therefore measure return on talent as well as return on investment.
- Knowledge is one of the most important factors for business success. If knowledge assets are increased, related factors such as sales will also increase.
- Talent—or intellectual capital—has fast become one of the most significant areas of business activity and competition.

Introduction

The performance of an organization is entirely determined by the performance of its employees. This bold statement deserves further study. If the determinant of corporate performance is not its employees, what is? Is it strategic intent? Core competencies? Manufacturing? Is it proprietary technologies? The best equipment and laboratories? A visionary C.E.O.? Yes, it's all of these things. And all of these things are created and constantly improved by employees. Talented employees are the change agents. Good employees join in to help implement new initiatives. Others follow at various times depending on when they can break the bonds of their comfort zone to enter the area of change, uncertainty, and opportunity. They fall by the wayside because they were in the wrong job.

It is broadly recognized that past performance is not a reliable indicator of potential or future success. Yet many organizations continue to use past performance to identify high-potential employees. How much true talent is overlooked by this practice?

Overlooked and misplaced high-potential employees stagnate. The problem of identifying, positioning, and compensating high-potential employees spans all disciplines and levels from the loading dock to the boardroom. Lost and underused employees represent enormous, largely unattended financial loss. A second problem is the difficulty in measuring the financial contribution of employees beyond global measures such as revenues per employee.

To focus a successful organization, managers must use a new tool called return on talent (ROT). Most organizations focus on return on investment (ROI) and fail to understand the key strategy of how to increase ROI by increasing ROT.

Harnessing Talent

ROT has the power to revolutionize business. ROT is calculated by dividing the knowledge generated and applied by the investment in talent. You need to address the dilemma of how to measure an intangible asset and how to generate high ROT value. For decades, organizations have used key metrics like ROI and ROA (return on assets) to determine value. But increasingly an effective new-economy organization will use ROT. Current business measurements merely measure the use of capital, but ROT is expressed as follows:

ROT = knowledge generated and applied ÷ investment in talent

If you have talented people, knowledge is just one component. The generation of knowledge is the most important thing talent can provide. Now you may realize that knowledge generated by the talent doesn't equal knowledge applied, right? And if knowledge isn't applied, the company loses most of the market value of that knowledge. Whatever knowledge a person generates in a year divided by how much is invested in that particular person is the value.

If an employee generates many innovative ideas but never implements any of them, that person fails to generate any value, because the return to the company is zero. Knowledge generated does not necessarily mean knowledge applied. So value is knowledge generated *and* applied. Knowledge becomes an asset only when it's captured and used effectively; if it isn't effectively applied, it can't generate any yield or ROI. Generating a lot of knowledge within organizations doesn't add any value unless that knowledge is used in effective strategy formulation. Knowledge assets, like money or equipment, are worth cultivating only in the context of strategy. You can't define and manage intellectual assets unless you know what you are trying to do with them. This is the backbone of the knowledge economy; success in this field depends on mastery of talent, just as success in manufacturing relies on the skillful employment of plant and supply chains.

The Value of Knowledge

1. Return on Talent

The value of knowledge generated increases with its effective deployment. Effective knowledge generated means high ROT. It leads to a creative work force, innovations, smooth processes, continuous product improvements, and improved communications. It helps management to be flexible, to capitalize on opportunities, and to keep pace with the changing business climate. Talented people influence those around them, and their knowledge is shared over time. Top knowledge generators should be rewarded. If managers expect top talent to achieve their maximum performance and produce maximum return, they must not place them in routine jobs.

ROT measures the payback from investment in people; it shows whether managers are hiring the right people and how effectively they use them to achieve business success. It can be a quantitative or qualitative measurement, based on management's viewpoint. Are managers getting the maximum payback on their investment? If managers want to see quantitative results, they need to put a price on knowledge generated, based on the results achieved. Talent generates knowledge, which is one of the greatest assets in the global economy. True knowledge brings creativity and innovation and adds value to the company. Knowledge has become a key production factor, along with traditional resources such as raw materials, buildings, and machinery. Companies that measure the knowledge generated and applied by their talent can make their investments in talent more profitable. Further, companies cannot improve what they do not measure.

Effective managers use ROT measurements to make their investments in talent more profitable. ROT measurements help monitor performance, forecast opportunity, and determine the profitability of their investment in talent. To make their investment more profitable, management must constantly measure ROT, continuously improve ROT, and nurture, develop, and refresh talent.

"There is no such thing as great talent without great will-power." (Honoré de Balzac)

2. RETURN ON KNOWLEDGE

Return on knowledge generated and applied is more difficult to calculate and track. Knowledge creates real wealth through multiple applications, for example, repeating the same application pervasively through a corporation, or finding new applications to new situations. Knowledge applications have breadth (across organizations) and length (in time). Years may pass between the generation of knowledge and its first application, let alone subsequent applications.

In order to properly account for the value of knowledge generated, initial estimates need to be made and refined yearly as applications appear on the horizon and then are realized. Leading indicators of return are based on projections of the probability of each anticipated application and the monetary value of each application summed over all anticipated applications.

Forward-looking projections and backward-looking allocations are both judgments, and there's no reason to believe that one is any better than the other. Indeed, projections made while focusing on the knowledge generated may be the more reliable of the two. It is certain that the combination of early projections, after-the-fact allocations, and annual updating and tracking between knowledge generated and the first of a series of applications, greatly improves the capability to measure and link return on knowledge generated and applied, and investment in talent.

MAKING IT HAPPEN

1. **Build a team focused on developing talent.** To reach high ROT scores, you need a talent team. Often you find one or two good people who can generate knowledge and perhaps even apply that knowledge, but you don't have a talent team that can leverage their ideas. Most of the individual talent in a company can be innovative if the team dynamics are right. If you have a low ROT score, you may have a dysfunctional team. ROT scores are not fixed; they change over time.
2. **Measure and monitor ROT.** If you are a manager who hires and invests in talent, you need to monitor ROT closely. In a company the size of General Motors or General Electric, you probably view salaries as a regular fixed cost that is standard. The portion that may vary is how much you invest in certain ideas. If you see that certain employees are not generating enough knowledge and success relative to your investment in them, that should be a big red flag, because your ROT value might become negative, or much lower than your competitor's ROT value.
3. **Decide how to increase ROT throughout the organization.** If you were hired to manage talent with a low ROT score (perhaps even a negative value), you need to do some things to boost the ROT fast. How do you turn around an organization and achieve higher ROT scores? You do it person by person, function by function. You have to assess the talent on your team and find out who and what is bringing the most profit to the company, who and what is winning and keeping the best customers. Your first task is to perform talent diagnostics. Youight easily spend six months identifying all your talent and determining which ones you can work with to turn the company around. But usually you don't have six months to do talent diagnostics. So you need to do it faster, even in a large company. There is much to be said for focusing on quick, high-profile actions that build support and momentum behind the need to increase ROT.

Many managers assess employees' talent intuitively—they don't necessarily need a measurement tool. Every manager, however, benefits from having a tool to measure and monitor ROT. Apple soared when Steve Jobs was C.E.O., and faded when he left. It doesn't mean that Jobs was a good or bad person. He was a very effective person in that environment. Many good C.E.O.'s fail in environments in which there is no structure. They go by intuition. After you identify the key talent, give them the authority and resources to boost the ROT team score. The talent diagnostic may show that in one division you have a lot of talented people, while in a different division you have very few. You have to cross functions, making sure you balance the talent according to the needs of the organization, and then challenge each talent and team to reach a financial goal.

CONCLUSION

Organizations that constantly improve ROT grow at a rapid rate. Management can monitor the performances of individuals as well as teams. Knowledge is one of the most important factors for business success. If knowledge assets are increased, then all other related factors like production and sales will be automatically increased. Consequently organizations should try to improve ROT continuously to sustain sales growth. ROT is a superb key performance indicator, and one that is set to be measured and managed in much the same way as financial issues.

For More Information

Books:

Becker, Brian E., Mark A. Huselid, and Dave Ulrich. *The HR Scorecard: Linking People, Strategy and Performance*. Boston, MA: Harvard Business School Press, 2001.

Kaplan, Robert S., and David P. Norton. *The Balanced Scorecard: Translating Strategy into Action*. Boston, MA: Harvard Business School Press, 1996.

See also:

☆ **The Balanced Scorecard (pp. 303–04)**
☆ **Finding and Keeping the Best Talent in the World (pp. 119–20)**
☆ **Human Capital (pp. 115–16)**
☆ **Retaining Employees (pp. 196–97)**
☆ **Snapping Managerial Inertia (pp. 257–58)**
✔ **Implementing the Balanced Scorecard (pp. 510–11)**
Benchmarking (pp. 1911–13)

"All our talents increase in the using, and every faculty, both good and bad, strengthens by exercise."

(Anne Brönte)

  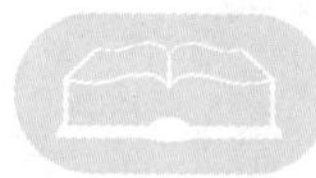    

COMPETING ON COSTS *by Dinna Louise C. Dayao*

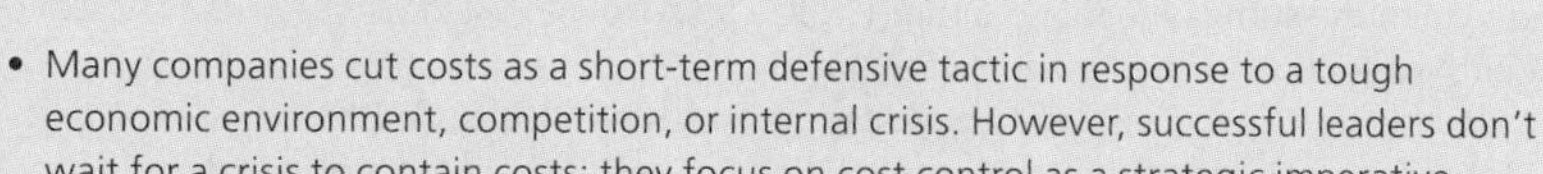

EXECUTIVE SUMMARY

- Many companies cut costs as a short-term defensive tactic in response to a tough economic environment, competition, or internal crisis. However, successful leaders don't wait for a crisis to contain costs; they focus on cost control as a strategic imperative.
- These companies rethink the very core of their companies' internal value chain, and as a result produce goods or deliver services for less money than their competitors. This translates into better profitability and potentially more cash flow.
- The position of low-cost leader assumes greater importance as more products and services become perceived as commodities. In markets in which price is the sole factor in the customer's purchase decision, why not be the leader?

INTRODUCTION

Nissan slashed 10% from its 2000 bill for auto parts by dropping its most inefficient suppliers and consolidating orders with the most cost-conscious ones. The resulting savings of at least $2.5 billion went straight to the automaker's bottom line. Minor Food Group, which owns franchises for pizza restaurants, ice-cream outlets, and steakhouses scattered all over Thailand, survived the Asian financial crisis through a strategy of price-cutting and streamlining. As a result, the fast-food company's net profits rose to a record 178 million baht in 1998, from 82 million baht in 1997. Electrolux has shed a third of its work force—40,000 jobs—since 1997. The tactic helped the Stockholm-based appliance giant boost its operating income by 8% in 2000, to $760 million, on sales of $12.4 billion.

Faced with a difficult economic environment, competitive pressures, or internal crisis, many companies switch to a cost-cutting mode as a short-term defensive tactic. However, low-cost leaders like Taiwan-based Quanta Computer, the Philippine fast-food company Jollibee Foods, the Indonesian retailer Ramayana Lestari Santosa (RLS), and Japan's Fast Retailing don't wait for a crisis to contain costs. They focus on cost control as a strategic imperative. This facilitates improvement in market position and drives bottom-line growth.

Instead of merely focusing on cost reduction, low-cost leaders rethink the very core of their companies' internal value chain—the distinct activities needed to create their products or services. They typically

- optimize the operating efficiency of facilities and resources;
- pursue cost reductions through tight procedural controls and avoidance or elimination of marginal customer accounts;
- minimize (but do not remove entirely) costs and increase efficiency in areas like research and development.

As a result they reap real and lasting breakthroughs, for example, increased productivity, reduced cycle time, and lower input costs, and they can produce goods or deliver services for less money than their competitors. This translates into better profitability and potentially more cash flow. Indirectly, it also provides other significant benefits, such as better customer service and enhanced customer retention and loyalty.

The position of low-cost leader assumes greater importance as more products and services, from cellular phones and computers to financial services and utilities, become perceived as commodities. In markets in which price is the sole factor in the customer's purchase decision, why not be the leader?

COMMON TRAITS OF LOW-COST LEADERS

How do low-cost leaders deliver products and services at the lowest prices? These companies share the following traits:

THEY ARE FANTASTIC AT CONTAINING COSTS

Fast Retailing, Japan's third-largest seller of clothing, cut costs drastically by focusing on a few core products and buying in bulk from low-cost manufacturers, mostly in China. The retailer's competitive prices help to build consumer loyalty. Its chain of 500 no-frills outlets is expected to rack up total sales of $3.3 billion in 2001.

RLS, which operates a chain of department stores across Indonesia, not only contains its recurrent operating expenses, it also uses capital in a very efficient manner. The company rents store space rather than owning it and uses supplier credit to fund working capital.

Askul, which supplies 1.5 million Japanese small businesses with office supplies ranging from paper clips to PCs, keeps costs low by buying direct from manufacturers. The company passes along savings of up to 40% to its customers. Combine that with a catalog of more than 12,000 items and guaranteed delivery within 24 hours, and you get a fast-growing company with sales of $615 million for the year ending May 2001.

THEY ARE OPERATIONALLY EXCELLENT AND EFFICIENT

How does the largest single provider of eye surgery in the world keep the cost of performing a cataract operation down to about $10 when it costs hospitals in the United States about $1,650 to perform the same operation? Aravind Eye Hospitals in India slashes costs by putting two or more patients in an operating room at the same time. Hospitals in the United States don't allow more than one patient at a time in surgery, but Aravind hasn't experienced any problems with infections.

Aravind's doctors have created equipment that allows a surgeon to perform one 10- to 20-minute operation, then swivel around to work on the next patient. They're so productive that the hospital has a gross margin of 40% despite the fact that 70% of its patients pay nothing, or close to nothing, and the hospital doesn't depend on donations. Crucially, this example highlights the fact that operational efficiency does not mean reducing quality standards.

Efficiency helped Quanta earn an estimated $3.8 billion in revenues in 2001. The Taiwanese electronics designer-manufacturer, which specializes in laptops, cellphones, and servers, boasts of flexible, round-the-clock manufacturing lines that mass-produce notebook computers with different product specifications and configurations for customers such as Dell, Compaq, and Apple. A computerized and automated warehouse feeds parts to the conveyor belts. Quanta fulfills orders received electronically from U.S. brands, sellers, or even end users within five working days (three for Japan)—two days to manufacture the machines, configured to specs, and three days for FedEx shipment. It's no wonder that Quanta shipped 4 million notebook units in 2001, 50% more than in 2000—and one-seventh of all the notebooks sold anywhere in the world.

THEY KNOW THAT CHEAP IS NOT NECESSARILY A SYNONYM FOR LOW QUALITY

Toyota is well on its way to becoming the world's lowest-cost producer of highest-quality automobiles. The Japanese automaker had just 115 problems per 100 vehicles, compared with 162 for Ford. Its average warranty cost per vehicle is a low $400, versus $650 at Ford and $550 at General Motors. As a result, Toyota enjoys a cost advantage of $1,800 per vehicle over Ford because of its greater efficiency and consequent ability to command high prices.

Nearly 90% of all items sold by Fast Retailing are made in China under exclusive contracts subject to strict quality standards. The company keeps strict tabs on quality and offers an unconditional money-back guarantee—still a rarity among Japanese retailers.

THEY KEEP LOYAL CUSTOMERS AND ATTRACT NEW ONES

When McDonald's Japan halved weekday hamburger prices in 2000, the move attracted a whole new clientele, instead of eating into earnings. What used to be a teen hangout is now frequented by businesspeople.

In the Philippines, fast-food market leader Jollibee achieved the same result. The company offered value meals at different price points during the financial crisis and pulled in new customers as high-income families switched from gourmet restaurants to fast food in order to cut spending.

THEY NURTURE A CULTURE THAT ABHORS WASTE AND IS CONSTANTLY AWARE OF THE NEED TO CONTROL COSTS

HSBC Holdings, one of the largest and most efficient banking and financial services organizations in the world, prides itself on being fanatical about expense discipline. Chairman John Bond sets the example for frugality. He's known to turn off the lights when he leaves his office, to fly economy, and to take the subway to work. Other HSBC executives follow his lead—when they travel they rarely fly first class, and they stay at middle-range instead of five-star hotels. The bottom-line benefits are considerable: a smaller and predominantly domestic U.K. competitor spends twice as much on travel and entertainment as does HSBC, which operates on every continent.

Cost consciousness is also a hallmark of the management of Singapore Airlines (SIA). SIA's unassuming C.E.O., Cheong Choong Kong, works in a small office at headquarters and sometimes travels economy class on his own airline. SIA executives get no stock options and no special dining room, not even a free parking space. Rigorous cost control has resulted in a strong balance sheet with very little debt and more than $1 billion in liquid assets. SIA's deep pockets enabled the company to expand its holdings, invest $300 million in an ambitious transformation of air-passenger service, and post significant earnings when other airlines were swooning at the height of the Asian financial crisis.

MAKING IT HAPPEN ▸▸

- Understand the bare bones of your company. Ask the most fundamental questions about each activity needed to create your product or service.
- Distinguish between low-cost and high-cost activities. Determine what controls the cost of each activity.
- Keep the activities that add value. Compress, eliminate, or outsource those that don't.
- Identify cost-reduction opportunities and implement those ideas. Aggressively pursue cost savings throughout the value chain.
- Consider how to build a culture of cost control within the organization. Making cost control a strategic imperative may help increase its prominence, as also leading by example.

CONCLUSION

These success stories demonstrate that low-cost leadership is a proven approach to successful competition in the marketplace. By asking fundamental questions about the processes that create your product or service, by grasping which activities are low-cost and which are high-cost, by eliminating process steps that truly do not add value, and by leveraging all cost-reduction opportunities, any company can compete with a low-cost advantage.

For More Information

Book:

Ludy, Perry J. *Profit Building: Cutting Costs Without Cutting People*. San Francisco, CA: Berrett-Koehler, 2000.

Journal Articles:

Gurley, J. William. "Above the Crowd: Why Dell's War Isn't Dumb." *Fortune* (July 9, 2001).

Slywotzky, Adrian J. "Managing Ahead of—and Through—a Recession." *Business Week* (February 13, 2001).

See also:

☆ **Infusing a Company with Cutting-edge Strategy (pp. 83–84)**
☆ **Outsourcing (pp. 89–90)**
☆ **Why EVA Is the Best Measurement Tool for Creating Shareholder Value (pp. 131–32)**
✔ **Controlling a Budget (pp. 546–47)**
✔ **Controlling Costs (pp. 548–49)**
Budgeting (pp. 1913–15)

"Too many companies are expending enormous energy simply to reproduce the cost and quality advantages that global competitors already have." (Gary Hamel)

ENVIRONMENTAL MANAGEMENT
by John Elkington

EXECUTIVE SUMMARY

Some management trends start at the top and cascade down; others evolve from the bottom up. Sustainable development has come from both directions. In the process it has caught a growing number of well-known companies off balance—among them Shell, Monsanto, and Nike. More positive has been the foundation of the World Business Council for Sustainable Development; and the World Economic Forum in Davos routinely covers sustainable-development issues. But in many respects the business story has only just begun. Meanwhile, the 2002 Earth summit in Johannesburg has spurred international stocktaking on progress since the 1992 summit in Rio de Janeiro. Among the key conclusions:

- Demographic pressures will create enormous new risks and opportunities. During the 20th century, the planet's human population rose from 1.6 billion to 6 billion. There is likely to be a further 50% increase by 2030.
- A growing range of environmental problems—including ozone depletion, climate change, the collapse of fisheries, and loss of forests—signals that today's economic and business models are unsustainable.
- The end of communism in many countries means that the one-third of humanity who used to live in the old communist world are now playing a growing role in the global economy. In total, there are some four billion people living in the poorer parts of the world; it will be necessary to meet their needs.
- Business is increasingly in the spotlight—and is expected to play a key role in defining and delivering sustainable development. Paradoxically, the governance vacuum created by accelerating globalization will increase the pressures on brand-name companies and on financial markets to act responsibly and effectively.
- At the same time, however, growing resistance to current forms of economic globalization represents a profound challenge to free market capitalism.
- As a result, growing numbers of companies are adopting *triple-bottom-line* strategies, focusing simultaneously on economic prosperity, social equity, and environmental protection.

THE SUSTAINABILITY AGENDA

Boardrooms have been buzzing with questions since the sustainable-development agenda first began to appear on corporate radar screens. Some business leaders see sustainable development as simply the environmental agenda in new colors, but others speak of a profound shift, with new forms of corporate responsibility and accountability emerging. Here are some key questions and answers.

WHAT IS SUSTAINABILITY?

The answer, first laid out in the 1987 report of the World Commission on Environment and Development, is that sustainability is the principle of ensuring that our actions today do not limit the range of economic, social, and environmental options open to future generations.

WHY IS IT IMPORTANT?

Simply stated, sustainable development is the emerging 21st-century business paradigm. It is increasingly proposed by governments and business leaders as a solution for problems now racing up the international agenda. These range from climate change to human-rights issues.

SURELY THIS IS A JOB FOR POLITICIANS AND LAWMAKERS?

In part, of course, it is, but industry's lobbying over the years for less regulation and in some cases active deregulation may now be coming back to haunt it.

WHAT HAS SUSTAINABLE DEVELOPMENT GOT TO DO WITH CAPITALISM?

Simply put, traditional capitalism dealt with financial and physical forms of capital. Increasingly, however, companies are expected to manage, account for, and grow multiple forms of capital, for example, financial, physical, human, intellectual, natural, and social capital.

HOW CAN WE SELL THIS TO THE FINANCIAL MARKETS?

It's tough, but in the coming decades the world's financial markets will adopt triple-bottom-line models to assess value creation. Insurers and reinsurers have been badly burned by issues like asbestos, contaminated land, and toxic and nuclear wastes. Leading banks are increasingly sensitive both to new forms of risk and to emerging opportunities created by new environmental and social standards. And while some financial analysts have been slow to wake up, the entry of players like the Dow Jones Sustainability Group is providing a wake-up call.

WHAT THE GURUS SAY

The ways in which the environmental and wider sustainable-development agendas have been engaged by business have reflected the priorities of those held responsible at the time in the corporate world. To help simplify the evolutionary history, let's focus in on three main phases:

PHASE 1—DENIAL

From the early 1970s, environmental and social issues were handled on the corporate periphery, by lawyers or PR people. Most companies were in denial: pollution problems either were not their fault or, if they were, were seen as the price of wealth creation. Key issues include compliance, a company's license to operate, and risk to reputation.

PHASE 2—CLEANING UP

From the late 1970s the spotlight shifted to plant siting, production processes, and products. As a result companies tended look to field planners, engineers, and new product development specialists, who used a growing range of tools such as impact assessments, audits, life-cycle assessments, and so-called clean technology. Ecoefficiency concepts introduced by the World Business Council for Sustainable Development were adopted by a growing number of companies. Phase 2 activity con-

---

"Economic activity should not only be efficient in its use of resources but should also be socially just, and environmentally and ecologically sustainable."
(Warren Bennis)

tinues to build, with the European Commission introducing new strategic impact assessment requirements for major industrial projects.

PHASE 3—GOVERNANCE

During the 1990s concepts like that of the triple bottom line began to draw in more senior business people. C.E.O.s and their boards began to pay attention, often because of the difficult tradeoffs involved. A water pollution control investment, for example, might result in higher carbon dioxide emissions, raising climate change issues. Accountants have also been increasingly involved. In the process, the sustainable-development agenda has begun to cross-connect with corporate and global governance agendas.

Most mainstream management writers have overlooked these trends. In their classic text *In Search of Excellence*, first published in 1982, Tom Peters and Robert Waterman made not a single reference to environmental issues. By 1991, however, Peters had published *Lean, Clean, and Green*. Other mainstream management gurus were soon nibbling at corners of the agenda, including Charles Handy (what is a company for?), James Collins and Jerry Porras (guidelines for long-lived companies), James Moore (business ecosystems), Francis Fukuyama (the role of trust and other forms of social capital), Peter Schwartz (the art of the long view, scenarios), Michael Porter (value chains, green competition), and Peter Senge (organizational learning).

However, the greatest impact has come from a number of sustainable-development experts whose books are beginning to be accepted as mainstream management texts. They include Claude Fussler (ecoefficiency, ecoinnovation), Ernst Ulrich von Weizacker (Factor 4–10), and Paul Hawken and Amory and Hunter Lovins (natural capitalism).

Organizations like the World Business Council for Sustainable Development now produce a huge amount of material on the sustainable-development agenda for business (***www.wbcsd.ch***). For those who want to see sustainable development in action, take a look at the work of ecoarchitect Bill McDonough and his colleague Michael Braungart (***www.mbdc.com***). Having designed buildings for companies such as The Gap and Nike, McDonough is working on a multibillion-dollar regeneration plan for the Ford Motor Company.

MAKING IT HAPPEN ▸▸

- Adopt a triple-bottom-line strategy, focusing simultaneously on economic prosperity, social equity, and environmental protection.
- Make environmental and social issues a central boardroom concern, with compliance, the license to operate, and reputational risk as key issues.
- Take the initiative by adopting policies that will meet the criteria of sustainable development.
- Use tools like impact assessments, audits, life-cycle assessments, and clean technology to obtain ecoefficient plant siting, production processes, and products.
- Consider what sustainable development may mean for your business: the areas to take action, the people to involve, and the benefits that may result.
- Closely monitor the new requirements for major industrial projects stemming from governmental bodies, including the European Commission.
- Accept that difficult tradeoffs may be required, and face up to the consequences sooner rather than later.

CONCLUSION

The floodgates are opening. The first major article in the *Harvard Business Review* on the sustainable-development agenda was by Professor Stuart Hart in 1997; the number has been growing ever since. Some key issues for the coming years include developing the business case for sustainable development (SustainAbility 2001); exploring the overlap between organizational learning and sustainable-development agendas (***www.solonline.org***), and engaging corporate boards in the governance dimensions of sustainable development. Sustainable development is set to become an increasingly significant strategic priority facing organizations. It offers a more efficient system for growth that is acceptable to stakeholders and is proven to be both viable and commercially advantageous.

For More Information

Books:

Fussler, Claude. *Driving Eco-innovation: A Breakthrough Discipline for Innovation and Sustainability*. London: Pitman, 1996.
Hawken, Paul, et al. *Natural Capitalism: Creating the Next Industrial Revolution*. New York: Back Bay Books, 2000.
Brown, Lester R., et al. *State of the World 2001*. New York: W. W. Norton, 2001.

Web Sites:

www.iisd.org: the International Institute for Sustainable Development, an organization that promotes the transition toward a sustainable future through information exchange, policy research, analysis and advocacy.
www.rmi.org: the Rocky Mountain Institute, an entrepreneurial nonprofit organization set up by resource analysts Hunter and Amory Lovins.
www.worldwatch.org: for other Worldwatch Institute *State of the world* annuals.
www.wri.org: the World Resources Institute, an environmental think tank that seeks practical ways to protect the earth.

See also:

☆ **Corporate Social Responsibility: Are You Giving Back or Just Giving Away? (pp. 291–92)**
☆ **SQ: Investing in Spiritual Capital (pp. 43–44)**
✓ **Taking Action on the Environment (pp. 520–21)**
Charles Handy (pp. 1000–01)
Anita Roddick (pp. 1134–35)
Environmental Management (pp. 1972–75)

"Many leading business people. . .are revelling in the opportunity to put new ranges on the market with 'eco-friendly' flashes and a 20 percent mark up."
(John Button)

HUMAN CAPITAL *by Edward E. Gordon*

EXECUTIVE SUMMARY

- Accountants and economists are struggling to find a way for a business to measure the intangible assets of human-capital development. What is their added value to the business?
- But what *is* human capital? It is the sum total of individual intelligence built on the acquisition of skills, training, and educational experience over a lifetime. It's the application of this human knowledge to the workplace that creates real value.
- The merging of three types of capital (''human,'' ''organizational,'' and ''customer'') creates the desired outcome—an organization so aligned and balanced as to produce the highest possible financial capital (value).

INTRODUCTION

The high performance workplace over the past two decades has been driven by two titanic forces: globalization and an increasing pace of technological change.

At the beginning of the 21st century these factors have combined to demand a new kind of well-educated knowledge worker, as profound a change as that wrought by the early Industrial Revolution on the role of manual labor in the 1800s.

In this environment, harnessing the human capital, the accumulated skills, experience, wisdom, and capabilities of all of the people employed in the organization is fundamental to success. This may seem obvious–after all, why pay for the most expensive resource in terms of results, than any other, without using them to the full? However, at a time when skills are more complex and transferable, traditional loyalty is reducing and at the same time the significance and value of knowledge is rising, there is a premium and renewed focus on managing human capital.

The U.S. departments of labor and education now estimate that 80% of all jobs in the high-tech workplace require at least 13th-grade reading, math comprehension, and applications skill levels. Unfortunately, the National Adult Literacy Survey (NALS) reported that 48% of U.S. adults fail to meet these criteria.

Though this problem can be found in many countries, it is most acute in the United States. The international Organisation for Economic Co-operation and Development (OECD) ranked the United States 15th out of 47 major industrial nations in the education and training levels of its citizens. This study showed about half of the U.S. adults reading below eighth-grade level, with much of the population performing below sixth-grade level.

In another comparative study of 18 nations, the OECD found that of U.S. high-school graduates who do not go on to acquire further education, nearly 60% perform below a literacy level that international experts consider necessary to cope with the complex demands of the modern workplace. That percentage was the highest among the nations studied, with Finland the lowest at 10% and other countries falling in between–20% in Germany, 35% in the United Kingdom, 50% in Poland. Instead of becoming knowledge workers, it would seem that many members of the current U.S. workforce, as well as students about to emerge from school, are in danger of becoming the new techno-peasants. Investment in human capital is necessary for any nation to reap the benefits from information technology says John Martin, director of education for the OECD. In this section, we will assess the importance of human capital: what it is, where it is and how it can be managed to best effect.

WHERE ARE THE KNOWLEDGE WORKERS?

As the world economy has grown during the past ten years, a demographic time bomb is in the making. The U.S. Census Bureau, Department of Labor, and Immigration and Naturalization Service concur that the population younger than 34 is declining. Increasing retirements will combine with this shrinking labor pool to produce a dramatic knowledge-worker shortfall until 2020. The same trends hold true throughout Western Europe and Japan. In some countries the total population may even decline.

With skilled workers in such high demand, U.S. companies have repositioned operations overseas, and they now lure up to 600,000 skilled workers to the United States on temporary H-1B visas.

The United States projects a shortfall of 2 million IT workers by 2005, while the European Union (EU) forecasts a 1.5 million worker labor gap. The United States and the EU share the same human-capital strategy–import the workers. But there aren't enough IT workers worldwide to fill the knowledge-worker gap. A so-called skill war is now starting, one that will see nations bidding up salaries just to attract these workers from a diminishing world supply.

To create real value, businesses must better leverage their human capital by helping develop larger numbers of their employees into better-educated workers capable of redesigning job and work processes. These workers will then be able to create more high-value-added products and services at extremely low cost.

DEVELOPING HUMAN CAPITAL: AVOIDING THE PITFALLS

The learning organization has largely failed in the boardroom for two reasons. First, presidents, C.E.O.s, and small-business owners still see no connection between company profit and investing in their human capital, because they believe you can't measure it. Second, training programs often don't improve employee performance, because they aren't based on the most recent advances in teaching critical-competency and problem-solving skills.

Complex and multilayered workplace performance issues need to be stated in a language and format that will move more business leaders to give them their personal support. Poll after poll now shows that people in the United States support the concept of better education in general, but it is in realizing the concept that support falls apart.

Many of the world's leading industrial powers are beating the United States at its own game simply by understanding that knowledge equals profit. Rather than ignoring the relationships, they are acting on the critical interactions among technology, smarter employees, and return on investment (ROI). They invest extensively in student career education and employee-retraining programs–and reap the short- and long-term profits.

The key is high-quality reeducation programs that motivate employees to use their own learning by applying innovative thinking on the job. This strategy will increase personal performance, better their

"Owning intellectual property is like owning land: You need to keep investing in it again and again to get a payoff; you can't simply sit back and collect rent." (Esther Dyson)

  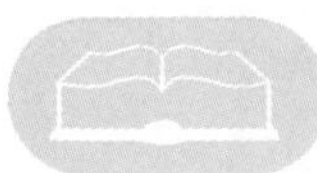    

lifetime careers, and, in turn, give business a high ROI in human capital.

TAKING RESPONSIBILITY FOR HUMAN CAPITAL DEVELOPMENT

Many organizations are abrogating this responsibility for human-capital development by empowering people to figure out what new knowledge they need and encouraging them just to go and get it. However, this do-it-yourself approach to training is a naive management strategy; for most people it's too scattered for any meaningful buildup of new personal skills.

Too many executives have followed the questionable supposition that Web- and video-based training can do it all. This confuses the delivery system with the content. It's a huge mistake to think of e-learning simply as a cheaper way to distribute knowledge, without taking into account the factors that really motivate people to learn. First comes acquiring new information; second, trying it out by applying it; third, reaching personal understanding. The social aspect of learning is vital for most people. A strong interpersonal relationship needs to exist between a good teacher/trainer to coach the learner through what went right or wrong. The teacher/trainer remains central to a successful learning experience, with the latest electronic teaching aids serving as supplemental tools, not a total system solution.

MINI-CASES

Trident Precision Manufacturing of Webster, New York, is one of the smallest companies ever to win a Malcolm Baldrige National Quality Award (in 1996). Over a period of six years, Trident invested 4.7% of the payroll in educating its employees. This custom-product sheet-metal company taught workers blueprint reading, trigonometry, and English as a second language (ESL). Product defect rates improved from 3% to 99.994% defect-free, turnover was reduced from 41% to 5% per year, annual revenue rose from $5 million to $19 million, and revenue per employee shot up by 73%.

Equimeter, based in the United Kingdom, invested its human capital in its Pennsylvania operations by providing a group of engineers with a *kaizen*-team-training program in order to improve the quality and productivity of a gas-meter assembly line. The company achieved a 16% productivity improvement and 22% space savings, reduced the work in process by 10%, and solved three safety issues. The estimated ROI of this training program was 31.6%.

Human-capital investment by thousands of other organizations, including Allied Signal, Elco Industries, Hampden Papers, Hardy Industries, Lumonics, MacLean-Fogg, the Northeast Illinois Metropolitan Transit Railroad Authority (METRA), Warner-Lambert, and Will-Burt, more clearly demonstrated the direct correlation of skills, training, and education with increased productivity and profit.

MAKING IT HAPPEN ▸▸

Investing in human capital produces better business returns; it provides cost savings and efficiencies, maximizes the use of available resources, and addresses specific performance and productivity issues. To succeed, it can help if:

- **Investments in human capital are measured in cash**—clearly highlighting the benefits of acting, and the perils of inaction.
- **The personal knowledge of employees across the organized is assessed**: this gives managers benchmarks for understanding its human capital strengths and weaknesses.
- **Relevant and appropriate performance development programs in skills, education, and training areas are selected.** These should be directly linked to productivity improvement needs and the strategy of the business. What skills are needed to progress towards the desired destination?
- **A human capital measurement system is applied**, so that the best return on investment is achieved in the short and long terms.

Such management strategies for human-capital investment encourage business innovation by leveraging structural capital and human capital in new combinations. The company benefits from a steeper learning curve at its critical cutting edge: the friction points where people grapple with operational productivity issues. Critical competencies are generated in-house that encourage people to innovate new procedures, new services, new products, new intellectual properties—the competitive ideas of business success that generate real profit.

CONCLUSION

Unless businesses invest in people, both technology and management systems will fail as they get more and more complex and require more people who can think for themselves and adapt information. By investing in their most critical intangible—human capital—businesses will rise to the challenges of technology and globalization and speed up the process of building a knowledge economy in their own communities and across the world.

For More Information

Books:

Becker, Brian E., Mark A. Huselid, and Dave Ulrich. *The HR Scorecard: Linking People, Strategy and Performance.* Cambridge, MA: Harvard University Press, 2001.

Conger, Jay A., and Beth Benjamin. *Building Leaders: How Successful Companies Develop the Next Generation.* San Francisco, CA: Jossey-Bass, 1999.

Edvinson, Leif, and Michael S. Malone. *Intellectual Capital: Realizing Your Company's True Value by Finding Its Hidden Brainpower.* New York: HarperBusiness, 1997.

Fitz-Enz, Jac. *The ROI of Human Capital: Measuring the Economic Value of Employee Performance.* New York: AMACOM, 2000.

Web Site:

www.astd.org: this American Society for Training and Development site publishes ongoing research regarding the return on investment of human capital.

See also:

- ☆ **Allocating Corporate Capital Fairly (pp. 123–24)**
- ☆ **Budgeting (pp. 117–18)**
- ☆ **Creating Value through People (pp. 121–22)**
- ☆ **Groundhog Management (pp. 194–95)**
- ☆ **Managing in a 24/7 Organization (pp. 200–01)**
- ☆ **Matching Pay to Achievement (pp. 297–98)**
- ☆ **Return on Talent (pp. 109–10)**
- ☆ **Snapping Managerial Inertia (pp. 257–58)**
- ☆ **Viewpoint: Christopher Bartlett (pp. 45–46)**
- ☆ **Viewpoint: Sumantra Ghoshal (pp. 190–91)**
- ☆ **Viewpoint: Jim Kouzes (pp. 309–11)**
- **Accounting (pp. 1899–1901)**

"Companies. . .have a hard time distinguishing between the cost of paying people and the value of investing in them."

(Thomas Stewart)

BUDGETING *by Jeremy Hope, Robin Fraser, and Peter Bunce, CAM-I Beyond Budgeting Round Table*

EXECUTIVE SUMMARY

- **The traditional performance management model.** This model was first developed in the 1920s to help financial managers control costs in such large organizations as DuPont, General Motors, ICI, and Siemens, and for the next 30 to 40 years it did the job reasonably well.
- **The changing environment.** In an age of discontinuous change, unpredictable competition, and fickle customers, few companies can plan ahead with any confidence. Yet most organizations remain locked into a traditional "plan-make-and-sell" management model that involves a protracted annual budgeting process based on negotiated targets and resources, and that assumes customers will buy what the company decides to make.
- **The barriers to change.** Organizations need to find a new model that effectively empowers frontline managers to make quick decisions based on fast, relevant information. But the annual planning and budgeting process acts as a barrier to change, both mental and systemic.
- **The BBRT model.** A number of companies have now broken through the budgeting barriers and devolved accountability to frontline managers, who use a range of new performance processes to monitor their progress. The Beyond Budgeting Round Table has studied these companies and developed a model of best practice known as the BBRT model.

THE TRADITIONAL MODEL

The traditional performance model was designed to execute a *producer-led* approach to business. The multidivisional organization (or M-form) coped with increasing complexity by placing the activities of each distinct product line, region, or technology into a separately managed compartment (for example, a business unit or division) and subjecting all these compartments to the financial discipline of a strong corporate staff. The underlying thread was control. The mission statement agreed on by senior executives was translated into the strategic plan by the planners and handed down the hierarchy to operational managers, who then prepared their plans and budgets. Once these were agreed on, all that was demanded was adherence to the plan. Head office did not like surprises. Control reports were constantly fed back up the line, and if they showed that performance was veering off track new directives would be issued.

THE CHANGING ENVIRONMENT

The traditional model worked well when market conditions were stable, competitors were known and their actions predictable, relatively few people made decisions, prices reflected internal costs, strategy and product life cycles were lengthy, customers had limited choice, and the priority of shareholders was good stewardship. But these conditions no longer apply. Today's competitive climate is far more uncertain, many people are required to make decisions, the pace of innovation is increasing, costs reflect market pressures, customers are fickle and shareholders more demanding. To compete more effectively in the information economy, firms must break free from the incremental planning and budgeting mentality and involve all their people in building a new platform for sustainable improvement.

THE BARRIERS TO CHANGE

While most senior executives want their organizations to be more adaptive (and thus more devolved), few know how to turn management rhetoric into operating reality. While they talk about fast response, empowerment, innovation, operational excellence, customer focus, and shareholder value, their management processes (for example, targets, plans, measures, and rewards) all too often remain stuck in a time warp of command and control. Fixed strategies prevent fast responses; rigid organizational structures turn off managers who seek challenge and development; bureaucracies stifle innovation; entrenched functions undermine cross-functional processes; an emphasis on product targets works against customer loyalty programs; and short-term performance contracts fail to support long-term value creation. Nor do the millions spent every year on reengineering, team-building, enterprise-wide systems, customer relationship management, value-based management, and balanced scorecards seem to overcome these problems. In fact, the vast majority of these initiatives fail for exactly the same reason—they support the rhetoric but get slaughtered by reality as they invariably collide with the immovable forces of the short-term planning and budgeting system.

THE B MODEL

The BBRT model is designed to overcome these barriers and create a flexible and adaptive organization. Twelve principles provide managers with a robust framework for implementation:

DEVOLUTIONARY FRAMEWORK

1. **Governance.** Establish a framework for devolution by clarifying purpose, principles, and values; don't enforce central control through rules and procedures.
2. **Empowerment.** Give people the freedom and capability to act; don't control and constrain them.
3. **Accountability.** Make people accountable for achieving competitive outcomes, not for meeting functional targets.
4. **Organization.** Organize around a network of interdependent customer-oriented units, not a hierarchy of functions and departments.
5. **Coordination.** Coordinate cross-company interactions through marketlike forces, not through central planning, budgeting, and control.
6. **Leadership.** Challenge and coach

"We didn't actually overspend our budget. The Health Commission allocation simply fell short of our expenditure."
(Keith Davis)

people, don't command and control them.

MANAGEMENT PROCESSES

1. **Goal setting.** Beat the competition, not the budget.
2. **Strategy process.** Make strategy a continuous and inclusive process, not a top-down annual event.
3. **Anticipatory systems.** Use anticipatory systems to inform strategy, not to make short-term corrections to keep on track.
4. **Resource utilization** Provide resources when (justifiably) required; don't allocate them on the basis of annual budgets.
5. **Measurement and control.** Provide fast, open information for multilevel control, not detail for micromanagement.
6. **Motivation and rewards.** Base rewards on company and unit-level competitive performance, not predetermined negotiated targets.

MINI-CASES

A number of companies have now broken through the budgeting barriers, though some are further down the path than others. Of the barrier-breakers we have identified, 14 have so far been the subject of visits and case studies by the Beyond Budgeting Round Table. Here are four examples:

Svenska Handelsbanken, a Swedish universal bank that since abandoning its centralized model in the 1970s has outperformed its Nordic rivals on just about every measure you can think of, including return on equity, total shareholder return, earnings per share, cost-to-income ratio, and customer satisfaction. And it has done this consistently, year in year out, for the past 30 years, a testament to the smooth performance sustainability of its radically devolved model. It is the most cost-efficient bank in Europe and has recently been voted one of Europe's best Internet banks.

Borealis, a Danish company that is at the leading edge of polymer research and development and is now Europe's largest producer (sales of $2.5 billion) and the fourth largest worldwide. Since it implemented its devolved model (and abandoned budgeting) in 1995, Borealis has met its ambitious return-on-capital targets and reduced costs by 30% over five years.

Bulmers, a British company with a clear leadership position (60% share) in the U.K. cider market. Since the adoption of a more devolved management approach in 1998 and adaptive management processes in late 1999, the early results have been impressive. The company is increasing revenue and profitability at a much higher rate than the industry average and has achieved significant cost savings. In 2001, the company was ranked as one of the best firms to work for in the United Kingdom.

AES Corporation, a United States-based global power company that, despite being one of the wonder U.S. stocks of the 1990s (total shareholder return was top of the *Fortune* rankings in the utility sector in 1999), places its values and principles above anything else, and has adopted a highly devolved management model.

Other cases that have adopted some or all of the BBRT model include Swedish roller bearings company *SKF,* U.K. retailer *Boots,* Swedish carmaker *Volvo,* U.S. eye-care company *Ciba Vision,* and U.K. charity *Sight Savers International.* A number of other firms have also made real progress. *General Electric* and *BP-Amoco,* for example, have adopted most of the BBRT philosophy and empowered frontline managers to make strategic decisions within clear values and boundaries.

MAKING IT HAPPEN ▸▸

- Devolve authority, substituting empowerment for central control exerted through rules and procedures.
- Organize around interdependent customer-oriented units, and make people accountable for achieving competitive outcomes.
- Coordinate cross-company interactions through market-like forces, not through central planning, budgeting, and control.
- Coach people and challenge them to beat the competition, not the budget, avoiding short-term corrections to "keep on track."
- Make strategy a continuous and inclusive process, not a top-down annual event, with resources allocated as required, not as budgeted.
- Base rewards on company and unit-level competitive performance, not on predetermined negotiated targets.

CONCLUSION

Devolving accountability for results and replacing plans and budgets with more adaptive systems will provide senior executives with an organization that:

- responds more quickly to change and is better able to deal with increasing levels of uncertainty;
- attracts more talented managers and potential strategic partners;
- generates a far better climate for generating breakthrough strategies aimed at improvement and growth;
- operates at lower cost;
- finds and keeps the right customers;
- creates sustained increases in shareholder wealth.

If organizations want their frontline managers to be more responsive to market demands and to be accountable for their actions, budgets provide the wrong performance drivers and control systems. They must be replaced by management processes and steering mechanisms that support a culture of responsibility and enterprise. The BBRT model is the way forward.

For More Information

Web Sites:

A white paper can be downloaded from the BBRT Web site at **www.bbrt.org**. You can also participate free of charge in the BBRT Benchmarking Project at **www.project.bbrt.org**.

See also:

☆ **Creating Value through People (pp. 121–22)**
☆ **Human Capital (pp. 115–16)**
☆ **New Yardsticks for Performance and Productivity in an E-world (pp. 285–86)**
✓ **Controlling a Budget (pp. 546–47)**
✓ **Drawing Up a Budget (pp. 554–55)**
Budgeting (pp. 1913–15)

Finding and Keeping the Best Talent in the World *by Richard J. Leider*

EXECUTIVE SUMMARY

- The growing effects of the innovation economy are creating a new era in business—the era of talent.
- Your company is only as good as its most talented people.
- Your ability to attract and retain talented, "on-purpose" people will determine whether you succeed.

Introduction

The era of talent has shifted power to talented people. As the world moves in the direction of an information economy, talented people will be able to demand purpose-driven work environments where they are free to contribute their motivated gifts and talents.

Is Talent One of Your Top Three Priorities?

Recently I listened to a powerful presentation on a company's new vision. The persuasive executive presenting it painted an inspiring picture of the operating model that she saw the company needed to execute the new vision. It was brilliant. But there was one thing missing: she never discussed talent. Talent is the make-or-break element the company needs to build the new vision. I see this often, and it perplexes me. Great vision requires great talent, but the pool of talent is shrinking. To create competitive advantage the company needs to attract talent, and to attract the best talent in the world the company will need to be seen as a great place to work.

When I coach executives most of them can articulate their business vision with great passion. Then I ask, "What keeps you awake at night?" They all tell me the same thing: How are we going to find the best talent to execute our vision? Yet there's rarely a talent strategy to address the cause of their sleeplessness. For these executives to sleep soundly, talent must be one of their top three strategic priorities.

What Do Employees Want to Know?

To attract talent, you must recognize the need for an engagement strategy. You have to engage employees emotionally if you want them to deliver big. In workshop discussions with employees from many companies, a major frustration they often cite is: Why should I go above and beyond what's required? They just want to get more and more and give less and less.

To address their frustration you need to answer the four core questions that every employee wants clarified:

1. Where are we going?
2. What are we doing to get there?
3. What do you want me to do?
4. What's in it for me when I do?

These are the common concerns on talented people's minds. What company, regardless of size, industry, or country, wouldn't benefit from clearly answering these four questions for their best employees? When it comes to answering them, there's one basic you can't afford to overlook: a feeling of purpose in the workplace. If you can create a culture of purpose you can attract the best talent to work at your company, even when talent is in short supply.

Does Money Matter?

Money matters. But competing for talent primarily by offering more money has rarely been enough to attract or retain the best people. Good pay is essential, but after a while the best people look for more from their work than just money. Talented people demand purposeful, challenging work, and they want the chance to express and develop their strongest talents.

The best people want to be part of something they can believe in, something that brings meaning to their work and their lives—something that involves a purpose bigger than themselves and their individual success. They want work that challenges them to make a difference. A powerful purpose is a magnet for attracting powerful people.

What Is the Power of Purpose?

The purpose I'm describing creates a psychological bond between employees and the company. This attachment is essential for you to execute your vision. Nancy Hutson knows that Pfizer's research pipeline depends on attracting and retaining the best talent in the world. As senior vice president and site head for the pharmaceutical company's 5,000-person Groton Research Laboratories in Connecticut, she also knows that great people can go anywhere today. That means her biggest competitive headache isn't companies like Merck or Johnson & Johnson. Her biggest worry is holding onto great people. "There's nothing more important than helping people succeed," she says. "That's my number one job."

Nancy is one of the company's leading advocates and models for creating a culture of purpose. She says, "I'm passionate about building an organization that allows people to be all that they can be and that exemplifies the Pfizer values. Helping others succeed is in my DNA!" Nancy knows it's a seller's market for talent. People with the right combination of talents, passions, and values can afford to shop for places to work. For example, the baby boomers, the largest and most significant part of the North American and European working population, are attracted to work that provides purpose and meaning. During this phase of their life they start to look inward and ask, Was it worth it? Did what I do make a difference?

In earlier eras meaning came from company identity. Today purposeful work has replaced company identity. What's important now is a source of meaning in the work itself. The intrinsic purpose of the work has to be powerful enough to make up for the eroding employer-employee identity of the past.

Are You Working on Purpose?

Several years ago Tom Schultz, a corporate vice president and director of financial planning for Motorola, issued a couple of simple questions to 25 of his colleagues: How do you see me? What's my legacy? He requested frank, honest responses from others about how they thought he might be remembered. Within 48 hours, 19 people responded. Tom was surprised by the feedback. Hardly anyone mentioned his "hard" skills, his financial accomplish-

"We would not knowingly hire anyone in our company that wasn't 'boundaryless.'" (Jack Welch)

ments. Everyone talked about his "soft" skills, his interpersonal contributions. Tom was, without knowing it, building a legacy.

"Today I always ask myself, What impact will this decision have ten years from now?" His answers help Tom manifest his purpose, which he defines as *making a difference with one person a day*. These days Tom also works to make a difference with his daughter, Kelly, who faces daily the challenges of spina bifida. Kelly's illness has at times tested Tom's resolve to keep making a difference at work. Exhausted by the pressures of caring for Kelly, he was ready to call it quits at Motorola. A senior executive shocked him by saying, "Don't do it! You need us and we need you right now".

Tom stayed and has taken the lead in creating a world-class leadership development process. Fueled by his interest in the long-term direction of people's lives, he's creating a role for himself in which he can make a difference in not just one life, but many people's lives each day. He says, "I love getting up in the morning to open up growth possibilities for people".

Picture the working lives of two people who do the same work. One has a job that pays the bills, while the other, like Tom Schultz, has a life's work that makes a positive difference in the lives of others. One drags out of bed most mornings feeling purposeless, tired, and stressed out. Tom has a reason to get up in the morning and feels a sense of purpose and energy most days. The difference is that Tom is *working on purpose* and the other person is not. Are you working on purpose? Are you creating a work culture in which the best people can work on purpose? (See the Working on Purpose Quiz below.)

Purpose is a deep concept. It is not a simple management or employee development technique. It's an issue reserved for the best talent in the world, those who are willing to engage the bigger questions that our work eventually presents to all of us. It's an issue for people who are not going to be sitting at their own retirement party wondering what it all added up to, why they worked so hard, and whether it was really worth it.

	Yes	No
1. I wake up most work days and feel energized to go to work.	_	_
2. I have a deep energy—feel a personal calling—for my work.	_	_
3. I am clear about how I measure my success as a person	_	_
4. I use my gifts to add real value to people's lives.	_	_
5. I work with people who honor the same values I do.	_	_
6. I speak my truth at work.	_	_
7. I am experiencing true joy in my work.	_	_
8. I am making a living doing what I most love to do.	_	_
9. I can speak my purpose in one clear sentence.	_	_
10. I go to sleep most nights feeling "This was a well-lived day."	_	_
Total Yes responses		
Total No responses		

Working on Purpose Quiz:

Are you working on purpose?

Does your current work feel like purposeful work?

Check the appropriate column.

The more Yes answers you have, the more purposeful you feel your work is. If you have fewer than five Yes answers, it becomes important to clarify what you believe your purpose is.

Making It Happen ▸▸

The following steps can help you get top talent to work for your company.

- Develop an *on-purpose* work culture in your company by first clarifying your own purpose and vision. Is it compelling? Are you passionate about doing that work?
- Create an engagement strategy by answering the four key questions that employees want to know.
- Communicate your answers to the four key questions relentlessly. Keep in mind that with every change, no matter how large or small, people start asking these questions all over again. Does your top talent know the answers to these key questions?
- Invite dialogue with your talent. What challenges them? What are their purposes and passions? What do they want out of their work? A key to retaining your top talent is the relationship that you as a leader develop with them.

Conclusion

It's a revolutionary notion: the most talented people are attracted to places where they can work on purpose. Purpose inspires creativity and innovation–the fundamental qualities of the successful company of the 21st century. The innovation economy is your invitation to create a company where people can work on purpose. That's what the best people want.

For More Information

Books:

Toms, Michael, and Justine Willis Toms. *True Work: Doing What You Love and Loving What You Do*. New York: Three Rivers, 1999.

Whyte, David. *The Heart Aroused: Poetry and the Preservation of the Soul in Corporate America*. New York: Doubleday/Currency, 1996.

See also:

☆ **Infusing a Company with Cutting-edge Strategy (pp. 83–84)**
☆ **Power Struggling and Power Sharing (pp. 95–96)**
☆ **Retaining Employees (pp. 196–97)**
☆ **Return on Talent (pp. 109–10)**
☆ **SQ: Investing in Spiritual Capital (pp. 43–44)**
☆ **Viewpoint: Christopher Bartlett (pp. 45–46)**
☆ **Viewpoint: John Seely Brown (pp. 137–38)**
✔ **How to Network and Market Yourself (pp. 758–59)**
Employee Relations (pp. 1964–66)

"If each of us hires people who are smaller than we are, we shall become a company of dwarfs."
(David Ogilvy)

CREATING VALUE THROUGH PEOPLE
by David H. Maister

EXECUTIVE SUMMARY

- The financial performance of a business is not something you can or should directly control. It is achieved by providing superior value to the marketplace.
- Marketplace value is a consequence of energizing and focusing employees to create and deliver value.
- To make money, managers should not spend their time managing money, but should instead devote their efforts to the things that produce the money: the enthusiasm, commitment, and drive of the labor force. Don't manage money. Manage people.

INTRODUCTION

Which of the following does your firm report on, monitor, and react to most frequently? Which consume the most management time?

- Client satisfaction levels.
- The strength of key client relationships.
- Employee motivation and energy.
- Levels of collaboration among staff.
- Financial results.

If you're like the overwhelming majority of businesses you will focus primarily on financial results. Consequently, you're making less money than you could!

Why? Because managing a business by looking at financial results is like trying to win a game by keeping your eye firmly fixed on the scoreboard. Financial results are just that: results. They are the *outcome* of excellence (or the lack of it) in the key processes that produce the value that your customers and clients pay for. What you must manage are the things that produce value: energized employees who deliver outstanding quality and service to the marketplace. Does this mean that you don't monitor financials in great detail? Of course not. Financial discipline is the bedrock of business success, but it's not all of it, and maybe not even the greater part of it. The real key is the ability to get your people sufficiently focused so that they eagerly and willingly strive for high standards.

CHALLENGES AND OPPORTUNITIES

Over the years, I've been trusted to see the strategic plans of many direct competitors. Remarkably, they are almost always identical. Everyone figures out correctly which client sectors are growing, which services are in rising demand, and which dimensions of competition, such as client service or innovation, clients are looking for. The strategy documents are the same because everyone's smart! Everyone knows what needs to be done.

If this is so, then what is competition really about? It's about who can best complete the work that need to get done. And this in turn is determined by the following set of closely related concepts:

- energy
- drive
- enthusiasm
- excitement
- commitment
- passion
- ambition

Where these exist the discipline can be found to engage in diligent execution and thereby outperform the competition. The role of the manager is to be a net creator of enthusiasm, excitement, passion, and ambition. Alas, all too often managers are destroyers of excitement. If all they ever talk about is finances (How are your billings? What's happening to receivables?), it can deaden the spirit. That doesn't mean they don't need to talk about these things—they do. But they shouldn't talk *only* about these things. It's the manager's job to inspire, cajole, exhort, nag, support, critique, praise, encourage, confront, and comfort, as individual people (and groups of people) struggle to live their work lives according to high standards.

All strategies, at some time or the other, involve a tradeoff between short-term cash and executing the strategy. If you're going to get the benefits of a strategy, you need to be willing to make hard choices and act as if you truly believe it. You must be willing to practice what you preach, both when it's convenient and, most importantly, when it is not.

Many people don't believe that their leaders truly want them to act strategically. Whenever a choice needs to be made between strategy and short-term cash—and it always does—most people feel under significant, if not irresistible, pressure from management to go for the cash. Usually the message from the firm's leadership is clear: strategy can wait for tomorrow (if we can get paid for competence, why strive for excellence?). Rather than leaders being a source of encouragement to execute the strategy, they're all too often the biggest obstacles to the implementation of strategy.

If you want to be known as excellent at something, you have to be reliably, consistently excellent at it. Business life is filled with daily temptations, short-term expediencies, and wonderful excuses for why we can't afford to stick to high standards today. We take in work that's off-strategy (after all, it's cash!), we defer training until some more convenient time (often never), we postpone investments until the ever-escalating profit goals are met, and the marketing principle is: we never met a dollar of revenue we didn't like!

There is nothing inherently wrong about making these choices, but you shouldn't fool yourself. If you're willing to sacrifice value to earn short-term cash, you won't create a market reputation for superior quality. It takes courage to believe that a reputation for excellence is worth more in the long run than incremental cash. In their vision, mission, and strategy documents, firms say that they are aiming for excellence, but that's not how they operate.

Managers must have the courage of the convictions they espouse, maintain a long-term focus, and intervene personally whenever there are departures from the values and vision that create excellence. The problem with the implementation of strategies is the absence of certain and recognizable consequences for noncompliance. If the manager doesn't have the courage to tackle individuals who aren't behaving in accordance with the strategy, others will quickly realize that the new strategy is not something they have to do. They'll quickly cease striving to comply, and the benefits of the strategy will never be attained.

Great managers give their people individually and collectively the confidence that greater success, fulfillment, accomplishment, and profits are indeed attainable. They give their people the courage to try.

"Trahey's Simple Rule: Would you hire you?" (Jane Trahey)

Change is threatening, however, and many, if not most, people operate well within their comfort zone, reluctant to abandon the old habits that brought them to their current success. If managers are often demanding, they must also be supportive. They must manage with a positive, supportive style.

Just as management involves a delicate balance between being supportive and being demanding, it also requires a style of insistent patience; it's the difference between saying Rome wasn't built in a day and insisting that we *are* building Rome. People must believe that the manager has the courage to believe in something and, more importantly, will stick with it. There's no greater condemnation of managers than to say that they're expedient, and no greater commendation than to say that a manager truly lives and acts in accordance with what he or she preaches.

BEING EFFECTIVE—AND SUCCESSFUL

An effective manager must be:

- articulate and vocal about his or her personal beliefs;
- disciplined about standards;
- even-handed and even-tempered;
- genuine and sincere;
- able to read people's characters and skill levels effectively;
- honorable, with high integrity.

What do the most successful managers believe?

- First you build your people, and the rest will come.
- Fun and discipline combined get the job done.
- It's important how people treat each other: monitor it and manage it.
- People have to trust management and trust each other.
- Success is about character, respect, integrity, trust, honesty, empowerment, confidence, loyalty, and keeping promises.
- You must bet on the long term and not get stampeded by short-term pressures.
- You need to balance your focus on people, clients, and finances.
- You should live up to your values every day.
- Your agenda as a manager is to create a great place to work, not to work at making your own star rise.

Finally, here are the rules on which the most successful managers model their behavior:

- Act as if not trying is the only sin.
- Act as if you want everyone to succeed.
- Actively help people with their personal development.
- Always do what you say you are going to do.
- Do what's right over the long term for clients and for your people.
- Don't regard yourself as separate and distinct from your people.
- Facilitate, don't dictate.
- Let people know you as a human being, not just as their manager.
- Show enthusiasm and drive; they're infectious and addictive.
- Speak regularly about your vision and philosophy so that people know where you stand.
- Take work seriously, but don't take yourself seriously.
- Understand what drives individuals.
- Know all your people as individuals.

MAKING IT HAPPEN ▸▸

To get started take out the documents that describe your company's mission, vision, values, and strategy. Turn them into a questionnaire and ask your people how well they think you're currently living up to the things you espouse. If you find out that there are some things that you're not doing so well, either fix them or drop them from your declarations: there's no point lying, pretending to advocate things you're not willing to live up to. Practice what you preach! Make it the short-term immediate priority to make the firm live up to its overarching vision.

Another vital step is to involve as many people as possible in the process of implementing, if not actually setting, strategy. The task of energizing, mobilizing, and motivating action is easier with people feeling involved, rather than being imposed on from above.

CONCLUSION

A person doesn't build a business. A person builds an organization that builds a business. Many managers are appointed because of their financial skills, their business development skills, or their technical excellence. However there comes a point where the central question is, Can you manage? Are you a net creator of energy, drive, and ambition in others? Can you cause others to strive to achieve high standards?

For More Information

Books:

Collins, James C., and Jerry I. Porras. *Built to Last: Successful Habits of Visionary Companies*. New York: HarperBusiness, 1997.

Heskett, James L., W. Earl Sasser, Jr., and Leonard A. Schlesinger. *The Service Profit Chain: How Leading Companies Link Profit and Growth to Loyalty, Satisfaction, and Value*. New York: Free Press, 1997.

Kaplan, Robert S., and David P. Norton. *The Balanced Scorecard: Translating Strategy into Action*. Boston, MA: Harvard Business School Press, 1996.

Pfeffer, Jeffrey, and Robert I. Sutton. *The Knowing-Doing Gap: How Smart Companies Turn Knowledge into Action*. Boston, MA: Harvard Business School Press, 2000.

See also:

☆ **Budgeting (pp. 117–18)**
☆ **Human Capital (pp. 115–16)**
☆ **New Yardsticks for Performance and Productivity in an E-world (pp. 285–86)**
☆ **Snapping Managerial Inertia (pp. 257–58)**
☆ **Viewpoint: Charles Handy (pp. 75–76)**
☆ **Viewpoint: Henry Mintzberg (pp. 241–42)**
☆ **Viewpoint: John Seely Brown (pp. 137–38)**
☆ **Viewpoint: Sumantra Ghoshal (pp. 190–91)**

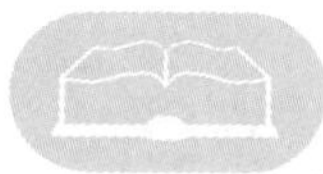

Allocating Corporate Capital Fairly
by John L. Mariotti

EXECUTIVE SUMMARY

- The principal job of management is the allocation of scarce resources—people, time, and money—to opportunities that yield the greatest returns.
- There is always a shortage of capital and an excess of worthy projects. There are many methods of capital allocation, but most do not fund the best opportunities.
- The key task is to allocate capital to support the greatest opportunities and match strategic objectives.

Introduction

The appetite of organizations for capital is insatiable. Understanding the nature of capital and its effective allocation is essential to organizational success. Classical economics defines land, labor, and capital as the determinants of wealth, each being exclusive to its owner. Now there is a fourth determinant of wealth–information–and it is nonexclusive. The more information is shared, the more valuable it becomes. Business is a game in which the score is kept in money, and thus allocation of capital is a critical decision.

The challenge is to decide which division, project, or acquisition gets the scarce capital. The challenge varies with the source of capital. Venture capitalists' tolerance for risk is offset by their high return expectations. The low risk of municipal bonds and banks is matched by low returns. Corporations, striving to enhance shareholder value, must match investment choices to their investors' expectations. Such is the world of being *your brother's banker*.

Allocating Capital

Investment models of prior eras are tested, changed, and then validated or proved flawed. The venture-capital driven dot-coms appeared to exist in a new reality where the old rules of finance were suspended. The reality of the situation re-emerged, and these returnless enterprises disappeared. Their mounting million-dollar losses with no profit in sight led to their inevitable and rapid demise. The principles of sound fiscal management and capital allocation still applied. If capital is allocated foolishly to poorly defined projects, it is wasted. The game is a simple one: invest in projects with the greatest return and the lowest risk, deciding which ventures to invest in has always occupied management. Corporations have developed many quantitative methods for allocating capital. Most of these remain valid, but they share one problem: they all depend on someone's forecast of the future, and this is risky. The challenge is to allocate capital to well-thought-out opportunities that have a reasonable chance of earning good capital returns.

The Plan: Allocation for Strategic Purposes

Capital allocation must be aligned with the strategic purposes and objectives of the corporation. The implication is that these are well defined and clearly understood. However, this is frequently not the case; too often their meaning is unclear or hidden from decision-makers.

The Typical Practice: A Capital Budget

Organizations develop capital expenditure budget needs for annual review by boards and banks. A common breakdown of capital budgets is by category or type of expenditure–for example, new products, new facilities, maintenance of existing products or facilities, infrastructure needs. This is a theoretically sound method since each category has a different strategic purpose, for example, sustaining current activities or revenue streams, creating new revenue streams, or providing infrastructure to support current or new business needs. These category splits are intended to allow senior management and boards to allocate capital fairly according to the company's strategic needs.

The problem with this approach is that there is an enormous gap between the theory of developing capital expenditure budgets and the actual practice of the process. This traditional route is a sure path to sustaining mediocrity.

The Capital Appropriation Process

When management has determined what it believes is an effective use of capital, it must find a means to communicate that need and its worthiness relative to other needs. Larger organizations use a formal capital appropriation process. This process involves documentation of the intended use, description of the assets to be acquired, time frames for the investments, and benefits to be gained. A financial analysis is a required part of the capital appropriation request.

The methods used to compare and evaluate capital investments use projections of future revenue streams and a calculation of some combination of:

- internal rate of return (IRR)
- net present value (NPV)
- breakeven
- economic value added (EVA)
- economic profit created (EP)
- risk adjusted return on capital (RAROC)

This approach will reward the best analysts, politicians, and sycophants, but not the best projects. The most innovative high-potential projects are seldom easy to quantify, analyze, and define. Yet these ideas turn out to be outstanding–but only in retrospect and only if they ever get funded.

For reasons of personal or organizational pride, differing goals, or political power, appropriation requests often do not match corporate goals. Competing executives or organizations will scuffle for scarce capital, and even if their intentions are good (which they usually aren't) the resulting conflicts can be ugly. Who resolves these conflicts?

Approvals and the Capital Appropriation Committee

In some companies the authority level for heads of business units is high–assuming funds have been budgeted–in the category needed. This means there is a chance that good, innovative ideas might receive financing. In central-control-oriented companies spending approval levels are kept low, forcing corporate review of most investments.

Appropriation requests go up the ladder to be approved by successively higher levels of management. The originator's chain of command is a normal path in addition to gatekeepers from finance and accounting. Other functions affected often have sign-off

  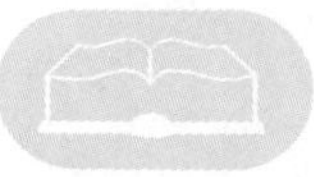    

rights, too. This time-consuming, bureaucratic, and often contentious. Such processes will wring the creativity out of any proposal, replacing it with conservatism, caution, and capital constipation.

After running the divisional bureaucratic gauntlet, the appropriation goes to the corporate capital appropriation committee, where it is subjected to more scrutiny. This review is supposedly based on alignment with corporate strategies, the return versus competing capital needs from other units, and the requesting unit's budget. The larger the organization the more levels there may be, but the process varies surprisingly little from company to company.

When the Cleveland, Ohio, manufacturing company Manco, Inc. was growing through the $100-million sales level, it implemented a formal but streamlined capital approval process. Since its acquisition by the Henkel Group this process now includes approval at corporate level in Dusseldorf, Germany. Some may consider this necessary; it is, however, slower. The successive layers of capital appropriation processes and committees can slow down or even kill good ideas.

Historically, depreciation was designed to replace assets by taking noncash charges to expenses, thereby reserving the money for new expenditures. Thus, it became normal for capital allocation to equal depreciation. To spend more is equivalent to putting in new money, and to spend less is in effect using up the business. Many lending agreements also contain restrictive covenants that limit capital spending to formulas—the right spending level is a function of what happened in the past divided by some accountant's factors. The obvious corollary is that, if the company is struggling, it will be starved of the necessary capital to rebuild.

Other Challenges in Capital Allocation

There are many other issues. Cash-rich companies also have a problem. A low return on conservatively invested cash reduces the return on assets. Corporations are expected to earn higher returns than banks (or bonds). A common alternative is to repurchase stock.

In other cases, company treasurers are tempted to use high-risk investments like derivatives. Multinational companies have another issue: currency fluctuations. Shifting exchange rates can negate the best analyses, making investments much better—or worse. Hedging currency by buying futures can protect the downside, but, like all insurance, this comes at a cost. This can often seem little better than gambling.

Then there are fiascoes in which capital allocation is based on equity markets and stock prices. The dot-com deals involving stock swaps quickly revealed the flaws here: huge profits disappeared overnight, replaced by unexpected write-offs. The pricing of deals is destroyed in a blink when stock prices fluctuate wildly. Carefully negotiated deals combining cash and stock might as well have been decided on a roulette wheel—long odds and large potential losses.

Furthermore, what happens to budgeted but unused money? The government model—use it or lose it—is often used. The rush to spend unused budgeted capital results in waste, misallocation, or both.

Nonmoney "Capital"

Finally, there are noncapital resources, such as people, knowledge, or time. If these were not available, all the capital in the world would not help. Capital must be spent wisely or else allocating it wisely is useless. People spend the capital. So if you are to be your brother's banker in allocating capital, the most important question you can ask is not what it will be spent on. Rather, it is who will be spending it and what their track record is. Choosing the right people to bet on is the critical decision. Then and only then are all the other processes useful and important.

Making It Happen ▸▸

An alternative to allocation?

In the new economy capital flowed freely to those perceived to deserve it (and the perceived undeserving were starved). Forget that many of the decisions were bad ones, and consider the concept. Instead of allocating capital, think in terms of earning it and deserving it. Unconventional ideas seldom survive the bureaucratic battles, particularly if they threaten to cannibalize existing businesses. Silicon Valley taught us that in a venture-capital-rich climate, an idea either attracts capital or it doesn't. No corporate committee says yea or nay. Then it must prove that the capital it attracted was deserved by succeeding with it.

Conclusion

Companies usually allocate capital on the basis of one of three mindsets.

- The first is *protecting the past*, in which case they will always be following the competition and reacting to a leader's moves, simply trying to hang on to past glories.
- The second mindset is the attractive trap of *perfecting the present*. Such moves are always easier to analyze, and make short-term strategic goals. The problems arise when a new, disruptive technology or a revolutionary competitor enters the fray, upsetting the applecart.
- The third mindset is the critical one, to allocate capital by investing in *finding the future*. This is harder and riskier, but it is the only true path to success.

Few traditional appropriation processes accommodate this approach, which is why so few companies succeed over the long term. Companies trying to find the future are often led by escapees from the other kinds of companies, people seeking outlets for creative brilliance, people thwarted by capital appropriations processes, restrictive policies, and countless committees.

The best rule for capital allocation is to allocate very little to protecting the past and just enough to perfecting the present, leaving plenty to spend on finding the future. That is where real wealth and excitement lies.

For More Information

Books:

Drucker, Peter F. *Management Challenges for the 21st Century*. New York: HarperBusiness, 1999.

Hamel, Gary. *Leading the Revolution*. Boston, MA: Harvard Business School Press, 2000.

Hamel, Gary, and C. K. Prahalad. *Competing for the Future*. Boston, MA: Harvard Business School Press, 1996.

Web Site:

www.amanet.org is the home site of the American Management Association, a leading membership-based management development organization that offers a range of business education and management development programs for individuals and organizations worldwide.

See also:

☆ **Human Capital (pp. 115–16)**
Competing for the Future (p. 899)
Warren Buffett (pp. 1066–67)
Gary Hamel (pp. 998–99)
C. K. Prahalad (pp. 1040–41)

"Capital as such is not evil; it is its wrong use that is evil. Capital in some form or other will always be needed."

(Mahatma Gandhi)

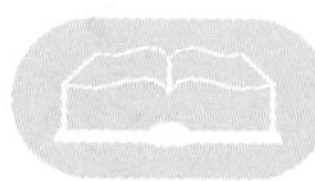

INTRAPRENEURIAL WARRIORS VERSUS TRADITIONAL MANAGERS *by Gifford Pinchot*

EXECUTIVE SUMMARY

- New ideas don't generally fit neatly within existing organizational boundaries; thus they require innovators to cross the boundaries in search of help, resources, and permission.
- Many good ideas are lost when progress is blocked by the need to use resources from other parts of the organization.
- Getting people from other parts of the organization to contribute time and resources to an innovation requires either raw power or the skills and mindset of an intrapreneurial warrior.
- The skills of the intrapreneurial warrior can be learned.

INTRODUCTION

As we leave the industrial era, work is increasingly about innovation and doing something different for customers. Dull repetitious jobs are being eliminated by machines and computers, leaving only the more human work of dealing with the shifting desires and needs of people in a world of rapidly emerging technical possibilities.

Almost all the good jobs now require using imagination and getting things done in new ways. Traditional bureaucratic expertise is not enough to achieve the rate of innovation needed to compete. What is needed are the skills of the intrapreneurial warrior.

TECHNIQUES FOR GETTING RESOURCES: THE QUIZ

Your project has come to a screeching halt because the people in another department don't understand its importance. You know the ROI for the company would be great. You need their help or their permission, but they are too busy to help. *What can you do?*

Which of these seven options would you select? Pick the top three, then let's score the effectiveness of each choice.

1. Plead with your boss to lobby the resource owners for what you need.
2. Explain all the glorious implications of the idea so resource owners recognize how important it is.
3. Ask resource owners for advice on your project before asking them for resources.
4. Express gratitude for whatever help you get.
5. Broadcast your idea and see who steps forward to help.
6. Build a network of friends and colleagues.
7. Seek out another project with more powerful sponsors.

Plead with your boss?

Well, you've probably tried asking your boss already. If it worked, fine, but before you ask your boss to spend precious political capital on your behalf, ask yourself if you have made the job as easy as possible.

When your boss requests project resources from someone in another area, it's going to be easier if you have pre-sold the idea to the people who will do the work. Have you converted those people to your cause—are they supportive and understanding? Getting someone to lobby others on your behalf may be part of the solution, but it is not the place to begin.

Intrapreneurial Warrior Score: 0 points

Explain the glorious implications?

It's tempting, when visualizing the positive impact of your project, to tell the world about it, but the effect of your excitement may be to scare people. If, in its fully realized form, the implications of your project will change everything—their department, their job, but the comfort of familiar ways of doing things, you cannot blame them for being cautious. If you make your project seem too world-changing, they will respond with delaying tactics and requests for more information, not action or help.

Intrapreneurial Warrior Score: -3 points

Ask resource owners for advice?

The danger of premature glorification is neatly matched by the danger of premature requests for resources. Ask too soon and there is a good chance that you will get some version of "No!" Once someone has denied you resources, rationalization sets in: if they refused to provide resources, then your idea must be bad. If it was good, then they, a good manager, would have found a way to help.

This vicious cycle of rejection can easily be turned around. Simply ask for some form of help that will not be refused. *The request for help least likely to be refused is a request for advice.* When someone gives you advice, they are contributing to your project. If they contribute to your project one of two things must be true:

1. Your project is worthwhile, so their helping makes them good managers.
2. Your project is worthless or destructive, in which case helping is a poor use of time, and therefore they are a poor manager.

The attraction of seeing oneself as good manager will win out almost every time. Keep asking for things they will say yes to and be careful not to ask for too much too soon. The more someone contributes, the more the project becomes their own. So start with advice and build your requests gradually until you can ask for resources. The intrapreneurial warrior gets people involved before asking them for anything of significance.

Intrapreneurial Warrior Score: +5 points

Express gratitude?

Gratitude cements the value of whatever help you have been given, and can even dissolve overt hostility to a project. When someone in a position of power criticizes the project of an intrapreneurial warrior, the intrapreneur takes careful notes. After some time to cool off and a bit of checking, the warrior finds a bit of truth in some of the criticisms. In some small way the plan is changed.

The intrapreneur then goes back to the critic and thanks him or her profusely for picking up on a problem that could have sunk the project. Your critic may have tried to define himself or herself as your enemy, but you have reframed the criticism as a form of support. To balance things out they rationalize that there must be good in your project. Few can resist the praise, *if it is delivered with total sincerity.* Thanking critics for their contribution sincerely requires the generosity of spirit to genuinely forgive and appreciate. Don't try it until you have genuinely done so.

Intrapreneurial Warrior Score: +4 points

Broadcast your idea?

It seems smart to "run your idea up the flagpole and see who salutes." It makes sense, but it doesn't work. Every innovation

"Risk is what an entrepreneur eats for breakfast." (Heather Robertson)

involves a bit of creative destruction, the new way replaces the old way. Those who will benefit from the new order don't really get the implications of the change; and those whose privileged positions will be challenged by the new order recognize it at once and come forward with spears sharpened. The lesson is this: premature promotion of your idea triggers the immune system. The grander you make your idea sound, the more widely you distribute the message, the more people it will frighten.

Intrapreneurial Warrior Score: –4 points

Build a network?

Gone is the era of the lonely innovator. The intrapreneurial warrior knows that when you are not in charge of everything you need, your success hinges on the quality of your relationships with the other players (and the referees). The warrior is alert to the feelings of others. He distributes credit widely. (The more you give away, the more comes back in the long run.)

The intrapreneurial warrior keeps everyone in the coalition fully informed. She takes time to check up on everyone. She even keeps many relationships alive when there is no need for help at the moment. Building a network of friends and colleagues is "Innovation 101."

Intrapreneurial Warrior Score: +3 points

Seek out another project?

Every innovation passes through dark and discouraging days. Intrapreneurial warriors don't give up easily. They find ways around obstacles; they don't knuckle under to them.

There are fake intrapreneurs who only want to head large projects with an impressive staff roster. They jump from project to project depending on what is in favor. If the project hits a political snag, they blame others and move on. This may be a good career strategy in some companies, but it will not lead to effective innovation.

Intrapreneurial Warrior Score: –5

POINTS SCORING

Add the points from your three choices; if the total is. . .

–4 or less: *Bureaucrat*: Stay in safe bureaucratic jobs or break out by starting a whole new career outside of large organizations.

–3 to 1: *In transition to the 21st century*: Take more time off from work and spend time learning to build relationships.

1 to 7: *Emerging Intrapreneurial Warrior*: Get an intrapreneurial mentor. Build your network. Get smart about handling the immune system.

7 or more: *Intrapreneurial Warrior*: Keep up the good work!

THE INTRAPRENEURIAL WARRIOR

To be an intrapreneurial warrior, one must have:

- an inspiring vision;
- integrity, trustworthiness;
- an inner compass guiding one toward the vision;
- the courage to follow this compass;
- the emotional intelligence to understand others;
- the wisdom to use diplomacy;
- the stealth and cunning to avoid organizational backlash;
- the generosity of spirit to make and keep allies across bureaucratic lines;
- the business judgment to make good use of resources.

MINI-CASE

DuPont's medical products department sold equipment to test for HIV. One of its customers, the New York Blood Bank, asked for help. If HIV is found, the source of the blood must be located. The Blood Bank needed a massive database to track all blood from collection to transfusion—and they wanted it in 90 days!

The department sought help from information technology and from corporate staff. Neither could meet the deadline. However, the medical products account executive had heard of a special intrapreneurial team within DuPont's fibers department. Traditionally, a staff group from one division does not do major jobs for another division. But, since this was considered an emergency, IEA got the job. It provided the blood-tracking database within deadline, and Medical Products solved its customer's problem successfully.

Furthermore, as IEA's reputation spread, the group found itself working with many other departments to solve their information problems. Ultimately, IEA became an intraprise (an independent enterprise within the corporation); it went on to provide new and better information technology services for every division of DuPont and spread learning across the organization.

MAKING IT HAPPEN ▸▸

The intrapreneurial warrior makes it happen by building relationships across the boundaries of the organization.

1. Build your network across organizational boundaries. Keep up with old friends when jobs change, and be curious about others' work; interest is a key currency.
2. Give credit widely: express gratitude and give others credit.
3. Always gauge requests for help so the answer you get is yes. Ask for advice before asking for resources, and build collaborative relationships gradually.
4. Be trustworthy and make sure your partners come out winners too.

CONCLUSION

Getting help and resources for your project is more about relationships and trust than it is about the quality of your ideas. The intrapreneurial warrior treasures a reputation for integrity, for without trust innovation is impossible. The intrapreneurial warrior is somewhat modest about the idea and its potential, lest others be scared by it. The intrapreneurial warrior asks for advice before resources, because advice is the form of help that people are most willing to give.

For More Information

Books:

Bellman, Geoffrey M. *Getting Things Done When You Are Not in Charge*. 2nd ed. San Francisco, CA: Berrett-Koehler, 2001.

Pinchot, Gifford. *Intrapreneuring: Why You Don't Have to Leave the Corporation to Become an Entrepreneur*. New York: Harper & Row, 1985.

Web Site:

www.intrapreneur.com: Pinchot & Company's site which is devoted to intrapreneuring.

See also:

☆ **Building Great Internal Partnerships (pp. 281–82)**
☆ **The Business Web (pp. 145–46)**
☆ **Corporate-level Strategy (pp. 101–02)**
☆ **Project Management (pp. 165–66)**
☆ **Viewpoint: Charles Handy (pp. 75–76)**
☆ **X-engineering Success (pp. 245–46)**

"Success is the result of perfection, hard work, learning from failure, loyalty to those for whom you work, and persistence."
(Colin Powell)

MANAGING 21ST CENTURY FINANCIALS
by Terry Carroll

EXECUTIVE SUMMARY

- C.F.O.s have to balance long-term planning with short-termist behavior in the markets.
- In order to do this, it's essential to have a good business model, a clear understanding of business risk, sustainable revenues, and proper communication.
- Failing to manage the financial information systems well can seriously damage your brand. Getting it right will please both short- and long-term investors.
- Value creation is top of the agenda. When investors are frightened or lose faith, they can destroy value much faster than you can create it.
- Relationship management is one of the most important new skills to acquire on the road to success.

INTRODUCTION

Corporate purpose, for most companies, is to create and sustain long-term shareholder value. However, markets are increasingly driven by fear, as the emergence of traded indicators such as "VXN" (and QQV) has shown in the U.S. Stuck in the middle are top managers, especially the C.F.O.s. They have to balance long-term planning with "short-termist" behavior in the markets. How can this be achieved? What are the new metrics for survival and sustainable prosperity?

For both quoted and private companies, it's about having a clear understandable business model that works; being able to explain it easily and consistently; understanding strategic business risk and making it work for you; generating sustainable revenues, income, and especially cash; and rapid, reliable reporting. It starts and ends with shareholder value creation.

MANAGING INVESTORS' EXPECTATIONS

It's not so much about managing shareholder value as expectations. The major long-term players (institutions, pension, investment and insurance funds) are advised by analysts. Short-term investors, traders and the public are more influenced by newsflow and market movements. How can we reconcile these forces? First, timely financial information; second, "no surprises"; third, always having cash; finally, having a credible, understandable business model.

FINANCIAL REPORTING IN THE COMMUNICATION AGE

Great companies produce rapid, reliable, succinct, simple, usable financial information. Internally, more than three days to report is too long. The Internet or intranets can provide "always-on," real-time connection for the whole company. Management and financial reporting tools and technology allow fast collection, collation, interpretation, and distribution of results. Now, three factors are converging internal with external reporting: urgency, transparency, and consistency.

Global markets and the pace of change mean management needs reliable financial feedback, fast. Meanwhile, external reporting periods are shortening. This is spilling into Europe. Information is a global property, especially when it "leaks." Global brand management demands control of your own destiny. The market wants information as fast as you get it. Too much conversion for external consumption takes time, unsettling management and investor alike. Meanwhile, market regulation requires transparency and "equality" of distribution.

Shareholders and investors want financial information consistent with expectations. The more frequently it is released, the smaller the "mismatch." Regular, progressive business and financial newsflow, augmented by rational enhancements to the business model can lead to outperformance. "No surprises" please, because markets wonder if management is competent.

Uneven information flow; profit warnings or their lack; information released to analyst briefings before the market; lack of comment on speculation. . .all these unsettle investors and regulators, often causing sharp movements in share prices. News and specialist market services supply corporate information 24 hours a day. Analysts interpret it as fast as it is produced.

Some C.F.O.s may need to wake up to the new paradigm. Others will see it as an opportunity for skilled relationship management, making the financial information systems work for the company as another weapon in the public relations armory. Brand is everything. Failing this new challenge can seriously damage yours. The right way will please both short and long-term investors.

CASH IS KING

Investors will demand that companies report quicker. This is a challenge for accounting standards and governance. Historic price/earnings multiples are being replaced by forecast revenues and EBITDA (earnings before interest, tax, depreciation, and amortization) as the currency of decisions. The new metric is cash. How much cash was generated last period; how much remains in the balance sheet; what is the NPV of sustainable future cash flows?

EVERYBODY NEEDS A BUSINESS MODEL

Apart from cash, the other factor that converges short and long-term interests is a credible, explainable business model. If you don't have one, analysts will create their own (or worse still, transport it from another company unlike your own). For example, good TMT stocks have floated up and down with bad on the waves of market volatility. Some values are absurd, for good or ill.

Both Nortel (U.S.) and Bookham (U.K.) have been a top 100 stock in their own market. They are both high-tech companies linked to building communications networks. Nortel has been around for 25 years and its market capitalization peaked at around £160 billion in 2000. It has not been immune from recession or the ebbing "dot.com" tide, falling 90% in the 18 months since.

Bookham Technology, on the other hand, was floated in July 2000 at £10. Its shares rocketed to £53 in a few months, based on the NPV of forecast revenues, for a business model that few people understood. The price was driven by over-optimistic analyst

---

"Successful investors, through good times and bad, focus a vigilant eye on managing risk."

(Arthur Levitt, Jr.)

estimates, blind faith, and greed. In a year it fell to 74p. Its market capitalization fell from £6.5 billion to less than £100 million (the £200 million cash in the balance sheet supported the growing stream of losses). Despite its disparity, its price fall correlated with Nortel, buffeted by fear and optimism.

In the TMT market in general, fear overtook logic as, for example, some telecoms companies which were quasi-utilities were lumped with their busted cousins. In a starved market, some companies ran out of cash because of oversupply to the cash-hungry cuckoos in their nest.

So it's the financial model that really counts, especially generating and sustaining cash. It's lack of cash that busts companies, not lack of capital. When you don't have enough cash to survive a recession and the market isn't receptive to new issues, you have to start slashing costs: "eating yourself" to stay alive. This can damage the business model, undermine the share price and become a vicious spiral towards expiry, or at best consumption by a sounder business model.

VALUING THE BUSINESS

There has been much theoretical talk in the past about "value added." What we really mean is that every company should be focused on protecting, creating, and sustaining value. Failure could mean stock price falls, cash calls, unwelcome bids, or business failure.

So the C.E.O., C.F.O., and colleagues need vision and courage. Value creation is top of the agenda. It involves generating the value and protecting it. Brand, fear, technical and fundamental analysis of markets have assumed more significance than the internal business plan, budgets, and the annual report. When investors are frightened or lose faith, they can destroy value much faster than you can create it.

This is why cash generation is critical. Share prices already eroding due to poor results or loss of confidence in a business model fall dramatically faster when you have to raise cash in an unreceptive market. Investors share your wish to sleep easy at night.

Some C.F.O.s cite short-termism as the real driver of value, therefore. They castigate "teenage scribblers" and analysts for not understanding their business. Some make errors of judgement, not only in their handling of such relationships but also in silence or worse still nasty surprises.

Marconi was a case in point. For months investors expected a profit warning. The company continued to make reassuring noises. Investors continued to sell against an expectation of bad news. Eventually the share price was suspended. Dreadful news was released. Returning from suspension the price was savaged. It had fallen from over £12 to under 20p in a year. Trust evaporated as investors tried to decide whether concealment or incompetence had been to blame. Marconi may never again be a FTSE 100 company.

MAKING IT HAPPEN ▸▸

Messages for managers

Creating and protecting shareholder value are even more important in the 21st century. Volatility, expectations, speed of reporting, and a hungry investor demand for "real-time" information have changed the dynamics. The C.F.O. needs new skills. These include: strategic thinking; proactive risk management; communication and interpersonal skills of a high order.

Value creation is about having a clear strategic and business focus, flexible and adaptable as appropriate. The C.F.O. and executive colleagues must recognize the importance of having a sound, understandable business model. The financial model must be based on value creation, ideally measured in sustainable revenues, income, and especially cash. Reporting should be rapid and transparent, using the speed of technology, with no surprises.

You can create long-term value, but investors can take it away in the short term when fear overrides faith, if you don't heed these messages. Relationship management with analysts, investors, and the media is the critical skill that wasn't mentioned when the C.F.O. trained as an accountant. When you understand and manage strategic business risk and the macro-economic factors, you may at least anticipate the challenge of analysts, whether or not they understand your own unique business model. If the unforeseen intervenes, report it rapidly and accurately, with a clear understanding of the factors and a plan to manage the consequences.

Finally, much of this message relates to private companies also. Investment of private capital is accelerating. A clear business model is fundamental to accessing the cash for investment and growth, especially if you plan eventually to come to market.

CONCLUSION

All companies can follow this best practice to prosper in the 21st century:

- fast, reliable reporting;
- proactively anticipating and managing investor interest;
- investing in relationships;
- being clear, informed and consistent;
- creating and sustaining long-term corporate value.

For More Information

Books:

Bierman Jr., Harold. *Corporate Financial Strategy and Decision Making to Increase Shareholder Value*. New York: John Wiley, 1999.

Conger, Jay A., Edward E. Lawler III, and David L. Finegold. *Corporate Boards: New Strategies for Adding Value at the Top*. San Francisco, CA: Jossey-Bass, 2001.

Moore, Geoffrey A. *Living on the Fault Line*. New York: HarperBusiness, 2000.

Murnighan, J. Keith, and John C. Mowen. *The Art of High-stakes Decision-making: Tough Calls in a Speed-driven World*. New York: John Wiley, 2002.

Read, Cedric. *eCFO: Financial Management for the 21st Century*. New York: John Wiley, 2001.

Silzer, Rob, ed. *The 21st Century Executive: Innovative Practice for Building Leadership at the Top*. San Francisco, CA: Jossey-Bass, 2002.

Web Site:

www.cfo.com: complete with numerous articles and resources, a market update, and a large directory, CFO.com has enough information for all of your 21st century financial needs.

See also:

☆ **Why EVA Is the Best Measurement Tool for Creating Shareholder Value (pp. 131–32)**
✓ **Shareholder Value Analysis (pp. 574–75)**

"I would argue that the information standard has replaced the gold standard as the basis of world finance."
(Walter Wriston)

Avoiding the Mistakes of the Past: Lessons from the Startup World

by James E. Schrager

EXECUTIVE SUMMARY

Congratulations if you didn't personally feel the hardship of the dot-com implosion. Many millions went to their demise but at least left behind a legacy of what not to do. Fear not if you won't be using the Internet in your next venture. Many of these lessons generalize well beyond their former faulty incarnations. For those of you with a new product, technology, or division to launch, most translate into corporate organizations.

Introduction

Failure is a wonderful teacher. The new-economy revolution had so many trappings of a genuine economic revolt: vast fortunes forged in a fortnight, dashing young heroes and heroines, rotten institutions brought to their knees. It held such great promise, yet today even the dreams feel thoroughly eviscerated. What to learn from the revolution that never was? What lessons can be applied to new ventures?

No better place to look for historical clues than the business plans presented by aspiring business managers. These serve as the revolutionary documents of record, holding within their propositions the seeds of ultimate success or failure. We will reassess these pillars of revolutionary wisdom.

The Lessons to Learn

We Will Establish First-mover Advantage

The problem with this mantra is that first mover by itself means little; what matters instead is the power of your strategy. The first team to execute a dumb idea has accomplished nothing. In some cases, when you have an exceptional new technology, being first brings power. In other cases—say, when your strategy is nothing more than another way to sell books—being first has little effect. Post revolution, you can safely ignore the first-mover boasts. Instead, worry about the inherent strength or weakness of the business strategy.

Amazon was concerned with being the first big player selling books on the Web. However, Amazon's profit struggle has shown that being first made little difference. If you have an invention, for example, the xerographic copy process, being first is wonderful. But note the difference: Xerox got a patent for its process, thereby making it not only the first, but also the only company to offer a plain-paper copier. Since no one could duplicate its service, it was able to charge a premium. Amazon will never be the only seller of books, so its margins will always be subject to pressure. First mover is fine when defensible, but meaningless without a way to stop competitors entering the market.

Our Strategy Will Be to Grow Quickly

Wrong. Growth isn't a strategy, it's a goal. But the hard part isn't making goals. Rather, it's developing a way to make those dreams come true.

Getting big is the goal of most companies. In some business models, however, it's a requirement: eBay had to get big fast because it needed lots of both buyers and sellers to be the auction site of choice. How to do this? eBay did it by buzz, by having a willing stock market, by being in the right place at the right time, and by sheer luck. Make your business plan rely on something other than perfect timing.

We Will Be the Technology Leader

Venture capitalists (VCs) are at their best when making carefully calibrated bets on technology companies. They have mostly ignored the rough-and-tumble world of retail business on their way to investments in computer memory chips, software codes, medical devices, pharmaceuticals, genomics, magnetic storage media, telecom satellites, optical bandwidth, and truly new technologies. In each case tech-company founders had to produce something new and wonderful that worked as promised, would be in great demand, and could be protected via patents, trade secrets, or switching costs. Internet retailers may claim to have some bits of technology in a one-click purchase screen or real-time chat lists, but these are hardly protectable. As such, e-retailing cannot be the basis of a technology strategy.

Claims of new technologies that cannot be protected are not worth much. Instead, strategies may center on building a brand; however, this is expensive to construct and requires constant maintenance to remain viable.

We Will Create a Powerful Image

Instead of worrying about technology that can be protected, retailers concentrate on the precise construction of a tailored image to appeal to a consistently fickle public. Priceline discovered how expensive it is to spend for a national audience and capture just a tiny slice. The overreach inherent in most mass-media advertising makes it a very dull tool for carving a startup's image. So how will the image be created? Post revolution business plans need to find a more efficient way than simply throwing money at the problem! Your marketing plan must also develop a carefully conceived media approach to allow for your image to be built in an economically efficient manner.

We Will Attract the Best VCs—with Their Reputations We Can't Fail

As long as VCs can sell the idea to Wall Street, they'll build the company. When they cannot, they'll do their best to be long gone. Post revolution, VCs who dabbled in e-commerce look just like other Wall Street pawns, appearing to be infallibly brilliant when the market goes up and hapless fools when the market collapses.

The final customer for your product rarely cares who was behind the financing. It's clearly better to have a brilliant idea funded by people no one has ever heard of than a specious idea promoted by a well-known VC shop.

We Plan a Full-scale National Rollout to Leverage Our First-mover Advantage and Ensure Our Ability to Grow

An accurate market test is your very best insurance against a giant belly flop. But

"The man who makes no mistakes does not usually make anything." (E. J. Phelps)

don't think you'll impress anyone by faking it. For example, a pacemaker distributor in Japan gauged demand for a new product by displaying it to its current customers. Even though the doctors involved in the test showed overwhelming approval of the new device, it didn't meet sales projections once launched. In looking at why the test failed, the distributor noticed that the new device sold almost exclusively to existing customers. The distributor failed to realize the extent to which doctors are brand-sensitive. Make it a real test or don't bother.

We Will Form Alliances with Key Players

This is a fine idea, except that in the early days no one knows who will win. In times of rapid change, even an alliance with a leading firm may not deliver the promised advantages. The underlying business strategy, not just its alliances, most be more carefully understood. Very few partnerships in which the giving and taking aren't balanced will survive.

The Internet Changes Everything

Well, not really. The information superhighway is certainly here to stay, and we'll use it more and more, but gone are the stories of TheStreet.com buying Dow Jones, e-STEEL buying Bethlehem, and Amazon buying Wal-Mart. Other than Wall Street bonuses last year, the immediate changes wrought by the Internet are fairly modest and will play out over a much longer period rather than the matter of weeks we were promised at the outset.

In fact, it's comforting to know that the Internet won't change everything overnight. But the pace of change continues, even though not all change is progress. The Internet does enable very rapid access to information and the rather carefree exchange of e-mail messages. If either of these two attributes can drive your business plan further or faster, by all means use the Internet to get there. But what the Internet will not do is take people out of the center of the business process.

Making It Happen ▸▸

- Protect any new technology with patents or trademarks—create barriers to market entry.
- Determine your strategy, then your goals. (Growth isn't a strategy; it's a goal.)
- Aim to reach your target market in an economical way.
- Promote your marketable idea, not your financial backers.
- Stage an accurate market test.
- Use the Internet if it can drive your business plan further or faster.
- Be realistic: by all means, consider different scenarios, but do not lose sight of reality.

Conclusion

The basic rules of business strategy remain intact and do indeed apply to the Internet. Like selling things in a store, selling products on a computer screen isn't about technology. A technology business develops something new that cannot be easily imitated. This is the great lesson of the Internet failures. New businesses can be understood by looking at success and failure patterns of the past. A careful review of the strategy you propose can help.

For More Information

Books:

Gupta, Udayan, ed. *Done Deals: Venture Capitalists Tell Their Stories*. Boston, MA: Harvard Business School Press, 2000.
Slywotzky, Adrian, et al. *Profit Patterns: 30 Ways to Anticipate and Profit from Strategic Forces Reshaping Your Business*. New York: Random House, 1999.

See also:

- ☆ **Delivering and Delighting—A New Spirit at Work (pp. 71–72)**
- ☆ **The Good, the Fad, and the Ugly (pp. 175–76)**
- ☆ **Infusing a Company with Cutting-edge Strategy (pp. 83–84)**
- ☆ **Managing 1:1 Marketing (pp. 55–56)**
- ☆ **Marketing: The Importance of Being First (pp. 61–62)**
- ☆ **The New Frontiers in Old-economy Industries (pp. 99–100)**
- ☆ **Project Management (pp. 165–66)**
- ☆ **Scenario Planning (pp. 267–68)**
- ☆ **Switching Strategies (pp. 93–94)**
- ☆ **Viewpoint: B. Joseph Pine II (pp. 69–70)**
- ☆ **Viewpoint: Patty Seybold (pp. 67–68)**
- ☆ **Viewpoint: Philip Kotler (pp. 53–54)**
- **Arthur Rock (pp. 1130–31)**
- **Venture Capital (pp. 2131–33)**

"The mistakes of the great, promulgated along with the discoveries of their genius, are apt to work havoc."
(Erwin Schroedinger)

WHY EVA IS THE BEST MEASUREMENT TOOL FOR CREATING SHAREHOLDER VALUE
by Erik Stern

EXECUTIVE SUMMARY

- Economic value added (EVA) has transformed the corporate finance scene and business practice by transferring modern business theory from classroom to boardroom.
- Traditional metrics, with their roots in accountancy, distort economic reality. For example, crucial long-term intangible investments often fall foul of traditional metrics.
- If shareholder value is the goal, then the key to any metric must be the cost of capital, or shareholders' required return.
- At its best, EVA is not just a financial metric, it is a complete management system focused on value creation.
- Incentive-based EVA uniquely aligns the interests of managers, employees, and shareholders. Studies show that EVA companies, after implementation, have increased their market value over peers by some 50% over five years.
- Bold implementation of EVA signals the beginnings of transparency and accountability, though it is too often the subject of lip service. Implementing EVA half-heartedly or without incentives spells disappointment.
- A balanced scorecard demands EVA as the balancing mechanism. EVA covers everything managers can influence, and therefore all drivers of value.

INTRODUCTION

Financial measuring tools are many and varied. The media and equity analysts focus on financial accounting metrics such as sales and sales growth, margin, operating profit and operating profit growth, bottom-line earnings and its partner earnings per share (EPS), market value, return on equity, and return on assets or cash flow.

Each of these metrics is flawed. Neither sales nor operating profit accounts for the financial requirements necessary to achieve them, in terms of either annual expenses or capital invested. Bottom-line profits and EPS take no account of the fact that equity has a cost. Market value ignores the capital employed to create it–invest more, and of course market value rises, without necessarily creating value. And yet each is popular.

Why is so fundamental a series of misapprehensions so widespread? The answer lies in the past. Accounting operating profit is conservative–literally. It focuses on collateral, or at least what would be left of a company after bankruptcy. This is a more than adequate measure for a bank, but it is misleading for an investor. The theory of modern business is founded on the blindingly simple insight that business is primarily about economics, not accounting.

THE PROBLEMS WITH EXISTING CORPORATE FINANCE MEASURES

Debt-inspired measures are misleading because they *expense*–write off as expenses–aspects of business that are becoming increasingly important. Long-term intangible investments (training, brand building, and so on), in particular, create much of the value of companies today. Yet traditional accounting procedures expense these rather than treating them as investments. Additionally, investments in acquisitions (goodwill) and in restructuring (extraordinary items) are expensed. This is a mistake. A focus on value demands that long-term investments should appear on the balance sheet for the current year, taking the cost of capital into account.

Unless they take into account the cost of capital, return measures can become inflated. Furthermore, concentrating on percentages can lead to a misguided focus–for example, reducing capital investments (especially intangibles) calculated to create profits in the future.

If the hurdle rate for returns is very high, increases may discourage optimal creation of value. If the hurdle for returns is very low, increases may destroy value. If return objectives are above the required returns of investors–the right benchmark–then managers may forgo investments that create value. If returns are the objective and an increase fails to meet this required return, value destruction results.

Of other measures, cash flow will not provide the right answers in growing businesses. When Wal-Mart was growing rapidly, new stores cost more than the existing cash flow, yet no one demanded that the company stop investing and growing. Furthermore, the net present value of free cash flow emphasizes success in the terminal value of the equation rather than the horizon that managers can visualize and experience. Free cash flow, in other words, is not a flow measure.

MVA

The best measure of corporate performance is market value added (MVA), because this measure differentiates between the total market value, including debt and equity, and the total capital invested: MVA is the difference. (MVA may also be viewed as management value added–the value managers have added to a company.)

The problem is that MVA is strongly affected by share price, which is notoriously independent of senior executives. This makes MVA less useful for encouraging the creation of value, since it has limited operational use.

THE NEED FOR A MEANINGFUL FINANCIAL MEASURE

An alternative is necessary, one that focuses on what managers can influence rather than what they cannot. The measure should differentiate between financial inputs–what enters a company over time–and outputs–the value created. Clearly our choice should not be a driver of value such as the financial accounting metrics that managers can influence. Consider instead output, on an annual basis, as operating

---

"Our fixation with financial measures leads us to downplay or ignore less tangible non-financial measures."

(Tom Peters)

  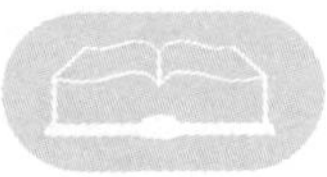    

profit after tax, with certain adjustments for intangible and other long-term investments and other accounting anomalies, and input as the annual rental charge on the total capital employed, both debt and equity. The rental charge or required return, known alternatively as the hurdle rate for investments or the weighted average cost of capital, is the true benchmark against which all investments and management should be measured. This is economic value added (EVA).

Understanding EVA

EVA covers all that managers can influence, all drivers of value. This is seen more easily if we view EVA as the capital investment multiplied by the difference between the actual return and the required return. If we think in addition about the required return as a mix of business risk and financial risk (where financial risk, or debt level, has a potential benefit also), then we have four of the major components of market value as defined by Merton Miller and Franco Modigliani. These are:

- the cost of capital for business risk
- the amount of debt
- the current level of operating profit
- capital expenditure

The other components look at future EVA (investor expectations for future growth) in the current level of EVA, what we call FGV, or future growth value: they are the expected return on new investment, and the time horizon for excess growth in profitability or EVA. Managers can influence more or less imperfectly the debt, operating profit, capital expenditure, and future returns. They influence the horizon and business risk little, if at all.

The Value and Scope of EVA

EVA covers profit and loss and the balance sheet, differentiating intangibles and growth, and thus covering all factors of production. Growing or improving EVA is the goal, with historic investments viewed as sunk. Hence, managers should focus on growing when the returns are greater than the cost of capital, redeploying capital when the returns are less than the cost, and improving returns on existing capital, as well as having an optimal capital structure (debt versus equity).

If value creation is key, then EVA is the answer, and EVA improvement is the goal. How managers achieve this or choose to accomplish this depends on what they think is victory for their business. Of course the answer may depend on the state of the economy. In reality, investing and containing costs are crucial everywhere on the economic cycle. However, criticism thrives in a falling market and falters in a rising one. A falling market puts failing companies under the microscope, and a rising market forgives all but the worst performers.

In other words, containing costs increases current and near-term EVA, and is always crucial. But investing determines near-term and future EVA and is also always crucial, if the cash is available.

Performance measurement is the bedrock of business. Since people manage what they measure, EVA can form the foundation for a more transparent and accountable management system, especially when combined with powerful incentives to improve EVA at every level, in every activity, across all functions, and independent of geography. With rights to make decisions accurately allocated, a fair system of transfer pricing in place, information flowing freely, and the appropriate tools and training offered, responsibility joins transparency and accountability through robust control and performance evaluation. Pay for the right performance, and value-based management results.

Under EVA, budgeting gives way to long-term planning. Control of the ends and the means is relinquished respectively to externally and objectively determined investor expectations and to management choice and opportunity that allow managers bet their own success on their meeting or beating shareholder requirements.

Making It Happen ▸▸

- Start using EVA as the key financial measure: subtract input (annual rental charge on the total capital employed) from output (adjusted operating profit after tax).
- Employ EVA as the foundation of a more transparent, responsible, and accountable management system, with robust control and performance evaluation.
- With the right to make decisions accurately allocated, put a fair EVA-based system of transfer pricing in place.
- Couple continuous restructuring of existing businesses to milk value with cautious investing in future businesses.
- Focus managers on growing where returns exceed cost of capital and on redeploying capital where returns are less than its cost.
- Insist on improving returns on existing capital as well as on having an optimal capital structure (debt versus equity).

Conclusion

EVA is, in short, the best measurement tool for creating shareholder value. A balanced scorecard of metrics allows for a big-picture view, but what is the balancing mechanism? If value creation over the long term is the goal—and if it isn't, shareholders should run—then EVA must be the balancing mechanism. Sales, margin, operating profit, and bottom-line profit simply fall short. Market value lacks levers. Return measures give the wrong answers. Only EVA can change companies.

Indeed, EVA correlates better with share price than any other measure: by 50%, compared with up to 30% for other metrics. Since EVA charges for all the factors of production, continuous improvement in EVA always furnishes investors with an increase in value.

Clearly if an organization pays lip service to EVA and blindly measures it without thinking about the behavioral consequences and the need to balance simplicity and accuracy, or else provides poorly considered or misguided incentives to create EVA, the outcome will disappoint. However, a robust system adhered to in times of boom and bust will provide the foundation of sound decision making and business practices.

For More Information

Books:

Ehrbar, Al. *EVA: The Real Key to Creating Wealth*. New York: John Wiley, 1998.

Stern, Joel M., and John S. Shiely. *The EVA Challenge: Implementing Value-added Change in an Organization*. New York: John Wiley, 2001.

Stewart, G. Bennett III. *The Quest for Value*. New York: HarperBusiness, 1991.

Web Site:

www.eva.com: a site set up by Stern Stewart & Co., the global consulting firm who pioneered the development of the EVA framework.

See also:

☆ **Competing on Costs (pp. 111–12)**
✔ **Calculating Economic Value Added (p. 841)**
✔ **Shareholder Value Analysis (pp. 574–75)**

"The great challenge of the twentieth century. . .is to create a new financial architecture in which private decisions produce a less degenerate capitalism." (Francis Hutcheson)

VIEWPOINT: PETER L. BERNSTEIN

The Case against the Long Run

The author of eight books in economics and finance, Peter Bernstein is a pre-eminent authority on capital markets and the real economy. His journal, *Economics and Portfolio Strategy*, is read by managers and owners of assets with a combined value of more than five trillion dollars.

Bernstein has been cited numerous times for his work and his thinking. In 1997, he received the Award for Professional Excellence from the Association for Investment Management & Research, AIMR's highest honor. In 1998 he was chosen to receive the annual Graham and Dodd Award for Excellence in Financial Writing. That same year, he was given the Clarence Arthur Kelp/ Elizur Wright Memorial Award from The American Risk and Insurance Association (ARIA) in recognition for an outstanding original contribution to the literature of risk and insurance.

"In the long run" is one of the most popular phrases in business and finance. It is also one of the most elusive, and has been used with contradictory meanings. Although many people assume the long run to be an essential part of both business and investment decisions, perhaps it deserves to be tossed into the dustbin.

Sometimes the long run shows up as a bad-weather friend. When business is bad or the stock market is depressed, we hear reassuring reminders that things always get better over the long run. Yet when business is great and the market is booming, emphasis on the temporary character of the short run is anathema. Everyone wants good business to last forever. The frequency with which people refer to the long run is a reliable measure of business and investor sentiment.

There is a more important meaning to the long run. Business decisions, where the rubber meets the road, also distinguish between the short run and the long run. Short-run decisions are those we can reverse without much difficulty. When we are locked into something, we are entering the deep waters of the long run. Accumulating inventory, executing a repo, or hiring a temp are clearly short-run decisions. Launching a new product, issuing a 30-year bond, building a new plant, and opening an office in Thailand are clearly long-run commitments.

The two uses of the concept of the long run appear to have nothing in common. The first says "This, too, shall pass." The second says we are locking ourselves in to this situation. Yet a common thread runs between the long run as a nostrum against bad news and the long run as a policy move reaching out in time: the key word is reversibility. This simple word reveals a great deal about the long run and how to put it to good use in shaping the future.

It is a truism to say that bad times will not last forever. Nothing lasts forever, including good times. Such a statement is little more than incantation, unless for forecasting or planning. John Maynard Keynes well understood this quality of incantation. He was not being facetious when he uttered his famous aphorism: "In the long run we are all dead. Economists set themselves too easy, too useless a task if, in the tempestuous seasons, they can only tell us that when the storm is long past the ocean will be flat." In a naturally volatile system characterized by uncertainty, we are inevitably trapped into the short run. Or, to put it another way, the long run is nothing more than a sequence of short runs.

Much of the appeal of the long run is in its resemblance to an average—the notion of regression to the mean over the long run appears to promise us that the good times will somehow come along after a while and bail us out of the bad times. But averages are dangerous things, useful in decision making only when they summarize a random sequence of events, like dice throws or spins of the roulette wheel. On the other hand, what happens today is the consequence of yesterday's decision, and what we do today determines what is going to happen tomorrow; hence, passive dependence on averages to hoist us out of trouble can lead to a perilous trap.

This little theoretical digression contains the moral of the whole story. History is notable for fluctuations from good times to bad, but history is not a random sequence of events. Nothing in the past happened without a cause. The great prosperity of the 1990s developed out of the 1980s—widespread deregulation combined with the flood of restructurings, takeovers, shutdowns, consolidations, layoffs, and, most of all, revolution in the boardroom and new emphasis on shareholder values. The impact of the high-tech revolution of the 1990s has been great, but I would argue that the dynamic of innovation would never have taken a grip on the economy without the intensely competitive environment created by the 1980s. Those

"Long-range planning does not deal with future decisions. It deals with the future of present decisions."

(Peter F. Drucker)

profound changes in both government and business in the 1980s were necessitated by the terrible errors of the 1970s, errors of both public policy and heedless over-expansion on the side of business. And so on and so on, all the way back to the beginning of time.

Which of these past heterogeneous states of the world are the ones we will have to confront over the long run that lies ahead? No one knows. Have we learned so little that we will replay the horrors of World War I, the 1930s, or the 1970s? Is the unique experience of the glorious 1990s likely to lead to anything that would closely resemble one of the eras of the past? But if the long-run past consists of nothing but experiences with no significance for today's world, then the long-run average derived from past events is also without significance.

We can learn from the past, but the experience of the 1990s is the launching pad of the future. Do not depend on the ocean being flat one day. Equilibrium is an economist's construct, effective in the textbook but irrelevant for executive planning. Even though nothing goes up or down forever, there is no predictable point, in space or time, to which matters regress.

When we enter the sacred precincts of the corporate boardroom, the context of the long run changes. Corporate leaders specialize in the search for empty space and disequilibrium, because that is where opportunity lies: undeveloped markets, products, or production and marketing techniques, waiting to be exploited. Great economic changes result in displacement, not more of the same.

Once taken, commitment to spend money filling empty spaces or capitalizing on disequilibrium does not readily lend itself to second thoughts. It is a scary business to decide to build a new factory, open a new market in a foreign land, launch a new drug, acquire a major company in another line, or redesign an entire production process. If you are wrong, embarrassing write-offs will confront you. People who cannot stand the heat of such largely irrevocable decisions tend to go to work on Wall Street or in the City, where assets are liquid and decisions more easily reversed.

Seen from this vantage point, long-run business decisions look a lot riskier than reversible ones. Yet, from other vantage points, long-run moves may be less risky than short-run moves. It all depends on how we manage the risks of irreversibility. Two elements are involved in that process: information and control. Both are essential in making the long run our servant.

The long run would be riskless if the future were known. And if the future were known, irreversibility would be irrelevant. But that is fantasy—we never have complete information. More information, however, is always better than less. Furthermore, we almost always have the option of postponing action while awaiting further information. Up to the point where we start actually writing checks, the arrival of new information has more value than the same information would have after the die has been cast. Decisiveness is admirable, but so is a sense of when to procrastinate before striding into the long run.

What is procrastination worth? Think of procrastination as an option to wait, or even not to act at all. The primary determinant of the value of an option is the volatility in the possible outcomes. Highly volatile outcomes add value to an option because a bad outcome would cost no more than the time spent waiting for information, while a good outcome could have enormous benefit. Consequently, the value of the option to procrastinate is a function of the uncertainty surrounding an irreversible decision. As the option expires at the moment when the corporation sinks its money into the new project, waiting for more information may often be preferable to a "damn-the-torpedoes-full-speed-ahead" approach. Indeed, the option of procrastination is properly part of the cost of capital or hurdle rate, justifying careful estimation of the long-run outlook.

The second element of risk management in long-run decisions is—rather, must be—control. In typical investment in a reversible asset like a stock or bond, owners or creditors play a passive role, in reality having no say over the management of the corporation involved. In contrast, the management of the corporation itself has the power after the fact to vary the fundamental parameters of irreversible decisions and illiquid assets for which they carry responsibility. For example, they can change their prices, redesign the product line, or replace executive personnel.

There are few decisions whose outcomes are so ironclad they are totally immune to revision. That matters. The ability to make revisions means the ability to break the long run into a series of short runs. The greater the control, the shorter the run.

Despite its irrepressible popularity, the concept of "the long run" is in many ways misleading and without substance. The long run of the past tells us almost nothing about the long run facing us in the years ahead. But the long run clearly matters in business decisions. Even here we should not over-estimate the apparently risky character of the sunk costs and irreversibility looming over long-range plans to build new facilities, open new markets, or launch new products. Given sophisticated employment of information and control, such moves will almost always open up opportunities to crack that long run into shorter time periods, providing enhanced flexibility and reduced risk to the ultimate outcome.

For More Information

Books:

Bernstein, Peter L. *Against the Gods: The Remarkable Story of Risk*. New York: John Wiley, 1996.

Dixit, Avinash K., and Robert S. Pindyck. *Investment under Uncertainty*. Princeton, NJ: Princeton University Press, 1994.

See also:

Risk Management (pp. 2107–09)

Managing by the Open Book *by John Case*

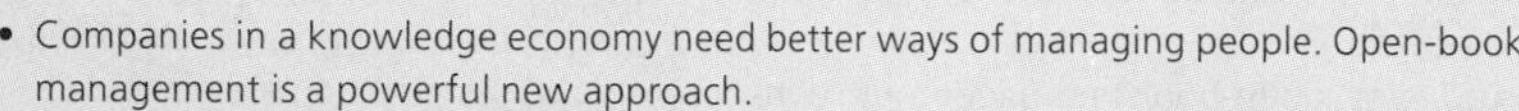

Executive Summary

- Companies in a knowledge economy need better ways of managing people. Open-book management is a powerful new approach.
- The open-book system focuses everybody's attention on business targets. Employees learn to be businesspeople rather than hired hands.
- Open-book management has caught on among only a few large companies for several identifiable reasons. But many young, entrepreneurial companies have adopted it and are now reaping the rewards.

Introduction

Companies in the 21st century are groping for new ways of helping people work together effectively. This is hardly surprising: the old hierarchical, command-and-control management systems were devised for industrial enterprises, where most people's jobs consisted purely of doing what they were told. Today's knowledge-intensive companies ask employees not only to do their assigned jobs, but also to take responsibility for world-class quality, impeccable service and continuous improvement and innovation. Thus employees find themselves in cross-functional groups and self-managing teams, charged with running their own projects or work areas as well as with solving their own problems.

But this situation presents a series of difficulties. Most employees don't really understand the business that they're in. They can't read a financial statement or a budget. They have never learned to understand the connections between operational performance and financial results. They don't have a good handle on the costs they incur (and must somehow manage) every day. They lack business acumen, because they have never had the occasion to acquire it.

The approach known as "open-book management," pioneered and developed over the past 20 years primarily by small and midsized companies is designed to solve this problem. Open-book companies teach *and expect* their employees to think and act like businesspeople, and to manage themselves accordingly.

The Essentials of Open-Book Management

"Open book" is a way of running a business; it means far more than just communicating financial results to employees. The following elements are essential.

Determine Critical Numbers

Every businessperson—every manager—has a few key numbers that he or she always keeps a close eye on. In small companies the critical numbers are usually financial: sales, margins, cashflow. In departments or divisions of larger companies, some key numbers are operational—they may include metrics such as units shipped, defect rates, machine uptime, and customer acquisition costs. Savvy managers and business owners know their critical numbers intuitively, and track them from week to week and quarter to quarter. They also understand the relationship between operational metrics and financial performance. Hotel executives know they make money when revenue per available room crosses a certain threshold. Seasoned plant managers estimate profitability simply by watching the number of trucks at the loading dock. Listen to J. Robert Beyster, C.E.O. of Science Applications International Corp. (SAIC), the big global research and engineering firm based in San Diego, California: "What are SAIC's critical numbers?. . .Time sold, or what is more commonly called labor utilization, drives our business. . .If our time-sold targets are not met, we face staff reductions."

Communicate and Explain Numbers

SAIC—one of a handful of large companies that practices open-book management—sends out biweekly reports on each division's time-sold performance. SRC Holdings Corp., a midsized remanufacturing company headquartered in Missouri, puts charts on the wall. For example, at an SRC subsidiary that rebuilds electrical equipment, a green chart shows plant-wide efficiency, and a red one shows how much of the finished product was composed of used parts (a larger percentage means more savings).

Teaching the "meaning" of the numbers essentially means explaining the connection between operational indicators and financial performance, and that, in turn, means providing people with a grounding in the basics of business. Employees of SRC, which has practiced open-book management since 1983, actually learn to read an income statement and a balance sheet; wall charts at the company show income and expense breakdowns as well as the operational indicators. A New York City marketing communications firm asks its employees to be "C.F.O. for a day," not only to learn the financial numbers but also to explain them to fellow employees. A Massachusetts manufacturer prepares profit-and-loss statements for each team of production employees, so they can learn to track their contribution to company profits, day in and day out.

Give Employees Power and Responsibility

Many companies these days claim to "empower" people. But empowerment for what? It doesn't do any good to empower people to halt an assembly line or solve a customer's problem unless they understand the business costs and benefits involved. Indeed, empowerment without such understanding can be counterproductive. One manufacturer empowered employees to do "whatever it took" to ensure on-time delivery of product. It wasn't long before managers discovered that the company's margins were being destroyed by expediting costs and overnight-delivery expenses.

For most companies, the best system of empowerment is regular unit meetings to review and discuss key numbers. If the numbers aren't moving in the right direction, what needs to happen? Who has an idea? At least some of the numbers discussed at these meetings must be financial, precisely to avoid the kind of problem created by the all-out effort for on-time delivery. Indeed, veteran open-book companies such as SRC actually build rudimentary income statements at such meetings: unit representatives report their results for the previous time period and discuss how to correct any unfavorable variances from plan.

Establish Rewards

Open-book management asks employees to learn new skills and take on new responsibilities. Employees naturally ask "what's in

"You've got to figure out a way to manage the complexity of large projects yet still allow your core teams to focus on the essentials."
(Steve Jobs)

it for me?" and if the answer is "nothing," the system won't work. Small and midsized companies committed to open-book management typically establish substantial bonus programs pegged to targets on key numbers. These targets can vary from year to year, since any business's priorities vary from year to year (for example, sales growth one year, profitability the next, quality improvements in a third). Whatever the target, the bonus must be transparent, equitable, and nondiscretionary. Employees must be able to see how they're doing on the key indicators over time. They must know that they will be paid the bonus if they make the targets.

Units of large companies may have to plead with the human resources department for flexible compensation plans, and unionized companies may need to negotiate bonus terms with the union. (The difficulties of both are one reason why relatively few large companies have been able to capitalize on the open-book approach.) Another useful tool for open-book management is an employee stock ownership plan or broad stock-option program. Insofar as employees *are* owners, they have a built-in incentive to think and act like owners, which is exactly what open-book management requires. The job for managers then is to spell out the connections between financial performance and the stock price.

Obstacles and Payoffs

Open-book management makes a good deal of sense on paper, but so far it has been adopted by a minority of small companies and only a few big ones. The reasons stem from both intrinsic difficulties and institutional obstacles. To "go open book" is a big change for a company. Managers, remembering the maxim that information is power, are accustomed to keeping what they know to themselves, and sharing it only when it suits them to do so. Many employees, for their part, still expect to come to work and do only what they're told, and don't want more responsibility or involvement. Open book is a system that must be learned, and changing people's expectations and behavior requires time and patience. In a large company, moreover, it involves change on many fronts—new training, new compensation arrangements, and new procedures for sharing and discussing information. Unit managers often must navigate a thicket of corporate policies and procedures just to reward employees for hitting a business target they all agree on.

And yet open-book management continues to spread, without much help from consultants or professors, primarily among new, growth-oriented companies. For example, a remarkable 53% of the companies on *Inc* magazine's year-2000 list of the 500 fastest-growing private companies in the United States practice open-book management. The reason is simply that the payoffs are substantial:

- It focuses employees' attention on the basics of the business
- It builds a collaborative environment—open-book companies report less of an "us versus them" attitude and less office politics
- It taps the wisdom and experience of employees at every level
- It helps create a more fun, more satisfying atmosphere in which everyone is working toward common goals.

Most of all it produces results. "By opening the books," writes Fay Wu, chief financial officer of Toronto-based Castek Software Factory, "we focused everyone's attention on business performance. . .Castek has successfully doubled its size every year by moving the 'numbers' in the right direction."

Making It Happen ▸▸

These are some first action steps you can take towards achieving open book:

- Determine your business's critical numbers. Chart the relationship between changes in these numbers and financial indicators (margins, costs, and so on)
- Put key numbers up on a chart or on your company's intranet. Hold lunchtime discussions to explain why these numbers are important to financial performance
- Set short-term targets for key numbers, and review progress at weekly meetings. Begin to involve employees in establishing longer-term targets
- Investigate your company's compensation plan to see how much flexibility you have. Meantime, see whether you can pay small bonuses or rewards out of your budget—and if so, set up a short-term, unit-wide "game" to hit a certain business goal. Pay the bonus if the goal is attained.

Conclusion

Companies searching for a new way of managing people in the knowledge economy can learn much from the small, entrepreneurial companies that have developed open-book management. Open book can be challenging to implement, particularly in a large corporation, but the payoffs are substantial.

For More Information

Books:

Case, John. *The Open-book Experience*. Cambridge, MA: Perseus, 1998.
Schuster, John P., et al. *The Power of Open-book Management*. New York: John Wiley, 1996.
Stack, Jack, with Bo Burlingham. *The Great Game of Business*. New York: Doubleday/Currency, 1992.

Web Sites:

www.greatgame.com: this site is based upon and accompanies the book *The Great Game of Business* by Jack Stack (see above).
www.saic.com/about/obm.html: this is the site of Science Applications International Corporation (SAIC), a research and engineering firm offering a broad range of expertise in technology development and analysis, computer system development and integration, technical support services, and computer hardware and software products.

See also:

☆ **Setting Objectives for a Business (pp. 305–06)**
The Practice of Management (p. 943)
Peter Drucker (pp. 982–85)

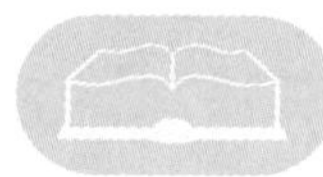

Viewpoint: John Seely Brown

Changing the Workplace into a Meaningful Community

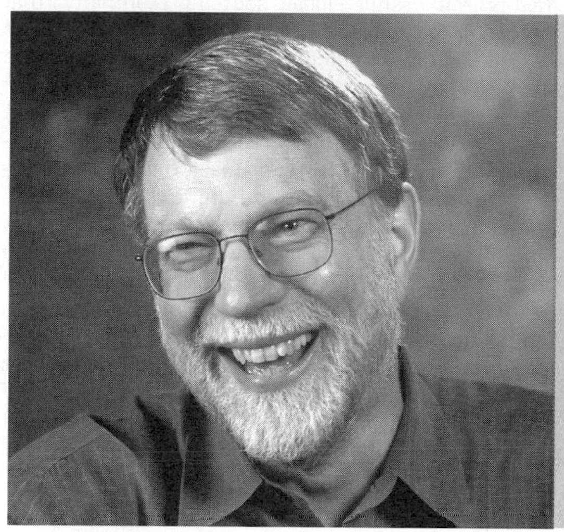

John Seely Brown is not your typical scientist, but rather a blend of scientist, artist, and strategist. Combining the worlds of digital culture, ubiquitous computing, and organizational learning, he serves as chief scientist for the Xerox Corporation and was director of the Xerox Palo Alto Research Center (PARC) from 1990 to 2000. His acclaimed *Social Life of Information*, a book he coauthored, is transforming the way people think about information. Offering a rare perspective on the human contexts in which technologies operate, he maintains change does not always represent genuine progress.

What is the most important thing and who is the most important person to have influenced your thinking on business and management?

Actually, two people come to mind–each operating in different domains from the other and both radically distinct in their views.

The first is Elizabeth Teisberg, at the University of Virginia's Darden Graduate School of Business Administration. Taking "real options evaluation" theory from the world of finance and capital management, she demonstrated how options thinking could be applied to the funding and evaluation of research and development initiatives. The concept is very dynamic and, truthfully, there's nothing I do any day that is not influenced by her model.

Real options analysis represents a merging of *investment* decision making with *strategy*. It enables us, in effect, to value two sources of *learning*: learning by *doing*, which allows us to determine if there are any unexpected problems with an undertaking; and learning by *waiting*–to see how the market develops and learn what customers really want.

By using these techniques companies can take calculated R&D risks, in the form of options on the future, without "betting the farm" or making full-scale strategic commitments initially. Indeed, it encourages the creation and exploration of opportunities, while providing a discipline for continuously assessing whether the options being created are *real*–having potential for significant returns and being worthy, therefore, of further investment. Most importantly, real options thinking strongly implies that viewing risk-taking as "betting" is a mistake!

As we begin to incorporate options thinking, we're continuously *staging* and *gating*–creating opportunities and determining checkpoints for making "go" and "no-go" decisions. This is a very useful concept in the world of R&D, particularly when you're concerned with cash flow. It establishes a dynamic system for scaling an investment as well as exiting a project altogether. The process effectively shapes conversation around managed risk-taking and the reserving of options for the future. It also favors a bias for innovative thinking, while eliminating much of the politics underlying the innovator's dilemma.

In a world of accelerating change and dynamic tension, we need disciplines in which we can be playful–frameworks for choreographing the delicate dances of opportunity and commitment. For me, the appeal has been in my being able to take the world of research management to a new plane–allowing for a sort of *creative abrasion* between acts of creation and evaluation.

The second person is Professor Lucy Suchman of Lancaster University's department of sociology. An anthropologist, ethnomethodologist, and author, Professor Suchman completely blew away a corner stone of artificial intelligence with her analyses of situated action. She elaborates on these findings in her book *Plans and Situated Actions: The Problem of Human-Machine Communications*.

Drawing on ethnomethodological studies of all types of work, from the seemingly mundane to the most complex and intellectually demanding, she successfully uncovered the specific culturally and materially embodied identities, knowledge, and practices that make up technical systems. Her research helps us to understand how work gets done and to honor the context and situations in which workers find themselves. For example, at Xerox we were interested in the role and importance of business processes. Dr. Suchman conducted analyses as a participant observer and then returned to ask that community of

"The joy and moral stimulation of work no longer must be forgotten in the mad chase of evanescent profits."

(Franklin D. Roosevelt)

practice if certain office procedures were helpful. They affirmed they were. But she found the procedures were not being used as originally intended. Workers did not follow the step-by-step instructions; instead, they improvised around the "unexpected," while ensuring the ensemble of improvisations created a result that looked like what they would have gotten had they followed the overall procedure.

I came to the conclusion that many practices in which employees are engaged in the workscape today are driven by improvisation and can't be reduced to written procedures—simply because workers are continuously problem solving, improvising, and dynamically interpreting what is going on in the contexts of their environment. That realization moved me to appreciate the inherent creativity of people "at work" and to conclude that *practice makes process* and not the converse.

What will business need to do differently in the 21st century?

We will need to transform the workscape into a place of *meaning*. It will be incumbent upon managers to view the work environment as "communities of practice." They must recognize their existence, understand them, and build environments that are genuinely supportive of continuous learning and identity formation. *Their challenge will be to architect the workscape of the future utilizing the triadic elements of social, physical, and informational space.*

I believe the pathway to the future will require "looking around"—managers will need to eschew the sort of tunnel vision that "sees" only *one* system or solution for getting there. Let's be frank! Real innovation is not born of logic, but of aesthetics based on a sort of playfulness and constant interpreting of the world in which we operate.

Creating joy, innovation, and meaning in the workscape requires that managers see and think contextually. They will have to unlearn old styles of managing and create, instead, workscapes that foster emergent communities of learning by honoring worker improvisation and knowledge formation.

What new skills will be needed to cope with these changes?

One's ability to unlearn is constrained by *tacit beliefs*. Successful managers must not assume they know someone else's frame of operation. Instead, they will have to appreciate the profound significance of seeing the environment through the eyes of the other person—whether employee, customer, or resource provider. They will have to determine what matters most to others and move to satisfy their needs.

As in sailing, it's a matter of "triangulation." When navigating through unfamiliar waters, managers need to reference various points continuously to get their bearings. Dead reckoning and triangulation are principal methods by which we can learn, but doing this is almost an art form. To be sure, in the corporate world there's a thin line between joy and terror, and it takes a skilled navigator to keep from going over the edge.

Managers must move increasingly to the mode of win-win. Consider Li & Fung Limited in Asia, a highly successful global sourcing company that orchestrates an entire network of some 6,500 shops in 100 countries to produce goods for their corporate clients. They can take an order from a retail customer and determine the best source according to craft skills, materials used, product quality, and turnaround times. Li & Fung have mastered a deep knowledge of their producer communities. By playing to individual strengths rather than forcing each to a uniform standard or to a least-cost basis, Li & Fung foster an environment where everyone wins and learns. Successful managers will need to become proficient in this regard and emulate the skills of orchestrators like Li & Fung rather than controllers of work practices.

Are there new management questions we should be considering?

Two questions relate to how well an organization is managing its own "periphery"—both *within* and *outside of* its own walls. The first periphery deals with finding the "radicals" who live on the fringes of the organization—customer contact people, for example, who make discoveries every day. Good ideas come from lots of different places. Managers need to honor those on the margins of the enterprise and centralize their knowledge for the sake of the business.

The second periphery has to do with looking and listening to the marketplace—looking at competitors, especially new entrants. It's so easy to discount the smaller players, but often they're only "small" relative to one's interpretation of the market.

A third consideration relates to how effectively managers challenge one another to think about strategic surprises they can launch at their competitors and, in turn, surprises the competition may be planning for them. This line of questioning is an effective way of getting people to think out of box.

How can companies best promote enterprises that are both profitable and good places for people to work?

The answer relates again to the idea of creating a learning milieu. By paying serious attention to *people* in an organization—on the fringes, serving customers, in the trenches—roles get reversed, as potentially marginalized ideas and competencies become central. Work becomes meaningful for everyone, and both individual and corporate intelligence grows. By understanding the contextual aspects of work, honoring the creative abilities of employees, and reserving opportunities for the future, managers can produce enterprises that are highly successful and enormously satisfying. Of course, the icing on the cake comes with building information systems that facilitate the flow of ideas and nurture the social capital of the enterprise.

"The chief problem of big business today is to shape its policies so that each worker will feel. . .a vital part of his company."

(William Cooper Procter)

ENTERPRISE INFORMATION SYSTEMS
by Thomas H. Davenport

EXECUTIVE SUMMARY

- Enterprise information systems are the backbone systems supporting business transactions all across an organization.
- They support broad business processes and cut across such organizational structures as business functions and business units.
- Increasingly the successful implementation and use of these systems is the key to organizational productivity, to customer and supplier relationships, to the successful execution of competitive strategy, and certainly to electronic commerce.

INTRODUCTION

Information systems have become an integral part of how organizations work and compete. They now support every business objective and process. Those systems that support core business activities for the entire organization are known as ***enterprise information systems*** or enterprise resource planning systems. Without them, no organization could easily take orders from customers, procure goods from suppliers, ensure that there is sufficient inventory, or keep track of employee compensation and vacation balances. Enterprise information systems, then, consist of some of the following types of systems, many of which are linked in the contemporary organization's technology architecture:

- accounting and financial
- human resource management
- sales and order management
- logistics and supply chain
- manufacturing
- inventory management
- customer relationship management

Enterprise information systems do not include those systems that serve only a small part of an organization—say, a standalone system to manage the legal department. They also would not generally include systems for analyzing data or supporting decisions, or for sharing knowledge within an organization. Enterprise systems are primarily focused on core business transactions. Because of their importance and complexity, enterprise systems have turned the usual formula for business change on its head. It used to be that firms decided what they wanted to do, then built systems to accomplish it. Now they must think first about what they can accomplish with systems, and then they proceed to do it. Of course this raises significant issues for how companies manage and compete.

MAKING IT HAPPEN

Getting Them in and Getting Value

Almost all firms that implement enterprise systems do so by buying and installing a package. Firms such as SAP, Oracle, and PeopleSoft (in descending order of current market share) supply application packages that are an integrated collection of modules—one for accounting, one for human resources, and so on. Firms attempt to configure the packages to fit their particular organizational situations. Because of the complexity of the packages, it is not generally advisable to modify them beyond the limits of the configuration process—hence the constraints that these systems impose on organizational flexibility. Some organizations, however, develop their own proprietary modules and interface them with their packages, although this can be a difficult undertaking as well.

The configuration process has been challenging historically, since both the packages and the organizations they support are complex. Vendors often provide a preconfigured set of choices that a particular organization can select from—for example, what currency to use, or whether revenue will be recognized across geographical units or product groups. The choices are complex, and deciding what options a particular company needs to fit its organization and way of doing business requires both business and technical decision making, and a high level of communication between technical and business managers. Many business executives do not understand these systems or the importance of not modifying them substantially. The idea that they should change their way of doing business to suit the limitations of an information system is often hard for them to understand. But for business people to withdraw from the configuration process almost ensures a system that will not meet business objectives.

One of the key challenges with these systems is to achieve real business value in the implementation process. These systems are capable of delivering such benefits as radically improved business processes, reductions in inventory, increased sales (through one-stop ordering and prevention of stockouts), and better management of financial and physical assets. Most organizations, however, fail to achieve these benefits—in part because simply installing the system often becomes the overriding objective. Yet these systems are expensive—usually costing in the tens or hundreds of millions of dollars to implement for a large organization—and managers of the projects must not lose sight of the potential benefits. The key to achieving benefit is to view the project not as a technical initiative, but as a business change project with clear objectives and measures.

Changing Everything at Once

The secret to both the opportunity and the difficulty of enterprise information systems is their tight integration with the business they support. Enterprise systems, to be effective, must be closely aligned to a company's business processes, information, organizational structure, and strategy. While this integration is positive in the sense that businesses can get higher-quality information than ever before, it is also challenging to deal with, both at the time of implementation and thereafter.

During implementation, the integrated nature of these systems means that organizations must "change everything at once." That is, they must ensure that all aspects of the organization that will be affected by the system are consistent with their objectives for them, and that the system fits each aspect. For example, most companies will have objectives for

"Only management can change the system." (W. Edwards Deming)

process improvement and for greater consistency of key processes across the organization. In most cases, some change is desired from the current state. An organization may wish or need in the course of its enterprise system project to develop greater consistency in definitions of key information across different business units, for example. At the same time it may want different units to share the same process for reporting financials. Identifying and bringing about these changes in the business may be much more difficult than simply configuring and installing a new system, but it is the system project and its managers that get saddled with the responsibility for making the changes happen.

Because the project involves business change as well as a new system, many organizations put a senior business executive in charge of the project, such as the chief operations officer or chief financial officer. If the desired changes primarily involve a single functional area, it may make sense to put a functional executive in charge, such as the head of logistics or manufacturing. Putting an IT executive in charge is a good way to ensure that little business change gets accomplished, even if the system gets installed.

The Implications for Competitive Advantage

It has been estimated that an enterprise systems package can support up to 70% of an organization's information needs. Since these systems come as packages and are similar from one company to another—even after the configuration process—the question arises how firms can obtain competitive advantage from their systems and the processes they support.

Some companies tailor their enterprise systems to fit the needs of their business, and rely on being the first to install the systems in their industry. Reebok, for example, added size and color information to the basic SAP system, and was the first company in the athletic shoe industry to implement a package with these capabilities. Its rival Nike also installed SAP, but completed its implementation several years later.

Another alternative is to implement enterprise systems only in those "commodity" business functions that are not associated with competitive advantage. Intel, for example, believes that its primary advantages over competitors come from its product design and manufacturing processes. When implementing an enterprise package, it did not use any package capabilities in these business functions, but rather developed its own systems internally.

What's Next for Enterprise Systems?

Enterprise systems have thus far been implemented primarily to support internal operations. In the future, it is likely that systems will be integrated across organizations. If a supplier's systems can interface with a customer's without human intervention, firms could better coordinate their logistical and production processes, and the costs of supply chains could be reduced. Some firms are already beginning to work on this integration.

Given the similarities across businesses in areas supported by enterprise systems, it is likely that we will begin to see new business arrangements wherein several firms collaborate on common business transactions and enterprise systems. For example, six oil exploration firms in the North Sea, including BP and Conoco, have combined their accounting and financial processes and enterprise information systems in a joint effort to share services. They have outsourced the operation of these services to an external professional services firm.

The other key direction for enterprise systems is for vendors and implementing firms to add increasing amounts of functionality to their systems. Today, for example, many firms are working at adding customer relationship management (CRM) and supply chain management (SCM) capabilities to their base enterprise systems. They have integrated their enterprise systems with the Internet so that core transaction systems can be employed in electronic commerce. They are also making enterprise systems information more easily available through portals and data warehouses. It is also likely that many firms will eventually add product lifecycle management functions to their core systems. The tight grip that enterprise packages have on business information systems is likely only to increase.

Conclusion

For an organization that has yet to implement a system, the following steps will help it get under way effectively:

- Create the project as a business change initiative, not a systems project.
- Select a package from a well-established vendor that has all the functionality your organization needs, and limit the changes to the configuration options provided.
- Don't put off the changes in business processes and organizational structure until after the system is installed.
- Tie incentive compensation of the project team, sponsoring executives, and any consultants used to the successful accomplishment of business objectives.

For companies that have already installed enterprise systems but did not receive sufficient value, it's not too late to optimize the system and deliver more benefits:

- Identify the areas of the business in which value from the system should have been achieved, but was not.
- Create a process improvement or reorganization initiative to bring about the desired business changes.
- Reset the configuration of the system to fit the new process and organization.

For More Information

Books and Articles:

Davenport, Thomas H. *Mission Critical: Realizing the Promise of Enterprise Systems*. Boston, MA: Harvard Business School Press, 2000.

Davenport, Thomas H. "Putting the Enterprise in the Enterprise System." *Harvard Business Review*, July–August 1998.

Norris, Grant, et al. *E-Business and ERP: Transforming the Enterprise*. New York: John Wiley, 2000.

Web Site:

www.cio.com/research/erp: the Web site of *CIO* magazine's Enterprise Resource Planning Research Center.

See also:

☆ **Data Mining (pp. 152–53)**
☆ **Managing the Challenge of E-service (pp. 188–89)**
✔ **Open Systems Thinking (pp. 568–69)**
Computers, Information Technology, and E-commerce (pp. 1931–33)

"Many individuals and organization units contribute to every large decision." (Herbert A. Simon)

  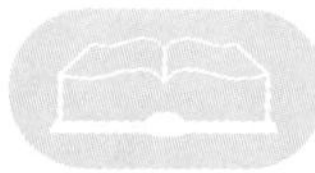    

DEVELOPING AN INTERNET-ERA MINDSET THROUGHOUT THE ORGANIZATION
by John Nirenberg

EXECUTIVE SUMMARY

- Because the Internet, telecommunications, and computer technologies enable us to behave so much more knowledgably and almost instantaneously, our organizations must mirror this behavior internally to remain effective and competitive.
- The Internet is changing the way we think about our environment and how we organize to stay competitive.
- The Internet-era mindset involves the integration of learning, imagination, and the capacity for radical innovation into the internal processes of the organization and the cognitive behavior of its work partners.

THE IMPACT OF THE INTERNET

It is now obvious that computer, electronics, and telecommunications technologies are influencing every aspect of our lives in dramatic and inescapable ways.

While we admire the Internet's presence, the hardware that connects us, and the enormous capabilities of the fiber-optic vine rapidly covering the planet, we have yet to integrate our observations of this new external world into the reality of our personal internal world and organizational processes. But our survival depends on coming to grips with how the Internet has fundamentally changed the way we compete, who we compete with, and how we'll need to organize even to stay in the game.

The new Internet environment is turning our traditional models of life and work upside down. While we've been used to linear time, incremental growth, slow face-to-face relationship building, top-down hierarchies of power, formal communications, and mostly centralized, unilateral command-and-control decision making, we now must adjust to an instantaneous world with massive, simultaneous, multitasking, parallel-processing capabilities made possible by technological innovation.

Add to that frequent surprises of new products and services that sometimes appear suddenly and from unexpected quarters, and we find ourselves in an unprecedented competitive environment. With the Internet we face a world of revolutionary change, viral growth, and instant intimacy with people we may never see; the new communications environment is a lateral, multinodal, collegial network activated by Web pages, e-mail, and instant messaging. The challenge to organizations today is therefore twofold:

1. to master the capabilities of an external Internet world;
2. to create an organization with the same internal qualities that reflect the Internet's driving forces.

Indeed, if we don't develop an Internet-era mindset, our organizations will fail.

THE INTERNET MINDSET

The Internet has three levels of impact. First is the now common but still incredible exchange of information globally, conveniently, and instantaneously. The second is building partnerships, creating synergies with suppliers and customers, and developing the ability to anticipate new competitive threats and solutions for emergent market needs and product/service efficiencies. The third level is the very reformulation of the nature of relationships and the creation of new realities that emanate from cyberspace.

In this new context a new nonlinear, nontraditional logic drives the development of meaning. Richard Ogle calls this the "Intercosm: a new kind of space for the creation of meaning and value, a space determined as it is by near-universal interconnection, interdependence, and the interplay of multiple emergent factors." This new arena for sense-making and world creation has profound effects as it overcomes geographic, cultural, and traditional forms of thinking, behaving, and creating meaning. All aspects of life become subject to intentionally constructing our reality, much like customizing a product or service to meet our individual desires. This postmodern idea that almost anything goes is tempered only by the agreements and negotiated outcomes of individuals freely choosing to associate. Harnessing this new force is one of the biggest challenges for organizations today.

HOW TO DEVELOP AN INTERNET-ERA MINDSET

If the impact of the Internet is obvious, unavoidable, and demanding of our adaptation, the implications for managerial behavior are equally revolutionary and transformational. There is simply no way to survive in this protean environment by conducting business as usual. Thus an Internet mindset must begin with the willingness to alter old hardwired patterns of human behavior. Organizations need to consider new ways for their members to communicate, build trust, share knowledge and experience, work together, and create a shared understanding of their reality. The Internet era requires that organizations become fully intentional—deliberate in their processes, inclusive of the contributions of each work partner, and responsive to all stakeholders.

This new environment demands teamwork, collaboration, a distribution of power to those closest to its application, accountability based on performance, expertise, and creativity freely used for the benefit of the group and not just oneself. The measure of success is defined by outcomes, not obedience. The purpose of controls is to ensure that resources are appropriately deployed toward meeting objectives, not conforming to a job description. Indeed, job descriptions become obsolete in an unpredictable world. These internal changes are necessary to successfully match the demands of the external world of constant change, innovation, and hyper-competitiveness.

How will it change? First, efficiency of resource use, speed of innovation, responsiveness to customer and employee needs, and intentional knowledge creation, management, and distribution will be essential. This will dismantle rigid hierarchies and conventional protocols and build networks of self-managing teams with access to whatever information they may need in order to respond as quickly as possible to customers and colleagues.

"Just having a great Web site is only one step in a company thinking of itself as an Internet company."

(Bill Gates)

Required organizational response to Internet-era mindset	
Driving Force	**Organizational Response**
Global opportunities	Global sourcing
Radical innovation	Flexibility/parallel processing
Competitiveness	Speed
Complexity	Teamwork
Accessible information and personal technologies	Decentralized decision making and personal responsibility
Continuous change	Continuous learning
Thorough professional socialization	Partnership/collegial orientation

We can understand how our managerial mindset and behavior need to shift by looking at computer hardware providers as an example of the global reach required to support corporate activities on a global scale by using intranets and the Internet.

In the case of, say, Apple or Dell, design may take place in California or Texas, while data is carried over intranets to a component manufacturer in Taiwan for chips, Hong Kong for housings, Peru for copper wiring to ship to a power-source manufacturer in Korea, all to be assembled in Malaysia and shipped to Guadalajara, Mexico, New Jersey, and Vancouver for warehousing and distribution.

Meanwhile logistic data is stored in Madras, human-resource administration is based in Dublin, and the worldwide sales and customer service headquarters is in South Africa, all connected through the company's intranet. The complexity of this arrangement—which is driven by the need to keep costs down, source where worldwide supply is available, and meet the demands of a global marketplace—is made possible by vast improvements in the Internet and other technologic, logistic, communications, and supporting infrastructure, from fiber-optic cables and communications satellites to state-of-the-art industrial parks and the availability of educated professional employees worldwide.

But the very complexity of this arrangement requires the power of a network itself driven by decentralized and self-managing teams that require a high level of professionalization, well-established working relationships, whether face-to-face or virtual, and the ability to manage the network for the mutual gain of the organization and its internal and external customers. Of course all of this must reflect the instantaneous nature of the Net.

Creating an Internet-era Mindset in Your Organization

Organize

- structures based on deliverables, not function;
- self-managing teams that take responsibility for their output.

Provide

- access to information;
- rewards based on team and individual performance;
- education and development opportunities to assimilate the necessary personal and organizational changes.

Create

- stimulating development experiences for each employee;
- off-line time to think;
- exposure to challenging input about changes in other organizations and the environment.

Convey

- a sense of shared meaning;
- authenticity and genuineness;
- respect.

Encourage

- innovation, creativity, and collaboration;
- consultative practices;
- personal and professional growth;
- career opportunities and challenges;
- fun.

Learn

- to communicate and lead in a virtual environment;
- to make sense of the Internet-era possibilities and create a shared reality with colleagues, including an intentional workplace of shared agreements, understandings, and commitments.

Making It Happen ▸▸

- Create an Internet mindset that includes developing divergent thinking skills—the ability to see new and different possibilities—and help each employee to become more curious, connected, inventive, trusting, and communicative.
- Integrate the Internet style of openness, accessibility, and knowledge sharing into your work life and your organization.

Conclusion

The Internet changes everything. The most obvious change is the ability to communicate and gather data instantaneously around the clock and around the world. Organizations need to create internal processes, structures, and procedures that mirror the world being created in the Internet era.

For More Information

Books:

Hamel, Gary. *Leading the Revolution.* Boston, MA: Harvard Business School Press, 2000.

Kelly, Kevin. *New Rules for the New Economy: 10 Radical Strategies for a Connected World.* New York: Penguin, 1999.

Levine, Rick, et al. *The Cluetrain Manifesto: The End of Business As Usual.* Cambridge, MA: Perseus, 2001. (See **www.cluetrain.com**.)

Ridderstråle, Jonas, and Kjell Nordström. *Funky Business: Talent Makes Capital Dance.* Upper Saddle River, NJ: Financial Times Prentice Hall, 2000. (See **www.funkybusiness.com**.)

See also:

☆ **The Business Web (pp. 145–46)**
☆ **Marketspaces (pp. 154–56)**
☆ **Virtual Collaboration (pp. 167–68)**
✔ **How to Establish an Enterprise Portal (p. 638)**
✔ **How to Generate Content and Build Loyalty through Online Communities (p. 629)**
✔ **How to Make the Most of an Intranet (pp. 636–37)**

"The electronic highway is not merely open for business; it is relocating, restructuring, and literally redefining business in America."
(Mary J. Cronin)

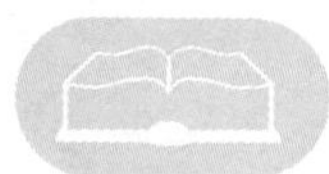

Integrating Real and Virtual Strategies *by David Stauffer*

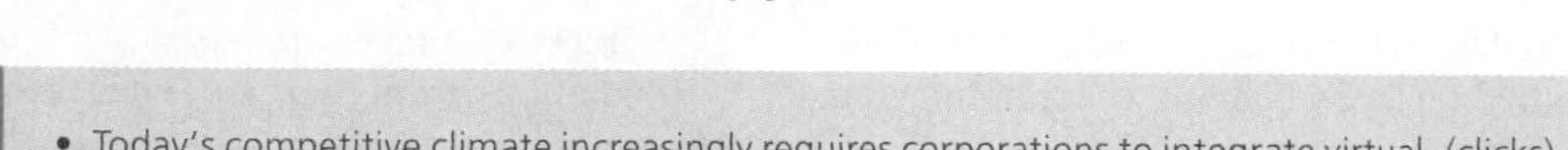

EXECUTIVE SUMMARY

- Today's competitive climate increasingly requires corporations to integrate virtual- (clicks) and physical-world (bricks) initiatives.
- Internally, the corporation's virtual units must drive more business to or through physical facilities, while bricks units must similarly boost virtual channels.
- Externally, customers must be able to interact with the corporation through virtual or physical channels, switch between channels, and receive the same products, services, and prices through any channel.

Introduction

Not long ago experts predicted the demise of long-established companies as relics of the Industrial Age. Then, as high-tech firms faltered, observers concluded that digital outfits weren't such world-beaters after all.

Today corporations young and old are demonstrating that success in the 21st century may most likely spring not from either old virtues or new technologies, but from a potent blend of the two. The ways in which any business effectively intertwines its real and virtual strategies—its bricks and clicks—uniquely reflect its history and its strengths. But an examination of companies that have successfully married clicks to bricks suggests that the key elements of a blissful union are:

- early and unflagging support from the top of the organization;
- meticulous strategic planning based in part on what other organizations have done;
- a clicks-side operation that strives to boost bricks-side business—and vice versa;
- technology employed not to replace workers, but to empower them;
- a structuring of products, services, and functionalities that allows customers to switch from clicks to bricks and back again at will.

How can you make each of these elements part of your powerfully integrated bricks and clicks strategies? Here are the essentials.

Taking It from the Top

Integrating bricks and clicks involves hard work, insight, and more than a few frustrations. Your effort won't necessarily succeed with the strong backing of corporate leaders. But it will certainly fail without that backing. Someone at the next level can, and probably should, be put in charge of implementing bricks and clicks integration. But the continuous, driving impetus must be exerted from the top.

One company with the right leadership chemistry is Eastman Chemical Company of Kingsport, Tennessee. Eastman has been one of the manufacturing sector's most prolific adopters of digital technologies, with an e-effort led by chairman and C.E.O. Earnest W. Deavenport, Jr. and chief information officer Roger K. Mowen, Jr. Both are career-long Eastman employees, with chemical engineering and sales and marketing backgrounds respectively. Yet Deavenport thinks way outside the chemical engineer's box. "Do you want to step back and wait until technology kills you?" he asks. "Or do you want to be out there on the leading edge?" And Mowen says his nontech background means that "business managers don't see me as the IT guy with wildly impractical ideas."

This high-tech odd couple implemented a bricks and clicks strategy by making a highly visible commitment to the effort. If managers—particularly those of the old school—don't see the top honchos leading the way, they're sure to play safe and stay where they are today.

Benchmarking and Best Practices

You've probably been advised more times than you can count not to reinvent the wheel. That's in part because it's sound advice endorsed by super-successful C.E.O.s. Ford C.E.O. Jacques Nasser has borrowed best practices from other industries in leading his organization's bricks and clicks integration. Among his initiatives was setting his managers' sights on emulating the build-to-order business model that made Dell successful. The Net-based enterprise FordDirect.com is structured along lines of Dell's build-to-order concept.

Do some exploring in business publications, on the Web, and by networking. Which companies are marrying clicks and bricks in a way you might emulate? Who's strongest where you may be weakest? What opportunities can you offer for a fair exchange of best practices? How can you encourage internal units to exchange their best ideas? Someone has already invented the wheel that's right for you. Find it.

A Virtuous Spiral of Mutual Aid

Provide incentives for your virtual-realm people to drive business to traditional outlets and for facility-based folks to generate online traffic. That's what Office Depot has accomplished. This Delray Beach, Florida office products retailer achieved its bricks and clicks synergy by getting things right when it first went online.

- *Office Depot made its Web unit an integral and equal part of its overall organization.* "That meant we weren't fighting over who got which customer or made which sales," says Monica Luechtefeld, the firm's e-commerce chief. By providing online access to information about store locations and inventory, Office Depot's Web sites have increased store traffic. The stores, in turn, promote the Web sites.
- *Office Depot committed additional time and expense to integrate Web functionality fully with its existing and proven information infrastructure.* Luechtefeld asserts that this is a largely unseen and often neglected strategy that can aid Net success. Now an Office Depot customer, even one new to Web purchasing, has online access to the past 18 months of purchasing history, from bricks as well as clicks.

Office Depot's experience suggests these strategies:

- Provide incentives for extending clicks efforts to the bricks side and vice versa. For example, tie part of sales reps' incentive pay to customer use of e-commerce, and so on.
- Make Net-based sales channels equivalent in structure and status to traditional channels.
- Tie Web functionality fully into existing systems as it's introduced.

"Stay one click ahead." (Anonymous)

Technology: It's a People Thing

New technology is often viewed as a way to reduce manpower. Some dot-coms even trumpeted the fact that they needed no employees at all (other than a few geniuses at the top). But some corporations that have achieved the most from emerging technologies view new capabilities as ways to further empower their people.

One of these is Inditex SA of La Coruña, Spain, a manufacturer and global retailer of hip clothes for fashion-conscious young people. Best known for its Zara stores, Inditex employs the clicks of digital technologies to link its people and operations worldwide and thereby boost sales from its bricks–some 1,000 stores on four continents.

Inditex starts with computers in every store, into which managers and sales reps enter notes on their sales-floor observations, not just on what's selling, but on the when, how, and why of selling. Fashion consultants similarly report from the favorite haunts of target customers. All of the input is analyzed in La Coruña by designers and production managers. They're empowered to make decisions on what to make, how to make it, and where to send it. Result: an incredibly short four-week lag between field observations and delivery of new fashions based on those observations.

Instant global communication is the enabler of Inditex's speed. But the key to its success is trusting and empowering employees.

Corporate leaders must provide their people with the technological capabilities that transform them from order takers or bean counters into insightful experts with a stake in contributing to the company's success.

Customers See Only Seamlessness

Do you see new technologies as strange and different channels for conducting business, channels used by strange and different people? If so, you're right–at least in the early stages of a digital initiative.

But experience has increasingly shown that companies make distinctions between bricks-customers and clicks-customers at their peril. For one thing, few customers now dwell in only one of these worlds. And even those who do deal with a corporation through only one channel want the same products and prices offered in the other.

Charles Schwab learned that lesson after the San Francisco-based investment services innovator set up its first online unit, e.Schwab, as a separate unit. Online customers got a break on stock-trading fees, but paid for that saving by having access to fewer services than those available to branch-office customers. E.Schwab succeeded at first, but soon stalled. Chairman Charles Schwab told *Forbes*, "Customers didn't feel good about the nonintegrated services."

So Schwab took a gamble by terminating e.Schwab and recognizing the online and offline customer as a single individual. That meant offering the lower online trading fee on the bricks side and extending enhanced services to the clicks world. Revenues plunged initially, but the gamble eventually paid off in new customers, new assets, and rocketing revenues.

The way to view customers, Schwab's experience shows, is holistically. Whether a customer interfaces with you by bricks, clicks, or both, that customer wants to be equally valued and get equal value. Make sure you provide it.

Mini-Cases

Combinations That Soar

Cemex SA, a Monterrey, Mexico cement maker that uses global positioning system (GPS) satellite technology to overcome the once-intractable obstacles of traffic and weather, delivering cement to construction sites within a 20-minute window.

Rosenbluth International, a Philadelphia corporate travel manager that used technology to pioneer the call-center concept. It has since incessantly applied technological innovations to automate the tedious aspects of workers' jobs and simultaneously serve customers better.

Snap-on Incorporated, a Kenosha, Wisconsin manufacturer and distributor of mechanics' tools that uses the Internet to make its dealers the main focus of digital initiatives. Its online catalog recruits new customers for dealers and provides dealer commissions on most sales.

Tesco, the United Kingdom's #1 supermarket chain, which is the world's sole example of a profitable purveyor of foods to customers who place orders online. It's simultaneously growing its bricks side by building ultramodern hypermarkets in Asia and Eastern Europe.

Making It Happen ▸▸

- Launch your bricks and clicks integration with an enthusiastic, ongoing commitment from the top of the organization.
- Explore what other firms have done to make clicks work with bricks. Avoid their missteps; adapt their successes.
- Insist that bricks and clicks become mutually supportive, with incentives on each side to boost business on the other.
- Implement new technologies not to replace employees but as a means of benefiting from their ground-level expertise and judgment.
- Blur customers' perceived distinctions between your bricks and clicks channels until they see no distinction.

Conclusion

We tend to view technological capabilities as something quite apart from the physical environment of factories, warehouses, trucks, and stores. Accordingly, most companies at first managed their clicks and bricks as nonintersecting universes. We know now that this distinction is not only incorrect, but it misses out on synergies. As bricks and clicks are treated as occupying one world, they can boost each other–and your business–to unprecedented success.

For More Information

Books:

Bovet, David, and Joseph Martha. *Value Nets: Breaking the Supply Chain to Unlock Hidden Profits*. New York: John Wiley, 2000.

Earle, Nick, and Peter Keen. *From.com to.profit: Inventing Business Models That Deliver Value and Profit*. San Francisco, CA: Jossey-Bass, 2001.

Seybold, Patricia B. *The Customer Revolution: How to Thrive When Customers Are in Control*. New York: Crown, 2001.

Web Site:

www.bricksplusclicks.com: the Web site of consultants Bricks Plus Clicks, which provides Internet tools enabling small bricks-and-mortar businesses to bridge the digital divide.

See also:

☆ **Viewpoint: Patty Seybold (pp. 67–68)**
✓ **Collecting Consumer Data on the Internet (pp. 624–25)**
✓ **Involving Customers in Product Development (pp. 706–07)**
✓ **The Key Issues of Implementing an E-commerce Strategy (pp. 580–81)**
▭ **Blur (p. 893)**

"Like the anthropologist returning home from a foreign culture, the voyager in virtuality can return home to a real world better equipped to understand its artifices." (Sherry Turkle)

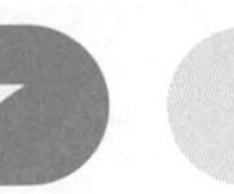

THE BUSINESS WEB *by Don Tapscott*

EXECUTIVE SUMMARY

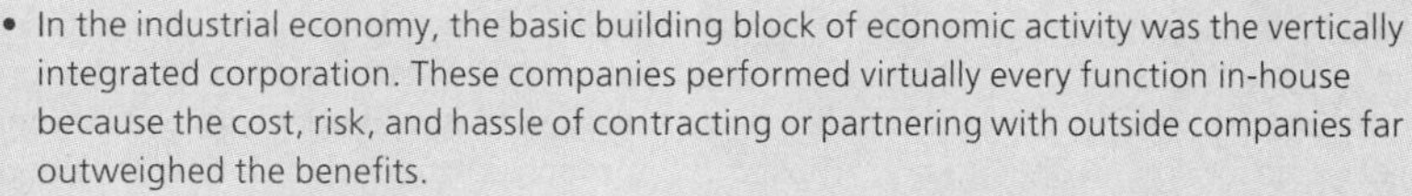

- In the industrial economy, the basic building block of economic activity was the vertically integrated corporation. These companies performed virtually every function in-house because the cost, risk, and hassle of contracting or partnering with outside companies far outweighed the benefits.
- Because the Internet slashes the cost of sharing knowledge, collaborating, and meshing business processes amongst corporations, companies can now focus on their core competencies and partner or outsource to do the rest.
- Together, in industry after industry, teams of companies—what I call a "business web"—are proving more supple, innovative, cost-efficient, and profitable than their traditional competitors.

INTRODUCTION

The headline-grabbing dot-com fireworks of the 1990s were largely a distraction, representing only a thin sliver of the businesses exploring the power of the Internet. Unfortunately, a get-rich-quick mindset distorted the assertion that "the Internet changes everything" (which is true) into the hope that "all things done on the Internet will prove lucrative" (which is rubbish).

It's now clear that a new vehicle of wealth creation is supplanting the corporation as the starting point for strategic thinking. It is a system of meshed entities–suppliers, distributors, service providers, infrastructure providers, and customers–using the Internet as the basis for business communications and transactions. Usually one company choreographs the activity and enjoys the lion's share of web profits, but all participants are essential, contributing according to their core competencies.

The key to competing in the digital economy is business model innovation that exploits business web power. Smart companies use the Net to achieve goals they have striven towards for 25 years, focusing on core competencies, reducing transaction costs, innovating more effectively, and gaining new ways to achieve deep customer relationships.

It's clear that profound changes are impacting corporate deep structures. LEGO, through its Mindstorm robot products, brings customers into its business web, enabling them to co-create products. Schwab moved from being a tightly integrated financial services provider to an Internet-based aggregator of financial services (and stole huge market share!). IBM is a computer company that doesn't manufacture computers–its partners do.

Yet most of this underlying restructuring has either been unnoticed or underappreciated by the financial media and business schools.

Many executives moving their companies incrementally (and often unconsciously) in the business web direction talk of closer links with customers and how they can now outsource more functions to suppliers because the Internet enables close collaboration. But these efforts fall short of their potential. Only by addressing the fundamental customer value proposition will the most effective business web construction be evident.

THE LESSONS OF COASE

To understand the superiority of business webs, one must first ask: Why do firms exist? If, as Economics 101 suggests, the "invisible hand" of market pricing is the epitome of efficiency, why doesn't it regulate *all* economic activity? Why isn't each person at every step of production and delivery an independent profit center?

Nobel laureate Ronald Coase asked these provocative questions in 1937. Coase blames *transaction costs* for the contradiction between the theoretical agility of the market and the stubborn durability of the firm. Firms incur transaction costs when, instead of using their internal resources, they go to the market for products or services. Transaction costs have three parts, which together–even individually–can be prohibitive.

1. **Search costs.** Finding what you need takes time, resources, and money. Determining whether to trust a supplier adds more costs. Intermediaries who catalog products and product information could historically reduce, but not eliminate, such search costs.
2. **Contracting costs.** If every exchange requires a unique, separate price negotiation and contract, the costs can be totally out-of-whack with the value of the deal.
3. **Coordination costs.** This is the cost of coordinating resources and processes. Coase points out that with "changes like the telephone and the telegraph," it becomes easier for geographically dispersed firms to coordinate their activities.

Coase says that firms form to lighten the burden of transaction costs. He then asks another good question: *If firm organization cuts transaction costs, why isn't everything one big firm?* He answers that the law of diminishing returns applies to firm size: big firms are complicated and find it hard to manage resources efficiently. Small companies often do things more cheaply than big ones.

All this leads to what I call "Coase's Law": A firm will tend to expand until the costs of organizing an extra transaction within the firm become equal to the costs of carrying out the same transaction on the open market. As long as it is cheaper to perform a transaction inside your firm, keep it there. But if it's cheaper to go to the marketplace, don't try to do it internally.

BEYOND THE CORPORATION

Despite the Net's dramatic growth in functionality, ubiquity, and bandwidth, it is still primitive. Nevertheless, any business that has tasted its benefits is hooked. No company has integrated the Internet into its business model and concluded the predigital way of doing business was better.

In every sector of the economy the competitive ground has shifted, and business webs are clearly established as the new mechanism for winning in the marketplace. To be sure, many companies–of both the Old and New Economies–have set up Web sites and been disappointed by the results. However, a Web site is the digital era equivalent of a business card–nothing more. Businesses that obsess about having "sticky" sites with elaborate multi-media content miss the point.

The power of the business web is that it allows companies to focus on their core competencies. Often the bulk of the employees in a given corporation have nothing to do with the firm's core competencies. They attempt to build up and "make do" with design, manufacturing, marketing, and other capabilities that are often not best of

"In the virtual economy, collaboration is a new competitive imperative." (Michael Dell)

breed. Now with the Net, business functions or large projects can be reduced to smaller components and farmed out (often simultaneously) to more specialized companies around the world with virtually no transaction costs.

This captures the enormous benefits brought on by the competitive environment. Suppliers strive to reduce costs and increase quality and innovation. They know there are other specialized workers and companies around the world keen to do the work.

By contrast, insisting a project stay in-house often means it is comparatively more difficult to mobilize resources, even with a high-performance intranet. Employees are pressed into jobs unrelated to their skills, as managers try to "make do" with the workers on hand. Alternately, adding new employees to the payroll is time-consuming and costly. Approvals must be sought, reporting structures developed, workspace arranged and so on. Every manager knows these internal rigidities increase corporate costs and stifle innovation.

MAKING IT HAPPEN ▸▸

How do you develop a high-performance business web? How do you know which functions to keep or shed? The first step is to disaggregate the value proposition that the end customer receives and experiences. Think about the genuine *customer needs* that your product or service addresses, not just the "thing you do" to get the business. Avoid preoccupation with the production or distribution channels that stand between you and the real customer. Dissect the end customer's experience in terms of your value proposition, as well as the enabling goods, services, resources, business processes and organizational structures, into individual components. Honestly face the weaknesses inherent in the Industrial Age mind- and tool-set. Reconfigure the components radically to transform the value proposition for the end customer's benefit.

Ask fundamental questions about the business system in question:

- Why does it exist at all and should it continue to exist?
- Who benefits from it?
- What are its strengths and weaknesses from the customer perspective?
- How could we improve it?
- Who can help us, or who could improve it and kill us?

A business value proposition differs from its products and services. The "value" that a customer needs endures, regardless of the particulars. When a traveler needs to get from A to B, how he gets there matters much less than actually getting there. For your marketspace, what value is offered, delivered, and consumed that justifies a business's right to exist? There are three guidelines:

- Focus on the essence, rather than on a small, fascinating or rarefied aspect of it. For example, in publishing, describe the underlying value of the publication to readers rather than the printed page or the table of contents.
- Begin with the end in mind, as in how to improve radically the value that the "real" end customer receives from your business. Nothing less will ensure your survival as a winner in the 21st century.
- Prepare and inform all steps of this process with a review and assessment of customer/market/channel trends; supply-side trends; competition; current and expected product/service innovations; industry use of human, relationship, and structural capital; business events (for example, consolidation); environmental issues; and regulation.

Ask the following four questions to drive a "customer-down" approach to the current value proposition:

- Who are your *end customers*, as opposed to intermediary customers? Define the customer categories and who else is serving them, regardless of value proposition.
- What *product* and *service* offerings does the current business system provide its customers?
- From the customer's standpoint, what *value propositions* can you attribute to these product and service offerings? List only the top ones that come to mind. Once you have listed several dimensions of the value proposition, construct a concise catch-all statement that accommodates all of them. This summary should nail your current business, its *raison d'être*.
- From the end-customer's perspective, what are the main *strengths* and *weaknesses* of the value proposition and the enabling products and services? Who else delivers more value, and in what ways?

CONCLUSION

With business webs, issues such as partnering, distribution channels, industry restructuring and strategic repositioning are suddenly much more complex. Strategists will no longer look at the integrated corporation as the starting point for value creation. Rather, they will start with a customer value proposition and a blank slate for the production and delivery system. They won't reject value proposals out of hand, because the art of the possible is dramatically changed through the business web.

For More Information

Books and Journal Article:

Coase, Ronald. *The Firm, the Market, and the Law*. Chicago, IL: University of Chicago Press, 1990.

Downes, Larry, and Chunka Mui. *Unleashing the Killer App: Digital Strategies for Market Dominance*. Rev. ed. Boston, MA: Harvard Business School Press, 2000.

Malone, Thomas, and Robert J. Laubacher. "The Dawn of the E-lance Economy." *Harvard Business Review*, Volume 76, Issue 5, 1998.

See also:

☆ **Building Great Internal Partnerships (pp. 281–82)**
☆ **Developing an Internet-era Mindset throughout the Organization (pp. 141–42)**
☆ **Managing 1:1 Marketing (pp. 55–56)**
☆ **Marketing to the "Real-time" Consumer (pp. 73–74)**
☆ **Viewpoint: Philip Kotler (pp. 53–54)**
☆ **Virtual Collaboration (pp. 167–68)**
☆ **X-engineering Success (pp. 245–46)**
✓ **Better Communication with Resellers (pp. 650–51)**
✓ **How to Add Value through E-alliances (pp. 640–41)**
✓ **How to Apply a Viral Marketing Approach on the Internet (p. 628)**
✓ **The Key Issues of Implementing an E-commerce Strategy (pp. 580–81)**
✓ **Understanding the Key Principles of Internet Marketing (pp. 622–23)**

"A sharing of control with local partners will lead to a greater contribution from them, which can assist in coping with circumstances that are unfamiliar to the foreign partner." (Yanni Yan)

VIEWPOINT: JEFFREY F. RAYPORT

Making Customer Satisfaction and Loyalty a Managerial Imperative

Jeffrey Rayport's academic background in international relations, American civilization, and business history has provided him with an unusual lens through which to explore and analyze the dynamics of an economy increasingly defined by technology. As an associate professor at Harvard Business School in the mid-1990s, his popular courses on e-commerce reflected pioneering research on the relationships between emerging information technologies and service and marketing strategies. Now serving as C.E.O. of Marketspace LLC, a business unit of Cambridge-based Monitor Group, he continues to research, write, consult, and educate on issues of doing business in the networked economy.

When I was just out of high school, I managed to secure what seemed the proverbial nightmare summer job–selling series books over the phone. As it happened, this job turned out to be bizarre and fascinating. The employer was Time-Life Libraries, a unit of what was then Time Inc. (now AOL Time Warner).

I was assigned to a small call center in Washington, D.C., where we "outbound telesales reps" would pitch series about gardening and collectibles. We worked in four-hour shifts; mine was 8pm to midnight. On that shift, we would change time zones every hour, moving progressively westward from Hartford to Honolulu to ensure that our calls came in just at or past the dinner hour. It was genius.

That telemarketing experience in the 1970s introduced me to business conducted through nonphysical, nontraditional channels. It was, in its own way, a version of electronic or technology-mediated commerce. And the striking thing was how effective it was: intimate, persuasive and cost-efficient.

The battle that was playing out was between the telemarketers and the direct mailers. This new approach was a powerful alternative to traditional direct-mail marketing. It was easier and more efficient than licking stamps or knocking on doors.

What I realized then is the power of technology-based interfaces to substitute for (or even eliminate) face-to-face interactions in business. Technology-mediated interactions enable companies to manage deeper and richer relationships with customers and markets than ever before, whether it's through the phone, the Web, or the ATM. In contrast to my Time-Life days, technology interfaces can do more than enable communication; they're often able to deliver the product or service itself, whether that's music, financial services, textbooks or any other information products (such as this encyclopedia). That's a radical, mind-bending shift, and we're still only beginning to understand the implications of it.

If the first half of the 20th century involved automation of physical processes (such as manufacturing, assembly, and transport of materials), then the second half involved automation of information processes (such as accounting and control functions, bill paying, and electronic communications). So where are we going from here?

The biggest change we're going to see is technology transforming the "front office" aspects of business enterprise. This may sound like a modest claim, but it is huge.

Most technology revolutions in business have been "back office" affairs until now—involving the automation or reengineering of existing back-office operations, from manufacturing processes on the factory floor to payment processing at corporate headquarters.

Most technology revolutions in business have been "back office" affairs until now—involving the automation or reengineering of existing back-office operations, from manufacturing processes on the factory floor to payment processing at corporate headquarters. Indeed, the application of technology to routine tasks is a still-amazing tale of productivity enhancements. The boosts to productivity come in two ways: machines often perform repetitive tasks better than humans; and their deployment in business results in lower operational costs.

And now the application of technology to business is entering its most profound phase: its substitution of capital for labor–of machines for people–not just in back offices, but in those aspects of business that

"A brand signals a set of expectations and a core understanding that drives everything."

(Shelly Lazarus)

touch customers and markets. Once marveled at machines' ability to build a car or assemble a PC; now we are entering an age where the machines will manage a company's relationships with us, their customers.

Some may find the idea of a future dominated by machine-mediated interfaces and services cold and impersonal, but smart companies won't let it evolve that way. Even now, it's clear that technology can create highly personal and satisfying service experiences that have a double productivity bonus: they are lower-cost channels than traditional service delivery, and more pleasant and satisfying than people-mediated services. ATMs, for example, have largely replaced the human teller, and few people miss the experience of visiting a bank. Likewise, smart ATM-like gas pumps have improved the gas station experience, Web sites have made booking travel a pleasure, and soon we'll see that a large-format, touch-screen interface will replace the teenage service worker who takes your order at McDonald's or Taco Bell.

This gets even more interesting in the context of faster data interchange. Broadband connections mean richer, smarter, more engaging virtual service providers. In a decade or two, the Taco Bell interface is likely to be more personable for many of us than the real person. The same thing will happen across every sector of services—from fast food to airlines, from medicine to law—in one way or another.

Looking ahead, we will surely mark 2001 as the year when graphics and animation became movie stars. We've long had special effects, but this year two blockbuster movies came to us from the synthetic world of electronic games, and one, "Final Fantasy," involved an entirely lifelike, but thoroughly virtual, cast. It was a big-screen version of what we can expect from many media experiences as they evolve, such as network news (watch Ananova, a virtual newsreader on the Web, who provides frequent updates on demand; if you don't like her hair, change it); operator services (Wildfire, a unit of mobile telephone operator Orange, provides a virtual assistant who lives inside your phone and responds to voice commands); directory services (a regional Bell telecommunications company, Verizon, uses voice-recognition-based services from TellMe.com to meet its subscribers' needs without human intervention), and even person-to-person remote communications (a California start-up just announced a holographic form of videoconferencing).

Some may find the idea of a future dominated by machine-mediated interfaces and services cold and impersonal, but smart companies won't let it evolve that way.

The use of technology to manage and mediate customer relationships can, in many businesses, give managers the tools and data they need to understand evolving customer needs and desires in real time.

Some might argue that delegating customer relationships to technology represents a wholesale abdication by managers of responsibility for customers' experiences. On the contrary, asking a machine to do anything—as any computer programmer knows—requires a deep understanding of the task in hand. To create compelling screen-to-face interfaces requires managers to anticipate much of what the customer will want. Managers need to shift from thinking "How do I sell my product?" to "How do I meet my customers' need?" to "What kind of experiences do I want to enable?"

It makes it essential for managers to be obsessed with the demand side of the business equation (customers and markets), while still maintaining the supply side (processes that deliver products and services).

Of course, the problem is that there is no one final answer regarding customer preferences and needs. They change constantly, just as the market context in which customers experience their preferences also is in a continuous state of dynamic flux. Hence, managerial obsession with customer needs must be continuous, not sporadic. And that is hard work.

There is good news, however.

Consider the TV home-shopping channel QVC, a virtual channel business long before there was a World Wide Web. QVC airs live 24 hours a day, displaying six to ten products an hour and taking incoming calls from viewers to register orders. The channel has little regard for audience ratings because viewership is not the measure of its success; phone calls to its call centers—and converting those calls to orders—is. That means that QVC managers have their finger on the pulse of customers' desires, literally every second. When the phones ring, they know they have a winning product; when the phones don't ring, they know they're marketing something no one wants, and they pull it off the air. Everyone in the company has a real-time awareness of, and ability to react to, the live pulse of the business. The culture and management is driven by demand, not supply.

And it's driven by customer desire in near real time. Real-time tracking of consumer need is the mainspring of the business. Imagine a two-hour delay in QVC's ability to respond to customer trends; this would mean leaving the wrong products on air for too long, promoting them with the wrong hosts and positioning them at the wrong price points. It is the ability to adjust in real time to the market that makes QVC so successful—and makes it an exciting place not just to shop but to work.

QVC has a winning model. It's also the model of the future—a demand-driven approach to business. That's why company and manager should aspire to respond in real time to customer demand.

Rational businesspeople have always asked, "What are my resources at hand, and how can I get the most out of my scarcest resource?" Traditionally, that question has been applied to physical and capital resources. As industrial history evolved over the last 100 years, firms developed strategies for maximizing returns, such as vertical and horizontal integration, which, in turn, aimed to maximize a company's access to scarce sources of supply.

"The Web attacks traditional ways of doing things and elites, and this is very uncomfortable for traditional businesses to deal with." (Martin Sorrell)

These days, supplies of goods and services are abundant. For the half century after World War II, the challenge for companies was making enough products to meet the rising tide of consumer and industrial need. The problem now is reversed; it's sourcing demand. Today, companies face rapid commoditization of products and brands; customers have an endless proliferation from which to choose. Simply put, now demand is the scarce resource.

As a result, it's time to measure success differently. For as long as business requires capital, return on investment and return on assets measures will remain relevant. But in a world where capital is more easily found than customer demand, we should measure success according to return on customer relationship or return on customer desire. In the first case, a company is measuring how much of the full theoretical value of a customer relationship it has successfully realized through a lifetime of interactions. In the second, a company would measure how completely it had harvested, in economic terms, the desires of the customers whose needs it met.

These new "return on" measures would give rise to an entirely new, customer-focused and demand-centric discussion about how companies plot strategy and establish competitive advantage. Measurements of this kind—and questions of this nature—will change the way we do business. And for our customers to get what they want, this kind of new thinking will be essential.

That means that every manager should ask, now and in the future:

- Who are my customers? How well am I doing at acquiring or retaining them?
- How much is each lifetime relationship worth?
- What share of the lifetime value of each customer is my company realizing?
- How can I raise that proportion?
- In what ways can I increase the duration or enhance the profitability of the relationship?

Companies are valuable because their customer relationships are valuable—and company valuations increasingly will reflect the full value of their portfolio of customer relationships. Paying attention to customer satisfaction and loyalty then becomes an obvious managerial imperative.

So there is no point in asking if you can do well by doing good, or if a company that puts its people first can also make money. Instead, the questions should be "How do we do it?" and "When do we start?"

Some people assume that "doing well by doing good" belongs only in the nonprofit sector. The truth is that it's the other way around. When was the last time you flew on an airline where all the staff were rude and then picked up the paper to read that the airline was insanely profitable? Good working environments and good business outcomes go hand in hand.

There are many reasons for this. The obvious is that most people who are happy in their jobs tend to have several attributes in common: they are in the right job; they know the goals; they want to, and do, learn on the job; they have shared values with those around them, and they are in a position to "win" for their customers or accounts.

All of this may seem simple, but it's amazing how few companies realize these basics effectively. Interestingly, it's even more amazing to consider this collection of attributes and identify any one that is not simultaneously good for people and good for business. Would anyone really want to work in a job where the fit was no good? Would anyone want to build a career among people without a shared vision, let alone shared values?

Yet the challenge here is more pertinent now than ever before. How people feel on the job matters much more for service businesses than for industrial operations. In the late 19th century, Andrew Carnegie and Henry Frick developed a technique for steel production in their Pittsburgh mills called "hard driving." It meant running furnaces at ruinously high temperatures and working men in the mills long shifts to harvest "abnormally" elevated output. Workers suffered to the point of staging massive strikes, ending in violence. But the steel produced by these workers did not suffer in quality as a function of poor conditions and outraged emotion—only their well-being did. Indeed, for Carnegie's steel business, hard driving made the operation more profitable than ever before, and it shaped industry practices worldwide as a result.

But that was in industrial businesses. In service businesses, there are higher prices to pay for hard driving; service businesses where employees are not happy usually fail. Why? Because success is highly dependent on human factors, the people who interact with the firm's customers. Trite as it may sound, happy employees—in a restaurant, hotel, airline, hospital, bank—make for happy customers. And disgruntled employees do the opposite.

So there is a lesson here: always in business, there is a human factor. And that means that goodness (how companies treat employees) should always correlate with wellness (how companies perform for stakeholders). Yet technology can sometimes make it easy to forget this.

These ideas are important to keep in mind especially regarding the service sector, not least because it represents more than four-fifths of gross domestic product output in the United States and a similar proportion in most other industrialized countries. Moreover, among industrial firms the largest numbers of jobs are generally in service positions. Put these together, and we are describing, pure and simple, a service economy. That means that we compete on people. And in service businesses this comes down to how they feel, what they find motivating and how well we equip them, with technology and otherwise, for success with their customers.

For More Information

Web Site

www.marketspaceglobal.com: the Web site of Marketspace consulting firm.

"We do not make very full value of the opportunities provided by technology because we prefer critical to constructive thinking, argument to design." (Edward de Bono)

Making B2B Your New Operational Standard *by Michael J. Cunningham*

Executive Summary

- Why should transaction and collaborative commerce systems co-exist?
- How can they be used to improve productivity across the enterprise and supply chains?
- How are work practices changing as a result of these technologies?

Introduction

Given the challenges of the marketplace today, executives are looking for solutions that will give them a key advantage over their competitors. Part of this advantage is clearly based on identifying ways to use technology and innovative work practices to improve productivity, reduce costs, and improve service to employees, partners, and consumers. Understanding business-to-business collaboration technologies and how they integrate with transaction systems is one way to gain a competitive edge.

Why Collaborative Commerce Is Important

Collaborative commerce technology is the glue that keeps employees, customers and partners communicating and informed. In particular, the rise of self-service applications that deliver relevant information to those that need it has created tremendous value over recent years.

Market Conditions

Market conditions are changing faster than they ever have, yet we seem to find it harder than ever to adapt and deal with these changes. Despite the fact that information technology solutions are mature and available, the gap between the organization that wins the first time out and the others continues to widen. How can operations such as COVISINT and Altra create tremendous value using technology to support their business needs, yet others spend millions and still fail to get it right?

Many organizations today are concerned about the possibility of failure with their e-business systems. Given the dramatic change in market conditions during 2000 and 2001, confusion has reigned supreme in many e-business decision cycles across the globe. Often, it appears that the very large benefits to be gained from e-business technologies are reaped when a combination of technologies are deployed in unison. For example, many firms now understand that implementing customer relationship management (CRM) technologies *without* a supporting knowledge base creates only another touch point for information, and not high-impact benefits. The latter are created only when technology and support systems work in harmony to provide all relevant information to the person who needs it.

Acceleration

The e-business economy, often cited initially as a separate market, is increasingly being recognized as a hybrid. Existing business operations and practices mutate into new forms, some recognizable from earlier business models, while others change much more dramatically. The successful systems that develop from this strategy focus on accelerating both the business relationship and the cycle.

Leading suppliers in today's economy not only embrace the concept of change; they aggressively try to modify the behavior of a marketplace. The successful ones mix a potent cocktail that includes:

- Knowledge of how their market (or supply chain) is currently working, and consequently what needs changing;
- A desire to collapse entire existing business processes and systems, or segments thereof (such as supply chains, work processes, decision cycles);
- Technology to effect the change;
- Marketing and distribution skills to deliver the new product;
- Partnership with others to gain rapid adoption of the new model;
- The ability to change and support new work processes and practices to build solutions.

The business benefits associated with these changes are not only desirable, they are also strategic weapons for e-business systems.

Collaborative Contact

By connecting the power of collaborative commerce tools with tools that build, deliver, and manage the procurement or sales process, significant benefits can be leveraged from buyer and supplier relationships. Many e-business relationships begin by automating the procurement process, so optimizing these relationships using additional tools may seem like a natural extension. However, because the entry points and reasons for collaborative commerce are often separate, many organizations miss out on the benefits of a more integrated strategy. Nevertheless, using collaborative commerce to support the procurement process often creates opportunities to improve the efficiency of business relationships, and can radically cut costs and unnecessary steps out of existing processes.

Over time, the effectiveness of any business relationship can be easy to measure. However, seeing what is failing and where improvements need to be made in the short term is much more difficult and is often only visible once serious problems arise and their repercussions felt.

Using collaborative commerce as a means of communication can help in identifying and resolving these issues rapidly. In addition, the development of the relevant content bases, training materials and support procedures can often accelerate the speed at which the buying, supply, and sales processes become integrated, reducing the potential for misunderstandings and problems along the way.

Transaction Systems

Over the last couple years, the use of the Internet as the basis for transaction tools has expanded. The transaction tools developed include dynamic marketplaces, portals, auctions, Web-based EDI, and electronic catalogs. Compared to traditional EDI, transaction systems affect a greater number of phases in procurement or selling life cycles.

The good news, however, is that the RFQ, proposal responses, and communication between purchaser and supplier can all be conducted electronically. This cuts the time required to complete the evaluation phases and the supporting tools allow the specialist to manage relationships with more suppliers or customers.

"Dotcom will become in our corporate language like Inc. or Co. or Corp.—a generic way of describing a company, in this case a company that does business on the Internet." (Clive Chajet)

Collaboration Tools

The tools discussed thus far support important phases in the transaction life cycle. They fit within an organization's processes and support certain tasks; in general, they do not require the company to make large process or organizational changes to utilize them. Collaborative tools extend beyond the task level to all the phases in the transaction life cycle. It is important to view them as modules that fit together to form solutions. These modules are often extensions of existing systems or other collaboration tools. For example, a workflow system will utilize e-mail to notify individuals that they need to take action. These are not a replacement for transaction systems. Rather, they are a way of extending the information and value of a transaction system throughout the enterprise and beyond to its trading partners. By implementing these tools to complement transactions systems, an organization will create a collaborative transaction network.

The collaborative transaction network gives all members of the trading network access to data. Even more importantly, it extends the knowledge of the specialist throughout the life cycle and in other major organization processes.

Until recently, most of the technology being implemented by corporations to aid transaction life cycles has been complementary to existing processes. Organizations have successfully implemented EDI and e-business systems without making significant organizational or process changes. This is no longer enough. In order to stay ahead, firms must also review and change their work processes and the supporting collaborative technology.

Making It Happen ▸▸

Work processes

Assessing the effect of new technologies on operational processes begins with a clear understanding of the capabilities being introduced. Most corporations understand that potential benefits can be achieved through systems that facilitate staff interaction with critical information and processes. However, enhanced or newly-enabled capabilities to access information, obtain status, self-serve, and collaborate can dramatically affect not only productivity of existing procurement processes, but the manner in which the work is conducted.

Best practices are emerging from the ability to apply one, or a combination, of these newly developed methods to existing transaction requirements. For example, proactive, real-time polling supports the ability to maintain point-of-use restocking and pay-on-consumption/receipt systems. Access to EDI or Web-linked information provides the ability to share demand forecasts and resource schedules. Self-service capabilities enable supplier-managed inventories and supplier self-qualification systems.

Procurement driven by function

At this state of development, transaction systems effectively increase a corporation's ability to procure high-quality items at the right time and place and at a fair price. Supply chain activities have evolved as a series of tasks integrated by processes and systems designed to take advantage of advances in connectivity and enterprise-wide databases.

Supply chain integration

More significant improvements often stem from enhanced capabilities in sourcing, procurement and materials management. Representative strategies include:

- Workflow facilitated and self-service processes that provide increased transparency and accessibility between purchasing, suppliers, and materials management
- Sole sourcing, supplier pre-qualification, and dynamic bidding processes that tend to lower the acquisition cost of procured items
- Coordinated forecasting, planning, and component replenishment processes that tend to lower the retained cost of procured items.

These benefits dramatically improve the efficiency and effectiveness of work processes required to attain business goals. As such, they can be characterized as "collaborative-based" processes that utilize the increased connectivity, accessibility, self-service, and parallel-processing capabilities of new transaction-based solutions.

These types of collaborative strategies tend to de-emphasize the impact and inefficiencies found in serial supply chain operations through the promotion and use of enhanced data accessibility, concurrent processing, and mutual accountability. Reflecting a more holistic supply chain approach, these systems and strategies increase productivity through the use of new processes that enable tasks to be accomplished simultaneously.

Trading partner benefits

Effective collaboration tends to reduce overall process cycles and costs by improving the level of accountability, and monitoring and controlling duplicate activities. All parties have to realize process efficiencies rather than bottom-line pricing as a primary source for operational savings. Once freed of historic concerns and boundaries, collaborative transaction systems establish the beachhead for a wide range of strategies leading towards the benefits of comprehensive supply chain integration. Among the most important will be those that link with back office ERP systems and real-time, automated transaction settlement. Ultimately, the benefits should result in lower inventories, faster processes, and higher-quality products and services.

The stakes are particularly high for systems like e-procurement and collaborative commerce that involve increased cooperation with clients and business partners. While traditional EDI has been at the leading edge for some businesses in the past, Internet-based systems open the door for almost any organization to revolutionize the way it does business. For many, changing the way they do things is more than just an opportunity—it will be a necessity for staying in business.

Conclusion

- It is essential for executives around the globe to understand the opportunity presented by the combination of collaborative commerce technologies and revised business processes.
- Just "waiting for it to happen around them" may produce very undesirable results.
- The competitive edge will go to those who understand and exploit these technologies and who change their business processes and practices to leverage them in the marketplace.

For More Information

Books:

Cunningham, Mike. *B2B: How to Build a Profitable e-Commerce Strategy*. Cambridge, MA: Perseus, 2000.

Koulopoulos, Thomas, and Nathaniel Palmer. *The X-economy*. New York: Texere, 2001.

"I would advise young companies, particularly the small dot-com companies, to pay close attention to their service levels."

(Lillian Vernon)

DATA MINING *by Michael Griggs and Maggie Kennedy*

EXECUTIVE SUMMARY

- In business, knowledge is power, but many companies don't know what information they possess.
- Data integration enables them to access this information.
- Technology can be used to ensure that the customer really is king.
- Data mining is the basis for multichannel distribution strategies, supply chains, e-procurement, knowledge management, and customer relationship management (CRM) initiatives.
- Information stored in a data warehouse is the fuel for a company's growth.
- Good segmentation of your customer base is essential.

INTRODUCTION

Put simply, data mining is the drilling down for lost data that has lain dormant, sometimes for years. Often a company has not been aware it possessed this data—usually because of decentralized database management, lack of relational database systems, or the existence of legacy systems with old and forgotten databases.

The real value of the data lies in analyzing it to reveal or create relationships that have been previously undiscovered. Having huge banks of data is of no value whatsoever if you don't bother to evaluate it.

Evaluation can relate to anything from sales records to seasonal correlations; it can be applied to any supplier-customer relationship, whether in the private or public sector or in industrial, commercial, or consumer markets.

The results of data mining can be grouped as follows:

- Association of events that can be correlated. A computer purchase, for example, is likely to involve the simultaneous purchase of a printer.
- Sequences as one event leads to another. Computer and printer purchase may be followed by the purchase of a scanner.
- Classification through the recognition of patterns. These can be based on any relevant data—income, sales, location, or even average summer rainfall! It all depends on how you see the data benefiting your business.
- Forecasting. This is a natural extrapolation from the other results and can facilitate more accurate projections. Projected beer consumption, for example, could also be related to future consumption of peanuts or potato chips.

MAKING IT HAPPEN ▸▸

In reality, successful data mining starts with data integration. The integration of disparate legacy systems and databases reduces operating costs by cutting out duplicate administration. Further, it provides closer control in forming the basis for more comprehensive customer information and tighter, more focused marketing strategies.

Nowhere is data integration more necessary than in established industries like insurance, telcos, and utilities. Frequently the established players have legacy systems dating back two decades or more. Their dominance of the market has been secure for a lot longer than that, yet it is now under threat from well-funded competitors with tailored systems that make them faster on their feet when it comes to accessing—and manipulating—data to benefit their business and customers.

The customer, of course, is king, and technology is now making a reality of customer-serving trends like e-commerce, customer relationship management (CRM), and enterprise application integration (EAI). For most organizations these areas are linked, because there is a need to understand, and make the best use of, the data that contains the customer information.

Achieving the Essentials

To ensure that customers are closely connected to them, organizations are now striving to establish multichannel distribution strategies, supply chains, e-procurement, knowledge management, and CRM initiatives.

Business development, whether along traditional lines or as e-business via PCs, television, or mobile communications, requires:

1. interactivity;
2. personalization;
3. secure transactional capability.

Refined data mining is essential to achieve the first two; by using it, business can stimulate the customer's desire to interact.

Digging for the Benefits

Suppliers as well as customers can benefit from data mining and analysis. Every business is a supplier of something, whether it's a service or a product.

From the data mined the supplier should be able to analyze internal trends that can be capitalized to benefit its own long-term CRM activity. Look to answer some very telling questions:

- Are all the company's service offerings relevant?
- If they are, are they reusable?
- Is customer service proactive? responsive? consistent?
- Is there evidence of steady improvement?
- What is customers' perception of the company?
- Is there a need for internal training?
- Is there evidence of persistent product failings?

Embarking on such a search prompts suppliers to take a long, hard look at their business. And such an exercise doesn't apply only to long-established businesses, although they may benefit the most at the beginning.

Reducing Customer Churn

In a sense we have arrived at a best-case scenario, with sophisticated integration leading to efficient and effective use of data, both internally and externally.

Evidence shows that in a free market companies can lose a very high

---

"While hard data may inform the intellect, it is largely soft data that generates wisdom."

(Henry Mintzberg)

percentage of their customers every five years—maybe as many as 45–50%. Other research indicates that a rise of just 5% in customer retention can result in an 80% rise in profit.

An overriding priority for any supplier is therefore how to retain its customers. Good CRM is central to customer retention, and CRM relies on a detailed understanding of customer profiles, together with the direct selling and cross-selling opportunities they reveal.

Good customer profiles within the existing base can also be used to identify areas for successful expansion into new ventures, new geographic areas, and new product launches.

In other words, your data provides you with knowledge—and in business, knowledge is power. Sound data analysis allows you to translate that knowledge into proactive marketing to existing customers and accurately-profiled prospects.

Ironically, companies often pay big money for information about their existing and prospective markets while the knowledge hidden in their own IT systems is overlooked.

Frequently they don't realize what they have because one set of data is held separately from another—on different systems, at different locations—and there are no means to collate and mine it. Once data is combined the knowledge extracted is usually greater than the sum of its parts.

As an example, imagine a scenario involving half-a-dozen companies operating under a group umbrella.

- Transaction 1: A customer has a store card and buys goods over the counter.
- Transaction 2: The same customer buys some Christmas presents through a seasonal mail-order catalog.
- Transaction 3: The customer decides to have a new central heating system installed. . .and so it goes on.
- A whole series of transactions, all for the same address, but all through different companies and logged on different databases.

With the tools to tie this information together and mine it intelligently, incredibly detailed customer profiles emerge that can put untold knowledge into the hands of marketers, sales executives, designers, engineers—looked at from different angles, the uses are legion.

Data Warehousing

With data mining the concept of data warehousing is fast gaining acceptance, and some research suggests that 50% of all companies are either using a data warehouse or planning to build one.

A data warehouse isn't simply for data mining, it's a resource susceptible to a variety of analytical processes. Data is first extracted from operational databases, cleaned up to remove redundant data and fill in blank and missing fields, and then organized into consistent formats.

Analysts can then drill down into the data using data access and data-mining tools as well as online reporting software, including online analytical processing (OLAP), statistical modeling tools, and geographic information systems (GIS).

With a data warehouse you have access to the information that fuels your company's growth. A profitable future depends heavily on extracting only data that has the potential to become useful, and with data mining you have the ability to extract data you didn't even know existed.

This will usually be information on customers, partners, and key business trends; the process can also be used for fraud protection, enhancement of customer satisfaction, analysis of product repositioning, discovery of profit centers, or corporate asset management. You can highlight loyal customers, then discover what it is that has kept them loyal—tailoring subsequent offers and benefits to retain them. Similarly you can spot reasons for churn, backtrack to discover the indicators leading to those reasons (frequently missed), and take the necessary steps to reduce it significantly.

CONCLUSION

Robert Richardson sums it up best: ". . . digging into the unknown and letting your algorithms find the patterns in the data is what mining is about. . .When you use data mining, the best [target] you may choose is a good segmentation of your customer base as it relates to likelihood of churn. Because, if you can figure out who's about to churn, plus the chances of dissuading them, then you can make appropriately targeted offers to keep the customers with real revenue potential in the fold."

He continues, "While the trick to knowing. . .who gets which special offer may frequently boil down to knowing which segment a customer belongs to, there's an added difficulty in discovering those segments in the first place. Often, companies trying to analyze their data arbitrarily decide that. . .they can simply divide everyone into a few round-number age groups—under 20 years, 21 through 30, and so on. This. . .may not produce any meaningful insights simply because these segments are arbitrary. They may actually mask the behavior of more meaningful age groupings. If all the customers aged 25 to 35 make similar buying decisions, for instance, you'll cut the group in half if you segment on 21-to-30 and 31-to-40 boundaries." ("Combing through the Cosmos," ***www.cconvergence.com/article/CTM20010402S0001***.)

For More Information

Web Sites:

www.KDnuggets.com: the Knowledge Discovery Web site was set up by one of the data mining industry's best-known practitioners.

www.acm.org/sigkdd: this Knowledge Discovery and Data Mining Society operates under the umbrella of the ACM (Association for Computing Machinery). The site defines the subject area and sets out codes of practice.

www.bscol.com: pointers on how to establish performance-measuring criteria so that you can scope your data-mining project.

www.emsl.pnl.gov:2080/docs/cie/neural/systems/shareware.html: one of many shareware resource sites.

For information on Neural Networks and the Kohonen model.

See the WEBSOM area of the above site for the largest application of self-organizing maps and their use in organizing large document collections.

"Most individuals, by the time they reach maturity, have built up an array of concepts which they use to interpret the data they observe."

(Charles Handy)

MARKETSPACES *by Jeffrey F. Rayport*

EXECUTIVE SUMMARY

- With the advent of new communications technologies, most notably the Internet, the traditional marketplace has expanded into a new, virtual sphere of management and commerce: the market*space*.
- The marketspace is exerting an increasingly profound impact on business strategy, particularly on the ways companies interact with their customers.
- Though technology enables the marketspace, successful companies will treat technology not as an end in itself, but as one among many components in their overall strategy to build and manage customer relationships.

INTRODUCTION

From the Athenian agora to the mall, the places where buyers and sellers negotiate their transactions have for thousands of years been just that: places. But over the past two centuries, and especially since the advent of the Internet and the World Wide Web, technology has given rise to an alternative to the marketplace: the virtual market*space*. More and more transactions that once took place only in the marketplace now occur in the marketspace, largely free from the bonds of space and time. As a result, there are exponentially greater opportunities for deeper, more frequent interactions between companies and customers. With the growth of a service-based economy in which products are increasingly commoditized and differentiation ever-harder to achieve, successfully managing company-to-customer interactions is critical. Indeed, there is a dialectic between the rise of the marketspace and the growth of the service-based economy: each feeds, and feeds off of, the other.

Thus, the marketspace presents both challenges and opportunities. Companies that either underestimate or overestimate its significance stand to suffer. On the other hand, firms that understand that the marketspace demands creative new strategies, yet relentlessly test those strategies against fundamental principles of service management, are likely to prosper. Even in the technology-enabled marketspace, using service to manage relationships with customers will only become a greater virtue.

FROM MARKETPLACE TO MARKETSPACE

A marketplace consists of three basic components:

- sellers, offering something of value (goods, services or information);
- buyers, offering something of value in return (cash or any of the above);
- a physical location (store, exchange) where the two come together.

In the marketspace, buyers, sellers and the value they exchange remain the same, but the time and space constraints disappear. In the marketspace, their transactions take place virtually any time, anywhere, thanks to a variety of technology-mediated interfaces (not just the Web) such as the telephone, wireless device, and personal computer. If a transaction takes place and you cannot say with confidence *where* it occurred, it happened in the marketspace.

One could say that the marketspace was born more than 150 years ago, the first time that a lone Morse code operator telegraphed an order to a supplier. Succeeding generations of communications technology—telephone, fax, pager, mobile phone, even fast-food drive-through microphone—expanded the universe of transactions that could take place outside of the marketplace.

The marketspace as we know it today is chiefly enabled by the kind of "screen-to-face" interactions offered by the Internet in general and the Web in particular. It should be noted, however, that the first (and still one of the most successful) screen-to-face technology predates the Web by more than a decade in the form of the humble ATM. In spitting out cash at more and more locales around the world, the automated teller machine performed first, on a widespread basis, what many marketspace interfaces are doing today: it represented a substitute of capital for labor, thus threatening to make bank tellers an endangered species.

Banks originally positioned ATMs as a service channel for their least profitable customers, assuming that account holders with substantial means would continue to talk with live tellers. They soon discovered, however, that customers of all stripes enjoyed banking at the machines—and the number of machines, networks linking them, and services they provided mushroomed. The result of retail banking's shift from marketplace to marketspace was nothing less than a transformation of the entire industry's competitive dynamics. As the ATM became the dominant interface between customer and company, consumer loyalty to individual bank brands eroded. The network trumped the brand as the locus of both customer relationships and economic value, which is why we are more interested in spotting Cirrus or NYCE on the side of an ATM than a placard for our particular bank.

By the early 1990s, even before the emergence of the Web, virtual channels were beginning to transform businesses and industries and create significant new sources of value. This is why, in 1992, fellow Harvard Business School professor John Sviokla and I, convinced that the old paradigms for teaching the first-year marketing course were increasingly outmoded, sat down and hatched a new term (and a new course) to describe the brave new business world: marketspace.

Since that afternoon, bubble economies and Wall Street manias have come and gone. But today, I have no doubt that the marketspace is a very real and powerful phenomenon—one that is here to stay.

THE MARKETSPACE *IS* TRANSFORMING BUSINESS

Just as the ATM changed the competitive dynamics of the banking industry, the emergence of the (so far) ultimate screen-to-face interactive medium—the Internet—represented an opportunity for radical reengineering and productivity gains across the full breadth of the economy. Today, it is the Internet that is the key technology enabling and propelling the explosive growth of the marketspace.

THE IMPACT OF THE INTERNET AND TECHNOLOGY

The Internet allows millions of customers to interact with a firm at any hour, from any place, via millions of distributed digital interfaces, on devices such as the PC. At any given moment, for example, thousands of people from around the world are simultaneously logged in to Amazon.com, buying CDs, selling food processors, browsing books, comparing prices, applying for credit

"You can have all the technology and global forces you want, but it's useless if basic trust does not exist."
(Arthur Levitt, Jr.)

cards, downloading music, registering for wedding gifts, sending electronic greeting cards. . .Much like the back-office reengineering revolution of the 1980s, the Internet represents a front-office reengineering revolution. It allows—in fact, it *mandates*—a ground-up rethinking of how companies interact with and create experiences for their customers. What drives this rethinking is clear from the success of automated-interface businesses, from banking with ATMs to bidding on auctions at eBay. It's no longer frontline service workers who have a monopoly on management of customer relationships in the service sector—it's machines that are increasingly doing the managing.

The widespread deployment of technology makes deep insight into customer experience possible, and necessary. Literally and figuratively, screen-to-face interactions augment the value of service, making it possible for companies to deliver service at lower cost and at higher quality. In a sector that has long been characterized by diseconomies of scale, machine-mediated interactions make scale economies possible. Given the importance of the service sector in the world's economies—it represents more than 80% of gross domestic product output in the United States, for example—this is a revolution of real magnitude and scope. Moreover, customer relationship management via machine gives businesses around the world a competitive weapon at a time in economic history when service is more crucial than ever.

The Rise of Mass Personalization

With the accelerating commoditization of products and brands, it is not supply, but customer demand, that is the scarcest and most valuable resource. As we continue to move toward a service-centered economy, firms are increasingly dependent on the quality of their customer relationships. Even for product-based businesses, service, more and more, is the key differentiator. Such iconic brands as IBM and Xerox that once made their money selling boxes (mainframe computers and copying machines) now sell those boxes at a loss; they rely almost exclusively on follow-on service, maintenance plans, financing, and even consulting services for their margins (indeed, the lion's share of IBM revenue is derived from services). Even Microsoft, famous for its ruthless pursuit of profit, has launched its game console, the Xbox, with a business plan for our times. Analysts estimate that every Xbox sold will cost Microsoft nearly $200 in negative margin, but that Microsoft will make up the difference—and ultimately reach profitability on the platform—by selling games, upgrades, and networking services.

That's why personalization has become such a hot concept; it's the ultimate frontier in the delivery of human-mediated or technology-mediated services. And, once again, technology can help marketers defy commoditization by enabling deeper and richer relationships with customers than ever before. For example, technology known as collaborative filtering allows online retailers to predict the products and services their customers may want to buy, based on their previous choices and on the preferences of other like-minded consumers. Or take Ritz-Carlton: the upscale hotelier can elevate its renowned personal service to new heights through its online customer database. A consumer who has stayed only at the Ritz in San Francisco, for example, can walk into its Washington, D.C., property to find that her credit-card and frequent-flier numbers, preference for nonsmoking rooms, and desire for an extra chocolate on her pillow have preceded her. Can other high-end hotel chains afford not to follow suit? Clearly, companies that fail to exploit the power of marketspace technology to make them more customer-centric are forfeiting a key competitive advantage.

. . .But Success in the Marketspace Means Paying Attention to the Fundamentals

The advent of the marketspace has already had a significant impact on business—particularly on the way that companies interact with their customers. However, that does not mean (as was famously proclaimed about the Web not long ago) that the marketspace exists independently of the fundamental laws of economics. In the end, the marketspace is not about new rules for a new economy, nor even about the Internet or the Web; it is about using the tools of digital technology to achieve a fundamental goal that is as old as the marketplace itself: the creation and nurturing of profitable customer relationships.

In the marketspace, just like the marketplace, the name of the game is providing value to customers; if anything, the marketspace makes the age-old business axiom "serve the customer" even more paramount. Technology must be used to create customer interfaces that deliver higher levels of customer-perceived value (relative to competitive offerings), thus driving rising levels of satisfaction and loyalty. The challenge for managers is to understand the full spectrum of interfaces available to them—both screen-to-face (online) and face-to-face (offline)—as well as how to manipulate those interfaces to optimize the customer's experience.

Technology, in other words, is simply another, albeit immensely powerful, business tool. Successful managers will seek out new and creative ways to integrate it into their firm's overall strategy to build and manage strong, loyal customer relationships in a high impact yet cost-effective manner.

Mini-cases

eBay

By bringing together buyers and sellers who would likely never meet in a physical place, the auction Web site eBay has become one of the best-known and most successful marketspace enterprises. Sellers list their wares in eBay's databases, which are then searched by prospective buyers. Technology facilitates the transactions: would-be buyers can sign up to be notified by e-mail when the object of desire comes up for auction, and they can have their bids automatically set (and reset and reset, as the bidding warrants). It makes little difference whether seller and buyer live across town or across the globe; they are linked by the electronic network of the Internet. In the end, eBay connects physical entities (people and products), but it does so in a highly efficient manner. It outsources to customers all the physical aspects of doing business—merchandising, inventory management, inventory carrying costs, shipping and handling, and logistics—thus keeping its margins extremely high. Moreover, eBay's reach and efficiency would be impractical, or even impossible, to realize in the physical world.

Charles Schwab

With the launch of Schwab.com in January 1998, discount broker Charles Schwab became one of the first companies in the brokerage sector—or in the general retailing sector—to create integrated online and offline offerings. When it did so, it kept its eye squarely on the customer, not the technology. Its Web site, for example, was designed not to showcase technological bells and whistles, but to provide easy-to-find, quick-to-download information to its core customer segment: the investor who wants to make fast, informed investment decisions without paying for advice. Ultimately, by embracing the Internet while staying focused on its customers, Schwab was able to use technology to offer superior service at lower prices to its target segment. Moreover, Schwab was the first to demonstrate unequivocally that the marketspace extends

"Any company, old or new, that does not see this technology as important as breathing could be on its last breath."

(Jack Welch)

and augments the marketplace, but seldom replaces it. A case in point: Schwab's success online was real, but research showed that two-thirds of new accounts, which would be accessed largely online, were nonetheless opened offline. As a result, even at the height of the Internet boom, when retail banks were closing branch offices by the dozen, Schwab was building new offices in key locations. Schwab drew the blueprint for the integration of the physical and the virtual—offline and online—for consumer-facing businesses.

MAKING IT HAPPEN ▸▸

As we have outlined, building and managing customer relationships is at the same time increasingly important, reliant on technology and complex. Some of the issues to consider may include:

- **How the Internet is shifting the balance of power to your customers.** It is important to realize that customers are now much more able than ever before to choose from a global marketspace, and as a result are often much more demanding in their expectations for service. The Internet offers customers richness and reach at the same time. E-commerce blurs the traditional trade-off between reaching large sections of customers with limited information, and only a few customers with large amounts of information.
- **The Internet is revolutionizing sales techniques and perceptions of established brands—**what are the consequences, either risks or opportunities, for your business in terms of such issues as the ability to sense customer needs and to build brand loyalty?
- **Modern marketspaces are now open 24/7.** The pace of business activity and change is rapidly accelerating, and the need to be flexible, adaptive, customer-focused, and innovative is now at a premium. The Internet compresses time and it is useful to consider how well-prepared and configured your business is. First, the Internet is always available and working; second, there is a culture of urgency and the ability to elicit immediate feedback, if required; and finally, the issue of immediacy means that issues, both trivial and important, need to be actioned swiftly as the trivial can fast become urgent.
- **There is a premium on managing knowledge.** Now more than ever, managing and leveraging knowledge is a key skill, and knowledge is a vital strategic resource that needs to be nurtured and developed.
- **Is it possible to extend the business in order to add value for current and potential customers?** Many organizations are now able to reevaluate factors as fundamental as their objectives, markets, and competencies, all of which may have been altered by the new marketspace opportunities and realities.
- **The Internet is increasing interactivity among people, customers, companies and industries.** It may help to assess the extent to which your business can—and could—forge new, valuable links with key groups.

CONCLUSION

Today, the traditional marketplace has a virtual counterpart: the marketspace. The advent of the marketspace fundamentally alters the ways firms can interact with, and manage, their customers. Companies must refine their corporate strategy accordingly. The proliferation of technology-mediated or "screen-to-face" service interfaces offers myriad opportunities for companies to manage customer relationships both more efficiently and more effectively. In this era of ever-accelerating competition and commoditization, service is the ultimate weapon.

For More Information

Books:

Gershenfeld, Neil A. *When Things Start to Think*. New York: Henry Holt, 1999.
Heskett, James L., et al. *The Service Profit Chain: How Leading Companies Link Profit and Growth to Loyalty, Satisfaction and Value*. New York: Free Press, 1997.
Kurzweil, Ray. *The Age of Spiritual Machines: When Computers Exceed Human Intelligence*. New York: Viking, 1999.
McLuhan, Marshall. *Understanding Media: The Extensions of Man*. New York: McGraw-Hill, 1964.
Rayport, Jeffrey F., and Bernard J. Jaworski. *e-Commerce*. New York: McGraw-Hill/Irwin, 2001.

See also:

☆ **Developing an Internet-era Mindset throughout the Organization (pp. 141–42)**
☆ **The New Frontiers in Old-economy Industries (pp. 99–100)**
☆ **Overcoming the Difficulties of Managing a Virtual Organization (pp. 208–09)**

"If [technology] keeps up, man will atrophy all his limbs but the push-button finger."
(Frank Lloyd Wright)

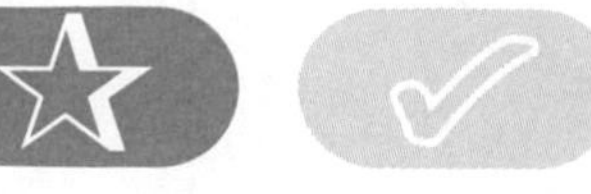    

CREATING A COMPANY WEB SITE TO REFLECT YOUR COMPANY *by Gerry McGovern*

EXECUTIVE SUMMARY

- Boom or bust, hype or not, the Internet has become a fundamental tool of business;
- Unfortunately, many organizations still treat their Web sites like a glorified brochure or a dumping ground for content;
- One of the best ways to think about your Web site is to see it as an interactive publication.

INTRODUCTION

Every day customers are leaving Web sites, turned off by out-of-date, poor quality content. People would never leave bowls of stinking fruit in their reception, yet they constantly leave out-of-date content on their Web sites. A 2000 survey by the NOP research group of large U.K. firms found that 77% admitted their Web sites contained out-of-date content.

Search and navigation is primitive on the Web. A 2000 Roper Starch Worldwide survey found that over 70% of respondents were frustrated when searching on the Internet. Online purchasing processes are poor. A 2000 survey by A.T. Kearney of retail Web sites, found that four out of five consumers abandoned attempts to purchase products online due to poor Web site design and functionality. Abandoned shopping carts are estimated to have cost e-tailers $3.8 billion in lost sales in 2000.

E-COMMERCE AND COMMERCE

The key difference between e-commerce and commerce is that commerce is selling with people, while e-commerce is selling with content. In traditional commerce there is a lot of flexibility because people are involved. The customer can ask questions. The sales person can support and guide. Often, the customer isn't sure what they want. It's said that great selling is having a customer walk into a store wanting to spend $100 on one item, and walking out happy having spent $500 on five items.

The problem with commerce is that it can involve a lot of inefficient and costly processes. The classic "old-time" commerce example is the local shop. This was the ultimate in relationship marketing. The friendly shop owner knew everybody and was always ready for a chat. The local shop was all well and good, but the big supermarket replaced it because it gave the customer more choice at cheaper prices.

E-commerce is like bringing the big supermarket idea to its logical conclusion. A professional e-commerce Web site has the content required to answer your questions. What price is it? Is there a discount if I buy ten? What size does it come in? What are its key features? When is it available? How long does it take to deliver? What do other customers think of it? What kind of reviews has it received in the media?

E-commerce is difficult to do right. An e-commerce Web site has to be as simple as possible to use, while having a robust and reliable back-end, and a depth of content that answers the huge variety of questions customers have. It has become clear that no matter how well designed the Web site is, customers are often wary of purchasing particularly high-ticket items online. They like to talk to or e-mail someone if only to know that there are "real" people running the operation. A 2001 survey by NFO Interactive found that over 40% of respondents said they would have more confidence in a Web site if they could e-mail someone.

An e-commerce strategy becomes more effective when:

1. The company is already an established brand;
2. The company can efficiently combine its offline assets with its Web site;
3. The product requires relatively little human support to sell;
4. The customer does not wish to touch and feel the product;
5. The product can be delivered electronically (software, music);
6. The product can be well described by written content and simple images;
7. The cost of delivery for the product is a small percentage of its price;
8. The product is targeted at an affluent, highly educated marketplace;
9. The product is niche with its customer-base geographically spread.

CLICKS 'N' MORTAR: THE BEST OF BOTH WORLDS

Launching a Web site is like opening a shop on the North Pole. Nobody knows you're there. A great many of the "dot-coms" found that the marketing costs to keep their brands in front of the consumer made their business models unworkable.

Those businesses that combined their offline business assets with their Web site, by and large, have had much more success. A survey by NielsenNetRatings found that during the 2000 holiday season in the U.S., established offline firms dominated the online retail market, accounting for 11 of the top 15 holiday e-tailers.

A clicks 'n' mortar strategy combines the distribution and physical presence strengths of the offline business with the convenience of online shopping. The result is better service and reduced cost of sale. Dell, for example, found that people who had visited its Web site and then rang Dell, were converted into purchasers quicker than people who had not visited the Web site.

MINI-CASES

America Online was the Web site that the Silicon Valley digerati loved to hate. It was boring, it was simple, it never implemented the latest "cool" technology. It was always "dumbing-down" for the average American. But America Online understood the Internet and people who used the Internet. Its founder, Steve Case, was quoted as saying that "the Internet makes every enterprise a publisher." People didn't want to wait for ages for pages to download. They wanted to get their e-mail, to chat, to quickly find content on products, services, and other areas of interest. Even before it became AOL Time Warner, *Wired* magazine grudgingly termed America Online as "unsexy and unstoppable."

Yahoo was built around the simple but powerful idea that people want limited rather than unlimited choice. That's why Yahoo used human editors to choose the best Web sites, rather than depend solely of search technology, as the other search engines did. Yahoo became a directory publisher, rather than a search engine Web site. It ensured that it had quality editors to choose the very best Web sites. It worked hard on creating a classification system that

---

"I could see the Internet was going to be massive so clearly having your own identity seemed obvious."

(Jason Drummond)

people would find easy to use. It focused on creating Web pages with minimal graphics that downloaded very quickly for its time-starved customers. It did the simple things well.

Microsoft is no slouch when it comes to the Web. Go to the Microsoft Web site and you might as well be picking up a copy of *Microsoft Daily*. It has a classic three-column layout. The left column is taken up with search and navigation. The rest of the page is filled with sharp content promoting the latest and greatest Microsoft offerings. On October 10, 2001, the lead story was titled, "Earn Your Stripes," encouraging engineers to become Microsoft certified professionals. Other stories covered .NET, Windows XP, special offers on Microsoft Office, information on the Code Red virus, etc.

E-BUSINESS: THE MEANING OF "E"

The Internet can make business operations more efficient. E-business is about doing just that. Oracle, for example, has claimed that implementing e-business processes has saved it $1 billion in 2000. General Electric has made similar claims. Perhaps these savings are exaggerated, nonetheless, it is clear that real savings can be made by implementing e-business processes.

An e-business strategy can deliver in the following areas:

- **Centralization**: Before the Internet, Oracle claimed that it had to go to sixty databases to find out how many people worked for the company. Implementing e-business processes allowed it to bring all its content into a few centrally managed databases.
- **Purchasing efficiencies**: General Electric has claimed that it has saved hundreds of million of dollars by creating online trading environments whereby its suppliers bid to supply materials and services.
- **Customer interaction**: The modern consumer is more educated. Time-to-market for products is ever-diminishing. These twin trends mean that the company needs to engage more than ever with the customer so as to get feedback that will help it quickly design products that more exactly meet consumer needs. The Internet can facilitate this type of closer interaction between company and consumer.
- **"The Internet is the computer"**: A key trend is to allow software to be accessed over the Internet. Properly done, this has major savings and efficiencies for the company. Software can be upgraded once and then accessed by all staff, thus saving time, reducing the cost of hardware, and minimizing support.

MAKING IT HAPPEN ▸▸

The Internet is here to stay. Properly used it can increase efficiency and drive profit. However, it is no magic wand that for little cost and effort will transform your company. A 2001 survey of U.K. businesses by Business Intelligence showed that business is only scratching the surface of the potential and challenges of the medium. It found that 64 percent of businesses were at least 12 to 18 months away from implementing a technology infrastructure for e-business.

Ask the following questions when you are developing your Internet strategy:

1. Is the Internet strategy being developed and driven from senior management level?
2. Is such a strategy fully integrated with the overall strategy of the company?
3. Is there buy-in from all levels of the organization, particularly those that need to implement it on a day-to-day basis?
4. Does the company have all the skills to implement the strategy?
5. Is appropriate training available to bring staff up to speed?
6. Have the technology issues been properly considered?
7. Is the company rolling out its Internet strategy on a step-by-step basis, rather than trying to change everything at once?
8. Is creating new value at the core of the Internet strategy, rather than simply focusing on reduced costs?
9. Are the needs of customers and staff always at the top of the agenda?
10. Is everyone totally and absolutely focused on keeping the Internet strategy as simple and straightforward as possible, rather than getting carried away on hype and bleeding-edge technology?

CONCLUSION: THINK PUBLISHING

A Web site is a publication. An intranet is a publication of vital content for staff, just as an extranet is for suppliers, and an Internet Web site is for customers. A quality Web site allows staff, customers, and all relevant stakeholders to quickly find the right content.

When all the hype is drained away, the day-to-day job of a Web site is about delivering the right content to the right person at the right time, at the right cost. Such content will help staff work smarter. It will make customers more educated about the organization's products, and thus more likely to purchase.

The best Web sites keep it simple. The best Web strategies are fully integrated with the organization's overall strategies.

For More Information

Books:

McGovern, Gerry and Rob Norton. *Content Critical*. Upper Saddle River, NJ: Financial Times Prentice Hall, 2001. (See **www.business-minds.com**.)

Nielsen, Jakob. *Designing Web Usability: The Practice of Simplicity*. Indianapolis, IN: New Riders, 2000. (See **www.useit.com**.)

Web Sites:

www.adventive.com/lists/isales/summary.html: this is one of the longest-running and best-managed discussion lists on the Internet e-mail discussion list. It is a must for those who want to understand sales and marketing on the Internet.

http://clickz.com: this site provides quality articles on a broad range of issues relating to doing business on the internet.

"The rush by marketers to establish World Wide Web sites at times resembled the Gold Rush that sent the 49ers west in search of riches."
(Stan Rapp)

  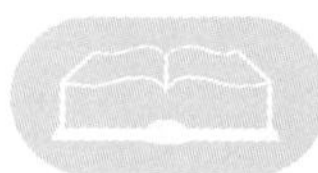  

INTELLECTUAL CAPITAL *by Thomas A. Stewart*

EXECUTIVE SUMMARY

- Intellectual capital is knowledge that transforms raw materials and makes them more valuable.
- To be considered intellectual capital, knowledge must be an asset.
- Intellectual capital's raw materials might be physical or intangible, like information.

INTRODUCTION

Intellectual capital is just that: a capital asset consisting of intellectual material. As such, it is one of three forms of capital: financial capital, that is, money; tangible or fixed assets, which include land, buildings, machinery, and other long-lived equipment; and knowledge.

To be considered intellectual capital, knowledge must be an asset—able to be used to create wealth. Thus intellectual capital includes: the talents and skills of individuals and groups; technological and social networks and the software and culture that connect them; and intellectual property such as patents, copyrights, methods, procedures, archives, etc. It excludes knowledge or information not involved in production or wealth creation. Just as raw material such as iron ore should not be confused with an asset such as a steel mill, so knowledge materials such as data or miscellaneous facts ought not to be confused with knowledge assets.

INTELLECTUAL CAPITAL AS AN ASSET

From the standpoint of traditional accounting, intellectual capital frequently does not fit the definition of an asset. Generally, under accounting rules, an asset must be tangible; it must have been acquired in one or more transactions so that it has a known cost or a market value; and it must be under the control of the party whose asset it is said to be. Thus scientific skill is not an accounting asset, but laboratory equipment is.

Intellectual capital theory argues that this definition is too narrow and hinders businesses from seeing, managing, or building knowledge assets. This in turn inhibits companies' ability to compete and prosper in an economy in which knowledge has become an important source of profits. The intellectual capitalists use a looser definition: an asset is something that transforms raw material into something more valuable. It is a magician's black box. Inputs get put in—a few handkerchiefs, say; the asset does something to transform them; and out come outputs worth more than the inputs—rabbits, maybe. The question of ownership and control matters less than the question of access. A corporation might not own scientific expertise (in the form of a cadre of employees, for example) but it has the use of it and can exert a quasi-proprietary influence over how it is used.

Intellectual capital, then, is knowledge that transforms raw materials and makes them more valuable. The raw materials might be physical—knowledge of the formula for Coca-Cola is an intellectual asset that transforms a few cents' worth of sugar, water, carbon dioxide, and flavorings into a dollar's worth of refreshment. The raw material might be intangible, like information. Knowledge of the law is an intellectual asset; a lawyer takes the facts of a dispute (raw material), transforms them through his knowledge of the law (an intellectual asset), to produce an opinion or a legal brief (an output of higher value than the facts by themselves).

Though financial accounting does not measure intellectual capital, markets clearly do. Shares of companies in the pharmaceutical industry, for example, generally trade at a high premium over the book value of their assets, and the companies' return on net assets is abnormally high; but if their spending on research and development is added to their capital, both their market-to-book ratios and their returns on assets come to resemble those of less knowledge-intensive companies. (There is a slowly growing movement to find ways to account for intellectual capital and report it to shareholders. Scandinavian countries, particularly Denmark, are leaders in the field.)

Indeed, it was the unusual behavior of the equities of knowledge-intensive companies that first drew the attention of analysts to intellectual capital. The term seems to have been employed first in 1958, when two financial analysts, describing the stock-market valuations of several small, science-based companies, concluded, "The intellectual capital of such companies is perhaps their single most important element" and noted that their high stock valuations might be termed an "intellectual premium." [Morris Kronfeld and Arthur Rock, "Some Considerations of the Infinite." *The Analyst's Journal*, November 1958, p. 6.] The idea lay dormant for a quarter of a century. In the 1980s, Walter Wriston, the former chairman of Citicorp, noted that his bank and other corporations possessed valuable intellectual capital that accountants (and bank regulators) did not measure.

INTELLECTUAL CAPITAL ANALYZED

Karl-Erik Sveiby, a Swede, intrigued by the anomalous stock-market behavior of knowledge-intensive companies, began an investigation that produced the first analysis of the nature of intellectual capital. Sveiby, his colleagues, and *Affarsvarlden*, Sweden's oldest business magazine, noticed that the magazine's proprietary model for valuing initial public offerings broke down for high-tech companies. Sveiby concluded that these companies possessed assets not described in financial documents or included in the magazine's model. With a likeminded group of associates, he sat down to puzzle out what these might be. In "Den Osynliga Balansrekningen Ledarskap" ("The Invisible Balance Sheet"), 1989, they laid the foundation stone for much of what has come after by coming up with a taxonomy for intellectual capital. Knowledge assets, they proposed, could be found in three places: the competencies of a company's people, its internal structure (patents, models, computer and administrative systems), and its external structure (brands, reputation, relationships with customers and suppliers).

After some tinkering by others—the pieces are now usually called human capital, structural (or organizational) capital, and customer (or relationship) capital—Sveiby's model still stands. It has made managing intellectual capital possible by naming its component parts. Shortly thereafter, Leif Edvinsson, an executive at the Swedish financial services company Skandia, persuaded his management to appoint him "Director, Intellectual Capital"; Skandia became the business world's most conspicuous laboratory for intellectual capital studies.

"Companies. . .have a hard time distinguishing between the cost of paying people and the value of investing in them."

(Thomas A. Stewart)

Ideas whose time has come flower everywhere at once. Ikujiro Nonaka and Hirotaka Takeuchi in Japan began investigations of how knowledge is produced that resulted in "The Knowledge-creating Company" (*Harvard Business Review*, November-December 1991) and Thomas A. Stewart synthesized American research in intellectual capital in "Brainpower: How Intellectual Capital Is Becoming America's Most Important Asset" (*Fortune*, June 3, 1991).

Every company or organization possesses all three forms of intellectual capital. Human capital consists of the skills, competencies, abilities of individuals and groups. These range from specific technical skills to "softer" skills like salesmanship or the ability to work effectively in a team. An individual's human capital cannot, in a legal sense, be owned by a corporation; the term thus refers not only to individual talent but also to the collective skills and aptitudes of a workforce. Indeed, one challenge faced by executives is how to manage the talent of truly outstanding members of their staffs: how to use it to the utmost without becoming overdependent on a few star performers, or how to encourage stars to share their skills with others. Skills that are irrelevant to a company's business—the fine tenor voice of an actuary, for example—may be part of the individual's human capital, but not of his employer's.

Structural capital comprises knowledge assets that are indeed company property: intellectual property such as patents, copyrights, and trademarks; processes, methodologies, models; documents and other knowledge artifacts; computer networks and software; administrative systems; and so forth. A data warehouse is structural capital; so is the decision-support software that helps people use the data. One knowledge-management process is converting human capital—which is usually available to just a few people—into structural capital, so it becomes shareable. This happens, for example, when a team writes up the "lessons learned" from a project so that others can apply them.

Customer capital is the value of relationships with suppliers, allies, and customers. Two common forms are brand equity and customer loyalty. The former is a promise of quality (or some other attribute) for which a customer agrees to pay a premium price; the value of brands is measurable in financial terms. The loyalty of a base of customers is also measurable, using discounted cash-flow analysis. Both are frequently calculated when companies are bought and sold. In a sense, all customer capital should eventually reflect itself either in a premium price or a sticky buyer-seller relationship.

Every organization possesses intellectual capital in all three manifestations, but with varying emphasis depending on its history and strategy. For example, a chemical company might have, as a knowledge asset, the ability to concoct custom chemical compounds that precisely match its customer's needs. That asset might be people-based, residing in the tacit knowledge of dozens of skilled chemists; it might be structural, found in an extensive library of patents and manuals, or databases and expert systems; it might be relationship-based, found in the company's intimate ties to customers, suppliers, universities, etc. Most likely, of course, the asset—skill at making custom chemicals—is a combination of the three.

At least three characteristics of intellectual capital give it extraordinary power to add value. First, companies that use knowledge assets deftly can reduce the expense and burden of carrying physical assets, or maximize their return on them. For example, transportation companies can use information networks and skill in logistics and load management to maximize their utilization of assets like rail cars and containers. Second, it can be possible to get enormous leverage or gearage from knowledge assets. The value of an aircraft can be realized over just one route at a time, whereas that of an airline's reservation system is limited only by the number of people in the world. In a study of the chemical industry that examined 83 companies over 25 years, Baruch Lev, professor of accounting at New York University, found that R&D spending (one form of investment in intellectual capital) returned 25.9% pretax, whereas capital spending earned just 15% (about 10% after tax, approximately the cost of capital).

Third, human and customer capital are the primary sources of innovation and customization. The increasing sophistication of machinery and information technology has led to the automation of more and more repetitive tasks. These manufacturing economies of scale are sources of competitive advantage in industrial processes. At a certain point, however, their value diminishes: The more it is possible to do a task the same way twice, the harder it is for one company to differentiate its offerings from its competitors'. When this happens the value of innovation, customization, and service increases; all are highly dependent on intellectual capital.

MAKING IT HAPPEN ▸▸

- Treat knowledge as an asset only if it is capable of yielding an economic return.
- Build human capital by developing skills, competencies, abilities of individuals and groups who deliver value to customers.
- Convert human capital into structural capital, by organizing the exchange and sharing of knowledge.
- Optimize customer capital—the value of relationships with suppliers, allies, and customers—by building brand equity and customer loyalty.
- Use knowledge assets to reduce the expense and burden of carrying physical assets, or to maximize return on those assets
- Look for competitive advantage from innovation, customization, and service rather than from economies of scale.

For More Information

Books:

Mayo, Andrew. *The Human Value of the Enterprise: Valuing People As Assets—Monitoring, Measuring, Managing.* Naperville, IL: Nicholas Brealey, 2001.

Sullivan, Patrick H. *Value Driven Intellectual Capital: How to Convert Intangible Corporate Assets into Market Value.* New York: John Wiley, 2000.

Teece, David J. *Managing Intellectual Capital.* New York: Oxford University Press, 2001.

Web Site:

www.intellectualcapital.nl: this is a truly global Web site with dozens of links off this page to IC resources around the world. Resources include articles, methods, online tools, best practices—and more.

"Owning the intellectual property is like owning land: you need to keep investing in it again and again to get a payoff; you can't simply sit back and collect rent." (Esther Dyson)

Viewpoint: David Weinberger

Explaining the Passion that Powers the Web

A key commentator on the Web and the way it affects our world today, David Weinberger sets forth here his views on how Web sites can both work for and against us.

Businesses make plenty of mistakes on the Web. They make users click 15 times to buy a single item. They get into price wars and cut prices below the profitability point. They put up sloppily secured sites that get hacked by teenagers with too much time on their hands. But the big mistake that businesses make isn't economic or technical. It's psychological or (dare I say it?) spiritual. They're not getting the biggest "it" there is to get: the Web isn't theirs. The Web is *ours*.

It's easy not to get this point–although, in another sense, you have to have your head inserted pretty far up a dark place to miss it. This is perhaps the biggest way businesses confuse the real world with the Web. In the real world, an unowned space, such as a new continent, is divided into owned parcels. If I own a piece of land, I build what I want on it and you may enter it only with my sufferance. So, companies assume that their Web sites are theirs in the same way. They think that visitors are entering the company's property. But, while that may be true legally, it's not true in any other way. Companies, typically, even make the Copernican mistake of thinking that the Web is about them. But it's not. The Web is ours. Profoundly ours. Ours in ways that transcend ownership. That is what gives the Web its power and appeal. Miss that fact and your Web presence will be worse than ineffective. It will alienate your customers. Heck, it's probably alienating them right now.

For example, I recently bought a washing machine. I went to some consumer review sites that confirmed my preference for a front loader and let me narrow the choices to Kenmore and Maytag. I checked some more customer sites and then at www.thathomesite.com stumbled on discussion boards devoted to the merits of these machines. The owners seemed to like both, so I was leaning towards Kenmore since it's considerably cheaper. But then I read a complaint about the Kenmore. It seems that the "done" buzzer is so loud that it wakes up the neighbors. There followed a flurry of messages confirming the complaint and suggesting various workarounds, including snipping the wires. Still, I decided to purchase the Kenmore because we'd be keeping it in the back corner of our basement. So, I went to our local store and bought it. (New models, by the way, have a volume control.)

If you were reading closely, you will have noticed that in my buying process I skipped a step: I completed the entire sales decision process without ever going to the Kenmore site. But why would I go there? I was getting great information from other customers. And I got from them not just honest reviews but information that I would never have gotten from the Kenmore site or store: it would never have occurred to me to ask how loud the buzzer is.

I then visited the Kenmore site, just out of curiosity. And it lived up to expectations: clean, crisp, professional. . .and totally boring and almost completely worthless. In other words, it was like the vast majority of corporate sites on the Web.

Boring and worthless would be bad enough. But it gets worse. The Kenmore site opens with a flash animation that portentously tells us that it is "introducing a revolutionary new washer that will change the way you think about laundry." Only then do you get to see the oh-so-professional home page that tells us in big print that Kenmore is "Smart. Stylish. Simple." This goes all the way beyond boring to off-putting. It's so unconnected with our interests and our way of talking that it alienates us. Alienating your customers is just about the worst thing you can do. Alienating them puts a gulf between you and them that is deep and is not only emotional, but intellectual. Alienated customers not only don't like you, they don't have the slightest idea what you're talking

---

"The Web is just going to be one more of those major change factors that businesses face every decade."

(Steve Jobs)

about and don't want to understand. Think about how you felt when your parents made you bring a rubber sheet to a sleep-over. That's alienation.

Alienation is an interesting phenomenon. It implies a sense of belonging that's been violated. But if the Web is a club, it's the least exclusive one since the People Who Type Society. What is this sense of belonging on the Web? Where does it come from?

In part it comes from the Web's origins in the minds of geeks. This antiauthoritarian subclass of humanity came to the Internet with a sense of "us against them," with the "us" being a set of rational contributors to a better world and the "they" perceived as a set of greedy, money-grabbing, technically inept morons. But the Web has spread far beyond the geeks, and their influence now is much more marginal. There is something about the Web itself that generates this sense of belonging, of shared community. The Web is a new persistent public place made of pages and links, both of which are expressions of human interest. We're on the Web because we have something to say or because we're interested in what other people say about an interest we share; we build the Web page by page and chat by chat because of this. The stuff of the Web is quite literally human passion.

This gives us a hint about the nature of the "ours." The Web isn't ours in most of the usual senses of the term. It is not ours legally. We don't own the Web the way we own our house. We don't own the contents of the Web the way we own what we have written. It would be closer to say that the Web is ours in the way that term is used in the Woody Guthrie song "This Land Is Your Land." Guthrie's song is a statement about the proper balance of values in a democracy—this land is not primarily about lining the pockets of the landed gentry but was established for the good of the everyone God created.

I think there is a further sense of "ours" that helps explain the deeper sense of alienation that we feel from the millions of sites like www.Kenmore.com. The real world, as it is affectionately known, is the one into which we are born. It existed before we were conceived and after we die we will be buried in it. It consists of atoms that form the landscape within which we are constrained to build our lives. If we were born near water and fig trees, we will have one type of life; if we were born into a land of ice-crusted caves, we'll have another type of life. The real world gives us distances and a geography spread out among those distances, and tells us to do the best that we can. Thus, the real world is fundamentally not human, although we humans take it up and transform it into livable lands—tilled, watered, leveled, planted, at times even exploded and remade. The Web, on the other hand, is made up of words and other forms of significance. It is human through and through. This is the sense in which the Web is ours. It is ours the way language is ours. It is *of* us.

Most businesses are too busy trying to sell us stuff to think even for a moment about why we are on the Web. We are there for lots of reasons, starting with gathering information, and including everything from downloading pornography to learning how to tie our Boy Scout neckerchiefs. But the palpable excitement about the Web comes not from a sudden desire of our species to become research librarians or Eagle Scouts, but from our excitement simply about being connected one to another. We are sharing interests, an act as fundamental to humanity as breaking bread together. Then we go on to the typical business site and suddenly a pitch man is yelling at us. All he wants to do is transfer money from our wallet to his. There's no recognition that we're on the Web to talk with other people who care about the same things as we do.

You don't have to be a psychologist to see that most sites are insultingly wrong about why you are visiting them. You can just to listen to the language they use. It's the language of marketing, an arcane cant never uttered by script-free human mouths, written by professionals feeding on one another in committees. The boasting, the inability to admit any flaws in their products, the slickness of the words designed to penetrate our defenses without ever actually being heard or thought about. . .the jargon tells us that the site has only one thing on its mind. To these sites we are nothing but targets.

You can't fix this simply by changing your rhetoric. Focus groups may tell you that a homier-sounding jargon will increase your sell-through rates by 1.4%, but you're still faking it and you will be discovered, chastised, and abandoned. . .just as you deserve to be. Instead you have to do the hardest thing for a business to do: give up the attempt to control your customers. Discover within your own borders the employees who still care about the products they're building. Those employees are already out on the Web, talking with your market, telling them the truth about your products, and doing so in the excited high-pitched tone of voice that conveys genuine enthusiasm. Build your Web presence around those people. Get used to the idea that the most important conversations about your products will occur among customers (and some of your employees) not on your own site. Learn how to take that as the most positive of signs; if people aren't talking about your product, then no one cares about your product. And if you can't trust your employees to tell the truth and still run a viable business, then in fact you don't have a viable business.

The very worst thing you can do is to build a site that you view as yours, a place that you imagine people come to in order to hear your marketing messages. It's bad marketing and, worse, it commits the spiritual mistake of thinking that the Web is a place to be divided into lots and owned by individuals, rather than as a new world made of the human stuff, a world that is fundamentally ours.

For More Information

Web Site:
JOHO: **www.hyperorg.com**

"I think one of the more interesting conclusions emerging from this ever more complicated business environment, is that values do matter."
(Mark Moody-Stuart)

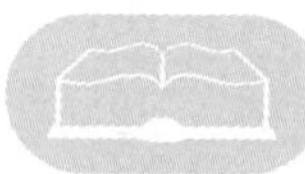

Viewpoint: Tom Petzinger

Pioneering a Biotech Business Model for Managing

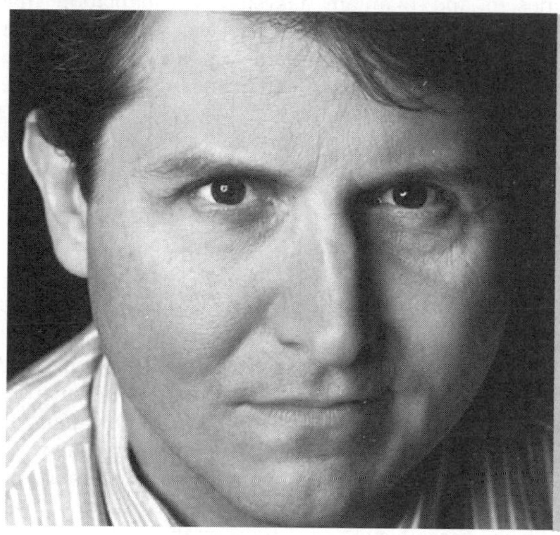

Readers of the *Wall Street Journal* knew Tom Petzinger for the observations on management that appeared in the regular columns that he wrote for that paper for four years. Ultimately, the direction of his columns led him to study the ways of small entrepreneurial firms and what big companies could learn from "the new pioneers," the term he used as the title for a best-selling book on the subject. Tom was so fascinated by the entrepreneurial world that in 2000 he left management writing to start a biotech company in his home town of Pittsburgh, Pennsylvania. Thus Tom became one of those rare management thinkers who have had to meet a payroll while striving to grow a sustainable business.

I guess what changed the field of management for me was biology. I now look at the profession of management with a totally different point of view.

Now, that may sound strange; but I really thought hard about the operations of businesses I knew in-depth and ultimately concluded that economic systems are not only *like* biological systems, they are really *an outgrowth of* biological systems. And the minute I comprehended this vividly in my mind, it changed everything. It influenced my thinking about how people should design companies and about how managers and employees should interact.

To be sure, I was influenced heavily by the writings of Stuart Kauffman, who has much to say about diversity and self-organizing systems, and by the thinking of William Frederick, who has focused heavily on business and ethics, and how business is (or should be) really an outgrowth of biological processes. But taking all that others have said and then filtering that through my own perceptions, the real point for me is this: How much of management, as a discipline, as a field of study, has been focused on hard and fixed boundaries, on highly rigid channels for sales and distribution? On legalities and policies? On organization charts that are more often than not assembled by a small band of "all-knowing" leaders locked away from the organization?

I'd say a very great deal of the discipline of management has been about such activities. And this strikes me now as artificial; it is *not* the way things happen in the natural world, which, without "management," often works with great efficiency and productivity. Management has much to learn about how matter and energy should naturally come together and flow—that having staff members come together and organize themselves is not only the "natural" thing to do, it may be the only organization chart that will really work! Leaders should, as I see things now, work primarily on values and goals and let their work teams decide how to make things work in the most natural, productive, and profitable ways.

Why all of this makes even more sense to me day by day is that the trend in business for the next 50 years is pretty clear.

Large organizations are going to be fewer in number and even more specialized, larger, and generally tied to even more narrow niches. Every time there's another big merger or acquisition making news headlines, there's one less big company to count in the corporate population. And, as we know, these big companies inevitably dwell on tightening distribution costs, or making their products more commoditized, or trimming the headcount.

So, where is there "life" in the marketplace? Where does the world turn for new thinking about businesses that may not exist today but that need to become a reality?

So, where is there "life" in the marketplace? Where does the world turn for new thinking about businesses that may not exist today but that need to become a reality? Without any doubt in my mind, we are going to see the trend toward ever-larger companies countered by a percolation of more and more small organizations, many of which will be purely entrepreneurial, developing totally new systems, products, or services. This is how, just as in nature, the marketplace will evolve, by new "life forms" in the shape of new businesses. One can see this happening in numerous industries. Consider the publishing world: there are far fewer, but larger, publishers than there were ten years ago; and these big publishing companies focus endlessly on logistics and

"Management that wants to change an institution must first show that it loves that institution."

(John Iusa)

distribution issues, all tied to streamlining operations and, hopefully, lowering costs. But there are more and more authors and writers working ever more independently and generating or supporting small publishing houses or e-publishing ventures. You see roughly the same thing in banking. Ditto the movie industry. In both the large-scale companies and in the small-scale enterprises, you simply can't manage anymore in the classic Frederick Taylor kinds of ways. It has to be more natural.

So, managers need to develop some new skills, and these are not going to be found in the tables of contents of today's Management 101 books. I'm not sure these skills are being stressed now in even Management 901 books.

First, managers will have to be able to sense and articulate patterns which are emerging—patterns of success—in either the marketplace, or in organizations, or in technology. But much more important than just sensing and articulating patterns (after all, academics often do these two things quite well), successful managers are going to have to be able to *translate* what they're seeing into meaningful action. Business in the future will demand managers with a new level of decisiveness so that a company can move in wholly new directions based on patterns that are happening in real time, patterns that others simply aren't observing or thinking about or acting upon. You know, if a manager can observe, think about, and act on emerging patterns—events that are happening *now*—that is almost as good as being able to see the future. Detect and act upon new patterns of market success and you are, in essence, inventing the future so that it favors your own initiative and risk-taking.

Business in the future will demand managers with a new level of decisiveness so that a company can move in wholly new directions based on patterns that are happening in real time, patterns that others simply aren't observing or thinking about or acting upon.

So opportunities abound for managers to ask new questions. To start with (and I say this without any kind of smirk), managers should ask why a company needs management at all.

I am not one of those advocating that we completely do away with management; but I am saying that, from where I sit, the reasons we had to establish and empower management in the past are not the same reasons to deploy management today. Look at it this way. As the world moved into the 1900s, management's goal seemed to be about designing an optimum—the perfect assembly line or what have you—and then maintaining it, forever! Today there is no optimum, just change. Today there is no value in establishing an unchanging optimum, as businesses need to be able to respond to change, not resist it. Perhaps the primary role of management in the future may be to design and maintain a system of adaptation that works reliably day after day because such a process or mindset is embedded into the organizational culture. I'd offer that as a good start point for discussing the future of management.

We can no longer afford to think about having either profitable companies or good places to work. It's an artificial distinction that's badly out of date.

Everything I've seen and every successful enterprise I've visited have shown me that the most consistently profitable places are companies where people enjoy working. Big businesses (and big b-schools) have regrettably reduced all aspects of management to financial terms and documented them that way. But there are so many other metrics tied to successful businesses, which are not financial: good attitudes, a healthy culture, improving the ways people treat one another, improving customer and vendor relationships, creating high trust among all levels—these factors *can and do* make a monumental difference in the character of a business. Leaders, thus, need to think hard and long about their corporate values, not as clichés but as drivers to the business, just as technology is a driver. And leaders need to be as concerned about "return on values" as they are about return on investment. I believe the best business leaders in the years ahead will be paid as much for their management of values as their management of capital. And I believe that the best business leaders will be more natural because they will have organizations that operate in tune with the same scientific principles that guide the natural world and which are revealed in the study of biology.

For More Information

Web Site:
www.petzinger.com

See also:

☆ **The End of Growth: Why Does It Always End? What Can You Do About It? (pp. 269–70)**
☆ **Groundhog Management (pp. 194–95)**
☆ **Keeping Control in Nonhierarchical Organizations (pp. 198–99)**
☆ **SQ: Investing in Spiritual Capital (pp. 43–44)**

"Dreams have their place in management activity, but they need to be kept severely under control."
(Arnold Weinstock)

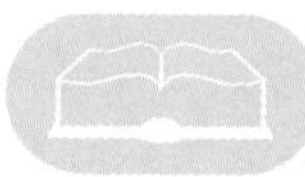

PROJECT MANAGEMENT *by Robert Buttrick*

EXECUTIVE SUMMARY

- Make sure your projects are driven by your strategy.
- Use a staged approach to manage your projects, and place high emphasis on the early stages.
- Engage your stakeholders and encourage teamwork and commitment.
- Ensure success by planning for it.
- Monitor against the plan.
- Formally close the project.

INTRODUCTION

Today, managers may spend as much time in interdisciplinary, cross-functional project teams as they do in their normal posts—project management has now become a core competence for all managers. This applies not only to projects undertaken for customers (external projects), but also to those undertaken for the development of the organization itself (internal projects).

Many factors have contributed to this. Among them is speed, coupled with the increased complexity of organizations and the closer relationships within and between companies, their customers, and suppliers. We now need evolutionary change at revolutionary speed, necessitating skillful project management.

As a vehicle of change, project management is well suited to meet these needs. However, it is too often perceived as a necessary technical discipline rather than the powerful business tool it really is. This section looks at the challenges of Project Management, and potential responses.

THE CHALLENGES TO BE FACED

All organizations have problems with the ways they tackle change within their businesses—these may be related to technology, people, processes, systems, or structure. During the late 20th century, there has been a variety of techniques and offerings available to managers to enable them to do this, most notably total quality management and business process reengineering.

Unfortunately, not all organizations secure the enduring benefits initially promised by these techniques. The initiatives often fail because they cost too much, take too long, are inadequately thought out and specified, or simply don't deliver the expected benefits.

This amounts to failure on a grand scale, costing billions every year, and results in the demise of some organizations. Organizations don't know *how* to tackle these initiatives: there's no company-wide way of organizing this. Also they don't know *what* they should be doing: there's no clear strategy driving decision making.

Project management gives you the environment to solve the first of these root causes, and by its proper implementation will prompt you to think about the second.

PRINCIPLES OF PROJECT MANAGEMENT

MAKE SURE YOUR PROJECTS ARE DRIVEN BY YOUR STRATEGY

You should be able to demonstrate explicitly how each project you undertake fits your business strategy. The screening out of unwanted projects as soon as possible is essential. The less clear the strategy, the more likely unsuitable projects are to pass the screening: hence there will be more projects competing for scarce resources, resulting in the company losing focus and risking its overall performance.

USE A STAGED APPROACH

Rarely is it possible to plan a project in its entirety. You should, however, be able to plan the next stage in detail and to the end of the project in outline. As you progress through the project you gather more information, reduce uncertainty, and increase confidence. The typical framework comprises the following progressive steps, or stages:

- *Proposal*—identifying the idea or need.
- *Initial investigation*—a brief overview of the possible requirements and solutions.
- *Detailed investigation*—undertaking a feasibility study of the options and defining the chosen solution.
- *Development and testing*—building the solution.
- *Trial*—piloting the solution with real people.
- *Operation and closure*—putting it into practice and closing the project.

You should use the same generic stages for all types of project. This makes the use and understanding of the process familiar and easier, avoiding the need to learn different processes for various types of project. What differs is the content of each project, the level of activity, the nature of the activity, the resources required, and the stakeholders and decision makers needed within each use of the framework. The *gates* are entry points to each stage, and are the key checkpoints for revalidating a project and committing resources and funding.

Placing high emphasis on the early stages of the project might mean that between 30% and 50% of the project's life cycle is devoted to investigative stages before any final deliverable is physically built. Research clearly demonstrates that placing heavy emphasis up front significantly decreases the time to market/completion. Good investigative work means clearer objectives and plans. Decisions taken at the early stages of a project have a far-reaching effect and set the tone for the remainder. In the early stages, creative solutions can slash delivery times in half or cut costs dramatically. Once development is underway changes can be very costly.

ENGAGE YOUR STAKEHOLDERS

A stakeholder is any person involved in or affected by a project. The involvement of stakeholders such as users and customers adds considerable value at all stages of the project. Engaging them is a powerful mover for change; ignoring them can lead to failure. When viewed from a stakeholder perspective, your project may be just one more problem they have to cope with in addition to fulfilling their usual duties; it may appear irrelevant to them, or even regressive. If their consent is required to make things happen, it is unwise to ignore them.

Be sure to encourage teamwork and commitment at all times. The need for many projects to draw on people from a range of functions means a cross-functional team approach is essential. The more closely people work and the more open the management style, the better they perform. Although this is not always practical, close-

"The chief executive. . .like a juggler keeps a number of projects in the air: periodically one comes down, is given a new burst of energy, and is sent back into orbit." (Henry Mintzberg)

ness can be achieved by frequent meetings and good communication, often through Web tools or videoconferencing.

Ensure Success by Planning for It

The more functionally structured a company, the more difficult it is to implement effective project management: project management by its nature crosses functional boundaries. To make projects succeed, the balance of power usually needs to be tipped toward the project and away from line management.

Monitor Against the Plan

There must be guidance, training, and support for all staff related to projects, including senior managers who sponsor projects or make project-related decisions. Core control techniques include planning, managing risk, issues, scope change, schedule, cost, and reviews. Planning as a discipline is essential. If you have no definition of the project and no plan, it will be virtually impossible to communicate your intentions to the project team and stakeholders, and terms such as "early," "late," and "within budget" have no real meaning.

Risk management is key: using a staged approach is itself a risk management technique, with the gates acting as formal review points. It is essential to analyze the project, determine which are the inherently risky parts, and take action to reduce, avoid, or, in some cases, insure against those risks while looking to exploit any opportunities that arise.

Monitoring and forecasting against the agreed plan ensures that events do not take those involved in the project by surprise. This is best illustrated by the "project control cycle," the frequency of which depends on the project, its stage of development, and the inherent risk. Monitoring should focus more on the future than on what has actually been completed. Completion of activities is not sufficient to predict whether milestones will continue to be met. The project manager should continually check that the plan is still fit for the purpose and likely to deliver the business benefits on time.

Many projects are late or never even get completed. One of the reasons for this is scope creep: more and more ideas are incorporated into the project, resulting in higher costs and late delivery. Changes, even beneficial ones, must be managed to guarantee that only those enabling the project benefits to be realized are accepted; you must communicate this to the team and stakeholders so they are absolutely clear what the current project comprises.

Formally Close the Project

Finally, every project must be closed, either because it has completed its work or because it has been terminated early. By explicitly closing a project you make sure that all work ceases, lessons are learned, and any remaining assets, funding, or resources can be released for other purposes.

Mini-case

One company that has a product leadership strategy terminated a new product before launch because a competitor had just released a superior product. It was better to abort the launch and work on the next generation product than with releasing a new product that could be seen by the market as inferior. If they had done so, their strategy of product leadership would have been compromised.

Making It Happen

Common mistakes include:

- intrafunctional thinking—not having a company-wide view;
- having too many rules—the more project rules you make, the more people will break them;
- disappearing and changing sponsors—continual changing of the driver will cause you to lose focus and forget why you are undertaking the project at all;
- ignoring the risks—risks don't go away, so acknowledge and manage them;
- rushing in prematurely to get something going; resist the temptation to confuse activity with progress;
- analysis paralysis—you need to investigate, but only enough to gain the confidence to move on;
- untested assumptions—all assumptions are risks, so treat them as such;
- executive's pet projects—make no exceptions. If an executive's idea is really so good, it should stand up to the scrutiny all the others go through.

Your project will run much more smoothly if you focus on a few basics.

- Define strategies clearly so you're better able to eliminate low-leverage, low-value projects.
- Plan through progressive stages: proposal, initial investigation, detailed investigation, development and testing, trial, operation, and closure.
- Concentrate on the early stages of the project, when the decisions taken have a far-reaching effect on the outcome.
- Analyze the project to reduce, avoid, or insure against the risks.
- To make projects succeed, tip the balance of power toward the project and away from line management.
- Focus progress monitoring more on the future than on completion of activities, which doesn't predict that future milestones will be met.

Conclusion

The success of an organization rests on its ability to manage projects effectively and efficiently. The interdisciplinary nature of project teams combined with the significance and sensitivity of their impact places considerable demands on management. Acquiring key skills will ensure that the process runs smoothly, minimizing costs and maximizing benefits, while securing stakeholder involvement and commitment. Responsive is an increasingly significant source of competitive advantage, and a fast, flexible and focused project management capability is essential for every organization. Tomorrow's successful corporations will reflect the efforts those organizations make to the way they research, plan and execute new initiatives and projects.

For More Information

Books:

Buttrick, Robert. *The Project Workout*. 2nd ed. with CD-ROM. Upper Saddle River, NJ: Financial Times Prentice Hall, 2000.

Obeng, Eddie. *All Change! The Project Leader's Secret Handbook*. Upper Saddle River, NJ: Financial Times Prentice Hall, 1996.

Web Site:

www.allchange.com is a portal to the Pentacle Virtual Business School, founded by Eddie Obeng.

See also:

☆ **Avoiding the Mistakes of the Past: Lessons from the Startup World (pp. 129–30)**
☆ **Intrapreneurial Warriors versus Traditional Managers (pp. 125–26)**
☆ **Keeping Control in Nonhierarchical Organizations (pp. 198–99)**

"Responsibility without control is at the core of management." (Paul Corrigan)

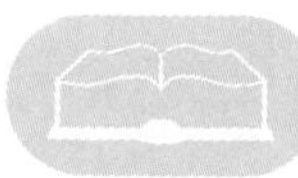

VIRTUAL COLLABORATION *by Stewart Clegg, Antoine Hermens, and Salvador Porras*

EXECUTIVE SUMMARY

- The Internet suits collaborative organizations.
- Customers want fast, flexible solutions rather than being hooked into a "single-vendor-provides-all" relationship.
- The value that e-business models creates resides in the network of partners.
- Collaborative e-business requires a win-win-win outcome for suppliers, companies, and customers.
- Governance of alliances needs to develop time and culture accounting.

INTRODUCTION

Bureaucracy won't last much longer. Today the new economy is generating strategic opportunities and organizational forms based on collaborative networks that defy bureaucracy's rationale. E-commerce is more than a way of Web-enabling existing business practices—it creates new opportunities and demands hitherto unknown organizational competencies. The business model for new economy firms is collaborative.

The Internet offers opportunities for smaller players to compete within global networks. Virtual villages are emerging in which small enterprises form and re-form alliances to provide high-tech services to larger companies. London-based Sohonet stretches such electronic adjacency further, sharing high-capacity data links to participate in the Hollywood and West Los Angeles creative milieu. High-speed digital exchange of film, video, and sound enables post-production operations to be carried out in London in direct competition with Californian companies. The open networked nature of the entertainment industry of southern California is a lower-tech version of the IT networks in northern California.

It's not only small businesses that use networked capabilities. Cisco's Global Networked Business Model enabled the company to build interactive knowledge-based relationships with potential clients, customers, partners, suppliers, and employees while saving more than $372 million annually in business expenses on an investment of less than $15 million.

THE PARADOX

- *Technologically*, the shift to e-commerce serves to drive transaction costs down.
- *Commercially*, where this occurs no organization has much advantage beyond that of being a first mover since every competitor drives down everyone's transaction costs.
- *Organizationally*, to obtain advantage organizations have to add value over and above the costs of transactions stripped out by the use of digital technology.
- *Paradoxically*, e-technology doesn't add value, but erodes it by driving transaction costs down, so the only way of increasing value in the e-economy is by reinstating transaction costs. Organizations must *turn transactions into relationships through collaboration*.

WHY DO FIRMS COLLABORATE?

Rapid economic and technological change, declining productivity growth and increasing competitive pressures, global interdependence, and the blurring of boundaries between distinct legal organizational entities, all facilitate collaboration. Collaboration is a response to turbulence that individual organizations are unable to manage because of a lack of resources or an inability to control externalities.

Low collaboration and high competition increase the risk that one party will act against others. The best strategy for organizations is high collaboration and high competition, with the major benefit of mutual learning for participants.

Trust plays an important role in collaborative networks. Transactions take place among organizations involved in reciprocal, preferential, mutually supportive actions. Such relationships are different from markets in that transactions involve joint, bilateral coordination of plans and activities. They differ from firms or hierarchies in having no single actor-participant; organizations maintain their independence, coordinating through negotiation and broad information interchange.

Successful collaborations combine the strength of two or more companies. They outclass competitors by establishing de facto standards, and avoid the risk of large stand-alone investments. One reason for forming such an e-network is to *co-market*. Members market products under a common brand name and portal while otherwise retaining their independence. The benefits of e-networking can include pool selling of products and services, pool buying of supplies and equipment, joint research and development resources, and improved quality objectives.

UNDERSTANDING THE BENEFITS

Collaborative arrangements aid organizational learning and the transfer of intangibles such as knowledge, organizational routines and skills, experiences, reputation, and goodwill. Firms gaining access to new technologies or markets are more likely to collaborate, benefiting from economies of scale in joint research, production, and marketing, and gaining complementary skills by tapping into sources of know-how located outside the boundaries of the firm. Other advantages include sharing risks in activities and gaining synergy by combining different strengths.

Strategic partnerships are a critical measure of a firm's ability to compete in the new economy. Paradoxically, interfirm differences, such as knowledge, skills, technologies, core competencies, and resources, usually form the underlying strategic motivation for entering into collaboration and remain essential for maintaining it. Differences in partner characteristics may have a negative impact on collaborative longevity and effectiveness. The erosion or convergence of these differences destabilizes the relationship. Confidence and trust in partners are recurring elements in successful collaboration.

MANAGING COLLABORATION

Collaboration has certain disadvantages. Sharing expertise with others can reduce management control. Increased dependence on external organizations can lead to greater need for more bureaucracy in order to manage what becomes virtual. Greater

"By 2020, 80 percent of business profits and market value will come from that part of the enterprise that is built around info-business."

(Stan Davis)

financial ties can lead to restricted access to other organizations and their capabilities.

Collaboration may increase one partner's competitive edge over the other(s). As e-businesses increasingly turn to *fast-alliance* strategy the vast majority of alliances will fail to deliver on their promises. Complementary objectives and learning are vital to the success of an alliance. When partners are equally intent on internalizing each other's skills, distrust and conflict may spoil the alliance.

What Are the Risks?

Participants may take advantage of a collaborative relationship and play side games: the relationship might finish and one partner benefit by copying others. There is the risk that one party will gain all the benefits from the venture.

A lack of understanding of partners can lead to resistance and conflict. If cooperation is lacking, opportunistic behavior will become the norm. Partners may relinquish their competitive position by loss or transfer of core competencies as a result of a sense of security or rationalization pressures. The most desirable alliance arrangements are with partners that are approximately equivalent in terms of their size, profitability, and status in their own industry and that possess complementary know-how and resources.

Some alliances have been criticized for being too flexible, thus causing a situation in which individual partners may have insufficient details on how to collaborate, little irreversible commitment, unclear property rights, or weak authority structure. Partners may join competing groups. The advantages of a high level of rigidity, especially through equity investment, include increasing incentives and commitment, aligning the partners' interests, and deterring opportunistic behavior. Such rigidity may seem especially paradoxical when the enabling technologies promise virtual flexibility.

The Framework for E-collaboration

Collaborative e-business models are crucial for value creation. The more codevelopers, the quicker problems and opportunities can be identified. Over the duration of the relationship partners can share benefits and control, contributing in one or more key strategic areas.

The loss of proprietary information, substantial organizational disruption, and conflict help to explain the structural instabilities of business-to-business relationships. Alliances involving access to knowledge or ability are more likely to dissolve as the party gaining access acquires its own internal skills through the partnership. Collaborations designed to gain benefits of scale or learning in performing an activity have a more enduring purpose.

Collaboration among businesses in the new economy with complementary resources, while creating substantial risks, is necessary for survival and growth. A realistic view of collaboration sees alliances as built on a foundation of dualities. Alliances are

- temporary *but* often produce long-lasting relationships;
- both cooperative *and* competitive weapons;
- strategically determined *and* emergent;
- may have emergent benefits that are more important than the intended purposes.

They are dialectical systems whose stability is determined by balancing multiple tensions within systems of accountability. These handle tension without stifling innovation.

Making It Happen ▸▸

Organizations need to create value for all participants including partners, suppliers, and customers. Partnering companies need to focus on the key value drivers, efficiency, complementarities, lock-in, and novelty. Success comes from:

- optimizing the value chain;
- achieving time to market;
- creating effective governance mechanisms;
- measuring progress and effectiveness;
- processing the inputs of environmental, market, and customer knowledge and expertise;
- delivering barriers that lock out competitors;
- following an open-system model;
- incorporating innovation and entrepreneurship;
- spanning boundaries between industries;
- blurring lines between suppliers, customers, and the firm.

There is a paradox, however: blurred lines lead to easy relations, easily broken. The paradox can be resolved by developing relations into ties that not only bind, but also add value. Ties that add value require inductive reasoning from past experiences, where no algorithm exists. In such situations organization members must work through reflexive capacities.

Conclusion

Organizations need to design virtual, reflexive strategies of interorganizational ties and self-governance. These must be managed by twin methods: accounting on a time basis (on a professional-practice model that delivers the best value for partners with a client focus) and cultural design of a meaningful context of collaboration that keeps the values of the collaboration uppermost. Managers with reflexive capacities account for their time and act in accordance with cultural values consciously designed to frame the specific collaboration project.

For More Information

Books:

Child, John, and David Faulkner. *Strategies of Cooperation: Managing Alliances, Networks, and Joint Ventures.* New York: Oxford University Press, 1998.

Ebers, Mark, ed. *The Formation of Inter-organizational Networks.* New York: Oxford University Press, 1999.

Hamel, Gary. *Leading the Revolution.* Boston, MA: Harvard Business School Press, 2000.

Web Site:

Amit, Raphael, and Christoph Zott. "Value Drivers of e-Commerce Business Models." Paper presented at the annual international conference of the American Academy of Management, Toronto, Canada, August 5–9, 2000, available online at **www.wharton.upenn.edu**.

See also:

☆ **Building Great Internal Partnerships (pp. 281–82)**
☆ **The Business Web (pp. 145–46)**
☆ **Developing an Internet-era Mindset throughout the Organization (pp. 141–42)**
☆ **Overcoming the Difficulties of Managing a Virtual Organization (pp. 208–09)**
☆ **Viewpoint: Philip Kotler (pp. 53–54)**
☆ **X-engineering Success (pp. 245–46)**

"The companies that fully capitalize on the promise of the Internet will be those that look at their businesses as more than building and selling products and services." (Michael Dell)

Integrating Technology into Business Processes *by Donryn Dewar and Melanie Ellis*

EXECUTIVE SUMMARY

- Integrating technology into business processes for the benefit of customers and the overall organization, is one of the biggest challenges managers face. Often, the weight of expectation is matched only by the practical, detailed complexity involved in making it happen.
- *Think, design, enable and run* is a proven approach that takes into account the critical factors determining success when harnessing IT. These factors include the soft issues of communicating, motivating and leading people, as well as the harder issues of managing projects, finances and technology.
- Among the many potential pitfalls of integrating technology into business processes are a lack of consideration of existing strategies, relationships and objectives; a lack of realism in the design, attention to the core needs, active ownership of the project, or the ability to lead what is often a major change management program. Finally, many projects fail because they are not dynamic and fail to address future as well as current needs.

Introduction

Resource constraints, budget limitations, and crowded market spaces are common issues facing manufacturing companies today. When it comes to implementing strategic enterprise information technology (IT) systems such as enterprise resource planning (ERP), immediate visibility of benefits, return on investment (ROI), and increased efficiencies are paramount. So, too, is the provision of a flexible platform for future growth.

Effective implementation is rarely straightforward, and ERP may not deliver the expected business benefits. Long project life cycles, unclear business requirements, and user resistance may result in disillusionment with ERP. Failure to realize the value of the investment often results in the reduction of further budget spends. Worse still, failure to deliver expected business benefits could result in business decline or closure.

Why does implementation of ERP cause so many headaches? By its nature ERP drills into the heart of the business engine and core business processes. It therefore disrupts business-as-usual and causes users multiple frustrations before the benefits are realized. Success is dependent on minimizing the extent and duration of disruption, ensuring that the change is managed with the user or stakeholder community (internal and external), and identifying a smooth path to realizing business benefits. Clear milestones and defined phases ensure control and transparency throughout the project life cycle.

Finally, adopting a tried-and-true approach and engaging seasoned expertise from day one is critical.

Think, Design, Enable, Run model is a tried-and-true roadmap, and is outlined in this section.

Think

Designing a Roadmap for Growth

Improved control, information at the touch of a button, and rationalization of route to manufacture and market are key components of employing a successful ERP strategy.

To capitalize on the benefits gained from an integrated back-office system, managers need to focus on the company's business strategy and growth objectives. They should also consider the stakeholder community to ensure their buy-in. Areas for consideration include:

- identification and development of new products and services;
- geographical markets;
- improved market share;
- criteria for measurement of objectives;
- ability to adapt quickly to compete;
- ERP—stakeholder benefits.

Employees

Provision of accurate and up-to-date information to allow empowered and fast decision making. Increased skill levels resulting in a greater sense of ownership.

Shareholders

Increased revenue and market share. Reduction of operating costs to provide an excellent return on capital employed and improved earnings per share.

Customers

Improved customer service levels through tightly controlled supply chain and accurate online stock availability information. Loyalty through increased global customer power.

Vendors

Standardization of processes and visibility across the group. Improved global buying power, supplier selection, and preferential pricing. Development of long-term relationships with suppliers.

Design

A Collaborative and Integrated Solution

Design effort is focused on aligning the core business processes that contribute directly to the bottom line and that will deliver increased business performance and responsiveness. Weighing up cost of solution vs. functionality match to deliver realistic and workable solutions.

Employing an effectively designed, integrated back-office system with aligned processes delivers:

- optimized and simplified view of material flows from planning and production through to sales and distribution. Having the right materials in the right place at the right time;
- operations planning and rationalization delivered through accurate product cost information—identifying optimal routes of manufacture across countries;
- improved manufacturing capability—global view of production capacities across production sites supporting load sharing and utilization of spare capacity, optimizing efficiencies;
- empowerment of remote support and sales offices. Improved efficiencies though the e-business workplace portal, allowing real-time access to the ERP system via the Web;
- global customer and account management through integration of the logistics and sales bases, allowing product rationalization, consolidated forecasting,

"The guy with the competitive advantage is the one with the best technology." (Walter Wriston)

pricing negotiation, and comprehensive reporting;

- global alignment and streamlining of processes across the organization to support performance evaluation against business objectives;
- collaboration end-to-end across the entire supply chain, utilizing proven ERP solutions and e-business developments.

ENABLE

Delivering the Solution

The keys to successful implementation in restricted timescales are:

- a change-management program—to work closely with stakeholders to understand the changes and impact that new systems and ways of working will bring;
- the engagement of best-practice solution providers;
- an industry best-practice template for fast-track implementations, providing a quick start to the project life cycle;
- a phased implementation approach for complex or global implementations to deliver quick wins with measurable benefits.

RUN

Support/Solution Management

Once you've gone live, supporting and managing ERP solutions is as critical as the implementation itself. There are two criteria for successful ERP operations. First, a well-managed system. Many companies are now moving away from in-house ERP system management to outsourced system/application hosting or ASP models. Outsourcing can cut IT management costs by up to one-third and ensure guaranteed efficiency improvements.

Second, comprehensive support offering. Companies that have adopted ERP must create a robust internal support infrastructure (competency center) that can support users, enhance deployed functionality, and respond to the changing demands of the business.

MINI-CASE

Titus is a midsize manufacturing organization specializing in the manufacture of connectors for self-assembly furniture and cabinetry. It operates in a mature, highly volatile, and competitive market. The company has manufacturing plants in the United Kingdom and United States, with warehouses across the globe.

The company's goal was to become a truly global business, keeping ahead of competitors, and providing an excellent return to shareholders.

Titus appointed Plaut to challenge the strategic thinking of the management team, advise on managing change, and implement and manage an integrated ERP and e-business solution.

Think

The project started with a comprehensive review of the company's strategic goals and identification of business objectives:

- Attain a 40% share of the worldwide connector market.
- Achieve at least 50% of revenue in any year from new products.
- Exceed 25% annual return on equity.
- Identify a solution and strategy to maximize Titus's differentiation of manufacturing customer-specific, innovative products, increasing sales threefold in five years.

Design

We used mySAP.com software to deliver:

- a single integrated global system using aligned business processes;
- remote Web-based access for sales and support offices;
- rationalization of product lines and manufacturing sites;
- product cost and profitability analysis to support management decision making and performance monitoring.

Enable

To support Titus's rapid six-month implementation requirements and budgetary limits, Plaut's templated mySAP.com solution, tailored for manufacturing companies, was implemented.

A phased approach to rollout across Titus' international operations was adopted. This allowed delivery of rollouts on time and within budget. This ensured realization of rapid business benefits and demonstration to the business users of delivery capability to business requirements.

Run

Titus opted for a cost-effective hosting solution from an SAP outsourcing center in Ireland for its system management. This incorporates a 24/7 support service providing application, software, hardware, communications, and infrastructure knowledge.

MAKING IT HAPPEN ▸▸

Think, Design, Enable, Run—a tried-and-true approach to rapid, successful ERP implementations.

Think

- Review business strategy and corporate objectives.
- Identify measurable business objectives and benefits.
- Define short-, medium-, and long-term objectives.
- Plan development of stakeholder relationships.

Design

- Define realistic goals.
- Focus on core, aligned business processes across the group.
- Consider cost vs. functional match for each business process.
- Define flows to provide accurate, timely information for decision making.
- Executive ownership and active involvement in process are critical.

Enable

- Create an effective solution.
- Use quick-win tools—best practice, industry templates, and phased approach to delivery.
- Adopt a change-management program.

Run

- Move into the future.
- Consider more cost-effective alternatives to in-house support and system management.

CONCLUSION

Virtually every industry is constantly reshaped by technology-driven changes affecting customers, suppliers and supply chains. These developments can increase costs and fail, or they can reduce costs, improve service and dramatically improve competitiveness and overall profitability. Furthermore, managing suppliers of technology is notoriously fraught with potential problems and difficulties. Finding an approach that integrates technology with business processes is therefore vitally important, and so is the ability for this process of change and adaptation to be constant. It cannot rely on a single shift or step-change—to succeed it needs to be a dynamic, ongoing process. The process of think, design, enable, and run provides a sound, tested approach to a permanent management challenge.

For More Information

Books:

Norris, Grant, et al. *E-business and ERP: Transforming the Enterprise*. New York: John Wiley, 2000.

Shtub, Avraham. *Enterprise Resource Planning (ERP): The Dynamics of Operations Management*. Hingham, MA: Kluwer Academic, 1999.

"People were skeptical about the new technology. They wanted it to be de-risked." (Jon Florsheim)

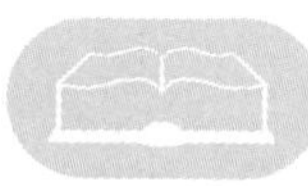

Managing by Individual Objectives
by Richard S. Handscombe

EXECUTIVE SUMMARY

- Managing by individual objectives (MIO) is imperative for all organizations in a competitive world.
- The generic concepts and processes can be applied to anyone's work and private life.
- MIO has maximum impact when introduced as *the way we manage and implement strategy.*
- The original ideas of Peter Drucker are timeless.
- Best practice is tough for even the best organizations.
- Successful MIO needs to be kept simple and constant.

The Need

For the last century there has been a general understanding that unless managers know where they are going and why, no one can expect them to perform optimally, either individually or as a team. But this does not always happen. There's a wide gap between best and average practice in both public and private sectors worldwide. Improvement is imperative in the competitive and complex world managers work and live in.

This article considers the evolution of MIO, what constitutes best practice, and the success factors for its effective introduction and operation.

A Generic Definition

At its simplest, MIO can be defined as *the proactive setting of individual objectives by a manager in order to understand, cope with, and benefit from the future.*

The benefits can be framed as personal satisfaction in terms of:

- contribution to the organization in which the manager works;
- use and development of personal capability;
- career, recognition, and rewards;
- private life and way of life;
- time management.

Most managers would not disagree with the concept. Many self-motivated managers have always striven to manage themselves that way, even applying the same discipline to their education and retirement. In reality the skills required for MIO are generic and apply to all people in all walks of life.

Managers, even the self-employed, do not work in isolation. But they may have different visions, priorities, and ambitions influenced by their status and function. Often the end result is not teamwork, but unproductive friction, frustration, and despair. The best-managed organizations have long recognized such problems. For decades they have provided managers with a common sense of purpose and direction and ensured that they had challenging careers based on clear objectives.

A Major Breakthrough

Although Peter Drucker's renowned *The Practice of Management* was first published in 1954, its insights, ideas, and ideals are as relevant today as they were 50 years ago. Drucker laid down basic guidelines for MIO that are still best practice:

- a continuous focus on current and future external and internal customer needs;
- focus through corporate and unit strategy. Achievement of strategy through management by objectives and self-control. A focus on key result areas;
- exceptional teamwork vertically, horizontally, and diagonally within the organization;
- reward in line with results.

Expansion of Drucker's Ideas

From the early 1960s many organizations sought to introduce MIO formally or informally, some on a worldwide basis. But often they were short of well-qualified managers, not only for line positions, but for the expanding functions of information technology, marketing, and human resources. These companies often sought outside help, and many academics and consultants started to research, write lectures, and consult in the area of MIO.

Drucker's most prominent early disciples were George Odione in the United States, John Humble (Europe), and William Reddin (Canada). Among them they developed approaches applicable to both small family businesses and major multinationals, charities, churches, governments, etc. In addition to Drucker's research they drew on the work of Grainger (hierarchy of objectives), Rensis Likert (integration of objectives), Douglas McGregor (theory X and Y), Abraham Maslow (hierarchy of needs and ambitions), and others.

Other consultants soon followed, and many brands of MIO were marketed in the 1960s and 1970s, such as achieving business results, managing by objectives, management effectiveness, action centers leadership, improving management performance, executive target setting and appraisals, and the one-minute manager. Each had its own processes, documentation, and terminology. The best programs worked because they were led by the chairman and chief executive, supported by internal or external change agents with a good grasp and experience of general management as well as MIO theory and practice. MIO has survived the decades in many well-run companies.

In others the result was less successful, often because top management support was merely lip service and MIO entered the organization as an objective-led management appraisal system via the human resources department. The links with the objectives of the organization were often slim, and as a result MIO died young.

In many cases the generic MIO processes and skills have been integrated into strategic leadership, total quality, and reengineering programs as the means of securing commitment to results.

MIO Best Practice—Where Are You Now?

The personal audit given in Table 1 overleaf includes a summary of best practice.

Use the questionnaire to:

- develop an appreciation of best practice;
- evaluate the effectiveness of your own current practices;
- identify where improvements are required.

Evaluate your position against each of the

"A good goal is like a strenuous exercise—it makes you stretch." (Mary Kay Ash)

Table 1					
I and all the members of my team have . . .	0	1	2	3	4
1. a clear understanding of the strategy, priorities, and key objectives of the total organization					
2. a clear understanding of the contribution expected from my unit in terms of its mission and key result areas					
3. agreement to support and receive support from other units in achieving our objective					
4. an agreed statement of personal objectives for the next 6, 12, or 18 months to which each is committed and dedicated					
5. consistently achieved agreed objectives over the last three years					
6. effective information/ intelligence for tracking progress and identifying emergent opportunities and risks					
7. effective scheduled and ad hoc team and pair meetings* to review progress, reduce risks, and update objectives (* pair relates to you and your superior and you and each of your team members)					
8. a personal development program to provide the knowledge, skills, and experience essential to achieving our objectives					
9. an annual performance review that is objective and fair					
10. rewards that reflect achievement of objectives directly and fairly					
Column Scores					

statements in turn and allocate a score as follows:

0 No evidence of concept.

1 Some evidence, but only lip service paid.

2 Exists but is not very effective.

3 Exists and company results demonstrate benefits.

4 I believe what we do is best practice.

Your unit may be the overall company, a subsidiary, business division, product group, or a department, branch, or project group.

What do you think should be changed over the next 12 or 24 months?

Success Factors for MIO

Numerous factors determine the success or failure of MIO systems. The following have been highlighted by many surveys (introducing and sustaining the system is not a soft option!).

- Visible management leadership.
- Continuity of senior management.
- Stability of the system.
- Ownership of the system and subprocesses by line management, not finance or human resources. Support from all functional heads.
- Challenging objectives set for all functions, whether line, service, or corporate support.
- Senior management acting as coaches, not prima donnas.
- Simplicity of documentation and guidance notes.
- A balanced set of objectives established for each manager that are specific, quantified, realistic, and measurable.
- Effective priority setting. The Pareto rule. Aiming for the things that matter.
- Tough objectives supported by a rigorous action plan and risk analysis.
- The objective-setting process for new managers introduced as a learning process with appropriate support.
- A direct link between objectives and budget, ensuring that funding is available to provide the resources required to achieve agreed objectives.
- Good baton passing between managers when changes occur due to promotion, special assignments, or departure to other companies.
- MIO update and reinforcement sessions included in internal conferences, leadership programs, and workshops.
- Managers empowered to act.
- Performance reviews happening when planned. They are coaching sessions, not courtrooms.
- Links between a manager's achievements and rewards are seen as fair.
- If tough objectives are set, the reward for achievement needs to be significant compared to that achieved with minimum effort by a nonperformer.
- Continuous reinforcement of the strategic direction and priorities of the organization.
- Participation used to stimulate and harness continuous challenges, vision, and imagination. Changing mindsets to think beyond the obvious and enrich reality.
- Regular audits to check that the MIO processes are still productive. If not, revive the system before disbelievers undermine MIO by declaring it the latest fad or merely an appraisal system.

Introducing an alternative approach can take years—if one in fact exists.

Making It Happen ▸▸

- Use MIO to enable managers to understand, cope with, and benefit from the future.
- Have the MIO system and subprocesses owned by line management, not by finance or human resources.
- Insist that senior managers act as coaches, not prima donnas.
- Establish for each manager in every unit or function a balanced set of objectives that are specific, quantified, realistic, and measurable.
- Set tough objectives supported by a rigorous action plan and risk analysis, and with significant rewards for achievement.
- Directly link objectives and budget to ensure funding of the resources required to achieve agreed objectives.

The Way Ahead

Whether you aim to improve your own objective-setting process, improve the processes of a total organization, or teach leadership and management, recognize that the core MIO concept and skills are generic, serving as foundation stones for good management. What makes or breaks the application is the manner in which MIO is institutionalized. Success requires leadership, insight, dedication, and a determination to keep it simple but rigorous.

For More Information

Books:

Blanchard, Kenneth, and Robert Lorber. *Putting the One Minute Manager to Work*. New York: Berkley, 1992.

Drucker, Peter. *The Practice of Management*. New York: HarperBusiness, 1993.

See also:

☆ **Avoiding Your Worst Career Nightmare (pp. 316–17)**
☆ **Choosing the Best Training Curriculum for You (pp. 336–37)**
☆ **Urbane Renewal: Trusting Your Own Wisdom—A Competitive (and Satisfying) Advantage (pp. 320–21)**
Stephen R. Covey (pp. 976–77)

"Despair is the prize one pays for setting oneself an impossible aim." (Graham Greene)

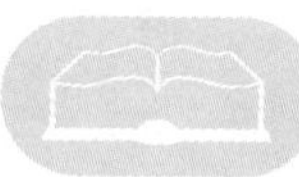

The True Total Quality *by Masaaki Imai*

Executive Summary

- It is important to recognize the importance of the commonsense approach of gemba (shop floor) kaizen to quality improvement, as against the technology-only approach to quality practiced in the west.
- The production system (batch production) employed by over 90 percent of all the companies in the world is one of the biggest obstacles to quality improvement. A conversion from batch to JIT/Lean production system should be the most urgent task for any manufacturing company today in order to survive in the next millennium.

Introduction

The differences between Knowledge and Wisdom are very important to our thinking about Total Quality Management. Knowledge is something we can buy. We can gain knowledge by reading books and attending seminars and classroom lectures. Knowledge remains just knowledge until we put it into action. On the other hand, wisdom is something we learn by doing. Practice is the best way of learning, and wisdom emerges from practice.

I have observed that Western management has tended to stress teaching knowledge in the classroom over wisdom through doing, whereas the Japanese approach for quality management has been to provide both knowledge and wisdom to employees. This latter approach is particularly effective in solving quality problems in gemba (shop floor).

Gemba Kaizen

"Gemba" means the place where real action occurs. In manufacturing "gemba" means the shop floor. In my book *Gemba Kaizen: A Common-sense, Low-cost Approach to Management* (McGraw-Hill, 1997), I pointed out the three major activities to support good gemba Management, namely: standardization, good housekeeping, and "muda" (waste) elimination. Let me explain the difference between wisdom and knowledge, citing an example from the housekeeping activities.

One of the five steps of housekeeping in gemba is "seiso," or cleaning, meaning the involvement of operators in cleaning the machines they work with. As they do so, operators often discover oil leaks or loosening of bolts on the machine This gives them the opportunity to take corrective actions and eventually develop maintenance standards. This is learning by doing, and the operators gain valuable wisdom about machine maintenance, which is an important step for quality improvement.

I have observed that many managers often neglect these three foundations of good gemba management and are interested in pursuing sophisticated approaches instead.

There are five Golden Rules of Gemba Management.

- When a problem (abnormality) arises, go to gemba first.
- Check with "gembutsu" (relevant objects).
- Take temporary counter-measures on the spot.
- Find the root cause.
- Standardize to prevent recurrence.

Fabricated Data

In managing gemba, the most critical part is for managers to go to gemba and have a good look, studying the data critically. Managers who stay away from gemba, and seldom take the trouble of going there, are in contact with the reality of gemba only through indirect means, such as reports and conferences. In such cases, managers are making decisions based on fabricated data.

When you go to gemba where an abnormality occurred, you do not need any data, because what you see there is the reality. A manager on the shop floor is right in the midst of reality, and chances are that the problem may be solved on the spot and in real time by following the five golden rules.

Collect and Analyze Data

Another effective approach for problem solving in gemba has been to collect and analyze data.

Generally speaking, when these down-to-earth activities in gemba are carried out, the reject rates should go down to a tenth of their original levels. And yet, I find most western managers do not take advantage of these effective gemba practices and pursue more academic and sophisticated approaches for quality improvement.

Conversion from Batch to JIT/Lean Production

The second and perhaps more acute issue facing most manufacturing companies today is the fact that their current production systems are the biggest hindrance to achieving quality management.

Today, most manufacturing companies subscribe to the traditional batch production system. I define batch production as an antiquated paradigm patterned after agriculture. In agriculture, farm products are sewn, grown, harvested, and stored in batches. The more grain you have in the warehouse, the better. Agriculture must take into account the shifting seasons, and it is taken for granted that the lead-time of growing and harvesting grain must be long.

When modern manufacturing emerged, it was patterned after this agricultural mentality. Raw materials were bought, processed, and stored in batches. Not much consideration was given to establishing a flow of work, and no effort was made to shorten the lead-time of production. Keeping a large inventory was taken for granted as a way of doing business. Even today, good inventory means high inventory to some managers.

As long as the varieties of products offered to customers were small in number, this type of production did not pose many problems. As customers have come to demand diversified products to be delivered on time and in different volumes, it has become increasingly difficult to develop flexibility to meet such demands in the context of the batch production system. To cope with the new demand, efforts have been made by management in such areas as shortening set-up time, quality improvement, adding more lines, and even building new plants.

Unfortunately, even to this day, more than 90 percent of all manufacturing companies in the world still subscribe to batch production, a system that is one of the biggest obstacles to establishing good quality management.

The Drawbacks of Batch Production

The following features of the batch production system stand in the way of quality management:

- **Large inventory**: As the name batch production suggests, the system is based on producing large batches of inventory

"Quality is not a program that can be simply imposed on an operation; instead it is a way of operating that permeates a business and the thinking of its employees." (Theodore B. Kinni)

at every production process. As a result, 100% quality-control inspection is nearly impossible. Even if quality defects are found at a later stage, it is almost impossible to go back to the previous process which produced the defects, seek out the root cause, and take corrective actions, since such rejects were made several days earlier. Also, the quality of products or parts deteriorates over time when stored in inventory, the only exceptions to this, of course, being red wine and whisky.

- **Long Lead Time**: The long lead time required by the batch production system makes it difficult to take prompt and flexible action to meet the customer requirements for quality and delivery. For instance, the batch production system is far less flexible when design changes are called for.
- **Isolated Islands**: Batch production is necessitated because each manufacturing process is separated from each other—each on its own isolated island. This necessitates transport between processes, causing damages. Again, the isolated islands make it difficult to diagnose quality problems in real time. When operators do their jobs surrounded by inventory, housekeeping is difficult to maintain, which in turn leads to lower morale and less self-discipline of employees.

It becomes clear from the reasons given above that no matter how much effort management may make towards improving quality, batch production destroys those efforts.

JUST-IN-TIME PRODUCTION SYSTEM

The JIT production system was developed as an antithesis to batch production by Taiichi Ohno at the Toyota Motor Corporation and, along with many other practical tools like kanban, poka-yoke (fail-safe device) and jidohka (automation), is supported by the following three pillars of production:

- takt time versus cycle time (theoretical time versus actual time for processing one work piece);
- pull production versus push production (producing only as many items as the next process needs versus producing as many as can be produced);
- establishing production flow (rearranging equipment layout and processes according to the work sequence).

Just-in-Time is really a revolutionary production system, and is in every sense just the opposite of the batch production. It employs minimum materials, equipment, manpower, utility, space, time, and money. It produces products within a shortest lead time and meets the diversified demand of customers and delivers the products just-in-time.

Quality is ensured by keeping small inventories and through the use of flow production. Small inventories eventually lead to one-piece flow, namely one work piece moving from process to process. This enables operators to make a 100% inspection of each piece. In flow production, unlike in the isolated islands approach of batch production, processes are arranged in a flow, and any quality reject created in one process can be identified in the next process immediately.

MAKING IT HAPPEN ▸▸

How many quality managers and engineers realize that the production system of their own company is a major cause for many quality problems they have to deal with? A review of the production system currently in use should be the first action taken by those engaged in quality improvement.

- To solve quality problems, help employees to gain wisdom, as well as knowledge.
- Base total quality on good "gemba" (shopfloor) management—meaning standardization, excellent housekeeping and effective elimination of "muda" (waste).
- When a problem (or abnormality) arises, always go to "gemba" first, and never rely on secondary information—reports, meetings, etc.
- When at "gemba," check with "gembutsu" (relevant objects), take temporary counter measures on the spot, find the root cause, and standardize to stop problems recurring.
- Recognize that batch production itself is one of the biggest obstacles to good quality management.
- Replace the batch system with Just-in-Time production, arranging processes in a flow, so that any quality reject created in one process can be immediately identified in the next.

For More Information

Imai, Masaaki. *Gemba Kaizen: A Common-sense, Low-cost Approach to Management*. New York: McGraw-Hill, 1997.

Imai, Masaaki. *Kaizen: The Key to Japan's Competitive Success*. New York: McGraw-Hill, 1986.

The Good, the Fad, and the Ugly *by Lucy Kellaway*

EXECUTIVE SUMMARY

- All senior managers despise management fads, yet most senior managers are guilty of following them.
- A few fads are valuable, many are not—and all are practical, frequently obvious, common sense approaches to business management.
- The ability to spot a fad and use it is as important as the ability to spot a fad and keep well clear. The ability to spot a peddler of fads is useful as well.
- Big fads often spawn little fads and fads should be treated carefully. There are many ways to treat a situation—and a one-size-fits-all approach may be anti-competitive.

Introduction

All senior managers despise management fads. Yet most senior managers are guilty of following them.

The attitude of business towards the management fad is a complex mixture of cynicism and optimism. This conflict is evident in the very language used to discuss them. The term "management fad" is derogatory. When managers use this term it is because they are going to say something cynical. They are going to talk about the sheep-like behavior of other companies, and other fads, or fads in general. But when they are describing their own recent adoption of the latest management fad, the f-word is replaced by the word "idea," "concept," "theory," or "solution."

Fads Don't Work

Most academics will tell you that management fads, in aggregate, do not work. Not only does the company that has implemented the fad not achieve the expected increase in productivity, profitability, staff retention or whatever, often the effect is actually negative. There are all sorts of reasons for this:

- The fad is not the right one for the company.
- The fad has been poorly or inconsistently implemented.
- It conflicts with other fads simultaneously being pursued.
- Management is not committed to it.
- Expectations of its likely effect are unrealistic.
- The fad was a stupid idea in the first place.

So Why Do Companies Use Them?

Partly they use them out of fear of being left behind. They use them because they are as fashion conscious as the average teenage girl. If their peers are using them they feel that they must too. They also use them because they crave concrete ideas; they want to have a story to tell. Senior managers are more likely to be highly rated by their shareholders, peers and employees if they are seen to be doing something. To set up a new system always looks more impressive than simply maintaining the status quo.

They also do it because they are seduced by the amazing success stories that come with every fad: Benchmarking–the measurement craze–comes complete with a story of what it did for Xerox; Six Sigma–a variant on Total Quality Management–comes with a glowing case study from Motorola and so on.

And if this is not enough to hook them, there will be a hard sell from armies of consultants who have a vested interest in making sure that yesterday's fad is smartly replaced by that of today.

How Many Fads Are There?

There are a lot, however you count them. The *Economist Guide to Management Ideas* covers 100 fads which have attracted mass followings over the last few decades. Yet this list is nowhere near exhaustive. Fads come in all shapes and sizes–hard, soft, big, small, reasonable, and stupid.

Whatever the exact number, there are far too many for any manager–even the most dedicated follower of fashion–to keep up.

Which Are the Good Ones?

There is–unfortunately–no correct answer to this question. Most of the fads are based on a solid idea or a reasonable assumption. The idea may not be new or original–indeed the most successful fads are based on ideas so achingly obvious it is amazing that they need spelling out at all.

Total Quality Management

This has been around since the 1950s. Its passage from pioneering idea to mass adoption to rejection is one that has been followed again by all the major fads.

Developed by W. Edwards Deming, it was practiced initially in Japan. By the 1980s and 1990s almost every Western manufacturer was doing it too. TQM is based on the rational notion that there is no point in just measuring the quality of the finished product. Every single process within a company should be monitored in terms of how it conforms to customer requirements. Managerial processes get measured in the same way as manufacturing ones, with the aim of reducing all errors to almost zero.

For a brief moment at the end of the 1980s TQM had the status of religion. Everyone believed it was the most important and beneficial management fad ever. The backlash set in at the start of the 1990s, as companies started complaining at the amount of paperwork and bureaucracy. Even companies that had successful TQM programs started having second thoughts. Florida Power & Light, which won an award for its quality program, subsequently abandoned it when it turned out just how much its employees hated it.

Reengineering

As TQM drifted out of fashion reengineering came in. It was the brainchild of two U.S. academics, Michael Hammer and James Champy. They argued that companies should go back to the drawing board, look at all their processes, and redesign them from scratch. This seemed to be a solution to all ills. Here was a way of cutting cost, and improving quality service and speed at the same time. It sounded unbeatable.

Only what actually happened was that reengineering became synonymous with the redundancies that almost always accompanied it. Within four or five years this fad had got such a bad name that even its creators distanced themselves from it. They noted that senior management tended to make itself exempt from any reengineering, thus rendering the whole exercise useless.

"I think one of the powers of fad surfing is that it really is a kind of managerial prozac."

(Eileen C. Shapiro)

This was one of the fastest trends to come and go. The time from the publication of the original article to the mass adoption of reengineering to its being largely discredited was barely five years.

KNOWLEDGE MANAGEMENT

This became the big idea of the late 1990s. It is based on the notion that the most valuable asset a company has is its knowledge: its intellectual property, ideas, and experience. This knowledge exists in files, databases, and in the heads of people. Knowledge management is about how to manage all this in a systematic way. Much of it is to do with creating better IT systems, so that one part of the company can know what other parts are doing. Some of knowledge management is cultural–about getting people to generate more ideas, and share their ideas and their knowledge with their colleagues.

The general idea of knowledge management is hard to argue with. Indeed few do argue with it, and it is still, broadly, in favor. However, many of the knowledge management schemes put in by different companies have come under attack for being needlessly complex, for saving too much useless information.

VISION, VALUES, AND MISSION

Aficionados might take these three categories separately, but all have a common theme. The idea once again is pretty simple. It is that by trying to define what a company is about, that company will learn something about itself. Odd as it might seem, this is often the case. If senior executives sit down and try to work out what their company is–and is not–trying to do, what it exists for, and what are its common values, then so much the better.

However, mission statements in fact have done little to change the corporate world for the better. In practice one company's mission looks uncannily like that of another–a predictable mixture of motherhood and apple pie. Even when the statement is appropriate and distinctive, taken alone it is powerless to bring about change. People do not change by dint of a statement, no matter how carefully drawn up it might be.

HARD FADS

For each of these big fads there are scores and scores of smaller ones. There are many other technical measurement fads like TQM–Six Sigma (a quality variant, hard to understand let alone implement), balanced scorecard, and benchmarking. All of these are about numbers, spotting your target and measuring it. All are sensible. Benchmarking yourself against other comparable companies is so sensible, it is extraordinary that it ever had any status as a fad. All companies should always benchmark–at least they should know roughly how they are doing relative to others. Measurement is important and necessary, but on its own it is not going to ensure much change in performance.

SOFT FADS

This is the biggest growth area among fads. It seems that every week there is a new pat solution that will help managers manage their people better. Management by Objective got replaced by Management by Walking Around, and then, still more ludicrously, with Management by Hanging Around. Senior managers started frequenting the cappuccino bars in the hope that this would lead to closer-knit teams.

Most soft fads are based loosely around the idea of personal growth. Since hierarchies went out of fashion twenty years ago, all management styles are meant to include coaching, mentoring.

MAKING IT HAPPEN

- Treat all fads with caution. Always act suspicious when introduced to a new fad.
- Never take up a fad because a management consultant has persuaded you it is a good idea.
- Never expect miracles from your fad.
- Always consider how well it fits with your company's culture. Any new fad in isolation is never going to change people's behavior.
- Never do it by half.
- Believe in the motto "If it ain't broke. . ." And even if it is broke, you don't need to mend it the same way as everybody else.

CONCLUSION

We know that happy employees are productive ones. According to the fashionable view, people are happiest when they are given responsibility and respect. Thus we have empowerment–the idea that everybody in the organization should be able to wield some power. This was all the rage in the 1990s, and is still fairly popular, especially with wide-eyed human resources people. The difficulty is that very few organizations can pull it off. Empowerment conflicts with some of the less positive aspects of human nature–senior managers do not want to let go, and many underlings do not want more responsibility.

For More Information

Books:

Dearlove, Des. *The Ultimate Book of Business Thinking*. San Francisco, CA: Jossey-Bass, 2001.
Hindle, Tim. *Guide to Management Ideas*. London: Hamilton with Economist Publications, 2000.
Shapiro, Eileen C. *Fad Surfing in the Boardroom*. Boston, MA: Addison-Wesley, 1995.

See also:

☆ **Avoiding the Mistakes of the Past: Lessons from the Startup World (pp. 129–30)**
☆ **Who's Guiding Your Corporate Destiny? (pp. 216–17)**
☆ **X-engineering Success (pp. 245–46)**

"A powerful new idea can kick around unused in a company for years." (Theodore Levitt)

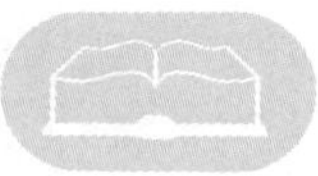

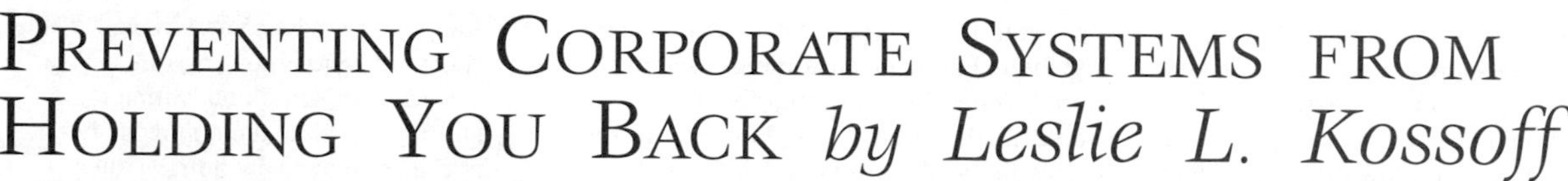

Preventing Corporate Systems from Holding You Back *by Leslie L. Kossoff*

Executive Summary

- Organizational systems, their policies, procedures, rules, and instructions, unintentionally limit the success of the organization.
- Since the organization's systems are owned by management, only management can make sure that appropriate review and action are taken.
- By establishing an ongoing dialogue, management can create an organization that never rests on its laurels and is designed to succeed.

Introduction

"No. We can't do that." Far too frequently managers return the ever-present and usually nonsensical "No" without thinking of the real consequences for the organization. This unarguable negative is based on policies, procedures, management, and other organizational systems that were designed by someone else at some other time for an organization that may no longer exist. Ultimately, that negative response can mark the beginning of the end of the enterprise. However, a modern organization that recognizes and values initiative and market change, avoiding yesterday's rules to govern today's challenges, is much more likely to succeed.

Assessing the Impact of Organizational Systems

Living in the technology era as we do, we have a tendency to equate organizational systems with information systems. In fact, there's a great deal of difference between the two. Information systems are those technological marvels that allow us to access and communicate information in ways never before possible. Organizational systems, on the other hand, develop in a patchwork over time. They constitute the regulatory infrastructure of the organization—the skeleton of policy, procedure, rules, and regulations that each employee is to follow.

The intent of these systems is positive; they're designed to protect the organization and its employees from harm and to create as fair and positive a workplace as possible.

Organizational systems run the gamut from security and disclosure edicts to dicta on compensation, attendance, vacation, and retirement programs. They address law and legal precedent as well as homegrown instructions on How things are done. They create a thinking process that allows management and employees to know the parameters within which they need to work.

The problem is that the systems are rarely correlated with the needs of the business. In the worst cases, they determine and direct how you are to operate as determined by someone in the organization who probably has no idea what you actually do and possibly does not even work there anymore.

Eventually organizational systems become embedded—and invisible—to almost everyone except those who are being adversely affected. It's conceivable that if all current employees were removed from an organization and replaced with people not at all familiar with the enterprise—but instructed to follow the same policies, procedures, rules, regulations, and instructions—the organization would continue to operate in exactly the same way.

Such is the unrecognized impact of organizational systems.

Techniques for Improving Corporate Systems

This situation leads to the questions all executives and managers should be asking themselves:

- Is my organization operating the way I want it to and the way it must for us to succeed?
- Which policies, procedures, rules, regulations, instructions within the organizational systems infrastructure support the organization's real goals? Which do not?
- Which systems cannot be changed, for example, because of laws or government regulations?
- Of those systems that can be changed, what must we do to make sure that the systems that direct and drive the organization are designed to help us succeed?
- Which systems have been unintentionally imposed or supported?

1. Understand the impact of organizational systems: in the form of rules, policies and procedures, systems give people a sense of security. Those same systems form a connection with the past for longer-term employees, who learned specific policies and procedures from people long gone from the organization. The rules represent the good old days.

Don't suppose that new organizations are immune from this syndrome. By the time a new organization has been in business a week or so, any new employee is likely to be instructed on "how we do business here."

As the organization grows and becomes more complex, more structure and systematization are necessary, to establish continuity and predictability across and between functions, departments, and employee activities. It's not that systems are bad, nor are they developed with ill intent. It's simply that they grow without consideration of their impact unless management takes an active role in seeing that the systems are designed for success.

Hence organizational systems should be treated organically as a reflection of the changing needs of the business.

2. Review your metrics: take a look at the various measures you use to track and monitor your organization. Determine where you see progress and where your performance doesn't meet the needs or expected goals for your area. Identify new measures needed to fully understand your performance and impact.

3. Assess your impact: using those same metrics as well as those of other departments or areas, look at how your organization is doing in supporting your internal customers and suppliers—as well as how it's forwarding ultimate organizational goals.

Wherever possible apply monetary figures to the processes and impact of your area—including its impact on the real and potential profitability of the larger organization.

4. Establish a systems dialogue within your organization: at scheduled staff, team, or communication meetings ask employees whether the policies, procedures, rules, and instructions they follow make sense to them. Also ask how the systems requirements of other departments affect their performance.

5. Make every employee a C.F.O.: using

"Running a company is a constant process of breaking out of systems and challenging conditioned reflexes, of rubbing against the grain."
(Mark McCormack)

the data you've collected and reviewed, incorporate the measures and their monetary impact into the ongoing dialogue. Explain how the financials of your particular department—and employees' individual jobs—affect the greater organization. Use this as a means of describing each employee's importance and contribution to the greater good and goals of the enterprise. Begin developing employees' financial understanding of their own jobs and garner their input on how those financials can be improved. (Do not use this as a means of berating any department's or individual's performance.)

6. Create an active systems redesign process: ask employees to discuss how they might be better able to perform—initially, with specific reference to changes they see as necessary to established organizational systems. Use existing teams, or form a team, to review current organizational systems, gain input from employees about their performance and financial impact, and recommend improvements.

Most important of all, implement the changes and continue the dialogue to address other embedded issues within the organization.

MINI-CASES

Because system implosion is usually invisible to the organization until it's too late, managers and executives need to look for signs that things aren't working as they should. Some examples of system implosions:

When *Hughes Aircraft Company* exclusively contracted with the government, its accounting departments had a policy that suppliers were paid 90 days after invoice. Even knowing that this policy was putting small businesses out of business (one department even posted a tally of the companies it had destroyed), it never occurred to anyone to consider the impact on Hughes' own manufacturing floor. Ultimately, because so few suppliers either could or wanted to continue doing business with Hughes, the line workers were constantly working with differing parts; supplier certification was overwhelmed and unable to adequately oversee and monitor suppliers. The quality of the product—and company profits—suffered.

Even a function as simple as newspaper circulation demonstrates how the system can affect customer retention. The *Financial Times* circulation department assures its customers that the paper can be delivered anywhere. However, customers based in the United States but wanting the paper delivered in the United Kingdom, where the FT has its headquarters, are informed that it can't be done. Even in this world of globalization, the FT's circulation system doesn't cross the Atlantic. This leaves the subscribing customers with broken promises—and a potential preference for competing publications.

Cisco Systems got caught in its own trap of cornering the market on supplied products to ensure that manufacturing could go forward without delays. While the technology sector was waning, Cisco continued to order supplied parts as if there were no foreseeable changes to production volume or scheduling. The technology downturn finally affected the company with the result that suppliers were paid late, orders were cancelled, and the company had to take a write-off for excess inventory.

These problems could have been avoided if managers had reviewed whether their systems were designed to support the organization's present needs and future goals especially in the context of market change. Taking that closer look could have avoided or addressed the existing system pitfalls before they adversely affected the enterprise.

MAKING IT HAPPEN ▸▸

Organizational systems are owned by management—which means that only management can do anything about them.

However, it really isn't difficult to ensure that the systems are in alignment with the organization's goals. The bad news is that this is a time-consuming process. This process is straightforward, whether applied on a cross-organizational or department-specific basis. The following measures can help to improve the situation:

- Understand the current position: the scope of the rules, why they are there, and the impact they have. Is the net effect of each rule positive?
- Consider how to mitigate the effects of necessary rules or systems which may have some challenging or potentially frustrating consequences.
- Involve people: systems are devised by people for people, so don't ignore them.
- Keep the process of reviewing, replacing, and enforcing rules dynamic. It is not an advantage simply to review the changes once and then leave well alone. Times change; so do systems.

CONCLUSION

The greatest win for the organization occurs when the initial systems review is complete and the less-structured systems become the center of management's and employees' attention.

An ongoing dialog within and between departments will keep the organization a living, growing entity focused on health, welfare, and profitability for all stakeholders. Whether it is communication systems and information movement or how departments coordinate with others, no part of the organization should remain unexamined over time. Every department should be subject to modernization.

Through this ongoing and expanding process management will ultimately create an organization designed to succeed, one that never rests on its laurels.

For More Information

Books:

Juran, J. M. *Juran on Leadership for Quality: An Executive Handbook*. New York: Free Press, 1989.

Kanter, Rosabeth Moss. *On the Frontiers of Management*. Boston, MA: Harvard Business School Press, 1997.

Drucker, Peter F. *Management Challenges for the 21st Century*. New York: HarperBusiness, 2001.

Web Site:

www.economist.com: the subscription information site from *The Economist* newspaper.

See also:

☆ **From Crisis Management to Crisis Leadership (pp. 293–94)**
☆ **Viewpoint: Christopher Bartlett (pp. 45–46)**
☆ **Viewpoint: Jim Collins (pp. 235–36)**
☆ **Viewpoint: Henry Mintzberg (pp. 241–42)**

"You can only raise individual performance by elevating that of the entire system."

(W. Edwards Deming)

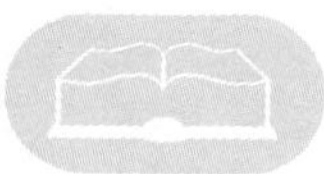

FACILITIES MANAGEMENT *by Keith Alexander*

EXECUTIVE SUMMARY

- Facilities management should be considered as a strategic business discipline.
- Organizations need greater flexibility, improved connectivity with customers and better working conditions for employees. Good facilities management can deliver on all these objectives.
- Managers need to consider not, "how do facilities benefit occupiers?", but more, "how do occupiers secure maximum benefits from facilities?"
- Research is now beginning to show the relationship between effective facilities management and improved share value.
- Facilities also play a leading role in fulfilling the social and environmental responsibilities of an organization.
- A business case can be made for facilities management either on grounds of efficiency and the ability to control costs or, alternatively, to improve the return on fixed assets.

INTRODUCTION

In order to respond to today's fast-moving and rapidly changing business environment, organizations need greater flexibility, improved connectivity with their customers, better working conditions and more choice for employees—all backed by a quality environment and excellent service. The concepts, discipline and practice of facilities management is evolving to meet these challenges, and is becoming increasingly sophisticated in offering "integrated workplace strategies" and in arranging the provision of "serviced accommodation" to meet these contemporary business needs.

THE IMPORTANCE OF CONTEXT

Facilities—a company's physical settings, support services and environmental conditions—must be used effectively to add value to business objectives, strategies and processes. This becomes increasingly important in this rapidly changing economic environment as organizations seek greater flexibility, seek to assimilate new workplace technologies and reconsider their strategies toward facilities and property. However the question is less, "how do facilities benefit occupiers?" and more, "how do occupiers secure maximum benefits from facilities?" It is a management issue rather than a design or technical issue.

Many organizations are still completely driven by shareholder return, and research is now beginning to show the relationship between effective facilities management and improved share value. But there are two other very significant factors in the business equation: corporate culture and motivational factors (for example reward, responsibility, job security). An organization's facilities and the services provided to support its operations should reflect that culture and must not disrupt motivational factors.

MAKING A BUSINESS CASE

The business case for facilities management can be made in a number of different ways. However, the emphasis is still generally on the contribution to financial performance and shareholder value. For many years, particularly in the 1990s, the emphasis has been on the office as an overhead cost, divorced from its contribution to output. The predominant trend has been to make a case on grounds of efficiency and the ability to control and reduce costs or, alternatively, to improve the return on fixed assets.

Clearly, facilities have an important impact on a company's profitability. As facilities are usually an organization's second largest expense, most facilities managers concentrate on seeking to reduce occupancy costs. Indeed, it is likely that their role and responsibilities in the organization are defined in this way. In many organizations, every facilities management decision must be justified in terms of impact on the profit and loss account. The emphasis is more on cost efficiency than on cost effectiveness.

Alternatively, in some organizations a business case will be built around the return on investment, and facilities are seen as a fixed asset or business resource, with a value on the balance sheet. Traditionally, buildings are seen as a capital asset. In this case the key measure is return on asset, and is an important determinant of shareholder value. However, research has shown that companies with lower property holdings derived superior stock-market value.

Facilities can also be considered as a factor of production. They can make a prime contribution in improving the effectiveness of individuals and teams and to enhancing productivity. Facilities managers have usually concentrated on reducing the office cost per employee and increasing the occupancy per square foot of office space, without sufficient regard to the impact this might have on people's performance and the all-factor productivity of their organization.

However, studies have shown that the total cost of providing office space is less than one-tenth of staff costs, and that operating costs are only one-hundredth of staff output. The importance of buildings in supporting the effectiveness and productivity of office workers has been underplayed, largely because of the lack of available evidence to support the business case. Organizations such as PricewaterhouseCoopers are collaborating in projects that develop tools for measuring the performance of facilities and for evaluating the productivity of office environments.

Facilities are important to public and industrial relations and play a large part in setting the corporate identity and image. Britain's National Health Service has had to reconsider the strategic role of hospital cleaning in recognition of how important cleanliness is to customer confidence in the healthcare received. It is increasingly recognized that facilities are a means of improving confidence and morale among employees, customers and visitors.

Other organizations recognize how essential it is to plan facilities in order to ensure business continuity and assess and manage business risk. There are increasing corporate concerns about the power, energy and transport infrastructures, and the consequences to business of failure. Contingency and disaster-recovery planning are essential elements of a coherent business continuity plan.

Facilities management strategies are developed around each of these dimensions of business performance, individually or in combination. Each will have an impact on share value. A more balanced approach is

"Communication is best achieved through simple planning and control." (Gerald M. Blair)

required, and methods and tools are needed to enable the facilities manager to maximize the output from an office and so contribute to the strategic performance of their organization. Many organizations are introducing a balanced scorecard approach in order to ensure they are driven by indicators of business performance other than merely financial ones.

INTELLIGENT CLIENT ROLE

From a practical perspective, facilities management is normally considered as the coordination of functions and integration of multi-disciplinary activities. Many definitions emphasize the practical and operational concerns. But as facility management has become aligned with the core business objectives of public and private organizations, it has had to become increasingly strategic and business oriented.

There are several strategies for dealing with facilities management. Over the past ten years there has been a significant shift toward the outsourcing of facility services in both the public and private sectors. Research suggests that global corporations are considering increasingly radical options for simplifying the facility supply chain. This increases the level of skill needed within an organization to create the conditions for innovation and continuous improvement.

Some organizations, both public and private, treat flexible working initiatives and new workplaces as a strategic issue—one which aims to create an organizational culture suited to the knowledge economy. Management theorists such as Peter Drucker argue that these trends form part of a wider economic restructuring linked to the growth of specialist knowledge-based organizations.

MINI-CASE

Abbey National has 750 branches across the United Kingdom but the portfolio numbers 1,400 sites in total. As well as major office sites, call centers and IT sites, many of these are offices above branches and are counted separately from the retail sites below. In 2000, Abbey National sold its entire property portfolio to a third party in order to guarantee operational and strategic flexibility, without the future risk of uncertainty over the cost of reconfiguring its property portfolio. The deal involved over 600,000 square meters of space. The transaction promised to deliver significant long-term value to the bank's shareholders and was another example of how the Abbey National Group was innovating to maintain and increase efficiency in its business.

Abbey National saw the project as a major step toward being able to alter its property requirements, radically if required, in order to meet its customers' future business needs, thereby significantly enhancing its competitive position.

The bank was keen to stress that it was not merely cashing in on its bricks and mortar for short-term gain. Abbey National intended to enter into a de facto partnership with the winning bidder via an innovative sale and leaseback structure, which would combine both freehold and leasehold properties. The deal was the first significant transaction of its kind in the private sector in the United Kingdom.

It was about a sustainable approach to property management over the long term—"we are in the banking business, not the property business." The project was also about the management of risk: "it means that we will limit a substantial area of liability from the start of the deal, without losing the flexibility that our business strategy requires." For Abbey National, the immediate and long-term benefits of the agreement will be the substantially reduced exposure to property risk, improved operational flexibility and secured property costs for the foreseeable future.

Abbey National has set new standards in property management. The bank is aligning its property strategy to that of the business, rather than looking at a property portfolio and its liabilities in isolation from its business strategy, as in so many other firms. Abbey National has also refused to accept that embarking on a 25-year lease is a given. Along with many other substantial organizations, its business-planning cycle is around three years in duration. This can shrink to months, of course, when it comes to new-economy enterprises. In short, Abbey National engineered a deal that will achieve the high level of flexibility its business requires.

MAKING IT HAPPEN ▸▸

- Make a business case by identifying the value added by facilities management.
- Plan facilities strategically to maximize the business benefit.
- Demonstrate the contribution facilities make to achieving organizational objectives.
- Manage change so that FM initiatives and workplace solutions fit the organizational culture.
- Develop the intelligent client role.
- Develop performance management systems consistent with the corporate climate.
- Create service partnerships to promote innovation and continuous improvement.

For More Information

Books:

Park, Alan. *Facilities Management: An Explanation*. 2nd ed. New York: Palgrave Macmillan, 1998.

Raymond, Santa. *Tomorrow's Office: Creating Effective and Humane Interiors*. London: Spon Press, 1996.

Robertson, Ken. *Work Transformation: Planning and Implementing the New Workplace*. New York: HNB Publishing, 1998.

Smith, Paul R., ed., et al. *Facilities Engineering and Management Handbook: Commercial, Industrial, and Institutional Buildings*. New York: McGraw-Hill, 2000.

Teicholz, Eric, ed. *Facility Design and Management Handbook*. New York: McGraw-Hill, 2001.

Web Site:

www.fdm.com: the Facilities Design & Management Web page is devoted to keeping facility managers informed about current issues and helping them track future developments. Along with the site, you can subscribe to their magazine of the same name.

WORKING FROM THE OUTSIDE IN
by Bill Jensen

EXECUTIVE SUMMARY

- Life is just too short. More to the point, it's just too damn precious.
- There is a great and grave difference between employee satisfaction and satisfying employees' work needs. The new covenant between employers and employees is about that difference.
- In the new war for talent, employees see themselves as investors. Every day, they invest scarce and precious assets—their time, attention, ideas, knowledge, passion, energy and social networks—to make our companies go. They will work wherever they get the best returns on those assets.

INTRODUCTION

Shortly after the September 11, 2001 attacks on New York's twin towers, I had a gut-wrenching conversation with a fellow airline passenger. She was angry and frustrated at having to be on the plane. Even though she is one of the most senior execs at a Fortune 50 company, she felt like she didn't have control of her own life. She was traveling 3,000 miles just because the C.E.O. said she had to. "What if something happens on this plane?" she said. "I don't want to leave my two girls believing that life is about sucking up and doing the right thing just for a paycheck or a career. This company just doesn't get that."

That same conversation is rippling across every workplace, in every sector, at every level of the organization. A lot of people are asking with new urgency, "Why am I doing this? Am I really making a difference? Is this what I want out of life? Out of my career?"

The events and aftermath of September 11 have altered forever the public conversation about how companies and individuals serve each other. The very covenant and rules of engagement between employee and employer are being questioned. However, the new rules were emerging long before we got that tragic wake-up call.

During the past decade I have studied how about a thousand companies get work done. And a startling shift and major inequity have occurred during that time. The people most companies want to attract and retain are bringing with them never-seen-before levels of sophistication and insights about the design of knowledge work. They know more than most leaders about how to collaborate, how to organize information, what they need to get stuff done, how to communicate and how decision making really works. Technology, marketplace, and social changes have trained, enticed and forced them to hone these skills.

Yet, for more and more employees, *the more they invest in their company, the more they lose control of their own destiny.* They have focused on customers. They have drunk the corporate Kool-aid, and they have worked hard. But the overwhelming majority of the tools, structures, and support they get are *still* designed to ensure corporate success—not necessarily theirs.

A NEW CONTRACT EMERGES

This inequity is forcing a new covenant. Under the new work contract, employees see themselves as investors. Every day, they invest scarce and precious assets—their time, attention, ideas, knowledge, passion, energy, and social networks—to make our companies go. They watch today's leaders wasting these assets and, like Wall Street, they want better returns.

Decent pay, appropriate benefits, feeling appreciated, being treated and rewarded fairly, and being part of a great team will always be important. But our best employees are moving beyond entitlements and nurturing. They know that they have to be more productive, more efficient and deliver more better and faster every day. They also know that each day contains only 1,440 minutes with which they can make a difference.

So, in return for those minutes, they're looking at:

- how easy it is to make a big impact;
- how much of their time is spent doing great and important work;
- how much and how fast they can learn;
- how challenging, rewarding, and exciting their work remains;
- how much personal success and balance they achieve—however they choose to define these things;
- how well, or poorly, your company uses their 1,440 minutes;
- how much control they have over their own destiny.

Since there are no guarantees with any employer, employees are beginning to see your firm as a middleman between them, their team mates, customers, and the marketplace. Your company is a tool to connect all these constituencies. And the new contract says it's time for you to start acting like an elegant tool.

Whoa, does this add a new dimension to the basic covenant! There is a great and grave difference between employee satisfaction and satisfying employees' work needs. The new contract is about that difference.

Wrenching uncertainty and tough economic times have not disguised the fact that—especially as you slash budgets and reduce headcount—you are using employees' time, attention, and energy as working capital to meet your company's short-term obligations. They know it. And your best talent is seeking more in return than just a job, a paycheck, or benefits—all of which may be yanked from them without notice.

People are seeking more in return for their time. . because life is just too short. More to the point, it's just too damn precious.

THE WAR FOR TALENT CHANGES

If we begin to think about our employees as investors, many efforts to attract and retain talent come up short.

Do you waste any of your talent's time, attention, ideas, knowledge, passion, energy, or social networks? What is the daily/weekly/monthly return your talent gets for investing their assets in your firm? The new war for talent will be fought over who provides the best returns on life's precious assets. Among the coming changes. . .

Employees are seeking to participate in infrastructure specs: Your technology, processes, information flows, and everything that connects your employees and organizes their work are being examined from the user's perspective. Sun Microsystems is one company where this is happening. They formed a Workplace Effectiveness

---

"A consultant is a person who takes your money and annoys your employees while tirelessly searching for the best way to extend the consulting contract."

(Scott Adams)

group to track how their workspaces and tools are viewed by the people who use them. Every six months, Sun surveys up to 6,000 employees worldwide on issues such as the factors behind personal productivity.

Employees are seeking more input into who manages them: IBM's Extreme Blue student interns have made it clear they won't tolerate "loser managers." And some companies, like PepsiCo, are allowing high-potential talent to select their own managers. For years, it has been established that many people do not leave their company, they leave because their manager impeded their progress or happiness. Smart companies are beginning to change the rules of how managers and employees are paired and developed.

Employees are seeking more input into how they collaborate: Smart companies also understand that new standards are being set daily for what is valued in work exchanges—for example, what content is most valuable, and what social connections, timing, tips and tools are needed, and what type of coaching would be most helpful. Companies like Cisco and Dell are designing entire learning structures based upon workforce feedback on what they say they need.

Making It Happen ▸▸

A new war for talent is emerging through tougher examination of work itself. For years, our companies have operated on the premise that there's *work* and there's *life* and it's up to employees to balance the two. Since September 11, it has become clear that this view is no longer acceptable. The very act of using someone's time assigns new accountabilities to each of us.

This creates new rules in how you fight the war for talent. Among them. . .

Great workplaces respect life's precious assets: Smart companies are beginning to attract and retain people with an amazingly simple idea: improve business results and create a great place to work by improving how they use employees' time and energy. This means embracing a bottom-up asset revolution.

Great workplaces get better results by giving people better control over their own destiny: Business must focus on personal, not just organizational, productivity. The future of work is increasingly customized, personalized and tailored to each individual.

This means the future war for talent will be anchored by My Work My Way—delivering business success by customizing more and more information, work tools and experiences to individual needs. As long as the future includes heavy knowledge work, where personal choices are integral to success, My-Way approaches will be critical.

Great workplaces get more out of collaboration by putting more into it: Today's centralized, top-down approaches to planning collaboration infrastructure and tools are simply not keeping up with the rate of change in how peers want and need to collaborate with each other. If you are going to add value to peer-to-peer exchanges, you must be willing to design budgets and strategies around what the people doing the work find most valuable. You need to focus a lot more on how you deliver peer-to-peer value.

The leaders of great workplaces accept accountability for life's precious assets: Those whom we will follow in the war for talent are "extreme leaders." What makes leadership "extreme" is greater accountability for performance through greater willingness to be challenged on, and address, work-level details. Partnering with employees who have no fear about pushing upward. Extreme leaders acknowledge that the route to corporate success includes changing the path employees must take for their personal success.

New metrics for great places to work

The SimplerWork Index™ tracks six new dimensions of great places to work. Beyond being nice to your employees, this index tracks what it takes to do great work in a knowledge-based economy. Each measure focuses on how well you enable people to work smarter and faster *while also* giving each employee greater control over his or her own destiny. Unfortunately, the percentages below* illustrate how much today's companies must still improve.

- **Competing on clarity 45%**—evaluates manager's effectiveness in helping individual employees work smarter and faster
- **Navigation 25%**—evaluates company's effectiveness in helping individual employees find who or what they need to work smarter and faster
- **Fulfillment of basics 25%**—evaluates company's effectiveness in work-oriented communication and knowledge management
- **Usability 15%**—evaluates company's effectiveness in all that it designs to help people get tasks done (tools, technology, training, instructions and so on)
- **Speed 12%**—evaluates company's effectiveness in enabling employees to work in a 24/7, ever-faster world
- **Time 10%**—evaluates company's respect for employees' time as an asset to be invested.

* 2001 survey of 7,500 individuals in 180 companies

Conclusion

No one has a crystal ball. Nobody knows perfectly how to juggle shareholder needs, customer needs, employee needs and corporate strategies. And certainly, the whole story of the war for talent is far more complex than space here allows.

Yet one signpost on the path ahead is undeniable. Our best employees will no longer tie themselves to any organization that doesn't give them greater control over their own destiny, or respect all of life's precious assets that they put to use each and every day.

The future of business success is tied to every individual's success. We win together, or not at all.

For More Information

Books:

Morris, Edmund. *Theodore Rex*. New York: Random House, 2001.
Orwell, George. *1984*. New York: New American Library Classics, 1990.
Toffler, Alvin. *Future Shock*. New York: Bantam Books, 1991.

"It is always easier to talk about change than to make it. It is easier to consult than to manage." (Alvin Toffler)

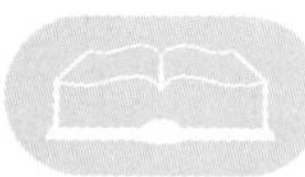

LEAN MANUFACTURING *by Daniel T. Jones*

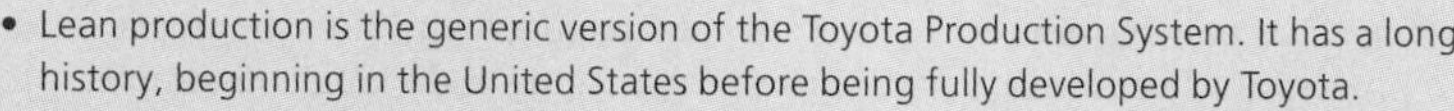

EXECUTIVE SUMMARY

- Lean production is the generic version of the Toyota Production System. It has a long history, beginning in the United States before being fully developed by Toyota.
- It is based on managing the product value stream from raw material to end customer, rather than focusing on managing separate assets and firms.
- The objective is to eliminate waste through reconfiguring operations into continuous flow cells linked by leveled pull systems.
- The gains are defect-free products, on-time delivery, big reductions in inventories, and freed-up people, machine time, and space.

INTRODUCTION

Although the terms "lean production" and "lean manufacturing" have only been in circulation since the publication of *The Machine That Changed the World* in 1990, the concepts and practices have a much longer history. Indeed, the core idea of lining production steps in process sequence can be traced back to Colt's armory in Hartford, Connecticut, in 1855. What Henry Ford later called "flow production" reached its peak at his plant in Highland Park in 1915, where every machine making parts and every step toward assembling them were lined up in single-piece flow, so that it took a matter of hours from raw casting to the finished product.

This system could not offer customers enough choice. So when Ford built his next plant at River Rouge in 1931, it was organized quite differently. Large machines able to make large batches of different parts were grouped together in separate departments, maximizing efficiency by ensuring there was always work waiting to be done. Batches of products wandered from department to department and throughput times stretched from several hours to several months. Long lead times entailed making to forecast and selling from several months' stock of finished cars in dealer lots. Thus the world of mass "production" was born and became the dominant model as long as producers could sell everything they made.

DISCOVERING LEAN PRODUCTION

Across the Pacific the founders of Toyota, Sakichi Toyoda and his son Kiichiro, were working on their own version of flow production in the 1930s. They formulated the two key pillars of what later became the Toyota Production System (TPS): automatic machine and line stopping whenever a mistake is made so that no bad parts are passed forward to interrupt the downstream flow (a system they called *Jidoka*), and a pull system in which only parts that are actually needed are made (called *just-in-time*). Later on the third pillar, involving leveling the workload in a mixed model production flow, was added (called *Heijunka*).

It was not until after World War II that Taiichi Ohno, the production chief at Toyota, implemented these principles. Ohno was determined to overcome all the obstacles to producing a range of products in low volumes, using simple equipment laid out in process sequence. His twenty-year experiment started in the engine plant before extending to pressing, body welding, and assembly. Only when Ohno needed to extend the TPS to the supply base in the early 1970s was it written down for the first time, though it was another decade before it was published in books and articles.

Toyota's steady and continuing rise to become the third largest carmaker in the world led others to try to follow its example. This could only be done by understanding the principles behind TPS and then selecting the right tools in the right sequence. Lean production is the generic version of TPS and lean thinking describes the principles behind not just TPS but the whole Toyota business system, including product development, supplier coordination, and customer management. These principles are based on five key insights.

THE FIVE PRINCIPLES OF LEAN THINKING

1. Specify value from the standpoint of the end customer.
2. Identify the value stream for each product family.
3. Link value-creating steps so the product can flow.
4. Enable your customers to pull what they need.
5. Manage toward perfection—where every action and asset creates value.

If you define value from the standpoint of the end customer, you realize that only a tiny fraction of actions and time actually create value. In a typical factory this might be 5% and in a whole value stream (from raw material to end customer) it is usually less than 1%. The rest of the steps are only necessary because of the way firms are currently organized and because of past decisions about assets and technologies. So the greatest opportunity for performance improvement is to reconfigure operations across the value stream to remove these wasted steps.

TAIICHI OHNO'S SEVEN WASTES THAT CONSUME VALUE

1. Overproduction
2. Inventories
3. Defects
4. Waiting
5. Excess Transport
6. Excess Movement
7. Excess Processing

If you identify the whole value stream for a given product (both the flow of orders upstream and the flow of products downstream) you see that optimizing each asset and activity in isolation creates huge amounts of waste elsewhere. It is only by optimizing the product value stream that you can identify ways of eliminating these interface wastes and can begin to rethink the appropriate equipment, technologies, and locations for the future.

The ideal way to organize waste-free production is to line up the value-creating steps so the product flows through them in the shortest possible time. This, in turn, means that every activity must be standardized and repeatable, and that every machine must be fully capable of delivering exactly what is needed and fully available to operate when needed. Where machines cannot be colocated and serve several product flows, then products need to be pulled directly as required from the upstream step. Time compression of every step is the only way to maintain these disciplines and to ensure that waste does not creep back when attention shifts elsewhere.

Multiple decision points and time lags in processing orders lead to amplification of the variance in orders passed upstream,

"No manufacturing company will ever do well if they are concerned only with calculating profits."

(Shoichiro Toyoda)

which in turn requires larger inventories and excess capacity to cover demand spikes. Time compression and direct pull systems are the key to eliminating this amplification and to being able to move away from make-to-forecast and sell-from-stock toward true build-to-order systems able to deliver what customers want within the time available.

The final insight is that reconfiguring the value stream to eliminate waste is a step-by-step process: the more waste you remove, the more you can see to remove next time. It starts by understanding the current state of your operations and defining an achievable future state in a short space of time, which then becomes the current state of the next improvement cycle. However, this cyclical process also needs to be guided by a vision of the perfect state to which you should be headed, in which every action and asset creates value for the end customer.

Implementing Lean Production

Lean production is by no means widespread, even in Japan. Indeed, it was only after 1973 that the rest of the Japanese auto industry recognized that Toyota was following a different path. By 1987 the first companies in the United States began to make serious progress with the help of several of Ohno's disciples, who had by then left to become consultants. The early lean conversion stories of Pratt & Whitney, Wiremold, and Lantech are described in *Lean Thinking*. Since then lean production has spread across the automotive, aerospace, and engineering industries and, following Alcoa's example, to raw material processing.

Many firms began implementing lean by involving the workforce in team-based problem-solving and *Kaizen* or continuous improvement activities. Putting the spotlight on operations should certainly lead to the removal of the most obvious wastes in the organization. However, lean production only really begins when you use value-stream mapping to learn to see the product flow from door to door, and when you give someone the responsibility for reconfiguring operations into continuous flow cells linked by leveled pull systems.

Once progress has been made within the plant then it is time to involve your suppliers by linking plants using simple pull systems and your customers by linking them directly to production using build-to-order systems. Beyond this it is possible to envisage rethinking and compressing the value stream using different technologies and right-sized tools colocated close to the point of use. We have in truth only just begun to realize the full potential of lean production.

Making It Happen

- Putting the spotlight on all of your operations should eliminate the most obvious wastes and deficiencies in the value chain—from the start of the process to the customer.
- For a more comprehensive assessment of the areas where your organization's processes may improve, use value stream mapping to clearly show product flows.
- Ensure that there is one person with overall responsibility for reconfiguring operations into continuous flow cells, linked by leveled "pull" systems.
- Knit together different parts of your value stream using build-to-order mechanisms.
- Compress your value stream through the development of new and ongoing strategies, and the application of new technologies, to eliminate wastage and continuously improve efficiency.
- Regularly review your activities—ideally from a customer or end user perspective—to make sure that they are delivered in an effective and profit-centered way.

Conclusion

Managing lean value streams is harder than managing individual operations. However, the gains are substantial, particularly when replicated across the whole value stream. First, your customers get defect-free products on time. Second, your suppliers get leveled orders and can deliver to you on time. Third, inventories at every point down the value stream can be cut in half. Fourth, you free up a lot of resources—people, machines and space—that will not appear on the bottom line until they are used. The challenge in sustaining progress towards lean is to grow the throughput and bring operations in house as you free up those assets.

For More Information

Books:

Womack, James P., et al. *The Machine That Changed the World*. New York: HarperCollins, 1990.

Womack, James P., and Daniel T. Jones. *Lean Thinking: Banish Waste and Create Wealth in your Corporation*. New York: Simon & Schuster, 1996.

Other lean manufacturing classics are listed at **www.lean.org**. Here you will also find an on-line community of those actively implementing lean production and the key workbook to help you get started in mapping your value streams: Shook, J., and M. Rother. *Learning to See*. Brookline, MA: The Lean Enterprise Institute, 1998.

See also:

Genichi Taguchi (pp. 1052–53)
Eiji Toyoda (pp. 1144–45)

"Large consumption is at the basis of saving in manufacture, and hence high wages contribute their share to progress."
(Thomas Brackett Reed)

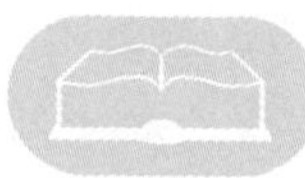

Getting All Your People Committed to Change and Transformation *by John Smythe*

Executive Summary

- The first age of internal communication: the application of external marketing techniques to internal employee audiences.
- The shift in the role of internal communication from one of replicating management's view of the world to one of creating work place cultures that help organizations achieve their ambitions, not least by creating a compelling place to work.
- The shift from an information-driven concept of communication—conveying messages—to one which releases the energy and creativity of employees; moving in dialog from compliance to commitment.
- Six practical insights to help leaders to create commitment in themselves, in management and all their colleagues.

Introduction

Internal communication as a management practice is probably no more than 15 years old. It came into vogue when "command-and-control" styles of leadership began to be questioned. Yet most of what is practiced under the banner of internal communication is the internal application of external marketing techniques—internal PR.

In the boardroom, communication is still the final item on the agenda. Directors ask, "What's our line on this?" The function of internal communication is to make sense of decisions after they've been made. Invariably, it's a matter of record of varying degrees of veracity. The driving metaphor is still largely that of the internal press officer, contriving sense about decisions post hoc and packaging them in a way which offends fewest around the top table. As such, internal communication has been useful in at least putting the communication needs of employees on the leadership team's agenda.

Current best practice enacts the belief that if you are able to communicate and mobilize people quickly and effectively around vision, strategy, change and transformation, then you have a robust internal marketing process. You will be rewarded by feedback which credits the leadership with keeping everyone on the same page as them.

Commitment Is Vital

The age of compliance at work is over and the essential task of internal communication has to change—in some organizations is changing—from one of replicating the view of the few to the many. Now it's about releasing people's energies in the interests of the organization.

The central challenge of leading people today is creating a work culture which releases people's creativity in a way which benefits both the employee and the organization. The organization which can score a 10/10 for strategy, 10/10 for effective organization and 10/10 for commitment will be a great place to work and commercially very powerful.

You can be sure that the style of internal communication in your organization faithfully reflects leadership style. Thus the organization which has chaotic communication processes and which is always behind the facts is telling you much about leadership style. So will the autocratically directed spin machine which whirrs into overdrive when the control freak sneezes. The only difference between the dumb control freak and the smart one is that the smart one has communication sewn up.

Like it or not, the leadership team is the most influential communication team.

The Chief Entertainment Officer

The C.E.O. could henceforth be called the Chief Entertainment Officer. The worst crime C.E.O.s can commit is being plain boring. The C suite is a massive influence on mood. You get to know the C.E.O.'s mood even when you are thousands of miles away.

Internal communication used to be about managing "news" and information. But with so many sources of information a company has to manage its information in a way that is accessible, timely, honest, and, maybe even entertaining, if it wants to win the war for employees' attention.

I use the idea of the C.E.O. as chief entertainer to bring attention to the fact that many employees are choosing between employment offers by asking themselves, "What culture will bring the best out in me?" It's not that one culture is necessarily "better," but that one will be more suitable.

What Have Mood, Style, Culture, and Commitment Got to Do with Commercial Success?

The answer is—plenty. Having the right strategy and a good organization isn't enough. Without commitment, strategy stays firmly on the ground.

Most C.E.O.s will tell you that turning around a failing business is difficult. It requires the making of hard decisions, made with people who may be part of the problem. These C.E.O.s will also tell you that change when the business is good is much tougher because people ask, "Why jump over that cliff, things are good here?"

Whether reductive or offensive change, the C suite needs to manage the mood around it. To manage it you need to read it. And so it's vital to be a fast listener who feels for the unstated. The prime job of a C.E.O. is to swing the mood behind them, which means:

- turning the instigators of change (often a bunch of gung-ho types in the program office) from robots into evangelists;
- seducing spectators and victims into being enthusiastic implementors;
- making converts of blockers;
- seeing themselves turning from lonely heroes to "becoming enablers" of the vision and energy of others.

Six Tips for Building Commitment

1. Agree the change/transformation story.
2. Map your change or transformation journey.
3. Be clear about who is to be involved.

"Changes are not without cost. . . We have found it possible to minimize resistance by establishing a culture based on core values."

(Charles G. Koch)

4. Model the desired change.
5. Engage and entertain.
6. Get your story told.

There are no easy answers to getting commitment, but some of the ideas below may bring value.

1. Agree the Change / Transformation Story

It is astonishing the number of leadership teams which believe that among themselves they share the vision or the story of change. So often a surface gloss of agreement hides real or imagined tensions and implementation plans are signed off with real agreement around the table merely assumed. The inevitable resulting tensions are felt by the whole organization.

Achieving real commitment in any team requires an investment in outing all the stories or pictures that individual team members have in their heads but may not know until they tell their version of the story to themselves and each other.

I liken this process to concluding a peace treaty. In the heat of apparent agreement around the table, the protagonists rush out to implement, each with their own story, which each is sure is the real truth. Alas, all too often the real negotiations then take place in the messy arena called implementation, and it seems to everyone that "decisions" keep getting opened up again.

This process of agreeing the story together saves much time. It can act as a teambuilding exercise and so avoids airing factionalism in a very public way.

2. Map Your Change or Transformation Journey

Too often the energy of the peace treaty is diluted in the environment of implementation. Deadly critical paths put paid to crusade of change. This is when the idea of a journey of rich experiences is more useful than a monochrome critical path. The instigating team should map the journey together, taking care to plot the mood swings likely to be encountered along the path.

This "journey" or "mood map" then becomes the basis for actively planning the journey to minimize the downs and maximize the ups, because the journey is mapped as it will be experienced by different constituents or stakeholders.

3. Be Clear About Who Is to Be Involved

Involvement is now a very hot topic. The key point for leaders is the development of a coherent approach to involving people in the design and implementation of change.

In my experience, and perhaps yours, most leadership or change teams take one of three approaches to involvement or consultation.

- They promise much, set false expectations and drive it all from one point.
- They involve endlessly but never implement.
- They promise little involvement and live up to it.

Increasingly, the wiser team will deliberate carefully about "the nature of the invitation" which will provide maximum benefit in terms of both the nature of the change and the extra motivation that results in better sustained implementation.

4. Model the Desired Change

The problem with "programs" or "projects" is that often a hit team is assigned which consists or is influenced by external advisers with entirely different values and with a very clear mission. Within hours of entering into the "chaos" of the client, the advisers are behaving like an alien nation, hellbent on delivering whatever the human cost.

On the one hand you're really happy that they are shaking the place up. On the other, a key team member has just walked to your biggest competitor because of the way he was treated by your pet project. It's all about behavior. Attempts at defining behaviors and getting people to live them are largely unsuccessful because they are seen as lip service and tokenism. Descriptions of "new behaviors" are rarely taken seriously by the leadership. An alternative route is to create a set of measurable service standards for the project. These are laid down as success criteria and are used to demonstrate that success is about the style of implementation as well as what is delivered.

Other approaches include that of basing desired behaviors on brand or corporate values. One thing is certain: "rolling out" behavior programs in the manner of a marketing campaign is unlikely to have an impact on the subsequent experiences of employees or external groups. Equally, intensive approaches to behavioral change, using group and individual coaching, can become wearisome processes. I believe that the secret here lies in personalizing the nature of the behavioral change required rather than trying to "infect" people with the jargon provided by an internal "brand/values/ behavior" team in association with consultants.

Avoiding the behavioral element is not the answer because the behaviors modeled by influential figures will soon become norms. And none more so than those modeled by individuals with any kind of power over others, be that specialist power, power over reward, network power, etc. The key is to think through what kind of program is likely to get take-up in your organization. It is highly unlikely to be an off-the-shelf formulaic approach.

Of all the ways of getting commitment, the behavioral must take account of past efforts, personalities and espoused barriers. A degree of experimentation may well be necessary. A formalized process including tools like coaching, 360 degree appraisals and so forth may be fine in some settings and laughed out of court in others, where, say, a shift in behavior by a significant figure does the trick.

5. Engage and Entertain

Leadership and change teams are competing with many entertaining stimulants, such as surfing the Internet, reading newspapers, watching CNN, and so on. The best thing we can do to make sure that the erudite vision, or strategy, or change process, or new product strategy stays in the files is to BORE everyone with a grimly corporate communication process.

The purpose of getting the change instigators to think through the journey milestones, and to keep change alive, is to create the basis for a lively engagement program which astutely allows for periods of reflection, moments of learning and outbursts of sheer exuberant fun. And I would emphasize the mix of learning, reflection, sometimes mourning, and fun. To engage correctly the activity must be sympathetic with the decisions which the organization is trying to make and implement.

Remember, participants in a change process see the experience as their own personal journey. If the organization can help employees make it a very personal journey on which they can take time to reflect and personalize, those employees are much more likely to identify with the process and help make it happen.

6. Get Your Story Told

Much has been written recently about the power of stories in conveying identity, work practices and social links between generations. In pre-modern times, story was the main social glue and the only method of learning aside from observation and experience.

"Anyone in a large organization who thinks major change is impossible should probably get out."

(John P. Kotter)

A characteristic of the story is that people listen and hear their own story. In turn, they internalize it and convey it onwards with their own interpretation. Which is of course what happens at work regardless of whether there is any effort to manage, influence or spin by management.

The lesson for management is that they have a responsibility to be a credible, fast and authoritative source of stories which affect people's motivation. But bearing in mind the countless other sources of data, the best you can do is be one source which, by virtue of its integrity, earns a readership and a dialog alongside other sources.

MAKING IT HAPPEN ▸▸

If you are planning to lead a major change initiative in your organization the following steps can be useful to consider:

- **Is it necessary to establish a sense of urgency?** This can often help to start overcoming apathy and inertia. It also highlights the need for attention and commitment. This might mean identifying and discussing crises or potential crises; examining recent market pressures and trends, as well as highlighting potential opportunities, and the benefits of rapid, urgent change.
- **Consider who will guide the change process.** A united, coordinated and respected group within the organization should have the authority to make decisions, lead, and ensure that the right things happen.
- **What is the vision that will guide the change effort?** It needs to be practical, simple, powerful, and consistent with the broader aims of the organization.
- **How will the vision for change be communicated?** This needs to be done in a way that gains people's understanding and commitment; initiates and drives change, unlocking people's energies and guiding their actions.
- **Are people empowered to act?** As we said, leaders alone cannot deliver change, it needs to come from the roots of the organization and people need to feel able—empowered—to make the necessary changes. To empower people it can help for the leader to remove obstacles in the organization, change systems that undermine the vision for change, and encourage risk-taking and innovative thinking.
- **Are there short-term wins that can be achieved?** These often help build enthusiasm, motivation, and momentum behind the change initiative. Successes and the people behind them need to be valued and recognized.
- **Are successes being consolidated and used as stepping-stones to more change?** The change process needs to move at the right pace, neither too slow nor too fast, and careful thought needs to be given to sustaining it. Hiring, promoting, and developing effective people can help, so too can reinvigorating the change process with new projects and themes.
- **Are the new approaches being anchored in the organization's culture?** A key danger is finishing too soon. This can be avoided by explaining the links between the new behaviors and organizational success. Supporting a climate of continuous improvement is also valuable in achieving success.

CONCLUSION

The new role of communication is no longer about spin. It is about helping bring about useful change, change which is good for the organization and productive and engaging for the individual. Organizations have managed to make change a dismal experience in which creativity is stifled. Communication should be employed to make the change experience stimulating and even fun.

For More Information

Books:

Maister, David H. *Practice What You Preach: What Managers Must Do to Create a High-achievement Culture*. New York: Free Press, 2001.

Wenger, Etienne, Richard A. McDermott, and William Snyder. *Cultivating Communities of Practice*. Boston, MA: Harvard Business School Press, 2002.

Yerkes, Leslie. *Fun Works: Creating Places Where People Love to Work*. San Francisco, CA: Berrett-Koehler, 2001.

Web Site:

http://knowledge.wharton.upenn.edu: a free service of the Wharton School of Business, this site contains current articles by top authors in many areas of business and management, including leadership and change, executive education, innovation, and entrepreneurship.

See also:

☆ **Now!—The Role of Urgency in Creating Positive Change (pp. 265–66)**
Philip Crosby (pp. 978–79)
Soichiro Honda (pp. 1094–95)

  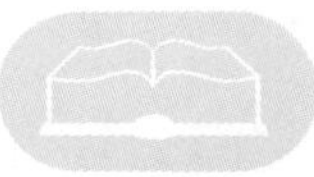    

MANAGING THE CHALLENGE OF E-SERVICE *by Chris Voss*

EXECUTIVE SUMMARY

- Customer expectations, in terms of service delivery and other key factors, have increased dramatically in recent years, as a result of the promise and delivery of the Internet. Even after the "dot-com crash" these raised expectations linger.
- The growth in the application and acceptance of Internet-driven technologies means that delivering an enhanced service is more achievable than ever before, however it is also more complex and fraught with potential costs and risk.
- The Internet introduces customers to a new perception of business time as always "on," available 24/7 and demanding an urgent and rapid response. The challenge for managers is to reconcile their business and their own personal perceptions of time with the perceived reality of Internet time.
- The Internet has decisively shifted the balance of power to the customer.
- The Internet is revolutionizing sales techniques and perceptions of leading brands, and the Internet is intensifying competition in all its forms.
- Companies are continuing to use the Internet to add value for their customers: but in order for this to work effectively—maximizing opportunities, reducing risks and overcoming problems—an e-service strategy is required.

INTRODUCTION

The growth of the Web and Internet as new channels, the growth in their use by customers, and the flood of companies entering the market, presents a series of key challenges to companies. It is easy and cheap to put up a Web site. But to create an environment delivering effective service on the Web to a significant proportion of your customer base requires an e-service strategy.

Any strategy must be based on understanding customers and markets. This means having arrangements for collecting data to help understand customers, to track their preferences, and to improve segmentation.

Technology provides the opportunity to track and interact with anyone contacting an organization via the Web and to explore customer needs in new ways.

TECHNIQUES FOR IMPLEMENTING AN E-SERVICE STRATEGY

The challenge is to develop a strategy for the right combination of value-added, personalized and proactive service. Keeping e-service customers will require high levels of service, a positive experience and trust in your organization. How can these be delivered? A strategy for e-service should be part of the overall electronic commerce strategy of the organization. In preparing for e-service, there are nine key steps:

1. Upgrade current service interaction.
2. Understand your customer segments.
3. Understand your customer service processes and interactions.
4. Define the role of live interaction (and hence areas for automation).
5. Make the key technology decisions.
6. Prepare to deal with the tidal wave of increased customer interaction.
7. Train customers and create incentives for them to use the appropriate channel.
8. Address the issue of channel choice and "brick versus click."
9. Exploit the Web to create relationships and a real customer experience.

MEETING THE TECHNOLOGICAL CHALLENGES–CHOOSING THE RIGHT CHANNEL

For many companies, the toughest stage is the fifth: *technology*. As one company said to our researchers: "one of our biggest implementation issues is the integration of Web-enabled technology with our legacy systems, both technology and business processes". Technology is moving rapidly so tough decisions need taking:

- Do we pilot now and learn and invest later, risking loss of position, or move quickly and risk major problems to gain market space today?
- Do we go for full integration, and if necessary throw out today's legacy systems?

There are two crucial questions regarding channel choice. The first is whether to offer the customer options, for example, face-to-face, post, phone and Web. In any industry there may be a variety of different approaches. For example, many retail banks allow the choice of managing current accounts through the branch, post or on the Web. Others have single channel accounts—for example, phone only. Others allow constrained choice, for instance, phone and Web, but enroll new customers only via the Web. The difficulty in getting high levels of service when adding new channels has led many in the past to start new ventures separate from existing channels and systems. Informing this decision are both the costs of the different channels, and importance of customer relationship management (CRM) databases. In most customer service environments, the quality and scope of the CRM database is central to the successful delivery of service. There is pressure therefore not to operate new channels separately, but to integrate existing channels around a single CRM database.

IMPLEMENTING AN E-SERVICE STRATEGY AND BUILDING CUSTOMER RELATIONSHIPS

No strategy can be effective without attention to implementation. Two of the main lessons from our research are as follows:

- business process and transaction analysis is essential for effective e-service design;
- you must get implementation right first time. If not, people will revert to the phone.

Important areas for implementation include organization and culture. Just as e-commerce changes the organization and power in markets, it can do the same within organizations. Another aspect of organization and culture is the need to realize that in the new environment, alliances and partnerships play a much-increased role.

Companies need to develop key metrics to set standards and measure performance in the following areas:

"E-commerce. . .is a means to an end. The objectives, as with IT, are to improve or exploit unique business propositions."

(Walid Mougayar)

  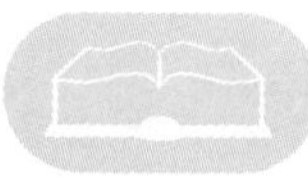    

- *Security/Trust*: measured through surveys and focus groups.
- *Response Time:* Internet customers may expect faster response.
- *Response Quality*: difficult to measure.
- *Navigability:* one of the most important determinants of service.
- *Download time*: the maximum time that a user will tolerate for any page may be less than 30 seconds!
- *Fulfillment*; is it fast and are the promised goods delivered?
- *Up to date*: out-of-date information may quickly turn off users.
- *Availability*: Can the user reach the site 24 hours a day, 7 days a week?
- *Site effectiveness and functionality:* Is the Web page intuitive and easy to use? What is the effectiveness of the site from the user's point of view?

Building an Investment Case

Many large companies have found building a case for investment in e-service and e-commerce extremely difficult. This difficulty arises from a number of factors—uncertainty over the data and trends, using the wrong baseline, lack of vision, and lack of knowledge and skills of senior management. One recent survey concluded that while in the United States directors took the competitive threat seriously, those in the United Kingdom and France were in "a state of denial." In building an investment case against a baseline of today's business, the investment costs are often high, whereas the returns are often not visible in the short term. There are two alternate baselines:

1. **Buying an option on the future.** In an uncertain world, investment in new media and channels could be viewed as buying an option on entry to future markets and in mastering future technologies. In the short term, this allows a company to build expertise and infrastructure without major investment or structural change. However, to profit from this, the option must be exercised before it expires.
2. **What will happen to your business without investment—the costs of not investing.** If your market is being attacked by new players, using new technologies and with different cost structures, and not bound by legacy systems or policies, then the baseline case for investment may be much lower than extrapolation of today's business.

In every market that we looked at, from utilities to banking, we found organizations wanting to break into the market or change the way the market operates by using new technologies. These organizations are quick to see both the weaknesses of the current marketplace and new ways of doing business, and to challenge underlying assumptions about customer behavior. Too often, the ability to change is constrained by an organization's unwillingness to make tough decisions about its legacy systems and procedures. That is no way to exploit the available dot-com strategies. Instead:

- ignore unattractive, expensive channels;
- cherry-pick segments, differentiate segments;
- pick products/services where Web adds value;
- offer services worldwide;
- capture or create intermediary roles;
- use strength of portal;
- create affiliate programs, selling products via other people's Web sites;
- use incentives.

Organizations must view their investment in e-service not just in cost/benefit terms, but also in comparison with doing nothing. By putting yourself in the shoes of a potential entrant, you can gain major insights into what might comprise a service vision.

Making It Happen ▸▸

- Use technology to track and interact with anyone contacting the organization via the Web and to explore customer needs and expectations in new ways.
- Ask "What is our strategy for e-commerce and e-service and how should it be implemented?", not "should we invest in e-Service?"
- Develop a strategy for the right combination of value-added, personalized and proactive service.
- Train customers and provide them with incentives to switch, or disincentives to continue using existing channels.
- Create relationships via tailor-made sites for customers; proactive service offerings; communities of users; and extension of relationships beyond the firm.

Conclusion

The Internet makes it easier to achieve three key elements of customer-loyalty: making it easy for customers to do business with you, satisfying your customers, and keeping them coming back to you. Furthermore, these can all be accomplished at a fraction of their normal cost, and by building greater customer loyalty, sales costs will often be reduced.

Customer care includes routine or mundane features (such as the need to provide a variety of payment methods), through more significant issues (such as responding to queries reactively or up-selling and cross-selling products proactively), to the downright vital—ensuring that customers' security and privacy are respected and maintained. Critical among these factors is the need to *support* customers and to instill *confidence*, and these can be achieved by:

- managing customers in a subtle and flexible way, for example by offering a variety of delivery options;
- ensuring adequate (meaning both capable and ever-present) customer support so that consumers and businesses find on-line shopping stress-free;
- providing security and privacy for on-line transactions.

For More Information

Books:

Evans, Philip, and Thomas Wurster. *Blown to Bits*. Boston, MA: Harvard Business School Press, 1999.

Swift, Ronald S. *Accelerating Customer Relationships*. Upper Saddle River, NJ: Prentice Hall, 2000.

Greenberg, Paul. *CRM at the Speed of Light*. New York: McGraw-Hill, 2001.

Godin, Seth, and Don Peppers. *Permission Marketing*. New York: Simon & Schuster, 1999.

See also:

- ☆ **Managing the Customer (pp. 65–66)**
- ☆ **Marketing to the "Real-time" Consumer (pp. 73–74)**
- ☆ **New Yardsticks for Performance and Productivity in an E-world (pp. 285–86)**
- ✔ **Building Partnerships with Business Customers (pp. 668–69)**
- ✔ **Communicating Customer Service (pp. 670–71)**
- ✔ **How to Deliver Quality Online Customer Service and Support (pp. 582–83)**
- ✔ **How to Implement Customer Relationship Management (pp. 584–85)**
- ✔ **Running a Customer Loyalty Program (pp. 678–79)**

"If I had a brick for every time I've repeated the phrase 'Quality, Service, Cleanliness and Value,' I'd probably be able to bridge the Atlantic Ocean with them."

(Ray Kroc)

Viewpoint: Sumantra Ghoshal

Taking Managers beyond Strategy, Structure, and Systems

Described by *The Economist* as a "EuroGuru," the Indian business academic Sumantra Ghoshal is now professor of strategic leadership at the London Business School. He is best known for his work with Harvard's Christopher Bartlett. Their books, *Managing Across Borders: The Transnational Solution* (1988)—named by *the Financial Times* as one of the 50 most influential business books of the century—and *The Individualized Corporation* (1997), have cemented their place among the world's most influential business thinkers. (In 2001, Ghoshal was ranked 12th in "The Thinkers 50," the first global ranking of business thinkers.) In their most recent work, Bartlett and Ghoshal anticipate the rise of a new organizational model based around purpose, people, and process. Integral to their thinking is the idea that the people who work for an organization should be viewed as volunteer investors rather than simply employees.

Who has had the most influence on your thinking on management?

C. K. Prahalad because of the perspective that he brings. I've known CK for a long time. He was my senior on the Harvard program, and then I have worked with him on consulting projects with companies.

I belong to what we normally call the strategy process school, as distinct from the content side. The focus is on the interaction of an organization's leadership in the things companies do, including the things that are strategic–and that link between leadership and management on the one side and strategic actions on the other. In that link, the ability to look at a phenomenon in a real company and ask truly insightful questions is vital. That has always been CK's amazing capability. So CK influenced me most.

But if I had to say who I have learned the most from, then I'd say Chris Bartlett–especially in terms of understanding why things happen the way they happen. I worked with Chris at Harvard. For the last 20 years most of what I've written has been with Chris. *Managing Across Borders* and *The Individualized Corporation* were both coauthored with Chris. In academe people don't tend to have particularly lasting partnerships, but my partnership with Chris is different. We have done hundreds of interviews together. After an interview we interpret what a manager is saying–why he is saying it. I really gained an understanding of administrative process from him.

The job of the leadership is to get the strategy right, and to design the right structure. And then to tie the strategy with the structure, through very defined systems, to be able to deliver performance.

What single thing or experience had the most influence?

I think the most influential thing for me was the experience of working closely with Digital Equipment Corporation through the 1980s, over almost eight years. At its very peak it was the second largest computer company in the world, growing at 30% per annum. At that time most people, and certainly those in the company, anticipated that Digital would become the world's number one computer company. From those heady days of success to the rapid decline and ultimate death of Digital as an independent entity–to watch that up close from inside that process has shaped a lot of my thinking, especially in terms of the difficulties of managing change and the challenges of leadership.

Compared to the last 50 years, how will business be different in the 21st century?

In the last 50 years a dominant philosophy has arisen that drives businesses. At its heart is the notion that a company is purely an economic entity; it is an economic instrument. That ultimately the job of management is to leverage the scarce resource capital. And we have created a whole doctrine of management based around those principles.

That premise has led to an overall leadership or corporate philosophy based around the notions of strategy, structure, and systems. The job of the leadership is to get the strategy right, design the right structure, and deliver performance. That's the core management philosophy that has driven companies over the past 50 years. It came basically from Alfred Sloan and his experiments at General Motors. That philosophy is no longer appropriate today.

"The oppressive atmosphere in most companies resembles downtown Calcutta in summer."

(Sumantra Ghoshal and Christopher Bartlett)

  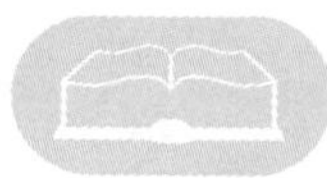  

The reason it is no longer appropriate is a basic shift in what is the scarce resource. We have seen trillions of dollars chasing what is really the scarce resource today and will be even more so in the next 50 years, which is ideas, knowledge, entrepreneurship, and human capital. This shift from financial capital to human capital as the scarce resource has enormous implications. The core management philosophy—the strategy, systems, structure doctrine—becomes bankrupt because it is designed to maximize the returns on financial capital and manage financial capital. You can't manage talent and people—if that is the source of competitive advantage—with that philosophy.

Chris and I argue in our last book that a very different management philosophy will become dominant—what we call the purpose, process, people philosophy. So we are moving beyond strategy to purpose; beyond structure to process; and beyond systems to people. All of which has occurred to allow the company to attract, retain, and then leverage this talent.

I think this shift will also shift the basic doctrine of shareholder capitalism, and moderate it so that if people are adding the most value then people will increasingly have to be seen as investors not as employees. Shareholders invest money and expect a return on their money and expect capital growth. People will be seen the same way. They will invest their human capital in the company, will expect a return on it, and expect growth of that capital. The notion that all the value is distributed to shareholders will have to change to accommodate this shift in the source of value creation.

What new skills set will be needed to cope with these changes?

Historically there has been a cognitive bias in management. When we talked about skills we talked about the knowledge—what do you know? People were largely seen as a seam of intellectual capital. Increasingly what we are seeing now is the importance of two other elements of human capital.

One is social capital—the ability of individuals to build and maintain long-term relationships with other people. Relationships based on trust and reciprocity. We've always known that relationships are important in business, but somehow we have not counted this factor in explicitly.

The other area is action-taking ability—call it emotional capital if you wish. In the vast majority of companies managers roughly know what they need to do. The trouble is that most don't do it. So the ability to act is another skill that is coming to the fore.

Are there new management questions we should be asking?

In the old world of strategy, structure, and systems, the questions were: What should our strategy be—in terms of market positioning, in terms of core competencies? What should our macro organization be—should we have a matrix, should we have a divisional structure, cross-functional teams? What should our systems be—should we have value-based management, should we get an EVA or whatever?

Increasingly we have to go much deeper into building the quality of management. How do we enhance the quality of management? How do we improve the quality of strategic thinking and quality of conversations around strategy inside the company? How do we improve the quality of analysis? How can we think of managerial action-taking? How can we enhance the capacity of individual and collective action-taking? These questions address issues at a much finer granularity.

How can companies best promote enterprises that are a) profitable and b) good places for people to work?

These two issues are totally symbiotic. Without profitability—success—it is very hard to create a good place to work; and if you don't have a good place to work you will not be able to attract, retain, and develop good people—which will make it very, very hard for you to be successful.

What can companies do to promote that? Visualize a company built around purpose, people, and process; a company that creates an overall sense of purpose—an umbrella that defines what you're going to do, what your vision of the future is, what your values are; a company that creates a sense of identity for each individual inside, that creates an organization built around entrepreneurship, integration, and continuous internal renewal, and that offers employees a contract that says: we cannot offer you a job for life, but if you work for this company we'll help you maximize your individual work potential. That's what is required for extraordinary performance.

Without profitability—success—it is very hard to create a good place to work; and if you don't have a good place to work you will not be able to attract, retain, and develop good people—which will make it very, very hard for you to be successful.

For More Information

See also:

- ☆ **Creating Value through People (pp. 121–22)**
- ☆ **How to Walk on the Leading Edge without Falling off the Cliff (pp. 229–30)**
- ☆ **Human Capital (pp. 115–16)**
- ☆ **Making the Workplace Flex, Not Break (pp. 31–32)**
- ☆ **SQ: Investing in Spiritual Capital (pp. 43–44)**

"It's important to pay people fairly, but managers also should heap on congratulations and feed people's souls."

(Kenneth Blanchard)

  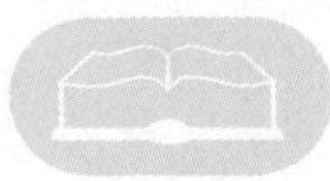    

The Critical Factors That Build or Break Teams *by Meredith Belbin*

Executive Summary

- "Team" and "teamwork" too easily become glib terms. Check their meaning.
- Find out what work really requires a team.
- Some people flourish in teams, others don't.
- Teams need to be empowered and enabled to work within boundaries to make things happen.
- Balanced teams need to be developed into mature teams.
- Effective teams need to understand both team roles and work roles.

Introduction

The problem about the word "teamwork" is that it has become too popular and has therefore lost its meaning. A person deemed good at teamwork is all too often someone who fits into a group and keeps out of trouble. Ideal behavior is often judged to mean complying with majority decisions and being willing to do anything that's required. Yet if everyone behaved like that, you'd have good reason to doubt that the team would function effectively. A flock of sheep may hang together well, but their only accomplishment is to eat grass.

For anyone interested in productive teamwork, it's often better to start with the work rather than the team. First of all, does the work call for a team? There are many types of repetitive operation, unskilled work, and specialist activities that are best performed by loners. Rounding up such people and making them members of a team risks producing a double disadvantage: their personal productivity falls and their privacy is invaded. Such social engineering may accord with the prevailing culture, but it's difficult to see any other benefit. Of course, it may be argued that isolated workers need a social dimension to their work. If this is true it implies that individuals engaged on such jobs have been wrongly placed. Introverts need work suitable for introverts, while extroverts need work appropriate to extroverts.

Designing Work to Fit the Person

It is important to ensure that people have the right fit in the organization, if not, difficulties may arise. The example below provides an illustration of this.

Introverts and extroverts look for different things in a job. Lighthouse-keeping and leading tour groups are contrasting jobs calling for different personalities. In the case of most jobs, of course, the relationship between work demands and personal characteristics is less pronounced. The reality is that most jobs entail some degree of individual work and responsibility along with a degree of liaison activity and some shared responsibilities. Such a mixture of demands not only makes it difficult to find candidates with the ideal profile, but there are intrinsic problems in setting up jobs encompassing such different constituents. Most employers make few attempts to define the boundaries, and even if they are laid down in advance, people who work in close association are inclined to move them at will. That's why colleagues are often cited as the biggest aggravation at work. When conflicts result, one party or another will be blamed as a poor team player.

The best starting point for establishing good teamwork is to begin with the principal demands of a broad work area. What are its structural characteristics? Do some responsibilities need to be shared? If so, which responsibilities, and with whom? Which responsibilities can be assigned to individuals and made subject to personal accountability? Which tasks are critical in their timing and mode of treatment and require a prescriptive approach based on best practice? These are all basic questions. They can either be asked and answered with the manager as the sole decision maker, or such decision making can be carried out in consultation with others. Either way, there's a risk that a busy manager will cut corners and make hasty decisions that are out of touch with operational realities. That's why it is often better to assign a group of workers to address these basic questions and seek to find answers. Those at the sharp end will be most familiar with the demands and pressures of the work. They are often better placed to decide how work should be shared out.

Mini-case

I was engaged on a project to facilitate the introduction of a cargo-handling computer system at a large airport. The perceived problem was that the workers whose jobs were to be converted were both computer-illiterate and highly unionized. Devising a suitable form of training proved a challenge, but once this had been accomplished the introduction went without a hitch. The main problem arose in the way in which the design engineers had devised the work itself. The physical arrangement required these sociable workers to sit in isolation at consoles. They soon tired of it and chose instead to bypass the information system by riding on the mechanical handling equipment in order to conduct personal inspections of the cargo bays. Such bravado may have been exhilarating, but it was also dangerous practice.

Clearly, it is not only vitally important to understand the nature of the work being undertaken, but also the skills, experience and approach of those doing the work. Taking account of people's strengths and motivations can certainly help to build or break teams.

Teams Need to Be Given Scope

The team approach for organizing work depends on empowerment; it relies on trust, the confidence that a manager places in the qualities and caliber of the work force. It also depends on how well members of a group have developed an understanding of each other's strengths and weaknesses. That's why training in teamwork is so important and why it helps to understand the language of team roles. People make different contributions to teams, and it's important that every team plays to the best strengths of its individual players. Diversity in the range of available team roles lays the foundation for a balanced team. But diversity does not automatically produce

"Dividing enemy forces to weaken them is clever, but dividing one's own team is a grave sin against the business."

(Henri Fayol)

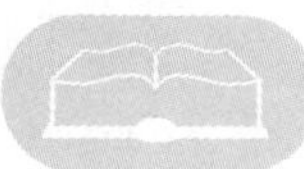

harmony or balance. It can just as well produce conflict as different individuals strive to do their own thing. This is where the manager becomes so important, in creating the vision and the ethos. The role of the manager is to turn a potentially balanced team into a mature team.

Mature teams have the capacity to make local decisions in distributing the overall workload and its various elements appropriately. This is impossible unless the manager has set the stage, believes in empowerment, and knows how to put it into effect. The key to success lies in managing the interface between team roles and work roles. The manager has to understand this before the team can be expected to respond with appropriate action. Managers sometimes fear that workers will lack the will to take tough decisions, for example, when one person is not up to a particular aspect of the job. The surprise is often that workers prove more intolerant of a slacker or a poor performer than the manager. The group builds up a body of opinion that's a powerful force in its own right. Such a force can operate against the interests of management, but it can equally well reinforce the policies and strategies that management favors. The more autocratic the management, the greater the likelihood that the group will combine to become a counterforce. The greater the level of empowerment, the more likely will be the team's sense of ownership and pride, and the greater its commitment to the responsibilities undertaken. Without empowerment balanced groups cannot be developed into mature teams.

Rewarding Teams Appropriately

All teams need to be assessed. The question is, how should it be done so that it is positive and constructive? One way is to set objectives for teams and judge how well these have been met. Such a view prevails in the top-down school of management and is given added impetus by performance-related bonuses. The argument put forward is that teams need fixed incentives to perform well, an assumption linked with the converse view that without such an incentive the team will not perform satisfactorily. This mechanistic view of human motivation is mistaken and is likely to backfire. Success in meeting given criteria depends partly on circumstances and contingencies. Success may not be commensurate with effort or skill. Objectives may be too easy to reach or too difficult. In the end, people may focus more on the shortcomings of the incentive than on the sense and purpose of their work. Retrospective awards for teams performing well are better received than prospective rewards for teams given set targets.

Making It Happen

- Start with the work, not the team. Ask first whether the work calls for a team at all.
- If a team is required, determine which responsibilities need to be shared and by whom.
- Decide which remaining responsibilities can be assigned to individuals, and make them subject to personal accountability.
- Use training in teamwork and team roles to ensure that every team plays to the best strengths of its individual players.
- Understand the team's strengths, weaknesses, and sense of "self-awareness" to improve.
- Maximize empowerment to develop ownership, pride, and maximum commitment to the team's responsibilities.
- Delegate work efficiently, and enable people to succeed.
- Understand what motivates the team, providing impetus and momentum.
- Give retrospective rewards for teams performing well rather than incentive rewards linked to set targets.

Conclusion

In recent years we have developed an approach to work that hinges on understanding and mastering two languages: the language of contributors to team effort—team roles—and the language of the work demands themselves—work roles. Essentially this approach offers a framework for deciding who does what. Unless people decide for themselves, or at least share in that decision making, there will be no commitment to the work itself.

For More Information

Books:

Belbin, R. Meredith. *The Coming Shape of Organization.* Woburn, MA: Butterworth-Heinemann, 1998.

Katzenbach, J. R., and D. K. Smith. *The Wisdom of Teams: Creating the High-performance Organization.* New York: HarperBusiness, 1994.

Film:

To facilitate an understanding of these issues, Belbin Associates have made three films in association with Video Arts: *Building the Perfect Team* (1991), *Selecting the Perfect Team* (1993), and *Does the Team Work?* (1999).

See also:

☆ **Keeping Control in Nonhierarchical Organizations (pp. 198–99)**

Meredith Belbin (pp. 966–67)

"One man can be a crucial ingredient on a team, but one man cannot make a team."

(Kareem Abdul-Jabbar)

GROUNDHOG MANAGEMENT *by Robert Fritz*

EXECUTIVE SUMMARY

- The most influential factor in organizational performance, both for individuals within the organization and the organization as a whole, is the underlying structure.
- Organizations typically exhibit either *oscillating* or *advancing* behaviors. In organizations that oscillate, success is eventually neutralized and reversed. In advancing structures, organizations build on previous successes; both success and failure evoke learning that translates into greater competence and effectiveness.
- We can redesign an organization's underlying structure so that it can move from oscillating to advancing.

INTRODUCTION

In the 1938 movie, *The Dawn Patrol*, Errol Flynn played an easy-going First World War pilot who, with his fun-loving buddy David Niven, flew dangerous missions during the day and caroused in town at night. He had another sport too: driving his serious squadron leader, Basil Rathbone, crazy. Ultimately, Rathbone took revenge, for he so hated the Errol Flynn character that he named him the new squadron leader when Rathbone was transferred. Soon, Flynn began to act as seriously as did Rathbone.

Now here's a movie that understands a common experience—one that all managers have encountered on occasion—*that a position sometimes seems to dictate the behavior of the people who fill it more than the people themselves do.* No matter the background, a new supervisor suddenly acts surprisingly like his or her predecessor. Here is the common pattern: A person is not working well; management does everything to help improve performance, but to no avail. Finally, the person is replaced. Six months later, the replacement is performing exactly like his or her predecessor.

THE IMPLICATION

This pattern contradicts our most cherished ideas about human motivations. How do we explain how such people act? Is it psychology, DNA, cultural background, education, life experiences, values, aspirations, talents, or abilities? Their astrology, numerology, biorhythms, age, gender, generation? We test the potential and predisposition of employees before we hire them and track their performance; yet, when it comes to replacements, though they are different in generation, gender, genetic code, temperament, experience, maturity, life situation, or work history, the pattern prevails.

The implication is that *no matter a person's individual traits, the architecture of the position is more causal that any of those traits.* This is not always the case. We can see that a change of individual can sometimes make a profound difference in performance. But we can learn something useful by thinking about how often good people and good professionals conform to "positional" behavior.

ELEMENTS OF PERFORMANCE

Performance has two dimensions. One is *execution,* and that's where talent, experience, know-how, and competence come into play. The other dimension is *design,* how organizational parts are put together. Since design and execution are independent, here are all the combinations that exist:

Good Design? Good Execution
Good Design? Bad Execution
Bad Design? Good Execution
Bad Design? Bad Execution

Often our bias is that weak performance is a matter of bad execution. Such bias comes from thinking we *can* control execution, and we are not used to thinking like architects or composers. So often we have seen what is obviously a very stupid policy or directive given to members of an organization which they have no possibility of achieving. "Increase production and reduce capacity" is the war cry of downsizing. "How can they do it?", one is prone to ask. "They will become more efficient and innovative," comes the answer, barely able to be said with a straight face. *Yeah, right.* And if you believe that I've got some land. . .

ORGANIZATIONAL PATTERNS

Just as individuals put into the same position can perform identically, so can entire organizations. Here, there are also two major patterns: *oscillation* and *advancement.* In an oscillating structure, the organization first moves in one direction but later moves in the opposite direction. It builds up capacity, then downsizes, then builds up capacity again. It decentralizes decision making, centralizes it again, but later decentralizes. The pattern is clear, but organizations often have trouble seeing it. When major change efforts are tried, the change (albeit successful elsewhere) is rejected. In oscillating organizations, success seldom succeeds. Come a reversal and success is soon neutralized—heroes and heroines become failures and villains.

An advancing organizational pattern is one in which each success creates a platform for future success. Every failure becomes a building block for learning and developing. As people learn, they become better performers: more capable, more team players, more creative, and more valuable.

CAN ORGANIZATIONS CHANGE?

When I began to work in organizations I asked why some oscillate and why some advance, and whether we could help an oscillating organization shift to an advancing one. The happy answer is, yes, organizations can actually change their fundamental pattern of behavior. But the type of change that is required is not on the same level as dictating new prescriptions for behavior or attempting to impose new systems on faulty structures.

For lasting change, we need to change the underlying structure. An oscillating structure contains critical conflicts of interests. As one interest is served, a competing interest is denied—creating a state of non-equilibrium which produces a shift, just as a rocking chair shifts from forward to backward movement. Typically organizations are fragmented and self-organize into competing interests often competing for the same resource base. If traditional management leads to fragmentation, which leads to self-organizing systems of conflict, then how do we change this condition?

Organizations are much like musical compositions, whether you think of them as Beethoven symphonies or works by Duke Ellington. Senior management has often not properly "composed" the organization, and people do not know what their parts are or how their parts fit with the other parts and with the whole. In fact, a telltale sign of bad management is that departments within the same organization are competing for the same resource base. Another sign is that there is no formal relationship and coordination between sales goals and capacity limitations in production. Another telltale sign

"The organization exists to restrict and channel the range of individual actions and behaviors into a predictable and knowable routine."

(Theodore Levitt)

  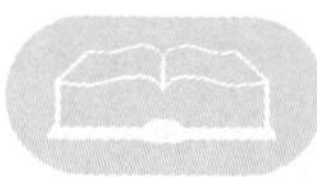  

is across-the-board percentage downsizing, an admission that management doesn't know how much its capacity is costing and doesn't know whether the real problem is to try to grow revenues or to blindly cut costs.

The enemy here is not "command and control" as it's often talked about; the enemy is *mindless* in the form of uncoordinated directives that are pushed down an organization's throat. They are often arbitrary rather than strategic, contradictory rather than reinforcing, and unfocused rather than focused. Bad design structure creates oscillation, with failure quickly chasing any short-term successes.

Redesigning the Organization

Organizations can be restructured from oscillation to advancement by a combination of clarity, design elegance, and discipline. Just as in writing music, the major theme is the purpose of the organization as expressed through business strategy which drives the management strategy which drives the various local-departmental strategies. And the local strategies support the management strategy which supports the business strategy which, in turn, supports the purpose.

Some talk about organizations as if they are *so* complex that they defy a compositional approach. But such enterprises only seem complex when you don't know how to design the parts, and then execute the performance. If I had to fix my auto's engine, it would seem complex; fortunately, there are mechanics in the world.

Making It Happen ▸▸

Over 20 years ago I created the model called *structural tension* (or as my friend and colleague Peter Senge liked to call it in his book *The Fifth Discipline*, "creative tension"). I was doing a lot of painting at the time, and I used the artistic process as the archetypal form of the creative process. How does a painter create a painting—and could managers use the same process? *Yes!* Structural tension is formed by the difference or contrast between the vision that we have—our goals—and the current situation that exists (current reality). A painter has a vision of the finished painting, but he or she must also be aware of the current state of the painting. The relationship between the desired state (the vision) and the actual state (current reality) is a structural dynamic formed by the tension between these two elements.

Tension *seeks* resolution, and the painter is managing structural tension throughout the painting process. He or she has the vision of the end result in mind, while also having a clear and accurate understanding of the current state of the painting. The painter takes action to change the current state so that eventually it conforms to the vision. At this point, the tension is resolved, and the actual state and the desired state for the painting are the same. When a painter signs the painting, he or she is saying, "This painting matches my vision."

Structural tension is not the same as psychological tension or stress. Instead, we can feel the dynamic energy that comes from the contrast between our desired state and the actual state. We translate that energy into actions, which become well motivated and have a sense of direction.

The way we can "compose" the organization is to establish "master structural tension charts" that include:

1. the major goals;
2. current reality relevant to those goals;
3. action steps that need to be taken to accomplish the goals;
4. the due dates of each action step, and;
5. the person who is accountable for accomplishing that action.

This is a simple "composition" to construct and understand. *But it is not simplistic.* It is elegant. The actions can be developed and managed, and the broad design can then be deployed throughout the organization.

In this system, we can understand the parts within the context of the whole. Details are developed by telescoping the charts. There is a high level of organizational control without having to be controlling or micro-managing. That's the beauty of it. People know what they need to do, how it fits within the broader frame, when it needs to be done, and why. They also begin to get into the habit of thinking in terms of relationships rather than fragments.

Mini-Case

Observing Design and Execution

Dell Computer Corporation's success is based on their very clear sense of business strategy, which generates all of their managerial decisions. They have a strict focus on minimal finished inventory, direct sales without any middlemen. This has led them to be one of the most successful companies worldwide. They have changed the face of the PC industry.

Gateway Inc. lost its once solid brand position when it expanded into the business computing market where it was not competitive. They lost focus on the home and family market, and their brand identity drifted.

Citicorp/Citibank has had a long history of understanding the relationship between a technological vision and current market trends. This understanding has led them to invest over $1.75 billion which has enabled them to become the largest integrated financial service company in the world.

Conclusion

Structure will lead to oscillation or advancement. Any change effort in an organization structured to oscillate will be neutralized. To accomplish change, the organization must first redesign itself to become an advancing structure. The parts must fit together, rather than work against each other.

For More Information

Books:

Mintzberg, Henry. *The Rise and Fall of Strategic Planning*. Upper Saddle River: Prentice Hall, 1994.

Senge, Peter, Art Kleiner, and Bryan Smith. *The Dance of Change*. New York: Doubleday, 1999.

Web Site:

www.solonline.org/connections: this is the Society for Organizational Learning's site. SoL is an international learning community dedicated to building knowledge about fundamental institutional change.

See also:

☆ **Human Capital (pp. 115–16)**
☆ **Keeping Control in Nonhierarchical Organizations (pp. 198–99)**
☆ **Viewpoint: Tom Petzinger (pp. 163–64)**
☆ **Viewpoint: Patty Seybold (pp. 67–68)**
Henri Fayol (pp. 986–87)
Alfred P. Sloan, Jr. (pp. 1140–41)

"Participative organizations tend to develop emotionally and socially mature persons capable of effective interaction, initiative, and leadership." (Rensis Likert)

  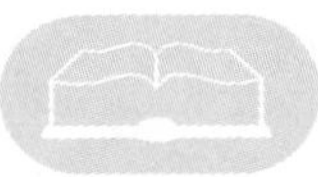    

Retaining Employees

by Sharon Jordan-Evans and Beverly Kaye

EXECUTIVE SUMMARY

- Regardless of whether the economy is booming, employee retention remains a major concern across all industries and countries.
- The keys to retaining talent are well researched. Most of them lie within the manager's control.
- Managers aren't using these keys. They need coaching, some focused accountability, and training.
- The emerging work force has different attitudes and expectations from the last generation. With the growth of self-reliance individuals are in charge of their own careers. Savvy leaders had better understand their new-millennium workers and shift the way they manage and mentor these golden assets.

Introduction

A decade ago the leaders of organizations seldom talked about the business issue that now reportedly keeps them awake at night: the challenge of attracting and retaining talent.

Research reveals that while pay and benefits matter, you can't count on money to retain talented people who have employment options. Key motivators include challenging and stimulating work, a chance to learn and grow, a good boss, and great people to work with. Managers can influence these major retention factors. The problem is that many managers don't believe they have the power to hang on to their best and brightest. Yet retention is hot for good reason:

- Talent is the only differentiator. It separates you from your competitors and ensures your company's place in the future. While capital is abundant and technology is easy to access, brainpower becomes the major asset for most businesses.
- The global talent shortage is expected to last for at least the next 15 years. In the United States there will be an estimated shortage of 10 million workers by 2006, and 40 million by 2015 (assuming 2% economic growth and current retirement conditions). In IT demand will outstrip supply by 20% through 2005. Fertility is now below replacement level in 61 countries.
- Good employees don't even have to leave their desks to find new jobs. The most popular log-on time for popular job-search sites like Monster.com is between 9 and 5. Headhunters and corporate recruiters practice a multifaceted science complete with firewall-breaking strategies to identify and steal top talent.
- Experts agree that replacing a talented employee costs at least two-and-a-half times his or her annual salary. The hard costs include search firms and sign-on bonuses. Softer opportunity costs include lost customers, contracts, or business. Replacing platinum employees (those with specialized professional skills) will cost you around four to five times their annual salary.
- You've seen talent loss following major organizational change or downsizing and know that you're at risk. Remember those talented employees who left 6 to 12 months after your last downsizing? They were overworked, demoralized, and pessimistic about the organization's future. If you're facing major change, you'd best double your retention efforts.

Techniques for Retaining Employees

Understand What Motivates People

We've asked over 10,000 people why they stayed in an organization for "a while." Here are the top five responses:

- exciting, challenging work
- career growth, learning, and development
- great people
- fair pay and benefits
- good boss

These answers are no surprise. For more than 50 years researchers have studied the factors that satisfy, motivate, or engage their talented workers, and their findings match ours. Abraham Maslow identified basic survival needs and found that, once those needs are met, people focus on social needs and self-actualizing work. Frederick Herzberg identified "hygiene factors" like decent work environment, pay, and benefits as potential dissatisfiers when they're inadequate, but these are not necessarily motivators.

Keep the Motivational Import of Remuneration in Perspective

If employees aren't challenged or growing, or if they don't get along well with the boss, their paycheck probably won't keep them for long. Even lucrative stock options (golden handcuffs) are being bought out today (golden hellos) by companies wanting to steal talent.

Know Where the Buck Stops

Nine out of ten managers will say that what keeps people is money. Some believe it; others hope it will absolve them of responsibility. They can then point the finger at senior management, human-resources professionals, or the compensation committee. Those players all have a role in retaining talent, but experts agree that the manager is central to attracting and retaining talent. How does a manager begin to do that?

First, you need to find out what individuals on your team really want. Don't guess, and don't assume they all want the same thing (like pay or promotion). Try this. Tell all your key employees, one at a time, how critical they are to you. Maybe you've told them before. If so, tell them again, "You matter so much to me and to this team. I can't imagine losing you. So, what will keep you here, and what might entice you away? What things do you want/hope for/need to stick around for a while?" You may not have opened that conversation for fear they'll ask for something you can't deliver.

So how will you respond if your top guy says he wants a 20% increase and you don't have the power to give it to him right now? Too many managers respond with something that shuts down the dialog and makes your key employee feel diminished. Instead try, "You're worth that and more to me. I'll have to think about how and when I can satisfy your request. Maybe you can help me figure out how to position it with senior management. Meanwhile, *what else*

"For us the core of management is the art of mobilizing and putting together the intellectual resources of all employees in the firm."
(Konosuke Matsushita)

  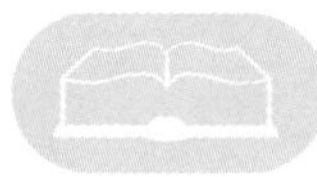    

matters to you?" Usually there will be at least one thing he wants that you can give.

Select the Right People and Support Their Growth

- Get the right people in the door in the first place and don't resort to desperation hiring. Remember that today's hiring mistake is tomorrow's problem.
- Enrich and enliven their work. When the thrill is gone, so are they.
- Allow employees to grow, or they'll find an employer that will. Think about how you can develop your workers' talents. Remember to ask individuals what and how they want to learn. Mentor them, and they're twice as likely to stay. Encourage, nurture, and teach them how to be successful in your organization. Link them to mentors, coaches, leaders, or colleagues.
- Identify options other than promotion or "up." Help your key employees uncover multiple options, including lateral moves, special projects, or growing while in place.

Develop a Management Style That Inspires Loyalty

- Loyalty is still possible but it is increasingly complex. New-millennium employees can be committed to the team, the project, the boss, the mission, and, yes, even to the company—that provides just what they want and need.
- Show respect in many ways. Treat people fairly "not identically" and trust them; they'll prove to be trustworthy. Create a culture of inclusion, valuing different experiences, and attitudes. Guard against negative behaviors that might turn off or turn away your talent.
- Provide feedback. Talented people want to know how they're doing and how you think they could improve and grow. Give feedback clearly, truthfully, and respectfully; in return get feedback from them about your own strengths and opportunities.
- Reward creatively. Use the universal reward: praise. Use it often and authentically with every one of your talented people. Then individualize rewards. Don't guess what people want—ask!

Create a Work Environment That People Love, Enjoy and Respond To

- Many busy, high-stress organizations admit they've become a fun-free zone. Ironically, fun may be just what they need to ease the pressure and stress. It's definitely what they need if they are to retain their fun-loving employees. Find ways to make the workplace enjoyable.
- Information is power. Give it as freely, openly, and often as you can.
- Give people space. Provide freedom to get the job done in ways that work best for them. Trust them, negotiate with them, and open your mind to really hear their requests and brainstorm creative solutions.
- Encourage people to have a life outside work. You'll get employees who show up refreshed and ready to work.
- Uncover and discover new opportunities inside your organization so employees don't have to seek them outside.

Mini-cases

Senior leaders at *Synopsys* are expected to spend 30% of their time on engaging and retaining talent.

At *Fleet* bank 1,000 managers have received retention training. They have significantly reduced their turnover rate.

The credit-card company *First USA* reduced staff turnover in its call centers with career-development conversations between managers and employees.

IT executives at *AT&T Network Systems* agreed to visit more sites, expanded their recognition services, and increased the amount of training employees are encouraged to take in response to feedback from their IT staff.

BryanLGH Medical Center of Nebraska involves managers and employees from all functions in specific retention assignments that apply across its organization.

The retailer *Macy's West* has focused on involvement, recognition, and celebration. All managers are held accountable for retention.

Making It Happen ▸▸

- Recognize the importance of retention. Understand how people feel now and what action is needed before it is too late.
- Remember: it's more than pay.
- Customize retention strategies to the needs and circumstances of each individual.
- Be accountable: it's no good blaming someone else; if you want the person to stay, then you need to act to retain them.
- Provide training, coaching, and feedback for the managers you count on.

Conclusion

Your success depends on keeping your best people. The keys to retaining talent are known, but are unfortunately seldom practiced. If you manage others, you have phenomenal influence over their decisions to stay or go. If you have managers reporting to you, they may need help in becoming retention-focused, retention-savvy leaders. Be clear about what keeps people. Customize your retention strategies to individual needs and wants—and pass the message and method on to anyone who manages others in your organization. The success or failure of many organizations is increasingly determined by this single issue.

For More Information

Books:

Buckingham, Marcus, and Curt Coffman. *First, Break All the Rules: What the World's Greatest Managers Do Differently*. New York: Simon & Schuster, 1999.

Catlette, Bill, and Richard Hadden. *Contented Cows Give Better Milk: The Plain Truth About Employee Relations and the Bottom Line*. Germantown, TN: Saltillo Press, 2000.

Gubman, Edward L. *The Talent Solution: Aligning Strategy and People to Achieve Extraordinary Results*. New York: McGraw-Hill Professional, 1998.

Harris, Jim, and Joan Brannick. *Finding & Keeping Great Employees*. New York: AMACOM, 1999.

See also:

☆ **Creating Fun in the Workplace (pp. 37–38)**
☆ **Finding and Keeping the Best Talent in the World (pp. 119–20)**
☆ **Finding and Keeping Top Talent (pp. 33–34)**
☆ **Fringe Benefits (pp. 21–22)**
☆ **Return on Talent (pp. 109–10)**
☆ **Viewpoint: Christopher Bartlett (pp. 45–46)**
☆ **Viewpoint: Jim Kouzes (pp. 309–11)**
✔ **Freelancing: Setting Up As a Free Agent (pp. 814–15)**

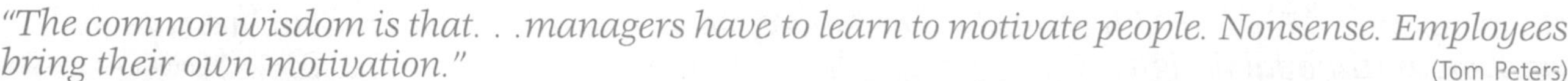
"The common wisdom is that. . .managers have to learn to motivate people. Nonsense. Employees bring their own motivation."
(Tom Peters)

KEEPING CONTROL IN NONHIERARCHICAL ORGANIZATIONS *by Karin Klenke*

EXECUTIVE SUMMARY

- The archetypal formalistic bureaucracy is increasingly outdated. Flatter organizations are now the norm.
- New organizational structures are constantly emerging that represent the antithesis of the traditional hierarchical form of organization.
- 21st-century organizations must be in tune with the business environment and take on a multitude of shapes, from entrepreneurial firms with no fat to elephants of the old economy with thick layers of excess fat.
- Keeping organizations controlled and focused is essential for an integrated, motivated, and effective organization.

INTRODUCTION

Nonhierarchical organizations have many advantages over their conventional, stratified counterparts. For example, experience and expertise are often shared; creativity and new ideas are fostered, tested and discussed. The organization is more cohesive; empowerment is a key feature; and it can be highly supportive.

However, there are several potential pitfalls. "Group think" or the herd mentality can prevail; implementing decisions can be difficult; and exercising control and bringing focus can be a significant challenge.

MANAGING IN HIERARCHICAL ORGANIZATIONS

1. UNDERSTAND THE VALUE OF FLATTER ORGANIZATIONS

Control is achieved through a number of classical management principles, including division of *labor*, *formalization* (the extent to which work rules are specified, written, and enforced), and *centralization* (the decision-making authority in the hierarchy of the organization). Centralization for the purpose of tight control provides stability, continuity, and predictable career paths and reward systems. In addition, each manager has a clear, unambiguous span of control (the number of employees they can effectively supervise), which creates a set of obligations and role differentiation, with the manager as the brain and the worker the hand. Control is reinforced by a dictatorial top-down, command-and-control leadership style.

The sheer size of the hierarchies in large traditional organizations, coupled with top management's distance from the market, makes this type of structure unresponsive. Many of the reasons for the failures of old-economy leaders in the steel, automotive, and consumer-electronics industries can be directly traced to the structure of fat organizations. Similarly, much of the renaissance of companies such as Xerox, Ford, and Hewlett-Packard can be attributed to throwing off the shackles of vertical integration.

In the new economy speed is of the essence and the time frame for decision making has been dramatically reduced. Hence, bureaucratic hierarchies are being deconstructed. What will tomorrow's organizations look like? What radical surgery may be necessary to transform the vertically integrated structures of the industrial paradigm into designs of the future? How can organizations learn today the skills they need for tomorrow? Answers to some of these questions are found in flat, or nonhierarchical, organizations.

2. BUILDING NONHIERARCHICAL ORGANIZATIONS

Twenty-first-century organizations tend to adopt the flatter structures enabled by more information going online. Instead of a managerial hierarchy with seven to ten or more layers of fat, flat organizations have three or four levels. Flat organizations are a cross between a spider's web (interconnected networks) and a leaping frog able to jump into innovations, reinvention, and renewal.

Flat organizations have been called boundaryless, networked, lattice, ameba, and virtual organizations or global heterarchies (the opposite of hierarchies). They are structured around self-directed or self-managed, multidisciplinary, cross-functional work teams in which power flows from expertise, not position. In flat organizations, a decentralized approach to management is emphasized, as is high employee involvement in decision making. Flat organizations are structured around customers, teams, problems and opportunities, adaptiveness, horizontal connections, and networking. They decentralize authority, share information, diffuse and distribute competency, and use reward systems that are primarily team-based. Their strategies consistently emphasize growth, innovation, product customization, and technological leverage, rather than cost containment and operating efficiency.

3. EXPLOIT THE BENEFITS OF NETWORKED ORGANIZATIONS

Worldwide networking within and across organizations, linking companies, suppliers, customers, designers, and sometimes even competitors, is common in building collaborative advantage and global connectivity. Although by definition competitors are fighting over the same bone, your competitors are probably the only people who know as much about your business as you do. Take Pomarfin, a Finnish shoe manufacturer that markets the Ten Toes brand. The linked company consists of five competitors that share their hidden knowledge in a way that strengthens their ability to compete. Such partnerships and strategic alliances blur traditional hierarchies.

The joint ventures and partnerships established through interorganizational networks are less formal, nonhierarchical, less permanent, and more opportunistic, since the companies within a network band together to meet a specific market opportunity. AOL Time Warner, Wal-Mart, and Procter & Gamble, and Disney's Celebration City have created conglomerates with fluid boundaries between the participating organizations for the purpose of sharing resources (financial, intellectual, and human) or inventing new businesses.

4. DEVOLVE RESPONSIBILITY AND SET PARAMETERS FOR ACTION

Control in flat organizations lies in the mutual agreements that establish the parameters of discretion and performance expectations. Control is dispersed throughout the organization, with emphasis on self-control and problem solving. People own their work—they are self-managing,

"In companies whose wealth is intellectual capital, networks, rather than hierarchies, are the right organizational design."

(Thomas A. Stewart)

self-organizing, self-designing. They take personal responsibility for work outcomes, continuously monitor their own performance, seek corrective action when necessary, and take the initiative to help others improve their performance. They also design and control their careers by defining the social contract with the organization, as opposed to having the organization determine individual career paths and progress. In short, in nonhierarchical organizations the main incentive of work is work itself.

Leadership in flat organizations constantly espouses the values of collaboration. It is shared, lateral (as opposed to top-down), and dispersed among organization members. It is a reciprocal investment process between leaders and collaborators. Through the processes of leadership making and team making, individual employees are integrated into cohesive adaptive units at the work level and larger competence networks at organization level. People take responsibility for the development of their leadership and collaborative skills, facilitate the leadership of others, and cultivate leadership processes, functions, and roles that maximize team performance. Leaders as designers, coaches, collaborators, and catalysts influence the workflow through coalition building and value consensus. In flat organizations, the larger-than-life, omnipotent individual leader is often replaced by executive teams, which form a key mechanism for managing the organization of the future.

5. Be Careful, Cautious, and Realistic When Building the Organization

Managers must design effective organizations and create superstructures within which the company's work takes place. In today's flatter companies trust is the glue that holds organizations together. Trust is important, because decentralized discretion implies that managers can no longer maintain the level of control they have been accustomed to in the past. When management does not control, but only monitors, it needs the trust of the workers, especially when they are geographically dispersed without face-to-face contact.

In both fat and flat organizations managers, as designers, must understand their industries' dominant technologies, economic prospects, and degree of organizational uncertainty. They must be capable of navigating in the fog, as Hewlett-Packard C.E.O. Carly Fiorina put it, in order to make effective choices about organizational design. Effective organizational structures are aimed at enhancing and maximizing the firm's capacity for innovation and change. Although the Internet is provoking companies to dynamically restructure their infrastructures, don't expect technology alone to radically change organizations and managerial practice.

Put simply, there's no such thing as a one-size-fits-all organizational design. Organizations must instead be in tune with their environments. A hierarchical organization will not work in a creative, rapidly changing e-commerce environment, although it may work in a standard business-as-usual environment. Similarly, large hierarchical organizations can be managed as if they were small, while mature conglomerates like General Electric can grow like startups. Organizational structures must change to facilitate growth.

Mini-cases

In the 1990s *General Motors* (GM), the world's largest automobile manufacturer, laid off 74,000 workers, closed 21 plants, and suffered from a staff bureaucracy that was in many places redundant. GM came to symbolize the bloated inefficiency of a contemporary hierarchical organization.

Before restructuring, *Motorola* had 12 layers of management. Even when the company decided to cut some of the fat by reducing the levels of management, top management was concerned with how such efforts would affect the organization's core values such as protecting employees who had served the company well in the past.

Saturn plants consist of semiautonomous teams of between 6 and 15 people, each of which is responsible for every aspect of its area. Showrooms guarantee no-pressure sales and eliminate haggling.

Edward Jones financial services has an organizational structure that has been called a confederation of highly autonomous entrepreneurial units bound together by a highly centralized core of values and services. The company is a network of thousands of brokers, each of whom works from a wired office.

Making It Happen ▸▸

Learn everything there is to learn about organizational forms; as organizational designers managers must know their design options and the full range of probable and possible structures, from the centrally controlled hierarchy to a totally flat organization with no control at all.

- Build strategic relationships and nurture them through collaborative efforts to compete in global markets.
- Learn the basic skills of collaboration—in your family, team, within and across organizations, and in your community.
- Develop an innovation culture.
- Don't let the old dinosaur eat you up.

Conclusion

Even the aging dinosaurs have to change and adjust to the rugged landscape of the global economy. Businesses can do so by decentralizing and splitting into smaller and smaller configurations and more adaptable units. Organizations of the future must innovate, therefore they must take risks. One of those risks is reinventing themselves when necessary. Leaders and managers must be able to create organizational environments that encourage out-of-the-box and contrarian thinking, cultural dexterity, knowledge sharing, and diffusion of ideas.

For More Information

Books:

Duck, Jeanie Daniel. *The Change Monster: The Human Forces That Fuel or Foil Corporate Transformation and Change*. New York: Crown, 2001.

Myers, David G., and Martin E. Marty. *The American Paradox: Spiritual Hunger in an Age of Plenty*. New Haven, CT: Yale University Press, 2001.

Web Sites:

www.fastcompany.com: a monthly e-zine with timely articles on a wide range of organizational phenomena.

www.workteams.unt.edu: this site covers education and research in all areas of collaborative systems.

See also:

☆ **The Critical Factors That Build or Break Teams (pp. 192–93)**
☆ **Groundhog Management (pp. 194–95)**
☆ **Project Management (pp. 165–66)**
☆ **Viewpoint: Henry Mintzberg (pp. 241–42)**
☆ **Viewpoint: Tom Petzinger (pp. 163–64)**

"Finding the right balance of hierarchical looseness versus control is a central task of leadership in the boundaryless organization."

(Ron Ashkenas)

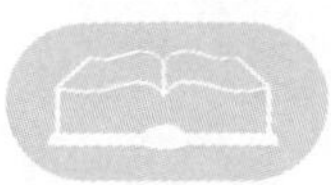

MANAGING IN A 24/7 ORGANIZATION
by Thomas M. Koulopoulos

EXECUTIVE SUMMARY

- Ubiquitous and portable computing, global operations, and increased competitive pressure have resulted in an around-the-clock mandate for nearly every industry.
- Companies will need to invest heavily in tools that ease the burden of connectivity by helping employees, customers, and partners to control, manage, and personalize their interactions.
- New approaches such as personalization, workflow, e-learning, and knowledge management will help us to cope with the 24/7 workplace.

INTRODUCTION

For better or worse, our work lives and our personal lives are entwined through electronic connections. Many employers expect—or even mandate—that their employees' work will be boundaryless. It's not unheard of for employment contracts to stipulate that certain employees responsible for critical business processes, projects, or clients be available around the clock through laptop, PDA, cellphone, and pager.

But it's not only a technology problem. The flattening of organizations and the personalization of desktop computing have resulted in a thinning of administrative support infrastructure, with 10 million fewer secretaries since 1989 in the U.S. workforce alone. We are being forced to become our own administrators and support staff. Like the fighter pilot whose airplane can exceed the G-force limits of physical endurance, we need to understand our limits and build enterprises that acknowledge them.

Yet how can any enterprise competing in a free market escape the gravity of 24/7? There's no substitute for time. If your competitors are open on Sundays, if their support lines are answered in the early hours of the morning, if their R & D works around the clock, you have little option but to follow suit. We may have little choice in the matter, as Dylan Thomas wrote, "Do not go gentle into that good night".

THRASHING—TOWARD TERMINAL VELOCITY

The acceleration of business cycles, increased attention to customer service as a competitive differentiator, and instant responsiveness to market volatility are all given as the upside of a 24/7 economy. What's not as often addressed is the very real human toll that 24/7 can exact from workers and consumers. But debating the merits of 24/7 does little to hasten or allay it. The question now is how to cope with what increasingly appears to be the *terminal velocity* of business.

The most profound effect of 24/7 has been the thrashing that results from our inability to manage and neatly compartmentalize the sheer quantity of information and resources to which we suddenly have instant and unabated access. Each of us is constantly juggling a multiplicity of priorities and tasks across what used to be solid boundaries. The result is a constant bouncing from project to project, application to application, information source to information source—in short, thrashing. The price of thrashing is high. It devours our attention, derails our focus, and compromises our creativity, by slicing our lives thinner and thinner.

Psychologists have long known that as the noise factor around us increases, our filtering mechanisms also increase. It's what scientists refer to as signal-to-noise ratios. As the background noise of our world increases, we need to become better at identifying relatively weaker and weaker signals. Yet filtering without accompanying focus can be a dangerous proposition—the equivalent of blinkers on an angry horse.

Compounding this volume and velocity of information are increasingly shorter windows in which to make decisions. We are weaving the web of our lives ever tighter by dedicating smaller and smaller intervals of attention to each task and responsibility. It's what I call the "X effect": the volume of opportunity increases and the time to act on each individual opportunity decreases proportionately.

Most of us walk through life tagged like wildlife with our pagers, PDAs, and cellphones latched to our belts—not just connected, but tethered. And this phenomenon is even more pronounced in Europe and Asia, where wireless technology is far more advanced and accepted than it is in North America, partly because the value of community is far better understood in these older cultures.

From an organizational standpoint the same principle seems to apply. Value chains are becoming far more intertwined, creating a level of complexity that makes discerning critical events and actions nearly impossible. It's as though we just built a superhighway and then put traffic lights at every on/off ramp.

The situation is not dissimilar from the early days of most new technologies. During its early years the automobile imposed a heavy burden on its owners by requiring that they spend as much as half of their time on maintenance. Keeping a car on the road meant a commitment far greater than just learning to drive. Although an automobile could get you to your destination faster than horse and buggy, the aggravation of getting there was rarely worth it. The image of a driver off the road in a ditch kicking his rims while the buggy driver disdainfully passes by is a familiar caricature. Although laughable in retrospect, it's not that far removed from the mixed feelings many workers have when it comes to the use of remote laptops, PDAs, and other devices intended to make work faster, but in the end just seeming to add more frustration to their lives.

MINI-CASE

Based on data from the U.S. Federal Communications Commission (FCC), over the past two decades telephone use has increased nearly tenfold, while simultaneously the length of a phone call has shrunk by nearly 30%! It could well be claimed that attention management, the exercise of capturing "mind share" against the ever-increasing din of background noise in the marketplace, is among the most pressing issues for the deluge of a 24/7 economy. It has now become the single most valuable and contested asset of any individual or organization.

MAKING IT HAPPEN ▸▸

Companies will need to invest heavily in tools that ease the burden of

"The key to running an entrepreneurial business with feet on four continents lies in constant access to information."

(Lycourgos Kyprianou)

  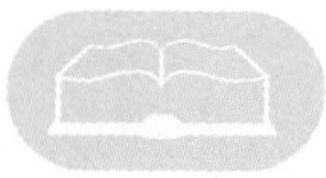    

connectivity by helping employees, customers, and partners control, manage, and personalize their interactions in the face of ever-increasing access. These tools are available and are becoming run on an increasing part of the landscape of highly competitive organizations.

Personalization

The question is not how to break away but, rather, how to better integrate and manage the accessibility and complexity that technology provides. Companies operating 24/7 take care to create environments that provide tools for personalizing every experience of their workers, customers, and partners, cutting through the clutter to the essence of what matters to each person. This paves the way for what has quickly become a new generation of *my*-based experiences. It's hardly a surprise, then, that one of the most popular prefixes for Web sites has become the word "my."

Technologies such as portals offer a single point of personalized access to myriad online resources and are a key factor in coping with a 24/7 world. With a personalized portal you can create anytime, anywhere, online access to all the information, people, processes, and applications you need for doing your job, making decisions, and collaborating with others. Personalization is essential to managing the increasing burden of 24/7 complexity and access.

Workflow

Since 24/7 often implies that we're juggling more individual activities than ever, we need more help with how we keep everything up in the air. Workflow provides the foundation for changes in the way we work by automating much of the routing, follow-up, and scheduling of activities. More importantly, workflow allows this change to occur in ways that improve the general quality and rhythm of our lives by alleviating much of the need for process administration.

Of greatest relevance is the use of roles in helping to define how work should be routed when a particular individual is not available. Most of our systems, from e-mail to organization charts, have used the individual as the designated recipient of work. As a result work often waits until a specific person can respond. Role-based workflow systems route work to the skills of the role, not to the individual. If we shift our focus from the *delivery* of work to the *coordination* of work, technologies such as workflow may actually improve our lives by proving that work is best accomplished when integrated with our lives.

E-learning

In a 24/7 economy we have less and less time to unplug from our tasks and take part in a formal training or education program. Since every task is sliced into smaller pieces of time, our learning has to be sliced into finer intervals. E-learning is a relatively new approach to just-in-time delivery of learning as an integrated part of a value chain. Unlike traditional forms of online learning that have simply delivered classroom materials and instruction on CD-ROM or through the Internet, e-learning synchronizes the learning needed for a given task with the performance of the task. The result is significant savings of time.

Knowledge management

Knowledge management was once summarized as, "My organization is just a bunch of answers all waiting for the right question to be asked." We've all had the experience of hopelessly navigating a large enterprise, bureaucracy, or community trying to get to the right person.

Knowledge management systems provide a mechanism by which organizations and industries can bridge the gap between those who know and those who need to know. In a 24/7 economy, making these connections will be the difference between organizations that succeed and those that fail. However, they will also yield enormous economy of time by connecting those who need to know with those who know.

CONCLUSION

By integrating personalization, workflow, e-learning, and knowledge management with a human-centered organization, the quality of life in a 24/7 economy and the opportunities it presents to individuals improve measurably. Rather than spending ever-increasing amounts of time administering, navigating, searching, and accommodating the 24/7 organization, workers are now able to focus their time and energy on the tasks that can most benefit from their intellectual capital.

Still, it's a difficult future to understand. As Dee Hock, founder and chairman emeritus of Visa International, said, "The old rules no longer apply, but the new rules are not yet known." Indeed, it's like trying to describe color to the inhabitants of a black-and-white world.

Imagine yourself going back in time and trying to explain the concept of jet lag to a citizen of the 19th century. They would have no framework for understanding what it meant to move at a rate of speed that could get you to your destination before you had even left.

For all our efforts there's a new generation who are going to regard the way we make decisions today in organizations as anathema. We wonder how we're going to survive at the pace of 24/7. They won't even question it.

For More Information

Books:

Davenport, Thomas H., and John C. Beck. *The Attention Economy: Understanding the New Currency of Business*. Boston, MA: Harvard Business School Press, 2001.

Rifkin, Jeremy. *The End of Work. The Decline of the Global Labor Force and the Dawn of the Post-Market Era*. Los Angeles, CA: JP Tarcher, 1996.

Schor, Juliet. *The Overworked American: The Unexpected Decline of Leisure*. New York: Basic Books, 1993.

See also:

☆ **Human Capital (pp. 115–16)**
☆ **Power Struggling and Power Sharing (pp. 95–96)**
☆ **Raising the Bar: Setting Effective Targets (pp. 283–84)**
☆ **Viewpoint: William Bridges (pp. 322–23)**
☆ **Viewpoint: Henry Mintzberg (pp. 241–42)**

"The parking is easy, there are no checkout lines, we are open 24 hours a day, and we deliver right to your door."
(Anonymous)

  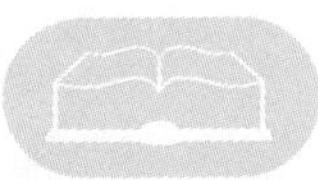    

Self-managed Teams: How They Succeed or Fail

by Andrew Leigh and Michael Maynard

EXECUTIVE SUMMARY

- Many companies have tried self-managed teams, with mixed results.
- When they're successful, self-managed teams can be 15–20% more productive than conventional teams.
- Despite the title, these teams usually have some form of official or unofficial leadership.
- It takes considerable effort and time to refine the concept to make it work well.
- In launching the self-managed concept it's important to understand the natural development cycle of groups.

Introduction

Procter & Gamble kept self-managed teams a commercial secret for years. Hundreds of companies have tried to make them work, with mixed results. Consultants extract large fees for either recommending them or unraveling the mess from the ones that failed.

Self-managed teams (SMT), often called self-directed work teams (SDWT), have acquired a momentum all their own. More than half of the largest companies in the United States now have them, from the carmaker Saturn to Federal Express. The United Kingdom is no slouch, either, with companies such as Land Rover and the Body Shop showing the way.

Such arrangements are not for the fainthearted. They represent a switch from the boss–worker relationship to a collaborative approach. Once the self-managed idea gets underway everything tends to be challenged, from supervision to setting wages, from existing production targets to persistent hierarchies. In principle these apparently leaderless teams are simple to understand. You empower everyone in a team to take responsibility. Instead of a supervisor or some distracted middle manager directing events, the team runs itself. Well, that's the theory. Now for the reality.

Creating Successful Self-managed Teams

1. Be Committed and Practical

Creating a self-managed team is a marathon, not a sprint. You stand a better chance of succeeding with an entirely new team than you do with a long-standing one. Managers who have introduced the self-managed principle usually say it's a time-consuming business that needs careful nurturing.

Self-management demands a new mindset, one where you stop thinking in terms of managing per se and focus on empowering or motivating. If you're fond of command and control as a management style, self-managed teams are definitely not for you.

So what exactly is a self-managed team? Broadly, it's a work group of around 5 to 15 people sharing responsibility for a task. It could be building an automobile or processing insurance claims. The assumption is that the members possess the skills and authority to supervise themselves. An important feature is that everyone tends to learn all the tasks required. In this it differs from the traditional team, in which jobs are broken into smaller elements, each assigned to an individual with specialist skills. When self-management works, productivity rises above conventional teams by anything from 10 to 20%. In addition, employee satisfaction increases and employee turnover falls (which explains why the originator, Proctor & Gamble, kept quiet about it for so long).

A particular challenge that this work arrangement poses for Western cultures is our passion for independence, self-sufficiency, and competitiveness. These often come at the expense of shared goals and collaboration.

2. Understand the Team Cycle

To make self-managed teams succeed you need to know some basic principles of groups and how they reach their peak performance.

Whenever someone leaves or joins, in effect you have a new group. A renewed effort needs to go into rebuilding relationships, clarifying working arrangements, establishing trust, and going through some or all of the development cycle. Teams switch between various stages of development as they encounter new issues.

There are different views concerning the evolution of successful teams, but most tend to follow the same pattern. The one that is used most frequently and perhaps most clearly defines the development of teams is the four stages of team development: forming, storming, norming, and performing.

- **Forming**–the team is a collection of individuals that are just starting to form into a single unit. The ice is carefully being broken, people are introducing themselves and are generally quiet, polite, and are getting the measure of others in the team.
- **Storming**–conflict starts to emerge as people display their attitudes and set boundaries. This is an inevitable phase as people get to know others in the team and find their own identity.
- **Norming**–norms are developed as people understand each other's strengths, weaknesses, and patterns of behavior. The group functions as a team and tasks are accomplished. Often teams settle at this level.
- **Performing**–the team starts excelling and performing at its very best. This largely results from a steady accumulation of trust, respect, and understanding, combined with a common sense of purpose and some successes.

To these four stages can be added a fifth–reforming–which refers to the process of renewing and reinvigorating the team, perhaps after failures, difficulties, or major changes.

3. Visit a Self-directed Team

If you like the idea of self-directed teams, visit some existing ones to gain a practical feel for the challenges you will inevitably encounter. For example, self-management implies that no one is really in charge, when in reality this is seldom true. Invariably there is someone providing leadership.

"A team is not a bunch of people with job titles, but a congregation of individuals, each of whom has a role that is understood by other members."

(Meredith Belbin)

4. Understand and Resolve Problem Areas

Mature teams can handle responsibilities that once kept the traditional line manager in business. For example, at Motorola, teams determine members' pay raises based on performance appraisals. At Honeywell, teams start by being responsible for such basic areas as material replenishment, quality at source, and on-the-job training. From there they progress to dealing with conflict resolution and scheduling vacations. Later they may take responsibility for selecting team members, cost control, and performance appraisal. This evolution depends on some early successes, which help motivate the desire to stick with it. There are, however, several issues that have to be resolved en route.

Many teams resist self-management, particularly when it's imposed by senior management. Employees, comfortable with conventional line management and having no desire to take on extra responsibility, can be intransigent. It's essential to offer them clear benefits and structured education.

5. Sustain Momentum

Newly created self-managed teams often produce quick results. Many problems emerge later once the excitement has worn off. Now the team faces the same challenge as any long-term group. It needs to focus on creating and maintaining self-motivation or creating a rota of people responsible for continually revitalizing the team.

How long it takes before the team is truly self-managing may depend on factors outside the team's own control; such factors influence teams no matter how they are managed. For example, in a U.S. survey of 400 organizations, about half complained of inadequate resources, just under half said they had no or low rewards, and a similar proportion reported lack of decision-making authority.

6. Allow Teams to Make Appropriate Decisions

Long-serving managers must learn to let go and trust people. They may also need to transform their style into a supportive and facilitative approach and learn to allow decisions to emerge naturally. Third, they need to respond to mistakes and crises by turning them into genuine learning opportunities instead of using them as an excuse to punish or even grab back decision-making control.

As companies increasingly rely on talent, brainwork, and virtual teams that hardly even meet, self-management has many attractions. The lessons so far are that self-managed teams can be highly productive and extremely satisfying to work in. Paradoxically, though, it takes particularly good management to allow them to succeed.

Five Myths about Self-Managed Teams

- **They don't need managers.** They need managing through coaching, facilitation, and other forms of support.
- **They don't need leaders.** Leadership is essential and is often shared ingeniously across the group.
- **They make leaders powerless.** Leaders must exercise power differently and rely more on influence than authority.
- **They're cheap.** They cost more in the short term and have high setup costs such as training and troubleshooting.
- **They're quickly established.** They can take years to get right, needing constant refinement.

Mini-case

When mining machinery manufacturer *Boart Longyear* opted for self-managed teams it had to learn the hard way. Team preparation involved at least 60 hours of training, but no single person emerged as the informal leader. The result was delays in decision making. One of the greatest sources of frustration was that employees felt comfortable only when they were told what to do. When they hit a problem their first reaction was to demand help from a supervisor. The benefits were:

- Individual team members really pulled their weight, because they didn't want to appear to be underperforming.
- Former supervisors shifted roles. They became resource providers rather than rationers and spent their time obtaining information and securing resources.
- Productivity rose by around 10 to 15%.

Making It Happen

- Stop thinking in terms of managing, focus on empowering and motivating.
- Visit some existing self-directed teams to gain a practical feel for the realities that you will inevitably encounter.
- To overcome resistance to self-management, offer employees clear benefits and education.
- Be sure to clarify what each person in the self-managed team does and where jurisdiction begins and ends.
- Invest time in developing communication skills and establishing best practice for conducting meetings and making decisions.
- Respond to mistakes and crises by turning these into genuine learning opportunities.

Conclusion

Self-managed teams and team-based working have developed into the normal way of structuring organizations and undertaking tasks, yet it is a difficult and complex aspect of leadership and is usually developed through experience. When developing a high performing, self-managed team it is valuable to have an understanding of:

- **the benefits of team building**—what it can achieve and what the leader should be striving for;
- **team roles and dynamics**—how teams work and achieve their greatest success;
- **the key stages of team development**—what they are and how to support the team in each stage;
- **the features of a successful team and team leader**;
- **how to avoid potential problems and pitfalls**.

Team building is a continuing process requiring energy, commitment, feedback, and review. Factors affecting the team change constantly, and the team needs to have the leadership and support that breeds flexibility and confidence. It is often useful to consider one's own career and reflect back to when you were in a successful team: what made it work and how could it have been better? Could your current team be improved?

For More Information

Book:

Orsburn, Jack D., et al. *The New Self-directed Work Teams*. 2nd ed. New York: McGraw-Hill Professional, 1999.

Web Site:

http://users.ids.net/~brim/sdwth.html is an informative site by the Self Directed Work Team providing useful links to other relevant sites.

See also:

☆ **Workers without Borders: Creating Bonds When Workers Have No Loyalty (pp. 204–05)**

"A good team is a great place to be, exciting, stimulating, supportive, successful. A bad team is horrible, a sort of human prison."

(Charles Handy)

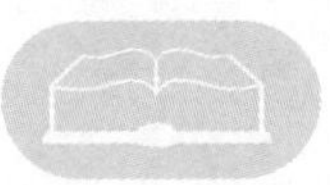

WORKERS WITHOUT BORDERS: CREATING BONDS WHEN WORKERS HAVE NO LOYALTY

by Perry Pascarella

EXECUTIVE SUMMARY

- The death of worker–company loyalty leaves business leadership grasping for ways to align people with the organization.
- Painful but necessary, this "death" gives birth to the possibility of more meaningful bonds for working effectively.
- Converging corporate and personal needs for creativity, collaboration, and commitment set the stage for stronger, though not lifelong, bonds.
- Leaders can take specific steps to create bonds for working together effectively—bonds built on person-to-person relationships.

INTRODUCTION

We see growing evidence from all quarters that many companies are not loyal to their employees and that employees are less and less likely to express loyalty to their companies. People in leadership positions are challenged to find some basis other than company loyalty to hold an organization together and accomplish its objectives.

On the corporate side we see sweeping organizational flux because of the application of new technologies by traditional and new competitors, the impact of globalization and the rapid flow of capital within and across national borders. Product lines are abandoned in the quest for greater profitability; corporate giants downsize, removing tens of thousands of workers from the payroll; companies relocate headquarters or plants; acquisitions and mergers result in redundancies.

Quite often such corporate measures have an impact on employment across national boundaries. Workers in Northern Ireland, Mexico, or France may lose their jobs when, for example, a U.S. company reduces its labor force.

MINI-CASES

LTV Steel, crippled by steel imports that exacerbated other difficulties, is seeking government assistance as it files for bankruptcy for the second time in recent years. Tens of thousands of workers, some of them third-generation steelworkers, are threatened with job loss; retirees face adjustments in their pensions.

Boeing, thriving in the world aircraft market, announces it will move its headquarters from Seattle to be better located for managing its other lines of business. About half of the 1,000 corporate employees are not expected to be taken to the new location.

LOYALTY VERSUS GLOBALIZATION

At the same time we see significant changes in behavior and expectations on the worker side of the loyalty equation:

- employees' willingness to relocate and change employers;
- a more entrepreneurial approach to careers, with the growing possibility of pursuing multiple careers over a lifetime;
- a search for the transcendent connection, community, and intimacy that people haven't found in traditional workplaces;
- resistance to the segmentation of work and personal life.

It has become obvious that companies can no longer promise lifelong employment and that fewer and fewer workers truly seek it. Workers and managers alike are increasingly apt to operate without borders, whether on the global map or on the organizational chart or in their mix of work and nonwork interests.

A TRANSITION TO SOMETHING BETTER

While it might be interesting to trace the causes of the death of the old loyalty or implicit contract in the hope of restoring it, there is little value in doing so. It's more valuable to recognize the present situation as a possible transition period between one kind of bond between worker and organization and something far more effective and rewarding to both parties. What we are experiencing is a painful aspect of the transformation in our concepts of work and organization.

Under the old loyalty system managers controlled and workers complied in organizations built on alliances of reluctant adversaries. Workers submitted to corporate demands in exchange for financial compensation. In such an atmosphere *loyalty* was a cruel misnomer. *Compensation* was truly that—a counterbalance or recompense to make amends for something given up—as employees separated their work from other aspects of their lives and performed tasks that required them to be less than their full selves. These conditions fostered competition and even hostility both between employees and the organization and among employees.

This kind of bond hardly optimized what people could do in an organization. It was tolerable only in situations in which the leader's primary function was maintaining the status quo. As we turn to the future, however, a premium will be placed on creativity and innovation. Leaders will be challenged to find or create a far more meaningful bond than the one forged by control and rigidity.

CONVERGENCE OF CORPORATE AND INDIVIDUAL NEEDS

The apparent parting of the ways between the organization and the individual masks the convergence of corporate and personal needs. The drive for innovation invites three key factors in organizational life:

1. **Creativity** arising out of an interplay of learning and doing in a risk-taking environment;
2. **Collaboration** that opens the way to innovation, from generating ideas to implementing them. It is widely recognized that innovation emerges through group process—"communities of practice"—more often than individual pursuits. Charles Ehin points out how this differs from the traditional workplace: "The production of intellectual assets depends primarily on voluntary relationships instead of competition."
3. **Commitment** to shared purpose. In an era of worker mobility and corporate

"Unless we develop a more sophisticated model of the organization, the corporation will become just a box of contracts with no commitment on anyone's part." (Charles Handy)

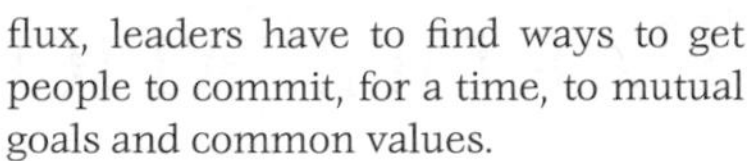

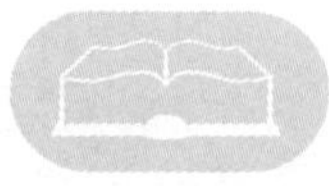

flux, leaders have to find ways to get people to commit, for a time, to mutual goals and common values.

These three ingredients match basic needs shared by most individuals; leaders do not need to inject them into people. To be creative, to collaborate with others, and to have something meaningful to commit to are common human desire. Leadership therefore implies discovering ways to capitalize on this convergence of needs and align people in ways that allow them to fulfill their inner needs while serving those of the organization.

Bonds Built on Trust

What will be the basis for building bonds, with others and with the organization that will allow personal and corporate needs to be met? To a large degree this will come primarily through personal bonds, between leader and follower and among followers. These bonds will depend on more than warm feelings toward others. They must be fashioned through working relationships in which individuals can rely on one another to work together toward some common purpose. People need something they can deeply commit to, even if only on a relatively short-term basis. They need a group purpose—something more substantive than the pins, pizza parties, and propaganda extended by so many quality and productivity improvement programs. Relationships won't be structured by corporate designers, but will have to grow naturally in human dimensions. This means that leaders face the challenge of revealing their humanity and recognizing the humanity of others in order to sow the seeds of trust.

Mini-case

Integrity establishes the trust that is so critical to the human relationships that make our values work. With that trust employees can take risks and believe us when we say a *miss* doesn't mean career damage.

In today's *General Electric*, the rewarded behavior has changed from being the exclusive originator of an idea as a vehicle for standing out among colleagues—to, more importantly, finding a better idea and eagerly sharing it across the entire company.

Making It Happen

A leader's ability to earn trust depends not simply on inner character, but on outward expressions—that is, what the individual does and how he or she does it. Here are some suggestions for being proactive about earning trust.

Be open about facts and feelings

- Share information. Work at informing others so that they can be more effective. Don't hoard information to build up personal power.
- Share your feelings. Admit your concerns and fears.
- Share the bad news as well as the good. Beat the grapevine in conveying bad news and put it into a perspective that will enable people to continue functioning effectively.
- Share what you know about where the organization is going. Explain strategy in terms people understand. Organizations need leaders who can give meaning to day-to-day activity. If you are operating without benefit of a clear corporate mission or strategy, you can at least explain what you know.

Explain how you make decisions

- Show consistency in the basic values that guide your decision making. Trying to please everyone increases the risk of straying from your basic values.
- Consider all the alternatives. Your colleagues are more likely to forgive wrong decisions based on careful consideration than those based on shooting from the hip.
- Describe how and why you're shifting management styles to fit a given situation. Depending on the situation, effective leaders shift among a variety of roles: team player, boss, leader, and individual player.

Be a resource

- Build your competence. Learn enough so you can speak the language and be part of the team.
- Prove your commitment. No matter how skilled you are, people will look first at your level of commitment to the endeavor.
- Earn the support of top management. Know what it considers important.

Respect and care for people

- Demonstrate that you're working in others' interests as well as your own. It won't surprise anyone that you want something from the organization, but peers, subordinates, and bosses will look at your track record to see if you generally work for the corporate good.
- Set high standards for all, including yourself. Being the object of high expectations raises people's performance. If you don't set appropriate standards, you will neither achieve maximum results nor keep everybody happy.
- Show that you value other people's ideas. Countless others may have information and viewpoints of value to you and the organization. Be a magnet for ideas.
- Support your subordinates' decisions. When subordinates err, follow up immediately to help them learn and improve.
- Clear bureaucratic roadblocks. Pay attention to what your followers need to do their work.

Conclusion

The strength of an organization will depend increasingly on its level of openness and risk taking. Rather than looking to formal organizational structures to provide energy and direction, leaders will have to nurture bonds among people who have no set borders for where they work, on where they fit into the group or on how their work fits into their lives. Earning trust is the first step in generating the bonds needed for strong, creative working relationships. The resulting loyalties will be more genuine than the old company loyalty despite the fact that in a fluid world they offer no lifetime guarantees. The new loyalty will go much further than the old in promoting risk taking and creativity.

For More Information

Books:

Ehin, Charles. *Unleashing Intellectual Capital*. Woburn, MA: Butterworth-Heinemann, 2000.

Stewart, Thomas S. *Intellectual Capital: The New Wealth of Organizations*. New York: Doubleday/Currency, 1999.

See also:

☆ **Business Ethics (pp. 231-32)**
☆ **Finding and Keeping Top Talent (pp. 33-34)**
☆ **Self-managed Teams: How They Succeed or Fail (pp. 202-03)**
☆ **SQ: Investing in Spiritual Capital (pp. 43-44)**
☆ **Viewpoint: Jim Collins (pp. 235-36)**
☆ **Viewpoint: Henry Mintzberg (pp. 241-42)**

"The bond between a man and his profession is similar to that which ties him to his country. . .it is understood completely only when it is broken." (Primo Levi)

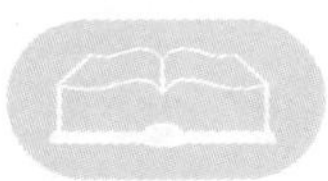

Converting Anonymity into Participation in a Membership Organization

by Jane Galloway Seiling

Executive Summary

- An informed and increasingly demanding workforce is insisting that working together has to get easier.
- Organizational members want to integrate their own beliefs and direction with those of their organization. They want to identify with its overarching design (mission, goals, strategy, culture).
- The principles of membership—contribution, motivation, decisioning, relationship, leadership, accountability, and advocacy—support the members' efforts to connect to other organizational members and the organization they represent.

Introduction

Organizations are learning that it is essential to value and develop the interests, skills, and abilities of each individual and to provide opportunities for learning to be used. Members who identify with their organization want to contribute to their own welfare and the welfare of those around them and their organization as best they can. They no longer want only to be hands, to do only what they are told to, to work in silence and in anonymity. They want to think and do.

They want to partner with workplace members at all levels, making it possible for all to benefit from a communally designed future. Being anonymous and doing mediocre work no longer satisfy the more demanding new workplace members. They want to *work with* instead of *work for*, in an environment in which their expertise, suggestions, and concerns are valued. They want to be given opportunities to perform at new levels of contribution. They want to work in a membership organization.

Looking at the Membership Organization

Membership suggests voluntariness: working here because I want to, not because I have to, heightens performance and enrollment to a degree impossible in the old disconnected way of working. In membership organizations people seek reliable ways of working beneficially with others. An overarching design creates an uncommon way of understanding and sustaining messages of why and what performance is in this place. All workplace activities are considered in the light of this overarching design.

The language of membership invites new understandings of beneficially working together. The old language of being an employee or boss signaled designated locations of power, control, and authority. Crossing the line uninvited was frowned upon, even punished, by superiors and coworkers alike. Successfully being together requires an atmosphere of partnering and working with instead of working for.

Membership recognizes the three common desires of workplace members: to be treated with dignity and respect, to be acknowledged and appreciated, and to know that what they do matters to the performance and success of their organization. By openly and authentically striving to address these desires, organizational leaders make it possible for members to connect to their organization and comembers. Failure to address these desires makes anonymity and disconnection inevitable.

Principles of Membership

In order to identify with the purpose and goals of their organization, members look for guidelines. Without a common understanding, personal responsibility and productivity suffer. In the membership organization the principles defined by the collective membership also define what a successful contribution is. An example of these principles might look like this:

- contribution–all members, wherever they are in the organizational circle, contribute to the well-being of the workplace community;
- motivation–members are personally and collectively empowered to take action and feel that they and their work are significant to overall achievement;
- decision making–long-term and short-term decisions are made with consideration for the three bottom lines: human, social, and financial;
- relationships–a relational approach is important to working with others; it's the responsibility of every member to establish connecting relationships that work, adding energy and respectful connection to relationships;
- leadership–leaders may be chosen or assigned, but leadership happens at all organizational levels;
- accountability–members are willingly and individually responsible and accountable for working toward organizational goals;
- advocacy–members' willingness to promote comembers and the workplace community positively influences the performance of individuals, groups, and the organization.

Through defined principles, membership takes participation and involvement to a higher level. New expectations become actualities when they are formed and performed together. Although formal leaders still exist, leading and following are no longer separate functions; all members share in the responsibility of running a successful organization. Organizations can no longer afford to separate, even isolate, the doers from the thinkers.

Heightened Responsibility and Accountability

Members make choices to sign on, get out, rebel, or be anonymous. These decisions are consciously and unconsciously shared with others. People recognize that the amount of energy put into a task is often adjusted by the amount of respect held for the person, organization, or process. A minimally responsible person (low-energy, nonparticipative, anonymous) doesn't identify with a group or an organization. This matters because a lack of identification with an organization stifles the drive and dynamism of the business, as well as disenfranchising people and bringing poorer performance.

"There is an idea, broadly held on Wall Street, that names with X's are more memorable and tend to capture the attention of analysts. It is not held by us." (Clive Chajet)

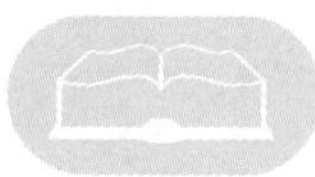

Responsibility

Within membership, actions of personal responsibility leading to informal leadership are normal occurrences, recognized as vital to the success of the group and the overall workplace community. Members' opportunities to perform are limited only by the extent of the individual's willingness to be personally responsible. Members are encouraged to question the status quo and are challenged to stretch and grow. It's potentially dangerous to be highly responsible and contributive in the hierarchical status-quo organization. In such organizations it may be best to choose anonymity.

Accountability

In the find-and-punish accountability of the old workplace, accountability is reserved for assigning blame, which kills the desire to participate at a higher level. Accountability as a process is important to the success of members and the organization alike. Constructive accountability as an ongoing tool for exchanging information is an opportunity for members to learn and serve together. Constructive accountability is the activation of ongoing conversations that indicate project status, questions, exchanges of learning, the checking of statements, and the search for resources. It is the involvement of others in accomplishment–the opposite of anonymity.

Constructive accountability provides vital performance parameters. It gives performers a way of openly seeking information while sustaining dignity and respect. It's the first step to real empowerment. Empowerment requires both hearing and telling the truth in a supportive environment in which decisions are made at the place of need. Constructive accountability that includes recognition of contributions as well as new learning provides opportunities for giving and getting support.

The Role of Leadership

Moving from anonymity to membership requires leaders to address safety and security issues. It requires a genuine willingness to step back from rigid control, a belief that giving up control is beneficial. Members must now believe there are leaders-of-the-moment everywhere, even change agents, and that deep participation is consistently supported and encouraged. Leaders (who are also members) are either facilitators or barrier creators in the process of moving toward becoming a membership organization.

Mini-cases

Southwest Airlines is often cited as an exemplary workplace. Southwest's goal is long-term employment of people who make a difference, while serving loyal customers–who are advocates for Southwest to other potential customers. Through these commitments to their members and their customers, according to Libby Sartain, vice president for people, "We get growth and profits. The result is a sustainable company where it is fun to work." This is a membership organization, one where employees share in the corporation's purpose and identify with its success.

The *Knowledge Capital Group* of Hout Bay, South Africa, is a new company with the goal of being a membership organization. Establishing this intention highlights the founders' awareness of the impact of working together to construct an inclusive organization. They are even now forming an overarching design and a hoped-for future for those who will be coming on board as the company grows. The entrepreneurs have created criteria for hiring members who desire to identify with a membership- and performance-oriented company. They see an exciting process ahead of them.

Making It Happen ⏵⏵

Considering membership as a new workplace reality raises important issues of belief, commitment, stamina, investment, and involvement. It derives from purposeful movement toward change. To make it a reality:

- involve, educate, and value member input in the overarching design of the future organization; provide extensive training and education opportunities;
- blur the lines of status and title; make it possible to become collaborative and cooperative–invite membership thinking;
- create new language, principles of performance, and deep involvement that indicate a valuing, respectful environment;
- encourage formal and informal leaders to reflect on and demonstrate these performance principles in all phases of their work performance and relationships;
- support personal and organizational change as a continuous, beneficial movement toward membership instead of a threatening, radical change that makes people fearful;
- move toward a genuine belief that all members understand the new philosophy and want to perform in responsible and accountable ways;
- understand that mistakes and setbacks will happen; acknowledge and understand what's happening. Be positive and consistent in the desire to forgive and move forward toward membership;
- be willing to take action when action is needed. It may be necessary to disconnect those unwilling to make the change.

Conclusion

Becoming a membership organization requires leaders to partner with organizational members at all levels to imagine and create an accomplishing, relationship- and performance-based organization. An overarching design anchors the process of steadfastly moving towards membership. The principles of membership, as designed by members, create new understandings of involvement, participation, and behavior. Anonymity, isolation, and mediocre performance are impossible when people choose to participate as members instead of employees. Membership creates and sustains hope in a beneficial future for the individual, group, and the organization.

For More Information

Books:

Goleman, Daniel. *Working with Emotional Intelligence.* New York: Bantam Doubleday Dell, 2000.
Handy, Charles. *The Age of Unreason.* Boston, MA: Harvard Business School Press, 1998.
Terez, Tom. *22 Keys to Creating a Meaningful Workplace.* Holbrook, NY: Adams Media, 2000.

See also:

☆ **Making the Workplace Flex, Not Break (pp. 31–32)**
☆ **Viewpoint: Christopher Bartlett (pp. 45–46)**
☆ **Viewpoint: Henry Mintzberg (pp. 241–42)**
☆ **Viewpoint: John Seely Brown (pp. 137–38)**
Mary Parker Follett (pp. 988–89)
Samuel Walton (pp. 1152–53)

"Identity shows up in our actions, our visions, our relationships inside and out of the organization. Identity gets deepened as we do the work." (Walter Wriston)

Overcoming the Difficulties of Managing a Virtual Organization
by Jim Underwood

Executive Summary

- In the new economy, accelerating rates of change and increasing levels of complexity pressure companies to move employees closer to the customer while at the same time keeping a close watch on costs.
- Emerging technologies will make virtual management easier; at the same time technology will create new management challenges.
- In the future more attention will need to be paid to how people are organized, motivated, and managed.

Introduction

The decades from 1980 to 2000 presented the business world with a sequence of serious challenges. In the early 1980s it was total quality. In the 1990s it was a new, connected world. By 2000 the problem was chaos: the reality was that managers of organizations had to learn to change with the technology-driving environment or be consumed by it. In response to each cycle of change, few, if any management theorists, produced a coherent system for success.

Another reality was the dispersion of the work force. Achieving the speed necessary for success required that either employees would be located closer to the customer or the customer would be brought closer through the use of technology. In either case many companies found themselves going virtual with no idea of how to maximize organizational performance. However, this brought significant problems. Customers seemed generally to prefer to deal with a human being, not an icon on a Web site. Similarly, dispersed employees seemed to miss the opportunity to interact with coworkers. Many felt their lack of interaction with managers did not bode well for their careers.

The changes brought about by the technological innovations of the 1990s and early 2000s have affected all aspects of business. There was a time when people had a choice as to whether they would be linked electronically. Today it's expected.

In the new wired world, technologies allow people to interact and deal with pressing issues electronically instead of attempting to find a common time and place for a group meeting. In fact, regardless of location, whether they're in close proximity or not, people tend to do business as if they were dispersed. This section will examine how organizations can take advantage of these changes, overcoming the difficulties presented by the changing business environment.

Mini-case

Going Virtual at Arthur Andersen

A short tour of the *Arthur Andersen* office in Dallas, Texas, reveals just how drastically technology has affected how companies do business. Entering the premises you're immediately aware of the fact that consultants have no offices. A consultant electing to work in the office selects an area that suits the immediate task, choosing among joint working areas with full computer and telephone access, large boardrooms for group meetings, and individual work areas.

The communications network is designed so that incoming phone calls follow consultants to their current work area; this is also true when they're working remotely. Cellphones and laptop computers allow consultants to work at home or on the road with the same connectivity and resources they would have in the office.

Competing Globally at the Lauck Group

In 1997 the *Lauck Group*, an interior architecture firm, was confronted with a challenge: to design ten offices in the United States and Europe for a major client, quickly. The team had to include professionals of different nationalities knowledgeable about the standards and requirements of their respective countries.

The Lauck team found top professionals in each country and then did something ingenious. They created a virtual workspace for all the constituents. During evening hours in the United States, the European teams would do their work and post it to the virtual workspace. When the U.S. teams came to work they'd log in and provide their input. The project—built on a 16-hour workday—was delivered on time and met every client requirement.

Challenges for the Virtual Organization

In spite of the advantages created by virtual organizations, there are also inherent problems. For example, managers at Nortel Networks and Sprint PCS talk about the difficulties of responding to between 100 and 200 daily e-mails. Subordinates become frustrated, feeling lost in their managers' inboxes.

If communication consists, on four levels—*spoken* or *written words*, *emotional pitch*, *nonverbals*, and *attitude*, the problems associated with communicating electronically with customers or coworkers become obvious. Three of the four are not easily discernible in an electronic message unless the author of the communication pays a great deal of attention to including them.

Les Carter and I have developed a concept we call the "significance principle." Every person has a driving need to be recognized, valued, and appreciated. There is a critical link between organizational performance and a firm's practice of this principle. It's no accident that companies like Southwest Airlines continue to perform well. Their people are committed to the company's success because the company is committed to each employee's success. Managers who don't recognize the significance of subordinates underperform at Southwest Airlines. This also appears to be the case at the "Top 100 Best Companies to Work For."

Today's virtual world does not lend itself easily to such recognition. Managers as well as coworkers must be acutely aware of the needs of others, and this may be achieved in a number of ways:

Managers

- Send a personal note recognizing

"Managing intellectual assets has become the single most important task of business."

(Thomas A. Stewart)

  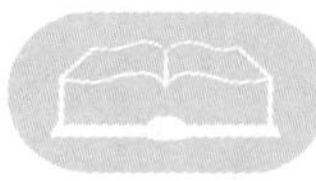    

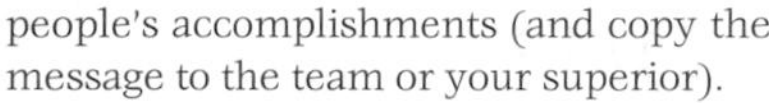

people's accomplishments (and copy the message to the team or your superior).

- Create special awards and recognition for team members who collaborate on corporate wins. Managers at Standard Aero of Canada found that their people preferred group incentives and awards for excellent work on team projects. This can be especially important for lower-profile remote contributors.

Colleagues

- Periodically post a comment about the contribution of a coworker.
- Communicate appreciation and value of coworkers.
- Try to avoid communication that might be misunderstood.

Emerging Technology

Many marvel at the new connected economy. Surprisingly, the change over the next three to five years is likely to be even more dramatic. Massive changes are about to hit the technology arena.

Many have heard of DSL (ADSL) Web access, which can easily be 10 times faster than a 56K modem. But many have not heard of DSVD, HDSL, VDSL, LMDS, MMDS, and other technological developments that could radically change how we work together. Add the light-spectrum technologies (using the light spectrum to significantly increase the capacity of a fiber-optic cable), or the emerging 3G networks (broadband wireless), and it quickly becomes apparent that we're standing at the edge of another megashift. These technologies will drive the virtual capabilities of the large corporation or the SOHO (small office, home office) to new levels of speed.

In the early 1990s Texas Instruments' senior executive team envisioned the world undergoing a massive technology shift. One of the key drivers, they concluded, would be DSP (digital signal processor) technologies. Basically, DSPs convert an analog signal such as a voice over a telephone into a digital signal that can be sent or forwarded to almost any device.

A DSP could take a voice message and convert it into a fax and send it. Or it could take a voice message or a fax, convert it into a digital format, and forward the message anywhere via e-mail. The implications of DSPs for the virtual world are overwhelming: geography no longer matters.

Home fax, home voice mail, office fax, office voice mail (plus cellphone messages), and pages can now all be forwarded to one common location. But it gets better—what about FIDs? FIDs, or fully integrated devices, are also going to play a major role in the virtual organization. Imagine this: a PDA (personal digital assistant), a pager, a computer (with full Internet capability), and a cellphone all rolled into one. Not only can remote or dispersed contributors receive all information anywhere, but they can also use the same devices to respond.

The new 3G networks will allow the FID to send and receive video streaming. These new networks will facilitate at least 30 frames per second (the same as broadcast-quality videoconferencing). The FID will double as a portable videoconferencing device and will be about the same size as existing PDAs.

Making It Happen ▸▸

Management has changed from traditional planning, organizing, leading, and controlling to learning, transformation, and performance. Leaders must be able to facilitate organizational learning, focusing on such things as the future of the organization, or competitive and technological challenges. Once the organization has learned, its derived knowledge must be actualized by transforming the organization from what it is into what it needs to be. Actualization of learning will produce maximum performance.

Some top-performing companies have leaders who understand this process: General Electric, Hewlett Packard, and Cisco Systems are three. The key steps allowing organizations and leaders to compete effectively in the new virtual world include the following.

- Focus on the basics: learning, transformation, and performance.
- Emphasize leadership, not management. Controlling approaches to managing a virtual organization will stifle performance. Organizations that genuinely value and appreciate their people will consistently outperform those that do not.
- Make technology transparent. Never implement a technology just because it's there.
- Recreate the workplace in the virtual world. In order to facilitate organizational learning, one company has a virtual brainstorming area on its wide-area network. Another has an intelligence board where people can post information on products and competitors.
- Never forget excellence! Great organizations are great because inspirational leaders establish clear standards of excellence and expect their team to win.

Conclusion

Technological change accelerates overall environmental change. Rapid technological change, combined with drastically changed market forces, has driven massive shifts through the competitive environment. Each shift changes the rules of the game. The rules of the game for managing change correspondingly: constantly and chaotically.

Since 1980 the business world has had to face a series of challenges. One of the most pressing has been how to manage employees in a virtual organization. Using new technologies and new ways to manage, a virtual organization can not only be successful but can also achieve an extraordinary level of excellence.

For More Information

Books:

Goldberg, Beverly. *Overcoming High-tech Anxiety: Thriving in a Wired World.* San Francisco, CA: Jossey-Bass, 1999.

Petzinger, Thomas, Jr. *The New Pioneers: The Men and Women Who Are Transforming the Workplace and Marketplace.* New York: Simon & Schuster, 1999.

Web Site:

www.soho.org provides lots of information about technologies for virtual organizations.

See also:

☆ **Delivering and Delighting—A New Spirit at Work (pp. 71–72)**
☆ **Marketspaces (pp. 154–56)**
☆ **New Yardsticks for Performance and Productivity in an E-world (pp. 285–86)**
☆ **The Second Coming of Service (pp. 77–78)**
☆ **Virtual Collaboration (pp. 167–68)**
✔ **Exploring Peer-to-Peer (P2P) Commerce (pp. 646–47)**
✔ **How to Deliver Quality Online Customer Service and Support (pp. 582–83)**
✔ **Setting Up an Extranet (p. 639)**

"The workplace is undergoing rapid change. So are American workers. Technology, globalization, and new demographics are constantly redefining what work is."
(Alexis M. Herman)

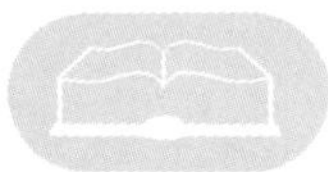

REORGANIZING THE FIRM WITHOUT DESTROYING IT *by Colin Price*

EXECUTIVE SUMMARY

- Pressures to change and compete frequently result in organizations needing to transform their structure. This transformation may occur quickly or over an extended period. Whether the organization is expanding, contracting, or simply refreshing its focus, the process needs to be handled very sensitively.
- Recent research has found that one year after a major reorganization, 70% of chief executives are disappointed or significantly concerned by the results of their efforts.
- Important factors influencing motivation among senior executives can be fundamentally affected by restructuring, impacting on issues such as the organization's values and culture, the need for differentiated compensation, and the level of freedom and autonomy enjoyed by managers.
- There are four adversarial mental traps to avoid when restructuring, as well as ten basic principles to observe in transforming performance.

INTRODUCTION

REORGANIZATIONS HAVE A BAD HISTORY

We all know that reorganizations have a bad history, not just at McKinsey and not just recently. A 1990 study found that more than 50% of firms reported stagnant or reduced productivity after downsizing. In 1995 a study by INSEAD Business School reported that only 46% of 1,005 downsized firms surveyed had actually cut expenses, and fewer had increased profits or productivity. In 1996 *The Economist* reported research by Monitor looking at firms that had outperformed their industry over a ten-year period. Researchers found that nine out of ten had stable structures with no more than one reorganization.

Despite these failures, the imperative to change is still with us. We need to transform the corporation without losing the things that made it work. I'll discuss the mental traps that I believe cause these failures and the elements you need to consider. The goal is to achieve a transformation that fundamentally shifts an organization's strategy, business system, and culture to deliver measurable and sustainable improvements.

THE AWFUL LAW OF ININTENDED CONSEQUENCES

The law of unintended consequences states that any change will be accompanied by a set of consequences that cannot be accurately predicted. The reason this law is awful is that the consequences have a strong tendency to destroy all the value of your planned change.

The problem stems from two sources: the objectives of the change and the process. Major programs of change are often begun for unpopular reasons–downsizing, business process reengineering, and takeovers all seem unattractive and threatening to staff. The process is often unpopular because it disenfranchises people within their own organization. Morale sinks, productivity drops, people lose their trust in management, and the value of the change is lost. If we're going to avoid these problems in our own programs, we need to understand the underlying causes and design our own process so that we can reorganize the firm without destroying its soul. This memo outlines four mental traps we need to avoid and ten rules we need to follow to avoid the awful law of unintended consequences.

FOUR MENTAL TRAPS

1. **People vs. Performance.** Many change programs are stuck in the old paradigm of improving despite people. Successful companies recognize that you can only improve *through* people. This recognition comes from two main forces. First, the move toward a service economy and the growth in the value of intangible assets mean that these days the people *are* the organization–you can't change without changing them. Jack Welch said of the merger with Honeywell that GE would be bringing its "social architecture" to bear in driving the integration. This is a real acknowledgement that the people and the program are inseparable in creating effective change.
2. **Structure vs. System.** Many change programs are overly focused on rearranging the formal organizational structure. The change will only be effective if the structure is part of a broader systemic transformation. In our ten-year survey of companies, structure was only one of several levers (with strategy, execution, culture, talent management, leadership, innovation, and growth through successfully managed mergers and acquisitions) that led to dramatic performance improvements.
3. **Us vs. Them.** The role of the leader in crafting a transformational process is to create an environment in which people can take leadership of the changes wherever they are able. Talented people are motivated by freedom, autonomy, and the opportunity to rise to challenges. They can bring your transformation to life, particularly if you have a strong story they can dramatize. This is more engaging and compelling than their simply rolling out your program for you.
4. **Concurrent vs. Consecutive.** Because the elements of the transformation program are complementary, you cannot achieve successful change by tackling them one at a time. Improvements to leadership, culture, and management processes will reinforce the changes you make to customer management, operational processes, and organizational design. Effective transformations work simultaneously on more than one element of the change to unfold a sequence of related chapters in the program.

MAKING IT HAPPEN ▸▸

Ten Golden Rules

Although every transformation is different, from our experience we have abstracted ten basic principles that you should observe in transforming performance.

1. **Confront the facts continuously.** Make sure you understand the reasons for your current situation, however good or bad. Take time and

---

"You can build a lasting competitive edge through the excellence of your organization structure."

(Percy Barnevik)

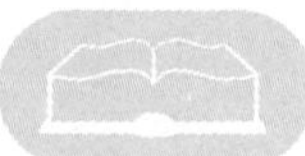

WHAT MOTIVATES TALENTED PEOPLE? Percentage of top 200 executives rating factor absolutely essential

Great company	%	Compensation and lifestyle	%	Great jobs	%
Values and culture	58	Differentiated compensation	29	Freedom and autonomy	56
Well managed	50	High total compensation	23	Job has exciting challenges	51
Company has exciting challenges	38	Geographical location	19	Career advancement and growth	38
Strong performance	29	Respect for lifestyle	14	Fit with boss I admire	29
Industry leader	21	Acceptable pace	1		
Many talented people	20				
Good at development	17				
Inspiring mission	16				
Fun with colleagues	11				
Job security	8				

be open-minded in analyzing the organization's current performance. Remember the world doesn't stop to wait for your transformation.

2. **Build a coherent and compelling transformation story.** Staff, customers, analysts, and investors need to see for themselves why the organization needs to change, where it is going, and how you plan to get there. Successful transformations are built on compelling stories that confront the existing facts, bring alive the point of inflection, threat, or opportunity that the company faces, and chart a clear course toward a new reality.
3. **Use the collective wisdom of the organization.** Transformation is far more effective when people discover a new reality for themselves and adopt new ways of working. No matter how convinced you are of the superiority of your business model, think carefully before imposing your views on the company—ultimately your transformation will take only if it taps into the organization's collective energies and insights. This isn't just a matter of buying in, it's one of genuine discovery.
4. **You can hold a few elements of your transformation sacrosanct, but be flexible about the rest.** As the organization changes its final form won't be clear. The process of revelation is a necessary part of change, and your design must be flexible enough to accommodate it; interim developments often reflect the changing reality of the business. But you need to be clear about the few elements that are nonnegotiable, and see that they're not compromised by any element of the transformation.
5. **Work through leaders at all levels.** Leadership is critical, but this is not just about your role as C.E.O. The transformation needs leaders throughout the organization building commitment to the new possibilities that emerge and engaging people in the story of the change.
6. **Get the right balance between action and reflection.** Action and reflection are both vital elements of the transformation process. Without sufficient action the process will lose momentum and fail, but you also need reflection to furnish renewal, check that the change continues to respond to the reality of the situation, and make sure that lessons are learned. Overemphasis on one or the other leads to failure.
7. **Demonstrate early success.** It's not enough to talk about change—people need to experience it. Inertia can often be overcome by demonstrating early progress in microworlds that deliver visible improvements in operating and financial performance, increase customer satisfaction, and spark enjoyment and motivation in employees participating in them.
8. **Make the change process unique.** Your organization is unique, your people are unique, and your transformation is unique. This means that you must follow a tailored, dynamic change process that meets your needs and responds to events as they unfold. You need to design the change process so that it works for your situation, leveraging the leaders available and the balance of action and reflection to allow you to learn and develop on the journey.
9. **Expect resistance—listen constantly, but be clear about the boundaries.** It's clear from this memo that transformation is not easy. People, probably including some members of the leadership team, will almost certainly undermine the process, either through active opposition or through passive but visible lack of support. Many transformations fail because top management refuses to listen to these people. Nonetheless, it's up to you to limit the space in which people explore and the degree of resistance that's acceptable. Ultimately people who refuse to join the process must be moved aside.
10. **Measure progress at every stage.** To be effective in your role as leader of the change, you need access to real information about how things are going. Constantly and rigorously measure progress against specific milestones, changes in organizational energy and alignment, operational performance, and financial performance. Make all of these results widely visible in the organization.

Conclusion

Don't Trade Off People and Performance

These principles are based on observation of organizational changes; they encapsulate lessons learned from the successes and failures of others. For the whole of the last century we were collectively stuck in the paradigm that insisted the role of leadership is to drive hard for performance and brush aside resistance. The time has come to abandon this limiting model. Our research on motivation and performance is conclusive: the best people are turned on by a strong performance ethic and an open, trusting, and supportive culture. A performance orientation and a people orientation are not opposites. They aren't even choices. Instead they're the two components that will enable us to achieve outstanding and sustainable results.

For More Information

Journal Articles:

Day, Jonathan D., and Michael Jung. "Corporate Transformation Without a Crisis." *McKinsey Quarterly*, no. 4 (2000). (See **www.mckinseyquarterly.com**.)

Kets de Vries, Manfred, and Katharina Balazs. "The Downside of Downsizing." *Human Relations* 50:1 (1996): 11–50.

"The inexorable forces of competition and change catch up again with companies that restructure but do not revitalize."

(Sumantra Ghoshal)

Viewpoint: Warren Bennis

Leading Managers to Adapt and Grow

Warren Bennis is practically synonymous with leadership. A student and protégé of Douglas McGregor, he was invited by McGregor in 1959 to establish a department of organization studies at MIT's Sloan School of Management. After serving in administrative positions in the 1960s and 1970s—as provost of SUNY Buffalo and president of the University of Cincinnati—he returned to research and teaching in 1979, joining the faculty at the University of Southern California, where he continues to pursue his groundbreaking work on learning, leadership, organizational life, and personal development. Here he reflects on the factors that have most profoundly influenced this thinking, as well as on the qualities that people and organizations must nurture in order to create meaningful work.

Like everyone else, I'd have to say that there's no one thing that has influenced my thinking. And that's probably true of life. In my own case, I think there were several factors that came out along the way and that, in looking back, seem like a set of eccentric precursors instead of kind of a singular willful, purposeful, I-know-what-I-want-to-do path. I'll start off from how I grew up. There were giants in the air. It was during World War II and these iconic figures dominated the world—some for great evil and some for great good. We happened to be on the side of great good, when you think about Churchill and Roosevelt. I'm reminded of how grateful we should be for their examples of leadership and how wary we should be of dictators and demagogues like the Hitlers and Mussolinis. In those days, very like as recently as September 11, 2001, we turned our eyes to public figures.

I happened to go to a college where the president was one of the men who laid the foundation for our field of organizational behavior and leadership. That was Douglas McGregor, who was the president of the college that I went to and had come from MIT.

This was true when I was a young person. As I was born in 1925, it was very clear that the Depression and World War II were influential in my development. Those of us growing up in those formative years saw horrors with Mussolini, Hitler and, later on, with Stalin. Listening to Hitler giving his speeches during the 1930s before World War II was very, very scary.

So, I grew up at a time when you saw how influential leaders could be and how influential their activities, their political entities, their organizations could be—potentially virulent and toxic; how much pathogen could be spread by one person and how many healthy white cells by the other. That was just part of it, part of the zeitgeist, part of the era. It was very important, though largely unconscious to us.

There were other things—of a more "micro," interpersonal nature. I happened to go to a college where the president was one of the men who laid the foundation for our field of organizational behavior and leadership. That was Douglas McGregor, who was the president of the college that I went to and had come from MIT. Well, it was no accident that I also became a college president and also did my Ph.D. at MIT. He was very interested in group dynamics and leadership-wrote a lot about it—and certainly the "McGregorian chants," as I called them, were very influential. Being at MIT, being in Cambridge, Massachusetts, during the 1950s and 1960s certainly influenced my thinking. I was fascinated by how, under certain conditions, groups can do the most creative, the most spectacular things and reach the most extraordinary heights of achievement—if they can create the right conditions for it. *Organizing Genius*, for example, was really the fruit, the result of those early years of thinking about groups. I became very interested to see how organizations, where we spend at least a third of our life, if not more, can be less toxic, more healthy, and provide more opportunities for people's growth, so that they can reach the frontiers of human possibility.

Three words leaders have trouble dealing with: "I don't know." I think good leadership will often start with questions whose answer is: "I don't know, but we're going to find out."

Even before September 11, we were living in a world characterized by mystery, doubt, complexity, un-

"Discrimination is the capacity to discern what is important." (Warren Bennis)

certainty, and chaos. Think about the transformation from an analog to a digital society. In 1989, for example, there were only 400 users of the Web; now, as Shakespeare wrote in the 16th century, "we are a girdled globe." Before September 11 there were something like forty ongoing border disputes around the world. Globalization. Disruptive technologies. People are going to have to deal with doubt and uncertainty.

Organizations, organizational leadership, and organizational culture will have to be people factories–generating, nourishing, and nurturing terrific talent. They have to be education factories where that talent will be continually going to school. They will have to be led by leaders with enough emotional intelligence and cognitive capacity to be able to hold two divergent ideas in their heads at one time. I think those are going to be the critical aspects.

I'm going to add from my own work what I consider to be four critical aspects of leadership, which came out of a study about leadership and learning. I think they're important. And I want to argue that these four factors, which I think are critical for leading in this new world, are context- and culture-free. One is the adaptive capacity, which I think is probably the *sine qua non*, absolutely the most essential and central aspect of leadership in this environment of complexity and turbo-change. The adaptive capacity has a lot of things under it. It means a sense of resilience, hardiness, and creativity. It means seizing opportunities. It means learning learning. The second critical ingredient is the capacity to engage followers in shared meaning–to align the stars around a common, meaningful goal. Not just any old goal. Think Henry V at Agincourt: "a mission from God." Third, leaders are really going to have to spend a long time–and it's a continual process–finding out who they themselves are: learning their own voice, learning how they affect other people, learning a great deal about emotional intelligence. And finally, leaders will have to rely on a moral compass, a set of principles, a belief system, a set of convictions. Every good leader is going to have to–one way or another–learn these capacities. Now, I do think there are contextual and cultural factors, but I'm saying that, regardless of culture and context, these four factors are essential. They are necessary, but not sufficient. For example, if you're interested in leading a ballet company, you must know something about choreography and about the art world. There's a whole ecology around ballet, around science, around being a baseball manager. Nevertheless, these four factors are, across the board, essential, whether talking about Shakespeare or the failure of Ivester at Coca-Cola.

Managers need to ask themselves: Do you really want to lead? Are you aware of the sacrifices, the time demands, the complexity? Do you have a true commitment to abandon your ego to the talents of others? Do you love what you're doing? Do you enjoy trying to understand the social etiquette of bureaucracy? Do you really enjoy engaging others?

Any great place to work can be profitable. In fact, the most profitable *are* great places to work. I remember a former president of MIT once said to me, without a trace of grandiosity, that MIT "has had the habits of success." There's something about being successful that tends to perpetuate itself. I think that what will make a workplace great is when people really feel down deep that the company is on their side, that they will be treated equitably and fairly, that they are being given many opportunities for self-development and organizational development, where people are encouraged to "talk truth to power." If they're going to be putting in a lot of work at a place, not only do people need to have a license to tell the truth, they want to be in a place where they really feel they're going to be learning. People want to feel nurtured, that they're growing, and that there are enormous developmental opportunities available to them. To use my friend, Charles Handy's, book title, I think we're all "hungry spirits." Deep down, we all want to make a difference; if there's no meaning at work, people will check their hearts at the door.

Organizations, organizational leadership, and organizational culture will have to be people factories—generating, nourishing, and nurturing terrific talent.

Emotional Intelligence and Leadership *by Rick Lash*

EXECUTIVE SUMMARY

- Effective leaders create organizational climates that foster superior performance.
- Creating climates for performance requires leaders to demonstrate high levels of emotional intelligence (EI)—the capacity to manage one's own emotions and the emotions of others.
- Developing EI is a journey demanding a commitment to personal growth and development.

Introduction

Most organizations are not the stable, predictable structures of the past. Keeping people motivated and committed in an era of unrelenting and accelerating change are among the most difficult challenges leaders at all levels now face. Companies need to be far more agile and flexible in how they operate both internally and externally. This changing nature presents a whole new challenge for those in positions of leadership. To meet these challenges, leaders must be able to create organizational climates that foster not only performance but also a sense of pride and purpose.

Research indicates that up to 30% of business results come from the climate a leader creates—defined as employees' perceptions of their work environment that impact their ability to do their jobs well. And up to 70% of organizational climate is driven by the competencies of the leader. These competencies can be wrapped up in a skills "package" called emotional intelligence (EI).

Defining Emotional Intelligence

To quote Daniel Goleman, best-selling author of *Working with Emotional Intelligence,* emotional intelligence is defined as "the capacity for recognizing our own feelings and those of others, for motivating ourselves, for managing emotions well in ourselves and in our relationships." Specific competencies that make up EI have been identified, including emotional self-awareness, empathy, self-confidence, self-control and listening skills.

For many leaders, EI is not an easy concept to accept. Yet studies have shown that EI has real impact on bottom-line results, sometimes doubling and even tripling productivity. For example, in a study done for the American insurance industry, the most successful companies (judged by growth and financial results) had C.E.O.s with a critical mass of emotional intelligence capabilities. By comparison, the C.E.O.s of companies with just average results lacked these strengths. The difference seems to have been in the climate created among those who worked in the companies, with the high-EI C.E.O.s creating a workplace where people gave their best.

In another study, sales agents with high EI competencies sold twice the amount as average performers. This same study has also shown that EI, unlike IQ, can be increased over time. The key to such improvement is the developmental approach that is used.

Developing Emotional Intelligence

Emotional intelligence is a complex set of skills and requires time to develop. There are seven critical factors in developing EI:

- Gauge readiness
- Motivate
- Make change self-directed
- Establish manageable goals
- Encourage practice
- Arrange support
- Provide models.

Gauge readiness: Many organizations pay little attention to whether someone they send for training is ready to learn and change. Frequently, only 20% of a group is committed to personal change at any given time. In truth, people will learn what they want to learn when they want to learn it. Learning requires interest, motivation and commitment. This requires an emotional investment in the process to make it happen.

Feedback tools that highlight EI competencies, such as 360-degree feedback, are particularly helpful in affirming what the individual does and does not know, and the level of interest in closing the gap between current state versus future state.

Motivate: People invariably want to know, "What's in it for me?" They are motivated when learning is aligned with their values, aspirations and goals. Personal and professional goals are major factors.

Meaningful and lasting change happens when participants have first identified their personal and professional values, goals and needs. People develop EI when goals are personally meaningful. Although all seven guidelines are important, this one is particularly important and requires time and attention. This can be done through exercises where people write down their ideal or dream job, or identify times in their lives when they felt engaged and truly alive. Their pictures of success will also include needs around family, community and leisure activities, as well as their work.

Make change self-directed: Learning EI is very personal, yet most training in organizations is designed as "one-size-fits-all." The commitment to learning—emotional investment—will increase with a greater opportunity for the individual to control the method and pace at which they learn. This honors the competencies of EI in respecting the individual's levels of achievement, self-confidence and need to "direct themselves." To support this, determining the person's "learning style" and then designing or adapting the program to match is critical.

Nor should EI training be limited to the classroom. Learning EI skills requires social interaction with others. Taking participants outside the classroom to environments that put them in real-life situations that require active listening, empathy and self-control skills is a highly-effective technique for achieving both a commitment to action and the retention of new knowledge, because the control sits with the student and not the trainer.

Establish manageable goals: Too often, people set goals that are too large and unwieldy. While their desired goal is not out of line, the sheer scope can be overwhelming and the individual can't see how they can get there. Goals should be specific and behavioral. Imagine a goal of achieving higher levels of empathy. At first glance, many would see the task as overwhelming and one may not know where to begin.

In developing empathy, the goal may be to have three conversations with people over the next week simply practicing listening without interrupting or jumping to

"In the new, stripped-down, every-job-counts business climate. . .human realities will matter more than ever."
(Daniel Goleman)

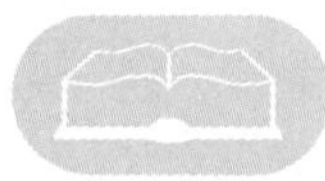

conclusions. Next, the goal may be to reflect back what you heard and check for understanding or seeking feedback from several trusted colleagues on your empathy skills. Small successes also build self-esteem and confidence.

Encourage practice and arrange support: Some believe that behavioral changes in EI will occur after a one, two or three-day program. It seems just a little ambitious to expect adults–usually with 20 or more years of life experience determining their current behaviors–to change to any great degree in a matter of days.

Good musician–practice. Good golfer–practice. Good public speaker–practice. The same applies to any desired result around behavioral change, although this is too frequently ignored in training programs. It requires support and direction from others, which can be delivered by establishing peer coaches, study groups and support networks or, in some cases, a trained personal coach.

To change complex competencies such as those found within EI can take three to six months for maximum effect.

Provide models: It's important to remember that those who teach should embody the behaviors they wish to see in others. Nothing is more demotivating than being asked to behave in a certain way by those who do not embrace the same behavioral practices.

People tend to model their behavior on those who are more senior within the organization, negative as well as positive habits. Leaders need a high level of self-awareness and skills in persuasion, and must demonstrate consistency and reliability.

Organizations utilizing EI for leadership:

- At Johnson & Johnson, all 20 EI competencies were significantly stronger in a group of "high potential" mid-career executives than in a comparison executive group.
- At a global division (with 400 branches in 56 countries) of the German electronics conglomerate Siemens, four EI competencies distinguished the star leaders, whose growth in revenues and return on sales put their performance in the top 15%. They were significantly stronger in the drive to achieve results, initiative, collaboration and teamwork, and leading teams. Not a single technical or purely cognitive competency emerged as the unique strengths of outstanding leaders.
- As part of a program to help the Defense Finance and Accounting Service of the U.S. Government prepare future leaders to handle a new organizational structure, downsizing and new technology, a program on Developing Competencies for Leadership Success (emotional intelligence competencies) was delivered to 20 high potential middle level managers. This program followed the principles for developing emotional intelligence put forth by the Consortium on Emotional Intelligence, and it included seven contact days over a period of 14 months. The outcome was overwhelming. Participants not only reported that the program was helpful in preparing them to deal with the challenges they were facing, but they increased significantly (from pre and post assessments) in 19 of the 20 EI competencies, as measured by a 360-degree assessment.

A Personal Journey

Emotional intelligence is developed by reflecting on experiences, learning about oneself and practicing new behaviors. This raises a key point–developing EI is a journey that unfolds in stages. It is all about personal transformation. Like all great stories of personal transformation, there is the call to adventure, crossing the threshold into the unknown, embarking on a road of trials and tests, coming face to face with one's greatest weakness, and ultimately transforming oneself.

The benefits that come from developing emotional intelligence are profound. Individuals gain new knowledge and skill, a deeper understanding of themselves, greater wisdom and, perhaps most importantly, a broader perspective.

People who have developed their EI tend to be less self-focused and more community focused; less concerned with their own needs and more concerned about positioning others for success and becoming catalysts for change in their organizations and communities. They are less fearful and more courageous, less blaming and more willing to take accountability.

Making It Happen ▸▸

- Start with developing a clear picture of your "ideal self"–what are your most important values? What are you passionate about? What would you most like to do? What is your unique contribution?
- Get feedback from others. How do they see you? Find out what impact your behavior has on others. Is there a gap between your "ideal self" and the way you really are in the world?
- Choose a personal development goal that is meaningful to you. Make it specific and behavioral. Remember, sometimes making a small change can have a big impact.
- Recognize your own journey–the transitions that forced you to learn and grow as an individual and a leader.
- Find a helper–someone who has been through the journey himself and who can give you that sense of perspective and roadmap for what you can expect along the way.
- Become more deliberate about your own learning. If you haven't failed lately, you're not learning.

Conclusion

In times of rapid change, leaders must possess the skills and knowledge that create a climate for outstanding performance. Emotional intelligence–the capacity to recognize and manage one's emotions and show empathy towards others–are the foundation upon which organizational leadership is based. Developing EI demands personal commitment to long-term growth. It's a journey worth taking, for becoming more emotionally intelligent enriches not just ourselves but the organizations and communities in which we live and work.

For More Information

Books:

Cherniss, Cary, and Daniel Goleman, eds. *The Emotionally Intelligent Workplace*. San Francisco, CA: Jossey-Bass, 2001.

Goleman, Daniel. *Working With Emotional Intelligence*. New York: Bantam Books, 1998.

Goleman, Daniel, Richard Boyatzis, and Annie McKee. *Primal Leadership: Realizing the Power of Emotional Intelligence*. Boston, MA: Harvard Business School Press, 2002.

Web Sites:

www.haygroup.com: this site contains numerous references on EI and other competency related topics and services.

www.eiconsortium.org: this site provides access to the latest research and references on EI in the workplace.

"Too seldom does the world pause to consider how much kinder and more humane business has become since women invaded the market-place."

(Edith Johnson)

WHO'S GUIDING YOUR CORPORATE DESTINY?
by Don Blohowiak

EXECUTIVE SUMMARY

- A shortage of organizational leadership looms on the horizon as economic and demographic forces converge to keep the pool of talented leaders small—just when they're needed most.
- Executives must act now to stop a leadership vacuum from developing and preventing their organization from competing in a most demanding and unforgiving marketplace.

INTRODUCTION

Organizations worldwide face a troubling demographic challenge. In blunt, politically incorrect plain talk: too many entrenched, old-style views, too few young leaders.

Population trends conspire to leave a huge hole in managerial ranks. Baby boomers, those born between 1946 and 1964, will soon retire from the full-time labor force, leaving a huge talent vacuum, with the greatest impact likely to be felt about 2010.

Throughout industrialized nations boomers have failed to replace themselves with a baby boomette. The 1970s pop-culture mantra of zero population growth apparently took root in fertile soil. The birthrate for nearly all developed countries continues to decline below the replacement rate of 2.1. This shrinking labor pool comes just as many nations see their economies cranking along at near-full throttle, straining the means of production to meet demand. Most companies already sense the coming shortage. McKinsey & Company surveyed nearly 7,000 executives and managers in 2000 and found only 7% who could strongly agree with the statement, "Our company has enough talented managers to pursue all or most of its promising opportunities."

DEBOSSED CAN'T MEAN AN END TO LEADERSHIP

But wait, isn't the "flat" organization, delayered of paper-shuffling, non-value-adding middle managers, solving the shortage problem? In short, no. Expectations for high performance results from customers and the financial markets alike mean that leadership is in increasing demand just as the labor pool evaporates.

Team- or process-oriented organizations may need fewer bosses, but they depend on bountiful cadres of *leaderful* people to make their teams and task forces productive. As Tom Peters recently opined, "We're going to see leadership emerge as the most important element of business—the attribute that is highest in demand and shortest in supply."

THE NEED FOR LEADERSHIP

A quick scan of the business landscape reveals a loud cry for leadership. Today's market decrees that an organization can survive only by consistently demonstrating increasing capacity for such hard-earned virtues as speed, innovation, responsiveness, value, productivity, quality, and teamwork.

The means to achieve such virtues lies in the province of leadership. They include:

- clarity of direction and priorities
- decisiveness
- adaptability to changes in technology, customer expectations, and society at large
- proficiency of the workforce
- consistency of execution

Leadership sustains life in an organization struggling to endure in a cruel market of demanding customers and ruthless competitors. Weak leadership condemns an organization to death.

LEADERSHIP VOID

This obvious need for leadership comes at a time when C.E.O. tenure is increasingly measured in months as impatient investors look for substantial results instantly and then constantly.

The irony, of course, is that results actually derive from leadership and competent execution by people who toil far from the executive suite. Most of them were sweating in the trenches before the latest C.E.O.'s arrival, and most will still be there when this one is replaced by yet another water-walking hopeful.

An organization that's going to be consistently successful must be led consistently well throughout its ranks. That means cultivating leadership skills deeply and broadly in the work force at large so that the whole organization can amplify, bring to life, and continuously make real the inspired musings of its visionary top leader. With fewer titular leaders at the very time that organizations need more leadership, the gap must be closed by more people, many without rank, being *leaderful*. And that means going beyond empowerment. It is not enough to empower employees; it may even be dangerous to do so. If empowered employees are not adequately prepared to exercise the rudiments of leadership as requisite underpinnings for their conferred power, they're tantamount to fully authorized but unguided missiles.

DEEP LEADERSHIP IN THE REAL WORLD

Some organizations grasp that leadership can't be the sole province of the executive suite, or even vested in the shrinking ranks of its heavily burdened middle managers. Others are beginning to uncouple the false relationship between position and leadership. We may never live in a bossless world—and that surely isn't the goal—but, as these organizations demonstrate, we should strive to create a world where more people act like leaders regardless of the hierarchy's depth.

MINI-CASES

With a leadership tradition spanning more than two centuries, the *Marine Corps*, operating in relatively small numbers, usually under hostile conditions, understands that its formal leaders can be lost just when they're needed most. So while vesting official authority in top ranks, the Marines make leadership development at all levels a priority. Personal leadership by all Marines is an ethic that is constantly on the agenda. It is reflected in continual training, in the culture of daily life, and in formal celebrations to mark what the Corps values most: honor, initiative, and accomplishment by the *team*. The Marines do not aggrandize their formal bosses. (Just try to name a famous Marine Corps general.)

Far removed from the Marines' frontline artillery, the finance organization of *Motorola* has put personal leadership on its agenda. It encourages its accountants, analysts, and other professionals at all levels to be leaderful in their work regardless of whether they have any personnel management responsibility.

"Control your destiny or die." (Jack Welch)

Likewise, *CUNA Mutual Group*, the financial services giant that supports credit unions worldwide, has created training and assessments to engage individual contributors in developing leaderful competencies. CUNA Mutual requires all its employees to understand its current challenges and opportunities and to know and apply the company's mission and vision to their own work. In addition, the company makes it clear that contributors can't merely be passive recipients of orders from their managers. "All employees are required to work with their manager and others to set goals and plan their workload—and to apply sound reasoning to make effective decisions and suggest process improvements where appropriate."

Building Leadership in Your Company

Because every individual works and learns differently, there is no universal leadership development panacea. And no one becomes a better leader instantaneously as the result of a singular event or experience, no matter how intense, memorable, or expensive.

But the author's experience, and studies conducted by Linkage, the Center for Creative Leadership, and Development Dimensions International, indicate that the following methods are most likely to build more leaderful associates from well-meaning people regardless of rank:

- opportunities to practice leading. Surgery, swimming, and leading are all developed by supplementing instruction and coaching with actual practice;
- evaluations (objective, from validated instruments; and subjective, through feedback from colleagues);
- instruction from credible leadership teachers, ideally including respected senior executives.

Making It Happen ▸▸

- **Identify the leadership capabilities you need to accomplish your organization's business objectives.** They may vary from those typically considered standard leadership competencies. If your organization doesn't truly value teamwork, preaching its virtues will ring hollow. Don't ask the middle to be better than the top, or you'll get two sure results: demoralized would-be leaders, and departing talent
- **Secure senior management support of and participation in the leadership development process.** If you can't readily point to he leadership qualities you're advocating in your company's own senior ranks, reconsider the development effort until it has registered an impact at the most visible level of management. Get top managers to put leadership development on their priority agenda and to become involved in the design and delivery of the leadership curriculum—not to talk about leadership theories, but to share their own very personal experiences with leadership challenges in their careers, especially their darkest and lowest moments. If you can't get senior managers to actively participate in the development program, it's not important. Save everyone a lot of time, energy, and money and avoid putting ambitious, hopeful people into a process that is bound to disappointment them.
- **Craft a uniquely tailored leadership development program.** It should:
  - tie in closely with your business needs. Don't try to build an idealized leader based on an overly generalized and unattainable model;
  - integrate multiple coordinated development mechanisms (see below);
  - welcome all interested associates;
  - teach and cultivate appropriate leadership skills. Someone wrestling with decisions about whether to merge with a competitor isn't drawing on the same leadership competencies as someone consumed with making sure a package gets shipped by 6 p.m.
- **Actually develop leadership capacity in your firm's people.** Use methods to increase the odds of delivering meaningful learning with tangible business results. Provide your associates with opportunities to:
  - participate in special assignments or work on special projects outside their normal work duties to give them exposure to new groups or departments;
  - rotate into new full-time assignments—a fresh view comes from a new vantage point;
  - teach or mentor others; a mentoring or teaching assignment provides great opportunities for people to pay greater attention to and reflect on what they do and why they do it that way;
  - receive coaching or mentoring; this personal, interactive learning experience could be in a one-on-one relationship with a more senior manager or could come through participation with a group of peers;
  - attend external development courses and learning events;
  - go to in-house training courses and leadership development programs;
  - volunteer for service to a charity or nonprofit organization to expose them to other perspectives and nonroutine challenges, some of which may well be bigger in scope than currently offered by their day job.

Conclusion

Leadership, like luck, is a secret ingredient in every successful enterprise. Unlike luck, leadership can be cultivated and grown. But it doesn't happen quickly. Given the growing need and the shrinking supply of future leaders, smart businesspeople will give immediate priority to intentionally and programmatically developing leadership skills at all levels of their organization.

The important elements of encouraging leaders at all levels include voicing and demonstrating your expectation for leaderful behavior and providing people with quality instruction, useful feedback, and rewards for practicing leadership. In the very near future a high-performing organization will be a leaderful organization. Build yours now.

For More Information

Books:

Conger, Jay A., and Beth Benjamin. *Building Leaders: How Successful Companies Develop the Next Generation.* San Francisco, CA: Jossey-Bass, 1999.

Tichy, Noel M., and Eli Cohen. *The Leadership Engine: How Winning Companies Build Leaders at Every Level.* New York: HarperBusiness, 2000.

See also:

☆ **Setting Objectives for a Business (pp. 305–06)**

"What I love about magazines is that an individual can change the destiny of an entire business."

(Duncan Edwards)

  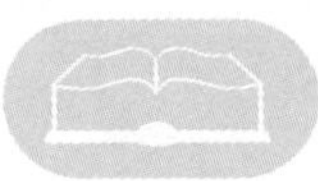    

DECIDING KEY OPERATIONAL QUESTIONS *by Mark Brown*

EXECUTIVE SUMMARY

- Think "white-light," not just "gray" goals.
- Think "future now"—create a "paradise paradigm."
- Nurture frames and not cages of mind.
- Encourage constructive dissent.
- Apply open-thinking tools.

INTRODUCTION

The information and knowledge latent within an organization are valuable resources for resolving key operational questions, making effective decisions, solving problems and ensuring success. Applying these resources to key operational issues is an important, valuable but challenging leadership task, and it is worth considering how best to harness the intellectual capital, knowledge, skills and experience of people within the organization for effective action. This needs to be done routinely and in a productive way, taking account of the needs of varied tasks, how people behave, time factors and the need for actions to be specific, achievable, dynamic and, very often, competitive.

This can be achieved by using the six-stage process outlined in the Executive Summary, which forms the focus for this section.

THE IMPERATIVE–THINK!

Think about thinking. Here's a simple and useful four-stage model of thinking:

1. goal
2. ideas or options
3. decision or selection
4. action

You go through these stages automatically time and time again.

For example,

- goal–to choose a vacation
- ideas–Mexico, Monaco, Morocco
- decision–Monaco
- action–off you go.

Or, in a business context,

- goal–to attract and retain customers
- options–new and improved products, packaging, new pricing strategy, etc.
- selection–new product
- action–launch the product.

The rate of change is exponential. Tom Peters named the 1990s the Nanosecond 90s. We now live in the mad mayhem of a new and probably crazier millennium.

Who will win in this new world? Those individuals and organizations that have the greatest passion for their work combined with an unremitting ability to think smartly and outthink their competitors.

To create passion, make work worthwhile and meaningful. To outthink others, start to "metathink," that is, think about thinking, and manage your own and your organization's thinking. What follows are some ideas for thinking about and managing thinking.

THINK "WHITE-LIGHT," NOT JUST "GRAY" GOALS

Think about *where* to think. You often automatically start to think when faced with a problem. Much thinking is problem solving–gray-driven, not opportunity-driven white light. You can solve numerous problems without particularly affecting your organization for the better. Or you can focus on one white-light opportunity–for example, to attract and retain substantially more customers–and have a real impact.

Although some problems do have to be solved, as a rule of mind you need to shift to more *white-light* thinking: what is it that would more radically shift or step-change the organization? *Gray* problem solving prefers to wait for necessity to be the mother of invention. White-light thinking says: Never allow necessity to be the mother of invention. Invent and think now.

THINK "FUTURE NOW"—CREATE A PARADISE PARADIGM

Think about the future now. Two of the more obvious white-light goals in many organizations are the vision and mission statements. Many such statements can be vapid, uninspiring, untransformational rather than step-changing or paradigm-shattering. Even if people do begin to think about the goal, that thinking will be largely *past now* thinking that takes their past experience and familiar patterns and build or extrapolate from there in an evolutionary manner. As a result you usually get more of the same.

If you want to engage people's hearts and minds to create a radically different and massively more positive future, generate a goal or image of the future that is *tinglingly tangible, head- and heart-grabbing.* It should be so stretching and challenging to the patterns of the past that people have no choice but to think in discontinuous, revolutionary ways.

Thereby you begin to nurture *future now* thinking, in which you work back from the future to the present. The *paradise paradigms*, also called BHAGS (big, hairy, audacious goals), shatter the old patterns. Incrementalism is simply not enough. The paradise paradigm encourages revolutionary breakthrough thinking. The impossible becomes possible–and, given enough revolutionary imagination, probable–and is then achieved.

"This nation should commit itself to achieving the goal, before this decade is out, of landing a man on the moon and returning him safely to earth."

John F. Kennedy, 1961

NURTURE FRAMES AND NOT CAGES OF MIND

Don't be a victim of your thinking. A paradise paradigm can usefully act to disrupt the patterns of the past. This is not to say the patterns of the past are always foes to be vanquished. Without past patterns, precedents, mindsets, or paradigms, the world would be frighteningly and incomprehensibly chaotic. Past patterns more often than not help us to make sense of today and in turn predict the future. I recall a history teacher who used to explain that we study the past to understand the present and so predict the future.

So mindsets are often useful. But here's the bad news: they're no longer as useful as they once were. The patterns are helpful only if the past is largely the same as the present. The danger arises when we rely on outdated frames of reference or models of the world. Our thinking and decision making can become limiting, and in retrospect

---

"I try to create an environment in which others make decisions. Success means not making them myself."

(Ricardo Semler)

even absurd. And as the world is changing, ever-faster models and frames need ever more challenging and rethinking.

"There is no reason for any individual to have a computer in their home." Kenneth Olsen, president and founder of Digital Equipment Corporation, 1977.

"We don't like their sound. Groups of guitars are on the way out." Decca Records, rejecting the Beatles, 1962.

"Computers in the future may . . . perhaps only weigh one-and-a-half tons." *Popular Mechanics*, forecasting the development of computer technology, 1949.

"Stocks have reached what looks like a permanently high plateau." Irving Fisher, professor of economics, Yale University, 17 Oct 1929.

"[Television] won't be able to hold onto any market it captures after the first six months. People will soon get tired of staring at a plywood box every night." Darryl F. Zanuck, head of 20th Century-Fox, 1946.

"Everything that can be invented has been invented." Charles H. Duell, U.S. commissioner of patents, 1899.

As Gary Hamel neatly summarizes:

"Experience is valuable only to the extent that the future is like the past. In industry after industry the terrain is changing so fast that experience is becoming irrelevant and even dangerous."

Never has it been such a challenging time for more mature managers. Their models and frames may be based on terrains long since perished.

Now you might think that surely once you become aware that the past pattern is no longer useful for making sense of the present or predicting the future, you'll drop the old frame and adopt a new one. This is often not the case. Frames of reference are very sticky and tricky, and once formed they easily become cages of reference within which we become prisoners. This is because the thinking system has a built-in confirmatory bias that works hard to subsume and make sense of now in the light of the patterns of the past. We selectively perceive and uniquely create our own worlds, constantly seeking evidence that confirms those constructs. What a coincidence so many people agree with themselves and yet often disagree with others!

Old-world, more autocratic organizations that may still encourage conformity of word and thought can exacerbate the problem of outdated mindsets in senior managers. Reporting staff may select and pass upward information that sits comfortably with and confirms their managers' outdated world view. The mind selects the easily fitting. People often communicate up the organization only that information that is acceptable.

Human beings and organizations find it only too easy to operate with closed minds. So how to deal with these self-sealing and unchanging mindsets?

Encourage Constructive Dissent

To think better, dissent more. First of all, encourage constructive dissent and debate. Our own consultancy, Innovation Centre Europe, has built on the groundbreaking organizational climate research of the Swedish psychologist Goran Ekvall. We've developed his work in the form of the Innovation Climate Questionnaire, which establishes how well you score on 13 critical dimensions that predict how clever and innovative your organizational climate is. One of the key dimensions is constructive debate, encouraging people to challenge and constructively knock around ideas (not people!).

Practically, you can encourage everyone to constructively challenge all the sacred cows, the way you do things around there, the way you think about things. If it ain't broke, break it!

I recall a client in a unit of General Electric who wanted a simple way to help people "work out" (in other words, get rid of) unhelpful processes and procedures. I came up with the following very simple routine.

ABC

Abolish.

How can we do away with this system, procedure, or process?

If you can't,

Blockbust.

Here's the opportunity for radical, revolutionary creativity. Think outside the square. Think back to the original purpose of the system, procedure, or process and go back to basics. Produce a much smarter/easier/more cost-effective alternative.

If you can't,

Change.

Here's the opportunity for incremental, evolutionary creativity. Think within the square. How can the system, procedure, or process be simplified and/or modified to be smarter/easier/more cost-effective?

Apply Open-thinking Tools

Think openly. As well as encouraging people to challenge other people's mindsets, you can also try to pull yourself up by your own bootstraps and challenge your own mindsets. Some of the following may help:

- If everyone sees it that way—beware.
- If everyone is doing it—think afresh.
- Pay attention to and read at the edge of your field and beyond.
- Assume a blip may signal a new trend.
- Make explicit every assumption you hold—and challenge each assumption.

Making It Happen ▸▸

Issues to consider when resolving key operational questions are:

- **What actions and additional resources may be needed** to increase the likelihood of success—who will do what, when, where and how.
- **How to mobilize and enthuse people** to take effective action.
- **What parts of the operational decision and response may be delegated**—and how.
- **The importance of timing** and the need to develop a sense of timing.
- **Where thoughtful analysis is required and where immediate, direct action is needed.**
- **The value of communication and empowerment**—an inclusive approach can often be the preferred method of deciding key operational questions, as it gives ownership of the answer to those people that will deliver the action.

For More Information

Book:

Collins, James C., and Jerry I. Porras. *Built to Last: Successful Habits of Visionary Companies*. New York: HarperBusiness, 1997.

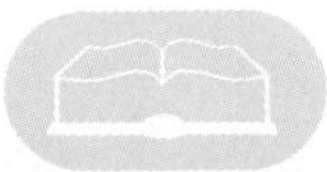

BOARDROOM ROLES *by Adrian Cadbury*

EXECUTIVE SUMMARY

- The role of the board is to direct not to manage.
- Balance of board membership and choice of individuals are key.
- The chair is responsible for the effectiveness of the board.
- Nonexecutive directors have a particular contribution to make to the work of a board.
- Board committees are important structurally and for the tasks they undertake.
- Executive directors should be appointed solely for the value they can add to the board.
- Board members have different roles; what matters is how they combine to form the board team.

ROLE OF THE BOARD

The crispest definition of a board's role is that of Sir John Harvey Jones, a well-known, British former C.E.O.: "to create tomorrow's company out of today's." A more extensive answer to "What is an effective board?" is provided in *Corporate Boards*, a book I cite more fully later: "The vast majority of U.S. governance practices are concerned with. . .shareholder value," though the authors of that book readily concede that a board only concerned with making profits for owners is a board with "too narrow" a perspective.

Boards are in place to direct and not to manage. They have the task of defining the purpose of their enterprises and of agreeing on the strategy for achieving that purpose. They are responsible for appointing chief executives to turn strategic plans into action, for supporting and counseling them on how to do so and, if necessary, for replacing them. Above all, boards are there to provide leadership, and it is in this context that the roles of board members need to be considered.

BOARD COMPOSITION

A single board at the head of a company is the commonest form of board structure. Unitary boards of this nature are made up of executive and nonexecutive, or outside, directors. (Two-tier boards separate these two kinds of director; their structure is covered briefly in Case Study). Given that both executive and outside directors sit on unitary boards, the first issue is the balance between them. Ten years ago the ratio for U.K. boards was around two-thirds executive directors and one-third outside directors. This has now moved closer to parity and in future I would expect outside directors to be in the majority. This is already the position in the United States where the chief executive is often the only executive on the board and is usually its chair as well.

In addition to the question of balance, there is the question of size. There is a clear move to smaller boards in both the United States and the United Kingdom. Martin Lipton and Jay W. Lorsch in their "Modest Proposal for Improving Corporate Governance" (*The Business Lawyer*, volume 48, pages 59–77) recommend a maximum board size of ten and favor eight or nine. The argument for smaller boards is that they enable all the directors to get to know each other and to contribute effectively in board discussions, thus arriving at a true consensus. The crucial point is that boards are teams and provide collective leadership. So the balance of membership and choice of individuals are key to forming the team.

MINI-CASE

TWO-TIER BOARDS

Two-tier boards constitute a supervisory board whose members are all nonexecutive and a management board made up of executive directors. The management board is responsible for strategy as well as for running the business. The supervisory board appoints and can dismiss the management board and no one can be on both boards. The legal responsibilities of the two boards and of their directors are different, whereas with a unitary board all directors have the same legal duties however the board is structured. Since supervisory boards often have employees as members, this raises the question of their role on boards. In Germany, for example, boards of companies of varying sizes include employees; by contrast, those in the Netherlands tend not to do so. My view is that employees can most effectively participate at levels below the board, where the decisions are taken that affect them most directly and to which they can contribute knowledgeably.

THE CHAIR'S ROLE

The chair is responsible for the effectiveness of the board. This responsibility rests with the chair whatever the other duties. It leads to the point that all companies are different and the issues they face are constantly changing. Individual boards have to follow accepted board principles, but in ways which meet their particular circumstances. It is the chair who has the responsibility of ensuring that the make-up of the board is appropriate for the challenges ahead. Similarly, it is the chair who has the task of welding their directors into an effective team. Effective boards are not brought into being simply by seating competent individuals around a board table. Creating effective boards requires effort by their members, but above all coaching and leadership by the chair. This is an argument for the chair not also being chief executive.

The chair is responsible for the running of the board. Responsibilities include the agenda, the provision of adequate and timely information to all directors and the actual conduct of board meetings. The chair is also, provided they are not chief executive, responsible for putting in place a means by which the board can evaluate their own performance. Where the chair is also chief executive, their duties in relation to their board remain the same, but their deputy or a senior outside director would be responsible for the appraisal of the chief executive and for the review of the board's performance.

ROLE OF NONEXECUTIVE DIRECTORS

All directors are equal in that they all carry the same legal responsibilities. Outside or nonexecutive directors are in that sense no different from their executive colleagues. They do however have particular contributions to make to their boards by virtue of standing further back from the business. One is in reviewing the performance of the chief executive and the executive team; clearly the outside directors are the only

"Top jobs are designed for people with wives." (Lucy Heller)

board members in a position to do this objectively.

Another contribution is in relation to potential conflicts of interest, such as those between the interests of the executives and those of the shareholders. Examples are directors' pay, dividends versus reinvestment and whether top appointments should be made from within or outside the company. Decisions on these matters are ultimately the decision of the whole board, but nonexecutive directors are well placed to offer direction on where the best interests of the company—to which all directors owe their duty—lie.

Nonexecutive directors bring with them their experience in fields which are different from those of the executive directors, and this external experience is of particular value in strategy formulation. The potential advantage which the unitary board has over the two-tier board is that it provides the opportunity to combine, in the same body, the depth of knowledge of the business of the executives with the breadth of knowledge of the nonexecutive directors. Once again, it is up to the chair to make the most of these different viewpoints by the way they structure board debates.

The role of these directors in helping to resolve conflicts of interest does not imply that they have higher standards than their executive colleagues. The difference is simply that they can judge these matters more objectively because their interests are involved less directly.

Role of Board Committees

As the responsibilities of directors have become more demanding, boards have increasingly formed committees to deal with some of their more detailed work. All quoted companies need to establish audit and remuneration committees and, unless they have a small board, nomination committees. These committees strengthen the position of the outside directors, of whom they are made up, and are important for the work they do. The essential point is that they are committees of the board. It is the board which appoints them, sets their terms of reference and turns their recommendations into decisions.

Role of Executive Directors

The duties of executive directors are the same as those of the outside directors. They are as responsible for the monitoring task of the board as the outside directors, who in turn are as responsible for the strategy and leadership of the company as the executives. This means that executive directors have to take their executive hats off upon entering the boardroom and put on their directorial ones. They should only be appointed for the contribution they can make to the board and they are there to further the company's interests—not those of their function or department. It is not an easy transition to make and executive directors can be helped in the adoption of their new nonmanagerial role through appropriate training or through a nonexecutive directorship elsewhere.

Role of the Company Secretary

The chair and board members should be able to look to the company secretary for impartial and professional guidance on their responsibilities and all directors should have access to the advice and services of a company secretary, who is responsible for ensuring that board procedures are followed.

Making It Happen

In their insightful book, *Corporate Boards: New Strategies for Adding Value at the Top* (Jossey-Bass, 2001), Jay Conger, Edward Lawler, and David Finegold note that "High performance boards can be created only if the right mix of talent is present on the board." [p.37] They then lay out the numerous and important considerations that should come into play whenever a board is being constituted—or reconstituted. What is perhaps most important to remember is that the process for arriving at the composition of a board is almost as important as the process of leading and managing the board itself.

Every aspect of board member selection—from how the nominating committee operates to determining what knowledge and expertise are needed to making sure that a true balance of stakeholder interests—is worth thinking about now. As noted in *Corporate Boards*, the board is a management unit and the strength of the corporation is heavily dependent on making sure that "the board's needs for knowledge, information, power, and opportunity" [p. 55] are addressed. Perhaps the first thing a corporate leader should do is to gain objective, outside assistance to ascertain the strengths and weaknesses of the current board and to develop a plan for developing the corporate board in a reasonable length of time, just as executives routinely do in developing any other corporate business unit.

Conclusion

Although board members have different roles, what counts is the way those roles are combined in the board team. This is why board selection is so fundamental. Directors should only be appointed for the value they can add to the board. All directors should have terms of office to enable renewal to take place, although I am against rigid rules tying retirement to age or length of board service. The search for outside directors should be purposeful, with the aim of filling gaps in the experience and backgrounds of the existing directors, and selection should involve the board as a whole. The chair, however, has a particular responsibility for the choice of board members since it is their responsibility to turn them into an effective team.

For More Information

Books:

Carver, John. *Reinventing Your Board*. San Francisco, CA: Jossey-Bass, 1997.

Conger, Jay, Edward Lawler, and David Finegold. *Corporate Boards: New Strategies for Adding Value at the Top*. San Francisco, CA: Jossey-Bass, 2001.

Demb, Ada, and F. Friedrich Neubauer. *The Corporate Board: Confronting the Paradoxes*. New York: Oxford University Press, 1992.

Shultz, Susan F. *The Board Book*. New York: AMACOM, 2000.

Ward, Ralph D. *21st Century Corporate Board*. New York: John Wiley, 1996.

Web Sites:

www.boardmember.com: this is the site of *Corporate Board Member* magazine—a useful resource for board members of U.S. public companies.

www.iod.com: the U.K. Institute of Directors offers practical advice on how to run boards.

"Leadership is practiced, not so much in words as in attitude and in actions." (Harold S. Geneen)

  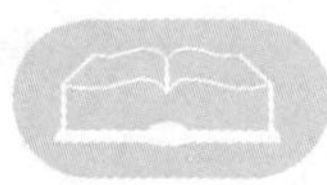    

REALLY LEADING: LEADERSHIP THAT IS AUTHENTIC, CONSCIOUS, AND EFFECTIVE

by Debashis Chatterjee

EXECUTIVE SUMMARY

- Leaders create reality when they challenge the prevailing constructs of convention.
- Conscious leadership is the art and science of the realization of reality.
- The first task of a leader is to define reality as the field of possibility; the final task of a leader is to lead people to their own possibilities.

INTRODUCTION

The leadership crisis is a crisis of perception. Imagine that you have to lead in a world that is vastly different not only from what you think it is, but also from what you think it can be. This world is changing faster than our thoughts can grasp. Consider that by 2037 only eight of the top 100 of the world's corporations are likely to be based in the United States. Today our timeworn notions are being seriously challenged. Consider what three corporate leaders have to say on the nature of the changing business environment:

- Leo Burke, former director of Motorola University, believes that "the future has already happened. However, this future is unevenly distributed."
- Michael Eisner, the C.E.O. of Disney, claims his organization brings a new product to the market every five minutes!
- Goran Lindahl, former president and C.E.O. of ABB, says, "Space is intellectual, space is not just physical space. Space is an environment that cultivates strong and useful ideas."

Reality as we know it is reshaping itself in countless nonlinear ways. Our thought-based linear models and plans are inadequate to contain this complex reality. What we need today are leaders with a quality of consciousness that can find coherence in this complexity. We need leaders with greater capability as well as "cope-ability."

THE THREE PARADOXES OF LEADERSHIP

1. PURSUING STABILITY AT A TIME OF INCREASING CHANGE

The first great paradox of leadership is that leaders must provide for stability in times of change. Change can be perceived only against an unchanging background. Each epoch of change has its unyielding frameworks, paradigms, and world-views.

Leaders shape reality. They do so by combining change and stability. This involves the synthesis of two innate human competencies: creation and construction. Whereas creation is a living and changing process, construction is a structure of stability that controls this process. Creation is multidimensional and dynamic; construction is sequential, progressing step by step. Any human organization has both a creative and a constructive aspect. Whereas the energy and vision of its members constitute the creative element of an organization, the functional division of the organization into design, manufacturing, and marketing constitutes the constructive element. Creation provides the organization with its core impulse, or the spirit of enterprise. Construction provides the tools and mechanisms for channeling impulse into activity.

During change, leaders have to challenge obsolete constructs, structures, systems, and procedures that sap the vital creative spirit of societies and organizations. Paradoxically, leaders have to clarify a consistent set of values or principles to make the process of change sustainable. Leaders have to ground themselves in certainty before they can lead people to an uncertain world of possibilities.

How do organizations on the bleeding edge of change maintain the integrity of a vital and creative organization while juggling with fleeting forms? The consulting firm, McKinsey, binds the unique spirit of enterprise of individual consultants with the integral purpose of the organization. McKinsey partners have developed "T-shaped" consultants. The vertical spike symbolizes the unique depth of expertise that each consultant brings, whereas the horizontal bar of the T stands for the need to integrate their expertise with the generalist perspective of the entire organization. Rajat Gupta, the managing director of McKinsey, says he builds a culture of flexibility and change without undermining the strong set of values governing McKinsey's ethos.

2. HANDLING AND COMBINING URGENT AND EMERGING ISSUES

The second great paradox of leadership is that leaders must develop the capacity to engage the urgent with the emergent. Change forces us to allow the urgent to dominate us: quarterly reports, market share, and tangible return on investment become paramount. In this paranoia, the emergent is often lost. Yet the emergent is the invisible face of a corporation's current reality. Roberto Goizueta, the former (and significant) C.E.O. of Coca-Cola, always believed that the future of the soft-drinks industry could be conceived as an emergent reality of infinite openings and possibilities. When the former Soviet Union was in political turmoil, Coke sent marketing experts to configure the country's emergent reality. Ed McCracken, the chairman and C.E.O. of Silicon Graphics, views emergence through the metaphor of farming. He says, "I grew up on a farm in Iowa, and I really appreciate the farming mentality, because you work really hard—and then you let the weather happen."

The urgent presents itself in tangible shape and form, whereas the emergent is subtler in its appearance. Leaders need to pre-sense emergent reality. In times of information overload leaders suffer from acute attention deficiency. They need to cultivate reflective moments in their work lives in order to restore the quality of attentiveness and see reality with greater clarity. A story from the Zen Buddhist tradition illustrates the point:

Three Zen masters are walking across a field. The youngest among them notices a flag tied to a pole. He draws the attention of his two companions and says, "Look how the flag moves." The middle-aged master pats the younger one on the back and says, "My boy, can't you see it is not the flag that moves, it is the wind that moves." The old master who has

 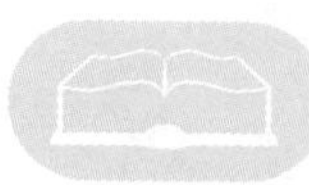    

been listening in silence softly says, "If you have attention enough you will see that it is neither the flag nor the wind that moves, it is the mind that moves."

3. Mutually Reinferring Knowledge and Action

The third great paradox of leadership is that leaders have to hold the tension of knowledge and action at the same time. The contemporary explosion of knowledge has far outstripped our capacity for action. Leaders today have to ask two fundamental questions:

1. Is this knowledge relevant?
2. Can this knowledge be put into practice and, if so, how?

Leaders need to operate through a framework of consistent values by which they can capture relevant knowledge and provide appropriate structures and tools to convert knowledge into action.

Knowledge is internal motion; action is external motion. Traditionally organizations could rely on the knowledge of the few at the top, who would strategize and plan for the actions of those below. Today an organization needs to be omniscient to be omnipotent. Organizational intelligence, which is simply knowledge-processing capacity, now needs to be distributed all along the organization's network in order for the organization to grow capacity for action. Ed McCracken of Silicon Graphics thinks that an Information Age company has to get as much connection as possible up to the nodes of the organization. This enables the company to have faster access to organizational intelligence and greater capacity for decision making at the grassroots.

Making It Happen ▸▸

How do conscious leaders make things happen? First, consciousness is not just about being aware of reality, it's also about influencing reality. This is truly an effective and integral view of leadership. Conscious leadership is a process that rests on two fundamental principles:

1. the principle of integration;
2. the principle of transformation.

Integration in the current climate of change implies *making the complex coherent*. Much of the complexity in the workplace comes from two sources: lack of attention and the loss of meaning. Leaders can restore lost attention through engagement with the minds and hearts of people they choose to serve. True integration is the orchestration of thought, feeling, and action. It is the process of connecting strategic intent with tools and techniques that evolve from people's own ingenuity and innovation. Loss of meaning occurs when leaders are unable to connect between the values of the organization and values-in-action, between knowledge infrastructure of the organization and its performance system.

As a leader, it can help to consider how the competing needs of the task, team and individual overlap.

- Achieving the **task** builds the team and satisfies the individuals.
- **If the team needs are not met** then the team lacks cohesiveness and efficiency, performance of the task is impaired and individual satisfaction is reduced.
- **If individual needs are not met** the team will lack cohesiveness and performance of the task can again be impaired.

Often leaders see charisma as being the defining skill of leadership. The difficulty is that charisma is frequently ineffective or inappropriate: it often dominates people and creates a reliance on the leader, instead of breeding initiative. Developing a successful workforce requires *empowering* leadership. This can be developed by fostering:

- a belief in constant learning rather than assumed mastery;
- the development of high self-esteem in others;
- a willingness to ask questions, admit weaknesses and listen to answers;
- strong interpersonal skills, including an appreciation of other people and sensitivity to individuals;
- an ability to engender trust, build relationships and inspire others; and the capacity to trust others;
- the ability and desire to develop leadership in others;
- the capacity to handle criticism by listening and drawing out people's concerns;
- a capacity to develop an effective vision for the future;
- an approach that possesses, values and nurtures innovation and initiative;
- the ability to communicate well at every level;
- integrity and trustworthiness;
- mentoring, coaching and counseling skills.

Conclusion

Transformation happens through sustained and sustainable change. It is a principle that creates so much synergy in a system that change happens spontaneously. Imagine an organization that captures relevant information from a swarming sea of data and quickly converts it into knowledge, creating one seamless flow of intelligence. That kind of organization must have the integrity and fluidity of a conscious system like the human body. When a certain part of the human body is in distress, the entire body's intelligence is activated to meet the contingency. Transformation happens through the unity of intelligence. In a human system leaders can bring about such unity of intelligence by trusting and acknowledging the essential magnificence of the human factor. A human being is a creation of life and not a construction of a machine-world. Conscious leaders therefore know that a human performs best as a factor of creation rather than as a factor of production. In this pursuit conscious leaders can do no more to lead people to their essential wholeness.

Conscious leaders learn to hold together the coordinates of stability and change, the urgent with the emergent, and knowledge with action. Authentic leadership is about restoring people to their full potential. Leaders accomplish this through the principles of integration and transformation. Conscious leaders lead people toward themselves.

For More Information

Books:

Heifetz, Ronald A. *Leadership without Easy Answers*. Cambridge, MA: Harvard University Press, 1994.

Senge, Peter M. *The Fifth Discipline: The Art and Practice of the Learning Organization*. New York: Doubleday, 1995.

See also:

☆ **Driving Fear from the Workplace (pp. 330–31)**
☆ **The Good, the Fad, and the Ugly (pp. 175–76)**
☆ **How to Walk on the Leading Edge without Falling off the Cliff (pp. 229–30)**
☆ **Viewpoint: Jim Kouzes (pp. 309–11)**
☆ **Viewpoint: Fons Trompenaars (pp. 27–28)**

"Leadership, unlike naked power wielding, is thus inseparable from followers' needs and goals."

(James MacGregor Burns)

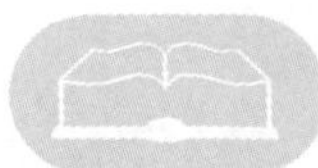

Viewpoint: Noel M. Tichy

Revealing How Management Is All About "Heart"

Anyone familiar with the history of General Electric will recognize Noel M. Tichy as one of the key advisors to C.E.O. Jack Welch. His relationship with Welch involved a two-year leave of absence from his faculty post at University of Michigan's Graduate School of Business to head up GE's Management Development Institute. His direct business experience and his extensive consulting, writing, and teaching career have shaped his views on transformational leadership. His unique perspective on 21st century leadership provides valuable insight for the business world as it forges ahead into the great unknown.

As much as I've learned in working with GE and consulting to Jack Welch, over the years, the person who has most influenced my thinking with respect to true leadership has been Eleanor Josaitis.

As a cofounder (and now executive director) of Focus: HOPE, Eleanor Josaitis joined forces with Father William Cunningham in 1968 to launch an initiative that has become a national model for change. Focus: HOPE began right after the Detroit riots of 1967. Eleanor was a housewife at the time and a mother of five children. Her concern was feeding the "hungry babies." As the program grew, she turned her attention to preparing young people for high-paying careers. She started a training program for students to become machinists, which led to the founding of MTI (the Machinist Training Institute). Her goal was to foster personal independence and self-sufficiency in an environment that would extend dignity and respect to every person.

Today we are in the midst of incredible change. Compared to the last 50 years, I think the future will be greatly influenced by the "enormously unexpected"—as in the case of terrorism.

Today this civil rights organization provides food to 43,000 seniors, mothers, and children monthly and operates a 40-acre college campus that grants bachelors degrees and boasts a $147 million factory of the future. It's a $90 million a year operation and a model of partnership that involves business, community, and some 51,000 supporters. Not bad for starting with no budget and a dream to feed the hungry!

What I've learned from Eleanor over the years has been how to *transform human beings*. The mission she and Fr. Cunningham crafted early on still guides the organization today, and I so believe in what she and her people are about, that I donate 20% of my own time to this initiative annually. What make her special are her qualities as a leader and teacher. She's the best I've ever met. . .and an excellent model for aspiring leaders. She is an advocate of capitalism, a champion for those she serves, and, at age 68, she has more spirit than most people half her age.

Today we are in the midst of incredible change. Compared to the last 50 years, I think the future will be greatly influenced by the "enormously unexpected"—as in the case of terrorism. There are those who would fractionalize the world—setting one nation against another, one ideology against another, one faction against another. As a capitalistic society, we cannot let this happen. We need to emulate Eleanor Josaitis's goal of uniting people of all races and ethnic origins in service to the greater good of helping others. We need to do everything in our power to figure out how everyone can benefit from sustainable development. Call it "enlightenment capitalism."

Distribution of wealth in the world is a problem. We have only to realize that all revolutions are the result of perceived deprivation and, furthermore, that societies cannot sustain themselves in situations where only a few benefit. Consequently, I think the challenge for business in the 21st century will be to ensure the equitable distribution of wealth. And, since the primary asset of every business is its intellectual capital, business leaders will be pressed to share the fruits of their intellectual wealth with others in ways that allow everyone to benefit. Those not doing this run the risk of being "overthrown" and their companies bested by the competition.

For the managers and leaders of the 21st century,

"The problem of our age is the administration of wealth, so that the ties of brotherhood may still bind together the rich and poor in harmonious relationship." (Andrew Carnegie)

the imperative will be to develop new skill sets—system-wide—that will enable their enterprises to cope with and manage change.

The whole game will be: how I as a leader can make the "brains" in my organization smarter and more aligned with the mission of what we are about. How will leaders do that? The answer is simple: teach! In a nutshell, the required skill, the hallmark of the successful leader of the future, will be that of continuously teaching and developing people. It will require the creation of what I regard as the "virtuous teaching cycle," which implies that "I teach you, but I create the situation where I learn from you, as well." Leaders will need to become better listeners and not just communicators.

As C.E.O. of General Electric, Jack Welch understood the importance of having managers in the classrooms of Crotonville who would challenge and teach *him* as much as he challenged and taught them. In fact, it was a group of young managers who pushed back on his strategy for the corporation of being #1 or #2 in their respective markets. Hearing their arguments as to the pitfalls of this strategy, he was prompted to rethink his direction for GE worldwide and return with a better, more refined strategy.

You might ask how managers will best be able to develop these required skills.

In my opinion managers will need to build very different kinds of environments for their people—environments that go beyond the creation of the "learning organization." That won't be enough. People will need to become teachers of others. In fact, it is in the process of teaching that we become both competent and confident in what we are about. And the more open we are to being taught by others, the more we learn.

David Novak, C.E.O. of Tricon Global Restaurants, owners of Taco Bell, KFC, and Pizza Hut, successfully transformed the culture of his organization after the restaurant group was spun off from PepsiCo. At Tricon people are encouraged to have fun, support one another, be committed to satisfying customers, and make a difference in their communities. Success is synonymous with personal growth and development.

At Accenture, the world's leading provider of management and technology consulting services, Mary Tolan, managing partner of the Resources Global Market unit, is driving virtuous teaching cycles deep into the organization. In a firm where intellectual capital is the stock in trade, you'd better believe teaching and learning are critical functions.

Terrorism in and of itself has redefined how we will go about globalization in the future as compared to our approach in the past. For example, from 1989 to 1998, after the end of the cold war, we'd take the top talent attending our Global Leadership Program at Michigan and send them out as teams to assess how to do globalization. We'd drop them into Japan, Russia, and China to let them figure what was the best way to approach business development in emerging markets. After a while the outcomes produced by the teams were fairly predictable. But, with the advent of terrorism as a global problem, all that has changed. I think we are in a world where we don't know what the playing field is going to look like. Yet the whole issue ties back to the distribution of wealth and its role as it relates to the environmental and human capital sides of the equation.

As I begin to watch Jeff Immelt, the "new guy" at GE, I find he is relating the business as a whole to its various communities globally. He appears to be rethinking globalization, in a way. And, I believe that's good, particularly for the emerging group of business leaders.

In my opinion managers will need to build very different kinds of environments for their people—environments that go beyond the creation of the "learning organization."

You know, for a long time the United States bought into the notion of destroying organizational structures and redeploying the assets. We need to take a hard look at that approach. The more serious issue is where people don't get to play at all, as distinct from what happens to those who get cut from payrolls.

When I think about how leaders can best promote enterprises that are both profitable and good places for people to work, it comes down to "heart."

That's another way of saying people have to care. If organizations are good places to work, they'll be profitable—the two are not mutually exclusive. The challenge for leaders in the 21st century will be how to bring about that combination. Jeff Immelt at GE certainly sees heart as important. He's getting the workforce and their communities more involved in working together. The way he sees it, if people are more in tune with one another then everyone benefits. But, no one has a lock on how to do this. For a period of time Hewlett Packard was this great model of the profitable enterprise and a great place to work, but their model was not sustainable. Getting heart into an enterprise is critical to its success, particularly in a global marketplace.

"The new theory of organization relates to a corporation as though it has characteristics of its own, such as intelligence, ability to learn, and a culture." (Michael D. McMaster)

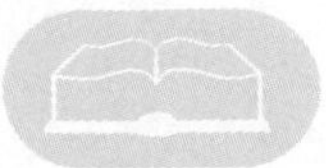

LEADERSHIP *by Peter de la Billiere*

EXECUTIVE SUMMARY

- Clarity without ambiguity is the essential ingredient in the executive mission statement.
- Communication is both lateral and up and down the chain of command. It is the lifeblood of an efficient company.
- Leadership is an extension of the personality and can be developed through training throughout a person's career.
- Delegation requires courage, but without it you will fail to exploit the potential of your managers.
- Change for change's sake spells disaster. The true leader sees necessary change as a challenge and as the foundation for growth and expansion.
- Moral courage is the backbone of a leader in peace or war.

INTRODUCTION

Leadership is exercised not only in a commercial business environment (although that is probably the biggest single area of activity where leaders are to be found), but in virtually every area of life, from the cradle to the grave. Principles of leadership apply in any sphere of activity, including public service, charitable work, the military, education, science, and other fields.

Nowadays leadership means getting the best from people—managing people so that they work together to move in the direction that the leader sets. Leadership is increasingly recognized as a transferable skill: it can be taught. This belief has gained enormously in popularity over the last thirty years, promoted by distinguished writers such as John Adair and Warren Bennis. By contrast, the so-called Great Man theories of leadership that used to predominate are now seen as largely irrelevant to the fast-moving, complex, and much less hierarchical world that has developed.

THE NATURE OF LEADERSHIP

The most effective leadership is example, and this kind of leadership is within the reach of anybody. I am told that in one of the now-crumbling concrete pillboxes that sprang up over the United Kingdom as that country prepared grimly and alone to hold it against the invader, was to be read this rough inscription:

> Hitler has taken Poland,
> Hitler has taken Denmark and Norway,
> Hitler has taken Holland, Belgium, and France,
> He will not take this pillbox.
> Signed J. Smith, Corporal, Home Guard

"We still have a lot of Corporal Smiths—and Mrs. Smiths. It doesn't matter what level a person is on from director to office boy, from works manager to factory hand, he can be a leader, a leader by example by the way he tackles the job."

This is a quotation from a radio broadcast given by that redoubtable leader in military, political, and civil affairs, Field Marshal Lord Slim. He spoke in England in 1947 when times were hard, yet after a long uphill pull the British people triumphed over their hardships and overcame their difficulties.

My leadership in the military was directed toward persuading others to implement plans in the face of death. Yours, perhaps less dramatically but not less importantly, is to persuade others to create profits for the success of your enterprise and your country. The ultimate aim of us all, however, is the same—we are today asking others to do for us, as their leader, something unselfish that is not necessarily in the immediate personal interest of those whom we lead. If you accept that, then the business and military objectives are identical and our means of obtaining them have many parallels.

MISSION STATEMENT

Nobody can lead anything effectively without a clear vision of where they are going. In the military every operation is preceded by an aim or objective, clearly stated, unambiguous, and undivided. From my first days in the army I was brought up to understand that a mission statement containing an *and* was a divided aim and therefore unlikely to succeed. A business or military operation, or even a small military patrol, must possess a clear aim, whether it be strategic or tactical. This aim must be clearly understood by everybody participating in the mission. In my first days at Robert Fleming as a merchant banker, John Manser, who had recently been appointed chief executive, collected together all the senior executives in the bank and told them that his aim was to make Fleming's the largest U.K. bank in the City of London with the best-paid employees within five years. This was clear, unambiguous, and easy to remember, and it caught the imagination. He did not achieve it by a short margin, but we all knew where we were going over the next five years and all played a part in making Fleming's one of the most expensive buys in the U.K. banking world when it was sold in 2000.

For myself, I always made everybody write down the aim when I issued it and I made sure that it was consistently repeated as frequently as possible. You would be surprised how short are people's memories.

LEADERSHIP TRAINING

In the services we select and promote people not only for their professional competence, but ultimately for their inherent demonstrative leadership skills and potential. Too often I have noticed in industry that people are promoted because of professional competence, and they are unable to manage the increased leadership responsibilities flowing from that promotion due to shortcomings in personality, training, or leadership experience. A successful business must ask itself questions concerning the value it places on leadership.

- Are you recruiting people of technical quality combined with the personality needed for senior positions?
- Is leadership an obligatory discussion subject in selection interviews? Do you offer training in, and discussion of, leadership during an executive's career? Leadership should be a thread throughout all training sessions.
- Is leadership given a place of importance in the annual review of employees aspiring to management?

COMMUNICATION

No leader is effective without being able to communicate and remember that communication is a two-way process consisting of listening as well as transmitting. Very

"Leadership can be felt throughout an organization. It gives pace and energy to the work and empowers the workforce."
(Warren Bennis)

  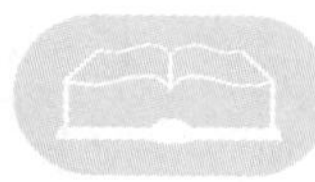    

often managers over-talk and under-listen. During the Gulf War my most valuable moments were those daily occasions when I traveled to ships, air bases, and military units to talk to audiences of all ranks. It was the question-and-answer session after an address or during the tour of a ship or unit when I had the opportunity to listen to individuals: it was then that I truly learned what the concerns, ideas, and views of my servicepeople were. An individual's views might not change the conduct of the war, but a consistent message from those who have to conduct the risky fighting business influences my own planning and thinking. Some of the best ideas come from the bottom up.

Leaders must communicate and listen with a daily consistency and an unambiguous clarity of purpose. This clarity of purpose must stretch to the very humblest in their business, and even to those who have recently joined. It is not an easy task, and is one that frequently goes unrecognized.

Delegation

People who cannot delegate deserve no further promotion. Delegation and risk-taking are close allies, for when you delegate you pass on to others the right to take decisions on your behalf. Sometimes mistakes will be made, and then the courage of the true leader is demonstrated when he or she backs a subordinate. If you are unable to do this when they make genuine mistakes, they will make sure they make no mistakes by failing to use the authority you may wish to give them, and you will have failed as a delegating leader. The effectiveness of your business and the power of command when you reach senior positions is not what you are able to do yourself, but what you are able to motivate others to do for you. Achieve this and you will have harnessed the energy, drive, and initiative of your senior management and your employees—and your company will prosper.

Managing Change

How often have we seen the new broom arrive in the business, instantly making changes before taking time to fully understand the complexity of the task ahead? Change for change's sake is the sign of a weak leader and a bully. This said, change should never be shirked, and a true leader will never accept things as they are simply because all is on an even keel and going well. It is too easy to leave the status quo unquestioned. A leader will see creative change as an opportunity and a challenge.

Change may be of a strategic nature, for example, our move from a defensive position after Iraq invaded Kuwait to one of offensive warfare designed to defeat Saddam's armies and eject him from Kuwait. On the other hand, change may be of a tactical nature. This was the case on my first patrol against the Chinese in Korea, a well-planned patrol designed to sweep the valley in front of our lines and to ensure that there were no Chinese battalions forming up for a dawn attack. Change was forced upon us when we walked into an ambush, found ourselves under heavy fire, and suffered a tactical defeat. Change, therefore, can be caused by forward planning and thinking, or it may be forced by the enemy or the business competitor. The former requires courage and leadership combined with vision; the latter requires instant response and leadership through decisive directions and initiatives.

Courage

There are two aspects of courage: physical and moral. In the services both are required to a high degree. In industry moral courage is the primary requirement. As Winston Churchill wrote, "Courage is a moral quality. It is a cold choice between two alternatives, the fixed resolve not to quit. Courage is willpower."

If your leaders lack the moral courage to stand up for their subordinates when they make genuine mistakes, or fail to confront their employees face-to-face with unpopular decisions, or fail to speak out clearly for what they believe to be the best interests of their company, then your leaders are not people of courage: they should be replaced.

Making It Happen ▸▸

Effective, consistent leadership relies on the following factors:

1. Avoiding the pitfalls of poor leadership. These include the danger that leaders can stifle innovation and reduce confidence by being too overbearing. Leadership can also lead to a cult of personality in which the leader is revered, usually to the detriment of the leader, the people he or she is leading, and the task they are all trying to accomplish. The final danger is that leaders who are too tough, ruthless, or macho will conflict with others, usually their peers, and split teams and the organization.
2. Empowering leadership. Developing an involved, committed, and ultimately successful work force requires empowering leadership, the key attributes of which are:
   - a belief in constant learning and the development of high self-esteem in others;
   - a willingness to ask questions, admit weaknesses, and listen to answers;
   - strong interpersonal skills, including an appreciation of other people and sensitivity to individuals;
   - an ability to engender trust, build relationships, and inspire others;
   - the ability and desire to develop leadership in others;
   - the capacity to handle criticism by listening and drawing out people's concerns;
   - a capacity to develop an effective vision of the future;
   - an approach that values and nurtures innovation and initiative;
   - the ability to communicate well at every level.
3. Being clear and focused on what you want to achieve. It is important to understand that leadership is a dynamic process and relies on leaders creating a vision and gaining people's commitment to that ideal. There are few certainties with leadership, and leaders therefore need to be clear about their goals.
4. Understanding present realities. It is easy for the leader to focus on a distant utopian vision—a dream—and ignore the immediate obstacles. Quite often these start with the leaders themselves. Initially many leaders may not feel comfortable with their role and may lack the confidence or respect vital for success. In general, therefore, leaders need to understand where they are starting from and what needs to be done immediately in order to start moving in the right direction. It is worth remembering that everyone can develop innate leadership potential, and trust and respect are there to be earned.
5. Understanding your own leadership style, and recognizing the different leadership needs of individuals. It is vitally important for successful leadership to match the leadership style to both the situation and the people involved. There are different times and situations for leading by

"Whoever is first in the field and awaits the coming of the enemy, will be fresh for the fight; whoever is second in the field and has to hasten to battle will arrive exhausted." (Sun-Tzi)

consensus, control, directing, or delegating, and they are best not confused!

6. Leading from the front, by example. It is important to confirm yourself as a leader, building trust and respect, by setting a clear example to your team. This means treating others as you would wish to be treated yourself, and it means developing and exhibiting a range of attributes and abilities such as demonstrating good work habits, understanding and valuing your staff's work, handling pressure, clearly demonstrating the values and aims that you hold dear, encouraging initiative and enthusiasm, providing regular, considered feedback, and listening and learning.

CONCLUSION

Decisiveness, vision, understanding, and confidence are at the core of successful leadership, and the leader needs to be able to use these qualities combined with additional skills relevant to each situation. The best leaders communicate their vision clearly and often: they are open to new approaches and ideas, but they know the direction in which the team and organization should be heading. They create a vision, communicate it, and guide their team to achieving their goal.

For More Information

Books:

Buckingham, Marcus, and Curt Coffman. *First, Break All the Rules: What the World's Greatest Managers Do Differently*. New York: Simon & Schuster, 1999.

Collins, Jim. *Good to Great: Why Some Companies Make the Leap . . . and Others Don't*. New York: HarperCollins, 2001.

Kotter, John P. *Leading Change*. Boston, MA: Harvard Business School Press, 1996.

Web Site:

www.hbsp.harvard.edu/products/hbr: this site contains an online version of the current edition of the *Harvard Business Review*, including a synopsis of many articles on leadership and management.

See also:

John Adair (pp. 960–61)

  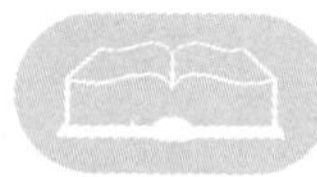    

How to Walk on the Leading Edge without Falling off the Cliff *by Judith A. Neal*

EXECUTIVE SUMMARY

- The complexity of today's world requires people to walk in many different worlds.
- Edgewalkers are leaders who sense the leading edge and have the courage to take action on their vision.
- It's important not to get too far ahead of the pack; walking on the edge only succeeds when others are motivated to follow.
- Walking on the leading edge is frequently the only way to succeed. Innovation, risk, and an ability to push beyond comfort zones can often be decisive.

Introduction

The complexity of the business world today is astounding. Nothing is predictable. The rules of the game are changing. Just when you think you've figured out how to have a competitive advantage, a competitor develops a new technology. Just when you think you've found the right motivation tool, the values in your workforce seem to shift. Just when you think you've found the right geographical area for the expansion of your internationalization efforts, political turmoil erupts.

Yet some people seem to have an uncanny knack for knowing what's going to happen before it unfolds. They're able to create new rules for the game instead of following the rules everyone else follows. They're able to plan a strategy that seems absurd to most people at first, and is later called brilliant when it's successful. They are a part of an unusual breed of leaders called edgewalkers.

An edgewalker is someone who walks between two worlds. In ancient cultures each tribe or village had a shaman or medicine man. This was the person who walked into the invisible world to get information, guidance, and healing for members of the tribe. This was one of the most important roles in the village. Without a shaman the tribe would be at the mercy of unseen gods and spirits, the vagaries of the cosmos. The skill of walking between the worlds hasn't died out, in fact it's even more relevant today. Organizations that will thrive in the 21st century will embrace and nurture edgewalkers. Because of their unique skills, they are the bridge-builders linking and facilitating different approaches, strategies, and techniques.

Walking on the Leading Edge

Five key skills form the hallmark of an edgewalker:

- visionary consciousness
- multicultural responsiveness
- intuitive sensitivity
- risk-taking confidence
- self-awareness

1. Visionary Consciousness

Edgewalkers begin with *visionary consciousness*. All their other skills are in service of a sense of mission about something greater than themselves. They feel called to make a difference in the world. The visionary skills arise out of a strong sense of values and integrity. Often these values are developed through some kind of painful experience or loss, and the edgewalker becomes committed to helping other people who may be going through similar kinds of experiences. Typically, the edgewalkers have gone through a major personal or career change that requires them to develop new skills that were never needed previously. Edgewalkers are the consummate integrators of seemingly unrelated ideas, skills, and fields.

2. Multicultural Responsiveness

Edgewalkers must have strong *multicultural responsiveness*. They're bilingual in the sense that they can understand the nuances of different worlds or cultures. They span conventional boundaries and act as translators. Edgewalkers know how to pick up on subtle cues that are different from their own. They pay minute attention to people different from themselves and have an open, warm curiosity about people from other cultures. They look for commonalities more than differences, and they want to know more about the worlds of others.

3. Intuitive Sensitivity

Edgewalkers have strong *intuitive sensitivity*. They're natural futurists. Because they're avid readers they are constantly integrating information from many sources and looking for underlying themes and patterns. Like the shamans of old, they've learned to pay attention to subtle, perhaps invisible, signs of potential change. They have an uncanny knack of making the right decisions, often taking action that seems counterintuitive to others. But when asked how they knew what to do in a particular situation, they have difficulty explaining. They reply, I just "knew." Intuitive skills are gained through the practice of deep listening. When listening to others, edgewalkers listen as much for the unsaid as the said. They also look for coincidences, patterns, or synchronicities that might provide clues to guide them in their decision making.

4. Risk-taking Confidence

Another strong skill that edgewalkers display is the skill of calculated *risk-taking confidence*. Edgewalkers have a strong sense of adventure and experimentation. They're always attracted to the next new thing. Like entrepreneurs, edgewalkers are easily bored with stability and are attracted to what's over the horizon. They're constantly asking what's next and trying to figure out how to be part of it. Because they're able to walk in two worlds, the world of practicality and the world of creativity, the risks they take to jump into the next new thing are based on information and intuition. Having a clear vision guided by strong values helps the edgewalker take risks that might not make sense to others.

5. Self-awareness

The most important edgewalker skill is that of *self-awareness*. A principle that edgewalkers understand is that each person is a microcosm of the whole. Leaders

"Corporate risk takers are very much like entrepreneurs. They take personal risks to make new ideas happen."
(Gifford Pinchot)

who are edgewalkers know that if they're experiencing a vision or dream or hunger, it's most likely arising in others as well. The challenge for the edgewalker is to find others who have the same passion and to work together to make a difference. Leaders who are edgewalkers have a strong sense of being connected to something greater than themselves.

These five skills can be taught. However, the leaders who tend to learn best strongly value their own personal development and have low control needs.

AVOIDING POTENTIAL PITFALLS

Edgewalkers can often get too far ahead of the pack. If this happens, they lose their credibility and the opportunity to influence others to do creative work. It's nice to have someone say you're ahead of your time, but there are few rewards for being too far out there. The most successful edgewalkers can remain in the real world and can remember established language and values so they can be a bridge to new ideas. For this reason, you should:

1. Watch for signs that you may be getting too far out on the edge; if this seems to be happening, revisit your own past experience, current priorities and future aspirations.
2. When you have a new idea that you want to implement, talk to people who are likely to disagree with you or try to block you.
3. Create relationships with people who may provide a good reality check.
4. Have patience with people who don't want to move as fast as you do; take time to build relationships with them and specifically ask for their support.
5. Cultivate the skill of honoring people who disagree with you; listen for any pearls of wisdom they have to offer.

If you feel blocked at every turn by people committed to the status quo, consider finding a different organization to work for, or even going out on your own. Being an edgewalker can feel very lonely. Connect with other edgewalkers for support and inspiration.

MINI-CASES

There are many interesting examples of people that successfully walk the leading edge.

Tom Aageson, the former executive director of Aid to Artisans, is now an independent museum consultant. When Tom turned 50 he was a highly successful executive at the Mystic Museum in Connecticut. For his birthday he went on a week's retreat to contemplate the rest of his life. He realized that his mission was to do whatever he could to eradicate poverty in the world. That led him to a position as the executive director at Aid to Artisans, which helps artists and craftspeople in developing countries to design and market products that respect their cultures and improve their economic situation.

Bill Catucci is the executive vice president and group executive for Equifax and former C.E.O. of AT&T Canada. When Bill first came to work for AT&T Canada, the company was losing a significant amount of money. His first act was to send a check for $75 to the home of every employee, saying that this wasn't much, but it was a token of appreciation for what they had already contributed to the company, he looked forward to working with them to turn the company around, and there would be more where that came from if they were successful. The company became successful and people were rewarded well.

John Lumsden is the C.E.O. of Metserve in New Zealand. John is originally from Scotland and served as an executive in Canada for a number of years; he's truly learned how to walk in different cultural worlds. Each month at Metserve there's an orientation for new employees that begins with a Maori welcoming ceremony. John holds regular "advances" (as opposed to retreats) for his management team, at which people spend time reflecting on deeper questions of life and work.

Jennifer Cash O'Donnell is director of organizational strategy and professional development for AT&T's Asia-Pacific group in China. Walking between the worlds of operations and organizational development, she helps AT&T achieve great results through a focus on human relationships and team-building, using Barry Heerman's Team Spirit process. Her success at AT&T Solutions with this team-based program led to her promotion to the directorship in Asia. This provides her with yet another opportunity to be an edgewalker.

MAKING IT HAPPEN ▸▸

- Write mission and values statements for the work you want to do in the world.
- Read professional material in fields that are unfamiliar to you.
- Listen carefully to what people and the world have to say.
- Trust your instincts about ways you can make a difference.
- Remember to take time to nurture your inner being and to pay attention to the signs you receive.
- Master practicality and common sense, as well as commanding the creative and visionary skills.
- Bring creative skills to scientific problems.
- Involve others in your ideas, recognizing different approaches and perspectives.

CONCLUSION

Edgewalkers are the leaders of the future. They are the corporate shamans who bring wisdom and guidance for their organizations. It's not an easy role to play, but it's one that's essential to the success of your organization—and one that can make you feel fully alive.

For More Information

Books:

Hock, Dee. *Birth of the Chaordic Age*. San Francisco, CA: Berrett-Koehler, 1999.
Moxley, Russ S. *Leadership & Spirit: Breathing New Vitality and Energy into Individuals and Organizations*. San Francisco, CA: Jossey-Bass, 1999.
Ray, Paul H., and Sherry Ruth Anderson. *The Cultural Creatives: How 50 Million People Are Changing the World*. New York: Harmony, 2000.

Web Site:

www.spiritatwork.com: this site has numerous resources for people who "walk between the two worlds."

See also:

☆ **Finding and Keeping Top Talent (pp. 33–34)**
☆ **Really Leading: Leadership That Is Authentic, Conscious, and Effective (pp. 222–23)**
☆ **Viewpoint: John Seely Brown (pp. 137–38)**
☆ **Viewpoint: Sumantra Ghoshal (pp. 190–91)**

"I am a risk taker but only within rules. I just like the support that an organization gives, combined with the freedom to express myself." (Guy Hands)

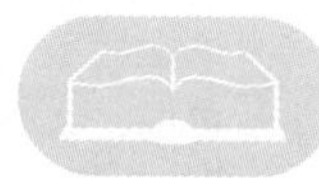

Business Ethics *by Sue Newell*

EXECUTIVE SUMMARY

- Business ethics focuses on identifying the moral principles by which we can evaluate business organizations.
- Corporations often behave unethically, having a harmful effect on people or the environment.
- Unethical behavior is typically not caused by a single bad apple, but is rather the outcome of complex interactions between individuals, groups and organizations.
- Ethical behavior can be defined either as behavior that maximizes happiness and minimizes harm or as behavior that is motivated by principles of duty.
- While behaving unethically may have some short-term benefit, in the long term it will harm stakeholder support.
- Long-term sustainability comes from concentrating on the *triple bottom line*: being concerned with the social and environmental as well as the economic impact of a business.

Introduction

Look in the newspaper on virtually any day of the week and you'll find at least one business scandal in which a corporation appears to have violated the rules or standards of behavior generally accepted by society. Toxic waste has been allowed to flow into a river, bribes have been paid in order to secure a business deal, child labor has been used to assemble a product, discriminatory practices have prevented the employment or promotion of members of a particular group, and so on. In other words, businesses regularly behave unethically, that is, they behave in ways that have a harmful effect upon others and in ways that are morally unacceptable to the larger community. Moreover, this impact is increasing as corporations become larger (indeed, global) and as profit-making concerns take over functions that were once publicly controlled such as the railroads, water utilities, and healthcare. Increasingly it is the private sector that determines the quality of the air we breathe, the water we drink, our standard of living, and even where we live and how easily we can move around.

Common Ethical Problems within Corporations

Given the increasing social impact of business, business ethics has emerged as a discrete subject over the last 20 years. Business ethics is concerned with exploring the moral principles by which we can evaluate business organizations in relation to their impact on people and the environment. Trevino and Nelson categorize four types of ethical problems common in business organizations (*Managing Business Ethics*, 2nd ed., John Wiley, 1999).

First are human resourcing ethical problems, which relate to the equitable and just treatment of current and potential employees. Unethical behavior here involves treating people unfairly because of their gender, sexuality, skin color, religion, ethnic background, and so on.

Second are ethical problems arising from conflicts of interest. Here particular individuals or organizations are given special treatment because of some personal relationship with the person or group making a decision. A company might get a lucrative contract, for example, because a bribe was paid to the management team of the contracting organization, not because of the quality of its proposal.

Third are ethical problems that involve customer confidence, with corporations behaving in ways that show a lack of respect for customers or a lack of concern with public safety. Examples here include advertisements that lie (or at least conceal the truth) about particular goods or services and the sale of products a company knows to be unsafe.

Finally, there are ethical problems surrounding the use of corporate resources by employees who make private phone calls at work, submit false expense claims, take company stationery home, etc.

Accounting for Ethical and Unethical Behavior

Despite popular belief, decisions harmful to others or the environment that are made within organizations are not typically the result of an immoral individual seeking to gain personal benefit. While individual influences such as the employee's level of moral maturity or the locus of control may be factors, we also need to explore the decision-making context in order to understand why an unethical decision was made. Group dynamics, as one example, very often influence the decision-making process.

A particularly important group-level influence is *groupthink*, a phenomenon identified by Irving Janis in his research on U.S. foreign policy groups (*Groupthink: Psychological Studies of Policy Decisions and Fiascoes*, Houghton Mifflin College, 1982). The research demonstrates the presence of strong pressures toward conformity in these groups; individual members suspend their own critical judgment and right to question, with the result that they make bad and/or immoral decisions. Janis defines groupthink as "the psychological drive for consensus at any cost that suppresses dissent and appraisal of alternatives in cohesive decision-making groups."

The degree to which decisions are ethical are also influenced by organizational culture. Smith and Johnson differentiate three general approaches that organizations take to corporate responsibility (*Business Ethics and Business Behaviour*, International Thomson Business Press, 1996):

1. **social obligation**: the corporation does only what is legally required;
2. **social responsiveness**: the corporation responds to pressure from different stakeholder groups;
3. **social responsibility**: the corporation has an agenda of proactively trying to improve society.

In a company in which the dominant approach to business ethics is social obligation, it is likely to be difficult to justify a decision based on ethical criteria; morally irresponsible behavior may be condoned as long as it does not break the law.

Ethical Dilemmas

In some instances it is clear that a business has behaved unethically, for example, where a drug is sold illegally or where client funds have been embezzled. Of more interest, however, and much more common, are

"A company's ethical conduct is something like a big flywheel. It might have a lot of momentum, but it will eventually slow down and stop unless you add energy." (William Adams)

situations that pose an ethical dilemma, those presenting a conflict between right and wrong or between values and obligations, so that a choice is necessary. For example, a corporation may want to build a new factory on a previously undeveloped site in a location in which there is large-scale unemployment among the local population. Here we have a conflict between the benefits of wealth and job creation in a location in which these are crucial and the cost of spoiling some naturally beautiful countryside. Philosophers have attempted to develop prescriptive theories providing universal laws that enable us to differentiate between right and wrong, good and bad. Essentially there are two schools of thought. The consequentialists argue that behavior is ethical if it maximizes the common good (happiness) and minimizes harm. Opposing nonconsequentialists argue that behavior is ethical if it is motivated by a sense of duty or a set of moral principles about human conduct—regardless of the consequences of the action.

Mini-case

Consequentialist Accounts of Ethical Behavior

Philosophers who adopt the consequentialist approach (sometimes also referred to as utilitarianism) consider that behavior can be judged ethical if it has been enacted in order to maximize human happiness and minimize harm. Jeremy Bentham (1748–1832) and John Stuart Mill (1806–73) are two of the best-known early proponents of this view. Importantly it is the common good, not personal happiness, that is the arbiter of right and wrong. Indeed, we are required to sacrifice our personal happiness if doing so enhances the total sum of happiness. For a person forced with a decision choice, the ethical action is thus to weigh up the impact on others of all the possible options and choose the one that maximizes happiness and minimizes harm. Common criticisms of this approach are that it is impossible to measure happiness adequately, and that it essentially condones injustice if this is to the benefit of the majority.

Nonconsequentialist Accounts of Ethical Behavior

Philosophers who adopt a nonconsequentialist approach (also referred to as deontological theory) argue that behavior can be judged as ethical if it is based on a sense of duty and carried out in accordance with defined principles. Immanuel Kant (1724–1804), for example, articulated the principle of *respect for persons*, which states that people should never be treated as a means to an end, but always as an end in themselves. The idea here is that we can establish moral judgments that are true because they can be based on the unique human ability to reason. One common criticism of this approach is that it is impossible to agree on the basic ethical principles of duty or their relative weighting in order to direct choices when multiple ethical principles are called into question at the same time.

Making It Happen ▸▸

While these two approaches to evaluating behavior are clearly different, they can be integrated to propose a checklist that will help an individual or group make sound ethical decisions.

- Gather the facts: what is the problem, and what are the potential solutions?
- Define the ethical issues. (This is a step that is often neglected, so that the ethical dilemmas raised by a particular decision are never even considered.)
- Identify the various stakeholders involved.
- Think through the consequences of each solution: what happiness or harm will be caused?
- Identify the obligations and rights of those potentially affected: what is my duty here?
- Check your gut feeling.

The last step is crucial. Those involved need to ask themselves what they would feel like if friends or family found out they had been involved in making a particular corporate decision, whether personally or collectively.

Why Behaving Ethically Is Important for Business

Choosing to be ethical can involve short-term disadvantages for a corporation. Yet in the long term it is clear that behaving ethically is the key to sustainable development. When you're faced with an ethical dilemma in which the immoral choice looks appealing, ask yourself three questions:

1. **What will happen when (not if) the action is discovered?** Increasingly the behavior of corporations is under scrutiny from their various stakeholders—customers, suppliers, employees, competitors, regulators, environmental groups, and the general public. People are less willing to keep quiet when they feel an injustice has been done, and the Internet and other media give them the means to make their concerns very public, reaching a global audience. Corporations that behave unethically are unlikely to get away with it, and the impact when they are discovered can be catastrophic. This leads to the second question.
2. **Is the decision really in the long-term interests of the corporation?** Many financial services firms in the United Kingdom generated short-term profits in the 1990s by misselling personal pensions to people who would have been better off staying in their company's pension plan. However, in the long term these firms have suffered by having to repay this money and pay penalties. Most significantly, the practice has eroded public confidence.
3. **Will organizations that behave unethically attract the necessary employees?** Corporations that harm society or the environment are actually harming their own employees, including those who are making the decisions. For example, corporations that pour toxins into the air are polluting the air their employees' families breathe. Ultimately a business relies on its human resources. If a company cannot attract high-quality people because it has a poor public image based on previous unethical behavior, it will certainly flounder.

Behaving ethically is clearly key to the long-term sustainability of any business. Focus on the triple bottom line—social and environmental as well as economic impact—provides the basis for sound stakeholder relationships that can sustain a business into the future.

For More Information

Books and Journals:

Brass, Daniel, Kenneth Butterfield, and Bruce Skaggs. "Relationships and Unethical Behavior: A Social Network Perspective." *Academy of Management Review*, 1998.

Elkington, John. *Cannibals with Forks: the Triple Bottom Line of 21st Century Business*. Gabriola Island, BC, Canada: New Society, 1998.

See also:

☆ **Workers without Borders: Creating Bonds When Workers Have No Loyalty (pp. 204–05)**
Frank and Lillian Gilbreth (pp. 994–95)
Konosuke Matsushita (pp. 1114–15)

"In recent years, public concern over the environment, human rights, and ethical issues has directly affected a wide range of household name companies." (Mark Moody-Stuart)

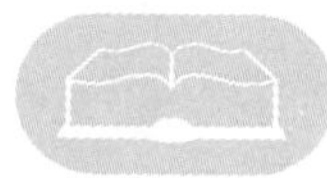

NEW ROLE MODELS FOR ENLIGHTENED LEADERSHIP *by Charles R. Day, Jr.*

EXECUTIVE SUMMARY

Role-model executives will be those leaders who are able to:

- reengineer the corporate realm so that working for large companies is fashionable again
- both enunciate core values and hold organizations accountable for living them
- align their organization's business goals with the needs of their communities to affirm that corporations are forces for good
- distinguish the full potential of e-commerce to fully harness its opportunities
- apply teaching skills and the art of persuasion to inspire individual creativity and innovation and build teams that appreciate a measure of structure and policy

We should make no assumptions about where we will find such role models.

INTRODUCTION

As much as we might like to believe that 21st-century corporate role models will emerge from among executives of high promise at, for example, Sony, Ford, ABB, or Bayer, the odds are that they won't. We might just as well find them among rapidly growing high-tech companies in developing countries. Nor are we apt to inspire the leaders we seek by holding up the most accomplished executives of the late 20th century and declaring, "Do exactly as they do." However, what has been done before may not be what needs doing now.

Political boundaries aren't what they were. Attitudes about globalization continue to shift. So do markets. World currencies now include legal tender that didn't even exist five years ago—the Euro.

Corporate changes are just as striking. DaimlerChrysler confronts vastly different challenges today from those it faced as Daimler-Benz five years ago. The success that India's up-and-coming technology companies enjoy prompts fresh challenges such as leveraging their success to improve the future of fellow citizens along with their businesses. Japan's political and economic difficulties leave its corporations with the formidable task of revising their long-held strategies, attitudes, and practices while preserving their competitive zeal and their renowned work ethic.

Almost any company in any country could offer identical scenarios. Collectively they affirm that the corporate role models of this century will emerge as they did in the last one: by tackling the challenges of circumstances with imaginative strategies that their peers will want to emulate. Role models emerge amid the circumstances that distinguish our times.

UNDERSTANDING HOW CORPORATIONS ARE PERCEIVED

What distinguishes corporate life at the start of this millennium is that so many executives want to avoid it. Striking out as an entrepreneur has never looked so appealing, notwithstanding the risks, long hours, and long odds against success. Mainstream corporations, by comparison, now appear as unsavory as they did in the days of Charles Dickens.

We have laws that enable executives to extend their careers, and advances in healthcare that help them maintain their vitality. Yet executives and professionals rush to retirement or depart the corporate world to launch new ventures. To be sure, new ventures are vital sources of ingenuity. But our corporations also nourish our well-being, and they, too, need leadership.

Two additional factors make this circumstance more alarming: the combination of basic demographics and ruthless dismantling of middle management that have left corporations with fewer executives to groom; and the rise of nongovernmental organizations that pester the corporate world, with the more radical inciting chaos at every opportunity.

Large corporations are derided as the source of the world's ills, not its solutions. This is preposterous. The true means of providing food, shelter, and economic opportunity and of solving energy and environmental problems lie in business tapping its creativity and technology, not in politicians enacting laws. Yet many individuals argue precisely the opposite, and the amount of attention they receive gives their contention legitimacy.

RESTORING APPEAL IS PARAMOUNT

Leaders who restore the appeal of corporate life and make it fashionable again will be our role models. They succeed not just with personal charisma and financial rewards, but by articulating core values worthy of support, by identifying an exciting mission, by painting an inspiring vision, and by arousing passion for their cause. It's noteworthy that this is hardly a new challenge. What business theorists and students yearn for today mirrors pleas of 25 years ago.

In this pursuit our new role models will need to reassess the role of the 21st-century business organization—and expand on it. This is a second area that needs attention.

The corporation's role in society has been studied almost as long as there have been corporations. Its importance often rises when economies falter as individuals discover that satisfaction in life isn't measured by income or stock options. Corporations and communities once enjoyed partnerships that nurtured each other. Our role-model leaders need to reconnect these partnerships for their mutual well-being. Certainly stockholders have legitimate interests, which may in fact take precedence over the interests of customers, employees, and communities. But these other stakeholders have valid interests, too. History shows that stockholders who support such initiatives will be rewarded far more handsomely than those who dismiss them as well-meaning but meaningless. Indeed, the opposition to corporations suggests how short-sighted and dangerous this can be.

Role models will also emerge in two other contexts. One is apparent and is the need to *explore the potential of e-commerce*. The other context that will produce role model leaders is *the need for teaching and team building*.

Certainly the notion that the Internet would suddenly challenge traditional retail channels was folly. But it's just as foolish not to discover just what the Net can do. For example, manufacturers envision harnessing e-commerce to deliver diagnostic services to customers and strengthen and

---

"The best leaders are apt to be found among those executives who have a strong component of unorthodoxy in their characters. Instead of resisting innovation, they symbolize it." (David Ogilvy)

extend business relationships far beyond initial purchase. Any number of marketers, meanwhile, are relying on the Internet to build personal relationships with consumers by learning more and more about their needs—after first obtaining their permission. Where this will end we can't imagine. But it starts with someone with the humility to acknowledge that they don't know, and the enthusiastic curiosity to find out.

The very top ranks of young talent may well be better educated and motivated than previous generations, but the masses are probably not. Moreover, a case could be made that many are not as eager to learn, in part because they've grown up more independently and learned to do things their own way. There's also evidence that suggests employees desire more balance in their lives. A study conducted recently by Jobtrak.com asked more than 2,000 college students and recent graduates, Which do you value most in your career decision? The largest number of respondents, 42%, chose balancing work and personal life. Just 26% said compensation, and 23% indicated advancement potential. Such attitudes may well make teaching and team building more challenging, but they also make them more important.

Mini-cases

RBMG of Columbia, South Carolina, is a modest financial institution with giant ideas. Its new management team spent its first 45 days identifying seven core values and articulating its mission. Under the direction of C.E.O. Doug Freeman, it's building its entire enterprise around these values. They're used as a recruiting tool and guide the development of technology.

Toyota's two-year-old Web site, Gazoo.com, helps Japan's leading automobile manufacturer speed up the disposal of used autos as it provides a wealth of customer data that may eventually lead to the development of a new vehicle. Gazoo.com is also helping Toyota retain young, restless employees who might otherwise strike out for careers in the computer industry.

Cemex, Mexico's leading producer of cement, is demonstrating that e-business has applications in the mature world of commodity products. It's relying on data both to manufacture cement and to deliver it on a just-in-time basis. The company's delivery vehicles are linked to its computers, enabling them to arrive with shipments at precisely the times they're needed. E-business has changed how Cemex conducts all its business and made it the most profitable competitor in its field.

Manco, a Henkel Group company headquartered in Avon, Ohio, musters as much enthusiasm as Duck Tape, its flagship product. Now in its second generation of family leadership, the company generates a plethora of ideas inspired by its duck mascot that inspire employees to say, I want to be part of that. Executives have leaped into icy ponds in March to celebrate milestones, and when the company hit $100 million in sales it treated the entire workforce to a musical performance at a restored downtown theater.

Two vehicle producers have put a new twist on a familiar idea. *Volkswagen* opened its Autostadt complex in Wolfsburg, Germany, in 2000. Adjacent to corporate headquarters, the museum helps VW's customers and community understand the company, its products, and its contributions. A fledging U.S. company has a similar plan for its new assembly plant in northern Florida, sited in the shadow of the famed Daytona International Speedway. *Corbin Motors* envisions a theme park that will show visitors both how its electric vehicles come to life and how they address environmental and energy concerns.

Making It Happen ▸▸

A manager needs to ask:

- What are the organizational core values that guide all your activities?
- What is your organization's mission? What is it in business to do?
- How do you envision your organization acting when it is older?
- Why does your organization matter? Why would it be missed if it disappeared?
- What *won't* your organization do in conducting business? What limits must be set?
- In addition to owners and stockholders, what stakeholders have a stake in the organization's success?
- What operations and procedures might be improved and benefit from e-commerce?

Conclusion

Human nature prompts us to believe that role models of 21st-century leadership will mirror those of today. Most likely they won't, because conditions and circumstances conspire to pose new challenges. Those challenges in turn breed a new generation of leadership.

We should begin our search for corporate role models by studying executives who strive to make corporations not only successful, but appealing. In all likelihood we'll be introduced to some heretofore unknown individuals from unsung organizations.

For More Information

Books:

Collins, James C., and Jerry I. Porras. *Built to Last: Successful Habits of Visionary Companies*. New York: HarperBusiness, 1997.

Downs, Alan. *Seven Miracles of Management*. New York: Penguin, 1998.

Levine, Rick, et al. *The Cluetrain Manifesto: The End of Business as Usual*. Cambridge, MA: Perseus, 2001.

Tichy, Noel M., and Eli Cohen. *The Leadership Engine: How Winning Companies Build Leaders at Every Level*. New York: HarperBusiness, 2000.

"The leader must know, must know that he knows, and must be able to make it abundantly clear to those about him that he knows."

(Clarence B. Randall)

  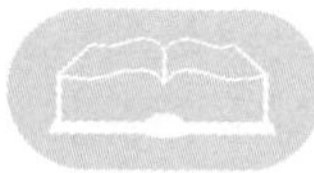    

Viewpoint: Jim Collins

Creating the Vision of Managers Growing from Good to Great

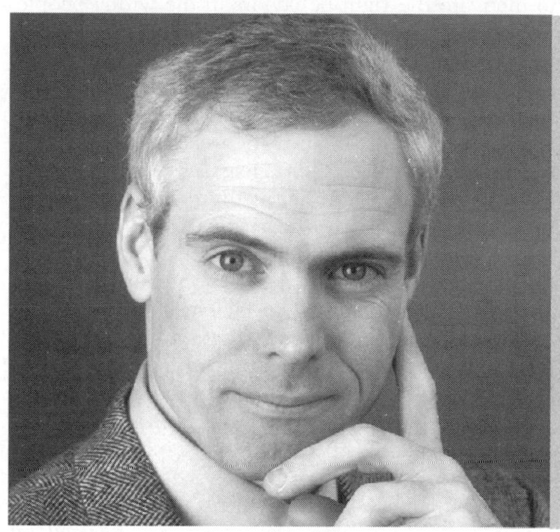

Jim Collins's career, since the publication of *Built to Last*, which he coauthored with Jerry Porras, has been meteoric. A bestseller for six years, that book has been through 70 printings and has been translated into 16 languages. More recently, Collins's book, *Good to Great*, has garnered an even wider audience. "Good is the enemy of great," Collins believes. But how a company achieves greatness is a lesson too few managers have taken the time to learn. Collins has dedicated the rest of his career to teaching that lesson to everyone he can. The following text is by Tom Brown; it is based upon one of his many conversations with Jim Collins.

What we have to keep in mind, when we think of what is "state-of-the-art" in management, is that this field is much more science than art. The conditions and the nature of business may change, but the principles of management really do not. So, if you want to think about the world in 2050, it's a sure thing that business will be different, but it's also a sure thing that many of the basic truths of management won't.

Think about the managers—that's what they were, whatever name they used—who built the pyramids. Given the tools and technology they had (and leaving aside labor relations practices we might frown on today!), those Egyptians were using sound management principles to get the work done. You could pick numerous events or personalities throughout history to make this same point. There was a great deal of management required of Christopher Columbus in his daunting expedition—essentially, the people managing NASA today are doing the same basic kinds of things that Columbus had to do. So, while the marketplace and organizational conditions under which you manage a group or a process may change, most of the fundamentals that define the superb manager remain the same, at heart, in 1350 and in 2050.

Why this is incredibly important to me is that my own mission in this field of study is to define what's immutable about management and leadership. Perhaps that's why many see my work as different from that of the many other authors who are writing today. Many management thinkers see themselves as engineers; I guess they see management as a form of engineering. Management, to many, is a series of "wheels and pulleys"—and people—that, if configured *just* right, will work! I'm much more of a physicist. I'm striving to research and write about the eternal laws, the unyielding principles, that inform sound management thinking.

I am indebted to Jerry Porras in so many ways, not only as a coauthor, but as a mentor. More than anyone else, he set me on a path that I hope to stay on as long as I can continue to make a contribution. But I am indebted to him in one fundamental way, in particular. What Jerry gave me was a lifelong gift—and it wasn't a set of ideas, a list of bullet points, or a point of view. Jerry didn't give me content; he gave me *method*.

Many management thinkers see themselves as engineers; I guess they see management as a form of engineering. Management, to many, is a series of "wheels and pulleys"—and people—that, if configured *just* right, will work!

Once I discovered the importance of method in the field of management, my career horizons changed. Jerry stressed—time after time, year after year—that the world will accept the answer to a truly major question only if one has a rock-solid method. So, on *Built to Last*, where Jerry and I spent years trying to outline the immutable laws of visionary leadership, it was the utilization of controlled comparisons that was the breakthrough.

Prior to *Built to Last*, no other piece of management research that I'm aware of tried to look at two sets of companies, one set visionary and the other could-have-beens. Each company under study was matched to a "peer" within its own industry, and we studied what they did and didn't do over their entire life span. What was truly great about the approach was that it developed a new kind of scientific method of inquiry in the field of management, in order to tackle major questions. And, as we all now know, the approach yields insights that can be breathtaking. So, the approach I now have used for years and that I am trying

"The new leaders face new tests such as how to lead in this idea-intensive, interdependent network environment."
(John Sculley)

to hone each day is quantitative and qualitative—but, most of all, it's scientific. It is a process that leads to true insights, and there is simply no way to cut the cycle time to arrive at compelling, confirmable insights about how to manage and lead.

What, then are the most important management "truths" today that people should be thinking about, reading about, and acting upon?

In an unsafe and uncertain world, managers must determine what their organization has to contribute to the world that no other institution can.

To answer that, let me go back to 1998. A group of people like me, authors and others who give a lot of thought to the world and leadership in general, came together to talk about our commonly held ideas, if any—or, at least, our commonly held concerns. As so often happens at these events, the discussion turned to what the future would be like 50 years out. When it came my turn to comment, I apologized and said that I really didn't know what the world would be like in 2050, but I also said that I had a wish. Wouldn't it be fascinating, I asked the group, if we could know what another group of thinkers—meeting in perhaps these very same chairs in this very same room in 50 years—would smile and shake their heads at when they thought about what we, today, hold to be truths about the world? Putting it a different way, I asked this: "What do we, today, take for granted, that in just 50 years our successors will marvel that we actually believed to be true?"

That meeting was held on the top floor of one of the towers of the World Trade Center in New York.

Now, think about that. In just three years, the assumption has been completely shattered that it would be risk-free to hold a meeting (any kind of meeting!) in the United States, because the United States is, after all, a safe cocoon. That's a world view that has been irreversibly changed. This all underscores the need for managers to be ever mindful of the value of adaptability: while you're operating at full tilt, you still have to be ready to confront new and perhaps quite unexpected (and, even, sometimes unwelcome) challenges.

If there is a new key management question for all of us to focus on, it might be this. How does one run—how does one lead—any business, government, company, university in an unsafe and terribly chaotic world? I believe the answer to that question inevitably brings leaders to address two priorities that are much closer to home and are, therefore, much more manageable.

In an unsafe and uncertain world, managers must determine what their organization has to contribute to the world that no other institution can. It is terribly important for managers to be emphatically clear about what it is that their enterprise can (1) be deeply passionate about, (2) be the best in the world at doing, and (3) have as a sufficient economic engine to keep the business going forward.

But there's another point to make. In an unsafe and uncertain world, managers must find the right people to help them make that special and unique contribution to the world. I commented once, and I meant it, that too many companies spend too much time trying to motivate the right behaviors in the wrong people, rather than getting the right people in the first place. In my most recent book, *Good to Great*, a team of researchers and I searched through 1,435 companies to find the small number that made the leap from average (or worse) results to truly great results and that sustained those results for at least 15 years. The good-to-great companies did not just hire anyone, then try to train them. Instead, they looked, and waited, and looked some more, in order to find the exact caliber of people they needed to make the company operationally strong and financially profitable.

Only then, when they had "the right people on the bus," did they start to fine-tune things like vision, strategy, and structure. By concentrating on finding only the right people for your organization and by giving those people liberal access to capitalize on your organization's best opportunities, you create an enterprise which can weather storms of uncertainty because the right people are, in general, focused on what your company does the best—and they are working at their own personal best. It's not an insurance policy against occasional setbacks, but it's the closest thing there is.

Don't settle for just being good. There's too much of that already. We have good schools, because people aren't committed to having great ones. There's good government, because people don't want to invest themselves in establishing great government. And too many companies miss the chance to be great simply because they sanction the attitude that "being good is good enough."

I fervently believe that nearly *any* company can become a great one. How greatness is achieved in the organizational world is the scientific breakthrough that I have been privileged to study and write about after investing more than a decade in research and thinking about what separates great from good. But greatness is not conferred, nor does it come by luck or through an inheritance. Greatness comes when leaders commit themselves and all who work with them to becoming the very best at what they collectively do. Deep, personal commitment precedes greatness. There is no other way.

For More Information

Web Site:
www.jimcollins.com

See also:
☆ **Preventing Corporate Systems from Holding You Back (pp. 177–78)**
☆ **Workers without Borders: Creating Bonds When Workers Have No Loyalty (pp. 204–05)**

"One of the most important tasks of a manager is to eliminate his people's excuses for failure."
(Robert Townsend)

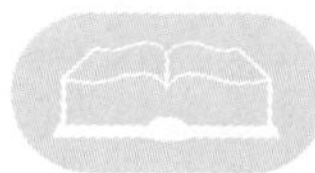

BREAKING THE LEAD CEILING

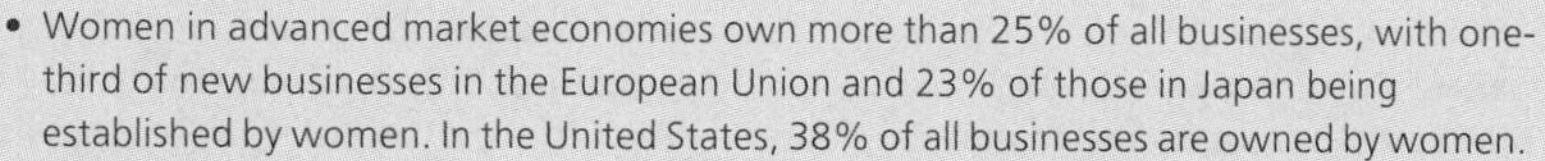

by Katherine Hammer

EXECUTIVE SUMMARY

- Women in advanced market economies own more than 25% of all businesses, with one-third of new businesses in the European Union and 23% of those in Japan being established by women. In the United States, 38% of all businesses are owned by women.
- Only 12.5% of the executive positions in U.S. *Fortune* 500 publicly traded companies are held by women. Only two Fortune 500 companies have women C.E.O.s or presidents, and 90 of those 500 companies don't have any women corporate officers.
- Between 1992 and 1997, the number of women-owned firms in the United States increased two-and-a-half times faster than businesses in general. Yet of the nearly 8 million women-owned businesses, only 1% have used venture-capital funding.
- To win in business women must not only be persistent and creative, but must learn to recognize and abandon a losing battle and become adventurers.

INTRODUCTION

A Catalyst survey of *Fortune* 1000 company C.E.O.s cited two major factors holding women back:

- a lack of line/management experience (82%);
- the fact that women haven't been in the pipeline long enough (64%).

These two factors seem related; it takes time in the pipeline to get significant management experience. However, since women now make up approximately half the labor force, you might believe that there are barriers to getting into the pipeline. That belief is bolstered by the fact that in 1999 only 8.8 million of the 19.6 million managers and professionals in the United States were women.

Of course, in part these figures may reflect choices made by women rather than as a result of discrimination. In a similar Catalyst survey, 1,251 women with titles of vice president and above in *Fortune* 1000 companies (37% response rate) largely attributed their success to several factors:

- consistently exceeding expectations (77%);
- developing a style their managers were comfortable with (61%);
- seeking out difficult assignments (50%).

Taking on difficult tasks and performing them exceedingly well are demanding enough, but having to transform your personal style may seem to be too much to sacrifice just to be one of the small proportion who reach executive standing.

Frustration with these conditions—and the desire for more personal autonomy—are at the heart of the huge growth of women-owned businesses. There is evidence that women fare better in the entrepreneurial climate. VentureOne found that 40% of the venture-backed companies in IT and 43% of those in healthcare that received funding in 1999 had women in senior management positions (various V.P. roles as well as C.F.O., controller, and C.O.O.). These figures were up from 20% and 21% respectively in 1995. However, only 4% of partners in the top 38 venture-capital firms are women; only 2.3% of their funds are invested in women-owned companies; and of all venture-backed companies only 5% are actually run by women.

BREAKING THE LEAD CEILING

COPING WITH SEXISM

There's little doubt that sexism plays some role in all this. I was once interviewed for a university teaching position sitting on the edge of a bed in a Chicago hotel while four male interviewers sat on chairs, asking whether I intended to have another child. Recently a woman with her own venture-capital firm told me that at board meetings of one of her companies, the other venture capitalists (all male) occasionally call a bathroom break to discuss something without including her. Incidents like these are outrageous; but if a woman decides to focus on fighting sexism, she becomes a social activist rather than a candidate for an executive position. A woman targeting an executive position should simply expect to work harder and smarter than the great majority of the competition. The upside to this is that if she achieves the position, she's much more likely to have the skills to be successful. But success will involve learning to play the game, staying the course, and, sometimes, walking away.

LEARNING TO PLAY THE GAME

Some companies promote the advancement of women. Deloitte & Touche has won numerous awards, including *Working Mother*'s 100 Best Companies for Working Mothers for seven years in a row and the 1998 Women in Technology International (WITI) C.E.O. Recognition Award. Such companies are clearly in the minority, though, and, as indicated by the VentureOne findings, women striving to obtain executive positions are more likely to find them in start-ups, since people who favor entrepreneurial environments are typically less conventional in general.

Yet the number of women C.E.O.s in venture-backed firms remains exceptionally low. Why? Venture capital is predominantly a man's game, but it's also a game in which success and failure are clearly delineated—and often success requires a public offering. Both in the process of taking a company public and in dealing with the financial analysts after the company is traded, the C.E.O. must consistently exude confidence and authority.

Most women who seek funding don't understand that venture-capital providers are judging how they would stand up to the street. Any nervousness, lack of conviction—any failing at all—contributes to their concern that a woman doesn't have what it takes. I recall that one of the partners in the firm that was to become my company's first venture investor was disturbed that my voice was shaky when I started to present. In short, even as an entrepreneur a woman must mind her manner.

Beyond image, a woman must command many business fundamentals to win venture-capital investors. In addition to understanding how private financing works, she must be able to:

- deliver a crisp business plan demonstrating the potential for substantial growth with a good go-to-market strategy;
- attract a strong management team;
- have a vision for a path to liquidity.

A number of organizations and forums exist for helping women attain these skills, including the San Francisco-based Forum for Women Entrepreneurs, and Springboard Enterprises, based in Washington, D.C.

"Anytime you have a fiercely-competitive, change-oriented growth business where results count and merit matters, women will rise to the top."

(Carly Fiorina)

Staying the Course

- **Accept that mishaps will occur.** The most important skill the ambitious woman must acquire is perseverance. Success grows out of the courage to learn from the misery of failure and come to terms with its major causes—mishap, malice, and miscalculation. There will be *mishaps*—downturns in the economic sector that change customers' spending, technical glitches with the product, unexpected competitors. Such failures will be recognized as coming from external factors and thus will have little long-term effect on a woman's career if she has otherwise performed effectively. The aspiring woman should simply learn from such events and resolve to be more diligent in trying to anticipate such turns on future projects.
- **Recognize the potential for malice.** Malice is another matter. There's much historical evidence that jealousy or fear is the cause of many conflicts. Sometimes colleagues may be jealous that the woman in question has been successful, even if she has done nothing to diminish their stature. In this case the harm will probably be slight—gossip in the coffee room—because if the malevolent colleagues had power or were in the game, they'd simply compete.

  Far more serious is malice that comes from a worthy contender threatened by the woman's success. However, if a woman is committed to beating the statistics, she should expect the path to be difficult.
- **Acknowledge miscalculations—and move on.** *Miscalculation* is one of the hardest sources of failure to acknowledge, because the woman must recognize that her instincts and judgments were flat-out wrong. While the term *mistake* suggests a simple act of omission or oversight, miscalculation suggests that your best efforts at solving a problem were flawed. A woman's success in learning from failures stemming from miscalculation frequently requires her to recognize shortcomings within herself—a tendency to lose her temper or reveal more than she should, a misjudgment about another person's capabilities or passion, or some behavior on her part that instilled malice in someone who could have been, if not a supporter, a bystander.

  Successful people transcend the impediments they encounter, whether self-made, external, or a combination of the two. If a woman wants to succeed in obtaining and retaining a top-level position, she should be committed to experiencing regular bouts of misery that force her to examine and modify her own beliefs, skills, and reactions.

Learning to Walk Away

While perseverance is key to success, so is the ability to recognize a losing battle and live to fight another day. Sometimes there's no winning, and if the woman is talented and performing, it may well be because the organization has a lead ceiling. In this case if she doesn't recognize the futility of her efforts and leave, she's likely to self-destruct and behave so negatively as to damage her reputation or to give up the fight altogether. The clue to recognizing a losing battle is when a woman continues to encounter resistance and experience frustration even after she has changed her own behavior and won multiple battles. In my own case at Texas Instruments, I had survived the hostility of my first boss and modified my style to deal successfully with my second boss—only to realize that the company's assumptions about how to approach the software marketplace were flawed. Only then did I realize that nothing I did would ultimately make a difference.

Making It Happen ▸▸

- Develop a plan to master the fundamentals of business. Whether inside a major corporation or with venture capital providers, a woman enhances her chances of success by being able to deliver a good business plan, and thus by knowing how to run a successful enterprise.
- Be willing to face mishap, malice, and miscalculation with perseverance. However, this doesn't mean tolerating the status quo. If you're in a losing battle, become an adventurer: look for the new path, new opportunity, new direction that can completely change your chances for achievement—success as *you* define it!

Conclusion

The statistics for women in business are not heartening. The path is long and hard, and it will be many more generations before things change. But the difficulty can be tempered by attitude. There are two paths to spiritual growth—that of the warrior and that of the adventurer. While both paths require courage and skill, the two result in very different lives. The warrior feels a duty to fight wrong wherever she encounters it, while the adventurer's focus is on the journey and the goal. The adventurer would rather avoid evil or move around or through it, fighting only as a last resort. Given the difficulty of succeeding in business regardless of sex, a woman will be best served if she adopts the path of the adventurer and finds another path to victory rather than spending her creative energy butting her head against a lead ceiling.

For More Information

Web Sites:

www.advancingwomen.com/intlinks.html: one of the top business and career sites for women. Advancing Women is a skills building organization providing mentoring, coaching, strategy and support to women in business.

www.abwi.org: Alliance for Business Women International is a nonprofit organization founded in 1995 to encourage and support business women.

www.nfwbo.org: National Foundation for Women Business Owners is one of the top sources of information about women business owners and their enterprises.

www.un.org/womenwatch: United Nations Women Watch is a site devoted to the advancement and empowerment of women.

See also:

☆ **Choosing the Best Training Curriculum for You (pp. 336–37)**
☆ **Mentoring (pp. 326–27)**
☆ **Taking Charge of Your Career (pp. 324–25)**
☆ **Viewpoint: Christopher Bartlett (pp. 45–46)**
☆ **Viewpoint: William Bridges (pp. 322–23)**
☆ **Viewpoint: Henry Mintzberg (pp. 241–42)**
✔ **Freelancing: Setting Up As a Free Agent (pp. 814–15)**
✔ **Working with Mentors: Developing Critical Relationships with Powerful People (pp. 780–81)**

GOVERNING THE CORPORATION
by Hugh Parker

EXECUTIVE SUMMARY

- It is often assumed that there is a direct and clear causal link between the actions of the board and the success of the organization, measured in terms of such factors as profitability, reputation and share price. In reality, this link to business performance is rarely strong, ranging from satisfactory to weak.
- There is renewed emphasis on corporate governance—not only how well the organization succeeds, but how well it is run and regulated, formally and informally.
- An extensive worldwide survey conducted by McKinsey & Company found compelling evidence that the shares of companies perceived by informed investors to have strong and effective boards of directors command a premium of as much as 20 percent on their share price.
- There are six specific ways by which board effectiveness can be enhanced, and one of these—and the most important —is to separate the roles of the chair and C.E.O.

INTRODUCTION

"Whenever an institution malfunctions as consistently as boards of directors have in nearly every major fiasco of the last forty or fifty years, it is futile to blame men. It is the institution that malfunctions." (Peter Drucker)

While it is difficult to prove conclusively that there is a direct causal relationship between the effectiveness of a company's board of directors and that company's performance in the marketplace, there is plenty of evidence to show that a weak and ineffectual board–especially one dominated by a powerful C.E.O.–will sooner or later commit strategic or other errors that will seriously damage the company's performance, and in some cases bring it to the brink of ruin.

Partly as a result of such well-publicized shipwrecks, and partly as the result of persistent initiatives by Robert Monks and other so-called shareholder activists, steps have been taken by some companies to obviate some of the more egregious boardroom malpractices. But many of these, like the 1994 "General Motors Board Guidelines of Significant Governance Issues," have been largely cosmetic changes aimed at improving the public perception of a board's effectiveness rather than attacking the problem at its root.

The real problem is that in most U.S. companies today there is a huge imbalance between the effective power of the C.E.O. on the one hand, and the nominal authority on the other hand of the board by which the C.E.O. is appointed and to which he or she is legally accountable. The C.E.O.'s delegated authority becomes absolute power, and the board's authority–vested in it by statute and bylaws–becomes effectively powerless.

WHY BOARDS ARE NOT INCREASING THEIR EFFECTIVENESS

In spite of all the attention focused in recent years on the quality of corporate governance–i.e., on the effectiveness (or not) of public company boards of directors–and in spite of efforts made to improve them, most boards are today only marginally more effective than they were ten years ago. There are several causes for this systematic weakness:

1. **For a long time–and largely by custom–boards have not been in a position to really govern the business.** Boards of directors on both sides of the Atlantic have almost never fully performed the trustee role for which they are legally accountable to the shareholders by whom they are elected. By tradition and long habit, boards of directors have always been more or less honorary bodies of which little action has either been expected or wanted. Board meetings have typically consisted of routine rituals through which members are led by a chair/C.E.O. who is equipped with information, inside knowledge, and staff support so that they can and generally do control the agenda absolutely. So while boards have the legal authority, it is the C.E.O.s who have the effective power.
2. **Combining the offices of chair and C.E.O. reduces effectiveness.** Combining the offices of board chair and C.E.O. in one person virtually guarantees that the board will be ineffectual. A board can only be as independent and effective as its chair wants it to be and is capable of making it. An independent chair must be able to look his or her C.E.O. in the eye and say "this is my board and I do not agree with you and your management on this issue." But clearly this will never happen if the two offices are combined. Yet this combination is still the norm in over 80% of U.S. companies (but less than 20% of U.K. companies).
3. **Most U.S. boards are simply too big.** In 1998, 70% of the *Fortune* 500 companies had boards with 12 or more members, and 20% had 15 or more. There are several reasons for these high numbers, not least being the realization by some C.E.O.s that the larger the board the less effective it will be in monitoring and controlling his or her performance. Experience has shown that beyond a total of about seven or eight members, a board's effectiveness tends to become inversely proportional to its size.
4. **Too many supposedly "independent" directors are just not qualified to do the job properly.** They often lack the experience, character, and basic financial and other skills required in today's environment. Even worse, although they are elected by the shareholders, in practice they have almost always been selected and nominated by the C.E.O. and rubber-stamped by the board and shareholders. So the wrong people get on corporate boards for the wrong reasons, and their supposed independence is a myth.
5. **Most external directors lack the motivation and/or the time to do the job properly.** Annual fees for directors tend to cluster around $50,000. For an active C.E.O. earning $500,000 or more (plus options) in another company this is too little to justify more than a day or two per month. But for an academic or retired admiral with an income of $100,000 or less, it is too much to put at risk by being too independent, so they

"Oratory is the power of beating down your adversary's arguments, and putting better in their place."
(Samuel Johnson)

  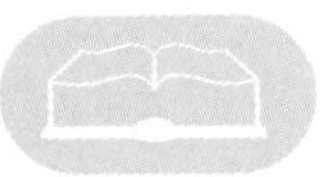    

tend to support the chair who appointed them.

6. **Lack of relevant information.** Nearly all outsider directors have less information and knowledge about the company and its problems than the C.E.O. whom they are supposed to monitor and judge, and they are entirely dependent on that C.E.O. and his or her management for what information they do have. Thus these outsider directors often only learn about critical strategic and policy issues when things go seriously wrong, by which time it is too late for anything but crisis management and damage limitation. This usually takes the form of replacing the C.E.O., whose successor must then do whatever he or she can to salvage the company.

Re-empowering the Leadership of the Board

Corporate governance has evolved differently in each of the major OECD countries. The governance system in each reflects the history, culture, economics, social values, and legal system in that country. One of these variables can be called the degree of "shareholder primacy"—i.e., putting the shareholders' interest first—which today ranges from very high in the United States, moderate in Germany, low in France, and virtually nil in Japan. In the United States and United Kingdom especially, there are growing pressures from shareholders—which nowadays means the institutional investors—to make the boards of their portfolio companies more responsive and accountable to their shareholders. Hence the current interest in improving corporate governance.

If there is one lesson to be learned by U.S. boards from recent British experience it is the emergence of the independent non-executive chair. During the 1970s and 1980s a number of corporate shipwrecks of some highly respected U.K. companies—e.g., Burmah Oil and Rolls Royce—raised serious questions about the competence of company boards in general, which in turn led to the appointment in 1991 of Sir Adrian Cadbury's "Committee on the Financial Aspects of Corporate Governance." In 1992 this Committee published its "Code of Best Practice" which proposed, among other things, that "There should be a clearly accepted division of responsibilities at the head of a company which will ensure a balance of power and authority, with no individual having unfettered powers."

The Cadbury "Code of Best Practice" was adopted by the London Stock Exchange. Companies listed on the Exchange are now required to state in their annual reports the extent to which they have complied with each of the code's provisions, and noncompliance must be explained. The growing practice in the United Kingdom of separating the roles of chair and C.E.O. has restored a better balance between them. It is time for more U.S. companies to adopt this practice.

The most common objection in the United States to this separation of roles is that it is "divisive": that it will lead to indecision and political infighting in the boardroom, that this will undermine the authority of the C.E.O., and that this in turn will weaken the leadership of the company. This view fails to understand that there are two quite different and distinct roles: one managing the board of directors, the other managing the company. The chair is responsible for the former and his or her jurisdiction is confined to the boardroom. The C.E.O. bears full responsibility for managing the company with the authority and powers delegated to the board to which he or she is accountable.

Making It Happen ▸▸

There are common issues on which the board needs now to focus their attention, and there is widespread agreement that the board needs to set the framework for action. Specifically, this involves the board in eight key activities:

- focusing on core activities and being pragmatic;
- adding value and reducing cost;
- building a business culture that embraces change;
- moving with the market, but not changing faster than the market;
- leading the business;
- integrating e-business activities, aligning and optimizing resources;
- managing risk;
- establishing and maintaining good corporate governance.

To help in considering how best to improve the effectiveness of the board, these activities can be grouped into three main areas:

1. The board needs to consider how best to **set the strategy and direction**. This needs to be more than an emphasis on cost-cutting or focusing on the core business. It needs to outline how the enterprise will create value and improve.
2. Recent developments mean that **managing financial performance** now requires an emphasis on cost reduction, but it also needs to be supplemented with an approach that will steady the share price. A critical issue that seems to be gathering in value and acceptance is that of measurement.
3. Crucially, it needs to be recognized that the role of the board in ensuring operational effectiveness is central to the business.

In short, the board must drive the company, and not the other way around.

For More Information

Books:

Conger, Jay A., Edward E. Lawler III, and David L. Finegold. *Corporate Boards: New Strategies for Adding Value at the Top*. San Francisco, CA: Jossey-Bass, 2001.

Garten, Jeffrey E. *The Mind of the C.E.O.* New York: Basic Books, 2001.

Web Site:

www.conference-board.org/expertise/gov.cfm: the Conference Board created this web page to list key links to resources on corporate board issues.

See also:

☆ **Boardroom Roles (pp. 220–21)**

VIEWPOINT: HENRY MINTZBERG

Taking Management on a Strategy Safari

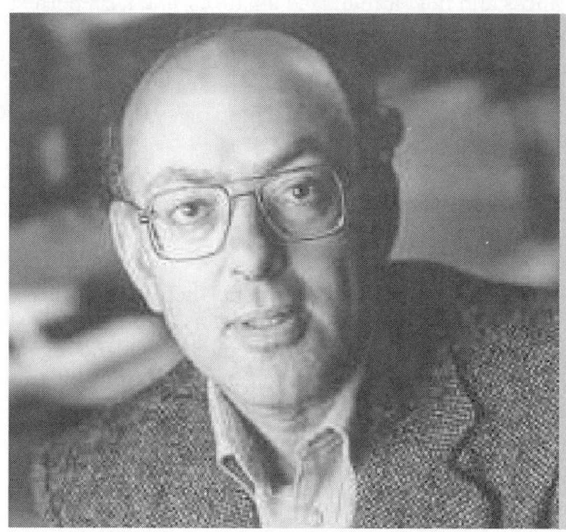

"The iconoclastic Henry Mintzberg" is the classic opening to any article about the Canadian strategy guru. Yet, in many ways, his career and work fit the traditional academic pattern. His Ph.D. research set him on his way. *The Nature of Managerial Work* was the result—one of the few (very few) books which actually examines what managers do rather than discussing what they should do.

Since then Mintzberg has set the agenda in the sphere of strategic management with a combination of academic rigor and a devotion to seeking out new perspectives, which has generally set him apart from his contemporaries. This reached a climax with the publication of *The Rise and Fall of Strategic Planning*, a coherent tour-de-force which sounded the death knell for the strategic planning orthodoxy that had long dominated management thinking and education. His most recent strategy book is *Strategy Safari*, coauthored with Bruce Ahlstrand and Joseph Lampel.

What is the most important thing and who is the most important person to have influenced your thinking on business and management?

I'm not sure I was so much influenced by any one individual. It's not as if I studied under somebody closely or something like that. But probably the most influential thinker for me was Herbert Simon.

He influenced me in two ways. He influenced me positively because his thinking about organizations was so far advanced and sophisticated that it had a very large impact on how I thought about things. And the other way because he eventually took an extreme view of intuition, such a narrow view of intuition, in fact, that his writing drove me in the opposite direction. He had such a strong belief in analysis and analytical processes that it drove me towards a much stronger belief in intuitive and soft processes and really questioning our obsession with analysis. I'm not opposed to analysis at all. I think it's a component. I think management is a practice and craft that uses science wherever it can. But it's not a science, and the emphasis on the analytical is very dangerous. So Simon influenced me both positively and negatively.

As far as the thing that influenced me—that's trickier. My wife was just reading an old article of mine, and she asked to borrow a book by Robert Ornstein, called *The Psychology of Consciousness*, which was the first book that put together key research about the left and right hemispheres of the brain. I think that research had a lot of influence on me.

The other thing that stands out is the whole experience around the IMPM—the International Masters Program in Practicing Management that I've been involved with over the last eight to ten years. That really grew out of the fact that I was criticizing MBA programs, and people were saying: what are you doing about it? The fact that we started doing something about it, and what we've learned from that, has had a big influence on me.

How will business be different in the 21st century?

My feeling about prediction is that anybody who could have predicted the September 11 events should feel free to predict other things. In other words nobody ever predicts anything with any accuracy. So it's simply not worth it. I discovered recently that this is the position that Peter Drucker has taken, but I've always believed that.

Basically, predictions are based on extrapolations. Optimists extrapolate what they like, and pessimists extrapolate what they don't like. And nobody ever gets it right. But nobody is ever held to account because nobody ever goes back and looks. So I think it's a waste of time to do those kinds of predictions. I can talk about trends that I find positive and trends that I find negative. Which ones are going to dominate? I don't know.

In the last ten years a trend that I've found extremely negative, for example, is shareholder value and the whole kind of mercenary view of management that has taken over completely. Economists have taken over the world. That's been a very negative factor because we've got completely out of balance. I would hope another trend, one that is broader, more humanistic, and open to human beings

Basically, predictions are based on extrapolations. Optimists extrapolate what they like, and pessimists extrapolate what they don't like. And nobody ever gets it right.

"The key managerial processes are enormously complex and mysterious, drawing on the vaguest of information and using the least articulated of mental processes." (Henry Mintzberg)

rather than simply interested in maximizing shareholder value, will redress the balance.

What new skills will be needed to cope with these changes?

I don't think they are new skill sets. I think they're probably very old skill sets. I don't think management changes that much. We're in a period of what I would call heroic management: a period where the great hero rides in on a white horse with the dramatic new strategy and the massive merger. These huge dramatic events impress the share market—at least the financial analysts first and then the market—and then the hero rides off into the sunset with the bonuses while the company collapses a year or two afterwards. Nortel is a classic example.

My hope is that we'll go back to some common sense. I think good managers are very thoughtful people. Some more thoughtfulness wouldn't be a bad idea. Social responsibility as opposed to shareholder value wouldn't be a bad idea. Not social responsibility in terms of sticking to the letter of the law and doing the minimum for everyone except the shareholders, but a responsible stance—nuanced management, where managers appreciate the different sides of arguments and don't just grab at simplistic techniques and simple-minded strategy. What I call "managing quietly." I wrote an article a few years ago about that. ["Managing quietly," *Leader to Leader*, Spring 1999 (***www.drucker.com***)]

I think good managers are very thoughtful people. Some more thoughtfulness wouldn't be a bad idea. Social responsibility as opposed to shareholder value wouldn't be a bad idea.

You said in that article that good management is often quite dull, and it is the business press that seeks dramatic leadership. Do you think that's still the case?

I'm not sure that dull is exactly the word; let's rather say quiet and steady and determined to make sure that things get corrected and function well and that organizations get strong. We had a presentation today by one of my colleagues, Meg Graham, who has just written a book on Corning with its 50 years of alliances and how it managed alliances, and it's a perfect example of that. Very, very solid. They just kind of worked at it and did it. The press would grab at the techniques, but really it's the culture of those alliances that has made that company so strong—how they approach things.

Are there new management questions we should be asking?

I'm back to my other comment: there are old management questions we should be asking. I think just looking more deeply at management itself, and organizations themselves, and getting away from all this hype about technique and heroic leaders and just understanding more in depth. We need to develop managers who are much more thoughtful and believe things and understand things much more deeply than happens now.

How can companies best promote enterprises that are a) profitable and b) good places for people to work?

I have to repeat what I've been saying. What's needed is more thoughtfulness. More of a social bonding process so there's a sense of community in the organization, a belief in what the organization is trying to achieve. Look at the organizations that have sustained high performance—that are just good, remain good, stay good, and keep going. Like Shell for example. There's a sense of depth, there's a sense of a culture, a sense of a deep understanding and belief in the business, a sense of commitment. These are all old-fashioned things, but they are important things.

For More Information

See also:

The Nature of Managerial Work (p. 932)

INVESTING IN TECHNOLOGY *by Steve Bone*

EXECUTIVE SUMMARY

- Four strategic questions need to be answered when you are investing in technology.
- The most rapid advances are in new valuation techniques for investing in technology.
- Whatever technology is being considered, it has to fit into your technology strategy.
- The readiness of the company to integrate the new technology is crucial. The management of the four critical areas is important.
- While the functional discipline of technology management has made enormous progress over the last ten years, it has much more to do.

INTRODUCTION

Businesses are now expected to fuel ambitious growth targets by marrying customer insights with relevant technologies to produce blockbuster products. Yet many business executives believe that product choices should be based upon the single dimension of technology. They leave technology decisions to engineering/process specialists, on the assumption that they are the custodians of the technical understanding and are therefore able to draw fine distinctions. The consequence is often a loss of objectivity in deciding on the correct technologies to invest in.

Without a clear technology management process driven by ambitious targets, it is very difficult to make informed and objective decisions on how to invest in the best fit-for-purpose technologies. The technical decision becomes disconnected from the end customer, the business direction, the location of technology (own R&D, geography, industry sector) and the timeliness of technology transfer.

STRATEGIC DECISIONS ABOUT TECHNOLOGY INVESTMENTS

It has been recognized that decisions about technology should be taken at a strategic level. Managers' understanding has advanced in recent years as a result of attempts to formulate a general theory of technology, common approaches to describing individual technology artifacts, and the taxonomy of technology.

There are several important questions that you need to ask about investing in technology (see Figure 1).

1. IS IT TECHNICALLY FEASIBLE?

It is crucial to conduct a due diligence of the technology prior to making decisions about investment. There are many books about assessment of technology, and you can find out more about technology audits from the sources listed in For More Information below.

2. WHAT IS ITS TRUE VALUE?

It is clearly important to value technology based on what it is worth to the company when integrated into products or used as part of services. A good valuation technique will get project managers, C.T.O.s, C.E.O.s, and investors on the same wavelength. Techniques have developed rapidly in recent years and have now met this need. They include qualitative evaluation, net present value, decision tree analysis, option pricing, and risk-adjusted, option-based valuation.

Traditional cash flow models that generate net present values (NPV) for technologies have been used for many years and work reasonably well for shorter-term projects with relatively certain outcomes. Where risk, uncertainties, and options are important, better techniques are needed, such as the real option approach for investing in highly uncertain, new technology projects. Using the Black-Scholes equations generates a distribution of likely NPVs that can be used to assess the value of a technology. However, real option techniques are difficult to use and are far from transparent. A numerical approach using Monte-Carlo techniques is more practical; it can be turned into a tool that can be used by project managers to both assess and improve their projects. This explicitly (and transparently) models all the relevant risks, uncertainties, options, and cash flows to produce outputs showing the probable range of outcomes.

3. DOES IT FIT WITH OUR TECHNOLOGY STRATEGY?

A technology strategy aims to answer two important questions so that the future technology position of the company is well defined (see Figure 2; *source: Arthur D. Little*).

To get a sense of the strategic importance of technology and help answer some of these questions, technology can be divided into four categories: base, key, pacing, and emerging. These indicate the scope of competitive impact on the market. The definitions for these categories are given in Figure 3 (*source: Arthur D. Little*); a more detailed description is given in Philip A. Roussel, et al., *Third Generation R&D* (1991).

4. CAN IT BE IMPLEMENTED?

Investing in the right technologies requires effort to address all aspects of the business at the same time. Companies that address only the business processes for assessing and investing in technology, for example, may have neither the correct vision nor the organizational culture to take on these new technologies. Managing technology investment therefore requires companies to ensure that the strategy, processes, resources, and organization are able to accommodate new technologies (see Figure 4).

Figure 1: **Strategic questions about investing in technology—SHOULD WE INVEST?**

Is it technically feasible?	What is its true value?	Does it fit with our technology strategy?	Can it be implemented?
Are the fundamental science and engineering credible?	What opinions are there?	Where does it fit on the technology road map?	Is it well understood and codified?
Are there any technically fatal flaws?	Are there competing technologies, and can it be protected?	Is it base, key, pacing, or emerging?	Do we have the right resources, processes, and organization?
Can it do what it claims to do?	What is the future market?	How much time do we have to acquire?	Are there external barriers to transfer?
Is there a clear route to a final product?	What are the risks and uncertainties?		

"In the era of globalization, plants tend to be focused in terms of product, robotized in terms of technology, and diversified in terms of markets served." (Paul W. Beamish)

Figure 2

WHAT TECHNOLOGIES?	HOW TO ACCESS?
Technologies to develop further	Leader or follower positioning
Technologies to hold down or phase out	Make—collaborate—buy choices
New technologies to acquire or grow	Strategic alliances retained or developed
New technologies to monitor or explore	Response to regulation and standards

Figure 3: **The categorization of technologies according to the competitive impact**

Base technology	**Key technology**	**Pacing technology**	**Emerging technology**
Essential to be in the business	Well embodied in products and/or processes	Under experimentation in the industry	At early research stage or entering other industries
Widely exploited by all in the industry	High competitive impact	Competitive impact likely to be high	Competitive impact unknown, but promising
Little competitive impact			

Making It Happen ▸▸

The following steps can help to focus thinking considering investments in technology:

1. How does the technology fit with the overall organizational strategy?
2. **Understand the technology available.** As well as the current functionality, it is also important to know how it might be enhanced in the future.
3. **Assess the costs.** Understanding the value has two components: assessing the costs and the benefits that will result. When it comes to cost, there is not only the initial capital spend but also the ongoing running and maintenance costs to consider, including any essential upgrades. Indirect costs, such as changes to other systems or processes, as well as training, should also be taken into account.
4. **Assess the value of the technology.** It is vitally important to understand and agree what the technology is for. This is the time to start asking people what they want and think—people that will need to make the system work and obtain the benefits.
5. **Plan the technologies' integration.** This can involve a range of issues and there is a need to consider:

- How much risk is there and how might this be minimized?
- Who is responsible for making the system work? What is the decision-making and management process? Is the implementation and management of the system adequately resourced?
- What are the consequences for other systems and processes? Is there a project plan to ensure that all the issues are considered, with adequate preparations made?
- Have all of the "soft" cultural factors been taken into account, as well as the "hard" technical and process issues?
- How will the decision and its implementation be communicated? This needs to be clear, inclusive and positive if the benefits are to be achieved.

Conclusion

Investing in technology is getting more and more expensive and specialized. The management of risk and the valuation of technology that takes account of all risks are a crucial part of the investment decision. It is also vitally important to understand what you are buying; is it a technology that is well codified or is it partly tacit knowledge? In this case the knowledge has to be transferred as part of the technology.

Companies that do all the necessary due diligence can still get the implementation wrong because they have not considered the organization's readiness for taking on technology. Finally, technology was once seen as being a major differentiator for products. In recent years it has been recognized that technology also plays a crucial part in service provision, and technology management has therefore had to deal with new problems. We are also seeing that more and more technology is outside the company investing in it, and the management of partners and ventures is crucial, as is the management of so-called virtual R&D communities.

For More Information

Book:

Roussel, Philip A., Kamal N. Saad, and Tamara J. Erikson. *Third Generation R&D—Managing the Link to Corporate Strategy*. Boston, MA: Harvard Business School Press, 1991.

Figure 4: **Are we managing technology as a strategic business asset so that new technology can be invested in and implemented?**

Do our technology strategy and vision support our business goals?	**Are our technology management processes effective and efficient?**	**Do we have the necessary internal and external technology resources?**	**Are our organization and culture appropriate to manage new technology introduction?**
Technology forecasting & foresight	Process design to fit strategic technologies?	Competence audit to ensure right skills/ knowledge?	Chief technology officer's role?
Technology intelligence	Technology management process?	Facilities correct?	Network of technology practitioners—internal and external?
Investment mapping	Process management infrastructure (IT)	External partner resources	Performance metrics
Technology road-mapping	Product creation process	Technology funds in place	Are there cultural barriers to new technology introduction?
Does the new technology fit the strategy?			

"Science, engineering, and technology are fundamental drivers. . .providing the foundation for business growth and overall improvement in the quality of life." (Mark Birrell)

X-ENGINEERING SUCCESS *by James Champy*

EXECUTIVE SUMMARY

- Partnerships are more important today than ever. Few companies can afford to invent, manufacture, sell, and service everything that they make without some help.
- So companies come together in relationships, typically called alliances, to complement each other's products and capabilities.
- With attention to harmonizing processes across organizations and with the good fortune of compatible cultures, alliances can work. But truth be told, most alliances now fail.

INTRODUCTION

An example of the joint venture is Concert, formed by AT&T and British Telecom to provide communications services to large multinational companies. The venture made sense on paper. Neither AT&T nor British Telecom had the global coverage that its big customers required. Rather than try to build this capability—at a cost of billions of dollars—and bang heads in competition, it made more sense for these companies to create a jointly owned company out of their combined resources. But in the end, these giants did bang heads, taking the venture apart. It would seem that someone forgot to put terms into the deal about what to do with assets and customers in the event that the alliance failed. About the only thing that the partners seemed to be able to agree on was that it hadn't worked. As Concert wound up its business, it was losing about $200 million each quarter.

What happened? Most observers attribute Concert's failure to a difference in cultures between the two partners. That's certainly plausible. The management styles of both companies are different, and each company has been distracted with its own struggle to maintain share in its local markets. A similar alliance formed by France Telecom and a number of other telecommunications companies also failed after much effort and millions of Euros. In fact, the business landscape is littered with alliance failures.

Research into these failures confirms that differing cultures and management styles are the principal causes for break-ups. But I believe that the problems go beyond different management breeding. Often alliances are the brainchild of sales organizations that are just looking to get access to each other's customers. The word *synergy* is freely used to justify a deal without much appreciation of what it will take to make the alliance work. Simply agreeing to jointly market products or services isn't enough to sustain an alliance. There is not enough value created for the partners or for their customers.

Even when an alliance is initially successful, it can fall apart when one partner becomes dominant and tries to exercise too much power. This often happens in the information technology industry when large software publishers or hardware manufacturers try to assert control over their smaller channel partners, the systems integrators and consultancies that use their products in delivering services. The big guys just assume that they know more and have superior processes. That behavior causes two problems:

1. Arrogance creeps into the relationship, forcing out the trust and good will needed to make it work.
2. Knowledge is lost.

There is a good chance that a smaller channel partner is closer to customers, knowing what they really want, and having a better process. When one alliance partner starts to assert power over another, the alliance is near its end. Recently I spoke with one large technology company that admitted that only 10 of its 400 alliances produced any significant business.

WHY BOTHER AND WHAT'S CHANGED?

The case for making alliances work goes beyond increasing a company's product offering or virtual size. Alliances can address the enormous inefficiencies that exist in many industries. Companies keep large and depreciating inventories because they don't have visibility into each other's operations. And because companies don't have processes that connect well together—such as your selling process not working well with my buying process—lots of unnecessary work and paper is produced. For example, it takes 26 separate electronic and paper documents to make many trans-oceanic shipments. Supply chain reengineering is just scratching the surface of what's possible if companies could work more closely together.

Up to now, it has been difficult to do the kind of collaborative work that a powerful alliance requires. Many economists have argued that the management and transaction costs outweigh the benefits, but that balance may well have shifted with the advent of the Internet. This ubiquitous network is not just about a new channel to market or a place to advertise. Its principal corporate benefit will be as an enabler of a new breed of cross-organizational processes that will dramatically improve business performance. To achieve this benefit will require what I call *X-engineering*. The "X" connotes the organizational boundaries that you will cross.

MAKING IT HAPPEN ▸▸

Making alliances work requires that the partners are culturally compatible. But the partners must do more than be polite to each other and throw resources, processes, people, and customers into a venture. A venture must be thoughtfully designed and implemented and the principles of X-engineering applied. Here's what to do.

- **Conduct an open assessment of cultures and management styles.** Studies that show cultural and management style differences to be contributors to failure are right. Probe each other's beliefs and values. Ask some simple questions, such as how will your partner handle a breakdown of relations with a customer? How do you both deal with issues of breach of integrity? How will you think about quality, innovation, profitability? Remember, there is no single company culture that is "right." The issue here is compatibility, and hopefully you and your partner will value the same things.

In the end, you must choose your partners carefully. Trust your intuition, and don't fool yourself into thinking that you can influence what your partner fundamentally believes. Company cultures, like country cultures, don't change easily.

- **Make your processes transparent.** Most companies operate under the premise that their processes are unique and should be kept secret. Just

"Where. . .one parent company has a special knowledge of technology, and the other a knowledge of the market, a shared management venture is the appropriate solution." (Yanni Yan)

the opposite is true. There are very few processes within a company that are unique. Maybe you have a secret formula or a proprietary manufacturing technique, but most of your and your competitor's processes are the same. To operate an alliance, companies must be open so that process relationships can develop. You cannot intimately connect unless you understand how each other operates.

A corollary principle is that you must share good ideas. Forget about who gets the credit. Just put good ideas into the alliance and go on and develop new ones. Just like any business, an alliance cannot be starved—especially by its partners. It may need innovation to maintain its competitiveness.

- **Harmonize your processes.** Being transparent isn't enough. Chances are that your processes and the processes of your partners won't connect easily. For example, if one partner contributes the sales processes to a venture and another partner the service processes, work will have to be done so customers experience these processes in a seamless way. Lots of problems occur in hand-offs. All the processes of an alliance have to be examined to be sure that they are harmonized—that is, that they act in concert with one another. In some cases, totally new processes will have to be developed.
- **Create a powerful business proposition for your customers.** An alliance is only worth doing if it can make one plus one equal three. The partners have to create a business proposition for their customers that neither could offer on its own. An alliance cannot be sustained because it's convenient for its partners. It requires steady revenues, and that will only happen if it offers a compelling business proposition for customers.

An improved business proposition can take many forms. It could be reduced costs and lower prices. That's what Dell and its product partners are doing in Dell's electronic marketplace. Alliances can offer variety and choice. Amazon.com is now a retail channel for Toys-R-Us. An alliance can make service more robust. Many computer hardware manufacturers partner with service providers to handle service problems. Unfortunately, customers don't always experience the benefits of such combinations because the partners haven't harmonized their processes.

The Ideal Is Possible

What does a great alliance look like? It's one that builds on the strengths of its partners, meets a customer need, and avoids the replication of resources or the redundancy of work. Yes, the venture must also make money, but I believe profits will come if the earlier three conditions are met.

Mini-case

The *Star Alliance* was formed by a number of major airlines. The Alliance members share few overlapping routes, but they do share information about their customers' travel preferences. This means that they can act as complementors, not competitors. They can offer the intelligent routes that their passengers want. The Alliance also wisely allows passengers to interchange and pool frequent-flier miles from individual member airlines. There is something in the deal for everyone. And because these airlines act as complementors, they will avoid spending billions of dollars on redundant jumbo jets to compete for routes. If the members can find ways to share more processes and eliminate redundant work, even more benefits will result.

Conclusion

More than ever, businesses need alliances to reduce costs, improve service, and feed innovation. Customers now expect that you can deliver anything, anytime, anywhere; but few companies can do that on their own. The Internet now enables the fundamental cross-organizational change required to reduce costs and create customer value. But relationships must be X-engineered—partners carefully selected, operations made transparent, and processes harmonized. Otherwise, relationships will consume enormous amounts of management time and yield little for companies and their customers. Enter alliances with your eyes and company wide open and expect that they will require an active, continuing negotiation between the partners. Only then will they be worth the effort.

For More Information

Books:

I believe in applying sound management principles to new conditions. So be sure to read the basics: read a Warren Bennis book on leadership; read *Management* by Peter Drucker; read a book by Richard Pascale; read a book by Stan Davis.

See also:

☆ **Building Great Internal Partnerships (pp. 281–82)**
☆ **The Business Web (pp. 145–46)**
☆ **Intrapreneurial Warriors Versus Traditional Managers (pp. 125–26)**
☆ **Marketing to the "Real-time" Consumer (pp. 73–74)**
☆ **Virtual Collaboration (pp. 167–68)**
✔ **Better Communication with Resellers (pp. 650–51)**

"Corporate intentions and capabilities to create cross-national strategic alliances are affected by the ongoing structural changes of the global and regional economy." (Richard Drobnick)

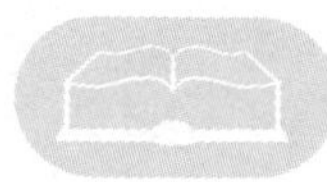

Creating Strategic Excellence *by Mike Freedman*

Executive Summary

- Organizations need strategy in order to prosper, rather than survive.
- The right environment is essential.
- Strategy, planning, and operational activities must be integrated.

The Need for Strategic Excellence

Survival or Prosperity?

Organizations can survive without a strategy, but that's about all they will do. They will never prosper over the long term and will always perform suboptimally–indeed, some may head in the wrong direction fast and finish up nowhere. With a clear strategy, effectively communicated, well planned, and carefully implemented, the chances of superior performance are enhanced immensely. Setting and implementing strategy, however, is not easy, requires considerable time and effort by an organization's leadership, and demands outstanding thinking skills by all involved.

The Right Environment

An appropriate performance environment is required to achieve strategic clarity, coherence, and coordination. The environment needs to encourage and stimulate those involved and balance strategic and operational imperatives, which are often in conflict for time, attention, resources, and thinking efforts. C.E.O.s must lead by example, for there is nothing more important in their role than to make sure that strategy is set and a leadership team is in place to help in that process and subsequently to direct its implementation.

Strategy Defined

Working on a global basis with many of the world's leading companies and government bodies, we have found that the following definitions have stood the test of time over the past 25 years.

Mission

The mission establishes the overall purpose of an organization in a simple, clear statement of intent. It guides strategy formulation but is not a substitute for it. It must be meaningful. One client had as its mission "to redefine, build, and own the greetings category globally." This provided direction and motivation and gave a sense of what needed to be covered in its strategic vision.

This compares favorably with the mission of a Japanese car manufacturer: to "kill Porsche." A dramatic statement, but somewhat simplistic.

Strategy

Strategy is defined as "a framework within which the choices about the nature and direction of an organization are made." *Framework* here means boundaries or parameters that help determine what lies inside or outside the scope of the organization's strategy. Clear criteria are developed to apply in this initial decision-making filter. The choices to be made are what products and/or services will and will not be offered, what markets (customers, consumers, and geographies) will and will not be served, and what key capabilities are needed to take products to markets. The *nature* of an organization is its very essence. McDonald's is defined by its fast-food essence, Dunhill by luxury goods, and Goldman Sachs by financial services. *Direction* refers to where an organization is headed and how it might retain or change its nature and/or the scope of its activities.

A Model for Strategy Formulation

Having a proven model and the processes to support it eases the burden of a C.E.O. and the top management team and produces a superior result. It also ensures that the necessary links are made and that the organization's mission, strategic vision, planning processes, day-to-day decision making, and human performance system are all aligned. Such an approach also facilitates continuous monitoring, review, and updating of the strategy, vital in today's climate of constant and rapid change.

A Five-phase Model

The model described below has been used effectively by many of the world's great corporations, including the Bank of Ireland, Corning, Hallmark, Hong Kong-based Towngas, the Venezuelan state oil company Lagoven, the Irish Development Agency, Kennametal, and Dunhill.

It has considerable advantages over many other well-known models such as those proposed by Michael Porter, Hamel and Prahalad, the Boston Consulting Group, General Electric, and McKinsey. Each of those focuses on only one or two elements of the Kepner-Tregoe model, typically omitting either planning the execution of the strategy or its actual implementation. They are thus incomplete. Our experience indicates that all five phases must be in place if there is to be a realistic chance of achieving strategic excellence. The model is as follows:

Phase 1: Strategic intelligence gathering and analysis;

Phase 2: Strategy formulation;

Phase 3: Strategic master project planning;

Phase 4: Strategy implementation;

Phase 5: Strategy monitoring, review, and updating.

The model is not linear, but iterative. A continuous feedback loop links each phase to the next.

Strategic Intelligence Gathering and Analysis

This phase ensures that the depth and breadth of information on which strategic decisions are based is up to date, accurate, and relevant; the quality of strategic decisions depends very largely on the quality of this information. The intelligence covered includes competition, technology, markets, macroeconomic, political, and social information and trends, and regulation, among other subjects specific to each organization. Key to this phase is determining the implications of this intelligence for the organization within its strategic time frame.

Strategy Formulation

Using our definition of strategy, this phase results in the creation of a strategic vision or profile that builds on the strategic mission developed as its starting point. Such a vision answers nine key questions:

1. What are our fundamental beliefs and values?
2. What are the assumptions on which we will make our future strategic decisions? (These are drawn from Phase 1.)

"Beware the manager who proclaims to the world he is a long-termer, beginning today."

(Thomas Boone Pickens, Jr.)

3. What products and/or services will we and will we not offer and what are their characteristics?
4. What customers and end-user groups (if they are different) will we serve and not serve and what are their characteristics?
5. What is our geographic scope?
6. What products/services and markets represent the greatest potential for growth and require the most investment and resource allocation?
7. What competitive advantage(s) will enable us to succeed?
8. What key capabilities do we need to ensure that we take our products/services to market and to support our competitive advantage(s)?
9. What financial and nonfinancial goals (for example, market share, technology leadership) do we aim to achieve?

STRATEGIC MASTER PROJECT PLANNING

This phase encompasses the development of the plan for strategy implementation.

A significant number of projects emerge (often several hundred), the execution of which leads to successful implementation. Creating a strategic master project plan and developing an optimal project portfolio help guide the organization in prioritizing, defining in detail, sequencing, scheduling, researching, executing, and monitoring these projects.

A strategic master project plan can contain projects covering a wide variety of activities, including:

- launching new products and markets;
- filling capability gaps;
- aligning organizational structure with strategy;
- reducing complexity;
- managing costs;
- synchronizing planning and budgeting with the strategy process;
- developing functional strategy;
- redefining and realigning IT hardware, software, and information requirements;
- repositioning the company externally;
- branding;
- managing merger, acquisition, and disposal activities;
- creating strategic alliances;
- training and developing middle managers in strategy;
- phasing out products and markets;
- establishing an appropriate performance system.

STRATEGY IMPLEMENTATION

This phase involves taking planned actions, monitoring implementation, and modifying the strategic master project plan as circumstances change and projects are amended, completed, or abandoned and new ones added. Involving significant numbers of employees in the implementation phase is a vital ingredient in successful execution. The more strongly employees feel ownership of the strategy, the more they will be committed to play their part. Ownership, commitment, and involvement begin with a major communications exercise to see that all employees fully understand the strategy and each can answer the question, What does this mean for me? Phase 4 often involves considerable training to empower employees to play their role.

STRATEGY MONITORING, REVIEW, AND UPDATING

Given the rate and pace of change in the 21st century, this phase is a vital requirement. Continuous monitoring of strategic progress, goals, and indicators of success is a full-time task and a key input to regular, generally quarterly, reviews. Such reviews not only evaluate ongoing implementation, but examine whether the assumptions used to underpin the strategy are still valid and whether the organization's strategic direction is still robust and viable. Strategic updates are an output of the monitoring and review process.

INTEGRATING STRATEGY, PLANNING, AND OPERATIONAL ACTIVITIES

Clearly the strategic dimension of an organization is not an isolated set of activities. Strategic alignment requires the integration of every organizational component. The following model is a guide.

Note: Constant internal and external communication is a key feature of successful strategic leadership and must accompany each phase of the process.

STRATEGY COMMUNICATION

What to communicate, to whom, by whom, when, how, and where are key questions in achieving strategic excellence. Many internal and external constituencies can and must play a role in effective strategy implementation. A precondition is that they all understand the message and know their role and what's in it for them. At Kepner Tregoe we use a communications matrix to guide this exercise. Each cell in the matrix requires a detailed project plan; this ensures that all key questions are answered. For more information about this, see *www.kepner-tregoe.com*.

Note: The elements of each matrix are different depending on the organization's stakeholders on the one hand and the subjects to be communicated on the other. Check marks indicate a definite need to know, question marks are for debate, and blank spaces represent no need to know.

MAKING IT HAPPEN ▸▸

As the glue to the whole strategic environment, creating a strategic culture helps an organization achieve its goals. Strategic culture is defined as "the combined effect of behaviors, norms, beliefs, values, heritage, thinking, and relationships and the way they manifest themselves in an organization and its strategic performance." Its facets are:

- basic beliefs and values;
- thinking patterns;
- organizational structure;
- management style;
- management processes and systems;
- education, training, and development;
- goal setting and appraisals;
- reward systems;
- myths, stories, legends, and symbols;
- information and knowledge;
- agendas and meetings;
- behaviors;
- external manifestations to outside constituencies.

When these align with, and support, an organization's strategy efforts, strategic success is assured.

For More Information

Books:

Johnson, Spencer. *Who Moved My Cheese?: An Amazing Way to Deal with Change in Your Work and in Your Life.* New York: Putnam, 1998.

Mintzberg, Henry, Bruce Ahlstrand, and Joseph Lampel. *Strategy Safari: A Guided Tour Through the Wilds of Strategic Management*. New York: Simon & Schuster, 1998.

Web Site:

www.kepner-tregoe.com: has many supplementary articles on strategic approach.

"Vision: Top management's heroic guess about the future, easily printed on mugs, T-shirts, posters, and calendar cards."
(Anonymous)

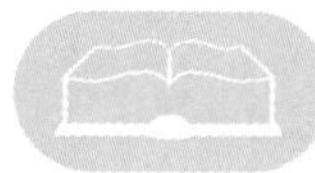

VIEWPOINT: MICHAEL HAMMER

Setting the Agenda for the Next Generation of Leaders

Michael Hammer has been, since the early 1990s, one of the most quoted management authors. He coauthored *Reengineering the Corporation*, which has worldwide sales of more than two million. No wonder, then, that *TIME* magazine included him in its first list of America's 25 most influential individuals. His latest book, *The Agenda*, delineates nine ways managers can compete more effectively in the 21st century.

The domain in which I specialize is different from that of most other management thinkers. I often refer to myself as "a plumber." I'm concerned with how companies do and should operate, how best to get work done, and how to organize an enterprise so that work will be done that way. Specifically, I am a believer in process: that it's better for a company to develop a system that will produce an unending stream of results, rather than hope for brilliant ideas and individual heroics.

While many of my colleagues are professors, consultants, or inspirational speakers, I think of myself as mostly a teacher. Trying to discover and communicate the best ways to get work done is what drives me, and is what underlies the educational programs that I present to thousands of managers each year. Instead of selling fish, I teach fishing.

I owe a lot to someone I've never met but respect immensely. David Halberstam and his milestone book *The Reckoning* moved me greatly. I still quote from that book, even though I first read it in the mid 1980s when I was a technology consultant.

At that time, I had recently left my MIT faculty position, and I was working with companies to help them use automation and technology more effectively. I ultimately concluded that technology utilization was only a fraction of the real problem, and that the best technology could not help a company that was organized ineffectively and had poorly designed processes. Without rethinking the basics, we would end up paving the cow paths. That's why *The Reckoning* grabbed me so strongly. What Halberstam did in that book was to track the parallel histories of Nissan and Ford. As he looked at the two companies over a long period (roughly 1947 to 1983), his chapters on Ford were a damning indictment of what was (and is) wrong with many enterprises.

The book was a revelation to me: it confirmed and elaborated my worst fears about large organizations. In the book Ford was depicted as a company more focused on financial issues rather than operational ones. How to design, make, and sell cars was less important than how to manage a balance sheet. Halberstam's insights made me face up to the fact that my technology advice would do little good unless companies rethought their priorities. I still have my copy with my marginal notations; some of the anecdotes in *The Reckoning* are burned into my memory.

Trying to discover and communicate the best ways to get work done is what drives me, and is what underlies the educational programs that I present to thousands of managers each year. Instead of selling fish, I teach fishing.

However, we can't be too critical of companies like Ford (whom I have worked with and, hopefully, helped since reading that book). After all, we still haven't had that much experience with large enterprises, and it is not surprising that we are still trying to figure out how they should be run.

The modern corporation as we know it is a very recent phenomenon, a creation of the 20th century. We're still just beginning to understand how to operate and manage these large enterprises. Furthermore, the world we face today is very different from the world in which the modern corporation was born. Therefore, nothing in conventional business practice should be regarded as set in stone. Indeed, the very identity of the corporation is now being called into question. Looking forward, the issue of enterprise boundaries will dominate much of our discourse.

Today most companies still try to be self-contained

"Every company has its own language, its own version of its own history (its myths), and its own heroes and villains (its legends), both historical and contemporary." (Michael Hammer)

enterprises. Today's typical corporation believes, as companies have done for the last 100 years, that it needs to do everything required to provide its product or service—and do it all inside the corporation. But that point of view is evaporating, and it will evaporate faster and faster as we move into the new century.

In other words, the question "What is a business?" is now in question.

As products have ever shorter lifetimes, we need to define our companies not in terms of what they produce, but in terms of what they do, focusing on process rather than product. To explain that distinction, let's think about a company that today considers itself in the jet aircraft business. Right now, that company does just about everything required to design, make, and sell jet aircraft. In the future, however, I can envision the managers in that company defining it as being in the business of assembling complex systems (for instance). They would assemble the components of a jet aircraft, but would work closely with other companies who would specialize in selling aircraft, or maintaining aircraft, or financing aircraft purchases by major airlines. In the past this idea was not very practical because of what economists call "transaction costs," the overhead of interfacing and coordinating with other companies. But with the advent of the Internet it is not much harder to work with others than it is to work with yourself—and the advantages of focus make doing so very worthwhile.

The way to shake off past traditions that are no longer relevant to tomorrow's business world is to make some hard choices.

As this trend develops, it will change people's perspective of what a business is and what it should be doing. Businesses become parts of systems rather than whole systems in themselves. More than that, it also says that the process by which you do business is the most important part of the business. In other words, your process is your business.

All that this means is that two management skills that today are largely absent will jump to the very top of the leadership agenda. Managers will have to be proficient in designing and instrumenting systems and processes and have an enormous capacity for teamwork and collaboration.

Managers will have to get a whole lot better at looking holistically at operational processes and systems, at designing ones that operate at maximum efficiency, at measuring system performance, and at improving a system once it's up and running. This is a very different emphasis from today's; management takes on much more of an engineering flavor, rather than a financial focus. I see this already starting to take place, as phrases like "business systems engineering" and "process management" enter the parlance and organizational charts of more and more companies. I also see an indicator of this shift in the increasing number of executives with engineering backgrounds. I don't think it is an accident that the most influential executive of modern times, Jack Welch, has a background in chemical engineering.

Managers have to shake off once and for all the sense that they are independent actors responsible for a self-contained unit. They will have to get used to the idea that it is only when all parts of a company work together that the company as a whole will perform effectively. It used to be that the grade-school child who came home with a report card that had an unsatisfactory grade in "playing well with others" was marked as one with executive potential. No longer. Companies can't afford the infighting and suboptimization that results from giving managers individual fiefdoms and letting them fight it out. Just as people on the front lines need to work collaboratively, so do their leaders. Nor can this collaboration end at company boundaries. As companies integrate their processes with each other, their managers will need to work together closely. To return to our jet aircraft example, the managers of the various companies that design, make, and sell the plane all need to work together.

We need to invoke new questions to guide our thinking. We should all be asking, every day, not only "What should I do?", but also "How can I do it better?" and "What should I not do?"

The way to shake off past traditions that are no longer relevant to tomorrow's business world is to make some hard choices. If your company is to move forward, which customers should you no longer serve? Which products should you discontinue? What things that your enterprise now does should be done instead by some other company?

This line of questioning will force companies to think about themselves in new ways. And it will also promote an environment in which everyone in the enterprise is thinking hard about how to sustain profitability and make the company the best possible place to work. Ultimately, good management tomorrow will come down to giving everyone in the corporation an understanding of the business, its customers and processes, and where each employee and manager fits. Good management tomorrow will give everyone a sense of connection and a real view of the opportunities that can be seized to generate success.

For More Information

Web Site:
www.hammerandco.com

See also:

☆ **Core Versus Context (pp. 255–56)**
☆ **New Yardsticks for Performance (pp. 285–86)**
☆ **X-engineering Success (pp. 245–46)**
✓ **Implementing Business Process Reengineering (pp. 506–07)**
Business Process Reengineering (pp. 1921–23)

"The revolution that has destroyed the traditional corporation began with efforts to improve it."
(Michael Hammer)

  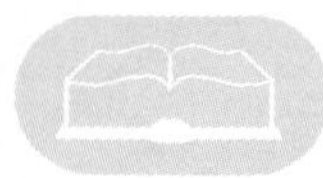    

TURNAROUND STRATEGIES *by Sir John Harvey-Jones*

EXECUTIVE SUMMARY

- In a crisis situation, the leader of a business tends to be the first casualty and outsiders are brought in to sort out the situation.
- However, remedies are usually best applied by those already within the organization.
- A turnaround situation is one of pointing out a new direction.
- The reason many companies find themselves in trouble is almost always due to problems right at the top.
- Any solution must be one to which all parties (particularly within the company) can offer their support.
- You only get one shot at trying to turn around a business.
- Everything has to be up for grabs, and fear and tradition must not be allowed to inhibit action.

INTRODUCTION

The area of business which, mercifully, few of us have any experience of is turning a business around before it goes under—but when the rocks ahead are clearly visible. In these situations, the first casualty tends to be the current leader. He or she is usually replaced by a hired in "hard man" to do the dirty work. The result is all too often far below what could be achieved by someone already within the organization, who would have been aware of the culture which has led to the decline in the first place.

The in-house candidate (a role I have personally filled) is desirable because he or she has the best chance of saving the largest proportion of what may be salvageable. After all insolvency practitioners, or at least the good ones, could be described as managing turnarounds, but at a cost which most of us would attempt to avoid. The greatest difficulty the in-house employee faces is the problem of analyzing the causes of the downfall with sufficient clarity and over a long enough time. The elapsed time from the first business mistake to eventual collapse varies enormously. Very large organizations can carry on for a surprising time before events overwhelm them, while in the case of the small business, retribution tends to strike much more quickly. What is certain is that both the stock market and the banks have less and less tolerance of business mistakes, and the time available to demonstrate an effective recovery plan is becoming ever shorter. Moreover the judgment of the chances of success is made by business analysts and the press, who probably have very little knowledge of the real situation which has led to the visible signs of failure. In reality, these are all too often symptoms rather than causes.

It is the people within the organization itself who know the myriad problems which must be overcome and the actions to be taken. Therefore the turnaround problem becomes one of pointing out the new direction. This is where being able to call on the knowledge, drive, and enthusiasm of existing employees can be so valuable. This is obviously far more difficult when all of your employees are worrying about the future, and the best and most self-confident are voting with their feet for a safer environment. The reason many companies find themselves in trouble is almost always due to problems right at the top. I have yet to meet such a situation which was caused by the employees. Employee dissatisfaction is largely caused by mismanagement or frustration. No employee actually wants to do a bad job, or to be seen to be doing one. Obviously no employee actually wants his company to fail or to find themselves faced with enforced redundancy on minimal terms.

DIAGNOSIS AND SOLUTION

If you find yourself managing a turnaround, the first two points on which you have to concentrate are your diagnosis of the problem and endeavoring to ensure that you have a reasonable time gap in which to implement your chosen solution. For the diagnosis, you need every scrap of information, opinion and statistical analysis you can lay your hands on. The views and openness of those on the shop floor are as—or in some cases, more—important than those at the top. Individuals in these situations are astonishingly honest with themselves, and it is from this apparently inchoate mass of opinion and fact that a first "rough cut" analysis will appear. The strategy has to be concise and simple, for it is essential that everyone inside or outside the company should understand the aims. The detail is best left to those who will have to deliver it.

Self-evidently you cannot turn around a company by doing more of what has already landed you in trouble, although it is extraordinary how often the existing management blame their own ineffectiveness and not the strategy which has so obviously failed.

Few individuals are so closed-minded that they won't give you a chance if you explain your thinking, and in any case, no recovery plan is a single unique solution. The eventual solution you decide upon can, and must, be one to which all parties (particularly within the company) can offer their support.

Remember that your advent has kindled hope in those who work for you, coupled with probably unrealistic assumptions of a miraculous and speedy change in the situation.

WHERE DOES EVERYBODY STAND?

A positive strategy with clear delegation for action and a lot of trust in your employees can change things surprisingly quickly. The next, and very difficult, action is entirely within your own outfit. It is absolutely vital that everyone knows where they stand. Start with the key 10%–20%, who you are sure need to be on board. Make clear that as long as you have a business, you need them and they are as secure as anyone in the year 2001 can be. Then address the 10%–15% most at risk. It is almost certain you will have to reduce cash, but generally a pay-out of under 20% will do the trick. Remember that starting at the top involves fewer people and releases more money. Those most at risk deserve the earliest warning and the

"Changing the direction of a large company is like trying to turn an aircraft carrier. It takes a mile before anything happens."
(Al Ries)

most help. Sharing the task of helping them to find alternatives eases the pain, as does the maximum affordable financial aid.

The remainder should be told that they are not at immediate risk, and that the risk to them depends almost entirely on the success of the turnaround.

The financial state of the company should be known to everyone, as should the direction and amount of change which will be required. Don't be trapped by the fear of lack of security on data. Bad news travels like lightning and all too often is far exceeded by the rumors and ill-concealed "schadenfreude" of those in the outside world. You only get one shot at trying to turn around a business, and concealment of the reality is not a help.

Delegation and Trust

Once you have decided the strategy, the aim and the team, delegate furiously. People have to know they are trusted and that all depends upon them.

Do not allow the inevitable attempts to "delegate upwards." You must keep on pushing the problem back to employees, while reiterating your commitment and support for their actions. The world is littered with examples of individuals who have achieved what you and others felt was impossible. Problems are only, and can only be, solved by those who "own" them, and your leadership role is to reinforce that ownership.

Leading by Example

You now enter what is probably the most personally difficult phase of all. Both inside and outside the company, you have to radiate confidence and realism while encouraging people to increase their speed of activity. This is helped by removing the brakes, simplifying the structure, reducing the senior management numbers and levels, and increasing the tempo.

Example is all. You cannot expect everyone else to throw themselves at the problem if you turn in late and go off early to enjoy a liquid lunch. The drum beat is taken from the top. In my own case, I have reduced my pay level and given back money I had been awarded until the business results had turned. You need a few dramatic examples from the top. Don't expect that stopping tea and biscuits will be greeted with anything other than cynicism. Selling the headquarters or the board cars is more likely to hit a responsive chord.

It is the board that has led the business into the mess, and it is the board who must be seen to take the medicine and be totally committed to the change. In my own case, a 50% reduction in the number of executive board members and a refusal to allow deputies both increased our speed of response and demonstrated that there were no sacred cows.

Everything has to be up for grabs, and fear and tradition must not be allowed to inhibit action.

The whole problem is to achieve ownership of a new plan and a new pace of action—and all must be results oriented. Turnarounds are difficult and test the imagination and courage, but once it is evident you have started on the way up again there is no limit to how far and how fast you can go.

Making It Happen ▸▸

- Act in the certainty that people within the organization itself know the myriad problems which must be overcome and the actions to be taken.
- Concentrate first on your diagnosis of the problem and ensure a reasonable time to execute your chosen solution.
- Ensure that the solution is one which all parties, particularly within the company, can support.
- Start your program by telling the key 10%–20% that you need them on board. Then address the 10%–15% whose jobs are most at risk.
- Once you have decided the strategy, the aim, and the team, delegate intensively to people who know they are trusted and that all depends upon them.
- Remove the brakes, simplify the structure, reduce senior management numbers and levels, increase the tempo—and implement a few dramatic examples from the top.

For More Information

Books:

Deming, W. Edwards. *Out of the Crisis*. Cambridge, MA: MIT Press, 2000.
Garr, Doug. *IBM Redux: Lou Gerstner and the Business Turnaround of the Decade*. Rev. ed. New York: HarperCollins, 2000.
Joiner, Brian L. *Fourth Generation Management: The New Business Consciousness*. New York: McGraw-Hill, 1994.

Web Site:

www.turnaround.org: this is the site of the Turnaround Management Association, an international nonprofit association that advocates the use of professional turnaround specialists in a crisis. The site includes a Journal of Corporate Renewal page and links to other sites.

See also:
☆ **Boardroom Roles (pp. 220–21)**
☆ **Leadership (pp. 226–28)**
☆ **Strategic Agility (pp. 103–04)**
✔ **Strategic Planning (pp. 484–85)**
Out of the Crisis (p. 939)
W. Edwards Deming (pp. 980–81)
Corporate Strategy (pp. 1944–46)

"No one has ever accused us of lagging behind. In fact, I am willing to turn an entire company upside down if it's time to do that. We're in perpetual evolution." (Richard Branson)

Tuning into the Harmonics of Management *by Dorothy Marcic*

EXECUTIVE SUMMARY

- Our organizations operate at 30% of capacity.
- Seeing employees as human beings with multiple intelligences can enhance productivity.
- Using harmonics in management education creates balance between rational, esthetic, and emotional approaches.

Introduction

Despite years of hearing about learning organizations and high-performing systems, we still aren't there. Even the best organizations operate at pitifully low levels of productivity. From over two decades of experience with hundreds of companies, I estimate we operate at 30% of possible output. That is based on asking people how many in their organization work at between 0 and 50% of their abilities. A typical answer: at least half. What I mean by the level of their abilities is this: think how much time is spent in meaningless conversations, the real aim of which is to take up time, rather than conversations that add meaning and purpose. Employees are required to be at work certain hours, or, as in professional firms with flexibility of hours, are expected to have a certain amount of "face time." Rather than doing real work, some choose to move from one office to another and waste time. Or how about the mindless meetings that are all one-way communication from the boss to the crew, with information that could as easily be put in e-mail? Or time lost in endless and unproductive conflicts, personal attacks, jealousies, power games, and other dysfunctional routines?

Why such organizational listlessness? It isn't because people are lazy. Given the chance, the typical employee welcomes challenge, a chance to have input, a means to feel energized. Very few get up in the morning hoping for another boring, grinding day at the office.

One Solution

One reason for this lack of engagement is our management paradigm, which assumes a purely rational world, one that responds effectively to analysis and data collection. If we realize, however, that organizations are ideas populated by groups of people, we conclude that those people have human needs. Unless their needs are met holistically, they will not respond with total dedication or energy.

Reasons for lower productivity include endless conflicts, hurt feelings, domination strategies and retaliations. Such behaviors do not emanate from our rational and orderly minds. They are emotional reactions to perceived threats. Whether those threats are real or not, the reactions and toxic waste they leave are very real, causing demotivation and cynicism.

To create a more productive work environment, then, requires some attention paid to the workers' other intelligences, which include those in the "Harmonics of Management":

Emotional: self-awareness, relationship skills, motivation and behavior management. Building these skills will reduce the combustible conflicts, difficult conversations, and antagonistic interactions too common at work.

Spiritual: focuses on the values people work from. An environment that allows employees to develop their capacities with integrity, trustworthiness, and service will, over the long run, create a more stable and motivated workforce.

Aesthetic: being able to appreciate arts increases the ability to help find underlying meanings, motivations, and insights, as well as helping find deeper meanings about work. British-born poet David Whyte, author of *The Heart Aroused*, counsels leaders that they will never reach their full potential until they find poetry in their work and their lives.

Much of management education uses the rational mind to find the most efficient route to solving a problem. Because organizations have become so much better at this in recent years, we've seen prices drop on consumer goods so that the average person in a developed country lives in the kind of luxury reserved for kings hundreds of years ago. If this push for efficiency is taken too far, however, it squeezes out the ability to tolerate and even appreciate the increasing complexity of the world. The success of business process reengineering came at the expense of the other intelligences.

"If I had my life to live over again, I would have made it a rule to read some poetry and listen to some music at least once a week; for perhaps the parts of my brain now atrophied would have thus been kept active through use. The loss of these tastes is a loss of happiness, and may possibly be injurious to the intellect, and more probably to the moral character, by enfeebling the emotional part of our nature." (Charles Darwin)

The new Internet world has changed the workplace and even workers themselves, as people are no longer willing to just show up for work they consider meaningless in order to get a paycheck. Younger workers particularly want their work to have some purpose, some impact, some meaning. Poetry and other arts can help sort through some of the complexity, so that underlying meanings, patterns, and our deepest yearnings emerge.

Shared Incompetency

Most leaders in organizations are not skilled in poetry, painting, sculpture, or music. In fact, if you asked them to participate in one of these activities, they would explain how irrelevant this was to their job or find some more pressing matter to attend to. Yet I believe it is the very fear these arts engender that makes them such a powerful teaching tool for managers. Much as the so-called "Ropes" courses work on the model of "shared incompetency," so too do programs using arts. Ask a group to write a song and the anxiety level goes up, ask them to draw a picture of their hand and nervousness appears. The growing number of trainers using arts in leadership programs report, though, that participants are able to find parts of themselves they had not accessed before, as shown below.

Mini-cases

Amy Stein: an artist who helps leaders draw their inner selves, thus accessing some parts of themselves which had been hidden and which now help them become fuller, more productive human beings.

Barry Scott: an actor who recreates Martin Luther King, Jr., and gives managers a deeper sense of organizational justice, pro-

"Conscience is the inner voice that warns us somebody may be looking." (H. L. Mencken)

foundly impacting their sense of the power they have for good or bad in their own decision making.

John Cimino: a musician who has gathered other musicians together to perform his "Concert of Ideas" in companies, helping people to reflect on their values and practices and bringing a sense of optimism.

Laura Derocher: a singer whose original music helps people remember what they want to be at work; she role models finding bliss and helps people evoke their former longings.

Gene Audette: a career counselor who uses pictures of sculpture to help clients figure out what their deepest desires are in terms of the types of work they wish to pursue.

Judi Neal: a singer whose music helps groups explore community, dissonance, conflict and harmony.

Roger Nierenberg: a musical conductor who teaches leaders how to manage a group of highly skilled and self-motivated individuals.

David Horth and others at the Center for Creative Leadership: teach managers the importance of complexity and underutilized capacities, as in the arts; participants in their programs report being able to speed up the strategic process or using poetry to develop marketing strategies.

Michael Jones: a pianist whose improvisational music for leaders and even Wall Street stands as a metaphor for the imagination companies need in the uncharted waters ahead.

LeeAnn Hearn and Amy Powell: sculptors and teachers who experiment with group-sculpting to increase interpersonal communication, cooperation, and conflict resolution.

Michael London: a musician who teaches team-building through helping groups write a blues song as a way of communicating their own struggles and having to overcome the obstacle of songwriting as a team.

The Harmonics of Management model is an underlying theory of employing the arts to make organizations more effective and fulfilling. Arts exploration helps people to access parts of themselves of which they were perhaps unaware. Imagine being able to sing or draw, something that had seemed impossible. That becomes a metaphor in organizations for learning new skills that seem too formidable, too difficult. Writing and performing a song, for example, not only highlights untapped talent, it also helps participants find their own courage to try something completely new. And in this fast-paced New Economy business world, which morphs into new configurations frequently, accessing capacities to be bold and the willingness to experiment with unknown structures or processes is needed if companies want to remain competitive.

MAKING IT HAPPEN ▸▸

- Invite artists in periodically for sessions on drawing, painting, or sculpture. Also have a facilitator to draw out the metaphors for organizational life. What can be learned from sculpture about being a leader, about molding the environment, yet learning to let the wheel and clay work their own process?
- Have musicians work with your people. On some occasions, have groups write a blues or other song as a means of learning team-building skills. Another time, individuals choose a song that describes their current life, another that articulates their dreams. What was learned that can bring greater productivity?
- As a group assignment, have people find popular songs that illustrate the culture of the company or have them find several songs that tell the firm's story. Present these songs in a general session, and then facilitate a discussion on how this music helps people better understand their environment and one another.

CAUTION: HANDLE WITH CARE

As with any tool, using the arts can be done ineffectively. To avoid wasted time, money, and increased cynicism, note the following concerns.

- Don't run a session without the right teachers. In other words, if you want to teach painting, only use skilled artists and also use facilitators to help guide discussion.
- Avoid doing arts sessions without ample time for discussion. People need time to make connections between the art and their worklife. Don't assume they will "get it" on their own. Often the artist will not be able to do this kind of facilitation, as it is an entirely different skill set.
- If you have a series of sessions, make sure they relate to one another and run in a meaningful pedagogical order. I once participated in a creativity and leadership session that was a grab bag of painting, drama, music, role playing, and dream analysis whose parts were totally disconnected. An hour of deep and often tearful analysis of poems written by participants was followed by a silly improv session, then, an hour later, everyone tried to focus on some deep and probing issue. In sum, the event was disjointed and not as effective as it could have been.

CONCLUSION

The Harmonics of Management helps people find the deeper part of their soul that yearns for higher purpose in their work. Getting away from the Old Economy linear-thinking, rational-only model, it helps workers be fully present in mind and spirit each day. Unlike the old Western movies, where the cowboys had to park their guns at the sheriff's office, we no longer have to park our values and inner essence when we get to the office. Using the arts in our organizations can help people bring their minds *and* their souls to work.

For More Information

Books and Journals:

Gardner, Howard. *Frames of Mind: The Theory of Multiple Intelligences*. 10th ed. New York: Basic Books, 1993.

Nicomacheus the Pythagorean. *The Manual of Harmonics*. Translation and commentary by Flora R. Levine. Grand Rapids, MI: Phanes Press, 1994.

Rosenfeld, Jill. "Speak Softly, but Carry a Big Baton." *Fast Company*, July 2001: 46–8.

Schuessler, Heidi A. "A Poet Taps into the Disillusionment of Managers." *New York Times*, June 20, 2001: C-2.

See also:

☆ **Creating Fun in the Workplace (pp. 37–38)**
☆ **Making the Workplace Flex, Not Break (pp. 31–32)**
☆ **Viewpoint: Henry Mintzberg (pp. 241–42)**
✔ **Downshifting: Working Less and Enjoying It More (pp. 812–13)**
Innovation and Creativity (pp. 2000–03)

"A nobler economics. . .is not afraid to discuss spirit and conscience, moral purpose and the meaning of life."
(Theodore Roszak)

Core Versus Context: Managing Resources in a Downturn

by Geoffrey A. Moore

EXECUTIVE SUMMARY

- *Core* processes create competitive advantage through differentiation.
- *Context* processes are necessary to meet competitive market standards, but do not differentiate.
- Investors wish the bulk of their capital to go to core processes, as only those can raise stock prices.
- It thus becomes imperative for executives to manage their firm's *core/context ratio.*

Introduction

Executives well understand the value of focusing on core business issues and activities, although they sometimes fail to distinguish between core as competitive advantage versus core competence. The former is what the market rewards, the latter what the company is good at. One of the toughest challenges in business occurs when core competence is no longer core. Competition has caught up with you to such an extent that what was once core has now become context. The market still demands the process, but it's no longer willing to pay a premium for it.

Companies thus find an increasing portion of their asset base—sometimes in equipment, always in personnel—no longer generates attractive returns. What was once differentiated and at a premium has now been commoditized. This in turn causes investors to bid down the value of their stock, since they see an increasingly large portion of their capital going to fund processes that are at best financially inert and are potentially a financial sinkhole.

Every company is subject to erosion of core into context; the very nature of competitive markets works to neutralize differentiation over time as competitors find ways to mimic or substitute for the value created. The knee-jerk response of most management teams is to make or find new core, which is necessary but insufficient. What they must also do is systematically work to shed themselves of context or face a perpetually deteriorating core/context ratio, with loss of attractiveness to investors and, ultimately, an uncompetitive cost of capital. In this section we will outline the impact of core versus context, and the actions that companies must take.

The Impact on Companies

Companies get trapped by context from various causes, many attributable to organizational inertia. Such processes were once their bread and butter, making it hard to abandon them. Moreover, if the alternative is to outsource the work (the fundamental domain in which context shedding is accomplished), there are inevitable concerns about cost. Rarely do in-house teams *not* assert that they can perform a given function cheaper, faster, and better than outsourcers.

Long-term, however, this is not the case. Where one company's context is another company's core, market dynamics ultimately favor the latter's position. That company can invest in productivity-improving systems and processes with full support of its investors, whereas the other company cannot. Moreover, it can attract the best people because it can provide them an upwardly mobile career path, whereas the latter company cannot. Finally, it can amortize investments across a broad base of customers, whereas the other company cannot.

Thus, in the long term, failing to outsource is a losing game. Only in the short term—specifically, in the current quarter—is it often more expensive, in part for reasons of transition costs, in part because prices and offerings are not as competitive as one would want until market forces have a chance to work. The end result: unless the outsourcer makes a short-term sacrifice, it's unlikely the deal goes forward.

Most executives are wise to this game, but few appreciate how pernicious it is to accede to it. They don't see how every context process not outsourced creates a tax on the asset base of the company. Worse, they don't see how failure to manage context aggressively leads necessarily to a loss of agility in their corporate culture and a corresponding rise in stifling administration. Why?

Context processes have no upside, but they do have downside. Context carries liability just as core does. The difference is that core also transfers competitive advantage, which context does not. Thus, if you're managing core, you're always in search of the efficient frontier of risk versus reward. But what is the best strategy for managing context?

Darwinian natural selection will drive context managers to increasingly risk-averse strategies, those being the most suitable for managing processes that have downside but no upside. As a company's core/context ratio deteriorates, its population of managers will thus become increasingly risk-averse. They are happy for other people to take risks, but not themselves (and not others if that's going to put their area in the line of fire). The result? Large corporations become stultified and unresponsive.

Successfully Managing the Core/Context Ratio

The proving ground for outsourcing context today is contract manufacturing in the electronics industry, with companies like Cisco and Dell, and outsourcers like Solectron and Flextronics, leading the way. What these companies are exploiting is the premise that whatever is one company's context can be another company's core. In this relationship, whenever a business process is transferred from one to the other, the investors of both companies applaud, one because it went off their balance sheet, and the other because it went on to theirs.

Drill down into the systems investments that have enabled these early adopters to steal a march on their competitors and we see that they focus on two critical issues: *control* and *visibility*. The following cases provide examples.

Beyond manufacturing, more companies are looking to outsource IT and financial and human resources services. Payroll has long been a function considered outsourceable. Now highly visible departmental outsourcing deals have been struck by General Motors with Arthur Andersen in accounts

"An economy based on knowledge is one where people are the greatest national resource."

(Tony Blair)

payable and British Petroleum with PricewaterhouseCoopers for human resources. Here, the best strategy is to determine for each function what is still core and what is legitimately context (particularly critical in the case of IT).

Early outsourcing relationships between EDS and General Motors and between IBM and Kodak provide some important lessons. In both cases, the corporations were fed up with their in-house organization and wanted a better substitute at a fixed price. They made no attempt to segregate core from context. Instead they focused on price, which was negotiated as low as possible. This in turn motivated the outsourcers to cut corners or nickel-and-dime the end users on change requests, leading to bad relationships and bad outcomes. The end result was annoying when it came to context processes, but it was devastating when it ended up holding core projects hostage.

Conversely, outsourcing IT infrastructure looks to be a major growth market, as companies like Exodus attest on the server farm side. Moreover, specialized services like 24/7 performance monitoring and security management both lend themselves to third-party provisioning. These functions, although frequently mission-critical, are almost never core. This is where outsourcing shines.

Key Points when Managing the Core/Context Ratio

1. **Be prepared to delegate core activities.** Top management can delegate core to middle management. Of course, it rarely wants to, because this is the fun stuff. The truth is that the middle of the organization has a better view of emerging market trends; if you empower it, it will do a better job than you.
2. **Outsource and manage context.** Top management's most powerful lever is the outsourcing of context. This is not the fun stuff. But middle management is never positioned to act on this directive, as it can't afford to put its political capital at risk. Only top management can drive these initiatives, always with an eye toward repurposing reclaimed resources into the next generation of core work.
3. **Distinguish between mission-critical and supporting activities.** To the distinction between core and context needs to be added the distinction between *mission-critical* and *supporting*. The former applies to processes that can directly damage customer outcomes or corporate capabilities. These must be kept under managerial control. The latter, by contrast, can be readily outsourced with only modest controls.

   The big challenge in core/context ratio management comes with the need to outsource mission-critical context. Indeed, executives often confuse mission-critical with core because they're sure they *can't* outsource such processes. But to manage their core/context ratio, they must. This demands new best practices in outsourcing, enabling customers to retain control and visibility while transferring the bulk of work to another organization.
4. **Harness the benefit of technology.** The technology key to the new best practices is for the company and its outsourcer to create information systems that give the company short-term adaptive controls and long-term visibility into its risk positions. The Internet provides a backbone for enabling such systems. The business logic that must ride on that backbone is just now coming to market. Early adopters may well have to write their own systems in order to get ahead of their competition.

Mini-Case

Dell has used IT to develop end-to-end visibility into their inventory positions and used their market power to force suppliers to hold that inventory until the last second. This would be intolerable for the supplier were it not for Dell giving them near-real-time visibility into the emerging order mix, which is made possible by configuration software, now Web-enabled, that funnels customer demand from an infinite array of selections into a finite and manageable set of options.

Making It Happen ▸▸

1. **Start with a questioning analysis of core and context activities, at three levels:**
   - **Top level**: which of our businesses are still core? Which have become context?
   - **Business unit level**: which of our line functions are the real basis for our competitive differentiation? Which are not?
   - **Function level**: which of our processes are the source of differentiation? Which are driven by more compliance?
   - **Departmental and, if useful, individual levels**: how much time is spent on context activities?
2. **Consider two key ideas to help guide this process, asking the questions:**
   - If we were entirely free of current obligations, what could we do to increase the competitive advantage of our company? This helps people to see the possible sources and types of core activity, and may help start the journey to get there. It also identifies the task work that should be passed on or left alone.
   - What work would we be willing to surrender if we were assured that someone else would handle it appropriately? This becomes a lightning rod to attract context processes that, once aggregated, can be analyzed for disposal.
3. **Implement and monitor the results.** It helps to understand from the outset that the process of detailed implementation will invariably result in a course correction later. Also, not only does the process of implementation need to be monitored to ensure that it remains on track, but the core/context ratio needs to be regularly assessed, as competitive markets are far from static. One of the keys to successful implementation is to assemble a sufficient amount of work to motivate an outsourcer to put their best efforts into the work.

Conclusion

Executives must learn to manage the core/context ratio. Regardless of how superior their core is, eventually its impact will be dwarfed by an ever-expanding context. It's like cholesterol: if you do not manage context, it will finish you.

For More Information

Book:

Christensen, Clayton M. *The Innovator's Dilemma*. New York: HarperBusiness, 2000.

See also:

☆ **Organic Growth Versus Acquisition (pp. 79–80)**
☆ **Outsourcing (pp. 89–90)**
✓ **Deciding Whether to Outsource (pp. 490–91)**
Outsourcing (pp. 2061–62)

"Companies, like people, cannot be skillful at everything. Therefore, core capabilities both advantage and disadvantage a company." (Dorothy Leonard)

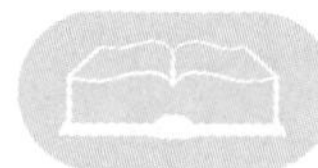

SNAPPING MANAGERIAL INERTIA
by Jeffrey Pfeffer and Robert I. Sutton

EXECUTIVE SUMMARY

- Despite the billions of dollars that industry spends on executive education, leadership development, and knowledge-management efforts each year, very little change takes place.
- Executives must use plans, analysis, meetings, and presentations to inspire achievement, not to substitute for action.
- To accomplish this, companies must eliminate fear, abolish destructive internal competition, measure what matters, and promote leaders who understand the work employees do.

INTRODUCTION

Why do so many managers understand so much about employee and organizational performance and work so hard, yet do so much to undermine performance? Why do so many companies sponsor training programs and knowledge-management initiatives, yet see no impact from those efforts? Knowing what to do isn't enough. Companies must inspire action to turn all of that individual and collective knowledge into achievements that affect the company's business results.

What happens in many companies is that managers spend so much time fighting internal battles that they have little time left to fight the company's competitors. In too many companies points are scored on the elaborateness of internal presentations (meaning that people spend inordinate amounts of time preparing those presentations to impress their bosses and peers) instead of tangible business results. In many other companies the penalty for failure is so great that managers spend their time preserving the status quo rather than trying to find new and better ways of affecting business results. Further, the "not invented here" (NIH) syndrome prevents people from learning from each other for fear that they'll give credit to some other person in the company who has developed a better method—for fear they'll admit the other person deserves more recognition and, perhaps, a greater share of the available rewards.

It doesn't have to be this way. Many companies are finding ways of overcoming the knowing-doing gap. Knowing how to bridge this gap will make a positive difference in your company's business results, your employee's morale and performance, and your effectiveness as a manager.

GUIDELINES FOR ACTION

RECOGNIZE THE IMPORTANCE OF PHILOSOPHY

Many companies have undertaken experiments in one division or location to implement high-performance work teams. While many such efforts have shown outstanding results, few of these companies have been successful in transferring these new work methods to other plants, divisions, or locations. A prime example of this is that few of the innovations from Saturn and NUMMI have ever been adopted by other parts of the General Motors organization. What's missing is a company-wide understanding of the basic philosophy of the new methods and a frank and open discussion of why the new methods are important and must be replicated throughout the company.

Companies that don't accept talk as a substitute for action often do one or more of the following:

- promote people who have developed a real-world understanding of the organization's work processes because they have performed them themselves
- build a culture that values simplicity (and doesn't reward complexity), uses simple, clear, and direct language, and values common sense
- use action-oriented language and follow up to ensure that decisions are implemented
- refuse to accept excuses for why things won't work, instead encouraging employees to reframe objections into challenges to be overcome

ACT AND TEACH OTHERS HOW TO ACT

Too many companies place great value on conceptual frameworks, fancy graphic presentations, and lots of words, but little value on action. Why are so many change efforts approved in the boardroom and never implemented? Honda puts employees into suppliers' organizations so they can see how the suppliers make parts and what work methods they use. Being closely involved with the supplier is imperative for real understanding and learning.

At IDEO Product Development, C.E.O. David Kelley walks the talk of learning through trial and error. Kelley and other top managers teach employees their method and students enact it by designing, building, demonstrating, and pitching their inventions to each other.

PLANS AND CONCEPTS COUNT LESS THAN ACTION

Too many companies are stymied by analysis paralysis, the feeling that plans must be complete and bulletproof before any action is taken. The more successful companies encourage action to foster learning by doing. In many of these companies it is believed that an 80% solution today is better than a 100% solution months or years from now. Continental Airlines C.O.O. Greg Brenneman speaks of the airline's turnaround in this way: "If you sit around devising elegant and complex strategies and then try to execute them through a series of flawless decisions, you're doomed. We saved Continental because we acted and we never looked back."

TOLERATE ERRORS AS A SIGN THAT LEARNING IS TAKING PLACE

Does your company treat mistakes so harshly that people continuously analyze and discuss plans instead of taking action? Thomas Edison tried thousands of materials for light-bulb filaments before discovering tungsten. When someone asked him how he overcame so many failures, he said that he never failed—he just learned. Roger Sant, cofounder and chairman of AES, fosters a culture of forgiveness, noting, "You would be amazed at how quickly people support and forgive one another here."

DRIVE FEAR OUT OF YOUR ORGANIZATION

If employees fear that any new idea that doesn't work perfectly at the first attempt will result in punishment or dismissal, they'll never try anything new. Rapid prototyping is a manufacturing design method in

---

"Sometimes I am forced to the conclusion that GM is so large and its inertia so great that it is impossible for us to be leaders."

(Alfred P. Sloan, Jr.)

which new ideas can be tried out quickly and relatively inexpensively and plans modified based on results. Failure of a new idea is viewed as part of the learning process, not as something to be feared. Successful companies encourage risk-taking and encourage employees to try new ideas without an overwhelming fear of retribution should they fail.

Companies that work to drive fear out of their organization often try some of these approaches:

- Rather than shooting the messenger, reward employees who deliver bad news. If the company doesn't know about a problem, it can't solve it.
- Punish inaction, not unsuccessful actions. An unsuccessful action should be viewed as a learning experience.
- Share failures. When leaders share their failures, they give permission to others to fail and encourage them to try.
- Banish anyone, at any level, who humiliates others.
- Learn from, and even celebrate, mistakes–especially when trying something new.

Fight the Competition, Not Each Other

Because competitive free enterprise has triumphed as an economic system, many companies have adopted internal competition as a way of life. This is typified by such practices as normal-curve performance rating systems, recognition for relatively few employees, and individual measurements and rewards that set people against each other. These practices take the focus away from the real opposition: external competitors. There are exceptions, however.

Measure Action and What Turns Knowledge into Action

Many companies are awash with data measuring every conceivable action. Amid so many measures employees spend far too much time focused on the numbers and how they'll look instead of on actions that can help improve the business and meet overall goals. More successful companies focus on a few key measures of company performance, believing that if those key measures are met, everything else will fall into line.

Leadership Is the Key

Successful leaders create a positive learning environment that not only helps employees learn but also helps them apply that learning to their work to make a positive difference in business results. They lead by their own example and teach others how to act.

Mini-cases

At *Men's Wearhouse* the emphasis is on team selling; employees succeed only as their colleagues succeed. Customers don't care who gets the commission, they want great service from every employee.

The *SAS Institute* has a very low turnover rate, based partly on employees' preference not to have to constantly look over their shoulder to see which colleague is getting ready to subvert their work in order to look better themselves.

Southwest Airlines focuses on key measures such as lost bags, customer complaints, and on-time performance.

AES focuses on uptime of their power plants, new business development, and environmental and safety factors.

Measurements that can help turn knowledge into action include those that are

- focused on organizational success rather than individual success. This encourages teamwork and interdependence.
- focused more on processes and means to ends, not on end products and final outcomes. This helps to facilitate learning and provides data that can better guide action and decision making.
- focused on the business model, culture, and philosophy of the firm. This means that measurements will vary from firm to firm and will generally depart from traditional accounting-based indicators.
- focused on a mindful, ongoing process of learning from experience and experimentation. No process is ever viewed as complete or final.

When David Kearns was C.E.O. at *Xerox*, he applied quality principles to the top management team as he encouraged their implementation throughout the company.

The C.E.O. of *General Motors* teaches in GM University, demonstrating his personal commitment to knowledge building and sharing.

Conclusion

Many readers will finish this article and start nodding: How'd they know what's happening in my company? But recognizing that the problems exist isn't enough. Going back twenty years, Peters and Waterman, in their book *In Search of Excellence*, recognized that the most successful companies have a "bias for action." And that's what you need to snap your company's managerial inertia. Start right now!

For More Information

Books:

Kelly, Patrick, and John Case. *Faster Company: Building the World's Nuttiest, Turn-on-a-Dime, Home-Grown, Billion-Dollar Business*. New York: John Wiley, 1998.

Tobin, Daniel R. *The Knowledge-Enabled Organization: Moving from "Training" to "Learning" to Meet Business Goals*. New York: AMACOM, 1997.

See also:

☆ **Creating Value through People (pp. 121–22)**
☆ **The Critical Factors That Build or Break Teams (pp. 192–93)**
☆ **The Good, the Fad, and the Ugly (pp. 175–76)**
☆ **Human Capital (pp. 115–16)**
☆ **Organic Growth versus Acquisition (pp. 79–80)**
☆ **Return on Talent (pp. 109–10)**
☆ **Viewpoint: Noel M. Tichy (pp. 224–25)**
Management Teams: Why They Succeed or Fail (p. 919)
R. Meredith Belbin (pp. 966–67)

"Pusillanimity disposeth men to irresolution, and consequently to lose the occasions and fittest opportunities of action."
(Thomas Hobbes)

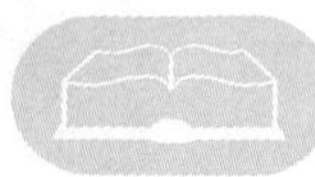

THE FUTURE OF MONEY *by Bernard Lietaer*

EXECUTIVE SUMMARY

Money is an agreement within a community to use something as a means of payment. A major shift is currently on-going in the power to create money, from the banking system to private currencies. This could create new possibilities in a wide variety of domains, including in the way business is done and social changes are facilitated.

WHAT IS MONEY?

Economic textbooks define money by what it *does*, that is, they describe its classic functions as a standard of value, means of exchange, and store of value. But what, in fact, *is* money?

Our working definition is as follows: money is an *agreement* within a *community* to use something as a *means of payment*.

From a business perspective, money is also the first objective of a corporation. If a business doesn't manage to have a higher money inflow than outflow, it is doomed to disappear.

Given the amount of effort that goes into trying to capture part of the money flow, it is intriguing that so little time is spent on thinking about where money comes from, or what it is.

TYPES OF MONEY

By our definition, there are already a number of different types of currency in widespread use today. We may distinguish between:

Legal tender "for all debts, public or private." Thus, if someone owes a debt and offers to pay with this currency, the debt can be declared void if the currency is refused. One important debt covered in this respect is tax payments. National currencies are typically the only legal tender in a country.

Commercial private currencies. The most common are loyalty currencies, the best known of which are "frequent-flyer miles." Barter currencies are another type of commercial private currency.

Complementary currencies. Currencies that are accepted in payment, but do not aim at replacing, merely at complementing, conventional national currencies. They are therefore designed to function in parallel with conventional currencies.

Social-Purpose currencies. Complementary currencies that aim at resolving a variety of social problems, such as elderly-care currencies, unemployment currencies, or environmental currencies.

TODAY'S NATIONAL MONEY

The secret of creating modern money is to be able to persuade people to accept one's IOU (a promise to pay in the future) as a medium of exchange. Whoever attains that status can derive an income flow from the process (for example, the interest on the loan that creates the money). Such income is called "seigniorage," a word derived from the right of the lord of the manor ("*Seignior*" in Old French) to impose the use of his currency on his vassals.

Four key features characterize conventional national money. Today, money is typically (1) geographically attached to a **nation-state**; it is (2) "**fiat**" **money**, i.e. created out of nothing, by (3) **bank debt**, against payment of (4) **interest**.

We now have trouble imagining any currencies *other* than those issued by a given country, or in the case of the Euro, a group of countries. However, the vast majority of historical currencies were, in fact, *private* issues made by the sovereign or some other local authority. Sharing a common currency creates an invisible, yet very effective, information boundary between "us" and "them." Thus national currencies are perceived as a distinctive attribute of nationhood.

The simple question "Where does money come from?" propels us into the world of magic. Today's money is "fiat" money. Every unit of every national currency in circulation started as a bank loan, either to the government or to a private entity. Just as the magician needs a handkerchief to wave above the hat before the rabbit can appear, bank money has an additional veil. In the process of creating money, attention will be drawn toward the boring technical aspects, such as mechanisms to foster competition among banks for deposits, reserve requirements, and the role of the central bank in fine-tuning the valves of the system. While these technical features all have a perfectly valid purpose (so does the handkerchief), they all simply regulate how much fiat money each bank can create (the number of rabbits that can be pulled out of which hat).

The last obvious feature of our money is interest. Here again, we tend to forget that for most of history interest was not a feature of money. In fact, all three "Religions of the Book" (Judaism, Christianity, and Islam) emphatically outlawed usury, defined as *any* interest on money. Applying interest on the loans creating money has a pervasive effect on society. For instance:

1. Interest indirectly encourages systematic competition among the participants in the system, because only the principal is created in a loan, while the interest isn't. When someone pays back interest he or she is using in fact someone else's principal.
2. Interest concentrates wealth by taxing the majority in favor of a minority. It is noteworthy that—when interest became legal—democratic countries felt the need to introduce progressive taxation to counterbalance that wealth concentration process.
3. Interest continually fuels the need for endless economic growth.
4. Finally, interest programs decision-makers to think short term. The "discounted cash flow" technique shows why future income or costs can be discounted into irrelevance when an interest-bearing currency is used.

THE FUTURE OF MONEY

In his massive study entitled *The History of Money from Ancient Times to the Present Day,* Glyn Davies remarks that over the past 5,000 years there have only been two fundamental innovations in the technology of money. The first was paper money, invented in China during the 9th century and spreading to Western Europe during the late Renaissance. It enabled the transfer of the power of money creation from kings and emperors to the banking system. We are now in the middle of the second fundamental innovation: electronic money. Already today, over 95% of the money existing in the world resides in the form of bits and bytes in computers at banks and brokers. All signs are that this new technology shift may also involve a change in the power of creating money.

While conventional bank-debt currencies will in most countries maintain their privileged status as legal tender, other types of currencies could become "common use tender."

Private commercial currencies have indeed already broken the monopoly of conventional money as medium of payment. Initially, airline frequent-flyer currencies were only a marketing gimmick issued by each airline individually. But today, for example, two-thirds of all British airline miles are cashed in for something else than purchasing air travel. Sainsbury, one of the largest supermarket chains in the United Kingdom, is now accepting them as payment in its shops.

Commercial barter, previously considered a "primitive" form of exchange, is now growing by 15% per year, three times faster than normal currency denominated transactions. *Barter News* estimates that broker-facilitated barter deals now amount to approximately $10 billion per year. More significant still is countertrade (international corporate barter). The U.S. Department of Commerce, the World Trade Organization (WTO), and *The Economist* all estimate countertrade to have reached a staggering volume of between $800 billion and $1.2 trillion per year. This represents between 10 and 15% of all international trade! *Fortune* reports that two out of every three major global corporations now perform such transactions routinely, and have specialized departments focusing on such deals. Social-purpose complementary currencies have similarly experienced explosive growth over the past 15 years.

There are a wide variety of social purposes pursued by such local complementary-currency systems. They vary from care of the elderly to unemployment, from the restoration of a spirit of community in a well-off neighborhood near Washington DC to getting kids off drugs and crime in ghettos in Chicago. They operate in Mexico City and in fishing villages in Canada. They have been designed for small groups of 50 people in Australia, a city of 2.3 million people in Brazil, or prefectures of 10 million in Japan.

While local activists on a shoestring budget started most of these systems, governments now actively support some of them as well.

- The city planning office of Curitiba, the capital city of Paraná in Southern Brazil, has launched and managed for 25 years a local currency that is now providing up to one third of all the income of its citizens, and has been a key to its remarkable development as the "most ecological city in the world" by UN standards.
- In Australia and New Zealand local authorities are funding local currency startups in high-unemployment pockets.
- In the United States, the IRS has declared one such system (Time Dollars) officially tax-free; and 31 States now pay their own employees to start up such systems.
- In Japan, the head of the services department of the Ministry of International Trade and Industry (MITI) has started 40 different experimental "eco-money projects," in order to choose the models that would be most appropriate for general application in the country.
- In the United Kingdom in 2001, the Blair government financed a £500,000 startup for a Time Bank in London.

What matters here is what they have in common:

- 95% of these systems are computer-driven.
- They have already proved that they can solve real-life social problems without burdening taxpayers or governmental budgets.
- The vast majority are small-scale affairs that are purposely kept on a local scale. But the only mature system today (the WIR in Switzerland) now has 80,000 members, including one quarter of all small and medium-sized businesses in the country, and enjoys an annual turnover of $2 billion.

Perhaps the most intriguing thing about this phenomenon is that it has proved wrong an implicit hypothesis in economics dating back to Adam Smith: that money is value-neutral. In fact, both empirical fieldwork and theoretical research have proved that *the use of different kinds of currency does significantly affect both the behavior and the relationships of the people who use them.*

These money innovations provide new possibilities for businesses to use their inventories as working capital, or for social issues to be addressed with less taxpayer's money.

We should leave the last word about the future of money to Georg Simmel, a German philosopher and author: "The debate about the future of money is not about inflation or deflation, fixed or flexible exchange rates, gold or paper standards; it is about the kind of society in which money is to operate."

For More Information

Books

Davies, Glyn. *A History of Money from Ancient Times to the Present Day*. Cardiff: University of Wales, 1994.
Lietaer, Bernard. *The Future of Money*. New York: Random House, 2001.
Simmel, Georg. *Philosophy of Money*. 2nd ed. New York: Routledge, 1990.

See also:

☆ **Why Managers Need Futurists (pp. 279–80)**
☆ **Viewpoint: Peter Bernstein (pp. 133–34)**
Social Responsibility of Management (pp. 2115–17)

"Money is not, properly speaking, one of the subjects of commerce. . .it is the oil which renders the motion of the wheels more smooth and easy."
(David Hume)

COMPETITOR ANALYSIS: FROM DATA TO INSIGHT *by Professor Liam Fahey*

EXECUTIVE SUMMARY

Competitor Analysis (CA) has emerged over the last decade as a distinct discipline or area of analysis in leading European, North American, and Asian firms. As it has become more sophisticated, CA has shifted from a pure data focus (gathering data about competitors) to a genuine analysis focus, that is, transforming data relating to competitors into "decision-relevant" insights.

INTRODUCTION: THE PURPOSE OF COMPETITOR ANALYSIS

Executives, amongst others, often misconstrue why competitor analysis is conducted. Its purpose and benefits are not just to learn about one's competitors.

Competitors are analyzed as one means of learning about the broader competitive environment–that is, in order to generate insights into customers, distribution channels, suppliers, technology, and competitive dynamics. In the same vein, CA is also used to reflect on and learn about one's own organization–its vulnerabilities, limitations, and capabilities relative to current and potential rivals.

WHICH COMPETITORS MERIT ATTENTION?

Potential insight is sometimes unnecessarily constrained in many firms because too much attention is devoted to *current* large-market-share competitors and far too little to other types of current and potential competitors. Critical insight into change in customers' buying behaviors often emanates from analysis of small(er) rivals or of functional substitute rivals. And, sometimes, it is especially useful to "invent" a competitor that is not yet in the marketplace–for example, one created by the alliance and integration of two smaller rivals, which would then develop and introduce a range of products new to the market–and use it as a reference point to challenge the firm's existing strategy or potential strategy alternatives.

THE PROCESS OF ANALYSIS

The core of the analysis process in CA can be simply stated: identify relevant indicators from competitors' behaviors, actions, and words, then draw inferences as to what change along those indicators would imply for what the competitor might do in the future (for example, how it might change its strategy), or what it might suggest about developments in the broader marketplace (such as how fast specific products might come to the market or how quickly other products might penetrate particular customer segments). It is especially important to emphasize that CA is always about detecting change in and around competitors and assessing what that change implies for the competitor itself, for the marketplace in general, or for your own organization.

THE FOCUS OF COMPETITOR ANALYSIS

A central competitor-analysis question confronts every organization: *what is it about our rivals that we should analyze?* Or, stated differently, what do we need know about our current and potential rivals? When competitor analysis is driven by a perspective that views it as a source of learning about both the competitive environment and our own organization, however, and not just as a source of learning about our rivals, then a number of other core focal points of analysis quickly surface.

We need to learn about:

- The competitor's *marketplace strategy*: how it tries to outmaneuver rivals in the marketplace.
- The competitor's *activity/value chain*: how it organizes itself to develop and execute its marketplace strategy.
- The competitor's *alliances and networks*: what other organizations it aligns with and how it manages its network of alliances.
- The competitor's *assumptions*: what the competitor assumes about the marketplace and itself.
- The competitor's *assets and capabilities*: what enables the competitor to compete.
- The competitor's *organizational infrastructure and culture*: the nature of the competitor's organization.

CAPTURING COMPETITORS' MARKETPLACE STRATEGIES

Let us take marketplace strategy to quickly illustrate some key points in how to conduct CA.

Understanding a competitor's marketplace strategy requires you to answer three fundamental, highly interrelated, questions related to the rival's marketplace scope, posture, and goals–the three central elements in any firm's marketplace strategy:

1. What product-markets does the competitor compete in (or want to compete in)?
2. How does it compete in those product-markets to attract, win, and retain customers?
3. What does it seek to achieve in those product-markets?

You can now think about the critical indicators associated with each question. Question (1) involves indicators associated with products and customers: the range of products offered; the variety within each product line; the segments of customers reached; differences across the segments, etc.

Indicators that allow posture to be identified depend upon the relevant dimensions associated with its key modes of competing or providing value to customers–product line width, product features, functionality, service, availability, image and reputation, selling and relationships, and price. For example, for a car manufacturer, functionality might involve a number of dimensions, each giving rise to specific indicators: take-off speed (how fast can the car go from zero to 60 mph); braking speed (how fast can you stop the car going at 40 mph); gasoline consumption (how many miles will the car go on a gallon of gasoline); reliability (on average, how often does this type of car have to be repaired).

Indicators that allow marketplace goals to be inferred are also specific to the particular type of goal: product, customer, market share, share of customer, etc.

One great merit of attention to indicators is that they guide you to relevant data sources. The overarching question is always: *What sources might provide data on this particular indicator?* You should always begin by asking which individuals or units within your own organization might possess the required data and what the external sources might be.

For example, a team of competitor analysts in one automobile manufacturer wished to know the terms and conditions associated with purchases of key components from specific suppliers, such as specific types of glass from a well-known international glass manufacturer and specific types of plastic from a local supplier. They discovered that their own internal purchasing department already possessed most of the required data.

The essence of the analysis task then becomes the derivation of inferences from the change detected along relevant indicators. For example, change along a number of indicators specific to the posture's modes of competition, as discussed above, could reveal that a competitor is moving its posture to increasingly add value for customers in terms of a broader range of service dimensions or through introducing new forms of functionality or by developing more intensive relationships with high-end customers.

Assessing Competitors' Marketplace Strategies

Analysis only generates real insight when it turns to assessing what change in the competitor's strategy indicates about current, emerging, and potential change in the broader competitive context, and what such change in turn implies for the firm's current and potential strategy, decisions, and actions.

Assessment begins by evaluating the performance of the rival's strategy. Is it resulting in market-share gain? Is it leading to a greater share of individual customers? Is it building greater brand name and reputation (that in turn could be the basis of further market-share gain)?

Assessment then addresses how well the rival's strategy is performing compared to other rivals or to our own firm's strategy. For example, with regard to specific customer segments, or even individual customers, is the competitor or our own firm providing greater value along the modes of competition? Based upon customers' judgments, who is providing superior functionality? Who is providing more useful services? Whose image and reputation is more appealing to customers? It is important to note that these assessments must be based in large measure on the judgments of the customers themselves.

Assessment then aims to determine what change in the rival's marketplace strategy might portend for change in the emerging and potential marketplace. For example, customers' positive responses to a rival's recently introduced product might suggest significant shifts in the value customers will increasingly demand from their suppliers. If the firm misses this signal, it could commit extensive investment to products that will be less appealing to the market.

To cite one more illustration, if a competitor appears to be committing extensive resources to introducing new product lines, to going after new customer segments, and to seeking a greater share of existing customers, then it may well significantly shift the dynamics of rivalry over time. Its rivals may find that their old ways of competing may no longer be sufficient to retain existing customers, much less attract new ones.

Assessment of change in competitors' marketplace strategy can also lead to strong judgments about what type of marketplace strategy might be required to win in particular product domains or specific geographic regions. For example, in one product area, one computer firm concluded from the analysis of a dominant rival's marketplace strategy change, and from the product initiatives of a recent entrant, that the only way any firm could succeed in this product/technology was to develop multiple alliances with a range of vendors (so that it could continue to develop state-of-the-art products) and with a range of value-added resellers and other type of retailers (so that it could guarantee rapid access to large segments of customer).

Assessment concludes by identifying specific implications for one's own firm. For example, do the marketplace implications of change in the rival's strategy suggest that one is missing an emerging marketplace opportunity or that one should be moving faster to penetrate a specific customer segment? Often, assessment reveals key vulnerabilities not just in one's own marketplace strategy but also in one's assets and capabilities.

In summary, competitor analysis can lead to significant new insights into the world around us, as well as into our own organization.

Making It Happen ▸▸

- Focus on analyzing the information gained on competitors in order to reflect on and learn one's own organization's vulnerabilities, capabilities, and future direction.
- Examine six areas of competitor activity: marketplace strategy; activity/value chain; alliances and networks; assumptions; assets and capabilities; and organizational infrastructure and culture.
- Ask what sources can provide the data you need. Look internally for sources of information first.
- Always consider what a change in competitor's activity indicates about the potential change in a broader competitive context.

Conclusion

While many managers feel it's all they can do to collect and analyze information about their own business, one cannot really compete in today's business environment without some understanding of what the competition is up to. Competitor Analysis is a new aspect of a manager's job, and it has rapidly become a respected discipline. However, analyzing the ways of one's competitors is valuable only when a company subsequently makes decisions about how it can perform better based on a wider view of what's happening in the marketplace.

For More Information

Books:

Fahey, Liam. *Competitors: Outwitting, Outmaneuvering and Outperforming*. New York: John Wiley, 1999.

Porter, Michael E. *Competitive Strategy: Techniques for Analyzing Industries and Competitors*. New York: Free Press, 1998.

Yoffie, David B., and Mary Kwak. *Judo Strategy: Turning Your Competitors' Strength to Your Advantage*. Boston, MA: Harvard Business School Press, 2001.

Web Site:

www.managementhelp.org/mrktng/cmpetitr/cmpetitr.htm: cited as a "free community resource" this Web page lists numerous links to resources that address the nature, scope, and advantages of competitive analysis. It also includes links to related subjects, such as customer service and intellectual property law.

See also:

☆ **The Balanced Scorecard (pp. 303–04)**
☆ **Benchmarking (pp. 295–96)**
✓ **Gathering Competitive Intelligence (pp. 560–61)**
Competitive Strategy (p. 901)
Michael Porter (pp. 1038–39)
Competition (pp. 1929–31)

"What do you do when your competitor's drowning? Get a live hose and stick it in his mouth."
(Ray Kroc)

VIEWPOINT: PETER SCHWARTZ AND PETER LEYDEN

The Next Scientific Revolution Is Now

The 1990s proved once again that new technologies can drive fundamental economic changes and that businesses need to tune in to these developments early in order to thrive, if not survive. But before the technologies appear, the basic science must emerge. Given the accelerating pace of change, a business person should not only keep an eye out for emerging technologies, but track key developments in science as well. As it happens, the scientific world is on the cusp of some revolutionary breakthroughs—particularly in the fields of biology, physics, and chemistry. Transformative technologies are sure to follow. The following conversation lays out what to expect in the next decade and beyond.

Leyden: How would you describe the state of science right now?

Schwartz: We are in a period of a major scientific and technological revolution akin to what happened at the beginning of the 20th century. In physics, chemistry, and biology we are seeing really revolutionary change, both theoretically and in terms of our capabilities. And as a result, we are going to see enormous advances in technology.

Significantly, the three sciences converge at the very small scale, the molecular and atomic scale. As a result, what we're seeing are developments in these realms coming together and creating revolutionary ideas and capabilities. And the ultimate form is nanotechnology, or molecular engineering, manufacturing at the atomic level.

Leyden: Could you give us a better time frame about where we are in this revolution?

Schwartz: It's different in the three disciplines. In many ways biology is further along, because we really have had a scientific revolution that began 20 years ago—in genetics and molecular biology. The clearest expression of it is the decoding of the human genome. But there are many other elements of it. They've given us a deep understanding of how biology works at a very fundamental level. We have new power over biology that was never imaginable—let alone doable.

Leyden: Like with recent stem cell research that points towards our eventual ability to grow replacement organs?

Schwartz: Stem cell work is a perfect example. And there are many, many others. The new drug Glivec is designed as a molecule targeting a particular molecule in a cancer cell. So in biology, we're very far along in the revolution. That's why it'll have such large effects in the near future, because a lot of the conceptual revolution has already happened.

Leyden: So then where are we in physics?

Schwartz: In physics we're about to go through a big conceptual revolution, just as relativity and quantum theory were a huge conceptual revolution over the Newtonian physics that came before.

Scientific revolutions are always preceded by two phenomena. One is that the old model gets weirder and weirder and weirder. That's what happened with the old model of the sun going around the earth. You could make the math work but, boy, it was hard, and it got weirder and weirder over time as we learned more.

The other phenomenon preceding a scientific revolution is that we find data that simply doesn't fit the old model. A perfect example of that was the recent discovery that the universe is expanding at an accelerating rate. That means there's another big force out there overcoming gravity by a lot. This is a whole new form of energy we never even imagined.

Leyden: Are you talking about "dark matter," the missing mass of the universe that scientists calculate must be out there but that we still can't see?

Schwartz: That's another whole weirdness. I'm talking about dark energy. Why do we call these things "dark?" It's because we can't see them, find them, or imagine them. But then we didn't know there were radio waves out there until we invented this device called a radio. We haven't invented the "radio" for dark matter and energy, though actually we have gotten little hints. We had a tweak of reception of dark matter recently. And we have huge evidence now that there is dark energy in the data on the accelerating expansion of the universe.

So in physics we are ripe for a new model. Does that mean we will necessarily get one? No. Because, of course, this requires a great leap of imagination.

Leyden: Could it be that the breakthrough is beyond humans, at least in this century?

Schwartz: No. The field is supersaturated; it's ready to break. But it might be 20 years. It might not be five years. But I think we're ripe. The world is ripe. One of the things that has to happen, and it was true with relativity and quantum mechanics: the mathematics has to advance and be able to support the new fields.

So higher-dimensional mathematics, computational abilities, simulation abilities need to continue to develop for us to be able to push these physics fronts. So where we are in physics is that we are ready to give birth to a new model. But we don't have it yet.

Leyden: What should we expect when the new model does pop out?

"Science means simply the aggregate of all the recipes that are always successful. The rest is literature."

(Paul Valéry)

Schwartz: When it happens, two things are likely, one really big and the other almost really big. First of all, we'll re-perceive the universe. Relativity had a huge impact on people's perception of human life and the human condition. What our re-perception will be this time, I don't know. But it's clearly going to shake things up again.

Secondly, it will create new technological capabilities. A good example that is very likely, but again unpredictable, is with energy. Suppose there is dark energy out there. Suppose there is a way to overcome gravity using that energy. Well, suddenly we could be in a world of completely new sources of energy, and maybe even antigravity vehicles.

And so all I'm saying is that because we know that one of the things that has to be explained is dark energy, and that dark energy is about overcoming gravity, then it is not implausible that the technological expression of this could be some combination of new energy sources or antigravity devices.

Leyden: What about the third field, chemistry?

Schwartz: In chemistry the real issue is that the fundamental basis of chemistry has been thermodynamics. We have an understanding at a theoretical level of how molecules are formed, but the real world of chemistry is millions and billions of molecules bumping into each other under various conditions.

What we're now talking about is understanding and getting control of individual bonds, individual molecules, individual connections between them. Not only do we understand these at a more fine-grained level, but our level of control is gaining enormously.

So it is the movement of chemistry from the realm of many large numbers of things bumping into each other to finite numbers of objects being controlled individually. This changes both our understanding and our capability fundamentally—for designing new materials, for example.

Leyden: Now, you're making a distinction between this molecular level chemistry and what lay people think of as nanotechnology.

Schwartz: Yes, nanotechnology is about machines, this is more about materials. But these then begin to overlap in the realm of nanotechnology, because you'll need to be able to do this kind of new materials manipulation to get to nanotechnology. And even before you get to nanotechnology, you get to new materials, new kinds of chemical processes.

Here's an example of something that has already been done, though it's just a step on the way. Today, if I want to take a rod of steel, put it onto a copper sheet, and weld the two together, I have a choice between the old welding techniques and new kinds of welding. I can use a hot welder and some metal that bonds the steel and copper together. Or I can take a superfine powder of the steel and the copper—and there's a way to align these molecules electrostatically so that one actually flows into the other. What you then have is steel, copper, and then a kind of flow between them of copper and steel merging into one.

Leyden: So you could imagine whole new classes of materials?

Schwartz: Exactly. So we might see new materials, new methods of manufacturing materials, new chemicals, and new kinds of chemical processes.

Leyden: What's your time frame here?

Schwartz: The next five years. Chemistry is closer because a lot of the theoretical work is far along, but the physical capabilities are hard to do, and there's a feedback between the theory and the technical capabilities that has to happen. There's still some more theoretical work that has to be done.

Leyden: That grounds us in time. How relevant are these developments to business?

Schwartz: I think they're huge. The implications are that we are moving fast toward a world of new science and technology. Just take a good example: energy. We're making all kinds of assumptions about the future of energy. These could turn out to be fundamentally wrong because we have really radical leaps in technology. Environmental issues are another. On the other side of these revolutions, the technical capabilities to deliver clean technologies would be very different. Manufacturing processes are another. The new materials and the new manufacturing methods could be extremely significant.

Leyden: So businesses should be watching these scientific developments today even if they have a ten- or twenty-year tail?

Schwartz: If you think about R&D, it has a five- to ten-year time horizon. So in terms of R&D activities, it means you've got to be pushing the frontiers of science and technology now.

For More Information

Web Site:
Global Business Network: **www.gbn.org**

See also:
☆ **Viewpoint: Stan Davis and Christopher Meyer (pp. 9–11)**

NOW!—THE ROLE OF URGENCY IN CREATING POSITIVE CHANGE *by John Reh*

EXECUTIVE SUMMARY

- Change happens. It always has happened. You cannot control change; you can only manage your interaction with it.
- Today change happens more quickly than ever before. You must be prepared for change at higher speed and be able to deal with it positively.
- Instilling a sense of urgency in an organization gives it a suite of tools with which to better relate to change and to adapt as necessary to survive.

INTRODUCTION

The speed and extent of changes in the dot-com space, while highly visible, are not unique. The Pony Express was forced out of business in only 18 months because of competition from the telegraph. Japanese automakers almost destroyed several U.S. giants in that industry. And the popularity of the PC pushed Dell and Microsoft past IBM, the company that developed it.

The strengths that got you to the top won't keep you there. Others are always pushing to move past you, to dominate your market, to steal your best customers. You need to stay ahead of them. You need to change with the times–or ahead of them. And that need is urgent.

Business organizations have always had to deal with change. That change now is simply coming faster. Change that occurred in the automobile industry over a period of 20 years starting in the 1960s occurred within less than 20 months in the Internet industry. Change will occur; management must make it as positive as possible.

Businesses are living organisms. Like animals they have certain characteristics that enable them to survive in their environment. When that environment changes the organism must evolve too, or it will die. If the organism is not able or willing to change fast enough, it will be unable to survive in the new environment. Those organisms that can change quickly can survive, however.

CHANGE IS NEVER UNANNOUNCED

Changes always give signs they're coming. Sometimes signs are obvious and we all see them. The more sensitive you are to your environment, the more likely you are to notice the changes. But being aware that change is coming is not enough: you have to be able to react in time.

The environment in which a business operates can change in innumerable ways. Some of the changes are obvious and happen over a long time. For instance, new government regulations that govern your industry are publicly announced, go through a public comment period, and are likely to be revised and republished before they take effect. Few are caught off-guard by such changes. We begin to prepare changes to our operations so that we can perform in compliance with the coming regulations.

Other changes can happen more quickly. A competitor may release a new product that captures significant market share almost overnight. A key supplier may suddenly go bankrupt. One of our facilities may be destroyed by a natural disaster. Our latest product may be more popular than expected and our plants unable to keep up with the demand. We develop contingency plans to cover such occurrences.

The better you are at tracking your markets and your competitors, the less likely you are to be surprised by a new product rollout. The more closely integrated you are with your supply chain, the less likely you are to be caught unprepared for a supplier's financial difficulties. The better attuned you are to your customers, the more likely it is that your product demand forecasts will be accurate.

SUCCESS BUILDS COMPLACENCY

Some companies are more sensitive to their environment and better equipped to deal with changes in that environment than their competitors. Sometimes it's an issue of size, sometimes an issue of longevity. Always it's an issue of leadership.

Success can breed complacency, dulling the sense of urgency around the need for change. Procedures that have outlived their usefulness survive because "that's how we've always done it." It's hard to let go of methods of doing things that have contributed to past successes, even though they now waste time and no longer create value.

GET THINGS MOVING

As a manager, you know change will occur. You saw, for example, how quickly the Internet became an essential part of business and how much more quickly businesses that had not properly understood it failed. You also know people have a natural tendency to resist change, a tendency you have to overcome. You have to act to initiate the process of change.

URGENCY: YOUR BEST WEAPON

Nothing is more important in creating positive change than a sense of urgency. It must start at the top, be communicated throughout the organization, and it must be felt by the entire organization.

Urgency is defined as "compelling immediate action; conveying a sense of pressing importance." If you want to blast people and organizations out of their inertia you have to get their attention, give them a compelling reason to act outside their comfort zone, and keep them moving. The sense of pressing importance helps you move ahead, and that gives you time to recover from mistakes or to change direction early enough, so that only minor corrections are required later.

Once you know a change is needed, urgency keeps you from wasting precious resources on the wrong choices. Failing to communicate a sense of urgency to your organization leaves an avenue open to continue with the status quo. This not only delays the implementation of the needed changes, it consumes resources that will be needed to make them. The most critical of these resources is time.

Those responsible for change must focus on the roles of the leader, not on the tasks of the manager. Leaders set direction, communicate the vision, and empower people to do what has to be done for the change to succeed. Managers plan how to make the changes happen. They organize, allocate resources, and help people perform more efficiently. Managers are necessary if a change is going to succeed, but the leader is critical.

"The tail tracks the head. If the head moves fast the tail will keep up the same pace. If the head is sluggish, the tail will drop."

(Konosuke Matsushita)

  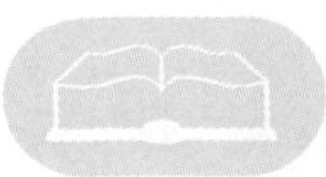    

Mini-cases

Urgency at Work

In the summer of 1999, Carlos Ghosn, new C.O.O. of *Nissan*, set a goal of profitability by 2001. Saying that a sense of urgency was key—"you should come to headquarters and the walls should be on fire"—he set in motion his Nissan Revival Plan (NRP). On May 17, 2001, Nissan announced its best financial results in a decade.

Wal-Mart has a Sundown Rule, founder Sam Walton's twist on the old adage, "Don't put off until tomorrow what you can do today." Observing that rule means striving to answer requests the day they're received. It's one reason that Wal-Mart associates are famous for their customer service.

AsiaTrak (Tianjin) is a joint venture of Caterpillar, Itochu, and SNT that provides undercarriage products to the excavator and tractor industries. The company culture recognizes time as a competitive advantage and aims to err on the side of moving too fast rather than too slowly.

Few industries are as time-sensitive as floral retailing. *1-800-FLOWERS.COM* uses a Web-based system for transmitting orders and scheduling deliveries. The system, called BloomLink, incorporates real-time chat capability so florists can ask questions about an order as they receive it.

Making It Happen ▸▸

Laying the groundwork for change requires leaders to:

- recognize that change isn't easy;
- determine what you want to change and what benefits change will create. Plan how you will communicate the change and the reasons it is necessary;
- communicate that message to the entire organization, in plain language, using enough different media to reach everyone;
- impress on everyone the urgency of making the change happen;
- share as much as you can, as early as you can, with as many as you can;
- insider-trading restrictions may limit your actions, but don't hide behind them;
- pushing people out of their comfort zone is high-risk, but can yield high reward;
- help people be brave. Brave people move faster;
- dare to dream. Planning change means visualizing a present that doesn't yet exist;
- reinforce the message by repeating it often and keeping it fresh in people's minds.

People do what they think is in their best interests. You need both positive and negative tactics to create a sense of urgency around your desired change. Show people why the status quo is bad for them. Then show them your vision of the future and why that will be better.

First:

- manufacture a crisis to start the ball rolling;
- allow a very visible (but not deadly) problem to blow up out of control;
- widely publish internal reports that support your position that the status quo is unacceptable;
- make information available that shows how quickly the situation is going from bad to worse.

Then:

- show people the significantly better state that will exist for them after the change;
- reinforce the need for urgency with a good slogan, like the UPS tag line, "Moving at the Speed of Business";
- use time-based metrics to keep up the sense of urgency;
- set targets that are unreachable without the change.

If your goal is to centralize the customer service staff in a single location to reduce costs, build and post graphs so people can track their progress toward the goal. A weekly step chart showing the savings planned from closing smaller facilities, for example, can help people visualize the goal. Superimposing actual savings on the same chart can vividly illustrate the value of closing one office a couple of weeks early and can help keep the sense of urgency high.

Conclusion

For business strategies to work in practice, organizations need to develop and change: business strategy is not about preserving the status quo, it is concerned with making progress, and this requires change. Combined with this is the fact that, whether it is welcome or not, change is the only constant in business: it is inevitable and needs to be harnessed. If it is not proactively managed, then the effects can be overwhelming.

Leading change is a vital aspect of leadership in general, because it requires dynamic, focused action. Without this proactive leadership, change will fail—or fail even to get started. Leadership is essential to delivering effective change as it provides vision—a clear idea of purpose and direction. Leadership and a sense of urgency are also important to communicate, facilitate, guide, and focus activity; to solve problems; to coordinate and make decisions. In general, to provide a framework that ensures success, creating a sense of urgency and the necessary motivation and support.

Change is happening more often and more quickly. The leader's job is to manage that change to create a positive outcome for the organization. Creating a sense of urgency is the best tool for making that happen.

For More Information

Books:

Bell, Chip R., and Oren Harari. *BEEP! BEEP!: Competing in the Age of the Road Runner*. New York: Warner, 2001.

Grove, Andrew S. *Only the Paranoid Survive: How to Exploit the Crisis Points That Challenge Every Company*. New York: Bantam, 1999.

Hanna, David P. *Designing Organizations for High Performance*. Boston, MA: Addison-Wesley, 1988.

Kossoff, Leslie. *Executive Thinking: The Dream, the Vision, the Mission Achieved*. Palo Alto, CA: Davies-Black, 1999.

Kotter, John P. *Leading Change*. Boston, MA: Harvard Business School Press, 1996.

Web Sites:

www.emeraldinsight.com/jocm.htm: this is the online home of the *Journal of Organizational Change Management*.

www.mapnp.org/library/org-chng/org-chng.htm: this Web site provides an *Overview of Organizational Change*, assembled by Carter MacNamara, MBA, Ph.D.

See also:

☆ **Getting All Your People Committed to Change and Transformation (pp. 185–87)**
☆ **Viewpoint: Henry Mintzberg (pp. 241–42)**
☆ **Viewpoint: Margaret J. Wheatley (pp. 273–74)**
✔ **Implementing Effective Change (pp. 504–05)**
📖 **The Change Masters (p. 897)**
🖱 **Change Management (pp. 1923–25)**

"Successful companies move quickly in and out of products, markets, and sometimes even entire businesses."

(George Stalk)

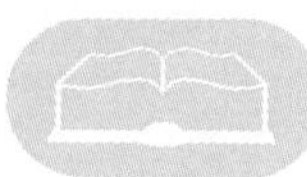

SCENARIO PLANNING *by Gill Ringland*

EXECUTIVE SUMMARY

- Scenario planning uses possible future outcomes (scenarios) to improve the quality of decision making (planning).
- The emphasis has moved in recent years from building scenarios to successfully using them.
- The techniques for building scenarios are well developed—the challenge is to incorporate an understanding and facility with possible futures into management thinking. This has led to an emphasis on using scenario planning for team development; improving the structural assumptions and data behind planning; and developing techniques for communication of scenarios.
- Scenarios are beginning to be widely used in the public sector as well as in business.

SCENARIOS AS MODELS OF FUTURE WORLDS

One of the best definitions of *scenario* is by Michael Porter:

"an internally consistent view of what the future might be, not a forecast but one possible future outcome."

At a time of volatility and change, managers need to be able to step out of their current framework and imagine future worlds–which may arrive sooner than expected. Scenario planning is a set of processes for creating several scenarios or mental models and using them to aid decision making. The scenarios explore a spectrum of different possible answers to core questions facing the organization.

- In 1985, what would the effect of the fall of the Berlin Wall be on the business of an Austrian insurance company?
- What new markets was a manufacturing company supplying copper cable to the telecom industry equipped to tackle?
- In a computer company, what would be the drivers of outsourcing, and what effect would this have?

The scenarios capturing possible answers to these and similar questions are used to improve the robustness of plans or to create new plans based on newly visible options.

FORECASTING AND SCENARIOS

Scenario thinking traces its history back to just after World War II, when Hermann Kahn pioneered *future now* thinking. This technique, put forward by Kahn to promote debate about nuclear weapons, aimed through the use of imagination and detailed analysis to produce a report about current events as it might be written retrospectively by people living in the future.

Most current uses of scenarios relate to Kahn's purpose in being used, for example, to

- stimulate debate about choices;
- develop strategy resilient against several futures;
- test business plans against futures;
- try to anticipate futures as an aid to decision making.

While forecasts or high-growth/low-growth forecasts (sometimes also called scenarios) can be used for any of these purposes, the use of imaginative and qualitatively different worlds is a central theme of most current uses of scenarios. Forecasts aim for accuracy, using techniques such as Delphi; scenarios explore the space of uncertainties in defining possible futures.

Questions often asked include

- How many scenarios?
- What timescale?

The number of scenarios is bounded on the lower end by the adoption of two qualitatively different worlds, at the upper by the ability of the team (and its intended audience) to be able to comprehend the differences, maybe up to five. In planning work with numerate groups it is usual to avoid three or five, because planners will often assume that the middle scenario is "right," that is, that it's a forecast. The timescale for the scenarios needs to be longer than the budget or planning cycle of the organization, and certainly longer than the job tenure of the team developing them, in order to avoid defensiveness. A longer timescale is easier to work with than the medium-term (for example, three years) since many of the defining trends will already be clear and the current complexities still confusing in the medium term.

CREATING SCENARIOS

The creation of scenarios is an excellent management development tool for a team, taking team members beyond defending their current role. It can be useful for management teams to take one or two days to develop scenarios for their business based on existing information within the group as a way of exploring shared perceptions. The classic method for developing scenarios, based on research and analysis by an in-house team or consultants, may take from three people-months to thirty people-years.

A significant advantage for an organization in creating its own scenarios is that wild cards will emerge during the research. These are events that would be calamitous but are judged unlikely to happen. Action to determine the process for dealing with these and the subsequent discussions are often beneficial, prompting new insights.

USING EXISTING SCENARIOS

The emphasis in most organizations, however, is moving away from developing new scenarios toward using and tailoring existing scenarios, working with management teams on the implications of the scenarios for their business or project.

A sample workshop outline to develop strategy-based scenarios is given in Table 1.

It is important that these workshops be held offsite to signal their difference from routine work. The two-day format is good to allow time for reflection and absorption.

PLANNING WITH SCENARIOS

SCENARIOS AND BUSINESS PLANS

Business plans always incorporate the assumptions of the management team, which are often implicit. For instance, will a characteristic that has added competitive advantage in the past continue to do so as markets change? By using scenarios the team can recognize the future world built into their plan and explore the implications of other possible—or probable—worlds.

Some organizations rework the entire business plan for all (usually two) scenarios. This may be a back-of-the-envelope sketch or a team effort. Back-of-the-envelope calculations can often capture the essential relative viability of a single capital project under different scenarios. Full reworking of the business plan may be needed in organizations in which many divisions and functions will be affected.

"By choosing occupations that you can get excited about you are likely to do your best work."

(Andrew Grove)

Table 1		
	Workshop	**Using existing scenarios with a team**
Day 1	Plenary	Brief on trends
	Groups	Discuss effect of trends on offerings; report back
	Plenary	Brief on scenarios
	Groups	Add depth for specific business; report back
	Groups	Communicate scenarios
Day 2	Groups	Discuss effect of scenarios on existing offerings, new offerings
	Groups	Develop time line for new offerings
	Groups	Develop time line for new threats
	Plenary	Report back, plan next actions

Portfolio Management

A market attractiveness/capability matrix is often used to manage a portfolio of businesses within a company (see Table 2).

Examining the portfolio as it would exist in the future under each scenario produces a new position on the matrix for each business. While the discussion of the factors affecting each business is useful, the improvement of the decision process is the main gain.

In assessing the likelihood of a scenario coming true, early indicators are used—events that will occur in the next year or so specifically under one scenario. These might be selected topics already watched by ongoing mechanisms, for example, the patents departments.

Scenarios in Public Policy

Since the time of Hermann Kahn, scenarios have been used to

- create a common language and understanding, for example, in South Africa at the time the African National Congress was poised to take power;
- develop strategy in the face of new challenges, for example, as Canada faced the implications of an information society;
- inform public debate, for example, in Norway on the use of oil revenues.

Workshops associated with building scenarios are widely used to develop public opinion.

Communication of Scenarios

When scenarios were mostly used within planning groups, the output was often expressed in tabular form, with a list of factors (for example, growth rate, dominant technology) in the left-hand column and the other columns describing the factors under each scenario. While these were good working tools, they were fatally bad communication tools.

Names are often used to communicate the essence of scenarios. The Chatham House Forum scenarios for the economics of the industrial world in 2020 are called Atlantic Storm and Market Forces; in Atlantic Storm Europe and the United States are at odds, while in Market Forces a free market dominates.

Newspapers written as if in the future, descriptions of role-model characters, a-day-in-the-life stories, and glossy booklets can all be used to communicate scenarios. Recent work has used film and video clips with interactive choice to explore scenarios with groups of decision makers.

Making It Happen ▸▸

1. Use scenarios for stimulating debate, developing resilient strategies, testing business plans against possible futures, and trying to anticipate futures.
2. Allow one or two days for management teams to develop scenarios, based on existing information within the company.
3. Hold workshops offsite to signal "different," with two-day residential formats to allow optimum reflection and absorption time.
4. For a single capital project, try back-of-the-envelope calculations o capture the essential differences in the viability of alternatives.
5. To assess the likelihood of a scenario coming true, use early indicators—events that should be seen in the next year or so.
6. Communicate scenarios graphically, for example, by imaginary newspapers written as if in the future.

Conclusion

Most people who work with scenarios find it to be stimulating and enjoyable. The next stage, making the most of scenario planning, depends on:

- deciding what problem the scenarios are intended to help solve. What are the crucial questions facing the organization, the questions whose answers imply, I wish I had known this seven years ago?
- creating or exploiting scenarios that explore the uncertainty space—often in-house scenarios focus on close-to-home and internal problems;
- giving the scenarios effort high enough status by offsite meetings, high-level sponsors, and management feedback;
- using the scenarios to drive decision making by stimulating debate, developing strategy, testing business plans, or anticipating futures;
- using imaginative and frequent communication to embed scenario thinking into discussion and decisions.

For More Information

Books:

Ringland, Gill. *Scenario Planning: Managing for the Future*. New York: John Wiley, 1998.

Schwartz, Peter. *The Art of the Long View: Planning for the Future in an Uncertain World*. New York: John Wiley, 1997.

See also:

☆ **Avoiding the Mistakes of the Past: Lessons from the Startup World (pp. 129–30)**
☆ **The End of Growth: Why Does It Always End? What Can You Do About It? (pp. 269–70)**
✔ **Strategic Planning (pp. 484–85)**
Business Plans and Planning (pp. 1920–21)

Table 2			
	Market attractiveness	**Capability**	**Matrix**
Market attractiveness	*weak*	*medium*	*strong*
high	Double or quit	Try harder	Leader
medium	Phased withdrawal	Proceed with care	Growth
low	Withdraw	Phased withdrawal	Cash generation

"We are self-activating organisms, and can, to some degree, control our own destiny and our own responses to pressures. . ."
(Charles Handy)

The End of Growth: Why Does It Always End? What Can You Do About It?
by Robert M. Tomasko

EXECUTIVE SUMMARY

- All growth trajectories follow a life cycle.
- Business growth invariably slows.
- If you anticipate the inevitable decline, you can push it further into the future.
- Sustained growth ultimately requires the courage to abandon one growth path for another.

Introduction

Why do bubbles burst? Because as they grow their surface area becomes so large that increasing amounts of energy are diverted to keeping the structure intact rather than expanding its size. Some bubbles find an equilibrium point and persist, but those that keep trying to grow collapse. This collapse has little to do with outside intervention. It's caused by trying too hard. Many businesses similarly try too hard, fighting the nature of their markets and organization, and find their growth trajectory coming to a crashing halt.

All growth efforts eventually slow. But neither your business nor your career has to decline in tandem with them as long as you stay alert to the dynamics that are in play and cultivate the ability to adapt.

The Laws of Gravity Also Apply to Business

Hitting the growth wall is a problem that eventually plagues every business.

- Wall Street analysts hate hearing from executives with no visibility about their next quarter's prospects.
- Underwater stock options demoralize.
- Unreachable sales quotas squash motivation.
- Just as rapid growth creates its own forward momentum, generating new fast-track career paths, ambitious top performers are often the first to jump ship at the prospect of a business slowdown. Net result: fewer seasoned business growers available to rebound the business.

The cumulative impact of poor publicity, talent loss, and demoralization serves only to reinforce this negative spiral. The dynamics behind the turn-of-the-millennium e-business slowdown aren't all that different from the forces that limited the expansion of the mainframe computer industry in the 1990s, energy companies in the 1980s, consumer-goods makers in the 1970s, and, a century ago, the steam railways.

Sudden, out-of-the-blue shocks are blamed for many business slowdowns. However, in reality these are few and far between. The Internet, a favorite scapegoat, has caused far more businesses to grow than it has destroyed. Every market runs on a life cycle. So does every business, in a cycle of:

- ramp-up
- rapid growth
- mature stability
- gradual decline

When the two cycles—the company's and its industry's—are out of sync, growth inevitably slows and economic performance suffers. But the enemy to be most wary of is lurking within. Most businesses don't need competitors to steal their growth opportunities. They do it to themselves, making errors of both omission and commission.

Understanding the Potential for Self-Inflicted Wounds

What's most commonly missing among executives of slow-growth companies is the ability to engage in systems thinking.

These people tend to

- treat each happening in the business as an isolated event rather than as part of a chain extending over a long time period;
- focus on the needs of their own company, department, or job rather than seeing their business as part of a network of interconnected players.

This mentality puts a brake on growth. It forgets that every driver of growth is accompanied by some kind of limiting process, such as:

- an awakened competitor
- an overtaxed supplier
- an extra-vigilant regulator
- an internal capacity constraint (usually cash or talent)

It's also important to be wary of growth substitutes. Among the most common are:

- **Accounting trickery**. Managing earnings instead of growth creates the appearance of profit increases through restructuring charges, hidden reserves, and changes in pension-funding policies.
- **Stock buy-backs**. Earnings per share do rise when the number of shares shrinks, but this is not the same as increases due to profitable revenue growth.
- **Merger mania**. Acquisitions and mergers, as Swissair and many other firms have learned, are often more of a long detour than a direct path to real growth.
- **Cost-cutting**. This source of short-term gain destroys more seeds of future growth than any aggressive competitor might.

Avoiding a Toxic Treatment

Why does cost-cutting bite back? There are times when it's the right remedy, but like some popular medicines it's overprescribed as a cure for stalled growth. Profits can grow in the short-term through cost-cutting, of course, at least until the business runs out of expendables. Profits resulting from creating hard-to-duplicate benefits that are conveyed to customers are a sustainable, renewable resource. But they are renewable only as long as the business growers who create them are kept in place and motivated. But when the cost-cutting fixer mentality dominates with its often mindless, across-the-board slashes, good growers run for cover. The growth mindset cultivates carefully nurtured, experience-based, invest-now-for-future-return behavior.

Responding to the End of Growth

If you're facing market collapse

- Remember that it's better to yield to some trends, instead of engaging in an unwinnable war.
- Even if you're facing total economic collapse, don't throw in the towel until you study the lessons of Brazilian and

"Growth does not always lead a business to build on success. All too often it converts a highly successful business into a mediocre large business."

(Richard Branson)

Lebanese businesses. Both are world-class improvisers—the best strategy when everything seems up in the air.

- If regulatory straitjackets seem insurmountable obstacles, look hard at the ways of northern Italy's virtual keiretsu and France's highly automated manufacturers.

If your market's life cycle is at war with your plans

- Sustain your growth by getting out ahead of the curve.
- Consider the first hints of growth deceleration as nature's way of telling you to shift gears. Nokia did this, growing in the same mobile phone manufacturing marketplace that was a quagmire for Ericsson and Motorola.
- When the market seems to have had enough of innovative products, consider reorienting around customer-defined requirements rather than inner vision.
- When growth slows because everyone in the industry seems to be following the same formula, follow the lead of upstarts like Southwest Airlines.
- When industry domination becomes too costly to sustain, pick off the most profitable segments, focus exclusively on customers' needs, and reap the high-margin rewards that come to specialist companies like Rolex.

If your company seems to be its own worst enemy

- Don't throw away that next invitation to a seminar on systems thinking. Go, and you'll never think about your business in the same way again.
- Don't confuse the kinds of growth accountants create with the real thing.
- Resist the urge to merge until it's crystal clear how the acquisition will enable growth.
- Never cut costs as an end in itself, only as a subordinate component of an overall growth plan.
- Never confuse stock-price growth with business growth.
- Don't waste energy whining when the market tanks your shares. High-tech manufacturer Seagate took advantage of a demolished stock price to divorce Wall Street, go private, and restore momentum away from the glare of the financial press.
- "Take no prisoners" is an order that belongs to the movie theater, not the boardroom. Taking a live-and-let-live perspective on the competition is a great way to expand the size of everyone's market. Coke and Pepsi need each other, and they both know it.

MAKING IT HAPPEN ▸▸

The following steps can help to ensure that successful growth continues, or is rekindled:

1. **Review current business activities**: this may involve analyzing strengths, weaknesses, opportunities, and threats, as well as assessing the business's relative market share. It can also mean answering the following questions:

- Where are the most profitable parts of the business?
- What are the prospects in the short-, medium- and long-term for those products and markets?
- How precarious is the business—for example, does it rely on too few products, customers, or distribution channels?
- How clearly focused is the business—is it over-burdened with too many products, markets, and initiatives, or is it running on empty with too few opportunities?
- What is likely to be the best method of expansion—is it affordable (not just in terms of money)?
- What are the advantages and disadvantages of expanding?

2. **Decide the best method of achieving growth**: discuss the options with senior managers and shareholders, refining potential opportunities and deciding how to approach problems.
3. **Plan for growth**: decide what action is needed to achieve growth. This will certainly involve leadership qualities to communicate and mobilize resources.
4. **Act decisively and consistently**: once the course has been set it needs to be rigorously followed. One of the greatest obstacles to growth is inertia, often in the form of attachment to heritage and past activities.

It is also necessary to pay attention to the details of any strategy for growth. Understand how the changes affect people. Decisive action is vital, but this needs to include an understanding of how to maintain people's commitment and motivation. If people feel threatened, or insecure then however sensible the strategy for growth and the plan for implementation it simply will not be achieved. It is vital to treat people with respect. It is also worth communicating what is happening to people so that they understand their role and how they can contribute. Also, monitor the situation: time lags need to be understood and planned for, and the strategy needs to be supported in the long term.

CONCLUSION

Growth always ends. For some businesses it comes with a bang, for others, with a whimper. The ideas here will assist in prolonging the endgame. Apply them, but do it with your eyes open. Ramping down is just as much a part of the business landscape as ramping up. Knowing when to let go, and recycling your efforts in a more promising direction, is the secret of long-term happiness in a business career. There are many market, industry, and organizational indicators you can watch for clues that bailout time is near. Look hard at them, but in the end the best litmus test is to ask yourself a simple question: Am I still having fun? If the honest answer is no, then you know what you need to do.

For More Information

Books:

Christensen, Clayton M. *The Innovator's Dilemma*. New York: HarperBusiness, 2000.
Hamel, Gary. *Leading the Revolution*. Boston, MA: Harvard Business School Press, 2000.
Foster, Richard, and Sarah Kaplan. *Creative Destruction: Why Companies That Are Built to Last Underperform the Market and How to Successfully Transform Them*. New York: Doubleday/Currency, 2001.

Web Sites:

www.mckinseyquarterly.com is the online journal of McKinsey & Co.
www.sustainer.org/meadows offers an overview and samples of Donella Meadows's insights on growth.
www.pegasuscom.com is the Web site of Pegasus Communications, a company dedicated to providing a wide range of resources on organizational change.

See also:

☆ **Scenario Planning (pp. 267–68)**
☆ **Finding and Keeping Top Talent (pp. 33–34)**
☆ **Viewpoint: Tom Petzinger (pp. 163–64)**

"Growth is like creativity, it doesn't go along very neat, precise plans. You get pollution before you figure out a way to fight it."
(Steve Forbes)

  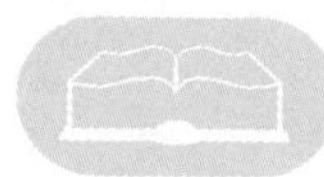    

CREATING CORPORATE CREATIVITY *by Edward de Bono*

EXECUTIVE SUMMARY

- Creativity is rapidly becoming the most important ingredient in business.
- Creativity is not a mystical talent that only a few people possess, but a skill that can be developed.
- Creativity is not a matter of waiting for inspiration, but a deliberate skill that can be used as needed.
- Feeling free and liberated as in traditional brainstorming is a weak approach.
- Formal creative techniques are based on an understanding of the brain as a self-organizing information system.
- Argument is a crude and primitive way of exploring a subject. Parallel thinking is far more effective.
- In any organization, if creativity is not an expectation it will be seen as a risk.

INTRODUCTION

In my experience with major multinationals and other organizations, the basic behavior is "maintenance and problem solving." This means running things as they are and solving problems as they arise. A great deal of lip service is paid to creativity but little is done. In surveys I have done at my seminars, 90% of people agree that creativity is important, and 80% claim that little is done in their own organizations.

Three things are becoming commodities in business. Competence is one of those things. If your only hope of survival is that your competitors will continue to be more incompetent than yourselves, you are weak, since there is nothing you can do to stop them from becoming competent. Information has already become a commodity available to anyone willing to pay for it. State-of-the-art technology is a commodity which can be bought or commissioned, with some exceptions such as pharmaceuticals.

When everything is a commodity, what is going to matter is the design and delivery of value created from these commodities. This requires creativity. Six chefs at a cooking competition each have the same ingredients and the same cooking facilities. Who wins? The chef who can create superior value from the basic commodities.

THE USE OF CREATIVITY

Creativity is used to solve problems, design ways forward, resolve conflicts, simplify procedures, cut costs, improve motivation, design new products and services, and fashion strategies. Any situations that require thinking demand creativity. Without it, we are condemned to repeating the standard routines.

In 1971, I suggested at a workshop with Shell Oil in London the concepts of horizontal drilling. Today, most oil wells in the world are drilled this way because the yield is three to six times that of a traditional well. (I am not claiming that this change came about as a result of my suggestion, but the chronological fact remains.) After a seminar to Ingwe Coal in South Africa, the senior engineer told me they had developed a new way of cutting coal—the first new way in 80 years. In both cases, there was not a problem, but applying creativity to the usual way of doing things developed powerful new ideas.

A major Scandinavian company used to spend 30 days on their multinational project discussions. Today they do it in two days through using parallel thinking instead of argument. After training in creative thinking, a U.K. television company said they had had more ideas in two days than they had had in six months before. One afternoon, Carole Ferguson (a certified trainer) put together 130 workshops for a steel company. Using just one of the techniques of lateral thinking, they generated 21,000 ideas that afternoon.

A person tied up with a rope cannot play the violin. If we cut the rope, does that make that person a violinist? If you are inhibited you cannot be creative. If you release yourself from that inhibition, does that make you creative? That is the essential weakness of processes such as brainstorming. Creativity can be a much more structured discipline with specific mental operations that can be used deliberately.

THE BASIS OF CREATIVITY

The purpose of the brain is to be non-creative. Instead, it is supposed to establish routine patterns for dealing with a stable world. If it were otherwise, life would be impossible (there are 39,816,800 ways of getting dressed in the morning with eleven items of clothing). As a self-organizing system the brain allows incoming information to organize itself into routine patterns. We should be grateful for these patterns (see *The Mechanism of the Mind*, 1969, Penguin Books, London). But there are side tracks which are suppressed. If, somehow, we manage to move "laterally" to the side track then, in hindsight, the new idea will be logical and obvious. This is why we have never appreciated creativity. Because every valued creative idea is logical in hindsight, we have assumed logic would be sufficient to reach this idea. This is simply not true in the asymmetric nature of self-organizing systems.

DELIBERATE CREATIVE PROCESSES

The techniques of "lateral thinking" are based directly on this understanding of brain behavior. The technique of "random entry" takes us away from the usual starting point to create a new "chance" starting point which allows us to open up tracks we could never have accessed from the usual starting point. That is why the history of science is full of examples of major discoveries that were triggered by an apparently random event.

In any self-organizing system there is a mathematical need for provocation. Otherwise we remain stuck in local equilibria instead of reaching a global equilibrium. The new word "po" signals that something is put forward as a provocation. "Po, you die before you die," sounds illogical but enabled Ron Barbaro of Prudential Insurance, Canada, to develop the concept of "living needs benefits." There are formal ways of setting up provocations. It would be

"In a restless, creative business with an emphasis on experiment and development, ideas are the lifeblood."
(Richard Branson)

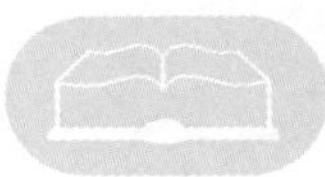

pointless to use "judgment" on provocations. We need to develop the very different mental operation of "movement." There are formal ways of getting "movement" from an idea.

"Challenge" is another aspect of lateral thinking. We challenge accepted concepts and perceptions, and then develop alternatives. This was the process that led to the suggestion of horizontal drilling of oil wells. We challenge traditional, accepted, and usual concepts, not because they are wrong or inadequate, but because the adequate can hide the better idea.

Alternatives are generated by extracting the concept that lies behind the existing approach. There follows a search for finding a better way of delivering this concept.

"Case Making" versus Creativity

In a court of law if the prosecuting lawyer thinks of a point which would help the defense case, that point is not going to be made. Conversely the defense lawyer would never mention a point that might help the prosecution case. This is not exploring the subject, but "case making." With parallel thinking, all parties at any one moment are looking and thinking in the same direction. The change in direction is signaled by the symbolic "six hats." Each hat indicates a mode of thinking: for example, white hat for information, red hat for feelings and green hat for creative possibilities. The result is a much quicker and much fuller exploration of the subject. Every person present is using his or her thinking and experience to the maximum instead of "making a case." This method is now widely used in schools and with senior executives. Why pay someone a large salary if you are not going to use that mind fully?

Creativity in the Organization

In any organization, creativity is either a risk or an expectation. If it is not an expectation, it is always a risk. In my experience the culture of creativity needs to be set by senior management. That way, creativity becomes an expectation. Executives and workers are now expected to come up with and explore new ideas. They receive "recognition" for doing that. Failure to explore new ideas means you are not doing your job properly. Training in creative methods then follows as part of the culture.

Making It Happen ▸▸

- Break out from the trap of "maintenance and problem-solving," or running things as they are and tackling problems as they arise.
- Recognize that competence, information and technology have become commodities, and that only creativity adds value.
- Use creativity to solve problems, design ways forward, resolve conflicts, simplify, cut costs, motivate, design new products and services, and strategize.
- Challenge traditional, accepted, and usual concepts and perceptions, because the adequate can hide the better idea.
- Use the "Six Hats" method for parallel thinking, with everybody looking and thinking in the same direction, and not arguing.
- Lead from the top to create the expectation that executives and other workers will come up with and explore new ideas.

For More Information

Books:

de Bono, Edward. *Lateral Thinking: Creativity Step by Step*. New York: HarperCollins, 1990.

de Bono, Edward. *Parallel Thinking*. New York: Viking, 1994.

Clegg, Brian, and Paul Birch. *Instant Creativity*. Milford, CT: Kogan Page, 1999.

Cooper, Robert G., Scott J. Edgett, and Elko J. Kleinschmidt. *Portfolio Management for New Products*. 2nd ed. Cambridge, MA: Perseus, 2001.

Firestien, Roger L. *Leading on the Creative Edge*. Colorado Springs, CO: Pinon Press, 1996.

Landau, Sy, Barbara Landau, and Daryl Landau. *From Conflict to Creativity: How Resolving Workplace Disagreements Can Inspire Innovation and Productivity*. San Francisco, CA: Jossey-Bass, 2001.

Locke, Christopher. *The Bombast Transcripts: Rants and Screeds of Rageboy*. Cambridge, MA: Perseus, 2002.

Web Site:

www.thinksmart.com: devoted to innovation, this site will help you, and your company or organization, become more creative and productive with information, articles, and even a creativity test.

See also:

☆ **Brainstorming (pp. 318–19)**
☆ **Creating Fun in the Workplace (pp. 37–38)**
☆ **Intellectual Capital (pp. 159–60)**
✓ **Managing Creativity (pp. 370–71)**
Innovation and Creativity (pp. 2000–03)

"We want worked out a relationship between leader and led which will give each the opportunity to make creative contributions to the situation." (Mary Parker Follett)

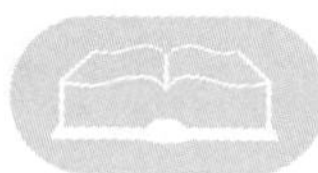

Viewpoint: Margaret J. Wheatley

Using New Scientific Thinking to Create a New Society

Margaret J. Wheatley is a graduate of the University of Rochester, New York, and University College, London. A Peace Corps volunteer in Korea, she was an educator and administrator from 1966–73 before earning a doctorate at Harvard. She worked as a consultant in Cambridge, Massachusetts, until 1989.

What I noticed early on, was that—for all the great efforts, for all the human energy expended, and for all the money spent—true organization change rarely succeeded.

I'd ask top consultants to tell me what their major successes were. It took a long time to get any kind of response, and their replies were quite shallow. That told me the paradigm about managing major organizations was dead; I was convinced that I did not want to spend my career doing more of the same kind of work that others in the field of management were doing. Then I read James Gleick's book about chaos (*Chaos: Making a New Science*) around 1989; it triggered whole new thoughts in me. I started connecting my liberal arts background—my interest in combining history, philosophy, and science—to the field of management. By 1990 I was writing *Leadership and the New Science*, and, upon its publication, I found that people were very receptive to my ideas. Their interest continues and grows.

If we don't change the way we manage business in the next ten years, we're dead.

The terrorism attacks that started in September 2001 are really "kindergarten," in terms of the kinds of changes we'll have to deal with in the future. It forces a major question: How do you behave as a leader when you don't have control over your own business? Think of it: the airline/hotel/car rental/travel industries have been socked—no matter how well they were managed in the past—by terrorists! Who had that prospect in their current business plans? More and more changes of this magnitude will affect managers in the future; we will all be facing extreme uncertainty and vulnerability. And it will not matter how good your planning systems are; you will have to lead under conditions of mega-change.

So the issue to focus on, to learn how to adjust to, is *change*. Managers are going to have to learn how to deal with exponential change, with cataclysmic events that affect all aspects of their work world.

Managers traditionally thought that understanding and managing systems was a luxury field of study. Not any more. Managers will only survive—their businesses will only survive—if they have developed, top to bottom, a trusting and cohesive workforce, people who can rapidly adjust organizational systems to unpredicted events. This means that everyone in the enterprise will need new levels of independence, flexibility, adaptability; and everyone must enrich their comprehension that every organization is part of an interconnected world. If you look at what's happening to businesses in light of recent terrorism and its mammoth impact, it's not surprising that a recent news story noted that companies were now preparing five different annual budgets, with the suggestion that (depending on events) one of those budgets might only be 40% accurate. *And that may be the best any business can do!* For those in management, business schools and corporate trainers will have to come up with courses which plainly don't exist today. We need courses with titles like "How to Lead When You Can't Be a Hero" or "How to Lead in Complete Uncertainty." Those are the new skills for managing in the next century.

Managers traditionally thought that understanding and managing systems was a luxury field of study. Not any more.

How can companies best promote enterprises that are profitable and good places for people to work? Even the question isn't quite right.

That question comes from a simpler time. Wouldn't it be great if that were the *only* major problem we

"Things we fear most in organizations—fluctuations, disturbances, imbalances—need not be signs of impending disorder. . .fluctuations are the primary source of creativity." (Margaret J. Wheatley)

faced in this new century? We must face the fact that we are living in an age where people can do great work, generate profits, and be quite pleased with the overall corporate culture—and *still* be critically challenged by enormous uncertainty. Managing a business is no longer like managing chess, even three-dimensional chess. You can't anticipate all the moves you are going to have to make in the future; there will be too much change. If anything, the game for tomorrow's manager is the Asian game of "Go!", where you can only determine your next move based on what your opponent has just done, and the range of options is limitless.

Yet this new reality presents managers with both challenge and opportunity. One need not become permanently depressed, because what exponential and unpredictable change demands is a greater appreciation of the human spirit and a greater reliance on human creativity. Managers need to focus on this and never forget it.

Look at any organization today and it's *people* who matter the most. I was touched when the C.E.O. of the Morgan Stanley financial powerhouse said, quite emotionally, that he was awestruck after the demise of the World Trade Center buildings on September 11, 2001. Unbelievably, out of 3,700 employees who occupied 25 floors of one of the buildings, only *six* were lost in the disaster. The C.E.O., realizing what true and permanent loss his firm might have had if more had perished, exclaimed, "This is a miracle!" He went on to extol how important the human element is to the management of the global financial services firm. To me, this is a new dimension to Morgan Stanley—and a new dimension to management, a new *emphasis* in management. Machines and computers are great for what they do, but they are linear by design; they can deal with mega-change in one way. Only the human element, spirited and creative, can face change head-on—*and adapt*. Managers who willingly acknowledge this and enhance their mastery of human systems have the best chance of surviving and prospering in the future.

For More Information

Web Site:
www.margaretwheatley.com

See also:

- ☆ **Avoiding Your Worst Career Nightmare (pp. 316–17)**
- ☆ **Corporate Social Responsibility: Are You Giving Back or Just Giving Away? (pp. 291–92)**
- ☆ **Driving Fear from the Workplace (pp. 330–31)**
- ☆ **From Crisis Management to Crisis Leadership (pp. 293–94)**
- ☆ **Managing Today's Angry Workforce (pp. 35–36)**
- ☆ **Now!—The Role of Urgency in Creating Positive Change (pp. 265–66)**
- **Organization and Organization Structure (pp. 2059–61)**

"We cannot hide behind our boundaries, or hold onto the belief that we can survive alone."
(Margaret J. Wheatley)

MANAGING NEW-PRODUCT PORTFOLIOS
by Robert G. Cooper and Scott J. Edgett

EXECUTIVE SUMMARY

- New-product portfolio management is about how you invest your business's product development resources through project prioritization and allocating resources across development projects.
- There are four goals in portfolio management: maximizing the value of the portfolio; seeking the right balance of projects; ensuring that your portfolio is strategically aligned, and making sure you have the appropriate number of projects for your limited resources.
- There are many tools—some quantitative, others graphical, some strategic—designed to help you choose the right portfolio of projects.

Your new-product process or ''stage-gate'' system must be working in order to achieve effective portfolio management. It must deliver data integrity and also weed out the bad projects early.

INTRODUCTION

How should you most effectively invest your product development resources? And how should you prioritize your development projects and allocate resources among them? These are crucial issues in new-product portfolio management.

Portfolio management is a critical senior management challenge. Here's why:

- A successful new-product effort is *fundamental to business success*. This logically translates into portfolio management—the ability to select today's projects that will become tomorrow's new-product winners.
- New-product development is the *manifestation of your business's strategy*. If your new product initiatives are wrong—either the wrong projects or the wrong balance—then you fail at implementing your business strategy.
- Portfolio management is about *resource allocation*. In a business world preoccupied with value to the shareholder and doing more with less, technology and marketing resources are simply too scarce to waste. The consequences of poor portfolio management are evident: you squander scarce resources and, as a result, starve the truly deserving projects.

MAKING IT HAPPEN ▸▸

There are four goals of portfolio management to aim for.

- **Goal 1. Maximize the value of your portfolio.** Here the goal is to select new product projects to maximize the sum of the values or *commercial worths* of all active projects in your development pipeline in terms of some business objective. Tools used to assess "project value" include:
- **Net Present Value (NPV).** Determine the project's NPV and then rank projects by NPV divided by the key or constraining resource (for example, the R&D costs still left to be spent on the project; that is, by NPV/R&D). Projects are rank-ordered according to this index until out of resources, thus maximizing the value of the portfolio (the sum of the NPVs across all projects) for a given or limited resource expenditure.
- **Expected Commercial Value (ECV).** This method uses decision-tree analysis, breaking the project into decision stages—for example, development and commercialization. Define the possible outcomes of the project along with probabilities of each occurring—for example, probabilities of technical and commercial success. The resulting ECV is then divided by the constraining resource (as in the NPV method), and projects are rank-ordered according to this index in order to maximize the *bang for buck*. This method also approximates *real options theory*, and thus is appropriate for handling higher-risk projects.
- **Scoring model.** Decision makers rate projects on a number of factors that distinguish superior projects, typically on 1–5 or 0–10 scales. Add the ratings for each factor to yield a quantified "project attractiveness score," which must clear a minimum hurdle. This score is a proxy for the "value of the project" but incorporates factors beyond just financial measures. Projects are then rank-ordered according to this score until resources run out. Typical factors are: strategic alignment; product/competitive advantage; market attractiveness; leverage or synergies; technical feasibility, and risk versus return.
- **Goal 2. Seek balance in your portfolio.** Here the goal is to achieve a desired balance of projects in terms of a number of parameters. For example, long-term projects versus short ones, or high-risk versus lower-risk projects. Balance can also be sought across various markets, technologies, product categories and project types. Pictures portray balance much better than numbers and lists, so the techniques used here are largely graphical in nature.
- **Bubble diagrams**: Display your projects on a two-dimensional grid as different-size bubbles (the size of the bubbles denotes the spending on each project). The axes vary but the most popular chart is the risk-reward bubble diagram, where NPV is plotted versus probability of technical success. Then seek an appropriate balance in numbers of projects (and spending) across the four quadrants.
- **Pie charts**: Show your spending breakdowns as slices of pies in a pie chart. Popular pie charts include a breakdown by project types, by market or segment, and by product line or product category.

Unlike the maximization tools described under Goal 1, bubble diagrams and pie charts are not decision models, but rather information display. They depict the current portfolio and where the resources are going—the "what is." These charts provide a useful beginning for the discussion of "what should be"—how your resources should be allocated.

- **Goal 3. Your portfolio must be strategically aligned.** Being strategically aligned means that all

---

"Truly great brands are far more than just labels for products. . .they are standards that are held aloft under which the masses congregate."

(Tony O'Reilly)

your projects are "on strategy," and that your breakdown of spending across projects, areas, markets, and so on must mirror your strategic priorities. Several portfolio methods are designed to achieve strategic alignment:

- **Top-down, strategic buckets**: Begin at the top with your business's strategy and from that, your product innovation strategy—that is, its goals, and where and how to focus your new product efforts. Next, make splits in resources: given your strategy, where should you spend your money? These splits can be by project types, product lines, markets or industry sectors, and so on. Thus, you establish strategic buckets of resources. Within each bucket, list all projects—active, on-hold and new—and rank these until you run out of resources in that bucket. The result is multiple portfolios, one portfolio per bucket. Another result is that your spending at year-end will truly reflect the strategic priorities of your business.
- **Top-down, product roadmap**: Once again, begin at the top, with your business and product innovation strategy. But now the question is, given that you have selected several areas of strategic focus (markets, technologies, or product types), what major initiatives must you undertake in order to be successful here? The end result is a mapping of these major initiatives along a timeline of several years—the product roadmap. The selected projects are 100% strategically driven.
- **Bottom-up**: "Make good decisions on individual projects, and the portfolio will take care of itself" is a commonly accepted philosophy. That is, make sure that your project gating system is working well—that gates are accepting good projects and killing the poor ones—and the resulting portfolio will be a solid one. To ensure strategic alignment, use a scoring model at your project reviews and gates (as in Goal 2), and include strategic questions in this model. Strategic alignment is all but assured: your portfolio will indeed consist of all "on strategy" projects (although spending splits may not coincide with strategic priorities).

Note that regardless of the strategic approach, all of these methods presuppose that your business has a product innovation strategy, something that many businesses lack.

- **Goal 4. Pick the right number of projects.** Most companies have too many projects under way for their limited available resources. The result is pipeline gridlock: projects take too long to reach the market, and key activities are omitted because of a lack of people and time. Thus an overriding goal is to ensure a balance between resources required for the active projects and resources available. The following are two ways of achieving this goal:
- **Resource limits**: The value maximization methods (Goal 1) build in a resource limitation. Using them means ranking your projects until you are out of resources. The same is true of bubble diagrams (Goal 2). The sum of the areas of the bubbles—the resources devoted to each project—should be a constant, and adding one more project to the diagram requires that another be deleted.
- **Resource capacity analysis**: Determine your resource demand by prioritizing projects and adding up the resources required by each department for all active projects (usually expressed in person-days per month). Project management software enables this roll-up of resource requirements. Then determine the available resources per department—how much time people have to work on these projects. A department-by-department and month-by-month assessment usually reveals that there are too many projects. It suggests a project limit (the point beyond which projects in the prioritized list should be put on hold), and it identifies which departments are the bottlenecks.

YOUR NEW-PRODUCT PROCESS MUST WORK

Before you charge ahead with portfolio management, put first things first: make sure that your new-product process or "gating system" is working well. An effective new-product process is central to portfolio management for the following reasons:

- Regardless of the sophistication of the portfolio models used, your input data must be sound. Look to your new-product process to deliver *data integrity*.
- Your gating process should at minimum kill or cull out the bad projects and, in so doing, yield a better portfolio.

Data integrity means that the up-front homework in projects must be done. Build two stages of homework into your process prior to the beginning of development:

- the scoping stage, which entails a preliminary market, technical, and business assessment;
- building the business case, which involves much more detailed market research (a user-needs-and-wants study, competitive analysis, concept tests) along with technical and manufacturing assessments.

An effective new-product process also means effective gates. In best-practice businesses, this translates into a menu of specified deliverables for each gate; visible "go/kill" and prioritization criteria at the gates (many companies use scorecards to rate projects at gate meetings); defined gatekeepers per gate; clear gate outputs, and even "rules of engagement" for the gatekeeping or leadership team of the business.

CONCLUSION

Portfolio management is fundamental to new-product success. But it's not as easy as it first seems. Not only must you seek to maximize the value of your portfolio, but the development projects in your portfolio must be appropriately balanced; there must be the right numbers of projects and, finally, the portfolio must be strategically aligned. No one model can deliver on all four goals, and so best-practice businesses tend to use multiple methods to select their projects.

For More Information

Books:

Cooper, R. G., S. J. Edgett, and E. J. Kleinschmidt. *Portfolio Management for New Products*. 2nd ed. Cambridge, MA: Perseus, 2001.

Cooper, R. G. *Winning at New Products: Accelerating the Process from Idea to Launch*. 3rd ed. Cambridge, MA: Perseus, 2001.

Web Site:

www.prod-dev.com: this is the official Web site of the widely used Stage-Gate™ Process Model developed by Robert G. Cooper.

See also:

New Product Development (pp. 2054–56)

"Sometimes I think we'll see the day when you introduce a product in the morning and announce the end of its life at the end of the day."

(Al Shugart)

  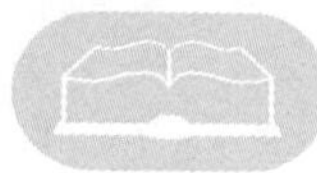    

MANAGING DYNAMIC CHANGE
by Robert Heller

EXECUTIVE SUMMARY

- Change management has become imperative in the competitive conditions of the early 21st century.
- Change means to pass from one form or phase into another, for which people are perfectly well prepared.
- "Strategic inflection points," demanding radical change, are likely to strike any company or industry.
- Change is synonymous with opportunity.
- The crucial task is to institute change when the company is prosperous, and change does not seem to be required.
- The true test of change management is perpetuating and renewing success.
- The more that change can be measured, the greater the likelihood of achieving successful change management.

INTRODUCTION

Change and its management loom very large in today's business requirements. Corporate success in the 21st century no longer rests simply on the old financial measures: earnings per share, profit growth, and return on capital employed. Shareholder value, service, quality, global market share—these are among the key objectives in world business as it moves forward in conditions of intense and intensifying competition. All the new objectives are inextricably intertwined, creating a dynamic of constant change.

The need to master change is becoming greater by the minute. In a world where Internet usage is doubling every 100 days (to give one phenomenal example of change), organizations and the people in them are most unlikely to succeed, even survive, unless they can manage change. In most cases the necessary changes—what must be done to improve quality, say, or generate added economic value—are obvious. By and large, everybody knows what needs to be done. But it is much easier to say than to do.

It is when an organization finds itself in this situation that change management skills are urgently required. Change management is not about pushing heavy stones uphill. Change means merely to pass from one form or phase into another, for which people are perfectly well prepared. That passage happens all the time, not only in organizational life, but in personal life. Much of today's need for business change springs from the rapid evolution of personal tastes, which alters markets both continuously and abruptly.

STRATEGIC INFLECTION POINTS

Andy Grove, the chairman of microprocessor leader Intel, calls monumental change of the Internet type a "strategic inflection point," which occurs when "10 x forces" alter a market with tenfold impact (see Mini-case). Faced with such a phenomenon, you have, in theory, three choices:

1. not to change
2. to change only as and when forced
3. to take charge of your destiny and seek to take advantage of change

In practice the three choices narrow to one—the third. Standing still in changing times is impossible; if you try to tread water in rapids, you'll be moved anyway and you'll probably drown. "Wait and see" or shunning the "first mover" advantage means you lose all control and are condemned to follow, not lead, very possibly forever: the faster the rate of change, the harder it is to catch up. Taking charge of your fate and thus of change, however, means seizing your opportunities.

Change is synonymous with opportunity. In a static market, dominated by established firms, newcomers have virtually no chance of breaking in. When Grove's 10 x forces strike, flux swamps everything. In case after case, industry after industry, newcomers adapt better to radically changed conditions than the existing players.

Strategic inflection points demand the ability to manage change on a dramatic scale. These drastic shifts are becoming less rare—you must constantly look for signs that they are affecting you. But sea-changes do not explain why the spotlight has turned on "how to manage change" in so big a way. Most change is evolutionary rather than revolutionary. All managers have always had to cope with change constantly. Customers, employees, bosses, rivals, products, technologies, regulations, markets, orders; you know that nothing lasts for ever.

MANAGEMENT AND MEASURABILITY

Understandably, however, managers prefer order and discipline to flux, and therefore seek to establish systems that provide predictability and control. That creates a perpetual tension between the real world, which is unpredictable and uncontrollable, and the corporate interior. To put that another way, it builds tension between creativity and organization, which mounts as the latter rapidly degenerates into bureaucracy. What people generally understand by "management of change" is combining chaos and order—changing, yes, but in a planned manner.

The definition of a good change management team is a group of people who know what to change, know how to accomplish that change and, above all, carry it out. It helps to operate technical change under a cultural banner. Total Quality Management, for example, can be described as a change program that lasts forever, with each year using a new theme (like "Putting the Customer First") to refocus and rejuvenate the program. Banners, themes, and exhortations are not the essence of change, but rather part of creating the atmosphere in which real change can take place.

In TQM programs, there is a clear correlation between success and the participation of the topmost management, not just as committed supporters, but as people whose own performance can be changed for the better by quality training and methods. It might seem difficult to find measures for boardroom performance—and TQM hinges

"The toughest thing about success is that you've got to keep on being a success." (Irving Berlin)

on improving measurable and measured statistics–but you can always find such measures. In fact, the more that change can be measured, the greater the likelihood of achieving successful change management.

Closeness to customers, or "customer focus," is a clear example of the importance of measurement. If your company seeks top ratings for RPQ and RPS (relative perceived quality and relative perceived service), it will be forced into continuous, continual change. Studies show that if it succeeds it will also generate increased market share and profitability. Customer satisfaction indices are mere statistics, but achieving the highest proportion of customers who rate your products and services as "excellent," or who call themselves "very satisfied," demands genuine market leadership, perpetually reinvented.

Change from the Bottom Up

You cannot manage such changes from the top. The prevailing view of change management has changed dramatically since the early 1980s. It was seen then as an inward-looking process ordained by chief executives who laid down the law from on high. By the end of the 1990s, change management had shifted to a bottom-up process encouraged by flat organization, relationships of trust, payment for performance, and training. These factors are all inner-directed, but they operate to create an outward-facing organization that is responsive, innovative, and dedicated to high RPQ and RPS performance.

Change Before the Crisis

Many managers are sure to find such shifts deeply uncomfortable, even intolerable. Often, as many as half the managers in an organization have to be changed (that is, moved or removed) before change can be achieved. Acceptance is especially hard to obtain at points below the crest of what Charles Handy presents as "the Sigmoid Curve." Similar to Grove's concept of the strategic inflection point, the curve charts the rise of an organization to peak power and profitability, and then the subsequent decline. Unless change management is set going well before the peak (which is difficult, because nobody thinks change is necessary), it will have to be enforced past the peak when the organization may be in crisis.

The key to change management is to manage the same way when you are not in crisis as you are forced to manage in crisis, and also to learn the striking lessons of surmounted crisis. Many turnaround cases show that any organization can be changed, for all intents and purposes overnight, even from total aversion to the essential trio–change, risk and action–to the opposite. The results are usually remarkable, but only in the context of recovery. Remember that turning around from incipient disaster is not good management of change. The true test of change management is perpetuating and renewing success.

Mini-Case

Intel

The strategic inflection point which nearly laid Intel low was the advent of more effective, massive competition in memory chips (its core business) from the Japanese. After a prolonged period of denial and indecision, Andy Grove and his C.E.O., Gordon Moore, asked what a new boss would do. The answer was to exit memory chips altogether. The change took a year to implement as Intel overcame internal resistance and switched all its efforts to the microprocessor. Grove's lessons from this failure turned into brilliant success are invaluable: (1) always have new projects under development as potential replacements; (2) act sooner rather than later; (3) argue out the change plan, but let opponents go rather than compromise the future; (4) treat crisis as opportunity.

Making It Happen ▸▸

- Decide to take charge of your destiny; learn to see change as opportunity–and always take advantage of the latter.
- Watch out for "strategic inflection points"–drastic shifts in the circumstances of your sector or industry–and respond early to their coming impact.
- Form a change management team of people who know what to change, know how to change it–and who, above all, will carry change through.
- Force your company into continuous, continual change by seeking top ratings for RPQ and RPS (relative perceived quality and relative perceived service).
- Shift from top-down to bottom-up by flattening the organization, establishing relationships of trust, and paying for performance.
- To perpetuate and renew success, manage out of crisis as you are forced to manage in crisis.

Conclusion

Study of turnarounds, however, does demonstrate a recurring pattern of eight elements that are also vitally needed for successful change management:

1. Leadership by a single person or united team is the fulcrum, both at the top and at lower levels.
2. Nothing is sacred. Everything is subject to challenge and, if necessary, change.
3. Decisions are taken decisively and rapidly.
4. Necessary action is also taken decisively and rapidly: the longer change is delayed, the less likely it is to be effective.
5. What's being done and why is clearly communicated inside and outside the company with maximum commitment.
6. Change is facilitated and symbolized by actions, above all by actions of top management.
7. The basics of the business are subjected to *kaizen* (continuous improvement) and, if needed, *kaikaku* (radical reform).
8. The future of the organization and its businesses is kept firmly in front of everybody's eyes and actions.

For More Information

Hammer, Michael, and James Champy. *Reengineering the Corporation: A Manifesto for Business Revolution*. New York: HarperCollins, 1983.

Pendlebury, John, et al. *The Ten Keys to Successful Management*. New York: John Wiley, 1998.

Price Waterhouse Change Integration Team. *Better Change: Best Practices for Transforming Your Organization*. New York: Irwin Professional Publishing, 1995.

See also:

☆ **Snapping Managerial Inertia (pp. 257–58)**
☆ **Turnaround Strategies (pp. 251–52)**
✓ **Implementing an Effective Change Program (pp. 504–05)**
Change Management (pp. 1923–25)

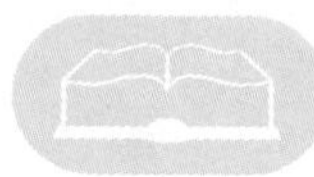

Why Managers Need Futurists
by Maria-Therese Hoppe

EXECUTIVE SUMMARY

- "Futurists are practical people enabling companies to navigate better and more securely in a world of turmoil."
- Managers need futurists to provide perspectives that clarify their view of the changes occurring today and their possible consequences tomorrow.
- Charting possible future changes enables managers to react proactively as soon as the first indications appear—to steer into the future competently and confidently.

Introduction

The future doesn't exist as a fixed entity. The moment future may be measured, when you can make statistics of a phenomenon, it's no longer future but the present. The past doesn't exist either. And the present is only a fleeting moment. The only constant we have is change. But change doesn't happen smoothly, it arrives in big rifts. Such a rift has taken place during the last five or six years: time becomes compressed; the pace of change intensifies; half a year becomes the past; one year medieval times, and two years ancient time. As time rifts happen, our concepts change rapidly and the world around us becomes unrecognizable. Strategies that looked like winning yesterday become obsolete tomorrow. Long-term planning seems a liability—because what will tomorrow bring? How to manage?

Interpreting the Future

When looking at the future, we always look at it and interpret it through invisible contact lenses: the past. Interpreting the traces from tomorrow through our experiences from yesterday is a sound strategy in a world that changes slowly, but deadly in a fast-changing environment.

Time rifts make discontinuities distinctly visible. They seem confusing but may in fact be traces from the future peeking through into today.

Futurists deal with change and discontinuities, with the uncertainties that make the job as a manager so challenging and, at times, dangerous. Futurists are practical people functioning in a company or corporation much as economists function—in a practical way. The intellectual discipline of reading economics at university does not mean that practicing economists are simply theoretical people who spin off beautiful constructions with no use. The same goes for futurists! Most futurists have a background in economics and social sciences, but have added skills that enable them to give management better decision tools to navigate in a fast-changing world. Such tools give companies and corporations better chances not only to survive, but to exist as winners. What's more, this goes not only for survival in the long term, but even more so in the short term!

The pace of change over the last five or six years has created tough competition, with chances of up- and downturns arriving like earthquakes. Futurists may function like seismologists, enabling companies not only to react by fleeing after the quake but to be proactive and avoid it.

Futurists May Act in Different Roles:

- **Futurists as "early warning."** In 1996, a research project called "Music of the future" was carried out for the music industry in Europe. Nine so-called "wildcards" were presented. One, called "Music like electricity," described how in a few years' time music could be downloaded from the Internet in a quality as good as the best CD, completely for free. Nobody in the music industry believed in that wildcard. Two years later, Napster happened. The music companies would have had two years to prepare for the event and would have come out as winners, had they believed the early warning.
- **Futurists as product developers.** A global chemical company involved a group of futurists in its product development. The problem was that the company had a lot of new chemical inventions, but wasn't sure which of them to market. Should it change course? Should it go for completely different products and ranges, or stick to the old traditional ways and perhaps lose new opportunities?

  A close cooperation between the internal development group and the futurists was established. The futurists provided tools to focus on changes in the world around the company, the company its product expertise. The collaboration produced four very different scenarios for the future, each of them concentrated on products and services for specific types of markets—all with sound economic bases and good perspectives. The project gave management the opportunity to choose and implement a new strategy, instead of just launching new products in a hit-and-miss way. The company consequently changed focus from being product centered to being customer centered, concentrating on how best to fulfill the needs and dreams of customers. Within half a year, the change started to be implemented and is still continuing to widen through the company. The consequences? The company's bottom line says it all!
- **Futurists as eye-openers to new concepts.** A big international furniture chain engaged a futurist to work with their store managers, challenging their concepts about customers and the classical segmentation according to age, gender, and income—as well as depicting the dream worlds of customers and focusing on the changes those are undergoing just now. The exercises enabled the managers to raise new questions about how their stores were seen by customers and the role of the employees in the stores, and opened their eyes to new opportunities. The managers created lists of new ideas and concepts challenging the old way of "this is how we do it in our company." Many of the ideas are already being implemented in stores.
- **Futurists thinking the unthinkable.** The world of technology changes faster than any other business: today's kings are tomorrow's beggars. Futurists may think the unthinkable for companies—but that still does not mean it is easy for management to believe in the unthinkable! In 1994 I wrote an article on the communication of the future, "Small is beautiful," in which I described the equivalent of what is today an advanced mobile phone.

"I never think of the future. It comes soon enough." (Albert Einstein)

I called it "the communicator." Most people thought I was off my rocker. I was mistaken in two points only: it didn't take ten years to get here, just seven. And the size was not two packets of cigarettes, but half a packet. But the description of the functionality, the range and the price was absolutely correct. The fact most impossible to believe for telco managers was that this new wonder would be a cheap commodity used by everybody.

An article on the future of the Internet from 1997, "It's not fantasy, it's future," has recently raised the interest of some telcos. It seemed to them a perfect description of their present visions, and they found it hard to believe that the article is four years old. Four years ago it was read as science fiction.

Managers need futurists to provide them with perspectives that clarify their view of the changes occurring today, and their possible consequences tomorrow. If possible future changes are charted, managers can react proactively—taking themselves and their organizations into the future confidently and successfully.

MAKING IT HAPPEN ▸▸

- It is impossible to manage effectively in the short term without forming a medium- and long-term view of the future. Doing the wrong thing, even efficiently, gets you nowhere.
- Short-term victories won at the expense of the future inevitably end up as defeats. That is why so few turnaround managements go on to longer-term success.
- The work of futurists begins with deep and thorough analysis and understanding of the present—without which management is doomed to fail, even in the short term.
- If management effectively orients the business towards a successful future, that automatically points the company towards opportunities for enhanced profitability, productivity, and customer satisfaction in the short term.
- Most major corporate difficulties stem, not from short-term errors, but from longer-term blunders. All major corporate success stems not from short-term action programs, but from accurately focused long-term strategy.

A classic example of the damage done by "future failure" is the U.S. car industry. Detroit failed to foresee the rise of the second car, or the increased role of women in purchase, or the relevance of revolutionary trends in Japanese car production. These failures led the industry to persist in uneconomic methods whose adverse impact on short-term results was greatly intensified by loss of domestic market share to the Japanese. Detroit has never fully recovered from this debacle.

In computer hardware, the failure of nearly all mainframe and mini-makers to build profitable PC businesses arose from missing the significance of clear trends towards distributed computing, miniaturization (Moore's Law), and falling mainframe prices. Even at IBM, initial dominance of the PC market was demolished by mistaken reading of the future. Efforts to achieve short-term improvements in IBM's performance consequently ended in failure and corporate upheaval. IBM, like Detroit, has never fully recovered.

CONCLUSION

As the above examples show, the future trends that were so fatefully ignored or misconstrued were in no sense "abstract," but firmly based on hard-nosed practical observation (such as more American women going out to work) and logical deduction from those facts (the consequent emergence of increased demand for smaller cars). The futurist is only interested in present and future realities.

For More Information

Books:

Cairncross, Frances. *The Company of the Future: How the Communications Revolution Is Changing Management*. Boston, MA: Harvard Business School Press, 2002.
Davis, Stan. *Lessons from the Future: Making Sense of a Blurred World*. Oxford: Capstone, 2001.
Gibson, Rowan, ed. *Rethinking the Future*. Naperville, IL: Nicholas Brealey, 1999.
Godin, Seth. *Survival Is not Enough*. New York: Free Press, 2002.
Jensen, Rolf. *The Dream Society*. New York: McGraw-Hill, 1999.
Williamson, Marianne, ed. *Imagine: What America Could Be in the 21st Century—Visions of a Better Future from Leading American Thinkers*. Emmaus, PA: Rodale/Daybreak, 2000.

Web Sites:

www.thegff.com: The Global Future Forum, an international think tank of prominent futurists.
www.viktoria.informatik.gu.se/~martin/future.htm: the Futurist's Cookbook is a site offering a number of links to organizations, individuals, projects, forecasts and publications devoted to futurist research.
www.gtalumni.org/news/magazine/sum93/sci.html: The Science & the Art of Futurism is a Web page by McKinley Conway. It describes what futurism is and how it could help your company foresee consumer needs and trends.

See also:

☆ **Managing Dynamic Change (pp. 277–78)**
☆ **Scenario Planning (pp. 267–68)**
Blur (p. 893)
The Third Wave (p. 952)
Alvin Toffler (pp. 1056–57)
Business Plans and Planning (pp. 1920–21)

"Managers who extensively plan the future get the timing wrong." (Shona L. Brown)

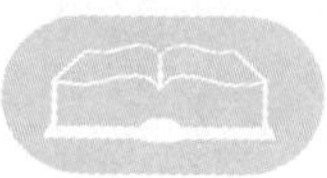

BUILDING GREAT INTERNAL PARTNERSHIPS
by Chip R. Bell

EXECUTIVE SUMMARY

- Organizational success is increasingly dependent on effective internal partnerships as organizations become more complex and as customer demands for improved service make excellence in communication and coordination a necessity.
- The difference between a great team and a great partnership substantially alters the way in which members approach leadership and accomplishment.

INTRODUCTION

When I was a little boy, the TV screen was the impetus for much of our backyard play. My friends and I would watch Batman and Robin and then race to the backyard to reenact what we'd seen on the TV. After what seemed like an hour of arguing over who would be the masked warrior, we'd settle in to battle against evil with our toy guns and pretend Batmobile. Whether it was cowboys and Indians, cops and robbers, or pitchers and batters, TV often shaped the form of our recreation.

A few weeks ago, I was consulting with the C.E.O. of a major high-tech corporation. His company had acquired a smaller software group six weeks earlier to bolster its IT capacity to provide more responsive sales support. The transition had been rocky, and he was now snarling about the infighting between operations and sales. Customer complaints were climbing, field salespeople were frustrated, and the new software enhancements the acquired company was supposed to produce were still stuck in applications development.

"We need better teamwork!" he snapped as he slammed his oversized desk. "Why can't these guys quit arguing in the huddle, just call the play, and get back to basic blocking and tackling?"

It was the Tuesday morning after a popular televised sports event. As I thought of Batman and Robin, I realized the appeal of his reenacting the athletic contest he'd watched on TV had seduced him into reaching for the wrong solution to a common work problem. His problem was not inadequate teamwork but ineffective partnering.

HOW TEAMS DIFFER FROM PARTNERSHIPS

Teamwork and partnership are not the same. Emulating the Dallas Cowboys within the operations department may heighten synergy and collective productivity. But it is the wrong model for how the operations department works with the sales department. An intact unit uses teamwork. However, synergy between units (whether an external vendor alliance or a relationship with the internal department down the hall) comes from partnership. Using teamwork tactics in a partnership context leads to flawed practices and counterproductive behavior. Here are a few of the key differences.

1. **A team is focused on accomplishing a task and uses an effective relationship as a tool for achieving it.** A partnership is focused on creating a relationship context from which all manner of outcomes can be accomplished. In a team the task is preeminent. In fact, the task a team is engaged on can be so compelling that even a less than excellent team can produce superior performance. In a partnership, excellence cannot be sustained without a superior relationship, no matter how compelling the mission.
2. **A team suspends the individuality of its members in the pursuit of interdependent action.** Collaboration (co-laboring) means *two become one*—like two horses harnessed to pull a wagon. In fact, teams work to tone down singleness in their quest to create a new whole; the focus is on mix or blend (as you'd mix yellow with blue to produce green: in green the individual root colors disappear). In a partnership individuality is as meritorious as jointness or union. Singleness is played just as loudly as togetherness, and the focus is on their amalgamation (as you'd create a fruit salad: no matter how hard you toss, apple stays apple and banana remains banana).
3. **Leadership is vital to the effectiveness of a team.** Generally a great deal of energy is devoted to leadership enlistment—getting associates to accept, value, and respond to followership induction. Even in leaderless teams or self-directed teams, groupings aimed at operating without the formal identification of authority, a sort of pack mentality encourages the emergence of a leader. In partnerships, followership is less person-centered and more spirit-centered. Partners follow a spirit or energy that may emanate from a partner but is not owned by that partner. It's energy owned by the partnership, providing a force that gives that partnership vitality and drive.

TECHNIQUES FOR BUILDING INTERNAL PARTNERSHIPS

Knowing the difference between a team and a partnership might win you an academic argument, but how does it help with the high-tech C.E.O.'s problem? The implications of these differences are profound. Trying to make a partnership a team is as flawed and problematic as using mules as breeding stock. Below are several key points about the difference between team and partnership that inform practice.

MATCHING VALUES, NOT JUST TALENTS

Teams depend principally on complementary talents more than congruent values. Partnerships can overcome a mismatch in capacities if the relationship springs from solidly congruent values. "We realized we were two left feet early on," said Frank Esposito, C.E.O. of the global power sport aftermarket distributor Tucker Rocky Distributing. Speaking of his company's alliance with a Taiwanese corporation working with Tucker Rocky on a major helmet project, he noted, "Because we shared the same values of honesty, fair play, and commitment, we were able to shore up our mismatch before it derailed our effort." The high-tech C.E.O. we visited earlier asked division heads to write down four work values their unit would refuse to compromise. When both divisions discovered that three of their four values were the same, they found new energy for collaboration and immediately set about working to accommodate the value that was different. The more they acknowledged values strength, the more their differences seemed minor or petty.

"I think making a name for yourself is a wrong objective. . .I would prefer to look for ways where you can make maximum contribution."

(Andrew S. Grove)

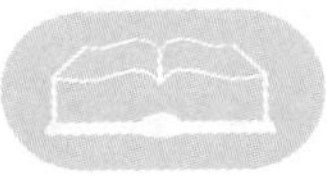

Nurturing Equality, Not Just Synergy

If partnerships are power-free alliances, effort must be devoted to nurturing and bolstering equality. The C.E.O.'s troubles with sales and operations were in part caused by their battles over turf, influence, and recognition. Operations didn't want sales encroaching on their territory; sales didn't want operations getting the right to influence certain decisions sales considered their purview. *Power over* was the driver, not *power with*. When the C.E.O. later reassured both groups (jointly) that turf, influence, and recognition were not relevant or in jeopardy, they gave up their tug-of-war to decide who was going to be Batman. "If our support staff at global headquarters thinks they have to lose their uniqueness in order to effectively partner with the regional staff in the field, they lose the fruitfulness of their diversity," said Steve Joyce, senior vicepresident of strategic alliances for Marriott International. "The reverse is equally true."

Negotiating Protocols, Not Just Objectives

Partnerships work because the relationships are anchored to a set of relationship protocols. "Successful partnerships are not built on deals and contracts," said Marriott C.E.O., Bill Marriott, Jr. "They work because of the heart and soul of the relationship." Teams may benefit from some fun-filled ropes course, but partnerships are spawned from hammering out the covenants that guide values and behavior, not just outcomes and results. Honesty, reliability, passion, and support are as vital as goals, roles, rules, and accountability. When the high-tech C.E.O. facilitated a meeting in which sales and operations staff revealed their expectations of each other as well as the no-nos that would sidetrack their relationship, the quality of their communication improved dramatically.

Valuing Early Warnings

Partnerships are purposeful relationships; success hangs on a perpetual focus on their mutual purpose or vision, overriding any zeal for an outcome at the expense of the relationship. Maintenance of the relationship is viewed as being as vital as a clear sense of direction. Great partnerships work out cues that signal hiccups in the relationship. Such gestures become the preamble to candid confrontation aimed at getting the relationship back on track. Feedback is seen as nurturance (a kind of performance fertilizer) rather than critique; advice is valued as supportive instruction rather than coercive superiority. A key question our high-tech C.E.O. asked the sales and operations departments was this: "How much time elapses between when your gut tells you there's tension in the relationship and when your partner hears you talk about that tension?" When both divisions agreed to work toward a zero time lapse, assumptions were quickly clarified and innuendoes were traded in for frankness.

Ending Rather Than Stopping

All work partnerships come to an end. Organizations are reshuffled, projects are completed, and new goals dictate new structural designs. The great partnership ends effectively through planning and attention to detail. Far too many internal confederations simply stop, with no consideration given to appropriate closure. This makes the next partnership more difficult and fails to capture the learnings important to growth and improvement. Great partnerships acknowledge when the configuration has achieved its purpose or when they have reached a point where continuation would be counterproductive. Debriefings reflect what worked and what didn't, celebrations highlight special people and milestones worthy of public affirmation, and commitments are made regarding ongoing support. The key is to acknowledge completion and bring the relationship to a productive end.

Making It Happen ▸▸

- Choose partners with complementary values, not just synergistic talents.
- Outline relationship agreements regarding communications, trust, and control.
- Assert the truth when behavior or performance wavers from what was agreed.
- Keep your promises or renegotiate them in good faith with ample lead time.
- Honor your partner by sharing credit and seeking ways to affirm contribution.
- Bring continuous passion and attentive energy to the relationship.
- Keep your sights tenaciously on the partnership purpose.
- When the partnership is over, implement a complete and comprehensive closure.
- If the partnership fails, don't burn bridges you may later need.

Conclusion

Partnering is the critical success factor of all relationships in today's world of enterprise—in boardrooms, conference rooms, shop floors, half-wall cubicles, and virtual liaisons. These alliances act very differently from teams. Their rise and fall is based far less on the efficacy of their efforts and far more on the success of their synergy. Greatness comes from managing the confederation more with the care of a marriage than with the discipline of a group of athletes.

For More Information

Books:

Dent, Stephen M. *Partnering Intelligence: Creating Value for Your Business by Building Strong Alliances*. Palo Alto, CA: Davies-Black, 1999.

Harbison, John R., Jr., and Peter Pekar. *Smart Alliances: A Practical Guide to Repeatable Success*. San Francisco, CA: Jossey-Bass, 1998.

Lewis, Jordan D. *Partnerships for Profit: Structuring and Managing Strategic Alliances*. New York: Free Press, 1990.

Lewis, Jordan D. *Trusted Partners: How Companies Build Mutual Trust and Win Together*. New York: Free Press, 2000.

Rackham, Neil, Lawrence Friedman, and Richard Ruff. *Getting Partnering Right: How Market Leaders Are Creating Long-term Competitive Advantage*. New York: McGraw-Hill Professional, 1995.

See also:

☆ **The Business Web (pp. 145–46)**
☆ **Corporate-level Strategy (pp. 101–02)**
☆ **Intrapreneurial Warriors versus Traditional Managers (pp. 125–26)**
☆ **Self-managed Teams: How They Succeed or Fail (pp. 202–03)**
☆ **Virtual Collaboration (pp. 167–68)**
☆ **Why Mergers Fail and How to Prevent It (pp. 81–82)**
☆ **X-engineering Success (pp. 245–46)**
Kurt Lewin (pp. 1014–15)
Interfirm Cooperation, Strategic Alliances, Joint Ventures (pp. 2005–07)

"We are self-activating organisms, and can, to some degree, control our own destiny and our own responses to pressure. . .we can select our goals and choose the paths toward them." (Charles Handy)

  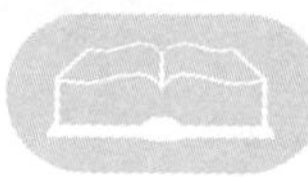    

Raising the Bar: Setting Effective Targets *by Matthew Budman*

EXECUTIVE SUMMARY

- Increasing demands on managers results in increasing demands on workers.
- Setting goals often produces higher achievement.
- Work/life shifts and changing technology complicate the issue of productivity.
- Getting more from employees requires more effort and skill on the part of managers.

Introduction

We want more productivity from workers; indeed, we often need more productivity. Often, as managers we have no choice—we must continue to raise the bar under pressure from all sides: enforced cost-cutting, tetchy labor markets, fresh competition from developing nations, increasingly in-charge customers, etc.

And we have to do it with fewer people and less leverage. Downsizing has led to fewer people being forced to do more work and to permanently heightened expectations of what employees are capable of.

But in asking for more from workers, we frequently make mistakes.

- We fail to understand adequately what workers are already doing, either during or outside the 9-to-5 routine.
- We ask for more while at the same time we undermine trust and commitment through paternalistic electronic supervision and demoralizing layoffs.
- We don't put the necessary thought and effort into managing people and the challenges of the 21st-century workplace.

Scoring with Goals

It's a well-established fact that setting concrete objectives raises workplace productivity; moving the bar upward is practically guaranteed to produce higher returns. People respond to targets by striving to reach them.

But moving goals is a double-edged sword. Workers who fail to meet their objective are likely to suffer disappointment and frustration, particularly if office mates have reached their respective targets. Yet if the goal is met before the specified date, an employee may slacken the pace since the pressure is off. Either case requires managerial attention.

With many jobs it's not easy to shift annual target numbers higher. Despite a post-reengineering emphasis on accountability and verifiability, knowledge-economy work is not readily measurable. (The Taylorist ideal of timing workers with stopwatches is often irrelevant in the modern office; work is now usually too complex to isolate tasks and measure efficiency in completing them.) Targets must be qualitative, and therefore somewhat subjective, rather than strictly numerical.

Goal setting must be considered regularly. Generally, the subject of new objectives is only raised annually, at performance appraisals—usually dreaded by all participants. Typically there's a space labeled "Goals for Next Year" that must be filled in, an automatic demand for more work.

It's important that new goals don't appear arbitrary or seem to take precedence over quotidian core tasks. They should be produced collaboratively, through manager-employee discussions. Incremental targets, or subgoals, are more effective than distant goals, which may seem daunting.

Setting goals constructively is a tall order. You don't want good people to stagnate; realistically there is no point at which you can tell anyone, "You're doing enough."

Longer Days, Longer To-do Lists

Don't consider asking more from your people until you understand how much they're already giving you. Many corporations have become "white-collar sweatshops." Your department or company may not fit this pattern, but it might, and you may simply be unaware of it. There's no question that a general culture of overwork has arisen, with Silicon Valley entrepreneurs sleeping on cots and working around the clock. U.K. workers report high levels of stress stemming from increasing demands and hours. Some have estimated that one-third of the working population in Japan suffers from chronic fatigue.

Why are so many people working so hard? Firstly, under the aegis of empowerment companies have shifted much of the burden of management to workers themselves.

Secondly, there are fewer people to do the work, and not all of them are top performers. Even after all the downsizings and reengineerings there's plenty of dead wood. Companies announcing layoffs obviously hope to prune only the worst performers, but invariably good people depart as well, partly because they dread the inevitable increase in workload.

Thirdly employees cite management's tolerance of below-par work as a cause of overwork. Managers' endless patience with mediocrity is easy to explain: it's difficult and unpleasant to fire individuals and expensive to hire and train new people. But unequal distribution of work is a crucial issue for managers to address.

Finally there is the issue of trust. Don't expect people to embrace new demands and goals while the company installs new electronic tools of managerial suspicion. Workers aren't primed to give their all to the company when they know their bosses are reading their e-mail, logging their lunch-hour minutes, counting their keystrokes, watching their Web site use, and recording their voice mail.

Taking Work Home

Technology has allowed both employers and employees to blur the distinctions between work and life; people are working more even as they're enjoying new freedom and flexibility. At the office people surf the Net for sports scores and make personal telephone calls without feeling as though they're exploiting the company.

But in return, they're accountable to the demands of work. They stay at the office later; on the commute home they return phone calls and study spreadsheets on their laptops; they block out time after dinner to read memos and prepare presentations; they check and reply to work-related e-mail and voice mail at all hours.

Managers know whether projects are completed by deadline, and whether people are physically in the office, but it's hard to look over an employee's shoulder and gauge how much work the person is actually getting done. It's especially difficult when

"To obtain the most from a man's energy it is necessary to increase the effect without increasing the fatigue."

(Augustin Colomb)

  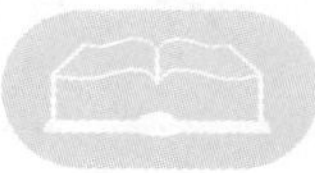    

that employee is working from home two or three days a week.

Some see this work/home trend as bad for employees, who find themselves not only carrying heavier workloads but, with beepers and electronic desk calendars, taking on work responsibilities around the clock. Others insist that workers don't necessarily resent the encroachment of the office on their personal lives, and that many people find more fulfillment and fun in the office than they do outside of it.

Either way, these shifts augur more challenges for managers. In conjunction with your input and in line with overall company policies, each worker can arrive at an individual best balance of efficiency and fulfillment. The more options, support, and coaching you can offer, the more productivity you'll get.

Playing Fair

Each worker performs at a particular level and a particular speed. Some thrive under heightened expectations; others grow sullen, believing their supervisor to be impossible to satisfy. The bottom line is that both want to be treated fairly.

What does *fairness* mean? Simply, fair treatment means something different to everyone. Some want special breaks, others no special breaks. For parents, allowing flexible scheduling to deal with children; for singles, ensuring that their workload doesn't rise disproportionately to compensate for the missing parents. Some demand that work be shared equally, others only that they don't have more than they can handle.

For U.S. workers in many industries, heavy workloads used to be an issue handled by union representatives, whose job it was to protect them from unreasonable demands. Today, as machinery takes more and more manual labor out of workers' hands, the strength of unions—both in numbers and by moral weight—continues to decline. This is a trend likely to continue even in countries with traditionally strong organized labor. In France, for instance, trade union membership has fallen below 10%, lagging behind even the U.S. figure of 14%.

And for white-collar workers, technology has rendered union-driven job protections less relevant than ever: productivity is usually measured not by piecework standards but by more intangible and individual methods. Even the issue of working conditions is fuzzy, since work often spills into out-of-office hours, and workspaces sometimes include commuter-train seats and living-room coffee tables.

Without the help of the unions, workers have little official bargaining power when it comes to telling their employers what they will or won't do; often their only defense against increasing demands is to threaten to resign. Obviously, it is best to avoid reaching that point.

Making It Happen ▸▸

- Familiarize yourself with current workloads and employees' feelings about their responsibilities. It is important to avoid burnout and resentment, especially as your most conscientious people are the ones likely to burn out first.
- Set goals, but be aware of the attendant complications. Collaborate with individual workers on their goals, keeping targets reachable but challenging enough to be interesting.
- In expanding responsibilities for employees, don't overemphasize tasks that aren't directly job-related. If the core fails, the rest doesn't matter.
- Don't assume that slogans or, worse, motivational posters or insincere rah-rah rallies will produce any effect other than cynicism.
- Through coaching and rewards, make it clear that slacking is unacceptable and that you're concerned about all employees feeling that they are treated fairly.
- Work with your staff to arrive at mutually beneficial schedules and workloads that satisfactorily balance work and home lives. A telecommuting option may be ideal for some; others need the structure of a 9-to-5 office.
- Don't ask for more without making it worth your people's while, either financially or through other means such as a job assignment or, when convenient for all, extra time off work.

Conclusion

Is it acceptable and productive to raise the bar through new targets? Empirically, the evidence suggests that where new targets are discussed and set in a realistic, achievable and trusting manner, these targets will be effective. Increasing targets requires greater effort from management; it's your responsibility to put that additional work in context. You can't simply raise the bar and assume everyone will rise to meet the new standards. No size fits all; pushing up standards in a knowledge-economy era of amorphous jobs requires more than cookie-cutter solutions.

The key to setting effective targets is to understand the needs of the team, the individual, and the tasks involved. Managers need to ensure that targets are both realistic and challenging. Nothing de-motivates like failure to meet expectations, while success in meeting targets will generate further confidence and productivity. Reinforcing a positive attitude to abilities will promote future success and a flexibility to engage new and more challenging targets. Setting a clear, unambiguous direction, ensuring that people are ready to meet the new challenges and that they remain on course is not easy. It requires a great deal of attention and keen leadership skills.

This necessitates leadership, not only by example, but also by making a real commitment to keeping staff engaged, productive, and flexible. You'll have to balance what is possible with how much of your people's lives you can legitimately ask for. No small task, but then no one ever said managing was easy.

For More Information

Books:

Ciulla, Joanne B. *The Working Life: The Promise and Betrayal of Modern Work*. New York: Random House, 2001.
Fraser, Jill Andresky. *White-collar Sweatshop*. New York: Norton, 2001.
Hochschild, Arlie Russell. *The Time Bind*. New York: Henry Holt, 2001.

Web Site:

www.workforce.com is home to the *Workforce Magazine* and is designed to give HR professionals sources to the trends and tools necessary to bring about business results.

See also:

☆ **Making Performance Appraisals a Win-win Experience (pp. 23–24)**
☆ **Managing in a 24/7 Organization (pp. 200–01)**
☆ **Preventing Your Work Problems from Causing You Stress (pp. 314–15)**
✓ **Managing Your Time Effectively (pp. 398–99)**
✓ **Setting Objectives (pp. 480–81)**
Stress and Stress Management (pp. 2117–19)

"I can charge a man's battery and then recharge it again. But it is only when he has his own generator that we can talk about motivation." (Frederick Herzberg)

NEW YARDSTICKS FOR PERFORMANCE AND PRODUCTIVITY IN AN E-WORLD

by Peter S. Cohan

EXECUTIVE SUMMARY

- Setting aside the wide mood swings of the stock market, the Internet remains a tool that lets managers enhance their firms' value to stakeholders.
- In an e-world, change takes place so quickly that managers cannot rely on traditional financial measures alone to chart their organizations' course.
- Several cutting-edge firms have developed more robust performance measurement and incentive systems that enable them to adapt more effectively to this rapid change.

INTRODUCTION

As we move beyond the dot-com bubble of 2000, it becomes clear that the Internet will not revolutionize all aspects of business. Despite the dot-com crash, the Internet—simply a relatively inexpensive wide-bandwidth global communications network—remains very relevant to the way business is conducted. However, the value of the Internet will not emerge from the technology itself. Rather, the value of the Internet will emerge from the ways in which managers use it to enhance the value their firms create for their stakeholders.

Managers need new yardsticks to succeed in a business world thus transformed. Traditional yardsticks such as profitability and productivity have been more important than ever since the market for IPOs shut down in 2000. However, business conditions change so rapidly in an e-world that managing through traditional accounting alone is dangerously akin to driving a car while looking in the rearview mirror. In an e-world, managers need predictive indicators that can pinpoint opportunities and threats to a business before they find their way into the firm's financial statements. Managers also need to create the right performance measurement and incentive systems to encourage their people to capture the stakeholder value referred to above.

NEW YARDSTICKS AND MEASURES IN AN E-WORLD

In an e-world, employees need to react thoughtfully—yet rapidly—to customers, suppliers, and shareholders. Consequently employees need new yardsticks to support their decision making. While employee performance measures must support those of managers, they must focus more specifically on helping employees to make decisions that improve the firm's competitive position.

Firms have four critical stakeholders:

- **Customers.** Firms can enhance the value they create for customers through initiatives such as lowering product price, increasing product performance to respond to changing customer needs, and/or enhancing customer service.
- **Suppliers.** Firms can enhance the value they create for suppliers through initiatives such as ordering a wider variety of products from a smaller number of suppliers, regular placing of orders, and/or lowering the joint costs of activities such as ordering, invoicing, and billing.
- **Employees.** Firms can enhance the value they create for employees through initiatives such as matching work assignments to an employee's interests and aptitudes, creating an environment that encourages a balance between work and personal activities, and/or offering competitive pay.
- **Shareholders.** Firms can enhance the value they create for shareholders by increasing their stock price, by consistently exceeding analysts' quarterly profit expectations.

Managers should consider three observations about enhancing the firm's value to these four stakeholders in an e-world.

Firstly, the Internet serves two roles in an e-world. It's a tool that can enable organizations to enhance their value to each of these four stakeholder groups. In addition the Internet can offer managers a way to measure the firm's performance in enhancing stakeholder value.

Secondly, the firm's posture toward these stakeholders is likely to change depending on the economic environment. For example, when revenues are growing a firm may invest more heavily in retaining employees, whereas when revenues are declining a firm may rank employee performance more rigorously and attempt to shed all but the top performers.

Finally, the firm's performance affects each of the stakeholder groups in tightly interrelated ways. For example, if a firm can enhance the value it creates for customers, revenue growth may accelerate, leading to beating analysts' earnings expectations, thereby raising the stock price. Conversely, if a firm creates an environment that frustrates employees, employee frustration may lead to behavior that dissatisfies customers—leading to lower revenues, lower profits, and a decline in stock price.

MINI-CASES

NEW YARDSTICKS IN ACTION

Raytheon (which generated 20% of its 2000 revenue outside the United States) manages the performance of its e-businesses using eight measurements:

- **Innovation and flexibility.** Average time from concept to start; speed to match a rival's site; speed at which the competition will match the site; time between new versions of a site.
- **Customer loyalty.** Percentage who return within a year; time between visits; duration of visits; conversion rate; percentage who give personal information.
- **Transactional excellence.** Unique visitors each month; online sales abandoned; percentage of orders correct; time to respond to a customer; percentage of orders filled on time.
- **Customer information.** Percentage of e-mail addresses collected from traffic.
- **Infrastructure reliability.** Time to load a page; network uptime; ease of system expansion.
- **Supply-chain excellence.** Inventory levels; inventory turns; order confirmation time; percentage of products built to order.
- **Valuation and financial performance.** Return on invested capital; market capitalization migration (the changing value of the overall business).

"Clearly, there is great potential to improve efficiency using Internet-based e-commerce strategies. . .But no one really knows how big those productivity gains will be." (Roger W. Ferguson, Jr.)

- **Digital quotient.** For complementary e-business channels, percentage of total revenue generated online.

Cisco Systems operates in 105 countries and generated over 80% of its $15 billion in revenue over its Cisco Connection Online (CCO). Cisco measures CCO's performance as follows:

- Register users and measure their CCO visit frequency by counting the days per month a registrant returns.
- Conduct random surveys among customers on their satisfaction with the site. Each page on the Cisco site includes a survey button. Any customer at any time can click on one and fill in comments.
- Survey customers on whether they were able to get their questions answered on the site or had to make a phone call to a company representative.
- Monitor the percentage of total sales that take place on the site.
- Measure the number of orders taken over the site, entered automatically into the ordering system, and forwarded to the factory without human intervention.
- Monitor the time it takes to access the site from 10 different locations around the world.
- Compare the money invested in the site with the revenue it generates.

Schneider National, a $2.7 billion trucking and logistics company, began measuring the IT department's overall performance to gauge internal stakeholders' satisfaction, not only to ensure that systems were performing the work business users requested, but also to rate the value and quality of that work. At the conclusion of any IT project, stakeholders fill out a report card that rates deliverables, timelines, requirements, and return on investment. An 18-month invoice-matching project received good marks, for example, in helping to facilitate reimbursement, reducing overheads by 15%, and enabling Schneider National to process 65% of all invoices electronically.

Key Success Factors

These examples of how systems-based organizations have implemented new yardsticks represent the vanguard of global business. The factors that led these companies to build new yardsticks in an e-world are valuable to general managers.

Successful new yardstick users share the following principles:

- **Involve the right people.** Involve the stakeholders who will produce, consume, and assess the output of the work. Typically, such stakeholders include customers (as Cisco's CCO does), suppliers, shareholders (as in Raytheon's measurement of market capitalization migration), and workers. Involving the stakeholders from the beginning of the process may cause work to proceed a bit more slowly, but the chance of doing the right thing efficiently increases dramatically.
- **Develop a broad set of measures.** Every organization has its own set of measures that are likely to lead to better performance. While all organizations should use traditional measures such as profit and productivity (as Cisco and NCR do), these should be supplemented with nonfinancial criteria that are significant to process stakeholders (such as Cisco's customer-satisfaction measures or Schneider National's measurement of the value and quality of IT work).
- **Understand the links between the measures.** Collect and analyze historical data on the selected measures to gain insights into their interrelationships. Specifically, organizations should identify which variables are leading indicators (customer satisfaction for Cisco and NCR) or financially measurable outcomes (incremental revenue per dollar invested in the system for Cisco, reduced overhead for Schneider National).
- **Tie incentives to performance.** It's a management axiom that what gets measured gets done, but measuring the right variables isn't enough. Managers must deliver more attractive incentives to employees who meet or exceed performance targets than to those whose performance lags. Winning users of new yardsticks put their money where their measurements are (for example, Cisco links employee bonuses to improvements in independently measured customer satisfaction).

Making It Happen ▸▸

Managing the transition from traditional performance measures to new yardsticks is challenging, but essential for companies navigating the e-world's choppy waters. The new yardsticks should include a firm's key stakeholders, not just executives; should incorporate nonfinancial measures; and should explicate the linkages between qualitative measures and financial results.

Here's how to make new yardsticks work for your firm:

- Understand how the Internet can improve the way your organization creates stakeholder value.
- Ask stakeholders how they measure your organization's success and how they would like your organization to improve along these lines.
- Assemble a team involving suppliers, customers, employees, and shareholders to identify and implement changes that realize that improvement.
- Track the impact of these changes on the stakeholder measures.
- Understand the relationship between these measures and financial results.
- Link incentives to performance on these measures.

Conclusion

The Internet remains a tool for enhancing the value a firm provides for its stakeholders. It's therefore helping managers to realize that they need to develop new ways to measure their corporate performance. The world is changing too quickly to rely solely on financial performance to chart an organization's course. Companies that use new yardsticks focus on enhancing the value they create for stakeholders—a focus that improves financial performance in a turbulent e-world.

For More Information

Web Site:

Shein, Esther. "Formula for ROI." *PC Week Online* (September 28, 1998). You can find this article at **www.zdnet.com/eweek/news/0928/28roi.html**.

See also:

☆ **Benchmarking (pp. 295–96)**
☆ **Creating Value through People (pp. 121–22)**
☆ **Making Performance Appraisals a Win-win Experience (pp. 23–24)**
☆ **Managing the Challenge of E-service (pp. 188–89)**
☆ **Overcoming the Difficulties of Managing a Virtual Organization (pp. 208–09)**
✔ **How to Deliver the Benefits of Affiliate Marketing on the Web (p. 626)**
✔ **The Key Issues of Implementing E-commerce Strategy (pp. 580–81)**
Benchmarking (pp. 1911–13)

"If you sit down and you ask, 'Where is the value center, where is the economic engine for e-commerce?' I guarantee you it is not in cost reduction." (Jay S. Walker)

  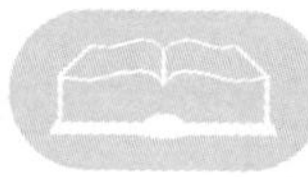    

USING MANAGEMENT CONSULTANTS EFFECTIVELY *by Steve Markwell*

EXECUTIVE SUMMARY

- Management consulting is a fast-growing industry that can promise more than it can deliver.
- The boundaries are blurring between types of consulting and in the relationships between consultants and suppliers.
- To be effective the consultant's role needs to be carefully defined and managed.
- Successful projects foster a partnership between consultants and their clients.
- Unless organizations feel confident that they can implement and maintain changes after the consultants have left, the project has been a failure.
- The true test of the consultants' worth is whether or not the organization would work with them again—although it may not choose to.

INTRODUCTION

Management consulting is one of the fastest growing, and most controversial, sectors of the service economy. Over the past five years, members of the London-based Management Consultancies Association (MCA) have seen their fee income treble to reach nearly £4 billion in 2000, while estimates suggest that the total market for U.K. consulting is somewhere in the region of £7 billion.

Management consulting may be lucrative for its practitioners, who unlike lawyers and accountants aren't bound by professional regulations. This can prove a mixed blessing for its clients, some of whom would recognize their own experiences in the description of the management consultant as someone who takes your watch and then uses it to tell you the time.

In order to use management consultants effectively, organizations need to think carefully about what type of consultant they wish to employ and why. They also need to pay close attention to how the relationship with the consultancy is managed, from its inception through to delivery of the completed project.

THE FIVE TYPES OF MANAGEMENT CONSULTANT

1. GENERALIST

These are the largest consulting firms, offering a wide range of services from strategy consulting to human resources and IT consulting on a global basis. They cover all the main industry sectors and may also have expertise in highly specialized areas such as Web design or complex project management. Examples are well-known names such as Accenture, PricewaterhouseCoopers, and PA Consulting. Clients often establish long-term relationships with these consultancies, using different services at different points in their development.

2. STRATEGY CONSULTING

This category covers smaller firms such as McKinsey, Bain, and Arthur D. Little. They are more likely to focus on individual industry groups. Their specialty is offering strategic board-level advice to companies as a onetime project.

3. HUMAN RESOURCE CONSULTING

These firms provide specialist advice on issues ranging from salary and benefit reviews to an analysis of pension planning. They include organizations such as Hay Management Consultants, Watson Wyatt, and William Mercer.

4. IT CONSULTING

Many former systems development companies and hardware suppliers have enlarged the scope of their operations to include more mainstream consulting advice. Examples are IBM, CSC, and CMG.

5. E-CONSULTING

The recent boom in e-business has led traditional bricks-and-mortar companies and startups alike to seek help with e-strategies, design, and implementation. Established consultancies founded new e-divisions, while the consulting market had its own startups with the arrival of new-style operations such as Razorfish and Scient.

BLURRED BOUNDARIES

Large accounting firms have begun to separate out their audit and consulting practices, partly as the result of regulatory pressure from the Securities and Exchange Commission. Accenture has now finalized its divorce from Arthur Andersen, while KPMG has recently floated on the NASDAQ; and Ernst & Young's consulting arm has been sold to Cap Gemini. PricewaterhouseCoopers has been in talks with Hewlett Packard, among other options.

While such moves are creating a firewall between firms' traditional accounting activity and consulting, other developments are more murky. An increasing number of consulting firms are entering into reseller or alliance partnerships with IT vendors, surely placing a question mark over their ability to provide truly independent advice to clients.

WHEN TO USE A CONSULTANT

Management consulting is by no means a universal cure-all. Some problems respond more positively to consulting advice than others, for example, when a company

- requires skills or knowledge that are in short supply or unusual or are needed for only a short period
- wants to facilitate and stimulate internal debate, perhaps prior to making significant changes
- is looking for an objective viewpoint free from company traditions, internal politics, and attachment to previous recommendations
- is contemplating a move into new areas and is seeking an informed view of current best practice.

Alternatively, some situations are unlikely to be improved by the introduction of management consultants, notably when a company

- is looking simply for confirmation of an existing decision
- suspects it may need to take unpopular actions and wishes to deflect responsibility for the decision onto a consultant
- finds its decision making paralyzed because views at senior management level have become polarized.

"Consultants eventually leave, which makes them excellent scapegoats for major management blunders."

(Scott Adams)

CHOOSING THE RIGHT CONSULTANT

Companies need to select a consulting firm that has the skills necessary to tackle the particular assignment and that has a good cultural fit with the organization's own attitudes. Prospective consultancies should be asked to

- describe how they would undertake the assignment;
- provide details of the names, qualifications, and industry experience of the staff who will work on the project;
- describe similar projects they have undertaken, plus names of referees;
- provide a draft work program and timetable with an estimate of the fees and other chargeable expenses;
- describe their client liaison and management procedures.

For a successful project outcome the consultants and the client have to be able to work together in partnership, sharing their expertise and resources. The company must be prepared to provide any information or personnel the consultants request, and the consulting firm must provide the staff and resources to which it originally committed.

Client organizations and consulting firms also need to be clear about how they will be managing the levels of risk associated with projects. While consultants will wish to propose solutions that have a reasonable likelihood of success, some companies will be willing to consider more ambitious proposals provided they can contribute the competitive edge they are seeking.

There should be a project committee that meets regularly to review progress and highlight problem areas. The committee should include a senior person from the client, tasked with providing information and assistance and resolving any operational difficulties.

Best practice and signs of success

- Staff members are happy to volunteer information to the consultants because they feel their views are understood and respected.
- Project reviews are held frequently and there is good visibility of progress.
- Action points arising from review meetings are addressed.
- Employees feel they are learning new concepts and adding value to their core skills.
- Project milestones and new concepts are clearly explained.

Warning signs

- Staff members find the consultants' questions time-wasting, irrelevant, or distracting.
- Consultancy project members appear unfamiliar with the industry sector or type of problem.
- It's hard to establish what point the project has reached in its life cycle.
- Consultants seem unwilling to hold review meetings.
- Problems are not remedied quickly.
- Employees feel the consultants are learning more than they are.
- Reports are full of jargon and peppered with acronyms.

VALUE FOR MONEY

Ultimately the best way to get value for money is to ensure that the consultants' recommendations are implemented. If the client-consultancy partnership has been successful, much of the implementation may be conducted before the consultants leave the company. So long as staff fully subscribe to the new plans and identify with the underlying concepts, they'll be happy to take the necessary actions.

However, once the consultants have left there is still a danger that the benefits of their work may be eroded through neglect, misunderstanding, or a lack of controls. To avoid this it may be helpful to arrange follow-up visits from the consultants to review the implementation process.

MAKING IT HAPPEN ▸▸

- Choose the type of consulting you need before picking a particular firm.
- Proceed with consultants to gain missing skills or knowledge, stimulate internal debate, seek an objective viewpoint, or find help in entering new areas.
- Don't proceed in order to get confirmation of an existing decision, avoid responsibility for unpopular actions, or cope with a polarized senior management.
- Make any consultancy you approach prove that it has the necessary skills and will be a good cultural fit.
- Put one of your senior people on a project committee that meets regularly to review progress and highlight problem areas.
- Get value for money by ensuring that the consultants' recommendations are implemented—with much of it done before the consultants leave.

CONCLUSION

Probably the clearest evidence of a successful consulting assignment is the client's willingness to work with the same consultant again—although any new requirement should be evaluated as rigorously as the original project. While some companies do favor a one-stop-shopping approach to purchasing consulting services and look for a single provider who can supply all requirements, others select on "best-in-class" criteria. One-stop-shop fans say their approach reduces management complexity, avoids turf wars between competing consultancies, and opens the way to pricing discounts. Those who favor best-in-class selections say that it leads to better overall performance and a wider choice.

Working successfully with consultants is a matter of planning, not luck. The relationship between consultant and client must be formally defined to ensure a watertight contract; however, it must also be sufficiently flexible during the work itself to enable the job to be done effectively.

For More Information

Books:

McGonagle, John J., and Carolyn Vella. *How to Find and Use a Consultant in Your Company*. New York: John Wiley, 2001.

Directory of Management Consultants 2002. Fitzwilliam, NH: Kennedy Information, 2001.

Web Site:

www.imcusa.org is the Web site for the Institute of Management Consultants of the United States of America, a nonprofit, national professional association founded in 1968 to set standards of professionalism and ethics for the industry.

See also:

✓ **Using Management Consulting Services Effectively (pp. 526–27)**

Consulting Services/Management Consultants (pp. 1937–39)

"Some firms hardly dare change the wallpaper without consulting a guru." (Anonymous)

Making Loyalty Work
by John Frazer-Robinson

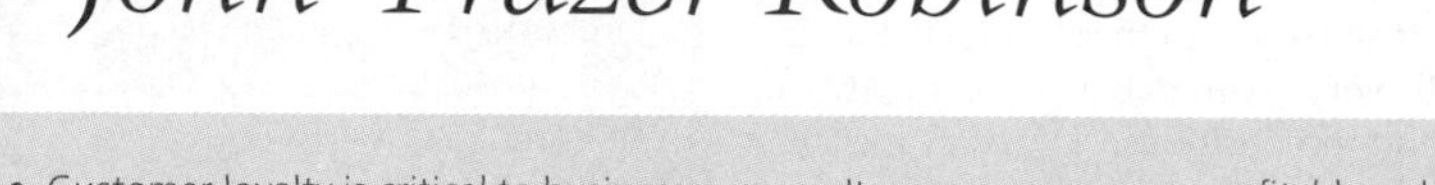

EXECUTIVE SUMMARY

- Customer loyalty is critical to business success. Its consequences are profitable, valuable, and of long-term benefit.
- Unlike customer satisfaction, customer loyalty measures customers' actual behavior. The company's goal is to gain—and keep—the maximum amount of each customer's available spend.
- This involves satisfying customers' emotionally based needs, explicitly recognizing their importance to you, and individualizing every contact with them. Managing the total relationship with customers is the business of everyone in the company.

Introduction

As the business world obsesses itself with customer relationship management, customer loyalty becomes a pivotal focus for those in sales, marketing, and service. It's right that professionals in these disciplines should have loyalty at the forefront of their minds, but it's unfortunate that customer loyalty is left predominantly to them, for just as customer loyalty is a measure of the business as a whole, it should be the concern of the whole business.

These fads come and go (take Total Quality Management as an example). And they generally depart from business-practice radar screens with mixed reputations and experiences. But customer loyalty will stand the test of time—and it will demolish the customer satisfactionists.

The fad of customer satisfaction was very annoying, leading as it did to a relentless barrage of mindless questionnaires attached to almost every customer experience. In truth measuring customer satisfaction is about as effective as dipping your toe in a pool.

Measuring customer loyalty is distinct from customer satisfaction in one important regard: it's not the measure of what people say, it's the measure of what they do. Activity—specifically, repurchasing more of the same or purchasing from across the product range—is an important ingredient of customer loyalty.

What Is Loyalty Made Of?

Customer satisfaction and loyalty do, however, have five strands in common:

- price
- product
- delivery
- service
- recognition

Each needs thought. Notice that price and product are based in logic, and that service and recognition are based in emotions. Delivery involves both logic and emotions. For the last 30 years, marketing has obsessed itself with the logical elements. Now, in order to concentrate on customer relationships, you have to get your business to become excellent at delivering the emotionally based issues. These should be focused on clearly and individually, as well as how they impact each other.

Price

While price is important, we very often overrate its importance—or worse still, we exacerbate it, simply eroding our own margins into the bargain. This doesn't stop you promoting on value. But get price in perspective. One of the long-term reasons for adopting a customer loyalty strategy is that it shrinks price as a customer priority and replaces it with value.

Product

There's no substitute for delivering a quality product. If the product fails, breaks down, doesn't last as long as it should, or is in any way imperfect, customers won't come back for more, nor will they feel inclined to buy other things from you. One of the stark realities of a customer-driven business is that there are no hiding places. Customer loyalty is built by exceeding customer expectations at every opportunity.

Delivery

If you're a traditional marketer or salesperson, this is what used to be called distribution. Delivery includes distribution, but it encompasses far more. Think of it as the delivery of the whole corporate promise to the customer—every facet of the way the customer feels, touches, and experiences your business.

The significant difference between distribution and delivery is that when you're in business to achieve a series of separate transactions, those transactions take place at the far point of your distribution channel. This is a product-driven process. It distributes your corporate product or service. When you're in business to achieve a managed customer relationship, then what we have is a means of delivering the corporate promise. Transaction marketing effectively switches on to standby between transactions; relationship marketing is permanently fully switched on 24 hours a day, seven days a week, ready for and alert to every customer interaction wherever, whenever, it touches the organization.

Service

In a customer-driven business service is paramount, which is why the whole business needs to be obsessive about a customer-loyalty strategy. Size and traditional structures inhibit larger businesses from delivering service. However, small businesses can profit from this. Smaller companies don't have nearly as many protocols as large ones and are much less set in their ways. If a customer wants something different or special, they will do it.

Does this mean a big business cannot become a customer-driven business? No! but it does mean it has more, and more serious, issues to address—management culture, organizational structure, human resources, to name but a few. In short, it has to retain the advantages of size and lose the disadvantages. Large corporations have to become as agile as their smaller competitors.

Recognition

Whether you're thinking about customer loyalty and becoming a customer-driven organization for business-to-business or business-to-consumer, the rudiments of developing and managing customer loyalty are the same. We all love to be recognized, not just for who we are, but for other things about us.

Some of the biggest contributions I've seen to the loyalty-building process have come from streaming consistent groups of employees to consistent groups of customers. The result is that the two groups

---

"With every decision we make, the last question we ask is what does the consumer think of this."

(Niall Fitzgerald)

become familiar and their relationships have a far greater chance of success. They know each other!

To boost customer loyalty, it is valuable to work on continuous improvement of the corporate promise, which means all five strands. It means adding to our previous logic-based experiences—product, price, and some delivery issues (essentially those to do with distribution)—and supplementing them with new, *soft-issue* experiences that are emotionally based—service, recognition, and those corporate delivery issues that surround the product at distribution and stay connected with customers throughout their relationship with you. Now we have to examine how we leave customers feeling.

To move from building satisfaction to creating loyalty, you must work on the emotional issues of the relationship. This will gain the most leverage and make the most difference. It is this recognition that exposes the fallacy in the vast majority of so-called loyalty programs.

Decide How to Measure Loyalty

Here's a list of the most popular means used to measure loyalty. If your business finds other ways, add or substitute them:

- customer satisfaction—what customers say
- recency—when did they last purchase?
- frequency—how often do they purchase?
- monetary value—how much do they spend?
- customer longevity—how long have they been with you?
- formal and informal (word-of-mouth) referral activity
- share of spend—how much to you and how much to competitors?
- willingness to repurchase

Share of Spend

Consciously work to build your share of the available and appropriate wallet for that family, household, or business and suddenly the whole picture is transformed. If most businesses had anything like 75% of the available spend of its customers, annual targets would be met in the first month! Most businesses neglect customers, and as a result customers place business elsewhere. When looking at how much they spend remember to look at current and recent transactions, but keep a cumulative figure, too.

Share of spend shares a characteristic with both customer satisfaction and customer loyalty. All three are comparatively fragile until you reach levels of approximately 70–80%. Up to that level, customers are still very vulnerable to competitive offers and propositions; lower than 50% there's no significant value. For businesses available spend is probably the budget for that product or service. For consumers it's their appropriate, affordable, or desired amount. Often this is a notional assessment, but you can easily ask the customer.

Consider How Far Will Customers Go to Help You

Another valuable piece of information is whether customers will do anything positive or negative to assist you, for example, whether they'll ever pass on positive or negative word of mouth or whether they're prepared to give solicited referrals or testimonials. You often find that customers are more open—more honest, in fact—about whether they would recommend you to someone else than they are about whether they would buy from you again.

Making It Happen ▸▸

- Measure repurchasing more or from across the product range as a key ingredient of customer loyalty.
- Continuously improve the corporate promise and what that means for price, product, delivery, service and recognition.
- Shape and direct your customer loyalty strategy to shrink price in the customer's priorities and replace it with value.
- Think of delivery as delivering the whole corporate promise in every way that customers feel, touch, and experience the business.
- Work on the emotional issues of the customer relationship to move from building satisfaction to creating loyalty.
- Seek to raise share of spend, customer satisfaction, and customer loyalty to solid levels of 70–80%.
- Consider how to move customers along the value chain, "cross-selling" and "upselling" products.
- Record information about customer intentions, and leverage this to provide a better, more efficient, and tailored service.
- Consider measuring a customer's lifetime value.

Conclusion

Understanding the external market and the internal strengths and weaknesses of the business are essential to making loyalty work. First, understanding clearly and monitoring continuously customer needs can enable the business to bond with individuals, retaining them as customers that are loyal and satisfied. Second, the realities of the market are constantly shifting, ranging from technological innovations to competitors' actions, and these need to be closely monitored and understood. It is worth considering the acquisition cost for each new customer, as well as the lifetime value of existing customers. This information may provide a useful target, as well as an indication of the significance of enhancing customer loyalty.

For More Information

Books:

Frazer-Robinson, John. *It's All About Customers.* Dover, NH: Kogan Page, 1999.
Reichheld, Frederick F. *The Loyalty Effect: The Hidden Force behind Growth, Profits, and Lasting Value.* Boston, MA: Harvard Business School Press, 2001.

Web Site:

www.crm-forum.com: an independent resource center for Customer Relationship Management.

See also:

☆ **Managing the Customer (pp. 65–66)**
☆ **Power Struggling and Power Sharing (pp. 95–96)**
☆ **Viewpoint: Patty Seybold (pp. 67–68)**
✔ **How to Get the Best from Loyalty Programs on the Web (p. 627)**
✔ **Increasing Lifetime Customer Value (pp. 676–77)**
Customer Relations/Customer Service (pp. 1948–50)

"Stop competing on price; compete on value. Deliver total consumer solutions, rather than just your piece of the solution."
(Faith Popcorn)

Corporate Social Responsibility: Are You Giving Back or Just Giving Away?

by Jim "Gus" Gustafson

Executive Summary

- Many 21st-century global corporations have become bigger and more powerful than the governments of the countries they do business in, and with this shift of resources necessarily comes a shift in responsibility to positively and proactively impact the world around them.
- Corporate social responsibility (CSR) is rapidly becoming an expectation of consumers worldwide that requires a fundamental and holistic change in the way that most businesses currently operate.
- Social and environmental accountability cannot be meaningless words on a dusty mission statement or an afterthought; they must be integrated into all aspects of everyday corporate life.
- Social responsibility and shareholder profitability don't need to be mutually exclusive propositions; if you give back, there's definitely a payback!

Introduction

Corporate social responsibility (CSR) is one of the most dynamic, complex, and challenging subjects that business leaders face today, and it is arguably one of the most critical. Fueled by the fall of communism and the enormous flow of capital, goods, and services across borders, business is now the most global of institutions. As governments around the world continue to withdraw from operating business enterprises, private-sector companies are increasingly under pressure to take a more active role in making the world a better place to live in, and not only for themselves.

In fact, several global corporations have become so enormous that they have overtaken many nation states as entities with the power and resources necessary to positively impact global change. Yet unlike governments that have been freely elected by and are accountable to a localized group of voters, these massive businesses answer primarily to their stockholders for most of their actions. This combination of enormous wealth and limited accountability makes today's companies extremely powerful.

All of this brings us to a central question. Why should these giant corporations—or any company, for that matter—whose primary reason for existence is to maximize profitability for their shareholders, be concerned with becoming good global citizens? The answer is, simply, that in addition to being the right thing to do, it is good business.

What Exactly Is CSR?

Although there is no single definition of CSR, the term generally refers to an ongoing commitment by business to behave ethically and to contribute to economic development while demonstrating respect for people, communities, society at large, and the environment. In short, CSR marries the concepts of global citizenship with environmental stewardship and sustainable development.

Good *corporate* social responsibility in practical terms means that organizational managers and leaders must:

- be sensitive to the issues that affect the lives of the people they live and work with;
- possess an understanding of the conditions in society that they could have a positive influence on;
- consider the social impact that their financial and business decisions have on a wide range of constituencies, stakeholders, and the environment;
- be conscientious about not only what the company produces, but also how it is produced.

Most important, being socially responsible means going beyond awareness of these social impacts by being willing to act on them.

The Case for CSR

The beginning of the 21st century has witnessed growing societal demand for increased corporate social responsibility and environmental accountability. No longer are companies obligated only to do no harm. Instead they're being called on to actively take responsibility for and positively engage with their communities, the global society, and the environment.

Consequently, today's business leaders are working hard to understand society's changing expectations of corporations in areas that were previously seen as the responsibility of government or nonprofit organizations. Since these leaders are also responsible for delivering profits to stockholders, their CSR efforts must also demonstrate a positive impact on the bottom line.

Many proactive and innovative companies have already discovered that a truly enterprise-wide commitment to CSR yields extremely positive results in both quantitative and qualitative terms. Several recent academic studies and case reports indicate that the value of CSR can be determined in a variety of ways, including:

- significant increase in sales
- increased ability to attract new customers
- improved customer retention rates
- reduced operating expenses
- more motivated and committed labor force
- enhanced brand image
- increased ability to attract talent
- enhanced cross-training of employees
- higher employee retention rates
- increased productivity
- reduced regulatory oversight
- improved quality of products and services

Furthermore, the Social Investment Forum reports that assets under management in portfolios that use screens linked to ethics, the environment, and corporate social responsibility are growing dramatically—thus allowing these socially responsible companies access to capital that might not otherwise have been available.

Global Consumers Care About CSR

Does the average consumer really care about CSR? The Millennium Poll on Corporate Social Responsibility, a study conducted in 1999 by Environics International, indicates an emphatic yes. Interviews with more than 25,000 average citizens of 23

"So long as commerce specializes in business methods which take no account of. . .social motives, so long may we expect strikes and sabotage. . ."

(Elton Mayo)

countries across six continents revealed three important points:

1. In forming impressions of companies, people around the world focus on corporate citizenship ahead of either brand reputation or financial factors.
2. Two out of three citizens want companies to go beyond their historical role of making a profit, paying taxes, employing people, and obeying all laws; they want companies to contribute to broader societal goals as well.
3. More than one in five consumers report either rewarding or punishing companies in the past year according to their social performance, and almost as many again considered doing so.

These findings reinforce what a number of companies have already found out the hard way: corporate reputation and sales are both at risk when customers have a negative perception of a company's social behavior.

MINI-CASE

Natura Cosmeticos (Brazil) is recognized as a leader in corporate social responsibility in Latin America for demonstrating commitment to the communities it operates in, creating an empowering workplace, and supporting human rights issues locally. The company focuses on creating partnerships with schools, government organizations, and nonprofits to enhance the quality of children's lives and the public educational systems in the regions it operates in. (**www.natura.com.br**)

BENCHMARKING CSR

Since the concept of social responsibility is as broad as it is complex, it is difficult to find any one standard or system that covers all aspects of CSR. There are, however, several emerging resources for companies to measure themselves against, including:

- **Keidanren Charter for Good Corporate Behavior.** Ten principles from the Japan Federation of Economic Organizations that articulate the kind of corporate behavior that they feel enriches and vitalizes society in the 21st century. (**www.keidanren.or.jp**)
- **Principles for Business.** Twelve principles from the Caux Round Table that aim to express a world standard of social responsibility against which business behavior can be measured. (**www.cauxroundtable.org**)
- **Principles for Global Corporate Responsibility.** Comprehensive benchmarking tool from the Interfaith Center on Corporate Responsibility to hold companies accountable to high standards of international human and labor rights conventions. (**www.iccr.org**)
- **Social Accountability 8000.** Standard created by Social Accountability International to enable organizations to develop voluntary standards of social accountability and to become accredited as such. (**www.cepaa.org**)
- **Sustainability Reporting Guidelines.** Common framework developed by the Global Reporting Initiative for reporting on the linked aspects of sustainability—economic, environmental, and social. (**www.globalreporting.org**)
- **Sustainability through the Market.** Seven keys from the World Business Council for Sustainable Development that offer companies a guide to implementing and benefiting from sustainable practices. (**www.wbcsd.org**)

MAKING IT HAPPEN ▸▸

To implement CSR, it is useful to consider the following:

- Clearly articulate a relevant CSR philosophy based on the scope and reach of your business, and incorporate it into your existing vision, mission, and guiding principles. Don't hesitate to use any of the benchmarking standards as a guideline or simply decide to adopt one in its entirety as your own.
- Create a social and organizational infrastructure that supports your CSR framework.
- Develop a reward and recognition system that officially supports socially responsible involvement and behavior throughout the organization.
- Appoint an executive leader as the CSR chief to be the cheerleader, watchdog, and subject expert for your initiatives.
- Make sure the entire senior management team embraces and supports the CSR program from the top down.
- Incorporate CSR into your long-range strategic planning to guarantee that it doesn't become just another flavor of the month.
- Constantly communicate the results of your ongoing efforts to all of your stakeholders and publicly celebrate your successes.
- Consider partnering with other corporations, community groups, or government organizations to multiply your impact and expand your reach.

And, most important,

- Use the same kind of energy, initiative, and commitment to develop, integrate, and implement your CSR program that you did to build your organization's other core competencies.

CONCLUSION

Today's global corporations have more capital and human resources at their disposal than many governments. As a result, business leaders are beginning to realize that this shift of power and resources also requires a shift in responsibility to becoming better global citizens. CSR is fast becoming a global expectation that is not only the right thing to do, but will also positively add to the bottom line.

For More Information

Book:

Tichy, Noel M., Andrew R. McGill, and Lynda St. Clair. *Corporate Global Citizenship: Doing Business in the Public Eye*. San Francisco, CA: Lexington, 1997.

Web Sites:

www.bsr.org, the Business for Social Responsibility site, is a worldwide information source on corporate social responsibility and provides a comprehensive links menu to other CSR resources.

www.environics.net/eil/esr, Environics International's Corporate Social Responsibility Monitor, builds on the results of the Millennium Poll and tracks citizens' changing expectations of companies with regard to social responsibility and accountability.

www.socialinvest.org, the Social Investment Forum site, offers comprehensive information, contacts, and resources on socially responsible investing.

See also:

- ☆ **Environmental Management (pp. 113–14)**
- ☆ **Viewpoint: Sumantra Ghoshal (pp. 190–91)**
- ☆ **Viewpoint: Noel M. Tichy (pp. 224–25)**
- ☆ **Viewpoint: Margaret J. Wheatley (pp. 273–74)**
- ✓ **Codes of Ethics (pp. 456–57)**
- **Social Responsibility of Management (pp. 2115–17)**

"In future, the most successful companies will be those who work hardest to make sure they are in tune with society."

(Mark Moody-Stuart)

FROM CRISIS MANAGEMENT TO CRISIS LEADERSHIP *by Ian I. Mitroff*

EXECUTIVE SUMMARY

- Some 20 years ago, the Tylenol poisonings prompted the field of crisis management. Although much has been learned since, many organizations still have not adopted proactive crisis-leadership programs.
- Until organizations do so, they will be crisis prone, susceptible to an ever-growing number of crises.

INTRODUCTION

Crisis management is no longer sufficient to respond to the crises today's organizations face. The difference between crisis management and crisis leadership is directional: crisis management is largely reactive, responding to crises after they have occurred. In contrast, crisis leadership is proactive, seeking to plan as carefully as possible before crises occur. Crisis management tends to consider individual crises in isolation, while crisis leadership considers the big picture–how individual crises interact.

Unless your organization takes a position of crisis leadership, you cannot respond properly when a crisis hits. Among the more important steps you can take now is anticipating the broadest possible range of potential crises. If your focus becomes too narrow you won't be able to respond appropriately when crises hit—and they will. If you aren't prepared to handle a crisis before it occurs, you won't be able to respond effectively when it arrives.

WHY EVERY ORGANIZATION NEEDS TO HAVE A CRISIS PORTFOLIO

Research demonstrates that crises fall into general categories or families (see table below). Within each general family, the specific crises share strong similarities. On the other hand, there are sharp differences between the general categories, families, or types of major crises.

This table (*Source: Pauchant and Mitrodd, 1992*) leads us to a number of key lessons that crisis-prepared organizations have learned.

Lesson 1: Prepare for at least one crisis in each of the families.

Research has demonstrated unequivocally how the best organizations plan and prepare for major crises. Most organizations consider only one or two crisis families, for example, natural disasters such as fires or earthquakes. This is undoubtedly a major focus because natural disasters not only occur with great regularity, but they're equally likely to strike all organizations. There's no blame associated with them as there is with other types of disaster, for example, workplace violence. Nonetheless, even earthquakes can attract some degree of human blame: humans are still charged with the responsibility of designing appropriate buildings that will withstand their worst effects and with designing appropriate recovery efforts for the survivors.

Lesson 2: It isn't sufficient to prepare only for industry-specific crises.

When organizations do broaden their preparations to cover crises other than natural disasters, more often than not it's to cover core or normal disasters specific to their industry. For instance, you rarely have to prod chemical companies to prepare for explosions and fires, which can easily arise from their day-to-day operating experience. No one has to prod fast-food companies to prepare for food contamination and poisoning, since such incidents are an ever-present threat in businesses that handle food. This kind of anticipation, while necessary, is too specific to count as complete preparation.

Lesson 3: Prepare for the simultaneous occurrence of multiple crises.

Major crises occur not only because of what an organization knows, anticipates, and plans for, but because of what it does not know and does not anticipate. Even if you've prepared for a particular type or form of crisis, major crises will still occur, because new environmental factors are constantly emerging to give a new wrinkle to old forms. It's not only the crises that you've planned and prepared for that constitute a threat–crises you've never even thought about may be even more serious.

Lesson 4: The purpose of definitions is to guide, not predict.

It isn't possible to give a precise definition of a crisis, because it isn't possible to predict

MAJOR CRISIS TYPES/RISKS

Economic	Informational	Physical (loss of key plants and facilities)	Human resources	Reputational	Psychopathic acts	Natural disasters
Labor strikes	Loss of proprietary and confidential information	Loss of key equipment, plants, and material supplies	Loss of key executives	Slander gossip	Product tampering	Earthquakes
Labor unrest	False information	Breakdown of key equipment, plants, etc.	Loss of key personnel	Sick jokes	Kidnapping	Fires
Labor shortage	Tampering with computer records	Loss of key facilities	Rise in absenteeism	Rumors	Hostage taking	Floods
Major decline in stock price and price fluctuations	Loss of key computer information relating to customers, suppliers, etc.	Major plant disruptions	Rise in vandalism and accidents	Damage to corporate reputation	Terrorism	Explosions
Market crash	Y2K		Workplace violence	Tampering with corporate logos	Workplace violence	Typhoons
Decline in major earnings						Hurricanes

"You need to plan the way a fire department plans." (Andrew Grove)

with exact certainty how a crisis will occur, when, and why. Nonetheless, as a guiding definition, a crisis is any adverse event that affects or has the potential to affect the *whole* of an organization. If something affects only a small, isolated part of an organization, it may not be a major crisis. In order for a problem to be judged a crisis, it must exact a major toll on human lives, property, financial earnings, the reputation, and the general health and well-being of an organization. Most often, all of these suffer damage simultaneously. A major crisis is something that *cannot be completely contained within the walls of an organization.* A single rogue trader at Barron's Bank had the potential to destroy the entire organization. The Firestone-Ford tire crisis also demonstrates this organizational ripple effect.

Lesson 5: Every type of crisis can happen to every organization.

Every organization needs to plan for the occurrence of at least one crisis in each family, because each type could actually happen. Further, you must consider all the types broadly and not literally. Consider, for instance, product tampering, which can impact a company in multiple ways.

Lesson 6: No type of crisis should be taken literally.

Product tampering doesn't apply only to food or to pharmaceutical companies. Any organization can be the victim of some form of product tampering. Computers, for example, are integral to every organization, yet the true value of computers is not the cost of the hardware or software: it's the information they contain about customers and other key stakeholders. If someone were to gain access and tamper with these records the company's products and services could be seriously affected. Consider the French publisher Larousse. The French are avid eaters of mushrooms; at times they search the forests with Larousse encyclopedias at their sides. One article in the encyclopedia has two facing pages of illustrations, one showing mushrooms that are safe to eat, the other those that are unsafe. Intentionally or not, the labels on the two pages were once reversed. The moral is clear: you ignore any or all of the types of major crisis at your peril.

Lesson 7: Tampering is the most generic form or type of all crises.

Tampering—significantly altering the properties of information or of an object, person, product, etc.—is the most important crisis type. Tampering essentially converts properties that are acceptable and safe into properties that are unacceptable or dangerous, thus threatening everything connected with an organization.

Lesson 8: No crisis ever happens in the precise way you plan for it, so it's not crisis planning per se that's important, it's thinking about the unthinkable.

Fortunately you don't have to prepare for every specific type of crisis within each of the families. If this were required, then crisis leadership would be overwhelming. It's acceptable to limit your preparations to one or more types of crisis within each of the families. Why? If a crisis seldom happens exactly according to plan, the critical thing is doing your best to think about the unthinkable. This exercise makes you better able to think on your feet when a crisis does hit, and hence to recover faster without being paralyzed. If the specific types of crises within a particular family share strong similarities, giving serious consideration to each of the families is the most helpful kind of preparation. It's still important to prepare for a broader and wider range of crises, although to start on the difficult road of crisis leadership it's not necessary to prepare for everything simultaneously. In fact, trying to prepare at once for every eventuality might well lead you to conclude that the task is overwhelming and hopeless—it's not.

Lesson 9: Every crisis is capable of being both the cause and the effect of any other crisis.

The best organizations don't prepare for a single crisis, they attempt to prepare for the simultaneous occurrence of multiple crises. Organizations that are well prepared study past crises, looking for patterns and interconnections. They generate visual maps to understand better how crises unfold over time and how they are interrelated. In today's world, no individual crisis ever happens in isolation and independently of any other crisis. You need to consider the potential impact of every crisis in your organization's crisis portfolio on every other crisis.

Lesson 10: Crisis leadership is systemic.

Like total quality management or environmentalism, if crisis leadership is not undertaken systemically, it is basically not being done, let alone being done well.

MAKING IT HAPPEN ▸▸

- Assemble and train a cross-functional, cross-divisional crisis team.
- Poll individual members of the team about the crises they can envision because of their distinct vantage points.
- Produce at least three or four general maps or big pictures showing how each of the individual crises that the various team members envision might interact so as to set off a chain reaction.
- Referring to the overall maps, determine what pieces of data can be used as early warning signals to announce the beginning stages of each individual crisis and indicate the likelihood that it will set off a chain reaction of other crises.

For More Information

Book:

Mitroff, Ian I., et al. *Essential Guide to Managing Corporate Crises: A Step-by-step Handbook to Surviving Major Catastrophes*. New York: Oxford University Press, 1997.

Web Sites:

www.compcrisis.com/company.html
www.usc.edu/dept/education/globaled/irl/irlcd8.html

See also:

☆ **Managing Today's Angry Workforce (pp. 35–36)**
☆ **Preventing Corporate Systems from Holding You Back (pp. 177–78)**
☆ **Viewpoint: Margaret J. Wheatley (pp. 273–74)**
✔ **Disaster Planning (pp. 492–93)**
Steve Jobs (pp. 1100–01)
Contingency, Crisis, Disaster Management (pp. 1939–41)

Benchmarking *by Paul Spenley*

EXECUTIVE SUMMARY

Understanding the scope and power of benchmarking is a strategic imperative in any business, as it allows existing businesses to defend their position, as well as to attack new business opportunities. Benchmarking is used at a number of levels.

- **Strategic benchmarking.** Strategic action teams use benchmarking to drive continuous improvement and refine the overall business strategy.
- **Competitive benchmarking.** For each major business driver, the competitive position is measured against the competition.
- **Customer benchmarking.** Customer perception is all there is—customers never buy just a product. Customer benchmarking enables a business to understand the views of their customers about the organization, relative to the competition.
- **Financial benchmarking.** Key performance measures and the establishment of rankings for each measure. Return on net assets (RONA) identifies which business drivers will deliver the greatest return on the investment needed.
- **Best practice benchmarking.** The minimum process to meet the business driver requirements for time and cost to meet the required outputs.

Introduction

Benchmarking is a management technique that is concerned with establishing performance measures for an organization, so that it can analyze its efficiency and compare itself to other, usually competing, businesses—notably, leading firms in the industry. The five benchmarking approaches can either be employed independently or together, and this section outlines how they can be used to best effect.

Strategic Benchmarking

Benchmarking is the practice of measuring and comparing key aspects of your organization relative to customer expectations. Ideally benchmarking achieves

- knowledge of competitive position
- knowledge of best practice
- a set of targets to achieve competitive advantage
- a customer-focused quality culture

To succeed, the operational and strategic team agrees on a clear mission statement for the business in terms of products and markets. This is done for the immediate one-year period and then for a longer, usually three-year, period. Often, the longer period is considerably more difficult to forecast. However, it is essential to identify the market requirements and product mix for the longer-term future, not just for next year.

Preparing a fishbone diagram is a helpful technique, as it provides a cause-and-effect analysis, breaking down the mission statement by identifying the key business drivers in a clear and concise manner. Figure 1 gives an example of a fishbone diagram used to identify the key business drivers of a global electronics company.

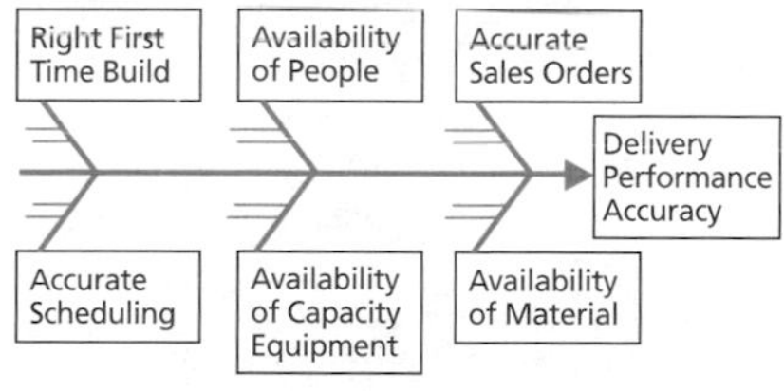

Competitive Benchmarking

For each major business driver, the firm's actual position is determined in measurable parameters, relative to the competition.

The key is to establish actual and target measures for each business driver. This establishes the degree of difficulty for the operational team in delivering all the customer benchmark elements contained within the business drivers.

The competitive benchmark matrix below provides an outline for this approach. The final, best practice column can include valuable information and ideas from competitors. After all, why reinvent the wheel when the wheel is best?

Performance Measure	Actual	Target	Competitor A (Market Leader)	Competitor B (Rising Star)	Competitor C	Best Practice

Customer Benchmarking

Total Product Concept

The total product concept is not new. It's based on the principle that customers never buy simply a product itself, but instead they buy a set of tangible and intangible attributes that they perceive as delivering value.

The total product concept tool is used for each product to identify clearly the things the organization needs to be good at with regard to product, service, added value, and "delight factors" (meaning those factors that really wow customers and help to build a strong customer relationship).

The most consistent business drivers are

- product quality
- delivery performance accuracy
- time to market
- response time to orders
- response time to inquiries, both technical and commercial
- accuracy and timeliness of information

The business drivers need to be reviewed by the strategic and operational teams for each product, then collated into a set of six dimensions such as those identified above.

Most managers realize that the more competitive the market, the more important the level of customer satisfaction. The message is clear. it is absolutely critical for a company to excel in defining its target customers and in delivering a product or service that completely meets their needs.

Customer Surveys As a Part of Benchmarking

The old-fashioned idea that you can measure customer satisfaction by unsolicited customer surveys often does more harm than good, and can actually alienate customers who value a relationship (at whatever level) with the supplier.

The best practice is the 3M top box system, which asks three questions:

1. Are you totally satisfied? If not why not?
2. Would you buy from us again? If not why not?
3. Would you recommend us? If not why not?

"Success should not be measured by earnings per share, but by market share." (Bruce Henderson)

The third question is the most important when developing a business—the fact is that word of mouth is the most effective means of persuading new customers to buy from you.

The levels of satisfaction among targeted customers are a good benchmarking indicator of the level of quality of the products and services they're receiving. Nevertheless, the way to raise the level of customer satisfaction from neutral to satisfied or satisfied to completely satisfied is not simply a matter of doing a better job of delivering the same value or experience that the company is currently delivering.

Comb Charts

Comb charts reconcile your customers' view of your performance with your own. These benchmark what is important to the customer and your relative performance against those expectations and against the competition. The information, which you have gathered, needs to be presented in a format that can easily be used to:

- contrast your performance with customers' requirements;
- compare one customer's responses with another;
- compare your strengths with those of the competition.

Comb charts are based on information gathered from surveys requiring your customers to rank areas of requirement in order of importance.

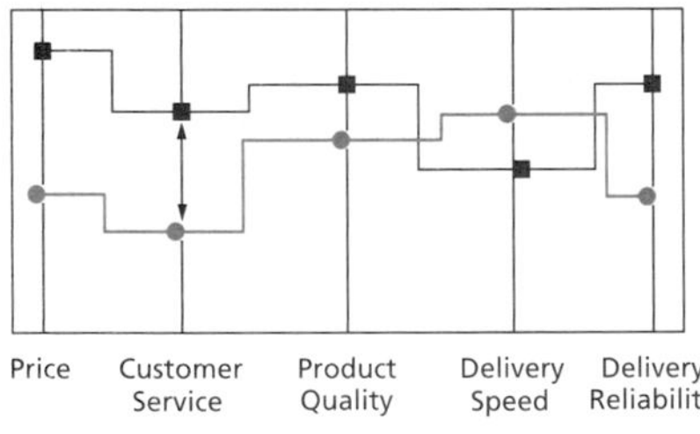

For each benchmark parameter ask the customer:

1. How important is this to you?
2. How do we measure up to your requirement?
3. Who is the best of your current suppliers?

Financial Benchmarking

Using the RONA model it is possible to identify which business drivers will deliver the greatest return on investment. For example, the effect on inventory turns, reductions in WIP (work-in-progress), and finished goods inventory can be calculated to achieve an ongoing financial saving.

Return on Net Assets (RONA)

It is necessary for the strategic and operational teams to establish the RONA plan together. This is crucial in agreeing on realistic performance improvements.

The process of working through the RONA analysis provides a deeper appreciation of the connections between the variables and a better idea of the most appropriate course of action. Reliable financial information is, of course, notoriously difficult to find: what matters here is understanding what seem to be the financial drivers of the industry in general and competitors in particular, and then setting realistic benchmarks and plans to achieve these.

Best Practice Benchmarking

Time and cost are, typically, the most significant drivers of business performance; benchmarking these factors can lead to significant operational improvements in efficiency and performance. The key task is to map out the minimum process required to deliver the product to the customer, and this can be achieved by assessing performance, setting targets, and following through on plans and initiatives focusing on improving the

- cost of waste (errors)
- cost of conformance (prevention)
- minimum process (added value)

Making It Happen ▸▸

The senior management team needs to structure benchmarking activities in such a way that they become a continuous process driving improvement and helping to build a sustainable business. For benchmarking to succeed:

1. The leadership of the organization should establish teams to lead the process, learning and acting on the results:
   - The **strategic action team** is responsible for the strategic direction of the business and needs to review this at monthly meetings
   - The **customer benchmarking team** should be cross-divisional and multilevel and include people at the sharp end of customer contact
   - The **business process teams** are the teams within the company that should have improvement targets.
2. Comprehensive and accurate information on competing businesses needs to be available.
3. The firm's internal auditing procedures need to be effective. First, the business needs to understand how they operate in relation to the organizations that are being benchmarked. Second, the organization needs to be able to understand how effective any changes have been.
4. The benchmarks—or performance measures—that are established need to be based on industry best practice. These may differ from the targets set by the firm's business units or departments which may be easily attainable or simply irrelevant. However, the benchmarks should directly relate to the company's overall business plans.
5. Finally, the benchmarks that are established must be flexible and able to change with the external environment.

Conclusion

Benchmarking is a fundamental requirement in building a sustainable business, particularly as it allows no room for complacency or "not-invented-here" thinking. The significance and value of benchmarking lies in the fact that building and sustaining a successful business is a battle to keep ahead of the competition. This is only achieved through constant vigilance and a policy from the top of continuous improvement at all levels of the company—and best practice benchmarking provides the framework for this to happen.

For More Information

Book and Journal Article:

Jones, Thomas O., and W. Earl Sasser. "Why Satisfied Customers Defect." *Harvard Business Review* (January 1995).

Kaplan, Robert S., and David P. Norton. *The Balanced Scorecard: Translating Strategy into Action*. Boston, MA: Harvard Business School Press, 1996.

See also:

☆ **The Balanced Scorecard (pp. 303–04)**
☆ **New Yardsticks for Performance and Productivity in an E-world (pp. 285–86)**
✔ **A Program for Benchmarking (pp. 488–89)**
✔ **Implementing the Balanced Scorecard (pp. 510–11)**
Benchmarking (pp. 1911–13)

"Management productivity is a more appropriate term than labor productivity. Improved productivity means less human sweat, not more." (Henry Ford)

MATCHING PAY TO ACHIEVEMENT
by Peter Brown

EXECUTIVE SUMMARY

- As the war for talent intensifies, the need to match pay to achievement is now greater than ever.
- The history of performance-related pay is variable, and even today, the efforts of many public sector service workers are not involved in performance-related bonuses. This trend is set to change.
- Performance-related pay and bonus schemes may vary between senior managers and other levels.
- There are several critical factors that determine the success, failure, or overall effectiveness of performance-related schemes, and these are reviewed in this section.

INTRODUCTION

David Ulrich talks about a workplace phenomenon all-too-familiar to anyone who's managed in today's corporate setting. He recalls one occasion [p. 140] when, upon meeting a new corporate group, he led a vigorous discussion about the company vision, its new products, reducing cycle times, and serving customers. To which, he says, one of the participants remarked quietly, "This is all well and good, but what's in it for me?" Matching pay to performance is a well-known issue in today's work world. But when did the trend begin?

The concept of matching reward to achievement took root in the 1960s as society changed due, particularly in the United Kingdom, to a much higher percentage of graduate workers and the outstanding success of young performers in areas such as sport and music, where rewards started to rise dramatically.

As the West moved from a manufacturing to a service-oriented society, the need to differentiate between average and outstanding performers became very apparent to employers in the professional, entertainment and general service industries. This led to the concept of the "bonus award" linked to the annual salary review.

Some of the old-fashioned systems, like Christmas bonuses that were in no way linked to personal performance and may have been paid in terms of a Christmas hamper or turkey, started to go and companies introduced an annual, often profit-sharing, bonus which, in a good year, might pay a bonus of between 5% and 10% of all employees' annual salary.

It is fair to say that the concept of trying to match pay to achievement arrived with Margaret Thatcher in 1970 in the United Kingdom as her government determined to free the United Kingdom from the union-dominated collective culture of the past and enthusiastically embraced tax systems to encourage a culture where increased productivity of whatever sort could be awarded with significant, after-tax rewards.

Since 1980, the private sector in the English-speaking democracies, led by the United States, has been moved towards altering pay systems to encourage pay for achievement concepts. In the United States, it is now common for senior executives in publicly quoted companies to have only 20% of their remuneration as salary, with the rest being paid out in performance options, cash bonuses, and preference or restricted shares which can only be encashed if certain predetermined profit or other targets are reached. The United Kingdom has followed this trend; the belief that this type of pay is likely to enhance the success of the nation as a whole has brought changes in tax policies and encouraged the concepts of performance-related pay of all varieties. Australia has also followed the trend, but the countries of the EU have been much slower to adopt this entrepreneurial culture. Most European countries are more socialist than the United Kingdom, and their philosophies of equality and redistribution have not encouraged high bonuses for those who are often already quite well paid. However, under pressure from multinational companies and the international employment environments, their resistance to the trend is breaking down and you now find that in France, probably the most recalcitrant of the European nations, even the managers in the semi-nationalized utilities are working within systems that allow them to earn a significant percentage of their pay via a performance element, often based upon options or shares in the companies for which they work.

The one area in which performance-related pay is still of relatively small importance is government service in all countries, including the United States and the United Kingdom. However, public employees including the armed services, like the police or fire brigade, increasingly use performance-related pay systems in countries like the United States and some of the more advanced Asian economies, and it is only a question of time before this concept spreads across most EU public sector areas.

In the United Kingdom, we have seen repeated attempts by the civil service to introduce performance-related pay. However, to date, their concept of how much of a total package should be related to performance—5–10%—is too small to influence the behavior of the people at whom it is targeted.

RULES FOR MATCHING PAY TO ACHIEVEMENT

"In the just-in-time workplace," says Bruce Tulgan [p.293], "you can't expect people to wait around to be rewarded once they've delivered. . .Managers need to reward desired performance consistently and with speed and creativity." This concept seems to be accepted by more organizations each day, but what are the rules for actually implementing such an ideal?

We now have about 20 years' experience of matching incentive pay to expected outcomes from different groups of staff, and it is fairly clear that certain rules need to be followed if the scheme is going to be successful. They are as follows.

1. **The relevance of the scheme to the individual.** The performance of the unit upon which the bonus is based must be one to which the individual can relate and whose output they feel they can influence. Bonuses based on the performance of a holding company make little impact on an individual working in one of the smaller subsidiaries.

   If you want to make staff feel they can actually benefit from a performance bonus culture, the targets they need to achieve must be broken down into departmental, divisional, or unit perform-

"Which of us. . .is to do the hard and dirty work for the rest—and for what pay? who is to do the pleasant and clean work, and for what pay?" (John Ruskin)

ance triggers where they can see that their personal input can make a difference.

2. **The scale and value of the performance-related element.** The scale of any performance-related pay needs to be significant in the eyes of the beneficiaries if it is going to affect the way they do their job. Performance-related pay will not necessarily make people work harder, but it will make them work in a more targeted way to deliver the outcomes which the bonus is designed to reward.

   It is generally understood that if you want to get individuals to align their personal targets with the organization's preferred objectives, you need to offer at least 10%, possibly 20%, of their salary as a potential bonus for achieving, or at least 90% achieving, these objectives.

3. **The reasonableness of the scheme—and in particular, the time frame.** For senior executives, increasingly you need to structure bonus schemes that pay out over time, as it is very difficult to assess their collective performance over a single 12-month period. For this reason, most consultants have been working on accumulator systems, option plans, or other approaches, whereby measurement of the increasing productivity or profit delivered is made over a rolling three-year period. Bonuses are then paid at intervals over time, with a percentage being banked on behalf of an individual rather than paid out in total; it is only on delivery of the three-year plan that the team involved gets the full bonus award to which it is entitled.

4. **The form of the performance-related bonus.** Because of taxation policy in most sophisticated countries and the need to try and ensure that senior executives feel they are members of the company, most private sector organizations prefer to pay part of their bonuses in shares or options in the company itself. These schemes, variously referred to as share option, restricted shares, preferred shares, share save schemes, or employee share owning plans, all have the same objective: to pay out a percentage of bonuses in the form of company stock so that the individuals feel part of the organization for which they work.

   Because of taxation rules in the United Kingdom, most people find it necessary to sell their shares the moment they are issued. The tax system is extremely detrimental to someone who takes up shares and holds them, rather than selling immediately, as they have to pay tax on any profit when they are issued.

5. **The need to make schemes inclusive, avoiding divisiveness.** One of the problems with incentive payment schemes is that many support staff who work in a cost rather than a profit center are left out of the scheme architecture. This can often lead to breakdowns in support units and communications behind the high-profile sales or dealing teams. It is therefore critically important to make performance-related pay inclusive, despite the difficulty of setting targets for administration and technical staff. If this doesn't happen, breakdowns will occur in vital, but relatively mundane, operations that have been overstretched by demands put on them by bonus-driven sales.

"Changing how a workforce is rewarded is difficult and not for the faint of heart," say Patricia Zingheim and Jay Schuster, who add that "Pay is a way of gaining understanding, acceptance, and commitment of what people can do to help make a company a success." For this and many other reasons, there seems no stopping the increasing use of performance-related pay in sophisticated democratic societies. To date, it is hard to prove just how effective it has been, but perceived wisdom is that most organizations using performance-related pay have in fact achieved higher levels of output than they would otherwise have attained. At the same time, this approach means that if there is a general downturn in demand, an organization is not necessarily saddled with very high fixed salary costs.

Making It Happen ▸▸

- Ensure that a bonus scheme is supported by the organization. The first step is for senior managers and the leaders of the organization to recognize that achievement will be rewarded in a way that will be valued by the employees.
- Relate the scheme directly to individual and team actions. The bonus needs not only to be meaningful, but achievable, and in this way affecting people's behaviors.
- The scheme can be imaginative, driving whatever behaviors are identified as priorities, but they must always be reasonable and fair.
- The type of bonus is significant, and it may be the case that external factors (such as taxation) reduce the benefit and value.
- Schemes must be inclusive: if people are excluded then everyone's performance can ultimately suffer.

Conclusion

We expect performance-related pay to increase in importance, though not at the rate it has over the past 20 years, and to spread into public sector areas such as health, education, social services, and the prison service. It is apparent that if the government cannot offer performance-related pay and does not outsource or privatize state services to organizations that use this approach, the public sector will have increasing difficulty in recruiting and retaining staff against private sector employers using increasingly sophisticated incentive and reward systems. It seems inevitable, therefore, that sophisticated industrial economies will move to systems in which almost everybody, excluding priests, judges, and politicians, is partially remunerated via performance-related pay.

For More Information

Books:

Berger, Lance A. *The Compensation Handbook*. New York: McGraw-Hill, 1999.

Martocchio, Joseph J. *Strategic Compensation: A Human Resource Management Approach*. Upper Saddle River, NJ: Prentice Hall, 2000.

Tulgan, Bruce. Interview in *Business Minds*. Upper Saddle River, NJ: FT/Prentice Hall (Pearson Education Limited), 2002.

Ulrich, Dave. *Human Resource Champions: The Next Agenda for Adding Value and Delivering Results*. Boston, MA: Harvard Business School Press, 1997.

Zingheim, Patricia K., and Jay R. Schuster. *Pay People Right: Breakthrough Reward Strategies to Create Great Companies*. San Francisco, CA: Jossey-Bass, 2000.

See also:

☆ **Human Capital (pp. 115–16)**
☆ **Making Performance Appraisals a Win-win Experience (pp. 23–24)**
✓ **Setting Up a Performance-related Pay Scheme (pp. 438–39)**
Remuneration (pp. 2103–05)

"The progress of human society consists [in] the better and better apportioning of wages to work."
(Thomas Carlyle)

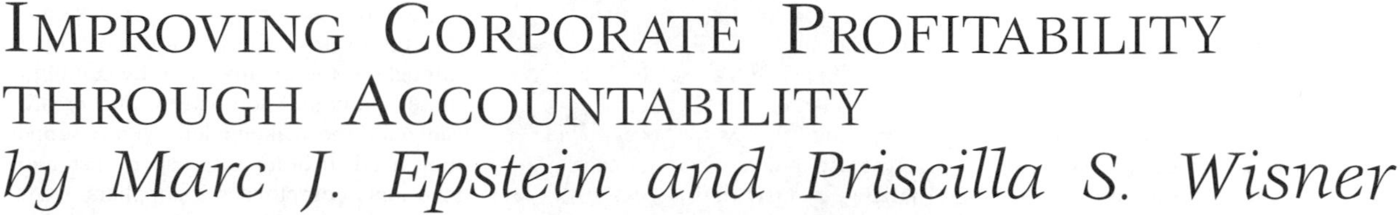

Improving Corporate Profitability through Accountability

by Marc J. Epstein and Priscilla S. Wisner

EXECUTIVE SUMMARY

- Traditional measures of performance are of limited use to modern businesses, being rooted in evaluating past performance. They are a poor guide to true value, often missing the key factors promoting long-term worth.
- It is essential to include the leading financial and non-financial indicators of performance driving long-term value. This provides broader and more sophisticated information that is better placed to highlight future trends.
- By effectively managing and communicating a broader set of performance measures, organizations enjoy improved financial performance, reduced uncertainty and better relationships with shareholders and analysts.
- Full accountability and disclosure combined with improved measures and new systems to drive the process throughout the organization, creates greater value for stakeholders, promoting future success.

Introduction

Improved governance requires the right employees, the right culture and values, and the right systems, information, and decision making. Unfortunately, most organizations are attempting to steer their information-age businesses using industrial-age measurements. Managers have struggled for decades with accounting systems that fail to measure many of the variables that drive long-term value. The historical lagging indicators of performance that are commonly used by accountants are of limited value in determining the value of businesses for external stakeholders, and are of little use in guiding the business internally. Financial data on profitability and return on investment are valuable measures of corporate performance, but they are lagging indicators that measure past performance. A broader set of financial measures is necessary (for example, measurement of intangible assets such as intellectual capital and research-and-development value), in addition to an expanded set relating to customers, internal processes, and organizational measures.

The metrics must include the *leading* financial and nonfinancial indicators of performance that are the drivers and predictors of future financial performance. For example, fines and penalties may be a leading indicator of corporate reputation, employee turnover is a leading measure of future recruitment and training costs, and product quality is a leading measure of customer satisfaction, which in turn is a leading measure of market share.

Improved Internal and External Reporting

Just as companies expand their performance measurement parameters, they must also expand their performance reporting models. Employees, shareholders, financial analysts, activists, customers, suppliers, government regulators, and others increasingly demand detailed information about corporate activities, and the Internet has made the dissemination of that information easier and faster. No longer can managers claim they don't have the information. The data are easy to collect, and it's essential to have broader and more forward-looking information to effectively manage the diverse issues that managers now confront daily. Managers should collect this broader array of information on activities and impacts both inside and outside the company and select a set of data to provide adequate disclosure to their various stakeholders. External stakeholders need a broader set of information to effectively evaluate corporate performance, and voluntary disclosure of this information is critical for corporate accountability. This accountability, both inside and outside the firm, through an effective corporate communications strategy, is an essential element of effective and responsible corporate governance.

Proactively managing external disclosures should be a fundamental part of corporate communications strategy. By externally disclosing a more comprehensive set of measures, company executives are seizing the initiative to describe the company's strategy, set expectations, increase transparency, and ensure goal alignment between the company and a broad set of stakeholders. Disclosing performance measures allows investors and other stakeholders to view the company through the eyes of management. A clear, comprehensive communications strategy is highly valued by shareholders and analysts alike.

Mini-cases

The *Campbell Soup Company* that has continually improved corporate governance.

Changes undertaken in the early 1990s required a majority of directors to come from outside the organization. All directors must stand for election every year and must own at least 6,000 shares of stock within three years of election. Among other provisions, interlocking directorships are not allowed and insiders are banned from certain key committees.

In 1995, the board began a rotating yearly performance evaluation of directors, board committees, and the board as a whole.

In 2000, the board approved a new director compensation program to closely link director compensation to the creation of shareholder value; only 20% is paid in cash (tied to attendance at meetings). The full set of Campbell Soup's governance standards and current performance review are disclosed in the annual proxy statement to shareholders.

The *Cooperative Bank*, based in the United Kingdom and with 4,000 employees, has won numerous awards for the high degree of transparency and accountability the company has exhibited. The bank has identified seven partners in its quest for corporate value: shareholders, customers, staff and their families, suppliers, local communities, national and international society at large, and past and future generations of co-operators. The company surveys all these stakeholder groups to determine the critical elements in creating value for each, and performance targets are set on the basis of

"We are responsible for actions performed in response to circumstances for which we are not responsible."

(Allan Massie)

this information. In 2000, 68 targets were established. The Cooperative Bank 2000 Partnership Report states that 47 targets were fully achieved, acceptable progress was made on 11, and 10 were not achieved. The bank reports progress on each target, providing data and management commentary, and establishes targets for the coming year. During 2000, the Cooperative Bank significantly improved ethical and ecological performance while achieving strong profitability.

MAKING IT HAPPEN ▸▸

The rewards from building the accountable organization are much like those from building the quality organization—the more committed the managers and workers and the better integrated the concept with company line operations, the greater the benefit. As a first step, managers must build accountable systems and practices within the company. Then they can build bridges to the outside. As they move toward full accountability—well-governed, measured, managed, and publicly responsive—they will position themselves to reap many benefits:

- Improving decision making: the accountable organization generates a wealth of information on performance, which in turn informs decision making with facts, not intuition. People inside and outside the company can make more effective decisions to further company strategy and goals.
- Accelerating learning: the accountable organization installs feedback systems that yield rapid-fire learning from people both across and outside the company. The company with the most feedback loops—internal and external—is the most successful.
- Empowering people: the accountable organization thins the ranks of middle managers that distill and convey information and apportions new decision-making authority to the front lines. As management articulates what it wants with concrete quantitative measures, workers have unmistakable guidance as they figure out how to deliver it.
- Communicating the story: the accountable organization delivers its story of value with credible financial and nonfinancial numbers. As senior managers report more numbers externally, exposing performance transparently, shareholders and analysts have less reason to undervalue their stock.
- Executing strategy: the accountable organization communicates each strategy and tactic with specific measures that align direction in ways that written objectives cannot. The hard measures then give managers a month-to-month reading on whether the strategy is working.
- Inspiring loyalty: the accountable organization markets its value on a basis of reliable performance measures. The no-smoke-and-mirrors approach spurs cooperation and inspires the loyalty of investors, customers, suppliers, employees, business partners, and communities.

CONCLUSION

Once a company has decided to improve corporate governance, measure a broader set of indicators of past and future success, and report internally and externally, managers must develop systems to drive these decisions through the organization. Leading companies are developing integrated, closed-loop planning, budgeting, and feedback systems to help align strategy implementation with corporate performance. While leadership at the top is critical, buy-in at the shop floor is essential for the success of any system implementation. Metrics must be linked to strategy and must be consistent throughout the organization. Companies are increasingly stating a desire to become more customer focused, yet many are still basing employee rewards on meeting revenue and profit goals. If companies expect employees to be more customer focused or more socially or environmentally responsible, part of overall performance evaluations and rewards should be on customer focus or social responsibility.

Accountable managers encourage not only continuous judgment, but continuous improvement. They insist that everyone in the organization participate in decision making. They implement a culture of constant learning and insist on building learning organizations. Accountable managers communicate constantly, setting a tone of forthright feedback and transparency.

Full accountability comes only when a company combines a strong governance structure, improved and broad measurement of relevant performance impacts, timely and full internal and external reporting, and comprehensive management systems to drive the accountability model throughout the organization. By combining these elements companies are creating value for the stakeholders whose support they need in order to prosper—customers, investors, employees, suppliers, communities, the public, regulators, and other government officials.

For More Information

Books:

Epstein, Marc J., and Bill Birchard. *Counting What Counts: Turning Corporate Accountability to Competitive Advantage*. Cambridge, MA: Perseus, 2000.

Monks, Robert A.G. *The Emperor's Nightingale: Restoring the Integrity of the Corporation in the Age of Shareholder Activism*. Cambridge, MA: Perseus, 1999.

Ward, Ralph D. *Improving Corporate Boards: The Boardroom Insider Guidebook*. New York: John Wiley, 2000.

Web Sites:

www.brt.org: The Business Roundtable is an association of C.E.O.s advocating policies that encourage economic growth and a dynamic global economy.

www.corpgov.net: The Corporate Governance site serves as a discussion forum and source of information and news for stakeholders.

www.irrc.com: The Investor Responsibility Research Center provides research, software products, and consulting services.

www.thecorporatelibrary.com: The Corporate Library is intended to serve as a central repository for research, study, and critical thinking about the nature of the modern global corporation, with a special focus on corporate governance. All site content is open to visitors at no cost.

See also:

☆ **Boardroom Roles (pp. 220–21)**
☆ **Corporate Social Responsibility (pp. 291–92)**
☆ **Governing the Corporation (pp. 239–40)**
Robert Owen (pp. 1032–33)
Anita Roddick (pp. 1134–35)
Social Responsibility of Management (pp. 2115–17)

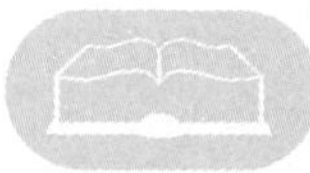

Organizational Learning and Performance *by Jerry W. Gilley and Ann Maycunich Gilley*

Executive Summary

- As strategic business partners, HR professionals are in a position to influence the direction of the organization as well as enhance the value of HR programs and services.
- Strategic business partnerships are synergistic, mutually beneficial, and long-term oriented. These relationships require HR professionals to develop a responsive, customer-service orientation better to understand and anticipate client needs.

Introduction

Some human resource (HR) professionals are not perceived as valuable because their programs and services are not linked to the organization's strategic business goals. Other programs falter because HR professionals do not properly communicate the value and benefits of their interventions and initiatives to decision makers within the organization. Although these are contributing factors, most HR programs suffer from a poor image because organizational leaders, managers, and employees do not view the HR department as a vital, contributing part of the organization. When this situation exists, HR is unable to help improve the organization's performance, quality, efficiency or productivity, or help it accomplish its strategic goals and objectives.

To address this dilemma, HR professionals need to become proactive. They need to discover ways of enhancing their credibility and thus, their effectiveness. One approach is for HR professionals to become strategic business partners. A strategic business partner is a person who "takes part" with others, and partnerships involve the "parts" we each play in our work. Partnerships are essential to the success of any organization.

Elements of Partnership

There are two primary elements of partnership—purpose and partnering. Purpose defines "why" a partnership is needed, and provides a focus and direction for the partnership. Without a purpose, no partnership exists. Purpose may be quite clear and explicit—as that imposed by an organizational leader or manager (client), or implicit—as a mutual exploration of a purpose about to be defined. Purpose, in essence, brings us together.

Partnering occurs when HR professionals and clients pursue a common purpose together. Partnering exemplifies the visible and invisible dynamics between HR professional, client and purpose, the result of clarifying roles and focus. Partnering also embraces underlying assumptions, trust and risk, shared values and expectations. Organizational consultant Geoffrey Bellman suggests that HR professionals and clients who attend to purposes but neglect partnering often fail in their work altogether.

Strategic business partnerships are intra-organizational alliances formed when HR professionals work closely with organizational leaders, managers, supervisors and employees to help the organization achieve its short-term business goals and objectives, as well as to ensure successful completion of the organization's overall strategic plans. These are long-term partnerships which create an interdependence between the HR department and the rest of the organization. They allow HR professionals to understand and anticipate their clients' needs better; to develop a responsive, customer-service oriented attitude toward the client, and to break down the walls between themselves and their clients. As a result, lasting relationships and commitments are forged and investments are made in learning, performance and change efforts.

Additionally, strategic business partnerships:

- give HR professionals the opportunity to develop personal relationships with clients;
- demonstrate the willingness of HR professionals to learn from clients;
- allow for more effective management of limited financial and human resources;
- produce economic utility, which is measured in terms of increased organizational performance, revenue, profitability, quality, or efficiency.

Making It Happen

There are four critical steps in becoming a strategic business partner:

Establish Credibility

The first and most important step in becoming a strategic business partner is to establish credibility within the organization. Improved credibility results from the ability of HR professionals to demonstrate professional expertise, as well as a good understanding of organizational operations and culture. In this way, HR professionals are able to provide real value to the organization.

David Ulrich points out in his book *Human Resource Champions* (1997) that HR professionals need to demonstrate a number of behaviors in order to enhance credibility. For example, HR professionals need to be accurate in all HR practices; to be dependable; to meet their commitments in a timely and efficient manner; to establish collaborative client relationships built on trust and honesty; to express their opinions in an understandable and clear manner; to behave in an ethical manner; to demonstrate creativity and innovation; to maintain confidentiality, and to demonstrate mutual respect.

In addition, HR professionals can establish credibility by:

- demonstrating the ability to solve complex problems, resulting in client needs and expectations being satisfied;
- exhibiting professional expertise, along with an understanding of organizational operations and culture, thus establishing respect for their insight and authority;
- securing third-party referrals. These usually come from a network, which is a collection of individuals who can introduce HR professionals to key organizational decision makers while keeping them informed.
- acquiring an excellent reputation, commonly by delivering results.

Credibility can also be established

"The ultimate power of a successful general staff lies, not in the brilliance of its individual members, but in the cross-fertilization of its collective abilities." (Reg Revans)

through an appropriate understanding of the HR professional's and the client's differing roles. Within a partnership, clients are accountable for results, clarity of vision, managing resources (time, energy, money, human talent, materials, equipment, environment), creating structures and systems, and strategic decision making. The HR professional's role combines competence and adaptability. He or she must demonstrate awareness of the organization's needs, assist in developing alternative solutions, reveal new perspectives, model risk-taking, and show knowledge of the consulting process—all while honoring his or her personal purpose and core beliefs. When appropriate roles are defined and maintained, trust and confidence emerge, which deepens relationships and bridges performance uncertainty. Over time, improved efficiency results as collaboration and cooperation replace competition and conflict.

Develop a Customer Service Strategy

The second step in becoming a strategic business partner is for HR professionals to develop a customer-service strategy that satisfies their stakeholders' needs. A stakeholder can be defined as anyone who has something to gain or lose as a result of an interaction with human resources. These gains and losses collectively frame needs and become the target for performance improvement interventions and change initiatives. The typical stakeholders of HR include:

- managers—the primary customer because they endure the cost of programs and services and reap the benefits;
- employees—who participate in programs and services;
- senior managers—who expect programs and services to return value and help the organization achieve its goals;
- organizations—which need the skills and abilities of all employees to produce and deliver high-quality products and services at a profit, and rely on employees' capabilities to remain competitive.

A strategy designed in accordance with the stakeholders' expressed interests ensures that the HR department is helping to maximize organizational performance. It also ensures that HR departments will be supported as well as defended by stakeholders during difficult economic periods, and viewed as essential to the organization's long-term success. A customer-service strategy that satisfies stakeholders' needs and expectations consists of six steps:

1. placing the business and professional needs of clients first
2. listening to clients, responding to their demands and collaborating with them
3. creating customer-service opportunities through face-to-face interaction
4. becoming active participants with clients rather than passive observers, using questioning, listening and facilitating skills that lead to viable recommendations and solutions
5. evaluating feedback from clients regarding their satisfaction with interventions and initiatives
6. implementing improvements in customer service, based upon the feedback received from clients.

Ultimately, an effective customer-service strategy is an important guiding principle for HR departments, and should direct HR professionals' decisions and actions.

Demonstrate Business Acumen

HR professionals must be able to demonstrate an understanding of business strategies, goals, tactics, and financial performance. Acquiring knowledge of business fundamentals, systems theory, organizational culture, operations, and politics enables HR professionals to think like their clients. In addition, HR professionals possessing business understanding are better able to facilitate change without disrupting the firm's operations.

Engage in Professional HR Sub-roles

The final step in becoming a strategic business partner is to engage in three sub-roles—influencer, strategist, and problem solver. Awareness of these sub-roles gives the HR professional the ability to respond to unforeseen contingencies; to provide appropriate solutions to complex, sensitive issues, and to conduct a wide range of activities designed to modify or enhance results.

As *influencers* HR professionals are directive in their efforts to influence client thinking, initiate change, or provide specific recommendations that address difficult performance problems. In order to be successful as an influencer, it is important to remain receptive to others' views, ideas, and recommendations. HR professionals should guard against letting their own personal biases and opinions overpower those of others. At the same time, a good influencer encourages organizational members to take risks to achieve their goals and objectives.

As *strategists* HR professionals are responsible for assessing organizational needs using quantifiable and qualifiable methodologies, developing and executing business initiatives, and evaluating the effectiveness of performance-improvement interventions and other change initiatives. Additionally, strategists incorporate the ideas of others into directive action plans.

When HR professionals take an active role in the decision-making and change-management process, they are serving as *problem solvers*. In this sub-role, they spend a majority of their time helping clients make decisions that are beneficial to achieving desired results. Problem solvers strive to make certain that the perceived problem is indeed the one critical to the organization.

These sub-roles are very common ones used by change management and organization development consultants such as Deloitte & Touche, William M. Mercer, Inc., and Towers Perrin.

Conclusion

Strategic business partnerships satisfy the needs of internal and external clients alike, while positioning HR professionals in a more positive light within the organization. The principal benefit for organizations is improved performance and efficiency, while HR professionals enjoy increased credibility and influence within the firm.

For More Information

Book:

Ulrich, David. *Human Resource Champion*. Boston, MA: Harvard Business School Press, 1997.

See also:

☆ **Building Great Internal Partnerships (pp. 281–82)**
Personnel Management and HR Management (pp. 2067–71)

"Because recruiting new leaders is difficult (if not impossible), it is important to use a process to transform the people whom companies already have in place." (David L. Dotlich)

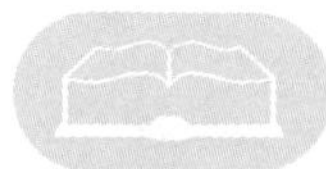

THE BALANCED SCORECARD
by Robert S. Kaplan and David P. Norton

EXECUTIVE SUMMARY

- The Balanced Scorecard is a powerful framework for aligning strategic objectives, management systems and corporate performance, resulting in robust long-term growth and value creation.
- Implementing the Balanced Scorecard successfully is a function of five core principles: mobilizing change through executive leadership; translating strategy into operational terms; aligning the organization to the strategy; making strategy everyone's everyday job; and making strategy a continual process.
- The Balanced Scorecard enables organizations to become more adaptive and responsive to the needs of both internal and external constituencies, resulting in greater opportunities for problem solving and innovation.

INTRODUCTION

The Balanced Scorecard is a performance measurement and management system using objectives and measures in four interrelated perspectives–financial, customer, internal process, and learning and growth. We introduced the Balanced Scorecard in the early 1990s because we believed that an exclusive reliance on financial measures in a management system would be insufficient for the 21st century. Strategies for creating value had shifted from managing tangible assets to knowledge-based strategies that created and deployed an organization's intangible assets, including customer relationships, innovative products and services, high-quality operating processes, and the skills, knowledge, and motivation of its workforce.

Organizations such as Mobil North American Marketing and Refining, Cigna Property and Casualty Insurance, Brown and Root Engineering Services, and Chemical (Chase) Bank implemented the Balanced Scorecard, embedded it into their management systems, and achieved breakthrough performance within two years. Our research has revealed a set of five principles, built around the Balanced Scorecard system, that enabled these and other organizations to execute their strategies rapidly.

PRINCIPLE 1: MOBILIZE CHANGE THROUGH EXECUTIVE LEADERSHIP

The single most important condition for success is the ownership and active involvement of the executive team. A Balanced Scorecard program starts with the recognition that it is not a "metrics" project; it's a change project. Initially executive leaders must *mobilize* the organization, creating momentum to get the process launched. Once mobilized, leadership focus shifts to *governance* to install the new performance model. Gradually a new management system evolves–a *strategic management system* that institutionalizes the new cultural values and processes into a new system for managing. Convergence to the system can take two to three years.

PRINCIPLE 2: TRANSLATE THE STRATEGY INTO OPERATIONAL TERMS

The objectives and measures on a Balanced Scorecard help executive teams better understand and articulate their strategies. The scorecard provides a framework for organizing strategic objectives into four perspectives:

1. *Financial*–the strategy for growth, profitability, and risk, viewed from the perspective of the shareholder
2. *Customer*–the strategy for creating value and differentiation from the perspective of the customer
3. *Internal Business Processes*–the strategic priorities for various business processes that create customer and shareholder satisfaction
4. *Learning and Growth*–the priorities to create a climate that supports organizational change, innovation, and growth.

From work done with an initial set of implementers, we developed a strategy map to provide a graphical representation of a well-constructed Balanced Scorecard. A strategy map, a logical and comprehensive architecture for describing strategy, specifies the critical elements and their linkages for an organization's strategy. It creates a common point of reference for all organization units and their employees.

Organizations build strategy maps from the top down, starting with the destination and then charting the routes that lead there. Corporate executives first review their mission statement (why their company exists) and core values (what their company believes in). From that information, they develop their strategic vision (what their company wants to become). This vision creates a clear picture of the company's overall goal.

Once the strategy map has been defined and agreed to by the executive team, the design of a scorecard with measures and targets is a straightforward process. The strategy map approach highlights that Balanced Scorecards should not just be collections of financial and non-financial measures organized into four perspectives. Balanced Scorecards should reflect the strategy of the organization. A good test is whether you can understand the strategy by looking only at the scorecard and its strategy map.

PRINCIPLE 3: ALIGN THE ORGANIZATION TO THE STRATEGY

The Balanced Scorecard is a powerful tool to describe a business unit's strategy. But organizations consist of numerous sectors, business units, and specialized departments, each with its own operations and often its own strategy. For synergy to occur across these diverse units, the strategies across these units need to be coordinated. The BSC helps to define the strategic linkages that integrate the performance of multiple organizations. Each unit formulates a strategy appropriate for its target market in light of the specific circumstances it faces–competitors, market opportunities, and critical processes–but that is consistent with the themes and priorities of the corporation or division. The measures at the individual business unit levels do not have to add to a corporate or divisional measure, unlike financial measures that aggregate easily from sub-units to departments to higher organizational levels. The business unit managers choose local measures that *influence,* but are not necessarily identical to, the corporate scorecard measures.

Beyond aligning the business units, strategy-focused organizations must also

"The balanced scorecard is. . .a way of understanding and checking what you have to do throughout the organization to make your strategy work." (Robert S. Kaplan)

  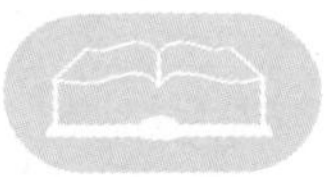    

align their staff functions and shared-service units, such as human resources, information technology, purchasing, environmental and finance. Often this alignment is accomplished with a service agreement between each functional department and the business units. The service agreement defines the menu of services to be provided, including their functionality, quality level and cost.

When this process is complete, all the organizational units–line business units and staff functions–have well-defined strategies that are articulated and measured by Balanced Scorecards and strategy maps. This alignment allows corporate-level synergies to emerge, in which the whole exceeds the sum of the individual parts.

Linkages can also be established across corporate boundaries to define relationships with key suppliers, customers, outsourcing vendors and joint ventures. Companies use such scorecards with external parties to be explicit about (1) the objectives of the relationship and (2) how to measure the contribution of each party to the relationship in ways other than just price or cost.

Principle 4: Make Strategy Everyone's Everyday Job

The C.E.O.s and senior leadership teams of organizations that adopted the Balanced Scorecard understood that they could not implement the new strategy by themselves. They wanted contributions from everyone in the organization. This is not top-down *direction*. This is top-down *communication* and bottom-up *implementation*. Three processes are required:

- **Use communication and education to create awareness**. A prerequisite for implementing strategy is that all employees understand the strategy. A consistent and continuing communication program is the foundation for organizational alignment.
- **Align personal objectives with the strategy**. Companies challenge individuals and departments at lower levels to develop their own objectives in light of the broader priorities; in some cases, personal scorecards are used to set *personal objectives*.
- **Link compensation to the scorecard**. To modify behavior as required by the strategy and as defined in the scorecard, change *must* be reinforced through incentive compensation. When the incentive compensation program becomes linked to the BSC, interest in the details of the strategy increases.

Principle 5: Make Strategy a Continual Process

Companies adopt a new "double-loop process" to manage strategy. The first step *links strategy to the budgeting process*. Managers use the Balanced Scorecard as a screen to evaluate potential investments and initiatives that will develop entirely new capabilities, reach new customers and markets, and make radical improvements in existing processes and capabilities. This distinction is essential. Just as the Balanced Scorecard attempts to protect long-term objectives from short-term sub-optimization, the budgeting process must protect the long-term initiatives from the pressures to deliver short-term financial performance.

The second step introduces a *simple management meeting* to review strategy. As obvious as this step sounds, such meetings didn't exist in the past. Now management meetings are scheduled on a monthly or quarterly basis to discuss the Balanced Scorecard, so that a broad spectrum of managers comes together to monitor organizational performance against the short-term targets for the scorecard's financial and non-financial measures. This process creates a focus on the strategy that did not exist before.

Information feedback systems change to support the new management meetings. Many organizations create an *open reporting* environment, in which performance results are made available to everyone in the organization. Building upon the principle that "strategy is everyone's job," they empower "everyone" by giving them the knowledge needed to do their jobs.

Finally, a *process for learning and adapting the strategy* evolves. As the scorecard is put into action and feedback systems begin their reporting on actual results, the organization tests the hypotheses underlying its strategy, to see whether the strategy is delivering the expected results.

A new kind of energy is created. People use terms like "fun" and "exciting" to describe the management meetings. One senior executive reported that the meetings became so popular, there was standing room only. . .he could have sold tickets to them.

Companies also use the meetings to search for new strategic opportunities that aren't currently on their scorecard. New challenges arise externally, and ideas and learning emerge internally from within the organization. Rather than waiting for next year's budget cycle, the priorities and the scorecards are updated immediately. Much like a navigator guiding a vessel on a long-term journey, constantly sensing the shifting winds and currents and constantly adapting the course, the executives of successful companies use the ideas and learning generated by their organization to fine-tune their strategies. Instead of being an annual event, strategy formulation, testing, and revision became a continual process.

Conclusion

The Balanced Scorecard enables organizations to introduce a new governance and review process–one focused on strategy, not tactics. The new governance process emphasizes learning, team problem solving, and coaching. Review meetings look into the future–exploring how to implement strategy more effectively, and identifying the changes to be made to the strategy–based on what has been learned.

This is a management process attuned to the needs of contemporary businesses. The essential ingredient is a simple framework–the Balanced Scorecard and its representation on a strategy map–that allows strategy to be clearly articulated. The Balanced Scorecard becomes the heart of the management system that strategy-focused organizations will use to build their future.

For More Information

Books and Journal Articles:

Kaplan, Robert, and David Norton. "The Balanced Scorecard–Measures That Drive Performance." *Harvard Business Review* (January-February 1992).

Kaplan, Robert, and David Norton. "Having Trouble with Your Strategy? Then Map It." *Harvard Business Review* (September-October 2000).

Kaplan, Robert, and David Norton. *The Strategy-focused Organization: How Balanced Scorecard Companies Thrive in the New Business Environment*. Boston, MA: Harvard Business School Press, 2001.

Kaplan, Robert, and David Norton. *The Balanced Scorecard: Translating Strategy into Action*. Boston, MA: Harvard Business School Press, 1996.

Web Site:

www.bscol.com: the Balanced Scorecard Collaborative's Web site.

See also:

☆ **New Yardsticks for Performance (pp. 285–86)**
☆ **Raising the Bar (pp. 283–84)**
✓ **Gathering Competitive Intelligence (pp. 560–61)**
Benchmarking (pp. 1911–13)

"It is an immutable law in business that words are words, explanations are explanations, promises are promises–but only performance is reality." (Harold S. Geneen)

 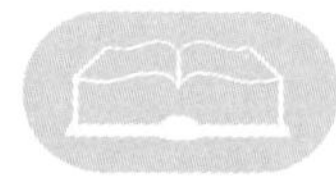    

SETTING OBJECTIVES FOR A BUSINESS
by Allan A. Kennedy

EXECUTIVE SUMMARY

- Managing inherently involves setting a goal or objective and then executing a series of actions to meet it. Establishing the right objective is critical to successful management of any business.
- Successful long-term businesses almost always started with a set of nonfinancial objectives (sometimes referred to as a vision or mission) and derived financial objectives consistent with pursuit of their broader goals.
- Setting only financial objectives is risky for business because single-minded pursuit of financial objectives can lead to actions that undermine long-term viability.

INTRODUCTION

Managing is the task of moving an enterprise toward a defined objective. Most of the disciplines of management–budgeting, strategic planning, performance monitoring take as a given that an appropriate objective has been set. Given the central role that objectives or targets play in most management actions, it is critical that they be set correctly. It may seem trite to point out, but it is nonetheless valid: if inappropriate objectives are set for a business, inappropriate outcomes will occur.

What constitutes appropriate objectives for a business? As business and management have evolved, thinking about what constitutes an appropriate objective has evolved as well. Throughout this evolution, there has been an ongoing tension between financial goals and objectives and nonfinancial objectives. If business exists primarily or solely to make a profit (a highly quantifiable outcome) then relatively simple financial objectives suffice, argue some. Others say that business exists to serve simultaneously the needs of various constituencies–shareholders, customers, suppliers, employees, communities. The interests of these various legitimate constituencies are not always quantifiable, leading to a school of thought that puts greater emphasis on nonfinancial objectives. The history of business would suggest that both types of objectives are important.

A BRIEF HISTORY OF BUSINESS OBJECTIVES

Most businesses that were launched in the 19th century began their life as some form of family enterprise. As family businesses, their objectives were quite clear: to provide an ongoing source of income and, where necessary, employment for current and future members of the family.

As the technology of management has evolved, ideas about what constitutes the right objective for a business have changed. In his book *Concept of the Corporation*, first published in 1946, Peter Drucker described the purpose of a corporation as generating the maximum profit achievable from its operations. He went on to comment on the potential conflict between this purpose and society's expectation that the job of business was to maximize the production of cheap goods and services for consumption. To a modern observer, Drucker's thinking seems simplistic.

Drucker based his comments on work he had done with General Motors (GM), then the largest industrial enterprise in the world. The people he worked with in GM were convinced he got it wrong. To set the record straight, the legendary leader of General Motors from 1923 until 1946, Alfred P. Sloan, Jr., wrote his own account of the GM system of management, which he called *My Years with General Motors*. In that book, Sloan described a high-level task force effort he led in 1920 to define the concept of GM's business. He articulated a purpose for GM's business quite different from Drucker's version. "We made the assumption. . .that the first purpose in. . . establishment of a business [is that it] will pay *satisfactory* dividends and *preserve* and *increase* its capital value" [emphasis added].

As a reflection of Sloan's influence in the business world, in the 1950s and 1960s most businesses sought to operate with a conservative balance sheet while showing steady signs of growth in sales, assets, profits, dividends and shareholder equity.

During the 1950s and 1960s, new types of companies emerged on the familiar business landscape. These companies were young, entrepreneurial and managed by hands-on practitioners, each on a mission. This new breed included the likes of Hewlett-Packard, a company set up to make useful technical contributions in a variety of engineering markets. It also included companies like Wal-Mart, whose driving rationale was providing superior value to its customers.

All of these new companies were in business to make a profit, both as a return to their investors and as a measure of the value of what they were doing as a company. These financial objectives were, however, secondary to their broader institutional objectives. Because many of these new companies grew very rapidly and became, relatively speaking, darlings of the stock market, many established companies modified their traditional objectives to focus on achieving specified levels of growth in revenues and profits in an attempt to keep pace.

In the late 1970s, a new theory about appropriate objectives for business was developed by academics specializing in the complex area of accounting. Their theory held that since shareholders owned companies, the real objective of business should be maximizing shareholder value. They went on to point out that conventional accounting measures of profitability, such as earnings per share of public companies, were very poor proxies indeed for the true value of a company. Instead they urged businesspeople to focus on the present value of future cashflow streams as a truer measure of value. Most managers ignored this advice for all practical purposes, but some specialized investment bankers, who came to be known as "corporate raiders" or "leveraged buyout bankers," took the insights of the academics very seriously.

The immediate result was an unprecedented wave of corporate takeovers during the 1980s. The longer-term result was a fundamental rethinking of what business was all about by most managers, as they adopted shareholder value thinking as a means of defending themselves from the corporate raiders.

Throughout the 1990s, maximizing shareholder value was the driving purpose of most businesses, and managers did virtually anything they could to ensure that their stock price–the most direct proxy for shareholder value–rose steadily.

"The goal of a big business person should be to create a new organization that feels and operates like a smaller business, yet retains the resource advantages of big business." (John Kotter)

  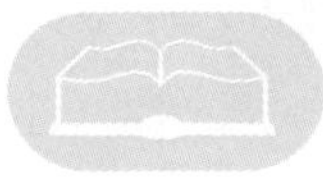    

LIMITATIONS OF RELYING SOLELY ON FINANCIAL OBJECTIVES

The stock market boom of the 1990s seemed to prove that focusing on shareholder value was the right way to run a business. But the boom of the 1990s gave way to the economic slowdown and stock market correction of 2000 and 2001. With the change in the business climate, the problems associated with over-reliance on maximizing shareholder value became apparent. With an exclusive focus on rewarding shareholders, many companies simply failed to take care of the legitimate needs of the other constituencies they depended on to provide them with a profitable future. As a result, these other constituencies rebelled.

Employees, having been treated as commodities by the companies they worked for, stopped being loyal to their employers and sold their services to the highest bidder. Especially for high tech companies in places like Silicon Valley, this change in the labor marketplace forced employers to pay top dollar to get the talent they needed, and left them saddled with the costs inherent in a high-turnover workforce.

Suppliers, who had been forced to accept lower and lower prices for providing ever-increasing amounts of service to their customers, banded together in a last-ditch effort to survive. In some very important sectors like the automobile industry, this led to more concentrated groups of suppliers who had more market power than the customers they served.

Customers, whose choices had been limited by companies intent on pruning product lines and closing outlets to produce higher immediate profits, responded by steadily reducing their loyalty to brands and increasingly shopping for the lowest price available, regardless of the consequences for the companies that supplied them.

Governments, which had once bent over backwards to entice companies to invest, increasingly eliminated investment subsidies and began negotiating tighter and tighter agreements and strictly enforcing the terms of these agreements.

The net effect of these changes in the business environment is that the path to future growth and profitability is compromised for many of the companies that so excelled in their pursuit of shareholder value.

THE STAYING POWER OF NONFINANCIAL OBJECTIVES

Why do some companies seem to thrive over a very long period of time, while others have a brief moment in the sun and then recede into obscurity? There are a number of factors that account for this long-term pattern of success, including leadership, the quality of management, and the dynamics of the markets they serve. James Collins and Jerry Porras in their landmark book, *Built to Last*, suggest there is one common element. Companies that thrive for a long time all have a nonfinancial vision of what they are in business to accomplish. The 3M company exists to create useful products through innovation. Boeing exists to be at the leading edge of the aeronautics field. Marriott has a mission to make its customers feel like they have a home away from home. Johnson & Johnson exists to help alleviate pain and suffering. All of these companies, and the others cited by Collins and Porras, also work hard to make a profit and return value to their shareholders. However, producing profits and generating value for their shareholders was a byproduct of the broader objectives each of these companies sought to pursue.

Why this should be so is actually quite simple. Most people who work for companies need a broader goal than purely a financial one to motivate them to perform at their best. The companies profiled by Collins and Porras provided their people with just such a broader mission, treated them as full partners in the pursuit of this broader goal, and as a result realized higher levels of commitment and motivation from them. The companies reward this higher level of commitment and loyalty with policies appropriate to maintaining an ongoing partnership. To be viable and successful, every business must set and work hard to achieve a series of financial goals and objectives. But having financial objectives alone will not produce superior performance over the long term.

MAKING IT HAPPEN ▸▸

How can a manager at any level of business decide whether or not the objectives set for the business are sound? There are no firm rules to rely on, but there are some common-sense tests any manager can apply to determine whether the objectives set are:

- compelling—capable of getting someone's attention;
- motivating—likely to inspire someone to put in extra effort;
- consistent—able to be met without compromise;
- achievable—reachable with reasonable levels of effort and commitment;
- distinguishing—something that when achieved will set the company or business apart from others;
- competitively superior—difficult enough to attain so that the achievement will produce superior rewards from the markets served and the investing public;
- satisfying—of such a nature that the achievement of the objective will produce a personal sense of satisfaction among those who contributed;
- lasting—likely to pass the test of time.

Tests like these are applicable to financial as well as nonfinancial objectives.

CONCLUSION

Making a profit and delivering value to shareholders is motivating indeed for anyone engaged in business. However, it is simply not a sufficient motivator to produce the kind of extra effort over a long period of time that produces superior long-term performance.

For More Information

Books:

Bower, Marvin. *The Will to Lead*. Boston, MA: Harvard Business School Press, 1997.

Collins, James C., and Jerry I. Porras. *Built to Last*. New York: HarperBusiness, 1994.

Drucker, Peter F. *Concept of the Corporation*. Reprint. Somerset, NJ: Transaction Publishers, 2001.

Sloan, Alfred P. *My Years with General Motors*. New York: Doubleday, 1996.

See also:

☆ **New Yardsticks for Performance and Productivity (pp. 285–86)**
☆ **Raising the Bar (pp. 283–84)**
☆ **Who's Guiding Your Corporate Destiny? (pp. 216–17)**
✔ **Setting Objectives (pp. 480–81)**
📖 **My Years with General Motors (p. 931)**

Profiting from Prices
by Michael de Kare-Silver

EXECUTIVE SUMMARY

- In an attempt to boost revenues, many companies have tried to reduce costs through reengineering, outsourcing, downsizing, etc.
- Companies are becoming aware of the opportunity and potential of the top line (as opposed to the bottom line).
- Pricing is an undiscovered weapon in the search for higher revenues.

Introduction

In recent years many companies have not found it easy to increase revenues. Economic conditions, government policies against inflation, increased competition on pricing (including producers from the less-developed countries), and globally more sophisticated customers have all put pressure on volume and price in many industries. Not surprisingly, companies have turned to levers more directly in their control—such as reducing costs and better process management—as sources of profit growth. Hence the fads and focuses on reengineering, downsizing, outsourcing, etc.

But reengineering can only go so far in boosting profits. As their markets strive for growth, companies are increasingly challenging revenue performance and realizing that the top line has not received the same close examination and insight as the bottom line in recent times. There is a growing awakening to the fact that more opportunity and potential may lie on the top line.

What can be realistically achieved? Is the search for higher revenues a futile battle against macro-economic forces and competitive pressures? Analysis shows the contrary. Pricing, especially, is an undiscovered weapon. There is significant profit potential for companies in challenging this area, and in "reengineering" their price position.

Opportunities in Pricing

Research shows two almost contradictory key facts. First, 21% of the top 100 U.K. companies have failed to grow revenues in real terms in the past five years. But, second, the majority (56%) of C.E.O.s in an interview program agreed that:

- insufficient attention is given to challenging revenue opportunities, especially in pricing;
- significant profit upside remains untapped in the pricing area.

Looking at pricing is, in principle, much more attractive than downsizing. There are no severance costs, no people/organization issues, an impact next Monday morning: a quick win flows straight through to the bottom line.

In any event, opportunities to improve profitability principally through cost and process management may have peaked for the time being. Many reengineering projects have disappointed. Research among U.K. and U.S. companies shows that:

- no more than two in ten companies achieve breakthrough improvements in performance;
- less than 30% claim to be satisfied with either the change process itself or the results.

Routes to Effective Pricing

The more you know about which products make money and which lose, the more you can adopt a better strategic and selective pricing policy. Three main routes can be identified that lead to more effective pricing:

- exploiting market advantages
- changing the decision-making process on pricing
- testing whether all the different pricing options are being proactively pursued

Of course, some companies enjoy market or structural circumstances that make pricing management easier. Have they just fallen by luck into those situations, or have their advantages been "engineered" more deliberately? Some companies have used strategic alliances to create market and structural barriers deliberately—by locking up a vital supply of raw materials, say, and making it hard for others to function. Procter & Gamble thus used an alliance to tie up the Japanese supplier of scarce polyacrylate material. As a result, it was able to block competitors and recover market leadership.

Even without market or structural advantage, significant untapped pricing potential exists. How can this be exploited? Many factors are *prima facie* within executive control, and can be changed to enable more effective pricing management. For example, internal structures could be adjusted to facilitate more effective pricing. Several roadblocks operate within the organization—such as:

- responsibility for pricing is left to the sales department (Who has ever seen a salesman who wanted to increase prices?);
- there is little or no finance department involvement to balance decision making;
- senior management's remoteness from the detailed market circumstances makes it difficult to challenge sales views;
- no systems/mechanisms are available to easily assess more aggressive pricing opportunities;
- data on the true net profitability of individual services/products to either company or customer is limited.

Indeed, not only could companies make structural moves that are more easily within their control; research shows that as many as 12 different pricing strategies are available. They often appear to be under-exploited. The challenge is frequently not lack of familiarity with the particular pricing option. It is more about:

- having enough management time to check whether the particular pricing options have been fully considered;
- understanding the pricing relationship to competitors and what drives it;
- examining price opportunities and developing insights on an *individual* product line basis, rather than across a range;
- management's ability to challenge sales-led pricing decisions;
- the effectiveness and rigor with which the pricing strategies are implemented;
- the information base and systems needed to do all this.

Pricing Strategies

Many of the 12 different pricing strategy options are geared to medium/long-term profit-building; few can have immediate effect. They fall into three main groups:

- customer information management
- exploiting structural advantages
- innovation and leadership

"Our policy is to reduce the price, extend the operations, and improve the article." (Henry Ford)

Customer Information Management

There are four approaches to consider.

1. **Category segmentation**: use detailed product-line profitability and pricing to achieve analysis and insight, developed separately for *each* product line.
2. **Customer segmentation**: use detailed customer segmentation to identify pricing opportunities.
3. **Bundling**: in medical products, as core product/service prices have come under pressure, companies have added related products and services where pricing is more robust (and which equally reinforce the core product/service value proposition). Similarly, some leading Internet software suppliers provide free access software but charge for use of related products and services.
4. **Trade terms management**: manage the level of discounts given to customers to get a better return.

Exploiting Structural Advantages

Four options are highlighted here:

1. **Lowest cost/lowest price**: cost advantages enable invaders to price lower and grow share rapidly.
2. **Supply and demand management**: as an illustration, better hotel occupancy/yield management systems have enabled leaders to quote more aggressive room tariffs.
3. **Supplier-customer "balance of power"**: this can be exploited to ensure that suppliers "contribute" to gross margin success. Tough management of the supply price provides greater flexibility in end-consumer pricing.
4. **"Open-book" and partnership-pricing**: the open-book approach was pioneered in the automotive industry. Sharing information about costs has enabled better suppliers to justify and push through selective price increases.

Innovation and Leadership

This area offers two zones of higher comfort:

1. **Branding**: consistent high levels of branding and advertising enable a company to maintain a price premium.
2. **Total value proposition**: where five strategies can be singled out:

- *Technology-driven*: continuous development of niche; technically advanced products can give strong gross margin advantages.
- *First in*: continual focus on being first to market gives initial pricing advantages, as well as other benefits.
- *Best at*: leadership on all features valued by the customer can give price leadership in both "value pricing" of certain products and "premium pricing" for certain others.
- *Share leadership*: restructuring the product portfolio to focus only on market share leaders where you have more control over pricing and other levers.
- *Innovative consumer value*: provide a clear mixing of quality, value and service to lead in the eyes of the customer.

There are at least a couple of shorter-term options, too:

1. **Price squeeze**: in one turnaround, the new C.E.O. insisted that each product line price be "squeezed" up 1%. Despite initial internal resistance, this was successfully implemented, immediately impacting the bottom line.
2. **Price elasticity**: is the price/volume equation effectively analyzed and balanced? For example, low-margin products can be priced up relatively aggressively with less impact on contribution from any volume lost.

Research shows that many of these pricing strategies are in fact applicable in most industries and most company situations, but that surprisingly few are being proactively investigated and implemented.

Using Pricing Opportunities

How can a company check whether it is fully utilizing its pricing opportunities? This initial checklist looks first internally—for example at the priority that pricing decision-making has in the organization:

1. What percentage of senior management time is spent on pricing?
2. How much senior management time is spent with customers?
3. Is there an information base in place which tracks pricing for each product line and its relationship with volume?
4. Is competitor pricing tracked in similar detail?
5. How frequently is pricing specifically and rigorously reviewed?
6. Is the company organized in a way that ensures that a "balanced" pricing decision is made?

The other questions are directed at the external market potential:

1. Are competitors' future pricing strategies and plans understood?
2. Is there a clear understanding and alignment between what the company sees as added value, compared to what the customer sees?
3. Does the company have a clear pricing strategy differentiated for the circumstances and market position of each product group and each customer?

As global competition intensifies, close attention to the detail, the "micro-management," will become increasingly important. "Discovering pricing" and systematizing its proactive exploitation in the business will become a key distinguishing factor among the more successful corporations.

Making It Happen ▸▸

- When seeking to boost financial performance, look at pricing possibilities before cutbacks in costs.
- Investigate three main routes: (1) exploiting market advantages; (2) improved decision-making process; (3) pursuing all pricing options proactively.
- Share responsibility for pricing between sales, finance, and a fully informed senior management.
- Develop high-quality data on true net profitability of individual services/products to both the company and the customer.
- Look for price opportunities on an individual product line basis, rather than across a range.
- Seek superior strategies by: (1) managing customer information; (2) exploiting structural advantages; (3) innovation and leadership.

Conclusion

Price decisions are too often made by too few people. Only by sharing the responsibility for pricing can managers begin to understand the importance that pricing can have on the success of any business. Ultimately, decisions on pricing must be measured against other critical factors, such as data on customers. In the final analysis, pricing can be an exercise in both innovation and leadership.

For More Information

Dolan, Robert J., and Hermann Simon. *Power Pricing: How Managing Price Transforms the Bottom Line*. New York: Free Press, 1996.

Nagle, Thomas T., and Reed K. Holden. *The Strategy and Tactics of Pricing*. Upper Sadle River, NJ: Pearson, 1994.

See also:
✓ **Running a Price Campaign (pp. 732–33)**
Pricing (pp. 2078–79)

Viewpoint: Jim Kouzes

Helping Managers Measure Up to the Leadership Challenge

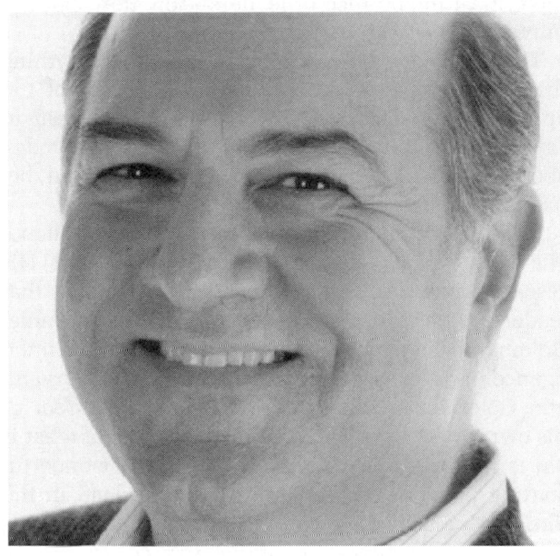

Jim Kouzes, along with Barry Posner, wrote *The Leadership Challenge*, which will be in its third edition in 2002. Based on years of research, involving over 250,000 individual leaders on whom more than one million observers provided feedback, it is the #1 textbook on leadership, bar none, and the winner of numerous awards and honors. What are the roots of Jim's own view of leadership and does he see the basic shape of leadership changing in the future? Times change, but Jim believes true leadership does not.

If there is one thing I've learned in over three decades of studying and teaching leadership, and in working with numerous outstanding leaders, it's this: *leadership is a relationship*.

All of us who write and speak and teach on leadership owe a profound debt of gratitude to an extraordinary group of men and women who toiled in the new field of behavioral science. Contemporary research on leadership began during World War II, and while we've learned a great deal since then, most of what we've learned has been built upon the foundations of that early work. So often we treat leadership and teamwork as if they were new phenomena, but we know they're not. Serious research has been going on for almost three-quarters of a century. Now, it may be a bit oversimplistic to try to summarize all of the leadership research in one phrase, but let me be bold enough to give it a try. What we learned in 1946 and what we've learned in the last year is this: leadership is all about how people influence other people to do something. It's all about human relationships.

So I smile when someone asks: "How will leadership be different 50 years from now?" My sense is that the practices of a leader have not been nor will be much different. The *context* will change, but the *content* will be pretty much the same. Our research indicates that leaders engage in five practices to get extraordinary things done in organizations. They "challenge the process," to make sure it's constantly improved. They "inspire a shared vision of the future" that followers deeply believe in and embrace with enthusiasm. They "enable others to act," fostering collaboration and strengthening individual capacity, to make a new vision a new reality. They "walk the talk"—or "model the way" as we call it—setting an example by their own behaviors to show others how the organization can best stay true to its vision and values. And, lastly, they "encourage the heart"—they recognize individuals for their contributions and then celebrate the community of people who care passionately about the destiny of the enterprise.

Each generation, then, has to redefine leadership for its own historical context.

It's so easy to confuse changing times with unchanging fundamentals. For example, today many seem to think that the Internet will change everything. Well, it makes sense in some ways, but not when it comes to leadership. For example, looking back to the time when the telephone was first invented, someone then might have said that bold leadership is connected to using the telephone. Put a phone on everyone's desk! Put a phone in everyone's home! Hook people up to long distance; enable them to converse across the globe, anytime, anywhere. That'll make them higher performers. That sounds silly now, but it's equivalent to what's been going on with the Internet. Are we better off because we have the telephone? Certainly. Are we better off because we have the Internet. Absolutely. Is the telephone or the Internet the secret to better leadership? Not in the slightest. The principles of leadership are the same; only the context is different.

It's so easy to confuse changing times with unchanging fundamentals. For example, today many seem to think that the Internet will change everything. Well, it makes sense in some ways, but not when it comes to leadership.

Leadership is about relationships. It's about working with and guiding people in new directions. It's about achieving the most positive interaction between customers, employees, shareholders,

"The leader. . .is the translator, facilitator, the articulating point between the group's genius, who is doing great things, producing big and innovative ideas, and the public, the market." (Warren Bennis)

vendors—whomever! One serendipitous reminder of this principle was the cover story on the issue of *TIME* magazine dated September 10, 2001. It was about U.S. secretary of state Colin Powell, and the general thrust of the story was that he was becoming an afterthought in the leadership of the United States on the world stage. Well, we all know what happened exactly one day after that. Terrorists struck New York, and Washington D.C., and in the skies over Pennsylvania. Immediately after those tragic events, Colin Powell had to reach out to leaders around the world and marshal a coordinated response to the insidious threat of worldwide terrorism. He had to ask the leaders of many countries (and their people) to do things they had not thought they would have to do, that perhaps they did not want to do. But they took the call from the U.S. secretary of state and then they acted. Why? I'm sure they said something like this (at least to themselves) as they responded to Secretary Powell's requests. "We'll do this," they probably said, "because it's *you*, Colin. We trust you." Leadership is all about relationships that are based on a person's credibility.

Leadership is all about relationships that are based on a person's credibility.

Where did I learn this? No one single person taught me my current point of view about leadership, but my father comes close to being the one who influenced me the most.

My father, Tom Kouzes, served the United States for over 30 years. In his final career assignment he was deputy assistant secretary of labor. In addition to his regular job, my dad always loved teaching and training, especially in the field of organizational management. Here I was, growing up in the Washington D.C. area during my earliest years, and my dad would bring home books by people like Peter Drucker and talk about them. He was also fascinated by short, experiential exercises that would help people in training classes "feel" the leadership lesson and not just think about it. I'll always remember that.

Everything that led me to my career followed the path of the applied behavioral sciences.

As I think about all this, *both* my mother, Thelma, and my dad strongly influenced me. At home, I would participate in all kinds of discussions about management and political science and world affairs. My mother was a volunteer at the United Nations and, beginning in 1961, we had foreign students live at our home year-round. She also was very active in the civil rights movement, and even took part with Dr. Martin Luther King in the great march on Washington. Now, it's worth noting that all this was happening before the term "diversity" was the hot concept it is now. I'm so thankful that I learned at a young age how important it is to see leadership issues through a global pair of glasses. Because of a combination of influences like the ones my parents provided (and from all the experiences I had becoming an Eagle Scout), I was determined to join the Peace Corps when I was young. There's no question that my service in Turkey helped me to see the critical importance of leaders—how they can improve the world through social action.

It's amazing how few leaders take the time to answer a very simple but key question: "What do I *really* care about?"

There was one other strong influence. Everything that led me to my career followed the path of the applied behavioral sciences. In fact, I think it's safe to say that everything that we read or hear or see today about leadership has its roots in the applied behavioral sciences.

I was especially influenced by David C. McClelland. His work on *The Achieving Society* was seminal. His research and writing definitely tie to the idea that leadership is about relationships. In fact, Daniel Goleman, who popularized the term "emotional intelligence," was a student of McClelland's at Harvard, and Goleman credits McClelland as the taproot of his own work. Here's just another example of what is old is new again. McClelland's work is a wonderful starting point for anyone who hopes to lead in the difficult and chaotic years ahead. A leader who is capable of managing relationships constructively must realize that there are basic skills that have to be mastered.

I have to add one other point, however. Leadership not just about skills, no more than any relationship is just about skills. Credibility is the foundation of all relationships. So, you can have all the skills in the world, but if people don't believe in you as a person, they simply won't want to follow you. We call it the First Law of Leadership: If you don't *believe in* the messenger, you won't believe the message. When we ask people what credibility is behaviorally, the response can always be summed up in the phrase "Do What You Say You Will Do," or DWYSYWD for short. In other words, for people to want to *willingly* follow someone, they have to observe two things: first, the leader has a clear set of values and beliefs, and, second, the leader's behavior is consistent with those beliefs.

Which leads to another practice that too many leaders discount. Leadership requires self-knowledge. This is a much a more significant point than many first assume. It's amazing how few leaders take the time to answer a very simple but key question: "What do I *really* care about?"

When a leader can answer what it is that he or she really cares about, then it's possible to see the actual leadership face that he or she presents to the rest of the world. Many, if not most leaders have some kind of speech about wanting their company to be both profitable and a great place to work. Yet great words in a nice speech are not the same as becoming fully aware of what you really care about. What keeps you awake at night? What ideas or issues grab hold of you and won't let go?

Learn what you really care about and you slowly but surely start to find your leadership voice, to discover your true vision and values.

John Robbins is the son of the cofounder of the

"A company requires a leader, but individually no one can pretend to be the driving force."

(Michel Bon)

Baskin-Robbins ice cream empire. He grew up in a household that sometimes served ice cream for breakfast; he swam in a backyard pool that was shaped like an ice cream cone. But John walked away from all of that. He rejected the lifestyle, and he rejected the production factory approach to how we treat animals. He embraced a whole new lifestyle structured around the profound idea that our diets can help save our lives and our planet. He is also an eloquent and passionate proponent for a saner approach to how we live, eat, and work in our environment. Now, John didn't wake up one morning with the revelation that this was the way his life should go. He spent 10 years after university on an island, in a one-room log cabin that he and his wife, Deo, built. By being with his thoughts and living a very simple life, he emerged with great clarity about his calling.

Now, I am not advocating that all leaders need to spend a decade alone on an island. But the point to stress is that today's work world is full of so much frenzy, so much noise, that it's nearly impossible for anyone to pause and reflect. But you have to! Winston Churchill, despite all the challenges that confronted him, found time to paint. Guess what he was thinking about when he painted? All great leaders find time to reflect: Lincoln, Gandhi, Martin Luther King. I believe this fervently. Any leader who says I don't have time to reflect is crippling his ability to lead. Why?

People who follow you want a leader who stands for a larger purpose. They want meaningful work, and connecting to a larger purpose ennobles and energizes everyone's efforts. Leadership is about relationships. It's about trust. It's about doing what you say you'll do. So I ask: what do *you* really care about? Find the answer to that question and you're on the path to becoming a better leader. Ignore that question, and you're on the road to an empty life. You can't pay people enough to care. People care when they have meaning in their work, when they can connect to a larger purpose. Find a worthy purpose for you and your constituents, and the profits will follow.

For More Information

Web Site:
www.theleadership.com

See also:

- ☆ **Boosting Business Success through Diversity (pp. 29–30)**
- ☆ **Human Capital (pp. 115–16)**
- ☆ **Really Leading: Leadership That Is Authentic, Conscious, and Effective (pp. 222–23)**
- ☆ **Retaining Employees (pp. 196–97)**
- **Leaders (p. 915)**
- **Leadership (p. 916)**
- **John Adair (pp. 960–61)**
- **Warren Bennis (pp. 968–69)**
- **Leadership (pp. 2020–24)**

"Effective leadership. . .including 'values for becoming', besides just 'skills for doing'. . .seems to demand continuous reflection and integral assimilation by a true leader." (S. K. Chakraborty)

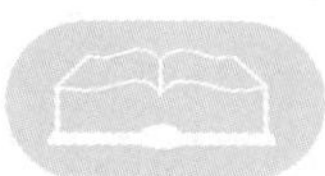

EMOTIONAL INTELLIGENCE
by Cary Cherniss and Daniel Goleman

EXECUTIVE SUMMARY

- Emotional intelligence (EI) is the ability to accurately identify and understand one's own emotional reactions and those of others, and to regulate one's emotions and to use them to make good decisions and act effectively.
- The competencies that make the biggest difference in individual performance at work are based on EI.
- EI can be improved at any age; in fact, several programs for doing so have been developed and found to be effective.
- However, improving EI takes considerable time and effort.
- To be effective, training and development efforts need to incorporate a number of elements.

INTRODUCTION

Ever since the publication of Daniel Goleman's first book on the topic in 1995, emotional intelligence has become one of the hottest buzzwords in corporate America. Many business leaders have found compelling the basic idea that success is strongly influenced by personal qualities such as perseverance, self-control, and skill in getting along with others. They point to sales persons who have an uncanny ability to sense what is most important to the customers and to develop a trusting relationship with them. They also point to customer service employees who excel when it comes to helping angry customers calm down and be more reasonable. Conversely, they point to brilliant executives who do everything well except get along with people, and to managers who are technically brilliant but cannot handle stress, and whose careers are stalled because of these deficiencies.

Many studies have confirmed that the so-called "soft skills" are critical for a vital economy. For instance, the influential report of the United States Secretary of Labor's Commission on Achieving Necessary Skills argued that a high-performance workplace requires workers who have a solid foundation not only in literacy and computation, but also in personal qualities such as responsibility, self-esteem, sociability, self-management, integrity, and honesty (Secretary's Commission on Achieving Necessary Skills, 1991). Emotional intelligence is the basis for these competencies.

But what exactly is "emotional intelligence?" What is the link between emotional intelligence and organizational effectiveness? Is it possible for adults to become more socially and emotionally competent? And finally, what is the best way to help individuals to do so?

WHAT IS EMOTIONAL INTELLIGENCE AND WHY IS IT IMPORTANT?

Emotional intelligence is the ability to accurately identify and understand one's own emotional reactions and those of others. It also includes the ability to regulate one's emotions and to use them to make good decisions and act effectively. EI provides the bedrock for many competencies that are critical for effective performance in the workplace. For instance, one's effectiveness in influencing others depends on one's ability to connect with them on an emotional level, and to understand what they are feeling and why. To effectively influence others we also need to be able to manage our own emotions.

CAN ADULTS BECOME MORE EMOTIONALLY INTELLIGENT?

Many managers and executives who accept the notion that emotional intelligence is vital for success are less certain about whether it can be improved. On the other hand, there are consultants and trainers who claim that they can raise the emotional intelligence of a whole group of employees in a day or less. Who is right? The truth lies somewhere in between. A growing body of research suggests that it is possible to help people of any age to become more emotionally adept at work. However, to be effective, programs need to be well designed, and the change effort requires months, not hours or days.

Several examples of effective change programs can be found in the Model Programs section of the CREIO Web site (www.eiconsortium.org). These models, all of which have undergone rigorous evaluation, show that well-designed training and development interventions can produce significant improvements in the so-called "soft skills," and these improvements in turn result in greater productivity and reduced costs. Unfortunately, while it is possible to improve workers' emotional competence, it is not easy to do so. Many programs intended for this purpose fail because they are poorly designed and implemented.

WHAT IS THE BEST WAY TO IMPROVE EMOTIONAL INTELLIGENCE?

To be effective, change efforts need to begin with the realization that emotional learning differs from cognitive and technical learning in some important ways. Emotional capacities like self-confidence and empathy differ from cognitive abilities because they draw on different brain areas. Purely cognitive abilities are based in the neocortex. But with social and emotional competencies, additional brain areas are involved, mainly the circuitry that runs from the emotional centers to the prefrontal lobes. Effective learning for emotional competence has to retune these circuits.

Unfortunately, these particular neural circuits are especially difficult to modify. Emotional incompetence often results from habits learned early in life. These automatic habits are set in place as a normal part of living, as experience shapes the brain. As people acquire their habitual repertoire of thought, feeling, and action, the neural connections that support these are strengthened, becoming dominant pathways for nerve impulses. When these habits have been so heavily learned, the underlying neural circuitry becomes the brain's default option at any moment—what a person does automatically and spontaneously, often with little awareness of choosing to do so.

Because the neural circuits that need to be modified extend deep into the nonverbal parts of the brain, the learning ultimately

"The conventional definition of management is getting work done through people, but real management is developing people through work." (Abedi Hasan)

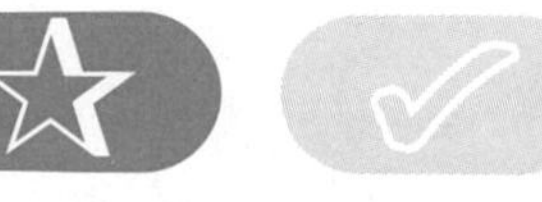     

must be experiential. Learning to control one's temper, for instance, is like learning to ride a bicycle. Understanding what needs to be done on a cognitive level only helps to a limited degree. It is only by getting on a bike and riding it, falling over, and trying again repeatedly, that one ultimately masters the skill. The same is true for most emotional learning. It usually involves a long and sometimes difficult process requiring much practice and support. One-day seminars just won't do it.

Implications for Training and Development

Because emotional learning differs from cognitive learning in a number of ways, training and development efforts need to incorporate a number of elements. Below are some of the most important ones:

1. **Practice**: There needs to be much more opportunity for practice than one normally sees in the typical work-based training program. Not only do there need to be many opportunities during the training itself, but also the learners need to practice new ways of thinking and acting in other settings—on the job, at home, with friends, etc. And this regimen needs to occur over a period of months.
2. **Ongoing encouragement and reinforcement from others**: Even with ample practice during the training phase, the old neural pathways can reestablish themselves all too easily unless learners are repeatedly encouraged and reinforced to use the new skills on the job. The best change programs continue to help participants to apply what they have learned after the formal training phase ends. They also provide periodic reinforcers and reminders to help the participants maintain the fragile new patterns of behavior that they have so recently learned. And effective programs provide social support to help individuals continue to work at strengthening the new competencies that they acquired in the training.
3. **Support from the boss**: A learner's bosses play an especially critical role in providing the support necessary for successful change. Reinforcement by one's supervisor can be especially powerful in helping new emotional competencies to take root. Also, supervisors influence transfer and maintenance of new competencies indirectly by serving as powerful models.
4. **Experiential learning**: In addition to sustained practice, feedback, reinforcement, and support, effective social and emotional learning needs to be based primarily on experiential activity rather than more intellectual, didactic approaches. Developing a social or emotional competency requires engagement of the emotional, non-cognitive parts of the brain.
5. **Emotionally intelligent trainers and coaches**. Because the competencies involved in social and emotional learning are so central to our personal identities, special care and sensitivity is required in the way that training is presented. The personal nature of what is involved in this kind of learning also makes it critical that there be a trusting and supportive relationship between the learners and trainers. Trainers need special skills and more than a little emotional intelligence themselves.
6. **Anticipation and preparation for setbacks**: Even when a training program has all of these elements necessary for successful personal change—ample practice and support, emotionally intelligent trainers, etc.—learners will inevitably encounter setbacks. The old emotional memories and social habits will tend to reassert themselves from time to time, especially when people are under stress. Thus, effective training programs also include "relapse prevention," which refers to a set of techniques that help people to reframe slips as opportunities to learn.

Conclusion

Emotional intelligence can make a big difference for both individual and organizational effectiveness. However, if the current interest in promoting emotional intelligence at work is to be a serious, sustained effort, rather than just another management fad, it is important that practitioners try to utilize practices based on the best available research. Only when the training is based on sound, empirically based methods will its promise be realized.

For More Information

Books:

Cherniss, C., and M. Adler. *Promoting Emotional Intelligence in Organizations.* Alexandria, VA: American Society for Training and Development, 2000.
Goleman, D. *Working with Emotional Intelligence*. New York: Bantam, 1998.

See also:

☆ **SQ: Investing in Spiritual Capital (pp. 43-44)**
✔ **Emotional Intelligence (pp. 354-55)**

"Too many companies believe people are interchangeable. Truly gifted people never are."
(Warren Bennis)

Preventing Your Work Problems from Causing You Stress *by David Allen*

Executive Summary

- Distracting internal conflict is produced by unexpected, unwanted, and unresolved circumstances, of any size and scope.
- Clarifying the successful outcomes desired and the specific actions next required in these situations eliminates internal conflict.
- Effective personal management of outcomes and actions maintains freedom from stress.

Introduction

If you're a knowledge worker, manager, or executive, you must constantly think creatively, make decisions, and manage what you and others are doing about it all. Every input triggers these behaviors, every opportunity invites them, and every crisis demands them. And when you avoid the appropriate thinking and decisions, or don't sufficiently manage the resulting actions, you pay a steep internal price—you lie awake at 3 a.m.

The volume of executive choices in a single day can be astonishing; the typical mid- to senior-level professional makes hundreds. Add the weight of several onerous problems—a 20% staff cut, a customer about to cancel a big deal, and a tax audit next week—and you wonder how anyone gets any sleep at all!

Unproductive worrying doesn't have to happen, however. If you apply a certain thought process and manage the results appropriately with good systems and reviewing habits, you can eliminate the distraction. You can get to sleep in the middle of even the most challenging of situations. But we aren't born knowing how to do this, nor is it taught in school or on the job. There is a learned set of behaviors that can be practiced and mastered. As with tennis, golf, skiing, or sailing, you must learn and apply the basic moves of work to play the game well. And you can continually improve how well you do this.

What Keeps Us Awake?

You can't eliminate challenging circumstances in life and work. What you can improve on is how you deal with them—and how much stress you're willing to allow and endure. There's a difference between stress and intensity. Intensity is concentrated energy focused on dealing with a situation. You can be intensely involved with something and still sleep five minutes later. Stress (the kind that usually keeps people up at night) is infinitely looping inner conflict caused by unfulfilled commitments to yourself.

The broken-agreement syndrome is subtle, though, and not often conscious. Unhealthy stress occurs when some part of you thinks something should be different, but you aren't yet appropriately engaged in making it happen. This kind of stress occurs when:

- you keep something you're paying attention to completely in your head, without acting on it;
- you don't decide and focus on what you want to be true about the situation;
- you don't decide the next physical actions required to move it forward;
- you don't organize reminders of those actions and outcomes to systematically trigger appropriate progressive motion.

Get It Out of Your Head

If you keep something only in your mind, you file it in psychic RAM, the short-term memory space that has limited capacity for filing and retrieval and operates with no sense of past and future. (You told yourself to clean your garage six years ago, and some part of you thinks you should have been cleaning your garage every day since then!) As soon as your RAM contains more than one current agenda item, it creates inner failure and stress, because you can only do one thing at a time, and RAM thinks it should all be happening *now*. If that were only two or three things, it might not be very noticeable. But most people have hundreds and sometimes thousands of woulds, coulds, and shoulds piled up internally, forming a kind of free-floating, unproductive tension and overreaction. Capturing something in writing will start to relieve pressure and facilitate intelligent focus.

Define the Game and Decide the Next Move

Even if you write down something that's bothering you, if you still haven't identified what you really intend to be true about it (the successful outcome), you won't resolve the frustrated feeling. For instance, if you've just found out that a key person on your staff is quitting, just writing down "key person leaving" probably won't make you relax. You must determine what you want to be true, for example, "reorganize staff" or "replace marketing VP." Then you'll have defined the loop that needs to be closed.

This still isn't sufficient, however, to relax your brain. You must also determine the next physical action required to move the situation forward toward closure. What has to happen first to replace your staff person? Send an e-mail? Converse with your partner? Call a recruiting firm? Or wait for someone else to do something?

Put the Results into a Trusted System

Once it's clear where you're heading with a situation and how to kick-start forward motion, it will feel much better. But there's one final critical element that has to be in place to allow you to let it go in your mind: you need to entrust the management of the outcome and the action to a system outside your own head. You have to know that you'll actually look at "replace marketing VP" written somewhere and think about it as often as you need to. And if your next action is to call about recruiting firms, you need to know that whenever you find yourself at a telephone with discretionary time, you'll see a reminder of that call as an option for what you need to be doing. Or if you've delegated the whole project to someone else, you must trust that the person will do it without fail, or at least that you have a reliable tracking mechanism to remind you in a progress report.

Even if you can't decide what to do about something, action is inherent in finding out what you need to know to make the decision. In the rare case that you really do simply need to sleep on it, you still need to trust that sometime in the future you'll be reminded about it. "Ready to decide about selling the company yet?" could go on your own calendar on a date you think appro-

"Brain cells create ideas. Stress kills brain cells. Stress is not a good idea." (Doug Hall)

priate, and you could then rest. You really just decided not to decide, and your own agreement with yourself is kept.

If you haven't engaged all these steps, your mind simply cannot let go. You can numb it or try to ignore it, but you can't fool it. Your mind knows whether you've made necessary decisions about a problem or situation and whether you have a system in place to manage the results. With anything less, some part of your psyche retains it.

But your head doesn't usually do a very good job of managing these distractions. That part of your mind hanging onto the issue doesn't seem to have innate intelligence. If it did, it would only remind you of a current issue when you could actually do something about it. (Most likely you remember you need batteries when you're trying to use a flashlight with dead ones, not as you're passing the battery display in a store!)

So when you think something needs to be different, you've implicitly made an agreement with yourself. If it remains unrecorded, undecided, and unmanaged objectively, your mind will not stop trying to get resolution, and it does that rather ineffectively. It can occupy your thoughts and still make no progress: you're awake at 3 a.m.

MINI-CASES

Carola Endicott, vice president of clinical operations at the 400-bed New England Medical Center in Boston, said: "A specific tool that has become a way of life for me is the simple question: what is the next step? In all of the hundreds of meetings I attend in the course of a year, I have learned the power of asking that simple question. Without it, the worry lingers—was I supposed to do something? Capturing and organizing my own next actions is also critical. By knowing these can be easily tracked and reviewed, I can free up my mind for being open to new ideas—and let it take a rest at night!"

Mike Verville, director of retail operations at L.L. Bean, described the dramatic results of learning and implementing these principles: "When I applied these principles [clarifying outcomes and next actions and tracking them appropriately] it saved my life. . .when I faithfully applied them, it changed my life. This is the vaccination against day-to-day firefighting (the so-called urgent) and an antidote for the imbalance many people bring upon themselves."

Robert Stiller, entrepreneur and C.E.O. of the fast-growing Vermont-based Green Mountain Coffee Roasters, has implemented a company-wide training program to instill these principles. He says: "Particularly exciting and successful for me has been training myself to decide the very next action steps on my projects on the front end. In the past I would list things; and when I'd go to do them, I would have to figure out what to do. I'd often get distracted or lose the energy I had for action. Changing my thought process and categorizing the possible actions appropriately really helps in dealing with the work. By collecting, processing, and organizing the things I have attention on, I'm able to look at the day-to-day flow and go on to the higher level context of the work. With my system working and keeping all the issues, projects, and action steps out of my head and before me, it's easy to sleep, and my sleep can actually help me problem solve."

MAKING IT HAPPEN ▸▸

- Get (and keep) everything out of your head. Whatever you have attention on, write it down. Even the little things.
- Analyze each thing you've collected: does it require action? If not, throw it away or archive it as reference. If it does require action, decide what the next action is and what the successful outcome is that you're committing to. If the action can be done in less than two minutes, do it now. If not, delegate it if you can.
- Organize reminders of the outcomes on a projects list. Organize reminders of work that cannot be delegated, and would take longer than two minutes in lists you can see when you can actually perform the action (for example, be able to see all the calls you have to make when you have a phone and some discretionary time).
- Bring your system current and review everything that represents outstanding outcomes and actions at least once a week.

CONCLUSION

You don't have to finish something to get it off your mind and sleep well. But stress-free is not free. You do have to stop a distracting thought from rattling in your head by tackling it, clarifying what you're committing to make happen, deciding the next action required to move it forward, and entrusting the results of that thinking to a seamless system.

Getting on top of things that are distracting you requires knowledge work—you must think. You need to discipline your focus to take a minute and answer the key questions—What's the outcome I want here? What's the next action? Then your brain can say, done! There's usually an inverse proportion between the amount of time something is on your mind and the degree to which it's getting done. The more relaxed you are, the more productive you'll be.

For More Information

Books:

Drucker, Peter F. *Post-capitalist Society*. New York: HarperBusiness, 1994.

Goldsmith, Marshall, et al., eds. *Coaching for Leadership: How the World's Greatest Coaches Help Leaders Learn*. San Francisco, CA: Jossey-Bass, 2000.

See also:

☆ **Managing Stress (pp. 18–20)**
☆ **Raising the Bar: Setting Effective Targets (pp. 283–84)**
☆ **Urbane Renewal: Trusting Your Own Wisdom—A Competitive (and Satisfying) Advantage (pp. 320–21)**
☆ **Viewpoint: William Bridges (pp. 322–23)**
✓ **Managing Dual Career Dilemmas (pp. 792–93)**
✓ **Stress Management (pp. 412–13)**
Stress and Stress Management (pp. 2117–19)

"I think in every country that there is at least one executive who is scared of going crazy."

(Joseph Heller)

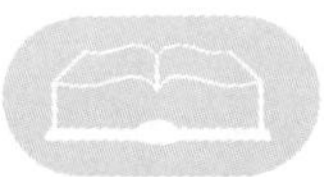

Avoiding Your Worst Career Nightmare by Martha I. Finney

EXECUTIVE SUMMARY

- Employees are more personally and emotionally invested in their work and the outcome of their efforts than at any other time.
- Repeated cycles of vision and failure can wear down resilience and the capacity for renewed hope for a successful outcome in the future.
- Loss of hope can result from the worst career nightmare—and at the same time be an invitation to revolutionary and beneficial change.

Introduction

What's your worst career nightmare? If you're tempted to say, "Why, losing my job, of course," you wouldn't be alone. Globally, with expanding and contracting economies squeezing once highly in-demand employees out of their careers, millions of productive, talented, and educated workers are dreading the notice that they are about to be fired, laid off, made redundant, or whatever term is in vogue for their particular company.

But losing your job is not your worst career nightmare. The moment you need to worry about is when you lose your hope—hope that you can pay for your basic needs, provide for your family's future, finally find an outlet for your potential, intelligence, and talent—and ultimately achieve success and fulfillment.

Hope on the Front Line of the Future

It's not just economic realities that pose a threat to hope. An accident may physically prevent you from being able to do the work you love. Or perhaps your talent might not be equal to the needs of a changing marketplace. War or political strife might force you out of your preferred cultural environment. Corporate politics might make you in conflict with powerful decision makers.

Hope is what drives us forward into our desired future. Hope is usually the last to fall—but when it does, the other side has won. When hope is finally laid down, the personal costs are high, perhaps including:

- loss of mission and vision;
- irrevocably closed doors and destroyed opportunity;
- anger and betrayal at the feeling of a promise broken;
- poor physical and psychological health;
- loss of sense of value and self-worth.

However, hope can be kept alive with a careful and mindful shift in perspective from a feeling of devastation toward one of invitation—invitation to a higher adventure, a more meaningful purpose. The threatened loss of hope frequently provides unexpected benefits: greater self-discovery, new worlds, creative opportunities, a new and more elevated role.

Mini-Cases

Growing up in a small village in northern England, *Carol Roberts* expected to be a hairstylist. She dedicated her young adult years to training in that field, which she loved, but only weeks into her new job a freak accident cut three tendons in her right hand. Her career was over before it had begun. After searching for unskilled work she became a salesperson. While selling video-game components she identified a need for a special joystick, which she then successfully developed and manufactured. Her new enterprise brought her an enviable and unforeseen life of world travel, creative satisfaction, and income beyond her earliest expectations.

Jack Zimmerman grew up poor in Chicago. His dream of becoming a trombonist in a symphony orchestra was born of joy-filled summer nights on the lawn of the amphitheater at the Ravinia Festival. Despite studying music for more than 15 years he failed as a professional musician, then briefly edited a music magazine, a job he loathed. Frustrated and depressed, he gave up music altogether and trained as a paralegal. The weekend of his graduation his phone rang: "Jack, I need a new public relations director who must know the media and love music. Will you come in for an interview?" The call was from the director of his childhood inspiration: the Ravinia Festival.

Franck Malegue graduated from a prestigious French business school and after a short career at L'Oréal realized his passion was to create businesses in Asia. He enjoyed almost a decade of successful startups—he was the first non-Chinese person to joint-venture with the Chinese government importing luxury products—before the Asian economies started to fail. He struggled to stay afloat, but eventually had to close his Asian enterprises. He later described the decision as a "deep release and lightness". Franck has embarked on a journey of self-discovery and rediscovered his passion for work. His new purpose: to help companies and governments work together for the public good.

Making It Happen ▸▸

The following ideas will help to turn a destructive loss of hope into creative, professional rebirth and success:

- **keep informed.** Know what's going on in your industry, community, and economic environment.
- **keep clued in.** Know what's going on in your heart: don't be afraid to understand your own aspirations, motivations, strengths, and weaknesses. What would be your ideal? Use this crisis in hope to understand your inner voice and see in what new directions it might be leading you.
- **keep connected.** Networking is a powerful and valuable tool: meeting people not only provides tangible help, but also helps to clarify one's thinking, providing perspective and a positive approach. It is also a two-way process; people are often happy to help when they can, treating others as they would wish to be treated. Attend professional chapter meetings, make new acquaintances, make appointments to meet people for coffee.
- **keep learning.** Learning new skills, facts, and technologies will do more than help you stay marketable in an alternately expanding and contracting economy. New learnings will help you connect concepts and relationships in new combinations, spark new ideas, and help you see your circumstances in new ways.

"For many wage earners work is perceived as a form of punishment which is the price to be paid for various kinds of satisfactions away from the job." (Douglas McGregor)

- **keep fit.** The psychological effects of exercising and healthy eating are well documented. Rhythmic, whole-body, aerobic exercising—like bicycling, running, or walking—not only releases mood-enhancing endorphins, but it also gives your mind the chance to relax and wander. This is when great ideas are born!
- **keep creative.** Take up a hands-on hobby that results in a tangible product—needlepoint, model-making, or woodworking. If you're caught up in a hope-challenging situation such as a layoff or a politically charged lose-lose environment, it's easy to start believing that nothing you do makes a difference. A craft that results in a tangible object of beauty uses different parts of your brain and gives you solid evidence that you can make a difference.
- **keep away from draining negative influences.** Many things—from people to TV advertisements—can act as a distraction or a debilitating influence that saps hope and energy. Avoid them.
- **keep contributing.** No matter what your skill or expertise there's a need for it in the volunteer community. You can restore hope by engaging your personal purpose in an environment in which it will be received and put to use gratefully!
- **keep moving.** This doesn't mean you should move away from home, it means you should stay active. Take the time you need to wallow in self-pity, fear, and despair—but then get up. Get out of the house. Get out of your head. Fill your calendar with appointments, even if the commitment is as seemingly inconsequential as taking someone to the airport or attending a book-signing. Only by living in the real world will you find opportunities to make progress.
- **keep the faith.** There are other forces at work to help you realize your ambitions, but you may not be able to see all of them. Imagine, for instance, a large clock. You can see its face and its hands. If you look carefully at those ever-so-slowly moving hands, you can even see the passage of time. But most clocks don't show you the wheels turning behind the scenes. You don't give much thought to what's not evident, to all the activity that's taking place in secret, but there's activity going on of which you are unaware. Perhaps certain other elements have to shift into place before your gifts and talents can be engaged again in the most productive and beneficial way. Perhaps while you've been forced to wait for your hope to manifest itself, you've been learning a skill—or gathering experience—that will be vital to your new call to action. Every day comes with its own surprises.

CONCLUSION

To manifest your hope and realize your professional objectives, you often need more than sheer, single-minded, determined effort. You need the efforts and influences of others. You also need the accumulation of skills, insights, and experiences that can only be acquired while you're playing the waiting game. And you need the necessary passing of time, while the rest of the world catches up with your vision and the time becomes right. Then the miraculous will happen. Just when you're about to give up all hope, the phone will ring. Or someone will drop by your office door with a proposal. Someone will say Yes, and hope will flare up again with a bright new light.

For More Information

Books:

Frankl, Viktor E. *Man's Search for Meaning: An Introduction to Logotherapy* Boston, MA: Beacon, 2000.
Pulley, Mary Lynn. *Losing Your Job—Reclaiming Your Soul: Stories of Resilience, Renewal, and Hope.* San Francisco, CA: Jossey-Bass, 1997.
Seligman, Martin E. P. *Learned Optimism: How to Change Your Mind and Your Life.* New York: Pocket Books, 1998.

Web Site:

www.heartlandatwork.com: this site tells the stories of the personal sagas and triumphs of ordinary people who have found work they love.

See also:

☆ **Choosing the Best Training Curriculum for You (pp. 336–37)**
☆ **Managing by Individual Objectives (pp. 171–72)**
☆ **Urbane Renewal: Trusting Your Own Wisdom—A Competitive (and Satisfying) Advantage (pp. 320–21)**
☆ **Viewpoint: William Bridges (pp. 322–23)**
☆ **Viewpoint: Henry Mintzberg (pp. 241–42)**
☆ **Viewpoint: Margaret J. Wheatley (pp. 273–74)**
✔ **Finding Your Calling and Living Your Passion: The Dream Job (pp. 744–45)**
✔ **Preparing for Retirement with Dignity and Grace (pp. 820–21)**
✔ **Working with Mentors: Developing Critical Relationships with Powerful People (pp. 780–81)**
Planning Your Career (pp. 2075–77)

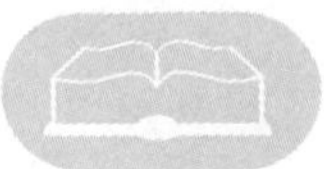

BRAINSTORMING *by Jules Goddard*

EXECUTIVE SUMMARY

- There is a paradox in modern organizational life: the demands placed on organizations to be creative and entrepreneurial are greater than ever; and yet what we observe today are organizations in the grip of profoundly conservative and risk-averse managerial styles.
- Today's corporations have built up a plethora of routines for administering, aligning, measuring, monitoring, and correcting organizational behavior—but a dearth of techniques for inventing, discovering, exploring, improvising, or inspiring new ways of working or new opportunities for wealth creation.

INTRODUCTION

Gary Hamel (2000), writing of the development of strategic thinking in corporate life, writes "New wealth creation is almost always the result of industry revolution. That in turn is the result of strategic innovation. I am as convinced as I can be that the capacity for strategic innovation will be the next competitive edge for companies around the world."

Since the 1950s, brainstorming has been put forward as a significant antidote to all forms of organizational rigidity and defensiveness–and an important catalyst for liberating organizational creativity. However, recent research has cast doubts on the efficacy of brainstorming and this has stimulated some exciting alternatives to it. Electronic brainstorming in particular has the potential to raise the organization's "capacity for strategic innovation."

THE ESSENCE OF BRAINSTORMING

Brainstorming is a particular way of using many brains to storm a singular problem creatively. Its adherents claim that individuals can get to a better solution if they act collectively than if they acted individually.

The virtue that is claimed for brainstorming is that it seeks to distinguish between the two cognitive activities that are intrinsic to all problem solving:

- free conjecture (having ideas)
- rigorous criticism (testing these ideas)

By separating these activities and dwelling exclusively on the conjectural dimension of problem-solving–uninhibited by the threat of destructive criticism–the brainstorming method claims to release the embedded creativity of the group.

Brainstorming is widely practiced–even though recent research has shown unequivocally that "brainstorming groups produce fewer and poorer quality ideas than the same number of individuals working alone" (Furnham 2001).

THE FOUR BASIC RULES

- **Suspend judgment:** refrain from judging the ideas of others as they are articulated and shared.
- **Record all ideas:** transcribe every candidate solution exactly as it is expressed, however half-baked or far-fetched or ill-formed it may seem at first sight.
- **Encourage "piggy-backing":** let each idea spontaneously spark further ideas and build on the creativity of others.
- **Think "out of the box":** encourage and pursue genuinely "contrarian" lines of thought.

THE STEP-BY-STEP PROCESS OF BRAINSTORMING

In its pure state, brainstorming takes the following form:

- The problem to which a solution is sought is stated in the form of a clear question.
- A group of people come together to address the problem.
- One member of the group takes the role of scribe, recording each idea as it is generated.
- Every member of the group is expected to "storm the problem" by contributing as wide a range of potential or tentative solutions as possible.
- No one is permitted to criticize or to challenge any of the ideas put forward, however impractical or irrelevant or nonsensical they may at first sight appear to be.
- Only when the flow of ideas dries up are the candidate solutions reviewed, clarified, amended, and evaluated.

In the event that a host of fruitful ideas emerge, a second stage of brainstorming–sometimes called "reverse brainstorming"–can be applied:

- Each idea deemed worthy of further consideration is posted in its strongest form.
- Group members take each idea in turn and generate all the reasons why the idea may not count as a fully satisfactory solution to the original problem.
- These reservations are then themselves reviewed, clarified, amended, and assessed.
- The reservations that survive are used to filter out the unsatisfactory solutions–leaving only those that have real merit and that are worth taking forward.

THE POPULARITY OF BRAINSTORMING

There are many features of brainstorming that its adherents find attractive:

- *It is inclusive:* it engages the interest and involvement of every member of a work group.
- *It is meritocratic:* it challenges the power structure by assuming that good ideas are not the monopoly of any one level.
- *It is efficient:* it focuses many minds on a single pertinent issue.
- *It is inspirational:* it acknowledges, champions, stimulates, and captures the creativity of each individual.
- *It is synergistic:* it recognizes that creativity is better for being a social activity, where one idea can easily trigger others, and where the total result ends up being greater than the sum of the parts.
- *It is productive:* it maximizes the number of ideas generated by a given group.
- *It is fun:* it promotes the virtues of conviviality and collegiality.

RECENT RESEARCH

The challenge to brainstorming has come from many experiments that have compared the productivity of "nominal" groups–that is, individuals working alone (whose ideas are only later combined and assessed)–with the productivity of "genuine" groups–that is, individuals generating ideas together in the same room. These experiments, conducted since the 1950s, have shown consistently that nominal groups outperform interacting groups (of whatever size) in terms of both the quantity and quality of their output.

How can this be explained? Which of the many assumptions that underpin classical brainstorming would seem to be at fault?

MISTAKEN ASSUMPTIONS IN BRAINSTORMING SESSIONS

Research has suggested that five particularly "unsafe" assumptions provide, in differing degrees, an explanation for

"Brains are becoming the core of organizations–other activities can be contracted out."

(Charles Handy)

the "failure" of groups to outperform individuals:

- The assumption that personal creativity is enhanced by the presence of others: evidence would suggest however that "social loafing"—the pathology by which the group provides an excuse for individual members to "opt out" and take it easy—often outweighs the opposite effect of "social energizing."
- The assumption that prohibiting is sufficient to encourage individuals to propose provocative and unusual ideas without fear of being judged or made to feel foolish or incompetent ("loss of face"): yet, however strongly the rules of brainstorming are espoused, there is evidence that many individuals are still not comfortable giving free rein to their imagination and remain inhibited.
- The assumption that creativity is contagious and that ideas spark further ideas, especially if group members are encouraged to build upon each other's thinking: but the reality would seem to be that "production blocking" is the stronger effect, as individuals are compelled to wait for others to express their ideas, by which time they will have forgotten their own ideas—or lost confidence in them.
- The assumption that group processes encourage divergent thinking and the confidence to explore uncharted territory: however, group processes can also have the opposite effect, sometimes called "anchoring," by which the creativity of the group is constrained simply to embroidering variations on the first theme to have emerged in the session, rather than inventing radically new themes.
- The assumption that time pressures enhance the creative process: but, if anything, the evidence suggests exactly the opposite—that "hot-housing" the process of discovery produces just the stressed state that generally reduces the capacity of people to think freely and imaginatively.

E-Brainstorming: A Remedy?

Electronic brainstorming—whereby individuals, each sitting at their own computer terminal, type in their own ideas (before sharing and appraising them) whilst having easy access to the ideas of others as they are generated—would seem to be an ingenious way of avoiding the problems of social loafing, loss of face, production blocking, anchoring, and hot-housing.

Social loafing becomes a less attractive option if individuals believe that their ideas are likely to be logged and counted; fear of loss of face is alleviated if the principle of anonymity is assured; production blocking ceases to be a problem if individuals can choose for themselves when to create their own ideas and when to attend to the ideas of others; anchoring cannot occur where most of the creative work is performed autonomously; and hot-housing is less likely in circumstances where individuals are not permanently fighting for airtime.

Making It Happen

The following techniques can help to ensure that brainstorming is fully effective:

- Make clear the aims of the brainstorm well in advance, giving people the chance to prepare their thoughts as well as avoiding too much tension at the start.
- Ensure that the people involved are the best ones; check that no one is omitted who could make a valuable contribution to the session.
- Ensure that people are relaxed, comfortable and focused—only then will they make their best contributions and generate ideas.
- Make clear the roles and ground rules (for example, avoid criticism of ideas, ensure that everyone contributes and understands the role of the facilitator)—and positively but firmly ensure that they are followed.
- As a facilitator, set the tone with a positive, energetic approach.
- Once ideas have emerged, look for patterns and links between ideas that may arise. Morphological analysis, which combines and blends elements from different ideas, often follows on from brainstorming.
- Be prepared to prompt discussion and draw people back to the key issues. Thinking about possible scenarios may help, so too can examples—anything that helps people to think innovatively and "outside the box."
- Agree the actions following the brainstorm: what will be done, who will do it and by when. Consider whether other people need to be informed of the results and actions arising from brainstorm.
- Conclude the session so that everyone emerges from the varied process with a clear sense of value and understanding of what has been achieved.

Conclusion

Successful brainstorming encourages people to give vent to all of their ideas on a specific topic, led by a facilitator, in an atmosphere of constructive suggestion rather than criticism, discussion, or even comment. After ideas have been generated, these are then discussed, explored, and prioritized—usually creating new solutions using elements from several suggestions.

The key to success is to ensure that the ground rules are clearly understood by everyone and are fairly applied. The facilitator must be expert and able both to draw out contributions and also to recognize where patterns may lie, while the group must possess (or be enthused with) the passion and commitment to actively participate.

For More Information

Books and Journal Articles:

Furnham, Adrian. "The Brainstorming Myth." *Business Strategy Review*, Volume 11, Issue 4: Winter, 2000.

Grant, John. "Goodbye, Pork Pie Hat." *Financial Times Weekend Magazine*, November 25, 2000.

Hamel, Gary. *Leading the Revolution*. Boston, MA: Harvard Business School Press, 2000.

Weatherall, Alan, and Jay F. Nunamaker. *Introduction to Electronic Meetings*. Chandlers Ford: Electronic Meetings Services, 1995.

See also:

☆ **Creating Corporate Creativity (pp. 271–72)**
✔ **Brainstorming (pp. 542–43)**
Innovation and Creativity (pp. 2000–03)

"Intelligence becomes an asset when some useful order is created out of free-floating brainpower."

(Thomas A. Stewart)

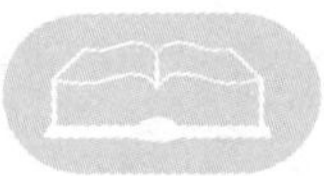

Urbane Renewal: Trusting Your Own Wisdom—A Competitive (and Satisfying) Advantage *by Cliff Hakim*

Executive Summary

- Whatever position you hold, you're struggling to manage and turn a pressing schedule and hectic pace into a productive focus: products and services. But the swirl of activity can thwart your diehard commitment.
- Urbane renewal can overcome this, providing a satisfying, valuable competitive advantage. *Urbane renewal* is your engagement in ongoing development that ushers forth your own wisdom. Act on your wisdom and you'll get lucky, feel satisfied, and add value to your customers.

Introduction

The challenge is learning to recognize and trust your own wisdom, not to defer to what your boss thinks, to what an analyst says, or to what the trend or general consensus is. Today you can't wait for the perfect moment for others to act, or for things to align seamlessly before you step forward. You must trust your own wisdom and commit to action—sooner rather than later.

Didn't your company hire you for your individual wisdom? Is your wisdom to lead or manage? To facilitate or advise? To build new systems or to operate them after they're built?

Your wisdom knows the gratifying and productive processes that you engage in to achieve, to produce a product or service. Your own wisdom is rooted in your vulnerability to know what you think, to understand what you believe, and to respond with meaningful actions. Your own wisdom runs deep. On the surface it may appear to be the expression of your skills and talents. Its beat, though, draws from your courage, and to be courageous is to be vulnerable.

There is no such thing as courage without a sense of vulnerability. It is only when you feel unguarded, exposed, challenged, and committed to action that you're really courageous. The people whom I cite below had courage, but first they were vulnerable—they opened themselves up to discovery personally and professionally to increase their satisfaction and significance. All recognized their need to grow and understood the benefits of their growth for their organizations. There are several reasons why organizations need continued wisdom:

Why Does Your Organization Need Your Wisdom?

- The world keeps demanding and changing. Yesterday's accomplishments are no guarantee for tomorrow's success.
- The marketplace is too competitive for dependence or complacency.
- Customers are looking for the highest-quality, lowest-price deal. They'll go elsewhere in this musical-chairs economy if you and your organization don't innovate or can't deliver.

Mutual Urbane Benefits

The benefits of embracing a program of urbane renewal are:

For the individual

- productive self-confidence
- an increased ability to trust your own wisdom
- courage, vulnerability, values, talents, and skills
- the ability to earn a living by expressing these qualities

For the organization

- innovative partners
- a resilient and confident work force better able to change and compete as the organization reinvents itself and the marketplace shifts

Real Wisdom

Popular public figures such as Duke Ellington, Steve Jobs, and Julia Child have all developed themselves and demonstrated their wisdom. Think about how such people have affected you. Each has contributed to your life, not because they followed a pied piper, but because they listened to and capitalized on their own wisdom. I doubt you'd argue with their satisfaction.

Similarly, organizations are filled with wise people. They're leading and managing and developing themselves despite the politics, competition, and chaos. The following mini-cases provide examples of such people and how they work.

Mini-cases

Natalie Bagdonas, vice president of Technology Systems Engineering at *Fidelity Investments*, taps into her wisdom, using it to lead. Natalie's role, critical to the company's e-business, is concerned with improving the customer's experience on the Fidelity Web site.

Executive coaching and, specifically, a leadership course called Positive Power and Influence have aided Natalie's development. But mostly she's relied on her experience and intuition to achieve her potential. For example, a challenging staff member was placed in her group. During her first conversation with Natalie, this employee announced that she was reluctant to work for her. Natalie could have covered her vulnerability and allowed the new employee to leave. Instead she knew her challenge would be to respond calmly, giving the staff member a chance. Natalie said, "It may take you months to find another job within the system. In the meanwhile I'd suggest that we talk about some ways to work together, at least temporarily." Natalie's manner and invitation began a planning process. She and her staff member talked about the mission of the group, tasks that the employee was best suited for, and educational programs that might best prepare her. Natalie commented, "I provided empathy and structure that set us both up for success." How could Natalie satisfy her external customers—you and me—if she weren't on a similar journey with her internal ones? Natalie benefited by summoning her intuition. The organizational benefit was a productive new staff member resulting in a congruence between serving internal and external customers.

In the world of consulting, Brad Sweet, senior partner at *Computer Sciences Corporation (CSC)*, recalled a mentoring partnership that influenced his development,

"Proficient is defined with one word: skilled. In order to become skilled you must have more than knowledge, you need to apply that information." (Jac Fitz-Enz)

leadership style, and ongoing contributions to CSC. Brad advanced to management early in his career. His new role put him in the position of managing several older consultants.

To learn how to manage in this environment more effectively, Brad partnered another staff member who had similar interests in running a productive organization but who had a very different set of skills. His colleague, a senior organizational development specialist, offered Brad his expertise in management, and Brad offered his colleague advice on technical, especially software, issues.

Their initial barter agreement turned into three-hour meetings. The first two hours were evenly split to talk about whatever business issues they brought to the table. During hour three they would eat lunch and socialize.

Twenty years later Brad now manages a larger group. He didn't realize it back then, but he and his colleague developed a mentoring relationship that he now considers to have fortified his management roots. One of Brad's primary management tools today is to set up formal mentoring partnerships in his division.

"I'm not herding my staff into some artificial training program," Brad says, "but ushering them into a highly relevant, practical relationship and process." Protégés are matched with willing and more experienced partners. They observe their mentors in everyday business interactions and vice versa. In addition they participate in the business at hand. Brad believes, "There's no better teacher than experience guided by a helping hand." Brad benefited by collaborating to learn and excel. The organization benefited from strong leadership and challenged and directed staff.

Steve Ruffing is senior human resource manager for *Medtronic*, the world's leading technology company providing lifelong solutions for chronic disease. He supports 450 salespeople for cardiac rhythm field sales. Steve's satisfaction and significance are derived from his passion—building highly functioning systems or a new organization from the ground up.

"As I evaluate my career history," Steve said, "whether at Honeywell, Northwest Airlines, or in my current role, my success was linked to being thrust into situations in which I had limited knowledge. Staying connected with my network—asking questions and digging and doing research—kept me going. I treated new opportunities like a hobby."

Steve's development wasn't fancy, it was consistent and anchored in his commitment and passion for innovation. He said, "I made a point to talk with others about what they were doing." Steve succeeded by honoring his zeal for building new systems. The organization benefited from his passion converted to innovation and managing others.

Making It Happen ▸▸

Wisdom is not the end goal, but the means you've engaged to achieve your goals. We both know what it takes—courage, boredom, excitement, uncertainty—to complete an event, produce a product, deliver a service, earn a certificate or diploma, or land a new position or job. You had to dig up your own wisdom to get there.

Right now, consider *when did your own wisdom work for you?* Was it when you satisfied a customer, set a personal-best record, received a standing ovation, supported a friend through a crisis, or wrote a topnotch proposal? Now that you have an example in mind, let go of the accomplishment or event and think about the process. The process—what you believed, thought, and did—contains your wisdom. In the process did you

- trust yourself?
- doubt yourself at first?
- focus?
- relax?
- ramble, staying open and flexible?
- talk with others?
- go one step at a time?
- use your special talents?
- say to yourself, I'll confront my fears?

To further deepen your own wisdom, ask yourself, what skills did I use? Did your skills include the following techniques?

- analysis
- influencing
- managing others
- organizing and prioritizing
- consulting and counseling
- seeing the bigger picture
- interviewing
- incorporating different ideas
- explaining and facilitating

Conclusion

As you become more familiar with your wisdom you can use it again and again, consciously, to create the worklife that you want and to make contributions to others. To guarantee the deepening of your wisdom, I encourage you to continue to reflect and dig. As you come to understand your wisdom you'll find it's a well you can draw from to make and sustain your worklife.

For More Information

Books:

Hudson, Frederic M. *The Adult Years: Mastering the Art of Self-renewal.* 2nd ed. San Francisco, CA: Jossey-Bass, 1999.
Rayman, Paula M. *Beyond the Bottom Line: The Search for Dignity at Work.* New York: St. Martin's Press, 2001.
Reich, Robert B. *The Future of Success.* New York: Knopf, 2001.

See also:

☆ **Avoiding Your Worst Career Nightmare (pp. 316–17)**
☆ **Choosing the Best Training Curriculum for You (pp. 336–37)**
☆ **Creating Fun in the Workplace (pp. 37–38)**
☆ **Emotional Intelligence (pp. 312–13)**
☆ **Managing by Individual Objectives (pp. 171–72)**
☆ **Preventing Your Work Problems from Causing You Stress (pp. 314–15)**
☆ **Taking Charge of Your Career (pp. 324–25)**
☆ **Viewpoint: William Bridges (pp. 322–23)**
☆ **Viewpoint: Fons Trompenaars (pp. 27–28)**
✓ **Finding Your Calling and Living Your Passion: The Dream Job (pp. 744–45)**
✓ **Getting Promoted: Forget Your Boss, Serve Your Customers (pp. 784–85)**
✓ **Identifying Your Marketable Skills (pp. 748–49)**

"A formal title and its placement on an organization chart have less to do with career prospects and success. . .than the skills and ideas a person brings to that work." (Rosabeth Moss Kanter)

  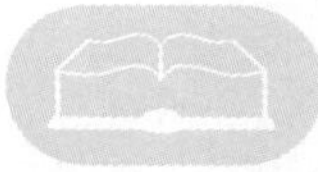    

VIEWPOINT: WILLIAM BRIDGES

"Work" and "Change"

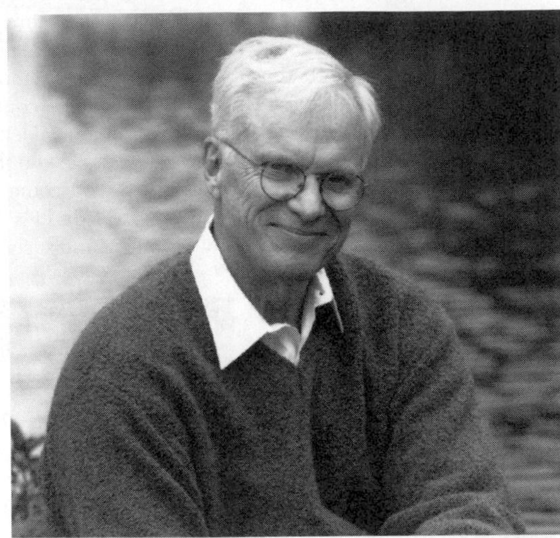

Americans share many of the nomadic traits of some of their Old World cousins. Yet, these New World pioneers, in particular, have long been regarded as people on the move. Even Alexis de Tocqueville noted in 1831, ". . .the American has no time to tie himself to anything, he grows accustomed only to change . . .regarding it as the natural state of man." With my original training in the field of American civilization and my extensive exposure to history, government, and literature, I have been able to draw from a wealth of resources over the years, like de Tocqueville, whose work, *Democracy in America*, is a brilliant study of the American culture.

Similarly, Edward P. Thompson's *Making of the English Working Class* provides extremely valuable information concerning the development of the historical artifact we call a "job." Originally, a "job" was an invention that could go away as easily as it came into existence. The word was first used as a verb, meaning something comparable to "doing." With the advent of the Industrial Revolution, the work people performed could be dissected into discrete tasks, and "job" came to mean something for which people took responsibility, like a possession. This perspective is useful in understanding why the "job" as we know it today—representing more of a function based on a set of activities—is literally imploding.

While I came to appreciate such *external* analyses of change, I was motivated to examine the thinking of others to formulate my own beliefs with respect to the *internal* experience of it. Those influencing my conclusions included: Arnold J. Toynbee, who helped us understand the process of renewal as it occurs in civilization and in a person; Dutch anthropologist Arnold van Gennep, who first coined the phrase *rites of passage*; and philosopher Mircea Eliade, whose analysis of religion assumed the existence of "the sacred" as the object of worship of religious humanity—providing a source of power, significance, and value.

Peter Drucker and Charles Handy, two organizational writers, and Ralph Waldo Emerson—all helped to enhance my perspective around what van Gennep referred to as the "neutral zone"—that period between the end of one phase and the beginning of the next in which the greatest opportunity for discovery and renewal is present. What I particularly came to appreciate is the absence of "focusing mechanisms" in our lives today that allow people to "know" where the end points and beginnings are. Our "transitions" are becoming all-consuming. They overwhelm everything rather than providing channeled influences that move us consciously in some new direction. Given the changing nature of work—with increased demands for knowledge, the disintegration of large corporations, and an accelerated pace of change—it is no longer appropriate to think of work as "fixed" jobs. To appreciate this, we have only to consider the dramatic example of the *Wall Street Journal*, whose offices were directly across from the World Trade Center in New York. The very next day following the destruction of the towers by terrorists, the publisher was able to go to press, utilizing an extensive network of cell phones, e-mail systems, fax machines, and remote sites of operation. With that magnitude of integrated technology, we can't think in terms of individual workers arranged in fixed work units producing a product. Instead, what we need to envision is whole communities of people agreeing to assume shifting roles in a highly flexible context.

All to say, these influences, combined with my own research, have shaped the way in which I view "work" and "change." You see, change is an *event*, whereas transition is a *process* that is always in flux, always disruptive. It forces people to go into a "neutral" role, and it is in this area that business and management have their most important work cut out.

As we begin the new millennium, I predict a dramatic intensification of the trends of the last 10 years. The pace of change has already given business many new advantages. Flexibility and responsiveness are the preeminent qualities of the new workplace. And, while technology enables us to work faster, with fewer jobs and greater productivity, business also has the ability to use more "outsiders." A new construct is well under way as traditional jobs continue to diminish.

Our work habits and lifestyles will change further. We'll need whole new systems of support for employees. To illustrate this: when Washington officials talk about a "safety net" of retirement security, unemployment benefits, and the like, their model is consistently predicated on the old concept of jobs. In the 21st century, *portability*—which allows workers to accrue benefits as they move from one assignment to another—will be terribly important. Business cannot continue to operate in an environment where health insurance, for example, acts as some huge counterweight to the migration of human capital across the workscape.

These are the *external* realities associated with change that I see. The *internal* realities are that people won't be able to keep pace—assimilating the turbulence of a process that gets protracted *ad infinitum*. They may go through the motions, but they won't be into the new work *emotionally*. They'll still be back in the old job. We're seeing this now, and I predict it will continue—slowed only by an occasional crisis—but it will be an unsustainable position leading to all kinds of meltdowns. At the end of the day, there is no end, as "home"—that safe haven from the world outside—is assaulted by beepers, cell phones, and unsolicited sales calls. Families are melting away. I predict other meltdowns, as well—psychological breakdowns, depression, constant fatigue. Even today, large numbers of people are running on empty.

To break this destructive trend, we must work on how the experience of transition can lead to personal renewal. Of course, in the midst of turbulence, usually the last thing we want is transition, especially when we're looking for renewal; but that's how renewal really takes place. We have to learn how to enjoy the ride more, by going *with* the transition—renewing on the fly, so to speak, without necessarily blowing the whistle for a timeout.

New skills will be needed to cope with these conditions. To begin with, *self-management of change* will be essential for everyone. Individuals, as well as businesses, will need to be able to make quick shifts. Leaders in every organization will have to realize how often the rules change, and they will need to assume hugely more responsibility for getting people through these changes successfully—especially for the well-being of the enterprise as a whole. This will involve every aspect of the change process—communication, timing, training, etc. The old way of "command and control" will be a formula for disaster, particularly if people are allowed to remain stuck in the unfinished mess of transition.

We will also need to reframe the concept of a *career* by incorporating elements that are "change-friendly." We must foster an entrepreneurial spirit that feeds on the change process. Indeed, the *new-style career* will require that everyone know:

- what resources, skills, and abilities they bring to the table;
- where the problems are that are yet to be solved and what the "market" needs;
- what new skills will be needed to bring solutions to these opportunities;
- that we are all "micro-companies," requiring strategic planning, training, financing, etc.;
- that transitions lead to renewal, and we need to be open to traversing many neutral zones.

We will have to find ways to make organizations even more flexible in the future. To do this we will have to facilitate the process by letting go of things that are not servicing us well anymore. We will also have to find ways of getting the most benefit from those who are not in the direct employ of the enterprise. This will involve new forms of recognition and reward sharing. And, finally, management will need to reinvent itself. Instead of assuming responsibility for assigning fixed duties, discrete tasks—like purchasing or human resource management—leaders will do better to shift the focus to cross-functional teams and/or outside workers who, in turn, will assume responsibility for getting work done and adjusting continuously—even more quickly—to change.

You see, change is an *event*, whereas transition is a *process* that is always in flux, always disruptive. It forces people to go into a "neutral" role, and it is in this area that business and management have their most important work cut out.

In the end, by involving people more in the design of their own work situations and tying rewards to results, people will become more aligned with the goals of the enterprise and more concerned with its welfare. Not only will this approach enable businesses to prosper, it will avert many of the costly meltdowns of human capital. But make no mistake, this will require a major shift from the old-style thinking of one "master" and one "job" to the new reality of *self-managing transitions*.

Our work habits and lifestyles will change further. We'll need whole new systems of support for employees.

For More Information

See also:

- ☆ **Finding and Keeping Top Talent (pp. 33–34)**
- ☆ **Viewpoint: Meg Wheatley (pp. 273–74)**
- ✔ **Finding Your Calling and Living Your Passion—The Dream Job (pp. 744–45)**
- **Planning Your Career (pp. 2075–77)**

  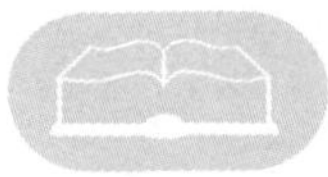    

Taking Charge of Your Career
by Andrew Lambert

Executive Summary

- In an increasingly uncertain world, build on your employability by accumulating skills and experience. Expect to change direction more than once.
- Don't expect to plan specific job moves far in advance. Be open to new opportunities that may arise, including events you can't control such as mergers and restructuring.
- Be clear about what you want out of life as well as work. Reevaluate this from time to time so that your career genuinely matches your needs as they change.
- Do something you enjoy (you won't succeed for long otherwise) and recognize when it's time to move on.
- Try to stay in control of your destiny—you're the only person who's likely to be concerned about your future. Market your talents with conviction.
- If you're a specialist, beware of dead ends. Alternatively, try not to be too much of a generalist, that is, a jack-of-all-trades but master of none.
- Be realistic about what an employer can offer you (for example, adding value to your résumé) and about whether you want to be your own boss: do you have what that takes?

Introduction

The quickening pace of market change means that both organizations and individuals need to focus harder than ever on how to adjust, or even reinvent what they do, if they are to continue to prosper. Just as the average life span of employing organizations is decreasing rapidly, with new corporations and public-sector bodies emerging to take the place of those that fail, so individuals face the danger of redundancy not only of their job, but of their knowledge and skills, if they don't attune to the needs of the future.

What is a career in this context? It *is* still valid to envisage a path that follows a broadly consistent direction. However, this is no longer likely to be with one employer, or even in the same industry and specialty. This means being flexible and adaptive, and adjusting any career plan regularly in the light of changing circumstances, both personal and market-related.

Choosing a Career

With or without economic, peer, and family pressures, some people find it easy to make up their minds early and pursue a path accordingly; others don't, and need time to find a path. Either approach is valid: if you're going to be successful it's important to do something you enjoy, something that will inspire your thoughts and energy.

If you're an early chooser, don't let enthusiasm blind you to some of the hard decisions you may have to make. Research your chosen area thoroughly, identifying the stepping stones and obstacles to making progress, and the life cycle of jobs in the field. Remember also that you may have to shift direction later.

There are advantages in being a late developer in that you can test the waters before committing yourself. Realistically, career planning is often about making opportunistic choices as you progress, not about sticking to a single idea. Many successful people had little idea at the outset that they would end up where they did. They learned from the positive and negative experiences they encountered and made their choices accordingly. However, once they did decide what to head for, they were single-minded.

The importance of academic credentials varies depending on the country you're in and whether or not you are following a specialist path. Some employers see degrees (even MBAs) primarily as a way of choosing among a large number of applicants. As you progress through your career, your track record assumes greater importance.

Specialists and Generalists

If you're expert in something, an employer has a good reason to hire and retain you—at any stage in your career. You will face choices both about how to maintain your specialist edge and how to broaden your managerial skills.

In a corporate context there tend to be two broad types of specialty. Some competences are core to what the organization does (for example, engineering, science, distribution and logistics, trading). Others are the classic support function competences (finance, marketing, IT, personnel, communications, facilities and property management, etc.). All of these have subsets that are more genuinely specialist.

If you continue to specialize, the availability of jobs on offer in companies will steadily reduce until you hit a dead end. You may then need to move into general management or consulting. As you climb the managerial ladder, it's increasingly important to acquire and display general management capabilities such as effectiveness in leading and motivating teams, managing change and projects, and understanding the commercial and systems context.

If you want to lead a support function, first become a generalist by experiencing a number of relevant specialties. If it's your ambition to be a consultant anyway, bear in mind that the real money and status derives from being an owner or partner, and that may not be easy if you enter the arena quite late.

Important Planning Factors

Whether you're moving within or between organizations, you need to provide evidence of your ability to handle varied challenges, demonstrate responsibility as well as initiative, learn from experience, motivate teams, and above all, achieve results. Whatever your level of ambition, be continuously aware of the qualities, knowledge, and skills that will be valuable in the future—don't let yourself become outdated.

Consider:

- what you're working for—job satisfaction, status, material comfort, real wealth, or the buzz of acquiring power;
- whether you intend to have a family at some point (and when);
- whether you feel the need to own a business (large or small), become the leader of an organization, or just be part of one;

"Bureaucratic and risk-averse environments are career killers because of their impact on learning."

(John Kotter)

- whether you want to stay in a certain geographical area or are willing to move;
- personal profiling to help you to understand your long-term capabilities and values.

Choosing an Employer

Building your résumé principally means two things: progressing steadily through professional roles, gathering experience and responsibility on the way; and doing so for recognized and well-respected employers. The competition to work for high-profile employers can be fierce.

Money is, of course, a key determinant of people's decisions, particularly early in their careers or when family finances are demanding. Benefits such as pensions and career development are important too, though. People choose to leave organizations more often because they're unhappy with the opportunities they face or with the attitude of their boss than on purely financial grounds.

So check out what life is really like inside a company, specifically in the department or division you are joining, before you accept an offer (especially if you're concerned about diversity). Some employers' reality doesn't match their reputation, and getting that name on your résumé can prove punishing, whatever the salary.

Staying in Control

It's ever more likely that an organization you join will undergo takeover, merger, or some other form of restructuring that will affect your career path directly or indirectly. Use any such event as an opportunity to learn—or make sure you move early before the rush. Remember that ultimately you can rely only on yourself to market your talent and achievements—no one else will be as interested as you are!

Making It Happen ▸▸

- Don't expect that your career will be with one employer, or necessarily in the same industry and specialty. Plan accordingly.
- Be rigorous in identifying ways to progress, and form an idea of the stepping stones and the life cycle of jobs in the field.
- Be prepared to make opportunistic choices as you progress instead of sticking to one single idea.
- It's important to become expert at something, and to maintain and expand your expertise, in order to give employers a good reason to hire and retain you.
- Learn how to lead and motivate teams as a manager of change and projects, and to deploy your specialist knowledge in a broad context.
- Fit your career plan to a realistic assessment of your abilities and potential. Be confident of your ability to achieve and succeed. It should also fit the level of your personal and financial ambition.

Conclusion

Taking charge of your career is increasingly important at a time when traditional loyalty from employees is much reduced, and when employers are learning (and having to learn) to show greater flexibility about employment patterns. Cradle-to-grave employment and automatic promotions are now, in virtually every area of life, a thing of the *recent* past. So, if your employer is now less likely to map out a career path for you, who will? The answer, of course, is the individual, and to take charge for the future requires a clear focus on oneself. There are several key points to remember when taking charge of your career:

- **Understand, value, and develop your own skills**—know what you do well, what you enjoy, and why. Letting these guide you will help to find a satisfying career path.
- **Recognize all of the factors that are important to you**—for example, geographical mobility, family time, vocational work.
- **Don't be afraid to discuss this with others**—friends and family can provide a useful sounding board, as they often recognize things about you that you may have missed yourself!
- **Plan your career—but not too much!** See opportunities and cope with change, positive or negative, that may arise and impact on this plan.

Finally, staying in control and making it happen are vitally important. Rarely will anyone else help you out or ensure that your career is looked after exactly as you would wish. The responsibility for acting, or reacting to changing circumstances, is yours.

For More Information

Books:

Berman Fortgang, Laura. *Take Yourself to the Top*. New York: Warner Books, 1998.
Brown, Duane. *Career Choice and Development*. 4th ed. San Francisco, CA: Jossey-Bass, 2002.
Ciulla, Joanne B. *The Working Life: The Promise and Betrayal of Modern Work*. New York: Times Books, 2000.
Hakim, Cliff. *We Are All Self-employed: The New Social Contract for Working in a Changed World*. San Francisco, CA: Berrett-Koehler, 1994.
Handy, Charles. *The Elephant and the Flea: Reflections of a Reluctant Capitalist*. Boston, MA: Harvard Business School Press, 2002.
Lore, Nicholas. *The Pathfinder*. New York: Simon & Schuster, 1998.

Web Sites:

www.careerbuilder.com: a comprehensive look at multiple career fields, Career Builder has many helpful resources.
www.monster.com: a global online career network featuring expert advice on job-seeking and career management.
www.careerplanning.org: a U.S.-based Web portal offering links to career planning tools and resources.

See also:

☆ **Breaking the Lead Ceiling (pp. 237–38)**
☆ **Choosing the Best Training Curriculum for You (pp. 336–37)**
☆ **Urbane Renewal: Trusting Your Own Wisdom—A Competitive (and Satisfying) Advantage (pp. 320–21)**
✔ **Finding Your Calling and Living Your Passion: The Dream Job (pp. 744–45)**
Planning Your Career (pp. 2075–77)

"Assignments that used to be seen in terms of their political value in the promotion game are now assessed for their résumé value."
(Rosabeth Moss Kanter)

MENTORING *by Max Landsberg*

EXECUTIVE SUMMARY

As the traditional career ladder crumbles and is replaced by an increasingly organic and fluid structure, individuals and firms are increasingly institutionalizing the once informal relationship known as mentoring, having noticeable impact on the way firms implement management and leadership.

- Mentoring is important in developing and retaining employees.
- Corporate mentoring schemes match seasoned employees with younger colleagues new to either the organization or a level of responsibility, designed to have measurable impact upon the organization.
- Mentors give advice on goal setting and strategizing, sharing their wisdom.
- Mentees gain advice, access to established networks and broader personal and professional perspective.

INTRODUCTION

Mentoring is defined as the process where the leader offers guidance and support to facilitate the understanding of another. Mentoring is vital to delegating and to a range of other management situations—e.g. team building, development of people and managing change.

Most of us probably acquired our mentors more by luck than through planning. But with the erosion of traditional career ladders and the increasingly unstructured composition of the modern firm, individuals and companies alike are seeing ever-greater merits to institutionalizing this once-informal relationship called mentoring.

THE SCOPE OF THE MENTORING RELATIONSHIP

In a corporate setting, a mentoring relationship focuses on skills and career and personal development. At the start of their relationship, neither mentor nor mentee can anticipate all the issues they'll end up discussing. Nevertheless, both parties should be aware of the topics that may emerge.

These topics fall into two broad categories: helping the mentee to achieve learning and career goals, and building the mentee's confidence and self-awareness.

Career issues most typically include:

- whether the mentee's career vision and goals seem relevant and viable;
- how to decode the organization's feedback to the mentee, for example, from an annual appraisal or from a promotion received or missed;
- what experience and expertise to acquire in the short and long terms;
- where to find role models the mentee can identify with;
- whether to accept an internal (or external) job offer;
- how best to promote a corporate initiative that the mentee has conceived;
- how the mentee can best interact with his or her line manager;
- how to react to unacceptable behavior experienced by the mentee, for example, apparent bias, favoritism, or harassment;
- how to deal with the effects of a family problem or disaster, for example, how best to ask for paid or unpaid leave.

Confidence and self-awareness issues may include:

- how the mentee can frankly review personal strengths and weaknesses;
- whether feedback about the mentee's personal style is accurate or not;
- how to overcome apparent career setbacks or feelings of isolation or depression;
- how the mentee can project greater charisma.

Despite this great breadth, mentoring relationships do have their limits. Organizations do not condone nepotistic relationships in which the mentor exerts undue influence in favor of the mentee. The mentor should focus on advice rather than rescue, and should direct the mentee to a professional counselor if needed.

THE FOUR OPTIONS FOR MENTORING

There are four main types of mentoring an individual may seek or an organization may wish to promote. It's important to recognize that these four models are not mutually exclusive. Furthermore, most people have more than one mentor, and those mentors may play complementary roles.

1. **Informal.** Informal mentoring takes place when an experienced person decides to take someone less experienced under his or her wing, often to give career advice.
2. **Positional.** Positional mentoring occurs when the mentor is the mentee's line manager.
3. **Formal.** Formal mentoring programs emerged during the 1990s in an attempt to gain the advantages of natural mentoring while recognizing the limitations of positional mentoring.
4. **Situational.** Situational mentoring provides advice for a specific circumstance, for example, when the mentee has to implement a new computer system or take up a foreign posting.

THE BENEFITS TO ALL PARTIES OF MENTORING

The benefits of mentoring accrue most obviously to mentees: advice, guidance, access to contacts and networks, reassurance, and a broader perspective.

But corporations also benefit through better recruitment, orientation, and retention of staff, better communication across vertical and horizontal boundaries, faster organizational learning, and a stronger corporate culture.

Finally, mentors often benefit by enhancing their interpersonal skills, gaining insight into the workings of their organization and teams, and enjoying the satisfaction of seeing others grow.

TECHNIQUES FOR ENSURING SUCCESS

The excellent mentor:

- helps the mentee to focus efforts and clarify goals;
- prompts the mentee to develop effective strategies, and acts as devil's advocate to challenge them;
- helps the mentee identify appropriate resources, contacts, and role models;
- shares knowledge and wisdom based on his or her own experiences;
- acts as a source of inspiration and motivation while maintaining confidentiality.

Mentors do this by asking penetrating questions that help mentees distinguish real issues from apparent ones; by accepting the mentees unconditionally, asking *how* or *what* rather than *why*; by listening actively to their mentees' feelings as well as their words; and by volunteering observations.

"I didn't particularly care that I was the role model, but I thought it was important that somebody should be."

(Sally Ride)

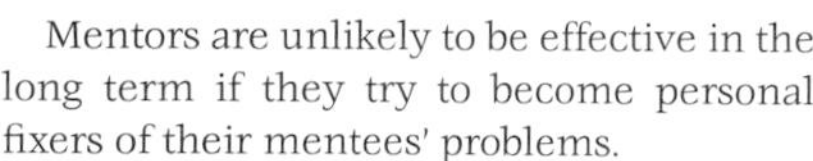

Mentors are unlikely to be effective in the long term if they try to become personal fixers of their mentees' problems.

In obtaining maximum value from the relationship, the three most important attributes of the excellent mentee are openness, initiative, and consideration for the mentor's time.

Mentees clearly need to be open about their objectives and aspirations. But they also need to be open to feedback or other observations by their mentor.

In taking the initiative, the excellent mentee is proactive in meeting with and relating to the mentor, arriving at meetings fully prepared with clear objectives, and taking the lead in suggesting new ways of viewing personal issues. Part of a mentee's task is to follow up on any ideas generated in the meetings and keep the mentor informed about progress.

Finally, the excellent mentee shows consideration for the mentor's investment of time. This involves identifying what the mentor wants to derive from the relationship, accommodating the mentor's schedule when arranging meetings, and providing feedback, praise, and thanks.

Establishing Mentoring Programs

Organizations increasingly aim to reap the benefits of mentoring by setting up formal programs. Contrary to natural mentoring, formal mentoring tends to focus on specific objectives and aim at a measurable impact, for example, employee retention. It usually runs for a limited period, involves professional discussions, and is based on pairing balanced in favor of the mentee.

Such programs typically aim to support employees who are new to the organization or a particular role, or who are part of a group that is in some way specialized or disadvantaged. Formal efforts to provide mentoring for all employees in an organization rarely succeed because of the lack of sufficient mentoring time.

When designing a corporate mentoring program:

- decide whether to adopt a formal program or one that includes an element of natural mentoring;
- develop simple criteria for eligibility to participate and for the maximum number of mentees per mentor;
- agree whether mentees are to choose mentors (recommended) or vice versa, and establish a matching process that is patently fair;
- explain the ground rules clearly, such as commitment to a duration of one year, ability to terminate the relationship at any time without blame or complete confidentiality;
- provide training for mentors and mentees and specify the expected benefits of the program.

Making It Happen ▸▸

- As a mentor, concentrate on helping the employee to achieve learning and career goals, and to build confidence and self-awareness.
- Some mentoring of team members is desirable, but recognize that the line manager, as a superior, can't provide an impartial view of the relationship.
- Use mentoring to enhance the mentor's own interpersonal skills and insights into the workings of the organization and its teams.
- Consciously move between six roles as needed: coach, motivator, guide, counselor, role model, and (possibly) provider of contacts.
- Ensure that the mentee arranges meetings with the mentor, comes fully prepared, and follows up on any ideas that emerge.

Use formal mentoring programs only for selected employees—there won't be enough mentoring time for everybody.

The following factors are critical to the success of corporate mentoring schemes:

- a supportive culture and work environment;
- visible top management commitment, support, and leadership;
- participants are volunteers;
- the mentoring scheme is designed to meet clearly envisioned, critical objectives within an effective time frame;
- agreed terms of reference and ongoing support is provided for mentors;
- that the scheme is regularly monitored and evaluated for successes and drawbacks and inadequacies, and that change is implemented on a sufficiently regular basis.

Key questions to consider when productively implementing a mentoring scheme are:

- what are the specific goals for the scheme?
- have all the people who need to be involved been identified?
- what are the metrics for the scheme's success and, accordingly, how shall the scheme be evaluated?
- is there commitment from the top management?
- what are the necessary resources and are they present?
- how will prospective mentors be trained?
- how will mentors and mentees be paired?
- have the guidelines for the scheme's operation been properly communicated to all parties involved?

Corporate mentoring schemes should be goal-focused and, providing the above points are recognized and effectively incorporated into the process, increase productivity and facilitate greater efficiency.

Conclusion

It is important to remember that corporate mentoring schemes should be clearly envisioned and constructed to meet the actual requirements of an organization. They are currently implementing in an increasing number of organizations where they act as an invaluable asset—a trend that is sure to continue in the future as old-fashioned management structures are eroded and replaced by organic and dynamic modern constructs. Corporate mentoring schemes are a crucial part of such constructs and the benefits of implementing them are certain to be reaped both short-term and in the future.

For More Information

Books:

Bell, Chip R. *Managers As Mentors*. 2nd ed. New York: McGraw-Hill, 2002.

Zachary, Lois J. *The Mentor's Guide: Facilitating Effective Learning Relationships*. San Francisco, CA: Jossey-Bass, 2000.

Web Sites:

http://152.121.2.2/hq/g-w/g-wt/g-wtl/mentoring.htm provides excellent expertise from the U.S. Coast Guard.

www.itstime.com/oct99a.htm offers up-to-date resources and links.

See also:

☆ **Breaking the Lead Ceiling (pp. 237–38)**

✔ **Working with Mentors (pp. 780–81)**

"I'm not an educator. . .I'm a learner."

(Bill Gates)

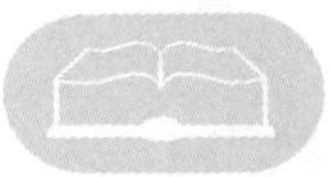

COACHING *by Max Landsberg*

EXECUTIVE SUMMARY

Coaching is an integrated set of actions, aimed at boosting the performance of an individual or team. Coaching includes:

- a context of trust and understanding
- use of "ask," not only "tell"
- agreement on the goals
- optimizing opportunities to perform
- ongoing, ad hoc, feedback
- periodically, coaching sessions of greater depth
- a recognition by the line manager of the obligation to coach, and the incentives to do so

INTRODUCTION

Coaching is an integrated set of actions aimed at boosting a colleague's performance—so that the person being coached (the "learner") reaches his or her full potential, or even redefines their view of their own potential. In the business world, coaching is a systematic form of on-the-job training, provided by professional outsiders, by peers, or (preferably) by the learner's line manager. Coaching typically aims to build skills in communications (written and oral), problem-solving, teamwork, and selling, or even to enhance personal characteristics such as "impact." In this section we will examine the very elements of successful coaching.

A CONTEXT OF TRUST AND UNDERSTANDING

For coaching to be effective, the coach and learner must first agree explicitly on how the coaching will be delivered. A brief discussion will normally suffice if the coach is the coachee's line manager. If the coach is an external professional, a written contract is advisable.

In addition, however, the coach and learner need to trust and understand each other.

Firstly, and most importantly, the learner needs to trust that the coach is not continually trying to evaluate him or her. In corporations or teams in which the culture is highly evaluative, junior people typically do not ask their line managers for coaching support—they avoid showing weakness or ignorance.

Secondly, the coach needs to understand what motivates the learner to perform strongly in the relevant areas—and whether any underperformance derives from a lack of skill, or from a lack of will (since the approach to coaching might differ in these two cases).

Finally, the learner needs to understand how the coach most likes to deliver coaching. This topic is often overlooked—but the truly great coach-cum-manager typically helps the learner understand his preferences.

ASK—DO NOT JUST *TELL*

In all aspects of coaching, the effective coach will more often ask questions than provide, or "tell," answers. This applies both when providing feedback about the learner's prior underperformance, as well as when generating ideas about how to improve that performance.

AGREE SPECIFIC GOALS

Crucial to the coaching process are explicit goals for the learner. This may spring from a recent annual appraisal, from the requirements of a new role, or from some new aspiration by the learner.

It is worth remembering that the best goals are specific, measurable, achievable, results-driven and time constituted—the memorable "SMART" acronym.

OPTIMIZE OPPORTUNITIES

Practice makes perfect—but feedback alone will not. Central to any increased performance by the learner is the opportunity to confront new challenges in the skill area on which he or she is working. This is why line managers are potentially the best coaches of their team members—they can directly assign tasks which will allow the learner to hone the relevant skills.

PROVIDE AD HOC FEEDBACK

Feedback is one of the coach's most important techniques. Ad hoc feedback means regular constructive and considered comments. Ineffective managers tend to provide feedback using generalities ("Your presentations lack impact"). Such negative forms of feedback leave the learner feeling blamed, defensive, uncertain, and lacking in confidence and self-esteem.

By contrast, constructive feedback focuses on specific skills and improvements needed. It clarifies "where the learner stands" and what to do next, and leaves the person feeling helped rather than merely judged. With this in mind, effective coaches deliver constructive feedback in three parts.

1. Firstly, the coach is specific in replaying actions that the learner took. ("During your last presentation you avoided answering a direct question and instead presented another chart.")
2. Second, the coach highlights the implications. ("This made the audience feel that you were uncertain about your material and uninterested in their concerns.")
3. Finally, the coach suggests a desired outcome. ("Next time try to allow time for questions and respond to them clearly.")

This three-part approach (*Action*, *Impact*, *Desirable outcome*—or *AID* for short), is the key to providing useful feedback. It is particularly effective if the three points can be elicited using "ask" mode, ("Which parts of your presentation worked best? Which parts of it worked least well? What was the impact of this? What could you do differently next time?")

Even when delivering positive feedback (that is, praise), effective coaches use the first two steps of this approach. By specifically highlighting the Action and the Impact, the coachee can more fully understand why he or she has "done a good job."

DELIVER IN-DEPTH SESSIONS

Periodically the coach and coachee will decide to complement ad hoc feedback with a 30–60 minute coaching "session."

To ensure a relevant focus and clear outcomes, effective coaches typically use a four-step agenda that covers **G**oals, **R**eality, **O**ptions, and **W**rap-up.

"There's nothing more demoralizing than having nobody notice good performance. . .the successful culture is one that provides constant recognition and applause." (Rosabeth Moss Kanter)

  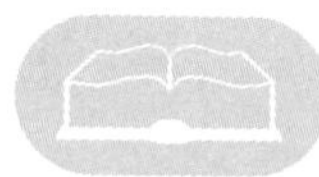    

In the first step (**Goals**), coach and learner agree on the topic for discussion and the objective for the session ("Let's find ways to further develop your presentation skills. Let's find at least three ideas in the next half-hour"). They might also review or amend the longer-term goal ("Let's establish as a goal that you feel able to present the division's results to the board meeting next month").

In the second step (**Reality**), the coach and learner take stock of the coachee's current strengths and weaknesses. The effective coach invites the learner to do most of the talking, starting with a self-assessment. If the coach does provide feedback, it takes the form of specific examples, either in ask mode ("What did you feel about the question-and-answer session at the end of your last presentation?") or in tell mode ("You could have allowed more time for questions").

In step three (**Options**), coach and learner both brainstorm ways forward. What can the coachee do to change the situation? What alternatives are there to that approach? Who could help? The coach's role is not primarily to provide answers. It is rather to stimulate creative ideas from the learner—possible actions that the learner will more naturally buy into.

Finally (**Wrap-up**), the coach helps the learner choose an option and commit to action. This involves identifying possible obstacles, making the next steps specific, agreeing timing, and identifying any support needed. In subsequent sessions the coach will naturally vary the length of each step as needed.

UNDERSTAND OBLIGATIONS AND INCENTIVES

The autocratic manager is fast becoming a dinosaur; all managers are now obliged to coach their teams. This stems from two changes in the business climate. Firstly, employees are now even more avid to acquire skills, and even more likely to change employer if they are disappointed. Thus, coaching is crucial to the retention of talented people. Secondly, the rapid pace of business and the greater prevalence of job rotation and cross-functional teamwork mean that traditional off-the-job training can rarely be scheduled in a timely way.

Strong managers recognize their obligation to coach. They also realize the benefits to themselves: more time because of having a stronger team to which to delegate; less time spent on recruiting replacements; a more positive and enjoyable work environment; and stronger interpersonal skills honed through coaching.

MAKING IT HAPPEN ▸▸

There are many questions that coaches can ask to focus the coaching process. The same questions can also be used for self-coaching—all you need to do is consider a major issue or ongoing behavior that you would like to resolve.

- What are you trying to achieve?
- How will you know when you have achieved it?
- Would you define it as an end goal or a performance goal?
- If it is an end goal, what performance goal could be related to it?
- Is the goal specific?
- In what way is it measurable?
- To what extent can you control the result? What sort of things won't you have control over?
- Do you feel that achieving the goal will stretch or break you?
- When do you want to achieve the goal by?
- What are the milestones or key points on the way to achieving your goal?
- Who is involved and what effect could they have on the situation?
- What have you done about this situation so far, and what have been the results?
- What are the major constraints in finding a way forward?
- Are these constraints major or minor? How could their effect be reduced?
- What other issues are occurring at work that might have a bearing on your goal?
- What options do you have?
- If you had unlimited resources what options would you have?
- Could you link your goal to some other organizational issue?
- What would be the perfect solution?

Once the position has been assessed, the time comes to select the best option and take action. The following questions may then be useful:

- What are you going to do?
- When are you going to do it?
- Who needs to know?
- What support and resources do you need, and how will you get them?
- How will the above help you to achieve your goals?
- What obstacles might hinder you and what strategies do you have for countering these?

CONCLUSION

Coaching has much to do with mentoring and it has a great deal to do with counseling. All three are about supporting an individual to overcome problems, achieve success, and realize their full potential. Common skills for coaches, mentors, and counselors are strong interpersonal skills, and include:

- good listening skills;
- good questioning—getting the learner to open up by asking open questions and avoiding yes or no answers;
- suspending judgement;
- giving constructive feedback;
- checking understanding;
- providing focus.

The value of all these attributes is that they: clarify issues; solve problems by creating options; change patterns of behavior; and help the individual to learn.

Coaching relies on the agenda being set by the learner. They should discover their own way forward, and should feel commitment to their course of action because they have been the one responsible for establishing it. Coaching can be seen as having four main phases:

1. Set **goals** both for the overall coaching relationship and for the individual session.
2. Explore the current position of the learner: the **reality** of their circumstances and their concerns.
3. Generate strategies, action plans, and **options** for achieving the goals outlined above.
4. Decide **what** is to be done, by whom, how, and when.

For More Information

Books:

Landsberg, Max. *The Tao of Coaching*. New edition. Santa Monica, CA: Knowledge Exchange, 1997.

Whitmore, Sir John. *Coaching for Performance*. New edition. Naperville, IL: Nicholas Brealey, 1996.

Web Site:

www.coachville.com: this site aims to be the definitive coaching portal.

See also:

✔ **Coaching for Better Performance (pp. 344–45)**
Coaching, Counseling, and Mentoring (pp. 1925–28)

"Run with your head the first two thirds of a race and with your heart the final one third."

(Jack Daniels)

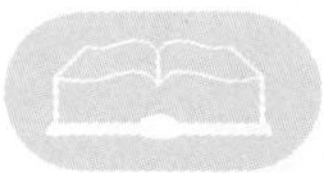

DRIVING FEAR FROM THE WORKPLACE
by Dick Richards

EXECUTIVE SUMMARY

- Disallowing or disowning fear extinguishes the passion needed to achieve organizational goals.
- Engaging human energy, including fear, and connecting it with organizational purpose is a fundamental task of management.
- Engaging human energy is an aspect of the art of management. It requires mastery of skills and techniques as well as intent to value the full spectrum of emotional energy.
- Human energy, particularly fear, can be oriented and employed as an effective tool for success.

INTRODUCTION

In the early 1980s management guru W. Edwards Deming admonished managers to "drive out fear so that everyone may work effectively for the company." He was referring to fear that causes people to distort or ignore unpleasant results. Deming held that such fear stifles learning. Despite Deming's admonishment, fear still stalks workplaces and remains a potent force. The Discovery Group, an opinion survey organization, concluded that "half of all employees do not feel free to voice their opinions openly."

Fear takes many more forms than the one Deming described. It is apparent when we retreat from speaking to someone who does not listen, or when we recoil from saying difficult things to people who are known to shoot messengers. Fear is present whenever we suspect a hidden agenda, or when we are summoned to find a better way of working. It shows up as job insecurity and as dread that our positions might be usurped. It is close by when we feel unwilling to take risks or do what we know is right, and whenever we masquerade as someone other than who we are. Startup companies frequently have an entirely distinct set of fears such as raising capital and making payroll.

Fear originates from different sources: as a consequence of the world we live in; or induced by people who want us to feel fearful; or self-generated in response to a challenge. Whatever its form or source, the effects of fear are insidious and pervasive; it corrupts learning, improvement, innovation, measurement, and relationships. However, fear itself is not the lone culprit. Disallowed or disowned fear, which I refer to as "unacknowledged fear," is another, perhaps more insidious, danger.

FEAR AND PASSION

While it seems that fear ought to have no home in our workplaces, we do want passion. We want excitement about visions. We want enthusiasm for strategic plans. We want the energy that people bring to work when they feel those emotions. It's obvious that emotions are sources of energy that compel action. That's why we welcome passion, excitement, and enthusiasm. When people experience those emotions things get done.

It's less obvious that emotions are inextricably connected to each other. We cannot readily isolate just one emotion. We cannot drive out fear, or any other so-called negative emotion, without the risk of driving out the energy we want—excitement and enthusiasm. Daniel Goleman, author of *Working with Emotional Intelligence*, writes, "When the dictates of a boss determine the emotions a person must express, the result is an estrangement from one's own emotions." For example, when a manager suggests, either directly or subtly, that he or she wants everyone to feel part of one big happy team, but never fearful, angry, or sad, people are likely to shut their genuine emotions down altogether and put on a happy face. Goleman calls this "emotional tyranny." When we fail to acknowledge fear, we also extinguish passion. The result is a robotic workplace.

ENGAGING EMOTIONAL ENERGY

A fundamental task of management is engaging human energy and connecting it with organizational purpose. One popular model posits four kinds of human energy. *Physical* energy is the energy of the body. Engaging physical energy involves deciding who does how much of what work and when. *Intellectual* energy is of the mind. Engaging it involves such activities as making sense of problems and finding creative solutions. *Spiritual* energy arises from feeling connected to something larger than the self—an idea, a cause, a place, a deity. Engaging spiritual energy is seen in attempts to gain commitment to a vision or mission; these are endeavors to enlist people in a higher calling.

Our concern is with the fourth of these—*emotional energy*, and specifically fear. Engaging emotional energy means, first, mobilizing the passion and commitment that spurs people into action and, second, dealing effectively with emotions that create barriers to such action. George Davis, cofounder of Davis & Dean, a global project-management education company, believes that our prevailing model of management fails when we deal with fear. Davis says, "We reward managers who are warriors. The warrior's orientation is toward short-term goals: win today's battle, take that hill." With such a mentality, Davis believes, induced fear becomes useful because it's a good short-term motivator. "The problem is," says Davis, "if you use it again and again the fear becomes replaced by a sense of helplessness. This is typical of many corporate cultures. It is what employees of large organizations express when they resist change, dismiss change efforts, or become passive and cynical. Induced fear, which seems to work great in the short term, eventually creates apathy, a sense of oppression, and hopelessness."

When induced fear loses its impact, the warrior's impulse is to induce more fear. In the hands of a warrior, Deming's injunction to drive out fear may become a license to make people afraid to be afraid, or at least afraid to admit to being afraid. Rather than engaging emotional energy, warrior managers are likely to kill it.

SELF-GENERATED FEAR

There is little human progress without fear. Psychologist Susan Jeffers said it this way: "The fear will never go away as long as I continue to grow." This is a different kind of fear from the induced fear used to threaten people. This fear is the self-generated consequence of accepting a meaningful challenge. It can be a friend, a harbinger of an important opportunity. It is stimulating

"Increasingly our society does not see social obligation as the primary obligation of the individual. The primary obligation is loyalty to the corporation." (John Ralston Saul)

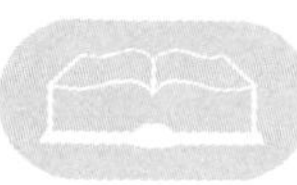

rather than paralyzing and can provide energy to meet the challenge.

Erik Sprotte, former director of human resources for Sears, accepted the challenge of helping to start a Web enterprise called FreeSamples.com. Self-generated fear arises from the challenge of "going where others haven't gone." Sprotte says, "I used to fear making a mistake like not having the facts at a meeting. This new kind of fear is good. It creates discipline and helps me focus on the important things that I really need to do."

The Art of Engaging Fear

While fear is an individual phenomenon, people collude with one another in order to allow it to remain unacknowledged. They agree, if only tacitly, that fear should be disallowed or disowned, that "we just don't talk about those things around here." Disallowing and disowning fear thus becomes a cultural norm. Managers can and should take the lead in encouraging people to allow and own their fear. Today's business environment is soaked in challenge. Managers need all the energy they can muster from themselves and from people they manage. They cannot afford to ignore or destroy emotional energy, even when it arrives in an uncomfortable form.

Management, like any other work, is part science and part art. Engaging emotional energy is an aspect of the art of managing. As painters engage the energy of paint and poets engage the energy of words, managers' artistic medium is the energy of the people they manage. So managers must be acquainted with human energy in the same way that a painter is acquainted with how paint behaves, or a poet with the rhythm of words.

Mini-cases

How Three Companies Deal with Fear

Many organizations are reluctant to have outsiders know they are fearful, so best practices aren't freely shared. However, Pfeffer and Sutton mention three companies that manage fear successfully:

PSS/World Medical, where managers work to get problems raised faster than they would be in a fearful environment, gives everyone the opportunity to communicate with others and does not punish honest mistakes.

SAS Institute, where David Russo, vice president of human resources said, "We punish nothing."

Men's Wearhouse, where senior managers believe so strongly in eliminating fear that a transgression such as stealing is often viewed as a signal that development is needed rather than that the transgressor ought to be fired.

Making It Happen ▸▸

Mastery of any art depends on developing certain skills and techniques. Consider the following:

- **Befriend your own fear.** There are three skills involved in befriending fear (or any other emotion): recognizing how it feels physically, putting it into words, and engaging it productively. None is easy in a work context, because most organizations discourage any emotion that seems negative. Find the people around you who are competent at managing their emotions. They are not those who overcontrol, but those who express emotions well and use them to create productive actions. Learn from those people.
- **Facilitate honest dialogue about fears of all kinds.** This requires developing a high level of trust. People won't talk about their fears if there are negative consequences for doing so. Once fear is in the open, treat it as a gift. Treat induced fear as a signal that someone must learn to challenge rather than threaten. Treat self-generated fear as a signal that growth is at hand. It is important to listen and cope with uncomfortable situations.
- **Challenge rather than threaten.** Drive out induced fear and befriend self-generated fear. George Davis argues: "It is far more valuable to challenge people than to induce fear. The person will then create his or her own basket of fears that will spawn creativity."
- **Connect people with purpose.** Erik Sprotte is convinced that people need to believe in what their organization is doing and need to know how their contributions make a difference. He says, "Good managers help others understand their role in keeping the boat afloat. When we know we have a common goal, and have owned our fear, we can keep each other inspired every day."

Conclusion

Mastering the art of management requires developing skills and learning techniques for engaging human energy, including fear. And it requires something more. In *The Art Spirit*, artist and art teacher Robert Henri wrote, "The technique learned without a purpose is a formula which, when used, knocks the life out of any ideas to which it is applied." If we employ skills and techniques to engage the energy of fear, they will work only when coupled with a heartfelt purpose to value the full spectrum of emotional energy. When this is accomplished, your team will have the motivation, discipline and cooperation required to reach ever more demanding organizational activities.

For More Information

Books:

Deming, W. Edwards. *Out of the Crisis*. Cambridge, MA: MIT Press, 2000.

Goleman, Daniel P. *Working with Emotional Intelligence*. New York: Bantam Doubleday Dell, 2000.

Henri, Robert. *The Art Spirit*. New York: Harper & Row, 1984.

Jeffers, Susan. *Feel the Fear and Do It Anyway*. New York: Fawcett Columbine, 1992.

Ryan, Kathleen D., and Daniel K. Oestreich. *Driving Fear Out of the Workplace: Creating the High-trust, High-performance Organization*. 2nd ed. San Francisco, CA: Jossey-Bass, 1998.

Web Sites:

www.articles911.com offers articles about managing difficult emotions such as anger and fear.

www.discoverysurveys.com/articles/itw-14.htm, the survey about workplace fear mentioned in this article.

See also:

- ☆ **Really Leading: Leadership That Is Authentic, Conscious, and Effective (pp. 222–23)**
- ☆ **SQ: Investing in Spiritual Capital (pp. 43–44)**
- ☆ **Viewpoint: Margaret J. Wheatley (pp. 273–74)**
- ✓ **How to Network and Market Yourself (pp. 758–59)**
- ✓ **Identifying Your Marketable Skills (pp. 748–49)**
- ✓ **Leaving with Style: How to Exit with Dignity (pp. 800–01)**
- ✓ **Making the Decision to Take a Risky Career Move (pp. 806–07)**
- ✓ **Managing Career Transitions: How to Enter an Entirely New Field (pp. 802–03)**

"If your employer starts upon a course which you think will prove injurious, tell him so, protest, give your reasons, and stand to them unless convinced you are wrong."
(Andrew Carnegie)

  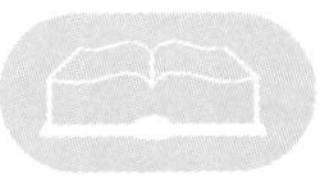    

Managing Internal Politics
by Kathleen Kelley Reardon

Executive Summary

- Advancing business and career goals often necessitates acting politically.
- Those managers who reject—or fail to understand—internal politics do so at their own peril.
- The nature of the political arena affects the productivity, morale, and success or failure of individual employees.
- Career success depends on matching the individual's political style to the firm's environment.
- Smart managers familiarize themselves with the warning signs of political pathology before it's too late.

Introduction

Many of the hurdles managers must face and overcome have little to do with technical competence. Rather, they have to do with politics. Internal politics is a fact of life in organizations, yet many managers and C.E.O.s will tell you their success is largely due to allowing "no politics" in their firms. They'll regale you with stories of how they use and encourage "people skills" to create a desired environment and accomplish organizational goals. What they're really talking about is how they use politics.

In common vernacular, "politics" is used to describe what people do to influence decision-makers, accomplish hidden agendas, and surreptitiously advance their careers, often to the detriment of others. But politics is not always so sinister. By its very nature, politics involves going outside usual, formally sanctioned channels to accomplish objectives, but not necessarily in a secretive manner and often to the benefit of all involved. When used to influence people in the service of valid company goals, politics becomes a positive tool indeed. The team leader who makes valuable connections with people who can advance the team's efforts is acting politically.

While a high level of field-based competence is required, given two competent persons, the one who has political savvy, agility in the use of power, and the ability to influence others is more likely to succeed as a senior manager. Indeed, to the successful senior manager in a competitive organization, day-to-day life *is* politics. That's why smart business people think like Caroline Nahas, managing director of Korn Ferry International, Southern California. To be politically astute, you need to "read where the trend lines are" and "be ahead of the game."

Of course, politics is not always positive. Sometimes, people must defend themselves from political maneuvering. When surrounded or targeted by coworkers playing underhanded political games, job survival may require one to act similarly. In organizations where biases or favoritism dictate who gets key assignments and promotions, political maneuvering is required to get into the loop. Here again, there's nothing unethical going on. The organizational political arena merely requires the use of relational strategies to advance oneself. In short, the astute manager must understand how politics functions in organizations and how to advance his or her and the firm's own goals.

Sizing Up the Political Arena

The first step in acquiring political acumen is learning to identify the kind of political arena in which you operate. Without this knowledge, managers operate in the dark, wondering why opportunities were lost. All four primary political arenas—minimal, moderate, highly political, and pathologically political—often coexist inside a large organization.

In a ***minimally politicized*** arena, the atmosphere is amicable. Conflicts rarely occur and don't usually last long. The atmosphere is camaraderous—there's an absence of in- and out-groups, and one person's gain isn't seen as another's loss. Rules may be bent and favors granted, but people treat each other with regard and rarely resort to underhanded political means. These are excellent environments for people uncomfortable with aggressive politics. Unfortunately, such organizations are more the exception than the rule.

Moderately politicized organizations operate on commonly understood and formally sanctioned rules. They often include smaller, fast-moving firms and large ones focused on organizational agility. Where customer focus, results, teamwork, and interpersonal trust are priorities, politics are rarely destructive, and often focus on surfacing worthwhile ideas. Achieving objectives via unsanctioned methods isn't unusual, but tends to be subtle and deniable. When conflicts get out of hand, managers will invoke sanctioned rules or shared mores for resolution.

As a manager, however, when such an arena becomes dysfunctional, you will see considerable denial before unspoken political rules surface to where you can identify and address them constructively.

In a ***highly politicized*** culture, conflict is pervasive. Instead of applying formal rules consistently, combatants only invoke them when convenient. In-groups and out-groups are clearly defined. Few people dare to communicate directly with senior managers. "Who" is more important than "what" you know, and work is often highly stressful, especially for those in out-groups. When there's conflict, people rely on aggressive political methods and involve others in the dispute. Highly political organizations are usually incapable of resolving conflicts constructively. They place blame and terminate losers. Such quick fixes rarely alter the dysfunctional pattern.

Pathologically politicized organizations are often on the verge of self-destruction. Productivity is suboptimal and information massaging is prevalent. People distrust each other, interactions are often fractious, and conflict is long-lasting and pervasive. People must circumvent formal procedures and structures to achieve objectives. They spend much time covering their backs. Management uses a carrot-and-stick approach to control people. Subordinates are seen as stubborn, willful—even stupid. In the classic *Harvard Business Review* article, "Asinine Attitudes toward Motivation," Harry Levinson described this as the "jackass fallacy."

"The least one can say about power is that a vocation for it is suspicious." (Jean Rostand)

Identifying Political Pathology

To avoid political pathology, managers must recognize its encroachment. Here are five indicators that it's time to alter the political environment to save it from self-destruction.

1. **Frequent flattery** of persons in power, coupled with abuse of people in weaker positions.
2. **Information massaging**. No one says anything that might rock the boat, and the common means of communication is hint and innuendo.
3. **Malicious gossip** and backstabbing are common, even where little overt conflict appears.
4. **Cold indifference**, where no one is valued and everyone is dispensable, indicates the area has been systemically polluted by people in charge. Survival is based on obsequiousness, and getting others before they get you.
5. "Fake left, go right." People, even entire departments, purposely mislead others in order to look good when they fail. Teamwork is absent. Managers sacrifice subordinates' careers to avoid looking bad.

Matching Political Style to Political Culture

The second crucial step in learning to manage politics is identifying individual political styles. The mix of styles and their "fit" with the predominant political arena exert considerable influence on goal achievement.

The Purist

The least political are "purists," who believe in getting ahead through hard work. They shun politics, and rely on following sanctioned rules to get things done. Purists are usually honest—sometimes naively so. They believe in getting ahead by doing their job well. Purists trust other people and prefer to work with those who do the same. Behind the scenes grappling for power and prestige is not of interest, hence purists are best suited to minimally political climates.

The Team Player

"Team players" believe you get ahead by working with others and using politics that advance the goals of the group. They rarely put career needs ahead of group needs. Team players prefer to operate by sanctioned rules, but will trade favors or engage in other relatively benign politics to achieve team goals. Focused on doing the job right and creating conditions for team member advancement, team players are best suited to moderately political environments.

The Street Fighter

An individualist, the "street fighter" believes the best way to get ahead is via rough tactics. The street fighter relies more on subliminal politics than the purist and the team player, but is just as likely to invoke sanctioned rules when they serve personal goals. Street fighters watch their backs, push hard to achieve personal goals, and are slow to trust others. They thrive on the "cut and thrust" of business, enjoy intrigue, and derive gratification from working the system. The street fighter is comfortable in highly political arenas and can survive in pathological ones as well.

The Maneuverer

The "maneuverer" is also an individualist, one who believes in getting ahead by playing political games in a skillful, unobtrusive manner. Subtler than the street fighter, but uninhibited about using politics to advance personal objectives and favored team objectives, maneuverers prefer to do so in deniable ways. They look for ulterior motives in others, have little regard for sanctioned rules, and rely largely on subliminal politics. These smooth operators are less committed to hard work than purists, and only operate as team players when it suits their agendas. People get in the way of a maneuverer at their own peril. The maneuverer is best suited to highly political and pathological arenas.

The task of all managers with regard to politics is to assess the arena prevalent in their division, and that of the larger organization. Is it becoming highly political or pathological? If so, is this because opinion leaders are of the street fighter or maneuverer styles? There's nothing inherently wrong with street fighters, and the occasional maneuverer may be an asset if he or she brings something valuable to the group. A predominance of these styles, however, can tip a division or organization closer to pathology, a condition that is difficult if not impossible to reverse. Savvy managers familiarize themselves with political warning signs and, as IBM C.E.O. Lou Gerstner did when he implemented a policy of straight talk, they take steps to stem the tide of political self-destruction.

Making It Happen

- Assess the degree to which your organization is politicized. Is the atmosphere amicable or distrustful? Is the workforce productive, or does conflict prevent work getting done?
- Recognize the signs of impending political pathology: flattery of superiors, malicious gossip, information massaging, indifference, and purposeful misleading.
- Take steps to detoxify the workplace: communicate more openly and directly, invoke sanctioned rules or shared mores to resolve conflict, emphasize solving problems over placing blame.

Conclusion

Politics are a reality in the workplace; and, consequently, one must manage the conflicts that arise from political behavior. Politics, in and of itself, is not bad if it works to serve company goals by making sure that the workplace is productive and that morale remains high. Politics must never be allowed to degenerate into a self-destructive process.

For More Information

Books

Jay, Antony. *Management and Machiavelli*. Upper Saddle River, NJ: Prentice Hall, 1994.

Reardon, Kathleen Kelley. *The Secret Handshake: Mastering the Politics of the Business Inner Circle*. New York: Doubleday, 2000.

See also:

✔ **Handling Conflict Situations (pp. 356–57)**
✔ **Managing Upward (pp. 778–79)**
The Prince (p. 944)
Machiavelli (pp. 1016–17)

"Brutally speaking, our scheme does not ask any initiative in a man. We do not care for his initiative."

(F. W. Taylor)

RESPONSE ABILITY—HOW MANAGERS STAY UP WHEN TIMES ARE DOWN *by Paul Stoltz*

EXECUTIVE SUMMARY

- Adversity in business is increasing. A poll of 45,372 managers in dozens of industries worldwide revealed that 98% predict a more difficult, chaotic, uncertain, and demanding future. A separate longitudinal, global survey of 57 different companies shows that the number of adversities a manager faces daily has climbed from seven in 1990, to 13 in 1996, and 23 today.
- Today, managers must have *Response Ability*—the ability to respond optimally to whatever happens the moment it strikes.
- The most important variable in unleashing and growing human capital is how people respond to growing levels of adversity.
- Adversity Quotient (AQ) is a measure of a person's hardwired pattern of response to adversity and a measure of Response Ability.
- AQ can be measured, permanently rewired, and strengthened, impacting individual and collective performance, agility, and resilience.

INTRODUCTION

Adversity, ranging from annoyance to tragedy, has become the rule in corporate life. Adversity is everything that gets in the way of, or blocks, an organization's quest to fulfill its vision, achieve its goals, and accomplish its strategic plan. To keep these imperatives alive requires greater resilience than most managers possess. Given that managing adversity lies at the heart of management's ability to unleash human capital, how can managers learn to harness adversity to launch new levels of opportunity and momentum? As adversity rises, every manager's and organization's resilience and effectiveness hinges on *Response Ability*, the ability to respond optimally to whatever happens the moment it strikes. Response Able managers thrive amid the same difficulties that paralyze their less Response Able counterparts.

MANAGING IN ADVERSITY

The Silent Toll

While today's workplace is arguably more dynamic and exciting, it is also exacting a growing toll. A Gallup Poll revealed that 19 percent of workers are "actively disengaged"—they are delivering a small fraction of their talents at work. Furthermore, 61 percent (or more) are at least partially disengaged. The estimated cost to corporations in the United States alone is $350 billion; multiply that several times over for a worldwide estimate.

As adversity rises, workers feel increasingly stretched. Their work and their lives become more complex, chaotic, uncertain, and demanding. Their entire world tasks them to do more, faster, and better. The physical toll adversity takes upon the majority of the workforce includes a multitude of dismal symptoms, including diminished immune functions (with increased sick days), sapped energy, insomnia, and stress. Inside most people, today's levels of adversity create a chronic and toxic biochemical reaction that holistically degrades their performance deeply.

The psychological toll of the adversity trend manifests as depression, restlessness, anxiety, and pessimism—all psychosocial phenomena which are occurring at epidemic levels and growing. These conditions are also symbiotic, feeding off and flourishing in each other's presence. Overall the grand-scale toll of adversity in organizations, their capacity, and human capital is inestimable. Fortunately, it is also largely unnecessary.

The Truth About Motivation

Nearly every manager perceives motivating others as an important and essential duty. Yet, intuitively, we know that we cannot motivate others: authentic motivation originates and is sustained from deep within the self. Attempting to motivate others can be like painting your car red to make it go faster. It may *feel* faster, but very little has happened to strengthen performance.

To fully understand the myth and challenge of motivation, we must consider three forms of capacity. A person's *Required Capacity* is what the world demands of them, or what is required of them to perform their job effectively. As adversity mounts, most people's required capacity is growing at an accelerated rate, making it harder to remain fully engaged and motivated.

When we motivate others, we are striving to help them tap and deliver their *Existing Capacity*—their talents, aptitudes, competencies, experience, knowledge, wisdom, and energy—to the challenge at hand. People are hired for their Existing Capacity under two assumptions: that they will tap most, if not all, of it on a regular basis and that they will grow it to meet or exceed the Required Capacity.

The portion of their capacity that a person actually taps and delivers is called their *Accessed Capacity*. Anyone who has hired someone knows that many people fail to access their best abilities at work. This is a chronic source of frustration among managers and the major source of lost or underutilized human capital. The quest of every manager must be to hire and grow Response Able people who can consistently tap and grow their Existing Capacities. Clearly traditional methods of motivation, screening applicants, and training employees fall critically short of what is required.

ACHIEVING SUCCESS AND RESPONSE ABILITY

Fortunately, there is a way to assess and strengthen how people respond to adversity, or their Response Ability. Beyond your IQ, experience, or skill-set, it is your Adversity Quotient, or AQ, that most directly predicts and determines your ability to weather and harness the current storm for future gains.

AQ is scientifically valid, a reliable measure of your hardwired pattern of response to adversity. More than 100,000 employees in dozens of companies representing a broad range of industries have measured their AQs and learned about how their CORE affects their Response Ability, capacity, and resilience.

A Response Able culture is one in which. . .

1. *People thrive on adversity.* The greater thechallenges,themoreenergizedandengaged people become. In fact, people get bored if things are too calm for too long.
2. *Challenges unleash greatness.* People are

at their best in trying situations and times. They consistently dig deep and bring out their greatest talents when faced with the impossible.

3. *There's calm in the storm.* There is a norm of cool-headed decision making. People are not easily fazed or thrown off by unexpected turns of events or adversities.
4. *There are stories of overcoming.* There is likely to be a history of resilience, with revered sagas of heroes who faced and overcame adversity to create pivotal advancements.
5. *Managers hire and keep the best.* Self-motivated, fully engaged people are attracted to and are likely to stay with the organization.

A low AQ culture is one in which. . .

1. *People crumble under pressure.* When adversity strikes, people are stunned, angry, resigned, and uninspired.
2. *Situations bring out the worst.* As adversity mounts, people act in selfish, distant, panicked, mean, disengaged, and dispassionate ways. Conflicts arise, panic spreads, helplessness grows, and problems fester.
3. *It seems like a blame game.* Adversity makes people point fingers and sidestep blame. The greater the adversity, the more accountability, trust, and agility suffer.
4. *The bleeding edge moves in.* Despite efforts to reward self-motivated top performers, there is a history of losing these people. Turnover remains a chronic, incalculable loss of human capital and potential.
5. *Excitement reduces to passionless pursuit.* People go through the motions, but the culture lacks passion, excitement, risk-taking, and a compelling sense of purpose. A mere five to 20 percent of the workforce drives the success of the entire organization.

Adversity Quotient: the CORE of Response Ability

AQ is comprised of four CORE dimensions, which together determine and drive Response Ability. Each dimension plays a unique role in a person's resilience, performance, innovation, and strength.

C = Control: *To what extent do I perceive I can influence the situation at hand?*

This dimension of AQ assesses perceived control, not actual control. It pinpoints your propensity for self-determination on the one hand and helplessness on the other.

O = Ownership: *To what extent can/should I play a role in improving this situation?*

This dimension assesses propensity for inner accountability. In contrast to blame, which is about pinpointing the source of the problem, ownership is about playing even the smallest role in improving the situation, regardless of its cause.

R = Reach: *How far does this adversity reach and affect other areas of work or life?*

This dimension pinpoints the perceived size or magnitude of the adversity, which has a dramatic impact on likelihood to take meaningful action.

E = Endurance: *How long can you continue to confront adversity in a positive way?*

This dimension provides a reading on how you will deal with the next challenge, obstacle, or difficult personality.

When we measure these four characteristics, individually and collectively, basic patterns emerge. A company can be seen as either having a Response Able culture, or not.

MINI-CASES

Organizations Building Response Ability

ADC Telecommunications successfully positioned itself to provide vital hardware and services to the prominent warriors (Lucent, WorldCom, Sprint, AT&T, etc.). Yet, when the entire sector lost 70 percent of its market value in a matter of a few months, ADC's stock plummeted, despite record earnings. ADC decided that creating a Response Able, resilient sales force would position them for a superior and quicker comeback against competitors. In classes in Singapore, Spain, China, Canada, and the United States, ADC's global sales force from 16 countries learned new ways to get, keep, and grow people who can thrive in a demanding, dynamic industry.

Marriott International recognized that the defining factor in sustaining their aggressive growth curve while maintaining their high standard of service during an economic downturn would be their associates' and leaders' Response Ability.

Many other organizations—including FedEx, Deloitte & Touche, Palm Pilot, and Qualcomm—have focused on how well their employees and managers handle adversity, resulting in improved performance, retention, agility, innovation, problem solving, resilience, and accelerated change.

MAKING IT HAPPEN ▸▸

Growing a Response Able workforce that can not only cope with but thrive amidst adversity-rich times requires a commitment to forgo the comforts of mediocrity and the courage to reinvent existing norms regarding Control, Ownership, Reach, and Endurance—the pattern of response to adversity. To start to build Response Ability, managers must:

- Assess the Adversity Quotient of their current workforce.
- Hire high AQ people.
- Grow high AQ, Response Able leaders.
- Pay attention to how people respond to adversity the moment it strikes, assessing Control, Ownership, Reach, and Endurance.
- Focus on what facets of a situation can be influenced, no matter how impossible it may seem.
- Establish norms of people stepping up to improve and address difficulties the moment they arise.
- Contain each adversity in scope immediately.
- Be the first to recognize and seize the opportunity embedded in each adversity.
- Strategize around worst case scenarios in a matter-of-fact way.

CONCLUSION

Adversity is on the rise, and that's the *good* news! Great companies and managers are and increasingly will be those who can harness the force of adversity to create even greater opportunity. They assess and strengthen their Adversity Quotients to become more Response Able. And they use their growing Response Ability to optimize their human capital and to stay up when times are down.

For More Information

Book and Video:

Collard, Betsy. *Building a Resilient Workforce As A Competitive Advantage.* Kantola Productions, 1998. See: **www.kantola.com/products/execbriefings/resil.html**

Seligman, M. P. *Learned Optimism: How to Change Your Mind & Your Life.* New York: Pocket Books, 1998.

See also:

☆ **Downsizing with Dignity (pp. 16–17)**
☆ **Emotional Intelligence (pp. 312–13)**
☆ **Viewpoint: Christopher Bartlett (pp. 45–46)**
✔ **Building an Awesome Contact List (pp. 760–61)**
✔ **Using Lateral Moves to Further Your Career (pp. 776–77)**

"When, in response to deteriorating business, a company blames outside forces or covers up its problems. . .it ensures failure."
(Charles G. Koch)

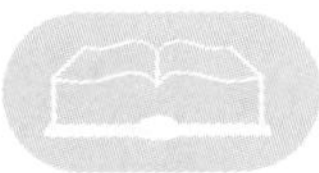

CHOOSING THE BEST TRAINING CURRICULUM FOR YOU *by Daniel R. Tobin*

EXECUTIVE SUMMARY

- Individuals cannot rely on their employers to provide lifelong employment or a full learning agenda keyed to career opportunities. You must take responsibility for designing your personal learning agenda and finding the learning resources you need to achieve that agenda.
- Within and outside of your company, there is an ever-increasing array of learning opportunities, ranging from traditional training programs and college courses to less formal learning methods.
- To get ahead you must understand your company's and your own personal goals and design a learning agenda that contributes to the company's goals while satisfying your own learning and achievement objectives.

INTRODUCTION

Companies are increasingly questioning their investment in employee education, seeing ever-increasing expenditures with no direct tie-in to the company's bottom line. As a result training is typically high on the list of areas to cut.

Many corporate training groups are rushing to convert their programs to e-learning, which they see as an opportunity to reduce costs in response to (or in advance of) corporate budget reductions. At the same, time e-learning has become a hot commodity on the open market, with dozens of e-learning companies springing up alongside new e-learning ventures from hundreds of universities around the world.

Employees face an ever-increasing array of learning options but receive less and less guidance on how to use these opportunities to advance their own careers. Now more than ever employees must take responsibility for their own learning and understand how that learning can contribute to their own career plans. In this section we will outline key issues relating to personal development planning.

THE FOUR BASIC QUESTIONS

The first step is to consider four fundamental questions:

1. HOW DOES YOUR WORK CONTRIBUTE TO ACHIEVING THE COMPANY'S BUSINESS GOALS?

Look at your company's business objectives for the next year and the next five years. What is your role in helping the company achieve those objectives? To answer this question you need to understand the company's major business processes and your role within those processes—you need to widen your perspective from your narrow functional area to the larger goals of the company. This is an interesting topic of discussion for your manager and your coworkers; you can gain a better understanding of your role in the company and achieve greater job satisfaction as you start making the connections between what you do and the company's business results.

2. WHAT CHANGES DO YOU NEED TO MAKE TO IMPROVE YOUR OWN, YOUR GROUP'S, AND THE COMPANY'S RESULTS?

Once you understand your role, ask what needs to change to meet individual, group, and corporate goals. Then identify what is necessary to learn. Not every change requires new learning—you may already have the necessary knowledge and skills but never have been given the opportunity to apply them to your work.

In most cases you can't act in isolation; you need to get the approval and support of your manager and/or your fellow workers. Major and even minor business processes rarely change through the efforts of a single individual. Look at both your own and your group's learning needs.

When you see a factory that shows year-to-year increases in productivity over a number of years, you will generally find that workers and managers are constantly assessing the need for change and working together to determine how best to make those changes, experimenting with work processes, inventories, and materials. This is the philosophy behind many Japanese manufacturing plants, and the results extend across the world to factories that have adopted similar team-working and learning environments.

3. HOW WILL YOU ACQUIRE THE KNOWLEDGE AND SKILLS YOU NEED?

Once you've identified your learning needs, you need to develop your learning agenda: how and from whom will you learn? Look at what your company offers in the way of formal training programs, and find out what opportunities are available from local colleges and professional associations.

E-learning opportunities are growing exponentially, with many colleges, universities, and e-learning companies providing courses through Internet-related technologies on virtually any technical, professional, managerial, or personal skills topic. However, little formal guidance exists on how to judge the quality of e-learning resources.

There are also many informal learning opportunities available. A learning coach (someone who has the knowledge or skills you want to acquire) within your company or in the community can be a valuable asset whether you're using traditional learning methods or studying on your own. If you can't locate a coach, team up with co-workers who are trying to master the same material so that you can coach each other, or join a discussion group on the Internet. You can find discussion groups on many company Web sites that allow you to team up with other workers at other company locations. There are also discussion groups on professional association Web sites and public discussion forums (for example, www.groups.yahoo.com).

With the large number of learning options available inside and outside the workplace, employees must also act as their own consumer advocates. It is unlikely that you will receive any recommendations. Most people enroll in training programs, which require a significant investment of time and money, without carrying out adequate research. Before undertaking any learning activity you should:

- get reviews from others who have already completed it;
- if possible, talk with the instructor to make sure the program covers what you feel you need to learn;
- ask the instructor to make changes if you find that the learning program isn't meeting your needs;

"If you want to be a champion, you have to train like a contender." (Linford Christie)

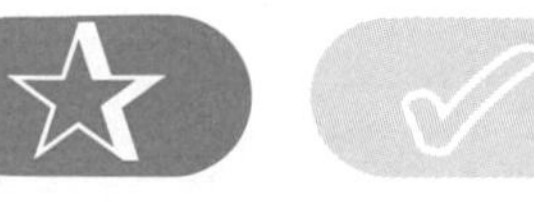     

- find out whether the instructor will be available by telephone or e-mail after the program ends to answer questions that may arise as you try to apply your learning to your work. Also ask other students in the class if they will be available, and offer yourself as a resource to others.

4. How Will You Apply Your Learning to Your Work?

Few employees work in isolation or can apply new learning to their work without affecting the work of others in the company. It's to your advantage to secure allies in your attempts to change the way you, your group, and the company work. Involve your manager, who ideally will be able to coach you and reinforce your learning as you apply it to your job. But even without having mastered the content, your manager can provide encouragement and allow you to experiment without fear of failure. If your manager can't play the coaching role, get one or more coworkers to learn along with you so you can try the new approach together, supporting each other and solving problems together as you apply your new knowledge and skills.

Before trying to apply your new learning to your job, it's important to negotiate an agreement with your manager recognizing that you need time to try out your new knowledge and skills and that some mistakes may occur initially; you should also set some goals for improved performance based on the new methods. This sets expectations on both sides. From the manager's point of view, this is the payoff for the investment in your learning, while for you it's the promise of support for that learning.

Finally, once you've mastered a new skill or acquired new knowledge, share it with others. Many people interpreted the old saying "knowledge is power" to mean that they should hoard their knowledge—in the belief that it makes them indispensable. But knowledge is a unique economic good. Most economic goods lose their value by being shared: if you give this book to someone you no longer have it. Knowledge is unique in that it increases in value the more it's shared. In today's business climate employees who are known to share their knowledge and bring along other employees are more valued and better rewarded than those who hoard their knowledge.

Making It Happen ▶▶

One of the biggest dangers a leader can make is to assume that there are one or two—or half a dozen—methods for learning; there are in fact many, depending on the situation. Whatever training approach is chosen, there are four useful principles to consider:

1. **Commitment**—a commitment from the senior managers right through the organization to actively train and develop new and existing employees.
2. **Planning**—a plan from the organization detailing how it will routinely include training into its business plan. This includes linking employees' training to the business's objectives and setting targets for training.
3. **Action**—evidence of how the organization has delivered on its plan: how staff training has been completed to meet the organization's objectives, and how development needs are being continuously assessed and met.
4. **Evaluation**—assessing the effectiveness of training activities is the final phase. It involves assessing the original plan against what is actually happening, and also assessing the quality of the training that is being provided and the benefits that result.

The following steps outline some actions that may be valuable when making progressing this initiative in the organization:

1. **Appoint a program champion** responsible for managing and overseeing the program.
2. **Undertake a self-assessment** of current training and development activities in the organization; in particular, consider
   - how well-trained staff are at all levels;
   - how you decide to train people—the criteria and process that is used;
   - the methods used to train and develop people;
   - the overall priority that training is given and the resources that are used.
3. **Produce a plan**, ideally derived from the overall business plan, that details:
   - the process for assessing and agreeing training needs;
   - how employees will be trained and developed within their organization;
   - the resources, including finance, that will be available.
4. **Implement the training program.**

Conclusion

Faced with an ever-increasing array of available learning options, you need to become much more adept at choosing the right learning activities, applying them to your work to improve business results, and planning your learning agenda to support your career with your current employer and into your future. By asking yourself the four basic questions given above you can create a personal learning agenda that will help you succeed in any company in any industry. Companies greatly value people who take the initiative to plan and accomplish their own learning agendas and then apply that learning to make a real difference in business results.

For More Information

Web Sites:

To find publicly offered e-learning and classroom programs, it is worth visiting two Internet portals that broker programs and materials from hundreds of different organizations:

THINQ **www.thinq.com**

TrainSeek **www.trainseek.com**

See also:

☆ **Avoiding Your Worst Career Nightmare (pp. 316–17)**
☆ **Breaking the Lead Ceiling (pp. 237–38)**
☆ **Managing by Individual Objectives (pp. 171–72)**
☆ **Taking Charge of Your Career (pp. 324–25)**
☆ **Urbane Renewal: Trusting Your Own Wisdom—A Competitive (and Satisfying) Advantage (pp. 320–21)**
☆ **Viewpoint: William Bridges (pp. 322–23)**
☆ **Viewpoint: Henry Mintzberg (pp. 241–42)**
☆ **Viewpoint: Fons Trompenaars (pp. 27–28)**
✔ **Creating and Balancing the Portfolio Career (pp. 804–05)**
✔ **Freelancing: Setting Up As a Free Agent (pp. 814–15)**
✔ **How to Network and Market Yourself (pp. 758–59)**
✔ **Identifying Your Marketable Skills (pp. 748–49)**
✔ **Staying Marketable: Identifying Your Transferable Skills (pp. 786–87)**
Management Development (pp. 2031–33)

"It takes less time to put up a factory than to train men of competence to run it." (Indira Gandhi)

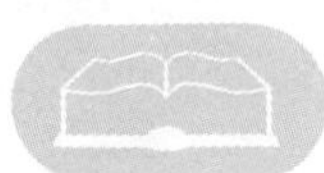

Developing Exceptional Problem-solving Skills *by Christopher Hoenig*

EXECUTIVE SUMMARY

- We live in an era where technology is our primary tool, knowledge is the strategic asset, and problem solving is the paramount skill.
- The best problem solvers in any situation or field rely on sophisticated knowledge of how to apply just six essential practices.
- These six practices also represent differing problem-solving preferences, or "personalities." You need all six of them for your problem solving to be complete and competitive.

Introduction

In the digital age business organizations are being challenged by global competition, as well as technological and social change, to solve bigger, tougher problems faster, better, and cheaper than ever. Improved problem-solving capability is the ultimate competitive advantage, and the best organizations are increasing the sophistication with which they systematize their problem-solving processes. Individuals who wish to lead organizations or build successful careers in the digital age will need to build their understanding of problem solving as a field in itself.

Sophisticated Problem Solving Is Based On Simple Essentials

Knowing how simple elements generate complex results is the ultimate source of power. Three primary colors blend to make up the paintings and films that capture our imagination. Two binary states are the foundation of the digital processing that underpins the information age.

In the same way, there are six essential skills involved in human problem solving: generating mindset, acquiring knowledge, building relationships, managing problems, creating solutions, and delivering results. The tougher, larger, and more demanding a problem or opportunity is, and the faster and more competitive your environment is, the more important these skills become.

I am not talking about the "old" problem solving—traditional cookbook approaches that are small-scale, linear, deficiency-oriented and tactical. I am talking about a "new," rapidly evolving definition of problem solving that encompasses large-scale, nonlinear, opportunity-oriented and strategic work. This is problem solving in the age of biotech, the Web, smart materials, and the global economy.

We live in an era when information technology is our primary tool, knowledge the strategic asset, and problem solving the paramount skill. Problem-solving ability is now the most sought-after trait in up-and-coming executives, according to a recent survey of 1,000 executives by Caliper Associates, reported in the *Wall Street Journal* by Hal Lancaster ("Managing Your Career.") To put it bluntly, if you're not a problem solver, your career potential is limited.

The Problem-solving Journey

I refer to the problem-solving journey because the mixture of problem solving and adventure blends two rich sources of knowledge into one. Exactly like an adventure, problem solving is a journey from a starting point to some distant destination. It is a journey into the unknown—through fear and exhilaration, confidence and disappointment.

Thinking of the solutions of problems (or opportunities) as journeys brings the topic alive. Professional knowledge about problem solving is, by definition, abstract. But the language, images, ideas, and principles of adventure and exploration make it accessible and invest it with the drama that real problem solvers experience: the disciplined planning, the long waits, and the moments of crisis and celebration. Moreover, since we have all traveled, this metaphor helps us tap into our own undiscovered sources of wisdom about the principles and practices of problem-solving journeys.

The Difference between the Best and the Worst Problem Solvers

The difference between the best and the worst problem solvers is how many of the six essentials they can marshal (by themselves or with others), and how deeply the skills are understood, individually and collectively. Poor problem solvers understand the skills incompletely and therefore cannot marshal a complete capability. Great problem solvers know the skills well enough to pull together and manage all six, or exhibit one in great depth as part of a team.

The journey from novice to world-class expert in any field begins by understanding the six essentials, practicing them, mastering them at one level, and then moving on toward the limits of your potential.

At some point in this process, the best problem solvers rise above their profession in a multidisciplinary fashion. Each of the six essentials represents a bundle of habits, skills, and knowledge that come together in problem-solving "personalities." Each personality draws its strength from a variety of specialties and professions.

The six personalities serve as a convenient way to assess yourself and others. They allow you to determine your own personal mix of strengths and weaknesses and how you can put together a complete problem-solving capability. Great problem solvers know their strengths and weaknesses, and they build teams to compensate for them, creating wholes that are equal to or greater than the sum of their parts.

The Six Essentials of Problem Solving

Generate the Mindset (the Innovator)

The **innovator** focuses on moving from self-doubt to innovation by developing potent ideas and attitudes, above all through seeking out alternative points of view. The ability to do this improves your effectiveness in moving creatively through a problem-solving effort. An innovator's potent mindset sets the stage for discovery, because the combination of commitment and open-mindedness generates the widest possible field of opportunities to consider.

Leading innovators such as Dee Hock, founder of VISA international, Jeff Bezos of Amazon.com, and John Seely Brown of Xerox PARC epitomize the innovator's mindset. Great companies known for a history of innovation, such as 3M, IDEO, and Procter & Gamble, have made it a pervasive part of their culture.

"The problem when solved will be simple." (Anonymous)

Know the Territory (the Discoverer)

The **discoverer** concentrates on moving from innovation to insight by asking the right questions and getting good, timely information. Better knowledge helps you define problems more effectively, choose the best routes, and identify what's at stake. A discoverer's knowledge of a territory brings understanding and insight, which reveal the most likely problems and opportunities in higher relief. With more investigation, the implications of those problems become more apparent as a foundation for action.

Leading discoverers such as Craig Venter of Celera Genomics, or Nobel Prize winner Dr. Eric Wieschaus are examples of what outstanding discovery can produce. Great companies and universities that have built a foundation on research and discovery include Bell Labs, MIT, and CalTech.

Build the Relationships (the Communicator)

The **communicator** deals with how to move from insight to community by cultivating quality interaction and so creating an ever-expanding circle of relationships based on service, loyalty, and identity. Communicators develop the support and human context needed to create and implement change effectively. Through their mastery of relationship building, communicators connect potential journeys to their actual implications for real people. They help determine whether a problem-solving effort is worthwhile, for whom, and why. Then they generate a core group that will tackle the journey and a network that will support the effort.

Great communicators like Franklin Roosevelt and Winston Churchill demonstrate the power of communication and relationship building in tackling historic problems. Companies that have built worldwide reputations for service because of their attention to communication include L.L. Bean, Hallmark Cards, and Dell.

Manage the Journeys (the Playmaker)

The **playmaker** focuses on moving from building a community to giving that community a sense of direction by choosing destinations and strategies. Fostering an understanding of the stages of any problem-solving journey helps people to set goals, define success, and develop effective plans. Playmakers take the attitude, knowledge, and people brought into play by innovators, discoverers, and communicators and shape the destinations, direction, and strategies to make the journey a reality.

Playmakers such as Nelson Mandela, Colin Powell, and Jack Welch demonstrate the power of leadership in directing problem-solving efforts. Companies like Kleiner, McKinsey & Company, and American Airlines have institutionalized that leadership in a way that has lasted over decades of business success.

Create the Solutions (the Creator)

The **creator** shows how to move from leadership to power by designing, building, and maintaining optimal solutions. Creators help to bring the best technology, people, and tools together in complete, flexible solutions that will fit the problem you're trying to solve. A creator takes the requirements and goals of a playmaker, which define the journey, and figures out what it will take to get the group where they want to go. When there is more innovation and better knowledge, when there are richer relationships and better-defined problems, then solution design and construction are more focused.

Great creators such as Bill Gates and Paul Allen, Steve Jobs, Steve Wozniak, and Thomas Edison exemplify the passion, talent, and will required to build new solutions. Companies such as Microsoft, Toyota, and General Electric have built corporate systems and cultures that sustain quality creative ability over long periods of time.

Deliver the Results (the Performer)

The **performer** concentrates on moving from power to sustainable advantage through intuitive and disciplined implementation, which allows you continually to exceed expectations. Performers can help to conquer complexity, friction, and scale with simplicity, discipline, and a competitive edge. Performers take the goals and strategies of the playmaker and the solutions of the creator, and work to achieve full resolution of the problem. Innovation, knowledge and well-developed relationships aid in their efforts. When all the other roles are done well, the performer is able to focus completely on achieving full resolution and not on redesign, unplanned maintenance or changing requirements.

Great performers such as Lou Gerstner in business, Reinhold Messner in mountain climbing and Isabelle Autissier in sailing, show the character and savvy it takes to deliver great performances. Companies like Federal Express and McDonalds have built empires on the precision and consistency of performance over time.

Making It Happen ▸▸

Master the six problem-solving essentials and the stages of any problem-solving journey so that you can locate yourself in problem-solving situations and organize your attack on the problem.
Diagnose yourself, to understand your strengths and weaknesses and how to compensate for them. Do a free diagnostic self-assessment to find out what type of problem solver you are at www.exolve.com.
Move in the new direction, and fill the gaps in your problem-solving team.

Conclusion

The new professional economy is placing an increasing premium on the mind, body, and soul of the adventurer—the problem solver—on people who can conceive, organize, and lead expeditions that add value to society, business, and humanity. These problem solvers have an adventurer's blend of innocence and wisdom, self-reliance and a willingness to collaborate, professional competence and the capacity to scale new peaks, as well as the resilience to persevere through uncharted territory.

And just as in the old economy or the next economy after this one, no amount of buzz, momentum, or technology will cover the lack of problem-solving essentials for long. True problem-solving capability is what drives enduring advantage in any field, at any time, in any place.

For More Information

Books:

Bradley, Bill. *Values of the Game*. New York: Broadway Books, 1998.
Dorner, Dietrich. *The Logic of Failure: Why Things Go Wrong and What We Can Do to Make Them Right*. New York: Metropolitan Books, 1996.
Senge, Peter. *The Fifth Discipline: The Art and Practice of the Learning Organization*. New York: Doubleday, 1990.

See also:

✔ **Solving Problems (pp. 408–09)**
✔ **Making Rational Decisions (pp. 566–67)**
The Fifth Discipline (p. 905)
Peter Senge (pp. 1046–47)
Decision Making and Problem Solving (pp. 1950–53)

"By blaming others, we fail to find the real solutions to our problems and we do not carry out our own responsibilities."
(Jeb Bush)

Management Checklists

  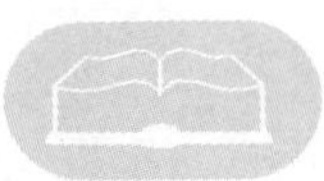    

Management Checklists

Finding Practical Solutions for Everyday Business Problems

The Management Checklists provide you with a comprehensive handbook of practical answers to everyday business challenges. Each list reflects current thinking and best management practice.

The Management Checklists come from the Chartered Management Institute—one of Europe's largest management organizations—and aim to answer the most pressing everyday problems that you will face at work. They provide step-by-step routes to success, from tasks such as **Conducting a Performance Appraisal** to **Handling Customer Complaints**. Each checklist includes a handy list of dos and don'ts, benefits and disadvantages, and thought starters to stimulate discussion and critical reflection.

Contents

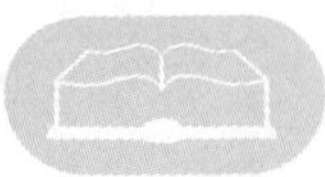

Coaching for Better Performance

This checklist describes the processes involved in coaching as a method of developing skills, potential, and performance.

Definition

Coaching is especially effective used as one of a range of learning activities and training processes when an individual or learner has potential that can best be developed through a focused relationship with a more experienced and senior colleague.

It is both a style and a method of conducting a one-on-one relationship in which a manager empowers and helps a more junior employee develop his or her skills through a series of planned work-based activities. In coaching, a manager works with the learner to identify where the learner could develop new skills to apply in either a current or a future job, and provides support, guidance, and advice to help in achieving the professional aims.

In coaching sessions the manager often works directly with the learner, offering the chance to try things out and supporting the learner in finding areas for further improvement. Coaching effectively may also involve bringing in others with appropriate skills and experience to run specific sessions, with the manager coordinating the overall coaching strategy.

Coaching can be part of mentoring, but they are different training techniques. Coaching is appropriate for passing on specific tasks, skills, or techniques that can be mastered and measured, while mentoring has more to do with longer-term development or progress within an organization.

Coaching also uses assessment skills, but adapts them to a more constructive purpose. Assessment is the neutral and objective observation of success or failure, while coaching is a helping relationship in which the coach provides tips, guidance, and support.

Advantages

When used selectively and appropriately, coaching:

- is a cost-effective approach to development that is tailored to individual employees;
- develops the skills of existing employees instead of requiring additional staff;
- provides the coach with a sense of achievement and value;
- sends a positive message to other employees about the value the organization places on staff;
- motivates employees, reducing staff turnover and the associated costs of recruitment and orientation;
- helps the learner reinforce and apply theoretical and knowledge-based learning acquired in courses and other training.

Coaches need to:

- be caring, supportive, and patient;
- have good listening skills;
- be aware of their own strengths and weaknesses;
- have good verbal and nonverbal skills;
- be good observers and counselors.

Disadvantages

- Because it is one-on-one, coaching can be a drain on limited resources.
- If there is no real structure to the activity, coaching can become nothing more than the senior person simply lecturing the junior.
- To provide coaching sessions, the coach/manager may need help from other people who may not be committed to coaching as a training technique.

Action Checklist

1. Plan the Approach

Hold a preliminary meeting with the learner to establish the ground rules.

- Identify, agree on, and prioritize the learning needs to be addressed by the coaching sessions.
- Agree on and set learning objectives—clearly state what the learner should achieve (for example, "By X date you will be able to explain/demonstrate how to do YZ.")
- Agree on success criteria, or task objectives, specifying the standard against which success will be judged ("By the end you will be able to weld two pieces of pipe to industry standard tolerances.")
- Review the options and make a detailed plan—this is where the coach prepares to demonstrate, explain, and review a task or skill.

2. Identify the Learner's Preferred Learning Style

Everyone learns in different ways. For coaching to be effective, it is essential to understand what these might be for the learner. Explore and test a mixture of methods, including watching, listening, thinking, reading, observing, reflecting, and trying things out, to identify the approach that gives the biggest payback, or the combination that seems most appropriate.

3. Identify Opportunities for Coaching

In coaching, the learner should try out skills in an actual task, so you need to plan the occasion and place to conduct a coaching session. From the identified list of priorities, agree on a time for the first session.

4. Carry Out the Coaching Session

Bearing in mind the learner's preferred learning styles:

- give a clear and easy-to-follow demonstration while explaining to the learner the detail of what is happening and why;
- watch for signs (for example, body language or revealing questions) that the learner has missed something;
- summarize and review at appropriate points to help the learner grasp the key points;

DOS AND DON'TS

For Coaching for Better Performance

DO

- Carry out a detailed task analysis of the activity you are going to coach, listing all the steps in the process, especially the most obvious (these are easy to overlook when you're experienced in an activity).
- Include all external restrictions and criteria such as health and safety requirements.
- Make sure that the approach, the detailed steps, and the actions within them are discussed and agreed on with the learner—coach and learner have an equal stake in success.
- Accept the learner's mistakes when tackling new tasks. Learning by doing means figuring out why something may not have worked, and planning better methods for the next time.
- Remember that coaching is more than instruction: the successful coach relies on a range of other skills, especially the communication skills of questioning, listening, and giving constructive feedback.

DON'T

- Don't confuse coaching with assessment.
- Don't jump in and tell the learner what to do or take over if the learner is experiencing difficulty.
- Don't assume that everyone knows the basics of a task just because you take them for granted.

- let the learner try out the task, offering support and, if necessary, reminders;
- actively encourage the learner in good performance.

5. Provide Feedback

Feedback is essential for the learner to get the most from the experience. In giving feedback, be honest but sensitive and critical but constructive, and always try to point to improvements.

6. Plan Interim Learning Activities

Plan development activities for the learner to undertake between coaching sessions. Don't spoon-feed the learner, but encourage the person to stay motivated and independently identify opportunities to practice newly learned skills. Agree on improvement targets for the practice sessions.

7. Close the Session

Discuss and review:

- the learner's success against the agreed criteria and standards;
- how well the learner handled the learning process;
- next steps. These may involve more coaching on this task if either the task or the learning objectives haven't been met in full.

THOUGHT STARTERS

- Think about who has coached you in the past and how effective it was—if it worked for you, it can work for others.
- Whom can you think of in your team at work who would benefit from coaching?
- Which tasks and skills would you be best at coaching?
- Who else has skills that others would benefit from developing?

For More Information

Books:

Buckley, Roger, and Jim Caple. *One-to-one Training and Coaching Skills.* 2nd ed. Sterling, VA: Stylus, 1997.
Hargrove, Robert. *Masterful Coaching: Extraordinary Results by Impacting People and the Way They Think and Work Together.* San Diego, CA: Pfeiffer, 1995.
Kinlaw, Dennis C. *Coaching for Commitment: Managerial Strategies for Obtaining Superior Performance from Individuals and Teams.* 2nd ed. San Francisco, CA: Jossey-Bass, 1999.
Parsloe, Eric. *The Manager as Coach and Mentor.* Woodstock, NY: Beckman, 2000.

See also:

☆ **Coaching (pp. 328–29)**
☆ **Mentoring (pp. 326–27)**
✔ **Empowerment (pp. 352–53)**
✔ **Mentoring in Practice (pp. 368–69)**

"Remember the finish line is at the end of a race. Don't use up all of your energy before reaching it."

(Jack Daniels)

CONDUCTING A PERFORMANCE APPRAISAL

CHECKLIST

This checklist is for managers responsible for conducting performance appraisals.

DEFINITION

The focus of performance appraisals has shifted in recent years away from evaluation and strict appraisal toward improving performance and developing the employee by means of a well prepared, honest, and open discussion. This checklist concentrates on the staff development approach.

A performance appraisal usually centers on a face-to-face discussion in which one employee's work is discussed, reviewed, and appraised by another using an agreed and understood framework. Although peers can appraise each other (upward appraisal by subordinate to superior is becoming accepted as a development method), usually line managers conduct appraisals of their staff, and this is the approach that this checklist takes.

The appraisal process focuses on behaviors and outcomes, not personality; issues and problems, not subjective gripes; constructive development to improve motivation; and the employee's growth and performance. It generally takes place every six to twelve months.

ADVANTAGES

Employees being appraised will:

- have a clear picture of what is expected of them;
- be able to discuss priorities;
- gain a platform to remove confusion when overload occurs;
- receive feedback on their performance;
- be heard and respected;
- be offered constructive guidance on attaining mutually agreed goals;
- receive help in constructing personal development plans and targets;
- take ownership of their performance.

Appraisers will use the appraisal discussion as an opportunity to:

- experience the jobholder's performance firsthand;
- better understand the jobholder's potential and needs;
- motivate the jobholder;
- develop a consistent approach to guidance and encouragement;
- tackle problems more effectively;
- improve the communication process.

Requirements for a successful appraisal include:

- thorough preparation by both appraiser and jobholder;
- the appraiser's skill and tact in not being offensive or drifting into personal attacks;
- reassurance by the appraiser that the jobholder's doubts, fears, or anxieties are unwarranted;
- clarification that the appraisal is not linked to pay (as long as it isn't).

ACTION CHECKLIST

1. PREPARE FOR THE MEETING

Much of the hard work of appraising performance should be carried out prior to the meeting itself. If there is an established program, this will provide a framework for action. If not, the following outline structure of discussion headings provides a starting point.

- Objectives for past 12 months—level of achievement/progress.
- Continuing or unresolved problems during this period.
- Evaluation of professional development during this period.
- Objectives for next 12 months.
- Support required in order to achieve these objectives.
- Personal development objectives that may vary from the above or provide a means to their attainment.
- Any anticipated major importance or worry in next 12 months.

2. ARRANGE FOR THE APPRAISAL DISCUSSION

In a premeeting briefing inform the employee of the purpose of the appraisal and the structure that it will follow.

- Inform the employee of any work to prepare in advance, for example, identifying personal strengths and achievements, weaknesses and failures over the past year.
- Get the employee to prepare a personal assessment of how well the past year's objectives have been achieved and what objectives should be adopted for the next year.
- Ask the employee to reflect on the value and practical application of training or development activities that have taken place in the past year.
- Explain that this is the opportunity to consider problems and set—and agree on—work directions and methods for the next year.
- Most importantly, explain that it is not linked to pay or promotion (unless it is).
- Introduce documentation for notes or record-keeping at this stage.
- Agree the time and place for the discussion.

3. PREPARE THE ENVIRONMENT

The environment for the discussion should be informal and friendly, private but comfortable, confidential and free from interruption, and nonthreatening. Don't seat the employee in front of your desk if you can avoid it—sit in chairs without a barrier between you.

4. USE A CONSULTATIVE APPROACH

Be conversational but positive, discussing specific activities and issues; the focus is on looking forward to improvements. Asking open questions, listening, reflecting back what you hear, and responding appropriately all enable you to exercise a control that is not overt and does not make the employee feel dominated.

"It's time for IBM to perform and then talk, instead of talk and then perform." (Lou Gerstner)

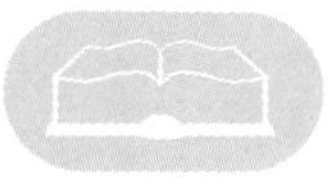

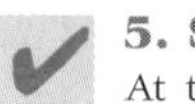

5. Start the Discussion

At the start of the discussion, it is important to relax the employee.

- Restate the purpose of the meeting and the structure that it will follow.
- Emphasize that the purpose of the discussion is to help the employee develop and improve.
- Restate the purpose of the documentation—it serves better than memory as a reminder of what is agreed, demonstrates that the meeting has taken place, and forms a basis for measuring progress.

6. Develop the Discussion

In theory and with thorough preparation by both parties, the discussion can follow the framework outlined. In practice this does not always happen. Try to

- encourage self-assessment and help—not lead—the diagnosis of problems;
- maintain and build the employee's self-esteem;
- offer help and suggestions but let the employee arrive at solutions independently;
- concentrate on job performance, not personalities;
- discuss specific examples, not generalities;
- summarize at critical or agreed action points;
- guide and agree on goals and plans.

7. Deal with Difficulties and Focus on Improvements

Ask the employee to point to any difficulties. Ask not only where, how, and when the employee might make improvements, but also what resources might facilitate the process. Be prepared to admit that you, as appraiser, might be the cause of problems yourself or could do more to help.

8. Agree on Areas for Improvement

Try to categorize those areas that may be in need of urgent remedial attention separately from those that are developmental and progressive. Agree on the preferred outcome of these training and development activities and encourage the employee to identify ways and means to achieving them.

9. Rate the Performance

Some appraisal procedures will use performance ratings. They can vary in nature and scope and can be useful or destructive, depending on how the rating is done and what the general understanding of such a rating is. If ratings are to be used, they should be:

- fair—reflecting performance against expectations, not other people's work;
- flexible—reflecting the level and extent of the individual's achievements;
- consistent—applying across different sectors of the organization.

10. Close the Discussion

Ensure that you have reached understanding and commitment in terms of objectives, the means to achieve them, and dates that serve as targets or review points. Ensure, too, that you know who is doing what to set up these activities. Agree on a follow-up date and ask the employee to write up the objectives and plans, preferably on a form that lays out the framework structure, so that you can both sign off on it. End on a positive note.

DOS AND DON'TS

For Conducting a Performance Appraisal

DO

- Remember the appraisal is a dialog/discussion.
- Invite the jobholder's comments.
- Get the jobholder to analyze his or her own performance.
- Highlight good performance and the reasons why it was good.
- Use the documentation to guide and record outcomes.
- Agree on a need for changed performance before planning action.
- Be aware of your use of language and the potential for misinterpretation.

DON'T

- Don't criticize personalities or try to change them.
- Don't skate around difficult moments.
- Don't fall into the trap of holding forth monolog-style.
- Don't use closed, rhetorical questions.
- Don't be afraid to call on specialist help or advice.

THOUGHT STARTERS

- Are you a good listener, able to extract salient points without making notes all the time?
- Are you satisfied with your own ability to coach and counsel?
- When were you last appraised? What went well? What went badly?
- Are you clear on objectives for your staff and the support they may need in achieving them?

For More Information

Books:

Fisher, Martin. *Performance Appraisals*. Milford, CT: Kogan Page, 1997.
McKirchy, Karen. *Powerful Performance Appraisals: How to Set Expectations and Work Together to Improve Performance*. Franklin Lakes, NJ: Career Press, 1998.
Toler Sachs, Randi. *Productive Performance Appraisals*. New York: AMACOM, 1992.

See also:

✔ **Managing Staff Turnover and Retention (pp. 364–65)**
✔ **Motivating Your Staff in a Time of Change (pp. 372–73)**
✔ **Setting Objectives (pp. 480–81)**

COUNSELING YOUR COLLEAGUES

CHECKLIST

This checklist is designed for managers who, in the context of their roles, may be required to help their colleagues by using counseling skills.

Becoming a professional counselor can take several years of training and supervised practical experience. Few managers have this level of qualification, but many of the skills employed by counselors can be put to use by managers of all levels in a work situation. Managers desiring this level of capability should consider some formal counseling training.

DEFINITION

Work often suffers when an employee is personally troubled. It may be work related or not, but even personal problems (family issues, debt, illness, and so on) may eventually become an issue of work productivity. Managers dealing with such issues may be able to assist the affected individual or individuals discover a solution—especially if it is a work-related issue (such as a personality clash or poor communication skills). However, many companies, as part of their employee medical benefits program, allow outside counseling for individuals and circumstances where added professional skills are necessary. Handled successfully, counseling is a process that helps individuals clarify their motivations, worries, and hopes. It also helps them come to terms with their feelings, and enables them to take responsibility for, and begin to resolve, their difficulties.

Counseling is not a process of advice-giving, nor does it involve the counselor providing or managing solutions to the problems experienced by the "client".

ADVANTAGES

Counseling your colleagues:

- may help solve issues that can hamper individual and business productivity.
- helps reduce employee loss time due to low morale, depression and illness.
- assists in building teams among people having divergent personality styles.

DISADVANTAGES

- It may create the need for more management training.

ACTION CHECKLIST

1. MAKE SURE YOUR COMPANY SUPPORTS PEER COUNSELING

Check your company's personnel policies to make sure that they support peer counseling. Some firms have formal procedures for initiating counseling; it is important to respect these procedures when that is the case.

2. FIND A SUITABLE ROOM

It is essential to choose somewhere that is quiet, free from interruption, and appropriate to the nature of the problem. Make sure you will not be disturbed by putting a "Do not disturb" sign on the door, and defer phone calls to avoid interruptions.

- Try to avoid a formal office setting with a desk between you and your colleague.
- If you need to keep an unobtrusive eye on the time, position a clock where you can easily see it.

3. ALLOW SUFFICIENT TIME FOR THE MEETING

If you know you have to end your meeting at a particular time, inform your colleague of that at the outset. To make sure there is enough time for the session it is sensible to block out the time for such a meeting in advance. Even if there are no time constraints, it is often useful to set a limit of about an hour, to prevent the discussion merely going over the same ground again and again.

4. ADDRESS YOUR FEELINGS TOWARD YOUR COLLEAGUE

Before the meeting, it is essential to assess your personal feelings toward your colleague and put them to one side. Whether or not you like the person is irrelevant.

5. OPEN THE MEETING BY EXPLAINING THE FRAMEWORK

It is important to lay down some ground rules at the beginning of the counseling session. These may include:

- the expectations of the discussion—for example, you may not be able to provide advice or guidance or solve all your colleague's problems;
- time limitations—state again what these are, and whether you will offer a follow-up session if needed;
- note taking—stress that any notes you take are for your own use and will not be revealed to a third party;
- confidentiality—assure your colleague that matters of confidentiality will be treated as such; otherwise the person may hesitate to be candid with you. Explain that the only exception to this will be if you both agree that something needs to be discussed with another party.

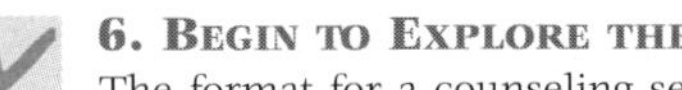

6. BEGIN TO EXPLORE THE ISSUES

The format for a counseling session is not set in stone; each is dependent on the needs of the individual. However, you will find the following skills essential in exploring your colleague's issues.

- Actively listen—what does this person feel? What point of view is being expressed? What seems to be happening to him or her to cause the issue to arise? What does this person do (or not do) in response to that situation? It is essential to understand that in emotional terms, your colleague's view of the facts or the situation is more important than the facts themselves and that people's behavior may not reflect their true feelings. By rephrasing the concerns your colleague expresses, you demonstrate that you have listened carefully, at

---

"I always pass on good advice. It is the only thing to do with it. It is never of any use to oneself."

(Oscar Wilde)

the same time you are seeking clarification of the issues involved. Throughout the conversation, occasionally summarizing what has been said will help both of you stay focused.

- Empathize—empathy is not the same as sympathy. Empathy means you recognize and understand the issues confronting your colleague without necessarily becoming an advocate or agreeing totally with the version you are hearing. Your empathy can help encourage your colleague to be more honest and precise in describing the issues.
- Question—there are many reasons for questions, and many types of questions. In a counseling situation, questions enable you to clarify your understanding of the issues, help focus on areas you think may be important, and demonstrate your interest in the other person.

Open, closed, and probing questions are all of value in a counseling session. Open questions can help your colleague begin to talk about an issue and the feelings it provokes. Closed questions help you to establish precise facts, but tend to lead to very short answers. Probing questions enable you to deepen your understanding of an issue and can help to draw out the whole picture.

- Challenge—by occasionally challenging a statement, you force your colleague to reconsider, and possibly rephrase the statement. It is useful to challenge if it appears that the discussion is going around in circles, if your colleague has an unrealistic self-image (either too positive or, more usually, too negative), or if there appear to be contradictions in what you are hearing.

Challenging statements may be based on phrases such as, "You say that you are struggling with your current project, yet I see you as meeting all its objectives and deadlines. Why do you think there is a difference in our views?"

7. Recognize Situations That Are Beyond Your Help

In certain circumstances it may be necessary to refer your colleague to trained counselors or organizations that may be better equipped to help. Be aware of outside resources—names of specific counselors, for example, or a list from the phone directory that you can share with your colleague. Your personnel department or human resources manager may have some information, but be sure not to break a confidence if you ask for a referral.

- Employee Assistance Programs (EAP) have been initiated by many organizations to provide external sources of help, guidance, and advice for their staff. The Employee Assistance Professionals Association Web site is an excellent source of help and a first point of contact if your organization does not have a program in place already.

DOS AND DON'TS

For Counseling Your Colleagues

DO

- Clarify what the realistic expectations of a counseling session are.
- Assure your colleague of confidentiality.
- Encourage your colleague to: explore his or her concern or problem; clarify the issue; and set objectives for action.

DON'T

- Don't let personal feelings intrude on the discussion.
- Don't take on the responsibility for solving problems.
- Don't be directive in what you say.

8. Help Your Colleague with Problem-Solving Skills

Counseling does not mean that the counselor provides solutions to the issues raised by the other person. The counselor can, however, help by bringing problem solving techniques to bear. The discussion should have served to identify the problem area and some possible causes. You can now encourage the individual to set specific objectives to tackle the problem and assign a timetable and means of monitoring progress.

9. Close the Session Constructively

Summarize what has been discussed and what actions have been agreed upon. If appropriate, arrange a follow-up session.

THOUGHT STARTERS

- The greater the perceived level of listening, the more likely the individual will be to accept comments and contributions from you.
- Recurring problems do not solve themselves.

For More Information

Books:

Carroll, Michael, and Michael Walton. *Handbook of Counseling in Organizations*. Thousand Oaks, CA: Sage, 1997.

Summerfield, Jenny, and Lyn Van Oudtshoorn. *Counseling in the Workplace*. Woodstock, NY: Beekman, 2000.

Web Site:

Employee Assistance Professionals Association: **www.eapassn.org**

"The glad hand is alright in sunshine, but it's the helping hand on a dark day that folks remember to the end of time."
(Amadeo Giannini)

Developing Passive People

This checklist is for line managers handling individuals who are too compliant, too conciliatory, or too self-effacing to make a positive impact. The checklist will help identify the problem and tackle it by making progress toward a more assertive and confident approach.

Definition

Passive people are often superficially very pleasant and eager to please—even too pleasant and too eager, since passive behavior is generally characterized by the desire to avoid conflict and the constant wish to please others. Passive people tend not to want to face up to difficult problems and situations because they are frightened of upsetting others.

They give in to unrealistic and unachievable demands, saying "yes" when they need to say "no" (or at least "but"). They promise deadlines that can't be met, promising to "do their best". They keep problems to themselves and play it safe to avoid any risks. This can lead to a spiraling effect—they gradually lose the confidence of those around them, including their manager. The manager's role is to help such people develop and become more assertive.

Advantages

There are many reasons for helping passive people change their behavior.

- Passive people become more confident, their self-esteem rises, and, as success breeds success, their newly learned assertive behavior starts to come naturally to them.
- Better communication means the productive airing of problems, fewer missed deadlines, and reduced potential for conflict.
- Passive people learn to make decisions and solve problems that they would previously have referred upward or sideways.
- Creative, decisive, and productive people get better results and cause fewer problems at work.

Disadvantages

The principal disadvantage of helping individuals develop is that it takes time, time, and more time. Passive people require sensitive handling, patience, and a genuine commitment from the manager.

But if you don't put in the time and simply avoid the problem, this may result in:

- the individuals themselves becoming less and less confident;
- a continuous cycle of low self-esteem, underperformance, acceptance of overwork and impossible deadlines, etc., leading to absenteeism and/or illness (often stress-related);
- the loss of their colleagues' confidence and respect, especially if their passivity affects colleagues' work;
- playing it safe or avoiding taking difficult decisions, which can have disastrous effects for the organization.

Action Checklist

1. Understand the Problem—Why People Are Passive

Reasons why people behave passively include:

- the mistaken beliefs that they will be disliked if they disagree and that others always like someone who agrees with them;
- the desire to please, sacrificing long-term realism for short-term compliance and agreement;
- the feeling that other people are threatening;
- the failure to understand that they have a right to their own views and ideas;
- a lack of confidence in their own views and ideas;
- a lack of familiarity with basic assertiveness techniques;
- an inability to see themselves as others see them.

Realize that for most passive people these attitudes and behaviors are deeply ingrained. They cannot be changed overnight, and simply telling a passive person to behave more assertively can make the situation worse. You need to empathize with the person's problems while staying committed to changing their behavior.

2. Understand the Problem—How Passive People React

All too often passive people confuse assertive with aggressive behavior and find it very difficult to act assertively themselves. They think if they make a firm statement they are being aggressive, and they equate passive behavior with politeness. It is important to spot these reactions—don't assume a polite smile means everything is fine.

3. Spot the Problem

Three key indicators of passive behavior are:

spoken language. People who behave passively tend to use expressions like, "I'm sorry to bother you, but. . . " or "I know I'm probably wrong, but. . ."

body language. Telltale signs of passive behavior include:

- an inability to make eye contact;
- stooping and keeping the head down;
- nervous gestures like fingering a collar or playing with a pencil;
- speaking abnormally quietly;
- excessive use of "um" and "er";
- stepping backward when spoken to.

work results. Passive people tend not to want to disappoint or upset people, so they take on too much work, get overloaded, and then can't keep up. They may become unreliable, miss deadlines, or habitually put off difficult decisions or refer them to a superior.

"People can place demands upon themselves that create uncertainty." (Rabi S. Bhagat)

4. Begin to Address the Problem

All too often managers allow passive behavior to continue unchecked because it poses no immediate problem. However, it is important to start getting to grips with it as soon as you recognize it. The first step is to communicate with the person, and in this case communication means more listening than speaking.

Find time to ask questions and listen—quietly and privately—to the person about their passive behavior. The idea is to start modifying behavior, which should help gradually to change underlying attitudes.

5. Explain Rights and Responsibilities

Emphasize that everyone has responsibilities and the right to:

- make mistakes;
- say how you feel and what you think;
- refuse certain requests;
- say you don't know, don't agree, don't understand, or need help;
- tell other staff members that their performance needs to be improved, and in what ways.

Help the passive person accept that it isn't helping anyone to relinquish rights and responsibilities; moreover, the team can suffer as a result.

6. Explain the Basics of Assertiveness

On a very basic level, assertiveness means:

- acknowledging the other person's point of view;
- expressing the facts, and your own thoughts and feelings, honestly and openly, without rancor;
- suggesting a constructive way forward when problems arise;
- standing up for yourself if you are being put upon.

7. Be a Role Model

Show how effective assertive behavior can be by demonstrating it yourself. If a passive employee can see that a manager acts assertively, listens to problems, and finds solutions without apportioning blame, the person is more likely to be encouraged to act the same way.

8. Give Your Approval and Encouragement

Make it clear always that the person has nothing to fear. One of the roots of passive behavior is that people are fearful of disapproval and of being wrong. Define your expectations. Make it clear that you will approve of assertive behavior and disapprove of passivity. Given that a passive individual wants to please and conform, establishing acceptable standards of behavior is helpful. Encourage a climate at work that actually allows people to release their fear. A person practicing assertiveness may actually behave aggressively to start with—discourage this carefully without squashing the effort to change.

9. Create the Right Environment

Help people leave passivity behind. Encourage assertiveness by:

- coaching them in techniques and approaches;
- setting up an easy way to increase confidence—for example, a situation in which the passive person can try out new skills and be assured of success;
- giving feedback regularly on the person's performance and progress, and praising assertive behavior;
- clamping down gradually on passive behavior.

10. Implement Training and Development

Training and development are key factors in helping passive staff change the way they behave. Informal coaching is one approach, but if an individual's passivity is particularly deep-seated the person may need to think about getting counseling. Videos or courses can also help.

DOS AND DON'TS

For Developing Passive People

DO

- Take the time to spot problems.
- Remember that each individual is unique.
- Explain that assertiveness is desirable and acceptable behavior.
- Continue to reinforce the message.

DON'T

- Don't ignore it and hope it will go away.
- Don't tackle only the aggressive people in your team.
- Don't become angry about the situation.
- Don't behave insensitively toward the person.

THOUGHT STARTERS

- Do you recognize any signs of passivity in your own behavior?
- Do you want to help individuals enjoy their work more and be more motivated by success?
- Do you ever blame people for their behavior instead of taking an effective management line and aiming to help them develop?

For More Information

Books:

Markham, Ursula. *How to Deal with Difficult People.* Lanham, MD: Thorsons, 1998.
Michelli, Dena. *Successful Assertiveness.* Hauppauge, NY: Barron's Educational, 1997.

Web Site:

American Management Association: **www.amanet.org**

See also:

✓ **Coaching (pp. 328–29)**
✓ **Counseling Your Colleagues (pp. 348–49)**
✓ **Empowerment (pp. 352–53)**
✓ **Handling Conflict Situations (pp. 356–57)**
✓ **Mentoring (pp. 326–27)**

"Most people live and die with their music still unplayed. They never dare to try." (Mary Kay Ash)

  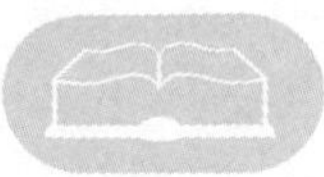    

Empowerment

CHECKLIST

This checklist has been designed to help line managers move toward a culture of empowerment in their companies.

Empowerment should be seen not as a single initiative, but rather as a climate, atmosphere, and culture in which responsibility and accountability for the job rest with the individual doing it. Empowerment can, however, be construed as a process or style by which people manage, requiring careful preparation, clear guidelines, and understood boundaries.

Definition

Empowerment is more than delegation, it is a genuine opening up of the creative power of your staff. It is based on the belief that employees' abilities are frequently under-used and that given the chance and the responsibility, people want to make a positive contribution.

The goal is to bring staff more into the action at work, in other words, to give them more power and choice to innovate, participate in problem solving and decision-making, and act and work with minimal intervention from their managers.

Empowerment is about:

- letting staff get on with the job;
- allowing staff to take responsibility for customers' experience;
- letting those closest to customers make decisions they feel are right;
- stripping away unnecessary bureaucracy;
- encouraging and helping staff to put their ideas for improvements at work into practice.

Advantages

Managed effectively, empowerment can:

- strengthen the commitment and motivation of staff as they take ownership of problems and generate their own solutions;
- generate ideas for improving services—staff feel their ideas count;
- help unearth staff talent that has previously lain dormant;
- reduce the amount of time managers spend sorting out other people's problems;
- improve customer service and organizational performance.

Disadvantages

If not handled effectively, the empowerment process may:

- stoke up resentment among managers who feel their role is being downgraded;
- cause anxiety among those you want to empower;
- lead to people innovating well beyond the normal control of their jobs;
- create expectations that cannot be fulfilled, and thus to frustration;
- breed resentment because extra responsibility is not accompanied by more pay;
- cause a breakdown in control of staff.

Action Checklist

1. Check Your Own Opinions, Assumptions, and Attitudes

Clarify what you mean by empowerment and what you expect to get out of it. Is it an improved consultative process? More active delegation? Is it extended responsibilities—with authority—for problem solving and decision making? Is your concern principally for developing people and expanding their skill base, or is it for improvements to the bottom line? Let colleagues and senior managers know what you are doing. Do their expectations meet your own?

2. Recognize the Barriers to Empowerment

Barriers may include:

- an unreceptive organizational culture—many organizations are inherently controlling, bureaucratic, and unreceptive to change;
- psychological factors—managers may feel that empowerment means losing control, while staff may fear responsibility;
- rigid routines that discourage people from taking responsibility.

3. Recognize the Need for a Conducive Culture

There is no single formula for a culture conducive to empowerment, but it is important to recognize that some corporate cultures lend themselves more than others to enabling staff to make a positive contribution free from fear or blame. Consider the following archetypes, adapted from the work of Charles Handy (*Understanding Organizations*, 1993) and Edgar H. Schein (*Organizational Culture and Leadership*, 1992).

1. The role culture, with defined functions and specialties and set procedures and job descriptions. This is most appropriate in a stable environment.

2. The task culture, job- or project-oriented, concerned to bring together the right resources and people and let them get on with the job. Reliant on the formation (and dissolution) of teams, the task culture is better equipped than the role culture to generate and respond to change.

3. The fear culture, in which:

- decisions—and truth—come from senior people;
- relationships are basically vertical and linear;
- each person has a niche that cannot be invaded;
- exchange takes place by agenda and appointment;
- deference is paid to rank and authority;
- people use the formal communication process to cover their backs.

4. The trust culture, in which:

- ideas come from individuals;

"Power can be taken but not given. The process of the taking is empowerment in itself."

(Gloria Steinem)

  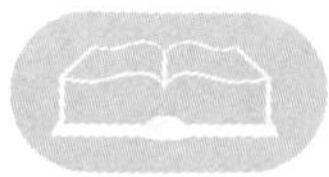    

- people are responsible and motivated;
- the prevailing atmosphere is of informality and few closed doors;
- mistakes are not met with blame or recrimination;
- opportunities for learning are plentiful.

4. Set Boundaries

Although empowerment allows staff extra autonomy, the boundaries should be clearly indicated (for example, at the level of consultation, participation, or full decision making). Set clear limits to the levels of responsibility and autonomy. Wherever the cutoff is defined, retain a mechanism allowing staff to refer problems and suggestions upward where necessary. After the boundaries have been set, it will still be necessary to establish them in practice on a case by case basis so that staff learn when to act without reporting, when to act and report, and when to ask before acting.

5. Raise Awareness

Before the process of empowerment begins, you need to raise employees' awareness of it. Hold meetings and discussion groups to inform everyone what is happening, what is expected of them, what the results are likely to be, and why the process is occurring.

6. Get Staff on Your Side

Reassure employees who are involved and win support from others. Staff who are used to doing what they are told instead of finding solutions for themselves or making independent decisions are likely to feel threatened, or even suspicious, about such a change in culture. Allow staff to air their anxieties and make sure that they are comfortable with the processes. They need to know that channels of communication are open and effective.

7. Audit Staff Skills

Investigate what hidden talents staff have. Draw up a roster of currently under-used talents, including those usually regarded as falling outside the working environment. Ask people about themselves instead of making assumptions.

8. Make Sure Staff Have Resources

Responsibilities for customers, complaints, and operational changes need to be rethought. So do new responsibilities and the levels and types of resourcing needed in order to allow people to perform their jobs.

Empowerment is working if your staff:

- seem able to run things without your daily or hourly involvement;
- take ownership of "their" customers;
- come up with ideas for improving the service;
- don't expect you to solve "their" problems.

9. Agree on Performance Objectives and Measures

Giving people real responsibility and resources to complete tasks is one thing, setting them adrift another. Empowerment encompasses agreeing objectives with your people and agreeing on the measures of efficiency (speed), effectiveness (accuracy, relevance), and cost effectiveness to deliver excellent customer service.

10. Launch the Initiative

Staff may need a good deal of support in the early stages if they are afraid to take responsibility, but support has to be distinguished from mothering. Managers may need careful handling, too, otherwise they may feel threatened and try to retain control by underhand means.

Once the ground has been prepared, empowerment can start to take effect. Encourage the empowerment process by acting on ideas suggested by the staff. Boost the success of the process by publicizing what is happening and reinforcing examples of good practice.

11. Monitor Developments

Hold meetings to check progress, give and receive feedback, and gather ideas and other support. Establish communication networks to build success and keep the initiative going. Be prepared to live with the mistakes. They are useful learning experiences for the future—as long as the same errors don't keep recurring.

THOUGHT STARTERS

- How much real authority do you want your people to have?
- Is there a climate of two-way trust in the organization?
- Are your people being under-used? Are you aware of all their skills and capabilities?
- Does your current reward system encourage empowerment?

For More Information

Books:

Handy, Charles. *Understanding Organizations.* 4th ed. Harmondsworth: Penguin, 1993.

Johnson, Ron, and David Redmond. *The Art of Empowerment: The Profit and Pain of Employee Involvement.* Upper Saddle River, NJ: Financial Times Prentice Hall, 1998.

Schein, Edgar H. *Organizational Culture and Leadership.* 2nd ed. San Francisco: Jossey-Bass, 1992.

See also:

✔ **How to Network and Market Yourself (pp. 758–59)**
✔ **Leading from the Middle (pp. 360–61)**
✔ **Managing Staff Turnover and Retention (pp. 364–65)**
✔ **Successful Delegation (pp. 380–81)**
Charles Handy (pp. 1000–01)
Edgar Schein (pp. 1004–05)

"I'm not wild about accepting responsibility without authority. Why should my people be?"

(Bill Creech)

Emotional Intelligence (EI)

CHECKLIST

This checklist explains the concept of emotional intelligence (EI, sometimes referred to as EQ or emotional intelligence quotient) and why it is becoming more important. It gives an overview of the basic principles and outlines why it is relevant for managers.

Emotional intelligence is increasingly being regarded as a major key to personal success and as being more important than IQ. Some of the most successful people in life today are those who are regarded as having a high level of emotional intelligence, whatever their IQ. Being able to manage themselves and others successfully is often a crucial factor in their success. With a growing emphasis on soft skills, managers need to be able to sensitively handle other people, both inside and outside the organization.

Definition

The ability to perceive, to integrate, to understand and reflectively manage one's own and other people's feelings.

(John D. Mayer, quoted in *People Management* (October 28, 1999))

Emotional Intelligence At Work

Most people experience a range of both positive and negative emotions at work, for example:

- satisfaction—you've done an excellent piece of work;
- exhilaration—you've won a major contract;
- pride—you've helped someone out of a difficult situation;
- anger—your work hasn't been appreciated;
- frustration—your recommendations have been shelved indefinitely;
- anxiety—you're having trouble meeting deadlines.

How Does Emotional Intelligence Work?

When an emotion like satisfaction, anxiety, or frustration is experienced, the human brain is programed to respond to the threat and an emotional response is triggered. However, acting on that first impulse can lead you to say or do things you later regret. Emotional intelligence means that while you acknowledge your instinctive emotional response, you don't act on it, but you step back from the situation and let rational thought influence your actions.

Advantages

Emotional intelligence can:

- improve your relationships with colleagues;
- help you keep yourself under control;
- help lower stress levels;
- help keep you motivated;
- enable you to communicate well and influence others without conflict;
- enhance your standing in the eyes of your colleagues.

Disadvantages

Emotional intelligence:

- cannot always be learned, though it can be developed;
- is sometimes dismissed as being just another management fad.

Action Checklist

1. Understand the Theories of Emotional Intelligence

Two U.S. psychologists, John D. Mayer and Peter Salovey, first defined the phrase "emotional intelligence" in the 1980s. Daniel Goleman, another U.S. psychologist, later built on their work and published his well-known books on the subject. He also produced a framework for emotional intelligence, which consists of five elements:

- self-awareness—an understanding of yourself, your strengths and weaknesses, and how you appear to others;
- self-regulation—the ability to control yourself and think before you act;
- motivation—the drive to work and succeed;
- empathy—how well you understand other people's viewpoints;
- social skills—the ability to communicate and relate to others.

Other important researchers into emotional intelligence include the British management professors Malcolm Higgs and Victor Dulewicz. They identified seven elements of emotional intelligence, which can be broken down into three main categories:

- drivers—motivation and decisiveness. These two traits energize people and drive them toward achieving their goals, which are usually set very high.
- constrainers—conscientiousness and integrity, and emotional resilience. In contrast, these two traits act as controls and curb the excesses of the drivers, especially if the drivers are very high and are undirected or misdirected.
- enablers—sensitivity, influence, and self-awareness. These three traits facilitate performance and help the individual succeed.

(Source: *People Management* (October 28, 1999))

2. Ask What This Means for You

The following competences are considered necessary for managers. They have particular relevance for emotional intelligence. Managers need to:

- be able to manage themselves (self-regulation, constrainers) and not vent their frustration on staff;
- have self-awareness of their real (not perceived) strengths and weaknesses;
- motivate others as well as themselves;
- counsel or coach others within the organization (social skills, enablers);
- encourage others and offer advice (social skills, enablers);
- develop good working relationships (empathy, enablers).

"You can be totally rational with a machine. But, if you work with people, sometimes logic has to take a back seat to understanding."

(Akio Morita)

DOS AND DON'TS

For Emotional Intelligence (EI)

DO

- Observe your emotional reactions to other people.
- Consider how you might test and develop your emotional intelligence.
- Ask yourself honestly how well you react to the concerns of others.

DON'T

- Don't assume you don't bring your emotions to work with you.
- Don't believe emotional intelligence isn't relevant for your job.
- Don't think your emotional intelligence needs no further development.

3. Test and Develop Your Emotional Intelligence

A major problem when testing for emotional intelligence is that there is no one agreed standard definition of the concept. Practitioners and trainers use a widely varying range of characteristics and assessment methods, and many of the tests available for measuring EI (on the Internet, for example) reflect this. These tests are, however, useful in making people aware of the issues involved and can give an indication of where an individual's emotional strengths and weaknesses lie.

Another question is whether EI can be developed. Certainly skills in team building or motivation can be developed—numerous books, seminars, and courses aim to do just that, or at least to give a better understanding of the issues involved. Until more academically rigorous and tested assessment outcomes are developed, it may be safest to say for the time being that only some facets of EI can be learned or taught. Others, like adopting a more understanding attitude or building drive and determination, can only come from within.

Examples of EI tests can be found at: **www.eip.org**; **www.eiconsortium.org**; and **www.eicentre.com**.

The tests usually take the form of questionnaires or psychometric testing, measuring competences or characteristics such as emotional energy, stress, assertiveness, sociability, attitudes, decisiveness, objective judgment, self-esteem, courage, and tolerance of and consideration for others. Some tests are wholly Web-based, others paper-based.

THOUGHT STARTERS

- Do you think your communication with your colleagues could be improved?
- When you're angry, do you say the first thing that comes to mind?
- Do you tend to ignore your emotional responses to events?

For More Information

Books:

Goleman, Daniel. *Emotional Intelligence: Why It Can Matter More Than IQ*. New York: Bantam, 1997.
Goleman, Daniel. *Working with Emotional Intelligence*. New York: Bantam Doubleday Dell, 2000.

See also:

☆ **Emotional Intelligence (pp. 312–13)**
Daniel Goleman (pp. 996–97)

Handling Conflict Situations

This checklist examines the approach to personal conflict and is designed to help line managers handle conflict when it arises.

Conflict can arise from a host of roots and causes, but principally it occurs from differences between people who disagree about ideas or find themselves in difficult situations. "Ideas conflict" can be desirable and creative when handled constructively; "situations conflict" can cause frustration and resentment if not dealt with. Personal conflict can be damaging and destructive unless it is managed with thought and care. Ultimately conflict can cost a great deal of time and money. Most organizations and individuals recognize the need to solve personal conflicts before they become destructive.

Definition

Personal conflict occurs when two or more parties have opposing attitudes or approaches to a particular situation, issue, or person. Sources of conflict range from a difference of opinion, problematic working conditions, or unrealistic work expectations to discriminatory behavior such as racism or sexism, poor communication, or noncompliance with organizational norms or values.

In some situations an ethical or practical issue emerges that you know should be confronted. Here conflict can be positive—you may even have to create it temporarily. For example, a member of staff turns up late every day and the manager fails to confront the individual. This avoidance may in the future lead to a development of conflict through the frustration and resentment of the other team members.

Conflict can occur between a member of staff and a manager, between two or more members of a team, or between departments, sections, or managers. Whether you are involved directly affects whether you negotiate with someone else, apply grievance or disciplinary measures, or mediate between other parties.

Conflict can be covert, taking the form of resentment from a team member passed over for promotion or irritation caused by an individual's personal habits. Such conflict is much harder to detect and easier to ignore. Whichever type it is, all conflict needs to be managed before it becomes a destructive force.

Advantages

The advantages of managing conflict situations are:

- better motivated staff; staff energies are directed toward work instead of emotions;
- a more positive image of the organization or staff;
- improved teamwork;
- better personal development of individuals.

Disadvantages

The disadvantages of avoiding or failing to manage a conflict situation may include:

- the escalation and spread of the conflict to others;
- the dissipation of staff energy;
- the misdirection of staff energy, contributing to falling productivity;
- the misperception that inaction is the easiest option—the problem will ultimately be harder to solve.

Action Checklist

1. Recognize Conflict

To handle conflict you have to spot it. Remember it can be overt, from an obvious or identifiable cause, clearly visible and defined, or covert, from a less obvious or apparently unrelated cause (for example, an employee could seem to be in conflict with colleagues, when the root cause is a perception that the supervisor's treatment of staff is discriminatory).

2. Monitor the Climate

Monitoring the climate at work gives you an early warning system, making it far easier to deal with conflict swiftly and efficiently before it gets out of hand. This does not mean constantly being on your guard; it simply means being prepared and keeping your eyes open. If you see a likely conflict situation, don't ignore it. Early action saves time and stress later.

3. Look into the Situation

Take time to find out the real cause of the conflict, who is involved, what the key issue is, and what its actual and potential effects are. Empathize—see the situation from other people's point of view instead of making a snap judgment.

4. Plan Your Approach

Don't take sides. Instead, encourage the parties concerned to examine the interests behind their position and try to create a climate of exchange so that the parties can deal with each other more constructively next time. Devise a strategy based on what this investigation has shown. Managers should decide on the result they want to achieve, bearing in mind that as different evidence emerges their preferred outcome may not always be possible.

5. Handle the Issue

Stay in control of the situation. Handling conflict is a difficult process that can create extreme emotions. Use the following techniques:

Stay calm. Take time to respond—don't give a knee-jerk reaction. If necessary declare a time out until people are calm enough to discuss the issues rationally and constructively.

Listen to the points of view of everyone involved and take time to understand all the issues raised by the conflict. Remember that people will be more open and honest if they feel they have a receptive and interested audience. Be aware of your body language and spoken language.

Avoid fight or flight. The instinctive human reaction to

"It's like breaking up a family row as an outsider." (Gerry Robinson)

conflict is either to run away or face it and fight. Neither of these approaches is constructive.

- Fighting back or being aggressive toward one or both parties when you are not personally involved causes greater long-term conflict and intimidates staff.
- Flight avoids solving the conflict and leads to loss of respect.

Stay assertive. This means avoiding being either passive or aggressive; neither is assertive and each is a short-term approach unlikely to solve the conflict.

- Passive behavior is characterized by apologizing, withdrawn body language, and always accepting the other person's point of view whether it is right or not.
- Aggressive behavior is characterized by being authoritarian and refusing to listen to reasoned argument.

An assertive approach is generally the best way to handle conflict. It means:

- acknowledging the views and rights of all parties;
- encouraging the parties to find the causes of the conflict—and solutions to it;
- trying to make sure that opinions and thoughts are expressed honestly and openly;
- suggesting a constructive way forward.

6. Let Everyone Have a Say

If you have managed to get the parties around a table for discussion in a climate in which exchange is possible, reaching a compromise solution may be feasible. Remember that your desired solution needs to hit a wide range of targets. It should:

- help to build good working relationships;
- be legitimate, nondiscriminatory, and compatible with organizational practice;
- recognize all parties' alternatives;
- help to improve communication;
- help to generate a lasting commitment to the solution.

7. Find the Way Forward

The most important aspect of handling a conflict situation is to find an acceptable way forward. Examine the options and decide what to do next. Can you reach a compromise acceptable to both or all sides? If not, what action needs to be taken to prevent the conflict from continuing? Make sure everyone knows what the conclusion is and what each person is expected to do.

The next steps need to be agreed and spelled out: they could include an individual's need for counseling, the likelihood of disciplinary proceedings, or an agreement to be implemented (even moving a member of staff to another department if there is a deep-rooted personal antagonism). Sometimes problems relate to health or psychology—you have to judge where your limits lie in resolving apparently intractable personal antagonisms.

8. Appraise, Don't Dwell

It is important to learn from conflict situations and move forward. Don't dwell on the past and reopen old wounds. Appraise the conflict and the way it was handled to see what you can learn. How can similar conflicts be avoided in the future? How could a similar situation be handled better? Learn from the experience and keep your eye on what has been resolved to stop it flaring up again.

DOS AND DON'TS

For Handling Conflict Situations

DO

- Tackle conflict early to keep it from escalating.
- Try to avoid instinctive reactions.
- Think the problem through and plan a way to deal with the conflict.
- Refrain from offering your own opinion before understanding the full picture.
- Stay assertive.

DON'T

- Don't avoid the issue and ignore the conflict.
- Don't take it personally (unless it is personal).
- Don't jump in without assessing and understanding the problem.
- Don't fight anger with anger.
- Don't run away.
- Don't handle conflict in public.

THOUGHT STARTERS

To resolve conflict, do you:

- encourage all parties to explore factors common to their respective positions?
- try to enable the parties to deal effectively with their differences?
- try to make it easier for the parties to deal with each other next time?
- encourage the parties to come up with ways of generating mutual gain?
- encourage the parties to come to realistic appraisals of their point of view?
- facilitate the questioning of inflexible attitudes?
- know which skills you need to work on?

For More Information

Books:

Crawley, John. *Constructive Conflict Management: Managing to Make a Difference*. Reprint. Naperville, IL: Nicholas Brealey, 1998.

Kindler, Herbert S. *Managing Disagreement Constructively*. Menlow Park, CA: CrispLearning.com, 1997.

Journal Article:

Holder, Roy. "How to Turn Conflict to Your Advantage." *Works Management* (March 1997): 28–30.

"When dealing with complexity and uncertainty, trust and openness become critical."

(David L. Dotlich)

INTRODUCING FLEXIBLE WORKING INTO YOUR ORGANIZATION

CHECKLIST

This checklist provides an introduction to the use of flexible working practices within an organization by considering alternatives to traditional working hours.

Employers are continually searching for ways to stay "lean and mean" but effective. Flexibility in working hours is increasingly viewed as a way to manage time and people more effectively within a volatile trading environment, and as a means of recruiting and retaining good people within a more competitive labor market.

DEFINITION

"Flexibility" covers any variation in working hours from the standard nine-to-five working day. The key variants are flextime, which may include a compressed work week, job-sharing, part time employment, comp time, and sabbaticals. These are defined in the glossary of terms.

ADVANTAGES

Flexible working can provide:

- recruitment and retention of qualified staff who may not be able to work traditional hours;
- equality of opportunity: standard hours often prevent individuals with family or caring responsibilities and disabled people from working;
- work patterns which can be tailored to accommodate swings in demand or new customer requirements;
- greater success in tackling skills shortages;
- higher return on training investment.

Flextime:

- reduces problems of punctuality and disciplining staff for late arrival;
- reduces one-day absenteeism: staff can use flextime to deal with minor crises or personal appointments;
- creates a greater sense of responsibility and better time management;
- improves efficiency in core times and reduces overtime;
- encourages people with family responsibilities to work;
- increases productivity by making it easier to manage seasonal labor requirements, while allowing control of total hours worked annually.

Compressed work week:

- may improve productivity by increasing the standard hours worked into fewer days;
- may improve employee morale by earning them more days off per month.

Job-sharing:

- brings two sets of skills and experience to one job;
- results in staff who are sometimes more energetic and committed than full-time workers;
- provides greater continuity in cases of sickness or leave.

Voluntary reduced work time:

- opens up jobs to a wider range of people.

Part time employment:

- opens up jobs to a wider range of people;
- encourages single parents, seniors, physically challenged people, and students to work;
- benefits the company's bottom line if no benefits are associated with part time work;
- benefits the employee if health and retirement package accompanies part time work.

Compensation "comp" time:

- avoids paying overtime;
- allows employee to "bank" a day off with pay at some other time.

Unpaid leave:

- retains the service of staff who would otherwise leave the organization altogether.

Sabbaticals:

- replenish employees' energy and creativity.

DISADVANTAGES

- Arranging cover and scheduling work require more management time than planning for standard working hours.
- If programs are not handled sensitively and made available to all employees, full time employees may become resentful.

Flextime:

- can encourage people to count the minutes rather than do the job.
- requires more managerial oversight to assure maximum work coordination during core working hours.

Compressed work week:

- requires more coordination of core working hours.
- sometimes creates excess stress on employees working longer days.

Part time work:

- requires more people and more coordination to get the work done.

Job-sharing:

- may lead to communications difficulties;
- can damage continuity if someone starts a task and then leaves it to another person.

ACTION CHECKLIST

1. SECURE THE COMMITMENT OF TOP MANAGEMENT

Reach agreement with senior managers on the extent of flexibility and make sure that they are committed to this.

2. ANALYZE YOUR WORK FORCE

Profiling your existing work force and analyzing its current work patterns may surprise you: you may not

"Nothing astonishes men so much as common sense and plain dealing." (Ralph Waldo Emerson)

  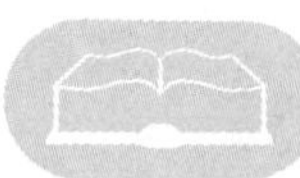    

realize the extent of informal flexible working already sanctioned by line managers.

3. Set Up a Working Group

Nominate a working group that represents all types and levels of employee. Use the group to steer through the changes and act as a sounding board.

4. Decide How Flexible the Organization Can Afford to Be

Are you willing to consider all options for flexibility, or do you want to limit employees to a fixed range? Flextime, for example, should apply to everyone at all levels. Keep in mind that once flexible working is adopted, it is difficult to go back to traditional practices. Pilot the program and expand it gradually.

5. Consult All Employees

Seek employees' views on any changes they would like to see, or ask their opinion on specific options. Use questionnaires, workshops, or discussion groups.

6. Have the Working Group Consider Options

- What system will there be for arranging cover?
- What effect will there be on pay?
- Will you allow line managers discretion in interpreting a broad policy, or will there be little scope for variation?
- How will you ensure parity of treatment in training and development, promotion and benefits?
- Will there be a qualifying period?
- Will any additional costs be offset by business benefits?

7. Secure Senior Management's Agreement

Make sure that senior managers are aware of the rationale and the business case for introducing flexibility. Confirm their commitment to the policy outlined by the working group.

8. Communicate the Policies

Publicize the new program to all staff. Use existing examples and role models. Be open and honest about terms and conditions of eligibility for each option and set clear guidelines for their use. Be specific about any particular times or circumstances under which flexible schedules will not be allowed, for example, during the annual parts inventory, harvest season, or at a particularly busy customer demand period.

9. Identify a Coordinator

You will need somebody to retain a general overview of the program and offer guidance on its implementation.

10. Train Line Managers/Team Leaders to Implement the Program

Continuing management control is vital as flexibility is introduced. It is the manager's job to ensure that work gets done; this may mean denying what staff prefer.

11. Monitor and Evaluate the Program

Set up a system to monitor and evaluate the program. Make sure you evaluate its success in terms of the business benefits sought.

12. Consider the Need for Complementary Programs

Think about how the flexible working program fits into the current corporate culture. Do you need to develop a program to change the culture or to support new working practices?

DOS AND DON'TS

For Introducing Flexible Working into Your Organization

DO

- Consult staff first.
- Assume that all jobs can be done flexibly unless a business case can be made otherwise.
- Target the program at all employees.
- Stress the business benefits to line managers at all stages of introduction and implementation.

DON'T

- Don't gear the program exclusively toward women with children.
- Don't make assumptions about employees' needs and wishes.

THOUGHT STARTERS

- Are you tackling flexible working at the three levels on which change needs to operate—culture, policies, and practice?
- Are you making assumptions about what your employees want?
- How will you evaluate the business benefits?
- How would you implement a working group to design the process?

For More Information

Books:

Bartl, Timothy J. *America Wants Flexible Work.* Washington, DC: LPA Inc., 1998.

Kane-Zweber, K. *Flexible Work Options: A Guide-book for Managers and Human Resource Professionals.* Schaumberg, IL: Motorola University Press, 1997.

Web Site:

www.hrsjobs.com

See also:

✓ **Managing Staff Turnover and Retention (pp. 364–65)**

"Many organizations view people as 'things' that are but one variable in the production equation."

(David M. Noer)

LEADING FROM THE MIDDLE

CHECKLIST

This checklist explains the fundamentals of leadership. In today's fast-changing business world, leadership is increasingly seen as a key to improved performance. It is needed at all levels of an organization, not just the top. Think about groups you have observed and you may be able to identify leaders who were at the bottom of the hierarchy or in positions with no formal authority.

Definable leadership skills exist that, when used purposefully, help managers get the most from their teams. Many companies sponsor programs to improve the leadership skills of staff at all levels, from supervisor to C.E.O. This underlines the point, increasingly understood by organizations in all industries, that leadership is not something we are either born with or not—it can be developed.

DEFINITION

Leadership is notoriously difficult to define, and the link with management is especially difficult. One way of looking at it is to say that "pure" leaders don't have to be good managers, but every manager has to be an effective leader. You may be given a managerial title, but you earn a leadership role. So what makes a good leader?

- Leaders have followers—without followers who trust, rely on, and feel supported by the leader there is no real leadership.
- Leaders have vision—they have a clear, exciting image of the future and set the agenda for their team.
- Leaders show commitment—they generate enthusiasm for the organization and help lead people through times of change.
- Leaders communicate—they are honest, open, and positive, and spend time talking and listening to their people.
- Leaders empower staff—they give staff the room and the confidence to get the job done.

John W. Gardner on leadership:

Although leadership and the exercise of power are distinguishable activities, they overlap and interweave in important ways. Consider a corporate chief executive officer who has the gift for inspiring and motivating people, who has vision, who lifts the spirits of employees with a resulting rise in productivity and quality of product, and a drop in turnover and absenteeism. That is leadership. But evidence emerges that the company is falling behind in the technology race. One day with the stroke of a pen the C.E.O. increases the funds available to the research division. That is the exercise of power. The stroke of a pen could have been made by an executive with none of the qualities one associates with leadership.

[John W. Gardner, *On Leadership* (Free Press, 1990)]

ADVANTAGES

Effective leadership:

- is a major factor in successfully bringing staff through turbulent times;
- helps to spread a common understanding of what the organization is about;
- generates enthusiasm and team spirit;
- can be a powerful motivator and get the best out of team members.

DISADVANTAGES

There are no disadvantages to effective leadership, but leaders can abuse their position.

- Domineering leaders tend to trample on other people and stifle innovation.
- Leadership can exert too strong a pull on followers—if the leader is too dominant or charismatic, people may go along blindly with policies or practices that are detrimental to themselves or the organization.
- Charismatic leadership can lead to a personality cult.
- Macho leaders who are in conflict with each other can split teams and the organization.

ACTION CHECKLIST

1. UNDERSTAND HOW LEADERSHIP DIFFERS FROM MANAGEMENT

If you are not clear about the distinction, it is difficult to isolate (and therefore improve) the skills unique to leadership.

- Management is really about the day-to-day running of a function, about getting the right people in the right place. It involves many administrative tasks.
- Leadership is more dynamic. It is about creating a vision for that function and gaining people's commitment. There are few certainties in leadership.

2. BE CLEAR ABOUT WHERE YOU ARE NOW

Are you comfortable with the idea of being a leader? If not, where do you think your weaknesses lie? Many people, especially those who have been promoted because they have a technical skill, feel uncomfortable with being leaders. You need to be clear about what you feel about yourself as a leader. Think about whether you feel that leadership is alien to your character, whether you lack the authority and respect to be a leader, or whether you believe that only more senior managers should be leaders.

Remember that everyone can learn how to develop leadership potential—authority and respect are there to be earned. In organizations today, people at all levels are expected to show leadership qualities.

3. DOWNPLAY CHARISMA

Charisma is often spoken of as the key to a leader's success. It is something of a blunt weapon, however, and one that is easily over-used. Charismatic leaders can be destructive. They tend to dominate people and can create slavish followers who are dependent on them for guidance and direction. Organizations need to empower employees to make their own decisions and to develop corporate leaders who have a broad range of leadership skills and styles.

 4. Recognize That People Have Different Leadership Needs

Work at developing a range of appropriate leadership styles and at matching your leadership style to specific situations and individuals. Different people need different kinds of leadership.

- People who are unwilling or unable to take responsibility need more supervision and direction with specific outcome-oriented work goals and constant monitoring.
- Staff who lack confidence but show potential need coaching. They need you to set goals and priorities, yet be supportive. You need to explain what needs to be done and then reinforce any positive behavior. The aim is to gradually get them to take responsibility.
- Talented but underachieving employees need you to lead by communicating with them. The key is to get them performing better, sharing in decision making, and taking initiative.
- Star performers who are already fully competent need to be left alone to get on with the job.

 5. Develop Leadership Qualities

Real leaders demonstrate a range of qualities that encourage others to follow. These include:

- developing and demonstrating good work habits;
- understanding and valuing your staff's work;
- working hard at handling pressure;
- clearly demonstrating the values you hold dear;
- encouraging your staff's enthusiasm;
- providing regular feedback;
- listening and learning.

6. Build Communication Channels

Develop and communicate your intentions and directions clearly, so people understand what you expect, know when they have done well or badly, and feel that they can give you feedback on your own performance. Most research into what makes a good leader stresses that leaders communicate—and communicate all the time. They create a vision of where the department and organization are going, and they communicate it clearly, and often, by demonstrating it through their actions and by listening to team members.

 7. Work Hard at Empowering Your Staff

You need to provide your staff with the support and confidence to achieve things for themselves. Effective leaders work at creating the right circumstances for employees to take real ownership of their work. Ask yourself if you are courageous enough to trust your people to do a good job and to show faith in them. If you are, and can still give them a sense of vision and guidance when they need it, they will begin to see you as their leader.

DOS AND DON'TS

For Leading from the Middle

DO

- Match your style to the situation.
- Be clear about your values.
- Keep communication channels open.
- Listen to your people.
- Empower your people.
- Encourage enthusiasm and show it yourself.

DON'T

- Don't be domineering.
- Don't think that leaders have to come up with all the ideas.
- Don't rely solely on your charisma.
- Don't mandate behavior for other people and do the opposite yourself.

THOUGHT STARTERS

- Have you tended to rely on one leadership style rather than using a range of styles?
- Do you over-use charisma?
- Are you clear about your values? Are your team members clear about them?
- Are you comfortable encouraging enthusiasm?
- Do you know who in your team needs space and who needs direction?
- Do you know how many of your people are with you?

For More Information

Books:

Adair, John. *Leadership Skills*. Woodstock, NY: Beekman, 2000.
Barrett, Jim. *Total Leadership: How to Inspire and Motivate for Personal and Team Effectiveness*. Milford, CT: Kogan Page, 1998.
Bennis, Warren, and Joan Goldsmith. *Learning to Lead: A Workbook on Becoming a Leader*. 2nd ed. Reading, MA: Addison-Wesley Longman, 1997.
Eales-White, Rupert. *How to Be a Better Leader*. Milford, CT: Kogan Page, 1998.

See also:

☆ **Emotional Intelligence and Leadership (pp. 214–15)**
☆ **Leadership (pp. 226–28)**
☆ **New Role Models for Enlightened Leadership (pp. 233–34)**
✓ **Empowerment (pp. 352–53)**

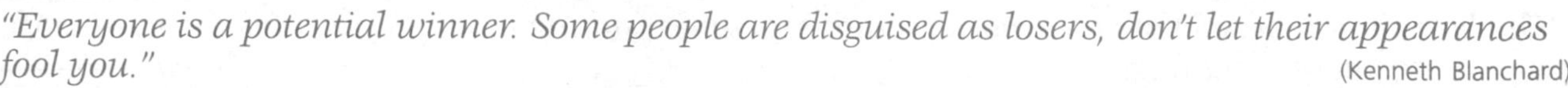

"Everyone is a potential winner. Some people are disguised as losers, don't let their appearances fool you."
(Kenneth Blanchard)

 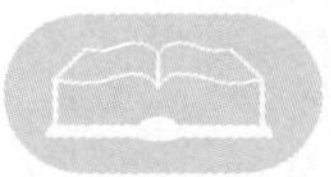    

MANAGING ABSENTEEISM

CHECKLIST

This checklist looks at the various options open to employers to minimize the amount of sick leave taken by employees.

According to the 2000 CCH Unscheduled Absence Survey, the average rate dropped to 2.1 percent of working time in 2000 from 2.7 percent in 1999 while the average cost of absenteeism remained at more than $600 per employee per year.

There is much that organizations can do and are doing to reduce staff absence due to sick leave.

DEFINITION

The term "sick leave" is generally accepted to cover all employee absences from work in which the employee pleads illness. While most employers believe that genuine illness accounts for the majority of days lost, it is also considered that other factors (poor management, lack of motivation, domestic difficulties, the low priority given to absence control by the employer) may contribute to employees' absence, particularly in the case of minor ailments.

ADVANTAGES

An absenteeism policy, in and of itself, may not reduce absenteeism. With a new management/staff awareness of the problem, however, and programs to address the underlying causes, the combination can produce the following results:

- reduce absence levels;
- minimize disruption to workflow and production;
- lower costs associated with absenteeism;
- produce a better motivated workforce;
- save co-workers from being subjected to unnecessary extra pressures and stress;
- ensure that absence is dealt with fairly and consistently throughout the organization;
- remove managerial subjectivity by specifying unacceptable levels of absence and procedures to deal with them;
- reduce the expectations of staff who regard sick days as additional vacation days.

DISADVANTAGES

An absenteeism policy has no real disadvantages, but it is important to make sure that staff who are genuinely sick or injured are not penalized, and that people are not pressured to work when they are not well. Overly stringent policies run the danger of disaffecting staff by giving them the feeling that they are not trusted. It may be wise to have a quarterly, or semi-annual evaluation to judge the efficacy and consistency of the policy-in-action.

ACTION CHECKLIST

1. KNOW THE LEGAL FRAMEWORK

Approach the case of each employee who is frequently sick or has a long-term illness on an individual basis, as each situation will be different. Do not treat an underlying medical condition on a disciplinary basis, but be sympathetic and thoroughly investigate the situation with the employee and doctors, following fair procedures. In the case of persistent, intermittent, unconnected illnesses, fair procedures should be followed, and the situation reviewed and discussed with the employee. Give the person the opportunity to improve and a warning that appropriate disciplinary procedures may be invoked if the situation continues. Fair and equal treatment and good record keeping will avoid legal action for alleged employee harassment and/or discrimination.

2. DEFINE UNACCEPTABLE LEVELS OF ABSENCE

Consider setting benchmarks for absenteeism, letting employees know that if they are absent more than a certain number of times within a given period, action will be taken (for example, counseling interviews). Don't allow a corporate culture in which absence is accepted without explanation. Without such measures employees may feel they are entitled to take as many days' sick leave as they like, and managers set bad examples.

3. RECORD ABSENCES

It has been proved that people are less likely to be absent in companies in which absence is recorded, monitored, and managed. Document absences and survey the extent of the problem. Analyze patterns of short-term absence, for example, by age, job level, and in which department(s). Focus on individuals whose attendance records need special attention, and identify recurring types of illness or accident that might indicate problems within the organization. Feed the information back to line managers so they know how effectively they are dealing with the problem. Encourage managers to keep absence levels under control by publishing comparative records of the performance of different parts of the organization. Consider publishing these figures to make employees aware of how much time the organization is losing through absenteeism. Finally, consider holding departmental or company meetings periodically to discuss the problem of absenteeism in a general way, soliciting feedback and corrective measures from employees.

Measure absence as the time lost due to sickness as a percentage of total working time in a defined period. To do this, divide the number of hours/days/shifts lost by the total number of working hours/days/shifts and multiply by 100.

4. ESTABLISH FORMAL REPORTING PROCEDURES

Require employees to notify either their supervisor or personnel department of their absence by 10 a.m. on the first day and to give some indication of the reason for the absence and how long it is likely to last. Make explicit what documentation (such as a doctor's letter) is needed to cover the employee's absence, especially if the absence is prolonged.

"The basic cause of sickness in American industry and resulting unemployment is the failure of top management to manage."

(W. Edwards Deming)

5. Interview Returning Employees

Determine the reason for the employee's absence and find out whether the illness is likely to recur. If appropriate, the supervisor could suggest the employee seek medical attention. The supervisor should also take the opportunity to update the employee on developments that may have occurred during the absence. This approach will not worry those who have been genuinely sick, but may deter others from taking avoidable absences. Try to learn whether there are underlying causes of absenteeism such as personal difficulties or problems of motivation.

6. Train Supervisors and Managers

Explain to supervisors and managers why they are key figures in controlling unwarranted absenteeism and then provide support and training for them. Recognize that the policy will succeed or fail by their efforts.

7. Don't Recruit Poor Attendees

When hiring, ask job applicants for references. When following up on references, make sure you ask about the applicant's previous attendance record. Don't assume that physically challenged and older applicants are at higher risk for poor attendance; it is often the reverse.

8. Maintain a Safe and Healthy Workplace

Make certain that you meet all legal requirements on health and safety at work. Entrust your company's workplace safety committee with managing the ongoing effort. Discourage employees from habitually working late and skipping lunch. Encourage people to take full advantage of their holidays and paid vacation. In any case, it is important for supervisors and managers to consult employees in a positive manner about health promotion activities and not to be prescriptive.

Employers should make sure that the absenteeism policy is included in the company's employee handbook, and that the employee health benefits plan is supportive of and reflects company policy on preventing illness.

9. Motivate and Gain Commitment from Employees

Find out what motivates employees and affects their commitment to the organization. Think in terms of the way people are managed, both individually and collectively. Take into consideration the function of their jobs, their individual role within the organization, and their working conditions. Remember that poor management can contribute to high absenteeism. Ask whether specific benefits might help improve attendance, for example, flexible working hours, defraying commuting costs, or support in caring for children or elderly relatives.

Research has shown that motivated and committed staff are less likely to be absent, particularly in the case of minor ailments.

10. Consider Offering Incentives

Consider offering bonuses or rewards for those with exemplary attendance records. Beware of the longer term implications of penalizing employees unduly for absenteeism, i.e. other than withholding wages for excessive sick leave. Such a move might force genuinely sick people to come to work, perhaps creating other problems. Being too heavy handed could also trigger employee complaints to union representatives or governmental agencies about slavish corporate policies. See that your corporate attorney reviews such policies before final adoption and publication. In any case, avoid placing too much stress on the economic relationship between employer and employee.

11. Evaluate the Absence Control Policy

Monitor the success of control efforts by regularly reviewing the trend and causes of absenteeism for each department, seeing whether absence levels are falling, whether (and why) the policy is more successful in some areas of the organization than others. Are you offering enough support and training to supervisors and managers? Adjust the program and bolster training accordingly.

DOS AND DON'TS

For Managing Absenteeism

DO

- Avoid a culture of leniency toward absenteeism.
- Monitor absence rates.
- Treat each case individually.
- Train and support supervisors and managers.

DON'T

- Don't accept absenteeism or brush it under the carpet; it can be reduced in all organizations.
- Don't create a climate of distrust.

THOUGHT STARTERS

- How much lost time and productivity does absenteeism cost your organization?
- What are the patterns of absenteeism?
- Do some employees feel resentment at having to regularly cover for others?

For More Information

Journal Articles:

"Sickness Absence." *IRS Employment Review*, no. 593 (October 1995): 2–9, blue.

Warr, Peter, and Shawn Yearta. "Health and Motivational Factors in Sickness Absence." *Human Resource Management Journal* 5:5 (Autumn 1995): 33–48.

"We spend most of our lives working. So why do so few people have a good time doing it?"

(Richard Branson)

MANAGING STAFF TURNOVER AND RETENTION

CHECKLIST

This checklist is designed to help managers analyze, understand, and manage staff turnover.

In a softening economy, labor turnover falls. One advantage of this, a reduction in recruitment costs, can obscure underlying problems such as the retention of dissatisfied staff who would like to move on or the inability of the company to bring in fresh blood. In a time of low turnover, therefore, it is important to manage these symptoms, even if they do not result in the actual turnover of staff.

Some labor turnover is inevitable and even desirable, particularly in today's flatter organizations. Some turnover may be beneficial, for example, because there are few promotion opportunities or because the company prefers to have a regular injection of new talent with fresh minds, enthusiasm, and knowledge and experience of up-to-date developments. Unnecessary turnover, however, is expensive in terms of recruitment costs, production and service inefficiencies, and lower staff morale.

DEFINITION

Turnover can be viewed as a whole or, more helpfully, can be classified in three ways:

- employer-controlled: dismissal, layoff, and early retirement;
- employee-led: dissatisfaction of varying kinds;
- employer and employee uncontrolled: long-term sickness, normal retirement, maternity leave, and death in service.

ADVANTAGES

Management leads to:

- more effective recruitment
- reduced costs
- better staff morale
- improved knowledge of the labor market as a whole
- more constructive development of the organization's knowledge base

ACTION CHECKLIST

1. DETERMINE THE EXTENT OF THE PROBLEM

Consider using one or more of the measurement techniques commonly used by employers.

- The global turnover rate, otherwise known as the crude wastage index, is the most frequently used measure. It is calculated as follows:
  (Leavers in year ÷ Average number employed in year) × 100

The advantage of this measure is that it is widely used, and comparisons can thus be made between companies. It has severe limitations, however, in that it includes all leavers, ignoring factors such as their reasons for leaving and their department, age, and length of service. This technique may leave you with an imbalanced workforce, for example, with all employees over 50 or under 30.

- The stability index is a frequently used additional measure, usually calculated as follows:
  (Staff with one year's service or more ÷ Total staff one year ago) × 100
- Cohort analysis takes a homogeneous group of employees who joined at the same time and tracks the way the group behaves over a period. The rate of leaving of this cohort can be plotted as a wastage curve.
- The census analysis method takes a snapshot of the total situation, rather than examining one group over a period. Leavers are studied in groups according to length of service and then plotted as a proportion of total staff in that group.
- Computer models for employment forecasting are used only in large firms and have recently declined in popularity.

2. BENCHMARK YOUR ORGANIZATION AGAINST OTHERS

One way of judging whether your turnover rates are reasonable is to compare them against national, regional, or industry figures. The American Productivity & Quality Center conducts best practice and benchmarking studies. In addition, the *Wall Street Journal*'s Web site maintains a database on industries and hiring trends as well as salary data (www.careerjournal.com/salaries/index.html). Some companies belong to informal employer networks where they exchange information on various personnel topics. If you trade statistics, make sure that you are clear on other firms' definitions, and that like is compared with like.

Monitor general labor market trends to assess how these will affect your organization. These include demographic factors, the number of women, minorities, and graduates in the workforce, and labor mobility.

3. FIND OUT WHY TURNOVER OCCURS

Although external forces such as short supply of some occupational groups may influence turnover, internal factors are usually more significant. Study the work of the motivation theorists. Maslow argued that people have a hierarchy of needs ranging from physical needs to self-fulfillment; Herzberg distinguished between two sets of factors: hygiene and motivation. McGregor proposed that bosses tend to treat subordinates according to their own prejudices, specifically their belief either that employees need to be ruled and controlled (Theory X), or that, given the opportunity, all employees can make a significant contribution if encouraged (Theory Y).

It is important to study physical or hygiene factors such as pay and working conditions, but other issues are just as important (some would argue more important) in determining people's attitude toward their employment. Motivation factors include:

"You cannot renew a company without revitalizing its people." (Christopher Bartlett)

  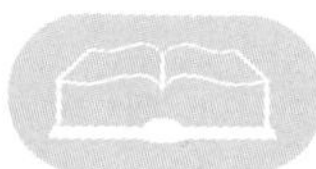  

- working for an efficient boss;
- thinking for yourself;
- seeing the end result of work and gaining a sense of achievement;
- getting interesting and challenging work assignments;
- being informed, listened to, and respected.

It is worth bearing in mind however, that organizations may appear to be following two apparently opposing directions: requiring more commitment and involvement of staff, while also being bent on cost reduction, which may include getting rid of staff. In such conditions it could be argued that while motivation factors may have come to the fore, there is a danger that the more fundamental hygiene factors or safety needs of employees are neglected.

4. Ask Leavers Why They Are Leaving

Consider conducting exit interviews with leavers or giving them questionnaires to complete. Either tool must be structured carefully and should not be relied on as the only way of collecting data. The trends behind involuntary turnover should not be ignored. For example, a rise in health-related departures may give rise to concerns about health and safety at work.

5. Assess the Effects of Turnover

The most obvious impact of turnover is that of increased costs. These fall into four tangible categories:

- separation costs
- temporary replacement costs
- recruitment and selection costs
- orientation and training costs

Turnover can be self-perpetuating in that it affects the morale of those who stay. Gauge employees' reactions through employee attitude surveys. Turnover also causes inefficiencies, not least because of the disruption caused by resignations.

6. Implement Retention Strategies

Take steps to:

- make sure that pay rates are competitive;
- offer a wider choice of benefits, for example, sabbaticals, career breaks, childcare, and eldercare arrangements;
- review your recruitment literature to make sure it gives an accurate picture of your organization;
- look at the quality of orientation and training you offer;
- improve job design and introduce flexible working practices such as job-sharing, flextime, and telecommuting;
- develop equal opportunity policies.

There are at least eight laws governing hiring policies.

Depending on its size, your organization may be exempt from some discrimination laws. For example, the Age Discrimination in Employment Act only applies to organizations with 20 or more employees.

- promote career advancement opportunities such as dual career ladders for technical and managerial staff;
- improve the quality of supervision and management;
- improve and offer training and education to your employees.

DOS AND DON'TS

For Managing Staff Turnover and Retention

DO

- Distinguish between different types of turnover.
- Understand the difference between hygiene and motivation factors, but make sure that you take account of both.
- Monitor the external labor market.

DON'T

- Don't measure and benchmark without knowing what you want to achieve.
- Don't throw money at the problem without knowing what the problem really is.

THOUGHT STARTERS

- Do you monitor turnover?
- Do you conduct exit interviews?
- Is turnover cyclical, seasonal, or departmentalized?

For More Information

Book:

Branham, F. Leigh. *Keeping the People Who Keep You in Business: 24 Ways to Hang on to Your Most Valuable Talent*. New York: AMACOM, 2000.

Journal Articles:

Bevan, Stephen. "Quit Stalling." *People Management* 3:23 (November 20, 1997): 32–35.
"Retaining Key Employees." *IRS Employment Review*, no. 650 (February 1998): 11–12.
Solomon, Charlene Marmer. "Keep Them: Don't Let Your Best People Get Away." *Workforce* 76:8 (August 1997): 46–52.

Web Site:

American Productivity and Quality Center: **www.apqc.org**

See also:

✔ **Attracting and Retaining People Reentering the Workplace (pp. 432–33)**
✔ **Conducting a Performance Appraisal (pp. 346–47)**
✔ **Empowerment (pp. 352–53)**
✔ **Implementing an Effective Change Program (pp. 504–05)**
✔ **Introducing Flexible Working into Your Organization (pp. 358–59)**
✔ **Motivating Your Staff in a Time of Change (pp. 372–73)**

"Very few people in the world can be relied upon to work without praise or recognition."

(Varindra Tarzie Vittachi)

Managing the Plateaued Performer

CHECKLIST

This checklist is concerned with managing employees who have apparently reached a plateau. It is aimed at managers who are immediately responsible for such people.

Plateauing is a familiar corporate phenomenon and is becoming more common with the proliferation of flat organizations, which offer less chance of promotion than traditional hierarchies. The performance of these plateaued employees may decline if it is not addressed, to the disadvantage of the organization and themselves.

Definition

A performance plateau is a leveling off of growth during which productivity flattens out and results remain stagnant.

(Theodore Kurtz, "Performance plateauing" (1989))

Plateaued performers are employees who have reached a certain level in the company and appear to be stuck there—they have neither the ambition nor the ability to progress further. There may be nothing wrong with their present performance, but they have no new ideas or initiatives and provide no inspiration to their own staff.

The experience of such employees can be very valuable as long as they maintain good performance levels—after all, not everyone can reach the heights. It's tempting to ignore their situation, since it poses no immediate threat. However, there's a serious danger of boredom and staleness setting in, with the result that they simply plod on doing their job in a routine way and cause demotivation in others. It's best to deal with the matter before it becomes a problem.

Staff members should have been plateaued for at least one year, maybe two, before you categorize them as plateaued performers. They are likely to have been in the same job or the same department for some time.

Advantages

Good handling should ensure:

- at the least, that the employee continues to make a significant contribution to the organization;
- at best, that the person makes new contributions;
- continued job satisfaction for the employee.

Disadvantages

There are many disadvantages of not handling the employee well.

On the part of the individual:

- poor motivation
- decreased job satisfaction
- infrequent generation of new ideas
- possibly declining performance

On the part of the organization:

- reduced productivity
- unoriginal thinking and uninspired ideas
- missing stimulation for other staff

Action Checklist

Remember throughout the process that the employee is not yet a problem—don't treat the person like one. Your only aim is to see if and how he or she can rise off the plateau.

1. Try to Spot the Signs

A plateau is an emerging process; it doesn't happen overnight. No one single incident will present itself as a benchmark or even diagnosis. Be careful not to confuse plateauing with the Peter Principle, the proposition that employees rise to their level of incompetence. Plateaued performers aren't incompetent, they just can't channel their energies or abilities into productive performance.

Ask yourself whether the employee's productivity declined consistently or sporadically. Have you observed a slackening in interest and commitment? Has the person's behavior altered from the norm?

2. Characterize the Plateau

Use the individual's attitude and level of activity to help you identify the type of plateau involved. Beverley Kaye has described four different types in "Are plateaued performers productive?" (1989).

- Passive: low in energy and activity, being trapped in personal inaction, with the apparent collusion of the employing organization.
- Productive: the opposite of passive, highly active, but busyness does not necessarily equal effectiveness.
- Partial: often concentrating on one small area of interest or responsibility, keeping a personal spark alive in the absence of prospects for promotion or challenge.
- Pleasant: happy with the status quo, doing the job well, in a comfortable groove, but wanting neither challenges nor risks and showing no desire to develop or improve.

3. Understand the Person

Try to understand what makes the person tick. Ask about outside interests, whether there are personal reasons for the plateau, and whether the person is actually content to stay there or whether, for example, earlier failure to get promotion had a demotivating effect. What are the individual's personal and professional ambitions? Only by knowing the person as a person can you hope to improve matters.

4. Examine Your Own Relationship with the Person

It may be that there is something in your relationship that is holding the individual back. It can be very difficult to find out if this is the case. It may be possible to ask directly; even if you don't get an answer, the person will appreciate your open and understanding approach. It is

"The moment you let avoiding failure become your motivator, you're down the path of inactivity."
(Roberto Goizueta)

often necessary, however, to consult other staff at your own level or above.

5. Identify the Problem

Be as precise as you can. There may be various causes for plateauing, for example:

- the company has not offered a stimulating environment;
- the person feels written off by you or other superiors;
- it's a long time since the person has been given a new challenge;
- colleagues largely ignore the person;
- there are problems at home.

There are many other possible causes, but a lack of stimulus is likely to figure among them.

6. Explore How You Can Improve Matters

Start with a positive assumption that improvement is possible, as it nearly always is. If you assume that you are unlikely to do much to help but have to go through the motions, your defeatist attitude is bound to communicate itself. The solution usually includes providing a new stimulus: very few people at any level do not respond to the right stimulus. This might mean nothing more than making the employee's present job more interesting (or pointing out how the person could make more of it), including a new challenge within the person's present responsibilities, or assigning the person to work with a team on a special project. It might mean suggesting a change of job within the company.

7. Continue to Show Interest and Give Support

At the same time you should emphasize that the person must take responsibility for his or her own future and make it clear that you will give your support. A plateaued performer may show a short-term improvement and then sink back again. Show continuing interest without being too obtrusive.

8. Make Supporting Plateaued Performers General Policy

Dealing with one person on your staff is not enough and might even appear to be singling out individuals for special treatment. Bring the matter to the attention of senior management and recommend that supporting plateaued performers be adopted as corporate policy. All managers should be able to identify plateaued staff members at an early stage and learn how they can be helped. This is after all an expression of the organization's concern for its main resource—its people. And success with one or two plateaued performers sends positive signals to other staff.

9. Recognize That You Can't Always Help

Although it is always worthwhile doing what you can to help plateaued performers and although you will achieve some surprising successes, you won't succeed every time. If you can't raise someone's sights after several attempts, you may at least be able to warn the person that his or her behavior is likely to be unsatisfactory to the organization sooner or later and might risk dismissal.

DOS AND DON'TS

For Managing the Plateaued Performer

DO

- Assume that something can be done.
- Get to know the person as well as you can and identify what is holding him or her back.
- Explore all possible ways of improvement and implement likely solutions.
- Make it clear that plateaued performers are responsible for their own future.
- Give continued support.
- Make identification and support for plateaued performers company policy.

DON'T

- Don't start with negative assumptions.
- Don't be too obtrusive.
- Don't give up too easily.

THOUGHT STARTERS

- People are much more likely to get stuck if an organization is stagnant and unstimulating.
- Have you ever been through a plateau phase? If so, how did you get out of it?
- What motivates you to do better?

For More Information

Books:

Brounstein, Marty. *Handling the Difficult Employee: Solving Performance Problems*. Normal, IL: Crisp Publications, 1993.

Kaufman, Roger, et al. *Guidebook for Performance Improvement: Working with Individuals and Organizations*. San Francisco, CA: Jossey Bass, 1996.

Zaccarelli, Herman, and David K. Hayes. *Training Managers to Train: A Practical Guide to Improving Employee Performance (50 minute series)*. Normal, IL: Crisp Publications, 1996.

Journal Articles:

Kaye, Beverley. "Are Plateaued Performers Productive?" *Personnel Journal* (August 1989): 57–65.

Kurtz, Theodore. "Performance Plateauing." *Supervisory Management* (December 1989): 19–22.

Savery, Lawson K. "Managing Plateaued Employees." *Management Decision* 28:3 (1990): 46–50.

Zaremba, Denise Karen. "The Managerial Plateau: What Helps in Developing Careers." *International Journal of Career Management* 6:2 (1994): 5–11.

"The people are not bad, but they have stopped questioning themselves." (Guy Hands)

 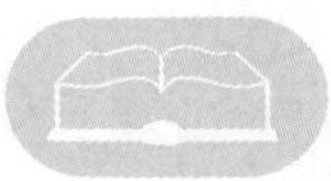    

MENTORING IN PRACTICE

This checklist is for managers wishing to explore mentoring as a process for developing people and their potential.

DEFINITION

Mentoring is a relationship in which one person (the mentor)—usually someone more experienced and often more senior in an organization—helps another (the learner) discover more about his or her personal qualities, capabilities, and potential. It can be an informal relationship, with the learner leaning on the mentor for guidance, support, help, and feedback, or a more formal arrangement between two people who respect and trust each other.

Mentoring need not bring together a trainer and a trainee or resemble line management with its attention to seniority and rank. Instead, the mentor's role is to listen, ask questions, and probe for facts and career choices; the mentor is a channel for information, experience, and opportunities from various sources that can benefit the learner.

Mentors are there not to instruct but to provide learners with input to help them form their own views, develop different perspectives, and develop as people and as potential managers.

ADVANTAGES

As a development tool, mentoring has advantages for the mentor, the learner, and the organization.

The organizational benefits of mentoring include:

- support for planning managerial succession and maximizing human potential;
- the likelihood of improving staff retention levels and recruitment prospects;
- improved communication and exposure of employees to the culture of the company;
- cost-effective, personalized staff development.

Mentoring offers the mentor:

- corporate recognition, higher status, and stronger job satisfaction;
- the development of leadership qualities and managerial skills;
- an opportunity to help others develop their careers.

Mentoring offers the learner:

- a sense of being valued by the company;
- an objective, supportive, nonthreatening source of support in developing new skills and exploring new directions;
- access to someone who understands the company's culture, personnel, and ways of working.

DISADVANTAGES

Mentoring has few disadvantages, but some cautions are in order.

- Mentoring does require corporate resources: the process takes time for learner and mentor, and both may need to work on appropriate skills such as planning, reviewing, and communication (particularly listening and constructive feedback).
- Mentoring is a complement to, not a substitute for, more formal training approaches.
- In the hands of an inappropriate mentor, a learner can develop in the wrong direction. You need to be very careful in selecting mentors and matching them to learners.
- A strong personal bond can develop between mentor and learner, to the detriment of both employees as well as to the organization.

ACTION CHECKLIST

1. MAKE CERTAIN THE MENTOR HAS THE RIGHT SKILLS

It is essential that the mentor has:

- good listening skills;
- sophistication in using different forms of questions—open, closed, probing, etc.;
- the maturity to suspend personal judgment and prejudice so that the learner can choose from a variety of directions;
- experience in giving constructive feedback, covering negative and positive aspects in a way that the learner can act on;
- skill in helping to define objectives and plan ways of achieving them;
- the initiative to use other people's skills and experiences to open up learning opportunities on the learner's behalf.

Consider having the skills of a potential mentor evaluated by an objective party, ideally someone with experience in mentoring. Individuals almost always either over- or underestimate their own competence (especially in communication, where most people believe they shine, even when they are barely adequate).

The mentor must be someone of authority in the organization, an experienced person who can open doors for the learner and offer viewpoints from a valued perspective. If necessary, arrange training and development for the mentor to sharpen and refine appropriate skills.

2. CLARIFY THE MENTORING RELATIONSHIP

Make sure that both the learner and the mentor are clear on what the relationship is—and is not—about. Early clarification can help avoid any later confusion and disappointment.

If appropriate, consider drafting a mentoring contract, specifying:

- the participants' respective roles, responsibilities, and commitment;

"Cheers hearten a man. But jeers are just as essential. They help maintain his sense of balance and proportion."

(Jay E. House)

 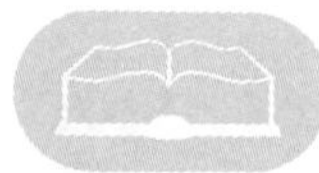     

DOS AND DON'TS

For Mentoring in Practice

DO

- Take the learner's views into account in selecting a well-matched mentor. The mentor needs to be someone the learner respects, trusts, and can open up to.
- Allow the mentor to take a flexible approach in order to focus on the learner's needs and aims.
- Remember that a key part of the mentor's role is to open doors to other people's experience and other learning opportunities.
- Make sure that each session starts with a review and ends with a clear action plan.
- Control the relationship and adjust it as necessary so the learner assumes increasing responsibility.

DON'T

- Don't assume that any line manager can be thrown in as a mentor.
- Don't believe that an individual's direct line manager is an appropriate mentor.
- Don't reveal information you learn during mentoring to people outside the relationship.
- Don't be afraid, as a mentor, to be open about yourself.
- Don't tell the learner what you know or try to supply all the answers—the mentoring journey is one of guided self-exploration.

- the planned number and frequency of meetings, to be reviewed and amended as necessary;
- the participants' obligation of confidentiality within the relationship.

Remember that the aim of the mentor is to help the learner develop, not adopt the mentor's ideas. The relationship should never become one of dependency—watch out for signs that this might be happening.

✔ 3. Open the Relationship

Recognize that in the early stages of the relationship the mentor needs to take a lead; later, as the learner's confidence and understanding grows, the balance shifts. Set objectives for what the mentoring process is to achieve; make the objectives relevant, specific, achievable, and time-limited.

✔ 4. Develop the Relationship

At the start of each mentoring session, and each time learners reach a milestone, review not just their current performance or success, but what lessons they learned about themselves and the process. Ask:

- What happened?
- Why?
- What was learned from the experience?

Mentor and learner should jointly identify what needs to be explored in order to achieve each objective. Compare the desired outcome with the current situation, identify the gaps, and outline what needs to happen to get from here to there.

Select and agree on a route to achieving each objective. Possible routes include learning experiences that can be provided or facilitated by the mentor, knowledge that can be passed from mentor to learner, and counseling and feedback to heighten the learner's self-awareness.

It can be hard to identify specific approaches for achieving a knowledge-based or attitudinal objective. In this case explore possible options, discuss experiences, and leave the learner to decide on a plan of action.

If the objective is skill-based, break down the required action into milestones. Hold regular progress reviews, and recognize and celebrate interim successes.

At the end of each mentoring session, articulate achievements so far and specify what needs to happen before the next session, especially if the mentor is to arrange something on the learner's behalf. Over the course of the mentoring, control of the learner's development should pass increasingly from the mentor to the learner: the goal is for the learner to be able to stand alone when the mentoring process ends.

✔ 5. End the Relationship

Mentoring relationships between people outside work may flourish for years. Inside the workplace, however, mentoring ends when the objectives are achieved. Having reached this point, celebrate the success of the relationship with a final review of the learner's progress.

THOUGHT STARTERS

- Who helped you make sensible decisions about your future, and how did they do it?
- Whom would you like to have as your mentor now? What qualities lead you to choose this person?
- Who in your company has potential and would benefit from working with a mentor?

For More Information

Books:

Bell, Chip R. *Managers As Mentors: Building Partnerships for Learning*. San Francisco, CA: Berrett-Koehler, 1996.

Hay, Julie. *Transformational Mentoring: Creating Development Alliances*. New York: McGraw-Hill, 1995.

Johnson, Harold E. *Mentoring for Exceptional Performance*. Torrance, CA: Griffin, 1997.

See also:

☆ **Coaching (pp. 328–29)**

☆ **Mentoring (pp. 326–27)**

✔ **Coaching for Better Performance (pp. 344–45)**

✔ **Training Needs Analysis (pp. 422–23)**

MANAGING CREATIVITY

This checklist distinguishes creativity from innovation and sets out the key steps for managing creativity in others.

DEFINITION

The terms creativity and innovation are often used interchangeably. The chief purpose here in distinguishing one from the other is to understand what each means so they can be managed better.

Creativity has been described as the organization of thoughts in a way that leads to different understandings of a situation. Innovation is more often associated with generating new products or services. This checklist is concerned with the processes, steps, and techniques of managing creativity in others rather than being creative yourself. For example:

1. Manager A is a highly creative individual who assails employees with ideas to the point where they can't keep up with the flow. As a result no one really knows what's going to happen from one day to the next—exciting and challenging, perhaps, but lacking in purposive direction and probably damaging to productivity.

2. Manager B has few creative ideas but is highly effective at listening, encouraging, and helping staff come up with ideas that can then be put to the test.

This checklist is mainly about Manager B.

ADVANTAGES

Every new product or service results initially from an idea that then follows an innovation cycle of testing, implementing, and marketing. It is generally accepted that the key to competitiveness is generating and successfully exploiting new ideas.

DISADVANTAGES

The environment in some organizations may prove hostile to creativity, and anyone managing creativity is likely to encounter obstacles, for example:

- free expression being stifled by a pervading culture of blame;
- general resistance to change;
- reluctance to think or move outside strict job descriptions;
- failure being regarded as a cause for penalties, not an opportunity to learn;
- a view that the best ideas come from the top;
- communication that is poor or moves only from the top down;
- rigid formalities and rules;
- inadequate or nonexistent incentives;
- slow decision-making.

ACTION CHECKLIST

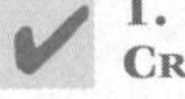

1. IDENTIFY POTENTIAL SOURCES OF CREATIVITY

- We tend to associate research with inventing new products, but it is just as likely to yield ideas for new processes. Sources of information include published academic research, newspaper reports, or articles in trade or professional journals.
- Employees are the ones who handle the day-to-day problems, processes, and plaudits. They are the best placed for spotting opportunities or threats, devising better ways of doing things, or thinking of ways of doing different things.
- Customers may not always be right, but listening carefully and exploring their comments, feedback, and complaints yields new ideas.
- Relationships with suppliers can develop beyond purchasing into partnerships exploring mutual benefit.
- Competitors have their own agenda for creativity; actively gathering intelligence on a competitor's activities can provide an early alert to new developments.
- Happenstance: a great deal of creativity seems to stem from unplanned and undirected circumstances.

2. SET AN EXAMPLE YOURSELF

This is a matter of attitude and style rather than being creative yourself, although that can obviously help. The idea is not to manage by visible face-time productivity, but by realizing that staff need downtime for chatting, thinking, and having sessions to explore different things in different ways.

- Encourage new ideas consistently, not just when (or if) you have the time.
- Discuss all ideas in open forum, not just those you think are good.
- Welcome new explorations and different directions instead of insisting on keeping the status quo.

3. FOSTER A CLIMATE OF CREATIVITY

A climate that fosters creativity is difficult to describe, but it is about:

- a sense of dynamism;
- a feeling of interest and mutual respect when people interact;
- an environment of controlled but flexible rules and procedures instead of blind conformance to the rules;
- an atmosphere of individual energy, enthusiasm, open-mindedness, and commitment.

4. USE TECHNIQUES FOR CREATIVITY

Brainstorming involves spontaneous open-ended discussion in the search for new ideas. It is invaluable for generating large numbers of ideas, however off-the-wall they may appear at the time.

Suggestion boxes gather ideas from employees to improve productivity, cut costs, or improve working conditions. The key to successful suggestion schemes is to give feedback and reward contributors so employees realize that management listens to and values them.

Focus groups explore a particular topic in some depth,

"Responsibility is what awaits outside the Eden of Creativity." (Nadine Gordimer)

allowing people to develop related ideas and build on others' views as they go along.

Lateral thinking, pioneered by Edward de Bono, takes us outside our familiar, even organizational, way of reasoning and suggests that there are many ways of thinking about a problem.

Mind-mapping, developed by Tony Buzan, mirrors the way the brain stores and retrieves information. It is a powerful way of expressing the thought patterns, pictures, and associations that exist in the brain.

5. Become a Team Member

Although you may be the team leader, become a team member as well. Challenge others in the way they do things, even what they are doing, and encourage them to challenge you. You need to adopt a number of different roles to get the best from teams—it's useful at various times to be:

- the manager who sits back, listens, and encourages and knows when to move away from an unprofitable track;
- the communicator who interprets input from different individuals;
- the devil's advocate who tries to get people to see that there is an alternative;
- the builder who makes links between a number of possibilities;
- the coordinator who sums up when a consensus begins to appear.

6. Build In Breathing Space

There's no secret here: if you want people to be creative, you can't expect to see them "doing" all the time. In fact you can't expect to see them all the time—they may be better at being creative out of your sight or hearing. If you trust people with space and time, generally they come up with the goods. Largely it's a question of trust, something that has to be given in order to be earned.

7. Build Systems for Creativity

Such systems will be based on the approaches outlined in Steps 1–6 above. They may include:

- 360-degree appraisal—in which constructive review and feedback from customers, subordinates, peers, and managers takes place on a regular, honest, and open basis.
- self-directed teams—small groups of people genuinely empowered to manage themselves and the work they do. They require flexibility and support from the organization and multiskilling and self-discipline from team members.
- flexible working—so that people are not disadvantaged by one-size-fits-all attendance requirements, which may no longer be appropriate or necessary for the type of work required. You can gain positive advantages by gearing the work to the employee instead of the other way around.

8. Devise Inexpensive Pilots

It is important to try out ideas that seem to promise much but may need significant investment. Plan how to pilot such ideas on a smaller scale to get information about whether they bear further development and learn from the initial phasing-in how to improve later, fuller implementations.

9. Feedback and Reward

No initiative will carry much value unless it is firmly supported with systems of feedback and reward. Letting employees know how their suggestions are turning out encourages them to be forthcoming with further ideas. Feedback should be constructive and supportive and should cover all the ideas employees have contributed, not just the ones an assessing panel has deemed worthy. Some successful suggestion programs reward all contributions in cash on a sliding scale depending on how far each idea can be developed.

THOUGHT STARTERS

- Do you believe that creativity will come of its own accord or that it needs to be nurtured?
- How often do you try out new ways of doing things in a spirit of inquiry?

DOS AND DON'TS

For Managing Creativity

DO

- Have a customer focus in order to produce goods or services that people want now or may want in the future.
- Understand the major business drivers—profitability, competitors, technology, demand, costs—against which ideas will be evaluated.
- Encourage trials and experiments and use failure to move on, not back.
- Weigh up the importance of creativity when recruiting new staff.

DON'T

- Don't accept that all conflict is negative.
- Don't accept that creativity takes second place to order and routine.

For More Information

Book:

Whatmore, John. *Releasing Creativity: How Leaders Can Develop Creative Potential in Their Teams*. Sterling, VA: Stylus, 1999.

See also:

☆ **Creating Corporate Creativity (pp. 271–72)**
Innovation and Creativity (pp. 2000–03)

"I don't think I am creative. I think I recognize creativity." (Michael Grade)

  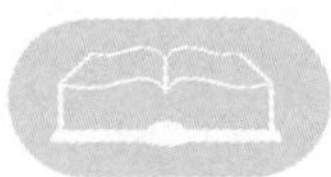    

Motivating Your Staff in a Time of Change

CHECKLIST

This checklist is designed for managers with responsibilities for managing, motivating, and developing staff at a time when organizational structures and processes are undergoing continual change.

In today's turbulent, often chaotic, environment, commercial success depends on employees using their full talents. Yet in spite of the myriad of available theories and practices available, managers often view motivation as something of a mystery. In part this is because individuals are motivated by different things and in different ways. In addition, these are times when delayering and the flattening of hierarchies can create insecurity and lower staff morale. Moreover, more staff than ever before are working part time or on limited-term contracts, and these employees are often especially hard to motivate.

Definition

Twyla Dell writes of motivation, "The heart of motivation is to give people what they really want most from work. The more you are able to provide what they want, the more you should expect what you really want, namely: productivity, quality, and service." (*An Honest Day's Work* (1988))

Advantages

A positive motivation philosophy and practice should improve productivity, quality, and service. Motivation helps people:

- achieve goals;
- gain a positive perspective;
- create the power to change;
- build self-esteem and capability;
- manage their own development and help others with theirs.

Disadvantages

There are no real disadvantages to successfully motivating employees, but there are many barriers to overcome.

Barriers may include unaware or absent managers, inadequate buildings, outdated equipment, and entrenched attitudes, for example:

- "We don't get paid extra to work harder."
- "We've always done it this way."
- "Our bosses don't have a clue what we do."
- "It doesn't say that in my job description."
- "I'm going to do as little as possible without getting fired."

Such views will take persuasion, perseverance, and the proof of experience to break down.

Action Checklist

1. Read the Gurus

Familiarize yourself with Herzberg's hygiene theory, McGregor's X and Y theories and Maslow's hierarchy of needs. Although these theories date back some years, they are still valid today. Consult a digest to gain a basic understanding of their main principles; it will be invaluable for building a climate of honesty, openness, and trust.

2. What Motivates You?

Determine which factors are important to you in your working life and how they interact. What has motivated you and demotivated you in the past?

Understand the differences between real, longer-term motivators and short-term spurs.

3. Find Out What Your People Want From Work

People may want more status, higher pay, better working conditions, and flexible benefits. But find out what really motivates your employees by asking them in performance appraisals, attitude surveys, and informal conversations what they want most from their jobs.

Do people want, for example:

- more interesting work?
- more efficient bosses?
- more opportunity to see the end result of their work?
- greater participation?
- greater recognition?
- greater challenge?
- more opportunities for development?

4. Walk the Job

Every day, find someone doing something well and tell the person so. Make sure the interest you show is genuine without going overboard or appearing to watch over people's shoulders. If you have ideas as to how employees' work could be improved, don't shout it out, but help them to find their way instead. Earn respect by setting an example; it is not necessary to be able do everything better than your staff. Make it clear what levels of support employees can expect.

5. Remove Demotivators

Identify factors that demotivate staff—they may be physical (buildings, equipment) or psychological (boredom, unfairness, barriers to promotion, lack of recognition). Some of them can be dealt with quickly and easily; others require more planning and time to work through. The fact that you are concerned to find out what is wrong and do something about it is in itself a motivator.

6. Demonstrate Support

Whether your working culture is one that clamps down on mistakes and penalizes error or a more tolerant

"The better people think they are, the better they will be. Positive self-image creates success."

(Liisa Joronen)

  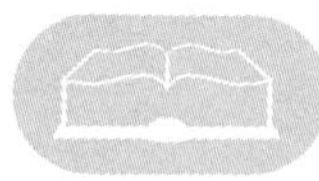    

one that espouses mistakes as learning opportunities, your staff need to understand the kind and levels of support they can expect. Motivation practice and relationship building often falter because staff do not feel they are receiving adequate support.

7. Be Wary of Cash Incentives

Many people say they are working for money and claim in conversation that their fringe benefits are an incentive. But money actually comes low down in the list of motivators, and it doesn't motivate for long after a raise. Fringe benefits can be effective in attracting new employees, but benefits rarely motivate existing employees to use their potential more effectively.

8. Decide On Action

Having listened to staff, take steps to alter your organization's policies and attitudes, consulting fully with staff and unions. Consider policies that affect flexible working, reward, promotion, training and development, and participation.

9. Manage Change

Adopting policies is one thing, implementing them is another. If poor motivation is entrenched, you may need to look at the organization's whole style of management. One of the most natural of human instincts is to resist change even when it is designed to be beneficial. The way change is introduced has its own power to motivate or demotivate, and can often be the key to success or failure. If you:

- tell–instruct or deliver a monologue–you are ignoring your staff's hopes, fears, and expectations;
- tell and sell–try to persuade people–even your most compelling reasons will not hold sway over the long term if you don't allow discussion;
- consult–it will be obvious if you have made up your mind beforehand;
- look for real participation–sharing the problem solving and decision making with those who are to implement the change–you can begin to expect commitment and ownership along with the adaptation and compromise that will occur naturally.

10. Understand Learning Preferences

Change involves learning. In their *Manual of Learning Styles* (1992), Peter Honey and Alan Mumford distinguish four basic styles of learning:

- activists–like to get involved in new experiences, problems, or opportunities. They're not too happy standing back, observing, and being impartial;
- theorists–are comfortable with concepts and theory. They don't like being thrown in at the deep end without apparent purpose or reason;
- reflectors–like to take their time and think things through. They don't like being pressured into rushing from one thing to another;
- pragmatists–need a link between the subject matter and the job in hand. They learn best when they can test things out.

As each of us learns with different styles, preferences, and approaches, your people will respond best to stimuli and suggestions that take account of the way they do things best.

11. Provide Feedback

Feedback is one of the most valuable elements in the motivation cycle. Don't keep staff guessing how their development, progress, and accomplishments are shaping up. Offer comments with accuracy and care, keeping in mind next steps or future targets.

DOS AND DON'TS

For Motivating Your Staff in a Time of Change

DO

- Recognize that you don't have all the answers.
- Take time to find out what makes others tick and show genuine caring.
- Lead, encourage, and guide staff—don't force them.
- Tell your staff what you think.

DON'T

- Don't make assumptions about what drives others.
- Don't assume others are like you.
- Don't force people into things that are supposedly good for them.
- Don't neglect the need for inspiration.
- Don't delegate work—delegate responsibility!

THOUGHT STARTERS

- People don't mind being in a rocking boat so much if they know where it's headed.
- Staff want a sense of direction, not directiveness.
- Your morale infects others, whether you like it or not.
- Trust your staff to perform 25 percent better than you expect.

For More Information

Books:

Dell, Twyla. *An Honest Day's Work: Motivating Employees to Give Their Best*. Los Altos, CA: Crisp Publications, 1988.

Holbeche, Linda. *Motivating People in Lean Organizations*. Woburn, MA: Butterworth-Heinemann, 1997.

See also:

✔ **Conducting a Performance Appraisal (pp. 346–47)**

✔ **Managing Staff Turnover and Retention (pp. 364–65)**

"The task of the leader is to get people from where they are to where they have not been."

(Henry Kissinger)

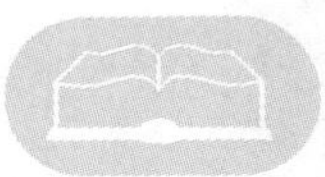

PLANNING OVERSEAS ASSIGNMENTS

CHECKLIST

This checklist provides planning guidance to companies sending employees, and to individuals being posted, on overseas assignments.

Selecting, appointing, supporting, and developing managers abroad can be highly complex. Failure rates or noncompletion of assignments have been put as high as 40 percent. Creating a positive sense of direction, purpose, and control and reducing uncertainty and ineffectiveness is greatly to the advantage of both the company and the individual manager.

DEFINITION

For the purposes of this checklist, working overseas means outside the United States. An assignment means a posting overseas with the current employer for a defined period of more than six months.

ADVANTAGES

- Employee and employer both benefit from minimizing culture shock and attending to detail.
- The potential for failure because of unsuccessful cultural adaptation is minimized.
- The cost of premature repatriation is reduced.

DISADVANTAGES

- The cost of such preparations can be high.
- Unforeseeable changes in political, economic, or environmental circumstances can counteract the preparation.

ACTION CHECKLIST

1. PREPARE FOR THE ROAD AHEAD

Be aware of local language requirements and cultural issues, and allow time to prepare for the transition. Preliminary visits for the employee and family are invaluable for gaining an initial perspective, making early introductions, and learning about local facilities, or the lack of them.

Just as the transition is the joint responsibility of both employee and employer, it is vital that both of them:

- understand the task to be accomplished;
- recognize the need for levels of adaptability, maturity, and technical competence;
- understand the need for organizational and family support.

2. BE AWARE OF RIGHTS ISSUES

Be aware of the rights of individuals and of the employing organization in the country of destination, especially those covered by existing or pending legislation. It is a good idea to contact the State Department before you plan your trip to find out as much as you can about your destination country. The State Department will be able to give you addresses of your destination country's embassies in the United States as well as contact details for U.S. embassies abroad. Additional resources within each state include the Secretary of State's office, International Trade office, and Small Business Development Centers, many of which are located at community colleges.

3. DEFINE THE PERSONAL CHARACTERISTICS AND REQUISITES FOR THE JOB SPECIFICATION

In *Managing Multinational Corporations* (1974), V. K. Phatak describes the personal characteristics of successful expatriate managers:

Ideally, it seems, he (or she) should have the stamina of an Olympic swimmer, the mental agility of an Einstein, the conversational skill of a professor of languages, the detachment of a judge, the tact of a diplomat, and the perseverance of an Egyptian pyramid builder. And if he is going to measure up to the demands of living and working in a foreign country, he should also have the feeling for culture; his moral judgements should not be too rigid; he should be able to merge with the local environment with chameleon-like ease; and he should show no signs of prejudice.

Obviously only very rare individuals can hope instantly to meet this description. Everyone else selected for foreign assignments must develop the following attributes.

- Knowledge of languages.
- International experience. Previous experience can help mental preparation and reduce culture shock. Preliminary visits and existing organizational networks can help the process of familiarization.
- Job experience, seniority, and qualifications. In some countries, qualifications–as a recognition and acknowledgment of expertise–are very important.
- Flexibility, learning, and lack of prejudice. Employees working overseas need to be aware of and overcome stereotypical U.S. superiority and insularity and to be able to cope with unfamiliar people in unfamiliar surroundings.
- Motivation factors:
  - the need to gain foreign experience for career advancement;
  - interest in other cultures;
  - interest in communication and language learning.
- Competence, effectiveness, and capabilities:
  - initiative and capacity for high levels of activity;
  - ability to handle stress;
  - respect for different opinions and values;
  - interest in and liking for people;
  - autonomy of action.

4. DRAW UP THE SHORT LIST FOR CANDIDATE SELECTION

Certain criteria are essential for the selection and elimination process.

- Is the candidate stable, self-reliant, and able to cope with crises?

"Planning is as natural to the process of success as its absence is to the process of failure."

(Robin Sieger)

- Is the candidate willing to adjust to a new way of life?
- Can he or she relate well to people and communicate effectively in the destination culture?
- Does he or she have the required technical knowledge and competence?
- What is the candidate's health record?
- Are problems likely to arise concerning family responsibilities?

The selection process should not focus solely on technical competence, but should also assess personal characteristics such as flexibility, emotional stability, and learning and relational skills.

5. Devise an Appropriate Training Program

Organizations may prefer job-related opportunities such as international transfers, assignments, or exchanges, but there can be no substitute for a practical, tailor-made, and flexible program that exposes the candidate to a variety of elements, including the following:

- Language training. Teach-yourself tapes and intensive crash courses such as Berlitz have good track records of success if the learner is willing and committed.
- General, national, and business orientation. Awareness of:
  - the global economic order and terms of trade.
  - trends in changing technology and communications, demography, religion, and the environment.
  - the country's historical, religious, ethnic, and political background.
  - the country's attitude toward foreign business.
  - the efficiency of transportation and communications.
  - facilities for health care, housing, education, and leisure.
  - social and cultural expectations and requirements.
  - international business strategies.
- Family consultation. A stable family life is generally regarded as an asset. Where the assignment is for two years or more, the family usually expects to move with the employee. Consider the whole range of domestic arrangements (which on home ground would remain the private preserve of the individual).
- Career development preparation. View this experience as a stage of development and not as the end of the road. Both employee and employer should give thought to how this experience will be of benefit and what will follow.

6. Support the Manager Overseas

An on-site line manager, subordinate, superior, or peer who acts as a troubleshooter, mentor, and guide in the early stages can be a boon during an otherwise traumatic, worrying, or frustrating experience.

7. Prepare for Repatriation

This is as important for the career path of the employee as for the avoidance of "reentry shock" for the family. Reintegration, or the "coming home" phase, may also require some training, familiarization, and updating in addition to personal effort.

THOUGHT STARTERS

- Have the political, economic, social, cultural, and market fronts been thoroughly researched?
- Have facilities and support lines in the foreign country been researched?
- Is a comprehensive training and familiarization program in place?
- Has adequate thought been given to what follows the foreign posting for the employee?

For More Information

Books:

Hachey, Jean-Marc. *The Canadian Guide to Working and Living Overseas*. Ottawa: Intercultural Systems, 1998.

Phatak, V. K. *Managing Multinational Corporations*. New York: Praeger, 1974.

Journal Articles:

Beeth, Gunnar. "Multicultural Managers Wanted." *Managerial Review* 86:5 (May 1997): 17–21.

Gaymer, Janet, and Hilary Belchak. "Posting Employees Abroad." *Company Secretary's Review* 20:18 (January 1997): 137–38.

Harvey, Michael. "The Selection of Managers for Foreign Assignments: A Planning Perspective." *Columbia Journal of World Business* 31:4 (Winter 1996): 102–18.

Web Sites:

Center for International Briefing: **www.cibfarnham.com**

Employment Conditions Abroad: **www.eca-international.com**

Expats International: **www.expats.co.uk**

See also:

✔ **Preparing for Business Abroad (pp. 514–15)**

"I never failed to convince an audience that the best thing they could do was to go away."

(Thomas Love Peacock)

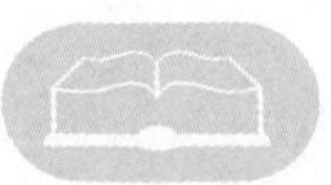

JOB CUTS—BREAKING THE NEWS

CHECKLIST

This checklist provides guidance to line managers who find themselves responsible for informing employees that their job is to be terminated.

The fact that there are to be job cuts rarely comes as a complete surprise to employees, but dismissing individuals is a difficult task that needs to be handled with great care. There are steps to follow, however, that can help make the process as painless as possible.

DEFINITION

This checklist concentrates solely on the termination interview itself, not the process leading up to it. It therefore excludes information about the statutory requirements of an company considering job cuts.

A job is considered to be cut if the employer:

- is ceasing to carry on the business the employment is in;
- is closing down the business at the site where the job is based;
- is transferring the business from the site where the job is based to another location (for example, a company with two offices decides to rationalize at one site);
- requires fewer employees to do a specific type of work (for example, one manager takes over a function formerly divided between two);
- needs fewer employees to perform the work at the place where it is conducted (for example, the divisional personnel function is closed, but the head office personnel department remains and a personnel manager is appointed for each site).

The basic test for job cuts is whether the employer now needs fewer employees either across the country or at a particular location. In theory, the amount of work need not have changed, but it must be capable of being performed by fewer people.

Termination interviews are conducted on an individual basis. Their purpose is to ensure that employees are:

- told the news in a clear and objective manner;
- made aware of the reasons for the termination;
- given information on the time frame of the termination process;
- provided with details of the severance package on offer;
- advised as to employment resources available for all unemployed workers; also about possible public benefits, such as unemployment compensation, available to workers laid off through no fault of their own;
- given a letter of recommendation (if it is deserved) so as to better their chances at being hired elsewhere;
- advised—if appropriate to the company's situation—that they could be re-hired by the company in the future, should conditions warrant future workforce expansion.

ADVANTAGES

Careful handling:

- helps to reduce possible animosity and ill will on the part of the terminated employee;
- helps to minimize damage to the company's reputation, by reducing the chances that the terminated employee will "bad mouth" the company in public;
- increases the chances that the terminated employee will have an easier time finding a new job.

ACTION CHECKLIST

1. PREPARE YOURSELF

All managers find it difficult to deliver bad news to their employees. Before breaking such news to an individual it is essential to address your own feelings on the issue, toward downsizing itself and its impact on the employee.

2. GATHER THE INFORMATION YOU NEED

Before you deliver the news of layoff to an employee, make sure you are aware of and understand:

- the reasons for the job cuts;
- the method of selecting employees for termination;
- the details of the severance package;
- the rights, responsibilities, and opportunities for laid-off employees.

Review the employee's personal details, particularly the person's employment record, before the meeting.

3. PLAN THE INTERVIEW

Plan the interview carefully in terms of its timing and location and what is to happen immediately afterward.

Timing. Decisions at higher levels may leave line managers with little leeway in choosing the timing of their announcements. Two rules of thumb, however, are:

- Avoid holding interviews on Fridays. Few (or no) professional support mechanisms are available to employees over the weekend.
- Allow sufficient time for each interview (while setting a clear time limit) and schedule a gap between interviews.

Location. Make sure that:

- the interviews are held in a quiet place, out of view and beyond the hearing range of other employees and free from interruptions;
- employees can leave via a different route to avoid embarrassment and to minimize upset between people who have been told what is happening and those still waiting to see you;
- the interview room is set up in an appropriate way—there are simple ways to avoid giving an overt message that it's "them" against "us". For example, furnish the room with chairs of equal size and have no desk in between you and the employee. Perhaps have water

"When this circuit learns your job, what are you going to do?" (Marshall McLuhan)

and tissues available, within easy reach, as an aid for employees who take the news hard and need a moment or two to compose themselves.

Aftermath. You must decide what you want employees to do immediately after they are told they are out. Some organizations require individuals to clear their desks (supervised by their manager or a member of the personnel department) and leave the premises immediately. Others expect employees to work a notice period, but send them home for the remainder of the day on which they are told. Clarify what your organizational policy is or whether special instructions apply to employees in particular positions of responsibility.

Supporting paperwork. Gather relevant information that employees can take away and read in their own time. This material should reinforce the information given in the interview and go into more detail on such issues as outplacement, support networks, and other services available to dismissed employees.

4. Give the News

It is essential to give news as momentous as dismissal in a clear and unambiguous manner. The individual should come away from the interview knowing that the decision is final.

The amount of information you supply is critical. There is a fine line between overloading an employee with information and leaving someone with unanswered questions. There can be no hard and fast rules about this; each person is different and will react to bad news in a different way.

5. Provide Details of What Is Available

Briefly explain:

- the redundancy package (including the financial settlement, outplacement, and other support);
- the time frame;
- contacts in organizations that may be of help (if no outplacement service is offered).

Give the employee the information you have prepared. If necessary, arrange a follow-up meeting to answer further questions or to help with any problems that arise.

6. Check the Employee's Understanding of the Situation and Close the Interview

Make sure that the employee understands the information you have given, and ask for any immediate questions. Invite the person to contact you again if (as often happens) further questions arise, but be firm about ending the interview to fit your schedule.

DOS AND DON'TS

For Job Cuts—Breaking the News

DO

- Address your own feelings and be prepared.
- Anticipate and prepare for negative reactions.
- Be firm, clear, and unambiguous.
- Demonstrate sympathy and empathy.
- Provide written details of both the situation and what is on offer.

DON'T

- Don't rush the interview.
- Don't lose control.
- Don't give employees conflicting messages.
- Don't patronize or insult employees ("We just got rid of some dead wood").

THOUGHT STARTERS

- Have you ever been laid off?
- If so, how was the news delivered?
- Could it have been handled in a better way?

For More Information

Books:

Steingold, Fred S., and Amy Delpo, eds. *The Employer's Legal Handbook*. 4th ed. Soquel, CA: Nolo Press, 2001.

Stiller, Richard, and Ron Visconti. *Rightful Termination: Avoiding Litigation*. Normal, IL: Crisp Publications, 1994.

Weiss, Donald H. *Fair, Square, and Legal: Safe Hiring, Managing, and Firing Practices to Keep You and Your Company out of Court*. 3rd ed. New York: AMACOM, 1999.

Web Sites:

HR Guide: **www.hr-guide.com**

HRnext: **www.hrnext.com**

"The shock of unemployment becomes a pathology in its own right." (Robert Farrar Capon)

STEPS IN SUCCESSFUL TEAM BUILDING

CHECKLIST

This checklist explores the essential aspects of planning, setting up, and maintaining an effective team for specific projects or assignments.

DEFINITION

Teams are not the same as other groups: they need to be planned, built, and maintained. A number of people who happen to work together in the same place may not operate as a team, and may not need to. A team has a distinct characteristic—it is a group working together to achieve a common purpose, and it may be composed of people drawn from different functions, departments, or disciplines. Increasingly, teams are groups set up for a specific project, are empowered to steer and develop the work they do, and are responsible for their achievements.

ADVANTAGES

Successful team building can:

- coordinate individuals' efforts as they tackle complex tasks;
- make the most of each team member's personal expertise and knowledge, which might otherwise remain untapped;
- raise and sustain motivation and confidence as individual team members feel supported and involved;
- encourage members to spark ideas off each other, to solve problems, and to find appropriate ways forward;
- help break down communication barriers and avoid unhealthy competition, rivalry, and point-scoring;
- raise the level of individual and collective empowerment;
- support approaches such as total quality management, just-in-time management, and customer service programs;
- bring about commitment to and ownership of the task in hand.

DISADVANTAGES

There are circumstances where teams may be inadvisable—for example, they may not fit in some organizational cultures where there are rigid reporting structures or fixed work procedures. A team approach may not be the answer especially:

- where one person has all the knowledge, expertise, and resources to do the job independently;
- when there is no real common purpose, and a group is wrongly called a team.

ACTION CHECKLIST

1. DECIDE WHETHER YOU REALLY NEED A TEAM

Just because it is fashionable to talk about team building, it does not mean that every job needs a team to complete it. It may be that a single skilled person working alone and properly supported can achieve the task more effectively than forming a group of people into a team. Consider whether you need a range of expertise and experience, shared workloads, brainstorming, and problem solving. If you do, a team will be your best option.

2. DETERMINE YOUR OBJECTIVES AND THE SKILLS NEEDED TO ACHIEVE THEM

Be clear about the broad outcome of the project. Identify the technical and team skills you need and bring together individuals with that range of skills. Whatever the range of personnel available, the key is to pick people with a mix of different skills. These include team skills, personal skills, and technical abilities.

3. PLAN A TEAM-BUILDING STRATEGY

Invest time at the outset in getting the operating framework right so that the team will develop and grow. There are various areas to consider:

- a climate of trust in which mistakes and failures are viewed as learning experiences, not occasions for blame;
- free flow of information to all those who need to integrate their work with business objectives;
- training in communication, interpersonal, and negotiation skills, and coaching to handle the tasks required and adopt responsibility for them;
- time, not only for regular meetings, but for coordinating activities, developing thoughts, and monitoring progress;
- objectives that are clearly understood by all team members. This is increasingly a case of involving team members in setting the objectives rather than dictating prescribed objectives to them;
- feedback focusing on the positive aspects and suggesting ways of dealing with the negative ones. Team members need to know how well they are doing and if and where improvements can be made.

4. GET THE TEAM TOGETHER

It is important at this early stage that you don't actually try to solve the problem you are confronted with. At the initial meeting you should aim to start to build the group into a team. Discuss and agree on the outcomes the team is to achieve. Clarify the common purposes and make sure that everyone knows what his or her personal contribution to the team's success is, its place in the project schedule, and its importance to the project's success.

5. EXPLORE AND ESTABLISH OPERATING GROUND RULES

There will be a need:

- to communicate openly and honestly, with team members feeling free to say what they think and feel without fear, rancor, or anger;
- to listen to others, including those voicing minority or extreme views;
- to agree on which decision-making, reporting, and other processes will be adopted for the life span of the team.

"To create human capital, a company needs to foster teamwork, communities of practice, and other social forms of learning."

(Thomas A. Stewart)

  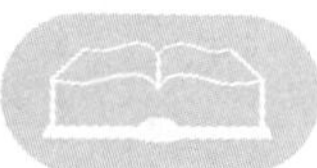    

DOS AND DON'TS

For Steps In Successful Team Building

DO

- Confirm that you actually need a team.
- Take the time and trouble to manage and facilitate the team's development and activity.
- Establish as a team the common aims, objectives, and success criteria for the task, project, or process.
- Clarify regularly who is to do what, and by what date, as their contribution to the team's targets.
- Remember that you can't win a team game on your own.
- Communicate freely with all members of the team.
- Manage team meetings so that everyone has a say and feels involved in decision making and planning.
- Disband the team when objectives have been met.

DON'T

- Don't expect a new team to fire on all cylinders from day one. A team is an entity in its own right, like a new employee who needs orientation and development.
- Don't dominate, however unintentionally or unconsciously.
- Don't exercise such tight management control that you squash creativity.
- Don't let individuals take the credit for the team's achievements.
- Don't let the team feel too exclusive, in case it shuts out other parts of the organization.

6. Identify Individuals' Strengths

Audit individuals' strengths so the team as a whole can benefit from all the skills and expertise available. Consider bringing in someone with team-building experience to help with the initial phases, especially if the team's task is important.

7. Include Yourself As a Team Member

Your role is as a member of the team, not just as the boss. Emphasize that everyone in the team has an important role and that yours happens to be the team leader. Act as a role model and maintain effective communication—especially listening—with all members.

It may be helpful for roles to remain fluid, adding to the flexibility of working relationships without team members losing the focus of their individual strengths or objectives. An effective leader may decide to cede project leadership temporarily to another team member when specific skills are required.

8. Check Objectives

Check the team's objectives regularly to make sure that members still have a clear focus on what they are working toward, individually and as a team.

9. Time Meetings Carefully

Inessential meetings are a bane, but if there are too few, the project—and the team—can lose focus. Meet regularly but purposefully:

- to provide an opportunity to ask, "How are we doing?";
- to review progress on the task;
- to reflect on how the team is working.

If any gaps or problems arise from the review, plan and implement activity and corrective measures.

10. Dissolve the Team

When the team has accomplished its tasks, acknowledge completion. Carry out a final review to see if the team has achieved the objectives and to evaluate the team's performance; individuals should learn, improve, and benefit next time from this exercise. If all the objectives have been met, the team can be disbanded.

THOUGHT STARTERS

- What excellent (or awful) teams have you worked in? What made them so good (or bad)?
- Does your natural management style fit a team approach, or do you need to adjust—maybe let go and trust individuals more?
- Do you use teams to the best advantage?
- Are you absolutely clear what you want your team to achieve?
- Have you thought through ways to resolve conflict if and when it arises?

For More Information

Books:

Colenso, Michael, ed. *Kaizen Strategies for Improving Team Performance: How to Accelerate Team Development and Enhance Team Productivity*. Upper Saddle River, NJ: Financial Times/Prentice Hall, 2000.

Romig, Dennis A. *Side by Side Leadership: Achieving Outstanding Results Together*. Marietta, GA: Bard Press, 2001.

Willcocks, Graham, and Steve Morris. *Successful Team Building*. Hauppauge, NY: Barron's Educational, 1997.

See also:

☆ **The Critical Factors That Build or Break Teams (pp. 192–93)**
☆ **Self-Managed Teams: How They Succeed or Fail (pp. 202–03)**
Meredith Belbin (pp. 966–67)

"Team management has been considered as the Chinese approach to enhance collective culture at work."
(Zhong-Ming Wang)

Successful Delegation

CHECKLIST

This checklist explains how to delegate effectively.

Delegation is a vital management skill that, like many managers, you may have avoided practicing. Perhaps you resist letting go of control, believing (mistakenly) that nobody else can do the job as well as you can. Or maybe you feel that you don't have time to delegate, and that it's easier to do everything yourself.

The key is to make sure that you delegate without abdicating on the one hand or interfering on the other.

Definition

Delegation is about entrusting others with appropriate responsibility and authority for performing certain activities or accomplishing specific goals. More simply, it is about getting other people to do part of your job—a job that is your responsibility but need not be done completely by yourself. It is not getting them to do something they are already responsible for doing. Delegation should be a positive action (for example, a means of developing staff) rather than a negative one (passing on a job you don't like).

There are various levels of delegation.

- You can delegate an activity but not accountability. Because you are delegating part of your job, you remain ultimately responsible for the outcome. You get the credit if you delegate effectively, but you also get the criticism if your delegation is less than successful.
- You can delegate responsibility and authority for the activity, leaving the other person to get on with it. In this case it is important not to abdicate, but to maintain a fine balance between interest, support, and motivation on the one hand, and interference or neglect on the other.

Advantages

Effective delegation:

- frees managers' time;
- encourages managers to prioritize their work;
- helps managers assess the potential of their people;
- motivates the people to whom work is delegated by giving them more challenging work;
- serves as a development tool by increasing the range of skills in a team;
- contributes to succession planning by exposing people to other levels of work.

Disadvantages

There are no real disadvantages to delegation, but you should consider that:

- delegation takes time and requires considerable effort and personal investment from managers;
- there is a certain level of risk—people take on part of the job, but effectively the buck stops with you;
- because of the recent spate of corporate downsizing, you may not have staff with sufficient resources, time, or competence to take on additional assignments.

Action Checklist

1. Be Consistent

Ask yourself if the task to be delegated is unique or is part of a general trend of assigning activities to others and developing their skills. Consistency allows your staff to know what to expect and develops a climate of trust.

You need to figure out—consulting both your boss and your staff—the boundaries of responsibility that enable your people to:

- make a decision independently with no need to report to you;
- make a decision and then report to you;
- make a decision only after discussion with you.

Vagueness about boundaries of responsibility, unfortunately very common, causes a great deal of confusion in organizations.

2. Identify the Task to Delegate

Be clear about what you want to delegate. Ask yourself what end result you want in terms of results and personnel development, and use this as the basis for deciding what to delegate.

Delegate whole tasks or activities rather than chunks. Having control of an entire process increases employee satisfaction, is good for staff development, and helps people really understand the job.

3. Enumerate the Benefits of Delegation

Think through exactly what the benefits of delegation are. Consider how it will benefit:

- you;
- the person to whom you are delegating the activity;
- the team;
- the department;
- the organization;
- customers.

Being clear yourself about the benefits to some or most of these constituencies will help you sell the idea that it is worth someone's taking on the delegated activity and gain commitment to delegation.

On the other hand, try to assess possible problems.

- What might happen if things go wrong?
- What is the worst-case scenario for the team, the organization, customers?
- What negative impact might this have on the individual?
- How much support should you give?

4. Select the Person

Shed your preconceptions and think creatively in selecting the right person for the job. It is all too easy to choose someone you have chosen before. Start afresh and really work through what the job is and what skills and

"Guidelines for bureaucrats: (1) When in charge, ponder. (2) When in trouble, delegate. (3) When in doubt, mumble."
(James H. Boren)

  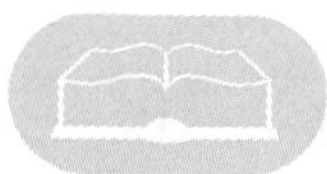    

qualities are required to complete it successfully. Ask yourself whether you want someone, for example:

- who is reliable and has plenty of experience;
- who will take a risk but bring about a quick result;
- whose development will benefit from the challenge;
- who will simply absorb the workload as a matter of routine.

5. Negotiate the Delegated Task

Delegation works best when the person taking on the job fully understands what is required and is enthusiastic and willing to take it on.

This process may require extremely detailed work. If you are delegating the writing of a report, you may need to specify the way the information should be presented, the arguments or hypotheses you want to expose, and even the number of pages it should contain.

Sit down with the individual and come to an agreement about what the person is going to do, when it is to be done, what resources are required, and what outcome is expected.

Sell the benefits. Explain exactly what's in it for the staff member and make sure that the person is happy to do it. Elicit, and listen to, the person's thoughts or fears and allow for them as you clarify and agree goals. Remember, staff members are entitled to say no.

6. Allocate Time and Be Supportive

Allocate the right amount of time. Agree on a schedule and arrange to meet and compare notes along the way.

Keep in mind that you are not simply dumping work on your staff—you are actually collaborating with them to make sure they can accomplish tasks you need to get done. Make yourself available for consultation in case they have problems or need advice.

7. Find the Appropriate Level of Responsibility with Authority

If you are delegating a part of your job that carries authority, make sure that the person undertaking the task and other staff members know that the person has your full support. If the delegated activity involves other departments, make sure that everyone concerned understands what is happening, why, and with whose authority.

8. Make It Happen

The person undertaking the work is responsible for deciding how best to accomplish it. Remember that you have delegated the task—don't specify how it actually has to be done. Once you have provided the necessary resources, don't interfere, but do be available and supportive.

9. Review and Evaluate

When the task is completed, conduct a review to see how well it went. Evaluate positive outcomes in terms of both accomplishment of the task and staff development. Address any failures constructively and make notes about what could be done better next time—for yourself as much as for the person who did the work.

DOS AND DON'TS

For Successful Delegation

DO

- Plan the delegation carefully.
- Negotiate with the person concerned. Be specific about the outcomes.
- Let go and allow the person to complete the job independently.

DON'T

- Don't leave people to sink or swim.
- Don't interfere or dictate how the job should be done.
- Don't delegate to the same people all the time.
- Don't take all the credit.

THOUGHT STARTERS

- Have you ever been guilty of dumping work on someone else and wondering why it went wrong?
- Have you failed to provide the resources needed to help the person complete the task successfully?
- Have you scheduled enough time to make sure the person can do it well?
- Have you delegated the right degree of authority?

For More Information

Books:

Heller, Robert, and Tim Hindle. *Essential Managers: How to Delegate*. New York: DK Press, 1999.

Maddux, Robert. *Delegating for Results*. 2nd ed. Menlo Park, CA: Crisp, 1997.

Nelson, Robert B. *Empowering Employees through Delegation*. New York: McGraw-Hill Professional, 1994.

See also:

✔ **Empowerment (pp. 352–53)**
✔ **Managing Your Time Effectively (pp. 398–99)**

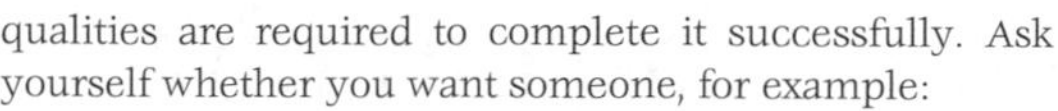

"The purpose of getting power is to be able to give it away." (Aneurin Bevan)

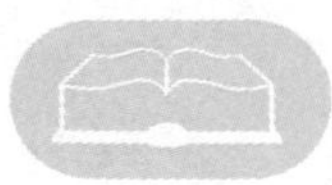

UNDERTAKING A DISCIPLINARY INTERVIEW

CHECKLIST

This checklist provides guidance for managers who are required to hold a formal interview with an employee to correct a disciplinary problem, such as unacceptable behavior or performance, as part of a disciplinary procedure. It should be read in conjunction with the related checklist Setting Up a Disciplinary Procedure.

DEFINITION

A disciplinary interview is a meeting between at least one manager and an employee (who may be accompanied by a colleague or union representative) to investigate and deal with an employee's misconduct in a fair and consistent manner.

ADVANTAGES

Effective handling of a disciplinary interview:

- tackles the cause of misconduct and provides solutions to remedy it;
- can prevent the need for further and more serious action to be taken against an employee;
- aids general morale (although an ineffective process will have the opposite effect).

DISADVANTAGES

Ineffective handling of a disciplinary interview:

- leaves the employee unclear about the problem or how to improve;
- can lead to claims of unfair dismissal if the employee is dismissed;
- lowers the respect of the manager in the employee's eyes.

ACTION CHECKLIST

✔ 1. PREPARE FOR THE INTERVIEW

Preparation and planning before the interview are essential in order to be fair and accurate in making a decision on the employee's conduct. The procedure—and the tone—should be as positive as possible in order to improve behavior and help prevent recurrence.

GATHER ALL THE FACTS

Obtain any written evidence (for example, attendance records or production figures) that highlights the employee's misconduct. To obtain a balanced view, look for any special circumstances inside or outside work that may help to explain the problem—low staffing levels, increased demand leading to work overload, or personal difficulties such as caring for a sick child.

CHECK THE EMPLOYEE'S RECORD

Find out if the employee has already received one or more warnings under the disciplinary procedure.

CHECK THE ORGANIZATION'S DISCIPLINARY PROCEDURE

Ascertain what options are available if the employee is guilty of misconduct, bearing in mind the person's disciplinary record and the seriousness of the offense.

LOOK FOR SIMILAR CASES AND OUTCOMES

Confer with colleagues to see whether they have dealt with similar cases and what the outcomes were. Also try to find out whether the employee is committing an offense that is widespread (for example, persistent abuse of smoking rules or bad timekeeping). Is the employee being singled out unfairly for an offense that should be tackled company-wide?

STRUCTURE THE INTERVIEW

Although no two disciplinary interviews will run exactly the same, you should map out a brief structure. Start by trying to define what you need to achieve from the interview. Note important points that you need to cover. Consider the reasons, mitigating circumstances, or excuses that the employee might make and how to record them so you can check them out later. Decide who should be present at the interview, including witnesses.

✔ 2. INFORM THE EMPLOYEE

The employee should be informed in writing of:

- the reason why the employee faces a disciplinary interview;
- the time and place of the interview;
- who will be present and who may accompany the employee to the interview.

Determine if everyone present should have access to all documents; in some cases this will not be in the employee's own interests.

Remember to give sufficient notice for the employee to prepare a case. Make sure that an appropriate room is available; it should be large enough to accommodate those attending without congestion. A phone is useful to call witnesses to the interview, but arrange for incoming calls to be diverted to avoid unnecessary interruptions.

Designate and inform a manager to be responsible for taking notes. Call witnesses so they can arrange to be available. If witnesses cannot be present, obtain written statements from them.

✔ 3. CONDUCT THE INTERVIEW

Disciplinary interviews are stressful for both the manager and the employee. Their ultimate purpose is to create a satisfactory environment for all employees.

Remember to try to stay calm; do not let the interview develop into a free-for-all. Make certain that the employee is aware that the interview is more than an informal reprimand.

The length of the interview depends on many factors, but it can become clear at any stage either that the problem has cleared up or that there needs to be further investigation; in either case you should adjourn the proceedings. Similarly, the interview should be called to a halt if the exchanges get heated or unconstructive.

"If people really liked to work, we'd still be plowing the ground with sticks and transporting goods on our backs."

(Vic Feather)

There is no set structure for a disciplinary interview; the following is one approach.

INTRODUCTION

- Introduce the people present and the reason for their being there (including the manager acting as a witness and taking notes, and any union representative).
- Communicate the reason for holding a disciplinary interview. Emphasize that it is part of the organization's disciplinary procedure that exists to ensure that all employees are treated equally and fairly.
- Describe how the interview is to be structured—that is, with the case against the employee being presented first, followed by the employee's reply.

PRESENT THE CASE AGAINST THE EMPLOYEE

- Detail the case against the employee, including specific dates and times that breaches of discipline occurred. If the case has already moved some way along the disciplinary procedure, present an outline of the previous stages, the actions taken, and the results to date.
- Call on any witnesses to state what they have seen or heard, or what they know. If witnesses are unable to attend, read their written statements aloud.

ALLOW THE EMPLOYEE TO REPLY

- Let the employee respond to the case, allowing the person to present evidence, call witnesses, and introduce statements.
- Listen carefully to what the employee has to say. Do not interrupt while the person is speaking.

DISCUSS THE CASE

Allow both sides to ask questions, particularly about ambiguous issues in the evidence. Ask open-ended questions to gain a general picture and more precise questions for specific information. It is important to ascertain whether there were any sound mitigating circumstances for the employee's behavior that you were unaware of. Allow the employee to suggest ways to overcome the problem.

SUMMARIZE THE CASE

After the discussion, reiterate the main points from both sides and summarize the whole case. When both sides have agreed the summary to be accurate, adjourn the interview so you can consider what action to take or whether the case requires further investigation. Try to do this as quickly as possible to keep the employee's anxiety or doubt to a minimum.

 4. INFORM THE EMPLOYEE OF THE ACTION TO BE TAKEN

Having conferred with colleagues and made a decision, meet with the employee and his or her representative and inform them what action is to be taken, if any. If appropriate, agree on actions for improving the situation. (Remember that these may involve the employer as well as the employee.) Both parties should sign a written copy of the actions to be taken. Set a date for review. If the employee disagrees with the result of the interview or feels unfairly treated, inform the person of the company's appeals procedure.

DOS AND DON'TS

For Undertaking a Disciplinary Interview

DO

- Follow your company's disciplinary procedure.
- Gather all the facts before the interview.
- Leave enough time for both sides to prepare for the interview.
- Make the interview a discussion; let the employee have a say and listen to it.
- Record the evidence, the minutes of the interview, and the outcomes.

DON'T

- Don't assume before the interview that the employee is guilty.
- Don't finish the interview without setting clear goals for the future.

THOUGHT STARTERS

- Do you understand the workings of the organization's disciplinary procedure?
- Have you ever had to discipline an employee before? How did it go?
- Have you ever been disciplined at work? Was it handled fairly?

For More Information

Books:

Fowler, Alan. *The Disciplinary Interview.* Woodstock, NY: Beekman, 2000.
Grote, Dick, and Richard C. Grote. *Discipline without Punishment: The Proven Strategy That Turns Problem Employees into Superior Performers.* New York: AMACOM, 1995.

Journal Articles:

"Disciplinary Hearings." *IRS Employment Review*, no. 675 (March 1999): 8–16, blue.
Fowler, Alan. "How to Conduct a Disciplinary Interview." *People Management* 2:23 (November 21, 1996): 40–42.

Web Sites:

HR Guide: **www.hr-guide.com**
HRnext (Human Resources): **www.hrnext.com**

"Stretch and discipline are the yin and yang of business." (Christopher Bartlett)

USING 360-DEGREE FEEDBACK

CHECKLIST

This checklist provides an introduction to the use of 360-degree feedback as an alternative to a traditional performance appraisal system.

Changes in organizational structure in recent years, with flattened hierarchies and greater employee empowerment, have had implications for the appraisal process. Individual managers now often have a greater span of control, so their colleagues may be in a better position to judge their performance than ever before. Hence the increasing interest in the technique of 360-degree feedback, which collects information from all around the employee. It is most often used as a development or training tool, and is not usually tied to pay. It can only work effectively in organizations that have, or are moving toward, an open, supportive, participative culture.

DEFINITION

Strictly speaking, 360-degree appraisal or feedback involves a paper-based appraisal by colleagues above, below, and to the side of an individual employee in addition to self-assessment. In practice it may not include all these elements. Feedback is communicated through a facilitator so opinions cannot be traced to individuals. Some commentators feel, however, that 360-degree appraisal should be an exercise in openness, and that views should not be anonymous.

ADVANTAGES

- Combined opinion gives an accurate, objective, and well-rounded view.
- Some skills (for example, leadership) are better judged by subordinates and peers rather than superiors who may not see their skills in evidence that regularly.
- A comment that is hard to accept can't be brushed off or ignored when a number of colleagues have expressed it independently.
- 360-degree appraisal can lead to positive behavior such as more openness and honesty.
- The technique can help motivate people who undervalue themselves.

DISADVANTAGES

- It is time-consuming and costly, so the technique is often restricted to management levels.
- If too many appraisers are used, the results can be hard to interpret.
- It can be destructive unless handled carefully and sensitively.
- It can generate an environment of suspicion unless it is managed openly and honestly. Transparency is vital to the process.

ACTION CHECKLIST

1. DECIDE WHICH BEHAVIORS TO MEASURE AND WHOM TO ASSESS

Decide which sets of knowledge, skills, and abilities you want to measure. Should they be competency-based, job-related, or behavior-related? Remember that 360-degree appraisal can be used at any level of the organization, so decide whether you want to assess specific individuals, particular teams, particular levels, or the whole organization. Is it important that everyone who takes part as an appraiser should also be subject to appraisal?

2. DESIGN A FEEDBACK QUESTIONNAIRE

In the interest of efficiency, written questionnaires are commonly used for collecting appraisals. Devise the detailed questions or, if you do not have the necessary expertise in-house, consider purchasing a questionnaire or employing a consultant. Make sure that the questions are phrased in a way that elicits descriptive rather than judgmental responses: descriptive comments are less likely to cause offense and more likely to provide useful information to the person being appraised. Avoid asking questions that the majority of the likely appraisers are not qualified to answer, or that contain wording that might be open to misinterpretation.

3. COMMUNICATE THE PROCESS AND PREPARE PARTICIPANTS

Explain the purpose of the process and encourage employees to air their concerns and objections. If necessary, circulate a pilot questionnaire, for example, asking employees for their views on managers in the organization in general. This trial run will demonstrate how the process works and reassure the staff. Appoint a manager to act as a facilitator, and publicize his or her roles and responsibilities. This person should be widely respected and have a reputation for fairness and honesty. If it is not appropriate to nominate an internal manager, consider using a consultant.

4. TRAIN YOUR STAFF TO GIVE, AND RECEIVE, CRITICAL FEEDBACK

Encourage appraisers to be constructive, positive, and specific instead of critical, negative, and general. In describing a colleague's behavior, for example, "I notice that you rarely acknowledge us when you arrive in the morning" is more helpful than "I think you are a bad communicator." "I know you need time and space to yourself, but when you get it you really produce the goods" pinpoints the message in an acceptable way, and is more palatable than "You're too much of a loner." Do not allow the appraisal to become an opportunity for subjective gripes. If the process degenerates, critically appraised people will tend to get their own back when appraising others, especially if they are identified or identifiable.

"Although colleagues provide high-quality input to multisource processes, they are often insufficient as the only source."

(Mark Edwards)

5. Let Employees Choose Their Appraisers

Allow employees to select their appraisers from an agreed pool. Since the aim is to achieve a rounded appraisal, make sure that each person being appraised chooses some appraisers they get along with and others they do not. Set limits on the number involved in each appraisal, otherwise the exercise can become an administrative nightmare. Instruct appraisers to return their questionnaires to the appointed facilitator. If you have agreed to treat comments anonymously, reassure the appraisers about confidentiality, and honor your commitment. Present the results as soon as possible after collecting the data.

6. Decide How to Present Feedback

Decide how the facilitator should collate and present the appraisers' comments. Is your objective to allow employees to be able to monitor their own performance over time, compare themselves with like employees, or measure themselves against specific competences? Consider whether feedback on a particular activity should be linked to an agreed estimate of how important that activity is to the job. If so, the results need to be weighted accordingly.

7. Provide Counseling and Assistance

Decide whether individuals should identify their own improvement actions or whether they should be offered solutions. If you wish to leave it to individuals, don't show the results to managers without their approval. The facilitator or another trained person such as a psychologist should be available to help employees deal with feedback, particularly to advise them on how to deal with divergent views. Consider holding development sessions in which the people who were appraised can support each other.

8. Set Individual Action Plans

Follow up each appraisal by agreeing on an appropriate program to help the individual improve. These may range from attending a course or shadowing a colleague to temporary internal or external placements. Remember that learners have different needs and preferences.

9. Evaluate the Process

Examine the appraisal process. Take into account the opinion of everyone who participated, including any feedback on completing the appraisal questionnaire or analyzing the data from it. Compare the results of using 360-degree feedback with previous appraisal techniques. Use what you learn from the evaluation to help you improve the next appraisal.

DOS AND DON'TS

For Using 360-degree Feedback

DO

- Remember that employees may find the prospect of 360-degree feedback threatening and challenging.
- Prepare and support people for their different roles in giving, receiving, and facilitating appraisals.
- Make the exercise nonthreatening by focusing on strengths as much as weaknesses.
- Respect the confidentiality of respondents' replies, if this has been agreed.

DON'T

- Don't allow appraisers to drift into personal attacks.
- Don't treat it as a onetime exercise or leave long gaps between appraisals.

THOUGHT STARTERS

- How effective is your current appraisal system?
- What is upward communication like in your company? How is it received?
- How good is your managers' morale?

For More Information

Books:

Edwards, Mark R. *360 Degree Feedback: The Powerful New Model for Employee Assessment and Performance Improvement*. New York: AMACOM, 1996.

Tornow, Walter W., and Manuel London. *Maximizing the Value of 360-degree Feedback: A Process for Successful Individual and Organizational Development*. San Francisco, CA: Jossey-Bass, 1998.

Ward, Peter. *360 Degree Feedback*. Woodstock, NY: Beekman, 2000.

Journal Articles:

Bracken, David N., Lynn Summers, and John Fleenor. "High Tech 360." *Training and Development USA* 52:8 (August 1998): 42–45.

Fletcher, Clive. "Circular Argument." *People Management* 4:19 (October 1, 1998): 46–49.

"No organizational action has more power for motivating employee behavior change than feedback from credible work associates."

(Mark Edwards)

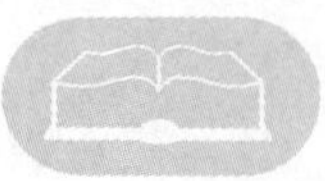

USING YOUR STAFF TO MUTUAL ADVANTAGE

CHECKLIST

This checklist is aimed at managers and looks closely at the building blocks of relationships between those who manage and those whom they manage.

Annual reports frequently pay tribute to ''our staff'', but practice seldom seems to match the written word. This checklist considers some of the major elements involved in getting the most out of working with others, including the changes in management practice in organizations, the ways in which change affects people, approaches to leadership and communication, and methods of consolidating and improving working relationships.

DEFINITION

"Staff" implies any people or group who are subordinate to a manager at any level.

"To mutual advantage" signifies to the advantage of the manager, to the advantage of the unit (whether company, department, or small firm), and to the advantage of the staff.

ACTION CHECKLIST

1. RECOGNIZE RECENT SHIFTS IN MANAGEMENT PRACTICE

In the 1980s and 1990s many organizations moved away from models based on differentiating workers from each other. They adopted instead more flexible organizational structures that more fully used the experience of their people, often described as the empowered, flatter organization. There are a number of elements involved in this shift away from practices that simply no longer work:

- the autocratic manager and the leader who energizes people
- authority by position and authority by merit
- domination and coordination
- control from the top along with participation and collaboration
- self-advancement and self-development
- individual responsibility and the shared responsibility of teamwork
- controlling the work force and giving employees freedom
- power and empowerment

With organizational culture based on trust and initiative rather than on dominance, blame, or fear, the onus is now on the manager to become a team member as well as a team leader.

2. MAKE CHANGE WORK FOR YOU

Change means moving from the familiar to the unfamiliar, from the known to the unknown. Be aware of the implications of change and its impact on individuals, particularly when it is imposed.

Psychologists have suggested that any substantial change in our lives involves a sequence of stages.

- Shock—emotional feelings of denial, confusion, and disbelief, a sense that everything is crumbling: "This can't be happening to me." Offer understanding and acceptance of the state of shock, convey empathy, create opportunities for grievances to be aired, and encourage the disclosure of feelings.
- Withdrawal or resistance—an attempt to keep the familiar world intact, a search for ways of avoiding the consequences of change, and a struggle to maintain the status quo. Counsel individuals to disclose frustrations and anxieties. Listen with attentiveness and sensitivity.
- Acknowledgment—a sense of inevitability is accompanied by the recognition of a need to keep in step, of a fear of isolation and rejection by others, of uncertainty and insecurity. Help individuals acknowledge change by reviewing their appropriate skills, competencies, and opportunities for development.
- Adaptation—emotional and psychological adjustment matching the rational acceptance of change. Inner confusion and uncertainty begin to give way as preparations for change get underway, anxieties are reduced, and practical steps forward identified. Help individuals by involving them in the design of new systems and procedures and in gaining familiarity with new resources and equipment, and by getting them to propose new solutions and methods.

Different individuals move through these stages at different rates and in different ways. Some people may assimilate the stages very rapidly; for others, one stage can prove an enormous obstacle. Understanding the individual nature of reaction to change will help you work with others and encourage them to take advantage of the constantly changing workplace.

Most people will accept change as long as they recognize why it is necessary and are involved in the process—it should be their change.

3. DEFINE THE BOUNDARIES OF EMPLOYEES' RESPONSIBILITY

Someone new to a job is dependent on the line manager, but this dependence normally diminishes as the jobholder gains in experience and learns the ropes. Allow newcomers to grow and feel their way.

As the person gains experience, the relationship becomes interdependent, and interactions arise when the manager needs information on progress or when consultation is required on specific issues. Get your people to report by exception and to present oral solutions to problems they encounter.

As time goes on, an increasing proportion of the person's job is characterized by a clear capacity to self-manage without supervision. Resist the temptation to oversupervise or interfere. Encourage the person's independence and the responsibility that goes with it. "Freedom with accountability" is the key phrase.

All three of these elements are present in all jobs. Good

"I've got an ego and all that, but I know I need help. So I go and hire the very best people."

(H. Ross Perot)

practice involves recognizing their shifting balance and behaving accordingly.

Whether your situation is rapidly changing or solid and stable, whether your culture is empowered culture or not, you must define the limits of the authority enjoyed by the people who work with you. To be wholly effective they need to know which sorts of decision:

- they can make independently, informing you afterwards;
- they can make only after consultation with you;
- they should pass on to you.

4. Identify Your Leadership Strategy

If leadership is about quality and effectiveness, change and development, and focus on the future, effective management is less and less about directing and instructing and more and more about supporting, coaching, and delegating to enable people to own their work and be committed to it. Various techniques or strategies can contribute to your effectiveness as a leader.

- Management by walking around (MBWA)—managers and leaders need to see their main activity as an interactive one, working alongside colleagues where tasks are carried out.
- Work review—this is a nondirected relationship designed to help colleagues develop professional skills through the regular process of reflection on experience.
- Critical friendship—this concept is sometimes used to describe the nature of the relationship between leader and team. It is essentially an active listening role for the leader in which colleagues can explore and clarify aspects of their work experience.

5. Give Feedback

One of the most effective ways of developing others is to help them reflect on their experience in order to learn from it. Feedback is an informal and highly effective way of promoting this process. It is, however, necessary to be aware of some of the psychological implications of giving others information about themselves and their behavior. Among the behaviors and responses managers may encounter are:

- difficulty in accepting responsibility for behavior;
- fear of making mistakes;
- difficulty with uncertainty and change;
- assuming that others know best;
- self-doubt and lack of confidence;
- reluctance to set personal goals for development;
- suspicion of experts and those in positions of authority.

Feedback can be of three basic types:

- Confirmatory—giving information that lets someone know he or she is on course and moving successfully toward their goals. It is vital, but often neglected.
- Corrective—giving information that helps someone get back on course when the person is experiencing difficulties or things are going wrong. Corrective feedback should always be positive, not negative.
- Motivating—giving information that tells someone about both successes and difficulties. This combines confirmatory and corrective feedback; the aim is to provide sufficient information to meet the development needs of the receiver and enable the person to make appropriate choices and decisions.

6. Practice Proactive Passiveness!

Getting the most out of relationships for all parties can be an exhausting process: you feel as if you're constantly monitoring employees for feelings of inadequacy, excessive cynicism, inability to express feelings, or a sense of being stuck. While MBWA, work review, and critical friendship may require you to change your behavior substantially, you should be employing other routine interpersonal techniques as a matter of habit:

- active listening, where the listener attempts to gain insights into the perceptual, intellectual, and emotional world of the speaker;
- undivided attention, away from telephones and other interruptions;
- support, using suggestions and prompts to check meanings, inviting the speaker to continue, and otherwise keeping quietly interested;
- conveying understanding, using body language to indicate understanding, acceptance, and agreement.

7. Review Your Relationships

Sit down from time to time and ask, "How are we doing?" Talk over work routines and objectives so that you know where you stand in relation to others, and they to you. Focus on moving forward so that the individual, the section, and the organization are all gaining mutual advantage.

THOUGHT STARTERS

- What do my people tell their friends and families about me as their boss?
- What do I do that makes it harder for them to do the job I want them to do?
- Am I using all their talents, skills, and capabilities?

For More Information

Books:

Honey, Peter. *Improve Your People Skills*. Woodstock, NY: Beekman, 2000.

Murdock, Alexander, and Carol Scutt. *Personal Effectiveness*. 2nd ed. Woburn, MA: Butterworth-Heinemann, 1997.

Web Site:

American Management Association: **www.amanet.org**

"The more time I spend with our people, the more I find out about our business." (Herb Kelleher)

The Psychological Contract

CHECKLIST

This checklist introduces the concept of the psychological contract from the employee's point of view. The psychological contract refers to the unwritten expectations that exist between employer and employee.

In the past the psychological contract implied that an employee could expect job security and adequate rewards from their employer in exchange for hard work and loyalty. Today's psychological contract relies more on an unwritten agreement that your employer will assist you in developing your skills in order to maintain your marketability.

The psychological contract is a subtle relationship that shifts over time and is subject to constant change. This checklist focuses on this aspect of continuous and delicate negotiation between employer and employee.

Definition

The psychological contract refers to the set of expectations and values that exist between you and your employer. It is most easily defined as "the set of unwritten expectations between an individual employee and the organization".

Everyone has some form of psychological contract. The concept addresses those relationships that are very hard to define clearly in a formal employment contract; it can cover:

- knowledge and skills development
- your work and motivation
- relationships with your bosses and coworkers
- the role that you are expected to fulfill
- the ethical code by which you and the organization will act
- the support you can expect from the organization and vice versa.

Action Checklist

1. Negotiate Your Psychological Contract from the Start

Both sides begin to explore the psychological contract at the job interview stage. The organization assesses how you might behave in your role and how well you're likely to fit in. You in turn have an early opportunity to judge whether you would feel comfortable working in the company.

This first psychological contract forms the basis of the others you create with the people you'll work with—colleagues, business partners (such as external suppliers, for example), and customers.

Think carefully about the organizational culture the company presents and the type of people you'll be working with. If their values and expectations initially appear questionable, it may be because you are seeing these as unfair or unsuitable to you.

2. Inform Yourself About the Organization's Culture and Values

For your first few weeks in the job, the psychological contract develops rapidly as you gather information about others' values and expectations. Watching when, where, why, and how staff talk and act is a good way to assess the realities of the organization's behavior. Don't be afraid to test your understanding by gently pushing against boundaries or asking questions.

3. Compare the Organization's Policies with Your Psychological Contract

The two should be complementary, not mutually exclusive. See whether what is explicit matches what is implicit—for example, does the job description acknowledge you or hours of work? Do managers really consult employees about change? Does the company actually fulfill its commitments to quality and customer service? Ask yourself: "Do they do what they say?" "Do they say one thing but expect another?"

If the answers to these questions seem unacceptable, you may have cause to question your future with the organization.

4. Examine the Psychological Contract

Psychological contracts have many parts. Among the most important are the following:

- Knowledge and experience—what are the expectations about what I know and can do, and how I use these? How will I be helped to improve my skills? How am I expected to share skills and knowledge—formally (for example, in reports) or informally (at team meetings)?
- Motivation—what are my real motivations for this job and how do these affect my performance? What motivates the people around me and how can knowledge of this improve my job? What are the rewards and disadvantages of working here?
- Goals (and means)—how do things happen in the organization? Do employees closely follow the rulebook or simply ignore it? Who do I go through to get things done? What happens if I don't follow the expected channels? Would I be happy with this?
- Role—who do I want to be in the organization? What is the real nature and content of the job? How do I avoid being a figurehead and get taken seriously? Do people have emotional expectations of me that weren't communicated at the start?
- Ethics—what are the moral principles that guide the organization? Am I happy with them? Is the company breaking any laws? What morals and principles must I exhibit when dealing with others (including customers and outside agencies)?

"One of the things that parents have taught me is never listen to other people's expectations."

(Tiger Woods)

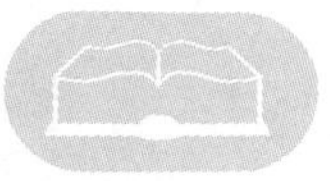

DOS AND DON'TS

For the Psychological Contract

DO

- Recognize that a psychological contract exists.
- Review the contract regularly and renegotiate when necessary.
- Realize that the old assumptions about employment relationships have changed.
- Be prepared to share your feelings and opinions with others so you fully understand your role.
- Be willing to adjust your opinions and how you work with others.

DON'T

- Don't expect everyone to share your expectations and values.
- Don't assume people will never change their expectations of you and your role.
- Don't form opinions of others or rely on expectations based on first impressions.

✔ 5. Review the Psychological Contract

A psychological contract is a description of how well you fit into the organization and how well the organization suits you. If both you and the organization agree on your role, what is expected of you, and what you expect of the organization, there's a good fit.

But things change. The business environment never stands still, people move on, the type of work changes, or the company implements new policies and practices. You may have negative reactions to any of these changes. If you do, group the factors in your working life and see where problems arise.

- Your boss—are the boss's expectations of you, your role, and your workload now different? Are you unhappy with your supervisor's methods of giving you work or communicating with you? Do you have too many bosses?
- Your coworkers—do you feel left out or sidelined? Are you happy with your colleagues' work? Do employees who have different personalities from yours seem more highly valued than you?
- The physical environment—is it unsafe, overcrowded, or otherwise unsatisfactory?
- Your work—are you bored, overworked, or underused?

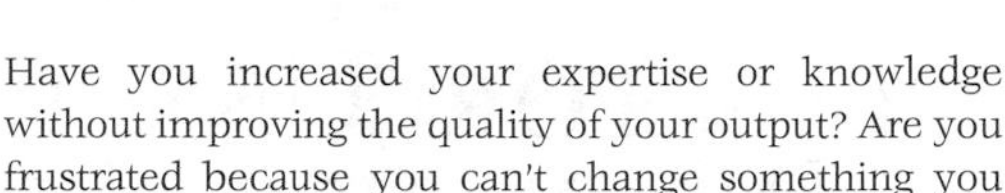

Have you increased your expertise or knowledge without improving the quality of your output? Are you frustrated because you can't change something you think needs changing?
- Your private life—is there something at work affecting your private life or vice versa?

✔ 6. Resolve Tensions in the Psychological Contract

Be honest with yourself and decide what it is you now want from your work. If you can, tweak or renegotiate the existing contract to reduce tension or conflict.

Use your psychological contract to judge:

- who can help you resolve your concerns and how both the people and the problems should be approached;
- how the organization expects problems to be recognized and dealt with.

THOUGHT STARTERS

- How well do you know your organization's values and expectations?
- What do you expect from your boss and colleagues? What do they expect from you?

For More Information

Books:

Hakim, Cliff. *We Are All Self-employed: The New Social Contract for Working in a Changed World.* San Francisco, CA: Berrett-Koehler, 1994.

Makin, Peter J., et al. *Organizations and the Psychological Contract*. Westport, CT: Greenwood Publishing, 1996.

Journal Article:

Altman, Wilf, and Cary Cooper. "New Deal Needed to Secure Commitment." *Professional Manager* 8:5 (September 1999): 38–40.

See also:

✔ **Starting a New Job (pp. 410–11)**
✔ **Stress Management: Self First (pp. 412–13)**
✔ **Succeeding As a New Manager (pp. 414–15)**

"Unhappiness is best defined as the difference between our talents and our expectations."

(Edward de Bono)

Arranging for Unemployment and Health Insurance After a Job Loss

CHECKLIST

This checklist is designed as a guide for those wishing to receive unemployment insurance and to continue getting health insurance through their employer after being laid off from work.

Definition

In broad terms, you can be laid off for one or more of these reasons:

- your employers are ceasing to carry on the business that employs you;
- your employers are closing down the business at the site where you work, for example, if a company with four distribution centers decides to close one;
- your employers are transferring the business from the site where you work to another location, for example, a company with two offices decides to consolidate at one site;
- your employers are selling the business and the new owners decide to "clean house," hiring new employees to replace those laid off;
- your employers need fewer employees to do your particular kind of work, for example, they decide to have one manager responsible for sales instead of two;
- your employers need fewer employees to do your particular kind of work at the place where you work, for example, the divisional personnel function is closed, but the head office personnel function remains and a personnel manager is appointed for each site.

The basic test of a layoff is whether your employers now need fewer employees, either across the company or at a particular location. In theory the amount of work need not have changed, but it must be capable of being done by fewer people.

Advantages

- Receiving unemployment insurance allows the ex-employee to get by, financially speaking, for at least one half-year.
- It protects the recently unemployed person from experiencing immediate distress, due to their inability to pay for food, shelter, and other basic needs.
- Having the ability to continue receiving health insurance benefits under the ex-employer's plan gives the laid-off employee the security of being covered temporarily, while seeking other health insurance alternatives.

Disadvantages

- Both unemployment insurance and continued health insurance under the ex-employer's plan are temporary benefits.
- Unemployment insurance is substantially less than what a normal pay check would be; it is also considered taxable income.
- While the unemployed person is eligible for health care coverage under their ex-employer's plan, they must pay for the cost of that insurance themselves.

Action Checklist

✔ 1. Check Eligibility

To be eligible for unemployment insurance, you must meet the following criteria.

- You must be a U.S. citizen, a registered alien, or have permission to work in the United States.
- You must have worked for a private employer or for state or federal government; unemployment benefits don't cover those who have been self-employed or who have worked for the railroad.
- You must be currently unemployed, and have lost your job due to no fault of your own.
- You must have earned sufficient wages during the past year; the exact details of determining your unemployment compensation (both the amount and the duration of benefits) may vary from state to state.
- In many states, you must also demonstrate that—if able—you are actively seeking employment.
- You must file an unemployment insurance claim with the state in which you reside.
- Unemployment compensation won't begin until after any employer-paid additional severance wages and bonuses are exhausted.

✔ 2. Determining the Amount of Payment

Determining the amount of time you may receive unemployment, as well as the amount of compensation, depends on the state in which you live, how long you have worked, and how much you earned. In general, benefits last at least 26 weeks (one half-year) but may be extended to a year under certain circumstances. It's best to contact the state department of labor or employment where you live, to be certain of the minimum requirements and benefits available.

Each state also varies in how it determines the amount of compensation someone may receive after being laid off. In general, the applicant for unemployment insurance must have worked at least two of the past four calendar quarters (six months or longer in the past year). The state will determine, based on the wages earned and length of employment, what the weekly benefit amount will be. That decision can be appealed if you think it unfair; you may choose to represent yourself during that appeals process, rather than hire an attorney.

✔ 3. Continued Health Coverage under the Employer's Plan

Losing your job, whether you were laid off, fired, or left for other reasons, doesn't mean you are immediately without medical and health insurance coverage. COBRA (the Consolidated Omnibus Reconciliation Act of 1985) is a federal law that requires your former employer to continue to offer you the same plan coverage you had while employed. If a company is small—less than 20 employees—they aren't required by federal law to follow the laws of COBRA. However, many state laws still require small companies to provide something like COBRA for ex-employees, or for those still employed there but working only part time.

COBRA is not a long term solution; rather, you can opt to receive coverage for between 18 and 36 months, depending on your particular circumstances. For specific details, check with your ex-employer's personnel office as well as the labor or employment department in the state you live in. The drawback to COBRA coverage provisions is that you must pay for the insurance coverage yourself. Before you decide to accept that proposition, consider the following options:

- the ex-employer may have alternative, less expensive, plans you could choose instead;
- you may be able to receive coverage under a spouse's plan for less;
- there may be other options available through a non-profit association or from independent insurance companies that would be as effective and perhaps less expensive.

Before deciding whether or not to request COBRA coverage, be sure to also check out the provisions of the HIPAA law (Health Insurance Portability and Accountability Act, of 1996). HIPAA regulates employer group health plans and health insurance companies, most notably in the area of "preexisting conditions".

4. Tax Consequences

Unemployment compensation is considered income by both federal and state governments, and is therefore taxable. You can elect to have the taxes taken out of each unemployment check, if you wish, but most states do not deduct the tax automatically. You will be sent a form (1099 G) at the end of January following the year in which you received unemployment payments. You are responsible for reporting unemployment compensation, filing the appropriate forms, and paying any taxes due on the income.

There are no negative tax consequences relative to continuing health care benefits under the provisions of COBRA and HIPAA. On the positive side, insurance payments are tax deductible, although they must be substantial to add up to more than the "standard deduction" allowed individuals and families each year.

5. Employers' Responsibilities

The only responsibility of the employer when you apply for unemployment insurance is to verify the timeframe and circumstances under which you were employed. They are also required to keep you on their health plan policy temporarily, if you make that request of them within 60 days of leaving the job.

DOS AND DON'TS

For Arranging for Unemployment and Health Insurance After a Job Loss

DO

- Fully understand your employee benefits package before you leave the job.
- Make sure you file for appropriate unemployment compensation and health insurance (COBRA) coverage in a timely fashion.
- Call the state departments that administer services to the unemployed for assistance and advice.

DON'T

- Don't assume your former employer will be acting on your behalf after you leave the job.
- Don't forget that you have reporting, record-keeping, and other paperwork responsibilities with these types of programs.

THOUGHT STARTERS

- How can you simplify your life with less income during the time between jobs? There are many resources for people in this situation. Start with local and state agencies that specialize in out-of-work issues.

For More Information

Book:

Okulicz, Karen. *Try! A Survival Guide to Unemployment.* Belmar, NJ: K-Slaw Inc., 1995.

Journal Article:

"1998 IRS Redundancy Survey: Part Two." *IRS Employment Review*, no. 659 (July 1998): 9–16.

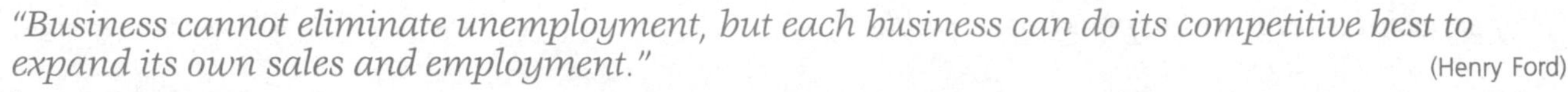
"Business cannot eliminate unemployment, but each business can do its competitive best to expand its own sales and employment." (Henry Ford)

Effective Communications: Preparing Presentations

CHECKLIST

This checklist is intended for those who are required to give any form of presentation. It covers all the stages of preparing a talk, from accepting the invitation to checking the site: the delivery of the presentation itself is covered in the following checklist. This checklist concentrates on how to develop an effective personal style rather than on the preparation of visual aids.

Definition

For the purposes of this checklist, a presentation covers any talk to a group, whether formal or informal, from giving a team briefing to delivering a major speech—the same rules and principles apply.

Action Checklist

1. Decide Whether to Accept

Ask yourself whether you are the right person to deliver this presentation. Do you have enough time to prepare? You may need to allow between thirty and sixty minutes for every minute of delivery. Are you excited enough about the topic to be enthusiastic? Do you know enough to answer awkward questions? If not, say no!

2. Clarify the Details

Find out how long you are to speak and the exact subject that is expected. Will there be questions at the end? If there are other speakers, what will they cover and how will you fit in with them?

3. Research Your Audience

View the audience as your customers. Try to gain a notion of their expectations: do they want to be informed, amused, or challenged? How many will there be? What is their level and background? Do they have any prior knowledge?

4. Define the Purpose

Tailor the presentation to meet the audience needs you identified. Is the aim of the presentation to:

- persuade—a sales pitch?
- instruct—if you know your topic?
- inspire—as part of a change program?
- entertain—if you are naturally funny?

5. Assemble Your Material

Assemble anything relevant to your topic: ideas, articles, quotes, anecdotes, references. Accumulate the material over time, but don't attempt to organize it while you are collecting it.

6. Organize Your Material

Review your collection. Group items into themes and topics. Are there metaphors or analogies that keep appearing?

7. Prepare an Outline

Structure the material into a rough plan. Aim for a beginning, a middle, and an end.

8. Write a Rough Draft

Use the outline to sketch a first draft. Write without stopping and don't impose a structure while writing. Aim to tell the audience what you are going to say, tell them, and end by summarizing what you have told them. Try to make only five key points, seven at the most.

9. Edit the Draft

Sleep on your first draft. Review it the following day. Convert the written word to speech: make the text more concrete, simpler, and more illustrative. Use anecdotes. Shorten your sentences and eliminate non-essential ideas and words. Cut all the jargon you can, and define any that is unavoidable. Make sure the timing is right—speaking to an audience is slower than talking to a friend.

10. Refine the Draft

Run through the draft several times, preferably in front of someone. Seek feedback and criticism on content, style, and delivery. Ask your listener not to interrupt but to make notes.

11. Select Your Prompts

If you want or need to deliver a spontaneous presentation, run through the draft again and begin to highlight prompts—key words and phrases. These will be the basis of your script and perhaps your visual aids. Practice using the prompts alone and learn the thoughts behind the words. When you are confident, transfer the prompts to numbered cards. Continue practicing and reducing the number of key words. (Sometimes you will need to use a full script—for example, if the press are present or if the occasion is very formal.)

12. Select Appropriate Presentation Aids

Presentation aids need to:

- integrate with your script—flow from your natural style;
- move the presentation on—add value to it and be clearly relevant to the content, or summarize what you are saying, allowing you to dispense with a script;
- look professional—clear, readable, and consistent;
- adopt an appropriate style—full-color slides may not be right for a small informal group;
- express their content simply—clearly legible from the back of the room;
- use graphics where appropriate—symbols, drawings, and charts help reinforce your words.

An increasing range of presentation aids is available,

"Pay especial attention to speaking in public." (Andrew Carnegie)

DOS AND DON'TS

For Effective Communications: Preparing Presentations

DO

- Practice as much as possible. Seek feedback and be open to criticism.
- Constantly review the purpose of your presentation against the text: are you meeting the customer's expectations?
- Remember that thorough preparation is a key factor in minimizing nerves and delivering a successful presentation.
- Put some enthusiasm into your presentation—stimulate the audience.

DON'T

- Don't sit in a room with a blank sheet of paper and try to write: look for external stimuli.
- Don't use a visual aid just because it is funny or striking and you can't bear to leave it out.
- Don't take anything for granted: the topic, the audience, the extent of your listeners' knowledge, the room, the equipment.

from flip charts and overhead transparencies to multimedia and computer-generated graphics. The most common presentation aid today is a set of images created using Microsoft PowerPoint and delivered using a personal computer and an LCD projector. Check with the presentation sponsor to determine if an LCD projector and screen can be made available to you.

✔ 13. Rehearse

Practice in your head, in front of a mirror, or in front of a partner (who will undoubtedly be your sternest critic!). Note any mannerisms you need to correct or anything you need constantly to remind yourself of as you talk: "Don't put your hands in pockets!", "Smile!" Keep these reminders on a cue card in front of you as you give the presentation.

✔ 14. Check the Room

Sit where the audience will sit and make sure your visuals are legible. Sit or stand where you will deliver the presentation and make sure you can work the equipment. Can you use the microphone?

THOUGHT STARTERS

- Have you agreed to speak just because you were asked? If so, do you really know and care enough about the topic to excite your audience?
- Are you trying to convey too much information in one presentation? Your audience can absorb a maximum of seven key points.

For More Information

Books:

Diresta, Diane. *Knockout Presentations: How to Deliver Your Message with Power, Punch, and Pizzazz*. Worcester, MA: Chandler House Press, 1998.
Owen, Michael D. *I Hate Giving Presentations: Your Essential Confidence Booster*. Sterling, VA: Stylus, 1998.
Zelazny, Gene. *Say It with Presentations: How to Design and Deliver Successful Business Presentations*. New York: McGraw-Hill, 1999.

See also:

✔ **Effective Communications: Delivering Presentations (pp. 394–95)**

"And adepts in the speaking trade/Keep a cough by them ready made." (Charles Churchill)

Effective Communications: Delivering Presentations

CHECKLIST This checklist is intended for anyone giving a presentation, whether formal or informal. It assumes that you have spent time in preparing an effective presentation (see related checklists below) and are now ready to deliver it.

Definition

For the purposes of this checklist, a presentation covers any talk to a group, whether formal or informal, from giving a team briefing to delivering a major speech—the same rules and principles apply.

Action Checklist

1. Choose the Right Style

The size of your audience and the purpose of the presentation will determine its style. Obtain precise information about audience size: an audience that one presenter thinks is large may be regarded as a small group by another.

- For five to ten, aim for an informal style with few visual aids. Sit or balance on the edge of a table or desk. Plan to establish relationships immediately and engage each individual.
- For ten to thirty, you need a more formal style, but you can still establish relationships. Stand up and expect to use some visual aids.
- For thirty to a hundred, you will need good presentation aids and a formal style. It will be difficult to engage with individuals.
- For over a hundred, view this as a theater-style presentation: you will be "on stage" and performing with a microphone. Your facial gestures and body language will need to be exaggerated to be effective.

2. Check the Room

Make a last-minute check of the equipment: can you manage the microphone and the projector? Are your visual aids legible? Who will introduce you and when? Is there a glass of water at hand?

3. Check Your Appearance

Make sure your appearance doesn't detract from your message. Dress conservatively and neatly. Check your tie, shoes, makeup.

4. Establish Your Presence

Once you have been introduced, pause. Take a deep breath, look at the audience, make eye contact, and acknowledge their presence. Relax your body and stand tall. Smile!

5. Establish Your Credentials

Explain why you are there and what gives you the authority to speak. Confirm the audience's expectations by announcing what you will speak about. Resolve any confusion or questions immediately: it is always possible you are in the wrong place!

6. Involve Your Audience

Get their attention immediately by using a visual aid or something unexpected. Ask a question, even if it is rhetorical. Say something that shows you understand their concerns or expectations. Deflecting attention to the audience removes some of the attention from you and helps with stage fright.

7. Let Your Personality Show

Remember that feelings, not facts, convince people. Put genuine conviction behind what you are saying and allow your emotions to show through. This will also help you overcome stage fright.

8. Use Positive Body Language

Remember to stand erect. Don't lean on the lectern and don't play with your hair, tie, jewelry, or clothing. For those who talk better on the move, walk around naturally and use your hands as you would in conversation for emphasis. Use ordinary facial expressions and, where appropriate, smile!

9. Take Control of Your Voice

Project your voice through standing straight and breathing deeply. Speak clearly and more slowly than usual. Speak naturally, but lower the pitch of your voice if you are nervous. Be aware of your speech mannerisms and consciously avoid repeating them. Avoid hesitating: if you have lost your place or your nerve, just pause—don't "um" or "er".

10. Introduce Variety

Vary the timing of your delivery and the pitch of your voice. Speed up or slow down and change tone in different sections. Use inflections and emphases even if they sound exaggerated to you. Occasionally pause or stop completely in a long presentation—the audience needs time to absorb the content and you need time to reflect: are you going too quickly? Have you put your hands in your pockets without realizing it?

11. Build On Your Rapport with the Audience

Maintain eye contact and play to the cheerleaders, people you know or sense to be sympathetic. Show how your presentation is relevant to them and avoid using "I" or "me" too often.

12. Introduce Humor

If you are confident, use humor to lighten or vary the mood. Use it only to support the text, not in its own right. Don't be cruel to anyone in the audience.

"If I am to speak for ten minutes, I need a week for preparation; if fifteen minutes, three days; if half an hour, two days; if an hour, I am ready now." (Woodrow Wilson)

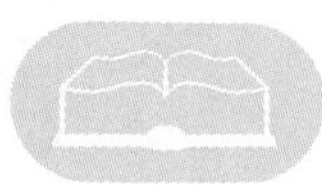

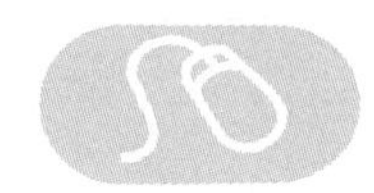

DOS AND DON'TS

For Effective Communications: Delivering Presentations

DO

- Be yourself: allow your own personality to come through rather than trying to emulate speakers you admire.
- Start and finish on time—or before time, if there will be questions—otherwise you will lose the audience's sympathy regardless of how good the content and your delivery are.
- Use handouts to convey detailed or complex ideas rather than cramming them into your presentation.

DON'T

- Don't try to cover too much in one presentation and end up rushing to finish by talking faster: the audience will find it hard to follow you.
- Don't use humor inappropriately or use it against your audience—you are the only legitimate target in the room.
- Don't use too many visual aids. They distract the audience and rarely add value.

✔ 13. Face Up to the Unexpected

The audience will notice disturbances or mistakes, but will remember only how you handled them. Acknowledge rather than ignore interruptions and try to deflect or make light of them through humor.

✔ 14. Improvise

Although thorough preparation is essential, it may be inappropriate to come over as overprepared, slick, or clinical. Remember to adjust to the mood and atmosphere of the audience.

✔ 15. Conclude

Bring the presentation to a conclusion. Be brief, don't repeat the main text, and end on a high in tone, energy, and content. Leave the audience wanting slightly more.

✔ 16. Be Positive About Questions

Actively encourage questions. Repeat each question so everyone can hear it. If you don't know the answer, admit it—but offer to take a name and address to respond later. Don't get into debate or argument.

THOUGHT STARTERS

- Is each part of your speech consistent with the title?
- Do your visual aids add something to the spoken word?
- Have you tried out your presentation on guinea pigs for length, humor, and interest?
- Have you ever used the particular visual aid you will be working with before?
- Do you know who your audience will be or how many there will be?

For More Information

Books:

Diresta, Diane. *Knockout Presentations*. Worcester, MA: Chandler House Press, 1998.
Owen, Michael D. *I Hate Giving Presentations: Your Essential Confidence Booster*. Sterling, VA: Stylus, 1998.
Zelazny, Gene. *Say It with Presentations*. New York: McGraw-Hill, 1999.

See also:

✔ **Effective Communications: Preparing Presentations (pp. 392–93)**

"I fear I cannot make an amusing speech. I have just been reading a book which says that 'all geniuses are devoid of humor.'" (Stephen Spender)

 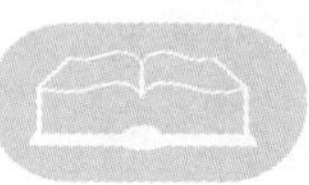    

HANDLING EFFECTIVE MEETINGS

CHECKLIST

This checklist is for anyone involved in planning and chairing meetings.

DEFINITION

For this checklist a "meeting" is defined as a face-to-face gathering of three or more individuals for a specific purpose at a specific time and place. Formal meetings, such as those covered here, are conducted by a chair, according to an agenda set in advance, and the proceedings may or may not be noted in a memo. This checklist does not, however, deal with the legal requirements of company board meetings or annual general meetings. Much of the guidance mentioned here will also apply to meetings held over the Internet or via videoconferencing, although there is no specific reference to them.

ADVANTAGES

Meetings may not always be necessary or efficient. It is important to make sure that they are justified before committing the time, effort, and other costs involved. Improved and cheaper technology is making remote videoconferencing a real possibility for many organizations, with substantial savings in traveling time, reduced travel and subsistence costs, and lower travel-related stress.

The general principles for holding a successful and productive meeting, however, are valid for all types of meetings, whether traditional face-to-face or electronically linked.

In the right circumstances, effective meetings can

- provide swift and effective communication among a number of people;
- be effective decision-making instruments;
- enhance the motivation and commitment of a team.

DISADVANTAGES

Ineffective or unnecessary meetings can:

- waste time and money;
- exacerbate factionalism and bad feeling;
- produce poor decisions.

ACTION CHECKLIST

To be fully effective, appropriate action will be necessary before, at, and after a meeting. Responsibility for success rests not only on the organizer and chair, but on all participants.

BEFORE THE MEETING

1. Ask "Do I really need a meeting?" Consider what the purpose of the meeting is: to exchange information, monitor progress on performance, deal with specific problems, brainstorm an issue, or develop plans. Only when you have done so can you decide the best timing, attendance, and format of the meeting.

2. Set clear, precise, overall goals for the meeting.

3. Keep creative and analytical discussion separate. Creative meetings need a more relaxed timetable and atmosphere. It is hard to switch from the routine to the creative and vice versa.

4. Decide who should be present; neither too many nor too few, and only those who can make a contribution.

5. Having a definite finish time helps concentration and may help to avoid time-consuming digressions. Make sure the data and time are suitable for all intended participants.

6. Select the format of the meeting, bearing in mind considerations such as the nature of the topic(s) under discussion, the number of participants, the amount of time set aside, and the goals you wish to achieve.

7. Make administrative arrangements:

- Choose and book a suitable room.
- Make sure that the necessary equipment and supplies will be available.
- Organize refreshments.
- Request secretarial help, including translation services if necessary, particularly if a memo is to be taken. The person taking the memo needs to be skilled at listening and taking notes.

8. Notify all involved as early as possible. The notification should include:

- full details of date, time, and place
- a list of participants
- the agenda
- copies of reports and other supporting papers

9. Complete your personal research, reading, and other preparation. This may include making advance contact with any participants whose contributions may be critical to the success of the meeting.

KEY ROLES OF THE CHAIR

1. Arrive in good time.

2. Check that all arrangements, including equipment, seating, and refreshments, are in place.

3. Welcome participants on arrival (especially newcomers).

4. Start promptly.

5. Deal with administrative items, such as introductions of any newcomers, and expressions of gratitude, congratulations, good wishes, condolences, or apologies received from absentees. Also deal with any domestic arrangements, including message-taking, car parking, catering, breaks, and the expected finish time.

6. Dispatch routine items.

7. Introduce each agenda item effectively, emphasizing the objectives.

8. You can shape and control the discussion by:

- encouraging the shy;
- restraining the verbose and opinionated;
- allowing only one discussion at a time;
- separating different subjects;
- "holding" on subjects that are not exhausted;
- balancing contributions on contentious subjects;
- keeping control of time;

"People can be themselves only in small comprehensible groups." (E. F. Schumacher)

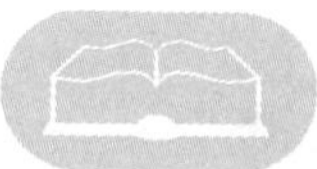

DOS AND DON'TS

For Handling Effective Meetings

DO

- Consider other ways in which the objectives of a proposed meeting can be achieved.
- Prepare thoroughly and well in advance.
- Arrive in good time.
- Consider participants' comfort and convenience (smoking, ventilation, acoustics and noise levels, breaks, etc.).
- Employ visual aids where useful.
- Focus on the objectives for each item.
- Make sure that all participants contribute what they can to the discussion.
- Maintain good but not oppressive discipline.
- Aim for consensus whenever possible.

DON'T

- Don't take notes if you are also the leader or a key contributor.
- Don't lose your temper.
- Don't get involved in purely personal disagreements.
- Don't talk too much or for too long.
- Don't insist on having the last word.
- Don't talk first, except to introduce a topic.
- Don't let the meeting run on and on.

- using visual aids where they can help make a point;
- refraining from expressing an opinion unless needed at the end;
- summarizing periodically;
- seeking clear decisions at appropriate points;
- expressing appreciation for participants' contributions.

9. Conclude firmly and concisely, emphasizing agreed action points.

✔ After the Meeting

1. Immediately write down decisions taken, actions agreed on (noting the persons responsible for each), and the date by which each action should be achieved.
2. Distribute the memo to all participants and other interested parties.
3. Monitor the progress of subsequent action.

✔ How to Assess Meeting Effectiveness

As with other activities, assessment of effectiveness requires you to have set clear objectives in advance for the meeting as a whole and for individual items. Measures of effectiveness include the following:

- Did all present contribute positively, according to their roles?
- Was the discussion lively but good-tempered?
- Were all aspects of the subjects thoroughly explored?
- Was consensus reached on all major decisions?
- Did the meeting cover the subjects within the time allotted?
- Did participants leave with clear knowledge of what had been achieved and their own responsibilities for future action?
- Ask participants to complete a brief evaluation. Besides providing feedback, this helps them perceive their own weaknesses and do better next time.

THOUGHT STARTERS

- Was the last meeting you called/attended really necessary?
- Do you always prepare for meetings, whether as chair or participant, thoroughly and in advance?
- Who is the best meeting leader you have worked with? Why was that person so effective?
- Who is the worst meeting leader you have worked with? Why was that person so ineffective?

For More Information

Books:

Kelsey, Dee, et al. *Great Meetings!: How to Facilitate Like a Pro.* Portland, ME: Hanson Park Press, 1999.

Smith, Taggart. *Meeting Management.* Upper Saddle River, NJ: Prentice Hall, 2001.

See also:

✔ **Managing Your Time Effectively (pp. 398–99)**

✔ **Planning a Workshop (pp. 426–27)**

"Time spent on any item on the agenda will be in inverse proportion to the sum involved."

(C. Northcote Parkinson)

Managing Your Time Effectively

CHECKLIST

This checklist is for managers who wish to manage their time more effectively.

Good time management has always been an important skill, but it is now essential. Factors such as widespread corporate restructuring, accelerating change, information overload, and the need to balance private and working lives have put the squeeze on managers to get much more from their working day.

Definition

Time management is a vital aspect of self management. It involves using time to create maximum personal effectiveness and efficiency. This is achieved by planning how best to use your time and successfully implementing the plan.

Advantages

Effective time management enables you to:

- achieve control over your activities;
- balance work, rest, and play;
- develop a management style that is proactive rather than reactive;
- deal with problems as they arise instead of letting them grow;
- build in time for constructive personal development;
- save money by increasing your efficiency and achieving more;
- complete important tasks on time and avoid wasting time on unimportant tasks;
- have time to listen to others;
- be regarded by others as a noticeably well-organized person and differentiated from less well organized colleagues;
- relieve pressure and stress;
- go home from the office on time.

Action Checklist

1. Find Out Where Your Time Goes

Look back through your appointment book or time sheets to find out how you spend your time. If you have never done so, log your activities over a two-week period to see where your time is going. Ask yourself:

- How much of your activity was a result of planning and how much was unplanned?
- How accurate was your planning—did you complete tasks in the time allowed?
- How much time was spent on routine activities that could be delegated?
- How often did interruptions divert you from your tasks?
- At what time of day did you accomplish most?

2. Identify Your Problem Areas

What is making you use time inefficiently? Split problems into "the enemy without" and "the enemy within". The enemy without includes external factors beyond your immediate control, for example, mistakes or inefficiencies of other departments, unexpected extra tasks, and complaints. The enemy within is personal inefficiency, and includes poor planning, lack of assertiveness in turning away unwanted callers, and putting off problems and unenjoyable activities.

3. Clarify Your Objectives and Priorities

Before you can successfully manage your time, you should make sure that you are familiar with your job description and with what you should and should not be doing as part of your job. Agree on your precise role, objectives, and targets with both your superiors and subordinates so that everyone knows what is expected of you, and put this in writing.

4. Tackle the Enemy Without

If you find that problem relationships, complaints, and reaction to situations beyond your control take up too much of your time, try to minimize this by:

- setting service level agreements that detail what each department expects from others, and improving interdepartmental communication;
- reviewing complaints procedures and setting up a more efficient system;
- examining personnel policies that might be giving rise to interpersonal tension or inefficient work practices;
- asking colleagues to be concise when giving written or oral reports.

5. Tackle the Enemy Within

Make more constructive use of your time by thinking about it in a structured way.

Plan

- Map out your activities a week in advance.
- Spend five minutes each morning reviewing your time plan; adjust it as circumstances change.
- Build slack time into your schedule so that you do not constantly overrun.
- Have a backup plan for contingency situations—decide which tasks can be dropped, who can be called on to help out, and who will need to be notified if you are consequently delayed with other activities.
- Plan time for relaxation and recreation as well as work.

Prioritize

- Rank tasks in order of importance. Try to be objective; avoid ranking highly the tasks that you enjoy but that are not vital.
- Be firm but polite in refusing to do tasks that are not your responsibility.
- Maintain clear objectives on what you are trying to achieve and allocate your time accordingly.

"Work expands so as to fill the time available for its completion." (C. Northcote Parkinson)

DOS AND DON'TS

For Managing Your Time Effectively

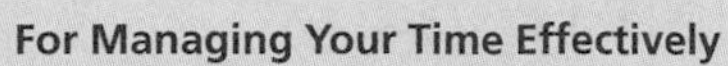

DO

- Clarify your objectives and targets.
- Make priorities and continually review them as circumstances change.
- Be firm and assertive with unwanted time-stealers.
- Make sure your time plan is efficient but realistic.

DON'T

- Don't equate being busy with being efficient.
- Don't attempt to do more than you are capable of.
- Don't give priority to the loudest claim on your time—it may not be the most important.
- Don't regard your plans as fixed. Environments and situations change, and you need to adapt.
- Don't see time management as purely a work issue. It is a personal issue, spanning work and home and the balance between them.

✔ Delegate

- Assess which tasks can be delegated to someone else.
- Choose carefully whom you delegate to. Is the person knowledgeable and competent in this area? Does he or she have the time and willingness to do the task? Will you be offending anyone else?
- Make sure you give clear instructions so the task is done well.
- Give routine tasks to your secretary—15 minutes spent showing a secretary how to perform a routine task can save you hours over the course of a year.
- Involve others in projects and share the workload.
- Train your employees to manage their time well.

✔ Review How You Work

- Plan to do important activities at the time of day when you function best.
- Break down complex tasks into manageable chunks.
- Avert unwanted interruptions. If necessary, ask your secretary to ward off unwanted callers, work somewhere other than your office, or simply put a Do Not Disturb sign on the door (make sure that people know it means what it says).
- Work at home for a day occasionally if this is allowed and if home is a quiet environment.
- Talk to people instead of writing—this can result in a quicker response and faster decision making.
- Avoid hopping from one task to another. Concentrate on one thing at a time.
- Batch similar tasks together.
- Have breaks or switch tasks when you feel tired or have a mental block.
- Keep accurate records and an organized filing system to save time locating information or having to compile documents again.
- Make use of new technology, but only if it really will save time.
- Minimize paperwork and avoid unnecessary duplication.
- Make sure the meetings you attend are really necessary, and if running one yourself, make sure it is well organized.
- Look at your travel arrangements for commuting or work trips. Can you shorten or eliminate unnecessary journeys?

✔ 6. Make Time to Play

Overwork is counterproductive. It can cause stress and unhappiness and decrease the time efficiency that you have worked hard to achieve. However well organized you are, there are still only 24 hours in a day, and you need to devote an adequate proportion of them to yourself. Don't be afraid to take 10 minutes for a coffee break or a walk around the block, or an hour to go to the gym. Try to maintain a healthy balance between your work and home life.

THOUGHT STARTERS

- Do you feel in control of your day?
- Do you have a plan of what you intend to accomplish each day?
- Do you keep both an appointment book and a record of what actually happened?
- Do you put off tasks you don't like doing?
- Are you frustrated by interruptions and unnecessary demands on your time?
- Do you agree to do things you know someone else should be doing?
- Are you kept waiting by other people? Do you keep others waiting?
- Is your social or family life suffering because of pressure at work and long hours?
- Do you get enough time to yourself?

For More Information

Books:

Allen, David. *Getting Things Done: The Art of Stress-free Productivity*. New York: Viking Press, 2001.

Jennings, Jason, and Laurence Haughton. *It's Not the Big That Eat the Small . . . It's the Fast That Eat the Slow*. New York: HarperCollins, 2001.

See also:

✔ **Handling Effective Meetings (pp. 396–97)**
✔ **Stress Management: Self First (pp. 412–13)**
✔ **Successful Delegation (pp. 380–81)**

"While we're talking, envious day is fleeing: seize the day, put no trust in the future." (Horace)

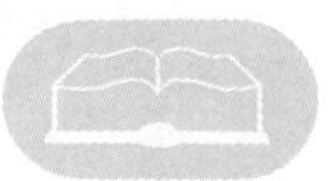

PERSONAL DEVELOPMENT PLANNING

CHECKLIST

This checklist promotes personal development planning (PDP) as a constructive approach to acquiring knowledge and skills throughout your working life.

The accelerating pace of market and technological change, the growth of information, and the shifts in economic and competitive pressures are all imposing demands on managers to continually renew their skills and capabilities.

Flatter organizational structures mean fewer promotion possibilities. Managers increasingly face a series of sideways moves within and between organizations instead of a steady upward progression. Managers can no longer rely on their initial training or qualifications to carry them through employment, or on their employer to provide everything they need to develop skills and experience—the old security, if it ever existed, has gone. More and more managers are having to take responsibility for their own lifelong, continuing development—the bottom line is that professional development is now up to the individual.

DEFINITION

Development is a lifelong process of nurturing, shaping, and improving your skills, knowledge, and interests in order to enhance your effectiveness and adaptability and minimize the chance that your skills might become obsolete or you might be laid off. It does not necessarily imply upward movement; rather, it is about enabling you to improve and use your full potential at each career stage.

A personal development plan involves establishing what you want to achieve or where you want to go in the short or long term and identifying your needs in terms of skills, knowledge, or competence. The plan also defines the development that is appropriate to meet those perceived needs. Scheduling and timing are important, but cannot be too regimented.

ADVANTAGES

PDP provides the structure of a schedule, facilitates motivation, and offers a framework for monitoring and evaluating achievements. It can lay the basis for:

- reappraising where you want to go and how you can get there;
- revitalizing technical skills that date very quickly;
- building up transferable skills;
- continuous learning;
- gaining satisfaction from a sense of achievement;
- ensuring your employability and survival in an age where very few jobs will be the same five years from now;
- taking advantage of opportunities that may arise, or that you can create.

DISADVANTAGES

Problems with PDP are usually associated with:

- getting started in a constructive way;
- assigning importance to development activities that may not have seemed so important in the past;
- being too modest, too demanding, or perhaps too unrealistic;
- getting the right balance between workaholism and inertia—between work, rest, and play.

ACTION CHECKLIST

PDP is a cyclical process—you don't have to start at the beginning if you have already decided where you are going and what you need to do to get there. The following diagram outlines the process.

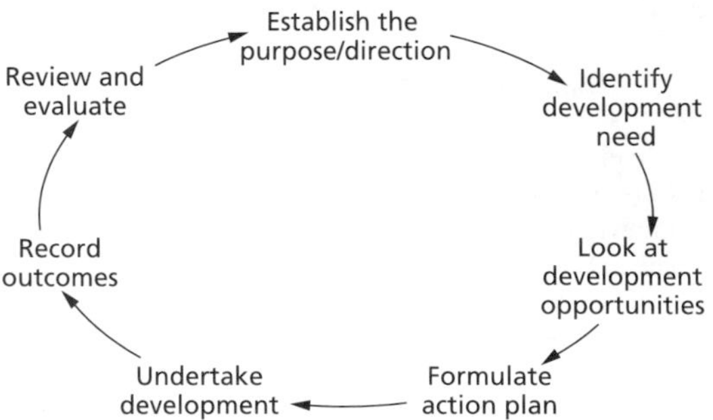

1. ESTABLISH YOUR PURPOSE OR DIRECTION

Identify the purpose of your development cycle. It involves:

- knowing what you are good at and interested in;
- getting a sense of your potential within your chosen sector;
- taking account of the organizational realities you encounter and linking your plans to organizational needs as much as possible.

Think about:

- your own value system: your family and private life, work and money, constraints and obstacles to mobility, now and in the future;
- the characteristics of work that fit with your value system.

2. IDENTIFY YOUR DEVELOPMENT NEEDS

These may emerge from intended or actual new tasks or responsibilities, discussions with your manager or others, or dissatisfaction with your current routines. Some of us may know what we are good at; many do not. Various instruments can help, including self-assessment tests, benchmarking exercises against management standards, or structured personal diagnostics that elicit your view of yourself.

Your development needs depend on your career goals. If you intend to remain in similar employment, do you want development to remotivate or reorient you, or is the

  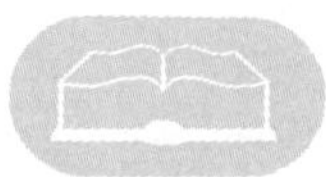    

aim to improve your current performance and effectiveness? Or do you intend development to prepare you for promotion, your next job, a new career, or self-employment?

3. Identify Learning Opportunities

On the basis of your self-assessment, draw up a list of the skills or knowledge you need to acquire, update, or improve. Compare this list to your current skills and knowledge base and identify the gaps. Consider:

- your learning style—some of us learn best from trying new things, while others prefer to sit back and observe; some prefer to put things to the test, others to carry out research. Honey and Mumford's *Manual of Learning Styles* (1992) includes an instrument that helps identify your preferred learning style;
- the resources available—think laterally in identifying sources of help. In addition to your own organization, consider government and private advisory agencies, literature and continuing education aids, multimedia packages, professional institutes, your peer groups, networks and colleagues, and family and friends;
- the range of learning options available. These can be broadly differentiated into three categories: education, training, and development. Education takes place over a sustained but finite period of time, usually leads to a qualification, and may lead you in a new career direction. Training takes place at a specific time and place, is usually vocationally relevant, and addresses specific aims and objectives. Development encompasses a large number of activities that offer learning potential but are neither education nor course-based, but are instead work-based (for example, work shadowing) or personal (private reading or authorship).

4. Formulate an Action Plan

For each of the gaps you have identified, set yourself development objectives. These need to be SMART: Specific, Measurable, Achievable, Realistic, and Timely. Make them challenging so they stretch you, but make sure they are attainable and viable.

5. Undertake the Development

Put your plan into action—your development is up to you.

6. Record the Outcomes

Keeping records serves to remind you of what you have done. Most importantly it helps you focus on what you have gotten out of the development activity. Record the date, the development need identified, the chosen method of development, the date(s) that development was undertaken, the outcomes, and further action.

7. Evaluate and Review

Evaluation is the key stage to the self-development cycle because it enables you to discover whether that development activity was worthwhile and applicable, and whether and how your skills or working behavior improved as a result. Evaluating development activities involves asking the following:

- What am I better able to do as a result of it?
- Has this experience thrown up further development needs?
- How well did this development method work?
- Could I have gotten more out of this activity?
- Would I follow this approach again?

Evaluation will also provide a key lead to the next stage of the continuing cycle. Goals change, tasks vary, and new needs emerge: it is important to revise your own plan accordingly. A plan that does not evolve and adapt is probably not being followed.

DOS AND DON'TS

For Personal Development Planning

DO

- Make sure your personal goals are balanced.
- Take time to evaluate learning experiences.
- Seek out feedback on your performance.
- Focus on development in two different directions at the same time for greater flexibility and adaptability in response to changing circumstances.

DON'T

- Don't be too ambitious; development is usually incremental.
- Don't be afraid of asking for help.

THOUGHT STARTERS

- "There were two stonecutters chipping away in a quarry. Asked what they were doing, one said, 'I'm cutting stone.' The other said, 'I'm building a cathedral.'" (Malcolm Kerrell, *Past Tense, Future Perfect*, 1997)
- "All men who have turned out worth anything have had the chief hand in their own education." (Sir Walter Scott, 1830)

For More Information

Books:

Ballback, Jane, and Jan Slater. *Managing Your Career in a Changing Workplace (Personal Growth and Development Series)*. Amherst, MA: Chang Association, 1996.

Kerrell, Malcolm. *Past Tense, Future Perfect: Successful Management and the Alice Principle*. London: Souvenir Press, 1997.

Planning Your Retirement

CHECKLIST

This checklist is designed to help managers planning for their own retirement. Good planning needs to start early if you are to enjoy many years of active and fruitful life after your formal employment ends. Taking personal responsibility for your retirement is becoming increasingly essential.

Definition

Retirement may mean the end of paid full-time employment, but with increased longevity and better health many more people can now look forward to 20 years or more in retirement. This is a large slice of life that needs to be planned for if it is to be comfortable and enjoyable. Planning, particularly financial planning, needs to be long-term.

Advantages

Planning your retirement can:

- reduce anxiety about your money, what you can do, and whether you can cope;
- permit you to look forward with confidence to a new phase of your life;
- enable you to develop yourself in ways you have not had the opportunity to do before;

Disadvantages

Failure to plan for retirement may result in:

- worrying about money;
- being anxious about losing your identity when you give up work;
- missing a secure daily routine and worrying about how to fill your spare time;
- finding it hard to change;
- lacking the personal contacts work provides;

Action Checklist

1. Adopt a Positive Attitude

Growing older happens to everyone and is something you have to accept. Retirement allows a fresh start in a new way of life, and so is an occasion for celebration rather than fear. However, it helps to be aware of the implications beforehand and make sensible plans.

2. Plan Your Finances

One of the commonest fears about retirement is whether you'll have enough money to enjoy it. You should aim to maintain the same standard of living in retirement that you enjoy during your working life. Take advantage of any preretirement counseling or courses offered in your area.

You need to know your likely retirement income. Find out:

- How much will your company pension be? You should receive regular statements of your account. If you have changed employers, make sure you also have statements from earlier plans. It is likely that you will have the option of taking part of the pension as a lump sum when you retire. This is generally regarded as a valuable option, particularly if you have a partner. But if your plan provides total or substantial inflation protection, think hard before you sacrifice it for a lump sum. Consider your health and your family record of longevity (you are statistically likely to live three to five years longer than your parents). If you are reinvesting the sum, will the yield from the investment and the protection of your capital be as good as the pension you've given up?
- How much is your Social Security income likely to be?
- There are varying laws covering the types of supplemental retirement plans: Keogh, 401(K) plans, 403B, defined benefit, money purchase plans, profit sharing, and IRA. Do they have any implications for you? A financial adviser could be helpful here in discovering exactly what effect they may have.
- What is the value and yield of your other investments?

If you start your planning early, say, ten years before retirement, you may be able to improve your position.

If you have a partner, look at your joint financial position. It is important to keep up to date with changes, particularly in taxation. It may, for example, be advantageous for the partner with the lower income to hold a larger slice of the investments. Your financial planning needs to take taxation into account, and you should have at least an elementary knowledge of allowances and tax brackets.

Unless you are an expert it is helpful to have a financial adviser. It's probably best to seek an independent financial adviser who isn't tied to the products of a particular company and whose income doesn't depend on commissions.

3. Make a Will

If you've already made a will, retirement is a good time to check it and make sure it is still appropriate. If you haven't made a will, retirement is a good time to do so. When you make a will you're thinking of others, not only in distributing your property, but in reducing your survivors' worry and anguish–dying intestate can make things difficult for your heirs. You can buy forms with simple instructions, but everyone's situation is different, and it's better to get a lawyer to draw it up for you. If you want to pass on substantial sums to your children, it may be best to pass some over earlier to avoid inheritance tax. Having made your will, make sure your executors and partner (or close relatives) know where it is kept.

5. Decide Where to Live

You may dream of retiring to some beloved vacation spot, returning to the place where you grew up, moving nearer your children, looking for somewhere warm, or retiring abroad. For some, these ideas may work out, but for many they can be a disaster. Spend some time in the chosen place and see it at its worst; think about

---

"Confidence is a plant of slow growth in an aged bosom; youth is the season of credulity."

(William Pitt)

whom you know there. While it might be wonderful to start with, consider how it will feel as you get older.

It may be better to stay put; in that case take a critical look at your home. Is it too big? People often think something smaller would be good for retirement, but you'll be there all the time. Is there room for your planned leisure activities? Do you need some kind of home office? Is it easy to run and to heat? Is it disabled accessible, or could it be easily adapted? Think about improvements or changes, safety (how old is your wiring?), taking care of your yard in 10 or 20 years (can you make it easier?), and transportation (what will you need?).

6. Plan for Your Leisure and Health

You have spent around 2,000 hours a year at work, and this may seem a daunting time to fill at first. You may want to think about some part-time work, at least to start with, particularly if you're retiring early. There is an increasing demand for the skills of older people on a short-term or part-time basis. The most essential ingredient is to be flexible in your approach.

Short-term or part-time earnings will affect your tax position, and you should check this when accepting a job or assignment.

There is great scope for those who wish to give their time to voluntary work. Many towns have organizations that serve as clearing houses for local groups needing volunteers. Many national organizations would like help at local level, and your management skills are likely to be welcomed.

You probably have some hobby or pastime you've been planning to develop in retirement. If you haven't, try to cultivate one, particularly one involving physical exercise. Walking and cycling are two obvious ones and both can be combined with other hobbies such as photography, sketching, or birdwatching. If you are already a golfer you'll be looking forward to playing more midweek.

If you want to exercise your brain, there are many opportunities for learning locally—try a local college or university—with organizations like Elderhostel, or through correspondence or residential courses.

Make sure you have plenty of social contacts. Even if you have a partner, each of you should have your own social life so your relationship doesn't go stale. Have a checkup on or before retirement. At best this will reassure you; at worst, it will guide you as to what you should and shouldn't do.

For a healthy, happy retirement a balance of activities seems to be best, but a reasonable amount of physical exercise is important. Pay attention to your diet.

7. Plan Vacations

Vacations are just as important in retirement as before. But now you can take them as you wish and have the advantage of off-peak prices, midweek travel, short-notice departure, off-season discounts, and longer-stay vacations. Check your home insurance policy to make sure you're covered if you are away for extended periods. Get a neighbor to keep an eye on your property

DOS AND DON'TS

For Planning Your Retirement

DO

- Plan your finances.
- Find something worthwhile to do.
- Consider your partner.
- Always have something to look forward to.

DON'T

- Don't rush into unwise decisions about finances or where to live.

If you are likely to take a number of vacations each year, consider taking out an annual travel insurance policy rather than paying a separate premium for each vacation.

8. Adjust

Remember that retirement is a new experience: you are doing it for the first time. Renegotiate the chores with your partner and work out a fair division of labor in the house. It is a good idea to do more things together, but each of you should plan to have some independent activities. Business matters, tax returns, and finances should be shared and understood by both partners.

Retirement is an opportunity, not a calamity! Enjoy it!

THOUGHT STARTERS

- Have you made a retirement budget?
- Have you set up a retirement planner for retirement activities?

For More Information

Books:

Brown, Rosemary. *Good Non-Retirement Guide 1997.* Milford, CT: Kogan Page, 1997.

Siegel, Alan M., et al. *The Wall Street Journal Guide to Planning Your Financial Future: The Easy to Read Guide to Planning for Retirement*. Rev. ed. New York: Simon and Schuster, 1998.

Web Sites:

About Retirement Planning: **www.retireplan.about.com**

Money & Investing: **www.quicken.excite.com/retirement**

Retirement Living Information Center: **www.retirementliving.com**

Senior Job Bank: **www.seniorjobbank.org**

See also:

✔ **Preparing for Retirement with Dignity and Grace (pp. 820–21)**
Planning for Retirement (pp. 2073–74)

"To be able to fill leisure intelligently is the last product of civilization." (Bertrand Russell)

Preparing for Appraisal

CHECKLIST

This checklist describes how you should prepare to receive a performance appraisal.

The focus of performance appraisals has shifted in recent years away from strict evaluation toward improving performance and developing employees by means of honest and open discussion.

With improvement and development as guiding principles, the appraisal process focuses on results and behavior, not personality; issues and problems, not subjective gripes; constructive development to improve performance; and the motivation and growth of the employee. Appraisals take place as often as is thought productive, perhaps every three to six months, certainly at least once a year.

Definition

A performance appraisal is more complex than a simple meeting. It centers on a face-to-face discussion in which an employee's work is discussed, reviewed, and appraised by another person, following an agreed and understood framework. Line managers usually conduct the appraisals of their staff. Objectives and targets for the coming year are also agreed on.

Advantages

Going into an appraisal you should expect to:

- know what is expected of you at the appraisal;
- be able to discuss priorities;
- receive feedback on your performance;
- be heard and respected;
- be offered constructive guidance on attaining agreed goals;
- get help in constructing personal development plans and targets;
- accept ownership of your performance;
- understand how your work relates to corporate objectives.

Disadvantages

A successful appraisal requires you to:

- clearly understand the purpose and the process of the appraisal;
- know the terms of reference of the appraisal (for example, if it is linked to pay, what are the evaluation criteria and how are they applied?);
- prepare thoroughly beforehand;
- resolve to tackle problems honestly;
- be as relaxed as possible, even if you have not achieved past objectives;
- maintain a positive attitude, especially in terms of further personal development.

Action Checklist

1. Understand the Objectives and Terms of Reference

If there is an established appraisal program this will provide a framework for action. Find out whether the appraisal is linked to pay. If it is, make sure you understand how the evaluation criteria apply to your work.

2. Agree On a Date for the Appraisal

Ideally, you should have at least two weeks to prepare and reflect. Don't agree to an early date simply to get it over and done with. You should be allowed reasonable time for preparation.

3. Prepare for the Meeting

Your manager should provide you with notes for guidance outlining the purpose of the appraisal process and the structure of the meeting. This will help both of you to prepare and focus on the same issues. Make notes on each point that you want to comment on. Broadly, the appraisal will be in two sections–reviewing your past year's performance, and agreeing on your goals and objectives for the coming year.

4. The Appraisal Itself

Although your manager will lead the appraisal, you should expect to contribute substantially to the discussion. Key areas to focus on include:

- tasks or projects that gave you particular satisfaction–and why
- tasks or projects that gave you the least satisfaction–and why
- your overall performance
- areas for possible improvement
- next year's output
- short- and long-term personal development

5. Ask For, and Give, Feedback

Feedback should be constructive, supported by specific examples and events to highlight aspects of learning and development. Feedback is invaluable, both to yourself and your manager.

6. Don't Be Reticent About Problems

Use the appraisal process to raise any issues or problems that may be affecting your performance. For example, a faulty piece of equipment may be hampering your efforts, or you may feel you need extra help. Whatever the issue, open discussion is an essential key to resolving such problems. Make sure to propose your own solutions to any problems. Even if they are not implemented, you're demonstrating a thoughtful approach to your job.

7. Establish Priorities

You and your manager may have differing views on what your key priorities are. There may be good reasons for this, for example, your manager will be trying

"Preparation is everything. Noah did not start building the ark when it was raining." (Warren Buffett)

DOS AND DON'TS

For Preparing for Appraisal

DO
- Look upon the appraisal as an opportunity, not a threat.
- Make sure you have enough time to prepare.
- Put together some development proposals for discussion.

DON'T
- Don't spend all your time taking notes—outcomes/action points are most important.
- Don't be overcritical of renegade departments or colleagues.
- Don't make personal comments about your colleagues.
- Don't try to skate around difficult moments.
- Don't be afraid to challenge any unfair conclusions or decisions.

to align the department's output with the company's goals and objectives, which is probably a different focus from yours. Discussion should help clarify these issues and help arrive at an agreed set of priorities.

8. Bring Departmental Relationships into the Open

Apart from breakdowns of equipment, systems, and relationships, other departments can cause difficulties. If other departments are a genuine and continuing source of operational or customer difficulty, raise the question of establishing a service level agreement with them. Give clear examples of how these departments are affecting your work.

9. Propose Objectives

Do not go into the appraisal meeting assuming that your boss will have already defined your next year's goals and targets. Plan your own proposals, your own tactics, and your own targets, and remember that you have an advantage that your boss should recognize—you are the one who is doing the job.

10. Agree On Goals and Targets

Setting goals and targets should not be a one-way process. At worst you can go on mechanically raising the figures from year to year, paying no attention to changing resources and markets. At best you can reassess the factors contributing to changes in the business environment. Don't be afraid to take a completely fresh look: you may need to establish completely different kinds of goals and targets. There is no point in hitting the bull's eye if you're shooting at the wrong target.

11. Agree On Further Training and Development

Besides airing specific problems and concerns, discuss aspects of continuing development that have not yet been addressed or that form part of a general program of skills acquisition. Make time to reflect on and plan a flexible development program that will benefit both you and your employer.

12. Explain Your Personal Development Requirements

Your boss will help you to identify your training needs, some of which may be more obvious than others. Take the opportunity to review your competence and capability, in terms of both technical competence and general management development.

13. Identify the Support You Need

With objectives set and targets agreed, assess whether you need extra support in order to move forward. Think in terms of training, resources, or even time for further clarification.

14. Agree On the Evaluation

If the appraisal process is primarily for evaluation rather than adopting the discussion focus this checklist has featured, be clear on what you can contribute to the process and how far the final evaluation is mutually agreed, how far imposed.

15. Sum Up

It is good practice for the appraiser to ask the employee to summarize the agreed action points and plans from the discussion. While it is important that you own the tasks and activities ahead, it is also to your advantage that they are clarified and expressed in a way that you understand. Write up the agreed action points and targets for both you and your boss to sign as a record for the future.

THOUGHT STARTERS
- Are you satisfied with your own performance?
- If you have not achieved your set objectives, where does the problem lie?
- When you were last appraised, what went well? What went badly?
- Are you clear on the objectives and the structure of the performance appraisal program?
- If you have appraised any of your staff, what have you learned from it?

For More Information

Books:

Fisher, Martin. *Performance Appraisals*. Milford, CT: Kogan Page, 1997.
Fletcher, Clive. *Appraisal: Routes to Improve Performance*. 2nd ed. Woodstock, NY: Beekman, 2000.
Gillen, Terry. *Appraisal Discussion*. Woodstock, NY: Beekman, 2000.

"Prepare your heart and mind before you prepare your speech." (Stephen Covey)

 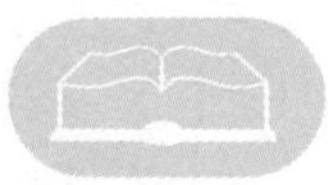    

REPORT WRITING

> CHECKLIST
> This checklist is intended both for those new to report writing and for experienced report writers who wish to review their own methods.

DEFINITION

A good report should be readable, interesting, and well presented, and it should be no longer than necessary. It should address the needs of its readership. As the readers are probably busy people who already have difficulty reading the volume of material that passes through their hands, a verbose or lengthy document is unlikely to be welcome. An obvious structure, with clear conclusions and a summary, is a must.

ADVANTAGES

Well written reports:

- help you communicate more effectively;
- improve your status and career prospects;
- contribute to business success by improving communication;
- reinforce a good corporate image;
- greatly assist in planning and decision making.

DISADVANTAGES

- Time is wasted as readers search for the information they require.
- Readers are frustrated because the information provided is incomplete.
- Misunderstandings result from ambiguity in the language.
- Readers lose confidence in the writer and the message being put across.
- The report may not be read at all.

ACTION CHECKLIST

1. PREPARATION

Putting pen to paper (or fingers to keyboard) is not the way to start the report writing process. You have to plan what you are going to say if you want to produce an effective document. In preparing for the actual writing process you should:

- consider the terms of reference or precise purpose—determine why the report is needed, the type of report it should be, the scope of the subject that is to be covered, and the timescale;
- identify the readership—is the person who requested the report the primary reader? Who else will see the report? What can the readers be expected to know about the subject? What do they need to know about the subject?
- establish the objectives in your own terms—present them as results to be achieved rather than intentions.

2. GATHER AND COLLATE INFORMATION

With most reports you will not have all the information you need close at hand, so some form of research or data collection will be required. This may entail identifying and reading other reports, interviewing people, carrying out primary research, or drawing together data from a number of different sources. Gathering too much information is not a bad fault; gathering too little definitely is—but bear in mind what you want the information for, otherwise you can bury yourself in a mound of data. Reports are much easier to write when you are able to choose from a good range of information. The important thing is to gain a balanced picture of the subject.

3. STRUCTURE YOUR INFORMATION

Referring back to your terms of reference and your readership, analyze the information to identify what is most important and what provides supporting evidence. For long documents you will need to write a detailed outline linking the main subjects with the topics they cover. Consider the order in which you are presenting the information. Restructure the outline if the order does not seem logical or it fails to portray the message you want.

Plan the layout of your report following the house style of your organization, if there is one. A simple framework for a format can form the basis of most reports. This should include:

- introduction (include your terms of reference and methodology)
- summary
- main report
- conclusions
- recommendations
- supplementary evidence (include full tables and figures that would interrupt the reading of the main report)

4. WRITE THE REPORT

View your first attempt at putting the report together as a draft. Your plan will provide a broad picture of what you want to achieve. By writing in a single sitting you are far more likely to retain your original concept. Setting yourself a deadline can help to focus your mind.

Make your writing as persuasive as possible by following a few simple rules.

- Keep your message simple without oversimplifying.
- Include only the information the reader needs to know.
- Organize your material in a logical way.
- Prefer short words and phrases for conciseness and clarity.
- Use long words only where they are necessary.
- Employ technical terms only where they are unavoidable or where you are sure that your audience will understand them—supply a glossary if necessary.
- Avoid long and complex sentences, especially those with several subordinate clauses.
- Use positive constructions—they are easier to understand than negative statements.
- Use the active voice—it is easier to understand than the passive.

"The only report we ask from all of our units is one page a month." (Alfred P. Sloan)

DOS AND DON'TS

For Report Writing

DO

- Stay focused on what you want to achieve.
- Write with your readership in mind.
- Express clearly and concisely what you have to say.
- Be complete.
- Provide a summary of the main issues and conclusions.

DON'T

- Don't write to impress.
- Don't include information only because you have found it.

Graphics and visuals are invaluable for expressing complex information. The forms available include tables, line graphs, bar graphs, divided bar graphs, pie charts, pictographs, and illustrations; figures are generally to be preferred to tables of data. They should be formatted with care, clearly numbered and titled, and introduced within the text. If the graphic is included to help explain a key point it should be placed as close to that point as possible. If it is supplied for documentary support it can be placed at the end of the report. It is often useful to include a simplified or summary figure or table in the main report and to relegate detailed data to an appendix.

✔ 5. Review What You Have Written

You should always allow time to review what you have written, but put the draft aside for a day or two first. Starting the revision after a short break can be more effective: the ideas are still clear in your mind, but you are fresher to analyze what you have written critically and you can view it with more perspective. You will often find simpler and shorter ways of saying what you intend.

Consider whether the report says what you want it to say. Does it fully cover the terms of reference? Analyze the readability of the text, making use of such techniques as the Gunning Fog Index. Check the organization of ideas. Make sure your spelling, punctuation, and grammar are correct.

Do your conclusions sufficiently differentiate between those drawn from information presented in the report, expressing your personal point of view, and recommending future action based on the report findings?

Ask a colleague to proofread the report and consider issues such as ease of understanding and structure.

✔ 6. Printing and Submission

If your organization's house style dictates how your report should be printed, make sure to follow it. In any case the layout should allow generous margins and make use of a readable typeface. For longer reports it is advisable to start each section on a new page.

Aim to submit your report ahead of schedule.

THOUGHT STARTERS

- When does the report have to be submitted?
- Who is the readership?
- What information do you need?
- Do you understand the brief for the report?
- Should you be following a house style?

For More Information

Books:

Blicq, Ron S., and Lisa A. Moretto. *Writing Reports to Get Results*. 3rd ed. New York: IEEE Press and John Wiley, 2001.

Leigh, Andrew. *Persuasive Reports and Proposals*. Woodstock, NY: Beekman, 2000.

"The biggest obstacle to professional writing is the necessity for changing a typewriter ribbon."

(Robert Benchley)

Solving Problems

CHECKLIST

This checklist outlines the systematic method of problem solving first put forward by Kepner and Tregoe in *The New Rational Manager* (1997).

With straightforward, common problems—for example, grubs killing the lawn—it is common sense to try a series of quick and tested solutions starting with the most simple or cheapest (applying insecticide) before moving on to those that take longer or cost more (replanting or laying new turf). With problems of greater complexity it may not be so easy, or indeed advisable, to try quick solutions. The answer may lie in any one of a number of directions and the quick fix may do more harm than good. The Kepner-Tregoe method enables far more complex problems to be tackled, for example, why staff morale is low, why sales are down, why complaints are up, or why industrial relations are worsening.

Definition

Kepner and Tregoe define a problem as a deviation from the norm. Problem solving differs fundamentally from decision making. A problem occurs when something is not behaving as it should: something is deviating from the norm; something goes wrong. Decision making is a case of choosing between different alternatives. Decision making is required for the question "Which computer shall I buy?" Problem solving is needed for the statement "My computer won't work."

Advantages

The process:

- is systematic and thorough;
- provides evidence to show how the problem was solved;
- helps avoid the rush to jump to a solution without knowing the cause of the problem;
- enables possible causes to be tested;
- is particularly effective for complex or fuzzy problems.

Disadvantages

The process:

- is time-consuming;
- relies on thorough investigation;
- requires disciplined information-seeking and collation.

Action Checklist

1. Define the Problem

Investigate exactly what has gone wrong. Do not be influenced by people with ready-made solutions. Try to identify the problem by looking for signals in routine statistical returns, progress meetings, suggestion programs, reports, and letters. A rising tide of complaints, for example, could stem from faulty machinery, poor packaging, staff absence, poor staff training, product deficiency, false marketing hype, or other causes not immediately obvious. Getting the definition accurate is crucial, otherwise you might find that you are solving the wrong problem and collecting possible answers to questions that have not been asked.

2. Gather Relevant Information

This is a key step, involving all factors which may have an influence on the problem. Go into detail on the people, activities, processes, equipment, systems, time scales, and conditions under which the problem occurs.

Ask the following:

- What is the problem? productivity on the shop floor (for example);
- What is not the problem? equipment, working conditions;
- What is different about the problem? the time it started;
- Who is affected by it? staff on the shop floor;
- Who is not affected by it? clerical, administrative staff;
- What is different about those affected? a continuing rise in absenteeism;
- What things are affected by the problem? failure to meet production targets, deadlines, quality requirements;
- What things are not affected? machine capacity, skill requirements;
- What is distinctive about those affected? rumblings of discontent, lack of cooperation.

3. Identify Possible Causes

Causes usually relate to people, systems, or equipment. Be careful not to blame the tool when it could be the operator. The question "What has changed from the norm?" helps identify the cause.

- When did the problem first occur? 6–7 weeks ago;
- When did it not exist? before then;
- What changed? new work teams were introduced;
- What changes might be relevant? new work practices.

4. Identify a Possible Solution

Once you have identified a likely cause, work out a hypothesis to test exactly what it is you are looking for and how you will know if you are right. The cause of a problem is always a change from the norm that has produced effects in some places but not in others. Find out where the effects are not happening.

- What changes might be relevant? new work practices;
- What causes might this suggest? imposition of new plan? lack of consultation? inadequate training? dominance of certain individuals? implementation too rushed?

5. Test the Possible Causes

Go back over the information you have assembled in steps 1–4 to test, on paper, if the cause finds a good match with how, where, and when the problem occurs, to what extent it occurs, and who is affected by it.

"It isn't that they can't see the solution. It is that they can't see the problem." (G. K. Chesterton)

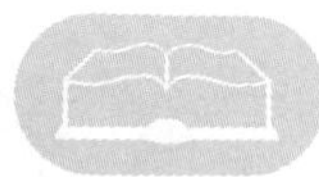

DOS AND DON'TS

For Solving Problems

DO

- Define the exact nature of the problem.
- Gather as much relevant information as possible.
- Keep asking the key questions: what, when, where, and who?
- Remember the key principle of opposites or negatives: what not? when not? where not? who not?
- Test possible causes against the data gathered.
- Keep a record of the information you collate for rechecking.

DON'T

- Don't jump to an apparently obvious solution without evidence.
- Don't evaluate ideas too quickly.

6. Come Up with Solutions

There may be a number of possible solutions (which may not be mutually exclusive), some more appropriate than others. This is the time to move from problem analysis to a method for decision making.

7. Make a Decision

Identify alternative solutions and assess the consequences of implementing each. Testing solutions against causes is one mechanism for doing this, group brainstorming another. Select the most promising alternative and produce a plan showing a schedule of actions to be performed by whom, when.

There may not be an ideal solution, but there should be a best one (even if "best" means "least worst").

8. Monitor the Results

Track the changes that occur because of what has been implemented. Take care to monitor how other changes might impact on the action you have chosen, and vice versa.

THOUGHT STARTERS

- When you have a problem, do you go for a choice or a cause?
- Do you come across complex, fuzzy problems?
- Do you have a systematic approach to tackling problems?
- Do you rely on flashes of inspiration?

For More Information

Books:

Cox, Geoff. *Ready-Aim-Fire Problem Solving: A Strategic Approach to Innovative Decision Making.* Dublin: Oak Tree Press, 2001.

Kepner, Charles H., and Benjamin B. Tregoe. *The New Rational Manager.* Princeton, NJ: Princeton Research Press, 1997.

Levine, Martin J. *Effective Problem Solving.* 2nd ed. Upper Saddle River, NJ: Prentice Hall, 1993.

Stevens, Michael. *How to Be a Better Problem Solver.* Milford, CT: Kogan Page, 1997.

See also:

✓ **Brainstorming (pp. 542–43)**
✓ **Performing a SWOT Analysis (pp. 468–69)**
✓ **Total Quality: Getting TQM to Work (pp. 522–23)**
✓ **Training Needs Analysis (pp. 422–23)**

"One's objective should be to get it right, get it quick, get it out, and get it over. . .your problem won't improve with age."

(Warren Buffett)

Starting a New Job

CHECKLIST

This checklist lists steps you may find useful prior to starting a new job and during the first few days on the job. This checklist is also relevant to organizations employing new recruits.

A new job does not begin on the day you take up your new position, but starts before you leave your current one.

Definition

Starting a new job may imply that:

- an individual is joining the company to fill a vacancy in an existing job or to assume the responsibilities of a newly created job;
- an existing employee has been appointed to fill a vacancy in an existing job or a newly created job.

An individual who is hired to start a new job generally has a harder time adjusting than an individual who is promoted or transferred within an organization. This checklist therefore focuses on new hires.

Advantages

Planning:

- reduces stress;
- enables you to become productive faster;
- leads new colleagues to accept you more quickly as a member of their group;
- prepares you to adjust to a new corporate culture;
- significantly reduces the potential for embarrassment in a new situation.

Action Checklist

1. Act Positively Before You Leave Your Present Job

Sort out personnel issues such as your pension and medical insurance. Hand in company property such as keys or passes.

Are there any contractual restrictions on your professional activities in the future? Will you be required to repay some or all of tuition assistance you have received?

Reconcile the demands, actual and potential, of the new job with your private life.

Whatever the level of the job, expect a settling-in period when you'll need extra support while you concentrate on work. Your private and working lives will change in ways that are going to affect your partner or your family; it is only fair to discuss potential changes with them beforehand.

2. Research the Company's Background

Arm yourself with as much information as you can obtain in advance: the more you know about your new employer the easier it will be for you in your early days on the job. Expand on the research you did prior to your interview.

If you don't already have a copy of the company's annual report, get one. Identify:

- the company's major competitors;
- its relative degree of business success;
- the basis on which it competes or is protected from competition.

Find out everything you can about the organizational structure, the corporate culture, the reputation of the department you'll be working in, and the people you'll be working with. Talk to people you know who already work there.

If you are new to the industrial sector, decide how you can best familiarize yourself with it. Learn its terminology—the people you work with may assume you're as accustomed to their jargon as they are. Try to get ahead of the game.

Consider what you've learned and its implications for a newcomer. Remember your learning process will continue after you join the company. Identify what you still need to know. Don't rely on getting this information at random, but resolve to seek it out quickly and systematically after you begin work—you'll gain the advantages that knowledge brings while impressing your superiors and colleagues with your willingness to work and learn.

3. If Your Job Was Recently Created, Find Out Why

Find out whether, and if so, why, the job was created. Find out its structural context, future plans for the position, and, most importantly, any special expectations of you as the newly appointed jobholder. Is the job unique in the company or are there others like it? Try to identify the qualities that made you the best person for the job; your performance will certainly be judged by your demonstration of those characteristics and deployment of those skills.

If the job fills a vacancy ask why the previous incumbent left. Was it to solve a problem? If so, what was the problem? Was it because of increased workload? If so, what caused the increase?

4. Fill In the Details

Your employer's orientation program should provide you with general background and information on your specific job. If it doesn't, ask or search for the information you need, especially:

- the purpose of the department you have joined
- the structure of your department
- the department's place in the organizational structure
- the purpose of your particular job
- your responsibilities
- the scope of your authority
- to whom you report and your boss's expectations
- who, if anyone, reports to you
- corporate and departmental culture and values
- the level of formality of working relationships

Clarify such practical matters as:

- working hours (formal and real)

"The people who get on in this world are the people who get up and look for the circumstances they want, and, if they can't find them, make them." (George Bernard Shaw)

- coffee break and lunch arrangements
- personal use of the phone, e-mail, and Internet
- performance appraisals
- the company's pension plan
- the company's medical plan
- employee assistance programs
- family-friendly policies such as parental leave and daycare
- tuition assistance
- dress (formal or informal)

What you need to know ranges from the obviously important to the apparently trivial, but matters that appear to be trivial are often integral to corporate culture, and if something helps you fit in, become accepted, and begin to achieve the purpose of your new job more quickly, it is worth knowing. This rule of thumb may apply more strongly if you have been appointed to a newly created job.

5. Feel Your Way into the Organization

You're the new kid on the block and your behavior will draw interested attention, especially if your new role involves managing others. Remember that junior employees may be savvier than their seniors in helping you find your way around. Be yourself, but leave yourself room for maneuver in light of what you may discover during your first few weeks.

Keep your eyes open: you'll notice things in those first weeks that you'll soon take for granted. Ask about them, but don't criticize them—yet! You'll get a chance to change some of them later.

Don't:

- form alliances too quickly;
- fall into the trap of joking around with the departmental clown;
- put yourself in a position you may later want to withdraw from;
- be overassertive;
- take the lead in discussions, formal or informal;
- take on too much in an effort to prove yourself.

Reserve your position until you see the lie of the land—it's easier to go forward than it is to retreat. Be polite to everyone and offer help where appropriate, but even in offering help, don't be overbearing.

6. Be Prepared for That Bewildered Feeling

Expect to meet a lot of new people and learn many new processes, from getting used to a different photocopier to the content of your job. Most people don't feel fully comfortable in a new job for at least six months, so don't worry too much if you're feeling overwhelmed after a couple of days

DOS AND DON'TS

For Starting a New Job

DO

- Spend as much time as possible preparing for your new job.
- Accept the fact that your life is going to change.
- Consider carefully what you can bring to the job that might distinguish you from others.
- Display a degree of humility.

DON'T

- Don't boast about your previous achievements.
- Don't keep referring to how you did things in your old company.
- Don't make comparisons between your former employer and your new one.
- Don't express initial impressions or opinions that you may live to regret.

THOUGHT STARTERS

- Recall some newcomers to your previous organizations. How did their behavior affect you?
- Why should they respect me?
- They know the rules—I don't.

For More Information

Books:

Allcock, Debra. *Your First Management Job: A Beginner's Guide*. Sterling, VA: Stylus, 1998.

Chapman, Elwood N., and Robert Maddux. *Your First 30 Days: Getting Started in a New Job*. 2nd ed. Menlo Park, CA: Crisp, 1997.

See also:

✔ **Planning the Recruitment Process (pp. 430–31)**
✔ **The Psychological Contract (pp. 388–89)**
✔ **Succeeding As a New Manager (pp. 414–15)**

"There were not enough men in senior positions who were prepared to give young women the break that they needed."

(Nicola Horlick)

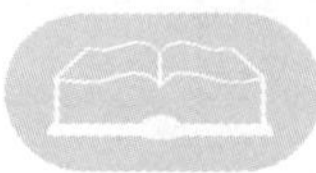

Stress Management: Self First

CHECKLIST

This checklist is designed to help individuals recognize symptoms of stress and sources of pressure and to identify coping strategies.

Successive waves of downsizing, closures, and reorganizations put pressure on managers and employees alike. Additionally, technological changes designed to improve the speed of communications in the form of fax machines, cell phones, and e-mail have created 24-hour accessibility. This is a potential recipe for disaster.

The detrimental effects of poorly managed pressures can be measured in terms of the cost to organizations and society as a whole. Corporations lose millions of working days and billions of dollars annually because of stress. The cost to individuals is less easy to measure, but its effects on the quality of life and relationships can be enormous.

Definition

In *Coping with Stress at Work*, J. M. Atkinson defines stress as "an excess of perceived demands over an individual's perceived ability to meet them".

Studies have shown that stress is closely related to the degree of control people have over their work. Self-controlled pressure, that is, pressure created by our own life's situations, can be tolerated at a very high level, while the threshold for imposed pressure from outside ourselves—say, from work—is low. The experience of stress is therefore very personal. Pressures come from many different directions, affecting us in different ways at different times. In some situations when we are under an enormous amount of pressure, we cope, feel stimulated, and on occasion positively thrive. In other situations we may suffer in some way, show signs of not coping, and feel unable to meet either the deadlines or the expectations. This is the experience of stress. Most people need a certain level of pressure to motivate them—it is when the pressure gets beyond this level that problems arise.

Action Checklist

✔ 1. Recognize Your Symptoms

Symptoms can alert you to the fact that you may be under stress. Commonly experienced symptoms include:

Health problems

- Headaches, sleep problems, changes in appe;tite, muscular tension, indigestion, exhaustion, stomach, intestinal, and skin problems, heart attacks.

Behavioral problems

- Feeling worried, irritated, unmotivated, or unable to cope and make decisions; being less creative; nailbiting; excessive smoking; alcohol abuse.

Work problems

- Reduced job satisfaction, communication breakdown, focusing on unproductive tasks, outbursts of anger.

All these symptoms may be experienced in normal life; they become symptoms of stress only when several occur together, when they do not have an obvious cause, or when you experience them more often than you would expect to. While the symptoms are often exhibited in your workplace behavior, they are not necessarily a reflection of workplace pressures.

✔ 2. Identify the Sources

We live in an ever-changing world and constantly need to adapt and adjust to technological and social changes. In addition, our lives are subject to recurring pressures that form predictable patterns of events, which can sometimes be a source of both stress and satisfaction.

In everyday life these may include:

- the death of someone close
- divorce
- injury or prolonged illness
- moving
- a large mortgage or excessive credit card debt
- vacations
- the birth of a child (especially the first)
- ongoing difficulties with a growing family

At work they may include:

- time pressures
- demanding deadlines
- relationships with colleagues
- having too much or too little work
- business or job changes
- the threat of job loss
- pressure from supervisors
- insensitive management

✔ 3. Know Your Response

Individuals respond to these external pressures by adapting and adjusting in a variety of ways, depending on their temperament and circumstances. Two broad categories of personality type have been identified. Type A people might be described as competitive, aggressive, or hasty, while Type B people are just the reverse. Type A people tend to take stress out on others, Type B to internalize it. Other characteristics such as age, gender, health, financial situation, and access to support can influence how we respond to change, regardless of our personality traits.

✔ 4. Identify the Strategies That Help You Cope

As individuals react differently to stress, so each person has different coping strategies. Identify for yourself those that have been successful in the past; they may have involved:

- removing or reducing the outside pressure;

"I try to only worry about things I have control over." (Steve Nash)

DOS AND DON'TS

For Stress Management: Self First

DO

- Recognize your symptoms and warning signs.
- Identify the sources of pressure.
- Accept yourself as you are.
- Pace yourself. Complete tasks rather than trying to keep too many balls in the air.
- Forget the near misses.
- Communicate effectively. It saves time and energy.
- Share work-related stress issues with your boss.
- Remove or reduce outside pressures.
- Take a break. Don't be afraid to relax—it is essential to regain your energy.
- Give yourself a special treat on occasion.
- Take care of your health and learn relaxation techniques.
- Talk to others.

DON'T

- Don't equate stress with weakness.
- Don't keep stress to yourself—talking helps.
- Don't ignore it, thinking that it will heal itself.
- Don't blame others or the environment.
- Don't stop activity completely. Doing something you enjoy is more therapeutic than doing nothing, which gives you more time to worry.

- accepting the things that can't be changed;
- breaking up big problems into smaller, solvable pieces.

✔ 5. Begin to Make the Necessary Changes

Change yourself: we can be our own worst enemies.

- Be realistic.
- Recognize your own weaknesses.
- Talk to others, at home and at work. Do not bottle up stress.
- Remember you are not the only one who is stressed. You are not alone.

  Change relationships: relationships can be both supportive and damaging.
- Invest in developmental and supportive relationships.
- Withdraw from damaging relationships.

  Change activities: activities create balance and an opportunity to release stress.
- Relax, if necessary, by using well established techniques.
- Develop interests that nourish you.
- Exercise regularly. It's a great way to relieve tension.
- Eat well—a sensibly balanced diet is important.
- Get enough sleep to ensure that you are refreshed.
- If doing all of the above still doesn't seem to be enough, seek professional medical or counseling assistance if the stress persists.

Your happiness and wellbeing depend on making changes. Accomplishing change will bring an easing of pressures, profound changes in personality and mood, and a fresh approach to life that will benefit you and those with whom you live and work.

THOUGHT STARTERS

- How would you advise a subordinate who is under stress?
- Where do you invest most of your time and attention—do tasks or people matter most?
- Often our greatest enemy in taking care of ourselves is ourselves. For example, do you place unrealistic expectations on yourself? How could you prevent this? How much pressure do you exert on the people who work for you?

For More Information

Books:

Cartwright, Susan, and Cary L. Cooper. *Managing Workplace Stress*. Thousand Oaks, CA: Sage, 1996.

O'Hara, Valerie, Ph.D. *Wellness 9 to 5: Managing Stress at Work*. Oakland, CA: Harbinger Publications, 1998.

Web Site:

International Stress Management Association: **www.stress-management.isma.org**

See also:

☆ **Managing Stress (pp. 18–20)**

✔ **Managing Your Time Effectively (pp. 398–99)**

✔ **The Psychological Contract (pp. 388–89)**

  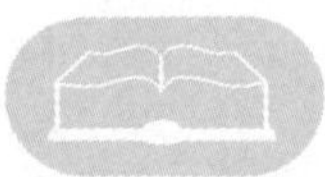    

SUCCEEDING AS A NEW MANAGER

This checklist examines the situation facing any manager newly chosen for a job that is more demanding than the previous one.

DEFINITION

For the purpose of this checklist, a new manager is someone who has recently been selected for a job with responsibility for a team of no more than 12 to 15 subordinates. This person may be taking on the responsibility of managing at this level for the first time, or indeed of managing at all for the first time. The relationship between the manager and the team is a new one, although the manager may previously have been a member of the team or a manager in another part of the same organization.

Such managers may represent a wide range of previous experience, but the principles outlined in this checklist apply to any new manager as defined above.

ACTION CHECKLIST

1. ANTICIPATE CHANGE

When you recover from the euphoria of your promotion, face the fact that even after you come to grips with your new role, life will probably be more demanding than it has ever been before.

Realistically, you'll need two things at home—support during a very stressful period and a lack of distraction to enable you to focus single-mindedly on your new responsibilities. At an early stage, discuss (and then continue to discuss) the ways that your new job is likely to affect your relationship with your partner and your family and change your domestic routines.

2. RESEARCH YOUR NEW JOB

Find out all you can about:

- the company (if it is one you have not previously worked for)
- the department you'll be working in
- your new job
- the history of the position
- your new subordinates, if you don't already know them

Don't prejudge what you're going to find in your new job. And don't be bound by what you did in previous jobs or how other companies you've worked for operated.

Find out as much as you can about your predecessor and his or her approach to the job. Establish:

- why the person left;
- what management style the manager preferred;
- what needs to be changed in the job.

Form at least a tentative plan in advance: it will be harder to plan once you are in position. Think about what you want to achieve and how you would like to develop yourself to match the demands of the job. Reflect on your strengths and weaknesses—how can you deploy your positive qualities and experience to advantage and compensate for your limitations? Don't assume your new team will welcome your style—even if your predecessor was unpopular, your subordinates may prefer the devil they know. Above all, don't depart too dramatically and quickly from established practice.

3. MAKE THE MOST OF YOUR ORIENTATION

On your first day you should be met by someone from the personnel department or perhaps your line manager, who will show you around, introduce you to colleagues, and attend to formalities. You'll be introduced to your team. Be proactive during this process—make sure you get the information you need.

4. GET TO KNOW YOUR TEAM

Learn the organizational purpose of your department, team, or unit—what work is being done, what is the current state of play, and what are your customers' expectations?

If your new team is based in an office, ask someone to get everyone together, introduce yourself, and tell them you are looking forward to working with them. Explain that you'll see them all individually as soon as you can. If they are scattered, aim to get them together quickly for the same purpose.

Meet your team members individually. Schedule a generous amount of time and plan a discussion framework for these talks—you want a spontaneous but structured exchange of information in a friendly but businesslike atmosphere. Be courteous and listen carefully, eliciting information about them as individuals. Take notes (and explain why you are doing so). Consider leaving them with a question to reflect on: "What should I do or not do to help you perform your job effectively?"

Evaluate your new team before you plan to enlarge it.

If you are aware that another team member wanted or expected to get your job, acknowledge the fact. Don't be patronizing, but express the hope that you can work together on a friendly basis and say that you look forward to his or her help. Be careful—the team has a yardstick to measure you against. And be especially careful if the rest of the team thinks the person in question should have got the job.

5. DEVELOP RELATIONSHIPS INSIDE AND OUTSIDE THE COMPANY

Introduce yourself to customers (internal and external), suppliers, and the people who make up the professional network surrounding your job. Begin to develop a relationship with your boss, but not too quickly. Find out how close he or she wants you to be before encouraging a close working relationship.

6. IDENTIFY LIKELY STANDARDS OF PERFORMANCE

Observe, listen, and note what is acceptable and what is not in the environment you have entered. Within a few

"A tough manager may never look outside his own factory walls or be conscious of his partnership in a wider world."

(Robert Menzies)

weeks you should have some idea of what your staff expects of you. Identify the criteria by which your boss, your peers, and your customers (internal and external) will judge you. Be honest with yourself—can you meet those standards? If not, what do you need to do? Consider who could help you and what the price might be.

7. Work On Your Relationship with Individuals

When you have met with your staff, follow up by initiating the process of developing individuals. Make a point of noticing and showing appreciation when someone puts in extra time and effort. Praise people's good qualities and achievements and foster self-belief.

Set yourself a code of management practice that includes staff development and progress, and make it known to your staff—but remember that people will judge you by the extent to which you deliver on your promises. Resolve to:

- listen to what staff members are saying;
- help people understand how their jobs contribute to team effectiveness;
- establish clear and specific goals and standards for individuals;
- sit down with individuals at least once a quarter to discuss overall performance;
- consider all relevant information when evaluating performance; discuss performance honestly and directly; work hard to reach mutual agreement on performance appraisals; and ensure that performance appraisals are consistent with informal feedback;
- help employees develop specific plans to improve their performance;
- make sure that each person's duties and responsibilities are clearly understood;
- provide training and guidance to improve performance and further individual development.

8. Develop a Winning Team

Research has repeatedly confirmed that good people management and good results are closely related. You will be judged by your team's results.

Lead by involving team members. Make a maximum effort from the very beginning to establish departmental and group goals. Seek staff participation in setting objectives and standards, prioritizing goals, and setting deadlines.

Set an example. Demonstrate strong personal commitment to achieving the team's goals. Communicate high personal standards informally in your conversation, appearance, and general conduct. Build warm, friendly relationships rather than remaining cold and aloof.

9. Take Stock Regularly

At the end of your first week as a new manager take time to reflect on your progress and identify issues that require particularly close attention. Make a plan for the following week. Get into the habit of setting aside time every week for review and planning. Don't let mistakes occasion self-doubt: everyone makes mistakes. Good managers learn from them, while bad managers repeat them.

The pattern of behavior you set in your first three months will be extremely hard to change later. As a new manager, your primary task is to listen and learn.

DOS AND DON'TS

For Succeeding As a New Manager

DO

- Use all the time at your disposal to prepare for your new role in advance.
- Leave yourself room to maneuver by not taking up rigid positions prematurely.
- Make your highest priority the development of your new staff.
- Recognize that first impressions of people may be replaced by more realistic ones.

DON'T

- Don't make promises that may be difficult or impossible to keep.
- Don't form alliances based on first impressions.
- Don't allow yourself to be trapped into accepting the status quo—reserve the right to postpone judgment.

THOUGHT STARTERS

- Have you defined your objectives? Do they need to be reviewed?
- What do you expect from a new boss?
- In your experience, which new bosses have impressed you most and why?
- Give yourself time to settle in—about six months is reasonable.

For More Information

Books:

Betof, Edward, and Frederic Harwood. *Just Promoted: How to Survive and Thrive in Your First 12 Months As a Manager*. New York: McGraw-Hill, 1992.
Carr, Clay. *The New Manager's Survival Guide*. New York: John Wiley, 1995.
Hill, Linda A. *Becoming a Manager: Mastery of a New Identity*. New York: Penguin USA, 1993.

Web Sites:

HR Guide: **www.hr-guide.com**
HRnext: **www.hrnext.com**
hrVillage: **www.hrvillage.com**

See also:

✔ **The Psychological Contract (pp. 388–89)**
✔ **Starting a New Job (pp. 410–11)**

"I've had enough success for two lifetimes. My success is talent put together with hard work and luck."
(Kareem Abdul-Jabbar)

  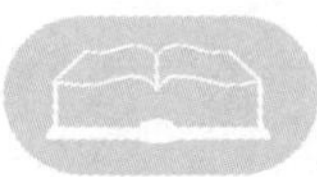    

Women Returning to the Workplace

CHECKLIST

This checklist is for women preparing to reenter employment.

Many women leave jobs and careers because of family responsibilities, but once these have changed or been resolved, they find that their confidence to return to work has been eroded or their skills are out of date. This checklist forms a step-by-step guide for addressing these problems.

Definition

Many women return to paid employment, whether full- or part-time, after a substantial period away from work, often to care for children or elderly relatives. This pattern is the norm among the female workforce: the full-time lifelong career woman with a family is still the exception.

Advantages

- Financial independence.
- New opportunities for broadening social contacts and work-related skills.

Disadvantages

- Less time for family and, perhaps, for voluntarism.
- New expenses for work-related clothing, transportation, etc.

Action Checklist

1. List Your Skills

If you are returning to work after a long absence, be imaginative in identifying skills you have already acquired: define the tasks you perform on a daily basis and the skills you use. Many of the skills you once used in prior employment may, indeed, still be completely up to date (for example, communications and computer skills). But even if some have grown rusty, running a home and caring for a family demand good management of time, projects, and finances, as well as the ability to organize and negotiate. Many employed people do not have this breadth of experience. Take into account any continuing education courses or training, you've taken, voluntarism, for example, with schools or local committees or boards. It will be useful here and throughout your job search to enlist the help of family and friends—they often see qualities in you that it is hard to identify yourself, and their different experiences of the working world can offer you a valuable perspective.

2. Translate Your Skills into Areas of Strength

Classify the skills you have identified into different functional areas (for example, communications, organizational development, clerical, supervisory, or financial). You can use these to emphasize your strengths with potential employers. Consider which skills you most enjoy; these might point you toward possible areas of work. If you have previous work experience in a certain industry, or a certain job classification, you may have a better response to your job search in that area than trying to enter a new career field.

3. Look At Areas of Weakness

When—and only when—you have built up your confidence by identifying your strengths, consider your weaknesses and limitations (for example, those imposed by family commitments). Be honest but positive. For every weakness you identify, think about ways of remedying it—through practice or training. Remember that no one in employment is perfect.

4. Identify Opportunities

Relate your strengths to areas of job opportunity. Be creative in identifying options. Have new companies moved into your area, or are they likely to? Use local sources of information such as libraries, directories, and employment agencies. Well over half of all jobs filled are from personal contacts rather than from job announcements in the newspaper. Ask friends, relatives, and acquaintances to help you gain access to people responsible for hiring in a variety of your "target" companies. Follow up by calling to schedule informational interviews, in which they find out about you and your skills.

5. Be Honest About the Barriers

Once you are clear about the opportunities, be honest at this stage about the potential barriers. These could include travel, childcare, family resistance, or lack of qualifications. Work through the list and be creative in thinking about how you might overcome each one, or be prepared to acknowledge that some will be formidable.

6. Set Goals and Priorities That Are Right for You

Set clear goals for what you want to achieve by returning to work and taking control of your own priorities. Your goals might include compensation, hours of work, or type of employment. Be realistic: set targets that are achievable in six months to a year rather than aiming too high initially.

7. Draw Up an Action Plan

From your set of goals list the actions you need to accomplish. Keep the steps simple. Set yourself a realistic but flexible timetable; assign dates and a cost associated with each action.

8. Consider Whether You Need Training

Will you need, or benefit from, training to achieve your goals? Consider all options, including:

- a job search skills course: a short course to prepare you for everything from how to search for the right job, to building interviewing skills and writing an impressive résumé. In many places, courses are available at little

"A woman is like a tea bag—only in hot water do you realize how strong she is." (Nancy Reagan)

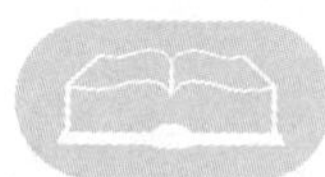

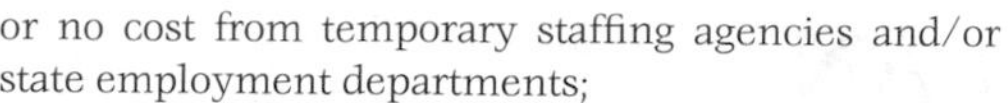

or no cost from temporary staffing agencies and/or state employment departments;

- a continuing education class: this might be basic skills in a new career path or perhaps an advanced course for a field of work in which you have some understanding and experience;
- higher education leading to a degree: this will be more time-consuming, involving a year or more at a community college or university, but will enable you to apply for a wider range of jobs. Grants and low-interest student loans are often available, especially for those with the greatest desire, aptitude and financial need;
- a course to help you acquire new skills: so you can change career direction;
- a course usually offered through community colleges and business schools to enable you to set up your own business.

You can seek guidance on any of these options from:

- temporary staffing or employment agencies in most cities;
- community colleges, business or technical training schools, and universities;
- employment offices and local job (or career) centers associated with state, or local governments;
- local, state or national women's associations;
- regional offices of the federal Small Business Administration.

9. Prepare Yourself

If you have been away from work for a long time, prepare yourself to return by doing voluntary work for a local non-profit organization, your church, or local government. Treat it as you would paid employment; learn from mistakes and experiences, and get used to working within time constraints.

10. Build Your Own Networks

Consider joining a network of working women. You will be able to share experiences and develop new contacts—particularly useful if some of the women are managers responsible for hiring, or if you are setting up your own business.

11. Draw Up a Résumé

Draft a résumé listing your education and qualifications, jobs to date, and relevant skills and experience. Seek help from family, friends, or a career adviser in refining the draft. Have the final version printed on quality paper. Consider having matching business cards made, with your preferred job title or skill listed, along with your phone and e-mail address.

12. Begin Searching for a Job

Begin looking at advertised and nonadvertised sources of employment: temporary staffing and employment agencies, newspapers and the Internet. Send your résumé and a cover letter to every potential employer in your geographic area and to people in businesses you've met (see steps 4, 10 above) through a variety of personal contacts and networking.

DOS AND DON'TS

For Women Returning to the Workplace

DO

- Be positive: take small steps initially to build your confidence.
- Get the support of your partner, family, and relatives.
- Develop a network of working women and men who can advise you, advocate on your behalf with their employer and even, perhaps, hire you.

DON'T

- Don't undertake extensive retraining or re-skilling before researching the local employment situation thoroughly.
- Don't sell yourself short, in terms of the valuable experiences you've had.
- Don't be easily discouraged; perseverance will be an added skill when you find that job.

13. Draw Up a List of Questions to Ask Employers

Focus on what is important to you, for example:

- onsite childcare;
- flexible leave arrangements to care for elderly or disabled relatives;
- training to help you develop;
- opportunities for promotion.

THOUGHT STARTERS

- Where would you like to see yourself in ten years? Will the goals you have set allow you to get there?
- What is your real priority in returning to work? Will your chosen route deliver this?
- What barriers are in your way? List them.
- How can you overcome these barriers?
- What would you do if you knew you could not fail?

For More Information

Books:

Figler, Howard E. *The Complete Job Search Handbook: Everything You Need to Know to Get the Job You Really Want.* Amawalk, NY: Owl Publishing Company, Owl Books, 1999.

Longson, Sally. *Women Returning to Work: How to Work Out What You Want and Then Go Out and Get It.* Oxford: How To Books, 2000.

Web Sites:

Equal Employment Opportunity Commission: **www.eeoc.gov**

Office of Personnel Management: **www. opm.gov/wrkfam/index.htm**

"I look forward to the day when we don't think in terms of a woman executive at all, but just an executive."

(Ellen Gordon)

Developing a Career Plan

CHECKLIST

This checklist is designed for anyone embarking on planning and managing a career.

Definition

Career planning is in itself a straightforward process of understanding, exploring, and decision making, reflecting on your life, family, and work in a wider context. What complicates it is that careers and organizations are constantly changing. Careers have been defined as "a set of improvisations based on loose assumptions about the future".

Advantages

- Understanding yourself. Time spent on reflection is never wasted, as everyone has a unique mix of skills, strengths, and limitations that change over time.
- Gaining clarity, so that when opportunities emerge you are able to make informed choices.
- Monitoring progress. A realistic and achievable plan helps you gauge your progress.

Disadvantages

There are no real disadvantages to planning your career—the only disadvantages arise if you plan badly.

- Impracticality. People often have unrealistic aspirations. Be sure to run your ambitions by other people—colleagues, mentors, family, and friends.
- Limited thinking. It is easy to view yourself as occupying the same type of job forever; this can narrow your career possibilities dramatically.
- Inflexibility. Overly detailed planning leaves you little or no scope for responding to the changes in circumstances that will inevitably occur.

Action Checklist

✔ 1. Who Am I?

The foundations of any plans for the future are based on your understanding of who you are, what is important to you, and what your dreams and plans are for the future. This understanding can help you begin a process of decision making about your future. Some simple questions can help you reflect on your career.

- What has triggered my moves in the past?
- What are the significant influences on my life, and how have they affected my career?
- What are my skills?
- What do I see as my strengths?
- What are my limitations?
- What have my successes and failures been?
- What are my core values?
- What are my current obligations and commitments?
- Do I have talents that I feel are underdeveloped?
- Do I feel as if I'm in a rut?
- Do my answers to these questions reflect an accurate picture? How do others see me?

✔ 2. What Do I Want?

Once you have completed a review of where you are, begin to focus on the future—where you see yourself going. You should not be restricted by the normal constraints of realism at this stage. Ask "Where do I see myself in the short, medium, and long term?"

✔ 3. What Options Do I Have?

There are two basic options—to make changes or to make no changes. But there are many more secondary options if, for example, you decide:

- to make a big change in one area;
- to make a small change in one area;
- to make several small changes;
- to plan changes over a long period;
- to make changes as soon as possible.

✔ 4. Make No Changes

You may decide that you don't wish to make any changes to your life at this stage. It could be that your current life matches your vision of your ideal life. Or, from reviewing your obligations and commitments, you may decide that this is not the right time to be making any changes, and that plans for the future should be deferred for a while. Whatever your reason for opting for no change, it should be a positive and conscious decision instead of one arrived at from feeling "but I have no choice!"

✔ 5. Change Your Current Job

Within your current job there are bound to be ways to enhance what you are doing and so increase the satisfaction you gain from it. Here is a list of suggestions. Not all will be appropriate for you, and you can probably add others.

- Undertake a new project.
- Organize a visit to another department.
- Participate in a job swap.
- Volunteer for new responsibilities.
- Look for alternative ways of doing things.
- Offer to coach new juniors.
- Negotiate for a redefinition of your job to include more challenge.
- Shadow a colleague.
- Investigate the options of part-time work, job-sharing, or flexible employment.

✔ 6. Change Yourself

The key to changing your situation may lie in changing yourself, for example, by learning new skills or updating rusty ones, by defining more realistic expectations for yourself, by setting yourself more ambitious targets, or by reexamining old attitudes. Here are a few suggestions.

- Attend a course or training program.
- Start working on an advanced degree.
- Encourage feedback.

"Make sure it isn't possible for a lesser man or woman to seize your clothes." (Dennis Stevenson)

DOS AND DON'TS

For Developing a Career Plan

DO

- Apply your management skills to managing your career.
- Audit where you are now.
- Evaluate how you can fill the gaps.
- Think about necessary changes.
- Ask for feedback.
- Talk to others and develop your network.
- Update your career plan regularly.

DON'T

- Don't depend on others to recognize your potential.
- Don't devolve responsibility for your career onto your organization.
- Don't take thoughtless risks—you should be making informed choices.

- Seek advice from someone you respect.
- Consult a career counselor.

7. Change Your Job

Within any organization there may be opportunities to find something nearer your ideal job. Given that we operate in the real world, you need to stay grounded when making career plans, but try to think creatively to find as close a match as you can between what you want and what is available.

- Can you identify gaps in your skills?
- Could you use your time constructively to update old skills or learn new ones?
- Should you polish up your interview techniques?
- Does your résumé need revising?

There are no guarantees that the right job will become available at the right time or, that when it does, your application will be successful. Don't limit yourself by thinking only about opportunities that offer promotion; it may be time to think about a sideways move to broaden your experience or to increase your job satisfaction. Looking internally for opportunities is not as simple as looking at internal vacancies. It may be useful to follow up contacts or establish new ones in the particular areas you are attracted to.

8. Update Your Plan

As time goes on you will probably find that you overestimated some of your abilities and underestimated others, that you have discovered capacities you didn't realize you had, that circumstances have made some skills redundant and others more important, and so on. Your plan will need revision—you should go through the processes outlined here at least every three years.

THOUGHT STARTERS

- It has never been as important as it is today to manage your career. Never devolve this responsibility onto anyone else—it is central to your well-being.
- It's not the most qualified people who get the best jobs—it's those who are most skilled at managing their careers and finding opportunities.
- Getting the perfect job is a job in itself.

For More Information

Books:

Bridges, William. *Creating You & Co.: Learn to Think Like the CEO of Your Own Career*. Cambridge, MA: Perseus, 1998.

Johnstone, Judith. *Building Your Life Skills: Who Are You, Where Are You and Where Do You Want to Go: A Personal Plan*. Hudson, MA: Pathways, 2000.

Web Site:

Career Web: **www.careerweb.com**

See also:

☆ **Taking Charge of Your Career (pp. 324–25)**
✔ **Finding Your Calling and Living Your Passion—The Dream Job (pp. 744–45)**

"Inventors and men of genius have almost always been regarded as fools at the beginning (and very often at the ends) of their careers." (Fyodor Dostoevsky)

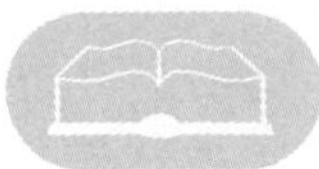

WORK-LIFE BALANCE

This checklist suggests ways in which managers can improve the work-life balance of employees. It focuses on an organizational approach, involving the assessment of the needs of employees, and the establishment of a work-life policy and benefits system.

DEFINITION

Work-life balance is an integrated and harmonious blending of the needs of an organization with the family and private commitments of its employees. There are clear business benefits to organizations in recognizing family and other external pressures on its employees, and in making provision to enable employees to deal with those pressures. The balance usually relates to flexible hours, times of work, and related working practices.

Achievement of a work-life balance is important for all staff, not just those with young children.

ADVANTAGES

If employees maintain a good balance between work and home life, this can result in:

- better employee performance and increased productivity
- higher morale and lower staff turnover
- lower absence and sickness rates
- reduction in burnout and stress
- better recruitment and retention of staff
- improved company image

DISADVANTAGES

- Improved company performance will take time to become apparent, and will take time and effort to get right.
- In downsized or delayered companies, flexible working arrangements may result in some employees taking on more in order for others to do less.
- If not introduced equitably, some employees may resent others.
- Flexible or remote working may make it difficult to maintain an organization's structure and culture.
- Once policies are introduced, it may be difficult to change them, even if the company runs into difficulties.

ACTION CHECKLIST

1. FIND OUT WHAT EMPLOYEES' NEEDS ARE, AND HOW FAR THEY ARE BEING MET

First establish what types of work/home conflicts your employees are experiencing. You might assess their home situation (for example, the proportion of employees with children or elderly dependents), and the consequences of home commitments (such as the amount of overtime worked, or number of days of missed work). Use exit interviews to find out if balance issues contributed to employees' departures. Set up focus groups or conduct surveys. Involving employees from the start will help overcome resistance to change.

Use the results to establish a business case for improving work-life balance. Relate it to the bottom line, and begin communicating your intentions to the most influential people in the organization, and to interested parties such as staff associations and trade unions.

Before proceeding, it is vital to identify financial resources and key personnel to carry out the implementation and to keep it running.

2. FOCUS ON ORGANIZATIONAL CULTURE

The culture and atmosphere of your organization must be conducive to flexibility, innovative work practices, and empowerment. Trust is a vital component. Not only will managers have to ensure that flexible benefits will not be abused, but employees must not be made to feel disloyal, resented, or poor performers if they take advantage of the benefits. Rather than putting an emphasis on presenteeism, it should be shifted on to performance and results.

Look at the organization structure, and consider if it enables or constrains work-life balance. A traditional hierarchy with a command-and-control approach may not be suited to effective implementation of the necessary new measures. A flatter organization, in which employees work in teams and are empowered, may make this easier. It is important that managers themselves set a good example, and that work-life balance becomes integrated into the culture of the organization at all levels.

3. IMPROVE PERSONAL AND ORGANIZATIONAL EFFICIENCY

An important part of achieving a work-life balance is ensuring that the "work" part of the equation is carried out as smoothly as possible. Time management, delegation, prioritizing, and handling information to avoid overload are all skills that can reduce both stress and hours worked, while maintaining the same level of productivity. This might impact on home life, for example, by eliminating the need to take work home, or making employees less tired and stressed in the evenings.

Consider also ways in which organizational procedures and activities could be improved in order to make employees' working lives less frenetic, stressful, or tiring.

4. SET UP WORK-LIFE POLICIES AND BENEFIT ARRANGEMENTS

There is no one approach that will create balance: a flexible set of policies should be set up to cover as many aspects and different situations as possible. Consider the following.

- Flexible working hours—allowing employees to organize working hours to accommodate important aspects of their home lives.

"The most successful people are those who take pride in their work, pride in their family. . ."

(Kemmens Wilson)

  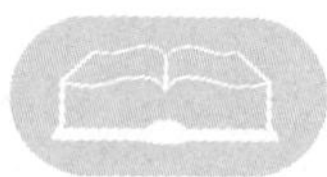    

DOS AND DON'TS

For Work-life Balance

DO

- Make sure that your work-life policy is inclusive and that every individual can benefit from it.
- Give the work-life initiative a catchy title.
- Communicate the policy and make sure everyone knows what is available.
- Make sure that supervisors are supportive and do not discourage employees from making flexible arrangements.
- Minimize red tape so that signing up to new arrangements is quick and easy.

DON'T

- Don't try to impose a work-life balance, or introduce it without consultation and cooperation.
- Don't assume that you only need to target parents or employees with elderly dependents.
- Don't think that flexibility is only appropriate to certain work settings.

- Self-rostering—teams of employees working out their own hours, accommodating each others' needs.
- Buddy system—pairing people up so that they can cover for each other, enabling each to take time off when necessary, knowing that someone else will take over their duties and responsibilities.
- Flexible working location—working from a different office or from home, either permanently or on an ad hoc basis, may help employees cope with family responsibilities and reduce or eliminate commuting time.
- Special leave availability—consider, for example, an allowance of paid or unpaid leave each year, to give employees time to cope with personal crises, and family and household emergencies, without using up their holiday allowance.
- Career breaks—these could be of varying length, and used for study, travel, bringing up children, voluntary work, or many other activities that can improve both home and working life.
- Counseling, advice, and information sources—not just confidential counseling on work-related issues, but also on family matters, such as childcare providers, and medical or financial advice, and so on.
- Childcare/eldercare subsidies—a workplace nursery may not be feasible, but subsidized places in local nurseries or nursing homes may be an option.
- Concierge services—these make it easier for employees to conduct their day to day household tasks.

It may not be possible to cater for every situation, in which case a cafeteria-style benefits system could be considered. This sets out a list of priced benefits, and each employee can "buy" whichever benefits they choose with their fixed annual allowance. Alternatively, certain benefits could be traded for a cut in salary.

Take into account employees' ideas. If an employee can make a business case for a change to his or her way of working, then the idea should be tested. This kind of suggestion scheme may prove more responsive to individual circumstances than a rigid set of policies.

Bear in mind at all times the legislation and best practice surrounding equal opportunities and diversity.

5. Inform and Train Managers

The achievement of balance depends not just on the policies chosen, but on their implementation. This must be consistent across the organization. Managers should receive training in the variety of benefits available, and in counseling employees to choose the right combination. Work-life issues could be incorporated into annual training plans and performance appraisals. Stress that take-up of flexible benefits in no way affects promotion prospects, recognition, or other job opportunities.

6. Communicate the Policies and Benefits

Inform employees of the options available. Consider incorporating the information into an employee handbook in an easy-to-understand way. Ensure all staff have access to the handbook, either in paper or electronic format.

7. Evaluate Work-life Balance Success by Measuring Employee and Customer Satisfaction

It is important to maintain the advantages of a good work-life policy by keeping it relevant and up-to-date. By measuring employee satisfaction and performance, and assessing factors such as retention rate, the effectiveness of the policies can be evaluated. Constant monitoring, feedback, and adjustment will ensure the policies and their implementation are working well.

THOUGHT STARTERS

- Do you know how many days taken as sick leave in your organization are genuine?
- If a member of staff is consistently late for work, do you know why?
- Do you feel your loyalty would be questioned if you discussed home or family commitments at work?

For More Information

Books:

Harvard Business Review on Work and Life Balance. Boston, MA: Harvard Business School Press, 2000.
Getting the Right Work Life Balance. London: Chartered Institute of Personnel and Development, 2000.

Journal Articles:

McBain, Richard. "Work, Family and Life: The Benefits of Achieving Balance." *Journal of General Management 26*, no. 3 (Spring supplement, 2001): 24–34.
"Work Life Balance." IDS Study no. 698 (November).

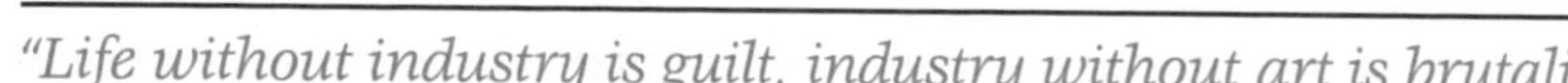

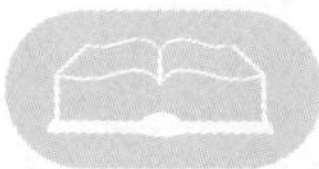

TRAINING NEEDS ANALYSIS

CHECKLIST

This checklist lays out the steps for implementing training needs analysis (TNA).

Effective training or development depends on knowing what results are required—for the individual, the department, and the organization as a whole. With limited budgets and the need for cost-effective solutions, all organizations need to feel secure that the resources invested in training are targeted at areas in which training and development is needed and a positive return on the investment is guaranteed. Effective TNA is particularly vital in today's changing workplace as staff exposed to new technologies and flexible working practices need to update their skills on a regular basis.

Analyzing and identifying training needs are prerequisites to any effective training program or event. Simply throwing training at individuals may miss the highest priority needs, and perhaps cover areas that are not essential. The analysis of training needs is not a task solely for specialists. Managers today are responsible for many facets of people management, including the training and development of their team; they should therefore understand TNA and be able to implement it successfully.

DEFINITION

A training need has two defining features.

- It is any shortcoming, gap, or problem that prevents an individual or organization from achieving its objectives.
- It can be overcome or reduced through training and/or development.

A training need can arise at either the organization, the activity, or the individual level. For our purposes an organization can be regarded not only as the whole company, but as any department, section, or team with its own objectives.

At the organizational level a training need is any behavior or lack of skill that hinders the achievement of corporate objectives; for example, a lack of customer service skills that harms the business or a lack of interpersonal skills that negatively affects staff retention.

At the activity level a training need applies to everyone doing the same work. All tire fitters in a company need to learn to use a new piece of machinery, for example, while the members of the sales team do not.

At the individual level a training need occurs when an individual lacks skills, knowledge, or understanding, or when certain behavior prevents someone from being successful. If receptionist A has a professional telephone manner while receptionist B, who does the same job, is abrupt and offhand, then B has a personal training need.

ADVANTAGES

Training needs analysis:

- targets resources at identified priorities;
- enhances organizational ability to plan for and adapt to changes in the workplace;
- helps individuals and teams perform better, improving their job satisfaction, morale, and motivation;
- flows naturally from the appraisal process, in which staff discuss which of their skills need to be improved and how;
- provides a constructive base for improving performance.

DISADVANTAGES

There are no disadvantages to the process, but TNA does require:

- time and energy to plan the analysis systematically and analyze the results;
- the coordination of the results among managers to ensure that an organizational plan reflects corporate priorities, allowing for economies of scale and avoiding duplication across departments;
- the full involvement of, and discussion with, potential trainees instead of faster but one-sided evaluation by their managers.

Ideally, it also means training managers in the process of TNA itself so that they understand what they are trying to achieve and what their approach should be.

ACTION CHECKLIST

Training needs can be sorted broadly into three types:

- those you can anticipate;
- those that arise from monitoring;
- reactions to unexpected problems.

1. COORDINATE TRAINING NEEDS

Training needs that exist in one department are likely to exist in others. It is pointless for individual managers to throw their own limited resources at each problem as it arises, duplicating efforts and dissipating energy. Most organizations have a personnel function that organizes training delivery. You may not be the person who coordinates the system, but you have an important role to play in gathering the best information you can about the training needs of your staff and passing it up the line. At the very least, cooperate with other managers to coordinate your training needs so the company integrates its training and development activities.

2. ANTICIPATE NEEDS IN YOUR OWN SPAN OF CONTROL

Anticipated needs often appear at the organizational or activity level. You know, for example, that a new machine coming into a workshop or office will almost certainly have training implications for everyone using it. Similarly, a company that decides to enhance customer service as part of its corporate strategy knows that a program of training and development is essential for its success.

"Education and training are decisive, and the single greatest long-term leverage point available to all levels of government."

(Michael Porter)

3. Develop Monitoring Techniques

Some problems that fall into the category of training needs can go unnoticed while they creep up on the organization. Active monitoring systems will help you spot these.

One approach to monitoring is variance analysis. This sounds technical, but it is a simple tool used by managers to monitor budgets, and it translates neatly to the identification of training needs. When a budget is agreed on, it is broken down into projected monthly expenditure. Any major variance from the forecast—upward or downward—triggers an investigation into why it occurred and what the results will be.

In TNA, the budget numbers are replaced by specific performance standards and indicators. Even in a "soft" issue like customer satisfaction, you can set a standard that 95 percent of customers should feel they received excellent service. Carrying out customer satisfaction surveys allows you to measure any deviation.

Asking questions in appraisal interviews is a form of survey since the same basic issues are addressed throughout the organization. A fundamental purpose of appraisal is to identify individuals' training needs.

It is also worthwhile to interview staff and customers to help identify specific problems. Regularly ask a random sample of people for their views on the same set of questions relating to general performance, for example, customer satisfaction levels.

4. Keep an Open Mind in Analyzing Problems

Monitoring will indicate where gaps and problems exist, but be careful not to rush into the wrong assumption to explain a particular set of circumstances. As an example, it may seem natural to conclude that unusually rapid staff turnover in a small section is due to shiftwork; however, exit interviews may indicate that cramped working conditions and poor ventilation are to blame. Training cannot resolve this problem, even though the monitoring process has helped you identify it.

5. Identify the Level

A training need might be limited to an individual or an activity, but it is more likely to impact on at least two, and perhaps all three, levels.

If the company generally treats customers as a nuisance, it needs to change its overall approach. Giving one or two people training addresses the training need at the wrong level; organizational development is needed, not individual training sessions.

6. Take Appropriate Action

If the training needs are within your own span of control, probably at individual or maybe at activity level, you can plan action to meet the needs.

If the needs appear to be at a wider level than the one you control, you need to make recommendations and proposals on a wider front.

DOS AND DON'TS

For Training Needs Analysis

DO

- Take TNA as seriously as you do the delivery of training.
- Coordinate your findings with those of other managers.
- Remember to consider potential needs at the organization, activity, and individual level.
- Include yourself as someone with potential training needs.

DON'T

- Don't arrange any training without first establishing that there is a clear need for it.
- Don't simply send everyone on the same training event that you found useful and enjoyable—individuals have different backgrounds and experiences, so they have unique training priorities.
- Don't concentrate on obvious training needs at the expense of those you need to search for (for example, with monitoring systems).

THOUGHT STARTERS

- How much of the training budget do you think was wasted last year—and why?
- What training do your people need that has not been arranged and is not likely to be? Why is this?
- Have you ever been sent on a course that you felt was irrelevant to your needs?
- Consider the motivational impact on your team of attending an engaging and worthwhile event.

For More Information

Books:

Hargrove, Robert. *Masterful Coaching: Extraordinary Results by Impacting People and the Way They Think and Work Together.* New York: Pfeiffer and Co., 1995.
Peterson, David B., and Mary Dee Hicks. *Leader As Coach: Strategies for Coaching and Developing Others.* Minneapolis, MN: Personnel Decisions International, 1996.

See also:

✓ **Evaluating Training (pp. 424–25)**
✓ **Mentoring in Practice (pp. 368–69)**
✓ **Solving Problems (pp. 408–09)**

"I must say that acting was good training for the political life that lay ahead of us." (Nancy Reagan)

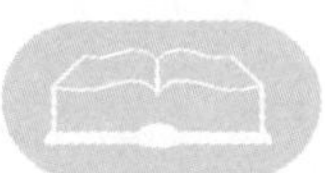

Evaluating Training

CHECKLIST

This checklist provides line managers with ideas and key points to incorporate in their employees' training programs and help assess the effectiveness of training. It should be read in conjunction with the related checklist on Training Needs Analysis. It is not written for trainers themselves.

Virtually all training events end with participants completing an evaluation form. Evaluations may fail to indicate, however, whether the participants actually learned anything useful or how that knowledge can be transferred to the workplace.

Evaluating training is a continuous process of defining training objectives, identifying training needs, delivering programs to meet those needs and objectives, evaluating trainees' reactions to the training, seeking evidence of skills or knowledge learned and their implementation in the workplace, and measuring the effects of training on bottom-line results.

It is not always possible to perform such evaluation in depth, but that is not to say that nothing should be done at all. The key is to have a training objective and put some indicator(s) in place to see whether that objective is met. In this way it should be possible to get some idea of your return on investment.

Definition

Evaluation is an analytical process of estimating the value of something. In the case of training, it focuses on whether the time and money spent on training have achieved the required results.

Advantages

- Broadly, evaluation can tell you whether what you have done has worked.
- It confirms that financial resources have targeted identified priorities.
- It tells you whether desired improvements in individual performance have been achieved.
- If training has not achieved its objectives, the evaluation provides information that should help you to improve it next time.
- The information gained feeds into the staff appraisal process and helps managers discuss progress with individuals.
- Individuals and teams know what results are expected from training before they start, raising their commitment to, and involvement in, the training itself.
- Evaluation shows clearly where the organization stands in terms of staff development and provides information about performance to use in planning future training.

Disadvantages

Successful evaluation of training requires:

- a commitment to training as an important and central business function rather than an optional or non-essential activity;
- the adoption of a disciplined and active planning approach rather than a reactive management style distracted by putting out fires;
- the allocation of valuable management time to a careful consideration of what is to be achieved and measured, and how to measure it, before training is planned;
- the commitment of time and resources to detailed analysis afterward.

Action Checklist

1. Define What You Want Training to Achieve

Remember the evaluation process starts as soon as you begin constructing a training plan. Having identified needs, quantify as specifically as possible what results and outcomes you expect. This can often be relatively easy to define, for example:

- to operate a machine safely;
- to use a graphics package;
- to set up a Web site;
- to construct widgets using new technology.

In many cases these outcomes can be specified and measured by occupational, organizational, or national standards.

It is much harder to set measurable targets when it comes to training designed for teaching skills, transferring knowledge, or changing behavior. Building up knowledge and experience in specific areas is fundamental to development, but it is difficult to quantify. It is essential to work with trainees to specify expected outcomes—for example, more effective selling behavior.

2. Turn Targets into Objectives

Objectives tell you what is to be achieved, by when. They should be SMART: Specific, Measurable, Achievable, Realistic, Time limited. A training objective specifies what you can realistically expect the trainee to know or be able to do as a result of the training.

If the training is to teach a skill, for example, the measure of success might be that within six weeks of the end of training, the trainee will be able to type a ten-page report containing no more than six mistakes within an hour.

In devising objectives for knowledge-based training, avoid the word "understand"—it is not a measurable concept. Say instead that the trainee should be able to "state", "explain", or "describe" the subject. These are checkable, and the trainee will need to have absorbed the knowledge in order to meet the objective.

"For the bold new world of the 21st century. . .every adult American must be able to keep on learning for a lifetime."

(Bill Clinton)

3. Publicize the Objectives

Make sure everyone knows the objectives from the start. "Everyone" includes:

- the trainees, whose should be advised of the objectives in briefings from their managers and any advance materials they receive;
- their managers, so they know what their staff should bring back from the training program;
- the trainers–this may sound obvious, but they need to design the training based on what it should achieve rather than which areas they have experience in (which may be different). Where the training is to be provided by an outside agency, make sure that the provider can meet the objectives you specify.

4. Design Methods for Comparing Results with Objectives

The best way to do this is to get people together to come up with one agreed and consistent approach. It may involve a post-training action plan, a debriefing session after trainees return to the workplace, forms, questionnaires, observation checklists, feedback meetings, or statistical data. The key point is that you must design the assessment procedures at an early stage.

Immediate feedback is important, but a realistic time span for evaluating performance improvements is often weeks or even months. You need to allow time for the training to be applied and practiced, leading to the actual outcomes you want to evaluate.

5. Evaluate the Input

Remind trainees to keep their objectives in mind throughout the training and to talk to the trainer if their needs are not being met. If the training is provided by an outside agency, ask the trainees for a summary of their response to the course at a debriefing session when they return. Encourage them to be honest in giving their opinion of the value of the training.

6. Evaluate the Impact of the Training on Performance

The process of evaluation is a matter of comparing results with expectations. Encourage trainees to produce a realistic action plan to implement what they have learned once they are back at work. In the longer term, perhaps three months afterwards, ask the trainees what the training has helped them to achieve.

7. Use the Results

Use the information provided by the evaluation in starting the training cycle again and planning what needs to be tackled next and how. Evaluation sets out key facts and measures of progress more clearly than any sort of gut reaction or guesswork.

DOS AND DON'TS

For Evaluating Training

DO

- Specify the outcomes and results required.
- Establish measurements for hard-to-measure activities. Even if the best available measurement is rough and ready, it remains the best one available, and it is much better than nothing.
- Design the evaluation procedures at the outset.
- Involve other managers with a stake in the training outcomes.
- Involve the trainees themselves.
- Review with an open mind what the evaluation tells you—mistakes and failures can be more helpful in making continuous improvements than convincing yourself it was really all right when it wasn't.

DON'T

- Don't try to justify poor results with excuses—if there is a lesson to be learned, value it.
- Don't rely on standard written evaluation forms.
- Don't give up—evaluating training is widely regarded as the most difficult aspect of the training function.

THOUGHT STARTERS

- How do you decide now whether training is achieving the right results?
- Wouldn't you like to know which training activities are effective and which can be improved?
- Aren't there some training activities that you already believe either don't work or could be improved, but you haven't got any evidence on which to base a case for improvement?

For More Information

Books:

Bramley, Peter. *Evaluating Training Effectiveness: Benchmarking Your Training Activity Against Best Practice*. 2nd ed. New York: McGraw-Hill, 1996.

Kirkpatrick, Donald L. *Evaluating Training Programs: The Four Levels*. 2nd ed. San Francisco, CA: Berrett-Koehler, 1998.

See also:

✔ **Training Needs Analysis (pp. 422–23)**

"When you consider something 'ideal', you lose the opportunity to improve it." (Shoji Shiba)

Planning a Workshop

CHECKLIST

This checklist describes how to plan and run a workshop.

Definition

Workshops are not just meetings, lectures, seminars, or discussions, although they may well contain elements of some or all of these things. They are principally gatherings called in order to tackle a problem or achieve an objective in an informal environment conducive to creativity. Workshops are appropriate for the study of broad issues that deserve deeper analysis than can be achieved in ordinary meetings, or of issues that require brainstorming or imaginative thinking.

Workshops do not have a chair or a leader as such, but a facilitator who creates an open, relaxed atmosphere to encourage contributions from those present. A typical workshop has from four to ten or more participants.

A workshop can therefore be a group event, learning occasion, or training session at which participants are the major contributors or learn from each other, or where the experience of those attending is more important than the knowledge of the facilitator.

Advantages

Workshops are useful when you need to:

- secure group ownership of the objective;
- get maximum contributions from people;
- involve people as fully as possible;
- brainstorm ideas;
- come up with the right questions and constructive alternatives;
- formulate a rough plan of action.

Disadvantages

Workshops are inappropriate if you need to:

- collate or analyze complex or detailed information;
- investigate mistakes or failure;
- make a final decision.

They do not work when some individuals dominate or when people do not want to be there.

Action Checklist

1. Select a Facilitator

Determine whether the facilitator should be internal or external. Internal staff can be used if the issue is not too contentious or complex and if you have a staff member who is an experienced facilitator. Otherwise, you should employ an external facilitator.

The facilitator should feel comfortable with running activity-based sessions and should be able to:

- indicate to participants what expected outcomes or targets are;
- formulate clear plans and tactics for moving the group toward them;
- persuade participants to own what they have achieved at the end.

2. Clarify the Necessary Outcomes

Identify the objectives of the workshop, deadlines to be met, and any opposing ideologies to reconcile. Ensure that objectives are measurable.

3. Identify the Participants

Each participant should be able to make a worthwhile contribution. Pay attention to the best mix of people and to any potential conflicts that will need to be managed.

4. Select a Site

The location you choose needs to have appropriate facilities; do not overlook basic features such as equipment, room size, and atmosphere. Look for space that can accommodate a flexible workshop structure, paying attention to appropriate space for group work. When it is important to step aside and think afresh, consider a location outside the workplace—this frees the participants' minds from preoccupation with work waiting for them a few yards away.

5. Gather Equipment

Think of all the small items that may seem trivial but can be enormously helpful when a session is in full swing, for example, glue, scissors, tape, flip charts and pens that work, paperclips, stapler, etc. Make sure the room layout suits your needs. Seating patterns can make a difference to discussion.

6. Establish Ground Rules

This is particularly important with brainstorming sessions and with groups of mixed seniority, but limit the number of rules—too many rules are likely to inhibit free discussion.

7. Prepare the Participants

You may like to set a pre-workshop task, but keep advance information to a minimum, as the focus should be on group activity. Be aware of preconceived ideas and fears, and be prepared to dispel them.

8. Set a Timetable

Workshops can last from half a day to two or three days, depending on the topic(s). Design the time flexibly, allowing for a comfortable proportion of plenary to small-group sessions. Take into account the concentration required of the participants. Try to work a balanced mix between active and passive sessions. Remain in control, but be flexible when events bypass or overrule your scheduling.

Allow adequate time for coffee breaks—participants need time to absorb ideas and chat informally. If the workshop lasts more than one day, it is often useful to start the first day with lunch so that people can relax and get to know one another.

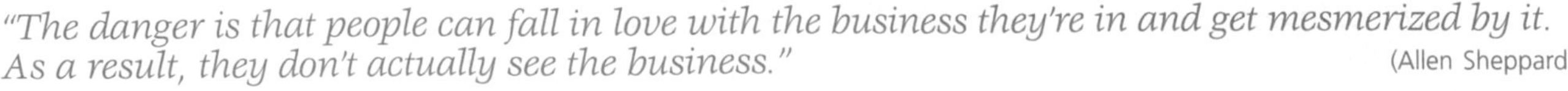

"The danger is that people can fall in love with the business they're in and get mesmerized by it. As a result, they don't actually see the business."

(Allen Sheppard)

  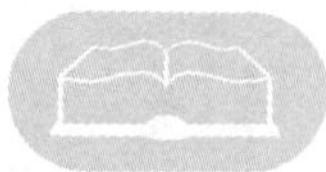    

DOS AND DON'TS

For Planning a Workshop

DO

- Create an informal atmosphere.
- Focus on getting the group to work collectively.
- Adopt tasks and activities that are meaningful to the participants.
- Allow and encourage participants to solve their own problems.
- Get the group to own their findings and recommendations.
- Finish with a summary of what has been agreed or achieved.
- Allocate responsibilities and arrange for a follow-up.

DON'T

- Don't allow things to become too relaxed.
- Don't worry about an individual's nonparticipation at the expense of overall group success.
- Don't spoon-feed participants.
- Don't seek to dominate or try to impress the group with your knowledge.
- Don't spend too much time lecturing or presenting.
- Don't indulge too many red herrings introduced by participants.

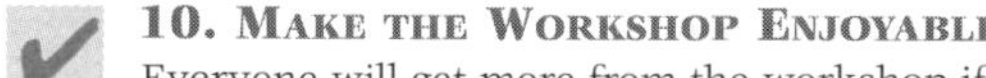

✔ 9. Plan an Opener

An immediate—but appropriate—icebreaker can help establish the atmosphere you wish to create and can also help with introductions. After the icebreaker sets the scene, clarify why you are there and explain the process so that everyone is comfortable with it.

✔ 10. Make the Workshop Enjoyable

Everyone will get more from the workshop if it is an enjoyable experience.

Measuring Workshop Output

Measuring the success or failure of a workshop goes beyond finding out whether participants experienced an enjoyable and constructive group experience. It is measured in terms of:

- the extent that measurable objectives were progressed, advanced, or achieved;
- the changes in thinking, behavior, or activity that have taken place, will take place, or have been confirmed;
- the action that results from the workshop.

THOUGHT STARTERS

- Do you have more than routine: questions to clarify? alternatives to construct? tactics to determine? proposals to clarify? initial decisions to test and agree? techniques to assimilate? skills to practice?
- Do you have people with appropriate experience who can help to achieve the required outcome?

For More Information

Books:

Jones, Ken. *Icebreakers: A Sourcebook of Games, Exercises and Simulations*. 2nd ed. Woburn, MA: Butterworth Heinemann, 1997.

Klatt, Bruce. *The Ultimate Workshop Training Handbook: A Comprehensive Guide to Leading Successful Workshops and Training Programs*. New York: McGraw-Hill, 1999.

Journal Articles:

Hargreaves, J. "How to Make a Workshop Work." *Industrial Marketing Digest* 13:4 (1988): 57–60.

Langley, Mark. "A Case for Workshops." *Training Officer* 24:4 (1988): 116–20.

Lusher, Brian. "Improving Working Relationships: Group Effectiveness Training." *Journal of European Industrial Training* 14:5 (1990): 4–20.

Peters, Bill. "Experiential Workshops for Managers." *Training Officer* 27:6 (1991): 179–81.

See also:

✔ **Brainstorming (pp. 542–43)**
✔ **Handling Effective Meetings (pp. 396–97)**
✔ **Performing a SWOT Analysis (pp. 468–69)**

"Curious people have an appetite for learning new things and they realize the necessity for change."
(Brad Frogger)

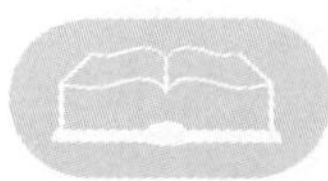

PLANNING CAREER ASSESSMENT AND DEVELOPMENT CENTERS

CHECKLIST

This checklist is for managers who are considering the use of career assessment or development centers in their organization. Although assessment centers have traditionally been used for selection and recruitment, companies are increasingly examining their potential role in training and development and even to help support potential candidates for layoffs.

Such centers typically employ such exercises as leaderless group discussions, formal exercises with rotating leaders, business games, role-play, fact-finding exercises, presentations, structured interviews, in-tray exercises, and paper-based and psychometric tests.

DEFINITION

A career assessment center offers a carefully designed program of job-related simulation exercises in which the performance of a group of participants is observed and appraised by specially trained observers who evaluate each participant against predetermined criteria.

Career development centers are similar in design and structure, but have a very different purpose. Because they are designed to help participants learn more about themselves, development centers generally provide much more feedback from observers.

ADVANTAGES

Career assessment and development centers:

- have a proven high level of reliability in predicting future job performance (three times as high as interviews);
- adhere to a clear structure and logic that are acceptable to participants and easily evaluated;
- offer a reliable and objective way of evaluating people against diverse criteria;
- present a proactive image of the company;
- provide insight into the nature of jobs and the culture of the organization;
- make it easier to present negative feedback to participants;
- prevent poorly qualified candidates from slipping through;
- support the company's strategic processes for human resource management.

DISADVANTAGES

Career assessment and development centers:

- are expensive and demanding to develop and maintain;
- require a high level of expertise;
- necessitate regular training and updating.

ACTION CHECKLIST

1. DEFINE THE OBJECTIVES

Clarify reasons for introducing a center and ensure that the necessary resources are available. Do a cost-benefit analysis on the basis of the current cost of poor selection and predicted improvements in selection success. Thus armed, you will need to sell the concept to the rest of the organization. Don't forget to develop some form of policy statement to provide guidance on future plans.

2. CONDUCT JOB ANALYSES

Effective job analysis is the key to successful assessment and development centers. If the behaviors and the criteria used by evaluators are general and unrelated to specific jobs, the probability of success is much reduced.

The special tools that can be used to analyze job roles include:

- direct observation and work study;
- structured interviews;
- critical incident analysis;
- repertory grid analysis;
- job analysis questionnaires.

3. DESIGN THE ACTIVITIES OF THE CENTER

Designing activities for a successful center is an art as well as a science. Designers need to take into account the following factors:

- the relevance of exercises to the job;
- the participants' backgrounds;
- the relative importance of criteria (weighting);
- an interesting and balanced mix of exercises;
- time and resource constraints.

Experienced designers like to create a matrix or grid of possible exercises mapped against the criteria. After selecting the most relevant items, they create a script for the center that presents the participants with a coherent experience (for example, the center might focus on a key issue or business simulation). The key stages in designing assessment and development centers are:

- establishing a design team;
- producing the first draft;
- trying out the exercises;
- reviewing and editing the exercises;
- developing guidelines for evaluators.

4. TRAIN YOUR EVALUATORS

No matter how well a center has been designed, its effectiveness ultimately depends on the quality of assessment. Evaluators must be carefully selected and prepared. They should be familiar with the requirements of the job, and are therefore often line managers. Key issues for the organization include:

- Who should be evaluators? How do we find evaluators for more senior positions?

"I am a big believer in insight and insightful people are hard to find." (Ric Simcock)

  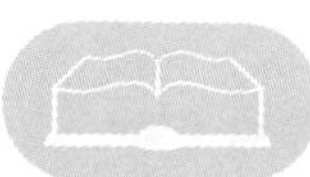    

- How many evaluators do we need? How many participants will there be? How often will centers be held?
- What qualities are we looking for in evaluators? (Commitment, observational acuity, analytical skills, attention to detail, reputation for fairness, counseling experience, etc.)
- What are our training objectives? (Technical knowledge, standards, ability to record behavior, feedback, objectivity, etc.)
- What should the content of the training sessions be?

5. Plan and Administer the Center

Career assessment and development centers require meticulous planning so that, in theory at least, they will run automatically on the day. Issues that need to be considered by the team include:

- the variety and number of people to be brought together, typically an administrator, evaluators, role-players and resource providers;
- the schedule for exercises, probably starting with a group exercise and incorporating variety, adjustable timing, and flexibility to alter the schedule;
- the master schedule or plan showing the time and location of all exercises and individuals;
- room and equipment allocations;
- procedures for briefing evaluators and participants on instructions and expectations;
- checklists for all concerned.

6. Run the Center

It is important to select an able administrator for the center who can deal with every eventuality smoothly. A typical program might go as follows:

- Start the center–check facilities, label rooms, finalize/adjust timetables, prepare rooms, provide photos of participants, brief evaluators, and check paperwork.
- Brief participants on the nature of the exercises, the roles of evaluators, expectations, and feedback arrangements.
- Administer exercises, providing periodic opportunities to review progress.
- Hold a closing session for participants. Hand out evaluation forms, explain feedback and follow-up arrangements, and say thank-yous.
- Hold a debriefing session for evaluators. Complete all work, review and reach agreement on overall ratings, document results, resolve disagreements in ratings, and allocate final responsibilities.

7. Write a Summary Report

The center's report should reflect the main purpose of the center. It normally contains:

- a summary of individuals' performance, usually including recommendations;
- a summary evaluation for each criterion, including ratings and justification;
- development needs and action plans

DOS AND DON'TS

For Planning Career Assessment and Development Centers

DO

- Involve key stakeholders in the process.
- Plan meticulously.
- Brief the participants carefully.
- Ensure that participants are provided with clear feedback on their performance.
- Assume that everything will go wrong on the day—plan for all contingencies.
- Question the design at regular intervals.

DON'T

- Don't initiate career assessment centers unless you are prepared to run them properly.
- Don't allow cost to put you off—career assessment and development centers may be cost-effective when compared directly with the hidden costs of traditional methods.
- Don't assume that good managers automatically make good evaluators.

8. Evaluate and Modify Centers

Career assessment and development centers should continually evolve if they are to serve the organization well. Every center should contain rigorous procedures for quality assurance and there should be regular reviews of the overall design. Jobs change, and new ways of assessing criteria are always emerging.

THOUGHT STARTERS

- Have you ever added up the real cost of unsuccessful recruitment?
- Have you ever considered direct assessment as a way of accurately identifying training needs? Or do you leave it to people to suggest training?
- Have you ever considered the possibility of using career assessment or development centers to identify future career paths for those faced with possible dismissal? Can you always afford to lose those who rush to accept voluntary layoffs?

For More Information

Book:

Ballantyne, Iain, and Nigel Povah. *Assessment and Development Centres.* Brookfield, VT: Ashgate Publishing Company, 1995.

"There's nothing wrong with people trying, but no one has a right to succeed because they think they are clever."

(Alan Sugar)

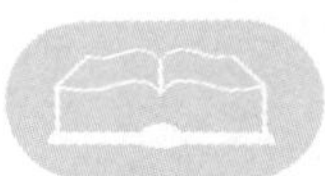

PLANNING THE RECRUITMENT PROCESS

CHECKLIST

This checklist deals with the recruitment process from the moment the current employee resigns or the hiring of an additional staff member is authorized to the drawing up of a short-list of candidates to interview.

Recruitment is an expensive process in its own right, but it can also have costly implications in terms of organizational performance and high staff turnover if recruitment fails to identify appropriate people. To minimize these problems, a planned approach to recruitment allows a systematic review of the organization's employment needs and the best way to achieve them.

DEFINITION

The first part of the recruitment process, before conducting interviews, is concerned with verifying that you have a vacancy. Next, identify the sort of person you are looking for and in what capacity. Finally, seek candidates and make a short-list of those who qualify.

ADVANTAGES

Planned recruitment:

- allows you to verify that you really do have a position to fill;
- offers an opportunity to reevaluate the existing position to see whether the job should be reconfigured;
- lets you decide on what basis you wish to employ somebody;
- ensures that you consider all possible avenues resources for finding the person.

DISADVANTAGES

The process:

- is time-consuming;
- may lead to delays in filling the position.

ACTION CHECKLIST

1. DECIDE WHETHER YOU HAVE A VACANCY

Determine whether you have a need for the work to be performed or whether it could be incorporated into another employee's job. If you have a vacancy, decide whether you need a permanent full-time member of staff. Would a temporary or part-time employee be sufficient? Consider using a staffing agency to supply personnel on the basis you want. Another option is to outsource the work altogether.

2. CONSULT STAFF WHO MAY BE INVOLVED

You will probably need to get authorization from senior management to hire or refill the position. Consider other departments in the organization that may have a vested interest in that position–you could decide to make it a joint effort. Talk to the previous holder of the position where possible, as well as to the relevant supervisor, and especially to the people with whom the new person will work. Consult staff in the personnel department, if you have one, and draw on their expertise. Decide who should interview applicants at various stages in the process.

3. DECIDE WHAT SORT OF PERSON YOU NEED

List the duties, responsibilities, authority, and relationships the job involves. If you are filling an existing position, decide whether the present job specifications are adequate, or whether this is an opportunity to make changes. Decide what qualifications you are seeking in candidates, what type and length of experience are required, and what personal qualities are important. On this basis you can update the job description and personal attributes desired. Fix a starting date and decide what training you are prepared to give and how soon the new hire is expected to be up to speed.

4. FIND OUT WHETHER YOUR EXPECTATIONS ARE REASONABLE

Ask yourself whether you are likely to find the qualities, qualifications, and experience that you are seeking in one person. If so, research the kind of pay and benefits package you will have to offer. This can be done by monitoring local and national advertisements, referring to salary surveys, and networking with other employers in your area and industry sector. This research will also give you a feel for whether you are likely to find qualified candidates locally or whether you will have to look further afield. Start thinking about whether people will want to join your organization and how to attract them.

5. PLAN THE SEARCH FOR APPLICANTS

Start within your own organization. Are there any employees ready for this opportunity? Even if your assessment is negative, make sure that you advertise the position internally, both as a courtesy to staff and because they may pass the information on to interested friends or relatives. Word of mouth can be a valuable recruitment method, but guard against the gender and racial imbalances that this practice may perpetuate. Check the files for previous applications, whether unsolicited or not. Draw on any appropriate contacts you have, for example, in relevant community colleges and universities. These can be useful whether you are looking for apprentices or MBAs. Decide at this point whether to use a recruitment agency to find and qualify applicants for you. Your decision will be based on the time and expertise you have available and the fees charged by an agency. Another source for candidates is job fairs. Many hundreds are held annually, all over the world. They can be targeted at particular audiences, such as recent college graduates, for example, or at the public at large. A good Internet search engine will indicate where upcoming fairs are to be held. Employers could then research how to become part of the fair's offering to job seekers.

6. Decide Where to Advertise

If you are going it alone, and you need to advertise, pinpoint the part of the press you need to contact. Do you want to use local or national newspapers? If the position is a specialist one, you may wish to advertise in professional journals or the trade press. Find out how much ads cost for various sizes and decide what you can afford. Use local job or career centers as well as new media such as the Internet, which has an immense number of job listings and employment opportunities.

7. Write the Advertisement

Decide if you and/or other staff are skilled enough to write an ad. If your organization's personnel department takes on this task, stay involved throughout the process. In the case of a senior position or if you are recruiting in large numbers, it may be appropriate to hire an advertising agency to draft the ad and select publications to place it in. It is better to name your organization in the ad instead of using a box number unless you have particular reasons for secrecy, as a box number may deter some applicants. The ad should state clearly:

- the duties and responsibilities of the job;
- the qualifications and experience required;
- the personal qualities sought;
- where the job is based;
- indications of the salary offered;
- what form of reply is required (letter and résumé or request for an application form);
- whether further information is available and in what form.

The ad should present a picture of an interesting and dynamic organization—it should be considered a public relations document with the potential to impact those who read it, candidates and non-candidates alike. More importantly, check that the ad does not contradict any civil rights legislation such as EEO or ADA for example, discrimination based on factors such as race, creed, sex, age, or physical capability. If you intend to ask applicants to use an application form, make sure this form requests all the details you need to assess the candidates. Complete the application form yourself, or get a colleague to do it, from the point of view of applicants and check its suitability. Prepare an information pack for those who ask.

8. Draw Up a Short-list

Decide on the length of the short-list, probably five or six people at most. You will probably need help reviewing and prioritizing the applications, either from an outside agency or from other staff, supervisors, or managers in your organization. Apart from the saving time, having feedback on the applicants from others is valuable. When reading an application look out for a close match between the candidate and your requirements, any unexplained employment gaps, the quality of presentation, and whether the applicant has tailored the reply to your particular job and organization.

9. Reply to Candidates

Those whom you have no intention of interviewing should be contacted as quickly as possible and dealt with courteously: they, and their relatives and friends, may be future customers or acquaintances of potential applicants. Those whom you do wish to interview should also be contacted quickly, to affirm that they are still interested in the job and, if so, to arrange a date and time to talk. Make sure they know where to find you and tell them whether you are willing to reimburse them for their expenses. You may wish to keep a small number of candidates in reserve.

DOS AND DON'TS

For Planning the Recruitment Process

DO

- Take the opportunity to review whether there is a job to be filled.
- Have a clear idea of who you are looking for.
- Use assistance from at least one other person.
- Assess the market before advertising.

DON'T

- Don't expose your organization to charges of discrimination.
- Don't forget that the recruitment process has public relations implications.

THOUGHT STARTERS

- Is there a high turnover of staff in your organization?
- What led to past recruitment mistakes?
- What is your own experience of being a candidate in the recruitment process?

For More Information

Books:

Ahlrichs, Nancy. *Competing for Talent: Key Recruitment & Retention Strategies for Becoming an Employer.* Palo Alto, CA: Davies-Black Publishing, 2000.

Roberts, Gareth. *Recruitment and Selection: A Competency Approach.* New York: Beekman, 2000.

Shreyer, Ray, et al. *Recruit and Retain the Best.* Waupaca, WI: Impact Publications, 2000.

Wood, Robert, et al. *Competency Based Recruitment and Selection.* New York: John Wiley, 1998.

Web Sites:

Chartered Institute of Personnel and Development: **www.ipd.co.uk**

Industrial Society: **www.indsoc.co.uk**

Institute of Management: **www.inst-mgt.org.uk**

See also:

☆ **Finding and Keeping Top Talent (pp. 33–34)**
✓ **Preparing and Using Job Descriptions (pp. 434–35)**
✓ **Starting a New Job (pp. 410–11)**

"One of the qualities I always seek in marketing people is curiosity." (Raoul Pinnell)

ATTRACTING AND RETAINING PEOPLE REENTERING THE WORKPLACE

CHECKLIST

This checklist is an introduction for organizations seeking to attract and retain people returning to the workplace after a prolonged absence.

Women reentering the workplace will continue to make up a large percentage of new entrants into the labor force over the next decade. From that standpoint, organizations will need to develop a range of policies in order to maximize the benefits that all existing and future employees can bring. So, while this action list deals more specifically with women, many of the same issues and policy solutions would also be applicable to men, regardless of the reason for their absence from the workforce.

DEFINITION

People reentering the workplace refers, in general, to anyone returning to paid employment whether full-time or part-time, after a substantial period away from work.

ADVANTAGES

- You can select from a wider pool of talent at a time of continuing skill shortages.
- Many of these people have maturity and experience, and are likely to be committed and motivated.
- They are likely to be relatively settled and to offer stability: recruitment costs are lower and retention rates higher.
- Women specifically are likely to have good organizational and time-management skills and be well focused.
- Women are especially skilled at multitasking, something many men find difficult.

DISADVANTAGES

- There may be initial costs to update skills or provide confidence-building measures.
- For people with special family or personal circumstances you may wish to offer flexible working practices that could be difficult to extend to all employees.

ACTION CHECKLIST

1. DEVELOP A BROAD HUMAN RESOURCES CORPORATE POLICY

Set out clear policies on recruiting and employing a variety of people, in accordance with federal Equal Employment Opportunity (EEO) laws. You may want to develop a subsection especially dealing with those returning to employment after a prolonged absence. With women, it might be because of caring for family, but for women and men alike, there are many other issues involved in having substantial breaks in an employment history. Where possible, try to obtain examples of comparable organizations' policies; learn from their experiences and those of people in your own organization. Emphasize that the policy is a way of meeting human resource needs and retaining specialist skills, and secure support for it at the highest management level. Communicate the policy to managers, then define and set up the mechanisms for implementing it.

2. ESTABLISH A PROFILE OF THOSE REENTERING YOUR WORKFORCE

Establish a profile of the jobs, levels, and occupations of women and men reentering your own workforce after a substantial break in employment. Use this as a benchmark and review these employees annually, as well as those hired subsequently.

3. WIN ACCEPTANCE FOR THIS TYPE OF EMPLOYEE

Your corporate culture may not fully support this initiative. If there are attitudinal barriers among your staff against employing this type of individual, provide training in equal opportunities (if it is not already available).

4. IMAGINATIVELY REVIEW WORKING PRACTICES

Investigate ways of introducing more flexible hours and flexible working practices to enable anyone with pronounced scheduling issues (for example, family needs, medical appointments, parole and probation meetings) to combine paid employment and other responsibilities: part-time, flextime, job sharing, telecommuting. Make flextime available to all employees, if possible.

5. IMPROVE EMPLOYEES' ACCESS TO CHILDCARE

Only large corporations can offer onsite subsidized childcare, but you can actively help employees to find good quality care elsewhere. Consider sharing day care facilities with other local employers, reserving a certain number of slots at private nurseries, or offering childcare vouchers. Don't neglect after-school care for older children: could you become a partner in local after-school and Boys & Girls Clubs or church programs, for example?

6. PROVIDE PARENTAL AND CAREGIVER LEAVE

Modify existing flextime and extended leave programs to take into account the needs of caregivers, whether for children or other family members. Provide a specific period of paid parental leave, with the opportunity for employees to take longer periods of unpaid leave.

7. PROVIDE APPROPRIATE TRAINING

Offer the opportunity for orientation to all those reentering the workforce to include confidence building and skills updating. Once they are working, provide training to enable these employees to develop and qualify for promotion. Consider family responsibilities when

---

"In politics if you want anything said, ask a man. If you want anything done, ask a woman."

(Margaret Thatcher)

arranging training times. Early morning and evening meetings are often difficult for women, especially single mothers with school-aged children.

8. Examine Your Rules for Promotion Make sure that the policies and procedures you adopt do not run afoul of federal and state EEO intentions (prohibiting discrimination based on race, color, religion, sex, national origin, or age).

9. Consider Extending Maternity Leave or Leave without Pay Provisions Can you provide maternity benefits beyond the minimum to encourage current employees to return after a break? Offer reasonable maternity leave with the option of additional leave without pay for special circumstances without loss of seniority.

10. Set Up a "Stay In Touch" Initiative Enable women on maternity leave and others with similar excused absences to follow developments at work. Provide a company contact person, and arrange regular phonecalls, mailings with copies of in-house newsletters, magazines, and other corporate communications. If appropriate, the arrangement could involve some telecommuting work, and you might consider allowing company computer equipment to be used outside the office for this purpose.

THOUGHT STARTER

- Are you a person who has experienced a long career absence? How did your organization help you? What more could have been done?

For More Information

Book:

Hirsh, Wendy. *Beyond the Career Break*. Springfield, VA: U.S. Dept. of Commerce, National Technical Information Service, 1992.

Web Sites:

Equal Employment Opportunity Commission: **www.eeoc.gov**

Office of Personnel Management: **www. opm.gov/wrkfam/index.htm**

See also:

☆ **Finding and Keeping Top Talent (pp. 33–34)**

✔ **Managing Staff Turnover and Retention (pp. 364–65)**

"For a woman to attain a high level in a male-dominated profession, she has to work twice as hard and/or be twice as smart."

(Elizabeth MacKay)

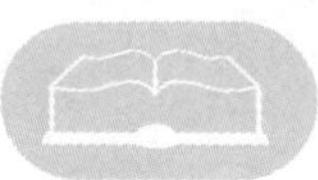

Preparing and Using Job Descriptions

CHECKLIST

This checklist provides guidance for anyone wishing to write a job description or update an existing one.

A job description gives an overview of the purpose of a job, what it contributes to the organization's aims and objectives, how it fits into the overall corporate structure, and, perhaps most importantly, what its main duties, responsibilities, and reporting lines are.

A well-written job description gives the jobholder and immediate line manager a clear overall view of the position, and the human resources department a recruitment tool to help match applicants with the skills, experience, and competencies required in the job. Job descriptions also form a useful basis upon which to conduct performance appraisals, job evaluation, and job grading, and can help identify the duplication or absence of particular functions or activities across the organization. It is important that the descriptions are structured to allow flexibility and forestall "That's not in my job description!" situations.

With constant change now a fact of life in the work world, job descriptions get out of date rapidly and must be revised regularly to reflect current practice.

Definition

A job description is a structured and factual statement of a job's functions and objectives. It should define the boundaries of the jobholder's authority and include the job title, department, job site, and reporting lines.

Advantages

Job descriptions:

- clarify duties and responsibilities;
- are useful in recruiting staff;
- help identify gaps or duplication in the company;
- provide an overview of the functions and activities undertaken by the department or organization.

Disadvantages

Job descriptions:

- can create a "That's not in my job description!" environment if they are too restrictive;
- need regular updating.

Action Checklist

1. Inform Staff of the Reasons for Reviewing and Amending Job Descriptions

When you are reviewing existing job descriptions, it is important that you keep staff fully informed. Explain that the exercise will be conducted with the full involvement of jobholders, the objectives being, for example, to:

- identify all interdepartmental working links;
- update existing job descriptions;
- help with job evaluation or job grading;
- give everyone a clear understanding of how the company is organized.

2. Assign Responsibility

Job descriptions have traditionally been prepared by the personnel department and agreed on with line managers and jobholders. However, many organizations are devolving this responsibility to line managers, with personnel offering guidance and checking for consistency and overlap. The following points should be taken into account:

- Are all key functions and activities listed in order of priority?
- Does each jobholder have a clear reporting line?
- Is there a balance between numbers of staff and any one manager?
- Are there too many reporting levels?
- Is there any overlap within departments or across the organization?
- Are all jobs grouped logically or are some scattered around?
- Are there any gaps or omissions in key functions?

3. Gather Information

The person responsible for compiling the job description should consider:

- what management wants from the job;
- what the jobholder thinks he or she is doing–and what he or she is actually doing;
- what other employees who interact with the jobholder professionally think he or she is doing–and ought to be doing.

You can most easily get this information from informal interviews. It is possible to use questionnaires, but it often takes longer to analyze written data than it does to interview people, and the results tend to be ambiguous.

4. Draft the Job Description

The job description should contain the following:

Basic information. Job title and department. The job title should be brief, descriptive, and clear. Remember that employees consider the status of people with similar job titles to be equal.

Reporting relationships. Give the job title of the person to whom the jobholder reports, and job title(s) and numbers of staff reporting to the jobholder.

Location. Specify the location of the job. If travel is involved, give clear and careful details.

Major functional relationships. Where appropriate, use an organizational chart to show how a job relates to other jobs and fits into the company's structure.

Principal purpose or objective of the job. This should be a short statement describing why the job exists, for

"Be nice to people on your way up because you'll meet 'em on your way down." (Wilson Mizner)

  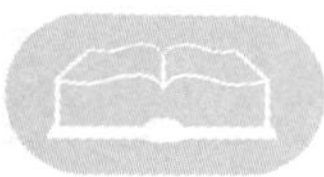    

DOS AND DON'TS

For Preparing and Using Job Descriptions

DO

- Let staff know why job descriptions are being amended or updated.
- Involve the current jobholder.
- Check job descriptions in surrounding areas of work to ensure integration without duplication.
- Update the job description regularly.

DON'T

- Don't restrict the employee's initiative by writing the job description too narrowly.

example, a sales manager's objective might simply read "making sure that sales targets are achieved".

Main duties/key tasks/key result areas. Key tasks or responsibilities are those that make a substantial contribution toward achieving the objectives of the job and the organization. They form the main part of the job. Ideally there should be no more than five or six main tasks. Some basic jobs may have only one or two main activities (for example, stocking shelves and working on the registers in a supermarket), though most may have several elements (bringing in new business, managing existing customers, managing staff, liaising with suppliers, etc.). Secondary duties and responsibilities should also be listed.

The description of each task should include three components:

- a "doing" verb highlighting the main activity (for example, to develop, design, implement, advise);
- the object of that activity (stock levels, existing suppliers, a new computer system);
- its purpose (to reduce costs, improve efficiency, generate new income).

An example of a task description incorporating these components might be "to advise on the selection and implementation of a new computer system to forge closer links with key account customers". Include outcomes ("to expand the existing customer base") in the task description, but not quantified targets. Targets are generally negotiated separately and are better incorporated into regular performance systems or reviews.

The key tasks are usually listed in order of importance or by other agreed criteria such as chronology, frequency of activity, or tasks related to a particular activity.

✔ 5. Update and Review

The job description must be kept up to date and should be examined at least:

- once a year when the jobholder is reviewed;
- whenever the job falls vacant, to ensure that the description still meets the department's requirements;
- after a new jobholder has been working for a few months, to take account of any significant changes in the duties assigned to the position.

THOUGHT STARTERS

- Do you know what's in your job description?
- Would you change your job description in any way?
- Is your job description up to date?

For More Information

Books:

Fowler, Alan. *Writing Job Descriptions*. Woodstock, NY: Beekman, 2000.
Roberts, Gareth. *Recruitment and Selection: A Competency Approach.* Woodstock, NY: Beekman, 2000.

Journal Articles:

Fondas, Nanette. "A Behavioral Job Description for Managers." *Organizational Dynamics* 21:1 (Summer 1992): 47–58.
John, Trevor. "Job Profiles." *Training Officer* 29:3 (April 1993): 86.
Moravec, Milan, and Robert Tucker. "Job Descriptions for the 21st Century." *Personnel Journal* 71:6 (June 1992): 37–38, 43–44.

Web Sites:

HR Guide: **www.hr-guide.com**
HRnext (Human Resources): **www.hrnext.com**

See also:

✔ **Planning the Recruitment Process (pp. 430–31)**

"It's good business for our people to have confidence that we will not lay them off just to help our profit short-term."
(Ken Olsen)

 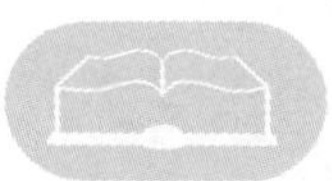    

Implementing Job Evaluation

CHECKLIST

This checklist offers guidance on implementing job evaluation or job analysis in an organization. It does not explain the detail of the various approaches to job evaluation.

Job evaluation aims to
- establish a fair and workable system of differentials between various jobs in the organization;
- eradicate anomalies between similar jobs in different parts of the organization;
- review the jobs that have changed over time;
- calculate the value of a job that is hard to fill.

Job evaluation is a specialized process usually handled by human resource specialists. Department managers and supervisors, however, have a large role to play in helping to define jobs and implementing the results.

Definition

Job evaluation is concerned with the value of a job, especially in relation to other jobs in the organization. It is not about individual employees or their competence or potential, nor is it primarily about pay rates, although it may influence pay structures.

Simple approaches to job evaluation tend to be non-analytical. One such method selects a single job as the benchmark against which all others are compared, and weighs certain factors in every job against the benchmark. Another method is to define a grading structure first, then review job specifications within that framework and make any necessary adjustments.

Analytical approaches involve factor-weighting and point-scoring systems. Each job is examined on a number of key factors such as the size of the budget controlled, the number of supervised employees, the level of direct contact with customers, the technical expertise required, and the potential for affecting the organization's success. Points are awarded for each factor from a predetermined set of specifications (for example, 5 points if 4 or fewer employees report to the position,12 points for 5–15 employees, etc.) and totaled to indicate the importance of the job. The total is then reviewed to take into account any additional factors that affect the value of the job.

Advantages

Formal job evaluation
- results in a relatively objective and unbiased view of the value of jobs;
- gives companies a method to establish a pay scale based on the value of the jobs (rather than on the job title), with more valued jobs getting paid more; simultaneously, it allows the company a means to compare wages paid internally with those elsewhere, for similar work;
- avoids favoritism or patronage as it takes no account of individual jobholders;
- irons out current discrepancies and helps to prevent future anomalies between jobs, which can cause bad feeling, resentment, and demands for parity from employees who feel undervalued;
- provides a transparent approach to valuing jobs once established.

Disadvantages

- The process can be lengthy and costly to plan, introduce, and implement, especially if you take an analytical approach or hire an outside consulting firm to do it.
- There can be an emotional backlash if the program is not introduced with adequate consultation and communication.
- Evaluation requires adequate representation from all levels and functions in the organization–individuals should have no grounds for complaining that they feel misunderstood, unrepresented, or neglected.

Action Checklist

1. Conduct Some Background Research

Before starting, think through all the implications of job evaluation and make sure that this is the route you wish to follow. If so, decide whether you are going to adopt an analytical or a non-analytical approach.

- Decide what you want job evaluation process to achieve (but keep in mind that it may bring other corporate issues to light).
- Consider whether there is an easier and more direct way of tackling this issue, especially if the inconsistencies between jobs in your company are minor, but make sure that any alternative solution is adequate.
- Try to find one or more colleagues in other organizations with experience of the process.
- If you are planning to use a detailed and analytical approach, research it thoroughly, talk to specialists, and read about it–this is not a route to be followed lightly.
- Once you have all the information, perform a cost-benefit analysis. If the benefits significantly outweigh the costs, move on to the next part of the checklist. If not, go back and think through more appropriate ways of achieving your objectives.

2. Decide On Your Approach

Based on the cost-benefit analysis, decide whether to bring in a consultant with an analytical process or to do what you can in-house, perhaps using a less complex methodology.

Plan the next steps carefully, considering essential details such as:
- whether job descriptions are all up to date or they need revision: they form a major element of job evaluation;

- who will be managing the process in-house, either as the prime mover or as the contact person for a consultant;
- how much time you can give this project;
- how much it will cost (job evaluation takes time and resources even if it is done in-house);
- whether you can afford it now or whether it is preferable to wait and build it in as a major project in the coming year.

3. Communicate and Consult

Think carefully about what impression any announcement will give to staff. Damage control at the start is preferable to damage limitation later. Consider what employees might read into the introduction of job evaluation and address possible concerns.

Consult wherever it is appropriate. If you need to talk to unions at some stage, start now: sell the benefits and try to work toward an agreement that both sides can live with.

Communicate so all employees are clear about what is happening, why, when, with what aim, and who will be doing it.

4. Draw Up a Project Plan

Remember that there are three basic elements to the process of job evaluation:

- project design
- data collection
- data analysis

List and time all actions so you know the timeline for each, what preparation is needed for each, what depends on it, and what are the key milestones along the way.

Implementing job evaluation is a significant initiative; draw up a separate plan for managing change. Consider the implications:

- What sort of resistance are you likely to encounter?
- Which factors will help you and which are going to block you?
- Whom can you pick as change agents or champions to help spread the word?

5. Implement the Program

An experienced consultant can advise you on what has to be done and how to go about it. If you are paying for expertise, make sure you use it.

If you are handling the project in-house, stay on top of developments in the project and change management plans; if they were well considered at the planning stage, they should ultimately work.

6. Monitor the Program

After the lengthy process of design and implementation, be wary of the program taking on a life of its own and becoming rigid. As jobs evolve or change, their content will impact on your evaluation framework.

Maintain the program as existing jobs change and new ones are created. You may need a panel or team trained in job evaluation techniques to meet regularly to carry out reevaluations.

DOS AND DON'TS

For Implementing Job Evaluation

DO

- Consider using a consultant—it may seem expensive, but they can take a great deal of the strain and work off your shoulders, and they contribute specialized knowledge and experience.
- Consult and communicate.
- Be aware that under equal employment opportunity (EEO) laws, there should be absolutely no unfairness or discrimination based on race, color, religion, gender, age, or disability.
- Remember that even the most analytical system needs judgment and a human touch to refine scientific results and make them workable.

DON'T

- Don't imagine that job evaluation will automatically save money; it is a process designed to sort out the relationship of value between jobs within an overall structure, not to limit pay.

THOUGHT STARTERS

- Have there been changes in the nature, structure, and design of the jobs in your organization?
- Are there people in your company who seem to have the same degree of responsibility but are paid differently?
- Would you have sufficient time and resources to tackle job evaluation yourself?

For More Information

Books:

Armstrong, Michael, and Angela Baron. *The Job Evaluation Handbook*. Woodstock, NY: Beekman, 2000.
Branuch, Michael T., and Edward L. Levine. *Job Analysis: Methods, Research and Applications for Human Resource Managers in the New Millennium*. Thousands Oaks, CA: Corwin Press, 2001.
Brown, Mark Graham. *Keeping Score: Using the Right Metrics to Drive World Class Performance*. Portland, OR: Productivity Inc., 1996.

Web Sites:

HR Guide: **www.hr-guide.com**
HRnext: **www.hrnext.com**

"The one thing I know through experience. . .is that people don't know why they come to work until they don't have to come to work." (H. Ross Perot)

  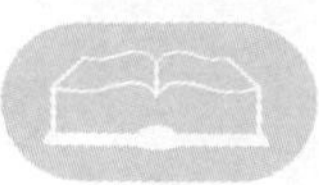    

IMPLEMENTING PERFORMANCE-RELATED PAY (PRP)

CHECKLIST

This checklist is for managers responsible for implementing performance-related pay.

Implementing performance-related pay (PRP) is by no means a total solution for motivating employees and increasing productivity: it is widely recognized that for most people money is not the most important aspect of a job. PRP should always be used in conjunction with other methods of improving employee performance.

DEFINITION

Performance-related pay (PRP) links additional payments to individual employees, over and above basic salary and cost-of-living increases, to appraisal of the individual's performance. Every employee is set objectives at the beginning of the year. Depending on how well the person has done in meeting those targets by the end of the year, the employee is awarded a sum of money that is paid on top of the next year's salary.

PRP is appropriate for both individuals and teams. This checklist concentrates on individual PRP.

ADVANTAGES

Relating pay to performance:

- enhances the performance of individual employees;
- creates a strong link between the company's goals and objectives and employees' goals and objectives;
- improves the retention and recruitment of staff–employees are seen to be rewarded for their efforts.

DISADVANTAGES

Performance related pay:

- may promote competition among employees and undermine team culture;
- can lead managers to ignore informal staff development and performance improvement;
- may award payments based on inconsistent methods and standards of assessment;
- requires substantial time and resources to administer.

ACTION CHECKLIST

1. DESIGNATE A PERFORMANCE-RELATED PAY COMMITTEE

The members of the PRP committee should be drawn from the levels of the organization that will be affected by the new system. Include staff or union representatives and at least one member from the personnel and accounting departments. Appoint a coordinator to oversee the process; this should be someone with project management experience who commands respect and can get things done.

2. DEFINE THE SCOPE AND COVERAGE OF PRP

Will all staff be eligible for PRP, or do you intend to cover a particular group–for example, middle to senior-level managers?

3. GATHER INFORMATION

Find out whether members of the committee or other members of your staff have been involved in PRP before; if so, take advantage of their experience. The coordinator should do some background reading and find out how such systems operate in similar organizations.

4. DRAW UP A PLAN

The five most important points of PRP are that it should:

- be simple and easily understandable by all employees;
- have a clearly defined relationship between the results of the performance rating and the amounts awarded;
- be consistently applied to all staff within departments and throughout the organization;
- include an appeals procedure for employees dissatisfied with their appraisal;
- contain a system of review and evaluation.

Consider the following areas in drawing up the plan:

A Method for Defining Performance Measures. Two approaches are available:

- qualitative–based on criteria for individual jobs (such as job specifications) or more general criteria that cover all jobs within an organization (such as customer service, repeat business, or lack of complaints);
- quantifiable–based on targets (usually financial, but can use other measures such as increasing the number of service-users or reducing processing time for invoices).

The method used will depend on the jobs in question–a combination of both methods can be extremely effective. Limit the number of performance measures on which an employee can be evaluated: ten is generally the maximum, otherwise rating becomes complicated and time-consuming.

A Scale for Rating Performance. Whatever method you use to define performance, you must produce a scale to rate it. Most rating systems use a 6-point scale, for example:

Exceptional
Very good
Good
Satisfactory
Poor
Unacceptable

"He that wants money, means, and content, is without three good friends." (William Shakespeare)

  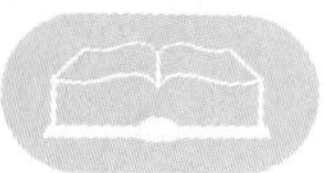    

Assign a numerical score to each division of the rating scale (for example, 6 = exceptional and 1 = unacceptable). The scale can be used to score each one of an individual's performance criteria or targets and the scores added to produce an overall performance rating.

A Link between the Rating and the Pay Award. Link the individual's rating directly to the percentage of the employee's salary to be awarded (for example, the award for a performance assessment of 2 is 4 percent of salary). Do not make awards for anything less than good performance. Inform employees of their awards in person.

A Timetable for Appraisal. Line managers should meet with every employee they supervise throughout the year. At the beginning of the year, they should discuss and set criteria or targets and agree on performance objectives. Regular reviews throughout the year can be used to identify and overcome problems. In final meetings at the end of the year, line managers can discuss performance and rate employees.

The first and final interviews should be formally documented, recording objectives and targets; one copy should be given to the employee and another kept on file.

An Appeals Procedure. It is very important that employees be able seek redress if they feel they have been appraised improperly or unfairly. Let each member of staff know whom to contact if such a situation occurs. This should not, obviously, be the same person who appraised them; the company's personnel officer is generally the most appropriate person.

5. Train Managers to Appraise Performance

Training of managers involved in setting targets and conducting appraisal interviews should:

- begin with the principles of PRP;
- cover in detail the organization's PRP plan;
- coach them in negotiating with employees to arrive at appropriate goals and objectives;
- demonstrate how to conduct an effective appraisal interview and include role-play of performance interviews.

Don't attempt to cover everything in one session. Run refresher courses after PRP is operational, and remember to provide full training for new recruits.

6. Communicate PRP to All Staff

Use team briefings and individual discussions to disseminate information about PRP. Produce a documented guide to the company's PRP plan and include it in the employee handbook. Provide the name of a PRP committee member whom an employee can contact for more information.

7. Pilot PRP

Depending on the size of your company, it may be advisable to concentrate initially on one department or level of management. You can use your experience from this pilot to improve the plan before implementing it more widely. Always start PRP at the beginning of your organization's financial year.

8. Review and Evaluate Your PRP Plan

The PRP committee should meet at the end of each financial year to review how well PRP is working. Obtain the views of the employees and the line managers to identify any problem areas. Do some managers feel unsure about setting objectives or conducting performance appraisals? Look at the award figures—does it appear that some managers are being more lenient or more strict than others? Are some managers featuring in the appeals procedure more than others? Take into account any legislative changes that affect PRP.

Most importantly, decide whether PRP is achieving its objective of improving employee performance. If it isn't, decide whether you can improve your particular plan or whether you should replace it with some alternative reward system. If PRP is succeeding, don't rest on your laurels—keep reviewing and modifying it as needed, and consider the possibility of expanding it to cover other departments or levels of staff.

THOUGHT STARTERS

- Do monetary incentives motivate employees?
- What are the performance objectives for your organization as a whole?

DOS AND DON'TS

For Implementing Performance-related Pay (PRP)

DO

- Design the most appropriate plan for your organization.
- Involve staff representatives or union officials.
- Communicate the advantages of PRP.
- Set clear links between objectives, effort, and reward.
- Train all staff involved in appraisal.
- Continually look for improvements.

DON'T

- Don't make the plan too complicated.
- Don't allow inconsistencies between managers in appraising performance and applying awards.

For More Information

Book:

Brown, Duncan, and Michael Armstrong. *Paying for Contribution: Real Performance-Related Pay Strategies.* Milford, CT: Kogan Page, 1998.

"Wages ought not to be insufficient to support a frugal and well-behaved wage-earner."

(Pope Leo XIII)

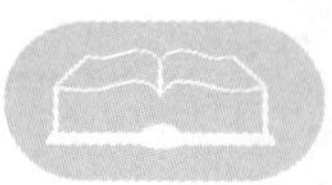

INTRODUCING AN EQUAL OPPORTUNITIES POLICY

CHECKLIST

This checklist provides managers with the basis for introducing an equal opportunities policy. Such a policy is a moral, legal, and business imperative for all line managers.

DEFINITION

An equal opportunities policy is a commitment by an organization to the development of procedures and practices that provide genuine equality of opportunity for all employees, regardless of sex, ethnic origin, age, religion, marital status, or disability. Its reach extends beyond strict compliance with the law and ensures the effective use of all human resources within the organization.

ADVANTAGES

- The ability to attract people with new ways of thinking, leading to a more diverse work force with a richer mix of skills and experience;
- The ability to attract the best talent;
- A more stable work force that retains the best people by seeing that their needs are fully met;
- An improved reputation marking the company as one with high ethical standards.

DISADVANTAGES

- A dissatisfied work force if raised expectations are not met in full;
- Higher recruitment and monitoring costs;
- Resentment or backlash among previously privileged groups in the work force.

ACTION CHECKLIST

1. SECURE THE COMMITMENT OF TOP MANAGEMENT

Demonstrate that the organization is serious about equal opportunities by giving overall responsibility to a senior manager, preferably at board level.

2. DESIGNATE AN EQUAL OPPORTUNITIES OFFICER

Appoint an equal opportunities officer to introduce and implement the policy and coordinate actions on a day-to-day basis. Define the assignment and level of responsibility clearly, even if the position is not full-time.

3. ESTABLISH A WORKING PARTY TO PROVIDE EMPLOYEE INPUT

Set up a working party drawn from representative groups within the organization, including union or staff associations, management, human relations, women, ethnic minority groups, and disabled staff members. Make it clear that the group is not a lobbying point for special interest groups.

4. REVIEW POLICIES OF OTHER ORGANIZATIONS

Obtain copies of the equal opportunities policies of other organizations in your sector. Draw on them to prepare a first draft of your own policy. Include only objectives and commitments that are appropriate to your culture and attainable within a realistic time scale.

6. CONDUCT AN EQUALITY AUDIT

Conduct a workplace audit to provide information about the composition of the work force in relation to gender, race, age, and disability, and use the information as a baseline for action. If the information is not already held in personnel records, conduct an employment survey, making it clear that any information collected will be used only for equal opportunity purposes. Review how many women and men you employ: in total, by grade and salary, by hours of work, by marital/family status, by age, and by ethnic origin. Use this information to identify existing patterns of employment and under-representation.

7. DRAW UP A PLAN OF ACTION

Use the information captured by the audit to identify the areas of the organization that need attention. Decide whether you will require positive action. At a minimum, the program needs to cover recruitment, selection, orientation, promotion, flexible working, and assistance for careers and training.

8. SET TARGETS FOR UNDER-REPRESENTED GROUPS

Set targets that are challenging enough to stretch the organization to change but are realistic enough to show existing employees they have a fair chance of promotion.

9. PROVIDE TRAINING

Provide specific equal opportunities training, first to priority groups such as senior executives, personnel specialists, recruiters, reception staff, and other gatekeepers. Where applicable, these groups should then transmit training through line managers to all employees.

10. OFFER FLEXIBLE WORKING ARRANGEMENTS

Assume that all jobs can be done on a flexible basis unless there is a clear occupational requirement for a full-time employee. Make sure that flexibility in hours is available to all employees.

11. REVIEW JOB DESCRIPTIONS

Rewrite job descriptions as positions become vacant. Be objective and base them on the organization's needs, not on the needs or preferences of the person currently doing the job.

"Inequality is not only about income, where real poverty has grown, it is about self-esteem."

(Will Hutton)

  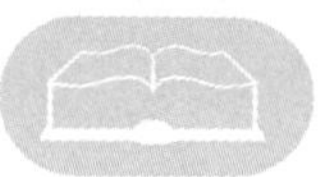    

12. Review Selection and Recruitment Practices

Short-list candidates only on the basis of whether they meet essential skills and knowledge requirements of the job, not on their personal characteristics. Remove personal details from applications before they are reviewed.

13. Adopt Family-friendly Policies

Offer plans for parental leave, childcare, and flexible working to all employees.

14. Monitor Employees' Qualifications and Training Needs

Monitor take-up of training among different categories and grades of employee. Where necessary, make special training available for employees from groups that have traditionally been discriminated against.

15. Offer Comparable Training Programs at All Levels

Your training programs should provide comparable on- and off-the-job training for all employees at every level. Distinguish between training to improve job performance and training to acquire new skills. Let employees know the link between acquiring new skills and the possibility of being regraded.

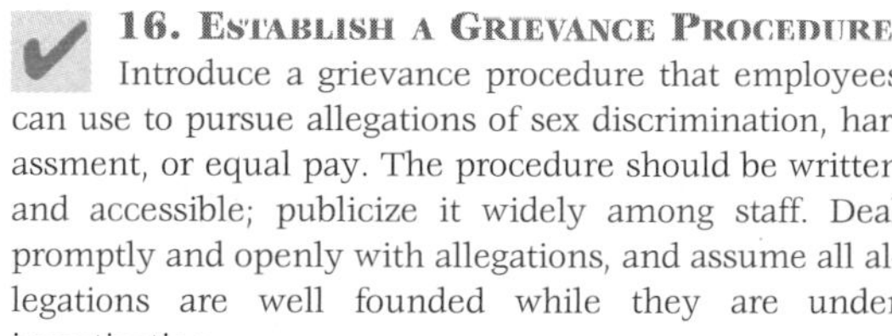

16. Establish a Grievance Procedure

Introduce a grievance procedure that employees can use to pursue allegations of sex discrimination, harassment, or equal pay. The procedure should be written and accessible; publicize it widely among staff. Deal promptly and openly with allegations, and assume all allegations are well founded while they are under investigation.

17. Monitor and Review Procedures

Your equality audit will give details only of your current work force. Set up monitoring systems to capture details of all job applicants and those recruited; establish performance indicators to review progress against your targets and action plan. Monitor internal and external appointments by gender and ethnic origin: you may also want to include age.

DOS AND DON'TS

For Introducing an Equal Opportunities Policy

DO

- Consult employees and union representatives.
- Use positive action measures to meet your equality targets.
- Monitor and review progress annually against the targets and consider whether positive action is needed.
- Beware of bias throughout the recruitment process, especially in interview techniques.

DON'T

- Don't set unrealistically high targets.
- Don't fall into the trap of positive discrimination.
- Don't target flexible working hours and childcare programs solely at women.

18. Communicate Policies and Practices

Send a copy of the policy to potential and actual applicants, new recruits, and current employees. Use every opportunity to publicize the policy (such as your company handbook or intranet, if you have one), and include a clear statement of it in the company literature.

For More Information

Books:

Clements, Phil, and Tony Spinks. *The Equal Opportunities Guide: How to Deal with Everyday Issues of Unfairness*. 2nd ed. Sterling, VA: Stylus, 1997.
Garrett, Helen, and Judith Taylor. *How to Design and Deliver Equal Opportunities Training*. Sterling, VA: Stylus, 1993.

Web Site:

U.S. Equal Employment Opportunity Commission: **www.eeoc.gov**

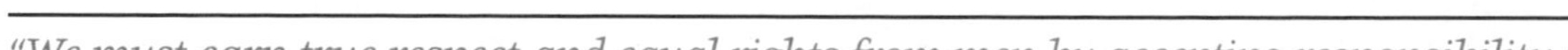

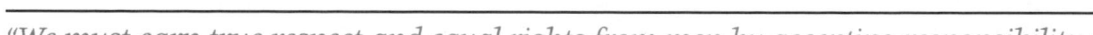

"We must earn true respect and equal rights from men by accepting responsibility." (Amelia Earhart)

 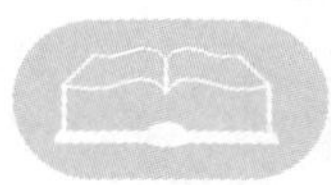    

Implementing a Diversity Management Program

CHECKLIST

This checklist provides a framework for setting up a diversity management program in an organization. It is aimed at managers in all areas and at all levels.

Definition

Diversity encompasses any sort of difference between two or more people. Differences might exist in terms of race, age, gender, disability, geographic origin, family status, education, social background—in fact, any factor that can affect workplace relationships and achievement. Diversity management involves the implementation of strategies through which a network of varied individuals is knitted together into a dynamic work force.

The approach goes beyond that of equal opportunities in that it recognizes an infinite number of differences between people and focuses on the individual rather than various disadvantaged groups.

Advantages

- A diversity management program enables an organization to keep pace with social and demographic changes such as increasing numbers of female, ethnic minority, and older workers in the labor market.
- Employee recognition can lead to empowerment, motivation, and commitment, and therefore to competitive advantage for the organization.
- By encouraging the individual talents of each person, diversity management strengthens the pool of human resources a company can draw on.
- Since diversity management leads employees to feel more valued, it reduces staff turnover, thus reducing recruitment and training costs.
- A diverse work force is better equipped to serve a diverse customer base and diverse markets, and facilitates entry into the global marketplace.
- Diversity management can create a flexible work force, increasing productivity.

Disadvantages

- If handled insensitively, a diversity management program may invade employee privacy.
- Implementation of a diversity management program may be expensive in the short term.
- Deep-seated prejudices may be brought into the open, causing short-term tension.
- Conflict and ill-feeling may result from a poorly handled program.

Action Checklist

1. Gain Support from Top Management

Approach the directors and managers in your organization and convince them of the advantages of diversity management. Present both the business and social cases for a diversity initiative. If necessary, conduct high-level diversity awareness training to develop the commitment of key decision-makers.

2. Commit Financial and Human Resources

Don't underestimate the time and money that will be needed. Take a long view—the program will spread over years, not months. At an early stage identify as many facilitators as possible who can act as change agents to lead the initiative.

3. Set Appropriate Goals

Decide what you want the program to achieve and set goals accordingly. You may want to use consultation, brainstorming, benchmarking, or literature reviews to help you establish goals. Goals should be specific, measurable, and achievable, for example:

- to increase the proportion of women in the work force to 50 percent;
- to enable parents to take time off to care for sick children;
- to draw from a wider geographical area in recruitment.

4. Establish Current Levels of Diversity Management in Your Organization

Plan and conduct a diversity audit to gauge existing levels of diversity management. Assess both qualitative and quantitative evidence, focusing on people, processes, and strategies. Find out:

- which kinds of difference affect the ability of individuals to achieve their working potential in your organization;
- to what extent these differences create disadvantages or advantages for employees;
- how the procedures and strategies of the organization affect different groups of employees.

Data-gathering methods might include:

- questionnaires—design these with your target audience in mind, and guarantee respondents anonymity and privacy;
- individual and group interviews—consider who should conduct these and how to create an informal and frank atmosphere;
- focus group discussions—you could, for example, talk to groups of female, disabled, older employees, or employees of color;
- unobtrusive observation—a discreet walk around the workplace can be very revealing;
- document surveys—examine written procedures, personnel records, customer complaints, publicity material, and any other documentary evidence in the company's files;

"Money, as a physical medium of exchange, has made a diversified civilization possible."

(Josiah Stamp)

  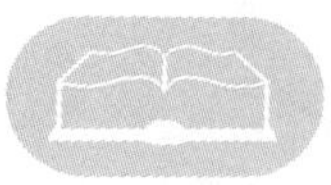    

- benchmarking–look in organizations similar to your own for examples of best practice to follow and bad practice to avoid.

5. Conduct a Gap Analysis

Review the audit results and establish how great the difference is between your current position and your goals.

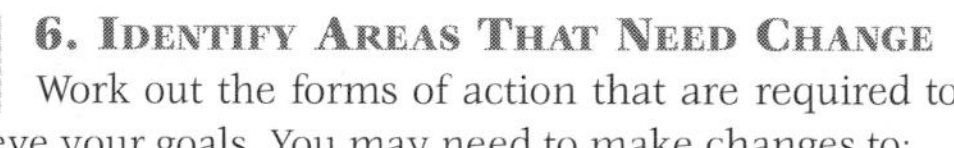

6. Identify Areas That Need Change

Work out the forms of action that are required to achieve your goals. You may need to make changes to:

- processes–for example, revising your recruitment procedure;
- working arrangements–for example, introducing flextime or childcare facilities;
- attitudes–for example, combating intercultural prejudice and improving intercultural communication;
- physical environment–for example, creating better access for disabled employees and customers.

7. Write a Diversity Policy

Use these broad change ideas together with your diversity goals to compile a concise written diversity policy. The policy should include:

- a definition of diversity
- reasons why it is important
- the goals of the diversity management program
- the ways in which the goals will be achieved

Communicate the policy to employees and all stakeholders. Post a copy on every staff bulletin board, in the staff handbook, and, if you have one, on the company intranet.

DOS AND DON'TS

For Implementing a Diversity Management Program

DO

- Communicate at all stages of the program. Keep employees, managers, customers, shareholders, and other stakeholders informed: their support is vital to the program's success.
- Involve everyone. This is not an issue for only the personnel department or senior managers: it should concern people throughout the organization.
- Use established change management processes to implement the program.
- Look to the long term. Changes involving attitudes don't happen overnight, and you should expect the program to last for years.
- Be prepared to invest money, time, and resources to achieve your goals.

DON'T

- Don't confuse equal opportunities with diversity management. The equal opportunity approach should form a part of any diversity initiative, but the program should go far beyond traditional equal opportunity issues.
- Don't design diversity goals and policies for "them." Think instead in terms of "us."

8. Compile a Diversity Action Plan

Spell out the finer details of the program, specifying exactly how the planned changes will be brought about. Hold brainstorming sessions to produce ideas for action, then compose an implementation plan that coordinates and timetables the actions to be taken. Make sure the plan includes regular reviews.

9. Set the Program in Motion

Communicate the plan to employees and put it into action. Appoint program coordinators and publicize their role, giving employees a point for feedback and information.

10. Monitor and Review

Monitor the program over 12 months and adjust the plan as necessary. Where problems occur, review the policy and decide whether it should be amended.

11. Establish an Ongoing Program

Schedule an ongoing diversity program for the long term. Allow for the program to be fluid and to change as the organization's internal and external contexts change. Diversity management should become a natural part of everyday life.

THOUGHT STARTERS

- List ten differences between yourself and a close colleague. Consider how these differences affect your working life.
- In what ways, if any, does your organization cater for these differences?
- Could your working arrangements, working environment, company policies, and procedures be improved to reduce any negative effects caused by these differences?
- Do you feel respected as an individual in your workplace? Is this respect evident from all levels of the organization?

For More Information

Books:

Thomas, R. Roosevelt, Jr. *Beyond Race and Gender: Unleashing the Power of Your Total Workforce by Managing Diversity.* New York: AMACOM, 1992.
Thomas, R. Roosevelt, Jr. *Redefining Diversity.* New York: AMACOM, 1996.

Web Sites:

National Association for Diversity Management: **www.nadm.org**
U.S. Equal Employment Opportunity Commission: **www.eeoc.gov**

See also:

☆ **Boosting Business Success through Diversity (pp. 29–30)**
Diversity (pp. 1955–57)

"Too many diversified companies strangle individual businesses with red tape in the form of financial and bureaucratic guidelines." (Kenichi Ohmae)

  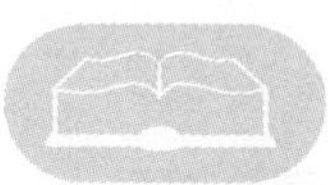    

IMPLEMENTING A SMOKE-FREE POLICY

CHECKLIST

This checklist provides guidance for those who wish to implement a smoke-free policy in their organization. It is primarily aimed at those implementing a corporate policy, although it is also relevant for single sites or departments.

Many firms have either totally or partially restricted smoking at work in response to legal requirements and pressure from employees. The federal Occupational Safety and Health Act (OSHA) of 1970 requires employers to protect the health of their employees. Smoking is entirely prohibited in most federal, state, and municipal government buildings throughout the United States. While smoking is not prohibited in private businesses, state and federal OSHA agencies do set standards for indoor quality, and many companies have adopted some form of smoking restrictions in the workplace to create a healthier environment for employees.

The addictive nature of nicotine makes limiting an employee's ability to smoke at work a sensitive issue, and it is important to help smokers adjust to restrictions by offering counseling on cutting down or stopping smoking. The aim of a smoking policy should not be to harass smokers, but should be to create an environment that is acceptable to both smokers and non-smokers.

A smoke-free policy provides guidelines for employees on where and when they can smoke, and states the disciplinary procedures to be used and disciplinary action to be taken against those who do not comply.

ADVANTAGES

By implementing a smoke-free policy, an organization:

- creates a healthier and cleaner working environment;
- complies with occupational health and safety legislation on safeguarding the health, safety, and welfare of employees;
- projects a caring attitude toward the health of employees;
- can reduce absenteeism through smoking-related illness.

DISADVANTAGES

A smoke-free policy:

- may make smokers feel they are being victimized;
- may cost employers significant expense in modifying ventilation systems or locating and equipping designated smoking rooms, should they choose to do so.

ACTION CHECKLIST

1. CREATE A SMOKE-FREE POLICY COMMITTEE

The members of the smoke-free policy committee should be drawn from all levels of the organization. If the employer already has an established Health and Safety Committee, they would probably be responsible for formulating such a policy. Check with state OSHA or the local health department about guidelines for designing and implementing such a policy. Appoint a coordinator to oversee the project. This person need not necessarily be from senior management, but should be someone with project management experience who commands respect, has excellent communication and negotiation skills, and can get things done. Include union representatives if your work force is unionized.

✔ 2. GET YOUR EMPLOYEES' VIEWS

Find out what your employees' opinions are on smoking at work and gauge the strength of feeling toward a policy. The survey should also provide information on the number of smokers in the company and their distribution among departments or areas. (Undertaking an employee attitude survey is covered in a related checklist.) The views of your employees should be taken into account in deciding what level of smoke-free policy to implement (a complete or partial ban); employees need to know that their opinions are important and valued on this delicate issue.

✔ 3. COMMUNICATE THE NEED FOR A POLICY

Provide feedback to employees, showing how many people support a smoking restriction—including smokers themselves.

Indicate the reasons why a smoke-free policy is needed, including, where applicable, complaints from customers and non-smoking employees. Use bulletin boards, newsletters, e-mails, and team briefings to get this message across.

✔ 4. DRAW UP A SMOKE-FREE POLICY

Decide on the level of smoking restriction.

- Total ban. A total ban, as is the practice in public buildings, forces smokers to leave the building to light up. A total ban may be possible if it is brought in gradually, allowing smokers time to adjust to the policy.
- Restricting smoking to designated rooms. Providing smoking rooms alleviates many of the problems of smoking at work, but assumes that spare rooms are available and that they can be ventilated directly outdoors and cleaned. Non-smokers may feel aggrieved if they see smokers disappearing to a smoking room for a break whenever they like. If this method is used it must be carefully supervised to avoid over-use or abuse. Make sure that such rooms are clearly marked as smoking areas.
- Restricting smoking to certain areas. This is less ideal

"I am extraordinarily patient, provided I get my own way in the end." (Margaret Thatcher)

  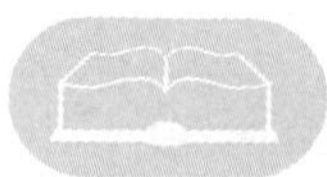    

than restricting smoking to certain rooms, as smoke can drift into non-smoking areas despite ventilation. OSHA and health department officials can levy fines and bring legal action if they determine–based on complaints–that the air quality in the building is substandard.

If the policy isn't company-wide, fashion it in such a way so as to avoid conflict between departments where smoking is allowed and those where it is not. The policy should also cover customers and visitors to the workplace.

Draw up a list of disciplinary procedures for those who do not comply with the policy. Designate who will be involved in any disciplinary proceedings.

5. Present the Policy to Senior Management

The backing of senior management is essential to the success of the plan, as they may have to deal with grievances raised by the employees.

6. Prepare to Help Staff Stop Smoking

Make every effort to help employees who want to quit smoking. Put them in touch with local "stop smoking/smoke cessation" classes, or hire a counselor who specializes in nicotine addiction.

7. Draw Up an Implementation Timetable

For many smokers, a restriction on smoking will have a major impact on their working life. They should be given time to adjust to the new policy, and it can be helpful to moderate disciplinary action during the implementation period.

8. Communicate the Policy

Send a letter (or e-mail) to every employee announcing the new policy. Spell out what the policy is, making sure to specify the areas or rooms where smoking is to be restricted or allowed, when the policy will come into effect, and the disciplinary consequences of noncompliance. Mention that the organization will have a smoke-free policy in future job advertisements.

9. Implement the Policy

Signs and posters should be put up in areas where smoking is restricted or not allowed. Likewise, a "Smoking Room" sign should be placed outside each specific room in which smoking may occur, alerting non-smokers. In workplaces that frequently have visitors, signs should be visible as soon as an individual enters the building. A member of the smoke-free policy committee should be available at all times to deal with any problems that arise related to smoking.

10. Evaluate the Policy

Check the numbers of policy infractions and complaints made by smokers and non-smokers. Act on infractions of the rules–a few can lead to widespread noncompliance. Remember that any evaluation procedure should be conducted regularly, at least once a year.

DOS AND DON'TS

For Implementing a Smoke-free Policy

DO

- Obtain your employees' opinions on smoking in the workplace.
- Remember to involve union representatives.
- Stress that the policy is for everyone's benefit.
- Offer smokers counseling to help them kick the habit.
- Enforce the disciplinary actions specified by the policy.

DON'T

- Don't make exceptions in the policy—for senior management, for example.
- Don't implement a policy all at once.

11. Modify or Revise the Policy

Use the information obtained from the evaluation to make any changes to the policy: for example, smoke may be drifting into non-smoking areas, requiring further restrictions or extra ventilation.

12. Provide Feedback

Report back to senior management and all employees the success of the policy and any changes that have been made. Distribute any comments made by suppliers, customers, visitors, or health and safety officials on the cleaner environment in your workplace.

THOUGHT STARTERS

- Have you ever smoked? What helped you quit?
- Have any of your previous workplaces had a smoking policy? Did it work?
- What are the penalties for smoking?

For More Information

Journal Articles:

Geldman, Adam. "Smoking at Work Still a Burning Issue." *Occupational Health Review*, no. 61 (May-June 1996): 27–36.

"Smoking at Work." IDS brief, no. 558 (February 1996): 7–11.

"Smoking at Work 2: Policy Content Enforcement and Development." *IRS Employment Review*, no. 607 (May 1996): 8–16, purple.

"Workplace Smoking Policies 1: Content and Motives." *IRS Employment Review*, no. 602 (February 1996): 10–16, purple.

"I believe that nicotine is not addictive." (Thomas Sandefur)

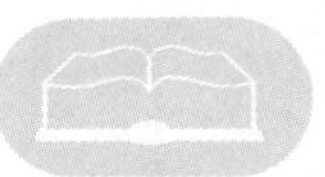

SETTING UP A SUGGESTION BOX

CHECKLIST

This checklist provides guidance for anyone setting up a suggestion box in their company or organization.

Suggestion boxes have been used by companies for a number of years as a way of gathering ideas from their employees to increase productivity, cut costs, and improve working conditions. A successful program has many positive effects: the most important is that employees believe that management cares and listens to them. Implementing a successful suggestion program is not an easy process. It requires careful planning, involving much staff time. A suggestion box should be regarded not as an alternative to regular communication and hands-on management, but as a supplement to them.

DEFINITION

A suggestion program is a planned procedure that enables employees to make known their ideas for improving any aspect of work, from cost savings and operational improvements to new product ideas and better customer service, and that may reward them for their initiative if their suggestions are implemented.

ADVANTAGES

Setting up a employee suggestion box can:

- lead to a reduction in costs and greater efficiency;
- encourage employee involvement, improving morale and motivation;
- help foster an environment in which creativity and innovation can flourish;
- enable employees at ground level (who can often see problems and solutions that management do not) to be heard.

DISADVANTAGES

- Suggestion programs need constant management to be effective.

ACTION CHECKLIST

1. DESIGNATE A SUGGESTION BOX COMMITTEE

The suggestion box committee provides input from its conception and helps manage the program. Committee members should represent all levels of the organization. Appoint a coordinator to oversee the project; this need not necessarily be someone from senior management, but should be someone with project management experience who commands respect and can get things done.

2. IDENTIFY ALTERNATIVE PLANS

Ascertain whether any members of the committee have had experience with suggestion programs, and if so make use of it. The coordinator should, if possible, undertake a literature search to find comparable case studies (remember, however, that a program that worked for one firm may not work for another). A small organization, for example, may not require a formal program at all if employees can communicate ideas directly and easily to the relevant person.

3. DRAW UP A PLAN

Plan the program, taking into account examples of other suggestion programs and the characteristics of your own organization. Include the following:

- Name of the program—the program should be given a name that will make it instantly recognizable to employees. Design a logo for the program that can be used for posters, leaflets, and suggestion forms.
- Length of program—running a program for set periods of time throughout the year allows you to gear publicity to specific startup dates—it can be difficult to keep a continuous program fresh in the employees' minds. Ideas do not, however, occur only at certain times of the year, so depending on your business cycle and the availability of resources, it is probably advisable to implement a continuous program. Make sure you readvertise it periodically—for example, after Christmas shutdowns.
- Format for suggestions—keep it simple. Encourage contributors to describe their ideas, even complex, technical ideas, in simple language. Details can be filled in later. Position prominently marked suggestion boxes at convenient sites throughout the workplace. Alternatively, invite employees to submit their suggestions to a designated address on the company's intranet. Some programs require that suggestions be signed, and do not accept anonymous contributions.
- Evaluation of suggestions—evaluate the suggestions on a regular basis—for example, monthly. The committee should discuss individual suggestions and develop the most promising ones. It might be helpful to prepare guidelines for the evaluation process. Important factors include the benefits to the organization or department, ease of implementation, originality, and overall cost.

Some suggestions may propose changes in administrative or production procedures, affecting many staff. Consider what retraining or retooling may be required and how and when this might be implemented. In such cases, a cost-benefit analysis may be useful.

Consider any possible effects on external stakeholders such as customers or suppliers.

Send a brief thank-you note to all contributors, successful or not.

- Rewards/awards—monetary rewards or gifts can be given to suggesters. The amount can be linked to cost savings or improvements in efficiency or can be a standard sum for each successfully implemented suggestion.

You can also link the award to the type of suggestion, for example:

- production–methods for reducing costs or increasing efficiency;
- health and safety–ideas for improving health and safety in the workplace;
- environmental–suggestions to make the organization more environmentally friendly.

Consider an award that recognizes the initiative of employees who make a suggestion, whether it is implemented or not. If a number of sites are involved, a "Suggestion of the Year" award could be made that covers the whole organization.

4. Publicity

Publicize the program widely and include details in the staff handbook. Communicate improvements made as a result of successful suggestions. Effective methods include:

- posters and leaflets on bulletin boards and on the company intranet;
- articles in staff newsletters and magazines (include stories about winners);
- inclusion as part of the orientation of new staff.

The initial publicity for the program should communicate the advantages for the employees and dispel any apprehension they may have.

5. Run a Pilot

Conduct a small-scale pilot program. Review it for problems in administration and make any necessary modifications.

6. Implement the Program

Implement the full program. The coordinator should note any problems that occur in running the suggestion box so they can be remedied immediately.

7. Evaluate the Program

At the end of a set period, evaluate the program, looking out for such points as:

- the number and types of suggestions made
- the number of suggestions taken up and implemented
- financial savings achieved
- increases in efficiency achieved
- costs incurred
- rewards/awards made
- problems
- feedback from employees.

If the program is under-used, investigate why this is the case.

The committee should discuss the evaluation and make any further modifications needed. Submit a report to management detailing the performance of the suggestion program.

The evaluation process should be carried out every year, and improvements and modifications continually made to the program.

DOS AND DON'TS

For Setting Up a Suggestion Box

DO

- Publicize the program regularly.
- Aim to get maximum participation.
- Try to give feedback to contributors as soon as possible.
- Recognize every suggestion, even those that can't be implemented.

DON'T

- Don't undersell the advantages of the suggestion box to employees.
- Don't implement a program without piloting it first.

THOUGHT STARTERS

- How many clever ideas are lying dormant in employees' minds?
- Have you ever wanted to make a suggestion to improve efficiency? What did you do?
- What would encourage you to make a suggestion?
- What would deter you from making a suggestion?

For More Information

Book:

Charles, Martin L. *Employee Suggestion Systems: Boosting Productivity and Profits (Fifty Minute Series).* Normal, IL: Crisp Publications, 1997.

Journal Articles:

"Any Ideas? A Survey of Suggestion Schemes." *IRS Employment Review*, no. 612 (July 1996): 9–14, purple.

"Suggestion Schemes Study," IDS Study, no. 638 (November 1997): whole issue.

UNDERTAKING AN EMPLOYEE ATTITUDE SURVEY

CHECKLIST

This checklist provides guidance for those who wish to undertake an employee attitude survey in their organization.

Employee attitude surveys are used by companies as a way of routinely or occasionally monitoring the views of their employees or of gauging the effect of a new policy. Surveys should not be carried out too often, perhaps no more frequently than every 18 months. Two very important parts of any such survey are to report the results back to employees and to act on those results.

DEFINITION

An employee attitude survey is a planned procedure that enables a company to learn its employees' opinions about a particular issue or the organization itself. The survey is usually carried out in order to be able to take employees' views into account in planning or to make changes that will benefit the firm and individuals alike.

ADVANTAGES

Employee attitude surveys:

- provide data that can be used in problem solving, planning, and decision-making;
- encourage employee involvement, improving morale and motivation;
- allow management to hear employees' opinions, of which they may not otherwise be aware;
- form an effective communication channel;
- act as a sounding board for corporate initiatives.

DISADVANTAGES

Such surveys:

- require a good deal of time to carry out and evaluate;
- incur significant costs in planning, implementation, and evaluation;
- can generate employee suspicion about hidden agendas or the "real" reasons behind the surveys.

ACTION CHECKLIST

✔ 1. DEFINE SCOPE AND COVERAGE

As precisely as you can, identify the subject on which employees' opinions are to be gathered. Be clear on how you will deal with their views once you know them. Bear in mind that a survey entitled, for example, "Introducing telecommuting" may give rise to all sorts of anxieties or expectations and think about how you might deal with these.

Decide who is to be included in the survey—all employees, one department or site, or one type of employee (for example, full-time permanent staff).

✔ 2. IDENTIFY AN ADMINISTRATOR

Appoint an agency to run the survey. This may be your own personnel department if yours is large enough, or a special working party drawn from all levels of the company. If your firm lacks the necessary expertise internally, you can contract the work out to an external consultant; this will probably be more expensive, but it may help persuade staff that the process is impartial and the results will be acted on.

✔ 3. SELECT A SURVEY METHOD

Two principal survey methods are available:

- questionnaire—questionnaires that the employees fill in are particularly useful when a large number of people are to be surveyed and when answers to the questions can be framed "yes/no";
- face-to-face interview—these can be on an individual or a group basis. The interactive format allows you to probe attitudes in some depth. But interviews are time-consuming, are impractical for surveying large numbers of people, can suffer from inconsistencies, and can produce results that are difficult to quantify.

The choice of method depends on the number of people to be surveyed, the type of information you need, and the resources that are available.

✔ 4. DETERMINE QUESTIONS AND PROCEDURES

Formulate the questionnaire (or guidelines for interviewers, in the case of face-to-face meetings). Ask yourself the following questions:

- Are the questions clear and unambiguous?
- Will this take the employee a long time to complete?
- Do the questions cover the subject thoroughly?
- Will the information obtained be easy to analyze?
- Is confidentiality assured?

Make certain that the questions are not discriminatory in any way; take into account any likely problems with literacy or in understanding terminology.

Devising questionnaires and holding interviews are not tasks for the enthusiastic amateur. Don't be afraid to seek advice.

✔ 5. PILOT THE SURVEY

Select a small number of employees to complete the questionnaire (or undertake an interview). Debrief them to see whether they had any problems completing the survey, ask them whether any of the questions were unclear or troublesome, and find out whether they would prefer to think about the issues at work or take the survey home. See whether the information you obtained is what you were looking for. If necessary, modify the questionnaire or provide extra training for the interviewers.

"Your attitude determines your altitude." (Stephen Covey)

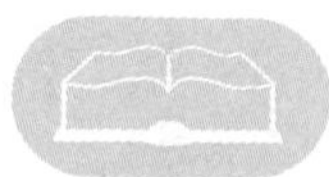

DOS AND DON'TS

For Undertaking an Employee Attitude Survey

DO

- Benchmark with employee surveys undertaken in other organizations if possible.
- Pilot the survey before full implementation.
- Report the results of the survey and plans of action to all employees.
- Note any problems in administering the survey so you can do better next time.

DON'T

- Don't use the survey for a hidden agenda.
- Don't implement the survey without careful planning.

6. Explain the Purpose of the Survey

It is crucial to make sure that all employees who will be involved understand the reasons for the survey and the benefits they will gain from it. Sharing information is the best way to alleviate fears and increase participation. Depending on the nature of the exercise, you may want to explain to employees who are not involved why the survey is being carried out.

7. Implement the Survey

Distribute the questionnaires (or arrange for interviews to be held). Maintain impetus by condensing the time frame, allowing sufficient time for employees who are traveling or on vacation. Make help available to deal with questions or problems. Having employees return completed questionnaires to an outside agency will reinforce your commitment to confidentiality and impartiality.

8. Collate and Report Results

Avoid distrust and suspicion by communicating the results of the survey to both senior management and employees. It is usually advisable to summarize the results for employees, who may not want to read a lengthy document. Be sure to include action plans resulting from the survey. Benchmark the results externally, particularly in the case of regular surveys that monitor trends. (Remember, however, that the survey may be so specific that comparison is impossible.) Survey analysis is a specialist task, and you may wish to contract this to an outside agency.

9. Evaluate the Survey

Evaluate the survey questions and your method both quantitatively and qualitatively, looking, for example, at the response rate, the information obtained, and problems in administering the survey. Take the findings into account in planning and designing a follow-up or future surveys.

10. Follow Up

Consider undertaking a second survey once the plans of action have had time to take effect, to see whether the changes have made improvements. This is obviously unnecessary in cases where little or no action was called for in the original survey.

THOUGHT STARTERS

- Have you ever taken part in an employee attitude survey yourself? Did anything productive come from it?
- What would motivate you to complete an attitude questionnaire?
- What would discourage you from taking part in an attitude survey?

For More Information

Books:

Oppenheim, A. N. *Questionnaire Design, Interviewing, and Attitude Measurement*. Herndon, VA: Books International, 1993.

Walters, Mike. *Building the Responsive Organization: Using Employee Surveys to Manage Change*. New York: McGraw-Hill, 1994.

Walters, Mike. *Employee Attitude and Opinion Surveys*. Woodstock, NY: Beekman, 2000.

Journal Articles:

Chaudron, David. "The Right Approach to Employee Surveys." *HR Focus* 74:3 (March 1997): 9–10.

"Employee Attitude Surveys Study." *IDS Studies Plus* (January 1998): whole issue.

Ettorre, Barbara. "The Unvarnished Truth." *Management Review* 86:6 (June 1997): 54–57.

Orpen, Christopher. "Our Survey Said." *Chartered Secretary* (January 1998): 29–30.

SETTING UP CHILDCARE POLICIES

CHECKLIST

This checklist provides guidance for those responsible for the implementation of a corporate childcare policy. It focuses on the general principles and considerations involved.

DEFINITION

A childcare policy is a voluntary program put into practice by an employer to provide, or to help to provide, care for employees' children during working hours. Such a policy allows primary caregivers to work despite childcare responsibilities. Care is available for children of various ages—all day programs for younger children, after-school care for older ones. To comply with equal opportunities legislation, childcare provision has to be made available to both male and female employees.

ADVANTAGES

Providing childcare:

- enables experienced and skilled employees to return to or continue in work, reducing recruitment and training costs;
- attracts a wider range of applicants for vacant positions;
- enhances the firm's reputation as a caring and employee-friendly organization;
- has positive tax implications (tax credits as well as deductions) for both the corporation and the employee.

Buying part of the capacity at local daycare centers:

- eliminates startup costs for employers;
- avoids the responsibility of managing a daycare center and its staff.

Childcare allowances:

- cost much less than paying for an onsite daycare center;
- can be used for any qualified daycare center in the parents' local area;
- allow parents to choose the form and location of childcare they prefer. Employers frequently offer childcare as part of a "cafeteria" benefits plan, whereby employees choose from a list of benefit options, including health care, for which they receive a lump sum allowance each year. The sum does not cover all possible benefits, so the employee must choose from a "menu." This type of plan has a tax advantage over other types of allowances or vouchers, in that the cost for daycare is deducted from employees' wages before taxes are calculated.

Childcare vouchers:

- can be used in much the same way as an allowance or "co-pay" to purchase childcare from qualified providers;
- can be cashed only in exchange for childcare;
- can be used in the parents' local area;
- like the other options, use of vouchers also qualifies the employer and employee for tax credits and deductions. Be sure to consult your tax advisor about the best options.

Workplace daycare centers:

- allow parents access to their children at lunchtimes or in emergencies;
- like other daycare options, offers a variety of tax benefits, depending on how the company and the employee work out the details of the cost for the daycare services;
- can provide a beneficial environment for children.

DISADVANTAGES

- If there is no "cafeteria" plan for benefits in place, employees without children may feel resentful of benefits for which they are ineligible.
- Buying part of the capacity at selected local daycare centers can be expensive for the company and may be considered a taxable benefit to the employee; while not as costly as building your own center, providing this benefit to employees will be an added expense, against which you must weigh the advantages.
- It may not be conveniently located for all families.

Childcare allowances:

- may be taxable benefits for employees, unless the allowance is part of a larger benefits plan;
- require administration.

Childcare vouchers:

- are of limited usefulness if recipients live in areas with inadequate childcare facilities.

Workplace daycare centers:

- are expensive to set up and run;
- must meet state and local licensing regulations and health codes on an annual basis;
- do not suit parents who don't wish, or find it impossible, to commute with their children to work every day;
- require the allocation of space in the company's own building or nearby, which may prove costly.

ACTION CHECKLIST

1. EXAMINE THE ORGANIZATION'S SHORT- AND LONG-TERM NEEDS

Will a childcare policy benefit the organization in the long term, justifying high initial costs? Is there a demand for a childcare policy?

2. OBTAIN TOP MANAGEMENT COMMITMENT AND APPOINT A PROJECT TEAM

Without strong commitment from the top, a childcare policy has little chance of success. Establish who will be responsible for the implementing and managing the policy. This is important; the implementation of a childcare policy is a long-term commitment and quality is essential. Consequently the individuals involved must be prepared to be project champions. Assemble a project team to collect and evaluate information and help formulate

"The first step in providing economic equality for women is to ensure a stable economy in which every person who wants to work, can work." (Jimmy Carter)

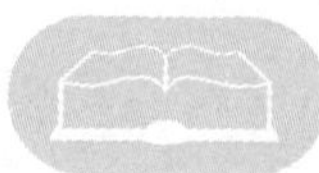

policy. Include a member of the human resources department.

3. Identify the Policy Options

Research the implications of each policy option, including costs, legal implications and local regulations, which options are workable, within a reasonable distance from the workplace, and where your employees live in relation to the workplace.

4. Consult Employees

Present the most practical policy options to employees and get their feedback. Which policy would they prefer, and why?

5. Formulate Policy

Taking the views of employees and the requirements and preferences of the firm into account, choose one or a combination of the options.

6. Draw Up a Business Plan Detailing Policy

Set a timeframe for project development, with a budget for setup and ongoing costs. Make sure that the company is adhering to all the laws and regulations that apply, and keep relevant organizations informed of the implementation of the policy. The plan should detail the scope of services provided, as well as the costs to employees, the company contribution, and the hours of coverage available under the plan.

7. Launch the Program

Inform employees of the final policy. Once the program is under way, allow time for parents to adjust to the service and for participation to increase.

8. Review the Program

Evaluate and monitor standards continuously to ensure that childcare policies meet the needs of the organization, the employees, and their children.

Glossary of Terms

Childcare allowances are paid directly to individual employees in the form of cash payments or are placed in a childcare fund.

Childcare vouchers are vouchers that are given to employees to pay for any form of childcare they choose. The provider then redeems them from the issuer at face value.

Flexible working means that employees can choose working hours that deviate from the nine-to-five norm. Options include flexible working hours, term-time working, a compressed work week (like 4 10-hour days), job sharing, voluntary part-time employment, and "comp" time, where employees who work—but aren't paid for—overtime, take the same number of hours later, when the schedule is less busy.

After-school provision is available for children awaiting a ride home with parents whose work day is longer than the school day. Generally, these services are provided by non-profit community organizations, including churches, YMCA, YWCA, and Boys & Girls Clubs. The cost to parents for these services is minimal, and is not usually covered by employers.

Purchased places in daycare enables employers to provide their employees with guaranteed places for their children in local daycare facilities. In some cases the costs are reimbursed by the firm, in others they are passed on to the employee.

Workplace daycare is usually onsite or located in nearby premises provided by the employer. It can be run in-house or by a contractor who specializes in childcare. Some organizations work in partnership with other firms to provide these facilities, sharing the costs and management responsibilities.

For More Information

Books:

Rosenbloom, Jerry S. *The Handbook of Employee Benefits*. New York: McGraw-Hill, 2001.

Sher, Margery Leven, and Madeline Fried. *Childcare Options: A Workplace Initiative for the 21st Century*. Phoenix, AZ: Oryx Press, 1994.

Journal Article:

"Employers and Childcare." *IDS Study, no. 633* (September 1997).

SETTING UP A GRIEVANCE PROCEDURE

CHECKLIST

This checklist provides guidance for those wishing to implement a grievance procedure in their company or organization.

Many grievances are too complex to be settled by a single meeting. A thorough grievance procedure goes further by providing a process, involving more than one level of management, through which the employer and employee can reach a mutually agreed conclusion to the problem. Settling grievances quickly and fairly means they do not fester and grow.

DEFINITION

A grievance procedure provides an employee with a hierarchical administrative structure for presenting and settling a grievance at work. The procedure defines:

- the type of grievance it covers;
- the individuals responsible at each stage;
- the presentation and documentation of a grievance;
- the time limits by which the grievance must be presented and dealt with at each stage.

ADVANTAGES

By implementing a grievance procedure, an organization:

- complies with, and sometimes surpasses, the requirements of employment legislation;
- can prevent a minor grievance from becoming a major problem;
- conveys a caring attitude toward its employees.

DISADVANTAGES

There are no real disadvantages to implementing a grievance procedure, but remember that such a procedure:

- requires time and resources to be effective;
- can deter an employee from presenting a grievance if it is too formal.

ACTION CHECKLIST

1. DEFINE THE TERMS OF REFERENCE

Decide which types of grievance the procedure will cover. Often, grievance procedures in such areas as sexual harassment, racial discrimination, intimidation or violence, and collective disputes have their own process for settlement. Identify at whom the procedure is aimed (for example, hourly workers only) and the levels of management that will be involved in settling grievances.

2. DRAW UP THE PROCEDURE

Consult with other members of the organization, including union representatives, to devise a procedure. Try to obtain copies of the procedures used in other companies. Write the procedure in simple, straightforward language that is easy to understand.

The procedure should contain the following:

Types of Grievance. List the types of grievances the process covers. Refer other types of complaint (such as sexual harassment) to the appropriate administrative or legal entities.

The Stages Involved. Initially the complainant should be encouraged to have an informal meeting with the immediate superior to discuss the problem and see if they can work it out without a formal proceeding. If this does not work, the first stage of the procedure should be a formal meeting with the complainant and the immediate superior. Provide an alternative—the personnel manager, for example—in case the supervisor is party to the complaint. If so, the alternative should not be one of the higher levels of referral. Making the immediate supervisor the first point of contact serves to uphold his or her level of authority.

The number of stages, in which the employee meets with progressively higher levels of management, will depend on many factors, including the size of the organization. There should be at least two stages to provide a minimum of one level of appeal, but too many stages can make the process lengthy and deter some employees. Give the name, or preferably the job title, of the person responsible for grievances at each level.

In the event that the grievance cannot be settled internally, the last stage should be referral to an external body such as an independent arbitrator or conciliator.

Representation at Meetings. A colleague or union representative should be allowed to accompany or represent the aggrieved at each meeting if desired. Specify at what stage the employee is entitled to representation—this can depend on the situation and the relationship between management and unions. The procedure represents the formal acceptance by management of the employee's representative as an equal partner in trying to settle the grievance.

Time Limits. Realistic time limits should be set (in working days) for the presentation of the complaint and the management response at each stage. Time limits should get longer as the grievance moves up the hierarchy to more senior management, since the problem will necessarily be more serious and will require more time to deal with. A proviso might be included permitting the extension of time limits by mutual agreement.

Presentation and Documentation of a Grievance. The initial presentation of a grievance need only be made verbally with the immediate supervisor. A written presentation might deter those who feel theirs is a minor grievance. Brief documentation should be kept of this meeting.

For each stage thereafter, a record of information and events, including supporting arguments and evidence, should be kept to pass up through subsequent stages for those not familiar with the grievance. The record should

"The microdivision of labor has fostered a basic distrust of human beings." (Charles Handy)

  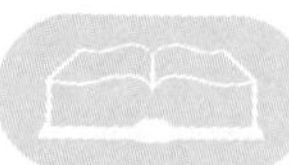    

be agreed by the manager concerned and countersigned by the employee and/or the employee's representative. This helps ensure that there are no misunderstandings when an agreement resolving the problem has been reached.

Guidelines for the Interviewer. Include instructions for the interviewer on the way in which he or she should prepare for and handle the grievance interview.

Status Quo Clause. Arrange a status quo clause with the unions so that any industrial action will be deferred until the grievance process is completed.

3. Draw Up an Implementation Timetable

In a large organization it is often better to pilot the grievance procedure on one site or large department before full implementation.

4. Provide Training for Managers and Supervisors

Conducting a grievance interview effectively is not easy. Training should be given to all managers and supervisors who may have to deal with a grievance. Make sure that they are aware of the limits of their and others' authority and that they understand the mechanics of the procedure, for example, the number of working days they have to reply to a grievance and the documentation they should keep. Training those responsible for holding interviews will help solve problems as close as possible to the point of their origin.

5. Communicate and Implement the Procedure

Make sure that everyone is aware of the procedure (a letter should be sent to all employees along with a copy of the procedure), the date the procedure will come into effect, and which managers are responsible for grievances at each stage. Explain that the procedure has been introduced to benefit employees by providing them with a systematic way of airing grievances and reaching an amicable agreement in as short a time as possible. The same information should be given to new recruits; a copy should be attached to every bulletin board and included in the employee manual. Name a contact person who can answer any questions employees may have about the grievance procedure.

6. Evaluate the Procedure

Regular evaluation of the procedure will help you improve it. Identify the number of grievances and settlements, the subject matter of individual grievances, and any levels of management that seem to have difficulties in handling grievances. Grievance records can help you analyze trends in the causes of grievance. Debrief employees who have used the procedure to settle grievances to see whether they experienced any problems with the process. It is essential to check that the procedure has been applied fairly and consistently in all cases.

7. Modify the Procedure As Needed

Alterations should be made to combat any of the problems highlighted in the evaluation. Changes may include offering extra training to certain managers or removing a stage in the procedure. Regularly update the names or job titles of managers responsible for grievances at each stage.

8. Provide Results Feedback

Communicate the success of the evaluation process to all employees and let them know of any changes to be made.

DOS AND DON'TS

For Setting Up a Grievance Procedure

DO

- Try to obtain copies of procedures used in other organizations.
- Define the types of grievance covered.
- Allow the aggrieved an alternative to the line manager in the initial meeting.
- Train those who will be involved at each stage of the procedure.

DON'T

- Don't make the initial stage too formal, otherwise some grievances may not be aired.
- Don't set unrealistic time limits.

THOUGHT STARTERS

- Have you ever been party to a grievance at work? What did you do?
- Do you know how to handle a complaint from an employee?

For More Information

Books:

Ewing, David C. *Justice on the Job: Resolving Grievances in the Non-Union Workplace.* Boston, MA: Harvard Business School Press, 1989.

Bringing ADR (Alternative Dispute Resolution) into Workplace 2000. Executive Special Reports. Brentwood, TN: M. Lee Smith Publishers & Printers, 1997.

Journal Articles:

Fowler, Alan. "How to Handle Employee Grievances." *Personnel Management Plus* 5:10 (October 1994): 24–25.

"Grievance Procedures." *Bargaining Report*, no. 149 (April 1995): 7–11.

Morgan, Philip, and H. Kent Baker. "The Complaint Interview." *Supervisory Management* (June 1984): 25–30.

Web Sites:

National Labor Relations Board: **www.nlrb.gov**

National Mediation Board: **www.nmb.gov**

"Many labor problems have spirit issues at their core, with lack of respect being perhaps the biggest."

(Kenneth Blanchard)

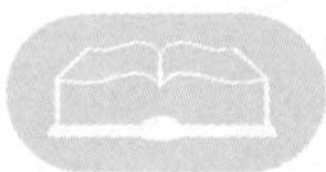

Setting Up a Disciplinary Procedure

CHECKLIST

This checklist is aimed at managers wishing to implement a disciplinary procedure in their company or organization.

It is essential for an employer to act reasonably in dealing with misconduct or indiscipline. A fair and thorough disciplinary procedure can protect an employer against unfair dismissal claims and their associated costs. Legislation aside, it is good personnel practice to deal with indiscipline quickly and fairly and to offer guidance on improving behavior so problems do not fester and grow.

Although this checklist focuses on the mechanics of a disciplinary procedure, it is important to remember that good management (for example, spotting problems before they become serious and identifying development needs to improve performance) can prevent many cases from reaching this stage.

Definition

A disciplinary procedure is a structured approach an employer uses to deal with indiscipline at work. The procedure defines the types of behavior it covers, the presentation and documentation of warnings, representation at disciplinary interviews, time limits for investigation, and rights of appeal.

Advantages

A disciplinary procedure:

- sets standards of conduct at work;
- ensures fair and consistent treatment for employees throughout the organization;
- may prevent minor problems from becoming major ones;
- helps protect the employer against claims of unfair dismissal.

Disadvantages

There are no real disadvantages of implementing a disciplinary procedure, but remember that:

- it requires time and resources to administer effectively;
- the objectives need to be explained thoroughly to staff so they don't worry unduly;
- the procedure should not replace informal warnings and performance monitoring systems.

Action Checklist

1. Designate a Disciplinary Procedure Management Committee

The committee should include, depending on the size of the organization, at least one person from the personnel department and from each level of management, as well as a person from every union representing employees. The committee will manage the design, implementation, and administration of the disciplinary procedure. Appoint a coordinator to oversee the project, preferably the personnel officer, but certainly someone with project management experience who commands respect, has excellent communication and negotiation skills, and can get things done.

2. Define the Terms of Reference

Identify the employees to be covered by the procedure (for example, shop-floor workers only) and the managers who will be responsible for the disciplinary interviews. Define indiscipline (both minor and serious misconduct), clarify legal obligations, and agree on the process to be used to lead up to dismissal.

3. Draw Up the Procedure

Use the experiences, soundings, and research of the committee to devise a procedure. Try to obtain samples of procedures used in other organizations. Remember to write the procedure as simply and clearly as possible so it is easy to understand.

The procedure should contain the following:

purpose. In an initial paragraph, give the reasons for having a procedure, highlighting the benefits to employees of a consistent set of rules and the importance of discipline in the workplace.

types of misconduct. This should spell out the kind of misconduct that would invoke the disciplinary procedure. Distinguish between minor offenses and those that are serious or may constitute gross misconduct, for example,

Minor	Serious
Smoking (where appropriate)	Vandalism
Timekeeping	Fraud
Dress	Alcohol/drugs

warnings. Depending on the seriousness of the offense, an employee will be faced with a series of warnings:

- oral (confirmed in writing)
- written
- final written

The ultimate penalty after this will be dismissal, although sanctions short of dismissal (such as transfer, demotion, or loss of pay) may be considered.

The warnings will be given to the employee after an interview, usually with the employee's line manager. Many procedures stipulate a length of time after which the warning lapses if the employee does not reoffend, but this leaves the system open to abuse. For this reason it is best not to set a time limit and to keep the warning on file. Remember that the disciplinary procedure should not be invoked unless informal warnings from the line manager have had no effect, or unless the offense is so serious that immediate disciplinary action must be taken. In cases of gross misconduct an employee may be suspended from work on full pay pending an investigation, then dismissed.

representation at meetings. A colleague or union representative should be allowed to accompany or represent the employee at each warning interview. Consider stipulating that the union should be involved unless the employee specifically objects. On occasions when the offense also constitutes a criminal offense, you should also allow a lawyer to be present.

investigations. All abuses of discipline should be investigated before a warning of any kind is issued. At the very least this involves hearing the employee's side of the story.

Set a time limit for investigating gross misconduct such as deliberate malpractice. This investigation should be completed within ten working days of the commission of the offense.

documentation. Take detailed minutes at all interviews and keep them together with copies of any investigation into the misconduct and any warnings issued. This documentation is useful for checking whether an employee's behavior improves; it also provides evidence that the company has followed correct procedures.

plans of action. In the case of minor offenses, the company should make every effort to help the employee overcome problems, obviating the need to pursue the disciplinary process further. The procedure should make it clear that plans of action will be agreed between the employee and the line manager at each interview to bring about improvements in discipline. An evaluation interview will be scheduled at which a more severe warning can be issued if progress has not been made.

appeals. Employees should have the right to appeal against any warning they receive as long as the appeal is made in writing to their line manager within five working days of the issue of the warning.

4. Draw Up an Implementation Timetable

In a large organization it is often better to pilot the disciplinary procedure on one site or in a large department before full implementation.

5. Train Managers and Supervisors

Provide training to all managers and supervisors who may have to deal with disciplinary issues. Make sure they understand the mechanics of the procedure, and try to ensure that they apply it consistently. Training should cover not only conducting a disciplinary interview effectively, but also general discipline and control; this will help solve as many problems as possible without going through the full procedure.

6. Communicate the Procedure

If you have disciplinary rules, the law requires that employees be notified. Make certain that staff are aware of the procedure; send a letter to all employees with a copy of the procedure. Explain that it is being introduced to benefit employees by providing a consistent method of dealing with indiscipline. Let them know when the procedure will come into effect. Include the disciplinary procedure in the staff manual and in the orientation of new recruits.

7. Implement the Procedure

Assign a member of the committee to answer questions, especially during the critical period following the communication of the procedure.

8. Evaluate the Procedure

Regular evaluation of the procedure will contribute to its improvement. Compile figures on the number of times the procedure is used, and identify managers who seem to have difficulty maintaining discipline. Ask for feedback from employees who have been disciplined under the procedure.

9. Make Changes and Give Feedback on the Results

Change the disciplinary procedure in the light of the evaluation. You may want to include extra training for some managers or rewrite some of the steps or phases. Communicate any changes to employees.

DOS AND DON'TS

For Setting Up a Disciplinary Procedure

DO

- Give examples of both minor and serious misconduct offenses.
- Train managers who will be conducting disciplinary interviews.
- Document every action taken under the procedure.

DON'T

- Don't take disciplinary action until the case has been investigated.
- Don't allow the procedure to replace the need for good management.
- Don't regard the procedure as unalterable—review it at regular periods.

THOUGHT STARTERS

- Have you ever been disciplined at work? What happened?
- Do you know how to handle a disciplinary problem involving one of your staff? Are you up to date with the law on unfair dismissal?

For More Information

Books:

Delpo, Amy, et al. *Dealing with Problem Employees: A Legal Guide*. Berkeley, CA: Nolo Press, 2001.

Weiss, Donald H. *Fair, Square, and Legal: Safe Hiring, Managing, and Firing to Keep You and Your Company out of Court*. 3rd ed. New York: AMACOM, 1999.

Web Sites:

HR Guide: **www.hr-guide.com**

HRnext (Human Resources): **www.hrnext.com**

"There could be no worse friend to labor than the benevolent, philanthropic employer. . .sooner or later he will be compelled to close."

(Lord Leverhulme)

CODES OF ETHICS

CHECKLIST

This checklist provides initial guidance for managers introducing a new code of ethics or updating an existing one. It applies equally to the public, private, and voluntary sectors.

There is a growing belief that organizations can succeed only if they are seen to observe high ethical standards. As a result, more are choosing to make a public commitment to ethical business by formulating and publishing a code of operating principles. The key difficulty they face in doing so is translating high-sounding principles into practical guidelines and thence into actual practice.

DEFINITION

Codes of ethics are guidelines to the moral principles or values used by organizations to steer conduct, both for the organization itself and its employees, in all their business activities, internal and external.

ADVANTAGES

A code of ethics:

- provides explicit guidance to managers and employees so they know what is expected of them in terms of ethical behavior;
- provides new employees with ethical guidance and a sense of common identity;
- enhances the organization's reputation and inspires public confidence;
- signals to suppliers and customers the organization's expectation of proper conduct;
- promotes a culture of excellence by demonstrating the commitment of the organization to ethical behavior.

DISADVANTAGES

- A corporate code can lead to employee cynicism if it is seen only as a paper exercise.
- Without explicit guidance, different parts of the organization may interpret the code differently, ultimately devaluing it.
- The effective introduction and implementation of a code demands a great deal of time from senior management.
- The code may raise public and employee expectations to a level that the organization is unable to live up to.

ACTION CHECKLIST

1. SECURE THE COMMITMENT OF TOP MANAGEMENT

Without the absolute and public commitment of top management, a code will not be taken seriously by employees. Commitment needs to be seen and felt.

2. GAIN ORGANIZATIONAL AGREEMENT ON THE PRIMARY PURPOSE OF A CODE

Is the code mainly for the benefit of employees, or is it to be directed at all stakeholders, including members of the board, shareholders, and even customers? Be clear on your major objectives, and be aware of all the changes that such a code may imply, from a shift in the organization's culture to whistle-blowing.

3. IDENTIFY AND DEFINE EXISTING SOURCES OF VALUES WITHIN THE ORGANIZATION

Consult existing codes, legal guidelines, policy memoranda, and founding statements, and involve both managers and employees in their evaluation. Review the standard codes (for example, those published by the Institute of Management) and those of organizations with operating policies similar to your own. Gain a consensus about the organization's traditions and unwritten rules.

4. INVOLVE YOUR EMPLOYEES

This is best achieved in a small group, but drafting the code should be a dynamic process, so don't exclude comments from employees at any level.

5. PREPARE A DRAFT CODE

The code should include:

- an introduction explaining the code's purpose, the need for such a code, and expectations about its use;
- a clear definition of the organization's mission and objectives;
- guidance on handling relations with each of the organization's constituencies: employees, shareholders, customers, suppliers, the outside community, etc.;
- expectations about acceptable behavior;
- operating principles (use realistic examples);
- a formal mechanism to resolve employees' questions.

6. CIRCULATE THE DRAFT

Consult widely within the organization, seeking feedback and comments. Be seen to take the feedback seriously. In addition to generating additional ideas, this process reinforces staff awareness of the code. If a significant amount of revision is necessary, circulate a second draft.

7. DEVISE AN IMPLEMENTATION STRATEGY

Once the draft is finalized, plan for its implementation. The implementation strategy must be dynamic and continuous. Incorporate the code into orientation, staff training, and management development programs. Bear in mind that implementation, like the preceding processes, may benefit from having a project management champion who can drive implementation forward with purpose, sensitivity, and consideration.

8. CIRCULATE THE FINAL CODE WIDELY

The code should be sent to all employees, accompanied by a letter from the head of the organization explaining the purpose of the code and expectations about its use.

"Most people sell their souls and live with a good conscience on the proceeds." (Logan Pearsall Smith)

DOS AND DON'TS

For Codes of Ethics

DO

- Make sure that the code reflects the organization's own values and traditions and that it is in line with staff handbooks and operating manuals.
- Seek employee input at all stages. Encourage a climate that promotes discussion of, and challenges to, the principles of the code without undermining it.
- Use plain language to write the code, avoiding platitudes, jargon, legal and technical phrases, or current buzzwords. Include realistic examples and factual situations to provide guidance.

DON'T

- Don't make the code either too vague or too narrowly prescriptive.
- Don't use the code to impose new or inappropriate values on the organization.
- Don't create an expectations gap between the principles of the code and the behavior of the organization in practice.
- Don't put ethical wallpaper on a decaying wall: an ethical code needs to be real, not cosmetic.

9. Establish a Procedure for Questions, Concerns, and Complaints

Who is responsible for responding to these—the line manager, human resources, or an ethics hotline? Make sure that an appeal process is built into the procedure.

10. Monitor and Evaluate the Code

Establish a mechanism to monitor and evaluate the code's effectiveness. There is no set formula or time frame dictated by good practice, but nine months to a year after implementation may be an appropriate time to get feedback and reactions and evaluate the impact of the code. Further consultation and one-on-one meetings are useful tools for this process. The code should be monitored regularly thereafter and evaluated for continued  relevance: circumstances change, and the code may need periodic amendment.

THOUGHT STARTERS

- Do you really have the commitment of senior management, or are they going to be distracted by other programs and initiatives?
- Does the code prompt employees to ask themselves the following questions before acting? Would I be willing to tell my family about this? Would I mind if the press found out about it?

For More Information

Books:

Chrysiddes, George D., and John H. Kaler. *An Introduction to Business Ethics*. Florence, KT: Thomson Learning, 1993.

Connock, Stephen, and Ted Johns. *Ethical Leadership*. Woodstock, NY: Beekman, 2000.

Journal Articles:

King, Hans. "A Global Ethic in an Age of Globalization." *Business Ethics Quarterly* 7:3 (1997) 17–32.

Navran, Frank. "12 Steps to Building a Best Practice Ethics Program." *Workforce* 76:9 (September 1997) 120–22.

Web Site:

International Business ethics institute: **www.business-ethics.org**

See also:

☆ **Business Ethics (pp. 231–32)**
Business Ethics and Codes of Practice (pp. 1918–20)

 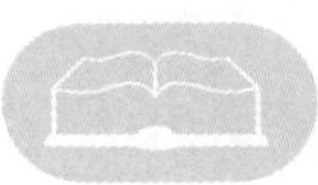    

DEVELOPING A MANUFACTURING STRATEGY

CHECKLIST

This checklist explains the basic steps in analyzing existing manufacturing operations and reviewing current manufacturing strategy.

Most organizations operate with a business plan and a broad corporate strategy. Not all manufacturing companies have a manufacturing strategy, however, and many that do fail to update it on a regular basis. A superior mix of people, technology, focus, and direction gives manufacturing a competitive edge: a manufacturing strategy addresses all these issues. The extended timescale required for completing a radical manufacturing change demands that you take a long-term view so you can plan investment and implementation.

DEFINITION

A manufacturing strategy is a working document outlining:

- the basis for your competitive advantage
- key issues affecting your organization
- your strategic manufacturing aims
- your broad strategic initiatives

The last should cover quality, technology, skill requirements, training, and make-or-buy decisions.

ACTION CHECKLIST

1. APPOINT A PROJECT TEAM

Planning strategy requires the full-time attention of a number of knowledgeable people from the management team. Team members need to have a detailed understanding of organizational, products, markets, and manufacturing technology. Skills in competitor analysis are also useful.

2. UNDERSTAND THE EXISTING MARKET POSITION

In order to formulate strategy you need a thorough understanding of your existing products. Ask:

- What strategy does your organization use to compete? The three generic strategies are to compete on cost (cost leadership), on superior features or service (differentiation), or in a subset of the market (niche market focus).
- What product families do you have? Use product life cycles as a framework for thinking about the manufacturing requirements of different products. Plotting product life cycles for existing key products and future projects will begin to fill in a picture of the size and shape your business needs to take on in the future.

In addition:

- Measure the performance of each of your products. Focus on their contribution, market share, and market growth.
- Identify the competitive edge of each product family.

Competitive features might include quality, delivery lead time, delivery flexibility, design flexibility, or price. What are the criteria that give you the greatest competitive advantage?

3. IDENTIFY THE DRIVERS OF CHANGE

Consider:

- business criteria (product performance, market demands, the evolution of manufacturing philosophies, and management structures)
- technological developments
- financial pressures

Analyze external influences on the organization, internal resources and capabilities, and the skills and competencies of staff by undertaking a SWOT analysis (see separate checklist).

4. ANALYZE YOUR CURRENT PERFORMANCE

Assessing your performance against competitive edge criteria can be difficult. Some factors are not easy to measure directly, while comparative data may be hard to obtain. Use techniques such as Pareto analysis and activity sampling to facilitate data collection. Focus on product performance features such as quality, delivery, flexibility, material costs, and capital costs. Obtain comparative data through published reports or databases, or by talking to customers and suppliers. Consider destructive analysis of a competitor's product. Participate in benchmarking studies.

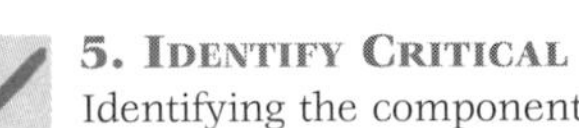

5. IDENTIFY CRITICAL COMPONENTS

Identifying the components that are most critical to your long-term success enables you to maximize the use of your investment capital. Range the components along a continuum of high to low business content, placing those of strategic importance at the high end of the scale. Include components with high added value on the list of strategic components; consider buying in those with a low business content.

- Identify the major part families and describe their manufacturing characteristics.
- List the key facilities needed to manufacture the strategic components.

6. EVALUATE YOUR MANUFACTURING OPERATION

This can be a complicated task, so give yourself plenty of time.

Examine current practice with regard to a range of criteria. The nine key areas most often covered are:

- facilities
- span of process (the degree of vertical integration)
- capacity
- processes and the way they are organized
- human resources
- quality

"The idea that commerce and profit may actually be pulling in the same direction is difficult for some people to accept." (Henry Ford)

  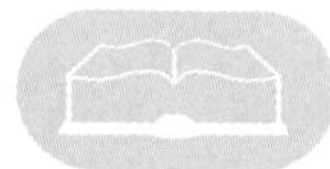    

- control policies
- suppliers
- new products

Compare the strengths and weaknesses of current practice with your established competitive edge criteria. Where are the gaps?

7. Set New Targets

Without tough targets it is difficult not only to measure achievement, but to maintain the necessary top-down pressure to achieve them. Targets can be wide-ranging; they cover such criteria as tooling costs, the utilization of equipment, defective materials, and inventory.

8. Develop a New Manufacturing Strategy

You are now ready to compile your new manufacturing strategy.

Using your knowledge of your most important product families, your competitive advantage criteria, and the existing performance gaps, identify the weaknesses of your existing policies. Discuss possible actions and strategic choices. Consider running a simulation to test these options.

9. Develop Your Supplier Network

For those components that you have decided to buy in, go through the process of identifying a potential supplier network and evaluating its ability to meet the demands of in-house manufacture. Consider your relationship with each supplier.

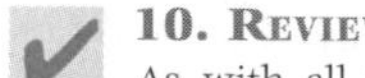

10. Review

As with all business plans, review your manufacturing plan annually against the developing business situation and set revised targets.

THOUGHT STARTERS

- Do you have a manufacturing strategy?
- Is it reviewed on a regular basis?
- What are the strengths, weaknesses, opportunities, and threats to your existing product line?

DOS AND DON'TS

For Developing a Manufacturing Strategy

DO

- Have a thorough understanding of your existing manufacturing strategy.
- Make sure you know the strengths and weaknesses of your existing product line.

DON'T

- Don't finish your strategy and leave it on the shelf—revise it to address changing market conditions.

For More Information

Books:

Greenhalgh, Garry R. *Manufacturing Strategy: Formulation and Implementation*. Reading, MA: Addison-Wesley Longman, 1991.

Hill, Terry. *Manufacturing Strategy: Texts and Cases*. 3rd ed. Boston, MA: Irwin/McGraw-Hill, 2000.

Web Sites:

Advanced Manufacturing: **www.advancedmanufacturing.com**

Manufacturing News: **www.manufacturingnews.com**

See also:

☆ **Lean Manufacturing (pp. 183–84)**

✓ **Performing a SWOT Analysis (pp. 468–69)**

"Those who invest only to get rich will fail. Those who invest to help others will probably succeed."

(Art Fury)

Developing a Strategy for World-class Business

CHECKLIST

This checklist provides an introductory framework for managers whose companies wish to pursue the route to world-class status. The responsibility for a world-class strategy usually rests with the chief executive and senior management.

Becoming a world-class company is not a simple process, and requires effort and commitment from the entire organization. Developing a strategy for action is essential if world-class status is to be achieved.

Definition

"World-class" is a concept that is difficult to define. However, an accepted working definition is that a world-class company should be able to compete with any other organization in its chosen markets and that it aspires to world-beating standards in everything it does, in every department or division. "World-class" also embraces the practice of, and excellence in, techniques such as Total Quality Management, continuous improvement, customer service, international benchmarking, flexible working, and training. World-class organizations also accept the necessity for continuous change.

Action Checklist

1. Consider Outside Influences

Identify the factors in the external environment that call for a strategic response from your business. These can be grouped under main headings such as economic factors, demographic trends, environmental factors, technology, suppliers, and competition.

2. Establish the World-class Vision

Determine the core business of your organization—that at which your organization should excel. Top management should make a vision of excellence clear in a brief statement that is impossible to misinterpret. In addition to helping form this vision, the chief executive's role is to clarify the message, push forward change, and champion the ideas and capabilities that will beat competitors.

3. Analyze Your Current Position

Benchmark your organization against your competitors as far as you can. This can be very difficult, as much of the necessary information may not be available. However, organizations exist that can help in this process.

Consider the following areas:

- your product
- its price
- its availability
- your customer service
- your policy for continuous improvement
- your costs
- your market share

Do you match your competitors in these areas, or is your organization well below or considerably superior to them? Don't limit this measure to competitors in your own country; compare yourself against worldwide competition. Identify which organizations are excellent within these areas and determine what makes them the best—in order to beat them!

Assess where you stand in customers' eyes. What is their perception of your status compared with the reputation of your competitors?

4. Focus on Core Capabilities

From the analyses of the external environment, the core business of the organization, and the standing of competitors, draw up a list of the core capabilities of your organization that will enable you to compete in world markets. Core capabilities include:

- product knowledge/service skills
- marketing skills
- innovation/research capacity
- financial planning and control
- human resource capabilities (including motivation as well as skills)

Determine which of these core capabilities need extra focus and resource their development.

5. Build a Corporate Strategy

Focus on achieving better products or services, better factories or service operations, better organization, better management, and better information and communication.

Ask yourself questions such as:

- Have the key business processes been defined and understood?
- Has a quality or customer focus ethic been established throughout the organization?
- Are quality and reliability of products and services measured?
- Are the key performance measures reviewed? Are they improving?
- Is everyone in the organization informed of results and developments?
- Is customer satisfaction monitored on a regular basis?
- Are employees multiskilled? Are they flexible and willing to adapt?
- Do your employees have continuing personal development plans in place?
- How are creativity and innovation encouraged and nurtured?
- How well does communication flow?
- Does it flow in all directions?

  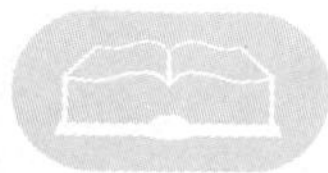    

6. Set High Targets for the Organization

Set imaginative and ambitious targets by identifying where you intend to be in one, three, and five years. If targets are easily achievable there is a danger that you will rest on your laurels. Being satisfied with these improvements means never becoming world-class.

- Make certain that organizational targets are translated into divisional and departmental goals that are incorporated into individual objectives.
- Get staff into the habit of setting their own targets—they will usually be higher than those you would set them yourself.

7. Develop Simple Performance Measures

Measurement processes, as simple and as straightforward as possible, allow you to continuously monitor what is happening and to continuously report on progress. Performance measures should be relevant to your aims: concentrate on customer service, time reduction, and quality, and remember that within a world-class company, financial measures are not the most important performance measure in terms of achieving your objectives.

8. Adopt Straightforward Reporting Procedures

Complex reports require a lot of preparation and take time to understand, and consequently tend to be produced monthly at best. World-class companies need to be able to act immediately on the results of performance measurement; if a report takes three weeks to generate, then this three-week lead time will impact on continuous improvement. Adopt the one-page management reporting rule.

9. Communicate Your Progress

Nothing inspires and motivates like success. Employees should be kept fully informed of the organization's progress (get your staff to produce their own progress charts if possible). By adopting simple measurement techniques, results can be given to employees on a daily basis, preferably in a graphic or pictorial form. Progress reports can be an inspirational form of communication; poor communication is responsible for many corporate failures and shortcomings.

10. Revise Your Performance Targets

As your organization raises its performance in the areas you have defined, identify new areas to be improved. As areas improve, their reports should reduce to exception reporting (reports showing only those items that deviate from plan or the established norm), allowing the organization to focus on new needs.

11. Assess Effectiveness

Becoming world-class, though an achievement, is not the end of the process. To be a world-class company you must continue to benchmark yourself against your competitors regularly. If you fail to do this, your organization will slip from the position it has achieved and be replaced by another. Staying world-class is just as hard as becoming world-class, if not harder.

DOS AND DON'TS

For Developing a Strategy for World-class Business

DO

- Continue to set challenging targets for your company.
- Remain flexible and adaptable—within limits.
- Have a bias toward action and controlled risk.
- Focus on continuous improvement.
- Keep a close and constant eye on major competitors.
- Be sensitive to the conditions, context, and methods of local cultures.
- Respect the importance of measures and reports.

DON'T

- Don't become complacent once you achieve world-class status.
- Don't attempt to impose your usual corporate practices across borders.

THOUGHT STARTERS

- Do you know the key performers in your industry?
- What approaches toward ensuring and measuring customer satisfaction do you have in place?
- Do you have the means of measuring the quality of your organization's performance?
- Do you set high targets that are measured, reviewed, and renewed?

For More Information

Books:

Meister, Jeanne C. *Corporate Universities: Lessons in Building a World-Class Work Force*. Rev. ed. New York: McGraw-Hill, 1998.

Schonberger, Richard J. *World Class Manufacturing: The Next Decade: Building Power, Strength and Value.* New York: Free Press, 1996.

Todd, Jim. *World-Class Manufacturing*. New York: McGraw-Hill, 1994.

Journal Articles:

Basu, Ron, and Nevan Wright. "Measuring Performance Against World Class Standards." *IIE Solutions* (December 1996): 32–35.

Markides, Constantinos, and John M. Stopford. "From Ugly Ducklings to Elegant Swans: Transforming Parochial Firms into World Leaders." *Business Strategy Review* 6:2 (1995): 1–24.

Smith, Steve. "World Class Competitiveness." *Managing Service Quality* 5:5 (1995): 36–42.

Web Site:

American Productivity & Quality Center: **www.apqc.org**

"In a global economy the challenges and changes are universal." (Robert Heller)

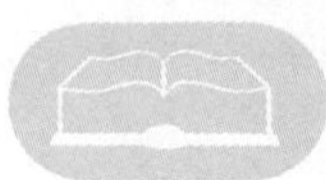

GETTING CLOSE TO THE CUSTOMER

CHECKLIST

This checklist is aimed at managers at all levels and explores the steps and principles involved in assessing customers' needs as the basis of any business operation. It focuses on how to identify your customers' needs, but does not extend to suggesting ways of meeting those needs.

DEFINITION

Getting close to the customer involves gathering facts and knowledge about your customers (current and potential) in order to develop an awareness of what customers want from you and how they perceive your organization and its products or services. This awareness in turn enables you to continuously strive to meet your customers' demands and secure your organization's long-term survival and profitability.

ADVANTAGES

Being close to your customers allows you to:

- respond to changes in demand and in the market;
- act on facts instead of hunches or intuition;
- develop products or services better tailored to your target market;
- achieve improved sales and increased profits.

DISADVANTAGES

The advantages of being close to your customers far outweigh any disadvantages, but you should take the following factors into account:

- The better you try to get to know customers, the more you risk intruding on their privacy.
- If you ask a customer to reveal personal or valuable information, you'll probably have to offer a reward or benefit in return.
- Customers may resist telling you personal information and may not always tell the truth.
- Surveys and research can be costly and time-consuming.

ACTION CHECKLIST

1. EXAMINE YOUR ORGANIZATIONAL CULTURE

You are unlikely to get close to your customers unless the culture of your organization encourages such a relationship. Staff should be trained to think "customer first"—those who are not customer-focused can jeopardize the success of the organization by making inappropriate decisions, failing to respond to changing situations appropriately or quickly enough, or neglecting to serve customers in a way that promotes their loyalty.

If the culture in your organization does not support a customer-focused approach, implement a program of long-term culture change.

Remember that every section of your organization has customers. Staff in direct contact with external customers cannot provide effective service without the internal support of colleagues all along the chain. To encourage internal service departments to adopt an outward-looking customer focus, their operators might work for a week or two in the department they service.

Customer focus needs to pervade every level of the organization. How often do your key decision-makers and strategy formulators deal face to face with customers? A period on the front line would increase their awareness.

2. IDENTIFY YOUR CUSTOMERS

Your customers are those who use the output of your work. They may be internal to your organization (for example, your personnel function has all employees as its customers) or external (members of the public, other businesses, or government or public bodies). In identifying customers, distinguish between purchasers, those who pay for your product (for example, the parent who buys the toy), and end users, those who actually use it (the child).

You will probably wish to compile a database of your customers so you can profile your customer base.

3. PROFILE YOUR CUSTOMERS

A wide range of factors influences customer behavior and choices, for example:

- gender—particularly where the purchaser or end user is not the sole decision maker;
- age—different age ranges being more susceptible to targeting by some products than others;
- marital status—especially combined with other factors such as children and disposable income;
- home ownership—indicating specific needs and responsibilities that relate to buying patterns;
- location—urban consumers differing from rural ones, and regions differing culturally and economically;
- lifestyle—since all customers have individual activities, interests, and opinions.

These factors become more useful when they are analyzed in combination—for example, home ownership, age, and number of dependent children can indicate the likely amount of a customer's disposable income.

Decide how to approach your customers to find out their basic characteristics. It may not be possible to ask every customer individually, but other fruitful approaches exist, for example:

- market research
- questionnaires
- user- or focus-group discussions
- customer audits
- attitude surveys

Take advantage of opportunities to meet business customers at their premises or at yours in a series of open houses or customer care programs or through membership of user groups, industry liaison meetings, or partnerships arising out of new product development.

"I look in my closet, and if I need it, I design it. If it works for me, it works for the customer."

(Donna Karan)

  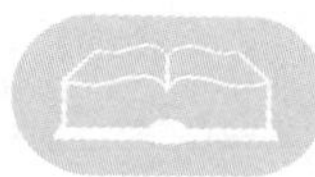   

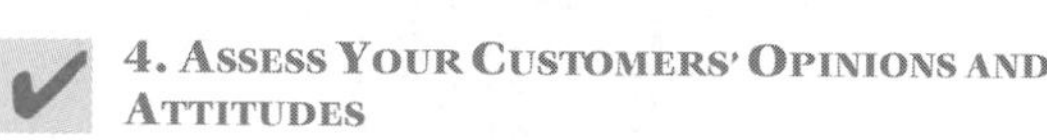

4. Assess Your Customers' Opinions and Attitudes

Organizations with an inaccurate perception of their customers' needs most likely:

- make untested and unwarranted assumptions about what customers think;
- rely on weak anecdotal evidence;
- accord too much weight to atypical complaints.

If you don't make the effort to find out what your customers think, you can be caught off balance when they go elsewhere. If you don't know why they are going elsewhere, you can't identify corrective actions. Besides basic factual information about your customers, find out:

- why customers buy your product or use your service;
- how they use it;
- what their opinion is of your product or service;
- why they choose your offering over the competition;
- what their experience is of your product or service in terms of performance and after-sales care.

Attitudes and opinions are hard to quantify, and many factors influence a decision to purchase or to remain loyal to a particular brand. Customers may be influenced as much or more by their impressions of service—courtesy, promptness, etc.—as by the quality of a product. Exploring these issues requires detailed research, and if you do not have adequate in-house expertise you may wish to use an external research agency.

Be sure to listen to your frontline staff, who are on the receiving end of firsthand comments from customers about their satisfaction and dissatisfaction. Consider setting up a procedure for reporting this information.

Channels usually employed for customer service can also be used to solicit customers' opinions by fostering an open dialog that is meaningful to the customer. Such channels include customer charters, extended warranties, statements (and monitoring) of performance standards, open and willing acceptance of penalties for noncompliance, and refunds in cases of nonsatisfaction.

5. Act On Your Findings

Analyze the results of your research, interpret the data, and publicize your findings. Use your findings to identify where you need to take action to maintain your competitive advantage. Involve all staff in this process; encourage everyone to think "customer first."

Paying attention to your customers' needs is an ongoing process. Consider setting up a regular research project, introducing methods of soliciting customers' suggestions and creating response mechanisms, or initiating procedures that constantly monitor your market.

6. Consider Using the Internet to Improve Customer Focus

The Internet is increasingly being used by customers to select items for purchase, specify designs, and submit comments and suggestions on products and services. Used judiciously, the Web permits an organization to get closer to its customers than ever before.

7. Give Feedback to Customers

Let your customers know that you value their needs and their ideas. This may mean publishing a revised mission statement reiterating your commitment to fulfilling their needs, or publicizing survey results and details of new products or product amendments made as a result of the research.

Feedback is not a onetime event. It needs to be a continuous process that informs customers of your organization's response to suggestions, mistakes, and new ideas and that encourages further dialog.

DOS AND DON'TS

For Getting Close to the Customer

DO

- Think of ways to reward customers for sharing their likes and dislikes.
- Make sure your organizational culture encourages staff to think "customer first."
- Integrate customer focus with other business activities—it should be a cross-departmental, cross-functional initiative.

DON'T

- Don't make assumptions about what people think without testing them.
- Don't rely on data from too small a sample of customers.
- Don't react too hastily to vociferous complainers—see whether other customers feel the same way.

THOUGHT STARTERS

- When was the last time you spoke to, or came into contact with, a customer?
- Do you know who buys your product and why?
- How easy is it for your customers to complain and give feedback?

For More Information

Books:

McQuarrie, Edward F. *Customer Visits: Building a Better Market Focus*. 2nd ed. Thousand Oaks, CA: Sage Publications, 1998.

Smith, Ian. *Meeting Customer Needs*. 2nd ed. Woburn, MA: Butterworth-Heinemann, 1997.

Web Sites:

Customer Care Institute: **www.customercare.com**

International Customer Service Association: **www.icsa.com**

"If the shoe doesn't fit, must we change the foot?" (Gloria Steinem)

 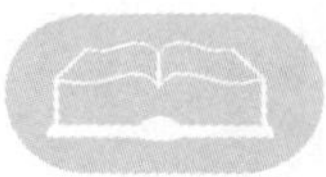    

HANDLING COMPLAINTS

CHECKLIST

This checklist outlines a procedure for handling complaints in small or large, manufacturing or service, or private- or public-sector organizations.

It is designed to establish a consistent company-wide approach to complaints that ensures that they are dealt with effectively to the advantage of both the customer and the organization.

DEFINITION

A complaint is an expression of lack of satisfaction with any product or service, whether orally or in writing, from an internal or external customer.

ADVANTAGES

A complaints procedure:

- provides a clear approach when a complaint occurs;
- engenders understanding and confidence about how to tackle complaints;
- helps to remove employees' personal guilt feelings when they receive a complaint;
- leads to a recognition of complaints as valuable feedback, not criticisms;
- can produce records for analyzing possible service improvements.

ACTION CHECKLIST

1. ESTABLISH A COMMON APPROACH TO HANDLING COMPLAINTS

The approach you decide on needs to have the widespread support of staff throughout the organization, including those who do not come into direct contact with customers. The corporate approach should be embedded in the corporate culture so that everyone is thinking about customers in the same way. This is primarily the responsibility of senior management.

Remember that when customers complain, they like to be:

- aware of who is dealing with the complaint;
- listened to and believed;
- treated fairly and efficiently;
- kept informed of progress;
- compensated if it is appropriate.

2. DRAW UP A COMPLAINT FORM

A standard form for recording complaints is a valuable tool. It should include the following information:

Receipt details

- date received
- received by
- department/division

Customer details

- name, address, identifier
- telephone/fax /e-mail

Complaint details

- action (to be) taken
- date completed
- sign-off
- line supervisor

3. SEE THAT COMPLAINTS ARE EVALUATED CORRECTLY

Any employee who receives a complaint should look on it as a second chance to satisfy the customer. Staff should:

- be courteous and empathize with the customer;
- make sure that all relevant details are obtained and recorded on the standard complaint form;
- be satisfied that the information is factual;
- not admit liability or fault at this stage.

Subject to getting more information and establishing the facts, the staff member who received the complaint should consult with the line manager if necessary and decide whether it is a major or minor complaint.

Minor complaints may result from misinterpretation, misunderstanding, detail errors, or straightforward carelessness. Major complaints may involve breach of the criminal law or have health and safety or financial implications.

4. ESTABLISH OWNERSHIP AND RESPONSIBILITY

Staff should be empowered to take appropriate action if the complaint is clearly justified, falls within their jurisdiction, and can be rectified immediately. If the complaint cannot be resolved right away, the staff member should record full details on the complaint form and pass it on quickly to the relevant area or level of responsibility. The customer should be told who is dealing with the complaint—nothing is more frustrating than dealing with a faceless corporation or being passed from one person to another—and assured that a reply will be forthcoming as soon as possible, and certainly within a specified time limit.

5. ESTABLISH ESCALATION PROCEDURES

In the case of major complaints, the manager should decide on appropriate action, for example:

- consulting a more senior member of staff;
- producing a detailed report on the events;
- contacting the organization's lawyer;
- contacting the police.

6. EMPHASIZE CUSTOMER CONTACT FOR COMPLAINT RESOLUTION

If the level of seriousness has been properly assessed and the relevant facts correctly ascertained, appropriate action should become apparent. Problem resolution is not a time for negotiation or bartering with a customer who has a genuine grievance and who should perhaps be compensated generously. If there is any delay in resolving a complaint, the customer should be given progress updates at regular, agreed intervals.

"I need problems. A good problem makes me come alive." (Tiny Rowland)

  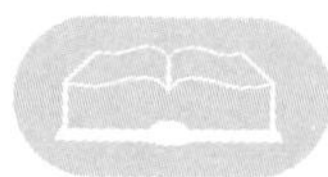    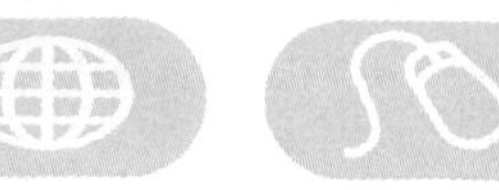

7. Make Sure That Complaints Forms Are Signed Off

When the problem has been resolved to the satisfaction of the customer, the staff contact or superior should sign off on the complaint form.

It may happen be that there is no satisfactory solution or that the customer requires something that seems unreasonable or is clearly beyond the responsibility of the company to deliver. If this occurs, it may be appropriate to:

- reaffirm the steps that can be taken;
- state that a report will be passed on to senior management.

8. Decide On Internal Corrective Action

Having dealt with the complaint, decide whether any system, equipment, or personnel-related improvement needs tackling. Deal with internal process improvements or training requirements as soon as possible after the complaint has occurred.

9. Build In Customer Satisfaction Checks

After an appropriate interval, say two weeks, get back in touch with the customer to confirm that the complaint was satisfactorily resolved–and to check that the organization still has a customer.

10. Analyze Complaints Periodically

All complaint forms should be returned to a central address where a manager should have responsibility for monitoring the level and nature of complaints. The results of this analysis and details of any corrective action should be reported to senior management on a regular basis.

THOUGHT STARTERS

- Do staff know what to do when they receive a complaint?
- Does the company receive many complaints?
- Does it receive many different kinds of complaints?
- Are they recorded?
- What happens to the records?
- When you last complained, how was the problem handled? Have you dealt with that company again?
- An organization that never has any complaints is probably a bad one—if no one bothers to complain, they just go elsewhere.

DOS AND DON'TS

For Handling Complaints

DO

- Make customer service part of the corporate culture.
- Empower staff to deal with complaints.
- Maintain contact with the customer to ensure that the complaint is dealt with satisfactorily
- Analyze the pattern of complaints and take action to make improvements.
- Treat complaints positively. Courtesy, speed of response, and a personal touch are essential. A complaining customer who gets all three will usually emerge a more satisfied customer than before the complaint.

DON'T

- Don't take the complaint personally or defensively.
- Don't blame the computer or a third party.
- Don't say it's not your department.
- Don't use paperwork to block a fast response to complaints.

Offhand, slow, or impersonal treatment is likely to lose you not only that customer, but many others besides—bad news spreads.

For More Information

Books:

Barlow, Janelle. *A Complaint is a Gift: Using Customer Feedback as a Strategic Tool*. San Francisco, CA: Berrett-Koehler, 1996.

Morgan, Rebecca L. *Calming Upset Customers*. Normal, IL: Crisp Publications, 1996.

Journal Articles:

Cook, Sarah, and Steve Macaulay. "Practical Steps to Empowered Complaint Management." *Managing Service Quality* 7:1 (1997): 39–42.

Eccles, Gavin, and Philip Durand. "Complaining Customers' Service Recovery and Continuous Improvement." *Managing Service Quality* 8:1 (1998): 68–71.

Horovitz, Jacques. "Managing Customer Complaints for Profit." *Perspectives for Managers* 27:11 (1996): whole issue.

See also:

☆ **Managing the Customer (pp. 65–66)**

✓ **Handling Customer Incidents (pp. 672–74)**

"In solving our problems, we should beware of creating worse ones." (Indira Gandhi)

  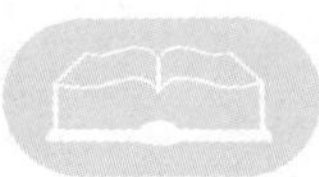    

Moving toward the Virtual Organization

CHECKLIST

This checklist is written for managers wishing to gain an understanding of the major philosophies underlying the concept of the virtual organization and the key factors involved in it.

The virtual organization embraces changes to traditional corporate structures and methods of working. Many of these changes are already established; others still seem futuristic. This checklist does not advocate revolutionary change, but describes the considerations involved in an evolutionary approach to creating a virtual organization. Some kinds of organization will find it easier to embrace virtuality than others, but all managers need to familiarize themselves with what has been described as the management model of tomorrow.

Definition

There is no single way to define a virtual organization. Most writers agree, however, that a definition should embrace the concept of organizational flexibility unconstrained by traditional barriers of place and time. Essentially the virtual organization relies on exploiting cyberspace, the electronic medium for data exchange brought about by the integration of telecommunications and computer software. It accepts the notion of a hidden reality behind the scenes, one in which results are not achieved in traditional ways. It implies that an organization, team, individual, service, or even product need not exist physically, although it may appear to be material; it is real but not real. "Virtual organization" is actually an umbrella term for various initiatives that organizations are exploring to make themselves more responsive to changes in today's marketplace.

Advantages

With a virtual organization:

- Distance does not hinder the accomplishment of work, meetings, collaboration, or conferences.
- Productivity rises significantly.
- Overhead costs are reduced.
- Work can be spread across time zones.
- Organizations can focus on what they are best at.

Disadvantages

The benefits of the virtual organization cannot be realized unless management:

- empowers and trusts staff members;
- establishes reciprocal loyalty between employees and employer;
- involves all employees, not just knowledge workers;
- questions older, accepted methodologies and explores new ways of working.

Action Checklist

Becoming Aware

1. Take Account of the Changing Marketplace

Evaluate what your organization is doing strategically to respond to change, remain competitive, and meet customers' demands. How will you:

- penetrate new markets and cut costs?
- meet ever-higher levels of quality and still increase speed-to-market?

2. Formulate a Corporate Vision

Thinking of your organization's future means analyzing where you are now and how you got there, and determining where you want to be in the future and planning how to get there. To do this you need to understand what your organization is best at and know how to deploy its skills and resources effectively.

Formulate a clear vision for the future that encompasses both a destination and a framework for planning, objective setting, decision making, and action.

3. Beware of Continual Downsizing

Try to analyze objectively where downsizing is taking you: leaner may not mean stronger. You should be considering new ways of working, not just reducing numbers and leaving others to fill the gaps. Downsizing should increase efficiency, and should come only after a reengineering effort involving due analysis of work processes and the capability of available technology.

4. Distrust Fixed Structures

Fixed, hierarchical structures are slow to respond to a fast-changing market. Think instead of flexible structures that can exploit opportunities more readily by allowing the company to pull together resources from both inside and outside the organization according to need.

Taking Steps

1. Join the Communications Revolution

Barriers to corporate adoption of IT are being dismantled by cheaper, ever more powerful hardware and software, and wider computer literacy. The convergence of IT and telecommunications has created an explosion of data sharing among individuals who are physically remote from each other. Take advantage of this revolution by:

- using e-mail as a cheap alternative to letters, fax, or phone;
- exploring computer-telephony integration (CTI), which allows a callers to be identified and their records to appear on the computer screen before, or as, the operator answers the phone;
- buying laptop computers so employees can be more mobile. With a laptop anyone can take the office anywhere at any time.

"The revolution people are talking about is one of form rather than substance." (Michael Perry)

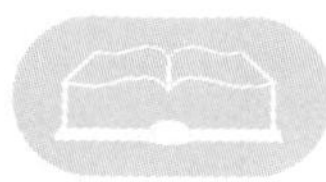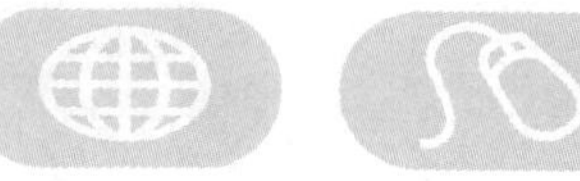

2. Consider New Ways of Working

Look at various options that give both employer and employee flexibility in where and how work is done. These options include:

- e-mail–allows people in different sites to work together;
- groupware–permits many people to participate in simultaneous on-screen dialogs while accessing the same corporate information;
- videoconferencing–connects people in remote locations by live audio and video links;
- telecommuting–connects home-based employees to the company's computer network;
- hot-desking–provides office space to mobile employees by maintaining a pool of unassigned workstations in the workplace;
- hoteling–provides office space to mobile employees by allowing them to reserve workstations in the workplace in advance.

Undertake a cost-benefit analysis. The added equipment costs may be insignificant compared with the potential savings on overheads such as office space and travel.

3. Consider Outsourcing

Decide whether outsourcing might enhance your competitiveness. Analyzing your company's core competencies will help you identify support functions for outsourcing: you may already have started with cleaning and catering services and may now decide to move on to training and IT. Before you do, consider potential problems outsourcing might raise as well as its benefits.

4. Identify Collaborative Partners and Alliances

Virtual organizations may extend beyond the boundaries of a traditional company in two ways:

- through strategic partnerships and alliances;
- through a temporary network of independent companies that share resources, skills, and costs in order to exploit market opportunities.

Finding the right partner may not be as easy as it seems. Considerations include:

- the right fit of competencies;
- shared values;
- mutual trust to stand alongside formal structures and agreements;
- the division of responsibility for marketing strategies;
- sharing financing for the project.

5. Add Value to Your Information Systems

Database systems can and should do more than store, handle, sort, and retrieve information. They can be integrated with other systems such as CTI and the Internet to expand customer service. Learn what is technically possible, decide what you want to achieve, and build a system that delivers what customers need. You no longer have to be in the office to deliver a first-class customer service–you can provide it through IT.

6. Manage the Human Implications

Think about instinctive human reactions to change and the investment your people have in the status quo. Employees may (with reason) feel that virtual working threatens the social aspects of work that they value, while managers fear (with equal reason) losing control of a work force they cannot see. Both organizations and individuals need to shift entrenched attitudes.

Such changes cannot happen overnight, however. Identify other organizations that have successfully implemented virtuality and see what you can learn from their experience.

DOS AND DON'TS

For Moving toward the Virtual Organization

DO

- Ask yourself where the organization will be in five years.
- Consider how IT and telecommunications can change the way you do business.
- Look at what your competitors are doing.
- Weigh up the cost implications of IT/communications technologies.

DON'T

- Don't think in terms of fixed structures.
- Don't underestimate the pitfalls in changing traditional ways of working.

THOUGHT STARTERS

- How do you manage people whom you do not see? (Handy, "Trust and the Virtual Organization" [1990])
- In the future, some organizational functions may exist solely in computer systems. (Barnatt, "Office Space, Cyberspace and Virtual Organization" [1995])

For More Information

Books:

Hedberg, Bo, et al. *Virtual Organizations and Beyond: Discover Imaginary Systems*. New York: John Wiley, 1997.

Lipnack, Jessica, and Jeffrey Stamps. *Virtual Teams: People Working across Boundaries with Technology*. 2nd ed. New York: John Wiley, 2000.

Journal Articles:

Barnatt, Christopher. "Office Space, Cyberspace and Virtual Organization." *Journal of General Management* 20:4 (Summer 1995): 78–91.

Handy, Charles. "Trust and the Virtual Organization." *Harvard Business Review* 73:3 (May-June 1990): 79–91.

"Knowledge building for an organization occurs by combining people's distinct individualities with a particular set of activities."

(Dorothy Leonard)

PERFORMING A SWOT ANALYSIS

CHECKLIST

This checklist is for anyone carrying out, or participating in, a SWOT analysis. SWOT is the acronym of Strengths, Weaknesses, Opportunities, and Threats. It is a simple, popular technique that can be used for preparing or amending plans, problem solving and decision-making, or making staff generally aware of the need for change. The usefulness of SWOT analysis, however, has recently been questioned, and it may be seen as an outdated technique.

DEFINITION

SWOT analysis is a general technique that can find applications across diverse management functions and activities, but it is particularly appropriate to the early stages of strategic and marketing planning.

Performing a SWOT analysis involves identifying and recording the Strengths, Weaknesses, Opportunities, and Threats concerning a task, individual, department, or organization. The analysis typically takes into account internal resources and capabilities (strengths and weaknesses) and factors external to the organization (opportunities and threats).

ADVANTAGES

SWOT analysis can provide:

- a framework for identifying and analyzing strengths, weaknesses, opportunities, and threats;
- an impetus to analyze a situation and develop appropriate strategies and tactics;
- a basis for assessing core capabilities and competences;
- the evidence for, and cultural key to, change;
- a stimulus to participation in a group experience.

DISADVANTAGES

Some commentators argue that SWOT analysis is an overview approach unsuited to today's diverse and unstable markets. They also suggest that it can be ineffective as a means of analysis because it tends to:

- generate long lists;
- rely on description instead of analysis;
- ignore prioritization;
- be overlooked in the later stages of the planning and implementation process.

ACTION CHECKLIST

1. ESTABLISH THE OBJECTIVES

The first key step in any management project is to be clear about what you are doing and why. The purpose of conducting a SWOT analysis may be wide or narrow, general or specific—anything from getting staff to understand, think about, and be more involved in the business to rethinking a strategy, or even rethinking the direction of the business.

2. SELECT APPROPRIATE CONTRIBUTORS

This is important if the final recommendations are to result from consultation and discussion, not just personal views, however expert.

- Pick a mixed group of specialist and "ideas" people with the ability and enthusiasm to contribute.
- Consider how appropriate it would be to mix staff of different levels.
- Think about numbers: 6 to 10 people may be enough, especially in a SWOT workshop, but up to 25 or 30 can be useful if one of the aims is to get staff to see the need for change.

3. ALLOCATE RESEARCH AND INFORMATION-GATHERING TASKS

Background preparation is a vital stage for the subsequent analysis to be effective, and should be divided among the SWOT participants. This preparation can be conducted in two stages: exploratory, followed by data collection; and detailed, followed by a focused analysis.

- Gathering information on strengths and weaknesses should focus on the internal factors of skills, resources, and assets, or the lack of them.
- Gathering information on opportunities and threats should focus on external factors such as social, market, or economic trends over which you have little or no control.

4. CREATE A WORKSHOP ENVIRONMENT

If compiling and recording the SWOT lists takes place in meetings, exploit the benefits of workshop sessions. Encourage an atmosphere conducive to the uninhibited flow of information and to participants openly expressing what they think, free from blame. The leader/facilitator has a key role and should allow time for free flow of thought, but not too much. Half an hour is often enough to spend on strengths, for example, before moving on. It is important to be specific, evaluative, and analytical at the stage of compiling and recording the SWOT lists—mere description is not enough.

5. LIST STRENGTHS

Strengths can relate to the organization, to the environment, to public relations and perceptions, to market shares, or to people. "People" elements include staff skills, capabilities, and knowledge that can provide a competitive edge or explain past successes. Other people strengths include:

- friendly, cooperative, and supportive staff
- a staff development and training program
- appropriate levels of involvement through delegation and trust

"Organizational" elements include:

- customer loyalty
- capital investment and a strong balance sheet
- effective cost control programs
- efficient procedures, systems, and well developed social responsibility

6. List Weaknesses

This session should not constitute an opportunity to criticize the organization, but should elicit an honest appraisal of the way things are. Key questions include the following:

- What obstacles prevent progress?
- Which elements need strengthening?
- Where are the complaints coming from?
- Are there any real weak links in the chain?

The list for action could include:

- a lack of new products or services
- a declining market for your main product
- poor competitiveness and higher prices
- noncompliance with or nonawareness of appropriate legislation
- a lack of awareness of the company's mission, objectives, and policies
- staff absenteeism
- the absence of methods for monitoring success or failure

It is not unusual for "people" problems—poor communication, inadequate leadership, lack of motivation, too little delegation, no trust, the left hand never knowing what the right is doing—to feature among the major weaknesses.

7. List Opportunities

This step is designed to assess socioeconomic, political, environmental, and demographic factors, among others, to evaluate the benefits they may bring to the organization. Examples include:

- the availability of new technology
- new markets
- a new federal administration
- new programs for training or monitoring quality
- changes in interest rates
- an aging population
- strengths and weaknesses of competitors

Bear in mind just how long opportunities might last and how the organization may take best advantage of them.

8. List Threats

The opposite of opportunities—all the above may, with a shift of emphasis or perception, have an adverse impact. Other threats may include:

- the level of unemployment
- environmental legislation
- political uncertainty or instability in offshore manufacturing sites or foreign markets
- exchange rate fluctuations

It is important to have a worst-case scenario. Weighing threats against opportunities is not an exercise in pessimism; it is rather a question of considering how possible damage may be limited or eliminated. A factor such as Information Technology may emerge as both a threat and an opportunity. Most external factors are in fact challenges, and whether staff perceive them as opportunities or threats is often a valuable indicator of morale.

9. Evaluate Listed Ideas against Objectives

With the lists compiled, sort and group facts and ideas in relation to objectives. It may be necessary for the SWOT participants to select the five most important items from the list in order to gain a wider view. Clarity of objectives is key to this process, as evaluation and elimination will be necessary to cull the wheat from the chaff. Although some aspects may require further information or research, a clear picture should start to emerge at this stage in response to the objectives.

10. Act On Your Findings

Make sure that the SWOT analysis is used in subsequent planning. Revisit your findings at appropriate intervals to check that they are still valid.

DOS AND DON'TS

For Performing a SWOT Analysis

DO

- Choose the right people for the exercise.
- Select an appropriate SWOT leader or facilitator.
- Be analytical and specific.
- Record all thoughts and ideas in steps 5–8.
- Take a wide-ranging view of external influences and trends.
- Be selective in the final report.

DON'T

- Don't try to disguise weaknesses.
- Don't merely list errors and mistakes.
- Don't allow the SWOT to become a blame-laying exercise.
- Don't ignore the outcomes at later stages of the planning process.

For More Information

Journal Article:

Hill, Terry, and Ray Westbrook. "SWOT Analysis: It's Time for a Product Recall." *Long Range Planning* 3:1 (February 1997): 46–52.

See also:

✓ **Brainstorming (pp. 542–43)**
✓ **Planning a Workshop (pp. 426–27)**
✓ **Preparing a Marketing Plan (pp. 472–73)**
✓ **Setting Objectives (pp. 480–81)**
✓ **Solving Problems (pp. 408–09)**
✓ **Strategic Planning (pp. 484–85)**
✓ **Writing a Business Plan (pp. 486–87)**

"Next to knowing when to seize an opportunity, the most important thing in life is to know when to forgo an advantage."

(Benjamin Disraeli)

PLANNING A CONFERENCE

CHECKLIST

This checklist is for anyone who is responsible for planning a conference. Conferences can be productive and memorable if they achieve the objectives of both the organization and the delegates. Alternatively, they can be disorganized, irrelevant, and wasteful of the delegates' time. The difference between the two is careful and detailed planning of the whole process, from the setting of objectives to the studious observation of protocol at the final dinner. If any detail is left to chance and something goes wrong as a result, the conference will be a failure for someone, and this can rebound on the organizers and the host organization.

DEFINITION

Conferences are held for a great variety of reasons—they can be promotional, in-house, educational, or sales-based, to name a few. This checklist concentrates on conferences run for profit.

Basically a conference is a gathering of speakers and delegates meeting to solve particular problems, make specific decisions, discuss or learn about issues of mutual interest, publicize services to potential markets, or discuss cooperation with other bodies.

ACTION CHECKLIST

1. ESTABLISH THE NEED FOR A CONFERENCE

If you have never organized a conference before, be warned: relative to some other methods of achieving your objectives, the planning of a conference can be very expensive and time-consuming. Ask yourself:

- Whom do you want to reach?
- What do you want to say (or ask or discuss), and why?
- How and where do you want to say it?

Your answers will help you determine whether a conference really is the most appropriate and cost-effective way of achieving your objectives, and will establish an initial set of objectives for planning the conference itself.

2. SET UP A PLANNING COMMITTEE

Conferences are best planned by a small committee, which will set detailed objectives and a business or promotional program. Remember, however, that the committee needs to be action-oriented.

3. APPOINT A CONFERENCE MANAGER

The committee should appoint a conference manager with full authority to solve problems, make decisions, and negotiate with external parties. This person should have experience in dealing with people at all levels and should like handling conferences, otherwise the work will not be done well. He or she should understand every detail of what is required and should cross-check with the conference committee regularly. The conference manager ultimately has responsibility for the success or failure of the conference.

It is possible to engage the services of a professional conference organizer. Although this can be expensive, it can also prove both desirable and cost-effective for large or complex conferences.

4. PREPARE A SCHEDULE

It takes time to organize a successful conference. Appropriate venues are often booked a year or more in advance. The committee and manager should plan a schedule that allows sufficient time to find the right venue, engage appropriate speakers, and send out publicity. The manager also needs to think of the multitude of other considerations that accompany a conference, for example:

- access and parking
- comfortable space for an unknown (although estimated) number of delegates
- presentation equipment and visual aids
- accompanying exhibition
- information desk
- access to phones, fax, and e-mail for delegates
- catering and special dietary requirements
- varying accommodation requirements

5. DRAW UP A PROGRAM

The business program, drawn up by the committee, should meet your objectives completely. Identify a range of speakers who are experienced, sincere, and convincing. Remember that poor presentation of first-class material can destroy a conference session. Plan the schedule so that the presentations hold the delegates' attention (people usually concentrate for a maximum of 25 to 30 minutes before needing a break). Make allowance in the program for:

- breaks between presentations
- extended refreshment breaks
- light lunches to prevent delegates from dozing off in the afternoon sessions (if you serve alcohol, do so in moderation)
- a few light relief presentations sandwiched between heavier ones
- the right balance between interactive, lecturing, and discussion sessions
- the right balance between work and leisure

Draw up a social program: it is to the organizer's and delegates' advantage to remain together most, if not all, of the time.

6. APPROACH AND BOOK SPEAKERS

Approach possible speakers and book them as early as possible. Once a booking is confirmed, agree on the content and format of the speaker's presentation. Approach and book reserve speakers, too, in case of last-minute problems.

Remember to stress (and re-stress) the timing of the presentations, as most speakers overrun. At least one dress rehearsal is advisable—schedule a date and make sure the speakers can attend.

"There is no better place in the world to find out the shortcomings of each other than a conference."

(Will Rogers)

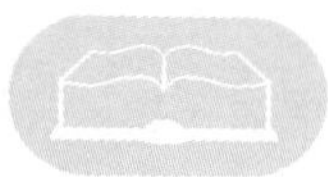

7. Identify Your Delegates

The choice of delegates is closely linked to the conference objectives and is not quite as straightforward as it may seem. A sales conference, for example, will have sales representatives as its delegates, but who else will attend? Will you invite partners? Who will help educate your sales force—the marketing department? Technical people? External consultants? Will you invite customers or potential customers?

8. Select a Venue

Once the format of the conference, the speakers, and the intended delegates have been determined, the conference manager should provide a list of appropriate venues that fall within the financial guidelines set by the committee. Venues can be identified through personal knowledge, word of mouth, or agencies.

The manager should visit the venues to compare them and ensure that they meet all specifications. It is worth remembering that hotels offer special conference rates and are often cheaper off-season and at weekends.

The conference room is of prime importance. The size of the room is the first consideration, but in addition it should have:

- pleasant overall surroundings
- ceiling height in proportion to the size of room (a low ceiling can depress delegates)
- a first-class PA system (if the system is inadequate, high-quality equipment should be hired)
- efficient but quiet air conditioning
- efficient room-darkening
- easy access to convenient exits and entrances
- comfortable seating

Inspect the bedrooms, both standard and executive, to check that they are clean and have the facilities your delegates will expect.

Are the catering facilities adequate to cope with the number of delegates who will be attending? Ask for some sample menus. Look at the dining area.

Find out how the hotel will deal with the sudden arrival and departure of your delegates. Ask how they will deal with people who arrive at 2 a.m. A separate conference reception desk can handle this efficiently and can also serve as a conference information desk throughout.

9. Advertise the Conference

Once you are clear about whom you wish to attend and details of the venue and speakers, it is essential to advertise the conference as widely (or as accurately) as possible. The committee should have identified possible advertisers at an early stage.

10. Assemble Information for the Delegates

As soon as arrangements allow, registered delegates should be sent a preconference packet containing:

- the objectives of the conference and an outline of the program
- arrival instructions
- hotel details (cost, contact information, map, etc.)
- details of what delegates are expected to pay for
- the name of the conference manager and assistant and their contact information

11. Create the Right Atmosphere

Achieving the right atmosphere is vital, although there is no magic formula for it. Panic and last-minute rush are obviously to be avoided; aim instead for calm efficiency, courtesy, friendliness. Even a very well planned conference can flop if the atmosphere isn't right.

12. Debrief After the Conference

During the conference, the manager should concentrate solely on the administration of the event and the domestic needs of the delegates. Finally, those involved should hold a briefing. Was your conference a success? What lessons did you learn? Add any action points to your checklist for the next conference.

DOS AND DON'TS

For Planning a Conference

DO

- Pay attention to details and recheck them with all concerned.
- Be a perfectionist to the extent of being a nuisance: your conference could easily fail on account of an avoidable error.
- Make contingency plans to deal with unexpected problems such as illness or guest speakers who are unavoidably delayed.
- Plan to collect feedback from delegates for analysis and review.

DON'T

- Don't leave things to chance or assumption.
- Don't be afraid to make changes or deviate from the plan when the conference will benefit, or survive, as a result of such action.

For More Information

Books:

Appleby, Pauline. *Organizing a Conference: How to Plan and Run an Outstanding and Effective Event*. Hudson, MA: Pathways, 1999.

Dodson, Dorian. *How to Put On a Great Conference*. Santa Fe, NM: Adolfo Street Publications, 1992.

Journal Articles:

Carrington, Lucie. "Meeting Points." *Personnel Today* (April 19, 1994): 35–36.

Churchill, David. "Hangovers Are Out and Cost-effectiveness Is In." *Management Today* (January 1993): 56–58.

Fowler, Alan. "How to Choose a Conference Venue." *People Management* 2:7 (April 4, 1996): 40–41.

"In preparing for battle I have always found that plans are useless, but planning is indispensable."

(Dwight David Eisenhower)

Preparing a Marketing Plan

CHECKLIST

This checklist focuses on the standard model of marketing planning endorsed by several writers in the field. The model contains formalized procedures, although the degree to which these are followed will depend on the culture and requirements of your organization.

The discipline of marketing planning has been widely debated. Depending on their standpoint, academics have defended the standard textbook model or proposed alternative versions. Malcolm McDonald, one of the principal writers in the field, acknowledges that "marketing planning is still the most enigmatic of all the problems facing management."

Definition

Marketing planning is simply a logical sequence and a series of activities leading to the setting of marketing objectives and the formulation of plans for achieving them.

(Malcolm H. B. McDonald, "Ten Barriers to Marketing Planning." *Journal of Marketing Management* 1989)

Advantages

- They encourage a rational approach to making business decisions.
- Everyone follows the same strategy, thus reducing potential conflicts, misunderstandings, and operational difficulties.
- They allow senior management to set out marketing strategy while leaving the day-to-day implementation to junior management.
- They help to highlight areas you might otherwise miss.

Disadvantages

- They form a complex process that requires basic knowledge and skills to plan.
- They are time-consuming and therefore costly to construct and follow.
- Firms composed of small business units lose some of their flexibility.
- Procedures can tend to take over and become an end in themselves.

Action Checklist

✔ 1. Set Strategic Objectives

Traditionally these have been set by top management, although current practice is to employ more democratic processes involving the key stakeholders, if not all the staff. They are not usually within the brief of the marketing planner alone. These objectives need to be kept firmly in mind and the strategies and action plans drawn up need to be broadly in line with them. The marketing process can't go forward without them. The written plan should include a copy of the strategic objectives and the organization's mission statement.

✔ 2. Conduct a Marketing Audit

This process enables a company to analyze and understand the environment in which it operates. It is the key to the SWOT analysis, the next stage in the marketing planning process. It is conducted in two parts: the external audit and the internal audit. The external audit should cover the business and economic environment, the market, and the competition; examine the important trends that have affected and will be affecting the market and the industry; and consider searching questions about competitors and customers, now and in the future. The internal audit should concentrate on the planner's own company and cover its operational efficiency and service effectiveness, its key skills, competences, and resources, its products or services, and its core business.

✔ 3. Conduct a SWOT Analysis

This is a summary of the audit listed under the headings Strengths, Weaknesses, Opportunities, and Threats, and should be included in the final written plan. Strengths and Weaknesses refer to the company and its internal environment. Opportunities and Threats are external factors over which the company has no control but which it must anticipate, evaluate, and try to exploit. Include only key data.

✔ 4. Articulate Your Assumptions

These assumptions are the strategic drivers of the marketing plan. They may relate to economic, technological, or competitive factors. Assumptions should be based on accurate information and sensible estimates of what can be achieved in the light of past performance. Sound information is problematic because the pace of change is making the future discontinuous from the past. Coming up with viable and challenging assumptions involves creative lateral thinking and breaking with the past. Only a few major assumptions should be included in the written plan.

✔ 5. Set Marketing Objectives

This is the central step in the marketing planning process. It is important not to confuse objectives (what you want to do) with strategies (how you are going to do it). Marketing objectives are concerned with which products are to be sold in which markets. The setting of achievable and realistic objectives is based on the analysis of the marketing audit; the objectives themselves drive strategy decisions. The objectives should be included in the written plan.

✔ 6. Estimate Expected Results

Marketing objectives should be SMART: Specific, Measurable, Achievable, Realistic, and Timetabled, for example, "to gain a 6 percent share of the overall market," or "to achieve 600 customers by the end of the year." Nonspecific terms such as "increase" or "maximize" should not be used unless they can be quantified.

"Running a media brand is about harnessing the value of people. . .journalists, DJs, editors—all of them are the brand."
(Vijay Solanhi)

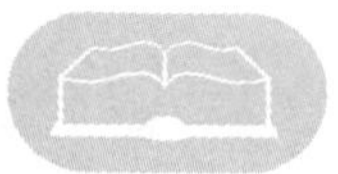

7. GENERATE MARKETING STRATEGIES
These describe the broad methods by which the marketing objectives will be achieved within a required time. They are generally referred to as the "marketing mix" or the "Four Ps": Product—what its benefits are to the customer; Price—how it is priced to attract the right, or appropriate, customer base; Place—who those customers are; and Promotion—how they can be reached. They should appear in the written plan.

8. DEVELOP PROGRAMS
The general strategies must be developed so that they have their own programs or action plans. The combination of these plans and their relative importance will depend on the company. A large company with several different functions or departments may have several plans covering advertising, sales promotion, pricing, etc. Other companies may have a single plan, for example, a product plan embracing the Four Ps. Details of the programs should be included in the written plan.

9. COMMUNICATE THE PLAN
Everyone should understand the plan. It is advisable to communicate it to employees by giving a presentation instead of circulating written copies. If the plan is not effectively communicated, it is likely to be implemented poorly and will probably fail.

10. MEASURE AND REVIEW PROGRESS
Monitor the plan as it progresses. Make sure the measures you collect are meaningful to its success. If circumstances change, revise the plan to include details of how you intend to take advantage of new opportunities or counter new threats; repeat steps 4–9 above in order to do this.

DOS AND DON'TS

For Preparing a Marketing Plan

DO
- Be clear on the organization's strategic objectives.
- Analyze information carefully.
- Adjust the plan to suit the size, culture, and circumstances of the organization.
- Consult on and communicate the plan.
- Remember that the plan is a means to achieve objectives, not a rigid control mechanism.
- Be aware that planning is a time-consuming exercise.

DON'T
- Don't confuse objectives (what you want to achieve) with strategies (how you are trying to achieve them).
- Don't spend too long projecting future markets from historical data.
- Don't let the planners alter the shape of the objectives.

THOUGHT STARTERS
- Is your marketing unsystematic, opportunistic, haphazard, or initiative-led?
- Have you set measurable market targets in the past?
- Are your marketing objectives and tactics known and coordinated throughout the organization?
- Do you really know what your customers think of you?
- Is your market stable and your market position secure?

For More Information

Books:

McDonald, Malcolm H. B. *Marketing Plans: How to Prepare Them, How to Use Them.* 4th ed. Woburn, MA: Butterworth-Heinemann, 1999.
Westwood, John. *The Marketing Plan: A Practitioner's Guide.* 3rd ed. Milford, CT: Kogan Page, 2002.

Journal Articles:

Cousins, Laura. "Marketing Plans or Marketing Planning?" *Business Strategy Review* 2:2 (Summer 1991): 35–54.
Griffin, Tom. "Marketing Planning: Observations on Current Practices and Recent Studies." *European Journal of Marketing* 23:12 (1989): 21–35.
McDonald, Malcolm H. B. "Ten Barriers to Marketing Planning." *Journal of Marketing Management* 5:1 (Summer 1989): 1–18.

Web Sites:

American Management Association: **www.amanet.org**
American Marketing Association: **www.marketingpower.com**

See also:

☆ **How to Plan Marketing (pp. 59–60)**
✔ **Performing a SWOT Analysis (pp. 468–69)**
✔ **Strategic Planning (pp. 484–85)**
✔ **Writing a Business Plan (pp. 486–87)**

"Grand business plans are all very well, but nothing beats dipping your toe in the water."
(Karan Bilimoria)

  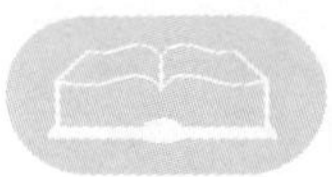    

Producing a Corporate Mission

CHECKLIST

This checklist is for senior managers charged with establishing a sense of mission within their organization. This may extend to implementing a cultural change and writing a mission statement.

Definition

There is a great deal of contradiction in the literature over the differences and similarities between vision and mission. It probably doesn't matter what you call it, or whether you treat them separately or as one and the same. It is the process that is important, and this checklist therefore focuses on that process.

In this checklist a corporate mission or vision is taken to mean a description of the road ahead. The mission statement:

- describes the purpose of the organization;
- identifies how an organization defines success;
- outlines the strategy that will be followed to achieve success;
- incorporates the shared values and behavior that the organization expects from employees.

The corporate mission may be known as a corporate philosophy, a credo, or a set of values. Whatever it is called, it should combine the inspiration of where we are going with the realities of where are we now and how are we going to get from here to there. The process of developing a corporate sense of mission incorporates such techniques as strategic planning, developing a corporate culture, internal communication, and empowerment. It involves writing a mission statement, from which appropriate goals and targets can be derived for specific business units and departments. (Strategic planning and setting objectives are dealt with in separate checklists.)

A mission statement does not create a sense of mission. Employees need to feel that they are part of the process, and they will respond to a mission statement only if they can understand it, relate to it, and own it. Developing a sense of mission is usually more successful if it is viewed as a long-term, evolutionary process. However, an organization can develop a mission statement and use it to focus the business. This approach is usually successful only if there has been close consultation with managers as the mission is developed.

Advantages

It is widely believed that an organization with a sense of mission will outperform those that don't have one.

A well produced mission:

- outlines clearly the way ahead for the organization;
- informs and inspires employees;
- identifies the business in which the organization will be operating in the future;
- defines success;
- serves as a living statement that can be translated into goals and objectives at each level of the organization.

Disadvantages

Missions fail when:

- the top management team lacks consensus;
- the organization's identity, goals, and strategies are poorly defined;
- communication with employees is ineffective;
- planning and focused implementation are neglected.

Action Checklist

The process of establishing a mission is a task for the senior management team. It involves a detailed analysis of the strategy and future of the company. Conducting a SWOT analysis can be helpful in identifying your company's strengths and opportunities. (Performing a SWOT analysis is the subject of a separate checklist.)

1. Create a Project Team

The mission team may comprise the complete senior management team in a small organization or a working group of a larger management team. An external facilitator is often useful in assisting the team to reach a consensus.

2. Gather Information

The project team should meet with all the senior managers and research internal and external information on the current strategy and image of the company.

Interview senior management, seeking to identify areas of agreement and conflicts in attitudes, opinions, and strategic thinking.

Obtain an internal view of the organization by talking to a number of influential managers. Research external opinion by consulting press files, analysts' reports, and customers and suppliers.

Compare the views. Use the acquired information to build a broad picture of the company.

The project team should collate this information and prepare a detailed report to present to the senior management team.

3. Build Consensus

The senior management team should work to reach a consensus of a clear vision for the company: an external facilitator can play an important role here. This vision may define direction—a clear declaration of where the management team wants to take the organization. It certainly constitutes a clear message of the firm's intentions to all stakeholders.

Explore barriers that may pose obstacles to the desired direction and agree on appropriate steps and responsibilities for dealing with them. This is the point at which the team begins to own the mission and take responsibility for it. Such obstacles may be perceived at the level of resources: they are probably at the level of core competencies, and appropriate staff development may be needed to overcome them.

"Our mission tritely is to change the world." (Donna Dubinsky)

4. Draft a Mission Statement

The mission statement should be written by the senior management team, as it needs to draw on the consensus already reached on the future of the organization. The mission statement is the guide to the company-wide evolution of the corporate sense of mission.

A good mission statement includes:

- a description of the business;
- the mission of the organization;
- the broad strategies to be pursued to fulfill the mission;
- a statement of the guiding values of the organization.

Mission statements often broadly declare the organization's goal of being the best; identify the importance of people, quality, and service; and emphasize the role of innovation, communication, and growth.

Mission statements should be assessed in terms of clarity, succinctness, memorability, credibility, and motivational power, and should be revised accordingly. The mission statement should be worded in such a way that all employees can relate to it.

5. Develop Action Plans and Set Objectives

Action plans should aim to build on the consensus and commitment developed among the senior management team and spread it throughout the organization. Set objectives by asking what needs to be done to realize the mission. Formulate plans to overcome the major barriers to achieving the vision—this is where the mission process meets the strategic planning process. Decide how to communicate the mission.

6. Communicate the Mission

Workshops, internal newsletters, and group meetings are all useful in communicating the corporate mission. It is important to develop a sense of ownership of the mission throughout the organization: it is the employees who bring it to life.

7. Monitor and Review

Developing a sense of mission should be viewed as a long-term process. Introduce mechanisms that allow you to continually monitor the views of all stakeholders so that you know how far the sense of mission has spread, how deep the relevance and understanding of the mission statement are, and to what degree corporate values have spread throughout the organization. Use regular group meetings to refine your corporate philosophy.

DOS AND DON'TS

For Producing a Corporate Mission

DO

- Develop a broad picture of the organization.
- Gain an understanding of the existing culture of the organization.
- Focus on the core activities of the organization.
- Listen to the views of all stakeholders.

DON'T

- Don't move without a consensus among the senior team.
- Don't see this as a quick process.
- Don't see this as a onetime activity.

THOUGHT STARTERS

- Is there a broad understanding of what the organization's values are and where the organization is headed?
- Is each staff contribution recognized as a key part in the mission?
- Do staff know what the mission of the organization is?

For More Information

Books:

Campbell, Andrew, and Kiran Tawadey. *Mission and Business Philosophy*. Woburn, MA: Butterworth-Heinemann, 1993.

O'Hallaron, Richard, and David O'Hallaron. *The Mission Primer: Four Steps to an Effective Mission Statement*. Richmond, VA: Mission Incorporated, 2000.

Journal Articles:

Bart, Christopher K. "Sex, Lies and Mission Statements." *Business Horizons* 40:6 (1997): 9–18.

Matejka, Ken, et al. "Mission Impossible? Designing a Great Mission Statement to Ignite Your Plans." *Management Decision* 31:4 (1993): 34–37.

Piercy, Nigel F., and Neil A. Morgan. "Mission Analysis: An Operational Approach." *Long Range Planning* 19:3 (1994): 1–19.

Raynor, Michael E. "That Vision Thing: Do We Need It?" *Long Range Planning* 31:3 (1998): 368–76.

Rigby, Rhymer. "Mission Statements." *Management Today* (March 1998): 56–58.

See also:

☆ **Who's Guiding Your Corporate Destiny? (pp. 216–17)**

PUBLIC RELATIONS PLANNING

CHECKLIST

This checklist is designed to help those with little or no background in public relations to begin to manage this area effectively in their organization. It provides a model for developing a public relations plan that supports the organization's overall aims and objectives and gives guidance on press and public relations activities. It is designed for use by managers in all types of organizations in the private, public, and nonprofit sectors.

ADVANTAGES

Effectively managing public relations can:

- influence public opinion of the organization and enhance corporate image;
- create awareness of a product, service, or brand, leading to sales;
- generate support for the organization's work;
- develop long-term business relationships;
- improve staff recruitment and retention.

DISADVANTAGES

There are no real disadvantages to public relations planning, but failure to manage public relations effectively can result in:

- misrepresentation of an organization's activities or products;
- damage to corporate image;
- boycotting of an organization's operations;
- lack of public understanding of the organization, leading to missed opportunities;
- loss of advantage to competitors;
- loss of business and sales.

ACTION CHECKLIST

In order to develop a public relations plan, you need to look at the overall business aims and objectives of your organization. The public relations objectives should support these and link to the overall business plan.

1. DEFINE TARGET AUDIENCES

These will depend on the nature of your business, but are broadly defined as:

- customers/clients—those who buy or use your products or services;
- the media—press, radio, TV, Internet;
- internal groups—current and future employees, suppliers, distributors;
- community groups and pressure groups;
- government—federal, state, local;
- investors, shareholders, potential sponsors.

2. CONDUCT RESEARCH

It can be valuable at this stage to undertake research among your customers or the groups you wish to influence to establish their current awareness and opinion of your organization, product, or service. The findings will reveal which areas you need to concentrate on, and can then act as a benchmark against which to measure your success in meeting your objectives.

3. SET PUBLIC RELATIONS OBJECTIVES

Objectives show what you plan to do, while strategies and programs describe how you plan to do it. Objectives should be realistic, measurable, and achievable within a specified time limit.

For example, if your organization has a marketing objective to increase purchases of Product X by consumer group Y by 10 percent over the next 12 months, you could set a public relations objective to improve awareness of the benefits of Product X among consumer group Y within the next 12 months.

4. DECIDE KEY MESSAGES

Decide on the messages that you wish to get across to the different groups your organization needs to communicate with. Outline the concepts you wish to convey—precise wording and presentation can only be determined later when you have chosen your media.

5. CLARIFY RESOURCES

Establish the financial and human resources available to commit to public relations. Your list should include budget, staff, time, equipment, IT, design, and printing facilities.

Indicate which are in-house resources and which may need to be bought in; then you will be in a position to make choices about where to spend your budget.

6. SELECT A PROGRAM OF ACTIVITY

The program describes the actions you intend to undertake to achieve your objectives. It should include a timetable detailing planned actions, perhaps classified by phases or activities, on a monthly, quarterly, and yearly basis. The program should clearly prioritize the communication channels you have chosen.

Below are examples of types of activity you might pursue. They are outlined under broad headings for ease of access, but some of these activities can often be used in communications with multiple audiences, although they might emphasize different messages. For example, a briefing could be used for public affairs and lobbying, but it could also be used to communicate with potential sponsors, staff, and community leaders.

Media Relations

Press releases/statements, articles, radio and TV interviews and discussions, press conferences and briefings, photo opportunities and photographs, press visits, and press interviews (telephone or face to face).

Internal Communications

In-house newsletters, staff briefings and seminars, bulletin boards, memos, briefing papers, training manuals,

"The public may be willing to forgive us for mistakes in judgment but it will not forgive us for mistakes in motive."

(Robert W. Haack)

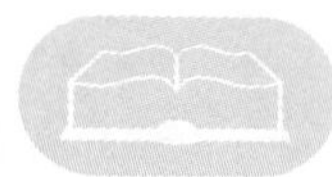

internal videos, open houses, conferences, intranets, and e-mails.

Public Affairs and Lobbying
Briefing documents for senators, members of Congress, and state legislators, submissions to government committees, briefings/presentations to senators, members of Congress, state legislators, and federal and state government officials.

Events Management
Exhibitions, conferences, talks, presentations, road shows, staffing a stand or leading workshops at trade shows, competitions, and awards.

Community Relations
Familiarization visits, community projects, sponsorship of local charities, open houses for community leaders and neighbors, information videos, consultation and discussion groups.

Investor Relations
Reports, accounts, annual general meetings, briefings and presentations, stockholder newspaper/magazine, corporate video.

7. Evaluate Successes and Failures

Making your public relations objectives measurable enables you to evaluate how well various activities have worked. You can measure success in terms of "output objectives"—for example, did you meet your original aim to release a given number of stories to the business media each quarter?

Measuring success by "impact objectives," however, is more valuable in the long term—for example, did you succeed in your original goal of raising awareness within a specific group and affecting its members' behavior? Impact can be harder to measure than output, but the results provide more accurate performance indicators.

You can also put systems in place to measure, for example, the number of leads and sales generated by media coverage or conduct follow-up research to determine changes in awareness and attitudes as a result of a public relations campaign.

THOUGHT STARTERS

- To whom are you talking?
- What message do you want to communicate?
- Why do you want to communicate it—what are the goals and objectives?
- Which activities are you going to use?
- When are you going to carry them out?
- How much will it cost in resources?
- How will you evaluate your success?

For More Information

Books:

Caywood, Clarke L. *The Handbook of Strategic Public Relations and Integrated Communications.* New York: McGraw-Hill, 1997.
Cutlip, Scott M. *Effective Public Relations.* Upper Saddle River, NJ: Prentice Hall, 1999.

Web Sites:

Institute for Public Relations: **www.instituteforpr.com**
Public Relations Society of America: **www.prsa.org**

"Whenever we have compromised on our principles, we and our customers have been the losers."
(Marcus Sieff)

Setting Up a Customer Service Program

This checklist describes the stages in establishing an organizational framework that maximizes the value offered to and derived from customers.

Definition

Successful customer service means making customers want to come back for more, and getting them to recommend products and services to others. Customer service is about not only meeting customers' expectations, but delighting customers by focusing staff energies on offering value, getting it right the first time, and yet improving it in the future.

Advantages

A comprehensive customer service program impacts on the organization through:

- increased success
- a developing and satisfied work force

Action Checklist

1. Secure the Commitment of Top Management

Unless top management is fully committed to the concept of customer service, there is very little chance of success. A formal customer service program with involved leadership helps clearly focus roles and responsibilities.

2. Know Your Customers

Excellence in customer service is wholly reliant upon knowing your customers' needs and expectations. Needs are not the same as demands: people don't ask for what they don't expect to get, even when it can be provided. Anticipating real needs can give competitive advantage.

While it is important to remember that most companies have internal customers in other departments, divisions, and sectors, establishing external customers' needs can be complex. A range of approaches is available, including:

- feedback directly from customers and staff
- direct discussion with customers
- analysis of customer complaints, inquiries, and thank-yous
- attitude surveys and questionnaires
- site visits
- focus-group discussions and customer audits

3. Assimilate the Major Elements of Customer Service

Customer service is more than just an excellent product or a first-class service; it involves a host of elements that contribute to genuine service and value for the customer. In the sales process these might include:

- clarity of literature on product features, price, payment methods, availability, and after-sales service
- the way the first contact takes place and is followed up
- simple ordering procedures designed to be convenient for the customer
- prompt order processing
- prompt notification of any changes to specifications or procedures
- clear invoicing with no hidden charges
- assistance when the product is delivered
- easy after-sales contacts

4. Develop Service Levels

It may be the case that performance standards do exist but are not formalized, recorded, or audited. It is not good enough to set indicators or levels that place the supplier's convenience in front of the customer's; such levels should be worked out, discussed, and agreed on with customers. Levels should be set that are challenging but have a realistic chance of attainment. Questions to help set service levels may include:

- How many times does the phone ring before someone answers?
- How many transfers take place before the customer gets an answer?
- How long does it take to process an order?
- How long does it take to respond to a complaint?

Measurements must not gain such a hold on processes that they become a time-consuming nuisance; they should be realistic and helpful in developing a relationship—however short-lived—between supplier and customer. Remember, what gets measured, gets done.

5. Recruit the Right Staff

Your service is only as professional as the people delivering it; attracting new customers and retaining existing ones are tasks for competent people. Focusing the recruitment process on customer service can mean introducing questions at the interview stage, covering, for example:

- candidates' experiences with customers
- service levels and customer expectations
- the prioritization of customer needs over in-house activities
- incentives to motivate frontline staff

Remember to include customer service in the orientation program.

6. Get Your Communications Right

Top management commitment to a customer service program is no good unless the right message is conveyed to all staff in the right way. If internal communications are not working as well as they should, then external communications cannot be expected to be successful. Communications have to be reliable, consistent, and regular. All people will then receive the same message and interpret it in the same way and end results will be the same.

"The important product comparisons come from people in the marketplace." (Regis McKenna)

7. Convert Complainants Back into Customers

Prompt and sympathetic handling of complaints can turn a disgruntled customer into a happy–and longer-lasting–one. People whose complaints are fully dealt with are more loyal than those who have no complaints.

Often, those who receive the complaint are not at fault, yet they bear the brunt of the customer's dissatisfaction. It is vital that all employees are familiar and comfortable with the company's procedure, and are fully prepared after receiving a complaint to start converting the customer's dissatisfaction into satisfaction. Bearing in mind that the complaint must be dealt with promptly, accurately–it may just be a misunderstanding or lack of information–and efficiently, individuals on the front line need to be familiar with seven rules for dealing with verbal complaints.

- Listen patiently–let the customer air the grievance without interruption.
- Acknowledge the customer's viewpoint–even if you don't agree.
- Apologize–say you are sorry if a mistake has been made, but don't overdo it.
- Find a solution–establish what needs to be done to rectify the problem.
- Keep the complainant informed–lack of ongoing information can exacerbate the problem.
- Reach a conclusion to resolve the problem for the customer quickly–a more permanent solution may take longer to find.
- Follow up–check that promised action happens.

8. Reward Service Accomplishments

Build excellent customer service into the culture by recognizing and rewarding staff for superior service performance. Try to recognize smaller accomplishments, not just the major ones.

Customers, too, appreciate rewards for their loyalty, and such rewards will make a significant contribution to their retention.

9. Stay Close to Your Customers

Staying close to customers means:

- carrying out continuous research in order to learn from them;
- asking questions about the quality and performance of the product at regular intervals after the sale;
- developing procedures to stay up to date with customer needs;
- listening.

10. Train Your People and Work toward Continuous Improvement

Recruiting the right staff is just one step in a customer service program. Training staff to understand customers' needs and tackle their problems, to turn threats into opportunities for the company, is also a prerequisite for effective and lasting customer service. Train staff on a continuing basis, especially in friendly telephone and face-to-face techniques that allow them to be sincere and genuinely helpful instead of parroting empty phrases; it will more than repay the investment.

Publicizing feedback from customers is especially motivating for staff behind the scenes who are not in direct customer contact. Feedback can help you make continuous improvements in how things are done as well as in what is done.

DOS AND DON'TS

For Setting Up a Customer Service Program

DO

- Make recruitment and selection customer-oriented activities.
- Involve all staff in discussions about customer service and customers' levels of expectation.
- Offer incentives to encourage customers to give feedback.
- Analyze complaints for any trends or patterns.
- Record customers' thanks as well as complaints.
- Stay close to your customers—the profile of your best prospect is the profile of your best customer.
- Celebrate and publicize good news and achievements.

DON'T

- Don't lose sight of your internal customers.
- Don't say, "It isn't my fault," or "I don't know who deals with that here."

THOUGHT STARTERS

- A service that receives no complaints may receive little else—a service that ignores complaints will receive less use.
- What irritates you as a customer? What delights you?
- How can you make ordering/purchasing more convenient for your customers?
- How can you develop more direct relationships with your customers?
- How can you reward loyal customers?
- How can you recognize customer (dis)satisfaction?

For More Information

Books:

Brown, Stanley A. *Strategic Customer Care: An Evolutionary Approach to Increasing Customer Value and Profitability*. New York: John Wiley, 1999.

Gerson, Richard F. *Beyond Customer Service*. Rev. ed. Menlo Park, CA: Crisp, 1998.

Wellemin, John. *Successful Customer Care*. Hauppauge, NY: Barron's Educational, 1997.

"If you're not happy with yourself, how can you make the customer happy?" (Liisa Joronen)

 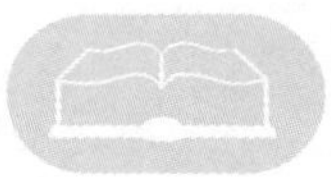    

SETTING OBJECTIVES

CHECKLIST

This checklist is designed for managers who participate in setting corporate objectives and who then have to interpret and apply such objectives to their own functional or departmental operation, including setting objectives with and for the people under their responsibility.

DEFINITION

An objective is an end toward which effort is directed and on which resources are focused. An objective should be specific (so that it is clear to those who are to work toward it), measurable (so that people will know when they have reached it or not), and, usually, tackled within certain time and cost constraints.

Setting corporate objectives means clarifying the strategic and policy requirements of the company and setting and agreeing on complementary operational objectives in relation to them. It is an integrated process that links corporate planning to business operations. As objectives are "rolled down" the organization, they are usually made more specific. Every department, every team, and every individual can and should have objectives.

Much ink has been spilled over the differences between aims, objectives, goals, and targets. There are no real differences except those of scale and time. The key is to use the terms that you—and the people you are dealing with—understand. Throughout this checklist we use the term "objective."

In order to succeed, objectives need to:

- identify a purpose and an area of responsibility such as improving performance or service;
- be specific and measurable;
- be achievable but challenging;
- be written down for both clarification and referral;
- be subjected to a process of discussion, compromise, and agreement between those setting the objective and those who are to tackle it;
- be agreed on with the performer—this is not always possible but is highly desirable because ownership leads to commitment.

ADVANTAGES

These include:

- a better understanding of corporate planning at operational level;
- a clear sense of direction;
- a better understanding of accountability throughout the organization;
- greater understanding in setting priorities;
- improved communication and motivation throughout the organization.

DISADVANTAGES

By failing to manage by objectives you risk:

- not knowing where you are going;
- never knowing what you have achieved;
- not knowing whether what you are doing is in tune with longer term plans or higher level objectives;
- confusion and demoralization.

ACTION CHECKLIST

1. DEVELOP AND COMMUNICATE THE ORGANIZATION'S MISSION/VISION STATEMENTS

People often confuse a mission with a vision statement. It is quite possible—even desirable—to have objectives relating to both.

The mission statement lays down the purpose for which the organization exists. It provides the umbrella statement for the organization's "standing" objectives.

The vision statement is the expression of an ultimate aim to which the organization aspires. It encapsulates the "change" objectives. For example:

- Our purpose is to make top quality cars (mission).
- Our aim is to become the largest-selling car manufacturer in the world by the year 2010 (vision).

Such statements should be clearly communicated to and reinforced with all personnel, not just senior management.

2. IDENTIFY CORPORATE OBJECTIVES FROM THE MISSION/VISION STATEMENT

It is important to link corporate objectives to mission and vision statements. This is usually the purpose of the strategic plan and the function of senior management, although this process is being increasingly decentralized throughout the firm in empowered organizations.

The strategic plan is formulated by an assessment of:

- what the company intends to accomplish and where it intends to be in terms of its market position in relation to the competition;
- how to be in the right markets at the right time with the right product(s) and service(s);
- how to ensure a sustainable and profitable growth.

Writing a strategic plan is the subject of another checklist.

Much will depend on the values of the organization: values may be challenged and reassessed when setting high-level objectives, and vice versa—the adoption of new objectives may well lead to a reappraisal of values. The organization's values will influence how it tackles its objectives in terms of the importance it attaches to the environment, the welfare of its staff, and job security and to its public image in general.

In many organizations, however, objective setting still remains a largely top-down exercise. In such cases, objectives should be set out in a plan and communicated to all staff.

3. AGREE ON THE OBJECTIVES FOR SENIOR MANAGERS

This is a process of splitting the corporate objectives by function, business unit, or by product or service. It will be necessary to rank the objectives in terms of priority, draw up time frames for achieving them, and identify the re-

"In business as on the battlefield, the object of strategy is to bring about the condition most favorable to one's own side."

(Kenichi Ohmae)

sources required to tackle them: this precedes the operational and financial (budgeting) planning of that function or business unit.

4. Make Sure Objectives Reach Departments and Individuals

Again, some organizations make this a two-way process, so that communication on key decisions is bottom-up as well as top-down. Don't wait forever for top-down objectives; establish your own at department level that reflect the organization's mission and are in harmony with what your customers need and what your resources are geared to deliver.

5. Agree On Objectives with Those Who Are to Tackle Them

Setting objectives should happen not by diktat or decree, but by proposing and seeking ideas, by discussion, negotiation, compromise, and agreement. That is an ideal situation. The minimum that both objective-setter and objective-performer should require from a one-on-one meeting is an answer to each of Kipling's six honest serving men: who, what, where, when, why, and how?

6. Identify Appropriate Performance Measures

Performance measures should allow progress against objectives to be measured. Performance measures (which can be employed on a team or individual basis) should indicate what is expected and how well people are doing in attaining their objectives. Performance measures should be clear, concise, easy to collect and interpret, and relevant in that they should provide information that tells you and your organization how well you are performing.

Measures are usually related to:

- efficiency (how quickly you deliver)
- effectiveness (how good/accurate/relevant the service delivery was for the customer)
- cost-efficiency
- cost-effectiveness

They usually cover information relating to:

- finance—costs as well as income;
- customers—new and lost;
- markets—penetration thereof;
- resources—consumed, saved, or required anew;
- processes—how efficiently and effectively tasks and activities are accomplished.

Performance measures should also be agreed on between job holder and manager and should be reviewed regularly, especially if there are significant changes to the work content. They are of benefit to the organization and the individual in terms of personal development. Managers may need time to help staff understand and interpret objectives for their department or their part of the organization, and even to help them determine what their own contribution to corporate objectives should be.

7. Set Up Procedures for Reviewing Performance

With step 6 above, this is the principal content of the performance appraisal. It is in the appraisal discussion that past performance is reviewed, learning opportunities are identified, and new or revised objectives are set for the next period.

THOUGHT STARTERS

- Are you clear on the "fit" between what you do and where the organization is going?
- Do your people have clear targets that are live issues in the workplace?
- Are targets measured for performance against financial, customer, and personal development indicators?

DOS AND DON'TS

For Setting Objectives

DO

- Focus on business logic, not short-term gain.
- Identify critical issues and potential obstacles.
- Recognize the importance of cultural fit.
- Build in flexible processes.

DON'T

- Don't ignore areas of potential conflict.
- Don't underestimate the resources required (money, time) for major projects.

For More Information

Books:

Rouillard, Larrie A. *Goals and Goal Setting: Planning to Succeed.* 2nd ed. Menlo Park, CA: Crisp, 1997.
Smith, Douglas K. *Make Success Measurable!: A Mindbook-Workbook for Setting Goals and Taking Action.* New York: John Wiley, 1999.

See also:

✔ **Conducting a Performance Appraisal (pp. 346–47)**
✔ **Making Rational Decisions (pp. 566–67)**
✔ **Performing a SWOT Analysis (pp. 468–69)**
✔ **Strategic Planning (pp. 484–85)**
✔ **Writing a Business Plan (pp. 486–87)**

"You establish some objectives for them, provide some incentive, and try not to direct the detailed way in which they do their work."
(David Packard)

STRATEGIC PARTNERING

> This checklist describes the planning phases of partnering: making the strategic decision to partner, structuring the strategic partnership, and selecting an appropriate partner. The principles apply equally to commercial partnerships and public-private sector partnerships.

DEFINITION

Strategic partnering agreements allow organizations to take advantage of market opportunities and respond to customer needs in collaboration, allowing them to do so more efficiently and effectively than they could separately. Such agreements may be for defined periods of time and may be nonexclusive.

Collaboration is the process by which partners adopt a high level of purposeful cooperation to maintain a trading relationship over time. The relationship is bilateral; both parties have the power to shape its nature and future direction over time. (Spekman)

Partnering means:

- spreading risk and trusting others to act in joint best interests;
- seeking a strategic fit between partners so that objectives match and action plans show synergy;
- finding complementary skills, competences, and resources in partners;
- sharing privileged or confidential information.

ADVANTAGES

Strategic partnering can help an organization:

- find an outlet for excess manufacturing capacity;
- gain quick, low risk access to new markets;
- strengthen its technological base;
- achieve economies of scale through high volume, low cost, and mass distribution;
- overcome geographic, legal, or trade barriers;
- speed up innovation and new product introduction.

DISADVANTAGES

Unsuccessful partnering may result in the following:

- a lack of strategic fit.
- an imbalance in the relationship between partners.
- implementation problems because of differing leadership styles.
- a lack of trust and confidence.
- slow decision making.
- key requirements for a market project are concentrated in one of the partners.

ACTION CHECKLIST

PHASE 1 MAKING THE STRATEGIC DECISION

1. CONSIDER YOUR PARTNERING NEEDS

Few organizations have all the resources or skills to tackle new market opportunities or other initiatives independently and maintain the economies of scale: low cost, high volume, and mass distribution. Going it alone can mean high investment, slower response to changing circumstances, and an infrastructure that may require dismantling, possibly soon afterward.

2. ANALYZE THE CHANGING MARKETPLACE

Take a good look at your organization in relation to its sector and market position. Understand who is emerging as a market leader and why, which market trends are beginning to dominate, and how the market is likely to develop in the future. The organization's stakeholders—customers, employees, stockholders, and suppliers—provide an invaluable resource to be tapped in this data-gathering exercise.

Carry out a SWOT analysis (see separate checklist) and look at how you got where you are. Do you need to invest in your technological base, your processing capacity, or new markets? Does market stability—or volatility—make that investment affordable or desirable? Look at what comparable organizations are doing to compete on innovation, service, and value for the customer.

3. IMAGINE THE FUTURE

This may well mean rethinking the business you are in or adjusting your business focus to concentrate on your core strengths. It is important not to be locked into the thinking of the past if you are to express a clear vision for the future. Such a vision should be owned by personnel throughout the organization as the driving force energizing the organization.

4. LOOK CLOSELY AT YOUR PROCESSES

When considering a strategic partner, remain conscious of what it is really like inside your own four walls. Try to gain a knowledgeable perspective on your company's:

- programs for continuing improvement and development;
- policies and practices of releasing authority to encourage initiative;
- generation, manipulation, and use of key information;
- ability to respond to market changes.

Identify the key processes that you are, or need to be, best at. Identify skills you need to develop and improve. Gaining excellence in a core competence requires years of consistent effort and application and continual renewal. A core competence, however, is probably your greatest bargaining chip in negotiating a strategic partnering agreement.

PHASE 2 STRUCTURING THE STRATEGIC PARTNERSHIP

1. DECIDE ON THE FIELD OF COOPERATION

A strategic partnership can take one of three forms: horizontal, vertical, or diagonal.

- Horizontal partnerships are usually formed with

"The Great Principles on which we will build this Business are as everlasting as the Pyramids."

(Gordon Selfridge)

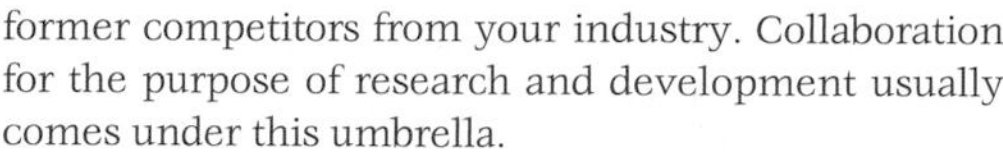

former competitors from your industry. Collaboration for the purpose of research and development usually comes under this umbrella.

- Vertical partnerships are usually formed with organizations in the supply-delivery chain such as suppliers, marketers, or distributors.
- Public/private partnerships are formed with organizations from other industries.

2. Decide On the Level of Cooperation

Consider:

- optimal time frames for making the project operational;
- resources available for the project;
- how formal the structure needs to be between partners—the legal form of organization, process and communication procedures, control processes, and organizational structure.

3. Decide On the Level of Involvement

It may or may not be a good idea to restrict the agreement to two partners. Innovation, production, and delivery, for example, may benefit strategically from partnerships with multiple partners, each bringing specific expertise and expanding the richness and the potential of the collaboration. In this case the partnership becomes a dynamic network of contributors. The addition of every extra partner, however, multiplies the possibility of something going wrong.

4. Decide On Measurement and Control

All strategic partnerships need some form of control. Determine:

- which activities which partner will control;
- how much control each partner will exercise;
- how partners will exercise control.

It would be ideal for partners to have similar measurement systems, but this is unlikely. Contribution to, and outcomes from, the partnership may be difficult to apportion when marketing and quality targets and learning objectives are key contributors to financial goals.

Phase 3 Selecting the Partner

1. Evaluate Intra- or Extra-industry Players for Basic Fit

This is largely a question of information gathering and analysis. Having decided on a horizontal, vertical, or diagonal approach, search out leading or emerging players that can add their strength to yours in a win-win partnership. Ask yourself questions like these:

- What are the risks of such a collaboration?
- Does this potential partner have a hidden agenda?
- How turbulent is the existing market? What does the future look like?
- Are other collaborators or associates in the game?

2. Establish a Partnering Champion

The partnering champion should be a senior manager who commands respect at all levels, has outstanding analytical ability, and gets things done. The champion is responsible for establishing the framework for the partnership agreement, promoting ownership of the partnership, and making it work in the startup phase.

3. Examine Strategic Fit

It is more important that partners share a broad business philosophy than short-term goals. The partnership needs to fit with the overall strategic plans of each organization; joint development of belief systems, business plans, partnership structures, and timescales flow from this agreement.

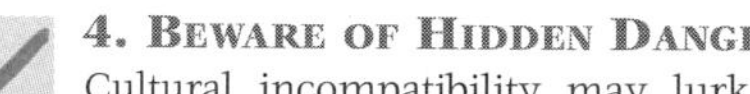

4. Beware of Hidden Dangers

Cultural incompatibility may lurk beneath the surface of many potentially successful partnerships. Management style, organizational feel, and the way things really get done are hard to quantify and often impossible to impose from the outside.

DOS AND DON'TS

For Setting Objectives

DO

- Focus on business logic, not short-term gain.
- Identify critical issues and potential obstacles.
- Recognize the importance of cultural fit.
- Build in flexible processes.

DON'T

- Don't ignore areas of potential conflict.
- Don't underestimate the resources required (money, time) for major projects.

THOUGHT STARTERS

- What changes are affecting your markets?
- How long will these changes last?
- How swiftly can you adapt to such changes?
- Is investment in your own resource levels the best answer?

For More Information

Books:

Child, John, and David Faulkner. *Strategies of Cooperation: Managing Alliances, Networks and Joint Ventures*. New York: Oxford University Press, 1998.

Mockler, Robert J. *Multinational Strategic Alliances*. New York: John Wiley, 1999.

Nooteboom, B. *Interfirm Alliances: Analysis and Design*. New York: Routledge, 1999.

Spekman, Robert E., Lynn A. Isabella, and Thomas C. MacAvoy. *Alliance Competence: Maximizing the Value of Your Partnerships*. New York: John Wiley, 2000.

"No business enterprise can succeed without sharing the burden of the problems of other enterprises."

(Ayn Rand)

 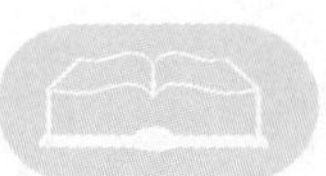    

STRATEGIC PLANNING

CHECKLIST

This checklist is for managers involved in planning the strategic position and direction of their organization for the first time. It provides a framework of practice to draw on and encourages strategic thinking rather than imposing a sequence of steps to follow.

Such is the pace of change, the growth of uncertainty, and the diversity of customer expectations today that the major risk to survival and success is in not planning. Strategic planning helps you manage the future—if you don't manage the future, the future will manage you.

DEFINITION

Strategic planning goes to the heart of what an organization does, why it does it, how it does it, and where it is going. In *The Strategy-Led Business* (1996), Kerry Napuk describes strategic planning as "a total concept of the whole business involving a framework and process that guides its future." Strategic planning addresses a number of basic questions:

- Where are you now?
- How did you get there?
- What business are you in?
- Where do you want to be in the future?
- How are you going to get there?

ADVANTAGES

Strategic planning provides an organization with a framework for:

- understanding the organization's position in the marketplace;
- moving forward with a sense of direction, purpose, and urgency;
- focusing on key issues such as quality, productivity, and customer satisfaction;
- improving motivation and communication throughout the organization;
- changing the organization to deliver required results and profitability.

DISADVANTAGES

Failing to plan makes an organization reactive, vulnerable to threats, and closed to opportunities. The strategic plan needs to be:

- flexible—adaptable to change (but too much change can cause havoc);
- responsive—taking account of the market and environmental conditions;
- creative—inspiring commitment and making the organization stand out;
- challenging—but realistic so that people can get to grips with it;
- focused—clear, defined, and understandable to staff and customers.

ACTION CHECKLIST

1. INVOLVE ALL MANAGERS AND STAFF

The planning process should not be restricted merely to contributions from senior representatives. All parts of the organization should play a part and all staff will have a contribution to make as stakeholders.

2. WHERE ARE YOU NOW?

Analyze recent performance to identify the current position of the organization in relation to its market and industry sector. Questions should include:

- What is your current market position in relation to your competitors?
- How do customers see you?
- What is your market share?
- What are your strengths (and weaknesses) in relation to your competitors?
- Are you on an upward or downward curve?

3. HOW DID YOU GET THERE?

Assess the reasons and factors that created this situation, for example:

- What did you do right (or wrong) to get there?
- What did you do well (or badly)?
- Were you in the right place at the right time?
- What does your success owe to market circumstances?
- What does your success owe to good planning, bad planning, or no planning?

4. EXAMINE YOUR CORPORATE IDENTITY

Try to gain a clear sense of identity by asking:

- What kind of people are you?
- What kind of values do you have?
- What people strengths (or weaknesses) do you have?
- What kind of leadership do you have?
- How would you describe morale?

It is important to gain a balanced view of the organization, not just the rosy side. Do not just see what you choose to—take a comprehensive look, seek evidence, and base your future planning on realism.

5. CONDUCT A SWOT ANALYSIS

Summarize your findings from the external and internal audits conducted in steps 2–4 above under the headings of (internal) Strengths and Weaknesses, and (external) Opportunities and Threats.

6. WHAT BUSINESS ARE YOU IN?

Question your own marketing literature. Does it convey the purposes for the existence of your organization? Think of your corporate focus—why you are there and what you are there to do. The business you are in is usually expressed in the organization's mission statement. There is a risk of limiting scope too much in an age of increasing specialization; equally there is a risk of broadening too far in an age that requires increasing diversification. Don't have such a narrow perspective that

"The essence of a strategy is not the structure of a company's products and markets, but the dynamics of its behavior."

(George Stalk)

  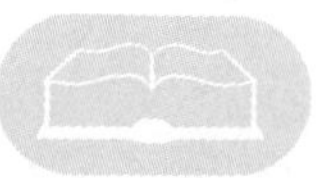    

you lose opportunities, but be wary of too broad a scope, which might lose focus and appeal.

✔ 7. Where Do You Want to Go?

Do you want to stay in the same business? Where do you want to be in the future? This consideration involves a vision for the future with objectives that, if you achieve them, will realize that vision. Do you want to expand into new areas? Why? Give priority to your core area? What is it? Deciding where you want the organization to be in the future means identifying a target destination that will shape all planning and decisions. Destination is usually expressed in terms of a vision statement.

There is some confusion and a good deal of overlap between missions and visions. Whatever distinctions are drawn, it is up to senior management to make a clear statement of what business the organization is in, where the organization is going, and how it is going to get there.

✔ 8. Establish a Time Frame

Visions usually take a rather long-term view. Although an organization needs time to change thinking and shift resources, targets are taking on ever-tighter time frames. As a general guide, visions may well take up to eight to ten years to achieve, but the strategic planning process should generate objectives or targets achievable within two to four years.

✔ 9. Set Objectives

Direction and destination need to be clarified, communicated, and agreed on, and be firm without being so rigid that modification causes failure. Set objectives by asking what needs to be done to contribute to the realization of the vision, covering:

- profitability and return on investment;
- market share and meeting market needs;
- product/service quality and customer service;
- growth and public responsibility;
- participation and commitment.

Your objectives may involve some or all of these elements and should be measurable. They should lead toward attaining the vision.

✔ 10. How Do You Get There?

Strategies need to account for the organization's weaknesses and provide the framework to put them right. The focus of the strategy, however, is on the outside world. Think of levels of empowerment and employee development; calculate plant and equipment and the investment needed; review flexible control systems and the information that you have available (or not) to make decisions. The SWOT analysis in step 5 related to the past and the present; now it is time to apply the following questions to the future.

Outside the organization:

- What changes are happening in today's markets?
- What is happening to customers' attitudes and demands?
- What is happening to technology?
- In which market areas will you have the best chance of success?
- What will customers want in the future?
- How will you tackle competitors?

And inside:

- What people skills do you need to develop?
- How can you improve your product(s) or service(s)?
- How can performance be improved to meet demand?
- What critical success factors do you have?
- How will you generate the resources to do all this?

✔ 11. Communicate and Seek Feedback

Communicate details of the emerging plan throughout the organization. Consultation and feedback are vital to widespread understanding and commitment, and your people on the ground are valuable sources of information about threats and opportunities.

✔ 12. Measure, Adapt, and Renew

The end point of strategic action is the combination of product(s), market(s), and technologies that produce results that realize the vision. The one constant is to stay close to the market. That means continuous change for the organization and continuous measurement of progress against the plan. Measurement is a key process that can indicate the levels of change and modification needed as the plan adapts to changing technologies and market forces and evolves to embrace new opportunities. Strategic plans need to be rolling plans: five-year plans should be rolled over every three years, three-year plans every two years.

THOUGHT STARTERS

- Have you looked at other organizations' strategic plans? If so, do they look credible?
- How well do you know your industry/market sector?
- How close are you to your customers?

For More Information

Books:

Johnson, Gerry, and Kevan Scholes. *Exploring Corporate Strategy*. 5th ed. Upper Saddle River, NJ: Prentice Hall, 1999.

Miller, Alex. *Strategic Management*. 3rd ed. New York: McGraw-Hill Higher Education, 1998.

Napuk, Kerry. *The Strategy-Led Business; Step by Step Strategic Planning for Small and Medium-Sized Companies*. Rev. ed. New York: McGraw-Hill, 1996.

Web Site:

Developing a Business Strategy: **www.planware.org/strategy.html**

See also:

✔ **Drawing Up a Budget (pp. 554–55)**
✔ **Performing a SWOT Analysis (pp. 468–69)**
✔ **Preparing a Marketing Plan (pp. 472–73)**
✔ **Setting Objectives (pp. 480–81)**
✔ **Writing a Business Plan (pp. 486–87)**

"The task of business strategy is to make the business more valuable by a specific route: that of targeting profitable customers."

(Shiv S. Mathur)

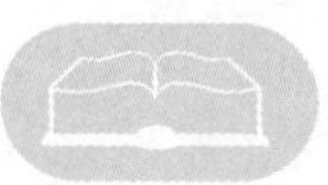

WRITING A BUSINESS PLAN

CHECKLIST

This checklist is designed as an aid to managers responsible for constructing a business plan, and provides a sequential framework for its compilation. The success of a business plan depends as much on the clarity and realism of the thought behind it as on how it is expressed and put together.

DEFINITION

A business plan is not only a requisite for seeking financing, it is also an essential document for describing aims and objectives and enabling the measurement of progress toward achieving them. The business plan provides the means to:

- appraise the present and future of the business;
- define short- and long-term objectives;
- establish a framework for action to achieve those objectives.

It consists essentially of three elements: a marketing plan, an operations plan, and a financial plan.

- The marketing plan covers how market intelligence will be gathered and ensures that the organization's strategies will meet market needs.
- The operations plan includes the supply of raw materials, technological requirements, key processes, resource needs, and production and delivery targets.
- The financial plan assesses fixed and variable costs and dictates minimum financial requirements.

ADVANTAGES

Clear business plans:

- form a yardstick by which to measure performance;
- are the starting point for departmental or divisional operational plans;
- provide a framework for offering incentives to managers;
- demonstrate that the organization knows where it is going;
- form the bridge between the organization's strategy and what people should actually do;
- can assist in attracting major customers, financing, and shareholders' support.

DISADVANTAGES

Business plans require:

- detailed thought, research, and application;
- absolutely clear expression that stands up to incomprehension and criticism;
- honest and realistic appraisal of the organization's shortcomings, problems, and obstacles as well as its strengths;
- writing from the reader's point of view, not the writer's;
- regular monitoring and modification if appropriate;
- acceptance by, not just imposition on, all the key players in the organization.

ACTION CHECKLIST

Before you start it is often valuable to carry out a SWOT analysis of your organization or industrial sector; this will help you focus on defining your objectives and drafting the plan. Remember too that the SWOT does not involve just an analysis of the past and present, but it also considers the future, especially in terms of markets, customers, and technology.

As a general rule the plan should be no more than about 25 to 30 pages, focusing most strongly on the management and financial elements. The executive summary should not exceed two pages.

1. SET THE CONTEXT

Describe the following:

- the background of the business, product, or service and a brief history of the organization
- who the customers are
- the past performance of the organization
- any key or influential elements that might dictate the success of the product or service

2. DEFINE CORPORATE OBJECTIVES

Develop a list of short-term, specific targets that will help to indicate progress toward longer-term ones. Measurability is important.

3. PERFORM A MARKET ANALYSIS

Persuade the reader/investor that the product or service will secure a substantial market. Include:

- a brief description of the overall market and the specific market segment targeted
- detailed information on current and proposed customers
- names of leading competitors, market share, and alternative products or services
- market influences—economic trends, seasonal fluctuations, legislation, social factors

Are you aware of who and where your target market is and of the changes affecting that market?

4. PROPOSE YOUR APPROACH TO MARKETING (THE MARKETING PLAN)

Describe the marketing strategy used to approach customers by detailing:

- the image of the organization you wish to convey;
- the key or unique features that will differentiate the product;
- a description of promotional and publicity material;
- the Four Ps of marketing;
- channels of distribution.

What marketing methods do your competitors use, and how effective are they?

5. DESCRIBE YOUR PLANS FOR DEVELOPMENT AND PRODUCTION (THE OPERATIONS PLAN)

Touch on all aspects of researching, developing, producing, and delivering your product or service. Describe

"After hard work, the biggest determinant is being in the right place at the right time."

(Michael Bloomberg)

  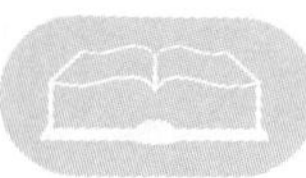    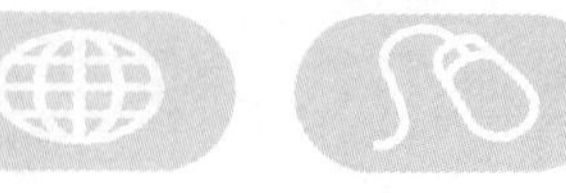

the research, development, and production processes with the expected costs of raw materials, labor, and plant and equipment. Include a brief section on contingency planning for possible scenarios that might disrupt your operations.

6. Clarify the Current Financial Situation (the Financial Plan)

Lay out exactly what is required of investors and lenders. The financial plan is composed principally of data documenting past, present, and projected performance, including startup costs, profit and loss statements, cash flow analyses, and balance sheets. Repayment will be of key interest to investors and lenders, so include accurate break-even projections. It is also important to demonstrate how sound financial control will be exercised over borrowed and incoming funds. Make sure you can support your sales forecast with reasons for your assumptions, and opt for caution rather than the rosiest scenario.

7. Demonstrate That Management Is Committed and Capable

Describe your strengths and skills. An organization chart should note managers' capabilities as well as responsibilities. If there are weaknesses, indicate how you propose to deal with them.

8. Describe the Ownership of the Organization

An investor or lender will need to know the legal constitution of the organization—partnership, limited liability, corporation. Show how much investment is already being made and by whom.

9. Discuss Critical Success Factors

Discuss risks and problems, not omitting actual and potential negative factors. Demonstrate that you are aware of likely changes in, for example, information technology, markets, or economic circumstances. Show that you will be ready to correct overspending or failure to meet deadlines.

Provide a brief account of critical success factors such as:

- the learning environment that generates success;
- specialists and technicians and their knowledge;
- how the team can respond to adversity and turn things around.

10. Conclude on a Positive Note

The conclusion summarizes the key features such as strategic direction, strengths and unique benefits, realistically projected sales, and returns. Include a proposed timetable of events to demonstrate sound planning. Write a strong conclusion that leaves the reader with a positive, dynamic impression.

11. Provide an Executive Summary

Written last, this nonetheless appears first in the final plan. Include the unique features of the product or service; the current, mid- and long-term direction of the organization; the benefits the product or service offers the defined market sector; the qualities and skills of the people who will make it all happen; a financial statement of assets, sales, and profit expectations and how much capital is required; and, as a conclusion, a statement of return for the investor.

DOS AND DON'TS

For Writing a Business Plan

DO

- Research the target readership and remember whom you are writing for.
- Consult as widely as is appropriate.
- Solicit help from appropriate sources such as accountants or bankers.
- Point out the "obvious" benefits of the product or service.
- Address fully any possible bones of contention.
- Remember the contingency aspects of the plan.
- Outline the qualities and skills of the management team.
- Keep it short, focused, and readable.

DON'T

- Don't make assumptions on the reader's behalf.
- Don't be too optimistic in estimating income potential or expecting an enthusiastic reaction.
- Don't use long words, technical jargon, or overcomplicated sentences.

THOUGHT STARTERS

- What is your main business?
- Who are your main customers?
- What is your main capability?
- How healthy—really—is your current financial situation?

For More Information

Book:

O'Donnell, Michael. *Writing Business Plans That Get Results: A Step-by-Step Guide*. New York: McGraw-Hill, 1991.

Journal Articles:

Sahlman, William A. "How to Write a Great Business Plan." *Harvard Business Review* 75:4 (July-August 1997): 98–108.

Schilit, W. Keith. "How to Write a Winning Business Plan." *Business Horizons* (September-October 1987): 13–22.

See also:

✔ **Drawing Up a Budget (pp. 554–55)**
✔ **Performing a SWOT Analysis (pp. 468–69)**
✔ **Preparing a Marketing Plan (pp. 472–73)**
✔ **Setting Objectives (pp. 480–81)**
✔ **Strategic Planning (pp. 484–85)**

"Planning, by its very nature, defines and preserves categories. Creativity, by its very nature, creates categories or re-arranges established ones." (Henry Mintzberg)

 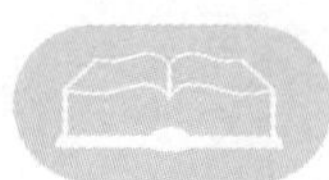  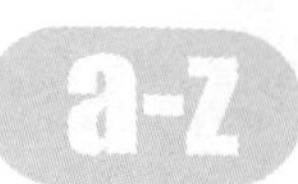  

A Program for Benchmarking

CHECKLIST

This checklist is for managers new to benchmarking or for those wishing to review current benchmarking practices.

Benchmarking is a powerful tool for organizations seeking continuous improvement. It is an essential part of many change programs, including total quality management and business process reengineering. A challenging technique to use, it requires careful management and a high level of commitment, but used effectively it can provide companies with a continuous competitive advantage.

Various types of benchmarking exist, including:

- internal benchmarking—the measurement and comparison of practices with similar practices in other parts of the company;
- industry or competitive benchmarking—industry-specific comparisons made either between direct competitors or with target companies with dissimilar products in the same industry;
- functional or noncompetitive benchmarking—the direct comparison of a function in two or more organizations, which may or may not be in the same industry;
- generic or best practice/world class benchmarking—benchmarking of the best practice of recognized world class companies;

Most organizations can use one or a mixture of these.

Definition

Benchmarking is the ongoing structured process of identifying, understanding, and adapting outstanding practices of industry leaders to help a company improve its performance and achieve and sustain competitive advantage.

Advantages

Benchmarking:

- aids the setting or stretching of performance goals;
- focuses on and accelerates change;
- motivates staff by showing what is possible;
- provides an early warning of competitive disadvantage.

Disadvantages

Benchmarking can fail for a number of reasons, including a lack of commitment, focus, or resources. There are no substantial disadvantages to benchmarking, however.

Action Checklist

1. Plan Your Study

Identify the critical performance factors at which you wish to excel; from these select the broad areas in which to benchmark. Focus on those activities that are of real importance to your company, avoiding activities that are irrelevant or are simply easy to measure.

Select a small number of related processes to benchmark. Do not be too ambitious at this stage, particularly if this is the first benchmarking project your company has undertaken. When selecting processes to benchmark, remember the critical success factors: benchmarking must be supported by senior management, be integrated with corporate strategy, and be based on a sound understanding of your own processes.

Consider the legal and ethical issues of competitive benchmarking. Confidentiality and data security are important issues for benchmarking partners and groups.

2. Identify Personnel

Select a benchmarking team and a team leader. Most benchmarking is done by teams to take advantage of the range of skills and knowledge they can offer–use either an intact work group, a cross-functional team, or a functional team. Six members is an average team size. Although much work will be conducted by the benchmarking team, it is advantageous to encourage the participation of all staff, as benchmarking may identify gaps in performance that may require radical change anywhere in the organization. The involvement of process owners ensures they are part of the evaluation process and can become the champions of change.

3. Examine the Process(es) to Be Benchmarked

Document the process(es) to be benchmarked to gain an understanding of the activities involved. Simple flow charts can be useful aids to help define the inputs to, and outputs from, the process. Any number of elements can potentially be measured, so it is important for the benchmarking team to determine which ones are true indicators of performance.

4. Plan Data Collection

Data is required in order to make comparisons between organizations or parts of an organization. This information may take the form of statistics, ratios, or detailed case studies and descriptions. As the key to the success of benchmarking projects, the data collection process should be carefully planned. Collect only the data required for decision making: collecting too much information can be as bad as collecting the wrong data.

5. Identify Benchmarking Partners

Consider internal sources (different departments, divisions, or companies within the organization) and external partners (competitors, similar industries, or best practice/world class performers). Sources that can help in identifying partners include trade and industry journals, market research reports, government studies, databases, suppliers, customers, corporate networks, and study tours.

"The most successful innovators are the creative imitators, the number two." (Peter F. Drucker)

Consider contacting a benchmarking clearinghouse or a joint interest group.

Solicit the participation of partners. Organizations are often willing to become involved if they can see that they will also benefit from benchmarking—after all, it should be a two-way process. Be willing to share data and findings and to respect requests for confidentiality.

6. Plan the Comparison Exercise and Gather Data

- Identify the "hard" and the "soft" issues that need to be measured. Hard issues include ratios, time, and costs. Soft issues might include management style, communications, or customer focus.
- Prepare an action plan. Identify who will collect the data, from where and when. The benchmarking team should develop an appropriate survey or interview guide. Questionnaires can be sent by mail or completed over the telephone or on site visits. Decide which is the most appropriate for your requirements.
- Collect the data. It is easy to underestimate the time that data collection requires—err on the side of caution when arranging fact-finding interviews

7. Use Data Analysis to Plan Improvements

Draw up a matrix of performance indicators from your benchmarking partners (using spreadsheets and databases can help the analysis).

Compare your current performance against the data. Identify where your company is missing certain elements, fails to match the targets of others, or generally needs to improve. The benchmarking team should try to identify the causes of these failures and, with relevant additional staff, plan to remedy them. It is useful to research case studies of best practice, which can form useful aids to help communicate the objectives of change.

Involve process owners in setting goals to close, meet, and exceed the gaps in performance. The benchmarking team should develop detailed action plans, including measures of success.

8. Action Improvements

Once the business benefits that would result from change have been identified, communicate the benchmarking findings. If you demonstrate benefits, employees are more likely to support change. Implement the plan, making use of "process champions" throughout the company as catalysts for change. It is at this stage that resources will need to be committed, so it is essential to have senior management support for the project.

9. Monitor and Review

Monitor the success of the benchmarking in reaching its objectives; the impact of the improvements on the organization; the evidence of a change in the process; the value of the changes to the organization; and the willingness and the barriers to change.

Evaluate the success of the project. Decide if further change is needed. Select the next process to benchmark. Maintaining momentum is one of the most challenging problems in benchmarking.

DOS AND DON'TS

For a Program for Benchmarking

DO

- Secure senior management support.
- Make sure that benchmarking is a team activity.
- Understand your own processes before starting to look at those of other organizations.

DON'T

- Don't be too ambitious at the start.
- Don't underestimate the need for corporate willingness to change and an openness to new ideas.
- Don't view benchmarking as a tool for providing short-term gains.

THOUGHT STARTERS

- Is the performance of your organization as good as it could be?
- How do you match up to the performance of competitors?
- Are you focusing purely on financial measures or have you considered all your key processes?
- How do your processes compare with those of other organizations?

For More Information

Books:

Finnigan, Jerome P. *The Manager's Guide to Benchmarking: Essential Skills for the New Competitive-cooperative Economy*. San Francisco: Jossey-Bass, 1996.

Harrington, H. James, and James S. Harrington. *High Performance Benchmarking: 20 Steps to Success*. New York: McGraw-Hill, 1995.

Journal Articles:

Hanman, Stephen. "Benchmarking Your Firm's Performance with Best Practice." *International Journal of Logistics Management* 8:2 (1997): 1–18.

Spendolini, M. J. "How to Build a Benchmarking Team." *Journal of Business Strategy* 41:2 (March-April 1993): 53–57.

Web Sites:

American Productivity and Quality Center: **www.apqc.org**

CFO.com Benchmarking Center: **www.cfo.com**

See also:

☆ **Outsourcing (pp. 89–90)**
✔ **Deciding Whether to Outsource (pp. 490–91)**
Outsourcing (pp. 2061–62)

"Whatever a great man does, others imitate. People conform to the standards he has set."

(Bhagavad Gita)

 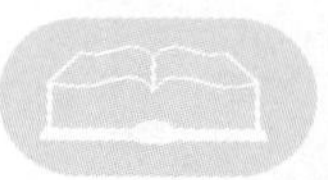    

DECIDING WHETHER TO OUTSOURCE

CHECKLIST

This checklist is for managers addressing the decision of whether to outsource or not, and if so, what and how to outsource. The checklist describes the stages in the process, leading up to drawing up and testing a contract.

Often seen as a threat by employees and an opportunity by companies, outsourcing is becoming more widely accepted. In addition to the inevitable driver of cost savings, many contributory elements lead a company to consider outsourcing, in particular the need for flexibility as demand for products or services rises and falls and as ways of delivering them improve.

DEFINITION

Outsourcing is increasingly understood to mean the retention of responsibility for services by an organization while the day-to-day performance of those services is devolved to an external organization, usually under a contract with agreed standards, costs, and conditions.

In this checklist the organization considering outsourcing some or part of its functions will be called the "Organization"; the external organization designated to take them on will be called the "Agency."

ADVANTAGES

The Organization generally makes the decision to outsource for a number of reasons, including:

- cost and efficiency savings
- greater financial flexibility through reduced overhead
- operational flexibility and control through contractual relationships
- a wish or need to focus on core activities
- access to better management skills for non-core activities
- staffing flexibility

DISADVANTAGES

Outsourcing can:

- reduce corporate robustness by changing support functions;
- require considerable care in coordinating information flow with the Agency;
- reduce the Organization's learning capacity by depleting its skill base;
- impair the Organization's ability to integrate processes;
- compromise the Organization's control over the functions that are outsourced;
- damage morale and motivation as jobs appear to be lost;
- increase employees' insecurity, whether staff remain in the Organization or are hired by the Agency.

ACTION CHECKLIST

1. CREATE A PROJECT TEAM

Treat the outsourcing proposal like a project. Select a project leader and team, establish terms of reference, a method of working, and an action plan.

2. ANALYZE YOUR CURRENT POSITION

Ideally you should have conducted a radical review of the Organization's processes—you don't want to outsource a function that might be better integrated with one of your core activities. Maintaining a clear vision of where the business is going, make sure you evaluate:

- what advantages you can gain by concentrating on core services;
- the minimum corporate involvement necessary to perform functions that don't affect the customer;
- how much control you require over nondiminishing, nonproductive overheads;
- which functions are more viable operated by an external agency.

3. PAY ATTENTION TO PEOPLE

As the contract stage approaches, your staff will suffer from anxiety and uncertainty. At best their working life will be transferred from one employer to another, at worst their job could be lost. Keep your people's welfare at the forefront of your thinking.

4. BENCHMARK

Someone somewhere is probably doing the same thing that you are in a better way, or in the same way at lower cost. Identify appropriate organizations to benchmark against, and establish which activities they are outsourcing.

5. COME TO A DECISION

Identify your core areas—Tom Peters says, "Do what you do best and outsource the rest." The principal questions are:

- What is core to the business and to the future of the business?
- What can bring competitive advantage?

Then decide whether outsourcing should become Organization-wide policy for non-core areas or whether it should be used only as the need arises.

6. DECIDE WHAT TO OUTSOURCE

Logically, what to outsource follows from the decision process. If you focus on the core competencies of the Organization, on your uniqueness, then targets for outsourcing become the support, administration, routine, and internal services of the company.

Areas that have traditionally been subject to outsourcing include legal services, transportation, catering, printing, advertising, accounting, and, especially, auditing and security. More recently these have been joined by data processing, IT services, information processing, public relations, buildings management, and training.

"In the past, business was the employer of all those who wanted to work. In the future, there will be lots of customers, but not lots of jobs."
(Charles Handy)

Staff are usually transferred with the function to the Agency. Obviously, this is an area that requires great consideration and sensitivity.

7. Tender the Package

The tender is an objective document detailing the services, activities, and targets required as well as a selling document designed to attract Agencies that can add to the Organization's capability. Outsourcing is not just a matter of getting rid of problem areas.

Once you have defined an attractive package, send an outline specification and request for information to the Agencies that are likeliest to be interested. The outline specification should contain the broad intention of the outsourcing proposal and the timescales the Organization has in mind. The request for information is a questionnaire-type eligibility test intended to establish the level of the Agency's competence and interest. The second stage is the invitation to tender, a precise document that spells out exactly what Agencies are required to bid for.

8. Choose a Partner

The tender process should be used to evaluate facts, but choosing an outsourcing partner is much more than choosing a new supplier, because the process involves a customized service, agreement on service levels, and a contract. At this stage the Organization is looking for an Agency with which it can agree on objectives and values, hold regular senior management meetings, and share otherwise confidential information. Harmony of management styles is a key requisite for success.

9. Introduce Your Staff to the Agency

Members of your staff scheduled for transfer to the Agency should meet their new management before any contracts are signed. Allowing employees to air their concerns and ask questions may help to reduce the feeling that they are being dumped or cast aside. On the other hand, glaring conflicts in style and personalities may emerge that could affect the contractual stage. Address other issues of terms and conditions of employment, including appropriate compensation if Agency employment is not available or not required.

10. Draw Up the Contract

If the project team draws up the contract, provide appropriate legal input. The contract should spell out:

- the minimum service levels that the Agency will provide, checks and controls that these are met and clauses including remedies or financial compensation if they are not;
- the demarcation of service responsibilities and boundaries so that both Organization and Agency are clear on who is doing what;
- who owns what in terms of equipment and hardware;
- the fate of the staff to be outsourced and details of their terms and conditions of employment;
- flexibility and allowance for change, for example, if the volume of business changes radically;
- a contract term with a review date and a provision for the outsourced function to revert to the Organization;
- a trial period before the contract becomes binding.

11. Test the Contract

Make certain that the contract will stand up to the rigors and complexities of actual operation. A trial period is ideal for making adjustments before the contract becomes final and for judging the likelihood of the partnership breaking down.

DOS AND DON'TS

For Deciding Whether to Outsource

DO

- Have a clear vision of what outsourcing should achieve.
- Understand the scope of the services to be outsourced.
- Outsource the performance of a function, not the responsibility for it.

DON'T

- Don't outsource strategic, customer, or financial management.
- Don't let the goal of cost savings dominate everything else.
- Don't think that outsourcing is the answer to every problem.

THOUGHT STARTERS

- Have you defined the core areas in which you need to excel?
- Do routine and support functions consume an ever larger slice of overhead?
- Will outsourcing be an extension of your organization's operations or an innovation?

For More Information

Books:

Bendor-Samuel, Peter. *Turning Lead into Gold: The Demystification of Outsourcing*. Provo, UT: Executive Excellence, 2000.
Greaver, Maurice F. *Strategic Outsourcing: A Structured Approach to Outsourcing Decisions and Initiatives*. New York: AMACOM, 1999.

See also:

✓ **Implementing a Service Level Agreement (pp. 502–03)**
✓ **Managing Projects (pp. 512–13)**
✓ **A Program for Benchmarking (pp. 488–89)**

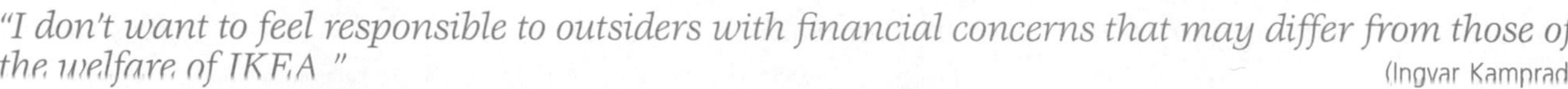
"I don't want to feel responsible to outsiders with financial concerns that may differ from those of the welfare of IKEA."
(Ingvar Kamprad)

Disaster Planning

CHECKLIST

This checklist aims to help managers putting together a disaster plan for their organization. It covers physical disasters such as fires, floods, or terrorist attacks. Crisis planning is the subject of a related checklist.

Having a disaster plan forces you to make decisions before a disaster strikes, allowing you to spend the first crucial days after a disaster dealing with the situation instead of deciding how to deal with it.

Definition

A disaster plan (DP) aims to prevent or reduce the likelihood of a disaster occurring by identifying threats and taking the necessary preventative action, and to ensure that if a disaster does strike, the organization is prepared to deal with it effectively.

Advantages

In the event of a disaster, a DP:

- supports the continuity of operations;
- mitigates the financial consequences.

Disadvantages

- Poor planning or an out-of-date plan may be worse than no plan at all.
- The planning process can be time-consuming.

Action Checklist

1. Establish a Disaster Planning Team

This team should include staff responsible for personnel, buildings, public relations, and IT, as well as someone with general management responsibility. You may want to include an external advisor experienced in disaster planning. Appoint of a team leader and a deputy. Senior management should clearly commit to the DP.

See that the needs of staff and other stakeholders are taken into account. Identify and prioritize the activities that are necessary to business continuity; consulting staff throughout the organization will help to establish a sense of ownership and commitment.

2. Carry Out a Risk Assessment

Identify particularly vulnerable aspects of your industry, operation, or service and potential internal and external risks to your company. Evaluate and analyze these and act to eliminate or reduce them. Distinguish between areas needing immediate action (the repair of broken windows, for example) and those that can be dealt with over a longer period (the installation of a burglar alarm or sprinkler system). List the extra resources required. Consider appointing a loss adjuster in advance so that the insurance claim process can start immediately in the event of a disaster.

Check and seek professional advice where necessary on your company's:

- insurance cover—is your existing cover adequate?
- maintenance of buildings and equipment
- security—do your detection and alarm systems work? If you don't have any, should you consider installing them?
- safety and fire precautions
- storage systems—are important documents held securely? Is adequate offsite storage available for IT backups?

3. Draw Up a Disaster Plan

The DP should be simple and easy to understand while containing all the necessary information. It must be developed with the worst case scenario in mind but be flexible enough to be used in less severe cases. Get copies of comparable companies' disaster plans and learn from them. Remember that recovery from a disaster can take a year or longer.

The DP needs to address the following personnel issues:

- key personnel—include out-of-hours contact details (draw up a roster if necessary)
- their responsibilities and limits of authority
- the location of the team's control center, preferably offsite

The DP should also contain:

- prioritized functions and activities
- floor plans
- evacuation procedures
- precautionary measures
- sources and locations of further information
- procedures for jobs to be done during the recovery period
- a directory of suppliers of emergency equipment and supplies

Anticipate the effects on employees, customers, suppliers, and others. Consider every part of your business operation.

Employees

- Make sure managers have employees' telephone numbers and home and e-mail addresses so that they can contact them out of work hours.
- Prepare to offer counseling and other help to deal with the aftereffects of a disaster.
- Communicate with staff—overcommunicate if necessary—about progress, moving back into the building, safety, etc. Make sure staff know whom to contact with problems.
- Make alternative arrangements for paying staff if the usual mechanisms are put out of action.

Alternative premises

- Investigate a reciprocal arrangement for sharing space with other organizations.

"Problems are only opportunities in work clothes." (Henry J. Kaiser)

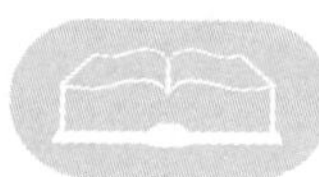

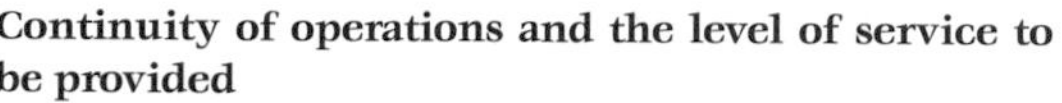

Continuity of operations and the level of service to be provided

- The company needs to be operational as soon as possible, preferably the next day.
- Inform customers and suppliers and let them know how to contact you. Customers will desert you if you are unavailable for weeks.
- Brief your PR spokesperson to deal with the media.

Physical communications

- Talk to your telephone company about forwarding calls.
- Plan for an ad hoc telephone directory and make sure your switchboard operators know what to tell callers.
- Decide where mail should be sent.

Equipment and resources

- Identify critical documents and their location so that vital material can be retrieved from damaged buildings.
- Store backups of important material, including IT information, offsite.
- Identify which resources would be needed during the recovery period and make sure they're available.
- Make sure cash is available at all times. Don't rush out and buy new equipment immediately—rental may be a better option.
- Consider establishing a resource network; identify cooperative partners with whom equipment, storage, and costs might be shared.

Keep copies of the DP in a number of locations for convenience and safety.

4. Pilot the Plan

A test run will reveal anything you've overlooked and indicate whether the plan is practicable. How long does it take to set up the control center? Will the communication systems work, even in the event of a natural disaster? Are the alternative premises suitable? Amend the plan as necessary to take into account any problems revealed by the pilot.

DOS AND DON'TS

For Disaster Planning

DO

- Be prepared.
- Learn from others' mistakes—and successes.
- Involve staff.
- Make sure that all staff are aware of the plan.
- Communicate—with staff, customers, suppliers.
- Keep copies of the plan in a number of locations—it's no use if the plan itself is destroyed in the disaster!

DON'T

- Don't be complacent—what if it did happen to you?
- Don't assume you've thought of everything; listen to comments and suggestions.
- Don't think of disaster planning as a onetime task. You must keep the plan up to date.

5. Communicate and Implement the Plan

A member of the disaster planning team should give a presentation to employees to ensure that everyone is aware of and understands the DP and its objectives and knows what to do in an emergency. The orientation of new staff members should include information about the DP. Rehearse emergency drills and reaction procedures at least once a year to remind existing staff. Deal with any worries staff may have.

6. Monitor, Revise, and Improve the Plan

The DP is not set in stone—it should change with circumstances. At intervals (at least annually) test out individual components and the whole plan and revise as necessary, taking into account the impact of new developments and new technology. Review reported disasters to see what you can learn to benefit your own DP. Communicate any changes to staff.

THOUGHT STARTERS

- Have you ever been involved in a disaster? What can you learn from that experience?
- If a disaster did hit, would your organization survive?
- What risks does your organization face? What can be done to minimize them?
- Can you afford not to have a disaster plan? The costs of a disaster are not just financial—they include interruption to business, wasted time, and lost opportunities.

For More Information

Books:

Bell, Judy K. *Disaster Survival Planning: A Practical Guide for Businesses*. Rev. ed. Portland, IN: DSP, 2000.

Kaplan, Laura G. *Emergency Disaster Planning Manual.* New York: McGraw Hill, 1996.

Journal Articles:

Dempster, John. "The Plan's the Thing When Disaster Strikes." *Professional Manager* 5:2 (March 1996): 21–23.

Hickman, Jennifer R., and William Crandall. "Before Disaster Hits—A Multifaceted Approach to Crisis Management." *Business Horizons* 40:2 (March-April 1997): 75–79.

"What a Disaster." *Management Accounting* 75:8 (September 1997): 54–55.

Web Sites:

Disaster and Emergency Management on the Internet (worldwide links): **www.keele.ac.uk/depts/por/disaster.html**

Federal Emergency Management Agency: **www.fema.gov**

"Science writers foresee the inevitable and, although problems and catastrophes may be inevitable, solutions are not."

(Isaac Asimov)

EFFECTIVE PURCHASING

> **CHECKLIST**
>
> This checklist is designed to help those responsible for purchasing adopt a more effective strategy. This checklist is not intended to itemize the steps in administering a purchase order process; rather it aims to present a proactive approach to purchasing. While directed at those involved in centralized purchasing, the principles apply equally to decentralized buying.

DEFINITION

Most textbooks state that purchasing is about buying the right goods, at the right time, at the right price, in the right quantity, and of the right quality. While these are indeed fundamental requirements, effective purchasing has to deliver more than this. Adopting an effective purchasing strategy turns a reactive buyer into a proactive buyer who adds value to the process.

ADVANTAGES

Effective purchasing:

- is proactive and adds value for your organization;
- improves communication with suppliers;
- gives you a deeper understanding of the marketplace.

DISADVANTAGES

There are no real disadvantages to effective purchasing, but it requires time to:

- gather and sort internal data;
- evaluate suppliers.

ACTION CHECKLIST

Your organization

1. UNDERSTAND YOUR OWN ORGANIZATION

Take time to learn how your own company functions and what is important to each department in terms of the supply of goods and services. What are the most crucial factors for each line manager in terms of quality, price, and delivery? Which items do they purchase most often, and what are they used for? How does each department determine its reorder levels?

Gather as much data as you can to provide a sound basis for formulating your strategy. Your internal customers will appreciate your professionalism and increase their sense of involvement in the process.

2. COMPILE A PURCHASE HISTORY

Use purchase orders and requisitions to compile a history of purchases. Gather data on product types, order quantities, lead times, pricing, order frequency, etc. Use this information to construct a purchasing pattern for key items.

3. BECOME A PROACTIVE BUYER

Negotiate better deals with suppliers by telling them what volumes they can expect over the year. Anticipate reorder dates and do the groundwork in advance. Reduce delivery charges by ordering like products at the same time. Arrange for suppliers to stock frequently used items free of charge, thus reducing your storage requirements, controlling lead times, and giving you the benefit of bulk purchasing. Monitor price fluctuations for seasonal trends.

Your suppliers

1. EVALUATE POTENTIAL SUPPLIERS

Evaluate suppliers using the following criteria:

- sales and profitability
- how long they have been in business
- who their major customers are (if they are dependent on one customer, what will happen to the business if they lose the account?)
- what percentage of their sales your business will represent
- whether they have any third-party certification
- their quality control policy
- their procedure for handling customer complaints
- their invoicing and administrative procedures
- their level of insurance coverage

2. VISIT POTENTIAL SUPPLIERS

Find out who would be dealing with your account and how your orders would be processed. Ask to meet the people with whom you will have day-to-day contact. Do they make you feel welcome?

3. GET REFERENCES

Take up references. Talk to buyers in organizations that are similar to yours and have similar purchasing patterns.

4. AUDIT YOUR MAJOR SUPPLIERS

Perform regular audits on your major current suppliers to evaluate their continued level of performance. Do they still meet the criteria you established at the beginning of the relationship? What improvements have you noticed in the service since then?

5. MAINTAIN GOOD COMMUNICATION

You expect your suppliers to keep you advised of delivery dates and problems associated with your orders. Make sure you reciprocate; advise them if you're expecting a sudden decrease in purchases—or indeed an increased requirement. Just as you should tell them exactly what you want from them, get them to tell you precisely what they expect of you.

Show an interest in your suppliers' other accounts. Have they won or lost any major contracts? How are they affected by the economy? Will shipping costs increase as a result of rising fuel prices? Will the price of paper affect the major print job you have scheduled for the end of the year—can you prepurchase the paper to minimize the damage? Good communication and understanding of

"A business must have a conscience as well as a counting house." (Montague Burton)

your suppliers' business will ultimately filter back into your own.

Get to know your suppliers as human beings. It's much easier to do business and especially to solve problems when you know the person at the other end of the phone (but don't let personal considerations outweigh organizational ones).

✔ 6. Use Your Suppliers' Expertise

You can't be an expert in everything. Use your suppliers' knowledge and expertise to help you draw up work specifications.

✔ 7. Maintain a Competitive Element

Always review the price and service your suppliers are offering. Let them know they have to remain competitive. Retain documentation proving you sought alternative prices; you'll need it for audits.

✔ 8. Compare Quotations

Make sure quotes are based on identical specifications. Check the exclusions such as delivery, installation, training, and insurance. Check the contract period, renewal dates, and how long the price is guaranteed. What provision is made to hold prices at the current level or within the realm of the RPI for long-term contracts? What are the payment terms?

✔ 9. Visit Trade Fairs

Visiting trade fairs and reading trade journals are essential for keeping up to date with the market.

✔ 10. When Prices Rise, Negotiate

When price rises are inevitable, try to negotiate other advantages such as longer payment terms, prompt payment discounts, quarterly instead of monthly invoicing, management reports, price stability for a fixed period, free delivery, or increased delivery frequency. Remember, your suppliers want to keep your business and may be able to help in other ways.

General hints/good practice

✔ 1. Establish a Code of Ethics

- Respect suppliers' confidentiality—don't disclose their prices and trading practices to their competitors.
- Declare any personal interest.
- Even though it is legally acceptable to receive gifts that would cost $25 or less, it is good practice not to accept gifts from suppliers or potential suppliers. Advise all suppliers of this in writing at the beginning of the relationship and prior to the Christmas period, when most suppliers traditionally send gifts.

✔ 2. Protect Yourself

- If you have a rollover contract, make sure you know when you have to give notice if you want to terminate.
- Be aware of the limits on your authority, and don't exceed them.
- Never make assumptions—clarify all details in writing.

✔ 3. Keep Your Side of the Bargain

See that your company pays suppliers in accordance with your agreements.

✔ 4. Maintain an Audit Trail

Always maintain an audit trail of all purchase documents.

DOS AND DON'TS

For Effective Purchasing

DO

- Involve your internal customers in the purchasing process.
- Assess and visit your suppliers regularly.
- Build relationships with suppliers based on mutual trust and good communication.
- Establish a clear code of ethics.

DON'T

- Don't allow yourself to be dragged into a Dutch auction by your suppliers.
- Don't stay with the same suppliers because you've always used them—be sure you're using them because they're the best.

THOUGHT STARTERS

- How much do you know about your organization's annual purchases?
- What is your organization's annual spend with major suppliers?
- How often have you visited your major suppliers?

For More Information

Books:

Cavinato, Joseph L., and Ralph J. Kauffmann. *The Purchasing Handbook: A Guide for the Purchasing and Supply Professional.* New York: McGraw-Hill, 1999.

Steele, Paul T. *Profitable Purchasing: A Manager's Guide for Improving Organizational Competitiveness through the Skills of Purchasing.* New York: McGraw-Hill, 1996.

See also:

✔ **Inventory Control (pp. 518–19)**

"Buy what's deliverable, not what could be." (Michael Bloomberg)

ESTABLISHING A PERFORMANCE MEASUREMENT SYSTEM

CHECKLIST

This checklist provides guidance on establishing a performance measurement system for an organization or department.

The primary purpose of performance measurement is to measure how well an organization or department is accomplishing its mission, goals, and objectives. Measuring performance is one of the key requisites in any continuous improvement program. The information gained from performance measures may be used to establish a program to benchmark against competitors, other organizations, or previous results.

DEFINITION

A performance measurement system provides an organized means of defining, collecting, analyzing, and making decisions regarding all performance measures within a process or activity.

A performance indicator is a level against which the management of any activity can be measured. Comparison with the indicator enables managers to assess how efficiently, effectively, and cost-effectively the operation is performing.

Performance measures provide a quantitative gauge of the degree to which you are meeting or exceeding the indicator set. They require the collection of raw data and conversion through a formula into a numerical unit.

For example, a target may have been set to reduce the number of customer complaints from 10 percent of total sales to 5 percent (the indicator). To calculate the percentage of complaints, divide the total number of complaints by the total number of sales and multiply by 100.

ADVANTAGES

Measuring performance enables an organization to:

- understand its current position;
- determine whether improvements have actually taken place;
- identify where improvements need to be made;
- be aware of its processes;
- make sure that decisions are made on the basis of fact;
- know whether or not it is meeting its targets.

DISADVANTAGES

The only drawback with measuring performance may be the resources (staff and time) that the process consumes. If you are considering introducing a performance measurement system, you should not underestimate the cost.

ACTION CHECKLIST

1. DESIGNATE A PERFORMANCE MEASUREMENT SYSTEM COMMITTEE

The committee will be responsible for the design, implementation, and review of the performance measurement system. The members of the committee should be drawn from all levels of the organization so that the whole process from beginning to end can be mapped. Appoint a coordinator to oversee the system.

2. IDENTIFY THE PROCESS TO BE MEASURED

Examples of processes in practice include purchasing raw materials, getting the finished product ready for delivery, invoicing, and handling complaints. Each process usually needs its own performance indicators and measures. Questions for the committee to consider in identifying processes for measurement include the following:

- What product or service do we produce?
- Who are our customers (internal and external)?
- What exactly are our processes?
- What do we do?
- How do we do it?
- What starts and what ends our process?

3. IDENTIFY THE ACTIVITIES TO BE MEASURED

By examining the process flow chart the committee can identify activities that are critical in terms of total process:

- efficiency and cost-efficiency
- effectiveness and cost-effectiveness
- quality, zero defects, or customer satisfaction
- timeliness
- productivity
- safety

Critical activities are those:

- that have to be watched closely and acted on if their performance does not meet specifications;
- that should be continuously improved;
- whose benefits exceed the cost of taking the measurement.

4. ESTABLISH PERFORMANCE INDICATORS

Establish a performance indicator for each of the critical activities selected for measurement. Remember there may in some cases be legislative standards to meet, for example, in the area of toxic emissions.

Good performance indicators are:

- realistic—meeting them does not require unreasonable effort;
- understandable—they should be expressed in simple and clear terms;
- adaptable—they can be changed if conditions change;
- economical—the cost of setting and administering them should be low in relation to the activity covered;

"Talent is cheaper than table salt. What separates the talented individual from the successful one is a lot of hard work." (Stephen King)

 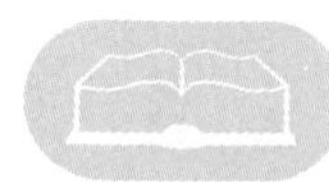     

- legitimate–they should at least meet legislative requirements;
- measurable–they should be communicable with precision.

5. Collect the Data

To determine how the data will be collected, ask yourself:

- What am I trying to measure?
- Where will I make the measurement?
- How accurate and precise must the measurement be?
- How often do I need to take the measurement?

For activities that are undertaken a number of times an hour, it may only be feasible for a sample measure to be taken, for example, every eighth event.

In many cases the data required for the performance measurement already exist, for example, in databases, logbooks, timecards, and checksheets. If additional data are required, the person in charge of that particular area of the activity is usually responsible for collecting it.

In some instances it may be appropriate to install an automated data collection system to provide accurate data without the need for human intervention.

Inform the individuals responsible when they should start collecting data and what format they should use to present it, for example, datasheets or spreadsheets. All data should be passed on to the committee for analysis.

6. Analyze and Report Actual Performance

Before drawing conclusions from the data, verify that:

- the data appear to answer the questions that were originally asked;
- there is no evidence of bias in the collection process;
- there are enough data to draw meaningful conclusions.

Once the data have been verified, the required performance measurement can be formulated.

Summarize the data and prepare a report. Be sure to:

- categorize the data and use graphs to show trends;
- make the report comparative to goals or standards;
- check that all performance measurements start and end on the same month or year;
- adopt a standard format by using the same size sheets and charts;
- add basic conclusions.

7. Compare Actual Performance to Indicators

Compare the results of the performance measures with the indicator set for each activity. You may need to prepare a further report to present to senior management for action.

8. Make Modifications to the Activity

Analysis will reveal whether:

- the activity is underperforming–leave the indicator as it is, but identify the reasons for failure and take remedial action;
- the variance is not significant–set a higher indicator to aim for continuous improvement;
- the indicator is easily achieved–review and raise the indicator. If indicators are not challenging, continuous improvement is unlikely.

9. Continue Measuring Performance and Evaluating the Performance Measures

Continue the process of collecting data and analyzing performance. Increase goals and standards as performance improves; change them as activities change, for example, a new plant may enable a component to be produced more quickly and efficiently.

DOS AND DON'TS

For Establishing a Performance Measurement System

DO

- Measure only what is important.
- Stress that you are measuring processes or activities, not people.
- Involve staff who are part of the activity to be measured.
- Act on the results of the performance measurement system.
- Review the indicators regularly to support continuous improvement.

DON'T

- Don't set performance measures in stone—modify them as processes and activities change.
- Don't be surprised if indicators are not met immediately—performance measurement should be used to drive continuous improvement.

THOUGHT STARTERS

- Did any company you have worked for measure performance? How?
- What are your organization's/department's key activities?
- How can you manage what you can't measure?

For More Information

Books:

Harbour, Jerry L. *The Basics of Performance Measurement*. Portland, OR: Productivity, Inc., 1997.

Kaydos, W. J. *Operational Performance Measurement: Increasing Total Productivity*. Boca Raton, FL: CRC Press/St. Lucie Press, 1998.

Journal Article:

Barchan, Margareta. "Measuring Success in a Changing Environment." *Strategy and Leadership* 27:3 (May/June 1999): 12–15.

Web Site:

Foundation for Performance Measurement: **www.fpm.com**

"When the effective leader is finished with his work, the people say it happened naturally." (Laozi)

 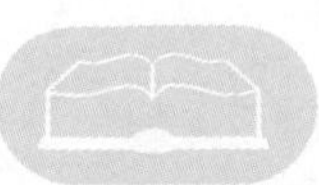    

Occupational Health and Safety: Managing the Process

CHECKLIST

This checklist provides an overview of the key issues to consider in managing the health and safety process in an organization. Effective workplace safety management is not just a corporate legal and moral obligation, but a personal one, as managers are increasingly being held personally accountable in law for the safety of their employees.

The success of a workplace safety initiative depends on the commitment of top management to a coherent strategy that is fully integrated into the general management of the organization.

Definition

Management of the occupational health and safety process involves setting a policy, creating a supportive organizational culture, developing and implementing a occupational health and safety plan, and evaluating the plan's performance.

Advantages

Managing health and safety in the workplace effectively not only ensures that you meet legislative requirements, but also:

- contributes to the positive well-being of the organization;
- decreases the risk of injury and ill health;
- reduces lost staff time;
- improves corporate image and averts negative publicity;
- contributes to a program of continuous improvement.

Disadvantages

The benefits far outweigh the disadvantages, but managing health and safety properly:

- takes up time and resources;
- requires constant review and updating.

Action Checklist

1. Get the Policy Right

The key to success is developing an effective policy that minimizes occupational health and safety risks to employees and others. Key actions at this stage include:

- undertaking a workplace safety assessment to identify areas that need attention and monitoring;
- familiarizing yourself with relevant legislation;
- allocating responsibilities for creating and revising health and safety policy and procedures;
- giving the health and safety policy the same priority as your other organizational goals;
- resourcing health and safety adequately, using a separate budget if appropriate.

2. Create a Positive Workplace Safety Culture

Create a corporate culture that involves and motivates all members of the organization in health and safety awareness. All employees need to think "safety first" and consider good health and safety practices a natural part of their working life.

Actions that foster a health and safety culture include:

- appointing health and safety champions to raise the profile and drive the project;
- setting health and safety objectives and performance standards for all staff (prevention is better than cure);
- involving employees and safety representatives at all stages, from planning through implementation to monitoring and review;
- providing adequate information on health and safety to all staff and keeping them up to date;
- offering refresher training for all staff at regular intervals;
- rewarding employees for good health and safety practice;
- including workplace safety as an agenda item at management meetings and team briefings.

3. Develop a Plan

You need to:

- produce a written plan for health and safety, coordinating and scheduling all health and safety activities in a single program;
- identify clear objectives and standards;
- set measurable targets;
- identify resources required;
- consider all personnel and all the processes in your organization, from purchasing materials to delivering the product or service, in drawing up the plan;
- review the plan regularly.

The plan may encompass such areas as:

- accident prevention—considering severe hazards such as chemicals and radiation as well as more common hazards such as heavy lifting and trailing electrical leads;
- physical working conditions—including factors such as light, heat, ventilation, seating, hygiene, and computer workstations;
- psychological health—covering areas such as stress reduction, shift working, rest breaks, prevention of bullying, and achieving a balance between work and family;
- health problems of employees—including alcoholism and drug addiction;
- health promotion—for example, exercise and healthy eating;
- emergency procedures—such as fire drills, equipment shutdown, and security procedures;
- specific groups of employees particularly at risk—

"Two basic values, autonomy and solidarity, serve as helpful prompters in any decision-making process."

(George Konrád)

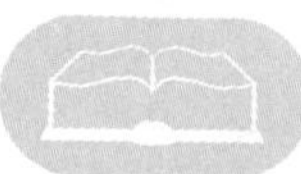

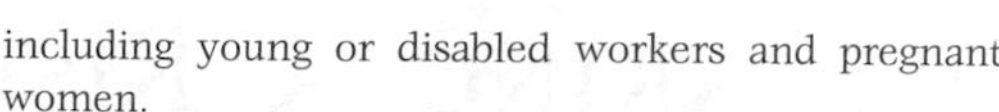

including young or disabled workers and pregnant women.

Depending on the nature of your business, you may also need to consider extending your workplace safety plan to suppliers and contractors. Any failings on their part will impact on your organization; you might want to introduce a written policy and penalties for noncompliance.

Remember also to consider the health and safety of customers using your products or services and of visitors to your premises.

4. Measure Performance

Once your plan is in place, evaluate its effectiveness. Performance can be measured both proactively and reactively. Proactive measures include:

- auditing your system to ensure that monitoring is in place and is effective;
- inspecting your workplace systematically;
- evaluating your training processes;
- talking to staff;
- reviewing relevant portions of minutes of management meetings.

Reactive measures include:

- examining data collected after incidents—accident books, sickness records, and records of near misses;
- checking damage to property, perhaps via insurance reporting.

DOS AND DON'TS

For Occupational Health and Safety: Managing the Process

DO

- Involve all your staff.
- Give health and safety the same priority as your organizational goals.
- Consider health and safety issues when carrying out organizational restructuring—if necessary, arrange training for those taking on new health and safety responsibilities.
- Aim for continuous improvement.
- Include temporary staff and contractors in your planning.

DON'T

- Don't assume health and safety is only for high-risk or hazardous environments.
- Don't believe health and safety is just common sense and therefore everyone understands it.

5. Review Performance

Evaluating the performance of the plan enables you to check that your policy and plans are working efficiently and continuing to meet objectives and respond to changing circumstances. The evaluation process might involve:

- comparing findings with objectives and standards;
- validating findings by talking to staff;
- benchmarking against similar organizations;
- giving feedback to staff and seeking commitment to improvements;
- changing your policy, plan, and procedures to reflect your findings, making sure to give priority to high-risk areas.

Review is a continuous process, but you should set a timetable for formally revising your health and safety plan every year or whenever new legislation or regulations require it.

THOUGHT STARTERS

- How much money are you losing by not managing health and safety effectively?
- Talk to your staff—how aware are they of health and safety risks and issues in your workplace?
- Who is responsible for health and safety in your organization? How accountable is that person?
- Are any incentives in place to encourage good health and safety practice?

For More Information

Book:

Hartnett, John. *OSHA in the Real World: How to Maintain Workplace Safety While Keeping Your Competitive Edge.* Morton, PA: Silver Lake Publishing, 1996.

Web Site:

Occupational Safety & Health Administration: **www.osha.gov**

"Developing a sound and healthy organization requires understanding the environment as much as understanding the organization."

(Gary Hamel)

WORKPLACE HEALTH: UNDERTAKING A RISK ASSESSMENT

CHECKLIST

This checklist provides a plan of action for those carrying out a workplace risk assessment in their company or organization.

By identifying hazards in the workplace and the likelihood (the risk) of an accident or illness occurring, employers can take action to remedy the hazardous conditions quickly. Reducing the incidence of workplace injuries and illnesses benefits both employer and employee by creating a safer working environment. It also leads to savings by minimizing illness and accident claims and loss of time and productivity. This checklist does not aim to cover the complex legal and medical issues of health and safety, for which expert advice should be sought.

DEFINITION

An occupational health and safety risk assessment is a planned procedure in which all hazards in the workplace are identified.

ADVANTAGES

Risk assessments:

- comply with health and safety legislation;
- make accident and work-related illness prevention easier by identifying hazards;
- help improve workforce morale by conveying a caring attitude.

DISADVANTAGES

There are no real disadvantages to carrying out a risk assessment, but remember that they:

- can require considerable resources in staff and/or consultants' time to undertake thoroughly;
- need to be updated each time a new piece of equipment or machinery is introduced, and each time an injury or work-related illness is reported.

ACTION CHECKLIST

1. DESIGNATE A WORKPLACE SAFETY COMMITTEE

The members of the workplace safety committee should be drawn from all levels of the organization. The committee will manage the implementation and running of the risk assessment. Appoint a coordinator (preferably but not necessarily from senior management—someone with project management experience who commands respect and can get things done) to oversee the project.

2. DEFINE THE SCOPE AND COVERAGE OF THE ASSESSMENT

Use the experience of committee members who have been involved in risk assessment before. All types of risk must be assessed: however, it can be easier (depending on the size of the organization) to identify and concentrate assessments on specific risks (for example, manual handling) at any one time. Decide who is to be included in the assessment at this stage—for example, all departments or one site or one floor. Indicate who will carry out the assessment—a large organization may need a number of individuals while in a small company one person may be sufficient.

3. DESIGN AN ASSESSMENT FORM

Create a form that the individuals involved in the assessment will use to record risks and/or incidents. Make wording simple and unambiguous. Include a rating scale for the severity of the risk, either in words (for example, "very severe" to "slight" risk) or numbers (for example, 1 = low risk and 5 = high risk). Identify which employees are at risk and, if applicable, any other individuals such as the general public. Leave space for suggestions of ways to minimize the risk. Include a list of common risks to point the assessor in the right direction. In a general risk assessment these may include:

- fire—are there any flammable materials near sources of heat?
- manual handling—are employees carrying items that should be left to machines?
- fork lifts or powered lift trucks—are operators certified? Is the work area well lit and well signed? Are pedestrians trained to work around such equipment? Is the racking system engineered properly to store heavy loads at substantial heights?
- power tools and equipment—are safety precautions, signage requirements and training of operators up to date?
- chemicals—are all hazardous substances stored correctly? Is the ventilation system adequate to take care of any noxious fumes?
- electricity—are any bare wires visible?
- dust—is the HVAC system doing its job?
- temperature (high and low)—do room temperatures reach abnormal levels?
- noise—are there areas of excessive noise? Are employees wearing protective equipment?
- tobacco smoke—are nonsmokers at risk from secondary exposure?
- electronic equipment—are users straining their eyes to see their computer monitors? Do employees have wrist support pads for their keyboards?
- office furniture—are chairs and desks ergonomic? Do they meet health and safety requirements? Is someone responsible for checking them regularly?

The basic U.S. legislation is the Occupational Safety and Health Act of 1970 (Public Law 91-596, 91st Congress, s.2193, December 29, 1970–84 stat. 1590).

There are many federal, state, and local regulations which govern the details. Information on federal legislation can be found at www.osha-slc.gov.

"Anything that promises to pay too much can't help being risky." (Dorothy Fisher)

If possible, use the accident book or log of close calls for actual examples.

4. Train Assessors to Identify Risk

Identifying risks in the workplace is not an easy task. If the individual assigned to carry out the risk assessment is not a health and safety officer, it is essential to provide appropriate training from either an internal source or an external agency. Suppliers of equipment, machinery, or chemicals can be a good source of advice.

It is important to train assessors to rate the severity of a risk. Examples of hazards should be discussed with the trainees to achieve some standardization.

5. Communicate the Assessment to Employees

Let all employees know (using newsletters, bulletin boards, e-mail, intranet, and team briefings) that a workplace safety assessment is to be undertaken and who the investigator(s) will be. Invite employees to identify hazards that should be included in the assessment and, if they find any, to inform their supervisor or the person responsible for the assessment in their area.

6. Draw Up a Plan for the Assessments

Plan a timetable scheduling the assessment of various areas and giving a completion date for the assessment. Build into the timetable a schedule noting the availability of risk assessment committee members to guarantee that at least one is always on hand to assist.

7. Carry Out the Assessment and Record the Results

The workplace safety committee should collate all of the completed assessment forms and analyze the results. Look for problem areas such as one department with a large number of high risks, recurring accidents, or illness. Create a list of all the risks and incidents in order of severity and report them to senior management. Keep this list as documentation for external occupational health and safety officials and as an internal record to check for changes made.

Look for any difficulties individuals had in completing the assessment; extra training may be needed for future assessments, or the assessment form may require modifications.

8. Report Back to Employees

Let your employees know the results of the assessment. Notify employees of any proposed changes to reduce the risk of accidents.

9. Take Action

Decide what action should be taken to eliminate or minimize the risks identified and draw up a plan for implementing the necessary changes, including budgetary implications.

DOS AND DON'TS

For Workplace Health: Undertaking a Risk Assessment

DO

- Make sure your company reviews all relevant laws and regulations for your industry.
- Involve all employees.
- Check the accident book or log of close calls.
- Seek advice from suppliers of any new equipment, machinery, or chemicals.
- Make sure that workplace assessment investigators are adequately trained.
- Keep written documentation of the assessment.

DON'T

- Don't think of the assessment as a onetime activity—action needs to be taken on the results and reviewed and updated.
- Don't ignore a risk because you assume it is too small.

THOUGHT STARTERS

- Have you ever been involved in an accident at work?
- Can you think of anything in your workplace that is potentially dangerous?
- How could you make your workplace safer?
- Has poor equipment ever caused damage/harm to personnel?

For More Information

Books:

Tompkins, Neville C. *A Manager's Guide to OSHA*. Normal, IL: Crisp Publications, 1994.

Viacoli, Jeffrey. *Making Sense of OSHA Compliance*. Rockville, MD: Government Institutes, 1997.

Journal Articles:

"Assess Your Business Safety." *Small Business Confidential*, no. 166 (June 1997): 2–3.

Hopkin, Paul. "Raising a Risk Profile." *Health and Safety at Work* 18:1 (January 1996): 16–18.

Waterman, Lawrence, and Rob Lane. "Health and Safety Risk Assessment." *Company Secretary's Review* 20.5 (April 16, 1997): 193–94.

Web Site:

Occupational Safety & Health Administration: **www.osha.gov**

"Confronting reality—no matter how negative and depressing the process—is the first step toward coming to terms with it."

(John Ralston Saul)

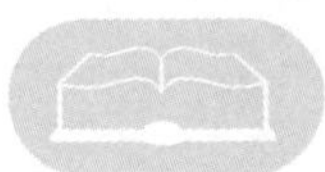

IMPLEMENTING A SERVICE LEVEL AGREEMENT

CHECKLIST

This checklist is for managers who need to draw up and implement a Service Level Agreement (SLA). Although this checklist draws on examples from Information Technology, it may be used for agreements in any context.

A surge of interest in SLAs has accompanied the growth of quality systems management, market testing, and benchmarking. SLAs themselves have also grown in importance as a result of the evolution of the computer control function from Data Processing Department to Information Technology Services.

The objective of an SLA is to improve the efficiency and effectiveness of the service provider for its customers through greater understanding of the needs and constraints of both sides and through greater accountability.

The SLA may not only benefit the interdepartmental arrangements of both private and public sector organizations, but may also provide a valuable baseline for partnership and outsourcing arrangements.

DEFINITION

Andrew Hiles defines an SLA as: "an agreement between the provider of a service and its users which quantifies the minimum quality of service which meets the business need." (*Service Level Agreements*, 1993)

Hiles stresses that this terminology is deceptively simple for several reasons.

- The agreement results from negotiations that recognize the needs and constraints on each side.
- The agreement records and measures the level of service to which both parties subscribe as the requirement to meet needs.
- The word "minimum" implies "adequate to meet quality needs" (serving the customer's needs and acceptable to the customer).

ADVANTAGES

Implementation of an SLA:

- clarifies understanding as to the basis of meeting expectations;
- requires the provider to be more accountable and responsible for the services delivered;
- commits the provider to plan for the development of services offered;
- commits the user to monitor and measure the efficiency and effectiveness of services from the provider;
- demands that the user be more conscious of the costs of service provision;
- forces the user to plan ahead for services required;
- should help to resolve difficulties in levels of user priority.

DISADVANTAGES

- An SLA can be seen as a threat by the provider.
- The provider may require extra resourcing to meet a minimum level of acceptable service, possibly increasing the cost of provision.
- It is not always easy to predict the level and nature of demand on the provider from all customers.

ACTION CHECKLIST

1. ASSESS CURRENT SERVICE PROVISION

Most agreements do not start with a clean slate. They often arise because of past problems. It is as important for the user to define the minimum levels of service required as it is for the provider to assess its current—and planned—resources and the current and planned demand on them. It is at this stage that levels of urgency and priority may be defined.

2. DRAW UP AN OUTLINE AGREEMENT

SLAs should identify at minimum:

- the purpose of the agreement;
- the parties to the agreement, typically the provider and user of the service;
- the service to be provided;
- the period of the agreement, with notice if appropriate;
- arrangements for monitoring, measuring, and review;
- the mechanism for resolving any conflicts;
- the procedure(s) in case of nonperformance (what happens if either party fails to meet the terms of the agreement?);
- procedures for change control;
- the degree of contribution and help from the user;
- lines of communication;
- any charges and insurance cover for both parties;
- means of arbitration for unresolved disputes.

The key elements that both provider and user need to clarify are:

- the precise nature of the service to be provided, including timeliness, relevance, accuracy, and format
- limits to the extent of the service
- response times, both expected and deliverable
- any exceptions to the rule
- agreed methods for monitoring and measuring

3. NEGOTIATE THE LEVELS OF PERFORMANCE

The SLA will usually emerge from discussions between both parties in the form of a compromise that recognizes the highest level of service feasible and the minimum that is acceptable. Although what constitutes unacceptable service should be obvious to both parties, it is still worth specifying to avoid possible misunderstandings. Equally, a "top-level" service should be discussed—what

"It is an economic axiom as old as the hills that goods and services can be paid for only with goods and services."
(Albert Jay Nock)

is desired may be impossible because of excessive costs.

The user must specify the levels of service required and response times for each, for example:

- Priority 1: must take precedence for immediate treatment;
- Priority 2: requires treatment within the hour;
- Priority 3: can wait for a maximum of 24 hours.

4. Include Change Control Procedures

Information technology will be renewed at an ever faster pace. While this will impact on agreement targets and measures, it should also influence the nature of the agreement itself. The agreement should take account of changing hardware and software, and the continuity and improvement of services to the user during the transition phase.

5. Consider Contingency and Backup Arrangements

Only in an ideal world can problems be solved in a flash and errors corrected at the touch of a button. The SLA needs to take this into account. At the same time due attention must be paid to risk management to provide a measure of contingency and backup, for example, for temporary operation of user services. Go a stage further and consider the eventuality of a disaster or crisis. Insurance may provide reassurance that things can be put right in due course, but can it answer the immediacy that users normally require?

6. Measure Performance and Monitor Faults

Agree on a mechanism for monitoring and measuring the actual performance of the provider against the agreement. This mechanism may oversee terms of speed or effectiveness as well as cost. Precise, mutually agreed performance targets or indicators are useful here in providing a benchmark to indicate whether the existing levels of service are satisfactory or not.

7. Pilot the SLA

The introduction of the SLA is important: lack of preparation or fine-tuning may well determine its fate. A sensible approach is to run an initial feasibility study with a pilot user group. This trial run should not have the potential to cause widespread damage if things go wrong, but it does need to be large enough to draw meaningful conclusions and make modifications for general implementation. It should be piloted by a user group with a clearly defined level of service need.

8. Review the SLA Periodically

Resources, demands, and targets will change over time; the SLA is not cast in stone and should be reviewed on at least an annual basis.

9. Measuring the Effectiveness of SLAs

Records of speed of response, length of computer downtime, and satisfaction with the solution can be rated against agreed performance indicators. The mean time between the failure and its repair or solution can provide an important indicator for the SLA. Response time can be reviewed against service objectives as agreed in the SLA.

DOS AND DON'TS

For Implementing a Service Level Agreement

DO

- Keep in mind the need to balance service against cost.
- Explore alternative service levels.
- Pay attention to detail during the initial assessment.
- Review the agreed performance indicators regularly.
- Recognize the resourcing and commitment required from both parties for success.
- Prepare to meet the cost of monitoring minimum quality service provisions.
- Pay attention to definitions with a potential for disagreement.

DON'T

- Don't be satisfied with inadequate measurements.
- Don't accept cumbersome, ill-defined documentation.
- Don't make the SLA too detailed or too difficult to monitor.
- Don't commit yourself to vague or impractical targets.

THOUGHT STARTERS

- Is dissatisfaction with a central support service department widespread but not heard?
- How is your central support service provider monitored and evaluated?
- Is the proposed SLA using a sledgehammer to crack a nut?

For More Information

Books:

Hiles, Andrew. *Service Level Agreements: Measuring Cost and Quality in Service Relationships*. New York: Chapman & Hall, 1993.

LaBounty, Char. *How to Establish and Maintain Service Level Agreements*. Colorado Springs, CO: Help Desk Institute, 1994.

Journal Articles:

Hiles, Andrew. "Service Level Agreements: Panacea or Pain." *TQM Magazine* 6:2 (1994): 14–16.

Small, Harry. "Getting Outsourcing Right." *Business and Technology Magazine* (September 1994): 50–51.

See also:

✔ **Deciding Whether to Outsource (pp. 490–91)**

"Men keep their agreements when it is an advantage to both parties not to break them." (Solon)

Implementing an Effective Change Program

CHECKLIST

This checklist is intended for managers who have mapped a change program for the organization and are now ready to implement it. It will serve as a guide to the issues involved in bringing in change rather than providing a detailed implementation schedule: the schedule will vary according to the organization and the nature of the change.

Definition

This checklist covers any type of major change program within an organization. These range from those driven by external forces (changes in the market, customer demands, legislation, or regulation) to those that are internally driven, for example, the decision to introduce a total quality management program.

Change results from the interaction between equipment (technology), processes (working procedures), organizational structure, and people. A change to any one of these elements inevitably causes changes in the others, because the organization is a living, evolving system.

Managing change involves accomplishing a transition from A to B and handling the problems that arise along the way.

Action Checklist

1. Agree on the Implementation Strategy

The details of the strategy need to be clear before you embark on change. Is implementation going to be top-down, bottom-up, or both? Will the change be made by division, by department, or in a "big bang?"

2. Agree on the Time Frame

Regardless of whether it is being introduced incrementally or simultaneously across divisions, every change program needs a start date and a finite time span. The timetable must be stretching enough to convey urgency but attainable enough to be motivating.

3. Plan for Implementation

Combine the strategy and timetable to draw up detailed implementation plans with each division or department head. Use the change team as a source of advice and consultation, but empower line managers to determine how they will implement the details of change against the overall goals.

The change program is unlikely to be the only corporate initiative underway. Make sure the strategy and goals behind the other initiatives all point in the same direction. Do employees receive consistent messages about the organization's core values and beliefs from each of the programs?

4. Set Up a Team of Stakeholders

This does not include top management but will benefit from top management sponsorship. The team should include the key people involved in designing and delivering the service as well as those receiving it. This group is responsible for defining and disseminating the benefits of the change.

5. Establish Good Project Management

Treat change like any project. Set goals and milestones and monitor progress to keep the project on schedule and on budget. Flag potential problems as early as possible and prepare contingency plans. Establish ground rules for the project team, especially on information sharing, decision making, and reporting.

6. Personalize the Case for Change

People will appreciate the case for change only if they can personalize it and relate it to their own job and team. Make sure that your line managers translate the corporate case for change into reality for every individual in the company. Consider what change will mean for each employee in terms of status (job title, budget responsibility), habits (changes to working time, new colleagues), beliefs (move to a customer focus), and behavior (new working practices).

7. Promote Staff Participation

Individual employees need to feel they can take ownership of the change program as it evolves. Change can be stressful if it is imposed. Introduce mechanisms that promote staff ownership. Allow criticism and feedback, but provide the means to take corrective action.

8. Tackle Known Blocks to Progress

Create a sense of purpose and urgency to tackle real problems that have prevented progress in the past. Ask what or who is preventing progress and who can really help in unblocking it.

Think of breaking the code of silence that engenders organizational protectiveness and maintains the status quo.

9. Motivate Your People

Sustained change requires very high levels of motivation. People need to feel valued, to be developed, to have their achievements recognized, and to be challenged. Recognize that different rewards motivate different people to change.

10. Be Prepared for Conflict

Change usually brings about conflict of one kind or another, simply because people have different views and reactions. Try to get conflict to surface rather than allowing it to fester; try to tackle it by dissecting and

"You can't permit a honeymoon of small changes over a year or two. A long series of small changes just prolongs the pain."

(Percy Barnevik)

analyzing it with those who are experiencing it. Conflict can often be put to positive use through open discussion and clarification.

11. Be Willing to Negotiate

When conflict cannot be resolved through improved explanation and discussion, you have to negotiate and persuade. This means avoiding taking entrenched positions yourself and deciding how to shift others from theirs. It means getting to an agreed "yes" without either side winning or losing face.

12. Anticipate Stress

It is uncertainty, not change itself, that really worries employees. Provide as much information as possible and quash rumors as soon as they arise.

Any change program is stressful. Fear of the unknown is the major contributory factor. Reduce its impact by being as open as possible about all the consequences of change. See that employees own the changes.

13. Build Skills

View the change program as a learning process and integrate it into the corporate training program. Build both technical and soft skills at all levels within the organization. Set an example by updating the skills of top management.

14. Build In Capability for Learning

Creating goals and plans that everyone subscribes to means that everyone can gain. Turn learning into something that people want to buy into, something that creates a buzz of discovery and involvement in new developments. Don't allow learning to become a chore.

15. Remember Change Is Discontinuous

Change is a long process made up of very small and often invisible modifications to behavior and attitudes. Seek innovative ways to remind staff of the overall case for change and to reinforce its value to them.

Accept that change will be a stop/start process. Plan for this and develop strategies to gear the organization up for renewed effort if there are setbacks.

16. Monitor and Evaluate

Monitor and evaluate the results of the change program against the goals and milestones established in the original plan. Are these goals still appropriate or do they need to be revised in the light of experience?

Existing performance measures may transmit the wrong signals and act as a block on change. Design measures that are consistent with the company's vision and goals.

Be honest in your assessment of progress. If the plan's goals and reality begin to diverge, take corrective action quickly. Be open about failure and involve employees in setting new targets or devising new measures.

THOUGHT STARTERS

- Which indicators will tell you if change has really been effected?
- What signals should top management send to employees to show the extent of their commitment to change?
- What messages will indicate successful staff ownership of change?

DOS AND DON'TS

For Implementing an Effective Change Program

DO

- Appreciate the depth of employees' resistance to change. Plan for resistance and cost it in terms of additional training and communications.
- Select priorities for change instead of attempting to address everything at once.
- Plan to deliver early tangible results and publicize successes to build momentum and support.
- Involve employees at every stage of designing and implementing change.
- Make sure top management sponsors and is fully committed to the agreed implementation.

DON'T

- Don't get lost in detail or lose sight of the vision: real change often comes through a simple breakthrough.
- Don't skimp on resources for training or communications.

For More Information

Books:

Hussey, David. *How to Be Better At Managing Change.* Dover, NH: Kogan Page, 1998.
Kanter, Rosabeth Moss. *The Change Masters: Innovation and Entrepreneurship in the American Corporation.* New York: Simon & Schuster, 1985.
Kotter, John P. *A Force for Change: How Leadership Differs from Management.* New York: Free Press, 1990.
Kotter, John. *Leading Change.* Boston, MA: Harvard Business School Press, 1996.
PriceWaterhouse Change Integration Team Staff. *Better Change: Best Practices for Transforming Your Organization.* New York: McGraw-Hill Professional, 1994.

See also:

✔ **Managing Staff Turnover and Retention (pp. 364–65)**
✔ **Total Quality: Getting TQM to Work (pp. 522–23)**

"Even the best leaders get submerged and stymied in organizations that are highly centralized and highly consolidated."

(Bill Creech)

Implementing Business Process Reengineering

CHECKLIST

This checklist provides a synthesis of best practice in the form of an outline guide to the key stages in implementing Business Process Reengineering (BPR).

BPR is multifaceted. At its heart are two fundamental approaches: the understanding that organizations are process-driven, not function-driven; and an appreciation of the far-reaching, quantum-leap approach encouraged by BPR.

BPR has many features in common with Total Quality Management (TQM): both require extensive commitment from staff and rely heavily on teamwork and problem solving to improve corporate processes in pursuit of customer satisfaction. But BPR differs from TQM in that its essence lies in discontinuous thinking and in rejecting the assumptions, received wisdom, and routine thinking that frame the way of doing things in many businesses. In this respect it is similar to Strategic Benchmarking, based as it is on the principle that the critical review of internal processes can reveal break points toward significant improvements in quality and competitiveness.

Definition

"Reengineering" is a method of initiating and controlling change processes through imaginative analysis and systematic planning.

Any organization, regardless of size, type, or desired objective, operates fundamentally by transforming a collection of inputs (for example, raw materials or raw data) into required outputs (products or services). This transformation involves one or more processes. In order to gain competitive advantage, an organization must transform inputs into outputs more efficiently than its competitors by concentrating on the efficiency of these core processes. This requires regular review and improvement of the relevant processes. Hammer and Champy define BPR as:

the fundamental rethinking and radical design of business processes to achieve dramatic improvements in critical contemporary measures of performance, such as cost, quality, service, and speed.

The improvements in process quality to be gained from BPR lie in three dimensions: process efficiency (for example, cost, cycle time); product quality (measured, for example, as customer satisfaction, scope, and quality of product); and product development time.

Advantages

- BPR often creates new markets through the identification of break points.
- BPR encourages creativity and innovation in teams.

Disadvantages

- BPR is effective for products and services that involve logical sequences in production. It may be less useful for highly variable processes.
- BPR initiatives often require a high investment in information technology (IT).
- The high cost of BPR initiatives can speed up the collapse of companies already in trouble.
- BPR requires good teamwork and a high level of expertise.
- The creation of a lean organization through downsizing may actually reduce its capacity to change.

Action Checklist

✔ 1. Develop the Vision—Think Big

Senior management needs to gain a perception of the problems in the current business. An awareness of customers' expectations, competitors' advantage, and opportunities resulting from IT lead this process.

Create a clear, grand vision. Thinking big and bold is the essence of BPR.

✔ 2. Establish a Steering Committee

Membership should be cross-functional. Specialists and consultants may be included, but a balance needs to be maintained. Senior managers should lead the project and provide strategic direction. The committee needs to understand the key leverage points in the organization. At an early stage it will need to decide whether it is going to undertake a pilot program or go for an all-embracing project.

The committee should outline a preliminary strategy and set goals for the organization. Use appropriate survey techniques to listen to customers, benchmark the competition, and analyze existing processes. Identify points at which there is a gap between performance and customers' expectations.

✔ 3. Prepare the Organization for Change

Communication is the key to success in managing change. Promote a sense of urgency. Present the business case for change, highlighting the objectives and goals of reengineering. Encourage feedback and input from all employees.

✔ 4. Analyze Existing Processes

Model current processes in detail. Reaffirm those processes that need to exist and their rationale. This reduces the likelihood that past mistakes will be repeated. Listen to the process owners to identify where problems exist. Document each and every helpful idea and make sure that these are widely circulated. Focus the redesign on the points that can provide the greatest return.

"Transformational change requires enormous energy." (Robert H. Miles)

5. Establish Performance Indicators or Baselines

Improvements in performance can be identified only if you know where you are starting from. Performance measures include:

- transaction volumes
- cycle times
- defect rates
- customer satisfaction levels

Make sure that the three dimensions of process efficiency, product quality, and product development time are examined comprehensively.

6. Redesign the Process

Start with the needs of your customers and redesign the process from the outside in. Apply the following guidelines to the redesign process.

- Collect information that is required throughout the life cycle of the process only once, at its point of origin, and make it available immediately to all who need it.
- Reduce the need for coordination by associating individuals with processes, not with departments or functions.
- Improve customer service through genuine empowerment, trust, and delegation of responsibility, allowing partnerships to develop with customers and suppliers.
- Identify the key business outcomes, the business processes required to produce such outcomes, and descriptions of how processes interrelate. It will also be necessary to lay out the infrastructure required to support the change by describing the management strategy, measurement systems, reward programs, organizational values, and individual belief systems that need to be adopted by all concerned.

7. Plan the Implementation

Once a process has been redesigned an implementation plan can be prepared. Changes need time to be implemented; although BPR aims to achieve dramatic improvement in a short time, the planned schedule of change should not be unrealistically short.

Reemphasize the need for change and communicate the vision to managers and employees to overcome the natural uncertainty that exists. Gain approval and popular support by outlining the expected benefits to be achieved by the proposed redesign.

An implementation plan should take the following into account:

- schedules, budgets, completion criteria, and economic justifications all need to be specified;
- training will be vital to smooth the transition;
- new control systems need to be established;
- immediate feedback on improvements is essential;
- contingency allowances are needed to allow for the problems that will inevitably occur;
- changes in physical location or layout, work flows and organization structures, plant and IT systems, testing and pilot projects, and a redefinition of roles and responsibilities will result from the process;
- the plan should deliver some significant but quick results in the early stages to build commitment.

8. Monitor and Evaluate Progress

Monitor the process continually to make certain that the expected benefits are being obtained. Feed back results to employees to let everyone gain by knowing what has and has not worked. This will help to identify further areas for improvement.

DOS AND DON'TS

For Implementing Business Process Reengineering

DO

- Question all assumptions.
- Choose your consultants carefully.

DON'T

- Don't assume you are on the right BPR track merely by introducing the latest IT.
- Don't settle for automating existing processes.
- Don't focus on individual tasks at the expense of the overall process.
- Don't embark on grand projects without the resources and support to complete them.
- Don't confuse BPR with rationalization.

THOUGHT STARTERS

- Do you know what proportion of resources is spent on the core processes in your organization?
- If you are considering BPR, examine your reasons very carefully—they will indicate your probable success.

For More Information

Book:

Hammer, Michael, and James Champy. *Reengineering the Corporation: A Manifesto for Business Revolution.* Rev. ed. New York: HarperInformation, 1999.

Journal Articles:

Aggarwal, Sumer. "Reengineering. A Breakthrough or Little New?" *International Journal of Technology Management* 13:3 (1997): 326–44.

Choi, Chung For, and Stephen L. Chan. "Business Process Reengineering: Evocation, Elucidation and Exploration." *Business Process Management Journal* 3:1 (1997): 39–63.

Hammer, Michael. "Reengineering Work: Don't Automate, Obliterate." *Harvard Business Review* 90:4 (July-August 1990): 104–12.

See also:

☆ **The True Total Quality (pp. 173–74)**
☆ **X-engineering Success (pp. 245–46)**
✓ **Total Quality: Getting TQM to Work (pp. 522–23)**
✓ **Total Quality: Mapping a TQM Strategy (pp. 524–25)**

"Power is the ability to influence individuals and institutions in ways that change ideas."

(Carl McCall)

Implementing Kaizen

CHECKLIST

This checklist is designed to introduce the concept of kaizen and explain its implementation.

In order to be successful, organizations are finding that they must continually improve their quality assurance, cost management, and delivery systems. Increasing competition has made it a priority for every organization to develop and seek an advantage over rivals. Many managers see a culture of continuous evaluation and improvement as an essential tool to achieve and maintain such an advantage. Kaizen is one of the main tools to develop such a culture.

Definition

Kaizen is a Japanese term, which roughly translated means "improvement"–kai means "change" and zen "good" or "for the better." Kaizen means "continuing improvement in personal life, home life, social life, and working life" (Imai, 1986). Essentially it means continuous improvement, seeking small improvements through the elimination of waste.

Kaizen is a philosophy that inspires the whole company with the instinct for improvement. The culture of seeking continuous improvement should involve everyone from the most senior manager to the most junior employee. Workers participate not for any particular financial reward, although rewards may be a part of the recognition process, but for the satisfaction of using their creative skills to improve the operations they perform and the goods and services they produce.

Kaizen incorporates a variety of techniques and principles into the overall culture and philosophy of improvement–improvement as a way of life, not simply the application of isolated techniques. It can help build employees' morale and self-respect. The company benefits from a more motivated workforce and improved financial returns resulting from more efficient operations. Customers benefit from the improved quality of product or service.

Advantages

- All functions of the organization come under continuous inspection.
- The employees most familiar with a particular operation on a day-to-day basis are the ones evaluating it.
- Employee morale and job satisfaction increase.
- Waste is eliminated throughout the organization, increasing efficiency and reducing costs.
- Product or service quality is improved and is monitored on a continuous basis.

Action Checklist

1. Understand the Processes

According to Imai, kaizen embraces three principal building blocks or keys to satisfying the customer:

- a continually improving quality assurance system to meet customer requirements
- a continually improving cost management system to provide the product or service at a favorable price to the customer
- a continually improving delivery system to meet customer requirements on time

These are known collectively as QCD–quality, cost, delivery.

2. Identify Corporate Objectives

The three most important elements to creating the spirit of kaizen are top management commitment, top management commitment, and top management commitment. "Without that, you had better forget the whole thing" (Imai). Kaizen is best introduced as a means of achieving business targets. Senior managers and the board should conduct a SWOT analysis on the company's business program. They should evaluate existing systems and structures for their support for cross-functional goals and plan necessary changes in organization, planning and control, and personnel practices. They should set targets for the next five years; commitment should be agreed on and shared. A statement of commitment by senior management to functional goals such as quality and cost, to the resourcing of the program, and to auditing its progress will demonstrate management's commitment to kaizen as a corporate strategy.

Kaizen is often introduced into organizations as a developmental step in total quality management (TQM). In such cases a culture of quality may have been achieved and quality is already part of all organizational planning. In order to move toward kaizen, evaluate:

- how successful the quality initiative has been;
- whether everybody understands the key importance of quality;
- whether improvements made have been publicized;
- how employees view quality.

3. Plan the Kaizen Program

A well-planned program of kaizen is often broken down into three segments–management-oriented, group-oriented, and individual-oriented kaizen–representing different levels of kaizen.

- Management-oriented kaizen focuses on the most important strategic issues, processes, and systems.
- Group-oriented kaizen is based on small-group activities that use statistical tools to solve problems.
- Individual-oriented kaizen is based on the assumption that each individual can work smarter and can contribute toward the improvement process.

Each segment requires particular consideration as it makes use of different management and personal skills.

4. Allocate Resources

Senior management must be prepared to allocate resources. You need to appoint a director in overall charge of the project and a manager to implement the program. Introduce training for all employees and allo-

"You can't change anything if you don't bring people with you." (Carolyn McCall)

cate sufficient funding (as well as other resources) to support this.

5. Develop a Training Plan

Explore the training requirements of your employees. A minimum requirement of kaizen is that they understand the continuous improvement process, cross-functional working, and problem-solving techniques. Work with your training department or consultant to draw up a training plan.

6. Communicate with Employees

Bring representatives from all functions and all levels of the organization into the planning process. Kaizen is about cultural change and employee participation, and ownership is an essential part of accepting the change process. Arrange meetings, briefing sessions, and newsletters to promote the objectives of kaizen.

7. Focus Training and Development on the Four Ps of Quality

The four Ps are as follows.

Process control. The management of processes ensures a consistent and reliable level of performance.

- Identify variations and their causes.
- Deal with assignable causes.
- Deal with random variation.
- Undertake process design reviews, making use as necessary of the range of analytical and quality improvement techniques.

Problem identification. Failure to understand the causes of process variation gives rise to incorrect identification of problems. Consider using a range of techniques to identify problems.

Problem elimination. Gain an understanding of problem-solving tools such as Pareto diagrams or cause-and-effect diagrams. Test solutions to see that they work, truly prevent the problem, and do not cause new trouble elsewhere. Implement the solution after gaining an understanding of the dynamics of change.

Permanence. Improvement is a continuous process. You need to ensure that the changes already made stick and that you go on improving. Processes such as policy deployment, TQM reviews, and quality function deployment are helpful here. Seeing to it that senior managers regularly attend quality improvement group meetings maintains momentum and commitment.

8. Set Up a suggestion Box

Involving employees is an integral part of individual-oriented kaizen. A suggestion box is a good way of encouraging employee contribution. Be prepared to listen to all suggestions and give recognition to employees' efforts.

9. Review

Plan to review the development of the kaizen program. Gauge the extent to which a process-oriented culture change has been achieved. Recognize champions and consider further training as required.

DOS AND DON'TS

For Implementing Kaizen

DO

- Gain the commitment of senior management.
- Involve everybody in the organization.
- Acknowledge that all organizations have problems.
- View the introduction of kaizen as a cultural change process.
- Remember that the search for improvement is never-ending.

DON'T

- Don't regard implementing kaizen as a onetime exercise; it must become part of the corporate culture.
- Don't underestimate the importance of constant communication to reinforce the cultural change.

THOUGHT STARTERS

- Can you afford not to be interested in improved quality and greater productivity?
- Are you making full use of the creative ability of all your employees?
- Do you use the full range of problem-solving techniques?

For More Information

Books:

Imai, Masaaki. *Kaizen: The Key to Japan's Competitive Success.* New York: McGraw-Hill, 1986.

Laraia, Anthony C., Patricia E. Moody, and Robert W. Hall. *The Kaizen Blitz: Accelerating Breakthroughs in Productivity and Performance.* New York: John Wiley, 1999.

Web Site:

Kaizen Institute: **www.kaizen-institute.com**

See also:

☆ The True Total Quality (pp. 173–74)

"There can be no major change in a complex organization unless there are both sufficient resources and substantial readiness."

(Robert H. Miles)

  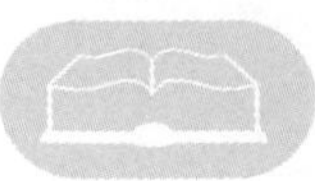    

IMPLEMENTING THE BALANCED SCORECARD

CHECKLIST

Traditionally managers have used a series of indicators to measure how well their companies are performing. These measures relate primarily to financial issues such as business ratios, productivity, unit costs, growth, and profitability. While useful in themselves, they provide only a narrowly focused snapshot of how a company has performed in the past and give little indication of likely future performance.

During the early 1980s the changing business environment prompted managers to take a broader view of performance, and a range of other factors started to be taken into account, exemplified by the McKinsey 7-S model and popularized by Peters and Waterman's business bible *In Search of Excellence*. These provide a broader assessment of corporate health for both the immediate and longer term. This checklist focuses on the balanced scorecard, developed by Robert Kaplan and David Norton in the early 1990s with the aim of providing a balanced view of a company's performance.

DEFINITION

The balanced scorecard is defined as a strategic management and measurement system that measures performance and links strategic objectives to comprehensive indicators. The key to the success of the system is that it must comprise a unified, integrated set of indicators that measure key activities and processes at the core of a company's operating environment.

The balanced scorecard takes into account not only the traditional "hard" financial measures, but also three additional categories of "soft" quantifiable operational measures. These include:

- customer perspective—how an organization is perceived by its customers;
- internal perspective—in which issues an organization must excel;
- innovation and learning perspective—in which areas an organization must improve and add value to its products or services or operations.

Measurements taken across these four categories are seen to provide a rounded balanced scorecard that reflects organizational performance more accurately than traditional financial indicators and helps managers focus on their mission instead of short-term financial gain. It also helps motivate staff to achieve the strategic objectives.

ACTION CHECKLIST

Kaplan and Norton have identified a number of stages for the implementation of the scorecard that make use of planning, interviews, workshops, and reviews. The type, size, and structure of an organization determine the detail of the implementation process and the number of stages it entails.

The main steps include the following.

1. PREPARATION

As the scorecard is inextricably linked to strategy, the first requirement is to clearly define corporate strategy and ensure that senior staff in particular are familiar with the key issues. Planning of any other action requires an understanding of:

- the strategy;
- the key objectives or goals to achieve that strategy;
- the three or four critical success factors (CSFs) fundamental to achieving each major objective or goal.

2. DECIDE WHAT TO MEASURE

Managers should identify the company's major strategic goals. As a guide, no more than 15 to 20 key measures in total should then be linked to these specific goals—significantly fewer measures may not achieve a balanced view; significantly more may become unwieldy and deal with noncritical issues.

Based on the four main perspectives suggested by Kaplan and Norton, a list of goals and measures may include some of the following:

Financial (Shareholder) Perspective

- Goals—increased profitability, growth, increased returns on assets.
- Measures—cash flows, cost reduction, economic value added, gross margins, profitability, return on capital/equity/investment/sales, revenue growth, working capital, sales.

Customer Perspective

- Goals—new customer acquisition, retention, satisfaction.
- Measures—market share, customer service, customer satisfaction, number of new/retained/lost customers, customer profitability, number of complaints, delivery time, quality performance, response time.

Internal Perspective

- Goals—improved core competencies, improved critical technologies, streamlined processes, better employee morale.
- Measures—efficiency improvements, faster development/lead/cycle times, reduced unit costs, reduced waste, amount of recycled waste, improved sourcing/supplier delivery, employee morale, and satisfaction, internal audit standards, number of employee suggestions, sales per employee.

Innovation and Learning Perspective

- Goals—new product development, continuous improvement, training of employees.
- Measures—number of new products and percentage of sales from these, number of employees receiving training, training hours per employee, number of strategic skills learned, alignment of personal goals with the scorecard.

"Modern industry seems to be inefficient to a degree that surpasses one's enduring powers of imagination."

(E. F. Schumacher)

Each organization needs to determine its own strategic goals and activities to be measured. A number of organizations have seen Kaplan and Norton's template as not meeting their particular needs and have either modified it or have devised their own scorecards. Public sector organizations, for example, may have different aims and objectives and may need to tailor the scorecard to reflect this.

3. Finalize the Implementation Plan

Further discussions, interviews, or workshops may be required to fine-tune the details and agree on strategy, goals, and activities to be measured, taking care that the measures selected focus on the critical success factors. Other important issues to be resolved before implementation include setting targets, rates, or other criteria for each of the measures and defining how, when, and where they should be recorded.

4. Implement the System

Produce an implementation plan and communicate it to the staff. The scorecard initiative should not come as a surprise at this point: staff should be informed at the beginning of the project and kept up to date on progress. Employees should be made to feel that they have an important part to play in achieving corporate goals. Conversely they should not feel threatened by the measures.

The system for recording and monitoring the metrics should be in place and tested well before the start date, and training in its use should be given to all users as far as possible. The system should automatically record all the data required, though some of the measurements may have to be logged manually.

5. Publicize the Results

Collate the results of all measurements on a regular basis—daily, weekly, monthly, quarterly, or as appropriate. The information is likely eventually to comprise a substantial amount of possibly complicated data. Decide whether to make complete data available to senior management, to divisional or departmental heads, or to all staff, or whether to circulate partial information on a need-to-know basis. Determine whether the results can best be publicized through meetings, newsletters, the organization's intranet, or other means.

6. Use the Results

Measurement is not an end in itself; it is a guide to organizational performance that may point to areas that need strengthening. Taking action on the information you obtain is as important as the data in the first place. Management follow-up action is an essential part of the balanced scorecard process.

7. Review and Revise the System

After the first cycle has been completed, review the quality of the information gathered and the success of subsequent actions, and modify the process as required.

THOUGHT STARTERS

- Do you know what measurements are currently taken in your company?
- Do the measurements in place give a holistic view of performance?
- What might be the consequences of not getting a balanced view of your company's performance?

DOS AND DON'TS

For Implementing the Balanced Scorecard

DO

- Define your goals clearly.
- Select measures that focus on the critical success factors of each goal.
- Limit yourself to a manageable number of measures.
- Reassure staff on the purpose of the scorecard.

DON'T

- Don't overmeasure your organization.
- Don't allow the measurement process to interfere with employees' ability to get on with the job.
- Don't adopt an off-the-shelf system not suited to your organization.

For More Information

Books:

Kaplan, Robert S., and David P. Norton. *The Balanced Scorecard: Translating Strategy into Action*. Boston, MA: Harvard Business School Press, 1996.

Kaplan, Robert S., and David P. Norton. *The Strategy-Focused Organization: How Balanced Scorecard Companies Thrive in the New Business Environment*. Boston, MA: Harvard Business School Press, 2000.

Peters, Thomas J., and Robert H. Waterman, Jr. *In Search of Excellence: Lessons from America's Best-run Companies*. New York: Warner, 1988.

Journal Articles:

Butler, Alan, Steve R. Letza, and Bill Neale. "Linking the Balanced Scorecard to Strategy." *Long Range Planning* 30:2 (April 1997): 242–53.

Van de Vliet, Anita. "The New Balancing Act." *Management Today* (July 1997): 78, 80.

Web Sites:

Balanced Scorecard Collaborative: **www.bscol.com**

Balanced Scorecard Institute: **www.balancedscorecard.org**

Foundation for Performance Measurement: **www.fpm.com**

See also:

☆ **The Balanced Scorecard (pp. 301–02)**

Robert S. Kaplan (pp. 1008–09)

"The leader is not just a scorekeeper. He is responsible for creating something new and better."

(Bill Creech)

MANAGING PROJECTS

CHECKLIST

This checklist outlines the steps in project management and provides a framework of sequential action for any manager undertaking a project.

Project management is recognized as a special process that differs in approach from general management or change management. The traditional project management focus has been that of completing defined work within given time constraints and cost limits. Recently the focus has shifted more to the quality of the final output delivered to the customer.

DEFINITION

Project management is a specialized management technique to plan and control projects. . .A project is generally deemed successful if it meets predetermined targets set by the client, performs the job it was intended to do, or solves an identified problem within the predetermined time, costs and quality constraints.

(Rory Burke, *Project Management: Planning and Control Techniques* (2000))

ADVANTAGES

Project management techniques provide:

- an appropriate way to bring about sudden, revolutionary, or purposeful change
- an effective approach for handling single tasks
- a realistic method for evaluating a proposed plan

DISADVANTAGES

- Projects often require an extraordinary use of resources—especially money and people—over a finite period of time.
- Projects usually consume more resources than expected.
- Projects can go over schedule by significant margins.

ACTION CHECKLIST

1. DEFINE THE OBJECTIVES

Fundamental to the management of any successful project are the understanding of and agreement on:

- what needs to be achieved;
- what is to be the outcome and/or what needs to be delivered as a result;
- dates and budgets for project completion by the project sponsor and project manager.

Lack of clear objectives will doom the project from the beginning.

2. APPOINT THE PROJECT MANAGER

The project manager should be someone who has a proven track record and can command respect and get action from the ranks of senior management. This person should be able to:

- plan and communicate all aspects of the project;
- motivate with integrity, sensitivity, and imagination;
- gain productivity and trust from shared decision making;
- lead both by example and by taking a back seat when appropriate;
- monitor costs, efficiency, and quality without excessive bureaucracy;
- get things done right the first time without being a slave driver;
- get the right people for the right task at the right time;
- use both technical and general management skills to control the project;
- see clear-sightedly through tangled issues.

3. ESTABLISH THE TERMS OF REFERENCE

The terms of reference specify the objectives, scope, time frames, and initial scale of resources required. They should also clarify risks, constraints, or assumptions. It is important to make early allowances for cost escalation and plans veering off course, and build in a level of contingency or safety margin.

4. CREATE THE WORK BREAKDOWN STRUCTURE DOCUMENT (WBSD)

Having established what the project should achieve, consider how to achieve it.

The WBSD forms the basis of much subsequent work in planning, setting budgets, exercising control, and assigning responsibilities. The key is to break the project down into identifiable phases, then into controllable units for action. Dividing a project into more approachable, discrete units makes it easier to estimate, plan, and control the work. As soon as possible allocate a timescale to each unit of work, being careful to distinguish sequential units (those that need to be accomplished before the next can be tackled) from overlapping units (those that can run in tandem).

5. PLAN FOR QUALITY

Planning for quality requires both paying attention to detail and ensuring that the project output or outcome does what it is supposed to, or is "fit for its purpose." The work breakdown structure should incorporate micro performance criteria or indicators for discrete units or phases, and macro indicators against which the final outcome can be assessed. Quality measures (systematic inspections against established standards) should be built into the process from the beginning, not later when things (may) have started to go awry. The following formula can run as a continuous sequence throughout the duration of the project:

establish standards > monitor performance > take corrective action.

The key is to guarantee effective quality control that acts as a prevention rather than a cure and enables you to get things right the first time.

"Beware the manager who proclaims to the world he is a long termer, beginning today."

(T. Boone Pickens)

6. Plan Costs

This is a key area, in which the most frequent error is to underestimate costs. Typical cost elements include:

- staff time and wages—usually the largest cost item
- overhead—general operating costs
- materials and supplies—the raw materials
- equipment—the relative advantages of leasing versus purchasing and taking depreciation
- administration—purchasing, accounting, record-keeping

One of the enabling functions of a good budget is to monitor costs while a project is in progress.

7. Plan Timescales

In order to calculate the shortest time necessary to complete the project you need to know:

- the earliest time a stage or unit can start;
- the duration of each stage;
- the latest time by which a stage must be completed.

Gantt charts, PERT diagrams, and the critical path method are prominent among a number of project management techniques that can help with effective planning of timescales.

8. Monitor and Report Progress

The monitoring of costs, timescales, and quality is a major consideration throughout the duration of the project. Quality is the hardest to measure and, as such, is prone to neglect.

In addition to progress reports, feedback sessions, and Management By Walking Around, various control tools can help you see that implementation is going according to plan.

- Control point charts ask you what is likely to go wrong in terms of time, cost, and quality.
- Project control charts provide status reports of actual costs against budget with variances.
- Milestone charts show stages of achievement as steps toward the project objectives.

It is important to know what to do when these or other control mechanisms indicate that something is going wrong. Contingency plans are also vital, as conditions change constantly.

9. Deliver the Output

Haynes writes that "the goal of project management is to obtain client acceptance of the project result" (*Project Management*, Crisp Publications, 1997). Steps before delivery of the project outcome may include the compilation of instructional documentation or training packages. The penultimate stage before project completion is ensuring that the outcome of the project is accepted by the customer or sponsor.

10. Evaluate the Project

Building in a final stage of evaluation allows you to gauge the project's success and see what lessons can be learned. Once again the three key areas for review are quality, time, and costs. Others include:

- staff skills gained or identified
- mistakes not to be repeated
- tools and techniques of particular value
- tasks or procedures to be tackled differently next time

DOS AND DON'TS

For Managing Projects

DO

- Take time at the beginning to define objectives, terms of reference, and the work breakdown structure.
- Appoint someone with the right skill mix as project manager.
- Facilitate access to resources needed as far as possible.
- Build in quality checks.

DON'T

- Don't let small changes creep in without assessing the implications.
- Don't lose sight of time targets and budget limits.

THOUGHT STARTERS

- Think of a job or task you have to do:
- Does it have a set start and finish date?
- Does it require a budget?
- Does it need other resources: people, equipment, raw materials?
- Does it involve changing something?
- Does it have a clear objective or target?

For More Information

Books:

Burke, Rory. *Project Management: Planning and Control Techniques*. 3rd ed. New York: John Wiley, 2000.
Cleland, David I. *Project Management: Strategic Design and Implementation*. 3rd ed. New York: McGraw-Hill, 1999.

See also:

✓ **Deciding Whether to Outsource (pp. 490–91)**

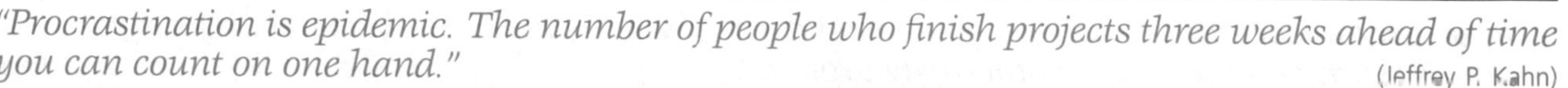

"Procrastination is epidemic. The number of people who finish projects three weeks ahead of time you can count on one hand."
(Jeffrey P. Kahn)

  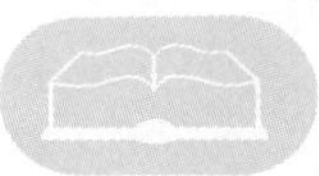    

PREPARING FOR BUSINESS ABROAD

CHECKLIST

This checklist aims to stimulate thoughts about some of the implications of doing business abroad—of doing business with people of other nationalities, races, and cultures. Success in doing business abroad often depends on getting the little things right—most importantly, recognizing and anticipating a multitude of cultural differences. The purpose of this checklist is to help you do that by pointing out some general guidelines and some specific examples. It is not a manual on foreign trade.

DEFINITION

For the purposes of this checklist "doing business abroad" involves either transacting business with people from other countries or transacting business in a country outside the United States. In doing business abroad you will be confronted with people of nationalities, races, and cultures other than your own, and probably with customs, practices, and legal systems that differ from yours.

ADVANTAGES

Preparing for business abroad:

- increases your self-confidence in potentially stressful situations;
- enables you to appear informed and international in outlook;
- reduces the chance of your being surprised by suddenly discovering that "they" do things differently;
- lessens the likelihood of you and your colleagues on the one hand, and of your potential business partners on the other, being embarrassed;
- reduces misunderstandings and increases mutual understanding.

ACTION CHECKLIST

1. IDENTIFY SOURCES OF INFORMATION

Write to, call, or even visit the U.S. embassy or consulate of the country you are visiting. Most have useful background literature about their countries. In the case of smaller countries, particularly those less economically developed, don't count on printed information being completely up to date.

Don't expect all embassies to be like those of the United States or other major powers. Some embassies consist of no more than two or three rooms on an upper floor. If you intend to visit an embassy, phone first and find out what hours it's open to visitors–not all of them are regularly open from 9.00 a.m. to 5.00 p.m. The employees of some embassies speak perfect English; in others they may not–be prepared for this.

Once you've arrived in the country you're visiting, remember the U.S. embassy as a source of information.

Other sources of information include the Internet and newspaper archives, and the *CIA World Factbook*. And don't avoid books intended for the tourist–they may contain useful information that is not available elsewhere (for example, on tipping or good places to eat). The best source may be someone who has recently been to the country.

2. LEARN ABOUT THE COUNTRY

- Identify the principal and minority languages of the country you are visiting–mistaken assumptions can be embarrassing. Spanish is the official language of most South American countries, for example, but Brazilians speak Portuguese.
- Learn something about the country's history, especially the past few decades. In complex regions like the Balkans this may seem daunting, but some knowledge of regional and international relationships will stand you in good stead.
- Discover whether there are significant minorities in the country: their presence can have a major impact on politics and on business and personal relationships. There are, for example, 600,000 ethnic Hungarians in Slovakia out of a population of five million. Don't forget you may be attempting to do business with a member of a minority or mixed group.
- Read up on the country's internal politics, but refrain from expressing your opinions, especially if you do not know the political sympathies of your local contacts. Remember that in some countries expressing dissenting political opinions can put you and/or your hosts in danger.
- Find out about the country's major religions (many countries have more than one). Don't assume that other countries observe the religious holidays that you're accustomed to or that the way a specific holiday is observed is the same in every country. Sundays are not always a day of rest (Israel is one case in point). Many countries have numerous public holidays; find out when they are so that you don't mistime your trip.
- Find out what the temperature and humidity are likely to be during your visit so that you can pack appropriate clothing.

3. ASK ABOUT VISA REQUIREMENTS

You may or may not need a visa (an authorization to visit that is attached to or stamped in your passport by a foreign government). Ask your travel agent or approach the country's embassy, which can issue a visa if you require one. Allow plenty of time for this: you are likely to have to submit forms, photographs, and your passport, and possibly a fee, and you may have to wait for days or weeks.

4. DECIDE HOW TO MANAGE FOREIGN CURRENCY

Ask your bank or travel agent what form of currency you should take. You may not always need to get local currency before your trip. U.S. dollars are accepted in some countries, and traveler's checks are still a good standby.

If you do take U.S. dollars, take only bills issued during the last five years. In some countries where large num-

---

"Chinese managers and employees perceive that they have as many problems with foreign business representatives as the other way around." (Jan Selmer)

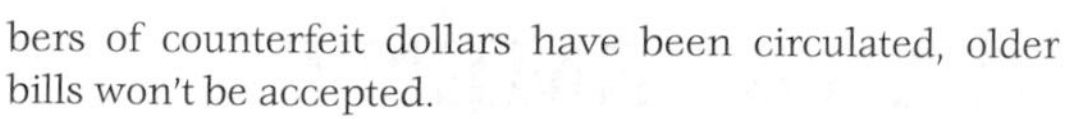

bers of counterfeit dollars have been circulated, older bills won't be accepted.

Unless you are a very experienced traveler, prepare a matrix giving at least approximate exchange rates of:

- the euro
- the pound
- the local currency (know its subdivision)
- the yen

Find out in advance whether, and which, credit cards are likely to be accepted in the country. Ask whether they are accepted in stores and restaurants, whether they can be used to obtain local currency at banks, and whether they can be used in ATMs. In addition:

- be prepared to pay a bank commission if you use your credit card to obtain currency;
- be prepared to produce your passport when you exchange money;
- don't get too much local currency at a time. Some countries do not permit you to take their currency out, and in countries with rapid inflation you can lose money by changing too much at once. Find out in advance what your own bank at home will accept if you bring foreign currency back.

✔ 5. Be Sensitive to Local Culture

To start with, educate yourself about a few basic cultural practices.

- Tips—local custom may or may not require them. The amount and way of giving a tip, especially in restaurants, may not be what you're used to. In some countries tips are given to taxi drivers but not in restaurants, in others it's the opposite. In any case different services usually require different sizes of tip. In some countries expectations differ according to the region or city you are in.
- Find out the locally acceptable practice for giving and receiving gifts.
- Don't be surprised by local restroom arrangements—mixed-sex restrooms with a female attendant are not unknown. Be prepared!
- Find out what is and what is not regarded as good manners. The belch that must be avoided at home may be obligatory in some countries to show appreciation of your meal. People are sometimes very critical of their own country—but can be offended if you agree with them. Learn as much as you can before your trip, and be tactful when you are traveling.
- Find out how to negotiate local transportation. It may be local custom to agree on taxi fares with your driver in advance, for example.
- Know something about the local police. Do they issue on-the-spot fines? For what?
- Humor doesn't always travel well; be cautious, especially about personal remarks. Some people laugh at themselves, others only at their neighbors. Some people who laugh at themselves don't expect (or like!) others to join in.
- Learn about common physical gestures—a nod in Bulgaria or Greece signifies lack of agreement.
- Don't make jokes about Communists or former nationalized institutions in Eastern Europe: you may be talking to a former Communist about an institution that he or she managed. Your listener's reaction may be reflected only in your order book.
- Accept hospitality carefully—pace yourself, especially when you're socializing over alcohol. Your hosts may be used to whatever you're drinking—you may not.

DOS AND DON'TS

For Preparing for Business Abroad

DO

- Remember that people from other countries and cultures are as proud of their histories, culture, and achievements as you are of yours.
- Remember the importance of listening.
- Know a few words in the language of your potential business partners—especially salutations.
- Try to know what is likely to be making the national news headlines of the country you're in as well as something of the background of those stories.

DON'T

- Don't make assumptions based on your own standards, customs, and practices.
- Don't criticize the country's politicians—your contacts may support them.
- Don't discuss religion.
- Don't patronize your contacts or anyone else.
- Don't disparage sanitary arrangements or standards of hygiene.

THOUGHT STARTERS

- What stereotypes come into your mind when you think of the foreign visitors you will be meeting?
- Do the stereotypes have any basis in reality?

For More Information

Books:

Axtell, Roger E., ed. *Do's and Taboos around the World.* 3rd ed. New York: John Wiley, 1993.

Earley, P. Christopher, and Miriam Erez. *The Transplanted Executive: Why You Need to Understand How Workers in Other Countries See the World Differently.* New York: Oxford University Press, 1997.

See also:

✔ **Planning Overseas Assignments (pp. 374–75)**

"A great many American managers are influenced by beliefs, assumptions, and perceptions about management that unduly constrain them."

(Richard Pascale)

SETTING UP AN ENERGY MANAGEMENT PROGRAM

CHECKLIST

This checklist provides guidance for managers wishing to control the amount of energy consumed by their company or organization.

Organizations, under pressure to reduce costs and protect the environment, are increasingly turning their attention on both counts to conserving energy. Some companies see energy as a fixed cost that cannot be reduced, but in fact almost all organizations can find ways to use less energy, and a successful energy management program produces benefits for both the organization and the environment.

DEFINITION

An energy management program provides a systematic and continuous method of analyzing, improving, and evaluating an organization's energy usage.

ADVANTAGES

An effective energy management program:

- saves money;
- conveys an environmentally friendly attitude;
- often makes for greater employee workplace comfort.

DISADVANTAGES

There are no real disadvantages to introducing an energy management program, but remember that it takes time to set up and can require a sizeable initial expenditure, and that savings or environmental benefits accrue over the long term.

ACTION CHECKLIST

1. DESIGNATE AN ENERGY MANAGEMENT COMMITTEE

The members of the energy management committee should be drawn from all levels of the organization. Your finance and purchasing departments should be represented, as should the transportation department, if you have one. The committee will manage the analysis, improvement, and evaluation of energy usage. Appoint a coordinator (someone with project management experience who commands respect and can get things done) to oversee the program. If in-house expertise or resources are limited, consider calling in an external energy management consultant.

2. DEFINE THE SCOPE AND COVERAGE OF THE PROGRAM

Depending on the size of the organization, it is advisable to concentrate initially on one site or building; you can build on this experience to improve energy efficiency throughout the organization. Alternatively, the committee may decide to look initially at only one type of energy usage, for example, heating or the use of company vehicles.

3. GATHER INFORMATION

Ask the committee's finance department representative to produce a report of all the company's energy bills over the last couple of years. Check the rates: do they look reasonable, or too high? Look for variations in consumption over the year. Ask an alternative energy provider for a quote using your own consumption data and compare the results.

If possible, try to compare your organization's energy usage figures with those of another organization.

4. UNDERTAKE AN ENERGY AUDIT

Examine the way the organization uses energy. Create checklists covering different systems and identify practices that are potentially wasteful.

Cover the following areas:

- Transportation
  Are vehicles regularly serviced, maintained, and tuned?
  Do employees share vehicles when they are traveling to the same place on business?
  Do some drivers appear to use too much gas? Do they need advice on fuel economy?
  In planning trips, is cost-effective transportation a consideration?
  Can diesel fuel or liquefied petroleum gas be used instead of gas?
- Lighting
  Are you using the most efficient light bulbs?
  Could you make more use of daylight by moving workstations nearer windows?
  Are lights switched off when rooms are not in use?
  Are windows cleaned regularly?
- Heating
  Is the heating system serviced regularly?
  Are thermostats functioning correctly, and are they set to the right temperature?
  Is the heating switched off or turned down when the building is empty?
  Are windows energy efficient?
- Air conditioning
  Do you really need it?
  Is the system kept clean and regularly maintained?
  Is it working against the heating system?
- Insulation
  Are wall and roof insulation materials of the correct type and thickness?
- Ventilation
  Do employees open doors or windows to cool the place down instead of turning down thermostats?
  Are badly fitting doors and windows causing excessive drafts?

"The measure of innovation is its effect on the environment." (Peter F. Drucker)

- Equipment and machinery
  Is machinery running efficiently?
  Could you reuse any of the heat/energy produced by processes?
  Are you using the right size of machine for each job?
  Do employees routinely turn off computers and machines when they are not in use?
  Every member of the committee should be actively involved in the audit. Members can be assigned to specific departments or sites, or each member can look at one particular aspect of energy use.

5. Analyze the Results and Make Improvements or Modifications

The results of the audit should highlight areas where action can be taken immediately (turning down thermostats, for example) and areas where investment may be needed to produce long-term gains (for example, buying a more efficient boiler). Instruct the purchasing department to take energy efficiency into account by asking suppliers about the energy consumption of every new piece of machinery or equipment. Ask the department to look for energy-efficient machines that could replace the present ones cost-effectively, and for innovatory products such as systems that switch lights off automatically.

If you don't already have such a system, it is essential to implement a schedule of regularly servicing and maintaining vehicles, machinery, and heating and cooling equipment.

DOS AND DON'TS

For Setting Up an Energy Management Program

DO

- Let all staff know about the importance of reducing energy usage.
- Remember to record the amount the company is spending on energy before the energy management program is launched.
- Make maintenance and servicing of machinery and equipment a regular program.
- Make sure that purchasing staff look at energy efficiency before making buying decisions.

DON'T

- Don't obscure the results of the program—inform all staff of its success.
- Don't stop after one audit and set of responses—continually look for improvements.

Keep a record of the committee's changes so that improvements in energy usage can be monitored.

6. Communicate and Train Staff

Communicate the benefits of improved energy management and reduced costs to all employees. Provide training on ways for employees to reduce energy usage—for example, by turning the heat down instead of opening windows to cool down an office. The checklists devised for the energy audit will help with this. Ask suppliers to provide training on the best ways to maintain and service specialist equipment. Reward staff who suggest successful ways to reduce energy usage.

7. Evaluate Changes and Look for Further Improvements

Check the energy bills after the program has been implemented and record reductions. Communicate successes to all employees. Hold regular meetings of the energy management committee to look for further ways to save on energy usage.

THOUGHT STARTERS

- Are lights switched off when a room is left empty?
- Are all the radiators functioning correctly?
- Does your company car use too much gas?
- Turning the heating down one degree saves fuel.

For More Information

Books:

Capehart, B. L., et al. *Guide to Energy Management*. Lilburn, GA: Fairmont Press, 2000.
O'Callaghan, Paul. *Energy Management*. New York: McGraw-Hill, 1993.
Romm, Joseph J. *Cool Companies: How the Best Businesses Boost Profits and Productivity by Cutting Greenhouse-Gas Emissions*. Washington, DC: Island Press, 1999.

Web Sites:

Department of Energy: **www.energy.gov/business**
ETSU (Energy Efficiency): **www.etsu.com**
Energy Efficiency and Renewable Energy Network: **www.eren.doe.gov**

INVENTORY CONTROL

CHECKLIST

This checklist deals with some of the major principles of stock control, as it has traditionally been called, or inventory control, as it has become more widely known.

Stock control is important at both ends of the supply spectrum. Too much inventory ties up cash, prejudices cash flow, and in extreme cases jeopardizes the very survival of the company. Too little inventory threatens prosperity and growth if goods cannot be provided to customers. Stock control is therefore very important, although paradoxically it is often neglected.

This checklist is not a manual on stock control. It suggests lines of inquiry for managers seeking to improve their company's management of inventory.

DEFINITION

Stock control is the sum total of the policies, practices, and procedures that a company follows to ensure that its inventory is kept at levels consistent both with meeting predetermined standards of services and with releasing funds for working capital.

Inventory is held by retailers (finished goods), wholesalers (finished goods), manufacturers (finished goods, part finished goods, parts, and raw materials), public bodies (a range of inventory for use), indeed every type of organization.

For the purposes of this checklist, strategic inventory is defined as inventory without which the organization cannot function, that is, essential inventory.

Nonstrategic inventory is defined as basic commodities that are not critical to the overall function of the organization and that can be readily sourced.

ADVANTAGES

The introduction of effective stock control requires the commitment of significant effort and resources. However, stock control:

- releases cash for the major functions of the organization;
- achieves a standard of service consistent with predetermined policy;
- minimizes the costs associated with holding inventory (finance, storage, insurance, handling, obsolescence, pilferage).

ACTION CHECKLIST

1. UNDERSTAND WHAT IS INVOLVED

Stock control systems can be extremely simple, from ledger books and card indexes to sophisticated computerized operating environments.

Establish a system that will provide you with regular reports about current inventory and that records supplies received and sales, deliveries, outputs, and usage. Your system need not be based on precise records for every item held in inventory. Use common sense: the cost of the system and its operation should not exceed the cost of the problem it is intended to solve. However, the following steps must be built into any stock control system:

- the reporting of current inventory levels;
- the recording of receipts/dispatches;
- the identification of reorder levels and quantities (through analysis of lead times, volume discounts, price stability)—this has a cost in itself in the form of higher ordering costs, loss of bulk discounts, and perhaps additional handling charges;
- the establishment of a schedule of regular auditing and inventory checking.

2. ANALYZE USAGE

Analyze usage of all items in terms of:

- volume
- strategic/nonstrategic status

It is important to:

- identify key products that must be available on demand;
- classify products in terms of their importance to sales, not in big product families or in other broad product groupings;
- analyze sales to identify the real money earners: 50 percent probably yields only 10 percent of the total value, so this half requires less attention;
- focus on the items that produce the most profit;
- resist giving equal attention to all inventory items.

Identify the level of inventory you need to hold to avoid the risk of missing core opportunities or failing to supply basic needs. Identify nonstrategic inventory and reduce it through:

- special offers
- nonreplacement
- repackaging
- scrapping for salvage value

In extreme cases, write it off.

Don't spend time monitoring items that yield 5 to 10 percent of annual revenue—reduce stocks of them. The 80/20 rule applies: monitoring the right 20 percent will give you control over 80 percent of the total value of your inventory. Arbitrarily reducing inventory by a fixed percentage across the board is likely to result in reduced service levels without identifying areas of wasted investment.

Identify the level above which excess inventory ties up money and diminishes your return on capital.

3. PLAN YOUR STOCKING AREA

- Locate frequently used items in an accessible place.
- Train staff in manual handling methods and the operation of mechanical handling equipment.
- Choose appropriate stacking methods—consider pallets, drums, bins, shelving, pipe racks. Do not try to store all items in the same environment.
- Consider storing large or bulky items with your sup-

"Our key words now are globalization, new products and business, and speed." (Tsutomu Kanai)

  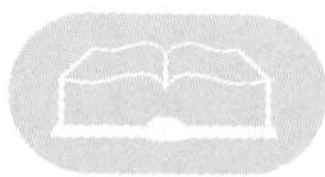    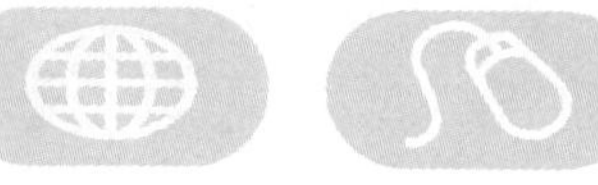

pliers if you have insufficient space, making sure that availability meets requirements.

- Use an appropriate labeling system for identifying inventory items (this might include bar coding or a simple handwritten label).
- Take shelf life into account and implement a stock rotation system.
- Review environmental conditions such as temperature and humidity.

4. Commit Adequate Personnel

Don't underestimate the staff required for running your stock control system in terms of numbers or quality—too few and you will lose control of your inventory, too many and the cost of running your system will be prohibitive.

5. Calculate the True Cost of Holding Inventory

Take into account the cost of:

- financing (the cost of funds or opportunity cost)
- storage, including equipment and labor
- protection from damp, cold, or damage
- insurance
- handling
- obsolescence
- losses through pilferage
- forgone rental income from your storage facilities

6. Use Common Sense

You cannot control every item by quantity—you wouldn't expect someone to count paper clips or screws. Consider classifying such items as consumables and make a policy decision not to count them. Some lines may be controlled by weight.

7. Coordinate with Other Departments

Try to link your stock control system to other departments. A system that works closely with accounting will reduce the workloads of both sections. Good communication with buyers and dispatch departments will lessen the risk of staff and plant being overworked one day and underoccupied the next.

DOS AND DON'TS

For Inventory Control

DO

- Understand that well-run companies plan inventory levels.
- Think of inventory as cash.
- Relate inventory to known or anticipated sales, deliveries, demand, and usage.
- Consider whether you are carrying excessive inventory.
- Establish and regularly review reorder levels and quantities.
- Designate someone in your company to coordinate the output of inventory, output forecasts, purchasing, and stock control.

DON'T

- Don't assume you aren't suffering from pilferage, excessive waste, or some other form of shrinkage.
- Don't exaggerate the potential consequences of running out.
- Don't assume that every quantity or early delivery discount offered is to your advantage.
- Don't let stock-taking become an annual nightmare—do it regularly on a partial basis.
- Don't think that a stock control system needs to be expensive and complex—a basic system may give you adequate control at a cost below the resulting savings.
- Don't hold inventory only to fill the store or warehouse.
- Don't buy on speculation.

THOUGHT STARTERS

- Who really controls our inventory levels?
- You conscientiously lock the safe because it contains $100. How much thought do you give to the warehouse containing $500,000 worth of inventory?

For More Information

Books:

Bolten, Ernst F. *Managing Time and Space in the Modern Warehouse: Practices and Procedures in Warehousing*. New York: AMACOM, 1997.

Jessop, David A., and Alex Morrison. *Storage and Supply of Materials*. Upper Saddle River, NJ: Financial Times Prentice Hall, 2000.

Tersine, Richard J. *Principles of Inventory and Materials Management*. 4th ed. Upper Saddle River, NJ: Prentice Hall, 1993.

Web Site:

Warehousing Management:
www.manufacturing.net/wm

See also:

✓ **Effective Purchasing (pp. 494–95)**

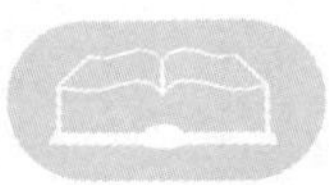

Taking Action on the Environment

CHECKLIST

This checklist is designed as an aid to the development of an action plan to comply with environmental regulations.

The environment has come to the forefront of industrial and commercial decision making in recent years. The onus and liability are increasingly on senior managers and directors to come to terms with environmental responsibilities by adopting environmental policies and initiating action plans.

This checklist is therefore aimed primarily at senior managers who have, or will have, responsibility for tackling environmental issues.

Definition

An environmental action plan brings together the key elements of environmental management, including:

- the organization's policy statement;
- the environmental audit;
- environmental management systems and standards, including the ISO 14001: Environmental Management Systems;
- the setting of targets and the measuring of performance against them;
- the identification and ordering of key responsibilities to set the system in motion.

Advantages

An environmental action plan will:

- demonstrate commitment to customers, shareholders, and legislators that action to reduce environmental damage is a priority;
- provide a coherent statement of policy and a plan for implementation;
- lead to reduced waste and cost;
- mandate closer examination of processes and raw materials that can contribute to cost savings and improved productivity;
- help to develop improved communications and management systems through better information on sources of environmental impacts;
- lay a foundation for effective management of environmental risk.

Disadvantages

- Staff may not see the need to change established practices.
- Stakeholders may see only the costs as opposed to an investment that will yield benefits.
- Benefits may be slow to accrue while costs are quickly incurred.

Action Checklist

1. Gain Top Management Commitment

Make sure that the implications of good—and bad—environmental practice are fully understood by top managers and key stakeholders.

2. Designate a Senior Manager

Allocate responsibility for environmental matters at senior level.

3. Identify Environmental Laws and Regulations

Do your homework on relevant legislation and codes of practice—liability usually means that the polluter pays.

4. Consider Applying for Registration under ISO 14001

Registration provides a recognized framework for environmental management and may give a competitive advantage where there is a need to demonstrate conformance.

5. Review the Environmental Impact of Your Organization's Operations

This will enable you to determine the issues that need to be addressed.

6. Identify the Environment–business Link

Focus on issues where environmental improvements can be directly related to financial and quality targets, for example, the generation of new or improved product lines by recycling waste, or the justification of price increases for more environmentally friendly products.

7. Establish Your Policy

Draw up a clear statement that covers objectives, improvement programs, audits, supplier and customer liaison, compliance with standards, and responsibility to the community.

8. Build In Measures and Records

These should cover not only outputs (damage to, or impact on, the environment) and inputs (damage created by raw materials), but also process measures (pollution created by outdated or worn-out machinery). Keep detailed records—ISO 14001 or legislation may require evidence of conformance.

9. Develop a Procedures Manual

The manual should be a "who does what and how" of operational control achieved through work instruction, performance criteria, measurements, tests, and verification.

10. Launch an Environmental Training Program

Build the environment into routine operational practice. The organization will benefit from the integration of environmental goals with financial, personal, and operational targets.

"While animals survive by adjusting themselves to their background, man survives by adjusting his background to himself."
(Ayn Rand)

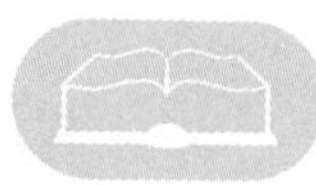

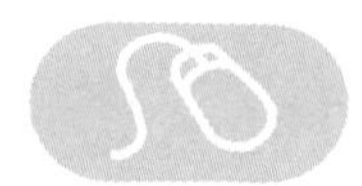

11. Involve Your Employees

Work on the commitment of staff by involving them directly rather than issuing remote instructions. Publicize your objectives and targets.

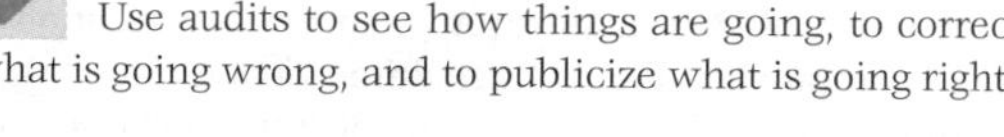

12. Conduct Regular Audits

Use audits to see how things are going, to correct what is going wrong, and to publicize what is going right.

13. Communicate Environmental Benefits

Make sure you communicate your successes both internally and externally. Where possible, express environmental benefits in terms of financial savings. The promotion of direct community benefits can also enhance the organization's image and reputation.

Measuring Environmental Damage

- Input measures should include indicators, targets, and measures of plant efficiency, materials quality and recyclability, and effectiveness of training in operational procedures.
- Process measures should aim at percentage improvements in reducing waste in manufacturing, finishing, and packaging.
- Output measures record impact on, or damage to, the community, and should measure reductions in waste or pollution discharge. Output measures are those that relate most to the organization's image and reputation and are the ones most likely to be reported outside the organization.

THOUGHT STARTERS

- "Businesses made a great deal of money fouling the world over the last 200 years. I have no doubt that there are many fortunes to be made cleaning things up over the next three generations." (Sir Crispin Tickell)
- Some 23 billion tons of carbon dioxide are pumped into the Earth's atmosphere every year.
- Tropical rainforests—the world's lungs—are being cut back by 170,000 square kilometers every year.

DOS AND DON'TS

For Taking Action on the Environment

DO

- Pay attention to ISO 14001.
- Focus attention on all stages of the product life cycle, not just the end.
- Take into account the environmental policies of suppliers, customers, and competitors.
- Try to spread the environmental message far and wide in the organization—action will follow more readily.
- Make sure that staff receive appropriate information and training.
- Communicate what you are doing to the outside world.

DON'T

- Don't assume the environment is irrelevant if you are not in manufacturing.
- Don't wait for legislation or bad press to force you to act.
- Don't impose complicated systems without full consultation and feedback.
- Don't equate measurement and records with bureaucracy. If it gets measured, it gets done.

For More Information

Books:

Tibor, Tom, and Ira Feldman. *ISO 14000: A Guide to the New Environmental Management Standards.* New York: McGraw-Hill Professional, 1995.

Winter, Georg. *Blueprint for Green Management: Creating Your Company's Own Environmental Action Plan.* New York: McGraw-Hill, 1994.

Journal Article:

Hormozi, Amir M. "ISO 14000: The Next Focus in Standardization." *SAM Advanced Management Journal* 62:3 (Summer 1997): 32–41.

Web Sites:

National Council for Science and the Environment: **www.cnie.org**

U.S. Department of Energy Office of Environmental Management (EM): **www.em.doe.gov**

U.S. Environmental Protection Agency: **www.epa.gov**

"Modern economic thinking. . .is peculiarly unable to consider the long term and to appreciate man's dependence on the natural world."

(E. F. Schumacher)

TOTAL QUALITY: GETTING TQM TO WORK

CHECKLIST This checklist provides guidance for those who have mapped a total quality management strategy for their organization and are now seeking to implement it.

DEFINITION

Total quality management, or TQM, is a way of managing that gives everyone in the organization responsibility for delivering quality to the final customer; quality being described as "fitness for purpose" or as "delighting the customer." TQM views each task in the organization as fundamentally a process in a customer-supplier relationship with the next process. The aim at each stage is to define and meet the customer's requirements, in order to maximize the satisfaction of the final consumer at the lowest possible cost.

ACTION CHECKLIST

1. DECIDE WHETHER TO RUN PILOTS

While you need to map a TQM strategy for the whole organization, you will usually introduce it in stages. Select for the pilots significant areas or functions in which you feel TQM will yield results within a year at most: short-term success will be critical in selling TQM to the skeptics.

2. MONITOR AND EVALUATE THE RESULTS OF THE PILOTS

Draw up a framework and appoint a management team to assess and evaluate the results of the pilots. What lessons can be learned, and how can these be applied in introducing TQM elsewhere in the organization?

3. SELECT TOOLS AND TECHNIQUES TO USE AT EACH STAGE OF IMPLEMENTATION

There are four key stages in the implementation of TQM: measurement, process management, problem solving, and corrective action. For each, you need to select the tools and techniques appropriate to the scale and environment of your organization.

4. SELECT MEASUREMENT TECHNIQUES

Measurement is critical to the success of TQM in quantifying situations and events and providing a benchmark by which to measure progress. The key is to make certain that measurement is a meaningful process leading to corrective action, not an end in itself. The main techniques are measurement and error logging charts, corrective action systems, work process flow charts, run charts, and process control charts.

5. SELECT PROCESS MANAGEMENT TOOLS

Many systems and tools can be used in process management. Some, for example, Gantt charts, flow charts, and histograms, may already be used in the organization for other purposes. Select those that are right for your organizational culture.

6. SET UP MECHANISMS FOR PROBLEM SOLVING

Plan to establish groups throughout the organization to look at improving quality from different angles.

- Improvement groups are regular sessions led by supervisors of natural work groups.
- Key process groups analyze the operation of important processes.
- Innovation groups cross departments and are drawn from different levels within the organization to look at totally new ways of working.

The groups will have a range of techniques available to help them, including brainstorming, fishbone diagrams, and Pareto analysis.

7. SET UP MECHANISMS FOR CORRECTIVE ACTION

The emphasis in TQM must be on identifying the causes of problems and solving them. At the planning stage, build in feedback loops with corrective action.

8. DRAW UP A COMMUNICATIONS PLAN FOR ANNOUNCING THE PROGRAM

Decide when and how to announce implementation of the program across the organization. Assume that staff may initially be cynical or skeptical, and devise strategies for overcoming employees' doubts. Use "converts" from the pilots to explain the benefits. Spell out the relationship of TQM to other initiatives within the organization.

9. PLAN TO CREATE THE RIGHT CULTURE FOR QUALITY

Successful TQM depends as much on cultural change as on process improvements. Be aware that TQM will probably need to be accompanied by a general program of information and education targeted at employees, supervisors, and managers.

10. IMPLEMENT THE EDUCATION PROGRAM

Introduce the education program mapped in your strategy. Target key groups first. Use these as agents of change to disseminate learning through the organization.

11. EMPOWER SUPERVISORS

The team leaders will be pivotal to the success of TQM. You need to give them the resources, time, support, and education to become leaders.

12. CONSIDER HOW TO MOTIVATE EMPLOYEES TO TAKE OWNERSHIP

Employees will need to take ownership of quality and act on their own initiative. To achieve this, you will need to create an open culture and drive out fears of failure, of taking risks, and of reprisals. You will also need to be prepared to deal with the possible insecurities of managers who discover that most or all of their work is unnecessary or can be done by staff at lower levels.

"We try to picture what the products will be and then say, what technology should we be working on today to help us get there?"

(John Sculley)

13. Establish a Program of Management Change

Employees will not be able to make the changes needed without profound changes in management style. A new approach based on collaboration, consensus, and participation will be needed under TQM. The largest single change for managers will be from telling to listening, from commanding to empowering.

14. Set Short- and Long-term Goals for the Implementation Program

Establish a means for monitoring progress. Combine short-term goals to demonstrate progress and more challenging long-term ones to stretch the organization. Include a mix of business and cultural indicators.

15. Maintain the Impetus

Cultural changes will take a long time to show results, but without results staff may be frustrated because they don't perceive much achievement through process improvements. Regularly review and report progress; recognize and publicize successes.

DOS AND DON'TS

For Total Quality: Getting TQM to Work

DO

- Spell out the relationship between TQM and other initiatives within the organization.
- Find out where the invisible barriers to change are. Be aware of them from the outset and develop a strategy for breaking through them.
- Make sure that systems concentrate on measuring the performance of work processes rather than the individuals engaged in them.
- Pay attention to the soft side of TQM. Changing culture is as important as changing processes.
- Make clear that TQM is not a quick fix, but an ongoing process of continuous improvement: you will never fully achieve total quality because the targets will constantly shift.

DON'T

- Don't view TQM as a precisely defined methodology or a prescribed series of actions to be completed one by one.
- Don't try to bring in TQM alongside other major initiatives if these already make heavy demands on management time.
- Don't lose sight of the ends by excessive concentration on the means.

THOUGHT STARTERS

- Do you need to make changes to the structure of the organization to make clear that quality is the responsibility of everyone?
- To what extent do current reward mechanisms promote employee involvement in quality?

For More Information

Books:

Bell, Desmond, Philip McBride, and George Wilson. *Managing Quality*. Woburn, MA: Butterworth-Heinemann, 1994.

Spenley, Paul. *Step Change Total Quality: Achieving World Class Business Performance*. 2nd ed. New York: Kluwer Academic Publishers, 1995.

See also:

✔ **Brainstorming (pp. 542–43)**
✔ **Implementing Business Process Reengineering (pp. 506–07)**
✔ **Implementing an Effective Change Program (pp. 504–05)**
✔ **Implementing Statistical Process Control (SPC) (pp. 562–63)**
✔ **Solving Problems (pp. 408–09)**
✔ **Total Quality: Mapping a TQM Strategy (pp. 524–25)**

 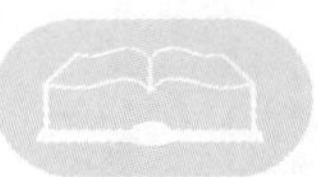  

TOTAL QUALITY: MAPPING A TQM STRATEGY

CHECKLIST

This checklist provides guidance on mapping a strategy for total quality management (TQM) for those seeking to introduce TQM to the organization for the first time. A quality strategy combines the "hard" edge of quality—its tools and techniques—with its "soft" side—the cultural changes you will need to achieve success. It is not just another management gimmick. It is a way of life.

The checklist is intended only as an aid to your initial thinking. Introducing TQM is a major strategic change that requires considerable research and planning. You are likely to need external advice or help to implement it.

DEFINITION

Total quality management, or TQM, is a style of managing that gives everyone in the company responsibility for delivering quality to the final customer, quality being described as "fitness for purpose" or as "delighting the customer." TQM views each task in the organization as fundamentally a process in a customer-supplier relationship with the next process. The aim at each stage is to define and meet the customer's requirements in order to maximize the satisfaction of the final consumer at the lowest possible cost.

ADVANTAGES

- TQM vastly improves the quality of the final product or service.
- TQM greatly decreases the waste of resources.
- Productivity rises sharply as employees use time more effectively.
- As products and services are improved, market share should show a long-term increase, leading to sustained competitive advantage.
- The workforce becomes more motivated as employees realize their full potential.

DISADVANTAGES

- TQM is extremely demanding of management and staff time
- TQM will help only if the organization is heading in the right direction. It is not a tool for turning an organization around
- TQM is not a quick fix: TQM takes years to implement and is in fact an unending process
- TQM can lead to too much attention being paid to the needs of final customers and not enough to those of employees
- TQM can become overly bureaucratic and mechanical, leading to an emphasis on consistency rather than improvement, or a focus on the means rather than the end
- TQM is likely to cause disruption at various stages, requiring careful handling.

ACTION CHECKLIST

1. ESTABLISH A PLANNING TEAM FOR TOTAL QUALITY

You will need a quality team to drive through the changes. In a small company this will be the senior management team; in a larger one, it will comprise senior managers representing the major functions. Include in the team known skeptics or mavericks, and make sure that minority views are represented.

2. EVALUATE THE NEED FOR CHANGE

Consider the competitive position of the organization. Establish who your key customers are and find out what they expect of you: don't assume that you are currently meeting all of their requirements. Finding out what customers need is a continuous process, not a onetime, exercise. Find out, too, how other groups—suppliers, competitors, and employees—view the quality of your product or service.

3. DEFINE YOUR VISION

Draw up a vision statement defining where the company wants to be in terms of serving its customers: this vision should be stretching but attainable. Define the principles and values that underpin the vision. Use comparable organizations as a model, but make sure your final draft reflects your own culture and circumstances.

4. DEFINE THE STANDARD OF SERVICE YOU AIM TO PROVIDE

Translate the vision into realistic outcomes. Establish what customers, suppliers, and employees expect the company to deliver in quality of product or service.

5. REVIEW HOW CLOSELY YOU MEET YOUR OWN STANDARDS

There will often be a large gap between customer expectations and reality. Determine the reasons for this across the organization. Key reasons are often external constraints, being let down by suppliers, and internal inefficiencies. It can happen that customers expect too little—you need to assess their needs, not only their expressed wishes.

6. AUDIT CURRENT LEVELS OF WASTE

Quantify quality failures by securing from heads of department an audit of current levels of waste. All employees should take part in this audit. Collect data as widely as possible, cost the results, and present the findings to the senior management team.

7. ESTABLISH THE CURRENT COST OF WASTE

Calculate how much is currently spent on rectifying internal failure (for example, reworking of substandard

---

"I could buy companies, tart up their products and put my name on them, but I don't want to do that. That's what our competitors do."
(James Dyson)

  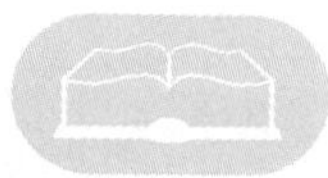    

goods) and external failure (such as handling customer complaints). Include appraisal costs and the time and money spent on inspection and checking.

8. Decide Whether to Seek Third-Party Certification

You need to decide whether to include a quality management system in your initiative. If you do, it will lead to third-party certification, which may bring benefits with customers and suppliers or even be demanded by them.

9. Draw Up Your Quality Strategy

Use the results of the waste audit to draw up your quality strategy. This will cover:

- the goals of the strategy, including the revised mission;
- the systems and tools needed to change processes;
- the cultural changes needed to create the right environment for quality;
- details of the resources that can be applied;
- time frames.

Secure senior management approval of the plan.

10. Draw Up a Management Structure for Change

The culture of the organization will be critical to the success or failure of TQM. Plan for the introduction of team-based working: strong, effective teams are essential.

11. Establish an Education and Training Program

Some staff will need training in depth, others less, but everyone should be given a thorough introduction to, and familiarization with, what TQM means. Analyze training needs in relation to TQM and cost the additional training required. The cost can be offset against the expected productivity gains. Plan for:

- general orientation and training of all employees in the principles of TQM;
- coaching of managers, supervisors, and team leaders in the soft skills needed to implement TQM;
- job-specific training in new techniques associated with TQM;
- additional training in customer relations.

An external trainer or facilitator is almost always essential, especially in the early stages.

12. Identify Opportunities and Priorities for Improvement

Set priorities for the introduction of TQM. Select key processes for early analysis and improvement. Start with three processes at the most, choosing at least one that is likely to demonstrate quick returns in business performance.

13. Establish Goals and Criteria for Success

You need both short- and long-term targets. Establish measures of success in both business and cultural terms.

DOS AND DON'TS

For Total Quality: Mapping a TQM Strategy

DO

- Secure commitment from top management from the very beginning.
- Make sure that this commitment is repeatedly conveyed.
- Involve all employees in assessing current failures.

DON'T

- Don't see TQM as a quick fix.
- Don't bring TQM in at the same time as other major new initiatives.
- Don't use TQM (or even appear to use TQM) as a means of downsizing.

THOUGHT STARTERS

- Is the climate really right for the introduction of TQM? In particular, do managers have the integrity and openness that TQM will demand of them?
- Does your strategy strike the right balance between the needs of your customers and your employees?

For More Information

Books:

Bell, Desmond, Philip McBride, and George Wilson. *Managing Quality*. Woburn, MA: Butterworth-Heinemann, 1994.

Kaydos, Will. *Measuring, Managing and Maximising Performance: What Every Manager Needs to Know About Quality Productivity to Make Real Improvements in Performance*. Portland, OR: Productivity Press, 1994.

See also:

✓ **Implementing Business Process Reengineering (pp. 506–07)**
✓ **Total Quality: Getting TQM to Work (pp. 522–23)**

"I admire the capacity of American executives to continually reinvent what they do; it shows they are never satisfied."

(Anonymous)

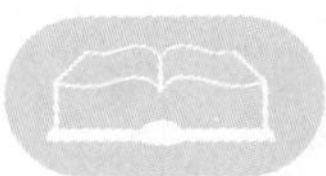

Using Management Consulting Services Effectively

CHECKLIST

This checklist is for prospective users of consultants. It suggests some of the questions you should ask yourself before approaching a consultant to undertake an assignment. There is little doubt that calling on the service of a management consultant can often prove to be a valuable investment, provided that:

- you allow enough time for the whole exercise;
- you have accurately defined the problem area;
- you know what you want the consultant to do and have identified the necessary steps for the task in hand;
- you exercise care in selecting the right consultant;
- you measure progress toward a solution.

Definition

Management consulting is an advisory service contracted for and provided to organizations by specially trained and qualified persons who assist, in an objective and independent manner, the client organization to identify management problems, analyze such problems, recommend solutions to these problems, and help, when requested, in the implementation of solutions.

(Greiner & Metzger, *Consulting to Management*, 1983)

Advantages

- Expertise. Since consultants are immersed in their specialty, they are well placed to advise on the state of the art. It may be impossible for an organization to tap such expertise in any other way.
- Short-term projects. It may be more cost-effective for a company to buy in skills as and when they are needed.
- Extra resources. A consultant can back up an overstretched management team or pursue a project that would otherwise not be completed.
- Independent viewpoint. An outsider can see things that are unclear to people on the inside or say things that members of staff may fear to articulate. Equally, employees may be more willing to agree to a course of action if they know that impartial advice has been taken.

Disadvantages

- They may be expensive. *Consultants News*, published by Kennedy Information, is a good source of information on industry trends.
- The end result may be unsatisfactory, though steps in the following action checklist will help you guard against this.
- The work may be left to junior consultancy staff once the assignment starts, or personnel may change during the project.
- There may be resentment from staff over the employment of consultants.

Action Checklist

1. Involve Senior Management from the Beginning

Gain their approval for the decision to use consultants and keep them informed during the selection process. This will help ensure that your choice of consultant will be accepted at the top level.

2. Be Aware of the Number and Scope of Management Consulting Firms

Some offer a wide range of services, while others specialize in particular industries, certain areas of business activity, or smaller or larger organizations.

3. Prepare a Short List of Possible Consultants

Personal recommendation is a common method of finding consultants; you can also consult directories and registers. Make sure you obtain references from previous clients to establish a consultant's track record.

4. Ask Short-listed Consultants for a Preliminary Survey

This should be free, although in certain circumstances a nominal charge may be made. It should enable you to establish the extent to which the consultant can help you, the likely benefits, and the duration of the job. It should also help you study the consultant's approach to the problem and to your organization. Ask for a written report of the survey.

5. Study the Consultancy Proposals Submitted

Each proposal should contain:

- an understanding of your situation or need;
- a program of work;
- an indication of the consultant's management style and approach;
- a timetable for the work;
- details of consultancy staff who will be involved, including relevant qualifications and experience;
- the resources required, for example, time, information, and equipment;
- estimates of fees and costs;
- a summary of the results and benefits to be achieved from the project.

6. Explain to Staff Why You Are Hiring a Consultant

All staff concerned should be fully briefed on why a consultant has been appointed, when the consultant will arrive, and what kind of cooperation is required. Appoint someone as the main contact with the consultant.

"Wall Street is the only place people ride to in a Rolls Royce to get advice from people who take the subway."

(Warren Buffett)

  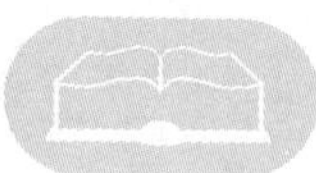    

7. Ask the Consultant for Regular Progress Reports

Measure actual progress against the agreed objectives of the assignment. Make sure that your requirements are not being overshadowed by the consultant's preferences.

8. Have a Debriefing Session Before the End of the Consultancy

Make sure the consultant summarizes the findings and conclusions of the project either in a report or in a presentation. Make certain that there are no misunderstandings or errors.

9. Assess the Consultant's Effectiveness

Check that the new development and procedures proposed are being implemented and applied appropriately, and that they are not being undermined by old methods and concepts. Discuss with staff concerned any particular difficulties that arise during implementation. Regularly examine the results being achieved and insist on follow-up visits from the consultant at appropriate intervals after completion of the project.

DOS AND DON'TS

For Using Management Consulting Services Effectively

DO

- Invest time in the whole process.
- Have a clear understanding of what you want to achieve.
- Prepare a checklist of requirements as a basis for reducing your short list to the final selection.
- Establish effective communication and coordination between consultant and staff.

DON'T

- Don't assume that you necessarily need to bring in an outsider.
- Don't accept friendly recommendations without investigating past performance.
- Don't presume that staff will readily accept an outside expert.
- Don't lose sight of your most important objectives.
- Don't become overly reliant on a consultant.

THOUGHT STARTERS

- Can you define clearly the problem or issue that needs to be tackled?
- Are you sure the expertise needed is not available internally?
- Have you worked with a consultant before? What was the outcome?

For More Information

Book:

The Directory of Management Consultants 2002. Fitzwilliam, NH: Kennedy, Information Inc., 2001.

Journal Articles:

Fowler, Alan. "How to Select an External Consultant." *Personnel Management Plus* 5:2 (February 1994): 26–27.

"Using Management Consultants." *IRS Employment Review*, no. 620 (November 1996): 7–12, purple.

Web Site:

Institute of Management Consultants USA: **www.imcusa.org**

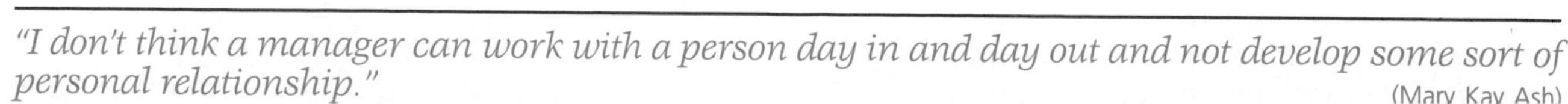

"I don't think a manager can work with a person day in and day out and not develop some sort of personal relationship."

(Mary Kay Ash)

 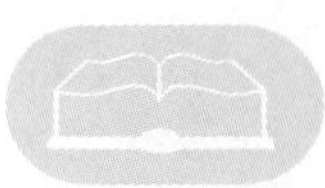    

Cash Flow for the Small Business

CHECKLIST

This checklist is designed to help you understand and control cash flow in your business.

Definition

The flow of cash through a business is roughly comparable to the flow of water through a central heating system. Too little cash/water, or obstruction to a smooth and continuous flow, creates problems. Without an adequate flow of cash, a company may be trading profitably in the shorter term, but it will nevertheless collapse. The figure below illustrates the flow of cash through a business. The flow starts at (1) when the owners or shareholders of the business invest funds, which go into the pool of cash (2).

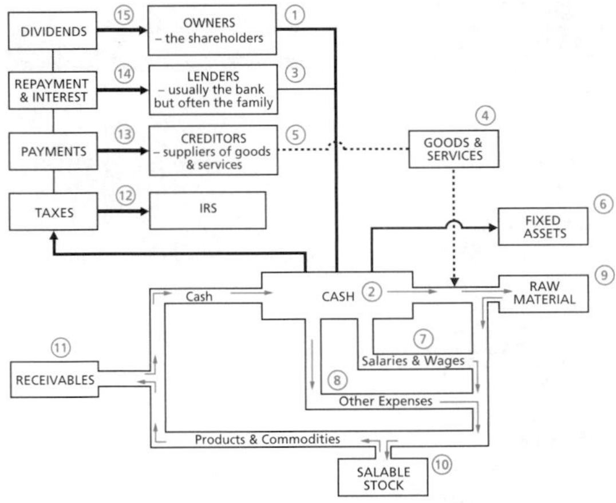

This investment may not be a one-shot occurrence. There may be subsequent injections of cash for a variety of positive (for example, business expansion) or negative (shortage of liquid funds) reasons. Lenders (3) may also put funds into the cash pool at any time. The lenders may be the company's bankers or, in some cases, members of the family or friends of the owners of the business.

Suppose that in order to start trading the company obtains goods and services (4) on credit from suppliers (5), who immediately become creditors. The business may also need to acquire fixed assets (6), perhaps real estate, office equipment, delivery trucks, or cars. If these assets are truly fixed, their purchase immediately immobilizes some liquid capital. Cash also flows out of the pool in the form of salaries and wages (7) and other expenses (8) such as stationery or computer software.

If the new business is in manufacturing, it buys raw materials (9)—another cash outflow, the timing depending on whether materials are paid for immediately or purchased on credit. The expenditure of wages and other expenses (for example, tools), together with some of the raw materials (7), (8), and (9), are used to produce salable stock (10). If the company does not manufacture products, it may purchase stock for resale. The stocks will rejoin the cash flow when they are sold, probably to customers buying on credit, whose debts immediately become receivables (11). They owe the company the price of the goods or services they purchased until they pay, whereupon cash flows back into the cash pool (2).

Periodically, the cash pool is reduced as cash is withdrawn to pay taxes (12) and creditors (13), repay capital and pay interest to lenders (14), and pay dividends or other rewards to the owners, the original investors (15). The cycle never ends. If it stops, the whole business process stops too. Without an injection of cash, trading ceases and the company goes out of business.

Advantages

Controlling your cash flow has important advantages.

- You know where your cash flow is tied up.
- You can spot potential bottlenecks and act to reduce their impact.
- You reduce your dependence on bankers and save interest charges by anticipating and managing your cash needs.
- You are in control of your business and can make informed decisions.

Action Checklist

1. Identify Potential Cash Bottlenecks

Examination of the figure above suggests some obvious bottlenecks:

- fixed assets (6)
- raw materials (9)
- salable stock (10)
- receivables (11)

Examine these bottlenecks in turn.

2. Reconsider Your Investment in Fixed Assets

- Is cash unnecessarily tied up in fixed assets?
- Is it tied up in assets that are not used, are underused, or could be disposed of?
- Is it tied up in necessary assets that could be replaced by leasing?
- Is it tied up in expensive assets that could be replaced by something cheaper?
- Has cash been invested in fixed assets for reasons of prestige rather than profit?

3. Reconsider Your Investment in Raw Materials

Have you tied up cash in raw materials to take advantage of special terms offered by suppliers?

Are you sure that the advantages outweigh the costs of holding raw materials that may not be used immediately? Consider:

- the cost of borrowing money to finance raw materials inventory;
- the loss of alternative uses for the capital;

"In the business world, everyone is paid in two coins: cash and experience. Take the experience first; the cash will come later."

(Harold S. Geneen)

- the cost of physical storage;
- the risk of shrinkage.

Similarly, reconsider your investment in finished goods.

4. Reconsider Your System of Inventory Control

An adequate system of inventory control does not necessarily require precise records for every line held in stock; common sense dictates the kind of records your company needs. Weigh the cost of the system against the costs and financial risks of the problems it is intended to help solve.

Some form of control is necessary to guard against theft, obsolescence, spoilage, and running out, or having too much, of a particular good, any of which can damage a business severely. The basic requirements of an inventory control system include:

- a forecast of what you expect to sell and when;
- a knowledge of your present inventory, provided via reports at regular intervals;
- a record of supplies received and shipments dispatched, which should be reconciled periodically with current inventory (this reconciliation need not be of every item, only of selected items in sequence);
- predetermined and regularly reviewed reorder levels and quantities;
- a knowledge of price trends and suppliers' quantity discounts and delivery times.

Check your inventory at least once a year. Have you considered a perpetual inventory system or a cyclical inventory check using staff as and when workloads permit?

5. Consider How Credit Works

The amount and length of credit allowed and potential return on capital are directly related. Some business owners assume that in most cases it is more important to turn over capital as quickly as they can instead of producing an additional return on capital made available (actually, lent) to a customer. Make sure your credit policy.

- recovers the cost of extending credit;
- gives customers strong incentives to pay promptly.

6. Consider Your Credit Policy

Policy.

- Is there one person in your business who is ultimately responsible for supervising credit and ensuring the prompt collection of monies due, and who is held accountable if your credit position gets out of hand? The exercise of this person's authority should not adversely affect individual sales reps' relationship with their customers—nor does it reduce individual reps' responsibility for seeing that the sales they make are paid for in accordance with the firm's credit terms.
- Do you have a clear-cut maximum credit policy? Is it written down? Is it known to all your sales staff?
- Are you clear in your own mind how you assess credit risks and how you impose your usual limits on each customer's total receivables and overdue accounts?

Bad debts.

- Did you know that—assuming you make 1.5 percent of net sales—a loss of $1,500 in bad debts nullifies the net profit on $100,000 sales and destroys all the effort involved in making those sales?
- Do you realize that an avoidable loss of $1,500 in bad debts almost certainly means that a lot of abortive effort has been expended trying to collect this money before it was written off—and that the cost of this effort is probably hidden and never identified?

Granting or extending credit.

- Do you methodically check the financial standing of all new customers before executing the first order?
- Do you recheck the financial standing of existing customers whose purchases have recently increased substantially?
- Do you check trade references by telephone? Suppliers will often tell you things over the phone that they would never put in writing.

Credit control and collection.

- How soon do your invoices go out after the goods are despatched? Can this be speeded up?
- How soon do monthly statements go out following the last day of the month? Can this be speeded up?
- Are the terms of sale clearly and precisely shown on all quotations, price lists, invoices, and statements?
- What is the actual average length of credit you are giving—or your customers are taking? What period do you generally allow?
- Do you have a collection procedure timetable? Do you stick to it?
- Are you politely firm but insistent in your collection routine?
- Do you watch the ratio of total debt on balances on the sales ledger at the end of each month in relation to the sales of the immediately preceding twelve months? Is the position improving, deteriorating, or static? Why?
- Are your sales staff aware that "It's not sold until it's paid for?"

For More Information

Book:

Dickie, Terry, and Beverly Manber. *Budgeting for a Small Business.* Normal, IL: Crisp Publications, 1994.

"Start small. If you can succeed with a few thousand pounds, then you can do much better with bigger sums."

(Reuben Singh)

DRAWING UP A CONTRACT OF EMPLOYMENT

CHECKLIST

This checklist details the steps involved in drawing up a contract of employment. It is primarily aimed at new contracts, but many points will also be useful in modifying an existing contract. As with any legal document, it is essential that you seek professional advice before putting a contract into effect.

Legislation does not require that an organization have a formal written contract with its employees, but such a contract can prevent later disputes over terms and conditions, whereas oral agreements are often called into question.

DEFINITION

A contract of employment is a legally enforceable agreement, either oral or written, between an employer and an employee that defines terms and conditions to which both parties must adhere. Areas covered include job title, remuneration, vacation days and holidays, sick pay, location, mobility, and the period of employment. Extra clauses can be added that make a certain qualification or confidentiality a prerequisite of the job, restrain the employee after termination of employment, and so on.

ADVANTAGES

Having well-drafted contracts of employment means that:

- employees can be clear about their rights;
- the employer can avoid the costs associated with disputes over terms and conditions;
- the employer can justifiably terminate employment if an employee does not meet the contract's requirements.

DISADVANTAGES

There are no real disadvantages to contracts of employment. Writing a contract that is watertight while allowing both parties some flexibility is difficult. Contracts require resources to draw up and review, and if they are badly written they can do the organization more harm than good.

ACTION CHECKLIST

1. ANALYZE THE JOB TO BE CONTRACTED

Look at the job description, if there is one, for information on what the job entails. Clauses in the contract must allow the employee to perform required duties without restrictions. The position may require the person to have a professional qualification—would the person be allowed to continue in the job if the awarding body were to withdraw professional status?

2. CONSIDER FUTURE PLANS AND OBJECTIVES

Do you expect the work force to be cut back in the future? If so, a permanent contract may be inadvisable. An overly specific job title may be inappropriate if the employee might be transferred to a different department—a general title such as "administrative officer" offers more flexibility. If you have plans to open further work sites, you may need to incorporate a mobility clause to cover employees who will be required at times to work away from their usual workplace. Including such clauses helps the company ensure that its work force will adapt to future corporate needs and developments.

3. LOOK BACK AT PROBLEMS

The organization may have had problems with contracts of employment in the past. Problems often arise from the nature of a company's work: departing employees might take some customers with them, might have created intellectual property of which the ownership is in dispute, or might resist relocation. Such problems are exacerbated when a contractual statement is poorly drafted or lacking.

4. GATHER INFORMATION AND CONFER WITH COLLEAGUES

Try to obtain some sample contracts of employment used in comparable organizations, and research the literature on the current requirements of personnel legislation. Colleagues can offer good advice over what has and has not worked in the past, in both the current organization and others they may have worked in. Union representatives can identify potentially contentious issues.

Consult your legal department, if your firm has one; if not, be prepared to go outside—incurring costs at this stage might well save you money in the long term.

5. INCORPORATE WRITTEN PARTICULARS

Neither federal nor state laws require an employer to provide an employment contract to new employees. Nor are employers required to provide an agreement, laying out the particulars of the job. Nevertheless, many employers do provide such things, and employment contracts have become more common. If you're considering an employee contract or agreement, here are some particulars to include:

- the employer's and employee's names;
- the date the employment started and will end (if fixed term), or the period it is expected to last if temporary. Some employers insert an "at will" provision, basically saying that the employer or employee may end the agreement at any time;
- the rate of remuneration, or how it is calculated, and when it is paid;
- terms and conditions relating to hours of work and benefits accrued;
- the notice required to be given by both employee and employer to terminate employment;
- an option to terminate, without discrimination, if a permanent disability keeps the employee from performing the duties for which he or she was hired;

"It is but a truism that labor is most productive where its wages are largest. Poorly paid labor is inefficient labor, the world over."

(Henry George)

- any collective agreements that affect the terms and conditions of employment—for example, those negotiated by a labor union;
- the job title and job description;
- an item related to employees agreeing to work in the employer's best interest, and that the employee will not simultaneously work for another company in the same industry;
- a nondisclosure clause, which prohibits the employee from divulging company information to anyone outside the business;
- a stipulation about the ownership rights of any inventions, discoveries, or intellectual property developed while the employee is a member of your staff;
- indemnification: the employer needs protection from legal action, should your company hire someone who has violated proprietary rights agreements from a former employer;
- policies and procedures that would include the appropriate steps used by an employee to appeal a disciplinary action taken against them;
- the name of the person or proper outside authorities, namely state or federal agencies, who can be approached, and the procedure to follow regarding any grievance related to employment;
- details of the place(s) of work;
- the length of time and currency in which remuneration will be made if the employee is required to work abroad for a period of more than one month.

The handbook must be accessible—a copy should be given to every employee as part of orientation.

6. Consider Extra Clauses

Any number of clauses may be included in a contract of employment depending on the nature of the job and the needs of the organization.

- Relocation expenses: It may be appropriate to include a clause requiring employees to repay any relocation expenses if they terminate their employment within a certain period.
- Qualifications: If the jobholder is required to obtain or hold a certain educational or professional qualification by a certain date, define the qualification and the consequences of failing to have it. Employees funded to obtain a qualification may be required to repay the cost if they terminate their employment within a certain period.
- Travel: Many jobs require travel to meet customers or clients; you may need to include a clause to cover this. Clerical workers are usually expected to be only as mobile as is reasonable on a daily commuting basis, whereas managers can be expected to travel as far as business requires.
- Probation: If you have a probationary period for new employees, specify its length and provisions to terminate the contract at the end or an earlier date, or to extend the length of the probation.
- Restraints: In some circumstances you can use clauses known as restrictive covenants to restrain the activities of an employee once employment has terminated. A common restraint is the prohibition on revealing trade secrets learned while working for a company. Some companies include a "non compete" clause, which restricts the employee from working for any of your company's competitors in the industry for a specified period of time after leaving your company.

7. Produce a Draft

Have it checked over, preferably by a legal professional. Make certain that all terms are clear and unambiguous and do not abridge any federal or state laws related to employee civil rights, wage and hour restrictions, health and safety regulations, worker's compensation laws, or family leave laws. Finally, make sure the contract or agreement doesn't restrict the employee from carrying out or further developing the role.

8. Review the Contract

Inform employees that the signed contract is legally binding. Generally, any subsequent changes to the contract or agreement must be confirmed in writing by both parties. Keep an eye on human resource literature for court cases and changes in legislation that may affect current or future contracts.

DOS AND DON'TS

For Drawing Up a Contract of Employment

DO

- Take time to prepare by examining the job and the future of the role.
- Get an idea of the law relating to contracts of employment, both federal and of the state in which you work.
- Use clear and unambiguous wording in the contract.

DON'T

- Don't cut corners—pay for legal advice if it is not available in-house.
- Don't try to restrain the employee too much—allow for some flexibility in the contract.

THOUGHT STARTERS

- Do you know what your contract of employment specifies?
- Have you ever had a problem with your contract of employment? What was it?

For More Information

Books:

Aikin, Olga. *Contracts*. Woodstock, NY: Beekman, 2000.

Bradley, John S., and Brian J. Youngman, eds. *International Handbook on Contracts of Employment*. New York: Kluwer Law International, 1988.

Web Site:

FindLaw Employment Agreements: **www.techdeals.biz.findlaw.com**

  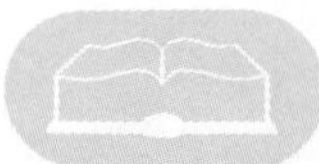    

Five Routes to Greater Profitability

This checklist identifies five routes that are frequently taken in pursuit of greater profitability. Many businesspeople and managers are familiar with them under a variety of labels, but many people fail to recognize their interrelationships. A change in any one of them has a potential impact on the others—a fact often ignored to the detriment of the business.

Definition

There are five basic ways in which a firm can have a direct effect on its profitability:

- increasing sales volume
- reducing costs and/or ensuring that costs are fully recovered where this has not previously been the case
- improving the product mix (varying the relationships between the volumes of individual products or groups of products sold)
- raising prices selectively or overall
- reducing the capital employed in the business

A change in any one of these affects the others. Any change, made or planned, voluntary or involuntary, must therefore be considered in the context of all the others; changes made in isolation may not have the expected impact on profitability. Other management strategies such as total quality management and customer service programs can also influence profitability, for example, by cutting out unneeded processes or motivating staff to greater productivity.

Advantages

- Financial planning takes all five factors and their interrelationships into account.
- You can assess the impact of changes on profitability systematically.
- You gain a more realistic view of the risks associated with changes.
- The line between risk-taking and recklessness may be clearer.

Action Checklist

1. Perform a Market Analysis

Take a close look at current and potential markets using focus groups, customer feedback, and commercial and commissioned market research. Bear in mind that in certain product and service sectors technological innovations can significantly change market structures and shift loyalty very quickly. Market analysis therefore has to be targeted to give rapid results. This research should reveal whether current markets can continue and new markets are available for penetration.

2. Consider Increasing Your Sales Volume

Increasing sales volume may appear to be an easy way of increasing profitability, but this is not necessarily the case.

- Selling more and more is not the key to increased profitability: profit requires sales, but sales does not equal profit.
- If you increase your sales volume, you must at the same time rigorously control costs, prices, capital employed, and your product/service mix. Be sure that none of these other four components of profitability increases disproportionately; if they do, increased sales reduce instead of increase profit.
- Trying to increase your sales by employing an additional sales rep or trading in a bigger geographic area only produces more profit if the extra sales produce at least enough extra profit (not revenue) to cover the extra costs.
- If you cut prices and margins to generate more sales, you need to achieve a considerable increase in sales volume—otherwise total revenue falls while costs remain the same.
- Increases in small-volume orders may hinder profitability instead of boosting it because of inherent administrative costs such as invoicing and dispatching.
- If you extend credit in order to encourage more sales, the company will have to bear the costs—with a knock-on effect on profitability.
- Selling more of all your existing product/service lines or introducing new ones may increase your sales volume, but be sure you know the contribution each line makes. Selling more of loss-making lines is bad business unless it is necessary in order to raise sales of profit-making ones.
- In some circumstances you can increase profits by reducing sales. Surveys have shown that a wholly disproportionate amount of cost and effort is sometimes invested to achieve a small amount of sales revenue. It is not uncommon to find that 50 percent of deliveries made account for only 15 percent of sales revenue. Or there's the 80/20 rule: 20 percent of your clients account for 80 percent of your profits. Consider what would happen if you reduced your sales by a selective 10 percent.

3. Look at Ways to Reduce Your Costs

Investigate and calculate your true costs in total and for unit sales. You cannot adjust your costs in relation to other parts of your business unless you know what they are. Consider the effects of specific cost reductions carefully—arbitrary reductions may not produce the desired results in the long term. Seek advice from your accountant, your auditors, and your bank manager.

4. Improve Your Product/Service Mix

Your product/service mix reflects the combinations in which the products or services you provide are sold. The mix is normally derived from a series of historical accidents rather than from careful planning and analysis, and consequently it may not be as profitable as it could be.

"Money is the seed of money. The first guinea is sometimes more difficult to acquire than the second million." (Jean-Jacques Rousseau)

Examine each product you sell in terms of the costs attributable to it and the net margin it makes. You may find that the products producing the highest unit gross profit and making the highest percentage contribution to your sales volume also attract a disproportionate amount of your selling costs.

You may find, for example, that you should aim to sell more of A and B, which you have found to be profitable, to supply less of C and D, which are of limited profitability, and to eliminate loss-making E and F from your sales portfolio. Consider the impact this will have on the other four factors—for example, a well-founded change in your product/service mix may lead to a reduced volume of sales but increase your profitability.

 5. Examine Your Selling Prices and Profit Margins

Raising selling prices is a potential route to increased profitability (or at least to maintaining the current level of profitability when it might otherwise fall), but there are of course pitfalls. Although customers may accept price increases if they are part of a general price adjustment in your business sector (in which case you are likely merely to maintain your overall level of profitability), raising prices in isolation without losing business (and thereby risking reduced profits) requires either a near monopoly, a vast difference between your products and your competitors', or a carefully thought out and implemented policy and sales strategy.

 6. Look at the Capital Employed in Your Business

Obtaining a good return on capital and reducing the capital tied up in your business normally improve profitability.

Identify the categories of capital employed in your business and consider whether the following strategies can apply to any of them:

- exercising tighter control of credit
- reducing inventory levels
- introducing outsourcing, or expanding its scope
- disposing of redundant buildings, or locating to a new site where better terms may be available
- exploiting information and telecommunications technologies more fully

Make sure you take professional advice.

7. Remember Balance

A healthy business in a competitive environment is always changing, and this is particularly true of the five components of profitability and their interrelationships. Change, particularly in the factors affecting profitability, always requires compromise; you should aim to achieve the best possible balance among sales volume, costs, margins, product mix, and capital employed, keeping in mind that the ideal balance is often impossible, and that this year's optimum will probably need to be recalibrated next year.

DOS AND DON'TS

For Five Routes to Greater Profitability

DO

- Identify which of the five categories any proposed change falls into.
- Carefully consider the impact of any change on all categories.
- Consider longer-term impacts, not only on profitability, but also on the capacity of the business to survive.

DON'T

- Don't ignore the result of analysis when it threatens a pet ambition such as expansion into other lines or into another country.
- Don't ignore changes that may be imposed on your business externally, for example, by legislation or your lender.

THOUGHT STARTERS

- Have you sometimes ignored the interrelationships in the past? What happened?
- The first priority of any business must be survival. Do proposed changes threaten the survival of yours?
- Is a proposed change based on necessity, opportunity, or vanity?

For More Information

Books:

Atkinson, Hawley, John Hamburg, and Christopher Ittner. *Linking Quality to Profits: Quality-based Cost Management*. Milwaukee, WI: ASQ Quality Press, 1994.

Oliver, Lianabel. *The Cost Management Toolbox: The Manager's Guide to Controlling Costs and Boosting Profits*. New York: AMACOM, 1999.

Web Site:

Foundation for Performance Measurement: **www.fpm.com**

"Pennies don't fall from heaven. They have to be earned on earth." (Margaret Thatcher)

FRANCHISING YOUR BUSINESS

CHECKLIST

This checklist provides guidance to anyone wishing to expand a business by selling franchises.

Franchising is a technique for business expansion appropriate for small, one-location firms and nationally active companies alike. It is often regarded as one of the safest means of achieving growth; although it does have many advantages, franchising requires careful planning to be successful.

Examples of large companies that use franchising include McDonald's, 7-Eleven, and Mail Boxes Etc. A large number and variety of small businesses have also used franchising.

DEFINITION

For the purposes of this checklist the term franchising refers to a business concept franchise. This involves a franchiser, a company that lends its trademark or trade name and its business system to the franchisee, who pays a royalty and often an initial fee for the right to do business under the franchiser's name and system.

ADVANTAGES

Franchising:

- provides an affordable means of accelerating expansion;
- spreads the financial risk of expansion;
- means that products or goods can be bought in bulk to cover the whole franchise network, thus increasing competitiveness and profit margins.

DISADVANTAGES

Franchising does have some drawbacks, in that the franchiser:

- relinquishes some control and profit by involving an outsider;
- risks conflict with franchisees;
- sees low returns until the franchise network has been built up.

ACTION CHECKLIST

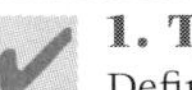

1. TAKE STOCK

Define what has made your business a success so far. Ask yourself:

- Is it a new or unique concept that has the potential to expand locally, nationally, or even internationally?
- Are the operating systems of the concept polished, efficient, and replicable?
- Would it be relatively easy to train others to use my systems and procedures?
- Are the profit margins built into the concept large enough to enable every franchisee to realize an attractive return on investment?
- Could franchises be affordable enough to attract a number of franchisees?

If you've answered "yes" to these questions, there's a good chance you can franchise your business.

2. OBTAIN LEGAL ADVICE

As what you are selling is really your trademark or trade name, make sure that it is legally yours and that anyone found copying it can be prosecuted. Your name or trademark must be registered with both USPTO and WIPO for you to assert legal ownership.

3. DRAW UP A BUSINESS PLAN

The business plan provides the means to:

- appraise the present and future of the business;
- define short- and long-term objectives;
- establish a framework for action to achieve those objectives.

Your bank should be able to help you with your business plan if you need assistance. Planning will help you identify how quickly you can expand, who your competitors are, and whether or not your system will be able to compete with them.

4. DEFINE THE FRANCHISE PACKAGE

Decide exactly what you will be offering franchisees, including:

- the concept (trademark and/or trade name)
- initial assistance (for example, finding premises)
- continuing training and advice
- bulk purchasing power
- sharing the cost of national advertising

You may also include other areas such as accounting advice and IT equipment.

The package should specify what each franchisee is required to pay. You may choose a royalty-only arrangement (leave plenty of room for franchisees to make a profit). Another option is to charge initial and annual fees (but if you set these too high you may discourage applicants).

5. DRAW UP A CONTRACT

Take professional legal advice to develop a watertight franchise contract. If a contracted franchisee does not perform to the required standard, you should need to make sure that you can regain control of the franchise.

6. PREPARE A PILOT

It is very important that you test out your franchise concept in one particular area. The pilot will tell you the best ways of recruiting and selecting franchisees and the kind of support they need to start operations. The lessons from the pilot will prove invaluable to the success of your franchising network.

7. ADVERTISE THE FRANCHISE

Advertise in the local newspapers of your pilot area and in national franchise journals such as *Franchise Times*. Highlight the attractions of running a franchise of your concept, including information about the market

"We cannot work for others without working for ourselves." (Jean-Jacques Rousseau)

need and your success so far. Develop a brochure to help sell the franchise. Obtain outside help if you do not have the resources in-house to produce a professional-looking document.

8. Select a Franchisee

Selecting the right franchisees is vital: no matter how catchy your trade name and sound your business concept, the franchisees will be the ones responsible for generating sales in their area. Increasing the number of franchises will be much easier if you can prove that the concept has been successful.

Carefully investigate the backgrounds of the applicants. Are they enthusiastic and hardworking, or are they likely to give up at the first sign of difficulty? Do they have a track record of successful management? Are they financially solvent? Honest? You'll never be 100 percent certain that an applicant has what it takes, but your business instinct should give you a good idea. Select the best applicant and sign a contract.

9. Start the Pilot

Provide as much support as you can to get the first franchise off the ground. Give advice when it is needed, but be prepared to let your partner exercise initiative without feeling crowded. Remember that once you have sold the franchise it is as much the franchisee's business as it is yours.

10. Monitor the Franchise

Learn from the results of the franchise pilot. You may have to revise elements of the franchise package such as royalties or training. Get the franchisee's opinion by asking about any startup problems with the franchise and finding out what other help would have been useful.

11. Advertise Again

You may wish to run further pilots or, if the initial one was successful, to expand as quickly as you can attract franchisees. Be realistic in anticipating the amount of help, advice, training, and resourcing your franchise network will require.

12. Review the Franchise Regularly

You should never allow your franchise to become static. Make changes to the concept and the package you offer as necessary. Review each franchisee annually and decide whether to renew the person's contract, look for another franchisee, or take control of the franchise yourself.

THOUGHT STARTERS

- What have been the secrets of your business success?
- What advice would have helped you when you first started your business?
- What were the most difficult periods in building up your business?

DOS AND DON'TS

For Franchising Your Business

DO

- Get legal advice about securing your trade name or trademark and drawing up a franchise contract.
- Pilot the franchise first.
- Select your franchisees and geographical markets with care.
- Remember how long it took for you to get a foothold in the market—be patient with franchisees.
- Make sure that you can take control of franchises if necessary at the end of the franchise agreement.

DON'T

- Don't abandon franchisees without advice and training.
- Don't be overly restrictive in the franchise contract—allow franchisees room to innovate.

For More Information

Books:

Bond, Robert. *Bond's Franchise Guide 2002*. Oakland, CA: Source Book Publications, 2002.
Bradach, Jeffrey L. *Franchise Organizations*. Boston, MA: Harvard Business School Press, 1998.
Dugan, Ann, ed. *Franchising 101: The Complete Guide to Evaluating, Buying and Growing Your Franchise Business*. Chicago, IL: Upstart Publishing, 1998.

Web Sites:

American Association of Franchisees and Dealers: **www.aafd.org**
This is a good resource and will save attorneys' fees: **www.franchise.org/resourcectr/mainmenu.asp**
Franchise Connections: **www.franchiseconnections.com**
Franchising Worldwide: **www.franchising.com**
Small Business Administration: **www.sba.gov**
Small Business Survival Center: **www.business-survival.com**

"Never let an opportunity pass by, but always think twice before acting." (Japanese proverb)

  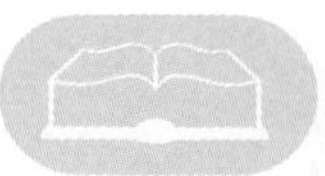    

Marketing for the Small Business

CHECKLIST

This checklist is designed to help you to identify which goods and services customers will buy and how you can best promote them to grow a successful business.

Mastering a few key aspects of marketing is essential if a small business is to survive and prosper. Too many small business owners believe that if they can't market like Coca-Cola or Nike they may as well not do any marketing at all. In fact there are many gradations in between that can benefit your small business.

Definition

Successful marketing ensures that you produce the right goods and services, at the right price, for the right people, at the right time, and in the right place.

Marketing is no more than identifying and profitably satisfying customers' needs. By studying the attitudes and needs of different kinds of customer, you can identify what existing or potential customers want and need; your business can then satisfy those needs at a profit in a cost-effective way.

Promotion (also called sales promotion) is the part of marketing in which you use advertising, publicity, and personal selling and offer incentives to publicize your products or services and persuade people to buy them. Marketing, promotion, and selling are not the same thing: selling is the final step in the marketing process.

For small businesses, marketing in its broadest sense may seem expensive and time-consuming. If you allow it to be expensive, it will be. Ineffective marketing will target the wrong people and convey incorrect messages about your company and its products or services.

Action Checklist

1. Subject Your Business to a SWOT Analysis

SWOT analysis requires you to identify the internal Strengths and Weaknesses of your business, its external Opportunities, and the Threats it faces in the business environment. Examples of SWOT factors that relate to marketing include the following.

Strengths

These could include:

- The unique selling proposition (USP) that diferentiates your products or services from the competition.
- Higher skill levels that give you an edge over your competitors.
- Your awareness of the market and potential opportunities.
- A well-developed business network that ensures that you and your products are well known.
- Effective cost control and highly competitive pricing.
- Well-trained staff.

Weaknesses

These could be:

- Inadequate working capital.
- Weak managerial skills.
- Poorly trained staff.
- Insufficient space for expansion to meet demand.
- Lack of new product development to meet customer demand.
- Ineffective marketing and promotion.
- Out-of-date plant and equipment.

Opportunities

For example:

- Changing consumer tastes that favor items that are, or could be, strongly represented in your product range.
- Recent legislation generating an increasing need for your goods or services.
- The arrival of a large company in your area that uses goods or services like those you supply.
- The closure of a competitor's business.

Threats

Such as:

- Price competition, usually in the form of lower prices or discounts offered by competitors.
- Higher prices for raw or finished materials or for services that you buy.
- Legislation imposing new obligations or restrictions.
- Poor performance by the national economy, raises in interest rates, or depressed consumer spending.

These threats are likely to have a more immediate effect on small firms than on larger companies with more resources and more opportunity to diversify. Consider whether you can turn any of your weaknesses into strengths or threats into opportunities.

2. Analyze Your Products, Services, and Market

- How much do you depend on suppliers and related businesses?
- Can your suppliers influence the way you do business?
- Are your services or products in a growth sector?
- Is consumer demand likely to increase, decrease, or remain stable?
- What is the nature of your competition—what do your competitors supply?
- How are your services or products similar to or different from those of your competitors?
- Can you generate more demand by promotion?

3. Look at Other Factors

You need to consider carefully:

- the geographic area you cover—the further you go from base the higher your shipping costs are likely to be and the less profit you make;
- the product mix you offer and how it affects your profitability—a high percentage of sales with low or negative margins can spell disaster;

"Small companies right down to the individual can beat big bureaucratic companies ten times out of ten."

(John Naisbitt)

  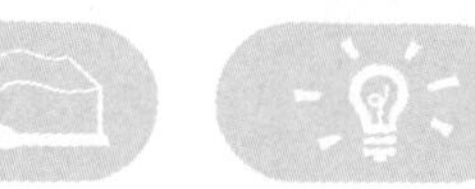    

- your target markets, whether individual or corporate—some customers want cheap goods and services; others regard cheapness as a sign of poor quality. You can't please everyone—decide whom you are aiming to satisfy;
- the products or services you offer—a decision that depends on your choice of customers. It is essential to keep your product line under regular review. All products have a natural life cycle, at the end of which sales and revenue tend to decline.

4. Identify Your Product

Think in terms of the specialist skills, knowledge, and capability that you have. Consider what you can do to improve existing products. Can you offer an obviously superior product at the same or a slightly higher price? Can you develop related products?

5. Set the Right Price for Your Products

You probably aren't after a reputation for the highest prices in the marketplace. By the same token, you may not want to be regarded as a price-cutter. You are looking to recover your costs and to make a satisfactory profit. Consider:

- your competitors' prices for similar products or services;
- the possibility of offering different prices to selected customers;
- individual costs—including overheads—for each of your products or services;
- whether to actively promote loss-making products or services;
- customers' perception of the value of your products or services. Will your customers pay a premium because your products best meet their needs?

6. Identify Your Prime Location

- How important is your location in marketing and promoting your products? Are visibility and accessibility important?
- Do your customers come to see you or do you go to them? Do you need to be physically near your customers? Do you need a storefront?
- How do your customers usually contact you—face to face, on the telephone, by fax, e-mail, Internet?
- Are public transportation or highway access important? Do you need close proximity to an airport?
- Could you work effectively from home?

7. Do Some Market Research

You need to know as much as possible about your competitors' activities. Sources of useful information include federal and state government statistics, trade directories, newspapers, the business and trade press, and personal contacts. If your business operates locally, try the Chamber of Commerce as well.

8. Conduct the Marketing and Monitor the Results

The result of your research will lead you to carry out a marketing campaign to a defined set of potential customers. This may involve advertising, publicity, press releases, setting up a Web site, or direct mail campaigns.

The design of promotional literature and the efficient use of marketing techniques can require professional guidance and advice. Marketing consultants may be beyond your budget, but check out the Web site for the U.S. Chamber of Commerce to find a local chapter in your area (www.uschamber.org).

Whatever you do (and however you do it), be prepared for customer reaction—and demand—and try to monitor where the strongest interest comes from to help you target more accurately the next time.

DOS AND DON'TS

For Marketing for the Small Business

DO

- Base your decisions on accurate information about your costs.
- Keep a careful eye on your product mix.

DON'T

- Don't fall into the trap of trying to compete on price alone.
- Don't make decisions except in the context of a planned strategy.
- Don't assume that because profit requires sales, sales equal profit.

THOUGHT STARTERS

- Why should anybody buy what you're offering?
- Are you sure you've correctly identified your competitors?
- What distinguishes you from the competition?
- What image do you think the public has of you and your business?

For More Information

Books:

Levinson, Jay Conrad. *Guerilla Marketing: Secrets for Making Big Profits from Your Small Business*. Boston, MA: Houghton Mifflin, 1998.

Putman, Anthony O. *Marketing Your Services: A Step-by-step Guide for Small Businesses and Professionals*. New York: John Wiley, 1990.

Web Sites:

American Marketing Association: **www.marketingpower.com**

Business Marketing Association: **www.marketing.org**

Small Business Administration: **www.sba.gov**

Small Business Survival Center: **www.businesssurvival.com**

"Is your company so small you have to do everything for yourself? Wait until you're so big that you can't. That's worse."

(Michael Bloomberg)

CONSIDERING WHETHER TO START A SMALL BUSINESS

CHECKLIST

This checklist is designed to help anyone who is considering setting up a small company.

DEFINITION

There are many ways to define a small business, most of which are more relevant to business statisticians than to would-be entrepreneurs. Anyone starting a business will of necessity be running a small business. By the time the size of the business meaningfully approaches any commonly used measures—number of employees, annual sales, total assets, and so on—the owner's problems will be those not of starting a business, but of sustaining its existence and growth.

However, according to the 1998 Annual Report of the U.S. Small Business Administration, "over 99.7 percent of the 5.5 million employer firms in the United States (all but about 16,000) had fewer than 500 employees. . . .In addition to employer firms, about 10 million individuals whose primary occupation is self-employment are by definition small businesses." These figures should offer would-be entrepreneurs some encouragement—you will not be alone.

ADVANTAGES

Benefits include:

- having control over what you do and how you do it;
- being your own boss;
- enjoying the satisfaction of succeeding by your own efforts;
- using your energy to promote your own interests.

DISADVANTAGES

- You're risking your own, or borrowed, capital.
- You have to work long hours with few, if any, vacations.
- Responsibility for success or failure rests with you and you alone.
- You give up the security of paid employment.

ACTION CHECKLIST

1. CONSIDER WHY YOU WANT TO BE SELF-EMPLOYED

Ask yourself whether:

- you really want to change your status, and why;
- your needs would be served by simply changing jobs;
- you have the support of your family or partner;
- you fully understand the risks you will be taking;
- you can work at and from home if necessary;
- your skills or experience could add value to products or services;
- you have the stamina to keep going in the face of difficulties;
- you have something to offer that people will pay for.

2. LIST YOUR ASSETS AND LIABILITIES

Every business requires capital. Whether you can finance your venture without borrowing depends on your existing assets. What is the value of your house, life insurance policies, savings and pension accounts, portfolio, material possessions, and other assets? What are your financial commitments over the next three to five years? What overhead do you need to cover and what liabilities need to be accounted for? Can any of your assets be turned into cash? How much cash can you put on the table? Would any family members or friends be willing to give or lend you money? Does your business idea lend itself to investment capital? Even at this preliminary stage, talk it over with your banker.

3. ASK YOURSELF WHAT YOU WANT

What are you really looking for? Freedom? Fortune? A chance to leave the corporate rat race behind? Opportunities to travel, to meet people, or to develop a pet idea? Less responsibility? More? Are your motives positive (to achieve something) or negative (to get away from something)? Set your requirements down on paper—be realistic.

4. IDENTIFY THE PRODUCTS OR SERVICES YOU INTEND TO DELIVER

- Assess your particular strengths and weaknesses, and determine the goals you want to achieve.
- Check out the startup costs for different kinds of business.
- Be cautious about becoming a consultant. Do you have the necessary expertise?
- Identify what goods and services local companies and other organizations buy from outside your area.
- Research the possibility of selling goods made by others.
- Consider how you could improve on someone else's ideas or enter into a partnership with an existing firm.
- Monitor your local newspapers—opportunities arise from the most unexpected and unusual situations.
- Check changes in legislation that might offer business opportunities you could take advantage of.
- Consider anonymously advertising your interest in investing in and sharing in the management of an existing business that is undercapitalized.

You could also check with your local Chamber of Commerce (www.uschamber.org) and the local office of the Small Business Administration (www.sba.gov). Also, see the Web site of the U.S. Department of Commerce (www.commerce.gov) and your state's Economic Development Office.

5. INVESTIGATE YOUR MARKET

- What is your product or service?
- Is it unique or are there many others like it?

"It's better to be the head of a chicken than the tail of a cow." (Stan Shih)

- Who will buy your product or service?
- Why should they buy yours and not someone else's?
- How many people will buy your product or service?
- Is the market stable, growing, or shrinking?
- How many competitors do you have?
- How price-sensitive are products and services like yours?

6. Consider the Legal Organization of Your Business

You may wish to become a sole proprietor operating alone and taking responsibility for every aspect of the business, including all taxes, debts, and day-to-day running of the business.

An alternative is to enter into a partnership. Partnerships combine the skills and experience of two or more people, who can share the workload and manage operations with some flexibility. Beware of proposing that friends join you in a partnership. Would they really make good business partners? Do you respect their judgment? What would they bring to the partnership?

Franchising is an easy and increasingly popular way of creating your own business by investing in a new branch of an established company. You get considerable support from the company and enjoy the advantages of a proven product or service, but the rewards are limited by the franchise agreement and you are committing yourself to operating according to someone else's policies and methods. Make thorough inquiries about any franchise before committing yourself to a contract.

Networking with business associates is an informal arrangement in which you retain control of your company, but you build relationships with others in the same kind of business to share some costs, for example, marketing or delivery. This arrangement has no legal foundation (unless you enter into specific contracts with associates), but depends on trust among associates. Networking can lead to a larger customer base and speed the growth of your business. You must be prepared, however, to give as well as take.

7. Test Your Ability to Manage

Running a business is enormously stressful. Measure yourself against the following criteria (preferably on a rising scale of 1–5):

- I am self-disciplined.
- I do not let things drift.
- I have the full support of my family.
- I can cope under pressure.
- I am ready to put in seven days a week if necessary.
- I get along well with people and I can motivate them.
- I can make quick decisions when necessary.
- I persist when the going gets tough.
- I can learn from mistakes and I can take advice.
- I am patient and I don't expect quick results.
- I am healthy, enthusiastic, and aware of the risks.
- I have specific goals, including the need to take care of myself and my family.

If you do not score well on these criteria (you need to score at least 3 on every item), take another look at your reasons for wanting to set up your own business.

8. Write a Business Plan

You've decided to go ahead. Numerous books, Web sites, and courses exist to help people write effective business plans. Your local Small Business Administration office or Small Business Development Center can offer personal help; if you live near a business school, students or faculty may be willing to help you. Your accountant, lawyer, and banker are also good sources of advice.

THOUGHT STARTERS

- What skills and experience do I have that will help me?
- What are my financial commitments, at least for the next three to five years?
- How realistic am I being?

For Considering Whether to Start a Small Business

DO

- Talk to others who have succeeded as entrepreneurs but have made mistakes and overcome setbacks along the way.
- Look at what startup help is available.
- Consult an accountant and lawyer before committing yourself irrevocably.
- Prepare a business plan.

DON'T

- Don't make any important decisions until you have talked them through with others.
- Don't try to set up a business just because it sounds like a nice idea.
- Don't overstretch yourself financially—borrowed money has to be repaid, usually with interest.

For More Information

Book:

Harper, Stephen C. *McGraw-Hill Guide to Starting Your Own Business: A Step-by-step Blueprint for the First Time Entrepreneur*. Reprint ed. New York: McGraw-Hill, 1992.

Web Sites:

Small Business Administration: **www.sba.gov**
Small Business Survival Center: **www.business-survival.com**

"Launching your own business is like writing your own personal declaration of independence from the corporate beehive."

(Paula Nelson)

CONDUCTING AN INFORMATION AUDIT

CHECKLIST

This checklist is concerned with the processes involved in an information audit.

The increasing problems caused by junk mail, information overload and indigestibility, and the need to make decisions ever more rapidly, mean that it is all too easy to take the wrong path in establishing systems for decision support. If accurate information is the key to effective decision making, an information audit will enable you to find out whether your information systems are up to the task.

The audit can take place on an organizational or individual level—approaches to both are presented here.

DEFINITION

An information audit requires an inventory of the way people and technology mix to make sure that the right information gets to the right people in the right form at the right time. It also requires measures to evaluate the costs and benefits of the operational system providing it.

Inventory checks include specialist, and perhaps untapped, human resource skills and processes and information flow charts as well as technological tools, databases, and knowledge stores.

ADVANTAGES

Your organization will discover:

- what information is being circulated but not used to advantage;
- what information is required but not available;
- the differences between what is needed and what is available;
- what needs to be done to match demand with provision;
- how information is best delivered to its potential users.

DISADVANTAGES

- It takes time, skills, expertise, impartiality, and honesty–in short, significant financial and specialist human resources–to gain a thorough, flexible, and updatable view of what is happening, where it is good and where bad, and what needs to be done now and continuously.
- Although it is a common practice, it is a mistake to assign value to information on the basis of cost alone. Information timeliness, relevance, and accuracy, its impact on efficiency and productivity, and its contribution to decision making are too often taken for granted or ignored altogether.

ACTION CHECKLIST

For Organizations or Departments

1. CONDUCT AN INITIAL INVESTIGATION

Establish the facts about your situation. Before you can find out where you are going it is essential to know your current position. Gain a picture of the importance information has in the organization and establish an understanding of the organization's objectives and targets, its management culture, and its organizational structure. This establishes a context and perspective for finding out what information resources the organization has and how it uses them, how information flows (or doesn't), and how it is valued.

2. SECURE SUFFICIENT RESOURCES TO DO THE JOB

Put together an audit team. You will need people with sufficient knowledge, experience, judgment, and standing in the organization to conduct the investigation. The team will need to establish a method of performing the investigation, securing access to the appropriate people and documentation, winning adequate time to carry out the requisite tasks, and securing support from the top.

3. ESTABLISH THE FRAMEWORK OF THE AUDIT

In order to guarantee consistency across the organization, set up a general framework of approach. Include the following considerations:

- What information do staff acquire, create, process, or transmit?
- Who and what are involved in these activities?
- What control procedures are in place?
- What is the nature of budget allocation and control?
- Which types of information are used a lot/partially/ not at all?
- Which types of information are required but not available?

4. ESTABLISH MEASURES AND VALUES IN ORDER TO ASSESS EFFECTIVENESS

Define ways of assessing the importance of the data to be gathered. For example, what significance or value can be attached to the fact that an office keeps files of information? What is done with them? To what use is the information put?

The cost of acquisition, processing, storage, and delivery is an undisputed primary consideration, but it will not necessarily indicate the effectiveness or even performance of the information resource, activity, or result that relates to it. Value or effectiveness may be assessed in more interpretive or qualitative terms such as accuracy, relevance and contribution to decision making, ease of use, and impact on efficiency, as well as return on investment in terms of the bottom line.

"At a certain speed, the speed of light, you lose even your shadow. At a certain speed, the speed of information, things lose their sense."

(Jean Baudrillard)

5. Get Down to the Detail of the Audit

An information audit should ascertain at least the following:

- What information do staff acquire? From which sources? At what cost? How is it used?
- What information do staff create? What happens to it? Where does it go?
- What information is stored and why? What purpose will it serve?
- What information is passed on or delivered? To whom? For what purpose? In what form?
- Is there a gap or a match between the information that is available and the information needed?
- What are the skills and responsibilities of the people who carry out these tasks?
- What equipment and tools do they have available?
- Are there any control documents such as policy statements or guidelines?
- Is any of the information superfluous to needs?
- Are any of the information-handling activities nonproductive?
- What budget is available? How was the budget figure reached? How adequate is it? Who controls it? What control measures exist for it?

6. Use the Data Gathered to Map Information Flows

Map out a flow chart to show the areas, processes, functions, and activities through which information passes, clarifying gaps or fault lines that need to be plugged or bottlenecks and overflows that need to be unblocked.

7. Evaluate the Effectiveness of Information Resources and Activities

When the data sets are assembled ask:

- To what extent does this activity or resource support objectives or help to meet targets?
- How efficient is it in terms of the time and cost required to do it?
- Are any positive or negative results directly or indirectly related to it?
- Does it need to be adapted to fit changing needs?
- Is there a good or a bad fit between the resources and the results they produce?
- Are there information gaps between different functions?
- Are there areas where information goes into a black hole?
- Are there gaping holes where results are not forthcoming because no one has identified responsibility for the information process?

8. Report the Findings

Focus on the gravest areas of mismatch—black holes where no useful outcome is visible—and the people, skills, and resources required to correct them. Conclude with recommendations for the next series of actions.

An Individual Audit

- Are your information needs structured or are they ad hoc, considered only when needs arise?
- Is anyone else aware of your needs or are they a secret?
- Do you review your information sources?
- Do you make do with what you already have?
- Do you add value to the information you process?
- Do you have a say in the hardware or software you use?
- Do you file most of the information you receive? For immediate or eventual reuse?
- When you send information on, do you know what will happen to it?
- Do you get information in the right form for your use?
- Is it reliable and accurate?
- Is it worth keeping for future use?
- Is it worth passing to someone else?
- Could you get hold of it again easily if the need arose?
- Would you know where to go for it?
- If it hadn't arrived, would you (or should you) have gone looking for it?

DOS AND DON'TS

For Conducting an Information Audit

DO

- Consider the needs of staff as a key indicator.
- Devise a method of relating resources and activities to objectives and targets.
- Evaluate levels of cooperation.
- Take the culture and structure of the organization into account.
- Think ahead—change is coming ever faster.

DON'T

- Don't be influenced by time-honored, fixed ideas, even when they seem persuasive.
- Don't make promises during the data-gathering stage.

THOUGHT STARTERS

- Do you add value to information or just file it, toss it, or pass it on?
- Can you identify specific information that you need but don't get?
- Can you identify specific information that you receive but don't want?

For More Information

Book:

Bentley, Trevor J. *Managing Information—Avoiding Overload.* Milford, CT: Kogan Page, 1998.

"An individual without information cannot take responsibility; an individual who is given information cannot help but take responsibility."

(Bill Gore)

BRAINSTORMING

The purpose of this checklist is to enable a busy manager, without previous experience of the technique and with a minimum of preparation, to introduce brainstorming to a group and then go on to brainstorm a specific problem or opportunity.

DEFINITION

Brainstorming involves a spontaneous, open-ended discussion in a search for new ideas. It is a means of getting a large number of ideas from a group of people in a short time. It can prove valuable for identifying opportunities, for example, for market development, tackling organizational problems, or problem solving in general.

ADVANTAGES

- Brainstorming rapidly generates a large number of fresh ideas and concepts.
- It actively engages people and allows them to feel they are making a positive contribution.

DISADVANTAGES

- Overbearing individuals can dominate or sidetrack the session.
- Getting people to be noncritical can be a problem.

ACTION CHECKLIST

PREPARATION

1. SELECT THE PROBLEM/OPPORTUNITY TO BE BRAINSTORMED

Select an issue important enough to justify the participation of others. It should lend itself to an imaginative approach and offer a number of possible solutions.

2. CONSIDER STRUCTURE, AIMS, AND OBJECTIVES

Although a brainstorming session is an open, no-holds-barred discussion, establish where you are going, what you want to achieve, and roughly how to get there.

3. CHOOSE THE FACILITATOR

Choosing the right facilitator is vital. Ideally, it should be an open, outgoing person with enthusiasm and the ability to communicate interest and enjoyment. The facilitator need not be the most senior person at the session, but will need to set the scene by relaxing the participants and creating an open, free atmosphere, controlling dominant people, getting and keeping the meeting on track by highlighting the issues, and creating a sense of fun. Perhaps most importantly, the person should be adept at keeping ideas flowing.

The facilitator should feel comfortable running activity-based sessions and should have clear plans and tactics for arriving at expected outcomes or targets. The facilitator must also ensure, as much as possible, that the group works as a team and owns what it has achieved at the end.

4. SELECT AN APPROPRIATE SITE

This depends largely on the time set aside for the session. If time is available, somewhere away from the usual place of work is often more appropriate. This often allows a fresh perspective on the business in hand.

5. INVITE A MIXED GROUP

Include people who have little or no knowledge of the problem to be brainstormed as well as those with a specialist contribution to make. Nonspecialists will not be concerned with detail and will offer a fresh approach.

6. DECIDE ON THE SIZE OF THE GROUP

There is no right number, although more than ten might be unmanageable when ideas really start to flow, and less than five might not be enough for generating creativity. Six to eight is usually about right, although this depends on the style of the facilitator and the nature of the problem to be tackled.

7. ORDER THE RIGHT EQUIPMENT

You will need to record the ideas that come up. A tape recorder smacks of Big Brother and may well inhibit the free flow of ideas. Use a flip chart—successive sheets can be fastened to the wall to help stimulate further ideas.

8. DESIGN A RELAXED SEATING PLAN

Do not use a room with fixed rows of seats. Something more relaxed is preferable; a circle or U-shape is fairly usual. A facilitator who is not familiar with the room should check it beforehand and prepare it.

9. SKETCH OUT A TIMETABLE

Think of your own powers of concentration and remember that brainstorming of ideas can go from dynamic to exhausted and back again. Between 10 and 20 minutes may be needed to get people relaxed. Two hours can be a long time to brainstorm—stop for a break if people show signs of tiredness. Arrange for a 20-minute break after an hour's uninterrupted flow or if and when the flow of ideas slows to a trickle.

10. SELECT A PRODUCTIVE TIME OF DAY

Unfortunately, advice is difficult here, as we are all different. Some people are better when their minds are less active and more relaxed and when their routine work has been dispensed with. Others may prefer the morning, when collective mental energy is at its highest, or at least is not dulled by the day's toil.

Provide sufficient notice of the session and an outline of the problem to be tackled.

"Our challenge is to stand out from the crowd when the crowd has much more money than you. Ideas are relatively cheap to have."

(Dave Hieatt)

THE SESSION

1. STATE THE PROBLEM/OBJECTIVE

State the problem and explain it to the group. Make sure everyone participating has a clear understanding of the purpose of the session.

2. RESTATE THE PROBLEM

Encourage the group to stand back from the problem, walk around it, and see it from every angle. Suggest rewording it in "How to. . ." statements. Some restatements may be close to the original; others may illuminate new facets.

3. BRAINSTORM THE PROBLEM

Keep to the following guidelines:

- Suspend judgment. Laugh with wild ideas, not at them.
- Use the following techniques for generating further ideas:
  - Call for a one-minute break, asking the group to look over ideas already noted before starting the flow again.
  - Offer a target, for example, "We only need six more to make fifty ideas!"
  - Look back at your restatements to pursue other lines.
- Freewheel: try to bring the subconscious into play—the wilder the idea, the better.
- Go for quantity, not quality. Suspend judgment; evaluation comes later.
- Cross-fertilize: pick up somebody's idea and suggest others leading from it.

4. TAKE OFF FROM A WILD IDEA

Ask the group to choose a really wild and apparently senseless idea from the lists you have generated. Using it as a starting point, see how many more ideas you can come up with.

5. CLOSE THE SESSION

About five minutes before the scheduled close, give a warning that the session will soon end. The participants will want to know what happens next. Explain that the lists will be typed up for circulation. Do this within 24 hours to retain freshness and familiarity.

EVALUATION

1. RANK YOUR IDEAS AND PICK OUT THE INSTANT WINNERS

When you circulate lists of the ideas generated at the brainstorming session, ask the team to rank them: 3 points for ideas that stand out; 2 points for those that have possibilities but need a little adjustment; 0 for those that are obvious nonstarters, clearly require too many resources, or do not meet the original objectives.

2. SIFT AND SHORT-LIST THE FEASIBLE IDEAS

Reduce the number of 2s to a minimum by applying such criteria as cost, practicability, acceptability, or timescale.

3. USE REVERSE BRAINSTORMING

- In how many ways can an idea fail?
- What are the negative factors?
- What is the potential downside for the organization?

4. APPLY THE KEY EVALUATIVE CRITERIA

- What will it cost?
- Will it be acceptable to management, staff, customers?
- Is it legal?
- Is it practicable?
- How long will it take?
- What competition will there be?
- How urgent is it? If it is not done now, will an opportunity be lost?

THOUGHT STARTERS

Does your organization need to:

- become more innovative?
- solve problems requiring creative or imaginative answers?
- get more involvement and participation from staff?
- generate ideas rapidly?

DOS AND DON'TS

For Brainstorming

DO

In the brainstorming session, the facilitator should:

- encourage an informal atmosphere;
- use a variety of techniques to generate further ideas;
- be sensitive to participants' fluctuating energy levels.

DON'T

The facilitator should not:

- use a tape recorder;
- allow critical or evaluative comments;
- allow interruptions;
- let the session go on too long;
- allow the session to become too "off-the-wall!"

For More Information

Book:

Clark, Charles. *Brainstorming: How to Create Successful Ideas.* Hollywood, CA: Wilshire Book Co., 1989.

Journal Article:

Buzan, Tony. "Constructive Brainstorming Can Jump the Gaps." *Business Marketing Digest* 18:1 (1993): 35–41.

See also:

✓ **Performing a SWOT Analysis (pp. 468–69)**
✓ **Planning a Workshop (pp. 426–27)**
✓ **Total Quality: Getting TQM to Work (pp. 522–23)**

"Intense concentration for hour after hour can bring out resources in people that they didn't know they had."

(Edwin Land)

  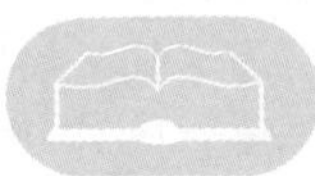    

COLLECTING DEBTS

This checklist deals with debt collection. All companies that extend credit to customers will be faced from time to time with situations in which payment is overdue. It is a matter for individual firms to decide at what point extended credit becomes a matter for debt collection and how urgently this is to be pursued. This checklist outlines sound principles for action from that point onward.

DEFINITION

Debt collection is the generic name for the processes and procedures adopted by organizations that have extended credit to customers for goods and services and find that payment is either not forthcoming or is overdue.

ACTION CHECKLIST

1. REMEMBER THAT PREVENTION IS BETTER THAN CURE

Think about the possible steps you might take to minimize the likelihood of bad debts. Decide who will operate your policy. Some common options include:

- a factoring agency
- a lawyer or agency—a letter on formal stationery sometimes gets a response
- your own staff—either dedicated to debt collection, or part of the accounts receivable or credit team

Be aware of the Uniform Commercial Code, which makes provision for claiming interest on outstanding debts. The legislation aims to deter late payment and penalize late payers.

2. IDENTIFY ORGANIZATIONAL NEEDS

The company needs:

- systems that identify arrears and potential bad debts at an early stage;
- good communication and understanding between departments;
- staff with procedural knowledge and good interpersonal skills;
- regular review of policies, procedures, and criteria for granting and extending credit;
- consistently applied policies, regularly reviewed, to ensure that debt collection procedures are initiated immediately when appropriate;
- regular training or refreshers in procedures and interpersonal skills.

3. CONCENTRATE ON BIG DEBTS

Remember that 20 percent of your receivables probably account for 80 percent of the debt outstanding at any one time. An even smaller percentage is involved in bad, or potentially bad, debts. Pursue the big debts first; while it may be easier to collect smaller past-due accounts, this is not necessarily the best approach. Evaluate the effectiveness of debt collection by the amount of money recovered, not the number of debts collected. Bear in mind, however, that:

- several smaller debts can add up to one large one;
- for a large debt a phone call before it falls due may be appropriate;
- for a small debt the process may start with a letter one month after payment is due;
- debts are seldom as simple as a single invoice or a month's transactions—they usually involve many transactions with invoices and credit notes over several months.

4. WRITE POSITIVE LETTERS

In the first instance an approach by letter is cheaper than approaching your debtors with a phone call. Be sure that your letters are addressed to a named executive and are courteous, clear, and specific.

Be concise and firm. Do not apologize, suggest a compromise, or refer to the possibility of partial payment. Stay focused on getting payment now; don't get sidetracked by asking why the debt hasn't been paid. An excuse is no substitute for your money. Don't make threats unless you are prepared to carry them out.

For maximum impact your letters should appear to have been written individually. Refer to previous correspondence, if appropriate, quoting dates. Avoid using "first," as in "first demand": it implies there are more to follow, which the debtor may seize upon as a further reason to delay payment. Avoid using "final" unless you mean it. Be polite, brief, and firm. Give the debtor a better reason for paying than for not paying, for example, by:

- pointing out the advantages of continuing to trade together;
- pointing out the advantages of enjoying credit terms, and of ensuring their continued availability;
- expressing the hope that you can avoid taking legal action.

Once a letter has been sent, reapply your credit control procedure before extending the customer further credit. Consider putting all business on a deposit in advance or cash on delivery (COD) basis until you receive payment and can satisfy your conditions for granting credit.

Many companies use a series of three or four letters escalating in tone and authority. These provide evidence in any subsequent legal proceedings, and should be sent regardless of any other courses of action you take.

5. FOLLOW UP LETTERS WITH PHONE CALLS

The telephone is an essential tool in debt collection, but you should not underestimate the cost and time involved in collection calls. Before calling the debtor, prepare yourself by gathering relevant files and copies of invoices. You should have:

- the debtor's correct name and legal status
- the name of the person you need to talk to
- the amount, date, and full details of the debt
- the agreed terms and conditions of the sale or supply

"Creditors have better memories than debtors." (Benjamin Franklin)

- details of previous communications, if any
- the date of the last payment received, if any
- ready responses to excuses, a request for more time to pay, or a suggestion of partial payment

Once you have the right person, identify yourself and personalize the discussion. You need persuasive skills to gain commitment, convert interest into action, and discover the reasons for the delay—they may be relevant to the customer's future credit relationship with you. If you can, find out whether a question, dispute, financial problem, or oversight is responsible for the delay in payment. If you are told that the check is in the mail, press for details. When and where was the check sent, and what were its number, date, and amount? If it wasn't for the full amount, ask why.

If the debtor fails to honor a commitment made on the telephone, consider what further actions to take. If after several attempts you cannot gain access to the person you wish to speak to, escalate the debt recovery chain.

6. Consider the Benefits of Fax and E-mail

Faxes and e-mails have a sense of immediacy, and both tend to be dealt with more quickly than letters. Remember that the contents may be public within the debtor's department or company—those concerned may be embarrassed into paying. Another advantage of faxes and e-mails is that they can be sent straight to the recipient and may therefore gain immediate attention.

7. If All Else Fails, Consider Visiting the Debtor

Visiting is the least cost-effective method of collection. Further, it is hard for those who wish to avoid confrontation, and you may feel you have lost face if you leave without a check. If you decide to visit the debtor, arrive unexpectedly and be firm, courteous, and unwavering. If you do not get a check, move quickly to the next stage.

8. Appoint a Debt Collection Agency

Use only agencies that have a good reputation. If in doubt, check with the Securities and Exchange Commission (SEC), which regulates the markets, or the Federal Trade Commission, which concerns itself with matters of debt and fair trade. Don't pay the agency up front or agree to a flat fee. Agree only to pay a percentage of what the agency recovers. Obtain a banker's reference and talk to other clients of the agency. Be sure you know and accept the agency's terms and conditions.

9. Think Carefully Before You Call in Your Lawyer or Start Legal Proceedings

Lawyers are expensive and require payment whether or not they achieve results—get a price before you make a commitment. Litigation is even more expensive. Be sure before you start legal proceedings that the debtor actually has sufficient money to pay, that you have reasonable evidence of the existence of the debt, and that the debt is less than six years old. Be sure that you have the full name and address and legal status of the debtor.

10. Don't Automatically Return a Postdated Check

A postdated check is better than no check. The check may be paid if presented, and if the bank does not honor it, the check at least provides proof of the debt. On the other hand, you are unlikely to want to do business routinely on this basis.

11. Be Aware of Consumer Protection Legislation

Be aware of the dangers of being charged with harassment. The Federal Trade Commission is there to protect consumers, and each State and many cities have a consumer protection office, which your debtor might call upon if you are too heavy handed.

THOUGHT STARTERS

- What percentage of your sales is represented by overdue receivables or bad debts?
- Do you know which customers have a history of late payment?
- Do your customers know when payment is due and what your procedures are in the case of overdue payments?
- Are your staff aware of customer credit limits?

DOS AND DON'TS

For Collecting Debts

DO

- Know your customers.
- Keep in mind all the effort that went into making the sale you haven't been paid for.
- Consider the consequences of not being paid.
- Remember that it's your money you're chasing, not theirs.

DON'T

- Don't start your collection process by offering a compromise.

For More Information

Books:

Posner, Martin. *Successful Credit Control*. 2nd ed. New York: John Wiley, 1998.

Sher, David, and Martin Sher. *How to Collect Debts (and Still Keep Your Customers)*. New York: AMACOM, 1999.

Web Site:

National Association of Credit Management: **www.nacm.org**

See also:

✔ **Controlling Credit (pp. 550–51)**

"A debt may get moldy, but it never decays." (Chinua Achebe)

CONTROLLING A BUDGET

CHECKLIST

This checklist is for all managers who have budgetary responsibility. Budgetary control is at the heart of many managers' jobs. Skilled budgetary control is increasingly valued in organizations. Further, the ability to control a budget is now seen as an important factor in measuring performance, and even as a passport to promotion.

Managers need to use a mix of approaches in controlling budgets—gathering and using information, setting up early warning systems, making decisions, and monitoring results—all key management skills.

DEFINITION

Budgetary control is achieved by comparing actual costs, revenues, and performance against a set budget. Such comparison is necessary in order for managers to take corrective action and change operational plans as required to keep them on budget.

ADVANTAGES

- It is the only way to monitor your organization's/team's financial performance.
- It allows you to understand your department's financial position.
- It gives you information to use as a basis for action.

DISADVANTAGES

If you fail to control your budget, you will:

- frequently overspend or underspend, not achieving what you planned;
- lack up-to-date information that might explain why the actual results are at variance with the budget;
- demonstrate that your team/department/work is out of control—a bad advertisement for your company and for yourself.

ACTION CHECKLIST

1. UNDERSTAND THE FIGURES

Make sure you understand how the figures in the budget are made up. You need to know which figures you control and will be held responsible for and which are outside your control. For instance, if staff costs are higher because you approved too much overtime, you may be held responsible for the overrun; but if the costs are higher because the union negotiated a higher than expected pay raise, you may neither be held responsible for the overrun nor exercise control over it. Only when you know which elements of the budget you are responsible for can you control it.

2. TALK TO YOUR ACCOUNTING DEPARTMENT

Find out what reports they can produce for you. This will save you extra work, provide accurate figures to work from, and help you keep in touch with the accountants—important, as they are key stakeholders.

3. SET UP A MONITORING/EARLY WARNING SYSTEM

This will help you keep track of your costs and income. A paper system (keeping a tally of costs incurred and checking them at the end of the month) works for small budgets, but budgets small and large benefit from the use of all available systems and information.

4. DECIDE ON APPROPRIATE INTERVALS TO MONITOR YOUR BUDGET

Choose intervals to monitor your budget that fit in with the other commitments of your organization and your team—most likely weekly, monthly, or quarterly. It is important to get the timescale right: overmonitor and you waste time, undermonitor and you won't stay in control of things. Stick to whichever review period you decide on, even when things are going well or you are swamped by other work.

5. IDENTIFY VARIANCES

Use the information you've gathered to identify positive and negative variances from your original budget. A negative variance means you have spent more than you planned; you need to look hard at the effect this will have on the year's performance and review your plans. A positive variance means you have underspent.

6. DON'T ASSUME A POSITIVE VARIANCE IS A GOOD THING

Analyze any variance—find out why it happened and what effect it will have on the year's activity. Was it a onetime payment that was not invoiced, a blip rather than a trend? Was it an unexpected drop in interest rates? If so, will it continue? Are you not carrying out the marketing activities you planned? Have you failed to recruit a key member of staff?

7. TELL THE RIGHT PEOPLE

If you find you have a problem, get information about it to the right people, for example, your boss, company accountant, or team members. People often don't know there's a problem until you tell them. And until everyone who needs to know does know, you can't act. Remember that communication is a two-way process, and your team members may be able to give you early warnings of problems. Discuss the variances with your team. They may have up-to-the-minute information on why things went wrong.

8. NOW ACT

You have a range of options, depending on the circumstances.

- Do nothing if you anticipate the budget will come back into line, but make sure you can justify this assump-

"Human beings were held accountable long before there were corporate bureaucracies. If the knight didn't deliver, the king cut off his head." (Alvin Toffler)

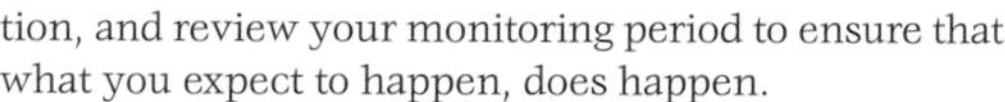

tion, and review your monitoring period to ensure that what you expect to happen, does happen.

- Prepare a forecast (or revise your forecast) projecting where you expect to be compared with your budget.
- Suggest corrective action to bring the figures back into line with the original budget (for example, cut back on costs, try to increase sales, or put in a bid for underspends elsewhere).

Once you have decided what to do, make sure that the appropriate people know what your plans are, understand them, and have time to comment if necessary. Then be seen to act.

✔ 9. Keep Monitoring

Monitoring is an ongoing process. Don't assume that because you've straightened out one problem there will never be another. Continuing to monitor the budget will help you make sure your performance is back on track, or at least that it hasn't gotten further out of control.

DOS AND DON'TS

For Controlling a Budget

DO

- Communicate–upward, downward, and across.
- Take action when you need to.
- Keep the appropriate people informed.
- Keep monitoring.

DON'T

- Don't act rashly without thinking through the implications.
- Don't go it alone—always involve others.
- Don't hide the problem or ignore it. It won't go away.

✔ 10. Communicate Any Changes

If you have amended your forecast, tell all the budget stakeholders, especially those who have to implement the change.

THOUGHT STARTERS

- Have you set up practical monitoring systems?
- Do your monitoring systems provide you with information you can act on to regain control?
- Have you gathered all the information you can about why things have gone wrong?
- Have you communicated thoroughly?
- Have you planned your action carefully?

For More Information

Books:

Droms, William G. *Finance and Accounting for Nonfinancial Managers*. 4th ed. Cambridge, MA: Perseus, 1998.

Welsch, Glenn A., Ronald W. Hilton, and Paul N. Gordon. *Budgeting: Profit Planning and Control*. 5th ed. Upper Saddle River, NJ: Prentice Hall, 1988.

Journal Article:

Finney, Robert G. "Budgeting from Pain to Power." *Management Review* 82:9 (September 1993): 27–31.

See also:

✔ Drawing Up a Budget (pp. 554–55)

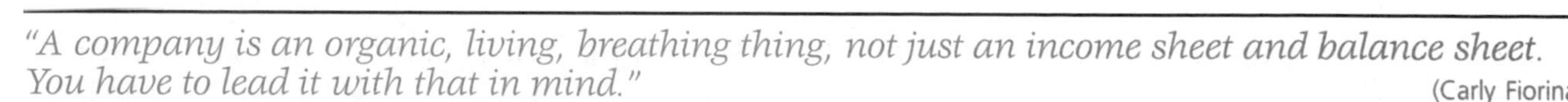
"A company is an organic, living, breathing thing, not just an income sheet and balance sheet. You have to lead it with that in mind."

(Carly Fiorina)

CONTROLLING COSTS

CHECKLIST

This checklist is for owners of small businesses or managers who wish to address cost control.

In a competitive business environment, getting the most from existing resources while keeping costs down is a key factor in business success or failure. Controlling costs is not the same thing as cutting costs. Naturally there are occasions when a period of belt-tightening is required, but frequent cost-cutting can adversely affect a company—quality may suffer, the reputation of the business be hurt, and customers, suppliers, and staff become unhappy. Controlling costs is, rather, an ongoing process of monitoring, analyzing, and accurately allocating costs and of promoting a culture of cost awareness.

DEFINITION

A cost is the value of something that must be given up to acquire or achieve something else.

Costs are the prices paid for the purchasing, processing, and delivery activities involved in turning raw materials into finished goods.

ADVANTAGES

- Cost control can supply essential management information.
- Effective cost control highlights inefficient practices.
- Cost data can provide a basis for formulating a pricing structure.

ACTION CHECKLIST

1. COLLECT DATA ON YOUR COSTS

Before you can implement cost control, you need to collect data on what your costs actually are. Costs are often broadly categorized as labor costs, materials costs, and general overheads. In general, labor costs in the service sector are the largest cost category; in manufacturing however, a typical cost breakdown might be 15 percent labor, 50 percent materials, and 30 percent general overheads.

2. COMMUNICATE COST AWARENESS

All employees should know the basic financial strategy of the company and understand the financial implications of their decisions: they should have enough information to be aware of the full costs of their activities and know what alternatives exist. Even if telephone and stationery billing are centralized, for example, true costing of all products and services should take account of this overhead on a departmental or activity basis. Open Book Management is one of the methods by which costs (and profits) are shared with employees. One of the major points is that employees must be educated to understand what the numbers represent.

Where the activities of cost centers are left unattributed, you should consider their levels of service use in allocating costs.

3. INVESTIGATE METHODS OF COST ALLOCATION

The budget is the most powerful instrument of cost control you have. Drawing up and controlling a budget are covered in related checklists. Controlling the budget is a self-evident factor in cost control, but additional approaches and techniques can also be used.

One method of discovering true costs is to restart the budgeting process from scratch and attempt to estimate—as if there were a blank sheet of paper—the current full cost of an activity. This is called zero-based budgeting. It works on the assumption that annual budget allocations should be justified from the ground up. Knowing the real cost of an activity may prompt the question, "Is this activity necessary in the first place?" Remember fixed costs. If you take one activity out, its share of fixed costs must be reallocated to the remaining activities.

Activity-based costing (ABC) involves looking closely at the key factors influencing a company's overheads and identifying the key cost factors. ABC requires that all costs associated with a product—from research and new product development to marketing and delivery—should either be identified as product costs or split up and traced to individual products or services.

Costs can be difficult to isolate, because they are often made up of multiple tasks and activities that from an organizational point of view may appear to be unrelated. Suppose, for example, you receive a service from another section or department. You know what its value is to you, but you are unaware of the cost attached to its supply. One method of tackling this is overhead value analysis, or the similar activities value chain analysis and process value analysis, which attempt to trace and quantify the workflows—increasingly these are information workflows—by which services are supplied to other parts of the organization.

4. IDENTIFY YOUR COST ELEMENTS

Costs are either fixed (for example, your office rent, which remains the same no matter what your volume of business) or variable (for example, raw materials, the cost of which fluctuates proportionately to your level of production). Some costs have elements of both and are classified as semi-variable.

Major cost elements include:

- space, rental, local business tax
- energy costs (heating and lighting, waste disposal, pollution cleanup)—is an environmental policy in force?
- salaries and wages (including the cost of recruitment, absenteeism, sick pay, pensions, and insurance)
- raw materials and services bought in
- travel and transportation—have you considered new telecommunications technologies?
- general costs of communication (postage, telephone, fax, Internet, stationery, supplies)

"Companies worry too much about the cost of doing something. They should worry about the cost of not doing it."
(Philip Kotler)

- security and insurance–without turning a disaster into a crisis, can you be without them? Is it worth investigating alternative services' rates? Do you have a disaster recovery plan?
- financial costs (interest, dividends, credit, bad debts)

5. Analyze Variable Costs

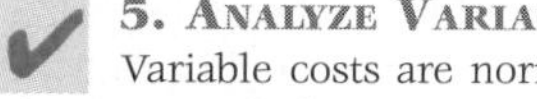

Variable costs are normally tied to sales volume. They may include:

- salaries and wages
- advertising
- selling expenses
- mailing expenses
- stationery supplies
- subscriptions
- heat, light, power, and water

What is the continuing relationship between your sales volume and costs? Is the trend healthy or unhealthy, positive or negative?

6. Monitor Your Costs and Expenses Regularly

Effective cost control can help you increase your profits on the same or even a reduced volume of sales. Keep a close watch on the pattern of your sales volume as well as your costs, and know the reasons for abnormal increases or decreases.

Regularly calculate the cost of goods sold as a percentage of net sales. Look for increases or decreases in the price of purchased items, transportation costs, wastage, and losses due to theft.

DOS AND DON'TS

For Controlling Costs

DO

- Reexamine your costs and expenses regularly.
- Remember that staff may have useful views on controllable costs.
- Understand that cost control may have an impact on staff morale—which may be good or bad.
- Recognize that it is easier to exercise control than it is to correct mistakes after the fact.
- Keep financial reporting systems up to date and publish financial targets regularly.
- Circulate key statistics to managers and keep all staff informed.

DON'T

- Don't equate cost control with cost-cutting.
- Don't use increased sales to justify an unwarranted rise in costs.
- Don't neglect quality in the pursuit of controlling costs.

7. Understand the Relationship between Cost Control and Profitability

Remember that costs are only one element of profitability. Others include:

- sales volume/value
- margins
- methods of financing
- product mix

A change in any one element affects all the others, for better or worse. If cost control leads to a dramatic change in costs, then be mindful of the likely impact on sales volume, margins, methods of financing, and product mix. There may well come a point where costs are reduced to such an extent, it has a negative effect on sales. You can't always have your cake and eat it.

8. Remember Quality

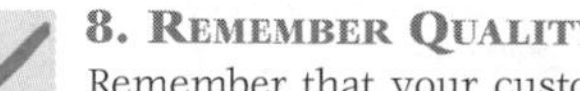

Remember that your customers' loyalty is to the best quality at the lowest price.

Initiatives such as total quality management, ISO 9000, and continuous improvement programs to improve quality in organizations have been proved to reduce costs by eliminating waste and duplication, largely by empowering the work force and pushing decisions down to where the work is actually done.

THOUGHT STARTERS

- Do you know the full costs of workflow processes in your organization?
- What discounts do you receive? Why?
- Does your budgeting process account for interrelated hidden costs?
- Do you involve staff in problem solving?

For More Information

Books:

Innes, John, and Falconer Mitchell. *Overhead Cost*. San Diego, CA: Academic Press, 1993.

Oliver, Lianabel. *The Cost Management Toolbox: The Manager's Guide to Controlling Costs and Boosting Profits*. New York: AMACOM, 1999.

Ruffa, Stephen A., and Michael J. Perozziello. *Breaking the Cost Barrier: A Proven Approach to Managing and Implementing Lean Manufacturing*. New York: John Wiley, 2000.

 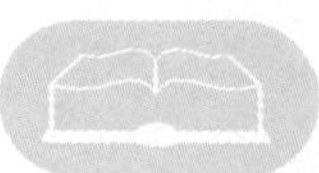    

CONTROLLING CREDIT

CHECKLIST

This checklist deals with controlling the credit a company allows to its customers and clients to pay for the goods and services they purchase. Credit control is essential to controlling cash flow. Many companies go out of business because of management's failure to distinguish between profitability and cash flow. An otherwise profitable enterprise can fold if it runs out of working capital to meet its commitments; this is frequently caused by poor credit control, since in effect the company's cash is tied up in financing customers' or clients' business. Even if working capital is adequate, overgenerous credit policies that allow customers too much credit or too long to pay can adversely affect profits.

DEFINITION

Allowing customers and clients to defer payment for goods and services is a common and often necessary practice. Credit control is the totality of the policies, procedures, and practices that guarantee that the total amount of credit extended and the period for which it is extended are consistent with corporate policy. Managers responsible for credit control make sure that the company grants credit systematically, recovers the costs of extending credit, and consistently meets its needs for liquid funds, and that customers pay in accordance with the terms they agreed. Remember: it's not sold until it's paid for!

ADVANTAGES

Credit control:

- prevents bad debts;
- plays a major role in controlling cash flow;
- contributes to improved return on capital and higher net profit;
- can make the difference between a company's ability or inability to grow;
- is a key factor in a company's ability to weather difficult periods.

DISADVANTAGES

Credit control:

- consumes a substantial amount of staff time;
- can sour relations with customers who have enjoyed uncontrolled credit in the past;
- can leave a company operating below maximum capacity;
- can result, in extreme cases, in a company not recovering its fixed costs.

None of these disadvantages, however, is a good reason not to control credit.

ACTION CHECKLIST

1. ASSIGN RESPONSIBILITY FOR CREDIT CONTROL

Appoint a suitably senior person in the firm to be responsible for negotiating, granting, and supervising credit and for seeing that receivables are collected promptly. Appoint a more senior person who can supervise the credit controller and assume responsibility if the credit position becomes questionable. The exercise of this authority should not undermine customers' relationships with individual members of staff, especially sales staff. Sales people are still responsible for ensuring that sales are made and goods and services paid for in accordance with the firm's terms and conditions.

2. INTRODUCE A CREDIT POLICY

Introduce a clear-cut maximum credit policy covering the amount and duration of credit. Write it down so that it cannot be changed arbitrarily, and make sure that all staff members involved in granting credit and all customers familiarize themselves with the policy.

3. REEXAMINE YOUR TERMS OF SALE

Reexamine every quotation, price list, invoice, statement, and similar document the company issues. Do they show your terms of doing business, especially your credit terms? Contracts are established and modified by each successive piece of paper prior to invoice; make certain that your credit terms cannot be replaced by those detailed on a customer's order document.

4. ASSESS CREDIT RISKS

Be clear in your own mind how you assess credit risk for new and existing customers and how you impose limits in terms of total indebtedness and payment schedules. You and your staff must perform this assessment systematically and impartially, without taking a customer's potential sales into account (remember that sales people are optimists by nature, especially if a commission is involved!). Consult other sources of information before establishing or increasing credit facilities for existing or potential customers. Sources include trade and bank references, credit agencies (such as Moody's, Standard & Poors, Fitch, Duff & Phelps), rating registers (Dun & Bradstreet, for example), trade sources (including your competitors), and online services.

5. REASSESS THE CREDITWORTHINESS OF EXISTING CUSTOMERS

Reassess the financial standing of all your customers regularly, and pay particular attention when a customer's purchases show a sudden substantial increase. Satisfy yourself that the increase is due to successful selling rather than to a competitor ceasing to supply—perhaps because of problems in securing payment.

6. UNDERSTAND THE EFFECT OF BAD DEBTS

Bad debts reduce bottom-line profits and undo the effort of achieving the sales volume required to generate those profits. Your staff need to expend a great deal of effort trying to collect overdue receivables before they are written off; the cost of this effort is probably hidden and

"It's time to make things ship-shape, to get rid of the debt, to get a bit of a cash box to work from, to enjoy life a bit more."

(Conrad Black)

never identified. On the other hand, if you have no doubtful—as opposed to bad—debts, you may have been missing out on profitable business by being overcautious.

7. Review Your Billing Cycle

The date on which customers receive an invoice or statement often determines when they make payment. Take a fresh look at the interval between the date the company supplies goods and services and the corresponding invoicing date. See whether you can speed up invoicing—you probably can. Likewise, find out how soon after the last day of the month you generally send monthly statements. Is the process ever delayed to enable work of lesser priority to be done? Can you establish a firm monthly date and stick to it?

8. List Overdue and Total Indebtedness

Every month you should prepare an aged receivables analysis, a list of customers whose payments are overdue, breaking down the amounts due from them month by month. List each customer's total receivables as well. If slow paying habits reflect financial difficulties, the whole debt may be at risk.

9. Monitor the Average Length of Credit

Calculate the average length of credit that your company is allowing—or which your customers are taking. This can be calculated whenever you choose, but ideally you should calculate and review this figure monthly. The only thing worse than bad news is bad news that arrives too late for remedial action.

The calculation required is to divide the total amount you are owed by the sales for the 12-month period ending at the same month end and multiply by 365.

DOS AND DON'TS

For Controlling Credit

DO

- Have a clear vision of what you hope to achieve with credit control.
- Remember that a businesslike approach is attractive to the right type of customer.
- Regard the credit control as a vital regular check on the financial health of your business.

DON'T

- Don't let credit control dominate everything else.
- Don't allow a customer's sales volume to influence your view of creditworthiness.
- Don't make excuses for bad payers.

For example, if you divide your total outstanding receivables of $10,000 by $100,000 sales for the 12-month period and multiply that by 365, you find that you are allowing an average 36.5 days credit to each customer. Establish this calculation as a regular routine,

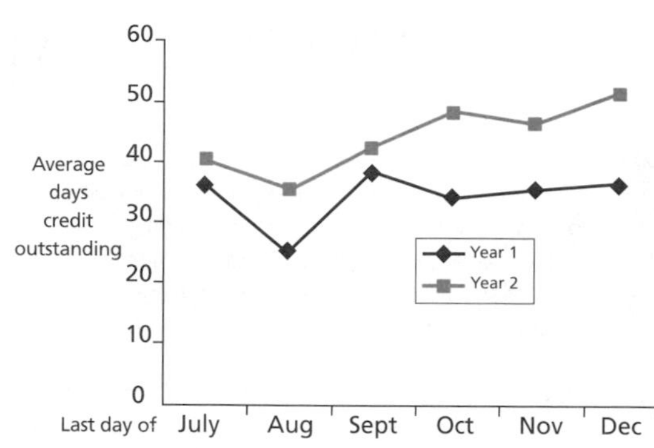

remembering to bring the sales figure up to date every time. Plot the result on a simple graph like the one above.

Look for any movement between the end of one month and the end of the next, and look for the trend revealed by the graph overall. This particular approach emphasizes the length of credit being allowed or taken rather than the amount. Both time and amount affect profit and liquidity.

10. Introduce a Collection Procedure

If you do not have a collection procedure timetable, introduce one. If you do have a timetable, see whether it is being followed systematically. Be politely firm in your collection routines. Attempt to get clear commitment to dates and amounts of payments. Remember to record details of every telephone call, including dates and the name of the person you talked to.

THOUGHT STARTERS

- How does the length of credit you receive compare with the length of credit you allow?
- What incentive do your customers or clients have to pay promptly?

For More Information

Books:

Dennis, Michael. *Credit and Collection Handbook.* Upper Saddle River, NJ: Prentice Hall, 1999.
Posner, Martin. *Successful Credit Control.* 2nd ed. New York: John Wiley, 1998.
Schaeffer, H.A., Jr. *Credit Risk Management: A Guide to Sound Business Decisions.* New York: John Wiley, 2000.

Web Site:

National Association of Credit Management: **www.nacm.org**

See also:

✓ **Collecting Debts (pp. 544–45)**

  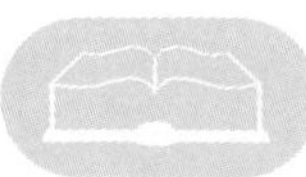    

Designing Questionnaires

CHECKLIST

This checklist is designed for anyone who needs to conduct a survey to determine the opinions or attitudes of a specific group. Questionnaires have applications in market research and in measuring employee attitudes and customer satisfaction.

It is a mistake to take a casual approach to designing a questionnaire; expert advice is not only desirable, but often essential.

Definition

A questionnaire is an instrument for obtaining specific information about a defined problem so that the data can be analyzed and interpreted to give a better appreciation of the issue in question.

Action Checklist

1. Define Your Research Objectives

The objectives provide the framework that determines the contents of the questionnaire. What topics are relevant to the decision-making task? Which information is essential and which would simply be nice to know? Questionnaires can be used to gather many kinds of information, including:

- consumption patterns/market trends/reasons for market changes
- beliefs about specific products or services
- expectations related to specific products or services
- general or specific attitudes
- economic, psychological, or social motivations for behavior
- influences on people's decision making
- competitors' activities
- media exposure and influence

2. Select the Appropriate Method

The most effective method of administration depends on the subject of the survey, the nature of the survey population, and your research budget. The traditional methods for administering questionnaires are by personal interview, telephone, and mail. Each has advantages and disadvantages (see table below).

Other methods of administering questionnaires include fax, e-mail, and the Web. The Web is most appropriate for lengthy surveys, complex routing, consumer research, and Web site tests. E-mail is appropriate for very short interviews, research on a low budget, employee research, recruiting for Web interviews, and business-to-business research. E-mail surveys benefit from being international in scope, cheaper than mail surveys, faster than the telephone, and automated for data collection, and they do not suffer from interviewer influence. There are, however, drawbacks, including technical incompatibilities, the lack of a universal e-mail directory, time delays in completion and return, and low penetration of the population, resulting in self-selecting samples.

3. Define Your Sample Population

Sources of names, addresses, and telephone numbers include databases, directories, and commercial lists. Consider the spread of customers to noncustomers, sex, socio-economic groups, and age, if relevant. You can choose to sample a specific population by quota or at random. In theory, random sampling is best, because you can calculate any error in the sample. Pressures of cost, convenience, and time, however, favor quota sampling, in which interviewers must meet numerical targets based on strata within the population.

4. Decide How to Analyze the Results

Even a low response rate may yield lots of paper to sort or plenty of data to key into a PC analysis package (such as SPSS or SNAP), spreadsheet, or database. Irrespective of whether the analysis will be done manually or electronically, think in advance of the logistics of data management and the facilities you have to analyze the responses. On the other hand, don't focus so much on ease of analysis that you compromise ease of use for the respondent or the relevance of the exercise. How you will use the responses helps determine the proportion of structured to unstructured questions and the decision whether to put all questions to all respondents—for example, do you need a filter question to establish whether or not respondents use the product or service being surveyed?

5. Order the Questions

It is good practice to:

- start with one or two general, bland questions that are easy to answer;

	Face to face	Telephone	Mail
Respondent acceptance	reasonable	doubtful	open choice
Recruitment	controlled	controlled	self-selecting
Response rate	fixed	fixed	variable
Speed	moderate	fast	slow
Variety of sample	poor	very good	very good
Interaction/rapport	very good	good	poor
Complexity of interview	possible	limited	impossible
Interviewer bias	present	present	absent
Interview length	up to 1 hour (prearranged)	10–15 minutes	30 questions (max.)
Demand on staff resources	heavy	substantial	moderate

"You know what charm is: a way of getting the answer yes without having asked any clear question."

(Albert Camus)

- explore present behavior (what is being used/done/bought now) before asking about the past or future;
- follow a logical order so that the respondent is not confused;
- put sensitive questions toward the middle or the end;
- make sure you don't broach ideas early in the questioning that might influence later answers;
- leave classification answers to the end (for example, "Which age range do you fall into?").

6. Design Precise Questions

Once you have determined which topics to cover and at what level of detail, consider the following:

- Open or closed questions? Questions can be closed or open-ended. The anticipated answers to a closed question are precoded with simple instructions to the interviewer or respondent, for example, "Circle number," "Please check ONE box only," or "Please check as applicable." Allow for "Don't know" or "Not stated." It is advisable to precode as many questions as possible—open-ended questions may provide richer data in that respondent answers in their own words, but the answers still have to be put into coding categories afterward.
- Confusion versus understanding. Avoid long, technical words and jargon. Watch out for possible ambiguity. Words such as "frequently," "often," "regularly," or "usually" need to be qualified. Avoid double negatives such as "Would you not drink a nonalcoholic beer?" Stick to one issue per question—avoid questions such as "What do you think of this administration's economic policies, and how should they be modified, if at all?"
- Attitude questions. The simplest approach is to put a statement to respondents and ask whether they agree or disagree, for example:

There is a sensible balance between my work and my personal life.

- Agree 1; Disagree 2; Neither agree nor disagree 3; Don't know 4.

This scale lacks subtlety, however: you have no idea how strongly those who reply "Agree" do agree, or how strongly others disagree. In order to measure the strength of respondents' attitudes, you need to construct rating scales. Two that are commonly used are the Likert scale and the semantic differential scale.

- Likert scale. A statement is put to respondents, who are asked, "Please tell me how much you agree or disagree with this statement," for example:

I have good opportunities for career development.

- Strongly agree 1; Slightly agree 2; Neither agree nor disagree 3; Slightly disagree 4; Strongly disagree 5.

The responses are analyzed by allocating weights to scale positions. You might allocate 5 to "Strongly agree," 3 for the midpoint, and 1 point for "Strongly disagree," or vice versa—but be consistent. If the scale battery includes both positive and negative attitude statements, then "Strongly agree" for a negative statement rates 1, not 5.

- Semantic differential scale. This is easier to administer and is more meaningful than the Likert scale in rating responses about specific attributes of named products and services. For example, if the product is an automobile, you might construct the following double-ended scale:

Acceleration:
Good................................Poor.

It is also common to use a point scale:

Reliability:	Good	1	2	3	4	5	Poor

Semantic scales can be either monopolar (bitter–not bitter; modern–not modern) or bipolar (modern–old-fashioned; strong–weak).

7. Consider the Page Layout

Don't cramp yourself—leave room for the answers! A questionnaire administered by an interviewer needs to have clear instructions that cannot be confused with the questions themselves. Instructions should in any case be in a different typeface. An attractive layout is especially important in a questionnaire to be mailed, as it has a significant effect on the response rate.

8. Pilot the Questionnaire

You may have to design a questionnaire without necessarily knowing the best questions to ask. If time permits, a group discussion or a number of in-depth interviews preceding the larger fieldwork program can be helpful. A questionnaire can be tested with as few as 10 to 20 interviews (but the more the better). The pilot identifies ambiguous questions and layout problems.

DOS AND DON'TS

For Designing Questionnaires

DO

- Keep it short, to the point, and easy to complete.
- Stress confidentiality.
- Minimize the nuisance factor for the recipient.
- Thank respondents for their cooperation.

DON'T

- Don't tell respondents the questionnaire will take five minutes if it takes 15.
- Don't use jargon or technical language your respondents won't understand.

THOUGHT STARTERS

- What was good about the last questionnaire you were asked to complete? What was bad?
- Don't reinvent the wheel—consult marketing and statistical sources to see whether what you want already exists.

For More Information

Book:

Walters, Mike. *Employee Attitude and Opinion Surveys.* Woodstock, NY: Beekman, 2000.

"That is the essence of science: ask an impertinent question, and you are on the way to a pertinent answer."

(Jacob Bronowski)

  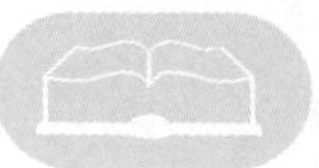  

DRAWING UP A BUDGET

CHECKLIST

This checklist is for managers who have responsibility for drawing up and presenting a budget.

Budgeting is at the heart of the way organizations measure what they want to achieve. It is a key planning device and one that companies are increasingly democratizing. Drawing up a budget is no longer the sole province of accountants and finance directors, but is a process likely to involve employees in many areas and at many levels. There is no longer room for financially naive managers in any kind of organization.

Drawing up a budget involves a mix of number skills and people skills like negotiation and listening. It is not a mechanical process, but a dynamic one.

DEFINITION

A budget is a statement of the expenditure or income that has been allocated under a set of headings for a set period of time.

ADVANTAGES

Budgets:

- serve as a key tool in achieving a company's strategic plan;
- help coordinate the activities of managers in different parts of the organization;
- encourage managers to take financial responsibility;
- allocate funds and planning effectively;
- communicate important financial information;
- motivate employees by setting clear goals;
- force managers to think about and plan for the future;
- provide criteria against which managers can measure their own performance and the performance of their team.

DISADVANTAGES

Poor budgeting or no budgeting at all presents a range of disadvantages, including:

- the generation of unreliable financial information;
- the breakdown of financial control.

ACTION CHECKLIST

1. IDENTIFY THE ORGANIZATION'S KEY PLANS AND OBJECTIVES

You need to identify these objectives so that you know what overriding factors to consider when preparing your budget. Budgeting is to some extent secondary to the strategic or business plans of the organization. Only when goals and broad strategies are clear can a meaningful budget be prepared.

Is it, for example, to be a budget for growth or for standing still? This will affect the way you draw up figures.

2. DETERMINE THE KEY OR LIMITING FACTORS

Every organization is subject to factors that limit its growth. In most cases this is sales volume, the number of customers, or the amount of manufacturing plant available. Whatever they are, these key factors have significance for planning and budgeting. There's no point drawing up a superb budget based on high sales volume if your sales department cannot realistically achieve this level of sales.

3. WHAT IS COMING IN?

Look at the range of sources—are you generating funds, or is money allocated at the beginning of each year? Will you really receive all the money you have projected, or will some come in the next financial year or fall through? How much of it is guaranteed income?

4. WHAT IS GOING OUT?

Estimate your expected costs. Break down costs under different headings. Cost headings usually include:

- staffing, wages, pensions, training, etc.;
- premises, rent, repairs, heating, etc.;
- the company's legal responsibilities;
- materials and equipment—stationery, telephones, raw materials;
- any other business costs—insurance, taxes, etc.

The general principle is to divide the budget up under whatever headings seem sensible to you—but, as organizations often group headings together, make sure your categories are roughly consistent with the rest of the company. Look at last year's budget and use the headings in it as a starting point.

5. THINK THROUGH YOUR FIXED AND VARIABLE COSTS

There are two types of costs:

- fixed costs—costs you have no matter how much extra work the organization handles, for example, permanent staff costs;
- variable costs—costs dependent on the organization's level of work, for example, raw materials or advertising costs.

Ask your accounting department to help you identify your fixed and variable costs.

6. DECIDE HOW TO DRAW UP THE BUDGET

There are several different methods of drafting a budget.

Incremental Budgeting

This method bases this year's budget on last year's budget figures, adjusting for factors such as inflation. This is a quick and simple way of putting together a first draft of a budget, but if last year's budget was inaccurate, you will be adding incrementally to past mistakes. It is a conservative approach, making the assumption that present objectives are correct and that there is a high degree of

"Enterprises are paid to create wealth, not control costs." (Peter F. Drucker)

continuity. If you are using an incremental approach, calculate how accurately last year's budget actually reflected reality. Write down:

- the budget;
- the corresponding final figures—what you actually spent;
- the variance—how far was the budget out, and why?

Zero-Based Budgeting

This method requires you to estimate every budgeted cost afresh at the start of each year. Analyze each cost as the picture looks now rather than referring to last year's budget. This is a fundamental approach, requiring you to justify every item and redefine your objectives.

✔ 7. Gather Information

Look at last year's budget and learn what you can for this year's. Make sure you speak to all the stakeholders before drawing up the budget to get maximum input. Look at the organization's objectives and targets to see whether and how your budget needs to be adjusted or reconstructed. Assess all external and internal factors that may have a bearing on your performance. These may include the rate of inflation, bank lending rates, trade prospects forecast for the following year, and whether you wish to stimulate the market. Budgeting for growth also means having the available resources to handle the increased levels of business if the marketing works, otherwise you will be stimulating a demand you cannot meet.

✔ 8. Ask Basic but Important Questions

- Am I clear about strategic objectives and how they affect my area of responsibility?
- Have I accurately forecast the number of people it will take to meet objectives?
- Are there likely to be any changes?
- Am I clear about income?
- Am I clear about outgoings?
- Are there any factors on the horizon that might throw the forecast into chaos?

✔ 9. Draw Up the Budget

Keep detailed notes on your rationale for the figures you include in your budget. It may seem obvious at the time you write them down, but six months later you might not remember how you arrived at your figures. Remember to build in a contingency allowance for things that may go wrong—the "what ifs." Contingency planning may reflect on revenue implications if levels of business do not meet expectations, or on controlling expenditure early in the financial year until you obtain a clearer picture of how your budget is performing.

✔ 10. Build In Budget Control Parameters

You or your accounting department will need to track income and expenditure against the budget. This may be monthly, weekly, or even daily, depending on the business.

✔ 11. Present the Budget

If you have to present the budget to senior managers or colleagues in addition to submitting a written statement, make sure you present a realistic forecast that allows for possible downturns and problems instead of attempting to impress them. If your forecast looks optimistic, say so and explain why you have made such an assumption; if it looks pessimistic, make sure you convey the appropriate message.

DOS AND DON'TS

For Drawing up a Budget

DO

- Be realistic.
- Take last year's budget and actual result into account.
- Be aware of fixed and variable costs.
- Develop budget headings that work for you and for the organization as a whole.
- Gather complete information.
- Decide whether to take a incremental or zero-based approach.

DON'T

- Don't make overoptimistic projections.
- Don't leave too little time to do a thorough job.
- Don't draw up a budget without involving others.

THOUGHT STARTERS

- Do you understand the major objectives laid down in your organization's current strategic plan?
- Do you know how your area of responsibility fits within the current strategic plan?
- Have you listened carefully to all the stakeholders?
- Have you checked last year's budget?
- Have you drawn up a list of budget headings?
- Have you left enough time for the process?

For More Information

Books:

Brookson, Stephen. *Essential Managers: Managing Budgets*. New York: DK Publishing, 2000.

Moore, Norman. *Forecasting Budgets*. New York: Lebhar-Friedman, 1999.

See also:

✔ **Controlling a Budget (pp. 546–47)**
✔ **Strategic Planning (pp. 484–85)**
✔ **Writing a Business Plan (pp. 486–87)**

"Some mistakes cost money, others have a more personal cost." (Peter de Savany)

Effective Business Writing

CHECKLIST

This checklist is an introduction to the basic principles of business writing. Business writing can take many forms, but what is common to each of them is the importance of conveying the right message to the right audience in the right way—and at the right time. The effectiveness of business writing is measured not by whether the recipient enjoyed reading the communication, but by whether it achieved its purpose.

In an age when business communications are increasingly transmitted in electronic form, it is just as important for ideas and information to be conveyed clearly and concisely. Technology does not remove the need to write well.

Definition

The term "business writing" is used to cover any form of written communication within the context of paid employment, including letters, memos, public relations or marketing materials, and reports. (Report writing is the subject of a separate checklist and is therefore mentioned only in passing here.) Although different organizations may have their own styles, the same principles apply whether the writer is in the public or private sector, a small business, or a large government department.

Action Checklist

1. Decide What You Are Trying to Achieve

What is your main aim? How does this relate to the broader context of the organization and the potentially conflicting aims of people within it? Unless you think about this, you will have no reference point by which to judge whether the communication is effective. Relate your objectives to the wider organizational picture.

2. Determine the Outcomes You Want

What do you want to happen as a result of your communication? This will be closely linked to its purpose. If you want to impart facts, how will you know you have been successful? Be explicit about the action, if any, you expect recipients to take.

3. See Whether a Written Communication Is the Most Appropriate Medium

Before you begin writing, decide and plan your message, and then choose the right communication strategy. Write only if:

- you need to address a number of people;
- the argument or explanation is complex or needs visual support;
- you need a considered response;
- you need an accurate and permanent record of the communication.

If the message is urgent or one-on-one or can be expressed simply and without visual aids, consider phoning. If you need to involve several people in an urgent decision, or if action is conditional on presenting an argument to several people, seek a meeting first.

4. Decide Who Should Sign the Communication

The usual assumption is that you are writing the communication. However, its effectiveness may depend on its being seen to come from someone else. Its message may be more powerful if it is signed by someone more senior—or more junior—than you. The important point is that someone with the right credentials for the target readers should sign.

5. Identify the Target Audience

Ensure that your intended audience is the right one to deliver the action you need and that the recipients will be motivated to respond. Do they represent the right constituencies within the organization? Will they have the authority to act? If you are targeting the public, how will you make sure that the right people see the communication?

6. Build a Rapport with Your Audience

Getting readers to deliver what you need, even if it is only their attention, depends on building a rapport with them. You can do this by setting the right tone, and you have three basic choices:

- Plead for the audience to do something on your behalf.
- Persuade them to do something by selling its benefits.
- Appeal to broader organizational interests and invoke the value of teamwork.

The last approach is usually the most effective. Try to establish common ground, and express the issue in terms of its shared effect on both you and the recipient.

7. Build a Convincing Argument

Develop a proposition that is compelling by spelling out the benefits and by anticipating and forestalling objections. See the issue from the recipients' perspective, understand their likely concerns, and show how the proposal addresses these while fitting in with overall organizational strategy. Be realistic about problems and the effort required to overcome them.

8. Prepare an Outline

Note down the key strands of your argument in a few words and build a structure around them. Group key relationships and themes. The structure can be logical (a discussion of the issue followed by evidence and conclusions) or declarative (the conclusion first, backed up by evidence).

"Later Marx was to recall his mother's words, 'If only Karl had made capital, instead of writing about it.'"

(Edna Healey)

  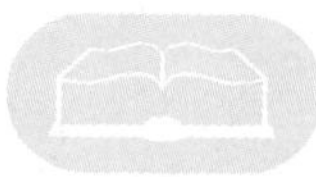    

9. Guide the Reader around Your Text

Use the outline to begin writing. Whatever the structure or formality of the document, use clear, eye-catching signposts and flags to guide the reader around. Provide an introduction that explains why you are writing and a summary that captures your key points. Separate out your conclusions and recommendations.

10. Make Your Text Easy to Read and Unambiguous

Think about readability. Use short paragraphs and short sentences and avoid long or unfamiliar words. Use simple, clear English. Avoid jargon where possible; where it is unavoidable, explain it. Spell out abbreviations the first time you use them, even if you think your reader will be familiar with them. Use tangible rather than abstract concepts. Use the active instead of the passive voice ("he decided," not "it was decided"), except where it is irrelevant or inappropriate to say who was responsible for the action. Use an occasional image to illustrate a point, but avoid language that is too flowery or informal. Use humor sparingly and tastefully. Be grammatical—grammatical lapses and misspellings irritate readers and hinder their ability to receive messages.

11. Enliven Your Text with Graphics

Use graphics to back up your arguments and convey your key messages—but only if they are clear and easy to read. Incorporate notes in the text telling your readers when to look at them and where to find them. Integrate graphics into the main body of the text, with the exception of detailed statistical tables: place these in an appendix. Don't be tempted to use visual or statistical tricks to bolster a weak argument (for example, by distorting the y-axis of a graph to paint an overly favorable picture of a sales increase). The size of a graphic should relate to the importance of the point you are trying to make.

12. Revise Your Text Once It Is Complete

Your communication will be effective only if it is authoritative. Read over your draft and be self-critical, or, if you have time, ask someone you respect to read the text. Check that your reasoning and arguments form a logical sequence; make certain that all your facts are right; give the source and authority for any opinions you cite; give due weight to contradictory arguments; and cover alternative conclusions or recommendations without being too dismissive of them. Be succinct.

13. Pay Attention to Presentation

As with oral communication, your audience will judge you as much on your presentation as the content of your message. Are you using a clear, easy-to-read typeface and font size, and good quality paper and ink? Use bold characters to give emphasis to key words and phrases instead of underlining them, and see that there is ample white space on every page. Use indentation, bullets, and one-line paragraphs to break up the text.

14. Follow Up

If the communication is important, follow it up with a telephone call where appropriate. Check that the reader really did receive the message you intended to convey. Make sure that there were no misunderstandings or ambiguities and that the action you needed is under way.

DOS AND DON'TS

For Effective Business Writing

DO

- If possible, find one or two vivid images or phrases that will convey the key element of your message and make it memorable.
- Establish common ground with your readers, and engage their attention and sympathy.
- Be self-critical of your work and be open to other people's comments and suggestions.

DON'T

- Don't undermine the effectiveness of your communication by grammatical, spelling, or typing mistakes. Always print and proofread a communication before sending it. Don't rely on the spell checker—mistakes show up more clearly in black and white than on the screen.
- Don't suppress arguments that do not wholly support your view, or your readers will distrust you. Confront them and say why you think they are not significant.

THOUGHT STARTERS

- Will a written communication alone be effective in securing what you need to achieve?
- Have you addressed the motivations and concerns of your audience as well as your own?
- Does the communication convey the best possible image of you—and the organization?

For More Information

Books:

Geffner, Andrea B. *Business English: A Complete Guide to Developing an Effective Business Writing Style*. New York: Barron's Educational, 1998.

Piotrowski, Maryann. *Effective Business Writing: A Guide for Those Who Can Write on the Job*. New York: HarperCollins, 1996.

"What do you want from me? Fine writing? Or would you like to see the goddam sales curve stop going down and start going up?"

(Rosser Reeves)

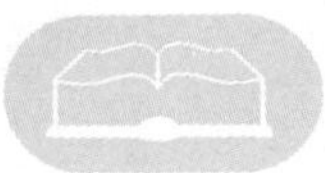

EFFECTIVE COMMUNICATIONS: COMMUNICATING WITH GROUPS

CHECKLIST

This checklist provides an introduction to group communication skills and techniques.

As formal hierarchies break down, managers are no longer able to get things done by passing on instructions to junior staff. The ability to make things happen increasingly depends on being able to adopt different roles, styles, and techniques and on the manager's effectiveness as a member of different groups both within and outside the organization.

DEFINITION

This checklist covers oral communications with all types of groups.

Within the organization, these range from large formal team briefings to casual encounters between two or three colleagues from different departments.

External groups comprise a very mixed universe, from customers and competitors to representatives of suppliers and regulatory authorities. In each context, managers may play a slightly different role, although the principles of effective communication stay the same.

ACTION CHECKLIST

1. DEFINE THE PURPOSE OF THE COMMUNICATION

Clarify the purpose of the communication at the outset: is it a meeting to make decisions, a briefing session to impart information, or a brainstorming session to generate new ideas? Some tasks are done better in groups—for example, sifting existing ideas, coming up with new ideas, or involving people in a key decision. Others are best left to individual or written communications, particularly when there is a need to impart large amounts of factual or sensitive information.

2. LIMIT THE EXTENT OF THE COMMUNICATION

Set a time limit, even for an informal encounter, and an agenda, even if it is an unwritten one. Be realistic about what you can expect to achieve within the group given its representation, and be sensitive to the pressures on other people's time.

3. MAKE SURE THAT THE RIGHT PEOPLE ARE THERE

Group communication works best when all the people present have a legitimate reason for being there, have something to contribute to the discussion, and have an interest in the outcome.

Postpone a discussion if the right people can't be present; delay is better than an inconclusive debate. Take the initiative in doing this yourself if a group leader is reluctant.

4. GET THE RIGHT NUMBER OF PEOPLE

For most group discussion, five is recognized as the optimum number for effective debate and decision making. In a group of this size members can adopt different roles, and a single member can be in the minority without undue pressure to conform.

Getting the right people is always more important than getting the right number.

5. FACILITATE INTRODUCTIONS

If you are leading a group, make clear what people's roles are, why they are there, and what they are expected to contribute. If your expectations turn out to be unrealistic, allow people to leave or suggest alternative members. As a member, define the contribution you expect to make and your authority for making it.

Make clear whether the authority is personal (a function of your own position) or vested (you have been asked to speak on behalf of someone else). Don't claim an authority that is not legitimate or that you can't substantiate.

6. BE ACTIVE

If you have agreed to be part of a group, be active in it. Take full responsibility for its success or failure, be energetic, and make positive contributions.

If you have nothing to contribute, admit it and step down: don't waste other contributors' time.

7. BE RATIONAL BUT OPEN-MINDED

Take up a clear position on issues, but be willing to listen to rational argument and be prepared to change your mind—if you do, explain why. Groups work effectively only if participants are open to new information and different points of view.

Give all members the opportunity to speak, even if you have doubts about the likely wisdom of their views. Don't put your own ideas ahead of the group's overriding objective.

Be aware of the dangers of unconscious domination. If the group leader always gives an opinion first, it is possible the others may:

- be unduly influenced from the start;
- be liable to think that this is all sewn up and they aren't required to contribute, only to react;
- get into the habit of not thinking for themselves.

8. BE BRIEF, BE SIMPLE, AND BE ORGANIZED

Speak slowly, clearly, and directly in short sentences. Structure your arguments logically. Think what you are going to say, say it, and summarize what you have said. Link your comments to what has already been said by other contributors. Clarify areas of support for their position or areas of disagreement.

"We could have over 520 brains connected in real time across time and space available for any problem."

(Robert Buckman)

9. Make Good Use of Nonverbal Communication

Use gestures to reinforce your key messages and nonverbal signals to convey attitudes and expressions. Make eye contact with each member of the group. Use nonthreatening but positive body language and convey an impression of calm and confidence. Pay close attention to other people's nonverbal signals: are you irritating them or patronizing them?

10. Stay Calm and Don't Argue

Even if you believe the group is making the wrong decision, stay calm and don't become emotional defending your own ideas. Stress points of agreement and minimize areas of disagreement with a view to finding a way forward.

11. Avoid Personal Attacks

The key to effective group communication is mutual respect. If you believe someone is wrong, criticize the idea, not the person.

- Make your criticism effective by making it palatable: preface it with a word of support or agreement on a related topic.
- Avoid being too negative, even if someone is deliberately putting forward unhelpful ideas.
- Resist the temptation to allocate blame for previous mistakes or failures, otherwise the group dynamics will break down.
- Remember that while group members may be competing to present individual positions, you are cooperating to find an overall solution.

12. Bring the Communication to a Conclusion

Casual encounters in particular often take longer than necessary because the purpose of the communication and its agenda are unclear at the outset.

- Review what you were expecting to get out of the communication and whether you have achieved it.
- If you have to postpone debate, make sure it isn't because the group lacks the people or authority to reach a conclusion.
- Write up a decision and action statement as soon as possible after the meeting and make sure everyone involved has a copy (including interested parties not present).

DOS AND DON'TS

For Effective Communications: Communicating with Groups

DO

- Be aware of the reference points of the other group members: how are they viewing an issue and what barriers will their views throw up to achieving your own objectives?
- Take part in any discussion with a genuinely open mind and good listening skills.

DON'T

- Don't dominate the discussion because you are convinced of the merits of your own argument and oblivious to others.
- Don't bring your own prejudices to the group and assume that certain members will react in a certain way.
- Don't allow groupthink. All groups have a tendency to say what they think the leader wants to hear. Define your contribution in terms of meeting the group's objectives, and stick to your position unless you are genuinely convinced by other members' arguments.

THOUGHT STARTERS

- How readily can you adapt your social style to the different roles required of you by different groups?
- Do you rely too much on the authority of your own position to persuade people of the merits of your arguments?

For More Information

Books:

Argenti, Paul A. *Corporate Communication*. 2nd ed. New York: McGraw-Hill Higher Education, 1997.

Boone, Louis E., David L. Kurtz, and Judy R. Block. *Contemporary Business Communication*. 2nd ed. Upper Saddle River, NJ: Prentice Hall, 1996.

See also:

✓ **Effective Communications: Communicating with Groups (pp. 558–59)**

"A lot of our communications have celebrated what we were not." (Rawdon Glover)

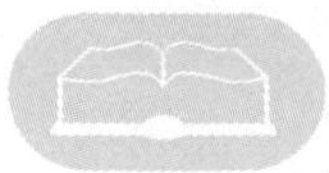

Gathering Competitive Intelligence

CHECKLIST

This checklist provides guidance for individuals or organizations wishing to take a structured and proactive approach to gathering competitive intelligence (CI).

Many companies gather information about competitors' activities informally—for example, through press coverage or conversations with clients. This approach is haphazard and reactive; the organization only learns about a competitor's activities after the event. A structured approach to gaining CI helps companies get advance notice and take appropriate action before the event.

Definition

Competitive intelligence (CI) provides organizations with actionable information about competitors' activities. It is a key aspect of analyzing the operating environment. Such information (which can range from new products or pricing to overall strategic direction) is used to make both short- and long-term plans in a number of areas, including strategy, mergers and acquisitions, pricing, marketing, advertising, and research and development.

Advantages

Taking a proactive approach to CI:

- minimizes surprises from competitors;
- identifies opportunities as well as threats;
- gives you hard information to use in formulating your company's plans;
- allows your organization to learn from competitors;
- permits more accurate assessment of the impact your company's actions will have on a competitor.

Disadvantages

Gaining a sound understanding of a competitor's activity has no real disadvantages, but remember:

- sources of competition are increasingly to be found in nontraditional sectors, so you need to keep an eye on the competitive environment as a whole;
- simply copying competitors or beating them fractionally to market is not the key to organizational success—differentiation from the competition is;
- some companies become so overwhelmed by the volume of data they collect about their operating environment that they are unable to reach strategic decisions. Management guru Igor Ansoff calls this "paralysis by analysis."

Action Checklist

1. Make the Commitment

The major resource requirement in gathering CI is that of staff time, but you will also incur costs in other areas such as traveling to conferences and exhibitions, searching online databases, and subscribing to journals. In purely financial terms CI rarely produces a direct return on investment, but improvements in softer areas will occur. Senior management needs to commit to developing a systematic CI program so that resources can be made available, even though gains may be intangible in the shorter term.

2. Identify Needs and Objectives

The overall aim of a CI program is to provide decision makers (for example, senior managers and heads of departments) with useful and accurate information. Survey these individuals and functions to find out what information they need and how they want it to be presented. Be clear on what you are attempting to find out through your competitor analysis. Are you trying to find the weak points of another company? Do you want to find out what the competition is like in a new market you plan to enter? Or are you aware of one particular organization that is posing a threat to your department or function?

Overall objectives for CI programs should include the provision of:

- information for strategic decisions
- early warnings of competitor activity

At the operational level you need to clarify exactly what the CI program will cover, including:

- individual or groups of competitors
- individual or groups of products or services

Specific areas can also be detailed, for example, a competitor's:

- pricing
- recruitment drives
- market behavior
- strategy

Clear and specific objectives for the CI program provide a focus and help reduce the amount of information that needs to be collected, but remember that they should not be set in stone: review them regularly.

3. Bring Together a Team and Assign Responsibility

The number of people involved in the CI program depends on your objectives; for example, comprehensive analysis of a company's competition requires more staff resources than keeping up to date with one or two competitors' activities. Assign responsibility for the CI program to one individual with good communication and information skills and the ability to work to deadlines.

4. Identify Sources of Information

Experts in the field of competitor analysis believe that most organizations already hold or have ready access to 80 percent of the information required for assessing the competition in the field.

Among the many published and unpublished sources of information on competitor activity that exist are:

- trade shows and conferences
- online databases and Web sites
- magazines and newspapers

"When the competition is moving at 200 miles an hour, every second you're in the pits matters a lot."

(Doug Nelson)

- product catalogs
- personal contacts in other companies

Don't overlook the importance of frontline staff as sources of CI—they pick up competitor information through their dealings with customers.

5. Use Technology

Use databases to keep an archive of the information you gather so that you can easily retrieve information about a specific subject or competitor. Be aware of copyright legislation—it is illegal to scan many documents, for example, press clippings, into an electronic format for storage and retrieval, but you may keep references or the newspaper in hard copy. Provide staff with training in using information storage and retrieval software.

6. Circulate Reports

Circulate regular reports of information gained from the CI program to all managers who need to see them. Decide how often the reports are to be produced; weekly may suffice in some environments, while other situations may require daily reports. Be brief: highlight the most important points and provide references to further information.

Remember that technology, particularly intranets and e-mail, can disseminate CI inside the organization more quickly than paper.

7. Take Action on the Results

CI gives strategic advantage only when it is analyzed and acted upon. Keep records of occasions when information was used successfully to gain advantage over competitors and when it arrived too late to take action.

Don't jump to counteract a competitor's movements without considering your own corporate objectives. Only the right action for you, at the right time, will bring you an advantage.

8. Evaluate against Objectives

Evaluate the success of your CI program against your initial objectives. Identify problem areas, for example, difficulty in obtaining information in one particular area or about one particular competitor, or failure to disseminate information quickly. Draw up recommendations for improving the program and present them to management, along with details of CI successes.

9. Make Changes

Take action on the recommendations for improvement and continue to evaluate the program regularly. Keep communicating CI successes.

10. Observe the Ethical Line

There are ethical and unethical approaches to gathering competitive intelligence. Information that is made publicly available, for example, in press releases or job advertisements, poses few ethical questions. On the other hand, sending employees to job interviews at a competitor organization to gather information about its plans is considered doubtful behavior. Spying or business espionage, for example, hacking into a competitor's computer system or going through a competitor's trash, is highly unethical.

DOS AND DON'TS

For Gathering Competitive Intelligence

DO

- Involve frontline staff who come into contact with customers and are at the cutting edge.
- Keep CI reports brief and regular, and direct the reader to more detailed information.
- Remember that your competitors will also be trying to gain intelligence on your organization.
- Recognize the importance of communicating the success of the CI program.

DON'T

- Don't spend money researching firms that are no longer your competitors—move with the market.
- Don't overstep the ethical line—check your organization's own code of conduct.

THOUGHT STARTERS

- Have you ever been taken by surprise by a competitor's activities?
- How much do you really know about your main competitors?
- What are the strengths and weaknesses of your competitors?

For More Information

Books:

Kahaner, Larry. *Competitive Intelligence: How to Gather, Analyze and Use Information to Move Your Business to the Top*. New York: Simon & Schuster, 1998.

Miller, Jerry P. *Millennium Intelligence: Understanding and Conducting Competitive Intelligence in the Digital Age*. Medford, NJ: Information Today, Inc., 2000.

Journal Articles:

Ettorre, Barbara. "Managing Competitive Intelligence." *Management Review* 84:10 (October 1995): 15–19.

Sawka, Kenneth A. "Demystifying Business Intelligence." *Management Review* 85:10 (October 1996): 47–51.

Web Sites:

Competitive Intelligence Guide: **www.fuld.com**

Society of Competitive Intelligence Professionals: **www.scip.org**

Implementing Statistical Process Control (SPC)

CHECKLIST

This checklist provides an outline of the techniques and benefits of SPC. The actual application of many of these techniques requires more detail than can be covered in a checklist.

SPC is usually understood to operate in a manufacturing context (for example, where production line machinery can be statistically monitored and controlled for deviations from the norm), but it can also apply to some service sector activities.

Definition

Outputs from a manufacturing process may vary from the exact specification, and deliveries from a service differ in quality and substance. These inconsistencies in quality require constant monitoring to see if they are random, regular, haphazard, important, or indicative of a problem. The monitoring and controlling should be applied to the process, not the product, and can be greatly facilitated by statistical process control (SPC).

Process control means controlling production by checking its quality while the work is still in process. Implementing SPC means applying statistical techniques and analysis to that control function. Since SPC is about measuring the quality of work in process, its implementation is usually allied to techniques related to quality systems management.

Advantages

Chaudhry and Higbie, in their paper " Quality improvement through statistical process control," report the following benefits from applying SPC in a chemical plant:

- increased production efficiency
- a more consistent product
- superior reliability
- greater ease in pinpointing problem occurrences
- provision of a usable measure of performance
- clearer communication of objectives
- improved customer relations

Disadvantages

SPC can take time to apply rigorously, but applications show that there are few, if any, disadvantages to SPC. Its application must remain relevant and useful, otherwise it risks becoming a system in place because of inertia.

Action Checklist

1. Plan and Communicate the Program

First approach the SPC project by addressing the elements essential to all successful change programs:

- securing proactive and continuous top management commitment;
- appointing the right project leader and obtaining the right expertise;
- establishing flexible time frames and broad resource requirements;
- communicating regularly with the implementation teams and everyone else involved;
- preparing an effective and continuous training program.

Then adopt a specific operational plan or process:

- locate the process to be tackled;
- research the extent of the problem to be controlled;
- specify objectives and identify the resources, data, and training required;
- select the appropriate technique(s) to control the problem;
- plan the equipment, materials, and expertise for the technique(s) chosen;
- identify possible causes of the problem;
- test possible solutions.

2. Identify Appropriate Tools and Techniques

In the toolkit of techniques at your disposal each approach has a particular application. It is important to choose the right technique for the right process: research your options carefully. Tools and techniques include the following:

- Checklists outline established best practice in a simple sequence so that a process may be checked and controlled for doing the right thing at the right time.
- Flow charts show the sequential steps in a process, how work flows from one area to another, and the when, how, and where (and where not) of activities.
- Cause-and-effect (fishbone) diagrams attempt to relate effects to causes. They examine all related possibilities of a process that is going wrong or a product or service that is not satisfactory.
- Scatter diagrams plot the occurrence(s) of failure, or deviations from the norm, enabling confirmation or dismissal of a suspected relationship between, for example, supply and production or production and delivery.
- Histograms, pie charts, and bar charts show how a process is performing at a moment in time. They are useful for showing the impact of one factor against another, such as faults against a process, or customer calls against sales.
- Run charts show the same data as a histogram but plot the values over time.
- Pareto analysis—according to Pareto, relatively few failure reasons are responsible for the many failures in a system; hence the 80/20 rule. A Pareto chart—a vertical bar chart with the bars representing complaints or defects ranked in descending order—shows the relative importance of a set of measurements, allowing you to focus on the most pressing problems.

"I realized that if you want to change something, nine times out of ten you can change it more effectively from within."

(Niall Fitzgerald)

- Process performance checks focus on the most recent observations from the process, offering a glance at a given moment in time.
- Process performance evaluations focus on past performance, using all available historical data to see how a process has been operating and suggest improvements.
- Process capability studies focus on current observations of the process, using control charts to determine the variability and thus capability of a specific process under statistical control.
- Control charts identify continuing and special causes of variation in a process. They can demonstrate that a process is (or is not) currently in control and can warn of causes of variation and signal the need for correction or improvement. Samples of data are needed to calculate limits, expectations, and norms. Different kinds of control chart include:
  - attributes charts: with only two values (right/wrong, pass/fail). Here you need to ask what is being counted, for example, defective items against total items;
  - variables charts: average, range (limited or unlimited), and median (the number in the middle of the set). Here you need to ask how many types of measures are to be controlled.
- Correlation and regression analysis are methods for determining the type of cause-and-effect relationship between variables.

3. Establish Norms and Indicators

You won't know if something is wrong unless you know what to expect when things are going right. Establish a sample of data from which you can determine acceptable limits, norms, or indicators of performance.

4. Resource Support and Prepare Procedures

Consult the hands-on practitioner and technical and procedural manuals to ensure that you've selected appropriate techniques and that the appropriate technical support is in place, not only for designing and constructing the control charts, but also for analyzing and adjusting the applications.

5. Integrate SPC into Your Quality Management System

Integration is vital if SPC is to succeed. While the tools and techniques used must be perceived to be of practical, operational value and not mere number-crunching exercises, the management of SPC must integrate it into the overall quality management system.

6. Select a Winning Pilot and Don't Rush

Choosing the first process for SPC implementation can be critical for success. Start SPC in a process with the most glaring quality problems and the best anticipated outcome. Poor production records, high costs, high complaints, and high failure levels will tell you where to look. Identify the critical variables to be the subject of the control.

Exercise patience in following through the implementation program. Trying to get results too quickly usually generates the wrong results. Gathering specific data meticulously and paying attention to detail will bring its rewards.

7. Use the Charts for Improvement, Not Just for Control

Assuming that your initial state was problem-free, solving a problem means getting back to where you were—control does not necessarily mean improvement. The evidence SPC produces can indicate what improvements can be made where and—with systematic selection of processes—how.

For Implementing Statistical Process Control (SPC)

DO

- Define clear objectives and pinpoint which process or part of a process you intend to tackle.
- Monitor the process—not the product.

DON'T

- Don't take shortcuts—expertise in whichever statistical method is used is vital.
- Don't seek to place blame on someone once you've solved the problem—fix the process that caused the problem.

For More Information

Books:

Bothe, Davis R. *Measuring Process Capability: Techniques and Calculations for Quality and Manufacturing Engineers*. New York: McGraw-Hill Professional, 1997.

Levinson, William A., and Frank Tumbelty. *SPC Essentials and Productivity Improvement: A Manufacturing Approach*. Milwaukee, WI: ASQ Quality Press, 1997.

Journal Article:

Chaudhry, Sohail, and J. Richard Higbie. "Quality Improvement through Statistical Process Control." *Quality Engineering* Vol. 2, No. 4 (April 1990) 411–19.

See also:

✓ **Total Quality: Getting TQM to Work (pp. 522–23)**

"You have more control and less ambiguity today than you are likely to have for the rest of your life."

(Daryl R. Conner)

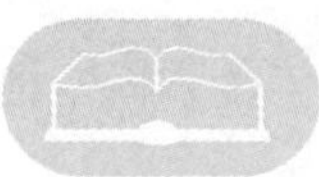

INTERNAL AUDIT

CHECKLIST

This checklist is designed to help managers tackle the process of an internal audit within their organization or department.

Internal audit is an essential part of business life, but not all companies are large enough to have a designated internal audit function. This checklist is aimed primarily at those who are undertaking an internal audit themselves or who are responsible for selecting and managing a member of staff who has this responsibility. It applies equally to organizations in the public and private sectors.

DEFINITION

Internal auditing is defined by the Institute of Internal Auditors as an independent appraisal function established within an organization to examine and evaluate its activities, the objective being to assist staff in the effective discharge of their responsibilities. To this end internal auditing furnishes staff with analyses, appraisals, and recommendations concerning those activities. Internal auditing is usually conducted by staff from within the organization.

ADVANTAGES

Internal audit should be a continuous process. Its advantages may include the following:

- Management's attention will be directed to the key business issues. The audit analyzes weaknesses in the system of control, which become the basis for practical recommendations for improvement.
- It gives management confidence when controls are operating satisfactorily.
- It identifies opportunities for improving efficiency and effectiveness.
- It gives early notice of potential problems. Management can then take action as necessary.

DISADVANTAGES

- Internal audit can be time-consuming and take managers away from their day-to-day work.
- If handled insensitively, internal audit can feel threatening to staff members who may feel that they are being scrutinized with the intention of finding fault.

ACTION CHECKLIST

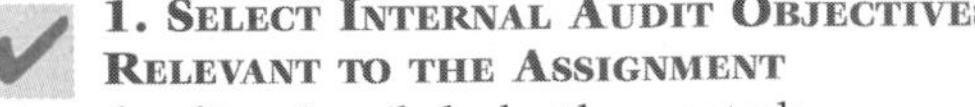

1. SELECT INTERNAL AUDIT OBJECTIVES RELEVANT TO THE ASSIGNMENT

Internal audits primarily look at key controls.

- Financial—how is money handled within the organization? Who authorizes payment, for example, and what are the checks and balances to stop unauthorized spending and fraud?
- Administrative controls—are these conducive to meeting strategic objectives?
- Systems—what systems are in place departmentally and across the organization, and how do they fit together?

They look, too, at value for money—is this being achieved through the systems currently in place, or do the systems fail to measure this?

The first step is to make sure your broad audit objectives reflect whichever of these are your priorities.

2. PREPARE A DETAILED BRIEF

An internal audit looks at a variety of aspects of the way an organization works. It does not focus solely on financial issues. Write an audit brief or strategy that sets detailed priorities in accordance with the main issues, and give some indication of the proportion of time you expect the auditor to spend on highlighted aspects.

3. CHOOSE YOUR AUDITOR

It is usual to appoint an individual from within the organization as the internal auditor. Depending on the issues to be examined, a formal qualification (for example, in accounting) may be appropriate.

4. BRIEF YOUR AUDITOR

Make sure you have all the background information you need before you brief your auditor. Include the following for your organization:

- strategic or business plans
- standing orders
- articles and memoranda of association
- internal procedure manuals
- lists of key personnel
- organization chart

Arrange a meeting with the auditor to confirm that you have provided sufficient information; even if the person is an employee, do not make assumptions about his or her level of knowledge.

The goal of the meeting is to agree on the objectives of the audit. Find out how the auditor plans to meet these objectives. Agree on a timetable and a plan of action and find out if further information is needed.

5. IDENTIFY THE KEY CONTROLS TO MEET AUDIT OBJECTIVES

The next stage is to start to look at the organization in detail. The auditor needs to look at the organization's existing procedures for controlling the key areas to be examined.

6. EVALUATE THE CONTROLS

Next, evaluate how effective the controls are. Could they be improved? Are there any omissions? Questions worth thinking about include the following:

- If someone wanted to commit fraud, where and how would they do it?
- If I had bought this product or service personally,

"When a company's profits slip, its position is tarnished. People are reluctant to buy from companies in financial trouble."
(Regis McKenna)

  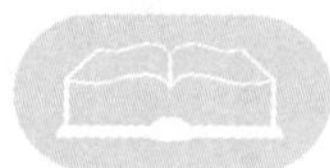    

would I be happy with the purchase price and the level of service offered?

7. Test the System

Now test the controls in action. Choose a number of activities or transactions at random, and trace back all the steps that took place. Ask:

- Are there any procedures or rules in place for this transaction?
- Did people follow the procedures?

This will show the degree of compliance with the existing rules and procedures.

8. Select Areas for Further Investigation

From random tests the auditor may find areas of concern that need thorough investigation. The audit should now examine these areas in depth, for example, every transaction of a particular type will be examined over a number of months to see whether the random, problematical sample was an exception or a recurring problem.

9. Consider Whether You Are Getting Value for Money

Whatever the overall audit objectives, it is always an internal auditor's job to test whether the organization is receiving value for money. Look at these kinds of questions:

- Has the market been tested by getting quotes and tenders for goods and services?
- Are the systems working in the most efficient way?

10. Draft a Report

Draft a report of all findings with a set of recommendations. Discuss it with everyone who participated in the audit to make sure that the auditor hasn't misinterpreted any information.

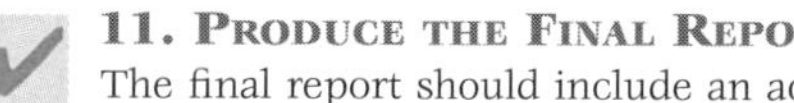

11. Produce the Final Report

The final report should include an action plan to tackle the areas requiring strengthening. Use the knowledge of the auditor as a guide to best practice, and make sure the recommendations are practicable. The report should include a timetable and an agreed time to meet again to monitor progress.

12. Take Action

Act on the findings to improve problem areas, and monitor how effective the remedial actions are. This may well involve changing written instructions, manuals, or procedures, alerting staff to the changes, and seeing that adequate training is given to staff in those areas.

DOS AND DON'TS

For Internal Audit

DO

- Brief staff on the benefits of internal audit.
- Concentrate on the high-risk elements identified.
- Set an action plan that is realistic.
- Keep staff informed of the findings of the audit and of any positive action that has been taken as a result of it.
- Monitor progress toward accomplishing the action plan.

DON'T

- Don't rely on internal audit as a day-to-day management control mechanism.
- Don't expect internal audit to pick up all the potential weak links in your systems.

THOUGHT STARTERS

- Have you defined the nature and scope of the internal audit?
- Have you established what the system is trying to achieve?
- Have you identified the key controls?
- Are your staff fully informed of what is happening and the actions you are going to take?

For More Information

Book:

Campbell, Lee A., ed. *Standards for the Professional Practice of Internal Auditing*. Altamonte Springs, FL: Institute of Internal Auditors, 2001.

Web Site:

The Institute of Internal Auditors: **www.theiia.org**

MAKING RATIONAL DECISIONS

This checklist provides an outline framework for making rational decisions. It is therefore relevant to all managers.

DEFINITION

A decision involves a choice between a set of alternatives. The key to the process of making rational decisions is generating the alternatives and then knowing how to select, or eliminate, them from the list. This method for making rational decisions was first proposed by Kepner and Tregoe in *The New Rational Manager*.

ADVANTAGES

The rational model:

- provides evidence and support for how the decision was made;
- works particularly well in complex or fuzzy situations;
- is thorough and systematic;
- relies on effective information gathering rather than preconceived ideas;
- provides an effective technique for determining a route through the mist and securing commitment to it.

DISADVANTAGES

Rational decision making:

- can be very time-consuming and resource-intensive, especially in fast-moving situations;
- relies heavily on information that may prove difficult to gather;
- requires fairly strict adherence if the outcome is to be a rational decision;
- highlights the possibility that a rational decision may not be the right one!

ACTION CHECKLIST

1. DEFINE THE DECISION TO BE MADE

Be clear on the exact decision that needs to be made. This first step helps to clarify thinking, aids communication, and provides a record for the future. It may lead to the discovery that previous assumptions have muddied the water.

Example—Decision: Which computer should I buy?

2. ESTABLISH THE OBJECTIVES

The objectives are the outcomes that you desire from the decision and should be measurable wherever possible. It is not necessary to worry at this stage if there are apparent incompatibilities between some objectives. This stage involves consultation, information searching, and checking.

Your objectives for a computer may be that it should be able to communicate with other computers, run CD-ROMs, handle word processing, spreadsheets, and graphics, and not run out of hard-disk space too quickly, and that it be affordable.

Objectives—The computer needs to have a modem, an expandable memory slot, CD-ROM drive, large hard disk, and standard software packages, and it has to stay within budget.

3. CLASSIFY THE OBJECTIVES

Differentiate between the essential requirements (the "musts") and the desirable (the "wants"). The fundamental difference between musts and wants is that if one of the decision alternatives does not meet a must, that option should be rejected. Failure to meet a want does not mean automatic rejection. The process for considering wants is dealt with in point 5.

Musts—maximum price, minimum processor capability, minimum hard disk capacity.

Wants—modem, CD-ROM drive, extra memory slot, software packages.

4. DEFINE THE MUSTS

To be a valid must, an objective should have a quantitative measure or an objective standard. Assign quantitative measures to the musts.

Musts—maximum price $2,200, minimum 600 MHz processor, minimum 10 gigabyte hard disk.

This means that if an option presented for purchase costs more than $2,200 or has a processor slower than 600 MHz or a hard disk smaller than 10 gigabytes, it should be rejected.

5. DEFINE THE WANTS

Examine the wants for importance and give a numerical weighting out of 10 (10 for the most important, less than 10 for those less important). For example, if the software packages are the most important feature after the musts, give software a 10. If an option includes spreadsheet, database, graphics, and word processing software, it may well score 10 out of 10; if one of these features is missing, it might score only 8. An extremely fast modem with built-in error correction may have a weight of 10; an option with a modem not so fast or sophisticated may score only 6.

The wants are not make-or-break points in the decision process like the musts. However, the more clearly defined they are, the better your decision will be.

Fast modem	10
Complete software package	10
Integral CD-ROM	9
Extra memory slots	8

6. GENERATE THE ALTERNATIVES

With information requirements established, you can research your alternatives. In the computer example, sources may include computer dealers, the trade press, and informed colleagues.

7. APPLY THE ALTERNATIVES TO YOUR REQUIREMENTS

The information—or options obtained—should be recorded for each alternative against each must objective.

"Nothing is so devastating as indecision and nothing is so futile." (Bertrand Russell)

8. Test the Alternatives against the Musts

Reject the options that do not meet the musts. Do any of the alternatives not meet the must criteria on price, processor, or hard-disk size? If negative, is it logical to reject that alternative?

If you do not wish to reject an alternative that has failed on musts or something else prevents your rejecting it, either the musts are proving unsatisfactory or you are not adhering to the rational process. In either case, restart at step 3.

9. Score the Remaining Alternatives against the Wants

Score the remaining options against each of the wants in turn. The alternative that meets the want best should be scored highest and others allocated proportionate scores. For example:

Slower modem	6
2 out of 4 software elements missing	5
No CD-ROM drive	0
2 extra memory slots	8

10. Multiply the Weights by the Scores

Weights should be multiplied by scores and the results added for each alternative. For example, from steps 5 and 9 above:

Slower modem	10 x 6 = 60
2 out of 4 software elements missing	10 x 5 = 50
No CD-ROM drive	9 x 0 = 0
2 extra memory slots	8 x 8 = 64
	Total = 174

11. Come to a Provisional Decision

The totals will enable you to come to a provisional decision. Comparing the totals of various alternatives usually allows you to make statements such as:

Alternative A is clearly the best.

Alternatives D and E are not worth considering.

There is little to choose between alternatives B and C.

12. Make a Final Decision

The analysis will not provide an automatic decision unless only one alternative meets all the musts. Where several alternatives have similar totals, it is particularly important to reexamine scores and weights and the evidence on which they have been based. The analysis will provide a sound framework for clear examination. It is not always necessary to use the entire process described above, especially for simple binary (yes/no) decisions. However, each element in the process can be used separately to improve the efficiency of a decision.

DOS AND DON'TS

For Making Rational Decisions

DO

- Make sure that your objectives will meet your needs.
- Take time in working out musts; make them measurable.
- Get sufficient information to be able to choose from a number of alternatives.
- Remain objective.
- Reexamine the process after the provisional decision to tighten or modify aspects.

DON'T

- Don't jump too quickly to an apparently obvious decision.
- Don't let personal preferences cloud the process.
- Don't let a preconceived conclusion influence the process.
- Don't cut corners, especially if the decision has far-reaching implications.
- Don't take the provisional decision as final.
- Don't use this approach for solving problems!

THOUGHT STARTERS

- Do you have a difficult or fuzzy decision to make?
- Do you need to impose order on a mass of data?
- Do you need to show evidence and method for how you made the decision?
- When you last bought a car, how did you come to your decision?

For More Information

Books:

Barker, Alan. *How to Be a Better Decision Maker.* Milford, CT: Kogan Page, 1996.

Kepner, Charles H., and Benjamin B. Tregoe. *The New Rational Manager*. Princeton, NJ: Princeton Research Press, 1997.

See also:

✔ **Solving Problems (pp. 408–09)**
✔ **Setting Objectives (pp. 480–81)**

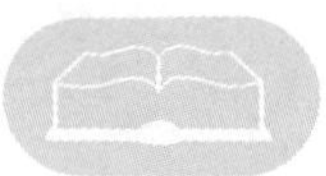

OPEN SYSTEMS THINKING

CHECKLIST

This checklist introduces an outline approach to open systems thinking; it does not replace the need for further reading or expert consultation. It is for managers who find that traditional problem-solving techniques are failing to deliver solutions in their organizations or who would simply like to know more about this rather vague term. The approach to open systems thinking presented here is just one way in which it may be used—by definition, open systems thinking should not follow a rigid series of tasks.

Systems thinking has always been valued in some disciplines like biology and information technology, but its scientific connections have tended to make it unattractive to practicing managers. However, systems thinking pervades many of the most radical approaches to modern management, for example, total quality management, environmental management, and the learning organization.

Three main reasons may explain why a traditional, mechanistic view of systems fails to work:

- system complexity;
- uncertainty in the environment—not knowing what the future may bring leads to difficulty in accurate forecasting and accounting for risk;
- conflict in human values—many perfect technical solutions have failed because their sponsors have failed to gain public acceptance.

Through open systems thinking, managers can support the strategic management of their organizations by taking advantage of the concepts, tools, and techniques available to systems analysts or management consultants who specialize in this area.

DEFINITION

In *The Fifth Discipline* (1994), Peter Senge describes systems thinking as:

"a way of thinking about, and a language for describing and understanding, the forces and interrelationships that shape the behavior of systems."

This checklist distinguishes between the wider approach adopted by Senge and some of the new breed of systems analysts (known as open) and the more traditional techniques used by engineers, information technologists, and systems analysts in the past (where the system in question is finite, or closed, and involves the use of traditional problem-solving techniques).

Traditional approaches are concerned with identifying the "correct" means to an end, defined at the start and taken as fixed. The pace of change, however, has demonstrated that while such an oversimplified view of life might work for engineering or scientific problems, it is totally inadequate for complex systems like organizations. Open systems thinking concentrates on describing the behavior of the system and associated problems before the possibilities for improving the behavior of the system and solving these problems are explored. Open systems thinking is also a learning approach compatible with modern quality philosophies.

ADVANTAGES

Open systems thinking:

- can encourage creative thinking and generate new ways of doing things;
- focuses on reality rather than the idealized mental maps people have of systems and processes;
- is probably the only way to deal with "wicked" problems;
- takes a longer-term, strategic view of organizations, not just a technical one;
- fits well with management practices such as teamwork and continuous improvement.

DISADVANTAGES

Open systems thinking:

- is intellectually challenging and can involve a great deal of time and effort;
- may produce more questions than answers in the early stages and can therefore be disconcerting;
- is not appropriate for situations where the structured problem-solving approach is guaranteed to produce results or where the culture is heavily technocratic;
- usually requires like-minded people to work together as a team.

ACTION CHECKLIST

✔ 1. FIND OUT ABOUT THE PROBLEM

Most managers rush into explanations for problems. Open systems thinking leaves explanations until the end. At this stage you should avoid the desire to find cause-and-effect relationships and simply collect the facts. Try to observe all the symptoms in a situation as a dispassionate observer in as wide an arena as possible.

✔ 2. DEFINE THE SYSTEM

- Describe the events that are relevant to the situation. Look at all the symptoms or changes that have occurred in this period, for example, accidents or crises, problems with customers or suppliers, or even apparently unrelated events. Pay attention to the department and organization as a whole.
- Pick out the main trends or patterns. Try to identify the most important variables and attempt to understand what is going on. Are there general trends like increasing levels of customer complaints, loss of customers, a slowing down of market penetration, or increased costs? Mapping changes on time lines will often reveal surprising relationships between key variables and events in time.
- Map the underlying systems or structures. This is a key stage in building effective models of systems. Its aim is to identify the relationships or interdependency between components, and in particular to focus on

"The first step toward change is acceptance. Once you accept yourself, you open the door to change."

(Stephen Covey)

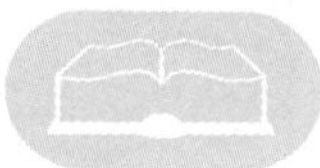

the feedback loops that control the behavior of the system.

The behavior of all systems, whether living or not, is controlled by feedback loops. Feedback loops tend either to resist change and maintain equilibria (negative feedback loops) or amplify the impact of change (positive or reinforcing loops). Although at this stage you're beginning to look for cause-and-effect relationships, it is important not to make up your mind yet, but to leave ample room for other possibilities. Example: A rise in customer complaints might be linked to a vicious circle in which increased pressure on sales staff may cause them to make unrealistic promises, thereby raising customer expectations that cannot be met.

3. Build Models from Your Definitions

Models are an important part of our everyday lives. We adjust our behavior according to a range of assumptions (models) about the world around us. If our world is not behaving according to plan, we can be sure of one thing—our current models are not appropriate.

Finding the right model to describe complex situations or systems is a real art form. Although technically trained managers often place a lot of emphasis on mathematical or computer-generated models to explain the performance of companies, sooner or later they're usually left scratching their heads when the model fails them in real life. On the other hand, mental models, or even metaphors, can often achieve remarkable results in conveying to others the essence of particular situations.

4. Compare the Models with the Real World

Having generated a model of the system in question, you need to check it out. Go back to the stakeholders and confirm that the model works and takes all the factors into consideration. At this stage you may find someone throws a monkey wrench into the works and forces you to change the model.

DOS AND DON'TS

For Open Systems Thinking

DO

- Avoid quick fixes.
- Test and retest your explanations for system behaviour throughout the process.
- Try to gain ownership and acceptance for your model before you look for solutions.

DON'T

- Don't place too much trust on the ability of your explanation to account for the behaviour of your organization.
- Don't take the rejection of your interpretation of events as personal criticism.
- Don't underestimate the importance of human beings in the system you're modelling.

5. Identify Possible Actions

It is only at this stage that you should identify possible actions; in systems terms these are not solutions, but ways of improving the behavior of the system.

Example: Customer complaints may be caused by imbalances in the relationship between the production, customer service, and sales departments. The solution may require shifts in these relationships instead of immediate short-term measures.

6. Implement the Action

In the true spirit of learning organizations, managers should spend a lot of time watching the effects of introduced change to see whether they learn any more about the effectiveness of their model.

7. Start the Cycle Again

Treating this approach to problem solving as cyclical is entirely consistent with the philosophy of continuous improvement.

Glossary of Terms

Structured systems analysis the use of formal problem-solving techniques to describe systems. Analysts tend to use a top-down approach to create their solutions. This approach is particularly associated with computer programming.

System a collection of units that interact to form a single operational unit.

Systems analysis the application of special techniques to study systems.

THOUGHT STARTERS

- If you were to draw up an organization chart based on the real power relationships within your enterprise, how would it differ from the official one?
- Many organizations consist of systems within systems (recursion). How many levels are there in your organization?
- Delayering attempts to simplify systems, but often fails to reestablish the right sort of feedback loops in the system to promote effective relationships between the units.

For More Information

Books:

Checkland, Peter B. *Soft Systems Methodology in Action.* Rev. 2nd ed. New York: John Wiley, 1999.

Gillan, Robert. *An Introduction to Systems Thinking and Models.* Waterlooville: Ethree Publishing, 1999.

Senge, Peter M. *The Fifth Discipline: The Art and Practice of the Learning Organization.* New York: Currency/Doubleday, 1994.

"The aim of science is not to open the door to infinite wisdom, but to set a limit to infinite error."

(Bertolt Brecht)

 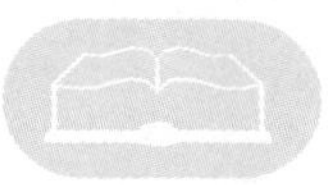    

Planning the Replacement of Software Systems

CHECKLIST

This checklist is a starting point for anyone who has to choose a new software package to replace an outdated or inadequate system.

Among numerous reasons for changing software packages are the need for increased flexibility, integration with other systems, greater employee productivity, and improved customer service. Costing should cater for data conversion, customization, installation, training, and the license agreement as well as the package itself. Although you may wish to form a small working party, you should also consult staff throughout the selection process, including those who will have to use the system and senior staff with line and budget responsibilities.

Action Checklist

1. Establish Objectives

It is important to have a clear idea of priorities before contacting suppliers. Priorities may change as the project unfolds and learning proceeds, but it is vital to work toward them. A checklist of firm requirements should start to emerge from answering questions such as the following:

- How does your current package hinder customer service improvements and flexibility for future developments?
- How does your current package impede integration?
- Are other systems within the organization going to be upgraded or replaced?
- Who is going to use the package and how?
- What degree of independence from the supplier is required?
- What degree of customization is required compared with a standard off-the-shelf package?
- Must the package fit the existing hardware and operating system you have?
- What improvements would you like to see from your old package?

2. Identify Potential Suppliers

Sources of names may include:

- suggestions from contacts, especially those in similar organizations
- visits to trade shows
- attendance at seminars and courses
- directories and the trade and professional press
- consultants

3. Create a Short-list of Potential Packages

Keep the checklist of requirements at hand and look at a number of systems. Decide which of these would be worth considering in detail. Try to match the size and capability of the package with the size of your organization or department.

4. Send Out Invitations to Tender (ITT)

The ITT is a formal statement of your requirements sent to the suppliers on the short-list, inviting them to reply with a formal proposal. It sets out a timetable for making a final selection, which should include visits to other users of the systems and to the offices of the suppliers.

5. Select the Software

Study each package in detail to assure yourself that the claims of the supplier can be substantiated and to check that it can meet your specific functional needs. Other questions concerning the package in general, the supplier, support, and training also need to be addressed.

The Package

- How old is it? Does it offer all that the present system offers?
- Is it modular?
- Are all modules easy to use? Are all modules compatible?
- Is it capable of data exchange? Receiving? Downloading?
- Can it integrate with a word processing package? With other packages within the organization?
- How often is it upgraded?
- What are the future plans for the package?
- What operating systems does it run on?
- How is it updated? Real time? Batch?
- What is the backup system?
- How many concurrent users can it support?
- How many installations are there? In North America? In Europe? In Asia?
- Can you visit other user sites, particularly migrations?
- What problems have other users encountered? How quickly were they resolved? How do the users react to the supplier and to the package?
- What are the capital and startup costs?

Support

- How long has the supplier been operating?
- Is the supplier financially sound?
- Can the supplier support all modules?
- What is the annual cost of maintenance?
- Do customer support costs appear to be value for money?
- Does the supplier offer on-site, dial-up, or telephone support?
- How much support is given prior to migration?
- How much work is left to the customer?
- How is the help desk organized?

Training

- Does the supplier offer training as part of the fee?

"Today, gone is craft, replaced by career. Instead of workers on our feet, we've become sedentary professionals, entering data into computers." (Clifford Stoll)

- Is preconversion training available?
- Can you rent a machine to train on in advance?

Migration
- What is the size of the migration team?
- What are the skills of the supplier's migration staff?
- Is the conversion process tried and tested?
- How many data migrations has the supplier performed?
- Can you have a trial data conversion?
- Have you planned enough contingency time to allow for mistakes?

6. Examine the Contract Terms

Look carefully at the responsibilities and liabilities of the supplier and question any terms that may be open to misinterpretation. Include in the contract details of any modifications you want made to the package and specify any tests you want run before you accept it. Question the level of support and service detailed in the contract and check that the final costs cover all aspects of the purchase, including items like delivery and training.

DOS AND DON'TS

For Planning the Replacement of Software Systems

DO
- Set up a team of users and consult widely.
- Remember the importance of forward thinking.
- Check out undemonstrated or unsubstantiated claims of the supplier.
- Be wary of too much customization on your particular application.
- See the products of at least four or five suppliers before short-listing.
- Visit sites where the package is up and running.
- Build in adequate contingency time.

DON'T
- Don't focus too much on your current application.
- Don't let the supplier deter you from your objectives.
- Don't take what the supplier says for granted.
- Don't make assumptions about what is stated or not stated by the supplier.
- Don't skip apparently minor details.

7. Plan for Implementation

Once you have chosen a package, a further objective will be to minimize the disruption of services upon conversion to a new system. Ways to do this include:
- running trial data conversions;
- planning for a period of parallel running;
- getting training from the supplier for all staff or for the trainer;
- choosing the timing carefully, for example, by avoiding peak vacation periods;
- managing modifications to the package.

8. Manage the "People" Side

From the start to the finish of the project, closely involve staff who will be using the system.
- Who is monitoring the views, reactions, and progress of staff?
- Who is checking that current and developing operational needs are being satisfied?
- Who is coordinating the emerging—as opposed to prescribed—training requirements?

THOUGHT STARTERS
- How old is your current package?
- How often is it upgraded?
- How much customization does your current package include?
- How long is it since you took a good look at alternative packages?
- How good is your current support?

For More Information

Books:

Collins, Tony, and David L. Bicknell. *Crash: Ten Easy Ways to Avoid a Computer Disaster*. New York: Simon & Schuster, 1999.
McConnell, Steve C. *Software Project Survival Guide*. Redmond, WA: Microsoft Press, 1997.

"A modern computer hovers between the obsolescent and the non-existent." (Sydney Brenner)

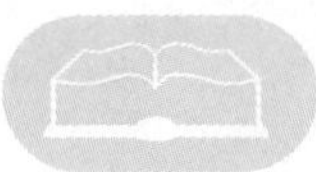

SIX SIGMA

CHECKLIST

This checklist introduces the Six Sigma quality technique and presents action points for its implementation.

Companies are increasingly adopting Six Sigma in a bid to improve the quality of their processes and products, and thus achieve competitive advantage. It has been estimated that poor quality, resulting in defects and wastage, can account for 20–40% of sales revenue. Six Sigma offers a structured and disciplined method for reducing that figure significantly: in fact, in a perfect Six Sigma state, a company would reduce it to only 10%. While many companies dismiss a zero defects state as unattainable, Six Sigma offers the potential to get very close.

DEFINITION

Six Sigma is both a technique and a philosophy based on the desire to eliminate waste and improve performance as far as is technically possible. At its heart is a statistical method that involves drawing up an optimum specification for each of the processes within the organization, then using statistical analysis to reduce defects in the processes, products, and services to almost zero. This is accompanied by an organization culture that focuses on creating value for the customer and eliminating any processes that do not make a contribution to this final goal.

Six Sigma is a registered trademark of Motorola, Inc., which implemented the technique successfully in the 1980s. It is based on the statistical tools and techniques of quality management developed by Joseph Juran.

ADVANTAGES

Implementing Six Sigma can mean that:

- quality, performance, productivity, and competitive advantage are improved;
- costs are greatly reduced;
- wastage and environmental impact are minimized;
- employees become motivated;
- customer satisfaction and retention is increased;
- improvements are sustained over time;
- visible performance goals are created;
- hard data is analyzed and quantifiable evidence of improvements provided.

DISADVANTAGES

- Claims of its potential are so great that it may be met with skepticism as unrealistic.
- It may be hard for employees to initially understand the technique.
- An investment in specialist high-level training will be required.
- It may require a culture change within the organization.
- It is a radical long-term project requiring deep commitment.
- It requires the collection and interpretation of data that may be difficult and time consuming.

ACTION CHECKLIST

1. UNDERSTAND SIX SIGMA

Before any organization can contemplate introducing Six Sigma, its managers need to understand exactly what it is. Sigma is the Greek letter used in mathematics to denote standard deviation, or the amount a process varies from the mean. As the level of sigmas rises, the level of variation decreases. A Three Sigma organization achieves 66,807 defects per million, whereas a true Six Sigma organization achieves just 3.4 defects per million. It is important to realize that perfect Six Sigma may not be achieved, but that even a rise from one sigma level to the next will produce significant benefits.

The Six Sigma technique hinges on a continuous reduction of process and product variation that results in defects. This is achieved by first of all defining and measuring variation in each process, and then discovering its causes. This enables the development of operational means to control and reduce the level of variation. Tools used in this stage include statistical process control, computer simulation, short cycle manufacturing, supplier qualification, and others.

Six Sigma involves not only reducing existing variation, but also avoiding any future variations that might develop. With this in mind, designers need to "design for producibility," making all new products and processes as little subject to variance as possible. This can be achieved by such methods as "poka-yoke," which aims to design products with minimum opportunity for error. In addition, any potential problems for the organization should be assessed and guarded against. Techniques such as total preventive maintenance and risk assessments are used for this. Before proceeding, the concept of Six Sigma and the goals of the initiative must be defined and communicated, both on a strategic and an operational level.

2. FOCUS ON ORGANIZATION CULTURE AND PREPARE FOR CHANGE MANAGEMENT

Six Sigma will be a major change initiative, so it is important that employee resistance is overcome and that the culture of the organization is supportive of radical change. Six Sigma is implemented through project teams, so teamworking will be a key to its success. A pervasive culture of creative thinking and innovation will also aid the process, since many stumbling blocks may have to be overcome.

3. DECIDE ON THE EXTENT OF IMPLEMENTATION

Although full Six Sigma is organization-wide, there are increasing numbers of companies implementing it in a limited way. Consider whether you might want to focus on manufacturing or engineering processes, or maybe on strategic projects critical to the organization.

4. Select and Train Key Personnel

Teams need to be formed with the brief of implementing Six Sigma in different areas. Key team members will need to be trained in leadership skills. Training traditionally involves three stages.

- Green belt—participants earn the status of green belt by completing a short course that introduces the Six Sigma methodology.
- Black belt—some green belts, usually of managerial status, proceed to complete a project exercise using the knowledge they have gained. Black belts will hold responsibility for leading and developing the teams, advising management, and teaching Six Sigma techniques to team members.
- Master black belt—a select few will need further training that will make them the organization's Six Sigma experts, leading the whole initiative, integrating it into the organization's strategic plans, and teaching the techniques to others.

Some companies use different terminology for these levels of training, and it is important to use names that create the right impression in your organization.

5. Bring the Six Sigma Teams into Action

Once personnel receive training, the teams need to begin to identify processes within the organization. Each process is earmarked as a Six Sigma project. The statistical techniques are applied to each project according to a framework. This usually consists of these key phases: definition of the problem; measurement; analysis; improvements; and control.

In the first phase the team focuses on identifying processes that customers perceive as value creating. They then need to work out what a "perfect" process would be. For example, a delivery company might aim to deliver all parcels by noon on the day after dispatch.

The next step is to measure how the process is performing in reality. The common measurement used is "defects per unit," which can be applied to virtually any product or process in any area of the company. For example, a unit might be a line of computer code, a sales invoice, a piece of raw material, a finished product, a delivery, or a record in a database. In the above example, a unit is a parcel delivered on schedule, and a defect occurs when the parcel fails to be delivered on time. In a service environment, as opposed to manufacturing, units and defects may be harder to measure. Tasks should be broken down and ways of quantitatively measuring defects should be created. Use data mining techniques and information technology to make this easier.

This is followed by an analysis that identifies the gap between current performance and the desired goal using statistical techniques. Reasons for this gap must be assessed, perhaps using root cause analysis, and some creativity may be involved in this phase.

6. Integrate Six Sigma into the Organization Infrastructure

If Six Sigma is a company-wide initiative, then it will need to be linked into existing company structures. Consider linking it to pay and rewards, departmental budgets, job descriptions, and documentation such as ISO 9001. Modify policies and procedures to reflect the improvements made.

7. Monitor and Evaluate Success

Ensure that projects are monitored and that failures are investigated while successes are publicized. Six Sigma is an ongoing, long-term initiative, so constant assessment is vital to make sure that it is heading in the right direction. Ascertain not only what cost savings have been made but also whether employee job satisfaction and customer satisfaction have improved. Remember to periodically reassess processes that have already been analyzed, to see if defects are creeping in again because of changed circumstances.

THOUGHT STARTERS

- Do you know what proportion of your costs goes on waste that produces no value to your customers?
- Are you aware of consistent errors with a piece of equipment or standard of customer service?
- What are the quality levels of your competitors, and why are they higher or lower than yours?

DOS AND DON'TS

For Six Sigma

DO

- Secure top management commitment.
- Keep things as simple as possible to make understanding clear and implementation easier.
- Make Six Sigma implementation the responsibility of everyone in the organization, not just black belts.

DON'T

- Don't let the seemingly mathematical nature of Six Sigma deter you, as it can be easily learned, and computer software can perform the calculations.
- Don't forget to teach the soft skills of handling meetings, teamworking, and facilitation that are needed for the statistical analysis to be conducted efficiently.

For More Information

Books:

Breyfogle, Forrest W., III, James M. Cupello, and Becki Meadows. *Managing Six Sigma*. New York: John Wiley, 2001.

Eckes, George. *The Six Sigma Revolution*. New York: John Wiley, 2001.

Pande, Peter S., Robert P. Neuman, and Roland R. Cavanagh. *The Six Sigma Way*. New York: McGraw-Hill, 2000.

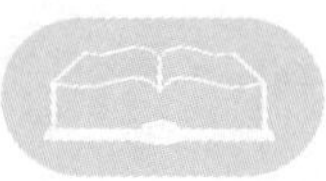

SHAREHOLDER VALUE ANALYSIS (SVA)

CHECKLIST

Shareholder value analysis (SVA) is one of a number of methods being explored as substitutes for traditional business measurements. SVA calculates the value of a company by looking at the returns it gives to stockholders and is based on the view that the objective of company directors is to maximize the wealth of the company's stockholders. This checklist introduces the financial calculations involved in carrying out SVA and advises on its implementation.

DEFINITION

Shareholder value analysis, or SVA, is a method of financial analysis that measures shareholder value by estimating the total net value of a company based on its present and future cash flows and dividing this figure by the value of its shares. The resulting figure indicates the company's value to stockholders. The fundamental principle underlying concepts of shareholder value is that a company adds value for its stockholders only when equity returns exceed equity costs. Once the amount of value has been calculated, targets for improvement can be set and shareholder value can be used as a measure for managing performance.

ADVANTAGES

Shareholder Value Analysis:

- takes a long-term financial view on which to base strategic decisions;
- offers a universal approach that is not subject to differences in companies' accounting policies. It is therefore applicable internationally and across sectors;
- forces the organization to focus on the future and its customers, particularly the value of future cash flows.

Other, more traditional, measures are cost-based, bearing little relation to the economic income generated during a period.

DISADVANTAGES

- Accurately estimating future cash flows, a key component of SVA, can be extremely difficult. Inaccurate projections can lead to strategic decisions being based on incorrect or misleading figures.
- Developing and implementing SVA can be a long and complex process.
- Communicating the SVA approach to managers can be difficult.
- Management of shareholder value requires more complete information than traditional measures.

ACTION CHECKLIST

1. UNDERSTAND AND CALCULATE THE COMPANY'S SHAREHOLDER VALUE

Before adopting shareholder value as a significant financial objective, you need to understand its implications and the best approach for your business. It can be helpful to plan the approach first with professional advisers such as accountants or consultants who specialize in this area.

A company's value to stockholders is calculated by subtracting the market value of any debts owed to the company from the total value of the company.

Total business value has three main components:

- the present value of future cash flows during the planned period;
- the residual value of future cash flows from a period beyond the planned period;
- the weighted average cost of capital.

Total business value is calculated by adding present value of future cash flows to residual value of future cash flows and dividing it by the weighted average cost of capital. If the result of this equation is greater than one, then the company is worth more than the invested capital and added value is being created.

- Future cash flows

Future cash flows are affected by growth, returns, and risk. According to Alfred Rappaport in *Creating Shareholder Value*, these factors can be explained by seven key value drivers that must be managed in order to maximize shareholder value: sales growth rate, operating profit margin, income tax rate, working capital investment, fixed capital investment, cost of capital, and value growth duration.

- Residual value

The residual value—the price at which a fixed asset is expected to be sold at the end of its useful life—is an important figure that represents cash flows arising after the normal planning period. It has been estimated that as much as two-thirds of the value of a business can be attributed to cash flows arising after the normal planning period (usually 5 to 10 years). Viewed another way, only one-third of the value of a business results from cash flows arising during the normal planning period.

- Weighted average cost of capital (WACC)

The WACC is the cost of equity added to the cost of debt. It represents the return a company needs to earn in order to justify the financial resources it uses; the WACC therefore expresses the opportunity cost of the assets in use. The WACC is entirely market-driven—if the assets cannot earn the required return, investors will withdraw their funds from the business.

2. GAIN TOP MANAGEMENT COMMITMENT

Underlying SVA is the belief that the creation and maximization of shareholder value is the most important measure by which to assess business performance. Top managers need to commit to this objective for the SVA approach to take root. They should also accept that traditional measures and approaches may fall short of achieving this objective.

3. IDENTIFY THE COMPANY'S KEY VALUE DRIVERS AND SET TARGETS

Unlocking shareholder value is about maximizing cash flows. In order to achieve this you need to identify the key value drivers of the business (the seven value drivers

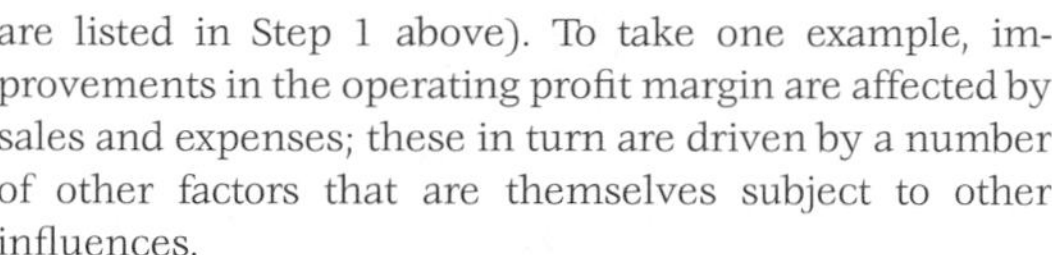

are listed in Step 1 above). To take one example, improvements in the operating profit margin are affected by sales and expenses; these in turn are driven by a number of other factors that are themselves subject to other influences.

This analysis of value drivers links financial and operational objectives and provides a framework for:

- setting performance targets;
- assigning responsibility to individual managers;
- reviewing the company's financial performance (and benchmarking against competitors);
- developing strategic plans.

Identifying the key factors influencing each value driver is invariably a process of trial and error. However, this process is fundamental to managing, controlling, and making improvements in the business, leading to improved cash flows.

4. Communicate the Approach and Train Staff

Managers need to understand the broad concept of creating shareholder value, particularly when appraising potential projects, but the technicalities of SVA are unlikely to be of concern to them. Managers should instead understand the importance of identifying, controlling, and improving the performance of the value drivers and the key factors that influence them.

Adopting SVA and setting new targets will probably challenge managers' ingrained habits and approaches and consequently may meet with resistance. Managers will be called on to reevaluate previous approaches and perhaps discard them in favor of new targets.

Unlocking shareholder value is essentially a change process, and it requires line managers (invariably the people making the key operational decisions) to be fully trained.

It is also important when implementing an SVA approach to achieve early, high-profile successes. As with any change process, early successes demonstrate the value of the new approach, highlighting its benefits and winning over skeptics.

5. Change the Company's Information Systems to Monitor and Measure Progress

The company's financial reporting systems and information systems in general usually need to be revised when SVA is implemented. Conventional reporting systems are unlikely to provide all the information required or to provide it in the most effective format. The implementation of SVA requires managers to regularly measure and monitor information about the company's key value drivers and targets.

6. Change Managers' Financial Incentive Packages

Review your incentive packages for managers and revise them to reward performance that adds shareholder value. Incentives for senior managers should reflect the need to increase shareholder value over realistic time periods instead of focusing simply on short-term profit growth or earnings per share.

7. Monitor and Review Progress

Creating sustained value requires continuous monitoring and redefinition of targets as circumstances change. Appraisals, performance reviews, management meetings, and key decisions should all focus on progress so far achieved and actions required to continue building shareholder value. Without consistent emphasis on value creation, managers may continue to focus on targets that have become irrelevant or are actually harmful to the long-term value of the business.

For Shareholder Value Analysis (SVA)

DO

- Take time to understand what will increase shareholder value in your company—what the value drivers are and what factors influence them.
- Review internal systems and make sure that they adequately and routinely provide the information you need to measure shareholder value.

DON'T

- Don't be impatient—unlocking shareholder value is likely to take time. Some estimates claim two years is the norm.
- Don't cut corners—adopting SVA takes time, energy, and commitment and may require a complete overhaul of the way the business is run.
- Don't be half-hearted or hesitant—make sure you know what improvements you are looking for and what needs to be done to achieve them, then take action.

THOUGHT STARTERS

- Have you set realistic targets for increasing SVA?
- Have you explained the new approach to the company's stockholders?
- Have you examined your company's strategy, procedures, and processes to make sure that nothing will hinder the adoption of SVA?

For More Information

Books:

Bachman, John E., Andrew Black, and Philip Wright. *In Search of Shareholder Value: Managing the Drivers of Performance*. 2nd ed. Upper Saddle River, NJ: Financial Times Prentice Hall, 2000.

Rappaport, Alfred. *Creating Shareholder Value: A Guide for Managers and Investors*. 2nd ed. New York: Free Press, 1997.

Web Site:

Association of Chartered Accountants in the U.S.: **www.acaus.org**

"MONEY n. A blessing that is of no advantage to us excepting when we part with it." (Ambrose Bierce)

ACTIONLISTS

ACTIONLISTS

The Actionlists, written by a team of international specialists, provide essential time-saving instructions for tackling tasks and solving problems. They address key management tasks in detail, and include in-depth coverage of e-business, marketing, accounting and finance, and personal development.

Actionlists include an **FAQ section**, as well as helpful suggestions on how to avoid **common mistakes**.

If you don't find the precise answer you are looking for, each list identifies a number of additional resources. Alternatively, you can turn to the **Business Information Sources** section to find a comprehensive listing of the best management materials from around the world.

CONTENTS

E-COMMERCE

MARKETING

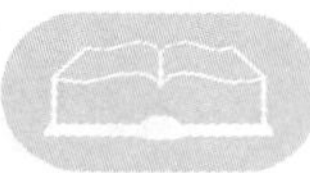

Personal Development

Accounting and Finance

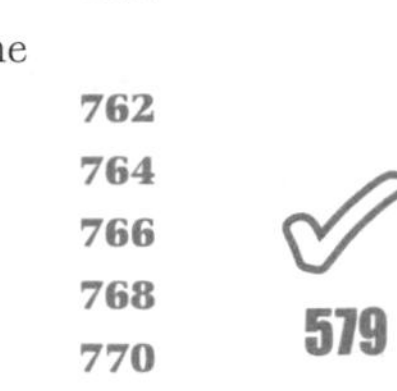

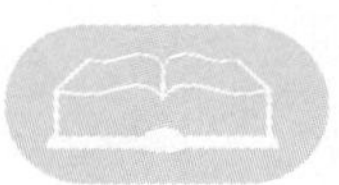

The Key Issues of Implementing an E-commerce Strategy

Getting Started

An effective e-commerce strategy combines many separate elements. E-commerce means selling online with content, and this requires a sophisticated content management system. E-commerce purchase, payment, and support systems are required, perhaps with customer relationship management and localization. Proper marketing will be needed for success. Underpinning all this will be a requirement for professional Web site development and management. In implementing e-commerce, keep the following in mind:

- e-commerce is not suitable for every product and service;
- the best e-commerce strategy is a clicks-and-mortar approach, combining offline retail resources with online capabilities;
- e-commerce is complex and expensive to get right: don't underestimate the difficulty involved in designing and managing an efficient e-commerce Web site.

FAQs

What products are best suited to e-commerce?

- Digital products such as software and information.
- Products with a high value relative to their cost of fulfillment.
- Products requiring a lot of information, such as books, music, travel products, and banking.
- Products that do not need to be handled or tried on.
- Products that are difficult to find locally.

How difficult is it to establish an e-commerce Web site?

Quite difficult, depending on the scope of what you want to do. You must be able to manage stock, fulfillment, payment, and security. You must be able to integrate your e-commerce Web site efficiently with your offline business. E-commerce software has improved and become more streamlined, but it is still neither cheap nor simple to get everything running smoothly.

If you set up an e-commerce Web site, will you suddenly be selling to a global marketplace?

No. Selling to a foreign marketplace involves more than setting up an e-commerce Web site.

Making It Happen

Make Sure You Have a Market

Who is going to buy your products online? The best place to start is your current customer base. Will going online make life easier for them? Are you going to save them time and money by allowing them to purchase online? You probably have a basic Web site already; are you getting requests for online buying from potential customers? It is never truly possible to judge in advance whether a market exists, but there should be at least some indications of a demand for an online presence.

Use a Clicks-and-mortar Strategy If Possible

The clicks-and-mortar approach is the most effective and economic. This combines offline resources, such as stores, brands, channels, with an online e-commerce presence. The other option—a pure play dot-com—is now rare. Consumers are looking for brands that they know and trust. They also like the fact that a business has a physical presence, a place where they can go if something goes wrong. Pure play dot-coms found that they had to spend a lot of money on marketing just to maintain awareness.

Integrate the Shopping Experience

Consumers look to the Web primarily for information; they may use the Web site initially to find out about the product, then buy by phone or in person. However, repeat purchasers more familiar with the Web are more likely to buy online. They will be able to do this more easily if their personal details and purchase history can be stored for use in subsequent purchases.

Plan How You Will Deal with Content, Pricing, Stock Management, Fulfillment, Payment, Returns, Support, and Security

These are the basics of any business, but there can be added complications online. You need to address the following:

- Content: This must be updated frequently.
- Pricing: If you are selling direct for the first time, you may have problems with your distributors and retailers, who will not want you to underprice them. If you are selling brands by other manufacturers there may be problems involved in selling in foreign marketplaces. Are you going to offer prices in a range of currencies? If so, which?
- Stock management: Are you going to use the same stock base to sell online and through your physical distribution channels? If so, you need an integrated stock management system.
- Fulfillment: Precise information on order status is essential. Each order should have a tracking number so that the customer can get information on the status of the order right up to the point of delivery. If you haven't sold by mail order before, you will have to plan for packaging and fulfillment. This can be a major cost, and needs careful management. If, for cost or other reasons, you decide not to fulfill to certain countries, you must make that very clear on the Web site.
- Payment: How will people pay? What credit cards will you accept? How will you manage fraud?

- Returns: What is your return policy? Studies indicate that returns can be a major cost for e-commerce.
- Support: How will you support the products you sell online? You must plan for a support section on your Web site to answer basic questions from customers. Will you also offer telephone and e-mail support?
- Security: Security will be a central issue in an e-commerce strategy. Fraud and hacking of computer systems are ever-growing problems.

Develop an Easy-to-use Purchase Process

An alarming number of consumers abandon their attempts to buy online. One of the reasons given is a badly designed purchase process. Your purchase process must be reliable and very easy to use; a good example is Amazon.com. It is a good idea to tell the consumer upfront how many steps there are in the purchase process, and to keep that information prominently displayed at the top of the Web page. An example of the purchase steps is as follows: "Shopping cart–Account–Shipping–Payment–Verify–Confirm."

Consider Localization Issues

If you want to sell seriously to foreign marketplaces, you will have to localize the Web site. Studies indicate that, without localization, sales will be minimal. More worryingly, returns are very high because of misunderstanding by people who are purchasing in a foreign language.

Consider Customer Relationship Management and Personalization

The Internet offers many opportunities for a better understanding of customers' behavior and for developing a closer relationship with them. Customer relationship management and personalization systems allow for the collection and application of comprehensive information to create a more customized environment for the consumer. While the potential of such systems is substantial, they are complex and difficult to implement, and, if not professionally managed, can lead to the abuse of consumer privacy.

Make Sure You Buy the Right Software

There is no need to do all the work internally, as there is now a wide range of quality software for e-commerce.

Make Sure You Have a Team in Place

An e-commerce Web site needs day-to-day maintenance. Technical problems must be fixed, new content must be published and old content removed, and the Web site must be constantly marketed.

If You Don't Market, They Won't Come

Opening up an e-commerce Web site is rather like setting up shop at the North Pole: nobody knows you are there. It is not enough just to register with search engines; you will need an aggressive marketing campaign to make your target market aware of what you have to offer. The ideal situation is a seamless integration with the marketing strategy of the offline business.

Common Mistakes

Thinking That It's Cheap to Set Up an E-commerce Web Site

It is not. Back-end infrastructure is expensive to set up and maintain. Without an existing business and brand, marketing costs will be very high.

Thinking That an E-commerce Web Site Has Failed Because It Didn't Deliver Direct Sales

Not necessarily: many businesses have found that their Web sites support the purchase process, but that consumers still like to complete the sale offline.

Thinking That E-commerce Is Just the Same As Ordinary Commerce

It is not, although it has many similarities with mail order. If you have never sold products by mail order before, e-commerce involves a steep learning curve.

A Poor-quality Purchase Process

A great many Web sites have poor-quality purchase processes. It is essential to test your purchase process thoroughly to make sure that it is reliable and easy to use.

Thinking That All You Have to Do Is Put Up a Product Catalog

E-commerce is selling with content, and you need a content-rich Web site that is constantly being updated if you want to make sales.

Not Dealing Professionally with Legal and Security Issues

Many consumers are wary of purchasing online because they feel they have better security in a physical store.

For More Information

Book:

Spector, Robert. *Anytime, Anywhere*. Cambridge, MA: Perseus, 2002.

Web Site:

OECD Electronic E-Commerce Resource, an extensive resource on worldwide e-commerce activity
www1.oecd.org/subject/e_commerce

See also:

☆ **Integrating Real and Virtual Strategies (pp. 143–44)**
☆ **New Yardsticks for Performance and Productivity in an E-world (pp. 285–86)**
✔ **How to Implement Effective Internet Security (pp. 602–03)**
✔ **How to Manage Payments Online (pp. 588–89)**
✔ **Understanding the Key Principles of Internet Marketing (pp. 622–23)**

How to Deliver Quality Online Customer Service and Support

Getting Started

Customer service is increasingly seen as a central concern for e-commerce. For many consumers it is a key differentiator between good and bad e-commerce Web sites. A wide range of online support options is now available to organizations, including e-mail, knowledge base systems, live chat, and phone-back. When designing an online support function, keep the following in mind:

- the first step in online customer support is a well-structured Web site with comprehensive information;
- organizations have a poor record in responding to e-mail queries from their Web sites; a lack of response damages your reputation;
- online support can cause a significant increase in queries, many of which are flippant or of little value. A strategy must be put in place to deal with these and sift out the important queries.

FAQs

Why offer customer support online?

The best-designed Web site in the world will never answer every question a consumer has. Studies in 2000 indicated that over half—and sometimes up to three quarters—of the people who started an online purchase did not complete it. Web sites that have added support facilities have found that the number of people completing transactions increases significantly.

When should you offer support online?

All Web sites should have at least some level of customer support. Cost is a central issue: the lower the margin on the product, the less support can be afforded.

Isn't online support expensive?

All support is expensive. The key is to target the support at the highest value customers. The ease of sending e-mails or clicking on a live chat increases the likelihood of bogus support requests. One way of dealing with this situation is to have a set of generic answers (to frequently asked questions) ready for general or vague queries.

Is online support more appropriate for some consumers than others?

It depends on the type of online support. Online support that is text-based, such as live chat and e-mail, is more appropriate for PC-literate consumers. Chat and e-mail are thus ideal for technology industry customers, who are frequent users of e-mail. New or infrequent computer users can often barely cope with learning to use the browser; asking them to use chat software might just confuse them. For such people, the option to have someone call them and talk them through the Web site can be very comforting.

Making It Happen

Ensure You Have Comprehensive, Well-organized Web Site Content

A Web site is often described as a library. Libraries have two key components: a selection of well-organized content and a support center where people can ask questions. Person-to-person support is expensive, and the Web site should seek to reduce unnecessary interaction by supplying content that will answer as many questions as possible.

It is widely recognized that quality Web sites can reduce the number of support calls an organization receives. While the entire Web site is there to answer questions, specific support functions include the following:

- Frequently Asked Questions (FAQs): a collection of the most frequently asked questions about a product or service. FAQs should be well written and concise. If there are a lot of them, they should be classified into logical groups, and perhaps provided with a search function.
- Comprehensive Help: a Help link should be prominent on every page. This should lead the person to a section containing information on all the support elements on the Web site. Where people are asked to carry out a complex task, such as using an advanced search function, or are carrying out a purchase process, context-sensitive help should be available: when they click on the Help link, they are brought to the specific page they need.
- Knowledge Based Systems: these approaches seek to take the FAQ model much further. The user can type in a question, rather than using keywords. The response may involve asking the person a series of questions in order to narrow down the area of interest. The Ask Jeeves Web site, www.ask.com, is an example of this approach.

E-mail-based Support

It is often sufficient to use e-mail as the main channel for support on a Web site. A response policy must be established, whereby e-mails are graded where appropriate, and a response time target is specified for each.

However, the ease of sending e-mails can often result in frivolous questions. Organizations receiving a high volume of e-mail and working on tight margins often make extensive use of auto-response. The auto-response e-mail, which is generated automatically, may contain an FAQ and links to support material on the Web site. More sophisticated auto-responders may connect to a knowledge base that will search for keywords in the e-mail and send back a response based on these keywords. It is advisable for these approaches to include a human-based option so that the enquirer can talk to someone if they need to.

Unfortunately, many organizations don't allocate

enough resources to e-mail response, and so messages are responded to late or not at all.

Live Chat

Also known as instant messaging, live chat allows a customer representative to chat with a Web site visitor in real time, using text. The benefits of live chat are:

- many people have only one phone line, so if they call support they will have to disconnect from the Internet: live chat means that they can receive text-based support without having to disconnect;
- support is sometimes complex and may take a long time; live chat can avoid the enquirer having to spend hours on the phone, and can solve the problem in a more logical manner;
- live chat can be an option for international customers who do not have access to a toll-free number;
- an experienced customer representative can handle several chat sessions at the same time.

Live chat can have drawbacks. Response times can be slow, depending on the connection, and novice computer users may not feel comfortable using it. In addition, the quality of the live chat support is dependent on the typing skills and knowledge of the support staff.

Call-back Support

With this option the Web site visitor is informed that if they enter their telephone number and details into a form someone will call them back. This option is expensive, and is most appropriate for high-value items. A related and popular option here is to offer the customer a free or low-cost telephone number that they can call.

Co-browsing and Page Pushing

Software is now available that allows the customer service representative to synchronize their browser with the person requesting support. Using live chat or the telephone, the rep can walk the person through a process, changing their Web page as they change their own. This is not appropriate for the sale of low-value items, but can be a valuable feature when complex processes and information have to be delivered.

The Importance of Graduating Customer Service

A fundamental objective of many e-commerce Web sites is to increase sales while reducing the need for person-to-person interaction, thus increasing profit. If there is too much customer interaction, especially with non-serious or low-value customers, the profit will be eaten away. For certain products, margins are so slim that person-to-person interaction must be kept to a minimum.

As a result, it is important that the customer service component of a Web site should be graduated. For example, a person seeking support should be guided to the FAQ section first; if they can't find an answer there, they should be offered the option of an e-mail, and finally the option of telephone support.

Outsourcing Customer Service

Customer service support functions such as live chat and e-mail support can now be outsourced to countries such as India and the Philippines, where well-educated English-speaking labor is available at low cost. While outsourcing support definitely reduces costs, it can have negative implications. The support staff may not have the in-depth knowledge required to answer complex questions.

Integration of Support Functions

When people are contacting the organization through a number of support channels, the support function can become dissipated. Planning is required to ensure that a single support knowledge base is used, and that all the technologies work in unison.

Training of Staff

Offering a range of support options requires a well-planned training approach and targeting of staff skills. Training will be required to raise skill levels.

Common Mistakes

Not Responding to E-mails

Surveys indicate that organizations have a poor record in responding to e-mail requests from their Web sites.

Too Many Queries

Online support makes it easier for people to communicate with the organization, and this can substantially increase the number of frivolous queries. Organizations are often not properly prepared to handle the increase in volume, and the important queries can be swamped.

Not Being Able to Answer the Question

A key problem with all customer service support is a lack of trained staff. When customers ask questions, they must be answered quickly and comprehensively; otherwise the whole purpose is defeated.

Lack of Proper Integration

Online support must integrate with the overall support structure. Adding numerous support options increases complexity, and this can lead to integration problems

For More Information

Web Sites:

Business2 E-business Customer Support Guide, links to articles, software and services relating to e-business customer support: **www.business2.com/webguide**

Customer Support Management, a magazine dedicated to customer support issues: **www.industryclick.com**

See also:

☆ **Managing the Challenge of e-Service (pp. 188–89)**

☆ **Marketing to the "Real-Time" Consumer (pp. 73–74)**

☆ **Overcoming the Difficulties of Managing a Virtual Organization (pp. 208–09)**

✔ **How to Establish an Enterprise Portal (p. 638)**

How to Implement a Customer Relationship Management Strategy

Getting Started

Customer relationship management (CRM) is about using people, processes and technology to develop long-term, profitable relationships with customers. The Internet is an important medium through which CRM services are delivered. CRM technology is generally best suited to organizations with a large customer base. CRM requires skilled staff to be able to exploit its features, in order to understand their customers better and deliver just the product or service that such customers require. CRM:

- is growing rapidly;
- has been over-hyped;
- is about a customer-centric view of the world;
- is about people as much as technology;
- is critical to successful e-commerce;
- is for medium and large organizations (smaller organizations should do CRM manually).

FAQs

What makes up a CRM system?

CRM generally includes some or all of the following: customer information systems; personalization systems; content management systems; call center automation; data warehousing; data mining; sales force automation; campaign management systems.

With the emergence of the Web we are seeing what is termed as e-CRM, where there is a strong customer self-service and personalization focus. Ideally, CRM and e-CRM should integrate seamlessly but, because they often use different technologies, this is not always easy to achieve.

Why is CRM so important to e-commerce?

The Internet is a fickle environment. There is no live interaction between the consumer and the Web site. Therefore, a Web site needs to work hard to develop relationships with its customers. It's about anticipating customer information requirements through personalization. It's about answering customer questions in a comprehensive and timely manner. It's about delivering exactly what the customer ordered, on time. It's about suggesting to customers new products that they will be genuinely interested in.

What are the key benefits of CRM?

The benefits of CRM include the following:

- better, faster information on customer needs;
- more cost-effective management of the customer relationship through automating and streamlining of customer processes;
- more empowered customers who can quickly find the information they need;
- more profitable and loyal customers.

Is CRM right for every business?

No. A small business should be able to know its customers without having to implement lots of technology. CRM is complex and expensive to install. It is best suited to organizations which have a large customer base, and are already customer-centric. They should have a significant sales force, run a variety of marketing and sales programs, and have strong internal IT resources and quality infrastructures.

Making It Happen

Develop a Long-Term Vision and Strategy

Because of the complexity and expense of CRM, it is not advised to implement an entire CRM system at one time. Rather, your organization needs to develop a vision of where it wants to go with CRM over the long term. Then, the CRM implementation should be broken down into manageable sections, prioritizing the technology that will deliver the most immediate benefits in the shortest time.

Develop a Return on Investment (ROI) Model

A significant number of organizations depend on intuition, rather than a clear ROI model, in deciding to implement CRM systems. This is not a good idea. To create an ROI model, establish appropriate metrics and see how they change with the implementation of CRM. CRM metrics include:

- revenue per sales rep
- cost and length of time it takes to close a lead
- revenue/profitability per customer
- length of time customers stay with you
- customer satisfaction ratings

Talk to Your Customers

In developing a vision and strategy, it's critical to talk to your customers. After all, CRM is about focusing on customer needs, and if you don't understand basic customer needs when designing a CRM solution, then chances are you'll get it wrong.

Talk to Employees

It's critical to survey employees internally: CRM covers a broad range of activities, including marketing, sales, support, and IT, so it's vital that key people in all of these areas are engaged. There will always be tradeoffs, but a rounded set of requirements should emerge.

CRM can be seen as an IT solution to a sales and marketing problem. Sales and marketing departments can resist such technology-based solutions unless they are brought fully on board and clearly convinced of the benefits of CRM. Getting everyone working together under a single CRM banner may be great in theory, but difficult in practice.

"The future will be a future of more and more intensified relationships." (Theodore Levitt)

Ensure That Employees are Properly Trained and Educated

Well-trained employees make for successful CRM. The key objective of CRM is not so much to train employees in how to use the new software, but rather to have a customer-centric view of the world. If employees are not open to embracing a philosophy of making the customer king, then CRM will become an expensive and wasteful exercise. Just as customers are becoming more information hungry, so employees also need to become more information hungry about their customers. Customer data must be analyzed by highly trained people.

Create a Single View of the Customer

A core objective of CRM should be to create a single view of the customer. Historically, organizations have held isolated pockets of information on individual customers. CRM should be about bringing all that information together into a single, well-organized environment. That means departments sharing and collaborating and ensuring that all relevant employees can make use of this single customer profile.

Carefully Consider Integration Issues

Because CRM can cover such a broad range of technologies and activities, integration becomes a key issue. There is likely to be a range of different software in the CRM solution and this will need to integrate properly. Also, the CRM solution will have to integrate with existing systems—trying to implement what are CRM technologies into an old or poorly managed IT infrastructure will cause serious problems.

Selecting a CRM Vendor

Your organization should have a detailed understanding of what it wants from CRM before approaching vendors. From there a detailed selection methodology should be developed so that all vendors are appraised on a consistent basis. Here are some key questions:

- Who are the vendor's customers? How happy are they with their implementations? Does the vendor have customers in your industry? (If so, talk to them about their experience.)
- What about support and training, which is just as important as the software itself? What are the means by which it is delivered? What support packages are available?
- How long has the vendor been in business? What's their financial situation? Have they been in the news lately? If so why?
- What are the skills and experience of the team that will be involved in implementing the solution?
- What's the pricing? Are payment options available?

The ASP Option for CRM

Technology vending is acronym city. An Application Services Provider (ASP) will offer basically to manage the CRM system for you, and will charge an ongoing fee for that service. Because of the complexity and ever-changing nature of CRM, this can be an attractive option. However, because a CRM system embodies the heart of what an organization does—dealing with customers—the choice of ASP vendor needs to be made very carefully.

Common Mistakes

Forgetting about the C in CRM

Much of the selling of CRM has focused on amazing technology and extraordinary features that do all sorts of fancy things. In all the excitement, the very reason CRM exists—to help organizations develop stronger customer relationships—is often forgotten.

Not Getting the Staff Approval

The best technology in the world is of little use if the people who are supposed to use it are not properly trained and motivated. CRM implementations have often ignored the core need of changing behavior within the organization. If employees do not have a customer focus, then CRM is dead on arrival.

Inability to Adapt CRM Solutions Quickly

Surveys indicate that a significant number of organizations have had problems in adapting CRM solutions quickly to changing customer needs. Often, because the systems are so complex, managers are dependent on the IT department to make even simple changes.

Lack of Senior Management's Understanding and Approval

A CRM implementation is crucial to core business functions. CRM projects will run into trouble if senior management is not fully engaged.

Poor Integration

Integration problems with CRM software have proven costly and time-consuming for organizations.

Automation without Common Sense

CRM can automate many sales and marketing processes, but that doesn't mean it shouldn't be carefully monitored. The story is told of a major car manufacturer whose sales department offered deep discounts to get rid of a backlog of lime green cars. The cars began to sell briskly. The CRM system noticed the trend and requested the manufacturing plant to make more lime green cars.

For More Information

Web Sites:
CRM Forum: **www.crm-forum.com**
ZDNET CRM Update: **www.techupdate.zdnet.com**

See also:
☆ **Delivering and Delighting—A New Spirit at Work (pp. 71–72)**
☆ **Making Loyalty Work (pp. 289–90)**
☆ **Managing the Customer (pp. 65–66)**
☆ **Managing 1:1 Marketing (pp. 55–56)**
☆ **The Second Coming of Service (pp. 77–78)**
✓ **Collecting Consumer Data on the Internet (pp. 624–25)**
✓ **How to Deliver Quality Online Customer Service and Support (pp. 582–83)**

How to Develop a Personalization Strategy for a Web Site

Getting Started

Personalization is the process by which a Web site presents customers with selected information on their specific needs. To do this, a personalization system is used to collect personal information on a particular individual. Used properly, personalization is a powerful tool that allows customers to access the right content more quickly, thus saving them valuable time. When considering personalization, keep the following in mind:

- personalization can only work well if the Web site has quality content that is well structured;
- true personalization is a complex and expensive process, and is financially worthwhile only if the Web site has a large quantity of information and many users;
- because personalization requires the collection of personal information it raises key privacy issues.

Privacy is a major concern on the Internet and needs to be addressed comprehensively.

FAQs

How can I encourage customers to provide the information that I need?

Most customers are willing to give personal information if they know it will benefit them. They need to be confident that the information they give will be properly protected, and that it will be used only for the reasons it was originally collected for.

Many studies indicate that privacy is a central issue for people using the Internet. People need to feel confident that they are dealing with a reputable organization that will not abuse their trust.

Can I use the information that customers provide for other sales and marketing activities?

The use of customer information is governed by legislation in each country. Collecting personal information on the Internet, and, in particular, moving that information between countries, can be very complicated because different countries have different laws. However, a basic principle is to tell the individual clearly why you are collecting the information, and what you will use it for. Only use it for that stated purpose.

Do personalized pages contribute to customer loyalty?

Yes. Studies have indicated that regular customers appreciate personalization options. New visitors are unlikely to use personalization because they are not sure whether they will want to come back to the Web site.

However, someone who visits regularly will probably have favorite sections of the Web site; personalization allows these sections to be brought together into a single environment for that user.

Making It Happen

Understanding How Personalization Works

In the basic model for personalization, personal information is collected on an individual, and used to customize the Web site for that person.

Personal information can be collected in two ways:

- a person fills out a personal profile directly, perhaps informing the organization of the type, or types, of products and services he or she is interested in;
- the organization uses software that tracks the way a customer uses the Web site; for example, if you looked at Product X last week, the next time you visit you may be told about a new feature for Product X. A popular method by which such tracking is carried out is the use of cookies, which reside on an individual's browser and collect information on that person's Web behavior.

Define Clear Objectives and Benefits

Personalization has failed to live up to its original promise of certain profitability. Many organizations spent large sums of money on personalization systems, only to see a very poor return on investment.

There should be a clear set of benefits for the organization and the customer before a personalization strategy is initiated. Personalization makes most sense if a Web site contains a very large quantity of information, which means that visitors are slow to find the information they seek. Personalization also requires a large number of Web site visitors, because systems are complex and expensive to install.

Personalization is a way of improving an already well-structured Web site with high quality information. It will not solve core problems such as a badly designed classification and poor-quality content.

Understand Where Personalization Works and Where It Doesn't

Personalization is not always suitable. A study by the Poynter Institute on how people read news-based information on the Internet found that, while many of the respondents had tried personalization, a great number had stopped using it. When asked why, the most common answer was that they felt they might be "missing something."

People are often not sure exactly what they want when they come to a Web site, and their needs can frequently change over time, so past behavior is not always a true indicator of present needs. The following example of a successful personalization strategy by Amazon.com shows where personalization works best.

Amazon.com offers millions of books and other products, so it can be hard for customers to find what they are looking for. However, Amazon.com's personalization approach, based on previous browsing or purchasing be-

  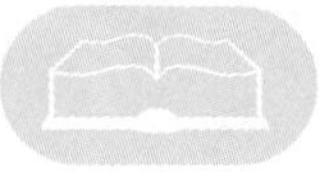    

havior, shows customers books or other items that reflect those previous choices. Customers may also be sent occasional e-mails informing them of new book or music releases in categories they have previously looked at. The objective is clear: helping the customer to find quickly the book or item they need, and giving them context for their purchase by providing information.

Don't Try to Do Too Much

Personalization can be complex, so start off by personalizing something that is easy to implement and that will deliver an immediate benefit. It is also important to understand that personalization depends on having a well-structured, well-classified Web site that has good-quality, up-to-date information. Without this, personalization is a waste of time and money.

Carefully Plan the Information You Need to Collect

It is essential to plan carefully the type of customer information you need, for two reasons:

- people hate filling out long forms, and are reluctant to provide too much personal information;
- too much information can be counterproductive by burying genuinely useful information under a mass of irrelevant detail.

When seeking to develop a customer profile ask for name and address, contact details, purchase history, personal interests, and product or service preferences.

Develop a Comprehensive Privacy Policy

A clear privacy policy is an essential part of any personalization strategy. It must be made clear why you are collecting the information and how it will be used. If you wish to use the information for purposes other than the personalization of the Web site, such as sending out e-mails on special offers, or sharing the information with partners, you should specifically inform the individual of that intention and give them the opportunity of opting out.

It is good policy to allow individuals to check at any time the information you have on them, and to allow them to delete information on themselves if they wish to do so.

Ensure Proper Security Procedures Are in Place

When collecting personal information on customers, a proper security procedure is essential. Internet security breaches are increasing, and hackers are particularly interested in breaking into systems containing personal information. An organization's reputation can be badly damaged by the theft of personal customer information.

Select a Software Vendor

While it is possible to develop custom-made software for personalization, it is not advisable unless the personalization system is a very simple one. There is a wide range of vendors selling personalization software. However, it is important not to be too influenced by what may be unnecessary features: keep your objectives clear, and always focus on real needs and benefits.

Common Mistakes

Assuming Personalization Is a Magic Formula

It is a mistake to think that personalization will turn a poorly designed Web site with poor-quality information into a winning success. Personalization is only as good as the foundations upon which it is built. In addition, it is not suitable for every Web site. The benefits must be very clear both from the point of view of the organization and of the Web site visitor.

Not Collecting the Right Information

Collecting the wrong information will ensure that personalization fails. Collecting too much information will frustrate the customer and will make the process of sifting through such information time-consuming and expensive.

Not Articulating a Clear Set of Benefits for the Customer

Many people are willing to give personal information once they can be shown that there are clear benefits in doing so. It is important to explain convincingly to customers why they should give their personal information to a Web site.

Not Having a Comprehensive Privacy Policy

There have been many instances of abuse of privacy on the Internet, and consumers are becoming increasingly wary of Web sites that seek to collect personal information on them. Before personalization can work you must establish credibility and trust. A way of doing this is to have a comprehensive privacy policy and honor it in every detail.

For More Information

Books:

Kasanoff, Bruce. *Making It Personal*. Cambridge, MA: Perseus, 2001.

Peppers, Don, and Martha Rogers. *Enterprise One-to-One: Tools for Competing in the Interactive Age*. New York: Doubleday, 1999.

Web Sites:

Inside Privacy: **www.insideprivacy.com**

Personalization Consortium: **www.personalization.org/index.html**

See also:

☆ **Managing 1:1 Marketing (pp. 55–56)**
✔ **Collecting Consumer Data on the Internet (pp. 624–25)**
✔ **How to Add Multimedia to a Web Site (pp. 596–97)**
✔ **How to Develop Appropriate Metadata and Classification for a Web Site (pp. 612–13)**
✔ **How to Get the Best from Loyalty Programs on the Web (p. 627)**

"When you are through changing, you are through." (Percy Barnevik)

 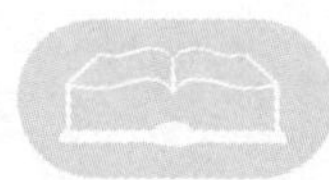    

How to Manage Payments Online

Getting Started

Getting your online payment system right is critical to the success of e-commerce. The system must be easy to use, as consumers dislike having to go through long, cumbersome processes to purchase products. However, it must be as secure as possible, since it is estimated that fraud costs an online business three times as much as an offline one. When considering online payment services, keep the following in mind:

- consumers are wary of giving credit card details and other personal information online. Your first step must be to gain their trust;
- fraud and chargebacks are critical issues that can seriously affect an online business;
- there is a wide range of online payment services available, so shop around.

FAQs

What is the most common form of payment on the Internet?

For consumer commerce it is the credit card. In the United States it is claimed that over 90% of all online payments are made by credit card. In Europe, the figure is estimated at 70%. For most business-to-business transactions, payment is usually made offline. New forms of payment are emerging, such as prepaid accounts and payments via mobile phone.

What are the key issues facing online payments?

- Fraud is a critical concern that must be addressed comprehensively.
- There is no cross-border integration of payment systems.
- People develop payment habits, and are reluctant to change them.
- Can traditional payment methods adapt to the new environment, or is a brand new system required?
- There is still no comprehensive hard data on how people pay online.

What is a payment culture?

Within any particular country, and sometimes within states or regions of a country, there are distinct approaches to payment, depending on the range of payment options available locally, local payment habits, and local/national payment regulations.

Making It Happen

Understand Your Marketplace

Depending on the country, or the region/state within a country, people pay for things in different ways. Different countries also have different payment processing approaches and legal obligations.

Types of Payment Options Available

It is important to understand the range of payment options available before choosing a particular payment method. The options available include the following:

- credit card payment
- credit transfer
- electronic checks
- direct debit
- smart cards
- prepaid schemes
- loyalty plan points-based approaches
- person-to-person payments
- mobile phone plans

The approach chosen will depend on the target market. For example, when a Web site targets young people, who often have no credit cards, a prepaid plan can work well. A particular Web site may use a variety of payment approaches, depending on its needs, but the ability to process all the major credit cards is almost always essential.

Characteristics of an Online Payment System

An online payment system should have these key characteristics:

- efficiency and ease of use: a central advantage of doing business online is that it saves time and cuts costs;
- stability and reliability: because payment is such a critical function, it is essential that a payments system is fully reliable. Payment systems cannot afford to be down for any length of time;
- authentication: much online fraud is caused by the absence of proper authentication;
- integration: a payment system must be able to integrate properly with relevant internal information systems, so that, for example, a record of the payment can be added to the account details;
- insurance: facilities such as escrow services must be available to ensure that the seller gets the money and the buyer gets the goods.

Selecting an Online Payment Service

The most suitable type of online payment service will depend on the volume of business you intend to do and the margins you make on each sale. There is a wide choice of payment services, so it is important to shop around to find the best one. However, whatever service you choose must be able to verify the credit card, process the transaction, and deposit the money in your account.

Key factors you must consider are setup fees, ongoing charges, and software and hardware expenses. Most banks offer some form of online payment service, and can be a good choice. When looking beyond banks, make sure you are dealing with reputable organizations. Those that advertise extremely low charges usually have expensive hidden extras.

Payment by Credit Card

There are two distinct methods by which credit card payments are made for Internet purchases: payment directly online, and payment by phoning or faxing credit card details. The first method is by far the most popular (88%), but it is advisable to offer both options to potential consumers.

When implementing an online credit card system, a comprehensive security system using a secure server with encryption technology is essential. It is equally important to have comprehensive security procedures for the storage of the information. A database containing confidential information on thousands of individuals is more attractive to a criminal than acquiring a credit card number as it is passed between consumer and seller.

Keep the Process Simple and Fast

Whatever the payment system you choose, make sure to keep the process as simple and fast as possible. Studies have indicated that many consumers abandon the online purchase process, often because it is too long and difficult to understand. Streamlining the purchasing process is extremely important where repeat business is concerned. Amazon.com, for example, has implemented a "1-Click" purchase process for repeat customers, avoiding a lot of form filling.

Business-to-business (B2B) Payment Options

While there is a wide range of effective business-to-consumer online payment options, payment for B2B transactions is generally made offline. One reason for this is that the amounts of money involved are usually large. However, one of the key reasons businesses embrace online B2B and join e-marketplaces is to reduce costs and to make transactions more efficient. Being unable to complete the payment online adds cost and inconvenience.

Running an Online Auction

If you intend to run an online auction for the general public, you encounter quite different payment issues: when consumers are trading with each other, the party selling the goods often does not have the capacity to accept credit cards. To overcome such problems, person-to-person (P2P) systems have emerged. Most of the larger auction Web sites, such as eBay and Yahoo, have such systems. However, P2P systems cause concern for legislators because of their potential for money laundering and other types of fraud, so choosing a system requires great care.

Online Escrow Services

Online escrow services offer to hold payments while the buyer examines the products purchased. If the buyer is satisfied with the products, they then authorize the payment. An online escrow service incurs extra cost because a fee is charged, but it may be worthwhile if it is essential to give the buyer as much confidence as possible.

The system operates by giving the escrow service a tracking number for the delivery. You must agree on the time period allowed to the buyer for examination of the merchandise; you must also establish who pays the shipping fees if the product is returned.

Fraud and Chargebacks Are Major Issues

Some studies estimate that e-tailers are losing as much as 5% of their margin to fraud—a rate three times higher than for businesses operating offline. For e-tailers on small margins this is a very serious issue. There are many different types of fraud, but a particularly common online form is identity theft, where fraudsters acquire confidential information on an individual and use it to purchase products. Clearly, e-tailers must take great care in this area, otherwise their profits will be eaten away. Fraud detection software is available and should be used.

Chargebacks (disputed payments) are also a major concern. MasterCard claims that, while online purchases represent 4% of total retail transactions, they account for 40% of all chargebacks. Credit card companies have initiated chargeback limits for e-tailers, and penalties are imposed for those who exceed them.

Common Mistakes

Not Understanding Payment Cultures

While credit cards may be very common in the United States, they are not as widely used in Europe. Different countries have different payment habits and payment legislation. Not understanding these is a serious obstacle to online business.

Not Securing Peace of Mind for the Consumer

Consumers are very concerned that their credit card numbers will be stolen on the Internet. They are equally concerned that confidential information that they give to a Web site will not be properly protected. Web sites that fail to show clearly the steps taken to protect customer information are likely to lose potential business.

Underestimating Fraud

Fraud is a pressing issue on the Internet, and can have a serious impact on profit margins.

For More Information

Web Sites:

Epaynews.com, information and news on the online payment industry: **www.epaynews.com**

E-payment Systems Observatory, a European Union-funded institute that carries out extensive studies on e-payment systems: **www.epso.jrc.es**

See also:

- ✓ **Exploring Peer-to-peer (P2P) Commerce (pp. 646–47)**
- ✓ **How to Implement Effective Internet Security (pp. 602–03)**
- ✓ **The Key Issues of Implementing E-commerce (pp. 580–81)**
- ✓ **Legal Issues in E-commerce (pp. 648–49)**
- ✓ **Setting Up a Subscription Process (pp. 618–19)**

"A credit card is a money tool, not a supplement to money." (Paula Nelson)

  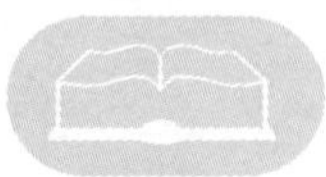    

The Key Issues to Consider When Designing a Web Site

Getting Started

For the majority of Web sites, Web site design is about information, not graphics. The most successful Web sites–Yahoo, AOL Time Warner, Microsoft, Amazon, eBay–have few graphics. Graphics and other high-bandwidth multimedia slow a Web site down, but most people view the Web as a library, not a source of entertainment, and they hate being kept waiting. Web site design should focus on:

- clean, simple, standardized design that helps people find the content they want without delay;
- good page layout that allows people to read the content as easily as possible;
- avoiding fancy graphics and multimedia experiences.

FAQs

What exactly is Web site design?

Web site design is information design. It's about organizing content so that it can be easily found and easily read. Web site design is a form of publishing: presenting content in a way that is attractive to visitors.

Why are so many Web sites still poorly designed?

Because many organizations still don't really understand what their Web sites are intended to achieve. In addition, if the Web site is controlled by graphic design or technical staff, the results may be essentially unusable from a consumer's point of view.

Why should an editor be in charge?

The Web is a publishing medium, and a Web site is a publication. The primary job of an editor is to understand content; the primary purpose of a Web site is to publish content.

What's the main thing people do on the Web?

They read, and the text that is easiest to read is black on white. Yet, even though it is already more difficult to read on a screen than on paper, many Web sites put colored text on colored backgrounds. If you think of your Web site visitors as readers, the function of Web site design will become far clearer.

Making It Happen

Design for the Reader/Visitor

Too few Web sites are designed for the needs of their visitors. Remember that the person who visits your site:

- is there to find some information;
- will scan read, moving quickly from one piece of text to another;
- is generally in a hurry, and may not wait for elaborate pages to download;
- may be skeptical because, on the basis of past experience, they expect a Web site to be full of useless material.

Make Sure the Content Is Well Written

When writing for the Web:

- keep it factual, with punchy, descriptive headings and summaries;
- keep it short. Documents should be between 500 and 700 words, paragraphs between 40 and 60 words. Sentences should be short. There should be no more than 9 to 12 words per line of text;
- keep it updated. Out-of-date content is no good.

Make Sure the Content Is Well Organized

Think of your Web site as a directory. If you have lots of products to sell, you must organize them so that people can browse through them easily. Web sites such as Amazon.com and eBay are successful because they organize huge quantities of products properly so that people can find what they want quickly and efficiently.

Metadata, navigation, and search are fundamental to the organization of content on a Web site. Metadata delivers essential information on a document or Web page: publication date, author, keywords, title, and summary. Search depends on metadata to be truly effective, and is one of the most common activities people do on a Web site. Search must be available on every page. Navigation is critical: if people can't easily find their way around a Web site, they will leave.

Make Sure the Web Site Is Interactive

Comprehensive contact details should be prominently available on the Web site, covering the appropriate range of e-mail and telephone contacts. Physical addresses, with location maps, should also be provided. Online community options such as chat, discussion boards, and e-mail discussion lists can enhance a visitor's understanding of the organization and its products. E-mail newsletters can allow the organization to keep in touch regularly and at low cost.

Ensure that Standards Are Developed and Adhered To

Newspaper designers have found that people follow a certain pattern when reading content in a newspaper. This is true of reading content on a Web site too: people navigate and search in a certain way. It is therefore confusing to have different designs within different sections of a Web site, or between Web sites in the same organization.

Some of the emerging standards and conventions for Web site design are included in the following list.

- Essential navigation: Every Web page should have a set of essential navigation that is visible when the first screen loads, containing key areas within the Web site.

  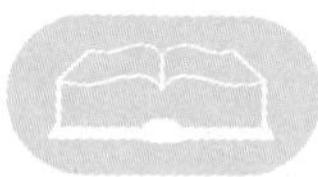    

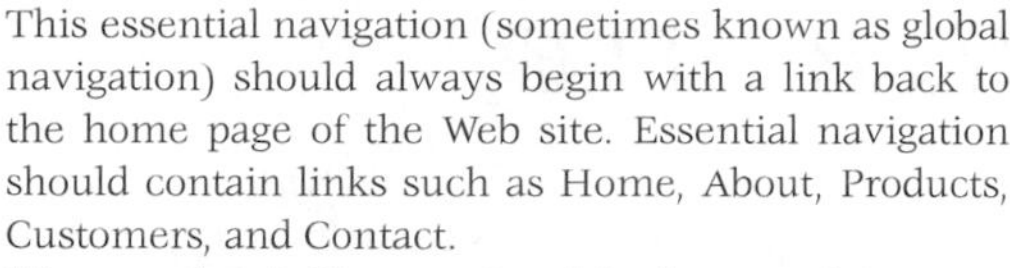

This essential navigation (sometimes known as global navigation) should always begin with a link back to the home page of the Web site. Essential navigation should contain links such as Home, About, Products, Customers, and Contact.

- Slim masthead: The masthead is the top of the page area, and should be slim, like the masthead of a newspaper. This makes the maximum amount of screen space available for the content—the main reason for a Web site visit. The masthead should contain the logo of the organization, and may also contain the search box and the set of essential links.
- Three-column layout: In the average Web site, a three-column layout is the best means of delivering maximum content in the most readable format.
- Footer on every page: A footer should go at the bottom of every page; it should contain a copy of the essential links, contact information (address, telephone, fax, e-mail), and links to copyright and privacy policy information.
- Maximum accessibility: Minimum accessibility standards for Web sites are increasingly becoming a legal requirement. In any case, implementing best practice in accessibility design generally leads to a more effective Web site.
- Effective home page layout and design: A home page has two central functions: firstly, to provide the visitor with the appropriate navigation and search options to allow them to find content quickly; secondly, to promote important content. This is done by using short, punchy headings and summaries.
- Consistent document page layout and design: In general, a three-column approach should be used for Web pages that display documents. Every document should have a heading and a summary. Include author and date of publication if appropriate.
- Large sans serif fonts: It is advisable to use sans serif fonts, such as Verdana and Arial, on the Web, because they are easier to read on a screen than serif fonts. Font sizes should not be lower than 8 point for summaries and headings on home pages. The minimum font size recommended for documents is 10 point. The ideal font color is black text on a white background.
- No italic, bold, or underline: Avoid using italic, which has a poor appearance on-screen. Avoid using bold in body text, as people may think it's a link. Never use underline, as people will definitely think it's a link.
- Small graphics: Graphics should be small, particularly on the home page. If a larger graphic is necessary, consider using a thumbnail approach, with a small graphic and a larger one linked from it, giving visitors the option to view the larger graphic if they want.
- Compatibility with all browsers: Although Internet Explorer now has the largest share of the marketplace, it is still important that the Web site can be viewed properly in Netscape Navigator. Test your Web site using both browsers, and different browser versions.
- Light pages: If your Web pages do not download quickly, people will simply leave. Keep pages under 50K in weight; this means small graphics.
- No frames: Frames break up a Web page into separate sections. In the words of Web usability expert, Jakob Nielsen: "Frames: just say no."
- No splash pages: A splash page is an introductory or initial page presented to visitors before they can get to the actual home page. It simply forces visitors to go through an extra, redundant stage before they can do what they came to do.
- Lots of hypertext: You should use hypertext liberally, but stick to the standard colors: blue for unclicked, purple for clicked. People are used to these colors. Hypertext is a navigation aid, and changing colors is confusing.
- No tricks: Swirling logos, animated e-mail postboxes, and page counters are signs of an amateur Web site.

Test, Test, and Test Again

Test out your Web site with potential visitors, and get as much feedback as possible. This is the best way to find out what's working and what isn't.

Common Mistakes

Thinking That a Web Site Is About Getting Attention

Many marketers are used to creating brochures and advertisements that seek to grab attention. However, when someone visits your Web site, you've already got their attention. They don't want to see a swirling logo; they want to find out something about your product or service.

Creating Brochure Ware

Too many people think that Web site design is just like brochure design. Large graphics simply slow down a Web site and turn visitors off. Web site design must allow you to update your Web site with new content easily, so it should be designed more like a newspaper.

Too Many Gimmicks

The majority of people come to Web sites to do things and find out information. Gimmicks may be fun and clever, but too often they get in the way.

For More Information

Web Sites:

Builder.com, a detailed source of information on Web design: **www.builder.com**

Webmonkey, detailed information on Web design: **www.webmonkey.com**

See also:

☆ **Creating a Company Web Site to Reflect Your Company (pp. 157–58)**
✔ **How to Add Multimedia to a Web Site (pp. 596–97)**
✔ **How to Develop Appropriate Metadata and Classification for a Web Site (pp. 612–13)**
✔ **How to Set Up a Basic Web Site (pp. 592–93)**
✔ **Making a Web Site Easy to Navigate (pp. 614–15)**
✔ **Writing Well for the Web (pp. 620–21)**

"Good design is good business." (Thomas J. Watson, Jr.)

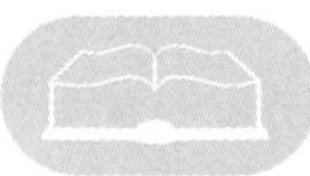

HOW TO SET UP A BASIC WEB SITE

GETTING STARTED

A Web site is a way of informing customers and other stakeholders of what you have to offer. A basic Web site involves delivering essential information that is easy to read and well laid out. In Web site design, simplicity is always best. A Web site must also be actively promoted to make people aware of its existence. When approaching Web site design, ask yourself the following important questions:

- Who are the people that I want to communicate with?
- How am I going to structure my information so it is easy to navigate and read?
- How am I going to let people know that my Web site exists?
- How am I going to keep my Web site updated and keep people informed of new content?

FAQs

HOW MUCH INFORMATION SHOULD I INCLUDE ON A WEB SITE?

Provide the information that your target market needs and is likely to read. Don't fill your Web site with irrelevant and/or repetitive information. It will clutter your site and make the important information hard to find.

HOW OFTEN SHOULD I CHANGE CONTENT?

You should change your content whenever you have something new and important to say, and whenever content already on the site is out of date. Ideally you should try to publish fresh content every week.

CAN I TRANSFER PRINTED COPY TO THE WEB SITE?

Printed copy can be used as a starting point for Web copy, but the structure and length would probably be unsuitable. People like to read short, punchy copy on the Web, so snappy headings and summaries are important. For a Web site to be truly effective, you must also use hypertext so that people can click for further information.

MAKING IT HAPPEN

KNOW WHO YOU WANT TO REACH

Before you do anything, decide who you want to reach. Prioritize your information for your most important audiences. Ask yourself:

- Do I want to reach new customers? In new markets?
- What can I say on my Web site that will turn a potential customer into an actual one?
- Do I want to offer support for existing customers?
- Do I want to provide information to attract new staff?

KEEP IT SIMPLE

Web site design is about the design and delivery of information. It is not graphic design. Lack of bandwidth means that fancy graphics and moving images slow a Web site down and frustrate visitors looking for information. Quality Web site design has simple layout and rich content that is well organized. The best, most successful Web sites in the world don't employ fancy gimmicks; neither should you. Keep it simple. Maximize the content and minimize the presentation.

STRUCTURE YOUR INFORMATION WELL

When people come to your Web site, they want to find information quickly. They are task-oriented, impatient, and skeptical. It is therefore essential to make your Web site as accessible and easy to navigate as possible.

IMPORTANT WEB SITE SECTIONS AND LINKS

You should have at least some of the following sections on your Web site. Links to these sections should be provided in a set of essential links placed prominently on every page of the Web site.

HOME PAGE

The home page is the first page on your Web site and the most important, as it is usually the first page visitors see. From a linking point of view, the home page is referred to as "Home." It should always be the first link in your set of essential links. The home page itself should be full of punchy, attention-grabbing headings and summaries that quickly inform the visitor of, for example, what you do, what you have to sell, or what special offers you have.

WHAT'S NEW

This section contains information on important news, events, and press releases. Always keep this section updated, and make sure that you date each entry. You should plan to add an entry for this section at least once a week, but remember to remove old items too.

ABOUT

This section should contain essential information about your business or organization. If the section contains a lot of information it should be broken down into manageable subsections. "About" information includes the following:

- mission: a short description of the organization and what it seeks to achieve;
- key strengths: key products, market position, manufacturing, skills, distribution;
- company background;
- management team;
- financial information: annual results, reserves, financial management, investment information;
- contact and location details: this should link to the Contact section on your Web site.

PRODUCTS

This is the core part of your Web site, containing the things you have to sell. It should contain a brief overview of products and services and links to detailed information on specific products or services, containing:

- product/services description
- product applications
- business case and ROI (return on investment): how

using your product can make and/or save money
- specifications
- purchase and delivery details
- FAQs
- pricing (be sure to specify currency)
- product reviews
- where you sell to; specify the countries or regions you do or do not sell to

Purchase
This is an essential link if you have an e-commerce facility that allows people to buy direct from your Web site. Ideally you should also create a small graphic to be displayed prominently, particularly on the home page, informing customers that they can purchase your products online.

Customers
People want to know who your customers are. Include a list of your key customers and a selection of quotes and case studies

Partners
If you have a number of partners and joint ventures, you should have a section describing them, explaining how they allow you to deliver a better service.

Contact
This section should contain all your essential contact information including:
- e-mail address
- physical address and map of location
- telephone and fax

Search
If your Web site has more than 50 pages, you need a search engine to enable visitors to find information. If you use search, put the search box on every single page of your Web site, preferably near the top.

Offer an E-mail Newsletter
Every Web site should offer an e-mail newsletter. If visitors give their e-mail address on their first visit, you can send them a regular weekly or monthly e-mail newsletter to tell them what's new.

Use Metadata
Every Web page should have a title. Where appropriate, content should have: classification, heading, summary, date of publication, author name, keywords. This is metadata; without it, search engines won't index your Web site properly, and people won't be able to find quickly what they are looking for.

Make Sure You Have the Proper Footer Information
The bottom of every page should have footer information containing:
- a list of the essential links for the Web site
- essential contact details: main address, telephone and fax, e-mail
- the copyright notice
- your privacy policy

Remember to Promote Your Web Site
A Web site needs promotion. Promotional strategies include:
- registering with the major search engines (Alta Vista, Google, Yahoo), as well as search engines specific to your industry or sector;
- making sure that your Web site and e-mail address is on all your promotional literature.

Do It Yourself or Get a Design Company?
If you are a competent computer user, you may well be able to do most of the work yourself, using packages such as Microsoft FrontPage or Macromedia's Dreamweaver, but you may require a graphic designer to help you with design issues.

Common Mistakes

Being Too Clever
Some sites try too hard to entertain without providing hard information. Animation, multimedia, video clips, and other tricks can obscure important data.

Poor Classification, Navigation, and Search
Good classification, navigation, and search are essential for a successful Web site. Customers expect easy access to the information they want. If they can't find it easily on your site, they will go somewhere else.

Content That Is Difficult to Read
Many Web sites try to impress by using lots of color, but the easiest text to read is black on a white background. Keep paragraphs, line lengths, and documents short.

For More Information

Web Sites:
Builder.com: **www.builder.com**
Webmonkey: **www.webmonkey.com**

See also:
✓ **The Key Issues to Consider When Designing a Web Site (pp. 590–91)**
✓ **The Key Principles of Web Site Management (pp. 598–99)**
✓ **Understanding the Key Principles of Content Management (pp. 608–09)**
✓ **Writing Well for the Web (pp. 620–21)**

How to Build a Web Site Team

Getting Started

All good Web publications are fueled by content, supported by an information architecture and technical infrastructure; the Web site must also be actively marketed and promoted. On a small Web site, all these functions will be carried out by a part-time resource, but a large Web site will require dedicated personnel. When building a Web site team, keep the following in mind:

- a Web site should be managed by an editor, who understands content and knows what readers want;
- information architecture skills are vital: the content must be well structured so that it can be quickly found and easily read;
- the need for technical support should not be underestimated, particularly in the area of Web security.

FAQs

Why should a Web site be run by an editor?

E-commerce means selling with content, so if the content isn't right, the customer won't buy. Content is not a technical issue but an editorial one. The primary job of the editor is to ensure that the right content is being created, and that it is being edited and published correctly.

What are the core functions of editing and publishing?

Publishing is about getting the right content to the right person at the right time, and the selection process is vital. Editing is therefore a critical quality control function, rejecting poor content and cutting out unnecessary text. Quality Web sites get the right content up quickly.

What is information architecture?

Information architecture deals with how content is organized and presented. It refers to the metadata, classification, navigation, search, layout, and design of the Web site. Maintaining an information architecture for a small Web site is a relatively simple job but is far more complex for larger Web sites.

What are the key technical resources required to support a Web site?

A Web site that doesn't load quickly and consistently is of little use. Large e-commerce Web sites require complex technical infrastructure that needs constant monitoring. Technical resources include HTML, programming, and systems administration; security is becoming an increasingly important issue.

Making It Happen

Define the Business Requirements

It is essential to establish the business requirements for the Web site and to manage how these requirements are being met. What is the Web site supposed to achieve? If it is modeled on a traditional publication, it will need to generate revenue through advertising and subscription. However, most Web sites exist to support the sale of the organization's products and to promote its brand.

Define the Scope of the Web Site

The people and skills required to run the Web site will depend on its scope.

Editorial Board

It is advisable to establish an editorial board within the organization to establish the content objectives and oversee their implementation. All the main departments and sections should be represented, and senior management should be involved.

The Role of the Managing Editor

A single individual, with an editorial background, should be given overall charge of running the Web site. Specifically the managing editor should:

- manage the content: decide what type of content is to be published, and how often updated;
- manage the staff: hiring, training, motivation, reward, assessment, and discipline;
- champion the visitor: make sure that the Web site focuses on its key visitors. The editor should encourage and make use of feedback from visitors;
- promote the Web site to senior management and within the organization;
- report to management on a regular basis;
- ensure that the Web site is achieving its objectives and evolving to meet changing needs.

Editor

Among other things, the editor should:

- commission and purchase content: make sure that it is delivered on time and to budget;
- edit the content: make sure that content meets editorial standards, clearly communicates its subject matter, and is well written. The editor should check for libel and other legal issues; make sure the metadata is correct; and review published content;
- publish the content: decide what is to be published and what is not. The editor should decide, in conjunction with the managing editor, what content should be highlighted on the home page and other relevant sections of the Web site;
- manage writers: for many people in the organization, writing is only a small part of their job, so they will require motivation and training. The editor will also deal with hiring, reward, assessment, and discipline;
- champion the visitor/reader: understand what readers want; note and reply to feedback.

Copy Editor

Copy editors check for spelling, grammar, and metadata. They ensure that the content is the right length, and rewrite where appropriate.

Writer

Writers must know their subject matter. They should have an ability and enthusiasm for writing, and should be able to suggest content ideas to the editor.

"Change is inevitable, but it is in us to control its content and directions." (Indira Gandhi)

CONTRIBUTOR

Where the writer is not responsible for adding the metadata to the content, contributors ensure that the content gets to the editor quickly with all the appropriate metadata. They may also be required to add proper headings and summaries.

MODERATOR

Where online community facilities are available (chat, discussion boards, mailing lists), moderators will be required. Moderators mix editorial and chairperson skills, and also champion a particular mailing list or chat forum.

INFORMATION ARCHITECT

The information architect is responsible for the information architecture of the Web site, which includes:

- metadata: metadata is crucial to the design of Web sites. How content is classified will directly affect how quickly and effectively it can be found. Defining content templates includes agreeing on vital elements that a particular document should have, such as date of publication, author name, summary, or keywords;
- navigation: the information architect should decide on the most effective options for navigation. Standards and consistency in navigation design must be maintained. The focus should remain on the main task of navigation—finding an item of content quickly;
- search: the information architect should design basic and advanced search options where appropriate. Search should be easy to use and deliver accurate results quickly;
- layout and design: the information architect should ensure that all content is laid out in its most readable format. Simple, elegant design delivers Web pages that are fast to download and easy to read. Consistency of design throughout the Web site is important;
- usability: the Web site must work for its visitors. Regular feedback and usability testing are essential.

IT MANAGER/PROGRAMMER

This skill will usually be supplied by the IT department or outsourced. Skills are needed most when the Web site design is being implemented, but there is an ongoing need for technical support, so have some sort of programming resource permanently available if possible. A key responsibility of the IT manager is to ensure that the Web site is secure.

SYSTEMS ADMINISTRATOR

A site with a lot of traffic requires constant monitoring. Responsibilities include maintaining the network and servers, day-to-day maintenance of all software, backing up the Web site, testing pages for download speed, and checking for broken links, or security breaches.

HTML CODER

This skill will vary depending on whether the Web site is being built in pure HTML or content management software is being used.

GRAPHIC DESIGNER

Graphic designers should support the information architect. They should be skilled in creating small, elegant, fast-downloading graphics that support the presentation and readability of navigation, content, and other Web site elements.

DEFINE THE MARKETING AND PROMOTION REQUIREMENTS

The marketing department will usually carry out marketing and promotion functions. Resources will be required to deal with specific Web-related marketing functions such as ongoing search engine registration, establishing links with third parties, promotion through e-mail newsletters, and development of banner ads.

COMMON MISTAKES

THINKING THAT A WEB SITE IS PURELY A TECHNICAL ISSUE

A Web site is about communication, and the communications department is where the Web site should reside, supported by the IT and marketing departments.

NOT HAVING AN EDITOR IN CHARGE

The job of the editor is to understand content—the central role in Web design and management. Sites that are run by graphic designers or technologists often push these aspects at the expense of readable content.

TREATING CONTENT AS A COMMODITY

Content is the most valuable resource a Web site has, but it must be handled with discretion. Overlong articles, badly written headings, poor metadata—all these reflect a Web site that doesn't care about its content or the person who is supposed to read it.

NOT REWARDING AND REMUNERATING WRITERS

Content is written by people. The creation of content should be part of the job function and remunerated accordingly, otherwise results will be poor.

For More Information

Book:

McGovern, Gerry, and Rob Norton. *Content Critical.* Upper Saddle River, NJ: Financial Times Prentice Hall, 2001.

See also:

- ✔ **Day-to-day Maintenance of a Web Site (p. 600)**
- ✔ **How to Make Sure Content Is Professionally Created, Edited, and Published (pp. 610–11)**
- ✔ **How to Use the Internet to Create Content Collaboratively (p. 617)**
- ✔ **The Key Principles of Web Site Management (pp. 598–99)**

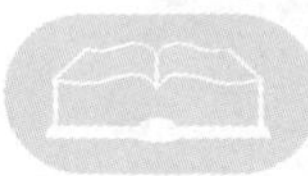

How to Add Multimedia to a Web Site

Getting Started

Multimedia has had problems on the Web, due mainly to limited bandwidth. While the overall environment for Web-based multimedia has improved significantly in recent years, it will still be a long time before rich multimedia can be delivered quickly to the majority of Web site visitors. However, the use of audio, and to a lesser extent video, is increasing steadily, particularly within office environments, where bandwidth tends to be more available. When considering using multimedia, keep the following in mind:

- never use it as a gimmick. Always make sure it has a clearly defined function that makes it easier for visitors to find and understand information;
- keep multimedia files as small as possible so that they download quickly;
- always offer an HTML alternative to multimedia that will deliver the information using text and simple images.

FAQs

Why isn't there more multimedia on the Web?

Many reasons: bandwidth, screen size and resolution, slow computers, the need for special software to view certain multimedia, and the inability of certain browsers to view multimedia. It will be a long time before people can have the same quality of experience from computer-based multimedia as they currently experience on their TVs. The Web is fundamentally an information-delivery medium. Where multimedia can deliver higher quality information than text and/or simple images reasonably quickly, it has a real purpose. On a low-bandwidth Web, however, this is difficult.

Isn't broadband access just around the corner?

People have been saying this since 1995, but many believe that it will be 2005, or even 2010, before a majority of people have access to sufficient bandwidth for truly rich multimedia experiences.

Why are plug-ins required to experience most multimedia?

Web browsers are not designed to view most multimedia, so extra software is required: a plug-in. The benefit of the multimedia experience has to be substantial before someone will make the effort to download a plug-in in order to view it.

What is streaming technology?

With streaming technology, you download just enough of the multimedia file to start viewing or listening to it, then the rest of the file is downloaded in the background, reducing, but not eliminating, download time. Streaming can be interrupted if there are bandwidth or server issues.

Making It Happen

Size Really Does Matter

If multimedia on the Web is complex, few people will be able or willing to make use of it. Smaller, but more limited, multimedia is accessible to more people. It depends on your target market: if you know they have the hardware, software, and bandwidth, and that they really want intricate multimedia, then give them exactly that. If, on the other hand, they have an average computer with average bandwidth, and simply need to find information quickly, be careful with multimedia.

Creating Animations with Animated GIFs

GIF (Graphics Interchange Format) is a straightforward method of animating a graphic on a Web site. Its major advantage is that it does not require a plug-in to view, so almost any browser can display it. It is ideal for animating small, simple icons and basic images, and for banner advertisements.

Creating Animations with Dynamic HTML (DHTML)

Dynamic HTML does not require a plug-in to view and, if properly designed, can be viewed by most browsers. However, the significant differences between the Microsoft and Netscape browsers mean that developing Dynamic HTML that will work perfectly across both browser platforms and multiple versions can be a complex task. Like animated GIFs, it is a relatively limited animation tool that often doesn't work well.

Creating Animations with Macromedia Flash

Despite the fact that it requires a plug-in, Macromedia Flash has become the most popular Web animation format. The majority of Web users have the Flash plug-in, but your design depends on the version they have.

Flash is flexible and easy to learn, but requires skill to master. It has a wide range of built-in animation features that will achieve a basic result quickly. For Web animation, Flash is a powerful tool. It uses streaming technology, so you can view the animation more quickly. It uses vector instead of bitmap graphics: smaller file size and more scalable, although vector graphics are not good at dealing with photographs. It also allows sound to be added to an animation effectively.

Creating Sound for the Web

High-quality sound results in a very large file, so sound must be compressed for delivery over the Web and then decompressed for listening. MP3 is a popular format that has emerged for doing this, achieving high-quality results. There are numerous software packages available for preparing audio for the Web, but the best way to get good quality is to record the audio properly in the first place. The leading audio plug-in is RealAudio. Apple QuickTime and Microsoft Media Player are also popular.

Be careful about sound. Never add it gratuitously to

your Web site, but only if it adds real value, for example, an important figure making a speech. (Make sure you provide a text transcript of the speech.) Always give the visitor the ability to stop the audio file.

Creating Video for the Web

Video is very bandwidth-intensive and should be used only when there is a specific need. Basic software-editing packages are available at reasonable costs, but doing the job properly requires very expensive software and equipment.

The frame rate that is used for delivering video on the Web is far lower than for television images, sometimes causing a jumpy and distorted picture. To avoid this, reduce movement as much as possible, and avoid zooming or panning.

Create Shortcuts around or Alternatives to the Multimedia Offering

Avoid multimedia intros, but if you must have them, always make sure that there is an obvious link that allows visitors to stop the multimedia and move on to find the information they need.

Many people have little interest in multimedia presentation: they are looking for information, and want to find it as quickly as possible. If a multimedia file contains important information, try to provide it also in an HTML text and simple image format. For example, publish a text transcript of an important interview.

Watch Out for Accessibility Issues

Ensure that your multimedia meets minimum accessibility standards; provide an accessible alternative where appropriate. Multimedia can be a support or a hindrance for people with disabilities: for example, audio files can help people with visual problems. However, when text is created as an image, text readers (which turn text into audio) will not work.

Test with a Range of Browsers and Computers

The advantage of HTML is its simplicity and open standards. However, even HTML needs to be carefully checked to make sure that it works properly on different browser platforms. Multimedia makes the situation more complex, as many problems can arise between browser platforms and browser versions. Careful checking is essential.

The type of computers also affects the multimedia experience. An old computer with a slow processor can make things happen very slowly. However, newer computers with very fast processors can sometimes have the reverse problem: the animation, for example, plays too quickly.

Inform the Visitor in Advance

When people click on a Web link, they expect to go to an HTML page. If this is not the case, tell them so in advance. If the link is an audio or video file, state this clearly. State the size of the file they need to download and the type of plug-in required, and provide a link to the plug-in, in case they wish to install it.

Common Mistakes

Pushing Boundaries Is Pushing Your Luck

Business is not about pushing boundaries but about making profit. Too many designers focus on creating exciting multimedia that many people are unable or unwilling to view.

Placing Text As an Image

As a rule, text in images should only be used for buttons and certain navigation links. One of the most common mistakes is to place substantial quantities of text as an image. The most readable text is black on a white background, and HTML is more than adequate to achieve this. Text in an image adds unnecessarily to download times, it cannot be searched, and it creates accessibility problems. The only text you should place as an image is, at most, a heading–and even that is not advisable.

Reading While an Animation Plays

Some Web sites seem to be designed to annoy people and distract them from the text they want to read. If there is a quantity of text to be read, avoid animation altogether, or have something animate a couple of times and then stop.

Scrolling Text

Scrolling text looks impressive but is often a gimmick. If you must scroll your text, make sure it moves at a suitable speed for reading.

For More Information

Web Sites:

Builder.com, Graphics & Multimedia, comprehensive technical-oriented advice: **http://builder.cnet.com/webbuilding**

Webmonkey, a good source of practical information on multimedia issues: **www.hotwired.lycos.com/webmonkey**

See also:

- ✔ **How to Develop a Personalization Strategy for a Web Site (pp. 586–87)**
- ✔ **How to Make Sure Content Is Professionally Created, Edited, and Published (pp. 610–11)**
- ✔ **The Key Issues to Consider when Designing a Web Site (pp. 590–91)**
- ✔ **Understanding the Key Principles of Content Management (pp. 608–09)**

  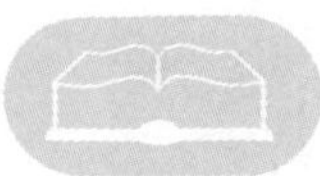    

The Key Principles of Web Site Management

Getting Started

A Web site has to be managed on a day-to-day basis. The work that needs to be done will depend on the size of the Web site and the amount of new content published. However, even small Web sites should be checked briefly each day to ensure that everything is in order. Keep the following in mind:

- Web sites are communication vehicles, and should be run primarily by people who understand content;
- security is a growing concern on the Internet; every site should have a comprehensive security policy;
- outsourcing can work well for Web site operations, but must be approached with care;
- visitor feedback should always be encouraged as it will help attune the Web site to visitors' needs.

FAQs

Why should an editor be in charge of the Web site?

Editors understand content, and content drives Web sites. Web site success does not depend on technical issues, important as they are. The ability to find the right content quickly is what makes a Web site work for a visitor. To achieve this, someone is needed who truly understands what the organization does and can consistently publish content on these activities.

Are Web sites a security risk?

Yes. Web sites can open a door into your computer system and require stringent security procedures that are actively policed. Hackers are an increasing threat on the Internet, and if your Web site is not properly secured, the consequences can be very serious.

Why is visitor feedback so important in Web site management?

Web site logs will give some indication of visitor behavior, but it is essential to encourage feedback. In this way, you can find out where visitors are having problems and what improvements they would like to see. A Web site should always be evolving, always seeking to make its processes and structures more customer-friendly.

Isn't outsourcing risky?

Web hosting is a solid and relatively mature business, with many excellent providers of hosting services, but more care is needed when considering outsourcing other Web and Internet functions. Make sure that you are dealing with a stable, well-funded outsource vendor, that you have a comprehensive contract with them, and that they offer quality service and support.

Making It Happen

Hosting Your Web Site

Hosting your Web site means putting it on the Internet so that people can visit it. There are two basic options: internal or external hosting. Internal hosting is often the option when dealing with an intranet, because most of the access to the intranet will be from within the organization. However, you must ensure that there is sufficient bandwidth so that staff working from home, or from hotel rooms, will be able to download pages quickly.

For most public Web sites, it makes sense to use a third-party hosting company. Such companies have mastered the complexities of Web site hosting and can offer excellent, good-value service. When choosing such a hosting company, consider the following:

- Do I need a domain name?
- How many visitors do I expect each month?
- How much space and what access speeds will I need?
- Will I need e-commerce facilities?
- Will I need special programming facilities such as CGI scripts?
- How do I want to deal with e-mail?
- What sort of support is offered?
- What are the price and payment options?

Outsourcing Your Web Site Operations

Hosting externally is a first step in outsourcing your Web site operations. Running a large Web site is a complex technical operation; the key advantage of outsourcing is that it allows you to focus on your core business, while giving you flexibility and removing the need to recruit your own technical staff. Keep the following in mind:

- Web site operation outsourcing is still a new industry with a high failure rate. Choose a company that is solid and well financed;
- it is important to develop a proper outsourcing strategy. This is a serious activity that can have serious consequences if done wrong;
- it takes time to choose the right vendor;
- a comprehensive contract must be in place. Assume that if something is not in the contract, it won't be done;
- proper metrics as well as a plan for day-to-day management of the outsourcing relationship must be in place;
- your outsourcer must have appropriate security practices;
- your outsourcer must have a good track record in providing quality service and support;
- outsourcing is not a technology strategy, so you will still need experienced technical staff to plan your future technology strategy.

Day-to-day Maintenance of a Web Site

Web sites are constantly evolving and therefore require continual maintenance. The level of maintenance will depend on the size of the Web site, and on which, if any, of the Web site's operations have been outsourced. To maintain a Web site professionally:

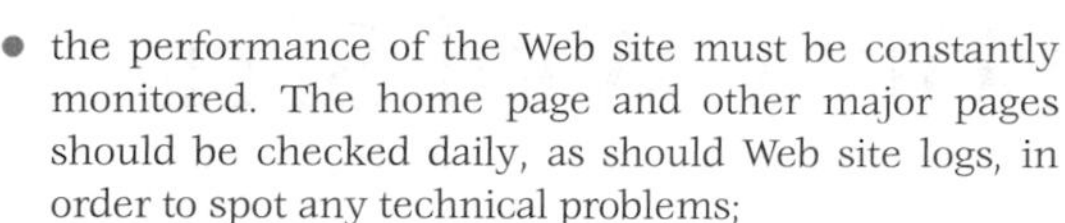

- the performance of the Web site must be constantly monitored. The home page and other major pages should be checked daily, as should Web site logs, in order to spot any technical problems;
- new content must be published regularly and old content removed. A Web site with out-of-date content makes a very bad impression;
- all links, forms, and programming elements must be checked regularly;
- standards established in the design of the Web site must be monitored, including navigation, search, layout, and graphic design;
- procedures should be in place to ensure regular feedback from visitors. Ideally, usability testing should be carried out regularly;
- Web site accessibility must be monitored;
- Web site security must be policed.

Managing Internet Security

The Internet is a network, and networks are, by definition, open. When approaching Internet security, keep in mind that if you don't have a defined and actively policed Internet security policy, you don't have Internet security. You should also:

- be ever-vigilant. There is no such thing as the perfect Internet security system. The security threat is constantly changing, so you must monitor the situation;
- combine software capabilities and human expertise. The best security software in the world still needs human experience and skills, particularly for larger systems;
- secure internally as well as externally: many security threats come from inside the organization;
- keep it simple. Less software and fewer options mean less opportunity for a hacker to find a weakness.

Dealing Effectively with Computer Viruses

Computer viruses are a constant and growing threat on the Internet, costing organizations billions of dollars every year. Every day they become more sophisticated and replicate more quickly. It is now possible to get a computer virus by visiting a Web site or opening an e-mail—previously, you had to open the e-mail attachment. The best approach to computer viruses is that prevention is far, far better than cure. To combat computer viruses:

- install the very latest antivirus software and keep it up to date;
- scan your entire computer system regularly with your antivirus software;
- get the latest software security patches for your computer; if you don't have them, your antivirus software may well not protect you;
- join an e-mail newsletter to get news on new antivirus and software upgrades;
- immediately delete suspicious e-mails;
- don't download anything from the Internet except from highly reputable Web sites;
- back up your data regularly;
- be vigilant.

Managing E-mail Professionally

Not treating e-mail seriously has two main results. First, there is so much e-mail around that its value as an effective communications tool is diminished. Second, many organizations are very lax in responding to e-mail enquiries from their Web sites or elsewhere. Not responding to an e-mail quickly is like leaving a phone unanswered. When managing e-mail, have policies and training in place to ensure that e-mail is used effectively, and implement a policy for responding to e-mails, particularly those received from the Web site.

Common Mistakes

Out-of-date Content

A Web site that has not been updated with fresh content, and/or that contains content that is no longer relevant, makes the organization look unprofessional.

Broken Links and Other Features

Many Web sites do not have procedures in place to check all the parts of the Web site to see if they are functioning properly. Broken links are common on the Web.

Poor Security Procedures

Many organizations do not realize how serious a security threat a Web site can be. Security has, in general, been poor on the Internet; the results of this are seen in the speed with which computer viruses can spread, and the frequency of Web site break-ins.

Not Responding to E-mails

Studies indicate that organizations perform poorly in their responses to people who have contacted them through the Web site. This gives a very poor impression to actual or potential customers.

For More Information

Web Sites:

Builder.com: **www.builder.com**

Google Web site Management Links, a comprehensive set of links relating to Web site management: **www.directory.google.com**

See also:

☆ **New Yardsticks for Performance and Productivity in an E-world (pp. 285–86)**

✓ **Day-to-day Maintenance of a Web Site (p. 600)**

✓ **Dealing Effectively With Computer Viruses (p. 601)**

✓ **How to Build a Web Site Team (pp. 594–95)**

✓ **How to Host or Select a Hosting Company (pp. 606–07)**

✓ **How to Implement Effective Internet Security (pp. 602–03)**

✓ **How to Set Up a Basic Web Site (pp. 592–93)**

Day-to-day Maintenance of a Web Site

Getting Started

The amount of Web site maintenance you will need will depend very much on the size of your Web site and the amount of new content that is being published on it. Web sites are not like brochures or other print material: they change, sometimes because of an action you have taken, and sometimes because of external factors. They must therefore be monitored constantly. Keep the following in mind:

- the performance of the Web site must be monitored;
- new content must be published regularly, and old content removed;
- all links, forms, and programming elements must be checked regularly;
- standards established in the design of the Web site must be monitored;
- procedures should be in place to ensure that regular feedback is obtained from visitors;
- Web site security must be policed.

Making It Happen

Test the Web Site from Different Environments

A Web site should be checked at least once a day to ensure that everything is working properly. It should also be regularly tested from different computers, browsers, and bandwidth access points, at different times of the day. Web pages may download quickly in the office environment over a fast connection, but how quickly are they downloading at home or in a hotel room? If pages are slow, it may be time to seek more bandwidth.

Managing Your Content

A Web site that doesn't regularly incorporate new content gives a very poor impression to visitors. Content must be created, edited, and published professionally on the Web site. Old content, or content that is found to be libelous or otherwise incorrect, must be removed quickly. The publication schedule for the Web site must be adhered to.

Optimize Graphics

New graphics should be checked for size. The objective is to have the graphic looking as good as possible, at the same time keeping it to the minimum possible file size. You must also make sure that the actual graphic size is being kept within agreed standards.

Web Page Weights

A Web page weight range should be established: 35K to 70K, with the objective of staying well below 70K, particularly for the home page.

Keep a Web Site Accessible

It is important that your Web site is accessible to people with disabilities. Minimum accessibility standards are increasingly required by law. The Web site must be checked regularly to ensure that it is accessible.

Check Links, Forms, and Programming Elements

Web site links, forms, and programming elements break, so it is important to check them regularly. Links may break because the page that you have linked to has changed or been removed. There is a wide selection of software that will check broken links. The page link may stay the same but the content that you originally linked to changes, so check key links manually.

Forms should be checked on a monthly basis. Put your e-mail address and dummy data into the form, and test that everything works properly. Programming should also be checked.

Manage Web Site Logs

Web site logs are important for tracking visitor behavior on the Web site. However, they can also provide very useful technical information. Check whether there are page errors or spikes in visitor behavior that may be causing bandwidth shortages.

Web Site Architecture and Management

A set of standards should be established with regard to the navigation, search, layout, and design of the Web site. It is important to monitor these standards to make sure that they are being implemented properly.

Usability and Feedback

Visitor feedback is critical in ensuring that a Web site continues to evolve to meet the needs of customers and other visitors. One of the best feedback methods is to get a small group of customers in a room and observe how they use the Web site.

Make Security a Priority

Computer security is an increasingly critical issue for Web sites. An Internet security policy should be in place, and this should be adhered to strictly.

For More Information

Book:

Nielsen, Jakob. *Designing Web Usability*. Indianapolis, IN: New Riders, 1999.

See also:

✔ **Dealing Effectively with Computer Viruses (p. 601)**
✔ **How to Build a Web Site Team (pp. 594–95)**
✔ **How to Host or Select a Hosting Company (pp. 606–07)**
✔ **How to Implement Effective Internet Security (pp. 602–03)**
✔ **The Key Principles of Web Site Management (pp. 598–99)**

  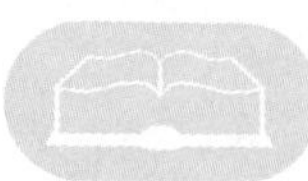    

Dealing Effectively With Computer Viruses

Getting Started

Computer viruses are a growing threat on the Internet. By September 2001, it was estimated that one in every 300 e-mails contained a virus, up from one in every 700 in October 2000. In addition, it is now possible to get a computer virus by visiting a Web site or simply by opening an e-mail. Computer viruses are costing organizations billions of dollars globally every year. To combat computer viruses:

- ensure that you have the very latest antivirus software and that you scan your entire computer regularly;
- ensure that you have the very latest software security patches for your computer;
- immediately delete suspicious e-mails and be very careful when opening unexpected attachments;
- don't download anything from the Internet except from reputable Web sites;
- back up your data regularly.

Making It Happen

Understand Computer Viruses, Trojan Horses, and Worms

In its simplest form, a computer virus attaches itself to computer files, and then seeks to replicate itself. Viruses can infect all sorts of files, from program and system files to Word documents and HTML files. The Internet causes viruses to spread with extraordinary speed.

A Trojan horse pretends to serve a useful function, such as a screen saver. However, as soon as it is run, it carries out its true purpose, which can be anything from using the computer as a host to infect other computers, to wiping the entire hard disk of the computer. Never download software over the Internet unless you are sure of its authenticity.

A computer worm does not try to damage the files it infects. Its objective is rather to replicate itself as quickly and as often as possible. Computer worms are a major drain on the Internet because they clog up bandwidth.

Prevention Is Much Better Than Cure

Viruses can be extremely difficult to get rid of. You may think you have cleaned them out with your antivirus software, but they may well have inserted hidden code in your operating system that is almost impossible to detect. It is, therefore, essential to stop viruses from getting into your computer in the first place. You do this by:

- making sure that you have the very latest antivirus software; popular antivirus software types include McAfee and Norton;
- joining an e-mail list that will inform you of new virus attacks. As soon as you hear of them, check your vendor for the latest updates;
- scanning your entire computer for viruses at least once a week;
- always making sure that you have the very latest security patches for your computer software. Viruses are always at their most potent in the first hours and days after their release, so it is vital to implement software patches as soon as they become available;
- if you use Microsoft Windows NT 4.0 and Windows 2000 software, regularly checking www.microsoft.com/security/ for news and updates. Microsoft also has a service that will check your computer for security weaknesses. It can be found at: www.microsoft.com/technet/mpsa/start.asp;
- only downloading software from reputable Web sites;
- deleting suspicious e-mails.

If You Become Infected

Deal with the threat immediately. Never wait, as the longer the virus is on your computer the more files it can infect. Some viruses, such as Code Red, open up your computer system to potential hacking. There is no guaranteed way to know that your system does not contain some malicious code that will be used at a future date, even when the offending virus has been deleted. If a virus such as Code Red has indeed infected your system, and if you want to be absolutely safe, reformat your hard disk and reinstall all your software again.

Coping with Virus Hoaxes

The Internet is full of virus hoaxes that waste time. If you get an e-mail about a new virus, go to the Web site of your antivirus software provider, and check if the warning is real. How to judge a hoax:

- Does the message come from a reputable source?
- Does it ask you to e mail it on to anyone you know? If it does, it's probably a hoax.
- Does it have a reputable link for more information?

For More Information

Web Sites:

McAfee Antivirus Software: **www.mcafee.com**
Norton Antivirus Software: **www.norton.com**

See also:

✓ **Day-to-day Maintenance of a Web Site (p. 600)**
✓ **How to Implement Effective Internet Security (pp. 602–03)**
✓ **The Key Principles of Web Site Management (pp. 598–99)**

"Short-term can be terminal." (Mark McCormack)

How to Implement Effective Internet Security

Getting Started

Internet security is a critically important issue. The Internet is a network, and is thus open to attack. A poor Internet security policy can result in a substantial loss of productivity and a drop in consumer confidence. Keep the following in mind:

- be eternally vigilant: the perfect Internet security system will be out of date the next day;
- combine software and human expertise: security software can only do so much; it must be combined with human expertise and experience;
- secure internally as well as externally; many security breaches come from inside the organization.

FAQs

What are examples of best practice in Internet security?

- Have an Internet security policy.
- If your system has been compromised, seek immediate independent expert help.
- For complete safety after an attack, the best course of action is to reformat the hard disk.
- Strip your computer down to its bare essentials. The more features, options, and software your computer has, the more open it is to attack. This is particularly true for Internet-related software and functions.
- For personal computers, be very careful about always-on connections provided by many broadband suppliers. An always-on connection to the Internet is always open to probing and attack by a hacker.
- Do not download software from the Internet unless you are totally confident about the source.

Are cookies a security threat?

Cookies collect information on how you browse the Web, and are a relatively low security risk. However, cookies can encourage lazy security practices, since they remember user-names and passwords.

Can you get a virus by opening an e-mail?

Yes. It used to be impossible to be infected by a computer virus transmitted by e-mail unless you opened the e-mail attachment. However, more recent viruses such as Nimda simply required the opening of the e-mail itself. Be very careful about unexpected e-mails from unfamiliar sources. If in doubt, delete without opening.

Making It Happen

Develop an Internet Security Policy

Keep the following in mind when developing your Internet security policy:

- many security breaches come from within an organization. The fewer people with access to the inner workings of the system, therefore, the better. Those who are allowed access must be recorded and given specific access rights. Immediately delete revoked and inactive users, or users who have left the organization;
- a rigorous procedure should be in place for granting and revoking rights of access;
- streamline hardware and software: a complex system is more open to attack. In your server software, for example, strip away as many of the optional features as possible;
- have a password policy. Do not allow simple or obvious passwords and change them regularly;
- have procedures for data backup and disaster recovery;
- have procedures for responding to security breaches;
- be vigilant. The Internet security threat is constantly changing, and constant vigilance is the best security;
- have your security policy audited by an external professional organization, and have them on call should a major breach occur.

The Benefits of Firewalls

A firewall is software that polices the space between your computer system and the outside world. The design and management of firewalls has become more complex since the advent of the Web because of the vast increase in activity between computers and the Internet. If the firewall is too stringent, it slows everything down and prevents people from carrying out certain legitimate activities; if too lax, the computer is open to attack.

Dealing with Viruses

Computer viruses are becoming more sophisticated and widespread. It is essential to have antivirus software and to keep it up to date. It is equally vital to upgrade your computer with the latest software security patches. For Microsoft software, more information on such patches is available at **www.microsoft.com/security**.

Dealing with Hackers

The main objective of a hacker is to gain unauthorized access to another computer, by probing for vulnerabilities on the computer, perhaps the result of flaws in the computer software and/or poor security procedures. Many hackers now focus on Web-based applications, which are still relatively new and have not developed reliable security measures. Security breaches can range from the hacker changing the pricing in a shopping cart to the theft of credit card numbers. The only way to deal with hackers is to implement rigorous security procedures and to monitor activity on the network constantly.

Reacting to a Security Breach

After a security breach there are two basic objectives. First, find out what happened so that you can stop it from happening again. Second, find out who did it so that you can prosecute or otherwise deal with them. It is very difficult to prosecute a security breach without hard evidence, and very easy to destroy such evidence. In dealing with security breaches, make sure that:

- you get professional advice, particularly if it is the first time your security has been breached;
- you protect all tracking activity on the system;
- the information collected is technically accurate;
- information is collected from various sources to develop an overall picture of what happened;
- no information is tampered with or modified.

In monitoring for security breaches:

- check access and error log files for suspicious activity;
- be alert for unusual system commands;
- be alert for repeated attempts to enter a password.

Denial of Service Attacks

Denial of service attacks do not seek to break into a computer system, but rather to crash a Web site by deluging it with phony traffic. Firewalls can be designed to block repeated and unusual traffic from a particular source. Distributed denial of service attacks, where the hacker takes over perhaps hundreds of other computers to carry out the attack, makes the job of the firewall more difficult. Firewalls can, however, be designed to guard against your computer becoming an unwitting host for such attacks on another computer.

Setting Up a Web Server

A Web server is potentially an open door into your network: if someone can break into your server, they are closer to breaking into your entire computer system. Before you set up a Web server you must ensure that you understand and deal effectively with the various security issues. By definition, Web servers interface with the Web and its potential hazards. They are large, complex software programs that embrace open architecture and that have often been developed at great speed.

From an e-commerce perspective, a secure server is a prerequisite. A secure server uses encryption when transferring or receiving data from the Web, turning it into special code that will then be decrypted only when it is safely within the server environment.

Equally important is what happens to the confidential information once it has reached the server environment. Once the information has been acted on, it should be stored in encrypted form. In the case of sensitive information, such as credit card details, it should be deleted.

Restricting Access to Your Web Site

You can restrict access to part or all of your Web site in a number of ways. The most common is by implementing a user-name and password system. However, you can also restrict access by IP (Internet) address, so that only people connecting from a certain address or domain can access information. Perhaps the most powerful approach is to use public key cryptography, whereby only the person with the assigned cryptography key can request and read the information.

Security and Outsourcing

Outsourcing creates an increased security risk. You must establish that the outsource vendor will adhere to your security policy, and that all work done adheres to proper security procedures. Ask your vendor:

- What is its security policy?
- What are its data backup and disaster-recovery procedures?
- How is your data safeguarded from that of other customers?
- How is your data safeguarded from the vendor's own employees?
- How is it insured with regard to security breaches?

Common Mistakes

Not Being Eternally Vigilant

There is no such thing as a perfect security system. Without constant vigilance, computer systems become an open invitation for hackers and viruses. An essential part of such vigilance is having the very latest security patches and antivirus software installed.

Thinking That You Won't Get a Virus

Viruses are becoming increasingly common. If you haven't had one so far, either you are tremendously lucky or you have excellent antivirus procedures.

Thinking That You Are Anonymous on the Internet

In general, you are not. When you visit a Web site, you will provide some or all of the following information:

- IP address
- time of access
- user-name (if a user-name and password are used)
- the URL requested
- the URL you have just visited
- the amount of data you downloaded
- the browser and operating system you are using
- your e-mail address

For More Information

Web Sites:

CERT Internet Security Center, a quality resource on Internet security issues: **www.cert.org**

Computer and Internet Security, a resource provided by the American Library of Congress: **www.loc.gov**

See also:

☆ **Viewpoint: David Weinberger (pp. 161–62)**

✓ **Day-to-day Maintenance of a Web Site (p. 600)**

✓ **Dealing Effectively with Computer Viruses (p. 601)**

✓ **Exploring Peer-to-peer (P2P) Commerce (pp. 646–47)**

✓ **How to Host or Select a Hosting Company (pp. 606–07)**

✓ **How to Manage Payments Online (pp. 588–89)**

✓ **The Key Principles of Web Site Management (pp. 598–99)**

How to Outsource Your Web Site Operations

Getting Started

Running a large Web site is a complex operation that requires substantial IT architecture and support. This can take the focus of your organization away from its core business of selling, marketing, and supporting your products and services. Outsourcing involves hiring third party professionals to manage and run your Web site's operations for an ongoing fee.

When approaching outsourcing, remember to:

- develop a proper strategy;
- ensure that a comprehensive contract is in place, and that there are proper metrics and management structures;
- make sure that you choose a stable, well-funded outsourcing vendor with a good track record for service and support.

FAQs

What are the key factors that drive outsourcing?

- The need to focus on core business activities rather than on building up a large IT function.
- Lack of sufficient skilled staff to run complex Web operations.
- Flexibility: a quality outsource vendor can respond more quickly to rapid changes in customer demand.

What are the advantages and disadvantages of Application Service Providers (ASPs)?

ASPs manage your software applications, which you then access over the Internet or a private network.

The advantages are:

- ASPs can save you money and time. Rented applications can be cost-effective and (in theory) can be up and running more quickly than buying an application;
- you have access to the best and latest software without worrying about upgrades and costly installations;
- the ASP option helps if you have a permanent IT skills shortage

The disadvantages are:

- outsourcing your applications involves considerable risk: the ASP industry is still young, and many ASPs have gone out of business;
- problems may arise because many applications were simply not designed to be accessed over a network, especially over the Internet;
- speed of access is very slow in many cases, which can be frustrating.

Has the outsourcing/ASP model been overhyped? Is it doomed?

Yes, it has been massively overhyped, but it is far from doomed. The fundamental offering is solid, and makes real economic sense. Renting software instead of purchasing it is expected to be a major development.

Making It Happen

Develop an Outsourcing Strategy

When considering the outsourcing of applications, or other Web and IT functions, you must ask yourself the following questions:

- Are my current applications proving very costly?
- Are there applications that would make my organization more productive but are simply too expensive?

Do you want to outsource:

- to reduce costs?
- to give greater flexibility?
- because you can't find the right IT skills?
- to guarantee a more reliable service?
- to focus better on your core business?
- to keep your IT department as small as possible?
- to reduce staffing levels?

You must also decide if there are certain elements of your IT infrastructure that you will never outsource.

Make Sure the Software Really Is Appropriate for Outsourcing

Many applications were simply not designed to be accessed over the Internet. Although upgrades can make such applications work in theory, in practice they can become excruciatingly slow and cumbersome. New software releases and increased bandwidth will solve these problems in time, but check if there are other customers successfully outsourcing the same thing.

Be Prepared

Deciding on an outsourcer is a complex and time-consuming process, so think about what you want to achieve and why. When developing your strategy, it is best not to be too open with outsourcing vendors. They will naturally want to sell you what they have, and may try to shape your thinking. It is better initially to go to a quality independent consultant who will help you think through all the issues and develop the comprehensive request for proposals (RFP).

When you finally engage with your shortlist of outsourcing vendors, they will have many detailed questions on how your operations are currently run. If you cannot answer these questions you will slow the whole process down, and will encourage the vendor to put forward a less fully and clearly defined contract than if it had had all the required information.

Choose a Stable, Well-funded Outsourcer

Choose a company that has a good reputation, is well funded, and has a good track record. When choosing an outsourcing partner, ask the following questions:

- How stable and well funded is it?
- Does it have a satisfied customer base?
- Has it successfully dealt before with the same needs as mine?

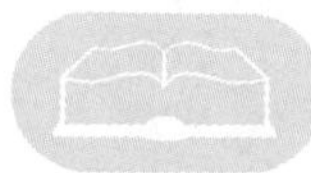

Service and Support Is Critical

The more you outsource, the more dependent you become on your outsourcer, so it is vital that your chosen vendor delivers comprehensive service and support.

Remember That Choosing an Outsourcing Vendor Takes Time

Outsourcing is a major strategic move involving much research and negotiation, so do not impose tight deadlines on yourself.

Ensure That a Comprehensive Contract Is in Place

An outsourcing contract should describe exactly what is to be delivered. It should state penalties for nondelivery. Legal expertise should be brought in early in the process, ideally when the RFP is being developed, so that everyone understands the legal implications of everything required and promised. However, the IT environment is constantly changing, and the contract must recognize this. Quality contracts are designed to facilitate later change and renegotiation.

Avoid long-term contracts. Vendors will argue that, because they have to bear a high upfront cost, you should sign a five to ten year contract with them. This does not make sense in a rapidly changing IT and e-commerce world; a two-year contract is reasonable to aim for.

Determine How This Relationship Will Be Managed and Measured

You must develop a set of metrics to measure how the outsourcer is meeting the objectives set by the contract. By doing this regularly, and addressing issues as they arise, major disputes, which benefit neither party, can be avoided.

Outsourcing is as much about managing the day-to-day relationship between you and the outsource vendor as it is about managing the technology. While a contract is important, prevention, by management that keeps a regular track of what is expected and what has been delivered, is better than cure.

Have a Corporate Technology Strategy

You are outsourcing your technology, not your technology strategy, and will always need skilled in-house resources to help you plan your direction from a technological point of view. Your outsourcer cannot do this; if they do, their recommendations will reflect their own strategy rather than yours.

Outsourcing Is Outsourcing

You cannot have the same level of control over the day-to-day running of your IT infrastructure after you outsource it, but some organizations forget that and try to achieve such control. Such an approach is counterproductive. You chose your outsourcer because they do the job better and more efficiently than you do.

Security Issues to Consider

Outsourcing creates an increased security risk. You must establish that the outsource vendor will adhere to your security policy, and that all work done integrates proper security procedures. Specific questions to ask are:

- What is the outsourcer's security policy?
- What are its data backup and disaster recovery procedures?
- How is your data safeguarded from its other customers?
- How is your data safeguarded from its own employees?
- How is it insured in relation to security breaches?

Common Mistakes

Outsource Vendors Who Promise Too Much

Outsource vendors have been known to over-promise and under-deliver.

Getting Rid Entirely of the Internal IT Web Operation

Some internal IT resource is necessary to take a more strategic view of the Web operation in order to plan its future evolution.

Going for the Lowest Price

Going for the lowest price rarely works out well. Service and support are critical elements in outsourcing, and the outsourcer that offers the lowest price is also, generally speaking, the one who will offer the least support. It is also the one most likely to go out of business.

Not Being Able to Deliver the Right Information

To deliver an outsourcing service, the vendor requires very detailed information on your current IT and Web setup. If you can't provide this information, you slow the whole process down, giving imperfect solutions.

Badly Framed Contracts

Long-term contracts are too often developed on the basis of short-term financial goals, such as cost cutting. Thus, the contract is unsuitable and renegotiation is required.

Poor Day-to-Day Management

Many IT departments do not have the management skills required to manage an outsourcing relationship.

For More Information

Web Sites:

Firmbuilder.com, good general resource on outsourcing: **www.firmbuilder.com/home.asp**

Outsourcing Center, provides extensive resources on outsourcing: **www.outsourcing-center.com**

See also:

☆ **Facilities Management (pp. 179–80)**
☆ **Outsourcing (pp. 89–90)**
✔ **How to Host or Select a Hosting Company (pp. 606–07)**

How to Host or Select a Hosting Company

Getting Started

Hosting your Web site means placing it on the Internet network so that it is available to people who want to visit it. There are two basic choices: internal or external hosting. Hosting a Web site internally is the general option for intranets, where visitors come only from within your organization. External hosting is the usual option for public Web sites.

FAQs

Should I host internally or externally?

External hosting has many advantages. Hosting is a complex activity, and there are many things that can go wrong. There are numerous specialist companies who are experts in the field of hosting, and are able to offer excellent service at a reasonable price because of the economies of scale.

What are the key issues to consider when choosing a hosting option?

Ask yourself:

- Do I need a domain name?
- How many visitors do I expect each month?
- How much space, and what access speeds, will I require?
- Will I need e-commerce facilities?
- Will I require special programming facilities, such as CGI scripts?
- How do I want to deal with e-mail?
- What sort of support is offered?
- What are the price and payment options?

What is the most popular and cost-effective hosting approach?

Virtual (shared) hosting. For between $20 and $30 a month there are excellent hosting packages that will work well for many small and medium-sized businesses. If, however, you want to add extra functionality, such as e-commerce, the costs begin to rise.

There are so many hosting companies. How do I choose the right one?

This is not easy. If you have quality technical expertise in-house you will be able to investigate the various options and choose the one that most closely fits your needs. If not, it is best to go with a big brand.

Key questions to ask are:

- How many customers do they have?
- How long have they been in business?
- How are they funded?
- What is their reputation for support?

Making It Happen

Basic Hosting Options

- Nonvirtual hosting: This is the most basic option, and is provided free by entities such as Geocities. You do not have your own domain name; instead, your address would be: www.hostingcompany.com/yourname. This sort of package is only advisable for very small businesses. A serious drawback is the lack of flexibility: you cannot change your hosting company without changing your Web address, whereas if you have your own domain name, it is yours forever (provided you pay your yearly registration fee), and you can move it wherever you want.
- Virtual hosting (sometimes known as shared hosting): You get space on a network vendor's server that is also used by other organizations. This is a popular and very suitable option for many small to medium-sized businesses. The hosting company agrees to deliver minimum access speeds and data transfer rates, and to carry out basic hardware maintenance, but you are responsible for managing the content and software.
- Collocation hosting: This involves placing your own servers with a hosting vendor. You manage everything that happens on your servers: content, software, and the hardware itself. The network provider supplies an agreed access speed to the Internet and an agreed amount of data transfer over a specified period. The network provider will also generally agree to some minimum service, such as ensuring that your server is running, and rebooting should it stop for any reason.
- Managed hosting: This is where the vendor has more responsibility. It can range from the vendor supplying and managing the hardware only, to also supplying and managing the software that runs on it. This type of vendor is called an application service provider (ASP).

Registering a Domain Name

If you are in business you should really have your own domain name. Most of the popular domain names have already been taken, particularly those connected with the .com suffix. Keep the following in mind when choosing a domain name:

- the name should be short and memorable;
- it's good to have a .com address, but if your primary markets are outside the United States, a domain name specific to these markets should be considered, for example, .co.uk for Britain; .de for Germany;
- to find out where to register your domain name, go to: http://directory.google.com/Top/Computers/Internet/Domain_Names

If you already have a domain name registered and are setting up with a hosting company, a transfer process will be required. This may take a couple of days, and if you already have a Web site up, or are using e-mail based on your domain, there may be a brief changeover period when your domain is inoperable.

Deciding on Network Speed

How quickly your Web pages download is very important. While the size of your Web pages is a major factor here, the network speed offered by your hosting company is another important element; as a rule, the cheaper the hosting package, the slower the speed. If you know that many of your customers are in, for example, the United Kingdom, it may make sense to host there so that pages download more quickly. Another key issue is whether the hosting company has backup and redundancy features, so that if one of their machines or lines to the Internet goes down, they can ensure that service is not interrupted.

Deciding on Disk Space

Most Web options provide plenty of disk space. If you have a substantial amount of content, estimate how many pages you expect to have. Multiply that by 50K average for each page. If you have 400 pages, the disk space you require will therefore be 20 megabytes.

Deciding on the Number of Web Site Visitors Expected

This is difficult to predict. A hosting company measures this by data transfer—the amount of data downloaded from your Web site. For example, if you expect 1,000 visitors a month, and the average visitor will look at four pages, a total of 4,000 pages will be downloaded. If the average size of a page is 50K, that gives a total data transfer of 200,000K, which would be well within the range of most hosting offers.

Access to E-commerce Facilities

While basic Web hosting can be very good value, it becomes more expensive if you want to add e-commerce functionality. E-commerce requires special software and programming, so you must ensure that your hosting package supports this. If you want to accept credit card information over the Internet, you will need a merchant account and a secure server over which such credit card information can be transferred.

Special Programming Features

If you want to do anything with your Web site that involves special programming, you must make sure that your hosting package supports it. It is essential to check whether your Web site is stored on a machine that supports the UNIX or Microsoft operating systems. Before you select a hosting package, discuss with your programmers or consulting company the potential programming that might be involved.

Extra Features That Must Be Considered

There are a number of features, over and above basic hosting, that must be considered when choosing a hosting package. These include:

- e-mail management: with your own domain you will want your own e-mail addresses, such as sales@mycompany.com. Depending on your hosting package, you may be allocated a certain number of e-mail addresses. Make sure that this allocation is sufficient;
- e-mail forwarding: check that the hosting package offers this;
- e-mail auto-responders: if you are away from the office you may want to use an auto-response function, whereby if someone sends you an e-mail they receive an automated response informing them that you are away. Check that the hosting company offers this;
- Microsoft FrontPage: if you are using Microsoft FrontPage as the tool to create your Web site, there are hosting packages set up specifically to support this;
- Web statistics: you need to access data easily so that you can use analysis software on it.

How the Hosting Will Be Paid For

Most hosting packages will require a setup fee. The payment structure can vary: some companies require payment monthly, others every 3 or 6 months, while some will ask for 12 months in advance. It is important to check the cancellation policy for any restrictive conditions.

Make Sure of Quality Support

The quality of support is critical. Occasional technical glitches will affect your site. The more you depend on your Web site, the more vital it is to get it back up quickly. If you can, find out what sort of reputation the hosting company has in this area. It is always better to pay a little more to ensure quality support.

Common Mistakes

Going for the Cheapest Option

The cheapest option is rarely the best choice. It is nearly always better to spend a little more to get better infrastructure and support.

Not Planning Ahead

You may not want e-commerce today, but will you want it in six months? If so, you must make sure that the hosting package you choose can provide it, or that you can easily migrate to another package with the hosting company. Changing hosting companies is a messy and time-consuming process.

For More Information

Web Sites:

Business2 Web Site Hosting Guide,
www.business2.com/webguide

HostReview.com, a site full of quality information on how to choose a Web hosting company:
www.hostreview.com

See also:

- ✓ **Day-to-day Maintenance of a Web Site (p. 600)**
- ✓ **How to Implement Effective Internet Security (pp. 602–03)**
- ✓ **How to Outsource Your Web Site Operations (pp. 604–05)**
- ✓ **The Key Principles of Web Site Management (pp. 598–99)**
- ✓ **Setting Up an Extranet (p. 639)**

Understanding the Key Principles of Content Management

Getting Started

When approaching content management, keep the following in mind:

- in an information economy full of information, workers, and consumers, content management is a critical function for a modern organization;
- content management is about the organization, classification, and storage of digital content, and the publication, navigation, and search of such content;
- content management includes processes that support the creation, editing, and publication of content.

FAQs

Why has content management become so important?

Because there is so much information in the world and so little time. Organizations are producing vast quantities of content every year, and the vast majority of this content is being produced in digital form. By 2001, it was estimated that there were over 550 billion documents on Internet, intranet, and extranet Web sites. Without professional content management it becomes almost impossible to find what you are looking for.

Why has the Web become such an important medium for the publication of content?

HTML, the layout language that is used to present content on the Web, has become the standard by which digital content is now published. The Web browser, through which HTML pages are viewed, is a simple yet powerful tool that is used by millions of people around the world every day.

What are the drawbacks of the Web?

As Steve Case, chairman of AOL Time Warner, has stated, the Web makes every enterprise a publisher. The problem is information overload. Much Web content lacks professional publishing standards. The early Web also depended on HTML for the management of content. HTML is to content management what hand-knitting is to the fabrics industry—beautiful results can be achieved for small amounts of content, but for large amounts of content it is a slow and expensive process. For large quantities of content, content management software is required.

Making It Happen

Develop a Core Business Case

Professional content management is an expensive process. Not all content has the same value. The organization needs to establish the business case for publishing content on its intranet or Internet Web site. A core business case will revolve around statements, such as "Getting the right content to our staff faster will make them more efficient" and "Quality content delivered to our customers will result in more sales and fewer support calls."

Carry Out a Situation Analysis

Before developing a content management strategy, it is important to understand how content is currently being managed within an organization and by the wider industry. If there is already a Web site:

- What content is being published on it?
- Is it up to date and accurate?
- Is it being read?
- What are our competitors doing on their Web sites?
- Are they being successful?
- Are there any standards emerging for content management within the industry?

Focus on Who Is Going to Read the Content

Too often, organizations think of content as a low-level commodity that merely needs to be stored. But content is a critical resource, and its value lies in being read. There is no point in having a great technical document if nobody knows it exists, or a Web site full of content that nobody uses. Thus, to make content management work, you really need to understand who the readers are. Who are the people that need to get your content? Ask them what content they need. Always remember that content is consumed by busy people.

Identify the Content You Need

How much content do you need to manage? What's the "must-have" versus the "like-to-have" content?

- How many other languages does it need to be published in?
- What are the media you want to publish it in (Web, e-mail, mobile)?
- What content forms will be required (text, audio, video)?
- Will you need to deal with PowerPoint slides and Word documents? How are these going to be converted?
- What is the sensitivity of the various items of content, and what will the security approach be?

Don't get carried away. You may have 50,000 documents, but maybe only 5,000 of them are relevant to the audience you want to reach.

Develop Professional "Create," "Edit," and "Publishing Functions"

There are a number of options available in relation to creating content, including:

- commissioning content, either from internal staff or from freelance authors;
- acquiring content from third-party sources such as commercial databases;
- online community-created content, whereby content is created from, for example, discussion boards, chat forums, or mailing lists.

Editing content refers to preparing it for publication. This will involve editing for tone and style, checking for correct grammar, and checking for such things as libel or copyright infringement. It will involve ensuring that the correct metadata is included. Editing also involves correcting content that is already published, and reviewing published content to ensure that it is up to date.

Define the Content Management Team

Content management software can underpin the publishing processes and make them far more efficient and cost-effective, but if you want quality content you need quality people to create, edit, and publish it. Someone with editorial and communication skills should run a content management project. Another core skill required is information architecture, and other skills will include moderating expertise (if there are online communities) as well as marketing, technical, graphic design, and usability expertise.

Design the Information Architecture

Good design of metadata and classification is crucial to the success of content management. Otherwise, content will end up being piled into a database and it will be almost impossible to find the right content quickly.

When designing metadata it is worth exploring how XML might be used. XML is an emerging metadata standard which facilitates the better organization and publication of content.

Navigation is like a signpost system. It is there to help people to find their way easily and logically around a Web site. Searching is a basic activity on the Web, and its professional design will be crucial to success. Graphic design and layout should ensure that content is presented in a way that is easy to read, view, or listen to. Other information architecture design issues include: multiple language design; content conversion (e.g. turning Microsoft Word documents into HTML); and integration with internal or external databases, subscription-based publishing design, and online community elements design.

Select the Content Management Software

If the Web site contains more than a couple of hundred pages and needs to be updated regularly, then it will make sense to acquire content management software. On the basis of the previous sections, a set of specifications can be drawn up covering the various content management processes required to achieve a professional result. These specifications will allow the organization to judge which content management software can best meet content management needs.

Define How Everything Is Going to Be Measured

A problem with content is that it is difficult to measure. However, that does not mean that measurables should not be put in place. Measures should be established with regard to how much content needs to be created each week, the quality of that content, and the time it takes to get content published. Information architecture measures include the quality of the metadata, how easy the site is to navigate, how well the search works, and how quickly pages download.

Common Mistakes

Not Having a Proper Business Case

While the Internet boom was in full swing, many content management projects did not have to show a strong business case. That reality has very much changed, and without having a clear business case and return-on-investment model it is unlikely that content management projects will receive the required funding.

Believing That All You Have to Do Is Buy Some Fancy Software and Your Problem Is Solved

Content management software is vital if large quantities of content are involved, but content follows the classic "garbage in, garbage out" rule. No amount of great software will turn poor quality content into good.

Allowing Out-of-date Content to Remain on Web Sites

A key problem on the Web today is out-of-date content. Many Web sites forget to remove old content. This results in a very poor experience for the visitor.

For More Information

Book:

McGovern, Gerry, and Rob Norton. *Content Critical.* Upper Saddle River, NJ: Financial Times Prentice Hall, 2001.

Web Site:

Business2.com, Web content management, an excellent selection of links to content management vendors, articles, and specialist Web sites: **www.business2.com/webguide**

See also:

- ✔ **How to Add Multimedia to a Web Site (pp. 596–97)**
- ✔ **How to Develop Appropriate Metadata and Classification for a Web Site (pp. 612–13)**
- ✔ **How to Make Sure Content Is Professionally Created, Edited, and Published (pp. 610–11)**
- ✔ **How to Set Up a Basic Web Site (pp. 592–93)**
- ✔ **How to Use the Internet to Create Content Collaboratively (p. 617)**
- ✔ **Making a Web Site Easy to Navigate (pp. 614–15)**

How to Make Sure Content is Professionally Created, Edited, and Published

Getting Started

If your content is not read by the people you want to read it, then your Web site has largely failed. Good content management software can help you create, edit, and publish quality content, but you need the people and processes in place to actually carry out the work. After you have identified the type of content and reader:

- establish processes that will ensure that this content is created and/or acquired;
- put editing processes in place that will ensure that the content is of the required standard;
- develop publishing processes that will allow the content to be published on time and presented in such a way that it is easy to find and easy to read.

FAQs

In editing, what is the key tradeoff?

In editing there is always a tradeoff between high-quality content and the time and expense it takes to achieve it. Publishing content to a very high standard is an expensive and time-consuming process. Such an approach becomes economically viable only if you have a large number of readers and/or can derive an appropriate return from a smaller number of readers. A balance needs to be struck between cost and the need to have content achieve a certain minimum standard of quality.

Can software make creating, editing, and publishing content more efficient?

Absolutely. However, whether you should buy content management software really depends on the quantity of content you are publishing. If there is a lot of content to be published, using an HTML approach with basic software can lead to bottlenecks. Content management software will make this process much faster and more manageable, but there will be significant setup costs.

Making It Happen

Create Content Internally

When creating content internally, keep in mind the following:

- content written with the Web in mind is far more likely to be read than content written for other sources. It may be more cost-effective to convert such content, but if nobody reads it, what good is it?
- it is necessary to consider what content creation tools are to be used. Is everyone going to standardize around a particular set of software, such as Microsoft Word?
- it is necessary to develop a style guide and glossary;
- if people are expected to create content regularly, it must be made part of their job function;
- an appropriate set of policies and procedures must be set in place for copyright and legal issues, and writers must be properly informed of the issues involved;
- a commissioning process must be established whereby editors can request that content be created.

Use Freelance Writers to Create Content

When there are gaps in the organization's ability to create content, freelance writers can be used. Remember that:

- a budget will need to be established, and authority given to the appropriate editors;
- freelance writers can plug gaps, but can become expensive if large quantities of content are involved;
- freelance writers will have the writing skills but not the in-depth knowledge of the organization.

Acquire Content through Purchase and/or Partnership

In purchasing and/or partnering to acquire content, keep the following in mind:

- for general content, such as industry news or trends, it makes a lot of sense to purchase;
- too much purchased content can give a generic feel to the Web site; it is important to get the balance right;
- partnering to acquire content usually works best in a traditional publishing setting. It is not always an option for an intranet or extranet publication, in which case it is usually better to purchase content if it cannot be created internally.

Acquire Content through Online Community Activities

Discussion boards, chat, and e-mail mailing lists can be effective ways of acquiring content for a Web site. Such online activities can help develop loyalty and a sense of community. The following should be considered:

- online communities need nurturing and encouragement;
- moderation is important, to see that the online community does not stray from its objectives, and that sensitive issues are properly monitored.

Establish Professional Editing Processes

Editing is about preparing content for publication. It is an essential though often neglected activity for content published on the Web. There are three editing functions that need to be considered:

- editing content awaiting publication;
- reviewing content already published;
- correcting published content for legal or other reasons.

Edit Content Awaiting Publication

Content that is awaiting publication needs to be thoroughly checked and edited for:

- metadata: this ensures that the content will be organized properly on the Web site so that it can be easily found. It includes such things as classification, date of publication, keywords, and author name
- quality and style: is the content written well and does it properly address its subject? Are the heading and summary snappy? Does it reflect the type of message the organization wishes to communicate? Are there any potential legal issues?
- accuracy and consistency: are the grammar, spelling, and punctuation correct?

Review Content Already Published

There are a number of ways content already published can be reviewed:

- an expiration date can be set for the content at publication so that it is removed from the Web site after that date. This is suitable for event-type content;
- related content can be reviewed as new content is published. For example, if a product specification changes then the previously published product specification should be removed from the Web site;
- it is a good policy to have a periodic review of all content on the Web site, perhaps once a year or more often, depending on the nature of the content.

Correct Content for Legal or Factual Errors

No matter how good the editing process, there will always be content that will get through with legal or factual errors. The important thing is to act quickly once these problems are isolated, as this will reduce the likelihood of legal action. Errors may be:

- minor: a date, or the name of a person, may be wrong; these errors should be changed immediately;
- more serious: an important fact may be wrong; a note may need to be attached to the document, explaining the error and the changes made;
- actionable: if charges of libel apply, an apology may need to be published and the document removed; act quickly and decisively in such situations.

Get Content Published

Publishing content on the Internet can occur in a number of ways:

- automatically: as a result of the metadata, the content is automatically placed within its classification. The heading and summary may be placed on the home page for a defined period of time;
- by editorial decision: the editor may decide to write special content to promote a particular piece of content on a home page; a number of articles may be grouped together to create a feature focusing on a particular topic or product;
- by subscription-based publishing: a selection of content may be delivered regularly by e-mail or other means to subscribers.

Whatever the means, the objective is to publish content in the most attractive manner possible, so as to ensure that the maximum number of people read it.

The home page is a critical part of any Web site. Studies show that, in the majority of situations, people are not sure exactly what content they want from a Web site. A well-organized home page, with good navigation and search facilities and punchy content, can guide the visitor in the right direction. Keeping that home page updated and lively is a key activity of publishing.

Common Mistakes

Not Having an Editor in Charge

At heart, content is not about technology but about people. Unfortunately, technical people tend to see content as a commodity. They don't really consider that someone somewhere may want to read it. Someone with editorial skills who truly understands the value of content, and how to create, edit, and publish it professionally should be in charge of the content management process.

No Reward for Creating Content

If content creation is not part of someone's job function, quality content will not be created, at least not on a consistent basis. Expecting people to create content and not rewarding them is a recipe for poor quality results.

Lack of Proper Editing Processes

Too often, Web sites become a dumping ground for content. Many organizations simply do not recognize the negative impact of poorly edited content.

Poor Metadata

The right content is becoming increasingly difficult to find on the Web. This is a result of poor metadata. Content is not being classified properly, keywords are not well thought through, headings and summaries are not descriptive. Add to that the fact that the search functions on many Web sites are poor, and it all adds up to an increasingly frustrating experience for the user.

For More Information

Book:

McGovern, Gerry, and Rob Norton. *Content Critical.* Upper Saddle River, NJ: Financial Times Prentice Hall, 2001.

Web Site:

Clickz content management and design:
www.clickz.com/design

See also:

- ✓ **How to Add Multimedia to a Web Site (pp. 596–97)**
- ✓ **How to Build a Web Site Team (pp. 594–95)**
- ✓ **How to Implement an Effective Search Process for a Web Site (p. 616)**
- ✓ **How to Use the Internet to Create Content Collaboratively (p. 617)**
- ✓ **Making a Web Site Easy to Navigate (pp. 614–15)**
- ✓ **Understanding the Key Principles of Content Management (pp. 608–09)**
- ✓ **Writing Well for the Web (pp. 620–21)**

" True creativity often starts where language ends."

(Charles G. Koch)

How to Develop Appropriate Metadata and Classification for a Web Site

Getting Started

If you have a large Web site—more than 100 pages—metadata is essential to ensure that your content is organized properly, so that it can be found quickly. Without metadata, the Web site becomes increasingly unusable as more content is included. Metadata includes such things as classification (which deals with how content is organized by subject matter), date of publication, keywords, heading, summary, author name, and copyright. The purpose of metadata is to:

- ensure that every document is properly classified so it can be found quickly;
- ensure that all relevant legal and administrative information on a particular document has been collected;
- maximize the chances of a document being indexed appropriately by internal and external search engines.

FAQs

What happens if you don't have good metadata on a Web site?

Without proper metadata it will take longer to find the right content. In fact, if it is a large Web site then it may be almost impossible to find what you are looking for. Time is the most valuable resource today. As information expands, time seems to be contracting. Waste your customers' time and you will lose their business.

What is XML and why is it so important?

XML (extensible markup language) is an emerging world standard for metadata. It has been described by Bill Gates, founder of Microsoft, as ushering in the third phase of the Internet. XML delivers a common approach by which metadata for content is collected. With metadata, organizations in a particular industry would agree to structure their documents in the same way. For example, organizations in the financial industry would agree to use the same methods of creating documentation such as morning notes, which are short analyses issued daily. The morning notes would all use the same layout structure, and would all have metadata such as: author name, date, ticker symbols, buy, hold, and sell rating. Because of this common structure, the person getting these morning notes would be able to search and interrogate them in a far more comprehensive manner.

What are examples of Web sites using quality metadata?

Perhaps the best-known example is Yahoo, which focused on creating a directory classification for the Web, instead of simply depending on search engine software. Yahoo became very popular because it had professional editors selecting and classifying Web sites for its directory. Visitors to the Yahoo Web site did not get an endless listing. Rather, they got a selection of the best Web sites under a particular classification. On the Web, that is what the majority of people want. All the best Web sites focus on quality classification and metadata; other examples are Amazon.com, eBay, and Microsoft.

Making It Happen

General Standards for Metadata Design

When designing metadata:

- always keep in mind the type of person that will be looking for the content. How would they like the content classified? When carrying out an advanced search, how would they like to refine their search?
- only collect metadata that is genuinely useful. Remember, someone has to fill in all the metadata. If you ask for too much metadata, then it will slow the publishing process down and make it more expensive;
- make sure that all essential information is collected. If copyright information is needed, then make sure that copyright is part of the metadata list;
- tell people not to abuse metadata. Some will put popular keywords in their metadata just to increase the chances of their documents coming up in a search. However, this is counterproductive, as the document will not be relevant to the search in question;
- remember that metadata should be strongly linked with advanced search. The metadata that you define becomes the parameters by which advanced search is refined.

Designing Document Templates

To collect metadata, some form of document template will be required which will contain all the relevant metadata fields. Examples of templates would be "Event Template," "Technical Paper Template," and "Personnel Details Template." You will require different templates when you have different metadata to collect. Avoid having too many templates, as it can be confusing. Give templates names that describe their function. Instead of "Template A," for example, call it "Event Template."

Getting Classification Right

Classification is a particularly important form of metadata. A Web site with poor classification is difficult to navigate. Visitors will not be able to find what they are looking for and will leave frustrated. Poor classification depresses them. Quality classification impresses them.

The top-level classification of your Web site expresses, in the fewest words possible, the nature of your business. Are you selling "products," "services," or "solutions"? Do you offer solutions for "home users," for "small business," or for "large business"? If you get your classification wrong, your Web site becomes a pointless exercise.

While it is relatively easy to design a classification for 50 documents, designing a classification for 1,000 or more documents is by no means simple. However, throw-

"If you file your waste basket for 50 years, you have a public library." (Tony Benn)

ing your hands up in the air and saying it can't be done is not acceptable. It must be undertaken, and professional advice must be sought where appropriate.

Things to Keep in Mind When Designing Classification

- Make sure that senior management is involved, particularly for the design of the top levels.
- Design from the point of view of the people who will be using the classification. Remember that classification terms that may be understood within the organization may not be nearly as clear to customers and potential customers.
- Focus on simplicity of design. Avoid using as classification terms jargon, ambiguous words, or complex terms.
- If possible, avoid going more than five levels deep for a classification design. Remember that the more levels there are, the more clicks are required to find what you are looking for. In addition, a classification with a lot of levels is prone to error in the classification process.
- As a general rule, aim for no more than 10 classifications at your top level, and certainly no more than 15. You have more flexibility at lower levels, but remember that if you have too many terms at a particular level, you risk confusing the visitor.
- Consider the number of documents you will have under any particular classification. If there are going to be more than 50 in any classification, then maybe that classification should be broken down further.
- Remember that the classification you create will be presented as navigation on the Web site. If possible, make sure that the classification terms at any one level—particularly the top level—are roughly the same length, otherwise the navigation will look awkward.
- Design the classification for the entire content environment, not simply the content you wish to publish at this time. You may have technical papers that you don't intend to publish on the Web site for another six months. However, create the classification term for them in the overall classification design.

Approaching Classification Design

When approaching the design of classification or other metadata:

- do your research. What sort of content do you have right now and in what way, if any, is it classified? How are your competitors classifying content on their Web sites? Are there any industry trends emerging? Make sure you get opinions from your customers on how they would like to navigate and search through your content;
- start at the top and design down. If you don't get the top level of the classification right, all other work is pointless. Make sure you involve senior management in the design of this level;
- mock it up and test it. Classification looks very dry and theoretical until you actually show how it will look on a Web page. It doesn't have to be a fancy design, just enough to illustrate how people might navigate through the classification. Keep changing and mocking up again until you are happy;
- get sign-off for the top level. Don't do any work on the lower levels until you have full agreement on how the top level is to be presented;
- design the lower levels. It may be that individual departments or sections will take on the job of designing the classification for the levels that relate to their areas. However, make sure that everything is coordinated so that the overall design is consistent;
- review and get final sign-off. The classification is the foundation for your Web site. It is essential, therefore, that it is properly reviewed and that the appropriate sign-off is obtained before any content is published that uses the classification. Work done in planning and designing a quality classification pays off handsomely.

Common Mistakes

Regarding Metadata as a Minor Activity

If content can't be found quickly, all the work and expense put into creating it in the first place will have largely gone to waste. Metadata is critical to the success of larger Web sites because it is the foundation upon which those Web sites are built.

Designing Classification for the Organization, Not the Visitor

A lot of organizations already have internal classification systems. Unfortunately, these may reflect obscure organizational structures rather than something that is useful for the customer or potential customer. When designing metadata, always keep in mind who will be using it.

Designing Too Complex a System

In an ideal world, it would be great to collect as much metadata on a document as possible. However, you have to be practical. If too much metadata is requested, people are unlikely to fill it out completely. Classification design can become very complex, but if it is too complex it will confuse both the visitor who is searching for content and the person who is charged with classifying the content. Remember, if content is continually being misclassified then the whole exercise becomes fruitless.

For More Information

Web Sites:

Business2 Information Architecture Links, a good selection of links on the subject of information architecture: **www.business2.com/webguide**

Google Metadata Links, links to Web sites carrying information on metadata by the Google search engine: **www.directory.google.com**

See also:

- ✓ **How to Develop a Personalization Strategy for a Web Site (pp. 586–87)**
- ✓ **How to Implement an Effective Search Process for a Web Site (p. 616)**
- ✓ **Making a Web Site Easy to Navigate (pp. 614–15)**
- ✓ **Understanding the Key Principles of Content Management (pp. 608–09)**

  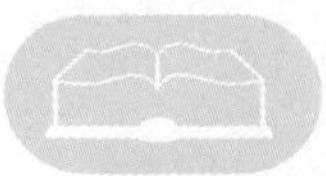    

Making a Web Site Easy to Navigate

Getting Started

Web navigation is like a signpost. Without it, a Web site becomes just a jumble of content. Keep the following in mind when approaching navigation design:

- navigation should provide context for content. It should show all the other content that is related to a particular category or item;
- navigation should be simple, unadorned, and consistent;
- people like to navigate through content in different ways, so a variety of navigation options should be provided.

FAQs

What is the key principle when designing navigation?

Functionality, not style. Functionality and plainness of design are what people want. What is important is the place they want to get to, not the navigation itself. Navigation should never be flashy and draw attention to itself. It should work in the background, making it easier for people to get to where they want to go.

What is the connection between navigation and classification?

Classification is how content is organized into manageable groups and subject areas. Navigation is how the classification is presented on a Web site. For a particular subject area there may be only one classification term, but it may be presented in a variety of different ways.

What is the connection between navigation and search?

There are two ways for people to find content on a Web site: one is through using search, the other is through using navigation. People often combine navigation and search: they might use search initially to narrow down their range of options, then use navigation to focus on the content in the subject area they wish to explore.

What would be the print media equivalent of navigation?

A publication's table of contents and index. It is unusual to find a publication without a table of contents. One of the key measures of the professionalism of a larger publication, such as a book or directory, is whether it has a good index. These navigation aids are thus seen as essential to quality publishing.

Making It Happen

Design for the Visitor

Navigation is about helping people to find content. Keep the visitor in mind at all times. Keep it simple, avoid being flashy, and test the navigation to see if people find it easy to use.

Give Visitors a Number of Options

Different people have different needs when navigating through content. Some may want to navigate geographically, some may have a particular subject in mind, some may want to get back to the home page as quickly as possible. A set of essential links (known as global navigation), placed near the top of the page, is always helpful. This allows the visitor to get quickly to key sections on the Web site, regardless of what particular page they are on. There are a variety of other navigation options that need to be employed, depending on the particular focus of the Web site. For example, if the Web site is e-commerce enabled, then it will require a prominent e-commerce navigation system.

Let Visitors Know Where They Are on the Web Site

Visitors may enter a Web site in a variety of ways. It is important that each page clearly displays what part of the overall classification it represents. If it is the home page, for example, this should be made clear. If it is a page dealing with pricing information for Product Z, then a heading at the top of the page should clearly state that. Such clear and unambiguous headings help put visitors at ease.

Let Visitors Know Where They Have Been

A primary function of hypertext is to indicate to visitors the places that they have already visited on a Web site. This is why hypertext links change color from blue to purple, with purple representing a link that has been clicked on. Avoid changing hypertext colors. People are familiar with blue for unclicked and purple for clicked.

Let Visitors Know Where They Are Going

Navigation should always support visitors in getting around the Web site, pointing them toward places they want to go and away from places they would like to avoid. There are a number of basic rules here:

- when visitors click on a link, they expect to be taken to a standard HTML page. They do not expect to be asked for a password, or to watch as a video or audio file starts downloading. If a link is to a nonstandard page, visitors should be informed in advance. For example, a statement such as "Password required" could be used if that is the case;
- if an image is a link, for example, a company logo linking to a home page, when visitors place their cursor over that image, text should appear with a statement such as "Company X home page";
- when visitors are asked to carry out a process, for example the purchase of something, navigation should appear that will indicate to them how many steps there are in the process, and how many steps they have completed.

Provide Context for Visitors

Studies show that only in a minority of cases do visitors know exactly the type of content they want. Visitors may be interested in buying laptop computers, but they may not know the exact make they require. Navigation as-

  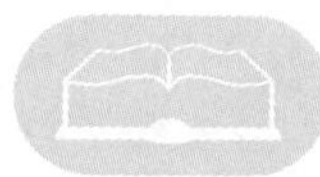    

sembles all the relevant content for a particular subject area into a well-presented environment. This is where navigation and classification are very much intertwined.

Keep Navigation Consistent

Avoid creating a Web site in which the navigation is constantly changing its structure. If the essential links are placed across the top of the page in one section of the Web site, then keep them across the top of the page in every other section unless you have a very good reason to change them. Lack of navigation consistency is particularly problematic if an organization has a number of Web sites, for example in an intranet environment. Departments and sections may feel a need to be distinctive, so they often make great efforts to create a navigation system that is totally different from those used by other sections. The result of this is confusion, and an environment that becomes increasingly chaotic, and so difficult and expensive to manage.

Where Possible, Follow Navigation Conventions That Have Emerged on the Web

People who use the Web instinctively see it as a single medium. They like familiarity of navigation design, because that means that what they have learned on one Web site they can carry over to another. Conventions that have emerged on the Web include:

- essential links (global navigation) that are placed on every page: these begin with a "Home" link and usually contain links to "About" and "Contact";
- the organization's logo on every page, usually in the top left, and linked back to the home page;
- a search box on every page, usually near the top;
- a footer on every page containing a copy of the essential links, contact information (address, e-mail, phone), and links to copyright and privacy statements;
- the use of standard hypertext colors: blue for unclicked, purple for clicked.

Never Surprise or Mislead Visitors

Never take visitors down paths that lead to a dead end. For example, if you don't sell to a particular country, inform people of this with a clear statement early on, not after they have ordered a quantity and filled in their address details. Some Web sites ask their visitors from other countries to call an 800 number, which is impossible to do from outside the United States. Also, not every country has ZIP codes. Give visitors an option.

Back Up Navigation with Quality Support

The Web is often compared to a library. If you visit a library, the bookshelves are the navigation system, but there are always librarians to get support from if you get lost. If the Web site is a large one, have a comprehensive help section. Make sure that if visitors e-mail the organization in search of a specific piece of content, someone gets back to them quickly. A surprising number of Web sites are extremely poor at responding to visitor queries. Subject-sensitive help is particularly important where you are asking visitors to carry out complex tasks. An example would be where a Web site offers advanced search. If visitors are asked to go through a process such as filling out a form, try to isolate any mistakes that are made. For example, if they didn't fill in the address, don't send them back the entire form, but rather isolate the exact mistake that they made.

Common Mistakes

Constantly Changing the Navigation

It is very frustrating to go back to a Web site and find that the navigation has been changed. Regular visitors get used to the way a Web site is laid out. The more regularly they visit, the more they get used to it (and the more likely they are to be valuable customers!). It is therefore important to plan your navigation well and to stick with it unless there is a compelling reason to change.

Designing Navigation from a Visual Point of View

Too many Web sites treat navigation as some visual branding exercise, rather than as a signpost system for helping visitors to find quickly the content they need. Navigation should be simple and functional. It should be one of the first things to download on a Web page.

Designing an Inconsistent Navigation

Navigation structures that change depending on the section of the Web site you are in, purely for the sake of being different, are of absolutely no help to the visitor. If a large organization with a number of Web sites does not provide consistent navigation, visitors may give up trying to use them. This leads to confusion and a sense of disorganization, thereby defeating the purpose of creating them in the first place.

For More Information

Book:

McGovern, Gerry, and Rob Norton. *Content Critical.* Upper Saddle River, NJ: Financial Times Prentice Hall, 2001.

See also:

✔ **How to Develop Appropriate Metadata and Classification for a Web Site (pp. 612–13)**
✔ **How to Establish an Enterprise Portal (p. 638)**
✔ **How to Implement an Effective Search Process for a Web Site (p. 616)**
✔ **The Key Issues to Consider When Designing a Web Site (pp. 590–91)**

How to Implement an Effective Search Process for a Web Site

Getting Started

Search is one of the most common activities that people carry out on a Web site. A quality search process allows people to find quickly the content they need. Getting your search working properly is thus one of the most important tasks you can undertake, particularly when you are dealing with large quantities of content. When designing a search function for your Web site:

- always make sure your search function is prominently displayed on your Web site; ideally, a search box should be available on every page;
- don't build your own; there are many vendors supplying quality search software;
- make sure your search function is effective. Despite search being such an important activity, a surprising number of Web sites do it badly. Don't be one of them.

Making It Happen

Types of Search

There are essentially two approaches to Web site search:

- basic search: this is sufficient for most smaller Web sites. Any Web site with more than 50 pages of content should consider having a basic search;
- advanced search: this is an additional option to basic search and is strongly recommended for Web sites with more than 500 pages of content.

General Standards for Search Design

The following general standards apply to search:

- the best font for search is Arial, as it is a narrow font that reads well while allowing the maximum number of characters to be entered into the smallest space;
- after entering their keywords or search term, visitors should be able to initiate a search with the touch of the return key as well as by clicking on a button marked "Search";
- all search functions create an index of the Web site. Make sure that indexing occurs regularly; otherwise recently published content will not be displayed in search returns.

Designing a Basic Search for a Web Site

Search is something people do all the time, so the basic search option should be available on every page of the Web site. Don't hide it behind a link. There are two common places where search boxes are found on Web sites today: at the top right of the Web page or near the top left of the page, directly underneath the organization logo. In a basic search:

- the search box must be sufficiently large to allow a minimum of 20 characters to be entered;
- the font should be Arial, and the font size should be 10 point, certainly no less than 8 point;
- there should be a button labeled "Search" at the right of the search box;
- if the Web site has an advanced search option, a text link labeled "Advanced Search" should be placed nearby.

Design an Advanced Search for a Web Site

Advanced search allows visitors to refine their search on the basis of various parameters. The larger the Web site, the more important advanced search becomes. Boolean search, a form of advanced search, allows you to search for a particular word while, for example, excluding another word. If metadata has been collected it may be possible to search by geographic region or subject area, or to search for documents by a particular author during a particular time period, and so on.

Display Search Results

Search is a very functional activity, and the search results page should not contain anything to distract the searcher; just give them the results. A particular set of search results should include the following:

- the title or heading of the Web page that the search result refers to. This should be shown in bold type and hyperlinked to that page;
- a two-line summary describing the content on that page;
- the URL for that page;
- the date of publication for that page.

Deciding on Search Software

There is a wide variety of excellent, well-priced basic search software available that is easy and quick to install. Dealing with search for larger Web sites is naturally more complex, with customization demanded where advanced search options are required.

For More Information

Web Sites:

Search Engine Watch, an excellent resource on search engines: **www.searchenginewatch.com**

Selection of Search Engine Software from Google: **www.directory.google.com**

See also:

✓ **How to Develop Appropriate Metadata and Classification for a Web Site (pp. 612–13)**

✓ **How to Establish an Enterprise Portal (p. 638)**

✓ **How to Make Sure Content Is Professionally Created, Edited, and Published (pp. 610–11)**

✓ **Making a Web Site Easy to Navigate (pp. 614–15)**

"Life is a search after power." (Ralph Waldo Emerson)

How to Use the Internet to Create Content Collaboratively

Getting Started

Collaborative writing has seen a steady increase since the coming of the Internet. E-mail, in particular, has been a driver of collaboration because it enables writers to communicate cheaply and regularly. When considering the collaborative creation of content, keep the following in mind:

- it is best applied to large, complex-content projects;
- quality results will not be achieved without proper planning and editorial management;
- the people involved must understand the objectives of the project clearly;
- appropriate rewards must be articulated in order to achieve proper motivation.

Making It Happen

Key Benefits of Collaboration in Content Creation

The key benefits are:

- in a complex, ever-changing world, very few people have all the expertise and knowledge required to publish the wide range of content required for an increasingly demanding readership;
- alliances, partnerships, and collaboration are seen as key characteristics of the new economy. Publishing collaborative content is an important result of collaboration and partnership;
- large-content projects can be published more quickly through collaboration;
- complex issues can be addressed by a range of experts;
- various skills and experience can be brought together to achieve superior results. For example, one person may be an expert in the subject area, while another may be a skilled writer who can translate this expertise into a readable format.

Collaboration Works Best for Large, Complex-content Projects

Collaboration is most suitable for large and complex-content projects that require the contribution of many kinds of expertise.

Make Sure Everyone Is on the Same Page

Before starting a collaborative writing project, it is important that everyone involved is clear on what the objectives are. While it is possible for people who have never physically met to collaborate, it is highly recommended that the collaborative group get together at least once so that people know each other better.

Make sure that a common style and tone are agreed. A short document should be prepared that will clearly articulate the intended style and tone. Some sample material should be presented that will illustrate these, such as a style guide and a sample document. A glossary of common words and phrases that will be used should also be prepared. This will establish spelling conventions as well as intended meanings.

Break the Project Up into Definable Segments

Ideally, the project should be broken up into definable segments, each being allocated to a particular individual. One writer may do research for a particular area and write the first draft, while another will take that draft and add to it. Editing functions may be swapped, depending on who has written what. However, be careful about oversegmentation. Simply giving a group of people different sections to write is not collaboration.

Put an Editor in Charge

If collaboration involves only two people, they may well be able to swap editorial functions and agree by consent. Where a larger group is involved, however, there should be an editor in charge who will ensure that the end result reflects the objectives, and that the style and tone are established at the outset.

Establish Clear Reward and Remuneration Structures

In a business setting—and in most other settings—people write for two basic reasons: pay and ego. Pay should be covered because it is part of their job. Ego is about making sure that everyone involved gets the proper credit.

Make Sure Version Control Is Properly Managed

It is frustrating to find that you have been working on the wrong draft of a document. Document management software can be used here, but if this is not available, then the editor should be in charge of keeping the master draft. A useful tool for tracking changes between versions is the Track Changes facility in Microsoft Word, which can be found in the Tools menu.

For More Information

Web Site:

Guidelines for collaborative writing, a short, informative article on collaborative writing:
www.uncp.edu/home/vanderhoof/syllabus

See also:

☆ **Virtual Collaboration (pp. 167–68)**
✔ **How to Build a Web Site Team (pp. 594–95)**
✔ **How to Generate Content and Build Loyalty Through Online Communities (p. 629)**
✔ **How to Make Sure Content Is Professionally Created, Edited, and Published (pp. 610–11)**

  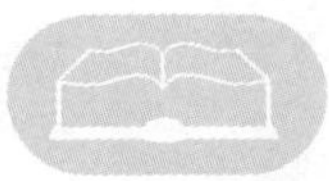    

Setting Up a Subscription Process

Getting Started

Subscription is becoming an increasingly important process if access to certain content on a Web site must be restricted, and/or an e-mail subscription service has to be established. Someone may become a subscriber as a result of giving personal information such as an e-mail address, or as a result of making a payment if the subscription service is directly revenue-generating.

FAQs

Why have paid-for subscriptions not worked on the Internet so far?

The early Internet promoted a culture that encouraged the free transfer of information. Traditional publishers subsidized their online publications from the money they were making offline. Others believed that they could become profitable using an advertiser-only model. It was also true that subscription processes were difficult to use. The time of free content is past and people are now realizing that a Web site must pay for itself, through subscription or advertising revenues, or by delivering valuable information that will further the organization's objectives. As the Internet evolves, many more Web sites will become subscription-based.

When should you consider using a subscription process?

Every Web site should have at least one e-mail subscription service, because that will enable the organization to keep in regular touch with its target market at minimal cost. Because intranets and extranets contain confidential information, a subscription process will be required to ensure that the right people are accessing the right information. It is also likely that certain parts of the public Web site will have restricted access. A subscription process defining access rights will be required here. If you are planning a paid-for publication on the Internet, you will need a subscription process.

Making It Happen

Clearly Define What the Person Is Subscribing To

Outline to potential subscribers what exactly they will get if they subscribe. If they are subscribing for access to a Web site, tell them what sort of content is available on it. If they are subscribing to an e-mail mailing service, tell them what type of content they will receive and how often it will be sent. Depending on the confidentiality of the information, it can be a good idea to offer a sample of the content, and/or a free period of access.

Have a Clear Privacy Policy

Clearly outline a privacy policy in relation to personal information that the potential subscriber is being asked to supply. Privacy is a critical issue for a great many people using the Internet. If they feel a Web site might sell on or otherwise abuse the personal information they give, they will be highly unlikely to subscribe. If a Web site wishes to track a subscriber's use of the site in order to personalize content for them, it must make it clear to the subscriber that this is going to happen.

Keep the Subscription Process As Brief and Simple As Possible

People hate filling out long subscription forms on the Internet, so if you want to maximize your subscription base you must keep the subscription process as short and simple as possible. It is often enough simply to ask for an e-mail address. However, if you do need to ask a number of questions, consider the following procedures:

- ask opinion-type questions first. People are more willing to answer opinion-type questions. Place the personal information questions after these;
- have mandatory and optional questions. Make sure that mandatory questions are clearly flagged. At the top of the form, make a statement such as "All questions marked * must be filled out";
- don't mandate answers to questions that some people cannot fill out. For example, not every country has a ZIP code. If you do want to mandate ZIP codes, advise those who don't have them to enter "None" in the field.

Support People Who Make Mistakes

People can make mistakes, particularly where they are asked to fill out longer forms. Don't just create a process that says "You have made a mistake." Instead, have the process isolate the error and state, for example, "You have not entered your telephone number. Please fill it in." In addition, have the process check for obvious errors where possible. For example, if someone mistakenly adds characters at the end of their e-mail address, isolate this. Make a statement such as: "The e-mail address you entered—mary@yourcompany.comp—seems to be incorrect. Please recheck."

Use a Double Opt-in Approach for Subscription

The double opt-in subscription approach is emerging as the industry standard for subscription management. The double opt-in approach ensures that someone is not maliciously subscribed to a service by a third party. It works as follows:

1. a request for subscription is sent using a Web form or e-mail process;
2. the system replies with a verification message, requesting an affirmative reply to the message;
3. only when an affirmative reply is received is that particular subscription completed.

Always Send a Confirmation Message

When someone has subscribed to a service they should be sent a confirmation message, including.

- a message welcoming them to the service:
- a description of the subscription service;
- how to unsubscribe from the service;
- the e-mail address the person subscribed with, and the username and password, if any, that were used.

"Nothing that costs only a dollar is worth having." (Elizabeth Arden)

The subscriber should be told to store this confirmation message carefully, so that they can access it in the future if, for example, they wish to unsubscribe or have forgotten their password.

Make Sure That There Is a Simple and Clear Unsubscription Process

People can get very irate when they find it difficult to unsubscribe. Ideally, a variety of options should be offered with regard to unsubscription, including:

- an unsubscription box on the Web site;
- a special e-mail address for unsubscribing;
- a contact for a real person who will carry out the unsubscription if the subscriber is having difficulties.

One of the most common mistakes that people make when trying to unsubscribe is that they forget the exact address they subscribed with. Without this exact address, most unsubscription systems will not allow users to unsubscribe. As part of the unsubscription process, the subscriber should be informed of this mistake before and after the fact so that they can avoid it. To overcome this problem, some e-mail subscription systems offer a feature whereby each mailing has information on the original e-mail address which was used to subscribe. When someone unsubscribes, they should be sent a brief message thanking them for having been a subscriber.

Spend Time Maintaining the Subscriber Base

As the subscriber base grows and matures, various maintenance problems will arise. People will move away from organizations and will forget to unsubscribe. There will be occasional network problems that will result in the nondelivery of e-mails. It is advisable to wait for a period to see if the delivery problems are temporary or permanent. After it is established that an address has permanent delivery problems, that address should be deleted.

Protect the Subscriber Base

A subscriber list is extremely valuable, and careful steps should be taken to protect it. Always make sure that the subscriber list is password-protected. Limit access to it to one or two people at most. Stolen subscriber lists can become a PR disaster, damaging the credibility of the organization. Make sure you create regular backup copies of the subscriber list.

Procedures for Managing Passwords

Remembering passwords is something that many people find difficult, but passwords are a necessary evil for Web-based subscription processes. Password-protected areas in Web sites should be clearly flagged with wording to such effect. It is very frustrating to click on a link, only to find that it requires a password to get to the content behind it. Cookie software can be used so that the subscriber is given an option for the Web site to remember their password, so that the next time they visit they will gain automatic access.

The ideal process for allocating a password is as follows:

- ask the subscriber to fill out a username: allow the subscriber to use their e-mail address as their username, as this will be easier for them to remember;
- if it is not possible to use the e-mail address as the username, ask them to fill out their e-mail address, as this will be required in order to communicate vital information to the subscriber;
- have the subscriber create a password that is a minimum of six characters long. Advise the subscriber not to use common words for their password. Ideally, they should mix characters and numbers. Show an asterisk for each character entered;
- present a second password field to fill out to ensure that the password has been filled in correctly;
- people regularly forget passwords. Provide a field which gives the subscriber the option of answering one of a selection of common questions: "What is the name of your pet? What is your mother's maiden name?" If the person forgets their password in the future they will be asked the question. A correct reply enables them to create a new password.

Common Mistakes

Making the Subscription Process Too Long

People hate filling out long forms. Some subscription processes ask for too much information, much of it not really useful. In most cases this has the effect of reducing the number of subscribers.

Not Reacting Quickly Enough to Requests to Unsubscribe

If someone gets in touch asking to unsubscribe, it is probable that they tried to unsubscribe themselves, using the automated process, and failed. They are thus already somewhat frustrated. Ignoring their request to unsubscribe can make them very angry. They may claim that you are spamming them, and this will not be good for your reputation.

Not Properly Protecting the Subscriber Lists

Hackers love to steal subscriber lists and publish them. Worse, spammers love to get their hands on subscriber lists and spam to them. Either way, it is a PR disaster.

For More Information

Book:

Seybold, Patricia B., with Ronni T. Marshak. *Customers.com*. New York: Random House, 1998.

See also:

✓ **Exploring Peer-to-peer (P2P) Commerce (pp. 646–47)**
✓ **How to Get the Best from Loyalty Programs on the Web (p. 627)**
✓ **How to Manage Payments Online (pp. 588–89)**
✓ **How to Use E-mail Marketing Effectively (pp. 632–33)**

Writing Well for the Web

Getting Started

People read differently on the Web, so you need to write differently for the Web. Surprisingly, very few Web sites take the time to lay out their content in a way that will maximize its readability. An important point is that it is more difficult to read on a screen than from paper. This means that if you want to be read on the Web, you must write and lay out your content in a more simple, straightforward manner than you would in print. If you want to ensure that your content has the best chance of being read, focus on:

- shorter sentences, shorter paragraphs and shorter documents;
- plentiful use of short, punchy, and descriptive headings and summaries;
- larger font sizes and sans serif fonts, because they are easier to read;
- straightforward, factual prose.

FAQs

In what way do people read differently on the Web?

They scan, moving quickly across text, always looking in a hurry for the content they need. They are very fact-oriented. People don't read on the Web for pleasure—they read to do business, to be educated, to find out something—so they like to read content that gets to the point quickly.

People like reading short documents, with links to more detailed information as appropriate. If a document is long, and people really have no choice but to read it, a significant number of them will print it out. In general, however, long documents tend to go unread.

Why do so many people regard Web content as poor quality?

People don't trust the content they read on the Web because they come across so many Web sites with poor publishing standards. The Web gives everyone access to the tools of publishing, but giving someone a word processor does not make them a good writer.

Too many Web sites lack proper editing standards. They also translate documents that were prepared for print directly to the Web; this may save money in the short term, but if people don't read the content, it is pointless. Some Web sites deliberately try to mislead people with their content. All this gives a poor impression to people who use the Web.

Is writing for the Web a difficult skill to learn?

It is not easy to write well, no matter what the medium is. However, writing for the Web is about concentrating on the facts. You don't need flowery prose; you must be able to communicate the really important stuff in as few words as possible. This is not an easy thing to do, but with practice most people can master the basics.

Making It Happen

If You're Not Read You're Dead

The connection between writing and reading is one that is not always considered: a surprising number of organizations create vast quantities of content without asking some obvious questions:

- Is anyone interested in reading this content?
- Is it written in a way that is accessible?
- How are we going to let people know that we have just published this content?

Less Is More

Writing is rarely about quantity, but it should always be about quality. Less is more, particularly on the Web. It is easier to write 5,000 words of waffle than 500 words that are succinct, but 500 words is what is needed on the Web.

Editing Is Essential

One of the primary functions of editing is to get a long draft into shape. As George Orwell put it: "If it is possible to cut a word, always cut it." We all have pet phrases that we love to put into sentences whenever we can. They may sound good to the writer, but very often add nothing to the meaning of what is being communicated. The Web is about functional writing. Get to the point, then stop.

Keep It Short

When writing for the Web:

- documents should rarely be longer than 1,000 words: 500 to 700 is a good length to aim for;
- paragraphs should be between 40 and 50 words;
- try not to let your sentences go over 20 words.

Write for the Reader, Not Your Ego

When writing, always keep in mind who it is you are writing for. Will they understand what you are writing about? Don't write to please yourself—write to please your reader. One mark of a poor writer is the use of big words and convoluted phrases. The good writer is clear and precise.

Focus on the Headings

Headings are important on the Web for two central reasons. First, people scan, so the first thing they often do is to look for headings; if the heading doesn't attract their attention, then they probably won't read any further. Second, people use search engines a lot, and the most prominent things in a page of search results are the headings. The heading really has to sell the Web page and convince the person to click for more information.

Writing headings well is an art, but here are a few rules that will help you get the basics right:

- keep them short. Ideally, a heading should not be longer than 5 to 8 words;
- make your point clear. For example, "Nasdaq crashes to record low" is more informative than "Apocalypse now for investors!" when talking about a severe stock market downturn;

- use strong, direct language. Don't be sensational, but at the same time don't be vague, and don't hedge;
- don't deceive the reader, for example by using "Microsoft" in a heading just because you think people will then be more likely to read it. The job of the heading is to tell the reader succinctly what is in the document.

Use Subheadings

In longer documents it is always a good idea to use subheadings, as they break up the text into the more readable chunks that readers like. Subheadings should be used every 5 to 7 paragraphs.

Summaries: the Who, What, Where and When

Next to the heading, the summary is the most important piece of text. It should be descriptive, not wandering or indirect. Tell the reader what the document is about, and who, where and when the information relates to.

Getting Down to Write

"No man but a blockhead ever wrote. . .except for money," according to Samuel Johnson. Sound advice. Writing is not easy but someone has to do it. The first rule of writing is reading: if you are asked to write a technical paper, read how other people write them. Read how they are written on your own Web site, on competitors' Web sites, in industry journals. Find a style that works well and copy it; use its techniques and approach to structure. Don't plagiarize, but never feel ashamed of finding quality writing and learning from it.

Learn How to Edit

Even if you have an editor, you still want to send them a draft that is well written. Here are a few steps to follow:

- Get a first draft written and don't throw it away.
- Leave it for a while, then print it out, or make the font size larger so that the text stands out more.
- Read it as if someone else wrote it. Is it written in a way that the reader can easily understand it? What is the writer trying to say? Is this sentence or paragraph necessary? Has the writer covered all the essential facts?
- First drafts are often too long. When preparing the second draft, cut ruthlessly, maybe by as much as half.
- Use your word count carefully. When you are asked to write something, always ask how many words are required. If you are not given a word count then decide on one yourself. Keep it as low as possible.

Explore Collaborative Writing

Computers and the Internet make collaborative writing far easier, and as a result it is becoming an increasingly popular approach to writing content. Collaborative writing works well if:

- the writers spend time working through the objectives of the writing exercise, and reach agreement on such necessary matters as the style, tone, and length of the piece;
- there is a lot of content to be written that can benefit from the input of multiple disciplines;
- people can be given defined segments of content to write, and/or the different skills of different people can be used, for example when one person understands the subject well, while another is a good writer;
- there are professional processes in place to facilitate collaboration;
- the writers know and respect each other.

Common Mistakes

Not Focusing on the Needs of the Reader

A surprising number of Web sites fail to consider who their reader is, simply adding content for its own sake. If you ignore the needs of your reader, then your reader will ignore you.

Putting Non-Web Formats onto the Web

Translating a 40-page Word document into HTML is a simple task; persuading someone to read it is another job entirely. Have you ever tried reading an Adobe PDF file on a screen? It's a painful experience. How many of your customers have read that PowerPoint presentation you translated into HTML?

Putting Every Piece of Content You Can Find on the Web

The Web is not a dumping ground for content. You might have 50,000 documents, with only 5,000 suitable for your Web site. Publishing the other 45,000 simply wastes your readers' time—not something you want to do.

Poor Editing

It is almost impossible to create quality content without sending it through a professional editorial process. No matter how good the writer, their content will always benefit by having it checked over by an editor.

Long, Rambling Documents

If, after reading the heading and summary, the average Web reader hasn't understood what exactly you are trying to communicate to them, then chances are they will click the Back button. Readers on the Web have become ruthless about their time.

For More Information

Book:

McGovern, Gerry, Rob Norton, and Catherine O'Dowd. *The Web Content Style Guide.* Upper Saddle River, NJ: Financial Times Prentice Hall, 2001.

Web Site:

Clickz Writing for the Web, a good selection of advice from web writing experts: **www.clickz.com/design**

See also:

✓ **How to Make Sure Content Is Professionally Created, Edited, and Published (pp. 610–11)**
✓ **How to Set Up a Basic Web Site (pp. 592–93)**
✓ **The Key Issues to Consider When Designing a Web Site (pp. 590–91)**

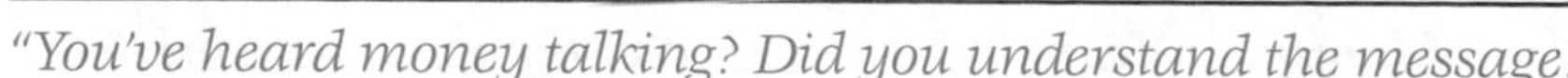

"You've heard money talking? Did you understand the message?"

(Marshall McLuhan)

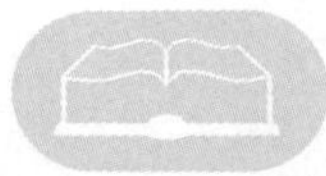

UNDERSTANDING THE KEY PRINCIPLES OF INTERNET MARKETING

GETTING STARTED

Internet marketing is about giving, rather than getting, attention. An adjunct to traditional marketing, it supports and enhances the overall marketing message by providing comprehensive information that answers consumers' questions about a particular product or service. Internet marketing also exploits the networking capabilities of the Web by leveraging online community activities, linking, affiliate marketing, viral marketing, e-mail marketing, and loyalty programs. When approaching Internet marketing, keep the following in mind:

- when visitors come to a Web site they are already aware of the brand. They want information;
- use Internet technology to understand the needs of your customers, so that you can offer them just the right information and products;
- remember that the Internet empowers the consumer. A dissatisfied consumer can use the networking capabilities of the Internet to undermine your brand.

FAQs

WHAT SORT OF PRODUCTS AND SERVICES IS INTERNET MARKETING BEST SUITED TO?

Internet marketing is best suited to:

- products and services that require a lot of information to sell. Travel is a very information-intensive product. People want times, prices, information about the destination. When buying books, they are strongly influenced by reviews, opinions of other readers, tables of contents, sample chapters;
- products and services that people feel strongly about, such as books, music, and movies. Fans network with other fans in online communities to discuss their favorite artists;
- products and services that are bought by the Internet demographic. Although the Internet demographic has broadened, it is still generally the domain of the well educated and better off. Those working in technology and academia are very well represented.

WHAT ABOUT ONLINE ADVERTISING? DOES IT WORK?

As a pure branding tool, online advertising does not have the same impact as television or glossy media, because of bandwidth restrictions. Studies indicate that most consumers avoid interactive ads because they simply take too much time to download.

However, the real power of online advertising is not from a mass marketing point of view but, rather, its ability to reach niche markets and target just the right consumer with just the right product. Advertising success is claimed by opt-in e-mail-based marketing, where consumers request information on a particular product or service. In online advertising, the scattershot approach is out and laser point focus is in.

MAKING IT HAPPEN

UNDERSTAND THAT INTERNET MARKETING IS PART OF THE OVERALL PACKAGE

The objective of Internet marketing should be to integrate it into the overall marketing strategy, where it supports and is supported by offline marketing activities. However, that is not to say Internet marketing doesn't have its own unique characteristics. Internet marketing is not about a big idea, some compelling graphics, and a killer catchphrase. Offline marketing brings consumers to the Web site with such approaches. Their interest has been aroused. They have questions. Internet marketing answers those questions by having comprehensive information on offer. Remember, people are not coming to the Web site to read the brochure again.

BACK IT UP WITH E-MAIL MARKETING

Since the Web was launched, perceptive marketers have been stressing that every Web site should have an e-mail marketing strategy. Consider that consumers must actively decide to go to a Web site, but with e-mail they join a database in which they can be regularly informed of products, services, and offers that the organization has. The key to e-mail marketing success is getting people who want the information to join a database in which they will receive regular e-mail alerts and newsletters. Of course, the information they receive needs to be of a type and quality that they signed up to get.

TAP INTO THE NETWORKING ABILITY OF THE INTERNET

The Internet is a community and it offers a tremendously powerful means for people and organizations to network. Linking is one of the simplest yet most effective Internet marketing devices there is. It underpins affiliate marketing efforts by Web sites such as Amazon.com. Linking is like embedded word of mouth. If another Web site links to you, it is essentially recommending you to its own visitors. Viral marketing is a network effect, whereby groups of consumers create a buzz about a product or service by e-mailing friends and/or creating their own Web sites. Consumers gain a power through Internet networking that they traditionally did not have. There are hundreds if not thousands of Web sites and activist groups set up by disgruntled consumers with the objective of attacking particular organizations.

UNDERSTAND THE CONSUMER BETTER

Quality Internet marketing focuses on getting to know the consumer better. The objective here is to understand consumers' exact needs so that exactly the right products and services can be offered to them at exactly the right time and in exactly the right way. The strength of the Internet is also its weakness. While people want information, they also suffer from massive information overload.

"The future of retail is the integration of Internet and digital services with the retail network."

(Charles Dunstone)

The Internet marketer that can cut through the overload and bring to time-starved consumers the information they need is much more likely to succeed. Find Web sites and e-mail databases that attract the exact type of consumer you wish to target. Analyze statistics generated as a result of consumers visiting your Web site and react appropriately to key trends. Customize consumers' experiences on a Web site through personalization systems, whereby a unique and finely targeted set of information and products is presented to a visitor.

Make Advertising and Promotion Highly Focused

A Web site, because it is not a physical store, faces a constant challenge to achieve and maintain awareness among its target market. Offline marketing plays a key role here, but so too do specific online marketing strategies. Search engine registration is an obvious one. This is not some simple, one-time task but a complex, ongoing activity in which the rules are constantly changing. Banner ads can be effective, if properly targeted. Banner ad design needs to apply the unique characteristics of the medium, and not simply apply traditional advertising principles. Getting other Web sites to link can be very effective, but this is a slow process, the rewards of which are delivered over time. E-mail signature files can effectively promote a Web site.

Remember that Affiliate Marketing and Loyalty Programs Can Deliver

There is no better example of the success of affiliate marketing than that of Amazon.com. Literally hundreds of thousands of Web sites offer books and other products to their visitors using Amazon's affiliate program. It's a win-win situation. The Web site in question offers an extra service that is easy to establish and delivers a certain amount of revenue. The affiliate sponsor opens up a new channel every time another Web site hooks into them.

However, like all marketing techniques, it's not some magic formula. It needs to be thought through properly and applied professionally.

Loyalty programs can work on the Internet, though they have been overhyped. Key elements in the management of loyalty programs are the use of customer databases and the tracking of customer purchasing behavior. The Internet facilitates such activities, and can thus be a medium through which loyalty programs can be run. Getting the incentive structure right is critical to the success of loyalty programs.

Use Online Communities to Build Loyalty

Using chat, discussion boards, and e-mail mailing lists to bring people together to discuss issues of interest can enhance brand loyalty. It can also be a source of unique and cost-effective content. However, it doesn't work in all situations, and online communities that are not properly managed can quickly lose momentum.

Remember that Some Old Marketing Tricks Still Apply

Discounts, competitions, and free offers work as well online as they work offline. While perhaps too much has been offered free on the Internet in order to build business, properly used, these traditional marketing techniques can be effective on Web sites.

Common Mistakes

Being Flashy

Although the Internet has been around since 1996, it is amazing how many marketers still think it's TV on a computer screen. On the Web, visitors don't really care about the graphics; they just want the information. Splash screens, audio, video and Macromedia Flash animations should be kept to an absolute minimum.

Not Building and Leveraging a Customer Database

Bringing people to a Web site without strongly encouraging them to join some sort of a database is a serious mistake. Studies indicate that many consumers will visit a Web site once, rarely if ever to return. It's vital to get them into a database so that ongoing communication can be set up.

Focusing on Volume of Visitors Rather than Quality Targeting

In the early years of the Web there was a frantic rush to build visitor traffic to a Web site, without any real focus on issues such as revenue per visitor, numbers who joined databases. Acquisition costs for visitors were high, and as the large number of visitors did not translate into valuable customers, many business models collapsed.

Focusing Purely on Purchase Activity

There is a need to understand how a Web site contributes to the overall purchase process. For example, a great many Americans visit car Web sites before they make a purchase, but very few will actually make the purchase online. The key is to forget about measuring by crude visitor volume numbers and focus on the quality of the targeting, along with the influence that the Web site and e-mail communications have on purchase behavior.

For More Information

Web Sites:

Adventive e-mail mailing lists, covering Internet marketing and selling: **www.adventive.com**

Web marketing information center: **www.wilsonweb.com/webmarket**

See also:

- ☆ **The Business Web (pp. 145–46)**
- ☆ **How To Plan Marketing (pp. 59–60)**
- ✔ **How to Apply a Viral Marketing Approach on the Internet (p. 628)**
- ✔ **How to Deliver the Benefits of Affiliate Marketing on the Web (p. 626)**
- ✔ **How to Promote Your Web Site Effectively (pp. 630–31)**
- ✔ **The Key Issues of Implementing E-commerce (pp. 580–81)**

Collecting Consumer Data on the Internet

Getting Started

Internet technologies offer a wealth of ways in which information on consumers can be gathered. Such information can either be collected directly as a result of consumers providing details, or indirectly by analyzing consumers' behavior while on a Web site. When gathering consumer information the following issues need to be kept in mind:

- privacy is a central concern of people who use the Internet, and they are becoming increasingly wary of Web sites that seek personal information;
- the benefit to the consumer needs to be made clear. Consumers are much more willing to offer personal information when a clear benefit to them can be articulated;
- it is one thing to gather information on consumers but another to analyze it and put it to productive use.

FAQs

Why has privacy become such a burning issue on the Internet?

The Internet has lacked a common and comprehensive legal infrastructure and this has led to an unfortunate situation in which basic consumer rights have been exploited. Web sites have gathered information on visitors in a surreptitious manner. Personal data has been sold on to third parties without making the consumer aware. This behavior has resulted in a consumer backlash. Study after study indicates that privacy is a key issue for those who use the Internet.

What are the key benefits of collecting consumer data?

Getting to know consumers better results in offering them products and services that are more in tune with their needs. This is a key competitive advantage in an information-driven economy. With more and more products becoming increasingly similar in their physical makeup, competitive advantage is achieved through finding out exactly what the consumer wants and meeting those needs precisely. The benefits to consumers are that they receive information and products that more accurately reflect their lifestyles and needs.

Why is it so important to collect information on how a Web site is performing?

A Web site is not like a bricks-and-mortar store in which a manager can walk around and observe what is happening. If there are always long lines at the checkout, and people are leaving the store because of these lines, this should quickly become obvious. However, people may be dropping out in the middle of a purchase process on a Web site, but unless proper data are coming through and being analyzed, no one will know. The number of people visiting the Web site may be dropping off. How will this be known without proper data? Web sites, like offline stores, need to monitor their performance continuously and adapt where appropriate. Without proper data and thorough data analysis this cannot be done.

Making It Happen

Using Web Site Logs to Analyze Consumer Behavior

Web site logs (server logs) track activity on a Web site. Log software is simple to install and can be purchased fairly cheaply, though for larger Web sites it is more complex and expensive. Using log software delivers vital information on Web site performance.

Unless the Web site is hooked into a personalization system, Web site logs are not able to identify who exactly has visited the Web site. Instead, such logs collect general Web site activity information, including:

- total number of visits to the Web site during a defined period of time.
- visitor frequency. Information on the number of people who visited only once during the period (unique visitors), and those who have visited more than once.
- page impressions/views. Information on the total numbers of complete Web pages visited during the period. This is a key measure for advertisers.
- hits. A totally unreliable measure of Web site visitor activity. Every Web page is made up of a number of components–graphics, text, programming elements. Some pages may have anything from 10 to 20 components. Each of these components is counted as a "hit." Therefore, the total number of hits is generally very high and bears little or no relation to the actual visitor activity.
- most frequently visited pages.

Web site logs can deliver a mind-numbing array of data. This will seem very exciting when you first install the software but can become tedious to wade through every day. Isolate what are the key measures required to deliver a better picture of how the site is performing.

Using Cookie Software to Track Consumers

Cookies are small files that are sent to reside in consumers' browsers in order to track those consumers the next time they visit the Web site. Cookies are an important component in personalization. A typical example of the use of cookies can be seen when people have subscribed to a service on a Web site. Cookies allow the Web site to remember the username and password information, so that they don't have to keep filling it out every time they revisit. This is clearly a benefit for most people. However, cookies have been abused, collecting information on people without their knowledge. When

"It is a capital mistake to theorize before one has data. Insensibly one begins to twist facts to suit theories, instead of theories to suit facts."
(Arthur Conan Doyle)

using cookies, clearly explain to people why they are being used and how they benefit them.

Web Bugs that Track Web Site Usage

An alternative technology to cookies is what has become known as Web bugs. Web bugs are not detectable by standard browsers, although there is software that can be downloaded to detect them. Web bugs have been controversial because their design reflects a desire not to let the person know that they are being tracked. Web bugs are adding fuel to the belief that people's privacy rights are being constantly abused on the Internet.

Collecting Information through the Use of Web Site Forms

Web site forms are used to collect information from a consumer in a structured manner. The following are guidelines to follow when designing a form:

- keep the forms as short as possible. If you make the form too long, consumers will simply not fill it out, or will skip over large sections of it.
- if forms have to be long, break them up. Inform the person clearly of how many sections there are.
- clearly mark mandatory fields. In every form there will be fields, such as e-mail addresses, that must be filled out. The convention is to mark the text associated with these fields in red and/or to place a red asterisk beside the field. At the top of the form, a clear statement needs to be made relating to the mandatory fields.
- don't mandate information a consumer can't give. Offer an alternative, for example: "If you don't have a ZIP code, please write 'None.'"
- ask opinion-type questions first. People tend to be more open to giving opinion rather than personal information.
- isolate errors that are made. Never say, "There's an error in your form. Go back and fill it out correctly". Rather say, "It seems you have not filled out your e-mail address. Please fill it out here".
- make sure the fields are of sufficient size. Don't, for example, give people a tiny field when you want their street address, which may be quite long.
- accessibility. Offer an alternative approach for people with disabilities to complete the information requested. Minimum accessibility standards are increasingly required by law.
- test regularly. It's not simply a good idea to test forms to see how user-friendly they are before they are launched. Forms break. As part of Web site maintenance, forms should be tested regularly with sample data.

Best Practice in Consumer Data Collection

People have become rightly uneasy about the abuse of personal information on the Web. To assuage fears and create a win-win situation, put into practice the following:

- clearly inform people of why the information is being collected and what purposes it will be used for;
- never use this information in a way that was not originally intended;
- allow the consumer to find out what information has been collected on them;
- allow them to delete any or all of this information;
- publish a comprehensive privacy statement in a prominent position on the Web site.

Protecting Consumer Data

Hackers—people who break into computer systems—love to target consumer databases. The reason is that these databases may contain credit card information (it is not advisable to store credit card numbers on a Web site). More usually, hackers know that publicizing the theft of consumer databases will be hugely damaging and embarrassing to the organization. It is therefore vital that any consumer data collected is properly protected and backed up.

Collecting Consumer Data on Children

The rules for collecting consumer data on children are quite naturally a lot stricter than for adults. While the law is evolving, numerous companies have been fined for collecting too much information on children who visit their Web sites. It's not enough simply to check your national legislation on this issue. The Web is international and your Web sites should adhere to international standards when it comes to children's privacy rights.

Common Mistakes

Surreptitiously Collecting Data

People have become very wary about their privacy on the Internet. Too many Web sites have collected data on consumers without them knowing. This may produce short-term benefit but has led to an inevitable backlash.

Collecting Too Much Data

Software today can deliver seas of data, and Web sites with large numbers of visitors can easily get flooded. Not focusing on what is the really important data to collect is a common problem. It's important to remember that analyzing data takes time, and that if tangible benefits are not delivered then it will be wasted time.

For More Information

Web Sites:

American Federal Trade Commission Privacy Initiatives—information on privacy and consumer data issues: **www.ftc.gov/privacy**

Yahoo Privacy Links: **www.dir.yahoo.com/ Computers_and_Internet**

See also:

☆ **Data Mining (pp. 152–53)**
☆ **Integrating Real and Virtual Strategies (pp. 143–44)**
☆ **Managing 1:1 Marketing (pp. 55–56)**
✔ **How to Develop a Personalization Strategy for a Web Site (pp. 586–87)**
✔ **How to Implement Customer Relationship Management (pp. 584–85)**

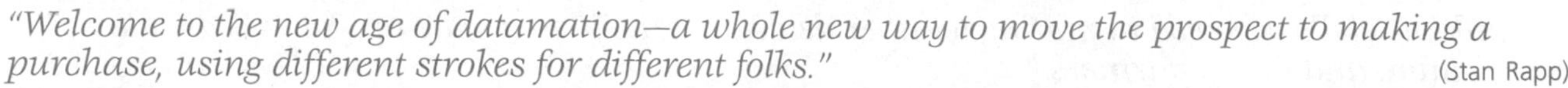

"Welcome to the new age of datamation—a whole new way to move the prospect to making a purchase, using different strokes for different folks." (Stan Rapp)

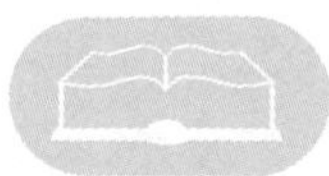

How to Deliver the Benefits of Affiliate Marketing on the Web

Getting Started

Affiliate marketing is about paying for performance. In short, it is a type of marketing in which one merchant induces others to place banners and buttons on their Web sites in return for a commission on purchases made by their customers. Amazon.com is the pioneer of affiliate marketing. It allows other Web sites to publish information of their own choices of books. When people click through to Amazon and buy these books, the Web site in question gets a commission. Affiliate marketing can open up new channels to market for the affiliate sponsor, and be a source of extra revenue for the affiliate Web site. When investigating affiliate marketing, consider:

- affiliate marketing is more suited to products than services;
- you'll need to work hard with your affiliates if you want it all to work;
- a well-designed compensation package will be critical to success.

Making It Happen

Figure Out If Your Business Is Suited To Affiliate Marketing

- There needs to be a substantial number of Web sites that are attracting your target market. These Web sites need to show a willingness to join an affiliate program. You might be selling medical supplies but that doesn't mean that hospital Web sites will become affiliates.
- Affiliate marketing is better suited to products than to services. It is much harder to track whether another Web site sent you visitors who, after prolonged negotiation, decide to pay you for your services.
- Is the market already saturated with affiliate programs? It would be difficult to set up an affiliate program today that offered commission on book sales.

Have a Strong Value Proposition

As with all good ideas, there are a huge number of merchants offering affiliate programs. How is your program going to attract new members? The level of compensation/commission you will offer will be important. However, on its own it will rarely be enough. You will need to work hard with your members by organizing regular competitions, special offers, and other incentives that make for an attractive value proposition both for your affiliate members and the end customer.

Keep in Regular Touch with Your Affiliates

Keeping in regular communication with your affiliates is essential in order to build their enthusiasm and trust. You should plan for an e-mail affiliate newsletter. Your affiliate members are your partners, and unless you treat them as such by working closely with them, they will drift away.

Agree a Compensation Approach

Critical to the success of your program will be how the affiliate is compensated. There are various compensation approaches:

- you might pay commission only; for smaller-price items such as books and music, commission is a popular option;
- for more expensive items such as cars, compensation may be based on paying for qualified leads;
- if brand building is also an important objective, then you also may offer compensation every time a visitor clicks through from an affiliate.

When making payments you will need to decide how often you do it. A problem you may face with partners is that some of them will have achieved very little revenue for a particular period, and it will not be cost-effective to send them a check. So you need to inform partners that there is a certain threshold before payment is made, and that commission earned in one period, if below the threshold, will be added to the commission for the next period. You will need an affiliate agreement that will cover these and other relevant issues.

Innovate, Analyze, Test, and Adapt

There is a need to innovate constantly so as to find the best approach. Affiliate software delivers substantial data and this needs to be carefully analyzed. New initiatives need to be properly tested and you need to be willing to keep adapting and refining your offer until you find something that works for both you and your affiliates.

Decide Whether to Outsource or Buy Software

Organizations can have the choice of outsourcing much of the running of the affiliate program or purchasing software and designing it in-house. It is better to outsource, as it allows you to focus on what you do best—selling and marketing your products and services.

For More Information

Web Site:
Affiliate Advisor: **www.affiliateadvisor.com**

See also:

- ☆ **New Yardsticks for Performance and Productivity in an E-world (pp. 285–86)**
- ✔ **How to Apply a Viral Marketing Approach on the Internet (p. 628)**
- ✔ **How to Promote Your Web Site Effectively (pp. 630–31)**
- ✔ **Understanding the Key Principles of Internet Marketing (pp. 622–23)**

"I think the skills involved in putting together deals are crucial to a start-up. You need wide distribution and many partners."

(Rob Herson)

  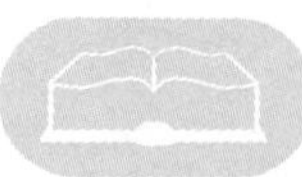    

HOW TO GET THE BEST FROM LOYALTY PROGRAMS ON THE WEB

GETTING STARTED

Loyalty programs reward customers who spend more and/or stay longer with an organization. Like much else about the Web, loyalty programs were a gigantic trend that crashed pretty severely. However, much of what went wrong does not reflect an inherent fault in the loyalty model itself, but rather in vastly overhyped expectations for what loyalty programs can deliver. When considering using loyalty programs on the Web, keep the following in mind:

- you should implement loyalty programs on the Web only after you have your e-commerce fundamentals solidly in place;
- loyalty programs are long-term projects: it can be disastrous to start a loyalty program and then stop it within six months;
- getting the level of incentive right is critical to success—too much and your profits will be hurt; too little and you won't attract members.

MAKING IT HAPPEN

MAKE SURE YOUR E-COMMERCE FUNDAMENTALS ARE IN PLACE FIRST

Top of the list for consumers are service, comprehensive information, appropriate returns policies, and quality support. Unless these fundamentals are fully addressed, consumers will see loyalty points only as gimmicks.

REMEMBER THAT LOYALTY PROGRAMS ARE LONG-TERM PROJECTS

A critical issue with regard to loyalty programs is that, by their very nature, they have to be there for the long term. Loyalty programs ask two key things of consumers: to collect points that will be redeemed at some future date; to give their loyalty. There is no better way to antagonize a consumer than to start a loyalty program and then six months later—as the member has collected half the points he needs for that coveted flight—to stop the program. Don't start a loyalty program unless you're in it for the long haul.

FIND OUT WHAT MAKES YOUR CUSTOMER LOYAL

If you don't know what makes your customers loyal then you cannot develop a program that will enhance their loyalty. It is also critical to focus on making your most profitable customers more loyal.

CHOOSE THE RIGHT TYPE OF LOYALTY PROGRAM

The following is a selection of approaches:

- points systems—a very popular approach that gives points to customers based on what they purchase;
- premium customer programs—customers who spend certain amounts of money and are repeat purchasers of a product or service gain special status. This may involve them receiving special service offers, discounts, exclusive offers, gifts, and so on. The important thing here is to make the customers feel special—make them feel that they are getting things that those who are not part of the program don't get;
- buyers' clubs—when a certain number of consumers get together to buy a particular product, they will be offered a special volume discount.

GET THE SWITCHING COST RIGHT

If you offer too much in your loyalty program then your margins will be squeezed, and you will be running to stand still from a profitability point of view. If your incentives are too low then the switching cost for your customer will remain low, and the very purpose of the loyalty program will have been negated. It would seem that the problem with a lot of loyalty programs on the Web was that—fueled by venture capital—major incentives were offered in the hope of attracting huge numbers of members.

CREATE A LOYALTY PATH FOR THE CUSTOMER

Customers can take loyalty programs very seriously. Some customers see it as an important achievement that they have a "Gold Card," or are seen as a "Premium Customer." Key in this sort of loyalty psychology is that there be a loyalty path for the customer. They need to see that the more they spend and the longer they stay with you, the more rewards and better treatment they get.

KEEP THE CUSTOMER INFORMED

Customers need to be able to check up on their status easily—to see, for example, how many points they have currently accumulated. Keep in touch. Send loyalty club members out a regular bulletin that creates a continuing buzz about the loyalty program, announcing competition winners, new competitions, special offers, and so on.

For More Information

Web Site:

Business2 magazine links to articles and resources from around the Web dealing with customer loyalty: **www.business2com/webguide**

See also:

☆ **Making Loyalty Work (pp. 289–90)**
☆ **Managing the Customer (pp. 65–66)**
✔ **How to Develop a Personalization Strategy for a Web Site (pp. 586–87)**
✔ **How to Generate Content and Build Loyalty Through Online Communities (p. 629)**

"Many people believe that we have entered the age of the Internet. Actually, it's more accurate to say that we're living in the age of the customer." (Anne Busquet)

How to Apply a Viral Marketing Approach on the Internet

Getting Started

Viral marketing is really another name for word of mouth, or in an Internet environment, word of e-mail. Viral marketing can work in mysterious ways, but what is clear is that the Internet is a medium that offers significant potential for such strategy. Yahoo did little or no advertising in its early years—people told other people that it was a great resource. News about music-swapping services such as Napster, and the independent movie *The Blair Witch Project*, grew like wildfire within universities. Viral marketing works well when:

- the product is new and genuinely different, and is something opinion leaders want to associate with;
- the benefits are real—people are telling their friends; they are putting their reputations on the line;
- the product is relevant to a large number of people, and it is relatively easy to communicate the benefits.

Making It Happen

Consider Incentives

Some viral marketing campaigns use an incentive-based approach. This involves rewarding people if they inform their friends and a percentage of these friends purchase the product, fill out a questionnaire, or whatever. It is important to have a cap on the number of people that the first person is asked to inform. For example, ask him or her to inform no more than five people. If the process is open-ended then it's very easy for spam to occur, where someone sends out thousands of e-mails to people they don't know in order to increase their rewards.

Create Useful Information That Will Be Quoted and Passed On

People see the Internet as an information resource. A powerful way of building a brand is to publish information that you allow people to quote and redistribute. There is no better way to enhance your reputation than for someone to pass your newsletter on to a friend, recommending that they should read it. The objective is that you be seen as an expert on a particular subject that is directly related to a product or service you offer. To facilitate such a process, create an "e-mail-to-a-friend" function on your Web site, which allows someone easily to e-mail information on something they have just read.

Linking Is Viral Marketing

Linking is embedded word-of-mouth. It's one thing for someone to send an e-mail praising your product or information. The effect is much better and longer-lasting if that person publishes a positive review on their Web site and links back to you. Linking is strongly connected with affiliate marketing, whereby rewards are delivered to Web sites that bring custom to other Web sites as a result of having links.

Viral Marketing Works Well When There Is Something Free

People love to tell their friends when there is some great new service that is free. The Hotmail free e-mail service and the Geocities free Web site service grew quickly with little or no marketing spend. The appeal of what is free may be losing some of its luster as the Internet matures, but it is still a powerful driver of behavior.

The Hotmail Approach

Hotmail was a pioneer of viral marketing. Its success was not simply based on the fact that it was a free service. It embedded viral marketing into the product itself. Every time someone using Hotmail sent an e-mail, at the bottom of the e-mail was the compelling message: "Get your private, free e-mail at http://www.hotmail.com." With Hotmail and other communications services such as ICQ, the very use of the product became a vehicle for marketing and promotion.

The Dangers of Viral Marketing

Done wrong, viral marketing can be seen as pyramid selling, chain-letter selling and/or spam. Every e-mail sent needs to make clear that the organization is not involved in spamming or other unethical practices. People complaining of spam can become extremely irate. It is important to respond to these people in a calm and reasoned manner.

Some viral marketing campaigns involve people sending e-mail addresses to the organization, which then carries out the actual communication. It's important that these e-mail addresses are only used for a one-time mailing, and that they are not added to a database for ongoing communication. Also, when sending out the e-mail, make it clear who the person is that referred the recipient. Remember, a referral does not mean that someone has agreed to receive ongoing communication from you.

For More Information

Web Site:

Business2 guide to viral marketing—a good source of articles and resources on viral marketing:
www.business2.com/webguide

See also:

☆ **The Business Web (pp. 145–46)**
✔ **How to Deliver the Benefits of Affiliate Marketing on the Web (p. 626)**
✔ **Understanding the Key Principles of Internet Marketing (pp. 622–23)**

"Marketing is not a function, it is the whole business seen from the customer's point of view."
(Peter F. Drucker)

How to Generate Content and Build Loyalty Through Online Communities

Getting Started

Online communities allow consumers to engage with one another and with your organization through use of interactive tools such as e-mail, discussion boards, and chat software. (Broader and more social online communities are not the topic of this Actionlist.) They are a means by which you can take the pulse of consumers to find out what they are thinking, and to generate unique content. As a standalone business, online communities have been found to be weak: they work best when they are supporting the need for the organization to get ongoing feedback. Online communities:

- allow the consumer an ongoing voice, thus facilitating greater feedback;
- require moderation and care if they are not to fizzle out, or turn negative;
- offer different options for interaction that reflect the varying ways in which people like to communicate.

Making It Happen

Keep It Moderated

Online communities rarely work if you simply install some discussion board software on a Web site and walk away. The discussion will either quickly dry up, or else drift off to topics that have nothing to do with the organization, and may well be libelous or otherwise illegal. Thus, to make a success of an online community, quality moderation is essential. Moderators need to combine editorial and chairperson-type skills. They need to be knowledgeable about the subjects being discussed, be enthusiastic, and encourage debate and quality discussion. They require an understanding of legal (particularly libel and copyright) issues, and should have the ability to deal with negative situations where members become overly virulent. Most of all, they need to care and want to make the community work for everybody involved.

Set Up E-mail Mailing Lists

E-mail mailing lists are an excellent way to discuss complex topics over a longer period of time. Members can be drawn from anywhere in the world and come together to share information and experience on a particular theme or subject area. The success of an e-mail mailing list is down to the quality of the contributions and moderation. Done right, it is a powerful way of transferring knowledge. An e-mail mailing list works as follows.

- a moderator establishes a list with mailing list software (this can be bought or rented; renting is usually the best option);
- the theme and focus of the list is published, and people join up, using a Web site form and/or e-mail address;
- the moderator invites contributions and these are duly published by e-mail;
- subscribers react to the initial publication with their opinions and feedback; a selection of these reactions then gets published in the next e-mail sent out;
- if successful, a feedback and opinion loop is created, with new topics of discussion being introduced as older topics have received sufficient discussion.

Set Up Discussion Boards

Discussion boards (also known as newsgroups, discussion groups, bulletin boards) are areas on a Web site that allow people to contribute opinions, ideas and announcements. They tend to be more general in nature than e-mail mailing lists, and are more suited for casual, one-off interactions. People require less commitment to participate in such boards. They can generally review a discussion topic without subscribing, although they do have to subscribe if they want to contribute something themselves. Moderation is not as essential here, although it is important to watch out for the emergence of "off-topic" subjects—contributions that are unnecessarily negative and perhaps libelous—and copyright infringement.

A prime example of the success of the discussion board approach is how Amazon.com uses it to allow consumers to publish book reviews. Discussion board software is relatively cheap and easy to install.

Set Up Online Chat

Online chat is real-time, text-based communication. Online chat can be effective when:

- there is a specific event occurring that is of interest to people;
- an expert can be made available to talk about a subject or product.

To be productive, online chat needs to be well moderated. It is really only suited to small groups of people (2 to 20) at any one time. Online chat software is relatively cheap and easy to install.

For More Information

Book:

Hagel, John, and Arthur G. Armstrong. *Net Gain: Expanding Markets Through Virtual Communities.* Boston, MA: Harvard Business School Press, 1997.

See also:

☆ **Converting Anonymity into Participation in a Membership Organization (pp. 206–07)**
✔ **How to Get the Best from Loyalty Programs on the Web (p. 627)**

"Consumers resent it when a company presumes to judge the quality of its products on their behalf."

(Andrew S. Grove)

  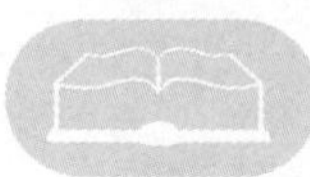    

How to Promote Your Web Site Effectively

Getting Started

Launching a Web site is like opening up a store in the middle of Antarctica or the Sahara Desert. Nobody will know that you are there unless you promote yourself! Web site promotion is not some one-time event that occurs at launch. It is an ongoing activity that demands a keen understanding of promotional techniques that are unique to the Web. It also requires full integration into offline marketing and promotional activities. When approaching Web site promotion, consider:

- it requires a range of promotional strategies, both online and offline;
- it demands skilled resources that are applied continually;
- it should be fully integrated into the overall promotional and marketing strategy.

FAQs

Why is Web site promotion of such importance?

In business, people talk about "location, location, location." Well, a Web site doesn't really have a location. It's not on a main street where thousands of people walk every day. Without such physical visibility, a Web site has a major problem attracting consumers. That is one reason why a clicks-and-mortar strategy (combining physical stores with an Internet presence) is deemed so essential for the success of a Web site. In a physical store, and in its marketing and promotional activity, consumers can be exposed to the benefits of the Web site constantly.

Is banner advertising an efficient and cost-effective way to promote a Web site?

The jury is still out on the effectiveness of banner advertising. However, prices for banner advertising have dropped significantly in recent years and there is certainly value to be had. It's really down to the target market you are after and whether that accurately matches the profile of visitors coming to a particular Web site. Online advertising systems allow for a level of targeting and measurement that is impossible in much offline media. So, if you can get to the right target market at the right price, then the equation makes sense.

Does online advertising and promotion have to cost a lot of money?

No. Online ads have dropped significantly in price and, with proper investigation, very good value can be had. Online promotion requires dedication, but a few hours spent every week can deliver real results.

Making It Happen

Get Linked

Linking is one of the most powerful means of promoting a Web site. A link from another Web site is essentially embedded word of mouth, a recommendation from that site to its visitors also to visit you. The Web is huge, with millions of Web sites, many of them of poor quality. People who use the Internet have become very skeptical and conservative in their behavior. Building credibility is critical. There is no better way to build such credibility than to have hundreds—ideally thousands—of other Web sites linking to you.

Google, perhaps the Web's most popular search engine, achieved popularity because its search results were seen as more relevant than those of other search engines. The way it achieved better results was by analyzing a Web site and seeing how many external Web sites had linked to it. The more links the Web site had, the higher in the results Google placed it. Thus, if you want your Web site to feature prominently with Google, the more links you can get the better.

But linking is not simply about getting placed higher in search engine results. Think of each link as another "road" to your Web site; another way that the visitor can get to you. Getting links is not easy. It involves finding Web sites that attract your target market and convincing them to include a link to you. Usually, they will not do this unless you have valuable content that could be of interest to their customers. Another approach is to pay for a link, either through monthly fees or through what is called "click through payments"—you pay for every visit that results from a particular link.

Get Registered with Search Engines

Because so many people use search engines, it is critical that your Web site is properly registered. Keep the following in mind:

- there are hundreds of search engines and directories but only a handful that really matter. These include: Yahoo, Google, Alta Vista, Microsoft Network, Excite, Lycos, Go, HotBot, All The Web, Direct Hit, Look Smart, and Northern Light;
- there may well be specialist search engines and directories for your particular industry. You should register with them;
- all search engines used to be free to register with, but this is no longer the case for an increasing number. You need to consider if the fee is worth it;
- an increasing number of search engines sell special placements in their search results. You can choose a keyword and when that keyword is input by a searcher, a short promotion for your Web site will appear;
- search engines need to be monitored regularly, as they can change the rules by which search results are presented. A set of keywords needs to be drawn up and the search engine regularly searched using these keywords. If you find your Web site is dropping down the results page, you may need to reregister. Also, if you launch a new product or service, you should consider registering that;

"We thought the creation and operation of Web sites was mysterious Nobel Prize stuff, the province of the wild-eyed and purple-haired." (Jack Welch)

- don't register popular keywords with a Web site just for the sake of increased visitors. It achieves very little, and some search engines will remove Web sites that continuously abuse search registration processes.

Use Banner and Other Online Advertising

Banner advertising should not be discounted, particularly where a new Web site, product, or service, is being launched. Banner ads can be paid for either on a cost-per-thousand (CPM) basis or per click through, where the seller gets paid wherever a visitors clicks on an ad. Online ads should be a call to action, with the key objective being to get the person to click on the ad. There are a variety of online advertising options:

- banner advertisements. These ads can go across the top or bottom of the page. A trend is where they go down the side, like wallpaper;
- interstitials. These are ads that appear before the actual Web page loads. They certainly get the visitors' attention but can be very frustrating;
- pop-under ads. These ads launch in a separate browser window and have been controversial.

Consider E-mail as a Form of Advertising

E-mail can be a very effective form of advertising, particularly when the advertiser is reaching a targeted list that has opted in to receive information on particular products or services. But beware of spam: mass distributed unsolicited e-mail. People are increasingly annoyed by spam, and antispam legislation has been enacted or is pending in many states and countries. It's not simply about whether spam is legal or not—but it is certainly unethical, and no reputable organization should use such an approach.

Remember E-mail Signature Files

An e-mail signature is the text at the bottom of an e-mail that contains information about the sender. It is also possible to place a short, two-line ad there (e-mail signatures should not be longer than five lines). E-mail signature promotion was used very effectively when Andersen Consulting changed its name to Accenture. For a period after the name change, every time one of Accenture's 60,000 employees sent an e-mail, there was a short e-mail signature ad notifying the receiver of the change of name.

Integrate with Offline Marketing

Every single piece of offline literature should contain the Web site address and, where appropriate, an e-mail address. This includes: all stationery (letterheads, business cards, compliment slips, receipts, invoices); all product packaging; training and support manuals; all ads that are placed in print, radio, or television. If the organization has physical stores, then promotional material should be placed prominently within these stores informing visitors of the Web site. When planning new offline promotional and marketing activities, you should seek ways to get consumers to go to the Web site. For example, entering a competition through the Web site.

Include Competitions and Giveaways

Consumers are as likely to react positively to quality Web-based competitions and special promotions as they do to such tactics in the offline world. Competitions and special offers give the Web site a sense of vibrancy. A key objective of such promotions should be to get consumers to join databases, used in the future to inform people of other special offers and relevant information.

Use Your Home Page

A key objective of a home page is to promote important content, products, and services situated deeper in the Web site. That's the job of sharp, punchy headings and summaries, supported on occasion by small graphics. The Microsoft Web site (www.microsoft.com) is a perfect example of how to use a home page to promote special offers, product launches, upgrades, and so on.

Common Mistakes

Seeking Quantity of Visitors over Quality

In the early days of the Web there was a mad rush—fueled by venture capital—to drive as many visitors as possible to Web sites. A stream of new brands emerged, each one seeking to outdo the next with ad spend. There is still a tendency to consider quantity over quality when it comes to building visitor numbers to a Web site. This is a serious and expensive mistake.

Focusing Purely on Search Engines

Search engines are important, but they should still be only a part of an online promotional strategy. Also, abuse of search engines by bombarding them with popular keywords and other visitor-generating techniques merely serves to bulk up visitor figures. It does little or nothing for the bottom line.

Lack of Integration with Offline Marketing

Organizations miss vital and cost-effective ways of promoting their Web sites through offline resources

Lack of Ongoing Commitment

Too many Web sites have been launched enthusiastically, only to be left to wither in the wilderness of cyberspace. To be successful, promotion must be an ongoing activity.

For More Information

Web Site:

Google's Web site promotion links—a comprehensive list: **www.directory.google.com**

See also:

- ✔ **How to Apply a Viral Marketing Approach on the Internet (p. 628)**
- ✔ **How to Deliver the Benefits of Affiliate Marketing on the Web (p. 626)**
- ✔ **How to Use E-mail Marketing Effectively (pp. 632–33)**
- ✔ **Understanding the Key Principles of Internet Marketing (pp. 622–23)**

"The Web site needs to be as sticky as a currant bun." (Carolyn McCall)

How to Use E-mail Marketing Effectively

Getting Started

E-mail should be an essential part of any Internet marketing strategy. If you have someone's e-mail address, you can send them information directly. But with e-mail it is important that the recipient wants the information you are sending. Keep the following in mind:

- e-mail is a relatively cheap, but powerful communications tool—you can send thousands of e-mail newsletters in a simple, cost-effective way;
- e-mail allows you to keep in regular contact with customers and to build up a rapport with them;
- never send unsolicited e-mails (spam). E-mail should only deliver worthwhile information.

FAQs

How often should you contact customers by e-mail?

E-mail is a fast, simple, and cost-effective form of communication, so it is tempting to use it at every opportunity. However, unless the information is valuable, this can become annoying for customers. As a general rule, you should not send e-mail to people more than once a week, unless there is a specific and defined need. People are overloaded and if they see too many e-mails from you they will turn off. Make sure that you stick to your schedule, as people will be expecting it.

Should newsletters be free or chargeable?

It depends on the focus of your business. If you are publishing information, then it is hard to see how a business model can be developed that is advertising only. However, if you are using the information you send to help sell some other product or service, it is highly unlikely that anyone will be willing to pay for it.

What is spam?

Spam is mass distributed, unsolicited e-mail. Spam is a major problem on the Internet today in that it is easy to buy a database of millions of e-mail addresses and send out unsolicited e-mails to them. If you want to be seen as a reputable business, you should avoid sending spam.

What do the terms "opt-in" and "double opt-in" mean?

An opt-in approach is where someone actively decides to give you their e-mail address so that you can send them e-mail. However, the emerging convention is double opt-in. What happens here is that when a person receives a request to subscribe to an e-mail address, they reply to that address for verification that the request did in fact come from there. This ensures that the e-mail address was not maliciously set up by a third party.

Is it better to buy software or can it be rented?

Very often it is better to rent. There are a number of organizations that offer professional e-mail management services. To get a list of such companies, go to a search engine, such as Google.

Making It Happen

Isolate the Information Need

The first step in any e-mail strategy is to isolate the information need of your target market. What sort of information would they find useful? Would they like information on new products and special offers? Would they like information on trends within your industry? What sort of information would make them want to give you their e-mail address?

Define Your Publication Scope and Schedule

Once you have defined an information need, you must make clear what the scope of your e-mail publication is. What exactly will the person get if they subscribe? Unless you are delivering very time-sensitive information, a weekly publication is usually sufficient.

Make the Subscription Process Prominent on Your Web Site

Getting people to subscribe is vital to the success of your e-mail strategy. There should therefore be a prominent subscription box on your Web site encouraging people to subscribe. Also, include subscription details in every mailing that you send out. Don't ask too many questions in the subscription process.

Many successful e-mail newsletter providers only ask for the e-mail address of the subscriber. That makes it a very easy and quick process for the potential subscriber. You can always ask for more information later on, when you have established a stronger relationship with the subscriber. As a rule, the more valuable the information is to the potential subscriber, the more information you can ask of them.

Make the Unsubscription Process as Easy as Possible

It is equally important to ensure that the unsubscription process is easy to use. People can get frustrated and angry if they find it difficult to unsubscribe from a service. Some might think you have started spamming them.

If You're Offering a Paid-for Subscription Service, Offer a Free "Teaser" Subscription

If you plan to offer a commercial service where you charge people to subscribe, then it is a good idea to offer a free e-mail that contains brief summaries of what is included in the commercial offering. It may also be an

"Electronic communication, as fast and efficient as it has become, does not automatically lead to better communication."

(Dan Dimancescu)

  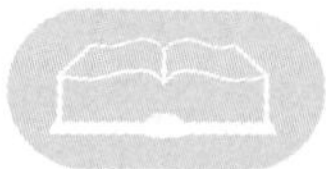    

idea to offer a free trial period, so that the subscriber can get an understanding of what you have to offer.

Decide Whether You Want a Plain Text or HTML Version of Your E-mail

There are two basic options for the format you can use when delivering an e-mail to your subscriber base: plain text and HTML. Plain text is just like a normal e-mail. It is the simplest and easiest to produce. HTML is like sending a Web page in an e-mail. It will deliver a lot more impact and color. However, it is more expensive to produce, and a number of older e-mail systems find it hard to read HTML. Thus, if you are going to use an HTML e-mail approach, offer a plain text version as well. Otherwise, a significant number of people may be unable to subscribe to your service.

For plain text e-mail layout keep the line length of text between 65 and 70 characters to avoid breaking lines, which make the layout look very ugly, and keep paragraphs nice and short—five to six lines is optimum. Use capitals for headings. Because plain text e-mails do not allow the use of bold or font sizing, capitalizing is the only way to give emphasis. Use a nonproportional font such as Courier, because it remains constant regardless of the e-mail package being used.

Keep the E-mail Short and Punchy

Think of what you are doing as delivering a publication. You're trying to get people to read something that will make them want to act—to buy your product, for example. Focus on having punchy headings and short summaries. Avoid having articles that are longer than 500–600 words. The entire e-mail should not contain more than 1,500 words, unless you have a dedicated audience that you know is willing to read longer pieces. So keep things short, and always have a call to action.

Have a Strong Subject Line

The subject line is what subscribers see first when they download their e-mail. Because people are so busy they often scan the subject line and, if it's not interesting, delete the e-mail. However, if you are sending out a regular publication you may wish to include the title of the publication and date in the subject line. In the body of the e-mail itself, it's a good idea to have a table of contents near the top that lets the reader know what to expect from the rest of the e-mail.

Using Hypertext and E-mail Addresses

It's a good idea to use a hypertext to link back to your Web site, in order to encourage the subscriber to get more information, purchase your product, and so on. However, when writing out a hyperlink (URL) always use the full URL. For example, don't use "www.mycompany.com"; instead, use "http://www.mycompany.com." The reason is that some older e-mail packages will not automatically turn the URL into a link unless you include the full URL. Also, if you have a URL that is more than 65 characters long, put in angle brackets (< >) on either side of the URL. Otherwise, a number of e-mail packages will break the URL onto two lines and make it unusable. If you are including an e-mail address, put in a "mailto": before the e-mail address, as this will turn it into a link to the subscriber's e-mail package. For example: "mailto:tom@-mycompany.com."

Include the Essential Things Every E-mail Mailing Should Have

Every e-mail you send out should contain the subject line (title) and date, subscription and unsubscription information, copyright and privacy policies (or links to these on the Web site), e-mail contact details (telephone and address may also be included), links back to the Web site, and brief information on the publication schedule and scope.

Common Mistakes

Using a "Bait and Switch" Approach

Be very clear to the potential subscriber about what exactly they are subscribing to. If you specialize in special offers, e-mail and tell them so. Don't pretend that you're going to send valuable updates on a particular industry, and then just send special offers.

Not Meeting a Real Information Need

Ask yourself the question: why would anyone want to read this? Too many e-mail mailings are full of useless, repetitive, or out-of-date information.

Not Keeping to a Publication Schedule

You're in the business of publishing and if you say you will deliver an e-mail every Wednesday, then you must deliver an e-mail every Wednesday or risk losing credibility and subscribers.

Not Managing the Subscription and Unsubscription Process Professionally

Make it difficult for someone to subscribe and they won't subscribe. Make it difficult for people to unsubscribe and they can become very irate.

Spamming People

Never subscribe people against their will or without them knowing. Sending unsolicited e-mail is a "get rich quick" strategy. It will damage your reputation.

For More Information

Book:

MacPherson, Kim. *Permission-Based E-Mail Marketing That Works!*. New York: Dearborn Trade Publishing, 2001.

Web Site:

Clickz e-mail marketing section—a good source of up-to-date information: **www.clickz.com**

See also:

☆ **Managing 1:1 Marketing (pp. 55–56)**
✔ **How to Promote Your Web Site Effectively (pp. 630–31)**
✔ **Setting Up a Subscription Process (pp. 618–19)**

"It is ironic but true that in this era of electronic communications, personal interaction is becoming more important than ever."
(Regis McKenna)

How to Get the Best from E-marketplaces

Getting Started

An e-marketplace is an Internet-based environment that brings together business-to-business buyers and sellers so that they can trade together more efficiently. E-marketplaces have been massively over-hyped. Fundamental issues were ignored, such as the fact that much trading is based on personal relationships developed over time. However, done properly, e-marketplaces can make for more efficient purchasing processes, saving time and money for everyone involved. Keep the following in mind:

- The technology is still relatively new, as are many of the companies involved. Caution is necessary.
- Which e-marketplace is right for you?
- E-marketplaces should not simply focus on getting the lowest price. Collaboration and the supply of quality information are key benefits they can deliver.

FAQs

What are the key benefits of becoming involved in an e-marketplace?

Reduced purchasing costs, greater flexibility, saved time, better information, and better collaboration.

What are the key drawbacks of e-marketplaces?

Inertia and resistance to change among key players, costs in changing procurement processes, cost of applications and setup, cost of integration with internal systems, and transaction/subscription fees.

What types of e-marketplaces are there?

There are three distinct types of e-marketplace:

Independent: These are public e-marketplace environments that seek to attract buyers and sellers to trade together. Many simply didn't attract a critical mass of buyers and sellers and folded quickly. Such marketplaces have found most success in commodity-based industries, where there are a large number of buyers and sellers.

Consortium-based: These are set up on an industry-wide basis, typically when a number of key buyers in a particular industry get together. They often drive an industry-wide move to achieve common standards for the transfer of information.

Private: These are established by a particular organization to manage its purchasing alone. The organization retains full control, though technology costs can be significant.

Making It Happen

More Than Buying and Selling

The early e-marketplaces were little more than auction environments. However, as they've evolved, they have sought to help organizations trade more efficiently with partners. This has involved optimizing communication and collaboration; improved time to market as information flows more quickly between parties involved in the product development process; and better inventory control, through better market feedback.

Consider Joining an Independent E-marketplace

The advantages of joining an independent e-marketplace are:

- you can find new trading partners that you might otherwise not have been aware of;
- it's useful if you need to alleviate an inventory pile-up;
- it can work well when dealing in commodities;
- independents should embrace open infrastructure standards, making them easier to plug into than private e-marketplaces, which may use more proprietary technology.

The disadvantages are:

- a volatile environment, with many independents going out of business;
- they are not really suitable for developing long-term trading relationships;
- confidentiality and security can be an issue;
- many suppliers see such marketplaces as a way to drive down price and are wary about getting involved. This limits the buying options.

Consider Joining a Consortium-based E-marketplace

The advantages are:

- less expense than establishing a private e-marketplace. Charges are usually in the form of subscription fees and/or commission;
- more choice of buyers and sellers;
- cheaper prices, though this isn't always the case;
- enhanced ability to work on industry-wide issues such as achieving common data standards.

The disadvantages are:

- you are setting up a trading environment with your competitors—so where's the competitive advantage?
- less control than with a private e-marketplace;
- it won't generally integrate as well into backend technology and processes as a private e-marketplace;
- it's more open and thus more generic. If buying/selling relationships are key to your competitive edge, then a consortium-based e-marketplace will not be a huge benefit;
- governments may view such e-marketplaces as cartels or monopolies, depending on the members and their power within the overall marketplace.

Setting Up a Private E-marketplace

The advantages are:

- relationships, information, and unique processes are protected from competitors;

"The greatest risk lies in not knowing what you don't know." (Walid Mougayar)

  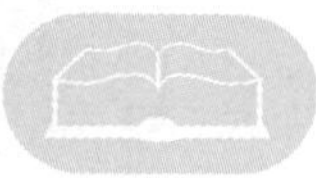    

- you can get the most out of unique business processes by integrating them more fully with your partners;
- proper integration with your backend systems and processes and those of trading partners;
- full control of the design and focus;
- it should make the trading process more efficient and thus cost-effective;
- it's more suitable when communicating highly confidential information with trading partners;
- owning an efficient e-marketplace infrastructure can give you a competitive edge.

The disadvantages are:

- it can be very expensive to establish and keep going. Costs may run into many millions of dollars;
- it's a complex undertaking that can take a long time to implement;
- it won't offer trading opportunities with new business partners;
- it won't necessarily drive down the price you pay for a particular product or commodity, so you must ensure cost savings are achieved through greater efficiencies in other processes.

You Don't Have to Stick with One Type of E-marketplace

You may decide to use a number of e-marketplaces. For example, a consortium-based one for most of your needs, and an independent to give yourself greater choice. A trading partner from an independent e-marketplace may end up migrating into your private e-marketplace.

Confidentiality Is Key

One of the major worries regarding involvement in either independent or consortium-based e-marketplace is confidentiality. Over time, a picture will be built up of how an organization trades; this is important information, which could be very valuable to competitors. It's essential that proper security procedures are in place.

Consider Content Management

Content management is an important part of an e-marketplace environment. The system will need to deal with requests for proposals (RFPs), quotations, product diagrams and specifications, pricing and delivery information. It will need to be able to archive everything in an accessible way, and to deal with version control to give users up-to-date information.

Training and Education Will Be an Issue

E-marketplaces invariably introduce new ways of doing things. There may be resistance within the organization and this will require ongoing education and evangelism. Training will be required for the staff who are expected to operate the e-marketplace.

Seller Beware

Sellers have been very cautious about getting involved in e-marketplaces because of their initial tendency to focus primarily on price. However, the right e-marketplace can have benefits for a seller, opening up new markets and customers, and providing a way of reducing excess stock.

General Issues to Consider

- What is the procedure if you want to develop a one-to-one relationship with a trading partner you meet within an e-marketplace?
- Will the e-marketplace have any role to play in shipping and logistics?
- What is expected of you as a participant? How, for example, do you deliver content and updates?
- What integration work is involved? If it doesn't integrate, what are the costs involved in new processes?
- How are payments to be made?
- How are the Request For Proposal (RFP) and quotations processes handled?
- Is there a certification process in place to ensure that you are dealing with reputable entities?

Common Mistakes

You Forget About Corporate Inertia

The expectation by e-marketplace providers that organizations would suddenly change their buying and selling habits upon the arrival of new technology was a serious mistake. Relationships and habits build up over years, and change only slowly in most situations.

There's More to Buying and Selling Than Price

Product quality, support and personal relationships are still key in business-to-business situations. E-marketplaces that simply focused on pitting seller against seller found that that approach simply didn't work.

Delays in Getting the E-marketplace Up and Running

E-marketplaces are complex. The more partners involved, the more difficult it is to synchronize the information and business processes between each entity. Delays in making some of the best-known e-marketplaces fully functional have hurt the image of the industry.

No Robust Payments Process

Many e-marketplaces lack a process whereby the participants can immediately settle the whole transaction. The fact that some of the trade must then be completed offline means that both offline and online processes need to be maintained, reducing efficiencies and cost savings.

For More Information

Web Site:
Google e-marketplace links to e-marketplace vendors:
www.directory.google.com

See also:

☆ **The Business Web (pp. 145–46)**
☆ **Making B2B Your New Operational Standard (pp. 150–51)**
☆ **The New Frontiers in Old-Economy Industries (pp. 99–100)**
✔ **How to Add Value Through E-alliances (pp. 640–41)**

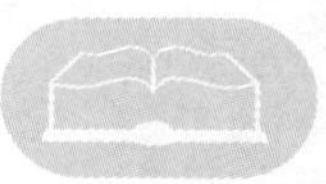

How to Make the Most of an Intranet

Getting Started

An intranet is a Web site for your employees. It should contain content and other resources that will make them more informed and productive. Many intranets have evolved in an ad hoc manner, with little approval from senior managers and few clear objectives. Instead of becoming valuable information resources, they have become information dumps. Consequently, staff are not using them and their potential is lost. When developing an intranet strategy, keep the following in mind.

- An intranet can combine internal and external information resources in a one-stop information shop.
- It can become the intellectual capital library of the organization, capturing staff knowledge, facilitating teamwork and collaboration, and providing an excellent induction vehicle for new employees.
- It can allow people to work remotely and still access key information.

FAQs

Should an intranet employ central standards?

Yes. Otherwise an intranet will become almost useless. Some larger organizations now have hundreds of intranets, each with different standards, creating an environment that's impossible to navigate and very expensive and time-consuming to maintain. The approach should be to control key standards centrally, while giving as much responsibility as possible to individual departments for the publication of relevant content.

Should employees be allowed to develop personal content?

Allowing staff space to create their own personal home pages can gain acceptance for the intranet and deepen the sense of organizational culture. However, care must be taken that such home pages are off the beaten track. They should not get in the way of the primary objective: to deliver content that helps employees do a better job. Nor should they take up too much time.

Should an intranet incorporate security measures?

Yes. Invariably, intranets will be accessed by staff from outside the physical organization—from home, hotels and so on. So a robust security system is crucial. Passwords need to be changed regularly and access to certain types of information managed properly. However, security should be planned carefully to maintain simple, open communication. If it's too difficult to access the intranet, a lot of people won't bother.

Making It Happen

Achieve Management Buy-in

Unless there is genuine management commitment to an intranet, it will quickly develop into a mess: underfunded, under resourced and underused. Experience indicates that employees behave in a "once bitten, twice shy" manner: if they go to an intranet and find it a waste of time, it's much harder to convince them to visit it a second time. It's better to have no intranet at all than one full of badly organized, out-of-date content.

Identify Who Needs Content Most

Organizations create a huge amount of content, not all of which is relevant or productive. The content that should go on the intranet first is that which is most likely to further the organization's objectives. Do salespeople require faster access to more accurate information? Do technical staff spend too long looking for documents that often end up being out of date? Are employee contact details kept in a little green book that nobody can find when they need it? Do support staff find that they're always asking around for answers to customer queries?

Develop Return on Investment Models

A primary reason intranets don't get proper funding is that no one has proved to the finance department that the extra budget should be allocated. Proving that a quality intranet can deliver a quantifiable return on investment (ROI) can loosen those purse strings. Here's a simple example:

Company X has 100 people working for it. On average they spend 12 minutes every day searching for content. The average hourly cost per employee is $50 and they work 250 days per year. Thus, the annual cost in lost productivity due to time spent searching is:

100 x 0.2 x $50 x 250 = $250,000.

If a well-organized intranet can reduce searching time by half, that would result in an annual saving of $125,000.

Start with Something Manageable and Likely to Deliver Real Benefit

It's important to start off with something manageable that delivers the most direct and measurable benefit. Find out who within the organization is most concerned about getting the right information. Is it the sales employees, support, research and development? Or is there a facility, such as an online phone directory or appointments diary, that people are screaming out for? Home in on the most burning need: once you prove that a success, it will be much easier to get budget and commitment to expand the intranet. There may also be some easy wins. Perhaps the canteen menu would get people checking the intranet every day?

Get Buy-in and Commitment from Staff

Where exactly is all this wonderful content going to come from? Some of it will be created already, certainly. Some may come in the form of subscriptions to magazines or commercial databases. But much of it will have to be created by people within the organization itself. There's no point in assuming that it will magically appear. You need to get approval and commitment from the staff expected to write the stuff.

Ensure That It Is Part of the Job Function

If the creation of content is not made part of someone's job function, and they are not measured on delivery, content quality will inevitably be poor. So reward and remuneration structures need to be put in place. It's not simply about money. If an employee knows their good technical paper may get a special feature on the intranet and be seen by their peers and managers, that's good motivation. Remember too, writing quality content takes time. If that time is not available, quality content won't get written.

Encourage Collaboration and Interaction

Consider setting up discussion forums, chat facilities and e-mail discussion lists that get people sharing issues and ideas. Encourage collaboratively created content, with several authors working on a document. Remember, collaboration and interaction don't happen on their own. Without quality moderation, discussion areas can quickly become stale and lifeless.

Put an Editor in Charge

An intranet is really a publication: it will live or die by the quality of its content. In the same way that a printer is not in charge of the *New York Times*, a programmer should not be in charge of an intranet. An editor understands content—what staff need or want to read, and how to write it in an accessible, readable way.

Get a Proper Commitment from the IT Department

Even though the central focus is quality content, there will always be technical issues that crop up from day to day. Without a sufficient commitment from the IT department, vital content may be delayed or the entire intranet may go down. Not a happy situation.

Focus Design on Metadata, Classification, Navigation, Search and Layout

Forget about fancy gimmicks and bandwidth-hungry applications. Remember that people will be accessing your intranet over those very slow lines from hotel rooms, or from home, and just want to get to the facts. Therefore quality classification and navigation, backed up by a robust search engine, are essential. To achieve this, you need the right metadata on every document and page.

Metadata is the content about the content, the who, what, where and when about each document or page. For example, metadata could include author name, date published, heading, summary and classification.

Consider Using a Content Management Application

An intranet that has several hundred pages, with more than 20 new pages being published every week, could well do with a content management application. Maintaining an intranet in HTML is fine if the site is small and is updated by only a few people. However if there's lots of content and lots of contributors, it may become unmanageable. Content management software can streamline the publishing processes, making them much more efficient and cost effective.

Promote It!

If you don't actively promote your intranet, many employees won't even know it exists. Send out a weekly newsletter to all staff informing them of what's new on the intranet. Put up colorful posters in the canteen.

Common Mistakes

You Don't Have Management Buy-in

In the early days, intranets grew in the wild, fed by the enthusiasm of a few dedicated staff. However, without proper planning, clear objectives and management buy-in, an intranet is doomed to failure. Staff will desert it and management will be left with an information dump.

No Budgets, No Staff Resources

An early Internet assumption was that information is cheap to create. This is far from the truth: quality content is expensive to produce and maintain. You can't expect consistent quality content from people if it's not part of their job function. It's better to have no intranet than one that is poorly funded and staffed.

A Big Launch and No Follow-up

The launch is the beginning, not the end. Too many organizations make a big effort to launch their intranet, only to ignore it. In ignored intranets, out-of-date content grows.

Poor Classification, Poor Standards

Without proper standards and well-planned classification, intranets can become a nightmare to navigate and manage. So when you do find the content you need, it turns out to be red text on a pink background!

No Encouragement of Intranet Use

An intranet is only valuable if employees use it. In many organizations people are not actually aware of the resources available on the intranet, because it has not been properly promoted.

For More Information

Web Site:

Intranet Journal Magazine, an online magazine dedicated to intranet issues, contains lots of how to information: **www.intranetjournal.com**

See also:

✔ **How to Establish an Enterprise Portal (p. 638)**

✔ **Setting Up an Extranet (p. 639)**

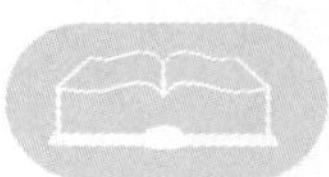

HOW TO ESTABLISH AN ENTERPRISE PORTAL

GETTING STARTED

Enterprise portals are Web sites that assemble a wide range of content and services for staff. Some of this content is published by the organization itself, and some will be acquired from third-party publishers. The principle is to bring together all the key information staff required to do a better job. When considering developing an enterprise portal, keep the following in mind:

- the word "portal" means different things to different people: to some, it's a souped-up intranet, to others it's a nascent e-marketplace: others will see it as part of a customer relationship management strategy;
- enterprise portals, while great in theory, are complex to develop and expensive to manage;
- an enterprise portal can easily fall into the trap of trying to provide all information staff could possibly need and providing none of it very well.

MAKING IT HAPPEN

AN EVOLUTION FROM AN INTRANET

In many ways, an enterprise portal (sometimes referred to as an enterprise information portal) is a fancy name for an intranet. The key difference is that an enterprise portal manages not just internal content, but also external content that may be useful to staff. Such external information could include, for example, specialized news feeds, or access to industry research reports.

LEARN FROM THE PUBLIC PORTALS

On the Web everyone is a publisher, but that doesn't mean that everyone is a good publisher or that people will want to read what they publish. Very few public portals have survived, because they have not been able to build a viable business case.

Another portal sector that has seen great change was the much-vaunted "vortal." A vortal, or vertical portal, provides information that is organized around a vertical market sector, such as pharmaceuticals or plastics. Vortals and e-marketplaces have a lot in common, and in many markets may be one and the same thing. Most of these vortals, if they haven't evolved into e-marketplaces, are probably no longer in business.

The lessons that need to be learned from public portals and industry vortals include:

- people are very conservative in the way they consume content. The majority of people go to a few trusted brands;
- running portals is expensive; many have not survived because they did not have a proper business model.

THE CAPTIVE AUDIENCE INSIDE THE ORGANIZATION

The enterprise portal would seem to have a captive audience—employees. But it's not as simple as that. Staff who use an enterprise portal demand high publishing standards. High publishing standards are expensive to maintain, and many enterprise portals are dying because they don't have enough quality content, the content is not being kept up to date, and the whole environment is not properly organized and structured. What many organizations are discovering is that providing all this related information is wonderful in theory, but expensive and difficult to manage in practice.

KNOW YOUR EMPLOYEES' CONTENT NEEDS

Ask the following questions:

- How are employees' information needs being met at present?
- Are any of these needs not being satisfied properly?
- Can I fill this gap cost-effectively?
- Will my staff trust me to fill this gap?
- Where's the return on investment?

Related information is all well and good, but the key question must be: where is the return on investment? If a member of staff can just as easily get this related information somewhere else, why duplicate the effort? Unfortunately, organizations rarely take the time to examine which of their content drives the business forward, and which has little effect. But having a Web site is being a publisher, and if you don't understand the impact of your content, you don't understand publishing.

For More Information

Web Site:

Business2 enterprise portal guide, links to articles on enterprise portal issues:
www.business2.com/webguide

See also:

☆ **Developing an Internet Era Mindset throughout the Organization (pp. 141–42)**
✔ **How to Deliver Quality Online Customer Service and Support (pp. 582–83)**
✔ **How to Implement an Effective Search Process for a Web Site (p. 616)**
✔ **How to Make the Most of an Intranet (pp. 636–37)**
✔ **Implementing Effective E-learning within the Organization (pp. 642–43)**
✔ **Making a Web Site Easy to Navigate (pp. 614–15)**

"Information networks straddle the world." (Günter Grass)

Setting Up an Extranet

Getting Started

An extranet is a private Web site between two or more business partners, which aims to enable the partners to share information in an efficient and timely manner. Because this is a work environment and partners will want to get to the information as quickly as possible, the design of an extranet should focus on minimal graphics and maximum content. An extranet will be password-protected in order to maintain confidentiality; security will be a key issue. When exploring the establishment of an extranet, consider the following:

- extranets are all about the speedy delivery of relevant information;
- supplying up-to-date, accurate and comprehensive information to a business partner is not a simple process;
- connecting partners into an extranet can make them more loyal and make it more difficult for them to switch to a competitor.

Making It Happen

When to Establish an Extranet

An extranet makes sense when you have business partners who continually require substantial information from you. By hooking them into an extranet, you are essentially offering them a self-service option. Instead of delivering the requested information by phone, fax, mail, or in person, an extranet allows your partners to get the information they need whenever they want it.

Examples of Extranet Uses

Extranets can range from the relatively simple to the very complex, as shown in these examples:

- a consultancy may be implementing a job for a client and use an extranet to keep the client fully informed on all aspects of the job;
- a private e-marketplace is essentially a complex extranet whereby products and services can be bought and sold;
- a product design may involve a number of partners. An extranet can be used to share design specifications and to allow effective collaboration to occur;
- an organization may sell a complex product to customers and offer them an extranet that will contain specific information on the product, including support, upgrades, and ways to use the product.

Confidentiality and Security in Extranets

By definition, an extranet will contain confidential information that you wish to share only with identified partners. From a security point of view keep in mind the following:

- an extranet often contains elements of your intranet. Make sure that it is properly locked off from other parts of your intranet;
- encryption should be considered: information transferred between parties is specially encoded so that only the relevant parties can read it;
- a joint security policy needs to be agreed with your partners, so that equal standards and procedures are maintained.

The Importance of Content Management

An extranet is only as useful as its information. If the content is not accurate, up to date and comprehensive, then the very purpose of the extranet is undermined. Therefore, quality content management procedures are required. Many extranets fall down because the content is not being updated and managed properly.

Simple, Lean Web Design

Your partners will not be happy if they are left waiting for a page to download because of some fancy animation containing a swirling logo. The design should be even more minimal than for other Web sites, to ensure that content can be navigated and downloaded as quickly as possible. Remember, an extranet is very much a work environment.

Bandwidth May Be an Issue

Extranets are often hooked into intranets, which are generally hosted internally. You will need to make sure that bandwidth is sufficient to allow external partners quick access.

The Need for a Contract

An extranet involves the communication of confidential information. This means a contract is required. Some extranets are designed and maintained jointly by a number of partners. In such a situation, a contract will need to cover who owns what, and who has what obligations from a maintenance point of view.

For More Information

Web Site:

Intranet Journal is full of practical advice that is equally relevant to extranet design and management: **www.intranetjournal.com**

See also:

☆ **Integrating Technology into Business Processes (pp. 169–70)**
☆ **Overseeing Invisible Employees in a Virtual Organization (pp. 211–12)**
✓ **How to Add Value Through E-alliances (pp. 640–41)**
✓ **How to Implement Effective Internet Security (pp. 602–03)**
✓ **How to Make the Most of an Intranet (pp. 636–37)**

"Capital, technology, and ideas flow these days like quicksilver across national boundaries."
(Robert H. Waterman, Jr.)

  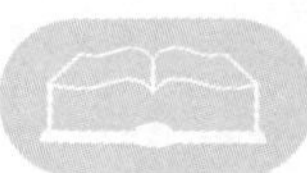    

How to Add Value Through E-alliances

Getting Started

E-alliances are partnerships forged between organizations in order to achieve e-business objectives more effectively. There has been a surge in such alliances since the Web took off in the mid-1990s. According to a 2001 McKinsey consultancy study, the most successful e-alliances were those involving traditional offline businesses and online entities—the clicks and mortar strategy. When examining e-alliance opportunities, consider the following:

- it is often faster and cheaper to set up an alliance than to build something from scratch to achieve a particular objective;
- you need to know exactly what you want to achieve from an alliance, how you will measure the objectives, and how to exit;
- about half of alliances end in failure, the key reasons being false expectations, lack of commitment of assets and resources, and unworkable management structures.

FAQs

Why are changes in technology facilitating more alliances and partnerships?

The reasons include the following:

- Internet technologies create a common platform upon which organizations and people can communicate and share information. Such collaboration was more difficult using traditional technologies and organizational structures.
- The huge changes brought by technology mean that modern organizations need to be much more flexible. Alliances can allow an organization to react quickly to an opportunity or threat.
- Trends such as outsourcing are fundamentally dependent on the partnership model.
- Modern technologies have made individuals more independent of the organization. They may work on contract, or go off and start a small company that will offer an alliance with the organization.

Is the trend towards more alliances and partnerships going to abate soon?

All the signs are that alliances and partnerships will be even more critical in the future. Internet use continues to grow, and is by definition a networked environment. Organizations and individuals will use the Internet to become more flexible, not less.

What does this all mean for a manager?

Instead of managing something fixed, like a department or factory floor, you are now managing objectives and relationships. The aim is to achieve the objective as quickly as possible. This should not be limited by organizational resources. Find a partner to fill the gap; form an alliance to get to market quicker than your competitor. You will be judged on achieving your objectives. How you achieve them may well require thinking outside the box.

Making It Happen

Understand Clearly What You Want to Achieve

If you approach alliance building merely because you think it's a "good thing," you may end up having some bad experiences. You really need to be clear about what you want to achieve from any alliance, and what your potential partner wants. Maybe you both want to achieve the same thing—more sales—but one of you wants much faster sales growth than the other. This will lead to a lot of pain down the line, so be careful that everyone's expectations are managed properly.

Use Alliances to Enter New Markets

Alliances are a key way by which organizations expand globally. Setting up alliances with established players in particular markets can be a much faster way of achieving market share than setting up a large physical presence.

What's in It for the Partner?

Partnership has to be attractive to both partners, or the relationship will go nowhere. Siebel produces sales and customer relationship management software. From day one it sought partners, such as Accenture and PriceWaterhouseCoopers, to implement its solutions. The logic was simple. For every $1 Siebel got paid for software, a consultancy would receive $5–7 for implementing it. Its partnership program has helped make Siebel one of the fastest growing companies in the world.

Competitors Can Form Alliances

Competitors may form an alliance to push a particular industry standard. However, in such situations you must be very clear about what the alliance wants to achieve and manage it carefully. A good example is consortium-based e-marketplaces, where competitors come together to achieve greater efficiencies in purchasing.

The Start-up and the Big Organization

Many start-ups seek to form alliances with larger organizations in order to gain more rapid access to markets, funding, and the credibility of being associated with a particular brand. The larger organization gets innovative products and services. The danger for the start-up is that it becomes too dependent on one major customer.

The Clicks and Mortar Alliance

A major study on e-alliances, published by McKinsey in 2001, found that partnerships between traditional offline companies and online business entities were most successful, such as that between Amazon.com and Toys R Us. Toys R Us had the physical infrastructure and brand, while Amazon.com had the online infrastructure and experience in making e-commerce work.

One Alliance Is Rarely Enough

It generally makes sense to have a network of alliances, some involved, some more casual, but all pushing forward your e-business strategy. The key is to be able to judge whether a potential alliance can add value or not, and to manage the network well. Of course, the risk in having too large an alliance network is that you spread yourself too thin.

Alliances Need Ongoing Management and Commitment

Because it is now so easy to establish alliances, many managers focus on the glitzy part—issuing the press release. Some alliances are treated merely as a PR exercise and are pretty much forgotten about after the immediate publicity. But without an ongoing commitment from management, these alliances are dead in the water.

Organizational Structures, Management and Metrics Need to Be in Place

Where do alliances and partnerships fit in the organizational chart? Who is responsible for them? Where is the strategy? What happens in the case of disputes? Some organizations treat alliances as if they are simply ancillary activities, but in this case, the benefits are likely to be negligible. Many partnerships fail because they don't have organizational or management structures in place.

You can't measure success by the number of your alliances. Rather, you need to know exactly what value each partner is delivering, so you will require a set of metrics that regularly measure the success or otherwise of a particular alliance. If negative, such information must be acted on quickly, rather than wait for the inevitable big bust-up.

Partnerships Aren't Necessarily About Equality

You don't have to be best buddies to make partnerships work, though a good relationship helps. Partnerships don't have to be with equals. Managing by consensus is all well and good, but if the wrong people are involved, decisions won't get made and momentum will be lost.

Think Long-term, Act Short-term

Because a great many alliances fail to deliver on their promises, it is not advisable to enter into long-term contractual arrangements. It is much better to establish a short-term arrangement with very defined goals. Once these goals have been achieved, a longer-term agreement can be considered.

Be Wary of Exclusive Deals

You need to be confident that a partnership will deliver substantial value before going into an exclusive deal. If your industry is subject to a lot of change, exclusivity is even more risky.

If your potential partner wants exclusivity, one option is to create a short-term agreement with very specific objectives: if these are achieved, an exclusive contract can be signed. Another option is to set triggers into the contract. Only if certain objectives—sales figures, for example—are met within a defined period, does the relationship remain exclusive.

Have an Exit Strategy

Part of knowing what you want to achieve from an alliance is knowing when it has fulfilled its objectives and how to close it down. This needs to be carefully thought through. Both partners should agree on a clear exit strategy, which will include such things as how assets and intellectual capital are to be shared out.

Common Mistakes

The E-alliance Press Release

Too often organizations have focused on forming an alliance just so that they can issue a press release and place the partner's logo on their Web site. In the early Internet buzz, such press releases often had an impact. However, since the technology downturn, cynicism is the more common reaction.

You Think an Alliance Is About Signing a Contract

Not making the proper commitment in time and resources is a key reason why partnerships fail. The real work begins after the contract is signed. Making the alliance work takes sustained effort, and it may well develop very differently from what was originally envisioned.

You Opt for the Glamor Alliance

Smaller start-ups often believe that an alliance with a large brand will solve all their problems. Big brands are very aware of their status and usually charge a heavy price either directly or indirectly for such associations. Rarely does the smaller player get a bargain.

For More Information

Book:

Segil, Larraine D. *Fast Alliances. Power Your E-Business*. New York: John Wiley, 2000.

Web Site:

McKinsey Quarterly: E-alliances will remain an intricate and necessary part of e-commerce strategies, according to McKinsey:
www.mckinseyquarterly.com

See also:

☆ **The Business Web (pp. 145–46)**
☆ **Making B2B Your New Operational Standard (pp. 150–51)**
✔ **How to Get the Best from E-marketplaces (pp. 634–35)**
✔ **How to Implement Customer Relationship Management (pp. 584–85)**
✔ **Setting Up an Extranet (p. 639)**

"Organizations based on trust have, on occasion, to be ruthless." (Charles Handy)

IMPLEMENTING EFFECTIVE E-LEARNING WITHIN THE ORGANIZATION

GETTING STARTED

E-learning over the Internet is flexible, cost-effective, and measurable. The global e-learning marketplace has grown rapidly, and is expected to be worth more than $20 billion by 2005. When investigating e-learning, consider the following:

- E-learning puts learners in the driving seat, allowing them to learn about specific subjects just when they need to.
- To be effective, e-learning needs to involve collaboration with other learners and mentoring from experts. The classroom should not be eliminated but rather introduced at strategic points in the learning process.
- The e-learning industry has matured very rapidly and there are many companies offering a broad range of e-learning content, technology and services.

FAQs

WHAT ARE THE KEY FACTORS THAT DRIVE E-LEARNING?

In the economic upturn, the logic for e-learning was compelling. Change was constant and there was an ongoing need to keep employees educated and up to date. Quality staff were hard to find, which had two major implications from a learning perspective. First, the best people tended to be focused on constantly improving their skills, so an organization with a comprehensive learning program was more attractive to them. Second, if appropriate staff couldn't be found for certain positions, an alternative was to train up current employees. This, again, required a learning program.

In the downturn, the need to train so many so quickly is not quite as compelling. However, the cost-effectiveness of e-learning becomes attractive here. Traditional classroom-based learning has a high cost in getting people to and from venues, much of which e-learning cuts out. In addition, the effectiveness of classroom-based learning has been difficult to measure. E-learning is seen as more accountable and measurable.

WHAT ARE THE DISTINGUISHING CHARACTERISTICS OF E-LEARNING?

The following are key characteristics of e-learning:

- e-learning is primarily delivered over the Web;
- it can adapt quickly to meet changing learning needs;
- learners can find what they want to learn, when they want to, at a pace that suits them. (However, some e-learning is instructor-led, when learners log-in at a specific time and are taken through a module by an instructor.)
- many e-learning modules are designed to be 20–30 minutes long, so learners can take them during a break period. By taking a series of modules over a period of time, learners build up an expertise;
- learners collaborate with instructors and other learners so as to learn better;
- compared to classroom-based learning, e-learning is a fast and cost-effective way to teach large numbers of people;
- it can deliver learning in multimedia format: text, images, audio, video, interactive and simulation tools;
- material that learners have accessed and completed can be accurately measured, allowing the organization to track who is learning what, and which resources are popular.

MAKING IT HAPPEN

UNDERSTAND WHAT E-LEARNING CAN DO

Organizations invest in learning so that their people can become smarter and thus more productive. The theory is great, but the reality has been described as the "great training robbery." Like the old advertising adage, organizations know that half of their training works, they just don't know which half. E-learning promises to make learning more efficient and accountable by getting the right training to the right people as quickly as possible, measuring the results to ensure it's achieving its goals, and making sure it's done in a cost-effective manner.

DEVELOP A LEARNING CULTURE

If there is no learning culture within the organization, e-learning is not going to make much difference. It can only work where staff and management are committed to it. Perhaps many employees feel the only way to learn is in a classroom: they will need to be won over to the benefits of e-learning. Simply installing an e-learning system and waiting for everyone to sign up is not likely to work.

IMPLEMENT THE COMPONENTS OF E-LEARNING

The following are necessary components of an e-learning environment:

- Personalized learning space: learners need their own customized environment within the overall e-learning Web site, so they can check such things as what modules they have completed and have yet to complete; who their mentors are; or what collaborative learning groups they are part of.
- Mentoring: without interaction and mentoring, e-learning can become very dry. Learners need to be able to access experts in order to ask questions and receive guidance.
- Simulation: quality e-learning offers simulated environments in which learners can practice what they have learned.
- Collaboration: interaction with other learners is a fundamental building block of all learning. E-learning needs to facilitate this by actively encouraging collaboration.

"Never let formal education get in the way of your learning." (Mark Twain)

- Assessment: important both for the organization and the learner. The organization needs to know if the e-learning is resulting in increased knowledge within its workforce; learners need to have targets and to know where they are doing well and where they need to work harder.

Manage and Administer E-learning

E-learning requires sophisticated administration if it is to be properly managed. The following elements will need to be in place:

- a registration process
- a payment process, or a process by which costs can be matched to budgets
- a monitoring process that allows the manager to track how learners are performing

In addition, a process must be established whereby managers and employees work together to plan and discuss what needs to be learned and how things are progressing. This was traditionally done during annual or biannual staff assessments, but because of rapidly changing learning needs, this now has to happen with greater regularity.

A method of measuring how the new skills learned contribute to a more productive workplace is also required. People may be learning lots of new skills, but if these are not applicable to their job or their future prospects, they will be wasted.

Mix Classroom-based Learning and E-learning

It is shortsighted to think e-learning will totally replace classroom-based learning. One of the critical functions of classrooms is that people get to know each other, and build up contacts. The classic way many people find out about things is to ring or e-mail someone. If they don't know who to contact, or don't feel comfortable doing so because they don't know the expert well, that can be a major drawback. A happy medium needs to be achieved: for example, learners could do most of a course through e-learning, but come together in a classroom environment at strategic points.

Create Your Own E-learning or Buy It in

The e-learning marketplace has expanded rapidly and there are many companies who have comprehensive and cost-effective e-learning offerings. E-learning technology is very complex and it will rarely make sense to build your own. A model that has emerged for organizations that have their own training content is to buy or rent e-learning technology.

Select an E-learning Company

The selection process will very much depend on your specific needs. However, in evaluating e-learning companies, the following questions will be useful:

- What are their reputation and brand like? Have they been around for a while, and do they look as if they'll be around in the future?
- What's the quality of their learning content? Is it highly interactive and engaging, with access to experts, or is it like a digitized textbook?
- How comprehensive is the offering? Will this organization meet all your e-learning needs, or will you have to go elsewhere for other courses?
- What is the technology like? Is it robust and scalable? Do the modules download quickly or do they hog bandwidth?
- What sort of global reach do they have? If the e-learning works well in one office, can it be quickly rolled out in other offices around the world?

Common Mistakes

Slow Bandwidth, Poor Machines

A multitude of technical issues often hobble the shining promise of e-learning. E-learning that uses a lot of multimedia elements–sound, video, animation–can cause a lot of delivery problems. Even within the internal network, bandwidth can be scarce.

Doing Training on the Cheap

E-learning does reduce training costs, but few believe that e-learning on its own will meet an organization's entire training requirements. People still need to get together to share ideas and develop friendships. Often, the socializing that occurs after classroom learning is as important as what happened in the classroom itself. Also, e-learning is less suitable for teaching soft skills and those that require a lot of hands-on activity.

Lack of Self-motivation

Not everyone is itching to learn. Some people will always find an excuse for not doing the course. Often the only way that you can get people to focus on learning is to get them into a classroom.

You Forget That Teachers Have Value

Some proponents of e-learning give the impression that teachers are the enemy of education and that getting rid of them is the answer to all training problems. E-learning without active input from mentors and experts can be a very shallow experience.

Lack of Recognition

The e-learning promise of learning when you want often translates into learning after work or at the weekend. Learners work away diligently, but there's no recognition of the effort. A sense of isolation sets in, and as the day-to-day workload increases, the need to do that e-learning course drifts into the background.

For More Information

Web Sites:

The e-learning jump page contains an extensive analysis of e-learning issues:
www.internettime.com
Google directory of e-learning companies:
www.directory.google.com

See also:

☆ **Organizational Learning and Performance (pp. 301–02)**
✔ **How to Establish an Enterprise Portal (p. 638)**

How to Use Videoconferencing Effectively

Getting Started

Videoconferencing allows a group of people in two or more physical locations to communicate using video and audio equipment. However, with cheaper, improved technology and an economic downturn, interest in it has been renewed. When considering videoconferencing, keep the following in mind:

- Videoconferencing has more benefits than simply saving money on air travel. It can save time and allow for more active collaboration.
- Many people do not understand the many uses of videoconferencing, and are nervous about using it for the first time. Training and education is vital if the expensive system is not to be left unused.
- Videoconferencing is still a complex activity, and it will never be of a high enough quality to eliminate the need for people to get together physically.

FAQs

Why has videoconferencing not been more widely used?

- The technology was very expensive and often failed. Many people who tried using it in the early days found it difficult to set up and awkward to use.
- Not enough people were using it. This is what is called the network effect. Videoconferencing is a network technology, and like other network technologies, such as fax or e-mail, requires a critical mass of users.
- Face-to-face meetings, which videoconferencing seeks to replace, are where relationships are built and deals are closed.
- Many people feel awkward in front of a camera, or hearing their own voice played back.

What are the new drivers of videoconferencing?

A number of factors have converged to make videoconferencing attractive. These include the following:

- the technology has become cheaper, more robust, and easier to use;
- broadband is becoming more widely available;
- PC/Web-based videoconferencing has developed;
- more people are telecommuting;
- the slowing economy has reduced travel budgets; videoconferencing is seen as an affordable alternative.

What are the key benefits of videoconferencing?

The key benefits are:

- it saves time and money;
- less relocation of staff is required, as people can work in virtual teams to a greater extent;
- it is often difficult to get a number of people in the same room at the same time. Videoconferencing makes this easier.

Making It Happen

It's Not All about Saving Money

If videoconferencing is viewed simply as a way to cut costs, then staff may develop a negative attitude toward it. They are likely to see it as something that takes away their perks, a secondhand way of doing business.

Videoconferencing should be promoted in a more positive manner. Staff should see it as a way to:

- get important decisions made more quickly because key people can be brought together more quickly;
- get key people together more often;
- allow people to collaborate and share knowledge more easily and frequently;
- still allow people to meet, even if they can't travel;
- carry out interviews;
- provide or receive training.

Training Is Critical

Videoconferencing is more than having what would have been a physical meeting by video. It can change the way people go about their work, organize their time, and plan their projects. Many people simply don't know how videoconferencing can help them. They are afraid of using it for the first time in case they appear foolish.

What must be emphasized again and again are the benefits for the people involved. Videoconferencing should be promoted as a tool that will make people more productive. Here are some ways of making it more easily understood and more acceptable:

- Make sure that senior management use it. Their presence can be a strong motivator.
- Find a videoconferencing enthusiast and give them scope to promote the technology to other people.
- Have regular demonstrations of videoconferencing to allow people to try it out in a relaxed environment.
- Promote its achievement of practical results by publishing articles and case studies.

Ask People to Examine Their Travel Plans

People should be reminded always to ask themselves: "Can I do this by videoconference rather than get on a plane?" If the trip involves meeting other people within the organization, they should be encouraged to have a premeeting videoconference. After this they can evaluate whether the trip still needs to take place. Even if it does, the meeting is likely to be more productive because of the preceding videoconference.

Get Feedback

Videoconferencing is new to most people, so it is important to track how people are using it and what sort of attitudes are emerging. People should be given evaluation forms to fill out after each meeting. Issues or suggestions should be followed up.

"Music you can see and pictures you can hear." (Walt Disney)

Videoconferencing Options

There are two basic options available for videoconferencing:

- full-blown videoconferencing using ISDN lines, dedicated equipment, and large screens. This is the more expensive option but guarantees a higher quality experience. However, this option is complex to set up, and quite expensive;
- PC/Web-based videoconferencing. Sometimes called Internet Protocol (IP) videoconferencing, this is a far cheaper option, since it piggybacks on PC and Internet technology. It is also far less reliable. It still requires an ISDN line, takes up a small box window on a PC, and is really more like videophone than videoconferencing. Be sure to check minimum processor speeds, video card, and operating system requirements.

Videoconferencing Components

The essential components in a videoconferencing system are as follows:

- a camera
- a monitor
- a microphone
- speakers
- a computer or specialized videoconference terminal, with the appropriate software and user interface
- a codec: a hardware or a software component that compresses and decompresses the audio and video signals (hardware codecs are generally faster)
- a network connection

The quality of each of these components has an impact on the overall quality of the videoconference. This is why videoconferencing is difficult to get right: everything else may be working well, but the microphone, for example, may be faulty.

Make Sure Security Is in Place

Confidential information will be communicated during many videoconferences. It is therefore important that a proper security process is in place. This is usually achieved by the use of encryption technologies.

Support from the Vendor

Videoconference equipment is liable to break down just at the moment you need it most. Because videoconferencing is so time-critical, having a number to call whenever you have a problem can be very helpful.

Tips for Running a Videoconference

The following are some things to keep in mind when participating in or running a videoconference:

- Get to the room at least 15 minutes before the meeting is supposed to start, to ensure that everything is working well. If this is the first videoconference in a particular location, a trial run is highly recommended.
- Make sure everyone has a proper agenda and all relevant documentation before the meeting.
- Make sure someone in each location is familiar with using the equipment for such techniques as camera zooming and audio control.
- The agenda should be accompanied by a page containing a list of all the relevant contact people and phone numbers in the videoconference locations.
- Make sure everyone gets a proper introduction and that the camera focuses on them as they are being introduced.
- Remember that there is often a slight delay in transmission, so it may be necessary to pause to allow people to digest and respond.
- Make sure people are not being left out.
- If you are showing any text, make sure it is in a large font. Keep graphics simple.

Common Mistakes

A Lot of Things Can Go Wrong

Videoconferencing requires a lot of components, cameras, microphones, and speakers, so there are a lot of things to go wrong. You are not depending on your own equipment alone, but on the equipment at the other end also. For example, if another room has a poor camera, then no matter how good your system, the picture will look poor in your room.

Lack of Training and Understanding

Many videoconferencing systems have been underused because of a lack of understanding among staff. Without training, the take-up of videoconferencing within the organization is likely to remain low.

Making Your First Sales Call by Videoconference

Videoconferencing will never replace the need for people to get together physically. If someone is selling a product, the golden rule is to get in front of the potential customer. It is unlikely that sales reps will rely on videoconferencing to make their first vital face-to-face impressions.

Disregarding Audioconferencing

In many situations, people feel that audioconferencing does the job fine. There needs to be a sufficiently compelling reason why you need to see as well as hear people at the other end. Often there is not, and the expensive videoconferencing equipment is underused.

For More Information

Book:

Wilcox, James R. *Videoconferencing: The Whole Picture.* Gilroy, CA: CMP Books, 2000.

Web Site:

Videoconference cookbook, a comprehensive and practical guide to videoconferencing
www.vide.gatech.edu/cookbook2.0

See also:

☆ **Project Management (pp. 169–70)**
☆ **Virtual Collaboration (pp. 167–68)**

 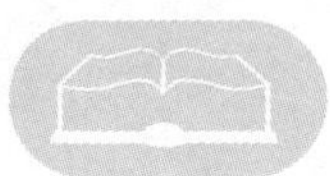    

EXPLORING PEER-TO-PEER (P2P) COMMERCE

GETTING STARTED

Peer-to-peer (P2P) embraces the networking capabilities of the Internet. It allows people to share and publish resources directly, and allows the unused processing capability of computers to be shared and used productively. While the concept of peer-to-peer has in fact been around for many years, it has gained a new lease of life with the advent of the Internet. The peer-to-peer model became particularly well known as a result of the Napster music swapping service.

FAQs

WHAT EXACTLY IS PEER-TO-PEER?

Peer-to-peer puts every computer on an equal footing in that every computer can be both a publisher and consumer of information. The traditional model on the Web is the client–server one. The client is a computer and browser that is able only to receive/consume information. The server, on the other hand, serves/publishes information on a Web site. Peer-to-peer makes a computer both a server and client.

WHAT ARE EXAMPLES OF PEER-TO-PEER?

Perhaps the best-known example of peer-to-peer is Napster (www.napster.com). Napster allows people to swap music files that reside on their computers. Person A could search for and download music from Person B's computer, while Person B could search for and download music from Person A's computer. (The problem with Napster was that the rights to the music being swapped did not belong to the people who were swapping it.)

WHAT SORT OF PEER-TO-PEER OPTIONS ARE AVAILABLE?

The following are distinct options for the use of peer-to-peer technologies:

- information/content: the content on your computer becomes accessible to everyone else in the peer-to-peer environment and vice versa;
- processing sharing: computers with spare processing capacity network together in order to combine their resources. Using a large number of computers, this can create very significant processing capabilities;
- services: a computer user can offer services to other people in the peer-to-peer network.

CAN CLIENT-SERVER AND PEER-TO-PEER SYSTEMS WORK IN HARMONY?

Yes. One does not exclude the other. The best scenario is to exploit the strengths of the client–server model—order, structure, management—and combine them with the flexibility and enabling capacity of peer-to-peer.

MAKING IT HAPPEN

MAKING BETTER USE OF PROCESSING POWER

Studies have indicated that 50% or more of a typical organization's processing power may be unused. Peer-to-peer is a way of tapping this unused resource for productive purposes. There are indications that commercial organizations see this as one of the most practical uses of peer-to-peer technology. However, it must be pointed out that such an application of peer-to-peer only becomes relevant when there are major processing needs that an organization is finding difficult to meet. Where such a situation arises, it can be more efficient and cost-effective to spread processing across the computers in the organization than to buy expensive mainframes.

The drawbacks here are that there will be a setup cost for installing the peer-to-peer technology. Education and training will be needed. When ongoing maintenance is added to this, the costs can begin to mount up. Whether peer-to-peer is genuinely cost-effective in such situations depends on the amount of processing that is going to be required. A careful analysis is required to establish when a peer-to-peer approach is worth considering.

COLLABORATION WITH PEER-TO-PEER

Driven by the rapid growth in partnerships and the need to be more flexible and adaptive, collaboration is now seen as a key attribute of a progressive organization. Peer-to-peer can prove useful where people are collaborating and sharing resources and content on an active basis. If there is a need to establish a group that might span several organizations, then peer-to-peer technology can be faster and easier to implement and run than traditional approaches.

CONTENT PUBLICATION WITH PEER-TO-PEER

It is true that most content today resides on individual computers rather than on servers that publish this content to Web sites. Peer-to-peer allows you to see all the content within the organization, rather than just what has been published on Web sites. This may be helpful when you are looking for something very specific, but there are some substantial drawbacks.

Much of the content that exists on an individual's computer is either private, in draft form, out of date, or simply not ready for publication or sharing. It is estimated that by 2001 there were already over 550 billion documents published on intranets, extranets, and public Web sites. This in itself is a vast, unimaginable quantity of content. The quantity of content that is on individual computers around the world would dwarf this massive amount. Having the capacity to access all this content may sound valuable in theory, but in practice it could make information overload a hundred times worse than it already is.

With regard to content publication, peer-to-peer thinking seems to miss some fundamental rules of publishing. Publishing is not, and never has been, about following an "as much as you can read" approach, but is about selecting the best content and publishing it. A quality publishing house will reject 90% of the content presented to it. It will then polish up the final 10%, and publish it in such a way that it is easy to find and easy to read.

"Nobody who has wealth to distribute ever omits himself." (Leon Trotsky)

File Sharing with Peer-to-peer

The classic model of file sharing occurs when someone downloads a file from a central server. This approach can put a lot of strain on bandwidth if there are a large number of people who need to download files. Peer-to-peer file sharing seeks to use bandwidth more effectively. Let's say Person A and Person B are close together on the network. Person A downloads an e-learning course. Later, Person B wants to download the same course. With peer-to-peer, instead of Person B's request being acted on by the central server, the system looks to see if there is anyone near B on the network who has downloaded the same course. The system finds that A has. So now, instead of B downloading from the central server, B will download from A's machine. This saves time and network resources.

Security and Privacy Are Major Issues

Peer-to-peer thrives in an open network environment. The problem is that hackers and viruses likewise thrive in that very same environment. Within an organization there may be a whole variety of operating systems and security protocols, and linking them all together in a cohesive and secure manner is not a simple task. Many believe that this is the Achilles heel of peer-to-peer.

A key aspect of peer-to-peer security is the authentication of users. Trustworthiness is critical. Many peer-to-peer interactions now use encryption, which ensures that the communication is secure as it is being passed from computer to computer.

Privacy is a major issue for people whose computers will be used in the peer-to-peer network. While enthusiasts tend to be technically competent, most computer users are novices from a technical point of view. What this means is that they become very dependent on their IT department to make sure nothing is going wrong. This situation is not welcomed by the average IT manager.

Equally, for the individual, the idea that someone else can root around within his or her computer can be unnerving. Making sure that their private files are fully protected is only part of the problem. In essence, it means thinking about the computer differently: looking at one part of it as being public domain and another private.

Peer-to-peer and Management

Peer-to-peer technology can allow the organization to investigate its computers and see what resources it has. This could allow an organization to monitor software continually and to distribute upgrades as they become available. It could also allow it to examine the content being created or downloaded by a particular individual, thus giving it more control. Some might describe this as a Big Brother situation.

Setting Up a Peer-to-peer Environment

Certain elements need to be in place for peer-to-peer to function. These include:

- publishing of resources: to make a resource available, it must be published on the computer. This requires that it be identified as a resource that can be shared. Part of this identification involves a proper description that will allow other users to identify it quickly and accurately;
- location of resources: the person who wants a resource must locate it. This can be a major problem in a large peer-to-peer environment where there could be many millions of resources available. Some form of directory classification becomes essential in such an environment;
- utilizing the resource: once the resource has been located, there must be a method by which it can be utilized. If the resource is content, such as music, then it can be simply downloaded. However, if it is processing power it will require a more complex interaction.

Common Mistakes

A Major Security Risk

Peer-to-peer works best in an open network. An open network is open to attack. The peer-to-peer structure can allow viruses to spread more easily. If accreditation and authentication of users is not carried out properly, then hackers or other malicious people can gain access to the network.

The Napster Example

Part of the Napster philosophy was that of bringing unsigned artists to the masses, but the reality was that the majority of people just wanted to hear the major acts. When Napster was stopped from illegally swapping commercial music, its usage dropped dramatically. The theory of peer-to-peer is that people are willing to wade through millions of pieces of content to find that precious gem; in fact, the vast majority of people just want what is popular.

Lack of Standards

Standards tend to vary widely in peer-to-peer technologies, thus making it more difficult to share resources. Without proper standards, a peer-to-peer environment can quickly become chaotic.

For More Information

Web Sites:

Business2 Peer-to-Peer Resources, an excellent selection of articles on peer-to-peer: **www.business2.com/webguide**

Peer Intelligence, a Web site dedicated to all things peer-to-peer: **www.peerintelligence.com**

See also:

- ☆ **Overcoming the Difficulties of Managing a Virtual Organization (pp. 208–09)**
- ✔ **How to Implement Effective Internet Security (pp. 602–03)**
- ✔ **How to Manage Payments Online (pp. 588–89)**
- ✔ **Setting Up a Subscription Process (pp. 618–19)**

Legal Issues in E-commerce

Getting Started

In any e-business strategy, it is important to address the key legal issues from the start and comprehensively. At a basic level, these are matters such as copyright and libel; at a more advanced level, such things as unique restrictions pertaining to the sale of your product within particular jurisdictions need to be dealt with.

When addressing legal issues on the Web, keep the following in mind:

- prevention is better than cure. Establishing a sound legal structure early on is much easier than trying to firefight legal problems as they occur;
- legal systems are getting a grip on the Internet. More and more laws are being passed that deal with doing business online;
- while you can't deal with the unique legal aspects of every jurisdiction, you still need to isolate the key jurisdictions for your online business and make sure you adhere to their relevant laws.

FAQs

Why should you address legal issues from the start?

Because it's important to guard against unpleasant consequences if you get legal things wrong, or just ignore them. Some early e-commerce businesses adopted the latter approach, believing that cyberspace was a kind of laissez-faire utopia beyond the reach of terrestrial governments. They were wrong, and paid the penalty in many cases.

Is it not the case that many laws do not apply online?

Nobody believes that fallacy any more. Which is fortunate, because courts and governments around the world have shown no hesitation about claiming jurisdiction over online activity—in some cases, even when the Web site in question is hosted on another continent. They have applied civil sanctions (such as injunctions and damages) and criminal penalties (fines and even imprisonment) in certain instances.

Is there a pragmatic approach to dealing with legal issues online?

Yes. The practical approach is to get legal advice on three specific types of territory for your Web site. They are as follows:

- the country (or countries) in which your Web operations are principally based, which will often, but not always, be where the site is hosted;
- the countries that are the primary target market of the Web site;
- any other countries which may claim authority over the Web site, and the breach of whose laws might cause unpleasant consequences. The United States is by far the best example of this: its legal regime has a dauntingly long reach.

Making It Happen

The Different Kinds of Web Sites

While there are many different types of Web sites, they can broadly be divided into those with the following attributes:

- shop window Web sites, which provide information about a company and its products, but without encouraging any significant visitor interaction—rather like an online company brochure;
- contributed content Web sites, which allow visitors to contribute content, such as information about their identity, or postings on message boards;
- full e-commerce Web sites, through which visitors can purchase goods or services, either physical products which are delivered offline, or digitized material which is available for download.

Shop Window Web Site Issues

Even shop window Web sites have legal issues to address. They comprise various types of digitized content, such as graphics, text, images, music and coding, that raise issues which apply to all forms of Web site.

Web site owners must assume that all such content is protected: either by copyright—which, in effect, disallows its inclusion in another Web site without the copyright owner's permission; or, in some cases, by moral rights—which require the author to be attributed, and that the work should not be significantly modified without the owner's permission.

These clearances can take the form of a license or an assignment of copyright from the relevant rights holder, which might be a third-party Web site designer, photographer, journalist, or (in the more difficult case of music) two or more rights-holding organizations.

In addition, you must ensure that content on your Web site satisfies other requirements, including:

- Using the registered trade marks of a third party as part of your Web site's metadata will generally constitute trade mark infringement. Even a straightforward reference on a Web site to a third party's trade mark can constitute an infringement.
- Hypertext linking, particularly by means of deep linking or framing, to third-party Web sites without the consent of those Web sites should be avoided.
- Misleading price indications, for example where online prices have not been updated, can incur penalties.
- Incorrect product descriptions, where inaccurate statements are made as to the quantity, size, fitness for purpose or performance of goods, can also cause repercussions.
- Unfair comparative advertising, such as comparisons between goods or services that are not intended for the same purpose, must be avoided.

As well as guarding against infringement of third parties' rights, it is important for owners to include wording in the terms and conditions of their Web sites which protects their own copyright and other rights. Usually this is done by means of terms which appear directly on the home page or, more commonly, are linked to/from the home page, as well as at the bottom of every other page on the Web site.

Contributed Content Web Site Issues

Web sites that encourage visitors to interact are exposed to several additional forms of legal risk. One of the most basic means of facilitating visitor interaction is a discussion board or chat room. Such environments can pose legal problems, as they are often unchecked and allow visitors to post information without any apparent restriction. You need to recognize that you can find yourself liable, either as a civil matter (where a third party's rights have been infringed) or, more extremely, under the criminal law, unless steps are taken to control material which appears on your Web site.

Some of the most obvious problems here include:

- defamatory statements
- infringement of copyright material
- obscene, blasphemous, threatening, racially discriminatory, and other legally objectionable material

To avoid liability for such material, you need to establish one or more of the following safeguards:

- proactive moderation of material before it appears on the Web site
- a documented "notice and take down" procedure, under which infringing content is removed from the Web site as soon as it has been notified
- regular reviewing of material which has been posted, and removal of any which appears problematic

These issues all need to be addressed in your Web site's terms and conditions, so that visitors (and potential third-party complainants) are aware of the steps taken to prevent infringement. Many prudent owners also require visitors to register with the Web site before they can post messages. This allows the owner to contact the visitor if a problematic posting is made by the visitor, and, in certain circumstances, to provide that visitor's personal and contact information to a wronged third party, or to a law enforcement authority.

Full E-commerce Web Site Issues

Clearly, there is a wide variety of goods and services which are capable of being traded through a Web site. Further, the seller can be either the Web site owner or a third party trading through the Web site, as in an online auction service.

It is impossible to cover here all the issues which the various kinds of products can raise. Many have specific regulations which have been imposed by governments for social, ethical and fiscal reasons. Examples of these include:

- sale of alcohol
- sale of medicines, particularly prescription-only medicines
- financial services
- betting, gaming and lotteries
- auctions, particularly in various European countries

Depending on the jurisdiction and type of product being sold, a Web site may need to adhere to regulations such as:

- provision of clear information to consumers before the conclusion of a contract, including: the identity of the supplier; the main characteristics of what's being sold; payment and delivery arrangements; and the principal terms and conditions of the contract between seller and purchaser;
- a minimum period during which a consumer may withdraw from the contract for any reason, and reject whatever has been purchased.

Whatever you sell through your e-commerce Web site, it is important that you form a legally binding contract with the purchaser. For example, you might ensure that such a contract is formed by requiring the visitor to scroll through your terms and conditions and click on an "I accept" button.

Common Mistakes

Doing Nothing Because You Think It's Just Too Complicated

It is certainly true that there is a dizzying array of legal issues to ponder when trading over the Web. However, that's not an excuse for doing nothing. There is a basic minimum that can and should be addressed. The key is to understand the legal issues that, if not addressed properly, can have a major impact on your business.

Assuming That the Long Arm of the Law Does Not Reach Online

This is a very false assumption. Yes, it is often more difficult successfully to prosecute an organization that is trading over the Web. However, that does not mean that governments and legal systems are ignoring those who they feel are breaking their laws, just because they happen to be on the Web.

Failing to Deal with Copyright and Libel Issues Quickly

If a third party accuses you of libel or copyright infringement, it is imperative that you deal with it urgently. In many courts of law, the longer the libel remains published on the Web site, the greater the penalties.

For More Information

Web Sites:

Guide to law online, a comprehensive resource from the U.S. Law Library of Congress that has a global focus: **www.lcweb.loc.gov/glin**

LLRX.com provides up-to-date information on Internet legal research and technology-related issues: **www.llrx.com**

See also:

✔ **How to Manage Payments Online (pp. 588–89)**

✔ **The Key Issues of Implementing E-commerce (p. 580–81)**

"Nothing is illegal if 100 businessmen decide to do it." (Andrew Young)

Better Communication with Resellers

Getting Started

To operate effectively, resellers need support. Help your resellers by making it easy for them to access technical support, and give them a helpline to your resources, skills and experience. Incentive programs can encourage resellers to do more business with you, and certification programs can help to improve reseller performance.

FAQs

Isn't reseller advertising a waste of money?

You have to strike a balance between investing in strong national or regional campaigns, and allocating funds to individual resellers to run their own smaller, local campaigns. If resellers just use funds to run occasional advertisements, the money can be wasted. If the individual local campaigns are well coordinated and planned, they can be extremely effective.

How tightly should you control the use of reseller identity?

Reseller identity is part of overall corporate identity and branding. It should therefore be used consistently throughout the reseller network. Some resellers may argue that their own identity is more important and try to modify your material. In such a situation, you need to stress the benefits of forming part of a nationally recognized brand.

Should you provide funds for specific marketing projects or a general reseller marketing fund?

This question tends to come up when there is a lack of trust between the two parties. Some companies believe that nonspecific marketing funds simply go into reseller profits and have no marketing benefits. They therefore exercise strict control over how the funds are spent. Others trust their resellers' local knowledge to use the marketing funds most appropriately.

Why don't resellers take responsibility for their own training?

Many larger reseller networks do operate their own training programs. However, the aim of training is to improve the performance of reseller staff in selling your product. You have to treat them as an extension of your own sales operation and that makes reseller training an important success factor.

Making it Happen

Support Is Vital

Resellers play a vital link in the supply chain. However, to operate effectively, they need support. Providing the right level of support has a number of important benefits:

- it contributes to high levels of customer satisfaction;
- it makes the company the preferred choice for local customers;
- it focuses the attention of sales staff on customer requirements;
- it improves the company's competitive position;
- it supports the effective launch of new products.

Resellers have the market awareness and experience to deliver added value, and they play a leading role in providing products and services. It's important for both parties to work together to succeed, so they should have access to your full range of products, services and support.

Scope of Support

A program could contain any or all of the following elements:

- advertising
- authorized reseller logo
- joint marketing
- financing
- services
- sales training
- technical support
- business education
- sales leads
- helpline
- rewards and incentives
- certification
- business and market information

Advertising

You can include resellers in your own advertising programs or allocate marketing funds to reseller advertising campaigns. Advertising like this typically generates awareness of resellers to small and medium-sized enterprises and features the reseller emblem.

Authorized Reseller Logo

Resellers can benefit directly from the strength of your own brand name. A reseller logo lets partners use the power of your brand as leverage, and helps them differentiate themselves from the competition when they communicate with potential customers. The logo can be used in brochures, direct mail, directory listings, exhibitions, trade shows, and Web sites.

Joint Marketing

You can help resellers by driving business in their direction. This can be as simple as generating leads, or running reseller advertising campaigns. Alternatively, you can get involved in marketing campaigns aimed at specific market sectors or individual customers.

Financing

Finance can help resellers market your products and services more easily. You can often help resellers close a deal by providing finance to their customers.

Services

Many resellers do not have the skills or resources to provide service and support to their customers. You can help them deliver services through your own resources in design, installation, and maintenance.

"I and each of my executives make it a hard and fast point to visit a minimum of 40 suppliers a year."

(Marcus Sieff)

Sales Training

Sales training should be a structured process designed to help your resellers build sales. It should help retailers:

- identify key customer business issues;
- create a solution based on your products and services;
- offer compelling, well-supported sales presentations.

Sales training can be delivered in your own training center, on the reseller's premises, or remotely through the Internet or other media.

Technical Support

Technical support can be crucial, particularly when your products or services are complex, so make it easy for resellers to access your technical support systems.

Business Education

A business education program will help your resellers keep up with the latest developments and maintain their product and business skills. Courses could cover:

- executive/management development
- leadership training
- product marketing skills
- sales and marketing tools

Sales Leads

A formal lead generation program simplifies lead management and delivers qualified leads from a single source in a consistent manner. You could generate leads through your own national advertising or direct mail programs and direct the leads to the local reseller. You should also monitor lead management to ensure that leads are used effectively.

Helpline

A helpline connects resellers with your resources, skills, and experience. It provides a quick response to sales and product customer queries, and can provide vital backup.

Rewards and Incentives

Reward programs encourage resellers to do more business with you, while incentive programs can increase revenue for both parties. Some reward programs are designed to provide business development funding equivalent to a percentage of the revenue generated from sales of your products. Resellers can use this funding for a wide variety of approved market development activities.

Certification

Like market development funding, certification programs can help to improve reseller performance. Certification should only be offered to resellers who meet agreed targets in terms of sales, training, skills levels, investment, technical resources and other factors essential to business success.

Business and Market Information

Resellers should be able to access information on products and availability, prices, order tracking, incentives, marketing campaigns, and sales information quickly and easily. The Internet makes it easy for you to offer resellers support and information electronically. You can offer information on products, pricing, and technical support, as well as various forms of electronic communication, online guides, and publication ordering.

Common Mistakes

Providing Support in an Ad-hoc Way

Many companies are faced with last-minute requests to support, for example, a one-off advertisement or a local trade show. While this may seem important to the local reseller, it may have little impact on the overall success of reseller marketing. It is better to provide funds and support for a support program with specific objectives.

Failing to Manage a Support Program at Local Level

Many companies provide only funds or marketing material to resellers, and leave them to do what they like with the resources. The results are often poor and inconsistent throughout the reseller network. It is far better to provide guidelines, or appoint a manager to work with resellers to develop and control local programs.

Inadequate Funds

Reseller support frequently has a low priority in the overall marketing budget. The result is that small funds are widely distributed and achieve little. If the available fund is small, it may be more effective to concentrate on a smaller number of more focused campaigns.

Poor Campaign Information

Resellers frequently complain that they are not kept informed of national marketing and advertising campaigns. As a result, they miss opportunities to benefit locally from those campaigns. Make sure you keep resellers up to date with all of your company's marketing activities and plans.

For More Information

Book:

Webb, Geoff. *The M-Bomb: Riding the Multi-channel Whirlwind.* San Francisco: John Wiley, 2000.

Web Site:

The Supply Chain Council: **www.supply-chain.org**

See also:

- ☆ **The Business Web (pp. 145–46)**
- ☆ **X-engineering Success (pp. 245–46)**
- ✔ **Managing Retailer Marketing Programs (pp. 740–41)**
- ✔ **Running Sales Meetings (pp. 734–35)**
- **Logistics and Distribution (pp. 2026–28)**

Getting Better Results from Your Agency

Getting Started

Agencies emphasize a number of factors when trying to win new business. It is important to review agency performance regularly to see that initial promises are being delivered and that the original selection criteria are still valid.

FAQs

Should I place all marketing tasks with a single agency or deal with specialists?

Full service agencies claim to integrate all aspects of a client's marketing operations so that clients get a better overall return for their marketing dollar. Specialists, on the other hand, claim to offer a more effective service in critical areas such as creativity, media buying, or below-the-line promotion. If you choose specialists, you have to make sure that they work to consistent standards and do not overlap. If you choose an integrated agency, you may need to compromise on the quality of some of the more specialist areas of activity.

Is agency commission better than a service fee?

Traditionally, agencies were remunerated by the commission received from the media in which they placed advertisements. Any creative, planning or buying services would be covered by that commission, which meant that these services were effectively free to the advertiser. However, the higher service content of most agency work meant that commission did not adequately cover agency costs. Agencies therefore charged fees to clients and passed some of the media commission to the client. In the absence of fees, agencies may have been forced to reduce service levels.

Making It Happen

Use the Right Criteria to Select an Agency

The most popular reasons for a client's choice of agency include:

- seeing advertising they like
- recommendation by a colleague
- information from the marketing/advertising press
- the agency winning an award
- using the services of a selection agency
- using a selection consultant

Agencies emphasize a number of factors when they are trying to win new business. It is essential to see that they are delivering on their initial claims and promises, which commonly include:

- a good understanding of the business
- quality thinking
- involvement of senior staff who will continue to work on the account
- evidence of sound business and account management skills
- a powerful creative idea

Concentrate on the Key Criteria

In reviewing your agency, you should concentrate on key criteria such as those identified in industry surveys:

- creativity
- value for money
- media buying
- quality of account management
- attentiveness and adaptability
- marketing strategy
- coverage of major world markets

According to other research, clients believe the ten most important factors in agency performance are:

- Does it take the trouble to understand your business?
- Can it use creativity effectively to sell your products?
- Does it have real creative flair?
- Does it get work done on time?
- Does it have a good understanding of your consumers?
- Does it believe in defining advertising objectives beforehand?
- Does it keep costs within budget?
- Does it use research to aid its creative work?
- Is it strong on media buying?
- Is it thorough and hard working?

Understand Why Agency/Client Relationships Fail

Reports in the trade press highlight a number of factors that create conditions for a breakdown.

- The agency is not devoting enough time or resources to the account.
- The agency is losing enthusiasm for the account.
- The agency may be faced with working on a conflicting account.
- There may be a personality clash.
- The client believes that advertising does not have the planned effect on the marketplace.
- The agency feels that poor results are caused by problems on the client side.
- The client does not like the advertisements for subjective reasons.
- The agency fails to understand the client's business.
- A failure of communication means the agency cannot respond to the client's real needs.
- Frequent changes in the agency team or client team make continuity difficult.
- Poor agency administration lets down good creative work.
- Relationships can become stale.

Schedule Regular Review Meetings

Review agency performance regularly. Many agencies and clients carry out reviews at three-, six-, or twelve-month intervals, or after each major campaign to assess both campaign and agency performance.

"Good copy can't be written with tongue in cheek, written just for a living. You've got to believe in the product."

(David Ogilvy)

  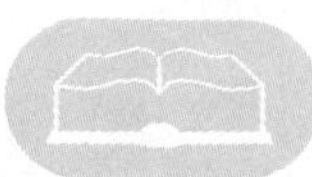    

Take Action to Improve Performance

If your agency shows poor performance in one or more areas, take remedial action. Suggest a change in remuneration that rewards performance or move part of your account into another type of agency offering specialist services.

Consider Paying Agencies by Results

With the increasing emphasis on accountability, a small but growing number of agencies are including an element of payment by results in their remuneration packages. Variations include:

- part fee and part results-based: for example, based on an increase in sales or awareness;
- part fee and part commission, with the fee based on achievement of agreed measurable objectives.

Although this orientation toward results is attractive to clients, it can be difficult to relate the contribution of the agency to a measurable result, and this trend seems unlikely to replace traditional forms of remuneration.

Switch to Creative Independents

If your agency is weak on creative work, you could consider working directly with an independent creative consultancy. Creative independents only handle creative work, such as copywriting and design. By specializing, the independents can often achieve more effective advertising than full service agencies. There are three types of creative independent:

- freelance staff, either combined writer/art director teams or individuals
- design consultancies offering advertising as part of a communications service
- specialist creative independents—small agencies with their own or freelance creative teams

Work with a Virtual Agency

As clients demand greater flexibility and an increasingly wide range of services, they are attracted by the concept of a virtual agency. In some cases, the agency may simply consist of a planning and management team with all creative, media, and specialist services bought in from independent suppliers. Other agencies maintain a central office with specialists based in satellite operations linked by telecommunications and videoconferencing.

Appoint a Brand Consultancy

The role of the advertising agency in creating and maintaining brand awareness is being challenged by a new type of marketing services organization known as a brand consultancy. The brand consultancy brings together skills from a number of different disciplines, including market research, marketing consultancy, management consultancy, and advertising.

The brand consultancy claims a number of advantages over the traditional advertising agency approach:

- longer-term perspective on the development of brands, because they are not limited by an annual advertising budget
- recognition and integration of the different elements that contribute to brand success
- closer working relationships with the whole client brand team

Choose a Media Independent

A media independent, as the name suggests, only handles media planning and buying. By concentrating on media, the independents can often negotiate better deals than full service agencies. In fact, many smaller advertising agencies use media independents to handle their media buying. You would have to handle campaign planning and creative work in other ways.

Appoint an Integrated Agency

Agencies offer integrated services in a number of forms:

- a single integrated agency where all campaigns are handled by the same team
- an agency group where nonadvertising campaigns are handled by specialist companies within the group

Common Mistakes

Failing to Review Agency Performance

Many companies appoint an advertising agency for a fixed period but do not build performance reviews into the agreement. Regular performance reviews provide opportunities to identify and resolve problems early.

No Performance Criteria

If you include performance reviews in your agency agreement, make sure you set out the criteria by which the agency will be assessed. The more precise and measurable the criteria, the easier it will be to carry out an objective assessment. It is too easy to say, "I don't like their creative work." If the creative work delivers results and meets targets, it must be judged successful, regardless of personal taste.

Expecting One Agency to Do Everything

Many agencies claim to be good at all types of marketing. They call themselves full service agencies. However, they may not be able to meet your requirements in all areas, so you should consider appointing specialists to handle specific tasks such as media buying, sales promotion, or product development.

For More Information

Book:

Sacharin, Ken. *Attention!: How to Interrupt, Yell, Whisper, and Touch Consumers*. New York: John Wiley, 2000.

Web Site:

American Marketing Association:
www.MarketingPower.com

See also:

✔ **Measuring Advertising Performance (pp. 660–61)**
✔ **Preparing an Agency Brief (pp. 658–59)**
✔ **Selecting an Advertising Agency (pp. 662–63)**
✔ **Setting Advertising Objectives (pp. 664–65)**
David Ogilvy (pp. 1124–25)
Advertising (pp. 1903–06)

"I want all our people to believe they are working for the best agency in the world. A sense of pride works wonders."

(David Ogilvy)

Integrating Advertising with Other Campaigns

Getting Started

Advertising is one of a series of interrelated marketing tools that support each other, and in an integrated campaign, advertising becomes a much more flexible medium and can be used wherever it is most effective.

FAQs

Why do some agencies avoid integrated campaigns?

It may be because they do not have the skills to handle the other marketing activities that fall outside the traditional advertising agency role. In some cases, they do not understand how the activities work together.

Is an advertising agency the best choice to handle an integrated campaign?

There are integrated agencies that offer all marketing services from within their own organization. Others may be part of a larger group who can offer the other, nonadvertising services. These types of agency are suitable for handling integrated campaigns. If advertising is not a major part of the integrated campaign, it may be more appropriate to talk to a marketing services company or group that offers all the relevant services.

Why is integration so important? Isn't it better to focus on getting the best results from individual marketing activities?

Results indicate that integration can save money and make better use of a budget. The savings come through multiple use of the same planning and creative work and more efficient use of the available funds. The other major bonus is that integrated activities support each other, improving the efficiency of individual campaign elements against overall objectives.

Making It Happen

Integrate Campaigns

Advertising is not a separate activity but one of a series of interrelated marketing tools that support each other. Although campaigns take many different forms, there are core elements that are crucial to the successful development of an integrated marketing strategy. The most important of these are:

- advertising
- direct marketing
- telemarketing
- press information
- relationship marketing
- sales support
- publications

In the integrated approach, the elements support each other. For example, an advertising campaign with reply coupon is integrated with a direct mail program, which is followed up by telemarketing. Without the support of the other marketing elements, the advertising and direct mail programs would have achieved results; but together they reinforce each other to achieve real impact.

Advertising

With an adequate budget and effective media planning, it would be possible to use advertising alone to launch and market a new product. In this situation, advertising would have a number of objectives:

- raising customer awareness of the new product;
- explaining the comparative benefits of the product;
- generating initial requests for information.

The success of the launch would be directly related to the size of the budget and how efficiently it is used. By integrating advertising with other marketing activities, however, the company can use advertising for specific tasks within the overall program and make more effective use of its budget. In an integrated program, advertising is just one of the marketing tools available, and it can be used in whatever capacity is most effective. This could be one of several ways:

- as a national direct response medium, to generate leads for a corporate direct marketing or telemarketing campaign;
- as a regional direct response medium, to generate leads for follow-up by local intermediaries;
- as part of a selective regional sales promotion campaign that offers prospects incentives for providing database information.

These options make advertising a much more flexible medium.

Direct Marketing

Direct marketing is one of the most flexible tools in an integrated marketing program. It can be used to reinforce the effectiveness of other marketing tools, or used alone in a variety of different ways. Direct mail advertising, for example, can be a viable alternative to press or broadcast media as a way of reaching specific sectors of the market. In an integrated campaign, it also can be used to follow up prospects who request further information. In addition, it can be employed to maintain effective contact and build long-term relationships with customers.

In an integrated campaign, however, direct marketing must be used to strengthen overall effectiveness. As a first stage, it can be integrated with the consumer advertising campaigns in the following ways:

- as a follow-up to the direct response advertising campaign. The advertisements provide information on warm prospects, which can be used to form a database for future direct marketing programs;
- to make differentiated offers to prospects who respond to the advertising campaign;
- to supplement the advertising campaign's coverage of different target markets;

"In good times, people want to advertise; in bad times, they have to." (Bruce Barton)

- to reach sectors that cannot be reached efficiently by other media, or to provide increased reach or frequency;
- to reinforce the impact of the advertising campaign by selective follow-up.

Telemarketing

Telemarketing can be used to supplement the advertising and direct marketing campaigns through inbound and outbound programs. It can be used to handle a number of different tasks:

- direct sales to prospects over the telephone
- maintaining contact with current customers
- using the relationship to launch new products
- generating leads from unqualified mailing lists
- following up direct marketing programs
- winning back lapsed customers by introducing them to new products that may be of greater interest
- following up leads generated through advertising or direct marketing, or via intermediaries
- carrying out market research, using surveys to establish consumer response to products or sales incentives
- maintaining contact with customers as part of a relationship marketing program

Telemarketing also can provide a point of response for queries generated through advertising or direct marketing campaigns, or to obtain information from respondents as a basis for future database marketing.

Press Information

Press activities can be used in the context of a wider public relations campaign. Sponsorship of sporting or entertainment events, for example, can increase awareness and build a high profile for a company, leaving advertising and direct marketing to focus on direct response and brand building strategies.

Sales Support

In an integrated campaign, leads can be generated for the sales force by advertising and direct marketing. Sales force productivity can also be improved by using telemarketing to handle routine customer communications. It is essential to back sales teams with information both on the products and on the marketplace to improve their overall effectiveness. The program includes:

- direct sales force and distributor support
- standard and customized presentations for different market sectors
- product/sales guides to improve product knowledge
- information on the advertising and direct marketing support available in each territory
- competitor profiles

Relationship Marketing

Relationship marketing builds on the leads generated by advertising and direct marketing. It also enhances the direct contact of the sales force by increasing customer loyalty. These are its key roles in an integrated program:

- maintaining existing customer base
- increasing account control
- issuing regular, planned flow of information
- increasing customer loyalty

Publications

Product publications do not normally form part of an integrated program. However, they form an important part of the communications program. Publications are used to:

- reinforce overall branding;
- provide benefits-led information;
- communicate positioning messages, as well as product information;
- act as sales presentation guides.

Common Mistakes

Running Integrated Campaigns through Separate Agencies

One of the key benefits of integrated marketing is that the client deals with a single agency for all marketing activities. Dealing with multiple agencies can lead to such problems as different creative solutions or duplicated costs. It is essential that one agency plans and produces the entire integrated campaign.

Defining Integrated Marketing Too Narrowly

Advertising, sales promotion, and direct marketing are viewed as the mainstream elements in an integrated campaign. However, sales support, telemarketing, public relations, exhibitions, and many other activities may have a key part to play.

Failing to Use Data to Plan and Control Campaigns

One of the key elements in an integrated campaign is the database. Information from all campaign activities should be used to identify communications needs, target individual communications, measure campaign effectiveness, and track customer responses. Without this underlying control, campaign funds may well be wasted.

For More Information

Book:

Engel, James F., et al. *Promotional Strategy: An Integrated Marketing Communication Approach*. 9th ed. Cincinnati, OH: Pinnaflex Educational Resources, Inc., 2000.

Web Site:

American Marketing Association: **www.MarketingPower.com**

See also:

✔ **Generating More Leads (pp. 698–99)**
✔ **Improving Direct Mail Response Rates (pp. 686–87)**
✔ **Planning an Advertising Campaign (pp. 656–57)**
✔ **Setting Advertising Objectives (pp. 664–65)**
✔ **Supporting Campaigns with Telemarketing (pp. 736–37)**
Advertising (pp. 1903–06)

"Marketing has displaced management as the industry's chief principle, and expenditures on investment advisory services are dwarfed by expenditures on advertising." (John Clifton Bogle)

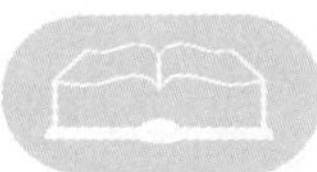

Planning an Advertising Campaign

Getting Started

An advertising campaign needs to have clear, measurable objectives, whether it is designed to communicate product benefits or to support an event. In order to achieve these objectives, it must also be planned carefully. There are eight main stages to consider, from defining the target market to setting a budget.

FAQs

Who is responsible for campaign planning–the client or the advertising agency?

Both parties contribute. The client sets the overall marketing and advertising objectives. The agency develops an advertising strategy based on those. Timings will be determined by the client's product and marketing plans, together with practical agency considerations such as publication dates and lead times.

Why is it necessary to plan a campaign in so much detail?

To be effective, advertising must meet specific measurable objectives. The objectives affect choice of media, creative strategy, overall budget, and lead times. Overlooking any of those details could weaken the effectiveness of the campaign.

Should planning be applied to the creative process?

There is an assumption that creative work takes place in a vacuum. Like any other marketing activity, it must be directed toward an objective. The more information a creative team has, the more focused its work.

Making It Happen

Set Campaign Objectives

It is important to set clear objectives for an advertising campaign. It is essential to identify a specific task for a specific campaign. This might be:

- raising awareness of a company, product, or service within a clearly identified target market;
- communicating the benefits of a product or service;
- generating leads for the sales force or retail network.

To insure you design a cost effective campaign that delivers results, advertising objectives should be translated into precise, measurable targets.

Identify Key Planning Activities

There are eight main stages in planning an advertising campaign:

1. Define the Target Market

Who is your campaign aimed at?

An understanding of your audience will influence the media you select and the creative treatment of your advertisement. To define your target market, you should ask questions like these:

- Who buys your type of product?
- Who influences the purchasing decision?
- In business buying, who are the important decision makers?
- Do you need to communicate with the actual buyers or those who influence the purchasing decision?
- How many potential buyers are there?
- How many users are currently buying your product and what is your share of the market?
- Which prospects do you want to reach with the campaign and where are they located?
- What are the characteristics of these people, for example, age, sex, income, job title and what are their most important considerations in choosing a brand or a supplier?
- What does research tell you about their attitudes toward your company and your products?
- How do they currently get information about your products?
- What is the role of advertising in reaching the target audience?

2. Select Media

There are four important factors to consider in selecting campaign media:

- how closely the audience profile of the medium matches your target audience;
- the comparative costs of reaching the target audience through different media;
- whether the frequency of the medium matches the timing of your campaign;
- the creative opportunities of the medium for the communication of your message.

3. Plan Campaign Timing

When should your campaign run? You have to consider a number of factors first in relation to the purchasing pattern of your products:

- When are your customers making their buying decisions?
- Do you know when your customers hold product/purchasing review meetings?
- If you are launching a new product, when will the product be available?
- Does your advertising campaign have to tie in with the timing of any other marketing activity, for example, an exhibition, direct marketing campaign, or sales force call?
- How quickly will you be able to follow up the campaign?

You also have to take into account production and media lead times:

- What is the next available publication or broadcasting date?
- When does the media owner require your advertisement?
- How long will it take to produce the advertisement?

4. Decide Campaign Frequency

Campaigns raise levels of awareness with each appearance and increase the number of opportunities to see the advertisement. They also move individual respondents further along the decision making process and maintain contact during an extended process. Campaigns reinforce the impact of the message by repetition and provide an opportunity to communicate multiple or complex messages about the company or the product range.

Frequency is determined by a number of factors:

- frequency of publication, that is, how often the publication appears;
- frequency of broadcast: radio or television commercials can be broadcast many times during the same day, if the budget allows;
- your budget, although a number of appearances in the same medium will earn a discount that makes the entire budget go further.

5. Plan Creative Treatment

To achieve good results, you must develop a comprehensive creative brief. These are the main elements:

- campaign objectives
- description of the target audience
- the main concerns of the target audience: why they buy; what they consider; how they view different products and suppliers
- the main benefits of the product or service: why the product is different from competitive offerings; what is new; why the benefits are important
- the proposition—what the prospect is being offered: opportunity to sample or buy; further information; a sales visit; an incentive; or a discount
- the planned response: should the prospect contact the company, send off an order, wait for a phone call, or simply absorb the information?
- the media—size and mechanical details
- the supporting activities—telemarketing, advertising, sales follow-up, tie-in promotions

6. Develop a Response Mechanism

Action is a vital ingredient of any advertising campaign and it is essential that you make it easy for your prospects to respond. First, decide which action your prospects are to take:

- place an order
- arrange a sales meeting
- request further information
- visit a retail outlet
- try the product

Review the cost, convenience, and practicality of response options, including telephone, mail, fax, e-mail, and Web site.

7. Set a Budget

A campaign budget will include direct, indirect, and variable costs:

Direct Costs

- production costs of advertisements, including design, writing and production
- media costs

Indirect Costs

- cost of setting up response handling, either by internal resources or an external supplier
- management costs of planning and controlling the campaign

Variable Costs

- the cost of handling the campaign response, for example, 800 number costs and telephone resources, or costs of postage-paid services
- the cost of meeting the response-supplying and distributing the material that is requested
- the cost of servicing the response-sales or telemarketing costs in dealing with the potential volume of new business

8. Set Schedules

To set a campaign schedule, work back from the launch date and work out how long each individual activity will take.

Common Mistakes

Failing to Integrate Advertising Plans with Other Marketing Activities

Advertising must be integrated with other related marketing tasks. Poor sales force performance, for example, could waste the contribution of a highly successful advertising campaign that provided a large number of sales leads.

Trying to Take Shortcuts on Lead Times

Advertising lead times are influenced by a number of factors including publication dates, production lead times, and product availability.

Trying to Achieve Advertising Objectives with Inadequate Resources

If companies try to achieve targets without committing the right budget, it will mean either that advertisements do not appear frequently enough to have impact, or that production quality is sacrificed.

For More Information

Book:

Sacharin, Ken. *Attention!: How to Interrupt, Yell, Whisper, and Touch Consumers*. New York: John Wiley, 2000.

Web Site:

The American Advertising Federation: **www.aaf.org**

See also:

✓ **Integrating Advertising with Other Campaigns (pp. 654–55)**
✓ **Measuring Advertising Performance (pp. 660–61)**
✓ **Preparing an Agency Brief (pp. 658–59)**
✓ **Selecting an Advertising Agency (pp. 662–63)**
✓ **Setting Advertising Objectives (pp. 664–65)**

"Unless your campaign has a big idea, it will pass like a ship in the night." (David Ogilvy)

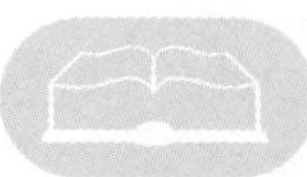

Preparing an Agency Brief

Getting Started

A comprehensive creative brief must cover all aspects of the project: background, objectives, research, competitors, product information, and the target audience at which it is aimed. Failure to draw up the brief properly will give unsatisfactory results with little impact.

FAQs

Why is a detailed creative brief important?

An imprecise brief would have limited benefits. For example, the work may be aimed at the wrong audience and may not take account of the client's understanding of the market. The brief should provide the creative team with as much information as possible so that they can produce a creative theme that achieves results.

Who should be involved in preparing a creative brief?

The people who evaluate a creative brief should also be involved in preparing or approving the brief. It can be difficult to deal with objections and criticism from someone who does not understand the brief. On the client side, the briefing team is likely to include the marketing executive, sales executive, and any relevant marketing specialists such as promotions or direct mail executives. The team should also include product or research specialists to provide detailed information on the product and prospective customers. The agency team should also be involved in preparing the brief, although this does not always happen in practice.

Should an agency brief always have measurable objectives?

The more specific the brief, the easier it is to assess the results of the creative work. It is not always possible to set a measurable objective, but this should be the aim. Agencies may argue that results depend on factors outside their control, but it should be possible to isolate the communications objectives and identify a way of measuring them. A direct response campaign, for example, can be measured by the number of responses, while a corporate campaign could be assessed through attitude surveys conducted before and after the campaign.

Making It Happen

Plan Creative Treatment

How will you present your message? Most publications and commercial broadcast media carry high volumes of advertising. Your advertisement must achieve immediate impact to succeed. There are three essential checks that can be applied to creative work in any media:

- it must have immediate impact;
- it must meet the needs of the reader or viewer;
- it must stimulate a response.

Produce a Comprehensive Brief

To achieve good creative results, you must develop a comprehensive creative brief. These are the main elements:

- campaign objectives
- description of the target audience
- the main concerns of the target audience: why they buy; what factors they consider; how they view different products and suppliers
- the main benefits of the product or service: why the product is different from competitive offerings; what is new; why the benefits are important
- the proposition: what the prospect is being offered—the opportunity to sample or buy, further information, a sales visit, an incentive or discount
- the planned response: Should the prospect contact the company, send an order, wait for a phone call, or simply absorb the information offered?
- the media: scope and practical details
- the supporting activities: telemarketing, advertising, sales follow-up, tie-in promotions

Information of this kind would enable writers and designers to approach the creative process in a disciplined, logical way. Great creative ideas may occur in a vacuum, but they are more likely to be a response to a clearly defined problem.

The creative brief is important whether you are using external suppliers or carrying out the creative work internally.

Provide Background Information

The brief should begin with the background to the project:

- What is the overall aim of the project?
- What threats and opportunities does the business face?
- Why is the project being produced?
- How does the project fit into the overall marketing program?
- How critical is the project to the overall success of the program?

The background material should ensure that the project works in context and is not produced in isolation. It should also list the other projects that form part of the overall program.

Set Out Objectives

The brief should set out a number of objectives, including the overall corporate objective and the marketing objective. The communications objective and the specific project task are derived from these objectives.

The project objectives should be detailed and specific. Examples could include:

- Convert 3% of prospects.
- Make sure that key decision-makers understand the product's business benefits.
- Raise awareness among 20% of the target audience.

Provide Access to Any Research Information

The creative team should be aware of any relevant research information, including:

- customer surveys

"Let us write as if we were writing to a skeptical aunt. All the rest of the world can look over our aunt's shoulder."

(Fairfax Cone)

- industry surveys
- competitor analysis
- product reviews
- press comment on the product or company
- customer satisfaction surveys
- feedback from focus groups
- results of previous campaigns

Include Information on Competitors

The brief should include detailed information on:

- Which competitors provide a similar product or service?
- How does the competitive offering compare?
- What are the product's key benefits against the competition?
- How are competitors perceived by customers?

This information can help creative teams identify some of the key benefits that will differentiate the product from competitors' offerings. It will also show how other companies have tackled the problem of describing the product.

Provide Comprehensive Product Information

The product or service should be described in detail:

- What is it?
- What is it used for?
- How does it operate?
- What are the main benefits for the customer?
- What are the advantages over competitive products?

Describe the Target Audience

Describing the target audience helps the creative team to focus on the key decision-makers:

- What types of company buy the product?
- Which business sectors are they in?
- How big are these companies?
- Who are the main decision-makers?
- What is their role in the decision making process?
- What are their business concerns?
- What is their perception of your company and its products?

Establish Target Perceptions

The creative team should be aware of any key messages that are important to the target audience. The task of the creative team is not to invent these messages; it is to communicate them as effectively as possible. The brief should therefore set out the perceptions that the target audience should hold once the project is complete.

Get Approval of the Brief

The brief should be circulated to all members of the group involved in briefing and approving the project. No creative work should begin until the brief has been signed off. Once the brief has been approved, members should not be able to change it without good reason.

Describe the Review Process

Let the creative team know how their work will be reviewed and evaluated. This can take place at a number of levels:

- review by the agency and client teams
- evaluation in focus groups
- pilot campaigns in test markets

Common Mistakes

Making the Brief Too Specific

It is possible to make a brief too specific, thereby ruling out creative approaches that may achieve outstanding results. For example, setting out the creative approach in the brief before the creative team has had an opportunity to consider it will produce very limited results. The creative team needs information to focus their attention on the problem, not suggestions on how the problem should be solved.

Creative Work Is Not Integrated

Although the brief should allow the agency creative team complete freedom, it is equally important that creative work across different media should be integrated. If advertising is the dominant medium, and a team is working on direct marketing, they should relate their approach to the advertising theme. Repetition of the same creative theme across different media reinforces the key messages and can improve overall awareness.

Award-winning Campaigns That Do Not Produce Results

Creative work should be accountable. The agency may have a great, award-winning creative idea, but if it fails to produce the intended results it may be a waste of money. The creative team should therefore be aware of the specific objectives of the campaign; it is not enough just to get attention.

For More Information

Book:
Ogilvy, David. *Ogilvy on Advertising*. New York: Vintage Books, 1987.

Web Site:
American Marketing Association:
www.MarketingPower.com

See also:

✔ **Getting Better Results from Your Agency (pp. 652–53)**
✔ **Selecting an Advertising Agency (pp. 662–63)**
✔ **Setting Advertising Objectives (pp. 664–65)**
David Ogilvy (pp. 1124–25)
Advertising (pp. 1903–06)

"The things we have to sell won't take the place of the Ten Commandments. . .Copy can be casually optimistic, but no more."

(Bernice Fitz-Gibbon)

MEASURING ADVERTISING PERFORMANCE

GETTING STARTED

Advertising is expensive, so it is important to make sure that it provides value for money in terms of effective results. Objectives should be clearly defined; results should then be measured and evaluated in order to establish that these objectives have been achieved.

FAQs

WHY IS IT SO IMPORTANT TO MEASURE ADVERTISING EFFECTIVENESS?

Advertising budgets represent a major investment for most companies. Measuring advertising allows you to measure the effectiveness of your advertising and your agency. The feedback obtained is invaluable in determining future strategies.

THE MEDIA PUBLISH RESEARCH ON THE EFFECTIVENESS OF ADVERTISING. CAN I USE THIS FOR MY OWN RESEARCH PURPOSES?

This type of research is unlikely to be completely objective, since it is designed to promote the medium. However, it can act as a useful guideline for carrying out a preliminary evaluation of the media. You must measure the results of your own advertising campaign.

SOME AGENCIES OFFER A PAYMENT-BY-RESULTS SERVICE. IS THIS THE ONLY WAY TO REWARD AGENCY AND ADVERTISING EFFECTIVENESS?

This type of agency typically runs a high proportion of direct response advertising, where results can be measured accurately. There are other important parameters, but they do not lend themselves to the same simple measurement.

MAKING IT HAPPEN

SET MEASURABLE OBJECTIVES

It is important to set clear, measurable objectives for an advertising campaign. There is no single advertising objective, so it is essential to identify a specific task for the campaign. This can take many different forms.

- Raise awareness of a company, product, or service in a clearly identified target market.
- Communicate the benefits of a product or service.
- Generate leads for the sales force or retail network.
- Encourage prospects to buy directly through a direct response campaign.
- Persuade prospects to switch brands.
- Support a special marketing event such as a sale or an exhibition.
- Make sure that customers know where to obtain the product.
- Build confidence in an organization.

Advertising objectives should be measurable for two important reasons: first, to make sure that advertising represents an adequate return on investment and, second, to measure the effectiveness of the campaign itself.

The objectives should be detailed and specific. Examples could include:

- Convert 3% of prospects.
- Make sure that key decision-makers understand the product's business benefits.
- Raise awareness among 20% of the target audience.

An effective campaign should have a single focus with a specific measurable result. By mixing objectives, you may achieve only a part of the results you want.

USE RESEARCH TO MEASURE ADVERTISING EFFECTIVENESS

Research should be used to assess how well your advertising has achieved its objectives. This will enable you to fine-tune your advertising plans. You should carry out research before and after a campaign to evaluate:

- changes in customer awareness of the product
- advertising recall
- attitudes to the product
- the responses to different creative approaches

TEST CREATIVE TREATMENT

There are three vital checks that can be applied to creative work in any media: it must have immediate impact, it must meet the reader's or viewer's needs, and it must stimulate a response.

Creative work can be tested in a number of ways, of which the most common are a panel of prospects and customers, test marketing, and measuring the response from pilot campaigns. Important variables to test are:

- size of advertisement
- layout
- creative approach
- position in the publication
- timing
- product offer
- price or discount offer
- response mechanism

MEASURE BRAND SWITCHING

Brand loyalty is a key marketing objective, helping companies to retain customers and increase their lifetime value. Brand switching advertising plays an important role in winning new customers as the first stage in a customer relationship program. It is an important objective that helps you to increase market share or maintain share against competitive actions. It is also important if you are introducing a new product that offers greater benefits than competitors' products.

MONITOR TARGET PERCEPTIONS

To find out what your customers consider important about your products and your company, carry out a survey or run a focus group. The survey should ask respondents how they rank the different brand values. It should also ask respondents how they believe your company and a number of competitors compare across a number of the brand values. The results should give you an indication of overall ranking as well as an insight

"A hard sell advertisement, like a diesel motor, must be judged on whether it performs what it was designed to do."

(Rosser Reeves)

  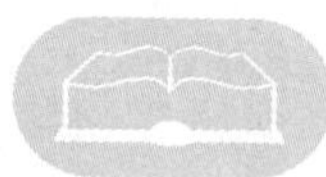    

into individual company perceptions. Advertising aims to change those perceptions so that customers hold a positive view of your company.

Customer perceptions change over a period of time, particularly if you are running targeted communications programs, so you should carry out continuous research to monitor changes in customer attitude. This type of research is known as tracking research and it helps you to measure the effectiveness of your advertising.

Monitor the Right Factors

The corporate reputation is the way a company is perceived by customers, suppliers, and other important groups. You should use your tracking research to monitor customer perceptions of factors such as:

- financial performance
- the quality of the management team
- clarity of direction
- market performance
- growth record and potential
- relationships with suppliers and employees
- manufacturing capability

Measure Response Levels

Direct response advertising is easier to measure than advertising that is designed to change perceptions over a period of time. Your advertisement will include a call to action, such as:

- send for more information
- reply within seven days and receive a free gift
- send for a free report
- take out an annual subscription now and get the first two issues free
- call for a free consultation
- reserve now at a special price
- order now and get a big discount
- visit our Web site and find out more

The most popular mechanisms for press advertisements are:

- Web site address
- e-mail address
- toll-free number

You should monitor the response levels from different sources to see which is the most effective.

Check the Cost of Your Response

You can measure the cost of your direct response campaign by dividing the cost of the advertising or marketing program by the number of responses. You can use the same type of measure to assess factors such as timing, offer, and creative treatment.

Measure Internet Advertising

The advantage of the Internet is that, at little or no cost, you can test your campaign on part of your target audience. You also can experiment with different banner ad sizes. The Internet is ideal for testing messages against your target, gauging the appeal of promotional offers and the type of message that attracts customers who buy. Some advertisers measure effectiveness on click-through rates (CTRs). The average CTR for banner advertising on the Internet is currently 0.2% to 0.4%. Commentators believe that banners that get high click-throughs may not be the best at getting conversions, where the user actually signs up for a subscription or makes a purchase. The real success of your campaign should be based on action, so it is more realistic to use conversions as your measure.

Consider Paying Agencies by Results

With the increasing emphasis on accountability, a small but growing number of agencies are including an element of payment by results in their remuneration packages. Variations include:

- part fee and part results-based, for example, based on an increase in sales or awareness;
- part fee and part commission, with the fee based on the achievement of agreed measurable objectives.

Although this orientation towards results is attractive to clients, it can be difficult to relate the contribution of the agency directly to a measurable result, and this trend seems unlikely to replace traditional forms of remuneration.

Common Mistakes

No Objective Performance Criteria

It is important to set objective criteria for measuring advertising performance. The more precise and measurable the criteria, the easier it will be to carry out an objective assessment.

Failure to Measure Advertising

Companies in consumer and business markets are prepared to spend millions on advertising campaigns but are reluctant to invest in research to measure the effectiveness of them. This has led to a lack of accountability and to problems in reaching a proper evaluation of advertising and agencies.

Using the Wrong Measures

The measures you use are determined by your advertising objectives. If you are running a corporate campaign, you should be measuring changes in perception. If you are working on a direct response campaign, you should be measuring response rates or direct sales.

For More Information

Book:

Sacharin, Ken. *Attention!: How to Interrupt, Yell, Whisper, and Touch Consumers*. New York: John Wiley, 2000.

Web Site:

American Marketing Association:
www.MarketingPower.com

See also:

✓ **Getting Better Results from Your Agency (pp. 652–53)**
✓ **Planning an Advertising Campaign (pp. 656–57)**
✓ **Setting Advertising Objectives (pp. 664–65)**
Advertising (pp. 1903–06)

"Never stop testing, and your advertising will never stop improving." (David Ogilvy)

SELECTING AN ADVERTISING AGENCY

GETTING STARTED

Choose an agency that can provide the right selection of services, including consultancy, strategy, creative work, media, and integration with other communications activities. Important factors in selecting an agency include its approach, reputation, and financial stability. Careful selection can avoid problems that cause breakdowns in the agency/client relationship.

FAQs

I WANT TO WORK WITH A SPECIFIC AGENCY, BUT THEY ALREADY HANDLE THE ACCOUNT OF A COMPETITOR. SHOULD I WORK WITH THAT AGENCY?

This problem occurs frequently, particularly when agency mergers occur, and the new group finds that its client lists include conflicting accounts. The decision to continue handling conflicting accounts is sometimes taken by the agency, and sometimes by the clients. It can be particularly difficult if the agency is seen as an industry specialist, with considerable expertise in a particular market. Sometimes the problem can be resolved by handling the conflicting accounts through separate agency teams.

HOW DO I KNOW THAT AN AGENCY CAN MAINTAIN ITS STANDARDS IN DAY-TO-DAY BUSINESS, ONCE THEY HAVE WON THE INITIAL PITCH?

Sometimes agencies field a special senior team to win new business, and then hand the day-to-day account to a completely different team. Since a good relationship between agency and client is so important, you should insist on meeting the team who will actually work on the business.

IS IT ESSENTIAL TO APPOINT AN AGENCY TO HANDLE ADVERTISING CAMPAIGNS?

A full-service agency may not be essential, particularly if you have the resources to handle part of the task internally. Creative consultancies, media specialists, or integrated agencies can take on specialist tasks.

MAKING IT HAPPEN

CHOOSE THE RIGHT TYPE OF AGENCY

Depending on the type of agency, you can use a comprehensive service or specific services including:

- initial consultancy;
- development of an advertising strategy;
- creative proposals, copywriting, design, and production of advertisements;
- media planning, negotiation, buying, and administration;
- integration of advertising with other communications activities.

WORK WITH A FULL-SERVICE ADVERTISING AGENCY

Full-service agencies handle all aspects of an advertising program. You should select a full-service agency if you do not have any internal skills or resources for handling advertising, or if advertising is important to the achievement of your marketing objectives and you want the campaign handled professionally.

USE A MEDIA INDEPENDENT

A media independent only handles media planning and buying. By concentrating on media, the independents can often negotiate better deals with them than full-service agencies. Many smaller advertising agencies use media independents to handle their media buying. You would have to handle campaign planning and creative work in other ways. Use a media independent if you can handle campaign planning and creative work in other ways but do not have any internal skills or resources for media planning and buying. A media independent could prove useful if you spend a large amount of your budget on media, and you want to take advantage of specialist buying skills to get better positions or lower rates. You may find that certain media will not deal with you, because you are an advertiser. In that case, a media agency can provide valuable support.

CHOOSE CREATIVE INDEPENDENTS

Creative independents only handle creative work such as copywriting and design. By specializing in this way, the independents can often achieve more effective advertising than full-service agencies. You would have to handle campaign planning and media in other ways. There are three types of creative independent:

- freelance staff, either combined writer/art director teams, or individuals;
- design consultancies offering advertising as part of a communications service;
- specialist creative independents: small agencies with their own creative teams, or that manage freelance teams.

You should consider using a creative independent if you can handle campaign planning and media in other ways but do not have any internal skills or resources for creative work. If advertising is a small part of your marketing activity, you could develop effective campaigns by taking advantage of specialist creative services.

WORK WITH AN INTEGRATED AGENCY

Integrated agencies handle all aspects of an advertising program and integrate advertising with other media. Agencies offer integrated services in two forms:

- as a single integrated agency, in which all campaigns are handled by the same team;
- as an agency group, in which nonadvertising campaigns are handled by specialist companies within the group.

An integrated agency may be suitable if other media, such as direct marketing, publications, and sales promotion are as important as advertising, and you want all of the activities integrated and handled professionally.

Evaluate Advertising Agencies

There are a number of important factors in selecting an agency:

- approach. What is the agency's philosophy, and how does it work in practical terms?
- track record. What campaigns has the agency produced, and how effective have they been?
- reputation. Does the agency have an established reputation in your market?
- accountability. How does the agency measure the performance of its campaigns?
- client relationships. What is the current client list, and how many of these clients are enjoying long-term relationships? What is the average length of account tenure?
- disciplines. Does the agency offer all disciplines from within its own resources, and can it offer the full range of services?
- staff. Does the agency have the staff to handle complex, large-scale programs? What is the consultancy's recruitment and personal development policy?
- financial stability. What is the agency's recent performance? Does it have the stability and resources to sustain an effective level of service over the long term?

Check Agency Performance

According to Henley Centre research, clients believe the ten most important factors in agency performance are:

- Does it take the trouble to understand your business?
- Can it use creativity effectively to sell your products?
- Does it have real creative flair?
- Does it get work done on time?
- Does it have a good understanding of your consumers?
- Does it believe in defining advertising objectives beforehand?
- Does it keep costs within budget?
- Does it use research to aid its creative work?
- Is it strong on media buying?
- Is it thorough and hard working?

Obtain Information about Advertising Agencies

There are a number of useful sources of information about agencies:

- the American Association of Advertising Agencies publishes information about agencies;
- individual agencies provide videos of their agency credentials;
- specialist magazines publish regular news about agencies and their clients.

Avoid Problems in Client/Agency Relationships

Reports in the trade press highlight a number of factors that create conditions for a breakdown:

- The client believes that the advertising has not delivered results, or not had the planned effect on the marketplace.
- The agency feels that poor results are caused by marketing, product, or management problems on the client side.
- The client does not like the advertisements for subjective reasons.
- The agency fails to understand the client's business.
- A failure of communication means that the agency cannot respond to the client's real needs.
- Frequent changes in the agency team or client team make continuity difficult.
- Poor agency administration can let down good creative work.
- Relationships can become stale.

Common Mistakes

Choosing the Wrong Size of Agency

A large agency may have the resources and scale to support national or international campaigns, but if your account is small, you may get poor service from a junior team. It may be more appropriate to work with a smaller agency, where you will get personal service from the senior people.

Choosing the Wrong Type of Agency

Agencies, like any other business, develop specialties. Their expertise may not coincide with your needs. The most important division is between a consumer and a business-to-business agency but, beyond that, agencies develop expertise in certain industries or markets. Look carefully at the agency's client list to find the right match.

Relying on a Creative Pitch

Agency selection is frequently made on the basis of a pitch—a presentation that shows how an agency would tackle a specific project. Although the presentation gives an insight into the agency's working methods, it is an artificial and limited guide to potential day-to-day performance.

For More Information

Book:

Ward, John. *Using and Choosing an Advertising Agency.* Henley-on-Thames: World Advertising Research Center, 2001.

Web Site:

American Association of Advertising Agencies: **www.aaaa.org**

See also:

✓ **Getting Better Results from Your Agency (pp. 652–53)**
✓ **Measuring Advertising Performance (pp. 660–61)**
✓ **Preparing an Agency Brief (pp. 658–59)**

"An advertising agency is 85 per cent confusion and 15 per cent commission." (Fred Allen)

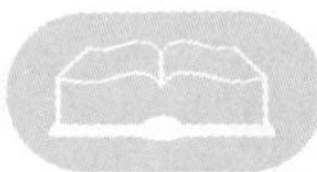

SETTING ADVERTISING OBJECTIVES

GETTING STARTED

It is important to set clear objectives for an advertising campaign, whether it is intended to generate leads or encourage brand switching. These objectives should be in place well before a campaign begins, to ensure that each campaign has a specific task. The results should be measurable, in order to ensure the campaign is worth the investment.

FAQS

SHOULD ADVERTISING BE JUDGED ON SALES RESULTS?

Advertising should certainly be measured, but there may not be a direct correlation between advertising and sales. Advertising may generate a large number of leads, but the sales force may not be able to convert those leads to sales.

SHOULD ADVERTISING AGENCIES BE JUDGED SOLELY ON THE RESULTS THEY DELIVER?

There has been a trend towards judging agencies on measurable results. This has been driven partly by the increasing importance of direct marketing agencies who claim to be driven by results, and partly by the desire of marketing executives to increase accountability. Some agencies have gone so far as to base their fees on results, rather than traditional agency payment. The problem is that results are dependent on so many other aspects of marketing. An agency could claim that it has no control over the performance of the sales force or the quality of the product.

IS IT POSSIBLE TO SET A NUMBER OF DIFFERENT OBJECTIVES FOR THE SAME ADVERTISING CAMPAIGN, PARTICULARLY WHEN BUDGETS ARE LIMITED?

It is possible, but it may not be a good idea. An effective campaign has a single focus with a specific measurable result. By mixing objectives, you may achieve only part of the outcome you want.

MAKING IT HAPPEN

SET THE RIGHT OBJECTIVE

It is important to set clear objectives for an advertising campaign. There are many different advertising objectives, so it is essential to identify a specific task for a specific campaign. This might be:

- raising awareness of a company, product, or service within a clearly identified target market;
- communicating the benefits of a product or service;
- generating leads for the sales force or retail network;
- encouraging prospects to buy directly through a direct response campaign;
- persuading prospects to switch brands;
- supporting a special marketing event such as a sale or an exhibition;
- ensuring that customers know where to obtain the product;
- building confidence in an organization.

MAKE THE OBJECTIVES MEASURABLE

To insure you design a cost-effective campaign that delivers results, advertising objectives should be translated into precise, measurable targets, as in the following examples:

CONSUMER PRODUCT

- Target market: 1 million ABC1 prospects.
- Marketing objective: achieve high level of product trial.
- Advertising objective: persuade 15% of target market to request a free sample.

BUSINESS PRODUCT

- Target market: 5,000 design specialists.
- Marketing objective: increase market share to 20%.
- Advertising objective: raise product awareness with 40% of design specialists.

RAISE AWARENESS

This objective is usually the starting point for advertisers. It is an important objective if your company is entering new markets where you do not have an established reputation, or you are trying to influence important decision-makers who may not be aware of your company. Awareness advertising can also be used if you are launching new products which appeal to specific sectors of your market, or if research shows that customers and prospects are not aware of the full extent of your products and services.

This type of objective would be important for a company launching a new range of products. For example, to raise awareness of its new range, one company planned to advertise in a group of special interest consumer magazines aimed at its target audience. The advertisements included the telephone number of an information line that generated a large number of inquiries. Editorial in the same group of publications backed up the advertising by providing more detailed information for consumers.

COMMUNICATE BENEFITS

Product advertising should lead on benefits. This type of advertising is important when research shows low awareness of product benefits. It should also be used if your products have recently been improved, or if you need to counter competitors who have introduced products with similar or better benefits.

For example, if research shows that your company's products are perceived as old-fashioned or poor value for money, you need to take action to correct this impression and communicate the real benefits of your products.

GENERATE SALES LEADS

Advertising's role is to provide leads that can be followed up by a field sales force or telemarketing team. Lead generation is important if marketing success depends on the performance of the sales force. Sometimes, customers or prospects have a complex decision-making structure and

---

"A desirable advertisement will be reasonable, but never dull. . .original, but never self-conscious. . .imaginative, but never misleading."

(Fairfax Cone)

you cannot identify some of the decision-makers. Advertising that generates inquiries can identify the right people and open the door for the sales team. It can also be used to identify prospects when you are entering new market sectors where you do not have an established customer base. The final use for this type of campaign is to generate leads for agents, distributors, or retailers who handle your local marketing.

Sell through Direct Response

Direct response advertising is the most measurable form of advertising. The advertising budget provides a direct return in terms of incremental sales. This objective can be important if customers can only buy direct from you. In an increasing number of markets, customers prefer the convenience of buying direct and you have to decide whether to bypass your existing distribution channels. If you are targeting niche markets which are not covered by retail outlets, direct response can be used to complement your distribution channels. Selling direct is not always a practical proposition. Where product inspection or demonstration is important, direct response may not be appropriate.

In the personal computer market, for example, manufacturers found that businesses and individuals were willing to buy personal computers "off the page" or via the Internet. The products were regarded as commodities and the resulting price competition put pressure on margins. The result was a considerable growth in the level of direct sales with manufacturers using large format advertisements or inserts in computer and business publications. Direct selling meant that the manufacturers could reduce prices by avoiding the cost of selling through retail outlets.

Encourage Brand Switching

Brand switching advertising plays an important role in winning new customers as the first stage in a customer relationship program. It helps you to increase market share or maintain share against competitive actions. It is also impportant if you are introducing new products that offer greater benefits than competitive products.

Support a Marketing Event

This objective can be important in a number of situations, for example, taking part in an exhibition where an important new product will be launched, or holding a sale, or promoting a seminar or other customer event at which you wish to insure customer participation. Advertising helps to build traffic for your event and insures that the event attracts the right prospects. A company that sponsors senior executive seminars as a way of building its credibility could run advertisements in the business press to promote a seminar.

Help Customers Obtain the Product

Advertising can help to drive business to retail outlets or distributors, or improve the performance of your distribution network by showing the range of services available from the outlets. It can also counter competitive action, if, for example customers are using other distributors to obtain spare parts and service. To win back this important business, advertising could show locations of retail outlets and explain why the authorized distributor should be the first choice for customers.

Build Customer Confidence

Capability advertising or corporate advertising is sometimes dismissed because it is difficult to measure. It is important when a company has been undergoing significant change, or is entering new markets where it is not known. It also provides support when a company is trying to win key account business or large contracts, or if competitors are threatening important business.

Common Mistakes

Setting Objectives That Cannot Be Measured

Advertising objectives should be measurable for two important reasons. First, to ensure that advertising represents an adequate return on investment. Second, to measure the effectiveness of the campaign itself so that future advertising can be improved or modified to deliver better results.

Setting Objectives That Are Too General

A general objective, such as raising awareness, is important, but often is seen as the only objective. Advertising objectives should be closely linked to marketing objectives so that advertising is used to carry out specific tasks within an overall marketing framework.

Failing to Integrate Advertising Objectives with Other Marketing Objectives

It is important that some advertising objectives, such as generating more leads, should be integrated with the other activities that will increase sales. It may be necessary to increase sales force training to improve the team's ability to convert leads into sales. Advertising alone cannot be expected to deliver sales.

For More Information

Book:

Broadbent, Simon. *Accountable Advertising*. Henley-on-Thames: Admap Publications, 1997.

Web Site:

American Association of Advertising Agencies: **www.aaaa.org/**

See also:

- ✓ **Generating More Leads (pp. 698–99)**
- ✓ **Getting Better Results from Your Agency (pp. 652–53)**
- ✓ **Measuring Advertising Performance (pp. 660–61)**
- ✓ **Planning an Advertising Campaign (pp. 656–57)**
- ✓ **Preparing an Agency Brief (pp. 658–59)**
- **Advertising (pp. 1903–06)**

"Advertising is the business of telling someone something that should be important to him. It is a substitute for talking to him."

(Fairfax Cone)

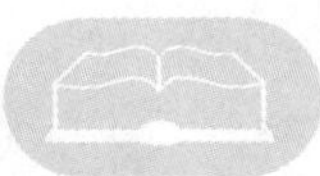

Building One-to-one Relationships

Getting Started

Building one-to-one relationships involves collecting and using information about actual and prospective customers as a basis for a customized selling approach. This provides an efficient and targeted means of maximizing sales.

FAQs

Do I have to tell customers that I am collecting personal information?

You may be bound by guidelines, rules, or legislation to advise customers about data collection and use. In any case, it is good commercial practice to publish a clear privacy policy explaining your procedures. You should also tell customers how you intend to use the data. Experience indicates that customers are happy to part with information if they see some tangible benefit. Concerns about security and privacy issues remain major barriers to the development of e-commerce.

Does one-to-one marketing guarantee customer loyalty?

It cannot guarantee loyalty, but it can make an important contribution. Customers will only remain if they continue to recognize the value of your products and the quality of your customer service. That means continually enhancing the customer experience.

Is one-to-one marketing always the best way to deal with customers?

For one-to-one marketing to work effectively, you need the right level of information on customers. You may not always be able to get that level of information on individual customers. However, if you have sufficient information on groups of customers with common needs, you can use techniques such as direct mail to communicate with a degree of precision. As your information on individual customers grows, you can move towards one-to-one communication.

Making It Happen

Refine Your Target Market

The more information you have about your target audience, the more precise you can make your campaign. In an ideal world, direct marketing techniques would allow you to communicate one-to-one with every prospect, but in practical terms you are more likely to be communicating with groups who share the same characteristics. This enables you to develop a unique relationship that competitors will find very difficult to match. It can also reduce your marketing and customer management costs by reducing wastage to a minimum.

Establish Clear Objectives

One-to-one marketing is designed to:

- improve the quality of customer service;
- strengthen customer relationships;
- maximize the profitability of each customer relationship;
- increase retention rates for customers;
- maximize the return on your investment in marketing and customer service.

Set Up a Database

At the heart of effective one-to-one marketing is a data networking solution that collects, stores, manages, and distributes all relevant customer information via a single, integrated customer database. The database is updated from all customer channels and is accessible by all customer-facing employees.

Keep Capturing Customer Data

The more you know about your customers, the better your chances of increasing lifetime value. Data capture must therefore be an integral part of all your sales, marketing, and customer service campaigns. You can build detailed profiles through campaign responses and customer research, and use the latest database and communications technology to manage, analyze, and distribute information. Take every opportunity to find out more about your customers so that you can build a real competitive edge, based on one-to-one personal relationships.

Invest in Personalization

The rapid development of data storage and data analysis tools means that it is now possible to know far more about your customers—with information well beyond details of income, spending patterns, service preferences, and frequency of use. The information available represents a quantum leap in the ability to profile customers.

Investing in personalization can increase value and loyalty even further.

At the heart of a personalized service is the customer's individual profile. A basic profile covers:

- name and address
- contact details
- purchase history
- personal interests
- product or service preferences

Let Customers Add Their Own Personal Details

If you offer personal pages on your Web site, you can allow customers to add further choices to the profile, using a special checklist. However, it is important to use customer information in appropriate ways. Attempts to increase customer interactions and provide more personalized information have made many consumers concerned about privacy issues. It is essential to let customers control the frequency and scope of interaction. Businesses must understand the difference between using and abusing the information they gather.

Information should be used to meet individual customer needs: customers are aware of the value of their

"Facts are available to everyone; it is interpretation and implementation that is key." (Ric Simcock)

information and are only willing to provide it when they see real benefits. That means giving customers control over their data and the way they interact with your company. To build trust, you must allow customers to choose how they want to interact and to use the information that they provide.

Develop a One-to-one Relationship

The contact between buyer and seller on the Internet is moving toward the ultimate one-to-one experience. Database technology supports a level of personalization that can deliver highly tailored products and services to specific individuals. Each time a customer logs on to a Web site, for example, the database can pull together purchase history and personal preferences as a basis for a highly personalized response. By giving customers a single point of entry, you can increase customer loyalty and learn more about their purchasing patterns. This provides an excellent basis for adding value and for the development of new products.

Maintain Regular, Targeted Communication

Once you have customer information, it is important to act on it. Maintain regular contact by sending customers information or special offers tailored to their individual needs.

Use E-mail to Maintain Contact

With e-mail you can deliver individual messages cost-effectively. E-mail also commands immediate attention. Most people check their e-mail routinely and generally read or quickly scan most messages. This makes e-mail a powerful marketing tool with a high potential return for a modest investment. Your e-mail goes straight into the customer's in-box, so you don't have to spend money attracting people to your site. When a customer elects to take regular e-mail from you, you have an opportunity to build a strong relationship. This makes online marketing more predictable and gives you the chance to develop a one-to-one relationship.

Allow Customers to Customize Products

Interactive facilities on a Web site allow customers to design their own customized products. Cars and computers are good examples. The customer chooses a basic model, and then selects features and options from a database. The system provides a price for the customized product, then gives the customer the choice of ordering now or storing the specification on a personal Web page for later modification. The high level of interaction gives customers greater choice and provides you with detailed insight into their needs.

Customize Information Services

You can use data on customer preferences as a basis for offering personalized information services. Customers specify the type of information they need, and you alert them by e-mail whenever relevant information is available.

Offer Different Service Levels

One-to-one service allows you to offer different levels of service to each category of customer. These could include:

- privileged rewards for top customers
- incentives for regular customers to spend more
- special offers to lapsed customers

Common Mistakes

Ignoring Privacy Issues

One-to-one marketing is based on the acquisition and use of high levels of personal information. You should publish a privacy policy on your site and you should also ensure that you comply with relevant guidelines, rules, and legislation. When you collect data, tell visitors what you do with the information, and follow best practice on privacy issues.

Failing to Develop Customer Relationships

The primary reason for collecting data is to find out more about customer needs so that you can build long-term relationships and increase customer loyalty. It is essential to act on the information you collect, analyze it, and develop strategies for building a personalized one-to-one service.

Targeting the Wrong People

Marketing programs work most effectively when they are aimed at a specific audience. The more you segment your target audience, the more precisely you can communicate. Different groups within your target market may have different purchasing needs or spending levels. By segmenting your audience and customizing your marketing material, you can address individual needs.

For More Information

Book:

Peppers, Don, and Martha Rogers. *Enterprise One-to-One.* New York: Doubleday, 1999.

Web Site:

The Peppers & Rogers Group's site:
www.peppersrogers.com

See also:

☆ **Managing 1:1 Marketing (pp. 55–56)**
☆ **The Second Coming of Service (pp. 77–78)**
✔ **Carrying Out Customer Research (pp. 702–03)**
✔ **Increasing Lifetime Customer Value (pp. 676–77)**
✔ **Making Better Use of Customer Data (pp. 708–09)**

"The more the data banks record about each one of us, the less we exist." (Marshall McLuhan)

BUILDING PARTNERSHIP WITH BUSINESS CUSTOMERS

GETTING STARTED

Partnership can increase your customers' dependence on you and strengthen long-term relationships. It requires long-term commitment by your company, combined with correct structuring and focus. Customer partners are looking for technical expertise, cooperation, and in some cases, total solutions.

FAQs

HOW CAN I USE PARTNERSHIP TO INCREASE CUSTOMER DEPENDENCY?

Put together a dependency checklist to develop a plan that shows how you could strengthen relationships with your customers. List the factors that are most important to your customers, describe how you could contribute to the achievement of their objectives, and prepare a plan for increasing your involvement.

MY CUSTOMERS WANT TO ACHIEVE MARKET LEADERSHIP THROUGH INNOVATION. HOW CAN PARTNERSHIP HELP THEM DO THAT?

Your technical skills and resources can help them develop the right level of innovation without investment in their own skills by using your technical resources to handle product development on a subcontractual basis. This provides them with new technology and allows them to diversify in line with your specialist skills.

IS PARTNERSHIP ONLY BASED ON TECHNICAL COOPERATION?

No: the scope of partnership is far wider, and its benefits can include reduced costs, increased capacity, nationwide distribution network, focus on core business, stronger supply position, and improved through-life costs.

HOW DOES PARTNERSHIP SAVE CUSTOMERS MONEY?

Through partnership, your customers can become value-for-money suppliers and succeed through competitive pricing. You can help them to reduce overall costs by improving design and manufacturing costs or by handling noncore activities cost-effectively.

MAKING IT HAPPEN

INCREASE CUSTOMER DEPENDENCY

Partnership can increase your customers' dependence on you and strengthen long-term relationships. It is important to understand a customer's business goals: by showing how your products or services can help them to achieve these objectives, you demonstrate that you can make an important contribution to their business.

DEMONSTRATE COMMITMENT TO THE BUSINESS

The partnership service should be your main business activity, and you have invested in its future growth and development. There must be no internal or external factors that could have an adverse effect on your performance or commitment. You will have a statement of direction showing your long-term plans for development of the business, and you must be able to demonstrate that you have the resources to achieve that development. You will have a record of innovation and excellence and are highly regarded by customers and competitors.

Your customer base will contain a high proportion of long-term customers, and you may demonstrate your readiness to make a major contribution to the future of your industry by means of involvement in industry associations or collaborative projects.

CLARIFY YOUR FUTURE DIRECTION

A company's future direction is closely related to its commitment to the business. What plans do you have for growth and for future developments? Information on your future range of products or services will help your partners to develop their own long-term plans.

FOCUS ON YOUR MARKET EXPERIENCE

Your track record is a key factor in any partnership, as it demonstrates that you are capable of understanding your partners' requirements and have already developed successful solutions in that market. You may be the market leader or have a growing market share. Your market knowledge may be specialized—focused on specific niche markets or sectors that are of interest to your partners.

OFFER TECHNICAL EXPERTISE

Gaining access to a partner's technical expertise is one of the major reasons for forming partnerships. Providing examples of technical innovation or leadership will demonstrate your existing capabilities, but partners are also interested in your potential for future development. Annual expenditure on research and development, a good track record in new product development, and technical and research resources all help to substantiate your claims of technical expertise.

PROVE YOUR MANAGEMENT CAPABILITY

Your partners will want to know that you have the resources to manage your business effectively and to insure that they are provided with the highest standards of service. You must have an experienced management team, with a management training and development program in position to insure ongoing development of skills to meet changing requirements. Your managers will have the right level of experience in the partners' business and understand their requirements.

STRESS FINANCIAL STABILITY

Partners must have confidence in your long-term ability to provide them with continuing high standards of

"If the U.S. and Japan cannot become partners, then there is a possibility that current trends could eventually make them enemies."

(Richard Drobnick)

service. Doubts about your financial stability will make them unwilling to commit themselves to a full partnership with you as the sole supplier. Make sure that your partners are fully aware of the financial structure and performance of your organization; if your company is part of a larger group, explain the financial relationship, and use the strength of the group's financial resources to demonstrate your own stability. Provide your partners with regular information on your financial performance.

Highlight Quality Processes

Quality processes insure that your partners enjoy the highest standards of service. You should demonstrate that quality is a key business strategy and that you have implemented recognized quality standards. Your staff should also be committed to quality and should be suitably qualified. Explain your quality principles and demonstrate how these principles are driven by customer needs. Explain how you use customer satisfaction indicators to measure the effectiveness of your quality processes and describe the customer surveys, user groups, or other customer response mechanisms that will form part of the partnership process. Describe how you might apply your quality processes to specific partnership activities and explain how you could integrate your quality processes with those of your customers.

Demonstrate Adequate Resources

Partnership is a long-term commitment, and you must demonstrate that you have the resources to provide the level of service your partners need, both now and in the future. The key facts about your organization—size, number of employees, location, turnover and profitability, national or international network, and infrastructure—will help your partners decide whether you can handle their target level of business. For example, if your customers operate a national or international network of branches, do you have a corresponding network to meet their local needs? Do you have the production resources to handle increasing volumes of business, and can you invest in or automate any processes to increase your capacity? How many staff do you have, and are you using training to develop their skills?

Get Organized for Partnership

It is important to explain to your customers how you will make partnership resources available to them. The structure of your organization must reflect customer needs, not internal requirements. For example, an organizational structure that reflects markets rather than internal divisions shows that you are focused on customer needs. Your organization should help your partners to make the best use of their own resources, and you should make it easy for them to use your services. A single point of contact for all your products and services provides your partners with rapid access. Quality staff who are committed to the highest levels of customer care demonstrate that your company is focused on your partners' interests.

Provide Total Solutions

As well as providing specific products and services, you can support your partners with other added-value services, enabling them to gain maximum business benefits. A total solution might include consultancy, project management, implementation, or training and facilities management, and you must demonstrate that you have the skills and resources to provide these services.

Demonstrate a Policy of Collaboration

To prove that you can make partnership work, quote other examples of collaboration or partnerships that you have been involved in. Describe the key success factors, and show how you have used your capabilities to insure the success of the partnership. By demonstrating involvement in user groups or industry liaison committees, you also can show that you are capable of working closely with other people to achieve joint objectives.

Common Mistakes

Mistaking Selling for Partnership

Selling a product or service does not create a strong relationship with a customer. It is the added-value benefits that increase customer dependency and provide the basis for an effective, long-term relationship.

Failing to Communicate Partnership Capability to a Customer

A partnership is a formal, long-term relationship, with high levels of collaboration and commitment on both sides. Your partners must have a full understanding of your capability and of any developments in your business that affect the partnership.

Focusing on a Narrow Area of Collaboration

Partnership covers a wide area of collaboration: technical cooperation, shared manufacturing resources, joint ventures and development programs, and shared distribution and logistics networks. The higher the level of collaboration, the greater the dependency of the relationship.

Neglecting Internal Partnership Processes

Partnerships can fail because people inside a company are not committed to the program. Internal communications should be used to explain the importance of the partnership and the contributions that different departments make. Quality processes and documented procedures can help to ensure that the company delivers on its partnership commitments.

For More Information

Book:

Doz, Yves L., and Gary Hamel. *Alliance Advantage: The Art of Creating Value Through Partnering*. Boston, MA. Harvard Business School Press, 1998.

Web Site:

U.S. Department of Commerce: **www.home.doc.gov**

"Mr. Morgan buys his partners; I grow my own." (Andrew Carnegie)

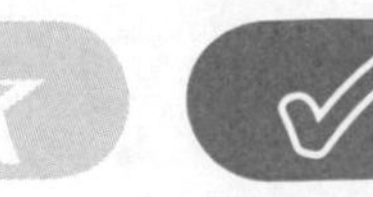

Communicating Customer Service

Getting Started

A clear, consistent, internal communications strategy is vital. Changes in strategy can create uncertainty, and customer service levels may be affected, but change can also demonstrate that an organization is committed to improvement and progress. Effective change requires commitment and involvement from all employees and each individual is responsible for achieving corporate standards and contributing to overall corporate success. Involve employees from the outset in customer service.

FAQs

Who is responsible for customer service?

Everyone in an organization contributes to overall customer satisfaction, even if their jobs do not involve direct customer contact. Broken delivery promises, inaccurate invoices or poor telephone handling can cancel out the benefits of a good product.

Why are award programs important to the success of customer service?

Customer service staff are in the front line, facing difficult customers and frequent problems. Award programs can help to maintain motivation and demonstrate that their contribution is important.

Isn't customer service the same as marketing?

Certain aspects of customer service–understanding customer needs, delivering a service, tailoring the offer to meet customer requirements–are the same, but the scope of marketing is much broader.

Is customer service just a set of personal skills?

Personal skills are important, but a company can put in place processes and programs that improve the customer's experience and make it easier and more convenient for the customer to do business.

Making it Happen

Communicate Clearly

When a company goes through a major change, a clear, consistent internal communications strategy is vital. Change creates an atmosphere of uncertainty so it is vital that everyone understands the important issues and feels that they can contribute to the success of the change. In an atmosphere of uncertainty, customer service levels can be adversely affected. A communications strategy that explains the positive benefits of the change is vital.

Build Understanding

Change is rarely simple, and effective communication is essential to ensure that change is handled successfully. Change may not always be driven by something as significant as a merger. Organizational changes or the introduction of new technology can have a significant impact on employees, suppliers, and distributors–so it is vital that they are thoroughly briefed. Change can be a powerful positive factor rather than a cause for concern, and change can demonstrate that an organization is committed to improvement and progress.

Identify the Influencers

Staff briefings, information packs, magazines, and other publications describing the rationale for change can all help to build understanding of the new organization. There are also key influencers within the organization–management groups, workteams, and key employees who can form the target of a direct marketing campaign. These key influencers can help to develop a communication channel throughout the organization and spread important messages.

Encourage Commitment

Achieving effective change requires commitment and involvement from all employees. Before implementing a major program, it is sensible to find what the level of commitment is, using a survey or other form of research. The most important part of the process is the follow-up. Too many employees believe their efforts to complete a survey would be wasted because nothing would happen.

Build Customer Focus

Introducing customer focus can have a major impact on many different parts of an organization. Internal communications should be structured to build understanding in all the departments contributing to customer care. These might include:

- design
- manufacturing
- distribution
- sales and marketing
- administration
- accounts

Many of these departments do not feel that they contribute directly to customer focus, but their role is vital in ensuring overall customer satisfaction. The communications program begins at the recruitment stage, when recruitment advertisements spell out corporate policy on customer care.

Involve Employees from the Outset

Recruitment advertisements and recruitment literature should stress that the company is committed to the highest standards of customer care, and that each individual is responsible for achieving corporate standards and contributing to overall corporate success. These recruitment messages can help to build confidence in employees that they have an important role to play in the success of the company, and this helps to build awareness and commitment throughout an organization.

Encourage Improvement

Training literature and programs should also reflect the importance of customer care and explain that training is

"Customers do not care about industry boundaries; they want service and convenience."

(Peter G. W. Keen)

available to each employee to improve standards. To help employees understand the importance of customer service and the practical implications of customer focus programs, customer satisfaction guides should be issued to all employees. These describe the main problems faced by customers and explain their main concerns about the service that should be provided. The guide should also describe the most important elements of customer service and the standards which apply.

Maintain Motivation

Motivation and award programs can help to maintain high levels of interest in the customer focus program and build a high level of commitment to the program's success. Award programs that reward continued improvement in levels of customer satisfaction maintain momentum and give customer service programs a high profile. They are therefore valuable in building team spirit and a commitment to excellence.

Provide a Vision

Clear visions and strong, motivating language focus attention on the importance of customer service programs. It is also essential that the program is led from the top. A key figure should be involved personally in every aspect of the programs—briefing senior management groups, talking to groups of employees, appearing in videos and using every public relations opportunity to raise the profile of the program. An effective, high-profile leader can put quality customer service on the corporate agenda and demonstrate a personal commitment to its success.

Develop Champions

The leader cannot achieve all the communications objectives alone, so it is essential that other people can take on the role of filtering the message through the organization. Management commentators call these people "champions." Their task is to utilize communications media to build commitment and enthusiasm for change. Champions make frequent presentations, they hold briefing meetings, they are regular contributors to employee magazines, and they take personal responsibility for the motivation and incentive programs that drive the changes forward.

Common Mistakes

Treating Customer Service As Departmental Function

Customer service is left to those staff who are directly involved with customers. This is too limited a view, because customer service is relegated to a sales or complaints handling process.

Managing Customer Service at Departmental Level

If customer service is treated as a line management function, staff will not appreciate its critical importance to the success of the organization. Customer service must be led from the top, with the direct involvement of a senior manager.

Failure to Develop Customer Service Skills

It's a common misconception that customer service quality depends solely on personal skills. Customer service standards can be improved through training and through the introduction of customer service programs.

Low Recognition

Customer service has long suffered from low recognition. Motivation and reward programs, together with leadership from the top, can help to redress the balance.

For More Information

Books:

Lovelock, Christopher H. *Services Marketing: People, Technology, Strategy*. 4th ed. Upper Saddle River, NJ: Prentice Hall, 2001.

McDonald, Malcolm, et al. *Creating a Company for Customers: How to Build and Lead a Market Driven Organization*. Upper Saddle River, NJ: Financial Times Prentice Hall, 2001.

Web Sites:

American Management Association: **www.amanet.org**

American Marketing Association: **www.MarketingPower.com**

See also:

☆ **Delivering and Delighting—A New Spirit at Work (pp. 71–72)**
☆ **Getting All Your People Committed to Change and Transformation (pp. 185–87)**
☆ **Managing the Customer (pp. 65–66)**
☆ **The Second Coming of Service (pp. 77–78)**
☆ **Viewpoint: Patty Seybold (pp. 67–68)**

"Above all, we wish to avoid having a dissatisfied customer. We consider our customers a part of our organization."

(L. L. Bean)

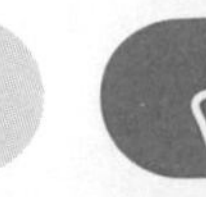     

HANDLING CUSTOMER INCIDENTS

GETTING STARTED

Customers who know that their problems are taken care of will be fully satisfied with the services that are available. A key factor in delivering time guaranteed services is the ability to reassure customers that help is on the way. An incident management strategy enables a company to deliver the highest standards of customer care at a time when the customer most needs it. Incident management is particularly valuable if the customer is likely to suffer a great deal of inconvenience because of the incident.

- The incident management approach is to appoint one person, trained in customer service skills, to deal with a customer throughout an incident.
- Incident management can be applied by any service led organization whose customers need to be kept informed.
- The role of the personal incident manager is to take responsibility for the provision of appropriate services.
- Many equipment manufacturers use incident management techniques to support their customers after a disaster.
- An incident management program has two main elements: the infrastructure to deliver the service and the personal skills to provide the right level of customer care.
- Skilled staff members are essential to the effective delivery of the service.

FAQs

SHOULD INCIDENT MANAGEMENT FORM PART OF ALL SERVICE OFFERINGS?

It depends on the type of service that is offered. If the service is critical to the customer's business process—telecommunications or computing, for example—incident management would be important. Disruption to those services could damage the customer's business.

WHY IS A PERSONAL INCIDENT MANAGER NECESSARY?

During an incident, effective coordination of support services and regular communication with the customer are essential. By appointing a single person to take responsibility for coordination and communication, you can guarantee continuity and reassure the customer by giving them a single point of contact.

IS IT POSSIBLE TO PLAN FOR FUTURE INCIDENTS?

It isn't just possible; it is essential. Industry research indicates that a high proportion of companies who did not have a documented plan failed to recover lost business. Planning is just as important as quality support services.

MAKING IT HAPPEN

DEAL WITH CUSTOMER INCIDENTS

Customers who know that their problems are taken care of will be fully satisfied with the services that are available and will be happy to deal with the same company in the future. Quality experts found that a key factor in delivering time guaranteed services was the ability to reassure customers that help was on the way. Customers would then be prepared to wait until help or support arrived, even if there was a long gap between reporting the incident and having it resolved.

IDENTIFY OPPORTUNITIES FOR INCIDENT MANAGEMENT

A number of scenarios can be used to identify situations where support like this could be valuable.

- The customer could suffer a great deal of inconvenience and stress as a result of the incident. Reducing the stress and inconvenience would help to demonstrate high levels of care and increase customer satisfaction.
- The incident could threaten the efficiency of the company business, and measures must be taken to limit the damage.
- The customer does not have the skills and resources to resolve the problems on the spot and is dependent on external forms of support.
- The customer has paid for a support package and has agreed to a certain level of response. The company must respond within the agreed levels.
- The speed of response is seen as a competitive differentiation and is positioned as an integral part of the service package.
- Failure to deal with the incident quickly could have a critical effect on the customer's business or personal activities.
- The incident could have legal implications, and the customer needs high levels of advice and guidance.

SET OBJECTIVES FOR INCIDENT MANAGEMENT

In developing a response and support strategy, you should set a wide range of business objectives:

- to provide the highest levels of quality response and customer support throughout an incident;
- to minimize inconvenience for the customer;
- to ensure that incidents are resolved promptly within agreed time scales;
- to ensure that support resources are deployed effectively to maximize customer satisfaction.

INTRODUCE INCIDENT MANAGEMENT

The incident management approach is to appoint one person, trained in customer service skills, to deal with a customer throughout an incident.

Incident management can be applied to any service led organization where the customer needs to be kept informed, for example, maintenance and support services for vital equipment or disaster recovery services where the customer faces difficult and unfamiliar decisions and needs support.

"When you stop talking, you've lost your customer. When you turn your back, you've lost her."

(Estée Lauder)

Appoint a Personal Incident Manager

The role of the personal incident manager is to take responsibility for the provision of appropriate services and to reassure the customer that help and support are on the way. The personal incident manager:

- takes the incoming calls from the customer, establishes the location, and identifies the form of support needed;
- provides individual guidance to the customer on action to be taken with an indication of the support that will be provided;
- deals with the customer's immediate queries;
- makes detailed arrangements to put support services into operation;
- monitors the progress of support services and keeps the customer up to date if possible.

Offer Disaster Recovery Services

Many equipment manufacturers use incident management techniques to support their customers after a disaster such as fire, accident, or system breakdown. If the customer loses essential equipment such as computers or telephones for an extended period, this could seriously threaten the future of their business. Industry research shows that only a minority of companies dependent on the computer have a formal disaster recovery strategy and points out that loss of a system for more than a few days could put them out of business.

Plan and Implement Disaster Recovery

A disaster recovery program has a number of stages:

- helping the customer identify critical activities that should be covered in the event of a disaster;
- training staff members and managers to prepare for a disaster by simulating the conditions of an emergency;
- preparing a contingency plan;
- providing replacement equipment and services in the event of an incident;
- providing support and project management resources during an incident;
- providing full support to restore normal service.

Throughout a disaster, the customer would have access to an incident manager who would coordinate the rescue and recovery activities, and provide advice, guidance, and support. The principle is similar to that of the personal incident manager, where customers are given reassurance that incidents will be resolved and that they can be sure of the highest standards of support throughout the incident.

Create the Infrastructure for Incident Management

The program has two main elements: the infrastructure to deliver the service and the personal skills to provide the right level of customer care. The infrastructure requires a significant investment to make sure that the service can be delivered rapidly and efficiently throughout the country. Depending on the complexity of the project, it might include:

- communications to provide a rapid response to customer questions, and put the service into operation;
- a trained support team to deliver the service;
- quality-controlled suppliers to support the direct response team;
- a control center to manage the operations and coordinate the response;
- a network of contacts and suppliers to provide the specialist services that form part of the response.

Develop the Right Skills

Skilled staff members are essential to the effective delivery of the service. The skills requirements would include:

- incident management skills, to deal with customers who may be in stressful situations;
- project management skills, to coordinate and implement a response;
- technical skills, to deliver the service;
- communications skills, to coordinate the elements of the program.

Common Mistakes

Failing to Communicate with the Customer During an Incident

Research shows that customers who receive regular progress updates feel reassured that they are getting the right level of support. Anxiety levels are high during an incident, but regular communication helps customers deal with the incident and contributes to overall customer satisfaction.

No Escalation Procedure

A company should have a formal escalation procedure for dealing with customer incidents. If support staff cannot resolve an incident within an agreed time scale, the incident should be reported to a more senior manager, who would then commit more resources. If there is no escalation procedure, the incident can get out of hand and damage customer relationships.

Failure to Train Staff in Customer Care

An incident creates high levels of stress in an organization, and support staff must be trained to deal with this.

For More Information

Book:

Lovelock, Christopher H. *Services Marketing: People, Technology, Strategy*. 4th ed. Upper Saddle River, NJ: Prentice Hall, 2001.

Web Site:

American Marketing Association:
www.MarketingPower.com

See also:

☆ **Managing the Customer (pp. 65–66)**
☆ **Viewpoint: Patty Seybold (pp. 67–68)**
✔ **Setting up a Customer Interaction Center (pp. 680–81)**

"If a brand screws up, honesty with the customer is the best way to recapture support."

(Michael Perry)

Handling Customer Inquiries

Getting Started

Helplines are essential for delivering support, service, advice, and information to customers. Use employees with extensive, up-to-date product knowledge and train them in customer service techniques to make sure they can deal effectively with different types of query or problem. To maximize the benefit to users of the service, deal with queries immediately where possible, or arrange to call the customer back on more complex queries and make sure that the customer is satisfied with the response at the end of the conversation.

FAQs

Should helpline services be offered free to customers?

Helpline services fall into a number of categories: support, help with problems, advice, and useful information. The support categories should be free because they are essential for customer satisfaction. The information services also can be seen as a customer service, something that adds value to the original purchase. You may feel it strengthens customer relationships to continue offering them free. Information services offered to the general public are valuable services that can be charged, usually through a premium rate number.

Which employees should work on the helplines?

Trained customer service employees can help customers report a problem effectively and may be able to offer advice or help up to a certain level. When the query goes beyond their level of knowledge, you should have a two-stage process in which the customer service representative takes the initial call and arranges for a specialist to call the customer back within an agreed time.

Can a helpline service be handled by an external organization?

Provided the external organization's team undergoes thorough training, there is no reason why the helpline cannot be outsourced. The practice is common in the computer industry.

Making It Happen

Set Up a Helpline

- Offer customers an 800 number facility to encourage contact.
- Set opening times to suit customer calling patterns.
- Use employees with extensive product knowledge and make sure that this knowledge is up to date.
- Train employees in customer service techniques to make sure that they can deal effectively with different types of query or problem.
- Provide employees with access to any existing product, technical, or service databases.
- Provide employees with guidelines on the actions they can take to deal with different types of complaint.
- Provide employees with lists of contacts for authorization of different types of action and information.
- Deal with queries immediately or arrange to call the customer back on more complex queries.
- Operate an escalation procedure to deal with complaints that cannot be resolved within agreed time scales.
- Record details of all queries and pass information to relevant employees for improvement action.
- Consider setting up a videoconferencing facility to handle complex queries and make best use of expertise.
- Check that the customer has received any callbacks within the agreed time scale.
- Make a follow-up call to make sure that the customer is satisfied with the response.

Plan Helpline Staffing Levels

- Ask your telephone supplier to provide a report on the number of calls to the helpline number.
- Determine the current and planned level of calls per day.
- Ask your telephone supplier to provide a report on the average waiting time for calls to the helpline number.
- Decide how many helpline employees you need.
- Work out the ratio of employees to calls.
- Analyze the pattern of calls during the day/week/month/year, using reports from your telephone supplier. Identify the peaks and troughs.
- Assess the number of employees required at peak and off-peak periods.
- Decide whether you can meet target staffing levels from current resources.
- Assess the potential benefit of using technologies such as voicemail to handle some of the incoming calls.
- Assess the potential benefit of using an external call handling service to handle overload or peak traffic.

Identify Helpline Skills

- Product knowledge.
- Technical skills.
- Product service skills.
- Administrative skills.
- Telephone technique.
- Customer service skills.

Develop Helpline Skills

- Assess the skills required for different types of helpline service.
- Review the current skills of your helpline employees.
- Compare the current skills profile with the skills requirement and identify the skills that need to be improved.
- If specific skills cannot be improved through training, consider using specialists to support the helpline employees.
- Implement training and monitor performance improvements.
- Obtain customer feedback to evaluate employee performance.

"Everything changes when there is a real customer yelling at you from the other end of the phone."

(Percy Barnevik)

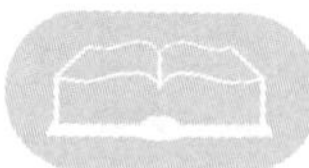

- Make sure that employees are trained in using any new technology.
- Obtain reports from your telephone supplier on average call time, average waiting time, and the number of calls answered.

Provide Customer Information for Helpline Employees

- Provide employees with customer information to ensure prompt response and personal service.
- Obtain customer information from existing customer records or from data generated by responses to advertisements or other promotional activities.
- Check, update, and take the opportunity to capture customer information each time a customer calls.
- Add further information that is appropriate to the helpline service, for example, service records.
- Use a simple code to access information quickly: for example, name, account number, and Zip code.
- Include prompts to contact customers with details of new products and services.

Set Up Helpline Escalation Procedures

- Identify critical types of helpline requests, including technical support, complaints, and breakdowns.
- Set target response times for critical activities.
- Appoint a supervisor with responsibility for monitoring conformance to target response times.
- Escalate any queries that exceed target times to a designated manager.
- Monitor the responses to escalated queries.

Record Helpline Usage

- How many calls does your helpline receive: per day; per week; per month; per year?
- What types of call does it receive and what is the volume of each type of call?
- Which customers are the most regular helpline users?
- Which media generate most inquiries to the helpline?
- What is the impact of promotional campaigns on helpline activity?
- Which products receive most/least: complaints, queries, and requests for support?
- What are the most frequent complaints, queries, and requests for support?
- Which type of request uses most resources?
- What is the average call time for different types of request?

Monitor Helpline Performance

- Determine the key measures and the measurement period.
- Identify the data required for measurement and its source.
- Record the number of calls per day to plan capacity and resource requirements.
- Analyze lost calls—the calls not answered—to plan an extension of opening hours or an increase in capacity.
- Analyze call waiting times to plan call handling capacity or to assess the potential contribution of new technologies.
- Contact helpline users by telephone or post to obtain feedback on satisfaction with the helpline service.
- Assess helpline productivity—the number of calls in relation to the number of employees—to plan the contribution of new technology or training.

Promote the Helpline Service

- Include the helpline number in advertisements, publications, Web site pages, and other promotional material.
- Ask sales and service employees to tell customers about the helpline.
- Include the helpline number on invoices, delivery notes, instructions, user guides, and other product documentation.
- Display the helpline number in branches or other customer facing locations.

Common Mistakes

Putting the Wrong People on the Helpline

The people who run the helpline should have good customer handling skills and a level of product and technical knowledge that enables them to provide the right answer or put the customer in contact with the right specialist.

Inadequate Resources on the Helpline

When customers call a helpline, they are looking for a quick response. Phones that go unanswered for long periods of time show poor customer service. Putting a customer in a queue of other callers is satisfactory only for a short period of time.

Giving Customers a Limited Choice of Contact Points

Although customers would probably choose telephone as their first point of contact, you could also offer them the choice of contact by fax or e-mail.

Failing to Call the Customer Back

If you cannot deal with queries immediately, let the customer know the likely time scale and check that the return call has been made.

For More Information

Book:

Blackwell, Roger, and Kristina Stephan. *Customers Rule! Why the E-Commerce Honeymoon is Over and Where Winning Businesses Go from Here.* New York: Crown Publishing Group, 2001.

Web Site:

CCNG International: **www.ccng.com**

See also:

☆ **Delivering and Delighting—A New Spirit at Work (pp. 71–72)**
☆ **Marketing to the "Real-Time" Consumer (pp. 73–74)**
✔ **Converting Leads into Sales (pp. 700–01)**
✔ **Setting up a Customer Interaction Center (pp. 680–81)**

"I probably spend some time once a month listening in on calls or talking to customers. I encourage my executives to do the same."

(Lillian Vernon)

Increasing Lifetime Customer Value

Getting Started

"Customer lifetime value" is a way of measuring how much your customers are worth, over the time they are your customers. Increases in customer retention can increase sales and profits significantly. It is important to retain customers, but not at the cost of other essential marketing activities.

Putting customers into key categories helps clarify analysis and acts as the basis for marketing activities designed to improve lifetime customer value.

FAQs

What's the difference between lifetime customer value and customer loyalty programs?

Customer loyalty programs are designed to retain as many customers as possible, regardless of their real value. The lifetime customer value calculation indicates the contribution individual customers make to profitability.

Why are lapsed customers important?

If they can be "revived," they tend to behave like new customers and become regular buyers once again, with good potential lifetime value.

Is customer retention more important than acquisition?

Acquisition should never be neglected, because existing business may decline for reasons outside your control. Industry experience indicates, however, that existing customers make a comparatively greater contribution when marketing costs are taken into consideration.

Can a company have too many customers?

You can have too many customers if it costs a lot of money to retain them. That money would include the cost of sales visits, contact, and marketing collateral. Using lifetime customer value, you can calculate the cost and contribution of each customer.

Making It Happen

Apply the Lifetime Customer Value Concept

Customer lifetime value is a way of measuring how much your customers are worth to you, over the length of time that they are your customers.

The lifetime for customers will vary from industry to industry, and from brand to brand, within a single organization. The lifetime of customers comes to an end when their contribution becomes so small as to be insignificant, unless steps are taken to revitalize them.

It is important to retain customers, but this should not be at the cost of other essential marketing activities. Ask yourself:

- Is it really sensible to keep as many customers as possible?
- Should retention activities take precedence over customer acquisition programs?

Benefits from Lifetime Customer Value

Industry experience indicates the following:

- A 5% increase in customer retention can create a 125% increase in profits.
- A 10% increase in retailer retention can translate to a 20% increase in sales.
- Extending customer lifecycles by three years can triple profits per customer.

Identify Categories of Customer

Before calculating lifetime customer value, it is important to break your customers down into four key categories. This can help to clarify analysis and act as the basis for marketing activities to improve lifetime customer value.

- A good customer is a long-term customer who regularly buys a profitable product.
- A new customer may be the best customer of all, since their lifetime value has yet to be realized.
- A long-term customer who does not buy regularly, and has not bought recently, is probably not a customer at all.
- A lapsed customer who has been rerecruited often behaves like a new customer.

Calculate Lifetime Value

In a consumer business, customer lifetime value is calculated, in practice, by analyzing the behavior of a group of customers who have the same recruitment date. The group could consist of:

- specific types of customers
- customers recruited from the same source
- customers who bought the same types of product

In a business-to-business environment, a similar approach can be used.

- Isolate particular customers, and examine them individually.
- Analyze the behavior of different groups, segmenting your customer database by factors such as industry, annual turnover, or staff numbers.

The basic calculation has three stages.

- Identify a discrete group of customers for tracking.
- Record (or estimate) each revenue and cost for this group of customers, by campaign or season.
- Calculate the contribution, by campaign or season.

Refine the Calculation

Other factors can be introduced to make the calculation more relevant. In a business-to-business environment, for example, it may be the sales representatives who generate sales. In this case, the calculation should include the representative's "running costs" and the cost of any centrally produced sales support material.

Evaluate a Campaign

The table shows the calculations for a group of customers who were recruited through a direct response advertising campaign that ran in the spring of year 1. The table tracks their expenditure over a five-year period.

"Good customers are an asset which, when well managed and served, will return a handsome lifetime income stream for the company."

(Philip Kotler)

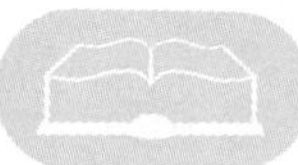

Campaign	Total Customer Expenditure	Total Marketing Costs	Total Contribution
Spring Year 1	$50,000	$45,000	$5,000
Total Year 1	$75,000	$60,000	$15,000
Total Year 2	$85,000	$65,000	$20,000
Total Year 3	$92,000	$68,500	$23,500
Total Year 4	$107,000	$81,000	$26,000
Total Year 5	$115,000	$86,000	$29,000
Overall Total	$524,000	$405,500	$118,500

Divide the total contribution by the number of customers in the group. Say there are one thousand customers: the average lifetime value per customer is $1,185.

Analyze the Results

A company may offer different products or brands, which are marketed under different cost centers. If a customer is a customer of more than one cost/profit center, there is a choice of approaches:

- examine customers of each brand and ignore multipurchases;
- build a more detailed model that combines and allocates the cumulative costs as well as the cumulative profit in the appropriate proportions.

Use Customer Lifetime Values to Improve Marketing Performance

There are four important applications:

- setting target customer acquisition costs
- allocating acquisition funds
- selecting acquisition offers
- supporting customer retention activities

Set Target Customer Acquisition Costs

If a customer is expected to generate more than one sale, the allowable cost can be greater than the cost allowed for the first sale—the classic loss-leader approach to customer acquisition. However, overspending on customer acquisition can also be ruinous. A reasonable calculation is to recruit only from those sources that yield new customers at less than half the estimated lifetime value. On that basis, the worst sources will have a cost per customer close to a lifetime value, while the average cost per customer should be far lower.

Allocate Acquisition Funds

Different recruitment sources will provide customers with different lifetime values. After identifying those values, spend more on the best sources.

Select Acquisition Offers

The lifetime value of a customer may depend on the type and value of their initial purchase. In turn, this can lead to decisions about which products and offers to use when advertising externally, or when considering how to upgrade existing customers.

Support Customer Retention Activities

Once the typical lifetime value of a group of customers is known, companies can decide how hard to work at retaining them. It is not a foregone conclusion that all customers are worth having. Activities should be tailored to the customers who are most valuable.

Increase Value with New Offers

A financial services company can increase lifetime customer value, by cross selling a range of different products and services.

Common Mistakes

Trying to Retain the Wrong Customers

Customer retention costs money in terms of sales and marketing funds. However, lifetime customer value analysis indicates that not all customers are worth retaining. You should carefully select the customers who are likely to yield the highest returns over a period of time.

Offering Customers a Limited Range of Products

When you have identified the most valuable customers, you need to have a wide range of products or services to offer them. Cross-selling and upselling are the best ways to increase lifetime customer value, but this can be difficult with a limited product range.

Spending Too Much on Acquiring New Customers

Lifetime customer value analysis reinforces a traditional marketing rule of thumb, that it costs less to retain existing customers than to acquire new ones. Overemphasis on new business development could be a bad move.

For More Information

Book:

Reichheld, Frederick F. *Loyalty Rules! How Today's Leaders Build Lasting Relationships*. Boston, MA: Harvard Business School Press, 2001.

Web Site:

"Treat Customers Right . . . They're Yours For Life!": **www.workplacemoxie.com/Customer-Service**

See also:

☆ **Delivering and Delighting—A New Spirit at Work (pp. 71–72)**
☆ **Making Loyalty Work (pp. 289–90)**
☆ **Managing 1:1 Marketing (pp. 55–56)**
✔ **Building One-to-one Relationships (pp. 666–67)**
✔ **Making Better Use of Customer Data (pp. 708–09)**

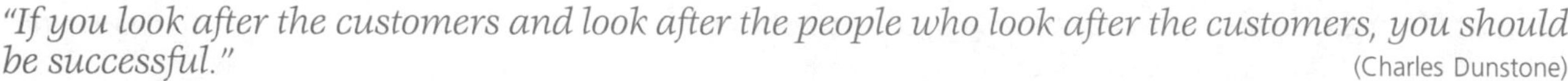

"If you look after the customers and look after the people who look after the customers, you should be successful."

(Charles Dunstone)

Running a Customer Loyalty Program

Getting Started

One of the most important marketing objectives is to retain customers over the long term, because the costs of winning new customers are far higher than those of servicing existing ones. A customer loyalty program is one way of doing this, although it cannot be regarded as a substitute for satisfactory product quality and service levels. Customer loyalty programs, however, do not simply reward customers for making repeated purchases; they are a powerful tool for gathering information on spending patterns and customer profiles. Because the costs and overheads of such a program are high, it is essential that it is structured and operated effectively.

FAQs

How important are loyalty programs?

It costs considerably more to attract new customers than to service existing ones, so loyalty programs can help to reduce the overall cost of sales. They also offer opportunities to increase the value of individual customers by encouraging them to continue to purchase from your company.

Can you run a loyalty program without investing in database management?

You could run a program simply by offering customers rewards for staying with your company and making occasional purchases. However, the data available from loyalty programs enables you to analyze your customers' purchasing patterns and identify the biggest spending customers. This information can be valuable in developing future marketing and customer service programs.

Isn't it better to invest money in improving quality and service?

Quality and service must be satisfactory before you even think about a loyalty program. If you don't attend to these first, the best you can expect is a temporary rise in sales. However, if these are satisfactory, loyalty programs can add an extra dimension to your marketing programs.

Making It Happen

Reward Loyal Customers

Retaining customers over the long term is a key marketing objective. Customers who are satisfied with the level and quality of service they receive are likely to continue buying from the same company. This can be reinforced by marketing programs that reward customers for their loyalty. The programs can take many different forms, from simple concepts such as discounts on repeat purchases and incentives for multiple purchases to more complex frequent user programs that provide multilevel rewards for customers who continue to use a service.

Set up a Loyalty Program

If you want to make your customers feel welcome, make them members of a loyalty program and offer them benefits that reward their loyalty. Loyalty programs meet a number of different marketing objectives.

- Your customers make regular high-value purchases and you want to retain their business.
- You have customers in a specific age group and you want to retain their loyalty for life.
- There is an opportunity to add value to basic support services.
- Members pay a single annual fee for a service and you want to retain their membership.
- There is an opportunity to make regular offers and sell related products to specific groups of consumers with special interests.
- There is an opportunity to differentiate a product or service by offering customers added-value services that enhance the basic product or service.
- There is an opportunity to offer regular subscribers special benefits.

Offer Customers Real Benefits

You must be certain that the benefits offered by the program are relevant and build the right perceptions. Ideally, they should reflect customer needs identified through research. The benefits should reflect appropriate standards of service, and they should have a degree of exclusivity. They also should add value to the basic product or service offer.

Identify the Costs

Running a loyalty program can represent a significant investment. The major cost areas are:

- recruiting members
- initial offers
- administration
- marketing costs
- full- and/or part-time staff and overheads
- customer offers
- administration
- database management
- cost of interaction, such as a helpline

Consider the Alternatives

Although a loyalty program offers powerful benefits, it may not be the only solution. Consider the following points carefully before committing resources to a program:

- Has customer research highlighted the need for a specific change to the product or service?
- Would such a change help to improve sales and market share?
- Would a loyalty program strongly differentiate your product or service?
- Do your competitors offer a similar program?
- Have you got the resources to set up and operate an effective program?
- Would the benefits justify the operating costs?
- Would the customer information available justify the costs?

Manage the Program Effectively

A loyalty program requires careful management to ensure that customers receive the highest standards of service, so training in program administration skills will be important. It is essential that adequate resources are committed to the program—quality customer relationships are essential to its success. The key tasks are:

- identifying the benefits of the program;
- assessing the cost;
- appointment of a program coordinator;
- research into customer requirements;
- refining the contents of the program;
- development of a launch strategy;
- introducing the concept of the program internally to build commitment;
- implementing the practical requirements of the program;
- implementing any training required to deliver quality service to customers in the program;
- development of a launch program to ensure high levels of awareness among prospects and customers;
- implementing a program to ensure that members continue to receive high levels of benefit.

Maintain Interest over the Long Term

A loyalty program is a long-term investment. This means ongoing commitment in terms of people and funding, and a program that will maintain members' interest over time. One way is to offer members increasing levels of benefit—for example, the frequent-flyer clubs run by major airlines.

Use the Program to Improve Understanding of Customers

Loyalty programs can provide you with high levels of information on your customers, and this can prove a valuable basis for future direct marketing.

- Ensure that you capture basic customer data on membership application forms.
- Track members' purchasing patterns and use this to make targeted offers.
- Consider using smart cards to improve data capture.
- Monitor the response to club offers.
- Segment your customer database where possible to improve targeting even further.

Collect Customer Buying Data

Retailers operate programs that issue points to customers based on their expenditure. The points can be accumulated via a smart card, and the customer can use the points to pay for other purchases. The use of technology like this can be used to build a more complete picture of your customers. A smart card can provide detailed information on purchasing patterns that provides a basis for cross-selling other products and services or for tailoring products and services to the customer.

Operate Frequent-Buyer Programs

Frequent-buyer programs that also accumulate information on customers are a powerful combination. An example is the frequent-flyer programs run by most of the major airlines. These provide regular travelers with points for every mile they fly which can be exchanged for free leisure travel. Some airlines add a privilege club that offers structured rewards to different groups of customers according to their overall use of airline services. The scheme includes access to preferential seating, arrangements with hotels and car rental companies, and access to executive airport lounges.

Common Mistakes

Offering Weak Benefits that Competitors Can Match

A loyalty program must offer real, long-term benefits that customers value. If the benefits are not sustainable, the investment will be wasted when customers take their rewards and move on to a competitor's program. Researching customer needs, getting feedback from customers, and monitoring program performance are essential to maintaining a program's success and retaining customers over the long term.

Ignoring the Alternatives

A loyalty program is just one approach to customer retention. The investment may be wasted if the real barrier to customer loyalty is poor product performance or poor customer service. You must research customer attitudes toward your products and your standards of service: if perception is poor, it is essential to put the basics right before setting up reward programs. In the long term, customers prefer quality to rewards.

Failing to Use Program Data

A loyalty program can provide large amounts of data on customer needs and buying patterns. These data should be used to build a better profile of individual customers and to create targeted offers that increase the lifetime value of the customer. The data should also be used to identify and remedy any recurring problems in product performance or customer relationships.

For More Information

Book:

Butscher, Stephan A. *Customer Clubs and Loyalty Programmes: A Practical Guide*. Brookfield, VT: Gower, 1998.

Web Site:

Peppers & Rogers: **www.peppersrogers.com**

See also:

☆ **Viewpoint: Patty Seybold (pp. 67–68)**

Setting up a Customer Interaction Center

Getting Started

The best way to retain customers is through proactive relationship management and outstanding customer service. An integrated approach to customer contact is essential and a customer interaction center integrates people, technology, and customer data. It brings together staff who deal directly with customers and support teams in a single, integrated location and gives customers the benefit of a single point of contact. The organization also benefits as it is able to create "virtual teams" that respond rapidly to requests or queries and is also better placed to share best practice more easily between business units.

FAQs

Why isn't a call center sufficient to handle customer contact?

Call centers were set up to handle telephone calls. They are staffed by people trained in telephone techniques and they are designed to deliver a personal service. Customers who communicate with a company via the Web or e-mail may not receive the same level of personal service because of the way electronic communications are routed through the company.

Isn't it best to concentrate resources on a call center because most contact is by telephone?

The trends are changing as more and more people recognize the convenience of ordering electronically, 24 hours a day, 7 days a week, when call centers may be closed. Companies who do not offer the full range of facilities may lose business opportunities.

Who should control the customer interaction center?

The customer interaction center should be more than an extension of the call center. It should be an integral part of the sales or marketing department and should be treated as a strategic resource that contributes to long-term customer retention.

Should the interaction center be limited to telephone and Internet technology?

Customer interaction is getting more and more sophisticated. Multimedia communication is becoming increasingly common in consumer and business markets. The interaction center should be capable of adapting to new technological developments.

Making It Happen

Retain Customer Loyalty

Increasingly, companies recognize that the best way to retain customers is through proactive relationship management and outstanding customer service. A key element in that strategy is an integrated approach to customer contact—a customer interaction center. The interaction center takes the traditional call center a stage further, integrating people, technology and customer data.

Deal with Multiple Contact

Customers can now contact organizations in many different ways, including the Internet, phone, e-mail, or fax. The integration of the Internet and telephony in multimedia call centers is taking the process even further. On the surface, that level of choice and convenience should lead to better customer service. But, in reality, the opposite is happening. When each channel has its own separate "information silo" of data on the customer, there is no integration.

Guarantee Consistent Service Standards

If you offer your customers different contact channels and you don't integrate your customer information, you could face problems. Here's a situation you might recognize. A customer enters a request via the Web, then calls a customer service representative in a call center to get a status report. If the call center only has access to its own departmental data, it may not even recognize the customer. This could result in an embarrassing phone conversation and possibly a lost customer.

Provide a Single Point of Contact

A customer interaction center brings together staff who deal directly with customers (customer-facing staff) and support teams in a single, integrated location. Staff, backed by sophisticated information and communication systems, provide customers with a single point of contact and access to the combined skills and resources of the whole company.

Bring Together All Customer-facing Staff

Staff from logistics, credit control, accounting, and administration—as well as customer service and technical support—can work together in a customer interaction center. By working more closely, the company can create "virtual teams" that respond rapidly to requests or queries and bring together the right combination of skills for the customer's business. This high level of integration will result in even better alignment between customer service, supply/demand planning and logistics operations. The company can also share best practice more easily between business units.

Speed Up Communication

The center should provide a sophisticated technology infrastructure that will make it easier for customers to do business with the company, by supporting a rapid response and a high quality service. Integrated telephony systems ensure that when a customer telephones, the call is directed to a named contact who speaks the appropriate language. If the first contact is busy, the customer will be transferred to another team member who also speaks the appropriate language. The team member who answers the call will have access to all of the customer's account information on screen, and this information will be updated automatically whenever a customer calls.

Integrate All Customer Information

At the heart of the infrastructure is an interconnected data networking solution that collects, stores, manages and distributes all relevant customer information via a single, integrated customer database. The database is updated from all customer channels and is accessible by all customer-facing staff. The aim is to make communications simpler and quicker by giving every member of the customer service team access to the most up-to-date information on a customer's business. The solution can also include business rules and workflow functions to ensure that the right level of resources is applied to different types of customer interaction. A solution like this could, for example, assign priorities to key account customers or escalate support requests that have not been resolved within agreed service levels.

Make It Easy to Do Business

Your customers will get consistent service, whatever way they contact your organization. Integrating the center with electronic commerce systems will simplify the purchasing processes even further. Customers who work with a number of different locations or divisions will now have a single point of contact for all their dealings with the company. This is important because customers are looking for ways of simplifying their own purchasing process. Centralized support is becoming more and more important to customers. By providing a single point of contact for sales and technical and service queries, the company can ensure a rapid, effective response to all customer support requirements.

Develop a More Personal Service

Many traditional personalization initiatives have been built on incomplete customer data. A personal Web page, for example, would probably have been based only on the customer's Internet interactions, completely ignoring any voice contact through a call center. With an integrated strategy, an organization can leverage all its customer interactions, giving it a significant competitive advantage in the drive for personalization.

Plan for Continued Improvement

The center infrastructure can be scaled up to accommodate growth in demand. It also provides a stable platform for developing advanced applications that will allow the company to improve customer service even further.

The interaction center co-ordinates all forms of customer interaction:

- consistently managing customer interactions through multiple communications channels, including phone, fax, e-mail, Web, and video;
- defining and applying business rules to customer interactions;
- routing customer interactions—according to business rules—to appropriate available resources;
- integrating disparate corporate data into customer interactions.

This approach brings together all the elements needed to strengthen customer relationships and retain loyalty.

Common Mistakes

Limiting the Scope of Communications

An interaction center should cover all forms of communication. It is not a telephone call center with other technology treated as an add-on. From the outset, the center should be capable of communicating via traditional and new media. Plans should also be in place to incorporate emerging media.

Concentrating on the Wrong Standards

If the center is treated as a technology-led function, customer service may suffer. Companies who want to maintain standards should set quality and performance standards that are focused on customer needs, not technical performance.

Failing to Develop a Personalized Service

A customer interaction center provides a great deal of valuable customer information that can be used to develop a personalized service. If the information simply stays on file, the company is losing a great opportunity for future business.

Limiting the Use of Information

The customer interaction center is only a starting point for information management. The information can be used to support decision making and business development throughout a company. Linking the information to what Microsoft calls a "digital nervous system" ensures that people throughout a company are able to act on the very latest information.

For More Information

Book:

Webb, Geoff. *The M-Bomb: Riding the Multi-channel Whirlwind.* New York: John Wiley, 2000.

Web Site:

International Call Center Benchmarking Consortium: **www.iccbc.org**

See also:

- ☆ **Integrating Technology into Business Processes (pp. 169–70)**
- ☆ **Marketing to the "Real-time" Consumer (pp. 73–74)**
- ☆ **The Second Coming of Service (pp. 77–78)**
- ✔ **Converting Leads into Sales (pp. 700–01)**
- ✔ **Handling Customer Incidents (pp. 672–73)**
- ✔ **Handling Customer Inquiries (pp. 674–75)**

"Make no mistake: Customers are in control today." (Anne Busquet)

Building a Mailing List

Getting Started

The most important element in a direct marketing program is the mailing list. You can use internal sources to compile a valuable mailing list of both customers and prospects. You may be able either to rent or purchase existing lists from sources such as list brokers, Web sites, publishers, or other organizations offering lists of their customers or you may wish to commission a specially tailored list that matches your requirements exactly. Three of the biggest problems in list management are duplication, incomplete addresses, and out-of-date information.

FAQs

My company has a mailing list of customers and prospects. Can I offer that list to other organizations?

You can market the list to other organizations. However, you should be aware of the implications of applicable legislation and regulations. Customers may have a right to know how their data is being used. Always include a clause asking customers if they are willing to allow their data to be passed to other organizations.

Is it better to buy or rent an external mailing list?

It depends how frequently you plan to mail. Rented lists are for a single use only, charged on a cost-per-thousand basis, and the owners have security techniques to counter unauthorized repeat use. A single campaign may be enough, but experience indicates that multiple mailings generally achieve better results. You would need to compare the cost of buying with renting the list for, say, three mailings.

Is a list compiled internally as effective as a list sourced from a direct mail list specialist?

An internal list is only as good as the sources you have available. However, if your target market is existing customers and good prospects, it may be adequate. An external list supplier may not have the same detailed understanding of that market. However, if you are moving into new markets where you have no existing contacts, it may be more effective to draw on the resources of a company with experience in the market.

Making It Happen

Create an Effective List

The most important element in a direct marketing program is the mailing list. In its simplest form, the list simply includes names, addresses, job titles, and telephone numbers. This can be refined by adding information on buying patterns, lifestyle, and many other factors to provide a comprehensive picture of customers and prospects.

Use Internal Sources of Information

You can use internal sources to compile a valuable mailing list of customers and prospects:

- customer records
- customer correspondence, including complaints
- warranty records
- service records
- sales prospect files
- sales force reports
- records of former customers
- market research surveys
- business information library

Segment Internal Lists

Customer records can quickly provide you with names and addresses of individuals, but to get more specific information, you will have to carry out further analysis. Simple segmentation might give you categories such as:

- customers who have bought in the last six months
- former customers
- customers who spend over X dollars per annum

Identify External Sources of Information

If you want to compile your own lists, you can use external sources to supplement internal information. External sources include:

- customers' and prospects' Web sites
- databases and information services available via the Internet
- general or industry-specific trade directories
- membership directories for associations and groups
- local telephone or chamber of commerce directories
- specialist magazines and yearbooks
- business reports and industry surveys in newspapers
- published surveys
- summaries or reports on consumer surveys
- government and industry statistics, including census, industry reports, and trade association statistics

Source External Lists

If you do not have the resources to compile your own lists or if you are moving into new markets, you may be able to make use of existing lists. Lists are available from several sources:

- list brokers who offer different categories of list
- Web sites
- magazine publishers
- directory publishers
- trade associations or professional institutes
- commercial organizations
- retailers

Assess External Lists

If you plan to use a ready-made list, you should check:

- How closely does the list match your customer profile?
- How much wastage will there be—that is, how much of the list falls outside your customer profile?
- Are there any restrictions on the use of the list? The

owner may wish to protect customers against direct mail overload, or to maintain an air of exclusivity.

Commission a List

Standard lists may not give you the degree of match you need, and you may wish to commission a specially tailored list. The success of such a list is directly related to the quality of the brief, and you should provide the supplier with a detailed description of your target audience.

Keep Refining Your Lists

Many standard lists and lists you have compiled yourself may not match your requirements exactly. To improve coverage or to make them more precise, you need to refine them continually. These are some of the actions you can take:

- Insure that new customer and prospect data is added to the list.
- Include coupons and other reply mechanisms with every form of communication and add the responses to your lists.
- Encourage the sales force to provide up-to-date customer and prospect information.
- Maintain an active search program on the Internet and in publications to identify new prospects for your list.

Segment Your Lists

The strength of direct marketing is that it can provide a high degree of precision—so your lists must be structured carefully. Below is a basic approach to segmenting consumer and business-to-business lists:

Consumer Lists:

- marital status
- income level
- occupation category
- home owner/home value
- car owner/car value
- personal interests
- credit card holder
- shopping patterns
- vacation preferences
- insurance status
- leisure interests
- brand preferences
- recent purchase history
- reading/viewing habits

Business Lists:

- type of business
- size of business
- number of employees
- annual expenditure
- average order size
- purchasing frequency
- head office/local purchasing
- purchasing history
- key contacts
- job title
- budget authority

Check the Accuracy of Lists

To reduce waste in your mailing campaigns, it is important that you regularly check lists for accuracy. Three of the biggest problems are:

- duplication, where the same individual appears several times, possibly in different guises, for example, Ron Smith, R. T. Smith, Mr. Smith. This is not only wasteful, it also irritates the recipient;
- incomplete addresses;
- out-of-date information, where the original recipient has moved or changed jobs.

Comply with Legislation and Regulations on Personal Data

The basic premise behind legislation and regulations on the use of personal data is, if you have data, use them properly. Laws and regulations work in two ways:

- They place obligations on data users. They must be open about how they use data and follow sound information handling practice.
- They may give every individual access to information held about them. They may also allow them to have the information corrected or deleted where appropriate, and may give the right to seek compensation for damage and associated distress through the courts.

Common Mistakes

Using Out-of-date Lists

A mailing list is out of date almost as soon as it is compiled. People change jobs, move, or change their interests. List maintenance must be a continuous process. You can use returned mail as a starting point, check your lists against updated sources, or use telephone research to check a prospect's current status.

Failing to Segment Lists

Direct marketing works most effectively when it is aimed at a specific audience. The more you segment your mailing lists, the more precisely you can communicate. Different groups within your target market may have different purchasing needs or spending levels. By segmenting your lists and customizing your marketing material, you can address individual needs.

Overlooking Internal Sources

Many companies choose to rent or buy external lists without even considering internal sources. Mailing present or past customers can reinforce the benefits of existing communications programs and deliver a high level of response.

For More Information

Book:

Fairlie, Robin. *Database Marketing and Direct Mail.* Dover, NH: Kogan Page, 1993.

Web Site:

The Direct Marketing Association: **www.the-dma.org**

See also:

☆ **Managing 1:1 Marketing (pp. 55–56)**
☆ **Marketing to the "Real-Time" Consumer (pp. 73–74)**
Direct Marketing (pp. 1953–54)

"GM reportedly has 14 million GM credit card holders being contacted, questioned, tabulated, tracked, and romanced each month when the credit card statement is delivered." (Stan Rapp)

Creating Direct Mail Material

Getting Started

Direct mail is an effective and precise marketing method that lends itself to personalization in order to more accurately reflect the needs of customers and prospects. Mailings can incorporate creative work, and can include different types of enclosure to provide additional details on the product or service being offered; eye-catching, perhaps three-dimensional, enclosures can also add impact.

The results of direct mail are easy to measure with precision, so the effects of a particular approach can be readily assessed. It is essential for a mailing to incorporate an easy response mechanism for the customer, such as a business reply envelope, or contact details such as an e-mail address.

FAQs

Is it possible to plan creative work in direct mail?

Like any other marketing activity, creative work must be directed toward an objective. The more information a creative team has, the more focused their work. Direct mail is a very precise medium, so it is possible to create highly customized mailings that meet the information needs of individual prospects.

How far can personalization go in direct mail?

Provided you have the budget, mailings can be personalized down to individual level (one-to-one marketing). As an example, you could write individual letters to each of your prospects, or include an incentive tailored to their individual preferences. Practical financial constraints usually prevent this degree of personalization, so most companies concentrate on limited customization, addressing specific sector concerns or tailoring special offers to different types of business.

Can the quality of direct mail creative work be measured?

Direct mail is an extremely accountable medium, and the results can be measured precisely, making it possible to judge whether or not a particular creative approach has worked. However, creative work is only one of the factors that influence campaign success, so many companies test different creative approaches to try to identify how they affect results.

Making It Happen

Create Quality Mailing Material

Direct mail is the most precise marketing medium, but campaigns will be effective only if they combine precise targeting with good creative work. In theory anything can be sent by post, but most mailings consist primarily of printed material — letters, leaflets, and brochures. Three-dimensional objects can be mailed and can stimulate interest, but they must be relevant and cost-effective. Creative envelope design can also add impact to a mailing.

Use Direct Mail Letters Effectively

Letters are a universal communications medium and an integral element of any direct mail campaign. They can be used on their own as a personalized form of communication, and can also be used to support and personalize other standard mailing items. Letters can be customized easily and cost-effectively to meet different sector marketing requirements.

Personalize Letters

Personalized one-to-one mailings are an ideal form of communication for companies with detailed information on their prospects. The letter should reflect the individual's main interests and concerns, and the offer can be tailored to the individual prospect. Subsequent mailings can build an individual relationship with the prospect.

The key features of this type of letter are:

- it is personalized to the individual reader;
- it offers direct and valuable benefits;
- it builds future relationships with the customer by promising regular offers.

Letters can also be customized by market sector, offering specific benefits to groups of customers.

Use Letters to Support Other Mailing Material

Direct mail letters can also be used to accompany other material—a product brochure or management guide, for example. The letter can customize the mailing by including information specific to the individual prospect or market sector, or by making a further offer to the prospect.

Include Enclosures

Enclosures can include:

- catalogs
- sales leaflets or brochures
- price lists
- management reports or surveys
- information on special offers

There are a number of criteria for selecting enclosures:

- they should be relevant to the prospect's needs.
- they should not make the mailing impractical or costly because of size or weight.
- they should not be used if the objective is to encourage further response from the prospect.

Create Three-dimensional Enclosures

Three-dimensional enclosures can add impact and novelty value to a mailing. They can be used to send product samples by mail, to send promotional items, or to improve response by creating interest. However, it is important that they be relevant to the prospect's needs, that they do not make the mailing too expensive, and that they do not contravene postal regulations.

Include a Response Mechanism

If your mailing is designed to stimulate action, it should

include an easy-to-use response mechanism such as a business reply card or envelope, or contact details such as a toll-Free telephone number, e-mail address, or Web site.

Treat Envelopes Creatively

Postal authorities specify a number of preferred envelope sizes which help them to handle mail more efficiently. Companies that wish to use specific postal response services such as Business Reply must use the preferred sizes indicated in the authority's design specification. However, using nonstandard envelope sizes can add greater impact to a mailing. Envelopes can be designed in a number of ways to achieve greater impact:

- they can include advertising messages;
- addresses can be handwritten to add a personal touch;
- they can incorporate corporate design elements such as logos or company colors.

Use Professional Creative and Production Services

Quality and impact are essential to the success of a direct mail campaign. Creating an effective direct mail item requires professional skills, and is best handled by a creative team. Although many of the direct mail processes are straightforward, a company may not have the skills or resources to achieve the best possible results. External specialists provide a range of direct mail services, including copywriting and design, printing letters, and producing three-dimensional enclosures.

Specialists include:

- direct mail agencies
- advertising agencies
- design consultancies
- creative consultancies
- printers

However, there may be occasions when you decide to create simple direct mail items yourself.

Write Persuasive Copy

Use a powerful headline to get the attention of the reader. Words such as "new" and "improved" attract attention, while price benefits such as "sale" and "reduced" are also useful. Keep your writing style simple, with short sentences and paragraphs; in longer mailing items, use headings and subheadings to make sure that the reader picks up key messages without having to read the complete text. Tell your prospects what they need to know in order to make a decision about your product or service. Your message should deal with your customers' most important concerns and requirements. Describe benefits to the prospect, not features of the product: for example, a power drill that features extremely high operating speeds may be technically interesting, but the benefits to a builder are greater productivity and the opportunity to finish a job quickly. Offer the prospect a clear, powerful proposition. Your copy should encourage the prospect to take action—contact the company for more information, ask for a demonstration, or order immediately to qualify for a promotional offer.

Create a Quality Layout

Design quality is also important in getting a message to prospects clearly and effectively.

- Keep the layout simple to ensure immediate comprehension.
- Use photographs, diagrams, or illustrations if they help to clarify a point or create impact.
- Use the most legible type faces and sizes to make text easy to read.
- Use bold headings or a larger type size for the headline or to emphasize important statements.

Common Mistakes

Producing Standard Mailing Material

Direct mail is a precise medium. You can use that precision to target specific sectors or individual prospects with tailored messages and offers. Too many mailings fail to address prospects' individual needs and concerns. Research will help you to identify the key messages for different prospects, and to build them into your creative work.

Failing to Measure Creative Work

Direct mail campaigns are measured on their results: they should deliver inquiries or sales. If they do not deliver results, even the most creative campaigns should be considered failures. Make sure that you set realistic targets for your campaign. If you do not reach the targets, change the creative approach until you find one that delivers the results you want.

Making Mailings Too Complex

Some mailings contain so much material they can be daunting to deal with, so the prospect may lose interest.

For More Information

Book:

Bird, Drayton. *Commonsense Direct Marketing*. 4th ed. Dover, NH: Kogan Page, 2000.

Web Site:

The Direct Marketing Association:
www.the-dma.org

See also:

Direct Marketing (pp. 1953–54)

"Time spent in the advertising business seems to create a permanent deformity like the Chinese habit of foot-binding."
(Dean Acheson)

Improving Direct Mail Response Rates

Getting Started

The simplest and most immediate measure of a direct marketing campaign is the response level it achieves. Many different factors can affect response rates; it is important to test the variables before committing all your resources to a particular approach, and you should aim for a realistic figure that is within your budget.

Define your target market precisely. The more precisely you target, the better your response rates will be. Make it easy for your prospects to respond, and test your approach before committing resources to the full campaign.

FAQs

Why are direct mail responses so low?

The figures quoted are industry averages. They can vary upward or downward depending on the industry and the type of mailing. Remember that a small percentage of a mass mailing can provide you with a reasonable level of new prospects. To put the response rates into perspective, compare the response and the cost of response with an equivalent amount of spending on advertising.

Should direct mailing always be tested?

If it is practical, test direct mail on a small proportion of the market. Although direct mail is a precise medium, testing can refine the process even further. With so many variables in a mailing campaign, you can test different elements individually and plan your full campaign on the basis of the best response rate.

Should direct mail effectiveness be measured by response or by sales?

The ultimate test of any marketing campaign is an increase in profitable sales. However, direct mail, on its own, cannot deliver sales. Sales depend on pricing, the quality of your products, sales representatives, customer service, competitive activity, and many other factors. Direct mail should be given a specific role and measured by how it fulfills that role.

Making It Happen

Set Target Response Levels

- Response levels as low as 1 or 2% are regarded as the industry norm.
- Response rates in the region of 5% are regarded as high.
- Response rates in the region of 10–20% have been reported by companies who have integrated other forms of marketing communications.

Define Your Target Market Precisely

Do you want to reach all customers and prospects, or are you targeting specific groups? Direct marketing is a precise medium, so your campaign could be aimed at one key decision-maker or thousands of potential users. The more precisely you target, the better your response rates will be.

Integrate the Campaign with Other Marketing Activities

Direct marketing campaigns can run at any time. However, performance can be improved by integrating the campaign with other marketing activities such as an exhibition, advertising campaigns, or sales force calls. With integrated campaigns, overall awareness levels among customers and prospects will be much higher.

Choose the Right Campaign Frequency

A mass mailing, telephone call, or direct response advertisement may produce results, but a series of quality contacts will have greater impact and insure you meet your response targets. Multiple direct marketing activities provide a number of benefits:

- they raise levels of awareness with each contact;
- they follow up contacts who have not responded;
- they move individual respondents further along the decision-making process.

Make It Easy for Prospects to Respond

If you want to improve response rates, it is essential that you make it easy for your prospects to respond. Web site or e-mail addresses, postage-paid envelopes, and 800 numbers provide easy-to-use response mechanisms that can boost response. You should monitor the response levels from different sources to see which is the most effective.

Test Your Campaign

To guarantee the success of your campaign, you should test your approach before committing resources to the full campaign. There are a number of variables that can be tested:

- the offer
- the creative approach
- the target audience
- the response mechanism
- frequency and timing
- integration with other communications programs

The most effective test campaign is the one that achieves the highest response levels.

Use Split Campaigns

If budget allows, you can develop a series of campaigns that vary by offer, creative approach, response mechanism, frequency, and timing.

Improve Your Mailing Lists

Getting the mailing list right is vital. Basic mailing lists simply include names, addresses, job titles, and telephone numbers of customers and prospects. The basic list can be refined by adding information about buying patterns, lifestyle, and many other factors—providing a comprehensive picture of customers and prospects.

Check All Internal Sources of Information

Your customer records are probably your most valuable

"I know half the money I spend on advertising is wasted, but I can never find out which half."

(John Wanamaker)

asset as they invariably generate the highest response rates when they are mailed with relevant information. The most important sources are:

- customer records
- customer correspondence, including records of complaints
- warranty records
- service records
- sales prospect files
- sales force reports
- records of lapsed customers

Simple segmentation of your internal lists might give you categories such as:

- customers who have bought in the last six months
- lapsed customers
- customers who spend over $X a year

Add External Sources of Information

Your internal lists are likely to yield high response rates. However, if you are moving into new market sectors, internal lists may not provide the information you need. External lists are available from a number of different sources, including list brokers, magazine publishers, directory publishers, trade associations or professional institutes, commercial organizations, and retailers. To achieve a high response rate, check how closely the list matches your customer profile.

Commission a Special List

Standard lists may not give you the degree of match you need. The successful preparation of a tailored list is directly related to the quality of the brief, and you should provide the supplier with a detailed description of your target audience.

Keep Refining Your Lists

- Make sure that the list is kept up to date with new customer and prospect data.
- Include coupons and other reply mechanisms with every form of communication, and add the responses to your lists.
- Encourage the sales force to provide up-to-date customer and prospect information.
- Maintain an active search program in appropriate Web sites, magazines, and newspapers to identify new prospects for your list.

Check the Accuracy of Lists

To improve response and reduce waste in your mailing campaigns, it is important that your lists are regularly checked for accuracy. The two main problems are:

- duplication, where the same individual appears several times on the same list, possibly in different guises, for example as Ron Smith, R. T. Smith, and Mr. Smith;
- out-of-date information, where the original recipient has moved, or, for business mailings, changed jobs.

Use Personalized Letters

Personalized one-to-one mailings are an ideal form of communication for companies with detailed information about their prospects:

- the letter reflects the individual's main interests and concerns;
- the offer can be tailored to the individual prospect;
- subsequent mailings can build an individual relationship with the prospect.

If the database or mailing list holds complete names and other information, direct mail letters can be personalized in a number of ways, such as including the name in the address and greeting or throughout the text.

Use Telemarketing

Direct mail response levels can increase significantly when telemarketing is used. It offers a wide range of benefits, being:

- selective: contact can be initiated and maintained with all or selected groups of customers and prospects;
- precise: the calls can be targeted;
- flexible: the offer and the message can be varied;
- fast: calls can be made immediately, provided the contact is available;
- responsive: because telemarketing is interactive, it encourages response;
- measurable: the effectiveness of a telemarketing campaign can be measured precisely.

Common Mistakes

Setting Unrealistic Response Rates

Direct mail is a precise medium. However, it is easy to set unrealistic targets for response. Figures such as 5% or 6% would be seen as extremely high in many industries.

Failing to Integrate Direct Mail with Other Marketing Activities

Direct mail works most effectively when it is part of an integrated marketing campaign. Advertising can be used to raise the company profile; direct mail would be used to reach specific prospects with a targeted offer, and telemarketing could be used to back up the mailing with follow-up calls.

Poor Mailing Lists

Good response rates depend on high quality mailing lists. If your lists contain duplicate addresses, out-of-date information, or incorrect data, response will be poor.

For More Information

Book:

Bird, Drayton. *Commonsense Direct Marketing*. 4th ed. Dover, NH: Kogan Page, 2000.

Web Site:

The Direct Marketing Association:
www.the-dma.org

See also:

✔ **Generating More Leads (pp. 698–99)**
✔ **Integrating Advertising with Other Campaigns (pp. 654–55)**

"It was something you only spoke of in hushed tones. Advertising is a bit of an anathema."

(Michael Bungey)

 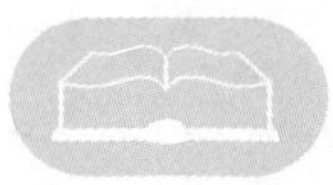    

Planning a Direct Marketing Campaign

Getting Started

Direct marketing works most effectively when it is aimed at a precise audience that cannot be easily reached by any other medium. A campaign should be carefully planned in accordance with the target market and the product or service concerned. Short-term results can be measured accurately and directly by the level of response, so the effectiveness of a campaign can be assessed quickly. There are, however, many different factors that can affect the outcome, such as product price or the quality of the campaign material. As with any direct approach, it is essential to make it as easy as possible for customers to respond.

FAQs

Can direct marketing be used to sell products?

There are many situations in which you can use direct mail to build direct sales. You may not have a sales force or a retail network, so customers can only buy direct from you. If you want to sell to niche markets, direct marketing may be the only cost-effective way of reaching them. If you decide to sell direct, you must insure that the products themselves are suitable for selling through direct marketing—that is, that they do not have to be demonstrated, or inspected by the customer.

How does direct marketing build relationships with customers?

The stronger your relationship with your customers, the more opportunities you have to influence the future direction and success of your business. If your company depends on a few key customers for most of its business, you can use direct marketing to improve customer loyalty by building long-term relationships with them. You may also need to use it if your customers want to rationalize the number of suppliers, and you want to remain on the approved list.

Is direct marketing only effective for reaching a small audience?

There are numerous examples of successful large-scale mailings. However, the key to direct marketing success is reaching the right people in a cost-effective way. Large-scale mailings based on poorly researched mailing lists may yield results, but there will also be a high level of wastage. The more precise your mailing, the more likely you are to succeed.

Making It Happen

The key stages of a direct marketing campaign are described below.

Set Campaign Objectives

Direct marketing objectives can be initially expressed in general terms.

- Encouraging prospects to buy directly in response to a direct marketing campaign.
- Generating leads for the sales force or retail network.
- Supporting sales force activity.
- Improving the effectiveness of other forms of communication.
- Raising awareness of a company, product, or service among clearly identified customers and prospects.
- Maintaining effective contact with customers and prospects.
- Building relationships with customers and prospects.

However, these general objectives should be translated into precise, measurable objectives, for example:

- Raising awareness of your product range among 35% of technical directors in the mechanical engineering sector.
- Insuring that purchasing managers in your ten top customers are contacted at least once every two weeks.
- Increasing direct sales of supplies by 15%.

Define the Target Market

Do you want to reach all customers and prospects, or are you targeting specific groups? Direct marketing is a precise medium, so your campaign could be aimed at just one key decision-maker or thousands of potential users. To plan your direct marketing campaign, you should ask questions such as:

- Who buys your type of product?
- Who influences the purchasing decision?
- How many prospects do you want to reach with the direct marketing campaign?
- How do they currently get information about your products?
- What is the role of direct marketing in reaching the target audience?

The more information you have about your target audience, the more precise you can make your campaign. In an ideal world, direct marketing would allow you to communicate one to one with every prospect, but, in practical terms, you are more likely to be communicating with groups that share certain characteristics.

Plan Campaign Timing

A direct marketing campaign can run at any time, so you do not have to consider advertisement publication dates. However, timing may be dictated by other factors—lead times for producing mailing material, seasonal purchasing patterns, product availability, or tender dates. These are some of the factors to consider in planning the timing of your campaign:

- When is your customer making the buying decision?
- If you are launching a new product, when will the product be available?
- Does your direct marketing campaign have to tie-in with the timing of any other marketing activity, such as an exhibition, advertising campaign, or sales force visit?
- How long will it take to produce the material that is to be mailed?
- When will you be able to follow up the campaign?

"I think editors are excellent marketers. They know their audience and produce copy to appeal to them—they just don't call it marketing."
(David Robinson)

Decide Campaign Frequency

A single mailing, telephone call, or direct response advertisement may produce results, but a series of quality contacts will have greater impact and insure you meet your objectives. There are several benefits from repeated contracts:

- raising levels of awareness with each contact;
- following up those who have not responded;
- moving individual respondents further along the decision making process;
- maintaining contact during extended decision making processes.

There is no hard-and-fast rule about the frequency of individual campaigns; a company trying to get a prospect to make a decision may make contact several times a week, while a company aiming to maintain long-term customer loyalty may need to contact customers only monthly or quarterly.

Develop a Response Mechanism

Action is a vital ingredient of any direct marketing campaign, and it is essential that you make it easy for your prospects to respond. First, decide if your prospects are to place an order, request a sales visit, or ask for further information. Then decide which of the five basic types of response mechanism are the most appropriate: mail, telephone, fax, e-mail, or Web site address.

Test the Campaign

Part of the flexibility of direct marketing is that you can test your approach before committing resources to the full campaign. There are several variables that can be tested:

- the offer
- the creative approach
- the target audience
- the response mechanism
- frequency and timing

The test campaign can be carried out in a number of ways:

- on a representative sample of the target market
- in a defined sales or geographical territory
- in a particular sector of the target market

The most effective test campaign is the one that achieves the highest response levels.

Plan Split Campaigns

Testing your campaign may reveal that different approaches work more effectively in different market sectors. If budget allows, you can develop a series of campaigns that vary the offer, the creative approach, frequency, timing, or other factors.

Set Target Response Levels

In the long term, a campaign may increase awareness, improve customer relations, or cut the cost of sales. However, the simplest and most immediate measure of a direct marketing campaign is the response level it generates. In setting your target response levels, you should aim for a realistic figure that is within your budget. Note that:

- response levels as low as 1% or 2% are regarded as the industry norm;
- response rates in the region of 5% are regarded as high;
- response rates in the region of 10–20% have been reported by companies who have integrated other forms of marketing communications.

Many different factors can affect the level of response, including price, quality of the mailing list, the promotional offer, and quality of copy and design.

Common Mistakes

Failing to Set Measurable Targets

The results of a direct marketing campaign can be measured precisely by the number of responses. This makes it a particularly accountable medium. It is therefore important to set realistic, measurable objectives. If your target is to generate leads from 2% of the target audience, this will determine how many people you mail, the type of offer you make, and the response mechanism you provide.

Poor Audience Selection

With direct marketing you can communicate with a single prospect or with 50,000. However, there may be more cost-effective ways of communicating with 50,000 prospects. Direct marketing works most effectively when it is aimed at a precise audience that cannot be easily reached by any other medium.

No integration with Other Communications

If your marketing budget is split between different communications activities such as advertising, sales promotion, and publications, it is essential that each activity works as effectively as possible. You can use integrated direct marketing in conjunction with the initial communications. If you place advertisements in publications that only reach a general audience, you can reinforce the advertisements with personalized communications to selected prospects. If your advertisements include a response mechanism, direct marketing will insure effective follow-up. You also can tailor your product and corporate literature to the information needs of different market sectors by including direct marketing material.

For More Information

Book:

Bird, Drayton. *Commonsense Direct Marketing*. 4th ed. Dover, NH: Kogan Page, 2000.

Web Site:

The Direct Marketing Association: **www.the-dma.org**

Planning a Customer Event

Getting Started

Desk research is no substitute for getting out and meeting customers face to face. Arranging visits or special customer events increases personal contact and improves customer relationships—although events need to be handled professionally to achieve the right results.

FAQs

Who should organize a customer event?

Few companies have the luxury of a specialist events department, so the task normally falls to the sales, marketing, or public relations department. Events generally form a small part of the overall customer relationship program, so they may not get the attention or the resources they require. Event organization is extremely time-consuming, so it may be better to appoint a specialist event company to work with an internal coordinator. Invitations and publicity could be handled internally, while the event company takes responsibility for venues, staging, and logistics.

Do events provide a good return on investment?

If events reach the right people and help to strengthen customer relationships, they provide a good return. However, many companies organize events simply to get together with customers. Without a specific objective, the event could be a waste of valuable funds.

How do you decide who should be invited to a customer event?

If resources are limited, you may have to select the most important contacts within a customer company. The sales force can provide advice, but you may still overlook influential people and create resentment. Asking customers to nominate their own delegates shifts some of the responsibility, but they may not choose the people you wish to contact. There is always likely to be a compromise, so make sure you check your records carefully and try to keep up to date with the power structure within a company.

Making It Happen

Become Familiar with Customers

How well do you know your customers' businesses, their markets, their plans, their competitors, and their strengths and weaknesses? The more you know, the more easily you can identify their real needs and develop a service that wins and keeps business.

Although you can find out a lot about your customers just by looking in your sales records, desk research is no substitute for getting out and meeting customers face to face. The sales team is doing that all the time, but it is unlikely that they will be responsible for delivering customer service. You need to meet the customers yourself by arranging visits or special customer events. These increase personal contact and improve customer relationships.

Manage Events Professionally

Events such as open evenings, trade shows, and customer receptions are a powerful method of building customer loyalty, but they need to be handled professionally to achieve the right results. By providing the right level of support, you can develop a program of events that is appropriate for the market. This can include:

- the development of suitable promotional and display material
- the theme for the event
- the invitations and generation of mailing lists
- support literature
- personal support by members of the head office team

Arrange an Informal Customer Visit

Many customers will appreciate the interest you are showing in their business when you arrange an informal visit. Alternatively, invite customers to visit your premises. It provides a good chance for employees who deal with customers to meet their opposite numbers, and meeting people face to face can help to improve working relationships.

Attend Customer Exhibitions, Seminars, and Conferences

You can find out what competitors are up to at the same time. Events like these are a good indicator of what customers believe is important to the success of their business and will give you a good sign of where they see themselves heading.

Make Customer Care Visits

Call on selected customers at intervals to discuss whether they are satisfied with the standard of service they are receiving from you. Ask if they have any specific concerns and insure that you contact them again with an appropriate response.

Set up Regular Review Meetings

This is a more formal process than the ad hoc customer care visits. Suppliers and customers agree to meet at regular intervals, for example every year or once a quarter, or monthly, according to the complexity and importance of the business. There is likely to be a set agenda for reviewing performance in specific areas, and there may be agreed standards that are used to measure performance.

Arrange Briefing Meetings for Your Customers

Briefings are not for reviewing progress or performance but for bringing your customers up to date with new developments in your business or industry that might benefit them. For example, you might brief them on a new technical development or on new legislation that is likely to have an impact on them. This type of meeting not only demonstrates your professionalism; it also helps to add value to the customer relationship.

"Quality is not a thing. It is an event." (Robert M. Pirsig)

Hold a Social Event

Many customers enjoy the chance to meet informally and talk shop. A social event could take place after a more formal meeting or it might be an event in its own right. Although the extravagant side of corporate hospitality has largely disappeared, social events remain an important aspect of business relationships.

Run Regional Events in Retail Outlets

When one manufacturer launches a new range of products, the central feature of the launch is a series of customer events run in conjunction with regional retailers around the country. The outlets are given detailed guidelines on the program and provided with letters inviting customers to the launch event. The outlets put together their own mailing lists using account information, local directories, and database information from head office.

Encourage Employees to Attend

At one event, one of the company's directors attended to make a brief presentation and talk to customers. A group of company sales and technical employees joined with retailer employees to host the evening and meet customers. The company also provided window displays and freestanding display units to insure consistent quality. By providing a professional support service, the company was able to insure a consistent standard and give the retailers the freedom to develop an event that was right for the local market.

Offer Events as Customer Incentives

An incentive scheme for a bank offered business customers a structured series of special sports prizes. Customers were awarded points for using different types of business banking services and could win a day's free participation and coaching in different sports activities, which had high levels of appeal to the target audience, such as gliding, water sports, auto racing. The local branches could tailor the awards to their own customer base, but they did not have to provide the resources to manage the events themselves. This was handled by a specialist organization that could set up the events in different parts of the country.

Sponsored Events

Sponsoring an event should be a positive marketing action, not an enforced response to a request for help. Depending on the type of event and its popularity, sponsorship can:

- build the image of an organization or product through association with an event that reflects corporate values;
- raise awareness of an organization or product through the exposure associated with an event.

There are different levels of sponsorship:

- international, national, regional, or local event
- whole event, with unique or joint sponsorship
- program or award sponsorship
- hospitality
- participants, as individuals or teams

Make the Most of Sponsorship

- Issue press releases about the organization's involvement.
- Advertise on the perimeter or program.
- Inform employees and customers.
- Use the event for customer hospitality.
- Consider other promotional activities tied in to the event.

Common Mistakes

Poor Organization

At a customer event, the company is on display. The event must be carefully organized and managed to insure that customers get the right impression of the company. If you are putting on a large or complex event, it may pay to use a professional event organizer. They have the resources and skills to manage all the services and logistics essential to success.

Failing to Set Objectives for the Event

An event must have a specific purpose: for example, to improve relations with key decision-makers or to reward loyal customers. The objectives determine the format of the event and the support services required.

Poor Internal Communication

The success of an event depends on the successful participation of employees. Make sure that employees who deal with customers are aware of the event, and keep them involved in the planning process. On the day, make sure that everyone is aware of individual responsibilities.

For More Information

Book:

Allen, Judi. *Event Planning: The Ultimate Guide to Successful Meetings, Corporate Events, Fundraising Galas, Conferences, Conventions, Incentives and Other Special Events*. New York: John Wiley & Sons, 2000.

Web Site:

Reed Exhibitions: **www.reedexpo.com**

See also:

Conferences and Exhibitions (pp. 1935–36)

RUNNING A NETWORKED CONFERENCE

GETTING STARTED

Networked conferencing brings people inside and outside an organization together. Although not as effective as live meetings, networked conferencing brings huge benefits in terms of convenience and time saving, and substantial savings on the costs of organizing and travel. Videoconferencing remains the most popular type of networked conference, but Web casting over the Internet is now becoming a viable alternative.

FAQS

IS NETWORKED CONFERENCING A SUITABLE SUBSTITUTE FOR LIVE MEETINGS?

Live meetings should always be the first choice if you need face-to-face contact or if you aim to motivate people through a dynamic experience. However, time constraints and the cost of staging live events mean that networked conferencing is a far more cost-effective solution for routine meetings or events that need to reach large numbers of people.

IS VIDEOCONFERENCING BETTER THAN WEB CASTING?

Each technique has specific benefits. Web casting over the Internet is a more cost-effective means of reaching a large audience and does not require the use of sophisticated videoconferencing equipment. However, it is not a secure medium, so there is some risk involved for events featuring confidential information.

Videoconferencing is probably more suitable for an internal audience, provided they have access to the necessary equipment. Low-cost, PC-based systems have made videoconferencing more accessible, but it is not such a universal medium as an Internet-based solution like Web casting.

DOESN'T NETWORKED CONFERENCING JUST ENCOURAGE EVEN MORE MEETINGS?

It certainly makes it easier to arrange meetings, and this can be a good or a bad thing. The reduction in traveling time and the problems of getting people together have to be offset against the increased frequency of meetings. Increasing the number of meetings may actually improve the quality of communication.

MAKING IT HAPPEN

BRING PEOPLE TOGETHER

Networked conferencing brings people inside and outside an organization together quickly and easily, wherever they are located. It supports effective teamwork when people operate in different locations or different countries, and it can help people meet key objectives efficiently and productively. It can also reduce the costs associated with traditional meetings.

Videoconferencing remains the most popular type of networked conference, but Web casting over the Internet is beginning to emerge as a viable alternative as new technologies develop.

IMPROVE TIME MANAGEMENT

Networked conferencing makes it easier to bring groups of people together, even at short notice. With a networked conference, all that is needed is the time for the meeting itself; travel time is eliminated, allowing busy executives and project team members to concentrate on important tasks.

REDUCE COSTS

The real cost of conventional meetings can be estimated by adding up the salaries of people traveling, the travel costs, and food and accommodation. In an organization that operates internationally, the potential cost savings of networked conferencing are enormous.

ENHANCE COMMUNICATIONS

The freedom and flexibility of networked conferencing means that the organization can arrange meetings whenever such communication is necessary. It is quick and easy to arrange meetings for briefing sales teams, reporting, training or coaching, reviewing progress, or dealing with project issues. Senior executives can communicate easily with people throughout an organization by broadcasting annual reports, for example, or news about significant corporate changes.

REDUCE TIME TO MARKET

Project teams can speed up the development process by using networked conferencing. Progress meetings, milestone reviews, technical evaluations, or routine meetings can be arranged to suit the team. Networked conferencing is ideal for simultaneous engineering projects where different specialists may work in separate locations. They can exchange information and work on problems at short notice. This eliminates project delays, and can reduce overall lead times, giving an organization a significant competitive advantage.

ENHANCE CONFERENCES WITH WEB CASTING

Businesses can now extend the reach of their meetings by using the Internet and a Web casting service. The service allows companies to stream traditional audio and video conferences over the Internet, incorporating multimedia content and adding interactive capability such as slides, polling, and messaging. Any unexpected increase in participant numbers is not a problem, as a Web cast can reach very large numbers of people in many different locations using sophisticated streaming media. Audio and video streaming is transforming conventional broadcasting and enhancing the distribution of multimedia material to consumer and corporate audiences.

USE THE POWER OF STREAMING

Streaming media allows users to view video and other content on the Web without having to wait for it to download completely on to a computer. Before streaming media was developed, the only way to view video or hear audio on the Internet was to download an entire file,

"Even a partial shift towards the electronic office will be enough to trigger an eruption of social, psychological, and economic consequences." (Alvin Toffler)

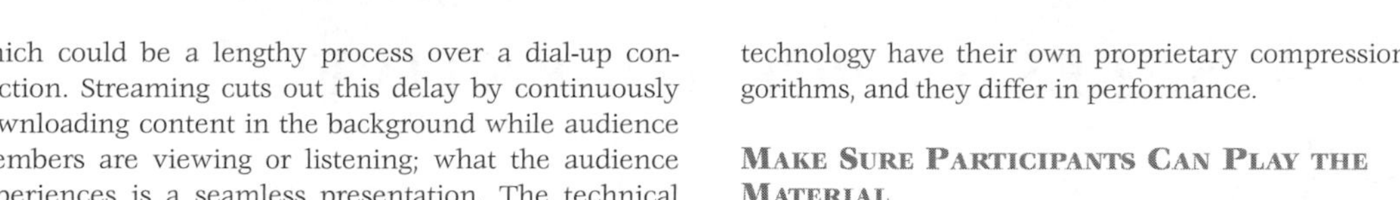

which could be a lengthy process over a dial-up connection. Streaming cuts out this delay by continuously downloading content in the background while audience members are viewing or listening; what the audience experiences is a seamless presentation. The technical requirements are simple, as audience members need no complex videoconferencing equipment; anyone with an Internet-connected computer, Web browser and media player can view a Web cast. New computers increasingly incorporate media players, and this makes Web casting a very accessible medium.

Include Interactive Multimedia Content

The latest Web casts combine live and recorded video, with multimedia content such as presentation slides or Web tours. Interactive capabilities, such as question-and-answer sessions and audience polling, create a rich and engaging experience for participants. These new capabilities can help businesses turn a standard videoconferencing system into an Internet broadcasting tool, ideal for conducting seminars, remote training, employee updates, and large meetings.

Reduce Distribution Costs

Because Web casting removes the problem of distance, it is a cost-effective way for businesses to extend the reach of their meetings by streaming their messages to hundreds or thousands of participants over the Internet. When its costs are compared with those of staging meetings or taking a roadshow to different locations around the country, Web casting becomes an attractive proposition. More and more companies are considering how they can use Web casting to improve their internal and external communications.

Identify Applications

Web casting is already being used for seminars, focus groups, investor relations, press conferences, financial reporting, training, employee announcements, and product launches. Nor is it confined to the corporate environment; it is being used to broadcast live and archived events such as sports, news, and concerts. One-time events can be broadcast live or prerecorded for later broadcast, while regular programs or items can be recorded and broadcast at specified times. Audio and video clips can be accessed on demand by users around the clock. The programs are broadcast over broadband, giving superb, TV-standard quality.

Check Performance over Different Internet Connections

Conference participants will have different types of Internet connection, modem speeds, and media players, so it is important to review the transmission in different environments to insure that participants are able to play the audio and video regardless of the technology they have available. Check performance over different types of connections using slower and faster modems, as well as broadband. The companies who provide streaming technology have their own proprietary compression algorithms, and they differ in performance.

Make Sure Participants Can Play the Material

Check what your participants have to do to play the material. In some cases, the preliminary processes may be prohibitive or their company may place restrictions on viewing.

- Do they have to download special software to play the content?
- If so, how long does it take to download?
- Does the Internet browser have the capability to play rich content? (Not all browsers do.)
- Do company Internet security systems prohibit rich content?

Common Mistakes

Poor Content

When companies stage live events, they aim to create an exciting experience. Networked conferencing rarely gets the same treatment, but the latest Web casting technologies support a wide variety of multimedia and interactive content. It is important to use the full potential of the medium, because the aim of many events is not just to inform but to motivate people to take action.

Creating Security Risks

Material distributed over the Internet poses security risks because the Web is a public medium. Although Web casting increases the range of a meeting, and is a cost-effective method of reaching large audiences, the event should not include confidential information. Although videoconferencing is more secure, it may also be broadcast over public networks. Only private links between individual sites can be regarded as secure.

Failing to Promote the Event

Simply putting an event on the Internet provides no guarantee of reaching the target audience. To attract specific customers or prospects, it is essential that they are aware of the Web cast. E-mail or conventional direct mail and telemarketing techniques can be used to keep people informed.

For More Information

Book:

Rhodes, John. *Videoconferencing for the Real World.* Woburn, MA: Butterworth-Heinemann, 2001.

Web Site:

Mshow: **www.mshow.com**

See also:

Conferences and Exhibitions (pp. 1935–36)

"No grand idea was ever born in a conference, but a lot of foolish ideas have died there."

(F. Scott Fitzgerald)

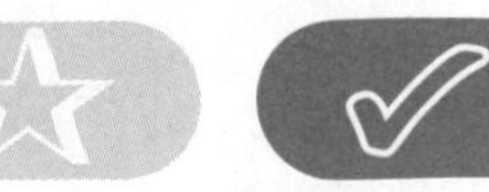     

Running a Sales Force Incentive Campaign

Getting Started

Incentive schemes are an integral part of sales management and can either provide general motivation of the sales force or improve performance in specific areas. They can also be used to achieve a new direction or to encourage sales employees to acquire new skills. The type and structuring of the incentive program depend on the desired objectives and the timescale involved.

FAQs

Why does a sales force need incentive programs?

A sales force can improve its general performance through training, encouragement, and higher levels of support. However, incentive programs can be used to improve performance in specific areas. Targeted programs are therefore the most effective form of incentive.

Should incentive programs be used to reward the top performers or the entire sales force?

That depends on the program objectives. If the aim is to encourage the highest levels of achievement, prizes should be restricted to top performers. However, this may act as a disincentive to some members of the sales force. It also may cause problems if some sales representatives appear to have unfair advantages, such as larger territories or customers in growth-market sectors. Incentive programs designed to raise overall standards should reward all members of the sales force who meet their personal targets, although top-performer prizes should be added to increase motivation.

Don't incentive schemes encourage sales employees to increase business at any cost rather than concentrate on improving customer relationships?

A poorly designed incentive scheme that focuses only on new business can cause problems. The new customers may not be creditworthy or offer long-term growth potential, and they may distract sales employees from existing customers. A good incentive scheme would take account of this.

Making It Happen

Improve Sales Force Performance

Incentive schemes are an integral part of sales management. They can be used to motivate sales employees to improve their overall performance or they can be structured to improve performance in specific areas, such as repeat sales, new accounts, or the acquisition of new skills.

Set the Right Objectives

Ask yourself why you are running the program. Is it because you want to increase overall volume or sales of specific products? Or, do you want to improve performance in other sales-related areas such as customer service, or participation in training schemes and other business programs?

Improve Customer Service

You can build both sales and customer loyalty by providing the highest standards of customer care. An incentive scheme should be carefully structured to improve performance in all the areas critical to achieving that objective. It should cover:

- participation in the relevant training program
- new accounts opened
- percentage of repeat business achieved
- achievement of major contracts
- sales of products identified for special promotion

Encourage Continuous Sales Effort

Sales representatives should be assessed on a series of long- and short-term objectives that help them build a specific type of business. The same approach can be used to encourage teams to focus on sales of a certain product line. The important point about incentive schemes of this type is that they are structured to encourage continuous effort over a period of time rather than achieving short-term objectives. Sales incentives have traditionally been geared to moving stock quickly for tactical reasons and, as such, they are an essential sales management technique, but they also can be used in a strategic way.

Achieve a Change of Direction

When a European vehicle paint manufacturer wanted to build a broader customer base rather than depend on a few large customers, it developed a year-long incentive program for its sales team. The organization wanted to encourage the sales team to win and retain business from independent garages, as well as the franchised car dealers who represented only a small part of the market. Under the program, points were awarded for opening new accounts with the independents, and a structured bonus system was applied to percentage increases in business with these new accounts. In addition, the sales representatives were also given points for increasing business with existing accounts, but these were weighted to count for less in the overall assessment.

The manufacturer also wanted to encourage the sales team to acquire new skills in business development, so that they could form closer working relationships with their customers at senior management level. To achieve this, additional points were awarded for participation in business skills training courses and for reaching different training levels. The incentive program also awarded points for participation in a number of business development programs designed to improve the quality of service to customers. In this way, the incentive program encouraged overall business development rather than short-term tactical sales.

Select the Right Incentive Program
Incentives have proved to be an effective form of motivation, but they must be managed carefully to provide long-term benefits. The wrong choice of prizes, unclear rules, or poor organization can undo all the good work.

Choose an Appropriate Program Format
- Prizes can be awarded to the biggest earners or the best performers against target.
- Programs that reward only top sales representatives can act as a disincentive to others; programs that reward performance against target give a wider opportunity to win, and can motivate a higher proportion of the sales force.
- A multilevel program that offers many lower-value prizes, with high-value prizes for top performers, can act as a strong motivator.

Make Sure the Prize Motivates People
- Achievable prizes can motivate large numbers.
- The prize structure should offer real variety.
- Quality prizes can be used to reflect the high standards set by a program.
- Popular prizes may have wide appeal but may not have much motivational value.

Define the Rules Clearly
- Set out the scope of the program and the awards.
- Explain what is required to win and how to collect the prizes.
- Include the closing date for the promotion.
- Set the specific targets for each participant.
- Indicate who is eligible for the award.
- State clearly the tax implications of any prize.

Offer Different Prize Levels
To maintain interest in the program, offer different levels of prize. A program like this has depth as well as breadth:
- regular monthly prizes for best sales performance;
- quarterly regional awards for best overall performance;
- regional winners go forward to a national incentive program that rewards high achievers with even more attractive prizes.

Maintain Momentum throughout the Program
- Send out teaser incentives or gifts during the program.
- Keep participants informed of their progress.
- Use secondary offers to encourage participants who are struggling.
- Publish results and distribute to all participants.

Reward Effort
A national conference or other event can be used to recognize high achievement. The highlight of this type of program is the individual presentation to the winner by a senior director, an event that represents real status to the winner. The high profile of the program's award ceremony can raise its importance among the whole sales force, and encourage high levels of participation and effort.

Manage the Event
Consider using a professional event management company or incentive specialist to handle the event, and appoint an event team with specific responsibilities for the event itself. If possible, obtain feedback from participants on attitudes to the venue and the event.

Common Mistakes

Putting Too Much Emphasis on the Incentive Program
While an incentive program may result in a short-term increase in sales, it may disguise underlying problems in sales force performance. More training, better regional management, different account allocation, or greater marketing support may lead to even higher levels of performance. An incentive program should not be treated as a short-term fix: it should be integrated with other aspects of sales force management.

Concentrating on Short-term Incentives
Incentive programs can be used to achieve long-term business objectives. If an organization wants to move into new markets, the sales force will have to acquire new product and market knowledge. The incentive program should then be structured to recognize achievement in those areas rather than to reward short-term sales.

Poor Program Management
An incentive program has to be carefully managed. Clear objectives and program rules, attractive prizes, a progressive structure, and sound administration insure high levels of motivation and achievement.

For More Information

Book:
Miller, William Skip. *Proactive Sales Management: How to Lead, Motivate, and Stay Ahead of the Game.* New York: AMACOM, 2001.

Web Site:
American Marketing Association:
www.MarketingPower.com

Designing a Response Mechanism

Getting Started

Response mechanisms make it easier for prospects to get information, place orders, and respond to offers. Every advertisement, mailing, or other customer communication should incorporate one.

There are five basic types of response mechanism:

- mail
- telephone
- fax
- e-mail
- Web site address

FAQs

Why should every communication include a response mechanism?

Although some advertisements or other customer communications are designed to impart information, it is a courtesy to include a response mechanism. Customers may want more information than you can provide. It is also important to collect customer data. The response mechanism allows you to capture basic details and measure the effectiveness of a campaign.

Why bother with other types of response mechanism when a Web site address is so simple and convenient?

A Web site is convenient. Customers can visit around the clock, download information, and sometimes place orders. However, if they do not register their details when they visit, you have no opportunity to contact them or develop a relationship. If the customer wants to ask questions or discuss a product in more detail, telephone contact may be more appropriate.

Doesn't using a call center take away the opportunity to deliver personal service?

Call center employees are trained to act as personal representatives of your company. They receive full product training and they will become familiar with your company culture and ways of doing business. Customers should notice no difference when they are linked to a call center.

Making It Happen

Include a Response Mechanism

It is important that any advertisement, mailing, or other customer communication incorporates a response mechanism. A response mechanism is a call to action that insures your prospect takes the next step in the buying process. It can also be an effective method of capturing customer data for use in future sales and marketing campaigns.

Encourage Response to Print Advertisements

You should include a coupon on print advertisements if you want to capture specific data on prospects, such as name and address, or business details. You can also encourage response by including a telephone number, mailing address, Web site, or e-mail address for further information, although this may not give you the same level of data capture. If you do not use coupons, try to capture data through telemarketing techniques. You should make it easy for the prospect to respond by offering a toll-free phone number. Capturing e-mail addresses can also be an important first stage in building customer relationships.

Build Response to Television and Radio Advertising

Include a telephone number or Web site address in television or radio commercials if you want prospects to ask for further information, and preferably make the number a toll-free number. If you want to include an address, allow viewers time to take the address down. Repeat the address at least once. If you are encouraging a telephone response, make sure that you have the resources to handle a high volume of calls. Television advertisements have been known to generate high response for a short period immediately after the commercial. If you do not have sufficient internal resources, you can hire a call center to handle the calls during the period of the campaign.

Use the Right Response Mechanisms

There are five basic types of response mechanism:

- mail
- telephone
- fax
- e-mail
- Web site address

Response mechanisms improve the effectiveness of advertising campaigns by making it easier for prospects to get information or place orders, and encouraging prospects to respond to offers.

Consumers feel comfortable with a reply mechanism because it allows more time for consideration and there is no sales pressure. Industry research indicates that customers respond to the range of response mechanisms in different ways. E-mail and the Internet are seen as fast and convenient. They involve little effort and can be used 24 hours a day, seven days a week. Telephone-based services are more immediate and can be more personal. Pay-per-minute information service numbers can be used to provide useful customer information and generate revenue. Business Reply is regarded as suitable for business and financial advertisements.

Encourage Telephone Response

With the toll-free number, prospects and customers call your company from anywhere in the country, free of charge. You can obtain a toll-free number from your telephone service provider and you pay for the calls you receive at the standard rate.

You can also offer customers local numbers. Prospects and customers call from anywhere in the country, and

---

"As you seek to change every procedure and job description to aid responsiveness, remember the bygone days when we whipped big competitors by being faster and fleeter of foot." (Ronald Reagan)

the call is charged to them at local rates. You can obtain a local call number from your telephone service provider and you pay the balance of the charge.

With a pay-per-minute number, prospects and customers call from anywhere in the country and pay a premium rate for prerecorded information. Revenue from each call is divided between your company and the telephone service provider. You can obtain pay-per-minute numbers from your service provider and charges for each call are at an agreed rate. You must publish the charge per minute to the customer, and any offers to children should include a warning to ask parents' permission before calling.

Offer E-mail Response

E-mail is a quick, convenient response mechanism. Prospects can either compose their own e-mail and send it to your e-mail address, or complete a form on your Web site. If you want prospects to complete an online form, you must include your Web site address in the original customer communication.

Direct Customers to Your Web Site

Including a Web site address on your customer communications provides an extremely flexible response mechanism. Customers can obtain detailed information direct from the site, reducing your information distribution costs. However, you may prefer to take greater control of the customer relationship. You can also ask customers to register on your Web site. This provides valuable customer data and allows you to choose how to follow up the inquiry.

Keep Data Requirements to a Minimum

Asking for minimal data is a courtesy to customers and increases response. Apart from name and position, the most important information is telephone number or e-mail address. That provides a basis for contact and collection of additional data. Long, complex forms or requests for large amounts of detail could put off potential respondents.

Maintain a Quality Response

Companies that have to handle large volumes of responses and distribute additional material may not have the resources to handle fulfillment internally. Fulfillment agencies specialize in high-volume response programs. The address or telephone number of the fulfillment agency should be included in the response mechanism. If you are selecting a fulfillment house, there are important criteria:

- quality and reliability of service
- capacity to handle the volume of responses
- aftercare service for customers
- management reporting systems

Common Mistakes

Asking Customers for Too Much Information

Customers may be willing to provide basic information, but lengthy questionnaires are time consuming and can deter people from responding. The most important elements are name, address, telephone number, and e-mail address. If you go beyond that point, you are moving into market research and customers may be less willing to co-operate.

Failing to Integrate Response Mechanisms with Relationship Programs

A response mechanism is simply a starting point for a customer relationship program. A customer may just ask for a leaflet, but that request gives you the opportunity to open a dialog, gather further information, and build a detailed customer profile as a basis for future campaigns.

Poor Follow-up

Your advertising is wasted if you capture customer details and fail to follow up effectively. Customers will feel frustrated if they have to wait a long time for a response. You will also lose the opportunity to develop a relationship while the customer is in buying mood. You should set time limits for responding to requests. If you cannot meet those targets, consider using external resources to handle fulfillment.

Failing to Offer Customers Choice of Response

Before the Internet became a popular medium, the mail and telephone were the only effective response mechanisms. Today, people expect the convenience of an e-mail or Web site address as well as telephone or postal mechanisms. Offering a choice of routes demonstrates good customer service.

For More Information

Book:

Hughes, Arthur Middleton. *Strategic Database Marketing: The Masterplan for Starting and Managing a Profitable, Customer-Based Marketing Program*. New York: McGraw-Hill Professional Publishing, 2000.

Web Sites:

American Marketing Association:
www.MarketingPower.com
The Direct Marketing Association:
www.the-dma.org

  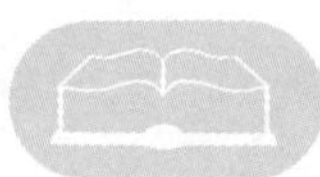    

Generating More Leads

Getting Started

The constant turnover of customers means that generating new leads is essential to keep a business growing. There are many ways of doing this, depending on the product and customer groups involved, but the primary purpose is to provide data on potential customers which can then be followed up.

FAQs

How important is lead generation?

Lead generation is vital to the development of new business. Customers just stop buying, or they move to competitors; this lost business must be replaced, and new customers added, if sales are to grow. Sales teams must have a constant flow of leads in order to maintain new business levels.

What is the best source of new leads?

The best source is the one that produces the highest-quality leads; some publications can produce large numbers of leads, but they could all be poor. A publication, a direct mail program, or an event that is precisely targeted is likely to produce the most effective source of leads.

Are incentives necessary to a lead generation program?

They are not essential, but they may help to encourage people to place inquiries. The incentive should not be too generous, since you may attract poor prospects who are more interested in free gifts than in your products.

Making It Happen

Make Direct Response a Priority

To generate leads from your marketing campaigns, include a response mechanism in every communication, and make it easy for prospects to reply. Getting names is a priority, so make sure your communications are designed to deliver.

Generate Leads from Press Advertising

If you want to generate leads, make sure your advertisement includes a call to action, such as:

- send for more information
- reply within seven days and receive a free gift
- send for a free report
- take out an annual subscription now and get the first two issues free
- call for a free consultation
- reserve now at a special price
- order now and get a big discount
- visit our Web site and find out more

Make It Easy for Prospects to Respond

To improve response rates, it is essential to make it easy for prospective customers to respond. The most popular mechanisms for print media advertisements are:

- Web site address
- e-mail address
- toll-free number

These facilities provide easy-to-use response mechanisms that can boost customer reaction. You should monitor the response levels from different sources to see which is the most effective.

Use Reader Response Cards

Many publications include a reader response card or helpline number. Readers send back the card to the publication, indicating the products that they are interested in. The usual method is to circle a number which is shown on the advertisement in the publication, for example, "For more information circle # 15." The publication then distributes the inquiries to individual advertisers for follow-up.

Run Advertorials in the Press

An advertorial with a prize is a cost-effective way of generating leads. The advertorial describes a product or service, and customers are offered the opportunity to win a prize in return for supplying basic data or completing a short questionnaire. The questionnaire might take the form of "Give three reasons why product X is the best on the market." The answers could be multiple choice, based on information in the advertorial, or the customer's own opinion. Open-ended questions provide added insight into customer attitudes.

Encourage TV and Radio Response

More and more television and radio commercials now include a response mechanism, such as a phone number or Web site address. Some direct the audience to a source of further information, others to a retailer or other outlet. The response mechanism must be clear, because the audience has only a short time to write down the details.

Use Direct Mail to Target Prospects

Direct mail can be used at a number of stages in a lead generation program. Mailings to lists that have not been qualified should include a response mechanism so that follow-up can begin.

Run Offers on Packaging

Your product packaging can feature special offers. Buyers send in a coupon or other proof of purchase, together with their name and address. Although the person contacting you is, strictly speaking, already a customer, you need to identify that person to build a relationship. Lead generation is just as important here.

Find Out Who Is Visiting Retail Outlets

Visitors to retail outlets are another potential source of leads. Many retail shoppers who buy from you may remain anonymous, so encourage shoppers to provide names and addresses by running competitions or making other special offers.

"Seize opportunity by the forelock and see where it leads you." (Armand Hammer)

Encourage Web Site Registration

Web site registration provides high levels of information. When customers visit your Web site, ask them to register their details. The registration form is completed online and submitted by e-mail. In return, you e-mail them regularly with details of products and services that are of interest to them. Incentives such as free reports or free software can encourage higher levels of registration.

Record Exhibition Visitors

Visitor registration should be an integral part of exhibition planning. Set up a process for capturing data on all stand visitors. Set up a database of exhibition contacts, and use it to plan and monitor a contact program after the exhibition.

Monitor the Business Press

Many business publications feature news about recent appointments or interviews with leading executives. This type of information can give you names of potentially valuable contacts. The appointments pages can also alert you to changes in personnel at one of your customer or prospect companies.

Use Telemarketing

Telemarketing can be used to generate new leads and qualify existing leads. The telemarketing team can call target companies and ask for the names of decision-makers for follow-up. The team can also call people who have made an initial inquiry, in order to qualify their interest and find out how good the prospects are. However, remember that some people may have placed their names on "don't call" lists and that contacting them by making unsolicited phone calls may lead to significant fines. Make sure you are contacting the right people from the outset.

Integrate Lead Generation with Other Marketing Activities

Lead generation programs can be improved by integrating the campaign with other marketing activities such as an exhibition, advertising campaign, or a call by a member of the sales force. With integrated campaigns, overall awareness levels among customers and prospects will be far higher. Your lead generation program will have an even greater chance of success.

Keep Refining Your Contact Lists

Many of the contact lists you have developed from internal or external sources may not match your requirements exactly. To improve coverage, or to make them more precise, you must make a continuous effort to refine them. These are some of the actions you can take to improve the coverage of your list:

- Make sure that new customer and prospect data are added to the list.
- Include coupons and other reply mechanisms with every form of communication, and add the responses to your lists.
- Encourage the sales force to provide up-to-date customer and prospect information.
- Maintain an active search program in appropriate Web sites, magazines, and newspapers to identify new prospects for your list.

Common Mistakes

Overlooking Lead Generation

Lead generation could be vital to your company's future. Without it, lost customers will not be replaced, and you may miss major opportunities in new or existing market sectors. Only a small proportion of leads become customers, so lead generation must be an ongoing process.

Paying Too Much for Your Leads

You can measure the cost of your lead generation program by dividing the cost of the advertising or marketing program by the number of leads. Media for lead generation should be assessed in the same way as media to meet other objectives.

No Integration with Other Marketing Programs

Lead generation programs do not work in isolation. Corporate advertising, for example, helps to raise awareness among the target audience, while direct mail and telemarketing can be used to back up lead generation advertising.

For More Information

Book:

Jobber, David, and Geoffrey Lancaster. *Selling and Sales Management*. 5th ed. Upper Saddle River, NJ: Financial Times Prentice Hall, 2000.

Web Site:

American Marketing Association:
www.MarketingPower.com

See also:

✔ **Converting Leads into Sales (pp. 700–01)**
✔ **Improving Direct Mail Response Rates (pp. 686–87)**
✔ **Integrating Advertising with Other Campaigns (pp. 654–55)**
✔ **Planning a Customer Event (pp. 690–91)**
✔ **Setting Advertising Objectives (pp. 664–65)**
✔ **Supporting Campaigns with Telemarketing (pp. 736–37)**

"Some people use research like a drunkard uses a lampost: for support, not illumination."

(David Ogilvy)

Converting Leads into Sales

Getting Started

Obtaining leads is only the beginning. Those leads must be converted into sales before they can benefit a business, so it is important to make sure that the leads are of the right kind in order to avoid wasted resources and to follow a systematic conversion process.

FAQs

How far can services such as telemarketing take over from the sales force?

These services can be used to handle many of the sales teams' routine functions: carrying out initial research, qualifying prospects, making appointments, and maintaining regular contact. They should not be used as a substitute for face-to-face selling where that is important to customer relationships. In addition, remember that some people may have placed their names on "don't call" lists and that contacting them by making unsolicited phone calls may lead to significant fines. Make sure you are contacting the right people from the outset.

What is the best way to measure lead conversion?

Measuring sales as a percentage of initial leads is too simplistic an approach; it is more effective to measure at each stage of the process. For example, only 50% of initial leads may turn out to be suitable prospects. If the leads have been well qualified, the sales team may be able to convert 20% of the final prospect list. Measuring results at each stage helps you focus the right level of resources and plan future lead generation programs.

Should we try to get as many leads as possible?

The quality of the leads is as important as the number. Following up a large number of unsuitable leads is a waste of resources, but getting as many good leads as possible is important to any company that wants to expand its business.

Making It Happen

Qualify Your Leads

Your lead generation program may have given you large numbers of leads, but not all of them will convert to sales. Some may be poor prospects, while others may simply be gathering information rather than planning a purchase. Good prospects have the following characteristics:

- the financial resources to purchase your product
- the authority to make a purchase decision
- a genuine need for your product or service
- the desire to learn more about your product
- plans to make a purchase in the near future

Telemarketing can be used to qualify the leads. Call the contact and ask for more details of their inquiry so that you can send information tailored to their needs. Just sending a brochure, with no accompanying letter and no understanding of the prospect's needs, is a waste of money. Qualifying questions can include:

- Is your company currently buying this product?
- What quantities do you buy, or how much do you spend on the service?
- When are you likely to make your next purchase?
- Are you the person who makes the purchasing decision? If not, who does?
- What information do you need on our product and company?

Choose a One-step or Two-step Program

In the case of some products and services, the lead generation and sales conversion programs can be combined. These are known as one-step programs, and are equivalent to direct selling operations. They are suitable for:

- inexpensive products
- information services such as newsletter or magazine subscriptions
- office supplies
- software
- low-value financial offers

In a two-step program, the prospect requests initial information. You send the information and then continue following up until the prospect is ready to buy. Two-step programs are suitable for:

- expensive offers
- complex technical products
- professional services
- high-value financial services

Plan the Conversion Program

Lead conversion can be a long-term continuous process, the duration of which depends on the complexity of the product and of the decision making process. The progress of the conversion process has been compared to a rail trip, with intermediate actions to move the prospect along the campaign track to a final decision. For a complex product, the process could be:

- identifying key decision makers;
- sending information to key decision makers;
- arranging meetings with decision makers;
- providing sample products for evaluation by the customer;
- bidding for a contract against competition;
- final negotiations;
- purchase.

You must decide how you will handle each stage of the process, who will be involved in the sales team, and how you will manage communications with the prospect.

Another example could be where the product and the purchasing process are simpler, but the prospect is reluctant to change suppliers. The conversion process could take a long time, so you must plan a program to maintain contact and move the prospect away from the existing supplier. Actions could include:

- personalized direct mail with product information
- regular updates on new developments in the company

"People do not buy much from a man who fails to command their respect." (William Wrigley)

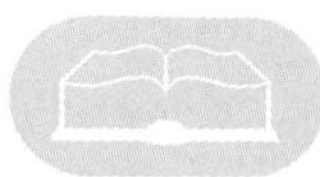

- targeted special offers to encourage the customer to try the product

Allocate Responsibility

Normally, the marketing department generates leads and the sales department follows up. It is important for the two departments to work together to integrate their activities and make sure that the company focuses on the kind of high-quality prospects it really needs. Sales departments frequently complain about the quantity and quality of leads. They want as many leads as possible so that the final number of new sales is high; however, they may also complain if too many of the leads are of poor quality and do not meet the right criteria. Collecting a large number of high-quality leads can be a difficult balancing act. Some sales teams prefer to do their own qualifying, while others prefer to leave that to others so that they can concentrate on face-to-face meetings with prospects.

Back the Sales Team with Telemarketing

Telemarketing can be used to enhance the performance and productivity of the sales force. The telemarketing team can be responsible for following up sales leads, qualifying prospects, setting up appointments, and maintaining contact with longer-term prospects. This frees the sales force for increasing the number of face-to-face meetings and for concentrating on the most likely prospects. The integration of telemarketing with the sales force can play an important part in reducing overall sales costs. The cost of keeping a sales team on the road continues to soar, and it may not always represent the most cost-effective way of reaching the right people.

Maintain a Contact Diary

A contact diary can help you plan the conversion process and make sure that the sales team does not miss any important contact opportunities. It also makes sure that the sales backup team integrates its follow-up activities with the field sales force. Computer software is available which allows sales teams to operate a sales diary and record details of meetings and other follow-up activities. The same software can be used by the management team to monitor progress and make sure that no important contacts are overlooked.

Track Progress

It is essential to track progress at each stage of the conversion process. If the prospect is important, you may wish to allocate additional resources to win the business. If a prospect is of only minor importance but is taking time and resources, you may want to refocus the efforts of the sales force. The progress from initial lead to customer goes through a number of stages:

- raw lead: an initial inquiry from any source
- suspect: an inquiry that has been qualified and has the potential to become a paying customer
- prospect: a lead that has been qualified in more detail
- inactive lead: a prospect who will not buy now but has future potential
- dead lead: a prospect that has little potential to become a customer
- customer

Choose the Right Contact Frequency

A single mailing, telephone call, or direct response advertisement may produce results, but a series of quality contacts will have greater impact and make sure you meet your response targets. Multiple direct marketing activities raise levels of awareness with each contact, follow up contacts who have not responded, and move individual respondents further along the decision making process.

Use Personalized Contact

Personalized one-to-one mailings are an ideal form of communication for companies with detailed information on their prospects. The letter reflects the individual prospect's main interests and concerns, and the offer can be tailored to the prospect's needs. Subsequent mailings can build or develop an individual relationship with the prospect.

Common Mistakes

Focusing on the Wrong Prospects

Sales teams have a natural tendency to deal with friendly prospects and avoid the difficult ones. From a business perspective, however, they may be dealing with the wrong people. The qualifying process should be used to identify the most important prospects in order to improve the targeting of the sales force.

Poor Management

Lead conversion can be a long, complicated process, so it is essential to monitor progress and manage the program carefully. Lead conversion can use a lot of sales force and telemarketing resources, and careful planning can make sure that it is carried out effectively.

Putting All the Burden on the Sales Force

In some organizations, the sales force is given total responsibility for generating leads, qualifying them, and converting them into sales. This may not represent the best use of sales force resources. Telemarketing can be used to supplement the sales force and take over routine tasks.

For More Information

Book:

Jobber, David, and Geoffrey Lancaster. *Selling and Sales Management*. 5th ed. Upper Saddle River, NJ: Financial Times Prentice Hall, 2000.

Web Site:

American Marketing Association:
www.MarketingPower.com

See also:

✓ **Generating More Leads (pp. 698–99)**
✓ **Handling Customer Inquiries (pp. 674–75)**
✓ **Supporting Campaigns with Telemarketing (pp. 736–37)**

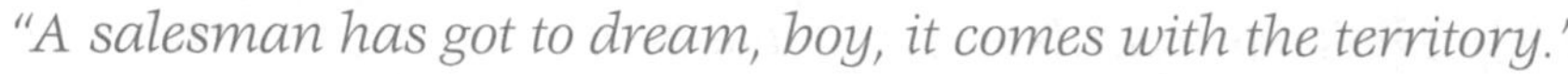

"A salesman has got to dream, boy, it comes with the territory."

(Arthur Miller)

  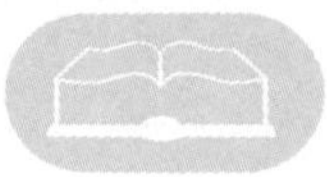    

Carrying Out Customer Research

Getting Started

Telephone interviews are a quick and cost-effective way to obtain opinions from a sample of customers. Telephone research can be used to assess customer reaction to a change in the product or service, or to measure awareness of a company or product. It can be difficult to reassure people that you are carrying out legitimate research.

Mail surveys are ideal for customer satisfaction surveys or detailed surveys that take time to complete. However, it can be difficult to obtain a worthwhile rate of response, and the researcher has no control over the process. Incentives may be needed to improve response and there is a risk of incomplete responses.

Group discussions or focus groups are ideal for identifying issues of concern to customers and assessing customer reactions to potential changes. This type of research is open-ended and can highlight important customer issues that the researcher may not be aware of. However, group discussions are not representative and can be influenced by a dominant member of the group.

The personal interview is ideal for obtaining detailed information on attitudes to products and services or getting feedback from specific individuals. Personal interviews allow in-depth discussion of complex topics and give you greater control over the response.

An omnibus survey is a cost-effective method of researching several topics at the same time. The same survey is used to carry out regular research on a number of different products by telephone or personal interview. You should check that the other topics in the survey are compatible with your own products.

FAQs

Can we carry out market research ourselves, or should we use a consultancy?

Market research is a professional discipline and you will get more meaningful results by using a consultancy. They are trained to detect possible errors in research results, and their independence is reassuring to people who are being interviewed.

You can carry out a limited amount of research yourself, developing and mailing questionnaires or carrying out limited telephone interviews. However, there is a risk that people may feel that your research is a thinly disguised sales pitch.

How reliable are the results from focus groups?

The results are as reliable as the quality of the participants and the people who run the sessions. It is easy for individual participants to dominate a group and influence the course of discussions. If the person running the discussion asks the wrong questions, the resulting discussion may prove worthless. Make sure those in charge are well briefed.

We have limited resources for research. Should we participate in an omnibus survey so that we can make the best use of our budget?

An omnibus survey is an ideal way to share expensive research resources and reach a large audience. However, you must be sure that the audience is relevant to your company's business. Ask for a profile of the research audience and check the names of other organizations which have used the survey. If there is a reasonable match to your own business, it could be a cost-effective solution.

Making It Happen

Interview Customers by Telephone

Telephone interviews are a quick and cost-effective way to obtain opinions from a sample of customers. They can be used to assess customer reaction to a change in the product or service, or to measure awareness of a company or product.

Speed Up Research

The main benefit of telephone research is speed. A large number of interviews can be conducted in a short space of time, and data can be gathered and processed quickly. Telephone interviews also cost considerably less than personal interviews. A customer may be too busy for a personal interview, but willing to spend time on the phone.

Don't Confuse Telephone Research with Selling

Telephone interviews have limited scope because people may not be prepared to spend a long period of time on the telephone. It can also be difficult to get across complex concepts by telephone.

Follow industry guidelines:

- define the target audience;
- draft a questionnaire and carry out pilot interviews;
- make the calls at times likely to be convenient for the target audience;
- identify the purpose of the call;
- use faxes, if necessary, to send more detailed information for discussion.

Use Mail Surveys

Mail surveys are a quick and relatively inexpensive method of obtaining information. They are ideal for customer satisfaction surveys or detailed surveys that take time to complete. However, it can be difficult to obtain a reasonable rate of response, and the researcher has no control over the process.

Assess the Value of Mail Surveys

Mail surveys are inexpensive. The costs include outward and return postage and stationery. They are precise and can be targeted at specific customers or prospects. They are also voluntary, because there is no pressure on the

"Research! A mere excuse for idleness; it has never achieved, and will never achieve any results of the slightest value."

(Benjamin Jowett)

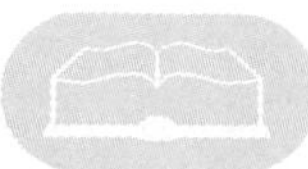

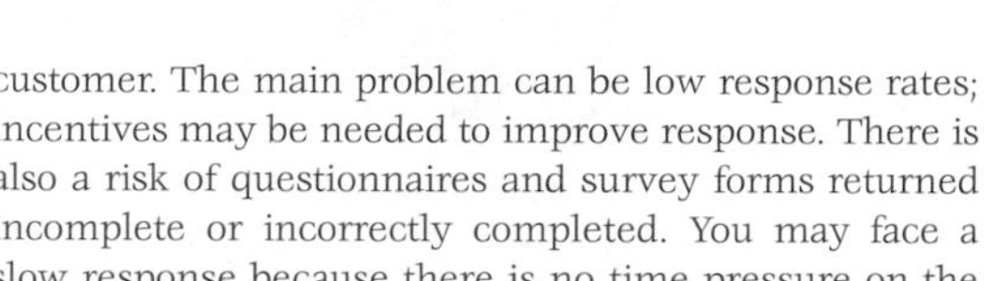

customer. The main problem can be low response rates; incentives may be needed to improve response. There is also a risk of questionnaires and survey forms returned incomplete or incorrectly completed. You may face a slow response because there is no time pressure on the customer. You also have little control over the research.

Improve the Response from Mail Surveys

Response rates can be influenced by many different factors; 5–10% would be normal and 15% or more would be extremely good. To improve response:

- offer an incentive for returned questionnaires;
- keep the questionnaire simple;
- reassure the customer that information will be kept confidential;
- enclose a stamped addressed or business reply envelope.

Hold a Group Discussion

In group discussions, or focus groups, customers and prospects are invited to discuss a particular topic, usually under the guidance of a researcher. They are ideal for identifying issues which concern customers, assessing customer reactions to potential changes, or identifying any problems customers are experiencing.

There is no limit placed on what the group can discuss, and this format can highlight important customer issues that the researcher may not be aware of. Many customers welcome the opportunity to discuss products and services with their colleagues and have an opportunity to contribute to change. The disadvantages are that group discussions are not representative, and they can be biased or influenced by a dominant member of the group. It is also difficult to quantify results.

Set up a group discussion:

- invite eight to ten customers;
- thank customers for participating and put them at their ease;
- record the discussion if possible, using a tape recorder;
- advise people that their comments are being recorded and that all material will be treated in confidence;
- to reduce the risk of bias, use more than one group and use an independent researcher to run the discussion.

Conduct Personal Interviews

In a personal interview, a customer and an interviewer work through a series of predetermined questions. The personal interview is ideal for obtaining detailed information on attitudes to products and services, or getting feedback from specific individuals. The interview can take place in a customer's home or office, or in a public place. It can be prearranged by telephone, mail, or personal contact.

Personal interviews allow in-depth discussion of complex topics and give you more control over the response. They offer greater accuracy, and results are easy to analyze. Meeting people in a working environment can give an indication of their real purchasing intentions. The main disadvantage is the time and cost of recruiting interviewers and conducting interviews and the risk of interviewer bias.

Use an Omnibus Survey

An omnibus survey is a cost-effective method of researching several topics at the same time. The same survey is used to carry out regular research on different products by telephone or personal interview. They are appropriate for measuring attitudes and behavior toward different types of products and services or monitoring changes in attitude among groups of consumers.

Generally, omnibus surveys are more appropriate for mass-market products. The use of shared resources makes them extremely cost-effective. They provide representative results by making it possible for large numbers of interviews to take place. They also allow you to make regular comparisons over time.

Before participating in the survey, you should check that the other topics in the survey are compatible with your own products and that the overall length of the survey is not excessive. It may reduce costs, but the audience may not give sufficient attention to all topics.

Common Mistakes

Choosing the Wrong Research Technique

Each research technique has different applications, benefits, and disadvantages. A market research consultancy can provide advice on an appropriate approach.

Relying on Limited Results

For reasons of cost or time, some research programs may provide limited results. It is important to put the research findings in context and take account of the limited findings when you are making important decisions. Market research consultancies use proven techniques to evaluate results and should advise you to use their findings with caution.

Using Research to Sell

Too many companies contact customers and prospects claiming to be carrying out market research. During the course of the research, the company then attempts to sell a product or service on the basis that the respondent has expressed an interest. This is a betrayal of trust and can prove damaging to valid research.

For More Information

Book:

Smith, D. V. L., and J. H. Fletcher. *Inside Information: Making Sense of Marketing Data*. New York: John Wiley, 2001.

Web Site:

Marketing Research Association: **www.mra-net.org**

See also:

☆ **Data Mining (pp. 152–53)**
✔ **Building One-to-one Relationships (pp. 666–67)**
Market Research & Competitor Intelligence (pp. 2042–44)

"The way to do research is to attack the facts at the point of greatest astonishment." (Celia Green)

Getting Competitor Intelligence

Getting Started

Competitor information helps you protect and grow your business. You need to build a detailed profile of your competitors, their strengths, weaknesses, and relationships with customers. To help you do this, compare the performance of your organization with that of your main competitors by measuring factors that are important to quality of service and use the comparison as the basis for a program of performance improvement.

The sales force can obtain competitor information from many different sources. Publications, the press, and the Internet have information readily available that can help you compile intelligence on competitors, and corporate brochures and annual reports are also excellent sources of published information. Maintain a file of press cuttings on your competitors' activities, using their trade publications as a source.

Published industry surveys can provide a useful insight into purchasing patterns and competitors' Web sites can provide valuable information on their resources, plans, and capabilities.

FAQs

Why is competitor intelligence so important?

Competitive activity can have a significant impact on your own plans. If you are about to run a marketing campaign or new product launch, competitive activity could limit its effectiveness–so you need to know about it. You may also identify growing threats to important accounts. Unless you monitor activity and take appropriate action, your business faces risk.

Should competitor research be carried out internally or by an independent research company?

You can carry out the research internally, provided you have the resources. Much of the source material is in the public domain, so you should be able to obtain it yourself. However, if you wish to research customer attitudes, you may need to use an independent research organization. Customers may not be open with your own representatives.

How reliable is published competitor information?

You have to make assumptions about the accuracy and quality of any published information that is used for research. Much of the material will be published to provide information for customers, so it is unlikely to be misleading.

Making It Happen

Identify the Competitive Threat

Competitor information helps you to identify how you can protect your most important business and, more positively, how you can strengthen your position with customers in situations in which your competitors are currently holding a larger share of the business than you. These are the main questions you should be asking:

- How many competitors do you have?
- Who are your major competitors?
- Are they direct or indirect competitors?
- Where are your main competitors located?
- How do they compare in size?
- How much of your business do they threaten?
- Which of your competitors has the strongest growth prospects?
- Which customers might switch to competitors?
- How strong are competitors' relationships with key decision-makers?
- How have levels of business changed over the past three years?
- Are there any significant developments that have affected these changes?
- How long have competitors been dealing with key customers?
- How do your products compare with competitive offerings?
- What are your competitors' main strengths?
- How do prices compare?
- What are their standards of customer service?
- Have they invested in links with customers that would make it difficult for other suppliers to make inroads?
- Have you got the skills and resources to overcome the competitive threat?
- Are any competitors making inroads into businesses in which you are currently the dominant supplier?
- What are customers' attitudes toward your competitors?
- How do these compare with attitudes toward your own organization?
- Who are your competitors' main customers?
- Which of your competitors' customers do you want to win?

Compare Key Competitive Factors

Listed below are a number of factors that are important to quality service. You can score these factors to see how your organization and your main competitors compare. The results should be used as the basis for a program of performance improvement:

- degree of commitment to quality service
- level of employee understanding and awareness of customer service
- level of customer focus within the organization
- existence of measurable service standards
- existence of suitable customer feedback mechanisms
- existence of suitable complaints management procedures
- degree of customer retention
- customer focus of product development processes
- commitment to quality service delivery
- scope of presales activity
- simplicity of inquiry and ordering
- quality of product/service delivery

"I don't meet competition. I crush it." (Charles Revson)

- efficiency of purchase administration
- effectiveness of sales follow-up
- quality of after-sales support

Use the Sales Force

The sales force can obtain competitor information from many different sources. By talking to customers, they can find out about competitors' direct sales calls, marketing campaigns, special offers, and new developments. They also can obtain similar information from retailers or distributors.

Analyze Published Information

Information is readily available from publications, the press, and the Internet that can help you compile intelligence on different aspects of competitors' business, including:

- main markets
- customers
- resources and financial performance
- product range
- new products
- plans for growth

Obtain Competitor Literature

Corporate brochures and annual reports are the best sources of published information. You can obtain copies from exhibitions and customers or as downloads from competitors' Web sites.

Monitor the Press

Maintain a file of press cuttings on your competitors' activities, using their trade publications as a source. Or you can use a press cuttings agency to gather material for you.

Analyze Industry Reports

Published industry surveys can provide a useful insight into purchasing patterns in different marketing sectors. You can obtain information on competitors, market share, and industry trends.

Check the Internet

Competitor Web sites can provide valuable information on their resources, plans, and capabilities. As well as checking the company information and product pages, you should read any customer case studies on the site and monitor the news section to find out about new developments. Trade publications are increasingly available in electronic editions, making it easier for you to monitor the press.

Visit Exhibitions

Competitors' exhibition stands can be valuable sources of information. Most organizations only participate in exhibitions that are important to their current or future business plans.

Monitor Competitors' Marketing Activities

Analyzing competitors' marketing strategies will help you to respond to their activities. By monitoring their advertising, promotions, exhibition presence, press activities, and Internet information, you can assess possible strategies. These are some of the possible scenarios:

- heavy advertising expenditure could indicate a competitor trying to win greater share;
- price promotions may indicate that your competitors want to be perceived as value-for-money suppliers;
- press announcements about new production facilities could indicate that your competitors are trying to increase their business significantly;
- announcements about new branch or dealership openings could mean that competitors are expanding into new territories.

Marketing publications can be useful sources of information on competitor marketing activity.

Appoint a Research Company

If you do not have the internal resources to monitor competitive activity, you can use an independent research company to carry out all the tasks outlined above. You also can ask them to explore customer attitudes to competitors. Customers may be more willing to provide this information to an independent organization.

Common Mistakes

Overlooking the Obvious Sources

Competitor intelligence is freely available from the Internet, the press, and other published sources. Information from these sources can provide a valuable starting point for developing detailed competitor profiles.

Ignoring Competitor Information

Competitor information is only valuable if you use it to refine your own strategies or take defensive action to protect your business. Simply gathering information without analysis or action is wasteful.

Acting on Incomplete Information

Be cautious about acting on competitor intelligence. Published sources can only provide a partial picture, and more strategic information is likely to be confidential. This means that you may make incorrect assumptions in planning your response to competitor action.

Using Out-of-date Information

Records should be carefully checked and maintained. Using poor quality data can ruin the best campaigns.

For More Information

Book:

Smith, D. V. L., and J. H. Fletcher. *Inside Information: Making Sense of Marketing Data*. New York: John Wiley, 2001.

Web Site:

Marketresearch.com: **www.marketresearch.com**

See also:

☆ **Benchmarking (pp. 295–96)**

Involving Customers in Product Development

Getting Started

Involving customers in product development can result in more targeted products with a greater chance of success, while at the same time strengthening relationships and creating mutual benefits.

FAQs

Is there a risk in letting customers evaluate new products before launch?

There are two risks. First, the customer may be extremely disappointed with the product if quality is poor. Second, there is a risk that competitors could find out about your plans indirectly. The quality issue is one that you should deal with: if a product is not right, it should not be given to customers in any form—it is not enough simply to promise future improvements. The security risk of a leak to competitors can be minimized through disclosure and confidentiality agreements, although these provide no real guarantee. However, the advantages of involving customers outweigh the risks, so evaluation is worthwhile.

How practical is it for customers and suppliers to collaborate on product development?

There are different levels of collaboration. Some may involve regular meetings to provide input and review progress. These meetings can be held on site or remotely, using videoconference links. In some cases, customer staff may work alongside the supplier team for all or part of the project. Secondment like this can provide other benefits for the customer by improving the technical knowledge of their staff.

Does preannouncement put new product launches at risk?

Some companies, particularly in the IT sector, have put themselves under unnecessary pressure by trying to meet a series of preannounced release dates. The schedule may not allow proper time for development, resulting in failure to meet the date, or the release of a product that is not ready. Both are potentially damaging.

Making It Happen

Ask Customers Before You Launch Your Product

If you are planning a new product or redeveloping an existing one, ask your customers for their views on the existing product and what they would like to see in a new one. By explaining your plans and involving customers in product development, you can strengthen relationships and provide a service that is mutually beneficial. Questions could include:

- How can we improve the current product?
- What problems need to be overcome?
- What new features would customers welcome?
- Do the plans represent an improvement?
- Would customers make greater use of a product that included the features they have highlighted?

Set Up a User Group

You can encourage feedback and build a sense of community by setting up a user group. The user group would operate as a forum for discussing issues of mutual concern to customers such as quality, performance, standards, future developments, and customer concerns. The group would include representatives from your own company and from a cross-section of your customers. Comments from the user group provide valuable feedback on current performance and help to identify needs that can be met through new product development.

Ask Customers to Evaluate New Products

Customer evaluation, or beta testing, is well established in the software industry. Customers test new products or upgraded versions before they are released to the market. They identify any problems in using the software, thus providing valuable feedback on product performance.

Issue New Product Announcements

Another valuable practice from the IT industry is to preannounce new products. For example, a company will set a number of release dates during the coming year when it will release new versions of products. The company outlines the new products and gives customers the opportunity to provide input to the development process. The major benefit for customers is that they can align their own business development plans to the release dates.

Work in Partnership with Customers

Product development can be a joint initiative where you work closely with specific customers to develop products that meet their specific needs. This approach is a valuable one where:

- your customers have developed partnership sourcing to take advantage of your technology;
- your customers have technology and technical skills that complement your own, and a joint project can produce more effective results; or
- you want to strengthen relationships with key customers by working in partnership on joint development projects.

Understand Your Customers' Markets

The new products you develop could enable your customers to improve their competitive performance, so it is important to understand their markets. Tell customers about your product plans and ask them for input to your development process. By building a de-

"If you pretest your product with consumers and pretest your advertising, you will do well in the marketplace."

(David Ogilvy)

tailed picture of their markets, you can align your own plans with them, and develop products that are tailored to their needs.

- What are their main markets?
- What is their position in the marketplace?
- Who are their main competitors?
- How are their products regarded in the marketplace?
- What are the key success factors in the market?
- What are the long-term product trends?
- What new technical developments will be needed to succeed?
- Could innovation by you help your customers to succeed?
- Are your customers considering entry into new markets?
- Do you have product development plans that are relevant to the new market?

Understand Customer Strategies

It is equally important to understand your customers' business strategies: their corporate direction and key objectives, and how they aim to succeed. By aligning your product development objectives with theirs, and showing how your products or services can help them to achieve their strategic business objectives, you can ensure that your new products will be successful.

There are two possible approaches to customer-focused product development. Where your customers want to become market leaders through innovation, your new product programs can help them develop the right level of innovation without investment in their own skills. Where they want to succeed through competitive pricing, you can help them reduce overall costs by developing cost-effective products.

Assess the Value of Your Products and Services

Products that help your customers to meet their strategic business objectives can increase the chances of new product success. The more your customers depend on your new product, the more likely you are to succeed.

For example, if your customer must develop new products quickly in order to retain and protect market share, your own new products can be critical to their product development program.

Analyze Your Customers' Technical Requirements

In assessing new product development opportunities, you should analyze how your products can help your customers. They can use your skills in a number of ways:

- improving the performance of their own products and services by using your design and development skills. They may gain privileged access to your technical skills to improve their own competitive performance;
- using your technical expertise to enhance the skills of their own technical staff, enabling them to make a more effective contribution to their own product development process;
- using your technical resources to handle product development on a subcontract basis. This provides your partners with access to specialist resources or to additional research and development capacity to improve the performance of their product development programs;
- using your technical expertise to develop new products that they could not achieve themselves. This provides your customers with new technology, and allows them to diversify in line with your specialist skills;
- using your design skills to improve through life costs (the total cost of owning and using a product, including purchase price, maintenance, and any other related costs). By carrying out value engineering studies on your customers' products, you may be able to reduce overall costs and improve reliability by designing components that are easier to assemble and maintain.

Common Mistakes

Insufficient Customer Involvement

Product development should be focused on customer needs. Although most companies carry out research before development, the research may not provide the detailed input that is essential. Product development may also be driven by technology, with no clear market focus. The more your customer depends on your product, the more likely it is to succeed, so involving customers can pay real dividends.

Ignoring User Groups

There are many examples of companies who have set up user groups in response to a crisis and then failed to use them. This can be frustrating for customers and wasteful for the companies. User groups provide a valuable perspective on products and service, and their feedback can provide real benefits for the product development process.

Failing to Understand Customer Strategies

Where the supplier/customer relationship is that of a partnership, products are developed and customized to help customers meet their business objectives. It is essential, therefore, to understand customers' markets and business strategies so that your product plans can be integrated with theirs.

For More Information

Book:

Morse, Stephen. *Successful Product Management*. 2nd ed. Dover, NH: Kogan Page, 1998.

Web Site:

American Marketing Association:
www.MarketingPower.com

See also:

☆ **Integrating Real and Virtual Strategies (pp. 143–44)**
☆ **Managing New Product Portfolios (pp. 275–76)**
☆ **Power Struggling and Power Sharing (pp. 95–96)**
✓ **Introducing a New Product to Market (pp. 720–21)**
New Product Development (pp. 2054–56)

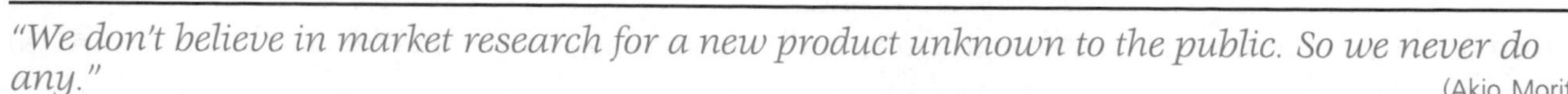

"We don't believe in market research for a new product unknown to the public. So we never do any."

(Akio Morita)

  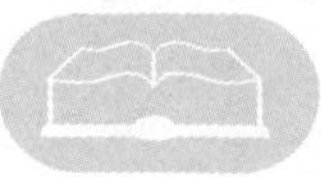    

Making Better Use of Customer Data

Getting Started

To get full benefit from customer data, analyze it, and make it available to the right people. Review data, and focus on questions important to your business. Where possible, create a data analysis team to be responsible for identifying the data required, collecting it, analyzing it, and distributing it.

FAQs

How do I carry out regular data analysis, when I don't have internal resources or the budget to use a research company?

Business intelligence software can speed up and simplify the process of analysis. You could also recruit a research and analysis team from different departments. This would have the added benefit of making sure that data was available and relevant to the company as a whole.

Can I carry out customer data analysis without sophisticated software?

You can use manual techniques to analyze and distribute customer information. Software speeds up and enhances the process. A good information network insures that everyone has access to the same, up-to-date, customer information.

Should I make the same information available throughout the company?

Too much data can overwhelm people. Good software programs include selective reporting processes, allowing you to select the right data for different audiences and to customize reports. In this way, people get the level of information that they need.

Should I put confidential customer data on an intranet or other internal network?

Provided the information is covered by security procedures, it is safe to do this. You could, for example, restrict access to a secure area of the network by issuing passwords to authorized users.

Making It Happen

Put Data in the Right Hands

Business and market data can provide a wealth of information about customers and about purchasing patterns. To get full benefit from the data, you need to analyze it and make it readily available to the people who need it.

Identify Data Requirements

Create a network of other people in the company who can tell you what questions need to be answered and quantified. Make these people responsible for reviewing data, and focus on the questions that are important to different groups within the company.

Create a Data Analysis Team

As well as creating a network of reviewers, you need to create a data analysis team, which is responsible for determining what data to collect and analyze. They should understand what metrics are important to the organization and how these are created and applied. They should also feed information to the rest of the organization.

Make Data Accessible

Make sure that the reports can be exported into tools such as spreadsheets, graphics, and slides, and decide how frequently you need to provide analysis. To save time, you may be able to automate the more frequent processes and keep the level of analysis simple. Most people really just want the key points. Your users can drill down through the data to obtain more detailed information.

Provide Self-service Reports

Create a secure area on an intranet for employees to access reports and look up the latest statistics. Store the reports in a format that can be easily imported to standard spreadsheets such as Excel.

Provide Flexible Archiving

Let other members of the company have access to your reports and data, and create a discussion group for reviewing the results. Use the feedback to help refine the analysis process and metrics used in analyzing the data.

Keep Analyzing Data

The data becomes more valuable as you continue analyzing it. As your analysis base broadens, you'll be able to track not only how profitable your company has become but also how profitable it can be in the future through best practice in data management.

Track Customer Satisfaction

Effective business intelligence allows you to identify early indicators of customer dissatisfaction and take action to retain customers for the long term. Customer retention depends on factors that cannot be tracked by mainstream indicators of customer dissatisfaction, such as revenue and growth.

Identify Warning Signs

Business intelligence can identify the early warning signs of customer dissatisfaction, such as late shipments, and the reasons behind complaints, returns, and claims. With this information, customer service teams can increase retention rates for high-profit customers, spot early indicators of customer dissatisfaction, and maximize the profitability of each service relationship.

Measure Delivery

Measuring on-time delivery lets customer service teams focus on one of the primary issues behind customer dissatisfaction–late shipments. Analysis should show performance by product line, by geographical area, or by individual customer. Using business intelligence

"I find more and more executives less and less well informed about the outside world." (Peter F. Drucker)

software, customer service teams can easily identify delivery issues before they become a problem.

Analyze Complaints, Returns, and Claims

Typically, most individual returns, claims, or complaints can be assigned to a relatively small number of reasons. Establishing categories of problem, rather than analyzing problems case by case, lets customer service teams quickly trace complaints to their source and identify trends. Problems related to a specific product, plant, or production run can be addressed before customer relationships are jeopardized. Analyzing the reasons behind customer complaints makes it easy for customer service teams to be more responsive.

Measure Cost of Service Relationships

Understanding the cost of service relationships lets companies adjust pricing, based on the information that flows through the company. Returns, orders changes, claims, and so on all have an impact on the bottom line. When the true cost of a service relationship is known, pricing can be adjusted to increase profitability.

Measure All Customer-facing Activities

The same measurements can be applied to marketing, customer service, or sales activities. The metrics should also be applicable to all customer channels and distribution mediums. This allows you to monitor the effectiveness of customer marketing or communication programs: for example, comparing the cost per lead on the Web versus direct mail, or cross-selling over the Web compared with the call center.

Develop High-profitability Strategies for Marketing

Business intelligence tools can be the key to developing highly profitable marketing strategies. Special software allows you to understand and analyze issues such as the effectiveness of marketing campaigns, or profit levels by customer. The software enables marketing teams to explore any combination of data—for example, revenues by customer, product, or region—making it easy to spot trends. It helps uncover significant, but often hidden, factors that have an impact on market share, such as price, product design, or packaging. It also provides access to transaction-level data, so that marketing teams can easily explore detailed information to find out what lies behind trends.

Analyze Strategic Marketing Activities

Strategic marketing analysis highlights product attributes and other information that is typically left out of marketing plans. For example, marketing teams can analyze revenue by products, distribution channel, materials, and other factors. This makes it easy to see which products are driving sales and profitability in each market and to focus strategies accordingly. Marketing can identify the factors behind profitability, from the product attribute level up.

Analyze Tactical Marketing Programs

Tactical marketing analysis lets marketing teams evaluate the effectiveness of marketing campaigns. They can explore the impact of marketing messages in different parts of the country by industry type, or by the buyers they are targeting. And, by comparing response profiles against the profile of high-profit customers, they can adjust messaging and media mixes for maximum impact.

Analyze Customer Portfolios

The customer portfolio analysis categorizes customers by profitability and charts their lifetime value to date. Marketing managers can analyze customers by profitability tier, view trends in the profitability mix, and develop strategies to address unprofitable customers.

Common Mistakes

Using Raw Data

Data is only valuable when it is both analyzed and used to address a specific question. Software tools allow you to carry out analysis quickly and easily to provide relevant data for important questions.

Measuring the Wrong Activities

It may be easy to collect data on a specific activity, but if the activity is unimportant the effort is wasted. By getting agreement from customer-facing groups throughout the company, you can identify important data.

Distributing Data in the Wrong Form

Make sure data is in a form that is useful to the recipient. People don't have time to go through masses of unsifted data to find the information they need.

Limited Analysis

The more you analyze data, the more valuable it becomes. You can uncover different levels of detail, spot trends, or identify recurring problems. You also should insure that the information is up to date, by continuing to collect data.

For More Information

Book:

Hatch, Denison. *Method Marketing: How to Make a Fortune by Getting Inside the Heads of Your Customers.* Chicago: Bonus Books, 1999.

Web Site:

Marketing Research Association: **www.mra-net.org**

See also:

- ☆ **Data Mining (pp. 152–53)**
- ☆ **Managing 1:1 Marketing (pp. 55–56)**
- ✔ **Building One-to-one Relationships (pp. 666–67)**
- ✔ **Carrying Out Customer Research (pp. 702–03)**
- ✔ **Increasing Lifetime Customer Value (pp. 676–77)**
- **Market Research & Competitor Intelligence (pp. 2042–44)**

"The importance of collecting data. . .cannot be too strongly pressed."

(Charles Babbage)

PROFILING DECISION MAKERS

GETTING STARTED

In business purchasing, more than one person influences the choice of supplier. A decision making team could include a wide range of key personnel, and the influence of team members varies at different stages during the purchasing process. It is important to identify the members of the team and communicate with each at the appropriate stage.

FAQS

HOW CAN I IDENTIFY A PURCHASING TEAM WHEN MY SALES REPRESENTATIVES ONLY EVER MEET THE PURCHASING MANAGER?

You need to find out who within your customer's company is interested in your products. Telephone research, direct mail, or advertising with a response mechanism can help to identify other team members. Be careful about direct approaches—purchasing managers may guard their status and resent approaches to other team members that appear to be undermining their position.

MY ORGANIZATION SELLS LOW-VALUE COMMODITY COMPONENTS. DO I NEED TO IDENTIFY A COMPLETE DECISION MAKING TEAM?

On the surface, your task should be simple. Just deal with the person who orders the products. However, there may be bigger opportunities. The technical manager may not be happy with the performance of commodity products. The research team or the marketing department may be planning new products, which could change the product specification. You need to monitor changing customer requirements.

MY ORGANIZATION NEEDS TO TALK TO SENIOR DIRECTORS ABOUT THE STRATEGIC IMPORTANCE OF OUR PRODUCTS. HOW CAN WE DO THIS WHEN OUR SALES TEAM NEVER GETS THE OPPORTUNITY TO MEET DIRECTORS?

It is unlikely that directors would have time during the normal working day to meet sales representatives or regard a sales meeting as high on their list of priorities. You could arrange a seminar or executive briefing session that would appeal to directors. That would insure you meet the right people and give you the opportunity to find out more about their needs.

MAKING IT HAPPEN

IDENTIFY THE DECISION MAKERS

In business purchasing, more than one person influences the choice of supplier. Individuals make different contributions to the decision making process and they have different information requirements. Many companies have adopted team purchasing structures to deal with high-value purchases and it is important that you communicate effectively with every member of the team.

Depending on the value and complexity of the purchase, a decision making team could include:

- senior executives
- purchasing professionals
- technical employees
- manufacturing managers
- service providers
- marketing employees
- departmental managers

ASSESS THE IMPORTANCE OF THE PURCHASE

As a rough guideline, you are likely to be dealing with a powerful purchasing organization if any of the following conditions apply:

- Your product is a vital component, or strategically important to your customers.
- Your product is technically complex.
- Your product is of high value.

If your product is of relatively low value, purchasing decisions are more likely to revolve around price and delivery and it is unlikely that a team would be involved.

The influence of team members varies at different stages during the purchasing process:

- Purchasing employees and departmental managers may have considerable early influence when a specification is being drawn up.
- When proposals are being evaluated, technical employees may be more influential.
- Senior executives are unlikely to be interested in detail, but they need an overview of the overall business benefits of the product or service.

SENIOR EXECUTIVES

Senior executives need an overview of the business benefits of a product or service and seek reassurance that your organization is capable of supplying their long-term needs—any risk could be detrimental to their own business. Many suppliers try to move discussion of their products and services to board level to demonstrate that they are of strategic importance. This can be a useful exercise in developing business, because it can build a level of dependency that is important to account control.

PURCHASING PROFESSIONALS

Purchasing professionals are usually the key figures in a purchasing team. While they may not take sole responsibility for decision making, they are likely to be the team leaders and will remain your main point of contact.

Many companies operate a preferred supplier program and, to be recognized, you may have to meet a detailed list of criteria. The purchasing department is instrumental in managing the list of approved suppliers. Many of the preferred supplier programs include rating schemes to measure suppliers' performance; these are part of a process of developing effective relationships, so that purchasing professionals can provide an even better service to their internal customers.

FINANCE EXECUTIVES

Finance executives have ultimate control over purchasing budgets and they're likely to be involved if purchases

are complex or entail major capital expenditure. They seek reassurance that they are getting value for money and that their purchase represents the best return on investment. They may consider alternative methods of financing, and you may be able to improve your competitive position by offering flexible schemes such as leasing or deferred payments.

Technical Employees

Technical employees are a vital part of the purchasing team. They are responsible for improving the performance of the company products in order to develop a competitive edge. You therefore need to be closely involved with the technical team at a number of stages. When they are developing new products, you should be involved at the planning stages so you can influence the design. When they are enhancing existing products, you should be developing proposals to improve product performance. If they are moving into new markets, you can support them by handling contract development services or by training their employees. You can provide them with a range of specialist technical services that enable them to provide a better service to their internal customers.

Manufacturing Managers

If you are introducing an innovative product, or you have identified an opportunity to improve your customers' manufacturing operations or reduce costs, you need to influence manufacturing specialists.

Service Providers

If you provide professional services rather than products, make sure that you are dealing with a service provider. Service providers are responsible for areas such as maintenance, training, administration, logistics, and computer and other services that enable business processes to operate efficiently. By working with them, you can improve relationships and increase customers' dependency on your organization.

Marketing Employees

Marketing specialists insure that a product or service adds value and helps the company to develop a stronger competitive position. They will play an important part in decision making if your customers are seeking to improve their market position or are entering new markets where you have a specific expertise.

Departmental Managers

Departmental managers are often the users of your products or services. They need to be reassured that they will benefit from dealing with a particular supplier. They play an important role in specifying the product and evaluating the performance of existing suppliers.

Research Decision Makers

Although it is simple to list potential decision makers, it is more complicated to identify who is actually involved in the process. Many decision makers may not have a direct role in a project team or may be involved in only part of the purchasing process, so you need to look carefully at your research processes.

Your sales team in regular contact with the customer should be best placed to identify the key decision makers. There are a number of other techniques for identifying other influencers:

- independent research into how companies buy different types of product or service; the survey may be limited to a specific group of customers, or carried out across a whole industry;
- published industry surveys on buying patterns; these provide broad guidelines to the key decision makers but need to be qualified by specific account research;
- direct response advertising, in which responses are analyzed to identify buying and decision making patterns;
- joint projects, in which members of the customer team work with members of your team; the relationships and approval procedures that emerge provide useful clues about who are the hidden decision makers.

Research like this should be carried out continuously because purchasing is a dynamic activity. Members of the decision making team may change their jobs and, as the process progresses through different stages, individual contributions change.

Common Mistakes

Concentrating on the Wrong People

Don't focus your sales team on the wrong decision makers. Companies rarely make it clear who influences the purchasing decisions. Meetings with the purchasing manager could be wasted if someone else draws up the specification.

Communicating at the Wrong Level

You may think you are just selling your customers a product or a service, but your product may make an important contribution to their business. If it is an innovative component that enables them to develop a new product or enter new markets, your company then becomes a potential strategic partner. Make sure that you communicate this to the right people.

Failing to Keep Up to Date

Purchasing requirements change and so do the people who make the decisions. Customers may launch new products, drop old ones, or acquire other companies. People come and go, and that influences the structure of the decision making team. Make sure you keep up to date with the latest developments.

For More Information

Book:

Parinello, Anthony, and Denis Waitley. *Selling To VITO (The Very Important Top Officer)*. 2nd ed. Avon, MA: Adams Media Corporation, 1999.

Web Site:

Marketing Research Association: **www.mra-net.org**

See also:

Selling and Salesmanship (pp. 2109–11)

"Good decisions come from wisdom. Wisdom comes from experience. Experience comes from bad decisions."

(Anonymous)

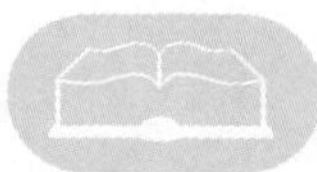

Branding a Business Product

Getting Started

Branding is as important in business markets as it is in consumer markets, and buyers feel more confident buying from a reliable company. Indeed, some buyers may be reluctant to buy new products that are not proven.

FAQs

How can I identify brand attributes?

Brand attributes are not always obvious. A good starting point is customer research. What do your customers feel is important when they buy? Compare their requirements against the performance of your own products and your company. Alternatively, look at your competitors and consider your comparative strengths.

What do I do if my brand attributes look poor?

Customers admire a company that is committed to continuous improvement, so start looking for improvements, particularly in the attributes that are most important to customers. Make sure you communicate any improvement.

Is it possible to measure the effect of branding?

In consumer markets, companies use tracking research to monitor changes in customer perceptions of the company. This research can indicate whether customers see your company in a more favorable light. This, in turn, can increase the likelihood of future sales.

My advertising budget is limited. Should I concentrate on product messages or brand-building messages?

Product messages are more likely to generate short-term revenue. That could increase your marketing budget over time. However, it would be wrong to neglect brand-building messages completely. You would be sacrificing long-term business development.

An increasing proportion of sales are coming via the Internet. Does this mean brand values are now less important?

With more and more crowding on the Internet, companies will have to work hard to stand out. Brand values will remain important.

Making It Happen

Why Business Branding Is Important

Branding is as important in business markets as in consumer markets. Business buyers, however, look for a different set of brand values. They ask what a product or service can do for their business.

Using the Brand Values

The following list covers the key attributes. Once you have identified the attributes that are most important to your customers and prospects, you can emphasize them in your communications. If an attribute is important to customers, but is currently weak, you should consider ways of improving performance.

Fitness for Purpose

The product should be fit for its purpose. Does it meet the buyer's specification or conform to industry standards? Approval by recognized authorities is important.

Value for Money

Value for money may be important to some buyers. That does not mean buyers will always look for the lowest price. Some customers may be happy to pay more for a product with an integral maintenance package.

Quality

Quality can be an important differentiator. Japanese companies led the way in transforming their brand values with massive improvements in quality. Companies that excel in quality build confidence.

Extendability

If you supply a range of products or services, brand values should be extendable to the entire range. This can help to build incremental business and strengthen customer loyalty.

Company Reliability

Buyers feel more confident buying from a reliable company. That means solid financial performance, a strong management team, a good industrial relations record and a track record in effective products.

Proven Products

Some buyers may be reluctant to buy new products that are not proven. They don't like to think that their companies are being treated as proving grounds for product development laboratories.

Investing in Product Development

Customers want to know that products are being continuously improved. They are not necessarily interested in leading-edge products, but they want to know that they are getting the best products currently available.

Distribution

If distribution is poor, customers can't buy the product. The importance of distribution varies by product and the recent growth of direct sales via the Internet is reducing its importance. However, certain products, such as components or supplies, continue to depend on effective national distribution.

Finance

The availability of finance may be important to some customers. Capital goods have long been marketed with a finance package, but finance is also available on many lower-value products. Attractive interest rates or payment terms can differentiate a product.

"I believe that if you're going to take someone on, you might as well take on the biggest brand in the world."

(Richard Branson)

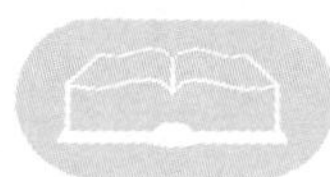

Service Backup
Service backup is vital to products that a customer depends on. The loss of a critical process can prove damaging so a customer wants to know that service response will be rapid. Quality of service can differentiate products that are almost commodities—computer systems, for example.

Training
Training helps customers make effective use of a product. Many companies operate their own training departments or develop distance learning packages, to ensure that customer staff become familiar with new products.

Customized Products
Customized products may represent higher value than standard versions. Customers have individual needs and a standard product may not prove an exact fit. By modifying, you can meet needs more effectively.

Partnership
Working in partnership with a customer can increase the value of the relationship. Partnership may mean working on joint development projects or providing a package of services that support a customer throughout the life cycle of the product.

Customer Service
Quality of customer service is a key measure of a company's values. Customer service takes many forms, from the way a customer's initial enquiry is handled to the quality of aftercare. In a number of companies, customer service is viewed as a strategic activity, with dedicated staff and documented procedures.

Consulting
Consulting can move a company from commodity supplier to valued partner. Presales advice is critical with complex or high-value products, and the quality of advice can determine where the order goes.

Technical Support
The scope of technical support ranges from advice on the right product for an application, to aftersales user support and problem solving. In complex products, the quality of technical support can be the most important differentiator.

Environment
Products must conform to environmental legislation, but companies are also measured by the effects of their processes on the environment. Using materials from nonrenewable sources or contributing to pollution can damage a company's image.

Ordering
Simple ordering procedures make it easier for customers to do business. Many companies have automated their ordering processes to reduce the time a customer has to spend on administration.

Product Information
Good quality brochures, detailed product guides, comprehensive information on the Internet, and clear presentations help buyers make informed decisions.

Customer Base
Buyers assess a product by the customers who already use it. A blue-chip customer list demonstrates product quality and approval.

Common Mistakes

Neglecting the "Soft" Issues
Many companies communicate their strengths in the "hard" attributes, such as quality, performance, and price. The "soft" attributes such as customer service or technical support, can prove to be key differentiators, however.

Ignoring Branding
Traditionally, branding has been seen as a consumer marketing discipline. Research has shown that business purchase decisions are more complex than thought, and companies base their decisions on a variety of factors. Business-to-business companies ignore branding at their peril.

Concentrating on the Wrong Attributes
Communicate what customers feel is important. In technology markets, quality of support and commitment to product development may outweigh price and delivery. In commodity markets, support and information can differentiate products with no performance advantage.

Failing to Communicate Brand Strengths
Marketing communications that focus only on the product may fail to communicate the important brand strengths. Customer presentations, corporate brochures, public relations activities and corporate advertising can be used to present a more balanced picture.

For More Information

Book:
Koehn, Nancy F. *Brand New: How Entrepreneurs Earned Consumers' Trust from Wedgwood to Dell.* Boston, MA: Harvard Business School Press, 2001.

Web Site:
Brand Chartering:
www.instituteforbrandleadership.org

See also:
☆ **Creating Powerful Brands (pp. 63–64)**
✔ **Planning an Advertising Campaign (pp. 656–57)**
✔ **Raising the Awareness of Business Brands (pp. 714–15)**

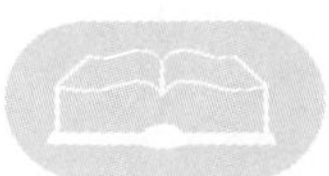

Raising the Awareness of Business Brands

Getting Started

Brand awareness is an important factor in customer purchasing decisions. Brand values relate to many areas, from product attributes to less tangible aspects of a company's operations. It is important to identify the key values of your brand and to establish how your products and company are perceived by different types of customer.

FAQs

How important are brand values in business markets?

Branding is frequently perceived as a consumer marketing discipline. However, industry experience indicates that business-to-business purchasing is a complex process influenced by intangible perceptions as much as by hard facts on product performance.

Do brand values carry equal weight across all markets?

Research indicates that different customers place different emphasis on individual brand values. Direct marketing that communicates individually significant brand values may therefore be more important than broadcast media such as advertising.

If our company is perceived as poor in critical brand values, should we concentrate our communications on those values?

Yes, but only when you are certain that your company can deliver on its promises. If your company is weak in important areas, take remedial action first.

Making It Happen

Identify the Key Business Brand Values

The key attributes of a business brand include:

- fitness for purpose
- value for money
- quality
- extendability
- company reliability
- proven products
- investment in product development
- distribution
- finance
- service backup
- training
- warranty
- customized products
- partnership
- administration
- customer service
- consultancy
- technical support
- environment
- ordering
- product information
- delivery
- customer base

Determine What Is Important to Your Customers

Although these brand values can be applied to business products in general terms, it is vital to understand how individual customers rank the values. This can be determined in several ways, described below.

Carry Out Customer Surveys

To find out what your customers consider important, carry out a survey; ideally, this should be done through a market research company so that respondents feel the survey is independent. It should ask respondents how they rank the different brand values and how they believe your company and a number of competitors compare across these values.

Run a Focus Group

A focus group can be used to cover the same ground as the customer survey, but it enables you to cover the subject in greater depth and to raise issues that would normally be outside the scope of a survey. Focus groups are ideal for identifying branding issues that concern customers, assessing customer reactions to potential changes, or identifying any problems customers are experiencing.

Review Industry Trends

Industry associations and publishers produce regular surveys into buying behavior in their industry sector. These surveys can highlight issues that concern the whole market.

Find Out about Customer Purchasing Requirements

An increasing number of business customers use formal criteria to evaluate potential suppliers and monitor their performance. These purchasing criteria indicate the factors that your customers believe are important and can help to identify the key messages you should include in your own brand communications.

Communicate through All Channels

Advertising and marketing communications are the most important media for raising awareness. However, there are several other direct and indirect channels, including:

- products
- services
- packaging
- distribution facilities
- Web sites
- customer service facilities

Product Branding

Do your products communicate your key brand values? The most important values are:

"You can get fame quickly but we're building a brand with depth and flavor." (Carl Lyons)

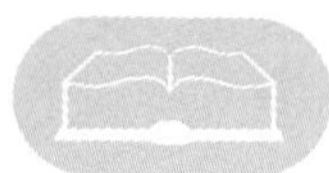

- fitness for purpose
- value for money
- quality
- extendability
- proven products
- investment in product development
- warranty
- customized products

If customer research shows that you are perceived as poor in any of these areas, or if customers are not aware of your strengths, you must look closely at your product development program.

Branding Your Services

Service capability can help to differentiate a company. The relevant brand values here are:

- service backup
- training
- warranty
- partnership
- consulting
- technical support

Many companies have underestimated the importance of service to their customers and have therefore not adequately communicated their service capability. Raising awareness of service capability is therefore an important aspect of brand communication. You can increase awareness through product advertising, product literature, direct marketing, and product public relations, as well as through service communications.

Communicating Brand Values through Packaging

Packaging raises awareness of brand values by the way in which it reflects the corporate identity. The right packaging communicates a number of important brand values including the use of environmentally friendly materials; quality and clarity of product information; ease of storage and handling; and delivery.

Branding Distribution Facilities

Your distribution facilities can raise awareness of a number of brand values:

- fitness for purpose
- quality
- company reliability
- distribution
- service backup
- partnership
- administration
- customer service
- delivery

Distribution is an area that is frequently overlooked in branding programs, but it can make an important contribution to customer perceptions of your company.

Building Brand Values through Your Web Site

An effective e-commerce Web site is one in which the various technical and design components all work together to generate customer interest, build trust, communicate product value, and support convenient profitable transactions.

Branding through Customer Service Facilities

Your customer service facilities have a major impact on the way your customers perceive your company. When inquiries, orders, or complaints are handled effectively, it creates awareness of positive brand values.

Monitor Levels of Brand Awareness

Customer perceptions change over a period of time, particularly if you are running targeted communications programs. Continuous research should be carried out to monitor customer attitudes. This type of research is known as tracking research, and it helps to measure the effectiveness of brand communications programs.

Common Mistakes

Failing to Monitor Customer Perceptions

Tracking research is critical. You must know how your customers perceive you so that you can plan your brand communications. Also track changes in perception to measure the effectiveness of your communications.

Overlooking Individual Customer Preferences

Industry research may give you a broad view of the brand values that are important to customers. However, it is more important to understand how individual customers rank individual values. This can be achieved only by continuous detailed research into individual customer needs.

Ignoring Important Communication Channels

Brand values are communicated through many different channels, not just advertising and marketing media. Make sure every aspect of your business reflects the brand values that are important to your customers.

For More Information

Book:

Cowley, Don (ed.). *Understanding Brands*. Dover, NH: Kogan Page, 1997.

Web Site:

American Marketing Association:
www.MarketingPower.com

See also:

☆ **Creating Powerful Brands (pp. 63–64)**
☆ **Marketing: The Importance of Being First (pp. 61–62)**
☆ **The Power Of Identity (pp. 91–92)**
✔ **Branding a Business Product (pp. 712–13)**
✔ **Planning an Advertising Campaign (pp. 656–57)**

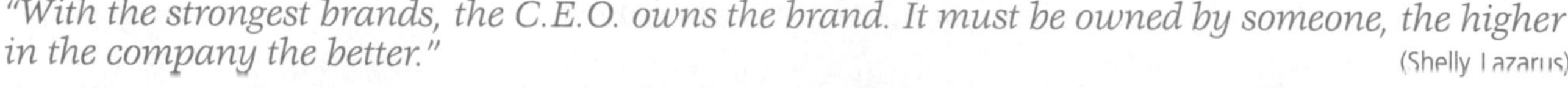
"With the strongest brands, the C.E.O. owns the brand. It must be owned by someone, the higher in the company the better."
(Shelly Lazarus)

  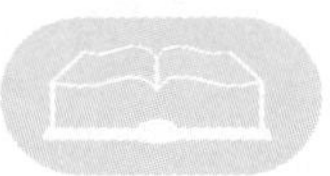    

Creating Product Literature

Getting Started

There are many different types of product publication, each of which has a different role in the sales and marketing process.

FAQs

Who should write product literature?

Product and technical specialists should provide the input and content for product literature. However, it is important that this content is edited or rewritten by a professional writer or communications specialist who understands the information needs of the market.

Isn't it easier to produce a single product catalog rather than a range of publications?

Not necessarily: for example, if the products change frequently, the cost of updating the catalog could be prohibitive. Where there is a wide range of products and customers in different market sectors, a single publication may not provide the depth of information needed.

Does the Internet make product publications redundant?

The Internet has made it easier to produce, update, and distribute product information. However, the comfort factor means that demand for printed publications remains high.

Making It Happen

Choose the Right Type of Publication

There are many different types of product publication, each with a different role in the sales and marketing process.

Leaflets

Leaflets or flyers are simple forms of communication used in the early stages of customer contact. They summarize the key benefits of a product or service and help to create initial interest. They are economical to produce and can be updated easily.

Catalogs

Catalogs give customers an indication of the scope of a product range. A catalog provides an overview and should point to other publications that provide more detailed information. It should be clearly laid out so that customers can find the specific information they want quickly and easily.

Product Brochures

The contents should cover:

- product description
- how the product is used
- main benefits to the customer
- important achievements
- market position
- related products or services
- company information
- commercial information such as price or availability

Data Sheets

Data sheets provide the detailed technical information that customers need in order to evaluate products. They should help customers to understand the benefits of a product and to compare it with competitors' offerings.

Product Guides

A product guide provides a highly detailed description of a product and can be issued to the sales force as well as to customers and prospects. It should include the same information as a product brochure but with a far greater level of detail. It should cover:

- description of the product and its main applications
- analysis of product features
- product operation and necessary skills
- accessories, replacement parts, and support services

Technical Updates

Technical updates are used to keep customers up to date with information on the products they have bought. They also communicate a policy of continuous improvement. The information that has changed may be important to customers, so it must be shown clearly. Any important safety information should be highlighted.

Help Customers Make Informed Decisions

Your customers may not evaluate a product in the way you want them to. You must explain benefits carefully, particularly those that are less obvious such as reduced maintenance costs.

Educate Customers

If your product is innovative, you may need to reinforce product description with customer education in order to explain the product and its potential benefits.

Provide Practical Guidelines on Usage

Your product literature may need to include instructions or guidelines on use to help customers get the best from the product. You should also include information on sources of technical help or other assistance.

Reassure Your Customers

Customers may be reluctant to change from an existing product or supplier. Case histories, testimonials from satisfied customers, lists of existing users, or approval by official bodies can help to reassure customers.

Stress Price and Quality

Customers don't necessarily want the lowest price: they are looking for value for money. Stress the quality of your product and show how it can save your customers money.

"Dull times are the very times when you need advertising most." (William Wrigley)

Present the Complete Product Range

Customers may be interested in one specific product, but you should refer to your complete range. It may generate cross-selling opportunities, and it also tells customers that they can obtain all their product needs from a single source.

Present Benefits, Not Features

When customers are making an initial assessment of your product, they want to know how it will benefit them. Features become more important when they are comparing your product with competitive offerings.

Recognize Your Customers' Needs

Your copy should demonstrate that you understand your customers' needs. Describe the business and technical issues facing customers, and show how your product helps customers deal with them.

Brand Your Products

It is important to build customer confidence in your products and your company. Reinforce the brand values that you have established in your advertising and direct marketing. Product literature should sell as well as inform.

Offer Related Services

You can add value to your products by offering customers services such as planning, installation, training, and maintenance. These services will help your customers make more effective use of your products and offer them the benefits of an all-in-one package.

Make Effective Use of Product Publications

A brochure may be the most obvious initial suggestion, but the idea should be carefully examined by laying down stringent requirements for in-house users.

- Ask them to make out a business case for the brochure.
- Levy an internal charge on the brochure which must be covered by an increase in revenue.
- Ask them to define a specific communications task for the brochure.

This process not only eliminates ill-considered requests, it also helps to ensure a precise brief that will improve the value and performance of the communication, whatever form it eventually takes.

Consider Alternatives to the Brochure

- Customized presentations, where your company has a small number of key customers. A presentation can be customized for each customer and easily updated. The presentation not only provides relevant, highly targeted information, it also increases personal contact with the customer.
- A customer magazine, where you have a larger customer base and your product range or technology changes rapidly. A regular magazine can easily be distributed to the larger target audience.
- A customer handbook, where you work in partnership with a small number of customers. A customer handbook, generally in looseleaf form, includes information on both supplier and customer to increase mutual understanding and awareness.
- A customized information pack, where you have a wide product range and a large customer base in many different sectors and where information requirements are therefore highly diversified. An information pack, consisting of a corporate folder or wallet with sector or customer specific inserts, provides a flexible communications tool.
- A targeted literature program, where you have a database that allows you to segment your customer base and track purchasing patterns and campaign response. Use the database to develop a contact strategy that begins with introductory literature and goes on to provide groups or individual customers with product information reflecting their specific needs and purchasing patterns.

Common Mistakes

Producing the Wrong Type of Publication

Different types of publication have specific roles in the sales and marketing process. Giving prospective customers detailed product guides when they are only carrying out a preliminary evaluation represents wasted effort.

Overlooking Alternatives to Publications

A publication may not always be the most appropriate communications solution. For example, if a prospect has specific product requirements, it may be more appropriate to develop a customized presentation tailored to that prospect.

Producing Information That Is Too Technical

Product information is read by a wide group of different decision-makers, including purchasing managers, general managers, technical specialists, and senior executives. The copy must relate to the information needs of each group. Content should reflect their interests.

For More Information

Book:

Yadin, Daniel. *Creative Marketing Communications*. 3rd ed. Milford, CT: Kogan Page, 2001.

Web Site:

American Marketing Association:
www.MarketingPower.com

See also:

✔ **Producing a Corporate Brochure (pp. 724–25)**
✔ **Running a Product Public Relations Campaign (pp. 728–29)**
Direct Marketing (pp. 1953–54)

 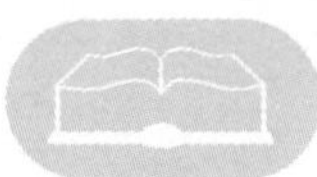    

Extending a Product with Service

Getting Started

Service is frequently relegated to maintenance and problem solving. However, done properly, service can be a key differentiator between you and the competition. Meeting customer requirements in the most appropriate and efficient way adds enormously to the perceived value of your product.

FAQs

My product is a market leader. Why would services be important?

Services can add further value to a product, providing incremental income and increasing customer loyalty. Services provide you with an opportunity to continue dealing with a customer long after the initial sale.

I already offer free installation and maintenance with my products. How does that add value?

Many companies have recognized the importance of service to their customers, and have changed their service strategy accordingly. Instead of offering free service, they have upgraded the services, widened their portfolio, and started charging customers for services. Although customers may initially object to being charged for something that was free, charging demonstrates the value of the service.

I don't have the skills or resources to deliver services. How can I offer my customers a service?

You can either build your own service team through recruitment and training or work in partnership with a specialist organization which will deliver service on your behalf.

My customers have their own internal service operations. Why should they want to use my services?

Many companies have internal service departments. They can be expensive to maintain, however, and are sometimes lacking in essential skills. By demonstrating the potential savings and benefits of outsourcing service, you can persuade them to switch to an external source.

Making It Happen

Differentiate with Service

Service is proving to be a key differentiator in many different market sectors. In many companies, however, the role of the service department is relegated to maintenance and problem solving. To take full advantage of the service opportunity, it is important to explain the benefits of effective service to customers, and present your service operations as convenient, cost-effective, and strategically important.

Meet Key Service Attributes

These are some of the key features that customers are looking for in a service offer:

- one contact point, simplifying contact and service administration;
- nationwide resources, ensuring support is available wherever the customer is located;
- direct contact with a technical specialist, providing an immediate response to problems or queries;
- quality support to ISO 9000, giving independent reassurance that service standards are high;
- support round the clock means that it is available when the customer needs it, and minimizes interruption of their business;
- complete support solutions provide support to meet all a customer's needs with consistent service standards;
- service options give a choice of service levels, which can be aligned to customers' needs;
- investment in support means long-term commitment to the customer.

Provide One Contact Point for Service Resources

Whether your customers have a technical query, a service request, or a product inquiry, or need advice, guidance, or information, they should be able to call one number for direct access to all your support resources. Ideally, you'll have specialists on the spot to deal with your requests. If they can't answer the query straightaway, make sure that the right person calls the customer back.

Offer Direct Contact with Technical Specialists

Your customers may have a technical query, and want to talk to an experienced specialist straightaway. When they call the technical help desk, they should be talking to a highly skilled person with extensive technical support and field experience.

Provide Quality Support

When your customers have a service request, they should contact the national service center, at any time of day or night, where service coordinators make sure that the right specialist is available to help. Service coordinators will use quality techniques to make sure that customers get the fastest and most effective response to their requests. In many cases, service centers can deal with requests directly, using advanced diagnostics. If not, they should assign an engineer to visit the customer site within agreed times. All of your service processes should be assessed to ISO 9001. If customers have any queries, there should be an escalation procedure (a service management procedure whereby customer complaints are "escalated" to a senior team member if the person dealing with the complaint initially cannot resolve the issue), guaranteeing a prompt resolution of any problems.

Develop Complete Support Solutions

Develop a comprehensive service portfolio including:

- consultancy

"A successful product merely gives us a head start in the race." (John Harvey-Jones)

- application development
- installation
- systems integration
- training
- planned maintenance
- technical support

Offer Flexible Service Options

Provide your customers with a choice of flexible service options to suit their operational needs. If your customers have an in-house support operation, support their team with an efficient spares delivery service, or manage their spares for them. Also offer to enhance the skills of your customer's in-house team with training, advice and guidance, technical support, and access to specialists.

Invest in Support

Quality service requires a significant investment in the service infrastructure; the right premises, efficient service communications, and a sophisticated service management system enable you to enhance your response and performance even further.

Add Value to a Product

Adding value to a product or service helps to differentiate products from the competition, and improves standards of customer service. By analyzing the products and services in your range, you can add value and improve a customer's perception of your organization. Some examples are:

- business services that free up customer staff to do more important tasks, or help managers perform their jobs better. Training, for example, can insure that staff make more effective use of the products the company buys;
- accessories to make a consumer product, such as a camera, more attractive;
- convenience services added to a basic service to enhance it. Insurance companies, for example, might add a helpline or list of approved repairers to help their customers recover more quickly from an accident.

Develop Product/Service Packages

To add value to products and to increase customer loyalty, put together "bundles" of products and services that reflect customer needs. The list below shows examples of this.

"Adding-in" Services

- Package holidays, including flights, hotel, and transport.
- Out-of-town retail sites, with greater convenience of parking and distribution.

"Leaving-out" Services

- "Fastfit" car repair centers, without nonessential services.
- Direct banking without premises.
- Direct insurance without intermediaries.

Changing Infrastructure Services

- Electronic newspapers.
- Home shopping.

Added Value Services

- Home delivery of fast food.
- Personal breakdown/recovery/onward transportation.
- Support and advice through helplines.
- Personal computers for home entertainment.

Changing Distribution Channels

- Direct sales, bypassing retailers.
- Electronic delivery, such as ATMs, replacing bank counter service.

Common Mistakes

Offering Only Basic Services

Basic services such as installation, maintenance, and upgrades are available from many different service organizations. They do not differentiate you and they do not add value. Higher-value services, requiring skill, knowledge, or experience, are the keys to success.

Failing to Invest in a Service Infrastructure

Customers expect a quality service. That means you have to invest in people and infrastructure. Ideally, your services should conform to recognized industry standards. If you fail to deliver the right standard of service, you could damage customer relationships.

Missing Service Opportunities

Customers require many different services during the time they own a product. Their requirements could include advice, consultancy, and design before the sale; installation, and training; followed by maintenance, upgrading, and other after sales services. Each of these represents an opportunity to earn incremental income and maintain contact with the customer.

For More Information

Book:

Gronroos, Christian. *Service Management and Marketing: A Customer Relationship Management Approach.* 2nd ed. New York: John Wiley & Sons, 2000.

Web Site:

U.S. Institute of Marketing: **www.usmktg.com**

See also:

☆ **Delivering and Delighting—A New Spirit at Work (pp. 71–72)**
☆ **The Second Coming of Service (pp. 77–78)**
✔ **Offering Customers Self-service (pp. 742–43)**

"Profit in business comes from repeat customers: customers that boast about your product and service, and that bring friends with them." (W. Edwards Deming)

INTRODUCING A NEW PRODUCT TO MARKET

GETTING STARTED

New product launches are crucial to the success of a business and need careful planning. Internal communications are vital to the early success of the program, as is the support of the senior management team.

FAQs

I'VE HEARD THERE IS A HIGH RATE OF NEW PRODUCT FAILURE. IS IT RISKY TO SPEND MONEY ON A HIGH PROFILE LAUNCH?

Failure to launch properly may be a contributory factor. Provided the product has been carefully researched and developed, an effective launch should contribute to success. It cannot, however, rescue a bad product.

WHY SPEND MONEY ON AN INTERNAL LAUNCH, WHEN IT IS THE CUSTOMERS WHO WILL DETERMINE SUCCESS?

Unless you have the commitment of the management team and the people who will be responsible for designing, producing, selling, and distributing the product, it is unlikely to get the support or resources it needs to succeed. Internal communication is key.

IF A PRODUCT IS GOOD ENOUGH, DO I NEED TO RUN SALES INCENTIVES DURING THE LAUNCH PERIOD?

Any product has to fight for attention from the sales team and resellers. An incentive may give the new product a vital push during the critical launch period.

MAKING IT HAPPEN

PLAN CAREFULLY

New product launches are crucial to the success of a business and reflect a considerable amount of investment. The product launch progresses through a number of important stages:

- internal communications, to ensure high levels of awareness and commitment to the new product;
- prelaunch activity, to secure distribution and insure that retailers have the skills, resources, and knowledge to market the product;
- launch events at national, regional, or local level;
- postevent activity to help sales force and retailers;
- launch advertising and other forms of customer communication.

COMMUNICATE THE LAUNCH INTERNALLY

Internal communications are vital to the early success of the program. The new product development team must sell its concepts to the senior management team who will commit resources to the project. They also need to win the support of a number of departments who will form part of the product launch process: manufacturing, design, research and development, distribution, and marketing. Sales and marketing departments involved in the practical launch of the product should be fully briefed on the product so that they can begin the external communications process. Sales staff should be issued with comprehensive sales and marketing guides so that they can identify the most important prospects. The marketing department will use the specification and objectives of the program to formulate other marketing programs and identify the most important sectors for development.

LAUNCH THE PRODUCT TO THE TRADE

If a product is sold through a distributor or retail network, prelaunch activity is important. The program should include a sales and distributor incentive program to generate high levels of initial interest. Incentives to build high levels of launch stock are essential. If a product is not available in the retail outlets, consumer launch material is wasted. Launch guides will help to give local outlets an indication of all the key activities.

PRODUCE A LAUNCH GUIDE

A launch guide insures that everyone involved in the launch process understands the product, and the launch itself.

EXPLAIN THE BACKGROUND

The first section of the guide should cover the background to the launch and the market opportunities:

- Why is the new product being launched?
- How does it fit into the company's overall strategy?
- What sort of people will buy the product and how do they differ from traditional customers?
- What new opportunities does this give the local outlet?
- How will competitors respond to this product?

HIGHLIGHT FEATURES AND BENEFITS

The second part of the guide should explain the features and benefits of the product. The guide:

- will act as a sales guide for the local outlet staff;
- will insure that they fully understand the product;
- should also include information about the training and product support available;
- will outline the key stages of any training that is to be an integral part of the launch program. The guide will identify the people who should be involved in the training program, together with a training schedule.

DESCRIBE LAUNCH SUPPORT

The third part of the guide should indicate the level of support available for the launch. This will include the launch event itself. Details should be given of national advertising and promotional programs, together with local marketing programs. Advance notice allows local outlets to order support material, and to plan their own local marketing program, so that it is fully integrated with the national launch.

OUTLINE LAUNCH ACTIVITIES

The final part of the guide should provide a schedule, and a list of key launch activities, so that the management team can meet all the requirements of the launch

"If I'm Philip Morris or R.J. Reynolds I'd go celebrate, because I know whatever brands I have now will never be seriously challenged by a new product."

(Clive Chajet)

program. These launch activities might include:

- stock and ordering details
- a training schedule
- launch events
- dates for national and local advertising
- suggested dates and formats for customer events
- a schedule for launch marketing activities

Arrange High-profile Launch Events

Hold a series of regional events for local retailers. Alternatively, you can introduce the new product to individual outlets through a series of sales calls, or send mailings to individual outlets.

Maintain Momentum through Postlaunch Activity

It is easy to overlook in the emotion of a major launch that the real sales effort has only just begun. Postlaunch sales activities can include: promotional support for retailers and ongoing incentives for retailers and sales force, as well as direct marketing programs to help retailers market the new products, and local events to reinforce the launch.

Communicate the Product to Customers

The customer launch can be achieved in a number of different ways, including advertising, direct marketing, trial offers, and exhibitions.

Use other forms of marketing to raise initial awareness and get customers to try the new product.

Use Advertising to Build Interest

Advertising can provide a high-profile launch platform. It can be used in a number of ways:

- announcing the new product to raise customer awareness
- advising customers where to obtain the new product
- offering customers further information, or a trial of the product, as a way of generating sales leads

Use Sales Promotion to Encourage Product Trial

Sales promotion activities can also be used to encourage sampling and product trial. Curiosity value and novelty are not sufficient to insure the success of a new product launch. The promotional campaign must incorporate strong consumer benefits, together with an incentive to buy that might include money off on trial packs.

Target Key Prospects with Direct Marketing

Direct marketing to key customer groups will allow the marketing group to target their most important prospects. It can be used to make special offers, or to provide detailed information about the new products and feedback on new product performance. The flexibility of direct marketing means that you can evaluate different launch and marketing approaches.

Communicate at the Point of Sale

Consumer information at the point of sale is essential for new products sold through retail outlets. It can be used to reach the prospects and customers who may have been missed in the advertising campaign and to reinforce other media. Point-of-sale material provides additional information to customers and prospects and supports sales development through retail outlets.

Use the Press

A press information program will ensure that the new product receives good coverage in the right publications. It can take a number of forms, including tie-in promotions such as reader offers, competitions tied to editorial, and product information in the form of press releases or feature articles.

Common Mistakes

Failing to Motivate the Sales Force

The sales force is critical to the success of a product launch. They need to be committed to the product so that they can communicate enthusiastically with customers and resellers. A new product will form just part of their overall sales target, so motivation is essential.

Overhyping a Poor Product

A new product is risky. It is tempting to oversell it to insure a successful launch. However, it is the long-term success of the product that determines a company's market position, so avoid launching for the sake of it.

Losing Momentum after the Launch

A great deal of effort and energy goes into a product launch, but many companies fail to maintain the sales and distribution momentum. After the initial period, sales may slump to a point where the product fails to recover.

For More Information

Book:

Cooper, Robert Gravlin. *Winning at New Products: Accelerating the Process from Idea to Launch.* Cambridge, MA: Perseus Books, 2001.

Web Site:

Journal of Brand Management:
www.henrystewart.com/journals/bm/

See also:

☆ **Managing New Product Portfolios (pp. 275–77)**
☆ **Marketing: The Importance of Being First (pp. 61–62)**
✔ **Involving Customers in Product Development (pp. 706–07)**

"The largest profits go to those businesses which most devotedly follow a policy of insisting on a competitive advantage, no matter how small, for every product or service they market." (R. H. Beeby)

  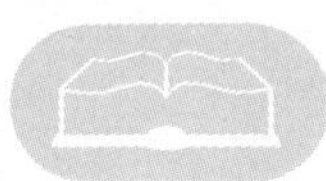    

Planning a Corporate Public Relations Campaign

Getting Started

Corporate public relations raises awareness of a company and builds confidence. It is important when a company has undergone change or is entering new markets. It can also overcome problems of poor reputation.

The corporate reputation is the way a company is perceived by customers, suppliers, and other important groups. Corporate public relations stresses the positive aspects of an organization and seeks to correct any misunderstandings.

The first stage in building a positive corporate reputation is to assess current perceptions. An audit identifies key areas for improving communications performance. A corporate press relations program should communicate:

- professionalism
- technical success
- market success
- corporate stability

It is essential that messages should be communicated consistently in every form of contact with the customer. The program should include information on:

- new appointments and management changes
- investments and other business developments
- business and financial performance

FAQs

If my company has a poor reputation in the market, can corporate public relations overcome that?

Corporate public relations can help to correct wrong perceptions. However, if the perceptions are based on poor corporate performance, the focus should be on improving performance. Trying to mislead the market can be dangerous. The press generally supports an improvement if it is genuine.

My company's products have an excellent reputation in the market. Why should I worry about corporate public relations?

Success depends on more than a good product range. Your company may have excellent products but a poor delivery record. If demand is growing, customers will ask if you have the capacity to meet new levels of demand. If your company is not making a good profit, customers will ask whether it can invest for the future or even survive in the long term. These are good reasons to keep customers informed about your company.

Who should deal with press inquiries about corporate matters?

Companies deal with this issue in different ways. Some companies appoint a single spokesperson who handles all inquiries. Others refer inquiries to a senior director. It is essential that telephone operators be aware of the correct press contacts. It can be frustrating for journalists to be passed from person to person. An alternative is to route all press inquiries to corporate public relations consultants. If they cannot deal with the inquiry directly, they can refer the question to the appropriate director.

Making It Happen

Plan Corporate Public Relations

Corporate public relations raises awareness of a company and builds the confidence of different groups in the company. It can be important in a number of different business scenarios:

- the company has undergone significant change;
- research shows that customers are not aware of the company's key strengths;
- the company is entering new markets and there is low awareness among potential customers;
- research shows that the company has a poor reputation in a number of areas important to its success;
- the company is building key account or partnership relationships and customers need to know that the company can maintain its standard of supply.

Identify the Elements of a Corporate Reputation

The corporate reputation is the way a company is perceived by customers, suppliers, and other important groups. It is based on a number of elements, including:

- financial performance
- the quality of the management team
- clarity of direction
- market performance
- growth record and potential
- relationships with suppliers and employees
- manufacturing capability

Build a Positive Corporate Reputation

Corporate public relations stresses the positive aspects of an organization and seeks to correct any misunderstandings.

Audit the Corporate Reputation

The first stage in building a positive corporate reputation is to assess current perceptions of the organization through research. This is the management summary of a research program into customer perceptions.

- The company is almost as visible as its competitors but is rated only third in all issues associated with image.
- Contact with the customer at all levels is less than professional. According to the customer, the company does not understand its business and its products, and does not communicate its future strategies.
- There is a legacy of poor reputation which has largely been overcome by increased product reliability, but the image persists in the minds of the customer's senior management team.

"Corporate values are a genuine competitive advantage. . .an enduring factor amid so many changes in products and services."

(Rosabeth Moss Kanter)

- The company is perceived as offering lower quality and lower performance than competitors, and its users are less satisfied than competitors' users.
- The company is seen as losing ground with important decision-makers.
- The company is identified more clearly than competitors with specific product lines, but is not rated most highly as the potential supplier of those products.
- The company's major weakness is perceived as its narrow product line and lack of expertise in certain areas.

An audit like this identifies key areas for improving communications performance and it is essential that these messages should be communicated consistently in every form of contact with the customer.

Communicate Professionalism

The company is a professional organization which understands the customer's business needs and can meet them with a wide range of high quality products and services. The sample messages below would support this perception:

- The company is investing $X in training over the next year.
- The company is organized into market-focused groups to offer the highest standards of service.
- X number of employees are dedicated to the customer's business.
- The company is committed to total quality.
- The company has developed a broad product range and a full range of support services.
- The new product development program is providing innovative new products.

Communicate Technical Success

The company is technically successful in major projects, developing total solutions and delivering value for money, on time, every time. The important messages to support this perception include:

- The company has an established reputation for innovation.
- The company's products have been selected for the following demanding applications: . . .
- Customers are saving money by using the company's products.
- The company's products conform to national and international standards.
- The company has a research and development budget in excess of $X, and has a team of X highly skilled people dedicated to technical support.

Communicate Market Success

The company is winning share from its competitors. The important messages to support this perception include:

- The company has been selected to provide products and services to the following customers: . . .
- The company has recently won a major order worth $X.
- The company has been selected as a strategic supplier to the following customers: . . .
- The company has gained X% market share in the last year, while competitors have lost X% share in the last year.

Communicate Corporate Stability

"The company is successful and financially stable, with a sound management team—a good prospective supplier and business partner." The important messages to support this perception include:

- The company's annual results show X% growth in orders, revenue, and profits.
- The company is expanding.
- The company is a member of the following international groups: . . .
- The company is the leading U.S. supplier.

Introduce a Corporate Press Relations Program

A wide variety of press relations techniques can be used to improve corporate relations. They include:

- regular press releases on new appointments and management changes;
- regular press releases on investments and other business developments;
- interviews with senior executives in important magazines;
- encouraging press visits.

Common Mistakes

Ignoring Corporate Public Relations

Many companies fail to recognize the problems caused by a poor corporate reputation. They concentrate on product public relations because corporate matters appear to be intangible. This can make it difficult for a company to rebuild confidence if problems occur.

Waiting until a Crisis before Investing in Corporate Public Relations

If a company hits a crisis, it may try to limit damage by issuing press information. Journalists usually recognize this type of crisis public relations and this can make the situation even worse. By adopting a policy of continuing public relations, it is possible to build effective relations with the press and gain understanding if there are problems.

Ignoring Certain Key Groups

Successful corporate communication depends on building understanding with all the groups that influence the success of your business. This might include investors, employees, pressure groups, distributors, and suppliers—as well as customers. In planning your campaign, make sure that you cover all the key groups.

For More Information

Book:

Treadwell, Donald, and Jill B. Treadwell. *Public Relations Writing: Principles in Practice*. Boston, MA: Allyn & Bacon, 1999.

Web Site:

Public Relations Society of America: **www.prsa.org**

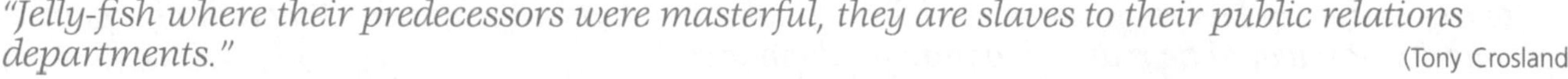

"Jelly-fish where their predecessors were masterful, they are slaves to their public relations departments."

(Tony Crosland)

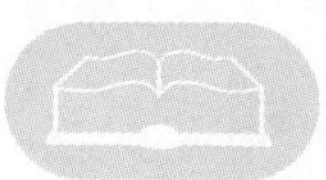

PRODUCING A CORPORATE BROCHURE

GETTING STARTED

A corporate brochure is a publication which is designed to provide customers with reassurance. Its aim is to present the company as a solid, well-managed business partner offering an excellent product range and possessing the attributes of financial stability, technological innovation, reliability, and customer focus.

FAQs

HOW IMPORTANT IS THE CORPORATE BROCHURE?

Many companies produce a corporate brochure before considering any other publication. It is seen as the face of the company and is particularly popular with the sales force. Despite its popularity, however, it is not necessarily the most effective form of communication. A corporate brochure has a role to play in communicating company information, but it should not be used as a substitute for targeted communications.

CORPORATE BROCHURES CAN BE EXPENSIVE TO PRODUCE. SHOULD THEIR USE BE RESTRICTED?

The feeling exists that corporate brochures should be high-quality publications because these will reflect a solid company. These expensive brochures are then often given away freely by members of the sales force. A growing number of companies have introduced internal charging for publications, so that internal customers must now prepare a business case for using publications; the result is that they are used more carefully.

WHO SHOULD RECEIVE CORPORATE BROCHURES?

Corporate brochures can be used as part of an integrated communications program aimed at customers (actual and prospective), suppliers, business partners, distributors, and investors. They can also be used, selectively, as part of an employee communications program.

MAKING IT HAPPEN

PRESENT A SUCCESSFUL COMPANY

A corporate brochure demonstrates corporate success with the result that the company is seen as a financially stable, long-term partner. Above all, the corporate brochure should be a statement of confidence: this is a publication that is designed to reassure customers.

A corporate brochure should include the following information:

- description of the product range
- location, resources, and international activities
- technical and research capability
- manufacturing resources
- success in handling complex projects
- success in terms of innovation or market leadership
- financial performance
- management skills

PRESENT THE PRODUCT RANGE

A company must show that its product range meets current requirements and can be developed in response to changing market conditions. The product range should contain a good balance of market leading established products and new products with good growth potential.

COMMUNICATE INNOVATION

Companies who supply technically advanced products must be seen to be at the leading edge of technology: they must convince their customers that their policy of continuous innovation enables them to offer more advanced products than their competitors.

DEMONSTRATE HIGH-PERFORMANCE PRODUCTS

When customers are trying to improve the performance of their own products, they need to work with companies that can comply with their requirements and meet new technological challenges. High-performance products have to meet stringent quality checks if they are to be accepted. They are often used in safety critical applications where the margin for error is extremely small. In presenting company capability, it is important to show how the company conforms to requirements.

COMMUNICATE INVESTMENT IN RESEARCH

Companies should point to their investment in research and development as evidence of their commitment to innovation. A company can enhance its reputation for innovation by becoming involved in industry research and helping to set industry standards. For example, membership of user groups or industry standards associations can help to demonstrate industry leadership and a commitment to progress.

A good research investment record demonstrates that the company is committed to providing increasingly higher standards of service and in turn to improving its long-term growth prospects. Investment does not necessarily mean capital expenditure on equipment: investment in people is seen as an increasingly important area for corporate development.

SHOW THAT YOUR COMPANY IS MARKET FOCUSED

Presenting a company as market focused can have a number of important benefits.

- It shows customers that you are concerned about their business.
- It tells investors that your company has the right priorities.
- It helps build staff commitment to customer service.

Market focus is demonstrated by:

- researching customer requirements;
- obtaining customer feedback;
- developing a new product program;
- appointing a senior executive responsible for customer service;
- focusing the organization on the customer;
- communicating customer benefits;
- the right levels of service;
- flexibility of production;

"If figures of speech based on sports and fornication were suddenly banned, American corporate communication would be reduced to pure mathematics."

(Jay McInerney)

- staff training in customer care;
- participation in user groups.

Explain Customer Focus

A market-focused company must first understand the needs of the market through research and consultation with the customer. New product programs are essential to any company, but in a market-focused company they are an integral part of the company culture. The whole organization must reflect the needs of the market, and the principles of market focus must be embodied in a senior executive. A key aspect of market-focused service is that it reflects key customer requirements such as convenience, cost-effectiveness, value for the money, and reliability. A product or service does not need to represent an industry as best in every aspect, but it should reflect the key perceptions identified by research.

Demonstrate Financial Stability

Presenting a company as financially stable can have important benefits.

- It reassures customers that you are a reliable supplier.
- It can help a company win long-term contracts.
- It can provide a company with access to funds.
- It tells employees that the company has good long-term prospects.

Several factors help to demonstrate financial stability:

- membership of a large group
- serving growing markets
- sound financial controls
- good investment record
- share price performance
- stable customer base
- broadly based product portfolio
- record of profitability
- low cost base

Communicate Size and Success

Being a member of a major group can help to reassure customers that your company will remain a reliable supplier. Customers need to know that you have the resources to finance work in progress and that you have access to funds for research and for growth investment. The backing of a major group provides the right credentials.

Market success is another indicator of good long-term prospects. For example, a company operating in sectors in overall decline, such as steelmaking or shipbuilding, is unlikely to have the same long-term prospects as a company in the high-technology sector.

Explain Company Management

A well-managed company should provide a cost-effective service and make reasonable profits to invest in future growth and the development of the service. There are a number of key factors in presenting a well-managed company:

- an experienced team
- commitment to excellence
- clear objectives
- customer-facing organization
- an effective recruitment process
- management development programs

Customers want to know that their suppliers are capable of running their own business effectively and that they understand the business of their customers. A well-managed company should be able to demonstrate a record of sustained growth and profitability and should have a clear sense of direction.

Explain Objectives

Good management begins at the top with effective leadership; if the board is committed, the rest of the management team will have clear guidelines to follow. A company should have a clear mission statement which is focused on service to the customer.

When a company has clear objectives, customers are reassured that future developments are in line with their needs. Many companies publish a statement of direction which tells customers how they intend to develop their business in the future; at the same time, it gives managers and staff a clear sense of direction.

Common Mistakes

Unbalanced Content

A corporate brochure should present a balanced picture of a company: its skills, products, resources, performance, and track record. Customers and prospects use corporate brochures to assess the suitability of a company as a supplier. The brochure should therefore cover all the factors that customers consider important.

Lack of Integration with Other Communications

The messages, treatment, and content of the corporate brochure should be integrated with advertising, product publications, a Web site, and public relations. It is just one part of the communications process.

Presentation before Content

Many companies concentrate on the presentation of a corporate brochure at the expense of its content on the assumption that customers judge a corporate brochure on its appearance. However, high-quality paper, excellent photography, and good print are no compensation for poor content.

For More Information

Book:

Yadin, Daniel. *Creative Marketing Communications*. 3rd ed. Milford, CT: Kogan Page, 2001.

Web Site:

American Marketing Association:
www.MarketingPower.com

See also:

☆ **The Power of Identity (pp. 91–92)**
✔ **Creating Product Literature (pp. 716–17)**
Public Relations (pp. 2090–92)

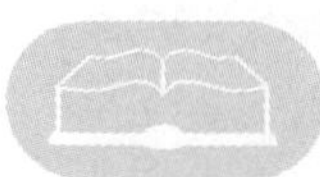

PRODUCING PRESS MATERIAL

GETTING STARTED

Newspaper, television, and radio journalists are always looking for stories. Supply information in the form of press releases, feature articles, or advertorials—in the right format and to the right person—and you can gain great publicity for your organization.

FAQS

SHOULD WE PRODUCE OUR OWN PRESS MATERIAL OR USE THE SERVICES OF AN EXTERNAL AGENCY?

An external agency can take a more objective view of your press material and may have experience of writing for the publications on your distribution list. That means they can tailor material for individual publications and make sure that it is printed. They may, however, lack product knowledge and require considerable training to achieve the right results. If your company produces complex technical products, you may split the task, keeping technical press releases in-house, and using an external agency to produce company or business material.

CAN WE USE THE SAME PRESS RELEASE FOR ALL THE PUBLICATIONS ON OUR DISTRIBUTION LIST?

You can issue a single release, but you will increase the chances of getting into print if you tailor information to the needs of individual publications. By reading previous issues and studying publishers' readership data, you can identify the type of material that is likely to be printed or broadcast.

WHAT SHOULD WE DO IF AN EDITOR DOES NOT PUBLISH THE INFORMATION IN A PRESS RELEASE?

There could be a number of reasons for nonpublication that are outside your control, such as lack of space, the release missing the copy date, or another story coinciding with your release. Your story may appear in the next issue if space allows. However, the editor may have decided that your information was wrong for the publication or not newsworthy. A quick call to the editor may help you find out the reason. If your material was unsuitable, you may be able to provide something more relevant for future issues.

MAKING IT HAPPEN

PLANNING PRESS RELEASES

A press release is a piece of information distributed to newspaper, television, or radio journalists which is published or broadcast as a piece of news. It can cover a variety of topics, including:

- information on new products or services
- information on developments in a company
- news of new appointments or promotions

An effective press release should contain news rather than thinly disguised advertising, and it should reflect readers' interests.

The release may be used without modification if it is newsworthy and if space permits. The press release may be cut to fit available space without any further reference to you. In some cases, a journalist or editor may contact you for further information and rewrite the item in the style of the publication. Sometimes the information may not be used, because it is not newsworthy or not relevant to the readership. Alternatively, although the main press release may not be used, an accompanying photograph may be used with a caption.

PRODUCING A PRESS RELEASE

The following guidelines will help you produce an effective press release:

- Press releases should be typed double-spaced.
- The source of the release should be clearly identified.
- A contact name for further information should be provided.
- Any limitations on use or timing of publication should be clearly highlighted, for example, "not for publication before. . ."
- The most important information should be included in the early paragraphs. If an editor is short of space, the press release will be cut as simply and quickly as possible, probably from the bottom upward.
- Quotes are useful and are frequently used by editors.
- Photographs or diagrams add value to the release and may help to insure publication.

DISTRIBUTING PRESS RELEASES

Press releases can be delivered by hand or by mail, depending on quantity. They can also be sent by e-mail or placed on a Web site so that they can be picked up by visiting journalists. Wherever possible, they should be sent to a named individual. Information on editorial contacts, with details of their special interests, is available in publications like *Public Relations Quarterly*, which is updated regularly. If you do not want the information published before a certain date for reasons of commercial security, include an embargo—"not for publication before. . ."

TIMING FOR PRESS RELEASES

Check the publication dates of magazines or newspapers on your distribution list. This information is available in publications such as *Public Relations Quarterly*. An editorial copy date will be indicated. Ensure that your release reaches the editor by that date at the latest.

PLANNING FEATURE ARTICLES

A feature article, which could be 500–2,000 words in length, is published in a magazine and credited to an organization. The article may be on technical or business developments in an industry, or on other subjects that provide practical or topical information for readers. The article may form part of an industry survey. This type of feature provides an opportunity for organizations to demonstrate their expertise and professionalism.

Feature articles can cover a variety of topics, including

surveys of new industry or technical developments, practical "how to" articles, or reviews of research projects.

If it is reasonably well written, the article may be used without modification; it will be published when space permits, or may be used as part of a special survey. In some cases, a journalist or editor may contact you for further information and rewrite the item in the style of the publication.

Producing Feature Articles

An effective feature article should reflect readers' interests and contain information that is useful to them. It should also bring them up to date with recent developments.

The following guidelines should help you prepare a feature article.

- Feature articles should be typed double-spaced.
- Length should be discussed with the editor, but is likely to be between 500 and 2,000 words, with 1,000 words as the average.
- A contact name for further information should be provided.
- Photographs or diagrams, with a caption for every item, add value to the article.

Distributing Feature Articles

Feature articles should only be sent to one publication at a time, although they can be modified for use in other markets. Wherever possible, they should be sent to a named individual. Information on editorial contacts, with details of their special interests, is available in the *PR Planner*, which is updated regularly. In some cases, the initiative may come from the publication and the editor will provide you with details of requirements.

Timing for Feature Articles

Check the publication dates of magazines or newspapers on your distribution list. An editorial copy date will be indicated. Make sure that your release reaches the editor by that date at the latest. You also should ask the editor for a list of special editorial features. The article may be suitable for inclusion in a survey.

Producing Advertorials

An advertorial is a special category of feature article, combining advertising and editorial, which is used to promote products and services. These are the key characteristics of an advertorial:

- may include a reader offer, such as a chance to participate in a competition
- should be identified as an "advertisement feature"
- the space is paid for, but it is produced in the form of editorial rather than in a conventional advertisement format.

The writing guidelines are similar to those for press releases and feature articles.

Common Mistakes

Writing Information That Is Not Suitable for a Publication

It is important to study the publications that are on your distribution list. Editors know very quickly what is relevant or interesting to their readers. If your material is not suitable, it will not be used. Study the editorial content and check the readership figures, which are usually available from the publication.

Providing News Stories That Are Out of Date

"Old news is no news" and that means a story could be wasted. It's easy to get the timing right with a daily or weekly publication, but it can be tricky to decide on the right date to send a news story to a monthly publication. The publication can provide you with the dates when your copy will be required, but you have to make sure that those dates tie in with your own schedules. If you have to release a sensitive news story early to catch a publication date, you can protect your interests by putting an embargo clause on the release, saying "not for publication before. . ."

Confusing Editorial with Advertorial

A press release or feature article should provide factual, newsworthy information. It should not be a blatant advertisement for the company. Editors are not keen on items that are thinly disguised advertisements.

For More Information

Book:

Treadwell, Donald, and Jill B. Treadwell. *Public Relations Writing: Principles in Practice*. Boston, MA: Allyn & Bacon, 1999.

Web Sites:

Institute for Public Relations: **www.instituteforpr.com**

Public Relations Society of America: **www.prsa.org**

See also:

☆ **Relating to the Public (pp. 57–58)**

✔ **Dealing with Press Inquiries (pp. 738–39)**

✔ **Running a Product Public Relations Campaign (pp. 728–29)**

Public Relations (pp. 2090–92)

Running a Product Public Relations Campaign

Getting Started

Product public relations is the most frequently used public relations activity, which can be used to support a number of different sales and marketing objectives. There are many different opportunities for improving product public relations across a variety of media.

FAQs

Should I hold a press conference every time I launch a new product?

You should only hold a press conference if the product being launched is critical to your company or will be seen as important in the market. Minor product developments or simple range extensions do not warrant a press conference.

Can I handle my own product public relations?

Many manufacturing companies handle product public relations internally. They have a detailed knowledge of products and services that an external consultancy would be unable to match.

Should technical specialists write their own product material?

Technical specialists are in the best position to write feature articles that require detailed product knowledge. However, they may write from a technical perspective, rather than a customer perspective, and this may reduce the value of the article. You can take the specialist's material and edit it as necessary.

Making It Happen

Plan Product Public Relations

Product public relations is the most frequently used public relations activity and can be used to support a number of different sales and marketing objectives:

- as part of a new product launch program
- to raise awareness of a company's product range
- to correct misunderstandings about a product
- to build understanding of product applications
- to encourage wider use of a product
- as part of a market education program

Identify Opportunities for Product Public Relations

There are many different opportunities for improving product public relations:

- contributing product information to regular product surveys
- issuing press releases on new products and new product developments
- contributing articles on complex product applications
- contributing how-to articles on different aspects of product usage
- contributing articles by technical specialists on new developments in the industry

Support a New Product Launch

A company marketing a new design software tool that will improve engineering design quality and productivity wants to raise awareness and understanding of the product among a group of decision makers, including:

- design engineers who would use the product
- managers and senior executives responsible for engineering, who would benefit from improved efficiency and productivity
- marketing directors who would benefit indirectly from better product performance

The program includes the following elements:

- press releases aimed at publications read by the target audience
- an interview with the company's engineering director, explaining how the product improved internal productivity and performance
- contributions to a number of product surveys on engineering design techniques
- a feature article on developments in engineering design
- a feature article submitted to marketing magazines showing how engineering design influences product and marketing performance

Improve Market Development

A professional services company marketing project services believes that lack of understanding is a barrier to market growth. The company develops a public relations program which includes the following elements:

- case histories of companies using a project management service
- feature articles on using project services to improve deployment of staff
- feature articles on the use of project services in outsourcing programs
- a press release including self-assessment questionnaire, helping prospects to identify the need for project services

Increase Use of a Product

A materials supplier wants to increase the usage of an advanced material which has not been widely used in general markets. The product was originally developed for use in demanding aerospace applications and is believed to be expensive and too good for conventional applications. The campaign is targeted at designers and application engineers in a wide variety of markets. The campaign includes the following elements:

- a press release on an information pack that describes applications of the product

---

"If someone thinks they are being mistreated by us, they won't tell 5 people, they'll tell 5,000."

(Jeff Bezos)

- a feature article, "How to design with the material," submitted to horizontal market design and engineering publications
- an editorial competition that enables readers to win a special design software package
- a series of application articles written specifically for vertical market publications

Run a Press Conference

A press conference provides an opportunity for an organization to meet journalists and editors in person and give them a detailed briefing on a new product development. However, unless the event is important and the press see a real benefit in attending, press conferences are a waste of time, so planning and preparation are important to ensure success.

- Invite journalists and editors from publications that reach your most important customers and prospects.
- Give the press plenty of notice, and try to plan the timing so that editorial coverage will appear in the next issue of the most important monthly publications.
- Provide press packs that include background information, specific information on the product, photographs, and other relevant material.
- If necessary, insure that senior executives or other specialists are available for interview or to answer detailed questions.
- If any important press contacts cannot attend, send a press pack and arrange a separate meeting if necessary.

Arrange Interviews with Key Product Specialists

An interview with a senior executive or product specialist provides an opportunity for an organization to meet selected or individual journalists and editors in person and to give them a detailed briefing on a new product development. The advantage to the press is that this process is more selective than a press conference, and it gives them an opportunity for an exclusive interview.

Put Information in Your Online Press Office

Set up a separate page on your Web site where journalists can get the latest news about your company's products and download press releases, background information, or feature articles. The press office should have a direct link from the home page, and new stories should be featured on the home page. The press page should also feature e-mail addresses and telephone numbers for key contacts.

Alert Journalists by E-mail

Journalists may visit your site regularly if it provides valuable information. You can also alert them to the latest product news by e-mail. Include a link to the press release or feature article on your site, so that it can be easily downloaded.

Issue Reprints of Published Material

If a story about your company's products is covered in the press, television, or radio, include a reprint of the item on your site. Also provide links to the publications that covered the story. Alternatively, e-mail the item to other journalists. This may increase coverage even further. Ask the publisher for permission before you reproduce a complete article.

Run an Online Press Briefing

The problem with conventional press conferences is usually time, but running an online press briefing can overcome that problem. Web casting allows companies to stream traditional audio and video conferences over the Internet, incorporating multimedia content and adding interactive capability such as slides, polling, and messaging. This enables journalists to attend a virtual press conference without leaving their desks, while the interactive facilities enable them to ask questions—just as they would at a traditional press conference.

Issue Material by Newsletter

If you issue a large number of product press releases, you can include brief summaries of the latest stories in a regular newsletter distributed to journalists or customers. The summaries should include a link to the complete release. The frequency of your newsletter depends on the volume of releases you produce each week or month.

Common Mistakes

Concentrating on Product News Rather than Information for the Market

Many companies simply write about their products from an internal point of view, ignoring the implications for the customer. Writing articles about applications or benefits for the market makes the press information more relevant and interesting.

Writing Information that is Not Suitable for a Publication

It is important to study the publications that are on your distribution list. Editors know very quickly what is relevant or interesting to their readers. If your material is not suitable, it will not be used. Don't assume that all industry publications will be interested in your product.

Failing to Keep Journalists Up to Date

Journalists may not be aware of your company's full product range or of its capabilities. They may receive the latest press releases, but that may give them a limited view of your company. It is important to provide background information as well as the latest product information.

For More Information

Book:

Cutlip, Scott M., Allen H. Center, and Glen M. Broom. *Effective Public Relations*. 8th ed. Upper Saddle River, NJ: Financial Times Prentice Hall, 2000.

Web Site:

Tradeworld: **pr.tradeworlds.com**

See also:

✔ **Dealing with Press Inquiries (pp. 738–39)**
✔ **Producing Press Material (pp. 726–27)**

"A happy atmosphere is something that customers pick up on." (Tom Farmer)

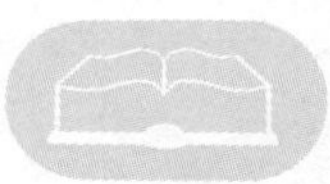

Planning Promotions

Getting Started

Consumer promotions account for around 20% of the value of the average shopping basket. Promotions are popular because they meet the demands of powerful retailers, and they help brand managers to meet volume targets. The strength of the retail trade puts increasing emphasis on trade and consumer promotions.

Consumers prefer instant win promotions to money-back or collector schemes. Instant win has a specific tactical role, but it may not be suitable for more strategic tasks such as brand switching. Cross promotion allows complementary products to be promoted in a cost-effective way.

FAQs

Is sales promotion more effective than advertising for building market share?

Sales promotion can deliver short-term gains in market share, but competitor promotions may wipe those out. Longer-term promotions such as collector schemes can encourage customer loyalty for the period of the promotion, but they may also be vulnerable to competitive activity. Advertising, on the other hand, can be used to build longer-term brand awareness and attract new customers. Ideally, the two activities should be integrated if budgets allow.

I sell my products through retail outlets. Should I run trade promotions rather than consumer promotions?

Trade promotions will help you sell into the retail outlets. If you also give retailers incentives to sell more to consumers, or to improve their standards of service, you may also increase sales to consumers. A consumer promotion may boost sales, but it may not increase sales through your retail outlets.

Who should plan promotions, my advertising agency or a specialist promotions company?

Sales promotion should be integrated with other marketing activities, so it is essential that your advertising agency is aware of the promotion. Your agency may not have the skills or resources to plan and implement the promotion. If you use a specialist company, make sure that the creative theme of the promotion reflects the themes of the advertising and other marketing programs.

Making It Happen

Take Advantage of Promotions

In the consumer sector, items under promotion account for around 20% of the value of the average shopping basket. The strength of the retail trade puts increasing emphasis on trade and consumer promotions. In the United States, the strength of the trade means that some retail-dependent brands allocate as much as 75% of budget on promotions. Promotions are popular because they meet the demands of powerful retailers and they help brand managers meet volume targets. They are also easy to justify financially because of immediate measurable results.

Identify Promotional Benefits

Promotions:

- attract attention of retail buyers and sales forces, particularly for smaller brands;
- generate excitement at the point of sale;
- simplify negotiations over margins; promotions may create better volumes than reductions in margins;
- increase the effectiveness of trialing. One survey indicated that 30% of consumers had not tried the brand in the last six months. Another reported that 44% of consumers said they would buy a brand they do not normally buy if it is part of a special offer.

Reflect Customer Views

An industry report indicates that consumers prefer instant-win promotions to money-back or collection schemes. The survey, which provides useful data for promotion of branded products, could also provide an insight for companies running business-to-business promotions. The report indicates that instant-win has a specific tactical role, but it may not be suitable for more strategic tasks such as brand switching. Key findings of the report include:

- instant win is most appropriate for products with a high purchase frequency.
- only 5% of consumers felt they would switch brands to participate in an instant-win promotion, compared with 41% of consumers who would switch brands for a price reduction promotion.
- the main reasons for liking instant-win promotions were: no waiting and immediate knowledge of success.
- the main dislikes were: unlikely to win and likely to be a waste of time.

Avoid Problems Created by a Promotional Culture

The pressure to run promotions can have an impact on overall marketing performance. A review by a major consumer goods company indicated that a great deal of time was required to design, implement, and oversee promotions. It accounted for 25% of sales force time and 33% of brand managers' time. Other problems included:

- supply inefficiencies
- cost of changing packs
- cost of promotional material
- cost of running the promotion
- impact on long-term brand building

Set the Right Promotional Objectives

Promotions must be managed carefully to provide long-term benefits. The wrong choice of offer, confusing rules, or poor organization can undo all the good work. In setting objectives, you should ask:

"You can't measure the value of being first." (Chris Moore)

- Why are we running the program?
- Do we want to increase overall volume, or sales of specific products?
- Do we want to improve performance in other sales-related areas, such as customer service or participation in training schemes and other business programs?

Choose an Appropriate Promotional Format

- Promotional offers can be awarded to the biggest spenders or to all consumers.
- Programs that only reward big spenders or large trade customers can act as a disincentive to others.
- Programs that reward performance against target give a wider opportunity to win.
- A multilevel program that offers many lower value prizes can act as a strong motivator.

Define the Rules Clearly

- Set out the scope of the promotion and the offer.
- Explain what is required to win and how to collect prizes.
- Include the closing date for the promotion.
- Specify the availability of the offer, for example, only available in selected retail outlets.
- Set the specific requirements for each participant.

Use Cross-promotion

Cross-promotion allows complementary products to be promoted cost-effectively. The project can be handled in-house, the samples are cheap, and the cost of the whole promotion is comparatively low. To be successful, this type of promotion should feature products that are complementary and noncompetitive. A database can be used to identify opportunities for cross-promotion—first identify the profile of a product, then look for products with a similar profile.

Maintain Momentum throughout the Promotion

If you are operating a long-term promotion or a promotion that involves a number of stages, you need to maintain momentum.

- Send out teaser incentives or gifts during the promotion to maintain interest.
- Keep participants informed of their progress.
- Encourage struggling participants with secondary offers.
- Publish results and distribute them to all participants.

Ensure Effective Fulfillment

If you are delivering promotional products to homes or businesses, you need to set up an efficient logistics operation. You can either operate your own fleet, tying up capital and personnel, or subcontract the operation to a specialist logistics company.

Appoint a Fulfillment Agency

If your promotion is likely to generate a large volume of requests, your company may not have the resources to handle fulfillment internally. Fulfillment agencies specialize in high volume response programs.

Assess the Effectiveness of Promotional Programs

- How do you justify spending money on promotions?
- What return on your promotional investment are you looking for?
- What are the related sales objectives?
- How will you quantify them?
- How will you isolate the effect of nonpromotional activities?
- Was the promotional impact evenly spread across your business?
- Were there significant account, sector, or regional differences in impact?
- Did the differences relate to techniques, premiums, value, customer appeal, or communications?
- Is it possible to profile people who used previous promotions as a basis for planning?

Common Mistakes

Setting Too Many Short-term Promotional Objectives

Sales promotion campaigns are judged on the way they change market share. However, any gains in market share can be lost when the promotion stops or competitive activity increases. It is also possible to create an environment in which consumers and the retail trade expect promotion to be a continuous activity.

Failing to Integrate Promotion with Other Activities

Sales promotion works most effectively when it is integrated with other activities. A consumer promotion, backed by a trade or sales force incentive, insures that all parties are aware of the promotion. A direct mail campaign in conjunction with a promotional offer can increase the direct mail response rate.

Choosing the Wrong Type of Promotion

If you run a promotional campaign, make sure that it reflects your brand values. If you can add value with your promotional offer, the campaign is more likely to be successful. You should also choose the right type of campaign. An instant-win campaign can have an immediate impact on market share, while a collection program encourages longer-term loyalty.

For More Information

Book:

Brown, Chris. *The Sales Promotion Handbook*. 2nd ed. Dover, NH: Kogan Page, 2002.

Web Site:

American Marketing Association:
www.MarketingPower.com

See also:

☆ **How to Plan Marketing (pp. 59–60)**

"Marketing goes wrong when it is perceived by companies as a bolt-on activity." (Michael Perry)

Running a Price Campaign

Getting Started

Promotional pricing can be used throughout the marketing process, in order to encourage brand loyalty and increase sales among customers. Pricing programs should be carefully matched to particular marketing tasks.

FAQs

Is pricing more important than brand building?

In the longer term, brand building is likely to be more important. However, price promotions can be used to win market share or quickly establish a new product. They can also be used to rapidly counter competitive activity that could have an impact on market share. Continuing to concentrate on price promotion alone is not a recommended strategy.

Should I always respond to a competitor's price promotion?

If the competitor's promotion is likely to damage your market share, it may be worth responding. However, you should weigh up the impact on profitability. It is easy to get drawn into a damaging price war that has no long-term benefit.

Retailers are demanding price cuts. Should I give in to their demands when I'd rather spend the budget on advertising?

It can be difficult to persuade retailers that advertising, direct marketing, and other brand-building strategies are going to benefit them. They frequently prefer a promotion that offers them an immediate return in terms of increased sales. Again, it is a question of balance, meeting both short- and long-term needs.

Making It Happen

Match the Promotion to the Marketing Program

Promotional pricing can be used throughout the marketing process, for:

- launching new products
- winning competitive business
- protecting market share
- entering new market sectors
- developing niche markets
- protecting volume and profit in mature markets

Choose the Right Pricing Program

There are five main categories of promotional pricing:

- money off current purchase
- money off next purchase
- cashback
- more product for the same price
- discounts on multiple purchase

Run a Money-off Promotion

This type of price promotion is one of the most commonly used tactics. It is immediate, easily implemented, and is easily understood by consumers. Results are measurable, and pricing levels can be modified for different market sectors. The program is also easy to modify in response to demand. Money-off promotions are acceptable to retailers, and easy to promote at the point of sale.

There are disadvantages. The promotion is easily imitated and competitors can respond quickly. It also has a potential long-term impact on manufacturer and retailer profitability. This type of promotion has no effect on long-term branding, minimal impact on customer loyalty, and does not differentiate the product.

Offer Money Off Next Purchase

This type of price promotion is designed to encourage repeat purchasing and to contribute to brand and customer loyalty. It is easily understood by consumers and can be measured accurately. The campaign is acceptable to retailers, and easy to promote at the point of sale. It helps to build a value for money reputation, and contributes to the development of long-term relationships. However, like promotions giving money off the current purchase, it is easily imitated by competitors and has no effect on long-term branding or on product differentiation.

Make a Cashback Offer

In this type of price promotion, the customer pays the full purchase price, and receives a rebate in the form of cash or a check. The customer also can be offered the rebate in a different form—for example, $400 worth of gas when you buy your next car—although this could be considered a free gift. This type of promotion is designed to encourage purchasers to switch brands, by offering them greater freedom of choice in the way they use the discount.

The promotion has perceived value for both consumers and retailers and encourages brand switching. It is easily understood by consumers and offers them greater flexibility. The offer can be modified for different market sectors and is easy to modify in response to demand. However, the offer is unrelated to brand values and does not encourage repeat purchase. Again, it is easily imitated and offers no product differentiation.

Offer More Product for the Same Price

This type of price promotion is designed to encourage brand switching or increase the volume of purchasing by offering the customer greater value for money. However, it can be difficult for customers to recognize the value of the offer when packs of different sizes are compared. Apart from this, it is easily understood and offers customers value for money. Competitors find it difficult to respond quickly to the offer, but it has a number of disadvantages. You may have to modify the product or the packaging, and that can have a potential long-term

"The funny thing is better TV shows don't cost that much more than lousy TV shows."

(Warren Buffett)

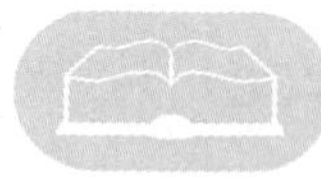

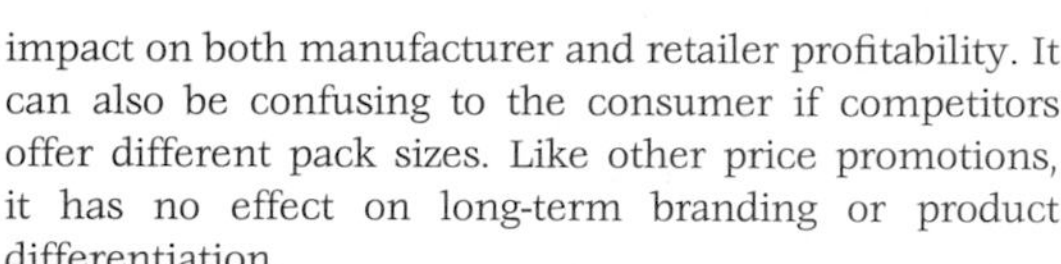

impact on both manufacturer and retailer profitability. It can also be confusing to the consumer if competitors offer different pack sizes. Like other price promotions, it has no effect on long-term branding or product differentiation.

Offer Discounts on Multiple Purchase

Although there is overlap between this and extra product promotions, this type of price promotion does not require any physical change to the product or packaging. It is designed to encourage repeat purchase, and to increase customer loyalty. The "Buy One, Get One Free" offer takes the promotion to its logical limit. A number of multiple retailers use this offer as the basis for long-term positioning as a value for money supplier. The promotion is easily understood, acceptable to retailers, and builds longer-term loyalty. It can, however, have a potential impact on retailer and manufacturer profitability.

Operate Credit Deals and Finance Schemes

Credit deals and finance schemes can increase sales by making it easier for customers to buy. Although the recession of the mid-1990s made consumers more cautious about unlimited credit, finance schemes remain an important method of increasing sales and building customer loyalty. In the business-to-business sector, finance schemes such as leasing are often an integral part of a marketing package.

Finance schemes can take a number of forms:

- storecards—credit cards that can be used only in named stores
- loan schemes–operated on behalf of stores or manufacturers by finance companies
- installment plans–operated on behalf of stores or manufacturers by finance companies
- business finance or leasing schemes–operated on behalf of companies by finance companies

Finance schemes make it easier for customers to buy and can increase customer loyalty. They can be used to encourage repeat purchasing, while reducing the impact of price competition. An important bonus is that they provide high levels of customer information as a basis for direct marketing. The disadvantage is that they can be complex to administer and they do not support product branding.

Common Mistakes

Relying on Price as the Only Weapon

Price promotions make little contribution to brand building or customer retention. Most promotions are easily imitated by competitors, and this can create a marketplace in which customers regularly switch brands to take advantage of the latest offer.

Running Price Promotions That Are Difficult to Understand

"Buy One, Get One Free" is a very simple concept. "Ten per cent off when you buy more than three in a two-week period" is confusing to customers and retailers. Price promotions must be immediately understandable.

Promotions That Are Difficult to Administer

Retailers prefer promotions that are simple to administer. If they have to return coupons, arrange refunds or rebates, or make complicated adjustments to their own pricing mechanisms, they will be reluctant to run the program.

Consumers, too, prefer simple offers. If the program involves redeeming coupons, or posting proof of purchase to claim a rebate, it will be less attractive.

Getting Caught in a Price War

When competitors make similar price offers, this can lead to larger and larger cuts. Although one competitor may gain market share, it may be at the expense of profitability. Since it is difficult to retain loyalty through price promotions, this can be a damaging strategy in the long term.

For More Information

Book:

Dolan, Robert J., and Hermann Simon. *Power Pricing: How Managing Price Transforms the Bottom Line*. New York: Free Press, 1997.

Web Sites:

American Marketing Association:
www.MarketingPower.com
Professional Pricing Society:
www.pricing-advisor.com

See also:

☆ **How to Plan Marketing (pp. 59–60)**
☆ **Profiting from Prices (pp. 307–08)**
Marketing Management (pp. 2045–48)
Pricing (pp. 2078–79)

"I will build a motor car for the great multitude. . .constructed of the best materials. . .so low in price that no man making a good salary will be unable to own one." (Henry Ford)

Running Sales Meetings

Getting Started

It is essential to maintain contact with all members of a sales force, wherever they are located, and a sales conference can help sales representatives understand business objectives, products, company policies, and what support is available to them. Conferences also play an important part in motivating sales teams.

National conferences are held for major events, such as the launch of a new product or a presentation of annual results, and because of their high profile, they can be used to generate high levels of enthusiasm, commitment, and effort. For example, the national conference could be used to reward high achievement by an individual or a team. In addition, they can raise awareness of the organization's overall strengths and help to build consistent standards and performance.

FAQs

Are sales meetings really that important? Isn't it better that sales representatives spend time with their customers?

It's true that sales representatives need to spend most of their time with customers, but if they are not fully aware of company policies, products, and support, that time may be unproductive. Good sales meetings equip representatives with the skills and knowledge to do their job effectively. They also play a key role in motivating sales teams and building team spirit, an important factor for people who spend most of their time working alone.

Should the emphasis in a sales meeting be on excitement or information?

It is easy to present an exciting, theatrical event that motivates but conveys very little hard information. However, such an event may succeed, because it is designed to create impact. Provided it is backed by simpler business presentations that communicate hard facts about new products or corporate development, the "experience" has a place. Sales representatives like to think that their organization cares about them, and a low-key meeting could give the impression that their meeting is not that important.

When networked conferencing makes communication so simple, is the live meeting dead?

Networked conferencing makes it easier to hold regular meetings, saving sales teams' time. For that reason, it will play an important part in the overall sales force communications program. However, personal contact and team building are important benefits of live meetings which means they should also remain an integral part of the program.

Making It Happen

Maintain Effective Contact

To make a sales force work effectively, it is essential to maintain contact with all team members. How many times has the local office accused head office of being remote and out of touch? Can head office employees be certain that local sales representatives are aware of the latest product information or the current operating policy? Is there a feeling that certain members of the team are better informed or supported than others?

Set Meeting Objectives

Formal and informal information channels are used to maintain effective contact with local sales representatives at all levels. The sales conference is a key part of that process, and it should help sales representatives to:

- understand your current business objectives;
- understand corporate operating procedures;
- be aware of the business and marketing support available to them;
- be committed to success;
- acquire up-to-date product knowledge;
- understand how to implement company policies;
- feel that they have a worthwhile career structure within the organization.

Run a National Conference

At national conferences, the entire sales team is invited to attend, and the event may last for a longer period than a normal meeting. The conference is usually held for a major event, such as the launch of a new product or presentation of annual results, and is designed to generate high levels of enthusiasm and commitment. A national conference has the additional benefit of bringing together people from around the country who would not normally meet each other, so it has a considerable team-building value.

Build Team Spirit

A national conference should have purpose and it should be handled effectively. Many product launches have a high theatrical content, because the intention is to create impact. The high point of the event is the launch itself, which needs to be impressive, but the remainder of the time can be spent in building the right level of team spirit within the sales force. A conference not only brings together employees who are separated by physical barriers but can also raise awareness of the organization's overall strengths and help to build consistent standards and performance.

Reward Effort

The national conference can also be used to reward high achievement. Many organizations run annual incentive and recognition programs for sales employees at different levels—the highlight being an individual presentation to the winner by a senior director, an event that confers real status on the winner. Using the national conference as the occasion for the award ceremony can raise the incentive program's profile and encourage high levels of participation and effort.

"In a good meeting there is a momentum that comes from the spontaneous exchange of fresh ideas and produces extraordinary results."
(Harold S. Geneen)

Run a Regional Business Meeting

National and international conferences have a role to play, but they can be expensive and time consuming. Unless such an event is important to business development or building team spirit, it may be more satisfactory to consider a regional business meeting.

With this type of event, busy sales representatives appreciate the fact that they need only commit part of a working day, and it cuts down on unnecessary traveling time. Regional business meetings are a valuable format for maintaining personal contact; they allow groupings of local outlets; and they enable an organization to hold a concentrated meeting to bring local sales teams up to date with key events.

Set a Meeting Format

Although regional meetings do not have the high profile of national conferences, they represent an opportunity to maintain regular contact at a high level. Such events should include presentations by senior management from the headquarters team and should concentrate on national policy as well as matters of regional interest.

Many organizations adopt a half day format for their regional business meetings. Delegates arrive at midday for an informal lunch before a series of afternoon briefings covering new products, corporate developments, management changes, promotional activities, pricing, marketing programs, and objectives for the next quarter. The meetings give the head office team an opportunity to update local sales employees on current activities and maintain contact between the teams.

Hold Local Branch Briefings

Although regional business meetings provide a convenient alternative to national conferences for events that do not need a high profile environment, they still have drawbacks. If an organization wants to brief a local sales team, or if the briefing is applicable only to one particular area, regional meetings may not be practical.

The solution is a presentation tailored to local needs, given at the local office. The location is convenient and the meeting does not take up much of the team's time. Wherever possible, the branch briefing should also be treated as a special event with a dedicated meeting room and professional presentation techniques. It should be formally structured and should resemble the main conference presentation in all but location.

Save Time with Networked Conferencing

A good addition to actual meetings of whatever kind is networked conferencing, which brings sales teams together quickly and easily, wherever they are located. It supports effective teamwork when sales representatives work in different locations or different countries, and it can help teams meet key objectives efficiently and productively. Videoconferencing remains the most popular type of networked conference, but Web casting over the Internet is beginning to emerge as a viable alternative.

With a networked conference unnecessary travel time is eliminated, which allows busy sales representatives to concentrate on customers. Add up the salaries of people traveling to meetings, the outlay on travel, food, and accommodation, and you can estimate the real cost of conventional meetings. If your organization operates internationally, the potential cost savings are enormous and networked conferencing may be an option.

Enhance Communications

The freedom and flexibility of networked conferencing means you can arrange more meetings, whenever you need to improve communications. It's a quick and easy way of briefing sales teams, reporting, training or coaching, reviewing progress, or dealing with specific customer issues. Senior executives can communicate easily with sales teams throughout an organization by broadcasting annual reports, for example, or news about significant corporate changes.

Common Mistakes

Too Many Meetings

Major events, such as a national conference, are beneficial when there is an important announcement, such as a new product launch or corporate reorganization. However, too many meetings cover routine matters that could be handled through written or networked communications. Networked communications make it possible for sales representatives to participate in meetings without time-wasting travel. You should look carefully at your meeting program to see where you can eliminate unnecessary meetings or arrange alternative virtual events.

Failure to Back Up Presentations

Many conference presentations are designed for visual impact rather than communication. As a result, sales teams may come away impressed but with little hard material to use. You can back up theatrical presentations with business presentations and documentation to guarantee longer term benefits.

One-way Communication

A sales conference should involve more than one-way presentations. It should give the sales force an opportunity to participate and contribute to corporate policy. Discussion groups, question-and-answer sessions, feedback forms, and forums encourage sales force participation.

For More Information

Book:

Miller, William Skip. *ProActive Sales Management: How to Lead, Motivate, and Stay ahead of the Game.* New York: AMACOM, 2001.

Web Site:

American Marketing Association:
www.MarketingPower.com

See also:

✔ **Better Communication with Resellers (pp. 650–51)**
Conferences and Exhibitions (pp. 1935–36)
Selling and Salesmanship (pp. 2109–11)

"A manager's ability to turn meetings into a thinking environment is probably an organization's greatest asset."

(Nancy Kline)

Supporting Campaigns with Telemarketing

Getting Started

Telemarketing can improve the effectiveness of other sales and marketing programs, providing opportunities to increase sales and customer contact; improve service levels; carry out fast, cost-effective research; and reduce overall marketing costs.

FAQs

Can I replace a sales force with a telemarketing operation?

Replacing the sales force would be a drastic move, particularly if face-to-face contact is important. If your company sells low-value products that do not require presales or aftersales support, telemarketing may be appropriate. However, if the sales process is protracted or complex, direct contact is likely to be more effective. Integrating sales force and telemarketing activities can optimize the sales process and reduce overall sales costs.

Can I use an external telemarketing company to contact key accounts?

External telemarketing operations are extremely professional. They would normally receive full training in your products and your company. They would also be briefed on your company's processes and standards. When they make telephone contact, they act as your own company, and the customer should not notice any difference.

Do customers believe telephone research is credible?

There is a risk that customers will feel that research is not independent or objective if it is carried out by an internal telemarketing department. However, this may be outweighed by the speed and simplicity of the research.

Making It Happen

Take a Systematic Approach

Telemarketing involves a systematic approach to campaign support, where the telephone is used as a tool for improving the effectiveness of other sales and marketing programs.

According to the Institute of Direct Marketing, telemarketing is twice as effective as direct mail, and the inclusion of a telephone number can increase response by up to 185%. The Henley Centre's Telebusiness Survey reports that consumers are becoming more and more aware of the benefits of doing business by phone, and up to 80% see it as both convenient and easy.

Improve Order Taking

Taking orders by telephone improves speed and accuracy and is more convenient for customers than filling in and posting forms. The use of fax or interactive voice systems means that orders can be handled around the clock.

Open New Marketing Channels

Telemarketing offers opportunities for "direct" sales to customers. This reduces administration costs and bypasses or supplements traditional distribution routes.

Increase Lead Generation

Offering customers 800 or 888 numbers can increase response. The call information enables campaigns to be monitored and evaluated and provides information for planning future campaigns.

Carry Out Market Research

The telephone provides a fast, cost-effective medium for carrying out market research interviews. It also provides a valuable channel for capturing database information from helplines, inquiries, and telesales operations.

Speed Up Market Testing

Telephone marketing provides an opportunity to evaluate different marketing and promotional routes and to carry out rapid telephone research.

Improve Sales Support

Telemarketing can be used to enhance sales force performance and productivity. The telemarketing team can take responsibility for following up sales leads, setting up appointments and warm-calling qualified prospects (potential customers who meet certain criteria: for example in a particular demographic group; able to afford the products being sold; bought similar products previously). This frees the sales force for increasing the number of face-to-face meetings and for concentrating on top prospects.

Increase Customer Contact

Courtesy calls add a personal touch to the sales process and increase customer contact. They provide an opportunity to offer additional products and services and help to overcome any initial problems.

Support Customers with Carelines

Carelines enable customers to report problems and complaints—a convenient route that demonstrates customer care. Helplines make expertise available to customers, allowing staff to handle minor technical problems and reduce customer downtime.

Integrate Campaign Support

Integration is the key to effective, profitable customer relationship management, with telemarketing services at the heart of integrated campaigns. Your customers receive a consistent, high-quality service on every contact, and the integration can reduce your overall costs. The integrated approach is designed to:

- insure high-impact marketing campaigns;

"If the public doesn't believe the message conveyed by your product and its promotion, the marketing game is lost." (Robert Heller)

- increase retention rates for high-profit customers;
- maximize the profitability of each service relationship;
- cultivate customers who generate high profit levels;
- maximize return on marketing investments.

REDUCE MARKETING COSTS

Integration can play an important part in reducing your overall marketing costs, particularly if you have relied on a traditional field sales team. The cost of keeping a sales team on the road continues to soar, and it may not always represent the most cost-effective way of reaching the right people. Research indicates that more and more people accept the telephone as a first choice for doing business. This means you can refocus your sales and marketing activities, using the power and flexibility of telemarketing. You should identify high-cost sales and marketing tasks and look at alternatives based on direct marketing or telemarketing. Wherever possible, set measurable targets so that you can see just how much you are saving.

FOCUS ON PROFITABLE SECTORS

You can refocus sales effort by identifying profitable segments, and achieving high penetration levels through direct marketing and telephone follow-up. The average cost of a sale is reduced. Industry research indicates that many consumers prefer the indirect approach to a doorstep sale, adding customer satisfaction to the list of campaign benefits.

SUPPLEMENT YOUR SALES AND MARKETING RESOURCES

You can use external telemarketing resources to supplement your own skills. This gives you the flexibility to tailor individual campaigns and to run fully integrated campaigns, even when you have no in-house resources. You also can pull in extra support when you need to get new products to market in the shortest possible time. By using external call center teams or other resources, you can achieve that vital edge, without investing in recruitment or training. Most reputable call centers employ people who are trained to deliver the highest standards of customer service and are fully immersed in your company's products and culture. They act as professional representatives of your company.

MEASURE EFFECTIVENESS

Start by identifying profitable business opportunities and developing suitable campaigns. You can use emerging technologies to develop new applications and services that can drive your business forward, reducing your costs and improving performance. To help you plan and evaluate your campaigns, look at the management information available from telemarketing records, including:

- campaign response rates
- regional patterns
- call flow patterns
- call patterns on helplines
- analysis of customer requests

Information like this makes your campaigns fully accountable and measurable, enabling you to integrate them with your marketing and corporate objectives.

COMMON MISTAKES

DUPLICATING EFFORT

Telemarketing can be used to supplement other sales and marketing resources. However, it is easy to fall into the trap of duplicating effort, for example when both the sales force and the telemarketing team contact the customer about the same thing. With careful planning, you can integrate activities to make the most effective use of resources.

FAILING TO MEASURE ACTIVITIES

Telemarketing records can provide a great deal of valuable information, enabling you to measure the effectiveness of campaigns and to identify sales and marketing trends. By measuring performance and comparing alternative communication channels, you can identify the most cost-effective routes to market.

NOT TAKING FULL ADVANTAGE OF TELEMARKETING

Telemarketing can be used to support a wide range of sales and marketing activities. However, departmental rivalries may mean that a company does not take full advantage of telemarketing. Incentive programs and commission schemes also can prove to be barriers to effective integration.

For More Information

Book:

Linchitz, Joel. *The Complete Guide to Telemarketing Management*. New York: PFS Press, 2000.

Web Sites:

ACD Call Center Learning Center: **www.call-center.net/fr-articles.htm**

Call Centers: **www.mapnp.org/library/customer/cll_cntr.htm**

See also:

✔ **Generating More Leads (pp. 698–99)**
✔ **Improving Direct Mail Response Rates (pp. 686–87)**
✔ **Setting up a Customer Interaction Center (pp. 680–81)**

"They don't understand that the cold face of the marketing business is about bringing in cash, not just about having big ad campaigns."
(Vijay Solanhi)

Dealing with Press Inquiries

Getting Started

Handling press inquiries promptly, honestly, and efficiently can help your organization to obtain fair coverage in the press. Lack of cooperation can reflect unfavorably on an organization, so respond promptly to press inquiries, because journalists have publishing deadlines. Wherever possible, appoint one spokesperson to handle all inquiries.

FAQs

Who should deal with press inquiries?

Some companies appoint a single spokesperson who handles all inquiries. Others refer inquiries to the most appropriate specialist. It is essential that telephone operators are aware of the correct press contacts. It can be frustrating for journalists to be passed from one person to another. Alternatively, route all press inquiries to a public relations consultancy. If they cannot deal with the inquiry directly, they can refer the question to a specialist.

Does the Internet make management of press relations any easier?

The Internet makes it easier for journalists to obtain information. It also puts the onus on companies to become more transparent in their dealings with the media.

Should we encourage senior executives to hold press interviews?

Interviews with key figures can be valuable for both the company and the press. Although it is important to encourage openness, it can be equally valuable to maintain a degree of exclusivity so that journalists value an interview.

Making It Happen

Deal Positively with Press Inquiries

Handling press inquiries promptly, honestly, and efficiently can help your organization to obtain fair coverage in the press. If there is nobody ready to supply information, the line "No one was available for comment" is used. In certain circumstances, this can reflect unfavorably on an organization. You will have to deal with inquiries when a news story breaks involving your organization or your industry, or some topical issue is affecting your area of expertise, and journalists are looking for clarification or comment. Press inquiries also occur when journalists need further information on products or the company, so they can use a press release or feature article sent to them.

Provide the Right Contacts for Journalists

You should always respond promptly to press inquiries, because journalists have publishing deadlines to meet. Journalists should be able to reach a named contact, and a substitute should be available when necessary. Wherever possible, appoint one spokesperson to handle all inquiries. This will guarantee that the organization speaks with a consistent voice. Include the name of the spokesperson in all press releases and make sure that the switchboard is aware of the press contact or any substitute.

It is important that the spokesperson is fully briefed on current activity. If they cannot provide all the necessary information, let the journalist know that either the spokesperson or someone with more specialist knowledge will call back within an agreed time. Journalists also should be given reasonable access to specialists or senior executives, if necessary.

Make Press Conferences Count

A press conference provides an opportunity for an organization to meet journalists and editors in person and give them a detailed briefing on a new product or corporate development.

Press conferences can be important in a number of situations:

- the launch of a major new product;
- a significant corporate event;
- a news story, such as a takeover, which will have an important impact on the market.

An effective press conference provides mutual benefit to the organization and the press. If journalists have the opportunity to meet contacts or get detailed information that would otherwise be difficult, they see a conference as valuable. From your own point of view, a good press conference provides your organization with direct access to journalists and editors who would normally only be accessible by telephone. It also insures that the event receives effective coverage in the right media.

Prepare for a Press Conference

Planning and preparation are important to insure the success of your conference. These guidelines will help you prepare for a productive event.

- Invite journalists and editors from publications that reach your most important customers and prospects.
- Give details of time and location and try to confirm who will be attending.
- Try to plan the conference so that editorial coverage will appear in the next issue of the most important monthly publications.
- Make sure journalists understand the importance of the event.
- Provide press packs that include background information, specific information on the subject, photographs, and other relevant material.
- If necessary, make sure that senior executives or other specialists are available to answer detailed questions.
- If necessary, provide facilities for journalists such as telephones, Internet connections, and working areas, so they can produce and transmit material quickly to meet deadlines.
- Provide appropriate refreshments.
- If any important press contacts cannot attend, send

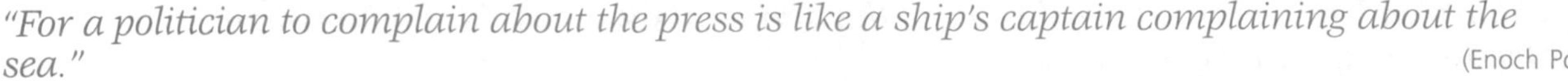

"For a politician to complain about the press is like a ship's captain complaining about the sea."

(Enoch Powell)

them a press pack and—if they're really important—arrange a separate meeting.

Arrange Interviews with Key People

An interview with a senior executive or specialist provides an opportunity for an organization to meet selected journalists and give them a detailed briefing on a new product or corporate development. The advantage to the press is that this process is more selective than a press conference and gives them an opportunity for an "exclusive." Ideally, there is mutual benefit for the organization and the press, because your company gets its message across to the right people in the right way, and journalists have open access to key figures.

Identify Opportunities for Interviews

An interview can be arranged either at the request of the press, or as part of a planned press relations program. Interviews can be important in a number of situations, including:

- the launch of a major new product;
- a significant corporate event, such as the opening of a new factory;
- a news story, such as a takeover, which will have an important effect on the market;
- the financial results of an important organization;
- the appointment of a new senior executive or specialist manager which might affect the prospects or future direction of your organization.

Prepare for an Interview

You should arrange the interview for selected journalists and editors from publications that reach your most important customers and prospects. If necessary, you can make the interview exclusive by limiting it to one publication only or one publication in each sector. Make sure that the person to be interviewed is fully briefed on the subject of the interview, and provide press packs. As with a press conference, provide facilities for journalists such as telephones, Internet connections, and working areas, so they can produce and transmit material quickly to meet deadlines.

Provide Background with a Press Pack

A press pack should contain background information on an organization and its products. It can be issued to press, television, or radio journalists in conjunction with press releases or feature articles, or distributed on its own.

Press packs can cover a variety of topics, including:

- the company, its products, and its services
- important recent developments
- key members of the management team
- financial and market information

The information can be used to fill in background if a journalist is writing a news item or editing a press release on the organization. It also can form the basis of a news item or feature article. Whenever you hold a press conference, launch event, interview, or press visit, make sure that journalists and editors have an up-to-date pack. Include any specific information that is relevant to the event. As a matter of routine, send a press pack to any new press contact.

Produce an Up-to-date Pack

Press packs are only useful if they are current and informative. These guidelines will help you produce an effective pack:

- Information should be typed, double-spaced.
- Names and telephone numbers of key personnel should be included.
- A contact name for further information should be provided.
- A selection of product or personnel photographs should be included.

Distributing them properly also is helpful:

- Press packs can be given directly to journalists and editors at events or press visits, or mailed.
- Wherever possible, they should be given to a named individual.
- Maintain a list of contacts who have received press packs and make sure that you send them updated information, whenever it is available.

Common Mistakes

Ignoring Press Inquiries

If a PR problem occurs, it's easy to ignore press inquiries and hope that journalists will go away. They rarely do, and the lack of cooperation from your company could lead to adverse reports in the press. If journalists don't have hard information, they have to rely on their own assumptions and this could create problems.

Calling a Press Conference for an Unimportant Event

Journalists cannot attend every press conference they are invited to. If your conference is not really newsworthy, you may lose their attention when it comes to later, more important events. You have to be ruthless about the value of the conference to journalists.

Failing to Keep Press Information Current

Journalists base their stories on the information they have. Press packs and other background material must be amended whenever information changes.

For More Information

Book:

Bland, Michael, Alison Theaker, and David Wragg *Effective Media Relations*. Dover, NH: Kogan Page, 2000.

Web Sites:

Institute for Public Relations: **www.instituteforpr.com**

International Public Relations Association: **www.ipranet.org**

See also:

✔ **Producing Press Material (pp. 726–27)**
✔ **Running a Product Public Relations Campaign (pp. 728–29)**
Public Relations (pp. 2090–92)

"The British Press is always looking for stuff to fill the space between their cartoons."

(Bernadette Devlin)

  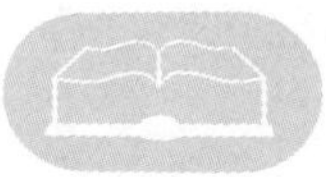    

MANAGING RETAILER MARKETING PROGRAMS

GETTING STARTED

If you are implementing retailer or distributor marketing programs, consistency across the board is important in order to insure the message is not diluted. Central support is therefore vital. There are many steps you can take to help make the program a success, and to make the best use of budgets.

FAQs

WHY SHOULD LOCAL ADVERTISING BE MANAGED?

It is easy for local outlets to develop and run their own advertisements. This can weaken a brand or corporate identity and give conflicting messages to different customers. A strong management program insures consistent standards and also makes better use of available funds.

SHOULD ALL LOCAL OUTLETS RUN THE SAME MARKETING PROGRAM?

It is not essential to run identical programs in all markets. However, consistent treatment helps local outlets to benefit from repeated communication of the same brand values. Campaigns should be tailored to local market conditions but should incorporate key visual standards and corporate messages.

WHO DECIDES HOW LOCAL MARKETING FUNDS SHOULD BE ALLOCATED?

Individual outlets have the best knowledge of their local markets, but they may not have the skills to plan and operate cost-effective marketing campaigns. By centralizing the management of advertising and marketing programs, local outlets benefit from professional advice and guidance and the cumulative effect of integrated national, regional, and local campaigns.

MAKING IT HAPPEN

HELP DISTRIBUTORS USE MARKETING PROGRAMS

Suppliers can produce a guide to support their programs which enables local outlets to select the ones that allow them to develop their own promotional strategies. The guides should explain the scope and benefits of individual programs; describe the support material available; explain how to order support material; and provide guidelines on running the programs.

SET UP A DISTRIBUTOR MARKETING DATABASE

The key to the success of local marketing programs is detailed knowledge of the local customer base, so that offers and information can be tailored. Maintain a central database of all local customers and use database management techniques to organize the mailing lists. Local outlets are unlikely to have the sophisticated equipment needed to carry out database management operations, so centralizing the exercise is probably more effective.

The database would contain the names and addresses of each outlet's customers, together with variable information such as purchasing patterns, size of expenditure, type of purchase, and number of employees.

KEEP DATABASE INFORMATION UP TO DATE

Information for the database can be gathered from a number of sources, including:

- local customer sales records
- replies to advertisements
- responses to special offers or invitations
- applications for membership
- market research

The initial database is unlikely to be complete or to provide information in the most suitable format, so companies who wish to benefit from direct marketing run special campaigns to gather appropriate information. For example, an invitation to an open evening or a prize draw would require customers to provide information that is essential for the database. Local outlets can be given guidelines on the way to build and maintain their own records so that they provide suitable input to the database. A series of mailings can then be carried out to meet business and marketing objectives. By managing the process centrally and working in close conjunction with retailers, suppliers can make sure that their local outlets enjoy a direct marketing service that is of professional quality, as well as being precisely tailored to their local market.

OPERATE A CUSTOMIZED ADVERTISING SERVICE

Local or regional advertising campaigns can be customized to suit the needs of the local market. Support can be delivered in a number of forms:

- funds to enable local outlets to produce and run their own advertisements
- contributions to the cost of joint supplier and local outlet advertisements
- contributions to the cost of advertisements run by regional groups of outlets
- production of national support advertisements that incorporate local information and are run on a regional basis
- support for advertisements run in conjunction with regional radio or television stations

OFFER FUNDING OPTIONS

The level of support depends on the funds available for local support and the outlet's own budget. For example, many independent outlets have substantial advertising budgets of their own and utilize the supplier's budget to supplement these, or to run specific campaigns. Other smaller outlets or franchised outlets without their own budgets rely entirely on the supplier's contribution to run local campaigns. The question of financial support is therefore usually subject to negotiation.

SUPPLY ADVERTISING MATERIAL

The more practical forms of support—complete advertisements, logos, artwork, photographs—can be supplied

---

"There is only one winning strategy. It is to carefully define the target market and direct a superior offering to that target market."
(Philip Kotler)

for inclusion in the outlet's own local campaigns. The supplier is likely to be more concerned about the consistency of advertisements than the local outlet and should issue clear guidelines on the use of different elements of corporate identity. Many suppliers provide advertising standards manuals which give examples of layouts for different sizes of advertisements, explain the position and size of the company name and logo, list the typefaces to use, and include sample advertisements for guidance.

Set Up a Centralized Advertising Service

Alternatively, the supplier can offer local outlets a central advertising service. This support policy enables suppliers to offer advertising to local outlets at consistent professional standards, incorporating local information (such as name, address, and map), priced offers, product variations, and special offers. Then the local outlet benefits from national advertising and strong branding, but also has advertisements that suit the local market.

Run Regional Advertising Programs

The regional approach also can be used to establish a cooperative advertising program between groups of local outlets. Local outlets pool their budgets and are able to build a higher profile by running larger advertisements or advertising more frequently. Each outlet includes its own name and address, but the advertisement promotes the generic benefits of the group. Some regional advertisements feature priced offers that are available at all the outlets in the group. This requires a high degree of cooperation between local outlets to set the target prices. However, suppliers should be aware that in the United States, the Federal Trade Commission (FTC) may regard this as a form of cartel. Suppliers should therefore seek guidance on the procedure for obtaining OFT approval for joint priced advertisements.

Providing a central form of support for local advertisements not only insures consistency and good branding but also can help to make the most effective use of limited budgets. By purchasing all advertising space or time centrally, the supplier can negotiate more effective rates based on volume purchase.

Take Advantage of Direct Marketing

The essence of an effective local support program is that local outlets understand their customers' needs and provide a level of service that is tailored to that market. In terms of customer satisfaction, the most powerful medium available to companies is direct marketing. The information in the marketing database provides a good basis for effective direct marketing programs. By operating them centrally in the same way as advertising, manufacturers can maintain quality and consistency.

Support Local Events

Local events such as open evenings, trade shows, and customer receptions are a powerful method of building customer loyalty, but they need to be handled professionally to achieve the right results. By providing the appropriate level of support, suppliers can help local outlets develop a program of events that suits their local market. The support includes:

- the development of suitable promotional and display material
- the theme for the event
- the design and production of invitations
- generation of mailing lists
- support literature
- personal support by members of the head office team

Common Mistakes

Failure to Control Local Spending

Local outlets frequently run marketing programs to meet ad hoc objectives. This can lead to fragmented communication and poor use of funds. The value of local marketing funds can be increased by integrating different campaigns and reinforcing local initiatives with national campaigns.

No Database

The marketing database is essential to the control of local marketing programs. It supports effective program administration and, more importantly, it allows companies to monitor and measure the effectiveness of programs. Response levels can be measured and compared across different regions and the effects of different spending levels assessed. The database also holds details of local marketing programs as a basis for direct marketing and telemarketing programs.

Poor Administration

Efficient administration is an important part of local marketing support, but it is frequently handled poorly. By setting up a process for ordering marketing support material, booking advertising space, invoicing local outlets, and recording responses, you can gain greater control over the marketing program and ensure that funds are used more effectively.

For More Information

Book:

Kotler, Philip. *Marketing Management: Millennium Edition*. Englewood Cliffs, NJ: Prentice Hall, 1999.

Web Sites:

Council of Logistics Management: **www.clm1.org**
The Supply Chain Council: **www.supply-chain.org**

See also:

✓ **Better Communication with Resellers (pp. 650–51)**
Logistics and Distribution (pp. 2026–28)
Marketing Management (pp. 2045–48)

 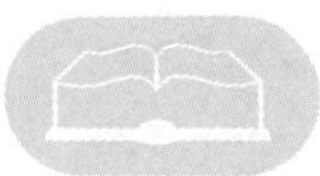    

Offering Customers Self-service

Getting Started

Offering self-service facilities to customers via the Internet has considerable benefits. For customers, being able to obtain information and place orders whenever they want is extremely convenient. And suppliers can obtain precise data on what customers want, as well as cutting down on administration costs. The only proviso is that the Web site must be constantly available and properly supported.

FAQs

Doesn't self-service weaken customer relationships?

Opinion is divided over the impact of self-service. In the professions, for example, some companies are concerned that their reputation for high-quality personal service is reduced. Other businesses argue that putting simple services online frees staff for more complex customer projects. In industry, the popularity of self-service among customers has convinced some companies that this is the most suitable way to deal with them. The quantity of customer information available from self-service sites is also important, provided it is used to strengthen relationships through tailored service.

If a customer makes a mistake as a result of using self-service facilities, whose fault is it?

Organizations which provide advice and guidance through a self-service facility must assess the risk of mistakes and include warning notices on the site. The warning might take the form of a phrase such as, "You should seek professional advice before taking any action."

Should self-service be the only form of support available to customers?

While self-service support benefits both parties, it may leave customers feeling vulnerable if they cannot get a satisfactory answer from the site. Including a backup telephone facility reassures customers that personal service is available if it is needed. You can discourage unnecessary use by charging a fee for the service.

Making It Happen

Identify Applications for Self-Service

The Internet enables companies to offer customers self-service facilities. Self-service reduces customer support costs and improves convenience for customers. It means companies can deliver service around the clock without tying up key staff. It also enables them to reduce their telephone-based support facilities by transferring support resources to a Web site. Self-service is important in delivery of information, direct sales, sales administration, customer support, and technical support.

Give Customers More Choice

With self-service, customers can obtain information on products, prices, features, and order status from a Web site, then place orders directly. The process is spreading throughout industry as manufacturers recognize the benefits of self-service in terms of cost, control, and customer satisfaction. Self-service gives manufacturers greater control over the sales process and customer relationships, and also reduces sales and distribution costs. Customers themselves recognize the value of these services; many have reported significant savings in productivity through improved support and better asset management. Having such a choice strengthens customer relationships and makes self-service a powerful differentiator.

Gain Better Customer Information

Self-service provides precise information on what customers want, so it is essential to tailor the service to meet those requirements and make self-service a rewarding experience. Support levels, for example, can be customized to individual user profiles, making service delivery more convenient and cost effective. Customer information can also be used to develop customized, added-value services. For example, business customers can be provided with personalized Web pages that include access to: their own product configurations; automated, paperless orders; order tracking; asset management facilities; and individual support tools. Components manufacturers offer services such as online design and specification to their customers, as well as high levels of technical support.

Improve Customer Convenience

Customers now expect service to be available 24 hours a day. They want a choice of services, personalized to their own requirements, and they want these services at competitive prices. Enabling customers to help themselves meets those criteria. Although it appears to reduce the element of personal service that is crucial to customer relationships, the convenience of self-service can add value and give a company even greater control. The challenge is to turn basic self-service into a highly differentiated product. The Internet allows companies to link products, businesses, and services into a database that customers can use to help themselves with routine tasks. By tailoring these products and using the customer information they contain, suppliers can offer a service that is even more personal than traditional face-to-face meetings.

Give Customers Automated Tools

A firm of brokers gives clients a personal minibroking system that they can use any time, day or night. Clients are offered a choice of tasks such as getting a quotation for car insurance. Many of the functions are highly automated, making it quick and easy for clients to get quotes—all they have to do is choose the type of cover they want. The system provides a selection of quotations and makes it easy to highlight and compare the benefits of different policies. Once the client has accepted a quotation, the system turns it into a live policy. Once credit card payment is completed, customers can print off their own certificate of insurance and policy details. This is self-service at its best and provides users with a quick, convenient, round-the-clock service.

Simplify Customer Support

Although support is a critical element in customer relationship management, many organizations see it as an expensive overhead. They want to reduce capital investment and operating costs, and to free skilled resources to focus on other activities. Many of them are therefore turning to self-service support as a cost-effective alternative. Online support tools use the speed and convenience of Web-based contact facilities to simplify support management and improve customer service. So customers can place support requests through various channels, including text, voiceover IP, e-mail, fax, and Web forms.

Speed Up Fault Resolution

Self-service support cuts the costs for the supplier and speeds up service for the customer. Customers can solve many problems themselves, by using frequently asked questions or interrogating an online service database. The latest support tools are using the power of data mining and knowledge management to improve fault resolution even further. They insure that all support knowledge and experience is captured and managed on a central database, which is continuously updated. This database insures that users get rapid access to the latest information. It can also distinguish trends as a basis for identifying emerging or recurring problems and providing alternative resources.

Encourage Customers to Help Each Other

A components manufacturer has made a significant saving in its customer support costs by enabling customers to serve themselves through an e-commerce site. Customers help themselves to technical support and order status information via personalized Web pages that hold full details of their own products, specifications, component requirements, and technical issues. The manufacturer has added value to this one-to-one service by encouraging community between all of its customers. Customers answer other customers' technical questions and help each other out publicly on the company's Web site. The site also provides shared access to design and technical tools that customers can use in their own projects.

Deliver Consistent Service

It is essential to offer the highest standards of service. In practical terms, that means a Web site that is constantly available, easily accessible information, and high levels of customer support behind the Web site. Although self service saves everyone time, experience indicates that customers need the reassurance that they can also talk to a specialist if they are having problems. You can provide this backup by including an automatic telephone callback facility on a Web page.

Common Mistakes

Failing to Use Customer Information to Enhance Self-Service

Self-service facilities provide vast amounts of data on customer purchasing habits, support requirements, and information needs. This information should be used continually to enhance the customer experience and develop services and processes that meet customer requirements more closely. Ignoring such data is a wasted opportunity.

Giving Customers Limited Choice

Self-service is just one method of delivering service. You should ask customers how they prefer to deal with you. You can then offer a range of service and support options with different charges for each level. For example, customer support packages can be offered at gold, silver, and bronze levels, with bronze as the most basic package. Self-service can be part of a portfolio, enabling customers to match your support to their operational needs.

Providing an Unreliable Service to Customers

Customers expect a service that is easy to use, as well as always available and reliable. It must be well supported with appropriate management, infrastructure, and staffing. Any loss of quality could damage your company's reputation.

Putting the Wrong Services Online

Not all services are suitable for online delivery. Simple queries, briefing material, news updates, and frequently asked questions are common, but more complex queries are best handled directly by specialists. Providing only what appear to be standard answers may create the wrong impression of your company.

For More Information

Book:

Seybold, Patricia. *Customers.com: How to Create a Profitable Business Strategy for the Internet & Beyond.* New York: Times Books, 1998.

Web Site:

Patricia Seybold Group: **www.psgroup.com**

See also:

☆ **The Second Coming of Service (pp. 77–78)**
☆ **Viewpoint: Patty Seybold (pp. 67–68)**
✔ **Extending a Product with Service (pp. 718–19)**

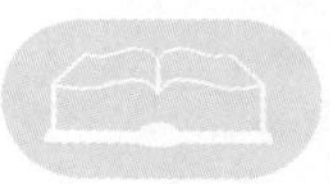

Finding Your Calling and Living Your Passion: The Dream Job

Getting Started

Do you wake up in the morning full of excitement and enthusiasm about your day? Or do you dread going to work? If your job is sapping the life out of you, then it is time to reassess your life and your work. If you feel like an old dream is stirring and just won't go away, then it is time to discover and pursue your calling. The following questions provide thoughts for reflection as you take the first steps in responding to your calling:

- What keeps you in your current job, even though you are unhappy?
- What skills and talents are unused?
- What dreams have you buried because they weren't "practical"?
- What would a "dream job" look like to you?
- What are you willing to sacrifice in order to have a dream job?

FAQs

Isn't work supposed to be painful? Isn't that why they call it work?

No, work is not supposed to be painful. If you believe that, then you will settle for less and never be completely satisfied. Work is as natural to human beings as breathing. We feel bored, dissatisfied, and empty if we cannot contribute to the world in some meaningful way. Freud said that there are two important things in life: work and love.

I'm just getting started in my career. Don't I have to pay my dues first before I can find work I truly love?

Certainly you shouldn't expect to jump into the job of your dreams straight out of school. Unless, of course, you started the company! You do need to spend time in a new job learning the ropes and making connections. But don't ever think of it as "Paying My Dues." This kind of thinking encourages staying in a job that may not really suit you. You should expect to be excited about going to work each day.

I'm getting near retirement. Isn't it a little late to be thinking about finding my calling?

Many people who are nearing retirement grew up in a culture where work was expected to be drudgery. You may have sacrificed your dreams for most of your life, but now is your chance to take the time to do something you really. love. You might consider volunteer work, being a mentor to someone getting started, or finding a company that really appreciates the wisdom of older people.

Making It Happen

Assessment

Begin by assessing your skills and talents. Make a list of all the things you have been good at. On this same piece of paper, make three columns. The first one is labeled "Current Job." In this column put a check next to all the skills and talents you are currently using. The second column is labeled "Joy and Meaning." Here put a check next to any skill that brings you joy and a sense of meaning when you are using it. This includes skills that you may not currently be using in your job. The third column is labeled "Dream Job." In this column put a check next to any skills that you would like to use in a "Dream Job." As you are doing this exercise, you may think of other skills and you can add them to the list. After completing the checklists, make some notes for yourself about any thoughts and ideas that came up about what a dream job might be.

Dream

Think about the dream you may have buried because it wasn't practical. Dreams can come true, but you have to be willing to believe in them. Read stories about people who have made their dreams come true. *Find Your Calling, Love Your Life* (see For More Information) is an excellent source of inspiration. The source of a "calling" often comes from difficult or painful experiences that we have experienced or overcome. It becomes our calling, then, to help other people with similar difficulties.

Be of Service

Focus on the principle of service. All vocational callings have a strong element of service in them. Whom do you serve? How can you use your gifts and talents to serve them? What issues in the community, in business, or in society do you care about? Have you ever wished you could make a difference? These are clues to your calling.

Do What Brings You Joy

In order to be of service to others, we first have to do what brings us joy. So do what pleases you, and you will probably find that you are acquiring knowledge and skills that will help you to be of service to others in the future. And sometimes it is enough just to know that if you do what brings you joy, even if it is not of service to anyone else, the world is a better place. The world could certainly do with a little more joy.

Make It Real

Make your dream real in some concrete way. Write down a description of your dream job. Write in your journal about what "calls" to you. Tell other people about your dream job. You will find that as you get more and more detailed about what you are looking for, opportunities will "coincidentally" appear. Make sure you are paying attention to these opportunities.

Talk to Others

Don't be afraid to tell others about your calling. The more you tell others about your dreams, the more real they

---

"Success can be attained in any branch of human labor. There is always room at the top in every pursuit."

(Andrew Carnegie)

become, and the more likely you are to notice opportunities that will help you fulfill your dreams. Also, by telling others about the job you would love to have, you are increasing the chances of finding someone who has just the right piece of information, or just the right connection for you.

Learn to Fly

Remember the rule of the bumblebee. According to the laws of mathematics and aerodynamics, it is physically impossible for bumblebees to fly. Fortunately, no one ever explained that to a bumblebee. Keep in mind that the most successful business people and entrepreneurs were frequently told that what they wanted to do was "impossible."

Let Go

In order to follow your calling, there are always necessary sacrifices that must be made. Before you make the move to another job or to starting your own business, spend some time thinking about what are absolute necessities in your life and work. Is it essential that you have high earnings, or are you willing to earn less money to do work that is more meaningful? Is it essential that you have a steady paycheck, or are you excited about the risk and potential in working for a small start-up organization? Is it essential that you work with people, or are you content to work alone? What things are absolutely necessary to you in your work, and what can you do without? Make a list of five things that are necessary and five things that you are willing to do without.

Look In Your Own Backyard

There's an old song that goes, "If you can't be with the one you love, love the one you're with." This can apply to your job too. Many people cannot easily leave their current job. The challenge, then, is how to see your current work as your calling. Once again, the principle of "Service" can be very helpful. If you need to stay with your current job, write yourself a brief reminder about how the work you do is of service to others, and keep it somewhere nearby.

Common Mistakes

Many people think that their dream job already exists, and that they just have to look around hard enough until they find it. The truth is that most people who have found their calling have actually created the work that they do. Don't go looking in the classified advertisements for the dream job. You must network, make connections, and tell other people about your dreams.

When you begin to follow your calling, there will always be people who will tell you that you are impractical, unrealistic, idealistic, or selfish. It would be a mistake to listen to them. They are the people who want to tell the bumblebee that it can't fly. Remember that just because it's never been done before, it doesn't mean that you can't do it.

Beware of a job that is too good to be true, especially if you are being asked to put in your own money, or to work for very little money at first. Scam artists understand the hunger that people have for a dream job, and they can play on that. If you are being offered a job that really seems to fit what you are looking for, make sure that you are going to be paid what you are worth.

Sometimes people get too attached to their idea of what a "perfect job" would look like. Beware of being too picky and of passing up opportunities that could turn out to be even better than the job you are looking for. Keep an open mind, but at the same time don't settle for something that doesn't fit your values, or that doesn't really use your most important skills and talents.

For More Information

Books:

Finney, Martha, and Deborah Dasch. *Find Your Calling, Love Your Life*. New York: Simon & Schuster, 1998.

Levoy, Gregg. *Callings: Finding and Following an Authentic Life*. New York: Harmony Books, 1997.

Web Sites:

Martha Finney's Web site, Working From the HeartLand: **www.heartlandatwork.com**

Fast Company: "Find Your Calling": **www.fastcompany.com/feature/00/act_corcazzini.html**

See also:

☆ **Avoiding Your Worst Career Nightmare (pp. 316–17)**
☆ **Taking Charge of Your Career (pp. 324–25)**
☆ **Urbane Renewal: Trusting Your Own Wisdom—A Competitive (And Satisfying) Advantage (pp. 320–21)**
✓ **Creating and Balancing the Portfolio Career (pp. 804–05)**
✓ **Succeeding As a New Manager (pp. 414–15)**
Planning Your Career (pp. 2075–77)

CHOOSING THE RIGHT FIRST JOB

GETTING STARTED

Your first job sets the tone for the rest of your career. It is extremely important to choose the right first job. If you aim low, your career path may be limited as a result. If you choose the wrong company, your choice could haunt you for years. The following points are questions to consider as you prepare to network and to market yourself:

- What kind of a career have you prepared yourself for?
- Are you financially able to hold out for the best job?
- How prepared are you to launch a professional job campaign?

FAQs

WHY IS MY FIRST JOB SO IMPORTANT?

The average person works for seven or more companies in their lifetime. When you are looking for your second job, employers will evaluate you by your job title and by the prestige of the company where you first worked. It is extremely difficult to go from a low-level position at an unknown organization into a much higher position in a well-known organization. However, it is much easier to go from a good professional position at a well-known company into a better professional position at an even more successful organization.

WHAT IF I WANT TO WORK IN A NON-PROFIT ORGANIZATION?

Your first job is still important. There is a hierarchy among non-profit organizations in terms of prestige, power, status, and success, just as there is in for-profit organizations. This hierarchy may not influence career choices so heavily, but it still has an effect. Ideally, you are better off establishing your career by working for a well-known and successful non-profit organization than by working for a small, idealistic, but unknown and unconnected organization. If you truly want to have a positive impact on the world (which is most people's motivation for working in a non-profit organization), you are probably better off if you can do that in an organization with resources and clout.

WHAT ABOUT THE IDEA OF BEING A BIG FISH IN A SMALL POND?

If you are not very ambitious, or are more comfortable in small organizations, then you might want to take a higher level position in a smaller organization as your first job. One of the benefits of doing this is that you learn more about the total organization than if you have an entry-level position in a large organization.

WHAT KEY QUESTION SHOULD I BE ASKING MYSELF IN ORDER TO PLAN MY CAREER STRATEGY WHEN I LOOK FOR MY FIRST JOB?

The key question you should be asking yourself is "Do I want to be a specialist or a generalist?" If you have chosen a particular field to pursue (such as biology, engineering, finance, music, or nursing) that you are really passionate about, then you probably are a specialist. If, on the other hand, you are interested in eventually becoming an organizational leader or an entrepreneur, you are probably more of a generalist. As a specialist, you would want to choose a first job that allows you in time to progress more deeply in your field. As a generalist, you would want to choose a first job that will offer you opportunities to learn more about other fields, and to expand your leadership abilities.

MAKING IT HAPPEN

TAKE TIME TO THINK ABOUT THE KIND OF LIFE AND CAREER PATH YOU WANT TO HAVE, EVEN BEFORE YOU BEGIN YOUR JOB CAMPAIGN

At this point, you have already done a great deal of career preparation through your education and perhaps through some additional training. Think back and remember why you chose this field. Is it still relevant? Will it give you the kind of lifestyle you want in terms of how you spend your time and how much money you want to make?

WRITE A "WORK PURPOSE STATEMENT"

The following exercise is adapted from *Zen and the Art of Making a Living* (see For More Information):

Complete each of the following sentences:

- The way I want to contribute is . . .
- The people I want to serve are . . .
- The scale I want to work at is . . . (e.g.: individual, community, national, global)

Now combine the essence of each of these sentences into one statement about your work purpose that includes who you want to serve, the way you want to serve them, and the scope of the impact you want to make.

EXPLORE POSSIBLE CAREER ROLES

Make a list of at least 10 different career roles that would be compatible with your "Work Purpose Statement." Now select the three that are most interesting to you.

LEARN ABOUT THE LIFESTYLE ASSOCIATED WITH EACH OF THESE CAREER ROLES

Use the Internet, the library, and personal contacts to get a better understanding of what it would be like to work in each of these potential career roles. Find out what a typical day is like for someone who does this career role.

ASSESS YOUR FINANCIAL SITUATION AND YOUR TIMESCALE

Determine how long you have to find your first job. If you do not have the financial support to wait for the "perfect" first job, then decide on your minimum criteria for accepting a position. These criteria could be financial, working conditions, geographic, or any other criteria. At the very least, if you are accepting a job that does not fit your "Work Purpose," then be sure that it gives you the time and opportunity to keep looking for a better position.

"In an economy where for the first time jobs are looking for people. . .ensuring that no American is left behind is as much an economic as a moral imperative." (Lawrence H. Summers)

Prepare to Launch Your Job Campaign

See other Actionlists in this section to create a professional CV, make your contact list, prepare for your interview, and create your networking plan.

Common Mistakes

You Choose a Career that Someone Else Thinks You Should Pursue

All too often, people choose a career path that their parents or a favorite teacher thinks they should pursue. Someone may say to you, "Your father and grandfather and uncle are all lawyers (or doctors, or teachers, or businessmen). Of course that is what you will do. It's family tradition." But this does not take into account your unique gifts and talents. It does not take into account what you feel called to do.

You Take a Job Because It Pays Well

If you are lucky enough to be offered several alternatives when you are looking for your first job, it is tempting to take the one with the highest salary. When you are starting your career, this is what seems to make the most sense. But it is short-term thinking. If the job does not fit your personality or your sense of purpose in life, you will either be looking for another job, or you will stay and be miserable. It's much better to take a long-term view when you accept your first job and to ask, "How will this job help me to develop my abilities so that I can best fill my work purpose and my personal and professional goals?"

You Jump at the First Offer

It is a mistake to take the first offer if you have applied for several jobs. But sometimes people lack confidence and think, "A bird in the hand is worth two in the bush." They are afraid that if they ask a potential employer to wait, they will lose that opportunity. But employers understand this situation, and are usually willing to give you some extra time while you wait for other offers. Also, even if you get an offer from your number one pick, it is usually a good idea to say to them, "Thank you so much. I'm really interested in your offer, but I would like to take a couple of days to think about it." If you eagerly accept a position without taking a little bit of cooling-off time, you may be jumping into something when you haven't considered some of the possible pitfalls.

You Go to Work for a Family Member or a Friend Because That's the Easiest Thing to Do

Everybody expects you to join the family business. Or your parents encourage a family friend to hire you. It seems so easy to fall into this. But that is putting your career and your life's direction into someone else's hands, and it is not taking responsibility for yourself. It may be that one of these opportunities is the perfect one for you. Take time to analyze and follow the steps above so that you are making a rational and informed decision.

You Avoid Trying to Find the Kind of Work You Would Really Love, Because People Tell You that the Job Market Is Bad or It's Not Practical

It is amazing what you can do if you are determined to make your dream come true. You can be incredibly creative and resourceful. It may be that you will have to work harder and take a little longer to find the kind of work you would really love to have, but it will be worth it in the long run.

For More Information

Books:

Boldt, Laurence. *Zen and the Art of Making a Living: A Practical Guide to Creative Career Design.* New York: Penguin USA, 1993.

Bolles, Richard. *What Color is Your Parachute? 2002.* Berkeley, CA: Ten Speed Press, 2001.

Web Site:

The Job Hunters Bible:
www.jobhuntersbible.com

See also:

✓ **Identifying Your Marketable Skills (pp. 748–49)**
✓ **Researching the Job Market (pp. 756–57)**
Job Hunting (pp. 2017–18)

"Whether it's choosing a career or deciding what charity to get involved with, the choice should come from your heart."
(Dave Thomas)

IDENTIFYING YOUR MARKETABLE SKILLS

GETTING STARTED

Most of us tend to think too narrowly about our marketable skills, and thus undersell ourselves when we are looking for a promotion or a new job. This Actionlist will provide you with a step-by-step approach to examining your life and work experiences, so that you can assess which of the many skills you have are the most marketable. As you read this, here are some questions for you to consider:

- What are your personal and professional goals?
- What educational, work and leisure experiences have you had that will help you reach your goal?
- Do you have a realistic picture of the match between your skills and your career goal?

FAQs

WHY IS IT IMPORTANT TO IDENTIFY MY MARKETABLE SKILLS?

There are two reasons for doing this. The first, and most pragmatic, is that it will help you to write a more powerful résumé. The second is that it will help you to present yourself more professionally to a potential employer. You will feel confident about what you have to offer and will sell yourself better.

WHAT IF I DON'T WANT TO KEEP ON DOING WHAT I AM SKILLED AT NOW?

The steps described below are designed to help you identify the skills that will get you the job you want. If you are planning to change careers, it is important to realize that you may have many transferable skills that will be marketable in a new position. Or you may have skills that you haven't used for some time that could be very useful in a new position.

MAKING IT HAPPEN

It takes a lot of time and energy to identify your marketable skills. It is not an easy task, but it is one of the most important you can undertake because it helps you to plan your job campaign and to target the best potential employers. It also gives you a strong sense of confidence in what you have to offer.

BEGIN WITH THE END IN MIND

In order to identify the marketable skills that you have, you must know what kind of a position you are looking for. This creates the context for thinking about the skills that you want to use in your next job. See the Actionlist on finding your dream job for guidance.

WRITE A BRIEF LIFE/WORK BIOGRAPHY

Take the time to sit down and write a 3–5 page history of your life that includes: significant events when you were growing up, important educational experiences, and a summary of your work experiences. As you write about each of these experiences, describe what you liked, what you didn't like, and what you accomplished. What were you most proud of? Also describe what you did during times when you were not working, and how you felt about those activities. Make sure that there are at least seven key events in your biography.

What, if anything, did writing your biography tell you about potentially marketable skills that you might have?

EDUCATIONAL ASSESSMENT

Whether or not you included much detail about your educational experiences, here is a useful assessment that may help to highlight some of your skills and interests:

- What teachers did you like best and why?
- What teachers did you like least and why?
- Which subjects did you like best and why?
- Which subjects did you like least and why?
- Which subjects did you get the best grades in and why?
- Which subjects did you get the worst grades in and why?

Based on what you have written, identify five key skills or knowledge areas that you might like to use in your next position.

WORK EXPERIENCE ASSESSMENT

Review each of the jobs that you have held and ask yourself the following questions:

- What was my favorite job and why?
- What was my least favorite job and why?
- Which of these jobs would I do even if I didn't get paid? Why?
- Which jobs really challenged me and helped me to develop personally and professionally? Why?

Based on what you have written, identify five key skills or knowledge areas that you might like to use in your next position.

LEISURE ACTIVITY ASSESSMENT

In the times you are not working (whether evenings and weekends, or longer periods of time when you have been between jobs), what do you really enjoy doing with your leisure time? Here are questions to consider:

- What skills have you developed from a hobby that might be marketable?
- What skills have you developed from your travels?
- What skills have you developed from other leisure time activities?
- Is there something you do for fun that you always dreamed of getting paid for?

Again, identify the five most marketable skills you have from your leisure activity assessment.

LIST ACHIEVEMENTS

Now go over what you have written and create a list of at least 10 major achievements in your life. Don't worry about whether or not they are work-related. When you have completed the list, rank your achievements in order, with number one being your most important achievement, number two being your second most important achievement, and so on.

"A professional is a man who can do his job when he doesn't feel like it. An amateur is a man who can't do his work when he does feel like it."

(James Agate)

Put It All Together

You can now create your final Skills Inventory by going over all that you have done so far and putting the information about your skills into the following categories. If you need help identifying other potential skills that you might have, visit the Web site listed below for ideas.

- Make a list of all your skills that are related to management in any way. Although your current job title may not classify you as a "a manager," you may still do some activities that are considered managerial. These can include policy formulation, policy implementation, conducting performance reviews, hiring, firing, project responsibilities, problem solving, budgetary responsibilities, planning, organizing, presenting, and so on.
- Make a list of all of your training skills, including any informal training you may have done. Training can be for individuals or for groups. Also list any certifications you may have received for programs you are certified to teach. Include any other professional training programs, seminars, and symposiums you have attended.
- Make a list of all of your documentation skills where you have prepared reports, manuals, summarized research, conducted studies, and so on.
- Make a list of all your technical skills which may include operating machines or computers, any specialized knowledge, any manufacturing, sales, engineering, human resources, or other skills that have not been mentioned in any of the categories above.
- Make a list of all your interpersonal skills. Although they are harder to define, these skills can "make or break" an application for a new position. This list could include any of the following skills: communication, facilitation, coaching, conflict resolution, negotiation, team building, and many others.
- Create a category of "other skills" for skills that don't fit into the above categories. Often, these skills are something unique that you have to offer, making you more attractive than other candidates.

Compare the List with Your Career Goals

By this time, you should have quite a long list of potentially marketable skills. Go back through this list and check or highlight the skills that most closely match your career goals. From this list, choose the ten skills that you think are most marketable. Ask yourself "If I were trying to hire someone for this job, are these the skills I would be looking for?" If you are lacking any essential skills for the job you desire, you should develop a plan to acquire these skills.

Take each of the top ten skills you have listed and write a sentence describing how you have actively used this skill. For example: "Used conflict resolution skills to solve a major problem between production and sales." Or "Conducted quality training in the billing department, leading to a 15% decrease in billing errors."

Reality Testing

Through your networking, identify someone who is doing the job that you would like to have. Ask him or her to review your list of skills and see if they agree that your skills are a match for this kind of position. If they do not think there is a match, ask him or her what skills you need to gain. Or you may wish to ask what kind of a job would be a better match for someone with your skills. Another reality check is to ask those closest to you to review your skills and to see if you may have left anything out.

Final Step

Your final step is to turn your list of marketable skills into valuable information in your cover letter and on your résumé.

Common Mistakes

You skip this process and jump into writing your résumé.

You may think that you already know all your skills, but this exercise always produces some surprising and creative results that help you market yourself better. Sometimes it even helps you to see that you may have chosen the wrong job objective, and you are able to alter your career goals to exploit all that you have to offer more fully.

You discount early life experiences.

You think to yourself, "It doesn't matter what I did in high school or in my first job. That was so long ago." But often there are clues to your strongest skills and to your life's purpose in these early experiences.

You are unrealistic about the match between your skills and your career goal.

You may want to change from a job in information systems to a job in human resources, but if you have not had any specialized training or experience in the new area, you will not be able to make the move. Make sure that you do the reality testing step of this process before you actually start your job search.

For More Information

Book:

Bolles, Richard. *What Color is Your Parachute? 2002*. Berkeley, CA: Ten Speed Press, 2001.

Web Site:

Skills Identification: **www.mnworkforcecenter.org/cjs/cjs_site/skill.htm**

See also:

☆ **Choosing the Best Training Curriculum for You (pp. 336–37)**
☆ **Urbane Renewal: Trusting Your Own Wisdom—A Competitive (and Satisfying) Advantage (pp. 320–21)**
✔ **Assessing Your Entrepreneurial Profile: Do You Have What It Takes? (pp. 818–19)**
✔ **Choosing the Right First Job (pp. 746–47)**
✔ **Staying Marketable: Identifying Your Transferable Skills (pp. 786–87)**
Planning Your Career (pp. 2075–77)

"Focus on operational positions where you have responsibility for profit and loss. That way it's easy to measure whether you're doing a good job." (Fabiola Arredondo)

Creating Cover Letters That Sell

Getting Started

A cover letter briefly describes the position you are seeking, why you are uniquely qualified for the job, and why you are interested in this company. It can provide a sense of who you are that may not necessarily come across in a résumé. You will use a cover letter when you know the exact position you are applying for, and when you know the name of the person you are sending your résumé to. Keep in mind the following as you prepare the cover letter:

- What tone do I want to convey in my letter?
- Have I done my research about this company and this position?
- What is unique about me that would interest this employer?

FAQs

Why is a cover letter important?

The cover letter is the very first thing a hiring manager reads. It must capture his or her attention and make him or her want to read your résumé.

Is the appearance of the cover letter important?

Yes, it is extremely important. Just as you put on your best professional clothes to go to an interview, you must use the best paper, the most professional looking fonts, and otherwise do what is necessary to convey the unspoken message that you are a quality person.

Do I use a cover letter in every job application situation?

No. In some cases you may send a letter to an organization inquiring about whether or not they have any job openings. You would also ask who to send your résumé to. You would not use a cover letter if you visit an organization in person and are asked to fill out a job application. You may or may not use a cover letter if you are conducting an Internet job search. Internet job searches are a new field—cover letters are not always necessary.

Making It Happen

The guidelines for writing a cover letter that really sells are fairly straightforward. But they do require you to do your homework. Each cover letter that you write should be uniquely tailored to the specific position that you are applying for. When you intersperse well-written letters with effective face-to-face and telephone networking, you will conduct a more successful job campaign.

Reasons for Writing a Cover Letter

You may write a cover letter and send a résumé to someone for a variety of reasons. Typically these include: responding to an ad; following up on a lead from your networking; advising a potential employer of your availability.

Identify a Specific Person to Receive Your Cover Letter and Résumé

Cover letters addressed to "Dear Sir," or "To Whom It May Concern," get quickly thrown into the wastebasket. If you do not know a specific person within the company, you can either call the company and ask, or you may be able to find out on the Internet or at a reference library.

Keep Your Letter Short and to the Point

An effective cover letter is typically two or three paragraphs long.

State the Position that You Are Seeking

In the very first line of your cover letter you will explain its purpose. It may read something like, "I am very interested in the position of Production Manager as described in your September 19th advertisement in the Big City Newspaper." Or, "I was given your name by Ms. Mary Bettencourt in connection with the position in Human Resource Information Systems."

Show Your Understanding of the Company's Business Issues

In order to stand out from the stack of letters and résumés that the hiring manager has on his or her desk, you must show that you have done your homework about the company and their current business issues and challenges. The Internet is a marvelous tool for learning more about a particular company. The first step is to go to the company's Web site. Most companies have a section for recent news articles about them, particularly their press releases. You should also be reading the best business newspaper and magazines available. They will give you a sense of the major industry issues, and they may also have particular information about companies that you are targeting.

It is a good idea to save these articles in a file for each company. They are valuable to review if you actually get an interview. You can also use your friendly reference librarian to help you research some basic information about the company in business reference books.

Describe Your Qualifications

Very early in the cover letter you must interest the hiring manager in your qualifications. Explain how your qualifications will help this organization achieve its goals. For example, "I understand that your company is planning on creating a Web presence to support your sales. In my current position as Director of Internet Sales for Speedy Sales Company, I have helped to increase our market share by 13% in the past year." Show how you specifically can help this organization with the issues or challenges it is facing.

Ask for an Interview

There are several ways to do this. You might say that you are going to be in their area during a specific time period and that you would be available for an interview. Or you

"Knowledge may give weight, but accomplishments add luster, and many more people see than weigh."

(Lord Chesterfield)

can simply say, "I look forward to discussing how my qualifications can help your organization to be more successful. I will call you within a week to set up an appointment."

Be Yourself

Résumés are cut and dried, and only convey your experiences and your accomplishments. Your cover letter is your one opportunity to convey something about your personality and your uniqueness before you actually go to the interview. Keep it professional, but don't be afraid to show your enthusiasm, your willingness to work hard, and your interest in the position. Potential employers are really attracted to job applicants who show an interest in them and who seem very eager to be a part of the company.

Present a Professional Appearance in Your Cover Letter

First of all, make absolutely certain that there are no grammatical or spelling errors. Fortunately, most word processing programs catch and correct these problems, but make sure that you proof-read the letter before you send it out. Use the highest quality paper that you can find. Unless you are applying for a very specialized job in the arts or advertising field, you will probably want to use a quiet, neutral toned paper such as ivory, light gray, or light beige. Use a standard and easily readable font such as Times New Roman or Helvetica.

If you are mailing the cover letter and résumé, send them in a large flat envelope. And send two copies. Many hiring managers will need to circulate your letter and résumé. Photocopies are better if the originals have not been folded.

Common Mistakes

You Use a Cover Letter Template from a Book

It's okay to read through cover letter samples in a cover letter book, such as the ones recommended below. You will get a feel for the kinds of information people include, the layout of the letter, and the tone of the letter. You can then customize letters to fit your particular need. Experienced managers have seen hundreds of cover letters, and they are tired of hearing the same old textbook phrases. Make sure you personalize each of your cover letters so that they are targeted to a particular person, and so that they represent you and your uniqueness.

You Use the Same Cover Letter for All Your Job Applications

A manager wants to know that you are interested enough to understand this particular company and that you have taken the time to write a personal letter.

For More Information

Books:

Krannich, Ronald L., and Caryl R. Krannich. *201 Dynamite Job Search Letters*. Manassas Park, VA: Impact Publications, 2001.

Wynett, Stanley. *Cover Letters That Will Get You the Job You Want*. Cincinnati, OH: Betterway Books, 1993.

Web Sites:

Yahoo Business Directories: **www.yahoo.com/business_and_economy/companies**

CareerWeb.com, 20 Deadly Letter Mistakes Job Seekers Make: **www.careerweb.com/rescen/car_advice/jobsearch/20dead.html**

See also:

- ✔ **How to Network and Market Yourself (pp. 758–59)**
- ✔ **Winning Résumés: Creating a Marketing Tool That Gets You the Interview (pp. 752–53)**
- **Job Hunting (pp. 2017–18)**
- **Planning Your Career (pp. 2075–77)**

"The truth is I started my own company because I could not fill out a job application." (Terri Bowersock)

WINNING RÉSUMÉS: CREATING A MARKETING TOOL THAT GETS YOU THE INTERVIEW

GETTING STARTED

The key thing to keep in mind is that a winning résumé is not one that gets you the job: it is one that gets you the interview. It is rare that anyone gets hired just from the résumé. You want to create a résumé that gets a potential employer interested enough to want to meet you in person. A hiring manager receives an average of over 120 résumés for every job opening. You want your résumé to stand out among the pack. And remember, you only have 10 seconds to capture his or her attention. Here are some things to think about as you prepare your résumé:

- Are you doing a targeted or a general career search?
- What is your career objective?
- Do you know what your potential employer is looking for?
- Which makes you more marketable, your experience or your education?
- What kind of a visual image do you want your résumé to portray?

FAQs

HOW IMPORTANT IS IT TO HAVE A DEFINED CAREER OBJECTIVE?

If you don't have a clear, defined, and specific career objective, you might as well not even send in your résumé. It's not enough to say, "Seeking a middle management position in a dynamic organization." Be more specific, and describe your ideal job. More details on this below.

WHAT IS THE KEY PURPOSE OF A RÉSUMÉ?

Many people are under the mistaken impression that employers make hiring decisions based on the résumé. They do not. Instead, they go through the pile and narrow it down to a manageable number that meet the basic job criteria. They decide how many people they want to bring in for an interview. Let's say they want to interview five people, so they pick the top five résumés that most closely match the job criteria. These people get invited in for the interview and then have a chance to sell themselves face-to-face.

IS IT TRUE THAT MY RÉSUMÉ SHOULD BE LIMITED TO ONE PAGE?

This is the "One Page Myth," and it is not true. It depends on the organization, on the industry, and on the complexity of your qualifications. You must grab the reader's attention very quickly, but that can be done in a two- or three-page résumé just as easily as in a one-page résumé. The key is to have an objective, or a summary statement at the beginning that really attracts the hiring manager's interest.

MAKING IT HAPPEN

Even if you are not looking for a job, you should update your résumé at least annually, if not more often. It is usually a good idea to add any new achievements or accomplishments as they occur. Otherwise they are easy to forget. The steps that are described here are aimed at people who are creating a résumé for the first time, but they can also be useful in considering how you might want to update and improve your current résumé.

DECIDE ON WHETHER YOU ARE DOING A TARGETED OR A GENERAL CAREER SEARCH

Let's say that you are currently working and that someone contacts you about a specific job opening at another company. Or you learn about a promotional opportunity within your current company. If that's the case, you are doing a targeted career search, and you will custom design your résumé to fit that particular job.

On the other hand, if you are just out of college, or you are unhappy in your current position, or you were recently laid off, then you are probably planning to contact a large number of potential employers in many different organizations and diverse industries. In this case, you are conducting a general career search, and you will probably want to have between one and three résumé formats. For instance, if you have a background in both electronics and photography, you might have one résumé that highlights your photographic skills for one set of employers, and another résumé that highlights your electronics skills for another set of employers.

SELECT A RÉSUMÉ TYPE AND LENGTH

Decide on the best type of résumé for your particular background and career goals. See pp. 754–55 for guidance on different types of résumé. Also, decide on the length of your résumé. Fast-moving industries such as advertising and Internet companies tend to respond more favorably to a short and concise résumé. More conservative and status-valuing organizations such as financial companies and stable manufacturing industries tend to want to know more details about your qualifications and won't be as put off by a two- or even three-page résumé. If you are uncertain, you can check with one of the résumé books focusing on particular résumés, or utilize the resources provided below in For More Information.

CREATE YOUR "CAREER OBJECTIVE" STATEMENT

Before you sit down to write your résumé, you should have a very clear idea of the kind of job you are looking for, and the kind of company you would like to work for. Your name and contact information will go at the very top of your résumé, and your Career Objective is the next major section. It is the statement that may make the difference between whether your résumé goes into the "Consider Further" pile or the "Send a Rejection Letter" pile. Here are some examples of Career Objective statements that start out too broad and are then made more specific. The amount of detail you provide in your Career Objective will also be based on whether you are doing a one-, two-, or three-page résumé. Look at these example texts to see how to turn statements that are too general into more focused descriptions.

Too general: Position in the broadcast industry.

More specific: A dynamic, multi-talented and experienced broadcast professional is seeking a position that will make full use of an in-depth background as a television producer, production manager, scriptwriter, and networker. Seeking a challenging production manager position that will provide an avenue for contributing creative talents and international experience in the broadcast industry.

Too general: Managerial position in a finance organization.

More specific: Highly motivated professional is seeking a position that will fully exploit advanced education in managerial accounting and experience in all areas of finance and cost control. Proven ability to define issues, propose solutions, and implement changes.

Create headings and prepare the order of the information that will be highlighted in your résumé.

Remember that your résumé is not a life history. Only include information that is most relevant to your reader, the hiring manager. Even if you are seeking a sales position, the hiring manager is not going to care that you ran a lemonade stand when you were ten years old.

The two major categories of information in the typical résumé are (1) professional experience and (2) education. Decide whether your work experience or your education is the thing that makes you most marketable. If you are just graduating from college and have not had a lot of professional experience, then you want to highlight your educational achievements first. If you have had a reasonable amount of work experience, then that is what you want to highlight first.

Other categories that might go in your résumé can include a few of the following:

- Academic honors
- Areas of study
- Professional honors
- Continuing education
- Internship
- Advanced training
- Professional affiliations
- Summary of skills and qualifications
- Computer expertise

Create Specific Action-oriented Statements for Each Heading

Educational accomplishments are very straightforward and usually consist of the degree you received, the university and city where you received it, and the date of graduation. Reporting on your professional experience is a much greater challenge. Whole books are written on this subject, and resources are offered at the end of this Actionlist. All the experts agree that résumé statements should begin with an action verb and, as much as possible, include measurable results. For example:

- Designed and developed ISO-9000 program that led to a 19% increase in international sales.
- Managed a 300-bed healthcare facility and improved patient satisfaction ratings by 24% over two years.
- Created a new process engineering method that saved manufacturing $64,000 per year.

Put It All Together

Use high quality paper and design the résumé so that it is easy to read and professional looking. Résumé books provide lots of examples, and you will notice that they make liberal use of white space. You may wish to ask other people's opinions about your résumé, but realize that if you ask 20 people you will get 20 opinions, and in the end you are the one who needs to feel comfortable with it.

Follow Up, and Always Say "Thank You"

When you send your résumé out, you will follow up with a call to set up an interview. Regardless of whether or not you get the job, always send a thank-you letter.

Common Mistakes

You Send an Old Résumé Because It's All You've Got

An opportunity comes up and you need to respond quickly, so you pull an old résumé out of file and send it off. But it doesn't really represent who you are now. Update your résumé on a regular basis so that you are never caught by surprise.

The Résumé Is Too "Busy" and Hard to Read

You think that the hiring manager wants as many details as possible, but they are really looking to see if you have at least the basic qualifications, and they want to find that information quickly. It's hard to do that if the résumé has long sentences, paragraphs, and a lack of white space. It's better to have a two-page résumé that feels more open than a one-page résumé that is solid text.

You Oversell

In an effort to get their attention, you make what might be interpreted as boastful or arrogant claims of success in your résumé. It is much better to let the results that you have achieved speak for themselves.

For More Information

Books:

Cochran, Chuck, and Donna Peerce. *Heart & Soul Résumés*. Palo Alto, CA: Davies-Black Publishing, 1998.

Jackson, Tom, and Ellen Jackson. *The New Perfect Résumé*. New York: Doubleday, 1996.

Web Site:

Monster Résumé Center:
www.resume.monster.com

See also:

✔ **Creating Cover Letters That Sell (pp. 750–51)**
✔ **Winning Résumés: Preparing Different Types of Résumé (pp. 754–55)**
Creating a Résumé (pp. 1946–48)
Job Hunting (pp. 2017–18)

"If you cannot communicate your many worthwhile achievements, no one will ever know what you have done."
(Jac Fitz-Enz)

Winning Résumés: Preparing Different Types of Résumé

Getting Started

Every person's career history is different. You want to design your résumé so that it puts your career history in the most marketable and attractive light. Your particular job search and career goals are also unique. All these factors play a part in deciding which type of résumé has the highest probability of getting you the interview that will lead to your perfect job. You should keep the following questions in mind as you decide which type of résumé to prepare:

- Are you planning on staying in the same field or are you changing careers?
- Have you had a fairly standard pattern of career development, or has your career been less traditional?
- Is this your first job?
- Are you targeting a specific job in a specific company?

FAQs

Doesn't everyone just do a chronological résumé?

Twenty years ago, that may have been true. But these days the average person has seven different major careers (not just jobs) in his or her life. And with all the restructuring and other changes going on in organizations, it has become almost impossible to have a traditional career that starts out in one field and steadily progresses through the ranks.

Would I ever do more than one kind of résumé?

Typically no. The only exception to this is when you have created one of the standard formats (either a chronological or a functional résumé), and a unique opportunity comes up for which one of the customized résumés (either a targeted or a capabilities résumé) is better for that situation.

Making It Happen

Understand When to Use Each Kind of Résumé

A chronological résumé is good when you are staying in the same field and are not making a major career change. This type of résumé also works well when you have steadily progressed up a standard career ladder. For example, beginning your career as a junior engineer, then progressing through senior engineer, manager of engineering before taking up your present position of vice president of engineering. You would also use this kind of résumé when you have worked for a well-known, highly respected company for most of your career, even though you may have had several different kinds of job within that company.

A functional résumé is the preferred choice when you are seeking your first professional job. It is also recommended when you are making a fairly major career change. If you have changed employers frequently, have followed a less traditional career path, or have some reason to think that your work history is not that impressive, then you will be better off with a functional résumé that focuses on your skills and accomplishments.

A targeted résumé works well when you are very clear about your job direction and when you need to make an impressive case for a specific job. It takes a lot of extra effort to write this kind of customized résumé, especially if you are targeting several jobs, but it can make your résumé stand out from the pack.

A capabilities résumé is used when you are targeting a specific job or assignment within your current organization. Again, you must be willing to take the time to customize your résumé for the situation.

Create Your Résumé to Fit the Situation

Here are basic guidelines for preparing each of the four types of résumé:

Chronological Résumé

- List your name and contact information at the top.
- State your job search "Objective" (See Action List #5).
- Start with your present or most recent position, and work backward.
- Only write about your last four or five positions, covering the last ten years or so.
- For each position listed, describe your major duties and accomplishments. Keep it short and sweet.
- Keep your career goals in mind as you write, and as you describe your duties and accomplishments, emphasize those which are most related to your desired job.
- Education is listed at the bottom of your résumé, in a separate section. Degrees are listed in reverse chronological order.

Functional Résumé

- List your name and contact information at the top.
- State your job search "Objective".
- Use from three to five separate paragraphs, each one emphasizing a particular skill or accomplishment.
- List the functional paragraphs in order of importance, with the one most related to your career goal at the top. Provide a heading for each paragraph.
- Within each functional area, emphasize your most directly related accomplishments or results produced.
- You can include information about your skills and accomplishments without identifying which employer or situation it was connected to.
- Put a brief synopsis of your actual work experience under the last functional area, giving dates (years), employer, and job titles only.
- Education is listed at the bottom of your résumé, in

"Enthusiasm and hard work are indispensable ingredients of achievement. So is stick-to-it-iveness." (Clarence Birdseye)

a separate section. Degrees are listed in reverse chronological order.

Targeted Résumé

- To develop the material for a targeted résumé, brainstorm a list of key points. For example, you could think about what you have done that is relevant to your job target and the results you have achieved. Are you proud of what you have achieved? Have you achieved anything in another field that is relevant to your job target? Think about what you do that demonstrates your ability to work with people.
- List your name and contact information at the top.
- State your job search "Objective".
- From the brainstormed list above, select 5–8 capabilities and accomplishments that are the most relevant to your job target. Make sure that the statements focus on action and results.
- Put a brief synopsis of your actual work experience under the capabilities/accomplishment area, giving dates (years), employer, and job titles only.
- Education is listed at the bottom of your résumé, in a separate section. Degrees are listed in reverse chronological order.

Capabilities Résumé

- To develop the material for the capabilities résumé, learn all you can about the internal job that you are applying for and make a list of 5–8 capabilities and accomplishments that you have achieved in your current position that are relevant to this job opening.
- List your name and contact information at the top.
- State your job search objective using words that come directly from the job posting. Use your cover letter to tell the hiring manager about your interest in this specific position.
- Place the list of 5–8 capabilities and accomplishments next, focusing on action taken and results achieved with this company, relevant to the position.
- Put a brief synopsis of your relevant work experience at this company next. If you have been at this company for just a short while, then you will want to provide a complete synopsis of your work experience as described above in the targeted résumé.
- Education is listed at the bottom of your résumé, in a separate section. Degrees are listed in reverse chronological order.

Common Mistakes

You Try to Include Every Skill, Capability, and Accomplishment You Have

It is common to want to tell the potential employer everything you have ever done so that they will be impressed. But regardless of the type of résumé you create, you must remember to keep it simple and focused on those things that are most likely to get your foot in the door.

You Don't Use Any Particular Format

(1) If you have not had much experience with résumés, you may create a résumé that is a mixture of job listings, skills, and accomplishments. This will confuse your reader. Go to the library or bookstore and get a book that provides sample résumés. When you have decided which type of résumé fits your situation, based on the steps in this Action List, then use the samples in the book to help you with the final organization of your material.

You Are Still Unsure What Type of Résumé to Use for Your Situation

If you still don't know which type of résumé to use, then you should consider hiring a professional career coach.

You Don't Follow Up

This is the most common and most serious mistake. In your cover letter you make a statement about when you will call to set up an interview. Put that date on your calendar and make sure that you follow up. If you do not keep your commitments, it does not look professional, and there will be less interest in you. It's hard to make the call because of fear of rejection, but you will never get the job if you don't.

Sales people have learned that you have to take a certain number of rejections before you get a "Yes." Finding a job is the same thing. If you receive a "No" after making a phone call for an appointment, tell yourself, "Well, that is one less 'No' that I have to hear before I hear a 'Yes.'"

For More Information

Book:

Jackson, Tom, and Ellen Jackson. *The New Perfect Résumé*. New York: Doubleday, 1996.

Web Site:

Career Builder Résumé Formats:
www.careerbuilder.com

See also:

✔ **Winning Résumés: Creating a Marketing Tool That Gets You the Interview (pp. 752–53)**
Creating a Résumé (pp. 1946–48)

"No one can possibly achieve any real and lasting success or 'get rich' in business by being a conformist."
(J. Paul Getty)

  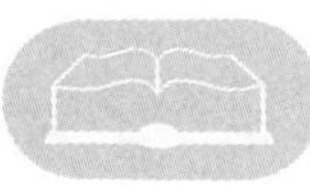    

Researching the Job Market

Getting Started

In starting your job search, you need to have several different kinds of information. You will need to research industry trends, find out details about the particular companies you are targeting, and perhaps even do some research on the hiring manager. You will want to keep in mind questions such as:

- What do I need to know about the industry I want to work in, that will help me to ask and answer intelligent questions?
- Where can I find out more information about the companies I have targeted?
- What kind of information do I want to know about each of these companies?
- What would I like to know about the hiring manager that will help me to write a more effective cover letter and to perform most effectively at my interview?

FAQs

Why do I have to research the job market? Isn't it enough to just read the help wanted ads in the newspaper?

Only a small percentage of people find jobs that they love through newspaper ads. If you research the job market thoroughly, you will have a clearer idea of what you are attracted to. You will also be able to design your résumé and cover letter more effectively and intelligently because of the information you have gathered.

Why do I need to research industry trends?

First of all, it will help you to decide whether or not you want to stay in the industry you have chosen, or if you want to move to something entirely new. If the trends show that you are in a declining industry, it may be time for a change. Secondly, when you have an interview, it will help you to ask informed questions (which always impresses hiring managers), and will help you to answer questions from a richer perspective.

How much time should I spend on this research?

It depends, of course, on the level of the job you are looking for. If you are seeking a very high level executive position in the same industry, you may already know most of the required information. If you are seeking a high level position in a new industry, you may need to spend several weeks on your job market research. If you are seeking an individual contributor position, you may not need to know as much about industry trends, but you will want to do several days' research on your targeted organizations.

Making It Happen

Start Broadly and Then Narrow Down Your Research

In the early stages of your research, you will begin by researching industry trends. The main things you will be looking for are:

- What are the major growth areas?
- Who are the major players?
- What are the major challenges and problems for this industry?

The first step in doing this research is to visit your nearest city or university library. Ask the reference librarian for help in finding reference guides and publications containing information about industry trends.

If you are not sure which industry you want work in, there are several good references and reports on attractive jobs and desirable companies. For instance, U.S. News & World Report has an annual ranking of the "20 Best Jobs in America." Ronald and Caryl Rae Krannich have written a book called *The Best Jobs for the 21st Century* that provides an overview of trends in different industries.

The major resource guide to information on types of jobs in the United States is the *Occupational Outlook Handbook* published by the U.S. Department of Labor. It describes more than 250 occupations and over 1 million jobs. You might also want to look at the *Encyclopedia of Associations*, which lists more than 100,000 professional and trade associations, organized by industry and the *Encyclopedia of Business Information Sources* which lists trade publications, newsletters, handbooks, associations, and online databases.

The Internet is another excellent resource in learning about industry trends. In the United States, two government Web sites provide very valuable information. The first is the Bureau of Labor Statistics at **www.stats.bls.gov** and the second is the U.S. Census Bureau at **www.census.gov**. In Canada, one of the most valuable Web sites for researching industry trends is **www.canadiancareers.com**. In the U.K., the Trade Partners U.K. Web site has well-organized information about trends in various business sectors at **www.tradepartners.gov.uk**.

Research Your Chosen Companies

The next step is to narrow your research by gathering information about the specific companies that you are targeting in your job search. The key facts you will probably want to know about each of these organizations are:

- size of the organization (sales, profits, market share, numbers of employees)
- strong and weak points
- key competitors
- organizational culture
- how the company is organized
- key strategic challenges

Go back to your friendly librarian and ask to see the business reference guides that provide background information on specific companies. The most popular guides to company information are *Moody's Industrial Manual* and Standard & Poor's *Register of Corporations, Directors, and Executives*. Once you have found an organization that you are interested in, it is a good idea to get a

"I wasn't satisfied just to earn a good living. I was looking to make a statement." (Donald J. Trump)

copy of their annual report. Find the company's Annual Report in the library, or call the company and ask them to send you a copy.

If you are targeting a local company, find ways to talk to employees about what it is like to work there and what its strengths and weaknesses are. You can also ask them about competitors, and about the key strategic challenges that the company is facing. If you don't know anyone who works there, you might consider attending local business meetings such as the Chamber of Commerce meetings, or other professional gatherings.

Large universities also have online databases with company information. For example, Columbia University in New York has an excellent site at **www.columbia.edu/cu/lweb/indiv/business/guides/cpny.html**.

Several "best company" Web sites are listed at the end of this Action List that will provide information about good companies to target, if you are not sure where to start.

Research Information about a Specific Job

The things you will typically want to know when you are looking for a specific job in a specific company are:

- What would my tasks and responsibilities be?
- What qualifications are needed? What is the typical salary for a job like this?
- What can I find out about the hiring manager?

Most of these questions will be answered when you are at the interview, but if you can gather information about them ahead of time, you are better prepared for your cover letter, your résumé, and your interview. If you saw the job advertisement, then the tasks and responsibilities were probably spelled out. If they were not, you can go back to the *Occupational Outlook Handbook* to find out more information about this type of job and what is expected. If you know for sure that there is a job opening, you can call and ask the company to send you a copy of the job description.

You will want to find out as much as you can about the hiring manager, and you may be able to do this through some of the business reference books mentioned above, if he or she is at a high enough level. You can also do an Internet search to see if he or she has been mentioned in any publications, or has written any publications in your field. Professional associations may have information on this person if he or she is active in your professional field. And if you know other people in the company, you can use your contacts to find out as much as possible about the hiring manager, before you contact him or her. You are looking for any information that shows that you may have something in common. This is valuable information for the cover letter, and also strengthens relationship-building when you are being interviewed.

Common Mistakes

Your Research Is Not Thorough Enough

If you do not do enough research about the industry, the company, and the job, you may say or do something that shows your ignorance and jeopardizes your chances. If you can demonstrate that you have done your homework, you will really stand out from the pack and will have a better chance of being hired.

You Do So Much Research that You Can't Keep Track of It All

It is helpful to create files for each of the industries and companies that you are researching. Systematize your information so that you can find what you need quickly. This is especially important when you are preparing for an interview. You might want to prepare a set of index cards listing key points that you want to remember. Carry these cards with you wherever you go to help you learn and remember important information.

For More Information

Books:

Wendleton, Kate. *Job-Search Secrets*. New York: Five O'Clock Books, 1997.

McDonnell, Sharon. *You're Hired! Secrets To A Successful Job Search*. New York: Macmillan, 1999.

Web Sites:

Fortune.com, best companies and most admired companies to work for: **www.fortune.com**

Global Edge: **www.globaledge.msu.edu/ibrd/ibrd.asp**

See also:

☆ **Taking Charge of Your Career (pp. 324–25)**
✔ **Choosing the Right First Job (pp. 746–47)**
✔ **Finding and Working with Search Organizations (pp. 810–11)**
✔ **Using the Web As a Career Resource (pp. 774–75)**

"By looking on each engagement as a part of a series. . .the commander is always on the high road to his goal."
(Karl von Clausewitz)

  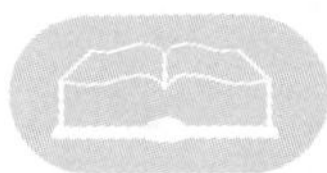    

How to Network and Market Yourself

Getting Started

No matter what your organizational position is, and no matter what your career goals are, you can always benefit from networking and marketing yourself. In today's world, business is driven by relationships. Networking and marketing yourself require you to build strong and meaningful relationships—many that will be long term. The following points are questions to consider as you prepare to network and to market yourself:

- Why are you networking? What is your personal or professional goal?
- What are your strengths that will help you to market yourself?
- What organizations or events will be valuable places for networking?
- How much time do you want to spend on networking, and when will you do it?
- How will you know when you've been successful?

FAQs

Why should I bother to network and to market myself?

Research has shown that people who have a vast network of contacts, who are involved in professional and community activities outside their organizations, and who look for opportunities to be visible are more successful in their careers and contribute more effectively to their organizations.

Isn't networking the same as politicking, and won't it look bad?

Politicking is done for personal gain. Networking is done for the good of the organization or your professional field. If you are a successful networker, people are drawn to you because they know you are well connected and that you have good resources.

When is the best time to network?

Networking should become a way of life, a way of being. You should be networking all the time. As you build professional relationships, be constantly thinking: "What can I offer this person?" "How can I be of help?" The more you try to be of service to others, the more people will want to do things for you.

Making It Happen

Clarify the Purpose of Your Networking and Why You Are Marketing Yourself

There are many reasons for networking and for marketing oneself. They can include finding a new job, seeking a promotion, or gaining support for a major project. Although it is important to continually build relationships, it is much more effective to know why you are building these relationships and what you hope to accomplish. Everyone has limited time, and this will help you to decide how to prioritize your networking activities.

Make a List of Your Strong Points

It is important to have a sense of who you are and what your strengths are when you are networking and marketing yourself. What are your special skills and abilities? What unique knowledge do you have? What experiences will other people find valuable? What characteristics and beliefs define who you are? Once you have made this list, make copies for your bathroom mirror, for your car dashboard, and for your wallet. Knowing your strengths helps you to remember that other people will value what you have to offer.

Never network from a position of weakness. Always network from a position of strength. Have something of value to offer; otherwise people will see you as an annoyance. And remember to begin networking before you need anything from other people. Join or create a network to build relationships, and do what you can to help others or the organization.

Make a List of Organizations and Events for Networking

Identify professional organizations and events that may be helpful to you in your career or with your project. Look for special interest groups like those for "entrepreneurial women" for example. Get involved. When you are at professional events, make sure that you attend social functions, that you join people for dinner, and that you seek out volunteer opportunities. If you are networking within your own organization, find special interest groups or social groups to join. Look for committees to be involved in, and don't be shy about asking questions and making suggestions.

If you are not sure where to begin on this step, ask for advice from a mentor, from your boss, and from trusted colleagues.

Create a Contact List

Keeping in mind your reasons for networking, brainstorm all the people you know who might be of help to you. Prioritize the list according to who is most likely to be helpful. Think about people you have done favors for in the past who might not be of direct help, but who may know someone who can be. After you have spoken to each one, ask him or her, "Who else do you know that can be of help to me?"

Create an Action Plan with a Schedule

Take your list of organizations and events and your contact list, and put together an action plan for making connections. Schedule networking events on your calendar, along with organizational meetings, conferences and so on. Using your contact list, set up a schedule for making a certain number of calls per day or per week.

Meet with People and Attend Events

Before you meet with someone or attend an event, review your list of strengths, and focus on your purpose

"The people we get along with, feel simpatico with, are the strongest links in our network."

(Daniel Goleman)

for networking and marketing yourself. It helps to visualize or picture a successful outcome. Be friendly and professional, but most of all, be yourself. Spend time connecting with people on a personal level before asking for help or sharing your reason for networking. If you are meeting in person with someone on your contact list, always bring a gift—something they can remember you by.

Networking on the Net

The Internet is a valuable place to make connections and to learn fruitful information from colleagues. If you have a special interest or a special field, there is sure to be a newsgroup or threaded bulletin board on your topic. If not, start one by setting up a listserve at **www.egroups.com**, **www.topica.com**, or at similar sites.

Market Yourself

The actions you take depend on why you are marketing yourself, but think of yourself as a brand, "Brand You." When marketers are marketing a product, they look for the "Unique Selling Proposition" (USP). A USP is something relevant and original that can be claimed for a particular product or service. The USP should be able to communicate: "Buy our brand and get this unique benefit." When marketing yourself, you need to define who your "customers" are and what your Unique Selling Proposition is. Your list of strengths above should give you some clues, but the USP needs to be stated in a short phrase. People who are closest to you can often give you suggestions. It might be something like: "I help people to realize their dreams," or "My leadership brings out the best in others," or "I solve problems quickly and simply."

Once you know your USP, brainstorm ways that you can market yourself and your uniqueness. The key is to let people know what you have to offer. Write an article for the company newsletter or a professional newsletter related to your USP. Volunteer to give a talk. Design a project that uses your unique talents and propose it to the right people. Be visible.

Assess Your Progress Toward Networking Goals

You may wish to keep a notebook of your action plans and your progress. It also helps to have someone as a sounding board. That person can be a friend, your boss, a mentor, or a professional coach. When we feel accountable for our actions to someone we trust, we are much more likely to follow through. It also helps to have someone who is willing to celebrate your successes and accomplishments with you.

Always Say "Thank You"

As you network, many people will offer you information, opportunities, and valuable contacts. In your notebook, keep track of the favors that people have done for you and make sure that you write each one a short and simple thank-you letter. People are always more willing to help someone who has been appreciative in the past.

Be Patient

Networking is a long-term activity. Steven Ginsburg of the *Washington Post* describes networking as "building social capital." You may not see results overnight, and at first should expect to give more than you get. But over time, your network will become one of your most valued assets.

Common Mistakes

You Don't Want to Bother Anyone

Remember that people love to help others. Don't take up too much of their time, and come well prepared. When you ask for someone's time, be specific. Say, "I'd like 30 minutes of your time," and then stick to it. Don't outstay your welcome. Whenever you meet with someone, always be thinking, "Is there something I can do to help this person?" Create a win-win situation.

You Come On Too Strong

Networking is not about selling someone something they don't want. You are looking for opportunities to create a mutual relationship, where there is give and take. In order for networking to be successful, you have to be interested in developing a long-term relationship. Remind yourself that your focus is on relationship building, not on immediate results.

You Don't Come On Strongly Enough

You put yourself in networking situations, but never talk about your needs or interests. This may be because you are not clear enough about why you are networking, or you are networking for reasons that are not particularly important to you. Go back to step one and clarify your purpose.

For More Information

Books:

Lowstuter, Clyde C., and David P. Robertson. *Network Your Way to Your Next Job*. New York: McGraw-Hill, 1995.

Michelli, Dena, and Alison Straw. *Successful Networking*. Hauppage, NJ: Barron's Educational Series, 1997.

De Reffele, Frank J., et al. *Successful Business Networking*. Worcester, MA: Chandler House Press, 1998.

Web Site:

The Vault Guide to Schmoozing: **www.vault.com**

See also:

☆ **Choosing the Best Training Curriculum (pp. 336–37)**
☆ **Driving Fear from the Workplace (pp. 330–31)**
☆ **Finding and Keeping Top Talent (pp. 33–35)**
✔ **Building an Awesome Contact List (pp. 760–61)**
✔ **Creating Cover Letters That Sell (pp. 750–51)**

"Forget loyalty. Or at least loyalty to one's corporation. Try loyalty to your Rolodex—your network—instead."

(Tom Peters)

Building an Awesome Contact List

Getting Started

Throughout your career, you will always need to have an awesome contact list. It is useful for job searching, for marketing and selling products and/or services, and for networking of all kinds. People who have good contacts in their profession are admired and considered powerful. It really is important who you know.

In preparing your contact list and setting up your system, here are some questions to keep in mind:

- What are your major career issues right now?
- What are your major career goals at this point in your life?
- What networks do you have that can be helpful to you?
- What networking activities can you participate in that will build up your contact list?
- What system do you have in place to record and maintain your contact list?
- What do you have to offer to people on your contact list?

FAQs

How can my contact list help me with my job search?

Contacts can help in many ways. They can provide information on industry trends; on the rewards and drawbacks of a particular kind of job; on the likelihood that a particular organization might be hiring; and other information about specific job openings. A contact list is integral to a successful job search.

I'm happy with my current job and am not involved in a job search right now. Why do I need a contact list?

First of all, these days you never know when you might suddenly find yourself looking for a job. If you have kept in contact with people while you are gainfully employed, they are more likely to help you when you are job hunting. And contact lists are useful for many reasons besides job hunting.

Your contacts can help you throughout your career. People in your field who are not in your organization can give you a broader perspective on your profession. People who are in your organization can provide important strategic information that will help you make effective career decisions. People who are in professional associations can encourage you to get more involved and can increase your visibility and help you gain more knowledge.

What is the best way to develop contacts outside my organization?

Generally, the best way to develop contacts is to join a professional association and to get involved by volunteering for committees or running for office. See **How to Network and Market Yourself (pp. 758–59)** for more information on networking.

People tell me that human resources professionals are the best point of contact in an organization. Is that true?

It is true if you are looking for a position in human resources. Otherwise, if you are job hunting, you should be developing contacts with people who make the hiring decisions.

Making It Happen

Identify Your Major Career Issues

It is important to understand your reasons for building an awesome contact list. The two key reasons people use contact lists are (1) job hunting and (2) professional development. If you are job hunting, your contact list will be focused on people who can provide you with information about the job market and who may be able to help you locate specific job openings. If you are not job hunting, you will most likely be using your contact list to help you learn more about your field, to solve particular professional problems, or to get mentoring from people in your profession.

Develop Relationships before You Need Help

Ideally, you want to begin building your contact list before you need to call on people for help or advice. In today's fast-paced climate, people have limited time to help others and are more likely to respond to someone they know and trust than to a stranger who is asking for help. As you begin to build contacts, keep in touch regularly with people just for the sake of keeping in touch. Then when you really need their help, they will be glad to give you their time and energy.

Identify Your Different Networks and Create a List of Everyone You Know for Each

We each belong to three basic types of networks: a personal network, a professional network, and a worklife network. Create a separate sheet of paper or computer document for each of these networks, and identify everyone you know within each one.

First make a list of people in your personal network, which includes your family, friends, neighbors, and others with whom you interact in your personal life. This might include people who are involved in community organizations in which you volunteer, people from your place of worship, and people connected to your children's school.

Next make a list of people from your professional network. This can include former and current coworkers and supervisors, teachers or professors, and colleagues who are members of professional organizations. You also might add suppliers or customers of your organization, consultants, speakers, and authors in your field.

Finally, make a list of people who are in your work-life network. These are people who are professionals in the career and outplacement field, such as

"The great body of managers. . .spend their whole careers climbing up inside one great Leviathan, with little contact with anyone outside."

(Anthony Sampson)

executive recruiters, college placement officers, and career counselors.

Create a System for Keeping Track of Your Contacts

There are several different types of system that you might consider. The most common systems are:

- index card or rolodex system;
- three-ring binder with tabs;
- computer software systems, such as Microsoft Access™ or Microsoft Outlook™;
- personal digital assistant (PDA) or electronic organizer systems.

You must decide whether you will do most of your contact work from your desk in the office or at home, or even when you're out traveling on the road. If you need to be more portable, the PDA is probably the best system to use. Otherwise, it is just personal preference.

Your system should allow you to record the person's name, address, phone numbers, e-mail, Web site address, pager number, and any other contact information that you might need. It also should allow you to include personal information such as birthday, names of family members, hobbies, or other details that will jog your memory about personal connections with this contact. Finally, you need room to include information about when you contacted the person, what transpired, and when you should get back to them.

Consider Creating a "Tickler File"

If you need to connect with people in your contact list on a regular basis, for example, once a month, you might want to create a "tickler" file. Let's say you are using an index card system. Instead of filing names alphabetically, you divide up your contacts into four groups, one for each week of the month. During week one, you call all the people in the first group. During week two, you call all the people in the second group, and so on. This system is particularly good for people who are in sales or public relations, but it also might be useful occasionally for people who are job hunting.

Have Something to Offer the People on Your Contact List

Remember that working with your contact list means working with relationships, and relationships are two-way streets. If you only call because there is something you want, people will eventually think of you as an energy drain and will avoid you. Always think about what you can give. When you ask a contact for help, also ask if there is anything that you can do in return. Each time you call, make sure you take the time truly to listen to the person you have called.

Don't Forget to Say "Thank You"

Every time you interact with someone on your contact list, make sure you find a way to say "thank you." People have so little time these days, and they are much more likely to be responsive to your calls in the future if they feel that their time is respected and appreciated.

Common Mistakes

You Use the "Shoebox" Method of Creating a Contact List

This is the method of writing people's contact information down on a slip of paper and then throwing it in a box or a drawer to look at later. Usually business cards get tossed into this pile as well. The difficulty is finding a particular piece of information when you want it. It's best to set a specific time aside to transfer the information from paper scraps and business cards to your master file on a regular basis.

You Have a Great System, But You Don't Use It

Some people love setting up wonderful systems with color-coding and dividers and cross-referencing and so on, but they find they freeze up when it comes actually to making the call or connection. Commit to a certain time of the day when you will make your calls, and give yourself motivational incentives for doing the work.

You Don't Follow Up

The worst thing in the world is making the initial contact with someone, getting their promise of help, and then not following up. All the hard work is in making the first call. If you don't follow up and keep your commitments to stay in contact, you lose credibility with the people in your networks. This is where the tickler file or a similar system can come in handy. Make sure that follow-up calls are on your calendar or on your daily to-do list.

For More Information

Books:

Baber, Anne. *Make Your Contacts Count: Networking Know How for Cash, Clients, and Career Success*. New York: AMACOM, 2001.

Fortang, Laura Berman. *Coaching: Take Yourself to the Top*. New York: Warner Books, 1998.

Michel, Alex, et al. *Schmoozing (Aka Networking): Insider Advice on Making Contacts and Building Rapport to Boost Your Career*. Boston, MA: Houghton Mifflin Co., 1999.

Web Sites:

Monster Career Center: **www.monster.com**

The Net Guide: sites to make contacts: **www.jobhuntersbible.com/contacts/contacts.shtml**

The Fourteen Ways to Look for a Job: **www.jobhuntersbible.com/library/hunters/fourteenways.shtml**

See also:

✔ **How to Network and Market Yourself (pp. 758–59)**

✔ **Identifying Your Marketable Skills (pp. 748–49)**

How to Win Friends and Influence People (p. 908)

Preparing for a Job Interview: How to Stand Out Above the Pack

Getting Started

Congratulations! You've made it through the first hurdle and have been invited to come in for an interview. That means that you have already found some way to stand out above the pack. Now you want to build on your successful strategy and continue to be seen as an outstanding candidate. As you prepare yourself mentally and emotionally for your interview, here are some questions to keep in mind:

- Why do you think you are the best person for the job?
- What is it about this job that attracts you?
- Who will interview you and what do you know about them?
- What is the appropriate dress and/or image for this organization?

FAQs

What is the most important thing for me to keep in mind in preparing for my interview?

It is important to remember that your interview is a two-way process. Not only is the organization trying to decide on the best candidate, you are also trying to decide on the best organization to work for. You will want to avoid appearing as if you are desperate for a job, so it is really helpful to remember that you also are interviewing them.

What are some typical questions that are helpful to prepare for?

There are some standard questions that interviewers often ask. They include such questions as:

- Where do you see yourself in your career five years from now?
- What are you most proud of in your career?
- What is your greatest strength?
- What is your biggest weakness?
- Describe a difficult situation and how you handled it.

A Web site with sample questions is listed at the end of this article.

Making It Happen

Review Your Résumé

Make sure that you are completely familiar with all the information on your résumé. Think about what questions someone might ask you based on your work history. Some examples of questions that might be difficult to answer have to do with why you left a job, or why you had a period of unemployment. Write yourself notes about what you are going to say and practice your answers.

Do Your Homework about the Organization

Before you go for the interview, you will need to know about things that affect the organization such as industry trends, competitive issues, strategic direction and particular challenges or opportunities.

Do Your Homework about the People Who Are Interviewing You

If possible, you should find out what you can about the people who are interviewing you. The purpose of this is to discover if there is anything you might have in common with them, such as attending the same school or being members of the same professional organization. If you learn as much as you can about the people you will be meeting, you can feel more comfortable with them and make some kind of emotional or intellectual connection.

Identify the Key Points You Want to Make about Your Strengths and Skills

When you prepared your résumé, you developed a list of key strengths and skills that you thought would be marketable to an employer. As you revisit that list, think of at least one example that allows you to demonstrate that strength or skill to an interviewer. If possible, focus on any concrete or measurable results that came out of your use of that strength or skill.

Prepare a List of Questions That You Would Like to Have Answered at Your Interview

In keeping with the philosophy that you are also interviewing the organization, you should be prepared with a list of things you can ask that will help you decide whether or not this job is a good fit for your personality and your career goals. Some examples of questions you might like to ask are:

- What are the key values in the culture here?
- What are the factors that would help me be successful here?
- What are the factors that will help this organization be effective?
- How fast are people promoted and what are the criteria for promotion?
- What is this organization's philosophy and policy on professional development?

Avoid asking questions about benefits and salary at this point, unless the interviewer brings them up. It is better to get the offer first, and then to negotiate your benefits and salary.

Be Enthusiastic

Know why you are interested in this job and communicate your interest clearly. People tend to hire candidates who are excited about the organization. Do not tell the interviewer that you are interested in this job because it pays well. Instead, be prepared to talk about what you can contribute, how it will expand your skills, and why this kind of work would be satisfying and meaningful to you.

"This is the age of intellectual capital, and the most valuable parts of jobs are the human tasks: sensing, judging, creating, building relationships." (Thomas A. Stewart)

Practice "Image Management"

It is important to look good and to sound professional when you are interviewed. A common rule of thumb for interviews is to dress at one level above the position you are seeking. For example, if you are at the supervisory level, you should observe the managers one level above you and base yourself on how they dress. This may not be true in some organizational cultures such as advertising, the arts, or in an Internet or high-tech enterprise.

Prepare Yourself Mentally

Athletes, salespeople, and many others prepare themselves for difficult or challenging situations by mentally picturing a successful outcome. You can use this technique in an interview as well. Plan to arrive 15 or 20 minutes early and to take some time while you are waiting to imagine yourself being very professional, interesting, and enthusiastic in your interview. Also imagine yourself leaving the interview with a very good impression about the company, and a good feeling about how you did. This will put you in a positive frame of mind and help you to come across in the interview at your very best.

Rehearse the Interview

If possible, enlist a friend or family member to role-play the interview with you. Career counselors and career coaches will also do this. Give this person a list of questions that you think you are likely to be asked. Role-play the interview and then get the other person's feedback. If possible, videotape the role-played interview so that you can see your body language.

Don't Forget to Say "Thank You"

You should follow up each interview with a brief and personal thank-you note to each person who interviewed you. It is a nice way to help them keep you in their minds.

Common Mistakes

You Misread the Culture or the Personality of the Person Interviewing You

The tendency is to underestimate the level of formality and professionalism that is required in an interview. Some interviewers even try to make the situation seem more like a social than a professional situation to catch you off your guard. If you come to the interview with a more casual approach than is appropriate, change your behavior as soon as you notice it. The interviewers are more likely to remember your behavior at the end of the interview than at the beginning. If the environment or the interviewer is more casual than you realized, don't worry. You are expected to look and act in a highly professional and even formal way in an interview. Use your intuition to judge how much you may need to change your behavior in order to show that there is a good cultural fit.

You Use Humor Inappropriately

In an effort to make the situation less tense, people sometimes try to use humor to lighten things up a bit. But if you have made a humorous statement and seem to get a negative reaction, you may want to find a way to recover from your mistake. Generally, it's best not to call attention to the situation by apologizing—if possible, act as if nothing happened and then go back to your professional demeanor. Whatever you do, don't follow inappropriate humor with more humor.

You Didn't Do Your Homework

You get to the interview and realize that you really know nothing about this organization. Hopefully, you showed up a little early and have some time in the waiting room. Often waiting rooms contain quite a bit of information about the company and its industry, possibly even on its products and services. Look around and learn everything you can. Feel free to talk to the receptionist and to ask him or her questions that may be helpful to you in the interview. It is possible to learn quite a bit about the organization on the fly, but nothing substitutes for doing your homework.

You Criticize Your Former Employer

Avoid this at all costs. It taints the interview with a very negative feeling, and will leave the interviewer wondering if you would say similar things about this organization if you left. This kind of criticism usually occurs when someone is asked why they are leaving (or have left) their former position. The best way to answer this is to talk about the future rather than the past, and to emphasize your strong desire for challenging career opportunities.

For More Information

Books:

Adams, Robert. *Job Interview Almanac* (and CD-ROM). Holbrook, MA: Adams Media Corporation, 1997.

Eggert, Max. *The Perfect Interview*. New York: Random House Business Books, 1999.

Jones, Alan. *Winning at Interview*. New York: Random House Business Books, 2001.

Web Sites:

Answering Tough Questions: **www.bio.com/hr**

Fifty Practice Interview Questions: **www.ivillage.com/work**

The job searchers' superstore.com: **www.thejobsearcherssuperstore.com**

See also:

✓ **Answering Tricky Interview Questions (pp. 766–67)**
✓ **Handling Inappropriate Questions in an Interview (pp. 768–69)**
✓ **Staying Cool in a Panel Interview (pp. 764–65)**
Job Hunting (pp. 2017–18)

"The person who knows 'how' will always have a job. The person who knows 'why' will always be his boss."
(Diane Ravitch)

Staying Cool in a Panel Interview

Getting Started

When you are on the job market, sooner or later you may experience a panel interview. Now becoming more popular, the panel interview allows several of an organization's representatives to meet a job applicant at one time and in one place.

While it can be intimidating to walk into a job interview facing several people, it also can be an excellent opportunity to showcase your strengths to various interviewers at one time. The key to success with a panel interview is to present yourself in a cool and confident manner. Here are a few things to consider before going to any job interview:

- How can I prepare myself mentally, in case this is a panel interview?
- What are my major selling points as a potential employee that I want to get across to each member of the panel?

FAQs

Why do organizations use panel interviews?

Organizations tend to use panel interviews for two major reasons. First, this type of interviewing can be timesaving and efficient. Several interviewers meet in one place at one time to interview a job applicant—and the applicant therefore does not need to be shuffled around from office to office. In a sequential interviewing process, if one interviewer runs late, the rest of the interview schedule is thrown off. In a panel interview, because all the interviewers are together, this does not often happen.

The second reason organizations may use a panel interview is for consistency of information. You, as the job applicant, only need to tell your story once instead of repeating it over and over in private meetings with interviewers. In addition, you receive consistent information from the organization's representatives, because they are all in one place at one time.

Should I send thank you notes to everyone on the panel?

Yes, thank you notes should be sent to each member of the panel individually, in the same way that you would send notes to each person if you had interviewed one-on-one with each. So be sure to get the names and titles of everyone on the panel. It is acceptable to write a similar note to the individual interviewers; it is not necessary to compose a completely unique note for each. Of course, each thank you note should be mailed individually.

Making It Happen

Prepare As You Would for Any Other Job Interview

As with any job interview, you should find out about the organization to which you are applying as well as the position available. To research the organization, start with its Web site and try to get a copy of its annual report. Talk with people who may be familiar with the organization. Go to the library and see if any recent articles have been written about it. These are some questions that you should look into before you get to the interview:

- How large is the organization?
- How is the organization structured?
- What is its main business?
- Who are its major competitors?
- What is the organization's work culture like?

Mentally Prepare for the Possibility of a Panel Interview

Before your interview, mentally rehearse a panel interview situation. Visualization can be a powerful technique to help you feel and appear relaxed and confident. Picture yourself in a conference room with several people sitting around a large table. Visualize yourself as being comfortable and open. In your mind's eye, see yourself answering each question easily, "connecting" with each interviewer, and having a successful interview.

Some people are uncomfortable using the visualization technique, but it is a very effective preparation tool. Remember, Jack Nicklaus claims that much of his golf success comes from mentally rehearsing each shot before he actually picks up a club. What has worked so well for him can work for you, too.

Take Each Question One at a Time, Even If It Feels As Though You Are Being Bombarded

Sometimes in a panel interview, it can feel as though questions are coming at you from all directions. One person may ask you a question and, before you have a chance to answer, another of the interviewers is adding to it or asking a different one. Try to take the first question, answer it, then build on that answer to incorporate what the second interviewer was asking. Make sure you answer every question. You do not want one of the interviewers to leave the room thinking that you either ignored or simply did not answer his or her question.

Clarify Questions If Necessary

If you find a question confusing, don't be afraid to seek clarification. Phrases such as, "Just to clarify. . ." or, "If I understand you correctly, you wanted to know. . ." can help you understand exactly what information the interviewers are trying to get from you.

You also may want to check that your answers were understood, or that you have answered the question fully. It might be a good idea, on occasion, simply to say, "Did I answer your question?" This should be directed at the individual who asked the particular question.

Common Mistakes

Not Being Prepared Mentally for the Possibility of a Panel Interview

Even if you don't think that your interview will be a panel interview, prepare for it mentally, just in case. You never know what an organization may choose to do in interviews. That way, if you walk into a panel interview, you

"One cool judgment is worth a thousand hasty councils." (Woodrow Wilson)

are prepared; if not, you haven't lost anything—you will be ready the next time (see "Mentally prepare for the possibility of a panel interview" above).

Letting the Panel of Interviewers Do All the Talking

You may feel more comfortable letting members of the panel do all the talking; it takes the pressure to perform from you. Resist this temptation. As in any interview situation, you are selling yourself, and to do that you need to get your point across. If the people on the panel do all the talking, all they will remember about you is that you may be a good listener.

While you should certainly not interrupt members of the panel, make sure you discuss your strengths and the reasons they should hire you. Sell yourself as you would in an individual interview.

Directing Your Comments Primarily at Only One of the Interviewers

As you are talking, make meaningful eye contact with each member of the panel. Meaningful eye contact usually entails catching the gaze of a particular member of the panel, holding it for about three seconds, and moving on to the next panel member. In reality, it is very difficult to look someone in the eye, count to three, and then move on, all while answering a challenging question—but practice the meaningful eye contact beforehand. It is also a useful skill for meetings and public speaking, and will become second nature after a while.

For More Information

Books:

Byham, William C., with Debra Pickett (contributor). *Landing the Job You Want: How to Have the Best Job Interview of Your Life*. New York: Three Rivers Press, 1999.

Deluca, Matthew J. *Best Answers to the 201 Most Frequently Asked Interview Questions*. New York: McGraw-Hill, 1996.

Kennedy, Joyce Lain. *Job Interviews for Dummies*. New York: Hungry Minds, Inc, 2000.

Levitt, Julie Griffin. *Your Career: How to Make it Happen*. 4th ed. Florence, KY: South-Western Educational Publishing, 1999.

Yeager, Neil M., with Lee Hough (contributor). *Power Interviews: Job-Winning Tactics from Fortune 500 Recruiters*. Revised and Expanded ed. New York: John Wiley, 1998.

Web Site:

Job Hunters' Bible: **www.jobhuntersbible.com**

See also:

✔ **Answering Tricky Interview Questions (pp. 766–67)**

✔ **Preparing for a Job Interview: How to Stand Out Above the Pack (pp. 762–63)**

ANSWERING TRICKY INTERVIEW QUESTIONS

GETTING STARTED

Job interviews are the single most important part of the selection process—for both you and your future employer. Once your résumé (or personal referral by someone whose opinion the hiring manager trusts) has established that you meet the basic skills and background requirements, it is the interview that establishes you as a candidate who will fit well into an organization's culture and future plans.

While most interview questions are generally straightforward, unambiguous inquiries, some interviewers will throw in surprises specifically intended to explore your thinking and expectations at a deeper level. Or they may be meant to throw you off guard to see how you react in high stress or confusing circumstances. Or they may not be intentionally tricky at all. They may merely be invented by the interviewer, or borrowed from lists of questions available on the Internet, with no idea what their value is, or how to assess your response as it relates to the requirements of the job.

How you answer tricky questions could determine whether you will receive an offer from the organization. But it's also important to remember that what those questions are, and how your answers are received, can tell you volumes about whether this is a company you want to work for.

Here are some of the most important questions you might want to consider as you're preparing yourself for a job interview:

- What aspects of your career do you feel especially good about, and how can you make sure those are discussed in the interview?
- What aspects of your career so far do you feel especially worried about discussing?
- Can you formulate answers to questions about those aspects in advance?
- How can you use the interview to learn about the potential employer?

FAQs

WHAT IF I DON'T UNDERSTAND HOW THE QUESTION RELATES TO THE JOB I'M APPLYING FOR?

Some questions—especially questions in which you are given a scenario and asked to think your way through to a solution—are designed to help the interviewer understand your ability to make tough decisions, or be a leader in high pressure situations.

True, it's reasonable to expect that you won't ever find yourself stranded in a lifeboat, charged with deciding which fellow survivor to throw overboard to conserve rations. But the way you reason out your decision may tell the interviewer much about you—for example, how you would choose which product to take out of inventory to conserve valuable warehouse space. Try to answer these kinds of questions based on business strategy and demonstrate your tactical thinking skills.

SOME QUESTIONS ASK ME TO DIVULGE MY GREATEST WEAKNESS. HOW CAN I ANSWER THESE QUESTIONS WITHOUT DISQUALIFYING MYSELF FOR THE JOB?

Such questions are usually designed to discover the extent of your self-knowledge. We all have weaknesses, and it's unreasonable to expect you to be perfect in every way. Keep your answer short and dignified. Identify only one area of weakness that you're aware of, but also describe what you are doing to strengthen that area. Don't try to be too clever by turning a negative into a positive, saying things like, "My biggest weakness is that I'm a determined worker and won't give up until the job is done well and completely." You aren't fooling anyone.

SOMETIMES I GET THE IMPRESSION THAT THE INTERVIEWER DOESN'T KNOW WHY I'M BEING ASKED A CERTAIN QUESTION, AND THAT MY ANSWER WOULD BE BEYOND HIS OR HER UNDERSTANDING. HOW DO I SALVAGE THAT SITUATION?

A company that hires unqualified interviewers to select qualified candidates may not be one you would like to work for—so you may not want to salvage such a situation. But if you're determined to give yourself the best chance to work at this organization, help the interviewer out by exploring the reasons behind the question and what exactly is being looked for in the way of response.

Even though you may not answer the question itself, you will still benefit from the conversation. You will position yourself in the interviewer's mind as someone who is not rattled by ambiguity, but instead works calmly and cooperatively with team members to arrive at the best possible outcome.

MAKING IT HAPPEN

UNDERSTAND THE PURPOSE OF THE INTERVIEW

The best job interviews are respectful encounters that allow mutual discovery. It may feel as if the employer has all the power—after all, it's the employer who will decide whether to offer you the job. Ultimately, however, it is you who holds the power, because it will be you who decides whether to accept the job. So interviews are just as important for you in the selection process as they are for the interviewer.

Keep that power balance in mind, and it will help you stay calm when tricky questions are asked.

ASSUME THAT THE INTERVIEWER IS PROBABLY AS UNCOMFORTABLE WITH THE PROCESS AS YOU ARE

Put yourself in the interviewer's shoes, and assume that he or she is slightly uncomfortable with the process as well. Few people relish meeting someone new and peppering them with probing questions. You may be the 25th candidate for a job, so the interviewer may feel tired of the same old questions and the same pat, rehearsed

"Bromidic though it may sound, some questions don't have answers, which is a terribly difficult lesson to learn."

(Katharine Graham)

answers. Remember also that the interviewer was once sitting in your seat, applying for his or her job within the company and worrying about the same surprise questions that you are. The resulting empathy will help break down barriers.

Prepare yourself in advance by identifying the topic areas that might be the trickiest for you. Then think carefully about how you might answer them. Broadly speaking, there are eight areas of questioning that could pose a challenge for you:

- your experience and management skills
- your opinion about industry or professional trends
- the reasons why you are leaving your current job
- financial or other value of your past achievements
- your work habits
- your salary expectations
- your expectations for the future
- your personality and relationship skills or problems.

Imagine which of these areas might be discussed and formulate in advance the general thoughts and responses you want to express. But don't rehearse answers to anticipated questions word for word.

Never Lie

Many interviewers do this work for a living, so they are more experienced at hearing the answers that candidates think they want to hear than you are at delivering them. Be candid and clear, and use lengthy answers only when you see that demonstrating your strategic thought process in detail will add valuable information.

When in Doubt, Try to Understand the Business Reason behind the Question. Ask Questions of Your Own

"What do you mean?" or "Could you rephrase that question?" are perfectly acceptable queries in any civilized conversation. Job interviews are no different.

Be Prepared to Answer Questions about Salary

During the interview process you want to keep the focus on your worth, not your cost. Early in the process, politely decline to go into details about past salary and future expectations. Many companies have a policy of offering salaries only at a certain percentage above a candidate's previous salary. If your previous salary, for whatever reason, was below market average or below your worth, you shouldn't have to be forced to accept a lower salary in the future.

If a question comes up about your salary expectations, make sure you have done your homework. You should have decided ahead of time on a salary range that is acceptable to you. Make sure the top of the range is well above the figure you would be thrilled to accept, and the bottom of the range slightly above your predetermined "walkaway" figure.

Study Question Lists

Many lists of questions are available online. Interviewers use them, and you can, too. Although you may not be asked those specific questions during the interview, the knowledge that you have done everything you can by preparing in advance will help you feel relaxed, confident, and capable.

Common Mistakes

You Criticize Your Former Employer or Coworkers

If you are asked why you are seeking new employment, focus on your positive ambitions, not any resentments or grudges you may harbor. Talk in terms of what has worked in your career, not what has failed.

You Get Angry or Defensive

A job interview is part gamesmanship, part blind date, part tea party. Use your social skills to smooth over edgy moments or bristly reactions to possibly offensive questions. And don't take anything personally.

You Give Away Your Power

You are at the interview to assess the desirability of the job, just as much as to sell your own desirability to the company. Remembering that will help you keep your dignity and protect you from feeling compelled to answer inappropriate, irrelevant, or intrusive questions.

You Use Scripted Answers to Anticipated Questions

These are inauthentic, and the interviewer has heard them all before. Original responses, even if they are slightly clumsy, will be more valuable to both you and the interviewer. They are a more accurate guide as to whether there is indeed a match between you and your potential new employer.

For More Information

Books:

Deluca, Matthew J. *Best Answers to the 201 Most Frequently Asked Interview Questions.* New York: McGraw-Hill Professional Publishing, 1996.

Fry, Ronald W. *101 Great Answers to the Toughest Interview Questions.* Franklin Lakes, NJ: Career Press, 2000.

Yate, Martin John. *Great Answers to Tough Interview Questions.* Dover, NH: Kogan Page, 2001.

Web Site:

Monster Career Center—tough interview questions: **www.content.monster.com**

See also:

✓ **Handling Inappropriate Questions in an Interview (pp. 768–69)**
✓ **Preparing for a Job Interview: How to Stand Out Above the Pack (pp. 762–63)**
✓ **Staying Cool in a Panel Interview (pp. 764–65)**

"To ask the hard question is simple." (W. H. Auden)

  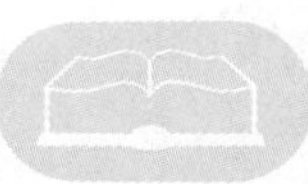    

Handling Inappropriate Questions in an Interview

Getting Started

Occasionally, you may get interviewed by someone who is less than politically correct. He or she may ask inappropriate questions, and this always creates a dilemma for the job candidate. Although this happens rarely, it is still useful to have worked through your strategy, just in case it should occur.

Here are issues that you will need to consider when preparing to deal with inappropriate questions:

- What kinds of question would feel inappropriate to me?
- If I get asked this kind of question, what does that say about the culture of the organization I am considering taking a job with?
- What are my options for dealing with inappropriate questions?
- Which of the strategic options fits my particular situation?

FAQs

How frequently do inappropriate questions get asked in an interview?

More than likely, this will never happen to you. Most hiring managers are very professional, and well trained in appropriate interviewing techniques. Nonetheless, it's much better to be prepared.

Is there any group of people who are more likely to get asked inappropriate questions?

Yes. Women are much more likely to get asked inappropriate questions than men, and the questions are generally of a sexual or gender-based nature.

Younger people are more likely to get asked these questions than older people. And people of a nondominant ethnic group may be more likely to be asked inappropriate questions.

Are inappropriate questions illegal?

It depends on the laws of the country in which you are working. However, many inappropriate questions are discriminatory, and are therefore likely to be illegal. Other questions are considered inappropriate simply because they are of a personal nature and have nothing to do with qualifications for the job.

Making It Happen

In order to prepare yourself for any interview, you need to think through all possible scenarios of what could happen and prepare yourself for those eventualities. Basically, there are two steps in preparing to handle inappropriate questions: deciding what is inappropriate or uncomfortable to you, and deciding how you will respond. The following pointers break this process up into more detailed steps.

Familiarize Yourself with the Law on Questions That It Is Illegal to Ask in an Interview

These are the worst type of inappropriate questions, and it is in order to try to prevent these questions from being asked that legislation has been created. In the United States, these questions fall under the Equal Employment Opportunity (EEO) laws. One of the simplest ways to find a list of these kinds of questions is to look in a human resource textbook. Some examples of illegal questions in the United States are:

- Why would a woman want a job like this?
- Are you planning to start a family?
- How old are you?
- Do you have any physical defects?
- Do you have any religious affiliation?
- Are you married, divorced, single?
- Do you have any children? How old are they?
- Will your husband/wife move if we offer you this job?
- How will you get to work?
- Have you ever been arrested?

There are complex reasons why each of these questions is inappropriate, but the underlying theme is that they might be discriminatory and, as such, illegal.

Make a List of Interview Questions That Would Feel Inappropriate to You

As mentioned earlier, these might be questions that have to do with your personal life. If you are married or cohabiting, they might be questions about your partner or children. If you are single, they might be questions about what you enjoy doing after working hours. But only you can decide if a question feels inappropriate to you. If it is not work-related and if it makes you feel uncomfortable, embarrassed, invaded, or angry, then it is an inappropriate question. By the same token, you also have to decide if the interviewer is just trying to make a human connection with you and is attempting to break the ice.

For example, let's say that your résumé says you worked for Shell Oil in Brazil. The interviewer asks, "What was your favorite thing to do on the weekends in Brazil?" This question has nothing to do with your job experience, but it probably won't make you feel uncomfortable. Perhaps you enjoyed hiking on weekends, and that allows the interviewer to tell you that this organization has a hiking club and that there are many good hiking trails nearby. By contrast, it could be that you worked as a volunteer in hospitals that care for children with AIDS on weekends, and you really don't want to get into a discussion about why you do AIDS volunteer work. In this case, the question might feel inappropriate to you.

Learn to Discern Why the Interviewer Is Asking This Kind of Question

There are two basic ways to discover the interviewer's motivation for asking a question that seemingly has

"Confidence is a mark of respect—and respect is appreciated by anyone of courage and honor."

(Anne-Marie-Louise d'Orléans)

nothing to do with the job you are applying for. The more subtle way is to watch for nonverbal cues. Pay attention to his or her body language and the way in which the interviewer uses his or her voice. Watch facial expressions, whether or not the interviewer's body seems tense and closed, and whether he or she makes direct eye contact. Most of us are reasonably good at interpreting these kinds of cues instinctively. You also should pay attention to your own responses. If you have a physical reaction to what is said—if you find yourself holding your breath, or your heart starts to pound, or you find your hands clenching—then your body is telling you there is something you don't trust about this person. The most overt way to discern why an interviewer is asking a question that makes you uncomfortable is simply to ask, "Why do you want to know?"

Be Aware of Your Options for Responding to Inappropriate Questions

Never let an interviewer intimidate you by asking inappropriate questions. You have a right to be treated professionally and with dignity. Your options for responding can include:

- humor: responding to the question as if it were a joke, giving the interviewer an opportunity to save face and to ask more appropriate questions;
- avoidance: ignoring the question and changing the subject;
- compliance: answering the question;
- gentle confrontation: this generally consists of asking the interviewer, "Why do you want to know?"
- strong confrontation: telling the interviewer that the question is inappropriate and that you are not going to answer it.

Decide Which Response Best Fits Your Situation

There are several factors to take into account in deciding how to respond. They include:

- the severity or outrageousness of the question;
- your sense of the interviewer's motivation in asking the question;
- how strongly you desire this job;
- the extent to which you believe that this kind of question is a reflection of the corporate culture.

You will have to weigh these factors and decide whether the question is fairly benign and can be safely ignored on the one hand, or whether the interviewer's behavior crosses ethical lines and must be confronted on the other. If you really want this job, you may overlook the interviewer's question. If the question is so awful that you know you could never work for this company, you may be more likely to be confrontational.

Common Mistakes

You Want the Job So Much, You Will Do Anything to Please the Interviewer

Therefore, you answer a question that you find inappropriate and end up leaving the interview feeling embarrassed, angry, or ashamed. You must avoid feeling this desperate when you are job hunting. Make sure that you have worked hard to create several attractive interview options. Also spend time preparing yourself mentally for the interview, so that you feel a sense of self-worth and self-esteem when you walk into the interview.

You Overreact to the Inappropriate Question

People who have a militant or political agenda tend to do this. A minority may see every comment as a potential insult: for example a woman candidate may perceive interview questions as sexist. With this kind of attitude, an interview is seen as an opportunity to right the wrongs of the world, and the result is that the candidate will not get the job. If you have a tendency to overreact, keep in mind that there are appropriate and inappropriate places to fight your battles, and a job interview is probably not the best place to make a point about your political values.

For More Information

Books:

Joel, Lewin G. *Every Employee's Guide to the Law: Everything You Need to Know About Your Rights in the Workplace and What to Do if They Are Violated.* New York: Pantheon Books, 1997.

Zigarelli, Michael. *Can They Do That? A Guide to Your Rights on the Job.* New York: Lexington Books, 1994.

Web Sites:

(General resources)
Illegal/inappropriate interview questions: **www.careerbuilder.com**
Ivillage: **www.ivillage.com**
(Legal resources)
U.S. Equal Employment Opportunity Commission: **www.eeoc.gov**

See also:

✓ **Answering Tricky Interview Questions (pp. 766–67)**
✓ **Preparing for a Job Interview: How to Stand Out Above the Pack (pp. 762–63)**
✓ **Staying Cool in a Panel Interview (pp. 764–65)**
Job Hunting (pp. 2017–18)

"You gain strength, courage and confidence by every experience in which you really stop to look fear in the face."
(Eleanor Roosevelt)

Understanding Psychometric Tests: A Survivor's Guide

Getting Started

Psychometric tests are often used to help in career guidance and counseling, and to help in selection decisions. There are two basic types of tests: aptitude tests and achievement tests. Aptitude tests measure a person's interests and their abilities to acquire or learn new skills. Achievement tests measure what a person already knows or can do right now. It is helpful to understand the different types of tests that you might run across in your job search and how to approach them. Here are some questions to ask yourself as you consider the implications of being tested:

- How should I prepare for the different types of psychometric test?
- Are there resources that can help me prepare for a particular kind of test?
- Are there test-taking skills that I can learn?
- What can I do if I don't like the results of the test?

FAQs

Why would an employer use psychometric testing?

Large organizations often use psychometric testing in their hiring and promotion processes as a way of ascertaining whether or not a candidate has the knowledge, skills, and personality characteristics needed to be a good fit for a job. It is frequently an important part of assessment center processes where candidates are identified for future leadership positions.

When can I use psychometric testing in my own career planning?

If you are just beginning your career, or if you are contemplating a major career change, psychometric testing can help you to identify different kinds of career that would fit your interests and personality (see John Holland's self-directed search Web site in "Best Sources of Help" below). University career development offices offer a battery of tests for students and alumni. Probably the most popular career instrument is the Strong-Campbell Index. This is sometimes used by career coaches as well.

How accurate are these tests?

None of these psychometric tests are 100% accurate, but any decent test should have background information on reliability and validity. Libraries have reference books on the various kinds of psychometric tests, what they measure, what research has been done on them, and statistical information on their reliability and validity. If you are taking these tests for career planning purposes, it is best to take several different tests, compare the results, and look for themes and patterns.

Making It Happen

Be Physically Prepared for Taking a Psychometric Test

This might seem like strange advice, since psychometric tests measure psychological and intellectual propensities. However, research has shown that people perform better in all kinds of psychometric tests when they are well rested and in good physical shape. Another interesting fact is that people do better in tests when they are slightly hungry, so eat lightly before taking one.

Prepare for Aptitude Tests

Since aptitude tests measure your interests and your ability to acquire and learn new skills, you can't really prepare for these tests in the way that you would for a math or history exam. Your best preparation is to spend time thinking about your life and career goals, and the things you love to do. Career-related aptitude tests are based on self-awareness, so the more you know yourself, the more likely the test results are to be useful to you. Richard Bolle's book, *What Color is Your Parachute?*, is full of great self-awareness exercises.

Skills-related aptitude tests generally test your problem-solving ability in a particular field. For example, if you are going to be working on equipment, designing with CAD-CAM tools, or doing architectural work, you might be tested on your ability to do spatial reasoning. The best preparation is to be well rested and relaxed so that you can focus clearly on the questions and provide your best answers.

Preparing for Achievement Tests

The two most common achievement tests are those that measure verbal reasoning and mathematical ability. These kinds of test have been used in schools and workplaces for decades and are considered valid and reliable tools. They also have been shown to be pretty good predictors of success in academic work and in certain job situations.

Before you go for the test, find out exactly what skills and knowledge are being examined. There are hundreds of test preparation books on the market, and it is a really good idea to use one for the kind of test you are taking. The books typically explain how the questions are structured, provide test taking strategies, and have sample tests you can take so that you can evaluate your own level of skills and knowledge. After taking a sample test, you can use the book's study guides to work on strengthening your weaker areas and then retest yourself to see if you have improved. This approach typically increases your score by a significant percentage.

Learn Test-taking Skills

The first lesson of test taking is to read the instructions very carefully. Make sure you understand them completely. Don't be afraid to ask for clarification from the

"The first steps to becoming a really great manager are simply common sense; but common sense is not very common."

(Gerald M. Blair)

person administering the test. You'd be surprised how many people just jump into taking tests, and end up getting a much lower score than they deserve because they missed some important information that could have been helpful.

For example, in some tests, unanswered questions do not count against you. The instructions may tell you that wrong answers will be subtracted from right answers to provide a ratio score for the test. If you understand this, you know that you should skip over questions where you're not sure of the answer, and that you shouldn't guess answers. Some tests are timed and, if so, it's important to know how much time you have left so you can focus on the questions that you are most likely to answer correctly.

One common test-taking strategy is to go through the test the first time answering only the questions you are sure of. When you have gone through the complete test, you can go back over the unanswered questions and tackle the ones that you are pretty sure of. If you still have time after that, you can go through the questions one more time, really taking the time to think them through and to provide your best answer.

Carefully Analyze the Results

If you are taking a test for career guidance, remember to take the results with a grain of salt. No test is completely accurate, and no one knows you better than you do yourself. If the career advice provided by the test seems too far afield, trust your intuition. You may want to take a different kind of career test as a kind of "second opinion."

If you are taking a test as part of a job application process, the organization should at least tell you if you passed or failed the test, even if they don't tell you the specific results. If you failed the test, or if the results lead to placement in a job that seems inappropriate to you, you have the right to question the test. In most organizations, a lot of work has been done to validate tests and make sure they measure what they're supposed to measure. But not all companies do this. As a result some tests have been shown to be discriminatory, and may therefore be illegal.

The human resources department of the organization is responsible for the quality of the tests, so if you have questions about your results that should be your first point of contact. If you are not satisfied with the response, and if you feel that the test might be being used as a way to discriminate against you, you may wish to consult a lawyer.

Common Mistakes

You Decide to Make a Major Career Shift Based on Your Test Results

Test results are only meant to be used as a guideline in decision making about careers, and should be part of a comprehensive career planning strategy. This strategy should include a lot of self-assessment exercises, plenty of personal soul searching, using trusted friends and family as sounding boards, and possibly employing the services of a professional career coach.

You Don't Take the Achievement or Placement Test Seriously

Your résumé looks good, you know some people in the organization, and you have a lot of confidence in your ability to charm the hiring manager—so you don't give much credence to the test you are told you have to take. But you really need to take it seriously. Organizations that use testing typically use the results as the first screen for job candidates. If you don't pass the test, you are not even considered for an interview. If there is a test, be as prepared as possible to do well on it.

You Stay Up All Night the Night Before, Cramming for the Test

This, and a lot of caffeine, was how you got yourself through college, so it has become your standard operating procedure for test taking. The truth is that it wasn't a good strategy then, and it's not a good strategy now. The students who did the best in exams in college were the ones who began preparing for the final exam right after the first night of class. Slow and steady wins the race. So if you are told you will need to take a psychometric test to measure your knowledge and skills, find out as much as you can about the test and study over a period of time on a regular basis. Then don't study the night before you take the test. Relax and make sure that you get a good night's sleep. That way you'll be clear headed and at your best.

For More Information

Book:

Bolles, Richard. *What Color is Your Parachute? 2002.* Berkeley, CA: Ten Speed Press, 2001.

Web Sites:

Careerzone online assessment center: **www.people-center.com/bydesin.htm**

The five rules about taking career tests by Richard Bolles: **www.jobhuntersbible.com**

John Holland's self-directed search: **www.self-directed-search.com**

The Net Guide: tests and advice: **www.jobhuntersbible.com**

SHL Group: **www.shlgroup.com/home.asp**

See also:

Psychological Tests (pp. 2086–89)

How to Negotiate Your Salary and Benefits

Getting Started

One of the most nerve-racking parts of the job search process is the moment when it's time to begin discussing salary and benefits. The way you handle this situation will make a major difference in your career. Don't leave these issues to chance. It's important to learn how to ask for what you think you really deserve. Here are some questions that will help you prepare to negotiate the best salary and benefit package possible:

- Do you know your market worth?
- Do you know the potential salary range of the job you are applying for?
- What stage of your career are you at?
- What questions is the interviewer likely to ask when you are discussing salary and benefits?

FAQs

What is the most important thing to remember when I am negotiating for salary and benefits?

Your sense of self-worth is the most important thing to keep in mind. You must do your homework, both mentally and emotionally, so that you feel confident when it comes to discussing what you are worth to the organization.

This will be my first job. Isn't the salary pretty much predetermined?

All jobs have a salary range. The hiring manager will probably try to offer you a starting salary at the low end of that range, but there is always room to negotiate.

Don't I have to take whatever they offer me?

When you go shopping for a box of pencils, you expect to have to pay the price marked on the box. When it comes to salaries and benefits, however, almost everyone acknowledges this as a negotiation situation, and that means that you are not necessarily expected to accept the first offer.

Making It Happen

Know Your Worth on the Market

There are many ways to discover your market worth. If you are just graduating from college, your university career development office will have lots of information on the starting salary ranges for people with various degrees and for different types of career. If you are currently working, it is a good idea to go on at least two job interviews per year, even if you are not looking to change jobs. It is a good way to find out whether your skills and experience are valued outside the organization that you work for, and you can get a sense of your worth from any salary offers you receive. These are external measures of worth.

However, it's also important to have an internal sense of your worth. In preparation for a job interview, you should have made a list of the strengths, skills, and experiences that you can offer this organization. Once the organization is ready to make you a job offer, you will be in a better mental and emotional position to negotiate your salary and benefits if you are confident that you have something of value to give.

Find Out What the Salary Range Is for the Position You Are Considering

There are several ways to do this. Some of the Web sites at the end of this article have salary calculators, but you have to take these with a grain of salt. Several other ways to discover what people doing this kind of job usually get paid are:

- read industry publications—most have an annual report on salaries in the field;
- join an industry or professional association and use that network to get an idea of the salary range for this type of job;
- talk to other people who work in a similar position to the one you are looking at, in person or by joining online discussion boards. Find out what they do and, if possible, how much they get paid or what salary range they are in.

Consider the Stage of Your Career When Preparing to Negotiate Salary and Benefits

The three basic stages of career are early, middle, and late. If you are in the early stages of your career, you may be willing to take a lower salary in exchange for the opportunity to work for an exciting and growing company, or the chance to learn valuable skills—or to work on a project that is deeply meaningful to you.

If you are in the middle of your career, you may be more interested in benefits such as healthcare and retirement than you are in salary. You also may be asking yourself questions about how much further you want to go in your career and how you want to balance work and family issues.

If you are at a late stage in your career, salary may or may not be that important to you, depending on how well you have been able to prepare for retirement. Like the person in midcareer, benefits may be more important than salary. But, often, even more important than either is the opportunity to make your mark and leave a legacy.

So keep your career stage in mind as you figure out what's important to you now and in the future.

Be Prepared to Handle Questions about Your Salary Expectations

You are asked, "What are your salary requirements?" and you don't know what to say. You must expect to face this question. You may have been advised to respond with a question such as, "What are you offering?" or, "I don't

"When a man says he wants to work, what he means is that he wants wages." (Richard Whately)

know, what does the job pay?" Throwing the question back into the interviewer's lap may seem like a good way to get yourself off the hook, but it can also appear a little too coy and may convey the message that you don't really know what you want. Salary negotiations are an opportunity to demonstrate your professional negotiating skills and, if you handle this well, you will gain the respect of the hiring manager. If you accept the first offer, you may actually convey a lack of self-confidence and an inability to go after what you deserve. If this is your first job, you also should be aware that raises are based on a percentage of current salary, so if you start low you limit your ability to increase your overall salary over time.

If you have done your homework on the job and the organization, you already have a pretty good idea of the range that they are likely to offer. You also should have an idea of your market worth and of the relative importance you put on salary level, benefits, and the work itself. When asked about your salary expectations, be prepared to suggest a range in which the lowest amount is slightly above the minimum you would accept, and the highest is more than you really expect them to offer. This amount shouldn't be too outrageous.

Watch the interviewer's body language closely to assess whether or not your stated expectations are reasonable. If the interviewer balks at the range, be prepared to remind him or her of the unique strengths, skills, and experience that you bring to the organization, and the results you expect to help them achieve. Remember to keep the focus on your worth, not your cost.

Receiving Their Final Offer

You may or may not receive a final offer during the interview. It's almost always a good idea to ask for a day or two to think about an offer, especially if you have concerns about it. You have the right to ask for time, because accepting a job offer is an important life decision. You also want to avoid appearing overly eager or desperate. If you have honest concerns about the offer, then be sure to state them when you call back.

Common Mistakes

You Are Told This Is the Final Offer, and You Accept That

The "final offer" usually refers to the salary offer, but there may be room to negotiate for better benefits. If that also seems like a closed door, then ask if you can come up for review within three to six months with the potential for a raise, based on your performance.

You Have Unrealistically High Expectations of What You Should Be Paid

This mistake is fairly common for young people who are fresh out of college. A visit to a university's career development center can be very helpful for setting realistic expectations, and can usually provide concrete information on typical starting salaries. Even if you have been out of school for a while, your alma mater will still be glad to help you with current salary information. It also helps to check out your salary expectations with other people in the field before you go in to negotiate.

You Accept the Highest Offer, Even Though the Job Is Not That Much to Your Liking

All too often, people think that job decisions should be based only on salary. However, you spend a very high percentage of your waking hours at work, and if you don't love what you do and care about the organization, it can really affect your overall quality of life. No amount of money can compensate for that. When making career and salary decisions, it is important to balance your financial requirements with your need for meaningful and fulfilling work.

For More Information

Books:

Fleming, Peter Ronald. *Successful Negotiating*. 2nd ed. Hauppage, NJ: Barrons Educational Series, 1997.

Wendleton, Kate. *Interviewing and Salary Negotiation: For Job Hunters, Career Changers, Consultants, and Freelancers*. Franklin Lakes, NJ: Career Press, 1999.

Web Sites:

Executive Compensation Database: **www.ecomponline.com**

The Job Hunters' Bible salary page: **www.jobhuntersbible.com/research/salaries.shtml**

The Riley Guide: **www.dbm.com/jobguide/salguides.html**

Salary.com: **www.salary.com**

See also:

✔ **Getting Paid What You're Worth: How to Assess Your Value in the Marketplace (pp. 788–89)**

✔ **Successfully Negotiating the Raise You Deserve (pp. 790–91)**

How to Win Friends and Influence People (p. 908)

Employee Benefits/Compensation (pp. 1959–61)

Finding Out What You're Worth: Remuneration/Salary (pp. 1982–84)

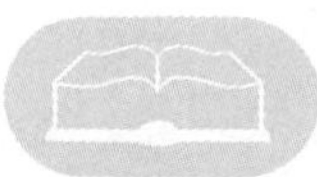

USING THE WEB AS A CAREER RESOURCE

GETTING STARTED

The Internet has completely changed the job search process, and savvy job hunters incorporate the Web as an important resource to explore. This action list assumes that you already have some basic computer knowledge, including the ability to create your résumé on the computer using a text program such as Microsoft Word; the ability to use a browser such as Internet Explorer or Netscape; and the ability to send and receive e-mail. It is also very helpful if you know how to create Web pages or have someone who can do that for you. As you prepare your Internet job search strategy, the following questions can help you get started:

- How important is knowledge of Internet technology in the job I am seeking?
- What skills and knowledge do I need to make the best use of the Internet in my search?
- What résumé format should I use on the Web?
- How can I use the Internet to learn about and target the perfect employer?

FAQs

WILL I BE ABLE TO FIND A GOOD JOB IF I DON'T KNOW HOW TO USE THE INTERNET?

The answer to this depends completely on the nature of the job you are looking for. For instance, if you are looking for a job as a graphics artist for Web pages, it is very important to know how to use the Internet. By contrast, if you are looking for a job as a chef, a musician, an accountant, or some other career that is not so Internet-based, it may be less important.

I AM LOOKING FOR A HIGH-TECH, INTERNET TYPE JOB. CAN I DO MY COMPLETE JOB SEARCH ON THE WEB?

It is possible to do your complete job search on the Web, but most employers prefer a mix of high-tech and traditional methods. For example, you can send your résumé by e-mail, but you should also follow up with a hard copy on quality paper.

IS THE INTERNET ONLY USEFUL FOR SEARCHING FOR HIGH-TECH JOBS?

No. Most large organizations use their Web sites to post information about job openings and have systems in place to interact with candidates who are using the Web for job hunting. This trend began in high-tech industries and is spreading rapidly into all kinds of organizations.

MAKING IT HAPPEN

BE CLEAR ABOUT THE KIND OF JOB YOU WANT, AND THE KIND OF COMPANY YOU WOULD LIKE TO WORK FOR

If you are considering using the Web in your job search, you should have already done your homework by being sure of what you want to do, identifying your marketable skills, and creating a winning résumé. The Web is a huge resource and if you are not completely clear and focused about what you are looking for, you could waste countless hours wandering around cyberspace.

One of the key things to think about is the importance of Internet knowledge in the job you are seeking. If your goal is to work in a high-tech organization, in a job that requires Internet knowledge and skills, then you will need to demonstrate your abilities in your approach, particularly in the choices you make about the way you present your résumé.

CHOOSE WHICH ELECTRONIC FORMAT OR FORMATS YOU WILL USE FOR YOUR RÉSUMÉ

Read through the following list to familiarize yourself with the various types of electronic format that exist for résumés. Contact potential employers to see which type of résumé they would prefer to receive. Generally, the more high-tech the organization, the more high tech your résumé should be:

- scannable résumé. A résumé that is typed in a traditional font such as Times New Roman or Arial that is easy for optical character readers (OCR) to recognize. Do not use bold or italics. It is strongly suggested that you include keywords related to the job position and to your field of expertise throughout the résumé;
- text format résumé. A résumé that can be attached to an e-mail, or included in the body of an e-mail, and read by any type of word processing software. It loses all formatting but is easy to send quickly to a potential employer;
- Web-based résumé. A nontraditional résumé that is posted on your Web site. Typically it is not just a posting of your résumé document but instead is broken up into several components such as work experience, specialized skills, education, and references. Each of these topics could have content on a separate page;
- CD-ROM résumé. A résumé that typically incorporates a multimedia presentation of your skills and qualifications for a particular position. The résumé is burned onto a CD-ROM and mailed to the potential employer.

(For more details on how to prepare each of these types of résumé, see the resources at the end of this action list.)

USE THE WEB TO TARGET POTENTIAL EMPLOYERS AND TO GET RELEVANT INFORMATION

Search functions on the Web can provide a gold mine of information about potential employers. Begin your search by using one of the search engines such as www.google.com or www.yahoo.com, or one of the Internet employer databases listed at the end of this action list. Make a list of your criteria so that you can narrow your search. Most databases are organized by industry type, organizational size, and location. These categories can help you to eliminate large numbers of potential employers.

Once you have a list of potential employers, you can begin to screen them by visiting their Web sites. These

"If politics is the art of the possible, research is surely the art of the soluble. Both are immensely practical-minded affairs."

(Peter Medawar)

may be in the database, or can be found through one of the search engines mentioned above.

Keep a Log of Potential Employers

Create your own database of organizations you are targeting, and keep track of information you have gathered about each. Also use this database to record any job search actions you take for each organization, such as dates of letters and résumés you have sent, what form of résumé you used, dates of phone calls, and who you spoke with and what was said.

Use the Web for Networking

One of the simplest ways to use the Web for networking is to e-mail people on your contact list. You can ask them about industry trends, potential job openings, or for specific contacts within an organization. Other possible ways to use the Web for networking include:

- e-mail lists or listservs. A technology for sending a simple e-mail to a large number of people. When someone responds to your e-mail, everyone on the list receives the message. This is useful for asking questions about what is going on in a particular field or industry, or to get information about an organization. Most listservs do not encourage direct job searches. It's best to participate in the listserv for a couple of weeks before you post any messages, so that you get a feel for what is acceptable;
- newsgroups, bulletin boards, or USENET. Each newsgroup is focused on a particular topic, and you must visit the Web site to see what information is posted before you can make a reply. However, it is fairly easy to locate a newsgroup that encourages job seeking and job posting. Visit www.liszt.com for access to many newsgroups and to search for particular topics;
- chat rooms. This is an excellent way to network in real time on the Web. Chat rooms are Web sites that allow several people to communicate interactively using text messages. If you find chat rooms that are based on your professional interests, you are likely to meet people who can provide you with valuable information and possible leads.

Create Your Own Web Page

You don't have to be a "techie" to create a Web page. These days, all the major Internet Service Providers (ISPs) offer free or inexpensive Web pages to their subscribers. If your ISP does not offer this service, you can get free Web pages on www.geocities.com. These are created by choosing simple templates and adding your own text—they are quick and easy and will provide some basic information about you. You can include your photo and your résumé. Depending on your background, you may want to include samples of your work or articles you have written in your professional field.

If you are seeking a high-tech job or a creative position in the arts or advertising, you may want to purchase your own domain name (www.nsi.com) and create a more complex and sophisticated Web site that could include video, audio, art, photos, and whatever else you think will portray your skills and abilities to potential employers.

Be sure to include your e-mail address and Web site address on all correspondence, in e-mail signatures, and on your business cards.

Common Mistakes

You Don't Have a Clear Goal and Plan

If you have not taken the time to narrow your focus and to design and target a job that you would really love, you will find that you will spend hours surfing the Web aimlessly. Many people who do this eventually feel drained, overwhelmed, and confused, and go back to searching the classified ads. But only a small percentage of jobs are found that way, and the future is on the Web, so learn to use it to support clearly defined goals. It may help to work with a career consultant if you don't feel you can do this on your own.

You Approach the Web with a Casual Attitude

Much of the interaction on the Web is quite casual, and it is common for people to use abbreviations and to not worry about typos or misspellings. However, if you are job hunting, you cannot afford to be this casual. Remember that hundreds or thousands of people may see your online communications. Make them as professional as possible.

For More Information

Book:

Cochran, Chuck, and Donna Peerce. *Heart & Soul Internet Job Search*. Palo Alto, CA: Davies-Black Publishing, 1999.

Web Sites:

Adams "Job Bank" Books (a list of prominent employers in a specific city or area): **www.careercity.com**
American Business Lists: **www.lookupusa.com**
CorpTech (a database of high-tech companies): **www.corptech.com**
Dun & Bradstreet Marketplace: **www.dbisna.com**
Hoover's: **www.hoovers.com**

See also:

✓ **Finding and Working with Search Organizations (pp. 810–11)**
✓ **Researching the Job Market (pp. 756–57)**
Job Hunting (pp. 2017–18)

USING LATERAL MOVES TO FURTHER YOUR CAREER

GETTING STARTED

Today's career environment requires more creativity, flexibility, and originality than ever before. The notion of a "job for life" has vanished. So, fortunately, has the rigid assumption that there is only one way to succeed in a company—that is, by promotion. Previously, if you were not moving up, you were almost certainly fast-tracked in another direction: out the door.

But today both employers and employees are discovering that lateral career moves are a creative way to build exciting companies and rewarding futures. For their part, individuals recognize that the more varied their skill sets and experiences, the more value they can bring to their employers. This translates into increased marketability, as well as additional job security in changing times. Your willingness to move laterally may protect you from being laid off as your company downsizes in one department while expanding operations in other more profitable divisions.

Employers, by contrast, are coming to recognize lateral moves as a way of retaining valuable employees (as well as protecting themselves from losing valued talent to their competitors). Top talent is difficult and expensive to identify, recruit, and retain. Top talent is also hungriest for new challenges and growth opportunities and will be quick to leave if not fed with them. Employers are beginning to understand that moving eager and interested employees within the organization is an extremely valuable approach to employee development, and one which will serve them well in the future.

The following points are key questions to ask yourself when considering the option to move sideways within the organization—perhaps, in certain circumstances, even down the ladder:

- If your company is downsizing, or if there are other elements in your life requiring more of your attention and energy, will a lateral move help you stay happily employed?
- Will a lateral move give you valued on-the-job exposure to business functions that will help you accelerate your upward mobility?
- How receptive is your employer to the principle of hiring from within and providing lateral experience as an employee development tool?
- Is there an oversight system in place within the management so that your career path will be tracked and your new skills set will be expanded further later on?

FAQs

WOULDN'T A LATERAL MOVE REFLECT NEGATIVELY ON MY RÉSUMÉ?

Not necessarily. As with almost every business decision, you get the best value if you make your choice for strategic reasons and then learn from the experience. A lateral move can be made for any number of reasons, and you may experience some surprising benefits in the process (understanding the ways other parts of the business are run, for example). Capture those benefits as added strategic value and you may actually boost your career prospects in the long run.

HOW CAN I BE SURE THAT MY COMPANY WON'T JUST ASSUME I BELONG PERMANENTLY ON THE SLOW TRACK?

Employers that support cross-functional communication and skills development are the most likely to understand the value of placing their high-potential employees in a wide variety of their business operations. After all, the best CEOs are the ones with the broadest exposure to the spectrum of corporate functions. However, if you observe that your company's most senior leadership have achieved their success via single channels of departmental experience, you might consider either staying on your departmental ladder or changing employers if your career plan involves wide variety.

MAKING IT HAPPEN

IDENTIFY THE REASONS WHY YOU WOULD LIKE TO EXPLORE THE OPTION OF A LATERAL MOVE

Does the next logical upward step in your career path require certain experience that you do not yet have? Have you just finished a protracted period of high-pressure productivity and need a lighter load for a short time? Are you taking demanding classes to increase your market value in the long run and need a less strenuous set of responsibilities during your workday? Are family needs preventing you from keeping up a demanding travel schedule? Are you committed to the company in the long run and want to understand as much of it as you can? Or do you simply desire some variety?

INVESTIGATE INTERNAL EMPLOYMENT POLICIES

Is there already a policy in place that supports lateral moves? Talk to employees who have made that choice to discover whether their long-term career ambitions are still being protected.

DISCOVER WHICH FUNCTIONS AND DIVISIONS OF YOUR COMPANY ARE GROWING

You want to seek out opportunities in areas in which your company is thriving or continuing to expand. Talk to other employees in those divisions to discover what the environment is like and whether senior management is supportive of individual ambition and career development.

CONSIDER THE DESIRABILITY OF THE OPENINGS THAT ARE AVAILABLE

Would you have to take a pay cut? How long do you think you would remain interested in that particular work?

"True motivation comes from achievement, personal development, job satisfaction, and recognition."

(Frederick Herzberg)

Does the new department show promise for continued growth and opportunity? Is the management team of your chosen department well received and respected among their own superiors?

Identify What You Enjoy about Your Current Work

Will you find the same elements in your prospective new assignment? How will you stay in touch with your current team members? Would you be able to return to your present assignment when and if you desire? If not, would that make an important difference to you?

Identify Your Potential for Success and Failure in Your Possible New Assignment

How long will it take to achieve your current level of proficiency in your new assignment? Are the measures of success acceptable to you? Are the requirements for upward mobility on this new ladder attractive to you?

Identify Your Prospects for Development Outside the Company

Does this new ladder present opportunities for expanding your marketability in the external job market? Will it provide you with technical training and experiences to boost your competence, therefore rewarding you sufficiently for the risk you would be taking now? Does it fit into your life plan?

Plan for Transitions

Be sure you and your new manager have worked out a plan to integrate you into the new team as smoothly as possible. You may have put a great deal of advance thought and work into making the transition, but your new coworkers may not be so ready for you as a new player.

Don't assume that just because you are a long-standing employee in the company, you are at home in this new division. If you are replacing a beloved former coworker, you may run up against additional resistance to your presence. Take whatever steps are necessary to make yourself welcome in the group.

Common Mistakes

You Leave a Secure Position Only to Discover that Your New Job Will Be a Casualty of a Downsizing Exercise

Thoroughly investigate the prospects of this new assignment, just as you would if you were applying for the job from the outside. Understand the roles this assignment and the department play in the company's long-term plans. If you cannot see how this work serves your employer's mission critical objectives, hold out for another opportunity.

You Become Unintentionally Slow-tracked

If you take a lateral move, especially if it is to reduce your stress load temporarily for a personal reason, you may find yourself accidentally on the list of expendable employees. You can halt this process, however. Be sure to invest time regularly to market yourself cross-functionally. Go to key meetings on a regular basis. Have lunch with your former manager to stay in touch with developments in your original department. Stay current with your company's developments and objectives and position yourself to make another jump into a more critical job as soon as you can.

You Make Too Many Lateral Moves with No Apparent Growth or Progression

Remember that, desirable as lateral moves may be, your career path must still show regular upward mobility. When you make lateral moves, try to take a job that pays, even though it is on the same level in the corporate organizational chart. Or take a lateral move to learn more management skills elsewhere, and then return to your original department at a higher rank.

Lateral career moves should not be used routinely as a preventative measure against losing your job, or as a way to tread water for longer than during a very short downturn in the economy or your industry. Lateral career moves should be used as a valuable strategic career management tool and when you are able to discuss your recent career path in those terms, you will find that a lateral move can be an excellent springboard to an even better future.

For More Information

Books:

Arthur, Michael B., and Denise M. Rousseau (eds.). *The Boundaryless Career*. New York: Oxford University Press USA, 1996.

Kaye, Beverly L. *Up Is Not the Only Way: A Guide to Developing Workforce Talent*. Palo Alto, CA: Consulting Psychologists Press, 1997.

Web Sites:

Emerald's response to downsizing and lateral moves: **www.managementfirst.com**

Monster Career Center: **www.monster.com**

See also:

✔ **Creating and Balancing the Portfolio Career (pp. 804–05)**
✔ **Making the Decision to Take a Risky Career Move (pp. 806–07)**

Managing Upward: Making Your Boss Your Strongest Ally

Getting Started

Scott Adams's comic strip *Dilbert* is popular and famous because the characters and situations—exaggerated though they may be—remind everyone of familiar examples from their own office lives.

Career ladders are crowded with superiors like Dilbert's who don't fit the image of the ideal manager. Inept, disorganized, power hungry, or downright mean—they come in all sizes and shapes. Often, they're so busy with their own careers that they're blind to your potential or goals. If you find yourself feeling unappreciated, dumped on, or frustrated at work, ask yourself:

- What's my goal with this particular job?
- What is my superior's style of managing, and what is his or her agenda within the organization?
- Can I work within his or her framework without losing my mind or my integrity?
- If I stay, what can I do to help my boss—and myself—to succeed?
- Would my interests be best served by looking for another job?

FAQs

When does the "difficult" boss become the "abusive" boss?

Definitions vary, depending on your threshold for intimidation. Abusive behavior can range from shouting or using threatening language and obscenities to more physical manifestations. Your organization should have grievance procedures for dealing with such behavior. If you feel unsafe, don't hesitate to get free of the situation immediately and report the incident to authorities. In no circumstances is it appropriate to fight fire with fire. You don't want to exacerbate the situation, and if formal proceedings arise from the dispute, you'll want to be the one who stayed calm and legally innocent.

What if I really can't afford to quit right away?

Staying, for however long you wish or need to, gives you an opportunity to gain marketable skills in the process. First, however, you'll have to adopt a new attitude. You'll have to be "bigger than they are," accepting insults, poor decisions, or slights with grace; learning how to appeal to your manager's best side and how to help him or her to succeed. If you can do that, you've gained things that will be valuable wherever you work next. More important, you will have developed a heightened sense of your own self and power.

What are the skills I need in order to get noticed and be successful?

Along the lines of "scratch my back and I'll scratch yours," you need to be an asset to your manager if you expect him or her to be an ally to you. Here are a few things that might help—but they call for a certain amount of swallowing your pride.

- Figure out your manager's blind spots and weaknesses, then see how your skills can help fill the gaps. Try to do this with genuine generosity and tactfulness, not letting on that you see these weaknesses.
- Take opportunities to play up your manager's strengths and successes. Building his or her credibility with others will eventually benefit you.
- Volunteer to take on jobs that your superior finds most disagreeable.
- Keep your boss informed. Managers need their employees' help to stay on top of what's going on in the organization.

Making It Happen

Have a Positive Attitude

It will be difficult to win your superior's admiration unless you can turn what you now view as a negative to a positive. Forget any ideas of retribution or "getting even." Recalibrate your sights on cooperation. You'll have to be sincere about it, though, or at least be a very convincing actor.

Your career is the end; your present job is the means to that end. Keeping your eye on your longer-term goal allows you to work at difficult short-term tasks.

Learn Who You're Dealing with and How He or She Works

Finding out what makes your boss tick—strengths, weaknesses, preferred style of work, and approach to problem solving—is a key to success in any job. Knowing these things allows you to adapt your own style to fit better with theirs. Is he aggressive or passive? Is she an innovative thinker or more conservative? Does he or she micromanage, or delegate? Be a good observer and a good listener.

Be Dutiful and Professional

Superiors depend on their employees to be helpful, resourceful, and loyal. Within reason, offer to take on additional responsibility, but don't let it get in the way of your primary job. Try to become the person others approach to get things done—in a quality manner and on time. If your manager is change resistant, suggest incremental steps.

When conflicts arise with your boss, try to figure out a few solutions before addressing the problem. Avoid whining or anger, especially if your boss uses his or her temper as a weapon. But neither should you feel fearful or intimidated. Learn to deal with conflict in a cool, professional manner, even if you have to excuse yourself from the heated moment. Then, when your superior has cooled down and you've rehearsed how to handle the situation professionally, you can both approach a meeting to solve the conflict. Advocate your ideas for

---

"Do not think a man has done his full duty when he has performed the work assigned him. A man will never rise if he does only this. Promotion comes from exceptional work." (Andrew Carnegie)

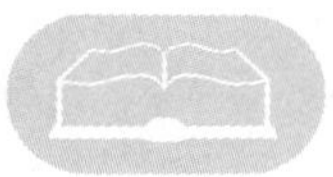

change from a positive position of "we" rather than "me," from a stance of "how this will help the organization," rather than "this is what I want."

Focus on the Bigger Picture—Look at the Organization

Your boss probably has a boss to whom he or she must report. Maybe your superior has the same difficulties with the next level of management as you do. Try to see what influences are outside of his or her control. Doing so will allow you to empathize better, and to position yourself as your manager's supporter.

Support the Organization with Individual Effort

Since organizations are social entities, the success of each department depends somewhat on its relation to other departments. Your value to your superior, as well as to the organization, increases as you attempt to make life easier for others. You can do that with your consistent good work, good communications, and by treating other department staff as valued customers. Build a network of constituents in your office and organization. The degree to which you can appear "selfless" should have a significant effect on the recognition you receive as a valued team player.

Leave Your Job in a Better Place

If, despite your best efforts, things just aren't improving for you, it may be that changing your place of work is your best option. If so, don't see this as a failure—it's important to acknowledge when it's time to move on, and to act on your convictions. Most times, moving on is a form of moving up. If you decide you need to leave, be sure to do so in a professional manner.

Common Mistakes

Getting Ahead of Yourself

Overachievers can sometimes be a threat to a supervisor. Eagerness is a virtue, but remember what you were hired for; if you appear dissatisfied with your present work and eager only for advancement, you won't win any points.

Being Critical and Combative

Somewhere in the heart of every lousy manager is a buried suspicion of his or her own inadequacy. Being overly critical, especially to someone's face or in their presence, reinforces that insecurity. But your superior, being the boss, will use their power to make you pay for your criticism.

A little bit of psychology and self-discipline goes a long way. Pick your fights carefully. If you decide to make a stand, do so on principles, not on personal gain. Show respect for your manager's authority, even if you disagree with a decision or action. Appeal to his or her ego. Ask advice. Make suggestions that you know will help the boss see you're interested in helping to solve a problem and help the organization. Don't expect miracles overnight—any movement is important, but a war isn't won in one battle.

Not Doing Your Homework

In this day and age, organizations count on fewer employees to do more. Thus, as each person's responsibility is increased, managers should treat employees accordingly. In a similar fashion, employees must be able to shoulder more responsibility and be willing to provide a creditable work performance every day. Part of that responsibility is to know more than you need to know, and to offer more than is required. In that way, you'll be showing your support, doing the best work anyone could expect, and gaining the confidence of supervisors, leading (hopefully) to raises and promotions. At least, that's the theory. But you'll never know if it's truc unlcss you're giving 100% to your job.

For More Information

Books:

Dobson, Michael S. and Deborah Singer. *Managing Up: 59 Ways to Build a Career-Advancing Relationship with Your Boss*. New York: AMACOM, 1999.

Weinstein, Bob. *I Hate My Boss! How to Survive and Get Ahead When Your Boss is a Tyrant, Control Freak, or Just Plain Nuts!* New York: McGraw-Hill Professional Publishing, 1997.

Web Site:

Careerbuilder.com: **www.careerbuilder.com**

See also:

✔ **Getting Promoted: Forget Your Boss, Serve Your Customers (pp. 784–85)**

✔ **Working with Mentors: Developing Critical Relationships with Powerful People (pp. 780–81)**

"It's just a very different way of thinking. My workers don't look at me as a boss, but as a friend, someone they can deal with in confidence." (Alberto Juantorena)

Working with Mentors: Developing Critical Relationships with Powerful People

Getting Started

Career success doesn't depend only on what you know and what you know how to do. It also depends on your ability to learn quickly the unwritten rules of the "system," the unmapped paths to rapid advancement, and the ways to handle yourself diplomatically and unemotionally during stressful or high-pressure times.

For those touchier areas of your working life, you need someone more advanced than you to turn to—someone to whom you can reveal your professional insecurities and inadequacies comfortably and confidently. Turning to your boss (or anyone else in your department, for that matter) for this kind of support is not always a safe or wise career move. This is where you need a mentor.

A mentor is someone who is committed to helping you find a path to success, helping you to gain the insight and contacts that you need in order to understand the steps to your future. He or she should also be able to provide wise advice for your incidental crises and decision crossroads.

The following points are questions for you to ask yourself when considering whether a mentor would be a valuable asset to your career path:

- How can having a mentor help my career progress?
- Wouldn't it be just as effective to depend on my boss for critical guidance in my performance and long-term career prospects?
- How can I be sure to choose the right mentor?
- What happens if my company doesn't offer a formal mentoring program? Do I have other options?
- At what point in my career can I actually be a mentor myself?

FAQs

Can I trust my mentor to keep what we talk about confidential?

You should be able to. How else would you be able to learn, if you didn't have someone to ask all those questions you're too embarrassed to discuss with your boss? The ideal mentor relationship is based on trust and candid communication.

What if there is no one at my company whose guidance I especially value?

Your mentor can come from anywhere: your organization, your trade association, your college. In fact you can have more than one mentor. It doesn't matter where they come from, as long as they're not your direct supervisors or in your department, and as long as they have the insight and experience that you value.

Do I have to pay for these services?

No. It's generally considered an honor to be asked to be a mentor. Accomplished individuals with significant achievement in their careers consider it good professional citizenship to participate in the process of helping those coming up after them.

Can I be a mentor, too?

Yes. From the time you leave kindergarten, you will always have "up-and-comers" following in your footsteps. Although your rank in your organization may be too junior for you to be officially considered eligible as a mentor, any time you're willing to share advice and information to benefit someone else, you are a mentor. Many organizations consider mentoring a valuable hallmark of leadership material. While you may be doing it out of kindness, others will take note and it will benefit your career in the long run.

Making It Happen

Decide What You Want Out of a Mentoring Relationship

Are you looking for guidance on building a career within one particular organization? Are you looking for help in developing your professional skills? Are you looking for introductions into seemingly closed circles of powerful people? The answers to these questions will help you decide whether you need a mentor within your company or elsewhere in your community or profession.

Assess What You Would Bring to the Relationship

Are you committed to developing the profession as well as your career? What will make the mentor glad to have invested time and energy in bringing you along? Do you listen carefully to expert opinions and follow advice? Or do you resist guidance?

Look for Candidates

Tell people you know that you would like a mentor in a specific area of your life and ask for recommendations. You can ask your boss for recommendations as well, but be careful that any mentor he or she suggests is not a close personal friend or golfing buddy. You won't be able to trust that your confidences on Wednesday will be kept come tee time on Saturday.

See if there is an official mentoring program sponsored by your company and let the organizer know that you'd like to participate. Eligibility for mentorship varies from one organization to another. If you're ineligible where you work, seek mentors elsewhere: your professional association, a community center, your place of worship, your local chamber of commerce or service organizations, your alumni association.

"Leadership is interpersonal influence, exercised in a situation and directed, through the communication process, toward the attainment of a specified goal or goals." (Lionel J. Beaulieu)

Interview Your Candidates

Just don't take the first candidate who comes along. The relationship you have with your mentor will be a working one. You need to know that you are personally compatible, with complementary values and shared ideas of what success looks like. Let the candidate interview you, too, without getting defensive or stressed. This is a low-pressure, getting-to-know-you step that, if done properly, will save a lot of time further down the road.

Establish Ground Rules

How often do you and the mentor want to meet? Does your mentor mind being called during the working day and/or at home? What will your mentor need to feel confident enough in you to start introducing you to his or her circles of influence? How often do the two of you want to review the relationship? How will you handle disagreements?

Consider Being a Mentor Yourself

Being a mentor is a rewarding way of building both your career and your profession in general. It can connect you with fresh ideas and ways of looking at the same old problems, and is an excellent way to network. As your mentees move on in their own careers, your network and sphere of influence expands as well.

Common Mistakes

You Look to Your Boss to Be Your Mentor

Avoiding that mistake is simple: Don't do it. Your boss may feel offended that you chose someone else, but you can explain diplomatically that it is common practice to go outside the employee's immediate working environment to seek a mentoring relationship.

You and Your Mentor Are Frustrated with the Lack of Progress Made

In your initial conversations, make sure the two of you share the same goals for the mentoring relationship. Also discuss your ideas of how quickly to expect projects to be done, and what kind of reporting system will work for both of you.

Misunderstandings Occur

In these situations, it is essential to know that both of you can speak freely, but always in the spirit of helping you grow your career: mentoring should be a positive process. This is especially important in cross-gender and/or cross-racial relationships.

If your mentor agrees with you that there are barriers to success for "someone like you," try to work with him or her on strategies to overcome those barriers, rather than giving in to a sense of mutual frustration. If your mentor refuses to help you overcome those barriers—whether they are real or perceived—you should look for another mentor.

For More Information

Book:

Zachary, Lois J. *The Mentor's Guide: Facilitating Effective Learning Relationships*. San Francisco: Jossey-Bass, 2000.

Web Sites:

Clutterbuck Associates:
www.clutterbuckassociates.co.uk (go to the Mentoring tab)
Institute of Leadership: **www.iofl.org**
Working Woman Magazine:
www.workingwoman.com

See also:

☆ **Avoiding Your Worst Career Nightmare (pp. 316–17)**
☆ **Breaking the Lead Ceiling (pp. 237–38)**
✓ **Managing Upward: Making Your Boss Your Strongest Ally (pp. 778–79)**
Coaching, Counseling, and Mentoring (pp. 1925–28)
Learning Organization (pp. 2024–26)

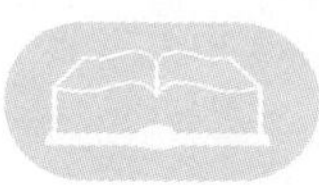

Developing an International Career

Getting Started

In the recent past, international careers were reserved for the stars of an organization. This might be an elite performer, in line for an exotic locale as a reward for a job well done; or an aggressive "closer," known for successfully developing important business in vital geographic locations; or an elegant, diplomat-type personality, assigned to a sensitive project abroad to smooth over feelings or gently open opportunities for future development.

Today, however, international experience is almost a necessity for ambitious career builders. Almost all organizations of any significant size consider themselves to be playing in the international arena—and even if they are not, they're well aware that their competitors are. So are their important customers. Consequently, having international experience on your résumé is a big help on your way up the career ladder. The following are questions to consider as you start planning to take your career international:

- How tolerant are you of different cultures and the feeling of being out of place?
- How eager is your family, especially your spouse, to join you in this new adventure?
- What is your organization willing to do to help you make the transition?
- How experienced is your organization in successfully reengaging employees once they come home from their assignment?

FAQs

Do I need to learn a foreign language to qualify for an international job?

It certainly helps, especially if there is a country or region you are particularly passionate about being assigned to. Knowing the area's native language gives you a useful extra tool and another argument in favor of sending you rather than your competitor, who doesn't know the language. But if you want to build an entire career based on international assignments, look for ways to improve your capacity for learning languages quickly as you need them, rather than studying them in advance of the assignment.

I've never lived abroad before. I wouldn't know how to set up my personal life once I'm there

If you work for an organization that has many employees assigned in foreign countries, the chances are good that it has a system in place to help you adjust to your new life. Your employer has invested a great deal of money, time, and expectation in your success, and is therefore likely to do whatever possible to help you do well. If that's not the case, take comfort in knowing that you will probably meet other people from your country—or at least from foreign lands—who will be happy to shepherd you through the confusions of getting a driver's license, finding an apartment, subscribing to a phone service, and understanding the true price of milk and eggs.

What if I get there and decide I don't like it?

That's a possibility with whatever assignment you accept, either domestic or foreign. Because of the extra expense your organization has incurred in arranging your move, you'd be wise to assume that much of the initial discomfort is homesickness and the stress of being in a totally foreign environment. Give yourself—and your family, if they're with you—the chance to become accustomed to the new life. The short, limited nature of an international assignment is easier to endure because you know there's an end in sight. If you give up too quickly, it may have an ill effect on your permanent record with the organization.

Making It Happen

Start Where You Are

If developing an international career becomes a driving passion, seek out employment opportunities that will be your passport abroad. The first thing to do is to research your current employer's opportunities and let it be known that you would welcome the opportunity to represent the organization overseas. Ask your employer what you need to know or do to position yourself for consideration.

If your organization's international presence is limited to only a few countries, and you want to stay with your present employer, start studying the languages of those countries. And let it be known that you have taken steps on your own to make yourself more useful and valuable abroad.

Volunteer for High-visibility, Short-term Projects Abroad

Even if your company has no full-term assignments abroad, it may have short-term projects in which you can participate. This will help you build a track record of meeting foreign objectives successfully, as well as giving you a low-risk opportunity to see what it's like to work in a different culture.

Try to select projects that have as high visibility and prestige as possible. This way, even if you should decide that the foreign life isn't for you or your family, you will still have moved your career forward by having accomplished significant goals for the organization.

Go Farther Afield

If staying with your present employer limits your prospects too much, start researching other organizations and their international opportunities. This research is easier with the Internet. The larger, international organizations will post their opportunities online, according to where those jobs are located.

If you care more about living and working in a specific country than you do about working for a particular indus-

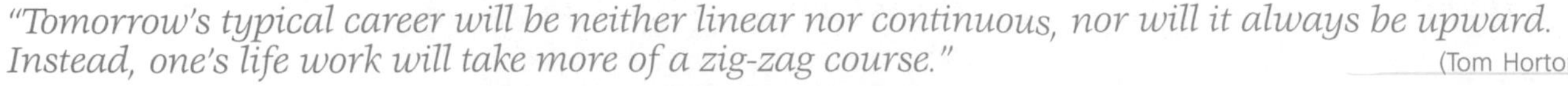

"Tomorrow's typical career will be neither linear nor continuous, nor will it always be upward. Instead, one's life work will take more of a zig-zag course." (Tom Horton)

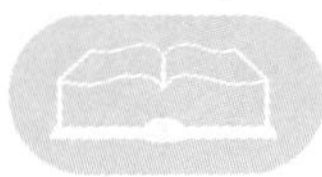

try or organization, there are excellent Web sites that list posted job openings by country rather than by employer.

Brand Yourself as an International Careerist

Read the international journals pertaining to your field of expertise. Contribute to them yourself, so you start building a bylined body of knowledge that is attributable to you. Instead of (or in addition to) renewing your local professional membership, join the international associations and societies that represent your profession or industry. Select the meetings that offer the best opportunities for meeting speakers and people attending from all over the world. Start speaking to these audiences yourself.

Move in this milieu and you will begin to cultivate a network of contacts that will build a bridge for you between where you are now and where in the world you want to be.

Keep Your Personal Risk Exposure at a Minimum

If you have a partner, see if your organization can help them find meaningful work in your new destination. Many companies have casual relationships with each other, especially in foreign postings, so that working partners relocate together without risking derailment of their own careers.

Try to get the company to incur the big expenses associated with moving your household goods abroad and providing excellent education for your children.

Common Mistakes

You Don't Consider Your Family—Especially Your Partner—When Making a Commitment to Work Abroad

Experts say that the single most common reason why overseas assignments fail is because the partner is unhappy. Many partners, especially those who don't work, find themselves isolated and lonely during the workday. Left alone to cope with the mundane aspects of trying to create a home life in a foreign environment, they don't have the same supportive team camaraderie that you enjoy at the office, nor the same prestige and excitement of working at a high-level, career-building job that you do. In fact, if they left their career behind to support you in your overseas adventure, they might actually miss the sense of purpose they enjoyed before they abandoned their jobs at home. Depending on the country you're assigned to, they may not even be able to obtain the right to work.

Many employers have programs designed specifically to help partners become accustomed to their new communities, including language classes; support and networking groups of other partners; even career counseling and referral services to help them find employment.

If no such support exists, be prepared to dedicate much of your time and energy to helping your partner find his or her way in the unfamiliar environment and to building both practical living systems and a healthy social life. This is a vital ingredient to a successful and rewarding experience for both of you. If you have children, they will take their cue from satisfied parents that this international adventure is an experience to treasure.

You Forget the Adage: Out of Sight, Out of Mind

It's too easy for the home office to get used to you being gone. As a result, you risk being passed over for other plum assignments and opportunities. Even though you're very busy thousands of miles away, you should continue to remind your superiors back home of your existence. Send updating e-mails regularly. Take frequent trips back to sit in on important meetings in person, and keep reminding key decision-makers that you are still a part of the team.

You're Not Prepared for Reverse Culture Shock

Coming home can be just as stressful as it was venturing out into the world at the beginning of the assignment. Abroad you may have had more leadership or entrepreneurial responsibilities, whereas back home you return to a much bigger pool of talent. Even though the international assignment will boost your career in the long run, the immediate effect of returning to the home office can feel like a loss of stature. Plan for that feeling and try to attract another high-visibility project to work on—only this time, make it at headquarters.

For More Information

Books:

Bell, Arthur. *Great Jobs Abroad.* New York: McGraw-Hill, 1997.

Francis, Huw, and Michelyne Callan. *Live and Work Abroad: A Guide for Modern Nomads.* Cincinnati, OH: Seven Hills Book Distributors, 2001.

Krannich, Ronald L. *The Complete Guide to International Jobs and Careers.* Manassas Park, VA: Impact Publications, 1992.

Roberts, Elisabeth. *The Directory of Jobs and Careers Abroad.* Oxford: Vacation Work Publications, 2000.

Web Sites:

Overseas Jobs: **www.overseasjobs.com**

Onexus—a unique self-publishing service available to employers and candidates at every level of commerce and industry: **www.onexus.com**

See also:

Working Abroad (pp. 2134–36)

"Global managers have exceptionally open minds. They respect how different countries do things."

(Percy Barnevik)

Getting Promoted: Forget Your Boss, Serve Your Customers

Getting Started

The common organizational wisdom is that if you want to get promoted, you need to make sure that you please your boss, do what you are told, keep your nose clean, and stay out of trouble. But in these turbulent times, the rules are changing and bosses no longer have the power they once had. Frequently, with the amount of turnover and churn in organizations, they aren't even around long enough to help you get promoted. So what do you do? Try a rather radical approach—focus your efforts on serving your customers. If you do this, you are much more likely to get promoted quickly and to see your career really take off. Here are some points to ponder as you consider your strategies for getting promoted:

- Who are your customers?
- Are they internal? External? Both?
- What are their needs, and how can you fulfill them?
- What does "service" mean to you?
- How can you make your work with your customers highly visible?

FAQs

Isn't it political suicide to ignore my boss?

Well, yes. You don't really want to ignore your boss, but if you are committed to adding value to the company and to investing in a successful career, then you should learn to focus primarily on your customers. At the same time, keep in mind that your boss may actually be one of your customers.

Our organization has a strong emphasis on customer service. But isn't that just for the frontline people? What if I don't have any direct contact with customers?

The majority of people in an organization do not have direct contact with external customers, but most people have an impact on the customer's experience of the organization in some way. If you keep the final customer in mind in everything you do, it will provide your work with a lot more meaning and purpose. And you will be seen as more of a leader.

My boss doesn't seem to value customers very much, and seems much more interested in just getting ahead. How should I handle this?

Ambitious and politically motivated people seem to do well in their careers for a while, but without a true emphasis on serving the customer, they reach a limit to how far they can go. There are several things you can do if you have a boss like this. You can talk to him or her about why customer service is important to you, and ask for the kind of support you need in order to serve the customer better. If that is not feasible, you may want to ask for help from Human Resources or the training department and bring in a customer service program to your area. Finally, if there is just too much of a values clash with your boss over the issue of serving the customer, you may want to think about transferring to another area. If your boss is not customer-service oriented, then he or she is not likely to be promoted, and that can have a negative impact on your career.

Making It Happen

Identify Your Customers

Who do you serve? Who are the people, both inside and outside your organization, who can be positively or negatively affected by your work? Internal customers may include people who are members of your team, internal clients, people in other departments, or certain managers. External customers could include the traditional customer who buys your company's products and services, but also could include vendors, government regulators, the media, or anyone else who may use information or services that you personally provide. Make a list of everyone you can think of, either by name, by category, or by role.

Complete a Customer Needs Analysis

For each customer, identify current needs that you help to fulfill. Then go back through the list and identify potential needs that you might be able to fulfill if you offered additional information, products, or services. When you have done this analysis, highlight the most entrepreneurial, useful, and creative ideas. These become potential projects that can further your career.

Think Deeply about What "Service" Means to You

In every religious and spiritual tradition in the world, wise people have taught us that being of service is one of the core values that gives meaning to our lives. In order to be of service, you must first become aware of the special gifts that you have to offer. What makes you unique? Perhaps it is a specific set of skills and knowledge. Perhaps it is a sense of humor, or the ability to listen deeply to a customer's concerns. Think about how you can bring more of your special qualities into your work so that you can be of service to others.

Don't Be Afraid to Make Your Work with Customers Highly Visible

Visibility is a very important factor in furthering your career. If you do good work and no one knows about it, it is pretty hard for them to develop you and promote you. Many of us are afraid of "tooting our own horn" and are afraid of being seen as egotistical, so we don't let people know about some of the creative and productive things we may have accomplished. But there are low-key ways to make your work with customers visible. Remember that the organization loves success stories if they are told in the right way.

"If the associates treat the customers well, the customers will return again and again, and that's where the real profit in the retail business lies." (Sam M. Walton)

Here are some possible ways to tell your success stories with customers, whether they are internal or external.

- Write articles for the company newsletter or intranet about what you or your team did for a customer and what results occurred.
- Write regular reports to your boss about what you have accomplished and highlight statements of customer appreciation.
- When an internal or external customer thanks you for something you have done, ask them if they would be willing to call or write your boss about their satisfaction.
- Conduct a customer satisfaction survey and report the results to people who can have a positive impact on your career.

Act with Integrity and Sincerity

If you are going to adopt a more customer-oriented way of being, it must be authentic and sincere. If you are only doing it to look good, people will see through that pretty quickly. You are better off being honest about being ambitious than to pretend to be customer-oriented just to get promoted.

Common Mistakes

You Are Focused on Goals That You Have Been Assigned to Complete

Most organizations are goal driven, and it is important to complete work that you are accountable for. However, if you are totally focused on goals that have been handed down to you, you are limiting your career potential. Organizations reward self-starters, and employees who take extra strides to fulfill customer needs tend to get more visibility over time.

All You Care about Is Your Own Career

One of the ironies of life is that if you spend all your time "looking out for Number One," you do not get as many opportunities and lucky breaks as someone who is more service-oriented. The more you focus on helping others to fulfill their needs and achieve success, the more successful you will be.

You Think That Your Boss Is Your Only Customer

All organizations are in business to serve customers. They have a product or service to sell, and satisfied customers return and bring their friends and family with them. Part of your job may be to help your boss and your team to be more customer orientated. The more that you and your fellow employees can adopt a sense of service, the more successful you all will be.

For More Information

Books:

Eisner, Michael D. *Be Our Guest: Perfecting the Art of Customer Service*. Orlando, FL: The Disney Institute, 2001.

Greenleaf, Robert. *On Becoming a Servant-Leader*. San Francisco, CA: Jossey-Bass, 1996.

Web Sites:

The Greenleaf Center: **www.greenleaf.org**

Team Spirit: **www.teamspirit123.com**

See also:

☆ **The Second Coming of Service (pp. 77–78)**

☆ **Urbane Renewal: Trusting Your Own Wisdom—A Competitive (and Satisfying) Advantage (pp. 320–21)**

✔ **Managing Upward: Making Your Boss Your Strongest Ally (pp. 778–79)**

"There aren't any categories of problems here. There's just one problem. Some of us aren't paying enough attention to our customers." (Thomas J. Watson)

Staying Marketable: Identifying Your Transferable Skills

Getting Started

On a global level, market demands are shifting and changing monthly, weekly, sometimes even from day to day. In recent years, thousands of individuals who trained specifically for sharply defined "hot careers" are discovering that those skills may not be in such strong demand that they warrant such a focused investment of time, money, and education. In such fields as information technology, for instance, disappointing downturns have dissolved what was previously assumed to be a "sure thing"—a "smart" career choice.

Staying marketable in shifting times requires more than a single channel approach to qualifying for certain jobs. It is not enough to have the skill sets required to complete certain tasks any more. To stay marketable, you must be willing both to update those skill sets continually and always to understand the many different roles your growing experience, critical thinking abilities, and interpersonal talents can play in many different market contexts throughout the rest of your career.

As a result, the most important skill that will keep you marketable is your ability to ask yourself fresh questions as circumstances change—and arrive at creative, dynamic answers that will lead you through a prosperous and relevant career. Staying marketable requires you to have enough motivation to invest extra and ongoing effort in keeping your skills not only up to date and transferable but also competitive. As such, your most marketable, most transferable skill is your passion to learn and acquire new skills.

The following points are key questions to ask yourself when considering ways to keep yourself marketable in an era of rapidly changing economic and business conditions:

- Why are you in the field you're in at the moment?
- What aspects of your current work give you the most satisfaction?
- What aspects of your current work give you the least satisfaction?
- Who are you meeting in the natural course of your work whose jobs may be a natural path of transition and growth for you?
- Would you be willing to leave your immediate career path to pursue a more promising or fascinating opportunity on an adjacent path?
- What topic areas fuel your natural, self-motivated curiosity?

FAQs

Why should I bother worrying about transferable skills?

Given the rapidly changing market and economic environments, it's essential to understand how your skill sets fit into your company's immediate objectives and future plans. If those plans don't agree with your own ambitions, you must know how to package and repackage your skills to build your career elsewhere. Transferable skills augment your core function skills to make you desirable across industries and functions.

Will I have to return to school to gain formal education?

Not necessarily. There are many different programs delivering skills training, including training that requires formal certification. Employers offer courses, as do distance-learning institutions. Additionally, old-fashioned "on-the-job" experience and training increase your transferable skill sets. Don't overlook that accomplishment, just because you didn't absorb this extra knowledge sitting in a classroom.

What do I do with an expanded transferable skill, once I have acquired it?

Market that skill. Put it on your résumé. Tell your boss.

Making It Happen

Make a List of All the Skills You Currently Have

Be sure to include skills you're not using at the moment, even those skills you think you'll never want to use again. This is a complete inventory of all your keys to your marketability now and in the future.

Analyze Those Skills

Highlight in one color the skills that help you do the work you love; circle in a separate color all the skills that require regular updating (for example, software, health care, continuing education requirements).

Prioritize Your Skills

Skills that are both highlighted and circled—those skills are your first priority for maintaining and cultivating so they stay current and relevant to the changing job marketplace.

Consider Your "Value Mesh"

Your value mesh is that network of connections and possible next steps for your own career progression (see also "Key Terms" above). Ask the people whose jobs appear in your value mesh what skills are most in demand for the positions you'd most like to consider as next steps.

Volunteer for "Stretch" Assignments That Will Develop Your Key Marketable Skills

Try to find assignments that are slightly beyond your immediate area of operation—in other corporate departments, for instance, where you can also expand your circle of contacts.

Develop References

Remember that in addition to actually having transferable, marketable skills, you must also develop a list of referees who will be happy to confirm that you indeed have those skills. So, as you complete "stretch" assignments, ask your new colleagues for letters of recommendation or introduction, if appropriate.

Document Your Skills

If you intend to continue working with the same employer, ask your "stretch" assignment supervisor to add a report on your performance to your personnel file.

Continue to Educate Yourself

Take advantage of all company-paid or reimbursed training programs to update and/or add to your technical and professional qualifications. Additionally, use whatever tax advantages may be available to support your continuing education.

Stay Involved in Professional Associations

Your skill sets include more than easily measurable technical expertise. It also includes your ability to come up with fresh ideas and innovations based on your overall knowledge and understanding of your industry or profession. For this reason, it is important to attend professional association meetings and development programs.

Make Your Professional Development a Top Priority

When selecting a new employer, choose companies that support ongoing employee development programs. High-quality employers understand that one of the best things they can do for their employees is give them the opportunity to keep their skills at the cutting edge. If potential employers exhibit indifference to this principle, this tells you that your personal potential for growth is likely to meet a dead-end while working for this company.

Common Mistakes

You Are So Busy Doing the Work That You Neglect Your Ongoing Development Needs

With rapidly changing technology and discoveries in almost every profession, it is easy to become obsolete very quickly. As work demands are intense and family needs absorb private time, it is also easy to ignore the need to stay current. It is important to develop and commit to a regular program of professional development (even if the program must be done during your private time) to stay competitive and marketable.

You Are Tempted to Focus Primarily on Acquiring Technical Skills at the Expense of More Conceptual Transferable Skills

Your continued marketability depends not only on your commitment to stay technically up to date but also on your commitment to upgrade continually all of your abilities, including interpersonal abilities such as persuasion or negotiation.

In Your Eagerness to Accept a New Job, You Sign a Noncompete Agreement That Is So Comprehensive It Effectively Takes You Out of the Marketplace

Your skills are transferable only as long as you can offer them in the open marketplace. Unfortunately, employers are currently tending to insist that new employees sign a noncompete agreement, reducing their ability to find new jobs later. Organizations have an obvious need to protect their intellectual property from competitors, and their competitors are a natural pool of future employers for you. So their interest in comprehensive noncompete agreements is understandable.

However, such an agreement could preclude you from working in your profession for an indefinite amount of time. Ask for time to review it with an attorney before signing. If the company makes immediate signing a condition of employment, consider that a negative signal. At the very least, carefully review all the wording in the contract and insist on altering any clauses that would prevent you from using your marketable skills in future jobs.

You Limit Your Own Prospects by Defining Your Potential Based on the Past, Not the Future

To stay marketable and develop your skills, it's important to build on your potential for the future and your passion for growth and learning. Every new experience is an opportunity for additional self-discovery and self-understanding. This is the foundation on which to build your plan for marketing and developing yourself in the future.

For More Information

Books:

Fallows, Stephen, and Christine Steven (eds.). *Integrating Key Skills in Higher Education: Employability, Transferable Skills, and Learning for Life.* Dover, NH: Kogan Page, 2000.

Pedler, Mike, et al. *A Manager's Guide to Self-Development.* New York: McGraw-Hill Publishing Company, 2001.

Web Site:

The Skills Zone: **www.pch.gc.ca/Cyberstation/html/szone2_e.htm**

See also:

☆ **Choosing the Best Training Curriculum for You (pp. 336–37)**
✓ **Identifying Your Marketable Skills (pp. 748–49)**

"If we simply do the job our bosses want us to do, we may soon find ourselves without any marketable skills."
(Tom Peters)

Getting Paid What You're Worth: How to Assess Your Value in the Marketplace

Getting Started

You may be at the beginning of your career, or you may be halfway through it. Wherever you are in your working life, your ability to be paid the salary you want depends entirely on your understanding of how much value you bring to your employer—and how effectively you are able to communicate that value to the person who controls what you are paid.

The subject of money carries with it a great many emotional and psychological issues, and we tend to get overwhelmed and even avoid the mysterious job of assessing what we bring to the marketplace. But just as a store periodically shuts its doors to count its inventory, a regular stocktake of all those things of value that you bring to your career and organization will help you decide how you need to supplement your skills and how to price them.

You should consider the following questions while you discover your worth to your employer, and decide how to translate that worth into compensation commensurate with your value:

- How can you capture the true value of what you have to offer the marketplace?
- Is there a logical design behind the way your organization pays its employees?
- How important is it to your future prospects to choose your boss when you agree to take a job?
- How much power do you have to position your job as a key contributor within your organization?

FAQs

Aren't salary structures a closely held secret?

Yes and no. Most organizations don't like to broadcast their pay structures. Many employers, in fact, consider their compensation and benefits plans to be a valuable, competitive tool. However, there are ways of finding out what your organization's salary structure is. Sometimes all it takes is simply to ask someone who does a lot of hiring and salary reviewing for the organization about the overall breakdown of the different levels and the reasoning behind them.

If my employer has a formal salary structure, doesn't that limit my ability to negotiate a higher salary?

Not necessarily. You can negotiate above the offered salary by emphasizing more intangible assets that you bring to the table. These might include, for example, the market supply and demand for your abilities, or your institutional knowledge (how long you've been at the organization and how much valuable information you have in your head), and so on.

Can I count on the organization offering me a salary within the range that is assigned to my job?

Again, not necessarily. As much as organizations want to attract and retain the best possible employees, they also want to save money. So your initial offer may be a figure that your employer thinks you will accept, not necessarily a figure that is "fair" in terms of the salary structure. Therefore, an initial offer to you could be well below the range that is officially assigned to your position.

Making It Happen

Inventory Your Assets

You have assets that carry with them intrinsic worth, regardless of what's going on in the marketplace, your profession, or your organization. They include your education, talents, track record for success (it helps to be able to quantify the financial value of your successes if you can), contacts, public recognition, and passions. This list shows your "fast-moving merchandise"—the goods that your employer already knows you have, and routinely relies on for the value that they bring to the organization.

Indicate on your list which of your assets aren't being used to their fullest potential at present. Then create another list of ideas you have had to benefit the organization's future, as well as interests you have related to the organization but not necessarily to your current job. This list represents your upward mobility, either within your existing range or into an entirely different range.

Inventory Those Behaviors, Skills, and Knowledge Sets That Your Organization Values

Look around you and observe how the "stars" within the organization work and behave. There you will find a clue as to what the informal, unwritten values are in your company. While, on paper, you may have all the necessary skills and knowledge required, you also might have to acquire certain behaviors (such as working late or going to official receptions) that will help you get noticed by the key decision-makers. It's when you are noticed by the people in power that you have the chance to market your worth to the organization. Likewise, if the organization values certain skills or levels of education—and if success within this particular organization is important to you—make plans to acquire them.

Understand How the Organization's Salary Structure Is Designed

The salary structure is not public knowledge, so you must ask around. Someone you know will know how the

"We're overpaying him, but he's worth it." (Samuel Goldwyn)

  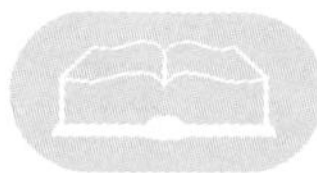    

compensation is arranged within the organization. If you are considering an offer within a new organization or new department, ask frankly where the offer falls within the range assigned to your job title. Expect an answer somewhere around the midpoint of the range. If the answer is vague or dismissive, that could be a sign that you are being offered a salary not within your range at all. Be prepared to negotiate.

Work for a Boss Who Is a "Star" within the Organization

Your prospects are limited by the prospects of your boss. Except in extremely rare circumstances, employees typically do not make more than their bosses. Find a positive, respectful, successful, and supportive supervisor, and your boat will rise with theirs. If, by contrast, you are stuck with a boss who is out of favor or in a department that is routinely under-funded, your own perceived value could diminish by association.

Know What Your Job Typically Pays in Your Marketplace

There are a wide number of variables that affect someone's salary, but, with a little research, general information is available. Trade and professional associations conduct salary surveys that reflect both local and national trends, or salary computation tools are available for free online. Or ask people you know and trust. Don't ask point blank for a specific figure, but talk in terms of ranges. Collect enough range information from enough people, and you will begin to get a picture of what your financial worth is, both to the organization and your bank balance.

Seize the Opportunity to Write Your Job Description

If someone asks you to write your own job description, it is a golden opportunity to position yourself as a valuable strategic player who is helping the organization to meet its objectives. Use verbs that emphasize the things you do to create change within the organization. The more strategic the role that you create for yourself, the higher you will be placed within your range—you might even be bumped up a grade.

Continue to Enhance Your Value in Four Different Ways

As you continue in your work, you can continue to improve your worth to the organization in these ways:

- You are a well-liked and trusted team player, who is both productive and cooperative.
- You are an acknowledged star performer among all the others who hold, or who have held, your job.
- You are irreplaceable—you possess unique skills, talents, contacts, or reputation in your industry.
- Your success track record is superior.

Common Mistakes

You Assume You Have No Power over the Salary You Can Command

You can almost always increase your salary, either by elevating your stature, perceived and real worth, and the respect you are held in within the organization, or by changing employers altogether. If you choose to stay with the same employer, you may have to wait for regularly scheduled increases. But when the time comes, you can take a proactive role in determining what your increase will be.

You Take Your Income Personally

Your salary is a reflection of your perceived worth to the organization, not your intrinsic value as a human being, or even as an employee. If you are dissatisfied with your salary, reflect calmly and systematically on the ways better paid employees managed to attract the higher incomes. Then follow their examples.

You Overlook the Worth of Nonfinancial Compensation

Remember that there are other valuable ways of being compensated: the opportunity to work with a prestigious or cutting-edge organization; the chance to do something that is meaningful and important to your personal set of values; tuition reimbursement while you are studying for an advanced degree; paid sabbaticals; the chance to learn important skills that will position you for an accelerated career progression later.

For More Information

Books:

O'Malley, Michael. *Are You Paid What You're Worth?* New York: Broadway Books, 1998.
Pinkley, Robin L., and Gregory B. Northcraft. *Get Paid What You're Worth: The Expert Negotiator's Guide to Salary and Compensation*. New York: St. Martin's Press, 2000.
Scudamore, Pat, and Hilton Catt. *Teach Yourself Getting a Pay Rise*. London: Teach Yourself Books, 2000.

Web Sites:

JobStar Central: **www.jobstar.org**
Salary Center at Monster.com: **www.salarycenter.monster.com**

See also:

✓ **How to Negotiate Your Salary and Benefits (pp. 772–73)**
✓ **Successfully Negotiating That Raise You Deserve (pp. 790–91)**
Employee Benefits/Compensation (pp. 1959–61)
Finding Out What You're Worth: Remuneration/Salaries (pp. 1982–84)
Remuneration (pp. 2103–05)

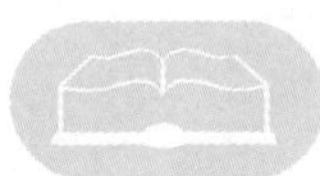

Successfully Negotiating the Raise You Deserve

Getting Started

You feel certain that you deserve a raise, but you are unsure about how to ask your boss. It is very important to think through a number of issues and to have lots of information available when you make your request. It is also important to know how to respond if you end up receiving a negative answer. Here are some questions that will help you prepare for your negotiations for a higher salary:

- When is the right time to ask for a raise?
- How has your performance been, and what is the evidence of your accomplishments?
- What is the typical salary range for a job such as yours?
- What is the best way to make the request?

FAQs

Why should I even bother to ask for a raise? Won't they give me a raise at my annual performance review if I have performed well?

Organizations have a trade off between paying enough money to keep people motivated to stay with the company and the need to keep down labor costs. You need to be your own agent and to promote your own case about why you should receive more money than you are currently making. It is helpful to learn about the salary philosophy of your organization. For example, does it pay the minimum it can to keep costs down, or does it pay higher than market rate in order to attract the best employees? Does it tend to give raises that are close to the cost of living increase for the year (which are really not raises)? Does it require managers to force a ranking among their staff and only give raises to the highest performers? If you have an understanding of the company philosophy, you can come to your performance appraisal well prepared to negotiate for a meaningful increase in salary. If you don't look out for yourself, the chances are pretty good that no one else will.

The company has not given many raises for quite a while. What should I do?

All companies go through boom times and difficult times, and they tend to retrench and cut costs when things are difficult financially. But that doesn't mean that you can't ask for a raise. If you have done a really outstanding job this past year and can point to concrete contributions, it is possible that the company might be able to find some money to reward your hard work.

I'm not good at asking for things for myself. How do I go about overcoming my own resistance?

If you go into the salary negotiation meeting with well-prepared documentation of your achievements (see "document your contributions to the company" below), you will have a stronger sense of your worth to the company and will feel more self-assured about asking for a raise. If you are really nervous about this, you might consider asking someone to role-play the situation with you so that you can practice beforehand. It is also helpful to visualize the meeting ahead of time and to picture what success would look like. And eliminate any negative talk in your head so that if thoughts come up such as, "No one ever appreciates what I do," or "I never get what I want," replace these ideas with something positive such as, "I have worked hard for this company this past year, and I can present a strong case for why I should receive a raise."

I was offered a promotion without a raise. Should I accept?

There are a lot of factors to take into account in this situation. If the promotion increases your skills, your responsibilities, and your visibility, and if the company is a start-up or is otherwise strapped for cash, you might agree to take the promotion. But you should also get written agreement from your supervisor that you will have a salary discussion at a predetermined time in the future, such as in three months.

Making It Happen

Decide on the Best Timing to Ask for a Raise

The most obvious time to ask for a raise is during your performance review discussion with your boss. However, it is not uncommon for supervisors to put off these discussions for quite a while. It is one of their least favorite things to do. If it has been more than a year since your last performance review and since your last salary increase, you should approach your supervisor about your performance and your salary.

Ask Your Supervisor to Meet with You

Give your supervisor time to prepare his or her thoughts for this discussion. Do not ask your supervisor for this meeting in front of other employees, because it puts him or her on the spot. Tell your supervisor that you would like to have a meeting to discuss your performance, your career plans, and your salary, and plan for it to last at least 30 minutes. Don't just drop into your supervisor's office and say, "I'd like to talk to you about giving me a raise."

Document Your Contributions to the Company

The best way to do this is to keep a job diary or a file of your achievements regularly throughout the year. It is so easy to forget all that you have done, but if you keep track of them along the way, you will have a great record of what you have contributed. When you ask for a raise, you need to build a business case for why the company should pay you more. You need to show what you have

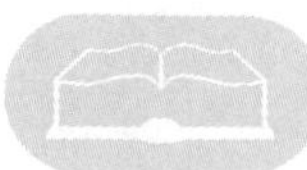

done for them and document why they should reward you. Be sure to keep track of measurable results from your actions, such as dollars saved, sales increased, level of quality improved, or percentage of employee retention. Prepare a one-page executive briefing on your accomplishments to take into your meeting.

Know Your Worth in the Marketplace

When companies calculate how much they typically pay for a job, they conduct wage surveys to compare salaries within the industry and geographic area. They also conduct internal pay analyses to make sure that comparable jobs within the company receive comparable pay. Such wage and salary information is now available on the Internet at sites such as **www.salary.com** and **www.rileyguide.com**. It is a little bit harder to find out information about the internal pay structure, but you can ask the human resource department for information on what jobs like yours typically pay.

Approach your meeting with your supervisor with a "win–win" attitude.

All successful negotiations end in both parties feeling like they received something of value. Your goal is to get a raise. Your supervisor's goal is to have a highly motivated and productive employee. Remember that raises are never given for potential or for what you are "going to do." Raises are given because of meeting and exceeding performance goals. When you meet with your supervisor, you should be thinking about how your actions and accomplishments have helped to fulfill your supervisor's own goals.

Discuss Both Performance and Salary

Begin your discussion with a description of your accomplishments and contributions. Next, discuss how you intend to build on those in the coming year, and what some of your key goals are. Describe your goals in terms of how they will support your boss and will make a difference to the company. Then ask for the amount and percentage of salary increase that you think you deserve and explain why.

Listen

As your boss responds, listen to any objections that are made. Consider this discussion as a mentoring session and keep an open mind about what you can learn that will help your progress in the company. Before trying to overcome any objections, make sure that you communicate your understanding of those objections through paraphrasing what you have heard. This is the first step in negotiation and objections are a normal response. Be prepared for objections and be prepared to explain why you still deserve a raise.

What If You Get a "No?"

If you are told that you will not be getting a raise at this time, then ask what it is you need to do in order to earn a raise. Write down everything you are told. After the meeting, write a memo thanking your boss for their time, and listing the actions you need to take in order to earn a raise.

Common Mistakes

You Threaten to Leave If They Don't Give You the Raise You Deserve

Unless you are really unhappy and were thinking of leaving anyway, this strategy can do you much more harm than good. If you threaten to leave, you are sending the message that you are not that committed to the organization and are basically out for yourself. This approach is not career enhancing.

You Complain to Coworkers about Your Salary

Most organizations prefer that all salary discussions take place only with your immediate supervisor. If you complain about your salary to your coworkers, you are seen as someone who is not a team player, and who is not politically astute. It is very unlikely that you would get promoted or get a raise under these circumstances.

You Ask Fellow Employees How Much They Make

Unless you are in an "open book" company, most organizations prefer that salary information be kept private. They are concerned that if employees begin to compare salaries with one another, it may lead some to think that they are being treated unfairly and therefore will lead to lower morale. You can get a better idea of your internal worth by benchmarking similar jobs in your organization and then doing a search on the Internet for salary ranges for those jobs.

For More Information

Books:

O'Malley, Michael. *Are You Paid What You're Worth? The Complete Guide to Calculating and Negotiating the Salary, Benefits, Bonus and Raise You Deserve*. New York: Broadway Books, 1998.

Pinkley, Robin L., and Gregory B. Northcraft. *Get Paid What You're Worth: The Expert Negotiator's Guide to Salary and Compensation*. New York: St. Martin's Press, 2000.

Web Sites:

The Riley Guide to Salaries: **www.rileyguide.com/salguides.html**

Salary.com: **www.salary.com**

See also:

- ✔ **Getting Paid What You're Worth: How to Assess Your Value in the Marketplace (pp. 788–89)**
- ✔ **How to Negotiate Your Salary and Benefits (pp. 772–73)**
- **Employee Benefits/Compensation (pp. 1959–61)**
- **Finding out What You're Worth: Remuneration/Salary (pp. 1982–84)**
- **Remuneration (pp. 2103–05)**

"A fair day's wages for a fair day's work: it is as just a demand as governed men ever made of governing."

(Thomas Carlyle)

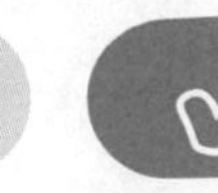     

MANAGING DUAL CAREER DILEMMAS

GETTING STARTED

There are many arguments in favor of dual career families. In most cases, two incomes enable partners to provide at least the basic comforts and modest pleasures of modern life. When both partners work, each is able to keep up with his or her career path, stay marketable and competitive, and contribute to postretirement financial security. Additionally, the knowledge that one partner is securely employed gives the other partner the opportunity to quit, if necessary, and seek a better position elsewhere.

However, there are also drawbacks: one member of the couple may have to subordinate their career interests in favor of the other's. Time and energy demands can distract dual career couples from their personal priorities: their marriage, their children, and their interests.

Fortunately, employers are increasingly recognizing the need to implement policies that promote flexibility and tolerance for balancing personal needs with work. As an example, many companies are offering flextime, telecommuting, and day care programs for children, among other initiatives to help working parents balance their jobs with their family life. But, as a member of a dual-career couple, you and your partner must still be the ones to make the choices and decisions that best reflect the values and priorities that you have agreed on as a couple.

Only you and your partner can prioritize the elements of your life together according to your values. But the following points are key questions to ask yourselves as you plan your dual career:

- Is each partner's career a primary career?
- How do family needs and career requirements conflict with each other?
- How do family needs and career requirements enhance each other?
- In the case of conflicting opportunities, how will the decisions be made equitably so that, in the long run, both partners will be able to look back with satisfaction?
- How can you make sure the long-term financial interests of the nonprimary career partner are protected?

FAQs

IS IT POSSIBLE TO BALANCE A CAREER THAT I DESIRE WITH A HEALTHY RELATIONSHIP?

Yes, but only if you manage each carefully. Have a clear idea in advance about what you want (and agree with your partner) and you will be able to make your choices consistently with your long-term mission. You will know later whether you achieved that mission.

HOW CAN I HAVE IT ALL AT ONCE?

Work–life balance experts say that you probably won't be able to have it all at once. But if you work together with your partner, you stand a better chance of having it all, even if it is only a piece at a time. How much you truly have all at once depends on your willingness to make tradeoffs.

I HAVE HEARD THAT DUAL CAREER DIVORCES ARE MORE COMMON THAN SINGLE CAREER DIVORCES. DO I HAVE TO SACRIFICE MY MARRIAGE FOR MY CAREER?

No. Communication, trust, flexibility, and creativity are important for every partnership and they are especially important for dual career couples.

WHAT SHOULD I DO IF IT'S NOT WORKING?

Take a businesslike approach to solving the problem. Living a rough and uninspiring life does not necessarily mean you're falling out of love—just as a failed product launch does not mean necessarily that your organization is doomed. It could merely mean that you simply need to alter the management of certain parts of your life.

MAKING IT HAPPEN

APPROACH YOUR DUAL CAREER AS YOU WOULD A COMPLEX BUSINESS

Understand there are various "departments" in your private life, and manage them effectively. This is not to suggest that you should not manage them with love and devotion. But budgeting and compartmentalizing certain aspects of your life and time could help you distribute your resources (time, money, attention) in the most effective way.

TAKE ADVANTAGE OF TECHNOLOGY WHEREVER YOU CAN

Many dual career homes have at least one computer. Install business management software that can also automate certain aspects of the business of your life. There are calendar, organization, and accounting software packages available for average consumers to give them the management advantages enjoyed by big business. You can even keep your grocery list on the family computer.

CONSIDER YOUR PERSONAL PARTNER TO BE YOUR BUSINESS PARTNER AS WELL

Just as a company defines long-term objectives and has a mission, work with your partner to determine what your relationship's mission and long-term objectives are. Using long-term missions and objectives as reference points will help the two of you make difficult decisions when an opportunity for one partner involves great sacrifice for the other.

COMMUNICATE

You can only expect your partner to serve your needs and your priorities if he or she knows them.

GET PROFESSIONAL HELP WHEN YOU NEED IT

Companies outsource services that are necessary but beyond their internal capability. Why not try this at

"I have yet to hear a man ask for advice on how to combine marriage and a career." (Gloria Steinem)

home if you need to? The services available to you can range from chores such as housekeeping and cooking to support services such as bookkeeping, financial planning, and even marriage counseling.

Use Your Business Skills Training to Help You Manage Your Work-Life Balance

One skill that could serve you well into the future is negotiation. When the two of you take the same course, you will then negotiate with each other according to the same rules and the same understanding of ultimate shared goals.

Recruit Your Children

There is no reason why dual career couples with children should shoulder the burden of all the little tasks of living. Give your children age appropriate responsibilities. Make them partners in your family's future as well as the beneficiaries of your hard work.

If There Is Going to Be a Primary Career and a Secondary Career, Agree Which One Is Going to Be Which

If you are not both going to put your careers first, make sure you both recognize this fact. With that understanding, you know who will be responsible for taking care of a sick child, while the other one makes that important meeting. If both careers are primary, it is important to understand that as well. Agreeing how your careers fit on the priority list will reduce the potential for major relationship straining disagreements.

Take Care of Yourself

You are also the CEO of your own life. Remember to fold in your own needs into the larger balance of family, work, and partnership obligations. You are no good to anyone if you are not good to yourself.

Make Dates and Make Appointments with Your Partner

Dates are for romance. Appointments are for managing the business of your lives together.

Common Mistakes

You Find That You Are "Ships Passing in the Night"

It's so easy to get absorbed with the daily details of living and working that you forget to appreciate the life you have built together. Schedule time for each other that is set aside exclusively for enjoying each other's company and remembering the joy of the relationship, regardless of what else is going on in your lives.

You Lose Control of the Small Details of Life

Keeping track of minor details could seem too trivial to prioritize. However, those details could mean the difference between whether or not you will have an argument over an empty gas tank or milk carton—or a forgotten child still waiting to be picked up at an empty school. Keep "To Do" and "To Buy" lists at a central location where everyone can keep them up to date. Make sure everyone knows whose responsibility it is to complete those "To Do" tasks.

You Feel As Though You Are Carrying the Whole Load, Both at Work and at Home

Be sure you continue to communicate with your partner on both daily needs and long-term career goals. If you find one of you continually is the one to subordinate personal goals and dreams in favor of the other's, check in with your partner to make sure that this trend is acceptable to both of you.

For More Information

Book:

Barnett, Rosalind C. *She Works/He Works: How Two-Income Families Are Happy, Healthy, and Thriving.* Boston, MA: Harvard University Press, 1998.

Web Sites:

Anglo Domus, International Relocation Services: **www.anglodomus.com**

Dual Career Couples: **www.workingmommall.com/resources**

Prospect Magazine: **www.prospect-magazine.co.uk**

See also:

✔ **Downshifting: Working Less and Enjoying It More (pp. 812–13)**

✔ **Managing Your Time Effectively (pp. 398–99)**

"In retrospect, for a full-time chief executive to do what is almost a full-time job is extremely difficult."

(Clive Thompson)

Getting the Most from Your Professional Career Consultant

Getting Started

Sometimes the best way to reach a goal is to call in professional help. Professional career consultants can help you figure out what kind of career you should be in, can help you set career goals for yourself, and can help you prepare for a job campaign or for seeking a promotion, if that is what you want. Career consultants come in many shapes and sizes, so you want to make sure that you select someone who is really right for your situation and with whom you feel a sense of compatibility and trust. And they are not inexpensive, so you want to make sure that you get the most for your money. You should consider the following questions as you set out to work with a career consultant:

- What is your goal in working with a professional career consultant?
- What are some of the services typically offered by career consultants?
- How do you find the right person?
- How do you manage the relationship effectively?
- How do you know when your goal has been achieved?

FAQs

When do people typically use a professional career consultant?

Career consultants are most frequently used when someone is considering changing careers or when they are between jobs and looking for a new position. However, career consultants can also be used as a sounding board for your current career. And some people use career consultants once or twice a year for career "tune-ups."

How much does a professional career consultant cost?

Career consultants usually charge by the hour, and their fees generally range from $70 to $200 per hour. Sometimes a consultant might ask you to pay a large fee upfront. Before you agree to do that, you may wish to interview several career consultants and find out what their fees are. The only exception to this is if the career consultant is going to offer you a battery of tests to help you understand your skills, your personality style, and self-assessment tests that can guide you in deciding what kind of career you will be successful in. The battery of tests will cost around $500, but these are not always necessary.

How do I find a professional career consultant?

The very best way to find a career consultant is through personal referral. If you know someone who has successfully used a career consultant, you can ask them to give you the person's name and number. Some people call themselves career coaches or career counselors rather than career consultants, so you can look these terms up in your yellow pages and on the Internet. One international source of coach or consultant referrals is **www.coachuniversity.com**

Making It Happen

Set a Concrete Goal for Working with Your Professional Career Consultant

Define your goal in results-oriented language. Be as clear and specific as possible so that you will know when you have met your goal. Some examples are:

- to find a new job
- to obtain a promotion and a raise
- to change careers to something more fulfilling

Become Knowledgeable about the Different Kinds of Services that Professional Career Consultants Offer

First of all, be skeptical of any career consultants who promise a quick fix, easy money, résumés that get speedy results, or other come-ons. Career issues are complex and often take time to work through. And professional career consultants require extensive training and education.

Make a List of Potential Career Consultants and Research Their Qualifications

After identifying sources for finding career consultants as described in the FAQs, narrow your list down by checking on the qualifications of each of the potential consultants. In the United States, career consultants are certified by the National Board for Certified Counselors: **www.nbcc.org** and the National Career Development Association: **www.ncda.org**. You also may call potential consultants and inquire about their training and experience.

Select a Professional Career Consultant from Your List

After screening candidates based on their background, conduct a telephone interview with the remaining people on your list and explain your goal to them. Ask them about their methodology, what their costs are, and how their background will help them to help you. Then pay attention to your comfort level with each person and to what your instincts or intuition tell you. You want to select someone that you can trust and who will challenge you to reach your full potential. If you are having difficulty deciding between two or three potential career consultants, then make a face-to-face appointment with each in order to make your final decision. Most pro-

"Don't be afraid to be unique or speak your mind because that's what makes you different from everyone else."

(Dave Thomas)

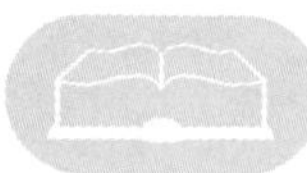

fessional career consultants will not charge you for an exploratory meeting.

Set Clear Goals and Expectations with Your Professional Career Consultant

Explain your goals to your career consultant. They will describe clear expectations about how they want to work with you and what they expect you to do between sessions. If you have any expectations about how you want to work together, make sure that you make them clear from the start. Also get clear on payment amounts and the payment schedule. Will you pay session by session, or will they bill you at the end of each month, for example? Usually, most career consultants expect you to pay something before the sessions as a sign of your commitment, and many will ask you to sign a contract. Only sign the contract if you are comfortable with all elements of it, and feel free to question any items that you don't understand or don't like.

Plan for the Ending of Your Engagement with the Professional Career Consultant

Since you have set a clear goal in the beginning, it will be obvious when your work together is done. However, sometimes new goals arise as a result of your work together, and you may decide to create a new contract. Or you may decide that you want to meet every six months, or on an "as needed" basis. Because the relationship with a professional career consultant can be very personal and rewarding, it's always nice to end with a little celebration or with a gift as a way of showing your appreciation.

Common Mistakes

You Don't Set Clear Goals

Some people go into this relationship because they have been laid off from their job and the company pays for them to have a career consultant as part of the severance package. The danger here is that you meet with your consultant regularly just because they are there, and nothing gets accomplished. A really good career consultant will guide you into setting goals right at the beginning, if you haven't done that already. If you find yourself meeting for over a month and not sensing any progress, then it's time to choose a new career consultant.

You Are Not Really Committed to Your Own Career Development

You meet weekly with your consultant and you agree to take certain actions such as working on your résumé or making five phone calls. But the following week when you meet again you have not done anything that you promised you would do. If this becomes a regular pattern, you need to take a serious look at your goal. You may have set a goal that is not really what you want to do. In your next meeting with your career consultant, ask them to help you evaluate the appropriateness of your goal.

You Don't Know How to Let Go

If the relationship has been really successful, you will have developed a powerful bond with your career consultant, and it will be difficult to terminate the relationship when your goal is met. But it is healthy for you to move on and to begin to apply on your own the things you have learned in this relationship. Having a celebration dinner is a nice way to symbolize the ending of your working together, and you can always schedule career "tune-ups" if you need them.

For More Information

Book:

Pickman, Alan (ed.). *Special Challenges in Career Management: Counselor Perspectives*. Mahwah, NJ: Lawrence Erlbaum Associates, 1996.

Web Sites:

Coach U referral service: **www.coachuniversity.com**

The Five O'Clock Club: **www.FiveoclockClub.com**

National Career Development Association: **www.ncda.org.about/polscc.html#careercounseling**

See also:

- ✔ **Creating and Balancing the Portfolio Career (pp. 804–05)**
- **Job Hunting (pp. 2017–18)**
- **Planning Your Career (pp. 2075–77)**

"*Get the advice of everybody whose advice is worth having—they are very few—and then do what you think best yourself.*"

(Charles Stewart Parnell)

Virtual Jobs: Staying Connected and Visible While Telecommuting

Getting Started

Telecommuting offers a delightful compromise between being employed full time (and enjoying the steady paycheck that comes with this arrangement) and experiencing much of the independence and privacy of self-employment. You can dress comfortably, saving substantially on your office clothing, and you can avoid the boring hours of commuting, saving substantially on gas, parking, and public transportation. As a telecommuter, you are also in a working environment that's all your own with no annoying coworkers nearby, which certainly promotes peace of mind.

Unfortunately, there are drawbacks to telecommuting. Among the most significant is falling "out of the loop"—being left behind, forgotten, or overlooked. You don't have access to the grapevine as you do in the workplace. And if you're not careful, you risk being ignored entirely when excellent, career-building assignments come up and you're not there to step forward to volunteer for them.

As a result, it's supremely important to build a plan for staying visible and connected with the people you work with, even if you spend much of your workday at your home office.

The following are key questions to ask yourself while considering whether to telecommute:

- How important is it to my boss to be able to track my performance and productivity firsthand?
- Can I trust myself to reach out to my coworkers on a regular basis, even if it's only for casual, social events?
- Does my organization offer built-in opportunities to return to the office and network?
- Does the environment already support telecommuters who are successful in their careers?

FAQs

Isn't it enough that I do my work and get the job done?

No. Work is about politics and perception, just as it is about productivity. So much work is done today in a teamwork environment that you must perform as a team member, even though you work largely in isolation.

What is the return for this extra investment in time and energy?

You will be remembered for promotions, raises, and important projects. When you market yourself as a key player in the organization, regardless of where you actually do your work, you are also less likely to be laid off in case of downsizing. By putting yourself forward, you also increase your chances of hearing incidental—but very significant—news and gossip that could change your future.

Making It Happen

Fit In with the Culture of Your Organization

Analyze how networks are built within your workplace and what behaviors are truly valued by your supervisors and the more senior members of your organization. If they have created casual, open-door environments where they welcome spontaneous visits, make a point of dropping in during the week. If they prefer formal appointments, set up lunch engagements or other dedicated times when you can regularly stay up to date with your department's news and projects.

Maintain a Presence in Your Company's Office

If possible, keep a desk and a direct phone line at the office. Furnish your workspace with pictures and business-related materials, so that there is no doubt that you remain an employee of the company.

Stay Visible "Virtually"...

Stay active and visible via your company's e-mail system, listserv, and other electronic communications. Try to answer all company e-mail within three hours of its delivery to you—immediately is best, whenever possible.

...and Physically

Attend all company-sponsored celebrations: birthdays, retirement parties, holiday festivities, cocktail parties, receptions.

Participate in Company-sponsored Community Events

Many companies are creating opportunities for employees to be directly involved with charitable and social projects. If your department is answering the phones during a telethon or repainting a home for the elderly, make sure you're there, too.

Market Yourself

Follow the example of independent consultants, who have to market themselves to build their business. You also must market yourself—even more so if you spend much of your time away from the office. Invite coworkers to lunch with you. Send them Web site references or clippings that would interest them, especially information that gives them ideas or surprise insights that will further their careers.

Get the Office to Come to You

Whenever possible, offer to use your home as a meeting place. Your comfortable living room might be regarded as a welcome "retreat" from the office's ringing telephones. It could be a great environment for group brainstorming sessions.

"Just as 'location, location, location' defines value in real estate, in business today it's connectivity that equals competitiveness."

(Mary J. Cronin)

Don't Forget the Bigger Picture

Remember to market yourself to your profession, as well as within your organization. Join your professional association's local chapter, as well as the national organization. Go to as many meetings as your budget and schedule permit. Keep your contacts current, both inside and outside the company.

Get into Print

Publish at every opportunity. Write articles and reports for your internal publications, employee communications vehicles, and intranet, if your organization has one. Contribute articles to your professional journal. When it's appropriate, invite your supervisor to be your "coauthor" on selected projects.

Common Mistakes

You Assume You Will Be Remembered

Just because your name is on the payroll, that doesn't mean you're on the minds of your fellow team members or supervisor. It is your job to make sure they don't forget you.

You Become Caught Up in the At-home Routine

This is easy to do. You start getting comfortable moving from bed to breakfast table to desk to sofa and then to bed again. Try to get to the office at least once a week. If that is impossible, make at least two outside appointments every week.

You Forget Your Coworkers

The best way to ensure that you will stay visible and remembered is by remembering the people you work with. Do the same things for them that you would have done if you were working in the same office. Remember their birthdays or work anniversaries; congratulate them on a job well done; pass on employment opportunities to them; ask them for advice.

You Lose Touch with What Your Superior Expects from You

Without maintaining a consistent presence in the office, you risk losing that instinctual sense of whether your boss is pleased or not. Likewise, your boss may be very uncomfortable with a telecommuting arrangement because they are not able to observe you working. Regular, one-on-one meetings with your boss, going over accomplished goals and agreeing to the next round of objectives, will make sure you both have the same definition of excellence. And you will have the opportunity to confirm that you are indeed achieving the goals set out for you.

You Lose Touch, Period

Suddenly you don't recognize the new jargon. The evolving technology has outpaced your ability to keep up. You performed some work based on an expired assumption or principle. The junior employee has been promoted far above you. You have never worked closely with any of the new faces immediately above or below you in rank.

Any of these signify one thing: it's time to return to the workaday world.

For More Information

Book:

Jackson, Paul, et al., eds. *Teleworking: International Perspectives: From Telecommuting to the Virtual Organization: The Management of Technology and Innovation*. New York: Routledge, 1998.

Web Site:

Telecommuting Jobs: **www.tjobs.com**

See also:

- ☆ **Overcoming the Difficulties of Managing a Virtual Organization (pp. 208–09)**
- ☆ **Virtual Collaboration (pp. 167–68)**
- ✔ **Moving toward the Virtual Organization (pp. 466–67)**
- ✔ **Setting Up and Maintaining Your Home Office (pp. 816–17)**
- **Flexible Working/Teleworking/Homeworking (pp. 1984–86)**

Losing Your Job: Survival Strategies for Starting Over

Getting Started

No matter whether you are suddenly laid off with no notice, or you know months in advance that your position is going to be eliminated, the actual event of losing your job can be a shock to your physical system, your emotional health, and, of course, your bank account. The steps you take as soon as you get a hint that your job is coming to an end will help cushion the impact of one of the most stressful times in your life.

The concept of "strategy" is extremely valuable at this period in your career. It invites you somehow to rise above your sensation of panic and, perhaps, the temptation to feel worthless in the marketplace. It will also help you take a new, bird's-eye view of your life and career, and see the potential for ultimately better work and greater success. You should consider the following questions as you take important steps to turn this upsetting news into a success story:

- How can you benefit in the long run?
- What can you do to prepare yourself in advance, so you're not taken by surprise?
- What power do you have to decide the terms of your departure?
- Can you be consistent with your own dreams, in the face of a marketplace that is urging you to build a career that doesn't interest you?
- How do your skills, talents, and drive fit into the larger business community?

FAQs

Why is it important to have a strategy in place before I lose my job?

If you are able to design your strategy in a calm environment, you can coolly select the steps and actions to take later when you are most likely to feel panicked and diminished by the event of discovering your employer no longer wants you.

If I'm laid off at my company, does that mean my relationship with my employer is over for good?

No. Many employers who are laying off their workers recognize that it's very likely that they will want to hire them back again when economic conditions improve. Even if that were not to happen, the business world is very small and you will likely run into your employer down the road at a convention, or even at a different organization. In fact, it's not unheard of for the laid-off employee to be the one to hire their former superior at a different organization months or years later. For this reason, it's important never to burn a bridge!

What should I tell my family?

Hundreds of thousands of excellent employees all over the world face unemployment through no fault of their own. If you aren't completely honest with your family, they won't understand the strain and tension that is suddenly in your home and you will rob them of the opportunity to support you in your time of crisis. Everyone—down to the smallest child—can contribute to the cause of thriving in temporarily reduced circumstances. This could be a golden opportunity to become closer through the teamwork needed to pull through.

Making It Happen

Try to Be Aware of Lay-off Potential Long Before It Actually Happens

Employers are often reluctant to announce to the workforce that there is a lay-off planned for fear that everyone will disappear en masse, leaving the organization in chaos. But it's still possible to be aware of trends that might be harbingers of unemployment. Is your local newspaper reporting lower profits out of your company? Is there a merger or acquisition rumored? Is there a sudden spate of "closed-door" meetings? Has your boss, or boss's boss, suddenly lost organizational power, no longer being invited to those closed-door meetings? Is your own job a vital link to the organization's profitability or is it a "cost center?" Is your overall industry—or local economy—suffering a downturn? The answers to these questions might help you assess how secure your position really is.

No Matter How Secure You Think Your Job Is, Always Take Time to Be a Recognized, Respected, and Active Member of At Least One Professional Organization or Association

Have a large and intricate network of contacts that you can always draw from, no matter what your employment circumstances. That network could be your advance warning system, or the conduit for information about other jobs and opportunities in good times and bad. Knowing you have that resource at your disposal will reduce the anxiety and panic, should the worst-case scenario of losing your job actually come true.

Understand You're Part of a "Value Mesh"

"Old economy" market equations would place you in a value chain, where you buy from one and sell to another, almost always in your immediate sphere of commerce or expertise. But in the "new economy" environment, you are actually one connection in an entire mesh—or network—of buyers and sellers from a wide variety of spheres and expertise. With a little imagination, what you do and what you know can be translated into a huge number of marketplaces, not just the one you're doing business in currently.

"Nothing bad's going to happen to us. If we get fired, it's not failure; it's a midlife vocational assessment."

(P. J. O'Rourke)

  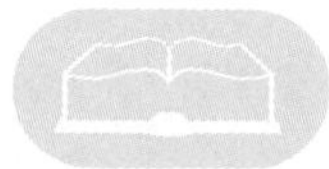  

Don't Sign the Severance Agreement While in a State of Shock

Most employers will tell you the terrible news and then slide a contract under your nose for you to sign before you go away. Remember, they have had plenty of advance warning to devise a separation agreement that benefits the organization. You deserve at least 24 hours to enable you to consider it carefully, perhaps even with an attorney.

Remember That Many Severance Agreements Are Negotiable

Perhaps you can convert your job to a contract position. In most cases, after all, the work still has to be done. By offering to do it on an outsourcing basis, you have found a way to generate cashflow for yourself while staying in touch and on good terms with your former employer. Other negotiable details can include the right to continue to use your office space while searching for new employment (the space exists whether you're there or not, and the illusion of being employed adds to your attractiveness to other possible employers); use of company equipment and services, such as the photocopy machine and voice mail; letters of recommendation or introduction from the organization's senior executives; or a larger severance pay package.

Take Advantage of Company-sponsored Outplacement Services

The best outplacement services are highly valuable benefits, largely unavailable to the average individual. This is a once-in-a-lifetime opportunity to have free professional help in designing your job search plan of action and to receive state-of-the-art aptitude and skills testing—as well as giving you a place to go to every day, where you will be in a professional office environment with your peers. Outplacement counselors also know the best and most powerful employers in the area, so you are plugged into a pipeline that's not available to individuals unaffiliated with organizations or outplacement services.

Keep Your Skills Up to Date

If your employer is offering free or subsidized skills training, take advantage of the offer. If you have been out of the job market for even as little as a year, it's likely that your technical and professional skills would benefit from a refresher course. Seize every learning opportunity that's placed before you. It will give you both a technical edge and the confidence to start your job search project.

Keep Your Spirits Up

The "pink slip party" is a new phenomenon of the current round of firings and closings. Throw a party for your fellow survivors, and invite local recruiters to enjoy the gathering as well. It's good to know you're not alone and, even if recruiters don't have any opportunities at the moment, they'll be glad to collect your résumé and contact information. The economy goes through cycles, and recruiters will always be glad to have a full file of excellent potential candidates.

Forget Those Lists of Promising, "Hot" Careers

They only ever promise a glut on the market of such careers in two to four years' time. Do what you love and build a career around your passions. There will always be a demand for employees who love what they do—they're the most innovative, self-starting, and constantly developing individuals.

Common Mistakes

You Fall into a Disempowered Despair

Don't tie your sense of self-worth to your career or job. You are who you are, regardless of where your salary is coming from. If you fall into a trough of low self-esteem, volunteer your professional expertise to a charity. The time spent with others will get you out of your malaise. Most important, you'll experience the real benefits of your gifts and knowledge, as they'll be received with no other payment than gratitude.

You Don't Take Care of Yourself Physically

Without routine and regular exercise, the sofa and the remote control become increasingly enticing. But if you maintain a regular routine and exercise program, your sense of purpose and minute-by-minute priorities will remain clear. The endorphins resulting from your physical exertion will also keep the blues and fear at bay. Eating sensibly will keep your body strong and resistant to the stress that comes with uncertainty.

You Let Isolation Overwhelm Your Life

Make a point of filling your calendar with business meetings every week. Put on presentable street clothes every day and go to a local coffee shop, if that's all that is available, just to be out among people. Meet at least one new person a week. Find a way to help that individual by introducing him or her to someone inside your own value mesh.

For More Information

Book:

Berman, Eileen L. *Dealing Effectively with Job Loss: A Unique Approach to Rebuilding Your Life.* Alpharetta, GA: Authority Press, Inc., 1999.

Web Site:

Laid Off Central: **www.laidoffcentral.com**

See also:

- ✔ **Leaving with Style: How to Exit with Dignity (pp. 800–01)**
- ✔ **Working in Interim Management (pp. 808–09)**
- ✔ **Working out Your Redundancy Package (pp. 390–91)**
- **Job Hunting (pp. 2017–18)**

"'You're fired!' No other words can so easily and succinctly reduce a confident, self-assured executive to an insecure, groveling shred of his former self." (Frank P. Louchheim)

Leaving with Style: How to Exit with Dignity

Getting Started

Probably several times during your career, you will leave one employer for another. Frequently, leaving the organization will be your choice; sometimes it will be the organization's. Either way, it is important for you to exit with style and dignity. Whenever you depart from a job, under whatever circumstances, you want to leave a lasting impression of professionalism. The following are questions you should contemplate as you get ready to leave your current employer:

- How do I want my supervisor and colleagues to remember me after I have moved on to the next job?
- What do I want my supervisor and colleagues to say about me after I leave the organization?
- What specific things can I do to demonstrate my professionalism, even when I know that I am leaving?

FAQs

Why should I worry about "exiting with dignity?" I won't be working there any more anyway

The phrase "never burn your bridges" became a cliché with good reason. You should always leave a job on the best possible terms. People from the organization you are leaving may be called to give you references for future jobs. You want to be able to use past employers for references, and to feel assured that they will speak highly of you.

Remember that, even in large industries, it is still a small world. People (especially at higher levels) know each other, and may casually inquire about a former employee. Staff from your former organization may go to conventions or conferences and meet people from your current organization. If you leave a negative impression at one company, your new employer may very well hear about it.

Also, suppose your new organization were to be bought by or merged with your old one? Mergers and acquisitions are becoming more common. You could end up working for and with some of the same people you left when you resigned from the company. Make sure you can face former employers with your head held high.

My boss has been impossible to work with. Should I discuss his or her management errors in the exit interview?

The simple answer is "no." What will you gain by badmouthing your (soon-to-be) former boss? When asked about working conditions or supervision, always begin and end with positive comments. For example, "I think we have a great team in the department, even though we've been under some real pressure lately. If there was a bit less pressure, I think the department could really capitalize on the creativity that's already there." Say as many positive, accurate things as possible.

Should I help my employer find my replacement?

If your boss asks you to interview candidates for your job, doing it well can go a long way to leaving a positive lasting impression. When talking to candidates for your job, do not discuss negative aspects of the job, coworkers, supervisors, or the organization. This is the time to be as affirming as possible. Talk about the positive facets of the work and the organization. Remember, the person you are interviewing may get the job, and you want his or her impression of you to be that of the consummate professional.

If the interviewee asks you why you are leaving the organization, never talk about how much more money you will be making, or how much better the working conditions are at your new job. Tell your potential replacement that you were offered an opportunity with some interesting challenges that will build on the skills that you have attained in your current position.

Making It Happen

Prepare Your Letter of Resignation

Always give notice to your employer in writing. Your letter should be brief and professional, and contain the date of your last day of work. End your resignation letter on a positive note by commenting briefly on the valuable learning, or challenging, or growth opportunities the position you are resigning from has afforded you. That's it. Do not go on about how much better the new job is.

Meet with Your Immediate Supervisor

Set up a time to meet with the person to whom you report directly. Your immediate supervisor always deserves the courtesy of a face-to-face meeting. During this meeting, you should tell your supervisor that you have decided to take another position, and when you will be leaving. This is not the time to tell your boss all the things that are wrong with him or her, how low your salary has been, or how awful the working conditions are in your present organization. When asked why you are leaving, simply state that an exciting new opportunity has presented itself, one that you just could not refuse.

Always be professional in this meeting. If you have had any problems with your supervisor, forget about them now. The best advice ever given about this meeting is, "let your supervisor save face." You want your boss to feel as comfortable as possible during this meeting. You also want to assure him or her that you will be finishing certain projects, or continuing to meet with customers, and so on. Perhaps one of the most difficult aspects of exiting with dignity is to keep this final meeting positive and upbeat.

"The final test of a leader is that he leaves behind him in other men the conviction and the will to carry on."

(Walter Lippmann)

Continue to Work As If You Were Staying with the Organization

This is the real key to exiting with dignity and leaving an excellent lasting impression. Continue to work as if you were trying for the next promotion. Finish as many projects as possible; attend all meetings; be an active participant in your work. This is not the time to let things slide.

One outstanding example of an impressive and dignified exit was set by a tutor who did not receive tenure at his university (the academic equivalent of being fired). He attended and actively participated in every meeting, put effort into his teaching, and continued to work enthusiastically with students. In short, he continued to work as if he would be in that job next week, next month, and next year. You should, too.

Leave Instructions for the Next Person Who Will Be Doing Your Job

If there are certain projects that are ongoing or you do not complete, leave detailed written instructions. Make the transition for the next person as easy as possible. In doing so, you are leaving the impression that you did not simply "blow off" the work you could not complete; you recognized it, and took the steps necessary to get the job done.

Common Mistakes

Not Giving Enough Notice When You Resign

In a number of professions, the two-week notice is a thing of the past. Many organizations expect a much longer notice. Check to see what the norm is in your industry or organization, and do it discreetly when you start looking for another job. Companies look very unfavorably on employees who give little or no notice before leaving. You should give your employer adequate notice to recruit someone to take over your position.

Talking Excessively about Your Great New Job and Salary to Coworkers

Coworkers will ask you about your new position, and talking about it is natural, but bragging about how much better your new position is than your old one only leaves coworkers feeling resentful and with an overall unfavorable impression of you. Tempting as it is to brag, and excited as you are about your new position, limit your discussions to comments such as, "well, this is a good opportunity for me."

Giving Your Notice or Resignation Via E-mail

Although we use e-mail more and more for office communication, always give your supervisor a formal letter of resignation (see "Prepare your letter of resignation" above). Also be sure to schedule a meeting to give your notice in person to your direct supervisor (see "Meet with your immediate supervisor" above).

For More Information

Book:

Levitt, Julie Griffin. *Your Career: How to Make it Happen.* 4th ed. Florence, KY: South-Western Educational Publishing, 1999.

Web Site:

Job Hunters' Bible: **www.jobhuntersbible.com**

See also:

- ☆ **Downsizing with Dignity (pp. 16–17)**
- ☆ **Driving Fear from the Workplace (pp. 330–31)**
- ✔ **Losing Your Job: Survival Strategies for Starting Over (pp. 798–99)**
- ✔ **Working in Interim Management (pp. 808–09)**
- ✔ **Working out Your Redundancy Package (pp. 390–91)**
- **Job Hunting (pp. 2017–18)**

"Handled creatively, getting fired allows an executive. . .to actually experience a sense of relief that he never wanted the job he has lost."

(Frank Pfeifer Louchheim)

Managing Career Transitions: How to Enter an Entirely New Field

Getting Started

It wasn't so long ago that employment stability was the hallmark of emotional maturity and reliability. Changing jobs frequently, even within the scope of a single career path, was generally frowned on, unless the transition was on a clearly upward path. Changing careers entirely was almost unthinkable. The prevailing wisdom was: "Pick one thing, do it well, and put away your childish notions of further adventures into discovery."

Now, however, most people are expected to change jobs several times during their working lives, and maybe their career. There are many reasons for this shift. We're healthier and more productive longer so we have time to build a body of several types of work, not just one. The marketplace changes so rapidly that many careers are unrecognizable from their forms even five years ago, and some have disappeared altogether. Some people are being forced into career transitions. But most can't resist the siren call of new discoveries and new opportunities to expand the frontiers of their potential.

The following points are key questions to ask yourself while considering whether you should make a career transition:

- What aspects of your current career do you especially enjoy?
- What attracts you to a different career prospect? Can you isolate those elements and find ways to experience them in your current work?
- Where are you in your career life? Do you expect to have enough working years ahead of you to become fully functional in your new career choice?
- Does the time required for education and training reduce your potential for seeing a return on your investment? If so, is there an alternative choice that can give you the same satisfaction without the necessary investment of years of training before you can start?
- Will the career transition be the change that will give you the happiness you seek? Or are there other issues that you must address as well?

FAQs

Is It Too Late to Change Careers?

This depends on what else you want to do with your life, and what you are willing to sacrifice. It's possible, for instance, to become a lawyer in your late 50s and early 60s, but that would require giving up or postponing the rewards of a leisurely retirement or the benefits of a senior executive position that you have earned in the years you have already invested in your current career.

What Happens If I Make the Change and Discover That I Don't Like It?

It's possible that you can find a way to return to your previous career. Or perhaps you can take your additional self-awareness and launch yourself into yet a third career. Continue thinking of this process as an ongoing journey.

Making It Happen

Focus On What Goes Right in the Career You Have Now

Make a list of the elements of your current work that give you satisfaction. Is it the people you work with? The tasks you perform? The way you feel about yourself when you have achieved a goal? The geographic location of your job? The nature of the industry? How your work benefits your customers?

Isolate Those Things You Dislike About Your Career

Consider the distasteful elements about your current work. Can you simply remove them or reduce them so that the positive elements are more prominent and you can renew your sense of satisfaction in your work?

Remember Your Earlier Dreams

Think back to those careers you dreamed about when you were young. You probably had some big, idealistic ideas for your future as a child, and you might have abandoned them prematurely in favor of more seemingly practical choices. But perhaps the time to realize your dreams has arrived. Refresh your memory of what those early dreams were and how they made you feel about yourself when you imagined doing your dream work. Now that you are equipped with more world knowledge and a more adult intellect, how many different real careers can you list that would realize those dreams?

Research Your Dreams

Use the vast resources available online. The Web continues to expand its content every day, so you should be able to discover the necessary information about any type of career you are interested in. Additionally, you can research the thousands of associations and professional groups that support and promote practitioners in careers that interest you. A good place to start is the American Society of Association Executives: **www.asaenet.org**.

Ask Around

Talk to the people who are already engaged in the work that interests you. Go to association receptions. Set up interviews with practitioners in the field of your dreams. Don't be shy. Most people who love their work consider it a pleasure and a welcome duty to promote their field to others. Encourage them to discuss their work on two levels: not only the practical how-tos and to-dos, but also the intangible rewards.

"The white collar job as now configured is doomed. Soon. So what's the trick? There's only one: DISTINCTION. Or as we call it. . .turning yourself into a brand. . .Brand You." (Tom Peters)

SEEK OUT THE NECESSARY FINANCIAL SUPPORT TO HELP YOU GET THE EDUCATION YOU NEED
It's possible that you will need to get additional education to prepare for your career transition. That could be an expensive proposition, but there are alternatives to paying for it entirely by yourself. There are sources of financial support available to you, and the Web is a good place to research sources of scholarships, grants, and other forms of financial aid. About.com offers a site that is comprehensive and informative at **www.financialaid.about.com/?once = true&rnk = r9&terms = Financial + Careers**.

KEEP THE FAITH
Once you have identified the next career transition that fires your imagination and your passion, continue to cherish that new excitement and vision for yourself and your future. You may go through moments of uncertainty or doubt, but try to consider those feelings as temporary dips in the transition process. Transition is a journey into the unknown, but the rewards will be well worth it.

COMMON MISTAKES

YOU ARE IN SUCH A HURRY TO MAKE A CHANGE THAT YOU NEGLECT TO MAKE AN IMPROVEMENT
Moving from one career to an entirely different one is more than simply changing jobs. It involves changing one of the most fundamental aspects of how you define yourself. You will be changing the environment you work in, many of your social and business contacts, much of your everyday vocabulary, your process of prioritizing conflicting demands. If you're like most people, you entered your first career in a hurry, without full knowledge about all the options available to you. Take this opportunity to make this a positive adventure in discovery, as well as a way of finding a new livelihood.

YOU RELY ON THE WRONG HELP OR ADVICE
Placement agencies and search firms, for instance, are in the business of filling positions, not helping you discover yourself and your new role. Many career counselors are underqualified and merely process you through questionable pencil-and-paper aptitude tests.

YOU RELY ON NO OUTSIDE HELP OR ADVICE
Do not try to process this adventure by yourself. If you have a high-quality outplacement firm available to you through your employer, be sure to make full use of its services. Additionally, many schools support alumni networking groups where you can investigate the pros and cons of possible new career paths with people already in those fields. Confer with those closest to you—people who have observed those things that have brought you satisfaction and joy throughout your recent years.

YOU PURSUE CAREERS MENTIONED IN "HOT CAREER" LISTS, THINKING THAT THEY WILL PROMISE FINANCIAL SECURITY
Recent history has shown that those "hot career" lists reflect the best of limited thinking for a limited time. As those lists are published, the market experiences a flood of candidates seeking those career options, and suddenly there is not quite the demand for qualified candidates that was originally expected.

If you are fortunate enough actually to land one of those hot jobs, you may discover that, financially lucrative as it might be, you are still left with that familiar discomfort that comes with the wrong fit.

YOU LOSE HEART
Try to keep in mind that you are in a far better position to seek out satisfying work the second or third time around than you were the first time you took on a new career. You are more mature, and you are equipped with deeper self-knowledge as well as with additional marketable skills and experience which will help you in all areas of your life.

Discovering and exploring career options that you might love should never be a one-time exercise. It should be an ongoing part of your life's journey, leading you to even more exciting revelations about your potential to contribute to the world and make a difference, while making a living.

For More Information

Book:
Lore, Nicholas. *The Pathfinder: How to Choose or Change Your Career for a Lifetime of Satisfaction and Success*. Columbus, OH: Fireside, 1998.

Web Sites:
Monster Career Center:
www.content.monster.com/careerchangers
American Society of Association Executives:
www.asaenet.org
Sources of scholarship, grants, and financial aid:
www.financialaid.about.com/?once = true&rnk = r9&terms = Financial + Careers.

See also:

☆ **Taking Charge of Your Career (pp. 324–25)**
☆ **Driving Fear from the Workplace (pp. 330–31)**
✓ **Making the Decision to Take a Risky Career Move (pp. 806–07)**
✓ **Working Out a Career Plan (pp. 418–19)**
Job Hunting (pp. 2017–18)

"If we don't change, we don't grow. If we don't grow, we aren't really living." (Gail Sheehy)

Creating and Balancing the Portfolio Career

Getting Started

Job satisfaction takes many forms. For some people, job satisfaction means a relatively secure income; for others, it means the opportunity to concentrate on a single, fascinating career. Then there are those for whom job satisfaction comes from having a variety of different careers (either all at once or end-to-end) that allow them to earn a livelihood exploring a wide world of interests.

To critical observers, this approach to career development may appear unfocused and directionless. However, it is an excellent approach to enjoying the many adventures, opportunities, and textures (sights, experiences, friends, diversities, and so on) of modern life. And because the so-called "job for life" is virtually extinct, the single most compelling argument for suppressing one's curiosity in favor of the illusion of job security has been negated.

In fact, portfolio career practitioners discover that their multiple sources of income provide them with a more secure feeling than depending on the continuing good will and loyalty of a single income source. And, even though you're self-employed and indulging your passions and spirit of adventure, that does not necessarily mean that you must trade away financial reward. With multiple sources of income, you may find that you make more money than you would in a traditional career.

The following points are key questions to ask yourself when considering ways to build a portfolio career:

- How high is your tolerance for uncertainty and insecurity?
- Are you self-motivated?
- Do you relish change and meeting new people?
- Do you depend on the social life and intimacy that being a regular member of a single workplace gives you?

FAQs

What protects me from being seen as a dilettante or someone who just can't keep a job?

An overall sense of purpose and big picture direction is what separates you from idle dabblers. You can dabble and experiment to your heart's content, but when you talk about your work, or even think about it in the privacy of your own mind, always regard your portfolio career in the context of a unified whole, rather than a diminishing perspective of a simple collection of "odd jobs."

Actually, I am between jobs. And my industry is in a recession at the moment, so it's not a good time to find a full time job. How can I use the portfolio career concept to improve my marketability later when I'm back on the job market?

Take a strategic approach to designing your portfolio career. Make sure that each assignment you accept gives you additional information, experience, or exposure to key players in your industry. The more varied your experience within a single industry, the better your understanding is of important trends in that industry. Therefore, you will be better qualified for strategic positions later.

Industry experts who have a bird's-eye view are often in a better position to command higher salaries.

Can I have a portfolio career even though I have a full-time job?

Yes. Your full-time job could be the keystone to your portfolio career as you build a lifelong résumé of ever-increasing experience, responsibility, and variety. Or you can build a portfolio career as a sideline, using your spare time and energy to develop passions that are either related or entirely unrelated to your full-time work.

Making It Happen

You Don't Have to Quit Your Job at First

Creating a portfolio career is more a matter of perspective and approach than needing to have the courage to "go public" with an all-or-nothing announcement that you're now a fully committed self-employed individual. While portfolio careers often entail at least one independent source of income, they don't require that you abandon a full-time source of financial security.

Explore the Big Picture View of Your Career

Your big picture approach to your portfolio career will probably evolve over time, but it's necessary to at least start out with a general idea of what the big picture looks like once you put all your job puzzle pieces together. Just as a collector gathers items according to some kind of theme, so a portfolio career also requires that ultimately your varied experience will piece together in some sort of unified idea. Ask yourself, "What do I want myself to be all about?" and keep that question centered in your mind as your career progresses and jobs accumulate.

Give Yourself the Best Chance of Success at Each of Your Portfolio Jobs

Always be businesslike to the extent that is appropriate to your job. Read industry publications and books. Stay current with trends and speak knowledgeably of the strategic issues facing your industry.

Market Yourself As a Management Consultant Would

Socialize, and volunteer to assist in situations that are likely to put you in front of leaders of industry and key decision-makers. Participate in local industry groups. Contribute as much as you can.

"A young person entering the work force in 2000. . .has almost no chance of working for the same company even a decade hence."

(Peter F. Drucker)

Don't Waste Time

Eliminate drains on your time whenever possible. Unnecessary hours spent in front of the television or reading may prove to be time-expensive luxuries that you can no longer afford.

Learn to Say "No" and Learn to Say "Yes"

As you become increasingly successful and popular in your variety of occupations, you'll have to learn to balance the temptations of pursuing exciting opportunities with staying focused on your overall career theme. Choose carefully, but do explore the most tempting offers. The reason why you say "Yes" may become apparent later; you may meet an important person or learn a new skill that will make the doors to other opportunities swing wide open.

Some career paths seem to be more like career trenches. You may not see exactly where they are leading you. By keeping a journal, you will be creating a map for retrospective analysis, and it will be in the looking back that you will understand the larger purpose of your journey.

Have Fun!

You may be the only person you know who is following a crazy, zigzag pattern of career progression. You may be alone in your values and the choices you make. There could be high costs in choosing this kind of work style. But there is one reward that you have total control over: the ability to enjoy the process. There will be benefits that are available to you only if you have a sense of independence, which often comes with knowing you have an independent source of income; the ability to pick and choose your assignments; the chance to live in beautiful parts of the world; the opportunity to travel, if you wish; and the chance to move freely through corporate hierarchies and meet exciting and powerful people up and down the ranks of organizations.

Common Mistakes

You Become Cash Strapped

Start this adventure with a cushion of six months' living expenses, if you can. Additionally, follow the practices of management consultants whenever possible: they sell their services by the value of results (not by tasks or time) and they insist on at least 50% in advance of the work.

You Become Bogged Down

It is possible to become overloaded. It's hard to turn down work, especially when you are unsure where and when the next opportunity will come, but overloading yourself robs you of the benefits of this kind of lifestyle and workstyle. It is important for the sake of your own mental and physical health to take time off and get plenty of exercise and rest.

You Become Isolated

Employees who work full-time in a congenial work environment have the advantage of everyday camaraderie, companionship, and creative synergy. As a portfolio careerist, it is very important to make sure your business and social networks are current and thriving. You must have friends you can turn to to share ideas with or simply to relax with.

You Become Obsolete

If you were working full-time for a company, you may have enjoyed tuition reimbursement benefits. As a portfolio careerist, you may be fully self-employed. It is up to you to make sure your skills are current and marketable, and you may be the one who must pay for the necessary training courses or schemes.

For More Information

Book:

Pink, Daniel. *Free Agent Nation, How America's New Independent Workers Are Transforming the Way We Live.* New York: Warner Books, 2001.

Web Site:

A Portfolio Career: **www.creativekeys.net/portfoliocareer3.htm**

See also:

☆ **Viewpoint: Charles Handy (pp. 75–76)**
✔ **Finding Your Calling and Living Your Passion: The Dream Job (pp. 744–45)**
✔ **Getting the Most from Your Professional Career Consultant (pp. 794–95)**
✔ **Using Lateral Moves to Further Your Career (pp. 776–77)**
Charles Handy (pp. 1000–01)
Planning Your Career (pp. 2075–77)

"People don't choose their careers; they are engulfed by them." (John Dos Passos)

  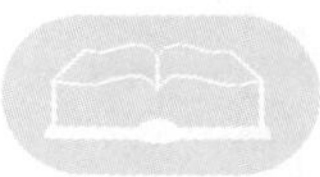    

Making the Decision to Take a Risky Career Move

Getting Started

Everything in business today is risky. There is no such thing as a safe bet. It is certainly risky to leave a familiar job with routines, expectations, and objectives that you're comfortable with to test the limits of your courage and skills in a strange environment, but, as over thousands of laid-off employees in global companies can attest, it's not exactly safe holding onto a job that is as dependable as a leaky lifeboat.

Whether you should decide to make that risky career move is entirely up to the nature of the risk and your ability to absorb the possible negative consequences. The risk itself may be made up of any number of factors, such as your ability to move into an unfamiliar job or your ability to move into an unfamiliar organization. Are you jumping from an Old Economy position to a New Economy one? Or are you leaping back into the Old Economy world after trying your luck in a high-tech, high-pressure, go-go New Economy environment? Are you considering leaving a stable, secure position that's limited in its prospects in favor of the white-knuckle environment of a bootstrap start-up? Are you about to move from a solid public organization into a family-owned business? Is the family that owns the business your own?

For some people, the notion of going into a shaky entrepreneurial environment after drawing a steady paycheck for years would be intolerable. For others, depending on only one income source, as opposed to the multiple sources of revenue available to an entrepreneur, may make them feel vulnerable.

The decision you make is entirely yours. The risk you take is entirely yours.

The following points are key questions to ask yourself while considering whether you should take the risk or not:

- Does the benefit outweigh the potential cost of the risk?
- How many people depend utterly on the regular income your current job provides?
- Is there a backup plan in case your gamble fails?
- Is it possible to return to your original position should you decide that your experiment was not as rewarding as you hoped?

FAQs

How can I be sure that I don't regret my ultimate decision?

Give yourself all the time you need to make your choice wisely and calmly. Think it through methodically, and then make the decision. Whatever the outcome, be sure to learn from it in some way.

I'm not comfortable in risky situations. Is there any way I can avoid this problem?

Not if you intend to grow in your career. Indeed, there are no guarantees in today's marketplace, so taking steps to avoid taking a risk might actually be the worst thing you could do.

Making It Happen

Identify What "Acceptable Risk" Means to You

If you are young and single (with no obligations other than to yourself), you can probably afford to take on a few risky career moves. These high profile actions can give you early boosts that could position you for more momentum-driven rewards later in your career.

If you are older, perhaps with a family, you may not be quite as willing to try your luck with a high-risk/high-reward venture, such as a start-up enterprise.

Your capacity to accept risk is entirely a personal one.

Know Your Goals

Make a list of your short- and long-term objectives. Is your current position more likely or less likely to help you achieve them? If your position is less likely to help you achieve these goals, can you make slight adjustments to your present job in order to position yourself better for achieving your dreams? Or is it necessary to depart from your position entirely, regardless of what you are heading for?

Know What You Value

List your less tangible values. Which opportunity is most likely to help you manifest those values? Your current job or your new possibility? Does one opportunity actually position you to behave in ways that are contrary to those values?

Conduct a Risk/Benefit Analysis

This is the process that will help you determine whether the potential reward outweighs the potential pain. There are several methods for analyzing your potential costs, but the easiest is simply to create two columns. List the potential pain in one column and the potential reward in the other. The column that has the longer list is the one that should receive serious consideration. A variation of this method is to assign points or anticipating dollar values to each item. You can then either compare the grand totals or assess each pain/reward item on its own merit.

Analyze and Compare the Relative Vitality of Prospective Companies

Consider the companies as an investor might. As an employee—even though you may not actually own stock—you are still an investor. You are putting in valuable time and talent in the hope of both short-term return and long-term gain. Is one organization receiving bad press attention which could erode investor confidence? Is one organization so heavily in debt that it threatens to collapse under the weight of this burden? Which organ-

"Risk means not knowing if, or when, you can pay yourself, or anyone else. It means working without health and pension plans, regular promotions, and paid vacations." (Heather Robertson)

ization is run by the best visionary who inspires confidence from both employees and conventional investors? Which organization creates the product that most directly and indispensably benefits the consumer? Which organization has the business model that you could most easily explain to a five-year-old?

Consider the People You Would Be Working With

Who do you have the most in common with? This is not a question of who you would be most comfortable spending an afternoon watching television or playing tennis with. Rather, whose visions and ideals are most compatible with your own? How does the corporate culture and environment appeal to you?

Consider Which Opportunity Is More Likely to Allow You to Develop Your Latent Talents

Almost all of us feel as though we carry an untapped treasure of talents, energies, and abilities. We are always looking for ways to express our genius. Which opportunity is more likely to give you the chance to develop in ways that you can take with you in the form of a much improved résumé should the worst-case scenario actually take place?

Common Mistakes

You Make a Choice That You Regret Later

As there are no guarantees, there is always a chance that you will make the wrong choice—or at least the choice that feels wrong to you as you begin to experience "buyer's remorse." Have faith in your risk assessment strategy, and carefully watch how that risk plays itself out. There is always something positive to be gained from every adventure.

You Don't Make Any Choice at All

Making no choice is still making a choice. And this is the one that is almost guaranteed to net you no gain at all.

Modern business is full of risky moves. Those who relish the thrill of the risk, shift, and change will be the ones who will ultimately benefit from the growth and added self-awareness that comes from the adventure of being engaged in contemporary commerce.

For More Information

Books:

Bolles, Richard N. *What Color is Your Parachute? 2002.* Berkeley, CA: Ten Speed Press, 2001.
Borge, Dan. *The Book of Risk.* New York: John Wiley, 2001.
Dilenschneider, Robert L. *The Critical 2nd Phase of Your Professional Life: Keys to Success from Age 40 and Beyond.* New York: Birch Lane Press, 2000.

Web Sites:

Executive Action International: **www.executive-action.co.uk**
Monster.com: **www.monster.com**

See also:

☆ **Driving Fear from the Workplace (pp. 330–31)**
✔ **Managing Career Transitions: How to Enter an Entirely New Field (pp. 802–03)**
✔ **Using Lateral Moves to Further Your Career (pp. 776–77)**
Charles Handy (pp. 1000–01)
Planning Your Career (pp. 2075–77)

Working in Interim Management

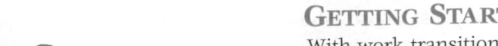

Getting Started

With work transitions, whether they be welcome or not, come new opportunities. One side product of modern employment turmoil and the end of the notion of a "job for life" is the opportunity for seasoned executives to move freely in the marketplace, practicing their skills in a wide variety of assignments. This is where market demand and supply have found happy accommodation. Where companies may not need certain permanent senior executives, they still have projects and initiatives to realize. As a result, many senior level executives are discovering that this sort of project employment suits their temperaments—providing income close to the equivalent of full-time salaries, as well as independence and the flexibility to choose the work they want and live the life they desire.

Whereas interim management providers are quick to say that these executives are not "between jobs," many practitioners find themselves doing this type of work when they are indeed terminated from their previous full-time job. As a result, interim management practitioners have a role at every career stage, including post-retirement if they want to stay involved in their field of business, at least to a limited extent. No matter how they arrive at this working arrangement, committed interim managers, however, often find themselves delighted with this solution that combines the best qualities of steady work and independence.

Interim management is not a work style that suits everyone. Ask yourself the following key questions when considering ways to work in interim management:

- Do you enjoy the temporary lifestyle, in which you change roles and responsibilities frequently, and often without seeing the long-term outcome of your initial efforts?
- Do you adapt easily to a wide variety of work environments and work teams that are already established and functioning when you arrive? Can you assume the leadership of such groups?
- Do you like challenge, variety, and unpredictability?

FAQs

Isn't an interim manager the same as a temporary worker or a consultant?

No. Interim management proponents are eager to distinguish this sort of practitioner from two other players on the market: temporary workers and management consultants. While many of the same agencies that place temporary workers also provide placement services for interim managers, they are quick to point out that the assignments are unquestionably senior level projects that drive the future of the client company. These assignments also last anywhere from a few months to a year or longer. Interim management practitioners also differ from management consultants in that they provide hands-on, day-to-day effort rather than the prescriptive, advisory support that management consultants deliver.

Can I make the same kind of income I once made as a full-time executive at my previous company?

Yes, maybe even more on an hourly or daily basis. As a practitioner in this particular marketplace, you are free to accept assignments, or reject them if they do not meet your requirements. Depending on the local demand for your particular range of skills, you can be as strict about your minimum salary requirements as you wish. You also can take unlimited time off between assignments for vacations, or writing books, or other personal projects.

What if I want to go back into the world of full-time employment?

Although interim management service organizations typically do not like to broadcast this fact, their contractors are frequently between jobs and are, in fact, in the market for another full-time position. Interim managers may discover that they enjoy the independence of this particular work style instead, however, and may not be interested in returning to full-time work.

Contractors committed to seeking a full-time position find that working in this environment has several advantages: fulfilling a contract is good for their self-esteem; they continue to feel needed and valued; they are learning new skills and gaining marketable experience in different industries. And, of course, the principle still holds true: it's easier to find a job when you already have one. This is an excellent way to already have one.

What if I find a permanent position before my contract is due to expire?

You will have to work directly with your interim management service company, as well as the client organization, to coordinate a transition that does not impact negatively on the client organization. In almost every conventional situation, both the new hiring organization and the incumbent employer understand and expect a moderately lengthy transition time. Especially among the most senior ranks, newly recruited talent is rarely available to start immediately. The same scenario applies in this circumstance. How you manage the transition, however, is extremely important. There are four affected parties in this situation: you, the client company, the interim management service provider, and your new employer. You will need to find a way to honor your commitment to all sides.

Making It Happen

Prepare Your Résumé As You Normally Would If You Were Applying for a Full-time, Permanent Position

Your résumé should include all the most senior and management level responsibilities you have fulfilled in your career.

"What is work and what is not work is a question that perplexes the wisest of men." (Bhagavad Gita)

Interview Interim Management Service Providers

Many of the leading international temporary staffing agencies have interim management service arms. Talk only to the best, the most dignified, and best established in your marketplace. Additionally, seek out agencies that specialize in your industry, if you wish to remain in your general field, such as manufacturing, aviation, or health care.

Sign with As Many Agencies As You Are Comfortable with

As with temporary help agencies, they typically do not expect an exclusive arrangement with you. They each hope to be the one that matches you with your next assignment, obviously, but it is generally understood that until you accept an assignment, you are a free agent, obligated to no one.

Be Clear What Types of Assignment You Will Accept and What Your Minimal Income Requirements Are

Depending on the marketplace, some contractors are even particular about the commuting time and distance from their home, or the amount of travel necessary to fulfill the requirements of the role. Indeed, in the most senior positions, you may also be able to specify certain perks, such as a car and driver.

Understand the Benefits Being Offered by the Interim Services Company, As Well As Your Responsibilities

Depending on the agency and/or the country in which you work, you may have all the basic benefits (health, life insurance, and so on) covered by your agency. However, you also may be required to provide your own liability insurance coverage, such as errors and omissions.

Assume the Leadership Role You Are Being Paid to Perform

Awkward as it may feel to jump into an organization and take over its management, if that is what you are being paid to do, then do it. You must be a fast study, and be fully functional in your role from day one.

Leave Your Work Behind You When You Are Done

You must be prepared to depart as quickly and unceremoniously as you arrived. Whether you complete the project you were hired to execute or the client organization has found the permanent replacement for the position you were temporarily filling, your services are no longer required. You may find this unsettling, especially if you have invested emotional energy, as well as time, in your work. Try not to take it personally, but do stay in touch with the contacts you have made during the assignment. You are building long-term equity—not in the participation of the company's long-term development but in the development of your own network of talent and contacts in your industry.

Common Mistakes

You Fail to Integrate Yourself into the Company's Leadership

Remember that while you are on contract with the client company, you are not an outsider. Although you may have to move carefully and sensitively according to the social and cultural climate of the organization, you need to accelerate the assimilation process as quickly as possible to be effective. The client company is paying for your short-term ability to get things done, not your aptitude for establishing and leveraging new long-term relationships.

You Forget that You Are Only Temporary at the Company

Some assignments last longer than some so-called permanent positions. After as many as 18 months on an assignment, it would be normal to become emotionally and professionally involved in the outcome of a project that may not occur until you are long gone. This is a frustrating fact of life for interim managers. But there is solace to be had from knowing that you will be well on your way to another fascinating project, or perhaps a lengthy, luxury vacation.

For More Information

Book:

McGovern, Marion, and Dennis Russell. *A New Brand of Expertise: How Independent Consultants, Free Agents, and Interim Managers are Transforming the World of Work.* Woburn, MA: Butterworth-Heinemann, 2001.

Web Sites:

Greenough Consulting Group: **www.greenoughgroup.com/home.html**

IMCOR: **www.imcor.com**

See also:

☆ **Viewpoint: Charles Handy (pp. 75–76)**
✔ **Losing Your Job: Survival Strategies For Starting Over (pp. 798–99)**
Charles Handy (pp. 1000–01)
Planning Your Career (pp. 2075–77)

"Ultimately, the job of the manager is to get ordinary people to create extraordinary results."

(Christopher Bartlett)

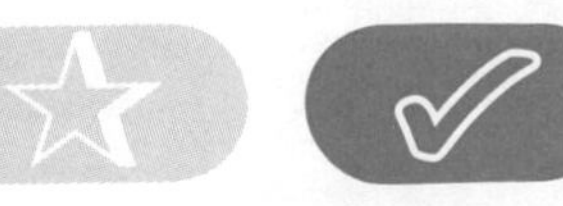
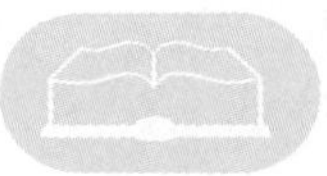

FINDING AND WORKING WITH SEARCH ORGANIZATIONS

GETTING STARTED

When you begin the job search process, it is common to feel haunted by the so-called "hidden job market," that exclusive club in which only a few people are connected with the very best job opportunities. This haunted feeling has legitimate reasons. Only a small percentage of open jobs are indeed publicly announced. The very best jobs usually require a special set of skills or background, and hiring companies use refined recruitment techniques to attract candidates for such unique positions.

One of those techniques is the retention of search organizations that specialize in ferreting out the best candidates for the open position. The trouble is that it is not easy to know about, much less apply for, these particular opportunities. And, among the very best search organizations, the general message to the public is: "Don't find us. We'll find you".

Indeed, the mere fact that you reach out to a search organization renders you undesirable in the eyes of many of these companies. Just as banks only like to loan money to people who do not really need it, search organizations like to recruit candidates who are not really looking.

With that closed-club impression, it is natural to feel as though actively setting out to attract the attention of search organizations is probably counterproductive. However, there are ways to use the connections and power of search organizations to promote your own career.

The following points are questions to consider as you prepare to look for your next job with the help of one or more search organizations:

- Do I need a search organization to help me find my next job?
- How quickly do I need a new job?
- Should I work with a contingency organization or a retained search organization?

FAQs

HOW MUCH SHOULD I EXPECT TO HAVE TO PAY A SEARCH ORGANIZATION FOR HELPING ME?

Nothing. The client is the hiring company. Never pay a search organization. Search organizations receive their fees from the company, valued at roughly 30% of the new employee's first year's salary.

WHAT'S THE DIFFERENCE BETWEEN A CONTINGENCY SEARCH ORGANIZATION AND A RETAINED SEARCH ORGANIZATION?

The contingency search organization only makes its money when it successfully places a candidate. Contingency organizations usually fill junior to middle-level executive positions, with salaries ranging from $50,000 to $150,000. A retained search organization works with more senior positions, receiving its fee regardless of whether certain positions are successfully filled. Both are legitimate forms of business; however, it is generally agreed that retained search organizations have a higher quality relationship with their client company—a long-term interest in which the mutual goal is the company's prosperity. With a contingency search organization, the emphasis is more likely to be on the individual placement. So both you and the hiring company could find yourselves in a wrong match.

CAN I WORK WITH MORE THAN ONE SEARCH ORGANIZATION AT A TIME?

In most cases, yes. You are the one still in charge of your own future. Seriously reconsider signing with a search organization that insists on an exclusive contract with you. Because you are not the paying client, your own personal interests are not part of the organization's business concerns. Therefore, you should be able to market and represent yourself freely elsewhere.

MAKING IT HAPPEN

IDENTIFY THE BEST SEARCH ORGANIZATIONS FOR THE TYPE OF POSITION YOU ARE SEEKING

Use word-of-mouth and other indirect marketing techniques for identifying the best search organizations and helping them find you. Ask your friends, colleagues, and college career centers to introduce you to the services they found to be satisfactory. Go where search organization consultants go. Attend high-end business receptions, go to human resource seminars in your community or industry. Participate as a speaker (or even a volunteer) at business symposia. Write articles for your industry journal.

CONTACT THE SEARCH ORGANIZATION

The best way to initiate contact with a search organization is to phone a search organization consultant specifically recommended to you by a friend or colleague. Have an expertly prepared résumé ready to send immediately. If you do not have a personal introduction, send the résumé with a covering letter describing your overall credentials and abilities.

BE PREPARED

You may be invited to come in for an interview immediately. Or you may be notified that your résumé has been keyed into the organization's database. Assuming that your résumé contains the important keywords associated with your career path, your information will then come up the next time a suitable position is researched.

Working with search companies is likely to be a long-term proposition, where both you and the consultant will find success if and when a compatible opening is available at a client company.

Know How to Evaluate a Search Organization

When you are contacted by a search organization that you are unfamiliar with, be sure to assess the organization's ability to serve your interests well. An excellent question to ask is who their client companies have been. The organizations you want to work with will freely offer a short list of prestigious client companies.

Select Only a Few Search Organizations to Work With

While you should never succumb to the pressure of signing an exclusive deal with only one organization, you also should sign with only a small number of organizations, so you can stay focused and in control of your schedule of interviews.

Follow Up

After the initial interview with the hiring company, follow up with that company in the standard ways, such as a thank you letter. Search organizations should not try to stand in the way of the relationship you cultivate with the hiring company. The successful hire will benefit all three parties, and it continues to be up to you to do your part to improve the chances of receiving an offer.

Listen to Consultant Feedback and Accept Recommended Advice

The consultant may see you as the best possible candidate for an ideal position; however, there may be a small element in your personal demeanor, grooming, or body language that could spoil your chances. If the consultant's recommendations do not require a fundamental shift in your basic nature or values, seriously consider following the advice.

Common Mistakes

You Waste Your Time with Low-quality Consultants and Search Organizations

Insist on a personal meeting at their offices. If they insist, in return, on a telephone relationship, or if you find that their offices are shabby, these are excellent indicators that their clients will probably not be top-market employment opportunities for you.

You Wait Until You Need to Find a New Job Before Cultivating a Relationship with a Search Organization Consultant

Some of the most successful search organizations receive up to 300 résumés a day, so you have to compete for their attention. Additionally, there may not be any openings for positions that you are best qualified for. The coincidence of availabilities is rare enough that you should be in the search organization's system long before you are desperate for a new job.

You Try to Camouflage a Spotty Past with Finessed Answers

Most consultants and hiring managers have heard the common language typically used to camouflage a downsizing or firing. If you are available now because you were downsized or fired, be as candid as possible.

You Drop Your Search Organization Consultant After You Have Accepted Your New Position

If you have achieved a mutually satisfactory relationship with your search organization consultant, stay in touch with that person. Send them excellent candidates for other positions that may become available. Meet for lunch now and then. You don't have to make that person your best friend. But the days of working for one company for the rest of your life are over. The chances are that you will be searching for a new position within a few years. Use that earlier relationship to keep moving forward along your career path toward your future.

For More Information

Book:

Gurney, Darrell W. *Headhunters Revealed! Career Secrets for Choosing and Using Professional Recruiters.* Los Angeles: Hunter Arts Publishing, 2000.

Web Sites:

Global Executive: **www.economist.com/globalExecutive**

Executive Grapevine: **www.askgrapevine.com**

See also:

✓ **Researching the Job Market (pp. 756–57)**
✓ **Using the Web As a Career Resource (pp. 774–75)**
Job Hunting (pp. 2017–18)

Downshifting: Working Less and Enjoying It More

Getting Started

The traditional definition of success is to work hard, get promoted, make more money, and give more and more of your life and your identity to your organization. Some call it "climbing the corporate ladder," or "making good." But in the last few years, there have been a growing number of people who are questioning common wisdom. Instead, they are looking for ways to get out of the rat race and to have a more balanced and fulfilling life.

There are many reasons why you might consider downshifting in your career. Quite often, the reason is family demands. Your children require more attention, or your marriage may be shaky because of the time you spend away from the family. Or perhaps an elderly parent requires more care. Conflicts of values can be another major reason for a desire to downshift. You may have been asked to do something by your organization that goes strongly against deeply held values, and it leads you to question why you are working so hard for this organization. And, finally, you may be near retirement and it feels as if it is time to begin disengaging from your career and building a new life outside of work.

Regardless of the reason for downshifting, it takes a lot of foresight, planning, and courage to make a move toward a simpler life. Some questions to consider as you think through the possibility of downshifting are:

- Why do you want to downshift?
- Do you feel called toward something new, or are you wanting to get away from something that no longer works for you?
- What is your current, and long-term, financial situation?
- What are the core values that you want to live by in your new life?
- Do you have a support network of like-minded people?
- What do you want to keep, what do you want to let go of, and what do you want more of?

FAQs

If I downshift, won't I be ruining my career?

If you have to ask this question, then you shouldn't even be considering downshifting. People who downshift generally are no longer interested in climbing the career ladder. It's just not relevant to them. They have emotionally detached themselves from the "corporate game" and are moving toward a slower, less demanding way of life. They are not motivated by the traditional definitions and trappings of success.

I am ready to get off the fast track, but won't everyone say I'm crazy?

Chances are very good that a number of people will say you are crazy. It's as if they are playing Monopoly and you have moved over to another table to play chess. You are each playing by a different set of rules, and if they think you are still playing Monopoly, then your behavior looks very strange to them. You must constantly check with your own inner voice and your own values to see if this is right for you. Don't worry about what other people think. It is your life to live. Paul Ray and Sherry Anderson (see "books" at the end of this action list) have done research on people's values in the United States and Europe. They found that about 26% of the adult population in these areas have a strong interest in living a slower, simpler life that is more in harmony with nature, family, and community life. So you are not alone.

If I decide that downshifting is not for me, will I be able to get back into my old career path?

You take a risk when you downshift. You are stepping into unknown territory and creating a new lifestyle for yourself. You may not be able to go back the way you came. However, chances are pretty good that this new adventure may lead you to other career paths you never even considered. If you decide that a simpler way of life just doesn't suit you, you can use the same risk-taking and imaginative skills you used in downshifting to create the next inventive step on your path.

Making It Happen

Be Clear about Why You Are Thinking about Downshifting and Involve Your Family

The decision to downshift is a major lifestyle decision. Take the time to do soul-searching about why you want to slow down and simplify your life. Then discuss it with your family and anyone else who would be directly affected by such a choice. Explain what you find attractive about this new way of life, and then be willing to listen to their concerns and fears.

Downshifting often occurs as a backlash to a corporate lifestyle that doesn't work for you any more. But be sure that you are not just running away from a difficult situation that perhaps you should face. Successful downshifting occurs when there is also a clear vision of a better and more meaningful life. It is important to be as concrete about the new vision as you can.

Make a Thorough Assessment of Your Short-term and Long-term Financial Situation

Downshifting requires some risk, but you should not be putting your health and your old age in jeopardy. Give careful consideration to what you might need in an emergency or in case of a long-term illness. But also don't turn so conservative that you become afraid to build a life that you've always dreamed of. Make sure that you have something in savings. And wherever possible, think of ways to develop passive income.

When you first make the move toward downshifting, it may mean leaving your organization and being on your

"If you work by the hour, you gently sail on the stream of Time, which is always bearing you on to the haven of Pay, whether you make any effort or not." (Charles Dudley Warner)

own for a while. You should have sufficient savings in place to pay your monthly expenses for six months to a year. As a part of downshifting, you will be dramatically reducing your expenses, so your savings should go quite a bit further

Conduct a Work-Life Values Assessment

Downshifting requires some major decision making about your life and your work. If you are going to be happy with your decision, you will need to be very clear about your core values and how your new life will be in alignment with those values.

Evaluate Your Living Situation and Consider a Move

A major way to reduce monthly expenses is to move to a smaller house or apartment. In the process, you will need to go through your possessions and decide what to keep and what to give away or sell. Also think about how a smaller home can simplify your life. Choose a place that requires minimal maintenance, is easy to clean, and has little or no yard work.

Make a Decision about Whether or Not You Want to Leave Your Organization

Downshifting often means leaving your job and becoming a free agent and working out of your home. But it can also mean moving to a lower-pressure less demanding job in the organization. Or you might consider moving to an organization that has a slower paced culture.

Decide What to Keep and What to Let Go of

You can simplify your life by getting rid of possessions you no longer need. There is less to keep track of and care for, and often you can do good by giving these things away. Clean out your closets. Give clothes to charity. Cancel magazine subscriptions. At the same time, be sure to keep things that have significant meaning and value for you. Even if it is not practical, you will want to keep those coffee cups that were passed down from your grandmother.

Create an Action Plan with a Schedule

Once you decide what living and working changes you are going to make, you can prepare a timetable of key actions. These might include putting your house on the market, selling furniture, giving notice at your company, and starting up your own business. As you begin to implement your plan, your life will actually get more hectic before it gets simpler. You will be still living your old life while planning for your new life. Be gentle with yourself and do not try to rush things too much. That would be defeating the overall purpose of having a slower, less stressful life.

Take an Annual Retreat and Continue Your Life-Work Assessment

At least once a year, take time off with your family to talk about how this new lifestyle is going. Analyze what is working and what you would like to change. Celebrate your courage for taking the risk to move toward a more balanced life.

Common Mistakes

You Get Excited about the Idea of Downshifting and Immediately Quit Your Job

Downshifting is a major life change, and requires a lot of thought and planning. Take your time to really think through the kind of life you want to build before doing anything drastic.

You Try to Do Too Much at Once

Changing jobs and moving are two of life's most stressful activities. If your downshifting plan calls for both of these actions, try not to do them both at once. Plan for gentle transitions where possible.

You Make Only Cosmetic Changes and Then Find Yourself Right Back in the Rat Race

Old habits are hard to break and many of us are addicted to hard work and stress. You might try to simplify your life by eliminating some of the things you normally do, only to find that you have filled up the spare time with new things to do. Revisit your core values assessment and spend time envisioning the simpler lifestyle you pictured. You may need to make a more dramatic change in order truly to have a slower lifestyle.

For More Information

Books:

Bolles, Richard N. *What Color is Your Parachute? 2002.* Berkeley, CA: Ten Speed Press, 2001.

Drake, John. *Downshifting: How to Work Less and Enjoy Life More.* San Francisco: Berrett-Koehler, 2001.

Web Site:

Downshifting: **www.labergerie.net/spirit/downshifting.htm**

See also:

☆ **Tuning into the Harmonics of Management (pp. 253–54)**

✔ **Managing Dual Career Dilemmas (pp. 792–93)**

Planning for Retirement (pp. 2073–74)

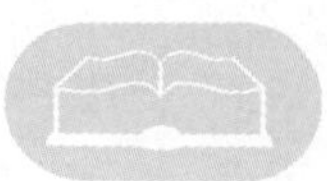

FREELANCING: SETTING UP AS A FREE AGENT

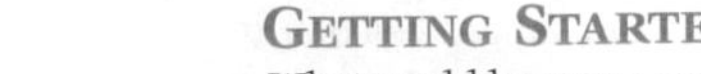

GETTING STARTED

What could be more appealing than to commute to work in your bathrobe and slippers to an office only a few yards away from your breakfast table? Think of it—the idea of being your own boss, of setting your own hours and workload. After winning the lottery, being self-employed is probably the next most intoxicating idea shared by working people today.

However, before you start shopping for an executive-style bathrobe, or turning the kids' bedroom into your world headquarters, you might ask yourself the following questions:

- How much of my freelance fantasy is based on being unhappy with my current situation?
- What is my "core competency," around which I will begin a freelance business?
- Who hires freelancers in my field of work and do I have enough experience?
- Who is my competition and what edge do I have?
- What are the costs of going into my own business, as well as the benefits?

FAQs

WHAT EXACTLY IS A FREELANCER?

The word "freelance" comes from the old days of knights for hire, but these days it refers to someone in the service of more than one employer. Nowadays, a freelancer can be a self-employed person in any number of industries, including writing, film and video, management consulting, software development, and Internet services.

WHAT SORT OF PERSONALITY TRAITS AND SKILLS MUST A PERSON HAVE AS A FREELANCER?

You must be—or quickly become—confident, resourceful, enterprising, adventuresome, flexible, and organized. As a business owner, you also must be a manager, a bookkeeper, and a promoter. You must be able to handle "multitasking"—juggling a number of diverse projects, each with different deadlines, for your clients.

HOW DO I DETERMINE WHAT TO CHARGE FOR MY SERVICES?

There are books and Web sites that give guidelines about the value of your profession on an hourly basis. Another way to determine your starting hourly rate is to figure out what people in that field earn per hour as employees, then add 25–50% to account for the overheads you'll have (taxes, retirement savings, insurance, equipment, supplies).

Remember, too, that as a business owner, at least a quarter of your workload will involve "nonbillable" activities such as research, marketing, promotion, and bookkeeping. If possible, find out what established freelancers in your field are charging. You may want to start at a reduced rate for the first year, especially if you're going to be competing against more established freelancers.

MAKING IT HAPPEN

CONDUCT YOUR RESEARCH

Making a jump to freelancing requires a kind of "inside-out" approach. First, be truthful with yourself about your motives for the move. If you feel more excitement about the future than dread of where you are now, you are on the right track. Then look at your personality assets: you'll need people skills, energy, promotional creativity, a love of your chosen profession, and a devotion to detail.

Your outside research should include canvassing the industry in which you will offer your services. Determine how big a "territory" you will initially serve, and what sort of companies. Seek the advice of those already in the field—through a professional association or business group. In the best of all worlds, knowing someone at those companies who knows you from a prior work relationship is a big asset.

DEVELOP YOUR BUSINESS PLAN

Once you decide to commit to a life as a freelancer—but before you quit your day job—develop a business plan. Even if you've lined up a client or two, a business plan will plot the first year's goals and activity.

It may be advisable to start your freelance business on a part-time basis, while you can still rely on your current income. This part-time approach may take on the dimensions of a second full-time job, but doing so will show you quickly if you have the determination and work ethic to persevere.

MARKET AND PROMOTE YOUR BUSINESS

Whether or not your freelance business is in the same industry you're currently employed in, you will need to develop a "target" list of companies that you wish to work for. Learn all you can about each company, its products and services, its financial health, its challenges, and its history with contract hiring. Learn who in those companies makes contract decisions (executive, department manager, or contracting officer, for example). Aim your marketing and proposals at them; invite them to lunch if they happen to live nearby.

Marketing can also include letters, brochures, or e-mails sent to potential customers, as well as personal networking, advertising and promotional activities, even a Web site. Hopefully, you will have built enough of a network before you start your business to reduce the amount of "cold calling" you must do.

FOCUS ON CUSTOMER SERVICE

Staying in the freelance world is largely a matter of time: the longer you are in business, the greater the chance you'll be successful. As the old saying goes: "It's far better to keep a client happy than to spend the same amount of time finding another one." Being prompt, and delivering a professional product or service for the proposed budget, are the cornerstones of a successful freelance business. And don't underestimate the value of being liked—being congenial and a good communicator often make up for

"Organizations have their essential core of jobs and people surrounded by an open and flexible space which they fill with flexible workers and flexible supply contracts." (Charles Handy)

the few flaws the client may eventually find in your work.

Maintain Good Business Practices and Organization

As a freelancer, it would be rare to have a consistent client, or set of clients, for a great many years. Business climates change, and freelancers are vulnerable to shifts in policy and personnel. Get used to the idea of losing clients and gaining new ones; it's part of the nature of the business, like an animal shedding a winter coat and growing a new one.

To protect themselves against this inevitability, freelancers usually have a bunch of irons in the fire. It often takes six months to a year to secure work with a new prospective client, so discipline yourself to plan at least six months ahead. Learn to anticipate when clients need more service, but also learn to predict when your tenure may be drawing to a close. Have the foresight to build enough diversity in your client base that the loss of one won't spell disaster for your business.

Common Mistakes

Being Cavalier about Your Home Office

Many freelancers begin at home and there's nothing wrong with that. But be very careful (for IRS purposes) to create a separate office that has no other purpose. Keep very good records of things you will want to list as itemized deductions on your business Schedule C. The IRS doesn't mind you having such a short journey to work (actually, it does mind a little), but it has some specific guidelines under which you may deduct home office expenses.

Overreliance on One Client

In the best sense, freelancers bring added value to a company, and companies are willing to pay top dollar for those who can deliver. But don't misunderstand—valued as you feel, freelancers are easier to lay off than employees, so when it comes to budget tightening or changes in administrative personnel be vigilant and be prepared. While having a contract may give you some security, it isn't a guarantee. For this reason, freelance work is often more volatile than being an employee, and the best advice is to insulate yourself against starvation by having a variety of clients.

Failure to Save for the Lean Times

Inevitably, there will be lean times in your freelance business. Putting aside a stash of cash is advisable to get you through, say, two or three months of basic expenses. Besides that, however, remember that as a freelancer, you are also responsible for paying quarterly taxes to the IRS and state government. Sometimes there are local business taxes, too. And don't forget to pay yourself first, including a tax-deductible set-aside for retirement purposes.

Being a Lax Business Manager

Just as you must be adept and professional about what you bill your client for, you also must become skilled at running your own business affairs. Plan to devote up to 25% of your time to various administrative and marketing-related activities. In fat times, it's especially easy to get complacent about record-keeping, credit card debt, payment of taxes, developing new business leads, and even collecting from your clients on time. If you don't stay on top of your own business details, you could be ruined very quickly in times of lesser bounty.

For tax purposes and others, it is well worth the $200–$350 a year to have a respected CPA look at your business. They can tell you how to avoid tax troubles and they'll often save you more in deductions than you'll pay them. They have lots of experience advising business people about a variety of issues, so feel free to pump them for information. If they are reluctant to share, ask around and find another one.

For More Information

Book:

Edwards, Sarah, and Paul Edwards. *Secrets of Self Employment: Surviving and Thriving on the Ups and Downs of Being Your Own Boss.* New York: Tarcher Putnam, 1996.

Web Sites:

Monster Career Center: **www.monster.com**
FreeAgent.com: **www.freeagent.com**

See also:

☆ **Breaking the Lead Ceiling (pp. 237–38)**
☆ **Choosing the Best Training Curriculum (pp. 336–37)**
✔ **Assessing Your Entrepreneurial Profile: Do You Have What It Takes? (pp. 818–19)**
✔ **Building an Awesome Contact List (pp. 760–61)**
✔ **Setting Up and Maintaining Your Home Office (pp. 816–17)**
Flexible Working/Teleworking/Homeworking (pp. 1984–86)

"The emerging work paradox is that in a post-job world, the only viable long-term career is to be a temp."
(Anonymous)

Setting Up and Maintaining Your Home Office

Getting Started

Commuting woes, getting laid off, pursuing personal freedom, raising children, having physical limitations, or scratching an entrepreneurial itch—there are dozens of reasons why having a home office appeals to most of us, especially those who have experienced the "real" office world and found it lacking.

But—whether you're starting your own business at home, or you're telecommuting—having an office at home calls for developing or honing skills to help you succeed there. To start, ask yourself the following questions:

- Can I handle the social isolation of a home office on a full-time basis?
- Am I a self-starter?
- How do I rate as a decision-maker, organizer, bookkeeper, and secretary?
- Could I separate business and personal life if both were under the same roof?
- Am I a workaholic and would an office at home worsen that problem?

FAQs

Is working from home as wonderful as it sounds?

Yes and no. For convenience, cost, and comfort, there's nothing quite like a home office. Low overheads, no commute hassles, no office politics, and setting your own hours are a few of the plusses. On the minus side, there's only you—and if you're not disciplined, you'll be spending more time with the kids, the pets, or snacking than working where you belong. It can be a simple formula for failure.

How can I make a home-based business seem professional to customers?

It depends on the type of business, but start with a professional attitude and then buy some good-looking business cards and stationery. Think about adding an attractive logo and using a two-color design on business cards, letterheads, and envelopes. Having a well-produced flyer or brochure that describes your business is also a plus. Quality customer service will do the rest.

E-commerce is relatively easy to conduct from a home office, especially with a Web site that attracts customers. Clients need not know whether you work at home or in a sophisticated office building, so long as you get the job done for them. As with your other materials, the Web site should reflect the personality and professionalism of your business.

What sort of investment is necessary to outfit a home office?

This, too, depends on the type of activity you will be doing—whether it will be business or telecommuting, or a personal or family office. But generally, spending between $2,000 and $4,000 should make you well equipped and comfortable. Make a list and a budget beforehand. You don't want to blow your entire savings on setting up the office, then have nothing to spend on attracting business.

Making It Happen

Plan the Layout of Your Office

Planning a home office involves decisions about where to locate the office, how to decorate it, and how to furnish it. Especially if the office will be the hub of a small business, you should give lots of thought to this. Some people even make a scale drawing of the room they intend to use, then place to-scale furniture in there to work out the best layout.

Take Account of Tax Considerations

If you plan to use the office for a small business, most government tax agencies allow you to deduct certain expenses connected to the business. For that reason, the office must be completely dedicated to the business and not merely a spare bedroom with a fold-up desk and your cordless phone. Good record-keeping is very important if you plan to deduct expenses and part of the mortgage interest, utilities, and phone bills for business activity.

Make Sure You're Comfortable and Have the Right Equipment

Office décor is important, whether you will use the office for business, for a hobby, or to write your next book of poetry. Besides getting the right atmosphere (lighting, paint/wallpaper, floor covering), you may need to run more phone and electrical outlets into the room to support the office equipment. Beyond that, having comfortable, functional furniture will allow you to work productively.

Your package of office equipment will depend on your level of activity, but will probably include computer(s) and peripherals, software, phones and phone service for voice, fax and computer, and maybe even a separate copier and/or scanner. Add a digital camera if you plan to put photos of yourself or your products on your Web site. Consider upgrading connections to the Internet, rather than relying on a computer modem to your Internet provider, especially if you are engaged in e-commerce.

Finally, there are the necessary office supplies and extra storage space for files and records to consider.

Impose Proper Discipline On Yourself

One of the most difficult aspects of the home office is the home itself. How easy it is to tend to house chores, watch TV, weed the garden, get involved with family things, snack, and otherwise avoid the work that awaits you in your office. Two factors will help avoid the home trap: being excited about your office space and the work—and discipline. Set regular office hours, have a separate business phone, organize your time, and stick to the schedules.

Don't Let Yourself Get Isolated

Being isolated in your home office, you may develop a tendency to cocoon yourself in there or to avoid reaching out, both of which can be unhealthy.

Having a business gives you plenty of opportunity to break away from the office to meet other people socially and professionally. Even if much of your business is conducted by phone and computer, it's still important to network. Invite customers and prospective customers to lunch, if they happen to do business nearby. Join a civic group or professional organization to stay connected and also to generate local interest in your business. Get physical exercise away from the home. Consider taking a class. All these things will help keep you connected, bring in new ideas, and generate lots of personal energy—things you'll value when working alone.

Common Mistakes

Going Halfway with the Office Arrangement

Starting a home office on the dining room table is not a good idea, nor is committing only half-heartedly to making a guestroom into a real office. If you don't treat the office seriously, there's a better than even chance you won't take your work seriously either.

Carve out a separate space and dedicate it as the office. You'll feel better and your work will benefit from that decision.

Succumbing to Workaholic Syndrome

If, while working in an office setting, you've had a tendency to stay there until the work is done, operating from home is a workaholic's dream come true. With the office only a few rooms away, there's a temptation to "get one last thing done" after dinner or on a weekend.

It's important to be professional about your business, but it's also important that you don't let the office become your new home. Set hours, try to manage your workflow into those hours, then shut the door and put up the "closed" sign.

Family Issues

Lots of women see working at home as the answer to two issues—making a living and raising a family. If it were easy to mix kids and work, parents would have been doing it at their business offices long ago.

That said, it isn't entirely impossible either. The trick is balance. You can't afford to be at the beck and call of your children, but you certainly don't want them to feel totally ignored. Racing from the office to untangle toys and do laundry every hour will soon turn your work world upside-down. Closing the door and ignoring the family will have an equally unfortunate effect.

Obviously, day care is an option. Consider it for the days that you might schedule your most critical tasks. On days you set aside for errands, such as paying bills, bookkeeping, research on the Internet, and so forth, you might more easily accommodate the family being around.

Lacking Certain Office Job Skills

When working for other companies, you relied on others with jobs that complemented your own. As your own businessperson, at your own business office, you have a lot more duties besides the specific ones that "bring in the bacon." You will be responsible for executive and marketing decisions, financial and administrative details and deadlines, as well as clerical and reception work. Until your business becomes profitable enough to employ other people, you're it.

This is where a business plan makes sense. You need to work out the details of how you'll charge for your products or services. Be careful to figure in the "cost of doing business," which includes the clerical and administrative things, too. Add in a "fudge factor" and some profit. Assuming that you'll work a 40-hour week, set your sights on making a living in 30 hours, then use the other 10 hours to take care of the other parts of the business—marketing, promotion, billing, bookkeeping, and business errands.

If you feel you lack the skills to juggle all of these things, or don't have the interest in becoming your own secretary, perhaps you're not cut out for a home business. But if you want to give it a try, you can certainly learn what you need to know about the care and feeding of a small business from books, the Internet, a local chapter of SCORE (Senior Corps of Retired Executives), or a nearby community college.

For More Information

Books:

Phillips, Barty. *The Home Office Planner*. San Francisco, CA: Chronicle Books, 2000.

Zelinsky, Marilyn. *Practical Home Office Solutions*. New York: McGraw-Hill Professional Publications, 1998.

Web Sites:

Entrepreneur: **www.entrepreneur.com**

Go Home: **www.gohome.com**

See also:

✓ **Freelancing: Setting Up As a Free Agent (pp. 814–15)**

Flexible Working/Teleworking/Homeworking (pp. 1984–86)

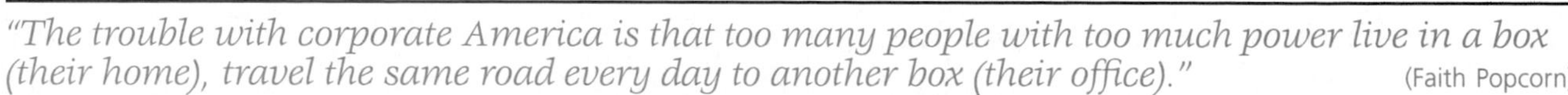
"The trouble with corporate America is that too many people with too much power live in a box (their home), travel the same road every day to another box (their office)."
(Faith Popcorn)

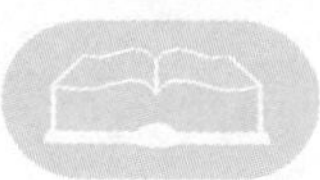

Assessing Your Entrepreneurial Profile: Do You Have What It Takes?

Getting Started

First, let it be said that, while there is a great deal of romance surrounding the notion of being an entrepreneur, not everyone has the aptitude. And it's important to understand that there's nothing wrong with *not* being an entrepreneur. This world functions well because of them, but it wouldn't be as successful if it were peopled solely with entrepreneurs.

Nevertheless, there are some general personality traits that are key for being an entrepreneur. If the following list seems to fit your personality, you may have what it takes:

- I am persistent, with a great deal of drive and stamina. I see problems as opportunities. I have a good intuitive sense and thrive on new ideas.
- I tend to rebel against authority. I want to be my own boss.
- I am positive, communicate well, and enjoy working with people.
- I have a strong need to succeed, financially and otherwise.
- I'm not afraid to make mistakes, and I learn from them.

FAQs

How can I be sure I've got what it takes?

Before quitting your job and using your savings to start a business, you owe it to yourself to approach your entrepreneurial venture with some practicality. Take a more in-depth personality test and talk to small business advisers—often available at no cost through business associations, community colleges, and organizations such as SCORE (Service Corps of Retired Executives).

How much money will I need?

Whether you want to buy an existing business, purchase a franchise, start your own company, or merely offer services to others from a home office, starting a business depends on first knowing the numbers. People in the same or similar business are a good source of information—use your ingenuity to find out what it cost them to get started, and where they got the funds to do so. Other sources include trade associations, franchise organizations, business articles in magazines and newspapers, Internet research, or business consultants.

Besides being an ideas person, what else do I need to be good at?

Success in a new enterprise depends on dedication and the consistent application of good business principles. Some of these principles include: being good with money; being good with people (investors, suppliers, employees, and so on); being a good promoter (marketing, sales, PR); and being good to yourself. Many entrepreneurs burn out before their businesses take hold. In this game, pacing yourself and your business is important.

Making It Happen

Check That You Have the Right Idea

If you've got a great new idea and no competition in sight, you must be sure that the product or service will be of value to customers—at a price at which you can afford to sell it. If your aim is to enter a field with established competitors, you have to know your own strengths and weaknesses, as well as those of your competition. You have to be certain that you can provide a better product or service for a competitive price. Finding out all these things is called "market research," and you'll have to do a thorough job of it to succeed.

Develop a Detailed, Professional Business Plan

This is the key to building a successful business. Having a well-considered and systematic plan allows you to recognize problems as they arise in time to be able to take corrective action. The plan should be a living document, flexible over time to adapt to changes in the marketplace and your industry. It should include sections on every facet of your business—whether you're a sole proprietor or the executive director of a new manufacturing venture.

Bankroll Your Idea

Take your ideas and business plan to a variety of people, starting with friends and close supporters. Be prepared for critical feedback, and be flexible. Take the inevitable first few comments of "no thanks" as opportunities to fine tune the next presentation. One of the hallmarks of an entrepreneur is the ability to regroup, rethink, and reach a goal in another way.

Seeking publicity for your business is a way not only to notify potential customers but also to get the attention of possible investors. The more people who know about your idea, the better the chances that you'll attract the right investor.

Be willing to share a portion of the company with the right partners, but be wary of finance companies and investors who want full control, or the lion's share of the proceeds.

Consider entering a joint venture with another company, or position your company to attract start-up funds from federal or state sources.

Practice Your Networking

Being entrepreneurial doesn't mean being a lone ranger. Being successful often depends on your ability to network with potential customers, suppliers, new investors, and even those in government who control certain aspects of the business environment.

"Entrepreneurs have no frontier other than their own ambition." (Robert Heller)

  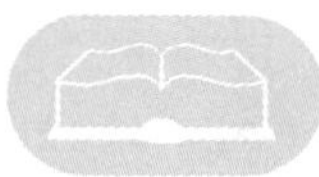    

Plan Your Marketing and PR

An integral part of your business plan involves a marketing plan—how you intend to create the demand for your product or service. While market research tells you the "what" and "where" of your opportunities, the marketing plan outlines the steps by which you will find potential customers and convince them to buy from you. Networking is a form of marketing and promotion, whereas advertising and PR (public relations) are others.

Make Sure You Have the Right Financial and Management Support

Sometimes entrepreneurs are better at ideas than at managing budgets, business operations, and employees. Anticipate that you'll need more capital than you figured at the start, and don't be lavish with spending beyond the company's means. If you find yourself in a questionable position, make sure you have a network of trusted and experienced advisers to help you see the proper perspective.

Common Mistakes

Setting up Equal Partnerships

Entrepreneurs often share the start-up responsibilities with a partner or partners. However, sharing 50–50 or by thirds or quarters is a big mistake, because conflicts will inevitably arise and need someone in a controlling position to make a final decision. Choose (or hire) a C.E.O.—someone with the experience and skills needed for success—and give that person a greater decision-making authority and a bigger salary, even if it is only bigger by a small margin.

Having Inadequate People and Planning

Entrepreneurs must become strong managers when the company gets going. Many businesses fail because the people in charge don't have the managerial qualities or strength to cope with the challenges. Business stress also can cause personal issues to arise which make the challenges doubly difficult. Personality assessments can determine if you're cut out for a managerial position, and managerial training can prepare you for your new role as an executive.

Without proper market research and a solid business plan, a business is more likely to fail. The more advanced preparation that is done, the better the chances for success.

Relying Too Heavily on One or Two Customers

Having too few customers makes your business vulnerable, because it ties your future to the decisions of other organizations. If their business falters, it puts your hard work and dedication at risk—through no fault of your own. The advice of personal financial consultants is appropriate here. Having lots of customers, even though none of them is gigantic, is healthier in the long run.

Causing Cashflow Troubles through Insufficient Financing

While some people are successful at jump-starting their own enterprise with little or no outside investment, they do so by being fortunate, being modest in their spending, and by plowing profits back into the business.

The majority of businesses, however, don't deliver the projected first-year sales volume. It's better to overestimate your need for capital resources at the beginning and to underestimate your projected sales figures. It's better to be pleasantly surprised at your success than to lose the business and your house because the money isn't there when it's needed.

When contemplating an expansion of your business, be wary of spiraling costs. If you're in a cyclical business, or one vulnerable to recession, be sure to be very calculating about your expenses—and develop "Plan B" well before you need to implement it.

Failing to Admit Mistakes

Entrepreneurs are sometimes the last to admit that their idea hasn't the sparkle it once did. Cut your losses and move on if your advisers all agree that you should. Doing so may save the company—if you can move quickly enough to capitalize on your mistakes, or shift the product or service to take advantage of other opportunities.

Underestimating the Competition

Your competition won't stand still for long, once you've demonstrated their weakness in the marketplace with your product or service. Expect them to plug the hole quickly and even try to outflank you in the process. Your business and marketing plans should anticipate how to deal with new initiatives from your competition. If you conduct ongoing research, product and service evaluations, and marketing campaigns, you should always be one step ahead of the competition.

For More Information

Books:

Kushell, Jennifer. *A Young Entrepreneur's Edge: Using Your Ambition, Independence and Youth to Launch a Successful Business*. New York: Princeton Review Series, 1999.

Stolze, William J. *Start Up: An Entrepreneur's Guide to Launching and Managing New Business*. Franklin Lakes, NJ: Career Press, Inc., 1999.

Web Sites:

Entrepreneur: **www.entrepreneur.com**
Entreworld: **www.entreworld.org**
Ewing Marion Kauffman Foundation: **www.emkf.org**
Internet Portal for Entrepreneurs: **www.new.innonet.ch**

See also:

☆ **Finding and Keeping Top Talent (pp. 33–34)**
✔ **Freelancing: Setting Up As a Free Agent (pp. 814–15)**
✔ **Identifying Your Marketable Skills (pp. 748–49)**

"Everything is always impossible before it works. That is what entrepreneurs are all about—doing what people have told them is impossible."
(R. Hunt Greene)

PREPARING FOR RETIREMENT WITH DIGNITY AND GRACE

GETTING STARTED

Building toward retirement is like building a good stereo system. Good input, amplifier, and speakers net you quality output. Add a CD read-write unit and you have got a way to accumulate a vast treasure of high-quality recordings. Retirement, too, takes consistent input and a variety of instruments that can store and amplify your investments over time. With preparation, your retirement will sound as good to you as your stereo!

Answer these few important questions:

- When do I want to retire, and what sort of lifestyle do I want?
- How much money will it take to maintain that lifestyle?
- How much short-term sacrifice can I make for a long-term payoff?
- What sorts of budgeting and investing am I already doing?

FAQs

HOW CAN I FIGURE OUT WHAT AMOUNT OF MONEY I'LL NEED TO RETIRE?

Financial planners and retirement-oriented Web sites have "calculators" that will give you a ballpark figure of what you'll need. They'll ask you: how much income will you want per year in retirement; how long after retirement will you need that income; what sources of income will you have to draw from? From this and other data, they can tell you the gap that exists between what you will need and what you predict you'll have. It's advisable to consult with a financial planner to help you close that gap with investments. Your bank may provide you with some consultation for free.

SHOULD I PAY OFF MY DEBTS FIRST OR START SAVING?

Generally, it's better to pay off debt first, especially credit cards. Why? Credit card interest is higher than the interest paid by most savings and investment accounts. Paying off debt saves you the future interest costs you'd be charged. And, when the debt is gone, you'll have made a habit of setting aside a certain amount. That same amount, or more, can then be earmarked for retirement.

There is one exception to that rule: If your employer has a company retirement plan and matches contributions made by employees, it's wise to put in as much as you can, because the employer's contribution is a bonus.

BESIDES THE FINANCIAL PART, SHOULD I BE PLANNING FOR OTHER THINGS IN RETIREMENT, TOO?

Retirement can be the life you never had as a working person and as a parent. Those who make the best of their "golden years" say that having interests beyond work is a key ingredient. Certainly, it may be desirable—or even important—to continue to work part time. But retirement also gives you the opportunity to do things you've never had the time for before—travel, volunteering, education, reading, physical conditioning, cooking, catching up with friends and family, or starting a hobby. It's probably best if you research a bit now into what may keep you happy and busy in later life, rather than maintaining a "wait and see" attitude.

MAKING IT HAPPEN

LEARN ABOUT HOW MUCH YOU CAN EARN

Do a little research on your skill level and job title. Look at both the private and public sectors, including the benefit packages available—insurance coverage, retirement account contributions, bonuses, and incentives. If you're not making what others in your category are, you can lobby for a raise or look for greener pastures.

Also consider additional education, if having college qualifications or other training will increase your worth with your employer. Just think, if you aim for a 3% raise each year, the difference in your earnings over a 40-year period is thousands of dollars more than if you get no increases whatsoever!

GIVE SOME THOUGHT TO WHERE YOU WANT TO BE IN FIVE YEARS, TEN YEARS, AND LONGER

Goal setting has a lot of value when it comes to career and retirement. It's important to separate wishful thinking from practical realities. Once you've decided on the priorities, for example, travel, children and their college fund, losing weight, buying a home or recreational vehicle, begin to put dollar signs to each of them. It may surprise you or shock you. Regardless, having those numbers is an important place to begin building a good life and a good retirement.

BUDGET PROPERLY

To some, the very thought of budgeting is like taking a cold shower. For those who do it religiously, however, budgeting can make the difference between comfort and catastrophe. In fact, budgeting is more apt to get you those things in life you most desire, and allow you to get there faster and more pragmatically, than buying on "impulse" as the desire arises. The primary rule of budgeting is to spend less than you earn and avoid debt.

Another rule is to pay yourself first, rather than paying all the bills and saving what's left. You probably know already that, often, there is nothing left if you pay yourself last. Start with 10% if you can, but start anyway and be consistent with your saving.

INVEST STEADILY

The benefit of investments—like mutual funds, stocks, bonds, a home, or even some "collectibles"—is that they'll almost always beat the interest rate paid by your bank's savings account. The only downside to investments is that there is some risk. However, reading about investing and talking to an investment planner about your particular comfort level with risk are ways to build your own knowledge and confidence.

Start with tax-deferred investments—either through your employer's retirement plan or with your own IRA, SEP, or Simple plan. Seek to diversify your investment portfolio across a spectrum of possibilities. Once invested, avoid micromanaging. Think of your investments—especially those invested for retirement—as being there for the long haul.

Protect Yourself and Your Family

Insurance, a will, and even a basic estate plan are also valuable assets to have when developing a lifelong strategy. "Whole life" insurance takes care of dependants in the event of your injury or death by replacing your lost income with insurance payments. "Term" insurance may be preferable for those without children or other dependants. "Disability" insurance replaces your income in the event of illness or injury. A will and estate plan make sure that your assets are not gobbled up in probate court and taxes but go instead to the people you want to leave them to.

As in the case of investments, shopping for and finding professional advice you can trust is important: get referrals and don't assume that one planner or agent is as good as the next. Don't buy more insurance than you need for your own particular situation.

Establish a Life Outside of Work

Statistically speaking, people whose lives revolve entirely around their careers don't fare as well in retirement as those who have a more well-rounded life. Never before have there been so many excellent choices and opportunities for retirees to stay active and engaged in life. How you view the element of time in retirement is largely an issue of attitude, but planning also plays a role.

Community nonprofit organizations, churches, schools, and even local government bodies, thrive on volunteers. Volunteering is a way to make a difference in the community, as well as being a way to socialize and continue to learn. Community colleges are designed to open new vistas to learners of all ages. But "getting a life" after your career takes practice, and if you're not doing so already, start practicing now.

Common Mistakes

Waiting Too Long to Begin Planning for Retirement

The "play as you go" attitude often leaves too little saved as retirement draws near. Get in the habit of budgeting and saving for retirement, even if you're in your 20s. If you're not investing in your employer's 401(k) plan, you're giving away free money.

If you've already waited longer than is advisable, don't despair—just get started right away. And get creative (legally!) about how to make up some lost time.

Getting in Too Deep with Consumer Debt

We all intend to pay off credit card balances each month, but it seldom works out that way. By accumulating more high-interest debt, you end up paying far more for a product or service than if you'd paid cash for it.

Renting Instead of Buying

Owning your own home is more than a status symbol—it's a great way to save money. As the mortgage is reduced, the value of your home is usually increasing. This "equity" translates into added cash when you decide to sell. Beyond that, however, the interest you pay on the mortgage is tax deductible which lowers your tax burden at each year's end.

There is one caution that should be added about home buying, however. If you buy "the house of your dreams" and that prevents you from saving additionally for your retirement, you've put too many eggs into the home basket. It's better to invest in a more modest house and continue to save for retirement simultaneously.

Keeping Poor Records

Failure to keep good records can translate into spending more on taxes than you should. Taking itemized deductions for legitimate expenses is not a privilege solely for the rich! But you must have records to back up the deduction claim, or the IRS will disallow those deductions should you be audited.

Investing with Your Heart, Not Your Head

It's sad how much hard-earned money is thrown away each year on bad investments. "Get rich quick" schemes have bilked thousands of investors of many hundreds of millions of dollars.

Be very wary of high-pressure sales from people you don't know, telling you about investments you know even less about. There's no such thing as high returns without a lot of risk. It is better to seek the advice of a professional planner, who can help you make reasoned decisions about investing in a diverse portfolio.

For More Information

Books:

Cantor, Dr. Dorothy, with Andrea Thompson (contributor). *What Do You Want to Do When You Grow Up: Starting the Next Chapter of Your Life*. New York: Little, Brown & Co, 2001.

O'Shaughnessy, Lynn. *Retirement Bible*. New York: Hungry Minds, 2001.

Web Site:

About.com: **www.retireplan.about.com**

See also:

☆ **Avoiding Your Worst Career Nightmare (pp. 316–17)**

Planning for Retirement (pp. 2073–74)

CALCULATING ASSET TURNOVER

WHAT IT MEASURES

The amount of sales generated for every dollar's worth of assets over a given period.

WHY IT IS IMPORTANT

Asset turnover measures how well a company is leveraging its assets to produce revenue. A well-managed manufacturer, for example, will make its plant and equipment work hard for the business by minimizing idle time for machines.

The higher the number the better—within reason. As a rule of thumb, companies with low profit margins tend to have high asset turnover; those with high profit margins have low asset turnover.

This ratio can also show how capital intensive a business is. Some businesses, software developers, for example, can generate tremendous sales per dollar of assets because their assets are modest. At the other end of the scale, electric utilities, heavy industry manufacturers, and even cable TV firms need a huge asset base to generate sales.

Finally, asset turnover serves as a tool to keep managers mindful of the company's balance sheet along with its profit and loss account.

HOW IT WORKS IN PRACTICE

Asset turnover's basic formula is simply sales divided by assets:

Sales revenue /Total assets

Most experts recommend using average total assets in the formula. To determine this figure, add total assets at the beginning of the year to total assets at the end of the year and divide by two.

If, for instance, annual sales totaled $4.5 million, and total assets were $1.84 million at the beginning of the year and $1.78 million at the year-end, the average total assets would be $1.81 million, and the asset turnover ratio would be:

4,500,000/1,810,000 = 2.49

A variation of the formula is:

Sales revenue /Fixed assets

If average fixed assets were $900,000, then asset turnover would be:

4,500,000/900,000 = 5

TRICKS OF THE TRADE

- This ratio is especially useful for growth companies to gauge whether or not they are growing revenue, for example, turnover, in healthy proportion to assets.
- Asset turnover numbers are useful for comparing competitors within industries. Like most ratios, they vary from industry to industry. As with most numbers, the most meaningful comparisons are made over extended periods of time.
- Too high a ratio may suggest overtrading: too much sales revenue with too little investment. Conversely, too low a ratio may suggest undertrading and an inefficient management of resources.
- A declining ratio may be indicative of a company that overinvested in plant, equipment, or other fixed assets, or is not using existing assets effectively.

For More Information

Web Site:
www.multimedia.calpoly.edu/development/busen gives good information on this topic.

See also:
✓ **Calculating Asset Utilization (pp. 845–46)**

CALCULATING APR

WHAT IT MEASURES

Either the rate of interest that invested money earns in one year, or the cost of credit expressed as a yearly rate.

WHY IT IS IMPORTANT

It enables an investor or borrower to compare like with like. When evaluating investment alternatives, naturally it's important to know which one will pay the greatest return. By the same token, borrowers want to know which loan alternative offers the best terms. Determining the annual percentage rate provides a direct comparison.

HOW IT WORKS IN PRACTICE

To calculate the annual percentage rate (APR), apply this formula:

APR = [1 + i/m]m – 1.0

In the formula, **i** is the interest rate quoted, expressed as decimal, and **m** is the number of compounding periods per year. For example:

If a bank offers a 6% interest rate, paid quarterly, the APR would be calculated this way:

APR = [1 + i/m]m – 1.0
= [1 + 0.06/4]4 – 1.0
= [1 + 0.015] 4 – 1.0
= (1.015) 4 – 1.0
= 1.0614 – 1.0
= 0.0614
= 6.14% APR

"No-one has a greater asset for his business than a man's pride in his work." (Mary Parker Follett)

Tricks of the Trade

- As a rule of thumb, the annual percentage rate is slightly higher than the quoted rate.
- When using the formula, be sure to express the rate as a decimal, that is, 6% becomes 0.06.
- When expressed as the cost of credit, remember to include other costs of obtaining the credit in addition to interest, such as loan closing costs and financial fees.
- APR provides an excellent basis for comparing mortgage or other loan rates; in the United Kingdom, lenders are required to disclose it.
- When used in the context of investment APR also can be called the "annual percentage yield," or APY.

For More Information

Web Site:
www.investorguide.com is a source of interest and mortgage calculators; it also offers information about financial markets, a detailed glossary, and links to other sites.

Calculating Bond Yield

What It Measures

The annual return on this certificate (the rate of interest) expressed as a percentage of the current market price of the bond.

Why It Is Important

Bonds can tie up investors' money for long periods of up to 30 years, so knowing their yield is a critical investment consideration. Similarly, bond issuers need to know the price they will pay to incur their debt, so that they can compare it with the cost of other means of raising capital.

How It Works in Practice

Bonds are issued in increments of $1,000. To calculate the yield amount, multiply the face value of the bond by the stated rate, expressed as a decimal. For example, buying a new 10-year $1,000 bond that pays 6% interest will produce an annual yield amount of $60:

1,000 × 0.060 = 60

The $60 will be paid as $30 every six months. At the end of 10 years, the purchaser will have earned $600, and will also be repaid the original $1,000. Because the bond was purchased when it was first issued, the 6% is also called the "yield to maturity."

This basic formula is complicated by other factors. First is the "time-value of money" theory: money paid in the future is worth less than money paid today. A more detailed computation of total bond yield requires the calculation of the present value of the interest earned each year. Secondly, changing interest rates have a marked impact on bond trading and, ultimately, on yield. Changes in interest rates cannot affect the interest paid by bonds already issued, but they do affect the prices of new bonds.

Tricks of the Trade

- Yield to call. Bond issuers reserve the right to "call," or redeem, the bond before the maturity date, at certain times and at a certain price. Issuers often do this if interest rates fall and they can issue new bonds at a lower rate. Bond buyers should obtain the yield-to-call rate, which may, in fact, be a more realistic indicator of the return expected.
- Different types of bond. Some bonds are backed by assets, while others are issued on the strength of the issue's good standing. Investors should know the difference.
- Zero coupon bonds. These pay no interest at all, but are sold at a deep discount, increasing in value until maturity. A buyer might pay $3,000 for a 25-year zero bond with a face value of $10,000. This bond will simply accrue value each year, and at maturity will be worth $10,000, thus earning $7,000. These are high-risk investments, however, especially if they must be sold on the open market amid rising interest rates.
- Interest rates. Bond values fall when interest rates rise, and rise when interest rates fall, because when interest rates rise existing bonds become less valuable and less attractive.

For More Information

Web Site:
www.azcentral.webpoint.com/finance offers exceptional explanations of bond yields.

See also:
✔ **Calculating Amortization (pp. 869–70)**

Calculating Book Value

What It Measures

A company's common stock equity, as it appears on a balance sheet.

Why It Is Important

Book value represents a company's net worth to its shareholders, based on the difference between assets and liabilities plus debt. Typically, book value is substantially different from market value, especially in high-tech and knowledge-based industries whose primary assets are intangible and therefore do not appear on the balance sheet.

When compared with its market value, book value helps reveal how a company is regarded by the investment community. A market value that is notably higher than book value indicates that investors have a high regard for the company. A market value that is, for example, a multiple of book value suggests that investors' regard may be unreasonably high—as was shown in the painful plunge of dot.com companies in 2000 and 2001.

The reverse is also true, of course; indeed, it may suggest that a company's stock is a bargain.

A companion measure is book value per share. It shows the value of the company's assets that each shareholder theoretically would receive if a company were liquidated.

How It Works in Practice

To calculate book value, subtract a company's liabilities and the value of its debt and preferred stock from its total assets. All of these figures appear on a company's balance sheet. For example:

	$
Total assets	1,300
Current liabilities	- 400
Long-term liabilities, preferred stock	- 250
Book value	**= 650**

Book value per share is calculated by dividing the book value by the number of shares in issue. If our example is expressed in millions of dollars and the company has 35 million shares outstanding, book value per share would be $650 million divided by 35 million:

650/35 = $18.57 book value per share

Tricks of the Trade

- Related terms include: adjusted book value or modified book value, which is book value after assets and liabilities are adjusted to market value; and tangible book value, which also subtracts intangible assets, patents, trademarks, and the value of research and development. The rationale is that these items cannot be sold outright.
- Book value can also mean the value of an individual asset as it appears on a balance sheet, in which case it is equal to the cost of the asset minus any accumulated depreciation.
- Though often considered a realistic appraisal, book value can still contain unrealistic figures. For example, a building might be fully depreciated and have no official asset value but could still be sold for millions, or four-year-old computer equipment that is not fully depreciated might have asset value but no market value, given its age and advances in technology.

For More Information

Web Site:

www.investopedia.com/dictionary has a user-friendly definition, interesting commentary, links to related terms, and ratios.

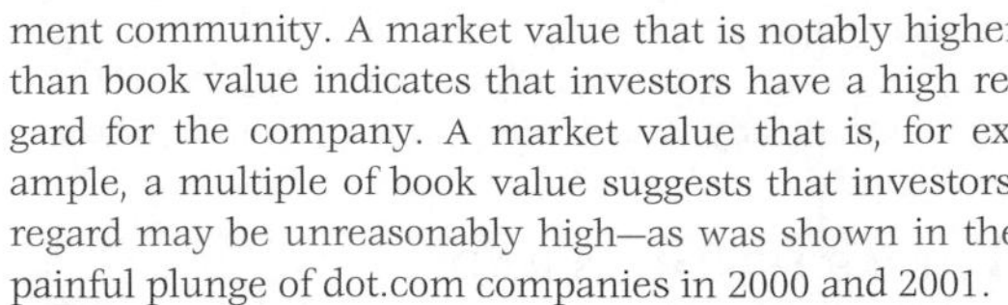

Calculating Contribution Margin

What It Measures

The amounts that individual products or services ultimately contribute to net profit.

Why It Is Important

Contribution margin helps a business decide how it should direct or redirect its resources.

When managers know the contribution margin—or margins, as is more often the case—they can make better decisions about adding or subtracting product lines, investing in existing products, pricing products or services (particularly in response to competitors' actions), structuring sales commissions and bonuses, where to direct marketing and advertising expenditures, and where to apply individual talents and expertise.

In short, contribution margin is a valuable decision-support tool.

How It Works in Practice

Its calculation is straightforward:

Sales price – variable cost = contribution margin

Or, for providers of services:

Total revenue – total variable cost = contribution margin

For example, if the sales price of a good is $500 and variable cost is $350, the contribution margin is $150, or 30% of sales.

This means that 30 cents of every sales dollar remain to contribute to fixed costs and to profit, after the costs directly related to the sales are subtracted.

Contribution margin is especially useful to a company comparing different products or services. For example:

	Product A $	Product B $	Product C $
Sales	260	220	140
Variable costs	178	148	65
Contribution margin	82	72	75
Contribution margin (%)	31.5	32.7	53.6

Obviously, Product C has the highest contribution percentage, even though Product A generates more total profit. The analysis suggests that the company might do well to aim to achieve a sales mix with a higher proportion of Product C. It further suggests that prices for Products A and B may be too low, or that their cost structures need attention. Notably, none of this information appears on a standard income statement.

Contribution margin also can be tracked over a long period of time, using data from several years of income statements. It can also be invaluable in calculating volume discounts for preferred customers, and break-even sales or volume levels.

Tricks of the Trade

- Contribution margin depends on accurately accounting for all variable costs, including shipping and delivery, or the indirect costs of services. Activity-based cost accounting systems aid this kind of analysis.
- Variable costs include all direct costs (usually labor and materials).
- Contribution margin analysis is only one tool to use. It will not show so-called loss leaders, for example. And it doesn't consider marketing factors like existing penetration levels, opportunities, or mature markets being eroded by emerging markets.

For More Information

Web Site:
www.toolkit.cch.com presents a concise explanation and rationale, plus a solid example.

Calculating Conversion Price

What It Measures

The price per share at which the holder of convertible bonds, or debentures, or preferred stock, can convert them into shares of common stock.

Depending on specific terms, the conversion price may be set when the convertible asset is issued.

Why It Is Important

The conversion price is a key factor in an investment strategy. Knowing it helps investors determine whether or not it is to their advantage to convert their holdings into shares of stock, sell them on the open market, or retain them until they mature or are called by the issuing company.

At the same time, existing stockholders of the issuing company need to know the point at which the value of their shares could be diluted by the creation of additional shares without the concurrent creation of additional capital.

For companies themselves, a conversion price represents an additional financing option: an opportunity to convert debt into equity, an action that itself has advantages and drawbacks.

How It Works in Practice

If the conversion price is set, it will appear in the indenture, a legal agreement between the issuer of a convertible asset and the holder, that states specific terms. If the conversion price does not appear in the agreement, a conversion ratio is used to calculate the conversion price.

A conversion ratio of 25:1, for example, means that 25 shares of stock can be obtained in exchange for each $1,000 convertible asset held. In turn, the conversion price can be determined simply by dividing $1,000 by 25:

$1,000/25 = $40 per share

Comparison of a stock's conversion price to its prevailing market price can help decide the best course of action. If the stock of the company in question is trading at $52 per share, converting makes sense, because it increases the value of $1,000 convertible to $1,300 ($52 × 25 shares). But if the stock is trading at $32 per share, then conversion value is only $800 ($32 × 25) and it is clearly better to defer conversion.

Tricks of the Trade

- Conversion ratios may change over time, according to the terms of the agreement. This is to ensure that a convertible asset holder is not unduly advantaged and that the value of existing stock is not diluted—which, of course, would anger existing shareholders.
- Shareholders, in turn, need to monitor closely a company that decides to issue a large number of convertible assets, since the value of their shares could ultimately be undermined.
- Convertible bonds closely follow the price of the issuing company's underlying stock. Often, in fact, the respective prices of the bond and the shares to be exchanged are almost equal.

For More Information

Web Site:
www.investopedia.com crisply defines conversion price, and presents a good analysis of its use.

See also:
✔ **Calculating Conversion Ratio (pp. 825–26)**

Calculating Conversion Ratio

What It Measures

The number of shares of common stock an investor will receive upon converting a convertible security—a bond, debenture, or preferred stock.

The conversion price may be set when the convertible security is issued, depending on its terms.

Why It Is Important

Like conversion price, the conversion ratio is an investment strategy tool which is used to determine what the value of a convertible security would be if it were converted immediately. By knowing a convertible's value, an investor can compare it with the prevailing price of the issuing company's common stock and decide whether it is best to convert or to continue holding the convertible.

By the same token, holders of common stock in the company issuing the convertible can use the conversion ratio to help monitor the value of their stock. For example, a relatively high ratio could mean that the value of their shares would be diluted if large numbers of convertible holders were to exercise their options.

How It Works in Practice

In the same way as conversion price, the conversion ratio may be established when the convertible is issued. If that is the case, the ratio will appear in the indenture, the binding agreement that details the convertible's terms.

If the conversion ratio is not set, it can be calculated quickly: divide by the par value of the convertible security (typically $1,000) by its conversion price.

$1,000 /$40 per share = 25

In this example, the conversion ratio is 25:1, which means that every bond held with a $1000 par value can be exchanged for 25 shares of common stock.

Knowing the conversion ratio enables an investor to decide quickly whether his convertibles (or group of them) are more valuable than the shares of common stock they represent. If the stock is currently trading at 30, the conversion value is $750, or $250 less than the par value of the convertible. It would therefore be unwise to convert .

Tricks of the Trade

- Although it is rare, a convertible's indenture can sometimes contain a provision stating that the conversion ratio will change over the years.
- A conversion ratio that is set when a convertible is issued usually protects against any dilution from stock splits. However, it does not protect against a company issuing secondary offerings of common stock.
- "Forced conversion" means that the company can make holders convert into stock at virtually any time. Convertible holders should also pay close attention to the price at which the bonds are callable.
- Conversion ratio also describes the number of shares of one common stock to be issued for each outstanding share of another common stock when a merger takes place.

For More Information

Web Site:

www.investopedia.com crisply defines conversion ratio, and presents a good analysis of its use.

See also:

✓ **Calculating Conversion Price (p. 825)**

Calculating Days Sales Outstanding

What It Measures

A company's average collection period, or the average number of days it takes a firm to convert its accounts receivable into cash. It is also called the collection ratio.

Why It Is Important

Knowing how long it takes a company to turn accounts receivable into cash is an important financial indicator. It indicates the efficiency of the company's internal collection, suggests how well a company's customers are accepting its credit terms (net 30 days, for example), and is a figure that is routinely compared with industry averages.

Ideally, DSOs should be decreasing or constant. A low figure means the company collects its outstanding receivables quickly. Typically, DSO is reviewed quarterly or yearly (91 or 365 days).

DSO also helps to expose companies that try to disguise weak sales. Large increases in DSO suggest that a company is trying to force sales either by accepting poor receivable terms or selling products at discount to book more sales for a particular period. An improving DSO suggests that a company is striving to make its operations more efficient.

Any company with a significant change in its DSO merits examination in greater detail.

How It Works in Practice

Regular DSO requires three figures: total accounts receivable, total credit sales for the period analyzed, and the number of days in the period (annual, 365; six months, 182; quarter, 91). The formula is:

accounts receivable/total credit sales for the period × number of days in the period

For example: if total receivables are $4,400,000, total credit sales in a quarter are $9,000,000, and number of days is 91, then:

4,500,000 /9,000,000 × 91 = 45.5

Thus, it takes an average 45.5 days to collect receivables.

Tricks of the Trade

- Companies use DSO information with an accounts receivable aging report. This lists four categories of receivables: 0–30 days, 30–60 days, 60–90 days, and over 90 days. The report also shows the percentage of total accounts receivable that each group represents, allowing for an analysis of delinquencies and potential bad debts—a figure that appears on a profit and loss account.

- A rarely used related calculation, Best Possible DSO, shows how long it takes a company to collect current receivables. Its formula is:

  current receivables/total credit sales for the period × the number of days in the period

So, current receivables of $3,000,000 and total credit sales of $9,000,000 in a 91-day period would result in a best possible DSO of 30.3 days (3,000,000/9,000,000 × 91).

- Only credit sales of merchandise should be used in calculating DSO; cash sales are excluded, as are sales of such items as fixtures, equipment, or real estate.
- Properly evaluating an acceptable DSO requires a standard for comparison. A traditional rule of thumb is that DSO should not exceed one-third to one-half of selling terms. For instance, if terms are 30 days, acceptable DSO would be 40 to 45 days.
- A single DSO is only a snapshot. A fuller picture would require at least quarterly calculations, and some companies review DSO monthly.
- DSO can vary widely by industry as well as company. For example, clothing wholesalers have to have the goods on retailers' shelves for months before they will be sold and the retailer is able to cover invoices. However, a computer wholesaler with a lengthy DSO suggests trouble, since computers become obsolete quickly.

For More Information

Web Site:
www.dnbcollections.com/kdso.htm, a Dun & Bradstreet site, provides explanation, analysis, and calculators for regular and best possible DSO.

Calculating Debt-to-Capital Ratio

What It Measures

The percentage of total funding represented by debt.

Why It Is Important

By comparing a company's long-term liabilities to its total capital, the debt-to-capital ratio provides a review of the extent to which a company relies on external debt finance for its funding and is a measure of the risk to its shareholders.

The debt-to-capital ratio is also a measure of a company's borrowing capacity, and of its ability to pay scheduled financial payments on term debts and capital leases. Bond-rating agencies and analysts use it routinely to assess creditworthiness. The greater the debt, the higher the risk.

However, it can be misleading to assume that the lowest ratio is automatically the best ratio. A company may assume large amounts of debt in order to expand the business. Utilities, for instance, have high capital requirements, so their debt-to-capital ratios will be high as a matter of course. So are those of manufacturing companies, especially those developing a new technology or new product.

At the same time, the higher the level of debt, the more important it is for a company to have positive earnings and steady cash flow.

How It Works in Practice

Although there are variations on exactly what goes into this ratio, the most common method is to divide total long-term debt by total assets (total long-term debt plus shareholders' funds), or

Total liabilities/total assets = debt-to-capital ratio

For example, if the balance sheet of a corporate annual report lists total liabilities of $9,800,000 and total shareholders' equity of $12,800,000, the debt-to-capital ratio is (calculating in thousands):

9,800/(9,800 + 12,800) =
9,800/22,600 = 0.434, or 43.4% debt-to-capital ratio

Some formulas distinguish different portions of long-term debt. However, that complicates calculations and many experts regard it as unnecessary. It is also common to express the formula as total debt divided by total funds, which produces the same outcome.

Tricks of the Trade

- If a company has minority interests in subsidiaries that are consolidated in the balance sheet, they must be added to shareholders' equity.
- Debt calculations should include capital leases.
- One rule of thumb holds that a debt-to-capital ratio of 60% or less is acceptable, but another holds that 40% is the most desirable.
- A high debt-to-capital ratio means less security for shareholders, because debt holders are paid first in bankruptcies. It still can be tolerable, however, if a company's return on assets exceeds the rate of interest paid to creditors.
- Do not confuse debt-to-capital with debt-to-capitalization, which compares debt with total market capitalization and fluctuates as the company's stock price changes.

For More Information

Web Sites:
www.multimedia.calpoly.edu is clear and concise. Debt-to-capital ratio is among the explanations presented within the "Credit Analysis: Banking" portion of **www.nyupress.nyu.edu**.

"Armaments, universal debt, and planned obsolescence—these are the three pillars of Western prosperity."

(Aldous Huxley)

CALCULATING DEBT-TO-EQUITY RATIO

WHAT IT MEASURES

How much money a company owes compared with how much money it has invested in it by principal owners and shareholders.

WHY IT IS IMPORTANT

The debt-to-equity ratio reveals the proportion of debt and equity a company is using to finance its business. It also measures a company's borrowing capacity. The higher the ratio, the greater the proportion of debt—but also the greater the risk.

Some even describe the debt-to-equity ratio as "a great financial test" of long-term corporate health, because debt establishes a commitment to repay money throughout a period of time, even though there is no assurance that sufficient cash will be generated to meet that commitment.

Creditors and lenders, understandably, rely heavily on the ratio to evaluate borrowers.

HOW IT WORKS IN PRACTICE

The debt-to-equity ratio is calculated by dividing debt by owners' equity, where equity is, typically, the figure stated for the preceding calendar or fiscal year. Debt, however, can be defined either as long-term debt only, or as total liabilities, which includes both long- and short-term debt.

The most common formula for the ratio is:

Total liabilities /owners' equity = debt-to-equity ratio

In our example, a company's long-term debt is $8,000,000, its short-term debt is $4,000,000, and owners' equity totals $9,000,000. The debt-to-equity ratio would therefore be (calculating in thousands):

(8,000 + 4,000) /9,000 =
12,000 /9,000 = 1.33 debt-to-equity ratio

An alternative debt-to-equity formula considers only long-term liabilities in the equation. Accordingly:

8,000 /9,000 = 0.889 debt-to-equity ratio

There is also a third method, which is the reciprocal of the debt-to-capital ratio; its formula is:

Owners' equity/total funds = debt-to-equity ratio

However, this would be more accurately defined as "equity-to-debt ratio."

TRICKS OF THE TRADE

- It is important to understand exactly how debt is defined in the ratio presented.
- Like all ratios, debt-to-equity must be evaluated against those of other companies in a given industry and over a period of time.
- When calculating the ratio, some prefer to use the market value of debt and equity rather than the book value, since book value often understates current value.
- For this ratio, a low number indicates better financial stability than a high one does; if the ratio is high, a company could be at risk, especially if interest rates are rising.
- A ratio greater than one means assets are mainly financed with debt; less than one means equity provides a majority of the financing. Since a higher ratio generally means that a company has been aggressive in financing its growth with debt, volatile earnings can result because of the additional cost of interest.
- Debt-to-equity ratio is somewhat industry-specific, and often depends on the amount of capital investment required.

For More Information

Web Site:
www.connex.bdc.ca.eng.ratio_dette.htm defines the ratio, and features a worksheet that guides its computation.

CALCULATING CREDITOR AND DEBTOR DAYS

WHAT THEY MEASURE

Creditor days is a measure of the number of days on average that a company requires to pay its creditors, while debtor days is a measure of the number of days on average that it takes a company to receive payment for what it sells. It is also called accounts receivable days.

WHY THEY ARE IMPORTANT

Creditor days is an indication of a company's creditworthiness in the eyes of its suppliers and creditors, since it shows how long they are willing to wait for payment. Within reason, the higher the number the better, because all companies want to conserve cash. At the same time, a company that is especially slow to pay its bills (100 or more days, for example) may be a company having trouble generating cash, or one trying to finance its operations with its suppliers' funds. Ultimately, companies whose creditor days soar have trouble obtaining supplies.

Debtor days is an indication of a company's efficiency in collecting monies owed. In this case, obviously, the

"The debt is like a crazy aunt we keep down in the basement. All the neighbors know she's there, but nobody wants to talk about her."

(Ross Perot)

lower the number the better. An especially high number is a telltale sign of inefficiency or worse. It may indicate bad debts, dubious sales figures, or a company being bullied by large customers out to improve their own cash position at another firm's expense. Customers whose credit terms are abused also risk higher borrowing costs and related charges.

Changes in both measures are easy to spot, and easy to understand.

How They Work in Practice

To determine creditor days, divide the cumulative amount of unpaid suppliers' bills (also called trade creditors) by sales, then multiply by 365. For example, if suppliers' bills total $800,000 and sales are $9,000,000, the calculation is:

(800,000 /9,000,000) × 365 = 32.44 days

The company takes 32.44 days on average to pay its bills.

To determine debtor days, divide the cumulative amount of accounts receivable by sales, then multiply by 365. For example, if accounts receivable total $600,000 and sales are $9,000,000, the calculation is:

(600,000 /9,000,000) × 365 = 24.33 days

The company takes 24.33 days on average to collect its debts.

Tricks of the Trade

- Cash businesses, including most retailers, should have a much lower debtor days figure than noncash businesses, since they receive payment when they sell the goods. A typical target for noncash businesses is 40–50 days.
- An abnormally high creditor days figure may not only suggest a cash crisis, but also the management's difficulty in maintaining revolving credit agreements.
- An increasing number of debtor days also suggests overly generous credit terms (to bolster sales) or problems with product quality.

For More Information

Web Site:

www.finance-glossary.com explains both terms and has links to additional information, including seminars and discussion papers.

Calculating Payback Period

What It Measures

How long it will take to earn back the money invested in a project.

Why It Is Important

The straight payback period method is the simplest way of determining the investment potential of a major project. Expressed in time, it tells a management how many months or years it will take to recover the original cash cost of the project—always a vital consideration, and especially so for managements evaluating several projects at once.

This evaluation becomes even more important if it includes an examination of what the present value of future revenues will be.

How It Works in Practice

The straight payback period formula is:

Cost of project /annual cash revenues = payback period

Thus, if a project cost $100,000 and was expected to generate $28,000 annually, the payback period would be:

100,000 /28,000 = 3.57 years

If the revenues generated by the project are expected to vary from year to year, add the revenues expected for each succeeding year until you arrive at the total cost of the project.

For example, say the revenues expected to be generated by the $100,000 project are:

	Revenue	Total
Year 1	$19,000	$19,000
Year 2	$25,000	$44,000
Year 3	$30,000	$74,000
Year 4	$30,000	$104,000
Year 5	$30,000	$134,000

Thus, the project would be fully paid for in Year 4, since it is in that year the total revenue reaches the initial cost of $100,000. The precise payback period would be calculated as:

[(100,000 – 74,000) /(1000,000 – 74,000)] × 365 = 316 days plus 3 years

The picture becomes complex when the time value of money principle is introduced into the calculations. Some experts insist this is essential to determine the most accurate payback period. Accordingly, present value tables or computers (now the norm) must be used, and the annual revenues have to be discounted by the applicable interest rate, 10% in this example. Doing so produces significantly different results:

	Revenue	Present value	Total
Year 1	$19,000	$17,271	$17,271
Year 2	$25,000	$20,650	$37,921
Year 3	$30,000	$22,530	$60,451
Year 4	$30,000	$20,490	$80,941
Year 5	$30,000	$18,630	$99,571

This method shows that payback would not occur even after five years.

"One way to make sure crime doesn't pay is to let the government run it." (Ronald Reagan)

  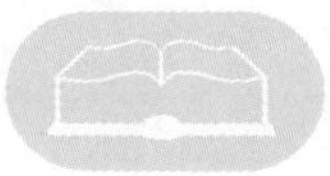    

TRICKS OF THE TRADE

- Clearly, a main defect of the straight payback period method is that it ignores the time value of money principle, which, in turn, can produce unrealistic expectations.
- A second drawback is that it ignores any benefits generated after the payback period, and thus a project that would return $1 million after, say, six years, might be ranked lower than a project with a three-year payback that returns only $100,000 thereafter.
- Another alternative to calculating by payback period is to develop an internal rate of return.
- Under most analyses, projects with shorter payback periods rank higher than those with longer paybacks, even if the latter project higher returns. Longer paybacks can be affected by such factors as market changes, changes in interest rates, and economic shifts. Shorter cash paybacks also enable companies to recoup an investment sooner and put it to work elsewhere.
- Generally, a payback period of three years or less is desirable; if a project's payback period is less than a year, some contend it should be judged essential.

For More Information

Web Site:
www.toolkit.cch.com has a thorough but concise analysis of payback period, including an example.

CALCULATING EFFICIENCY

WHAT IT MEASURES

The portion of operating revenues or fee income spent on overhead expenses.

WHY IT IS IMPORTANT

Often identified with banking and financial sectors, the efficiency ratio indicates a management's ability to keep overhead costs low. This measurement also is used by mature industries, such as steel manufacture, chemicals, or auto production, that must focus on tight cost controls to boost profitability because growth prospects are modest.

In some industries, the efficiency ratio is called the overhead burden: overhead as a percentage of sales.

A different method measures efficiency simply by tracking three other measures: accounts payable to sales, days sales outstanding, and inventory turnover, which indicates how fast a company is able to move its merchandise. A general guide is that if the first two of these measures are low and third is high, efficiency is probably high; the reverse is likewise true.

HOW IT WORKS IN PRACTICE

The efficiency ratio is defined as operating overhead expenses divided by fee income plus tax equivalent net interest income. If operating expenses are $100,000, and revenues (as defined) are $230,000, then:

100,000/230,000 = 0.43 efficiency ratio

However, not everyone calculates the ratio in the same way. Some institutions include all non-interest expenses, while others exclude certain charges, and intangible asset amortization.

To find the inventory turnover ratio, divide total sales by total inventory. If net sales are $300,000, and inventory is $100,000, then:

300,000/140,000 = 2.14 inventory turnover ratio

To find the accounts payable to sales ratio, divide a company's accounts payable by its annual net sales. A high ratio suggests that a company is using its suppliers' funds as a source of cheap financing because it is not operating efficiently enough to generate its own funds. If accounts payable are $50,000, and total sales are $300,000, then:

42,000/300,000 = 0.14 × 100 = 14% accounts payable to sales ratio

TRICKS OF THE TRADE

- Identifying "overhead" to calculate the efficiency ratio can itself contribute to overall inefficiency. Some financial experts contend that efficiency can be measured equally well by reviewing earnings per share growth and return on equity.
- Some banks identify amortization of goodwill expense, and pull it out of their non-interest expense in order to calculate what is called the cash efficiency ratio: non-interest expense minus goodwill amortization expense divided into revenue.
- In banking, an acceptable efficiency ratio was once in the low 60s. Now the goal is 50, while better-performing banks boast ratios in the mid 40s. Low ratings usually indicate a higher return on equity and earnings.

For More Information

Web Site:
www.bizval.com/publications/articlelibrary offers a thorough discussion.

CALCULATING EXPECTED RATE OF RETURN

WHAT IT MEASURES

The projected percentage return on an investment, based on the weighted probability of all possible rates of return.

Why It Is Important

No self-respecting businessperson or organization should make an investment without first having some understanding of how successful that investment is likely to be. Expected rate of return provides such an understanding, within certain limits.

How It Works in Practice

The formula for expected rate of return is:

$$E[r] = \Sigma_s P(s) r_s$$

where $E[r]$ is the expected return, $P(s)$ is the probability that the rate r_s occurs, and r_s is the return at s level.

A simple example, as given below, is far easier to grasp, and adequately illustrates the principle which the formula expresses. It will also probably be of more practical use to most of those who need to calculate ERR:

The current price of ABC, Inc., stock is trading at $10. At the end of the year, ABC shares are projected to be traded:

- 25% higher if economic growth exceeds expectations—a probability of 30%;
- 12% higher if economic growth equals expectations—a probability of 50%;
- 5% lower if economic growth falls short of expectations—a probability of 20%.

To find the expected rate of return, simply multiply the percentages by their respective probabilities and add the results:

(30% × 25%) + (50% × 12%) + (25% × –5%) = 7.5 + 6 + –1.25 = 12.25% ERR

A second example:

- if economic growth remains robust (a 20% probability), investments will return 25%;
- if economic growth ebbs, but still performs adequately (a 40% probability), investments will return 15%;
- if economic growth slows significantly (a 30% probability), investments will return 5%;
- if the economy declines outright (a 10% probability), investments will return 0%.

Therefore:

(20% × 25%) + (40% × 15%) + (30% × 5%) + (10% × 0%) =
5% + 6% + 1.5% + 0% = 12.5% ERR

Another method that can be used to project expected return is the Capital Asset Pricing Model (CAPM), which is explained separately.

Tricks of the Trade

- The probability totals must always equal 100% for the calculation to be valid.
- Be sure not to overlook any negative numbers in the calculations, or the results produced will be incorrect.
- An ERR calculation is only as good as the scenarios considered. Wildly unrealistic scenarios will produce an equally unreliable expected rate of return.

For More Information

Web Site:
www.teachmefinance.com/probabilitydistribution.html presents explanations and links to further analysis.

Calculating Elasticity

What It Measures

The percentage change of one variable caused by a percentage change in another variable.

Why It Is Important

Elasticity is defined as "the measure of the sensitivity of one variable to another." In practical terms, elasticity indicates the degree to which consumers respond to changes in price. It is obviously important for companies to consider such relationships when contemplating changes in price, demand, and supply.

Demand elasticity measures how much the quantity demanded changes when the price of a product or service is increased or lowered. Will demand remain constant? If not, how much will demand change?

Supply elasticity measures the impact on supply when a price is changed. It is assumed that lowering prices will reduce supply, because demand will increase—but by how much?

How It Works in Practice

The general formula for elasticity is:

Elasticity = % change in x /% change in y

In theory, x and y can be any variable. However, the most common application measures price and demand. If the price of a product is increased from $20 to $25, or 25%, and demand in turn falls from 6,000 to 3,000, elasticity would be calculated as:

- 50% /25% = – 2

A value greater than 1, as in this case, means that demand is strongly sensitive to price, while a value of less than 1 means that demand is not price-sensitive.

Tricks of the Trade

There are five cases of elasticity:

- E = 1, or *unit elasticity*. The proportional change in one variable is equal to the proportional change in another variable: if price rises by 5%, demand falls by 5%.
- E is greater than 1, or just *elastic*. The proportional change in x is greater than the proportional change in y: if price rises by 5%, demand falls by 3%.
- E = infinity, or *perfectly elastic*. This is a special case of

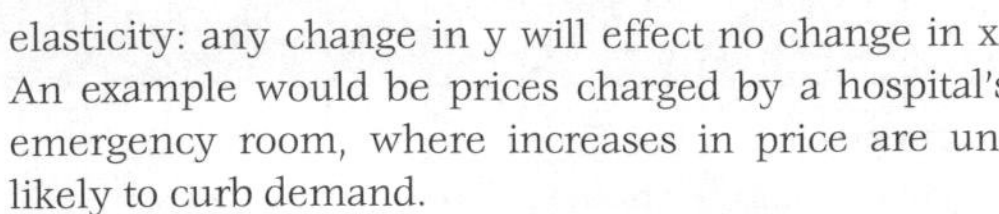

elasticity: any change in y will effect no change in x. An example would be prices charged by a hospital's emergency room, where increases in price are unlikely to curb demand.
- E is less than 1, or just *inelastic*. The proportional change in x is less than the proportional change in y: if prices are increased by 3%, demand will fall by 30%.
- E = 0, or *perfectly inelastic*. This is another special case of elasticity: any change in y will have an infinite effect on x.

There are more complex formulae for determining a range of variables, or "arc elasticity."

Elasticity can be used to affirm two rules of thumb:
- demand becomes elastic if consumers have an alternative or adequate substitute for the product or service;
- demand is more elastic if consumers have an incentive to save money.

For More Information

Web Site:
www.hadm.sph.sc.edu includes a well-presented interactive tutorial developed by Samuel Baker of the University of South Carolina.

CALCULATING FUTURE VALUE

WHAT IT MEASURES
Any amount of any currency.

WHY IT IS IMPORTANT
Future value is a fundamental of investment. Understanding it helps any organization or individual determine how a sum will be affected by changes in inflation, interest rates, or currency values. Inflation, for instance, will always reduce a sum's value. Interest rates will always increase it. Exchanging the sum for an identical amount in another currency will increase or decrease it, depending on how the respective currencies perform on the world market.

Armed with this knowledge, an organization can make more informed decisions about how to generate the maximum value from its funds in a given period of time: would it be best to deposit them in simple interest-bearing accounts, exchange them for funds in another currency, use them to expand operations, or use them to acquire another company?

HOW IT WORKS IN PRACTICE
Start with three figures: the sum in question, the percentage by which it will increase or decrease, and the period of time. In this case: $1,000, 11%, and two years.

At an interest rate of 11%, our $1,000 will grow to $1,232 in two years:

> **$1,000** × **1.11** = **$1,110** (first year) × **1.11** = **$1,232** (second year, rounded to whole dollars)

Note that the interest earned in the first year generates additional interest in the second year, a practice known as compounding. When large sums are in question, the effect of compounding can be significant.

At an inflation rate of 11%, by comparison, our $1,000 will shrink to $812 in two years:

> **$1,000/1.11** = **$901** (first year)/**1.11** = **$812** (second year, rounded to whole dollars)

TRICKS OF THE TRADE
- Express the percentage as 1.11 and multiply and divide by that figure, instead of using 11%. Otherwise, errors will occur.
- Calculate each year, quarter, or month separately, as our example illustrates.
- It is important always to use the **annual** rates of interest and inflation.
- A more useful tool is "present value," which estimates what future value cash flows would be worth if they occurred today.

For More Information

Web Site:
An excellent Web-based calculator can be found at **www.xfcu.org**.

CALCULATING INTERNAL RATE OF RETURN

WHAT IT MEASURES
Technically, the interest rate that makes the present value of an investment's projected cash flows equal to the cost of the project; practically speaking, the rate that indicates whether or not an investment is worth pursuing.

WHY IT IS IMPORTANT
The calculation of internal rate of return is used to appraise the prospective viability of investments and capital projects. It is also called dollar-weighted rate of return.

Essentially, IRR allows an investor to find the interest rate that is equivalent to the monetary returns expected from the project. Once that rate is determined, it can be compared to the rates that could be earned by investing the money elsewhere, or to the weighted cost of capital. IRR also accounts for the time value of money.

"Most economists. . .are reluctant to make predictions, and the ones who make them are seldom accurate."
(Alice M. Rivlin)

  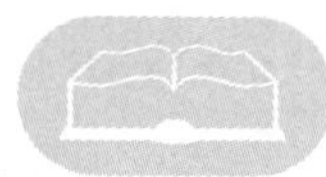    

How It Works in Practice

How is IRR applied? Assume, for example, that a project under consideration costs $7,500 and is expected to return $2,000 per year for five years, or $10,000. The IRR calculated for the project would be about 10%. If the cost of borrowing money for the project, or the return on investing the funds elsewhere, is less than 10%, the project is probably worthwhile. If the alternate use of the money will return 10% or more, the project should be rejected, since from a financial perspective it will break even at best.

Typically, management requires an IRR equal to or higher than the cost of capital, depending on relative risk and other factors.

The best way to compute an IRR is by using a spreadsheet (such as Excel) or financial calculator, which do it automatically, although it is crucial to understand how the calculation should be structured. Calculating IRR by hand is tedious and time-consuming, and requires the process to be repeated to run sensitivities.

If using Excel, for example, select the IRR function. This requires the annual cash flows to be set out in columns and the first part of the IRR formula requires the cell reference range of these cash flows to be entered. Then a guess of the IRR is required. The default is 10%, written 0.1.

Now	-2,500
Year 1	1,200
Year 2	1,300
Year 3	1,500

If a project has the following expected cash flows, then guessing IRR at 30% returns an accurate IRR of 27%, indicating that, if the next best way of investing the money gives a return of -20%, the project should go ahead.

Tricks of the Trade

- IRR analysis is generally used to evaluate a project's cash flows rather than income, because, unlike income, cash flows do not reflect depreciation and therefore are usually more instructive to appraise.
- Most basic spreadsheet functions apply to cash flows only.
- As well as advocates, IRR has critics who dismiss it as misleading, especially as significant costs will occur late in the project. The rule of thumb "the higher the IRR the better" does not always apply.
- For the most thorough analysis of a project's investment potential, some experts urge using both IRR and net present value calculations, and comparing their results.

For More Information

Web Site:
www.hadm.sph.sc.edu/courses/Econ is a thorough and well-written tutorial on IRR.

Calculating Marginal Cost

What It Measures

The additional cost of producing one more unit of product, or providing service to one more customer.

Why It Is Important

Sometimes called incremental cost, marginal cost shows how much costs increase from making or serving one more, an essential factor when contemplating a production increase, or seeking to serve more customers.

If the price charged is greater than the marginal cost, then the revenue gain will be greater than the added cost. That, in turn, will increase profit, so the expansion in production or service makes economic sense and should proceed. Of course, the reverse is also true: If the price charged is less than the marginal cost, expansion should not go ahead.

How It Works in Practice

The formula for marginal cost is:

Change in cost /change in quantity

If it costs a company $260,000 to produce 3,000 items, and $325,000 to produce 3,800 items, the change in cost would be:

$325,000 – $260,000 = $65,000

The change in quantity would be:

3,800 – 3,000 = 800

When the formula to calculate marginal cost is applied, the result is:

$65,000 /800 = $81.25

If the price of the item in question were $99.95, expansion should proceed.

Tricks of the Trade

- A marginal cost that is lower than the price shows that it is not always necessary to cut prices to sell more goods and boost profits.
- Using idle capacity to produce lower-margin items can still be beneficial, because these generate revenues that help cover fixed costs.
- Marginal cost studies can become quite complicated, because the basic formula does not always take into account variables that can affect cost and quantity. There are software programs available, many of which are industry-specific.

"Economics limps along with one foot in untested waters and the other in untestable slogans."
(Joan Robinson)

- At some point, marginal cost invariably begins to rise; typically, labor becomes less productive as a production run increases, while the time required also increases.
- Marginal cost alone may not justify expansion. It is best to determine also average costs, then chart the respective series of figures to find where marginal cost meets average cost, and thus determine optimum cost.
- Relying on marginal cost is not fail-safe; putting more product on a market can drive down prices and thus cut margins. Moreover, committing idle capacity to long-term production may tie up resources that could be directed to a new and more profitable opportunity.
- An important related principle is contribution: the cash gained (or lost) from selling an additional unit.

For More Information

Web Site:
www.xrefer.com gives a concise analysis of marginal cost and its relationship to pricing.

Calculating Net Present Value

What It Measures

The projected profitability of an investment, based on anticipated cash flows and discounted at a stated rate of interest.

Why It Is Important

Net present value helps management or potential investors weigh the wisdom of an investment–in new equipment, a new facility, or other type of asset–by enabling them to quantify the expected benefits. Those evaluating more than one potential investment can compare the respective projected returns to find the most attractive project.

A positive NPV indicates that the project should be profitable, assuming that the estimated cash flows are reasonably accurate. A negative NPV, of course, indicates that the project will probably be unprofitable and therefore should be adjusted, if not abandoned altogether.

Equally significantly, NPV enables a management to consider the time value of money it will invest. This concept holds that the value of money increases with time because it can always earn interest in a savings account. Therefore, any other investment of that money must be weighed against how the funds would perform if simply deposited and saved.

When the time value of money concept is incorporated in the calculation of NPV, the value of a project's future net cash receipts in "today's money" can be determined. This enables proper comparisons between different projects.

How It Works in Practice

Let's say that Global Manufacturing Inc. is considering the acquisition of a new machine. First, its management would consider all the factors: initial purchase and installation costs; additional revenues generated by sales of the new machine's products, plus the taxes on these new revenues. Having accounted for these factors in its calculations, the cash flows that Global Manufacturing projects will generate from the new machine are:

Year 1:	-100,000 (initial cost of investment)
Year 2:	30,000
Year 3:	40,000
Year 4:	40,000
Year 5:	35,000
Net Total:	145,000

At first glance, it appears that cash flows total a huge 45% more than the $100,000 initial cost, a strikingly sound investment indeed.

Alas, it's not that simple. But time value of money shrinks return on the project considerably, since future dollars are worth less than present dollars in hand. NPV accounts for these differences with the help of present value tables. These user-friendly tables, readily available on the Internet and in references, list the ratios that express the present value of expected cash flow dollars, based on the applicable interest rate and the number of years in question.

In our example, Global Manufacturing's cost of capital is 9%. Using this figure to find the corresponding ratios on the present value table, the $100,000 investment cost, expected annual revenues during the five years in question, the NPV calculation looks like this:

Year	Cash flow	Table factor (at 9%)	Present value
1	($100,000) ×	1.000000 =	($100,000)
2	$ 30,000 ×	0.917431 =	$27,522.93
3	$ 40,000 ×	0.841680 =	$33,667.20
4	$ 40,000 ×	0.772183 =	$30,887.32
5	$ 35,000 ×	0.708425 =	$24,794.88
	NPV =		$ 16,873.33

NPV is still positive. So, on this basis at least, the investment should proceed.

Tricks of the Trade

- Beware of assumptions. Interest rates change, of course, which can affect NPV dramatically. Moreover, fresh revenues (as well as new markets) may not grow as projected. If the cash flows in years 2–5 of our example fall by $5,000 a year, for instance, NPV shrinks to $5,260.89, which is still positive but less attractive.
- NPV calculations are performed only with cash receipts payments and discounting factors. In turn, NPV is a tool, not the tool. It ignores other accounting data, intangibles, sheer faith in a new idea, and other factors that may make an investment worth pursuing despite a negative NPV.

- It is important to determine a company's cost of capital accurately.

For More Information

Web Site:
www.toolkit.cch.com/text, site of the Business Owners' toolkit, has both tables and additional information about net present value.

Calculating Rate of Return

What It Measures

The annual return on an investment, expressed as a percentage of the total amount invested. It also measures the yield of a fixed-income security.

Why It Is Important

Rate of return is a simple and straightforward way to determine how much investors are being paid for the use of their money, so that they can then compare various investments and select the best—based, of course, on individual goals and acceptable levels of risk.

Rate of return has a second and equally vital purpose: as a common denominator that measures a company's financial performance, for example in terms of rate of return on assets, equity, or sales.

How It Works in Practice

There is a basic formula that will serve most needs, at least initially:

[(Current value of amount invested – Original value of amount invested)/Original value of amount invested] × 100% = rate of return

If $1000 in capital is invested in stock, and one year later the investment yields $1,100, the rate of return of the investment is calculated like this:

[(1100 – 1000)/1000)] × 100% = 100/1000 × 100% = 10% rate of return

Now, assume $1,000 is invested again. One year later, the investment grows to $2,000 in value, but after another year the value of the investment falls to $1,200. The rate of return after the first year is:

[(2000 – 1000)/1000] × 100% = 100%

The rate of return after the second year is:

[(1200 – 2000)/2000] × 100% = –40%

The average annual return for the two years (also known as average annual arithmetic return) can be calculated using this formula:

(Rate of return for Year 1 + Rate of return for Year 2)/2 = average annual return

Accordingly:

(100% + –40%)/2 = 30%

Be careful, however! The average annual rate of return is a percentage, but one that is accurate over only a short period, so this method should be used accordingly.

The geometric or compound rate of return is a better yardstick for measuring investments over the long run, and takes into account the effects of compounding. As one might expect, this formula is more complex and technical, and beyond the scope of this article.

Tricks of the Trade

- The real rate of return is the annual return realized on an investment, adjusted for changes in the price due to inflation. If 10% is earned on an investment but inflation is 2%, then the real rate of return is actually 8%.
- Do not confuse rate of return with internal rate of return, which is a more complex calculation.
- Some mutual fund managers have been known to report the average annual rate of return on the investments they manage. In the second example, that figure is 30%, yet the value of the investment is only $200 higher than it was two years ago, or 20%. So, read such reports carefully.

For More Information

Web Site:
www.ricefinancial.com/calcs is a calculator that computes rates of return required for an investment to reach a desired amount, based on amount invested and time.

Calculating Return on Sales

What It Measures

A company's operating profit or loss as a percentage of total sales for a given period, typically a year.

Why It Is Important

ROS shows how efficiently management uses the sales dollar, thus reflecting its ability to manage costs and overhead and operate efficiently. It also indicates a firm's ability to withstand adverse conditions such as falling prices, rising costs, or declining sales. The higher the figure, the better a company is able to endure price wars and falling prices.

Return on sales can be useful in assessing the annual performances of cyclical companies that may have no earnings during particular months, and of firms whose business requires a huge capital investment and thus incurs substantial amounts of depreciation.

How It Works in Practice

The calculation is very basic:

Operating profit/total sales × 100 = Percentage return on sales

So, if a company earns $30 on sales of $400, its return on sales is:

30 /400 = 0.075 × 100 = 7.5%

Tricks of the Trade

- While easy to grasp, return on sales has its limits, since it sheds no light on the overall cost of sales or the four factors that contribute to it: materials, labor, production overhead, and administrative and selling overhead.
- Some calculations use operating profit before subtracting interest and taxes; others use after-tax income. Either figure is acceptable as long as ROS comparisons are consistent. Obviously, using income before interest and taxes will produce a higher ratio.
- The ratio's operating profit figure may also include special allowances and extraordinary non-recurring items, which, in turn, can inflate the percentage and be misleading.
- The ratio varies widely by industry. The supermarket business, for example, is heavily dependent on volume and usually has a low return on sales.
- Return on sales remains of special importance to retail sales organizations, which can compare their respective ratios with those of competitors and industry norms.

For More Information

Web Site:
www.xrefer.com offers a concise explanation of return on sales, plus many other performance liquidity ratios.

Calculating Return on Assets

What It Measures

A company's profitability, expressed as a percentage of its total assets.

Why It Is Important

Return on assets measures how effectively a company has used the total assets at its disposal to generate earnings. Because the ROA formula reflects total revenue, total cost and assets deployed, the ratio itself reflects a management's ability to generate income during the course of a given period, usually a year.

Naturally, the higher the return the better the profit performance. ROA is a convenient way of comparing a company's performance with that of its competitors, although the items on which the comparison is based may not always be identical.

How It Works in Practice

To calculate ROA, divide a company's net income by its total assets, then multiply by 100 to express the figure as a percentage:

Net income/total assets × 100 = ROA

If net income is $30, and total assets are $420, the ROA is:

30 /420 = 0.0714 × 100 = 7.14 %

A variation of this formula can be used to calculate return on net assets (RONA):

Net income/fixed assets + working capital = RONA

And, on occasion, the formula will separate after-tax interest expense from net income:

Net income + interest expense/total assets = ROA

It is therefore important to understand what each component of the formula actually represents.

Tricks of the Trade

- Some experts recommend using the net income value at the end of the given period, and the assets value from beginning of the period or an average value taken over the complete period, rather than an end-of-the-period value; otherwise, the calculation will include assets that have accumulated during the year, which can be misleading.
- While a high ratio indicates a greater return, it must still be balanced against such factors as risk, sustainability, and reinvestment in the business through development costs. Some managements will sacrifice the long-term interests of investors in order to achieve an impressive ROA in the short term.
- A climbing return on assets usually indicates a climbing stock price, because it tells investors that a management is skilled at generating profits from the resources that a business owns.
- Acceptable ROAs vary by sector. In banking, for example, an ROA of 1% or better is a considered to be the standard benchmark of superior performance.
- ROA is an effective way of measuring the efficiency of manufacturers, but can be suspect when measuring service firms, or companies whose primary assets are people.
- Other variations of the ROA formula do exist.

"Never invest your money in anything that eats or needs repainting." (Billy Rose)

For More Information

Web Site:
moneycentral.msn.com/investor offers tips about assessing ROA.

See also:
✔ **Calculating Return on Shareholders' Equity (pp. 837–38)**

Calculating Return on Investment

What It Measures

In the financial realm, the overall profit or loss on an investment expressed as a percentage of the total amount invested or total funds appearing on a company's balance sheet.

Why It Is Important

Like return on assets or return on equity, return on investment measures a company's profitability and its management's ability to generate profits from the funds investors have placed at its disposal.

One opinion holds that if a company's operations cannot generate net earnings at a rate that exceeds the cost of borrowing funds from financial markets, the future of that company is grim.

How It Works in Practice

The most basic expression of ROI can be found by dividing a company's net profit (also called net earnings) by the total investment (total debt plus total equity), then multiplying by 100 to arrive at a percentage:

Net profit / Total investment × 100 = ROI

If, say, net profit is $30 and total investment is $250, the ROI is:

30 / 250 = 0.12 × 100 = 12%

A more complex variation of ROI is an equation known as the Du Pont formula:

(Net profit after taxes / Total assets) = (Net profit after taxes / Sales) × Sales / Total assets

If, for example, net profit after taxes is $30, total assets are $250, and sales are $500, then:

30 / 250 = 30 / 500 × 500 / 250 =
12% = 6% × 2 = 12%

Champions of this formula, which was developed by the Du Pont Company in the 1920s, say that it helps reveal how a company has both deployed its assets and controlled its costs, and how it can achieve the same percentage return in different ways.

For shareholders, the variation of the basic ROI formula used by investors is:

Net income + (current value – original value) / original value × 100 = ROI

If, for example, somebody invests $5,000 in a company and a year later has earned $100 in dividends, while the value of the shares is $5,200, the return on investment would be:

100 + (5,200 – 5,000)/5,000 × 100 =
(100 + 200)/5,000 × 100 =
300 /5,000 = 0.06 × 100 = 6% ROI

Tricks of the Trade

- Securities investors can use yet another ROI formula: net income divided by common stock and preferred stock equity plus long-term debt.
- It is vital to understand exactly what a return on investment measures, for example assets, equity, or sales. Without this understanding, comparisons may be misleading or suspect. A search for "return on investment" on the Web, for example, harvests everything from staff training to e-commerce to advertising and promotions!
- Be sure to establish whether the net profit figure used is before or after provision for taxes. This is important for making ROI comparisons accurate.

For More Information

Web Site:
www.return-on-investment.net lists links to a wealth of ROI sites for calculating return on investments and a variety of business projects.

Calculating Return on Shareholders' Equity

What It Measures

Profitability, specifically the percentage return that was delivered to a company's owners.

Why It Is Important

ROE is a fundamental indication of a company's ability to increase its earnings per share and thus the quality of its stock, because it reveals how well a company is using its money to generate additional earnings.

It is a relatively straightforward benchmark, easy to calculate, and is applicable to a majority of industries. ROE allows investors to compare a company's use of their equity with other investments, and to compare the performance of companies in the same industry. ROE can also help to evaluate trends in a business.

Businesses that generate high returns on equity are businesses that pay off their shareholders handsomely and create substantial assets for each dollar invested.

How It Works in Practice

To calculate ROE, divide the net income shown on the income statement (usually of the past year) by shareholders' equity, which appears on the balance sheet:

Net income /owners' equity × 100% = return on equity

For example, if net income is $450 and equity is $2,500, then:

450/2,500 = 0.18 × 100% = 18% return on equity

Tricks of the Trade

- Because new variations of the ROE ratio do appear, it is important to know how the figure is calculated.
- Return on equity for most companies certainly should be in the double digits; investors often look for 15% or higher, while a return of 20% or more is considered excellent.
- Seasoned investors also review five-year average ROE, to gauge consistency.
- A word of caution: financial statements usually report assets at book value, which is the purchase price minus depreciation; they do not show replacement costs. A business with older assets should show higher rates of ROE than a business with newer assets.
- Examining ROE with return on assets can indicate if a company is debt-heavy. If a company owes very little debt, then it is reasonable to assume that its management is earning high profits and/or using assets effectively.
- A high ROE also could be due to leverage (a method of corporate funding in which a higher proportion of funds is raised through borrowing than share issue). If liabilities are high the balance sheet will reveal it, hence the need to review it.

For More Information

Web Site:
www.fool.com has an interesting discussion of ROE, analysis of ROE, and variations of its basic formula.

See also:
✔ **Calculating Return on Assets (pp. 836–37)**

Calculating the Alpha and Beta Values of a Security

What They Measure

A security's performance, adjusted to risk, compared to overall market behavior.

Why They Are Important

Just as coaches would expect their most accomplished athletes to perform at a higher level than others, investors expect more from higher-risk investments. Alpha and beta give investors a quick indication of just how risky a stock or fund is.

Alpha is defined as "the return a security or a portfolio would be expected to earn if the market's rate of return were zero."

Beta is a means of measuring the volatility (or risk) of a stock or fund in comparison with the market as a whole. The beta of a stock or fund can be of any value, positive or negative, but usually is between +0.25 and +1.75.

Alpha expresses the difference between the return expected from a stock or mutual fund, given its beta rating, and the return actually produced. A stock or fund that returns more than its beta would predict has a positive alpha, while one that returns less than the amount predicted by beta has a negative alpha. A large positive alpha indicates a strong performance, while a large negative alpha indicates a dismal performance.

How They Work in Practice

To begin with, the market itself is assigned a beta of 1.0. If a stock or fund has a beta of 1.2, this means its price is likely to rise or fall by 12% when the overall market rises or falls by 10%; a beta of 0.7 means the stock or fund price is likely to move up or down at 70% of the level of the market change.

In practice, an alpha of 0.4 means the stock or fund in question outperformed the market-based return estimate by 0.4%. An alpha of -0.6 means the return was 0.6% less than would have been predicted from the change in the market alone.

Both alpha and beta should be readily available on request from investment firms, because the figures appear in standard performance reports. It is always best to ask for them, because calculating a stock's alpha rating requires first knowing a stock's beta rating, and calculating beta is a challenge! It is based on linear regression analysis, the week-to-week percentage changes in the given stock's price and the corresponding week-to-week percentage price change in a market index, over a given period of time, often 24 to 36 months. In short, beta calculations can involve mathematical complexities.

If it's any consolation, calculating alpha is far less taxing, provided requisite data is available. The formula is:

(Actual return – Risk-free return) – [Beta × (Index return – Risk-free return)] = Alpha

If a mutual fund with a beta rating of 1.1 returned 35%, while its benchmark index returned 30%, and a U.S. Treasury bill returned 4% (T-bill returns are usually used as the "risk-free investment"), then the fund's alpha would equal 2.4, based on the formula:

(35% – 4%) – 1.1 × (30% – 4%) = 31% – 1.1 × 26% = 31% – 28.6 % = 2.4 alpha

Tricks of the Trade

- The underlying rationale for both alpha and beta is that the return of a stock or mutual fund should at least exceed that of a "risk-free" investment such as a U.S. Treasury bill.
- Stocks of many utilities have a beta of less than 1. Conversely, most high-tech NASDAQ-based stocks have a beta greater than 1; they offer a higher rate of return but are also risky.
- Alpha is often used to assess the performance of a portfolio manager. However, a low alpha score doesn't necessarily reflect poor performance by a fund manager, any more than a high alpha score means that a manager's performance is outstanding. At times factors beyond a manager's control affect alpha values.

For More Information

Web Site:
The Education Center on **www.zurich.com** discusses alpha and beta in greater detail and offers links to additional sites.

Calculating the Future Value of an Annuity

What It Measures

The value to which a series of fixed-amount payments made at regular intervals will grow over the specified period of time.

Why It Is Important

The calculation enables companies to determine the future value of a fund receiving regular payments, such as contributions to a pension fund. Individuals in companies may find the calculation equally useful if they want to establish a fund to pay the cost of future college education: they will know what their annual payments will grow to in a given number of years.

How It Works in Practice

There are several types of annuity. They vary both in the ways they accumulate funds and in the ways they disperse earnings.

A **fixed annuity** guarantees fixed payments to the individual receiving it for the term of the contract, usually until death.

A **variable annuity** offers no guarantee but has potential for a greater return, usually based on the performance of a stock or mutual fund.

A **deferred annuity** delays payments until the individual chooses to receive them.

A **hybrid annuity**, also called a combination annuity, combines features of both the fixed and variable annuity.

Financial calculators and spreadsheet programs will compute annuity calculations automatically. Manual calculations require a future value of annuity table that contains figures based on the interest rate and period in question. The basic formula is:

Amount invested × table value [interest, period] = future value

If, for example, a pension manager puts $1,000,000 at the end of every year into his company's pension fund, the fund earns 8% interest, and there are no withdrawals, at the end of five years it will be worth:

$1,000,000 × 5.867 [table value] = $5,867,000

Tricks of the Trade

- The formula assumes that payments are made at the end of a given period.
- If a stated interest rate is not an annual rate, it must be adjusted to reflect an annual rate.
- Although their yields are low, annuities are relatively safe investments that provide level streams of cash flows for fixed periods of time.
- In the United States, annuities are tax-deferred, but also often carry an early withdrawal penalty.
- If you are calculating manually, be sure to use the designated future value of an annuity table, and not the future value table; there is a significant difference.
- The mathematical expression for the numbers appearing on a future value of an annuity table is $[(1 + i)^n - 1]/i$; **i** is the interest rate, and ^{n} is the number of years in question.

For More Information

Web Site:
www.getobjects.com/Components/Finance/TVM/fva.html offers useful examples along with further explanation.

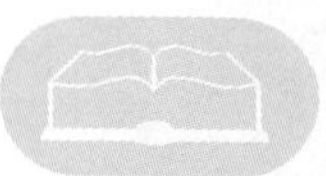

CALCULATING WORKING CAPITAL PRODUCTIVITY

WHAT IT MEASURES

How effectively a company's management is using its working capital.

WHY IT IS IMPORTANT

It is obvious that capital not being put to work properly is being wasted, which is certainly not in investors' best interests.

As an expression of how effectively a company spends its available funds compared with sales or turnover, the working capital productivity figure helps establish a clear relationship between its financial performance and process improvement. The relationship is said to have been first observed by the U.S. management consultant George Stalk while working in Japan.

A seldom-used reciprocal calculation, the working capital turnover or working capital to sales ratio, expresses the same relationship in a different way.

HOW IT WORKS IN PRACTICE

To calculate working capital productivity, first subtract current liabilities from current assets, which is the formula for working capital, then divide this figure into sales for the period.

Sales/(Current assets – Current liabilities) = Working capital productivity

If sales are $3,250, current assets are $900 and current liabilities are $650, then:

3250/(900 – 650) = 3250/250 = 13 working capital productivity

In this case, the higher the number the better. Sales growing faster than the resources required to generate them is a clear sign of efficiency and, by definition, productivity.

The working capital to sales ratio uses the same figures, but in reverse:

Working capital/Sales × 100% = Working capital to sales ratio

Using the same figures in the example above, this ratio would be calculated:

250/3250 = 0.077 × 100% = 7.7%

For this ratio, obviously, the lower the number the better.

TRICKS OF THE TRADE

- By itself, a single ratio means little; a series of them, several quarters' worth, for example, points to a direction over time, and means a great deal.
- Some experts recommend doing quarterly calculations and averaging them for a given year to arrive at the most reliable number.
- Either ratio also helps a management compare its performance with that of competitors.
- These ratios should also help motivate companies to improve processes, such as eliminating steps in the handling of materials and bill collection, and shortening product design times. Such improvements reduce costs and make working capital available for other tasks.

For More Information

Web Site:
www.bcg.com/publications/publications_splash.asp is a perspective on working capital and asset productivity.

CALCULATING RISK-ADJUSTED RETURN

WHAT IT MEASURES

How much an investment returned in relation to the risk that was assumed to attain it.

WHY IT IS IMPORTANT

Being able to compare a high-risk, potentially high-return investment with a low-risk, lower-return investment helps answer a key question that confronts every investor: is it worth the risk?

By itself, the historical average return of an investment, asset, or portfolio can be quite misleading and a faulty indicator of future performance. Risk-adjusted return is a much better barometer.

The calculation also helps reveal whether the returns of the portfolio reflect smart investment decisions, or the assumptions of excess risk that may or may not have been worth what was gained. This is particularly helpful in appraising the performance of money managers.

HOW IT WORKS IN PRACTICE

There are several ways to calculate risk-adjusted return. Each has its strengths and shortcomings. All require particular data, such as an investment's rate of return, the risk-free return rate for a given period (usually the performance of a 90-day U.S. Treasury bill over 36 months), and a market's performance and its standard deviation.

Which one to use? It often depends on an investor's focus, principally whether the focus is on upside gains or downside losses.

Perhaps the most widely used is the **Sharpe ratio**. This measures the potential impact of return volatility on expected return and the amount of return earned per unit of risk. The higher a fund's Sharpe ratio, the better its historical risk-adjusted performance, and the higher the number the greater the return per unit of risk. The formula is:

(Portfolio return – Risk-free return) /Std. deviation of portfolio return = Sharpe ratio

Take, for example, two investments, one returning 54%, the other 26%. At first glance, the higher figure clearly looks like the better choice, but because of its high volatility it has a Sharpe ratio of 0.279, while the investment with a lower return has a ratio of 0.910. On a risk-adjusted basis the latter would be the wiser choice.

Meanwhile, the **Treynor ratio** also measures the excess of return per unit of risk. Its formula is:

(Portfolio return – Risk-free return) /Portfolio's beta = Treynor ratio

In this formula (and others that follow), beta is a separately calculated figure that describes the tendency of an investment to respond to marketplace swings. The higher beta the greater the volatility, and vice versa.

A third formula, **Jensen's measure**, is often used to rate a money manager's performance against a market index, and whether or not a investment's risk was worth its reward. The formula is:

(Portfolio return – Risk-free return) – Portfolio beta × (Benchmark return – Risk-free return) = Jensen's measure

Tricks of the Trade

- A fourth formula, the **Sortino ratio**, also exists. Its focus is more on downside risk than potential opportunity, and its calculation is more complex.
- There are no benchmarks for these values. In order to be useful the numbers should be compared with the ratios of other investments.
- No single measure is perfect, so experts recommend using them broadly. For instance, if a particular investment class is on a roll and does not experience a great deal of volatility, a return per unit of risk does not necessarily reflect management genius. When the overall momentum of technology stocks drove returns straight up in 1999, Sharpe ratios climbed with them, and did not reflect any of the sector's volatility that was to erupt in late 2000.
- Most of these measures can be used to rank the risk-adjusted performance of individual stocks, various portfolios over the same time, and mutual funds with similar objectives.

For More Information

Web Sites:

www.captive.com presents a detailed discussion of risk-adjusted return and lists the formulas used to calculate it.

www.cpadvantage.com discusses the Sharpe ratio and related concepts.

www.finportfolio.com has definitions and detailed information.

www.sortino.com presents a lengthy and technical discussion of the Sortino ratio.

Calculating Economic Value Added

What It Measures

A company's financial performance, specifically whether it is earning more or less than the total cost of the capital supporting it.

Why It Is Important

Economic Value Added measures true economic profit, or the amount by which the earnings of a project, an operation, or a corporation exceed (or fall short of) the total amount of capital that was originally invested by the company's owners.

If a company is earning more it is adding value, and that is good. If it is earning less the company is in fact devouring value, and that is bad, because the company's owners (shareholders, for example) would be better off investing their capital elsewhere.

The concept's champions declare that EVA forces managers to focus on true wealth creation and maximizing shareholder investment. By definition, then, increasing EVA will increase a company's market value.

How It Works in Practice

EVA is conceptually simple and easy to explain: from net operating profit, subtract an appropriate charge for the opportunity cost of all capital invested in an enterprise—the amount that could have been invested elsewhere. It is calculated using this formula:

Net operating profit less applicable taxes – Cost of capital = EVA

If a company is considering building a new plant, and its total weighted cost over 10 years is $80 million, while the expected annual incremental return on the new operation is $10 million, or $100 million over 10 years, then the plant's EVA would be positive, in this case $20 million:

$100 million – $80 million = $20 million

An alternative but more complex formula for EVA is:

(% Return on invested capital – % Cost of capital) × Original capital invested = EVA

Tricks of the Trade

- EVA is a measure of dollar surplus value, not the percentage difference in returns.
- Purists define EVA as "profit the way shareholders define it." They further contend that if shareholders expect a 10% return on their investment, they "make money" only when their share of after-tax operating profits exceeds 10% of equity capital.
- An objective of EVA is to determine which business units best utilize their assets to generate returns and maximize shareholder value; it can be used to assess a company, a business unit, a single plant, office, or even an assembly line. This same technique is equally helpful in evaluating new business opportunities.

For More Information

Web Sites:

www.sternstewart.com is the web site of Stern Stewart & Co., now regarded as the leading authority on EVA. Additional information about EVA and related concepts is available at **www.evanomics.com**

See also:

☆ **Why EVA Is the Best Measurement Tool for Creating Shareholder Value (pp. 131–32)**

Calculating Exchange Rate Risk

What It Measures

The risk of a gain or loss in the value of a business activity or investment that results from changes in the exchange rates of world currencies.

Why It Is Important

Exchange rates can be highly volatile and this clearly poses risks to any enterprise conducting business in foreign markets, and any investor holding either stock in a foreign-based company, or an interest in a mutual fund that invests in foreign companies. The effects on a firm's earnings, cash flow, and balance sheet can be significant.

The main exchange rate risk to an operation or investment is that any profits realized will be partially reduced—or wiped out altogether—when they are exchanged for the domestic currency, be it U.S. dollars, U.K. pounds, the Euro, or Japanese yen.

More often, exchange rate risk will affect a company's price competitiveness in a product or service also offered by a competitor whose costs are incurred in a foreign currency. If the competitor's currency weakens, its relative competitive position improves because its costs decline, enabling the competitor to reduce its price and attract a larger share of a market.

How It Works in Practice

There is a simple way to avoid the risk posed by exchange rates: don't do business abroad! A second defense against exchange rate risks is almost as unrealistic: conduct all business in your home currency. Requiring foreign customers to pay up only in, say, dollars, puts the burden of currency fluctuations squarely on the customer's shoulders and completely insulates the selling firm from any shrinkage of profits from exchange rate differences. The price for such insulation, however, is likely to be a steady loss of customers.

The practical course of action, then, is to gain a basic understanding of exchange rate risks, if only enough to sort out the reams of opinions on the subject, and to select knowledgeable advisors and use their counsel wisely. Exchange rates, interest rates, and inflation rates have been linked to one another via a classic set of relationships that can serve as leading indicators of changes in risk. These relationships are:

- The **Purchasing Power Parity** theory (PPP). While it can be expressed differently, the most common expression links the changes in exchange rates to those in relative price indices in two countries:

  Rate of change of exchange rate = Difference in inflation rates

- The **International Fisher Effect** (IFE). This holds that an interest-rate differential will exist only if the exchange rate is expected to change in such a way that the advantage of the higher interest rate is offset by the loss on the foreign exchange transactions. Practically speaking, the IFE implies that while an investor in a low-interest country can convert funds into the currency of a high-interest country and earn a higher rate, the gain (the interest rate differential) will be offset by the expected loss due to foreign exchange rate changes. The relationship is stated as:

  Expected rate of change of the exchange rate = Interest-rate differential

- The **Unbiased Forward Rate Theory**. This holds that the forward exchange rate is the best and unbiased estimate of the expected future spot exchange rate.

  Expected exchange rate = Forward exchange rate

Other than these yardsticks, defending against exchange rate risk is largely a matter of observation. In the floating exchange rate environment that has existed for nearly the past 30 years, currency exchange rates respond to a host of factors: political climates, the flow of imports and exports, the flow of capital, inflation rates in various countries, consumer expectations, and confidence levels, to name a few. Frequently, limits are placed on exchange rate fluctuations by government policies—actions that themselves can arouse controversy or debate.

Even so, the exchange rate risks these factors create can be arranged into three primary categories:

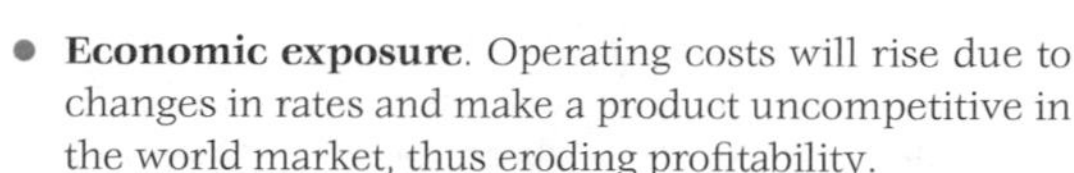

- **Economic exposure**. Operating costs will rise due to changes in rates and make a product uncompetitive in the world market, thus eroding profitability.
- **Translation exposure** The impact of currency exchange rates will reduce a company's earnings and weaken its balance sheet. In turn, the denominations of assets and liabilities are important, although many experts contend that currency fluctuations have no significant impact on real assets.
- **Transaction exposure**. There will be an unfavorable move in a specific currency between the time when a contract is agreed and the time it is completed, or between the time when a lending or borrowing is initiated and the time the funds are repaid. This is the most common problem that confronts most companies. Requiring payment in advance is rarely practical, and impossible, of course, for borrowing and lending.

To reduce translation exposure, experienced corporate fund managers use a range of techniques known as currency hedging, which amounts to diversifying currency holdings, monitoring exchange rates, and acting accordingly, depending upon specific conditions. Its advocates contend that taking appropriate action can greatly reduce translation risks, if not avoid them altogether. Currency hedging, however, is also technical and sophisticated.

Transaction exposure can be eased by a process known as factoring. Major exporters, in particular, transfer title to their foreign accounts receivable to a third party factor ing house that assumes responsibility for collections, administrative services, and any other services requested. The fee for this service is a percentage of the value of the receivables, anywhere from 5% to 10% or higher, depending on the currencies involved. Companies often include this percentage in selling prices to recoup the cost.

Commercial and country risks can affect exchange rates, too. Commercial risks include the default or bankruptcy of major foreign customers. While this risk mirrors what can also occur at home, foreign-based firms operate under different laws and relationships with their governments. More worrisome are country risks: political or military interventions and currency restrictions that less stable nations might impose. Insurance is available to address such risks, but it can be costly.

Tricks of the Trade

- Any number of models has been created to explain and forecast exchange rates. None has proved definitive, largely because the world's economies and financial markets are evolving so rapidly.
- A forward transaction is an agreement to buy one currency and sell another on a date some time beyond two business days. It allows an exchange rate on a given day to be locked in for a future payment or receipt, thereby eliminating exchange rate risk.
- Foreign exchange options are contracts which, for a fee, guarantee a worst-case exchange rate for the future purchase of one currency for another. Unlike a forward transaction, the option does not obligate the buyer to deliver a currency on the settlement date unless the buyer chooses to. These options protect against unfavorable currency movements while allowing retention of the ability to participate in favorable movements.
- A producer facing pricing competition caused by fluctuations in exchange rates can also use currency contracts to try to match competitors' cost structures and reduce costs.
- Firms doing larger volumes of business in a foreign country often establish a local office there to pay expenses and collect revenues in local currencies to reduce the impact of sudden and pronounced exchange rate fluctuations.
- Private-sector subscription services monitor currencies and publish alerts. One U.S.-based service has established numerical ranges that indicate risk, starting from 100 (no risk) to 200 (extreme risk or an outright currency crisis).
- The U.S. Export-Import Bank (Eximbank) may be a source of advice for companies, especially smaller and medium-sized firms, seeking assistance.

For More Information

Web Site:
www.stern.nyu.edu/ ~ igiddy/fxrisk.htm is a lengthy but well-written analysis that urges companies to engage in currency management.

Calculating Total Returns

What It Measures

The total percentage change in the value of an investment over a specified time period, including capital gains, dividends, and the investment's appreciation or depreciation.

Why It Is Important

Total return furnishes fundamental information that every investor seeks sooner or later: all things considered, just how much did my investment return?

That in itself makes total return rather important. In addition, there are several sound reasons for paying close attention to each of its components. For those who invest to maximize income, dividends will be very important. For those who invest for long-term growth, capital appreciation will be equally important.

Knowing how much of an investment's total return is attributable to each of the components can help in assessing how volatile the fund is likely to be, how tax-efficient it is, and how much steady income it can be expected to produce.

How It Works in Practice

The total return formula reflects all the ways in which an investment may earn or lose money: dividends as income, capital gains distributions, and capital appreciation—the increase or decrease in the investment's net asset value, or simply NAV:

(Dividends + Capital gains distributions +/- Change in NAV) /Beginning NAV = Total return × 100%

If, for instance, you buy a stock with an initial NAV of $40, and after one year it pays an income dividend of $2 per share and a capital gains distribution of $1, and its NAV has increased to $42, then the stock's total return would be:

(2 + 1 + 2) /40 =
5 /40 = 0.125 × 100% = 12.5%

Tricks of the Trade

- The total return time frame is usually one year, and it assumes that dividends have been reinvested.
- If a fund's capital gains exceed its capital losses for the year, most of the net gain must be distributed to shareholders as a capital gains distribution.
- Total return measures past performance only; it cannot predict future results.
- Total return generally does not take into account any sales charges that an investor paid to invest in a fund, or taxes they might owe on the income dividends and capital gains distributions received.
- Rules of the U.S. Securities & Exchange Commission require a company to show a comparison of the total return on its common stock for the last five fiscal years with the total returns of a broad market index and a more narrowly focused industry or group index.
- Total return can be a key yardstick in selecting funds once an investor has set objectives and a time horizon, and made decisions about risk and reward.

For More Information

Web Site:
www.fool.com presents a definition, and links to related concepts.

Calculating Price/Earnings Ratio (P/E)

What It Measures

The price/earnings ratio (P/E) is simply the share price divided by earnings per share (EPS). While EPS is an actual amount of money, usually expressed in cents per share, the P/E ratio has no units, it is just a number. Thus if a quoted company has a share price of $100 and EPS of $12 for the last published year, then it has a historical P/E of 8.3. If analysts are forecasting for the next year EPS of, say, $14 then the forecast P/E is 7.1.

Why It Is Important

Since EPS is the annual earnings per share of a company, it follows that dividing the share price by EPS tells us how many years of current EPS are represented by the share price. In the above example then, the P/E of 8.3 tells us that investors at the current price are prepared to pay 8.3 years of historical EPS for the share, or 7.1 years of the forecast next year's EPS. Theoretically the faster a company is expected to grow, the higher the P/E ratio that investors would award it. It is one measure of how cheap or expensive a share appears.

How It Works in Practice

The P/E ratio is predominantly useful in comparisons with other shares rather than in isolation. For example, if the average P/E in the market is 20, there will be many shares with P/Es well above and well below this, for a variety of reasons. Similarly, in a particular sector, the P/Es will frequently vary quite widely from the sector average, even though the constituent companies may all be engaged in broadly similar businesses. The reason is that even two businesses doing the same thing will not always be doing it as profitably as each other. One may be far more efficient, as demonstrated by a history of rising EPS compared with the flat EPS picture of the other over a series of years, and the market might recognize this by awarding the more profitable share a higher P/E.

Tricks of the Trade

- Take care. The market frequently gets it wrong and many high P/E shares have in the past been the most awful long-term investments, losing investors huge amounts of money when the promise of future rapid growth proved to be a chimera. In contrast many low P/E companies, often in what are perceived as dull industries, have proved over time to be outstanding investments.
- The P/E then is an investment tool that is both invaluable, and yet requires extreme caution in its application, when comparing and selecting investments. It remains though by far the most commonly utilized ratio in investment analysis.

For More Information

Web Site:
The Motley Fool: **www.fool.com**

See also:
✔ **Reading the Financial Pages (pp. 875–77)**
✔ **Calculating Yield (p. 864)**

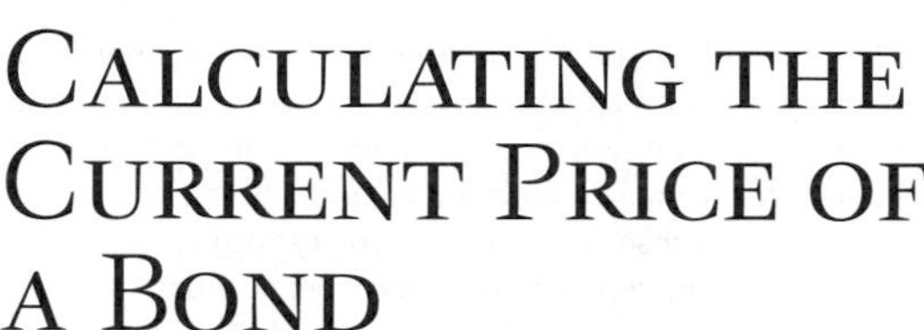

Calculating the Current Price of a Bond

What It Measures

The narrow range within which a given bond price falls, based on that bond's current asking price and bid price.

Why It Is Important

Current prices of comparable bonds are strong indicators of a bond's buying or selling price. Changes in bond prices are also indicators of economic strength and direction.

How It Works in Practice

The price of a bond depends on several factors:

- interest rates: as rates rise, a bond's price falls, because it pays less interest than current offerings and is thus less attractive. Conversely, a bond becomes more attractive as interest rates fall.
- the risk perceived for the issuing entity, reflected in its credit rating from one of the major rating agencies. The price of a bond of a company in bankruptcy, for instance, will be low because the company may never be able to redeem it. The price of a bond from a strong company may include a premium over its face or "par value" because it is considered a reliable investment: a bond with a face value of $1,000 might sell for $1,050, indicating a $50 premium.
- the issuing of new bonds by corporations or other bodies (and the ratings they receive) affects the prices of existing bonds.

Daily bond tables vary in format, but list the basic information necessary for comparing prices. Only a small fraction of the outstanding bonds trade on any given day, but these representative prices provide sufficient information to estimate what a fair price would be for the bonds being considered.

When considering bonds, several pieces of information are essential:

- the bond's coupon rate: what it will pay in interest
- how long before the principal amount of the bond matures, or if there is a call date
- its recent price and current yield.

Essentially, all the tables provide this basic information. The U.S. Treasury table, for example, would be listed as follows:

Rate	Maturity	Bid	Ask	Chg	Yld
$7^{3/4}$	Feb. 03	105:12	105:14	?	5.50
$5^{3/8}$	Feb. 03	99:26	99:27	?	5.44

In the first row, the security is paying its bondholders $7^{3/4}$% interest and is due to mature in February 2003. Prices in the bid and ask columns are percentages of the bond's face value of $1,000. A bid of 105:12 means that a buyer was willing to pay $1053.75, compared to the seller's lowest asking price, 105:14, or $1054.38, a difference of 63 cents per thousand.

Bond quotes follow certain conventions. Prices are given as percentages of face value, but the digits appearing after the colons are not decimals, being expressed in terms of 1/32. So 12/32nds, for example, would equal $3.75, which is appended to the 105 before the colon.

The bid and ask prices indicate that an investor who bought the bond at par when it was first issued can make a profit of more than 5% if it were sold now. The last column gives the yield to maturity, an interest rate summarizing the bond's overall investment value.

Common Mistakes

- A bond's yield and its price are not the same. Price is what is paid for a bond; yield expresses the percentage return on the investment. Yield is most useful for comparing fixed income investments for planning purposes, rather than as an exact measure of the return expected from an investment.
- The number of bond issues outstanding at any given time is far greater than stocks, and most bondholders buy with the intent of holding them until maturity, so the amount of trading is limited.
- There are several bond-rating agencies. A bond's rating indicates its level of risk.
- Listing tables also show the volume traded along with the current yield.
- The Internet offers many calculators for quickly determining bond prices and yields.

For More Information

Web Site:

www.investinginbonds.com offers an excellent and well-written explanation, with examples, of several different kinds of bonds.

See also:

✓ **Calculating Amortization (pp. 869–70)**

Calculating Asset Utilization

What It Measures

How efficiently an organization uses its resources and, in turn, the effectiveness of the organization's managers.

Why It Is Important

The success of any enterprise is tied to its ability to manage and leverage its assets. Hefty sales and profits

  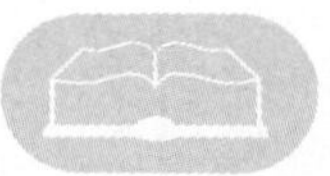    

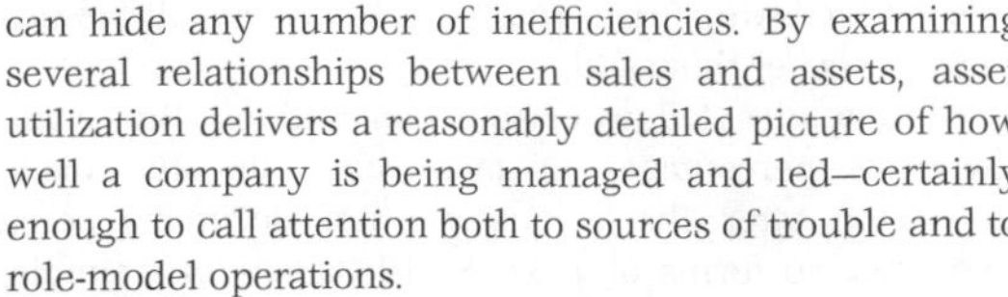

can hide any number of inefficiencies. By examining several relationships between sales and assets, asset utilization delivers a reasonably detailed picture of how well a company is being managed and led—certainly enough to call attention both to sources of trouble and to role-model operations.

Moreover, since all the figures used in this analysis are taken from a company's balance sheet or profit and loss statement, the ratios that result can be used to compare a company's performance with individual competitors and with industries as a whole.

Many companies also use this measure not only to evaluate their aggregate success but also to determine compensation for managers.

How It Works in Practice

Asset utilization relies on a family of asset utilization ratios, also called activity ratios. The individual ratios in the family can vary, depending on the practitioner. They include measures that also stand alone, such as accounts receivable turnover and asset turnover. The most commonly used sets of asset utilization ratios include these and the following measures.

Average collection period is also known as days sales outstanding. It links accounts receivable with daily sales and is expressed in number of days; the lower the number, the better the performance. Its formula is:

Accounts receivable/Average daily sales = Average collection period

For example, if accounts receivable are $280,000, and average daily sales are 7,000, then:

280,000/7,000 = 40

Inventory turnover compares the cost of goods sold (COGS) with inventory; for this measure, expressed in "turns," the higher the number the better. Its formula is:

Cost of goods sold /Inventory

For example, if COGS is $2 million, and inventory at the end of the period is $500,000, then

2,000,000/500,000 = 4

Some asset utilization repertoires include ratios like debtor days, while others study the relationships listed below.

Depreciation/Assets measures the percentage of assets being depreciated away to gauge how quickly product plants are aging and assets are being consumed.

Depreciation /Sales measures the percentage of sales that is tied up covering the wear and tear of the physical plant.

In either instance, a high percentage could be cause for concern.

Income/Assets measures how well management uses its assets to generate net income. It is the same formula as return on assets.

Income/Plant measures how effectively a company uses its investment in fixed assets to generate net income.

In these two instances, high numbers are desirable.

Plant/Assets expresses the percentage of total assets that is tied up in land, buildings, and equipment.

By themselves, of course, the individual numbers are meaningless. Their values lie in how they compare with the corresponding numbers of competitors and industry averages. A company with an inventory turnover of 4 in an industry whose average is 7, for example, surely has room for improvement, because the comparison indicates it is generating fewer sales per unit of inventory and is therefore less efficient than its rivals.

Tricks of the Trade

- Asset utilization is particularly useful to companies considering expansion or capital investment: if production can be increased by improving the efficiency of existing resources, there is no need to spend the sums expansion would cost.
- Like all families of ratios, no single number or comparison is necessarily cause for alarm or rejoicing. Asset utilization proves most beneficial over an extended period of time.
- Studying all measures at once can devour a lot of time, although computers have trimmed hours into seconds. Managements in smaller organizations may conduct asset utilization on a continuing basis, tracking particular measures monthly to stay abreast of operating trends.

For More Information

Web Sites:

www.powerinvestor.com lists several asset utilization ratios, with examples.

www.indiainfoline.com gives a lengthy analysis, including diagrams and two lesser-known financial formulae.

www.users.penn.com features analysis and links, and also explores other measures that can be used to appraise asset utilization.

See also:

✔ **Calculating Accounts Receivable Turnover (pp. 846–47)**
✔ **Calculating Asset Turnover (p. 822)**

Calculating Accounts Receivable Turnover

What It Measures

The number of times in each accounting period, typically a year, that a firm converts credit sales into cash.

  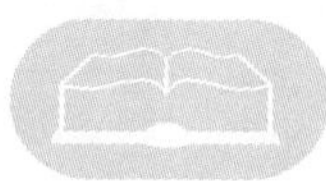    

WHY IT IS IMPORTANT

A high turnover figure is desirable, because it indicates that a company collects revenues effectively, and that its customers pay bills promptly. A high figure also suggests that a firm's credit and collection policies are sound.

In addition, the measurement is a reasonably good indicator of cash flow, and of overall operating efficiency.

HOW IT WORKS IN PRACTICE

The formula for accounts receivable turnover is straightforward. Simply divide the average amount of receivables into annual credit sales:

Sales/Receivables = Receivables turnover

If, for example, a company's sales are $4.5 million and its average receivables are $375,000, its receivables turnover is:

4,500,000/375,000 = 12

TRICKS OF THE TRADE

- It is important to use the average amount of receivables over the period considered. Otherwise, receivables could be misleading for a company whose products are seasonal or are sold at irregular intervals.
- The measurement is also helpful to a company that is designing or revising credit terms.
- Accounts receivable turnover is among the measures that comprise asset utilization ratios, also called activity ratios.

For More Information

Web Site:

www.xrefer.com offers a definition and links to related Web sites.

See also:

✔ **Calculating Asset Utilization (pp. 845–46)**

CALCULATING CAPITAL ASSET PRICING MODEL

WHAT IT MEASURES

The relationship between the risk and expected return of a security or stock portfolio.

WHY IT IS IMPORTANT

The capital asset pricing model's importance is twofold.

First, it serves as a model for pricing the risk in all securities, and thus helps investors evaluate and measure portfolio risk and the returns they can anticipate for taking such risks.

Secondly, the theory behind the formula also has fueled—some might say provoked—spirited analysis among economists about the nature of investment risk itself. The CAPM model attempts to describe how the market values investments with expected returns.

The CAPM theory classifies risk as being either diversifiable, which can be avoided by sound investing, or systematic, that is, not diversified and unavoidable due to the nature of the market itself. The theory contends that investors are rewarded only for assuming systematic risk, because they can mitigate diversifiable risk by building a portfolio of both risky stocks and sound ones.

One analysis has characterized the CAPM as "a theory of equilibrium" that links higher expected returns in strong markets with the greater risk of suffering heavy losses in weak markets. Otherwise, no one would invest in high-risk stocks.

HOW IT WORKS IN PRACTICE

CAPM holds that the expected return of a security or a portfolio equals the rate on a risk-free security plus a risk premium. If this expected return does not meet or beat a theoretical required return, the investment should not be undertaken. The formula used to create CAPM is:

Risk-free rate + (Market return – Risk-free rate) × Beta value = Expected return

The risk-free rate is the quoted rate on an asset that has virtually no risk. In practice, it is the rate quoted for 90-day U.S. Treasury bills. The market return is the percentage return expected of the overall market, typically a published index such as Standard & Poor's. The beta value is a figure that measures the volatility of a security or portfolio of securities, compared with the market as a whole. A beta of 1, for example, indicates that a security's price will move with the market. A beta greater than 1 indicates higher volatility, while a beta less than 1 indicates less volatility.

Say, for instance, that the current risk-free rate is 4%, and the S&P 500 index is expected to return 11% next year. An investment club is interested in determining next year's return for XYZ Software, Inc., a prospective investment. The club has determined that the company's beta value is 1.8. The overall stock market always has a beta of 1, so XYZ Software's beta of 1.8 signals that it is a more risky investment than the overall market represents. This added risk means that the club should expect a higher rate of return than the 11% for the S&P 500. The CAPM calculation, then, would be:

4% + (11% – 4%) × 1.8 = 16.6% Expected Return

What the results tell the club is that given the risk, XYZ Software, Inc. has a required rate of return of 16.6%, or the minimum return that an investment in XYZ should generate. If the investment club doesn't think that XYZ will produce that kind of return, it should probably consider investing in a different company.

TRICKS OF THE TRADE

- As experts warn, CAPM is only a simple calculation built on historical data of market and stock prices.

"First get in, then get rich, then get respectable."

(Bernie Eccleston)

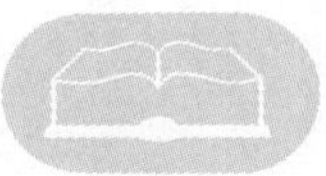

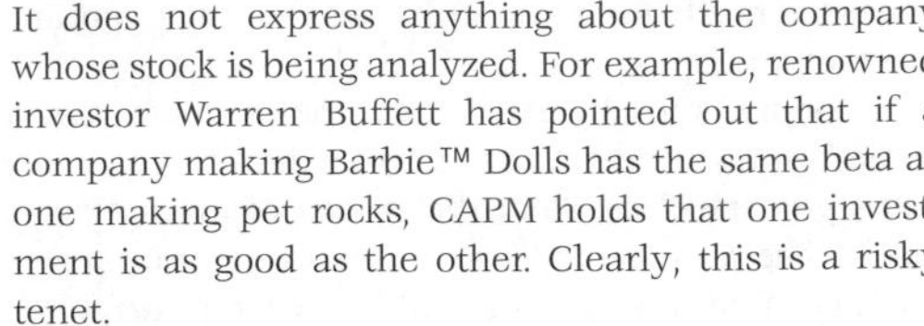
It does not express anything about the company whose stock is being analyzed. For example, renowned investor Warren Buffett has pointed out that if a company making Barbie™ Dolls has the same beta as one making pet rocks, CAPM holds that one investment is as good as the other. Clearly, this is a risky tenet.

- While high returns might be received from stocks with high beta shares, there is no guarantee that their respective CAPM return will be realized (a reason why beta is defined as a "measure of risk" rather than an "indication of high return").
- The beta parameter itself is historical data and may not reflect future results. The data for beta values is typically gathered over several years and experts recommend that only long-term investors should rely on the CAPM formula.
- Over longer periods of time, high beta shares tend to be the worst performers during market declines.

For More Information

Web Sites:
www.xrefer.com and
www.contingencyanalysis.com have analysis, definitions, and links to additional references.

See also:
✔ **Calculating the Alpha and Beta Values of a Security (pp. 838–39)**

Calculating Current Ratio

What It Measures

A company's liquidity and its ability to meet its short-term debt obligations.

Why It Is Important

By comparing a company's current assets with its current liabilities, the current ratio reflects its ability to pay its upcoming bills in the unlikely event of all creditors demanding payment at once. It has long been the measurement of choice among financial institutions and lenders.

How It Works in Practice

The current ratio formula is simply:

Current assets/Current liabilities = Current ratio

Current assets are the ones that a company can turn into cash within 12 months during the ordinary course of business. Current liabilities are bills due to be paid within the coming 12 months.

For example, if a company's current assets are $300,000 and its current liabilities are $200,000, its current ratio would be:

300,000/200,000 = 1.5

As a rule of thumb, the 1.5 figure means that a company should be able to get hold of $1.50 for every $1.00 it owes.

Tricks of the Trade

- The higher the ratio, the more liquid the company. Prospective lenders expect a positive current ratio, often of at least 1.5. However, too high a ratio is cause for alarm too, because it indicates declining receivables and/or inventory—signs that portend declining liquidity.
- A current ratio of less than 1 suggests pressing liquidity problems, specifically an inability to generate sufficient cash to meet upcoming demands.
- Managements use current ratio as well as lenders; a low ratio, for example, may indicate the need to refinance a portion of short-term debt with long-term debt to improve a company's liquidity.
- Ratios vary by industry, however, and should be used accordingly. Some sectors, such as supermarket chains and restaurants, perform nicely with low ratios that would keep others awake at night.
- One shortcoming of the current ratio is that it does not differentiate assets, some of which may not be easily converted to cash. As a result, lenders also refer to the quick ratio.
- Another shortcoming of the current ratio is that it reflects conditions at a single point in time, such as when the balance sheet is prepared. It is possible to make this figure look good for this occasion alone and, therefore, lenders should not appraise these conditions by the ratio alone.
- A constant current ratio and falling quick ratio signal trouble ahead, because this suggests that a company is amassing assets at the expense of receivables and cash.

For More Information

Web Site:
www.toolkit.cch.com
discusses current ratio in detail, and offers examples and useful tips.

Calculating Reserve Ratio

What It Measures

In the United Kingdom and in certain European countries, there is no compulsory ratio, although banks will

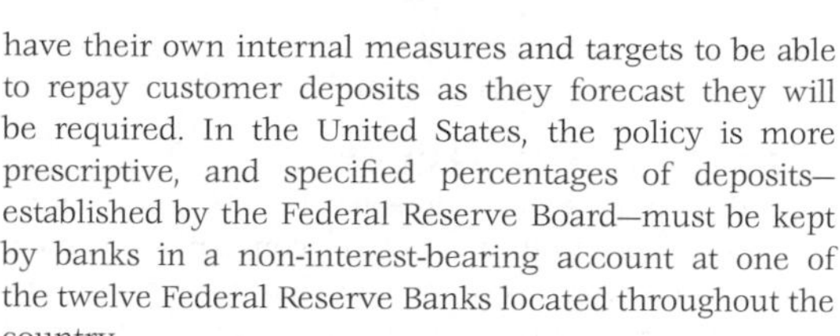

have their own internal measures and targets to be able to repay customer deposits as they forecast they will be required. In the United States, the policy is more prescriptive, and specified percentages of deposits—established by the Federal Reserve Board—must be kept by banks in a non-interest-bearing account at one of the twelve Federal Reserve Banks located throughout the country.

Why It Is Important

To provide stability. In view of the volume and unpredictability of transactions that clear through their accounts every day, banks and financial depositories must maintain a cushion of funds to protect themselves against debits that could leave their accounts overdrawn at the end of the day, and thus subject to penalty.

As a result of the creation of reserve ratios, periods of financial stress are no longer characterized by runs on banks by depositors.

How It Works in Practice

In Europe, the reserve requirement of an institution is calculated by multiplying the reserve ratio for each category of items in the reserve base, set by the European Central Bank, with the amount of those items in the institution's balance sheets. These figures vary according to the institution.

The required reserve ratio in the United States is set by federal law, and depends on the amount of checkable deposits a bank holds. The first $44.3 million of deposits are subject to a 3% reserve requirement. Deposits in excess of $44.3 million are subject to 10% reserve requirement. These breakpoints are reviewed annually in accordance with money supply growth. No reserves are required against certificates of deposit or savings accounts.

The reserve ratio requirement limits a bank's lending to a certain fraction of its demand deposits. The current rule allows a bank to issue loans in an amount equal to 90% of such deposits, holding 10% in reserve. The reserves can be held in any combination of vault cash and deposit at a Federal Reserve Bank.

A bank facing a reserve deficiency has several options. It can try to borrow reserves for one or more days from another bank, sell marketable assets such as government securities, or bid for funds in the money market, such as large CDs or Eurodollars. As a last resort, it can pledge collateral and borrow at the Federal Reserve's discount window.

In order to meet deposit withdrawal contingencies, many banks maintain a margin of excess reserves above the required reserve ratio, since the required reserves are really not available to meet withdrawal liquidity needs. Excess reserves are higher than those needed to meet reserve and clearing requirements, and provide extra protection against overdrafts and deficiencies in required reserves.

Tricks of the Trade

- Because reserves earn no interest, they have an adverse effect on bank earnings.
- In practice, the required reserve ratio has been adjusted only infrequently by the U.S. Federal Reserve Board.
- U.S. depository institutions hold required reserves in one of two forms: vault cash on hand at the bank or—more significant for monetary policy—required reserve balances in accounts with the Reserve Bank for their respective Federal Reserve District.

For More Information

Web Site:
www.furman.edu/~stanford/mbnote6b.htm discusses a rationale for a "desired" reserve ratio in the absence of central banking authorities.

Calculating Capitalization Ratios

What They Measure

By comparing debt to total capitalization, these ratios reflect the extent to which a corporation is trading on its equity, and the degree to which it finances operations with debt.

While not the focus here, capitalization ratio also refers to the percentage of a company's total capitalization contributed by debt, preferred stock, common stock and other equity.

Why They Are Important

By itself, any financial ratio is a rather useless piece of information. Collectively, and in context, though, financial leverage ratios present analysts and investors with an excellent picture of a company's situation, how much financial risk it has taken on, its dependence on debt, and developing trends. Knowing who controls a company's capital tells one who truly controls the enterprise!

How They Work in Practice

A business finances its assets with either equity or debt. Financing with debt involves risk, since debt legally obligates a firm to pay off the debt, plus the interest the debt incurs. Equity financing, on the other hand, does not obligate the firm to pay anything. It is apt to pay investors dividends—but at the discretion of the board of directors. To be sure, business risk accompanies the operation of any enterprise. But how that enterprise opts to finance its operations—how it blends debt with equity—may heighten this risk.

Various experts include numerous formulas among capitalization financial leverage ratios. Three are discussed separately: debt-to-capital ratio, debt-to-equity ratio, and interest cover ratios. What's known as the capitalization ratio per se can be expressed in two ways:

= Long-term Debt /Long-term Debt + Owners' Equity

and

= Total Debt /Total Debt + Preferred + Common Equity

For example, a company whose long-term debt totals 5,000 and whose owners hold equity worth 3,000 would have a capitalization ratio of:

= 5,000 /5,000 + 3,000 =
= 5,000 /8,000 = 0.625 capitalization ratio

Both expressions of the capitalization ratio are also referred to "component percentages," since they compare a firm's debt with either its total capital (debt plus equity) or its equity capital. They readily indicate how reliant a firm is on debt financing.

Tricks of the Trade

- Capitalization ratios need to be evaluated over time, and compared with other data and standards. A gross profit margin of 20%, for instance, is meaningless—until one knows that the average profit margin for an industry is 10%; at that point, 20% looks quite attractive. Moreover, if that the historical trend of that margin has been climbing for the last three years, it strong suggests that a company's management has sound and effective policies and strategies in place.
- All capitalization ratios also should be interpreted in the context of a company's earnings and cash flow, and those of its competitors.
- Take care in comparing companies in different industries or sectors. Figures that appear to be low in one industry can be very high in another.
- Some less frequently used capitalization ratios are based on formulas that use the book value of equity (the stock). When compared with other ratios, they can be misleading, because there usually is little relation between a company's book value and its market value—which is apt to be many times higher, since market value reflects what the investment community thinks the company is worth.

For More Information

Web Site:
www.sba.muohio.edu/kehrjb/RATIOS981.doc
concisely lists a series of financial leverage ratios, along with dozens of other commonly used financial ratios.

Calculating Acid-test Ratio

What It Measures

How quickly a company's assets can be turned into cash, which is why assessment of a company's liquidity also is known as the quick ratio, or simply the acid ratio.

Why It Is Important

Regardless of how this ratio is labeled, it is considered a highly reliable indicator of a company's financial strength and its ability to meet its short-term obligations. Because inventory can sometimes be difficult to liquidate, the acid-test ratio deducts inventory from current assets before they are compared with current liabilities—which is what distinguishes it from the current ratio.

Potential creditors like to use the acid-test ratio because it reveals how a company would fare if it had to pay off its bills under the worst possible conditions. Indeed, the assumption behind the acid-test ratio is that creditors are howling at the door demanding immediate payment, and that an enterprise has no time to sell off its inventory, or any of its stock.

How It Works in Practice

The acid-test ratio's formula can be expressed in two ways, but both essentially reach the same conclusion. The most common expression is:

(Current assets – Inventory)/Current liabilities = Acid-test ratio

If, for example, current assets total $7,700, inventory amounts to $1,200 and current liabilities total $4,500, then:

(7,700 – 1,200)/4,500 = 1.44

A variation of this formula ignores inventories altogether, distinguishes assets as cash, receivables, and short-term investments, then divides the sum of the three by the total current liabilities, or:

Cash + Accounts receivable + Short-term investments/Current liabilities = Acid-test ratio

If, for example, cash totals $2,000, receivables total $3,000, short-term investments total $1,000, and liabilities total $4,800, then:

(2,000 + 3,000 + 1,000)/4,800 = 1.25

There are two other ways to appraise liquidity, although neither is as commonly used: the cash ratio is the sum of cash and marketable securities divided by current liabilities; net quick assets is determined by adding cash, accounts receivable, and marketable securities, then subtracting current liabilities from that sum.

Tricks of the Trade

- In general, the quick ratio should be 1:1 or better. It means a company has a unit's worth of easily convertible assets for each unit of its current liabilities. A high quick ratio usually reflects a sound, well-managed organization in no danger of imminent collapse, even in the extreme and unlikely event that its sales ceased immediately. On the other hand, companies with ratios of less than 1 could not pay their current liabilities, and should be looked at with extreme care.
- While a ratio of 1:1 is generally acceptable to most creditors, acceptable quick ratios vary by industry, as

do almost all financial ratios. No ratio, in fact, is especially meaningful without knowledge of the business from which it originates. For example, a declining quick ratio with a stable current ratio may indicate that a company has built up too much inventory; but it could also suggest that the company has greatly improved its collection system.

- Some experts regard the acid-test ratio as an extreme version of the working capital ratio because it uses only cash and equivalents, and excludes inventories. An acid-test ratio that is notably lower than the working capital ratio often means that inventories make up a large proportion of current assets. An example would be retail stores.
- Comparing quick ratios over an extended period of time can signal developing trends in a company. While modest declines in the quick ratio do not automatically spell trouble, uncovering the reasons for changes can help find ways to nip potential problems in the bud.
- Like the current ratio, the quick ratio is a snapshot, and a company can manipulate its figures to make it look robust at a given point in time.
- Investors who suddenly become keenly interested in a firm's quick ratio may signal their anticipation of a downturn in the firm's business or in the general economy.

For More Information

Web Site:

www.toolkit.cch.com/text/P06_7145.asp offers a concise but solid definition, tips, examples, and links.

Calculating Convertible Preferred Stock

Getting Started

- Evaluating convertible preferred stock is principally an analysis of risk rather than of a company.
- Preferred stocks are listed as equity on a balance sheet, but perform more like bonds than common stock, since most of these issues pay a fixed dividend set at the time of issue.
- While holders of preferred stock are entitled to a fixed dividend, they do not usually have voting rights.
- Preferred stocks are usually repayable at par value, and rank above the claims of ordinary shareholders but behind bank and trade creditors.
- An expensive form of capitalization, preferred stock is typically used to finance growth opportunities and capital expenditures, and to repay bank debt and non-bank short-term debt.
- Preferred stocks are often preferred by venture capitalists because they protect their investments better, and offer them greater leverage and growth opportunities.
- U.S. income tax considerations severely limit the appeal of preferred stock among individual investors, but enhance it among corporations.

FAQs

1. Officially, what is convertible preferred stock?

It is a share of corporation ownership that give holders a claim prior to the claim of common stockholders on earnings and, generally, on assets in the event of liquidation. It may also be exchanged for a fixed number of shares of common stock. Because no maturity date is stipulated, preferred stock is priced based on a stated dividend yield—in, for example, dollars, pounds or marks—or as a percentage of par value.

2. How does preferred stock compare to common stock?

The dividend on common stock is uncertain and variable: high when a company performs well, low or non-existent when it fares poorly. Holders of preferred stock, however, get a fixed dividend—and one which, if not paid, accrues until it can be. On the other hand, preferred stockholders are not usually able to vote on pertinent resolutions unless dividends fall into arrears, while holders of common stock have voting rights based on the number of shares owned.

3. Are there different kinds of preferred stock?

Yes. For example, callable preferred stock may be repurchased by the issuing company, typically at par value or slightly higher, while an indirect convertible may be exchanged for another convertible security, such as a bond that can be exchanged for convertible preferred stock. There are also participating preferred stocks, which entitle holders both to receive specified dividends and to participate along with holders of common stock in receiving additional dividends.

4. Any other important distinguishing features of preferred stock?

First, there may be an option to receive cash for those who decline to exercise their conversion rights. Most preferred stocks also carry lower interest rates than similar fixed-interest securities, since the investor has the opportunity to convert his holdings to common stock and, in turn, to realize a capital gain if its price rises above its conversion price. Some preferred stocks also permit the investor to require the issuing company to redeem the shares after a predetermined time for an amount that gives the investor a modest profit.

5. Venture capitalists are known to prefer preferred stock. Why?

It gives them preference in the event of a company's liquidation or sale. A typical convertible preferred stock also enables venture capitalist investors to convert their shares into common stock at a predetermined formula and to vote the preferred stocks on major shareholder issues such as the election of directors and a change of the company's core business activity.

6. How are repeated conversions of preferred stock prevented from diluting the value of common stock?

The formula used to convert the convertible preferred stock into shares of common stock typically includes an adjustment mechanism—an "anti-dilution provision"—that protects the investor against any dilution in his percentage ownership caused by sales of cheaper stock to later investors. The nature and extent of the protection afforded also can be very important to the holders of the company's common stock: the greater the protection against dilution given to the holder of convertible preferred stock, the more dilution common stockholders are likely to suffer.

Making It Happen

Like virtually any stock consideration, evaluating convertible preferred stock opportunities and transactions is based on research, market knowledge, and past experience.

It is essential firstly to understand what a company does and how it generates cash. The next question is determining the likelihood of the company being able to pay its preferred dividends. The tools of choice are, first, a common "coverage ratio" like EBIT or EBITDA and, second, preferred stock ratings.

EBITDA is the acronym for "earnings before interest, taxes, depreciation, and amortization." It usually measures a company's ability to handle debt service (interest payments), but can easily be adapted to include preferred stock dividends. The ratio is:

EBITDA/Interest expense + Preferred dividends

The higher the coverage ratio, the better.

Like corporate bonds, most preferred stocks are rated by such services as Standard & Poor's and Moody's. Each rating service uses a slightly different rating system, but they have a similar basis: "A" is good, "AAA" is better, and so on. A "B" or above is considered investment grade, but anything below that is regarded as very high risk.

Another warning point is that if a preferred stock is rated only by one of the second-tier rating agencies, the likelihood is that the company's management was unable to get a favorable rating from Standard & Poor's or Moody's. The investor relations offices and Web sites of most corporations will provide the ratings. If they do not, beware—although the Web sites of the rating services themselves will probably list them.

There are also some guidelines to follow. For instance, preferred stocks should have a higher yield than the issuing company's comparable debt (yield is the annual dividend divided by the price). This must be gauged on a case-by-case basis.

There is another long-held contention that higher-quality firms issue standard convertible preferred stock, while lower-quality firms issue convertible exchangeable preferred stock. Similarly, it is maintained that only the "best" firms are consistently able to issue straight debt cost-effectively, while medium-quality firms issue convertible securities, and lower-quality firms or high-risk firms tend to issue additional common stock.

Conversion ratios and prices are other key facts to know about preferred stock. This information is found on the indenture statement that accompanies all issues. Occasionally the indenture will state that the conversion ratio will change over time. For example, the conversion price might be $50 for the first five years, $55 for the next five years, and so forth. Stock splits can affect conversion considerations.

In theory, convertible preferred stocks (and convertible exchangeable preferred stocks) are usually perpetual in time. However, issuers tend to force conversion or induce voluntary conversion for convertible preferred stock within 10 years. Steadily increasing common stock dividends is one inducement tactic used. As a result, the conversion feature for preferred stocks often resembles that of debt securities. Call protection for the investor is usually about 3 years, and a 30- to 60-day call notice is typical.

About 50% of convertible equity issues also have a "soft call provision." If the common stock price reaches a specified ratio, the issuer is permitted to force conversion before the end of the normal protection period.

Converting preferred stock risks diluting common stock, of course, and among mature companies that is a valid concern. Where a company has a good track record and aggressive growth plans, however, it may benefit both investors and the company, especially if the management can maintain (or increase) profit margin.

Tricks of the Trade

- In any country, tax considerations invariably accompany exercising convertible preferred stock transactions. Here are considerations based on U.S. laws:
- Like common stock, preferred stock comes with a prospectus that should answer such basic questions as: Are the dividends cumulative? Are the shares redeemable; if so, when? What is the likelihood of redemption? Has the board of directors ever suspended dividends? (If it has, this is a bad sign indicating cash flow problems.)
- At least in the U.S., many companies dislike issuing preferred stock because it is an expensive form of capitalization. Preferred stock pays dividends from after-tax profits, while bonds pay interest from pre-tax dollars, thus delivering a tax break that preferred stock cannot match.
- Owning preferred stocks of other companies is another matter, however: corporations are exempt from taxes on up to 80% of preferred dividend income.
- Missing preferred stock dividends is not legally a default, but a company that omits a preferred stock dividend may not pay common stock dividends. Moreover, if subsequent preferred stock dividends are missed, preferred stock shareholders may gain board seats (or more of them), and in some cases also accrue special voting rights.
- Most preferred issues are cumulative, so dividends accrue even if they are not actually paid in a given quarter. Once the dividends are resumed, and before

common dividends can be paid, cumulative preferred shareholders must be paid their accrued dividends.

- If a company is liquidated, holders of preferred stock are entitled to receive their investment back before the holders of any common stock receive anything. In other words, "investment" means the amount paid for the preferred plus any accrued and unpaid dividends—an important consideration.

Preferred stocks and other convertible securities offer investors a hedge: fixed-interest income without sacrificing the chance to participate in a company's capital appreciation.

When a company does well, investors can convert their holdings into common stock that is more valuable. When a company is less successful, they can still receive interest and principal payments, and also recover their investment and preserve their capital if a more favorable investment appears.

For More Information

Web Site:
www.e-analytics.com presents thorough but very readable descriptions and analyses of preferred stock issues and considerations.

CREATING A BALANCE SHEET

WHAT IT MEASURES

The financial standing, or even the net worth or owners' equity, of a company at a given point in time, typically at the end of a calendar or fiscal year.

WHY IT IS IMPORTANT

The balance sheet shows what is owned (assets), what is owed (liabilities), and what is left (owners' equity). It provides a concise snapshot of a company's financial position.

HOW IT WORKS IN PRACTICE

However they are presented, assets must be in balance with liabilities and shareholders' equity. In other words, assets must equal liabilities and owners' equity.

Assets include cash in hand and cash anticipated (receivables), inventories of supplies and materials, properties, facilities, equipment, and whatever else the company uses to conduct business. Assets also need to reflect depreciation in the value of equipment such as machinery that has a limited expected useful life.

Liabilities include pending payments to suppliers and creditors, outstanding current and long-term debts, taxes, interest payments, and other unpaid expenses that the company has incurred.

Subtracting the value of aggregate liabilities from the value of aggregate assets reveals the value of owners' equity. Ideally, it should be positive. Owners' equity consists of capital invested by owners over the years and profits (net income) or internally generated capital, which is referred to as "retained earnings"; these are funds to be used in future operations.

As an example:

ASSETS $	
Current:	
Cash	8,200
Securities	5,000
Receivables	4,500
Inventory & supplies	6,300
Fixed:	
Land	10,000
Structures	90,000
Equipment (less depreciation)	5,000
Intangibles/other	
TOTAL ASSETS	**129,000**

LIABILITIES $	
Payables	7,000
Taxes	4,000
Misc.	3,000
Bonds & notes	25,000
TOTAL LIABILITIES	**39,000**
SHAREHOLDERS' EQUITY (stock, par value × shares outstanding)	80,000
RETAINED EARNINGS	10,000
TOTAL LIABILITIES AND SHAREHOLDERS' EQUITY	129,000

TRICKS OF THE TRADE

- The balance sheet does not show a company's market worth, nor important intangibles such as the knowledge and talents of individual people, nor other vital business factors such as customers or market share.
- The balance sheet does not express the true value of some fixed assets. A six-year-old manufacturing plant, for example, is listed at its original cost, even though the price of replacing it could be much higher or substantially lower (because of new technology that might be less expensive or vastly more efficient).
- The balance sheet is not an indicator of past or future performance or trends that affect performance. It needs to be studied along with two other key reports: the income statement and the cash flow statement. A published balance sheet needs to include prior period comparatives.

For More Information

Web Site:
www.conetic.com offers definitions and samples of balance sheets, along with other software programs.

Creating a Profit and Loss Account

What It Measures

A company's sales revenues and expenses over a period, providing a calculation of profits or losses during that time.

Why It Is Important

Reading a P&L is the easiest way to tell if a business has made a profit or a loss during a given month or year. The most important figure it contains is net profit: what is left over after revenues are used to pay expenses and taxes.

Companies typically issue P&L reports monthly. It is customary for the reports to include year-to-date figures, as well as corresponding year-earlier figures to allow for comparisons and analysis.

How It Works in Practice

A P&L adheres to a simple rule of thumb: "revenue minus cost equals profit."

There are two P&L formats, multiple-step and single-step. Both follow a standard set of rules known as Generally Accepted Accounting Principles (GAAP). These rules generally adhere to requirements established by governments to track receipts, expenses, and profits for tax purposes. They also allow the financial reports of two different companies to be compared. Note that in the United Kingdom and several other nations, sales, revenues, and receipts may all be designated as turnover.

MULTIPLE-STEP PROFIT & LOSS ACCOUNT ($)			
NET SALES			750,000
Less: cost of goods sold			450,000
Gross profit			300,000
LESS: OPERATING EXPENSES			
Selling expenses			
Salaries & commissions	54,000		
Advertising	37,500		
Delivery/transportation	12,000		
Depreciation/store equipment	7,500		
Other selling expenses	5,000		
Total selling expenses		116,000	
General & administrative expenses			
Administrative/office salaries	74,000		
Utilities	2,500		
Depreciation/structure	2,400		
Misc. other expenses	3,100		
Total general & admin expenses		82,000	
Total operating expenses			198,000
OPERATING INCOME			102,000
LESS (ADD): NONOPERATING ITEMS			
Interest expenses	11,000		
Interest income earned	(2,800)		8,200
Income before taxes			93,800
Income taxes			32,360
Net Income			**61,440**

The multiple-step format is much more common, because it includes a larger number of details and is thus more useful. It deducts costs from revenues in a series of steps, allowing for closer analysis. Revenues appear first, then expenses, each in as much detail as management desires. Sales may be broken down by product line or location, while expenses such as salaries may be broken down into base salaries and commissions.

Expenses are then subtracted from revenues to show profit (or loss). A basic multiple-step P&L is shown in column 1.

P&Ls of public companies may also report income on the basis of earnings per share. For example, if the company issuing this statement had 12,000 shares outstanding, earnings per share would be $5.12, that is, $61,440 divided by 12,000 shares.

Tricks of the Trade

- A P&L does not show how a business earned or spent its money.
- One month's P&L can be misleading, especially if a business generates a majority of its receipts in particular months. A retail establishment, for example, usually generates a large percentage of its sales in the final three months of the year, while a consulting service might generate the lion's share of its revenues in as few as two months, and no revenues at all in some other months.
- Invariably, figures for both revenues and expenses reflect the judgments of the companies reporting them. Accounting methods can be quite arbitrary when it comes to such factors as depreciation expenses.

For More Information

Web Sites:

www.bized.ac.uk provides explanations of individual entries and a worksheet for practice exercises.

www.askltd.com/askjava/WatPandL.html provides additions, definitions, and sample exercises.

Creating a Cash Flow Statement

What It Measures

Cash inflows and cash outflows over a specific period of time, typically a year.

Why It Is Important

Cash flow is a key indicator of financial health, and

it demonstrates to investors, creditors, and other core constituencies a company's ability to meet obligations, finance opportunities, and generally "come up with the cash" as needs arise. Cash flow that is wildly inconsistent with, say, net income, often indicates operating or managerial problems.

How It Works in Practice

In its basic form, a cash flow statement will probably be familiar to anyone who has been a member of a club that collected and spent money. It reports funds on hand at the beginning of a given period, funds received, funds spent, and funds remaining at the end of the period.

That formula still applies to a business today, even if creating a cash flow document is significantly more complex. Cash flows are divided into three categories: cash from operations, cash-investment activities, and cash-financing activities. Companies with holdings in foreign currencies use a fourth classification: effects of changes in currency rates on cash.

A standard direct cash flow statement looks like this:

CRD, Inc.

Statement of Cash Flows

For year ended December 31, 20__

CASH FLOWS FROM OPERATIONS $	
Operating Profit	82,000
Adjustments to net earnings	
Depreciation	17,000
Accounts receivable	(20,000)
Accounts payable	12,000
Inventory	(8,000)
Other adjustments to earnings	4,000
Net cash flow from operations	**87,000**

CASH FLOWS FROM INVESTMENT ACTIVITIES	
Purchases of marketable securities	(58,000)
Receipts from sales of marketable securities	45,000
Loans made to borrowers	(16,000)
Collections on loans	11,000
Purchases of plant and real estate assets	(150,000)
Receipts from sales of plant and real estate assets	47,000
Net cash flow from investment activities:	**(121,000)**

CASH FLOWS FROM FINANCING ACTIVITIES	
Proceeds from short-term borrowings	51,000
Payments to settle short-term debts	(61,000)
Proceeds from issuing bonds payable	100,000
Proceeds from issuing capital stock	80,000
Dividends paid	(64,000)
Net cash flow from financing activities	**106,000**
Net change in cash during period	72,000
Cash and cash equivalents, beginning of year	27,000
Cash and cash equivalents, end of year	**99,000**

Tricks of the Trade

- A cash flow statement does *not* measure net income, nor does it measure working capital.
- A cash flow statement does not include outstanding accounts receivable, but it does include the preceding year's accounts receivable (assuming these were collected during the year for which the statement is prepared).
- Add to a cash inflow any amounts charged off for depreciation, depletion, and amortization, since cash was actually spent.
- Cash equivalents are short-term, highly liquid investments, although precise definitions may vary slightly by country. These should be included when recalculating the movement of cash in the period
- There are alternative ways to present cash flow from operations. Some texts, for example, omit earnings and adjustments, and list instead cash and interest received, cash and interest paid, and taxes received.

For More Information

Web Site:

"Moneychimp," **www.datachimp.com**, offers a cash flow sample, plus a glossary of financial and investment terms.

Reading a Balance Sheet

Getting Started

A balance sheet will tell us something about the financial strength of a business on the day that it is drawn up. That situation changes constantly, so you could say it is more like a snapshot than a movie. Although the method of producing a balance sheet is standardized, there can be a certain element of subjectivity in interpreting it. Different elements of the balance sheet can tell you different things about the how the business is doing.

This actionlist gives an overview of a balance sheet and looks at a brief selection of the more interesting figures that help with interpretation. It's important to remember that a lot of these figures do not tell you that much in isolation, it is in trend analysis or comparisons between businesses that they speak more lucidly.

FAQs

What is a balance sheet?

A balance sheet is an accountant's view, the book value of the assets and liabilities of a business at a specific date and on that date alone. The term "balance" means exactly what it says—that those assets and liabilities will be equal. In showing how the balance lies, the balance sheet gives us an idea of the financial health of the business.

What does a balance sheet not do?

A balance sheet is not designed to represent market value of the business. For example, property in the balance

  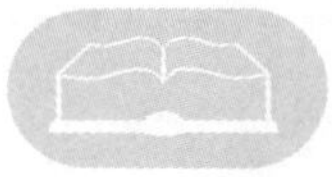  

sheet may be worth a lot more than its book value. Plant and machinery is shown at cost less depreciation, but that may well be different from market value. Stock may turn out to be worth less than its balance-sheet value, and so on.

Also there may be hidden assets, such as goodwill or valuable brands, that do not appear on the balance sheet at all. These would all enhance the value of the business in a sale situation, yet are invisible on a normal balance sheet.

Making It Happen

Here is a very simple company balance sheet:

Fixed Assets		1,000
Current Assets	700	
Less Current Liabilities	400	
Net Current Assets		300
		1,300
Less Long-Term Loans		200
Net Assets		1,100
Profit and Loss Account		500
Share Capital		600
Shareholders' Funds		1,100

Defining the Individual Elements

- *Fixed Assets*—items that are not traded as part of a company's normal activities but enable it to function, such as property, machinery or vehicles. These are tangible assets (meaning you can kick them). This heading can also include intangible assets (you cannot kick them). A common example is "goodwill," which can arise upon the acquisition of one business by another.
- *Current Assets*—items that form the trading cycle of the business. The most common examples are stock, debtors, and positive bank balances.
- *Current Liabilities*—also items that form the trading cycle of the business but represent short-term amounts owed to others. Examples will be trade creditors, taxes, and bank overdrafts—broadly, any amount due for payment within the next 12 months from the date of the balance sheet.
- *Net Current Assets*—not a new figure, but simply the difference between current assets and current liabilities, often shown because it may be a useful piece of information.
- *Long-Term Loans*—debt that is repayable more than one year from the date of the balance sheet.
- *Net Assets*—also not a new figure, but the sum of fixed assets plus net current assets less long-term loans. In other words, all of the company assets shown in its books, minus all of its liabilities.
- *Profit and Loss Account*—the total of all the accumulated profits and losses from all the accounting periods since the business started. It increases or decreases each year by the net profit or loss in that period, calculated after providing for all costs including tax and dividends to shareholders.
- *Share Capital*—the number of shares issued, multiplied by their nominal value. The latter is the theoretical figure at which the shares were originally issued and has nothing to do with their market value.
- *Shareholders' Funds*—not a new figure, but the sum of the profit and loss account plus the share capital. It represents the total interest of the shareholders in the company.

How to Interpret Them

Note that balance sheets differ between one industry and another in the sense of the range and type of assets and liabilities that exist. For example, a retailer will have little in the way of trade debtors because it sells for cash, or a manufacturer is likely to have a far larger investment in plant than a service business like an advertising agency. So the interpretation must be seen in the light of the actual trade of the business.

Reading a balance sheet can be quite subjective—accountancy is an art, not a science and, although the method of producing a balance sheet is standardized, there may be some items in it that are subjective rather than factual. The way people interpret some of the figures will also vary, depending what they wish to achieve and how they see certain things as being good or bad.

Look First at the Net Assets/Shareholders' Funds

Positive or negative? Our example, being a healthy business, has net assets of a positive $1,100. Positive is good. If there were 600 shares in issue, it would mean that the net assets per share are $1.83.

If it had negative assets (same thing as net liabilities), this might mean that the business is heading for difficulty unless it is being supported by some party such as a parent company, bank, or other investor. When reading a balance sheet with negative assets, consider where the support will be coming from.

Then Examine Net Current Assets

Positive or negative? Again, our example has net current assets of a positive $300. This means that, theoretically, it should not have any trouble settling short-term liabilities because it has more than enough current assets to do so. Negative net current assets suggest that there possibly could be a problem in settling short-term liabilities.

You can also look at NCA as a ratio of current assets/current liabilities. Here, a figure over one is equivalent to the NCA having a positive absolute figure. The ratio version is more useful in analyzing trends of balance sheets over successive periods or comparing two businesses.

A cut-down version of looking at NCA considers only (debtors + cash)/(creditors) thus excluding stock. The reasoning here is that this looks at the most liquid of the net current asset constituents and again a figure over one is the most desirable. Also a ratio that is more meaningful in trends or comparisons.

The Significance of Trade Debtor Payments. . .

Within current assets, we have trade debtors. It can be useful to consider how many days' worth of sales are tied up in debtors—given by (debtors × 365)/annual sales. This provides an idea of how long the company is waiting to get paid. Too long, and it might be something requiring

investigation. However, this figure can be misleading if sales do not take place evenly throughout the year. A construction company might be an example of such a business: one big debtor incurred near the year end would skew the ratio.

...AND TRADE CREDITOR PAYMENTS

Similar to the above, this looks at (trade creditors × 365)/ annual purchases, indicating how long the company is taking in general to pay its suppliers. This is not so easy to calculate because the purchases for this purpose include not only goods for resale but all the overheads as well.

DEBT

Important to most businesses, this figure is the total of long and short-term loans. Too much debt might indicate that the company would have trouble, in a downturn, in paying the interest. It is difficult to give an optimum level of debt because there are so many different situations, depending on a huge range of circumstances.

Often, instead of an absolute figure, debt is expressed as a percentage of shareholders' funds and known as "gearing" or "leverage." In a public company, gearing of 100% might be considered pretty high, whereas debt of under 30% may be seen as on the low side.

COMMON MISTAKES

BELIEVING THAT BALANCE SHEET FIGURES REPRESENT MARKET VALUE

It is completely incorrect to assume that a balance sheet is a valuation of the business. Its primary purpose is that it forms part of the range of accounting reports used for measuring business performance—along with the other common financial reports like profit and loss accounts and cash flow statements. Management, shareholders, and others such as banks will use the entire range to assess the health of the business.

FORGETTING THAT THE BALANCE SHEET IS VALID ONLY FOR THE DATE AT WHICH IT IS PRODUCED

A short while after a balance sheet is produced, things could be quite different. In practice there frequently may not be any radical changes between the date of the balance sheet and the date when it is being read, but it is entirely possible that something could have happened to the business that would not show. For example, a major debtor could have defaulted unexpectedly. So remember that balance sheet figures are valid only as at the date shown, and are not a permanent picture of the business.

CONFUSION OVER WHETHER IN FACT ALL ASSETS AND LIABILITIES ARE SHOWN IN THE BALANCE SHEET

Some businesses may have hidden assets, as suggested above. This could be the value of certain brands or trademarks, for example, for which money may not have ever been paid. Yet these could be worth a great deal. Conversely, there may be some substantial legal action pending which could cost the company a lot, yet is not shown fully in the balance sheet.

For More Information

See also:
✓ Reading a Cash Flow Statement (pp. 859–61)

READING A PROFIT AND LOSS ACCOUNT

GETTING STARTED

A profit and loss account is a statement of the income and expenditure of a business over the period stated, drawn up in order to ascertain how much profit the business made. Put simply, the difference between the income from sales and the associated expenditure is the profit or loss for the period. "Income" and "expenditure" here mean only those amounts directly attributable to earning the profit and thus would exclude capital expenditure, for example.

Importantly, the figures are adjusted to match the income and expenses to the time period in which they were incurred—not necessarily the same as that in which the cash changed hands.

FAQs

WHAT IS A PROFIT AND LOSS ACCOUNT?

A profit and loss account is an accountant's view of the figures that show how much profit or loss a business has made over a period. To do this, it is necessary to allocate the various elements of income and expenditure to the time period concerned, not on the basis of when cash was received or spent, but on when the income was earned or the liability to pay a supplier and employees was incurred. While capital expenditures are excluded, depreciation of property and equipment is included as a non-cash expense.

Thus if you sell goods on credit, you will be paid later but the sale takes place upon the contract to sell them. Equally if you buy goods and services on credit, the purchase takes place when you contract to buy them, not when you when you actually settle the invoice.

WHAT DOES A PROFIT AND LOSS ACCOUNT NOT SHOW?

Most importantly, a P&L account is not an explanation of the cash coming into and going out of a business.

MAKING IT HAPPEN

Here is a simple example of a profit and loss account for a particular year:

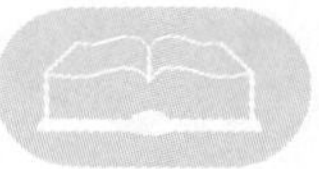

Sales		1,000
Opening Stock	100	
Purchases	520	
	620	
Closing Stock	80	
Cost of Sales		540
Gross Profit		460
Wages	120	
Other Overhead	230	
		350
Net Profit before Tax		110
Tax		22
Net after Tax		88
Dividends		40
Retained Profit		48
Retained Profit Brought Forward		150
Retained Profit Carried Forward		198

Note that the presence of stock and purchases indicates that the business is trading or manufacturing goods of some kind, rather than selling services.

Defining the Individual Elements

- *Sales*—the invoiced value of the sales in the period.
- *Stock*—the value of the actual physical stock held by the business at the opening and closing of the period. It is always valued at cost, or realizable value if that is lower, never at selling price.
- *Purchases and Other Direct Costs*—the goods or raw materials purchased by the business for resale—not capital items used in the business, only items used as part of the direct cost of its sales. In other words, those costs which vary directly with sales, as distinct from overhead (like rent) which do not.

When a business holds stock, the purchases figure has to be adjusted for the opening and closing values in order to reach the right income and expenditure amounts for that period only. Goods for resale bought in the period may not have been used purely for that period but may be lying in stock at the end of it, ready for sale in the next. Similarly, goods used for resale in this period will consist partly of items already held in stock at the beginning of it. So take the amounts purchased, add the opening stock and deduct the closing stock. The resulting adjusted purchase figure is known as "cost of sales."

In some businesses there may be other direct costs apart from purchases included in cost of sales. For example, a manufacturer may include some wages if they are of a direct nature (wages of employees directly involved in the manufacturing process, as distinct from office staff, say). Or a building contractor would include plant hire in direct costs, as well as purchases of materials.

- *Gross Profit*—the difference between sales and cost of sales. This is an important figure as it measures how much was actually made directly from whatever the business is selling, before it starts to pay for overhead.

The figure is often expressed as a percentage ratio, when it is known as the "gross profit margin." In our example the GPM is 460:1,000—or 46%. Ratios are really only useful as comparison tools, either with different periods of the same business or with other businesses.

- *Overhead*—the expenses of the business which do not vary directly with sales. They include a wide range of items such as rent, most wages, advertising, phones, interest paid on loans, audit fees and so on.
- *Net Profit before Tax*—the result of deducting total overhead from gross profit. This is what the business has made before tax is paid on that profit.
- *Tax*—this will not actually have been paid in the year concerned, but is shown because it is due on the profit for that period. Even then the figure shown may not be the actual amount due, for various reasons such as possible overpayments from previous years. Tax can be a very complex matter, being based upon a set of changeable rules.
- *Net Profit after Tax*—the result after deducting the tax liability—the so-called bottom line. This is the amount that the company can do with as it wishes, possibly paying a dividend out of part of it and retaining the rest. It is the company's reward for actually being in business in the first place.
- *Dividends*—a payment to the shareholders as a reward for their investment in the company. Most publicly listed companies of any size pay dividends to shareholders. Private companies may also do so, but this may be more for tax reasons. The dividend in the example shown is paid out of the net profit after tax, but legally it is not permitted to exceed the total available profit. That total available profit is made up of both the current year's net profit after tax and the retained profit brought forward from previous years.
- *Retained Profit*—the amount kept by the company after paying dividends to shareholders. If there is no dividend, then it is equal to the net profit after tax.
- *Retained Profit Brought Forward*—the total accumulated retained profits for all earlier years of the company's existence.
- *Retained Profit Carried Forward*—the above figure brought forward, plus the current year's retained profit. This new total will form the profit brought forward in the next accounting period.

How to Interpret the Figures

A lot of accounting analysis is valid only when comparing the figures, usually with similar figures for earlier periods, projected future figures, or other companies in the same business.

On its own a P&L account tells you only a limited story, though there are some stand-alone facts that can be derived from it. What our example does show, even in isolation, is that this business was successful in the period concerned. It made a profit, not a loss, and was able to pay dividends to shareholders out of that profit. Clearly a pretty crucial piece of information.

However, it is in comparisons that such figures start to have real meaning.

The example figures reveal that the gross profit margin was 46%, an important statistic in measuring business performance. The net profit margin before tax was 110:1,000, or 11%. You could take the margin idea further and calculate the net profit after tax ratio to sales as 88:1,000, being 8.8%. Or you could calculate the ratio of any expense to sales. In our example, the wages:sales ratio is 120:1,000—12%.

If you then looked at similar margin figures for the preceding accounting period, you would learn something about this business. Say the gross margin was 45% last year compared with 46% this year—there has been some improvement in the profit made before deducting overhead. But then suppose that the net profit margin of 8.8% this year was 9.8% last year. This would tell you that, despite improvement in profit at the gross level, the overhead has increased disproportionately. You could then check on the ratio of each item of the overhead to sales to see where this arose and find out why. Advertising spending could have shot up, for example, or perhaps the company moved to new premises incurring a higher rent. Maybe something could be tightened up.

Another Commonly Used Ratio

Another ratio often used in business analysis is return on capital employed. Here we combine the profit and loss account with the balance sheet by dividing the net profit (either before or after tax as required) by shareholders' funds. This tells you how much the company is making proportionate to money invested in it by the shareholders—a similar idea to how much you might get in interest on a bank deposit account. It's a useful way of comparing different companies in a particular industry, where the more efficient ones are likely to derive a higher return on capital employed.

Common Mistakes

Assuming That the Bottom Line Represents Cash Profit from Trading

It does not! There are a few examples where this is the case: a simple cash trader might buy something for one price, then sell it for more; his profit then equals the increase in cash. But a business that buys and sells on credit, spends money on items that are held for the longer term such as property or machinery, has tax to pay at a later date, and so on, will make a profit that is not represented by a mere increase in cash balances held. Indeed, the cash balance could quite easily decrease during a period when a profit was made.

For More Information

Web Site:
The Motley Fool: **www.fool.com**

See also:
✔ **Reading a Cash Flow Statement (pp. 859–61)**

Reading a Cash Flow Statement

Getting Started

In their annual report, most public companies must publish a cash flow statement—together with the profit and loss account and a balance sheet. As the name suggests, the purpose of a cash flow statement is to explain the movement in cash balances or bank overdrafts held by the business from one accounting period to the next.

The balance sheet shows the assets and liabilities at the end of the period, with comparative figures for the start of it. The profit and loss account shows how much profit was generated by the business in the period. The cash flow statement is the third part of the financial picture of the business over the period.

FAQs

What Is a Cash Flow Statement?

Over an accounting period, the money held by a business at the bank (or its overdrafts) will have changed. The purpose of the cash flow statement is to show the reasons for this change. If you look at the previous actionlist on profit and loss, one of the common mistakes illustrated was the erroneous belief that the profit was equal to the cash generated by a business. It is not, but the cash flow statement is the link between profit and cash balance movements. It takes you down the path from profit to cash. The figures are derived from those published in the annual accounts, and notes will explain how this derivation is arrived at.

What Does a Cash Flow Statement Not Show?

In the same way that a profit and loss account does not show the cash made by the business, a cash flow statement does not show the profit. It is entirely possible for a loss-making business to show an increase in cash, and the other way round too.

Making It Happen

Here is a simple example of a cash flow statement for a particular year:

Net Cash Inflow from Operating Activities		7,020
Returns on Investments and Finance Costs		
Interest Paid	820	
Less Interest Received	90	
Net Cash Outflow from Finance Costs		(730)
Taxation		(1,060)
Capital Expenditure		
Sale of Fixed Assets	760	
Less purchase of fixed assets	4,420	
Net Cash Outflow from Capital Expenditure		(3,660)
Dividends Paid		(1,530)
Net Cash Inflow before Financing		40
Financing		
New Loans	1,000	
Loan Repayments	(300)	
Finance Lease Repayments	(100)	
Net Cash Inflow from Financing		600
Increase in Cash		640

Defining the Individual Elements

- *Net Cash Inflow from Operating Activities*: broadly this is the profit of the business, before depreciation plus the change in debtor and creditor balances. There may also be other items included here. In the statutory

  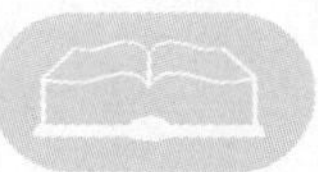    

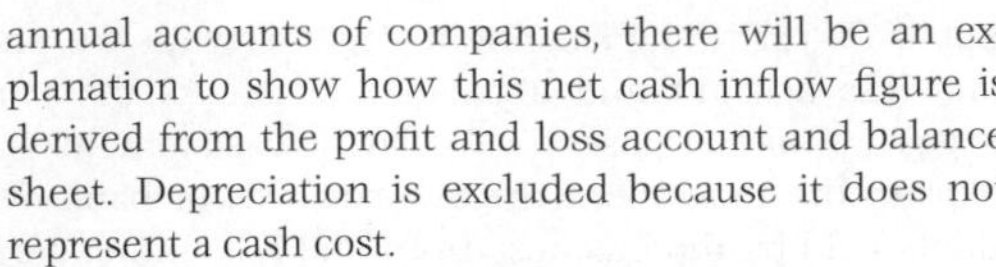

annual accounts of companies, there will be an explanation to show how this net cash inflow figure is derived from the profit and loss account and balance sheet. Depreciation is excluded because it does not represent a cash cost.

Debtor and creditor balance changes are included here because they represent an inflow or outflow of cash to the business. Thus if customers owe you less or more at the end of a period than at the beginning of it, it follows that there must have been cash flowing in or out of the business as a result. A reduction in debtors means that cash has come in to the business, and the reverse for an increase in debtors. The same applies to the creditor balances of suppliers. An increase here means a cash inflow, with a decrease denoting an outflow.

- *Returns on Investments and Finance Costs*: these figures comprise interest received on cash balances, less interest paid on debt. There could be other forms of investment income here, such as dividends on shares owned.
- *Net Cash Outflow from Finance Costs*: this is not a new figure but the net result of the above items, identified as returns on investments. In our example the result is an outflow of cash. That is, the interest paid on debt exceeded the interest received on cash. It could in some circumstances be the other way around, where for example a business has substantial cash balances earning interest.
- *Taxation*: self explanatory, this is the outflow of cash arising from corporation tax paid by the business. It can on occasion be an inflow, where the company has obtained a repayment of corporation tax for some reason.
- *Capital Expenditure*: this is cash expended on fixed assets bought for the business, less cash received from the sale of assets no longer required by the business.
- *Net Cash Outflow from Capital Expenditure*: this is not a new figure but the net result of the above items, identified as expenditure on new fixed assets less receipts from the sale of disposals of such items. In our example there is a large outflow, which generally would be the norm. It can happen sometimes though that a business realizes more from the sale of fixed assets in a particular period than it expends on items acquired.
- *Dividends Paid*: self explanatory, this is the outflow of cash arising from paying dividends to shareholders.
- *Net Cash Inflow before Financing*: this is not a new figure but a subtotal of the items above. In our example, the figure of $40 shown happens to be an inflow but it could just as easily have been an outflow. There is no typical figure here, it is just as common to see net inflows as outflows.

  It is important to understand what this figure represents. It is the net cash result of running the business in the period concerned, after paying tax to the government and dividends to the shareholders. However, as its label indicates, it doesn't include any financing.
- *Financing*: this term includes the raising of new loans, the repayment of old ones and other methods of financing such as issuing new shares. In the example the company borrowed $1,000 in new loans, which creates a cash inflow of that sum, and repaid 300 on old debt plus a further $100 on equipment leases (which are another form of finance), making a net inflow on finance of $400.
- *Increase in Cash* (the bottom line): adding the net inflow of $600 from finance to the $40 generated by business operations gives us an overall net cash inflow of $640. This is the bottom line. It means that we have $640 more in the bank at the end of the accounting period than at the beginning of it.

How to Interpret the Figures

As suggested above, the cash flow statement is the third section of the primary set of accounting documents used to explain and analyze businesses. It is a "derived schedule," meaning that the figures are pulled from the profit and loss account and balance sheet statements, linking the two.

Its purpose is to analyze the reasons why the company's cash position changed over an accounting period. For example, a sharp increase in borrowings could have several explanations–such as a high level of capital expenditure, poor trading, an increase in the time taken by debtors to pay, and so on. The cash flow statement will alert management to the reasons for this, in a way that may not be obvious merely from the profit and loss account and balance sheet alone.

The generally desirable situation is for the net position before financing to be positive. Even the best-run businesses will sometimes have an outflow in a period (for example in a year of high capital expenditure), but positive is usually good. This becomes more apparent when comparing the figures over a period of time. A repeated outflow of funds over several years is usually an indication of trouble. To cover this, the company must raise new financing and/or sell off assets which will tend to compound the problem, in the worst cases leading to failure.

Cash is critical to every single business, so it is important for the management to understand where its cash is coming from and going to. The cash flow statement gives us this information in an abbreviated form. You could argue that the whole purpose of a business is to start with one sum of money and, by applying some sort of process to it, arrive at another and higher sum, continually repeating this cycle.

Common Mistakes

Confusing "Cash" and "Profit"

As mentioned previously, the most common mistake with cash flow statements is the potential confusion between profit and cash. They are not the same!

Not Understanding the Terminology

It is clearly fundamental to an understanding of cash flow statements that the reader is familiar with terms like "debtors," "creditors," "dividends" and so on. But more than appreciating the meaning of the word "debtors," it is quite easy to misunderstand the concept that, for example, an increase in debtors is a cash outflow, and equally that an increase in creditors represents an inflow of cash to the business.

For More Information

Web Site:
The Motley Fool: **www.fool.com**

See also:

✔ **Reading a Profit and Loss Account (pp. 857–59)**
✔ **Reading a Balance Sheet (pp. 855–57)**

DEFINING ASSETS

WHAT THEY MEASURE

Collectively, the value of all the resources a company uses to conduct business and generate profits.

Examples of assets are cash, marketable securities, accounts and notes receivable, inventories of merchandise, real estate, machinery and office equipment, natural resources, and intangibles such as patents, legal claims and agreements, and negotiated rights.

WHY THEY ARE IMPORTANT

No business can continue for very long without knowing what assets it has at its disposal, and using them efficiently. Assets are a reflection of organizational strength, and are invariably evaluated by potential investors, banks and creditors, and other stakeholders.

Moreover, the value of assets is also a key figure used to calculate several financial ratios.

HOW THEY WORK IN PRACTICE

Assets are typically broken down into five different categories:

- Current assets include cash, cash equivalents, marketable securities, inventories, and prepaid expenses that are expected to be used within one year or a normal operating cycle. All cash items and inventories are reported at historical value. Securities are reported at market value.
- Noncurrent assets, or long-term investments, are resources that are expected to be held for more than one year. They are reported at the lower of cost and current market value, which means that their values will vary.
- Fixed assets include property, plants and facilities, and equipment used to conduct business. These items are reported at their original value, even though current values might well be much higher.
- Intangible assets include legal claims, patents, franchise rights, and accounts receivable. These values can be more difficult to determine. Accounts receivable, for example, reflect the amount a business expects to collect, such as, say, $9,000 of the $10,000 owed by customers.
- Deferred charges include prepaid costs and other expenditures that will produce future revenue or benefits.

TRICKS OF THE TRADE

- Assets do not necessarily include everything of value, such as the talents of individuals, an organization's collective expertise, or the value of a customer base.
- Classic definitions of assets also often exclude or undervalue trademarks, even though there is universal agreement that these, for example, the three-point star of Mercedes-Benz or Coca-Cola's red logo, can have enormous value.
- Fixed assets are valued at their original cost, because of the prevailing opinion that they are used for business and are not for sale. Moreover, current market value is essentially a matter of opinion.
- Determining the value of patents can be challenging, because a patent has a finite life span, its value declines each year, and its useful life may be even shorter.
- Some scholars contend that the principal assets of "knowledge-based" businesses such as consulting firms or real estate development companies are, in fact, its people. In turn, their aggregate value should be calculated by subtracting the net value of assets from market value.

For More Information

Web Sites:
www.investorwords.com presents concise and cross-referenced definitions of assets and related terms.
www.sveiby.com presents an intriguing analysis of intangible assets, prepared expressly for the era of the "knowledge-based" economy.

CALCULATING COST OF GOODS SOLD (COGS)

WHAT IT MEASURES

For a retailer, COGS is the cost of buying and acquiring the goods that it sells to its customers.

For a service firm, COGS is the cost of the employee services it supplies.

For a manufacturer, COGS is the cost of buying the raw materials and manufacturing its finished products.

WHY IT IS IMPORTANT

Cost of goods sold may help a company determine the prices to charge for its products and services, and the volume of business that it needs to maintain in order to operate profitably.

For retailers especially, the cost of the merchandise sold is typically the largest expense, and thus an abso-

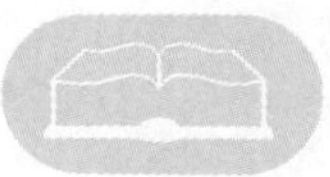

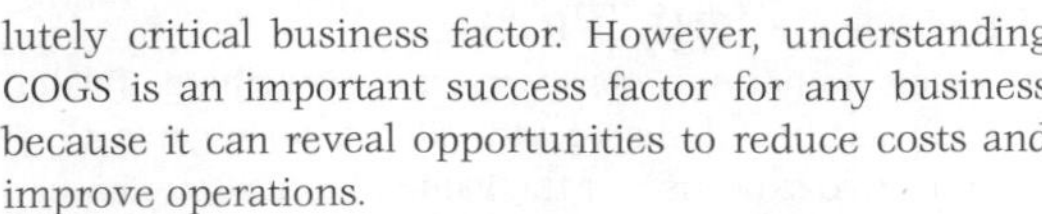

lutely critical business factor. However, understanding COGS is an important success factor for any business because it can reveal opportunities to reduce costs and improve operations.

COGS is also a key figure on an income statement (also called the profit and loss account), and an important consideration in computing income taxes because of its close relationship to inventories, which taxation authorities treat as future income.

How It Works in Practice

Essentially, COGS is equal to a company's opening stock of goods and services, plus the cost of goods bought and direct costs incurred during a particular period, minus the closing stock of goods and services.

A critical consideration is the accounting policy that a company adopts to calculate inventory values, especially if raw materials prices change during the year. This may happen often, particularly when inflation is high. Inventory values under a First In First Out (FIFO) policy reflect original or older prices of materials, while a Last In First Out (LIFO) policy reflects current (and often more expensive) prices. Somebody computing COGS first needs to know which policy is being used, because this will affect inventory values.

COGS for a manufacturer will include a variety of items, such as raw materials and energy used in production, labor, benefits for production workers, the cost of raw materials in inventory, shipping fees, the cost of storing finished products, depreciation on production machinery used, and factory overhead expenses.

For a retail company such as Wal-Mart, COGS is generally less complex: the total amount paid to suppliers for the products being sold on its shelves.

COGS is calculated as follows:

Because the counting of inventory is an exhaustive undertaking for retailers, doing it quarterly or monthly would be open to error. Accordingly, taxation authorities allow them to estimate cost of goods sold during the year.

Stocks at beginning of period	$20,000
Purchases during period	= $60,000
Cost of good available for sale	= $80,000
Less inventory at period end	– $15,000
Cost of goods sold (COGS)	= $65,000

Determining these estimates requires details of the gross profit margin (retailers typically use the preceding year's figure). This figure is then used to calculate the cost ratio:

Begin by assuming that net sales are 100%, then subtract the gross profit margin, say 40%, to produce a cost ratio of 60%: 100% – 40% = 60%. A monthly COGS calculation then looks like this:

Inventory at beginning of month	$10,000
Purchases during month	+ $25,000
Cost of goods available for sale	= $35,000
Less net sales during month	– $28,000
Cost ratio 100% – 40%	= 60%
Estimated cost of goods sold	= $16,800 ($28,000 x 60%)

There is one sample to review, because calculating COGS for manufacturers requires additional factors:

Inventory at beginning of year	$20,000
Purchases during year	+ $50,000
Cost of direct labor	+ $15,000
Materials and supplies	+ $12,000
Misc. costs	+ $3,000
Total product expenses	= $100,000
Less inventory at year-end	- $15,000
Cost of goods sold (COGS)	= $85,000

Tricks of the Trade

- Anyone who wants to determine COGS must maintain inventories and know their value!
- Because good returned affect inventory values and, in turn, cost of goods sold, returns of goods must be reflected in COGS calculations.
- Merchandising firms may use different inventory accounting systems, but the choice has no bearing on the actual costs incurred; it only affects allocation of costs.
- COGS should not include indirect costs, which may include factors like administration and marketing costs, and other activities that cannot be directly attributed to producing or acquiring the product.

For More Information

Web Sites:

www.bized.ac.uk presents a sample COGS worksheet, plus definitions and related theories.

www.tax.gov/operating_cogs is an uncluttered site that offers crisp, well-presented definitions, samples, and links to more references.

Calculating Working Capital

What It Measures

The funds that are readily available to operate a business. Working capital comprises the total net current assets of a business, which are its stocks, debtors, and cash—minus its creditors.

Why It Is Important

Obviously, it is vital for a company to have sufficient working capital to meet all of its requirements. The faster a business expands, the greater will be its working capital needs.

If current assets do not exceed current liabilities, a company may well run into trouble paying creditors who want their money quickly. Indeed, the leading cause of business failure is not lack of profitability, but rather lack of working capital, which helps explain why some experts advise: "use someone else's money every chance you get and don't let anyone else use yours."

How It Works in Practice

Working capital is also called net current assets or current capital, and is expressed as:

Current assets – current liabilities

Current assets are cash and assets that can be converted to cash within one year or a normal operating cycle; current liabilities are monies owed that are due within one year.

If a company's current assets total $300,000 and its current liabilities total $160,000, its working capital is:

$300,000 – $160,000 = $140,000

The working capital cycle describes capital (usually cash) as it moves through a company: It first flows from a company to pay for supplies, materials, finished goods inventory, and wages to workers who produce goods and services. It then flows into a company as goods and services are sold, and as new investment equity and loans are received. Each stage of this cycle consumes time. The more time the stages consume, the greater the demands on working capital.

Tricks of the Trade

- Good management of working capital includes actions like collecting receivables faster and moving inventory more quickly; generating more cash increases working capital.
- While it can be tempting to use cash to pay for fixed assets like computers or vehicles, doing so reduces the amount of cash available for working capital.
- If working capital is tight, consider other ways of financing capital investment, such as loans, fresh equity, or leasing.
- Early warning signs of insufficient working capital include: pressure on existing cash; exceptional cash-generating activities such as offering high discounts for early payment; increasing lines of credit; partial payments to suppliers and creditors; a preoccupation with surviving rather than managing; frequent short-term emergency requests to the bank, for example, to help pay wages, pending receipt of a check.
- Several ratios measure how effectively and efficiently working capital is being used. These ratios are explained separately.

For More Information

Web Sites:

www.planware.org/workcap.htm is dedicated to working capital issues, and includes calculations, spreadsheets, definitions, and software packages.

www.studyfinance.com was created for students of finance at the University of Arizona, but its wealth of financial information benefits and serves managers also.

Calculating Goodwill and Patents

What It Measures

The value of two intangible assets.

Why It Is Important

Since both goodwill and patents are intangible assets, their values will be whatever negotiators conclude. Still, their values need to be reflected in financial statements.

Goodwill is created in the aftermath of an acquisition, and must appear on a balance sheet. The acquisition of a patent has a cost of its own, be it the price of internal development costs or the purchase price paid to an inventor.

How It Works in Practice

Ultimately, the assigned values of both assets are matters of opinion, however learned the opinions may be. Each must be considered separately.

Ordinarily, goodwill is completely ignored by accountants. Only when a company has been acquired by another does goodwill become an intangible asset. It then appears on a balance sheet in the amount by which the price paid by the acquiring company exceeds the net tangible assets of the acquired company. In other words:

Purchase price – net assets = goodwill

If, for example, an airline is bought for $12 billion and its net assets are valued at $9 billion, $3 billion of the purchase would be allocated to goodwill on the balance sheet.

The buyer will attribute the difference to any number of reasons that give a competitive advantage, such as a loyal and long-standing customer base, a strong brand, strategic location, or productive employees.

A patent's value, meanwhile, will probably be the sum of its development costs, or its purchase price if acquired from someone else. It is usually to a company's advantage to spread the patent's value over several years. If so, the critical time period to consider is not the full life of the patent (17 years in the United States), but its estimated useful life.

For example, let's say that in January 2000 a U.S. company acquired a patent issued in January 1995 at a cost of $100,000. It concludes that the patent's useful commercial life is 10 years, not the 12 remaining before the patent expires. In turn, patent value would be $100,000, and it would be spread (or amortized in accounting terms) over 10 years, or $10,000 each year.

Tricks of the Trade

- Accounting for goodwill can vary by country, an issue to be considered when evaluating or negotiating acquisitions of foreign-based companies. Moreover, the rules may change from time to time. In the United

States, for example, goodwill no longer has to be amortized over 40 years.

- The total value of a patent's development costs may stretch over several years.
- The cost of a patent ultimately may have little bearing on the future revenues and profits it brings.

For More Information

Web Site:
www.patentcafe.com offers a wealth of patent valuation services and information, including links to the U.S. Patent & Trademark Office, and to fee-based evaluation services. Searching for "patent valuation" can produce more than 50,000 additional sites.

See also:
✔ **Calculating Amortization (pp. 869–70)**

Calculating Yield

What It Measures

Shares that pay dividends (note that not all do) will produce an annual cash return to the investor. Simply dividing this cash return by the current share price and expressing that as a percentage is known as the "yield"—that is, the annual percentage income at the current price. As far as newspapers are concerned, the yield figure published there is usually the historical one.

Analysts will often provide forecasts for dividends in terms of earnings per share (EPS) and thus the forecast yield can then be calculated. Forecasts can of course go wrong and consequently there is some risk in relying on them.

Why It Is Important

Yield, after the price/earnings ratio (P/E), is one of the most common methods of comparing the relative value of shares and that is why it is so widely quoted in the press. The majority of investors like to see a cash income from their shares, although to some extent this is a cultural thing. There are more companies in the United States, for example, that pay no dividends than in the United Kingdom.

How It Works in Practice

You can compare yields against the market average or against a sector average, which in turn gives you some idea of the relative value of the share against its peers, much like other ratios. Other things being equal, a higher yield share is preferable to that of an identical company with a lower yield. The higher yield share is cheaper. In practice of course, there may well be good reasons why the market has decided that the higher yielder should be so—possibly it has worse prospects, is less profitable, and so on. This is not always the case; the market is far from being a perfectly rational place.

An additional feature of the yield (unlike many of the other share analysis ratios), is that it enables comparison with cash. When you put cash into an interest-bearing source like a bank account or a government stock, you get a yield—the annual interest payable. This is usually a pretty safe investment. You can compare the yield from this cash investment with the yield on shares, which are far riskier. This produces a valuable basis for share evaluation. If, for example, you can get 4% in a bank without capital risk, you can then look at shares and ask yourself how this yield compares—given that, as well as the opportunity of long-term growth of both the share price and the dividends, there is plenty of capital risk.

Tricks of the Trade

Care is necessary, however, because unlike banks paying interest, companies are under no obligation to pay dividends at all. Frequently, if they go through a bad patch, even the largest, most well-known household name companies will cut dividends or even abandon paying them altogether. So, share yield is greatly less reliable than bank interest or government stock interest yield.

Despite this, yield is an immensely useful feature of share appraisal. It is the only ratio that tells you about the cash return to the investor, and you cannot argue with cash. Earnings per share (EPS), for example, is subject to accountants' opinions but a dividend once paid is an unarguable fact.

For More Information

Web Sites:
Securities and Exchange Commission: **www.sec.gov**.
The Accounting Standards Board U.K.: **www.aicpa.org**.

See also:
✔ **Reading the Financial Pages (pp. 875–77)**
✔ **Calculating Earnings per Share (pp. 879–80)**
✔ **Calculating Price/Earnings Ratio (P/E) (p. 844)**

Reading an Annual Report

Getting Started

Every company must publish an annual report to its shareholders as a matter of corporate law. The primary purpose of this report is to inform shareholders of the company's performance. As a legal requirement, the report usually contains a profit and loss account, a balance sheet, a cash flow statement, a directors' report, and an auditors' report. The different elements tell you about different aspects of the company's performance and can be read in a particular order to build up a true picture of how it is doing.

Many companies also provide a lot of other nonstatutory information on their affairs, in the interests of general communication. In some cases, this may be little more than gloss, contrived to illustrate the company's wonderful achievements while remaining strangely silent on negative features.

FAQs

Is there any difference between annual reports from private and public companies?

The main difference is usually length. Privately held companies will have far smaller contents because their mandatory reporting requirements are much reduced. Additionally they will be less concerned with image and consequently will tend to omit the noncompulsory public relations features that are present in public company reports.

What guarantee is there that an annual report is a true picture of a company's performance and not just propaganda put out by directors?

All annual reports have to include a report from the auditors, independent accountants charged with investigating a company's financial affairs to ensure that the published figures give a true and fair view of performance. Their investigation cannot extend to examining every single transaction (impossible in a company of any size), so they use statistical sampling and other risk-based testing procedures to assess the quality of the company's systems as a basis for producing the annual report. They are not infallible, but they stand between the shareholders and the directors as a way of trying to ensure probity in the running of the company.

Making It Happen

Understanding the Main Contents of an Annual Report

The best way to look at this is to take an example. Standard sections in annual reports can vary from country to country, but the following is the contents list of a medium-sized U.S. public company—let's call it X, Inc.

- X World
- Chairman's Statement
- Chief Executive's Review
- Financial Review
- Board of Directors
- Board Report on Remuneration
- Directors' Responsibilities
- Report of the Auditors
- Financial Statements
- Five-Year Record
- Shareholder Information

X World—belongs in the PR area. It tells you about the company, its products and markets.

Chairman's Statement—comments on the group results for the year and upon future developments. It also provides detail on earnings per share and dividends.

Chief Executive's Review—goes into more detail about individual divisions, breaking down the operating results from areas around the world. It tells us a bit about discontinued businesses and new ones acquired.

Financial Review—expands on the two previous section in a more quantitative way, looking at things like cash flow and how it affected group debt; interest charges; the effect of exchange rate fluctuations on profits, assets and liabilities; exceptional items that affect the profits (such as the disposal of a subsidiary company), and so on.

Board of Directors—lists the directors, with a brief description and photo of each.

Board Report on Remuneration—describes the work of a committee of nonexecutive directors, who decide the directors' income and that of other senior employees. Their remit includes looking at service contracts, bonus and share option plans, plus pension plans. It includes an analysis of the pay of each director, with comparable figures for the previous year plus details of share options and so on.

Directors' Responsibilities—is a mandatory statement showing exactly what the directors are obliged to discharge with regard to the annual report, maintaining accurate accounting records and so on.

Report of the Auditors—is simply what it says. Their findings are published using standard language in this report.

Financial Statements—are the main purpose of the annual report. In the example of X Inc., these consist of:

- Consolidated Profit and Loss Account. The profit and loss account of all the group as one;
- Consolidated and Company Balance Sheets. The former is the group balance sheet and the latter shows the parent company alone;
- Consolidated Cash Flow Statement. A guide to how the money flowing in and out of the company was utilized;
- Management's Responsibility for Financial Reporting;
- Management's Discussion and Analysis;
- Notes to the Accounts. These amplify numerous points contained in the figures and are usually critical for anyone wishing to study the accounts in detail.

Five-Year Record—shows a very abbreviated set of profit and loss and balance sheet figures for the current and previous four years. Some companies provide a ten-year record.

Shareholder Information—deals with matters such as the registered office, share registrars, brokers, solicitors, dates for meetings, and dividend payments.

Choosing the Right Order in Which to Read the Report

One way is simply to read the report from cover to cover, like a book. However, if you are not experienced in these things, that may lead you to giving equal weight to all the contents and, perhaps, overvaluing the glossy PR bits at the expense of the hard facts shown by the figures.

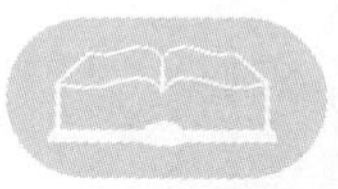

Start with the Auditors' Report

Remember that this thin gray line of accountants is all that stands between the outside shareholder and the directors. To speed up matters, look at the final paragraph, their opinion. Does that statement give a true and fair view? If so, fine. If not, then it is said to be "qualified." Qualifications vary from the disastrous, meaning that the company has gotten something seriously wrong, to perhaps a difference of opinion between the auditors and the board over some accounting matter. Most auditors' reports are unqualified, but if there is a qualification present, you will have to judge how much the accounts can be relied upon as a measure of the company's performance.

Next, Turn to the Five/Ten-Year Review

This is where you build up a mental picture of the company's financial history. Look at earnings per share (EPS)—is it increasing, decreasing, fluctuating wildly? This gives you an idea of how it has been doing over the period. Look at dividends, if any, and consider their pattern. Do they follow EPS or, as is likely, are they showing a smoother picture? Look at company debt, if the information is there, and compare it with shareholders' funds. How is it changing over the years?

Generally, try to build up a view as to whether the company is doing better, worse, or perhaps has no particular pattern over the period. Depending on your reasons for reading the report, a set of prejudices will have begun to develop from this historical picture. If it shows a declining financial situation, this could be a good thing from some points of view—if you wish to acquire the company, for example. If you are an employee, though, it would not be very encouraging. So reading reports depends to some extent upon which angle you are coming from.

Now Read the Chairman's and Directors' Comments

These will give a deeper feel for the company's business, over and above the raw numerical data. Try to exercise a degree of skepticism in some areas, because it is natural for directors to attempt to play up the good points and play down the less good ones.

Get to the Heart of the Matter

The kernel of the report comprises the financial statements and the huge number of notes that accompany them. A lot of it is in highly technical accounting terminology, but it gives you the intimate financial detail on the year. Never ignore the notes—they are critical. In fact some investment analysts read the report from the back, because the notes are so important.

Notes have increased dramatically over the years as new legal and accounting standards have been introduced, primarily to enforce standardization so that accounts are more comparable, but also to avoid "creative accounting" whereby some companies have tried to conceal (legitimately) financial undesirables.

Relax with the Glossy Stuff

Having absorbed all that really matters, settle back and read the glossy parts that tell you how wonderful the company is. Just remember to exercise a mild degree of cynicism here—this is the least important, though no doubt the most visually attractive, part of the annual report. The real picture of the company is the numbers, not the photo of the guy in the hard hat standing on an oil rig!

Common Mistakes

Paying Too Much Attention to Pretty Pictures and Directors' Comments and Too Little to the Accounting Data

This can give a false view of how well, or badly, the company is doing. Understandably, a large number of people have difficulty in comprehending the figures. But if you want to appreciate annual reports properly, then learning to read accounts is essential.

Some cynics among investment analysts have even expressed the view that there is an adverse relationship between the number of glossy pages in an annual report and the company's actual performance. Maybe that's a little harsh but. . .there might be something in it.

For More Information

Web Site:

Securities and Exchange Commission: **www.sec.gov**

See also:

✔ **Calculating Earnings per Share (pp. 879–80)**

Calculating Depreciation

Getting Started

Depreciation is a basic expense of doing business, reducing a company's earnings while increasing its cash flow. It affects three key financial statements: balance sheet, cash flow, and income (or profit and loss). It is based on two key facts: the purchase price of the items or property in question, and their "useful life."

Depreciation values and practices are governed by the tax laws of both national governments, and state or provincial governments, which must be monitored continuously for any changes that are made. Accounting bodies, too, have developed standard practices and procedures for conducting depreciation.

Depreciating a single asset is not difficult: the challenge lies in depreciating the many assets possessed by even small companies, and is intensified by the impact that depreciation has on income and cash flow statements, and on income tax returns. It is essential to depreciate with care and to rely on experts, ensuring that they fully understand the current government rules and regulations.

FAQs

What is depreciation?

It is an allocation of the cost of an asset over a period of time for accounting and tax purposes. Depreciation is charged against earnings, on the basis that the use of capital assets is a legitimate cost of doing business. Depreciation is also a non-cash expense that is added into net income to determine cash flow in a given accounting period.

What is straight-line depreciation?

One of the two principal depreciation methods, it is based on the assumption that an asset loses an equal amount of its value each year of its useful life. Straight-line depreciation deducts an equal amount from a company's earnings throughout the life of the asset.

What is accelerated depreciation?

The other principal method of depreciation is based on the assumption that an asset loses a larger amount of its value in the early years of its useful life. Also known as the "declining-balance" method, it is used by accountants to reduce a company's tax bills as soon as possible, and is calculated on the basis of the same percentage rate each year of an asset's useful life. Accelerated depreciation also better reflects the economic value of the asset being depreciated, which tends to become increasingly less efficient and more costly to maintain as it grows older.

What can be depreciated?

To qualify for depreciation, assets must:

- be used in the business;
- be items that wear out, become obsolete, or lose value over time from natural causes or circumstances;
- have a useful life beyond a single tax year.

Examples include vehicles, machines and equipment, computers and office equipment and furnishings, and buildings, plus major additions or improvements to such assets. Some intangible assets also can be included under certain conditions.

What cannot be depreciated?

Land, personal assets, inventory, leased or rented property, and a company's employees.

Making It Happen

In order to determine the annual depreciation cost of assets, it is necessary first to know the initial cost of those assets, how many years they will retain some value for the business, and what value, if any, they will have at the end of their useful life.

For example, a company buys a truck to carry materials and finished goods. The vehicle loses value as soon as it is purchased, and then loses more with each year it is in service, until the cost of repairs exceeds its overall value. Measuring the loss in the value of the truck is depreciation.

Straight-line depreciation is the most straightforward method, and is still quite common. It assumes that the net cost of an asset should be written off in equal amounts over its life. The formula used is:

(Original cost – Scrap value)/Useful life (years)

For example, if the truck cost $20,000 and can be expected to serve the business for seven years, its original cost would be divided by its useful life:

(30,000 – 2,000)/7 = 4,000 per year

The $4,000 becomes a depreciation expense that is reported on the company's year-end income statement under "operation expenses."

In theory, an asset should be depreciated over the actual number of years that it will be used, according to its actual drop in value each year. At the end of each year, all the depreciation claimed to date is subtracted from its cost in order to arrive at its "book value," which would equal its market value. At the end of its useful business life, any undepreciated portion would represent the salvage value for which it could be sold or scrapped.

For tax purposes, some accountants prefer to use accelerating depreciation to record larger amounts of depreciation in the asset's early years in order to reduce tax bills as soon as possible. In contrast to the straight-line method, the declining-balance method assumes that the asset depreciates more in its earlier years of use. The table below compares the depreciation amounts that would be available, under these two methods, for a $1,000 asset that is expected to be used for five years and then sold for $100 in scrap.

While the straight-line method results in the same deduction each year, the declining-balance method produces larger deductions in the first years and far smaller deductions in the later years. One result of this system is that, if the equipment is expected to be sold for a higher value at some point in the middle of its life, the declining-balance method can produce a greater taxable gain in that year because the book value of the asset will be relatively lower.

The depreciation method to be used for a particular asset is fixed at the time that the asset is first placed in service. Whatever rules or tables are in effect for that year must be followed as long as the asset is owned.

Depreciation laws and regulations change frequently over the years as a result of government policy changes, so a company owning property over a long period may have to use several different depreciation methods.

	Straight-Line Method		Declining-Balance Method	
Year	Annual Depreciation	Year-end Book Value	Annual Depreciation	Year-end Book Value
1	$900 × 20%=$180	$1,000-$180=$820	$1,000 × 40%=$400	$1,000-$400=$600
2	$900 × 20%=$180	$820-$180=$640	$600 × 40%=$240	$600-$240=$360
3	$900 × 20%=$180	$640-$180=$460	$360 × 40%=$144	$360-$144=$216
4	$900 × 20%=$180	$460-$180=$280	$216 × 40%=$86.40	$216-$86.40=$129.60
5	$900 × 20%=$180	$280-$180=$100	$129.60 × 40%=$51.84	$129.60-$51.84=$77.76

  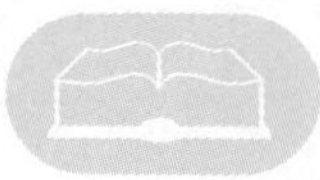    

Tricks of the Trade

- With rare exceptions, it is not possible to deduct in one year the entire cost of an asset if that asset has a useful life substantially beyond the tax year.
- To qualify for depreciation, an asset must be put into service. Simply purchasing it is not enough. There are rules that govern how much depreciation can be claimed on items put into service after a year has begun.
- It is common knowledge that if a company claims more depreciation than it is entitled to, it is liable for stiff penalties in a tax audit, just as the failure to properly allow for depreciation causes an overestimation of income. What is not commonly known is that if a company does not claim all the depreciation deductions it is entitled to, it will be considered as having claimed them when taxable gains or losses are eventually calculated on the sale or disposal of the asset in question.
- While leased property cannot be depreciated, the cost of making permanent improvements to leased property can be (remodeling a leased office, for example). There are many rules governing leased assets; they should be depreciated with care.
- Another common mistake is to continue depreciating property beyond the end of its recovery period. Cars are common examples of this.
- Conservative companies depreciate many assets as quickly as possible, despite the fact that this practice reduces reported net income. Knowledgeable investors watch carefully for such practices.

For More Information

Web sites:
www.toolkit.cch.com offers a thorough and well-written tutorial on depreciation, as does **www.encyclopedia.com**.

See also:
✔ **Calculating Amortization (pp. 869–70)**

Calculating Enterprise Value

What It Measures

It measures what financial markets believe that a company's ongoing operations are worth.

Some people also define enterprise value as what it would actually cost to purchase an entire company at a given moment.

Why It Is Important

Enterprise value is not a theoretical valuation but a firm and finite value, logically determined. It tells an individual investor the underlying value of his stake in an enterprise. For potential acquirers considering a takeover of a company, enterprise value helps to determine a reasonable price for their desired acquisition.

How It Works in Practice

Although it is a finite figure, enterprise value can be calculated in two ways. One method is quicker, but the other is more thorough and thus more reliable.

The quick way is simply to multiply the number of a company's shares outstanding by the current price per share. Using this approach, the enterprise value of a company with 2 million shares outstanding, and a share price of 25, would be:

2,000,000 × 25 = 50,000,000 enterprise value

However, this value is based on the market's perception of the value of shares; it also ignores some important factors about a company's fiscal health. The second, more complete, method is therefore preferred by many experts. This method calculates enterprise value as the sum of market capitalization, plus debt and preferred stock, minus cash and cash equivalents:

Market capitalization + long-term debt + preferred stock − cash & equivalents = enterprise value

In turn, if market capitalization is 6.5 million, debt totals 1 million, the value of preferred stock is 1.5 million, and cash and equivalents total 2.5 million, enterprise value would be:

(6.5 + 1 + 1.5) − 2 = 7 (million) enterprise value

This more thorough calculation recognizes the existence of both a company's debt and of the amount of cash and liquid assets on hand. No matter how a stock may fluctuate, these sums are relatively constant, and the amount of debt can be very significant. Debt—and cash, too—can be just as important during a company's sale, since new owners both assume existing debt and receive any cash on hand. Indeed, more than a few acquisitions are financed in part with funds of the acquired company.

Tricks of the Trade

- Financial markets often use the market capitalization figure for enterprise value, but they really are not the same thing.
- Experts will occasionally refer to "total enterprise value," but its definition and formula are virtually identical to this second-formula enterprise value. Total enterprise value is only meaningful to those who use the quick method to compute enterprise value.
- A company's value is sometimes expressed as "the total funds being used to finance it." This is increasingly used in place of the price/earnings ratio, and indicates the economic rather than accounting return that the company is generating on the total value of the capital supporting it. Companies that have borrowed heavily to finance growth, or that have paid

"Total commercial honesty always costs something, but total or partial dishonesty will cost more."
(Robert Heller)

large premiums for acquisitions or assets, are more frequently evaluated by this method.

For More Information

Web Site:
www.fool.com describes enterprise value and assesses the different ways of measuring it.

Calculating Amortization

What It Measures

Amortization is a method of recovering (deducting or writing off) the capital costs of intangible assets over a fixed period of time. Its calculation is virtually identical to the straight-line method of depreciation.

Amortization also refers to the establishment of a schedule for repaying the principal and interest on a loan in equal amounts over a period of time. Because computers have made this a simple calculation, business references to amortization tend to focus more on the term's first definition.

Why It Is Important

Amortization enables a company to identify its true costs, and thus its net income, more precisely. In the course of their business, most enterprises acquire intangible assets such as a patent for an invention, or a well-known brand or trademark. Since these assets can contribute to the revenue growth of the business, they can be—and are allowed to be—deducted against those future revenues over a period of years, provided the procedure conforms to accepted accounting practices.

For tax purposes, the distinction is not always made between amortization and depreciation, yet amortization remains a viable financial accounting concept in its own right.

How It Works in Practice

Amortization is computed using the straight-line method of depreciation: divide the initial cost of the intangible asset by the estimated useful life of that asset. For example, if it costs $10,000 to acquire a patent and it has an estimated useful life of 10 years, the amortized amount per year is $1,000.

Initial cost / useful life = amortization per year
$10,000 / 10 = $1,000 per year

The amount of amortization accumulated since the asset was acquired appears on the organization's balance sheet as a deduction under the amortized asset.

While that formula is straightforward, amortization can also incorporate a variety of noncash charges to net earnings and/or asset values, such as depletion, write-offs, prepaid expenses, and deferred charges. Accordingly, there are many rules to regulate how these charges appear on financial statements. The rules are different in each country, and are occasionally changed, so it is necessary to stay abreast of them and rely on expert advice.

For financial reporting purposes, an intangible asset is amortized over a period of years. The amortizable life—"useful life"—of an intangible asset is the period over which it gives economic benefit. Several factors are considered when determining this useful life; for example, demand and competition, effects of obsolescence, legal or contractual limitations, renewal provisions, and service life expectations.

Intangibles that can be amortized can include:

- copyrights, based on the amount paid either to purchase them or to develop them internally, plus the costs incurred in producing the work (wages or materials, for example). At present, a copyright is granted to a corporation for 75 years, and to an individual for the life of the author plus 50 years. However, the estimated useful life of a copyright is usually far less than its legal life, and it is generally amortized over a fairly short period.
- cost of a franchise, including any fees paid to the franchiser, as well legal costs or expenses incurred in the acquisition. A franchise granted for a limited period should be amortized over its life. If the franchise has an indefinite life, it should be amortized over a reasonable period not to exceed 40 years.
- covenants not to compete: an agreement by the seller of a business not to engage in a competing business in a certain area for a specific period of time. The cost of the not-to-compete covenant should be amortized over the period covered by the covenant unless its estimated economic life is expected to be less.
- easement costs that grant a right of way may be amortized if there is a limited and specified life.
- organization costs incurred when forming a corporation or a partnership, including legal fees, accounting services, incorporation fees, and other related services. Organization costs are usually amortized over 60 months.
- patents, both those developed internally and those purchased. If developed internally, a patent's "amortizable basis" includes legal fees incurred during the application process. Normally, a patent is amortized over its legal life, or over its remaining life if purchased. However, it should be amortized over its legal life or its economic life, whichever is the shorter.
- trademarks, brands, and trade names, which should be written off over a period not to exceed 40 years. However, since the value of these assets depends on the changing tastes of consumers, they are frequently amortized over a shorter period.
- other types of property that may be amortized include certain intangible drilling costs, circulation costs, mine development costs, pollution control facilities, and reforestation expenditures. They can even include intangibles such as the value of a market share or a market's composition: an example is the portion of an acquired business that is attributable to the existence of a given customer base.

TRICKS OF THE TRADE

- Certain intangibles cannot be amortized, but may be depreciated using a straight-line approach if they have "determinable" useful life. Because the rules are different in each country and are subject to change, it is essential to rely on specialist advice.
- Computer software may be amortized under certain conditions, depending on its purpose. Software that is amortized is generally given a 60-month life, but it may be amortized over a shorter period if it can clearly be established that it will be obsolete or no longer used within a shorter time.
- Under certain conditions, customer lists that were purchased may be amortized if it can be demonstrated that the list has a finite useful life, in that customers on the list are likely to be lost over a period of time.
- While leasehold improvements are depreciated for income tax purposes, they are amortized when it comes to financial reporting—either over the remaining term of the lease or their expected useful life, whichever is shorter.
- Annual payments incurred under a franchise agreement should be expensed when incurred.
- The Internet has many amortization loan calculators that can automatically determine monthly payments figures and the total cost of a loan.

For More Information

Web Site:

www.fasb.org is the Web site of the U.S. Financial Accounting Standards Board, which provides the latest information on amortization and other accounting topics.

See also:

✓ **Calculating Depreciation (pp. 866–68)**
✓ **Calculating Goodwill and Patents (pp. 863–64)**
✓ **Calculating Bond Yield (p. 823)**
✓ **Calculating the Current Price of a Bond (p. 845)**

CALCULATING ACTIVITY-BASED COSTING

GETTING STARTED

- Activity-based costing (ABC) identifies the relationship between a business activity and all the resources needed to conduct it by assigning costs to each of those resources, thus presenting the true total expense of the entire activity.
- ABC can account for so-called "soft" or indirect operating costs, and thus produce a more revealing, and perhaps startlingly different, financial picture than other accounting methodologies such as standard costing might offer.
- Used properly, ABC helps management better to distinguish operations that add value from those that do not, permitting more informed decisions about such matters as pricing, product mix, capital investments, and organizational change.
- In turn, ABC's advocates praise it as a more effective tool to identify and control costs, improve productivity, and increase profits.

FAQs

WHEN DID ABC START?

ABC came of age in the 1980s amid manufacturers' furious efforts to raise the quality of their products while simultaneously eliminating every unnecessary cost from their operations. The dramatic improvements realized by manufacturers have led to ABC becoming a widely used tool, especially in the manufacturing industry.

WHAT ARE THE BASIC STEPS OF ABC?

There are five:

- identify the product or service to be studied;
- determine all the resources and processes that are required to create the product or deliver the service, and their respective costs;
- determine the "cost drivers" for each resource: the cost of labor as well as raw materials;
- collect cost and other data such as time taken, data for each process and resource;
- use the data to calculate the overall cost of the product or service.

WHAT ARE ABC'S PRINCIPAL ADVANTAGES?

First, ABC can gauge virtually any activity, be it a manufacturing process, a business process, the performance of a service, or an administrative operation. Second, it considers a much wider range of resources and materials than more traditional accounting methodologies, and can thus present a more complete picture.

WHAT ARE ABC'S PRIMARY WEAKNESSES?

It can be an very time-consuming exercise because of the volumes of data it demands. Also, if not managed properly, ABC can transform every manager into an accountant whose energies become fixed on tracking the costs of the activity, rather than on tracking and perfecting the activity itself.

WHAT KIND OF BUSINESS SECTORS USE ABC?

The list ranges from accountants to zoologists. It may be especially helpful to knowledge-based businesses that rely primarily on human services and related resources, whose total costs may be difficult to measure with more traditional accounting yardsticks.

WHAT IS CRITICAL TO ABC'S SUCCESS?

Without gaining and maintaining the enduring commitment of all individuals, even a modestly detailed initia-

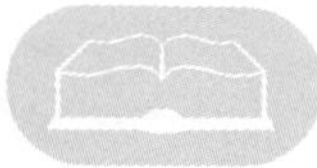

tive will probably fail. It's also best to start with pilot projects to demonstrate success.

What preliminary steps are needed?

First, an organization needs to understand its activities and the resources that these require. Second, it needs to understand thoroughly the amount of information required, and the expense of generating that information. It must also first determine what level of accuracy will be acceptable.

Making It Happen

Creating an ABC cost accounting system requires three preliminary steps:

- converting to an accrual basis of accounting;
- defining cost centers and cost allocation;
- determining process and procedure costs.

Businesses have traditionally relied on the cash basis of accounting, which recognizes income when received and expenses when paid. ABC's foundation is the accrual-basis income statement. The numbers this statement presents are assigned to the various procedures performed during a given period. Cost centers are a company's identifiable products and services, but also include specific and detailed tasks within these broader activities. Defining cost centers will of course vary by business and method of operation. What is critical to ABC is the inclusion of all activities and all resources.

Once these steps have been taken, the results are often more than satisfying.

Banks and financial services firms have long used ABC-like methods to confirm that investments in automated teller machines would be both cheaper than continuing to rely on tellers and clerks and in their customers' best interests.

Railroad companies have used the methodology to determine the cost of processing bills of lading by hand, fax, and the Internet. Studying such costs confirmed the wisdom of using e-commerce, generating annual savings of up to $1 million.

Publishers launching "new media" services can more accurately calculate the true costs of creating material for them, then compare such costs to those required to produce traditional publications and draw more accurate conclusions about what best serves their long- and short-term interests.

Law firms are better positioned to confirm that the hourly fees they charge—no matter how princely they may at first appear—do, in fact, enable them to provide their services profitably.

Finally, healthcare providers use ABC to measure profitability, eliminate unnecessary costs, and plan for change. A medical practice that knows the actual cost of providing a specific service, for example, can make far better decisions about the price of managed health care.

For instance, let's say the Apple-a-Day Medical Clinic includes three physicians, Drs. Peel, Core, and Stem. Their clinic has an in-house laboratory and a radiology department. All direct revenues and expenses are allocated to the physician who performs the service and incurs the expense. Indirect variable overhead costs are allocated to each physician based on the proportion of total revenues that each generates in a given period. Fixed overhead costs are divided equally among physicians. Because of their respective incomes and expense allocations, each physician would represent a separate cost center.

Additional cost centers for this medical practice could be laboratory, radiology, and administration. As cost centers are defined, they could further be classified as, say, "patient service centers" or "support centers." In this example, laboratory, radiology, and each individual physician's activity would be patient service centers, while administration would be a support center.

Once cost centers are identified, management teams can begin studying the activities each one engages in and allocating the expenses each one incurs, including the cost of employee services. In this healthcare scenario, activities would range from actual treatment by physicians and nurses, X-rays, medical tests and assessments of their results, plus such administrative support services as personnel, bookkeeping, rent, utilities, property insurance, office supplies, advertising, telecommunications expenses, and equipment costs related to the administrative function. Rent, utilities, and property insurance are usually allocated on the basis of the square footage that the particular activity covers.

Tracking and allocating the detailed costs of individual activities and procedures can be accomplished by different methods, with various degrees of accuracy. The more detailed the cost analysis, of course, the greater the accuracy of the data. Then again, as the detail increases, so does the time and expense.

The most appropriate method is developed from time studies and direct expense allocation. Management teams that choose this method will need to devote several months to data collection in order to generate sufficient information to establish the personnel components of each activity's total cost. The cost of this exercise itself can be significant, but also worthwhile. Proponents say ABC has resulted in cost savings worth as much as 14 times the cost of the exercise. More importantly, the exercise has provided solid documentation for decisions that "seemed correct," as a Chrysler Corporation team once reported "but could not be supported with hard evidence."

Time studies establish the average amount of time required to complete each task, plus best- and worst-case performances. Only those resources actually used are factored into the cost computation; unused resources are reported separately. These studies also can advise management how best to monitor and allocate expenses which might otherwise be expressed as part of general overhead, or go undetected altogether.

Notably, determining how much of an operation's personnel is underused or unused can significantly help management planning, specifically by exposing activities that are overstaffed or understaffed. This can be especially helpful to any knowledge-based business, since payroll is almost always its highest cost. Moreover, in any business, the more efficiently an enterprise deploys its personnel, the more profitable it will be.

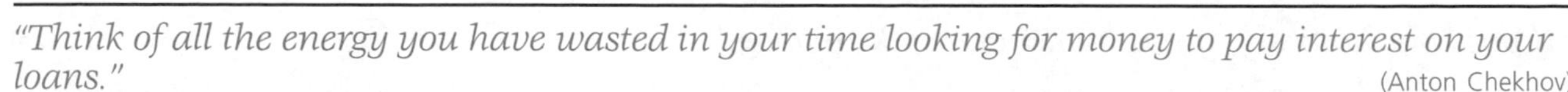
"Think of all the energy you have wasted in your time looking for money to pay interest on your loans."

(Anton Chekhov)

In addition, this type of analysis can also establish useful performance benchmarks within an operation, and might even allow for a comparison of procedure costs with industry averages.

COMMON MISTAKES

YOU GET CAUGHT UP IN THE DETAILS

Notwithstanding its successes, ABC remains a tool, not an end in itself. Organizations can lose sight of that fact if they are not careful, and end up allowing it to dominate their working lives.

The enormity and complexity of such a project should never be underestimated. The data requirements alone are daunting. It is all too easy to get caught up in ABC's details and mechanics. In turn, estimating some costs is often recommended, to reduce the level of detail.

At the same time, however, some details are important prerequisites of objectivity and success. For example, if time studies are not used, some other measure must be used to allocate personnel and related costs, as well as indirect costs such as percentage of revenues or income, or the number of customer calls. These methods require far less time for compiling data and are less costly, but drawbacks abound. For one thing, accuracy suffers, and they are almost always subjective, potentially to the point of compromising the entire initiative. Being far less precise, these alternative methods also do not differentiate between used and unused personnel resources, and will not provide information on unused capacity or trends in procedure costs.

Without the aid of computer software that has been developed to automate the process, ABC can be hopelessly time-consuming. Indeed, unaided by technology, ABC might well be hoist with its own petard and exposed as an outrageous waste of time.

Like any cost-accounting system, activity-based costing is not static. Once established, it needs to be maintained and updated as business conditions and organizations change.

Finally, in delivering its crystal-clear pictures, activity-based costing also has the potential to make individual champions of particular products or services squirm, because it may reveal them to be far more expensive than they might otherwise appear. All the more reason for advocating caution: "Watch out what you wish for!"

If a management team is to reduce and eliminate costs, it must first identify them and grasp their impact on specific processes or products. Because activity-based costing can paint a single picture that reveals all the individual direct and indirect costs a business incurs in a given operation, it can be a powerful tool for both assessing current operations and guiding prompt and intelligent reactions as circumstances change. In fact, it's also known as activity-based management (ABM).

For More Information

Journal article:
Ness, Joseph A., and Thomas G. Cucuzza. "Tapping the Full Potential of ABC." *Harvard Business Review*, July/August 1995.

Web Site:
www.abcbenchmarking.com is the Web site of the Activity Based Costing Benchmarking Association (ABCBA™), currently a free association of companies and organizations that use activity-based costing. The association conducts benchmarking studies to identify practices that improve the overall operations of its members.

CALCULATING PRICE/SALES RATIO (P/S)

WHAT IT MEASURES

The price/sales ratio (P/S) is another measure, like the price/earnings (P/E) ratio, of the relative value of a share when compared with others.

WHY IT IS IMPORTANT

Like many such price-based ratios, it does not mean too much in isolation but acquires worth when making comparisons. So the above the figure of 0.33 does not say a lot on its own, until you start to look at how this matches up to the market average or the sector average, for example.

HOW IT WORKS IN PRACTICE

The P/S ratio is obtained by dividing the market capitalization by the latest published annual sales figure. So a company with a capitalization of $1 billion and sales of $3 billion would have a P/S ratio of 0.33.

P/S will vary with the type of industry. You would expect, for example, that many retailers and other large-scale distributors of goods would have very high sales in relation to their market capitalizations—in other words, a very low P/S. Equally, manufacturers of high-value items would generally have much lower sales figures and thus higher P/S ratios. Like anything to do with share analysis (this being more of an art than a science), it is not always that clear cut. . .but that would be the general trend. If you rank companies by ascending P/S, you will find usually that supermarket chains figure amongst the lowest ones.

A company with a lower P/S is cheaper than one with a higher ratio, particularly if they are in the same sector so that a direct comparison is more appropriate. It means that each share of the lower P/S company is buying you more of its sales than those of the higher P/S company.

Note though, that it is cheaper only on P/S grounds. . . that does not mean it is necessarily the more attractive share. There will frequently be reasons why it has a lower ratio than another ostensibly similar company, most commonly because it is less profitable. As far as corporate efficiency goes, this ratio considers only sales, the top line of the profit and loss account. It is a long way from there to the bottom line, the bit that really counts (that is, how much profit the company has made).

Tricks of the Trade

- A loss-making company would thus still have a P/S ratio, even though it would have no P/E ratio. In consequence, like all investment analysis tools, P/S has to be used with care—but it can be of use for investors. P/S was cited in an extensive study of the New York Stock Exchange as one leading indicator for selecting very long-term shares that perform well.

Calculating Capital Lease

Getting Started

Determining whether a lease obligation is an operating or capital lease, for financial reporting purposes, requires that it be evaluated according to four criteria established by the FASB. The criteria are objective rules for making a judgment about who, the lessor or lessee, bears the risks and benefits of ownership of the leased property. If a lease is determined to be a capital, an asset and corresponding liability is recorded at the present value of the minimum lease payments. The capital asset is depreciated over time, while the liability is amortized as lease payments are made. Rental payments under operating leases are simply expensed as incurred. Due to the complexity of lease agreements, management judgment still plays a large role in distinguishing between operating and capitals.

FAQs

What is the definition of minimum lease payments?

The minimum lease payments are the rental payments to be made during the lease term, plus the amount of the bargain price, guaranteed residual value or penalty for failure to renew the lease at the end of its original term.

In determining whether a lease should be classified as an operating or capital lease, what interest rate should be used to discount the minimum lease payments?

The interest rate used to discount the minimum lease payments to their present value is the incremental borrowing rate of the lessee. The incremental borrowing rate is the interest rate that the lessee would have been charged if the assets had been acquired by borrowing the purchase price. If the lessor's implied interest rate for the lease is known and is lower than the estimated incremental borrowing rate of the lessee, then the lessee uses the implied rate to discount.

Making It Happen

The Four FASB Criteria

Until the 1970s, many companies used leasing as a means to purchase tangible assets without recognizing their ownership or the lease obligation on the balance sheet. In substance, leases were off-balance sheet financing. Although all leases were required to be disclosed in the footnotes to the financial statements, even long-term finance leases did not appear as a liability. Because the basic measures of leverage, such as debt-to-equity or debt-to-capital ratios, do not consider off-balance sheet obligations, the accounting profession and the investment community believed that there needed to be more stringent guidelines for classifying leases as operating or financing. To promote consistency in the accounting treatment for leases, in 1976 the FASB issued statement no. 13, "Accounting for Leases." The statement contains four criteria for distinguishing between an operating and capital (finance) lease:

1. The lease agreement transfers ownership of the assets to the lessee during the term of lease.
2. The lessee can purchase the assets leased at a bargain price (also called a bargain purchase option), such as $1, at the end of the lease term.
3. The lease term is at least 75% of the economic life of the leased asset.
4. The present value of the minimum lease payments is 90% or greater of the asset's value.

If a lease agreement does not meet any of these criteria, the lessee treats it as an operating lease for accounting purposes. If, however, the agreement meets one of the above criteria, it is treated as a capital lease.

Accounting for a Capital Lease

Capital leases are reported by the lessee as if the assets being leased were acquired and the monthly rental payments as if they were payments of principal and interest on a debt obligation. Specifically, the lessee capitalizes the lease by recognizing an asset and a liability at the lower of the present value of the minimum lease payments or the value of the assets under lease. As the monthly rental payments are made, the corresponding liability decreases. At the same time, the leased asset is depreciated in a manner that is consistent with other owned assets having the same use and economic life.

Accounting for an Operating Lease

If the lease is classified as an operating lease, the monthly lease payments are simply treated as rental expenses and recognized on the income statement as they are incurred. There is no recognition of a leased asset or liability.

Clearing Up Remaining Confusion

The FASB's attempt to establish objective criteria for distinguishing between operating and capital leases was a good first step. This has enabled companies to make prudent financial decisions in lease versus buy situations, based on the accounting treatment afforded a specific lease structure. Furthermore, financial professionals now have a framework within which to determine what lease terms create a capital lease. However, the use of

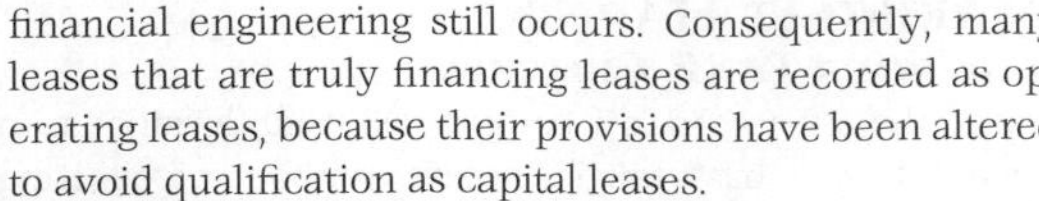

financial engineering still occurs. Consequently, many leases that are truly financing leases are recorded as operating leases, because their provisions have been altered to avoid qualification as capital leases.

When in doubt, a manager should always ask whether the risks and benefits of ownership have truly been passed from the lessor to the lessee. Facts that indicate the transfer has occurred are when maintenance, insurance and property tax expenses are born by the lessee or when the lessee guarantees a specific residual value on the leased property. Otherwise, managers are left with the four criteria outlined by the FASB and their own judgment.

For More Information

Web Site:
Securities and Exchange Commission: **www.sec.gov**

Calculating Borrowing Costs and Capital Structure

Getting Started

The costs of borrowing are primarily made up of interest and issuance expenses. The interest rate assigned to a particular debt instrument is based on the level of default risk assumed by the investor. Several rating agencies assess the default risk of public debt issuances and provide a rating that is indicative of credit quality. The credit quality is greater for secured/collateralized senior debt than for unsecured subordinated debt issued by the same company, and hence, the former typically carries a lower rate of interest. Firms that have higher levels of debt must typically pay higher interest rates to investors to compensate them for the increased risk of default. Capital-intensive businesses can usually maintain greater debt-to-capital ratios for the same level of borrowing costs as businesses that are less capital intensive.

FAQs

What are debt issuance costs and are they always incurred when borrowing money?

Debt issuance costs are the underwriting, legal, and administrative fees required to issue the debt. These fees are significant when issuing debt in the public markets, such as bonds. However, other types of debt, such as private placements or bank loans, are cheaper to issue because they require less underwriting, legal, and administrative support. Consequently, the public issuers of debt are typically Fortune 500 firms, while middle-market companies tend to issue debt through private placements.

Do borrowing costs increase or decrease for callable bonds or bonds with detachable stock warrants?

When debt securities are issued with a call feature, the debt can be retired at the discretion of the company until some specified future date. The call feature represents value to the issuing company, much like a call option on equity. The issuer must compensate investors for providing this option. Therefore, the interest rate on callable bonds is typically higher than those on non-callable bonds of the same credit quality. That is, the borrowing costs increase on bonds with a call feature.

The opposite is true of bonds with detachable stock warrants. A stock warrant provides the bondholder the right to purchase shares of common stock in the issuing company at a specified price during a defined period of time. The warrant's strike price is typically at, or higher than, the current market price of the company's stock. Nonetheless, the warrant provides value to the bondholder in the form of a call option on the company's equity. Because these warrants add to the potential total return on the debt, the stated interest rate is usually lower than that on debt issued without warrants of similar credit quality. Borrowing costs are typically lower on bonds with detachable stock warrants.

Making It Happen

When companies borrow money, they enter a formal obligation to make periodic payments of interest and to repay the principal balance outstanding, according to an agreed schedule. The interest payments are typically based on a stated, annual percentage of the original amount borrowed. The interest paid on such obligations represents the cost of borrowing, along with the costs to issue the debt.

The Difference between Funded and Unfunded Debt

The debt can be classified as funded or unfunded. Funded debt is long-term debt or debt that has a maturity date in excess of one year. Unfunded debt is short-term debt requiring repayment within a year from issuance. Funded debt is usually issued in the public markets or in the form of a private placement to qualified institutional investors. Most unfunded debt is commercial paper or bank lines of credit.

Senior and Subordinated Debt

Debt can also be classified as senior or subordinated, based on its preference to assets in the event of default by the lender. Subordinated lenders have a junior claim to assets in the event of bankruptcy and are paid only after senior creditors' claims have been satisfied.

Senior credit can be secured or unsecured. Much of the corporate debt outstanding is referred to as a bond.

However, a true bond is secured by claims against the firm's property, plant, and equipment. For example, many airlines secure their public debt by mortgaging their airplanes. In this example, an airline could be forced to sell its airplanes to pay its public debt if it defaults on the bonds. Most public debt is secured by the good faith and credit of the issuing company, and is more accurately called a debenture. A firm can also pledge certain assets, like accounts receivable, inventory, or property, as collateral for a loan or debt.

Differing Levels of Risk

Even when debt is secured or collateralized, it still does not guarantee repayment by the issuer. A company's underlying asset value and its earnings may be very volatile, increasing the risk of default in a down business cycle. Because this risk can be different from one business to another, there are several national rating agencies that rate public debt based on the credit-worthiness of the borrower. Investment-grade debt securities are securities that are rated in the top four categories of credit-worthiness by Standard and Poor's or Moody's rating agencies. All debt securities rated below investment-grade are considered to be junk bonds.

Different Types of Interest Rate

Debt can have a fixed or floating rate of interest. Fixed-rate debt pays the same interest rate over its term. Most long-term debt is issued with a fixed rate. Many short-term loans are floating-rate instruments based on the prime lending rate, LIBOR (London Interbank Offered Rate) or some other U.S. Treasury security. When the rates on these securities change, the loan rate changes. For example, a line of credit whose current interest rate is 6%, based on one percentage point above the three-year LIBOR rate, will change to 6.25% if the LIBOR rate increases by a quarter of a point. Floating-rate debt is typically used to support a business's working capital requirements.

The Determinants of Credit Quality

The interest rate and, consequently, the borrowing cost is determined by credit quality. Credit quality depends on the type of debt security, the amount of debt relative to total capital, and the capital intensiveness of a company's business. All other things being equal, a secured or collateralized debt security is less risky than an unsecured obligation. Therefore, investors require a greater return for the additional risk assumed by investing in unsecured debt. Likewise, an investor will require a greater return for subordinated debt than for senior credit.

Credit quality also deteriorates as the level of debt grows on the balance sheet of a company. Intuitively, the greater the debt-to-capital ratio—debt plus the value of equity—the greater the risk of default. By continuing to add financial leverage to its business operations, a firm increases the risks that in a bad year it may not be able to cover its debt service. In studies on cost of capital, it was determined that companies experiencing debt-to-capital ratios between 25% and 45% saw their cost of capital increase exponentially, indicating greater risk of financial distress.

Debt-to-Capital Ratios

Finally, firms that are more capital intensive tend to have greater debt-to-capital ratios. For example, automobile and airline manufacturers typically maintain greater leverage than professional services and software companies. The academic explanation given for this circumstance is the degree of industry maturity, lower earnings volatility and the ability to secure more debt with tangible assets. Consequently, companies within more capital-intensive industries tend to have lower borrowing costs at a given debt-to-capital ratio than those in less capital-intensive industries.

Tricks of the Trade

- The costs of borrowing are composed of interest payments and issuance costs. Interest paid on outstanding debt is a function of the credit-worthiness of the borrower. The greater the interest rate on a debt security relative to other, similar securities, the lower the credit quality of the issuer. As credit quality falls below investment-grade, the risk of default becomes ominously greater and the costs of borrowing become more exorbitant.
- The firm's capital structure is another major determinant of credit quality. There is a direct relationship between debt level and default risk. At a given debt to capital ratio, incremental borrowing costs increase dramatically as the firm's risk of financial distress reaches its peak.

For More Information

Web Site:
The Motley Fool: **www.fool.com**

Reading the Financial Pages

Getting Started

There are two broad areas to the financial pages of newspapers. One consists of a simple listing, primarily of stocks quoted on the stock exchange, shown alphabetically with certain details on each stock.

The other area will contain reports by journalists on individual stocks and other general economic and financial information. Often the article will end with an opinion upon whether or not the stock should be purchased as an investment. How much credence is attached to such opinion is a matter of individual judgment.

To be able to appreciate the data shown in NYSE stock market share listings, you do need to have a little understanding of some basic financial analysis—particularly yield and price/earnings ratio (P/E)—the two most common measures of the value of a share. We suggest you read the two actionlists on these subjects first.

FAQs

What information is included in the financial pages?

The financial pages of the papers publish tabular price and statistical information about stocks listed on the stock exchange, together with a series of articles on individual stocks and the economy in general. The latter could include an enormous range of subjects, such as unemployment and interest rates, the effects of technologies on particular types of share, and so on. Individual company stocks will also be discussed, usually around the time when important information about the company is published—such as results or other corporate activity, perhaps a takeover, a profits warning or a new product development.

The statistical listings of financial data may cover more than just stocks quoted on one local stock exchange. They could, for example, include overseas stock exchanges and commodity exchange prices, though the latter are of far less general interest than stock prices.

Are there any rules about how to read these pages?

No. The financial pages are there to provide people with information on the general economy, particular industries, and individual companies. All of these are changing constantly so that there is a perpetual stream of news being published. How much of it is relevant to an individual reader is something that each person will decide for him or herself.

Making It Happen

General Information about Stock Listings

Here is an actual extract from the stock listing pages of a paper, for a Monday. The actual entries will contain a lot more information than this, but we have selected the key elements.

52 Week High	52 Week Low	Stock	Div.	Yield %	P/E	Close
53.9	22.15	Honeywell	.75	2.3	dd	32.90
119.75	63.27	Goldman Sachs	.48	.6	20	86

The abbreviations at the heads of each column stand for:

- 52 Week High/Low: indicators of the highest and lowest price of the stock over the past year
- Stock: the name of the company
- Div: the annual dividend per unit of stock, based upon the company's last declaration
- Yield: the dividend per stock, expressed as a percentage of the closing share price
- P/E: price/earnings ratio

The sample companies have been chosen from different sectors (IT and banking). Note that different papers may have a slightly different choice of data for each stock but all will have the price—that being the most important fact.

How to Interpret the Figures

What is this information telling us about these stocks? You could separate the data into two broad groups, one of which tells us something absolute about the particular stock and the other which enables us to compare the stock with others, although some data falls into both groups.

52 Week High/Low

This gives you an indication of the range within which the share price has been fluctuating. A big range might indicate that the company concerned is operating in a volatile market. It should only be used as an indicator of a stock's value in conjunction with a number of other facts about the company.

Dividend

This is paid by the company to its shareholders. The amount of dividend paid to shareholders is dependent upon a number of factors, but is one important indicator of the long term profitability of a company. Companies with a long history of consistently rising dividend payments and earnings per share are generally considered to be safer bets than companies offering no dividends at all. In the case of Honeywell, dd indicates that the company made a loss over the most recent four quarters.

Price

This is simply the closing market price of the share, in dollars, from the last day of trading. For a Monday edition, this would be the previous Friday.

Yield and Price/Earnings Ratio (P/E)

Briefly, yield represents the historical annual dividend income paid by the share as a percentage of its current price. P/E shows how many years of current earnings are represented in the current price. Both of these ratios will therefore fluctuate with the price of the stock—P/E in direct proportion and yield in inverse proportion.

These are two of the most common ratios used by investors and market commentators in evaluating a stock as a potential investment, both on its own merits and as a comparison with other stocks. For this reason they are widely quoted in the press and almost every serious newspaper will show these figures alongside the price of each stock in the listings.

Common Mistakes

Believing That Share Price Alone Is Indication of the Value of the Stock

It seems logical to believe that stock for company A, with a share price of $200, is twice as expensive as that of company B, with a share price of $100. This is completely incorrect. The share price alone tells you almost nothing about the stock, which is why P/E is so critically important.

Suppose in the above example, A has a P/E of 12 and B a P/E of 24. Now you can see that in fact B is twice as costly as A, even though it has half the share price. It means that collectively, investors have decided that it is worth paying 24 years' earnings for B but only 12 years' earnings for A. This does not mean that the collective

market view is right or wrong, in that a higher P/E is better or worse than a lower one. That is a matter for the individual to decide.

What we are doing when using P/E is relating the price to some other fact about the company, in this case its earnings. Similarly, yield relates the price to the annual dividends paid. There are several other measures that relate the price to something about the stock, examples being assets and sales. It is really only by reference to these that one stock can be compared with another to ascertain which is cheaper or costlier.

Thinking That the Yield Will Apply in the Future

In most cases, the yield figures shown in papers are historical. The exact method varies between papers, but generally it is based on taking the last year's dividends paid, dividing by the share price and expressing the result as a percentage. But it must be borne in mind that no company is obliged to pay dividends at all.

Assuming That Yield Figures Will Always Be Sustainable

If you look through the tables, you can occasionally discover stocks that appear to give enormous yields like 20%—which on the face of it, seem to be a fantastic investment. But if you look behind the figures at announcements from the company, you will very likely find that it is going through a bad time and will probably cut, or eliminate, its dividend in the future. The huge historical yield appears only because the share price has collapsed following the bad news, and a falling share price drives up the yield in inverse proportion. So do not make the mistake of assuming that the yield figures are always sustainable in the future, particularly those that appear astronomically high in relation to the rest of the market.

For More Information

Web Sites:
The Motley Fool: **www.fool.com**
The Wall Street Journal: **www.wsj.com**

See also:
✔ **Calculating Price/Earnings Ratio (P/E) (p. 844)**
✔ **Calculating Earnings per Share (pp. 879–80)**
✔ **Calculating Yield (p. 864)**

Calculating EBITDA

What It Measures

A company's earnings from ongoing operations, before net income is calculated.

Why It Is Important

EBITDA's champions contend it gives investors a sense of how much money a young or fast-growing company is generating before it pays interest on debt, tax collectors, and accounts for non-cash changes. If EBITDA grows over time, champions argue, investors gain at least a sense of long-term profitability and, in turn, the wisdom of their investment.

Business appraisers and investors also may study EBITDA to help gauge a company's fair market value, often as a prelude to its acquisition by another company. It also is frequently applied to companies that have been subject to leveraged buyouts—the strategy being that EBITDA will help cover loan payments needed to finance the transaction.

EBITDA, and EBIT, too, are claimed to be good indicators of cash flow from business operations, since it reports earnings before debt payments, taxes, depreciation, and amortization charges are considered. However, that claim is challenged by many—often rather forcefully.

How It Works in Practice

EBITDA first appeared as leveraged buyouts soared in popularity during the 1980s. It has since become well established as a financial-analysis measure of telecommunications, cable, and major media companies.

Its formula is quite simple. Revenues less the cost of goods sold, general and administrative expenses, and the deductions of items expressed by the acronym, or:

Revenue – Expenses (excluding tax and interest, depreciation, etc) = EBITDA

or:

Revenue – Expenses (excluding tax and interest) = EBIT

This formula does not measure true cash flow. A communications company, for example, once reported $698 million in EBIT but just $324 million in cash from operations.

Tricks of the Trade

- A definition of EBITDA isn't as yet enforced by standards-making bodies, so companies can all but create their own. As a result, EBITDA can easily be manipulated by aggressive accounting policies, which may erode its reliability.
- Ignoring capital expenditures could be unrealistic and horribly misleading, because companies in capital-intensive sectors such as manufacturing and transportation must continually make major capital investments to remain competitive. High-technology is another sector that may be capital-intensive, at least initially.
- Critics warn that using EBITDA as a cash flow indicator is a huge mistake, because EBITDA ignores too many factors that impact true cash flow, such as: working capital, debt payments, and other fixed expenses. Interest and taxes can and do cost a company cash, they point out, while debt holders have higher claims on a company's liquid assets than investors do.
- Critics further assail EBITDA as the barometer of

  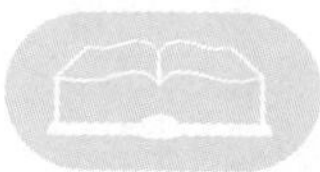    

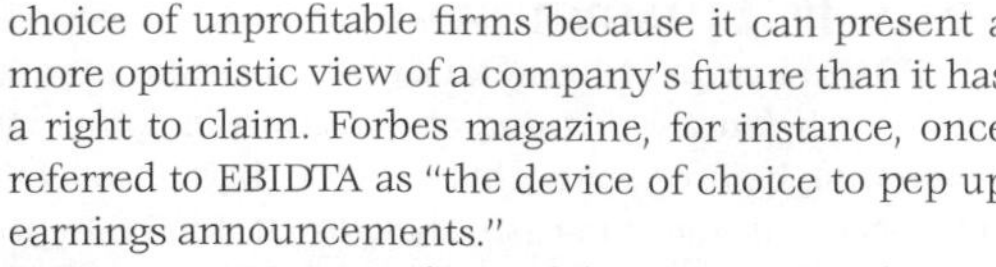

choice of unprofitable firms because it can present a more optimistic view of a company's future than it has a right to claim. Forbes magazine, for instance, once referred to EBIDTA as "the device of choice to pep up earnings announcements."

- Even so, EBITDA may be useful in terms of evaluating firms in the same industry with widely different capital structures, tax rates and depreciation policies.

For More Information

Web Site:
The Motley Fool: **www.fool.com**

Calculating Dividend Cover and Payout Ratio

What It Measures

Dividend cover expresses the number of times a company's dividends to common stockholders could be paid out of its net after-tax profits.

Payout ratio expresses the total dividends paid to shareholders as a percentage of a company's net profit in a given period of time.

Why It Is Important

Whether defined as dividend cover or payout ratio, it measures the likelihood of dividend payments being sustained, and thus is a useful indication of sustained profitability. However, each ratio must be interpreted independently.

A low dividend cover suggests it might be difficult to pay the same level of dividends in a downturn, and that a company is not reinvesting enough in its future. Negative dividend cover is unusual, and a clear sign of trouble.

The payout ratio, expressed as a percentage or fraction, is an inverse measure: a high ratio indicates a lack of reinvestment in the business, and that current earnings cannot sustain the current dividend payments.

How It Works in Practice

Dividend cover is so named because it shows how many times over the profits could have paid the dividend. To calculate dividend cover, divide earnings per share by the dividend per share:

Earnings per share/dividend per share = dividend cover

If a company has earnings per share of 8, and it pays out a dividend of 2.1, dividend cover is:

8/2.1 = 3.80

An alternative formula divides a company's net profit by the total amount allocated for dividends. So a company that earns 10 million in net profit and allocates 1 million for dividends has a dividend cover of 10, while a company that earns 25 million and pays out 10 million in dividends has a dividend cover of 2.5:

10,000,000/1,000,000 = 10 and 25,000,000/10,000,000 = 2.5

The payout ratio is calculated by dividing annual dividends paid on common stock by earnings per share:

Annual dividend/earnings-per-share = payout ratio

Take the company whose earnings per share is 8 and its dividend payout is 2.1. Its payout ratio would be:

2.1/8 = 0.263 or 26.3%

Tricks of the Trade

- A dividend cover ratio of 2 or higher is usually adequate, and indicates that the dividend is affordable. By the same token, the payout ratio should not exceed two-thirds of earnings. Like most ratios, however, both vary by industry.
- A dividend cover ratio below 1.5 is risky, and a ratio below 1 indicates a company is paying the current year's dividend with retained earnings from a previous year—a practice that cannot continue indefinitely.
- The higher the dividend cover figure, the less likely that the dividend will be reduced or eliminated in the future should profits fall. Companies that suffer sharp declines or outright losses will often continue paying dividends to indicate that their substandard performance is an anomaly.
- On the other hand, a high dividend cover figure may disappoint an investor looking for income, since the figure suggests directors could have declared a larger dividend.
- A high payout ratio clearly appeals to conservative investors seeking income. However, when coupled with weak or falling earnings it could suggest an imminent dividend cut, or that the company is short-changing reinvestment to maintain its payout.
- A payout ratio above 75% is a warning. It suggests the company is failing to reinvest sufficient profits in its business, that the company's earnings are faltering, or that it is trying to attract investors who otherwise would not be interested.
- Newer and faster-growing companies often pay no dividends at all in order to reinvest earnings in the company's development.

For More Information

Web Site:
www.finance-glossary.com explains not only dividend cover, but also dividends and dividend yield, and its U.S. equivalents.

"It's one of life's ironies that the more you can prove you don't need a loan, the better your chances usually are of getting one."
(Lillian Vernon)

UNDERSTANDING INTEREST COVER

WHAT IT MEASURES

The amount of earnings available to make interest payments after all operating and non-operating income and expenses—except interest and income taxes—have been accounted for.

WHY IT IS IMPORTANT

Interest cover is regarded as a measure of a company's creditworthiness because it shows how much income there is to cover interest payments on outstanding debt. Banks and financial analysts also rely on this ratio as a rule of thumb to gauge the fundamental strength of a business.

HOW IT WORKS IN PRACTICE

Interest cover is expressed as a ratio, and reflects a company's ability to pay the interest obligations on its debt. It compares the funds available to pay interest—earnings before interest and taxes, or EBIT—with the interest expense. The basic formula is:

EBIT / interest expense = interest coverage ratio

If interest expense for a year is 9 million, and the company's EBIT is 45 million, the interest coverage would be:

45 million / 9 million = 5:1

The higher the number, the stronger a company is likely to be. Conversely, a low number suggests that a company's fortunes are looking ominous. Variations of this basic formula also exist. For example, there is:

Operating cash flow + interest + taxes / interest = Cash-flow interest coverage ratio

This ratio indicates the firm's ability to use its cash flow to satisfy its fixed financing obligations. Finally, there is the fixed-charge coverage ratio, which compares EBIT with fixed charges:

EBIT + lease expenses / interest + lease expense = Fixed charge coverage ratio

"Fixed charges" can be interpreted in many ways, however. It could mean, for example, the funds that a company is obliged to set aside to retire debt, or dividends on preferred stock.

TRICKS OF THE TRADE

- A ratio of less than 1 indicates that a company is having problems generating enough cash flow to pay its interest expenses, and that either a modest decline in operating profits or a sudden rise in borrowing costs could eliminate profitability entirely.
- Ideally, interest coverage should at least exceed 1.5; in some sectors, 2.0 or higher is desirable.
- Interest coverage is widely considered to be more meaningful than looking at total debt, because what really matters is what an enterprise must pay in a given period, not how much debt it has.
- As is often the case, it may be more meaningful to watch interest cover over several periods in order to detect long-term trends.
- Cash flow will sometimes be substituted for EBIT in the ratio, because EBIT includes not only cash but also accrued sales and other unrealized income.
- Interest cover is also called "times interest earned."

For More Information

Web Site:
www.fool.com presents an explanation of interest cover that is both informative and witty.

CALCULATING EARNINGS PER SHARE

WHAT IT MEASURES

The portion of a company's profit allocated to each outstanding share of a company's common stock.

WHY IT IS IMPORTANT

Earnings per share (EPS) is simply a fundamental measure of profitability that shows how much profit was generated on a per-share-of-stock basis. Were the term worded as profit per share, the meaning certainly would be much clearer, if not self-evident.

By itself, EPS doesn't reveal a great deal. Its true value lies in comparing EPS figures across several quarters, or years, to judge the growth of a company's earnings on a per-share basis.

HOW IT WORKS IN PRACTICE

Essentially, the figure is calculated after paying taxes and dividends to preferred shareholders and bondholders. Barring extraordinary circumstances, EPS data is reported quarterly, semiannually, and annually.

To calculate EPS, start with net income (earnings) for the period in question, subtract the total value of any preferred stock dividends, then divide the resulting figure by the number of shares outstanding during that period. Or:

Net income – Dividends on preferred stock / Average number of shares outstanding

By itself, this formula is simple enough. Alas, defining the factors used in the formula invariably introduces complexities and—as some allege on occasion—possible subterfuge.

For instance, while companies usually use a weighted average number of shares outstanding over the reporting period, shares outstanding still can be either "primary" or "fully diluted." Primary EPS is calculated using the number of shares that are currently held by investors in the market and able to be traded. Diluted EPS is the result of a complex calculation that determines how many shares would be outstanding if all exercisable warrants and options were converted into common shares at the end of a quarter. Suppose, for example, that a company has granted a large number of share options to employees. If these options are capable of being exercised in the near future, that could alter significantly the number of shares in issue and thus the EPS—even though the E part (the earnings) is the same. Often in such cases, the company might quote the EPS on the existing shares and the fully diluted version. Which one a person considers depends on their view of the company and how they wish to use the EPS figure. In addition, firms can report extraordinary EPS, a figure which excludes the financial impact of unusual occurrences, such as discontinued operations or the sale of a business unit.

Net income or earnings, meanwhile, can be defined in a number of ways, based upon respective nations' generally accepted accounting principles.

For example, "pro forma earnings," tend to exclude more expenses and income used to calculate "reported earnings." Pro forma advocates insist these earnings eliminate all distortions and present "true" earnings that allow pure apples-to-apples comparisons with preceding periods. However, "non-recurring expenses" seem to occur with such increasing frequency that one may wonder if a company is deliberately trying to manipulate its earnings figures and present them in the best possible light, rather than in the most accurate light.

"Cash" earnings are earnings from operating cash flow—notably, not EBITDA. In turn, cash EPS is usually these earnings divided by diluted shares outstanding. This figure is very reliable because operating cash flow is not subject to as much judgment at net earnings or pro forma earnings.

TRICKS OF THE TRADE

- Given the varieties of earnings and shares reported today, investors need to first determine what the respective figures represent before making investment decisions. There are cases of a company announcing a pro forma EPS that differs significantly from what is reported in its financial statements. Such discrepancies, in turn, can affect how the market values a given stock.
- Investors should check to see if a company has issued more shares during a given period, since that action, too, can affect EPS. A similar problem occurs where there have been a number of shares issued during the accounting period being considered. Which number of issued shares do you use: the opening figure, the closing figure, the mean? In practice the usual method is to use the weighted mean number of shares in issue during the year (weighted, that is, for the amount of time in the year that they have been issued).
- "Trailing" earnings per share is the sum of EPS from the last four quarters, and is the figure used to compute most price-to-earnings ratios.
- Diluted and primary shares outstanding can be the same if a company has no warrants or convertible bonds outstanding, but investors should not assume anything, and need to be sure how "shares outstanding" is being defined.

For More Information

Web Site:
www.investopedia.com/articles/analyst/091901.asp presents a complete but also concise analysis of earnings-per-share, pointing out the many variations and circumstances to be considered.

See also:
✔ **Reading the Financial Pages (pp. 875–77)**
✔ **Calculating Yield (p. 864)**
✔ **Reading an Annual Report (pp. 864–66)**

Recommended Reading for Accounting and Finance Actionlists

Droms, William G. *Finance and Accounting for Nonfinancial Managers*. 4th ed. Cambridge, MA: Perseus, 1998.

Johnson, H. Thomas, and Robert S. Kaplan. *Relevance Lost: The Rise and Fall of Management Accounting*. Boston, MA: Harvard Business School Press, 1991.

Kaplan, Robert S., and Robin Cooper. *Cost and Effect*. Boston, MA: Harvard Business School Press, 1997.

Livingstone, John Leslie. *The Portable MBA in Finance and Accounting*. 3rd ed. New York: John Wiley, 2001.

Keiso, Donald, Jerry J. Wygandt, and Terry D. Warfield. *Intermediate Accounting*. New York: John Wiley, 2001.

McKoen, Paul, and Leo Gough. *The Finance Manual for Non-Financial Managers: How to Make Confident Financial Decisions*. Philadelphia, PA: Trans-Atlantic Publications, 1999.

Rice, Anthony. *Accounts Demystified: How to Understand and Use Company Accounts*. Upper Saddle River, NJ: Financial Times Prentice Hall, 1999.

Tracey, John A. *How to Read a Financial Report*. 5th ed. New York: John Wiley, 1999.

Recommended Reading for Accounting and Finance Activists

Management Library

Management Library

Summarizing the Most Influential Business Books of All Time

There is a vast literature covering business and the world of work, and thousands more new publications emerge every year. Separating the fad-of-the-day from ideas of lasting value can be a daunting prospect. The Management Library distills the main lessons from the most important works ever published. They include both influential new titles such as ***The Age of Unreason*** and ***Blur***, as well as time-honored classics such as Peter Drucker's ***The Practice of Management*** and Frederick W. Taylor's ***The Principles of Scientific Management.***

Each summary includes an analysis of the book's contributions to management thinking and practice, as well as a list of the key points emerging from the work, and a short reading list of related works by the author.

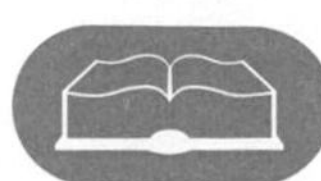

Contents

  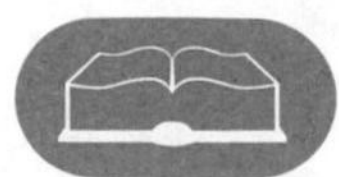    

ACTION LEARNING

Reg Revans

WHY READ IT?

What is the difference between a puzzle and a problem? According to Revans, there is an existing solution to a puzzle and it simply needs to be found. There is no existing solution to a problem. The solution has to be worked out by a process of inquiry that begins at the point where one does not know what to do next and expertise is no help. *Action Learning* explains that process and offers an alternative method of learning to the traditional one, which is based on programmed knowledge instead of encouraging students to ask questions and roam widely around a subject..

GETTING STARTED

As a young man, Reg Revans competed in the 1928 Olympics and worked in the famous Cavendish laboratories at Cambridge, England, alongside such fathers of nuclear physics as Ernest Rutherford and J. J. Thompson. Action learning is his systematization of the methods used by the Cambridge team to deal with problems. He developed them further when working for the National Coal Board after World War II. He also later went on to become Britain's first professor of industrial administration at the University of Manchester.

Action Learning is all about an alternative to traditional education and training. The method it sets out is a form of "learning by doing," but its proponents are careful to distinguish it from simply "learning on the job" or "learning by experience." It involves a collaborative effort, humility, a "trading of one's confusion with that of others," and deep reflection on one's experience and on the nature of the problem. Its outcome is personal growth as much as a way out of a current difficulty.

CONTRIBUTION

1. ACTION LEARNING

The concept of "action learning" is based on a simple equation: L = P + Q. Learning (L) occurs through a combination of programmed knowledge (P) and the ability to ask insightful questions (Q).

It does not deny all usefulness to existing knowledge, but its focus is on asking questions. Learning must be opened up. Programmed knowledge is one-dimensional and rigid; the ability to ask questions opens up other dimensions and is free-flowing.

The first step towards asking constructive questions is to acknowledge one's own ignorance. Too many people are concealing their ignorance under a veneer of knowledge. Instead of hiding our ignorance, according to Revans, we should be bartering it.

The essence of action learning is to become better acquainted with the self through observing what one actually tries to do, endeavoring to ascertain the reasons for attempting it, and tracing the consequences that result from it. Revans said he sought "to focus [his] own doubt by keeping away from experts with prefabricated answers."

2. THE IMPORTANCE OF SMALL TEAM LEARNING

The structure linking the two elements in the equation is the small team or set. The central idea of this approach is collaboration within the set; its members strive to learn with and from each other as they confess failures and expand on victories.

3. A BETTER WAY TO DEVELOP MANAGERS

Action learning is also the antithesis of the traditional approach to developing managers. We keep solving the same problems because we do not learn from them. We bring in consultants to provide solutions or send managers on courses where they are taught a lot but learn little. Action learning is about teaching little and learning a lot.

4. COLLABORATION COUNTS

In industry, managers and workers need to acknowledge the problems they face and then attempt to solve them. When doctors listen to nurses, patients recover more quickly. If mining engineers pay more attention to their workers than to their machinery, the pits are more efficient. It is neither books nor seminars from which managers learn much, but from here-and-now exchanges about the operational job in hand.

According to Revans, "The ultimate power of a successful general staff lies not in the brilliance of its individual members, but in the cross-fertilization of its collective abilities."

CONTEXT

For a long time Revans's ideas were comparatively little known and comparatively undervalued—at least in the English-speaking world. His ideas were received much better in mainland Europe (and in Belgium in particular), however, and he himself spent the final period of his working life abroad. Many management ideas that are currently fashionable, however, such as teamworking, reengineering, and the learning organization, contain elements of "action learning."

One of the critical points about action learning is its relation to action. In a way it appears misnamed. The name at first sight suggests learning in practical situations or performing tasks rather than studying theory. It tends to conceal the centrality of reflection, questioning, especially questioning one's own actions in a deliberate and precise way, ignorance-bartering, and collaborative effort to the process. The solutions that are eventually arrived at must be tested in action, but that is very much the final stage.

Interest in Revans's ideas nevertheless continues to grow. The Pentagon is said to be enthusiastic; the ANC has taken up action learning; General Electric uses action teams to tackle particular problems. There is also a Revans Centre at the University of Salford in England, where the theory and practice of action learning are particularly studied.

For More Information

Revans, Reg. *Action Learning*. London: Blond & Briggs, 1974.

See also:
☆ **Action Learning (pp. 12–13)**
Reg Revans (pp. 1042–43)

"Unless your ideas are ridiculed by experts they are worth nothing." (*Action Learning*)

ADMINISTRATIVE BEHAVIOR

Herbert Simon

WHY READ IT?

Decision making, according to Simon, is synonymous with management. But what is decision making, how are decisions made? Simon realized that most people's assumptions were hopelessly unrealistic. He set out to inject some realism into the subject, but not in a merely reductive way; he also elaborated a very modern concept of the organization as an interrelated and intercommunicating body. He also said that the ability to make decisions effectively made the difference between effectiveness and ineffectiveness in organizations. On that basis alone, his book must be worth reading.

GETTING STARTED

Herbert Simon, the son of German immigrants to Milwaukee and a graduate of the University of Chicago, won the Nobel prize for economics in 1978 for his work on administrative behavior, the subject of his doctoral thesis and this book. He is said to have been inspired to write it by observations made while working part-time for the Milwaukee local authority while a student. He is also said to have told the Nobel committee, when collecting his award, that his real interest was in artificial intelligence—the field into which his interest in how decisions and choices are made ultimately led him.

In *Administrative Behavior: A Study of Decision-making Processes in Administrative Organization* (to give the book its full title), he developed a theory of human choice or decision making that aimed to be sufficiently broad and realistic to accommodate both the rational views of economists and the human concerns of psychologists and practical decision makers.

CONTRIBUTION

1. THE PROBLEMS OF ORGANIZATIONAL THEORY

According to *Administrative Behavior*, the way in which administration is usually described suffers from superficiality, oversimplification, and a lack of realism. Theorists have refused to undertake the tiresome task of studying the actual allocation of decision making functions. Instead, they have been satisfied with talking loosely about authority, centralization, span of control, function, and the like, without seeking operational definitions of these terms.

Classic economic theory also suggests that decisions are made by obtaining all the available information, assessing it, and coming to an objective and rational conclusion as to how the best result can be achieved. In reality, nobody has the time and the mental resources to do this. Instead of aiming for "the best," administrative man is content with what is "good enough," a solution that is "satisficing" (that satisfies and suffices).

2. ORGANIZATION IS IMPORTANT

Organization is important, first, because in our society, people spend most of their waking adult lives in organizations, and this environment provides much of the force that molds and develops personal qualities and habits.

Second, because it provides those in responsible positions with the means for exercising authority and influence over others.

3. THE COMPLEXITY OF ORGANIZATIONAL INTERACTION

It is not sufficient to regard organizational behavior as a matter of understanding people or measuring the performance of people more effectively. Each act in an organization exists in a complex interaction with the organizational system as a whole.

4. UNDERSTANDING DECISION MAKING

A complex decision is like a great river, drawing from its many tributaries the innumerable component premises of which it is constituted.

Many individuals and organization units contribute to every large decision, and the problem of centralization and decentralization is a problem of arranging the complex system into an effective scheme.

5. THE IMPORTANCE OF RELATIONSHIPS

An organization is not an organizational chart, but a complex pattern of communications and other relationships in a group of human beings.

This pattern provides the members of the group with much of the information, assumptions, goals, and attitudes that enter into the decisions made by each and every one of them. It also provides them also with a set of stable and comprehensible expectations as to what the other members of the group are doing and how they will react to what any individual says and does.

CONTEXT

Simon later observed that he must have had a prophetic gift when he included the words "behavior," "decision-making," and "organization" in the book's full title, as they quickly became the fashionable phrases of social science.

Organizational theory had remained deeply bedded in vagueness before the publication of *Administrative Behavior*. Its clearest proponent up to that time had been Chester Barnard who contributed the foreword to Simon's book.

In response, Simon developed a theory of human choice or decision making that aimed to accommodate:

- the rational aspects of choice that have been the principal concern of the economist;
- and the properties and limitations of the human decision-making mechanisms that have attracted the attention of psychologists and practical decision makers.

He thus formed a bridge between the humanists and engineers in management thinking.

His views were ahead of their time. For the next 40 years, organization, in the West at least, continued to be seen as an act of ordering, simplifying, and categorizing rather than as a powerful dynamic and ever-changing force.

Only in the early 1990s, partly through the success of Senge's *The Fifth Discipline*, did systems thinking make the leap from academic obscurity to the executive agenda.

For More Information

Simon, Herbert. *Administrative Behavior: A Study of Decision-making Processes in Administrative Organization.* New York: Free Press, 1997.

"Organization is not an organizational chart, but a complex pattern of communications and other relationships in a group of human beings." (Administrative Behavior)

  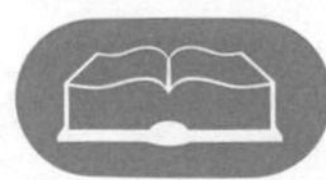    

The Age of Discontinuity

Peter Drucker

Why Read It?

Drucker predicted the rise of the knowledge worker long before the term came into common usage. His definition is much broader than the IT-led version that is currently used. The book gives a valuable insight into the changing nature of management roles and responsibilities in the knowledge economy.

Getting Started

According to Drucker, the manager as knowledge worker was a new breed of thoughtful, intelligent executive. The manager was reincarnated as a responsible individual, paid for applying knowledge, exercising judgment, and taking responsible leadership.

The knowledge worker sees him or herself as another professional. While dependant on the organization for access to income and opportunity, the organization equally depends on him or her.

Knowledge, rather than labor, is the new measure of economic society—and the knowledge worker is the true capitalist in the knowledge society.

Knowledge is not only power, but also ownership of the means of production.

Contribution

1. The Manager As Knowledge Worker

Drucker coined the term "knowledge worker." This was a new breed of executive—a highly trained, intelligent managerial professional who realized his or her own worth and contribution to the organization. Drucker bade farewell to the concept of the manager as mere supervisor or paper shuffler. The manager was reincarnated as a responsible individual.

Though the knowledge worker is not a laborer, and certainly not proletarian, he or she is not a subordinate (in the sense that he or she can be told what to do). The knowledge worker is paid, on the contrary, for applying his or her knowledge, exercising judgment, and taking responsible leadership.

2. The Nature of the Knowledge Worker

According to Drucker, the knowledge worker sees him or herself just as another professional, no different from the lawyer, the teacher, the preacher, the doctor, or the government servant of yesterday. He or she has the same education, but more income—and probably greater opportunities as well.

The knowledge worker may well realize that he or she depends on the organization for access to income and opportunity, and that without the organization, there would be no job. But there is also the realization that the organization depends equally on him or her.

Drucker effectively wrote the obituary for the obedient, gray-suited, loyal, corporate man and woman. The only trouble was, it took this corporate creature another 20 years to die.

3. The Impact of Knowledge Workers

The social ramifications of this new breed of corporate executive were significant. If knowledge, rather than labor, was the new measure of economic society then the fabric of capitalist society had to change. The knowledge worker is both the true capitalist in the knowledge society and dependent on his or her job.

Collectively, the knowledge workers—the employed, educated middle class of today's society—own the means of production through pension funds, investment trusts, and so on.

Knowledge was not only power, but it was also ownership.

Context

The book effectively mapped out the demise of the age of mass, labor-based production and the advent of the knowledge-based, information age.

Drucker's realization that the role of the manager had fundamentally changed was not a sudden one. The foundations of the idea of the knowledge worker can be seen in his description of management by objectives in *The Practice of Management* (1954).

Knowledge management, intellectual capital, and the like are now the height of corporate fashion. The modern idea of the knowledge worker is a creature of the technological age, the mobile executive, the hot-desker.

Drucker provided a characteristically broader perspective. He placed the rise of the knowledge worker in the evolution of management into a respectable and influential discipline.

Drucker has since developed his thinking on the role of knowledge, most notably in his 1992 book, *Managing for the Future*, in which he observed, "From now on the key is knowledge. The world is becoming not labor intensive, not materials intensive, not energy intensive, but knowledge intensive."

The Age of Discontinuity was startlingly correct in its predictions. Much of it would fit easily into business books of today.

Management guru Gary Hamel said, "Peter Drucker's reputation is as a management theorist. He has also been a management prophet. Writing in 1969, he clearly anticipated the emergence of the knowledge economy. I'd like to set a challenge for would-be management gurus: try to find something to say that Peter Drucker has not said first, and has not said well. This high hurdle should substantially reduce the number of business books clogging the bookshelves of booksellers, and offer managers the hope of gaining some truly fresh insights."

For More Information

Drucker, Peter. *The Age of Discontinuity*. Woburn, MA: Butterworth-Heinemann, 1969.

See also:
Peter Drucker (pp. 982–85)

"If knowledge, rather than labor, is the new measure of economic society then the fabric of capitalist society must change."
(*The Age of Discontinuity*)

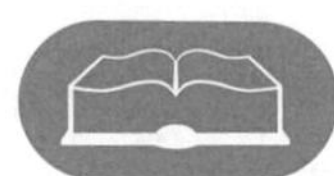

The Age of Unreason

Charles Handy

Why Read It?

Written in 1989, this book includes a number of incisive predictions about the way work would develop. The author provides valuable insights into changing organizational structures and developments such as knowledge working, outsourcing, and strategic alliances—the hallmarks of the new economy.

Getting Started

The age of unreason is a time when the future is shaped by us and for us. At such a time, a number of organizational forms will emerge, as will new working patterns, such as outsourcing, telecommuting, the intellectual capital movement, and the rise of knowledge workers.

The portfolio worker will become more important, contributing to a greater work/life balance. A work portfolio is a way of describing how the different bits of work in our lives fit together to form a balanced whole. Portfolio work includes wage work and fee work, homework, gift work, and study work.

The social changes resulting from these developments will be reflected in changing patterns of business, with a mix of small enterprises and large conglomerates. There will also be temporary alliances of large and small organizations to deliver a particular project.

Contribution

1. The Concept of an Age of Unreason

The age of unreason is a time when the future, in so many areas, is to be shaped by us and for us. The only prediction that will hold true is that no predictions will hold true. It will be a time for thinking the unlikely and doing the unreasonable.

2. New Organizational Forms

A number of organizational forms will emerge in an age of unreason:

- the shamrock organization
- the federal organization
- the Triple I organization

The shamrock organization is a form of organization based around a core of essential executives and workers supported by outside contractors and part-time help.

The federal organization is a form of decentralized set-up, in which the center's powers are given to it by the outlying groups; the center therefore coordinates, advises, influences, and suggests rather than directs or controls. Federalism is the way to combine the autonomy of individual parts with the economics of coordination.

The Triple I organization is based on Information, Intelligence, and Ideas. This type of organization will resemble a university and will seek to make added value out of knowledge. To achieve this, the Triple I organization increasingly uses smart machines, with smart people to work with them.

3. New Working Patterns

Handy anticipated the growth of outsourcing, telecommuting, the intellectual capital movement, and the rise of knowledge workers. He also foresaw how these developments might affect the individual. His concept of the portfolio worker helped redefine the nature of work, as well as questions of work/life balance.

4. Portfolio Working

A work portfolio is a way of describing how the different bits of work in our life fit together to form a balanced whole. There are five main categories of Portfolio work:

- wage work and fee work, which are both forms of paid work;
- homework, gift work, and study work, which are all free work.

Wage (or salary) work represents money paid for time given.

Fee work is money paid for results delivered. Employees do wage work; professionals, craftspeople and freelancers do fee work. Fee work is increasing as jobs move outside the organization. Some employees now get fees (bonuses) as well as wages.

Homework includes that whole catalog of tasks that go on in the home, from cooking and cleaning, to children and carpentry. Done willingly or grudgingly, it is all work.

Gift work is work done for free outside the home, for charities and local groups, for neighbors or for the community.

Study work done seriously is a form of work, not recreation.

5. A Broader Portfolio

In the past, for most people, the work portfolio has had only one item in it-their career. This was a risky strategy. Few people would put all their money into one asset, yet that is what most people were doing with their lives. The career had to provide many things at once—interest or satisfaction in the work, interesting people and good company, security, money, and the opportunity for development.

6. Funding the Portfolio

Portfolio people think in terms of portfolio money, not salary money. Money comes in fits and starts from different sources, for example a bit of a pension, some part-time work, some fees to charge or things to sell. They lead cash-flow lives not salary lives, planning always to have enough in-flows to cover out-flows.

Portfolio people think in terms of barter and know that most skills are saleable if you want to sell them.

7. Changing Patterns of Business

It will be a world of "fleas and elephants"—large conglomerates and small individual entities, or large political and economic blocs and small countries.

A small enterprise can be global as easily as a large conglomerate, but can more easily be swept away. Conglomerates are a guarantee of continuity, but small enterprises provide the innovation.

There will also be ad hoc organizations, temporary alliances of large and small organizations to deliver a particular project.

Context

The book predicts many of the important changes in working patterns which are now commonplace, including outsourcing, telecommuting, and virtual project teams from different organizations.

It also recognized the rapidly growing importance of knowledge workers and intellectual capital.

For More Information

Handy, Charles. *The Age of Unreason*. London: Hutchinson, 1989.

See also:
☆ **Viewpoint: Charles Handy (pp. 75–76)**
Charles Handy (pp. 1000–01)

"The age of unreason is a time for bold imaginings, for thinking the unlikely and doing the unreasonable."
(*The Age of Unreason*)

The Art of Japanese Management

Richard Pascale
Anthony Athos

Why Read It?

This book was one of the first business bestsellers. It played a crucial role in the discovery of Japanese management techniques. In its comparisons of Japanese and U.S. companies, it provides rare insights into the truth behind the mythology of Japanese management and the inadequacy of much Western practice.

Getting Started

By the late 1990s, growing Japanese superiority threatened the United States' dominant position in world markets. A major reason for the superiority of the Japanese is their managerial skill. Japanese managers have vision, something notably lacking in the West. In Japan, visions are dynamic, rather than generic statements of corporate intent. U.S. managers are constrained by their beliefs and assumptions. The seven S framework (strategy, structure, skills, staff, shared values, systems, and style) represents the key categories requiring managers' attention. The Japanese succeeded through attention to the "soft" Ss—style, shared values, skills, and staff, while the West remained preoccupied with the "hard" Ss of strategy, structure, and systems.

Contribution

1. Growing Japanese Superiority

In 1980, Japan's GNP was third highest in the world. Extrapolating trends at the time, it looked likely to be the highest by the year 2000.

For the U.S. readership, *The Art of Japanese Management* contains some hard-hitting truths.

If anything, the extent of Japanese superiority over the United States in industrial competitiveness is underestimated.

2. Managerial Skills

A major reason for the superiority of the Japanese is their managerial skills.

Among the key components of Japanese management is vision, something they found to be notably lacking in the West.

The tools are there but vision is limited.

Beliefs, assumptions, and perceptions about management frequently constrain U.S. managers. The Western vision of management circumscribes our effectiveness.

In Japan, managers enhance their modus operandi via dynamic visions rather than pallid or generic statements of corporate intent.

3. The Seven S Framework

The book is best known for its central concept: the seven S framework.

As a generic statement of the issues facing organizations the seven S framework is unremarkable, though it did gain a great deal of attention. It simply lists the seven important categories that managers should take into account—strategy, structure, skills, staff, shared values, systems, and style.

According to Pascale, the value of a framework such as the seven Ss is that it imposes an interesting discipline on the researcher.

4. Comparing Management Styles

The seven Ss presents a framework for comparing Japanese and U.S. management approaches.

The Japanese succeeded largely because of the attention they gave to the "soft" Ss—style, shared values, skills, and staff.

The West remained preoccupied with the "hard" Ss of strategy, structure, and systems.

Since the book's publication, the general trend of Western managerial thinking has been directed towards the soft Ss.

Context

The book played a crucial role in the discovery of Japanese management techniques.

The authors considered how a country the same size as Montana could be outstripping the U.S. industrial juggernaut in terms of performance.

The roots of the book lie in Pascale's work with the U.S. National Commission on Productivity. Having initially thought that lessons from Japan were limited for cultural reasons, Pascale decided it would be more productive to look at Japanese companies in the United States. The research for the book eventually covered 34 companies over six years.

The authors' championing of vision proved highly influential. It was Athos who really started the entire "visioning" industry in the United States.

Soon after *The Art of Japanese Management*, a flurry of books appeared highlighting so-called visionaries. Today, corporate visions are a fact of life.

Leading author Gary Hamel commented, "Japan-phobia has subsided a bit, helped by a strong yen, inept Japanese macro economic policy, and the substantial efforts of many Western companies to rebuild their competitiveness. While Pascale and Athos undoubtedly overstated the unique capabilities of Japanese management (is Matsushita really that much better managed than Hewlett-Packard?), they successfully challenged the unstated assumption that the United States was the font of all managerial wisdom. Since *The Art of Japanese Management* hit the bookstores, U.S. companies have learned much from Japan. Pascale and Athos deserve credit for setting the learning agenda."

For More Information

Pascale, Richard Tanner, and Anthony Athos. *The Art of Japanese Management*. New York: Simon & Schuster, 1981.

See also:
Richard Tanner Pascale (pp. 1034–35)

"The Western vision of management circumscribes our effectiveness." (The Art of Japanese Management)

THE ART OF WAR

Sun Tzu

WHY READ IT?

When the postwar achievements of Japanese industry began to make a significant impression in the West, and Western businesspeople began to inquire into the thinking that underlay the success of their Eastern counterparts, Sun Tzu's *The Art of War* was a book that was often mentioned. This may seem surprising as it was probably written some 2,500 years ago. But military language and imagery have played an important role in the development of management thinking, and if you wish to gain an insight into strategy, leadership, and survival in a hostile, competitive environment, who better to turn to than a general whose name is a byword for sagacity?

GETTING STARTED

Sun Tzu is thought to have lived over 2,400 years ago, at roughly the same time as Confucius. Historians are generally agreed that he was a general who led a number of successful military campaigns in present-day Anhui Province; the state of Wu, under whose sovereign he served, became a dominant power at that time. Since then, it has become standard practice for Chinese military chiefs to familiarize themselves with his writings.

The Art of War (the book's actual title is *Sun Tzu Ping Fa*, literally "The Military Method of Mr. Sun") is a compilation of the legendary general's thinking on the strategies that underlie military success. His anecdotes and thoughts, which fill no more than about 25 pages of text in all, are divided into 13 sections. Not all of them are relevant to modern-day concerns, but some strike a significant chord. Rather like a proponent of judo, Sun Tzu particularly recommends using the momentum of your enemy's own moves to defeat him.

CONTRIBUTION

1. GET THE STRATEGY RIGHT

Sun Tzu, like most good and seasoned generals, is anything but an adventurer and anything but gung-ho. "Why destroy," he asks, "when you can win by stealth and cunning? To subdue the enemy's forces without fighting is the summit of skill."

His advice shows subtlety and restraint: "A sovereign should not start a war out of anger, nor should a general give battle out of rage. While anger can revert to happiness and rage to delight, a nation that has been destroyed cannot be restored, nor can the dead be brought back to life."

He continues: "The best approach is to attack the other side's strategy; next best is to attack his alliances; next best is to attack his soldiers; the worst is to attack cities."

2. GET INFORMATION FROM THE RIGHT SOURCES

Sun Tzu also gives sound advice on knowing your markets, saying: "Advance knowledge cannot be gained from ghosts and spirits, but must be obtained from people who know the enemy situation."

3. STAY FOCUSED

His view on strategy leaves no room for sentiment or distraction.

"Deploy forces to defend the strategic points; exercise vigilance in preparation, do not be indolent. Deeply investigate the true situation, secretly await their laxity. Wait until they leave their strongholds, then seize what they love."

CONTEXT

So what does *The Art of War* have to offer the manager of a small components factory in, say, Peoria or Nottingham? Sun Tzu's admirers argue that his pithy sayings encapsulate basic and eternal truths. According to Gary Hamel, "Strategy didn't start with Igor Ansoff; neither did it start with Machiavelli. It probably didn't even start with Sun Tzu. Strategy is as old as human conflict. . ." Anyone, therefore, who has to devise a plan, anyone who has to give a lead, can do with all the help they can get.

Hamel goes on to add ". . .and, if the stakes are high in business, they're rather higher in the military sphere." One of the attractions of the military analogy and the military role model in business is that they elevate proceedings to a loftier plane. Not only are the issues larger, and the scale more heroic, but it is clear who your enemy is, and when your enemy is clear, the world appears clearer whether you are a military general or a managing director.

Embattled managers, in particular, may benefit from the stimulus that military authors, like Sun Tzu, Clausewitz, or Liddell-Hart, and the writings of modern military leaders, like Colin Powell or Norman Schwarzkopf, can give to their civilian imaginations.

Finally, as has often been pointed out, Sun Tzu has long been revered in the East. He is said to be required reading not only for Eastern military tacticians but also for Eastern businesspeople. To know your enemies—or indeed to know your friends, partners, and colleagues—it is useful to have read what they read.

For More Information

Sun Tzu. *The Art of War* (trans. Sawyer). Boulder: Westview Press, 1994.

See also:
Sun Tzu (pp. 1050–51)

"Water flows in accordance with the ground; an army achieves victory in accordance with the enemy."

(*The Art of War*)

A BEHAVIORAL THEORY OF THE FIRM

Richard Cyert
James March

WHY READ IT?

The book is useful introduction to the complex world of decision making. One of its authors, James G. March, is one of the foremost decision making theorists of the 20th century. The book evaluates traditional approaches to decision making and puts forward real-world alternatives.

GETTING STARTED

An entire academic discipline, decision science, is devoted to understanding management decision making. Early thinkers believed that the decision process could be rationalized and systematized. However, reality is often more confused and messy, and managers make decisions based on a combination of intuition, experience and analysis.

CONTRIBUTION

1. THE EVOLUTION OF DECISION-MAKING THEORY

Early theories were based on the premise that, under a given set of circumstances, human behavior is logical and therefore predictable.

A profusion of models, software packages and analytical tools followed, seeking to distil decision making into a formula. The danger is in concluding that the solution provided by a software package is the answer.

2. THE RATIONAL THEORY OF DECISION MAKING

The rational, or synoptic, model of decision making involves a series of steps:

- identifying and clarifying the problem;
- prioritizing goals;
- generating and evaluating options;
- comparing predicted outcomes of each option with the goals;
- choosing the option that best matches the goals.

These models rely on a number of assumptions about the way in which people will behave when confronted with a set of circumstances. The assumptions allow mathematicians to derive formulae based on probability theory. The decision-making tools include such things as cost/benefit analysis, which aims to help managers evaluate different options.

3. PROBLEMS IN THE RATIONAL THEORY

Reality is often more confused and messy than a neat model can allow for. Underpinning the mathematical approach are a number of flawed assumptions. The model assumes that decision making is:

- consistent;
- based on accurate information;
- free from emotion or prejudice;
- rational.

4. REAL-WORLD DECISION MAKING

The reality is that managers make decisions based on a combination of intuition, experience and analysis. As intuition and experience are impossible to quantify, the temptation is to focus on the analytical side of decision making.

5. THE RELEVANCE OF DECISION-MAKING MODELS

This does not mean that decision theory is redundant or that decision-making models should be cast to one side.

A number of factors mean that decision making is becoming ever more demanding. The growth in complexity means that companies no longer encounter simple problems. Complex decisions are now not solely the preserve of senior managers but the responsibility of many others. Managers are having to deal with a flood of information: a 1996 Reuters survey of 1,200 managers worldwide found that 43% thought important decisions were delayed and their ability to make decisions affected as a result of having too much information.

Decision theory and the use of models is reassuring, as they lend legitimacy to decisions that may be based on prejudices or hunches. However, no model is foolproof; none is universally applicable, and none can yet cope with the idiosyncrasies of human behavior.

6. THE CHALLENGE FOR ORGANIZATIONAL DECISION MAKING

Business decision-making theory faces a crucial and immediate problem: individuals have goals; collective groups do not. There is a need, therefore, is to create useful organizational goals, while not believing there is such a thing as an organizational mind.

Organizations should be regarded as coalitions that negotiate goals.

Creating goals requires three processes:

- bargaining, which establishes the composition and terms of the coalition;
- internal organizational control, which clarifies and develops the objectives;
- adjustment to experience, which alters agreements in accord with changing circumstances.

Goals are inconsistent for three reasons:

- decision making being decentralized;
- short-term goals taking most managerial attention;
- the resources available to the organization being insufficient to maintain the coalition.

7. A NEW DECISION-MAKING MODEL

The five principal goals of the modern organization are production, inventory, sales, market share, and profit. There are nine steps in the decision process: forecast competitors' behavior; forecast demand; estimate costs; specify objectives; evaluate plans; reexamine costs; reexamine demand; reexamine objectives; select alternatives. To work successfully, this decision-making model demands that there are standard operating procedures. The procedures can be divided into general ones based on avoiding uncertainty, maintaining the rules, and using simple rules. There are also specifics, such as task performance rules, continuing records and reports, information-handling rules, and plans.

CONTEXT

Much of decision science is built on the foundations set down by early business thinkers, such as computer pioneer, Charles Babbage, and scientific management founder, Frederick W. Taylor, who believed that, under a given set of circumstances, human behavior was logical and predictable. Based on this premise, models emerged to explain the workings of commerce which, it was thought, could be extended to the way in which decisions were made.

For More Information

Cyert, Richard, and James March.
A Behavioral Theory of the Firm.
Upper Saddle River, NJ: Prentice Hall, 1963.

"Managers make decisions based on a combination of intuition, experience and analysis."

(*A Behavioral Theory of the Firm*)

BLUR

Stan Davis
Christopher Meyer

WHY READ IT?

Blur is a book about the future, but the authors do not offer prescriptions. Instead they offer a starting point: provocative ideas, observations, and predictions to get you to think creatively about your business and your future.

GETTING STARTED

At the heart of *Blur* are three forces—connectivity, speed, and intangibles—that are redefining businesses and destroying solutions that worked for the industrial world. The forces are known as the blur of desires, the blur of fulfillment, and the blur of resources.

A product offer and exchange were once clear cut, but buyers and sellers are now in a constantly evolving relationship. The entire theory and practice of competitive strategy is changing, and intellectual capital has emerged as the key resource.

Change no longer carries the huge weight it did only a few years ago, and connectivity is speeding the economy up and changing the way it works.

CONTRIBUTION

1. THE NATURE OF *BLUR*

At the heart of the authors' Blur theory are three forces: connectivity, speed, and intangibles. These forces are blurring the rules and redefining our businesses and our lives.

They are destroying solutions, such as mass production, segmented pricing, and standardized jobs, that worked for the relatively slow, unconnected industrial world.

The three forces are shaping the behavior of the new economy.

They are affecting what Davis and Meyer label the blur of desires; the blur of fulfillment, and the blur of resources.

2. THE BLUR OF DESIRES

The blur of desires has two central elements—the offer and the exchange that were once clear cut.

In the product-dominated age, a company offered a product for sale. Money was exchanged and the customer disappeared into the distance.

Now, products and services are often indistinguishable from each other. Buyers and sellers are in a constantly evolving relationship—a mutual exchange—which is driven by information and emotion as well as by money.

3. THE BLUR OF FULFILLMENT

As organizations change to meet changing demands, so too must the entire theory and practice of competitive strategy.

Connectivity produces different forms of organization operating to different first principles.

The blur of businesses has created a new economic model in which returns increase rather than diminish; supermarkets mimic stock markets, and you want the market, not your strategy, to price, market, and manage your offer.

4. THE BLUR OF RESOURCES

Intellectual capital has emerged as the key resource.

Hard assets have become intangibles; intangibles have become your only assets.

5. CHANGE IS LESS CRITICAL

Built to last now means built to change. However change, and the ambiguity it brings, no longer carries the huge weight it did only a few years ago.

6. THE IMPACT OF CONNECTIVITY

In the information economy, small things are connected in myriad ways to create a complex adaptive system.

Instantaneous, myriad connections are speeding the economy up and changing the way it works. The problem is that the connections are so many and so complex, that they can bring things to a grinding, inexplicable halt.

CONTEXT

From Dale Carnegie to Stephen Covey, Frederick Taylor to Michael Porter, business book readers have been weaned on a diet of prescriptions for success. Books are distilled down to a handful of key points or simple models. The trouble is that lists of the essential ingredients for success are becoming increasingly more questionable.

Uncertainty is uncharted territory and *Blur* is a book of the new breed. *Blur* would not even have been considered as a possible title just a few years ago when blind faith and certainty ruled. It would have been too weak, too suggestive of managerial confusion and impotence, too realistic.

For More Information

Davis, Stan, and Christopher Meyer. *Blur*. Cambridge, MA: Perseus, 1998.

See also:
☆ **Viewpoint: Stan Davis and Christopher Meyer (pp. 9–11)**

"Built to last now means built to change." (*Blur*)

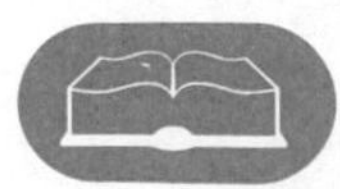

THE BORDERLESS WORLD

Kenichi Ohmae

WHY READ IT?

Like *The Mind of the Strategist*, the book gives valuable insights into the strategic thinking behind Japanese corporate success. The author adds new elements to the structure of business strategy, showing how it operates on a global scale.

GETTING STARTED

In the global marketplace, the concepts of country and currency are important to business strategy. Fluctuations in trade policy or exchange rates can affect an otherwise brilliant strategy. Strategy is about more than being better than the competition. Big companies must relearn the art of invention in global industries. Customers are not driven to purchase things through nationalistic sentiments, therefore strategy should be formulated around a determination to create value for customers. Global business balances world-scale economies with products tailored to key markets. The role of central governments must change to allow individuals access to the best and cheapest goods and services from anywhere in the world.

CONTRIBUTION

1. THE KEY ELEMENTS OF BUSINESS STRATEGY

To the three Cs of his previous works (commitment, creativity, and competitiveness), Ohmae adds:

- country—the government-created environments in which global organizations must operate;
- currency—the exposure of such organizations to fluctuations in foreign exchange rates.

These two additional elements are now key to the formulation of any strategy.

An otherwise brilliant strategy can be ruined by a sudden fluctuation in trade policy or exchange rates, leading to a seemingly irreparable hemorrhage of cash.

Making arrangements to deal with fluctuations must lie at the very heart of strategy.

Strategy is creating sustained values for the customer more effectively than the competitors.

2. INVENTION IS CRITICAL

Invention and the commercialization of invention are essential. Most people in big companies have forgotten how to invent.

It's time for big companies to relearn the art of invention.

This time they must learn to manage invention in industries or businesses that are global, where it is necessary to achieve world-scale economies and yet tailor products to key markets.

3. GOING BEYOND THE COMPETITION

Strategy is about more than simply being better than the competition, which only encourages companies to become fixated on the competition. This fixation drives them to formulate their strategy according to the strategy of their competitors.

Possible strategies should be tested against competitive realities.

Tactical responses to what competitors are doing may be appropriate, but they should come second to your real strategy.

Before you test yourself against the competition, your strategy should encompass the determination to create value for customers.

3. THE INTERLINKED ECONOMY

Countries are merely government creations.

In the Interlinked Economy (made up of the Triad of the United States, Europe and Japan) consumers are not driven to purchase things through nationalistic sentiments, no matter what politicians may say.

At the cash register, people don't care about country of origin or country of residence. They don't think about employment figures or trade deficits.

This also applies to industrial consumers.

4. DECLARATION OF INTERDEPENDENCE

The role of central governments must change to:

- allow individuals access to the best and cheapest goods and services from anywhere in the world;
- help corporations provide stable and rewarding jobs anywhere in the world, regardless of the corporation's national identity;
- coordinate activities with other governments to minimize conflicts arising from narrow interests;
- avoid abrupt changes in economic and social fundamentals.

Governments must deal collectively with traditionally parochial affairs, including taxation.

CONTEXT

The Borderless World explores the new logic of the global marketplace as well as what Ohmae calls power and strategy in the interlinked economy.

This manifesto for the future is as broad ranging as it is, in political reality, unlikely.

The Borderless World has, however, fueled debates about the role of governments, as well as the relationship between governments and the business world, which have yet to be resolved.

Ohmae has since gone on to explore the role of nations still further and now suggests that we have reached a time when the end of the nation state is imminent (see *The End of the Nation State*, Free Press, 1996, and *The Invisible Continent*, HarperBusiness, 2001).

Leading business author Gary Hamel commented, "So the world is becoming interdependent. Hardly news to companies like Dow Chemical, IBM, Ford, or Nestlé. But in 1990 this was still news to Japanese companies (and politicians) who typically defined globalization as big open export markets, and maybe a factory in Tennessee. Kenichi challenged Japanese companies, and myopic executives elsewhere, to develop a more sophisticated view of what it means to be global. Just what balance will ultimately be struck between the forces of globalization and the forces of nationalism and tribalism remains to be seen."

For More Information

Ohmae, Kenichi. *The Borderless World: Power and Strategy in the Interlinked Economy*. New York: HarperBusiness, 1990.

See also:
Kenichi Ohmae (pp. 1028–29)

"It's time for big companies to relearn the art of invention."

(*The Borderless World*)

Built to Last

James Collins
Jerry Porras

Why Read It?

According to the authors, companies that enjoy enduring success have core values and a core purpose that remain fixed, while their business strategies and practices endlessly adapt to a changing world. The book shows the importance of developing and sticking to a set of guiding principles, and identifies the qualities essential to building a great and enduring organization.

Getting Started

Values are important in the context of business and corporations, and many companies have long recognized the importance of possessing a set of guiding principles.

Enduring organizations with strong guiding principles have outperformed the general stock market by a factor of 12 since 1925.

Core values are the organization's essential and enduring tenets, and drive the way the company operates at a level that transcends strategic objectives. Such values don't change, although strategies and practices adapt endlessly to change.

Core ideology defines what the company stands for and why it exists. It complements the envisioned future—what the company aspires to become. Any effective vision must embody the core ideology of the organization.

Contribution

1. The Importance of Corporate Values

Honesty, integrity, wealth, fairness are all values that we may be able to relate to on an individual personal basis. But what about values in the context of business and corporations?

While the term "corporate values" is a relative newcomer to the business lexicon, the concept of values as an important aspect of corporate life is not. Many companies have long recognized the importance of possessing a set of guiding principles, and the evolution of the concept can be traced through some of the most influential business books over the last 50 years.

Thomas Watson, Jr., C.E.O. of IBM, observed that any great organization that has lasted over the years owes its resiliency to the power of its beliefs and the appeal these beliefs have for its people.

2. The Qualities of an Enduring Organization

The book sets out to identify the qualities essential to building a great and enduring organization—the successful habits of visionary companies.

The 18 companies chosen as subjects had outperformed the general stock market by a factor of 12 since 1925.

Core values are the organization's essential and enduring tenets. These are a small set of guiding principles (not to be confused with specific cultural or operating practices) which are never to be compromized for financial gain or short-term expediency.

Values are timeless guiding principles that drive the way the company operates at a level that transcends strategic objectives. For Hewlett-Packard, for example, values include a strong sense of responsibility to the community. For Disney, they include creativity, dreams, and imagination and the promulgation of wholesome American values.

3. Core Values Don't Change

Companies that enjoy enduring success have core values and a core purpose that remain fixed while their business strategies and practices endlessly adapt to a changing world. This is a key factor in the success of companies such as Hewlett-Packard, Johnson & Johnson, Procter & Gamble, Mercke, and Sony.

4. A Model for Core Values

The authors recommend a conceptual framework to cut through some of the confusion swirling around the issues.

In their model, vision has two components—core ideology and envisioned future.

Core ideology, the Yin in their scheme, defines what the company stands for and why it exists.

Yin is unchanging and complements Yang, the envisioned future.

The envisioned future is what the company aspires to become, to achieve, to create—something that will require considerable change and progress to attain.

Core ideology provides the glue that holds an organization together through time.

5. An Effective Vision

Any effective vision must embody the core ideology of the organization. This has two components—core values (a system of guiding principles and tenets) and core purpose (the organization's most fundamental reason for existence).

Context

Built to Last set out to identify the qualities, or corporate values, essential to building a great and enduring organization.

The evolution of the concept of corporate values can be traced through some of the most influential business books over the last 50 years.

In *A Business and Its Beliefs*, published in 1963, Thomas Watson, Jr. observed, "Consider any great organization—one that has lasted over the years—I think you will find it owes its resiliency not to its form of organization or administrative skills, but to the power of what we call beliefs and the appeal these beliefs have for its people."

In the early 1980s, Tom Peters and Robert Waterman thought corporate values important enough to warrant an entire chapter in *In Search of Excellence*.

For More Information

Collins, James, and Jerry Porras. *Built to Last*. New York: HarperBusiness, 1994.

"Companies that enjoy enduring success have core values and a core purpose that remain fixed while their business strategies and practices endlessly adapt to a changing world." (Built to Last)

  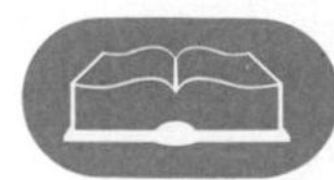    

A BUSINESS AND ITS BELIEFS

Thomas Watson, Jr.

WHY READ IT?

A Business and Its Beliefs: The Ideas that Helped Build IBM was written by the son of the founder of IBM's commercial greatness, who himself led the company into the computer age. It describes the origins of one of the world's most successful corporations and shows how its achievements were built on a strong corporate culture and a passionate commitment to customer service.

GETTING STARTED

Thomas Watson, Jr. went to work for IBM in 1946 as a salesman. He was appointed chief executive in 1956 and retired in 1970, after presiding over IBM's rise to international preeminence at the beginning of the computer age.

IBM's origins lay in the Computing-Tabulating-Recording Company, which Thomas Watson, Sr. joined in 1914. The company initially made everything from butcher's scales to meat slicers, but gradually concentrated on tabulating machines that processed information mechanically on punched cards. It changed its name to International Business Machines in 1924.

IBM's development was helped by the 1937 Wages-Hours Act, which required U.S. companies to record hours worked and wages paid. The existing machines couldn't cope; Watson, Sr. developed a solution, the Mark 1, followed by the Selective Sequence Electronic Calculator in 1947. By then IBM's revenues were $119 million and it was set to make the great leap forward to become the world's largest computer company.

As far as management thinking is concerned, what IBM stood for is more important than what it did. Thomas Watson, Jr. took on a hugely successful company with a strong corporate culture built around salesmanship and service. Thomas Watson Sr. had emphasized people and service obsessively. IBM was a service star in an era of machines that performed badly. This is where the heart of the message of *A Business and Its Beliefs* lies.

CONTRIBUTION

1. CORE VALUES ARE CRITICAL

A company's central beliefs (what would now be called its core values) are central to its success. Watson believed that these beliefs help people find common cause with each other, and sustain this common cause and sense of direction through the many changes that take place from one generation to another.

Success, in his view, comes through a sound set of beliefs, on which the corporation premises all its policies and actions. Beliefs must always come before policies, practices, and goals. The latter must always be altered if they are seen to violate fundamental beliefs.

Not only should the beliefs be sound, they should be stuck to through thick and thin. The most important single factor in corporate success is faithful adherence to those beliefs. Beliefs never change. Change everything else, but never the basic truths on which the company is based.

However, Watson argued for flexibility in all other areas. If an organization, he asserted, is to meet the challenges of a changing world, it must be prepared to change everything about itself except beliefs as it moves through corporate life. The only sacred cow in an organization should be its basic philosophy of doing business.

2. DEVELOP A CORPORATE CULTURE

The beliefs that mold great organizations frequently grow out of the character, the experience, and the convictions of a single person. In IBM's case that person was Thomas Watson, Sr.

The Watsons created a corporate culture that lasted. IBM, Big Blue, became the archetypal modern corporation and its managers the ultimate stereotype, with their regulation somber suits, white shirts, plain ties, zeal for selling, and company song.

3. A PASSION FOR COMPETING

Behind the corporate culture lay a belief in competing vigorously and providing quality service. Later, competitors complained that IBM's sheer size won it orders. This was only partly true. Its size masked a deeper commitment to managing customer accounts, providing service, building relationships, and to the values laid out by the Watsons.

4. PEOPLE MATTER

The real difference between success and failure in a corporation can very often be traced to the question of how well the organization brings out the great energies and talents of its people. Giving full consideration to the individual employee was one of the enduring beliefs on which IBM's success was built.

CONTEXT

In this book, the author codified and clarified what IBM stands for. The book is a statement of business philosophy, an extended mission statement for IBM.

Though it was published in the same year as Alfred P. Sloan, Jr.'s *My Years with General Motors* it could not be more different. While Sloan sidelines people, Watson celebrates their potential; while Sloan espouses systems and structures, Watson talks of values.

Guru Gary Hamel commented, "Never change your basic beliefs, Watson argued. He may be right. But the dividing line between beliefs and dogmas is a fine one. A deep set of beliefs can be the essential pivot around which the company changes and adapts; or, if endlessly-elaborated, overly-codified, and solemnly worshipped, the manacles that shackle a company to the past."

For More Information

Watson, Thomas, Jr. *A Business and Its Beliefs: The Ideas That Helped Build IBM.* New York: McGraw-Hill, 1963.

"The secret I learned early on from my father was to run scared and never think I had made it."

(*A Business and Its Beliefs*)

  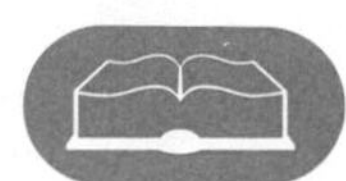    

THE CHANGE MASTERS

Rosabeth Moss Kanter

WHY READ IT?

This book is regarded as an authoritative work on the factors behind successful corporate change. Kanter's work takes a human relations perspective, and was one of the earliest books to focus on the importance of empowerment.

GETTING STARTED

"Change masters" are adept at anticipating the need for, and leading, productive change. Companies with a commitment to human resources were significantly ahead in long-term profitability and financial growth.

Growth problems in U.S. companies are due to suffocation of the entrepreneurial spirit—innovation is the key to growth. New skills are required to manage effectively in innovation-stimulating environments: power skills, the ability to manage employee participation, and an understanding of how change is managed. Empowerment is critical to corporate success.

CONTRIBUTION

1. THE NATURE OF CHANGE MASTERS

Change masters are those people and organizations adept at the art of anticipating the need for, and leading, productive change. Change resisters are intent on reining in innovation.

2. THE IMPORTANCE OF MANAGING PEOPLE

A research program asked 65 human resource directors in large organizations to name companies that were progressive and forward-thinking in their systems and practices, in relation to people. Forty-seven companies emerged as leaders in the field. They were then compared to similar companies. The companies with a commitment to human resources were significantly ahead in long-term profitability and financial growth.

The message is that if you manage your people well, you are probably managing your business well.

3. INNOVATION AS THE KEY TO GROWTH

Kanter places responsibility for company growth problems on the quiet suffocation of the entrepreneurial spirit in segmentalist companies. She identifies innovation as the key to future growth. The way to develop and sustain innovation is to adopt an integrative approach rather than a segmentalist one.

Three new sets of skills are required to manage effectively in such integrative, innovation-stimulating environments:

- the ability to persuade others to invest information, support, and resources in new initiatives driven by an entrepreneur
- the ability to manage problems associated with increased use of teams and employee participation
- an understanding of how change is designed and constructed in an organization: how the microchanges introduced by individual innovators relate to macrochanges or strategic reorientation.

4. THE IMPORTANCE OF EMPOWERMENT

The extent to which individuals are given the opportunity to use power effectively influences whether a company stagnates or innovates. In an innovative company, people are at center stage.

CONTEXT

Rosabeth Moss Kanter began her career as a sociologist before her transformation into international business guru. *The Economist* (October 15, 1994) commented, "Kanter-the-guru still studies her subject with a sociologist's eye, treating the corporation not so much as a micro-economy, concerned with turning inputs into outputs, but as a mini-society, bent on shaping individuals to collective ends."

Kanter's work is a development of the Human Relations School of the late 1950s and 1960s. Through *The Change Masters* (1983) and *When Giants Learn to Dance* (1989), she was partly responsible for the increased interest in empowerment, if not its practice.

The Change Masters has been called "the thinking man's *In Search of Excellence*."

U.S. author Gary Hamel said: "In a turbulent and inhospitable world, corporate vitality is a fragile thing. Yesterday's industry challengers are today's laggards. Entropy is endemic. Certainly *The Change Masters* is the most carefully researched, and best argued, book on change and transformation to date. While Rosabeth may not have discovered the eternal fountain of corporate vitality, she certainly points us in its general direction."

For More Information

Kanter, Rosabeth Moss. *The Change Masters*. New York: Simon & Schuster, 1983.

See also:
Rosabeth Moss Kanter (pp. 1008–09)

"The companies with a commitment to human resources were significantly higher in long-term profitability and financial growth."
(*The Change Masters*)

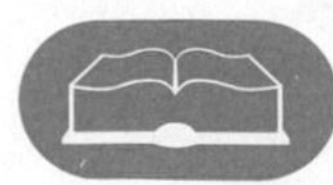

THE CHANGING CULTURE OF A FACTORY

Elliot Jaques

WHY READ IT?

This book is based on an extensive study of industrial democracy in practice at the United Kingdom's Glacier Metal Company between 1948 and 1965. The company introduced a number of highly progressive changes in working practice that were ahead of their time and set a pattern for future practice.

GETTING STARTED

The Glacier Metal Company introduced a number of highly progressive changes in working practice, resulting in a form of industrial democracy that was ahead of its time. The emphasis was on granting people responsibility and giving them a say in every problem. The project highlighted the shortcomings of conventional industrial relations practice, and showed that managers should be measured by the long-term impact of their decisions.

CONTRIBUTION

1. INTRODUCING INDUSTRIAL DEMOCRACY

The Glacier Metal Company introduced a number of highly progressive changes in working practice:

- a works council was introduced. This was far removed from the usually toothless attempts at worker representation;
- no change of company policy was allowed unless all members of the works council agreed. Any single person on the council had a veto;
- "clocking on," the traditional means of recording whether someone had turned up for work, was abolished.

Contrary to what experts and observers anticipated, the company did not grind to an immediate halt.

2. INCREASING PERSONAL RESPONSIBILITY

The emphasis was on granting people responsibility and of understanding the dynamics of group working. Everybody should be encouraged to accept the maximum amount of personal responsibility, and should be allowed to have a say in every problem in which they could help.

3. ANTICIPATING ORGANIZATIONAL DEVELOPMENTS

The project was a decade ahead of any form of organizational development. It highlighted a number of issues:

- the redundancy of conventional organization charts;
- the potential power of corporate culture (a concept then barely understood);
- the potential benefits of running organizations in a fair and mutually beneficial way.

4. THEORY OF THE VALUE OF WORK

"The manifest picture of bureaucratic organization is a confusing one", according to Jaques. "There appears to be no rhyme or reason for the structures that are developed, in number of levels, in titling, or even in the meaning to be attached to the manager–subordinate linkage."

A solution, labeled "the time span of discretion," contended that levels of management should be based on how long it was before their decisions could be checked. Managers should be paid in accordance with that time, and measured by the long-term impact of their decisions.

CONTEXT

The practices introduced at the Glacier Metal Company were almost a decade ahead of their time. However, they did not ensure the company's survival.

Other authors such as Mary Parker Follett and Frederick Herzberg have dealt with the issue of motivation at work. Jaques' work was based on long-term scientific observation, in contrast to what he terms the "fantasy fads," the "waffle and fiddling around" of management consultants.

For More Information

Jaques, Elliot. *The Changing Culture of a Factory*. London: Tavistock Publications, 1951.

See also:
Mary Parker Follett (pp. 988–89)
Frederick Herzberg (pp. 1002–03)

"I'm completely convinced of the necessity of encouraging everybody to accept the maximum amount of personal responsibility." (*The Changing Culture of a Factory*)

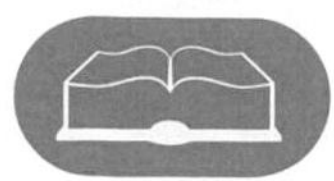

COMPETING FOR THE FUTURE

Gary Hamel
C. K. Prahalad

WHY READ IT?

Competing for the Future, named by *BusinessWeek* as the best management book of 1994, is regarded as the definitive book on strategy for contemporary business. It criticizes the narrow mechanistic view of strategy and calls for a broader approach that recognizes a company's core competencies.

GETTING STARTED

This book argues that traditional strategy is too narrow in its perspective. Far from being a simple annual exercise, strategy is multifaceted, emotional as well as analytical, and concerned with meaning, purpose, and passion. Few managers spend enough time looking to the future. They should adopt "strategizing"—a new approach for developing complex, robust strategies, focusing on core competencies.

Today the onus is on transforming not just individual organizations, but entire industries. The true challenge is to create revolutions when you are large and dominant. Small entrepreneurial offshoots are not the route to organizational regeneration. Downsizing is an easy option—growth comes from creating a difference, and vitality comes from within, if only executives would listen.

CONTRIBUTION

1. THE NARROW FOCUS OF TRADITIONAL STRATEGY

Strategy has tied itself into a straitjacket of narrow, and narrowing, perspectives:

- a huge proportion of strategists, perhaps 95%, are economists and engineers who share a mechanistic view of strategy;
- strategy is multifaceted, emotional as well as analytical, concerned with meaning, purpose, and passion;
- strategy should be looked on as a learning process.

2. STRATEGY IS NOT SIMPLE

Executives perceive that the problem with strategy is not creating it, but implementing it. Strategy is not a ritual or a once-a-year exercise. As a result, managers are bogged down in the nitty-gritty of the present-spending less than three percent of their time looking to the future.

3. ADOPT STRATEGIZING

Instead of talking about strategy or planning, companies should talk about strategizing and ask, "What are the fundamental preconditions for developing complex, variegated, robust strategies?"

Strategizing is part of the new managerial argot of strategic intent, strategic architecture, foresight (rather than vision), and the idea of core competencies.

4. FOCUS ON CORE COMPETENCIES

Core competencies represent the collective learning in the organization, especially how to coordinate diverse production skills and integrate multiple streams of technologies.

Organizations should see themselves as a portfolio of core competencies as opposed to business units. Core competencies are geared to growing opportunity share whereas business units are narrowly focused on market share.

5. DIFFERENT APPROACHES TO STRATEGY

There is a thin dividing line between order and chaos. Neither Stalinist bureaucracy nor Silicon Valley provides an optimal economic system. Silicon Valley is extraordinarily good at creating new ideas, but in other ways is extraordinarily inefficient.

6. SMALL OR LARGE ORGANIZATIONS?

Small entrepreneurial offshoots are not the route to organizational regeneration. They are too random, inefficient, and prone to becoming becalmed by corporate indifference. Smaller companies have had a revolutionary impact (IKEA, Body Shop, Swatch, and Virgin), but the true challenge is to create revolutions when you are large and dominant. American companies such as Motorola and Hewlett-Packard are more successful at this than their European counterparts. We are moving to more democratic models of organization, to which U.S. corporations appear more attuned. In Europe and Japan there is a more elitist sense of knowledge residing at the top—a hierarchy of experience, not of imagination.

7. RULES FOR SUCCESS

- A company surrenders today's businesses when it gets smaller faster than it gets better.
- A company surrenders tomorrow's businesses when it gets better without getting different.
- Downsizing is an easy option.
- Growth (the authors prefer to speak of vitality) comes from difference, though there are as many stupid ways to grow as there are to downsize.
- The pressure for growth is usually ignited by a crisis.
- Vitality comes from within, if only executives would listen.
- Companies will pay millions of dollars for the opinions of McKinsey's bright 29-year-old, but ignore their own 29-year-olds.

CONTEXT

The debate on the meaning and application of strategy is long-running. The 1960s gave us the resolutely analytical Igor Ansoff; the 1970s Henry Mintzberg with his cerebral and creative crafting strategy; the 1980s, Michael Porter's rational route to competitiveness.

Nominations for the leading strategic thinkers of the 1990s would certainly include Gary Hamel and C. K. Prahalad. *Competing for the Future* has been called the blueprint for a new generation of strategic thinking. *BusinessWeek* (September 19, 1994) said: "At a time when many companies continue to lay off thousands in massive re-engineering exercises, this is a book that deserves widespread attention. It's a valuable and worthwhile tonic for devotees of today's slash-and-burn school of management."

The surge of interest in core competencies has tended to enthusiastic oversimplification. Commentators believe companies need to be cautious about where core competencies will lead. They are a very powerful weapon, but can encourage companies to get into businesses simply because they see a link between core competencies rather than ones where they have an in-depth knowledge.

The authors' strategic prognosis falls between two extremes. At one extreme are the arch-rationalists, insisting on a constant stream of data to support any strategy. At the other is the thriving-on-chaos school, with its belief in freewheeling organizations where strategy is a moveable feast.

For More Information

Hamel, Gary, and C. K. Prahalad. *Competing for the Future*. Boston, MA: Harvard Business School Press, 1994.

See also:

C. K. Prahalad (pp. 1040–41)

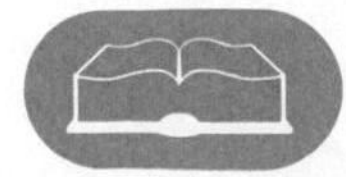

The Competitive Advantage of Nations

Michael Porter

Why Read It?

Many consider *The Competitive Advantage of Nations* to be one of the most ambitious books of our times. Said to do "for international capitalism what Marx did for the class struggle," it re-examines the nation state, suggesting that its basic role in the modern world is an economic one, and that, even in a global economy, it has a key role to play by ensuring the competitiveness of the companies operating within its borders who are the actual wealth producers for the population.

Getting Started

Michael Porter, author of the modern business classic *Competitive Strategy*, has a good deal of experience as a consultant to national governments. *The Competitive Advantage of Nations* emerged from his work on Ronald Reagan's Commission on Industrial Competitiveness. The research for the book encompassed ten countries: the United Kingdom, Denmark, Italy, Japan, Korea, Singapore, Sweden, Switzerland, the United States, and Germany (then West Germany).

The book can be read on three levels:

- as a general inquiry into what makes national economies successful;
- as a detailed study of eight of the world's main modern economies;
- as a series of prescriptions about what governments should do to improve their country's competitiveness.

It asks crucial questions. What makes a nation's firms and industries competitive in global markets and what propels a whole nation's economy to advance? Why are firms based in a particular nation able to create and sustain competitive advantage against the world's best competitors in a particular field? Why is one nation often the home for so many of an industry's world leaders? Why, for example, is Switzerland the home base for leaders in pharmaceuticals, chocolate, and trading?

At its heart is a radical new perspective of the role of nations. From being military powerhouses they are now economic units whose competitiveness is the key to power.

Contribution

1. Nations, Competition, and Productivity

"Nations don't compete. Companies compete. Nations can make it hard or easy for them to do so." When governments deliberately set out to help companies compete, however, their efforts are often counterproductive. The principal economic goal of a nation is to produce a high and rising standard of living for its citizens. The ability to do so depends not on the amorphous notion of competitiveness but on the productivity with which a nation's labor and capital resources are employed.

2. The Paradox of Globalization

Companies and industries have become globalized and more international in their scope and aspirations than ever before. This would appear to suggest that the nation has lost its role in the international success of its firms. Companies, at first glance, seem to have transcended countries.

While the globalization of competition might appear to make the nation less important, instead it seems to make it more so. With fewer impediments to trade to shelter uncompetitive domestic firms and industries, the home nation takes on growing significance because it is the source of the skills and technology that underpin competitive advantage.

In addition, it is the intensity of domestic competition that often fuels success on a global stage.

3. The National Diamond

To make sense of the dynamics behind national or regional strength in a particular industry, Porter developed the concept of the national diamond.

This is made up of four forces.

- Factor conditions—these would once have been largely restricted to natural resources and plentiful supplies of labor; now they also embrace data communications, university research, and the availability of scientists, engineers or experts in a particular field.
- Demand conditions—if there is strong national demand for a product or service, this can give the industry a head start in global competition. The United States, for example, is ahead in health services due to heavy national demand.
- Related and supporting industries—industries which are strong in a particular country are often surrounded by successful related industries.
- Firm strategy, structure, and rivalry—domestic competition fuels growth and competitive strength.

Together, these four determine whether a nation has competitive advantage or not.

4. Clusters

"Nations succeed not in isolated industries, but in *clusters* of industries connected through vertical and horizontal relationships." Groups of interconnected firms, suppliers, and related industries arising in particular locations contribute substantially to national success. Porter shows how such clusters come into being.

Context

According to *The Economist* (October 8, 1994), "The book that projected Mr. Porter into the stratosphere, read by aspiring intellectuals and despairing politicians everywhere, was *The Competitive Advantage of Nations*."

Not everyone, however, agrees with Porter on the relationship between the nation and the globalized economy. Kenichi Ohmae believes that the nation state is on its way out, and Gary Hamel commented: "While *The Competitive Advantage of Nations* provides a good account of why particular industry clusters emerged in some countries and not others, it is essentially backward-looking. In a world of open markets, and mobile capital, technology, and knowledge, no firm need be the product of its geography."

Yet on balance, readers around the world have embraced the challenges outlined in Porter's book, and its status and impact as a classic business text cannot be underestimated.

For More Information

Porter, Michael. *The Competitive Advantage of Nations*. New York: Free Press, 1990.

"Productivity is the prime determinant in the long run of a nation's standard of living."

(The Competitive Advantage of Nations)

  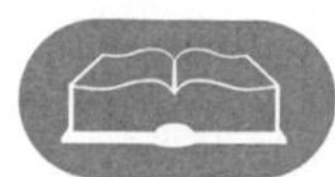  

Competitive Strategy

Michael Porter

Why Read It?

Competitive Strategy is a modern classic. It claims to provide a solution to a long-running strategic dilemma, and certainly put strategy at the forefront of management thinking.

Getting Started

In 1973 Michael Porter became one of the youngest professors ever at the Harvard Business School. He has since acted as a strategy counselor to many leading U.S. and international companies, besides playing an active role in economic policy with the U.S. Congress, business groups, and as an adviser to foreign governments.

Competitive Strategy is one of those books that bases its message around significant numbers—in this case three and five, the three generic strategies (every company must adopt one or lose out to its competitors) and the five competitive forces (that determine what a company must do to remain competitive). Over 20 years after its first publication, the current critical consensus seems to be that the competitive forces are truer to reality than the generic strategies. But strategy, having gone out of fashion in the 1980s and 1990s, may be making a comeback.

Contribution

1. Resolving the Strategy Dilemma

Competitive Strategy presents a rationalist's solution to a long-running strategic dilemma. At one end of the spectrum are the pragmatists, who contend that companies have to respond to their own specific situations. Competitive advantage emerges from immediate, fast-thinking responsiveness. There is no pat formula for achieving sustainable competitive advantage.

At the other end are those who, like the Boston Consulting Group, think that market knowledge is all-important. Any company that masters the intricacies of a particular market can reduce prices and increase market share. Porter proposes a logical compromise, arguing that there are three generic strategies for dealing with competitive forces: differentiation, overall cost leadership, and focus.

2. Differentiation

Differentiation entails competing on the basis of value added to customers (quality, service, differentiation) so that customers will pay a premium to cover higher costs. It requires creative flair, research capability, and strong marketing.

3. Overall Cost Leadership

Cost-based leadership involves offering products or services at the lowest cost. Quality and service are not unimportant, but cost reduction provides focus to organization.

4. Focus

Focus involves combining elements of the previous two strategies and targeting a specific market intensively.

5. Combining the Strategies

Companies with a clear strategy outperform those whose strategy is unclear or those that attempt to achieve both differentiation and cost leadership.

Sometimes the firm can successfully pursue more than one approach, though this is rarely possible. Effectively implementing any of these generic strategies usually requires total commitment, and organizational arrangements are diluted if there is more than one primary target.

6. The Risks of Ignoring Generic Strategies

If a company fails to focus on any of the three generic strategies it is liable to encounter problems. The firm stuck in the middle is almost guaranteed low profitability. It either loses the high-volume customers who demand low prices or must bid away its profits to get this business away from low-cost firms. It also loses high-margin businesses, the cream, to the firms who are focused on high-margin targets. In addition, it will also probably suffer from a blurred corporate culture and a conflicting set of organizational arrangements and motivation systems.

7. The Five Competitive Forces

In any industry, whether domestic or international or product- or service-oriented, the rules of competition are embodied in five competitive forces.

- The entry of new competitors. New competitors necessitate some competitive response, which will inevitably use resources and reduce profits.
- The threat of substitutes. If there are viable alternatives to your product or service in the marketplace, the prices you can charge will be limited.
- The bargaining power of buyers. If customers have bargaining power they will use it. This will reduce profit margins.
- The bargaining power of suppliers. Given power over you, suppliers will increase their prices and adversely affect your profitability.
- The rivalry among the existing competitors. Competition leads to the need to invest in marketing or R&D, or to price reductions. These will reduce profits.

The collective strength of these five competitive forces determines the ability of firms in an industry to earn, on average, rates of return on investment in excess of the cost of capital.

Context

When *Competitive Strategy* was published, it offered a rational and straightforward method for companies to extricate themselves from strategic confusion. The reassurance proved short-lived. Less than a decade later, companies were having to compete on all fronts. They had to be differentiated, through improved service or speedier development, and be cost leaders, cheaper than their competitors.

Porter's other contribution proved more robust. The five forces are a means whereby a company can begin to understand its particular industry. Initially passively interpreted as statements of the facts of competitive life, they are now usually seen as the rules of the game, which may have to be changed and challenged if an organization is to achieve any impact.

Influential author Gary Hamel commented, "In *Competitive Strategy*, Michael Porter did a masterful job of synthesizing all that economists know about what determines industry and firm profitability. While *Competitive Strategy* isn't much help in discovering profitable strategies, it is an unfailing guide to whether some particular strategy, once articulated, can be counted on to produce worthwhile profits. What distinguishes *Competitive Strategy* from many other contemporary business books, is its strong conceptual foundation. Every MBA graduate in the world can remember Porter's five forces. How many can recall the eight rules of excellence?"

For More Information

Porter, Michael. *Competitive Strategy*. New York: Free Press, 1980.

(Competitive Strategy)

CORPORATE STRATEGY

Igor Ansoff

WHY READ IT?

In *Corporate Strategy*, Ansoff codifies and generalizes his experiences as a strategist at Lockheed. The book develops a series of concepts and procedures that managers can use to develop a practical method for strategic decision making within an organization.

GETTING STARTED

Corporate Strategy integrated strategic planning concepts invented independently in a number of leading American firms. The book provided a powerful, rational model by which strategic and planning decisions could be made. Ansoff saw strategic planning as a complex sequence, or cascade, of decisions and defined two main concepts which are essential to understanding its nature, and therefore to implementing it successfully. The first of these was "gap analysis"—the "gap" being the difference between the current position of an organization and its strategic objectives. The second was "synergy"—the concept that 2 + 2 = 5.

CONTRIBUTION

1. INTEGRATING STRATEGIC PLANNING CONCEPTS

Corporate Strategy integrated strategic planning concepts which were invented independently in a number of leading U.S. firms, including Lockheed.

Ansoff saw strategic management as a powerful applied theory, offering a degree of coherence and universality lacking in functionally-dominated management theorizing.

2. NEW THEORETICAL CONCEPTS

The book presented several new theoretical concepts such as partial ignorance, business strategy, capability and competence profiles, and synergy. One particular concept, the product-mission matrix, became very popular, because it was simple and—for the first time—codified the differences between strategic expansion and diversification.

3. A RATIONAL MODEL FOR PLANNING DECISIONS

Corporate Strategy provided a rational model by which strategic and planning decisions could be made. The model concentrated on corporate expansion and diversification in particular, rather than on strategic planning as a whole.

The Ansoff Model of Strategic Planning was a complex sequence, or cascade, of decisions. The decisions started with highly aggregated ones and proceeded towards the more specific.

4. THE INTRODUCTION OF GAP ANALYSIS

Central to the cascade of decisions is the concept of gap analysis, which can be summarized as: see where you are; identify where you wish to be, and identify the tasks that will take you there.

The procedure within each step of the cascade is similar.

- A set of objectives is established.
- The difference (the gap) between the current position of the organization and the objectives is estimated.
- One or more courses of action (strategy) is proposed.
- These are tested for their gap-reducing properties.

A course is accepted if it substantially closes the gap; if it does not, new alternatives are tried.

5. THE CONCEPT OF SYNERGY

Corporate Strategy introduced the word "synergy" to the management vocabulary. Although the term has become overused, Ansoff's explanation (2 + 2 = 5) remains memorably simple.

CONTEXT

Corporate Strategy was published at a time of widespread enthusiasm for strategic planning, and an increasing number of organizations were joining the ranks of its users.

Until *Corporate Strategy*, strategic planning was a barely-understood, ad hoc concept. It was practiced, while the theory lay largely unexplored.

Ansoff also examined corporate advantage long before Michael Porter's dissection of the subject in the 1980s.

While *Corporate Strategy* was a remarkable book for its time, its flaws have been widely acknowledged, most honestly by Ansoff himself.

Corporate Strategy is highly prescriptive and advocates heavy reliance on analysis.

Some companies have encountered what Ansoff calls "paralysis by analysis"—the more information they possess, the more they think they need. This vicious circle dogs many organizations that embrace strategic planning with enthusiasm.

Ansoff regards strategic planning as an incomplete invention, though he is convinced that strategic planning was an inherently useful management tool.

He has spent the last 40 years attempting to prove that this is the case and that, rather than being prescriptive and unwieldy, strategic management can be a dynamic tool able to cope with the unexpected twists of turbulent markets.

Business guru Gary Hamel described Ansoff as "Truly the godfather of corporate strategy," and said, "Though Ansoff's approach may now appear overly-structured and deterministic, he created the language and processes that, for the first time, allowed modern industrial companies to explicitly address the deep questions of corporate strategy: how to grow, where to coordinate, which strengths to leverage, and so on."

For More Information

Ansoff, Igor. *Corporate Strategy*. New York: McGraw-Hill, 1965.

See also:
Igor Ansoff (pp. 962–63)

(*Corporate Strategy*)

CORPORATE-LEVEL STRATEGY

Michael Goold
Marcus Alexander
Andrew Campbell

WHY READ IT?

Although large conglomerates claim to add value through synergy and economies of scale, the authors suggest this is not the case. They recommend that multibusiness organizations should aim for a tighter fit between individual company strategies and the overall corporate strategy. The book introduces the concept of heartland businesses and shows how it can help corporations improve their overall performance.

GETTING STARTED

Most large companies are now multibusiness organizations. Research indicates that the benefits of economies of scale and synergy do not, in reality, exist.

While individual businesses within the organization often have strategies, the corporation as a whole may not. Only a tight fit between the parent organization and its businesses will add value.

There must be a clear insight about the role of the parent organization. "Parents" must concentrate on heartland businesses that they understand. The parent must only intervene on limited issues, and corporate strategy should be driven by parenting advantage.

CONTRIBUTION

1. THE VALUE OF MULTIBUSINESS ORGANIZATIONS

Multibusiness companies, by virtue of their very size, should offer economies of scale and synergy between the various businesses, which can be exploited to the overall good. The authors' research suggests that in reality this is not the case.

They calculate that in over half of multibusiness companies, the whole is worth less than the sum of its parts. Instead of adding value, the corporation actually detracts from its value. Its influence, though pervasive, is often counter-productive.

This condemnation is not restricted to conglomerates. The influence of the corporate parent is also felt in companies with portfolios in a single industry, or in a series of apparently related areas.

2. LACK OF OVERALL STRATEGY

A primary cause of this phenomenon is that while individual businesses within the organization often have strategies, the corporation as a whole may not. The proclaimed strategy is often an amalgam of the individual business strategies given credence by general aspirations.

3. NEED FOR A TIGHT FIT

If corporate-level strategy is to add value, there needs to be a tight fit between the parent organization and its businesses.

Successful corporate parents focus on a narrow range of tasks and create value in those areas, and align the structures, processes, and central functions of the parent accordingly. Rather than being all-encompassing and constantly interfering, the center is akin to a specialist medical practitioner intervening in its areas of expertise when it knows it can suggest a cure.

4. SUCCESS FACTORS FOR MULTIBUSINESS ORGANIZATIONS

From their analysis of 15 successful multibusiness corporations, the authors identify three essentials for successful corporate strategies:

- there must be clear insight about the role of the parent. If the parent does not know how or where it can add value, it is unlikely to do so;
- the parent must have distinctive characteristics. They, too, have a corporate culture and personality;
- it must be recognized that each parent will only be effective with certain sorts of business—described as their "heartland."

5. THE IMPORTANCE OF HEARTLAND BUSINESSES

"Heartland businesses are well understood by the parent; they do not suffer from inappropriate influence and meddling that can damage less familiar businesses," say the authors. "The parent has an innate feel for its heartland that enables it to make difficult judgments and decisions with a high degree of success."

Heartland businesses are broad ranging and can cover different industries, markets, and technologies. Given this complexity, the ability of the parent to intervene on a limited number of issues is crucial.

6. CORE BUSINESSES

The concept of heartland businesses is distinct from core businesses. "A core business is often merely a business that the company has decided to commit itself to," they say. Though core businesses may be important and substantial, the parent may not be adding a great deal to them.

7. BUILDING PARENTING ADVANTAGE

The authors continue: "In contrast, the heartland definition focuses on the *fit* between a parent and a business: do the parent's insights and behavior fit the opportunities and nature of this business? Does the parent have specialist skills in assisting this type of business to perform better?"

Corporate strategy should be driven by "parenting advantage" to create more value in the portfolio of businesses than would be achieved by any rival. To do so requires a fundamental change in basic perspectives on the role of the parent and of the nature of the multibusiness organization.

CONTEXT

Most large companies are now multibusiness organizations. The logic behind this fact of business life is generally assumed rather than examined in depth.

The authors' research runs counter to the findings of authors such as Alfred Chandler in *Strategy and Structure* and Peter Drucker in *The Practice of Management*.

Gary Hamel said: "Chandler and Drucker celebrated large multidivisional organizations, but as these companies grew, decentralized, and diversified, the corporate center often became little more than a layer of accounting consolidation. In the worst cases, a conglomerate was worth less than its break-up value. In writing the definitive book on corporate strategy, Goold, Alexander, and Campbell gave hope to corporate bureaucrats everywhere. Maybe it really was possible for the corporate level to add value."

For More Information

Goold, Michael, Marcus Alexander, and Andrew Campbell. *Corporate-level Strategy*. New York: John Wiley, 1994.

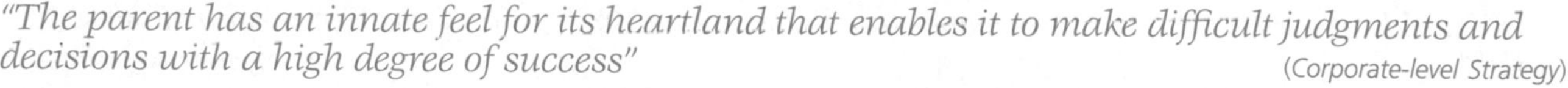
"The parent has an innate feel for its heartland that enables it to make difficult judgments and decisions with a high degree of success"
(Corporate-level Strategy)

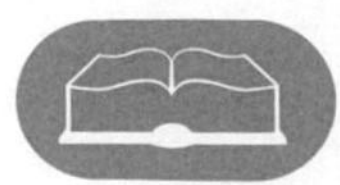

Dynamic Administration

Mary Parker Follett

Why Read It?

The book provides one of the earliest perspectives on business from the point of view of human relationships. It was written at a time when workers were seen simply as part of the mass-production process. The book provides useful background on the development of concepts such as empowerment and visionary leadership.

Getting Started

Management is a social process and should have a special human dimension. The process is based in human emotions and in the interrelations created by working. The working environment has human problems, with psychological, ethical, and economic dimensions.

Workers should be given greater responsibility, which is the great developer of people—and successful leaders must offer a vision of the future and train followers to become leaders.

Relationships, not just transactions, are important in organizations. Knowing this involves recognizing that conflict is a fact of life that we should use to work for us—but integration is the only positive way forward.

Contribution

1. Management As a Social Process

"We can never wholly separate the human from the mechanical sides," says Follett. "The study of human relations in business and the study of the technology of operating are bound up together." The everyday incidents and problems of management reflect the presence or absence of sound principle.

Management has a special human character. Its nature as a social process is deeply embedded in the emotions of man and in the interrelations to which the everyday working of industry necessarily gives rise—both at manager and worker levels and, of course, between the two.

2. Toward Empowerment

Mary Parker Follett believed that, "we should undepartmentalize our thinking in regard to every problem that comes to us."

She continued, "I do not think that we have psychological and ethical and economic problems. We have human problems, with psychological, ethical, and economical aspects, and as many others as you like."

Follett advocated giving greater responsibility to people at a time when the mechanical might of mass production was at its height. "Responsibility is the great developer of men," she said.

3. Leadership through Vision

The most successful leader of all is one who sees another picture not yet actualized—who sees the whole rather than the particular, organizes the experiences of the group, offers a vision of the future, and trains followers to become leaders.

Leading should be a two-way, mutually beneficial process. "We want worked out a relation between leaders and led which will give to each the opportunity to make creative contributions to the situation," Follett wrote.

4. Relationships Matter

Relationships, not just transactions, are important in organizations. The reciprocal nature of relationships means that a mutual influence is developed when people work together, however formal authority is defined.

Conflict is a fact of life that we should use to work for us. There are three ways of dealing with confrontation: domination; compromise; or integration. Integration is the only positive way forward. This can be achieved by first uncovering the real conflict and then taking the demands of both sides and breaking them up into their constituent parts.

Outlook is narrowed, activity is restricted, and chances of business success largely diminished when thinking is constrained within the limits of what has been called an either-or situation. "We should never allow ourselves to be bullied by an either-or," said Follett. There is often the possibility of something better than either of two given alternatives.

Context

Published eight years after her death, *Dynamic Administration* is a collection of Mary Parker Follett's papers on management gathered from 12 lectures given between 1925 and 1933. Her work stands as a humane counterpoint to that of Frederick Taylor and the proponents of scientific management. Follett was a female, liberal humanist in an era dominated by reactionary males intent on mechanizing the world of business.

Bearing in mind she was speaking of America in the early 1920s, her thinking can be described as little less than revolutionary, and certainly a generation ahead of its time.

During her life, Mary Parker Follett's thinking on management was generally ignored—though in Japan there was a great deal of interest in her perspectives.

Leading commentator Gary Hamel said, "The work of Mary Parker Follett is refreshingly different from that of her peers. She was the first modern thinker to get us close to the human soul of management. She had the heart of a humanist, not an engineer."

To some, Follett remains a utopian idealist, out of touch with reality; to others, she is a torchbearer of good sense whose ideas have sadly not had significant impact on organizations.

Henry Mintzberg commented, "Integration requires understanding, in-depth understanding. It requires serious commitment and dedication. It takes effort, and it depends on creativity. There is precious little of all of these qualities in too many of our organizations today."

For More Information

Dynamic Administration. Follett, Mary Parker. New York: Harper & Bros., 1941.

See also:
Mary Parker Follett (pp. 988–89)

"We should remember that we can never wholly separate the human from the mechanical sides."
(*Dynamic Administration*)

THE FIFTH DISCIPLINE

Peter Senge

WHY READ IT?

This is the book that popularized the concept of the learning organization. More philosophical in tone than the majority of business-oriented books, it adopts a holistic approach. Learning is an individual and a group experience, something, Senge would claim, much deeper than just taking information in. "It is about changing individuals so that they produce results they care about, accomplish things that are important to them."

GETTING STARTED

Peter Senge is director of the Center for Organizational Learning at MIT. *The Fifth Discipline* emerged from extensive research by Senge and his team, but Senge said the "vision that became *The Fifth Discipline*" came to him one morning during his meditation, when he realized that "the 'learning organization' would likely become a new management fad."

The "fifth discipline" of the title is systems thinking. Of the five building blocks of a learning organization, systems thinking connects the other four and enables them to work together for the benefit of business.

CONTRIBUTION

1. LEARNING IS VITAL

As the world becomes more interconnected and business becomes more complex and dynamic, work must become more "learningful." It is no longer sufficient to have one person learning for the whole organization, a Ford, say, or a Sloan or a Watson. It is no longer possible to figure it out from the top, and have everybody else follow the orders of the grand strategist.

The organizations that will excel in the future will be those that can tap the commitment and capacity to learn of people at all levels within them.

Managers should therefore encourage employees to:

- be open to new ideas;
- communicate frankly with each other;
- understand thoroughly how their companies operate;
- form a collective vision;
- work together to achieve their goal.

2. THE FIVE DISCIPLINES

There are five components to a learning organization:

- systems thinking
- personal mastery
- mental models
- shared vision
- team learning

3. SYSTEMS THINKING

Systems thinking is a conceptual framework to make patterns clearer. It requires a shift of mind to see interrelationships rather than linear cause and effect. It can help managers spot repetitive patterns, such as the way certain kinds of problems persist, or the way systems have their own in-built limits to growth.

4. PERSONAL MASTERY

This idea is based on the familiar competencies and skills associated with management. But it also includes spiritual growth–opening oneself up to a progressively deeper reality and living life from a creative rather than a reactive viewpoint.

As part of this discipline, one must continually learn to see current reality more clearly; the ensuing gap between vision and reality produces the creative tension from which learning arises.

5. MENTAL MODELS

These are the organization's driving and fundamental values and principles. Senge alerts managers to the power of patterns of thinking at the organizational level and the importance of nondefensive inquiry into the nature of these patterns.

6. SHARED VISION

Senge stresses the importance of cocreation and argues that shared vision can only be built on personal vision. He claims that shared vision is present when the task that follows from the vision is no longer seen by the team members as separate from the self.

7. TEAM LEARNING

The discipline of team learning involves two practices: dialog and discussion. Dialog is characterized by its exploratory nature, discussion by the opposite process of narrowing down the field to the best alternative for the decisions that need to be made. The two are mutually complementary, but the benefits of combining them only come from having previously separated them.

8. CREATING LEARNING ORGANIZATIONS

Transforming companies into learning organizations has proved highly problematical, principally because it involves managers surrendering their traditional spheres of power and control to the people who are learning. If people are to learn, they must be allowed to experiment and fail. In a blame-oriented culture, this requires a major change in attitude.

The learning organization demands trust and involvement. Again, this is usually notable by its absence. Real commitment is rare in today's organizations. Experience indicates that 90% of the time what passes for commitment is compliance. One man reported to Senge that by adopting the learning organization model, he made what he called "job-limiting choices." What he meant was that he could have climbed the corporate ladder faster by rejecting the theories and toeing the company line.

CONTEXT

Although the learning organization sounds like a product, it is actually a process. Phil Hodgson of Ashridge Management College commented: "Processes are not suddenly unveiled for all to see. Academic definitions, no matter how precise, cannot be instantly applied in the real world. Managers need to promote learning so that it gradually emerges as a key part of an organization's culture."

The Fifth Discipline has proved highly influential. Though the learning organization has rarely been converted into reality, the idea has fuelled the debate on self-managed development and employability, and has affected the rewards and remuneration strategies of many organizations.

Gary Hamel observed that: "While Professor [Chris] Argyris put organizational learning on the management agenda, Peter Senge married it with system thinking and created a language and approach that makes the whole set of ideas accessible to managers. Peter is no mere theorist, his organizational Learning Centre at MIT has helped launch thousands of in-company learning experiments. *The Fifth Discipline* would certainly be on my short list of the half dozen best business books of the last 25 years."

For More Information

Senge, Peter. *The Fifth Discipline: The Art and Practice of the Learning Organization.* New York: Doubleday, 1990.

"The harder you push the system, the harder the system pushes you." (*The Fifth Discipline*)

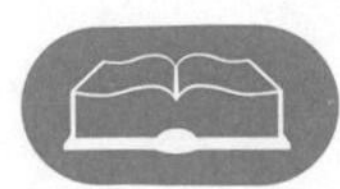

The Functions of the Executive

Chester Barnard

Why Read It?

Barnard is regarded as an important management thinker, who, according to Tom Peters and Robert Waterman in *In Search of Excellence*, created "a complete management theory." Though his language is dated, much of his thinking—particularly on the importance of communication—is relevant to modern management.

Getting Started

An organization allows people to achieve what they could not achieve as individuals, as they and their actions are interconnected. One essential ingredient for a successful organization is good, short lines of communication because communication enables everyone to be tied into the organization's objectives. It is also vital that chief executives nurture goals and values and translate them into action; executives should not just ensure conformance to a code of morals, they should create moral codes for others.

Contribution

1. People Are Interconnected in an Organization

Barnard rejected the concept of an organization as comprising a rather definite group of people whose behavior is coordinated with reference to some explicit goal or goals. "In a community" he argued, "all acts of individuals and of organizations are directly or indirectly interconnected and interdependent."

2. The Importance of Communication

Barnard highlights the need for communication. He argues that everyone needs to know what and where the communications channels are so that every single person can be tied into the organization's objectives.

Lines of communication should be short and direct. "The essential functions are, first, to provide the system of communications; second, to promote the securing of essential efforts; and third, to formulate and define purpose," he writes.

3. The Need to Nurture Goals and Values

The chief executive is not a dictatorial figure geared to simple, short-term achievements. Part of his or her responsibility is to nurture the values and goals of the organization. Values and goals need to be translated into action, rather than meaningless motivational phraseology—"strictly speaking, purpose is defined more nearly by the aggregate of action taken than by any formulation in words," he writes.

4. A Holistic Approach to Management

An organization is simply a means of allowing people to achieve what they could not achieve as individuals. An organization is a system of consciously coordinated activities of forces of two or more persons.

5. A Code of Management Morality

The distinguishing mark of the executive responsibility is that it requires not merely conformance to a complex code of morals, but also the creation of moral codes for others.

Context

Chester Barnard was a rarity: a management theorist who was also a successful practitioner. He won an economics scholarship to Harvard but, before finishing his degree, he joined American Telephone and Telegraph, eventually becoming President of New Jersey Bell in 1927.

The Functions of the Executive collected together his lectures on management. "It is doubtful if any other book since Taylor's *Scientific Management* has had a deeper influence on the thinking of serious business leaders about the nature of their work," observed Barnard's contemporary, Lyndall Urwick.

Although the language is dated, much of what Barnard argued strikes a chord with contemporary management thinking. His ideas on communication and the importance of short lines of communication remain relevant. In arguing that there was a morality to management, Barnard played an important part in broadening the managerial role from one simply of measurement, control, and supervision, to one also concerned with more abstract notions, such as values.

For More Information

Barnard, Chester. *The Functions of the Executive*. Boston, MA: Harvard University Press, 1968.

"In a community, all acts of individuals and of organizations are directly or indirectly interconnected and interdependent." (*The Functions of the Executive*)

General and Industrial Management

Henri Fayol

Why Read It?

Fayol created one of the first systems of management that put management at the center of the organization. His system divides a company's activities into six groups, in which managerial activities are distinct from the other five. The book provides a systematic analysis of the process of management, in which he anticipated most of the more recent analyses of modern business practice. His brief resumé of what constitutes management has largely held sway throughout the 20th century.

Getting Started

Fayol created a system of management in which management was the basis of the organization. His system focused on acceptance of, and adherence to, six different functions: technical, commercial, financial, security, accounting, and managerial activities.

He believed that to manage is to forecast and plan, to organize, to command, to coordinate, and to control. His view of forward planning was one of the first examples of business planning in practice.

Contribution

1. A System of Management

Fayol created a system of management encapsulated in *General and Industrial Management.*

"Management plays a very important part in the government of undertakings; of all undertakings, large or small, industrial, commercial, political, religious or any other," he writes.

2. Division by Function

Fayol's system was based on acceptance of, and adherence to, different functions. He said that all activities to which industrial undertakings give rise can be divided into six groups. These are:

- technical activities
- commercial activities
- financial activities
- security activities
- accounting activities
- managerial activities

3. The Nature of Management

The management function is quite distinct from the other five essential functions. To manage is to forecast and plan, to organize, to command, to coordinate, and to control.

Fayol's view of what constitutes management has been highly influential throughout the 20th century, and has only recently been challenged.

4. Principles of Management

From his observations, Fayol also produces general principles of management:

- division of work
- authority and responsibility
- discipline
- unity of command
- unity of direction
- subordination of individual interest to general interest
- remuneration of personnel
- centralization
- scalar chain (line of authority)
- order
- equity
- stability of tenure of personnel
- initiative
- esprit de corps

5. Forward Planning

Fayol talks of ten-yearly forecasts, revised every five years—one of the first instances of business planning in practice.

The maxim "managing means looking ahead," gives some idea of the importance attached to planning in the business world. It is true that if foresight is not the whole of management, it is at least an essential part of it.

Context

Fayol created a system that put management at the center of the organization in a way never envisaged by contemporaries such as Frederick W. Taylor, author of *Scientific Management.*

Fayol's championing of management was highly important. While Taylor regarded managers as little more than overseers with limited responsibility, Fayol regarded their role as critical to organizational success.

In his faith in carefully defined functions, Fayol was systematizing business organization in ways that worked at the time, but proved too limiting and restraining in the long term.

In *The Principles and Practice of Management*, a 1953 study of early management thinking, E. F. L. Brech notes, "The importance of Fayol's contribution lay in two features: the first was his systematic analysis of the process of management; the second, his firm advocacy of the principle that management can, and should, be taught. Both were revolutionary lines of thought in 1908, and still little accepted in 1925."

Igor Ansoff has noted that Fayol anticipated imaginatively and soundly most of the more recent analyses of modern business practice. His brief resumé of what constitutes management has largely held sway throughout the 20th century. Only now is it being seriously questioned and challenged.

An extrapolation of Fayol's methods was later exposed by Peter Drucker who observed, "If used beyond the limits of Fayol's model, functional structure becomes costly in terms of time and effort."

For More Information

Fayol, Henri. *General and Industrial Management*. Rev ed. New York: IEEE, 1984.

See also:
Henri Fayol (pp. 986–87)

"To manage is to forecast and plan, to organize, to command, to coordinate, and to control."
(*General and Industrial Management*)

  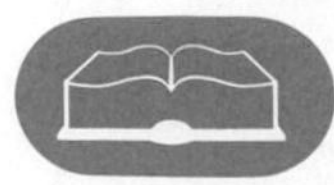    

How to Win Friends and Influence People

Dale Carnegie

Why Read It?

Dale Carnegie was a highly successful public speaker and author of books on public speaking and confidence development. *How to Win Friends and Influence People* provides practical advice on the universal challenge of face-to-face communication. As the familiarity of the title proves, the book has had a great impact. The first edition had a print run of a mere 5,000, but the book has since sold over 15 million copies.

Getting Started

Carnegie holds that it is essential to handle people effectively, and to make them like you to ensure your own success. His book is littered with illustrative anecdotes from the lives of the famous—Clark Gable, Marconi, Franklin D. Roosevelt, Mary Pickford—and the not so famous.

Contribution

1. Handle People Effectively

Carnegie presented the fundamental techniques in handling people:

- don't criticize, condemn, or complain;
- give honest and sincere appreciation;
- arouse in the other person an eager want.

2. Make People Like You

He added advice on other ways to make people like you:

- become genuinely interested in other people;
- smile;
- remember that a person's name is to that person the sweetest and most important sound in any language;
- be a good listener;
- encourage others to talk about themselves;
- talk in terms of the other person's interests;
- make the other person feel important, and do it sincerely.

Context

How to Win Friends and Influence People is the original self-improvement book, and Carnegie was the first superstar of the self-help genre. Cashing in on his success, he wrote a plethora of other titles on similar themes, including *Public Speaking and Influencing Men in Business, How to Stop Worrying and Start Living, How to Enjoy Your Life and Your Job*, and *How to Develop Self-confidence and Influence People by Public Speaking*. His successors included Anthony Robbins and Stephen Covey, who studied American success literature (of which Carnegie is a prime example) before coming up with *The Seven Habits of Highly Effective People*.

Carnegie had done much the same 50 years before, and his principles have a similar homely ring to those of Covey. Carnegie's books and his company's training programs continue to strike a chord with managers and aspiring managers, because they deal with the universal challenge of face-to-face communication.

Carnegie was notable in being the first to create a credible long-term business out of his ideas. In creating a flourishing business, Carnegie ensured that his name and ideas should continue to live on and make money after his death.

For More Information

Carnegie, Dale. *How to Win Friends and Influence People*. New York: Simon & Schuster, 1937.

See also:

✔ **How to Network and Market Yourself (pp. 758–59)**

Dale Carnegie (pp. 972–73)

"The application of these principles literally revolutionize the lives of many people."

(How to Win Friends and Influence People)

THE HP WAY

David Packard

WHY READ IT?

David Packard was half of the partnership that created one of the business and management benchmarks of the 20th century—Hewlett-Packard. In 1937, with a mere $538 and a rented garage in Palo Alto, Bill Hewlett and David Packard created one of the most successful corporations in the world. This book tells the story behind the company.

GETTING STARTED

Their secret lay in a simple approach to business. The HP way reflected the culture of the company and the management style they used to run it. It was based on openness and respect for the individual, which was key to the company's success. Management was always available and involved. Conflict had to be tackled through communication and consensus rather than confrontation. Their commitment to people fostered commitment to the company, and HP people at all levels show boundless energy and enthusiasm. The recipe for growth was to make products leaders in their markets. They kept divisions small and didn't do anything too risky. These values worked to save the company when times were hard.

CONTRIBUTION

1. A SIMPLE APPROACH TO BUSINESS

Their secret lay in the simplicity of their methods.

"Professors of management are devastated when I say we were successful because we had no plans. We just took on odd jobs," said Bill Hewlett.

Their legacy lies in the culture of the company they created and the management style they used to run it—the HP way.

From the very start, Hewlett-Packard worked to a few fundamental principles:

- it did not believe in long-term borrowing to secure the expansion of the business;
- its recipe for growth was simply that its products needed to be leaders in their markets;
- it got on with the job.

"Our main task is to design, develop, and manufacture the finest [electronic equipment] for the advancement of science and the welfare of humanity. We intend to devote ourselves to that task," said Packard in a 1961 memo to employees.

The duo eschewed fashionable management theory: "If I hear anybody talking about how big their share of the market is or what they're trying to do to increase their share of the market, I'm going to personally see that a black mark gets put in their personnel folder."

2. RESPECT FOR THE INDIVIDUAL

The company believed that people could be trusted and should always be treated with respect and dignity.

"We both felt fundamentally that people want to do a good job. They just need guidelines on how to do it."

HP believed that management should be available and involved—"Managing by wandering about" was the motto.

Rather than the administrative suggestions of management, Packard preferred to talk of leadership.

If there was conflict, the company decided, it would be tackled through communication and consensus rather than confrontation.

Their legacy, and Packard's proudest achievement, is a management style based on openness and respect for the individual.

3. KEEPING IT SMALL

Hewlett-Packard was a company built on very simple ideas. While competitors were turning into conglomerates, Hewlett and Packard kept their heads down and continued with their methods.

When their divisions grew too big (around 1,500 people) they split them up to ensure that they didn't spiral out of control.

They didn't do anything too risky or too outlandish. Packard was skeptical about pocket calculators—though, in the end, the company was an early entrant into the market.

They didn't risk the company on a big deal or get into debt.

4. COMMITMENT TO VALUES

Their values worked to save the company when times were hard.

During the 1970s recession, Hewlett-Packard staff took a 10% pay cut and worked 10% fewer hours.

If the company hadn't had a long-term commitment to employee stock ownership, perhaps employees wouldn't have been so willing to make sacrifices.

Commitment to people clearly fostered commitment to the company.

CONTEXT

Hewlett-Packard has pulled off an unusual double—it is admired and successful.

When they were assembling their list of excellent companies in the late 1970s, Tom Peters and Robert Waterman included Hewlett-Packard.

When Jerry Porras and James Collins wrote *Built to Last*, their celebration of long-lived companies, there was no doubt that Hewlett-Packard was worthy of inclusion.

In 1985, *Fortune* ranked Hewlett-Packard as one of the two most highly-admired companies in the United States.

The company is ranked similarly in virtually every other poll on well-managed companies or ones that would be good to work for.

"Wherever you go in the HP empire, you find people talking product quality, feeling proud of their division's achievements in that area. HP people at all levels show boundless energy and enthusiasm," observed Tom Peters and Robert Waterman in *In Search of Excellence*.

According to Louise Kehoe in the *Financial Times*, "Their legacy, and the achievement that Packard was most proud of, is a management style based on openness and respect for the individual."

For More Information

Packard, David. *The HP Way*. New York: HarperBusiness, 1995.

See also:
David Packard (pp. 1126–27)

"Management by wandering about." (*The HP Way*)

THE HUMAN PROBLEMS OF AN INDUSTRIAL CIVILIZATION

Elton Mayo

WHY READ IT?

The author was part of the team conducting the Hawthorne Studies at Western Electric's Chicago plant between 1927 and 1932, early studies on motivation in the workplace. The book shows the important link between workforce morale and organizational performance, and paved the way for policies and management theories based on teamwork and effective communication.

GETTING STARTED

The Hawthorne Studies offered important insights into the motivation of workers:

- people and their motivation were critical to the success of any business;
- there was a link between morale and output—changes in working conditions led to increased output;
- it is important to restore humanity to the workplace.

Workers selected for a test felt that more attention was being paid to them. They felt chosen, and so responded positively. The feeling of belonging to a cohesive group led to an increase in productivity. Informal organizations between groups are a potentially powerful force.

CONTRIBUTION

1. THE HAWTHORNE STUDIES

The studies offered important insights into the motivation of workers. It was found that changes in working conditions led to increased output, even if the changes didn't obviously improve working conditions.

Whatever the dictates of mass production and scientific management, people and their motivation were critical to the success of any business.

2. THE LINK BETWEEN MORALE AND OUTPUT

The researchers were interested in exploring the links between morale and output. Five women workers were removed to a test room and observed as they worked. The research was initially restricted to physical and technical variables. Sociological factors were not expected to be of any significance. The results proved otherwise.

Removed from their colleagues, the morale of the "guinea pigs" improved. By virtue of their selection, the women felt that more attention was being paid to them.

3. THE IMPORTANCE OF GROUP COHESION

The feeling of belonging to a cohesive group led to an increase in productivity. "The desire to stand well with one's fellows, the so-called human instinct of association, easily outweighs the merely individual interest and the logic of reasoning upon which so many spurious principles of management are based," commented Mayo.

Mayo champions the case for teamworking and for improved communications between management and the workforce.

The Hawthorne research revealed informal organizations between groups as a potentially powerful force, which companies could make use of to their benefit or ignore at their peril.

3. RESTORING HUMANITY TO THE WORKPLACE

Mayo's belief that the humanity needed to be restored to the workplace struck a chord at a time when the dehumanizing side of mass production was beginning to be more fully appreciated.

"So long as commerce specializes in business methods which take no account of human nature and social motives, so long may we expect strikes and sabotage to be the ordinary accompaniment of industry," Mayo notes.

The research assumed that the behavior of workers was dictated by the "logic of sentiment" while that of the bosses was by the "logic of cost and efficiency."

CONTEXT

The author is known for his contribution to the famous Hawthorne experiments into the motivation of workers.

The experiments were carried out in 1927–32 at the Chicago division of Western Electric. Although they were celebrated as a major event, their significance lay not so much in their results and discoveries but in the statement they made—that people and their motivation were critical to the success of any business.

The findings influenced the human relations school of thinkers, including Herzberg, McGregor, and Maslow, which emerged in the 1940s and 1950s.

The work of the Hawthorne researchers redressed the balance in management theorizing, and the scientific bias of earlier researchers was put into a new perspective.

For More Information

Mayo, Elton. *The Human Problems of an Industrial Civilization*. New York: Macmillan, 1933.

See also:
Elton Mayo (pp. 1020–21)

"The desire to stand well with one's fellows, the so-called human instinct of association, easily outweighs the merely individual interest." (*The Human Problems of an Industrial Civilization*)

THE HUMAN SIDE OF ENTERPRISE

Douglas McGregor

WHY READ IT?

McGregor was a key member of the Human Relations School of Management whose work significantly influenced management styles from the 1960s on. His most famous concept is "Theories X and Y" which describe two extreme approaches to managing people. The book highlights the potential for a more enlightened approach to human relations management and paved the way for approaches such as empowerment and the learning organization.

GETTING STARTED

Management assumptions about controlling human resources determine an organization's character. Theory X assumes that workers are inherently lazy, needing to be supervised and motivated. Authority is the central, indispensable means of managerial control. Theory Y assumes that people want and need to work and organizations should develop employees' commitment. The average human being learns, under the right conditions, not only to accept but to seek responsibility.

CONTRIBUTION

1. THE IMPORTANCE OF HUMAN RESOURCES

The assumptions management holds about controlling its human resources determine the whole character of the enterprise.

2. THEORY X—A TRADITIONAL MANAGEMENT APPROACH

Theory X is built on the assumption that workers are inherently lazy, need to be supervised, and motivated, and regard work as a necessary evil.

3. THE ASSUMPTIONS BEHIND THEORY X

- People inherently dislike work and will avoid it if they can.
- People need to be coerced, controlled, directed, and threatened with punishment into making adequate effort toward the organization's ends.
- People lack ambition, preferring to be directed and to avoid responsibility. Above all they want security.

4. THE INFLUENCE OF THEORY X

The assumption that authority is the central, indispensable means of managerial control pervades U.S. industry. This is a consequence not of man's nature, but of management philosophy, policy, and practice. It is not people who have made organizations, but organizations that have transformed the perspectives, aspirations, and behavior of people.

5. THEORY Y—A HUMANIST APPROACH

Theory Y is based on the principle that people want and need to work. An organization needs to develop the individual's commitment to its objectives, and then to liberate his or her abilities on behalf of those objectives.

6. THE ASSUMPTIONS BEHIND THEORY Y

- Work is as natural as play or rest—the typical human doesn't inherently dislike work.
- External control and threat of punishment are not the only means for bringing about effort.
- Commitment to objectives is a function of the rewards associated with their achievement.
- The most important reward is the satisfaction of ego, which can be the direct product of effort directed toward an organization's purposes.
- The average human being learns not only to accept but to seek responsibility.
- The capacity to use imagination, ingenuity, and creativity in the solution of organizational problems is widely distributed in the population.

7. TOWARD THE LEARNING MANAGER

Four kinds of learning are relevant for managers:

- intellectual knowledge
- manual skills
- problem-solving skills
- social interaction

8. ASSESSING BEHAVIOR

The skills of social interaction are outside the confines of normal teaching and learning methods. "We normally get little feedback of real value concerning the impact of our behavior on others. If they don't behave as we desire, it is easy to blame their stupidity, their adjustment, their peculiarities. Above all, it isn't considered good taste to give this kind of feedback in most social settings. Instead, it is discussed by our colleagues when we are not present to learn about it," says McGregor.

CONTEXT

Despite publishing little in his short life, McGregor's work remains significant. His classic study of work and motivation reflected the concerns of the middle and late 1960s, when the monolithic corporation was at its most dominant and the world at its most questioning. The common complaint against Theories X and Y is that they are mutually exclusive. To counter this McGregor was developing "Theory Z" when he died in 1964: a theory that synthesized the organizational and personal imperatives. William Ouchi later seized on the concept of Theory Z. In his book of the same name, he analyzed Japanese working methods. Here he found fertile ground for many of the ideas McGregor was proposing:

- lifetime employment;
- concern for employees including their social life;
- informal control;
- decisions made by consensus;
- slow promotion;
- excellent transmittal of information from top to bottom and bottom to top with the help of middle management;
- commitment to the firm;
- high concern for quality.

Leading author Gary Hamel commented: "Over the last forty years, we have been slowly abandoning a view of human beings as nothing more than warm-blooded cogs in the industrial machine. People can be trusted; people want to do the right thing; people are capable of imagination and ingenuity—these were McGregor's fundamental premises, and they underlie the work of modern management thinkers from Drucker to Deming to Peters, and the employment practices of the world's most progressive and successful companies."

For More Information

McGregor, Douglas. *The Human Side of Enterprise*. New York: McGraw-Hill, 1960.

See also:
Douglas McGregor (pp. 1022–23)

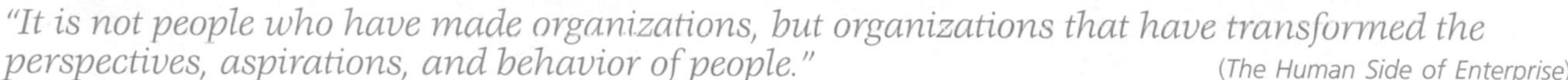

"It is not people who have made organizations, but organizations that have transformed the perspectives, aspirations, and behavior of people." (The Human Side of Enterprise)

  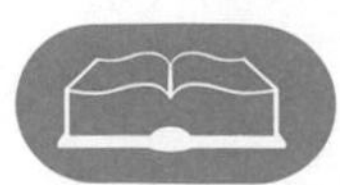    

In Search of Excellence

Tom Peters
Robert Waterman

Why Read It?

In Search of Excellence is the most popular management book of recent times. Appearing when Japanese competition had brought Western business low, it gave managers new heart and a new direction, reminding them, in Gary Hamel's words, "that success often comes from doing common things uncommonly well."

Getting Started

The book emerged from research conducted by Peters and Waterman with the consulting firm, McKinsey. They identified excellent companies, then sought to distill lessons from their behavior and performance.

The sample was eventually whittled down to 62 (which were not intended to be perfectly representative). The choices were largely unsurprising, including the likes of IBM, Hewlett-Packard, Wal-Mart, and General Electric. The emphasis was exclusively on big companies.

There is a certain irony here. Although it celebrated big manufacturing businesses, the book condemned the excesses of dispassionate modern management practice and advocated a return to simpler virtues. The authors later came to feel that their ideas were better embodied in smaller companies.

Contribution

1. Success Builds on First Principles

The book attacks the excesses of the rational model and the business strategy paradigm that had come to dominate Western management thinking.

It counsels return to first principles:

- attention to customers;
- an abiding concern for people (productivity through people);
- the celebration of trial and error (a bias for action).

"The excellent companies really are close to their customers. That's it. Other companies talk about it; the excellent companies do it."

2. Achieve Productivity through People

The authors quote a General Motors worker laid off after 16 years making Pontiacs: "I guess I was laid off because I make poor quality cars. But in 16 years, not once was I ever asked for a suggestion as to how to do my job better. Not once."

Excellent companies encourage and nurture an entrepreneurial spirit among all employees.

3. The Management Role

The real role of the chief executive is to manage the values of the organization. Executives nurture and sustain corporate values. Rather than being distant figureheads, they should be there making things happen.

The word "manager" in lip-service institutions often has come to mean not someone who rolls up his or her sleeves to get the job done right alongside the worker, but someone who hires assistants to do it.

4. Keep Things Simple

Excellent companies "stick to the knitting." They remain fixated on what they know they are good at and are not easily distracted.

One of their key attributes is that they have realized the importance of keeping things simple, despite overwhelming pressures to complicate things.

The authors explain what they call the "smart–dumb rule" as follows.

"Many of today's managers. . .may be a little bit too smart for their own good. The smart ones. . .shift direction all the time, based upon the latest output from the expected value equation [and] have 200-page strategic plans and 500-page market requirement documents that are but one step in product development exercises. Our dumber friends are different. They just don't understand why every customer can't get personalized service, even in the potato chip business."

5. Become Simultaneously Loose and Tight

The debate about how to become loose and tight (controlled and empowered; big yet small) has dominated much subsequent business writing. The authors recommend new concepts that should be added to the management vocabulary. Each one turns the tables on conventional wisdom, implying both the absence of clear directions and the simultaneous need for action. They include:

- temporary structures
- ad hoc groups
- fluid organizations
- internal competition
- product champions
- skunk works

Context

Peter Drucker suggested that the book's simplicity explained its appeal: "The strength of the Peters book is that it forces you to look at the fundamentals. The book's great weakness—which is a strength from the point of view of its success—is that it makes managing sound so incredibly easy."

Gary Hamel said, "The dividing line between simple truths, and simplistic prescription is always a thin one. For the most part, Peters and Waterman avoided the facile and the tautological. Indeed, the focus on operations research, elaborate planning systems, and (supposedly) rigorous financial analysis had, in many companies, robbed management of its soul—and certainly had taken the focus off the customer."

For such a trailblazing book, it is surprisingly uncontroversial. Peters and Waterman admit that what they have to say is not particularly original. They commented that the ideas they were espousing had been generally left behind, ignored, or overlooked by management theorists.

The criteria for selecting excellence were debatable, as all criteria are, and set the authors up for criticism when their excellent companies fell from grace. In 1984 *BusinessWeek* revealed that some had speedily declined into mediocrity and, in some cases, abject failure. But Peters and Waterman had already provided a warning: "We are asked how we know that the companies we have defined as culturally innovative will stay that way. The answer is we don't."

In Search of Excellence created the impetus for the deluge of business books and, in the business world, established customer service as a key form of differentiation and advantage.

For More Information

Peters, Thomas, and Robert Waterman. *In Search of Excellence*. New York: Harper & Row, 1982.

See also:
Tom Peters (pp. 1036–37)

"Do it, fix it, try it, is our favorite axiom." (*In Search of Excellence*)

Innovation in Marketing

Theodore Levitt

Why Read It?

Levitt's views on the importance of marketing are highly regarded. His article "Marketing Myopia" (reprinted in the book) was one of the most popular *Harvard Business Review* articles ever published. It highlights how narrow perspectives result from companies focusing on production rather than customers.

Getting Started

Historical success encouraged the belief that low-cost production was the key to success, but this inevitably leads to narrow perspectives. Companies must broaden their view of the nature of their business, and should be marketing-led rather than production-led. The emphasis is on providing customer-creating value satisfactions.

There is no such thing as a growth industry: success comes from being perceptive enough to spot where future growth may lie. Companies fail because they assume continued growth, believe that a product cannot be improved, and concentrate on improved production techniques to deliver lower costs. Mass-production industries aim to produce all they can and marketing gets neglected.

Contribution

1. A Focus on Customers

The central preoccupation of corporations should be with satisfying customers rather than simply producing goods. Companies should be marketing-led rather than production-led. Management must think of itself not as producing products but as providing customer-creating value satisfactions. The lead must come from the chief executive and senior management.

2. Problems of Production-led Companies

Henry Ford's success in mass production fueled the belief that low-cost production was the key to business success. Ford continued to believe that he knew what customers wanted, long after they had decided otherwise.

Production-led thinking inevitably leads to narrow perspectives.

3. Narrow Perspectives

Companies must broaden their view of the nature of their business; otherwise their customers will soon be forgotten. The railroads are in trouble today not because the need was filled by others, but because it was not filled by the railroads themselves. They let others take customers away from them because they assumed they were in the railroad business rather than in the transportation business—they were product-oriented instead of customer-oriented.

The railroad business was constrained by a lack of willingness to expand its horizons. Similarly, the film industry failed to respond to the growth of television because it regarded itself as being in the business of making movies rather than providing entertainment.

4. Taking Growth for Granted

Growth can never be taken for granted. There is no such thing as a growth industry—growth is a matter of being perceptive enough to spot where future growth may lie.

History is filled with companies that fall undetected into decay for these reasons:

- they assume that the growth in their particular market will continue for as long as the population grows in size and wealth;
- they believe that a product cannot be surpassed;
- they tend to put faith in the ability of improved production techniques to deliver lower costs and, therefore, higher profits.

5. Problems of Mass-production Industries

Mass-production industries are impelled by a great drive to produce all they can. The prospect of steeply declining unit costs as output rises is more than most companies can usually resist. The profit possibilities look spectacular, so all effort focuses on production.

Concentration on the product also lends itself to measurement and analysis. The result is that marketing gets neglected.

6. Distinguishing Selling and Marketing

There is a distinction between the tasks of selling and marketing. Selling concerns itself with the tricks and techniques of getting people to exchange their cash for your product—it is not concerned with the values that the exchange is all about. It does not, as marketing invariably does, view the entire business process as consisting of a tightly integrated effort to discover, create, arouse, and satisfy customer needs.

Context

Ted Levitt's fame was secured early in his career with "Marketing Myopia"—a *Harvard Business Review* article which enjoyed unprecedented success and attention, selling over 500,000 reprints.

It has since been reproduced in virtually every collection of key marketing texts. "Marketing Myopia" is a manifesto rather than a deeply academic article. It embraces ideas that had already been explored by others (Levitt acknowledges his debt to Peter Drucker's *The Practice of Management*).

In the 1980s when marketing underwent resurgence, companies began to heed Levitt's view that they were too heavily oriented toward production. Levitt's article and his subsequent work pushed marketing to center stage. In some cases it led to what Levitt called marketing mania, with companies obsessively responsive to every fleeting whim of the customer.

Many of today's leading thinkers, such as Pascale and Peters, continually re-emphasize Levitt's message that there is no such thing as a growth industry.

Influential writer Gary Hamel said: "If Ted Levitt had done nothing else in his career—and he did plenty—he would have earned his keep on this planet with the article 'Marketing Myopia.' Managers get wrapped up inside their products (railroads) and lose sight of the fundamental benefits customers are seeking (transportation). Equally provocative was Ted's 1983 *Harvard Business Review* article, 'The Globalization of Markets.' While some argue that markets will never become truly global, there are few companies that are betting against the general trend."

For More Information

Levitt, Theodore. *Innovation in Marketing*. New York: McGraw-Hill, 1962.

See also:
Theodore Levitt (pp. 1012–13)

"The central preoccupation of corporations should be with satisfying customers rather than simply producing goods."

(*Innovation in Marketing*)

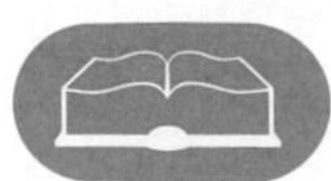

INTELLECTUAL CAPITAL

Thomas Stewart

WHY READ IT?

The author is widely regarded as the world's leading authority on knowledge management, and his views are valuable to any organization that wants to improve the return on its "intellectual capital." The book is a useful guide to the strategic and practical issues of identifying, capturing, and using knowledge to improve competitive advantage.

GETTING STARTED

Traditional capital had financial or physical characteristics. The emphasis now is on an intangible asset, intellectual capital, consisting of human capital, customer capital, and structural capital.

Human capital resides in the heads of employees; customer capital represents the value of a company's ongoing relationships with customers; and structural capital is the knowledge retained within the organization.

The real value comes in being able to capture and deploy intellectual capital. However, you cannot define and manage intellectual assets unless you know what you want to do with them.

Knowledge working will change the pattern of individual careers in the 21st century.

CONTRIBUTION

1. THE NEW CONCEPT OF CAPITAL

Traditionally, capital could be viewed in purely financial or physical terms. It showed up in the buildings and equipment owned, and could be found in the corporate balance sheets.

Recently, the emphasis has switched to an intangible form of asset, intellectual capital. Intellectual capital can be broken down into three areas: human capital; customer capital; and structural capital.

2. HUMAN CAPITAL

Human capital is the knowledge residing in the heads of employees that is relevant to the purpose of the organization.

Human capital is formed and deployed, when more of the time and talent of employees is devoted to activities that result in innovation. It can grow in two ways: when the organization uses more of what people know; or when people know more that is useful to the organization. Unleashing it requires an organization to minimize mindless tasks, meaningless paperwork, and unproductive infighting.

3. CUSTOMER CAPITAL

This represents the value of a company's ongoing relationships with the people or organizations to which it sells. Indicators of customer capital include market share, customer retention and defection rates, and profit per customer.

Customer capital is probably the worst managed of all intangible assets. Many businesses don't even know who their customers are.

4. STRUCTURAL CAPITAL

Structural capital is the knowledge retained within the organization. It belongs to the company as a whole and can be reproduced and shared.

Structural capital includes technologies, inventions, publications, and business processes.

5. MANAGING INTELLECTUAL CAPITAL

The real value comes in being able to capture and deploy intellectual capital. Knowledge assets exist and are worth cultivating only in the context of strategy. You cannot define and manage intellectual assets unless you know what you want to do with them.

There are ten principles for managing intellectual capital.

- Companies don't own human and customer capital. Only by recognizing the shared nature of these assets can a company manage and profit from them.
- To create usable human capital, a company needs to foster teamwork, communities of practice, and other social forms of learning.
- Organizational wealth is created around skills and talents that are proprietary and scarce. Companies must recognize that people with these talents are assets to invest in.
- Structural assets are the easiest to manage but those that customers care least about.
- Move from amassing knowledge "just in case" to having readily available information that customers need.
- Information and knowledge can and should substitute for expensive physical and financial assets.
- Knowledge work is custom work.
- Every company should reanalyze its own industry to see what information is most crucial.
- Focus on the flow of information not the flow of materials.
- Human, structural, and customer capital work together. It is not enough to invest in people, systems, and customers separately.

6. KNOWLEDGE WORKING AND INDIVIDUAL CAREERS

Careers in the 21st century will have a number of characteristics.

- A career is a series of gigs, not a series of steps.
- Project management is the furnace in which successful careers are made.
- Power flows from expertise, not from position.
- Most roles in an organization can be performed by either insiders or outsiders.
- Careers are made in markets not hierarchies.
- The fundamental career choice is not between one company and another, but between specializing and generalizing.

CONTEXT

Thomas Stewart pioneered the field of intellectual capital in a series of articles that earned him an international reputation, with the Planning Forum calling him in 1994 "the leading proponent of knowledge management in the business press."

Intellectual Capital has proved itself as the definitive guide to understanding and managing intangible assets. It explains not only why intellectual capital will be the foundation of corporate success in the new century, but also offers practical guidance to companies about how to make best use of their intangible assets. Since it first appeared, there have been a flood of books on knowledge management.

The term "knowledge worker" is not a new one. In 1994, Peter Drucker wrote that, "the true investment in the knowledge society is not in machines and tools but in the knowledge of the knowledge worker. In the knowledge society the most probable assumption for organizations. . . is that they need knowledge workers far more than knowledge workers need them."

For More Information

Stewart, Thomas A. *Intellectual Capital: The New Wealth of Organizations*. New York: Doubleday, 1997.

See also:
☆ **Intellectual Capital (pp. 159–60)**

"You cannot define and manage intellectual assets unless you know what you want to do with them."
(*Intellectual Capital*)

Leaders: Strategies for Taking Charge

Warren Bennis
Burt Nanus

Why Read It?

Warren Bennis is an academic and regular presidential adviser who brought leadership to a new, mass audience. He is regarded as one of the most important contemporary thinkers.

Burt Nanus is the founder and director of the Center of Futures Research at the University of Southern California.

The book uses an eclectic selection of America's leaders to learn how to become successful. The message is that leadership is open to all.

Getting Started

Leaders commit people to action and convert followers into leaders. They are usually ordinary people rather than particularly charismatic, as leadership is all-encompassing and open to all.

Successful leaders also have a vision that other people believe in, and communicate it effectively. Instead of being an individual problem solver, they achieve greatness through working with groups. Devising and maintaining an atmosphere in which others can succeed is the leader's creative act.

Contribution

1. The Ordinary Leader

The new leader is one who commits people to action, who converts followers into leaders, and who may convert leaders into agents of change. Leadership is not a rare skill—leaders are made rather than born. They are usually ordinary people, or apparently ordinary, rather than charismatic. Leadership is not solely the preserve of those at the top of an organization—it is relevant at all levels. Leadership is not about control, direction, and manipulation.

2. Common Abilities of Leaders

From a survey of 90 U.S. leaders (including Neil Armstrong, the coach of the LA Rams, orchestral conductors, and businessmen such as Ray Kroc of McDonald's), Bennis and Nanus identified four common abilities:

- management of attention
- management of meaning
- management of trust
- management of self

3. Management of Attention

This is a question of vision. Leadership is the capacity to create a compelling vision, translate it into action, and sustain it. Successful leaders have a vision that other people believe in and treat as their own.

4. Management of Meaning

A vision is of limited practical use if it is encased in 400 pages of wordy text or mumbled from behind a paper-packed desk. Effective communication relies on use of analogy, metaphor, and vivid illustration as well as emotion, trust, optimism and hope.

5. Management of Trust

Trust is the emotional glue that binds followers and leaders together. Leaders have to be seen to be consistent.

6. Management of Self

Leaders do not glibly present charisma or time management as the essence of their success. Instead, the emphasis is on persistence and self-knowledge, commitment and challenge, taking risks and, above all, learning. The learning person looks forward to failure or mistakes, which means that the worst problem in leadership is basically early success. There's no opportunity to learn from adversity and problems.

7. A Positive Self-regard

Leaders have a positive self regard, known as emotional wisdom. This is characterized by an ability to accept people as they are. They also have a capacity to approach things in terms of only the present, and an ability to treat everyone, even close contacts, with courteous attention. They need an ability to trust others, and to do without constant approval and recognition.

8. Leaders and Group Working

Greatness starts with superb people. Great groups don't exist without great leaders, but they give the lie to the persistent notion that successful institutions are the lengthened shadow of a great woman or man. It's not clear that life was ever so simple that individuals, acting alone, solved most significant problems. Instead of the individual problem solver, we have a new model for creative achievement.

9. Changing Leadership Qualities

The leader is a pragmatic dreamer, a person with an original but attainable vision. He or she knows that this dream can only be realized if others are free to do exceptional work. Typically, the leader is the one who recruits the others, by making the vision so seductive that they see it too, and eagerly sign up.

Inevitably, the leader has to invent a leadership style that suits the group. The standard models, especially command and control, simply don't work. The heads of groups have to act decisively, not arbitrarily. They have to make decisions without limiting the autonomy of other participants.

10. The Idealistic Leader

Most organizations are dull and working life is mundane, so groups can be an inspiration. Individual leaders can create a human community that will, in the long run, lead to the best organizations. "A Great Group is more than a collection of first-rate minds. It's a miracle," say the authors. Every person has to make a genuine contribution in their lives and the institution of work is one of the main vehicles to achieving this.

Context

With the torrent of publications and executive programs on the subject, it is easy to forget that leadership had been largely overlooked as a topic worthy of serious academic interest until it was revived by Bennis and others in the 1980s. Since then, leadership has become a heavy industry. Concern and interest about leadership development is no longer an American phenomenon: it is truly global. The book stands as a humane counter to much of the military-based hero worship which dogs the subject.

For More Information

Bennis, Warren, and Burt Nanus. *Leaders: Strategies for Taking Charge*. New York: Harper & Row, 1985.

See also:
☆ **Viewpoint: Warren Bennis (pp. 212–13)**
Warren Bennis (pp. 968–69)

(*Leaders: Strategies for Taking Charge*)

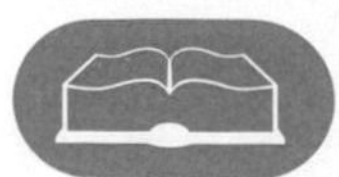

Leadership

James MacGregor Burns

Why Read It?

In his book *Leadership* Burns makes an important contribution to management literature by refocusing interest on the nature of leadership. He brings practical insights from both business and politics and has used those insights to identify two key strands—transactional and transformational leadership.

Getting Started

Burns believes we know too much about our leaders, but too little about leadership. It is a structure for action. It is not the preserve of the few or the tyranny of the masses.

Burns identifies two vital strands of leadership—transformational and transactional leadership. Transactional leadership is built on reciprocity—the relationship between the leader and their followers develops from the exchange of some reward. The secret of effective leadership appears to lie in combining the two elements so that targets, results, and procedures are developed and shared.

Contribution

1. Problems in Defining Leadership

If we know all too much about our leaders, we know far too little about leadership. There are literally hundreds of definitions of leadership and, as a result, the concept "has dissolved into small and discrete meanings," Burns claims.

2. Leadership As a Structure for Action

Leadership is exercised when persons with certain motives and purposes mobilize—in competition or conflict with others—institutional, political, psychological, and other resources so as to arouse, engage, and satisfy the motives of followers.

Leadership is not the preserve of the few or the tyranny of the masses. The leadership approach tends often unconsciously to be elitist, it projects heroic figures against the shadowy background of drab powerless masses. The followership approach tends to be populist or anti-elitist in ideology, perceiving the masses, even in democratic societies, as linked with small, overlapping circles of conservative politicians, military officers, hierocrats, and businessmen.

Leadership is a structure for action that engages people, to varying degrees, throughout the levels and among the interstices of society. Only the inert, the alienated, and the powerless are unengaged. It is also intrinsically linked to morality—moral leadership emerges from, and always returns to, the fundamental wants and needs, aspirations, and values of the followers.

3. Transformational Leadership

Burns identifies two vital strands of leadership—transformational and transactional leadership.

Transformational leadership occurs when one or more persons engage with others in such a way that leaders and followers raise one another to higher levels of motivation and morality. Their purposes, which might have started out separate but related, become fused. Power bases are linked, not as counterweights, but as mutual support for common purpose. Various names are used for such leadership: elevating, mobilizing, inspiring, exalting, uplifting, exhorting, evangelizing.

Transformational leadership becomes moral in that it raises the level of human conduct and ethical aspiration of both the leader and the led, thus having a transforming effect on both. It is also dynamic, in the sense that the leaders throw themselves into a relationship with followers who will feel elevated by it and often become more active themselves, thereby creating new cadres of leaders.

Transformational leadership is concerned with engaging the hearts and minds of others. It works to help all parties achieve greater motivation, satisfaction, and sense of achievement. It is driven by trust, concern, and facilitation rather than direct control. The skills required are concerned with establishing a long-term vision, empowering people to control themselves, coaching and developing others, and challenging the culture to change. In transformational leadership, the power of the leader comes from creating understanding and trust.

4. Transactional Leadership

Transactional leadership is built on reciprocity. The relationship between the leader and his or her followers develops from the exchange of some reward, such as performance ratings, pay, recognition, and praise. It involves leaders in clarifying goals and objectives, communicating well in order to plan tasks and activities with the cooperation of their employees, so that wider organizational goals are met.

The relationship depends on hierarchy and the ability to work through the mode of exchange. It requires leadership skills such as the ability to obtain results, to control through structures and processes, to solve problems, to plan and organize and work within the structures and boundaries of the organization.

5. Combining Transformational and Transactional Leadership

In their apparent mutual exclusiveness, transformational and transactional leadership are akin to Douglas McGregor's theories X and Y. The secret of effective leadership appears to lie in combining the two elements so that targets, results and procedures are developed and shared.

Context

Burns' book provides an important link between leadership in the political and business worlds. For all the books on leadership, the two have usually been regarded as mutually exclusive. His examination of transformational and transactional leadership also stimulated further debate on leadership at a time when it was somewhat neglected. In the 1980s, it returned to prominence in management literature as a subject worthy of study.

Business guru Gary Hamel commented, "There is no theme in management literature which is more enduring than leadership. Among the many contributions which Burns makes to our understanding of leadership, two seem central: leadership must have a moral foundation; and the responsibility for leadership must be widely distributed. Self-interested autocrats, whether political or corporate, ignore these truths at their peril."

For More Information

Burns, James MacGregor. *Leadership*. New York: Harper & Row, 1978.

"If we know all too much about our leaders, we know far too little about leadership." (Leadership)

The Living Company: Habits for Survival in a Turbulent Business Environment

Arie de Geus

Why Read It?

The book looks at the problem of corporate failure, presenting alarming statistics on the relatively short life of European and Japanese enterprise. The author argues that short-term focus on profits, rather than nurturing people, is a key factor in failure. *The Living Company* is the testimony of someone who practiced the human side of enterprise and who believes that companies must be fundamentally humane to prosper.

Getting Started

Corporations should last as long as two or three centuries. The reality is that companies usually die young. A focus on profits rather than on human issues lies behind the high failure rate. However, like all organisms, the living company exists primarily for its own survival and improvement.

A successful company is one that can learn effectively, and senior executives must dedicate a great deal of time to nurturing their people.

Contribution

1. The Problem of Corporate Morality

Companies may be legal entities, but they are disturbingly mortal. The natural average lifespan of a corporation should be as long as two or three centuries—for example, the Sumitomo Group and the Scandinavian company, Stora.

The reality is that companies usually die young. A Dutch survey indicated 12.5 years as the average life expectancy of all Japanese and European firms. The average life expectancy of a multinational corporation—*Fortune* 500 or its equivalent—is between 40 and 50 years.

2. Reasons for Longevity

The high company failure rate is attributed to the focus of managers on profits, rather than on the human community that makes up their organization.

In an attempt to get to the bottom of this mystery, de Geus and a number of his Shell colleagues carried out some research to identify the characteristics of corporate longevity. As you would expect, the onus is on keeping excitement to a minimum. The average human centenarian advocates a life of abstinence, caution, and moderation; and so it is with companies.

The research team identified four key characteristics. The long-lived companies were:

- sensitive to their environment;
- cohesive, with a strong sense of identity;
- tolerant;
- conservative in financing.

3. The Importance of People

There is more to a company and to its longevity than mere money making. The skills, capabilities, and knowledge of people are paramount; capital is no longer king.

4. The Learning Company

A successful company is one that can learn effectively. Learning means being prepared to accept continuous change, and a company can only change if its community of people changes.

Individuals change through learning—requiring senior executives to dedicate a great deal of time to nurturing their people. The author recalls spending around a quarter of his time on the development and placement of people; while C.E.O. of GE, Jack Welch claimed to spend half of his time on such issues.

According to de Geus, all corporate activities are grounded in two hypotheses:

- the company is a living being;
- the decisions for action made by this living being result from a learning process.

Like all organisms, the living company exists primarily for its own survival and improvement. It aims to fulfill its potential and to become as great as it can be.

Context

With its faith in learning, *The Living Company* represents a careful and powerful riposte to corporate nihilism.

The book proposes that the wisdom of the past be appreciated and used, rather than cast out in the manner of a cultural revolution.

Contrast this with reengineering, which sought to dismiss the past so that the future could begin with a blank piece of paper. De Geus suggests that the piece of paper already exists, and notes are constantly being scrawled in the margins as new insights are added.

De Geus's arguments are probably at their weakest when he contemplates why companies deserve to live long lives. The average entrepreneur would probably accept a life expectancy of 12.5 years.

The Living Company is the testimony of someone who practiced the human side of enterprise, and who believes that companies must be fundamentally humane to prosper—whatever the century.

For More Information

de Geus, Arie. *The Living Company: Habits for Survival in a Turbulent Business Environment*. Boston, MA: Harvard Business School Press, 1997.

"Learning is tomorrow's capital." (The Living Company)

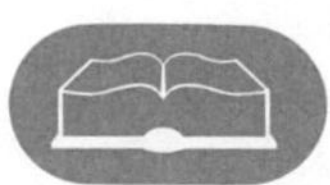

Made in Japan

Akio Morita

Why Read It?

Made in Japan is the story of Sony and reflects the changes that took place in postwar business history. Morita and Sony's story parallels the rebirth of Japan as an industrial power. When Sony was first attempting to make inroads into Western markets, Japanese products were sneered at as being of the lowest quality. Surmounting that obstacle was a substantial business achievement.

Getting Started

Sony's story parallels the rebirth of Japan as an industrial power. It helped change the image of "Made in Japan" from shoddy goods to high quality. Sony invented new markets with a pioneering spirit by bringing out product after product, innovation after innovation. Sony's most famous success was the Walkman, the development of which was based on instinct, not research. Analysis and education do not necessarily help you to reach the best business decisions; sometimes understanding must come before logic. "Japanese people tend to be much better adjusted to the notion of work, any kind of work, as honorable," says Morita. Recruitment is "management's risk and management's responsibility."

Contribution

1. The Japanese Renaissance

Morita and Sony's story parallels the rebirth of Japan as a major industrial power.

They helped change the image of "Made in Japan" from something shoddy to something reputable and desirable.

At the time when Sony first tried to break into the Western electronics market, Japanese products were considered fifth-rate. Morita helped Sony not only to overcome this prejudice but to reverse it.

2. Inventing New Markets

Morita and Sony's gift was to invent new markets with a pioneering spirit. "Sony is a pioneer and never intends to follow others," says Morita.

"Through progress, Sony wants to serve the whole world. It will always seek the unknown. Sony has a principle of respecting and encouraging one's ability. . .and always tries to bring out the best in a person. This is the vital force of Sony."

3. The Power of Innovation

While companies such as Matsushita were inspired followers, Sony set the pace with product after product, innovation after innovation.

Sony brought the world the handheld video camera, the first home video recorder, and the floppy disk.

The blemishes on its record were the Betamax video format, which it failed to license, and color television systems.

3. Instinct and Research

Sony's most famous success was the Walkman, the brainchild of Morita. Morita noticed that young people liked listening to music wherever they went. He put two and two together and made—a Walkman.

He did not believe that any amount of market research could have told the company that this would be successful.

"The public does not know what is possible, we do," he has famously said.

4. Analysis Doesn't Always Pay

Brilliant marketing by instinct was no mere accident.

Morita believes that, if you go through life convinced that your way is always best, all the new ideas in the world will pass you by.

Analysis and education do not necessarily help you to reach the best business decisions. You can be totally rational with a machine but if you work with people, sometimes understanding has to come before logic.

5. Japanese Culture Encourages the Work Ethic

Morita has emphasized the cultural differences in Japanese attitudes toward work. The Japanese tend to have a much stronger work ethic, and see work as an honorable occupation.

Morita believes that management has ultimate responsibility for its staff. If a recession is looming, profit should be sacrificed rather than employees be laid off.

Context

The book tells the story of the rise of Sony and it reflects the rise of Japan as a postwar industrial power. It looks at the role of quality and innovation as key factors in the success of Japanese companies. Many Western authors have focused on the role of quality in Japan, particularly the influence of people like Deming and Juran.

Richard Pascale and Anthony Athos look at the phenomenon in *The Art of Japanese Management*.

Morita and Sony took the attitude that global markets were important from the outset. Ken Ohmae writes on that subject from the Japanese perspective in *The Borderless World*.

For More Information

Morita, Akio. *Made in Japan*. New York: Dutton, 1986.

See also:

Akio Morita (pp. 1118–19)

"The public does not know what is possible, we do." (*Made in Japan*)

Management Teams: Why They Succeed or Fail

R. Meredith Belbin

Why Read It?

Effective teamworking is now seen as key to the success of all types of organization. Meredith Belbin identified the characteristics of people needed to make a successful team. His recommendations are still used, and the book can therefore help anyone who needs to develop a team.

Getting Started

Corporations have been preoccupied with the qualifications, experience, and achievement of individuals—but it is not the individual but the team that is the instrument of sustained and enduring success in management.

Team performance is influenced by the kinds of people making up a group, and testing indicates that certain combinations of personality-types perform more successfully than others. Nine archetypal functions make up an ideal team—plant, coordinator, shaper, teamworker, completer, implementer, resource investigator, specialist, and monitor evaluator. Unsuccessful teams can be improved by analyzing their composition and making appropriate changes.

Contribution

1. The Preoccupation with Individuals

Corporations have been preoccupied with the qualifications, experience, and achievement of individuals, and have applied themselves to their selection, development, training, motivation, and promotion. However commentators believe that the ideal individual for a given job cannot be found, because he or she cannot exist. It is not the individual but the team that is the instrument of sustained and enduring success in management.

2. The Contribution of Individuals in Teams

Belbin was interested in group performance and how it might be influenced by the kinds of people making up a group. He asked members engaged in a business school exercise to undertake a personality and critical-thinking test and, based on the test results, discovered that certain combinations of personality-types performed more successfully than others.

Belbin realized that given adequate knowledge of the personal characteristics and abilities of team members through psychometric testing, he could forecast the likely success or failure of particular teams. Unsuccessful teams can be improved by analyzing their team design shortcomings and making appropriate changes.

3. Identifying Team Characteristics

A questionnaire completed by team members was analyzed to show the functional roles the managers thought they performed in a team. From this research, Belbin identified nine archetypal functions which go to make up an ideal team.

4. Successful Team Composition

- Plant—creative, imaginative, unorthodox; solves difficult problems. Allowable weakness: bad at dealing with ordinary people.
- Coordinator—mature, confident, trusting; a good chairman; clarifies goals, promotes decision making. Not necessarily the cleverest.
- Shaper—dynamic, outgoing, highly strung; challenges, pressurizes, finds ways round obstacles. Prone to bursts of temper.
- Teamworker—social, mild, perceptive, accommodating; listens, builds, averts friction. Indecisive in crunch situations.
- Completer—painstaking, conscientious, anxious; searches out errors; delivers on time. May worry unduly; reluctant to delegate.
- Implementer—disciplined, reliable, conservative, efficient; turns ideas into actions. Somewhat inflexible.
- Resource investigator—extrovert, enthusiastic, communicative; explores opportunities. Loses interest after initial enthusiasm.
- Specialist—single-minded, self-starting, dedicated; brings knowledge or skills in rare supply. Contributes only on narrow front.
- Monitor evaluator—sober, strategic, discerning. Sees all options, makes judgements. Lacks drive and ability to inspire others.

Context

The explosion of interest in teamworking during the last decade has prompted greater interest in Belbin's work. The teamworking categories he identified have proved robust and are still used in a variety of organizations. Gary Hamel commented, "High-performing companies increasingly believe that teams, rather than business units or individuals, are the basic building blocks of a successful organization. Belbin deserves much credit for helping us understand the basic building blocks of successful teams".

Antony Jay commented, "Corporations have been preoccupied with the qualifications, experience, and achievement of individuals. . .it is not the individual but the team that is the instrument of sustained and enduring success in management."

For More Information

Belbin, Meredith R. *Management Teams: Why They Succeed or Fail.* Oxford: Butterworth-Heinemann, 1984.

See also:
R. Meredith Belbin (pp. 966–67)

"It is not the individual but the team that is the instrument of sustained and enduring success in management."
(*Management Teams: Why They Succeed or Fail*)

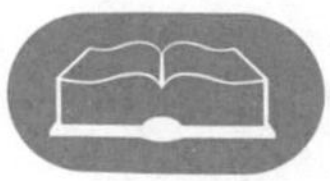

THE MANAGERIAL GRID

Robert Blake
Jane Mouton

WHY READ IT?

The book made an important contribution to the measurement of management performance. It challenged existing theories and provided organizations with a grid for assessing the types of manager they needed for different positions.

GETTING STARTED

In the early 1960s there was a sizeable gap in management theorizing, especially in terms of leadership and motivation. Douglas McGregor's Theory X and Y had a number of shortcomings in reality, and Blake and Mouton found that a management performance model was a more accurate representation of reality. The important axes were concern for productivity, concern for people, and motivation. Accurate measurement is important because of managers' capacity for self-deception.

CONTRIBUTION

1. CHALLENGING MANAGEMENT PERFORMANCE THEORIES

During consultancy work for Exxon, Blake and Mouton concluded that there was a sizeable gap in management theorizing, especially in terms of leadership and motivation. Popular among theories of the time was that of Douglas McGregor and his motivational extremes of X and Y. However, Blake and Mouton believed that many behaviors and motivations fell in the middle of these extremes. Theories X and Y were only a part of the overall picture of organizational behavior.

2. A NEW MODEL OF MANAGEMENT PERFORMANCE

Blake and Mouton's conclusion was that a model with three axes was a more accurate representation of reality. The three crucial axes they determined were: concern for productivity, concern for people, and motivation.

Concern for production and people were both measured on a scale of one to nine, with nine being high. The reason a people axis was necessary is that managers achieve things indirectly. They don't produce nuts and bolts themselves, they organize others so that the production line can be productive.

Motivation was measured on a scale from negative (driven by fear) to positive (driven by desire).

3. FLAWS IN PERFORMANCE MEASUREMENT

Blake and Mouton found that, when left to rank themselves, some 80% of people give themselves a 9,9 rating. Once this is discussed and considered, this figure is routinely reduced to 20%. Given the capacity for self-deception, it is little wonder that change programs fail.

4. KEY MANAGEMENT STYLES

From the grid emerge five key manager styles:

- 1 (production); 1 (people): Do nothing manager. The leader exerts a minimum of effort to get the work done, with very little concern for people or production;
- 1 (production); 9 (people): Labeled the Country Club Manager. This manager pays a lot of attention to people, but little to production. Can be seen in small firms that have cornered the market and some public sector organizations;
- 9 (production); 1(people): This manager emphasizes production and minimizes the influence of human factors;
- 5 (production); 5 (people): Organization man who diligently fosters mundanity;
- 9 (production); 9 (people): Managerial nirvana. The ultimate, with an emphasis on team working and team building. Personal and organizational goals are in alignment; motivation high.

CONTEXT

When Blake and Mouton examined the behavior of people at Exxon, they concluded that there was a sizeable gap in management theorizing, especially in terms of leadership and motivation. They found that many behaviors and motivations fell in the middle of Douglas McGregor's X and Y extremes. They observed that Theories X and Y were only a part of the overall picture of organizational behavior.

Blake and Mouton's conclusion was that a model with three axes—concern for productivity, concern for people, and motivation—was a more accurate representation of reality.

For More Information

Blake, Robert, and Jane Mouton. *The Managerial Grid.* Houston, TX: Gulf Publishing, 1964.

See also:
Douglas McGregor (pp. 1022–23)

"Managers. . .don't produce nuts and bolts themselves, they organize others." (The Managerial Grid)

  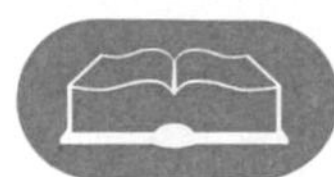    

MANAGING

Harold Geneen

WHY READ IT?

Geneen joined the board of ITT in 1959 and set about turning the company into the world's greatest conglomerate. Along the way he became, according to *BusinessWeek*, the legendary conglomerateur. The book relates the management style and culture that helped ITT to achieve that success. In particular, it highlights the importance of knowing the numbers in minute detail.

GETTING STARTED

Geneen's success was based on knowing every single figure possible. He did not invent the conglomerate, but he had an obsessive belief that it could be made to work. ITT bought 350 companies and appeared to be a managerial nightmare—Geneen made the nightmare work by fanatical attention to detail.

He only micro-managed the numbers; the people were generally overlooked. However, his success meant that people followed his methods without question. Over 200 days a year were devoted to management meetings held throughout the world.

Success was based on amassing all the facts so that decisions became self-evident—Geneen wanted no surprises.

CONTRIBUTION

1. A RIGOROUS MANAGEMENT STYLE

Geneen was the archetypal workaholic. His style was unforgiving, built on a degree of intellectual rigor that bordered on ruthlessness. He pinned his managerial faith on hard work and knowing every single figure possible. For Geneen, detail was everything. Once an accountant always an accountant.

2. MAKING CONGLOMERATES WORK

The conglomerate was not Geneen's invention. But he brought an obsessive belief that it could be made to work. He believed that ITT could manage any business in any industry if it knew the figures.

His career with ITT, described in *Managing*, is a pageant of acquisition and diversification. Under Geneen, ITT bought companies as casually as a billionaire buys trinkets. One acquisition funded another. ITT bought 350 companies, including Avis Rent-A-Car, Sheraton Hotels, Continental Baking, and Levitt & Sons, among many others. By 1970, ITT was composed of 400 separate companies operating in 70 countries. With such huge numbers of companies in such vastly different fields, ITT was hopelessly diversified. To contemporary eyes, the company was a managerial nightmare. Yet, Geneen made the nightmare work by fanatical attention to detail.

3. MANAGING THE NUMBERS

Geneen only micro-managed the numbers, however; the people were generally overlooked.

"The very fact that you go over the progression of those numbers week after week, month after month, means that you have strengthened your memory and your familiarity with them so that you retain in your mind a vivid composite picture of what is going on in your company," he wrote.

4. MANAGEMENT CULTURE

Geneen inculcated a remarkable culture within ITT. His success meant that people followed his methods with the unquestioning faith of true believers.

Between 1959 and 1977, ITT's sales went from $765 million to nearly $28 billion. Earnings went from $29 million to $562 million, and earnings per share rose from $1 to $4.20.

As part of Geneen's formula, over 50 executives flew every month to Brussels to spend four days poring over the figures. It was calculated that over 200 days a year were devoted to management meetings held throughout the world.

5. SUCCESS BASED ON FACTS

The point was to amass all the facts available so that the decisions became self-evident. If you knew everything, you would then know exactly what to do. Facts were the lifeblood of the expanding ITT.

"The highest art of professional management requires the literal ability to smell a real fact from all others," Geneen believed. "Managers should have the temerity, intellectual curiosity, guts and/or plain impoliteness, if necessary, to be sure that what they do have is indeed what we will call an unshakable fact."

Geneen wanted no surprises. He also hoped to make people as predictable and controllable as the capital resources they must manage.

CONTEXT

Much of Geneen's managerial philosophy and practice would appear to be anathema to the contemporary executive.

However, his fundamentalist style of management remains. Management consultants, for example, continue to trade their rational models—pour in all the figures you can find and the right decision will emerge. There is still a temptation to manage by numbers rather than through and with people.

On the positive side, Geneen can be said to have elevated management to a new level. His system required a team of highly numerate, professional managers who had to take responsibility.

The Geneen legacy is most notably evident in the conglomerates that continue to survive. General Electric, under Jack Welch and now Jeff Immelt, may be the most lauded corporation of our age, but it is also a conglomerate with interests in everything from financial services to nuclear reactors and washing machines. Harold Geneen would have regarded the survival of such companies as vindication of his methods.

Others point to the decline of ITT on his departure as a true measure of the long-term validity of Geneen's approach to management.

For More Information

Geneen, Harold. *Managing*. New York: Doubleday, 1985.

See also:
Harold Geneen (pp. 1084–85)

"Putting deals together beats spending every day playing golf." (*Managing*)

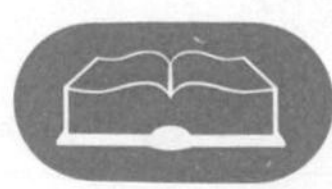

MANAGING ACROSS BORDERS

Christopher Bartlett
Sumantra Ghoshal

WHY READ IT?

Bartlett and Ghoshal map out the new business reality of globalization and the kinds of organizations a "borderless" business world requires. The book is regarded as a classic, and has helped many companies to focus on the type of organization they need for global success.

GETTING STARTED

Changing patterns of international management have led to a new global model, in which enabling innovation and disseminating knowledge in globally dispersed organizations is a major challenge.

A number of organizational forms are now prevalent among global companies: multinational firms offer a high degree of local responsiveness; global firms offer scale efficiencies and cost advantages; international firms have the ability to transfer knowledge and expertise to overseas environments that are less advanced; and the transnational firm combines local responsiveness with global efficiency and the ability to transfer know-how better, cheaper, and faster.

Integration and the creation of coherent systems for value delivery are the new drivers of organizational structure.

CONTRIBUTION

1. CHANGING PATTERNS OF INTERNATIONAL MANAGEMENT

The traditional international management model was simply to export your own way of doing things elsewhere, and companies believed that global operations were simply a means of achieving economies of scale. Local nuances were overlooked in the quest for global standardization: global and local were mutually exclusive. In general, organizations either gave local operations autonomy or controlled them rigidly from a distance.

2. A NEW GLOBAL MODEL

Global presence with local responsiveness is now key. Companies face the challenge of enabling innovation and disseminating knowledge in globally dispersed organizations. Bartlett and Ghoshal identify a number of organizational forms prevalent among global companies.

3. MULTINATIONAL COMPANIES

The multinational or multidomestic organization offers a very high degree of local responsiveness. It is a decentralized federation of local businesses, linked together through personal control by expatriates who occupy key positions abroad.

4. GLOBAL COMPANIES

Global organizations offer scale efficiencies and cost advantages. With global scale facilities, the global organization seeks to produce standardized products. It is often centralized in its home country, with overseas operations considered as delivery pipelines to tap into global market opportunities. There is tight control of strategic decisions, resources, and information by the global hub.

5. INTERNATIONAL COMPANIES

International companies have the ability to transfer knowledge and expertise to overseas environments that are less advanced. They are coordinated federations of local businesses, controlled by sophisticated management systems and corporate employees. The attitude of the parent company tends to be parochial, fostered by the superior know-how at the center of the organization.

6. THE TRANSNATIONAL COMPANIES

Global competition is forcing many businesses to shift to a fourth model, which they call the transnational. This organization combines local responsiveness with global efficiency and the ability to transfer know-how better, cheaper, and faster. The transnational company is made up of a network of specialized or differentiated units, which focus on managing integrative linkages between local businesses as well as with the center. The subsidiary becomes a distinctive asset, rather than simply an arm of the parent company. Manufacturing and technology development are located wherever it makes sense, and there is an explicit focus on leveraging local know-how in order to exploit worldwide opportunities.

7. THE IMPORTANCE OF INTEGRATION

Integration and the creation of a coherent system for value delivery are the new drivers of organizational structure. Companies cannot be left to their own devices, but have to be brought within the fold—while also keeping in touch with their local business environment.

What binds the companies together is a set of explicit or implicit shared values and beliefs that can be developed and managed effectively. There are three techniques crucial to forming an organization's psychology: 1) clear, shared understanding of the company's mission and objectives; 2) the actions and behavior of senior managers are vital as examples and statements of commitment; 3) corporate personnel policies must be geared up to develop a multidimensional and flexible organization process.

CONTEXT

Managing Across Borders is one of the few business books of recent years that deserves recognition as a classic. When it was published in 1989, understanding of globalization was in its infancy. With its emphasis on networking across the global organization and transferring learning and knowledge, the book effectively set the organizational agenda for a decade and created a new organizational model.

Bartlett and Ghoshal effectively signal the demise of the divisional organization—which gives divisions independence—first developed by Alfred P. Sloan of General Motors.

For More Information

Bartlett, Christopher, and Sumantra Ghoshal. *Managing Across Borders*. Boston, MA: Harvard Business School Press, 1989.

See also:
☆ **Viewpoint: Christopher Bartlett (pp. 45–46)**
☆ **Viewpoint: Sumantra Ghoshal (pp. 190–91)**

"Integration and the creation of a coherent system for value delivery are the new drivers of organizational structure."
(*Managing Across Borders*)

MANAGING ON THE EDGE

Richard Pascale

WHY READ IT?

This book challenges traditional management thinking, which Pascale feels is too complacent for an environment driven by change. He sets out a new perspective for "contention management" which seeks to harness the conflicting energies in an organization to achieve positive change. The book set the management agenda for a decade after its publication.

GETTING STARTED

U.S. managerial history is largely inward-focused and self-congratulatory. Change is a fact of business life, but complacency can cause problems. It is essential to change the management perspective. The incremental approach to change is no longer effective. The new emphasis should be on asking questions. Successful organizations undergo continual renewal by constantly asking questions.

Four factors drive stagnation and renewal in organizations:

- fit
- split
- contend
- transcend

"Contention management" is essential to orchestrate tensions that arise between these four factors. Forces locked in opposition can be used to generate inquiry and adaptation and the manager's job is to maintain a constructive level of debate.

CONTRIBUTION

1. THE DANGERS OF MANAGEMENT COMPLACENCY

Nothing fails like success. Great strengths are inevitably the root of weakness.

Of the companies listed in *Fortune* 500 of 1985, 143 had been dropped by 1990.

U.S. managerial history is largely inward-focused and self-congratulatory.

2. THE NEED FOR CHANGE

According to Pascale, change is a fact of business life. We are ill-equipped to deal with it and the traditional approach to managing change is no longer applicable. The incremental approach to change is effective when the goal is to obtain more of the same thing. Historically, that has been sufficient. The United States' advantages of plentiful resources, geographical isolation, and absence of serious global competition defined a league in which Americans competed with each other and everyone played by the same rules.

3. GROWTH OF MANAGEMENT FADS

There have been more than two dozen management fads since the 1950s.

A dozen emerged in the five years prior to 1990.

4. DRIVING STAGNATION AND RENEWAL

Four factors drive stagnation and renewal in organizations:

- fit—pertains to an organization's internal consistency (unity);
- split—describes a variety of techniques for breaking a bigger organization into smaller units and providing them with a stronger sense of ownership and identity (plurality);
- contend—refers to a management process that harnesses (rather than suppresses) the contradictions that are inevitable by-products of organizations (duality);
- transcend—alerts people to the higher order of complexity that successfully managing the renewal process entails (vitality).

5. CHANGING MANAGEMENT PERSPECTIVE

Pascale calls for a fundamental shift in perspective.

Managerial behavior is based on the assumption that people should rationally order the behavior of those they manage. That mindset needs to be challenged.

Orderly answers are no longer appropriate.

The new emphasis should be on asking questions. Strategic planning, at best, is about posing questions, more than attempting to answer them.

Successful organizations undergo a continual process of renewal.

Central to achieving this is a willingness to ask questions constantly and to harness conflict for the corporate good, through systems that encourage questioning.

Companies must become engines of inquiry.

6. CONTENTION MANAGEMENT

Managers are ill-equipped to deal with the contention that arises when fundamental questions are posed.

Contention management is essential to orchestrate tensions that arise. Around 50% of the time when contention arises, it is smoothed over and avoided.

The forces that we have historically regarded as locked in opposition can be viewed as apparent opposites that generate inquiry and adaptive responses.

Each point of view represents a facet of reality, and these realities tend to challenge one another and raise questions.

If we redefine the manager's job as maintaining a constructive level of debate, we are, in effect, holding the organization in the question. This leads to identifying blind spots and working around obstacles.

Truth—personally and organizationally—lies in the openness of vigorous debate.

Organizations are, in the last analysis, interactions among people.

CONTEXT

Managing on the Edge presents a formidably researched and argued challenge to complacency and timidity.

Pascale criticizes Peters and Waterman's *In Search of Excellence* saying, "Simply identifying attributes of success is like identifying attributes of people in excellent health during the age of the bubonic plague."

Passions and obsessions frequently degenerate into simplistic formulae—for example, acronyms such as KISS (Keep it simple, stupid).

Managing on the Edge set the tone for much of the management thinking of the decade. Its emphasis on the need for constant change has since been developed by Pascale. He now argues that the issue of managing the way we change is a competence rather than an episodic necessity.

The capability to change is a core competence in its own right.

Influential critic Gary Hamel commented, "In *Managing on the Edge*, Richard Pascale provides a number of useful observations on the sources of corporate vitality. One of the things I've always admired about Richard Pascale is that he focuses not on tools and techniques, but on principles and paradigms. While management bookshelves groan with the weight of simplistic how-to books (for example, *The One Minute Manager*), Pascale challenges managers to think, and to think deeply. Pascale forces managers to deconstruct the normative models on which they base their beliefs and actions."

For More Information

Pascale, Richard. *Managing on the Edge.* New York: Viking Books, 1990.

(*Managing on the Edge*)

  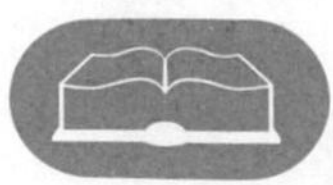    

Marketing Management

Philip Kotler

Why Read It?

Kotler is one of the leading authorities on marketing. *Marketing Management* is the definitive marketing textbook, covering the full scope of contemporary marketing. It is the most widely used marketing book in business schools.

Getting Started

Marketing continues to evolve and expand its scope exponentially. The emphasis is shifting from transaction-oriented marketing to relationship marketing-retaining customer loyalty through continually satisfying their needs. Marketing management is the process of planning and executing functions that satisfy customer and organizational objectives.

Customer-delivered value is the difference between total customer value and total customer cost.

Organizations encounter three common hurdles to marketing orientation:

- organized resistance;
- slow learning;
- fast forgetting.

Contribution

1. Marketing Continues to Evolve

The marketing discipline is redeveloping its assumptions, concepts, skills, tools, and systems for making sound business decisions.

Marketers must know when to:

- cultivate large markets or niche markets;
- launch new brands or extend existing brand names;
- push or pull products through distribution;
- protect the domestic market or penetrate aggressively into foreign markets;
- add more benefits to the offer or reduce the price;
- expand or contract budgets for sales force, advertising, and other marketing tools.

The scope of marketing is expanding exponentially as is demonstrated by the size and scope of *Marketing Management*. Its contents range over:

- industry and competitor analysis;
- designing strategies for the global marketplace;
- managing product life cycle strategies;
- retailing, wholesaling, and physical-distribution systems.

2. The Change to Relationship Marketing

The emphasis is shifting from transaction-oriented marketing to relationship marketing. Good customers are an asset which, when well managed and served, will return a handsome lifetime income stream.

In the intensely competitive marketplace, the company must retain customer loyalty through continually satisfying their needs in a superior way.

3. Defining the Role of Marketing

Marketing is the social and managerial process by which individuals and groups obtain what they need and want through creating, offering, and exchanging products of value with others. A market consists of all the potential customers sharing a particular need or want, who might be willing to exchange in order to satisfy that need or want.

Marketing management is the process of planning and executing the conception, pricing, promotion, and distribution of goods, services, and ideas, to create exchanges with target groups that satisfy customer and organizational objectives.

4. Analyzing Products

A product is anything that can be offered to a market for attention, acquisition, use, or consumption that might satisfy a want or need.

A product has five levels:

- the core benefit (marketers must see themselves as benefit providers);
- the generic product;
- the expected product (the normal expectations the customer has of the product);
- the augmented product (the additional services or benefits added to the product);
- the potential product (all the augmentations and transformations that this product might undergo in the future).

5. Customer Value

Customer-delivered value is the difference between total customer value and total customer cost. Total customer value is the bundle of benefits customers expect from a given product or service. It consists of product value, service value, personnel value, and image value. Total customer cost consists of monetary price, time cost, energy cost, and psychic cost. Combined, the two produce customer-delivered value.

6. Barriers to Marketing Orientation

In order to become marketing oriented, organizations encounter three common hurdles:

- organized resistance—entrenched functional behavior tends to oppose increased emphasis on marketing, as it is seen as undermining functional power bases;
- slow learning—most companies only slowly embrace the marketing concept;
- fast forgetting—companies that embrace marketing concepts tend, over time, to lose touch with the principles. Various U.S. companies have sought to establish their products in Europe with scant knowledge of different marketplaces.

7. Achieving Market Leadership

Good companies will meet needs; great companies will create markets. Market leadership is gained by envisioning new products, services, lifestyles, and ways to raise living standards. There is a vast difference between companies offering "me-too" products and those creating previously unimagined product and service values.

Ultimately, marketing at its best is about value creation and raising the world's living standards.

Context

Marketing Management is the definitive marketing textbook. Tightly argued and all-encompassing, its content has been expanded and brought up to date through various editions. The eighth edition, published in 1994, maps out the emerging challenges to all those involved in marketing.

The very size and scope of *Marketing Management* demonstrates the exponential expansion of marketing. Gary Hamel commented: "There are few MBA graduates alive who have not plowed through Kotler's encyclopedic textbook on marketing, and have not benefited enormously from doing so. I know of no other business author who covers his (or her) territory with such comprehensiveness, clarity, and authority as Phil Kotler. I can think of few other books, even within the vaunted company of this volume, whose insights would be of more practical benefit to the average company than those found in *Marketing Management*."

For More Information

Kotler, Philip. *Marketing Management: Analysis, Planning, Implementation, and Control.* Upper Saddle River, NJ: Prentice Hall, 1996.

"Good companies will meet needs; great companies will create markets." (*Marketing Management*)

  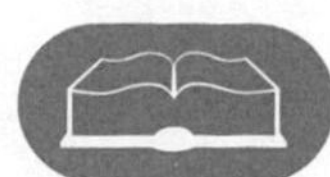    

MEGATRENDS

John Naisbitt

WHY READ IT?

Megatrends was written in 1982 before the technology revolution took hold. It attempts to predict the key changes in business and society. Naisbitt correctly anticipated a number of factors such as globalization, empowerment, and the rise of an information economy.

GETTING STARTED

We have changed to an economy based on the creation and distribution of information. Speed is a competitive weapon.

We must now acknowledge that we are part of a global economy. The bigger the world economy, the more powerful its smallest player—and in small organizations, we have rediscovered the ability to act innovatively and to achieve results from the bottom up. Big bureaucratic organizations can be beaten. Economies of scale are giving way to economies of scope. The acceleration of technological progress has created an urgent need for a return to human scale.

Empowerment, with responsibility, has become more important for every individual in an organization. We are more self-reliant and less hierarchical. Society is moving toward much longer-term time frames.

CONTRIBUTION

1. TOWARD THE INFORMATION ECONOMY

Although we continue to think we live in an industrial society, we have in fact changed to an economy based on the creation and distribution of information.

In the early 1980s however, traditional issues, such as production methods, still held sway. The technological possibilities in information exchange and transfer were contemplated by a small group in West-Coast laboratories.

2. TECHNOLOGY WITH A HUMAN SCALE

We are moving in the dual directions of high tech/high touch, matching each new technology with a compensatory human response. Heart transplants led to new interest in family doctors and neighborhood clinics; jet aircraft resulted in more face-to-face meetings.

High touch is about getting back to a human scale. All change is local and bottom-up. If you keep track of local events, you can see the shifting patterns.

You can't stop technological progress, but by the same token, you can hardly go wrong with a high touch response. FedEx has all the reliability and efficiency of modern electronics, but its success is built on a form of high touch hand delivery.

3. THE EMERGENCE OF A GLOBAL ECONOMY

We no longer have the luxury of operating within an isolated, self-sufficient, national economic system. We must now acknowledge that we are part of a global economy.

We have begun to let go of the idea that the United States is and must remain the world's industrial leader as we move on to other tasks.

The global paradox is that the bigger the world economy, the more powerful its smallest player.

4. A LONGER TIME FRAME

We are moving away from a society governed by short-term considerations and rewards to one which deals with things in much longer-term time frames.

5. THE GROWTH OF EMPOWERMENT

In cities and states, in small organizations and subdivisions, we have rediscovered the ability to act innovatively and to achieve results from the bottom up.

Naisbitt anticipated the fashion in the late 1980s and early 1990s for empowerment with responsibility being spread more evenly throughout organizations, rather than centered on a small group of managers.

6. GREATER SELF-RELIANCE

We are shifting from institutional help to more self-reliance in all aspects of our lives.

Trends in working patterns, such as employability, suggest that this is becoming the case for a select few professionals with marketable skills.

7. CHANGING FRAMEWORK OF DEMOCRACY

We are discovering that the framework of representative democracy has become obsolete in an era of instantaneously shared information. Alvin Toffler was suggesting this in his 1970 book *Future Shock*, though there are few signs of reform.

8. INFORMAL NETWORKS REPLACING HIERARCHY

We are giving up our dependence on hierarchical structures in favor of informal networks. This will be especially important to the business community.

This has become one of the great trends of the last decade as networks are developed in a bewildering variety of ways—with suppliers, between competitors, internally, and globally.

Technology has enabled networks never previously anticipated, with important repercussions. When everyone hears about everything at the same time, we all know that everyone is equally well-informed.

9. SPEED AS A COMPETITIVE WEAPON

Linked to this is the entire question of speed, which Naisbitt identified early on as a competitive weapon.

Economies of scale are giving way to economies of scope, finding the right size for synergy, market flexibility, and above all, speed.

10. MORE CHOICE FOR SOCIETY

From a narrow "either/or" society with a limited range of personal choices, we are exploding into a free-wheeling, multiple-option society.

11. THE POWER OF SMALL BUSINESSES

Naisbitt championed the role of small business in generating the wealth of the future. Small companies, right down to the individual, can beat big bureaucratic companies every time.

Unless big companies reconstitute themselves as a collection of small companies, they will just continue to go out of business.

It's the small companies who are creating the global company.

CONTEXT

Megatrends identified ten critical restructurings. Some have proved accurate predictions of what has happened in intervening years, others have proved less accurate.

Naisbitt predicted the rise of the information economy when the technology was still a laboratory product, and he identified the emergence of factors such as globalization and empowerment.

Naisbitt's predictions can be compared with those of Alvin Toffler in *The Third Wave*.

For More Information

Naisbitt, John. *Megatrends*. New York: Warner Books, 1982.

(*Megatrends*)

THE MIND OF THE STRATEGIST

Kenichi Ohmae

WHY READ IT?

The book illuminates the strategic thinking behind Japanese corporate success. The author shows how and why it differs from the Western approach to strategic thinking and explains that Western companies can adapt to this successful model.

GETTING STARTED

To a large extent, Japanese success can be attributed to the nature of Japanese strategic thinking. Japanese businesses tend not to have large strategic planning staffs. The customer is at the heart of the Japanese approach to strategy. There are three main players in any business strategy—the corporation itself, the customer, and the competition—collectively called the strategic triangle. Just as events in the real world do not always fit a linear model, the Japanese approach to strategy is irrational and nonlinear.

CONTRIBUTION

1. STRATEGY DETERMINES JAPANESE SUCCESS

Japanese success can be attributed to the nature of Japanese strategic thinking. This is basically creative and intuitive rather than rational, but the necessary creativity can be learned.

Unlike large U.S. corporations, Japanese businesses tend not to have large strategic planning staffs. Instead they often have a single, idiosyncratic, naturally talented strategist.

From the dynamic interaction of the company, customers, and competition, a comprehensive set of objectives and plans eventually emerges.

2. THE CUSTOMER AT THE CENTER

In contrast to the West, the customer is at the heart of the Japanese approach to strategy and the key to corporate values.

3. STRATEGIC TRIANGLE

In the construction of any business strategy, three main players must be taken into account: the corporation itself, the customer, and the competition. Collectively they are called the strategic triangle.

The job of the strategist is to achieve superior performance. At the same time, the strategist must be sure that his strategy matches the strengths of the corporation with the needs of a clearly defined market. Otherwise, the corporation's long-term viability may be at stake.

4. STRATEGY IS IRRATIONAL

The central thrust of the book is that strategy as epitomized by the Japanese approach is irrational and nonlinear.

In strategic thinking, one first seeks a clear understanding of each element of a situation, and then makes the fullest use of human brain power to restructure the elements in the most advantageous way.

Events in the real world do not always fit a linear model. Hence the most reliable means of dissecting a situation into its constituent parts, and reassembling them in the desired pattern, is not a step-by-step methodology, but the ultimate nonlinear thinking tool, the human brain.

True strategic thinking thus not only contrasts sharply with the conventional mechanical systems approach, but also with the purely intuitive approach, which reaches conclusions without any breakdown or analysis.

5. GAINING GROUND THROUGH EFFECTIVE STRATEGY

An effective business strategy is one by which a company can gain significant ground on its competitors at an acceptable cost to itself.

There are four main ways of achieving this:

- focusing on the key factors for success (KFS);
- building on relative superiority;
- pursuing aggressive initiatives;
- utilizing strategic degrees of freedom.

The principal concern is to avoid doing the same thing, on the same battleground, as the competition.

6. FOCUSING ON KEY FACTORS FOR SUCCESS

Certain functional or operating areas within every business are more critical for success in that particular business environment than others.

If you concentrate effort into these areas and your competitors do not, this is a source of competitive advantage. The problem lies in identifying these key factors for success.

Today's industry leaders, without exception, began by bold deployment of strategies based on KFS.

7. BUILDING ON RELATIVE SUPERIORITY

When all competitors are seeking to compete on the KFS, a company can exploit any differences in competitive conditions.

For example, it can make use of technology or sales networks not in direct competition with its rivals.

8. PURSUING AGGRESSIVE INITIATIVES

Frequently, the only way to win against a much larger, entrenched competitor is to upset the competitive environment, by undermining the value of its KFS.

That means changing the rules of the game by introducing new KFS.

9. UTILIZING STRATEGIC DEGREES OF FREEDOM

This means that the company should focus upon innovation in areas that are untouched by competitors.

CONTEXT

The author is Japan's only successful management guru. The book was published in the West at the height of interest in Japanese management methods.

Ohmae challenged the simplistic belief, that Japanese management was a matter of company songs and lifetime employment. Instead, Japanese success could be attributed to the nature of Japanese strategic thinking.

Bestselling author Gary Hamel commented, "I loved this book! At a time when most strategy savants were focused either on the process of planning (Ansoff and his followers) or on the determinants of successful, that is, profitable, strategies (Michael Porter), Kenichi Ohmae challenged managers to think in new ways. Strategy doesn't come from a calendar-driven process; it isn't the product of a systematic search for ways of earning above-average profits; strategy comes from viewing the world in new ways. Strategy starts with an ability to think in new and unconventional ways."

For More Information

Ohmae, Kenichi. *The Mind of the Strategist: The Art of Japanese Business.* New York: McGraw-Hill, 1982.

See also:
Kenichi Ohmae (pp. 1028–29)

"The job of the strategist is to achieve superior performance, relative to competition, in the key factors for success of the business."

(*The Mind of the Strategist*)

Moments of Truth

Jan Carlzon

Why Read It?

Jan Carlzon is a Swedish businessman who shot to international prominence by leading a turnaround at the Scandinavian airline, SAS. The turnaround was based on excellence in customer service, and the book contains many practical examples of the way this can be applied. The SAS story is one of the most frequently-used case studies in customer service training and literature.

Getting Started

Carlzon used customer service as a vehicle for turning the SAS airline around. He held that quality service is built around moments of truth—the critical transactions at each stage of the ownership or use cycle. These critical transactions occur at initial contact; first use; problem solving; ongoing support; further purchases: and recommendations to others. Customer satisfaction and value are affected at different points in the cycle. They also vary by customer type.

This approach owes much to the Scandinavian management style—humane and people centered. Scandinavian companies embraced team working and employee participation before they became fashionable: their leaders are anti-authoritarian; they make very effective use of coaching and mentoring, and they also communicate consistently and continually.

Contribution

1. Making Customer Service Work

Carlzon actually made customer service work and used it as a vehicle for turning the SAS airline—formerly an indifferent performer—into a world class organization.

Carlzon came up with the phrase "moments of truth"—the sequence of critical transactions across each stage of the ownership or use cycle. Any time a customer comes into contact with any aspect of a business, however remote, is an opportunity to form an impression.

2. Identifying Moments of Truth

The critical transactions are broken down into:

- initial contact;
- first use;
- problem solving;
- on-going support;
- further purchases;
- recommendations to others.

The key to understanding customer behavior is to: 1) evaluate the degree to which satisfaction and value are affected at these different points in the cycle; 2) understand how they vary by customer type. Carlzon decided dramatically to prove the company's dedication to moments of truth by sending tens of thousands of SAS managers on training programs.

3. The Success of the Scandinavian Approach

Like most stereotypes, the image of highly motivated, well-rewarded, hard-working, and contented Scandinavians is only partly true. However, Scandinavian companies have a track record of managing their human resources in innovative ways. Their management style tends to be humane and people centered, and they were champions of team working and employee participation long before they became the height of managerial fashion.

Scandinavia has a very stable political system and a fairly homogeneous society, and problems typically are solved through negotiation. Historically there has been little unrest—but the counter to this is that often, without a crisis, advancement is not achieved. The Scandinavian business culture shares some characteristics with that of the Japanese. Saving face is important and, rather than direct frontal attack, Scandinavians prefer a more obtuse and subtle approach.

4. A Scandinavian Leadership Style

Old-fashioned virtues are in. Typically, in one survey, American executives rated honesty as the prime business virtue. Swedish executives did not include honesty at all—it was assumed.

The Scandinavian leader tends to be decidedly anti-authoritarian. Highly personal and practical theories, such as coaching and mentoring, find fertile ground; being upfront and communicating openly is expected. With Carlzon and others there is a certain amount of showmanship—they play their roles to perfection. They stand in the middle of their strategy. They don't preach the strategy; they are the strategy. They communicate consistently and continually. They repeat the same messages again and again. But they never grow tired of saying them—there is no sign of boredom, no cynicism, no sarcasm. They give words real meaning. This appetite for communication is clearly linked to a more humane style of management.

Context

Carlzon set in train SAS's revival, which became a benchmark for international best practice in customer service. The achievement was celebrated, among many others, by Tom Peters in *A Passion for Excellence*.

After Carlzon left SAS, the company's halo slipped a little and Scandinavian role models were thin on the ground for a number of years. During the 1990s, however, there was a steady stream of corporate benchmarks. The new Scandinavian role models—IKEA, Skandia, Oticon, and ABB remain indebted to Carlzon's example.

For More Information

Carlzon, Jan. *Moments of Truth*. New York: HarperBusiness, 1987.

See also:

Ingvar Kamprad (pp. 1102–03)

"All business is show business." (*Moments of Truth*)

  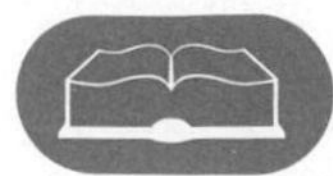    

MOTIVATION AND PERSONALITY *Abraham Maslow*

WHY READ IT?

Maslow introduced the concept of a hierarchy of needs which has formed an integral part of marketing, human resource, motivational, and management literature ever since. The book makes an important contribution to the emergence of human relations as a professional discipline.

GETTING STARTED

There is an ascending scale of needs that provides the basis for motivation. Basic physiological needs come first; once these are met, other needs dominate. At the top of the scale is self-actualization, where individuals achieve their personal potential. Also high up are social or love needs, and ego or self-esteem needs. The hierarchy of needs provides a rational framework for motivation, and human nature determines that motivation is intrinsically linked to rewards.

CONTRIBUTION

1. THE HIERARCHY OF NEEDS

There is an ascending scale of needs, which must be understood if people are to be motivated. First are the fundamental physiological needs of warmth, shelter, and food. It is quite true that man lives by bread alone—when there is no bread.

But what happens when there is plenty of bread?

2. EMERGING NEEDS

Once basic physiological needs are met, others emerge to dominate. These can be categorized roughly as the safety needs. If man's state is sufficiently extreme and chronic, he may be characterized as living almost for safety alone.

Next on the hierarchy are social or love needs, and ego or self-esteem needs.

3. SELF-ACTUALIZATION

As each need is satisfied, eventually comes self-actualization—the individual achieves their own potential.

4. FROM MOTIVATION TO REWARD

While the hierarchy of needs provides a rational framework for motivation, its flaw lies in the nature of humanity. Man always wants more. When asked what salary they would be comfortable with, people routinely—no matter what their income—name a figure that is around twice their current income.

Instead of being driven by punishment and deprivation, motivation became intrinsically linked to reward.

CONTEXT

Abraham Maslow was a member of the Human Relations School of the late 1950s, which also included McGregor and Herzberg.

Motivation and Personality is best known for its hierarchy of needs—a concept that was first published by Maslow in 1943. He argues that there is an ascending scale of needs, which must be understood if people are to be motivated. While the hierarchy of needs provides a rational framework for motivation, its flaw lies in the nature of humanity.

Maslow's hierarchy of needs contributed to the emergence of human relations as a discipline, and to a sea-change in the perception of motivation.

Gary Hamel commented: "However subtle and variegated the original theory, time tends to reduce it to its most communicable essence: hence Maslow's hierarchy of needs, Pascale's seven Ss, Michael Porter's five forces, and the Boston Consulting Group's growth/share matrix. Yet there is no framework that has so broadly infiltrated organizational life as Maslow's hierarchy of needs. Perhaps this is because it speaks so directly to the aspirations each of us holds for ourself."

For More Information

Maslow, Abraham. *Motivation and Personality*. 3rd ed. New York: Harper & Row, 1987.

See also:
Abraham Maslow (pp. 1018–19)

The Motivation to Work

Frederick Herzberg
Bernard Mausner
Barbara Bloch Snyderman

Why Read It?

Herzberg's work has had a lasting influence on human resource management. Concepts such as job enrichment, self-development, and job satisfaction have evolved from his insight that motivation comes from within the individual, rather than from a policy imposed by the company. It has also influenced organizations' rewards and remuneration packages.

Getting Started

Employee motivation can be improved through greater emphasis on human relations.

Research indicates that motivation at work takes two forms—hygiene factors and motivation factors. Hygiene factors, which cover basic needs at work, include working conditions, benefits, and job security. Motivation factors, which meet uniquely human needs, include achievement, personal development, job satisfaction, and recognition. Improvements in hygiene factors remove the barriers to positive attitudes in the workplace, although hygiene factors alone are not sufficient to provide true motivation to work.

Employers should aim to motivate people through job satisfaction, rather than reward or pressure.

Contribution

1. The Importance of Employee Attitudes

"People are our greatest assets" has become one of the most over-used clichés in business. However, before Herzberg, "people issues" took a low priority in management literature. Management thinkers rarely sought the opinions of employees, or considered them worthy of study. Herzberg and his colleagues, Mausner and Snyderman, highlighted the importance of employee attitudes through a study of 203 Pittsburgh engineers and accountants. By asking what pleased and displeased people about their jobs, he raised the wider question: "How do you motivate employees?"

2. Identifying Factors That Motivate Employees

Herzberg made a critical distinction between factors that cause unhappiness at work and factors that contribute to job satisfaction. This distinction was based on his earlier work in public health, where he had concluded that mental health was not the opposite of mental illness. Transferring that concept to the workplace, he suggested that the reverse of the factors that make people happy did not make them unhappy. His research indicated that motivation at work takes two forms—hygiene factors and motivation factors.

3. Hygiene Factors

Hygiene factors cover basic needs at work. They include working conditions, supervision levels, company policies, benefits, and job security. If these are poor or deteriorate, they lead to poor job attitudes and dissatisfaction with work. Conversely, improvements in hygiene factors remove the barriers to positive attitudes in the workplace. However, improvement in hygiene factors alone is not sufficient to provide true job satisfaction.

4. Motivation Factors

Herzberg discovered that the factors that lead to dissatisfaction are completely different from those that provide satisfaction. He called the positive factors "motivation factors." These meet uniquely human needs and include achievement, personal development, job satisfaction, and recognition. Improving these factors can make people satisfied with work.

3. Challenging the Reward Process

Herzberg concluded that organizations should aim to motivate people through job satisfaction, rather than reward or pressure.

This led to the concept of job enrichment, which would enable organizations to liberate people from the tyranny of numbers and expand the creative role of an individual within the organization.

Context

Herzberg was one of the humanist school of management thinking, emphasizing the human aspects of organizations, in contrast to the mechanistic views of scientific thinkers. The humanist tradition includes Mary Parker Follett, Elton Mayo, Douglas McGregor, Abraham Maslow, Charles Handy, and Tom Peters.

Maslow's hierarchy of needs, formulated in 1943, influenced industrial psychologists like Herzberg by showing that work can be made more satisfying by giving greater emphasis to affection, ego, and self-actualization needs.

Herzberg's breakthrough was to identify hygiene and motivation factors. His work has had a lasting influence on human resource management: concepts such as job enrichment, self-development, and job satisfaction have evolved from his insight that motivation comes from within the individual, rather than from a policy imposed by the company. It has also influenced organizations' rewards and remuneration packages.

The trend toward "cafeteria benefits" reflects Herzberg's belief that people choose the form of motivation that is most important to them. Many organizations believe that money is the sole motivation for workers; Herzberg's work offers a more subtle approach. There has been much subsequent academic debate on the extent to which pay or other factors are the most important motivators.

Guru Gary Hamel commented: "Too many organizations believe that the only motivation to work is an economic one. Treating knowledge assets like Skinnerian rats is hardly the way to get the best out of people. Herzberg offers a substantially more subtle approach—one that still has much to recommend it."

Critics of Herzberg argue that pay plays an important part in the motivational equation, and can be used to reinforce other motivational levers. Others point out that people frequently describe good work experiences in terms that reflect credit on themselves—success, greater responsibility, or recognition. Conversely, they will blame bad work experiences on factors that are outside their control, such as poor working conditions or a difficult boss.

Recent commentators believe that the main application of Herzberg's theories has been to nonmanual workers, where the hygiene factors are normally well satisfied. They believe that employees who were reasonably well rewarded would tend to emphasize motivational factors as more important.

For More Information

Herzberg, Frederick, Bernard Mausner, and Barbara Bloch Snyderman. *The Motivation to Work*. New York: John Wiley, 1959.

"If you have someone on a job, use him. If you can't use him, get rid of him." (The Motivation to Work)

My Life and Work

Henry Ford

Why Read It?

My Life and Work is an account of Henry Ford's life and business philosophy. It provides unique insights into the man who took mass production to new levels and opened up mass markets through consistently low pricing and standardization. It also highlights the risk of a single-product strategy and the problems of autocratic control.

Getting Started

Ford's policy was to reduce the price, extend the operations, and improve the article. He did not bother about the costs. Price forces the costs down. Ford reduced prices by 58% at a time when demand was such that he could easily have raised them. Mass production was the result, not the cause, of his low prices.

Ford was both the most brilliant and the most senseless marketer in American history. He refused to offer anything but a black car—but he built a production system designed to fit market needs. At the center of his thinking was the aim of standardization.

Management and managers were dismissed by Ford as largely unnecessary—but his lack of faith in management, along with its total reliance on the Model T, later proved the undoing of the company.

Contribution

1. Pricing and Costs

Ford stated his policy as being, "to reduce the price, extend the operations and improve the article. The reduction of price comes first. We have never considered any costs as fixed. Therefore we first reduce the price to the point where we believe more sales will result. Then we go ahead and try to make the prices. We do not bother about the costs. The new price forces the costs down. The more usual way is to take the costs and then determine the price, and although that method may be scientific in the narrow sense, it is not scientific in the broad sense. What use is it to know the cost, if it tells you that you cannot manufacture at a price at which the article can be sold?"

Ford's commitment to lowering prices cannot be doubted. Between 1908 and 1916 he reduced prices by 58% at a time when demand was such that he could easily have raised them.

2. Marketing

In a sense Ford was both the most brilliant and the most senseless marketer in American history. He was senseless because he refused to give the customer anything but a black car. He was brilliant because he fashioned a production system designed to fit market needs.

We habitually celebrate him for the wrong reason, his production genius. His real genius was marketing.

3. Standardization

Ford realized that the mass car market existed—it just remained for him to provide the products the market wanted.

Model Ts were black, straightforward, and affordable. At the center of Ford's thinking was the aim of standardization—something continually emphasized by the car makers of today.

4. Problems of a Single Product

The problem was that when other manufacturers added extras, Ford kept it simple and dramatically lost ground.

Henry Ford is reputed to have kicked a slightly-modified Model T to pieces, such was his commitment to the unadulterated version. But the company's reliance on the Model T nearly drove it to self-destruction. The man with a genius for marketing lost touch with the aspirations of customers.

5. Mass Production

Ford is celebrated for his transformation of the production line into a means of previously unimagined mass production.

He calculated that the production of a Model T require 7,882 different operations. Production was based around strict functional divides or demarcations. Ford believed in people getting on with their jobs and not raising their heads above functional parapets. He didn't want engineers talking to salespeople, or people making decisions without his say so.

6. Authoritarian Control

Management and managers were dismissed by Ford as largely unnecessary, and he made a systematic, deliberate, and conscious attempt to run the billion-dollar business without managers.

Ford's lack of faith in management proved the undoing of the huge corporate empire he assembled. Without his autocratic belligerence to drive the company forward, it quickly ground to a halt.

7. Innovation in Business

In some respects Ford remains a good role model. He was an improviser and innovator who borrowed ideas and then adapted and synthesized them. He developed flow lines that involved people; now, we have flow lines without people, but no-one questions their relevance or importance.

Though he is seen as having dehumanized work, Ford provided a level of wealth for workers and products for consumers which weren't previously available. He introduced the $5 wage for his workers which, at that time, was around twice the average for the industry.

He had an international perspective that was ahead of his time. His plant at Highland Park, Detroit, produced. But the world, not just the United States, bought.

Ford was acutely aware that time was an important competitive weapon. "Time waste differs from material waste in that there can be no salvage," he wrote.

Context

My Life and Work is a robust account of Ford's life and business philosophy, although it is notable for the dominance of the former and the lack of the latter. Ford's business achievements and contribution to the development of industrialization are likely to be remembered long after his theories on politics, history, motivation, or humanity.

Leading author Gary Hamel said, "Henry Ford may have been autocratic and paranoid, but he brought to men and women everywhere a stunningly precious gift—mobility. Whatever his faults, Henry Ford was driven by the dream of every great entrepreneur—to make a real difference in people's lives—and to do it globally."

For More Information

Ford, Henry. *My Life and Work*. New York: Doubleday, Page & Co., 1923.

See also:
Henry Ford (pp. 1080–81)

"I have no use for a motor car which has more spark plugs than a cow has teats." (My Life and Work)

My Years with General Motors

Alfred P. Sloan, Jr.

Why Read It?

Alfred P. Sloan, Jr. is one of the very few figures who undoubtedly changed the world of management. He was also one of the first managers to write an important theoretical book. *My Years with General Motors* is an account of his remarkable career and the creation of a new organizational form, the multidivisional form, that spawned a host of imitators.

Getting Started

Alfred P. Sloan, Jr., a leading figure at General Motors from 1917, became its chief executive in 1946 and honorary chairman from 1956 until his death in 1966.

When he joined, the automobile market was dominated by Ford, and GM's market share was a mere 12%. GM was then an unwieldy combination of companies with eight models that competed against each other as well as against Ford. Sloan cut the eight models down to five and targeted each at a particular segment of the market. The five ranges were updated regularly and came in more than one color–unlike Ford's Model T. He also reshaped the organization so that it was better suited to deliver his aspirations.

He created eight divisions–five car and three component divisions. In the jargon of 50 years later, these were strategic business units. Each had responsibility for its own commercial operations and its own engineering, production, and sales department. The divisions were supervised by a central staff responsible for overall policy and finance.

The main interest of *My Years with General Motors* for modern management thinkers lies in how Sloan managed to coordinate the semi-autonomous divisions with the center and balance flexibility with control.

Contribution

1. Balancing Flexibility with Control

The policy that Sloan labeled "federal decentralization" marked the invention of the decentralized, divisionalized organization.

The multidivisional form enabled Sloan to utilize the company's size without making it cumbersome. Executives had more time to concentrate on strategic issues and operational decisions were made by people in the front line rather than at a distant headquarters.

By 1925, with its new organization and commitment to annual changes in its models, General Motors had overtaken Ford. More than that, however, Sloan's segmentation of the company changed the structure of the car industry and provided a model for how firms could do the same in other industries.

2. Commitment to Employees

The book reveals that Sloan was committed to what at the time would have been regarded as progressive human resource management. In 1947 he established GM's employee-research section to look at employee attitudes, and he invested a large amount of his own time in selecting the right people for the job.

3. Problems in Decentralaization

The decentralized structure built up by Sloan revolved around a reporting and committee infrastructure that eventually became unwieldy.

As time went by, more and more committees were set up. Stringent targets and narrow measures of success stultified initiative. The organization proved quite incapable of creating and developing new businesses internally. This inability to manage organic expansion into new areas was caused by many factors:

- operating responsibilities and measurement systems focused on profit and market share in existing markets;
- business unit managers were not expected to look for new opportunities;
- the boxes in the organization chart defined their product or geographic scope;
- small new ventures could not absorb the large central overheads and return the profits needed to justify the financial and human investments.

As Sloan himself put it: "In practically all our activities we seem to suffer from the inertia resulting from our great size. There are so many people involved and it requires such a tremendous effort to put something new into effect that a new idea is likely to be considered insignificant in comparison with the effort that it takes to put it across."

Context

Sloan established General Motors as a benchmark of corporate might, a symbol of American strength and success. "What's good for GM is good for America," ran the popular mythology. Peter Drucker and Alfred Chandler celebrated his approach, but the deficiencies of the model were apparent to Sloan himself, have become more so since the publication of his book, and are most obviously manifested in the decline of GM.

By the end of the 1960s the delicate balance, which he had brilliantly maintained between centralization and decentralization, was lost. Finance emerged as the dominant function, and GM became paralyzed by what had once made it great.

Gary Hamel commented: "Can you be big and nimble? The question is as timely today as it was when Sloan took over General Motors. Despite divisionalization and decentralization, Sloan's organizational inventions, GM still fell victim to its size. . .[T]he corporate superstructure that emerged to manage GM's independent divisions was more successful in creating bureaucracy than in exploiting cross-divisional synergies. The challenge of achieving divisional autonomy and flexibility on one hand, while reaping the benefits of scale and coordination on the other, is one that has eluded not only GM, but many other large companies as well."

One thing that should not be forgotten is that Sloan believed in managers and management in a way that his great rival Henry Ford did not. Nevertheless, as *The Economist* said: "Alfred Sloan did for the upper layers of management what Henry Ford did for the shopfloor: he turned it into a reliable, efficient, machine-like process."

Of the book as a whole, Peter Drucker remarked: "It is perhaps the most impersonal book of memoirs ever written. And this was clearly intentional. Sloan's book knows only one dimension: that of managing a business so that it can produce effectively, provide jobs, create markets and sales, and generate profits."

For More Information

Sloan, Alfred P., Jr. *My Years with General Motors*. New York: Doubleday, 1963.

"I had learned that increased productivity would support higher wages." (*My Years with General Motors*)

The Nature of Managerial Work

Henry Mintzberg

Why Read It?

Mintzberg is regarded by many as a leading contemporary management thinker, and this book was the first to explore what managers actually do at work. It goes behind the myths and the self-perceptions to describe the day-to-day work of a manager.

Getting Started

What managers actually do, how they do it and why, are fundamental questions. Managers believe they deal with big strategic issues—in reality they move from task to task dogged by diversions. Managerial work is marked by variety, brevity, and fragmentation.

Managers have three key roles. The prominence of each role varies in different managerial jobs.

Contribution

1. What Managers Do—The Myth

What managers actually do, how they do it, and why they do it, are fundamental questions. There are a number of generally accepted answers.

Managers believe:

- that they sit in solitude contemplating the great strategic issues of the day;
- that they make time to reach the best decisions;
- that their meetings are high-powered, concentrating on the meta-narrative rather than the nitty-gritty.

The reality largely went unexplored until Henry Mintzberg's book.

2. What Managers Do—The Reality

Mintzberg went in search of the reality. He simply observed what a number of managers actually did. The resulting book blew away the managerial mystique.

Managers did not spend time contemplating the long term. They were slaves to the moment, moving from task to task with every move dogged by another diversion, another call. The median time spent by a manager on any one issue was a mere nine minutes.

3. The Characteristics of the Manager at Work

Mintzberg's observations were that the typical manager:

- performs a great quantity of work at an unrelenting pace;
- undertakes activities marked by variety, brevity, and fragmentation;
- has a preference for issues that are current, specific, and nonroutine;
- prefers verbal rather than written means of communication;
- acts within a web of internal and external contacts;
- is subject to heavy constraints but can exert some control over the work.

4. Managers' Key Roles

From these observations, Mintzberg identified the manager's work roles as:

- interpersonal
- informational
- decisional

Interpersonal Roles

- Figurehead: representing the organization/unit to outsiders.
- Leader: motivating subordinates, unifying effort.
- Liaiser: maintaining lateral contacts.

Informational Roles

- Monitor: overseeing information flows.
- Disseminator: providing information to subordinates.
- Spokesman: transmitting information to outsiders.

Decisional Roles

- Entrepreneur: initiating and designing change.
- Disturbance handler: handling nonroutine events.
- Resource allocator: deciding who gets what and who will do what.
- Negotiator: negotiating.

All managerial work encompasses these roles, but the prominence of each role varies in different managerial jobs.

Context

Henry Mintzberg is perhaps the world's premier management thinker, according to Tom Peters. His reputation has been made not by popularizing new techniques, but by rethinking the fundamentals of strategy and structure, management, and planning.

His work on strategy—in particular his ideas of emergent strategy and grass-roots strategy making—has been highly influential.

Influential author Gary Hamel commented: "Five reasons I like Henry Mintzberg: He is a world class iconoclast. He loves the messy world of real companies. He is a master storyteller. He is conceptual and pragmatic. He doesn't believe in easy answers."

The Nature of Managerial Work has produced few worthwhile imitators, but Mintzberg's rigor and originality have given his ideas staying power.

For More Information

Mintzberg, Henry. *The Nature of Managerial Work.* New York: Harper & Row, 1973.

See also:
☆ **Viewpoint: Henry Mintzberg (pp. 241–42)**

"The manager undertakes activities marked by variety, brevity, and fragmentation."

(*The Nature of Managerial Work*)

New Patterns of Management

Rensis Likert

Why Read It?

The author was a pioneer of attitude surveys and introduced an attitude scale that is now widely used in business research. The book explains how he used his research tools to identify patterns of participative management and organization that would bring success in an increasingly competitive environment.

Getting Started

Rensis Likert was a pioneer of attitude surveys and poll design, as well as social research as a whole. According to Likert, there are four types of management style:

- exploitative and authoritarian
- benevolent autocracy
- consultative
- participative

Participative management is the best option, as increased participation and individualism is essential to meet increased competition. Participative groups can improve management and performance. The greater the loyalty of a group, the greater the motivation to achieve its goals.

An organization's style can be linked directly to its performance. The route to understanding managerial performance is improved measurement.

Contribution

1. Measuring Attitudes

In his doctoral thesis, written in 1932 while Likert was at Columbia University, and entitled *A Technique for the Measurement of Attitudes*, he introduced a straightforward five-point scale by which attitudes could be measured. The now well-known scale ranges from "strongly agree" to "strongly disagree" and is known as the Likert Scale.

2. The Contribution of Participative Groups

Likert's business research focused on the ways in which participative groups could improve management and performance. It also examined the human systems that exist in organizations.

The greater the loyalty of a group, the greater is the motivation among members to achieve the goals of the group, and the greater the probability that the group will achieve its goals.

3. Management Styles

Likert identified four types of management style, each of which tends to mold people in its own image. Authoritarian organizations tend to develop dependent people and few leaders. Participative management was seen by Likert as the best option, both in a business and a personal sense. Participative organizations tend to develop emotionally and socially mature people capable of effective interaction, initiative, and leadership.

4. Organization Style and Performance

"Managers with the best records of performance in American business and government are in the process of pointing the way to an appreciably more effective system of management than now exists," Likert wrote in the book's opening. With the assistance of social science research, it is now possible to state a generalized theory of organization based on the management practices of these highest producers.

5. The Importance of Participation

Increased participation in the workplace and individualism are necessary consequences of increased competition and fast-accelerating technological improvement. There is much greater need for cooperation and participation in managing the enterprise than when technologies were simple and the chief possessed all the technical knowledge needed.

6. The Importance of Measurement

Management can make a difference, and the route to understanding managerial performance is improved measurement. An organization should be outstanding in its performance:

- if it has competent personnel;
- if it has leadership which develops highly effective groups and uses the overlapping group form of structure;
- if it achieves effective communication and influence, decentralized and coordinated decision making, and high performance goals coupled with high motivation.

Context

Likert's research highlights the importance of participative styles of management. This book bids farewell to the world of blind obedience and corporate man. Likert picks up the mood of individualism, which was to sweep the world later in the 1960s. The book provides a blueprint for the ideal organization, which has largely stood the test of time.

For More Information

Likert, Rensis. *New Patterns of Management*. New York: McGraw-Hill, 1961.

"Authoritarian organizations tend to develop dependent people and few leaders."

(*New Patterns of Management*)

  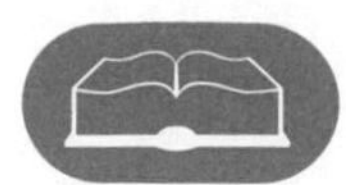    

ON THE ECONOMY OF MACHINERY AND MANUFACTURES

Charles Babbage

WHY READ IT?

Charles Babbage was one of the great minds of the first industrial revolution. He is credited with pioneering the computer, and wrote extensively about the importance of data and manufacturing. The book offers fascinating insights into the early development of manufacturing techniques.

GETTING STARTED

In an age of economic theory, Babbage argued for a highly scientific approach. His emphasis on fact-finding influenced not only the practical elements of factory management in the early industrial era, but the formation of interpretive theory. Mechanical principles govern manufacturing, and merchants and manufacturers are the best people to supply the data on which all the reasoning of political economists is founded. People should not fear bad deductions from good facts.

Good factory organization is important, and factories require an entire system of operation.

The most important principle of manufacture is the division of labor.

It is vital to calculate the life expectancy of capital equipment. In five years capital equipment ought to have paid for itself, and in ten it should be superseded by a better version.

CONTRIBUTION

1. MECHANICAL PRINCIPLES GOVERN MANUFACTURING

Babbage's fundamental approach was highly scientific. He held that mechanical principles regulate the application of machinery to arts and manufacture.

First, he said, it is essential to gather the evidence. Babbage did so through touring factories exhaustively in the United Kingdom and Europe. The book provides helpful hints and a checklist of questions on how to find the best information when touring a factory.

2. MAKE USE OF FACTS

Political economists have been reproached with too small a use of facts, and too large an employment of theory. "If facts are wanting, the closet-philosopher is unfortunately too little acquainted with the admirable arrangements of the factory," Babbage wrote. "The merchant and manufacturer are the best people to supply readily, and with so little sacrifice of time, the data on which all the reasoning of political economists are founded."

3. COLLECTING DATA IS ESSENTIAL

People should not fear that erroneous deductions may be made from recorded facts. The errors which arise from the absence of facts are far more numerous and more durable than those which result from unsound reasoning based on true data.

Babbage encourages managers to follow his example and gather their own data. Collecting data is essential for the manufacturer who wants to know how many additional customers he will acquire by a given reduction in the price of the article he makes.

4. GOOD FACTORY ORGANIZATION IS IMPORTANT

The arrangements that should regulate the interior economy of a factory are founded on deeply-rooted principles. Babbage recognized that the factory requires an entire system of operation. It needs to be organized in a vastly different way to the conventional means of production.

Babbage provides insights in two central areas. First, economies of scale and second, the division of labor.

5. CALCULATING THE RIGHT DIVISION OF LABOR

Perhaps the most important principle on which the economy of manufacture depends is the division of labor among the people who perform the work. "The number of operations performed in a given time may frequently be counted when the workman is quite unconscious that any person is observing him," Babbage said. "For example, the sound made by the motion of a loom may enable the observer to count the number of strokes per minute, even though he is outside the building in which it is contained."

6. LIFE EXPECTANCY OF CAPITAL EQUIPMENT

Machinery for producing any commodity in great demand seldom actually wears out. New improvements, by which the same operations can be executed either more quickly or better, generally supersede it long before that time arrives. To make such an improved machine profitable, it is usually reckoned that in five years it ought to have paid for the cost of purchase, and in ten to be superseded by a better machine.

CONTEXT

The book was a bestseller of its times. It is one of the first to recognize the importance of factories, economically and socially. In that sense, it is like the first book on the potential of the Internet.

Babbage was a pioneer of modern management. His approach bears more than a passing resemblance to that later adopted by the American champion of scientific management, Frederick Taylor. He beckoned in the industrial era and, in doing so, laid the intellectual groundwork for Marx, Engels, and John Stuart Mill. Contrasts can be made with Adam Smith whose economic viewpoint remained stuck in the agricultural era.

Joseph Schumpeter called the book, "a remarkable performance of a remarkable man."

For More Information

Babbage, Charles. *On the Economy of Machinery and Manufactures*. London: Frank Cass & Co., 1963.

"Political economists have been reproached with too small a use of facts, and too large an employment of theory." (On the Economy of Machinery and Manufactures)

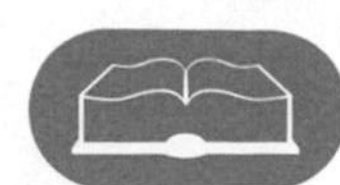

ONWARD INDUSTRY

James Mooney
Alan Reiley

WHY READ IT?

The book provides insights into early thinking about the nature of organizations and their impact on the performance of industry. The authors argue that organization is a universal phenomenon and has a benefit on the overall standard of living.

GETTING STARTED

Organization is a universal phenomenon that has occurred throughout history. The organization of businesses is crucial to prosperity and living standards.

Production without distribution is worthless; the emphasis must be on finding and exploiting markets. Industry should encourage participation in business so that purchasing capacity can be created and extended. Organizational size is less important than knowing what to do with the organization.

CONTRIBUTION

1. ORGANIZATION IS A UNIVERSAL PHENOMENON

People love to organize, and organization is as old as human society itself. Consider the scalar organization of the Catholic Church, governmental organization, and the evolution of different forms of organization from Roman times to Medieval times, through to the company of the early 20th century.

2. ORGANIZATION IS CRUCIAL TO STANDARDS OF LIVING

The organization of businesses is crucial to overall standards of living. There is a direct link between industrial prosperity, built on modern management techniques, and the affluence of society as a whole.

"The highest development of the techniques both of production and distribution will be futile to supply the material wants of those who, because of poverty, are unable to acquire through purchase," they write. The final task of industry, therefore, is to organize participation in these activities, even in the poorest communities and countries, through which purchasing capacity can be created and extended.

3. PRODUCTION WITHOUT DISTRIBUTION IS WORTHLESS

Before the 1930s, production was the overarching driving force. Later the emphasis shifted to finding new markets and enhancing and expanding distribution to make inroads into these markets.

4. THE VALUE OF SIZE

Size isn't everything. Modern business leadership has been generally characterized by the capacity to create large organizations, but by failure in knowing exactly what to do with them.

5. KEY ORGANIZATIONAL PRINCIPLES

Mooney and Reiley's theory of organizations identified three central organizational principles:

- the coordinative principle, leading to effective coordination;
- the scalar process, resulting in functional definition;
- the functional effect, leading to interpretative functionalism.

CONTEXT

The book provides an organization model that is firmly of its time. It applies the reasoned science of Frederick W. Taylor to the broader organizational canvas.

The argument that production without distribution is worthless marks something of a watershed. Before the 1930s, production was the overarching driving force. From World War II, the emphasis shifted to finding new markets and enhancing and expanding distribution to make inroads into these markets.

For More Information

Mooney, James, and Alan Reiley. *Onward Industry*. New York: Harper & Bros., 1931.

"Organization is as old as human society itself." (*Onward Industry*)

  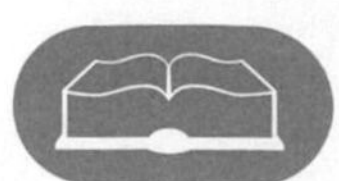    

THE ORGANIZATION MAN

William Whyte

WHY READ IT?

From the point of view of the age of uncertainty, the age of downsizing, reengineering, and "discontinuous change," the 1950s and 1960s can easily seem like a golden age. The careers enjoyed by corporate executives were built on solid foundations, workers had jobs for life, suburbia was heaven, and everything seemed set to go on and on and on. William Whyte showed the downside to this corporate utopia. Read his brilliant, witty, and often poignant analysis to get both the postwar past and the present in perspective.

GETTING STARTED

William Whyte joined the staff of *Fortune* magazine in 1946 after graduating from Princeton and serving in the U.S. Marines during World War II. *The Organization Man* is based on articles he wrote for the magazine. He subsequently left *Fortune* and, in his later years, wrote mainly on the subject of urban sprawl, urban planning, and human behavior in urban spaces.

Nineteen-fifties America still publicly and privately subscribed to the idea that rugged individualism was the hallmark of the American character and the foundation stone of American success. According to Whyte, this was a delusion. Average Americans in fact subscribed to a collectivist social ethic that was turning them into organization people—and they needed to realize the fact and do something about it.

CONTRIBUTION

1. THE SOCIAL ETHIC

Whyte believed that the condition he was analyzing did not affect America alone: he referred to "a bureaucratization that has affected every country."

The bureaucratic or collectivist ethic rested on three major principles:

- a belief in the group as the source of creativity;
- a belief in "belongingness" as the ultimate need of every individual;
- a belief in the application of science to achieve belongingness.

And above all that, "the fundamental principle of the new model executive is. . .that the goals of the individual and the goals of the organization will work out to be one and the same."

2. THE IMPORTANCE OF LOYALTY

Gray-suited and obedient, corporate man was unstintingly loyal to his employer. He spent his life with a single company and rose slowly, but quietly, up the hierarchy.

Loyalty and solid performance brought job security. This was mutually beneficial.

The executive gained a respectable income and a high degree of security. The company gained loyal, hard-working executives.

But while loyalty is a positive quality, it can easily become blind. What if the corporate strategy is wrong or the company is engaged in unlawful or immoral acts? The corporation becomes a self-contained and self-perpetuating world supported by a complex array of checks, systems, and hierarchies. The company is right.

In a remark reminiscent of George Orwell's *1984*, Whyte suggested that the organization man "must not only accept control, he must accept it as if he liked it."

3. LOW-RISK ENVIRONMENT

Customers, who exist outside the organization, are often regarded as peripheral.

In the 1950s, 1960s, and 1970s, it sometimes seems, no executive ever lost their job by delivering poor quality or indifferent service. In some organizations, executives only lost their jobs by defrauding their employer or insulting their boss. Jobs for life was the refrain and, to a large extent for executives, the reality.

Clearly, such an environment was hardly conducive to the fostering of dynamic risk-takers. It rewarded the steady foot soldier, the safe pair of hands, the organization man living with his organization wife.

CONTEXT

Reviewing the book in the *New York Times*, C. Wright Mills wrote: "Whyte understands that the work-and-thrift ethic of success has grievously declined, except in the rhetoric of top executives; that the entrepreneurial scramble to success has been largely replaced by the organizational crawl."

Chester Barnard noted in *The Functions of the Executive*: "The most important single contribution required of an executive, certainly the most universal qualification, is loyalty [allowing] domination by the organization personality."

Twenty years after the publication of Whyte's book, things had not changed very much. When she came to examine corporate life for the first time in her 1977 book, *Men and Women of the Corporation*, Rosabeth Moss Kanter found that the central characteristic expected of a manager was dependability.

Fortune founder Henry Luce commented: "It was *Fortune*'s William H. Whyte, Jr. who made the 'organization man' a household word, and the organization wife too. His was a fine achievement in sociological reporting. In it he related the phenomenon of the business organization to questions of human personality and values. The kind of people who are eager to hear the worst about American society assumed that Mr. Whyte was predicting the destruction of individualism by the organization."

Whyte was uneasy about corporate life, which seemed to stifle creativity and individualism. He was uneasy about the subtle pressures in the office and at home that called for smooth performance rather than daring creativity. However, he did not urge the organization men to leave their secure environment. Rather he urged them to fight the organization when necessary, and he was optimistic that the battle could be successful.

For More Information

Whyte, William. *The Organization Man*. New York: Simon & Schuster, 1956.

"The fault is not in organization, in short, it is in our worship of it." (*The Organization Man*)

Organizational Culture and Leadership

Edgar Schein

Why Read It?

Edgar Schein's *Organizational Culture and Leadership* clarified the entire area of corporate culture in a way no previous book had. It brought culture into the management debate and paved the way for a plethora of further studies. Even today, its perspectives on culture as a constantly changing force in corporate life remain as disconcerting as they are valuable.

Getting Started

Schein is sometimes seen as the inventor of the term "corporate culture"; he is, at the very least, one of its originators. After a long and distinguished academic career, he is currently the Sloan Fellows' Professor of Management Emeritus at the MIT Sloan School of Management.

In this book, he not only provides a sophisticated definition of culture, but he turns the abstract concept into a tool to assist managers in understanding the dynamics of organizations. In addition, he tackles the vital question of how an existing culture can be changed—one of the toughest challenges for leadership.

Contribution

1. The Basis of Corporate Culture

Culture is a pattern of basic assumptions invented, discovered, or developed by a given group as it learns to cope with its problems of external adaptation and internal integration. These assumptions have worked well enough to be considered valid and, therefore, to be taught to new members as the correct way to perceive, think, and feel in relation to those problems.

They can be categorized into five dimensions:

- humanity's relationship to nature—while some companies regard themselves as masters of their own destiny, others are submissive, willing to accept the domination of their external environment;
- the nature of reality and truth—organizations and managers adopt a wide variety of methods to reach what becomes accepted as the organizational truth;
- the nature of human nature—organizations differ in their views of human nature. Some follow McGregor's Theory X and work on the principle that people will not do the job if they can avoid it. Others regard people in a more positive light and attempt to enable them to fulfill their potential for the benefit of both sides;
- the nature of human activity—the West has traditionally emphasized tasks and their completion rather than the more philosophical side of work. Achievement is all. Schein suggests an alternative approach—"being-in-becoming"—emphasizing self-fulfillment and development;
- the nature of human relationships—organizations make a variety of assumptions about how people interact with each other. Some facilitate social interaction, while others regard it as an unnecessary distraction.

These five categories are not mutually exclusive, but are in a constant state of development and flux. Culture does not stand still.

2. Shaping Organizational Values

Key to the creation and development of corporate culture are the values embraced by the organization. A single person can shape these values and, as a result, an entire corporate culture. The heroic creators of corporate cultures include such people as Henry Ford and IBM's Thomas Watson, Sr.

3. Development of Corporate Culture

There are three stages in the development of a corporate culture:

- birth and early growth—the culture may be dominated by the business founder. It is regarded as a source of the company's identity, a bonding agent protecting it against outside forces;
- organizational mid-life—the original culture is likely to be diluted and undermined as new cultures emerge and there is a loss of the original sense of identity. At this stage, there is an opportunity for the fundamental culture to be realigned and changed;
- organizational maturity—culture, at this stage, is regarded sentimentally. People are hopelessly addicted to how things used to be done and unwilling to contemplate change. Here the organization is at its weakest, as the culture has been transformed from a source of competitive advantage and distinctiveness to a hindrance in the marketplace. Only through aggressive measures will it survive.

4. Changing Corporate Culture

Each stage of the culture's growth requires a different method of change.

If culture is to work in support of a company's strategy, there has to be a level of consensus covering five areas:

- the core mission or primary task;
- goals;
- the means to accomplish the goals;
- the means to measure progress;
- remedial or repair strategies.

Achieving cultural change is a formidable challenge, one that well-established executives in strong cultures often find beyond them. The exceptional executives who achieve cultural change from within a culture they are closely identified with (such as GE's Jack Welch) are rarities, and are known as cultural hybrids.

Context

Schein's findings gave rise to a host of other studies of the subject. His basic assumptions are rephrased and reinterpreted elsewhere in a variety of ways. Perhaps Chris Argyris comes closest to him when discussing "theories-in-use."

Gary Hamel says: "It is impossible to change a large organization without first understanding that organization's culture. Ed Schein gave us an ability to look deeply into what makes an organization what it is, thus providing the foundation of any successful effort at transformation or change. *Organizational Culture and Leadership* remains essential reading for all aspiring change agents."

For More Information

Schein, Edgar. *Organizational Culture and Leadership*. 2nd ed. San Francisco, CA: Jossey-Bass, 1997.

See also:
Edgar Schein (pp. 1044–45)

"Through debate, dictatorship, or through simple acceptance, if something achieves the objective, it is right."
(*Organizational Culture and Leadership*)

Organizational Learning

Chris Argyris
Donald Schön

Why Read It?

This book shows why organizational learning is the ultimate competitive advantage. It also explains two of the central paradoxes of business life—how individual initiative and creativity can work in an organizational environment, where rules will always exist, and how teamworking and individual working can coexist fruitfully.

Getting Started

Learning is a key business activity. Many organizational models only achieve single-loop learning, which—while this permits a company to carry on its present policies and achieve its current objectives—is limited to detection and correction of organizational error.

Double-loop learning, however, enables organizations to detect and correct errors in ways that involve the modification of underlying norms, policies, and objectives. With double-loop learning, managers can act on information and learn from others. Most organizations do quite well in single-loop learning, but have great difficulties with double-loop learning.

Deutero-learning is the process of inquiring into the learning system by which an organization detects and corrects its errors. It underpins the concept of the learning organization.

Increasingly, the art of management is managing knowledge—and effective leadership means creating the conditions that enable people to produce valid knowledge. Success in the marketplace increasingly depends on learning, yet most people don't know how to learn.

Contribution

1. The Weakness of Single-loop Learning

The authors investigate two basic organizational models.

Model 1 is based on the premise that we seek to manipulate and form the world in accordance with our individual aspirations and wishes. In Model 1, managers concentrate on establishing individual goals. They keep to themselves and don't voice concerns or disagreements. The onus is on creating a conspiracy of silence in which everyone dutifully keeps their head down. Defense is the prime activity in a Model 1 organization, though occasionally the best means of defense is attack. Model 1 managers are prepared to inflict change on others, but resist any attempt to change their own thinking and working practices.

Model 1 organizations are characterized by single-loop learning—the detection and correction of organizational error that permits the organization to carry on its present policies and achieve its current objectives.

2. The Importance of Double-loop Learning

Model 2 organizations emphasize double-loop learning—where organizational error is detected and corrected in ways that involve the modification of underlying norms, policies, and objectives.

In Model 2 organizations, managers act on information. They debate issues and respond to change—as well as being prepared to change themselves. They learn from others. A virtuous circle emerges of learning and understanding.

Most organizations do quite well in single-loop learning, but have great difficulties with double-loop learning.

3. The Challenge of Deutero-learning

Deutero-learning offers even greater challenges. This is the process of inquiring into the learning system by which an organization detects and corrects its errors. The examination of learning systems is central to the contemporary concept of the learning organization.

4. The Importance of Managing Knowledge

Learning is powerfully practical and increasingly, the art of management is managing knowledge. Organizations should not manage people per se, but rather the knowledge that they carry.

Leadership means creating the conditions that enable people to produce valid knowledge, and to do so in ways that encourage personal responsibility. Knowledge must relate to action, rather than knowledge for the purpose of understanding and exploring.

5. The Learning Imperative

There is a natural temptation for organizations and individuals to limit themselves to single-loop learning rather than its more demanding alternatives. However, the need better to understand learning in all its dimensions is now imperative. Any company that aspires to success in the tougher business environment of the 1990s and beyond must embrace learning—yet most people don't know how to learn. Those members of an organization who are assumed by many to be the best at learning are, in fact, not very good at it.

Context

If you wished to trace the roots of the learning organization, you would invariably find yourself reading *Organizational Learning*.

Organizational Learning grew out of Argyris and Schön's 1974 book, *Theory in Practice*.

Chris Argyris was part of the human relations school of the late 1950s and involved in the work of the National Training Laboratories. He was drawn to the riddles of human nature—in particular, why do people fail to live up to their own professed ideals? Why is so much human behavior so self-frustrating, particularly within organizations?

In the last decade, Argyris's ideas have become fashionable. This is most apparent in the upsurge of interest in the concept of the learning organization.

Organizational Learning appeared in 1978, but it took the 1990 bestseller from Peter Senge of MIT (Massachusetts Institute of Technology), *The Fifth Discipline*, to propel the learning organization from an academic concept to mainstream acceptance.

Charles Hampden-Turner of the University of Cambridge's Judge Institute of Management says, "There is an urgent need for alternative visions of science and Schön's work, along with that of Argyris, provides some of the best ideas and answers. Few have gone so far in reconciling the vigor of relevance and in building a bridge between the isolated academic fortresses of the sciences and the humanities."

Gary Hamel concurs, "If your organization has not yet mastered double-loop learning, it is already a dinosaur. No one can doubt that organizational learning is the ultimate competitive advantage. We owe much to Argyris and Schön for helping us learn about learning."

For More Information

Argyris, Chris, and Donald Schön. *Organizational Learning*. New York: Addison-Wesley, 1978.

"Increasingly, the art of management is managing knowledge."

(*Organizational Learning*)

OUT OF THE CRISIS

W. Edwards Deming

WHY READ IT?

This book is regarded as a classic of literature on quality management. It reflects Deming's experience in introducing quality to Japan, and its aim was to transform the style of U.S. management. Deming is regarded as the leading figure on quality and this book sets out the methods that taught industry the power of quality.

GETTING STARTED

Profit comes from repeat customers—and they respond to good quality.

Statistical quality control produces spectacular results, so senior managers must take charge of quality, and quality training should begin at the top of the organization.

Quality is a way of living: it is not the preserve of the few but the responsibility of all. Deming argued that factory workers already understood the importance of quality, but were stymied by managers focused on increasing productivity regardless of quality.

Japanese culture is uniquely receptive to the quality message.

CONTRIBUTION

1. THE IMPORTANCE OF QUALITY

Profit in business comes from repeat customers, customers who boast about your product and service, and who bring friends with them.

Quality is more than statistical control, though this is important. Statistical quality control produces spectacular results by using tools to improve processes in ways that minimize defects and eliminate rejects, rework, and recalls.

Deming's work bridges the gap between science-based application and humanistic philosophy.

2. THE QUALITY GOSPEL

The book's quality gospel revolves around a number of basic precepts:

- if consistent quality is to be achieved senior managers must take charge of it;
- implementation requires a cascade, with training beginning at the top of the organization before moving downwards through the hierarchy;
- the use of statistical methods of quality control is necessary so that, finally, business plans can be expanded to include clear quality goals;
- quality is a way of living, the meaning of industrial life and, in particular, the meaning of management.

3. DEMING'S FOURTEEN POINTS

- Create constancy of purpose for improvement of product and service.
- Adopt the new philosophy.
- Cease dependence on inspection to achieve quality.
- End the practice of awarding business on the basis of price tag alone. Instead, minimize total cost by working with a single supplier.
- Improve constantly and forever every process for planning, production and service.
- Institute training on the job.
- Adopt and institute leadership.
- Drive out fear.
- Break down barriers between staff areas.
- Eliminate slogans, exhortations, and targets for the workforce.
- Eliminate numerical quotas for the workforce and numerical goals for management.
- Remove barriers that rob people of pride of workmanship. Eliminate the annual rating or merit system.
- Institute a vigorous program of education and self-improvement for everyone.
- Put everybody in the company to work to accomplish the transformation.

4. THE IMPORTANCE OF EMPOWERMENT

The simplicity of the Fourteen Points disguises the immensity of the challenge, particularly that facing management: quality is not the preserve of the few but the responsibility of all. In arguing this case Deming was anticipating the fashion for empowerment.

People all over the world think that it is the factory worker that causes problems. He or she is not your problem. "Ever since there has been anything such as industry, the factory worker has known that quality is what will protect his job. He knows that poor quality in the hands of the customer will lose the market and cost him his job. He knows it and lives with that fear every day. Yet he cannot do a good job. He is not allowed to do it because the management wants figures, more products, and never mind the quality."

5. THE PROBLEM OF MANAGEMENT

Management is 90% of the problem, a problem caused in part by the Western enthusiasm for annual performance appraisals. Japanese managers receive feedback every day of their working lives.

The basic cause of sickness in American industry and resulting unemployment is failure of top management to manage. He that sells not can buy not.

The Japanese culture was uniquely receptive to Deming's message for a number of reasons. Its emphasis on group rather than individual achievement enables the Japanese to share ideas and responsibility. It also promotes collective ownership in a way that the West often finds difficult to contemplate, let alone understand.

CONTEXT

W. Edwards Deming has a unique place among management theorists. He had an impact on industrial history that others only dream of.

Deming visited Japan after World War II on the invitation of General MacArthur, and played a key role in the rebuilding of Japanese industry. During the 1950s, Deming and the other U.S. standard bearer of quality, Joseph Juran, conducted seminars and courses throughout Japan.

Deming, and Japanese management, was eventually discovered by the West in the 1980s.

British management journalist Robert Heller says, "Deming didn't invent quality but his sermons had a uniquely powerful effect because of this first pulpit and congregation: Japan and Japanese managers. Had his fellow Americans responded with the same intense application, post-war industrial history would have differed enormously."

Management guru Gary Hamel adds, "Of all the management gurus. . .there is only one who should be regarded as a hero by every consumer in the world—Dr. Deming. He may have taken the gospel of quality to the Japanese first, but thank God his message finally penetrated the smug complacency of American and European companies. No senior executive ever sat through one of Dr. Deming's harangues without coming away just a little bit more humble and contrite—a good beginning on the road to total quality."

For More Information

Deming, W. Edwards. *Out of the Crisis.* Cambridge, MA: MIT Center for Advanced Engineering Study, 1982.

"Quality is not the preserve of the few but the responsibility of all." (*Out of the Crisis*)

  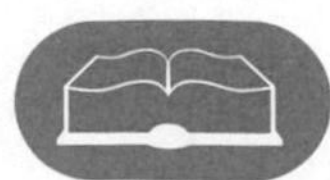    

Parkinson's Law

C. Northcote Parkinson

Why Read It?

Parkinson's Law, like *The Dilbert Principle*, takes a cynical look at business. The book treats the growth of bureaucracy in a humorous way, but the findings reflect real life situations, particularly in government organizations.

Getting Started

Companies grow without thinking of how much they are producing and without making any more money. The time to complete a task depends on the person doing the job and their unique situation. Work expands to fill the time available for its completion and officials make work for each other.

Contribution

1. How Organizations Grow

Parkinson's Law simply states that work expands to fill the time available for its completion.

As a result companies grow without thinking of how much they are producing.

Even if growth in numbers doesn't make them more money, companies grow and people become busier and busier.

An official wants to multiply subordinates, not rivals.

Officials make work for each other.

2. Work Expands to Fill the Time

The notion of a particular task having an optimum time for completion is wrong. There are no rules—it depends on the person doing the job and their unique situation.

An elderly lady of leisure can spend an entire day in writing and dispatching a postcard to her niece at Bognor Regis.

The total effort which would occupy a busy man for three minutes may, in this fashion, leave another person prostrate after a day of doubt, anxiety, and toil.

3. Administration Expands

Faced with the decreasing energy of age and a feeling of being overworked, administrators face three options:

- resign;
- halve the work with a colleague;
- ask for two more subordinates.

There is probably no instance in civil service history of choosing any but the third alternative.

The number of admiralty officials in the British Navy increased by 78% between 1914 and 1928 while the number of ships fell by 67% and the number of officers and men by 31%.

The expansion of administrators tends to take on a life of its own.

The conclusion drawn is that officials would have multiplied at the same rate had there been no actual seamen at all.

Context

Parkinson's Law is an amusing interlude in management literature.

It is a kind of *Catch-22* of the business world, by turns irreverent and humorous, but with a darker underside of acute observation.

The book was written in the late 1950s when the Human Relations School in the United States was beginning to flower and thinkers were actively questioning the bureaucracy that had grown up alongside mass production.

Max Weber's model of a paper-producing bureaucratic machine appeared to have been brought to fruition as the arteries of major organizations became clogged with layer upon layer of managerial administrators.

Gary Hamel has this to say, "Yes, I know that bureaucracy is dead. We're not managers any more, we're leaders. We're not slaves to our work, we've been liberated. And all those layers of paper-shuffling administrators between the C.E.O. and the order-takers—they're all gone, right? Well then, why does a re-reading of *Parkinson's Law*, written in 1958, at the apex of corporate bureaucracy, still ring true? *Parkinson's Law* was to the fifties what *The Dilbert Principle* is to the 1990s."

For More Information

Parkinson, C. Northcote. *Parkinson's Law*. London: John Murray, 1958.

"Work expands to fill the time available for its completion." (*Parkinson's Law*)

THE PETER PRINCIPLE

Laurence Peter

WHY READ IT?

This book is one of the most enduring books to take a cynical view of management. It is a humorous book that sets the tone for later works like *The Dilbert Principle.*

GETTING STARTED

In a hierarchy, every employee tends to rise to his or her level of incompetence. There are no exceptions to the Peter Principle. In time, every post tends to be occupied by an employee who is incompetent to carry out his duties. If at first you don't succeed, you may be at your level of incompetence. There are two kinds of failures: those who thought and never did, and those who did and never thought. There are two sorts of losers—the good loser, and the other one who can't act.

CONTRIBUTION

1. FINDING A LEVEL OF INCOMPETENCE

In a hierarchy every employee tends to rise to his level of incompetence.

A position of incompetence is the apotheosis of a corporate career—or, indeed, of any career in any profession in which there is a hierarchy.

No one is exempt from the Peter Principle.

For each individual, for you, for me, the final promotion is from a level of competence to a level of incompetence. So, given enough time—and assuming the existence of enough ranks in the hierarchy—each employee rises to, and remains at, his level of incompetence.

In time, every post tends to be occupied by an employee who is incompetent to carry out his duties.

2. DEALING WITH FAILURE

If at first you don't succeed, you may be at your level of incompetence.

If you don't know where you are going, you will probably end up somewhere else.

An economist is an expert who will know tomorrow why the things he predicted yesterday didn't happen.

Human inadequacy is universal, as is the human capacity to build vacuous power structures. In our supposedly leaner and fitter times, there are still hierarchies aplenty. The difference is, perhaps, that we have simply become more adept at disguising them.

There are two kinds of failures in the corporate world: those who thought and never did, and those who did and never thought.

Similarly, there are two sorts of losers—the good loser, and the other one who can't act.

Fortune knocks once, but misfortune has much more patience.

3. COMPUTERIZED INCOMPETENCE

Computerized incompetence is the incompetent application of computer techniques or the inherent incompetence of a computer.

CONTEXT

Cynicism about the way businesses and managers operate is nothing new. For example, *The Dilbert Principle* is simply an accurate and amusing portrayal of corporate cynicism, 1990s-style.

From *Murphy's Law* to *Parkinson's Law*, from Pudd'nhead Wilson to Stanley Bing, a steady infusion of comic skepticism has been injected into the corporate canon.

The Peter Principle is perhaps the most enduring, cynical classic.

The book carries many echoes of that other humorous classic of the 1960s, *Catch-22.*

The Peter Principle remains a poignant antidote to the blind optimism and sugary reality of most business books. It is a reminder that corporate reality is not usually about grand designs and great decisions. It is more mundane and frustrating. Too mundane and too frustrating to be taken seriously.

Dilbert creator Scott Adams commented, "Now, apparently, the incompetent workers are promoted directly to management without ever passing through the temporary competence stage. When I entered the workforce in 1979, *The Peter Principle* described management pretty well. Now I think we'd all like to return to those Golden Years when you had a boss who was once good at something."

The book remains relevant today. When Peter refers to codophilia (defined as speaking in letters and numbers instead of words), he could be talking of today's consultants.

Microsoft's Bill Gates echoes Peter saying, "The art of management is to promote people without making them managers."

For More Information

Peter, Laurence. *The Peter Principle*. New York: William Morrow & Co., 1969.

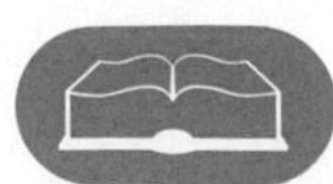

PLANNING FOR QUALITY

Joseph Juran

WHY READ IT?

Juran, like W. Edwards Deming, was one of the key figures in the quality revolution. In this book he stresses that the human aspect of quality management is as important as statistical control. The book underscores the contribution that quality teams and empowerment give to the quality process.

GETTING STARTED

Unlike the West, the Japanese have made quality a priority at the top of the organization.

The key elements in a quality philosophy are:

- quality planning;
- quality management;
- quality implementation.

Quality is nothing new, but it has become ignored in the West where it is treated as an operational issue. There is more to quality than specification and rigorous testing: it cannot be delegated and has to be the goal of each employee, individually and in teams. Quality can be seen as an invariable sequence of steps. Planning consists of developing processes to meet customers' needs; the human side is just as important.

CONTRIBUTION

1. NATIONAL ATTITUDES TO QUALITY MATTER

Talking to Japanese audiences in the 1950s, Joseph Juran's message was enthusiastically absorbed by groups of senior managers-the Japanese have made quality a priority at the top of the organization. In the West, Juran's audiences were made up of engineers and quality inspectors. Quality was delegated downward—an operational rather than a managerial issue.

In the postwar years, U.S. businesses were caught unawares for two reasons:

- they assumed their Asian adversaries were copycats rather than innovators;
- chief executives were too obsessed with financial indicators to notice any danger signs.

2. THE QUALITY TRILOGY

Juran's quality philosophy is built around a "quality trilogy" based on "Company-Wide Quality Management" (CWQM), which aims to create a means of disseminating quality to all. Juran insisted that quality cannot be delegated, and he was an early exponent of what has become known as empowerment.

Quality has to be the goal of each employee, individually and in teams, through self-supervision.

3. THE HISTORICAL CONTEXT OF QUALITY

Manufacturing products to design specifications and then inspecting them for defects to protect the buyer was something the Egyptians had mastered 5,000 years previously when building the pyramids. The ancient Chinese set up a separate department of the central government to establish quality standards and maintain them.

Juran's message is therefore that quality is nothing new. But if it is so elemental and elementary, why had it become ignored in the West?

4. THE HUMAN SIDE OF QUALITY

There is more to quality than specification and rigorous testing for defects; Juran regarded the human side of quality as critical. He developed all-embracing theories of what quality should entail.

5. THE QUALITY PLANNING PROCESS

Quality planning consists of developing the products and processes required to meet customers' needs. Quality planning includes the following activities:

- identifying the customers and their needs;
- developing a product that responds to those needs;
- developing a process able to produce that product.

Quality planning can be produced through an invariable sequence of steps:

- identify the customers;
- determine their needs;
- translate those needs into our language;
- develop a product that can respond to those needs;
- optimize the product features to meet our needs as well as customers' needs;
- develop a process which is able to produce the product;
- optimize the process;
- prove that the process can produce the product under operating conditions;
- transfer the process to the operating forces.

CONTEXT

Juran is critical of Deming (*Out of the Crisis*) as being over-reliant on statistics. Juran's approach is less mechanistic than Deming, and places greater stress on human relations. It is based on Company-Wide Quality Management (CWQM), a means of disseminating quality to all. Juran was an early exponent of what has become known as empowerment and believed that quality should be the goal of each employee.

Gary Hamel commented: "The impact of Juran, and of Deming as well, went far beyond quality. By drawing the attention of Western managers to the successes of Japan, they forced Western managers to challenge some of their most basic beliefs about the capabilities of their employees and the expectations of their customers."

For More Information

Juran, Joseph. *Planning for Quality*. New York: Free Press, 1988.

See also:
Joseph Juran (pp. 1006–07)

"Quality planning consists of developing the products and processes required to meet the customers' needs."

(*Planning for Quality*)

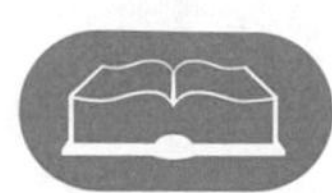

THE PRACTICE OF MANAGEMENT

Peter Drucker

WHY READ IT?

Peter Drucker is regarded as the major management and business thinker of the century. *The Practice of Management* is a book of huge range, encyclopedic in its scope and historical perspectives. It laid the groundwork for many of today's accepted management practices and is an excellent primer in management thinking.

GETTING STARTED

Management will remain a basic and dominant institution, with managers being at the epicenter of economic activity.

A business's purpose is to create a customer; and the two essential functions of business are marketing and innovation. Organization is a means to achieving business performance and results.

There are five basics of the managerial role—to set objectives; organize; motivate and communicate; measure; and develop people. Management has a moral responsibility, and must be driven by objectives.

CONTRIBUTION

1. THE IMPORTANCE OF MANAGEMENT

Management will remain a basic and dominant institution perhaps as long as Western civilization itself survives. Drucker places management and managers at the epicenter of economic activity.

Rarely has a new basic institution emerged as fast as has management since 1900, and never before has a new institution proved indispensable so quickly.

2. A MARKETING ATTITUDE IS CRITICAL

There is only one valid definition of business purpose: to create a customer.

Markets are created by businessmen. The want they satisfy may have been felt previously by the customer, but it was theoretical. Only when the action of businessmen provides a means to satisfy that want is there a customer, a market.

Since the role of business is to create customers, its only two essential functions are marketing and innovation. Marketing is not an isolated function, it is the whole business seen from the customer's point of view.

3. THE NATURE OF ORGANIZATIONS

Though indispensable, organization is not an end in itself, but a means to achieving performance and results. The wrong structure will seriously impair performance and may even destroy the business.

The first question in discussing structure must be: what is our business and what should it be? Organization structure must be designed in such a way that it's possible to achieve business objectives for 5, 10, 15 years hence.

4. THE MANAGERIAL ROLE

There are five basics of the managerial role. These are to:

- set objectives;
- organize;
- motivate and communicate;
- measure;
- develop people.

The function that distinguishes the manager above all others is to give others vision and ability to perform.

5. THE IMPORTANCE OF MORAL RESPONSIBILITY

It is vision and moral responsibility that, in the last analysis, define the manager. This morality is reflected in five areas.

- There must be high performance requirements; no condoning of poor or mediocre performance, and rewards must be based on performance.
- Each management job must be rewarding in itself, not just a step on the ladder.
- There must be a rational and just promotion system.
- Management needs clear rules on who has the power to make decisions affecting a manager; and there should be some way to appeal to a higher court.
- In its appointments, management must realize that integrity is the one quality that a manager has to bring to the job and cannot be expected to acquire later on.

6. MANAGEMENT BY OBJECTIVES

A manager's job should be based on tasks, the performance of which will help attain the company's objectives. The manager should be directed and controlled by these, rather than by his or her boss.

The manager must know and understand what the business demands in terms of performance, and his or her superior must judge the manager accordingly.

7. TASKS FOR THE MANAGER OF THE FUTURE

Drucker identified seven new tasks for the manager of the future. Given that these were laid down over 40 years ago, their prescience is astounding. Tomorrow's managers must:

- manage by objectives;
- take more risks and for a longer period;
- be able to make strategic decisions;
- be able to build an integrated team, each member of which is capable of managing his or her own performance in relation to the common objectives;
- be able to communicate information fast and clearly;
- be able to see the business, and the industry, as a whole and to integrate his or her function with it.

CONTEXT

The Practice of Management laid the groundwork for many of the developments in management thinking during the 1960s, and is important for the central role it argues management has in 20th-century society.

Drucker coined phrases such as "privatization" and "knowledge worker," and championed concepts such as management by objectives. Many of his innovations have become accepted facts of managerial life.

The Economist commented, "In a field packed with egomaniacs and snake-oil merchants, he remains a genuinely original thinker."

Influential author Gary Hamel says, "No other writer has contributed as much to the professionalization of management as Peter Drucker. Drucker's commitment to the discipline of management grew out of his belief that industrial organizations would become the world's most important social organizations—more influential, more encompassing, and often more intrusive than either church or state. Professor Drucker bridges the theoretical and the practical, the analytical and the emotive, the private and the social more perfectly than any other management writer."

For More Information

Drucker, Peter. *The Practice of Management*. New York: Harper & Row, 1954.

See also:
Peter Drucker (pp. 982–85)

"Management will remain a basic and dominant institution perhaps as long as Western civilization itself survives."

(*The Practice of Management*)

  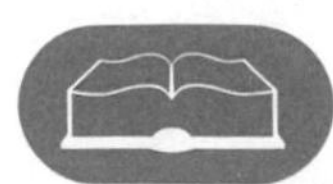    

THE PRINCE

Niccolò Machiavelli

WHY READ IT?

Although written over 300 years ago, Machiavelli's advice to leaders remains relevant to managers today, and covers many popular topics such as motivation, dealing with change, and leadership qualities.

GETTING STARTED

Change management, leadership style, motivation, and international management were just as relevant in the 16th century as they are today. Executives continue to see themselves as natural rulers of an organization, and to the leader, presentation is as important as ability.

Introducing change is extremely difficult. It's essential to keep motivation high-success is not the result of luck or genius, but happy shrewdness. Leaders who rise rapidly often fall just as quickly, and people ruling foreign countries should be on the spot to prevent trouble. Sometimes leaders have to practice evil when necessary.

CONTRIBUTION

1. EXECUTIVES HAVE NOT CHANGED

Machiavelli covers topics as apparently contemporary as change management, leadership style, motivation, and international management. Like the leaders Machiavelli sought to defend, some executives tend to see themselves as the natural rulers in whose hands organizations can be safely entrusted.

Theories abound on their motivation: is it a defensive reaction against failure, or a need for predictability through complete control? The effect of the power-driven Machiavellian manager is usually plain to see.

2. PRESENTING THE RIGHT IMAGE

According to Machiavelli, "It is unnecessary for a prince to have all the good qualities [I have] enumerated, but it is very necessary to appear to have them. It is useful to be a great pretender and dissembler."

3. MANAGING CHANGE AND MOTIVATION

"There is nothing more difficult to take in hand, more perilous to conduct, or more uncertain in its success, than to take the lead in the introduction of a new order of things. A leader ought above all things to keep his men well organized and drilled, to follow incessantly the chase."

4. MANAGING INTERNATIONALLY

"When states are acquired in a country with different a language, customs, or laws, there are difficulties; good fortune and great energy are needed to hold them. It would be a great help if he who acquired them should go and live there. If one is on the spot, disorders are seen as they spring up, and one can quickly remedy them; but if one is not at hand, they are heard of only when they are great, and then one can no longer remedy them."

5. THE QUALITIES OF LEADERSHIP

In the author's opinion, success is not the result of luck or genius, but happy shrewdness. He felt that a Prince ought to have no other aim or thought, nor select anything else for his study, than war and its rules and discipline; for this is the sole art that belongs to him who rules.

"In addition, those who solely by good fortune become princes from being private citizens have little trouble in rising, but much in keeping atop," says the author. "They have no difficulties on the way up, because they fly, but they have many when they reach the summit."

It is all very well being good, but the leader "should know how to enter into evil when necessity commands."

CONTEXT

The Prince is the 16th-century equivalent of Dale Carnegie's *How to Win Friends and Influence People*. Many of its insights are as appropriate to today's managers and organizations as they were half a millennium ago. Antony Jay's 1970 book, *Management and Machiavelli*, developed the comparisons.

The book offers something for everyone. It covers topics as apparently contemporary as change management, leadership style, motivation and international management.

Gary Hamel has said: "We occasionally need reminding that leadership and strategy are not twentieth century inventions. It's just that in previous centuries they are more often the concerns of princes than industrialists. Yet power is a constant in human affairs, and a central theme of Machiavelli's *The Prince*. It is currently out of fashion to talk about power. We are constantly reminded that in the knowledge economy, capital wears shoes and goes home every night. No place here for the blunt instrument of power politics? But would Sumner Redstone, Bill Gates, or Rupert Murdoch agree? What is interesting is that after 500 years, Machiavelli is still in print. What modern volume on leadership will be gracing bookstores in the year 2500? Does Machiavelli's longevity tell us anything about what are the deep, enduring truths of management?"

For More Information

Machiavelli, Niccolò. *The Prince*. New York: Penguin, 1967.

See also:
Niccolò Machiavelli (pp. 1016–17)

"It is unnecessary for a prince to have all the good qualities I have enumerated, but it is very necessary to appear to have them."
(The Prince)

THE PRINCIPLES OF SCIENTIFIC MANAGEMENT

Frederick Winslow Taylor

WHY READ IT?

At the time *The Principles of Scientific Management* was published, "business management as a discrete and identifiable activity had attracted little attention" as Lyndall Urwick, the British champion of scientific management, said. The book put management on the map, and its influence on working methods and managerial attitudes for most of the 20th century, especially in mass-production industries, was enormous. Taylor's principles have been alternately reviled, rejected, and rediscovered. They remain undeniably significant even today.

GETTING STARTED

Frederick Winslow Taylor was a U.S. engineer and inventor, whose fame rests chiefly on this book. He shares with Henry Ford the dubious distinction of founding an "-ism." Taylorism is the practice of the principles of scientific management, which emerged from Taylor's work at the Midvale Steel Works, where he was chief engineer. It involves rigorous measurement of work processes, total objectivity in the assessment of which methods work best, and the consequent mechanization of work and elimination of the human element. The objective standards arrived at, however, are as binding on managers, who have to enforce them, as on the workers who have to meet them. Like the unstoppable assembly line, scientific management imposes its discipline on everyone. Not surprisingly, to most members of the humanistic school of management it is the enemy *par excellence*.

CONTRIBUTION

1. MEASURING WORK

Taylor's science consisted in the minute examination of individual tasks. Having identified every single movement and action involved in doing something, he could determine the optimum time required to complete a task.

Armed with this information, the manager could determine whether a person was doing the job well.

2. PUTTING SCIENCE BEFORE OPINION

The most obvious consequence of scientific management is a dehumanizing reliance on measurement.

The experts, who first analyze and then accurately time the various ways of doing each piece of work, will finally know from exact knowledge, and not from anyone's opinion, which method will accomplish the results with the least effort and in the quickest time.

The exact facts will have in this way been developed and they will constitute a series of laws, which are destined to control the vast multitude of our daily personal acts which, at present, are the subjects of individual opinion.

3. A SYSTEM WITH NO INITIATIVE

The Taylorist system envisages no room for individual initiative or imagination. People are labor, mechanically accomplishing a particular task and doing what they are told.

According to Robert McNamara: "those who were so important in the early stages of American manufacturing, the foremen and plant managers were disenfranchized. Instead of being creators and innovators, as in an earlier era, now they depended on meeting production quotas. They could not stop the line and fix problems as they occurred; they lost any stake in innovation or change" (quoted in *Promise and Power* by Deborah Shapley).

Taylor's schemes for objectively determining best practices for every imaginable job could, on the other hand, be said to have freed front-line workers from the capricious discipline of unscientific, turn-of-the-century foremen.

CONTEXT

While Taylor's concepts are now usually regarded in a negative light, the originality of his insights and their importance are in little doubt. He himself announced that he was ushering in a revolution, "a complete mental revolution on the part of the working man engaged in any particular establishment or industry, a complete mental revolution on the part of these men as to their duties toward their work, toward their fellow men, and toward their employees."

Peter Drucker observed in *The Practice of Management*: "Few people had ever looked at human work systematically until Frederick W. Taylor started to do so around 1885. Work was taken for granted and it is an axiom that one never sees what one takes for granted. *Scientific Management* was thus one of the great liberating, pioneering insights."

Lyndall Urwick adds: "At the time Taylor began his work, business management. . . was usually regarded as incidental to, and flowing from knowledge of. . ., a particular branch of manufacturing, the technical know-how of making sausages or steel or shirts. The idea that a man needed any training or formal instruction to become a competent manager had not occurred to anyone."

The legacy of Taylor's work is most obvious in companies that tend to emphasize quantity over quality. His ideas were enthusiastically taken up by Henry Ford in the development of mass-production techniques.

Drucker goes on to identify two fundamental flaws in scientific management.

"The first of these blind spots is the belief that, because we must analyze work into its simplest constituent motions, we must also organize it as a series of individual motions, each if possible carried out by an individual worker; the second that it divorces planning from doing."

Gary Hamel sums up the position thus: "The development of modern management theory is the story of two quests: to make management more scientific, and to make it more humane. It is wrong to look at the latter quest as somehow much more enlightened than the former. Indeed, they are the yin and yang of business. The unprecedented capacity of twentieth century industry to create wealth rests squarely on the work of Frederick Winslow Taylor. While some may disavow Taylor, his rational, deterministic impulses live on. Indeed, reengineering is simply late twentieth century Taylorism. Though the focus of reengineering is on the process, rather than the individual task, the motivation is the same: to simplify, to remove unnecessary effort, and to do more with less."

For More Information

Taylor, Frederick Winslow. *The Principles of Scientific Management*. New York: Harper & Row, 1911.

"The determination of the best method of performing all of our daily acts will, in the future, be the work of experts."

(*The Principles of Scientific Management*)

  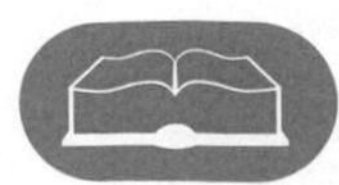    

QUEST FOR PROSPERITY

Konosuke Matsushita

WHY READ IT?

This book describes how Konosuke Matsushita built a global business—Panasonic—from nothing. It contains lessons on customer service, business ethics, and marketing that would benefit any business.

GETTING STARTED

According to the author, customer service is critical to success—customers want goods that will benefit them. After-sales service is more important than assistance before sales.

Business with a conscience cements loyalty. We are using precious resources that could be better used elsewhere unless we make a good profit. Production efficiency and quality products are key. The mission of a manufacturer should be to overcome poverty, to relieve society as a whole from misery, and to bring it wealth.

CONTRIBUTION

1. BUILDING A WINNING BUSINESS

The Matsushita story is one of the most impressive industrial achievements of the 20th century.

The company's first break was an order to make insulator plates. The order was delivered on time and was high quality. Matsushita began to make money. He then developed an innovative bicycle light. Initially, retailers were unimpressed. Then Matsushita had his salesmen leave a switched on light in each shop. This simple product demonstration impressed the retailers, and the business took off.

2. THE IMPORTANCE OF CUSTOMER SERVICE

The company understood customer service before anyone in the West had even thought about it:

- don't sell customers goods that they are attracted to. Sell them goods that will benefit them;
- after-sales service is more important than assistance before sales. It is through such service that one gets permanent customers.

3. EFFICIENCY AND QUALITY

Matsushita emphasized efficient production and quality products.

To be out of stock is due to carelessness. If this happens, apologize to the customers, ask for their address, and tell them that you will deliver the goods immediately.

4. RISK-TAKING PAYS

Matsushita took risks and backed his beliefs at every stage.

The classic example of this is the development of the videocassette. Matsushita developed VHS video and licensed the technology. Sony developed Betamax, which was immeasurably better, and failed to license the technology. The world standard is VHS and Betamax is consigned to history.

5. BUSINESS WITH A CONSCIENCE

Matsushita advocated business with a conscience, reflected in his paternalistic employment practices. During a recession early in its life the company did not lay any of its workers off. This cemented loyalty.

It is not enough to work conscientiously. No matter what kind of job, you should think of yourself as being completely in charge of and responsible for your own work.

6. THE ROLE OF THE LEADER

Big things and little things are the leader's job. Middle-level arrangements can be delegated.

Matsushita also explained the role of the leader in more cryptic style: "The tail trails the head. If the head moves fast, the tail will keep up the same pace. If the head is sluggish, the tail will droop."

7. THE BROADER AIMS OF BUSINESS

Matsushita mapped out the broader spiritual aims he believed a business should have. Profit was not enough. The mission of a manufacturer should be to overcome poverty, to relieve society as a whole from misery, and bring it wealth.

He outlined his basic management objective as follows: "Recognizing our responsibilities as industrialists, we will devote ourselves to the progress and development of society and the well-being of people through our business activities, thereby enhancing the quality of life throughout the world."

Failure to make a profit was regarded as a sort of crime against society: "We take society's capital, we take their people, we take their materials, yet without a good profit, we are using precious resources that could be better used elsewhere."

Business is demanding, serious, and crucial: "Business, we know, is now so complex and difficult, the survival of firms so hazardous in an environment increasingly unpredictable, competitive, and fraught with danger, that their continued existence depends on the day-to-day mobilization of every ounce of intelligence."

CONTEXT

Matsushita created a $42 billion revenue business from nothing. He also created Panasonic, one of the world's most successful brands, and amassed a personal fortune of $3 billion.

The book explains the principles that made his business a success.

For More Information

Matsushita, Konosuke. *Quest for Prosperity*. Kyoto: PHP Institute, 1988.

See also:
Konosuke Matsushita (pp. 1114–15)

"We are going to win and the industrial West is going to lose out; there's not much you can do about it because the reasons for your failure are within yourselves." (Quest for Prosperity)

  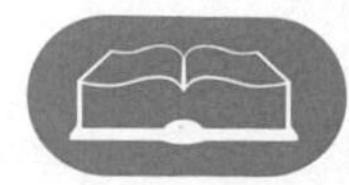    

REENGINEERING THE CORPORATION

James Champy
Michael Hammer

WHY READ IT?

Reengineering the Corporation is seen as the key book in the reengineering revolution. It encourages organizations to take a fresh look at inefficient and outdated processes, and to focus on dramatic improvements in cost, quality, service, and speed. Although the message has been misinterpreted, reengineering remains a powerful tool for change.

GETTING STARTED

Reengineering must focus on the fundamental rethinking and radical redesign of key business processes. Dramatic improvements in cost, quality, service, and speed are the aim, and organizations must make key processes as lean and profitable as possible, discarding peripheral processes and people if necessary.

Reengineering should go far beyond altering and refining processes: the aim is "to reverse the Industrial Revolution." Organizations should start with a blank piece of paper and map out processes to identify how their business should operate. They should then attempt to translate the paper into concrete reality.

Reengineering puts a premium on the skills and potential of the people at the center of the organization, and should also tackle three key areas of management–managerial roles, styles, and systems.

CONTRIBUTION

1. FOCUS ON IMPROVING CORE PROCESSES

In the context of a fiercely competitive environment and the ability of IT to transform business processes, the book encourages organizations to take a fresh look at inefficient and outdated processes. Reengineering, according to the authors, is the fundamental rethinking and radical redesign of business processes.

2. CREATE A LEAN ORGANIZATION

The authors argue that organizations need to identify their key processes and make them as lean and profitable as possible. In some cases, peripheral processes and people need to be discarded.

Unfortunately, many organizations have taken this advice literally and downsized without reengineering. CSC, the consultancy founded by Champy and Hammer, surveyed more than 600 companies involved in reengineering projects in 1994. In the United States, an average 336 jobs were lost on each project. In Europe, the figure was 760 jobs per project.

3. ACHIEVE A COMPLETE CORPORATE REVOLUTION

Simple business process reengineering is not enough, say the authors. True reengineering is a recipe for a corporate revolution, and should go far beyond altering and refining processes: the past is history; the future is there to be coerced into the optimum shape.

The authors believe that reengineering is concerned with rejecting conventional wisdom and received assumptions about the past. However, this can mean ignoring the experience of the past. Companies are discouraged from trying to understand why they have been successful and building on that.

4. TRANSFORM THE FUTURE

The authors suggest that organizations should start with a blank piece of paper. They should map out their processes to identify how their business should operate, and then attempt to translate the paper into concrete reality.

In practice, this has proved difficult to achieve. The authors now believe that companies tend not to cast the reengineering net widely; they find processes that can be reengineered quickly and stop at that point. They lack a vision for the future and the revolutionary approach to take reengineering forward.

5. REENGINEER MANAGEMENT AS WELL

Part of the problem, they now believe, is that managers fail to impose change on themselves–they concentrate on tearing down processes, but they leave their own jobs and management styles intact. However, the old ways of management could eventually undermine the very structure of their rebuilt enterprise. The reengineering process should therefore tackle three key areas of management–managerial roles, styles, and systems.

6. REENGINEERING SHOULD BE BUILT ON TRUST, RESPECT, AND PEOPLE

The authors believe that reengineering actually puts a premium on the people at the center of the organization. Once peripheral activities have been cut away, the new environment puts a premium on skills of the people who are left. Experience suggests that this has not happened so far: downsizing creates a difficult environment in which trust is frequently absent.

CONTEXT

Reengineering is seen by some as an old concept with a new label. Frederick W Taylor's *Scientific Management* advocated similar change, but at an individual rather than an organizational level. Gary Hamel pointed out that reengineering followed a line from scientific management, industrial engineering, and business process improvement.

The mechanistic theme has been a key focal point for critics, who have made the point that reengineering owes more to visions of the corporation as a machine, rather than a human system. Peter Cohan, a former colleague, said the authors ignored the importance of people, describing them as objects who handle processes. Christopher Lorenz of the *Financial Times* believed that the authors failed to state whether organizations should undertake behavioral and cultural changes in parallel with reengineering.

It has also been easy to take the book's messages too literally. Reengineering has been seen as a synonym for redundancy, and the book has been blamed for a wave of downsizing.

For More Information

Champy, James, and Michael Hammer. *Reengineering the Corporation*. New York: HarperBusiness, 1993.

See also:

☆ **X-engineering Success (pp. 245–46)**

"I tell them what I really do is I'm reversing the Industrial Revolution."

(Reengineering the Corporation)

Riding the Waves of Culture

Fons Trompenaars
Charles Hampden-Turner

Why Read It?

Riding the Waves of Culture is an examination of the cultural imponderables faced by managers in the global village. Based on exhaustive research, it systematically "dimensionalizes" cultural differences, identifying seven areas, such as attitude to rules and awareness of time, in which different nations have fundamentally different conceptions. Anyone whose work involves dealing with people from other cultures would benefit from reading it.

Getting Started

Fons Trompenaars studied at a top U.S. business school, where he started thinking about cultural differences. "I started wondering if any of the American management techniques I was brainwashed with in eight years of the best business education money could buy would apply in the Netherlands, where I came from, or indeed in the rest of the world."

Charles Hampden-Turner is an international authority on cross-cultural communication who taught for many years in the United States and, like his coauthor, worked for Shell.

The book is based on meticulous quantitative research (over 15 years 15,000 people from 50 countries were surveyed) and more than 900 seminars presented in 18 countries. Its main contentions are that basic to understanding other cultures is the awareness of cultural difference, that cultural difference can be systematically analyzed, that flexibility, humility, and a sense of humor are needed in dealing with cultures other than our own, and that the reconciliation of difference is the supreme managerial art.

Contribution

1. Culture

Culture is a series of rules and methods that a society has evolved to deal with the recurring problems it faces. They have become so basic that we no longer think about how we approach or resolve them.

People should be aware, first, that they belong to a culture and have a specific way of doing things, and they should be prepared, second, for a different response from the one they are accustomed to receiving when they do business with someone whose culture differs from theirs.

2. Seven Dimensions of Culture

In analyzing cultural differences, the authors identify seven dimensions in which different or contrasting attitudes are particularly crucial. There are:

- universalism vs. particularism
- individualism vs. collectivism
- neutral vs. emotional
- specific vs. diffuse
- achievement vs. ascription
- attitude toward time
- attitude toward the environment

3. Universalism and Particularism

There are two fundamentally distinct ways of dealing with situations that the book labels "universalism" and "particularism." Universalists (including Americans, Canadians, Australians, and the Swiss) advocate one best way, "what is good and right can be defined and always applies." They focus on rules and procedure. Particularists (South Koreans, Chinese, and Malaysians) feel that circumstances dictate how ideas and practices should be applied. They focus on the peculiar nature of any given situation and on particular relationships.

Universalists doing business with particularists should be prepared for meandering or irrelevancies that do not seem to be going anywhere.

Particularists doing business with universalists should be prepared for rational and professional arguments and presentations and little else.

4. Collectivist and Individualist

The book also contrasts the collectivist mindset with the individualist one.

The United States again comes at one extreme of the spectrum emphasizing the individual before the group. Countries such as Egypt and France are at the other end.

Individualists working with collectivists must tolerate time taken to consult and negotiators who can only agree tentatively and may withdraw an offer after consulting with superiors.

5. The Role of the International Manager

Given the wide range of basic differences in how different cultures perceive the world, it is evident that the international manager is moving in a world riddled with potential pitfalls. There are also profound differences between those who show their feelings (such as Italians) and those who hide them (such as the Japanese), and those who accord status on the basis of achievement and those ascribe it on the basis of family and age.

The international manager needs to go beyond awareness of cultural differences.

He or she needs to respect these differences and take advantage of diversity through reconciling cross-cultural dilemmas. The international manager reconciles cultural dilemmas.

In the end, the only positive route forward is through reconciliation. Those societies that can reconcile better are better at creating wealth.

Context

Tom Peters called *Riding the Waves of Culture* a masterpiece. "What's not okay is cultural arrogance. If you come to another's turf with sensitivity and open ears. . .you're halfway home."

Gary Hamel takes the authors to task for their criticisms of American cultural inflexibility: "So Americans will never understand foreign cultures? Funny how American companies are out-competing their European competitors in Asia and Latin America. . .Where I agree with Trompenaars is that the future belongs to the cosmopolitans."

The cultural aspects of managing internationally are likely to gain in importance as the full force of globalization affects industries and individuals. In this respect the value of the book's contribution is undeniable. It has been argued, however, that its stress on cultural relativism and adaptability might become outmoded if capital markets were to enforce "global rules of the game" independent of different cultures.

For More Information

Trompenaars, Fons, and Charles Hampden-Turner. *Riding the Waves of Culture*. 2nd ed. New York: McGraw-Hill, 1997.

See also:
☆ **Viewpoint: Fons Trompenaars (pp. 27–28)**

"Culture is the way in which people resolve dilemmas emerging from universal problems."
(*Riding the Waves of Culture*)

The Rise and Fall of Strategic Planning

Henry Mintzberg

Why Read It?

Mintzberg shows how over-emphasizing analysis and hard facts limits strategic planning. Planning should be something visionary and creative. The book has become an influential classic.

Getting Started

Planning is concerned with analysis; strategy making is concerned with synthesis. Strategic planners tend to make false assumptions that discontinuities can be predicted; the future will resemble the past; and strategy making can be formalized. They tend to be detached from action and the reality of the organization.

Planners typically gather hard data on their industry, markets, and competitors. Soft data–such as networks of contacts, talking with customers, suppliers, and employees–have been ignored. Strategy formulation has been dominated by logic and analysis. Intuition and creativity need to become part of the process.

Contribution

1. Strategy and Planning

Planning codifies, elaborates, and operationalizes existing company strategy. In contrast, strategy is either an emergent pattern or a deliberate perspective, and cannot be planned. While planning is concerned with analysis, strategy making is concerned with synthesis.

2. The Nature of Planners

Planners do have value, but only as strategy finders, analysts, and catalysts. At their most effective, they unearth strategies in unexpected pockets of the organization, whose potential can then be explored.

3. Problems with Planning Practices

The three main pitfalls are:

- the assumption that discontinuities can be predicted;
- planners are detached from the reality of the organization;
- the assumption that strategy making can be formalized.

4. The Assumption That Discontinuities Can Be Predicted

Forecasters often assume that the future will resemble the past. This gives artificial reassurance, and creates strategies that disintegrate as they are overtaken by events.

5. Detachment from the Reality of the Organization

If the system does the thinking, strategy must be detached from operations, and thinkers from doers. This disassociation of thinking from acting lies at the root of strategic planning's problem.

6. Hard Data and Soft Data

Planners typically gather hard data on their industry, markets, and competitors. Soft data–networks of contacts, talking with customers, suppliers, and employees, using intuition, and using the grapevine–have all but been ignored.

Hard data are often anything but. There is the fallacy of measuring what's measurable. There is a tendency to favor cost-leadership strategies (emphasizing operating efficiencies, which are generally measurable) over product-leadership strategies (emphasizing innovative design or high quality, which tends to be less measurable).

To gain useful understanding of an organization's competitive situation, soft data need to be dynamically integrated into the planning process. They may be difficult to analyze, but they are indispensable for synthesis–the key to strategy making.

7. The Assumption That Strategy Making Can Be Formalized

The emphasis on logic and analysis creates a narrow range of options. Alternatives that do not fit into the predetermined structure are ignored.

The right side of the brain needs to become part of the process, with its emphasis on intuition and creativity. Planning defines and preserves categories. Creativity creates categories or rearranges established ones.

Thus strategic planning can neither provide creativity, nor deal with it when it emerges. Mold-breaking strategies grow initially like weeds–they are not cultivated and can take root anywhere.

8. The Nature of Strategy Making

Mintzberg defines strategy making thus:

- it is derived from synthesis;
- it is informal and visionary, rather than programmed and formalized;
- it relies on divergent thinking, intuition and using the subconscious. This leads to outbursts of creativity as new discoveries are made;
- it is irregular, unexpected, ad hoc, and instinctive. It upsets stable patterns;
- managers are adaptive information manipulators–opportunists, rather than aloof conductors;
- it is done in time of instability characterized by discontinuous change;
- it results from an approach that takes in broad perspectives and is, therefore, visionary, and involves a variety of actors capable of experimenting and then integrating.

Context

The book reflects a general dissatisfaction with strategic planning. Research by the U.S. Planning Forum found that only 25% of companies considered their planning was effective.

The book attracted much attention and debate. It also brought a spirited response from the defenders of strategy. Andrew Campbell, coauthor of *Corporate-Level Strategy*, wrote: "Strategic planning is not futile. Research has shown that some companies–both conglomerates and more focused groups–have strategic planning processes that add real value." Campbell further argues that the corporate center must develop a value-creating, corporate-level strategy and build the management processes needed to implement it.

Management guru Gary Hamel commented: "Henry views strategic planning as a ritual, devoid of creativity and meaning. He is undoubtedly right when he argues that planning doesn't produce strategy. But rather than use the last chapter of the book to create a new charter for planners, Henry might have put his mind to the question of where strategies actually do come from!"

For More Information

Mintzberg, Henry. *The Rise and Fall of Strategic Planning*. New York: Free Press, 1994.

See also:
☆ **Viewpoint: Henry Mintzberg (pp. 241–42)**

(*The Rise and Fall of Strategic Planning*)

STRATEGY AND STRUCTURE

Alfred Chandler

WHY READ IT?

Chandler's book is regarded by many commentators as a masterpiece. It demonstrates the critical link between a company's strategy and its structure, and played an influential role in the profitable decentralization of many leading corporations. The book's findings remain relevant to new forms of organization such as the federated organization, the multi-company coalition, and the virtual company.

GETTING STARTED

Structure should be driven by strategy—and if it isn't, inefficiency results. The structure of many corporations is driven by market forces: recognition that production had to be market-driven led large organizations to change to a looser divisional structure.

Increases in scale also led to business owners having to recruit a new breed of professional manager, as professional management coordinates the flow of product to customers more efficiently than market forces.

A planned economy is important to long-term organizational success.

CONTRIBUTION

1. STRUCTURE SHOULD BE DRIVEN BY STRATEGY

Strategy is the determination of the long-term goals and objectives of an enterprise, and the adoption of courses of action and the allocation of resources necessary for reaching these goals.

A firm's structure is dictated by its chosen strategy—and unless structure follows strategy, inefficiency results.

A company should establish a strategy and then seek to create the structure appropriate to achieving it.

2. STRUCTURE DRIVEN BY MARKET FORCES

Organizational structures in companies such as Du Pont, Sears Roebuck, General Motors, and Standard Oil were driven by the changing demands and pressures of the marketplace.

The market-driven proliferation of product lines in Du Pont and General Motors led to a shift from a functional, monolithic organizational form to a more loosely-coupled divisional structure.

3. THE RISE OF THE MULTIDIVISIONAL ORGANIZATION

The multidivisional organization removed the executives responsible for the destiny of the entire enterprise from the more routine operational responsibilities.

It gave them the time, information and even psychological commitment for long-term planning and appraisal.

4. THE PROFESSIONALIZATION OF MANAGEMENT

The managerial revolution was fueled by the rise of oil-based energy, the development of the steel, chemical, and engineering industries, and a dramatic rise in the scale of production and the size of companies.

Increases in scale led to business owners having to recruit a new breed of professional manager. The roles of the salaried manager and technician are vital, as the visible hand of management coordinates the flow of product to customers more efficiently than Adam Smith's "invisible hand" of the market.

5. THE IMPORTANCE OF A PLANNED ECONOMY

Organizations and their managements require a planned economy rather than a capitalist free-for-all dominated by the unpredictable whims of market forces.

CONTEXT

The book is based on Chandler's research into major U.S. corporations between 1850 and 1920. Its subtitle is "Chapters in the History of the American Industrial Enterprise," but its impact went far beyond that of a brilliantly-researched historical text. Alfred Chandler's *Strategy and Structure* is a theoretical masterpiece which has had profound influence on both practitioners and thinkers.

Chandler was highly influential in the trend among large organizations for decentralization in the 1960s and 1970s. While in 1950 around 20% of *Fortune* 500 corporations were decentralized, this had increased to 80% by 1970. In the 1980s, Chandler's thinking was influential in the transformation of AT&T from what was in effect a production-based bureaucracy to a marketing organization.

Until recent times, Chandler's conclusion that structure follows strategy has largely been accepted as a fact of corporate life. Now, the debate has been rekindled.

Tom Peters said, "I think he got it exactly wrong. For it is the structure of the organization that determines, over time, the choices that it makes about the markets it attacks."

In *Managing on the Edge*, Richard Pascale said, "The underlying assumption is that organizations act in a rational, sequential manner. Yet most executives will readily agree that it is often the other way around. The way a company is organized, whether functional focused or driven by independent divisions, often plays a major role in shaping its strategy. Indeed, this accounts for the tendency of organizations to do what they best know how to do—regardless of deteriorating success against the competitive realities."

Gary Hamel, author of *Leading the Revolution*, said, "Those who dispute Chandler's thesis that structure follows strategy miss the point. Of course strategy and structure are inextricably intertwined. Chandler's point was that new challenges give rise to new structures. The challenges of size and complexity, coupled with advances in communications and techniques of management control, produced divisionalization and decentralization. These same forces, several generations on, are now driving us towards new structural solutions-the federated organization, the multi-company coalition, and the virtual company. Few historians are prescient. Chandler was."

For More Information

Chandler, Alfred. *Strategy and Structure*. New York: Doubleday, 1962.

"Unless structure follows strategy, inefficiency results." (Strategy and Structure)

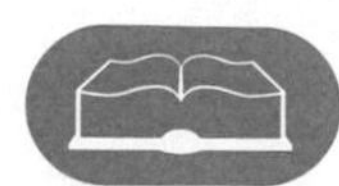

THEORY OF SOCIAL AND ECONOMIC ORGANIZATION

Max Weber

WHY READ IT?

It is quite easy to make Weber's book sound as if it was intended to be a source text for Franz Kafka's novels and Charlie Chaplin's film *Modern Times*, not to mention George Orwell's *1984*. Weber is often incorrectly assumed to have been an advocate of bureaucracy and a mechanistic society, rather than someone who described bureaucracy—with at least some degree of correctness—as the most efficient and rational means of organization. In fact, as R. J. Kilcullen puts it "bureaucracy was for Weber what capitalism was for Marx, the admired enemy." No understanding of the way modern organizations work would be complete without a study of this book.

GETTING STARTED

Max Weber was a versatile thinker who was a professor of political economy at the universities of Freiburg and Heidelberg in Germany. He is best known today as one of the founding fathers of modern sociology.

The Theory of Social and Economic Organization grew out of his philosophical inquiries into the nature of authority and how it is transmitted. Weber identified three types of authority, the "charismatic," based on the individual qualities of a leader and reverence for them among his or her followers, the "traditional," based on custom and usage, and the "rational-legal" based on the rule of objective law. Bureaucracy is the most efficient way of implementing the rule of law.

CONTRIBUTION

1. HOW BUREAUCRACY WORKS

There are four main principles identified by Weber as characteristic of a rational-legal bureaucracy.

- The organization is structured around official functions which are bound by rules, each area having its own specified competence.
- Functions are structured into offices organized into a hierarchy that follows technical rules and norms for which training is provided.
- The administration is separated from the ownership of the means of production.
- The rules, decisions, and actions of the administration are recorded in writing.

2. THE IMPERSONALITY OF BUREAUCRACY

The most important feature of bureaucracy—its main strength as well as its main weakness—is its impersonality.

Impersonality is a strength in that it minimizes the abuse of power by leaders because:

- offices are ranked in hierarchical order;
- operations are conducted in accordance with impersonal rules;
- officials are allocated specific duties and areas of responsibility;
- appointments are made on the basis of qualifications and suitability for the post.

It is a weakness in that:

- their characteristic information processing and filtering to the top makes bureaucracies cumbersome and slow to react;
- their machinery makes it difficult to handle individual cases, because rules and procedures require all individuals to be treated as if they were the same;
- bureaucratization leads to depersonalization, because the roles of officials are circumscribed by written definitions of their authority, and there is a set of rules and procedures to cater for every contingency.

3. TOWARD ULTIMATE EFFICIENCY

The purely bureaucratic type of administrative organization is, from a purely technical point of view, capable of attaining the highest degree of efficiency. It is, in this sense, the most rational known means of carrying out imperative control over human beings. It is superior to any other form of organization in precision, in stability, in the stringency of its discipline, and in its reliability.

CONTEXT

Bureaucratic organization as expounded by Max Weber became the model for the 20th-century organization, and was encapsulated in Alfred Sloan's General Motors and Harold Geneen's ITT. Strictly implemented, and in combination with regimented mass-production as practiced by Henry Ford, who echoed some of Weber's thoughts in his faith in strict demarcations and his fervently mechanistic approach to business, it could produce a nightmare scenario for the world of work in the 20th century.

Weber himself could see no realistic substitute for bureaucracy. He regarded its triumph with distaste, but as inevitable. Only in the latter part of the 20th century did new and more humane concepts of the organization emerge and start to win adherents. The roots of some of the latest are in biology and the new sciences of chaos and complexity, areas unknown to Weber. Today's organizations are talked of in terms of fractal and amoebae—they are imagined as elusive and ever-changing rather than efficient and static.

The regularity of the machine age has given way to the tumult, ambiguity, and complexity of the information age.

Even so, Max Weber remains important. In his book *Gods of Management*, Charles Handy chose as one of the gods Apollo, who is characterized by a Weber-like faith in rules and systems. Aspects of the bureaucratic model remain alive and well in a great many organizations where hierarchies, demarcations, and exhaustive rules dominate.

The influential author Gary Hamel notes: "Every organization wrestles with two conflicting needs: the need to optimize in the name of economic efficiency, and the need to experiment in the name of growth and renewal. Authoritarian bureaucracies, of the sort that rebuilt the Japanese economy after the war, serve well the goal of optimization. While there is experimentation here, it is tightly constrained. Anarchical networks, of the sort that predominate in Italy's fashion industry, allow for unfettered experimentation, but are always vulnerable to more disciplined competitors. Weber staked out one side of the argument; Tom Peters the other. As always, what is required is a synthesis."

For More Information

Weber, Max. *Theory of Social and Economic Organization*, trans. A. M. Henderson and T. Parsons. New York: Free Press, 1947.

See also:

Max Weber (pp. 1060–61)

"Large organizations require that the people involved put the cause of the organization before their own aspirations."

(*Theory of Social and Economic Organization*)

  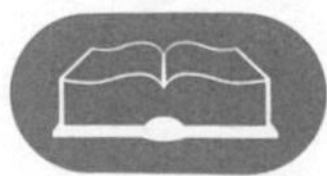    

THE THIRD WAVE

Alvin Toffler

WHY READ IT?

The obvious reason for reading a work of futurology more than 20 years after its publication is to see if the futurologist got it right. In many respects Toffler did. But there is a danger there also. Toffler predicted the electronic office and its effects. Now that most people work in electronic offices and live with their effects, perhaps it seems redundant to read a book simply in order to be able to congratulate the author on his foresight. What is startling about *The Third Wave* is that it was written so recently, and yet the technological leaps made since its publication have been so immense. The intriguing thing now is whether the author's broader analysis encompassed the developments that flowed from the developments he immediately foresaw. For many people Toffler's ideas are still intriguing.

GETTING STARTED

Alvin Toffler began his career as a journalist but shot to international fame as a futurologist with the publication of his first book, *Future Shock*, in 1970. *The Third Wave* appeared ten years later, and *Power Shift* ten years after that.

The "Third Wave" referred to in the title is the super-industrial society that emerged toward the end of the 20th century and is still taking shape. It succeeded the "Second Wave," the industrialized society produced by the Industrial Revolution, which itself succeeded the agricultural phase of human development, the "First Wave." Each new wave was ushered in by the development of new technology. Electronics brought in the third.

Though the various waves followed one another in time, they did not affect the whole of the human race simultaneously-many people are still living under First Wave conditions. Toffler's main concern is with the transition from the Second to the Third Wave in advanced societies, but he also deals with possible areas of friction between people coexisting at different stages of development.

CONTRIBUTION

1. TOWARD MASS CUSTOMIZATION

The Third Wave, according to Toffler, is characterized by mass customization rather than mass production.

The essence of Second Wave manufacture was the long run of millions of identical standardized products. By contrast, the essence of Third Wave manufacture is the short run of partially or completely customized products.

The Second Wave strictly separated consumer and producer. The Third Wave will see the two become almost indistinguishable, as the consumer becomes involved in the actual process of production, expressing choices and preferences.

2. THE GROWTH OF FLEXIBLE WORKING

Toffler predicted the demise of the nine-to-five working day.

Machine synchronization shackled the human to the machine's capabilities and imprisoned all of social life in a common frame. It did so in capitalist and socialist countries alike. Now, as machine synchronization grows more precise, humans, instead of being imprisoned, are progressively freed. They are freed into more flexible ways of working, whether it is flexitime or working at home.

3. CHANGES IN WORKING RELATIONSHIPS

A partial shift towards the electronic office will be enough to trigger an eruption of social, psychological, and economic consequences. The coming word-quake means more than just new machines. It promises to restructure all the human relationships and roles in the office.

The Third Wave will produce anxiety and conflict as well as reorganization, restructuring, and, for some, rebirth into new careers and opportunities. The new systems will challenge all the old executive turfs, the hierarchies, the sexual role divisions, the departmental barriers of the past.

4. THE IMPACT ON THE CORPORATION

Instead of clinging to a sharply specialized economic function, the corporation, prodded by criticism, legislation, and its own concerned executives, is becoming a multipurpose institution.

The organization is being driven to redefinition through five forces.

- Changes in the physical environment. Companies must take greater responsibility for the effect of their operations on the environment.
- Changes in the line-up of social forces. The actions of companies now have greater impact on those of other organizations such as schools, universities, civil groups, and political lobbies.
- Changes in the role of information. As information becomes central to production, as information managers proliferate in industry, the corporation, by necessity, impacts on the informational environment exactly as it impacts on the physical and social environment.
- Changes in government organization. The profusion of government bodies means that the business and political worlds interact to a far greater degree than ever before.
- Changes in morality. The ethics and values of organizations are becoming more closely linked to those of society. Behavior once accepted as normal is suddenly reinterpreted as corrupt, immoral, or scandalous. The corporation is increasingly seen as a producer of moral effects.

The organization of the future will be concerned with ecological, moral, political, racial, sexual, and social problems, as well as traditional commercial ones.

CONTEXT

Other studies of the future of working tend to plunge head-first into celebrations of the miracles of technology with little attempt to understand the human implications. Toffler is aware of them.

Many of his ideas have since been developed further by others. Charles Handy, for instance, has done a lot of work on the rise of homeworking.

Gary Hamel, author of *Leading the Revolution*, commented: "The post-industrial society is here! And Alvin Toffler saw it coming in 1980. . .One of the challenges for anyone reading Toffler, or any other seer, is that there is no proprietary data about the future. Your competitors read Toffler, Naisbitt, and Negroponte too! The real challenge is to build proprietary foresight out of public data!"

For More Information

Toffler, Alvin. *The Third Wave*. New York: Bantam, 1980.

See also:
☆ **Alvin Toffler (pp. 1056–57)**

"Old ways of thinking, old formulas, dogmas, and ideologies, no matter how cherished or how useful in the past, no longer fit the facts."

(*The Third Wave*)

TOYOTA PRODUCTION SYSTEM

Taiichi Ohno

WHY READ IT?

During the last 40 years, Western carmakers have lurched from one crisis to another. They have always been one step behind. The company they have been following is the Japanese giant Toyota, and the reasons for this are explained by Taiichi Ohno in his brief book *Toyota Production System: Beyond Large-scale Production.*

GETTING STARTED

The Toyota Production System was developed to help the company catch up with the United States. U.S. car workers were producing nine times as much as their Japanese counterparts. The Toyota system differed from the Western approach, emphasizing a reduction in costs rather than an increase in selling price.

Acording to the author, the company should be seen as a continuous and uniform whole, including suppliers as well as customers. Asking the question "why?" five times at each stage helps identify and solve problems before moving on.

CONTRIBUTION

1. CATCHING UP WITH THE WEST

The roots of the Toyota Production System lie in the immediate postwar years.

Toyoda Kiichiro, president of Toyoda Motor Company, demanded that the company should catch up with the United States. He gave his company three years to do so. Otherwise, he anticipated, the Japanese car industry would cease to exist.

At that time in the car industry, an average U.S. worker produced around nine times as much as a Japanese worker.

2. A DIFFERENT APPROACH TO PRODUCTION

The Toyota Production System evolved by Ohno was strikingly different from approaches used in the West.

In the West, selling price was regarded as the combination of actual costs plus profit.

Toyota, believing that the consumer actually sets the price, concluded that profit resulted when costs were subtracted from the selling price. Their emphasis therefore was on reducing costs rather than increasing the selling price.

3. THE PRINCIPLES OF THE TOYOTA SYSTEM

The three simple principles of Toyota are:

- just-in-time production;
- wider responsibility for quality;
- concept of value stream.

4. JUST-IN-TIME PRODUCTION

There is no point in producing cars, or anything else, in blind anticipation of someone buying them; production has to be closely tied to the market's requirements.

5. WIDER RESPONSIBILITY FOR QUALITY

Responsibility for quality rests with everyone.

Any quality defects need to be rectified as soon as they are identified.

6. CONCEPT OF VALUE STREAM

The company should not be seen as a series of unrelated products and processes.

It should be seen as a continuous and uniform whole, a stream including suppliers as well as customers.

7. THE FIVE WHYS

Another central element in Ohno's system was the process of the five whys.

This suggested that by asking "why?" five times and discovering the answer at each stage, the root of any problem can be discovered and solved.

CONTEXT

These concepts were brought to mass Western audiences thanks to work carried out at the Massachusetts Institute of Technology as part of its International Motor Vehicle Program. The MIT research took five years, covered 14 countries, and looked exclusively at the worldwide car industry.

The researchers concluded that U.S. carmakers remained fixed in the mass-production techniques of the past. In contrast, Japanese management, workers, and suppliers worked to the same goals as each other-resulting in increased production, high quality, happy customers, and lower costs.

This research was the basis for the 1990 bestseller by James Womack, Daniel Jones, and Daniel Roos, *The Machine That Changed the World.* From lean production, Womack and Jones went on to propose the lean enterprise (based on research covering 25 U.S., Japanese, and German companies) and lean management. As with most management fads, it was wilfully misinterpreted. It became linked to reengineering and, more worryingly, with downsizing.

The reality is that lean production as introduced by Ohno and Toyota is a highly effective concept. It can provide the economies of scale of mass production; the sensitivity to market and customer needs usually associated with smaller companies, and job enrichment for employees.

The West continues to see lean production as a means of squeezing more production from fewer people. This is a fundamental misunderstanding. Reducing the number of employees is the end rather than the means. Western companies have tended to reduce numbers and then declare themselves as lean organizations.

Womack argues that while lean production requires fewer people, the organization should then accelerate product development to tap new markets to keep the people at work.

Inevitably, lean production has its downside. The most obvious one is that its natural home is the mass-manufacturing world of car making. It can be more difficult to apply in other industries.

The second obvious problem with lean production is that it fails to embrace innovation and product development. It is one thing being able to make a product efficiently, but how do you originate exciting and marketable products in the first place?

Womack and Jones would suggest that the critical starting point for lean thinking is value, but this is effectively one stage beyond the initial one of generating ideas. Even so, lean production has raised awareness, provided a new benchmark, and brought operational efficiency to a wider audience.

Harvard Business School's Michael Porter argues, "Organizations did well to employ the most up-to-date equipment, information technology, and management techniques to eliminate waste, defects, and delays. They did well to operate as close as they could to the productivity frontier. But while improving operational effectiveness is necessary to achieving superior profitability, it is not sufficient."

For More Information

Ohno, Taiichi. *Toyota Production System.* Cambridge, MA: Productivity Press, 1988.

"Toyota's emphasis therefore was on reducing costs rather than increasing the selling price."

(*Toyota Production System*)

  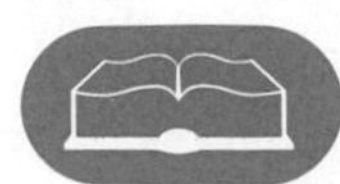    

THE WEALTH OF NATIONS

Adam Smith

WHY READ IT?

Many books are claimed to be classics or seminal works: *The Wealth of Nations* is indisputably both. It is a broad-ranging exploration of commercial and economic first principles. In it Adam Smith laid the philosophical foundations for modern capitalism and the modern market economy. There are few economists over the last 200 years—and fewer politicians of a free-market persuasion—who have not been influenced by it. Smith has helped shape the economic policies of British prime ministers and chancellors of the exchequer from the days of Lord North (1770–82) to those of Margaret Thatcher—and even Tony Blair.

GETTING STARTED

Adam Smith was a Scottish philosopher. He was professor of logic and professor of moral philosophy at Glasgow University, but left his university posts in order to travel on the continent as tutor to a young nobleman. In France he was greatly influenced by a school of philosophical economists known as the "physiocrats." Returning to his native town of Kirkcaldy in Fife, he spent ten years preparing *An Inquiry into the Nature and Causes of the Wealth of Nations*, which was published—a significant coincidence perhaps—in the year of the signing of the Declaration of Independence, 1776.

His central thesis is that capital can best be used for the creation of both individual and national wealth in conditions of minimal interference by government. The "invisible hand" of free-market competition ensures, in his view, both the vitality of commercial activity and the ultimate good of all a nation's citizens.

CONTRIBUTION

1. THE INVISIBLE HAND

According to Smith, conscious and well-meaning attempts to better the lot of a nation and its population are generally doomed to failure. The unintended cumulative effects of self-interested striving are far more effective. As he puts it: "Every individual is continually exerting to find out the most advantageous employment for whatever he can command. . .[and] necessarily labors to render the annual revenue of the society as great as he can. He generally neither intends to promote the public interest nor knows how much he is promoting it. He intends only his own gain, and he is in this, as in many other cases, led by an invisible hand to promote an end which was no part of his intention."

2. VALUE AND LABOR

The value of a particular good or service is determined by the costs of production. If something is expensive to produce, then its value is similarly high.

"The real price of everything, what everything really costs to the man who wants to acquire it, is the toil and trouble of acquiring it. What everything is really worth to the man who has acquired it, and who wants to dispose of it or exchange it for something else, is the toil and trouble of which it can save himself, and which it can impose on other people."

"What is bought with money or with goods is purchased by labour, as much as what we acquire by the toil of our own body. They contain the value of a certain quantity of labour which we exchange for what is supposed at the time to contain the value of an equal quantity."

3. THE DIVISION OF LABOR

Smith's legacy to scientific management was the concept of the division of labor.

"The division of labor occasions in every art a proportionable increase of the productive powers of labor. The separation of different trades and employments from one another seems to have taken place in consequence of this advantage."

"Men are much more likely to discover easier and readier methods of attaining any object when the whole attention of their minds is directed towards that single object than when it is dissipated among a great variety of things."

CONTEXT

For a book that is over 200 years old, there is a surprisingly modern-sounding ring to a great deal of what *The Wealth of Nations* has to say. This is mainly owing to the acuteness and lasting value of Smith's analysis—the book was the first comprehensive exploration of the foundations, workings, and machinations of a free market economy—but also to the familiarity of many of its basic concepts. *The Wealth of Nations* continues to have a role as a right-wing manifesto, a gloriously logical exposition of the beauty of market forces. And the appeal is not only to the right wing in politics.

Smith's system of demarcation and functional separation provided the basis for the management theorists of the early twentieth century, such as Frederick Winslow Taylor, and practitioners such as Henry Ford. They translated the economic rigor of his thinking to practices in the workplace, though in ways and to a scale that Smith could never have imagined.

History has, however, put its own limitations on Smith's theorizing.

- Physical labor is no longer so important.
- The 20th century saw the emergence of management as a profession. It is barely acknowledged by Smith.
- Smith wrote without knowledge of the power and scope of modern corporations, let alone the power of brand names and customer loyalty.
- He also wrote in harder times where self-interest was not a choice but a necessity.

Nevertheless, as Gary Hamel commented: "Revisionists be damned. Citizens from Prague to Santiago to Guangzhou to Jakarta owe much of their new-found prosperity to the triumph of Adam Smith's economic ideals. [He] laid the philosophical foundations for the modern industrial economy. Enough said."

For More Information

Smith, Adam. *The Wealth of Nations.* Amherst, NY: Prometheus Books, 1991.

See also:
Adam Smith (pp. 1048–49)

"The real and effectual discipline which is exercised over a workman is not that of his corporation, but that of his customers."

(*The Wealth of Nations*)

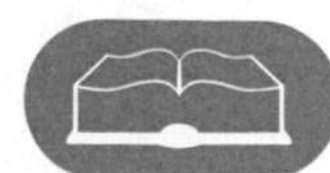

The Will to Manage

Marvin Bower

Why Read It?

Marvin Bower is the man who did more than anyone else to create the modern management consulting industry. The book gives a valuable insight into the management practices that made McKinsey and Company such a long-lasting success.

Getting Started

Marvin Bower's success grew on his principle that building trust with clients is critical to consultancy success. The interests of the client should precede increasing the company's revenues: if you look after the client, the profits look after themselves.

He also believed that using values to help shape and guide an organization is extremely important. One of those values is that regard for the individual is based not on title, but on competence, stature and leadership. Instead of experienced consultants, McKinsey recruited graduate students who could learn how to be good problem solvers and consultants. The company also developed "virtual" project teams, bringing in the best people in the organization wherever they were based in the world. Clear, simple employment policies and change through empowerment helped to maintain high professional standards.

Contribution

1. A New Way of Looking at Consultancies

Bower did not change the name of his company, McKinsey, as he shrewdly decided that clients would demand his involvement in projects if his name was up in lights. His vision was to provide advice on managing to top executives and to do it with the professional standards of a leading law firm. Due to a belief that in all successful professional groups, regard for the individual is based not on title but on competence, stature, and leadership, McKinsey consultants were associates who had engagements, rather than mere jobs, and the firm was a practice rather than a business.

2. Building Trust with Clients

The entire ethos of McKinsey was to be very respectable, the kind of people C.E.O.s naturally relate to. Bower's gospel was that the interests of the client should precede increasing the company's revenues: unless the client could trust McKinsey, the company could not work with them. If McKinsey looked after the client, the profits would look after themselves. High charges were not a means to greater profits, but a simple and effective means of ensuring that clients took McKinsey seriously.

Other central principles were that consultants should keep quiet about the affairs of clients, should tell the truth, and be prepared to challenge the client's opinion. They should only agree to do work which is both necessary and which they could do well. Using values to help shape and guide an organization was extremely important.

3. New Patterns of Recruitment

Instead of hiring experienced executives with in-depth knowledge of a particular industry, Bower recruited graduate students who could learn how to be good problem solvers and consultants. This changed the emphasis of consulting from passing on a narrow range of experience to using a wide range of analytical and problem-solving techniques.

4. Developing Virtual Project Teams

Another element of Bower's approach was the use of teams. He thought of McKinsey as a network of leaders. Teams were assembled for specific projects, and the best people in the organization were brought to bear on a particular problem, no matter where they were based in the world. McKinsey's culture fostered rigorous debate over the right answer, without that debate resulting in personal criticism.

5. Clear, Simple Employment Policies

The company's policy remains one of the most simple: seniority in McKinsey correlates directly with achievement. If a consultant ceases to progress with the organization, or is ultimately unable to demonstrate the skills and qualities required of a principal, he or she is asked to leave McKinsey.

6. Change through Empowerment

"There have been thousands of changes in methods, but not in command and control. Many companies say they want to change, but they need to empower people below. More cohesion is needed rather than hierarchy," Bower said in 1995.

Context

Under Bower's astute direction, McKinsey became the world's premier consulting firm. Recent years have also seen the structure and managerial style of the company receiving plaudits. McKinsey is special because it has developed a self-perpetuating aura that it is unquestionably the best. Marvin Bower was the creator of this organizational magic.

American Express chief, Harvey Golub, says that Bower led McKinsey according to a set of values, and it was the principle of using values to help shape and guide an organization that was probably the most important thing he took away.

For More Information

Bower, Marvin. *The Will to Manage*. New York: McGraw-Hill, 1966.

"If you looked after the client, the profits would look after themselves." (*The Will to Manage*)

Business Thinkers and Management Giants

Business Thinkers and Management Giants

Profiling the Top Management Thinkers and Pioneers

This section provides over one hundred profiles of the most influential or controversial business writers, entrepreneurs, and managers. The Business Thinkers and Management Giants range from pioneer and professor to performer and pundit. One factor links them all—they have all had an impact on current business practice.

Business Thinkers includes summaries of the career and thinking of the most important and influential writers on management, as well as an assessment of their contribution to business theory and practice. **Management Giants** is a highly selective and controversial gallery of some of the most successful business leaders—those mavericks in a range of industries who by their efforts have transformed the way a business is conducted. Being nice is not one of the main criteria for selection; being effective is.

CONTENTS

JOHN ADAIR

Action-centered Leadership

John Adair, best-known for his three-circle model of "action-centered leadership," is widely regarded as Britain's foremost authority on leadership in organizations. He believes that leadership can be taught, and his works have been instrumental in overturning the "great man" theories of leadership. He draws a distinction between leadership and management. Adair's ideas are practical and relevant to all managers. Many of his ideas on the practical aspects of leadership were ahead of their time.

1934	Born.
1963–1969	Senior lecturer in military history and leadership training advisor, Royal Military Academy, Sandhurst.
1969–1973	Assistant director at Industrial Society; pioneered "action-centered leadership."
1978	Becomes the world's first professor in leadership studies, at the University of Surrey, England.

LIFE AND CAREER

John Adair's early career was varied and colorful, and undoubtedly formed the basis for his views on leadership. After joining the Scots Guards he became the only national serviceman to serve in the Arab Legion, where he was adjutant in a Bedouin regiment. Before going to college he qualified as a deckhand and worked on an Icelandic trawler. He also worked as an orderly in a hospital operating room. After studying at Cambridge University, he became senior lecturer in military history, and leadership training advisor at the Royal Military Academy, Sandhurst. He went on to become the director of studies at St. George's House in Windsor Castle, and two years later was appointed assistant director of the Industrial Society, where he pioneered action-centered leadership.

In 1978, Adair became the world's first professor in leadership studies at the University of Surrey. He is currently visiting professor in leadership studies at the University of Exeter, and a consultant to many organizations around the world in business, government, education, health, and the voluntary sector.

For over three decades his overlapping, three-circle model of action-centered leadership has been integrated into company cultures and individual leadership styles, and is an established hallmark of management training for many organizations.

KEY THINKING

ACTION-CENTERED LEADERSHIP

This simple and practical model is based on three overlapping circles, representing the task, the team, and the individual. The model has endured well, probably because it is a fundamental description of what actions leaders must take in order to be effective:

- achieve the task;
- build and maintain the team;
- develop the individual.

Adair's concept asserts that the three needs of task, team, and individual are the building blocks of leadership, as people expect their leaders to help them achieve the common task, build the synergy of teamwork, and respond to individuals' needs.

- The task needs work groups or organizations to come into being because one person alone cannot accomplish it.
- The team needs constant promotion and retention of group cohesiveness to ensure that it succeeds. The team functions on the "united we stand, divided we fall" principle.
- The individual's needs are the physical ones (such as salary) and the psychological ones of recognition, sense of purpose and achievement, status, and the need to give and receive from others in a work environment.

For Adair, the task, team and individual needs overlap as follows:

- achieving the task builds the team and satisfies the individuals;
- if the team needs are not met (if the team lacks cohesiveness) performance of the task is impaired and individual satisfaction is reduced;
- if individual needs are not met, the team will lack cohesiveness and performance of the task will be impaired.

He holds that leadership exists at three different levels:

- team leadership, of teams of between 5 and 20 people;
- operational leadership, where a number of team leaders report to one main leader;
- strategic leadership, of a whole business or organization, with overall accountability for all levels of leadership.

Regardless of the level at which leadership is being exercised, Adair's model remains the same: task, team, and individual needs must constantly be considered.

The strengths of the concept are that it is both timeless and independent of situation or organizational culture. It can also help a leader to identify where he or she may be losing touch with the real needs of the group or situation.

THE FUNCTIONS OF LEADERSHIP

In order to fulfil the three aspects of leadership and achieve success, Adair believes that there are eight functions that must be performed by the leader:

- defining the task: Individuals and teams need to have the task distilled into a clear objective that is SMART (Specific, Measurable, Achievable, Realistic, and Time Constrained);
- planning: Planning requires a search for alternatives, best done with others in an open-minded, positive, and creative way. Contingencies should be planned for and plans should be tested;
- briefing: Team briefing is viewed as essential for creating the right atmosphere, promoting teamwork, and motivating each individual;
- controlling: Excellent leaders get maximum results with the minimum of resources. To achieve this, they need self-control, good control systems in place, and effective delegation and monitoring skills;
- evaluating: Leaders need to be good at assessing consequences, evaluating team performance, appraising and training individuals, and judging people;

"Leadership is about a sense of direction. . .It's knowing what the next step is." (John Adair)

- motivating: Adair distinguishes eight principles for motivating others: Be motivated yourself; select people who are highly motivated; treat each person as an individual; set realistic and challenging targets; remember that progress motivates; create a motivating environment; provide fair rewards; and give recognition;
- organizing: Good leaders have to be able to organize themselves, their team, and the organization (including structures and processes). Leading change requires a clear purpose and effective order to achieve results;
- setting an example: Leaders need to set an example both to individuals and to the team as a whole. Since a bad example is noticed more than a good one, providing a positive pattern to follow must be worked at constantly.

These leadership functions need to be developed and honed constantly to improve the leader's ability.

Motivating People

In many ways, Adair's ideas in the area of motivating people are in line with those of the classic motivational theorists, such as Maslow, McGregor, and Herzberg.

The 50:50 Rule

Just as the Pareto principle (or 80:20 rule) is the ratio of the vital few and the trivial many, the Adair 50:50 rule (from *Effective Motivation*) states that: "50% of motivation comes from within a person and 50% from his or her environment, especially from the leadership encountered therein."

Adair's view is that people are motivated by a number of complex factors. So, for example, he does not dismiss the "carrot and stick" approach, but sees it rather as one stimulus-response factor among many that might influence a person's actions.

The strength of an individual's motivation, is affected by what outcome the person expects from certain actions—and also what he or she would prefer that outcome to be (as demonstrated by Victor Vroom in the 1960s). Conditions in the working environment and the individual's own perceptions and fears are also factors that have an impact on strength of motivation.

Adair's Eight Rules in Motivating People

Adair proposes that understanding what motivates individuals is fundamental to engaging their interest and focusing their efforts. The will that leads to action is governed by motives, and motives are inner needs or desires that can be conscious, semiconscious or unconscious. In *The John Adair Handbook of Management and Leadership*, the point is made that "motives can also be mixed, with several clustered around a primary motive."

Adair emphasizes the importance of a motivating environment and a motivated individual. Another crucial factor is the role of the leader who must, he believes, be completely self-motivated. In *Effective Motivation*, eight basic rules are outlined to guide leaders in motivating people to act:

- be motivated yourself;
- select people who are highly motivated;
- treat each person as an individual;
- set realistic and challenging targets;
- remember that progress motivates;
- create a motivating environment;
- provide fair rewards;
- give recognition.

Developing a Personal Sense of Time

Adair's view of time management accords closely with Peter Drucker's, in that he argues that it is essential to manage time in order to manage anything else. He was one of the first management thinkers to emphasize the critical importance of time management and its central role in focusing action and helping leaders to achieve goals. Time management is not simply about being organized or efficient, or completing certain tasks, Adair states. It is about focusing on achievement: time management should be goal-driven and results-oriented.

Success in time management should be measured by the quantity of productive work achieved, and the quality of both the work and the person's private life. Ten principles of time management given in *How to Manage Your Time* are:

- develop a personal sense of time;
- identify long-term goals;
- make medium-term plans;
- plan the day;
- make the best use of your best time;
- organize office work;
- manage meetings;
- delegate effectively;
- make use of committed time;
- manage your health.

Of these 10 principles, developing a personal sense of time and increasing personal effectiveness are central to Adair, again highlighting his emphasis on individual characteristics.

John Adair in Perspective

Adair's ideas were very "different" when they first appeared, and for many people their main value lay in the successful challenge they offered to the "great man" theories that dominated then. These theories, because they insisted that leaders were born and not made, eliminated the possibility of training or developing people in leadership skills. So Adair's new ideas were welcomed and quickly became established.

Given the pace and scale of changes in the work environment during the last 20 years, however, it is perhaps not surprising that there has been something of a backlash against Adair, with critics claiming that his approach (developed in the 1960s) has itself now become outdated.

One major criticism of action-centered leadership is that it takes little account of the flat structures that are now generally advocated as the best organizational form. It is also judged to be too "authoritarian"—applicable in a formal, military-type environment but less relevant to the modern workplace, where the leadership emphasis is on leading change, empowering, enabling, managing knowledge, and fostering innovation.

Another criticism leveled at Adair's approach in recent years is that his ideas are too simplistic, merely stating the obvious, common sense view. For many people, however, it is exactly this simplicity and clarity about what a leader should do that is so valuable.

For More Information

Key works by Adair

Books:

Action-centered Leadership. New York: McGraw-Hill, 1984.
The Skills of Leadership. New York: Nichols Publishing Company, 1984.
Effective Motivation. Guildford: Talbot Adair Press, 1987.
The Action-centered Leader. London: Industrial Society, 1988.
Effective Leadership. Burlington, VT: Ashgate Publishing Co., 1983.
Great Leaders. Philadelphia: Trans-Atlantic Publications, 1997.
Understanding Motivation. Guildford: Talbot Adair Press, 1990.
How to Manage Your Time. Guildford: Talbot Adair Press, 1990.
Thomas, Neil, ed. *The John Adair Handbook of Management and Leadership*. London: Thorogood, 1998.

See also:

☆ **Leadership (pp. 226–28)**
Frederick Herzberg (pp. 1002–03)
Warren Bennis (pp. 968–69)

"The capacity to create a compelling vision and translate it into action and sustain it."

(Warren Bennis)

Igor Ansoff

Father of Corporate Strategy

Igor Ansoff was the originator of the strategic management concept, and was responsible for establishing strategic planning as a management activity in its own right. His landmark book, *Corporate Strategy* (1965), was the first text to concentrate entirely on strategy, and it remains one of the classics of management literature.

The John Carter Brown Library at Brown University, Ansoff's alma mater.

1918	Born.
1936	Family emigrates to the United States.
1950	Joins the Rand Corporation.
1957	Publishes article "Strategies for Diversification" that presents the Ansoff Matrix.
1963	Appointed professor of industrial administration at the Carnegie Institute of Technology, Pittsburgh.
1965	*Corporate Strategy* published.
1983	Joins U.S. International University as professor of strategic management.
2000	Retires from academic life.

Life and Career

H. Igor Ansoff was born in Russia in 1918 and his family emigrated to the United States in 1936. His early academic focus was on mathematics, and he obtained a Ph.D. in applied math from Brown University, in Rhode Island. He joined the Rand Corporation in 1950, and moved on to the Lockheed Aircraft Corporation, where he eventually became vice president, plans and programs, and then vice president and general manager of the industrial technology division.

In 1963 Ansoff was appointed professor of industrial administration at the Carnegie Institute of Technology in Pittsburgh. He went on to hold a number of positions in universities in both the United States and Europe. Although he still acts as a consultant, he retired from academia in 2000 and, on his retirement, was named Distinguished Professor Emeritus at the United States International University.

Key Thinking

Until the publication of *Corporate Strategy*, companies had little guidance on how to plan for, or make decisions about, the future. Traditional methods of planning were based on an extended budgeting system that used the annual budget, projecting it a few years into the future. By its nature this system paid little or no attention to strategic issues. With the advent of greater competition, higher interest in acquisitions, mergers, and diversification, and greater turbulence in the business environment, however, strategic issues could no longer be ignored. Ansoff felt that, in developing strategy, it was essential to anticipate future environmental challenges to an organization systematically, and draw up appropriate strategic plans for responding to these challenges.

He explored these issues in *Corporate Strategy* and built up a systematic approach to strategy formulation and strategic decision-making through a framework of theories, techniques, and models.

Strategy Decisions

Ansoff identified four standard types of organizational decisions as related to strategy, policy, programs, and standard operating procedures. The last three of these, he argued, are designed to resolve recurring problems or issues and, once formulated, do not require an original decision each time. This means that the decision process can easily be delegated. Strategy decisions are different, however, because they always apply to new situations and so need to be made anew every time.

Ansoff developed a new classification of decision-making, partially based on Alfred Chandler's work, *Strategy and Structure* (Cambridge, MA: MIT Press, 1962). This distinguished decisions as either: *strategic* (focused on the areas of products and markets); *administrative* (organizational and resource allocating), or *operating* (budgeting and directly managing). Ansoff's decision classification became known as Strategy-Structure-Systems, or the 3S model. (Sumantra Ghoshal has since proposed a 3Ps model—purpose, process, and people—to replace it.)

Components of Strategy

Ansoff argued that within a company's activities there should be an element of core capability, an idea later adopted and expanded by Hamel and Prahalad. To establish a link between past and future corporate activities (the first time such an approach was undertaken) Ansoff identified four key strategy components:

- product-market scope—a clear idea of what business or products a company was responsible for (predating the exhortations of Peters and Waterman to "stick to the knitting");
- growth vector—as explained in the section below on the Ansoff matrix, this offers a way of exploring how growth may be attempted;
- competitive advantage—those advantages an organization possesses that will enable it to compete effectively—a concept later championed by Michael Porter;
- synergy—Ansoff explained synergy as "2 + 2 = 5," or how the whole is greater than the mere sum of the parts; it requires an examination of how opportunities fit the core capabilities of the organization.

Ansoff Matrix

Variously known as the "product-mission matrix" or the "2 x 2 growth vector component matrix," the Ansoff Matrix remains a popular tool for organizations that wish to understand the risk component of various growth strategies including product versus market development, and diversification. The matrix was first published in a 1957 article called "Strategies for diversification" and the example below illustrates what such a matrix may look like:

	Present	New
Present	1. Market penetration	2. Market expansion
New	3. Product expansion	4. Diversification

"History consists of the tracks made by strategy and includes the risks players take, whether they win or lose."

(George Konrád)

Of the four strategies given in the matrix, *market penetration* requires increasing existing product market share in existing markets; *market expansion* requires the identification of new customers for existing products; *product expansion* requires developing new products for existing customers; and *diversification* requires new products to be produced for new markets.

Ansoff's article focused particularly on diversification as a potentially high-growth but also high-risk strategy that necessitates careful prior planning and analysis before any decision is taken. In Ansoff's view it requires organizations to "break with past patterns and traditions" as they enter on "uncharted paths" where, generally, new skills, techniques, and resources will be required. His matrix offered a method of carefully analyzing and evaluating the profit potential of diversification strategies.

Paralysis by Analysis

It has sometimes been suggested that the application of the ideas in *Corporate Strategy* can lead to an over-heavy emphasis on analysis. Ansoff himself recognized this possibility, however, and coined the now famous phrase "paralysis by analysis" to describe the type of procrastination caused by excessive planning.

Turbulence

The issue of turbulence underlies all of Ansoff's work on strategy. One of his key aims in establishing a better framework for strategy formulation was to improve the existing planning processes of the stable, postwar economy of the United States, since he realized these would not be sufficient to cope with the pressures that rapid and discontinuous change would place on them.

By the 1980s change, and the pace of change, had become a key issue for management in most organizations. Ansoff recognized, however, that if some organizations were faced with conditions of great turbulence, others still operated in relatively stable conditions. Consequently, although strategy formulation had to take environmental turbulence into account, one strategy could certainly not be made to fit every industry. These ideas are discussed in *Implanting Strategic Management*, where five levels of environmental turbulence are outlined as:

- repetitive—change is at a slow pace, and is predictable;
- expanding—a stable marketplace, growing gradually;
- changing—incremental growth, with customer requirements altering fairly quickly;
- discontinuous—characterized by some predictable change and some more complex change;
- surprising—change that cannot be predicted and that both develops, and develops from, new products or services.

Igor Ansoff in Perspective

Although Ansoff's work is frequently referred to by strategists, it has not become as generally recognized as that of other theorists. The complexity of his work, and its reliance on the disciplines of analysis and planning, are perhaps among the reasons why Ansoff is not popularly viewed as belonging within the top echelons of management thinkers.

Other theorists were working on similar themes to Ansoff at similar times. In the 1960s Ansoff's notion of competence (which was later developed by Hamel and Prahalad) was not unique, and although Ansoff seems to have been the originator of his 2 x 2 growth vector component matrix, a similar matrix had been published earlier. It is likely that much work done during the 1980s and 1990s by other theorists on strategy formation under conditions of uncertainty or chaos owed something to Ansoff's theory of turbulence, though it is difficult to evaluate the extent of the debt.

A debate between Ansoff and Henry Mintzberg over their differing views of strategy has been reflected in print over many years, particularly in the *Harvard Business Review*. Ansoff has often been criticized by Mintzberg, who dislikes the idea of strategy being built from planning that is supported by analytical techniques. This criticism is based on the belief that Ansoff's reliance on planning suffers from three fallacies: that events can be predicted, that strategic thinking can be separated from operational management, and that hard data, analysis, and techniques can produce novel strategies.

Ansoff was one of the earliest writers on strategy as a management discipline, and laid strong foundations for several later writers to build upon, including Michael Porter, Gary Hamel, and C. K. Prahalad. He invented the modern approach to strategy, and his work pulled together various ideas and disparate strands of thought, giving a new coherence and discipline to the concept he described as strategic planning. During the 1970s and 1980s, this concept shaped more ideas about management as other writers took up ideas of Ansoff's such as core competence or "sticking to the knitting."

For More Information

Key works by or about Ansoff

Books:

Corporate Strategy. New York: McGraw-Hill, 1965.

Ansoff, Igor, with Roger P. DeClerck and Robert L. Hayes. *From Strategic Planning to Strategic Management*. New York: John Wiley/Interscience, 1975.

Strategic Management. London: MacMillan, 1979.

Implanting Strategic Management. Upper Saddle River, NJ: Prentice Hall, 1984.

The New Corporate Strategy. New York: John Wiley, 1988. (Revised edition of *Corporate Strategy*.)

Journal Articles:

"Strategies for Diversification." *Harvard Business Review*, Sept./Oct., vol. 35 no. 5, 1957, pp. 113–124.

"The Firm of the Future." *Harvard Business Review*, Sept./Oct., vol. 43 no. 5, 1965, pp. 162–174.

Hussey, David. "Igor Ansoff's Continuing Contribution to Strategic Management." *Strategic Change*, Nov., vol. 8 no. 7, 1999, pp. 375–392.

See also:

☆ **Viewpoint: Christopher Bartlett (pp. 45–46)**
Corporate Strategy (p. 902)

"Structure will become a dynamic enabler of both change and unchange, the ultimate model of organizational chaos."
(Igor Ansoff)

Chris Argyris

The Manager's Academic

Chris Argyris's career may look more like that of a classical academic than that of a management guru but a stuffy academic he is not. His passionate interest in management and organizational problems makes him one of the most respected management thinkers of our time. He is also as much at home in the factory and boardroom as in academia. Argyris is first and foremost a behavioral scientist, with a career devoted to understanding how organizations behave and how managers learn.

1923	Born.
1960	Publication of *Understanding Organizational Behavior.*
1968	Moves from Yale to Harvard Business School.
1971	Appointed James Bryant Conant Professor of Education and Organization Behavior, Harvard Business School.
1978	Publication of *Organizational Learning.*

Life and Career

Chris Argyris was born in 1923 and at an early age developed an interest in how people learn. "It sounds corny, but I love learning for its own sake," is how he explains it. After service in World War II he returned home and, like so many young men at that time, felt a strong determination to help create a better world. Fortunately for us, he chose to direct his interest in education toward the needs of organizations and the individuals working in them. His great energy and formidable academic qualifications—a baccalaureate in psychology, a Masters in economics, and a Doctorate in organization behavior—equipped him perfectly for the task, and by the early 1950s he was teaching and carrying out research at Yale University.

By the mid 1960s he was Professor of Industrial Administration at Yale and in 1968 he moved to the Harvard Business School where, in 1971, he became the James Bryant Conant Professor of Education and Organization Behavior.

His consulting work has been wide-ranging and highly influential. Clients have included IBM, DuPont and Shell, along with the U.S. State Department, other U.S. government bodies and several overseas governments.

Key Thinking

A staunch supporter of job enrichment, Argyris has always challenged the extremes of Taylorism, especially the suggestion that one "hires a hand," rather than a whole person. Underlying virtually all his thinking is a fundamental belief in people, and he tirelessly reminds us of the mutual benefit that comes when organizations assist and encourage individuals to develop their full potential. He believes that each person already has the "psychological energy" that provides motivation. The challenge, he suggests, is not to find ways of artificially motivating people; it is to recognize and channel this innate energy.

T-Groups

Chris Argyris was the main force behind the groundbreaking T-group experiments in the 1960s. "T-group training" is a phrase used to describe a number of similar training methods, the purpose of which is to increase the trainee's skills in working with other people—and a considerable proportion of time on such a training course is spent in discussing the trainees' relationships with one another. Argyris was not alone in being elated by the success of T-groups, by their power to unfreeze the rigid, authoritarian behavior of so many managers and to generate a feeling of liberation and excitement. However, as we now know, for most people these positive effects are short-lived. Once back in the turmoil of life in their organization, mixing again with those who have not been trained, the resolution and ideas are quickly forgotten, and people revert to their old ways of doing things.

This rapid return to their original behavior patterns by people who had been extremely enthusiastic about the "new approach" generated by T-group training led Argyris to formulate an idea that has affected people's views about organizational behavior for many years. The way people behave in organizations, he suggests, shows that there is a sharp difference between the beliefs they profess and the beliefs on which they appear to act.

"Espoused Theories" and "Theories-in-use"

Argyris coined the term "Espoused Theories" for things that people profess to believe, and the term "Theories-in-use" for those that they appear to believe when faced with problems in the real world, concluding, after much research, that, no matter how genuinely we believe in some approach to a situation, at the first sign of threat, embarrassment, or loss of face, most of us fall back on a deep-rooted "master program" of behavior. This behavior, which is characterized by a powerful defensive attitude and a tendency to blame others while struggling to maintain control and save face, is surprisingly consistent across different cultures and classes.

Not only do people slip easily into defensive routines, but they also remain totally unaware that they are doing so. It is a reflex action, an automatic response to any threat or challenge. Argyris argues that the organization can inhibit learning because it imposes—perhaps unconsciously—rules over the ways in which people relate to one another. He maintains that problem solving and decision making can be dominated by an almost unconscious drive to "save face," "protect others," or maintain the status quo. What concerns him most about this behavior is that it blocks any opportunity people have to learn from experience and provides an all too effective strategy for avoiding change.

Single-loop and Double-loop Learning

Concern at people's failure to learn from experience has led Argyris to the theory for which he is best known: the concept of single- and double-loop learning. Developed in collaboration with Donald Schön, and

---

"Individual learning is a necessary but insufficient condition for organizational learning."

(Chris Argyris)

described in their book *Organizational Learning* published in 1978, the theory stresses the importance of human reasoning as a basis for decisions and action.

Their work also produced the idea of a "learning organization." An organization, Argyris and Schön suggest, differs from a mob by having procedures for making collective decisions, by delegating authority to individuals to act for the "collectivity," and by setting out boundaries and rules. Norms and strategies are developed for all this activity, but in a healthy organization these are constantly being tested and challenged as people interact and learn new ideas. When the constant learning of people within an organization is reflected in the way the organization itself changes and develops, then the organization itself can reasonably be described as learning—hence the term "learning organization."

The two types of learning—single-loop and double-loop—refers to the way people respond to changes in their environment. Single-loop learning occurs when a manager responds to a problem with a simple "application of the rules." For example: problem, budgets are being exceeded; solution, cut costs. Argyris uses a thermostat as an analogy for single-loop learning; the thermostat switches the heating on and off in response to temperature changes.

Double-loop learning goes beyond this simple feedback response and questions the assumptions on which the response is based. In the thermostat model, the double-loop approach would be to question the validity of the selected temperature. In the example involving exceeded budgets, the double-loop approach would be to check the appropriateness of the budget figure and the basis on which it was calculated. Speaking to a conference in 1982, Argyris described the theory thus:

"Learning can be defined as occurring under two conditions. First, learning occurs when an organization achieves what it intended; that is, there is a match between its design for action and the actual outcome. Second, learning occurs when a mismatch between intention and outcome is identified and corrected; that is, a mismatch is turned into a match. . . Single-loop learning occurs when matches are created, or when mismatches are corrected by changing actions. Double-loop learning occurs when mismatches are corrected by examining and altering first the governing variables and then the actions."

Chris Argyris in Perspective

Argyris's work is rarely a comfort to managers. He raises profound questions about how we run organizations and frequently throws into doubt much of what is widely accepted to be "good practice." And when he does outline solutions they are never simple or easy. What he offers, and what makes his contribution to management thinking so important, is a profound and detailed exploration of the fundamental principles of organization behavior and human interaction in the workplace. He pulls no punches when showing us how hard we will have to work, and how much we will have to change if we are to achieve our full potential; but he is equally convincing when describing the rewards we will receive for our efforts.

Future

In recent years Argyris has been looking at leadership and, after considerable research, he claims the massive literature on this overworked subject has failed to produce anything practical. Such strong views should make his forthcoming book on leadership compelling reading.

He is also taking a lively interest in IT, something he feels will play a key role in learning within organizations. He says, "In the past the one-way, top-down approach gained strength from the fact that a lot of behavior is not transparent. IT makes transactions transparent so that behavior is no longer hidden. It creates fundamental truths where none previously existed."

For More Information

Key works by Argyris

Books:

Personality and Organization: The Conflict between the System and the Individual. New York: Harper & Row, 1957.
Understanding Organizational Behavior. Homewood, IL: Dorsey Press, 1960.
Reasoning, Learning, and Action: Individual and Organization. San Francisco: Jossey-Bass, 1982.
Overcoming Organizational Defenses: Facilitating Organizational Learning. Boston, MA: Allyn and Bacon, 1990.
Knowledge for Action. San Francisco: Jossey-Bass, 1993.
On Organizational Learning. Cambridge, MA: Blackwell Business, 1994.
Argyris, Chris, with Donald Schön. *Organizational Learning II: Theory, Method, and Practice* (2nd edition). Reading, MA: Addison-Wesley, 1996.

Journal Articles:

"Teaching Smart People How to Learn." *Harvard Business Review*, May/June 1991, pp. 99–109.
"Education for Leading Learning." *Organizational Dynamics*, Winter 1993, pp. 5–17.
"Good Communication That Blocks Learning." *Harvard Business Review*, July/August 1994, pp. 77–85.

See also:

☆ **Action Learning (pp. 12–13)**
Organizational Learning (p. 938)
Kurt Lewin (pp. 1014–15)
Peter Senge (pp. 1046–47)

"Managers who are skilled communicators may also be good at covering up real problems."
(Chris Argyris)

R. Meredith Belbin

Team Builder

R. Meredith Belbin is acknowledged as the father of team-role theory. As a result of research carried out in the 1970s, he identified eight (later extended to nine) useful roles that are necessary for a successful team. His contribution has gained in significance because of the widespread adoption of teamworking in the late 1980s and 1990s.

1926	Born.
1981	Publication of *Management Teams: Why They Succeed or Fail.*
1987	Founds Belbin Associates.
1990	Publication of *The Job Promoters: A Journey to a New Profession.*
1993	Publication of *The Coming Shape of Organization* and *Team Roles at Work.*
1997	Publication of *Changing the Way We Work.*
2000	Publication of *Beyond the Team.*
2001	Publication of *Managing without Power.*
	Visiting Professor of Leadership at the University of Exeter, United Kingdom.

Life and Career

Belbin, who was born in 1926, is an academic who has also spent periods working in industry and who now has his own consulting company. It was while working at the Industrial Training Research Unit in Cambridge that he was asked by Henley Management College to conduct some research into the operation of management teams. The college's approach to management education was based on group work, and researchers there had noticed that some teams of individually able executives performed poorly and others well. This impression was reinforced when a business game was introduced to one of the courses. Belbin discovered that it was the contribution of particular personality types, rather than the merits of the individuals themselves, that was important to the success and failure of such teams.

Key Thinking

There has been a continuing interest in Belbin's work because teamworking is an increasingly important strategy for organizations. There are many reasons for this. Teamworking is variously seen as a means of:

- providing greater worker flexibility and cooperation;
- helping to achieve cultural shifts within an organization;
- improving problem-solving and project management;
- tapping the talents of everyone in the organization.

There are also different types of teams involved in working together, for example, temporary teams, cross-functional teams, top management teams, and self-directed teams. Because of this interest in teams, the issue of team building, including team selection, group dynamics, and team performance, has become particularly vital. Although there are many models of team relationships, such as the Team Management Systems (TMS) developed by Margerison and McCann, Belbin's model is probably the best known.

Team Role Theory

It is important to remember that Belbin's findings relate to teams of managers rather than other types of teams. They were first published in *Management Teams: Why They Succeed or Fail* and later refined in *Team Roles at Work*. In Belbin's own words, a team role "describes a pattern of behavior characteristic of the way in which one team member interacts with another where his performance serves to facilitate the progress of the team as a whole."

The essence of his theory is that, given knowledge of the abilities and characteristics of individual team members, success or failure can be predicted within certain limits. As a result, unsuccessful teams can be improved by analyzing their shortcomings and making changes. But it is also important for individuals within the team to understand the roles that others play, when and how to let another team member take over, and how to compensate for shortcomings. Although each of the eight roles have to be filled for a team to work effectively, the eight roles are not needed in equal measure, nor are they needed at the same time. There can be fewer than eight people in a team, since people are capable of taking on back-up roles where there is less need for them to fulfil a primary team role.

The roles themselves are determined largely by the psychological makeup of individuals who instinctively adopt them. Four principal factors are involved: intelligence, dominance, extroversion/introversion, and stability/anxiety. Each role demands a particular combination of the four. Any individual can be rated in terms of them. In the list of team role contributions, the ratings for each particular trait are shown.

The Self-perception Inventory and the Interplace System

Belbin devised a self-perception inventory, which has been through several revisions, as a quick and easy way for individual managers to work out what their own team roles should be. It was taken up by organizations and used to determine employees' team types, and it has been questioned whether it is psychometrically acceptable for this purpose. Academics were concerned that it was too subjective and recommended that feedback should come instead from a range of sources. Belbin answered this criticism by reiterating that the inventory was never designed for this purpose and by developing a computerized system called *Interplace* to cater to the wider needs of organizations.

Interplace is a more sophisticated approach to role analysis than the self-perception inventory because it incorporates feedback from other people, not just the individual concerned. The main inputs to the *Interplace* system use data from self-perception exercises, observer assignments, and job requirement evaluations. *Interplace* filters, scores, stores, converts, and interprets the data gathered. It offers advice based on the three inputs with respect to counseling, team role chemistry, career development, and the behaviors needed in certain jobs and team positions. The system works as a diagnostic and development tool for organizations.

Later Theories

In the 1990s Belbin extended his work on teams to explore the link between teams and the organizational environment in which they operate. He suggested that an effective model for the new flatter organization might be a spiral or helix in which individuals and teams move forward on the basis of excellence rather than of function.

He has also very recently devised a system for defining jobs which he calls "Workset." The aim of the concept is to define the boundaries and content of a job through an interactive communication process between the manager and the jobholder. The system uses color to denote different aspects of the job. There should be five key outcomes:

- the facilitation of empowerment;
- the encouragement of greater job flexibility;
- the promotion of teamworking;
- the support of cultural change;
- a continuous improvement process for jobs and job holders.

It is too early to say what impact the Progression Helix theory or Workset system will have. They are undoubtedly a contribution, however, to management in today's delayered organizations and flexible working environments, with their associated need to involve and communicate with staff.

R. Meredith Belbin in Perspective

Although independent recent research has thrown doubt on the existence of nine separate team roles, Belbin's broad findings have not been questioned, nor has the popularity of his theories been disputed. There has been an enduring interest in team role categories on the part of practicing managers in a wide variety of organizations. This is because:

- there is an increasing interest in teamworking
- Belbin made his ideas accessible to the lay person
- Belbin is recognized as the first to develop our understanding of the dynamics of teams.

For More Information

Key works by Belbin

Books:

Management Teams: Why They Succeed or Fail. Woburn, MA: Heinemann, 1981.
Team Roles at Work. Woburn, MA: Butterworth-Heinemann, 1993.
The Coming Shape of Organization. Woburn, MA: Butterworth-Heinemann, 1996.
Changing the Way We Work. Woburn, MA: Butterworth-Heinemann, 1997.

Journal Articles:

Belbin, Meredith, Barrie Watson, and Cindy West. "True Colours." *People Management*, 6 March 1997, pp. 36–38, 41.
Senior, Barbara. "An Empirically-based Assessment of Belbin's Team Roles." *Human Resource Management Journal*, vol. 8 no 3, 1998, pp. 54–60.
Furnham, Adrian, Howard Steele, and David Pendleton. "A Psychometric Assessment of the Belbin Team Role Self-perception Inventory." *Journal of Occupational and Organizational Psychology*, vol. 66 no 3, 1993, pp. 245–261. (This article includes Belbin's criticism of the research and the response of the authors.)

Web Site:

www.belbin.com contains a useful list of answers to frequently asked questions about team role theory, as well as an online team analysis and reports service. It also contains helpful information on Belbin's latest work on Work Roles.

See also:

☆ **The Critical Factors That Make or Break Teams (pp. 192–93)**
Management Teams: Why They Succeed or Fail (p. 919)
Teams and Team Building (pp. 2121–23)

"Corporations have been preoccupied with the qualifications, experience, and achievements of individuals."
(Anthony Jay)

WARREN BENNIS

Leadership Guru

Warren Bennis has worked as an educator, writer, administrator, and consultant, besides authoring or coauthoring many books on different topics. He has carried out highly respected work in the areas of small group dynamics, change in social systems, T-groups, and sensitivity training, and during the 1960s became a recognized futurologist. Bennis wrote his first article on leadership in 1959, and he has become a widely accepted authority on the subject since 1985, when *Leaders* was published.

1925	Born.
1959	Sets up department for organizational studies at MIT.
1967	Appointed Provost of State University of New York (SUNY).
1971	President of the University of Cincinnati.
1979	Professor of Management at the University of Southern California.
1985	Publication of *Leaders: The Strategies for Taking Charge*.
1989	Publication of *On Becoming a Leader*.
1997	Publication of *Organizing Genius*.

LIFE AND CAREER

Bennis was born in New York in 1925 and educated at Antioch College and the Massachusetts Institute of Technology (MIT). Later, he studied group dynamics, and during the 1950s was involved in the U.S. National Training Laboratories teamworking experiments. His early field of work was organizational development.

Bennis was a great admirer of Douglas McGregor and his "Theory Y" approach to motivation. In fact, Bennis became very close to McGregor and was strongly influenced by him. His career path even followed McGregor's to some extent. First, he was an undergraduate student at Antioch College while McGregor was President there, and later, in 1959, he was recruited by McGregor to set up a new department for organization studies at MIT. From the late 1960s, Bennis's career moved for a time from academic research and teaching to administration. He became Provost at the State University of New York (SUNY), Buffalo, in 1967, staying there until 1971, when he moved to take on the post of President of the University of Cincinnati.

As an administrative leader from 1967 to 1978, Bennis attempted to put McGregor's motivation theories into practice, and found them unworkable without some adaptation in the form of strengthened structure and direction.

During the 1960s, Bennis became known as a student of the future, and predicted (with coauthor Philip Slater in a March 1964 article for the Harvard Business Review called "Democracy Is Inevitable") the downfall of communism. By the mid-1960s, he was predicting the demise of bureaucratic organization. His 1968 book *The Temporary Society* explored new forms of organization, advocating an "adhocracy" of free-moving project teams as a future necessity. This idea has since been taken up by other writers, such as Toffler and Mintzberg.

In an adhocracy, responsibility and leadership are distributed to groups or task forces on the basis of the relevance of members' qualifications or abilities for the specific task or purpose of the group. For Bennis, adhocracy was an important concept as a counter to hierarchy, centralized control, and bureaucratic organization.

KEY THINKING

In his early book on leadership, *The Unconscious Conspiracy* (1976), Bennis highlights how leaders can positively influence others to bring about change. His most distinctive ideas on the subject, however, partly grew out of the broad, general response to a landmark *Harvard Business Review* article of 1977 by Abraham Zaleznik (then Professor of the Social Psychology of Management at Harvard).

The Zaleznik article was entitled "Managers and Leaders—Are They Different?" Bennis's research and writing were extreme in emphasizing a complete, qualitative difference between management and leadership, and he drew up a list of sharp distinctions that ended with the now familiar aphorism: "Managers do things right, leaders do the right thing." While Bennis considers that managers can become leaders through learning and development, he is firm about the functional differences between the roles and the approaches involved, and the distinctions he draws echo throughout most of his writings on leadership.

THE LEADERS STUDY

In 1979, on his return to research and teaching as Professor of Management at the University of Southern California, Bennis sought to unravel the lessons of his practical experience of leadership. He explored the subject through a 1985 serial study that was published as a book coauthored with Burt Nanus, called *Leaders: The Strategies for Taking Charge* (1985). While Bennis has written or co-written many other books relating to leadership, these largely expand on the ideas developed in *Leaders*.

Leaders aimed to identify common characteristics among 90 successful American leaders who had all, the authors considered, demonstrated "mastery over present confusion" in their careers. The leaders ranged from an orchestra conductor to Ray Kroc, the founder of McDonald's, and included a baseball player and a tightrope walker, as well as the astronaut Neil Armstrong. It was Bennis's second book on leadership, selling over 300,000 copies, and is still considered an important text on the subject.

In *Leaders*, Bennis and Nanus identify four common factors amongst the participants, and these form the core of their ideas about leadership.

- Attention through vision—all had an agenda, an intense vision and commitment that drew others in. The leaders also gave much attention to other people.
- Meaning through communication—all had an ability to communicate their vision and bring it to life for others, sometimes using drawings or models as well as metaphor and analogy.
- Trust through positioning—through establishing a position with a set of actions to implement their vision, and

"Successful executives are great askers." (Warren Bennis)

staying the course, the leaders established trust.

- The deployment of self through positive self-regard—the creative deployment of self is essential to leadership, involving an honest appreciation of oneself and one's own worth, and instilling confidence in others.

Positive self-regard is related to "emotional wisdom," and five key skills in emotional wisdom are given as the abilities to:

- accept others as they are;
- approach things in terms of only the present;
- treat others, even familiar contacts, with courteous attention;
- trust others, even where the risk seems high;
- do without constant approval and recognition.

One quality common to these leaders that Bennis and Nanus particularly distinguished was their way of responding to failure as a learning experience. Karl Wallenda, the great tightrope aerialist, was taken as a main example. The authors illustrate his manner of putting his energies completely into his task, thinking of failure as a mistake from which he could learn, and viewing this experience (of learning based on failure) as a new beginning, rather than the end, for a project or idea.

"Transformative" Leadership

The style of leadership discussed by Bennis and Nanus is termed "transformative," in that it is said to have an empowering effect on others, enabling them to translate intentions into reality. A transformative leadership style is described as one that motivates through identification with the leader's vision, pulling rather than pushing others on.

Four elements of empowerment are distinguished as:

- significance—a feeling of making a difference;
- competence—development and learning "on the job";
- community—a sense of interreliance and involvement in a common cause;
- enjoyment—capacity to have fun at work because it is enjoyable and involving.

The four major characteristics of transformative leaders identified earlier are linked to strategic approaches through which a leader leads.

- The creation of a compelling vision: a leader must develop and communicate an image, or vision, of a credible and attractive future for the organization.
- The translation of meaning into social architecture: social architecture is the intangible variable that translates the buzz and confusion of organizational life into meaning. While similar to culture, social architecture is more precise in meaning, in that it can be defined, assessed and, to some extent, managed. Three styles of social architecture are distinguished as formalistic, collegial, and personalistic.
- The position of the organization in the outside world: positioning of an organization is described as the process by which it establishes a viable niche in its environment. It encompasses all that must be done to align the internal and external environments of the organization.
- The development of organizational learning: good leaders are experts at learning within an organizational context, and their behavior can help to direct and energize innovative learning within the organization as a whole.

The end result of transformative leadership is, Bennis and Nanus consider, an empowering environment and accompanying culture, enabling employees to generate a sense of meaning in their work. Higher profits and wages, the authors suggest, inevitably accompany this sort of culture, if it is genuinely established.

At the end of the book, five myths about leadership are identified and contradicted:

- That leadership is a rare skill—it is not.
- That leaders are born—they are not.
- That leaders are charismatic—most are ordinary.
- That leadership can exist only at the "top"—it is relevant at all levels
- That leaders control, direct, and manipulate—they do not. Transformative leaders align the energies of others behind an attractive goal.

Later Work

A later, prominent book by Bennis, *On Becoming a Leader* (1989), looks at learning to lead, developing leadership qualities, and how leadership can be taught. It uses 29 well-known Americans as case studies to illustrate leadership qualities. Its main message suggests that becoming a leader involves continual learning, development and the reinvention of the self.

Bennis has since written or co-written many books and articles that expand on and develop his ideas on leadership. His more recent works focus on the important roles of followers and groups, as well as on leadership. In *Organizing Genius* (1997), a collaborative work with Patricia Ward Biederman, Bennis almost returns to his roots in group work. The book looks at the history of seven well-known groups in action, including Walt Disney's animation studios, President Clinton's 1992 election campaign, and Lockheed's "skunk works." Common features of these successful groups are highlighted, and the mutually interdependent relationship between great leaders and great groups is stressed.

Warren Bennis in Perspective

The importance of Bennis's work in the field of leadership is indisputable and his informal and easy-mannered style of writing and use of practical illustrations have made his books very approachable. The management writer Stuart Crainer emphasizes Bennis's humane approach to leadership. Bennis views leadership as a skill that can be developed by ordinary people and that centers on enabling and empowering others rather than on control and direction. He is sometimes criticized as a romantic in his approach and has himself affirmed (in *The Director* of October 1988), that he is indeed a romantic, if that term accurately describes someone who believes in possibilities, and is optimistic.

For More Information

Key works by Bennis

Books:

The Unconscious Conspiracy: Why Leaders Can't Lead. New York: AMACOM, 1976.

Leaders: The Strategies for Taking Charge. New York: Harper & Row, 1985.

On Becoming a Leader. Cambridge, MA: Perseus, 1989.

Why Leaders Can't Lead: The Unconscious Conspiracy Continues. San Francisco: Jossey-Bass, 1989.

Bennis, Warren, with Patricia Ward Biederman. *Organizing Genius: The Secrets of Creative Collaboration*. Cambridge, MA: Perseus, 1997.

Managing People is like Herding Cats. Provo, UT: Executive Excellence Publishing, 1998.

Managing the Dream: Reflections on Leadership and Change. Cambridge, MA: Perseus, 2000.

See also:

Charles Handy (pp. 1000–01)

Abraham Maslow (pp. 1018–19)

Douglas McGregor (pp. 1022–23)

Henry Mintzberg (pp. 1024–25)

"Empowerment is the collective effort of leadership." (Warren Bennis)

Kenneth Blanchard

The One Minute Manager

The One Minute Manager was first published in in 1982. Lambasted as trite and shallow by academics, it has since sold over 7 million copies, been translated into over 25 languages, and is frequently found on managers' bookshelves. It launched a new genre of management publishing, providing the model for a host of imitations.

1939	Born.
1982	Publication of *The One Minute Manager*.
1984	Publication of *Putting the One Minute Manager to Work*.

Life and Career

Kenneth Blanchard graduated from Cornell University in Government and Philosophy and went on to complete his Ph.D. in Administration and Management. In the early 1980s he was Professor of Leadership and Organizational Behavior at the University of Massachusetts, Amherst. He wrote and researched extensively in the fields of leadership, motivation, and the management of change and his *Management of Organizational Behavior: Utilizing Human Resources* (coauthored with Paul Hersey) is now in its 7th edition and has become a classic text. Blanchard and his coauthor of *The One Minute Manager* (OMM), Spencer Johnson, MD, describe the book as an allegory, a simple compilation of what "many wise people have taught us and what we have learned ourselves" (Introduction to OMM).

Key Thinking

One-minute Management

The framework story of *The One Minute Manager* imagines a young manager going off in search of that holy grail of the aspiring newcomer—an effective manager on whom to model his own thinking and actions. The novice—a cross between Le Petit Prince and Candide—is caught between the two extremes of the Scientific and Human Relations schools: some managers get good results (but at a price that few colleagues and subordinates seem willing to support), while others (whose people really like them) have results which leave much to be desired. Our hero, however, soon comes across a manager who gets excellent results as a result of—apparently—very little effort on his part—the One Minute Manager. The OMM has three simple secrets that bring about increases in productivity, profits, and satisfaction—one-minute goal-setting, one-minute praising, and one-minute reprimanding.

One-minute Goal-setting

Although staff cannot know how well they are doing without clear goals, claims the OMM, many are not clear on priorities, and many are spoken to only when they make a mistake. The OMM requires managers to make it clear what tasks people are to do and what sort of behavior or performance is expected of them, and to get staff to write down their most important goals on a single sheet of paper for continued clarification.

One-minute Praising

The second secret—one-minute praising—is the key to improved performance and increased productivity. Instead of criticizing people for doing something wrong, the opposite is recommended: "the key to developing people is to catch them doing something right." There are three steps in one-minute praising.

- Praise someone as close in time to the good behavior as possible. If you can't find someone to praise every day, then you should wonder why.
- Be specific. Make it clear what it was that was performed well.
- Share feelings—tell them how you feel about what they did, not what you think about what they did.

One-minute Reprimanding

The third secret of the One Minute Manager is the key to changing the attitude of the poor performer. There are four aspects to it:

- Immediacy—when a reprimand is necessary, it is best to deliver it as soon as possible after the instance of poor performance that led to it.
- Be specific—don't tell people about your reactions or give vent to your feelings, tell them what they did wrong; admonish the action, not the person.
- Share feelings—once you have established what was wrong, share your feelings.
- Tell them how good they are—the last step in the reprimand. If you finish on negative feedback, they will reflect on your style of behavior, not on their own performance.

The Development of One-minute Management

Putting the One Minute Manager to Work was a follow-up in 1984 by Blanchard and coauthor Richard Lorber (an expert in performance improvement) to flesh out some of the basic ideas which had met initial success in *The One Minute Manager*. Subtitled *How to Turn the Three Secrets into Skills*, the 1984 follow-up focuses on the "ABCs" of management, "effective reprimanding," and the "PRICE" system.

The ABCs

- Activators—those things that a manager has to do before anyone else can be expected to achieve anything, such as goal-setting, laying down areas of accountability, issuing instructions, and setting performance standards.
- Behavior—or performance—what a person says or does, such as filing, writing, selling, ordering, buying, etc.
- Consequence—what a manager does after performance, such as sharing feelings, praising, reprimanding, supporting, etc.

Effective Reprimanding

A manager has to distinguish between a situation where an employee can't do something—which implies a need for training and signals a return to the activator of goal-setting—and one where an employee won't do something—which implies an attitude problem and a case for a reprimand. Reprimands do not teach skills, they can only change attitudes. Positive con-

"Managers should work for their people. . .and not the reverse." (Kenneth Blanchard)

sequences on the other hand can influence future performance to the good, so it is important, as *The One Minute Manager* had already suggested, to end a reprimand with praise, making the employee think about his or her own behavior, not that of the reprimander.

The PRICE System

PRICE takes the three basic secrets of one-minute management and turns them into five steps:

- **P**inpointing—defining key performance areas in measurable terms—part of one-minute goal-setting;
- **R**ecording—gathering data to measure actual performance and keep track of progress;
- **I**nvolving—sharing the information recorded with whomsoever is responsible;
- **C**oaching—providing constructive feedback on improving performance;
- **E**valuating—part of coaching, also part of reprimanding or praising.

Later Works

Leadership and the One Minute Manager stresses that there is no single, best method of leadership, but that there are four styles: directing, delegating, coaching, and support. Whichever style is employed depends on the situation to be managed. "Situational leadership is not something you do to people, but something you do with people." Blanchard turns conventional leadership thinking on its head, using the analogy of turning the organizational pyramid upside down; instead of staff working for their boss, the boss should work for the staff.

The One Minute Manager Builds High-performing Teams can be seen as a companion to *Leadership* and concentrates on integrating the simplicity of the one-minute techniques into understanding group dynamics and adjusting leadership style to meet developing circumstances.

The One Minute Manager Meets the Monkey deals with the problems of time management and overload. Paying tribute to Bill Oncken, Blanchard's coauthor who created the monkey analogy, Blanchard points the finger at the concept of the manager as the "hero with all the answers," stressing that bosses are not there to tackle every problem themselves, rather to get others to come up with solutions. The monkey is the problem being passed from subordinate to superior, making the superior rapidly ineffective; the one-minute manager is not a collector of monkeys, rather a facilitator and coach helping others to solve their own problems.

Kenneth Blanchard in Perspective

So where does Blanchard sit in the Hall of Fame of management thinkers?

In the early years of the 21st century, much of what Blanchard et al. have to say in the One Minute Manager series no longer seems earth-shattering. Countless publications and endless seminars on leadership, change, delegation, and time management have, unsurprisingly, rendered a glance back to Blanchard an entertaining experience, yes, and a comforting one in its confirmation of what one has learned elsewhere, but—like the key message of a contemporaneous publication *In Search of Excellence* (Peters and Waterman, 1982)—one-minute management is no longer the inspiration it was.

When asked why *In Search of Excellence* did so well, critics and commentators argued that its timing was impeccable: It was published at a time when Western business concepts were being trashed in favor of analyses of the Japanese business boom. If Peters and Waterman were largely about reinvigorating pride in successful American organizations, Blanchard's book was excellently timed for its impact on individual skills and techniques.

It is important to remember that before Blanchard, Peters, and the host of others following in their wake, management—as far as the hard-nosed manager was concerned—was a stuffy, dry subject reserved for lengthy academic treatises and exposés. Most books—not that there were many of them—focused on building the arguments of the human relations school and tackling the monstrous scientific/bureaucratic establishment so convincingly constructed by Taylor, Ford, and Weber. Books on management were not popular, not widely read, and certainly not best-sellers. It is often claimed that Peters and Waterman changed all that. But Ken Blanchard's contribution was also hugely influential. *The One Minute Manager* may have been panned by the academics, but it did more to make management digestible, readable, and accessible to a wide audience than any of its predecessors. By means of allegory, anecdotes, and allusions, it brought management to a level where many believed they could do it and do it well. Others have followed the story-telling format of OMM, *One Page Management* (Khadem) and *Zapp! The Lightning of Empowerment* (Byham) to name but two.

So what is the appeal of the One Minute Manager, rejected (like Maslow) by academia, but wholeheartedly adopted (as was Maslow) by practicing managers around the world? Blanchard's book was, first and foremost, short and to the point. Moreover, it was written in everyday language, offering practical, everyday solutions to practical, everyday problems. This was no dry, stuffy theory, but a collection of honest sensible techniques to try out straight away. This is where Blanchard scored a first.

Any author who sells over 7 million copies deserves a place in the Management Hall of Fame. For Blanchard, that place has to be broadly in the Human Relations School alongside the great popularizers of empowerment on the one hand and the self-help school, stretching from Samuel Smiles and Dale Carnegie to present-day figures like Stephen Covey and, recently, with Tom Peters, on the other. Blanchard's message may not be original but few have spread the simple messages more effectively, or to such a wide audience.

For More Information

Key works by Blanchard

Books:

Blanchard, Kenneth, with Spencer Johnson. *The One Minute Manager*. New York: Berkley Publishing Group, 1983.

Blanchard, Kenneth, with Robert Lorber. *Putting the One Minute Manager to Work*. New York: William Morrow & Co., 1984.

Blanchard, Kenneth, with Patricia Zigarmi and Drea Zigarmi. *Leadership and the One Minute Manager*. New York: William Morrow & Co., 1985.

Blanchard, Kenneth, with William Oncken and Hal Burrows. *The One Minute Manager Meets the Monkey*. New York: William Morrow & Co., 1989.

Blanchard, Kenneth, with Donald Carew and Eunice Parisi-Carew. *The One Minute Manager Builds High-performing Teams*. New York: William Morrow & Co., 1980.

Blanchard, Kenneth, with Terry Waghorn. *Mission Possible*. New York: McGraw-Hill, 1997.

Blanchard, Kenneth, with Sheldon Bowles. *Gung Ho*. New York: William Morrow & Co., 1998.

(Kenneth Blanchard)

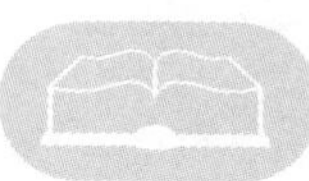

Dale Carnegie

How to Win Friends and Influence People

Dale Carnegie's main focus is on dealing with people successfully. His best-known work, *How to Win Friends and Influence People* (1936), puts forward the essential principles for doing this in the form of commonsense advice, such as that you should never criticize, complain about, or condemn another person, you should give sincere appreciation to others, and that in order to motivate people, you need to stimulate a specific desire in them.

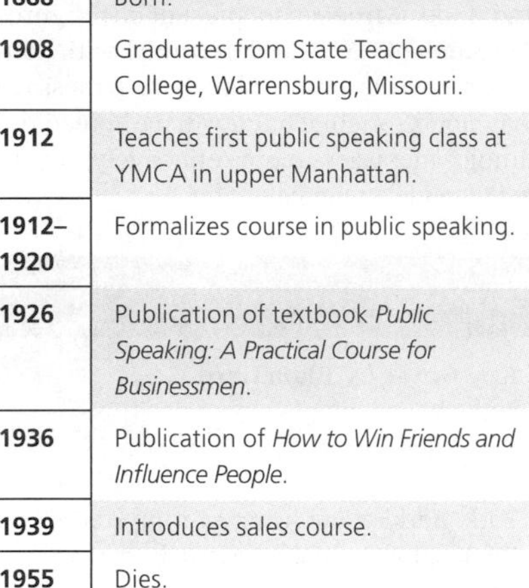

1888	Born.
1908	Graduates from State Teachers College, Warrensburg, Missouri.
1912	Teaches first public speaking class at YMCA in upper Manhattan.
1912–1920	Formalizes course in public speaking.
1926	Publication of textbook *Public Speaking: A Practical Course for Businessmen*.
1936	Publication of *How to Win Friends and Influence People*.
1939	Introduces sales course.
1955	Dies.

Life and Career

Dale Carnegie (1888–1955) came from a poor, farming background and had to struggle through college. Looking for a way to distinguish himself, he began to enter speaking contests and, despite a shaky start, was soon winning every contest he entered. On leaving college he worked for some time as a salesman, making his territory the most successful one in the company, before deciding to train and work as an actor. This was another false start, however. He gave up the stage to run his own business, then eventually decided to write novels and support himself by teaching at night.

Carnegie's first courses on public speaking for businessmen at the YMCA schools in New York were run purely on a commission basis, as he was initially refused any pay. The courses did well, however, and their popularity made him a great success. They were so successful, in fact, that he was able to turn them into a series of popular books that extended beyond his initial sphere of public speaking into the realm of human relations in general. Providing simple rules on how to achieve success with people and illustrated from his own and others' experiences and with stories about people historical figures such as Roosevelt and Lincoln, the books became runaway successes in their turn. Carnegie went on to found the Dale Carnegie Institute of Effective Speaking and Human Relations to spread his ideas yet further. In 1997, over 40 years after his death, *How to Win Friends and Influence People*, the book that made him internationally famous, was still on the bestseller list in Germany.

Key Thinking

Carnegie believed that criticism was counterproductive and should never be used to try to change or motivate people. In his view, people who are criticized tend to respond by justifying themselves and condemning the critical person in return. Great leaders such as Abraham Lincoln achieved their success partly because they never criticized others. Carnegie recommended instead the practice of self-control, understanding, and forgiveness. Most importantly, he advised that you should always try to see the other person's point of view.

In order to influence people and achieve your aims, Carnegie suggests, it is necessary to understand individual motivation. You need to ask yourself what will motivate a person to want to do a task for you, before you attempt to persuade them to do it. He considers most people to be interested only in their own desires, but suggests that, if they are given what they want, they can help the giver to achieve great success in business.

People may simply want to drive a better car or buy a bigger house. For most people, however, the desire to be important is a main, if not the main motivator. It can inspire them to do great things, such as become important leaders or make their fortune in business. It can also take morbid forms. Sometimes individuals become invalids to gain attention or become insane so that they can live in a dream world where their importance is exaggerated by imagination. In any event the urge to be important should not be ignored. Using very human, anecdotal evidence, Carnegie illustrates how nourishing a person's self-esteem can achieve far better results than criticism.

The Rules

How to Win Friends and Influence People has "In a nutshell" conclusions at the end of each section. In them Carnegie summarizes the main messages each section offers in terms of behavior. Some of these are paraphrased below.

Six ways to make people like you:

1. Show a genuine interest in other people.
2. Be happy and positive.
3. Remember that people love hearing the sound of their own name.
4. Listen to other people and develop good listening skills.
5. Talk about others' interests rather than your own.
6. Give others a sincere sense of their importance.

Twelve ways to win people to your way of thinking:

1. To get the best of a situation, avoid arguments.
2. Always listen to others' opinions and never tell anyone they are wrong.
3. Admit it if you are wrong.
4. Show friendliness.
5. Make statements that the other person can agree with.
6. Let the other person talk more than you.
7. Make the other person feel that an idea is their own.
8. See the other person's point of view.
9. Show empathy with others' ideas and desires.
10. Infuse some drama into your ideas.
11. Appeal to the better nature of others.
12. Finish with a challenge.

"Don't criticize, condemn, or complain; give honest and sincere appreciation; and arouse in the other person an eager want."

(Dale Carnegie)

Nine ways to change people without arousing resentment:

1. Start with genuine praise and appreciation.
2. Draw attention to people's mistakes gradually.
3. Admit that you have made mistakes and then talk to other people about theirs.
4. Don't give direct orders but ask questions.
5. Never humiliate anyone, and let people keep their pride intact.
6. Use plenty of genuine praise and encouragement when there is the slightest improvement.
7. Give people a reputation to maintain.
8. Encourage people. Show them that their task is easy to correct.
9. Suggest what you want them to do and make them happy about it.

Becoming a Good Public Speaker

Some of the advice given by Dale Carnegie at the start of his career, when he trained and wrote to help people to make speeches in public, is summarized below.

Preparation

From the beginning, Carnegie suggested, you should generate an enthusiasm within yourself for public speaking, whether you have a financial or a social goal in view. Prepare as much as possible for the speech, and have it ready well in advance. Begin planning as soon as you can, and look for a topic that you know a lot about. Always try to use your own ideas, but bring the topic of your talk into conversation, so that you can explore any interesting stories on the subject that others may be able to tell you. Think about your talk at every possible opportunity, and research it thoroughly, using libraries and other sources and collecting more material than you will need.

Do not memorize the talk word for word, as you will then be more likely to forget it. It may also lose much of its effectiveness if it seems too studied. While having plenty of material prepared, you should not try to say too much in the talk itself. Your material needs to be structured simply, so that you can talk as if you were in ordinary conversation.

Most people are nervous about talking in public. If you try to act bravely and pretend that you feel more confident than you really do, you will often actually gain in confidence. Practice will help you to feel more certain of yourself, and it is a good idea to rehearse your speech as much as possible, maybe in front of the mirror, or with family and friends as an audience.

Delivery

Dress the part for your speech. Smile, and make sure you are clearly visible to your audience. Show respect and affection for the audience, and let the first sentence capture their attention. Examples of techniques to help you to achieve this are:

- start with a striking incident or example;
- state an arresting fact;
- ask for a show of hands;
- use an exhibit;
- do or say something to arouse suspense;
- promise to tell the audience how they can get something they want.

You should not, however, open a talk with either an apology or a funny story. Humorous stories often fail to work, and this is particularly likely to be the case when you are nervous.

Use statistics or the testimony of experts to support your main ideas, but know your audience, and do not use technical terms if you are addressing a lay audience. Be eager to share your talk with your listeners, putting passion into your way of speaking and using your emotions without fear. Represent things visually when possible, turning a fact into a picture to help your audience to understand what you are talking about and using specific instances and concrete cases.

Stress important words, and avoid any hackneyed expressions or clichés. Once your talk is launched, you may feel more free to be humorous when appropriate, but take care to target any fun at yourself rather than others.

Your talk should have some marked form of closure. Summarize what you have said, then use a finalizing climax or close of some sort that is appropriate within the context, for example:

- make an appeal for action;
- pay the audience a sincere compliment;
- raise a final laugh;
- use a fitting verse of poetry or a quotation.

Carnegie's Concluding Advice

- Remember that many famous speakers were originally terrified of speaking in public and that a certain amount of stage fright is useful.
- Predetermine your mind to success and seize every opportunity to practice.
- Remember that as you increase your experience your fear will lessen, so seek opportunities to speak in public, and believe in yourself.

Dale Carnegie in Perspective

Carnegie claimed that his theories do really work and that he had seen them transform the lives of many people. Some management writers have, however, dismissed Carnegie's ideas as being simple wisdom dressed up in a commercial coating.

Certainly, Carnegie's ideas are based on common sense and are hardly revolutionary. All his self-help books are based on down-to-earth and simply illustrated basic principles. Despite this simplicity, Carnegie has expressed many general truths which people acknowledge and, whatever his critics may say, the books he wrote are still popular.

In fact, Carnegie created a highly successful business out of his ideas, and his books have sold millions. Even today, much money is still being made from his work, which suggests that people still find him very relevant. Certainly, it is possible to see Carnegie's influence in some of today's ideas about management, particularly in discussions on the treatment of customers, and in approaches to interpersonal skills development.

For More Information

Key works by Carnegie

Books:

How to Win Friends and Influence People. Reissue. New York: Pocket Books, 1994.

How to Enjoy Your Life and Your Job. New York: Pocket Books, 1986.

How to Stop Worrying and Start Living. Rev. ed. New York: Pocket Books, 1985.

See also:

How to Win Friends and Influence People (p. 908)

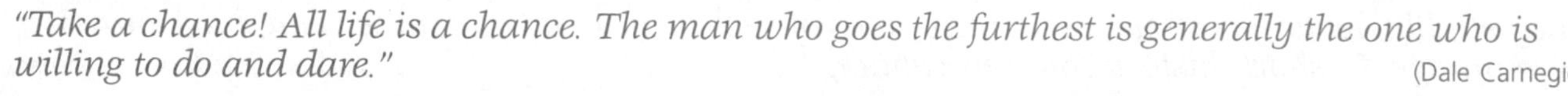

"Take a chance! All life is a chance. The man who goes the furthest is generally the one who is willing to do and dare."

(Dale Carnegie)

 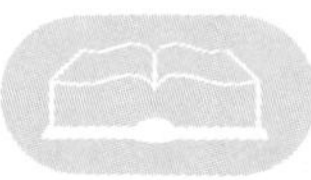    

Alfred D. Chandler, Jr.

Business History As a Management Tool

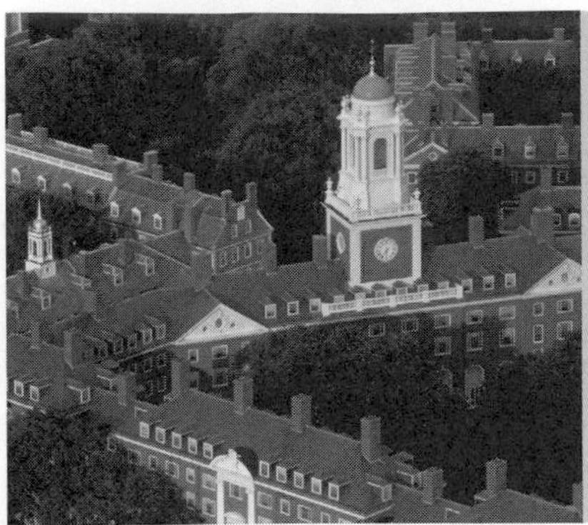

The U.S. academic Alfred D. Chandler, Jr. is the first historian in the modern era to both forge his own subject area and dominate it for almost half a century. When he stumbled on the genre after World War II, business history was just a virgin cousin of economic history, a largely theoretical discipline that dealt with macrofiscal issues as they affect national and international economies.

Harvard University, where Chandler completed his Ph.D.

1918	Born.
1952	Completes Ph.D. at Harvard.
1962	Publication of *Strategy and Structure.*
1970	Isidor Straus Professor of Business History, Harvard Business School.
1977	Publication of *The Visible Hand: The Managerial Revolution in American Business.*

Life and Career

Chandler was born in 1918 and acquired his first interest in history from Wilbur Fiske Gordy's *Elementary History of the United States*, which his father gave him at the age of seven. He was educated at Phillips Exeter Academy, Harvard College, the University of North Carolina, where he received his M.A., and Harvard University, where he completed his Ph.D. in history in 1952. His wartime experience was with a unit responsible for analyzing photographs of gunnery exercises by the Atlantic Fleet and bombing raids in the Pacific.

He acquired an interest in sociology and saw the value of explicit concepts, generalizations, and theories in analyzing human behavior, but it was when he came to choose his dissertation topic that his interest in business history was initially sparked. His great-aunt died suddenly, and Chandler and his family moved into her house, in which were stored the personal papers of his grandfather, Henry Varnum Poor. Poor, whose name survives as one half of the business information company Standard and Poor's Corporation, had been one of the people most knowledgeable about American railroads, having edited the *American Railway Journal* for nearly 20 years. Using Poor's personal papers, together with the extensive backfiles of his newspapers and related publications in the Baker Library at Harvard, he produced a classic series of articles, his dissertation, and a book entitled *Henry Varnum Poor: Business Editor, Analyst, and Reformer*. This treatise, a seminal work on American railroad companies during their formative years, enabled him to develop what—through his genius at widespread comparative analysis—became his characteristic way of extracting clear historical patterns that tended toward inductively derived theory.

His career as a working business historian was spent at the Massachusetts Institute of Technology, where he had the opportunity of working on the individual histories of Du Pont, General Motors, Standard Oil (now Exxon), and Sears, Roebuck & Co., a course of study that culminated in *Strategy and Structure*; at the Johns Hopkins University, where he wrote the biography of Pierre du Pont; and later at the Harvard Business School, where in 1970 he was appointed the Isidor Straus Professor of Business History, the world's only endowed chair in the field at the time. Since then he has led a growing field of teachers and studies; about 200 American academics now work on the subject.

Key Thinking

Until Chandler turned to business history as his principal interest, mainstream economic history predominated as the subject matter of business education. There was, admittedly, a detour, the result of imported Western European attitudes, when both popular journalism and academia started to take an interest in the corrupt practices of businessmen. The perception emerged that they were "robber barons," a viewpoint that only started to change when Joseph Schumpeter's *The Theory of Economic Development*, which depicted the businessman as a force for positive advancement, was translated from German into English in 1934. Several notable academics started to reevaluate the same robber barons as constructive, daring, and far-seeing "industrial statesmen," who deserved credit for making the United States a predominant economic power able to defend itself and its allies from the totalitarian assaults on freedom of the 20th century. Nevertheless, it was Chandler who made business history a linchpin of the curriculum.

His work was pioneering in several other respects. It was conducted in front of a largely unreceptive audience: The majority of management educators long resisted the concept of using the real example of corporate and business history as a teaching tool. With an attachment to the more empirical methodologies dominated by macroeconomics and quantitative analysis, they believed that business historians painted with too broad a brush on too wide a canvas and lacked a solid or explicitly stated methodology. They also accused the genre of being largely irrelevant given the perceived pace of change. Chandler's work did much to change these attitudes, although it is instructive to note that business and management teachers—unlike educators in disciplines such as the military, politics, music, architecture, sociology, and so on—still widely resist both the concept and development of history-based experiential learning in their own discipline. Chandler also spent his life challenging economic thinking, in particular the static equilibrium theory. Although he used the results of quantitative research, he did not employ mathematical notation, remaining skeptical of highly theorized arithmetical manipulations that, he says, while elegantly logical, distort intelligible generalizations about the past.

In shifting the focus of business history, Chandler's work, which in fact specifically addresses the process of evolution and change, uses a systematic and analytical approach that has evolved from an intellectual outlook, which he labeled "managerial enterprise." As he explains it, this concept moves in two directions—forward from the past to the present and backward

"Regrettably, history is strewn with the visions of such "new eras" that, in the end, have proven to be a mirage. In short, history counsels caution."
(Alan Greenspan)

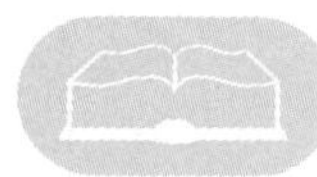

from the present to the past. Using the former perspective, for example, he examined why early 19th-century industry did not employ any managers, a phenomenon which changed decisively and forever in the second half of the 19th century. Using the latter perspective, he questioned the 1950s moves by industry toward decentralization of their functionally-specialized and multidepartmentalized organizations. His answers–in a landmark book entitled *Strategy and Structure* published in 1962–took business history into a new dimension by establishing a fresh framework and rationale for the subject. He introduced the feature of making comparisons within and between industries and over time, and enabled business history to acquire relevance in a wide range of related fields.

In *The Visible Hand*, another milestone book, Chandler used the concept of managerial enterprise to illustrate how Germany became the most powerful industrial nation in Europe before World War II, the United States became the most productive country in the world for 40 years until the 1960s, and Japan became its most successful competitor thereafter. For this book he won the Pulitzer Prize. These and other works–including, with Richard Tedlow, *The Coming of Managerial Capitalism*–are routinely used in at least 30 higher educational establishments in the United States and many more abroad.

Business history's role at the operational level, Chandler explains, is not about teaching specific management techniques. It has a more strategic function. Any meaningful analysis of an organization today, he says, must be based on an accurate understanding of its past. "Such data has to come from business history based on company records or from historically based case studies. Certainly a restructuring of enterprises to meet changing conditions requires an understanding of both why and how the existing organization evolved and how and why competitive conditions changed. Managers facing such problems can get insights by observing the working out of such processes in other enterprises." Companies such as McKinsey & Co and AT&T have applied *Strategy and Structure* to this end. The former, for example, has used it to teach its clients about the timing of strategic change and how to adjust their organizational structures, while the latter put it to use in one of its reorganizations.

At the wider education level, Chandler believes that business history can provide insights into the processes of businesses such as the development of competitive strategy, the restructuring of organizational forms, and the effectiveness of investment and monitoring techniques. His view is that the value of teaching business histories in universities is to make MBA students and those in more advanced management courses aware of recent as well as long-term changes in functional activities such as production, marketing, research and development, finance, labor relations, and the like; also in monitoring and coordinating the activities of the current operations of an enterprise as well as in locating resources for future production and distribution. "Not only can the students learn something about the nature of the functions but also the complexities of carrying out change," he says.

Alfred D. Chandler, Jr. in Perspective

For students and practitioners alike, Chandler's name may be remembered principally as the pioneer who placed strategy before structure in his seminal work published in 1962. Not only did he champion the systematic study of modern bureaucratic administration in an original way, he also turned what is often dismissed as an artless medium into a valid and powerful educational tool. Using the conglomerate history of individual companies to arrive at a historical theory of big business instead of the mainstream–economic–discipline of the day, he revolutionized the fledgling discipline by refocusing attention away from individual entrepreneurs and seeking patterns in the rise of large-scale modern business. Almost uniquely, his work–which has spawned the nomenclature Chandlerianism–has had a profound effect on historians and business thinking all over the world, particularly in Japan and Germany. Some of his books have been translated into Chinese and Russian.

Following his lead, American business historians have moved to more thematic areas: for example, how companies formulate and implement policy, how industries evolve, the impact of administrative hierarchies on the modern economy, industrial evolution across national boundaries, the interaction of business with governmental institutions and regulatory bodies, and organized labor and the consumer.

History will no doubt endow him with the distinction of giving modern management educators a less theoretical way of teaching the business of business. In essence, he has skillfully recycled the tried and tested past to provide both practicing and aspiring managers with an inheritance that has practical corporate application in today's highly competitive world. In truth, history is the only way individuals and companies can learn from experience. And learning from experience is the only way to increase productivity and competitiveness.

For More Information

Key works by Chandler

Books:

Strategy and Structure. Cambridge, MA: MIT Press, 1962.

The Visible Hand: The Managerial Revolution in American Business. Cambridge, MA: Harvard University Press, 1977.

Managerial Hierarchies. Cambridge, MA: Harvard University Press, 1980.

Chandler, Alfred, with Richard Tedlow. *The Coming of Managerial Capitalism*. Homewood, IL: Richard D. Irwin, 1985.

Scale and Scope; The Dynamics of Industrialized Capitalism. Cambridge, MA: Harvard University Press, 1994.

Big Business and The Wealth of Nations. New York: Cambridge University Press, 1997.

The Dynamic Firm. New York: Oxford University Press, 1998.

REFERENCES: Both quotations are extracts from private correspondence with Chandler.

See also:

Strategy and Structure (p. 950)

Henry Mintzberg (pp. 1024–25)

Kenichi Ohmae (pp. 1028–29)

Michael Porter (pp. 1038–39)

STEPHEN R. COVEY

The Seven Habits of Highly Effective People

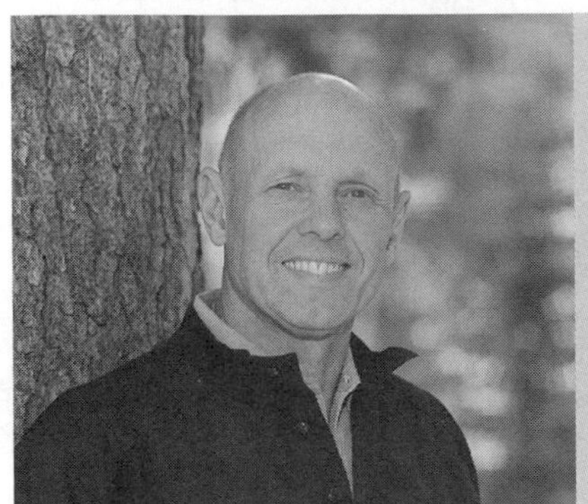

In *The Seven Habits of Highly Effective People*, Stephen Covey offers a holistic approach to life and work that has struck a significant chord with the perplexed manager working in turbulent times. The recurring themes in his various works are: the transforming power of principles rooted in unchanging natural laws that govern human and organizational effectiveness; the necessity of adapting every aspect of one's life to accord with these principles; effective leadership; and empowerment.

1932	Born.
1985	Founds Covey Leadership Center.
1989	Publication of *The Seven Habits of Highly Effective People*.
1997	Covey Leadership Center merges with Franklin Quest.

LIFE AND CAREER

Stephen Covey is founder and chairman of the Covey Leadership Center (1985)—now part of Franklin Covey—and the Institute for Principle-Centered Leadership in Utah. Born in 1932, he received an MBA from Harvard Business School and a doctorate from Brigham Young University, where he was subsequently Professor of Organizational Behavior and Business Management.

At the Covey Leadership Center, through his writing—chiefly *The Seven Habits of Highly Effective People* (which has sold over five million copies)—and through consulting (he was invited to Camp David by President Clinton), his message has reached millions of individuals in business, government and education.

KEY THINKING

The Seven Habits of Highly Effective People

The Seven Habits is addressed to readers not only in their capacity as managers but also as members of a family, and as social, spiritual, sporting, and thinking individuals. It offers a "life-transforming prescription," which calls for a reappraisal of many fundamental assumptions and attitudes (paradigms), and builds on the fundamental concept of interdependence. Covey traces a personal development outline from:

- dependence in childhood (many people never grow out of a dependency culture), through. . .;
- independence in adolescence—self assurance, a developing personality, and a positive mental attitude, to. . .;
- interdependence—recognition that the optimum outcome results from everyone giving of their best, each aiming for a common goal, sharing the same mission and vision, but having the freedom to use their best judgment as to how to go about achieving that common goal.

HABIT 1

Be proactive.

Covey distinguishes between proactive people—those who focus their efforts on things which they can do something about—and reactive people, who blame, accuse, behave like victims, pick on other people's weaknesses, and complain about external factors over which they have no control (for example, the weather).

Proactive people are responsible for their own lives. Covey breaks down the word *responsibility* into two parts: response (especially choosing a response) and ability. Proactive people recognize their responsibility to make things happen. Those who allow their feelings to control their actions have abdicated responsibility and empowered their feelings. When proactive people make a mistake, they not only recognize it as such and acknowledge it, they also correct it if possible and, most importantly, learn from it.

HABIT 2

Begin with the end in mind.

Leadership is about effectiveness—the vision of what is to be accomplished. It calls for direction (in every sense of the word), purpose, and sensitivity. Management, on the other hand, is about efficiency—how best to accomplish the vision. It depends on control, guidance, and rules.

To identify the end, and to formulate one's route or strategy to achieving that end, Covey maintains the need for a "principle-centered" basis to all aspects of life. Most people adopt something as the basis (or pivotal point) of their life—spouse, family, money, church, pleasure, friends (and, in a perverse way, enemies), sports, etc. Of course all of these have some influence over the life of every individual. However, only by clearly establishing one's own principles, in the form of a personal mission, does one have a solid foundation.

HABIT 3

Put first things first.

Covey's first major work *First Things First* set out his views on time management. It argues that the important thing is not managing time, but managing oneself, focusing on results rather than on methods when prioritizing within each compartment of work and life.

He breaks down life's activities into four quadrants:

Quadrant 1: Urgent and important—for example, crises, deadlines, unexpected opportunities.

Quadrant 2: Not urgent, but important—for example, planning, recreation, relationship-building, doing, learning.

Quadrant 3: Urgent, but not important—for example, interruptions, meetings.

Quadrant 4: Not urgent and not important—for example, trivia, time-wasters, gossip.

Essentially all activity of effective people should focus on the second quadrant, apart from the genuinely unpredictable quadrant 1 events. However, effective planning and doing in Quadrant 2 should minimize the number of occasions on which crises occur.

The outcomes of a Quadrant 2 focus include: vision, perspective, balance, discipline, and control. On the other hand, the results of placing one's main focus on the other quadrants are:

Quadrant 1: stress, burnout, inability to manage time (and thus loss of control of one's own life).

Quadrant 3: short-termism, loss of control, shallowness, feelings of being a victim of circumstances.

"If offended, take the initiative to clear it up." (Stephen R. Covey)

Quadrant 4: irresponsibility, dependency, unsuitability for employment.

Habit 3 is therefore about managing oneself effectively, by prioritizing according to the principles adopted in Habit 2. This approach transcends the office diary or day-planner, embracing all roles in life—as manager, mentor, administrator, strategist, and also as parent, spouse, member of social groups, and as an individual with needs and aspirations.

Habits 1–3 are grouped under the banner "Private Victory." They are about the development of the personal attributes that provide the foundations for independence. Habits 4–6 are described by Covey as the "Public Victory," as they are the basic paradigms of interdependence.

Habit 4

Think win/win.

Interdependence occurs when there is cooperation, not competition, in the workplace (or the home). Covey holds that competition belongs in the marketplace.

Covey points out that, from childhood, many people are conditioned to a win/lose mentality by school examinations, by parental approval being related to "success," by external comparisons and league standings. This results in a "Scarcity Mentality," a belief that there is only a finite cake to be shared: A "Scarcity Mentality" is evident in people who have difficulty in sharing recognition or credit, power or profit. It restricts their ability to celebrate other people's success, and even brings about a perverse satisfaction at others' misfortune.

By contrast Covey advocates an "Abundance Mentality" that:

- recognizes unlimited possibilities for positive growth and development;
- celebrates success;
- understands and seeks a win/win solution.

Covey argues that to be true to your ideals, it is sometimes necessary to walk away if the other party is interested only in a win/lose outcome: Covey describes this as "win/win or no deal."

Habit 5

Seek first to understand, then to be understood.

"I just can't understand my son . . . he won't listen to me." The absurdity of this statement is highlighted by Covey in emphasizing the importance of listening in order to understand. Clearly, the parent needs to stop and listen to the son if he or she truly wants to understand him.

However, most people want to make their point first, or are so busy looking for their opportunity to butt into the conversation that they fail to hear and understand the other party. Covey defines the different levels of listening as:

- hearing but ignoring;
- pretending to listen ("Yes," "Oh," "I see. . .");
- selective listening (choosing to hear only what we want to hear);
- attentive listening, without evaluation (e.g., taking notes at a lecture);
- empathic listening (with intent to understand the other party).

True empathic listening requires a great deal of personal security, as one is vulnerable to being influenced, to having one's opinions changed. "The more deeply you understand other people," Covey says, "the more you appreciate them, the more reverent you feel about them."

Likewise, when you feel that someone is genuinely seeking to understand your point of view, you recognize and share their openness and willingness to negotiate and to reach a win/win situation.

Habit 6

Synergize.

The essence of synergy is where two parties, each with a different agenda, value each other's differences. Everything in nature is synergistic, with every creature and plant being interdependent with others.

We also have personal effectiveness where there is synergy at an individual level—where both sides of the brain are working in tandem on a problem or situation: the intuitive, creative, visual right side and the analytical, logical, verbal left side combining to achieve the optimum outcome.

Synergy is lacking in insecure people: they either clone others, or else try to stereotype them. Of such insecurity is born prejudice—racism, bigotry, nationalism, and any other form of prejudging others.

Habit 7

Sharpen the saw.

The seventh and final habit relates to renewal. Just as a car or any other sophisticated tool needs regular care and maintenance, so too do the human body and mind.

Covey uses the metaphor of a woodcutter who is laboring painfully to saw down a tree. The saw is obviously in need of sharpening, but when asked why he doesn't stop and sharpen the saw, the woodcutter replies, "I can't stop—I'm too busy sawing down this tree."

The warning is quite clear. Everyone can become so engrossed in the task in hand that the basic tools are neglected:

- "the physical self"—which requires exercise, a sensible and balanced diet, and management of stress;
- "the social/emotional self"—which connects with others through service, empathy, and synergy, and which is the source of intrinsic security;
- "the spiritual self"—which through meditation, reflection, prayer, and study helps to clarify and refine our own values and strengths, and our commitment to them;
- "the mental self"—building on to our formal education through reading, visualizing, planning, writing, and maintaining a coherent program of continuing personal development.

Stephen R. Covey in Perspective

Commentators have both attacked and applauded Covey's approach for mixing the self-help message, which can be traced back to Samuel Smiles, with the positive self-drive of winning friends and influencing people (Dale Carnegie), current management theories, and religious fervor.

In times of change and confusion, however, when failure, redundancy, and unemployment dominate individual thinking and lead to stress, Covey's message offers the individual something to hang on to. *First Things First*, coauthored with Roger and Rebecca Merrill, has achieved twice the sales of *The Seven Habits* over the same time period.

He is undoubtedly a philosopher for our times, highlighting the significance of changing industrial and human relations in this post-confrontational era, and recognizing the potential of the untapped resources within each individual.

For More Information

Key works by Covey

Books:

The Seven Habits of Highly Effective People. New York: Simon & Schuster, 1989.

Principle-centered Leadership. New York: Summit Books, 1991.

Covey, Stephen R., with A. Roger Merrill and Rebecca R. Merrill. *First Things First*. New York: Simon & Schuster, 1996.

The Seven Habits of Highly Effective Families. New York: Golden Books, 1997.

See also:

Tom Peters (pp. 1036–37)

"Avoid fight or flight, talk through differences." (Stephen R. Covey)

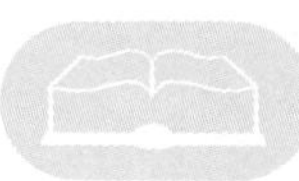

Philip B. Crosby

Zero Defects

Philip Crosby wrote the best-seller *Quality is Free* at a time when the quality movement was a rising, innovative force in business and manufacturing. In the 1980s, his consultancy was advising 40% of the Fortune 500 companies on quality management.

His popularity as a consultant can be partly attributed to his ability to talk about quality management ideas in terms that were easy to understand.

1926	Born.
1952	After war service, begins his career working on an assembly line.
1961	Establishes "zero concepts" while working for Martin-Marietta.
1965	Joins ITT.
1979	*Quality Is Free* published. Leaves ITT to found Philip Crosby Associates Inc.
1984	*Quality without Tears* published.
1988	*The Eternally Successful Organization* published.
1991	Launches Career IV Inc.
2001	Dies.

Life and Career

Crosby was born in West Virginia in 1926. A graduate of Western Reserve University, he saw service in the Korean War, and started his working life on the assembly line in 1952, becoming quality manager for Martin-Marietta where he developed the "zero defects" concept. After working his way up, Crosby was corporate vice president and director of quality at ITT for 14 years.

As a result of the interest shown in *Quality Is Free* (1979), he left ITT to set up Philip Crosby Associates II, Inc. and started to teach organizations quality principles and practice as laid down in his book. In 1985, his company was floated for $30 million. In 1991 he retired from Philip Crosby Associates to launch Career IV Inc., a consultancy advising on the development of senior executives. He died in August 2001.

Key Thinking

Quality, Crosby emphasized, is neither intangible nor immeasurable. It is a strategic imperative, something that can be quantified and put to work to improve the bottom line. "Acceptable" quality or defect levels produced by means of traditional quality control measures, for Crosby, represent evidence of failure rather than assurance of success. The goal is to meet requirements on time, first time, and every time. The emphasis, therefore, should be on prevention, not inspection and cure.

Crosby's approach to quality was unambiguous. In his view, good, bad, high, and low quality are meaningless concepts in the abstract; the meaning of quality is "conformance to requirements." What that means is that a product should conform to the requirements that the company has itself established based on its customers' needs. He also believed that the prime responsibility for poor quality lies with management, not with the workers. Management sets the tone for the quality initiative from the top.

Nonconforming products are ones that management has failed to specify or control. The cost of nonconformance equals the cost of not doing it right first time, and not rooting out any defects in processes.

"Zero defects" does not mean that people never make mistakes, but that companies should not begin with "allowances" or substandard targets with mistakes as an inbuilt expectation. Instead, work should be seen as a series of activities or processes, defined by clear requirements and carried out to produce identified outcomes. Systems that allow things to go wrong–and that result in those things having to be done again–can cost organizations between 20% and 35% of their revenues, in Crosby's estimation.

His seminal approach to quality was set out in *Quality is Free*, and is often summarized as the "Fourteen Steps."

The Fourteen Steps

1. Management commitment: the need for quality improvement must be recognized and accepted by management, who then draw up a quality improvement program with an emphasis on the need for defect prevention. Quality improvement equates to profit improvement. A quality policy is needed which states that "...each individual is expected to perform exactly like the requirement or cause the requirement to be officially changed to what we and the customer really need."

2. The quality improvement team: representatives from each department or function should be brought together to form a quality improvement team. Its members should be people who have sufficient authority to commit the area they represent to action.

3. Quality measurement: the status of quality should be determined throughout the company. This means establishing and recording quality measures for each area of activity in order to show where improvement is possible and where corrective action is necessary. Crosby advocated delegation of this task to the people who actually do the job, thus setting the stage for defect prevention on the job, where it really counts.

4. The cost of quality evaluation: the cost of quality is not an absolute performance measurement, but an indication of where the action necessary to correct a defect will result in greater profitability.

5. Quality awareness: this involves making employees aware of the cost to the company of defects, through training and information, and the provision of visible evidence of the results of a concern for quality improvement. Crosby stresses that this sharing process is a key, or even *the* key, step in the progress of an organization toward quality.

6. Corrective action: discussion of problems will result in the finding of solutions and also bring to light other elements that are in need of improvement. People need to see that problems are regularly being resolved. Corrective action should then become a habit.

"Quality has to be caused, not controlled." (Philip B. Crosby)

  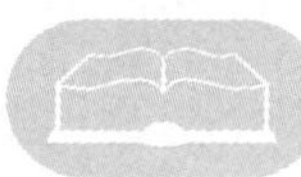    

7. Establishing an ad hoc committee for the zero defects program: zero defects is not a motivation program: its purpose is to communicate and instill the notion that everyone should do things right first time.

8. Supervisor training: all managers should undergo formal training on the Fourteen Steps before they are implemented. Managers should understand each of the Fourteen Steps well enough to be able to explain them to their people.

9. Zero defects day: it is important that the commitment to zero defects as the performance standard of the company makes an impact, and that everyone gets the same message in the same way. Zero defects day, when supervisors explain the program to their people, should make a lasting impression as a "new attitude" day.

10. Goal setting: all supervisors ask their people to establish specific, measurable goals that they can strive for. Usually, these comprise 30-, 60-, and 90-day goals.

11. Error cause removal: employees are asked to describe, on a simple, one-page form, any problems that prevent them from carrying out error-free work. Problems should be acknowledged and begin to be addressed within 24 hours by the function or unit to which the memorandum is directed. This constitutes a key step in building up trust, as it will make people begin to grow more confident that their problems will be attended to and dealt with.

12. Recognition: it is important to recognize those who meet their goals or perform outstanding acts with a prize or award, although this should not be in financial form. The act of recognition itself is what is important.

13. Quality councils: the quality professionals and team leaders should meet regularly to discuss improvements and upgrades to the quality program.

14. Doing it over again: during the course of a typical program lasting from 12 to18 months, turnover and change will dissipate much of the educational process. It is important to set up a new team of representatives and begin the program again from the beginning, starting with zero defects day. This "starting over again" helps quality to become ingrained in the organization.

Putting Quality to the Test

Crosby often used stories to convey his message, and audit techniques and questionnaires to clarify organizational and individual understanding.

Below we reproduce a quick "true or false" questionnaire that features in *Quality is Free*. (The answers are given at the end of this piece.)

1. Quality is a measure of goodness of the product that can be defined as fair, good, excellent.
2. The economics of quality require that management establish acceptable quality levels as performance standards.
3. The cost of quality is the expense of doing things wrong.
4. Inspection and test should report to manufacturing so manufacturing can have the proper tools to do the job.
5. Quality is the responsibility of the quality department.
6. Worker attitudes are the primary cause of defects.
7. I have trend charts that show me the rejection level at every key operation.
8. I have a list of the ten biggest quality problems.
9. Zero defects is a worker motivation program.
10. The biggest problem today is that customers don't understand.

Later Work

In his 1984 book, *Quality without Tears*, Crosby developed the idea of a "quality vaccination serum," which would be made up of the following ingredients.

- Integrity for the chief executive officer, all managers, and all employees.
- Systems for measuring conformance, and educating all employees and suppliers so that quality, corrective action, and defect prevention become routine.
- Communications that enable problems to be identified, progress to be conveyed, and achievement to be recognized.
- Operations organized in such a way that procedures, products, and systems are proven before they are implemented and are then continually examined.
- Policies that are clear, unambiguous, and establish the primacy of quality throughout the organization.

The Eternally Successful Organization (1988) presented a broader approach to improvements. In it Crosby identified five characteristics essential for an organization to be successful.

- People routinely do things right first time.
- Change is anticipated and used to advantage.
- Growth is consistent and profitable.
- New products and services appear when needed.
- Everyone is happy to work there.

Philip Crosby in Perspective

Throughout his work, Crosby's thinking was consistently characterized by four absolutes.

- The definition of quality is conformance to requirements.
- The system of quality is prevention.
- The performance standard is zero defects.
- The measurement of quality is the price of nonconformance.

The importance of the contribution made by Crosby to management thinking is indicated by the fact that his phrases "zero defects," "getting it right first time," and "conformance to requirements" have now entered not only the vocabulary of quality itself, but also the general vocabulary of management.

When Crosby's name is not mentioned in the very same sentence as the best-known quality thinker of them all, Deming, then it is almost certain to be mentioned in the next. Crosby's practical and easy-to-read books on quality became—and remain—bibles for many, demystifying a great deal of the jargon formerly associated with quality management. His timing was perfect for the quality movement, and his writing has marketed quality to a wide audience.

Answers to Questionnaire

1. F; 2. F; 3. T; 4. F; 5. F; 6. F; 7. T; 8. F; 9. F; 10. F

For More Information

Key works by Crosby

Books:

Quality Is Free: The Art of Making Quality Certain. New York: McGraw-Hill, 1979.

Quality without Tears: The Art of Hassle-free Management. New York: McGraw-Hill, 1984.

The Eternally Successful Organization: The Art of Corporate Wellness. New York: McGraw-Hill, 1988.

See also:

☆ **Get All Your People Committed to Change and Transformation (pp. 185–87)**
W. Edwards Deming (pp. 980–81)
Joseph Juran (pp. 1006–07)

(Philip B. Crosby)

W. Edwards Deming

Total Quality Management

W. Edwards Deming is widely acknowledged as the leading management thinker in the field of quality. He is credited with being the most influential catalyst of Japan's postwar economic transformation, although it wasn't until much later that the value of his ideas and practices began to be recognized by the U.S. manufacturing and service industries.

1900	Born.
1928	Completes Ph.D. at Yale.
1950	Begins teaching management quality in Japan.
1986	Publication of *Out of the Crisis*.
1987	Receives National Medal of Technology.
1993	Founds W. Edwards Deming Institute.
1993	Dies.

Life and Career

Deming obtained a Ph.D. in mathematical physics from Yale University in 1928 and concentrated on lecturing and writing in mathematics, physics, and statistics for the next ten years. It was only in the late 1930s that he became familiar with the work of Walter Shewhart, who was experimenting with the application of statistical techniques to manufacturing processes. Deming became interested in applying Shewhart's techniques to nonmanufacturing processes, particularly clerical, administrative, and management activities. After joining the U.S. Census Bureau in 1939, he applied statistical process control to their techniques, which contributed to a sixfold improvement in productivity. Around this time he also started to run courses for engineers and designers on his—and Shewhart's—evolving methods of statistical process control.

Deming's expertise as a statistician was instrumental in his posting to Japan after World War II as an adviser to the Japanese Census. At this time, the United States was the leading economic power, with products much envied by the rest of the world; it saw no need for Deming's new ideas. The Japanese, on the other hand, recognized that their own goods were shoddy by international standards. Moreover, after the war, they could not afford the wastage of raw materials that postproduction inspection processes brought about and were consequently looking for techniques to help them address these problems. While in Japan, Deming became involved with the Union of Japanese Scientists and Engineers (JUSE) and his career of lecturing to the Japanese on statistical methods and company-wide quality, a combination of techniques now known as Total Quality Management (TQM), had begun.

It was only in the late 1970s that the United States became aware of his achievements in Japan. The 1980s saw a spate of publications explaining his work and influence. In his American seminars during 1980, Deming talked of the need for the total transformation of Western-style management. In 1986 he published *Out of the Crisis*, which documented the thinking and practice that had led to the transformation of Japanese manufacturing industry. His ideas gained acceptance in the United Kingdom following the foundation of the British Deming Association in 1987. Deming died in 1993.

Key Thinking

Deming's work and writing constitute not so much a technique as a philosophy of management, one that focuses on quality and continuous improvement, but that has also—justifiably—had a much wider influence.

Below we consider Deming's interest in variation and his approach to systematic problem-solving, which led on to his development of the 14 points that have gained widespread recognition and are central to the quality movement.

Variation and Problem Solving

The key to Deming's ideas on quality lies in his recognition of the importance of variation. In *Out of the Crisis* he states that "the central problem in management and in leadership. . .is failure to understand the information in variation."

Deming was preoccupied with why things do not behave as predicted. All systems (be they the equipment, the process, or the people) have variation, but, he argued, it is essential for managers to be able to distinguish between special and common causes of variation. He developed a theory of variation: that special causes of variation are usually attributable to easily recognizable factors such as a change of procedure, change of shift or operator, and so on, but that common causes will remain when special causes have been eliminated and are normally inherent in the design, process, or system. These common causes often are recognized by workers, but only managers have the authority to change them to avoid repeated occurrence of the problem. Deming estimated that management was responsible for more than 85% of the causes of variation. This formed his central message to the Japanese.

Deming's 14 Points for Management

Deming created 14 points that provided a framework for developing knowledge in the workplace and guiding long-term business plans and aims. The points constitute not so much an action plan as a philosophical code for management. They have been extensively interpreted, both by commentators on quality control and by experts on other management disciplines.

- Create constancy of purpose toward the improvement of products and services, with the aim of becoming competitive, staying in business, and providing jobs.
- Adopt the new philosophy. Western management must awaken to the challenge, learn its responsibilities, and take on leadership for change.
- Cease dependence on mass inspection. Build quality into the product from the start.
- End the practice of awarding business on

"Only management can change the system." (W. Edwards Deming)

the basis of price tag alone. Instead, minimize total cost. Move toward a single supplier for any item, based on a long-term relationship of loyalty and trust.

- Improve constantly and forever the system of production and service to improve quality and reduce waste.
- Institute training and retraining.
- Institute leadership. The aim of supervision should be to lead and help people to do a better job.
- Drive out fear so that everyone may work effectively for the company.
- Break down barriers between departments. People in research, design, sales, and production must work as a team, to foresee and solve problems of production.
- Eliminate slogans, exhortations, and targets, for the workforce as they do not necessarily achieve their aims.
- Eliminate numerical quotas in order to take account of quality and methods, rather than just numbers.
- Remove barriers to pride in workmanship.
- Institute a vigorous program of education and retraining for both the management and the workforce.
- Take action to accomplish the transformation. Management and workforce must work together.

These principles are relevant to management in general, not simply to quality and process control. They contributed to Deming's status as a founder of the Quality Management movement, and attracted an audience much wider than the quality lobby.

W. Edwards Deming in Perspective

Naturally enough, no one as universally acclaimed as Deming escapes without criticism. Some have criticized his approach as being good for improvement but uninspiring for creativity and innovation. Others say his approach is not effective in generating new products or penetrating new markets.

Others—particularly Juran, another quality guru—accuse him of overreliance on statistical methods. Deming's American lectures in the 1980s, however, point time and time again to a mistaken preoccupation with the wrong type of statistics. He argued against figures that focused purely on productivity and control and argued for more evidence of quality, a message that Tom Peters adopted in the 1980s and 1990s.

Deming also stirred up wide interest with his rejection of management by objectives and performance appraisals. Similarly, his attitude toward integrating the workforce led TQM to be perceived as a caring philosophy. Paradoxically, however, his focus on cost-reduction has been pointed to as a cause of downsizing.

Although in the 1980s America paid tribute to Deming—not only for what he did in Japan, but also for his thinking and approach to quality management—few American companies use his methods today. One reason for this is perhaps that, by the 1980s, Deming was selling a system that worked, and implying that he had discovered the only way to achieve quality; thus he was no longer alert to changes in the problems. In Japan, in the beginning, he had listened to Japanese needs and requirements, showed them respect, and developed his thinking with them. In the United States of the 1980s, he appeared to try to dispense his philosophy rather than readapt it to a different culture.

In 1951, in early recognition of their debt to Deming, the JUSE awarded the Deming prize to Japanese organizations that excelled in company-wide quality. It was not until the 1980s that the United States recognized Deming's achievements in Japan and elevated him to guru status. In 1987 the British Deming Association was founded in the United Kingdom to disseminate his ideas. From the 1990s it seemed as if Deming's legacy was likely to have both a lasting and significant impact on management theory. Why is this?

The first reason must lie in the nature of his achievement. Deming has been universally acclaimed as one of the Founding Fathers of Total Quality Management, if not the Founding Father. The revolution in Japanese manufacturing management that led to the economic miracle of the 1970s and 1980s has been attributed largely to him.

Second, if the 14 points make less of an impact today than they did just after World War II in Japan, it is probably because many aspects of those points were adopted, assimilated, and integrated into management practice in the 1990s and have been continuously debated and taught in business schools around the world.

The third reason is more complex, and lies in the scope of his legacy. Deming's 14 points add up to a code of management philosophy that spans the two major schools of managerial thought that have predominated since the early 20th century: scientific (hard) management, on the one hand, and human relations (soft) management, on the other. Deming succeeds—despite criticisms of his overuse of statistical techniques—in marrying them together. Over half of his 14 points focus on people as opposed to systems. Many management thinkers veer towards one school or the other. Deming, like Drucker, melds them together.

The originality and freshness of Deming is that he took his philosophy not from the world of management, but from the world of mathematics, and wedded it with a human relations approach that did not come from management theory but from observation and from seeing what people needed from their working environment in order to contribute of their best.

For More Information

Key work by Deming
Book:
Out of the Crisis: Quality, Productivity, and Competitive Position. Cambridge, MA: MIT Press, 2000.

Further Reading
Book: Bendell, Tony. *The Quality Gurus*. London: Department of Trade and Industry, 1991.

See also:
Philip Crosby (pp. 978–79)
Quality and Total Quality Management (pp. 2096–98)

Peter F. Drucker

The Father of Postwar Management

Peter Drucker is accepted by both practicing managers and writers throughout the world as the management guru. He himself prefers to be known as a writer. He does not claim to have invented management—but does concede that he discovered it as a way of life central to the well-being of society. With more than 33 books published over seven decades Drucker is, by common consent, the founding father of modern management studies.

1909	Born.
1927	Commences study at University of Hamburg.
1931	Doctorate in Public & International Law, University of Frankfurt, Germany.
1933	Moves to London to work as an investment banker.
1937	Leaves for United States to become investment advisor and correspondent for Financial News.
1939	Publication of *The End of Economic Man*.
1940	Private consultant to business and on government policy; teacher at Sarah Lawrence College; Professor at Bennington College, Vermont.
1943	Spends 18 months interviewing senior management at General Motors, which results in the best-selling *The Concept of the Corporation*.
1950	Professor of Management at New York University Graduate School of Business.
1969	Publication of *The Age of Discontinuity*.
1971	Marie Rankin Clarke Professor of Management, Graduate School, Claremont.
1974	Publication of *Management: Tasks, Responsibilities, Practices*.
1975	Columnist for *Wall Street Journal*.
1990	Founding of The Peter F. Drucker Foundation for Non-Profit Management.
1999	Publication of *Management Challenges for the 21st Century*.

Life and Career

Peter Ferdinand Drucker was born in Vienna in 1909 into a high-achieving, intellectual family and was surrounded, in his early years, by members of the prewar Viennese cultural elite. He began his studies at the University of Hamburg, but transferred to the University of Frankfurt, where he obtained a Doctorate in Public and International Law in 1931.

While still a student in Frankfurt, he worked on the city's *General Anzeiger* newspaper and rose to the posts of foreign and financial editor. Recognized as a talented writer, he was offered a job in the Ministry of Information. Observing the Nazis' rise to power with abhorrence, he wrote a philosophical essay condemning Nazism; this was probably instrumental in hastening his departure to England in 1933. It was in 1937 that he left for the United States to become an investment adviser to British industry and correspondent for several British newspapers, including the *Financial Times*, then called the *Financial News*.

His first book, *The End of Economic Man*, appeared in 1939. In 1940 he set up as a private consultant to business and government policy-makers, specializing in the German economy and external politics. From 1940 to 1942 he was a teacher at Sarah Lawrence College, and this was followed by the post of Professor of Philosophy, Politics, History, and Religion at Bennington College, Vermont.

It was in the early stages of this appointment that he was invited by the vice president of General Motors (GM) to investigate what constitutes a modern organization, and to examine what the managers running it actually do. Although Drucker was relatively inexperienced in business at the time, his analysis led to the publication, in 1946, of *The Concept of the Corporation*, which had a mixed reception but nonetheless confirmed Drucker's future as a management writer.

The period 1950–1972 was a time of prolific writing, teaching, and consulting while he was Professor of Management at New York University Graduate School of Business. In 1971 he was appointed the Marie Rankin Clarke Professor of Social Science and Management at the Graduate School in Claremont, a school that was subsequently named after him. In 1994 he was appointed Godkin Lecturer at Harvard University.

Drucker holds decorations from the governments of Austria and Japan as well as 22 honorary doctorates from universities in Belgium, Japan, Spain, Switzerland, the United Kingdom, and the United States. He is also a Fellow of the American Association of Science, an Honorary Member of the National Academy of Public Administration, a Fellow of the American Academy of Arts and Sciences, and a Fellow of the American, British, Irish, and International Academies of Management. He lives in Claremont, 40 miles east of Los Angeles, and has four children and six grandchildren.

Key Thinking

Drucker's management writings are phenomenal in their coverage and impressive in their clarity. With over 33 books to his credit, we can provide only a snapshot of his thinking here. His earlier works made a significant contribution to establishing what constitutes management practice; his later works tackle the complexities–and the management implications–of the postindustrial 1980s and beyond. It is that range and development that we have tried to represent in our comments on the books covered here.

The End of Economic Man–1939

The End of Economic Man concentrates on the politics and economics of the 1930s in general and the rise of Nazism in particular; Drucker signaled a warning about the Holocaust and predicted that Hitler would forge an alliance with Stalin. This was his first book in English as sole author; J.B. Priestley said of it: "At once the most penetrating and the most stimulating book I

"Whenever anything is being accomplished, it is being done, I have learned, by a monomaniac with a mission."

(Peter F. Drucker)

have read on the world crisis. At last there is a ray of light in the dark chaos."

This was followed by *The Future of Industrial Man* (1942), which assumed Hitler's defeat and started to look ahead to peacetime, warning of the dangers of an approach to planning founded on the denial of freedom. It attracted the interest of critics, who argued that it mixed economics with social sciences; it was, in fact, the first book to argue that any organization is both an economic and social organ. As such, it laid the foundations for Drucker's interest in management in general and, as it turned out, General Motors in particular.

The Concept of the Corporation—1946

When General Motors invited Drucker to write about the company, it was expected that the invitation would result in a glowing description of GM's success. What in fact emerged was something different, something that recognized success but also looked to the future.

General Motors provided Drucker with the opportunity to test in practice the theory he had propounded in *The Future of Industrial Man*, that is, that an organization was essentially a social system as well as an economic one. *The Concept of the Corporation* questioned whether what had worked in the past—a foolproof system of objective policies and procedures throughout every layer of the organization—would continue to work in a future of global competition, changing social values, automation, the drive for quality and the growth of the knowledge worker.

The assembly line, he argued, actually created inefficiency because activity took place at the pace of the slowest. Demotivation was rife because no one saw the end result, and initiative was stifled by the minutiae of checks, rules, and controls. The layers of bureaucracy slowed down decision making, created adversarial labor relations, and did nothing to create a "self-governing plant community" (the phrase Drucker used for an empowered workforce). Drucker reported the benefits of decentralized operations—an issue that critics were quick to praise and organizations quick to mimic—but suggested that the GM hierarchy of commands and controls would be slow to respond in a rapidly changing future.

The fundamental difference between Drucker and GM was that GM saw the workforce as a cost in the quest for profits, whereas Drucker saw people as a resource who would be better able to satisfy customers if they had more involvement in their jobs and gained some satisfaction from doing them. *The Concept of the Corporation*, consequently, was decades ahead of its time in terms of its espousal of empowerment and self-management. Although Alfred Sloan—the chief executive and powerhouse behind General Motors' success—had no time for Drucker's book, Drucker was, in the early 1950s, to advise Sloan on setting up a School of Administration at MIT. His criticism of Sloan was implicit rather than explicit, saying he had vision rather than perspective, and implying that leadership had been sacrificed to the rulebook. Sloan was measured in his reply—after all, at the time, General Motors was the largest and arguably one of the most successful companies in the world. His response came in 1963 with the publication of *My Years with General Motors*, which sets out the scientific credo of GM's philosophy, yet talks little of people, transparently because they had comparably little importance relative to the systems they were following.

Another effect of *The Concept of the Corporation* was the establishment of management as a discipline, bringing to the fore the notions of:

- the social and environmental responsibility of the organization;
- the relationship between the individual and the organization;
- the role of top management and the decision-making process;
- the need for continual training and retraining of managers with the focus on their own responsibility for self-development;
- the nature of labor relations;
- the imperatives of community and customer relations.

It is interesting that Japanese industry listened to these messages and American industry did not.

The Practice of Management—1954

The Practice of Management was Drucker's second book on management, and it established him as a leader in his field. It set trends in management for decades, and reputations were built by adopting and expanding on the ideas that he set out in it. It is still regarded by many as the definitive management text.

Drucker states that there is only one valid purpose for the existence of a business, that is, to create a customer. It is not, he argues, the internal structure, controls, organization, and procedures that keep a business afloat; rather, it is the customer—who pays, and decides what is important—who fills this role. He sets out eight areas in which objectives should be set and performance should be measured:

- market standing
- innovation
- productivity
- physical and financial resources
- profitability
- managers' performance and development
- workers' performance and attitude
- public responsibility

The Practice of Management is probably best remembered for setting out the principles of Management by Objectives and Self Control (Drucker's term, although he didn't coin it)—a management process that has become the accepted basis for management theory and practice.

The book also identified the seven tasks of the manager of tomorrow. He or she must:

- manage by objectives;
- take risks and allow risk-taking decisions to take place at lower levels in the organization;
- be able to make strategic decisions;
- be able to build an integrated team whose members are capable of managing and measuring their own performance and results in relation to overall objectives;
- be able to communicate information quickly and clearly, and motivate employees so as to gain commitment and participation;
- be able to see the business as a whole and to integrate his or her function within it;
- be able to relate the product and industry to the total environment, to find out what is important and what needs to be taken into account. This perspective must embrace developments outside the company's particular market or country and the manager must begin to see economic, political, and social developments on a worldwide scale.

Management: Tasks, Responsibilities, Practices—1974

Much of the work in *The Practice of Management* is updated, expanded, and revised in *Management: Tasks, Responsibilities, Practices*, which establishes where management has come from, where it is now and where it needs to go. It draws upon a wide range of international examples and sets out principles for managers and management. Effectively, it is a complete management handbook.

Moving on from his earlier work, Drucker defines the manager's work in terms of five basic operations. He or she:

- sets objectives;
- organizes;

"Leadership is all hype. We've had three great leaders in this century—Hitler, Stalin, and Mao."

(Peter F. Drucker)

- motivates and communicates;
- measures;
- develops people, including him/herself.

Top management's tasks are to:

- define the business mission;
- set standards;
- build and maintain the human organization;
- develop and maintain external relationships;
- perform social and civic functions;
- know how to get on with the task in hand if and when necessary.

Management: Tasks, Responsibilities, Practice is regarded by many as Drucker's finest book.

THE AGE OF DISCONTINUITY—1969 (REISSUED 1992)

It is in *The Age of Discontinuity* that Drucker describes the very changes that he had signaled to General Motors 23 years earlier. He writes in the preface: "This book does not project trends; it examines discontinuities. It does not forecast tomorrow; it looks at today. It does not ask: 'What will tomorrow look like?' It asks instead: 'What do we have to tackle today to make tomorrow?'"

The book deals with the forces changing society as new technology impacts on old industries, changing social values impact on consumer behavior, and markets become international. Drucker advocates privatization, pointing out the ineffectiveness of government in leading and stimulating change; he examines the role of organizations in society in an age of discontinuity and looks at different ways of managing the knowledge worker.

MANAGING IN TURBULENT TIMES—1980

The issues raised in *The Age of Discontinuity* were revisited a decade later in *Managing in Turbulent Times*. Change, uncertainty, and turbulence are the underpinning themes as Drucker highlights the new realities of changing population demographics, global markets, and a "bisexual" workforce.

Drucker issues challenges to junior, middle, and senior management.

- In the knowledge organization, the "supervisor" has to become an "assistant," a "resource," a "teacher."
- The very term "middle management" is becoming meaningless [as some] will have to learn how to work with people over whom they have no direct line control, to work transnationally, and to create, maintain, and run systems—none of which are traditionally middle management tasks.
- It is top management that faces the challenge of setting directions for the enterprise, of managing the fundamentals. It is top management that will have to restructure itself to meet the challenges of the "sea-change," the changes in population structure and population dynamics.
- It is top management that will have to concern itself with the turbulences of the environment, the emergence of the world economy, the emergence of the employee society, and the need for the enterprises in its care to take the lead in respect to political process, political concepts, and social policies.

DRUCKER SAID IT FIRST

Part of Drucker's success and longevity as a management expert was that he had a remarkable knack of spotting trends that were later picked up and made fashionable by others. Invariably, research will trace the origin back to something Drucker wrote ten years—sometimes 20 years—ago. It is interesting that Drucker noted that one of the key aspects of leadership is timing; he, in fact, upbraided himself for being ten years ahead with his forecasts.

The following section is adapted from work by Clutterbuck and Crainer, who summarized the work of James O'Toole, Professor of Management at the University of Southern California. O'Toole said that Drucker was the first to:

- define the role of top managers as the keepers of corporate culture;
- advocate mentoring, career planning, and executive development as top management tasks;
- say that success hinges on the vision expressed by the CEO;
- show that structure follows strategy;
- suggest a reduction of management layers between the top and the bottom;
- argue that success comes from sticking to the basics;
- state that the primary purpose of the organization is to create a customer;
- say that success boils down to sensitivity to the consumer and the marketing of innovative products;
- suggest that quality is a measure of productivity;
- describe the coming knowledge worker;
- state that new approaches to management would be needed in the post-industrial age.

It must be said, however, that Drucker also prophesied the continuing growth of the middle manager as he or she evolved into the knowledge worker of postindustrial society. It has not quite happened like that and the massive delayerings of the early 1990s suggest that Drucker may well have got it wrong. . .so far.

"DRUCKERISMS"

On business:

A business is not defined by the company's name, statutes, or articles of incorporation. It is defined by the want the customer satisfies when he buys a product or service. (*Management: Tasks, Responsibilities, Practices*)

On leadership:

There is no substitute for leadership. But management cannot create leaders. It can only create the conditions under which potential leadership qualities become effective; or it can stifle potential leadership. (*The Practice of Management*)

On management:

The function which distinguishes the manager above all others is his educational one. The one contribution he is uniquely expected to make is to give others vision and ability to perform. It is vision and moral responsibility that, in the last analysis, define the manager. (*The Practice of Management*)

On decision making:

[In] these specifically managerial decisions, the important and difficult job is never to find the right answer, it is to find to find the right question. For there are few things as useless—if not as dangerous—as the right answer to the wrong question. (*The Practice of Management*)

On the knowledge worker:

Increasingly, the knowledge workers of tomorrow will have to know and accept the values, the goals, and the policies of the organization—to use current buzzwords, they must be willing—nay, eager—to buy into the company's mission. ("Drucker speaks his mind," *Management Review*).

[The knowledge worker]. . .may realize that he depends on the organization for access to income and opportunity, and that without the investment the organization has made—and a high investment at that—there would be no opportunity for him. But he also realizes, and rightly so, that the organization equally depends on him. (*The Age of Discontinuity*)

PETER F. DRUCKER IN PERSPECTIVE

Critical of the business school system in general, Drucker always set himself apart from mainstream management education. He said of himself: "I have always been a loner. I work best outside. That's where I'm most effective. I would be a very poor manager. Hopeless. And a company job would bore me to death. I enjoy being an outsider."

An outsider maybe, but commentators point consistently to his gentlemanly old-world charm, his humility, and the fact that he has never criticized negatively, always politely and constructively.

Drucker's earlier works no longer strike the new reader with the same force that they did in the 1950s, 1960s, and 1970s. But this is entirely to his credit. His thinking has become absorbed and adopted as the prevailing wisdom behind the philosophy and practice of modern management.

What does strike the modern reader, however, is the sheer force of his writing, his clear mastery of the subject matter, and the clarity of his expression. It is as well to remember that readable books on management were very few and far between when Drucker wrote *The Concept of the Corporation* and *The Practice of Management*. Texts for managers concentrated usually on technical and industrial engineering and were too complex to have either a wide readership or the impact or influence that Drucker has had.

"For many business leaders across the world. . .he remains the doyen of modern management theory, not so much because he can lay claim to being the founder of any particular concept such as business re-engineering, or total quality management, rather because he has demonstrated a rare ability to apply common sense understanding to the analysis of management challenges and their solutions." ("Interview with Peter Drucker," the *Financial Times*)

One of Drucker's achievements lies in the fact that he, a devotee of the Human Relations school, recognized the value of Taylor's scientific, work-study approach, and succeeded in striking a balance between the two approaches. Management by Objectives, when carried out properly, is an effective marriage of both schools, which attaches significance to culture and to the fact that organizations are held together not just by a dictated vision but by a shared vision of the future.

So, although Drucker awards the accolade of "guru's guru" to F. W. Taylor, the world of management will always attribute it to Drucker himself. His ability to see management with a long historical perspective and in a broad social and political context is very rare in management writers. With his capacity for demystifying the apparent complexities of management for millions worldwide, he stands, as he said of himself, quite alone.

For More Information

Key works by Drucker

Books:

The Future of Industrial Man: A Conservative Approach. New York: The New American Library, 1965.

The Practice of Management. New York. Harper & Row, 1954.

Managing for Results: Economic Tasks and Risk-taking Decisions. New York: Harper & Row, 1964.

The Concept of the Corporation. New York: New American Library, 1964.

The Effective Executive. New York: Harper & Row, 1967.

The End of Economic Man. New York: Harper & Row, 1969.

Technology, Management, and Society. New York: Harper & Row, 1970.

Management: Tasks, Responsibilities, Practices. New York: Harper & Row, 1973.

Managing in Turbulent Times. New York: Harper & Row, 1980.

The Changing World of the Executive. New York: Times Books, 1982.

Innovation and Entrepreneurship: Practice and Principles. New York: Harper & Row, 1985.

The Frontiers of Management: Where Tomorrow's Decisions Are Being Made Today. New York: Truman Talley Books/ Dutten, 1986.

Managing the Non-profit Organization: Practices and Principles. New York: HarperCollins Publishers, 1990.

Managing for the Future: the 1990s and Beyond. New York: Truman Talley Books/Dutten, 1992.

Managing in a Time of Great Change. New York: Truman Talley Books/Dutten, 1995.

Further Reading

Books: Beatty, Jack. *The World According to Peter Drucker.* New York: Free Press, 1998.

Clutterbuck, David, and Stuart Crainer. *Makers of Management: Men and Women Who Changed the Business World*. London: Macmillan, 1990.

Kennedy, Carol. *Managing with the Gurus: Top Level Guidance on 20 Management Techniques*. New York: Century Business Books, 1994.

Micklethwaite, John, and Adrian Wooldridge. *The Witch Doctors: What the Management Gurus Are Saying, Why It Matters, and How to Make Sense of It*. New York: Times Books, 1996.

O'Toole, James. *Leading Change: Overcoming the Ideology of Comfort and the Tyranny of Custom*. San Francisco: Jossey-Bass, 1995.

Journal Article: Donkin, Richard. "Interview with Peter Drucker." *Financial Times*, 14 June 1996, p.13.

See also:

Charles Handy (pp. 1000–01)

Henry Mintzberg (pp. 1024–25)

Alfred P. Sloan, Jr. (pp. 1140–41)

"No other area offers richer opportunities for successful innovation than the unexpected success."

(Peter F. Drucker)

HENRI FAYOL

Planning, Organization, Command, Coordination, Control

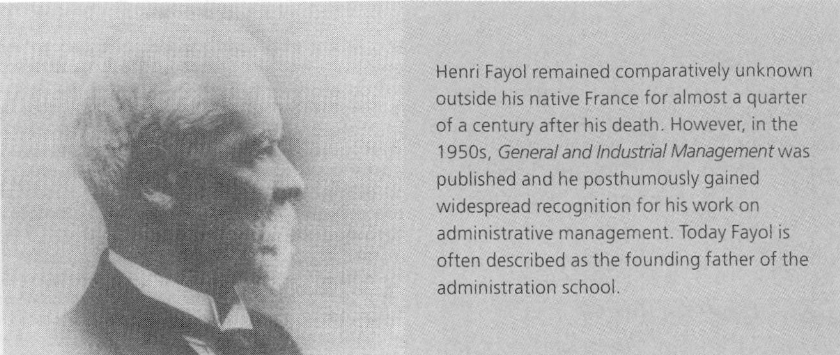

Henri Fayol remained comparatively unknown outside his native France for almost a quarter of a century after his death. However, in the 1950s, *General and Industrial Management* was published and he posthumously gained widespread recognition for his work on administrative management. Today Fayol is often described as the founding father of the administration school.

1841	Born.
1872	Appointed as director of a group of mines.
1918	Retires.
1925	Dies.
1950s	*General and Industrial Management* published; Fayol's reputation as "the founding father of the administration school" established.

LIFE AND CAREER

Fayol spent his entire career in one company, the French mining and metallurgical combine Comentry-Fourchamboult-Decazeville. He began as a mining engineer, was appointed director of a group of mines in 1872, and became managing director in 1888—a post which he held until his retirement in 1918. He retained the honorary title until his death.

When Fayol began his career, the financial health of the mining combine was poor. By the time he retired, however, there had been a complete turnaround and the company was prospering. Fayol's success is often attributed to his development and championing of the "functional principle." This involved:

- preparing yearly and 10-yearly plans, and acting on them;
- preparing organization charts to demonstrate and encourage order;
- recruiting and training carefully to ensure each employee was in the right place;
- adhering to the principle of the chain of command;
- arranging regular meetings with heads of departments and divisions to ensure coordination.

KEY THINKING

Administration Industrielle et Générale—Prévoyance, Organisation, Commandement, Contrôle (General and Industrial Management—Planning, Organization, Command and Control)

In his writing, Fayol attempted to construct a theory of management that could be used as a basis for formal management education and training. First, he divided all organizational activities into six functions:

- technical: engineering, production, manufacture, adaptation;
- commercial: buying, selling, exchange;
- financial: the search for optimum use of capital;
- security: protection of assets and personnel;
- accounting: stocktaking, balance sheets, costs, statistics;
- managerial: planning, organizing, commanding, coordinating, controlling.

Although well understood in their own right, none of the first five functions takes account of drawing up a broad plan of where the business is going and how it will operate; organizing people; coordinating all of the business efforts and activities, and monitoring to check that what is planned is actually carried out. Fayol's sixth function, therefore, acts as an umbrella to the previous five.

Fayol argued that to manage is to:

1. Plan. A good plan of action should be flexible, continuous, relevant, and accurate. Its function is to unify the organization by focusing on the nature, priorities, and condition of the business; longer-term predictions for the industry and economy; the intuitions of key thinkers; and strategic sector analyses from specialist staff.

For effective planning, managers should be skilled in the art of handling people, and possess considerable energy and a measure of moral courage. It is also important that they have some continuity of tenure; be competent in the specialized requirements of the business; have general business experience; and be able to generate creative ideas.

2. Organize. Organizing is as much about lines of responsibility and authority as it is about communication flow and the use of resources. Fayol lays down the following organization duties for managers:

- ensure the plan is judiciously prepared and strictly carried out;
- see that human and material structures are consistent with objectives, resources, and general operating policies;
- set up a single guiding authority and establish lines of communication throughout the organization;
- harmonize activities and coordinate efforts;
- formulate clear, distinct and precise decisions;
- arrange for efficient personnel selection;
- define duties clearly;
- encourage a liking for initiative and responsibility;
- offer fair compensation for services rendered;
- make use of sanctions in cases of fault and error;
- maintain discipline;
- ensure that individual interests are subordinated to the general interest;
- pay special attention to the authority of command;
- supervise both material and human order;
- have everything under control;
- fight against excess regulation, red tape, and paperwork.

3. Coordinate. Coordination involves determining the timing and sequencing of activities so that they mesh properly; allocating the appropriate resources, time, and priority; and adapting means to ends.

4. Command. Managers who are in charge should:

- gain a thorough knowledge of their personnel;
- eliminate the incompetent (this is not as final as it sounds! Fayol takes pains to point out that any decision to part with employees should be the result of careful thought; that the employees should have

"There is no merit in sowing dissension among subordinates; any beginner can do it." (Henri Fayol)

had fairly assigned work for which they were trained; that they should have been appraised fairly and objectively and provided with honest feedback; that they should have been given every opportunity for additional training, offered guidance and—where possible—reassigned to alternative work. Fayol also mentions procedures involving written warnings and protection against bias and "inequities");
- be well versed in the agreements between the business and its employees;
- set a good example;
- conduct periodic audits of the organization;
- bring together senior assistants to ensure unity of direction and focus of efforts;
- not become engrossed in detail;
- aim at making energy, initiative, loyalty, and unity prevail among employees.

5. Control. Controlling means checking that:

- everything occurs according to the plan adopted, the principles established, and the instructions issued;
- appropriate corrective action is taken;
- weaknesses, errors, and deviations from the plan have not slipped in;
- the plan is kept up to date (it is not cast in stone but adapts to changing developments).

Fayol's Principles of Management

Fayol's five-point approach advises managers on their tasks, duties and activities. From his own experience, he established a number of general principles of management, which lend definition to this approach.

- division of work: specialization allows the individual to build up expertise and therefore be more productive
- authority: the right to issue commands, along with the appropriate responsibility
- discipline: two-sided—employees obey orders only if managers play their part by providing good leadership
- unity of command: one man, one boss—with no other conflicting lines of command
- unity of direction: staff involved in the same activities should have the same objectives
- subordination of individual interest to the general interest: the good of the organization must come first over any group, just as the interests of any agreed team should come first over the individual
- remuneration: should be fair and equitable, encouraging productivity by rewarding well-directed effort; it should not be subject to abuse
- centralization: there is no formula to advocate centralization or decentralization; much depends on the optimum operating conditions of the business
- scalar chain: Fayol recognized that although hierarchies are essential, they do not always make for the swiftest communication; lateral communication therefore is also fundamental
- order: avoidance of duplication and waste through good organization
- equity: a "combination of kindliness and justice" in dealing with employees
- stability of tenure: the more successful the business, the more stable the management
- initiative: encouraging people to use their initiative is a source of strength for the organization
- esprit de corps: management must foster and develop the morale of employees and encourage each person to use his or her abilities.

Henri Fayol in Perspective

It is hard to overestimate the influence Fayol has brought to bear on management thinking and management thinkers. Labeled "the founding father of the administration school," he was the first author to look at the organization from the "top down"; to identify management as a process; to break that process down into logical subdivisions; and to lay out a series of principles to make best use of people—thereby establishing a syllabus for management education.

The fact that Fayol's influence has endured is expressed no better than in the influential classic management formula, POSDCORB, a notion directly derived from his writings. It directs that managers should Plan, Organize, Staff, Direct, Coordinate, Report, and Budget.

Looking more closely at the detail of Fayol's five management activities, it is obvious that the conflicts and concerns, responsibilities and duties, styles, and problems that he identified a century ago are still just as relevant today. How do we "ensure that individual interests are subordinated to (harmonized with) the general interest?" How do we "encourage a liking for initiative and responsibility?" And if the "fight against an excess of regulation, red tape, and paperwork" was problematic enough for Fayol to regard as a management duty in his day, he would surely be disappointed at how little progress has been made.

Fayol's last two management activities, command and control, have been taken to describe the hierarchical structure and management style that large organizations adopted from the 1950s through to the 1980s. But again, if we look closely at what Fayol actually says—especially about command—it is not too distant from a description of an empowering, rather than a "commanding," manager today.

Fayol's views have been criticized for weakness of analysis and assessment; for the overlap in his principles, elements, and duties; for confusing structure with process; and for an overreliance on top-down bureaucracy. However, his principles of management do not differ greatly from the characteristics of formal organizations as set out by Max Weber. Fayol's influence as the first to describe management as a top-down process based on planning and the organization of people will ensure his prominence among students and practicing managers alike.

For More Information

Key works by Fayol

Book:

Revised by Gray, Irwin. *General and Industrial Management*. New York: IEEE Press, 1984.

Further Reading

Books: Brech, Edward. *The Principles and Practice of Management*. 3rd ed. London: Longman, 1975.

Crainer, Stuart. *Financial Times Handbook of Management*. 2nd ed. Upper Saddle River, NJ: Financial Times Prentice Hall, 2001.

Pugh, Derek S., and David J. Hickson. *Great Writers on Organizations*. 4th ed. Thousand Oaks, CA: Sage, 1989.

See also:

General and Industrial Management (p. 907)

Frederick Winslow Taylor (pp. 1054–55)

"To manage is to forecast and plan, to organize, to command, to coordinate, and to control."

(Henri Fayol)

 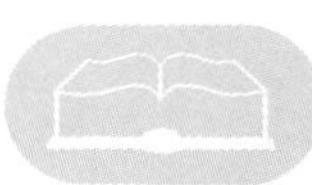    

MARY PARKER FOLLETT

Prophet of Management

Mary Parker Follett was one of the first people to apply psychological insight and social science findings to the study of industrial organization. Her work focused on human relations within industrial groups. She viewed business as a pioneering field within which solutions to human relations problems were being tested out. After World War II, Follett's ideas were largely neglected, except in Japan. Yet her work foreshadowed current Western approaches emphasizing involvement and cross-functional communications.

1868	Born.
1888	Attends Society for Collegiate Instruction of Women, Harvard.
1890	Spends a year at Newnham College, Cambridge University.
1896	Publication of *The Speaker of the House of Representatives*.
1918	Begins writing *The New State*.
1933	Gives inaugural series of lectures for Department of Business Administration (now Department of Industrial Relations) at the London School of Economics (LSE). Dies.

LIFE AND CAREER

Born in Massachusetts to a well-off Boston family, Follett was a brilliant scholar who graduated from high school at the age of 12. She was educated at the Thayer Academy, Boston, and Radcliffe College, Massachusetts. At 20 she attended an annex of Harvard University called the Society for Collegiate Instruction of Women. In 1890, as a student of 22, she spent a year at Newnham College in Cambridge, England, and went on to Paris as a postgraduate student. Pauline Graham describes Follett as a polymath, and records that she studied law, economics, government, and philosophy at Harvard, and history and political science at Newnham. While at Cambridge, Follett gave a paper that she later developed into her first book, *The Speaker of the House of Representatives*. This was taken seriously enough to be reviewed by Theodore Roosevelt in the *American Historical Review* of October 1896.

Follett's family life was difficult. Her father, to whom she was close, died when she was in her early teens. Her mother was an invalid with whom Follett did not get along very well. From an early age Follett ran the household, and later she also ran the family housing business.

Eventually, Follett broke all family ties and went to share a home with her friend, Isobella Briggs. Over the next 30 years, Isobella provided a stable domestic background, while her social connections were helpful to Follett's work. When Isobella died in 1926, Follett lost her home life as well as her closest friend. Later that year she met Dame Katherine Furse, an Englishwoman who was strongly involved with the Girl Guide scouting movement. Follett later moved to England to share a house in Chelsea with Furse.

FOLLETT THE SOCIAL WORKER

Follett was expected to become an academic, but instead went into voluntary social work in Boston, where her energy and practicality (as well as her financial support on occasions) achieved much in terms of community-building initiatives. For over 30 years, she was immersed in this work, and proved to be an innovative, hands-on manager whose practical achievements included the original use of schools as centers for community education and recreation after the normal school day. This was Follett's own idea, and the resulting community centers became models for other cities throughout the United States.

Follett set up vocational placement centers in Boston schools, and represented the public on the Massachusetts Minimum Wage Board. From 1924 she began to give regular papers relating to industrial organization, especially at conferences of the Bureau of Personnel Administration in New York. She became, in effect, an early management consultant, as businessmen began to seek her advice about their organizational and human relations problems.

In 1926 and 1928, Follett gave papers for the Rowntree Lecture Conference and to the National Institute of Industrial Psychology. In 1933, she gave an inaugural series of lectures for the newly founded Department of Business Administration (now the Department of Industrial Relations) at the London School of Economics. Later in 1933, Follett returned to America, where she died on December 18 of that year at age 65.

KEY THINKING

The New State was written during 1918, and argues for group-based democracy as a process of government. Through this book, Follett became widely recognized as a political philosopher. It was based on her social work experience rather than on business organizations, but the ideas it contains were later applied in the business context.

The New State presented an often visionary interpretation of what Follett viewed as the progress of social evolution, and the tone is occasionally infused with poetical religious feeling. The text argues that democracy "by numbers" should give way to a more valid process of group-based democracy. This form of democracy is described as a dynamic process through which individual conflicts and differences become integrated in the search for overall group agreement. Through it, people will grow and learn as they adapt to one another's views, while seeking a common, long-term good.

The group process works through the relating of individuals' different ideas to each other and to the common interests of the group as a whole. Appropriate action would, Follett held, become self-evident during the consultation process. This would eventually reveal a "law of the situation," representing an objective that all could see would be the best course for the group as a whole to pursue. Conflict and disagreement were viewed as positive forces, and Follett considered social evolution to progress through the ever-continuous integration of diverse viewpoints and opinions in pursuit of the common good.

The New State envisions the basic group democratic process following right through to the international level, feeding up from

"The most successful leader of all is one who sees another picture not yet actualized."

(Mary Parker Follett)

neighborhoods via municipal and state government into the League of Nations. Sometimes, Follett refers to an almost autonomous group spirit, which develops from the community between people.

The Creative Experience was also written during 1918, and again focused on democratic governance, using examples from business to illustrate ideas. *Dynamic Management—The Collected Papers of Mary Parker Follett* and *Freedom and Coordination* were both published posthumously and edited by L. Urwick. *Freedom and Coordination* collects together six papers given by Follett at the LSE in 1933, and these represent the most developed and concise distillation of her thoughts on business organization.

Follett's business writings extended her social ideas into the industrial sphere. Industrial managers, she saw, confronted the same difficulties as public administrators as regards control, power, participation, and conflict. Her later writings focused on management from a human perspective, using the new approach of psychology to deal with problems between individuals and within groups. She encouraged businessmen to look at how groups formed and how employee commitment and motivation could be encouraged. The participation of everyone involved in decisions affecting their activities is seen as fundamental, in that Follett viewed group power and management through cooperation as the obvious route to achievements that would benefit all.

Views on Power, Leadership, Authority, and Control

Follett envisioned management responsibility as being diffused throughout a business rather than wholly concentrated at the hierarchical apex. Degrees of authority and responsibility are seen as spread all along the line. For example, a truck driver can act with more authority than the business owner in terms of knowing most about the best order in which to make his drops. Leadership skills are required of many people rather than just one person, and final authority, while it does exist, should not be overemphasized. The chief executive's role lies in coordinating the scattered authorities and varied responsibilities that make up the organization into group action and ideas, and also in foreseeing and meeting the next situation.

Follett's concept of leadership as the ability to develop and integrate group ideas, using "power with" rather than "power over" people, is very modern. She understood that the crude exercise of authority based on subordination is hurtful to human beings, and cannot be the basis of effective, motivational management control. Partnership and cooperation, she sought to persuade people, were of far more ultimate benefit to everyone than hierarchical control and competition.

Follett viewed the group process as a form of collective control, with the experience of all who perform a functional part in an activity feeding into decision making. Control is thus realized through the coordination of all functions rather than imposed from the outside.

Follett's Four Fundamental Principles of Organization

Follett identified four principles of coordination that she considered basic to effective management.

- Coordination consists in the "reciprocal relating" of all the factors in a situation.
- Coordination should be by direct contact, operating by means of direct communication between all responsible people involved, whatever their hierarchical or departmental positions.
- Coordination should begin in the early stages. It should involve all the people directly concerned, from the initial stages of designing a project or forming a policy.
- Coordination should be a continuing process, based on the recognition that there is no such thing as unity, but only the continuous process of unifying.

Mary Parker Follett in Perspective

The Context of Evolutionary Progress

Follett's thinking was ahead of her time, yet was founded on a conviction of social, evolutionary progress, which the course of subsequent history has shown to be flawed. She lived through momentous times, when social and technological change seemed to make a new order inevitable. The destruction caused by World War I also seemed to dictate the clear need for a determined effort to create a social order that would not break down so disastrously. Simultaneously, the war created pressures in both England and America for labor participation in management, and led to a growth in internationalist ideas and to the birth of the League of Nations. Like other writers of the time, Follett made leaps of the imagination that grew out of the factual changes that were actually taking place. Her view was rational and progressive, and she could not know the degree to which some things would remain constant, undermining the apparently inevitable dynamic of social "progress."

Looking back on the whole of the 20th century, of which Follett saw only the beginning, we have only too full a knowledge of World War II and countless other conflicts, of the discrediting of Russian Communism, and of worsening ethnic divisions and continuing human barbarities. The progressive, internationalist vision seems to be, from our contemporary perspective, a fast-receding dream.

Yet, while Follett's optimistic expectations of radical social change were largely mistaken, she drew from it the imaginative vision to transform at least some of her convictions into ideas about ways of living and working that have contributed much to both social and management practice. In fact, it is almost disheartening to read Follett and realize that she clearly and strongly stated, so many years ago, ideas that are being proffered as "new" today and that are still rarely practiced in any sustained way.

For More Information

Key works by Follett

Books:

The Speaker of the House of Representatives. New York: Longmans, Green, & Co., 1896.

The New State: Group Organization—The Solution for Popular Government. New York: Longmans, Green, & Co., 1920.

Creative Experience. New York: Longmans, Green, & Co., 1924.

Urwick, L. F., ed. *Freedom and Coordination: Lectures in Business Organization*. New York: Garland Publishing, 1987.

Fox, E. M., and L. F. Urwick, eds. *Dynamic Administration: The Collected Papers of Mary Parker Follett*. New York: Pitman Publishing, 1973.

Further Reading

Book: Graham, Pauline, ed. *Mary Parker Follett: Prophet of Management—A Celebration of Writings from the 1920s*. Boston, MA: Harvard Business School Press, 1995.

See also:

Dynamic Administration (p. 904)

Anita Roddick (pp. 1134–35)

"Responsibility is the great developer of men." (Mary Parker Follett)

Henry Laurence Gantt

The Gantt Chart

Henry Laurence Gantt's legacy to management is the Gantt chart. Accepted as a commonplace project management tool today, it was an innovation of worldwide importance in the 1920s. But the chart was not Gantt's only legacy; he was also a forerunner of the human relations school of management and an early spokesman for the social responsibility of business.

1861	Born.
1884	Qualifies as mechanical engineer.
1887–1893	Employment at Midvale Steel Company, Philadelphia.
1901	Introduction of task and bonus system.
1917	Contributes to war effort for Frankford Arsenal and for the Emergency Fleet Corporation. Creates Gantt chart.
1919	Dies.

Life and Career

Henry Gantt was born into a family of prosperous farmers in Maryland in 1861. His early years, however, were marked by some deprivation as the Civil War brought about changes to the family fortunes. He graduated from Johns Hopkins University and was a teacher before becoming a draftsman in 1884 and earning a degree as a mechanical engineer. From 1887 to 1893 he worked at the Midvale Steel Company in Philadelphia, where he became Assistant to the Chief Engineer (F. W. Taylor) and then Superintendent of the Casting Department.

Gantt and Taylor worked well in their early years together and Gantt followed Taylor to Simonds Rolling Company and on to Bethlehem Steel. From 1900 Gantt became well known in his own right as a successful consultant as he developed interests in broader, even conflicting, aspects of management.

In 1917 Gantt accepted a government commission to contribute to the war effort in the Frankford Arsenal and for the Emergency Fleet Corporation. He died in 1919.

Key Thinking

Gantt is often seen as a disciple of Taylor and a promoter of the scientific school of management. In his early career, the influence of Taylor—and Gantt's aptitude for problem-solving—resulted in attempts to address the technical problems of scientific management. Like Taylor, Gantt believed that only the application of scientific analysis to every aspect of work could produce industrial efficiency, and that improvements in management came from eliminating chance and accidents.

Gantt made four individual and notable contributions.

The Task and Bonus System

Gantt's task and bonus wage system was introduced in 1901 as a variation on Taylor's differential piece-rate system. Under Gantt's system, the employee received a bonus in addition to his regular daily pay if he accomplished the task for the day; he still received the daily pay even if the task was not completed. Taylor's piece-rate system, by contrast, penalized employees for substandard performance. As a result of introducing Gantt's system, which enabled workers to earn a living while learning to increase their efficiency, production often more than doubled. This convinced Gantt that concern for the worker and employee morale was one of the most important factors in management, and led him eventually to part company with Taylor on the fundamentals of scientific management.

The Perspective of the Worker

Gantt realized that his system offered little incentive to do more than just meet the standard. He subsequently modified it to pay according to time allowed, plus a percentage of that time if the task were completed within the specified time or less. Hence a worker could receive three hours' pay for doing a two-hour job in two hours or under. But here Gantt brought in an innovation, by paying the foreman a bonus if all the workers met the required standard. This constituted one of the earliest recorded attempts to reward the foreman for teaching workers to improve the way they worked. In *Work, Wages, and Profits* Gantt wrote:

"Whatever we do must be in accord with human nature. We cannot drive people; we must direct their development. . .the general policy of the past has been to drive; but the era of force must give way to that of knowledge, and the policy of the future will be to teach and lead, to the advantage of all concerned."

Gantt was interested in an aspect of industrial education which he called the "habits of industry"—habits of industriousness and cooperation that entailed carrying out work to the best of one's ability, and taking pride in the quality as well as the quantity of work performed.

From his experience as a teacher, Gantt hoped that his bonus system would help to convert the foreman from an overseer and driver of workers to a helper and teacher of subordinates.

The Chart

Gantt's bar chart started as a humble but effective mechanism for recording the progress of workers toward the task standard. A daily record was kept for each worker—in black, if he met the standard, in red, if he didn't. This expanded into further charts on quantity of work per machine, quantity of work per worker, cost control, and other subjects.

It was while grappling with the problem of tracking all the various tasks and activities of government departments on the war effort in 1917, that Gantt realized he should be scheduling on the basis of time and not of quantities. His solution was a bar chart that showed how work was scheduled over time through to its completion. This enabled management to see, in graphic form, how well work was progressing, and indicated when and where action would be necessary to keep on time.

Gantt charts have been applied to all kinds of projects to illustrate how scheduling may be best achieved. To illustrate the

principle we might take the miniproject of redecorating an office. The operation would be broken down into the following steps:

- establishing the terms of reference and standards of quality, the cost, and the time;
- informing all appropriate personnel and customers;
- arranging alternative accommodation;
- preparing the office;
- redecorating.

Each step would be allocated a specific amount of time that would be represented on the chart. The Gantt chart provided a graphic means of planning and controlling work and led to its modern variation—PERT (Program Evaluation and Review Technique).

The Social Responsibility of Business

After the death of Taylor in 1917, Gantt seemed to distance himself further from the core principles of scientific management and extended his management interests to the function of leadership and the role of the firm itself. As his thinking developed, he believed increasingly that management had obligations to the community at large, and that the profitable organization had a duty toward the welfare of society.

In *Organizing for Work*, he argued that there was a conflict between profits and service, and that the businessman who says that profits are more important than the service he renders "has forgotten that his business system had a foundation in service, and as far as the community is concerned has no reason for existence except the service it can render." These concerns led him to assert that: "the business system must accept its social responsibility and devote itself primarily to service, or the community will ultimately make the attempt to take it over in order to operate it in its own interest."

Gantt was hugely influenced by the events in Russia in 1917 and, in fear that big business was sacrificing service to profit, he began to attack the profit system itself, calling for public service corporations to ensure service to the community.

Henry Laurence Gantt in Perspective

Gantt was a prolific writer and speaker. He addressed the American Society of Mechanical Engineers on a number of occasions. One of his papers—"Training Workmen in Habits of Industry and Cooperation" (1908)—has been noted by several commentators as giving a unique insight into the human relations dimension of management at a time when scientific management was at its peak.

His approach to the foreman as teacher marks him as an early contributor to human behavioral thought in a line that stretches back to Owen and forward with Mayo to the present day. His approach to the duty of the firm towards society also singles him out as one of the earliest spokesmen on the social responsibility of business. But it is as the inventor of the Gantt chart that he will be remembered.

It has been suggested that his thinking became somewhat vague shortly before his death, as he began to situate the work of the firm in a broader national and political context. It seems that there was a struggle in his later years between service and appropriate rewards, on the one hand and socialist control policies, on the other.

Gantt never profited from his enduring innovation, and his books are illustrated with examples of charts showing "work in progress" rather than the lateral project bar chart with which we are more familiar today. He did receive the Distinguished Service Medal from the government, but it was a member of Gantt's consulting firm, Wallace Clark, who popularized the idea of the Gantt chart in a book that was translated into eight languages.

For More Information

Key works by Gantt

Books:

Work, Wages, and Profits. New York: Engineering Magazine Co., 1910.

Industrial Leadership. New Haven, CT: Yale University Press, 1916.

Organizing for Work. New York: Harcourt, Brace and Howe, 1919.

Further Reading

Books: Clark, Wallace. *The Gantt Chart: A Working Tool of Management*. New York: Ronald Press, 1922.

Duncan, W. Jack. *Great Ideas in Management*. San Francisco: Jossey-Bass, 1989.

George, Claude S. *The History of Management Thought*. 2nd ed. Upper Saddle River, NJ: Prentice Hall, 1972.

Urwick, Lyndall. *The Golden Book of Management*. London: Newman Neame, 1956.

Wren, Daniel A. *The Evolution of Management Thought*. New York: John Wiley, 1987.

See also:

Frederick Winslow Taylor (pp. 1054-55)

"I've often thought that after you get organized, you ought to throw away the organization chart."

(David Packard)

GHOSHAL AND BARTLETT

Managing Across Borders

Pioneering research with collaborator Christopher Bartlett into what makes large global organizations tick, and an enquiring mind committed to management as the wealth creator, have contributed to the emergence of Sumantra Ghoshal (left) as one of the most respected management thinkers of his generation.

Already a sought-after consultant, teacher, speaker, and prolific writer, his research will continue to play an important role during this era of globalization.

GHOSHAL: LIFE AND CAREER

Born in India in 1946, Sumantra Ghoshal studied physics before spending 12 years (1969–81) at the Indian Oil Corporation. He demonstrated his appetite for understanding what makes organizations work by obtaining two doctorates, one from MIT, champion of the rigorous scientific method, the other from more pragmatic Harvard, whose approach is based on case studies, observation, and practice.

After lecturing at MIT and INSEAD, Ghoshal became professor of business policy at INSEAD in 1992, and professor of strategic leadership at the London Business School in 1994. In 1999, he began plans for a new business school in India. He first came to international prominence with the publication in 1989 of *Managing Across Borders*, coauthored with Christopher Bartlett.

BARTLETT: LIFE AND CAREER

Christopher Bartlett is Thomas D. Casserly, Jr. Professor of Business Administration at Harvard Business School where he obtained both his masters (1971) and doctorate (1979). Before joining the faculty of Harvard in 1979, he was a marketing manager with Alcoa in Australia, a management consultant in McKinsey and Company's London office, and general manager at Baxter Laboratories' subsidiary company in France.

His research interests have focused on the strategic and organizational challenges which managers face in running multinational corporations, and these interests have been reflected in his most successful books.

Managing Across Borders was cited by *Financial Times* as one of the 50 most influential business books of the century.

KEY THINKING

MANAGING ACROSS BORDERS

Ghoshal and Bartlett's thinking begins with two fundamental questions:

- What does strategy mean?
- Why do the time-honored business models—exemplified by Alfred Sloan's General Motors—no longer work?

Their initial research involved asking over 250 managers in nine multinational companies how their companies were facing up to the complexities of international competition and the growing global marketplace. They identified a pervasive organizational inability to cope, survive, and succeed in the face of growing diversity and accelerating change.

They found three types of organizational model in operation:

- the multinational model, exemplified by Philips or Unilever—a decentralized federation of local firms held together by posting key people from the center;
- the global model, exemplified by Ford and Matsushita—benefiting from large-scale economies and conduits into new market opportunities;
- a more widespread international model—focusing on technology and the transfer of knowledge to less advanced environments.

They concluded that a fourth model was necessary—the transnational—which would combine all the elements of the other three and, in addition, exploit local know-how as the key weapon in identifying opportunities, not operate overseas sites as outposts of the center.

EFFICIENCY VERSUS ECONOMIC PROGRESS

To understand why the old models no longer worked, Ghoshal examined Alfred Sloan's General Motors, the pioneer of the three Ss (Strategy—Structure—Systems), emulated by other companies for decades.

The three Ss were designed to make the management of complex organizations systematic and predictable. The top people in the organization crafted the strategy, then designed the structure that enabled it to unfold and the systems that made it operational. The information systems they relied on dealt with facts and reduced the human element to a minimum. Employees on Ford's assembly lines, for example, were viewed as replaceable parts; ITT, under Harold Geneen, abolished the possibility of surprise by constantly establishing "unshakeable facts."

For years, this systematic approach worked. It started to break down only in the 1980s, when converging technologies, fluctuating markets, overnight competition, and technological innovation combined to make its control systems cumbersome, unresponsive, and ultimately a risk to the survival of the organization itself. An article by Ghoshal, Christopher A. Bartlett, and Peter Moran in the *Sloan Management Review*, Spring 1999 ("A New Manifesto for Management," pp. 9–20) pointed out that criticisms of these systems for stifling initiative, creativity, and diversity were valid: "They were designed for an organization man who has turned out to be an evolutionary dead end." (p. 11)

In the same article, the authors implicitly attacked Michael Porter's work. Porter had influenced strategic thinking for over a decade by arguing that organizations must beat the competition by gaining a stranglehold on value, that is, by either reducing competitors' value (perhaps through competitive incremental cost or quality improvements) or buying them out. Ghoshal wrote: "Porter's theory is static in that it focuses strategic thinking on getting the largest possible share of a fixed economic pie." (p. 12) For Ghoshal, companies exist not to appropriate value, but to create it—and they get themselves into a position to be able to create value by "changing the smell of the place."

FONTAINEBLEAU AND CALCUTTA: THE "SPRINGTIME THEORY"

Ghoshal developed his "springtime theory" while teaching business policy at INSEAD in

"Satisfactory under-performance is a far greater problem than a crisis." (Christopher Bartlett)

the forest of Fontainebleau, south of Paris. During a summer visit to his home city of Calcutta, he found the humidity oppressive and draining, and likened this to the stultifying atmosphere in control- and system-oriented corporate climates. Later, walking in the woods at Fontainebleau, he realized that the fresh, energizing forest reminded him of the cultural atmosphere of more open and dynamic organizations. From this, he went on to propound his "springtime theory," arguing that managers and approaches to management strongly affect cultures, and can create or change the organizational context, "the smell of the place." But how?

The Three Ps

Ghoshal considers that today's leading companies are built around the "three Ps": Purpose, Process, and People. In an interview in *Management Skills and Development*, he claimed that, as shapers of purpose, senior managers need ". . .to create a shared ambition among their staff, instil organizational values, and provide personal meaning for the work their staff do." Creating that shared ambition is an active management process that challenges poor performance, establishes a common goal, demonstrates managers' commitment, and provides "meaning for everyone's efforts." (p. 40)

In the same interview, Ghoshal also stresses the need for organizations to:

- start thinking outside the "strategic planning" box and examining how they actually learn;
- complement vertical information flows with horizontal personal relationships;
- build a trust-based culture by spreading a message of genuine openness;
- share all the information that has traditionally been a source of power.

He says: "You cannot have faith in people unless you take action to improve and develop them. The success of businesses depends now more than ever on the talent of people working for them." (p. 39) In short, organizations need to forge a "new moral contract" with their people.

The New Moral Contract

In the past, the contract between organizations and employees promised relative security in return for conformity. In the 1980s and 1990s, however, this changed: job security was undermined by downsizing and reengineering, while managerial approaches such as Total Quality Management and Customer Focus demanded more involvement and initiative from employees. The new contract Ghoshal proposes is based on developing employability, and providing challenging jobs rather than functional boxes. It should be viewed neither as altruism on the company's part nor as something imposed on employees. It is, rather, a new management philosophy that recognizes that personal development both improves employees' performance and makes them more employable in their future working lives, and that market performance stems from the initiative, creativity, and skills of all employees, and not just the wisdom of senior management.

Such a contract involves a great leap for both organizations and employees. Employers must create a working environment with opportunities for personal and professional growth, within a management environment in which it is understood that talented, growing people mean talented, growing organizations. Employees must make greater commitment to continuous learning and development, and accept that, in a climate of constant change and uncertainty, the will to develop is the only hedge against a changing job market.

Companies As Value Creators

Ghoshal feels strongly that organizations must stop focusing on squeezing out every last cost saving, waste reduction, or improvement in quality or efficiency. Organizations with that sole aim are only good at improving existing activities. Their emphasis is wholly on conservation, which, as Ghoshal points out, Jack Welch of GE described as a "ticket to the boneyard."

The main message of Ghoshal and Bartlett's more recent book, *The Individualized Corporation* (1998), is that the key to competitive advantage in a turbulent economy is a company's ability to innovate its way out of relentless market pressures. As companies shift emphasis from acquiring value to creating it, managers should shift their focus away from obedience, control, and conformity to initiative, relationship building, and continuous challenge of the status quo. Instead of being cogs in a system, they should become facilitators, drawing creativity from others.

In an interview published in the *Professional Manager*, Ghoshal points out that the modern world has brought about an enormous improvement in the quality of our lives and that this improvement—this value—has been created by business. Politicians create the context, they do not, in Ghoshal's view, create value: this comes from companies and managers. From this perspective, management is the most important profession today: "The quality of BT's management matters, perhaps matters more than a quarter per cent change in interest rates, because it creates value. The most important source of a nation's progress is the quality of its management." ("Professor of the Spring Strategy." *Professional Manager*, May 2000, pp. 20–23.)

Ghoshal and Bartlett in Perspective

In the 10 years or so since Ghoshal came to prominence, his focus has shifted from international strategy to the importance of putting people, creativity, and innovation at the top of the agenda and an emphasis on high-quality management as an important social and moral value-creating force.

It will be interesting to see where the "smell in the air" takes him next, especially in the light of a 1999 article in the *Financial Times* ("Guru with a teaching mission for his country," 12 April, p.14) in which he describes his plans to open a new business school for India.

For More Information

Key works by Ghoshal (all cowritten with Christopher A. Bartlett)

Books:

Managing Across Borders: The Transnational Solution. 2nd ed. Boston, MA: Harvard Business School Press, 1998.

The Individualized Corporation: A Fundamentally New Approach to Management. Collingdale, PA: DIANE Publishing Co., 1997.

Journal Articles:

"Changing the Role of Top Management: Beyond Strategy to Purpose." *Harvard Business Review*, Nov./Dec., 1994, pp. 79–88.

"Changing the Role of Top Management: Beyond Structure to Processes." *Harvard Business Review*, Jan./Feb., 1995, pp. 86–96.

" Changing the Role of Top Management: Beyond Systems to People." *Harvard Business Review*, May/June, 1995, pp. 132–142.

See also:

☆ **Viewpoint: Christopher Bartlett (pp. 45–46)**
☆ **Viewpoint: Sumantra Ghoshal (pp. 190–91)**
Managing Across Borders (p. 922)

"It is possible for a business venture to be an island of efficiency in a sea of sloth." (Indira Gandhi)

  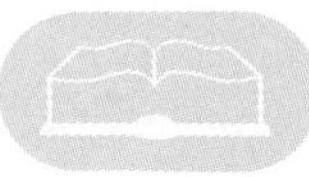    

Frank and Lillian Gilbreth

Motion Study Pioneers

Management practitioners today largely ignore the Gilbreths, possibly because motion study is now unfashionable. However, through Frank's concerns that the efficiency of employees should be balanced by economy of effort and minimization of stress, and Lillian's interest in the psychology of management, they laid the foundations for modern concepts of job simplification, meaningful work standards, and incentive wage plans.

1868	Frank born.
1878	Lillian born.
1885	Frank develops theory of work simplification.
1895	Frank founds engineering consulting company, Gilbreth Inc.
1890s	Frank founds Society to Promote the Science of Management, in conjunction with F. W. Taylor.
1904	Frank and Lillian marry; go on to produce 12 children.
1912–1913	Lillian's book, *Psychology in the Workplace*, published in installments by the Society of Industrial Engineers.
1915	Lillian awarded a Ph.D. in applied management by Brown University.
1921	Lillian becomes first woman member of the Society of Industrial Engineers; later becomes first woman member of the American Society of Mechanical Engineers.
1924	Frank dies. Lillian presents a paper of his shortly after his death at the International Management Conference in Prague.
1925	Lillian continues the work of Gilbreth Inc., conducting seminars on motion study and accepting consulting jobs.
1972	Lillian dies, having been the first and, to date, only female recipient of the Gilbreth Medal, the Gantt Gold Medal, and the CIOS Gold Medal.
1995	Lillian included in the National Women's Hall of Fame in the United States.

Life and Career

Frank B. Gilbreth (1868–1924) began his career as a bricklayer and, by the age of 27, had worked his way up through the profession to found his own engineering consulting company, Gilbreth Inc. He had a particular interest in the development of people to their fullest potential through training, work methods, and improving the working environment and tools, as well as through the creation of healthier working conditions. An adherent to the principles of scientific management, Frank was one of the first to find practical applications for it. Although he had disagreements with F. W. Taylor (mostly through Taylor's claiming Frank's work as his own, and then implying that it was nothing new), Frank was an advocate of Taylor's methods and founded the Society to Promote the Science of Management (renamed the Taylor Society after Taylor's death).

Frank and Lillian married in 1904, and were the parents of 12 children (one daughter died of diphtheria at the age of five). Frank apparently informed Lillian that he wanted six sons and six daughters. In an interview with the *New York Post* in 1941, Lillian was quoted as having once asked him, "How on earth could anybody have 12 children and continue a career?" To which Frank had replied, "We teach management, so we'll have to practice it."

Lillian Moller Gilbreth (1878–1972) was an inspirational woman. In what was very much a man's world at the time—particularly in the area of engineering consulting work, which she entered with Frank—Lillian achieved an astounding amount. When she completed a thesis on the psychology of management, the University of California refused to award her a doctorate unless she returned to campus for a year's residency. This was impractical, so the family moved to the East Coast, where Lillian undertook a Ph.D. in applied management at Brown University, writing a new thesis entitled, "Some Aspects of Eliminating Waste in Teaching." Her Ph.D. was finally awarded in 1915.

Lillian worked closely with Frank in Gilbreth Inc., as well as running their household and bringing up their children. Within a few days of Frank's death in 1924, she traveled to Europe to present a paper that he had intended to give at the International Management Conference in Prague. As Frank's widow, Lillian continued the work of Gilbreth Inc. through conducting seminars on motion study and accepting any consulting jobs that she was not barred from taking simply because she was female.

Often called "the first lady of management," Lillian became the first woman member of both the Society of Industrial Engineers (1921) and the American Society of Mechanical Engineers. She was also the first and, to date, only female recipient of the Gilbreth Medal, the Gantt Gold Medal, and the CIOS Gold Medal. In 1995, Lillian Gilbreth was included in the National Women's Hall of Fame in the United States.

Key Thinking

Work Simplification

Work simplification was based on respect for the dignity of people and work, and was developed by Frank Gilbreth from the age of 17, when he began work as a bricklayer. He documented the different ways that individuals laid bricks and, from these observations, determined the most efficient way to carry out this task. For Frank, efficiency was of benefit both to the employer through an increase in the number of bricks laid, and to the employee, through minimizing the levels of exertion required, and so reducing tiredness and risk of injury. Through his extensive analysis, Frank pioneered a new system of laying bricks that increased output per worker from 1,000 to 2,700 bricks per day.

Another application of Frank's efficiency studies can be seen in operating rooms in hospitals around the world today. Prior to the efficiency study he carried out, surgeons would find all the instruments they needed for operations for themselves, wasting precious minutes as the patient lay on the table. Frank introduced the procedure of having a nurse assist the surgeon by passing instruments into an open hand, as they were required.

Frank took his efficiency systems very seriously, even at home. In *Cheaper by the Dozen*, it is stated that he used two shaving brushes to lather his face in order to save 17 seconds on his shaving time. He abandoned attempts to shave with two razors however: While it saved 44 seconds in shaving time, he also had to spend an extra two minutes bandaging his cuts.

Neither were the Gilbreths' children exempt from their parents' efficiency methods. They were all given their own tasks and became individually responsible for duties such as buying the family's birthday presents, or being chairperson of the house budget committee.

Therbligs

In their study of hand movements, the Gilbreths found that terms such as "move hand" were too general to allow detailed analysis. They split hand movements into 17 basic units of motion that could then, through various combinations, form the hand movements being monitored. These units were known collectively as "therbligs"—Gilbreth spelled backwards, with the "th" transposed.

Microchronometer

In the course of their motion study work, the Gilbreths used photographs to record and then analyze workers' movements. To aid in the clear analysis of their films, they developed the microchronometer—a clock that could record time to 1/2000 of a second—which was placed in the area being photographed. This device is still sometimes used today.

Process and Flow Charts

Around the time that the Gilbreths began working, Henry Gantt developed the ideas that grew into what came to be known as the "Gantt chart"—a system of recording the planning and controlling of work in progress. Frank and Lillian used a Gantt chart in their work and, in their turn, added process charts and flow diagrams. These new tools graphically demonstrated the constituent parts that need to be carried out to complete a task.

Psychology of Management and Personnel Issues

The importance of employee welfare was reflected throughout the work of both the Gilbreths, ranging from Frank's concern over the minimization of employee fatigue and stress to their mutual interest in incentives, promotion, and employee welfare. Although not the originator of the discipline of industrial psychology, Lillian's research for her doctoral thesis raised awareness of the importance of the human element in industry. Many publishers refused to publish a book by a woman on such a technical subject, but *Psychology in the Workplace* was eventually published in installments by the Society of Industrial Engineers in 1912 and 1913. The Gilbreths' interest in industrial psychology continued throughout their lives and was demonstrated by Lillian's participation in various U.S. government committees, on subjects ranging from unemployment and war production to problems related to aging and disability.

Frank and Lillian Gilbreth in Perspective

The Gilbreths are largely unknown and uncelebrated in today's modern corporate world, which tends to minimize the importance of measurement minutiae and favors the space and thinking time needed for creativity and innovation. Earlier in the 20th century, however, management writers from the 1940s on, such as Lyndall Urwick and Edward Brech, had lionized the Gilbreths, along with Taylor and Fayol, as scientific management became the popular gospel.

As we move into the 21st century, any glory for original time and motion work is largely assigned to Taylor, and the work of the Gilbreths is often forgotten or ignored. As the human relations school of management gained in momentum, with the Hawthorne studies and the work of motivational theorists such as McGregor, Maslow, Likert, and Herzberg, people rather than processes slowly became the central pivot for many management thinkers.

The overwhelming influence of scientific management faded from the 1960s onward. The work of the Gilbreths, however, combining the disciplines of both motion study and industrial psychology, deserves to be recognized for its lasting contribution to management thought, and to the ways in which we work today.

For More Information

Key works by the Gilbreths

Books:

Spriegel, William R., and Clark E. Myers, eds. *Writings of the Gilbreths* (A compendium of various books and papers by the Gilbreths including: *Field System, Concrete System, Bricklaying System, Primer of Scientific Management, Motion Study, Applied Motion Study, Motion Study for the Handicapped, Fatigue Study, Psychology of Management*). Homewood, IL: Richard D. Irwin, 1953.

Further Reading

Books: Gilbreth, Frank B., Jr., and Ernestine Gilbreth Carey. *Cheaper by the Dozen*. New York: Thomas Y. Cromwell, 1948. (New edition: published by Yearling, September 2000)

Wren, Daniel. *Evolution of Management Thought*. 3rd ed. New York: John Wiley, 1987.

Yost, Edna. *Frank and Lillian Gilbreth: Partners for Life*. New York: American Society of Mechanical Engineers, 1949.

See also:

☆ **Business Ethics (pp. 231–32)**

Frederick Winslow Taylor (pp. 1054–55)

 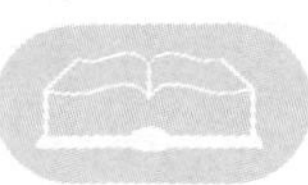    

Daniel Goleman

Emotional Intelligence

Daniel Goleman is usually credited with challenging the traditional view of the IQ (intelligence quotient) by drawing together research on how the brain works and developing this to promote and popularize the concept of emotional intelligence. In *Working with Emotional Intelligence* (1998), Goleman defined emotional intelligence as a capacity for recognizing our own and others' feelings, for motivating ourselves, and for managing our emotions, both within ourselves and in our relationships.

1946	Born.
1984	Joins editorial staff of *New York Times*.
1995	Publication of *Emotional Intelligence*.
1997	Founds Consortium for Research on Emotional Intelligence at Rutgers University.
1998	Publication of *Working with Emotional Intelligence*.

Life and Career

Goleman, born in 1946, gained his Ph.D. in psychology from Harvard, where he also taught. His best-selling book, *Emotional Intelligence: Why It Can Matter More Than IQ*, was published in 1995 and in 1998 this was followed by *Working with Emotional Intelligence*. Goleman has frequently written for the *New York Times* on behavioral science, and currently acts as the chief executive of Emotional Intelligence Services in Sudbury, Massachusetts, which is affiliated with the Hay Group and offers courses in training and assessment for emotional intelligence. Goleman is also co-chairman of the Rutgers-University-based Consortium for Research on Emotional Intelligence.

Goleman's interest in EI arose from a realization that a high IQ is not necessarily a prerequisite for having a successful life. In *Emotional Intelligence* he identifies many people who, while brilliant academically, were nevertheless failures socially or in corporate life. Conversely, he identifies others who were not well qualified or distinguished in academic terms, but were still highly successful in terms of their lives and business achievements. Goleman went on to relate business acumen to emotional intelligence. In the later *Working with Emotional Intelligence* he identified 25 EI competencies, or surface behaviors, and discussed how high emotional intelligence can make all the difference between success and failure.

Key Thinking

Emotional Intelligence and the Brain

In *Emotional Intelligence*, Goleman describes how the evolution of the brain has implications for our emotions and behavioral responses. He outlines how, during its evolution over millions of years, the brain has now come to comprise three main areas:

- the brain stem is situated at the base of the brain and at the top of the spinal cord. It controls bodily functions and instinctive survival responses, and is the most primitive part of the brain;
- the hippocampus evolved after the brainstem and is situated just above the latter. It includes the amygdala region, the importance of which was identified by Joseph LeDoux during the 1980s. Here, the brain stores emotional, survival-linked responses to visual and other inputs. The amygdala seems able to "hijack" the brain in some circumstances, taking over people's reactions literally before they have had time to think, and provoking an immediate response to a situation. Mammals or human beings who have had their amygdala removed show no signs of emotional feeling at all. The amygdala can catalyze the sort of impulsive actions that may sometimes overpower rational thought and the capacity for considered reactions;
- the neo-cortex is the large, well-developed, top region of the brain which comprises the center for our thinking, memory, and reasoning functions.

Because of this course of evolution, our emotions and thinking intelligence—the two main functions of the brain regulating our behavior—are situated in separate areas. Furthermore, our emotional centers receive "input" before our thinking centers, and can react very quickly and very strongly in some situations. The results of this for human behavior can be catastrophic in that, unless we are aware of the situation and practiced in controlling our initial feelings, we may allow inappropriate emotional responses to pre-empt behavior based on consideration of more appropriate options. Our emotions have a "wisdom" of their own that we should learn to use more, particularly in terms of the intuitive sense they offer. Yet, when people first confront stimuli that prompt, for example, extreme fear, anger, or frustration, their first impulse to active response comes from the amygdala. Unless intelligent control is exerted, the brain moves into survival mode, stimulating instinctive actions that, while possibly right for the situation, are not rationally considered, and may be very wrong.

Today, we usually have no need to fight or run away from dangers of the sort faced by prehistoric people. While some instinctive reactions may be wise in given circumstances, we need to be aware of how the primitive response in the brain's emotional center precedes all rational evaluation and response. Emotional intelligence is largely about understanding this and making use of our EI, while also controlling our responses to take account of it.

Goleman's Framework of Emotional Intelligence

Goleman developed a framework to explain emotional intelligence in terms of five elements he described as self-awareness, self-regulation, motivation, empathy, and social skills. Each of these elements has distinctive characteristics, as outlined below:

- *Self-awareness*: examining how your emotions affect your performance; using your values to guide decision-making; looking at your strengths and weaknesses and learning from your experiences (self-assessment); and being self-confident and certain about your capabilities, values, and goals.
- *Self-regulation*: controlling your temper;

"Emotional intelligence is a different way of being smart." (Daniel Goleman)

controlling your stress by being more positive and action-centered; retaining composure and the ability to think clearly under pressure; handling impulses well; and nurturing trustworthiness and self-restraint.

- *Motivation*: enjoying challenge and stimulation; seeking out achievement; commitment; ability to take the initiative; optimism; and being guided by personal preferences in choosing goals.
- *Empathy*: the ability to see other people's points of view; behaving openly and honestly; avoiding the tendency to stereotype others; and being culturally aware.
- *Social skills*: the use of influencing skills such as persuasion; good communication with others, including employees; listening skills; negotiation; cooperation; dispute resolution; ability to inspire and lead others; capacity to initiate and manage change; and ability to deal with others' emotions—particularly group emotions.

Goleman claims that people who demonstrate these characteristics are more likely to be successful in senior management, citing research from various sources that suggests senior managers with a higher emotional intelligence rating perform better than those without. He gives several anecdotal case studies to illustrate ways in which emotional intelligence can make a real impact in the workplace.

THE EMOTIONAL COMPETENCE INVENTORY

Goleman believes that emotional intelligence can be developed over a period of time and he developed an Emotional Competence Inventory (ECI), in association with the Hay Group, to use in assessing and developing EQ competencies at work. The ECI reduces the original five components of emotional intelligence to four:

1. SELF-AWARENESS

- being aware of your emotions and their significance;
- having a realistic knowledge of your strengths and weaknesses;
- having confidence in yourself and your capacities.

2. SELF-MANAGEMENT

- controlling your emotions;
- being honest and trustworthy;
- being flexible and dedicated.

3. SOCIAL COMPETENCE

- being empathic, being able to perceive another's thoughts and points of view;
- being aware of and sensing a group's dynamics and interrelationships;
- focusing on others' needs, particularly when they are customers.

4. SOCIAL SKILLS

- helping others to develop themselves;
- effective leadership;
- skill in influencing others;
- excellent communication skills;
- change-management skills;
- ability to resolve arguments and discord;
- ability to build good relationships;
- team-player skills.

LEADERSHIP STYLES

Goleman, in association with Hay/McBer, has more recently been involved in researching leadership styles, as he reported in a 2000 *Harvard Business Review* article. On the basis of findings with 3781 executive participants, the research suggests that leaders gain the best results by using a combination of six leadership styles, each of which has a central characteristic feature and uses different components of emotional intelligence:

- *Coercive leaders*—demand instant obedience. Coercive leaders are self-motivated, initiate change, and are driven to succeed.
- *Authoritative leaders*—energize people toward a goal. Authoritative leaders initiate change and are empathetic.
- *Affiliative leaders*—build relationships. Affiliative leaders are empathic and have good communication skills.
- *Democratic leaders*—actively encourage team involvement in decision-making. Democratic leaders are good at communication, listening and negotiation.
- *Pacesetting leaders*—set high standards of performance. Pacesetting leaders use their initiative, and are self-motivated and driven to succeed.
- *Coaching leaders*—expand and develop people's skills. Coaching leaders have the ability to listen well, communicate effectively, and motivate others.

The research evidence suggests that the six leadership styles identified are each appropriate for different types of situations, and also that leadership styles have a direct influence on the working atmosphere of an organization, which, in turn, influences financial results.

DANIEL GOLEMAN IN PERSPECTIVE

The conviction that success depends to a high degree on interpersonal skills is not new, and Goleman has often been criticized for taking others' ideas, to some extent, and repackaging them as a new concept. Goleman himself, however, freely discusses the origins of his ideas, and acknowledges fellow academics when he uses their work.

A critical article by Charles Woodruffe in 2001 reviewed Goleman's version of EI, and suggested that:

- Goleman contradicts himself in claiming that emotional intelligence is inherent and biologically based, yet is a skill that can be learned and developed;
- the self-report measures of emotional intelligence used by Goleman have considerable limitations, particularly in terms of accuracy;
- the EI behaviors or competencies put forward by Goleman, such as self-confidence and leadership, are not at all new, and are factors that have often been recognized as commonly associated with high achievement levels.

Whatever truth there might be in these criticisms, Goleman has certainly promoted management thinking on the subject of EI. He has taken some quite complex ideas relating to human behavior and biological evolution, and put these into a more simple and comprehensible format that, under the label of "emotional intelligence," is easy to understand. As a result, many people have found his core proposition, that we can use intelligence to better manage our emotions and draw on our emotional intuition to guide our thinking, to be a helpful approach in both their lives and their work.

For More Information

Key works by Goleman

Books:

Emotional Intelligence: Why It Can Matter More Than IQ. New York: Bantam, 1995.

Working with Emotional Intelligence. New York: Bantam, 1998.

With Richard Boyatzis and Annie McKee. *Primal Leadership: Realizing the Power of Emotional Intelligence*. Boston, MA: Harvard Business School Press, 2002.

Journal Article:

"Leadership That Gets Results." *Harvard Business Review*, vol. 78 no 2, Mar./Apr. 2000, pp. 78–90.

See also:

☆ **Emotional Intelligence (pp. 312–13)**

✔ **Emotional Intelligence (pp. 354–55)**

"A common core of personal and social abilities has proven to be the key ingredient in people's success: emotional intelligence."
(Daniel Goleman)

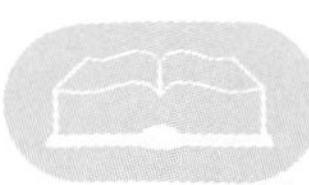

Gary Hamel

The Search for a New Strategic Platform

Professor Gary Hamel (1954–) is one of the most respected contributors to the debate on strategy of the late 20th century. His fresh and often hard-hitting approach to organizational innovation has brought wide acknowledgment from academics and practitioners alike. His reputation developed from the early 1990s when, with C. K. Prahalad, he began to communicate his revolutionary views on strategy.

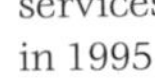

1954	Born.
1980	Gains a Ph.D. in international business from the University of Michigan, where he meets C. K. Prahalad.
1983	Starts teaching at the London Business School.
1990s	Comes to prominence through journal articles containing revolutionary views on strategy.
1994	Cowrites *Competing for the Future* with C. K. Prahalad.
1995	Sets up Strategos Inc. with C. K. Prahalad; is currently chairman.
Present	Visiting professor in strategic and international management at London Business School; research fellow at Harvard Business School.

Life and Career

Hamel worked as a hospital administrator until 1978, when he began to study for a Ph.D. in international business at the University of Michigan. While there, he met C. K. Prahalad, who later became his mentor, collaborator, and colleague in research, writing, and business. Hamel first came to prominence through journal articles in the early 1990s, and as the coauthor of the 1994 book *Competing for the Future*, written (like most of the articles) with Prahalad.

Now at the forefront of thinking on strategy, Hamel is visiting professor in strategic and international management at the London Business School, distinguished research fellow at Harvard Business School, and chairman of Strategos Inc., the strategy services company he set up with Prahalad in 1995.

Key Thinking

Why a new approach to strategy?

At the beginning of the 1980s, Hamel argues, organizational development was no longer driven by strategic forces but by incrementalism. Companies were concerned with getting bigger and better through downsizing, delayering, reengineering, and continuous quality improvement, and their goal became to mimic best practice. The result of all these incremental improvements was to squeeze cost efficiencies to the point where there was nothing left to gain.

At the same time, there were various new forces at work that were changing the nature of competition and the base of traditional industries that had enjoyed primacy in the past. These forces included:

- deregulation and privatization, particularly in the airline, telecommunications, and financial services sectors
- blurring, fragmentation, and increase in newcomers to the computer and telecommunications industries
- changing customer expectations, in terms of price, quality, and service
- continuous technological growth, particularly with the Internet
- shifting boundaries of control and authority, as workforces become more widely distributed, more empowered, and less layered
- changes in traditional loyalties as people became simultaneously the most valuable, but also the most expendable, asset
- the lowered value of experience, as change undermines its relevance for the future.

Strategic Questions to Address

Hamel argues that a compelling view of the future is necessary if one is not to be tied to the orthodoxies of the past, and highlights the number of companies that lost money because they stuck too long to the same game instead of trying to get ahead. Although no view of the future can be accurate or perfect, a view of some sort is essential. This can be developed through addressing questions about the possibility of unleashing the corporate imagination, turning technicians into dreamers, turning planners into strategists, and creating an organization that really lives and makes its decisions in the future.

In a 1996 article Hamel states that, while we can all recognize a great strategy once it is proved to be successful in action, we find it difficult to generate a great strategy in the first place. He argues that strategy generation is not a purely analytical process, but is multifaceted and involves risk, gut feelings, intuition, and emotion, as well as analysis. ("Competing in the New Economy: Managing out of Bounds," with C. K. Prahalad, *Strategic Management Journal*, vol. 17, pp. 237–242.)

Strategy As Core Competence

The concept of corporate competencies was highlighted by Hamel and Prahalad in journal articles and in the book *Competing for the Future*. In the latter they argued that, for too long, organizational focus had been on returns from individual business units, as opposed to the conditions, processes, and competencies that enabled those returns. They define "core competencies" as the collective learning in the organization and, especially, the coordination of diverse production skills and integration of multiple streams of technologies.

Hamel and Prahalad ask organizations to look on themselves as portfolios of core competencies by analyzing what it is that they do better than others. Viewing the organization as systems of activities and building blocks means asking:

- How does activity X significantly improve the end product for the customer?
- Does activity X offer access to a range of applications and markets?
- What would happen to our competitiveness if we lost our strength in activity X?
- How difficult is it for others to imitate activity X and compete with us?

In order to realize the potential that core competencies create, the organization's

"Perseverance may be just as important as speed in the battle for the future." (Gary Hamel)

people must have the imagination to visualize new markets and the ability to move into them, ahead of the competition. One of the keys to core competencies and effective competition is, therefore, the process through which an organization releases corporate imagination. And one of the words that recurs increasingly through Hamel's writing is "revolution."

Strategy As Revolution

In a seminal article, "Strategy As Revolution" (*Harvard Business Review*, Jul/Aug 1996, pp. 69–82), Hamel sets out 10 principles that strategy generators should bear in mind.

- Strategic planning is not strategic: Rather, it is a calendar-driven ritual involving plans and subplans, instead of something challenging and innovative that might lead to discovery.
- Strategy making should be subversive: Great strategies come from challenging the status quo and doing something different. Anita Roddick, of the highly innovative Body Shop, is quoted as saying, "I watch where the cosmetics industry is going and then walk in the opposite direction."
- The bottleneck is at the top of the bottle: The most powerful defenders of strategic orthodoxy are senior management, and strategy making needs to be freed from the tyranny of their experience.
- Revolutionaries exist in every company: Let everyone have their voice, so that new and young as well as tried and tested contributors are part of strategy making.
- Change is not the problem—engagement is: People will support change and welcome the responsibility for engendering it, if this gives them some control over their own future.
- Strategy making must be democratic: The capability for strategic thinking is not limited to senior people, and it is impossible to predict where a good, revolutionary idea may be lurking.
- Anyone can be a strategy activist: People who care about their organization do not wait for permission to act.
- Perspective is worth 50 IQ points: Subversive strategy means gaining a new perspective on the world, and looking at potential markets through new eyes.
- Top-down and bottom-up are not alternatives: If top-down can achieve unity of purpose among the few involved, bottom-up will bring diversity of perspective. Bring the two together.
- You can't see the end from the beginning: Surprises do not appeal to everyone, but delving into discontinuities and identifying potential competencies will bring about unpredictable outcomes. These will probably not fit the orthodox strategic mold—but strategy making is about letting go.

So how do we begin to put these principles into a framework for creating strategy as a systemic capability?

Creating Strategy

"Strategy innovation is the only way for newcomers to succeed in the face of enormous resource disadvantages, and the only way for incumbents to renew their lease on success." ("Strategy Innovation and the Quest for Value." *Sloan Management Review*, Winter 1998, pp. 7–14.)

While some strategies result from analysis and others from inspiration and vision, many strategies also evolve and emerge. To achieve strategies that are neither too random nor too ordered or ritualistic, Hamel suggests we look to the roots of strategy creation, which he regards as a relatively simple phenomenon amid the complexity of organizational life. In "Strategy Innovation and the Quest for Value" (cited above), Hamel turns his revolutionary principles into action points, and urges organizations to adopt a new stance through:

- new voices—top management relinquishing its hold on strategy and introducing newcomers; young people and people from different groups bring richness and diversity to strategy formulation
- new conversations—the same people discussing the same issues over and over again leads to sterility; new opportunities arise from juxtaposing formerly isolated people
- new passions—people will go for change when they can steer it and benefit from it
- new perspectives—search for new ways of looking at markets, customers, and organizational capabilities; think different, see different
- new experiments—small, low-risk experiments can accelerate the organization's learning and will indicate what may work and what may not.

Gary Hamel in Perspective

While it is not possible to pigeonhole Hamel, we can place him roughly in the progressive (if sometimes ragged) line of strategic thinking stretching back to Chandler and Ansoff and including Porter and Mintzberg, as well as Hamel's collaborator and colleague, Prahalad. Hamel's curiosity and tendency to challenge the status quo make it difficult to predict where his future research interests may take him next. However it is likely that he will continue to move in tune with, if not ahead of, the rapidly changing business environment. His recent book, for example, *Leading the Revolution*, is about throwing away the old rule book, imagining a future that others have not seen, and then taking the initiative to act on it.

For More Information

Key works by Hamel

Books:

Hamel, Gary, with C. K. Prahalad. *Competing for the Future*. Boston, MA: Harvard Business School Press, 1994.

Hamel, Gary, with Yves Doz. *Alliance Advantage: The Art of Creating Value through Partnering*. Boston, MA: Harvard Business School Press, 1998.

Strategic Flexibility: Managing in a Turbulent Environment. New York: John Wiley, 1998.

Leading the Revolution. Boston, MA: Harvard Business School Press, 2000.

Journal Articles:

Hamel, Gary, with C. K. Prahalad. "Strategy As Stretch and Leverage." *Harvard Business Review*, Mar./Apr. 1993, pp. 75–84.

Hamel, Gary, with C. K. Prahalad. "The Core Competence of the Corporation." *Harvard Business Review*, May/Jun. 1990, pp. 79–91.

See also:

Competing for the Future (p. 899)

C. K. Prahalad (pp. 1040–41)

"Neither Stalinist bureaucracy nor Silicon Valley provide an optimal ecosystem." (Gary Hamel)

CHARLES HANDY

Understanding the Changing Organization

Charles Handy is well known for his work on organizations. This work has culminated in the formation of a vision of the future of work and of the implications of change for the ways in which people manage their lives and careers. His observation of work in modern society has identified discontinuous change as the (paradoxically) continuing characteristic of working lives and organizations. He has forecast a future—so far, with a good deal of accuracy—where half of the United Kingdom's workforce will no longer be in permanent full-time jobs.

1932	Born.
1967	Founder of Sloan Program, London Business School.
1972	Professor, London Business School.
1974	Governor, London Business School.
1976	Publication of *Understanding Organizations*.
1977	Warden, St. George's House, Windsor Castle.
1985	Publication of *Gods of Management*.
1989	Publication of *The Age of Unreason*.
1994	Publication of *The Age of Paradox*.

LIFE AND CAREER

Born in Ireland, Charles Handy is a self-employed writer, teacher, and broadcaster. He is visiting Professor at the London Business School and consultant to a wide range of organizations in government, business, and the voluntary and educational sectors.

After he graduated from Oxford, his working life began in the marketing and personnel divisions of Shell International and, as an economist, with Anglo-American Corporation. He then returned to academia at the Sloan School of Management of the Massachusetts Institute of Technology. In 1967 he was founder director of the Sloan Program at the London Business School, where he also taught managerial psychology and development. Appointments as professor and governor of the School followed in 1972 and 1974 respectively. In 1977 he was appointed Warden of St. George's House in Windsor Castle, a private conference and study center with a strong focus on the discussion of business ethics. As a teacher he later concentrated on the application of behavioral science to management, the management of change, the structure of organizations, and on the theory and practice of individual learning in life.

He is a past Chairman of the Royal Society of Arts; in 1994 he was U.K. Business Columnist of the Year. He has also been a regular contributor to Thought for the Day (a daily brief religious talk) on the Today Program on BBC Radio 4.

KEY THINKING

Four of Handy's books in particular consider the structure of organizations in detail, and offer a perspective on the ways in which they work. These are: *Understanding Organizations* (1976), *Gods of Management* (1985), *The Age of Unreason* (1989), and *The Age of Paradox* (1994).

UNDERSTANDING ORGANIZATIONS

Handy's *Understanding Organizations*—described by publishers and commentators alike as "a landmark study"—is equally valuable for the student of management and for the practicing manager. Among the subjects with which it deals are motivation, roles and interactions, leadership, power and influence, the workings of groups, and the culture of organizations. They are dealt with both as "concepts" and "concepts in application." A "guide to further study" points the way for further examination of each concept.

GODS OF MANAGEMENT

Handy identifies some established structures in organizations and suggests new forms that are emerging. He perceives that, currently, organizations embrace four basic "cultures." These are:

- *Club Culture*. This is represented metaphorically by Zeus, the strong leader who has, likes, and uses power, and graphically by a spider's web. All lines of communication lead, formally or informally, to the leader. Such organizations display strength in the speed of their decision making; their potential weakness lies in the caliber of the "one man bands" running them.
- *Role Culture*. This is personified as Apollo, the god of order and rules, represented by a Greek temple. Such organizations are based on the assumptions that people are rational, and that roles can be defined and discharged with clearly defined procedures. They display stability and certainty, and have great strength in situations marked by continuity; they often display weakness in adapting to, or generating, change.
- *Task Culture*. This is likened to Athena, the goddess of wisdom, and is found in organizations where management is concerned with solving a series of problems. The structure is represented by a net, resources being drawn from all parts of the organization to meet the needs of current problems. Working parties, subcommittees, task forces, and study groups are formed on an ad hoc basis to deal with problems. This type of culture is seen to advantage when flexibility is required.
- *Existential Culture*. This is represented by Dionysus, the god of wine and song. Organizations characterized by a culture of this type are those that exist to serve the individual and in which individuals are not servants of the organization. They consist of groups of professionals, for example, doctors or lawyers, with no "boss." Coordination may be provided by a committee of peers. Such structures are becoming more common as more conventional organizations increasingly contract out work to professionals and specialists whose services are used only as and when required.

THE CHANGING ORGANIZATION

The link between this analysis of organizational structures and Handy's later work is, in part, provided by the development of "contracting out"—one of a number of

"Brains are becoming the core of organizations—other activities can be contracted out."

(Charles Handy)

changes that he observes in the world of employment. Another major change is the basing of the quest for profit on intelligence and professional skills rather than on manual work and machines. Yet another is that the days of working for one employer and/or in one occupation may be over.

The Shamrock Organization

An example of Handy's changing perception of organizations is provided by his use (in *The Age of Unreason*) of the shamrock. He uses this symbol to demonstrate three bases on which people are often employed and organizations linked today. The people linked to an organization are beginning to fall into three groups, each with different expectations of it, each managed and rewarded differently.

The first group is a core of qualified professional technicians and managers. They are essential to the continuity of the organization, and have detailed knowledge of it, and of its aims, objectives, and practices. They are rewarded with high salaries and associated benefits, in return for which they must be prepared to give commitment, to work hard, and, if necessary, to work long hours. They must be mobile. They work within a task culture, one within which there is a constant effort to reduce their numbers.

The second group consists of contracted specialists who may be used, for example, for advertising, R&D, computing, catering, or mailing services. They operate in an existential culture; and are rewarded with fees rather than with salaries or wages. Their contribution to the organization is measured in output rather than in hours, in results rather than in time.

The third group—the third leaf of Handy's shamrock—consists of a flexible labor force, discharging part-time, temporary, and seasonal roles. They operate within a role culture; but, Handy observes, while they may be employed on a casual basis, they must not be managed casually but in a way that recognizes their worth to the organization.

The Federal Organization and the Inverted Doughnut

The concept of the federal organization was first explored in *The Age of Unreason* and expanded in *The Age of Paradox*. In it, subsidiaries federate to gain benefits of scale. Federal organizations should not be confused with decentralized organizations, in which power lies in the center and is exerted downwards and outwards. In the federal organization, the role of top management is redefined as that of providing vision, motivating, inspiring, and coordinating; initiative comes from the components of the organization. Handy observes and describes the principle of "subsidiarity"—not handing out or delegating power, but ruling and unifying only with the consent and agreement of equal partners.

In *The Empty Raincoat* Handy uses the metaphor of the inverted doughnut to demonstrate how those in the subsidiaries must constantly seek to extend their roles and associated activities. The hole in the conventional doughnut is filled by the core activities of the subsidiary; the substance of the doughnut represents a diminishing vacuum into which the subsidiary can expand its activities given the necessary drive, will, and ability.

Portfolio Working and Downshifting

Following on from his work on organizational change, Handy studied the effects of such change on the individual. He coined the concept "portfolio working," based on the assumption that full-time working for one employer will soon be a thing of the past. Embedded in this is the notion of downshifting—the idea that it is possible to exchange some part of income for a better quality of life.

Although Handy has gone on record as saying that more and more individuals will opt out of formal organizations and sell their services at a pace and at a price to suit themselves, he has also admitted that comparatively few may find themselves in a position to take real advantage of this. He argues, however, that there is much that the organization can do to help the individual to get to grips with the new uncertainty. It was in discussion with the Japanese that Handy coined the "theory of horizontal fast track." In Japan, the most talented people are moved around from experience to experience as quickly as possible, so that their talents can be tested in different situations, with different managers and different cultures. This ensures that they discover what they are really good at and provides a lot of experience.

Charles Handy in Perspective

With his imaginative use of analogy and metaphor, the Handy of the 1990s moved us from the past into the future. He argues that federalist and shamrock organizations can really be successful only if businesses are prepared to invest in their workforces and build relationships of trust.

While he is as much concerned with individuals as organizations, his messages are sometimes disquieting. In *The Hungry Spirit*, he assesses the effects of the competitiveness of capitalism on the individual, suggesting that people can become not only stressed but also selfish and insensitive. But his message is not confined to pessimism about the future. On the contrary, the new capitalism consists of intellectual property—know-how, not merely physical and financial resources; the new knowledge markets enable low-cost entry to those with "a bit of wit and a bit of imagination" and the new products of the knowledge world are not nearly so destructive on the environment as the industrial products of the past.

Handy stands apart from many other management writers by his breadth of vision, his setting of management in a wide social and economic context, and the sheer readability of his writing. He is also ready to modify his views in the light of experience and further thought (he has admitted that some of his expectations have been proved wrong). He is not merely an observer of change but increasingly a catalyst who forces people to stand back from their daily routine, take stock, and view the future through different glasses, acknowledge change, and address its implications.

For More Information

Key works by Handy

Books:

Understanding Organizations. New York: Oxford University Press, 1985.

Gods of Management. London: Souvenir Press, 1985.

The Age of Unreason. Boston, MA: Harvard Business School Press, 1989.

The Age of Paradox. Boston, MA: Harvard Business School Press, 1994.

Beyond Certainty. Boston, MA: Harvard Business School Press, 1998.

The Hungry Spirit: Beyond Capitalism—A Quest for Purpose in the Modern World. New York: Broadway Books, 1998.

See also:

☆ **Viewpoint: Charles Handy (pp. 75–76)**
The Age of Unreason (p. 889)
Stephen R. Covey (pp. 976–77)
Peter F. Drucker (pp. 982–85)
Tom Peters (pp. 1036–37)

"Profit has to be a means to other ends rather than an end in itself." (Charles Handy)

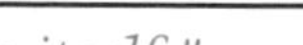

FREDERICK HERZBERG

The Hygiene-Motivation Theory

Herzberg is best known for his "hygiene-motivation" or "two factor" theory of what motivates workers, formulated in the late 1950s. He invented the acronym KITA (Kick In The Ass) to explain why personnel practices such as wage increases, fringe benefits, and job participation often fail to instill motivation and prove to be only short-term solutions. He also coined the term "job enrichment" to describe a process in which the positively motivating factors he had previously identified are deliberately built into the design of jobs.

1923	Born.
1945	Enters Dachau concentration camp with U.S. liberating forces.
1946	Graduates from City College of New York.
1951–1957	Research director of psychological services in Pittsburgh, Pennsylvania.
1957	Appointed professor of management at Case Western Reserve University, Cleveland, Ohio.
1959	*The Motivation to Work* published.
1966	*Work and the Nature of Man* published.
1968	"One More Time: How Do You Motivate Employees?" published in the *Harvard Business Review*.
1972	Joins University of Utah's College of Business.
2000	Dies.

   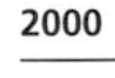

LIFE AND CAREER

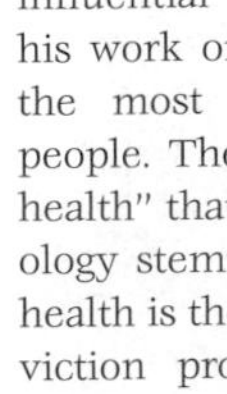 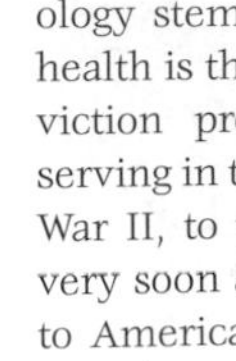 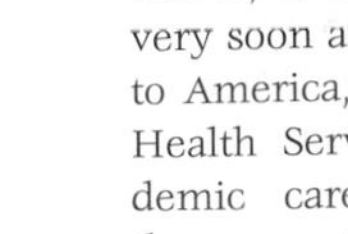 

Frederick Herzberg (1923–2000) was a U.S. clinical psychologist who became an influential management thinker through his work on the nature of motivation and the most effective ways of motivating people. The "overriding interest in mental health" that led him into a career in psychology stemmed from a belief that "mental health is the core issue of our times," a conviction prompted by his posting, while serving in the American forces during World War II, to the Dachau concentration camp very soon after its liberation. On his return to America, he worked for the U.S. Public Health Service before beginning an academic career. His "hygiene-motivation" theory was first set forth in *The Motivation to Work*, published in 1959. From 1972 until his retirement he worked at the University of Utah Business School.

KEY THINKING

THE HYGIENE-MOTIVATION THEORY

The "hygiene-motivation" or "two factor" theory that made Herzberg's name grew out of research he undertook with two hundred Pittsburgh engineers and accountants in the late 1950s.

He asked his subjects to recall times when they had felt exceptionally good about their jobs, then why they had had these positive feelings, and also what effect those feelings had had both on their performance at work and on their lives outside work. In a second question, he asked them to recall times when their experiences at work had resulted in negative feelings.

Herzberg was struck by the fact that, in the answers to his questionnaire, the positive things that the respondents had to say about their work experiences were not the opposite of the negative ones. From this, he concluded that there were two factors at work.

He postulated first of all that human beings have two sets of needs:

- lower-level needs as an animal to avoid pain and deprivation;
- higher-level needs as a human being to grow psychologically.

These needs have to be satisfied at work as much as in any other sphere of life. He concluded from the results of his survey that some factors in the workplace meet the first set of needs but not the second, and vice versa. The former group of factors he called "hygiene factors" and the latter, "motivators."

"Hygiene factors" have to do with the context or environment in which a person works. They include:

- company policy and administration
- supervision
- working relationships
- working conditions
- status
- security
- pay

The most important thing about these factors is that they do not in themselves promote job satisfaction; they serve primarily to prevent job dissatisfaction, in the same way that good hygiene does not in itself produce good health, but a lack of it will usually cause disease. Herzberg also spoke of them as "dissatisfiers" or "maintenance factors," because their absence or inadequacy causes dissatisfaction at work, while their presence simply keeps workers reasonably happy without motivating them to better themselves or their performance. Some factors are also not to be regarded as true motivators because they need constant reinforcement. Once introduced, they increasingly come to be regarded as rights to be expected, rather than incentives to greater satisfaction and achievement.

"Motivators" (also referred to as "growth factors") relate to what a person does at work, rather than to the context in which it is done. They include:

- achievement
- recognition
- the work itself
- responsibility
- advancement
- growth

Herzberg explains that the two sets of factors are separate and distinct because they are concerned with two different sets of needs. They are not opposites.

Herzberg's hygiene-motivation theory is derived from the outcomes of several investigations into job satisfaction and job dissatisfaction, studies that replicated his original research in Pittsburgh. The theory proposes that most of the factors that contribute to job satisfaction are motivators, while most of the factors that contribute to job dissatisfaction are hygiene factors.

Most of the evidence on which Herzberg based his theory is relatively clear-cut. This is particularly the case with regard to achievement and promotion prospects as potential job satisfiers and with regard to

"If you have someone on a job, use him. If you can't, get rid of him." (Frederick Herzberg)

supervision and job insecurity as factors that contribute principally to dissatisfaction.

The element that continues to cause some debate is salary/pay, which seems as if it might belong in either group. Herzberg himself placed salary with the dissatisfiers, although the evidence was not so clear in this instance. This would seem to be the more appropriate classification. Although pay may have some short-term motivational value, it is difficult to conceive of it as a long-term motivator of the same order as responsibility and achievement. Most experience (and the history of industrial relations) would point to pay as a dissatisfier and therefore a hygiene factor along with supervision, status, and security.

KITA

In his extremely influential 1968 article for the *Harvard Business Review*, "One More Time: How Do You Motivate Employees?", Herzberg basically lumped all the hygiene factors together with the less pleasant aspects of work experience under the heading KITA (Kick In The Ass). To explain why managers are unable to motivate employees, he demonstrated again that employees are not motivated by being kicked (figuratively speaking), or by being given more money or benefits, or by a comfortable environment, or by reducing the time they spend at work. These things merely produce movement, the avoidance of pain. What genuinely motivates are things that are intangible, or intrinsic to the work.

Adam and Abraham

Herzberg used biblical allusions to illustrate his theory, especially in his book *Work and the Nature of Man*, first published in 1966 and intended as a psychological underpinning to his workplace-oriented studies. He depicted humanity's basic needs as two parallel arrows pointing in opposite directions. One arrow represents the "Animal-Adam" nature of human beings, concerned with the basic need to avoid physical deprivation (the hygiene factors); the other represents their "Human-Abraham" nature, which is driven by a need to realize their potential for perfection (the motivation factors).

Job Enrichment

Job enrichment was a logical extension of Herzberg's hygiene-motivation theory. Still working on the basic premise that a satisfied workforce is a productive workforce, he proposed that motivators of the type he had always advocated should be built into job design. They included:

- self-scheduling
- control of resources
- accountability
- undertaking specialized tasks in order to become expert in them

He saw it as a continuous function of management to ensure that people were given the opportunity to become more responsibly and creatively involved in their jobs.

Frederick Herzberg in Perspective

Herzberg's work—in common with that of Elton Mayo (known for the Hawthorne Experiments), Abraham Maslow (developer of the hierarchy of needs), and Douglas McGregor (creator of Theory X and Theory Y)—can be seen as a reaction to F. W. Taylor's scientific management theories. These last focused on techniques which could be used to maximize the productivity of manual workers and on the division of mental and physical work between management and workers. In contrast, Herzberg and his contemporaries believed that workers wanted the opportunity to feel part of a team and to grow and develop.

Although Herzberg's theory is not highly regarded by psychologists today, managers have found in it useful guidelines for action. Its basic tenets are easy to understand and can be applied to all types of organization. Furthermore, it appears to support the position and influence of management.

More specifically, it has had a considerable impact on reward systems, first, in a move away from payment-by-results systems, and today in the growing proportion of cafeteria benefits schemes, which allow individual employees to choose the fringe benefits which best suit them.

Job enrichment was more theorized about than put into practice. Many schemes that were tried resulted only in cosmetic changes or led to demands for increased worker control and were therefore terminated. Nowadays the concept is more one of people enrichment, although this still owes a great deal to Herzberg's original work. His greatest contribution has been the knowledge that motivation comes mainly from within the individual; it cannot be imposed from the outside by an organization in accordance with some formula. Many of today's trends—career management, self-managed learning, and empowerment—have their basis in Herzberg's insights.

For More Information

Key works by Herzberg

Books:

Work and the Nature of Man. New York: Ty Crowell Co., 1966.

The Managerial Choice: To Be Efficient and To Be Human. Homewood, IL: Dow Jones-Irwin, 1976.

Herzberg, Frederick, with Bernard Mausner and Barbara Bloch Snyderman. *The Motivation to Work*. 2nd ed. New York: John Wiley, 1959.

Journal Articles:

"One More Time: How Do You Motivate Employees?" *Harvard Business Review*, Jan./Feb. 1968, pp. 53–62.
(This article was republished in *Harvard Business Review*, Sep./Oct. 1987, pp. 109–120, with a retrospective commentary by the author. By the time of this republication, the article had sold over one million reprints, making it the most requested article in the Harvard Business Review's history.)

Further Reading

Journal Article: Cameron, Donald. "Herzberg—Still a Key to Understanding Motivation." *Training Officer*, Jul./Aug. 1996, pp. 184–186.

See also:

☆ **Retaining Employees (pp. 196–97)**

✔ **Managing Staff Turnover and Retention (pp. 364–65)**

Abraham Maslow (pp. 1018–19)

Geert Hofstede

Cultural Diversity

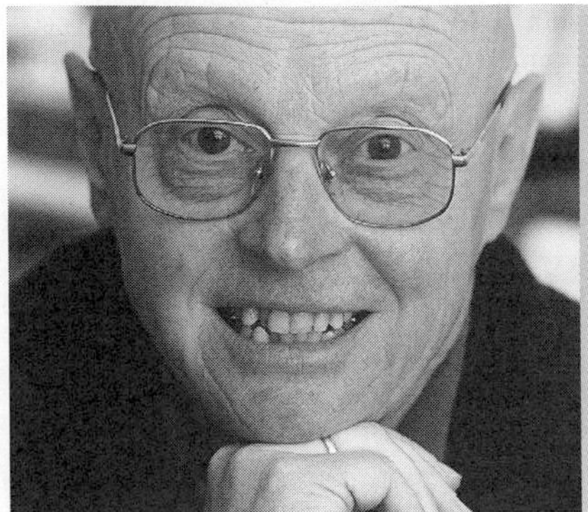

Hofstede identified four "dimensions" (commonly known as "Hofstede's dimensions") for defining work-related values associated with national culture: power distance; individualism/collectivism; masculinity/femininity; and uncertainty avoidance. He also devised the "values survey module" for use in researching cultural differences, which has been adopted by many other researchers in their work.

1928	Born.
1953	Graduates from Delft Institute of Technology.
1967	Receives Ph.D. from University of Groningen.
1967–1973	Undertakes massive research project into IBM.
1980	*Culture's Consequences* published.
1991	*Cultures and Organizations* published.

Life and Career

Geert Hofstede is a Dutch academic who has also spent long periods in industry, most notably at IBM. He is emeritus professor of organizational anthropology and international management at the University of Limburg in Maastricht in the Netherlands, and he founded the Institute for Research on International Cooperation. He has become known for pioneering research on national and organizational cultures. Much of his subsequent thinking was based on a monumental six-year research project in the late 1960s and early 1970s into the workings of a giant international corporation, originally known by the pseudonym HERMES and later revealed as IBM.

The management of cultural diversity is becoming a significant issue for companies of all sizes, not just multinationals. The rise of global business–leading to an increase in the number of joint ventures and cross-border partnerships, greater cooperation within the European Union, and business's need to embrace people from a variety of ethnic backgrounds and cultures, have all contributed to the need to develop cultural sensitivity. Ignorance or insensitivity in cultural matters can cause serious problems to international operations. The transfer of Western values to the East, for example, may be inappropriate, and corporate culture and management practices may need modifying to suit local conditions. Hofstede's work has provided a framework for understanding cultural differences.

Key Thinking

Theory of Culture

Hofstede defines culture as being collective, but often intangible. Nonetheless, it is what distinguishes one group, organization, or nation from another. In his view, it is made up of two main elements: internal values, which are invisible, and external elements, which are more visible and are known as practices. The latter include rituals (such as greetings), heroes (a broad concept that includes not only people but also such things as television shows), and symbols (such as words and gestures). The cultures of different organizations can be distinguished from one other by their practices, while national cultures can be differentiated by their values.

Values are among the first things that are programmed into children. These are reinforced by the local environment at school and at work. It is, therefore, difficult for an individual to change them in later life, and this is the reason why expatriate workers often experience difficulties when faced with another national culture.

The Dimensions of National Culture

Hofstede carried out his research using a questionnaire called the values survey module. From the results, he drew up indices that reflected the national cultural characteristics or dimensions of a country. (All the quotations in this section are taken from Hofstede's *Cultures and Organizations*, 1991.)

Power Distance: How a Society Handles Inequalities

Power distance is defined by Hofstede as "the extent to which the less powerful members of institutions and organizations within a country expect and accept that power is distributed unequally."

In nations with a low power distance, such as the United Kingdom, inequalities among people will tend to be minimized, decentralization of activities is more likely, subordinates will expect to be consulted by superiors, and privileges and status symbols are less evident. In high-power distance nations, conversely, inequalities among people are considered desirable, there is greater reliance by the less powerful on those who hold power, centralization is more normal, and subordinates are likely to be separated from their bosses by wide differentials in salary, privileges, and status symbols.

Individualism/Collectivism: Behavior toward the Group

"Individualism pertains to societies in which the ties between individuals are loose: Everyone is expected to look after himself or herself and his or her immediate family. Collectivism as its opposite pertains to societies in which people from birth onward are integrated into strong, cohesive in-groups, which throughout people's lifetime continue to protect them in exchange for unquestioning loyalty."

In some societies, people need to belong to a group and have a loyalty to the group. Children learn to say "we." This is true of countries such as Japan, India, and China. In other societies, such as in the United Kingdom, individualism is more important, and there is a lower emphasis on loyalty and protection. Children learn to say "I." In strong collectivist countries, there tend to be greater expectations of the employer's obligations toward the employee and his or her family.

Masculinity/Femininity: Behavior According to Gender

"Masculinity pertains to societies in which social gender roles are clearly distinct;

"Management in a global environment is increasingly affected by cultural differences."

(Geert Hofstede)

femininity pertains to societies in which social gender roles overlap."

In a masculine society (Hofstede gives the United Kingdom as an example), there is a division of labor in which the more assertive tasks are given to men. There is a stress on academic success, competition, and achievement in careers. In a feminine society such as France (according to Hofstede), there is a stress on relationships, compromise, life skills, and social performance.

The last 10 to 15 years have seen enormous changes—a "feminization" process—in the behavior of Western democracies. It has also been said that the emergence of developing countries is as much about feminization, as it is about dealing with harder business and economic realities.

Uncertainty Avoidance: The Need for Structure

Uncertainty is "the extent to which the members of a culture feel threatened by uncertain or unknown situations."

In some societies there is a pronounced need for structure. This is because those societies tend to fear the unknown and to possess a high degree of uncertainty. Countries characterized by a low level of uncertainty (such as the United Kingdom) do not perceive something different to be dangerous, whereas, in strong uncertainty-avoidance societies, people will seek to reduce their exposure to the unknown and limit risk by imposing rules and systems to bring about order and coherence. The same thing can be seen in organizations: for example, where there is a need for rules and dependence there will tend to be a pyramidal organizational structure.

Dimensions in Practice

Hofstede is keen to emphasize that his "dimensions" are not a prescription or formula but merely a concept or framework. They equip us with an analytical tool to help us understand intercultural differences, and a very useful one now that, with the rise of global business, many people are working with, or managing, individuals and groups from cultures other than their own. Multinational companies, for instance, building international teams, can make use of Hofstede's framework to make sense of the cultural differences they encounter in their practical experience. Knowing about such differences can help to avoid conflict in international management. Using the framework shows that it is always not safe to assume that apparently similar countries in the same region, for example, Holland and Belgium or Austria and Hungary, have similar cultures.

The dimensions also provide us with a convenient shorthand method of defining the cultural characteristics of a particular organization or country. For example, if someone refers to a country as having a "high feminine index," it suggests that its inhabitants characteristically value having a good working relationship with their supervisor and with their coworkers, living somewhere they and their family want to live, and having job security.

Geert Hofstede in Perspective

Hofstede's theory has been extensively validated, although the point needs to be made that cultures change and the specific country examples that Hofstede used in the past may no longer be valid today. His framework has been used by other researchers to determine the suitability of certain management techniques for various countries or to make comparisons between countries to understand cultural differences in various areas of management. Mo Yuet-Ha used Hofstede's framework to assess the cultural differences and similarities between East Asian countries. The findings were then used to underpin the understanding of competency-based behaviors in these countries.

Hofstede's original research focused on middle-class workers. Other writers have extended his work by looking at different groups of workers and different countries. Michael Bond took Hofstede's work into Hong Kong and Taiwan, using a Chinese values module devised by Chinese social scientists to test whether Hofstede's work was conditioned by his Western outlook and methods. The cultural dimensions were confirmed, except that of uncertainty avoidance, which may be a theory applicable only to the West. (Other researchers have also cast doubt on this dimension, suggesting that it may have been merely a product of the time at which Hofstede did his original research and may not be as relevant today.) Bond's work led to the discovery of a fifth dimension, long-term/short-term orientation. This dimension measures the extent to which a country takes a long- or short-term view of life. The long-term orientation of Confucian dynamism and thrift correlated strongly with economic growth.

Fons Trompenaars, another noted writer on cultural diversity, has carried out work that shows how national culture influences corporate culture. For Trompenaars, the major types of culture—the Family (a power-oriented culture), the Eiffel Tower (a role-oriented culture), the Guided Missile (a project-oriented culture), and the Incubator (a fulfillment-oriented culture)—are comparable with Hofstede's model. Hofstede himself has also extended his work into this area by collaborating with Henry Mintzberg, linking Mintzberg's five organizational structures with his own cultural dimensions. This link is intended to show that some organizational structures fit better in some national cultures that in others.

For More Information

Key works by Hofstede

Books:

Culture's Consequences: International Differences in Work-related Values. Thousand Oaks, CA: Sage, 1980.

Cultures and Organizations: Software of the Mind. New York: McGraw-Hill, 1991.

Hofstede has pointed out that *Culture's Consequences* was a scholarly book, whereas *Cultures and Organizations* was written for practicing managers and students. The latter book revisited the basic material of the former and also included some new information.

Journal Article:

Hofstede, Geert, with M. H. Bond. "Confucius and Economic Growth: New Trends in Culture's Consequences." *Organisational Dynamics*, vol. 16 no. 4, pp. 4–21.

Further Reading

Journal Articles: Hodgetts, Richard. "A Conversation with Geert Hofstede." *Organizational Dynamics*, vol. 21 no. 4, 1993, pp. 53–61.

Brown, Andrew D., and Michael Humphreys. "International Cultural Differences in Public Sector Management: Lessons from a Survey of British and Egyptian Technical Managers." *International Journal of Public Sector Management*, vol. 8 no. 3, 1995, pp. 5–23.

Morden, Tony. "National Culture and the Culture of the Organisation." *Cross-cultural Management: An International Journal*, vol. 2 no. 2, 1995, pp. 3–12.

Yuet-Ha, Mo. "Orienting Values with Eastern Ways." *People Management*, 25 July 1996, pp. 28–30.

See also:

Henry Mintzberg (pp. 1024–25)

"One of the greatest challenges to international business today is how to manage business operations across cultural boundaries."
(Jan Selmer)

Joseph M. Juran

Quality Management

Dr. Joseph M. Juran is a charismatic figure and a legend in his own time, recognized worldwide for his extensive contribution to quality management. He has been instrumental in shaping many of our current ideas about quality. While he is often referred to as one of the leading figures of total quality management, much of his work actually preceded the total quality concept. Regarded as one of the architects of the quality movement in Japan, his influence on manufacturing throughout the world has been substantial.

1904	Born.
1912	Family joins father in United States.
1920	Enrolls at University of Minnesota.
1924	Goes to work for Western Electric at Hawthorne Works in Chicago.
1926	Chosen for inspection training program by visiting Bell Laboratories team.
1928	Produces first work on quality—the training pamphlet—*Statistical Methods Applied to Manufacturing Problems.*
1937	Head of industrial engineering at Western Electric's corporate headquarters in New York.
1941	Assistant administrator for Lend-Lease program.
1945	Leaves Western Electric for New York University.
1951	Publication of *Quality Control Handbook.*
1954	Invited to lecture in Japan.
1964	*Managerial Breakthrough* first published.
1979	Founds the Juran Institute.

Life and Career

Juran was born in 1904 in a small village in part of the Austro-Hungarian Empire that is now Romania. He was the third of four children and lived in poverty for much of his childhood. His father left the family in 1909 to find work in America and some three years later there was enough money for the rest of the family to join him in Minnesota.

Juran excelled at school in America and his affinity for mathematics and science meant that he was soon advanced the equivalent of three year-grades. He enrolled at the University of Minnesota in 1920 and became the first member of his family to enter higher education. By 1924 he had earned himself a B.S. in Electrical Engineering and in 1936 a J.D. in Law at Loyola University.

During his career Juran has produced many leading international handbooks, training courses, and training books that have all been widely read and have collectively been translated into 16 languages. He has been awarded more than 40 honorary doctorates, honorary memberships, medals, and plaques around the world. For his work on quality in Japan he was awarded the Second Order of the Sacred Treasure for "the development of quality control in Japan and the facilitation of U.S. and Japanese friendship," and in the United States he has been awarded the National Medal of Technology.

Starting out as a professional engineer in 1924, Juran worked in the inspection department of the famous Hawthorne works of Western Electric, and this first job stimulated his interest in quality. The plant was vast, with some 40,000 workers, 5,000 of whom were in inspection. Juran's unfailing memory soon allowed him to develop an encyclopedic knowledge of the place. His intellectual and analytical abilities were recognized early and he quickly progressed through a series of line management and staff jobs.

In 1926 a team of statistical quality-control pioneers from Bell Laboratories came to the Hawthorne plant to apply some of their methods and techniques. Juran was selected as one of 20 trainees to participate in the training program and was later appointed as one of the two engineers in the newly formed inspection statistical department. It was while in this role that he authored his first work, *Statistical Methods Applied to Manufacturing Problems.*

By 1937, Juran was head of industrial engineering at Western Electric's head office in New York. He became the equivalent of an in-house consultant, visiting other companies and discussing ideas about quality and industrial engineering. Indeed, it was on one such visit to General Motors in Detroit that he realized how relevant Pareto's idea of "the vital few and the trivial many" was to quality management. He eventually described this idea as the "Pareto principle" in his *Quality Control Handbook* (1951) (see below, under Key Thinking).

In 1941 Juran was seconded as an assistant administrator to the Lend-Lease Administration in Washington. This assignment was to last for four years, during which he streamlined the shipment process to reduce the number of documents required and to cut costs significantly. Today such an approach might be called business process re-engineering; Juran has long claimed that there is nothing new about BPR!

Juran left Washington and Western Electric in 1945 with the aim of writing, lecturing and consulting. In 1951 he published his *Quality Control Handbook*, and this established his reputation as an authority on quality and increased the demand for his lecturing and consulting services. In 1954 he delivered a series of lectures in Japan at the invitation of the Union of Japanese Scientists and Engineers. Though Juran himself plays down their significance, in Japan it is widely held that these lectures formed the basis of the country's shift towards an economy based on quality principles. The ideas from these lectures were published in his book, *Managerial Breakthrough*, in 1964.

In 1979 Juran founded the Juran Institute with the aim of increasing awareness of his ideas. It was through this Institute that the widely acclaimed video series *Juran on Quality Improvement* was produced, and he continued to write and publish into the 1990s. He played a part in setting up the Malcolm Baldrige National Quality Award and only retired from leading the Institute in 1987.

"In the language of the industrial leader, quality is primarily a business problem, not a technical problem."

(Joseph M. Juran)

Key Thinking

Pareto Principle

In his early days as a young engineer Juran noted that when defects were listed in the order of the frequency with which they occurred, a relatively small number of types of defect accounted for the bulk of those found. As his career in management progressed he noted the occurrence of this phenomenon in other areas. The idea of "the vital few and the trivial many" was forming.

In the 1930s Juran was introduced to the work of Vilfredo Pareto, an Italian economist, who had produced a mathematical model to explain the unequal distribution of wealth. Pareto had not promoted his model as a universal one and did not talk of an 80:20 split, but in preparing the first edition of the *Quality Control Handbook* Juran needed a form of shorthand to describe his idea. Remembering Pareto's work he captioned his description "Pareto's principle of unequal distribution." Since then "the Pareto Principle" has become a standard term to describe any situation where a relatively small percentage of factors are responsible for the substantial percentage of effect. Juran later published an explanation of his error in attributing more to Pareto than the latter had originally claimed, at the same time recognizing the contribution of another economist, M. O. Lorenz.

Juran was, in reality, the first to identify and popularize the 80:20 rule (as it has colloquially become known) as a universal principle.

Breakthrough

In his classic work *Managerial Breakthrough* Juran presents his general theory of quality control. Central to this is the idea of an improvement breakthrough.

Juran defines a breakthrough as "change, a dynamic, decisive movement to new, higher levels of performance" (Juran 1994, p. 3). This he contrasts with control, which means "staying on course, adherence to standard, prevention of change" (Juran 1994, p. 1).

Not all control is viewed as negative, and not all breakthroughs are expected to be for the good. Breakthrough and control are seen as part of a continuing cycle of events. Juran highlights the importance of managers' understanding of the attitudes, the organization, and the methodology used to achieve breakthrough, and of how they differ from those used to achieve control.

The Juran Trilogy and Quality Planning Road Map

Juran's message on quality covers a number of different aspects. He focused on the wider issues of planning and organization, managerial responsibility for quality, and the importance of setting targets for improvement. Intrinsic to these, however, was his belief that quality does not happen by accident and needs to be planned. The process of quality improvement is best summarized in his "trilogy" concept, based on the three financial management processes of financial planning, financial control, and financial improvement. Various interpretations of the trilogy have been published, and the following represents one version.

Quality planning

- Identify who the customers are.
- Determine the needs of those customers.
- Translate those needs into our language.

Quality control

- Optimize the product features so as to meet our needs and customer needs.
- Develop a process which is able to produce the product.

Quality improvement

- Optimize the process.
- Prove that the process can produce the product under operating conditions.
- Transfer the process to operations.

Juran's "road map" provides a more detailed approach to the steps within the quality planning element of the trilogy. It is made up of a series of actions with corresponding outputs, and emphasizes the need for measurement throughout. In his book *Juran on Quality by Design* Juran describes six activities in the road map: establish quality goals; identify the customer; determine customer needs; develop product features; develop process features; establish process controls; and transfer to operations.

Quality campaigns

Juran has never been a fan of quality campaigns based on slogans and praise. He viewed the Western quality crisis of the early 1980s as being a result of too many quality initiatives based on campaigns with too little planning and substance. In his view, planning and action should make up 90% of an initiative, with the remaining 10% being exhortation.

Juran's formula for success is:

- establish specific goals to be reached;
- establish plans for reaching those goals;
- assign clear responsibility for meeting the goals;
- base the rewards on the results achieved.

Joseph M. Juran in Perspective

Juran's contribution to the revolution in Japanese quality philosophy helped to transform that country into a market leader. Add to this his influence on Western manufacturing and management in general, and you emerge with a guru who has been influential for more than half a century.

Juran has had a varied career in management and, while his fame centers upon his ideas and thinking on quality issues, his influence in the field of management is far wider. He has played a number of roles—writer, teacher, trainer, and consultant—and has contributed a great deal, over many years, to the field of management. Many of the thousands of managers who have learned from him hold him in near reverence, and management today is infused with his techniques and ideas, even though the name of their creator is not always recognized.

For More Information

Key works by Juran

Books:

Managerial Breakthrough. New York: McGraw-Hill, 1964.
Juran's Quality Control Handbook. New York: McGraw-Hill, 1988.
Juran on Planning for Quality. New York: Free Press, 1988.
Juran on Leadership for Quality. New York: Free Press, 1989.
Juran on Quality by Design. New York: Free Press, 1992.
Juran, Joseph M., with Frank M. Gryna. *Quality Planning and Analysis*. New York: McGraw-Hill, 1993.
Managerial Breakthrough. Rev. ed. New York: McGraw-Hill, 1994.

Further Reading

Book: Butman, John. *Juran: A Lifetime of Influence*. New York: John Wiley, 1997.

See also:
Planning for Quality (p. 942)
Philip Crosby (pp. 978–79)
W. Edwards Deming (pp. 980–81)

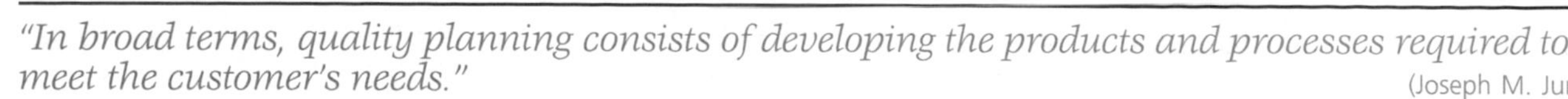

"In broad terms, quality planning consists of developing the products and processes required to meet the customer's needs."
(Joseph M. Juran)

Rosabeth Moss Kanter

Pioneer of Empowerment and Change Management

It is difficult to classify Rosabeth Moss Kanter as a specialist in any particular area, as her prolific writings encompass a wide range of topics. She views herself, however, as a thought leader and developer of ideas, and is best known for her work on change management and innovation.

Much of Kanter's success is due to a combination of rigorous research, practical experience, and her ability to write in a clear and concrete way, using many illustrative examples.

1943	Born.
1977	Publication of *Men and Women of the Corporation*.
1983	Publication of *The Change Masters: Corporate Entrepreneurs at Work*.
1986–present	Professor of business administration, Harvard Business School.
1989	Publication of *When Giants Learn to Dance: Master the Challenge of Strategy, Management, and Careers in the 1990s*.
1989–1992	Editor, *Harvard Business Review*.

Life and Career

Kanter was born in 1943, in Cleveland, Ohio, and attended the top women's academy, Bryn Mawr. She earned her Ph.D. at the University of Michigan and was associate professor of sociology at Brandeis University from 1966 to 1977. Between 1973 and 1974 she was on the Organization Behavior Program at Harvard, and she was a fellow and visiting scholar of Harvard Law School between 1975 and 1976.

From 1977 to 1986, Kanter was professor of sociology and professor of organizational management at Yale, and from 1979 to 1986, she was a visiting professor at the Sloan School of Management, Massachusetts Institute of Technology (MIT). In 1986, she returned to Harvard as the "class of 1960" professor of entrepreneurship and innovation, and she still holds the post of professor of business administration at Harvard Business School.

Between 1989 and 1992 Kanter was editor of the *Harvard Business Review*, and she acted as a key economic adviser to Michael Dukakis during his 1988 Presidential campaign. She has traveled widely as a public speaker, lecturer, and international consultant. In 1977, she and her future husband Barry Stein set up a management consultancy called Goodmeasure, which has some large and well-known multinational companies as clients.

Key Thinking

Kanter has authored or coauthored several books and well over 150 major articles. Her doctoral thesis was on communes, and her first books, written during the early 1970s, were sociological. The three books for which she is best known are *Men and Women of the Corporation*, *The Change Masters* and *When Giants Learn to Dance*. There is a logical progression within them, in that the first studies the stifling effects of bureaucratic organization on individuals, while the subsequent titles go on to explore ways in which "post-entrepreneurial" organizations release, and make use of, individuals' talents and abilities. Later books include *The Challenge of Organizational Change* (with Barry A. Stein and Todd D. Jick), *World Class: Thriving Locally in the Global Economy*, *The Frontiers of Management*, and *Evolve.*

Men and Women of the Corporation

Men and Women of the Corporation won the C. Wright Mills Award in 1977 as the year's best book on social issues. It is a detailed analysis of the nature and effects of the distribution of power and powerlessness within the headquarters of one large, bureaucratic, multinational corporation (called Industrial Supply Corporation, or Indsco, in the book). The effects of powerlessness on behavior are explored and the detrimental effects of disempowerment, both for the organization and individual employees, are made clear. Women were the most obvious group affected by lack of power, though Kanter emphasizes that other groups outside the white, male norm, such as ethnic minority members, were also affected.

Three main structural variables explained the behaviors observed within Indsco:

- the structure of opportunity;
- the structure of power;
- the proportional distribution of people of different kinds.

Before this book was published, it was generally assumed that behavioral differences underlay women's general lack of career progress. Kanter's findings made structural issues central, however, and the implications for change management were significant. If all employees were to become more empowered, organizations rather than people would need to change. Accordingly, the book ends with practical policy suggestions to create appropriate structural changes.

While working on this book, Kanter identified the need for organizational change to improve working life, create more equal opportunities, and make more use of employees' talents within organizations.

The Change Masters

The Change Masters puts forward various approaches to achieving these ends. Kanter compares four traditional corporations like Indsco with six competitive and successful organizations, described as "change masters." All findings were weighed against the experiences of many other companies, and much other material. From the six innovative organizations, Kanter derives a model for encouraging innovation.

Innovative companies were found to have an "integrative" approach to management, while firms unlikely to innovate were described as "segmentalist" insofar as they were compartmentalized by units or departments. The difference begins with a company's approach to problem-solving, and extends through its structure and culture. Entrepreneurial organizations:

- operate at the edge of their competence, focusing on exploring the unknown rather than on controlling the known;
- measure themselves by future-focused visions (how far they have to go) rather than past standards (how far they have come).

"You've no future unless you add value and create projects." (Rosabeth Moss Kanter)

Individuals can also be change masters. "New entrepreneurs" are people who improve existing businesses rather than start new ones. They can be found in any functional area and are described as, literally, the right people, in the right place, at the right time:

- the right people—those with vision and ideas extending beyond the organization's normal practice;
- the right place—an integrative environment fostering proactive vision, coalitions, and teams;
- the right time—a moment in the historical flow when change becomes most possible.

The ultimate change masters are corporate leaders, who translate their vision into a new organizational reality.

The Change Masters advocates "participation management" as the means to greater empowerment. Some major "building blocks" for productive change are identified, and practical measures to remove "road blocks" to innovation are discussed.

When Giants Learn to Dance

When Giants Learn to Dance completes Kanter's trilogy on the need for change which, she considered, United States corporations had to confront in order to compete more effectively. The book is based on observation from within various organizations, through consultancy projects. The global economy is likened to a "corporate Olympics" of competing businesses, with results determining which nations, as well as organizations, are winners.

The games differ, but successful teams share some characteristics such as strength, skill, discipline, good organization, and focus on individual excellence. To win, American companies would have to become progressively more entrepreneurial and less bureaucratic. Kanter suggested as a model for the 1990s the "post-entrepreneurial" corporation, in which three shaping forces would play the key roles:

- the context set at the top
- top management values
- project ideas and approaches coming up through the organization

An "athletic" organization of this kind would be lean, flexible, and would seek to create synergies through the use of team and partnership approaches. The organization would be built on empowerment, and employees would be highly valued within team-based or partnership relationships.

Kanter picks out seven skills or sensibilities that characterize individual "business athletes." These are:

- the ability to operate and get results without depending on hierarchical authority, position, or status;
- the ability to compete in a way that enhances cooperation, and aims to achieve high standards rather than destroy competitors;
- the high ethical standards needed to support the trust that is crucial for cooperative approaches when competing in the corporate Olympics;
- a dose of humility, basic self-confidence being tempered by the understanding that new things will always need to be learned;
- process focus, that is, respect for the process of implementation as well as for the substance of what is implemented;
- a multifaceted approach that makes possible cross-functional or cross-departmental work, the forming of alliances where appropriate, and the cutting of ties where necessary;
- a temperament that derives satisfaction from results, and a willingness to be rewarded according to achievements.

World Class: Thriving Locally in the Global Economy

World Class: Thriving Locally in the Global Economy focuses on world class companies with employees described as "cosmopolitan" in type. These people are rich in the "three Cs"—concepts, competence, and connections—and carry a more universal culture to all the places in which their company operates.

This knowledge-rich breed is compared with "locals" who are set in their ways, and the two groups are viewed as the main classes in modern society. Globalization, it is argued, offers an opportunity to develop businesses and give new life to the regions. From her studies of regenerative areas, Kanter suggests that business and local government leaders can work together to draw in the right sort of companies to create prosperity.

Later works

The Challenge of Organizational Change: How Companies Experience It and Leaders Guide It, coauthored with Barry A. Stein and Todd D. Jick, on the management of change, draws a distinction between evolutionary and revolutionary change, here described as the "long march" and "bold stroke" approaches.

Rosabeth Moss Kanter on The Frontiers of Management collects Kanter's essays and research articles for the *Harvard Business Review* together into one volume.

Rosabeth Moss Kanter in Perspective

Overall, Kanter's books present some fairly complex ideas in a way that many people seem to find approachable. They are well-argued and supported with a wealth of practical research evidence. Some of her central ideas, once viewed by some as unrealistic, have now become absorbed into general management wisdom. These include empowerment, participative management, and employee involvement. In *The Frontiers of Management,* she is presented as a groundbreaking explorer who has initiated a revolution in terms of new ways of working. It is also pointed out, however, that some managers have still not crossed the frontiers, or do so in aspiration rather than actuality.

For More Information

Key works by Kanter

Books:

Men and Women of the Corporation. New York: Basic Books Inc., 1977.

The Change Masters. Corporate Entrepreneurs at Work. New York: Simon & Schuster, 1983.

When Giants Learn to Dance: Master the Challenge of Strategy, Management, and Careers in the 1990s. New York: Simon & Schuster, 1989.

The Challenge of Organizational Change: How Companies Experience It and Leaders Guide It (coauthored with Barry A. Stein and Todd D. Jick). New York: Free Press, 1992.

World Class: Thriving Locally in the Global Economy. New York: Simon & Schuster, 1995.

Rosabeth Moss Kanter on the Frontiers of Change. Boston, MA: Harvard Business School Press, 1997.

Evolve. Boston, MA: Harvard Business School Press, 2001.

Further Reading

Book: Crainer, Stuart. *Key Management Ideas: Thinking That Changed the Management World.* London: Pitman, 1996.

Journal Articles: Golzen, Godfrey. "World Class Guru." *Human Resources,* May/June 1996, pp. 38–40, 42–44.

Dickson, Tim. "Interview with Rosabeth Moss Kanter." *The Financial Times,* May 17, 1996, p. 17.

"Power is the ability to get things done." (Rosabeth Moss Kanter)

Kaplan and Norton

The Balanced Scorecard

Robert S. Kaplan (left) and David P. Norton jointly introduced the "balanced scorecard" to the business world in the early 1990s. They argued that adherence to quarterly financial returns and the bottom line alone could not provide the organization with an overall strategic view. The balanced scorecard was a breakthrough precisely because it enables the organization to describe its strategy adequately. It shows how nonfinancial factors—intangible assets—tied in with the financial ones.

Lives and Careers

Robert Kaplan is Marvin Bower Professor of Leadership Development at Harvard Business School in Boston. He was previously based at Carnegie Mellon University, where he was Dean of the Graduate School of Industrial Administration in Pittsburgh. Kaplan's research work has focused on performance measurement systems, in particular activity-based costing and the balanced scorecard.

David P. Norton is a founder and president of the Balanced Scorecard Collaborative based in Lincoln, Massachusetts. He also founded and was president of Renaissance Solutions, a balanced scorecard consulting firm.

They are jointly recognized as the popularizers of the balanced scorecard concept. Their approach to it was first introduced in a 1992 *Harvard Business Review* article "The Balanced Scorecard: Measures That Drive Performance" which began with a variation of the saying "What gets measured gets done;" Kaplan and Norton took as their starting point "What you measure is what you get."

As the story goes, David Norton coined the term "Balanced Scorecard" after a conversation with John Thompson, who was then president of IBM Canada. John Thompson, returning from a round of golf, announced he needed a scorecard just like the one he used during his game to measure the performance of his company. The balanced scorecard grew out of that conversation.

Key Thinking

Setting up the balanced scorecard, Kaplan and Norton argued that strategies often fail because they are not converted successfully into actions that employees can understand and apply in their everyday work. The problem comes with the search for realistic measures that are meaningful to those doing the work, relate visibly to strategic direction, and provide a balanced picture of what is happening throughout the organization, not just of one facet of it. It is this aspect that the balanced scorecard addresses.

It concentrates on measures in four key strategic areas–finance, customers, internal business processes, and learning and innovation-and requires the implementing organization to identify goals and measures for each of them. Research and experimentation have come up with the following, which seem to be regularly applied in many organizations.

Financial Perspective

- Goals: survival, success/growth, prosperity.
- Measures: return on capital, cash flow, revenue growth, liquidity, cost reduction, project profitability, performance reliability.

Customer Perspective

- Goals: Customer acquisition, retention, profitability, and satisfaction.
- Measures: Market share, transaction cost ratios, customer loyalty satisfaction surveys/index, supplier relationships, key accounts.

Internal Business Process Perspective

- Goals: Core competencies, critical technologies, business processes, key skills.
- Measures: Efficiency measures of working practices and production processes, cycle times, unit costs, defect rates, time to market.

Learning and Innovation Perspective

- Goals: Continuous improvement, new product development.
- Measures: Productivity of intrapreneurship, new ideas and suggestions from employees, employee satisfaction, skill levels, staff attitude, retention, and profitability, rate of improvement.

The scorecard provides a description of the organization's strategy. It will indicate where problems lie because it shows the interrelationships between goals and the activities that are linked to the achievement of those. It creates an understanding of what is going on elsewhere in the organization and shows all employees how they are contributing. As Kaplan has said: "The business scorecard seeks to empower all levels of the workforce by educating them about their company's strategy and the small steps they can take to achieve their goals." Providing that accurate and timely information is fed into the system, the scorecard also helps to focus attention where change and learning are needed through the cause and effect relationships it can reveal. Examples of the types of insight achieved were detailed in "Linking the Balanced Scorecard to Strategy":

- If we increase employee training about products, then they will become more knowledgeable about the full range of products they can sell.
- If employees are more knowledgeable about products, then their sales effectiveness will improve.
- If their sales effectiveness improves, then the average margins of products they sell will increase.

Implementing the Balanced Scorecard

In "Putting the Balanced Scorecard to Work" Kaplan and Norton identify eight steps toward building a scorecard:

1. Preparation. Select/define the strategy/business unit to which to apply the scorecard. Think in terms of the appropriateness of the four main perspectives defined above.

2. First interviews. Distribute information about the scorecard to senior managers along with the organization's vision, mis-

sion, and strategy. A facilitator will interview each manager on the organization's strategic objectives and ask for initial thoughts on scorecard measures.

3. First executive workshop. Match measures to strategy. The management team is brought together to develop the scorecard. After agreeing the vision statement, the team debates each of the four key strategic areas, addressing the following questions:

- If my vision succeeds, how will I differ?
- What are the critical success factors?
- What are the critical measurements?

These questions help to focus attention on the impact of turning the vision into reality and what has to be done to make it happen. It is important to represent the views of customers and shareholders, and to gain a number of measures for each critical success factor.

4. Second interviews. The facilitator reviews and consolidates the findings of the workshop and interviews each of the managers individually about the emerging scorecard.

5. Second workshop. Hold a team debate on the proposed scorecard; the participants should discuss the proposed measures, link ongoing change programs to the measures, and set targets or rates of improvement for each of the measures. Start outlining the communication and implementation processes.

6. Third workshop. Final consensus on vision, goals, measures, and targets. The team devises an implementation program to communicate the scorecard to employees, integrate it into management philosophy, and develop an information system to support it.

7. Implementation. The implementation team links the measures to information support systems and databases and communicates the what, why, where, and who of the scorecard throughout the organization. The end product should be a management information system that links strategy to shop-floor activity.

8. Periodic review. Balanced scorecard measures can be prepared for review by senior management at appropriate intervals.

Kaplan and Norton in Perspective

Kaplan and Norton published their first article on the balanced scorecard in early 1992. Since then, elaborating, explaining, and applying the basic concept seems to have become a small industry. The jury is, nevertheless, still out on whether it will be an innovation of lasting importance or merely a passing fad. But an increasing number of organizations are trying it out. David Norton has claimed that 60% of large U.S. companies are now using some sort of scorecard that combines financial with nonfinancial measures.

The balanced scorecard should not be regarded as a panacea. In "The design and implementation of the balanced business scorecard: an analysis of three companies in practice," Stephen Letza states that the balanced scorecard should highlight performance as a dynamic, continuous, and integrated process, act as an integrating tool, function as the pivotal tool determining the organization's current and future direction, and deliver information that forms the backbone of its strategy.

Letza also highlights some of the major drawbacks that may be encountered when using the balanced scorecard and points out the need to:

- avoid being swamped by the minutiae of too many detailed measures and make sure that measures do genuinely relate to the strategic goals of the organization;
- make sure all the organization's activities are included in the assessment—this ensures that everyone is contributing to the organization's strategic goals;
- watch out for conflict as information becomes accessible to those who were not formerly in a position to see it or act on it, and try to harness conflict constructively.

The balanced scorecard can be seen as the latest in a long line of attempts at management control, descending from Taylor through to work measurement systems, quality assurance systems, and performance indicators. Commentators claim that the balanced scorecard could become the management tool of the early 21st century, given that it is flexible and adaptable to each organization's use, and that it is practical, straightforward, and devoid of obscure theory. Most importantly, it responds to many organizations' requirements to expand strategically on traditional financial measures and points to areas for change.

For More Information

Key works by Kaplan and Norton

Books:

The Balanced Scorecard: Translating Strategy into Action. Boston, MA: Harvard Business School Press, 1996.

The Strategy-focused Organization. Boston, MA: Harvard Business School Press, 2000.

Journal Articles:

"The Balanced Scorecard: Measures That Drive Performance." *Harvard Business Review*, Jan./Feb. 1992, pp. 71–79.

"Putting the Balanced Scorecard to Work." *Harvard Business Review*, Sept./Oct. 1993, pp. 134–147.

"Using the Balanced Scorecard As a Strategic Management System." *Harvard Business Review*, Jan./Feb. 1996, pp. 75–85.

"Linking the Balanced Scorecard to Strategy." *California Management Review*, Fall 1996, pp. 53–79.

"Strategic Learning and the Balanced Scorecard." *Strategy and Leadership*, Sept./Oct. 1996, pp. 18–24.

See also:

☆ **The Balanced Scorecard (pp. 303–04)**
✔ **Implementing the Balanced Scorecard (pp. 510–11)**
Frederick Winslow Taylor (pp. 1054–55)

Theodore Levitt

Marketing

Theodore Levitt has made a key contribution to management theory in the marketing field, stimulating debate on the importance of a pervasive marketing mindset within an organization. He has analyzed the benefits and shortfalls of marketing in a series of journal articles and books over four decades. His talent for expounding his views clearly and for illustrating his arguments with company examples and metaphors makes his work highly accessible.

1925	Born.
1935	Leaves Germany for the United States.
1959	Lecturer of business administration at Harvard Business School.
1960	"Marketing Myopia" appears in *Harvard Business Review.*
1965	Edward W. Carter Professor of Business Administration, Harvard Business School.
1990	Resigns post as editor of *Harvard Business Review.*

Life and Career

Born in Volmerz in Germany, Levitt moved with his parents to the United States in 1935, where he later studied economics. In the late 1950s he worked as a consultant in Chicago before being approached by the Harvard Business School. In his very first year there he began to teach marketing, although at the time he had reportedly never read a book on the subject.

Levitt's first article was published in 1956. His tenure at Harvard as an academic lasted for more than 30 years. This period included a spell as a somewhat controversial editor of the *Harvard Business Review*, a post from which he resigned in 1990 following an argument over an article on women in management.

Key Thinking

Levitt emphasizes the need for a company to achieve a balanced orientation by including marketing in its strategy; he focuses on the need for a marketing outlook to pervade an organization and provide a necessary counterbalance to a preoccupation with production. His landmark article expounding this theory, "Marketing Myopia," appeared in the *Harvard Business Review* in 1960 and is one of the most requested reprints from that journal, having sold over 500,000 copies. Subsequently, Levitt reiterated and expanded his theory in several articles and books. These partly focus on the methodology of implementing the marketing mode, including the proposition of a "marketing matrix" for assessing the degree of marketing orientation existing in a company. They also explore the theory behind the marketing concept and delineate some of its limitations and problems. Other works concentrate on such topics as "the industrialization of service" (examining the potential benefits of applying the production line and quality control methods of industry to service provision), the nature of the product, advertising, and globalization.

"Marketing Myopia" Explored

Levitt himself described his article "Marketing Myopia" as a manifesto. It challenged the conventional thinking of the time by putting forward a persuasive case for the importance of the marketing approach and the shortsightedness of failing to incorporate it into business strategy.

In an era in which post-war shortages contributed to a concentration on production, most companies had developed a product orientation, which, Levitt believed, was too narrow a philosophy to allow continued business success. A drive to increase the efficiency and volume of production took place at the expense of monitoring whether the company was actually producing what the customer wanted. "Marketing Myopia" stressed that customer wants and desires should be a central consideration of any business. "The organization must learn to think of itself not as producing goods or services but as buying customers, as doing the things that will make people want to do business with it."

In order to achieve this, ". . .the entire corporation must be viewed as a customer-creating and customer-satisfying organism. Management must think of itself not as providing products but as providing customer-creating value satisfactions. It must push this idea (and everything it means and requires) into every nook and cranny of the organization."

Levitt highlighted the need for companies to define what business they are in, as this concentrates attention on customer needs. He used the now famous example of the railroads, which, rather than thinking of themselves as being in the business of running trains, should instead have defined themselves as providing transportation. Self-definition along those lines would have helped the railroad companies to be aware of changing customer demand; if they had had that awareness, they might not have suffered so greatly from the rise of road and air transportation. Focusing on the satisfaction of customer needs, Levitt argues, is a better path to continued business success than concentration on the actual product on offer.

Also presented in "Marketing Myopia," as a warning against complacency, is Levitt's belief that "in truth there is no such thing as a growth industry." There are growth opportunities, which can be created or capitalized on, but those companies which believe they are ". . .riding some automatic growth escalator invariably descend into stagnation." The belief that a company is in a growth industry and is therefore secure must never be allowed to overshadow or replace awareness of the need to practice marketing and assert a customer orientation. This is the only route through which a company can hope to achieve sustained expansion.

Of a more practical nature is the "marketing matrix," a device presented by Levitt in *Marketing for Business Growth* to aid the measurement of a company's marketing orientation. A horizontal scale of 1–9 records the degree of customer orientation, and a vertical scale of 1–9 records the degree of company orientation. A score of 9 on both scales is the ideal. Using this method,

"Ideas are useless unless used." (Theodore Levitt)

organizations can assess their incorporation of marketing thinking and determine where steps are needed to improve their strategy and to become more marketing-oriented.

Ways of doing this include the "industrialization of service," which involves the measuring and standardizing of customer service to a predetermined quality level, in other words, applying industrial-style quality controls to the service process. For example, a production line can be set up for service delivery, and service encounters can be standardized and monitored to ensure that they are of a similar quality. This has been accomplished with great success By the McDonald's fast food chain ("The Industrialization of Service"). To recognize this concept is, writes Levitt, ". . .to introduce a potentially emancipating new cognitive mode and operating style into modern enterprise" (*The Marketing Imagination*). Another factor that is important in enhancing a marketing orientation is relationship marketing. (See "After the sale is over.") This revolves around the need not only to acquire customers, but also to keep them and form mutually beneficial long-term relationships with them.

In a 1983 article, "The Globalization of Markets," Levitt once more produced a forward-looking "manifesto" with a view of the changing nature of the marketplace and the trend, fuelled by technological advances, towards globalization. His thesis is that, in order to survive and prosper, companies must offer standardized products around the world, products that incorporate the best in design, reliability, and price. The efficiency of such an approach will outweigh, in his opinion, the benefits of taking into account varying cultural preferences and tailoring products to different national markets. The reason for this is the overlying trend toward world homogenization. "Two vectors shape the world—technology and globalization. The first helps determine human preferences; the second, economic realities. Regardless of how much preferences evolve and diverge, they also gradually converge and form markets where economies of scale lead to reduction of costs and prices."

Thinking About Management, Levitt's latest book, contains a distillation of his thinking on effective management, presented in nuggets in the three categories of Thinking, Changing, and Operating. Many of his theories are here reiterated, and the work forms a useful guide to his collected thought.

Theodore Levitt in Perspective

A major influence on Levitt's work was the writing of Peter Drucker, who was among the first to see marketing as all-pervasive: "Marketing is not a function, it is the whole business seen from the customer's point of view." (*The Practice of Management*)

However, although influenced by academic thought, Levitt seems to have drawn his greatest inspiration from the real world, examining the companies around him and distilling the examples of good and bad practice that illustrate much of his writing.

Levitt's influence contributed to the rise of the marketing concept in the 1960s and its increasing incorporation into management thinking, initially in the United States but later also in Europe. His subsequent works may not have achieved the fame of "Marketing Myopia," but they are nevertheless an important part of the evolving pattern of marketing writing that has gathered impetus through recent decades. By pointing out the myopic vision of many managers, Levitt set in motion a vigorous new way of thinking that was taken up by other management writers and practitioners and culminated in the rebirth of marketing in the 1980s. Other marketing gurus such as Philip Kotler acknowledge the influence of Levitt's work, and he is regularly quoted.

In retrospect, Levitt has been proven to have had remarkable foresight in his anticipation of the importance of marketing to organizations, his initial work predating the marketing boom by two decades. He also successfully predicted the value of relationship marketing, a topic which only became an identifiable discipline in the early 1990s, and the concept of the global village, which is now commonplace.

Levitt's assertion that there is no such thing as a growth industry is another tenet that proved influential, and was taken up by writers such as Tom Peters and Richard Pascale in the 1990s.

For More Information

Key works by Levitt

Books:

Innovation in Marketing: New Perspectives for Profit and Growth. New York: McGraw-Hill, 1962.

Marketing for Business Growth. New York: McGraw-Hill, 1974. (First published in 1969 as *The Marketing Mode: Pathways to Corporate Growth*.)

The Marketing Imagination. New York: Free Press, 1983.

Thinking about Management. New York: Free Press, 1991.

Journal Articles:

"Marketing Myopia." *Harvard Business Review*, Jul./Aug. 1960, pp. 45–56.

"The Industrialization of Service." *Harvard Business Review*, Sept./Oct. 1976, pp. 63–74.

"After the Sale Is Over." *Harvard Business Review*, Sept./Oct. 1983, pp. 87–93.

"The Globalization of Markets." *Harvard Business Review*, May/June 1983, pp. 92–102.

Further Reading

Book: Drucker, Peter. *The Practice of Management*. New York: HarperBusiness, 1986.

See also:

☆ **How to Plan Marketing (pp. 59–60)**

✔ **Preparing a Marketing Plan (pp. 472–73)**

Innovation in Marketing (p. 913)

Marketing Management (pp. 2045–48)

KURT LEWIN

Change Management and Group Dynamics

Kurt Lewin's extensive output included studies of leadership styles and their effects and work on group decision-making, and he was responsible for the development of force field theory, the "unfreeze—change—refreeze" model of change management, the "action research" approach to research, and the group dynamics approach to training (especially in the form of T Groups).

The Dome at MIT, where Lewin cofounded the Research Center for Group Dynamics.

1890	Born.
1910	Begins formal training in psychology in Berlin.
1914	Graduates as Ph.D. from the University of Berlin.
1914–1916	Active service with the German army; is wounded and awarded the Iron Cross.
1916–1932	Teaches at the University of Berlin.
1932	Leaves Germany to escape persecution by the Nazis.
1935	Appointed professor of child psychology at the University of Iowa.
1939	Researches leadership styles in Iowa.
1944	Cofounds the Research Center for Group Dynamics at MIT.
1946	Pioneers T-Group approach.
1947	Dies.

LIFE AND CAREER

German-born, Lewin was professor of philosophy and psychology at Berlin University until he fled to the United States in 1932 to escape from the Nazis. There, he taught at Cornell University, and then at Iowa, becoming professor of child psychology at the latter's Child Research Station. In 1944 he went on to cofound a research center for group dynamics at the Massachusetts Institute of Technology.

KEY THINKING

LEADERSHIP STYLES AND THEIR EFFECTS

With his colleagues L. Lippitt and R. White, Lewin studied the effects of three different leadership styles on the outcomes of boys' activity groups in Iowa (1939). Those three styles were classified as "democratic," "autocratic," and "laissez-faire." It was found that in the group with an autocratic leader, there was more dissatisfaction and behaviors became either more aggressive or apathetic. In the group with a democratic leader, there was more cooperation and enjoyment, while those in the laissez-faire group showed no particular dissatisfaction, although they were not particularly productive, either.

Significantly, when the respective leaders were asked to change their styles, the effects produced by each leadership style remained similar. Lewin was aiming to show that the democratic style achieved better results. The possibility of social and cultural factors influencing the results undermined his findings to some extent; nevertheless, the studies suggested the benefits of a democratic style in an American context. They also showed that it is possible for leaders and managers to change their approach, to improve their leadership through training, and to adopt management styles appropriate for their situation and context.

GROUP DECISION MAKING

After World War II, Lewin carried out research for the U.S. government, exploring ways of influencing people to change their dietary habits and eat less popular cuts of meat. He found that, if group members were encouraged to become involved, discussed the issues themselves, and were then able to make their own decisions as a group, they were far more likely to change their habits than if they simply attended lectures where they were given information, recipes, and advice.

FORCE FIELD ANALYSIS

Lewin put forward the theory that people's activity is affected by forces in their surrounding environment, or "field." Its three main principles are that:

- behavior is a function of the existing field;
- analysis starts from the complete situation and distinguishes its component parts;
- a concrete person in a concrete situation can be mathematically represented.

A particular feature of Lewin's method of analyzing behavior within a given field, for example, within a situation or an organization, is its identification of the forces at work there as either "driving forces," which will tend to promote change, or "restraining forces," which will tend to hinder it. Such things as ambitions, goals, needs, or fears, that drive a person toward or away from something, constitute driving forces. Restraining forces are different in nature, according to Lewin, in that they act to oppose driving forces rather than constituting independent forces in themselves.

Force field analysis is used extensively for purposes of organizational and human resources development, because it can help to indicate when the driving and restraining forces affecting people are not in balance, thus creating a situation in which change can occur.

The interplay of the two types of force can produce either stability or instability. Where activities and situations go on from day to day in a regular, stable routine—that is, in what Lewin calls "quasi-stationary processes"—the forces are more or less balanced out and equalized; they fluctuate around a state of equilibrium. Achieving change, therefore, involves altering the forces that maintain this equilibrium. To bring about an increase in productivity, for example, the forces currently keeping production at its existing quasi-stationary levels would have to be changed. This can be done by taking one of two alternative routes:

- strengthening the driving forces, for example, paying more money for more productivity;
- restraining inhibiting factors, for example, simplifying production processes.

"There is nothing so practical as a good theory." (Kurt Lewin)

Strengthening the drives would seem the obvious route to take, but analysis would show that this could lead to the development of countervailing forces, concern among employees about tiredness, or worry about new targets becoming a standard expectation. Reducing restraining forces, for example, through investment in machinery or training to make the process easier, might be a less obvious, but more rewarding approach, bringing about change with less resistance or demoralization.

Lewin identified two questions to ask when seeking to make changes within the framework of force field analysis:

- Why does a process continue at its current level under the present circumstances?
- What conditions would change these circumstances?

For Lewin, "circumstances" is a concept with a very broad meaning; it covers anything from the social context and wider environment to subgroups and communication barriers between groups. The position of each of these factors determines a group's structure and "ecological setting" while the structure and setting together determine a range of possible changes that are dependent on, and can to some degree be controlled by, the pacing and interaction of forces across the entire field.

Model of Change: Unfreeze—Change—Refreeze

Lewin believed that, to achieve change effectively, it was necessary to look at all the options for moving from the existing state to a desired future one, then to evaluate the possibilities of each option and decide on the best one, rather than simply identifying a desired goal and taking the straightest and easiest route to it. His change management model is linked to force field analysis and encourages managers to beware of two kinds of force of resistance, the first deriving from "social habit" or "custom," and the second from the creation of an "inner resistance." These two different kinds of force are rooted in the interplay between a group as a whole and the individuals within it, and only driving forces that are strong enough to break the habits, challenge the interests, or "unfreeze" the customs of the group will overcome them. As most members will want to stay within the behavioral norms of the group, individual resistance to change will increase as a person is induced to move further away from current group values. In Lewin's view, this type of resistance can be lowered either by reducing the value the group attaches to something, or by fundamentally changing what the group values. He considered that a complex, stepped process of unfreezing, changing, and refreezing beliefs, attitudes, and values was required to achieve change, with the initial phase of unfreezing normally involving group discussions in which individuals experience others' views and begin to adapt their own.

Since Lewin's death, "unfreeze—change—refreeze" has sometimes been applied more rigidly than he intended, for example, by discarding an old structure, setting up a new one, and then "fixing" the latter into place. Such an inflexible course of action fits badly with more modern attitudes to change as a continuous and flowing process of evolution. Lewin's change model is now often criticized for its linearity, especially from the perspective of more recent research on nonlinear, "chaotic" systems and complexity theory. The model was, however, process-oriented originally. Lewin himself viewed change as a continuing process, recognizing that extremely complex forces are at work in group and organizational dynamics.

T-Groups

What is now known as the "T-Group" (or Training Group) approach was pioneered by Lewin when, in 1946, he was called in to try to develop better relations between Jewish and black communities in Connecticut. Bringing such groups of people together was, Lewin found, a powerful way of exposing areas of conflict, so that established behavior patterns could "unfreeze" before potentially changing and "refreezing." He called these learning groups T-Groups. This training approach became particularly popular during the 1970s. Some interpreters of the method, however, have used it in a more confrontational way than Lewin may have intended.

Action Research

Lewin's "action research" approach is linked to T-groups. Introduced during the 1940s, it was seen as an important innovation in research methods and was especially used in industry and education. Action research involves experimenting by making changes and simultaneously studying the results, in a cyclic process of planning, action, and fact-gathering. Lewin's approach emphasized the power relationship between the researcher and those researched, and he sought to involve the latter, encouraging their participation in studying the effects of their own actions, identifying their own biases, and working to transform relationships within their communities.

"Action research" centered on the involvement of participants from the community under research and on the pursuit of separate but simultaneous processes of action and evaluation. Different variations of this approach have evolved since Lewin's day, and its validity as a scientific research method for psychology is often questioned. Its strengths, however, in offering groups or communities an involving, self-evaluative, collaborative, and decision-making role are widely accepted.

Kurt Lewin in Perspective

Lewin is widely recognized as a seminal figure in social psychology, although his early death obscured his central role in the development of the managerial human relations movement. In the United States and the United Kingdom (especially through the work of the Tavistock Institute), much subsequent management thinking and research has been influenced by Lewin's approaches and ideas. These, following in the tradition of Mayo's 1920s and 1930s Hawthorne studies, underlie the whole current field of organizational development and change management.

For More Information

Key works by Lewin

Books:

Resolving Social Conflicts and *Field Theory in Social Science*. Washington, D.C.: American Psychological Association, 1997.

Journal Articles:

Lewin, Kurt, with R. Lippitt and R. White. "Patterns of Aggressive Behavior in Experimentally Created 'Social Climates'." *Journal of Social Psychology*, vol. 10, 1939, pp. 271–299.

"Action Research and Minority Problems." *Journal of Social Issues*, vol. 2, 1946, p. 65.

"Frontiers in Group Dynamics." *Human Relations*, vol. 1, 1947, pp. 5–41.

See also:

Douglas McGregor (pp. 1022–23)

"If you want truly to understand something, try to change it." (Kurt Lewin)

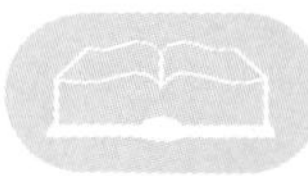

Niccolò Machiavelli

The Patron Saint of Power

Throughout most of the five centuries since his death Niccolò Machiavelli has not been a popular figure. There have always been a few people who appreciated his genius, but most have so closely associated him with intrigue and dark deeds. Fortunately, in the last 100 years or so, a more reasoned view of his work has developed and the enormous value of Machiavelli's philosophy, and its remarkable relevance to modern society, has emerged progressively.

1469	Born.
1489	Secretary of Second Chancery, Florence.
1512	Falls from grace as Medici family returns to power.
1513	Publication of *The Prince*.
1527	Dies.

Life and Career

Niccolò Machiavelli was born in 1469, the son of a Florentine lawyer. He first came to public notice when in 1498, at the age of 29, he was appointed Secretary of the Second Chancery—part of the complex bureaucracy that ran Florence as a city state. His appointment came after the execution of Savonarola, the friar-politician who, after leading a revolt that expelled the Medicis and established a democratic republic, dominated Florentine life until he ran afoul of the papacy and was burned for heresy.

Machiavelli held the post of Secretary for 14 years, during which time his influence was significant. He took part in 30 foreign missions, meeting most of Europe's key politicians and rulers. This opportunity to learn about government, politics, and economics must have been unique. Unfortunately, it was not to last. In 1512 the Medicis returned to power, and Machiavelli lost his post immediately. He was then suspected, quite wrongly, of plotting against the Medicis, for which he was arrested, imprisoned, and tortured. Although eventually found innocent, he was expelled from Florence and forced to spend the rest of his life in exile on an isolated farm. His many attempts to reenter political life failed and he died in 1527 still struggling to regain his lost influence. It was more than 300 years later that Italy became unified, as Machiavelli had wanted it to be.

While Machiavelli may not have enjoyed his time in exile, the world has gained immeasurably from it. The enforced idleness allowed him to write prodigiously about his experiences and ideas. His written works include a history of Florence, several plays, and two books that established him as a great authority on power politics: *The Prince* and *The Discourses*. Professor Max Lerner, in his introduction to the 1950 Random House edition of *The Prince* describes the book as *"a grammar of power*." There can be no more fitting description of this seminal work.

Key Thinking

Machiavelli presents no instant management theories, no clever techniques for solving day-to-day problems. He deals mainly with broad strategies and to get value from his writing one needs to interpret it and make comparisons. Perhaps the best approach is to first read Jay's introduction on the art of making such comparisons and then to read Machiavelli with a personal checklist of interests and questions.

Some Pertinent Insights

The following examples show how certain passages in Machiavelli's writing bridge the seemingly huge gap between sixteenth-century politics and twenty-first-century business.

Leadership

Machiavelli provides several examples of good leaders and leaves his readers in no doubt about the importance of skillful leadership to the success of any enterprise. He dismisses luck and genius as the key to successful leadership and goes for "shrewdness." The dangers and risks a leader faces are dramatically illustrated (happily for us these are less terrifying today than in Renaissance Italy), and comparison is made between the relative ease of getting to a position of leadership and the difficult task of staying there.

Centralization versus Decentralization

Anyone who thinks that the problem of choosing between centralized or decentralized control is a modern dilemma will be quickly persuaded otherwise by reading *The Prince*. Machiavelli's examples are drawn entirely from government and from military history, but the comparisons with today's business world are easy to make. Perhaps his best advice comes when he is talking about the government of colonies and outposts. Poor communications in Renaissance times usually made decentralization the only option in such cases, and Machiavelli's recommendations center on what today we would call selection and training. A colonial governor must be carefully selected for his experience and loyalty, trained thoroughly in the state's way of doing things and made so familiar with "best practice" that however isolated from "head office" guidance he may be, the job will still get done in a highly predictable way. Is it possible to detect here shades of William Whyte's *Organization Man?*

Takeovers

The equivalent of a takeover in Machiavelli's world was the conquest of another country or the establishment of a colony. In such matters his advice is very clear. One either totally subjugates the original inhabitants, so that rebellion is unlikely and the cost of garrisoning the place reduced to a minimum, or, and Machiavelli makes clear this is his preference, the conqueror puts in a small team of "key managers." This team will only displace a small number of the original inhabitants, who being scattered cannot rebel, and the remainder will quickly toe the new management line since they have everything to gain from cooperation and a clear indication of what happens to those who do not cooperate. Parallels with business takeovers are frighteningly stark.

"All empire is no more than power in trust." (John Dryden)

  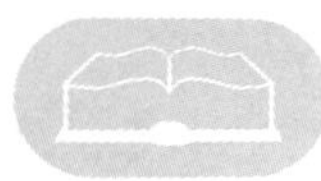    

Change

Machiavelli has little to offer in the way of ideas for coping with change, but shows clearly that the problems of introducing change were just as in the sixteenth century as they are today. In *The Prince* he says: "It must be considered that there is nothing more difficult to carry out, nor more doubtful of success, nor more dangerous to handle, than to initiate a new order of things."

Federations and Bureaucracies

Machiavelli compared the "management" of sixteenth-century France and Turkey. He saw France as a "federal organization;" a collection of independent baronies in which the retainers regarded their baron, and not the king, as the "key manager." Such organizations are difficult to control, impossible to change, and the ruler is easily overthrown. Turkey was in Machiavelli's time a classic bureaucracy with a highly trained civil service. Civil servants were frequently moved around, hence they developed no local loyalties, and had a strict, hierarchical relationship with "top management." The ruler in such a state, being appointed by the "system" was secure, respected, and powerful. The points of comparison with today's large organizations need little emphasizing.

Niccolò Machiavelli in Perspective

The impact of Machiavelli's writing on politics has been accepted for some time, but the relevance of his ideas to business had to wait until the second half of the nineteenth century, when companies began to operate as large, complex organizations—the equivalent in Machiavelli's terms of a move from a tribal society to a corporate state. An English parson, writing in 1820, compares Machiavelli unfavorably with the devil, yet by the 1860s Victor Hugo was able to say, "Machiavelli is not an evil genius, nor a cowardly writer, he is nothing but the fact. . .not merely the Italian fact, he is the European fact."

Machiavelli's image is not helped by what many see as an amoral attitude toward power. It is easy to take offense when he says, "A prudent ruler ought not to keep faith when by so doing it would be against his interest, and when the reasons which made him bind himself no longer exist."

Such statements are easier to accept if we remember they were made in times very different from our own. They were also the words of a man who was a true observer; he reported what he saw and measured results dispassionately in terms of practical success or failure. He had moral views, as can be seen in his other writing, but on political issues he is a cold realist. He had, as Professor Lerner so aptly observed ". . .the clear-eyed capacity to distinguish between man as he ought to be and man as he actually is—between the ideal form of institutions and the pragmatic conditions under which they operate."

By being so linked with intrigue, cruelty, and opportunism, Machiavelli remains rooted in his own age. However, if we set him aside from the harsh realities of sixteenth-century Europe and look at how he observes human nature and organizations, we see a man who was centuries ahead of his time.

For More Information

Key works by Machiavelli

Books:

The Prince and *The Discourses* (introduced by Max Lerner). New York: Random House, 1950.

A number of editions of *The Prince* and *The Discourses* are currently in print.

Further Reading

Books: Fisher, Robin. *Beyond Machiavelli: Tools for Coping with Conflict*. New York: Penguin USA, 1996.

Jay, Antony. *Management and Machiavelli*. London: Hodder and Stoughton, 1967.

McAlpine, Alistair. *The New Machiavelli: The Art of Politics in Business*. New York: John Wiley, 1999.

Whyte, William. *The Organization Man*. Philadelphia: University of Pennsylvania Press, 2002.

See also:

✔ **How to Network and Market Yourself (pp. 758–59)**

The Prince (p. 944)

"It is a common fault of men not to reckon on storms in fair weather." (Niccolò Machiavelli)

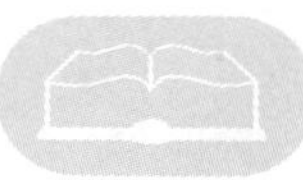

ABRAHAM MASLOW

The Hierarchy of Needs

Maslow, known principally for his theory of the "hierarchy of needs," was one of the first people to be associated with the humanistic—as opposed to task-based—approach to management. As people have increasingly come to be appreciated as a key resource in successful companies, Maslow's model has remained a valuable management concept.

1908	Born.
1934	Receives Ph.D. from the University of Wisconsin.
1935	Returns to New York to work at Columbia University.
1937–1951	On the faculty of Brooklyn College.
1943	"Hierarchy of needs" first presented in an article in the *U.S. Psychological Review*.
1951	Becomes head of the psychology department at Brandeis University.
1954	*Motivation and Personality* published.
1970	Dies.

LIFE AND CAREER

Abraham Maslow (1908–1970) was a U.S. psychologist and behavioral scientist. He was born in Brooklyn, New York, to poorly educated immigrant parents from Russia. He spent part of his career in industry as well as working as an academic. He liked to say that, whereas most early psychologists studied people with psychological problems, he devoted his attention to successful people. The "hierarchy of needs" theory, on which his fame chiefly rests, was first presented in 1943 in the *U.S. Psychological Review*, and later developed in his book *Motivation and Personality*, first published in 1954. His concepts were originally offered as general explanations of human behavior, but quickly came to be regarded as a significant contribution to workplace motivation theory. They are still used by managers today to understand, predict, and influence employee motivation.

KEY THINKING

Maslow grouped human needs into classes and arranged these classes in the form of a hierarchy, ascending from the lowest to the highest. When one set of needs is satisfied, it ceases to be a motivator; motivation is then generated by the unsatisfied needs further up the hierarchy. The classes of needs identified by Maslow are: survival or physiological needs, safety or security needs, social needs, ego-status needs, and self-actualization needs, and they appear in that order in the hierarchy. Today the hierarchy is usually represented as a pyramid, although Maslow himself did not present it in that way.

The five levels within the hierarchy can be broken down as follows.

- Survival or physiological needs. These are the most primitive of all needs, comprising all the basic animal requirements such as food, water, shelter, warmth, and sleep.
- Security or safety needs. In earlier times, these needs expressed themselves in the form of a desire to be free of physical danger. In the modern context, they have been refined and are now felt in mainly social and financial terms; purely physical requirements have been replaced by the need for things such as job security or a living wage.
- Social needs. Most humans need to belong and to be accepted by others. They are essentially social beings and therefore seek membership of social groups, such as work groups.
- Ego-status needs. Most humans also need to be held in esteem by both themselves and others. This kind of need is satisfied by power, prestige, and self-confidence.
- Self-actualization needs. The most sophisticated type of need is the desire to maximize one's skills and talents. This embraces self-realization, self-expression, and self-fulfillment.

There are certain conditions, Maslow wrote, that are immediate prerequisites for satisfying needs, such as the freedom to speak, the freedom to express oneself in other ways, the freedom to defend oneself, justice, fairness, and honesty. Any danger threatening these is perceived almost as if it were a danger to the satisfaction of the needs themselves.

The hierarchy is usually referred to as if it were a fixed order, but Maslow explained that it is not necessarily rigid or universally applicable in its usual form. While most people do experience their basic needs in the order indicated, there are a number of exceptions. Creative people, for example, are often driven by a desire for self-actualization and give it precedence over the satisfaction of "lower" needs in a way that the average person perhaps would not.

The hierarchy is often presented in simplified terms, giving the false impression that one need must be fully satisfied before the next need emerges. In fact, as Maslow pointed out, man is a continually wanting animal, whose basic needs are for the most part partially satisfied and partially unsatisfied at the same time. Needs continually overlap; for example, social needs are felt by almost everyone, including those people whose basic physiological needs are not being met. As soon as a need is satisfied, however, it will drop out of the equation and cease to be a motivator.

Maslow's intention all along was to define an aspect of the human condition, but his insights are obviously applicable within a business context. If, for example, a manager is able to recognize which level of the hierarchy a worker has reached, then he or she can motivate the employee in the most appropriate way. Peter Drucker, in his book *Management: Tasks, Responsibilities, Practices* (New York: Harper & Row, 1973), pointed out that although it becomes less satisfying to obtain economic rewards as one moves up the hierarchy, the need for economic reward does not necessarily become less important. This is because, as their impact as a positive incentive decreases, their ability to create dissatisfaction and act as a disincentive increases. Economic rewards

"In order for an ideal to become a reality, there must be a person, a personality to translate it."

(Jesse Jackson)

come to be seen as entitlements and, if they are not looked after, can act as deterrents.

Abraham Maslow in Perspective

Maslow often is mentioned in connection with his contemporaries, Douglas McGregor and Frederick Herzberg, who also were developing motivation theories at about the same time. Maslow admired McGregor, the author of Theory X and Theory Y, although he had strong reservations about the validity of Theory Y. Herzberg suggested that hygiene factors—those that may be causes of job dissatisfaction (for example, working conditions, salary, job security, or company policy) but are not in themselves incentives to improve performance—should be separated from motivators—those that lead to positive job satisfaction (such as achievement, recognition, responsibility, or advancement). Herzberg's hygiene factors can be compared with Maslow's levels one, two, and three, and the motivators to levels four and five.

Maslow's influence continues through the work of later psychologists and writers, such as Chris Argyris and Blake and Mouton. Argyris looked at how individual initiatives and creativity can coexist with organizational rules. Blake and Mouton were the authors of the *Managerial Grid*, which created the concept of the manager who balanced a concern for people with a concern for the task.

Practicing managers have also, on the whole, found Maslow's concept a valuable and sensible one, which helps to clarify their thoughts. It often is used as a basis for questionnaires and checklists to discover an individual's level of motivation, or cited in support of the idea of empowerment. Twyla Dell, in *How to Motivate People* (London: Kogan Page, 1988), listed the ten qualities that people most want from their jobs and included two questionnaires to help readers judge how many of the ten qualities they were receiving and giving in their work. She then matched the ten qualities to Maslow's hierarchy.

Maslow's theory fully makes sense only when applied, as he originally intended, to life in general rather than to the workplace in particular. This is because some of the needs of the individual, particularly the higher needs, may be satisfied outside the workplace. This holistic view is nonetheless important within the workplace, as employers increasingly come to realize that individuals have a life outside their job that impinges on their performance at work. Although Maslow's theory is now over 50 years old, it is still referred to by managers and it offers them useful insights. Along with Herzberg and McGregor, he is recognized as one of the founding fathers of motivation theory.

For More Information

Key works by Maslow
Books:
Motivation and Personality. 2nd ed. New York: Harper and Row, 1970.
The Farther Reaches of Human Nature. New York: Viking Press, 1971.

Further Reading
Books: Frick, Willard B. *Humanistic Psychology: Interviews with Maslow, Murphy, and Rogers*. Columbus, OH: Charles E. Merrill, 1971.
Lowry, Richard J. *A. H. Maslow: An Intellectual Portrait*. Monterey, CA: Brookes Cole, 1973.
Hoffman, Edward. *The Right to be Human: A Biography of Abraham Maslow*. Wellingborough: Crucible, 1989.
Journal Article: Berman Brown, Reva. "Abraham Maslow and Self-actualization." *Organizations and People*, Jan. 1994, vol. 1 no. 1, pp. 42–45.

See also:
Frederick Herzberg (pp. 1002–03)

"True motivation comes from achievement, personal development, job satisfaction, and recognition."
(Frederick Herzberg)

  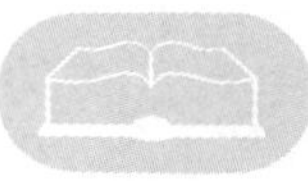    

ELTON MAYO

The Hawthorne Experiments

Professor George Elton Mayo (1880–1949) has secured fame as the leader in a series of experiments that became one of the great turning points in management thinking. At the Hawthorne plant of Western Electric, he discovered that job satisfaction increased through employee participation in decisions, rather than through short-term incentives.

1880	Born.
1911	Appointed lecturer in logic, ethics, and psychology (later Professor of Philosophy) at University of Queensland.
1923	Moves to United States and takes a post at Pennsylvania University; conducts experiments on productivity in a spinning mill, related to working conditions.
1927–1932	Experiments are carried out at the Hawthorne plant.
1928	Moves to Harvard as associate professor of industrial research; becomes involved with Hawthorne experiments.
1929–1930	Deduces that a more listening, caring style of supervision raises morale and boosts productivity.
1930–1945	Develops TWI program.
1947	Retires from Harvard.
1947–1949	Advisor to British government on problems within industry.
1949	Dies.

LIFE AND CAREER

An Australian by birth, Mayo studied psychology at Adelaide University and, in 1911, was appointed lecturer in logic, ethics, and psychology (and later Professor of Philosophy) at the University of Queensland.

Anxious to move to the United States for professional reasons, he took a post at Pennsylvania University in 1923. Here, he became involved in one of the investigations that acted as a dry run for Hawthorne. In one department at a spinning mill in Philadelphia, labor turnover was 250%—compared with an average of 6% in other parts of the company. A series of experimental changes in working conditions was introduced in the department, most notably rest pauses. These changes led to successive increases in productivity and the raising of morale. After one year, labor turnover was down to the average level for the company. It was assumed that this improvement was due to the introduction of rest pauses—a conclusion that was to undergo substantial modification as a result of Hawthorne.

The Hawthorne experiments began in 1924 and Mayo's involvement in them in 1928, after he had moved to the Harvard University School of Business Administration as associate professor of industrial research. Later he became a professor and remained at Harvard until his retirement in 1947. During World War II, Mayo contributed to the development of supervisor training with his Training Within Industry (TWI) program, which was widely adopted in the United States. The last two years of his life were spent in the United Kingdom, as an advisor to the British government on problems within industry.

KEY THINKING

Mayo wrote about democracy and freedom, and the social problems of industrialized civilization. It is as the author of *Human Problems of an Industrial Civilization*, which reports on the Hawthorne experiments, that he is known for his contribution to management thinking, even though he disclaimed responsibility for the design and direction of the project.

HAWTHORNE

The Hawthorne plant of Western Electric was located in Chicago. It had some 29,000 employees and manufactured telephones and telephone equipment, principally for AT&T. The company had a reputation for advanced personnel policies and had welcomed a study by the National Research Council into the relationship between workplace lighting and the efficiency of individual workers.

THE EXPERIMENTS

The study began in 1924 by isolating two groups of workers in order to test the impact of various incentives on their productivity. Improvements to levels of lighting produced increases in productivity, but so, too, did reversion to standard lighting and even below-standard lighting in both groups. The initial assumption therefore was that increased output stemmed from variation alone.

Other incentives—including payment incentives and rest pauses—were manipulated at regular intervals and, although output levels varied, the trend was inexorably upwards. Whatever experimentation was applied, output went up. Although it had been fairly conclusively determined that lighting had little to do with output levels, the assistant works manager (George Pennock) agreed that something peculiar was going on, and that experimentation should continue.

EARLY DEDUCTIONS—SUPERVISION AND EMPLOYEE ATTITUDES

In the winter of 1927, Pennock invited Clair Turner, professor of biology and public health at Massachusetts Institute of Technology (MIT), to contribute. Turner quickly resolved that rest pauses in themselves were not the cause for increased output, although longer rest pauses gave rise to more social interaction, which in turn affected mental attitudes. Turner attributed the rise in output to the small group; the type of supervision; earnings; the novelty of the experiment; and the increased attention to the workers generated by the experiment.

Pennock had been among the first to note that supervisory style was important. The supervisor involved in the illumination experiment had been relaxed and friendly; he got to know the operators well and was not too worried about company policies and procedures. Discipline was secured through

"You can't treat your people like an expense item." (Andrew S. Grove)

enlightened leadership, and an esprit de corps grew up within the group. This was in stark contrast to standard practice before the experiment.

When Pennock invited Turner to participate, he also invited Mayo—although it is not known whether this was as a result of Mayo's achievements at the Philadelphia spinning mill, or because of a desire to involve Harvard. Visits in 1929 and 1930 indicated to Mayo "a remarkable change of attitude in the group." Mayo's view was that the test room workers had turned into a social unit, enjoyed all the attention they were getting, and had developed a sense of participation in the project.

In order to understand this further, Mayo instituted a series of interviews. These provided the workers with an opportunity to express their views. It emerged that they would feel better for discussing a situation, even if it did not change. Further exploration revealed that some complaints had little or no basis in fact, but were actually indicators of personal situations causing distress.

By focusing on a more open, listening and caring interview approach, Mayo had struck a key which linked the style of supervision and the level of morale to levels of productivity.

Further Research—Social Groups

A third stage in the research took place in the bank wiring room, with a similar application of incentives to productivity. Here it emerged that output was restricted:

- the group had a standard for output that was respected by individuals in the group;
- the group was indifferent to the employer's financial incentive scheme;
- the group developed a code of behavior of its own, based on solidarity in opposition to the management;
- output was determined by informal social groups rather than by management.

Mayo had read the work of F. W. Taylor, who had already established that social groups were capable of exercising very strong control over the work behavior of individual members (Taylor had called it "systematic soldiering"). The interesting development that Mayo noted, however, was that whereas in the first set of experiments productivity went up as the project progressed, in the other—the bank wiring room—productivity was reduced.

In *The Human Problems of an Industrial Civilization*, Mayo wrote: "Human collaboration in work. . .has always depended for its perpetuation upon the evolution of a non-logical social code which regulates the relations between persons and their attitudes to one another. Insistence upon a merely economic logic of production. . .interferes with the development of such a code and consequently gives rise in the group to a sense of human defeat. This. . .results in the formation of a social code at a lower level and in opposition to the economic logic. One of its symptoms is 'restriction.'"

The question which needed to be asked, therefore, was, "What was different between the two groups?" The answer was found to lie with the attitude of the observer—where the observer encouraged participation and took the workers into his confidence, productivity went up; where the observer merely watched and adopted the trappings of traditional supervisory practice, output was reduced.

Interpreting Hawthorne

For industry to benefit from the experiments at Hawthorne, Mayo first concluded that supervisors needed training in understanding the personal problems of workers, and also in listening and interviewing techniques. He held that the new supervisor should be less aloof, more people-oriented, more concerned, and skilled in handling personal and social situations.

It was only later, after a period of reflection, that Mayo was able to conclude that:

- job satisfaction increased as workers were given more freedom to determine the conditions of their working environment and to set their own standards of output;
- intensified interaction and cooperation created a high level of group cohesion;
- job satisfaction and output depended more on cooperation and a feeling of worth than on physical working conditions.

In Mayo's view, workers had been unable to find satisfactory outlets for expressing personal problems and dissatisfactions in their work life. The problem was that managers thought the answers to industrial problems resided in technical efficiency, when actually the answer was a human and social one.

Mayo's contribution lies in recognizing that the formality of strict rules and procedures spawns informal approaches and groups with their base in human emotions, problems, and interactions. The manager, therefore, should strive for an equilibrium between the technical organization and the human one, and hence should develop skills in handling human relations and situations. These include diagnostic skills in understanding human behavior and interpersonal skills in counseling, motivating, leading, and communicating.

Elton Mayo in Perspective

Mayo has been acclaimed by his followers as the founder of the human relations school of management, and criticized by sociologists for not going far enough in his interpretations.

Reading Mayo's conclusions causes no surprise—let alone discovery—at the end of the 20th century; his findings are increasingly commonplace among social scientists, labor unionists, and managers alike. But that is perhaps a measure of his achievement, because most commentators agree that he was the first to demonstrate, infer, and provide evidence for the benefits of a shift in management thinking, away from the widespread dominance of Taylor's scientific management. F. J. Roethlisberger said of Mayo that the data were not his; the results were not his; but the interpretations of both were indeed his. Without those interpretations, the results of Hawthorne might still be collecting dust in the archives.

The experiment also gave rise to the term "Hawthorne effect"—a situation that arose because people were "singled out" for special treatment, or a "special situation" was created, in which workers could feel free to air their problems.

Mayo's ideas on the emergence of "informal" organizations were read by Argyris and others as they developed theories about how organizations learned and developed. The discrediting of the "rabble hypothesis" theory led directly to the work of McGregor.

The conclusions drawn by Mayo from the Hawthorne studies recognized that management style is a major contributor to industrial productivity; that interpersonal skills are as important as monetary incentives or target-setting, and that a more humanistic approach is an important means of satisfying the organization's economic and social needs.

For More Information

Key works by Mayo

Books:

The Human Problems of an Industrial Civilization. 2nd ed. Boston, MA: Harvard University Press, 1946.

The Social Problems of an Industrial Civilization. NewYork: Macmillan, 1945.

See also:

Chris Argyris (pp. 964–65)

Douglas McGregor (pp. 1022–23)

DOUGLAS MCGREGOR

Theory X and Theory Y

Developer of Theory X and Theory Y, which describe two views of people at work and two opposing management styles, Douglas McGregor's relatively short career has been a key influence for many of today's management commentators. *The Human Side of Enterprise* marked a watershed in management thinking, and laid the foundations for the modern, people-centred view of management.

1906	Born.
1932	Graduates from Wayne University.
1935	Receives Ph.D. in Experimental Psychology from Harvard University.
1948–1954	President, Antioch College.
1954	Professor of Management, Massachusetts Institute of Technology.
1960	Publication of *The Human Side of Enterprise.*
1964	Dies.
1993	Listed as one of the most popular management writers alongside Henri Fayol.

LIFE AND CAREER

Douglas McGregor (1906–1964) followed a mostly academic career lecturing at Harvard University, Massachusetts Institute of Technology (MIT) and Antioch College, becoming the first Sloan Fellows professor at MIT. Although, because of his early death, he wrote only a few publications, they have had a great impact. In 1993 McGregor was listed as one of the most popular management writers alongside Henri Fayol (in *Management Gurus—What Makes Them and How to Become One*). Major American writers such as Rosabeth Moss Kanter, Warren Bennis, and Tom Peters, whose writings have much influence on current learning and practice, agree that much of modern management thinking goes back to McGregor, especially the implications of his writing for theories on leadership.

KEY THINKING

McGregor believed that managers' basic beliefs have a dominant influence on the way that organizations are run, and central to this are managers' assumptions about the behavior of people. McGregor argues that these assumptions fall into two broad categories—Theory X and Theory Y. His findings were detailed in *The Human Side of Enterprise*, first published in 1960.

Theory X and Theory Y describe two views of people at work and may be used to describe two opposing management styles.

THEORY X: THE TRADITIONAL VIEW OF DIRECTION AND CONTROL

Theory X is based on the assumptions that:

- the average human being has an inherent dislike of work and will avoid it if at all possible;
- because of this human dislike of work, most people must be coerced, controlled, directed, and threatened with punishment to get them to make adequate effort toward the achievement of organizational objectives;
- the average human being prefers to be directed; wishes to avoid responsibility; has relatively little ambition; wants security above all else.

A Theory X management style therefore requires close, firm supervision with clearly specified tasks and the threat of punishment or the promise of greater pay as motivating factors. Managers working under these assumptions will employ autocratic controls that can lead to mistrust and resentment from those they manage. McGregor acknowledges that this approach constitutes a damning statement about the "mediocrity of the masses." He acknowledges, too, that the "carrot and stick" approach can have a place but will not work when the needs of people are predominantly social and egoistic.

THEORY Y: THE INTEGRATION OF INDIVIDUAL AND ORGANIZATIONAL GOALS

Theory Y is based on the assumptions that:

- the expenditure of physical and mental effort in work is as natural as play or rest. The average human being does not inherently dislike work. Depending on controllable conditions, work may be a source of satisfaction, or a source of punishment;
- external control and the threat of punishment are not the only means for bringing about effort toward achieving organizational objectives. People will exercise self-direction and self-control in the service of objectives to which they are committed;
- commitment to objectives is a result of the rewards associated with their achievement. The most significant of such rewards, such as the satisfaction of ego and self-actualization needs, can be direct products of effort directed toward organizational objectives;
- under proper conditions, the average human being learns not only to accept but to seek responsibility. Avoidance of responsibility, lack of ambition, and emphasis on security are generally consequences of experience, not inherent human characteristics;
- the capacity to exercise a relatively high degree of imagination, ingenuity, and creativity in the solution of organizational problems is widely, not narrowly, distributed in the population;
- under the conditions of modern industrial life, the intellectual potential of the average human being is used only partially.

Theory Y assumptions can lead to more cooperative relationships between managers and workers. A Theory Y management style seeks to establish a working environment in which the personal needs and objectives of individuals can relate to, and harmonize with, the objectives of the organization.

In *The Human Side of Enterprise*, McGregor recognizes that Theory Y is not a panacea for all ills. But by highlighting such ideas, he hopes instead to achieve an abandonment by management of the

"The process of developing heterogeneous resources must be continuous; it is never completed."

(Douglas McGregor)

  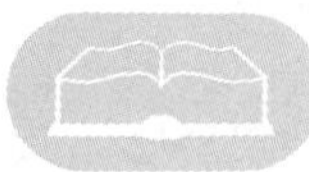    

limiting assumptions of Theory X and a consideration of the techniques involved in Theory Y.

Theory into Practice

Abraham Maslow viewed McGregor as a mentor, and was a strong supporter of theories X and Y. So he decided to put Theory Y (that people want to work, achieve, and take responsibility) into practice in a Californian electronics factory. However, he found that an organization driven solely by Theory Y could not succeed, as some sense of direction and structure was required. Instead, Maslow advocated an improved version of Theory Y that involved an element of structured security and direction taken from Theory X.

Maslow's negative experience with implementing Theory Y must be balanced against that of McGregor himself at a Procter & Gamble plant in Georgia, where he introduced Theory Y through the concept of self-directed teams. This plant was found to be a third more profitable than any other Procter & Gamble plant; it was kept a trade secret until the mid-1990s.

Before he died, McGregor began to develop a further theory that addressed the criticisms made of theories X and Y—that they were mutually incompatible. Ideas he proposed as part of this theory included lifetime employment; concern for employees (both inside and outside the working environment); decision by consensus; and commitment to quality. He tentatively called it Theory Z. Before it could be widely published, McGregor died and the ideas faded.

Theory Z

The work on Theory Z that McGregor began was not completely forgotten. During the 1970s, William Ouchi began to expound its principles by comparing and contrasting Japanese (Type J) and American (Type A) organizations.

Type A organizations, he proposed, tend to offer short-term employment, specialized careers (with rapid promotion), and individual decision making and responsibility. Type J firms, on the other hand, mirror the ethos of Japanese society—collectivism and stability rather than individuality. Those American firms that share Type J characteristics, and indeed have more in common with Type J organizations, were described as Type Z (examples included Hewlett-Packard and Procter & Gamble).

Leadership

Before McGregor, the thrust of writing about leadership focused on the qualities and characteristics of "great people," in the hope that, if those qualities were identified, they could be emulated.

McGregor argued that there were other variables involved in leadership, including the attitudes and needs of the followers, the nature and structure of the organization itself, and the social, economic, and political environment. For McGregor, leadership was not a property of the individual but a complex relationship among these variables. He was one of the first to argue that leadership was more about the relationship between the leader and the situation he or she faced, than merely the characteristics of the leader alone.

Douglas McGregor in Perspective

The Human Side of Enterprise marked a watershed in management thinking that had previously been dominated by the scientific approach of Taylor, and formed the foundations for the current, people-centered view of management.

Theory Y has been criticized for being too idealistic, but if we examine each of the six tenets of Theory Y in turn, we can trace much modern thinking back to McGregor:

1. Work, as a source of satisfaction, means accepting that people need to know not just what or how, but why; the adoption of meaningful objectives is one of the keys to self-motivation.

2–4. Ownership, commitment, and responsibility are three of the cornerstones of empowerment.

5–6. The encouragement for people to be fully exercised in the solution of organizational problems is central to action learning, total quality management, strategic thinking, and knowledge exploitation.

As mentioned above, Moss Kanter (writing on empowerment), Bennis (on leadership), and Peters (on excellence as well as chaos) all acknowledge their debt to McGregor.

Contemporary and subsequent commentaries on McGregor's theories have tended to see them as black and white. Harold Geneen, former president and CEO of ITT, commented that although Theories X and Y propose a neat summary of business management, no company is run in strict accordance with either one or the other. Peter Drucker said that Theory X sees people as immature, whereas Theory Y sees them striving towards adulthood.

The two contrasting theories are best seen perhaps as two polarizing forces with which managers have to grapple. Blake and Mouton expressed this in terms of the managerial grid, where managers constantly have to balance the drives and forces between task—getting things done, and people—how best to get them done for the benefit of the organization and the individuals doing them.

Although Theory Y has been held up as an unachievable aim—with the individual and the organization having convergent aspirations—the successful cases in which this aim is being attempted are growing. It is precisely such a goal that organizations are hoping to achieve through continuous improvement, continuous professional development, and participation schemes, operating in climates of empowerment.

It is not going too far to say that *The Human Side of Enterprise* recognizes that although we cannot actually motivate people, we do have a responsibility to acknowledge the elements involved in motivation. What we can do is to attempt to create the right climate, environment, or working conditions for motivation to be enabled.

For More Information

Key works by McGregor

Books:

The Human Side of Enterprise. New York: McGraw-Hill, 1960.

Leadership and Motivation. Cambridge, MA: MIT Press, 1966.

The Professional Manager. New York: McGraw-Hill, 1967.

Further Reading

Books: Huczynski, Andreas. *Management Gurus—What Makes Them and How to Become One*. London: Routledge, 1992.

Ouchi, William G. *Theory Z: How American Business Can Meet the Japanese Challenge*. Reading, MA: Addison Wesley, 1981.

See also:
Elton Mayo (pp. 1020–21)
Kurt Lewin (pp. 1014–15)

"Commitment to objectives is a function of the rewards associated with their achievement."

(Douglas McGregor)

  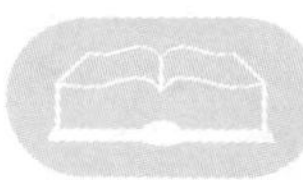    

HENRY MINTZBERG

A Great Generalist

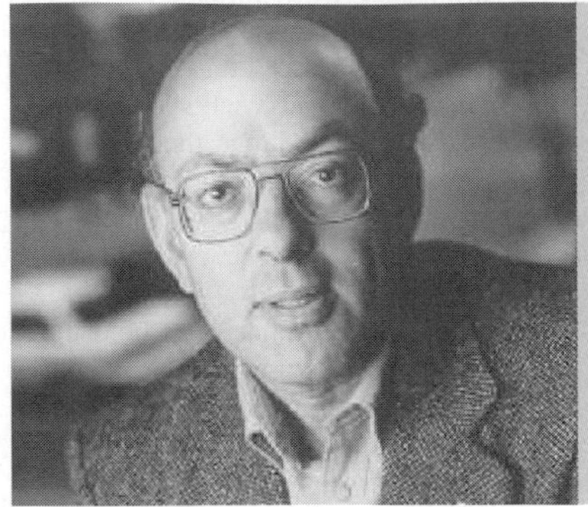

Often regarded as an iconoclast and a rebel, Henry Mintzberg (1939–) has certainly challenged many traditional ideas. But he does not attack people with whom he disagrees; he simply sets about proving them wrong, with devastating clarity. In his writing—the product of a career devoted to understanding how people actually manage—he resists every temptation to pontificate about how anyone ought to manage.

1939	Born.
1961	Receives a B.Eng. from McGill University.
1961–1963	Operational Research with Canadian National Railways.
1968	Receives a Ph.D. and becomes professor at McGill University; also subsequently becomes director of the Center for Strategic Studies.
1973	Publication of *The Nature of Managerial Work*.
1975	Wins the McKinsey Prize for best article.
1988–1991	President of the Strategic Management Society.
1991–	Holds other positions in management institutions, including that of visiting professor at INSEAD in France.
1995	*Academy of Management* receives the George R. Terry best book of the year award.
1995–2000	Director of International Masters Program in Practicing Management.
1996	Appointed Cleghorn Professor of Management Studies at McGill University.

LIFE AND CAREER

Henry Mintzberg was born in Canada and has spent virtually all his working life there. He studied at McGill University and, after further study at MIT, returned to Canada to take up an appointment with Canadian National Railways in 1961. In 1963 he moved into the academic world and by 1968 was back at McGill University as a professor, a post he holds to the present day. He is also director of the Center for Strategic Studies in Organization at McGill and has held several important positions in other management institutions, including that of visiting professor at INSEAD, the international business school at Fontainebleau in France. He has been a consultant to many organizations throughout the world and from 1988 to 1991 he was president of the Strategic Management Society.

Mintzberg's major impact on the management world began with his book *The Nature of Managerial Work*, published in 1973, and a seminal article in the *Harvard Business Review*, "The manager's job: folklore and fact," written two years later. Based on detailed research and thoughtful observation, these two works established Mintzberg's reputation by showing that what managers did, when successfully carrying out their responsibilities, was substantially different from much business theory.

KEY THINKING

Unlike many gurus, Mintzberg's contribution to management thinking is not based on one or two clever theories within some narrow discipline. His approach is broad, involving the study of virtually everything managers do and how they do it. His general appeal is further enhanced by a fundamental belief that management is about applying human skills to systems, not applying systems to people, a belief that is demonstrated throughout his writing.

HOW MANAGERS WORK

In "The Manager's Job: Folklore and Fact," Mintzberg sets out the stark reality of what managers do. "If there is a simple theme that runs through this article, it is that the pressures of his job drive the manager to be superficial in his actions—to overload himself with work, encourage interruption, respond quickly to every stimulus, seek the tangible and avoid the abstract, make decisions in small increments, and do everything abruptly," he writes.

Mintzberg uses the article to stress the importance of the manager's role and the need to understand it thoroughly before attempting to train and develop those engaged in carrying it out.

"No job is more vital to our society than that of the manager. It is the manager who determines whether our social institutions serve us well or whether they squander our talents and resources. It is time to strip away the folklore about managerial work, and time to study it realistically so that we can begin the difficult task of making significant improvements in its performance." In *The Nature of Managerial Work*, Mintzberg proposes six characteristics of management work and ten basic management roles.

The six characteristics are:

- the manager's job is a mixture of regular, programmed jobs and unprogrammed tasks;
- a manager is both a generalist and a specialist;
- managers rely on information from all sources but show a preference for that which is transmitted orally;
- managerial work is made u;p of activities that are characterized by brevity, variety and fragmentation;
- management work is more an art than a science and is reliant on intuitive processes and a "feel" for what is right;
- management work is becoming more complex.

Mintzberg places the 10 roles that he believes make up the content of the manager's job into three categories.

INTERPERSONAL

- Figurehead—performing symbolic duties as a representative of the organization.
- Leader—establishing the atmosphere and motivating the subordinates.
- Liaiser—developing and maintaining webs of contacts outside the organization.

INFORMATION

- Monitor—collecting all types of information that are relevant and useful to the organization.

"Society has become unmanageable as a result of management." (Henry Mintzberg)

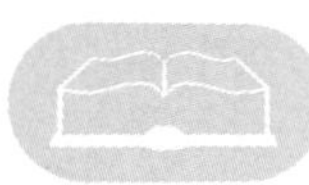

- Disseminator—transmitting information from outside the organization to those inside.
- Spokesperson—transmitting information from inside the organization to outsiders.

DECISION MAKING

- Entrepreneur—initiating change and adapting to the environment.
- Disturbance Handler—dealing with unexpected events.
- Resource Allocator—deciding on the use of the organization's resources.
- Negotiator—negotiating with individuals and dealing with other organizations.

THE STRUCTURING OF ORGANIZATIONS

In his 1979 book, *The Structuring of Organizations*, Mintzberg identified five types of "ideal" organization structures. These were: simple structure; machine bureaucracy; professional bureaucracy; divisional; and adhocracy. The classification was reexamined ten years later in *Mintzberg on Management* and the following, more detailed, view of organization types drawn up:

- the Entrepreneurial Organization—small staff, loose division of labor, little management hierarchy, informal, with power focused on the chief executive;
- the Machine Organization—highly specialized, routine operating tasks, formal communication, large operating units, tasks grouped under functions, elaborate administrative systems, central decision making, and a sharp distinction between line and staff;
- the Diversified Organization—a set of semiautonomous units under a central administrative structure. The units are usually called divisions and the central administration referred to as the headquarters;
- the Professional Organization—commonly found in hospitals, universities, public agencies, and firms doing routine work, this structure relies on the skills and knowledge of professional staff in order to function. All such organizations produce standardized products or services;
- the Innovative Organization—this is what Mintzberg sees as the modern organization: one that is flexible, rejecting any form of bureaucracy and avoiding emphasis on planning and control systems. Innovation is achieved by hiring experts; giving them power; training and developing them; and employing them in multidisciplinary teams that work in an atmosphere unbounded by conventional specialisms and differentiation;
- the Missionary Organization—it is the mission that counts above all else in such organizations, and the mission is clear, focused, distinctive, and inspiring. Employees readily identify with the mission, share common values and are motivated by their own zeal and enthusiasm.

STRATEGY AND PLANNING

In his 1994 book *The Rise and Fall of Strategic Planning*, Mintzberg produces a masterly criticism of conventional theory. His main concern is with what he sees as basic failings in our approach to planning. These failings are:

- processes—the elaborate processes used create bureaucracy and suppress innovation and originality
- data—"hard" data (the raw material of all strategists) provides information, but "soft" data provides wisdom. "Hard information can be no better and is often at times far worse than soft information."
- detachment—it is no use producing strategies in "ivory towers." Effective strategists are not people who distance themselves from the detail of a business ". . .but quite the opposite: they are the ones who immerse themselves in it, while being able to abstract the strategic messages from it."
- strategy is not "the consequence of planning but the opposite: its starting point." Mintzberg has coined the phrase "crafting strategies" to illustrate his concept of the delicate, painstaking process of developing strategy—a process of emergence that is far removed from the classical picture of strategists grouped around a table predicting the future. He argues that while an organization needs a strategy, strategic plans are generally useless as one cannot predict two to three years ahead.

HENRY MINTZBERG IN PERSPECTIVE

Henry Mintzberg remains one of the few truly generalist management writers of today. Different readers see him as an expert in different areas. For some people, he is an authority on time management, and he has written some of the most practical advice on this subject; for others he is the champion of the hard-pressed manager, surrounded by management theorists telling him or her how to do their job; and for yet another group, he is a leading authority on strategic planning.

For most people, however, Mintzberg is the man who dared to challenge orthodox beliefs and who, by the scholarly presentation of research findings and some truly original thinking, has changed our ideas about many key business activities.

For More Information

Key works by Mintzberg

Books:

The Nature of Managerial Work. New York: Harper & Row, 1973.
The Structuring of Organizations: a Synthesis of the Research. Upper Saddle River, NJ: Prentice Hall, 1979.
Structures in Fives: Designing Effective Organizations. Upper Saddle River, NJ: Prentice Hall, 1983.
Power In and Around Organizations. Upper Saddle River, NJ: Prentice Hall, 1983.
Mintzberg on Management: Inside Our Strange World of Organizations. New York: Free Press, 1989.
The Rise and Fall of Strategic Planning. Upper Saddle River, NJ: Prentice Hall International, 1994.
Mintzberg, Henry, with J. B. Quinn. *The Strategy Process: Concepts, Contexts, Cases*. 3rd ed. Upper Saddle River, NJ: Prentice Hall International, 1996.

Journal Articles:

"The Manager's Job: Folklore and Fact." *Harvard Business Review*, Mar./Apr., pp. 163–176. (Originally published in 1975, the article includes a retrospective commentary by the author.)
"Crafting Strategy." *Harvard Business Review*, Jul./Aug. 1987, pp. 66–75.
"The Fall and Rise of Strategic Planning." *Harvard Business Review*, Jan./Feb. 1994, pp. 107–114.
"Rounding Out the Manager's Job." *Sloan Management Review*, Autumn 1994, pp. 11–26.
"Musings on Management." *Harvard Business Review*, Jul./Aug. 1996, pp. 61–67.

See also:

☆ **Viewpoint: Henry Mintzberg (pp. 241–42)**
The Nature of Managerial Work (p. 932)
The Rise and Fall of Strategic Planning (p. 949)
Alfred D. Chandler, Jr. (pp. 974–75)
Kenichi Ohmae (pp. 1028–29)
Michael Porter (pp. 1038–39)

"Strategy is not the consequence of planning but the opposite, its starting point." (Henry Mintzberg)

IKUJIRO NONAKA

Knowledge Creation

The work of Ikujiro Nonaka is best known for its focus on the creation of knowledge within organizations. Nonaka believes that this is the most meaningful core capability for a company, particularly because it leads to innovation. He argues that the knowledge generated becomes the key source of competitive advantage for the firm.

Many industries have felt the benefit of Nonaka's work.

1935	Born.
1958	Graduates from Waseda University
1995	Publication of *The Knowledge-creating Company*.
1995	Joins Japan Advanced Institute of Science and Technology (JAIST).
1997	Becomes dean of the school of knowledge science at JAIST.

LIFE AND CAREER

Ikujiro Nonaka (born 1935) is the first professor of knowledge at the Haas School of Business, University of California, where he previously received his MBA and Ph.D. degrees. He is also dean of the graduate school of knowledge science at the Japan Advanced Institute of Science and Technology (JAIST) in Japan. He was formerly a professor and director of the Institute of Innovation Research at Hitotsubashi University, Tokyo.

Professor Nonaka has described his work as comparative research on knowledge-creating processes in companies around the world, and also research on the characteristics of innovative activities in Japanese companies. He seeks to answer questions about what knowledge is, how organizations create knowledge, and how we can promote knowledge creation.

KEY THINKING

THE KNOWLEDGE-CREATING COMPANY

In their book *The Knowledge-creating Company: How Japanese Companies Create the Dynamics of Innovation*, Ikujiro Nonaka and Hirotaka Takeuchi argue that the success of Japanese companies is due to their skill and expertise in organizational knowledge creation, especially with respect to bringing about continuous business innovation. They use the metaphor of a journey, warning that there are new and foreign road signs to follow on the way. The book, which combines theoretical and philosophical analysis with practical case studies, attempts to convey the complex forces at work within creative organizational systems. It is not straightforward to read, but the authors justify this with the declaration that ". . .managers can no longer afford to be satisfied with simplistic ideas about knowledge and its creation."

EXPLICIT AND IMPLICIT KNOWLEDGE

Nonaka and Takeuchi's starting point is a contrast between Western and Eastern philosophies. In the West knowledge is formal, unambiguous, systematic, falsifiable, and scientific, and a quest for knowledge normally involves the analysis and interpretation of data and information. New knowledge is documented and then transferred by means of formal training. The authors describe this form of knowledge as "explicit." It is primarily managed through databases and manuals. Human expertise, experience, and insights are, they claim, generally ignored as sources of knowledge.

In the East, however, knowledge is intuitive, interpretive, ambiguous, non-linear, and difficult to reduce to scientific equations. Instead of being created through data analysis and interpretation, it grows from the expertise and experience of many people, whose minds are probed for insights. New knowledge is distributed and retained through experience. The resulting Eastern form of knowledge is described as "implicit."

In the authors' view, implicit and explicit knowledge are not totally separate but complementary entities. Successful Japanese companies are able to convert implicit knowledge to explicit knowledge, so that knowledge acquired by individuals becomes organizational knowledge shared among colleagues, and explicit knowledge is converted into implicit knowledge by individuals. Nonaka and Takeuchi refer to this interaction as knowledge conversion. They suggest four methods of knowledge conversion, otherwise known as the SECI process:

- socialization
- externalization
- combination
- internalization

These are described as the mechanisms by which implicit knowledge is "amplified" throughout the organization, creating a spiral model of knowledge creation.

MIDDLE-UP-DOWN MANAGEMENT STYLE

Nonaka and Takeuchi argue that the two traditional Western management styles, "top-down" and "bottom-up," fail to foster the dynamic interaction necessary to create organizational knowledge.

Successful Japanese companies acknowledge the vital role played by middle managers in taking the top management vision of "what should be" and the frontline employees' realistic sense of "what is," and developing midrange concepts. Middle managers are, in effect, the real "knowledge engineers" of the knowledge-creating company, serving as facilitators between top and bottom as well as between theory and reality, and playing a key role in innovation.

A "hypertext" organization consisting of interconnected layers is suggested as the ideal structure for knowledge creation. It combines two traditional structures—the hierarchy and the task force. Surprisingly, the model for this is the U.S. military, which is bureaucratic in peacetime but highly task-oriented in war. Nonaka and Takeuchi provide two case studies of Japanese companies that have attempted to implement a hypertext structure—Kao and Sharp.

TRANSFERRING KNOWLEDGE

The Knowledge-creating Company is rich in case studies, which are mostly based on large, well-established Japanese companies, including Matsushita, Canon, Honda, and

"Bureaucratic administration means fundamentally the exercise of control on the basis of knowledge."

(Max Weber)

Nissan. Many of the case studies describe a "transferring process," in which the organizational knowledge created during new product development in one division becomes transferred to other parts of the company. For example, the knowledge created within Canon while developing the mini-copier in the early 1980s was subsequently used in other areas. The product knowledge generated was applied to other equipment such as printers; the knowledge gained from the manufacturing process led to the automation of copier production; and the organizational knowledge gleaned, especially with respect to the role of middle managers and cross-functional working, influenced the way the company was managed.

The transfer of knowledge can also take place across national boundaries, and one example given is of Nissan's experience of developing a car in the United Kingdom. The case of Shin Caterpillar Mitsubishi, a U.S.-Japanese alliance, shows how knowledge creation can cut across company as well as national boundaries. It refers to the experience of Mitsubishi of Japan and Caterpillar of the United States when they pooled their resources to develop and market hydraulic shovels. Nonaka and Takeuchi show that using the four stages of knowledge conversion within the alliance averted potentially damaging clashes of culture, overcame the weaknesses of both sides in knowledge creation, and led to effective knowledge creation and innovation.

Practical Implications

The authors finish with recommendations as to how Western companies can become knowledge-creating companies. They should:

- create a knowledge vision (top management should define the boundaries of organizational knowledge and outline what kind of knowledge ought to be created);
- develop a knowledge crew (of employees with diverse talents);
- build a high-density field of interaction (an environment in which frequent and intensive interactions take place) at the front-line;
- piggyback on the new product development process;
- adopt middle-up-down management;
- switch to a hypertext organization;
- and construct a knowledge network with the outside world (meaning external stakeholders such as customers).

The Concept of "Ba" or Shared Spaces

Since the publication of *The Knowledge-creating Company*, Nonaka has developed the theory of "Ba," which provides a platform for creating knowledge. Ba means "place" or "shared spaces" and can be physical (for example, an office), virtual (for example, e-mail) or mental (for example, shared experiences, ideas, and, by extension, organization culture). Nonaka argues that knowledge cannot be separated from its context and is embedded in these shared spaces.

Nonaka describes four kinds of platform corresponding to the four stages of knowledge conversion mentioned above. Each space supports a particular conversion process and thereby speeds up overall knowledge creation.

- Originating (supports the socialization stage)—physical face-to-face experiences which provide the environment in which individuals share feelings and experiences. These are the key to the transfer of tacit knowledge.
- Interacting (supports the externalization stage)—a team-based environment, where individuals' mental models and skills are converted into common terms and concepts. This assists the process in which tacit knowledge is made explicit.
- Cyber (supports the combination stage)—interaction in the virtual world of cyberspace. This facilitates the exchanging and combining of different forms of explicit knowledge.
- Exercising (supports the internalization stage)—focused training with senior mentors and colleagues which assists the conversion of explicit knowledge into tacit knowledge.

"Knowledge Activists"

Knowledge activists support platforms and cultures by enabling knowledge creation. A knowledge activist can be an individual, group, or department that takes on a particular responsibility for energizing and coordinating knowledge creation throughout the organization. The activist has three roles: to act as a catalyst of knowledge creation, to coordinate knowledge creation initiatives, and to provide overall direction to these efforts.

Ikujiro Nonaka in Perspective

Peter Drucker first used the terms "knowledge worker" and "knowledge society" in the 1960s and more recently stated that knowledge has become the only meaningful resource. Nonaka acknowledges Drucker's contribution and takes it a stage further by looking at how knowledge is created and examining the processes and mechanisms involved.

The second half of the 1990s saw a huge surge of business interest in knowledge, led primarily by practitioners rather than academics. Nonaka, while not responsible for the attention given to knowledge management, provided ideas that gave purpose and direction to practitioner initiatives. No other writer in this field has made such a forceful business case for knowledge creation. Also, in contrast with much of the organizational thinking on knowledge management prevalent today, Nonaka reminds us that information technology is not enough and that human experience and implicit knowledge are important in creating new knowledge. Lastly, Nonaka emphasized the importance of middle management in organization information creation as early as 1988, and this was a significant departure from the Western view of middle management as a deadweight, potentially expendable part of the corporate structure.

In these respects Nonaka's ideas have been absorbed into the mainstream of management thinking and are almost taken for granted. Few organizations, however, have embraced his vision in its entirety, or attempted the kind of cultural and organizational restructuring to improve knowledge creation which he advocates.

For More Information

Key works by Nonaka

Book:

Nonaka, Ikujiro, with Hirotaka Takeuchi. *The Knowledge-creating Company: How Japanese Companies Create the Dynamics of Innovation*. New York: Oxford University Press, 1995.

Journal Articles:

"The Knowledge-creating Company." *Harvard Business Review*, vol. 69 no. 6, Nov./Dec., 1991, pp. 96–104.

Nonaka, Ikujiro, with Georg von Krogh and Kazuo Ichijo. "Develop Knowledge Activists!" *European Management Journal*, vol. 15 no. 5, Oct. 1997, pp. 475–483.

Nonaka, Ikujiro, with Noboru Konno. "The Concept of 'Ba': Building a Foundation for Knowledge Creation." *California Management Review*, vol. 40 no. 3, Spring 1998, pp. 40–54.

Nonaka, Ikujiro, with Ryoko Toyama and Noboru Konno. "SEC Ba and Leadership: A Unified Model of Dynamic Knowledge Creation." *Long Range Planning*, vol. 33 no. 1, Feb. 2000, pp. 5–34.

"To make knowledge productive. . .requires the systematic exploitation of opportunities for change."

(Peter F. Drucker)

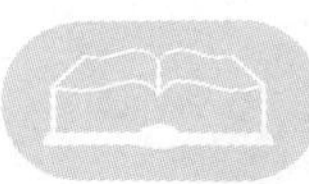

KENICHI OHMAE

The Art of Japanese Business

Ohmae's fresh approach to business strategy challenged business leaders to think in innovative, simple, and unconventional terms. His work in the late 1970s and 1980s heralded the arrival of Japanese management techniques in the West. Ohmae was the messenger for the Japanese way of doing business, urging managers to think "out of the box," and challenge accepted norms with clear, simple ideas in order to gain, and sustain, competitive advantage.

1943	Born.
1972	Joins McKinsey & Co.
1975	Publication of *The Mind of the Strategist.*
1987	Publication of *Beyond National Boundaries.*
1990	Publication of *The Borderless World.*
1995	Stands as candidate for governorship of Tokyo.
1995	Publication of *The End of the Nation State.*

LIFE AND CAREER

Kenichi Ohmae was born in 1943 on the island of Kyushu, and graduated from Waseda University and the Tokyo Institute of Technology before obtaining a Ph.D. in nuclear engineering from the Massachusetts Institute of Technology. In 1972 he joined the consulting firm McKinsey & Co. becoming managing director of their Tokyo office. As well as being a nuclear physicist he is an accomplished clarinettist, and a politician. In 1995, he ran for election as governor of Tokyo and also acted as an adviser to Japan's then prime minister, Nakasone.

Ohmae lives in Yokohama and advises some of Japan's most successful international companies in a wide spectrum of industries. His special interest, and area of expertise, is in formulating creative strategies, and developing organizational concepts to implement them.

Ohmae's seminal book, *The Mind of the Strategist*, was published in Japan in 1975. It was, however, only when interest in Japanese management methods increased during the early 1980s that the book was published in the United States. This 1982 American edition was given the subtitle *The Art of Japanese Business.* In *The Mind of the Strategist* Ohmae argues that the success of Japanese companies can be attributed to the nature of Japanese strategic thinking. This, contrary to the Western stereotype of Japanese management, was largely creative, intuitive, and vision-driven. Ohmae went on to explain what this creativity involved, and how it could be learned.

The view presented by Ohmae overturned traditional Western perceptions of Japanese managers, and the idea that their success was founded on brilliantly rational, farsighted thinking. Ohmae heralded a revolution based on creativity and innovation, and showed how, in the hands of a single, talented strategist, creativity could transform a major corporation.

In 1990, Ohmae's book *The Borderless World* challenged Japanese companies and corporations around the world to take account of globalization in their strategic planning. He urged businesses to focus less on the competitive aspects of strategy (promoted so effectively by Porter and others), and instead to give greater focus to "country" and "currency," two key elements that in an interdependent world economy can make or break a business strategy. This approach reflected Ohmae's increasing focus on global business and the relationship between business and the nation state. The latter was also the subject of two other books, *Beyond National Boundaries* (1987) and *The End of the Nation State* (1995).

Just as *The Mind of the Strategist* had encouraged innovation in strategy in the 1980s, so *The Borderless World* highlighted the importance of the global interdependence that has dominated trade in the 1990s.

KEY THINKING

THE ROLE OF THE STRATEGIST

Ohmae has explored a number of features of successful business strategies (usually Japanese), and compared them with their typical counterparts in the West. He identified several key differences.

- *Vision and dynamic leadership.* Japanese businesses tend to have a single, driving force in the form of an effective strategist, a leader or visionary who possesses what Ohmae has described as an idiosyncratic mode of thinking. Through this, company, customers, and competition (described as the strategic triangle) merge into a dynamic interaction from which, eventually, a comprehensive set of objectives and plans for action emerges. This approach was in marked contrast to the large, strategic planning bureaucracies that were typical of many large Western corporations of the time (the early 1980s).
- *Customer focus.* The customer is at the heart of Japanese strategy and is virtually enshrined as central to corporate values. The focus of the business needs to be on delivering what the customer wants, or there will be no business.
- *Methodology.* Ohmae perceived that to develop effective strategies, managers must first gain a detailed understanding of the characteristics of each element in a situation, and then develop a holistic plan tying each part of the business, each separate resource, into a competitive and efficient operation. This is not a systems approach based on linear thinking, but instead relies on detailed analysis ("the starting point") and knowledge, combined with innovation, intuition, and creativity.

THE STRATEGIC TRIANGLE

Ohmae claimed that, in constructing any business strategy, the three main players to be taken into account are the corporation itself, the customer, and the competition. Each of these three Cs is a living entity with its own interests and objectives, while collectively they form the strategic triangle. The three Cs influence strategy

"In Japan, organizations and people in the organizations are synonymous." (Kenichi Ohmae)

and planning in a number of important ways.

1. *Strategic business units (SBUs)*. The need for strategic business units that understand all three elements and to which strategic decisions can be delegated is held to be essential, in order to take adequate account of the strategic triangle. This is particularly the case for a large company made up of a number of different businesses selling to different customer groups (probably with different competitors). The definition of a business unit is always likely to be in dispute, so Ohmae suggests asking three key questions as a test:

- Are customer wants well defined and understood by the industry, and is the market segmented so that differences in those wants are treated differently?
- Is the business unit (an aspect of the corporation) equipped to respond easily to customer wants and needs?
- Do competitors have different sets of conditions that give them a relative advantage over the business unit?

If the business unit seems unable to compete effectively, then it should be redefined to better meet customer needs and competitive threats.

2. *Freedom of operation*. For Ohmae, the SBU must have full freedom of operation across the strategic triangle in order to develop and implement an effective strategy. In devising a strategy the SBU must be able to:

- address the total market for its customers;
- encompass all of the critical functions of the corporation, i.e., procurement, design, manufacturing, sales, marketing, distribution, and service, in order to respond with maximum freedom to the total needs of the customer;
- understand all key aspects of the competitor so that the corporation can seize an advantage when opportunities arise, and exploit any unexpected sources of strength.

3. *Matching the corporation with the market*. In the context of the strategic triangle, Ohmae sees the role of the strategist as matching the strengths of the corporation to the needs of a clearly defined market. Such matching, however, is relative to the capabilities of the competition. For this reason, Ohmae defines a successful strategy as one that ensures a better or stronger matching of corporate strengths to customer needs than that provided by competitors.

Four Routes to Strategic Advantage

In *The Mind of the Strategist*, Ohmae identifies four ways in which a corporation can gain advantage over its competitors.

- A business strategy based on Key Factors for Success (KFS). The business is required to identify what it does to give it an advantage over its competitors, or where the potential for advantage is greatest, and then concentrate resources there.
- Relative superiority. If a business is still unable to gain an advantage over its competitors and the KFS struggle is being waged equally, then any difference between the two competing businesses can be exploited. This might, for example, mean linking products together through the sales network to provide customers with better offers.
- Aggressive initiatives. When a competitor is established in a stagnant, low-growth industry, then Ohmae advocates an unconventional strategy aimed at upsetting the competitor's KFS. This can be achieved by challenging the accepted ways of doing business in the industry—upsetting the status quo.
- Strategic degrees of freedom. Success in the competitive struggle can be achieved by a business strategy based on the use of innovations. This may involve the vigorous opening up of new markets or the development of new products in areas untouched by the competition.

In each case, Ohmae believes that the main concern is to avoid taking the same approach in the same market as the competition.

Kenichi Ohmae in Perspective

Gary Hamel, among others, has recognized Ohmae's immense influence and contribution, emphasizing the impact of his challenge to managers to think in new and unconventional ways. It is a testament to the strength and appeal of Ohmae's work that, although the growth of the Japanese economy faltered during the 1990s, his ideas are still regarded as fundamental contributions to strategic management.

It might be argued that Ohmae's emphasis on strategic creativity helped to lay the foundations for the radical, transforming management approaches of the 1980s and 1990s. Certainly, if one accepts the need for an intuitive, innovative strategist, then it seems likely that there will be widespread changes in the ways that organizations are managed. So it was with the arrival of lean production, business process reengineering, and strategies for innovation and empowerment. Ohmae's view of the strategist, in fact, is now the widely accepted norm, and the need for a questioning approach that is not constrained by tradition, fear, or habitual patterns of behavior has filtered down from the strategists themselves to all layers of organizations.

Later works by Ohmae have focused on the rise of the global business and the relationships between business and governments. In a sense, Ohmae has grown away from his starting point and now prefers to write about a time when the end of the nation state is imminent. For many this emphasis on the distant future—rather than on business approaches for the medium-term—is of more relevance to politicians and academics than companies competing today. Even so, his legacy of startlingly simple, unconventional, and effective approaches is still required reading for many executives.

For More Information

Key works by Ohmae

Books:

The Mind of the Strategist. New York: McGraw-Hill, 1982.
Japan Business: Obstacles and Opportunities. New York: John Wiley, 1983.
Triad Power: The Coming Shape of Global Competition. New York: Free Press, 1985.
The Borderless World: Power and Strategy in the Interlinked Economy. New York: HarperBusiness, 1990.
The End of the Nation State: The Rise of Regional Economics. New York: Free Press, 1995.

See also:

The Borderless World (p. 894)
Alfred D. Chandler, Jr. (pp. 974–75)
Sumantra Ghoshal (pp. 992–93)
Henry Mintzberg (pp. 1024–25)
Richard Tanner Pascale (pp. 1034–35)
Michael Porter (pp. 1038–39)

"The strategist's method is very simply to challenge the prevailing assumptions with a single question: Why?"
(Kenichi Ohmae)

Taiichi Ohno

Toyota Production System

Japanese manufacturing has gained a reputation for innovative thinking and developments, and the current Western focus on quality, just-in-time delivery, waste and defect reduction, and kanban systems all have their origins in Japanese manufacturing companies. Taiichi Ohno was responsible for much of the thinking that created the now widely recognized Toyota Production System.

A Toyota production line, much influenced by the work of Ohno.

1902	Sakichi Toyoda invents power loom.
1912	Taiichi Ohno born.
1932	Ohno joins Toyoda Automatic Loom Works.
1936–1937	Toyoda starts manufacturing automobiles.
1945–1973	Development of Toyota Production System.
1947	Toyota producing 100,000 vehicles per year.
1956	Ohno visits United States to study production methods.
1990	Dies.
2000	Toyota produces 5.8 million vehicles internationally.

Life and Career

The history of the Toyota Production System goes back to the Toyoda Spinning and Weaving Company, set up by Sakichi Toyoda in 1918. This company later became the Toyota Automatic Loom Works. From the outset Sakichi recognized that his main competitors were based in the United Kingdom—an early observation of global competition. By 1929 the company had gained a reputation for innovative looms that stopped when there was a quality problem, such as a break in the thread. A British company, Platt Brothers, bought the production and sales rights for this loom for £100,000, a deal that was to have far-reaching consequences. This money was given to Sakichi's son Kiichiro to expand the company and to develop automotive technology. The first passenger car, the Model AA, was launched in 1936. A year later the Toyota Motor Company was formed.

Kiichiro traveled widely in his search for the best infrastructure for his company and Detroit was a place where he learned a great deal. Ford's assembly line system provided the framework upon which Kiichiro based his early car production, but he recognized the need to adapt it to the particular market conditions in Japan. Toyota was producing cars solely for the internal market, which meant supplying small numbers with high variety. This contrasted with the Ford approach of large numbers "in any color you like as long as it is black." Operating with only limited funds, Toyota was forced to work with supplier partners to generate the necessary capital investment.

It was under these conditions that Taiichi Ohno was brought into the company and one of his initial assignments was to increase the productivity of the Japanese company, which was behind that of Ford by a factor of ten. At the end of World War II Kiichiro had decreed that the company must "catch up with America in three years." Ohno realized that Japanese workers could not realistically be working ten times less effectively than their American counterparts. Waste and inefficiency must be prevalent and if this could be eliminated from the system productivity could increase by a factor of ten—or even more! The elimination of waste marked the start of the Toyota Production System and remains the basis from which it has evolved to this day.

Key Thinking

Ohno's early experiments in waste elimination were based within the manufacturing machine shops of which he was in charge. The "one man one machine" approach was seen as the only cost-effective system that a heavily unionized American industry could adopt. The production of large quantities of parts on high-speed, expensive machines creates the potential for an abundance of waste. Ohno experimented with different machine layouts, encouraging workers to become multiskilled and stopping machines when a job was finished. He encountered many problems during these early stages and learned the need for patience to allow workers to adapt to change.

Later he traveled widely in America looking at automobile plants. The knowledge he gained about Ford's assembly line was later to be applied in his ideas on continuously flowing processes. However, according to company lore, his "most important discovery in the U.S. was the supermarket." This has been explained by the fact that he came from a country that, at the time, was unused to self-service. The way customers chose exactly what they wanted impressed Ohno, as did the way stores supplied goods in a simple, efficient, and timely manner. In his later years Ohno often described his production system in terms of a supermarket. Like a supermarket, each production line sets out its produce for the next line to choose from. Each line becomes the customer for the preceding one and a "supermarket" for the following one. Such an approach represents a radical rethink of the production systems of the time. These were primarily "push" systems where the rate of output of the preceding line governed the running rate of the factory. Ohno's ideas amount to a "pull" system whereby demand pulls through resources from the previous line.

The Toyota Production System was developed between 1945 and 1973 and is still evolving. Its basic elements are *muda* (waste control), just-in-time, *ninben no tsuita jidoka* (automation with a human touch), *jidoka* (the quality principle), *heijunka* (production leveling), and *kanban* (the "signboard"—a stock-control system).

Muda

The philosophy of the Toyota Production System is based on obtaining cost reductions through the elimination of wasteful operations. Ohno divides waste into the following seven categories:

- overproduction
- transporting
- unnecessary stock on hand
- producing defective goods

"Automation does not make optimism obsolete." (Keith Funston)

- waiting (idle/nonproductive time)
- processing itself
- unnecessary motion

The key to eliminating waste is first to find it and then to ensure that it is recognized as waste by all.

Just-in-Time

The concept of just-in-time (often shortened to JIT) was invented by Kiichiro Toyoda, but it was Ohno who developed its full potential and made it into the system we know today. JIT means supplying to each process what it needs when it needs it and in the quantity that it needs.

Ohno's ideas about just-in-time implementation flowed once again from his experience of the supermarket. Customers visit the supermarket to buy as much of what they want as they happen to need. When he arrived at Toyota he found that, as in most assembly production at the time, lines producing an item usually pushed their output on to the next stage, whether the next stage needed it or not. Ohno proposed turning this around so that the "process that needs the parts [goes] to get what is needed, when it is needed and in the quantity needed." Thus, the output of a process is replaced as it is transported and consumed by the next process. Storage (inventory) becomes the responsibility of the producer, not the user. Thus workers and their supervisors can clearly see whether they are working too fast or too slowly and can act to reduce the waste.

Ninben no tsuita jidoka

"Autonomation" is the second pillar of the Toyota Production System and results from Sakichi Toyoda's earlier invention of the auto-activated weaving machine. The machine would automatically stop if a problem occurred, thus preventing the production of defective products. At Toyota the same principle was carried forward so that all machines were equipped with various safety devices, fixed-position stopping, and poka-yoke foolproofing systems to eliminate defective products.

The concept, however, is applied not only to machinery, but also to the production line and workers. It basically allows workers to stop the production line if a problem occurs. This enables each problem to be fully explored using Ohno's "five whys" (asking the question "Why?" five times to get to the heart of a problem), and makes sure that everyone understands the reason why it has arisen. In the long term this creates an efficient production line.

Jidoka

Jidoka means building quality into the process itself and is a natural extension of autonomation. Inspection teams were the traditional answer to quality control in most manufacturing systems. Ohno believed that quality must flow from production and not inspection. He achieved this by developing the most efficient and safest method of doing every task and training each team member to carry it out in this manner.

Heijunka

Work leveling or load smoothing is the major premise for the elimination of waste. Peaks and troughs in demand create waste capacity; it should be possible to rearrange the production plan and schedule to level out its effects. In this way a process with less work can help a process with excess work. In the complex production systems of the car industry the only viable solution, which most manufacturers adopted, was to maintain inventory, itself a waste.

A production line may have cars with different engine sizes, of different colors and with a mix of left- and right-hand drives. Toyota's solution was to equalize not only the quantities but also the types of parts used. This creates an even demand for the different types of components throughout the production cycle. Peaks and troughs are avoided, even in the most minute parts of the process.

Kanban

The kanban system evolved at the same time that Toyota was experimenting with just-in-time and is the method by which the system runs smoothly. Ohno recognized the need for a method of exchanging information between processes in a pull manufacturing environment. By taking the finished product as the starting point, Ohno developed a system of tags or signboards for controlling the transportation of a finished assembly and the production of replacement parts.

A kanban is used for managing and assuring just-in-time production. It is a simple and direct form of communication that is always located at the point where it is needed. Kanbans can be of various shapes as designed by the particular plant. Normally they are a small piece of paper on which is recorded how many of what part to pick up or which parts to manufacture. Ohno built the Toyota kanban system around six rules.

- Do not send defective products to the next process.
- Subsequent processes come to withdraw only what is needed.
- Produce only the exact quantity withdrawn by the subsequent process.
- Equalize production (load smoothing).
- Use *kanban* as a means of fine tuning.
- Stabilize and rationalize the process.

Taiichi Ohno in Perspective

Taiichi Ohno was an excellent originator of new ideas with his own unique management style. The Toyota Production System is remarkable because it was developed in completely the opposite direction to the traditional ways of thinking about production at the time. Ohno was able to build in the quality and the flexibility required in a small but demanding home marketplace by developing a "pull" manufacturing system. The combination of the early example set by his senior managers, his own conscientious research and study of the best of America's assembly line production systems, and his Japanese patience and logic enabled the fledgling Toyota motor company to survive, against its large American competitors.

For More Information

Key works by Ohno

Books:

Workplace Management (translated by Andrew P. Dillon). Cambridge, MA: Productivity Press, 1982.

Toyota Production System: Beyond Large-scale Production. Cambridge, MA: Productivity Press, 1988.

Ohno, Taiichi, with Setsuo Mito. *Just-in-Time for Today and Tomorrow*. Cambridge, MA: Productivity Press, 1988.

Further Reading

Books: Japanese Management Association (translated by David J. Lu). *Kanban Just-in-Time at Toyota: Management Begins at the Workplace*. Cambridge, MA: Productivity Press, 1986.

Monden, Yashuhiro. *Toyota Production System: An Integrated Approach to Just-in-Time*. 2nd ed. Norcross, GA: Industrial Engineering and Management Press, 1993.

See also:

Toyota Production System (p. 953)

 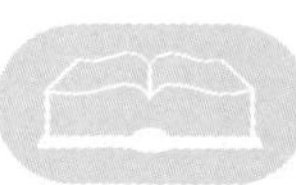    

ROBERT OWEN

Pioneer of Personnel Management

Robert Owen (1771–1858) is perhaps best known for his model textile factory and village at New Lanark in Scotland. Conditions in early factories were harsh, with hazardous working conditions. Long working hours were the norm, with children as young as five or six working under the same conditions as adults. Unlike other factory owners, Owen's strength was that he saw his employees as every bit as important to the success of his enterprise as the machines he owned.

1771	Born.
1781–1790	Works in various drapery businesses in Stamford, London, and Manchester.
1790	Becomes joint owner of textile factory in Manchester.
1799	Purchases mill in New Lanark from his father-in-law, David Dale, and sets about creating a "model" mill and village.
1808	Keeps the mill open, in spite of the U.S. trade embargo on British goods; mass unemployment elsewhere.
1813–	Tries to persuade other manufacturers to follow his example in employment practices.
1815	Attempts to introduce a bill to legislate on working conditions in factories.
1819	Legislation finally introduced, although limited to banning employment of children under nine.
1825	Leaves for the United States; founds New Harmony in Indiana.
1828	Returns to England after project fails due to internal disagreements and bad planning, leaving the settlement in his sons' hands.
1834	Founds the Grand National Consolidated Trades Union.
1858	Dies.

LIFE AND CAREER

OWEN THE FACTORY OWNER

By the age of 19, Owen was joint owner of a textile factory in Manchester, England. Being new to the responsibilities of management, he learned about the workings of the factory by observing his employees as they carried out their work. He wrote: "I looked very wisely at the men in their different departments, although I really knew nothing. By intensely observing everything, I maintained order and regularity throughout the establishment, which proceeded under such circumstances much better than I had anticipated."

In 1799, Owen (with a group of partners) purchased the New Lanark mill from his father-in-law, David Dale. Even though Dale was recognized as a progressive employer, conditions in and around the factory were still very poor. Children from five or six years old were employed through contracts with the local poor house, and working for 15 hours per day was common. Owen immediately withdrew from accepting any further children from the poor house and raised the minimum age of employment to 10. He also banned the beating of children.

KEY THINKING

Although a paternalistic employer, Owen was a businessperson above all else. He made no changes to employment conditions that could not be justified on economic grounds—all social improvements at New Lanark were funded through the profits of the factory. To achieve this, he required improved productivity from his workforce through changes to the working practices and methods of the factory.

For a workforce that was already working very hard, this was not popular. Owen (uniquely for the time) realized he had to gain the trust of his employees in order to get them to cooperate with the changes to the working environment he wished to achieve. He did this (in the language of today) by persuading "champions." He wrote: "I. . .sought out the individuals who had most influence among [the workforce] from their natural powers or position, and to these I took pains to explain what were my intentions for the changes I wished to effect."

Owen further won the trust of his employees when, in 1808, the United States passed a trade embargo on British goods. Most mills closed and mass unemployment occurred. Unlike other mill owners of the time, Owen kept his employees on full pay just to maintain the factory machinery in a clean, working condition.

This approach of fair management proved to be successful and, as returns from the business grew, Owen began to alter the working environment. Employment of children gradually ceased (as no further children were indentured from the poor house) and those still in employment were sent to a school built for the purpose in New Lanark. The housing available to his workers was gradually improved, the environment was rid of gin shops, and crime decreased. The first adult night school anywhere in the world also operated in New Lanark. Finally, Owen set up a store at New Lanark, and the principles behind this laid the basis for the later retail cooperative movement.

OWEN THE INNOVATOR

Owen's innovations, however, did not merely extend to improving working conditions for his employees. The Industrial Revolution (which began in the mid-to-late 1700s) led to a belief in the supremacy of machines. Owen opposed this growing view by seeking to humanize work.

"Many of you have long experiences in your manufacturing operations of the advantage of substantial, well-contrived and well-executed machinery. If, then, due care as to the state of your inanimate machines can produce such beneficial results, what may not be expected if you devote equal attention to your vital machines, which are far more wonderfully constructed," he wrote.

As already indicated, Owen was one of the first to "manage" rather than order his workforce, and the first to attempt to gain agreement for his ideas rather than impose them on others (a worker could not be fired

"Wealth may not produce civilization, but civilization produces money." (Henry Ward Beecher)

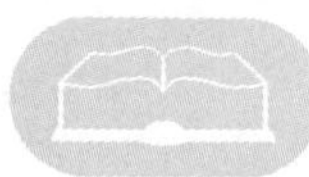

for disagreeing with Owen). Additionally, he required his managers to behave with some autonomy (possibly the first example of empowerment at work); managers (or superintendents) were selected carefully and trained to be able to act in Owen's absence.

Owen developed an aid to motivation and discipline—the silent monitor system—which could be described as a distant ancestor of appraisal schemes in practice today. Each machine within the factory had a block of wood mounted on it with a different color—black, blue, yellow, or white—painted on each face. Each day, the superintendents rated the work of their subordinates and awarded each a color that was then turned to face the aisle so that everyone was able to see all ratings. The intention of this scheme was that high achievers were rewarded and slackers were motivated to improve.

Owen the Reformer

The factory at New Lanark was spectacularly profitable, with returns of over 50% on investment, and Owen held this to be proof of the validity and importance of his theories. Strengthened by his profitability, he tried to persuade other manufacturers to follow his example in employment practices. This was first attempted through those of influence who visited New Lanark (estimates put the number of visitors at 20,000 between 1815 and 1825) and then, in 1815, via his attempt to introduce a bill to legislate on basic working conditions in factories.

The aims of the bill were to ban the employment of those aged under 10; to ban night shifts for all children; to provide 30 minutes' education a day for those under 18; and to limit the working day to 10.5 hours. This would have been enforced by a system of government factory inspectors. The bill failed to be introduced in its intended form, as its opponents argued that it would be bad for business and that in any case most employers were voluntarily doing what the bill would require. By the time it was finally introduced in 1819, the legislation was limited to banning the employment of those under nine.

In 1825, disillusioned with his failure successfully to introduce far-reaching employment legislation but still enthusiastic about his ideals, Owen left for the United States, where he founded New Harmony in Indiana. This, along with other projects, failed because of internal disagreements and bad planning. He returned to England, where in 1834 he founded (and briefly chaired) the Grand National Consolidated Trades Union and continued to push for social reform and the growth of the co-operative movement. Robert Owen died at the age of 87 in 1858.

Robert Owen in Perspective

Owen occupies a curious position in the history of management thinking. Dismissed by his contemporaries and now little recognized apart from the linking of his name with that of New Lanark, his vision and foresight place him as the pioneer of management practices that are taken for granted today.

Although many influential people visited the sites of New Lanark and New Harmony, the ideas Owen propounded failed to win him immediate followers. There is much debate about the reasons behind this. The New Lanark factory was obviously very profitable (although, as Frank Podmore argued, almost any personnel policy could have been profitable then because profits in the cotton spinning industry at the time were so large), but still none of his factory-owning contemporaries adopted his ideas. Possibly the radical nature of his views contributed to this—if he had instead advocated a step-by-step approach toward improving working conditions and relations with employees instead of an "all-or-nothing" approach, he might have been more successful.

Although it is not too surprising that resistance to his ideas came from factory owners (who may indeed have felt they had much to lose from following them), antipathy was also expressed from across the political spectrum. Some of the most longlasting criticism was expressed by Marx and Engels in their Communist Manifesto. The label of "Utopian" that they applied to Owen is one by which he is still well known. The manifesto expressed the view that his ideas could not work in practice; his success at New Lanark was, they argued, due to luck rather than judgment.

Against these negative views must be set the experiences of those followers Owen did inspire. Although Owen's own partnership with Quakers and nonconformists at the end of his time at New Lanark failed (due to their wish to impose religious instruction on all), it was this sector of society that produced the people who were most influenced by his ideas. They included Titus Salt, George Palmer, and Joseph Rowntree.

The foresight Owen demonstrated in areas such as motivation of employees, industrial relations, and management by observation was not appreciated until a century later, in the work of F. W. Taylor and Mary Parker Follett, among others. In 1949, Urwick and Brech wrote of Owen: "Generations ahead of his time, he preached and practised a conception of industrial relations which is, even now, accepted in only a few of the most progressive undertakings."

Owen's lasting contribution may be best seen in the fact that it would be unthinkable for modern employers not to meet the practices he advocated.

For More Information

Key works by Owen
Book:
A New View of Society. London: n.p., 1817.

Further Reading
Books: Clutterbuck, David, and Stuart Crainer. *Makers of Management: Men and Women Who Changed the Business World*. London: Macmillan, 1990.
O'Toole, James. *Leading Change: Overcoming the Ideology of Comfort and the Tyranny of Custom*. San Francisco: Jossey-Bass, 1995.
Podmore, Frank. *Robert Owen*. London: Appleton, 1906.
Urwick, Lionel, and Edward Brech. *Making of Scientific Management: Volume II, Management in British Industry*. London: Management Publications Trust, 1949.
Wren, Daniel. *Evolution of Management Thought*. New York: John Wiley, 1987.

See also:
Mary Parker Follett (pp. 988–89)

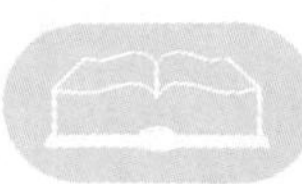

RICHARD TANNER PASCALE

Change, Agility, and Complexity

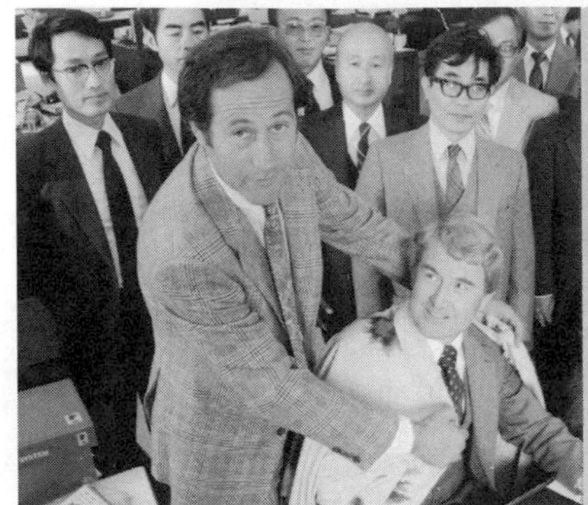

Richard Tanner Pascale came to prominence in the early 1980s at the time when Peters and Waterman's *In Search of Excellence*, published in 1982, was aiming to redefine the route to corporate success. His *The Art of Japanese Management* (coauthored with Anthony Athos), expounding the virtues of the McKinsey Seven-S model, has become a classic, and he has remained at the forefront of management thinking ever since.

1938	Born.
1982	Publication of *The Art of Japanese Management*.
1984	Publication of "Perspectives on Strategy: The Real Story behind Honda's Success," *California Management Review*.
1999	Publication of "Surfing the Edge of Chaos," *Sloan Management Review*.

LIFE AND CAREER

Born in 1938, Pascale was educated at the Harvard Business School. In the late 1970s he was heavily involved in the evolution of the Seven-S model developed by Peters and Waterman at McKinsey. As a member of faculty at Stanford's Graduate School of Business, Pascale acted as an advisor to the White House and as a consultant to many Fortune 500 companies. More recently he became an associate fellow at Templeton College, Oxford University.

A critic of fads, Pascale, like many of his contemporaries, does not want to be known as a "guru" or "expert." Such labels, he believes, evoke the image of a "hero with all the answers," and he would rather be recognized as someone who keeps addressing questions as they occur and recur. To that end, Pascale spends a number of days every year focusing on questioning, and learning from discussions with, business leaders.

KEY THINKING

JAPANESE MANAGEMENT AND THE 7 Ss

A spirit of inquiry brought Pascale and Athos into contact with Peters and Waterman in the late 1970s when Waterman was driving a McKinsey initiative to seek out new models of corporate success. Peters and Waterman went on to cite American examples of success in their 1981 bestseller, while Pascale and Athos looked at lessons from Japan and how they were being applied in corporate America. What brought the four of them together was the accelerating pace of business change and the increasing inadequacy of corporate information systems that had been sufficient in the past. Both *In Search of Excellence* and *The Art of Japanese Management* expounded the 7-S theory, but it was Pascale and Athos who explored it in greater depth, tracing many of its origins to working practice in Japanese organizations, and particularly in the Matsushita Electric Company.

Comparing Matsushita to ITT, Pascale and Athos found that the two organizations were differentiated more by "softer" elements of management style, staffing policies, skills, and shared values than by their systems, structure, or strategy.

In the early 1980s, the 7 Ss—usually presented in the shape of a circle or diamond—were as original for their juxtaposition of concepts not previously trumpeted as important, as for their communicability through alliteration.

- Strategy—how the organization gets from where it is to where it wants to be.
- Structure—how the firm is organized.
- Systems—how information moves around.
- Style—the patterns of behavior of senior management.
- Staff—not just numbers, but the characteristics of those who live and work at the organic center of the organization.
- Skills—the distinctive capabilities of individuals or of the organization as a whole.
- Superordinate goals (shared values)—not so much bottom-line targets as the meanings and values that are pervasive throughout the organization and "genuinely knit together individual and organizational purposes."

AMBIGUITY AND UNCERTAINTY

In *The Art of Japanese Management*, Pascale and Athos describe how managers are increasingly faced with situations which are neither clear-cut nor susceptible to resolution by the application of rational analysis. These situations are born out of the conflicts, ambiguities, and uncertainties that stem from the four Ss of style, staff, skills, and shared values. In such circumstances, the East has something to teach us. Rather than forcing a final solution, the authors suggest, it may be better to accept the lack of clarity in the situation, and simply "decide" to proceed. "Proceeding" should yield further information, and the best course may be to move toward the goal by a sequence of tentative steps rather than by bold, striking actions.

THE HONDA EFFECT

Pascale published "Perspectives on Strategy: The Real Story behind Honda's Success" in the Spring 1984 issue of *California Management Review*. This article juxtaposed two contrasting views on the rise of Honda in the United States: the Boston Consulting Group's (BCG's) account and Honda executives' own explanation. The article stimulated much debate, which was later summarized in "The Honda Effect Revisited," another *California Management Review* article (vol. 38, no. 4, Summer 1996) by Henry Mintzberg and others.

BCG attributed Honda's success to long-term investment in technology and economies of scale instead of in short-term profitability. Pascale did not aggressively dispute this, but found it did not explain why the then still young Honda had embarked on an apparently reckless U.S. strategy in the first place. Interviewing a number of Honda executives, Pascale became aware that the story was characterized more by miscalculation, chance, and learning-on-the-spot than by a logical, analytical progression of the sort that emerges from BCG's rationalized account.

"Our problem today is that the tools are there but our vision is limited." (Richard Pascale)

Pascale explained BCG's interpretation of the "Honda effect" as the result of a Western preference for the oversimplification of reality and linear explanations of events, an approach that overlooked the process through which organizations experiment, adapt, and learn. This preference leads to a failure to appreciate that the ways in which an organization deals with miscalculation, mistakes, and chance events outside its defined plan are often crucial to its success over time.

The key to Honda's success, concluded Pascale, was organizational agility. He continually returns to this theme, believing agility to be a core organizational competence.

Agility

Pascale's five conclusions summarizing the Honda debate propose that:

- Organizational agility is increasingly important as a source of renewable competitive advantage.
- Agility resides in what an organization is rather than what it does. In *The Art of Japanese Management*, Pascale cites Harold Geneen's attempt, while chief executive at ITT, to reduce uncertainty through quantification and controls. Matsushita, on the other hand, he pictures as a Pied Piper, more in tune with the uncertainty and imperfection that exist in all organizations, and operating on a basis of shared values and beliefs created by a philosophy linking work to social as well as productive ends.
- The interaction of four key dimensions makes an organization what it is:
  (i) power—can employees really influence the course of events?
  (ii) identity—do individuals identify with the organization as a whole?
  (iii) contention—how is conflict brought out into the open and used creatively?
  (iv) learning—how does the organization handle and develop new ideas?
  Within Honda, for example, employees are empowered to take pioneering action and they share an enterprise-wide identity in cross-functional teams, while debate, experimentation, and inquiring attitudes are actively encouraged.
- Strategic intent and agility depend on the norms, values, and behaviors inculcated within the social system of the organization. Pascale refers to Honda's efforts to institutionalize responsiveness, adaptability, and external focus.
- Agility depends on certain organizational disciplines, such as continuing dissatisfaction with the status quo, managing back from the future, uncompromising straight talk and the bringing of differences out into the open, and harnessing adversity by learning from setbacks and adapting to move forward.

Complexity, Chaos, and Letting Go

In an article called "Surfing the Edge of Chaos" in *Sloan Management Review* (Spring, vol. 40, no. 3, 1999), Pascale addresses what he considers to be the biggest challenge facing organizations today—how to increase the number of workable and winning strategic initiatives. He builds on the principles of the science of complexity.

- A complex adaptive system is at risk when it is interfered with and controlled. Equilibrium precedes extinction.
- Complex adaptive systems are capable of self-organization and of generating new methods of operating.
- Some complex adaptive systems can move toward the brink of chaos before new patterns emerge and new forms of organization take shape.
- Complex adaptive systems cannot be directed or strictly controlled.

In drawing parallels between the world of complex scientific systems and the world of organizations, Pascale tests out these four principles against a period of change at Shell, through interviews with Steve Miller, the director driving Shell's renewal initiative. He concludes the article by quoting Miller's words—that is, not by summarizing and generalizing, but by going into the depth and individuality of the organizational context itself. It is interesting to look at some of Miller's comments (quoted below) and relate them to the above four principles:

- "you have to recognize that the top can't possibly have all the answers";
- "the actual solutions about how to best meet the challenges of the moment, those thousands of strategic challenges. . . have to be made by the people closest to the action";
- "the leader becomes a context setter";
- "once the grassroots realize they own the problem, they also discover that they can help create and own the answers";
- "There's another kind of risk to the leaders. . .the risk of exposure. Before, you were remote from them, now, you're very accessible";
- "Finally, the scariest part is letting go. . . you get more feedback than before. . . you know more through your own people about what's going on in the marketplace. . . but you still have to let go of the old sense of control."

Richard Tanner Pascale in Perspective

Pascale's research, consulting, and exploration continue to lead him to redefine what makes organizations tick, at a time when uncertainties grow at an accelerating pace. He does not fit easily into any predefined category of management theorist and remains both at the front and at the edge in seeking new ways of understanding organizations. Pascale has sought to explore the processes of change by trying to understand their complexities and interdependencies, and not by trying to reduce his findings to mechanistic formulas. In line with his own advice to organizations, he himself exhibits a lack of complacency in his efforts to understand the right pieces, before fitting them into the organizational jigsaw.

He describes his recent work on complexity as a "big idea" and, although it builds on established principles of complexity theory, it will no doubt seem a little strange at first, particularly to those who want to eradicate uncertainty.

For More Information

Key works by Pascale

Books:

Pascale, Richard Tanner, with Anthony Athos. *The Art of Japanese Management*. New York: Simon & Schuster, 1981.
Managing on the Edge: How Successful Companies Use Conflict to Stay Ahead. New York: Simon & Schuster, 1990.
Pascale, Richard Tanner, with Mark Millemann and Linda Gioja. *Surfing the Edge of Chaos*. New York: Crown Business, 2000.

Journal Articles:

Pascale, Richard Tanner, with Mark Millemann and Linda Gioja. "Changing the Way We Change." *Harvard Business Review*, Nov./Dec. 1997, pp. 127–139.
Pascale, Richard Tanner, with Tracy Goss and Anthony Athos. "The Reinvention Roller Coaster: Risking the Present for a Powerful Future." *Harvard Business Review*, Nov./Dec. 1993, pp. 97–108.

See also:
The Art of Japanese Management (p. 890)
Managing on the Edge (p. 923)
Konosuke Matsushita (pp. 1114–15)
Kenichi Ohmae (pp. 1028–29)
Tom Peters (pp. 1036–37)

"If it ain't broke, break it." (Richard Pascale)

 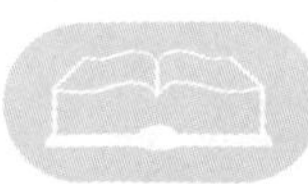    

Tom Peters

The Guru As Performer

Tom Peters has probably done more than anyone else to shift the debate on management from the confines of boardrooms, academia, and consulting organizations to a broader, worldwide audience. Peter Drucker has written more and his ideas have withstood a longer test of time, but it is Peters—as consultant, writer, columnist, seminar lecturer, and stage performer—whose energy, style, influence, and ideas have shaped the new management thinking.

1942	Born.
1966–1970	Naval service, including a term of duty in Vietnam and being assigned to the Pentagon.
1973	Leaves Stanford with Ph.D. in organizational behavior; works for White House as senior drug abuse advisor.
1974–1981	Joins consulting firm, McKinsey, becoming a partner in 1977.
Late 1970s	Various collaborative research projects; development of the McKinsey 7-S Model.
1982	Publication of *In Search of Excellence*.
1982–present	Writing, lecturing, touring, and changing his mind; formulates ideas for a management agenda for the 1990s and beyond.

Life and Career

Born in Baltimore in 1942, Peters repaid a navy scholarship to Cornell with a degree in civil engineering and four years' service in the navy, spending a term of duty in Vietnam in 1966 before being assigned to the Pentagon in 1968. He left Stanford in 1973 with a Ph.D. in organizational behavior and worked for the White House for a short while as senior drug abuse adviser. In 1974 he joined the top consulting firm, McKinsey.

Exposed to consulting assignments in America's blue-chip companies, Peters's curiosity and imagination led him in the late 1970s into various aspects of collaborative research, which brought about the development of the McKinsey 7-S Model. This model focuses on shared values, staff, systems, strategy, structure, skills, and style. It was in fact the first expression of the shift—characterizing all of Peters's work—away from the traditional numbers-centered, rational, analytical, and bureaucratic notion of management of McKinsey and many others toward a more innovative, intuitive, and people-centered approach.

In 1982, Peters copublished with Bob Waterman *In Search of Excellence*, which brought him worldwide fame, and set him off on a new career expounding his theories of excellence. Since then, his life has been a whirlwind of writing, lecturing, touring, and changing his mind.

Peters describes himself as gadfly, curmudgeon, champion of bold failures, prince of disorder, maestro of zest, corporate cheerleader, and irritator. *Fortune* Magazine calls him the Ur-guru (the original guru) and *The Economist* the Über-guru. He is the founder of the Tom Peters Group and lives on his farm in Vermont, or on American Airlines, or on an island off the Massachusetts coast.

Key Thinking

In Search of Excellence resulted from the application of the 7-S model in an attempt to discover models of excellence in corporate America. Peters and Waterman identified eight lessons from their research.

- A bias for action—excellent companies got on with doing the job, unconstrained by the bureaucratic trappings.
- Be close to the customer—this has since become a key business "must."
- Autonomy and entrepreneurship—the entrepreneur has freedom to think, act, and invest effort in the organization.
- Productivity through people—it was previously believed that large organizations held the key to productivity because only they could handle the economies of scale required for profitability.
- Be driven by hands-on values—the shared values of the 7-S model that matter to employees, as well as making the business tick with managers who are not afraid to get their hands dirty.
- Stick to the knitting—companies should stay with their core competencies, not diversifying for the sake of it.
- Simple form, lean staff—successful companies were not preoccupied with their size or procedures but with keeping things simple.
- Simultaneous loose-tight properties—examples of excellence derived from the faster-moving, more flexible features of smaller organizations, not the more cumbersome aspects of large ones.

When Peters declared in 1987, at the beginning of *Thriving on Chaos*, that there are no excellent companies, it was not only in recognition of the fact that many of the companies he had cited earlier had foundered. It was also because the rules had changed again; there was no single consistent route to excellence. Times change, so companies need to change their approach in order to continue to be successful. Peters has argued consistently that the eight lessons from *In Search of Excellence* remain valid—the companies he cited that later foundered merely failed to follow the lessons through.

A Passion for Excellence was published in 1985, intended as a sequel to *In Search of Excellence*, but this time with the focus on leadership. According to Peters (and his coauthor Nancy Austin) the successful leader becomes passionate about getting the most out of people, takes to heart the full people-centered implications of the 7 Ss, and lays the basis for the culture of empowerment. It is also in this book that Peters starts to return time and again to the centrality of the customer.

In *Thriving on Chaos*, Peters was one of the first to describe the emerging world of uncertainty and accelerating change. He was lucky with his timing: it was published in the same month (October 1987) that the stock market crashes in Wall Street, London, and Tokyo brought chaos to the world's money markets. The book was in fact a rejection of the secure world of the past, and a description of the uncertain world of the future. Some of the book's themes were

"Progress is mostly the product of rogues." (Tom Peters)

already there in *In Search of Excellence*, customer responsiveness and flexibility through empowerment, for example. But already in 1987, the world was a fast-changing place where increased competition meant speed to market, and that meant fast-paced innovation. Most of all, Peters understood that organizations would need flexible systems to deal with a topsy-turvy world.

Thriving on Chaos encouraged managers to cast off their old thinking and be prepared for a world of change and uncertainty. But Peters had not yet drawn a map of how to get there. *Liberation Management* was his attempt to draw such a map. He advocated flexible, flowing structures that are antihierarchical and based on building up relationships with customers. As he had done in *Thriving on Chaos*, Peters quoted examples of companies that represent the lean, flatter, and responsive organization required now that the old rule-book had been torn up. Again, he focused on the need to innovate, on closeness to customers, and on empowerment. In *Liberation Management* it was Peters who asserted that knowledge is becoming the key asset, the working capital of the organization.

Peters the Writer

Drucker may have written more, but Peters is beginning to catch him up. *Thriving on Chaos* is over 500 pages long; *Liberation Management* is over 800. In addition, Peters wrote a column for ten years as a channel for his thoughts, ideas, observations, and continuing flow of examples of companies.

His style of writing, as well as the content of his work, has changed over the years. One of the attractive features of *In Search of Excellence* was its accessible style. Peters's later works take this style to an extreme and reduce the language of management to monosyllabic expressions designed to shock, excite, provoke, and stir the reader out of conventional thinking. Hence his 1994 title—*The Pursuit of Wow!*

In *The Circle of Innovation*, this lightness and accessibility of expression may be construed by the traditionalist to have gone beyond levity and entered the realms of eccentricity, with striking illustrations and word collages.

The Guru As Performer

This is an area that Tom Peters has made his own. Many gurus are academics or writers, but few would claim to have the impact of Peters on stage. He has been universally described as a brilliant performer, with great stage presence and unbeatable delivery technique. Sometimes delivering two seminars a day in different cities, Peters is acknowledged for his genuine interest, concern, even passion for getting people to reflect on the way they manage.

The Tom Peters Seminar: *The Circle of Innovation*

The message that comes over in *The Circle of Innovation* is one that has taken between 15 and 20 years to develop, with Peters continuously adding to and refining the first lessons of *In Search of Excellence*. The book attempts to push the management of organizations to anticipate the topsy-turvy markets that are emerging with global markets, the Internet, and the ever greater closeness of customer and producer.

- Beyond change—be prepared to try things out, but do not expect to get things right first time. Peters acknowledges the role of stability and regularity but attaches far greater importance to agility.
- Beyond downsizing—aim to be big and small at the same time, so that you get the benefits of a large organization (economies of scale, networking, and knowledge-sharing) along with those of the small (speed, independence, and responding to opportunities).
- Beyond empowerment—make every job entrepreneurial.
- Beyond loyalty—everybody learns to think about the future, the customer, and the bottom-line.
- Beyond reengineering—the conversion of units or departments into full professional service firms with responsibility and accountability.
- Beyond disorganization—as the organization spots and responds to opportunities, it becomes a network of partners, distributors, suppliers, and customers with transparent boundaries.
- Beyond the learning organization—stimulating curiosity and creativity everywhere in the organization.
- Beyond TQM—toward sustainable product/service differentiation to escape the sameness of today's markets through design.
- Beyond management—from management to revolutionary leadership.

Tom Peters in Perspective

Peters did not actually discover the concept of customers with *In Search of Excellence*, but he and Waterman bucked the dominance of strategy to remind management that customers come first. If he seems all for discontinuity and disorganization, it is principally to remind people not to get stuck in the rut of procedures and routine.

Peters has been criticized for not being thorough or academic enough in support of his assertions, for relying too much on his charisma as a performer, and for "dumbing down" management to a level of mundaneness and banality However, his antennae have sensed where the world of business is heading before it arrives. It is also widely acknowledged that his approach, style, and energy have popularized management ideas to a wider audience than ever before.

Managers from all levels say that Peters's influence has been positive rather than negative, and he is spoken of in the same league as Porter, Ohmae, Hamel, Handy, and even Drucker. If he has changed his mind, it is because the world of the 1990s and 2000s has altered radically from that of the 1970s. If he has been inconsistent, he has nonetheless stayed ahead of the management times and foreseen—or helped to set—the management agenda for the fast-changing world of the future.

For More Information

Key works by Peters

Books:

Peters, Tom, with Bob Waterman. *In Search of Excellence: Lessons from America's Best-run Companies*. New York: Harper & Row, 1982.

Peters, Tom, with Nancy Austin. *A Passion for Excellence: The Leadership Difference*. New York: HarperCollins, 1985.

Thriving on Chaos: Handbook for a Management Revolution. New York: A. Knopf, 1987.

Liberation Management. New York: A. Knopf, 1992.

The Tom Peters Seminar: Crazy Times for Crazy Organizations. New York: Vintage Books, 1994.

The Pursuit of Wow! Every Person's Guide to Topsy-turvy Times. New York: Vintage Books, 1994.

Further Reading

Book: Crainer, Stuart. *Corporate Man to Corporate Skunk: The Tom Peters Phenomenon, A Biography*. San Francisco: Jossey-Bass, 1997.

See also:

In Search of Excellence (p. 912)

Stephen R. Covey (pp. 976–77)

"The world's best poker players don't hanker for jobs in casino management." (Tom Peters)

MICHAEL PORTER

What Is Strategy?

In an age when management gurus are both lauded by the faithful and hounded by the critics, Michael Porter seems to be one of the few who is both academically fireproof and largely without criticism from the business world. Porter has been at the leading edge of strategic thinking since his first major publication, *Competitive Strategy*, in 1980.

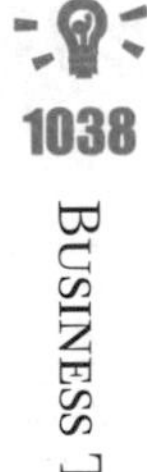

1947	Born.
1969	Completes a degree in aeronautical engineering at Princeton University.
1971	Receives an MBA from Harvard Business School.
1973	Receives a Ph.D. from Harvard University. Joins the Harvard Business School faculty.
1980	Publishes *Competitive Strategy*, which sets him at leading edge of strategic thinking.
1994	Founds The Initiative for a Competitive Inner City, and becomes Chairman and C.E.O.

LIFE AND CAREER

Born in 1947, Porter completed a degree in aeronautical engineering in 1969 and joined the Harvard Business School faculty at the age of 26. Like many academics, he has set up a consulting company, Monitor, advising both leading-edge companies and governments on strategy.

His thinking on strategy has been supported by precision research into industries and companies. Over a period of almost 20 years, his thinking remains consistent as well as developmental—it has not stood still since *Competitive Strategy* became a corporate bible for many in the early 1980s.

KEY THINKING

Before *Competitive Strategy*, most strategic thinking focused either on the organization of a company's internal resources and their adaptation to meet particular circumstances in the marketplace, or improving an organization's competitiveness by lowering prices to increase market share. These approaches, derived from the work of Igor Ansoff, were bundled into systems or processes that provided strategy with an integral place in the organization.

In *Competitive Strategy*, Porter managed to reconcile these approaches and provide management with a fresh way of looking at strategy—not just from the point of view of markets, or of organizational capabilities, but from the point of view of industry itself.

INTERNAL CAPABILITY FOR COMPETITIVENESS—THE VALUE CHAIN

Porter describes two different types of business activity—primary and secondary. Primary activities are concerned with transforming inputs (raw materials) into outputs (products), and in delivery and after-sales support. These are usually the main "line management" activities and include:

- inbound logistics—materials handling, warehousing;
- operations—turning raw materials into finished products;
- outbound logistics—order processing and distribution;
- marketing and sales—communication and pricing;
- service—installation and after-sales service.

Secondary activities support the primary and include:

- procurement—purchasing and supply;
- technology development—know-how, procedures and skills;
- human resource management—recruitment, promotion, appraisal, reward and development;
- firm infrastructure—general and quality management, finance, planning.

To survive competition and supply what customers want to buy, the company has to ensure that all these value-chain activities link together, even if some of the activities take place outside the organization. A weakness in any one of the activities will impact on the chain as a whole and affect competitiveness.

THE FIVE FORCES

Porter argued that in order to examine its competitive capability in the marketplace, an organization must choose between three generic strategies:

- cost leadership—becoming the lowest-cost producer in the market;
- differentiation—offering something different, extra, or special;
- focus—achieving dominance in a niche market.

The skill is to choose the right one at the right time. These generic strategies are driven by five competitive forces that the organization has to take into account. These are the:

- power of customers to affect pricing and reduce margins;
- power of suppliers to influence the organization's pricing;
- threat of similar products to limit market freedom and reduce prices and thus profits;
- level of existing competition that impacts on investment in marketing and research and thus erodes profits;
- threat of new market entrants to intensify competition and further impact on pricing and profitability.

In recent years, Porter has revisited his earlier work. Such is the acceleration of market change that companies now have to compete not on a choice of strategic front, but on all fronts at once. Porter has also said that it is a misconception of his approach for a company to try to position itself in relation to the five competitive forces. Positioning is not enough. What companies have to do is ask how the five forces can help to rewrite industry rules in the organization's favor.

DIVERSIFICATION

Instead of going it alone, an organization can spread risk and attain growth by diversification and acquisition. While the blue-chip consulting companies such as Boston Consulting Group (market growth/market share matrix) and McKinsey (7-S

"National and economic prosperity is created, not inherited." (Michael Porter)

framework) have developed analytical models for discovering which companies will rise and fall, Porter prefers three critical tests for success:

- the attractiveness test. Industries chosen for diversification must be structurally attractive. An attractive industry will yield a high return on investment, but entry barriers will be high; customers and suppliers will have only moderate bargaining power, and there will be only a few substitute products. An unattractive industry will be swamped by a range of alternative products, high rivalry, and high fixed costs;
- the cost-of-entry test. If the cost of entry is so high that it prejudices the potential return on investment, profitability is eroded before the game has started;
- the better-off test. How will the acquisition provide advantage to either the acquirer or the acquired? One must offer significant advantage to the other.

Porter devised seven steps to tackle these questions:

- as competition takes place at the business unit level, identify the interrelationships among the existing business units;
- identify the core business that is to be the foundation of the strategy. Core businesses are those in attractive industries and in which competitive advantage can be sustained;
- create horizontal organizational mechanisms to facilitate interrelationships among core businesses;
- pursue diversification opportunities that allow shared activities and pass all three critical tests;
- pursue diversification through a transfer of skills, if opportunities for sharing activities are limited or exhausted;
- pursue a strategy of restructuring if this fits the skills of management, or if no good opportunities exist for forging corporate partnerships;
- pay dividends so that shareholders can become portfolio managers.

The National Diamond

Why do some companies achieve consistent improvement in innovation, seeking an ever more sophisticated source of competitive advantage? For Porter, the answer lies in four attributes that affect industries. These attributes are:

- factor conditions—the nation's skills and infrastructure capable of enabling a competitive position;
- demand conditions—the nature of home-market demand;
- related and supporting industries—presence or absence of supplier/feeder industries;
- firm strategy, structure and rivalry—the national conditions under which companies are created, grow, organize, and manage.

These are the chief determinants that create the environment in which businesses flourish and compete. The points on the diamond constitute a self-reinforcing system, in which the effect of one point often depends on the state of the others, and any weakness at one point will impact adversely on an industry's capability to compete.

The New Strategic Wave

Sometime between 1980 and 1990 a new wave of more subversive strategic thinking—with Gary Hamel and *Strategy as Revolution*, and Mintzberg with "The Fall and Rise of Strategic Planning" (*Harvard Business Review*)— emerged to replace the old rulebook. Porter's main contribution to date, *Competitive Strategy*, argues that strategic planning lost its way because managers failed to distinguish between strategic and operational effectiveness and confused the two.

The old strategic model was based on productivity, increasing market share, and lowering costs. Hence, total quality management, benchmarking, outsourcing, and reengineering were all at the forefront of change in the 1980s as the key drivers of operational improvements. But continuing incremental improvements to the way things are done tend to bring different players up to the same level, rather than differentiating them. To achieve differentiation therefore means that:

- strategy rests on unique activities, based on customers' needs, customers' accessibility, or the variety of a company's products or services;
- the company's activities must fit and link together. In terms of the value chain, one link is prone to imitation but with a chain, imitation is very difficult;
- it is important to make trade-offs. Excelling at some things means making a conscious choice not to do others—it's a question of being a "master of one trade" to stand out from the crowd, as opposed to being a "jack of all trades" and lost in the mass. Tradeoffs deliberately limit what a company offers. The essence of strategy lies in what not to do.

Michael Porter in Perspective

It is a mark of Porter's achievement that much of his work on *Competitive Strategy*, researched in the 1970s, still has high value and relevance, and still shapes mainstream thinking on competition and strategy.

While his work is academically rigorous, his ability to abstract his thinking into digestible chunks for the business world has given him wide appeal to both the academic and business communities. It is now standard practice for organizations to think and talk about "value chains," and the five forces have entered the curriculum of every management program.

For More Information

Key works by Porter

Books:

Competitive Strategy: Techniques for Analyzing Industries and Competitors. New York: Free Press, 1980.
Cases in Competitive Strategy. New York: Free Press, 1983.
Competitive Advantage: Creating and Sustaining Superior Performance. Rev. ed. New York: Free Press, 1985.
Competition in Global Industries (ed.). Boston, MA: Harvard Business School Press, 1986.
The Competitive Advantage of Nations. Rev. ed. New York: Free Press, 1998.

Journal Articles:

"Corporate Strategy: The State of Strategic Thinking." *The Economist*, May 23,1998, pp. 21–22, 27–28.
"The Competitive Advantage of Nations." *Harvard Business Review*, Mar./Apr. 1990, pp. 73–93.
"From Competitive Advantage to Corporate Strategy." *Harvard Business Review*, May/June 1987, pp. 43–59.
"What Is Strategy?" *Harvard Business Review*, Nov./Dec. 1996, pp. 61–78.

Further Reading

Book: Crainer, Stuart. *Key Management Ideas: Thinking That Changed the Management World.* Upper Saddle River, NJ: Prentice Hall, 1998.
Journal Article: Jackson, Tony. "Dare to Be Different." *Financial Times*, June 19, 1997.

See also:
The Competitive Advantage of Nations (p. 900)
Competitive Strategy (p. 901)
Alfred D. Chandler, Jr. (pp. 974–75)
Henry Mintzberg (pp. 1024–25)

"Overall size is largely irrelevant for competitive advantage." (Michael Porter)

C. K. Prahalad

A New View of Strategy

C. K. Prahalad is regarded as one of the most influential thinkers on strategy in the United States. His work is concerned with the ability of large organizations to maintain competitive vitality when faced with international competition and changing business environments. Many of his ideas on competitive analysis argue against the supremacy of traditional strategic thinking and focus upon the concepts of "strategic intent," "core competence," and "strategy as stretch and leverage."

1941	Born.
1960–1964	Works as an industrial engineer.
1966	Completes an MBA at the Indian Institute of Management.
1975	Completes a DBA at Harvard Business School.
1975	Visiting Research Fellow, Harvard Business School.
1975–1977	Professor and Chairman, Management Education Programme, Indian Institute of Management.
1981	Visiting Professor, INSEAD, Fontainebleau, France.
1986–	Professor, University of Michigan Business School.
1994	Cowrites *Competing for the Future* with Gary Hamel.
1994	Receives award from Indo-American Society for promoting goodwill, understanding, and friendship between India and the United States.
1995	American Society for Competitiveness recognizes his contribution to competitiveness in business.

Life and Career

Prahalad came to management thinking from the field of physics. He worked as an industrial engineer before completing an MBA at the Indian Institute of Management in 1966 and a DBA at Harvard Business School in 1975. Since then he has been a visiting research fellow at Harvard, a professor at the Indian Institute of Management, and a visiting professor at the European Institute of Business Administration (INSEAD). He is Harvey C. Fruehauf professor of corporate strategy and international business at the Graduate School of Business Administration, University of Michigan. Over the years he has consulted for many large, multinational firms, including Eastman Kodak, AT&T, Honeywell, Philips, Motorola, and Ahlstrom.

Prahalad's contributions to strategic thinking have been widely acknowledged. *Business Week* wrote ". . .a brilliant teacher at the University of Michigan, Prahalad may well be the most influential thinker on corporate strategy today." In September 1993 the *Wall Street Journal*'s Special Report on Management Education named him as one of the top ten teachers in the world. In 1994 he received the annual award presented by the Indo-American Society for his outstanding contribution toward the promotion of Indo-American goodwill, understanding, and friendship, and in 1995 the American Society for Competitiveness recognized his outstanding academic contribution to competitiveness in business.

Key Thinking

Competing for the Future

Prahalad sees this book as presenting a new view of competitiveness, strategy and organizations. It takes the ideas of strategic intent, core competence and strategy as stretch and leverage, and builds on them to create a new strategy model.

Strategic Intent

Strategic intent is described as a way of creating an obsession with winning at all levels and across all functions of the organization. It is a shared competitive agenda for global leadership. Strategic intent uses stretch targets to create competitive advantage. For example, landing a man on the moon by the end of the 1960s provided the stretch target that gave the United States global leadership in space. It is the role of senior management to develop the organization in a way that closes the gap between ambition and ability. This involves active management processes, which include focusing the organization's attention on the urgency of winning; motivating people with challenges that require personal effort and commitment; using these challenges to create midterm competitive advantage, and applying intent consistently to guide resource allocation. Strategic intent provides the focus for "barrier-breaking" initiatives.

Core Competencies

Core competencies are often confused with core capabilities and core technologies. A core competence is an ability that transcends products and markets, and it results when an organization learns to harmonize multiple technologies, learning, and relationships across levels and functions. Core competencies feed into core products, which themselves can become business units. A core competence provides access to a wide variety of markets, makes a significant contribution to the customer's perceived benefit, and is difficult for competitors to imitate. Examples include Sony's competence in miniaturization, Philips's optical-media expertise, and Black & Decker's knowledge of small electrical engines. Viewing the organization as a portfolio of competencies is seen to lead to strategic advantage.

Strategic Architecture

A strategic architecture is a framework for leveraging corporate resources toward the strategic intent. It draws upon a variety of information to present a view of the evolution of an industry. A strategic architecture identifies the core competencies to build, and their constituent technologies. It provides a framework within which innovation can be planned and managed.

Corporate Imagination

In order to realize the potential that core competencies create, organizations must have the imagination to visualize new markets and the ability to move into them ahead of the competition. The key to com-

"You might merge with another organization, but two drunks don't make a sensible person."
(Gary Hamel)

petitive advantage is the process through which organizations release corporate imagination, identify and explore new competitive space, and consolidate control over emerging markets. Prahalad suggests that four elements combine to quicken an organization's imagination:

- escaping the focus on served markets;
- searching for innovative product concepts;
- overturning assumptions about price and performance relationships;
- leading customers rather than following them.

Escaping Served Markets

Traditionally, organizational concern for existing markets blurs the view of new markets. Such a defensive policy is fine up to a point, but it should not be at the expense of new and potentially lucrative markets.

Innovative Product Concepts

Dramatic innovations in product concepts reshape markets and industry boundaries, creating new competitive space. Such innovations take one of three forms:

- the addition of a new function to a successful product;
- the development of a new form for delivering a proven functionality;
- the delivery of a proven functionality through an entirely new product concept.

Product innovations flow from organizations that view a market in terms of needs and functionalities. This logical process of dissecting a product or service into its functional components is rare in most organizations.

Price/Performance Tradeoff

Most organizations view products and services as price/performance tradeoffs. Radical innovation can be achieved where an organization pursues those products labeled "unattainable dreams." New competitive space can be created by understanding how emerging technologies might allow customers' unmet needs to be satisfied, or their existing needs to be better satisfied.

Leading Customers

Leading customers requires a deep insight into the lifestyles, needs, and aspirations of today's and tomorrow's customers. Traditional modes of market research fail to provide such insights; it is through creative human science studies that such an understanding can be gained. Leading customers to where they want to go, before they know it themselves, provides a huge competitive advantage. This approach involves all functions of the organization. It creates marketeers with technological imagination and technologists with marketing imagination, overcoming the debate about whether an organization should be market- or technology-led.

Expeditionary Marketing

On the premise that being first to market provides a competitive advantage, expeditionary marketing is identified as a tool used by organizations that create competitive space. Expeditionary marketing helps organizations gain an understanding of the particular features, price, and performance of new products that will successfully penetrate the market. Such learning can be gained only when a product—imperfect as it might be—is launched. Expeditionary marketing increases the number of successful products an organization achieves by increasing the number of market opportunities, niches, and product variations explored.

C. K. Prahalad in Perspective

The strength of Prahalad's writing lies in the fact that much of it has resulted from debate and development with his joint authors. His belief that there was more to strategy than existing theories portrayed caught the attention of academics and practicing managers alike. Couple this with a strong belief in the need for business school research to have a strong managerial significance, and you begin to realize why Prahalad is held in such high regard.

Consultancy work in corporate America and beyond continually raised the question of how smaller rivals, new to a market, could prevail against much larger, richer organizations. "Existing theories of strategy and organization, while providing a solid base for discovery, do not fully answer these questions," Prahalad argues. These theories help us to understand the structure of an industry, identify the attributes of a transformational leader, and provide a scorecard for monitoring relative competitive advantage. But they do not provide insight into what it takes to redesign an industry, help us understand the role of the leadership team in visualizing the future, or explain the process of competence-building. *Competing for the Future* is a work which aims to fill the gap between theory and reality.

Prahalad's ideas developed at a time when corporate strategy was in crisis and in need of a new face. Organizations were more concerned with improving operational efficiency than focusing on the future, and downsizing for short-term gain meant that many businesses were failing to focus on the potential of tomorrow. It was the recognition that such an approach could not continue that has made large organizations receptive to Prahalad's thinking.

For More Information

Key works by Prahalad

Books:

Prahalad, C. K., with Gary Hamel. *Competing for the Future*. Boston, MA: Harvard Business School Press, 1994.

Journal Articles:

Prahalad, C. K., with Yves L. Doz. "An Approach to Strategic Control in MNCs." *Sloan Management Review*, vol. 22 no. 4, 1981, pp. 5–13.

Prahalad, C. K., with Gary Hamel. "Do You Really Have a Global Strategy?" *McKinsey Quarterly*, Summer 1986, pp. 34–59.

Prahalad, C. K., with Gary Hamel and Yves L. Doz. "Collaborate with Your Competitors and Win." *Harvard Business Review*, Jan./Feb. 1989, pp. 133–139.

Prahalad, C. K., with Gary Hamel. "Strategic Intent." *McKinsey Quarterly*, Spring 1990, pp. 36–61.

Prahalad, C. K., with Gary Hamel. "Core Competence of the Corporation." *Harvard Business Review*, May/Jun. 1990, pp. 79–91.

Prahalad, C. K., with Gary Hamel. "Corporate Imagination and Expeditionary Marketing." *Harvard Business Review*, Jul./Aug. 1991, pp. 81–92.

"A Strategy for Growth. The Role of Core Competencies in the Corporation." *EFMD Forum*, no. 3–4 1993, pp. 3–9.

Prahalad, C. K., with Gary Hamel. "Competing for the Future." *Harvard Business Review*, vol. 72 no. 4, Jul./Aug. 1994, pp. 122–128.

Prahalad, C. K., with Gary Hamel. "Competing in the New Economy: Managing out of Bounds." *Strategic Management Journal*, Mar. 1996, pp. 237–242.

See also:

Competing for the Future (p. 899)
Gary Hamel (pp. 998–99)
Henry Mintzberg (pp. 1022–23)
Michael Porter (pp. 1038–39)

"There is nothing more short term than a 60-year-old C.E.O. holding a fistful of share options."

(Gary Hamel)

  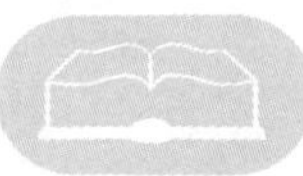    

Reg Revans

Action Learning

Professor Reginald Revans (1907–) has been involved in education throughout his long and varied career. He is scathing about the value of traditional "chalk and talk" management education that prevailed during the 1960s and 1970s, arguing that people learned most effectively not from books, lecturers, or teachers, but from sharing real problems with others.

Revans was director of education for the U.K. mining industry.

1907	Born.
1926–1929	Studies at Cambridge.
1928	Represents Great Britain in the long jump at the Olympics.
1929	Sets undergraduate long jump record; held until 1962.
1935	Appointed chief education officer for Essex.
1938	Becomes director of education for the mining industry (later the National Coal Board).
1950	Returns to academia to research management of coal mines; develops theories of action learning.
1950–present	Holds range of professorial positions in the fields of industrial administration and management; campaigns around the world to spread his ideas and has had influence in countries as diverse as Belgium, India, and Egypt.
1970s–1980s	National output in Belgium surpasses that of many major competitors; credit laid at Revans's feet.

Life and Career

Revans studied at Cambridge (where he held the undergraduate long jump record between 1929 and 1962) and, during his time there, represented Great Britain in the long jump at the 1928 Olympics. After he obtained his degree, Revans became a research fellow at Emmanuel College and in 1935 he was appointed chief education officer for Essex. At the end of World War II, he became director of education for the mining industry (later the National Coal Board), but by 1950 he had returned to academia to research the management of coal mines. Since the mid-1950s, Revans has held a range of professorial positions in the fields of industrial administration and management. At the time of writing he retains an interest in the Centre for Action Learning and Research, established at the University of Salford.

Key Thinking

Action Learning Processes

While director of education for the National Coal Board, Revans spent two years living and working with miners trying to identify what their problems really were (rather than what people thought they were). His experiences led him to understand that people learn most effectively through "doing" in groups, and this realization helped him develop the theories to support "action learning."

The learning process may be expressed as:

Learning = Programmed knowledge + the ability to ask "insightful" Questions or L = P+Q.

Programmed knowledge (P) is conveyed through books, lectures, and other structured learning mechanisms. It is an accessible format for knowledge, but it may take time to find exactly what we need, and in isolation is not sufficient to fulfill all learning needs. Revans argues that it is overvalued in management learning.

Insightful questions (Q) are those questions that are asked at the right time and are based on experiences or an attitude about ongoing work projects, as well as on creativity that goes beyond acceptance of ready-made solutions. Revans maintained that P is the domain of experts, while Q is the domain of leaders who wish to drive projects forward by getting answers. Revans noted also that P was the initial letter of poppycock, platitude, and professor, while Q initiates query and quiz.

Insightful questions are the key to Revans's process. P will not take you very far unless you focus on the reflective side of what you do. Revans argues that it is not just "doing" but learning to learn by doing—Q—that is much more important.

Revans suggests that each participant should have the following (deceptively simple) questions at the forefront of their thinking.

- What are we really trying to do?
- What is stopping us from doing it?
- What can we do about it?
- Who knows about (understands) the problem being tackled?
- Who cares (genuinely wants something done) about the problem?
- Who can (has enough power to) get something done about it?

Action learning requires solutions to be implemented, not just recommended. Because it demands probing and sensitive questions, it can also require levels of tact and diplomacy.

Principles of Action Learning

Action learning is a process that, to work, must be owned by its participants. This is because (Revans argued) the participants need to make their own decisions about tasks, in order to learn how to help each other. Besides the important issues of ownership, action learning has other principles that must be adhered to:

- the learning context must be a real working situation, or a defined project meaningful to the participants—not a simulation. Learning to take action involves taking it, not merely making a recommendation on someone else's problem;
- members of the learning set (the group or team involved) should all be able to make a contribution from their experience;
- the team members need to be ready to continue to learn from one another as they discuss problems and test out ideas through regular meetings. The learning process is not one of isolation: managers learn best from each other;

"Unless your ideas are ridiculed by experts, they are worth nothing." (Reg Revans)

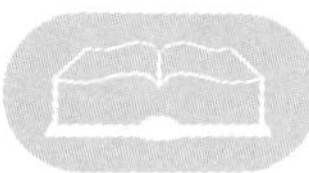

- scheduled input of knowledge (P) should be kept to a minimum;
- an adviser needs to be present for the life of the team to facilitate, help, steer, or guide when needed, but not to teach or lecture;
- top management support must be available to respond to the team's findings.

To be successful, action learning also requires:

- commitment from the top—no hidden agendas in which time spent will produce an outcome that has been rejected before it is announced;
- the full commitment of everyone iinvolved—action learning must be voluntarily embraced; it cannot be imposed;
- time for meetings and questions, which necessitates flexibility in terms of scheduling;
- good communication to facilitate enthusiasm and commitment from all participants;
- an atmosphere of trust and openness—team members should be able to feel relaxed about confronting sensitive internal issues.

These are onerous requirements for a learning program, but the benefits offered through action learning make the undertaking worthwhile. Action learning:

- encourages self-reliance and develops people, especially in times of uncertainty and discontinuity;
- is an aid to management development because it helps individuals to prepare for the future by helping themselves;
- develops the organization by changing the way it behaves;
- produces results because it requires team members to take decisions;
- can be a powerful problem-solving tool.

Reg Revans in Perspective

Accepting Revans's distinction between knowledge or didactic learning (P) and insightful questioning (Q), research has revealed those situations in which action learning may be most appropriate. These are where:

- knowledge is changing rapidly;
- a body of knowledge is applied to specific problems;
- the individual is acquiring self-knowledge;
- processes and concepts for thinking and learning are applied.

By contrast, action learning may prove less appropriate where knowledge is relatively stable; when you are building up a body of knowledge, or where the body of uncontested knowledge is well established.

Revans's position of influence on modern-day management remains undefined, and he varies from being underestimated and ignored to being described as a management genius. He has campaigned around the world to spread his ideas and has had influence in countries as diverse as Belgium, India, and Egypt. In Belgium, his ideas were applied with particular success—national output during the 1970s and 1980s surpassed that of many major competitors, and credit for this was laid at Revans's feet. He has his detractors as well as his devotees, and this is probably as much for his uncompromising style as for his apparently simplistic thinking. But it is on his thinking that posterity should judge him, and there are a number of discernible developments in the domain of business learning that have been influenced by Revans.

Learning Cycle

Developed by David Kolb, this ensures that a learner cannot assume a passive role. Instead learning is active, following a continuous, cyclical process of: experience; evaluation; conceptualization; experimentation.

Learning Preferences

All learners have different levels of comfort or difficulty in relation to the phases of Kolb's learning cycle. Some may need to practice more than others; some may prefer reading; some observation. Peter Honey and Alan Mumford have identified four basic styles of learning—the activist, the theorist, the reflector, and the pragmatist—which take account of Revans's great emphasis on learning to learn by doing.

Competence Movement

The competence movement in management education is principally about being able to do things better in the workplace, by using work-based problems and situations for projects and assignments. Along with the growth of National Vocational Qualifications and the rise of mentoring schemes, the movement must surely acknowledge Revans as one of its main forerunners.

For More Information

Key works by Revans

Books:

Action Learning: New Techniques for Management. London: Blond & Briggs, 1974.

The ABC of Action Learning: A Review of 30 Years of Experience. Bromley: Chartwell-Bratt, 1983.

Further Reading

Books: Bennett, R., and J. Oliver. *How to Get the Best from Action Research—A Guidebook*. Bradford: MCB University Press, 1988.

Honey, Peter, and Alan Mumford. *Manual of Learning Styles*. 3rd ed. Maidenhead: Peter Honey Publications, 1992.

Kolb, David A. *Experiential Learning: Experience as the Source of Learning and Development*. Upper Saddle River, NJ: Prentice Hall, 1984.

Journal Article: Bourner, Tom. "What Can Be Learned Using Action Learning." *Organizations and People*, vol. 3 no. 4, 1996, pp. 18–21.

See also:

Chris Argyris (pp. 964–65)
Peter Senge (pp. 1046–47)

"Seek to understand each others' problems and develop a sense of responsibility for each other through working in small groups."
(Reg Revans)

EDGAR SCHEIN

Careers, Culture, and Organizational Learning

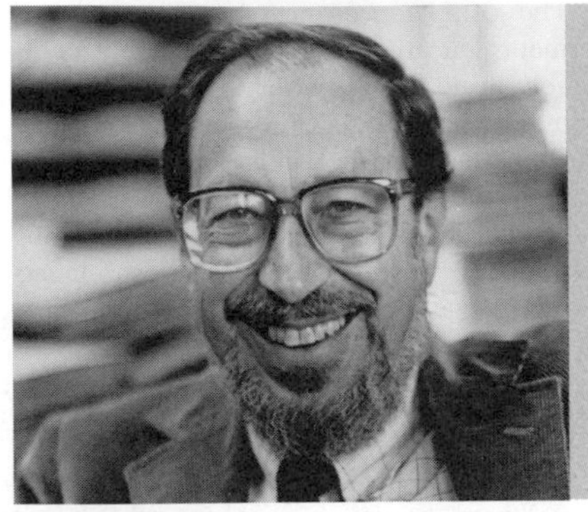

Edgar Schein pioneered the concept of corporate culture with his landmark book *Organizational Culture and Leadership* (1985), which sparked off much research into the subject. He also coined the now much-used phrases "psychological contract" and "career anchor."

1928	Born.
1949	Masters Degree in Psychology, Stanford.
1972–1982	Chairman of the Organization Studies Group of Sloan School of Management, Massachusetts Institute of Technology.
1978–1990	Sloan Fellows Professor of Management, Massachusetts Institute of Technology.
1985	Publication of *Organizational Culture and Leadership*.

LIFE AND CAREER

Now the Sloan Fellows Professor Emeritus of Management and senior lecturer at the MIT Sloan School of Management, Professor Schein has had a long and distinguished academic career. He received his Ph.D. in social psychology from Harvard University, collaborated with Douglas McGregor at MIT, and worked for many years with the National Training Laboratory. In addition, he has made a strong contribution to the "helping" professions, mainly in the areas of organization development, career development, and organizational culture.

Schein has researched and written extensively about the factors that influence individual and organizational performance. The main themes underlying his work are the identification of culture(s) in the organization, the relationship between organizational culture and individual behavior, and the importance of organizational culture for organizational learning. Douglas McGregor invited him to MIT on the basis of his work on the repatriation of POWs following the end of the Korean War. This work strongly influenced Schein's whole career, and reemerged forcefully in an article for *The Learning Organization* on brainwashing and organizational persuasion techniques in 1999 ("Empowerment, Coercive Persuasion, and Organizational Learning: Do They Connect?", vol. 6 no. 4, pp. 163–172).

KEY THINKING

CORPORATE CULTURE

Early in his career Schein found traditional approaches to understanding work behavior and motivation first too simplistic to explain the range of experiences of individuals in organizations, and, second, too restrictive, since human and organizational needs vary widely from person to person, place to place, and time to time. In *Organizational Culture and Leadership*, he became the first management theorist to define corporate culture and suggest ways in which culture is the dominant force within an organization.

In his view, culture is a mix of many different factors, such as:

- observed behavioral regularities when people interact;
- norms that evolve in working groups;
- dominant values pushed by the organization;
- the philosophy guiding the attitudes of senior management to staff and customers;
- organizational rules, procedures, and processes;
- the feeling or climate that is conveyed without a word being spoken.

In *Organizational Culture and Leadership*, Schein defines culture as a pattern of basic assumptions, and discusses how these fall into five, often oppositional, categories:

- humanity's relationship to nature—some organizations seem want to dominate the external environment, while others accept its domination;
- the nature of reality and truth—the ways and means by which organizations arrive at the "truth;"
- the nature of human nature—some people seem to avoid work if they possibly can, while others embrace it as a way of fulfilling their potential, to both their own and the organization's benefit;
- the nature of human activity—a focus on the completion of tasks on the one hand, and on self-fulfillment and personal development on the other;
- the nature of human relationships—some organizations seem to facilitate social interaction, others to regard it as an unnecessary distraction.

ORGANIZATIONAL SOCIALIZATION

Schein's thoughts on organizational socialization were triggered when, after arriving at MIT, he asked McGregor for guidance in the form of previous outlines and notes for a course he was preparing. McGregor suggested that Schein should make up his own mind. This lesson in acclimatizing to MIT led Schein to argue that companies should be conversant with their socialization practices, and recognize the conflicts they can create for new recruits.

In "Organizational Socialization and the Profession of Management" (*Sloan Management Review*, Fall 1988, pp. 53–65), Schein discusses how, when a new recruit enters the organization, a process of socialization—adaptation or "fit"—takes place. He argues that this process has more to do with recruits' past experience and values than their qualifications or formal training.

Usually, Schein suggested, organizations create a series of events that work to undo the new recruit's old values to some extent, so that he or she is more open to learning new values. This process of "undoing" or "unfreezing" can be unpleasant, and its success may therefore depend on either a recruit's strong motivation to endure it, or the organization's perseverance in making recruits endure it. There are three basic responses to this socialization process:

- rebellion—outright rejection of the organization's norms and values;
- creative individualism—selective adoption of key values and norms;
- conformity—acceptance of the organization's norms and values.

"Success goes to those with a corporate culture that assures the ability to anticipate and meet customer demand."

(Tadashi Okamura)

  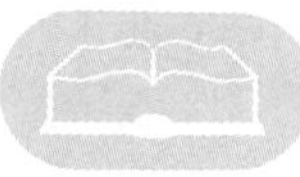    

Noting similarities between brainwashing experienced by servicemen captured during the Korean War and the socialization of executives on programs at MIT, Schein argues that many forms of organizational development involve restructuring and change, and have serious implications for the way people work and their relationship with management.

Schein likens such processes to a form of coercive persuasion, or brainwashing, giving people little choice but to abandon, for example, older norms and values that fit badly with the new learning. If we are in tune with the goals and values of the change this will not be a problem, but if we dislike the values, we are likely to disapprove of the brainwashing. Schein concludes that, because the very concept of organization involves some restriction of individual freedom to achieve a joint purpose, the concept of a continually learning, innovative organization is something of a paradox, since creativity and learning are related to individual freedom and growth.

Organizational Learning

Organizational learning, Schein considers, needs to be fast in order to cope with growing market pressures, yet seems to be obstructed by a fear of, or anxiety about, facing change, particularly on the part of senior executives. This feeling is associated with reluctance to learn what is new, because it appears too difficult or disruptive. Schein argues that only a new anxiety greater than the existing one can overcome this, and his "anxiety 2" is the fear, shame, or guilt associated with not learning anything new.

Schein emphasizes the need for people to feel psychologically safe, if change is to happen. Achieving organizational learning and transformation therefore depends upon creating a feeling of safety, and overcoming the negative effects of past incentives and past punishments—especially the latter. To learn, people need to feel motivated and free to try out new things.

Psychological Contract and Career Anchors

In *Organizational Psychology* Schein highlights a "psychological contract" (attributing the original concept to Chris Argyris) which he defines as an unwritten set of expectations operating between employees and employing managers and others in an organization. He stresses how essential it is that both parties' expectations of a contract should match, if a long-term relationship that will benefit both parties is to develop.

Closely linked to the notion of the psychological contract is the concept of the "career anchor," a guiding force that influences individuals' career choices and is based on their self-perceptions. Schein proposes that, from their varying aspirations and motivations, individuals—perhaps unconsciously—develop one underlying career anchor, which they are unwilling to surrender. On the basis of 44 cases, he distinguishes career anchor groups such as technical/functional competence, managerial competence, creativity, security or stability, and autonomy.

The Three Cultures of Management

Rather than a single culture, Schein identifies three cultures (or communities of interest) within an organization: the operator culture, which evolves locally within organizations and within operational units; the engineering culture of technicians in search of "people-free" solutions; and the executive culture, which is focused on financial survival.

The three often conflict rather than work in harmony. For example, while the executive culture requires systems and reporting relationships for evidence that operations are on track, the engineering culture attempts to design systems that cut across lines of control and the people manning these.

In his article "Three Cultures of Management: The Key to Organizational Learning" (*Sloan Management Review*, Fall 1996, pp. 9–20), Schein suggests that, in many cases, either operators assume executives and engineers do not understand their work needs, and covertly do things in their own way; or executives or engineers assume a need for tighter control over operators and force them to follow policies and procedure manuals. In either case, there is no commonly understood plan, and efficiency and effectiveness suffer.

Schein stresses the need to take the concept of culture more seriously and accept how deeply embedded are the assumptions of executives, engineers, and employees. He proposes that helping executives and engineers learn how to learn about, analyze, and evolve their cultures may be central to organizational learning.

Edgar Schein in Perspective

Schein's work now spans more than four decades and his great contribution has been in linking culture with individual development and growth, putting the accent on organizations as complex systems and on individuals as whole beings.

Schein was aware that the concept of corporate culture was no cure-all for ailing organizations. The fact, however, that culture is now generally recognized as a central factor in organizational change and development is largely attributable to his work.

For More Information

Key works by Schein

Books:

Career Dynamics: Matching Individual and Organizational Needs. Reading, MA: Addison-Wesley, 1978.

Organizational Psychology. 3rd ed. Upper Saddle River, NJ: Prentice Hall, 1980.

Organizational Culture and Leadership. 2nd ed. San Francisco: Jossey-Bass, 1997.

The Corporate Culture Survival Guide. San Francisco: Jossey-Bass, 1999.

Journal Article:

"How Can Organizations Learn Faster? The Challenge of Entering the Green Room." *Sloan Management Review*, Winter 1993, pp. 85–92.

See also:

Organizational Culture and Leadership (p. 937)
Chris Argyris (pp. 964–65)
Warren Bennis (pp. 968–69)
Douglas McGregor (pp. 1022–23)

"Market competition is the only form of organization which can afford a large measure of freedom to the individual."

(Frank H. Knight)

  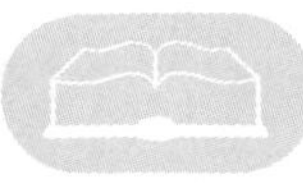    

Peter Senge

The Learning Organization

Popularizer of the theory of the learning organization, first suggested by Chris Argyris and Donald Schon, Peter Senge studied how organizations develop adaptive capabilities in a world of increasing complexity and change. His work culminated in the publication of *The Fifth Discipline: The Art and Practice of the Learning Organization.*

1947	Born.
1975–1990	Research at the Sloan School of Management into ways of learning.
1990	Publication of *The Fifth Discipline.*
present	Director of the Center for Organizational Learning at the Sloan School of Management, MIT.

Life and Career

Peter Senge is the director of the Center for Organizational Learning at the Sloan School of Management, Massachusetts Institute of Technology (MIT). He graduated in engineering from Stanford before earning a Ph.D. in social systems modeling at MIT. For many years, Senge studied how businesses and organizations develop adaptive capabilities in a world of increasing complexity and change, but the success of his book *The Fifth Discipline* popularized the concept of the "learning organization."

Published in 1990, *The Fifth Discipline* brought the attention of the world to bear on this rather unassuming man, who suddenly found himself the modern equivalent of a medieval crusader seeking dramatically to change corporate America, and indeed the rest of the world, against all the odds. Senge's message was simple—the learning organization believes that competitive advantage derives from continued learning, both individual and collective. Furthermore, the new challenges of the information age demand that not only businesses, but also educational institutions and governments, transform themselves radically. Senge describes himself as an "idealistic pragmatist" and spends much time building learning organizations with the top leaders of companies, education, and government.

Although Senge's ideas are utopian, his Center for Organizational Learning has attracted an impressive list of corporate sponsors who have dug deep into their pockets to fund pilot programs.

Key Thinking

The Fifth Discipline

In *The Fifth Discipline*, Senge suggests that there are five basic ingredients for a learning organization.

Systems thinking: Senge's whole approach to organizations is a "systems" approach that views the organization as a living entity, with its own behavior and learning patterns. He introduces the idea of "systems archetypes" to help managers spot repetitive patterns that lead to recurrent problems or limits to growth.

Personal mastery: Every modern manager recognizes the importance of developing skills and competencies in individuals, but Senge takes this notion further by stressing the importance of spiritual growth in the learning organization. True spiritual growth exposes us to a deeper reality; it teaches us to see the current reality more clearly and, by highlighting the difference between vision and the current reality, generates a creative tension, out of which successful learning arises. In Senge's own words, a learning organization is "a group of people who are continually enhancing their capability to create their future" by "changing individuals so that they produce results they care about, accomplish things that are important to them."

Mental models: The systems approach is continued with Senge's emphasis on mental models. This discipline requires managers to construct mental models for the driving forces behind the organization's values and principles. Senge alerts his readers to the impact of acquired patterns of thinking at the organizational level and the need to develop nondefensive mechanisms for examining the nature of these patterns.

Shared vision: According to Senge, true creativity and innovation are based on group creativity, and the shared vision the group depends on can only be built on the personal vision of its members. Shared vision occurs when the vision is no longer seen by the team members as separate from the self.

Team learning: Effective team learning involves alternating processes for dialogue and discussion. Dialogue is exploratory and widens possibilities, whereas discussion narrows down the options to find the best alternatives for future decisions. Although these two processes are complementary, they need to be separated. Unfortunately, most teams lack the ability to distinguish between these two modes and to move consciously between them.

Senge's basic premise can be stated very simply: people should put aside their old ways of thinking (mental models); learn to be open with others (personal mastery); understand how the company really works (systems thinking); form a plan everyone can agree on (shared vision); and then work together to achieve that vision (team learning).

Practical Tools—*The Fifth Discipline Fieldbook*

Recognizing that the ideas contained in *The Fifth Discipline* needed to be made more accessible to practicing managers, Senge and his colleagues produced a more practical guide—*The Fifth Discipline Fieldbook.* Throughout the book, the authors stress that anyone who wants to be part of a learning organization must be willing to go through a personal change. To help this process, Senge and his coauthors provide a set of elaborate personal awareness exercises. The *Fieldbook* was designed as a resource for dipping into and it contains many good ideas and case studies. Even if you find Senge's thinking too general, the *Fieldbook* is well worth scrutinizing for references and new ideas. Here are just a few:

System archetypes and causal loops: The *Fieldbook* devotes a lot of time to mapping processes in organizations, analyzing feedback loops and identifying typical

"A mistake is an event, the full benefit of which has not yet been turned to your advantage."

(Edwin Land)

organizational problems (the system archetypes). This process-mapping tool can help employees to work out how complex systems interact, and to develop their "mental models" of the organization. The "beer game" described in *The Fifth Discipline* is a simulation based on these models.

Left- and right-hand columns: By writing down in meetings what you really think (left-hand column) and what you actually said (right-hand column), you can analyze and identify those personal prejudices that get in the way of really productive work.

The ladder of inference: This exercise provides a step model for analyzing our values, beliefs, and actions. Climbing down the ladder helps us to discover why we behave the way we do, and helps us to avoid jumping to dangerous conclusions. The steps on the ladder are as follows:

- I take ACTIONS based on my beliefs;
- I adopt BELIEFS about the world;
- I draw CONCLUSIONS;
- I make ASSUMPTIONS based on the meanings added to my mental models;
- I add MEANINGS (cultural and personal);
- I select DATA from what I observe;
- I OBSERVE data and experiences.

The container: This is a dialogue tool that has proved very effective (if not explosive!) in some organizations. People at a meeting are encouraged to imagine a container that holds everyone's hostile thoughts and feelings. As everyone speaks out, putting their fears, prejudices, and anger on the table, the hostility between different factions is neutralized, because it is exposed in a safe place for all to discuss. In the early days of such experiments, a good facilitator is probably essential.

Learning labs and flight simulators: The *Fieldbook* provides useful references for all those who wish to design effective simulations for training sessions.

Peter Senge in Perspective

Although Senge's *The Fifth Discipline* was a bestseller, its basic concepts had emerged from extensive research carried out at the influential Sloan School of Management at MIT over 15 years. The success of the "learning organization" concept is a reflection of the times. None of the book's concepts are new, but Senge was able to put them all together and to create a simple but very powerful concept.

Senge is a product of his age, probably greatly influenced by the culture of the 1960s in the United States. His systems approach toward organizations shows the same maturity displayed in the systems analysis tools developed by thinkers such as Peter Checkland at Lancaster University. Here the organization is viewed as a "super-organism" with its own behavior patterns, but also profoundly influenced by the nature of its constituent members. The sad fact is that Senge was one of the first management gurus to make the accepted beliefs of a whole generation of social scientists, biologists, and environmentalists credible to the corporate world.

In his own words, Senge says: "We live under a massive illusion of separation from one another, from nature, from the universe, from everything. We're depleting the earth and we're fragmenting our spirit. The symptoms are pollution, anger, and fear. Everything in our culture is about the management of impressions and appearances, from physical fitness to the way we dress. And yet on another level we know it's all bullshit." Even having just passed the millennium, there is little evidence that the change in attitude needed to achieve Senge's ideals—of long-term corporate sustainability and freedom for all to achieve personal mastery—is in sight: there are very few organizations that have been able to implement his ideas successfully.

The main criticism that can be leveled at Senge's work is the inherent difficulty of applying his models. Senge was trained as an engineer and then became involved in social research. Both require a systems approach, but this cannot be developed easily. In fact systems thinking is about as easy as learning brain surgery on a three-day seminar. Nor can most companies afford the luxury of their top executives learning to "crash land" for too long.

Breaking old corporate habits is very hard, and therefore transforming an enterprise into a learning organization is highly problematical and not for the faint-hearted. The reason for this is simple—in order to move forward to a new, co-operative learning model, managers have to give up their traditional areas of power and control. They have to hand over power to the learners and allow them to make mistakes. In a blame-orientated culture, this change in attitude remains a major obstacle.

Despite the elusiveness of its ideals, *The Fifth Discipline* has proved highly influential. Its concepts have stimulated the debate and acceptance of issues such as self-managed development, empowerment, and creativity. Its practical impact can be seen in modern human resource management strategies, teamwork principles, and in quality models.

It is more important perhaps to recognize that in life all the most profound truths are deceptively simple, yet almost impossible to apply in practice. The difficulty experienced in applying Senge's ideas does not invalidate them—if anything, it confirms their importance for companies in the next millennium.

For More Information

Key works by Senge

Books:

The Fifth Discipline: The Art and Practice of the Learning Organization. New York: Doubleday, 1990.

Senge, Peter, et al. *The Fifth Discipline Fieldbook: Strategies and Tools for Building a Learning Organization*. New York: Currency Doubleday, 1994.

Journal Articles:

"The Future of Workplace Learning and Performance." *Training and Development USA*, vol. 48 no. 5, 1994, pp. S36–S47.

"Mr Learning Organization." *Fortune International*, October 17, 1994, pp. 75–81.

"Looking Ahead: Implications of the Present." *Harvard Business Review*. Sept./Oct. 1997, pp. 18–32.

Further Reading

Books: Checkland, Peter. *Systems Thinking, Systems Practice!* New York: John Wiley, 1981.

Gibson, Rowan, ed. *Rethinking the Future*. Naperville, IL: Nicholas Brealey, 1997.

Kleiner, Art. *The Age of Heretics: Heroes, Outlaws, and the Forerunners of Corporate Change*. Naperville, IL: Nicholas Brealey, 1996.

See also:
The Fifth Discipline (p. 905)
Chris Argyris (pp. 964–65)

"Dividing an elephant in half does not produce two elephants." (Peter Senge)

ADAM SMITH

Founder of Political Economics

Adam Smith (1723–1790) published his best-known book, fully entitled *An Inquiry into the Nature and Causes of the Wealth of Nations* but commonly known as *The Wealth of Nations*, in 1776. This is often described as one of the most important texts of our time, and its two main philosophical points stressed the supreme value of individual liberty, and the pursuit of self-interest as ultimately beneficial for society as a whole.

1723	Born.
1748	Appointed lecturer in literature at Edinburgh University, Scotland.
1751	Appointed professor of literature at Glasgow University.
1763	Publication of *The Theory of Moral Sentiments.*
1776	Publication of *The Wealth of Nations.*
1778	Accepts post of commissioner of customs in Scotland.
1787	Elected lord rector at Glasgow University.
1790	Dies.

LIFE AND CAREER

Smith was brought up in Kirkcaldy, Scotland by his widowed mother. He went, on a scholarship, to Glasgow University at 14, to study mathematics and moral philosophy; and then, at 17, to Balliol College, Oxford. In 1748, he was appointed to a lectureship in literature at Edinburgh, and in 1751, became professor of literature at Glasgow University. One year later, he was appointed professor of moral philosophy and, despite a nervous disorder, faltering speech and a tendency to forgetfulness, became a teacher of high repute. His lectures focused on theology, ethics and jurisprudence.

In 1763, following the publication of his first book, *The Theory of Moral Sentiments*, Smith was asked to act as tutor and companion to the young Duke of Buccleuch during his "grand tour" of Europe. Through this he met several great philosophers and thinkers, including Voltaire and Rousseau, and his own ideas took firmer shape. On his return from Europe he retired to Kirkcaldy to concentrate on writing *The Wealth of Nations*.

In 1778, Smith accepted the post of commissioner of customs in Scotland, and was elected lord rector at Glasgow University in 1787. Although Smith had plans to add a third volume (on jurisprudence) to follow the other two, his writings remained limited to reissuing editions of *The Wealth of Nations*.

Smith never married and, despite his impressive mind, became known as somewhat eccentric, largely due to his tendency to forget everyday things, such as changing from his nightclothes into day wear. After the death of Smith's mother, he was looked after by a maiden aunt until his death in 1790.

HISTORICAL BACKGROUND

To understand Smith's thinking fully, it is helpful to know a little about his background. He knew many of the most influential contemporary thinkers, and spent much time debating in the gentlemen's clubs of London. He was a friend of both John Locke and David Hume and was, for a time, a disciple of Quesnay, the leading French physiocrat. *The Wealth of Nations* undoubtedly drew ideas from many such sources.

In the later 17th and 18th centuries, there was increasing interest in the theory of "natural" law. The natural sciences had become established since the publication of Newton's *Philosophiae Naturalis Principia Mathematica* (1687) and there was a strong drive to uncover the natural laws that were thought to guide people's actions.

At the same time, burdensome government regulations were increasingly criticized, and the theory of natural order was being drawn into ideas about society and government. For example, John Locke's *Treatise on Civil Government* (1691) proposed that men are born free and equal, and are governed by "natural laws," arguing that, while executive power is necessary, this should be only by consent.

Such revolutionary ideas were taken up by many great thinkers, including Hume, Hutchison, the French physiocrats, and Smith himself. It was, however, impossible to prove the existence of a benevolent "natural order," ordained by God for men's happiness. While proponents of the concept considered it to be self-evident, it was always, in fact, an intangible hypothesis wide open to challenge.

The idea that human society should be based on a natural order encouraged ideas about individualism to develop further. The concept of an economic system founded on individual self-interest rather than government control is central to *The Wealth of Nations*, and to later social, political and economic change.

THE WEALTH OF NATIONS

NATURAL LAW AND "LAISSEZ FAIRE"

The Wealth of Nations followed the French physiocrats in arguing that all human powers are subject to immutable, natural moral and physical laws. These laws, divine in origin, were thought to offer a basis for government that could leave things to work naturally, with results that would satisfy both individual and state interests.

Smith never actually used the term "laissez faire," but his book popularized associated arguments for government nonintervention in social, economic and commercial matters. "Laissez faire" was first used by the French, and essentially meant that the government should let things alone, specifically in terms of trade, production of goods, and quantities or quality of products. This philosophy dominated much 18th and 19th century government, and assumed that:

- natural laws, if left to work freely, would create the best possible society;
- enlightened individual selfishness was ultimately in the public interest;
- men are born equal.

The Wealth of Nations took ten years to write, and the ideas within it challenged Smith's contemporary, mercantilist government and its protectionist laws. The author realized that his book would outrage vested interests in business or government, be-

"The propensity to trade, barter and exchange. . .is common to all men and is to be found in no other race of animals."

(Adam Smith)

cause of its arguments for government-enforced competition and against price-fixing.

Although often castigated as such, Smith was neither inhumane nor a proponent of "the law of the jungle" as an approach to social organization. He recognized the worst tendencies of some businessmen who ". . . love to reap where they never sowed," and was extremely aware of how greed could lead to excesses of monopoly and corruption. Smith did, in fact, support some forms of intervention, especially in public areas such as defense. He did not, however, have our benefit of hindsight, or know how the Industrial Revolution would change society, creating some extremely wealthy businessmen, and a mass of extremely poor industrial workers, who would suffer greatly because of their lack of protection from regulatory laws.

The Law of Labor

Natural law was considered by Smith to encompass a "law of labor." According to this, the external environment could provide men with the products necessary for subsistence, in return for their labor, and all men should therefore have the right to carry out activities to preserve their existence. Government's only role should be to promote the existence of natural law, and to enable its free working.

The natural laws were assumed to work in the same exacting way as mathematical laws. Left to themselves, they should establish an order that would benefit both individuals and society. Individualism, for Smith and the other economists and philosophers of his time, meant relief from the constraints of mercantilism, the right to economic freedom, and the right of a people to legislate for themselves and be taxed by the government they chose.

The Division of Labor

Smith gives many examples of the advantages of the division of labor, with each worker focusing upon a single stage of manufacture rather than, as in traditional crafts, being involved in every stage. His ideas were based on life before 1760, and he did not foresee how the introduction of machinery would make the division of labor even more logical, and sometimes a harsh necessity.

The Free Market

Smith's main thesis throughout *The Wealth of Nations* was the inefficiency of government interference, which he demonstrates with reference to the markets for both national and international trade. He envisions a free market as a customer-driven, democratic mechanism through which, by exercising their free choices about purchase or sale prices, people would act to regulate resources fairly. Although it was Dudley North who first related supply to demand and extolled the benefits of free trade, Smith recognized that buyers as well as sellers profit from trade, and saw international commerce as a source of wealth for both importers and exporters.

Smith had a very positive vision of how a free market would eventually realize a state of "universal opulence" for everyone. He argued that each nation should concentrate on those industrial areas where it enjoyed a "comparative advantage." These ideas were taken up by subsequent economists such as Riccardo and Malthus, and can be traced within the thinking of some contemporary strategists, particularly in Michael Porter's work on competitive advantage.

Morality

Smith is often criticized for a lack of moral focus in *The Wealth of Nations* but he did assume that its readers would already know of the moral base given in *The Theory of Moral Sentiments*. The earlier book sought to explore moral judgments within the context of Smith's assumption that people are essentially driven by self-interest, and proposed that we all have "social propensities" for sympathy, justice and benevolence.

Adam Smith in Perspective

The Wealth of Nations had a profound influence on English history, leading to the end of the mercantilist era, and catalyzing a social and economic order based on individualism and the "natural laws" supposedly underlying competition and free market forces.

Smith's ideas have often been castigated for the support they gave to later businessmen, who grew very rich while rejecting any regulations to protect industrial workers. He wrote his masterpiece, however, before the Industrial Revolution began to take effect, and it was intended as a polemic against restrictive government policies and monopolistic abuses, rather than as a panegyric for unregulated business. Also, just as Smith's first book on *The Theory of Moral Sentiments* supplies a moral aspect to complement *The Wealth of Nations*, it is probable that his intended, but unwritten, third volume on jurisprudence could have contributed ideas for legal safeguards to protect the public from abuses resulting from greed and collusion, since he considered these typically to arise out of people's business activities and contacts.

For his time, Smith was actually a social radical, promoting liberty and equality, and denouncing various pillars of the existing establishment. From our modern perspective, it is clear there was no factual base for his ideas about natural law and harmony, and that perfect competition could not erase social problems, particularly when factors from a future that Smith could not have imagined (including giant corporations, economic cycles and depressions, mass unemployment, and mechanical warfare) became more pertinent. Despite this, however, *The Wealth of Nations* remains a "milestone" book offering a composite analysis that shaped our social and economic world.

For More Information

Books:

Haakonssen, Knud, ed. *The Theory of Moral Sentiments*. New York: Cambridge University Press, 2002.

Smith, Adam. *An Inquiry into the Nature and Causes of the Wealth of Nations* (abridged). Indianapolis, IN: Hackett Publishing Company, 1993.

See also:

The Wealth of Nations (p. 954)

"There is no art which one government sooner learns of another than that of draining money from the pockets of the people."

(Adam Smith)

 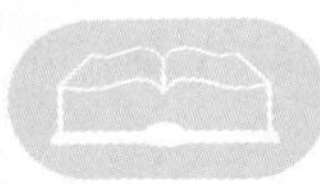    

SUN TZU

Strategy and *The Art of War*

Sun Tzu is the author of an ancient Chinese military treatise known as *The Art of War*. It contains ideas on leadership and strategy that Asian business leaders in the second half of the 20th century found relevant and helpful in their work. Impressed by the success of Eastern, particularly Japanese, business methods, Western business people began to investigate the sources of that success and, in the process, rediscovered Sun Tzu.

c. 400 BC	Sun Tzu lived and wrote.
1780	First European translation of *The Art of War* published.
1910	English translation published.

LIFE AND CAREER

Although the precise dates of his birth and death are not known, Sun Tzu is thought to have lived over 2,400 years ago, at roughly the same time as Confucius. Raised in a family of army officers, he became familiar with, and eventually expert in, military affairs. Historians are generally agreed that he was a general who led a number of successful military campaigns in the region currently known as the Anhui Province. It is recorded that the state of Wu, under whose sovereign he served, became a dominant power at that time. Since then, it has become standard practice for Chinese military chiefs to familiarize themselves with Sun Tzu's writings.

KEY THINKING

THE ART OF WAR

Sun Tzu's *The Art of War* (the book's actual title is *Sun Tzu Ping Fa*, literally "The Military Method of Mr. Sun") is a compilation of his thinking on the strategies that underlie success in war. It has been translated into many languages, and there are several English versions. This account is based on the translation by Thomas Cleary, published by Shambhala Pocket Classics and available on the Internet. Two further editions, published by Tuttle and Wordsworth Editions respectively, also were consulted.

Sun Tzu's anecdotes and thoughts, which fill no more than about 25 pages of text in all, are divided into 13 sections:

1. strategic assessments
2. doing battle
3. offensive strategy
4. formation
5. force
6. emptiness and fullness
7. armed struggle
8. adaptations
9. maneuvering armies
10. terrain
11. nine grounds
12. attack by fire
13. use of spies

Some of these have less current relevance than others, but they are all worth at least a glance. Hidden among advice such as not to dally in salt marshes when retreating or attacking (11), there is the odd gem that is striking in its modernity. For example: "when a leader enters deeply into enemy territory with the troops, he brings out their potential." (11) The advice given in section 10 on how to proceed in narrow or steep terrain (occupy the high and sunny side to await your opponent) can be quickly passed over, but a little further on in the same section Sun Tzu's castigation of poor leadership is much more pertinent: "When generals are weak and lack authority, instructions are not clear, officers and soldiers lack consistency, and they form battle lines every which way; this is riot."

ON STRATEGY

Many commentaries focus on the first section, Strategic Assessments, at the expense of the others. It is certainly there that, helped by a little lateral thinking, Sun Tzu seems best to relate to the spirit of modern business. He refers initially to five key factors that determine the result of war:

- politics—that which causes people to be in harmony with their ruler;
- weather—the seasons;
- terrain—distances, difficulty or ease of travel, opportunities or safety;
- leadership—a matter of intelligence, trustworthiness, humaneness, courage, and strictness;
- discipline—organization, chain of command, logistics.

There are also seven issues to be appraised (the postscript following each question has been added to indicate the line most interpretations take).

- Whose moral influence is the stronger? (Whose followers are more willing to subscribe to common goals?)
- Which leader is the more able? (Who has the ability to combine benevolence and compassion with boldness and strict discipline?)
- Which army has greater advantage of nature and terrain? (Whom do politics, economic cycles, investment, and social and cultural factors favor? Who understands the bigger picture?)
- Whose laws and rules are more effective? (Do people understand what is expected as a result of clear instructions and procedures?)
- Whose troops are stronger? (How can things be arranged so that small can compete effectively with large?)
- Whose soldiers are better trained? (Who uses delegation and training for organizational effectiveness?)
- Whose system of rewards and punishments is clearer? (Who is therefore able to generate higher performance and a better competitive position?)

The theme of strategy is picked up again and again, apparently at random. One interpretation stretches section 6 to make it relate to market presence and strategies of deception employed to fool competitor intelligence. Sun Tzu argues that "there is no constant good or bad, right or wrong: therefore victory in war is not repetitious, but adapts its form endlessly. . . so a military force has no constant formation, water has no constant shape: the ability to gain victory by changing and adapting according to the opponent is called genius." (6)

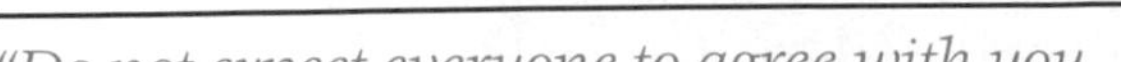

"Do not expect everyone to agree with you. . .Do not consider all opponents to be enemies."

(Wess Roberts)

On Information and Intelligence

"...to fail to know the conditions of opponents because of reluctance to give rewards for intelligence is extremely inhuman, uncharacteristic of a true military leader... so what enables an intelligent government and a wise military leadership to overcome others and achieve extraordinary accomplishments is foreknowledge...[which] must be obtained from people who know the conditions of the enemy." (13)

On Tactics

"Making the armies able to take on opponents without being defeated is a matter of unorthodox and orthodox methods." (5)

"The difficulty of armed struggle is to make long distances near and make problems into advantages." (7)

On Competition and Competitor Intelligence

"So if you do not know the plans of your competitors, you cannot make informed alliances." (7)

"So the rule of military operations is not to count on opponents not coming, but to rely on having ways of dealing with them; not to count on opponents not attacking, but to rely on having what cannot be attacked." (8)

On Leadership and People Management

"If they rule armies without knowing the arts of complete adaptivity, even if they know what there is to gain, they cannot get people to work for them." (8)

"If soldiers are punished before a personal attachment to the leadership is formed, they will not submit, and if they do not submit, they are hard to employ." (9)

"Look upon your soldiers as you do infants, and they willingly go into deep valleys with you; look upon your soldiers as beloved children, and they willingly die with you." (10)

"If you are so nice to them that you cannot employ them, so kind to them that you cannot command them, so casual with them that you cannot establish order, they are like spoiled children, useless." (10)

On Communication

"When directives are consistently issued to edify the populace, the populace accepts... when directives are consistently issued, there is mutual satisfaction between the leadership and the group." (9)

Sun Tzu in Perspective

Historians tell us that the *Sun Tzu Ping Fa* is the oldest existing military treatise in the world, predating Clausewitz by 2,200 years. But so what? Does it have any relevance for people in business today? How can the thoughts of a Chinese general who lived two and a half millennia ago possibly inform, enlighten, or inspire a modern manager, or have any bearing on his or her day-to-day concerns? And even if there are interesting links, do they do any more than show us that ancient Chinese strategists did not differ fundamentally from modern businesspeople?

Sun Tzu's supporters, however, insist that his concepts are ageless. Although it is easy to stretch interpretation too far and find meaning anywhere if you look hard enough, such things as strategic intelligence, planning, attention to detail, cunning, deception, and theories of leadership in which the leader earns authority with the led, have universal value and are appropriate to any human arena and any period.

If part of Sun Tzu's modern appeal derives from the constant search for any nuggets of intelligence that may give an organization an edge over the competition, another part lies in the fact that the *Ping Fa* offers an opportunity to gain insights into the Oriental mind that do not come from someone with a modern ax to grind or reputation to make. In addition, the insights are couched in direct, no-nonsense, hard-hitting language that makes them seem more, not less, pregnant with meaning.

As globalization brings East closer to West, business relationships will hinge on understanding cultures and attitudes that may appear strange at first. And wherever managers set strategic goals, sell their goods abroad, or interrelate with their workforce, *The Art of War* may still have something to say to them. It is finding its way into many MBA programs.

For More Information

Books:

The Art of War. Translated by Yuan Shibing, interpretation by Tao Hanzhang, foreword by Norman Stone. Hertfordshire: Wordsworth Editions, 1993.

The Art of War. Translated by Thomas Cleary. Boston, MA: Shambhala Pocket Classics, 1991.

Kaufman, Stephen F. *The Art of War: The Definitive Interpretation of Sun Tzu's Classic Book of Strategy for the Martial Artist*. Rutland, VT: Charles E. Tuttle, 1996.

Commentaries:

Chen, Min. "Sun Tzu's Strategic Thinking and Contemporary Business." *Business Horizons*, Mar./Apr. 1994, pp. 42–48.

Crainer, Stuart. "Braingain." *Management Today*, April 1998, pp. 68–70.

See also:

The Art of War (p. 891)

Richard Tanner Pascale (pp. 1034–35)

  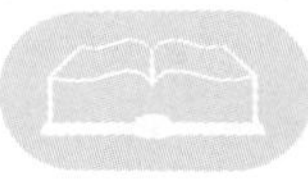    

GENICHI TAGUCHI

Veteran Design and Development Engineer

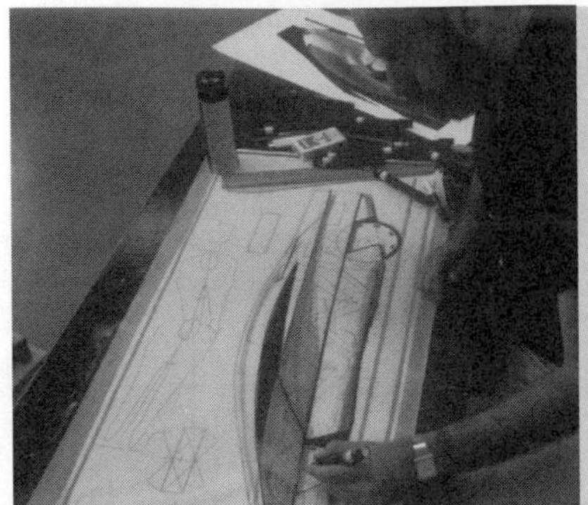

Taguchi is famous for his pioneering methods of modern quality control and low-cost quality engineering. He is the founder of what has come to be known as the Taguchi method, which seeks to improve product quality at the design stage by integrating quality control into product design, using experiment and statistical analysis.

Taguchi's methods have influenced design and engineering around the world.

1924	Born.
1942–1945	Serves in Japanese navy during World War II.
1945	Works in Ministry of Public Health and Welfare and Ministry of Education.
1950	Joins Electrical Communication Laboratory (ECL) of Nippon Telephone and Telegraph Company.
1960	Wins Deming prize for contribution to field of quality engineering (later wins it three more times).
1962	Awarded doctorate by Kyushsu University.
1964	Takes up professorship at Aoyamagokuin University in Japan.
1970s	Develops concept of the quality loss function.
1980s	Visits AT&T Bell Laboratories in the United States; American interest in his methodology established.
1983	Becomes executive director of the Ford Supplier Institute.
1986	Receives Indigo Ribbon from the emperor of Japan for contribution to economics and industry; medal from International Technology Institute.
1986	Institute of Statisticians organize conference in London; Taguchi's ideas become known in Europe.
1987	U.K. Taguchi Club formed (now the Quality Methods Association); ideas adopted widely in the West, particularly in the car industry.
1998	Honorary member of the American Society for Quality (ASQ).

LIFE AND CAREER

Genichi Taguchi, born in Japan in 1924, served in the Navigation Institute of the Japanese navy during World War II. He then worked in the Ministry of Public Health and Welfare and in the Institute of Statistical Mathematics of the Ministry of Education, meeting the renowned statistician, Matosaburo Masuyame, who nurtured his statistical skills.

In 1950, Taguchi joined the Electrical Communication Laboratory (ECL) of Nippon Telephone and Telegraph Company, gaining six years' experience in experimentation and data analysis while developing telephone switching systems. The commercial benefits resulting from his ECL work helped Taguchi to earn the Deming prize in 1960, for his contribution to the field of quality engineering. He went on to win this award, one of Japan's most prestigious commendations, three more times.

In 1962, Taguchi was awarded a doctorate by Kyushu University, after working with industrial statisticians (and beginning his work on the signal-to-noise ratio) at Bell Laboratories in the United States. He continued working for ECL in a consulting role and became part of the associate research staff of the Japanese Standards Association, where he founded the Quality Research Group. In 1964, he took up a professorship at Aoyamagokuin University in Japan, where he spent the next 17 years developing his methods.

Throughout this time, Taguchi was largely unknown outside Japan. He developed his concept of the quality loss function in the early 1970s, but it was during the 1980s that Taguchi's methods became established, when he revisited AT&T Bell Laboratories in the United States, as director of the Japanese Academy of Quality.

After that, interest from U.S. companies such as Xerox, Ford, and ITT in Taguchi's methodology increased. In 1982, Taguchi was involved in seminars for Ford executives, and the following year he became executive director of the Ford Supplier Institute (later known as the American Supplier Institute). He was also further honored in 1986, receiving the Indigo Ribbon from the emperor of Japan for his contribution to Japanese economics and industry, and the International Technology Institute's medal for his work on statistical methods to achieve cost and quality improvements.

Throughout much of this time, Taguchi was also operating as a full-time consultant to various major companies in the United States, Japan, China, and India. Apart from occasional work with, for example, Lucas Industries, Taguchi's ideas only became known in Europe from 1986, when the Institute of Statisticians organized a conference in London. The U.K. Taguchi Club (now the Quality Methods Association) was formed the following year and, since then, Taguchi methods have been in regular and widespread use in the West, particularly in the car industry. Taguchi himself is now in semi-retirement.

KEY THINKING

TAGUCHI METHODS

Taguchi developed methods for both online (process) and offline (design) quality control, which formed the basis of his approach to total quality control and assurance within a product's development life cycle. His approach emphasized improving the quality of product and process prior to manufacture (that is, at the design stage) rather than the more traditional approach of achieving quality through inspection.

QUALITY LOSS FUNCTION

Taguchi's approach differed from the traditional one of manufacturing a product within a specification based on tolerances, equally spaced around a target value. He developed a concept of "quality loss" occurring as soon as there is a deviation away from the target value, and worked in terms of quality loss rather than just quality. He defined quality loss as "the loss imparted

"The excellent companies treat the rank and file as the root source of quality and productivity gain."

(Tom Peters)

to society from the time the product is shipped," and this related the loss to society as a whole. Thus, it included both company costs, such as reworking, scrapping, and maintenance, and any loss to the customer through poor product performance and reduced reliability.

A loss function curve can be calibrated by using information from the customer. A target value is identified as being the best possible value of a quality characteristic. Taguchi associates a simple, quadratic loss function with deviations from the target. Thus:

- the smaller the performance variation, the better the quality of the product;
- the larger the deviation from the target value, the larger the loss to society.

A loss will occur even when the product is within the specification allowed, although it is minimal when the product is on target.

After the design engineer has determined the cost of parts being manufactured out of specification, this information can be used to justify expenditure on quality improvement, enabling decisions to be made on firm cost and quality grounds. Thus, it is possible to estimate whether the "quality gain" from changing a design is worthwhile—although ensuring that a product is produced at a quality level acceptable to the customer remains an important consideration.

Signal-to-Noise Ratio

One of Taguchi's most innovative ideas was to use a quality measure called the "signal-to-noise ratio," which communications engineers could employ to find the strength of an electrical signal. Taguchi applied this measure to everyday products, and used it as a measure to choose control levels that could best cope with changes in operating and environmental conditions, or noise.

Robust Quality of Design

On the basis of the signal-to-noise measure, Taguchi was able to develop the concept of robustness, which enables a product to be designed to be less affected by noise. Given normal variations in process operations, the product in question would be less likely to fail acceptable quality criteria.

Product Design Improvement

During the product design and production engineering phases, Taguchi set out three steps that must be followed.

1. System design. This may involve the development of a prototype design, and will determine the materials, parts, and assembly system to be used. The manufacturing process has also to be considered

2. Parameter design. Taguchi's parameter design aimed to find the most cost-effective way of controlling noise. Taguchi process and design improvements are gained by identifying easily controllable factors and settings that minimize performance variation. Controllable factors are design factors that a designer can set or easily adjust. The specified value becomes the signal. Uncontrollable factors are noise, or external variations, and a higher signal-to-noise ratio means better quality. Taguchi found that if controllable factors were set at optimal levels, the product would be robust to external changes. This was achieved through parameter design applied at the design (offline) stage to reduce or remove the effect of noise factors.

Experiments were designed using orthogonal arrays that (rather simply described) were a series of rows and columns allowing the effects of different factors to be extracted and separated out. Taguchi was not the inventor of the orthogonal array, but this type of experimentation moved away from the traditional approach of testing one factor at a time. His new approach dramatically reduced the number of experiments and prototypes required and, in consequence, costs were much lower. He developed various experimental designs that allowed the variability of the noise factors on each controllable factor setting to be simulated. The settings that minimized variability could then be determined.

3. Tolerance design. If parameter design failed, Taguchi suggested using tolerance design to identify the most crucial noise factors. Tolerances could be reassigned so that the overall variability was reduced to acceptable levels.

Invest Last not First

Taguchi placed much emphasis on optimizing the product and process at the beginning, in order to engineer product quality (parameter design) into the system. Using low-cost materials and components was a vital feature of this, and money was spent on higher cost items only when necessary (tolerance design).

Genichi Taguchi in Perspective

It was W. E. Deming who first recognized the importance of moving quality control backward from inspection to proper process control, notably via statistical process control (SPC). Taguchi moved quality control even further back, to the design stage, thus completing the total quality loop. Taguchi's techniques and statistical experimental designs for offline quality improvement complemented SPC, to achieve online quality improvement. Deming's philosophy regarding management quality improvement encompassed both.

It has been said that Deming's work inspired a revolution in the old management culture, while Taguchi inspired evolution. Certainly Deming provided a theory mainly for management, while Taguchi provided important techniques for improving a process at every stage, from design to production, and for keeping the improved processes under control.

For More Information

Key works by Taguchi

Books:

Offline Quality Control. Nagoya: Central Japan Quality Control Association, 1980.
Introduction to Quality Engineering: Designing Quality into Product and Processes. Tokyo: Asian Productivity Organization, 1986.
Online Quality Control. Tokyo: Japanese Standards Association, 1986.
The System of Experimental Design, vols. 1 & 2. New York: Kraus International Publications, 1987.
Ohno, Taiichi, with Elsayed A. Elsayed and Thomas C. Hsiang. *Quality Engineering in Production Systems*. New York: McGraw-Hill, 1989.

Further Reading

Books: Bendell, A., et al. *Taguchi Methodology within Total Quality*. Kempsten: IFS Publications, 1990.
Bendell, A., et al. *Taguchi Methods: Applications in World Industry*. Kempsten: IFS Publications, 1990.
Logothetis, Nickolas. *Managing for Total Quality: From Deming to Taguchi and SPC*. Upper Saddle River, NJ: Prentice Hall, 1992.

See also:
W. Edwards Deming (pp. 980–81)

"In broad terms, quality planning consists of developing the products and processes required to meet the customer's needs."
(Joseph M. Juran)

FREDERICK WINSLOW TAYLOR

Father of Scientific Management

Peter Drucker is often called "the guru's guru." Drucker himself would suggest that the accolade should be given to Frederick Winslow Taylor (1856–1915). "On Taylor's 'scientific management' rests, above all, the tremendous surge of affluence in the last 75 years which has lifted the working masses in the developed countries well above any level recorded, even for the well-to-do," Drucker wrote in *Management: Tasks, Responsibilities, Practices.*

1856	Born.
1874	Becomes an apprentice pattern-maker and machinist at Enterprise Hydraulic Works.
1878	Takes unskilled job at the Midvale Steel Works.
1881	Gains master's degree in mechanical engineering.
1890	Becomes general manager of Manufacturing Investment Company (MIC).
1898	Becomes joint discoverer of the Taylor-White process, a method of tempering steel.
1911	Publication of *The Principles of Scientific Management.*
1915	Dies.

LIFE AND CAREER

Although Taylor passed the entrance examination for Harvard College, failing eyesight meant that he could not become a student there. Instead he took the unusual step, for someone of his background, of becoming an apprentice pattern-maker and machinist at the Enterprise Hydraulic Works in Philadelphia.

Following his apprenticeship, Taylor took up an unskilled job at the Midvale Steel Works. After several different jobs and a master's degree in mechanical engineering, he was appointed chief engineer there. In 1890 he became general manager of Manufacturing Investment Company (MIC), eventually becoming an independent consulting engineer to management.

In 1881, Taylor won the doubles championships of the United States Lawn Tennis Association and a year later, the doubles in the Young American C. C. Lawn Tennis Tournament. Later in his career he developed a passion for golf and, in keeping with his love of experiment, attempted to make a putting green that was reliant on water below the surface rather than on natural rainfall. By the time of his death, Taylor's experiments had led to him filing at least 50 patents and had made him an extremely wealthy man.

KEY THINKING

SCIENTIFIC MANAGEMENT

Taylor's seminal work—*The Principles of Scientific Management*—was published six years before his death. In it, he put forward his ideas of "scientific management" (sometimes referred to today as "Taylorism"), which differed from traditional "initiative and incentive" methods of management. These ideas were an accumulation from his life's work, and included several examples from his places of employment. The four overriding principles of scientific management are as follows:

- Each part of an individual's work is analyzed "scientifically," and the most efficient method for undertaking the job is devised—the "one best way" of working. This consists of examining the implements needed to carry out the work, and measuring the maximum amount a "first-class" worker can do in a day. Workers are then expected to do this much work every day.
- The most suitable person to undertake the job is chosen, again "scientifically." The individual is taught to do the job in the exact way devised. Everyone, according to Taylor, has the ability to be "first class" at some job. It is management's role to find out which job suits each employee and train them until they are first class.
- Managers must cooperate with workers to ensure the job is done in the scientific way.
- There is a clear "division" of work and responsibility between management and workers. Managers concern themselves with the planning and supervision of the work, and workers carry it out.

Taylor summed up the differences between his principles of management and the traditional method as follows: "Under the management of 'initiative and incentive,' practically the whole problem is 'up to the workman'; while under the scientific management, fully one-half of the problem is 'up to the management'. . .The principal object of management should be to secure the maximum prosperity for the employer, coupled with the maximum prosperity for each employee." Taylor could justify his methods because he felt that his long-term goal would lead to "diminution of poverty, and the alleviation of suffering."

His main reason for developing scientific management was that he wished to do away with "soldiering" or "natural laziness," as he believed that all workers spent little time putting in full effort. To do this, Taylor aimed to analyze every job in a scientific way so that no one could be in any doubt about how much work could and should be done in a day. He felt that "every single act of every workman can be reduced to a science." Much inconclusive argument has ensued as to whether he was the pioneer of time and motion study. Certainly, time study played as important a part in Taylor's scientific job and task analysis as the examination of a worker's movements and the implements he used.

Inherent in Taylor's management style was the setting up of planning departments, staffed by clerks who ensured that "every laborer's work was planned out well in advance, and the workmen were moved from place to place. . .very much as chessmen are moved on a chessboard, a telephone and messenger system having been installed for this purpose." He concluded that, in this way, "a large amount of the time lost through having too many men in one

---

"In the past the man was first. In the future the system will be first." (Frederick Winslow Taylor)

place and too few in another, and through waiting between jobs, was entirely eliminated." Such a policy did, however, require the setting up of a more "elaborate organization and system," which sowed the seeds for Max Weber's bureaucratic organization structure. Taylor's approach constituted one of the first formal divisions between those who do the work (workers) and those who supervise and plan it (managers).

Management and Workers

For workers on the shop floor, scientific management brought a dramatic loss in skill level and autonomy. As well as being subject to increased supervision, workers were no longer able to use their own tools, which they might have spent many years modifying to suit their own style. In many cases, however, Taylor's ideas were extremely effective. In the case of shovelers at the Bethlehem Steel Works, workers earned higher wages and the company saved between $75,000 and $80,000 per year through greater efficiency.

Although Taylor believed that disputes between managers and workers would be eliminated because what "constitutes a fair day's work will be a question for scientific investigation, instead of a subject to be bargained and haggled over," there were numerous occasions when his ideas came into conflict with labor organizations. His opinion of such unions was invariably derogatory, as he was convinced that their objective was to limit the output of their members. Because of this, Taylor focused on the individual, believing that where a group of workers was formed, peer pressure would be used to ensure each man did not work to his full capacity. In the Bethlehem Steel Works, he decreed that no more than four men could work together in a gang without a special permit.

Even the way he wrote about unskilled workers was condescending. "Now one of the very first requirements for a man who is fit to handle pig iron as a regular occupation is that he shall be so stupid and phlegmatic that he more nearly resembles in his mental make-up the ox than any other type" is a typical example.

Although Taylor's manner often appeared inhumane, he also wrote: "If the workman fails to do his task, some competent teacher should be sent to show him exactly how his work can best be done, to guide, help, and to encourage him and, at the same time, to study his possibilities as a workman. So that, under the plan which individualizes each workman, instead of brutally discharging the man or lowering his wages to make good at once, he is given the time and the help required to make him proficient at his present job, or he is shifted to another class of work for which he is either mentally or physically better suited."

Contemporary Reaction to Scientific Management

It is easy to see why Taylor's work was regarded as inhumane. However good his motives of bringing about the greater good for the worker on the shop floor, the alleviation of poverty, and the elimination of waste, his methods were extremely hard and sometimes had the opposite effect.

It took him three years to implement some of his methods in the Midvale Steel Works. The men resorted to breaking their machines in an attempt to prove to management that Taylor was overworking them. In response, he fined any man whose machine broke, until eventually "they got sick of being fined, their opposition broke down, and they promised to do a fair day's work."

Frederick Winslow Taylor in Perspective

Many of Taylor's ideas are relevant to the modern day. Three in particular, taken from *The Principles of Scientific Management*, stand out:

- Rewards: "A reward, if it is to be most effective in stimulating men to do their best work, must come soon after the work has been done. . .The average workman must be able to measure what he has accomplished and clearly see his reward at the end of each day if he is to do his best." In Taylor's view, it was pointless to involve the shop floor workers in end-of-year profit sharing schemes.
- Quality standards: The use of written documentation for each part of a worker's job, inherent in scientific management, is strikingly prescient of the procedural documentation used in the ISO 9000 series of quality standards. "In the case of a machine-shop which is managed under the modern system, detailed written instructions as to the best way of doing each piece of work are prepared in advance, by men in the planning department. These instructions represent the combined work of several men in the planning room, each of whom has his own speciality, or function. . .The directions of all of these men, however, are written on a single instruction card, or sheet." The main difference is that today's best practice means involving staff in drawing up their own procedures.
- Suggestion schemes: Taylor proposed a form of incentive for employees to make suggestions if they felt an improvement could be made, either to the method or the implement used to undertake a task. If, after analysis, the suggestion was introduced into the workplace, the person suggesting it "should be given the full credit for the improvement, and should be paid a cash premium as a reward for his ingenuity. In this way the true initiative of the workmen is better attained under scientific management than under the old individual plan."

At the time of his death in 1917, Taylor's work was the subject of much debate, both for and against. His approach is now frowned on as "Victorian," but it should not be forgotten that he was a man of his times and sought solutions to the problems of his times. The main criticism of Taylor is that his approach was too mechanistic—treating people like machines or as unthinking creatures to be trained like dogs, rather than as human beings.

However, he was one of the first true pioneers of management through his scientific examination of the way work is done, and his thinking led directly to the achievements of other management gurus such as Max Weber and Henry Ford.

For More Information

Key works by Taylor

Books:

Shop Management, 1903 in *Scientific Management* (comprising *Shop Management, The Principles of Scientific Management, Testimony before the Special House Committee*). New York: Harper, 1947.

The Principles of Scientific Management. New York: W.W. Norton, 1967.

Further Reading

Books: Kakar, Sudhire. *Frederick Taylor: A Study in Personality and Innovation*. Cambridge, MA: MIT Press, 1970.

Nelson, D. *Frederick W. Taylor and the Rise of Scientific Management*. Madison: University of Wisconsin Press, 1980.

See also:

The Principles of Scientific Management (p. 945)

Henry Laurence Gantt (pp. 990–91)

Frank and Lillian Gilbreth (pp. 994–95)

"You know as well as I do that a high-priced man has to do exactly as he is told from morning to night."

(Frederick Winslow Taylor)

ALVIN TOFFLER

The Futurologist's Futurologist

Widely recognized as one of the world's leading authorities on change, Alvin Toffler very carefully avoids words like "trend" and "prediction" in his writing, and insists that nobody can tell for certain what will happen in the future. Toffler's special gift is an understanding of the effects of change. It comes from a knowledge of science, technology, and the arts, and a capacity to deduce what might result when complex technological and social changes impact on entrenched attitudes and vested interests.

1928	Born.
1965	Coins the term "future shock" in an article in *Horizon.*
1969–1970	Works as consultant for AT& T.
1970	Publication of *Future Shock.*
1977	Cofounds Institute for Alternative Futures with Clement Bezold and James Dator.
1980	Publication of *The Third Wave.*
1986	Helps set up Issyk-Kul Forum, the first non-Communist, nongovernmental organization in the former USSR.
1990	Publication of *Powershift.*
1993	Publication of *War and Anti-War.*
1996	Founds Toffler Associates, an executive advisory firm.

LIFE AND CAREER

Alvin Toffler was born in 1928. Though he has traveled widely, he gained all his education and working experience in the United States. He has been a visiting fellow at the Russell Sage Foundation, a visiting professor at Cornell University, a faculty member of the New School for Social Research, and a highly successful business consultant. He has several honorary degrees, and his books have won many awards.

Much of Toffler's work has been created in collaboration with his wife Heidi—as he is always the first to point out. Theirs is a longstanding partnership: both studied English at New York University and then entered the heady Bohemian world of postwar Greenwich Village, where their interests were mainly in writing poetry and planning novels.

Not a scientist by first choice, Toffler understood from a very young age the importance of science and technology in the modern world, and took a course in the history of technology.

The Tofflers spent several years in journalism, writing for publications ranging from *Fortune* and *Playboy* to the leading political, scientific, and economic journals of the day. In 1960 an invitation from IBM to write a paper on the long-term social and organizational implications of the computer gave them a lengthy exposure to high technology. From this seminal experience grew the all-consuming interest in change for which they are now world-famous. *Future Shock*, the first book in Toffler's great trilogy on change, was begun shortly after completing the IBM paper.

KEY THINKING

Though he has published many books and countless articles and papers, Toffler's philosophy, and most of his key ideas, are encapsulated in three books: *Future Shock* (1970), *The Third Wave* (1980), and *Powershift* (1990). Each is a self-standing work in its own right, but they combine to form a trilogy that develops Toffler's ideas about change in a seamless dialogue.

Toffler gives his own brief summation of what the trilogy is all about in the Preface to *Powershift*: "...the central subject is change—what happens to people when their entire society abruptly transforms itself into something new and unexpected. *Future Shock* looks at the process of change—how change affects people and organizations. *The Third Wave* focuses on the directions of change—where today's changes are taking us. *Powershift* deals with the control of changes still to come—who will shape them and how."

Besides giving a painstaking analysis of change and the many challenges and problems it brings, the trilogy is full of hope. The books argue, convincingly, that the rapid change all around us is not so chaotic or random as it first appears; there are patterns and recognizable forces behind it. Understanding these patterns and forces will allow us to cope "strategically" with change, and to avoid haphazard responses to individual events as they are encountered.

THE TRILOGY: *FUTURE SHOCK*

Toffler has described the effect of too much change occurring too quickly so well, that the expression "future shock" has entered the world's vocabulary and is now widely used to define the disorientation, confusion, and breakdown of decision-making capacity that afflicts individuals, groups, and whole societies when they are overwhelmed by change.

In his preface to *Powershift*, Toffler contends that "...the acceleration of history carries consequences of its own, independent of the actual direction of change. The simple speed-up of events and reaction times produces its own effects, whether the changes are perceived as good or bad."

Future Shock was written over thirty years ago, and we are now able to test the accuracy of Toffler's foresight. What we find is quite remarkable; he anticipated the break-up of the nuclear family, the genetic revolution, the "throwaway" society, the resurgence of emphasis on education, and the increased importance of knowledge in society.

THE THIRD WAVE

This book explores perhaps Toffler's most elegant theory, adding a "third wave" to the other two great and generally recognized surges in human development.

The first came with the introduction of agriculture, and humankind's revolutionary shift from hunter-gatherer to settled farmer. This released it from the constant struggle for subsistence, providing the stability and security needed to develop the arts and technology that are the basis of civilization as we know it today.

The second was the industrial revolution,

"The advanced economy could not run for thirty seconds without computers." (Alvin Toffler)

the remarkable leap forward in manufacturing methods and the organization of labor that created the industrialized world. The exploitation of raw materials, mass production, and an ever more ingenious application of technology brought prosperity and comfort to those countries that could embrace the necessary changes.

Toffler's third wave is the post-industrial, information-based revolution that began, he suggests, in the 1950s, with a number of major technological and social changes.

In *The Third Wave*, Toffler predicted with an uncanny foresight both the profound effects of information technology and biotechnology on the economy, and the changes we can now see taking place in manufacturing methods, marketing, and working patterns. He showed particular prescience in foreseeing the development of niche marketing and the increased power of the consumer. He even invented a new word—"prosumer"—to designate the fusion of producer and consumer.

In his introduction to the book, Toffler talks of the seemingly chaotic changes of the 1960s that produced "a culture of warring specialisms, drowned in fragmented data and fine-toothed analysis," and a climate in which synthesis "is not merely useful—it is crucial." It was to address this need for synthesis that Toffler conceived *The Third Wave*. It is, he claims, "a book of large-scale synthesis [that] describes the old civilization in which many of us grew up, and presents a careful, comprehensive picture of the new civilization bursting into being in our midst."

He goes on to say: ". . .the world that is fast emerging from the clash of new values and technologies, new geophysical relationships, new life-styles and modes of communication, demands wholly new ideas and analogies, classifications and concepts. We cannot cram the embryonic world of tomorrow into yesterday's conventional cubby holes."

Powershift

In this, the final book of the trilogy, Toffler carries forward his earlier analysis with an exploration of how individuals, organizations, and nations will be affected by inevitable changes in the way power is perceived and applied. He talks of a "new power system replacing that of the industrial past."

The word "powershift" in the title means something very different from the usual two-word term "power shift." Toffler says that, while a power shift is a transfer of power, a "powershift" is "a deep-level change in the very nature of power." A powershift does not merely transfer power, but also transforms it.

In *Powershift* we are reminded of the three basic sources of power: violence, wealth, and knowledge. All businesses work in what Toffler describes as a "power-field" where these three "tools of power" constantly operate. The rising importance of knowledge, so eloquently argued throughout the trilogy, has brought about a profound change in the balance between them.

Powershift gives no hint of an early solution to the problems associated with change. Toffler talks about the struggles to come as individuals, businesses, and national economies move away from their traditional sources of power toward a new dependence on knowledge. In his view, the problems will not be over when these power conflicts are resolved. He sees even greater challenges ahead as divisions develop between "fast" and "slow" economies.

Another idea, explored throughout the trilogy but most strongly in *Powershift*, is what Toffler calls "de-massification." By this he means a reversal of the trend toward "mass" solutions prevalent in the late 20th century. He sees mass marketing giving way to niche and micro-marketing; mass production being replaced by increasingly customized production; and large corporations being broken down into small, autonomous units. Even politics and the concept of nationhood, Toffler believes, will be affected by the pressure to "de-massify," created by the increasing awareness of better-informed individuals and made effective by the unstoppable development of information technology.

Alvin Toffler in Perspective

Influential as Toffler's trilogy continues to be, it must be remembered that the last of the three books was published in 1990; it would be misleading to imply that Toffler's work started or finished at that point. *The Adaptive Corporation*, for example, published in 1985, was built around the report resulting from Toffler's 1969–70 consultancy work for AT&T. Ignored by senior management at the time, this report became influential later, at the time of the Bell divestiture. The book deals with questions of organizational change and adaptation through focusing on the case of AT&T.

Other books and articles have appeared since the trilogy and, from the time of the publication of *Powershift*, Heidi Toffler has allowed her role to be more formally acknowledged; the Tofflers' more recent publications have been under explicit joint authorship.

Their contribution to world politics is something many management commentators neglect. Respected by many world leaders, they have played a significant part in improving east-west relations. Mikhail Gorbachev is an admirer whom they have met several times and greatly influenced.

The Tofflers also visited China and were having a positive effect on Chinese politics until the disastrous reversals following the Tiananmen Square episode. Their books are now banned in China though, of course, banning books often merely serves to increase their influence.

Of the Tofflers' major publications in the last ten years, *War and Anti-War* is usually regarded as the most important. It focuses on warfare, suggesting that changes in the way we do business are matched by a parallel revolution in how we make war—and that, like so many in commerce and manufacturing, these military changes derive directly from advances in information technology. Their ideas have already been proved correct in the Gulf War and elsewhere, but Alvin Toffler's most chillingly accurate prediction came in an interview he gave for the *New Scientist* magazine of March 1994, where he spoke of the inadequacy of conventional military force in controlling terrorist action. To illustrate his point, he quoted a former U.S. intelligence officer as saying that, if he had 20 people and a million dollars, he could shut down America. Seven years later the events of September 11, 2001 provided appalling evidence of this statement's credibility.

For More Information

Key works by Toffler

Books:

Future Shock. New York: Random House, 1970.

The Third Wave. New York: Bantam, 1980.

Powershift. New York: Bantam Books, 1990.

Toffler, Alvin, and Heidi Toffler. *War and Anti-War*. New York: Little, Brown & Company, 1993.

"It is always easier to talk about change than to make it. It is easier to consult than to manage."

(Alvin Toffler)

VICTOR H. VROOM

Motivation and Leadership Decision Making

Victor H. Vroom (1932–) is acknowledged as a leading authority on the psychological analysis of behavior in organizations. His major contributions include work on motivation in the workplace, illustrated by his expectancy model, and research into leadership styles and decision making. From the latter, he and Philip Yetton developed a model for selecting appropriate methods of problem solving for different situations.

1932	Born.
1955	Receives M.A. from McGill University.
1958	Receives Ph.D. from the University of Michigan.
1964	Publication of *Work and Motivation*.
1972	Appointed chairman of the department of administrative science at Yale.
1973	Publication of *Leadership and Decision-Making*, coauthored by Philip Yetton and containing the Vroom/Yetton model.

LIFE AND CAREER

Born in Canada in 1932, Victor Vroom gained his bachelor's and master's degrees at McGill University and a Ph.D. at the University of Michigan. He taught at the universities of Michigan and Pennsylvania and the Carnegie Institute of Technology before being appointed John G. Searle professor of organization and management and professor of psychology at Yale University's school of management. He has also acted as a consultant to many large organizations.

Vroom's work spans the two disciplines of management and psychology. He first applied psychology to organizations in a prize-winning doctoral dissertation in 1960. This examined the effects of personality on participation in decision making. His theories were further developed in a 1964 book, *Work and Motivation*, which applied expectancy theory to work for the first time. Expectancy theory maintains that people will be motivated to behave in certain ways if they believe that doing so will bring them rewards they seek and value.

Vroom's study of the causes of people's decisions to act in certain ways at work continued with his collaboration with Philip Yetton to develop what became known as the Vroom/Yetton model of leadership decision-making (*Leadership and Decision-Making*, 1973). This is a contingency model that identifies styles of leadership appropriate to different situations. Specifically, it can be used by managers to assess the degree to which they should encourage people to participate in the decision-making process. With Arthur Jago, Vroom further developed this model in *The New Leadership: Managing Participation in Organizations*.

KEY THINKING

EXPECTANCY THEORY

In *Work and Motivation* Vroom defines the central problem of motivation as "the explanation of choices made by organisms among different voluntary responses" (p. 9). To understand how these choices are made, he defines three concepts—valence, expectancy, and force—and describes how these work in conjunction to determine how people will decide to act, given possible routes of behavior leading to possible outcomes.

Valence is a term referring to a preference for one outcome over another. An outcome is said to have positive valence when a person prefers attaining it to not attaining it; when he or she prefers not to attain an outcome, then it has a negative valence; and when he or she is indifferent to whether an outcome is attained or not, it has a valence of zero. If a manager particularly wants a promotion, for example, and thinks that successful completion of a certain project will earn that promotion, then he or she will attach a positive valence to completing the project, and be motivated to do so by the perceived value of the reward.

A person's behavior, however, is affected not only by preference for one outcome over another, but also by how likely he or she believes these outcomes to be. Vroom defines expectancy as "a momentary belief concerning the likelihood that a particular act will be followed by a particular outcome" (p. 17). Expectancy can be assigned a value from zero (the belief that the outcome will not follow on from the action) to one (the belief that the outcome certainly will follow on from the action). If someone wants a cup of coffee, for example, and knows that there is a drinks machine in the staff room, that person will walk straight there. The act of walking there has a high expectancy value in terms of obtaining coffee, whereas the act of walking to, say, the post room has a low expectancy value, as the person does not expect to find coffee there.

The third concept that Vroom outlines is force. He argues that a person's behavior is the result of a field of forces, each of which has direction and magnitude. Mathematical values assigned to the valences and expectancies for acts are combined to produce their hypothetical force, and the act that produces the highest level of force is assumed to be the one that the person will choose. The highest levels of force will be produced by actions with high levels of both valence and expectation.

Vroom's model is summed up by:

$M = (E \times V)$

where M is the motivational force resulting from the sum of expectancy and valence, E is the expectancy measure and V represents the valence for the individual of a particular outcome. (Source: Martin, J. *Organizational Behavior*. Boston: International Thompson Business Press, 1998.)

Vroom's theory can be put into practice by interviewing individuals or giving them questionnaires to assess their expectancies and valences. These are then scored, and the expectancy score is multiplied by the valence score. The results for all outcomes that could be produced by a particular behavioral alternative are added together to give the expected value (EV) of that alternative. Each possible course of behavior can be assigned an EV in this way, and the model predicts that the one with the highest EV will be a subject's most likely choice.

The primary implication for managers is that, since motivation is closely tied to reward, they should aim to encourage high work performance by tailoring rewards to those things which employees value most–and some research will be needed here to find out just what these might be for each individual. Incentives and benefits should be explicitly linked to actions which are in line with the organization's strategy and which will contribute to its success.

This is a normative model: it can only predict how people should make decisions to act, rather than how they actually do make such decisions. In reality, few people are well enough informed about all the possible choices and all the possible outcomes to make balanced judgments as to which behavior it would be best for them to adopt. As a theory explaining a general approximation of an individual's behavior, however, it has gained much support.

In 1968 Vroom's expectancy theory was extended by L. W. Porter and E. E. Lawler in their book *Managerial Attitudes and Performance* (Homewood, IL: Richard D. Irwin, 1968). Their model emphasized that performance is also affected by factors other than motivation.

Subsequent research has focused on showing that expectancy models can be used quite accurately to predict choice of occupation, levels of job satisfaction, and levels of work effort. An extensive review of recent research on expectancy theory can be found in "Old friends, new faces: motivation research in the 1990s," by Maureen L. Ambrose and Carol T. Kulik (*Journal of Management*, May/June 1999).

Vroom/Yetton Model of Leadership Decision Making

Vroom's second major model, developed with Philip Yetton, shows how different leadership styles can be harnessed in solving different types of problems.

In *Leadership and Decision-Making* (1973), they developed a set of rules that can be used to determine the level and form of participation in the decision-making process that will support the best solution in different problem-solving situations. New managers may think they must make decisions alone, but Vroom clearly believes that this is not the case. He outlines types of decision-making involved in both group problems that affect a manager's workgroup, and in individual problems that affect only the manager. The following list from *Leadership and Decision-Making* (p. 13) shows the types of management decision methods for group problems:

- authority decisions–made by the manager alone without involving others. A1–the manager makes the decision on his own using information available at the time. A2–the manager makes the decision alone but obtains his information from subordinates or other group members first.
- consultative decisions–made by the manager after consultation with a group. C1–the manager approaches several other people individually to obtain their suggestions, then makes his own decision. C2–the manager brings several other people together at the same time as a group and collectively obtains their suggestions, then makes his own decision.
- group decisions–made by a whole group in consensus. G2–the manager brings together several other people at the same time and they discuss the problem to arrive at a consensus decision between them.

Five similar methods are defined for individual problems. The Vroom/Yetton model then proposes a decision tree based on seven rules, which managers can use to pinpoint the most appropriate method for a given situation.

By means of a sequence of questions, each requiring a yes/no answer that advances the manager along a decision tree path, the problem is ultimately defined as one of 14 types. Vroom and Yetton then recommend suitable methods of decision-making (from methods A1–G2 above) for each problem type.

Since some types of problem can be solved by more than one method, further means of choosing between them are needed. When Vroom and Arthur Jago revised the model in 1988, they suggested that time is one important factor to consider: person-hours carry a financial cost, and a swiftly made decision may be best; also, a decision might be required urgently, and participative processes may slow down the decision-making process.

The Vroom/Yetton model has been progressively developed by its original authors, and by Vroom and Jago, since its inception. Further factors examined include:

- the extent to which participation benefits the organization by offering development opportunities for participants;
- the influence of a manager's position in the organizational hierarchy on his or her problem-handling style;
- the styles adopted by women managers.

Victor H. Vroom in Perspective

Vroom has made valuable contributions in the fields of both management and psychology. His models have been tested and extended, and remain important landmarks in the discipline of industrial psychology. Vroom has explored other, neighboring aspects of industrial psychology, but the two theories outlined above remain his most famous and enduring work. The models proposed by Vroom, and by Vroom and Yetton, have contributed much to managers' understanding of behavior, and to their ability to mold behavior to produce the most favorable outcomes, and so to manage more effectively.

The Vroom/Yetton model of leadership decision making, however, was at the height of its fame a quarter of a century ago and management thinking has changed since then. There is now more emphasis on delegation, empowerment, flatter structures, and matrix management, all of which have implications for managers' choices of leadership style. Vroom himself is not oblivious to change and development, and has actually used it to justify the relevance of his work on the Yale Web site: "Managers seldom live in a static world. They change jobs, change organizations, move from one country to another, from sector to sector. [Such changes]. . .spur new challenges, new opportunities, and place new situational demands on leadership. . .Old habits must be discarded if one is to respond to today's challenges and opportunities."

For More Information

Key Works by Vroom

Books:

Work and Motivation. New York: John Wiley, 1964.

Vroom, Victor, with Philip Yetton. *Leadership and Decision-Making*. Pittsburgh: University of Pittsburgh Press, 1973.

Vroom, Victor, with Arthur Jago. *The New Leadership: Managing Participation in Organizations*. Upper Saddle River, NJ: Prentice Hall, 1988.

Journal Article:

"Reflections on Leadership and Decision Making." *Journal of General Management*, vol. 9 no. 3, Spring 1984, pp. 18–36.

"True motivation comes from achievement, personal development, job satisfaction, and recognition."

(Frederick Herzberg)

  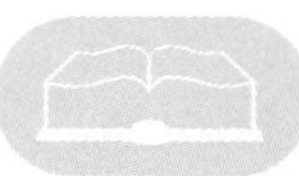    

MAX WEBER

The Conceptualization of Bureaucracy

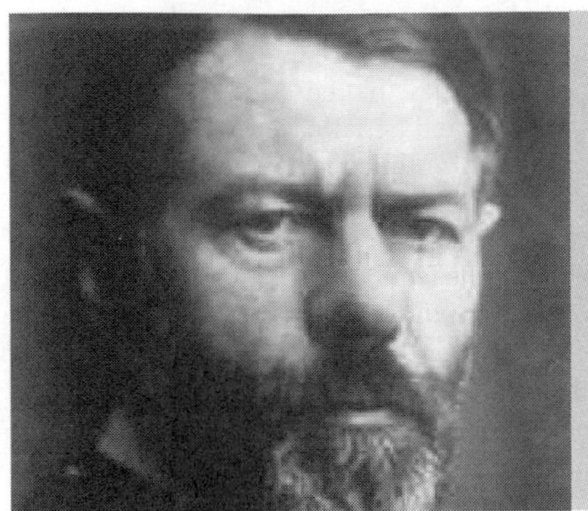

Since the early 1980s it has become fashionable to criticize bureaucracies for being out of touch with rapidly changing market conditions. Any understanding of the way modern organizations work would be incomplete without at least a cursory study of Weber, who is commonly described as a founding father of sociology. Weber's thoughts on the concepts of leadership, power, and authority are closely linked to his description of bureaucracy.

1864	Born.
1894	Professor of Political Economy, University of Freiburg, Germany.
1897	Professor of Political Economy, University of Heidelberg, Germany.
1904	First publication of *The Protestant Ethic and the Spirit of Capitalism.*
1919	Professor of Political Economy, University of Munich, Germany.
1920	Dies.

LIFE AND CAREER

Max Weber was born on April 21, 1864, the first of seven children, and grew up in a cultured bourgeois household, ruled by a strong authoritarian father. At university in Heidelberg, Weber studied economics, medieval history, and philosophy as well as law. A period of military service brought him under the care of his uncle, Hermann Baumgarten, a historian, and his wife. Both uncle and aunt acted as mentors to Weber, the former as a liberal who treated him as an intellectual peer, the latter as a person who impressed him with her deep sense of social responsibility toward her charitable work. Both offered a stark contrast to Weber's father, who treated his son with patronizing authoritarianism.

It was probably during this formative period that Weber developed an aversion to the way people then most often gained positions of power and authority—through nepotism and accident of birth—factors he considered were lacking in legitimacy. He started to think of ways to free the individual as much as possible from personal judgments or from judgments clouded by emotion or self-interest.

After periods as a legal scholar at Heidelberg and then at the University of Berlin, Weber became professor of political economy, first at the University of Freiburg, and later at Heidelberg.

His principal contribution to the study of organizations stemmed from his interest in understanding why people obeyed commands. This interest led him to distinguish between power as the ability to force obedience irrespective of resistance, and authority as the ability to get orders obeyed as a matter of course, apparently voluntarily.

KEY THINKING

Weber describes power as the probability of carrying out one's own will despite resistance or, at its extreme, as the ability to force people to obey. It is not necessarily the same as leadership or authority, but is invariably linked to them. Organizational power he links to structure and authority and considers inherent in any hierarchy or bureaucracy. Invariably the effects of power depend on who has it, how that person is perceived, and the particular situation in which power is invoked. Weber identified three types of legitimate authority.

CHARISMATIC AUTHORITY

The leader is obeyed because of followers' faith in his or her special, "supernatural" qualities. Weber proposed in his *Theory of Social and Economic Organization* that the term "charisma" was associated with someone who possesses exceptional, supernatural qualities and who is thus set apart from ordinary people. These qualities constitute the basis on which that individual is considered to be, and is treated as, a leader.

Commentators at the beginning of the 21st century might conclude that very few business leaders could be said to have supernatural qualities. We must remember, however, that Weber was arguing from a philosophical standpoint, not a current, pragmatic management one; we may therefore understand "supernatural" as being "supernormal" and at the opposite end of a scale balanced by "rational." Although not considered supernatural, many business leaders have been deemed special in some way, and have had attributed to them qualities that set them apart from "ordinary people." Indeed, research in the 1970s and 1980s by Warren Bennis suggested that leaders do have qualities which set them apart, although he did not use the word "supernatural" and went on to suggest that leadership qualities can be developed.

Of his three models of legitimate authority, Weber thought charisma the least stable because its inspirational and motivational qualities disappear when the leader relinquishes the post. For Weber, charisma was not a sustainable option as the basis for authority. He advocated locating legitimacy in something more lasting and systematic.

TRADITIONAL AUTHORITY

Leaders have authority by virtue of the status they have inherited—the extent of their authority is determined by birth, custom, precedent, and usage. Although Weber derives his theory from a study of history, we can still sometimes witness today how many positions of authority are handed from one generation to another, as firms establish dynasties, and appointments have more to do with family ties than competence. Another characteristic of organizations based on traditional authority is that things tend to be done in a particular way just because "they have always been done like that."

In the competitive world of today, the dangers of this approach are only too apparent: larger organizations get caught up in their own systems and either fail to spot when competitors are catching them up or markets are slipping away, or else simply become trapped by their own inertia. Precedent, rather than rational analysis, becomes the reason in itself for doing things.

Weber's search for a sustainable form of organizational authority based on rational

"Man is dominated by the making of money, by acquisition as the ultimate purpose of his life."

(Max Weber)

analysis led him to distinguish a third authority system.

Rational-legal Authority

Authority within a bureaucracy is both legal and rational when it is exercised through a system of rules and procedures attached to the "office"—the job role—which an individual occupies.

Weber described how bureaucracy-based, rational-legal authority works:

- the organization is structured around official functions that are bound by rules, each area having its own specified competence;
- functions are structured into offices organized into a hierarchy that follows technical rules and norms for which training is provided;
- the administration is separated from the ownership of the means of production;
- the rules, decisions, and actions of the administration are recorded in writing.

Weber stated that the bureaucracy was technically the most efficient form of organization because, within it, work is conducted with precision, knowledge of files, continuity, discretion, unity, strict subordination, and reduction of friction.

Bureaucracies

Within bureaucracies organized along rational lines, the abuse of power by leaders is minimized because:

- offices are ranked in hierarchical order;
- operations are conducted in accordance with impersonal rules;
- officials are allocated specific duties and areas of responsibility;
- appointments are made on the basis of qualifications and suitability for the position.

Weber was, however, also aware of the shortcomings of bureaucracy, inasmuch as:

- their characteristic information processing and filtering to the top makes them cumbersome and slow to react;
- their machinery makes it difficult to handle individual cases, because rules and procedures require all individuals to be treated as if they were the same;
- bureaucratization leads to depersonalization, because the roles of officials are circumscribed by written definitions of their authority, and there is a set of rules and procedures to cater for every contingency.

Weber recognized that the more efficient a bureaucracy becomes, the more it succeeds in excluding the personal, the irrational, and the incalculable in favor of emotional detachment and "professionalism." Perhaps this goes a long way toward explaining why Weber is held in low esteem in today's business climate of change and uncertainty.

Max Weber in Perspective

Weber recognized the dangers of bureaucratization and spoke of how measurement processes could turn people into cogs in a machine. In this respect his reflections are not too distant from Marx's theories of alienation. Although organizational bureaucratization increases efficiency and productive capability, its mechanical efficiency also threatens to dehumanize its participants. Weber also believed, however, that the only way people could make a significant contribution was to subjugate their personalities and desires to the impersonal goals and procedures of large scale organizations. Paradoxically, he believed that the only way to escape such a mechanical future was for a charismatic leader to transform the organization into something new.

Bureaucracy became the model for the 20th-century organization, and was encapsulated in Alfred Sloan's General Motors and Harold Geneen's ITT. Perhaps the mundaneness and regularity of bureaucratic, corporate life was best described in William Whyte's *The Organization Man* (1956), in which the individual is taken over by the bureaucratic machine, in the name of efficiency. A more recent and humorous interpretation of life in a bureaucracy has been depicted by Scott Adams in *The Dilbert Principle*.

The bureaucracy may have outlived its age of supremacy, but it is still hard to foresee a future without any need for the order, procedures, levels of authority, and controls that constitute a bureaucracy. The problem is how to develop systems that combine necessary bureaucratic features with a people-centered, flexible, and imaginative style.

As the foremost social scientist of his day—with little interest in management—Weber would have found it hard to believe that he was to exercise such a dominant influence on the way organizations have been managed. He would have also found it hard to credit the notion that he would be quoted as one of a trinity of management pioneers, along with Henri Fayol and F. W. Taylor, contemporaries whom he would not have known or read.

For More Information

Key works by Weber

Books:

The Protestant Ethic and the Spirit of Capitalism. New York: Routledge, 2001.

Theory of Social and Economic Organization (trans. by A. M. Henderson and T. Parsons). New York: Free Press, 1947.

Further Reading

Book: Pugh, Derek, and David J. Hickson. *Great Writers on Organizations.* 2nd ed. Burlington, VT: Ashgate Publishing, 1999.

See also:

- **Managing Today's Angry Workforce (pp. 35–36)**
- **The Theory of Social and Economic Organization (p. 951)**
- **Warren Bennis (pp. 968–69)**
- **Henri Fayol (pp. 986–87)**
- **Frederick Winslow Taylor (pp. 1054–55)**

"Bureaucratic administration means fundamentally the exercise of control on the basis of knowledge."

(Max Weber)

JOHN JACOB ASTOR

Born in Germany, John Jacob Astor emigrated to America in 1780. Arriving with a few dollars and seven flutes, he amassed a fur and property empire that made him one of the richest men of his day. Astor's story is a lesson for all entrepreneurs: provide excellent customer service; be close to markets; buy cheap, and sell wherever the price is best. In a battle with Astor, the state-subsidized fur trade looked as if it would surely be the winner, but Astor won by a knockout.

Then, in his smartest career move, Astor dumped his fur trading interests, just before fur became old hat. Moving onto something more fashionable, he bought up property—lots of it—in the way that most people buy groceries. In doing so, he helped shape the development of one of the greatest cities on the planet—New York. When he died in 1848, he was worth over $20 million.

Astor fashioned a fortune from his exploits in the fur trade.

1763	Born.
1783	Sets sail for the United States. Takes $24 and seven flutes.
1784	Arrives in New York.
1785	Marries.
1786	Opens shop selling pianos and buying furs.
1808	Consolidates holdings and incorporates American Fur Company.
1810	Founds Pacific Fur Company.
1811	Establishes Astoria at the mouth of the Columbia River.
1820s	Fur trade begins to slow down.
1834	Sells entire holdings in fur trade and retires. Develops property.
1848	Dies.

BACKGROUND AND RISE

Born in Walldorf, Germany in 1763, John Jacob Astor was the third son of a butcher. His brother George, the eldest son, left Germany for England to set up a business making and selling musical instruments. His brother Henry departed for New York City. In 1780, John Jacob too left the family farm, made his way down the Rhine Valley and set sail for England, where he joined his brother in business.

By 1800, Astor was the leading American fur trader. It was a considerable achievement.

In London, Astor learned to speak English, assisted his brother, and saved enough money to take a ship across the Atlantic. In November 1783, at the end of the American Revolution, he set sail for the United States. With him he took $24 and seven flutes. The journey took the standard eight weeks, arriving in Chesapeake Bay in January. Astor's berth was in the crew's quarters and on the crossing, so the story goes, he befriended another German emigrant who told him about the fur trade and the opportunities it offered.

DEFINING MOMENTS

Arriving in New York in March 1784, aged 21, Astor soon married and set up a shop selling pianos and buying furs. His wife would mind the store while Astor ventured into the northern territories, building a network of contacts among the fur traders.

The lucrative fur trade was important not only commercially, but politically. Canada's patronage from France was dependent on its revenues. American, French-Canadian and British companies–like the Hudson Bay Company and the Northwest Company–dominated the fur trade. In 1796 a treaty between the United States and Great Britain demarcated trading boundaries along national borders, excluding the Canadians from American territories. Into the vacuum left by the Canadians moved Astor.

By 1800, Astor was the leading American fur trader. It was a considerable achievement. As well as dealing with competition from other private traders, Astor was competing with the American government. Eager to make a show of strength to the Native Americans and to keep out the French and English, President George Washington had approved funds to set up the Office of Indian Affairs and a series of state-sponsored fur factories. The problem was that when it came to the actual trading, private traders won hands down. Government representatives like Thomas McKenney insisted on foisting plows, and other implements that were deemed to be intrinsically good or useful, on the Indians. The Indians, uninterested in sanctimony or agricultural equipment, wanted kettles and muskets. Like all good entrepreneurs, Astor gave the Indians what they wanted and got what he wanted in return–furs. He refused to sell the Indians liquor, figuring that drunk Indians were unlikely to make good trappers. Astor also out-competed on service. The government maintained trading posts some distance from the Indians, so Astor's men went upriver to deal with them directly. It was customer service at its best.

At the other end of the supply chain, Astor got better prices for his furs than the government did. While the government sold the furs immediately on the local market, regardless of demand or oversupply, Astor shipped his furs around the world to whatever market paid the best price. The folly of the government's attempts to control the fur trade was revealed when it passed legislation to close down the fur factories and sell their assets.

Already wealthy, Astor expanded his commercial horizons. He obtained permission to trade through ports owned by the East India Company; sent a ship to China in a joint venture, and pocketed $50,000 in profit. The profit was plowed into New York property.

In 1808 Astor consolidated his holdings and incorporated the American Fur Company. This was a precursor to an attempt to control the developing fur trade in the West. Most companies planned to extend their territories to the West. The key would be finding and controlling a route through to the Pacific. A Canadian expedition had set out cross-country and was rumored to be making good progress. Astor thought it would be more sensible to make his way around the Cape of Good Hope by ship and head for the mouth of the Columbia River. To finance his enterprise, he took up with some of the members of the Northwest Company and founded the Pacific Fur Company in 1810.

Astor's party arrived at the Columbia River in 1811. Six weeks after they raised the U.S. flag over a hastily erected stockade, christened Astoria, the Canadian expedition arrived. Astoria was to be an essential cog in Astor's international trading plans. No one could accuse him of lacking ambition. His intention was to send goods from New York to Astoria; trade them for furs with the Indians; ship the furs to the Orient to be traded for goods; ship the Oriental goods to Europe and trade them for European goods, and ship the European goods to America, taking a profit at every stage. It was a brilliant plan that fell at the first hurdle when one of his ships sank, and the 1812 war between the United States and England broke out. The British forced Astor to hand over his fort in Astoria for $58,000.

Other than this setback, Astor did well out of the war. Even in his worst year during the war, his revenues were $50,000. By the end of the conflict he had substantially increased his property holdings. After the war, with the help of some friendly government officials and some handy legislation that forbade Canadian involvement in the American fur trade, Astor gained control of all the Northwest Company's holdings that lay within American borders. He continued to take over the interests of other companies, inching his way West. But by the late 1820s, fashions had changed, silk was all the rage, and profits were falling. Never failing to spot a trend, Astor got out while he could. In June 1834, he sold all his fur trading holdings and retired.

For the rest of his years, Astor dabbled in property speculation. He had always bought parcels of land in New York City when they became available. Now he bought up vast tracts of land on the urban fringes of New York, figuring—correctly—that at the current rate of population growth, the city would soon swallow up his plots. As usual he figured right. He became one of the largest property owners in New York City and, as a by-product, one of the main landlords. He died in 1848, the richest man in America. His fortune was some $20 million.

For the rest of his years, Astor dabbled in property speculation.

Context and Conclusions

What Astor considered legitimate trade, modern sentiment labels amoral and unethical. The fur trade, an industry of considerable commercial and political importance at the time, is now considered anathema in many parts of the world. Astor's dealings with the indigenous Indian population and the tenants of his property empire also left much to be desired by today's standards. Nevertheless, Astor is an important figure in business history for a number of reasons. As a champion of private enterprise, his endeavors clearly illustrated the shortcomings of state monopolies. Ultimately he demonstrated that the disincentivized, bureaucracy-ridden, heavily subsidized, state-run fur factories were no match for an agile private enterprise that paid close attention to its customers' needs and promoted innovation as a means to increasing profitability. Astor's actions also helped open the western frontiers of America for development. Finally, regardless of his motivation, he was responsible for shaping the development of Manhattan and New York City.

For More Information

Books:

Houghton, Walter R. *Kings of Fortune or the Triumphs and Achievements of Noble, Self-made Men.* Chicago: The Loomis National Library Association, 1888.

Irving, Washington. *Astoria; or, Enterprise Beyond the Rocky Mountains.* London: Richard Bentley, 1839.

Smith, Arthur D. Howden. *John Jacob Astor: Landlord of New York.* Philadelphia: Lippincott, 1929.

Terrell, John Upton. *Furs by Astor (John Jacob Astor).* New York: Morrow & Co., 1963.

  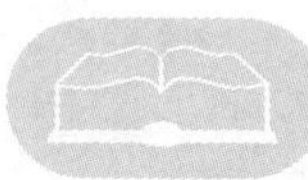    

Jeffrey Bezos

Jeff Bezos, the founder and C.E.O. of Amazon.com, is the most famous son of the e-commerce revolution. The company he created became the best known online brand in the world.

After graduating from Princeton University in 1986, Bezos worked for a variety of investment firms, notably D.E. Shaw & Co., where he helped set up one of the most successful quantitative hedge funds on Wall Street. By 1992 he had made it to vice president, yet he gave up this glittering career to chase a dream. Amazon.com opened for business on the Internet in July 1995, and with relentless hype soon became the flagship for the New Economy. When the tide turned against dot-com stocks in 2000, Amazon.com looked as if it might be washed up. Yet Bezos rode the storm and is floating high once more.

Amazon has gone from strength to strength under Jeff Bezos.

1964	Born.
1986	Graduates from Princeton.
1990	Youngest vice president at Bankers Trust.
1992	Senior vice president at D.E. Shaw & Co.
1995	Amazon.com opens for business.
1998	Net sales of $252.9 million, an increase of 283% over the same period in 1997.
1999	Amazon.com, Inc. has a market capitalization of $6 billion. Voted *Time* magazine's person of the year.
2001	Amazon.com, Inc. posts first quarterly profit.

Background and Rise

Born on January 12, 1964 in Albuquerque, New Mexico, Jeffrey Preston Bezos was a clever child. At a very early age he took a screwdriver to his crib and dismantled it into its component parts. This set a pattern. A few years later, when his grandfather bought him a Radio Shack electronics kit, he concocted a "burglar alarm" to keep his siblings (one brother, one sister) out of his bedroom. Moving on to the garage, the venue of choice for so many budding entrepreneurs, the ingenious Bezos proceeded to build a microwave oven driven by solar power. There is, by all accounts, no record of how well it cooked.

Amazon.com opened for business on the Internet in July 1995, and with relentless hype soon became the flagship for the New Economy.

Mike Bezos was an engineer with Exxon, and the family moved several times because of his work. Jeff attended high school in Miami and spent most summers on his grandfather's ranch, living the life of a cattle farmer and driving the tractors.

Defining Moments

In 1986, after graduating in electrical engineering and computer science from Princeton, Bezos headed for Fitel, a high-tech start-up company in New York, where he built a computer network for financial trading. After Fitel Bezos joined Bankers Trust, becoming their youngest vice president in February 1990. From there he moved to D.E. Shaw & Co. The Wall Street firm interviewed him on the strength of a recommendation from one of its partners, who suggested, "he is going to make someone a lot of money someday."

At Shaw, Bezos described his role as a "sort of an entrepreneurial odd-jobs kind of a person," effectively looking for business opportunities in the insurance, software, and Internet sectors. He excelled in the role, helping to set up one of the most successful quantitative hedge funds on Wall Street, and becoming senior vice president in 1992.

Then came his epiphany. Sitting at his computer in the office one day surfing the Internet, Bezos came across an astounding fact. According to usage statistics, the Internet was growing at a rate of 2,300% a year. He sensed an opportunity. Online commerce, he realized, was a natural next step. Being a combination of Wall Street insider and computer nerd, he was perfectly positioned to cash in.

Bezos compiled a list of 20 products that were suitable for selling online. On the list were items such as CDs, magazines, PC software and hardware–and books. The shortlist was quickly whittled down to two contenders–books and music. In the end, he decided on books. His logic was twofold. With more than 1.3 million books in print as against 300,000 music titles, there was simply more to sell. And, perhaps more important, the major book publishers appeared less intimidating than their record company counterparts. The six major record companies had a stranglehold on the popular music distribution business, but the biggest book chain, Barnes & Noble, had only 12% of the industry's total sales.

Quitting his job, Bezos headed out to Seattle. "I will change the economics of the book industry," he is

"We are pioneers and the history of pioneers is not that good." (Jeff Bezos)

reputed to have told one venture capitalist. Ironically, some of the fundraising was carried out from the coffee shop of a Barnes & Noble bookstore.

With no state tax, a wealth of high-tech talent, and a major book distributor on the doorstep—Ingram's warehouse, Oregon—Seattle seemed a perfect place to start his new business. In the garage of his rented home, Bezos and his first three employees set up their computers and began writing software for the new business. He originally planned to call the company Cadabra—a reference to the magic incantation. Fortunately for him, his friends convinced him that, while the name might have spellbinding connotations, it also sounded very similar to "cadaver." Instead, Bezos opted for Amazon, after the world's largest river.

The company, according to its Web site, "opened its virtual doors in July 1995 with a mission to use the Internet to transform book buying into the fastest, easiest, and most enjoyable shopping experience possible." By the beginning of 1999, Amazon.com, Inc. had a market capitalization of an astonishing $6 billion—more than the combined value of Barnes & Noble and Borders, its two largest bookstore competitors. The fourth quarter of 1998 brought net sales of $252.9 million, an increase of 283% over the same period in 1997. With Amazon awash with revenue, analysts and e-commerce commentators seemed unperturbed by the absence of profits.

Bezos, meanwhile, was a model of reassurance. Amazon would reach $1 billion in sales by 2000, he confidently asserted, and sure enough it did. Yet details about when Amazon would make a profit were hazier. Amazon was, said Bezos, in "an investment phase," as might be expected of a company that had only just celebrated its fourth birthday. For a while, investors were more than happy to go along for the ride.

Then, in June 2000, cracks began to appear in the almost unanimous support enjoyed by the star child of the Internet revolution. Holly Becker, e-commerce analyst at Lehman Brothers and a longtime Amazon believer, switched her recommendation on the company from a buy to a neutral. She was, she said, "throwing in the towel on Amazon." Many saw Becker's change of heart as a turning point in the company's fortunes.

Yet Bezos may well have the last laugh. With some 21 million satisfied customers in the year to June 2001, revenue over the same period up by 16%, and a strategic alliance with Internet Service Provider AOL in the bag, Warren Jenson, Amazon.com's chief financial officer, correctly predicted operating profitability in the fourth quarter of 2001. Whether, in the final analysis, Bezos will go down in the business history books as the creator of a viable and long-lived Internet business, or simply as an e-business pioneer, remains to be seen.

Context and Conclusions

Amazon is the totem stock of the Internet evangelists. What the critics will tell you is that through smoke and mirrors, PR, and puff, one man has succeeded in making a fortune through hyping his online business to previously unthought-of heights. What he has created, after all, is nothing more or less than a virtual bookshop, and one that in its first five years didn't turn a profit. But Amazon.com isn't a bellwether stock without reason. Bezos is the quintessential dot-com icon. He proved to the business world that the Internet was about more than the dissemination and exchange of knowledge. He proved that it was possible to overcome fears about purchasing online, that it was possible to drive down transaction costs, and that it was feasible to build an international e-commerce business over the Internet. Bezos is one of the great business pioneers. He had the courage to attempt something that people doubted could be done. Amazon has firmly entrenched itself as a dominant force in e-commerce and as a result of product additions and strategic alliances is now a virtual marketplace. The question is whether it can profitably exploit its position.

Holly Becker, e-commerce analyst at Lehman Brothers and a longtime Amazon believer, switched her recommendation on the company from a buy to a neutral. She was, she said, "throwing in the towel on Amazon."

Close But No Cigar

Scott Blum
A colorful character, Blum survived a brush with the SEC while at his company Pinnacle Micro and went on to found buy.com. buy.com epitomized the gung ho, blindly optimistic philosophy of dot-com mania with its "make money by losing money" strategy. The idea was to sell goods on the Internet at a loss and make money through advertising. Critics sniggered. The "losing money" part went well; unfortunately the "make money" element was lacking. Critics laughed openly. Meanwhile Blum stepped down as C.E.O. in March 1999, and as chairman in October of the same year. He put his less than 50% of shares into a blind trust, raised $100 million in finance, and moved on to Enfrastructure.com, providing "scalable, full-service technology, and infrastructure for high-growth companies."

For More Information

Books:

Saunders, Rebecca. *Business the Amazon.com Way: Secrets of the World's Most Astonishing Web Business.* 2nd ed. New York: John Wiley, 2002.

Spector, Robert. *Amazon.com: Get Big Fast—Inside the Revolutionary Business Model That Changed the World.* New York: HarperBusiness, 2000.

Web Site:

Amazon.com: **www.amazon.com**

"I believe we can still be a footnote in the history of e-commerce." (Jeff Bezos)

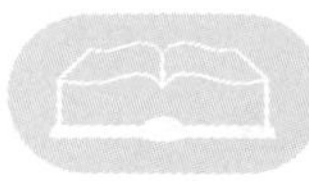

WARREN BUFFETT

Warren Buffett (1930–) had an eye for a deal from an early age. He progressed from childhood race tipster and paper-route king to property owner and stock picker extraordinaire. By the age of 14 the young Buffett had already accumulated enough money to buy 40 acres of farmland. Now in his seventies, he is a multibillionaire—though not one to flaunt his wealth. The Coca-Cola-swilling, ukulele-playing Buffett lives a modest life, occupying an average house and preferring to drive an older car rather than the latest model even though his personal fortune makes him one of the richest men in the world. He is justly one of the most influential people in the finance world.

Buffett's advice on the stockmarkets has been invaluable to millions.

1930	Born.
1934	Publication of *Security Analysis* by Ben Graham and David Dodd.
1950	Attends Columbia Business School.
1951	Graduates from Columbia, starts to invest for a living.
1965	Acquires Berkshire Hathaway (invests $10,000; it is worth $51 million by 1999).
1967	Berkshire Hathaway buys National Indemnity Company and National Fire & Marine Insurance Company.
1969	Winds up investment partnership to concentrate on Berkshire.
1995	Buys major stake in McDonald's.
1996	Acquires GEICO, the sixth-largest U.S. automobile insurer.
1998	Buys Executive Jet Corporation.

BACKGROUND AND RISE

In 1952, an aspiring 21-year-old money manager placed a small advertisement in an Omaha newspaper, inviting people to attend a class on investing. He figured it would be a good way to accustom himself to appearing before audiences. His preparation even involved investing $100 for a Dale Carnegie course on public speaking. Twenty others showed up that day. If that same young man were speaking today, the building would be besieged. He was Warren Buffett, one of the greatest investors of all time.

At the age of six, he would buy six packs of Coca-Cola for a quarter, break them up, and sell the individual bottles for a nickel each.

Born on August 30, 1930, in Omaha, Nebraska, Warren Buffett exhibited the talents that were to make him wealthy at an early age. At the age of six, he would buy six packs of Coca-Cola for a quarter, break them up, and sell the individual bottles for a nickel each. When the young Buffett was stricken with a mysterious illness, he lay in bed figuring out how to get rich. On his recovery he roped his friends into a number of money-making enterprises he had thought up.

He looked for lost golf balls, packaged those he found, and sold them. He also became one of the youngest racing tipsters in the United States when he published *Stable Boy Selections*—his information on the hot horses of the moment. His record for picking winners is not known, but if it was anything like his later talent for picking stocks, he must have made a few gamblers very rich.

When Warren was 12 his father, Howard Buffett, won a seat in Congress and the family moved to Washington, D.C. The move was initially unpopular with Buffett. However, he changed his mind when he realized the commercial potential of the U.S. capital. He took on five paper routes at once, delivering a staggering 500 papers each morning and earning the equivalent of a man's full-time salary of $175. When he was still only 14 he had earned $1,200—enough to enable him to buy 40 acres of farmland in Nebraska and rent it out for farming.

DEFINING MOMENTS

After another business foray in high school, installing overhauled arcade games in barbershops, Buffett decided to enhance his natural flair for commerce with a formal business education. He was admitted to the Wharton School at the University of Pennsylvania.

But Buffett did not complete his studies at Wharton. He found the theoretical aspects of business dull and discovered nothing in the curriculum to slake his thirst for practical knowledge. He finished his studies in business and economics at the University of Nebraska, in the meantime organizing paper routes for the *Lincoln*

"Never is there just one cockroach in the kitchen." (Warren Buffett)

Journal on the side. At 19 he applied to Harvard Business School, but was refused admission. He turned to Columbia Business School, where he studied finance under investment guru Ben Graham.

It was in reading the stock market that Buffett found his true vocation. His first foray into stocks had been as a boy of 11 (of course it helped that his father was a stockbroker). Young Buffett bought three shares in Cities Service preferred at $38 a share; the stock promptly fell to $27. When it had recovered to $40 he sold, making a small profit. The stock then rose to $200, leaving the boy kicking himself and teaching him the value of long-term investment.

Determined to make a living by investing, Buffett plowed his energy and all the savings amassed from his various enterprises into the stock market. From 1951 to 1956 he turned $9,800 into $140,000. News spread about the new whiz kid investor, and more and more people asked him to invest their money for them. What started with friends spread to the general public, and soon Buffett was forming limited partnerships and taking a 25% cut of any return above 4%.

Once Buffett started investing as a career, he developed his own personal investment strategy. He began by looking for stocks that offered outstanding value—those that were relatively cheap given their asset value—and then holding those shares for the long term. "Lethargy, bordering on sloth, should remain the cornerstone of an investment style," he has said. He was heavily influenced by the theories of Ben Graham, his former teacher at Columbia and the coauthor of the investment classic *Security Analysis* (1934). Buffett eventually took Graham's investing strategies a step further by seeking out companies whose shares were inexpensive compared to their growth prospects. This approach required assessing a company's intangible assets, such as brand value. In this Buffett was ahead of his time. The area of intangible assets is now the subject of growing interest from business academics, but in the 1950s it was largely neglected. Buffett, however, was not unduly interested in theoretical niceties.

Theory was all very well, as Buffett had noted at Wharton, but how would his strategy work in practice? The answer proved to be, phenomenally well. Between 1957 and 1966 the investment partnership that Buffett managed posted an amazing 1,156% return—against 122.9% over the same period for the Dow Jones Industrial Average. A partner's investment of $10,000 would, after deducting Buffett's share, have returned $80,420. Buffett continued to outperform the market, making a 36% return in 1967 and a 59% return in 1968 in a speculative market, which was not particularly suited to his particular investment strategy.

In 1969, to the surprise of his managers, Buffett called it a day. Concerned about maintaining his performance in an uncongenial investment climate, he decided to wind up the partnership.

Since 1969 his attentions have been focused entirely on his investment vehicle Berkshire Hathaway, the publicly listed company he acquired in 1965. The markets may go up or down, but over time Buffett has delivered consistently for his shareholders. His legendary, almost uncanny, knack of picking stocks has earned him the epithet "the Sage of Omaha." On the strength of his company's performance, it's a tag he undoubtedly deserves. A $10,000 investment in Berkshire Hathaway in 1965 would have been worth over $50 million by the end of 2000. Investors who backed the S&P 500 Index would have accumulated some $500,000, a paltry amount by comparison. Along the way, Buffett has picked stocks such as Coca-Cola and American Express when they were at a low ebb. On the other hand, he has resisted the temptation to be drawn into media-fueled stock bubbles such as the Internet boom of the 1990s. "As a group, lemmings have a rotten image," notes Buffett, "but no individual lemming has ever received bad press."

The markets may go up or down, but over time Buffett has delivered consistently for his shareholders. His legendary, almost uncanny, knack of picking stocks has earned him the epithet "the Sage of Omaha."

Buffett himself has remained relatively unaffected by the plaudits heaped upon him. A modest man, he has few indulgences other than a corporate jet. Even then he bought a small, used plane for Berkshire; when he traded up to a more expensive model, he named it "the Indefensible." He lives in an average home in Omaha, famously drives an old car, and maintains a fairly small office with few staff. His main hobby, it seems, is reading company reports, in which he reportedly maintains an avid interest despite the many thousands he's undoubtedly plowed through.

Context and Conclusions

Warren Buffett is one of the greatest investors of all time. What lifts him above his peers is a determination to stick to his investment principles. Companies have risen and fallen, one minute at the height of fashion, the next on the bankruptcy pile. Buffett has steadfastly refused to jump on any bandwagon. Unlike so many other investors who are nursing their burns, Buffett let the dot-com train roll on by. Famously, he refuses to invest in businesses that he doesn't understand—which includes most high-tech companies. Instead Buffett has made a fortune for himself and his shareholders by investing in undervalued companies for the long term. It's Buffett's willingness to buck the trend that makes him worth his "Sage of Omaha" tag.

For More Information

Book:

Lowenstein, Roger. *Buffett: The Making of an American Capitalist*. New York: Doubleday, 1996.

 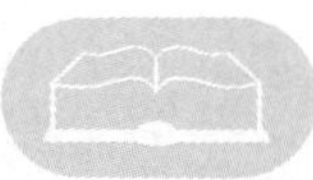    

ANDREW CARNEGIE

Andrew Carnegie (1835–1919) was one of the finest businessmen of his generation. A significant proportion of his achievements fell within the 19th century, yet his impact on the commercial revolution that took place in the United States as the 19th century gave way to the 20th is huge. Carnegie was arguably the first of a generation of businessmen who pioneered industrial growth in the United States and throughout the world on the back of steel manufacturing and the building of railroads. At the end of his long career he had built the largest steel company in the United States and amassed a vast personal fortune.

Carnegie forged a business empire from steel.

1835	Born.
1848	Family moves to Allegheny near Pittsburgh, Pennsylvania. Carnegie, aged 12, takes job in cotton mill.
1870	Builds first blast furnace. Experiments with the Bessemer process.
1874	Opens steel furnace at Braddock.
1880	Plant operating for 24 hours a day with profits of $2 million.
1881	Company reorganizes as Carnegie Bros. & Co.
1882	Carnegie acquires coke-producing interests of Henry C. Frick.
1886	Writes *Triumphant Democracy*.
1889	Moves to New York to conduct R&D into the steel manufacturing process. "Gospel of wealth" article published. Steel production 332,111 tons.
1899	Steel production 2,663,412 tons. Carnegie buys out Frick.
1901	Frick and J. Pierpont Morgan purchase the Carnegie Company for $500 million.
1919	Dies.

BACKGROUND AND RISE

Carnegie was arguably the first of a generation of businessmen who pioneered industrial growth in the United States. . .on the back of steel manufacturing and the building of railroads.

Andrew Carnegie was born in Dunfermline on November 25, 1835. In 1848 economic depression persuaded Carnegie's father to emigrate with his family to the United States. The family settled in a colony of Scots gathered at Slabtown, Allegheny, near Pittsburgh, and the 12-year-old Andrew took work in a local cotton mill.

Leaving the cotton mill, he got a job at the Pittsburgh Telegraph Office as a messenger boy. Thomas A. Scott, superintendent of the western division of the Pennsylvania Railroad at the time, spotted Carnegie's potential and appointed him as his secretary at $50 a month, in those days a handsome salary for one so young. It was Scott who set Carnegie on the path to riches by showing him the likely gains of investing in startup companies. Acting on a tip from Scott, Carnegie bought stock in the Adams Express Company using money from his mother, who remortgaged her house. Shortly afterward he borrowed money to invest in a venture commercially exploiting the invention of the sleeping car for the railroad.

During the Civil War, Carnegie served with Scott in Washington. Then, with the Union victory secured, he took Scott's old position as superintendent of the western division of the Pennsylvania Railroad. But his entrepreneurial instincts were not satisfied, and he soon left the railroads to set up an iron bridge building firm, the Keystone Bridge Company. He was also involved in several other speculative ventures that proved successful.

DEFINING MOMENTS

While Carnegie was busy hustling in the United States, Henry Bessemer, an inventor and businessman, was working on a manufacturing process in England that would change industry the world over. The Bessemer process allowed the industrialized production of steel from iron. Carnegie often visited the United Kingdom, and on one visit he came across the Bessemer converter. It was a revelation.

Hurrying back to the United States, Carnegie formed Carnegie, McCandless, & Co., built his first blast furnace in 1870, and began experimenting with the Bessemer process. He opened a steel furnace at Braddock and, by 1880, the plant was operating 24 hours a day and producing annual profits of $2 million. In 1881 the company reorganized, becoming Carnegie Bros. & Co. Carnegie

"The man who dies rich dies disgraced." (Andrew Carnegie)

  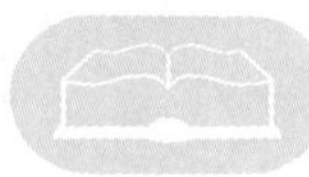    

held the controlling interest. In 1882 he acquired the coke-producing interests of Henry C. Frick, who became his most trusted associate.

In 1889 Carnegie moved to New York to continue his research into the steel manufacturing process. He also spent six months of the year with his family in Scotland. In his absence Carnegie left Frick, as chair of Carnegie Bros., in charge of the day-to-day running of the company. When Frick took over, the company was a collection of disparate threads—the threads being individual mills and furnaces dotted about Pittsburgh. Frick wove these threads together into a fabric: an organization that would become the biggest steelmaking enterprise in the world. He centralized the management structure and integrated production. The firm was transformed into the Carnegie Steel Company, valued at $25 million.

Unfortunately for Carnegie, Frick also presided over one of the most notorious incidents in U.S. corporate history. In an attempt to drive down costs and boost profits, Frick reduced piecework rates. Incensed, the Amalgamated Iron and Steel Workers Union called its members at the Carnegie Homestead plant out on strike. Instead of settling through negotiation, Frick inflamed the situation by arranging to bring in 300 strikebreakers.

When the day came and the strikebreakers arrived on barges down the Monongahela River, complete with armed guard, all hell broke loose. At the end of a day of pitched battle, ten men lay dead and a further 60 were wounded. Homestead was placed under martial law.

Carnegie, in Scotland at the time, was irate. It was not just the disruption to the company that he rued; Frick had gone against his explicit instructions not to use strikebreakers. For Carnegie it was a matter of personal ethics. Nevertheless, being the controlling owner and, as such, ultimately responsible, he had to bear the dark stain of the workers' blood on his reputation for many years after the debacle.

Although Carnegie refrained from criticizing Frick in public, their relationship never recovered. The company continued to thrive, improving annual production of steel from 332,111 tons in 1889 to 2,663,412 in 1899, and profits from $2 million to $40 million. But, because of the deteriorating relationship between them, Carnegie took the opportunity to buy Frick out for a handsome $15 million in 1889. Even this act of severance failed to quell the personal animosity between the two men. In 1901 Frick returned with the backing of the notorious J. Pierpont Morgan and purchased the Carnegie Company for $500 million, establishing the U.S. Steel Corporation which, valued at $1.4 billion, was the biggest steel company in the world.

Context and Conclusions

Carnegie played a leading role in the industrialization of the United States. As a poor Scottish boy who became one of the wealthiest men in the world, his rise from rags to riches was extraordinary. In his time he was criticized and praised in equal measure. Some saw him as a smug, tyrannical, autocratic, arrogant slave driver; others as a wise, benevolent, enlightened entrepreneur. Of the many qualities Carnegie possessed, one in particular stands out: he was an opportunist who acted on his instincts. He took any opportunity to promote his business interests. When he invited the Prince of Wales to ride a Pennsylvania Railroad engine, for example, he did it to secure business favors rather than to increase his social standing.

Some saw him as a smug, tyrannical, autocratic, arrogant slave driver; others as a wise, benevolent, enlightened entrepreneur.

Carnegie will be remembered as much for his philanthropy as for his business adventures. In later life, guided by his ethical beliefs, he gave away the greater part of his fortune. He set up a trust fund "for the improvement of mankind." The Carnegie Institute of Pittsburgh, the Carnegie Institute of Technology, the Carnegie Institution of Washington, and three thousand public libraries were built with this trust money.

When the "King of Steel" died in August 1919, he had already given away $350 million of his fortune.

For More Information

Books:

Carnegie, Andrew. *The Empire of Business*. New York: Doubleday, Doran, & Co, 1902.

Mackay, James. *Andrew Carnegie: His Life and Times*. New York: John Wiley, 1998.

Web Site:

Carnegie Corporation of New York: **www.carnegie.org**

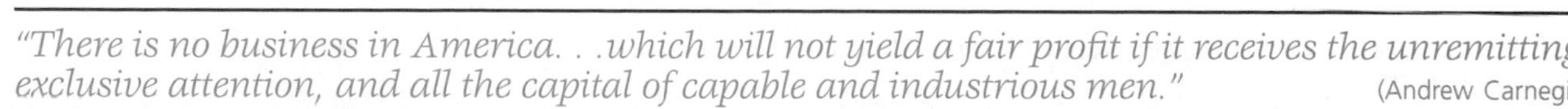
"There is no business in America. . .which will not yield a fair profit if it receives the unremitting, exclusive attention, and all the capital of capable and industrious men." (Andrew Carnegie)

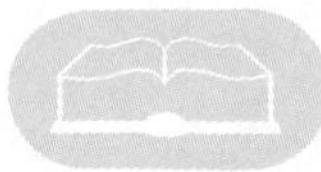

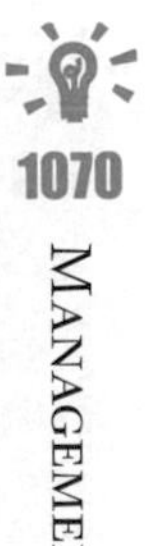

STEPHEN CASE

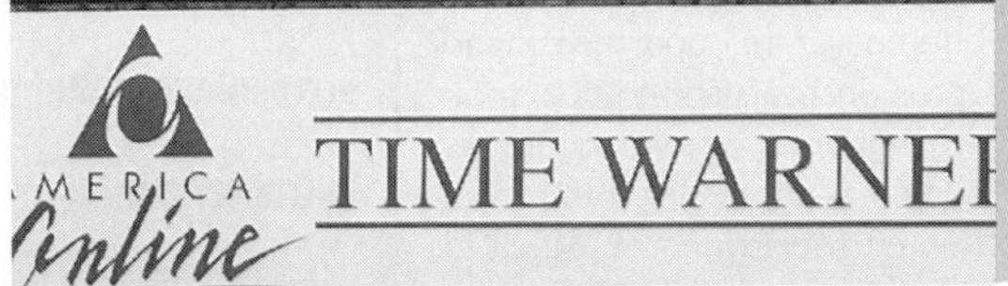

Steve Case, born in 1958, former C.E.O. and cofounder of America Online (AOL) is Chairman of the Board of AOL Time Warner. A political science graduate, he worked in various marketing and sales positions before eventually starting up Quantum Computers, which offered online services to users of Commodore computers.

Renamed America Online (AOL) in 1989, the company went public in 1992 with 150,000 subscribers. By 1996 that figure was 4.6 million. In 1998 Case wiped out a chunk of the competition by buying CompuServe and its 2.5 million subscribers, as well as Netscape.

The pinnacle of Case's deal making came in early 2000 with the shock announcement of a $166 billion merger with media giant Time Warner. By 2001 AOL had 30 million subscribers worldwide.

Case at the height of his success.

1958	Born.
1979	Graduates from Williams College, joins Procter & Gamble.
1983	Gets job at Control Video.
1989	Quantum Computers renamed America Online (AOL).
1991	Case becomes C.E.O. of AOL.
1992	America Online I.P.O.
1996	4.6 million subscribers.
1998	Acquires CompuServe.
2000	Announces merger with Time Warner.
2001	AOL has 30 million subscribers. Launches new improved AOL 7.0.

BACKGROUND AND RISE

Steve Case, born August 21, 1958 in Honolulu, Hawaii, is a world apart from the Marc Andreessens (Netscape) and David Filos (Yahoo!) of the New Economy. Instead of taking the standard geekster's path to billionaire status by studying computer sciences or engineering in some West Coast tech hotspot like Stanford—he majored in political science at Williams College, Massachusetts.

The pinnacle of Case's deal making came in early 2000 with the shock announcement of a $166 billion merger with media giant Time Warner.

He followed this by working in marketing and sales, first at Procter & Gamble (haircare products) and then at PepsiCo (the Pizza Hut division). It was only then that Case paid any attention to the Internet.

Recalling the first time he logged on, Case said: "I thought it was magical then, I still think it's magical today. The center of my world is consumers. Every day I wake up and say, 'How can we make America Online more interesting, more useful, more fun, more affordable, so that it will attract a broader audience?' Because I still remember that excitement 13 years ago when I first connected to an online service."

After his taste of the corporate world, Case joined a small video games service company, Control Video, in 1983. He had always had a touch of the entrepreneur about him. As a kid he sold lime juice from his backyard at two cents a cup, took charge of the obligatory paper route, and started a mail-order company, Case Enterprises, with his brother Dan.

While the video company wasn't a storming success, it did introduce Case to Jim Kinsey and Mark Seriff. It was the perfect combination: Seriff had technology in his blood (he had worked on Arpanet, the forerunner of the Internet), Kinsey was a finance man, and Case provided the sales and marketing know-how. Together the trio founded Quantum Computers. The company provided online services to users of the soon-to-be defunct Commodore computer. Commodore imploded, but America Online (AOL), as the Quantum business was renamed in 1989, went from strength to strength.

DEFINING MOMENTS

Case instinctively knew what the customer wanted. Not burdened with a technological background, he could pitch the product at the average consumer, and make the consumer experience as simple and as user-friendly as possible. "Our strategy has always been crystal clear," he said in a 1998 interview. "Consumers want one place where they can find good Internet content and meet interesting people. And they want someone to make it easy for them."

America Online entered the market in 1992. At the time it had a membership of some 150,000. By 1996, with the help of an innovative marketing strategy involving the shipping of AOL CDs offering a free trial, 4.6 million

"The Internet is an elite organization; most of the population of the world have never made a phone call." (Noam Chomsky)

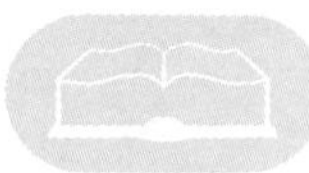

had signed up. The company's marketing guru, Jan Brandt, even put disks on the office wall bearing the message, "Resistance is futile."

AOL dominated its main rivals, CompuServe and Prodigy, although Microsoft's MSN was still a distant threat. Yet success brought its problems. AOL replaced usage charges with a flat-fee structure and usage figures shot up. People spent more time online, the systems couldn't cope, and the service caved in under the pressure.

Case hired Bob Pittman, cofounder of MTV, to take over the day-to-day running of the company. Pittman was a media man who understood content delivery. He also knew how to deal with a corporation the size of AOL. Making money out of the subscriptions, however, proved a tough nut to crack. The more users AOL signed up, the more AOL spent on infrastructure and maintaining quality of service. Case and Pittman formulated a business model in which content sucked in subscribers who then spent money. Surely if they had a captive audience, advertisers would be falling over themselves to get onto AOL. That's what they figured, and they were right.

Pittman attacked costs, driving down customer acquisition costs from close to $400 per new subscriber to below $100. Concessions were sold to bring in money: 1-800-Flowers bought the flower concession for $25 million; Amazon paid $19 million to be the exclusive bookseller on the external aol.com Web site; Barnes & Noble went one better, paying $40 million to be the exclusive bookseller inside.

Active on the acquisitions trail, Case engineered a takeover of rival CompuServe in 1998 (adding 2.5 million subscribers), and in the same year took the opportunity to acquire Netscape for $4.2 billion. Then, in early 2000, AOL made the shock announcement of a planned $166 billion merger with media giant Time Warner. Case is now Chairman of the Board of AOL Time Warner, Inc.

Roughly 80% of the world's online users log on to AOL in some way. And while they are there, traipsing around the online shopping malls, they part with over $10 billion dollars a year. AOL itself saw revenues of over $4.5 billion in 1999 and nearly $6.9 billion in 2000. As of September 2001, AOL had 30 million subscribers worldwide.

Context and Conclusions

Steve Case did not pore over circuit boards in the garage to build a tech empire! He took an alternative route to IT stardom. When he saw the Internet, he figured there would be plenty of people who would struggle to get to grips with the technology. Until the advent of the Internet, most home entertainment involved turning on a switch and choosing a channel. If you could read the television schedules, then you had pretty much mastered the art of TV use. The Internet changed the rules. For a start, access was via a computer, which had to be correctly configured, and then there were the browser and the URLs, the server addresses, the e-mail protocols, and much, much more. For the uninitiated, logging on to and navigating the Internet was the equivalent of string theory and quantum mechanics. Case changed all that with the AOL CD. He made the Internet experience easy for millions worldwide, and in so doing built a company that was effectively able to take over one of the world's largest media companies, Time Warner.

> **"Consumers want one place where they can find good Internet content and meet interesting people. And they want someone to make it easy for them."**

CLOSE BUT NO CIGAR

Jeffrey Wilkins/William Von Meister
Trading a job in the burglar alarm business for one in the IT industry, Wilkins founded CompuServe in 1969 to provide excess computer capacity to other corporations. It shifted in 1978 to providing services to the owners of personal computers, and shifted again in the age of the Internet to become a provider of online services. The first service to offer e-mail and real-time chat, the company was bought out by competitors AOL in 1998. Wilkins meanwhile had left to found Metatec International, "a full-service information distribution company offering businesses optical disk manufacturing, supply chain solutions, and Internet-based information and software distribution services."

Von Meister was the entrepreneur who founded a phone-in data service for PC owners—the first purely consumer online service—called The Source. The Readers Digest Association bought it in 1980 for $6 million and in 1988 sold it on to CompuServe, who closed it down. Ironically, von Meister also founded Control Video Corporation in 1981. The company was funded, among others, by Dan Case II, Steve Case's brother, a banker at Hambrecht & Quist. Von Meister was ousted from the company by its backers in 1983 on the day Steve Case arrived. He died in 1995.

For More Information

Book:
Swisher, Kara. *Aol.com: How Steve Case Beat Bill Gates, Nailed the Netheads, and Made Millions in the War for the Web*. New York: Random House, 1998.

Web Site:
Aol Anywhere: **www.aol.com**

(John A. Roth)

MICHAEL DELL

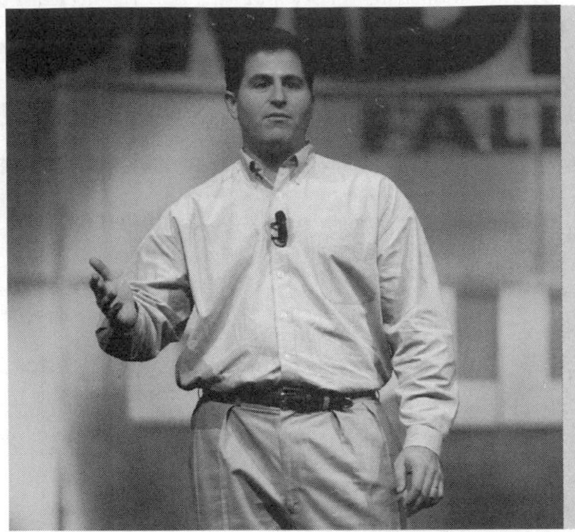

Michael Dell (1965–) was always going to be a winner. After all, how many high school students earn more than their teachers? Dell progressed from selling newspaper subscriptions to selling computers.

Yet it wasn't the product that made him wealthy, it was the way he sold it. The Dell corporation pioneered direct selling of computers. It is also an excellent example of a company succeeding by sticking to its founding principles: build to order, keep low stocks, sell direct, understand your customer. And the Internet was a godsend for Dell. What better way of reaching the global consumer? Dell's success with the direct selling business model has made him the youngest C.E.O. ever of a Fortune 500 company.

Dell's direct approach was a hit with his customers.

1965	Born.
1977	Aged 12, sells stamps by catalog.
1983	Enters the University of Texas at Austin.
1984	Drops out of college to found Dell Computer.
1988	Dell Computer's first year revenue $257.8 million.
1994	www.dell.com launched.
1997	Dell's online sales, begun in 1996, exceed $3 million a day.
2000	Online sales reach $50 million.

BACKGROUND AND RISE

Michael Dell started his business career as a boy. Born in Houston, Texas, on February 23, 1965, he came across his first commercial opportunity when he was just 12 years old. Like many children his age, Dell was an enthusiastic collector of stamps. Where he differed from his peers was in his approach. Dell didn't trade stamps with his friends at school, he contacted the auction houses and sent them his catalog. When anyone placed an order he went out to find the required stamps. His direct sales method and entrepreneurial acumen were an early sign of what was to come.

Dell brought new focus and intensity to his early commercial forays. As a summer job he sold newspaper subscriptions for the *Houston Post*. He quickly realized that calling people at random using the list of telephone numbers supplied by the company was not the best way to win new business. Instead he targeted two distinct groups, newlyweds and new homeowners. He obtained lists of applicants for wedding licenses from the local courthouse. From another source he compiled a list of people who had recently applied for mortgages. He then wrote a personalized message and carried out his own direct mail campaign. Subscriptions poured in. When the new school term began Dell was asked as part of an economics assignment to complete a tax return. After calculating his profits Dell estimated his income at $18,000. His teacher, assuming a mistake, corrected his return by moving the decimal point. She was dismayed to discover that the mistake was hers. Dell earned more than she did.

Low costs and high profit margins are a recipe for an exceptional business. In its first eight years Dell Computer grew at an astonishing annual rate of 80%.

DEFINING MOMENTS

Dell's career really started while studying at the University of Texas at Austin. By then the boy who had dismantled and reassembled the motherboard of his Apple II computer at 13 had grown into a fledgling entrepreneur, making money from his computing hobby. Dell would rebuild computers and sell them. Still at college, he started a company called PCs Limited, headquartered in his dorm room. Ignoring his parents' advice to concentrate on his studies, he decided the lure of business was too great and concentrated his efforts on his PC company.

In 1984 the Dell Computer Corporation was founded with just $1,000 in capital. With such a small investment Dell was forced to develop a business model that required little capital outlay. He decided to build to order. This eliminated the need to tie up working capital in inventory. The company carried only around 11 days' worth of inventory—and still does. Compare this to the 45 days' worth of inventory in an average, nondirect distribution channel and the cost savings are obvious. Building to order also allowed Dell to cut out the middleman, retaining more profit and reducing selling costs from a typical 12% of sales to a mere 4–6% of sales.

Low costs and high profit margins are a recipe for an exceptional business. In its first eight years Dell Computer grew at an astonishing annual rate of 80%.

"Ideas are a commodity. Execution of them is not." (Michael Dell)

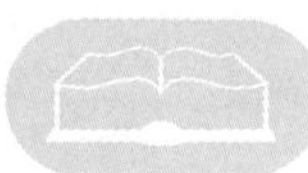

Even when it slowed down, it was still growing at over 50% a year. By the middle of 2000 its yearly sales were up to $27 billion.

Such a successful business model has attracted its imitators. Companies such as Compaq and Gateway have adopted a similar model. None, however, seem to be able to capture the Dell magic. "There is a popular idea now that if you reduce your inventory and build to order, you'll be just like Dell. Well, that's one part of the puzzle, but there are other parts too," Dell has said. He explains the company's success as "a disciplined approach to understanding how we create value in the PC industry, selecting the right markets, staying focused on a clear business model, and just executing."

Dell has built more than a simple direct selling company. His company's success is closely linked to its relationship with the customer. He knows that the company must not only sell but deliver. Dell Computer has made good use of its direct communication with the consumer. The result? A strong brand, low customer acquisition costs, and high customer loyalty. Dell asks his customers to complain so he can keep the company at the cutting edge of consumer needs. The company once ran an ad that said, "to all our nit-picky, over-demanding, ask-awkward-questions customers. Thank you, and keep up the good work." Few computer companies—or any other company, come to that—would have the confidence to run an ad like this.

With his innate enthusiasm for technology Dell was quick to realize the potential of the Internet. Harnessing its power to reach a wide audience at little cost, the company swiftly moved its selling operations online. "The Internet for us is a dream come true," Dell has said. "It's like zero-variable-cost transaction. The only thing better would be mental telepathy." The figures support the point. Dell began e-commerce in 1996. By 1997 the company's online sales exceeded $3 million a day. The comparable figure for 2000 was $50 million. Half the company's sales are Web-enabled.

When it comes to strategy Dell is no slouch. As the year 2000 approached all the talk in the industry (apart from Y2K worries) was about the imminent demise of the PC. Analysts predicted that PC sales would slump as consumers sought mobile computing solutions. Donald Selkin, chief investment strategist at Joseph Gunnar, the New York securities and banking firm, said of Dell Computer, "I believe its glory days are over; I hate to say it, but it's old technology."

Others believe that Dell's success is founded on a business model rather than a particular product. As if to prove the point, Dell has expanded into areas such as servers and storage network devices. In the quarter ending April 30, 2000, for example, sales of these products accounted for 48% of the systems sales total. There was a 100% increase in sales of storage products, and Dell's machines accounted for 40% of the worldwide industry growth in the server market. Michael Dell says, "I believe we have the right business model for the Internet age. We have a significant lead in dealing direct with customers and suppliers."

The youngest C.E.O. ever to run a Fortune 500 company, Michael Dell has joined the ranks of the most revered entrepreneurs in America.

The Dell Computer Corporation had been consistently ranked number two in the world in terms of liquidity, profitability, and growth among all computer systems companies, and number one in the United States. With that sort of performance, many a C.E.O. would be pleased to take a bow and enjoy the applause. Michael Dell merely describes it as "a great start."

Context and Conclusions

The youngest C.E.O. ever to run a Fortune 500 company, Michael Dell has joined the ranks of the most revered entrepreneurs in America. He is credited as the man who took the direct sales model and elevated it to an art form. Dell Computer may not be the biggest company in the world—yet. Nor are its products the most innovative. Yet Dell has built a benchmark company, demonstrating how best to structure a business in order to reap the most reward from new technologies.

For More Information

Book:

Dell, Michael, with Catherine Fredman. *Direct from Dell: Strategies That Revolutionized an Industry*. New York: HarperInformation, 2000.

Web Site:

Dell: **www.dell.com**

"When a business goes wrong, look only to the people who are running it." (Michael Dell)

WALTER ELIAS DISNEY

Walt Disney (1901–1966) started with an idea for a cartoon and finished with a film studio. Over a 43-year career in Hollywood, he and his studio won 48 Academy Awards and 7 Emmys as well as a host of other awards. He pioneered the cartoon as an entertainment medium with full-length cartoon features like *Snow White and the Seven Dwarfs*, *Dumbo*, and *Fantasia*. Under his guidance the Disney entertainment machine also produced family film favorites such as *Mary Poppins* and wildlife features such as *The Vanishing Prairie* among its 100-plus films. Today the company that Disney created spans a huge entertainment industry that even his, the most fertile of imaginations, could never have conceived.

Disney and one of his most popular creations.

1901	Born.
1918	Tries to enlist for World War I, at age 16, but is rejected.
1920	Creates his first original animated characters.
1925	Marries employee Lillian Bounds.
1928	Creates Mickey Mouse.
1937	First feature-length musical animation, *Snow White and the Seven Dwarfs*, premieres.
1940	Disney and over 1,000 staff occupy the Burbank Studios.
1955	Disneyland opens.
1964	Conceives Experimental Prototype Community of Tomorrow (Epcot).
1966	Dies.
1971	Disney World opens in Orlando, Florida, with Epcot to follow in 1982.

BACKGROUND AND RISE

When World War I arrived, Disney tried to enlist in the U.S. Army. Unable to produce his birth certificate, he was rejected as being too young.

Born in Chicago, Illinois, on December 5, 1901, Walt Disney was raised by his parents on a farm near Marceline, Missouri. As a child he showed above average ability. At the tender age of seven he sold sketches to neighbors. His interest in the arts continued at McKinley High School in Chicago where he concentrated on drawing and photography. In the evenings he studied at the Chicago Academy of Fine Arts.

When World War I arrived, Disney tried to enlist in the U.S. Army. Unable to produce his birth certificate, he was rejected as being too young. Instead he traveled to France with the Red Cross and spent his time driving an ambulance decorated with his own cartoons.

Settling in Kansas City after the war, Disney embarked on a career as a cartoonist. In 1920, while working for Kansas City Film Ads, he created his first original animated characters. In May 1922 he started his own company, Laugh-O-grams. The laughs were short-lived as the company quickly ran into financial difficulties, and Disney decided to skip town. Emboldened by the spirit of youth, he left for Hollywood armed only with his drawing equipment, an idea for a cartoon, and the suit he stood up in.

DEFINING MOMENTS

Disney's new venture began where so many great U.S. corporate dreams have started—in a garage. Together with his brother Roy, Disney launched Disney Brothers Studio. He started out with $500 borrowed from his uncle, $200 from Roy, and $2,500 from his parents, who mortgaged their house to find the money. Before long Disney was out of the garage and into the back of a Hollywood real estate office. The first work that he sold was a series of featurettes based on Lewis Carroll's Alice character.

Mickey Mouse was born in 1928. There are several versions of how Disney came up with the idea of the little mouse. The most frequently recounted story is that a flash of inspiration came to him on the way home from a disastrous business meeting in which he was forced to relinquish control of his most successful character at the time—Oswald the Rabbit. Daydreaming on the train to Hollywood, he recalled the mice that had been frequent visitors to his old office. Disney wanted to call his new character Mortimer. His wife—displaying a more acute instinct for marketing—persuaded him to christen his creation Mickey Mouse. Mickey made his debut in the first ever sound cartoon *Steamboat Willie*. It was November 1928 and Disney was just 26.

Disney continued to innovate within the cartoon medium. *Silly Symphonies* introduced Technicolor to cartoons, and in 1937 he premiered the first feature-length

"Of all the things I've done, the most vital is coordinating the talents of those who work for us and pointing them towards a certain goal."

(Walt Disney)

musical animation, *Snow White and the Seven Dwarfs*. Disney took a huge risk with *Snow White*. The film was the first of its kind. The $2 million it cost to make was a huge amount in the 1930s, particularly in the middle of the Great Depression. Fortunately for Disney, the gamble paid off, and the studios followed *Snow White* with other full-length animated classics including *Pinocchio*, *Dumbo*, and *Bambi*.

By 1940 Disney and over 1,000 staff had occupied the Burbank Studios. For some time Disney's role had been that of a catalyst; he no longer drew any of the studio's output, nor had he done so since the early 1920s. In his own words he was "a little bee. I go from one area to another, and gather pollen and sort of stimulate everyone." The worker bees in Disney's hive weren't always impressed with Disney. Many resented his reluctance to acknowledge the contribution of the studio artists. Indeed, he wasn't an easy man to work for. Frequently neurotic and obsessive, he imposed strict rules at his studio. Anyone caught cursing in mixed company was fired on the spot, and despite Disney's own preference for a pencil mustache, facial hair was forbidden for all male employees.

During the 1940s the Disney studio became embroiled in a series of labor disputes. He was also a member of the Motion Picture Alliance for the Preservation of American Ideals—an organization which sought out "communists, radicals, and crackpots" in the movie business. In 1947 he testified before the House Un-American Activities Committee, denouncing a number of employees at his studios as communist sympathizers. The fallout from these events took years to dissipate.

World War II had temporarily sidelined the Walt Disney studio's output. During the war most of the Disney facilities were given over to the making of propaganda and health films commissioned by the U.S. government. The studio's small nongovernmental output consisted of comedy shorts to pep up morale. After the war Disney continued to hone his craft and vary the studio's productions. Cartoons were joined by films combining live action and animation, and "true-life adventures" portraying animals in their natural habitat.

In 1955 Disney took his brand in a new direction. The Disneyland theme park in Anaheim, California, was to be a living embodiment of the Disney movies; a magical land where children and adults could mingle with their favorite cartoon stars from the big screen. Disney's investment was $17 million. It was another big risk for him, but Disneyland was a great hit, with Mickey and his friends greeting a million people in its first seven weeks and many millions more since.

At the same time, Disney continued to push Disney products on television. He supplied television with the *Wonderful World of Color*, exploiting the lack of programming in what was still a comparatively new medium—color television.

From the mid-60s onwards one project consumed the final years of Disney's life. The plan was to build a Disney World with a social dimension. Disney was interested in solving the problems afflicting urban living in America. His answer was the Experimental Prototype Community of Tomorrow (Epcot)—the equivalent of a gigantic Ideal Home Exhibition for urban life.

The Disneyland theme park in Anaheim, California, was to be a living embodiment of the Disney movies; a magical land where children and adults could mingle with their favorite cartoon stars from the big screen.

Disney World opened in October 1971. Located in Florida, it was built over 43 square miles and included an amusement theme park, hotel complex, airport, and, 11 years later, the futuristic Epcot Center. Like its Californian relation, Disney World was a success. Disney, however, was not present to witness the fruition of his plans. He died on December 15, 1966.

Context and Conclusions

Walt Disney is an icon of the 20th century and an American folk hero. To many, his name conjures up an image of wholesome homespun entertainment laced with good old-fashioned American family values. While this may have been true of his studio's output, Disney himself was a tough, tenacious, and driven businessman with a sizeable ego.

His innovative work ranged from celebrated animated feature films to futuristic amusement parks. The magic of Disney is, however, nowhere more evident than in the fact that such a complicated and often difficult man could attract such talented individuals to his studios and somehow persuade them to produce their very best work. Critics may carp about his management style, but the vision and drive that spawned a billion dollar international entertainment company was down to one man—Walt Disney.

For More Information

Books:

Byrne, Eleanor, and Martin McQuillan. *Deconstructing Disney*. London: Pluto Press, 1999.

Giroux, Henry A. *The Mouse That Roared: Disney and the End of Innocence*. Lanham, MD: Rowman & Littlefield, 1999.

Nardo, Don. *Walt Disney*. San Diego, CA: Lucent Books, 2000.

Schickel, Richard. *The Disney Version: The Life, Times, Art, and Commerce of Walt Disney*. Chicago: Ivan R. Dee, 1997.

Sherman, Robert B., and Richard M. Sherman. *Walt's Time: From Before to Beyond*. Santa Clarita, CA: Camphor Tree Publishers, 1998.

Web Site:

Disney.com: **www.disney.com**

(Walt Disney)

George Eastman

"You push the button, we do the rest." The well-known advertising phrase was coined by George Eastman (1854–1932), the U.S. industrialist who brought photography to the masses. Before Eastman's intervention, photography was the province of a small number of specialists who could both understand and physically maneuver the cumbersome technical machinery necessary to take a small picture. Eastman reduced photography to a simple process, making it accessible to all. In addition to his role as an innovator, he brought enlightened management practices to his company, the Eastman Kodak Company—practices that were far ahead of their time. During his tenure the Eastman photographic empire grew from one assistant to over 13,000 employees and from a small room to the 55-acre, 95-building Kodak Park Works in Rochester, New York.

Eastman developed a portable camera. The world did the rest.

1854	Born.
1874	Starts work at the Rochester Savings Bank on $15 per week.
1878	Takes up photography.
1880	Patents a dry plate and a machine for mass-producing it.
1881	Takes Henry A. Strong as partner.
1884	The Eastman Dry Plate and Film Company incorporated.
1885	Advertises his revolutionary new photographic film.
1888	The word KODAK registered as a trademark.
1899	"Wage dividend" strategy implemented.
1919	Hands one-third of his company holdings—$10 million—to his employees.
1932	Dies.

Background and Rise

The youngest of three children, Eastman was born in the village of Waterville, 20 miles southwest of Utica, in upstate New York. Aged five, Eastman moved with his family to Rochester. Sadly, his father died unexpectedly, leaving the Eastman family in financial straits.

Eastman never made it to Santo Domingo. Instead he became obsessed with photography.

Finishing school at 14, Eastman was forced to get a job to contribute to the family finances. After a period with an insurance firm, he decided to study accounting at home in the evenings to increase his chances of earning more than $5 a week. In 1874, five years after starting in insurance, his studies paid off when he was offered a position as a junior clerk at the Rochester Savings Bank on a weekly salary of over $15.

Defining Moments

Eastman's life-changing moment came at age 24. He was planning a vacation in Santo Domingo when a colleague suggested making a photographic record of the trip. Eastman bought the equipment needed to take a photograph using state-of-the-art wet-plate technology. This comprised a camera the size of a 21-inch computer monitor and tripod, together with the glass plates on which the images were captured, and the chemicals, glass tanks, plate holder, and other paraphernalia required for developing them. There was also a tent in which the developing had to take place before the wet plates with the photographic emulsion on could dry out. To learn how to use all the equipment cost $5—a week's wages for Eastman only a few years earlier.

Eastman never made it to Santo Domingo. Instead he became obsessed with photography. Before long he was busy perfecting a dry-plate process in which a photographic plate was covered with a veneer of a special gelatin emulsion. This emulsion remained sensitive even when it was dry, enabling the plate to be exposed whenever the photographer wished, unlike the wet-plate process in which the print had to be developed immediately. It was an idea that Eastman had read about in a British magazine. He took the idea, perfected it, and in 1880, after three years of experimentation, patented a dry plate and a machine for mass-producing it. He gave up his job at the bank and at the beginning of 1881 took on a partner, Henry A. Strong.

Quick to recognize the commercial possibilities of his innovation, Eastman leased a building on State Street in Rochester and began to turn out dry plates for other photographers. Early on the company was faced with a crisis when the dry plates provided to dealers proved defective. Eastman recalled all the faulty plates and replaced them with good ones. "Making good on those plates took our last dollar," he later said. "But what we had left was more

"Every man's occupation should be beneficial to his fellow-man as well as profitable to himself. All else is vanity and folly."
(P. T. Barnum)

important–reputation." In 1884 the Eastman Dry Plate and Film Company was incorporated.

It dawned on Eastman that he could do more than make life easier for professional photographers. He could, in his own words, "make the camera as convenient as the pencil."

When Eastman perfected the transparent roll film and roll holder, the days of cumbersome plate photography were numbered. Photography was at last within reach of the amateur. Eastman took a hand in all aspects of promoting his new photographic film. He wrote the ads and came up with the famous slogan: "You push the button, we do the rest." He even dreamed up the word Kodak, registering the trademark in 1888, and devised the yellow color scheme associated with it. Its origins have been a subject of speculation ever since, but Eastman appears to have invented the name out of thin air. "I devised the name myself," he told his biographer. "The letter 'K' had been a favorite with me–it seems a strong incisive sort of letter. It became a question of trying out a great number of combinations of letters that made words starting and ending with K. The word Kodak is the result."

The KODAK camera was released in 1888 and before long KODAK advertising was inescapable. One of the first electric advertising signs in Piccadilly, London, bore the legend KODAK. In 1892 the company was renamed the Eastman Kodak company of New York.

Eastman built his business using an enlightened humanitarian management style far removed from that of some of his contemporaries. In 1899 he distributed to his entire work force a substantial sum from his own pocket. It was the first act of Eastman's "wage dividend" strategy, a plan to reward employees in proportion to the dividend paid on the company stock. Continuing in the same vein, in 1919 he handed a third of his company holdings–worth some $10 million–to his employees. At the same time he instituted retirement annuities, life insurance, and disability benefits.

George Eastman's philanthropy extended beyond the confines of his corporation. The Massachusetts Institute of Technology (MIT) was particularly favored as two of its graduates, Frank Lovejoy and Darragh de Lancey, had become valued assistants to Eastman. He gave the institute $20 million under the name of "Mr. Smith"–and for years after there was intense speculation over the identity of the mysterious benefactor. Eastman was confident enough of his anonymity to join in a toast to Mr. Smith at an annual MIT alumni dinner.

On one day alone in 1924 Eastman signed away $30 million to the University of Rochester, MIT, Hampton University, and Tuskegee Institute. As he laid down the pen he said, "Now I feel better."

In his final years Eastman was plagued by disability resulting from damage to the lower spinal cord. His inability to lead an active life frustrated him so much that he shot himself on March 14, 1932. He was 77.

Context and Conclusions

Eastman took a cumbersome scientific process and turned it into a commercial mass-market product. Through his pioneering and innovative work on photographic technology he brought the means of capturing the moment on film to the general public at a price it could afford. Eastman was also the father of a particular type of branding: "Trust what's in the box" branding. With its suggestion that consumers simply need to provide their imagination to complement its technology, Microsoft's "Where do you want to go today?", for instance, is a modern echo of that first Kodak promise, as is "Intel Inside." Both draw on Eastman's early inspiration that consumers could be persuaded to trust the brand to take care of the technological side, leaving them free to personalize the product to suit their own lives.

An enlightened manager, Eastman introduced business practices well ahead of his time.

Eastman's slogan captured a turning point in the history of consumerism unlike any other. Previously consumers had understood–even if only at a rudimentary level–how the products they bought worked. But in the late 19th and early 20th century, an explosion of new and technically complex inventions–which included the telephone, the electric light bulb, and film processing–changed the situation forever.

An enlightened manager, Eastman introduced business practices well ahead of his time. He recognized the importance of crisis management when faced with complaints from customers. He also understood that acknowledging the contributions of the work force with remuneration above and beyond their basic salary would in turn benefit the company. Few companies the size of Eastman Kodak were forward-thinking enough to implement employee stock ownership programs and the variety of employment benefits he instituted.

For More Information

Books:

Ackerman, Carl W., and Edwin R. Seligman. *George Eastman: Founder of Kodak and the Photography Business*. Boston, MA: Houghton Mifflin Co., 1930.

Brayer, Elizabeth. *George Eastman: A Biography*. Baltimore, MD: Johns Hopkins University Press, 1996.

Collins, Douglas. *The Story of Kodak*. New York: H.N. Abrams, 1990.

Web Site:

Kodak.com: **www.kodak.com**

Thomas Alva Edison

"Genius is one percent inspiration and ninety-nine percent perspiration," declared Thomas Alva Edison (1847–1931), the inventor and entrepreneur. It was a maxim Edison clearly lived by. Unlike many inventors, Edison was a great businessman. By the end of his extraordinary career Edison had accumulated 1,093 U.S. and 1,300 foreign patents. The inventor of the phonograph and the incandescent light bulb also found time to start up or control 13 major companies. Directly or indirectly, his endeavors led to the creation of well-known corporations like General Electric and RCA. Consolidated Edison is still listed on the New York Stock Exchange.

Edison's genius lit up the world.

1847	Born.
1854	Family moves to Port Huron, Michigan.
1859–62	Sells newspapers on the Grand Trunk Railway.
1863	Works as a telegraph operator; travels across the United States.
1868	Patents his first invention, an electric vote recorder.
1869	Takes up inventing full time, moves to New York City, and starts his first business, making telegraph equipment.
1871	Opens a factory and laboratory in Newark, New Jersey.
1874	Develops a quadruplex system for the telegraph.
1876	Moves to Menlo Park, New Jersey.
1877	Invents the phonograph.
1879	Develops the first commercially viable electric light bulb.
1882	Opens Pearl Street Central Power Station in New York City.
1889	Forms Edison General Electric, and invents the kinetograph (an early motion picture camera).
1892	Edison General Electric merges with Thomson-Houston to create General Electric. Edison sells his interest.
1910	Invents a nickel–iron–alkaline storage battery.
1931	Dies.

Background and Rise

Thomas Edison was born in the town of Milan, Erie County, Ohio, of Dutch and Scottish extraction. The youngest of seven children, he was effectively an only child since his siblings were much older. His schoolteacher mother was loath to let the young Edison out of her sight and educated him mainly at home.

He was a voracious reader. Newton's *Principia Mathematica*, Parker's *Natural and Experimental Philosophy*, and Gibbon's *Decline and Fall of the Roman Empire* had all been devoured before he reached the age of 12. It was a pattern that continued as Edison embarked on a lifetime of discovery and self-education.

From an early age he displayed an entrepreneurial spirit. When, due to economic hardship, the family was forced to move to Port Huron, near Detroit, he sold vegetables from his home garden, operated a newspaper concession on the Grand Trunk Railroad, and eventually printed his own paper, the *Grand Trunk Herald*. In his spare time he conducted chemical experiments. In one particular episode, he set fire to a train's boxcar. This mishap aroused such anger in the guard, who had to put out the fire and burned his hands in the process, that he struck Edison on the ear, bursting his eardrum and leaving him partially deaf.

Defining Moments

Telegraphy turned out to be the catalyst for Edison's greatness. He was a natural with the Morse key, becoming one of the fastest transcribers of his day. As a night-duty telegrapher, he was required to key the number six every hour to confirm he was still manning the wire. Instead he invented a machine that automatically keyed the number and he spent the nights indulging himself at local bars. Fired from a succession of jobs, he crossed the United States working as a freelance telegrapher, finally coming to rest in New York. He had by this time filed his first patent—an automatic vote recorder for the Massachusetts Legislature.

It was in New York that Edison formed his first partnership, with Frank L. Pope, a noted telegraphic engineer, to exploit the potential of their inventions. The partnership was subsequently absorbed by Gold & Stock, a company controlled by Marshall Lefferts, former president of the American Telegraph Company, who paid $20,000 to

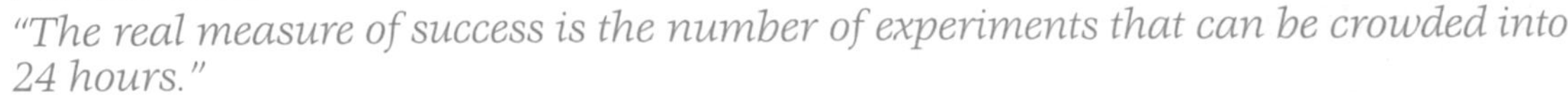

"The real measure of success is the number of experiments that can be crowded into 24 hours."

(Thomas Edison)

the two partners for this privilege. Recognizing Edison's ingenuity, Lefferts conducted a side deal with him, securing Edison's independent patents for the then princely sum of $30,000.

In 1870, with the benefit of some financial security, Edison hired the talents of Charles Batchelor, an English mathematician, and John Kruesi, a Swiss machinist. He signed patent agreements with Gold & Stock and Western Union, took on a business partner, William Unger, moved into a four-story building at Ward Street, Newark, New Jersey, and started inventing on a grand scale. The fertile mix of minds at Ward Street quickly produced a stock printer, quadruplex telegraphy, and a machine to enable the rapid decoding of Morse.

By 1876 the 29-year-old Edison had 45 inventions to his name and was worth some $400,000. Domestic life did little to change his work habits. Indeed he appeared to work even longer hours. Edison was notorious for his devotion to seeking a solution to the problem in hand. Not only would he work, sleep, and eat at the company premises, but he would lock the lab doors and tell his staff they were staying until they arrived at an answer.

The 1870s were the most creative phase of Edison's life. Needing to expand his premises he moved into buildings at Menlo Park, New Jersey. It was there that he and his team perfected the phonograph. The patents were filed in December 1877, but developing a commercially viable product proved difficult. Finally the phonograph came to market in a selection of models from large to miniature, motordriven or handcranked. The product was a huge success—so much so that Edison's creditors began creeping out of the woodwork.

Barely pausing to draw breath, Edison continued to invent. In early 1877 he began experimenting with incandescent filaments and glass bulbs. Some time before developing the light bulb, he managed to persuade a consortium that he could design a marketable lighting system based on such a product. As a result he signed a rights and remuneration agreement that laid the foundation for the Edison Electric Light Company.

In reality he was far from developing this product. Time passed with Edison making favorable noises about progress while actually making little headway in the lab. Feeling the pressure, at one point he retired to an understairs closet, took a dose of morphine, and slept for 36 hours.

It was on Wednesday, November 12, 1879 that Edison finally lit a bulb that lasted long enough to be considered of commercial value. It lasted for 40 hours 20 minutes and within two months Edison had extended its lifetime to 600 hours. Countless visitors trekked to Menlo Park to gaze in wonder at the lights that lit the roadway. Sadly, what followed for Edison was not the triumph of invention but a period of protracted patent litigation that lasted over ten years.

The invention of the light bulb and the formation of the Edison Electric Light Company mark the pinnacle of Edison's achievements. He did continue to invent. In the years that followed, a succession of innovations emerged: DC generators, the first electric lighting system, electrical metering systems, alkaline storage batteries, cement manufacturing equipment, synchronized sound and moving pictures, and submarine detection by sound. His labs also hosted a great number of prodigious minds, most notably Nikola Tesla, famed for his work on the Tesla coil and AC induction motors. The wizard of Menlo Park, however, never quite recaptured the brilliance of his earlier years. Edison died, working to the last, on Sunday, October 18, 1931.

He was a voracious reader. Newton's *Principia Mathematica*, Parker's *Natural and Experimental Philosophy*, and Gibbon's *Decline and Fall of the Roman Empire* had all been devoured before he reached the age of 12.

Context and Conclusions

Part of Edison's genius lay in the realization that innovation alone was insufficient for commercial success. Edison focused on creating a commercially viable product. To do so, he assembled a team of brilliant minds at Menlo Park. In effect he created the first product research lab—a forerunner of facilities such as the celebrated Xerox PARC at Palo Alto, California. It was a practical and commercial approach to invention that proved immensely successful.

Edison's pragmatism also extended to patenting his ideas. He understood the value of intellectual property and the importance of being able to assert ownership of ideas.

A legend in his own lifetime, his achievements were acknowledged shortly before his death in a nationwide celebration attended by luminaries such as President Hoover, Henry Ford, John Rockefeller, and George Eastman. He remains an inspiration for inventors and entrepreneurs to this day.

Domestic life did little to change his work habits. Indeed he appeared to work even longer hours.

For More Information

Books:

Baldwin, Neil. *Edison, Inventing the Century*. New York: Hyperion, 1995.

Israel, Paul. *Edison: A Life of Invention*. New York: John Wiley, 1998.

Jenkins, Reese V., et al., eds. *The Papers of Thomas A. Edison*. Baltimore, MD: Johns Hopkins University Press, 1989.

Josephson, Matthew. *Edison: A Biography*. New York: John Wiley, 1992.

Millard, Andre. *Edison and the Business of Innovation*. Baltimore, MD: Johns Hopkins University Press, 1990.

Web Site:

Con Edison Inc.: **www.conedison.com**

Henry Ford

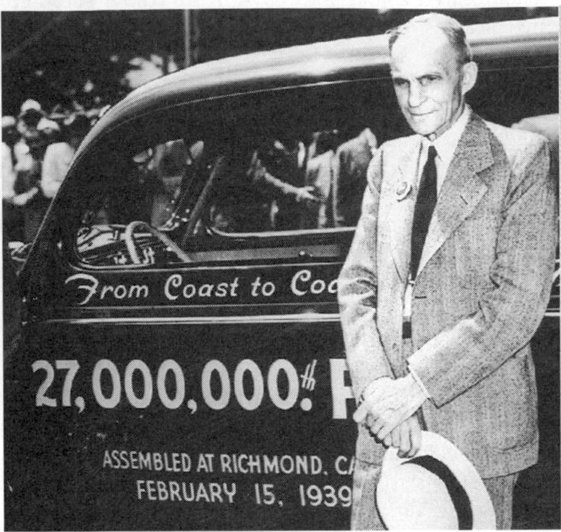

Henry Ford (1863–1947) was part engineer, part inventor, and part entrepreneur. A talent for engineering and curiosity drove Ford to develop a prototype automobile in his garden. His flair helped him found the Ford Motor Company to develop his prototype. By 1924 Ford had sold ten million Model T Fords—the car famously available in a choice of colors—"so long as it's black." On his way to ten million sales Ford broke the land speed record and the mold of manufacturing. During his lifetime his introduction of mass production assembly line methods irrevocably changed the nature of manufacturing, something for which, for once, the use of the phrase "paradigm shift" is wholly justified.

Ford on the road to another great achievement.

1863	Born.
1884	Attends business school for three months.
1896	Chief engineer at Edison electric factory in Detroit. Drives first vehicle out of garden shed.
1901	Ford drives to victory in Grosse Point car races.
1903	Founds Ford Motor Co.
1905	Model A Fordsmobile produced.
1908	The first Model T rolls off the production line.
1914	Ford introduces wages for unskilled workers at a minimum of $5.
1918	The River Rouge plant built.
1919	Ford's son, Edsel, becomes president of the company.
1924	Ten millionth Model T produced.
1928	Brings out second Model A.
1945	Hands over power to his grandson Henry II.
1947	Dies.

Background and Rise

Ford was born in 1863 on his father's farm at Greenfield, near Detroit, Michigan. As a boy he showed great interest in mechanics and engineering. He delighted in dismantling his friends' watches and then reassembling them, and while still a schoolboy built an engine from junk. He was always looking for ways to improve things. "Even when I was very young I suspected that much might somehow be done in a better way," he later observed. "That is what took me into mechanics."

His first prototype automobile was the Quadricycle built in his garden shed.

Leaving school at 16, Ford went to work as an engineer for James Flower & Co. in Detroit. To supplement his meager $2.50 a week, he worked at a jewelers in the evenings. Nine months of grueling hours later, Ford moved to the Dry Dock Engine Works to try his hand at a different type of engineering. By 1896, he was chief engineer at the Edison electrical factory in Detroit, but finding himself unable to confine his engineering to work, Ford continued to tinker with engineering projects at home.

Ford's strategic planning skills appear to have been underdeveloped at this early stage in his career. His first prototype automobile was the Quadricycle built in his garden shed. The Quadricycle was too big to drive out of the shed, which forced him to dismantle part of the shed to remove the innovative horseless carriage.

For eight years Ford continued to work 12-hour days and then come home to improve his invention. Yet despite the potential of his automobile, no one could be persuaded to invest in it. The turning point came when Ford built a car for the Grosse Point automobile races. Although inexperienced, Ford entered the races, drove the car himself, and won emphatically. He repeated the feat the following year, in 1902. The victory attracted financiers and, after a couple of corporate false starts, the Ford Motor Company was up and running. On the way Ford broke the world land speed record for a four-cylinder automobile, driving a mile over the frozen Lake Sinclair in 39 and one-fifth seconds, seven seconds faster than the existing record.

Defining Moments

Ford's idea was to produce a car for "everyday wear and tear," suitable for the masses. "Anything founded on the idea of the greatest good for the greatest number will win in the end," said Ford. Competitors like Cadillac were expensive, at many thousands of dollars, and so beyond the reach of the majority of ordinary people. Ford's first commercial automobile was the Model A Fordmobile, in 1905. Priced at $850 it undercut its rivals and, in its basic but solid design, it appealed to the mass market. It was followed in 1908 by the Model T.

"A business that makes nothing but money is a poor kind of business." (Henry Ford)

The overwhelming demand for the Model T forced Ford to modify the production process and make it more efficient. Initially the cars moved along the production line on cradles. At each stop, men climbed over the cars attending to different tasks. Ford simplified the process and made it more predictable. First, he delineated tasks so that one man performed one task repeatedly, instead of several. Second, he roped the cars together so that they travelled at a steady speed through the plant. These simple but effective measures resulted in an increase in production from 100,000 to 200,000 with, at the same time, a reduction in the workforce of nearly 1,500 men.

Production line work was arduous and monotonous; staff turnover was high. In 1914 Ford reluctantly increased wages for unskilled workers to a minimum of $5, a move that brought in workers from far and wide. Tens of thousands joined the Ford automobile company.

So many prospective employees queued up at the factory gates that the fire brigade had to use its hoses to disperse the crowd. Ford's management style was not, however, benevolent. The company had its own Sociological Department to nanny the workers—making sure, among other things, that they were mindful of good personal hygiene. Ford's coercive managerial style grated among the workforce. To sweeten this Ford introduced profit sharing and an extensive welfare program.

He stopped short of allowing the workers to form a labor union, however. When Roosevelt introduced the Wagner Act of 1935, allowing the unionization of the motor companies, Ford resisted the legislation bitterly, refusing to let labor unions operate at Ford auto plants. It was only after adverse publicity, as a result of the infamous Battle of the Overpass in May 1937, when several United Auto Workers' officials were badly beaten, allegedly by Ford employees outside the River Rouge plant, that Ford was forced to back down and permit union organization at the company.

By 1924 Ford had manufactured 10 million Model Ts and built a new plant at River Rouge, with wages raised to $6 a day. Increasingly he spent less time managing—his son, Edsel, had become president in 1919—and more time pursuing his socially idealistic interests. He built an experimental rural idyll, a model U.S. village named Greenfield Village. He also launched the Peace Ship in an attempt to end World War I and hobnobbed with other magnates and entrepreneurs such as his good friend Henry Firestone. Although a pacifist, Ford was drawn into war manufacturing after Pearl Harbor when the Willow Plant was built to produce B-24 bombers. This gigantic production works with its mile-long assembly line produced one plane every hour, with a total of 86,865 aircraft between May 1942 and the end of the war. In 1943 Ford returned as C.E.O. after Edsel died.

So many prospective employees queued up at the factory gates that the fire brigade had to use its hoses to disperse the crowd.

More at home on the factory floor addressing engineering problems, Ford lacked the managerial skills and flexibility necessary to keep the company ahead of the competition. He was unable to keep pace with the beast he had created. Fixated on the Model T, he waited too long to develop the company's next model, the revamped Model A (launched in 1927), and so lost the initiative forever to General Motors. Like many entrepreneurs Ford was reluctant to give up his company. A poorly managed succession further damaged the company, with Ford finally handing power to his grandson Henry II in 1945. Ford died at the age of 84 on April 7, 1947.

Context and Conclusions

Henry Ford is frequently cited as one of the most important and influential businessmen of the 20th century. Although Ford didn't invent that icon of modern society, the motor car, he was responsible for turning it into a mass-market commodity. Once the sole province of the wealthy, the car was, in its pre-Ford incarnations, a toy—unreliable, poorly engineered, impractical, and above all expensive. Ford changed all that. The champion of mass production, Ford started an entire industrial revolution of his own, founded on his Model T. It was a revolution that made Ford $1 billion richer and made travel a reality for millions.

For More Information

Books:

Doubleday, Ralph H. *The Triumph of an Idea: The Story of Henry Ford.* New York: Graves, Doran & Company, Inc., 1934.

Ford, Henry, and Samuel Crowther. *My Life and Work.* New York: Doubleday, Page & Co., 1923.

Web Site:

Ford Motor Company: **www.ford.com**

"Sometimes it is the men 'higher up' who most need revamping—and they themselves are the last to recognize it."

(Henry Ford)

BILL GATES

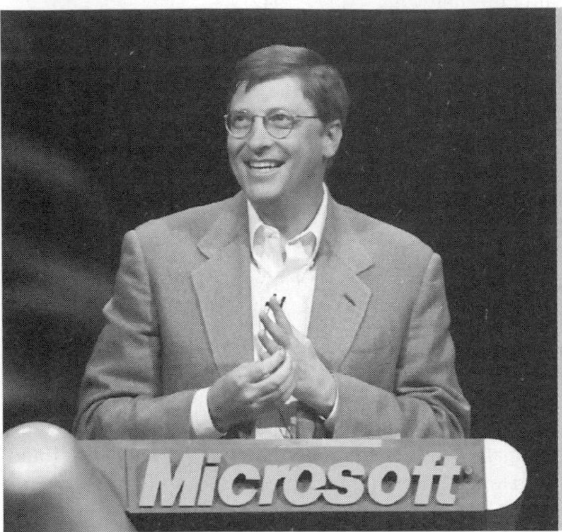

Bill Gates's contribution to the development of computer technology is beyond dispute. At the age of 13 he was already plotting his business future, forming the Lakeside Programmers Group with some school friends. Its aim was to seek commercial opportunities for their computer skills. His early programming brilliance, his alliance with Microsoft cofounder Paul Allen, and his departure from Harvard to start Microsoft are well known.

Microsoft went on to become one of the most successful companies the world has ever seen. As the Internet market exploded, he beat off Netscape in the browser wars. But perhaps his biggest challenge to date has come from the Department of Justice and its antitrust lawyers. Despite protracted litigation Gates has so far managed to keep Microsoft intact, and enabled it to hold on to its dominant position.

Bill Gates—cyber visionary.

1955	Born.
1977	Drops out of Harvard to start up computer software company with Paul Allen.
1980	Agrees to license operating system to IBM.
1995	Windows 9X series introduced.
1997	Microsoft ordered to supply Windows 95 without a browser.
2000	Microsoft found guilty of anticompetitive behavior. Judge orders break-up of Microsoft.
2001	Break-up ruling set aside by appeal court. Launch of XP generation of OS and Xbox game console.

BACKGROUND AND RISE

William Henry Gates III was born in Seattle on October 28, 1955. He was a precociously brilliant boy. Before his tenth birthday he had read the family's encyclopedia from beginning to end.

He was a precociously brilliant boy. Before his tenth birthday he had read the family's encyclopedia from beginning to end.

At Lakeside, the exclusive private school he attended in Seattle, he developed an obsession with computers. Gates, then still only 13 years old, and some of his computer friends formed the Lakeside Programmers Group, dedicated to using their programming skills to make money.

At Lakeside he developed a friendship with another boy two years his senior. The boy, whose obsession with computers matched Gates's, was Paul Allen.

The intellectually driven Gates left Lakeside in 1973 to study law at Harvard. Law was a lot less appealing to him, however, than computing. He contacted Allen and the two teamed up to develop a version of an early computer language—BASIC. Gates dropped out of Harvard in 1977 to start up a small computer software company with Allen. They called it Microsoft.

DEFINING MOMENTS

A brilliant strategic decision in 1980 set Microsoft on the road to global dominance. At that time IBM dominated the IT industry through its mainframe business. By the late 1970s Microsoft was licensing its software to a number of customers. But the prevailing wisdom was that hardware was the business to be in and software merely an adjunct. Apple at the time was developing a proprietary in-house operating system (OS) that would provide a competitive advantage. Its strategy was to maintain control over what it regarded as its superior hardware by running it with its own software. Gates thought differently. As far as he was concerned the more people that used Microsoft software on their machines the better. So when IBM approached Microsoft to develop the operating system for its first PC, Gates recognized what an enormous opportunity this presented. IBM's dominance of the IT market meant that its PCs were destined to set the standard—both for hardware and for the OS. IBM failed to realize that, when the end user switched on the machine, the part of the computer he or she interacted with would be the OS, supplied by Microsoft. Gates capitalized on the situation, cannily retaining the right to license its OS to other PC manufacturers.

The decision by IBM to use Microsoft's MS-DOS was a turning point for both companies. From that point onward, the fortunes of IBM, which singularly failed to grasp the significance of the OS, would inexorably decline, until Lou Gerstner came to its rescue as C.E.O. in 1993. For Microsoft the only way was up. Endorsed by IBM, MS-DOS displaced other competing OS offerings regardless of their technical merits, in much the same way that VHS had vanquished Betamax in the battle of the video standards. Yet in those early days the rest of the world still failed to understand the importance of Gates's coup. Even in 1984, *Fortune* magazine was criticizing Gates for failing to develop the management depth that would turn a temporary victory into long-term dominance. Not for the last

"If the 1980s were about quality and the 1990s were about reengineering, then the 2000s will be about velocity."
(Bill Gates)

time the media underestimated Gates's drive, ambition, and strategic vision.

When ill health forced Allen to leave Microsoft, Gates's position as leader was confirmed. Microsoft's rapid growth soon made it the darling of Wall Street. From a share price of $2 in 1986, Microsoft stock had soared to $105 by the first half of 1996, making Gates a billionaire.

Microsoft has launched a succession of successful products. But Gates hasn't had things all his own way. When the Internet revolution took off in the early 1990s, Microsoft was momentarily caught off balance. A company called Netscape sprang up, giving away a nifty piece of software called a browser that transformed the Web from a techie's playground to a mass-market phenomenon. Microsoft desperately responded by licensing Mosaic browser technology from a company called Spyglass, tweaking it, and repackaging it as the Microsoft browser Internet Explorer. To cover all the bases, Microsoft also bought WebTV, eShops, Hotmail, and Vermeer, the original developers of the Front Page HTML editing software.

Critics regularly deride the company for buying technology rather than developing its own solutions. Microsoft has countered that it has developed a number of important technologies and is still doing so.

Criticism has also constantly been leveled at Microsoft, alleging that it abuses its dominant market position. Matters came to a head when the U.S. Justice Department investigated Microsoft to establish whether the company was in breach of antitrust law. In June 2000, after a lengthy trial and a mountain of depositions, U.S. District Judge Thomas Penfield Jackson ordered Microsoft to be split into two companies, holding that it had violated the nation's antitrust laws by using monopoly power to push aside potential competitors to the detriment of consumers. Microsoft took the case to the appeal court in February 2001, and in June of that year the court decided to overturn part of the original decision, withdrawing the requirement for Microsoft to be broken up.

Ultimately it may not be the antitrust ruling that poses the biggest threat to Microsoft's bottom line. Microsoft risks being sidelined by the sheer pace of technological progress. Handhelds and mobile phones may be the PCs of the future, and those markets are not dominated by Microsoft. Even on its home ground of PC operating systems, open-source software such as Linux poses a threat. Gates hit back with the launch of Microsoft's next generation XP operating system toward the end of 2001. On this occasion it was the closer integration with the Internet and, in particular, the "smart tags" feature that worried some commentators. In the event, the feature was dropped, although that doesn't mean it won't resurface. Another big product for Gates in 2001 was the Xbox. This new gaming system, due out in time for Christmas 2001, was Microsoft's shot at breaking into a lucrative market on the hardware side. It is too early to tell, however, whether the combined forces of XP and the Xbox, plus the numerous partnership agreements Microsoft has forged with dot-com companies, will be enough to preserve its hegemony. But Gates, the architect of the world's greatest software company, won't go down without a fight.

Context and Conclusions

Bill Gates is lauded and reviled in almost equal measure. The secrets that lie behind Microsoft's spiral of success have been dissected from every possible angle. Whatever you think of the dominance of Microsoft or Gates's methods, it cannot be doubted that when it comes to building and retaining a competitive advantage he has few peers. His technical skills, while not to be underrated, are not his greatest attribute. Far more important is his strategic thinking. It is this that has enabled him to outsmart his opponents at every turn. His other great attribute is the ability to hire the best talent and then motivate it to work at high tempo. He may appear awkward, geeky even, in public, but Gates is as sharp as a box of razors.

Yet in those early days the rest of the world still failed to understand the importance of Gates's coup. Even in 1984, *Fortune* magazine was criticizing Gates for failing to develop the management depth that would turn a temporary victory into long-term dominance.

CLOSE BUT NO CIGAR

Ken Olsen
Olsen was once hailed by *Fortune* magazine as the "most successful entrepreneur in the history of American business." Founding Digital Equipment Corporation (DEC) in 1959, he spent the next 35 years riding the IT roller coaster at the helm of his company. Olsen, the man who pioneered the minicomputer, was heavily influenced by the writings of Alfred Sloan and organized DEC along similar lines to GM (small business units) when under Sloan's control. He left in 1992 to found Advanced Modular Solutions Inc. After a disastrous spell in the early 1990s, DEC was finally bought by Compaq in 1998.

For More Information

Books:

Dearlove, Des. *Business the Bill Gates Way*. New York: AMACOM, 1999.

Gates, Bill. *Business @ the Speed of Thought: Using a Digital Nervous System*. New York: Warner Books, 1999.

Wallace, James, and Jim Erickson. *Hard Drive: Bill Gates and the Making of the Microsoft Empire*. New York: John Wiley, 1992.

Web Site:

Microsoft: **www.microsoft.com**

"Take our 20 best people away, and I will tell you that Microsoft would become an unimportant company."

(Bill Gates)

  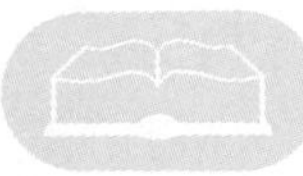    

Harold S. Geneen

Harold Geneen is the classic example of the C.E.O. as analyst. He joined the board of ITT in 1959 and set about turning the company into the world's greatest conglomerate. His basic organizational strategy was that diversification was a source of strength. Under Geneen, ITT's spending spree amounted to 350 companies. By 1970, ITT was composed of 400 separate companies operating in 70 countries.

By sheer force of personality, Geneen's approach worked. Between 1959 and 1977, ITT's sales went from $765 m to nearly $28 billion and earnings per share rose from $1 to $4.20. Geneen stepped down as chairman in 1979. But a company built around the drive and energy of one man will not last longer than that man's career. His followers were unable to sustain Geneen's uniquely driven working style. In the month of Harold Geneen's death, ITT was taken over.

Geneen spread the word about ITT.

1910	Born.
1934	Obtains a degree in accounting.
1934–1959	Works for number of firms including American Can, Bell and Howell, Jones and Laughlin Steel, and Raytheon.
1959	Joins ITT.
1966	ABC merger blocked.
1971	Acquires Hartford Insurance.
1977	Steps down as chief executive.
1979	Steps down as chairman.
1983	Resigns as director.
1997	Dies.

Background and Rise

Son of a Russian Jewish father and an Italian Catholic mother, Harold Sydney Geneen was born in Bournemouth, England in 1910. His family moved to the United States before his first birthday, but his parents separated soon after they arrived. As a result, Geneen's childhood was spent at boarding schools and summer camps. When Geneen started work as a runner for the New York Stock Exchange, he continued to study at night at New York University. In 1934 his hard work was rewarded with a degree in accounting.

For the next 25 years his career took in a string of companies, starting with the forerunners of Coopers & Lybrand, followed by Montgomery (an accounting firm), then the American Can Co., Bell and Howell Co., Jones and Laughlin Steel Co., and Raytheon. After Raytheon, where Geneen was vice president, came the biggest challenge of his career and the job that made him famous: the International Telegraph and Telephone Company, more commonly known as ITT.

Fortunately for ITT, Geneen was no slouch; on the contrary, he was a fiercely driven workaholic.

Defining Moments

When Geneen arrived at ITT in 1959, the corporation was a ragbag collection of businesses, loosely focused around telecommunications, with revenues of $800,000. During the 1960s the predominant organizational trend was one of diversification and conglomeration. C.E.O.s went into a purchasing frenzy, raiding the corporate aisles for any company, no matter what business it was in, so long as it turned a profit. Geneen was no exception.

Over the ensuing decade Geneen purchased over 300 companies, operating in over 60 different countries. There was no rationale to these purchases, no common thread, other than that of profit. Sheraton hotels, Avis car hire, Continental Baking were all tucked away in ITT's roomy locker. "I never met a business that I didn't find interesting," said Geneen, and the ITT balance sheet certainly bore him out.

It was a mammoth undertaking to manage so many disparate companies. Fortunately for ITT, Geneen was no slouch; on the contrary, he was a fiercely driven workaholic. His ITT office in New York was equipped with eight telephones and a clock that showed which parts of the world were in daylight and which were in darkness. Ten suitcase-sized leather attaché cases crammed full of documents were stacked along the window ledges. Six of the cases, stuffed with reports, communiqués, and memos from over 400 reporting corporations, followed Geneen around the country and the world. "If I had enough arms and legs and time, I would do it all myself," said Geneen. Well into his eighties, long after he left ITT, Geneen was still working a ten-hour day at his office in New York's Waldorf-Astoria hotel. A typical Geneen story is recounted by an old ITT executive. Dragging a group of executives in for an evening meeting, Geneen worked them late into the night. At 11:45 p.m., the last of the

"The worst disease which can afflict business executives in their work is not, as popularly supposed, alcoholism; it's egotism." (Harold S. Geneen)

executives made his way out of the office, pausing to wait for Geneen. Instead the C.E.O. peeled off his jacket, pulled on a sweater and kept on working—the last executive in the building.

Even so, it required all his energy to control the ITT conglomerate. To keep it together, Geneen employed rigorous financial accounting methods. Each month, 50 or more executives flew to Brussels to spend several days examining the figures. "I want no surprises," was one of Geneen's mantras. Full information was paramount, as was the ability to tell real facts from details masquerading as facts. "The highest art of professional management requires the literal ability to smell a real fact from all others," asserted Geneen.

And his approach seemed to work. From 1959 to 1977, ITT sales rocketed from some $765 m to approaching $28 billion, with earnings up from $29 m to $562 m. It was a success by most people's standards, not just Geneen's. Yet the more companies he acquired, the harder it was to keep all the plates spinning in the air. In 1974 and 1975 profits fell: Geneen may have been able to keep up a relentless pace, but his followers were either unable or unwilling to match it.

Geneen's efforts to support his company's share price sometimes strayed outside the boundaries of acceptable practice. In 1972, America's Securities and Exchange Commission discovered $8.7 m had been sunk into nefarious and illegal activities around the world. This allegedly included bribery, and colluding with the CIA in an attempt to undermine the Allende government in Chile.

Geneen stepped down as chief executive in 1977, as chairman in 1979, and as a director four years later—not that such a relentless man could ever retire to a life of quiet contemplation and gentle pastimes. He carried on working in a number of different companies of his own creation until his death from a heart attack in 1997.

ITT, however, was a different proposition. Without Geneen to support it, the house of cards collapsed. ITT limped on but eventually, after selling many of the companies acquired by Geneen, it was split up into three separate companies.

Context and Conclusions

Harold Geneen was one of the last of his breed. He came to power at ITT at the height of the mania for conglomerates. Size mattered, and if size mattered then Geneen was very, very important. It is doubtful if any other C.E.O. in corporate history acquired more companies—over 300—with less rationale. Of course acquisition is one way to grow earnings, but eventually the relentless growth has to stop and increased earnings must come from existing operations. Even a man with Geneen's drive and boundless energy will struggle to keep 300 plates in the air, and so it proved. In the decade following his departure from ITT, the cry from the boardroom was "stick to the knitting." Companies slimmed down, shed noncore business, and left ITT looking like a bloated dinosaur. Yet Geneen deserves his place in the pantheon of business greats. Why? Because he was the best of his type, the paragon of his age, the king of the conglomerates.

Harold Geneen was one of the last of his breed.

CLOSE BUT NO CIGAR

Charles G. Bludhorn

Who today remembers Charlie Bludhorn? Yet in the 1960s and 1970s, Bludhorn—then head of conglomerate Gulf and Western—was one of the most fashionable C.E.O.s of his time. Along with conglomerate kings such as James Ling, Henry Singleton, Charles "Tex" Thornton, and of course Harold Geneen, Bludhorn was fêted as a business visionary. Among the many corporate baubles he accumulated were Music Corporation of America, Madison Square Garden, and Paramount Studios. When conglomerates fell out of fashion, so did Bludhorn. Gulf and Western was whittled down to size until Paramount was pretty much all that remained.

For More Information

Books:

Sampson, Anthony. *The Sovereign State of ITT*. New York: Stein and Day, 1973.

Shoenberg, Robert J. *Geneen*. New York: Norton, 1985.

"Every company has two organizational structures: The formal one is written on the charts; the other is the everyday relationships of the men and women in the organization." (Harold S. Geneen)

KING CAMP GILLETTE

King Camp Gillette, the safety-razor entrepreneur, made his fortune by taking a mundane everyday product and improving it. So confident was he of his invention that he formed the American Safety Razor Company in 1901 and persuaded investors to back him before he even had a commercial product. In the first year of production Gillette sold 51 razor sets and 168 blades. By 1905 the figure was 250,000 razor sets and 100,000 blade packages. Part of the secret of Gillette's success was his modern attitude towards branding. With his picture on the wrappers of his disposable blades he was soon known the world over. By the time he had moved on to improving the world through his social theories, the Gillette safety razor was a permanent fixture in the grooming habits of a large proportion of the world's male population.

Gillette was at the cutting edge of shaving technology.

1855	Born.
1871	Gillette family hardware business burns down.
1890	Holds four patents.
1894	Writes *The Human Drift*.
1895	Works for the inventor of cork-lined bottle caps.
1901	Gillette and Nickerson form the American Safety Razor Company.
1903	Production begins on the new safety razor.
1904	The renamed Gillette company is awarded the patent for the new invention. Invents the double-edged blade—a concept still used to this day.
1905	Twelve million blades sold to date, generating revenues of $90,000.
1915	Sales of seven million blades a year.
1932	Dies.

BACKGROUND AND RISE

King Camp Gillette was born in Fond du Lac, Wisconsin, into a family of innovators. His father was a patent agent and small-time inventor. His mother wrote a cookbook based on a lifetime of culinary experimentation; the book was still in print a century later. When Gillette was four, his family moved to Chicago to start up a hardware business. Unfortunately, the business was ravaged by the Great Fire, and in 1871 the family moved once again, this time to New York City.

His father was a patent agent and small-time inventor. His mother wrote a cookbook based on a lifetime of culinary experimentation; the book was still in print a century later.

Gillette took a job as a traveling salesman. Not content with merely selling his products, he couldn't resist improving them. By 1890 he had accumulated four patents. In 1895 he was working for the man who had invented cork-lined bottle caps. He had some simple advice for Gillette: "Invent something people use and throw away." Gillette took his words to heart and turned his attention to the safety razor.

Traditionally, men of the time used the straight-handled razor blade to shave. The increasing use of the railroad, however, had prompted a rethinking of the design of this basic implement. The swaying of the carriages made it downright dangerous to use the traditional cut-throat. Safety razors had been invented—a heavy blade fitted at right angles to a short handle—but they still had major shortcomings. Gillette used a Star safety razor. This required continual sharpening on a leather strop just as the traditional razor did. Eventually the blade wore out.

Gillette had an idea. What if it were possible to take a small square of sheet steel and put a permanently sharp edge on it? Such a product would be sufficiently affordable to throw away when it became dull.

DEFINING MOMENTS

To help him in his quest for a new improved safety razor, Gillette turned to metallurgists at the Massachusetts Institute of Technology. They assured Gillette that his idea was impossible. Undaunted, Gillette continued to search for someone who shared his belief and vision. That person was William Emery Nickerson, an inventor who, ironically, had been educated at MIT.

Gillette's search had taken six years. His doggedness was rewarded in 1901 when, together with Nickerson, he formed the American Safety Razor Company. Then in 1903 production began on the new safety razor. Razor blades were bundled up and sold as a package. The razor handle was sold as a one-time purchase. In 1904 the renamed Gillette Safety Razor Company was awarded the patent for the new invention. Initial sales were disappointing. After an intensive advertising campaign in men's magazines and newspapers in the United States

"Don't study the idea to death with experts and committees. Get on with it and see if it works."

(Kenneth Iverson)

and Europe, however, things improved. By 1906 12 million blades had been sold generating revenues of $90,000.

The inevitable patent battles ensued. With a large proportion of the world's population as a potential market, sharp practices were rife. Competitors came to the market with modified versions of Gillette's product. Gillette responded with litigation or, in many cases, by buying the competition. And all the while he continued to tinker with his invention. In 1904 he came up with the double-edged blade, a concept used to this day. With his face plastered over the wrappers of his razor blades, Gillette became a celebrity, recognized throughout the United States.

Although the Gillette razor made King Camp Gillette a millionaire, he remained unfulfilled. He had strong philosophical and political beliefs. With his newly made millions he was now a powerful figure in North American commerce. He had an idealistic vision of a utopian society based on universal cooperation, and as a result of his high profile and success, he now had the means to attempt to make it a reality.

Gillette wrote several books outlining his vision, beginning with *The Human Drift* (1894) that predated the invention of the Gillette razor. In a reaction against the mass pollution and sprawling urban development of the Industrial Revolution, he planned pollution-free cities contained in giant glass domes. In this new utopia, one company would carry out all production with the citizens as the shareholders. "Selfishness would be unknown, and war would be a barbarism of the past," he wrote.

One interesting byproduct of Gillette's obsession was his meeting with Henry Ford. In the years before World War I Gillette attempted to set the wheels of his World Corporation in motion. First he asked Teddy Roosevelt to be president. When Roosevelt unsurprisingly declined, Gillette approached the writer Sinclair Lewis, who in turn arranged a meeting between Gillette and Ford. The outcome of this meeting between two dogmatic, strong-willed millionaires should have been no surprise. At first the two merely talked over each other then, growing angrier, they began to shout at one another.

Context and Conclusions

Gillette's attempts at social engineering came to nothing. The stock market crash of 1929, coupled with boardroom machinations and constant patent litigation, wiped out his personal fortune. He spent a lot of time during his final years trying unsuccessfully to extract oil from shale. In the end he died, unfulfilled and frustrated, in 1932. The Gillette Safety Razor Company, however, thrived, carrying on its founder's tradition of innovation and remaining at the cutting edge of safety razor development. The company introduced foam shaving cream (Foamy), anti-perspirant (Right Guard), and continued to do what Gillette had always done—improve the safety razor with the twin-blade, pivoting-head, disposable, and triple-blade razors.

The stock market crash of 1929, coupled with boardroom machinations and constant patent litigation, wiped out his personal fortune.

King Camp Gillette will be remembered for creating a product used daily by people the world over. Not only did he pioneer the market for disposable products, but he also showed an early and prescient awareness of the power of both celebrity and the brand. His image on the packaging of his product made him famous and helped reassure the consumer about the product's quality. This in turn boosted sales and helped make the Gillette Safety Razor Company the leader in its market.

For More Information

Books:

Adams, Russell B., Jr. *King C. Gillette: The Man and His Wonderful Shaving Device.* Boston, MA: Little, Brown & Co., 1978.

McKibben, Gordon. *Cutting Edge: Gillette's Journey to Global Leadership.* Cambridge, MA: Harvard Business School Press, 1997.

Web Site:

The Gillette Company: **www.gillette.com**

ANDREW S. GROVE

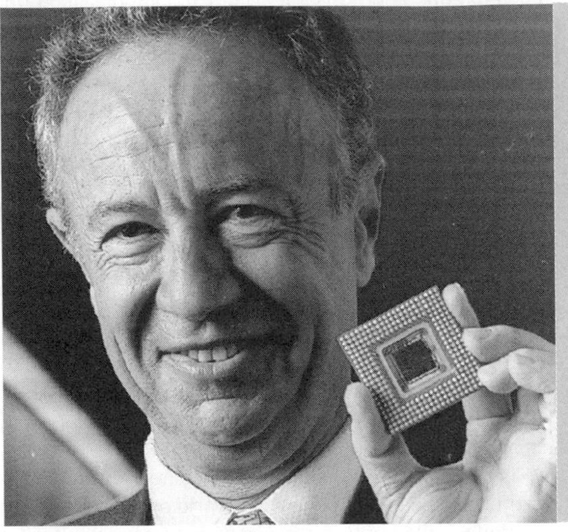

Andy Grove (1936–) managed to survive a childhood in Nazi-occupied Hungary only to find himself a victim of the Cold War. He escaped to the United States in 1957. After educating himself in New York and California, Grove joined Fairchild Semiconductor. In 1968 he followed colleagues Bob Noyce and Gordon Moore to form a new company, Intel. By 1979 he was chief operating officer.

In the 1980s Grove concentrated the company's efforts on manufacturing microprocessors. He was made C.E.O. in 1987. In 1994 he faced a crisis when a flaw was discovered in the company's flagship product, the Pentium processor. Under pressure, Grove made the decision to replace the chips rather than try to tough it out, reinforcing Intel's reputation.

Andy Grove with one of the keys to his success.

1936	Born.
1957	"Traitorous eight" start Fairchild Semiconductor. Grove escapes to United States.
1963	Gains Ph.D. from University of California, Berkeley.
1968	Gordon Moore and Bob Noyce start Intel.
1979	Becomes Intel's president and chief operating officer.
1981	IBM decides to use Intel microprocessors.
1985	Shifts Intel's focus to microprocessors.
1987	Becomes C.E.O. of Intel.
1994	Flawed Pentium microprocessors recalled.
1998	Steps down as Intel's C.E.O.

BACKGROUND AND RISE

Illness, discrimination, poverty: Andy Grove, born Andras Grof in prewar Hungary on September 2, 1936, suffered them all as a child. At the age of four he contracted scarlet fever which left him with impaired hearing. Then another, more sinister, threat cast its shadow: as the Nazis swept to power in Europe, the Jewish Grof family feared for their lives. Grof and his mother assumed false identities and were sheltered by friends. The young Grof became Andras Malesevics.

Miraculously he and his family avoided the death camps and survived the war. Their celebrations were short-lived however, for in 1956 communist Russia invaded Hungary; Grof and the rest of his family found themselves on the wrong side of the Iron Curtain. Weighing up his options Grof, by now used to playing for high stakes, decided to escape.

He fled to Austria and from there to the United States, changing his name to Andrew S. Grove along the way. Arriving in the United States in 1957, he enrolled at City College of New York, graduating in 1960 with a degree in chemical engineering. After City College, he studied at the University of California, Berkeley, receiving his Ph.D. in 1963.

His first job after graduation was at Fairchild Semiconductor, a young company formed by several research scientists including Robert Noyce and Gordon Moore.

DEFINING MOMENTS

Fairchild Semiconductor was the cradle of the computing revolution. It was formed by a disaffected group of researchers from William Shockley's research team at Shockley Semiconductor Laboratory in Palo Alto, California. Shockley had received the Nobel Prize for his work developing the transistor, and his academic reputation attracted some of the finest minds in electronics to his company, including Bob Noyce, Gordon Moore (of Moore's Law fame), Julius Blank, Victor Grinich, Eugene Kleiner, Jean Hoerni, Jay Last, and Sheldon Roberts.

Fairchild Semiconductor was the cradle of the computing revolution. It was formed by a disaffected group of researchers from William Shockley's research team at Shockley Semiconductor Laboratory in Palo Alto, California.

Shockley's poor management style bred disaffection among his research team. The eventual exodus from his company of the so-called "traitorous eight" was one of the landmarks of computing history. The company they founded, Fairchild Semiconductor, revolutionized the world of computing with its work on the silicon transistor. The drain of talent from Shockley's lab went on after Fairchild to start up some of the best-known companies in Silicon Valley. Intel (Bob Noyce and Gordon Moore), Advanced Micro Devices (Jerry Sanders), and National Semiconductor (Charlie Sporck) were all spinoffs from Fairchild.

When Gordon Moore and Bob Noyce left Fairchild in

"Columbus didn't have a business plan when he discovered America." (Andrew S. Grove)

1968 to start Intel, they asked Grove to come with them. Noyce and Moore's original business plan involved manufacturing a new kind of computer memory using semiconductor technology, and in 1970 the first dynamic random-access memory (DRAM) for commercial use rolled off Intel's production lines. Intel had also been approached by a Japanese company, Nippon Calculating Machine Corporation (NCM), to produce logic chips. Intel had already been working on a smaller single chip and offered its own solution. A chip was eventually developed. Instead of the patent rights passing to NCM, Intel retained ownership and licensed manufacturing and selling rights. It was this key decision by Grove and the management team that paved the way for Intel to become the microprocessor giant it is today.

Intel's success was founded not only on its innovative skills but also on its skillful repositioning of what had previously been a commodity computer component into a household-name brand. TV commercials elevated the mundane microchip to an aspirational product. Encouraged by the "Intel Inside" ad campaign, consumers insisted on having an Intel chip inside their PCs. The Intel Pentium processor became as strongly associated with PCs as Microsoft's Windows operating system, another marketing success story.

Andy Grove's vision was instrumental in Intel's success. Grove steered the company from a fledgling producer of memory chips into a giant of the microprocessor industry. He got things done. In the early days he was the man who organized the office space and manufacturing capacity. He played a key role in the 1981 negotiations with IBM that saw Intel beat off competition from Motorola to supply the microprocessors for IBM's PCs.

In many ways Grove's childhood experiences in war-torn Europe had prepared him well for business life. He was a man who didn't avoid tough decisions. In the 1980s, when microprocessors looked as if they might be a better bet than memory, Grove made the bold and risky decision to refocus the company's efforts. It was a tough call that meant laying off thousands of employees. In 1987 Grove became the C.E.O. of Intel. The decisions didn't get any easier. Grove averted a potential crisis when a flaw was discovered in the company's flagship Pentium microprocessor. With a technical problem probably discernible only by mathematicians threatening to balloon into a public relations disaster of epic proportions, Grove acted decisively. He could have used Intel's muscle to pass on the burden of replacement to the retailers and consumers. Instead Grove offered to replace the processors. The move may have cost a fortune—$475 million—but it safeguarded the Intel brand. Profits went up.

Grove was a godsend to the company's stockholders. During his tenure as C.E.O. Intel's stock value increased 24-fold. In May 1998 Grove resigned as C.E.O., remaining as chair of the board.

Since Grove took a back seat at Intel the company has been wrestling with a number of difficult issues, not least a likely future decline in demand for microchips. Moore's Law (originated by Intel cofounder Gordon Moore) states that microprocessing power will double every 18 months. It has held true for over a decade, delivering revenue growth to Intel through consumer chip upgrades. Eventually, though, Moore believes that the rate of increase will slow, and he should know. Grove appears to be prepared for this. He is on record as saying that "all companies will be Internet companies." Backing this view, Intel has diversified its operations to embrace the Internet.

Since Grove took a back seat at Intel the company has been wrestling with a number of difficult issues, not least a likely future decline in demand for microchips.

Context and Conclusions

Just as all companies need an entrepreneur to make things happen in the formative stages of a new venture, so too they need an organizer and steady hand to help guide a company from startup through the growth phase and beyond. Andy Grove is such a man. With resolve, vision, and an ability to take risks based on hard facts, Grove came from behind the Iron Curtain to become C.E.O. of one of America's technology bellwether stocks. As a child in war torn Europe, Grove learned to assess a situation using all available information and then make a decision. It is a skill that has served him well throughout his life, both business and personal. Whatever his future achievements, his accomplishments at Intel alone merit a place alongside the great business leaders of the 20th century.

For More Information

Books:

Grove, Andrew S. *Only the Paranoid Survive: How to Achieve a Success That's Just a Disaster Away*. New York: Doubleday, 1999.

Grove, Andrew S. *Swimming Across: A Memoir*. New York: Warner Books, 2001.

Jackson, Tim. *Inside Intel: Andy Grove and the Rise of the World's Most Powerful Chip Company*. Collingdale, PA: DIANE, 2001.

Web Site:

Intel: **www.intel.com**

"Much as we talk about Internet companies today, in five years' time there won't be any Internet companies. All companies will be Internet companies or they will be dead." (Andrew S. Grove)

William Randolph Hearst

Arguably the most famous media mogul of the 20th century, William Randolph Hearst (1863–1951) took the silver spoon of his inheritance and fashioned it into a gold one. Despite his patrician upbringing, he succeeded in keeping his finger on the pulse of his industry. Through a combination of media savvy and extraordinary stamina and persistence, he built an ailing newspaper, the *San Francisco Examiner*, into a billion dollar media empire. At his peak, Hearst owned over 40 major newspapers and magazines, not to mention a handful of radio stations and movie companies. In 1951 he died an immensely wealthy and powerful man, immortalized ten years previously, and much to his chagrin, in Orson Welles's movie, *Citizen Kane*.

Hearst knew how to handle the media.

1863	Born.
1887	Takes control of the *San Francisco Examiner.*
1889	The *San Francisco Examiner* makes a profit.
1895	Heads for New York to save the *New York Morning Journal.*
1896	Acquires New York's *Evening Journal.*
1902	Becomes a Democratic congressional representative for New York.
1920s	Builds a fabulous castle on San Simeon estate.
1930s	Forced to consolidate empire following the Great Depression.
1951	Dies.

Background and Rise

Hearst was born in San Francisco on April 29, 1863. His father was a wealthy industrialist and speculator, and his mother a socialite and philanthropist. It was a potent cocktail of wealth, commerce, and culture that was to have a profound effect on him. An only child, he spent his early years shuttling between the family's huge estate at San Simeon, California, and their home in New York.

The classical academic route for the privileged awaited: a first-class prep school—St. Paul's Preparatory School in Concord, New Hampshire—followed by an Ivy League university—Harvard. At Harvard Hearst excelled in social activities. He was a member of the Hasty Pudding Theater and, more notably, business manager for the college magazine, the *Harvard Lampoon*. So much energy was put into his social life that he neglected his academic work. Hearst was eventually expelled and he never received his degree.

An only child, he spent his early years shuttling between the family's huge estate at San Simeon, California, and their home in New York.

Shrugging off his academic failure, he took a job instead at the *New York World*. Joseph Pulitzer's newspaper was one of the leading newspapers in New York at the time. Hearst may not have paid attention in his Harvard classes, but at the *New York World* he received a first-class education in how to run a newspaper. However, he was soon summoned back to San Francisco by his father.

Defining Moments

In contrast to media moguls like Louis B. Mayer who worked their way up from the bottom of the pile, Hearst was handed his first newspaper as a gift. The *San Francisco Examiner* had been purchased by Hearst's father to provide him with a voice when he was running for the U.S. Senate. With the senate seat secured, the paper was surplus to requirements. Neglected, its circulation dwindled. The younger Hearst was desperate to take charge of it. His father was less enthusiastic and offered him as alternative inducements a one-million-acre ranch in Chihuahua, the 275,000-acre San Simeon ranch north of San Luis Obsipo, the Anaconda copper mines in Montana, and the Homestake gold mine in South Dakota. Hearst refused them all saying: "You are very kind but I would rather have the *Examiner*." Reluctantly, his father relented.

On March 4, 1887 Hearst took up residence at the *San Francisco Examiner*. He had discovered his métier. He was a brilliant newspaper owner. Thanks to a radical overhaul, by 1889 the *Examiner* was in profit. The staid format Hearst had inherited was replaced with hard-hitting investigative reporting, coupled with sensationalist attention grabbing headlines. Increased sports coverage, serialized stories by well-known authors, banner headlines like "Huge Frantic Flames," biographical sketches, and exposés of the seedy underbelly of Californian life all contributed to the heady populist mix.

As circulation and profits rose, Hearst expanded the business. In 1895 he returned to his old hunting ground

"Accuracy is to a newspaper what virtue is to a lady, but a newspaper can always print a retraction."
(Adlai E. Stevenson)

on the East Coast to save the *New York Morning Journal*. It was a decision that put him in direct competition with his onetime mentor, Joseph Pulitzer. Hearst pulled no punches in the ensuing circulation war. He added the *Evening Journal* to his collection in 1896 and poached some of Pulitzer's top writers. It was a period that gave rise to the term "Yellow Journalism," where newspapers assumed the role of opinion formers and determiners of morals. In scenes commonplace today, rival newspapers vied for scoops and used their front pages to boast of their achievements.

The most famous example of Hearst's proactive stance to newspaper reporting is the comment attributed to him when the illustrator Frederick Remington informed him that he wished to return from an uneventful Havana. Hearst supposedly responded: "Please remain. You furnish the pictures and I'll furnish the war."

His methods may have been controversial, but they worked. Hearst was unstoppable. He soon acquired newspapers in major cities throughout America. Following in his father's footsteps he became involved in politics. In 1902 Congress welcomed Hearst as a Democratic representative for New York. In all he served two terms in Congress and also became Mayor of New York City.

With his newspaper empire firmly established, Hearst expanded into other areas of the media. As a publisher he produced titles that included *Cosmopolitan*, *Good Housekeeping*, and *Harper's Bazaar*. He also moved into the movie business, cutting his teeth with Hearst-Metronome News. Ultimately it was the movie industry, coupled with his infatuation for the actress Marion Davies, that was to prove his downfall.

He formed W. R. Hearst's Cosmopolitan Productions as a vehicle for Davies, his Brooklyn-born mistress and a former Ziegfeld Follies girl. Abandoning his political career after failed attempts at the Senate and the presidency, Hearst focused solely on films. Of the hundred films Hearst sanctioned over the next 20 years, half featured his mistress. As well as sinking millions of dollars into making movies, Hearst spent more millions on a Beverly Hills mansion for Davies. Finally he embarked on the folly that was to prove his undoing, the construction of the Hearst Castle estate at San Simeon. The 25,000 acres of the estate and castle contained rare and priceless works of art, antiquities, a zoo, an airfield, and guest houses which were chateaux dismantled in Europe and flown to California to be reassembled stone by stone.

Hearst might have survived such profligate extravagance had it not been for the Great Depression. During the 1930s he was forced to consolidate his empire, selling newspapers and works of art to remain afloat. By the end of the decade he had halved his business interests and plundered the treasures at San Simeon. Marion Davies too, liquidated her personal assets and pumped $1 million into her lover's business. His final years were spent trying to prevent the release of Orson Welles's film *Citizen Kane*, a thinly disguised biopic of him. He failed. In the end, in ill health and bitter at the Welles episode, he retreated to San Simeon, handing over control of his empire to lawyers and managers. He died at the home of Marion Davies on August 14, 1951.

His final years were spent trying to prevent the release of Orson Welles's film *Citizen Kane*, a thinly disguised biopic of him. He failed.

Context and Conclusions

Although Hearst's final years were marred by what must have been for him a humiliating fall from grace, he will still be remembered as one of the greatest media barons of all time. While he was born with all the advantages wealth brings, Hearst turned around the *San Francisco Examiner*, invented a new style of popular journalism, and fashioned a media empire through hard-nosed determination, incredible stamina, and a common touch that belied his background. Hearst was truly a paradox. A man with wealth beyond the dreams and understanding of most, he was blessed nevertheless with the innate ability to appreciate the hopes and fears of ordinary people.

To the last he saw himself as the people's champion. He believed that the criticism and misfortunes that had befallen him were the result of his willingness to take a stand on behalf of the masses. "Any man who has the brains to think and the nerve to act for the benefit of the people of the country," he said, "is considered a radical by those who are content with stagnation and willing to endure disaster."

For More Information

Books:

Davies, Marion. *The Times We Had: Life with William Randolph Hearst*. New York: Ballantine Books, 1975.

Proctor, Ben. *William Randolph Hearst: The Early Years 1866–1910*. New York: Oxford University Press, 1998.

Nasaw, David. *The Chief: The Life of William Randolph Hearst*. Boston, MA: Houghton Mifflin Co., 2000.

Web Site:

The William Randolph Hearst Foundations: **www.hearstfdn.org**

Milton Snavely Hershey

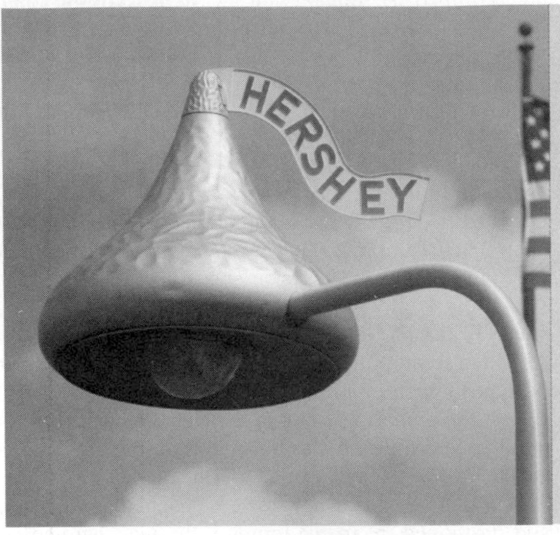

Milton Snavely Hershey (1857–1945) is the entrepreneur who brought the world the Hershey chocolate bar. He was a late starter in business, his first attempts in the confectionery industry ending in failure. Real success finally came in his late thirties with the Lancaster Caramel Company, a business he eventually sold to a rival for a large sum. The break that put Hershey in the history books came in 1893 when he stumbled across chocolate-manufacturing equipment at the World's Fair in Chicago. Hershey concentrated on chocolate, perfected a recipe for milk chocolate, introduced mass production, and built a thriving chocolate business as well as a town called Hershey.

Milton Hershey enjoyed the sweet taste of success with the innovative Hershey Kiss.

1857	Born.
1871	Drops out of school at age 13.
1872	Apprenticed at Joe Royer's Ice Cream Parlor and Garden.
1876	Opens a store making and selling candy in Philadelphia.
1882	Closes business in Philadelphia; opens and fails in Chicago.
1883	Opens candy store in New York City, which closes in 1886.
1886	Starts the Lancaster Caramel Company.
1893	Visits Chicago World's Fair and orders chocolate making equipment.
1895	Starts selling chocolate.
1900	Hershey's Chocolate Bar introduced. Lancaster Caramel Company sold for $1 million.
1906	Derry Church becomes Hershey Town.
1916	Builds sugar mill in Cuba.
1920	Loses $2.5 million on sugar futures. Forced to borrow from banks.
1942	U.S. Army asks Hershey to develop chocolate bar for field rations.
1945	Dies.

Background and Rise

Born on September 13, 1857, Milton Snavely Hershey was brought up in Hockersville, Pennsylvania. It was a small rural town and he was educated in a one-room schoolhouse. His parents were farmers and, from a very early age, Hershey was expected to help out on the farm tending the livestock and doing other chores.

Hershey put his caramel making skills to work. From the outset his business was based on quality of product.

After attending a string of schools—including a private high school, the Village Academy of Green Tree, where he did not do well—Hershey gave up on education and took a position as an apprentice with a German-language newspaper based in Gap, Lancaster County. It was soon clear that his talents did not lie with either journalism or publishing. He left the paper and joined Joseph H. Royer of Lancaster as an apprentice confectioner.

He was an ambitious young man. Aged 19 he founded his own company, M.S. Hershey, Wholesale and Retail Confectioner. The business failed and was sold in 1882. Over the following few years Hershey traveled the country trying to set himself up in the candy business. In Denver, Colorado, he learned how to make caramels. In New York City he sold his candy on the street. None of these ventures prospered, so he headed back to Lancaster. It was in Lancaster, the scene of his first business failure, that Hershey finally met with some success.

Defining Moments

Hershey put his caramel making skills to work. From the outset his business was based on quality of product. "Give them the quality, that's the best kind of advertising in the world" was his motto. The business took off when Hershey's caramels came to the attention of a candy importer who bought some to sell in England.

In 1893, however, while visiting Chicago, Hershey met the manufacturer of a German-made chocolate-making machine. He ordered one of the machines and had it shipped to Lancaster. The eventual result was a change of direction and the development of his most famous product, Hershey Chocolate.

With the caramel business, Hershey had excelled in creating a diverse range of candies. Now he concentrated on perfecting a single product—chocolate. In 1900 he sold his caramel business for $1 million to the American Caramel Company of Philadelphia. With the proceeds, he

"You have to love the products if you are going to sell them." (Barbara Thomas)

  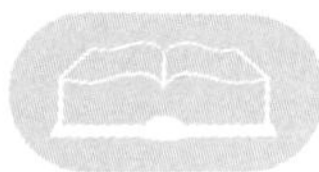    

invested in a new chocolate factory near his family home—he was married by now—in Derry Church.

When it came to making chocolate, Hershey had no recipe book or magic formula to rely on. Together with a few trusted colleagues he locked himself away and labored over the perfect milk chocolate recipe. "Nobody told Mr. Hershey how to make milk chocolate. He just found out the hard way," recalled one of his employees. Hard work though it was, Hershey struck chocolate gold. The result of his research—the Hershey chocolate bar—soon became a byword for quality in the United States.

Hershey continued to consolidate his chocolate business. He produced variations on the standard bar including: Mr. Goodbar, a milk chocolate and peanut candy bar, in 1925; Krackel, a chocolate bar filled with crisped rice, in 1938; and Hershey miniatures—small versions of all Hershey's chocolate bars—in 1939. To secure his sugar supply and guarantee its quality he built a sugar mill and small town in Cuba along the lines of Hershey, Pennsylvania.

In 1920 Hershey suffered a setback when he lost $2.5 million on the sugar futures market. He was forced to borrow from the bank, and, as a condition of the loan, the bank put a representative in Hershey's factory. It took him two years to pay the loan off and eject the overseer.

As Hershey's business grew, so too did the town surrounding the factory. Hershey wanted to build a town in keeping with his social philosophy in the same way that other chocolate philanthropists, like Joseph Rowntree and George Cadbury, had done in England. He drew up plans for an idyllic community that would not only house its inhabitants but provide for their every need, including employment at the Hershey chocolate factory. When the town was completed it contained parks, churches, a school, a hotel, a golf course, and even a zoo. Townsfolk would walk along streets such as Areba, Caracus, and Para, all named after cocoa-bean-producing regions. Hershey held a competition to name the new town. The winning entry, Hersheyoko, was vetoed by the U.S. Post Office, so he settled for plain old Hershey Town. He also constructed a mansion, High Point, overlooking the chocolate factory, to house his family.

Shortly before his death, one last act assured the name of Hershey a place in business history. When the United States entered World War II, the U.S. military instructed him to develop a chocolate bar for the troops—one that wouldn't melt. He once again set about chocolate innovation. The resulting Field Ration D Chocolate Bar formed an essential part of the army's personal kit. Not only was it a great favorite of the U.S. personnel, but with the stationing of American troops in England and the subsequent D-Day invasion of Europe, it became part of World War II folklore. Hershey died on October 13, 1945 at age 88.

CONTEXT AND CONCLUSIONS

First and foremost Hershey pioneered the mass production of food and in particular chocolate. It may only have been milk chocolate, but Hershey manufactured it on an unprecedented scale. Besides his single-minded approach, Hershey possessed a number of other qualities that contributed to his success. He was innovative, creating the Hershey Kiss and inventing his own recipe for milk chocolate. He was a bold risk-taker, making decisions like the one to build a sugar plant in Cuba. Perhaps his defining characteristic, however, was his enlightened attitude toward corporate social responsibility. It makes sense to keep the work force happy, but few can claim to have gone to such lengths as Hershey to do so. The business history books tell how successful the Hershey chocolate bar was and still is. Hershey Town with its schools, parks, churches, and chocolate factory is a more permanent record.

Hershey wanted to build a town in keeping with his social philosophy in the same way that other chocolate philanthropists, like Joseph Rowntree and George Cadbury, had done in England.

For More Information

Books:

Brenner, Joël Glenn. *The Emperors of Chocolate: Inside the Secret World of Hershey and Mars*. New York: Random House, 1999.

McMahon, James D. *Built on Chocolate: The Story of the Hershey Chocolate Company*. Santa Monica, CA: General Publishing Group, 1998.

Web Site:

Hershey Foods Corporation: **www.hersheys.com**

SOICHIRO HONDA

Soichiro Honda started in business as a car mechanic and then, bypassing the time-honored Japanese networking system or *gakubatsa*, he made his own way in business with no help from cronies. The Honda Company was founded in 1948 and its first motorcycle—the Dream—was produced a year later. Success followed success. In 1959 Honda became the leading motorcycle manufacturer in Japan, and the Honda sports motorcycle team won the team prize at the Isle of Man TT races. In the same year the first Honda motorcycles were sold in the United States; soon they were outselling every other brand. The company went into the automobile business in the 1960s. Until Soichiro Honda's death in 1992 the company continued to be the most popular motorcycle manufacturer in the world and remained high in the international rankings of leading automobile manufacturers.

Soichiro Honda rides onto the world stage.

1906	Born.
1937	Founds Tokai Seiki Heavy Industry (TSHI).
1948	Cofounds Honda with Takeo Fujisawa.
1949	D Type motorcycle—the Dream—manufactured.
1952	Production of Cub begins.
1954	Honda motorcycle team is founded.
1959	Opens dealership in United States. Super Cub goes into production.
1963	Honda becomes top-selling motorcycle brand in United States.
1973	Officially retires.
1984	Ten million Honda 50s sold in United States.
1992	Dies.

BACKGROUND AND RISE

Born in the small Japanese town of Komyo in 1906, Soichiro Honda spent his early childhood helping his father with his bicycle repair business. At 15, without the benefit of a formal education, Honda traveled to Tokyo to look for work. He secured an apprenticeship at a garage, but ended up babysitting for the garage owner. Frustrated and dispirited, he returned home, only to be called back within six months. This time he stayed for six years, working as car mechanic before returning home once more to start his own car mechanic business. He was 22.

Born in the small Japanese town of Komyo in 1906, Soichiro Honda spent his early childhood helping his father with his bicycle repair business.

Honda's love of cars extended to racing them, and he set a new average speed record in 1936. Unfortunately he suffered a bad crash, breaking several bones, including both wrists. His wife, fearing for his safety, persuaded him to give up his hobby. Without the distraction of racing Honda concentrated his energies on his business, and in 1937 he expanded into piston ring manufacture, founding Tokai Seiki Heavy Industry (TSHI). He was still conscious of his lack of education, however, and enrolled at the Hamamatsu School of Technology. As it turned out, he needn't have bothered.

Honda made a poor student. The demands of his business made it difficult to keep up with his classwork. He was reluctant to pay attention to engineering lectures that didn't involve piston rings, and he refused to take notes or attend written examinations. When the school's principal warned Honda that if he did not submit to examination he would not receive his diploma, Honda was unrepentant. "I am not impressed by diplomas. They don't do the work," he later said. "My marks were not as good as those of others, and I didn't take the final examination. The principal called me in and said I should leave. I told him that I didn't want a diploma–it had less value than a cinema ticket. A ticket at least guaranteed you would get in. A diploma guaranteed nothing."

Giving up on the diploma and therefore shunning the *gakubatsa*, the Japanese old-boy networking system, the maverick Honda set out to make his fortune on his own terms.

DEFINING MOMENTS

By 1948 Honda had sold TSHI to Toyota for 450,000 yen (worth about $1 million today). He had established the Honda Technical Research Institute in 1946 and had tried to retire but found he couldn't resist the lure of engineering.

In 1948 Honda met a kindred spirit in financier Takeo Fujisawa. The two men had similar opinions on Japan's postwar industrial strategy. Both believed in long term investment, and in partnership with Honda, Fujisawa agreed to invest in a new company to manufacture engines. Honda retained responsibility for engineering, while Fujisawa dealt with marketing and sales.

"To me success can only be achieved through repeated failure and introspection." (Soichiro Honda)

  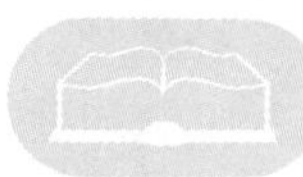    

By the 1950s Honda had signed a contract to sell the company's entire output of motorcycle engines to a company called Kitagawa. This wasn't as good a deal as it first appeared: Honda was geared up to produce 100 engines a month, while Kitagawa only produced 80 motorcycles at the most during the same period. Honda addressed the resulting cash flow problem by tearing up his contract with Kitagawa and replacing it with deals to supply complete motorcycles to distributors.

The company's first big hit was the Cub, which offered customers the choice either of buying an engine to fit to their bicycles or buying a complete motorcycle. In less than a year the Cub was selling 6,500 units a month and had captured over 70% of the Japanese domestic motorcycle market.

While Honda's reluctance to play by the rules caused problems in some areas, particularly with the Japanese Ministry of International Trade and Industry, it served the company well in others. Honda adopted a refreshingly open recruitment policy. Although the company had problems recruiting graduate students because of Honda's unwillingness to play the *gakubatsa* game, it attracted many high caliber employees who had been rejected by other Japanese corporations.

Honda was a perfectionist when it came to product design. He traveled the world conducting market research in person. He attended motorcycle races, taking notes on the competition. By using the best of the competition as a benchmark, Honda managed to turn the Honda motorcycle from an average product into the best racing motorcycle in the world. Success in motorcycle racing (Honda launched its own motorcycle racing team in 1954) raised the public profile of the company, added to the brand value, and enabled racing technology to filter down to the standard production model.

A big year for Honda came in 1959, when the company went into large scale production of a new model that would sweep all before it, the Super Cub. To manufacture it Honda constructed the world's largest motorcycle plant in Suzuka City, which turned out 30,000 machines a month. In the same year the Honda team won first prize in the Isle of Man motorcycle races. Success on the track translated into sales.

In 1959 Honda Motorcycles opened its first dealership in the United States. Instead of selling through the existing U.S. motorcycle distributors, Honda took a more unconventional approach. He sold the small Honda motorcycles wherever he thought he might attract customers. At the time, total motorcycle sales in the United States were less than 5,000 a month. But by 1963 the company was selling 7,800 units; by 1984 Honda had sold some ten million Honda 50s. This remarkable success was due to the quality of the product and a brilliant advertising campaign. Instead of targeting its product at conventional motorcycle enthusiasts, Honda authorized a campaign with the slogan "You meet the nicest people on a Honda." The campaign targeted the family market and was a huge success.

The company Honda built went on to dominate the motorcycle market and make a big impact in the car market. At the end of the 20th century the company was still the world's number one motorcycle manufacturer. Honda retired on October 1973, taking an office in Tokyo where he busied himself with work connected with the Honda Foundation. He died in 1992.

Honda was a perfectionist when it came to product design. He traveled the world conducting market research in person.

Context and Conclusions

Along with Konosuke Matsushita, Akio Morita, and Eiji Toyoda, Soichiro Honda was one of Japan's greatest industrialists. Notable for his independent streak, Honda spurned the traditional methods of building a business, deciding instead to go it alone. Turning a hobby into a business, he built a billion dollar company that produced the best selling motorcycle in the world. So good were their design and build quality that Honda motorcycles were soon outselling Triumph and Harley-Davidson in the U.K. and U.S. markets. To achieve this Honda used a combination of excellent engineering and clever marketing. By making a sports motorcycle that was faster than its competitors, the Honda company gained cachet for its consumer models and stayed at the cutting edge of technological development.

Above all, Soichiro Honda was determined to make his dreams a reality. "Many people dream of success," he said. "To me success can only be achieved through repeated failure and introspection. In fact, success represents 1% of your work which results from the 99% that is called failure."

For More Information

Web Site:
Honda: **www.honda.com**

See also:

- **Konosuke Matsushita (pp. 1114–15)**
- **Akio Morita (pp. 1118–19)**
- **Eiji Toyoda (pp. 1144–45)**

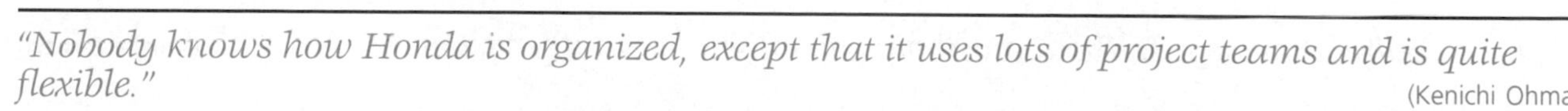

"Nobody knows how Honda is organized, except that it uses lots of project teams and is quite flexible."

(Kenichi Ohmae)

 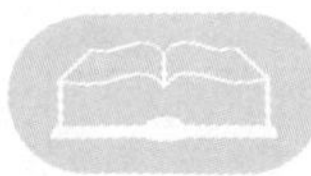    

Howard Robard Hughes, Jr.

Howard Robard Hughes, Jr. (1905–1975) was born into wealth. His father founded a company that exploited a new design of oil drill. The Hughes Tool Company was to provide a safety net of wealth throughout Hughes's life that made it possible for him to indulge his every whim. Indulge he did. Before the age of 25 he had moved to Hollywood and made several successful movies, founded a new drill bit company, bought over a hundred movie theaters, and learned to fly. By the time of his death in 1975, he had a built a successful airline (TWA), run a movie business, bought a piece of the gaming action on the Strip in Las Vegas, broken several airspeed records, survived three plane crashes, and become a legendary recluse. Few people have packed as much into one lifetime as Howard Hughes.

Howard Hughes on the way up.

1905	Born.
1909	Father forms Sharp-Hughes Tool Company.
1925	Hughes moves to Hollywood, California. Starts making movies.
1927	*Two Arabian Knights* wins the Academy Award for comedy.
1934	Sets up Hughes Aircraft Company.
1935	Breaks airspeed record.
1936	Aged 30, breaks U.S. transcontinental speed record in a self-built plane.
1938	Smashes record for New York–Paris flight with time of 16 hours and 35 minutes.
1939	Obtains majority share in Transcontinental & West Airline.
1948	Saves airline (now renamed Trans World Airlines) from bankruptcy.
1954	Sells large part of RKO and concentrates on TWA.
1955	Establishes the Howard Hughes Medical Institute in Miami, Florida.
1966	Sells TWA shares for $750 million.
1975	Dies.

Background and Rise

Hughes's first movie, *Swell Hogan*, was a flop. His third, *Two Arabian Knights*, made money and won the 1927 Academy Award for comedy.

There is much disagreement about the facts surrounding the life of Howard Hughes. The disagreement even extends to his birthplace. Was it the city of Houston or the oil town of Humble? But there is no argument that Hughes was born on December 24, 1905 in Texas. His father was a wealthy man with a business degree from Harvard and a law degree from Iowa State University. In 1909 Howard Sr. formed the Sharp-Hughes Tool Company, manufacturing drilling bits for the oil industry. It was his invention of a new oil drill bit that propelled the Hughes family to the kind of wealth that even his noted profligacy could not dent.

As a boy, Howard Jr. was especially interested in engineering. He showed an impressive knack for building machines, constructing his own radio set as well as his own motorcycle. Away from engineering, Hughes's Uncle Rupert, a novelist and playwright, would take the boy to visit the Goldwyn studio where he developed a fascination with the movies.

Both Hughes's parents died before he was 20. On the death of his father, he somehow persuaded his relatives to sell him the Hughes Tool Company. Then, in 1925, he married a wealthy woman, Ella Rice, and moved to Hollywood, California.

In Hollywood Hughes began to exhibit the almost maniacal energy and drive that sustained him throughout his varied career.

Defining Moments

By 1925 Hughes had created the Caddo Rock Drill Bit Company, bought a controlling interest in Multi-Color, Inc., moved into a house on Muirfield Road in Los Angeles, and hired Noah Dietrich, ostensibly as an assistant. Dietrich was to become the "fixer" for the Hughes empire in the coming years. Hughes also purchased over a hundred movie theaters to assist him in his latest venture—moviemaking.

Hughes's first movie, *Swell Hogan*, was a flop. His third, *Two Arabian Knights*, made money and won the 1927 Academy Award for comedy. Hughes had another hit with *Scarface* and followed it with *The Front Page*. The difficulties involved in making *Scarface*, which stemmed partly from antagonism toward his anti-Semitic beliefs, took their toll on him and he temporarily abandoned moviemaking. For a time he restricted his interest in the

"I have a feeling there is just about one more good flight left in my system." (Amelia Earhart)

movies to dating some of the most beautiful women of the time, including Ida Lupino, Katharine Hepburn, Ginger Rogers, Ava Gardner, and Lana Turner. Instead of making movies he turned his attention to the aviation business.

Hughes decided to form an aircraft company, so he hired a brilliant aeronautical engineer, Glen Odekirk, and set up business in a hangar in California. In the interval between shooting *The Front Page*, and setting up the Hughes Aircraft Company in 1934, he disappeared from sight. At about the same time, however, there appeared on the scene a gangly employee of American Airways, 6 feet 3 inches tall, called Charles Howard, who, irritatingly, asked endless questions about the airline's operations. Charles Howard, it transpired, was none other than Howard Hughes himself. Hughes also spent some of this "missing" period traveling as a hobo, and as a society photographer, a business he started from scratch in Huntsville, Texas, under the name R. Wayne Rector.

In 1939 Hughes helped finance Transcontinental & West Airline, obtaining a majority share in the process. The airline was later renamed Trans World Airlines (TWA). By 1940 a dynamic Hughes was running several businesses simultaneously, in different fields. He still owned the tool manufacturing company he had bought from his father's estate, which made him $2 million a month. In addition he was back in the movie business, running an airline, and gearing up for wartime manufacturing.

In the first half of the 1940s Hughes ordered commercial aircraft from Lockheed, made and released the film *The Outlaw*, created a new starlet in Jane Russell, opened a manufacturing plant to assist the U.S. war effort, and crashed yet another aircraft. He had already crashed two planes, killing two passengers.

In 1946, after another period of absence, Hughes reappeared to test his experimental reconnaissance aircraft, the XF-11. At 400 mph the plane became unstable. To the consternation of the members, he tried to land on the Los Angeles Country Club golf course. Luckily for the club, but unluckily for him, he didn't make it, plowing into a house on the way down. He was admitted to the Cedars of Lebanon Hospital, and the doctors predicted he would not last through the night. His injuries were extensive: a crushed chest, 12 broken ribs, a collapsed left lung, fractured shoulder, crushed vertebrae, and third-degree burns. Remarkably, the apparently indestructible Hughes made a good recovery. He was left with burn scars and a deformed left hand, but very much alive.

Discharged from the hospital, he set about turning TWA around. He saved the ailing airline by obtaining a subsidy from the Civil Aeronautics Board in 1948, and a $10 million loan from the Reconstruction Finance Corporation. He also bolstered his movie business, buying the struggling RKO studio (Radio-Keith Orpheum) for $9 million. In 1954 Hughes sold most of RKO to concentrate on TWA. In 1955 he established the Howard Hughes Medical Institute in Miami, Florida, in an attempt to reduce his tax liabilities. On May 3, 1966 he sold 78% of his TWA stock for $750 million. It made him, temporarily, the richest man in the world.

The remainder of Hughes's career, until his death in 1975, was characterized by obsessive-neurotic behavior and flight from the IRS. Yet, despite his continual dislocation—moving from one hotel to another, one country to another—his increasingly bizarre behavior, and his dependence on pain-killing drugs, Hughes somehow managed to control his businesses from the end of a phone. He even expanded into hotels and casinos, buying the Desert Inn, Sands, Castaways, New Frontier, and Silver Slipper on the Strip in Las Vegas, as well as thousands of acres of land and over 500 mining concessions in an incredible spending spree.

The remainder of Hughes's career, until his death in 1975, was characterized by obsessive-neurotic behavior and flight from the IRS.

The fact that Hughes's disparate collection of companies fell apart within 12 years of his death is evidence, if any were needed, that his bizarre personality was the glue that bound his business empire together.

Context and Conclusions

Of all the business leaders and entrepreneurs of the 20th century, Howard Hughes is one of the most colorful, controversial, and bizarre. An examination of his life reveals a man driven by the most basic of instincts: power, greed, lust, enmity. He ended his days a compulsive-obsessive, drug dependent hypochondriac, but consistently conducted business deals with a shrewdness beyond most of his peers. His achievements encompass movie making, aviation, and the hotel and gaming industry. In the movies Hughes notoriously pushed back the boundaries of decency and showed that it was possible to make successful movies outside the studio system. In Nevada he succeeded in loosening the Mob's grip on Las Vegas. In aviation he was among those who pioneered commercial airflight.

For More Information

Books:

Brown, Peter Harry, and Pat H. Broeske. *Howard Hughes: The Untold Story*. Brentwood, CA: Dutton, 1996.

Keats, John. *Howard Hughes*. New York: Random House, 1972.

Rummel, Robert W. *Howard Hughes and TWA*. Washington, D.C.: Smithsonian Institution Press, 1991.

Thomas, Tony. *Howard Hughes in Hollywood*. Secaucus, NJ: Citadel Press, 1985.

LEE IACOCCA

The lionization of chief executive officers began in earnest with Lee Iacocca. In the 1980s his remarkable turnaround of car giant Chrysler made him a corporate hero. The myth he helped to create culminated in the extraordinary worship of GE's Jack Welch in recent years. Arriving at the Ford Motor Corporation as a trainee engineer in 1946, Iacocca received the best education available in the industry. He worked his way up through Ford, not in engineering but in sales. Iacocca always claimed he wasn't a natural salesman, but he made a big impact at Ford with his revolutionary financing plan. He introduced the Ford Mustang, and was promoted to president of the company. After an internal power struggle, instigated by Henry Ford II, Iacocca was fired in 1978. He switched sides, joining Chrysler and becoming C.E.O. in 1979.

Iacocca was the driving force behind Chrysler's turnaround.

1924	Born.
1946	Joins Ford as a trainee engineer.
1949	Becomes sales manager.
1956	Introduces a new finance plan called the "56 for '56."
1970	Becomes president of Ford.
1978	Fired by Henry Ford II.
1979	Iacocca becomes chairman and C.E.O. of Chrysler.
1983	Writes out check for $813,487,500 to clear Chrysler's federal debt.
1992	Retires from Chrysler.
1999	Starts E.V. Global Motors.

BACKGROUND AND RISE

Lee Iacocca was born on October 15, 1924 in Allentown, Pennsylvania. Iacocca's father ran a small hot dog business. For the Iacoccas, as for many other families during the late 1920s and 1930s, times were hard. Iacocca Sr. lost all his money and nearly lost the family home. Even though Lee Iacocca was only seven at the time, the harshness of the Depression ingrained frugality so deeply that, while he may not have been risk-averse in his business dealings, he always invested money conservatively and to this day dislikes waste.

Iacocca received the best education available in the industry. He worked his way up through Ford, not in engineering but in sales.

DEFINING MOMENTS

As a trainee at Ford's famous River Rouge plant, Iacocca got to see every stage of automobile production, from the extraction of coal and limestone, through the production of steel, to the manufacturing of the cars on the assembly line. It represented the best training the auto industry had to offer. Graduating from his trainee course, Iacocca decided against engineering and instead went to work in the Ford sales office in Chester, Pennsylvania. He was not a born salesman, yet through practice and experience he improved quickly, moving from a bashful, stammering sales clerk to become sales manager in 1949.

The 1950s were good years for Iacocca. In 1956, to combat poor sales of Ford motor cars, he introduced a new finance scheme called the "56 for '56." Credit financing was just beginning to take hold as a way of purchasing cars. The scheme allowed the cash strapped purchaser to make a modest down payment of 20% and then follow up with three further payments of $56. The scheme was a success, and was adopted company-wide, making Iacocca an overnight star within the Ford ranks. One promotion quickly followed another. By 1960 he was head of the Ford division. Aged 36, Iacocca was general manager of the largest division in the world's second biggest automobile company.

He soon stamped his authority on the company, playing an influential role in the decision to abandon a proposed new model, the Cardinal, which was dropped despite the company incurring a $35 million loss. In its place, the first Ford Mustang rolled off the assembly line. The new car had been designed from scratch and was priced at an affordable level. Its launch created a wave of publicity, simultaneously featuring on the covers of *Time* and *Newsweek* magazines. The Mustang was the car the market had been waiting for. In its first year it sold a record 418,812, making a profit of $1.1 billion.

For Iacocca, who had championed the Mustang, the car's popularity had certain unwelcome side effects. There was no such thing as a private life anymore for the man who had brought Ford's most popular car to market. When Iacocca was returning from a trip to Europe on the Ford company plane, the pilot was contacted by two other pilots and a radio operator from a ship below, all of them wanting to speak to his celebrated passenger.

"If you're not scared, you're too stupid to work here." (Lee Iacocca)

"Is nothing sacred? It's Sunday morning. I am in the middle of nowhere, and I can't get away from this Mustang mania!" was Iacocca's reply. But Iacocca had much to thank the Mustang for. In January 1965 he was promoted to vice president of the corporate car/truck group, and on December 10, 1970 he became president of the Ford empire.

President he may have been, but Iacocca was not the most powerful person at Ford. That honor was reserved for the founder's grandson, Henry Ford II. Ford operated an unorthodox management style; he ruled through fear. Executives could find themselves clearing their desks for the most unlikely reasons. For several years Iacocca managed to walk the tightrope, on the one hand not seeming to threaten Ford's authority yet, on the other, doing a good enough job to avoid being fired. It is to his credit that Iacocca managed to stay in the job as long as he did.

In ill health, with his marriage strained, Ford became increasingly paranoid and his decisions increasingly bizarre. There was even an internal investigation within the company at Ford's request into Iacocca's activities which allegedly cost over $1,500,000 and came up with nothing damaging. Then, in 1977, Ford turned to the management consulting firm McKinsey & Company, calling them in to reorganize the company's management structure. McKinsey recommended a new structure with a chairman/C.E.O., vice chairman, and president at the top. Iacocca now became number three in the ruling triumvirate, and to humiliate him further, Ford insisted on parading this apparent demotion in public. Then in 1978 Ford fired Iacocca. The reason—in Ford's own words—was: "Sometimes you just don't like somebody."

Iacocca was 54. He could have retired. Yet a few months later he joined the Chrysler Motor Corporation, becoming chairman and C.E.O. in September 1979. During his time at Chrysler Iacocca executed one of the most impressive turnarounds in automobile history. When he arrived, the Detroit press was full of gloomy headlines such as "Chrysler losses are worst ever." The company was struggling, but, when he joined, Iacocca had not realized how serious its problems were. He soon found out—Chrysler was running out of money, and fast. Iacocca took swift remedial action: he eradicated excess inventory, renegotiated contracts with car rental companies Hertz and Avis, recruited a slew of top talent, and made substantial layoffs. Most important of all, he went cap in hand to the government and applied for a loan guarantee for $1.2 billion. It required new legislation. To secure government support Iacocca had to give testimony in Washington before the House of Representatives and Senate hearings. But the request was granted.

That it was attests to Iacocca's powers as a salesman. As he cut costs at Chrysler (he cut his own salary to $1), and the automobile market picked up, Chrysler's flagging fortunes revived. In 1983 Chrysler made a profit of $925 million and not long after a new stock offering, Iacocca wrote out an historic check for $813,487,500 to clear the balance of the debt outstanding on the government loan.

Iacocca went on to steer Chrysler to greater success. He engineered the company's $1.5 billion acquisition of American Motors, and incorporated the Jeep into Chrysler's product offering. Iacocca retired from Chrysler in 1992, but his enthusiasm for business remained undiminished. Leaving the motor giants behind him, he founded a small start-up company, E.V. Global Motors, selling electric powered bicycles.

Context and Conclusions

Brilliant businessmen such as Henry Ford, Walter Chrysler, and Billy Durant long ago earned their place in the auto hall of fame. But among the postwar generation, few deserve to sit alongside the founding fathers. Lee Iacocca is one of them, successfully running not one but two of the big three U.S. motor manufacturers.

A rare combination of talented salesman and empathetic man-manager, Iacocca had an instinctive feeling for which models would sell and which would not. He introduced the Ford Mustang and revitalized Ford's prospects when the company was drifting directionless following the death of the first Henry Ford. At Chrysler Iacocca performed one of the most breathtaking turnarounds in corporate history; in the process he became a corporate icon.

CLOSE BUT NO CIGAR

Bob Lutz
Ex-Marine fighter pilot Lutz paid his dues in the motor business, working his way through General Motors, BMW, and, finally, Ford, where he was vice president. After Ford he became Iacocca's right-hand man at Chrysler and played a big part in the company's revival. Many think he should have gotten the C.E.O. job when Iacocca left. In 2001 he left Chrysler to join General Motors as vice president.

For More Information

Books:

Iacocca, Lee, with William Novak. *Iacocca: An Autobiography*. New York: Bantam Books, 1984.

Iacocca, Lee, with Sonny Kleinfield. *Talking Straight*. New York: Bantam, 1989.

Wyden, Peter. *The Unknown Iacocca*. New York: Morrow, 1987.

Web Site:

Chrysler 2001: **www.chrysler.com**

"We at Chrysler borrow money the old-fashioned way. We pay it back." (Lee Iacocca)

STEVE JOBS

Steve Jobs, cofounder of Apple Computer, is one of the folk-hero C.E.O.s. The company was started in a garage by Jobs and his cofounder Steve Wozniak—and its Apple PCs changed the face of computing. Unfortunately, Apple got its strategy wrong, tying the Mac operating system software to Apple hardware. Microsoft went in the opposite direction, licensing the MS-DOS operating system to any and every PC manufacturer. The rest is history.

In 1985, former Pepsi chairman John Sculley, brought in to add beef to Apple, removed Jobs from the company he had founded. Sculley himself was removed in 1993, and Jobs was eventually asked to return.

Since his comeback, Jobs has breathed new life into the company. To his many fans, Apple's revival confirms Jobs's status as one of the greatest technology entrepreneurs ever.

Steve Jobs, folk-hero founder of Apple.

1955	Born.
1974	Takes a job with Atari.
1976	First product, the Apple I, marketed.
1977	Apple II. Apple incorporated; Mike Markkula buys shares in the company and becomes chairman.
1980	Apple goes public.
1982	$1 billion sales; John Sculley becomes C.E.O.
1984	Launch of Apple Macintosh.
1985	Jobs leaves Apple.
1986	Founds NeXT. Cofounds Pixar.
1993	Sculley leaves Apple.
1996	Jobs returns as consultant.
1997	Becomes "interim C.E.O."
1998	iMac launched.
2000	Drops "interim" from job title.

BACKGROUND AND RISE

In February 1955 Paul and Clara Jobs adopted an orphan, Stephen Jobs. Jobs was brought up in Los Altos, California.

> **The Apple I computer was designed in Jobs's bedroom and the prototype constructed in his garage.**

Out of school, Jobs attended lectures at the Hewlett-Packard electronics company, and it was while working at Hewlett-Packard one summer that he met Stephen Wozniak, a University of California dropout. Wozniak was an engineering whiz kid who was continually inventing gadgets.

Once again he hooked up with Wozniak, attending meetings of the "Homebrew Computer Club." Most of the members were geeks, interested only in diodes, transistors, and the electronic gadgets they built from them. Jobs was different; he had an eye for style, utility, and marketability. Jobs persuaded Wozniak to work with him to build a personal computer. The Apple I computer was designed in Jobs's bedroom and the prototype constructed in his garage.

After moderate success selling their first computer, a local electronics retailer ordered 25. Some helpful advice from a retired C.E.O. of Intel inspired Jobs and Wozniak to start their own company. To do so they sold their most treasured possessions, in Jobs's case his Volkswagen microbus. For Wozniak it was his prized Hewlett-Packard calculator. With the $1,300 they raised, the two started a new company, which they named Apple.

DEFINING MOMENTS

The company's first product, the Apple I, was marketed in 1976, priced at $666. As members of the local computing fraternity, Jobs and Wozniak were well positioned to drum up interest in their new machine. Sales of the Apple I brought in $774,000 and soon the two entrepreneurs were working on the Apple II. The second incarnation of the Apple computer was a resounding success. This was not just down to its engineering, it was also due in large part to Jobs's marketing savvy. In an inspired move he brought in Regis McKenna, the best public relations man in Silicon Valley, the man who went on to popularize relationship marketing.

In 1980 Apple went public. Originally priced at $22 per share, the stock rose on the first day to $29, capitalizing the company at $1.2 billion. Between 1978 and 1983, in the absence of any real competition, Apple forged ahead in the personal computer market; its compound growth rate was over 150% per annum. Then, in 1981, IBM introduced its first PC, using an operating system called MS-DOS, licensed from a small software company called Microsoft. Within two years, IBM had exceeded Apple's dollar sales of PCs. Furthermore, Microsoft was causing a stir in the PC market, even though it didn't manufacture

"I want to put a ding in the universe." (Steve Jobs)

PC hardware. Microsoft licensed its operating software to PC producers. Jobs realized that if IBM and Microsoft were allowed to dominate the market then Apple could become marginalized.

To restore Apple's fortunes, Jobs turned to John Sculley, C.E.O. at Pepsi.

The result of this unlikely alliance between the corporate suit, Sculley, and the counterculture kid, Jobs, was the personal computer that cemented Apple Computer's status as the computer enthusiast's favorite computer company—the Apple Macintosh.

Instead of writing commands in computerese, Macintosh owners used a mouse to click on easily recognizable icons—a trash can and file folders, for example. Suddenly, you didn't need a degree in computer science to operate a personal computer. Other companies followed where Apple led, most significantly Microsoft. Apple became the darling of the creative world with an iconic status that Bill Gates and his crew never achieved. But what Microsoft did do was to dominate the PC software industry, commanding 80% market share as against Apple's 20%. In the end that proved critical.

The Apple fairy tale came to a sticky end in 1985 when white knight Sculley did the unthinkable and removed Jobs from the company he had founded. A fired-up Jobs proceeded to plow $250 million of investors' money into another start-up, NeXT Computer. It disappointed, selling only 50,000 units. Pixar Animation Studios, in which he invested $60 million of his own fortune, was a different story, however. This investment eventually paid out with the computer-animated blockbusters *Toy Story* and *A Bug's Life*. Back at Apple, Sculley himself was booted out in 1993 after a disastrous period that saw Apple's market share plummet from 20% to just 8%. He was replaced by Michael Spindler who lasted until 1996, by which time Apple's market share had fallen to just over 5%. Apple was staring oblivion in the face as even its long-term devotees began to switch to the Microsoft-powered PCs in droves. Spindler was shown the door; Gil Amelio took over in the hot seat. After 500 days in the job, and with Apple's market share unmoved, Amelio invited Jobs back to help in a consulting role. It wasn't long before Amelio was on his way out too, and Jobs, now Apple's self-styled interim C.E.O., was back where he started.

With Jobs back at the helm, Apple looked more like its old self. He dumped the NeXT operating system that he had sold to Apple, ditched loss-making licensing contracts, and most significantly launched the new iMac. The iMac was the embodiment of everything Jobs believed in: eye-catching design and simple operation. It was also the product of a different vision of the computer itself. It had no disk drive because Jobs believed they had been superseded by external storage devices such as zip drives and the Internet. The stylish Internet-ready machine, which Jobs hoped would restore the company's fading fortunes, was launched with the slogan "Chic Not Geek" blazed across advertising posters. The iMac, a vision in translucent blue, sold 278,000 units in the first six weeks, an achievement that had *Fortune* magazine describing it as "one of the hottest computer launches ever." Wall Street, too, recovered its confidence in Apple: the company's share price doubled in less than a year. Fiscal 2000 revenues were some $7.98 billion, with net earnings of $786 million, and Apple has started to open a series of retail stores across the United States. Since then Apple's share price has been caught up in the same vortex as other technology companies. What the future holds is unclear, but with Jobs back on the Apple throne, at least the company looks more like its old successful trailblazing self.

The iMac was the embodiment of everything Jobs believed in: eye-catching design and simple operation.

Context and Conclusions

Described by one newspaper as a "corporate Huckleberry Finn," Steve Jobs is one of a select group of IT whiz kids that includes Bill Gates, Larry Ellison, and Scott McNealy. Where Jobs differs from his tech peers is in his sense of style. IBM brought computers to the business world, Microsoft gave the PC its MS-DOS operating system, but Jobs made computing easy. By taking the graphical user interface that he had first seen in a Xerox PARC laboratory and incorporating it into the Apple Mac, Jobs enabled the technologically nonliterate to use a computer by simply pointing and clicking.

And if that wasn't a sufficient contribution to the history of the PC, Jobs developed one of the first computer animation film studios, Pixar, and then returned to Apple just in time to save it from rotting. With the introduction of the iMac, Jobs once again demonstrated the imagination and design flair that made him a multimillionaire and made Apple the computer of choice for millions of devoted followers.

For More Information

Books:

Carlton, Jim. *Apple: The Inside Story of Intrigue, Egomania, and Business Blunders*. New York: Random House, 1997.

Deutschman, Alan. *The Second Coming of Steve Jobs*. New York: Broadway Books, 2000.

Young, Jeffrey S. *Steve Jobs: The Journey Is the Reward*. New York: Lynx Books, 1988.

Web Site:

Apple: **www.apple.com**

"I'm just a guy who probably should have been a semi-talented poet on the Left Bank. I got sort of side-tracked here."

(Steve Jobs)

  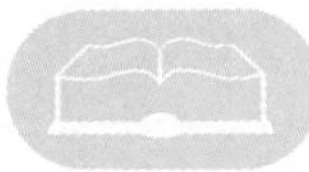    

Ingvar Kamprad

The flat pack king of furniture, Kamprad is a brilliant if unorthodox businessman. Like Richard Branson, Kamprad enjoys challenging the establishment and upsetting the odds. Industrious from an early age, Kamprad took on the furniture cartel in Sweden and neatly outsmarted it. In the end, as he always predicted they would, customers got what they demanded: low prices and good quality. Kamprad continued to deliver value for money to ordinary people through innovations such as flat-pack furniture and self-service. Shopping the IKEA way became a family day out, a fun experience, long before the advent of the out-of-town super mall. When Kamprad officially took a back seat from line management at IKEA in 1986, he had changed the nature of retailing and provided inspiration for thousands of entrepreneurs.

IKEA, Kamprad's home base.

1926	Born.
1943	Registers company, Ikéa (letters don't become uppercase until much later).
1948	Advertises furniture for the first time.
1951	Publishes first catalog. Revenue exceeds one million kronor ($95,000).
1953	Opens factory combined with furniture exhibition center in Älmhult.
1956	Introduces flat packaging.
1958	Opens first store in Älmhult.
1965	Introduces self-service in stores.
1982	Ownership transferred to Dutch Foundation—Stichting INGKA.
1986	Officially retires, handing day-to-day running to Anders Moberg.
1995	Stichting INGKA buys Habitat chain.
1999	150th store opens. Turnover reaches Kr60 billion ($5.689 billion).

Background and Rise

Ingvar Kamprad was born on the family farm, Elmtaryd, in 1926, in the harsh countryside of Småland, Sweden. His was a tough upbringing. Sweden in the late 1920s and early 1930s was a difficult place in which to grow up. Outside the Swedish cities, the cold unforgiving landscape of the country offered few opportunities for advancement. Yet Kamprad was resourceful, committed, and full of the enthusiasm of youth.

He made his first real money selling garden seed. It was enough to buy a new racing bike and a typewriter.

He began in a small way by selling matches to neighbors. He was five years old. He graduated to catching fish and selling them, as well as picking lingonberries which he dispatched by bus to a local buyer. He made his first real money selling garden seed. It was enough to buy a new racing bike and a typewriter.

Defining Moments

Kamprad was still only 17 when, in 1943, he started his own company. He called it Ikéa: IK from his initials, E and A for Elmtaryd, the farm he grew up on, and Agunnaryd, his home village. By 1945 Kamprad was selling a hodgepodge of products. His business had outgrown local delivery and he began to sell by mail order. Newspaper advertisements stimulated demand and the local milk cart and train network solved his distribution problems. Soon pens, pencils, picture frames, wallets, watches, and other assorted goods were wending their way across Sweden, courtesy of IKEA. Astonishingly Kamprad was still working full time, as well as running this business. It was only after completing his national service in 1946 that he began to focus solely on his business.

Kamprad advertised furniture for the first time in 1948. His decision to sell furniture was initially a result of matching his main competitor. The furniture was sourced from local manufacturers; it was cheap, and sales were promising—so much so that four years later he abandoned his other products to concentrate on affordably priced furniture and domestic articles.

Until 1953 the business had operated as a mail order business only. The problem was that competition in the mail order industry was driving down prices and product quality. Kamprad was engaged in a vicious and unsustainable price war on several fronts, and delivery of shoddy goods by competitors was also adversely affecting the reputation of the industry. The solution was to allow the customers to see and touch the products themselves. Kamprad bought a local joinery in Älmhult that was about to close and informed his customers that IKEA was now a furniture company. If the customers wished to see the products in the catalog close up, then they could visit

"How the hell can I ask people who work for me to travel cheaply if I am traveling in luxury."

(Ingvar Kamprad)

IKEA's furniture exhibition when it opened on March 18, 1953. It was a gamble. On the opening day, nervously Kamprad threw back the doors of his new display store-cum-furniture factory. The sight that greeted him took his breath away. There were at least 1,000 people waiting patiently outside. Maybe it was the coffee and buns that he had rashly promised to all first-day visitors.

It was in those early days that the principles that underpin IKEA's business today were developed. Cost awareness was one fundamental rule. Kamprad saved on string, boxes, paper, and whatever he could. Another feature was the provision of food. IKEA's stores may have progressed from the provision of buns and coffee to restaurants with extensive menus, but the idea that you can get something tasty to eat remains. For Kamprad it was always a practical decision to provide food, since people were traveling long distances to reach the Ämhult factory.

In 1955, Kamprad encountered his first major setback. IKEA was doing well; but business was too good, as it turned out. Unable to compete fairly with Kamprad, competitors turned to less savory methods. Suppliers suddenly found themselves under pressure not to supply IKEA. The company was mysteriously banned from trade fairs. On one occasion, Kamprad had to resort to entering a trade fair hidden under a carpet, in the back of a friend's Volvo. But he had the last laugh. Facing difficulties in obtaining supplies, Kamprad decided to build and design his own furniture. Banned from trade exhibitions, he bought his own exhibition centers. Whatever the competition did, Kamprad outfoxed them.

IKEA milestones followed swiftly, one after another. Flat packaging was introduced in 1956, so customers could get the furniture into their cars more easily. A 6,700 square meter IKEA store was opened in Älmhult in 1958, and the company signed on its 100th employee. Self-service was introduced in 1965. By the 1970s, IKEA was an international company with stores right across Europe. By 1999 the company had 150 stores in 30 countries, employing 44,000 people. Revenues were over $7 billion and the IKEA catalog's circulation was a staggering 100 million.

Although Kamprad is officially retired from day-to-day management, he is still seen by many as the company's totemic leader. Despite his phenomenal wealth—taxation and legal issues mean that he resides in Switzerland—Kamprad appears to be fundamentally the same person who started out selling matches all those years ago. He is still famously cost conscious—he once described himself as a "Swedish Scotsman." He flies economy, eats modestly, dresses casually, and has been known to haggle at his local market. IKEA is the same: suits are conspicuously absent, there is minimal hierarchy, the advertising is a little oddball.

As for succession, Kamprad shows no signs of acceding to his sons—he has three. Statements like, "I don't think any of my sons are capable of running the company, at least not yet," reinforce the impression that Kamprad believes there is still an important role for him to play at IKEA. As does his biography, *Leading by Design*, in which he says, "The demon in me says that there is so much to do. . .I'm never satisfied."

Context and Conclusions

Kamprad's unique approach to management is encapsulated in "A Furniture Dealer's Testament," the list of concepts Kamprad wrote down for his coworkers before he emigrated from Sweden. This creed says as much about Kamprad himself as it does about his company. It is based on some simple statements: "The product range is our identity; the IKEA spirit is a strong and living reality; profits give us resources; reaching good results with small means; simplicity is a virtue; doing it a different way; concentration is important to our success; taking responsibility is our privilege, and many things remain to be done—a glorious future." IKEA is a company made in Kamprad's own image. He has taken his values, carved from the harsh terrain of Småland, and assembled them into an international furniture company. He has done things his way, the different way. He has taken the road less traveled. It is a lesson for all entrepreneurs.

He flies economy, eats modestly, dresses casually, and has been known to haggle at his local market.

CLOSE BUT NO CIGAR

Terence Conran

With a similar idea at a similar time, Conran first started selling furniture from his basement in London's Notting Hill in 1952, just as Kamprad was about to open his factory store. The first store in the Habitat chain opened on the Fulham Road in 1964. Conran was always strongly design-led. The Conran Design Group was founded in 1956, and he was instrumental in shaping the look and feel of London's "swinging sixties." Selling affordable, stylish furniture, Habitat stores flourished and were joined by The Conran Shop. In the early 1990s, Conran sold the Habitat chain to IKEA. He continues to control the chain of Conran Shops and has successfully branched out into restaurants.

For More Information

Book:

Torekull, Bertil. *Leading by Design: The IKEA Story*. New York: HarperBusiness, 1999.

Web Site:

Ikea: **www.ikea.com**

"My answer is to stay close to ordinary people because at heart I am one." (Ingvar Kamprad)

 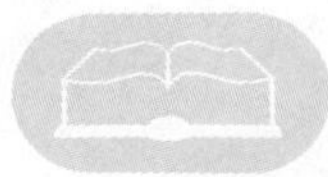    

HERB KELLEHER

It was 1966 when lawyer Herb Kelleher sketched the plans for a low-price, no frills airline on the back of a napkin. It was another five years until the first Southwest Airlines plane taxied down the runway carrying passengers. Ever since, Kelleher has been tearing up the management rule book. With singing flight attendants, practical jokes, and costumes, a Southwest ticket is worth its price just for the onboard entertainment— forget the fast turnarounds, reliability, convenience, and low cost. But what else would you expect from a Harley-riding, bourbon-drinking C.E.O. who dresses up as Elvis and arm wrestles executives from competing carriers? From nowhere, Kelleher has created a company with $5 billion in annual revenues and a record of over 25 years of profitability. Maybe it doesn't seem so crazy after all.

Kelleher & Southwest Airlines fly to success.

1932	Born.
1956	Graduates from New York University.
1960	Starts to practice law in San Antonio, Texas.
1966	Discusses plan to start airline with Rollin King.
1968	Competing airlines sue Southwest.
1971	Southwest starts flying in Texas. Has its IPO.
1973	Southwest turns first profit.
1978	Becomes chairman.
1982	Becomes president and C.E.O.
1989	$1 billion in revenues.
1992	Arm wrestles Kurt Herwald.
2001	Steps down as C.E.O.

BACKGROUND AND RISE

Born on March 12, 1932 in New Jersey, Herb Kelleher was an exceptional scholar. An undergraduate at Wesleyan University in Connecticut, he was one of those lucky students who excel at both sports and studies, and he racked up an impressive list of achievements. From Wesleyan, Kelleher went on to New York University where he studied law, graduating in 1956.

In hindsight, the resignation of Muse was the making of Southwest: it brought Kelleher in as president.

After law school, Kelleher had a stint as a clerk in the Supreme Court of New Jersey and then practiced law in San Antonio, Texas, starting in 1960. Over the next six years he built his law practice up, until in 1966 a chance conversation with one of his clients set him on an entirely new career path.

In a downtown bar—the St. Anthony's Club—Kelleher's client Rollin King explained his idea for a budget airline service to connect three of Texas's main cities, Dallas, Houston, and San Antonio. The two of them drew up a business plan and jotted down the flight pattern on the back of a paper napkin: it was the outline for Southwest Airlines. The napkin is now framed and hanging on the wall in the company HQ. Kelleher put in $10,000 (for a stake worth over $200 m by 2001), and the company was incorporated in March,1967.

DEFINING MOMENTS

With three airlines dominating the air traffic in Texas—Braniff, Texas International, and Continental—breaking up the cozy status quo was no easy task. Neither was it cheap. Over the next four years, Kelleher and Southwest Airlines sunk over a million dollars into fighting moves to block the company's application for airline certification. It was a bitter fight. A newspaper reported, "Don't bother spending your money on a movie or going to see a play or attending a concert. Just come over and watch Herb Kelleher and the lawyers for Braniff and Texas International cut each other into little bits and pieces." Colleagues and friends told Kelleher to give up, but Kelleher, a born fighter, won a final appeal to the Texas Supreme Court.

With Kelleher as chief legal counsel and Lamar Muse, a veteran of the airline business, as C.E.O., Southwest Airlines opened for business in 1971. Under intense pressure from the competition, Southwest toughed out the early years. Smarting from their legal defeat, the competing airlines embarked on a savage price war, which at times turned into physical violence. "We were the bar room brawlers of the airline industry," said Kelleher. It wasn't until the third year in business that the company turned a profit. But, in 1978, Southwest Airlines flew into more turbulence when Muse resigned. In hindsight, the resignation of Muse was the making of Southwest: it brought Kelleher in as president. In 1982 he became C.E.O. He was to prove one of the most unorthodox, innovative, and successful C.E.O.s of any major American corporation.

"There are a hundred roads to Rome; the important thing is to get there, not to use the same road."

(Herb Kelleher)

Kelleher had no time for existing airline business practice unless it supported his two principal aims: keeping the customer happy, and keeping costs down. He instigated a raft of measures designed to keep costs to a minimum. For example, customers choose seats on a first-come, first-served basis. And those hoping for a meal will be disappointed, as there are no in-flight meals—only peanuts—thus saving time and speeding up turnaround.

Kelleher's no frills service is backed up with excellent customer care, driven by even better employee care. The key to this is the corporate culture that Kelleher has inspired. As far as he is concerned, working for Southwest Airlines should, above all else, be fun. At Southwest headquarters, casual dress is the norm, practical jokes are encouraged, employee birthdays are celebrated, and any excuse to have a party is a good one. It is no different on the planes. Passengers are likely to be greeted by flight attendants dressed as leprechauns on St. Patrick's Day, have their safety instructions delivered in a Southwest Airlines version of stand up comedy, and jump when the flight attendants pop out of the overhead luggage compartments.

Nor is Kelleher is above these bizarre pranks either. There can be few C.E.O.s of major American companies who have settled a high-level dispute with another corporation by arm wrestling their opposite number (Kelleher arm wrestled Kurt Herwald, chairman of Stevens Aviation, instead of going to court over an advertisement; he lost). Or who, when faced with a complaining customer who was clearly in the wrong, authorized a letter to the offending party advising them to fly with another airline. Or who have dressed up as Elvis for a recruitment ad that helpfully suggests résumés should be marked "Attention Elvis."

But despite what many may think, there is method in Kelleher's madness. The staff turnover rate at Southwest—below 7%—is one of lowest in the industry. And the company has never lost at any time because of union disputes. When Kelleher took over as C.E.O. in 1982, revenues were $270 m, there were 2,000 employees and 27 planes. By 2001, revenues had soared to over $5 billion, with 30,000 employees and 344 planes.

Kelleher's unique brand of management continues to dazzle in an intensely competitive business. There is no doubt that Southwest Airlines' success is principally down to its C.E.O.. . .The question is, what happens when Kelleher steps down? Southwest is about to find out. In 2001, Kelleher retired as C.E.O. When asked what he would be doing with his new-found free time he replied, in his characteristic but offbeat style, "I might write about science. I might write about astronomy."

Context and Conclusions

Southwest took a risk when it named a lawyer with no practical airline experience as president, and then C.E.O. The gamble paid off. Kelleher has inspired a unique corporate culture of fun and family at Southwest. Employees want to work for Southwest, and don't want to leave. Passengers want to fly Southwest because they know that, as well as a quick, on-time, low-cost flight, the likelihood is they will have a light-hearted, amusing trip.

Success didn't come overnight. Kelleher had to do battle with the competing carriers in the courts. He then had to convince the people at Southwest that the zany and offbeat can work, if it is underpinned by sound business practice. It may seem a little crazy on board, but the planes are full and the company is turning a profit every year. Along with C.E.O.s such as IKEA's Ingvar Kamprad, Kelleher has pioneered unconventional management practices and shown you can "do it different" and win.

Kelleher's unique brand of management continues to dazzle in an intensely competitive business.

CLOSE BUT NO CIGAR

Sir Freddie Laker
Laker started the U.K. version of Southwest Airlines, Laker Airways Ltd., in 1966. He followed up with Laker Skytrain in 1977, flying across the Atlantic for rock-bottom prices. The cut-price, no frills, no reservations approach was the same as Southwest, but Sir Freddie was no Kelleher. When the competition ganged up on Southwest Airlines, Kelleher beat them off—just. Sir Freddie was less fortunate. After a vicious price war, Laker Airways was grounded when the receivers were called in in 1982. Resolutely, Laker bounced back in 1992 with Laker Airways (Bahamas) Ltd., a small carrier that flies tourists to the Bahamas. Off the major carriers' radar, Laker has been operating profitably ever since.

For More Information

Books:

Freiberg, Kevin, and Jackie Freiberg. *Nuts! Southwest Airlines' Crazy Recipe for Business and Personal Success.* Austin, TX: Bard Press, 1996.

Goddard, Larry, and David Brown. *The Turbo Charged Company: Igniting Your Business to Soar Ahead of the Competition.* Cleveland, OH: The Parkland Group, 1995.

Web Site:

Southwest Airlines: **www.southwest.com**

  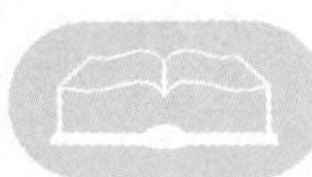    

Ray Kroc

Ray Kroc (1902–1984) was looking forward to retiring after a comfortable career selling milkshake mixers. All that changed one day in 1954 when he walked into a small restaurant in San Bernardino, California. It was called McDonald's Famous Hamburgers, and Kroc's visit was the catalyst for a global food revolution. He cut himself a deal with the McDonald brothers and set about creating a franchise network. In 1961 he bought out the brothers for a bargain $2.7 million.

The company went public in 1965. By the 1970s Kroc had turned a $2.1 million investment into a $500 million fortune. The public bought McDonald's burgers by the million. By the time of Kroc's death in 1984, the McDonald's golden arches were recognized the world over as a symbol for convenient and cheap fast food.

Ray Kroc on the way to a fast food fortune.

1902	Born.
1922	Begins work as sales representative for Lily Tulip Cup.
1954	Visits McDonald's burger restaurant in San Bernardino, California.
1955	Opens his first McDonald's in Des Plaines, Illinois.
1961	Buys out the McDonald brothers for $2.7 million.
1963	Number of hamburgers sold reaches one billion. Ronald McDonald introduced.
1967	First overseas branch opened.
1974	Buys the San Diego Padres.
1984	Dies.

Background and Rise

Raymond A. Kroc was born in Oak Park, Illinois, on October 5, 1902. His life and career can be divided up into two periods–before McDonald's and after it. Before McDonald's Kroc tried a variety of jobs before carving out a role as a milkshake-mixer sales rep.

Kroc was convinced that fast food, McDonald's style, could be the next restaurant revolution.

At 15 he lied about his age so he could take part in World War I as a Red Cross ambulance driver. Disappointingly for him, the nearest he got to Europe was Connecticut. He was still finishing his training the day the war ended.

Having missed out on the war, Kroc looked for a job. He spent some time playing the piano for a living, and in 1922 landed a job selling paper cups for Lily Tulip Cup Company. Kroc was good at sales and had an eye for business. When one of his customers, Earl Prince, patron of Prince Multimixers, showed Kroc the five-spindle mixer he had invented, Kroc switched companies. He got a contract to sell the mixers nationally, and for the next 17 years that was exactly what he did. At 52 Kroc had spent most of his working life selling mixers. He was comfortably off and was thinking about his retirement, until, that is, the fateful day in 1954 when he walked into the small burger restaurant in San Bernardino run by the McDonald brothers.

Defining Moments

What impressed Kroc about the burger restaurant run by brothers Dick and Mac McDonald, apart from the large number of mixers they ordered and the lines of customers down the street, was the way the business was run. It was as if Henry Ford had applied his mass-production formula to the food business. The brothers ran a burger assembly line. There were eight five-milkshake mixers churning out 40 milkshakes at a time. To speed up the cleaning, the brothers dispensed plastic utensils and paper napkins. So efficient was the McDonalds' operation that customers received their meal within 60 seconds. Furthermore, the brothers offered a very limited menu at extremely competitive prices. For Kroc it was commercial love at first sight. "I felt like some latter-day Newton who'd just had an Idaho potato caromed off his skull," he later wrote.

Kroc was convinced that fast food, McDonald's style, could be the next restaurant revolution. Using all the skills he had acquired in 25-plus years of selling, he sold himself to the McDonald brothers, persuading them to license their name to him. In return they would receive a percentage of the sales for each franchise he created. To the McDonald's model Kroc brought dynamism and a homespun business philosophy. "Luck is a dividend of sweat," he once observed. "The more you sweat, the luckier you get."

The four pillars on which Kroc built the McDonald's empire were quality, service, cleanliness, and value. He introduced some innovations of his own such as standardizing the size of the burger and the amount of onions

"I believe in God, family, and McDonald's and, in the office, that order is reversed." (Ray Kroc)

served with each one. He even built a laboratory in Chicago to research the ultimate french fry. Kroc's obsession with perfecting the McDonald's business formula cost him his marriage.

Kroc's first restaurant opened in Des Plaines, Illinois, in 1955. Several others quickly followed. Kroc insisted that franchisees run their restaurants according to his strict guidelines. Although he had little trouble convincing franchisees to open McDonald's restaurants, Kroc still encountered severe financial problems that nearly bankrupted him in the early years. In 1960 sales of $75 million translated into a profit of $139,000. His solution was to buy the land where the restaurants were to be located and then lease them to the franchisees. In this way Kroc retained closer control over the business and made more money.

Soon Kroc's financial problems were a thing of the past and he was eyeing a bigger prize. In 1961 he bought out the McDonald brothers for just $2.7 million. It was one of the best deals in business history—for Kroc at least. He then embarked on a massive advertising campaign. The McDonald's landmarks kept coming: a billion hamburgers by 1963; the five hundredth restaurant; the brilliant concept of the burger clown, Ronald McDonald, universally appealing to children. In fact, so popular was Ronald McDonald that not long after his first national ad appearance in 1965, more children knew his name than that of the U.S. president.

When the company went public in 1965, Kroc was $3 million richer. It was a fortune that grew to $500 million by the mid-1970s as McDonald's franchises sprang up everywhere. With the company firmly established in the United States, Kroc expanded overseas. In 1967 he took the golden arches to Canada, followed by Europe, Asia, and the rest of the world.

Kroc's great wealth affected him very little, since he spent much of his time ensuring that the McDonald's franchises maintained his high standards. One small indulgence was his acquisition of the San Diego Padres in 1974. He died at the age of 81 in San Diego, California.

Context and Conclusions

Few people can claim to have changed the way the world eats. Ray Kroc is one such individual. It took vision and courage to turn his back on a comfortable retirement for a new business opportunity at the age of 52. Kroc's idea was perfect for his time. The United States was suburbanizing, prospering, and depending more and more on the automobile; Kroc provided an increasingly mobile nation with fast, cheap, convenient food. His genius was not only to spot the opportunity but to package the experience carefully. Through franchises, strictly-regulated service and food production values, and innovative marketing, Kroc single-handedly invented the modern concept of fast food. He also pioneered the global brand, cooking up a McDonald's-style food revolution across the world.

Few people can claim to have changed the way the world eats. Ray Kroc is one such individual.

For More Information

Books:

Kroc, Ray, with Robert Anderson. *Grinding It Out: The Making of McDonald's.* New York: St. Martin's Press, 1992.

Love, John F. *McDonald's: Behind the Arches.* Rev. ed. New York: Bantam, 1995.

Web Site:

McDonald's™: **www.mcdonalds.com**

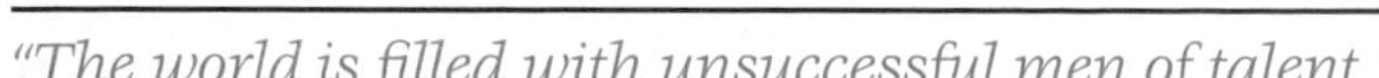

"The world is filled with unsuccessful men of talent." (Ray Kroc)

ESTÉE LAUDER

Much of the U.S. cosmetic queen Estée Lauder's (1908–) early life is shrouded in mystery. What is known is that she started in the cosmetics business selling her uncle's Six-in-One cold cream in 1924. By 1944 she had acquired a husband, an office in New York City, and a cosmetics concession in Saks Fifth Avenue. Lauder formally incorporated Estée Lauder Inc. in 1947. Resisting calls to go public, she kept her company in family hands and used her formidable sales and marketing talents to drive the business forward. In 1968 revenues were an estimated $40 million with profits of $4 million. Lauder ceded control to her son, Leonard, in 1972. By 1999, Estée Lauder Inc. was earning over $3 billion in revenue from over a hundred products.

Cosmetics before Estée Lauder.

1908	Born.
1924	Uncle founds New Way Laboratories.
1944	Lauder sets up her own office.
1947	Estée Lauder Inc. founded.
1948	First retail account at Saks Fifth Avenue, New York City.
1960	First international account at Harrods, London.
1968	Revenues of $40 million.
1972	Son Leonard made president. Lauder becomes chair.
1980s	Lauder steps back from running the company.
1995	Company I.P.O.

BACKGROUND AND RISE

Estée Lauder was born Josephine Esther Mentzer in Queens, New York City, in 1908, the youngest of nine children. Her father ran a hardware store, and Lauder went to school nearby.

The young Lauder was introduced to the cosmetics business through her uncle Dr. Schotz, a chemist. His business, New Way Laboratories, was founded in 1924. Among the various potions and lotions he made—which included a poultry-lice killer, paint stripper, varnish, and embalming fluid—were several beauty treatments. Lauder helped her uncle out by selling products with names like Six-in-One Cold Cream and Dr. Schotz Viennese Cream.

In 1930 she married Joe Lauder, but by 1939 the couple had separated. A subsequent reconciliation led to their remarriage in 1942, at which time Lauder vowed to direct all her energies to selling cosmetics products. She continued to sell her uncle's products, setting up her own office at 39 East 60th St. in February 1944.

Soon afterward Lauder won a sales concession in the Bonwit Teller department store. She then set her sights higher. The prize concession was in Saks Fifth Avenue. When she told Bob Fiske, cosmetics buyer at Saks, that the department store should give her a concession, Fiske demurred, explaining that there was no demand for her products from his customers. Undeterred, Lauder created a demand by giving her products away at a talk at the Waldorf-Astoria Hotel. When she returned to Fiske, he relented.

In the late 1940s, with $60,000 or so at her disposal, Lauder was unable to persuade the BBD&O advertising agency to create a campaign for Estée Lauder. Instead she chose a more direct route to her customers. Using Saks's mailing list, Lauder sent out samplers and gifts as an enticement for customers to visit her store concessions.

DEFINING MOMENTS

Lauder's breakthrough came with the invention of her first fragrance, the bath oil Youth Dew. Her principal competition, firms like Arden and Rubenstein, had all started with skincare products and gravitated to fragrances.

Accounts of how Lauder created her first fragrance differ. It seems that an old friend, A. L. van Amerigan, president of van Amerigan-Haebler (which subsequently became International Flavors and Fragrances), was involved. Similarly Ernest Shiftan, an employee of IFF and one of America's top perfumers, may well have been responsible for the development of the fragrance. Whether Amerigan gave the fragrance to Lauder is unclear. What is certain is that Youth Dew, introduced at Bonwit's as bath oil, was an instant success. For $8.50 customers got a perfume that lasted a whole day.

Shrewdly, Lauder used the demand for the new perfume to sell her other cosmetics. The Youth Dew line was eventually extended across a range of cosmetics including a pure fragrance. With Lauder shamelessly promoting it at every opportunity, it wasn't long before

"If you can't smell it, you can't sell it." (Estée Lauder)

Estée Lauder was the third-largest cosmetics business in the United States behind Arden and Rubenstein.

Lauder's marketing acumen was again evident when a new breed of skincare products making dubious scientific claims began to spread from Europe to the United States. In France an emphasis on "feeding" the skin had given rise to products that made various health claims about their effects. The Food and Drug Administration, however, imposed tough regulations on products making any such claims. There were, for example, a host of placental-based products that ran afoul of the FDA and were withdrawn. Lauder, instead of making scientific claims for her new skin product, simply named it Re-Nutriv. The product's health enhancing attributes were implied in the name. She was also careful not to cross the line in her advertising. It focused instead on the high price of the product, and how a price of $115 a pound was justified by the inclusion of the "costliest" ingredients.

At the time Estée Lauder's headquarters were at 666 Fifth Avenue, on the second floor—Lauder had a fear of heights. Competitors were close at hand. Charles Revson, founder of Revlon, was on the top floor of the same building and Helena Rubinstein was across the street. As Lauder made progress commercially she was also climbing socially. Her house in Palm Beach, Florida, afforded her the opportunity to meet rich people from the upper echelons of U.S. society. Lauder's efforts at networking were not entirely without mishap. One story has it that, arriving for dinner at the home of Dorothy Munn, wife of financier Charles Munn, she gave a box of cosmetics (presumably her own) to her hostess. This was viewed as a gauche gesture as Dorothy Munn was wealthy enough to have her cosmetics made privately—a kind of haute-perfume.

By the 1970s Estée Lauder had bested its corporate competition and added the Clinique brand to its beautifying armory. Lauder herself had outlasted her personal rivals as both Elizabeth Arden and Helena Rubenstein had died within a year of each other in the 1960s. Lauder had since moved her headquarters to the new General Motors Building (with the ever-present Revlon camped on the top floors); she had also, by virtue of her friendship with the Duchess of Windsor, firmly placed herself at the pinnacle of the social scene. Her son Leonard became president of the company in 1972, with Lauder becoming chair.

The "little business" that Leonard Lauder once said his mother was growing now controls over 40% of the cosmetics market in U.S. department stores. Available in 118 countries, Estée Lauder products bring in over $3 billion in revenue.

Context and Conclusions

Estée Lauder Inc. is an astonishing example of how an international business can be built up from humble beginnings through one woman's relentless drive, networking, belief in her own products, and brilliant marketing. In particular, Lauder was responsible for a number of innovative marketing techniques for the cosmetics business, most notably the free gift with purchase.

The "little business" that Leonard Lauder once said his mother was growing now controls over 40% of the cosmetics market in U.S. department stores.

Her strength of leadership was emphasized through her determination to keep the company in the control of her family. Estée Lauder remained an entirely private company until its IPO in 1995. The Lauder family still holds a significant proportion of the shares. Although Lauder has progressively taken a back seat since the 1980s, her sons Leonard and Ronald, daughter-in-law Evelyn, grandson William, and great-granddaughter Aerin remain actively involved in the company.

For More Information

Books:

Israel, Lee. *Estée Lauder: Beyond the Magic: An Unauthorized Biography*. New York: Macmillan, 1985.

Lauder, Estée. *Estée: A Success Story*. New York: Random House, 1985.

Web Site:

Estée Lauder: **www.esteelauder.com**

Henry Robinson Luce

Henry Robinson Luce's strict Presbyterian upbringing at a missionary station in China seemed to do him no harm. His early academic record was outstanding, and his performance at Yale University no less impressive. When he graduated in 1920 he had already shown a talent for editing by radically overhauling the Yale newspaper, the *Daily News*. Following a whistle-stop tour of Europe, he worked on the *Chicago Daily News* and then the *Baltimore News*, where he linked up with fellow Yale alumnus Briton Hadden. Together they were unstoppable, launching a new publication *Time, the Weekly News Magazine* in March 1923 and nursing it from a paltry circulation to one of 118,000 in its third year. In 1929 they followed this success with the launch of the business magazine *Fortune* to chronicle the ups and downs of the Wall Street Crash and the ensuing Great Depression.

Fortune smiled on Henry Luce.

1898	Born.
1920	Graduates from Yale. Voted "most brilliant student."
1922	Leaves Baltimore for New York. Time Inc. incorporated on November 28.
1923	The first issue of *Time* hits the stands.
1927	First profit posted—$3,860.
1928	Profits of $126,000.
1929	*Fortune* magazine launched.
1936	*Life* magazine launched.
1954	*Sports Illustrated* magazine launched.
1958	Suffers heart attack.
1967	Dies.

Background and Rise

Henry Robinson Luce was born on April 3, 1898 in Tengchow, China, where his Presbyterian missionary parents were teaching at a Christian mission. The first of four children, Luce's upbringing was an austere one. His daily schedule began at six in the morning with a cold bath followed by half an hour of Bible study. With six hours of Chinese lessons a day, the young Luce was fluent in the local tongue before he was able to speak English.

Barring a brief visit to America in 1906, Luce was to remain in China until he was 14. A precocious scholar, he attended the British-run boarding school in Chefoo. It was a tough environment with strict discipline. Fortunately for Luce, a strong work ethic, combined with a keen mind, kept him at the top of the class and away from the master's cane. The school's pupils were predominantly English, and Luce frequently found himself sticking up for the United States. "My Anglo-Americanism is deeper than any words," he once said. "Indeed, it is written in the blood of that shameful, and futile, endless two hours one Saturday afternoon, when I rolled around the unspeakably dirty floor of the main schoolroom with a British boy who had insulted my country."

With catastrophic timing, the first issue of *Fortune*, 30,000 copies in all, rolled off the presses just three months after the spectacular stock market crash of October 1929.

After Chefoo came the Hotchkiss School in Connecticut. There Luce continued his excellent scholastic record: outstanding marks in his Greek exams and leader of the class in most subjects. Outside his classes he discovered a new talent as editor-in-chief of the *Hotchkiss Literary Monthly* and assistant managing editor of the weekly school newspaper, the *Record*. Luce had found his vocation.

Defining Moments

It was at Yale that Luce started his career in publishing in earnest. Together with fellow student and ex-Hotchkiss pupil Briton Hadden, Luce revolutionized the Yale newspaper, the *Daily News*. On graduation in 1920 Luce was voted "most brilliant" and Hadden "most likely to succeed." The combination proved irresistible. After Yale, Luce continued his tour of the world's most prestigious educational establishments, heading for Oxford, England, where he studied history. Then, after a whistle-stop tour of Europe, he returned to the United States, obtaining work first on the *Chicago Daily News* and then on the *Baltimore News*. It was in Baltimore that Luce rejoined his old friend Hadden and together they developed a plan to launch a new weekly news magazine called *Facts*. When the magazine was finally launched it was called *Time the Weekly News Magazine*.

The pair left Baltimore for New York in February 1922. There they rented a small one-room office, acquired a third partner in Culbrith Sudler, who was reportedly an expert at selling advertising, and spent the next few months seeking advice and capital. Advice was forthcoming–mostly along the lines of "don't do it"–but

"What I love about magazines is that an individual can change the destiny of an entire business."

(Duncan Edwards)

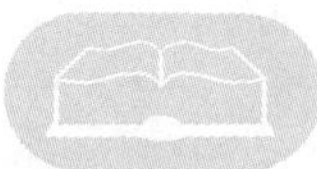

capital was less plentiful. Eventually, however, they managed to raise sufficient funds (partly through a share issue) and incorporated the business on November 28, 1922, having moved to a small loft in the printing trades building on Eighth Avenue. To decide who should edit the magazine and who should manage the business side of things, Hadden and Luce tossed a coin. It was to Luce's everlasting chagrin that he lost and, in the intervening three-year period before he was able to take up the post of editor, Hadden had the opportunity to stamp his mark on *Time* magazine. The first issue of *Time* hit the newsstands in March 1923, with a cover price of 15 cents.

The distribution of the first issues was farcical. A string of debutante acquaintances was entrusted with the task of addressing the first three issues and dispatching them to subscribers, who could read all three before making a financial commitment. In the ensuing mix-up some subscribers received three copies of the same issue, only one issue, or no issue at all. Of the 25,000 who agreed to take a look, only 9,000 ever received a copy. And of the 5,000 sent to the newsstands, 3,000 were returned unsold.

After this inauspicious start, however, circulation grew steadily. By the third year it had reached 110,000, with advertising revenue of $283,000, yet a profit remained elusive. Indeed, it wasn't until 1927 that the new magazine made a profit, and then it was just $3,860. In 1928 a more respectable figure of $126,000 was posted, and from that point onward figures improved rapidly. By then, Luce was editor. He ensnared his readers with an array of literary devices: compound words such as "sexational" and the more successful "socialite" made their debuts on the pages of *Time*. Foreign words such as tycoon—from the Japanese *taikun*, meaning prince and pundit from the Hindu *pandit*, meaning sage—were popularized by Luce; and he also made common the use of euphemisms such as "great and good friend"—meaning mistress—to skirt around potentially libelous issues.

By 1927 *Time* had moved again, not once but twice, coming to rest eventually in Manhattan, just off Fifth Avenue. Luce's lifelong friend Hadden had always said his aim was to make one million dollars by the age of 30. As it turned out he made more than that, but in February 1929, nine days after his 31st birthday, he died from a streptococcus infection. Luce was left in full charge of the magazine.

Fortune magazine was the second major venture under the Time Inc. banner. Founded in 1929, it was Luce's idea, based on his instinct that "business is obviously the greatest single common denominator of interest among the active leading citizens of the United States—our best men are in business." *Fortune* was two years in the planning. The magazine owes its name to Luce's wife Lila, who preferred *Fortune* to *Power*. To head up the editorial staff, Luce chose Parker Lloyd Smith, a brilliant Oxford graduate who did an excellent job in the magazine's early days, until in 1931 he threw himself to his death from a hotel window, for no apparent reason.

With catastrophic timing, the first issue of *Fortune*, 30,000 copies in all, rolled off the presses just three months after the spectacular stock market crash of October 1929. In spite of, or perhaps because of, its timing, the first issue was well received, and the magazine managed to survive the economic depression that followed. By 1937 revenues were up to $500,000 and circulation in excess of 460,000. Through the ensuing decades *Fortune* magazine cataloged the ups and downs of U.S. business life.

Over the next 30 years, Luce built a publishing business with a worldwide circulation of over 13 million. To *Time* and *Fortune* he added the even more successful *Life* magazine, founded in 1936. In 1954 when *Sports Illustrated* was introduced, it broke the circulation records set by *Life*. Luce successfully steered the company through World War II, adroitly negotiated the communist witch hunts that swept postwar America, and fended off hundreds of threats to sue the company for invasion of privacy or libel each year.

A brilliant scholar, a brilliant editor, Luce did much to change the nature of reporting.

In 1967 the circulation of Luce's flagship magazine was some 7,500,000. Advertising, which was twice as much as for any other magazine, brought in $170 million to Time Inc. *Time* magazine itself sold some 3,500,000 copies, yielding $86 million in advertising revenue. The company that Luce founded on a budget of $86,000 had total revenues in excess of $500 million, with profits of $37 million. For much of his later career Luce regularly threatened to retire; "At 40 I will retire and let the young take over," he used to say. But it was always the same story; even after his heart attack in 1958, Luce could not drag himself away. In February 1967 he was still in command of his empire when he finally succumbed to another heart attack.

Context and Conclusions

Flamboyant media moguls such as William Randolph Hearst, Lord Beaverbrook, and Lord Thomson are better remembered today than Henry Robinson Luce, especially outside the United States. Luce, the man with a Presbyterian upbringing, was content to remain in the shadows. He neither sought political power, as Beaverbrook did, nor did he go in for ostentatious shows of wealth like Hearst's mansion in San Simeon. Yet Luce's contribution to publishing was just as important as, if not more important than, that of his peers. He created a number of magazines that have survived him and gone on to become national institutions.

For More Information

Books:

Cort, David. *The Sin of Henry R. Luce: An Anatomy of Journalism*. Secaucus, NJ: Carol Publishing Group, 1974.

Swanberg, W. A. *Luce and His Empire*. New York: Scribner, 1972.

Web Sites:

Fortune.com: **www.fortune.com**

Time: **www.time.com/time/**

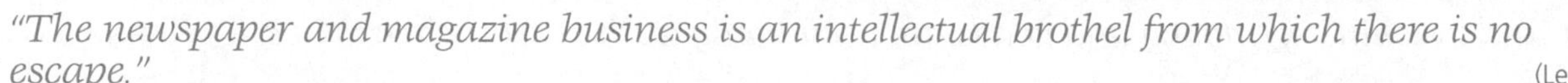
"The newspaper and magazine business is an intellectual brothel from which there is no escape."

(Leo Tolstoy)

Cyrus Hall McCormick

Cyrus Hall McCormick had invention in his blood. He grew up with a father who was constantly inventing strange contraptions. On the family farm in Virginia, McCormick perfected the design of one of his father's crazy ideas—the mechanized reaping machine. Aged only 22, he started a small-scale home manufacturing operation in Virginia Valley, producing two machines in 1840. It ended up as a massive manufacturing concern, based in Chicago. In 1884, the McCormick Harvesting Machine Company sold 54,841 harvesting machines to farmers from the United States to Australia.

A millionaire by the age of 50, McCormick paved the way for an agrarian revolution through the invention of his reaping machine and a host of innovative marketing techniques, from the installment plan to the money-back guarantee.

McCormick was a leader in his field.

1809	Born.
1830	Given ownership of his father's prototype reaper invention.
1831	Produces viable working machine.
1834	Receives 14-year patent for the threshing machine.
1843	Head-to-head showdown with rival Obed Hussey.
1847	Moves business to Chicago.
1851	Awarded prize at Crystal Palace Grand Exhibition.
1859	Production at 4,119 machines a year.
1861	Beginning of American Civil War.
1870	Production of 10,000 machines year.
1871	Great fire of Chicago destroys McCormick's manufacturing plant.
1873	New production plant opens.
1884	Dies.

Background and Rise

The son of a farmer and inventor, Cyrus Hall McCormick was the oldest of eight children. Born on February 15, 1809 in Rockbridge County, Virginia, McCormick grew up on the 532 rolling acres of farmland belonging to the family. His father Robert, in addition to running the farm, spent a lot of time tinkering with inventions aimed at easing the burden of farming. The most significant of his inventions was a horse-drawn reaping device, abandoned when he failed to perfect it. McCormick's father lacked the business sense, the will and the drive necessary to turn any of his various inventions into a commercial venture.

He arranged a head-to-head showdown with his rival in 1843, in which the McCormick reaper cut down 17 acres in the time it took Obed Hussey to clear just two.

The young McCormick had already demonstrated an ability for invention when, at the age of 15, he built a light-weight cradle for harvesting grain. When he was still 21, his father gave him a head start in life, handing over the ownership of his reaper invention. In 1831, McCormick worked six weeks nonstop to perfect the invention, to produce a viable working machine.

Defining Moments

In the summer of 1831, the 22-year-old McCormick used his horse-drawn reaper to mow down the field of wheat at John Steele's farm in Rockbridge County, Virginia. The assembled audience—farmers, laborers and slaves—had witnessed the beginning of the mechanization of agriculture. Quality control would come later.

McCormick wasn't the first to invent the reaper. Others, such as Obed Hussey, were also thinking along the same lines. In 1834, McCormick applied for and received a 14-year patent for his threshing machine. Hussey had obtained a patent for his reaping device a year earlier. In the end it was McCormick's marketing genius that would make his product the standard for mechanical threshing.

Despite the obvious advantages of the reaper, developing the business proved difficult. McCormick swiftly set about remedying the situation. He started by eliminating the competition in the minds of the consumer. He arranged a head-to-head showdown with his rival in 1843, in which the McCormick reaper cut down 17 acres in the time it took Obed Hussey to clear just two. Word soon traveled through the farming community about the disparity in performance between the two machines.

Next, McCormick developed a licensing system. Manufacturers close to market were granted a license to produce the McCormick reaping machine. In some cases the agreement operated like a franchise, demarcating area in return for a franchise fee; in others it was simply a question of paying McCormick $20 for each reaper produced and sold.

To obviate the need to walk alongside his machine, McCormick designed a seat so the operator could sit above the reaper. This design, known as the "old reliable," became the standard model.

In 1840, from his Walnut Grove base, McCormick sold two machines—they both broke down. The following year, he sold seven. In 1844, still in the Virginia Valley, production had risen to 75 machines, 25 manufactured under license. In Chicago in 1849, before completion of the factory, McCormick's company produced 1,500 reapers. By 1859, in a new factory premises, production had rocketed to 4,119 machines a year.

In 1847, McCormick moved to Chicago. The decision was motivated by the knowledge that, although he had manufactured 75 reapers in 1846, this was still a long way short of the demand. Devotion to his father, Robert, had kept McCormick in his hometown. When his father died in 1846, there were few reasons for him to remain in the backwoods of Walnut Grove. In Chicago, McCormick built a plant on the banks of the Chicago River. Over 7,500 square feet of factory space and river frontage meant completed machines could be loaded onto river transport. This allowed McCormick to expand production rapidly.

By 1860, some 70% of the country's wheat harvest was gathered using McCormick's reaper. Before the reaper, it took a man 40 hours to harvest an acre of wheat. With the McCormick reaper, two people could harvest an acre of wheat in a day. In the decade leading up to 1859, United States production of wheat boomed from 100 m bushels to 173 m. The agricultural revolution made McCormick a millionaire. It also made him a worldwide celebrity. The machine, first described by the *London Times* as a "contraption seemingly a cross between a wheelbarrow, a chariot and a flying machine," won the main prize at the Grand Exhibition at Crystal Palace in 1851. This award was followed by prizes at the Hamburg Exposition, the Vienna Exposition and the Paris Exposition.

McCormick continued to manage his business well into his 70s. It was quite a feat, considering some of the severe setbacks the business suffered. Production was slack for the duration of the American Civil War, starting in 1861, during which time McCormick took the opportunity to promote his machine in Europe. By 1870 his factory was producing a staggering 10,000 machines year. Then in 1871 a devastating blow was dealt to his business when the great fire of Chicago destroyed $188 m worth of property at his manufacturing plant. The resilient McCormick built an even bigger factory and production complex that sprawled over a 160-acre site. It opened in 1873.

McCormick died in 1884, with the business safely in the hands of his enterprising son Cyrus McCormick Jr. In the final years of his life McCormick successfully promoted his business abroad, taking the reaper to the both the Pacific and South America.

Context and Conclusions

In 1831, the year that McCormick invented his mechanized reaping machine, 80% of all workers in the United States worked in farming. By the 1930s this figure was down to just 2%. That dramatic reduction, which freed up the workforce to better mankind in other ways than through the drudgery of manual agricultural work, is largely due to Cyrus Hall McCormick and his "Virginia Reaper." The effects of his achievements cannot be overstated. The commercial success of his machine accelerated the colonization of America's West Coast, and allowed for the wholesale exploitation of the bread basket of the Midwest, which in turn allowed for a rapid expansion in the United States population. This growth, coupled with the release of workers from work on the land was a significant factor in the growth of the United States as the biggest economy in the world.

McCormick continued to manage his business well into his 70s. It was quite a feat, considering some of the severe setbacks the business suffered.

Would this have happened without McCormick? Possibly, but McCormick was blessed with talents that many of his competitors lacked. His inventiveness extended beyond the creation of machines. He pioneered marketing innovations such as installment plans, commission sales and money-back guarantees, that ensured every farmer who wanted a McCormick reaper could have one.

CLOSE BUT NO CIGAR

John Deere/Obed Hussey

Inventor and entrepreneur John Deere was a contemporary of Cyrus Hall McCormick. A blacksmith by trade, Deere invented the first self-polishing steel plow in the 1830s, just as McCormick was testing his reaping machine. In the end, McCormick's invention proved the more significant of the two. By 1855 Deere was selling 13,000 plows a year. He went on to found Deere & Company in 1868, today a million-dollar company.

The "almost-ran" of agricultural invention, Hussey could justifiably lay claim to the invention of the reaping machine. A former whaler, Hussey patented his device in 1833, a year before McCormick. However his big mistake was to stay in Baltimore, Maryland, miles from his market. McCormick bit the bullet and moved from Virginia to Chicago in the Midwest. Hussey also lacked McCormick's flair for marketing and was unwilling to accommodate improvements to his design suggested by others.

For More Information

Books:

Casson, Herbert N. *Cyrus Hall McCormick: His Life and Work*. Chicago: A.C. McClure & Co., 1909.

Dobler, Lavinia. *Cyrus McCormick: Farm Boy*. Indianapolis, IN: Bobbs-Merrill Co., 1961.

McCormick, Cyrus. *The Century of the Reaper—Cyrus Hall McCormick & Business*. Boston, MA: Houghton Mifflin Co., 1931.

"Only a real lazybones can produce labor-saving inventions." (Günter Grass)

KONOSUKE MATSUSHITA

For a man who never left his native country before the age of 56, Konosuke Matsushita (1894–1989) made a big impact on the world. Matsushita started work at the age of nine. After spells as a coal worker and at an engineering company, Matsushita started his own company, Matsushita Electric Appliance (later Matsushita Electric Industrial, or MEI) in 1918. Through a combination of product innovation, clever marketing, and forward-thinking management, Matsushita developed the company into one of the largest of its kind in prewar Japan.

After a difficult postwar period, Matsushita rejoined his company in 1950. Reasserting his business values, he transformed MEI into an industrial giant that today consists of over 300 subsidiaries.

A key subsidiary of Matsushita's MEI.

1894	Born.
1918	Starts Matsushita Electric Appliance Factory.
1929	Formulates the "basic management objective."
1933	Introduces the "five guiding principles."
1935	Matsushita Electric Appliance renamed Matsushita Electric Industrial Company (MEI).
1937	Adds two more guiding principles.
1946	Founds the Peace and Happiness through Prosperity (PHP) Institute.
1950	Returns to the company.
1961	Becomes chairman of MEI.
1965	Introduces five-day workweek.
1973	Steps down as chairman.
1989	Dies.

BACKGROUND AND RISE

The youngest of eight children, Konosuke Matsushita was born in 1894 in the farming village of Wasa in Wakayama Prefecture, Japan. His father was a landlord who received income from the local tenant farmers, enabling the family to live in reasonable comfort. That changed in 1898 when Matsushita's father decided to speculate on the rice market. The investment was spectacularly unsuccessful and left the family in financial ruin. The changed circumstances spelled the end of Matsushita's rudimentary schooling. At the tender age of nine, he was asked by his father to go to Osaka to work in a charcoal brazier shop. This was followed by an apprenticeship in a bicycle shop.

Matsushita's first socket design turned out to be a dud. But the next product, an electrical attachment plug, sold well, especially since Matsushita undercut the competition by up to a third.

In 1910 the young Matsushita was taken on as a wiring assistant at the Osaka Electric Light Company (OELC). He was a quick learner and despite his age, just 16, his skill at wiring earned him rapid promotion. But in 1917 he decided to leave OELC, partly due to health problems. Matsushita suffered from a debilitating lung condition and frequently took days off from work to rest. He decided that if he could start his own business he would be able to accommodate his poor health. He also wanted to market a new light socket he had invented, and his employers at OELC had done little to encourage his inventiveness.

DEFINING MOMENTS

In 1918, at the age of 23, he founded Matsushita Electric Appliance Factory (the company became Matsushita Electric Industrial Company—MEI—in 1935). He had three employees, the equivalent of $50, and a prototype for a new type of electrical socket. Matsushita's first socket design turned out to be a dud. But the next product, an electrical attachment plug, sold well, especially since Matsushita undercut the competition by up to a third. Business was tough at first. The product that kept the company going, though, was a battery powered bicycle lamp shaped like a bullet. The lamp was unique in being able to run for up to 40 hours. Some Japanese even used it to light their houses.

Matsushita was a good engineer, but he was even better at marketing. He used the demand for his bicycle lamp to build a sales network throughout Japan. Once he had established countrywide distribution, he put the trademark "National" on Matsushita products and lowered prices to make his lamp a mass-market product. He also pioneered the use of national newspaper advertising, a relatively rare sight in Japan in the 1920s.

In 1929, with the company firmly established, Matsushita put into practice the management practices and philosophy for which he was to become famous. He was

"Big things and little things are my job. Middle level management can be delegated."

(Konosuke Matsushita)

an extremely enlightened manager for his time. This much is evident from the slogan he adopted for the company: "harmony between corporate profit and social justice." Matsushita followed this in 1933 with his "five guiding principles" (two more were added in 1937), which shaped the conduct of the company. The principles, still adhered to today, are service to the public, fairness and honesty, teamwork for the common cause, untiring effort for improvement, courtesy and humility, accord with natural laws, and gratitude for blessings.

During the 1930s Matsushita made a number of decisions illustrating the leadership style that was to earn him the nickname "the god of management." During the recession of 1930 Matsushita refused to make wholesale layoffs. Instead he recruited underemployed factory workers to go out and sell stockpiled inventory. Later in 1931 he bought the rights to a radio patent, which he then made freely available to the market. This was an expensive ploy, but it had the effect of stimulating the market and so ultimately profited the company. It presaged a similar move by David Sarnoff, the head of RCA, with the patent for building color television sets, and anticipated the stance taken much later by the open source movement in computing. In 1932 Matsushita declared that entrepreneurs and manufacturers should aim "to make all products as inexhaustible and as cheap as tap water."

Somehow Matsushita managed to hold the company together during World War II. In postwar Japan, MEI came under the severe restrictions imposed on certain Japanese companies by the Allies. Matsushita was almost removed as president, but was saved in part by a petition from 15,000 employees. For a time he devoted his energies to the Peace and Happiness through Prosperity Institute, which he founded in 1946, returning to his company duties only in 1950. He reinvigorated the company, reorganizing it along divisional lines. At the same time he reassessed processes to make them more efficient and refocused the company on the core values he had expressed in the 1930s.

From 1950 until his retirement as chairman in 1973, Matsushita oversaw a huge expansion of the company as its "three treasures"—washing machines, refrigerators, and televisions—as well as other electrical goods were exported around the world. The company grew to become one of the world's largest manufacturers of electric goods, contracting a stable of global brand names including Panasonics, Technics, and JVC.

A measure of the man's attention to his business is revealed by an incident at the Matsushita Pavilion during the Osaka World's Fair in 1970. The exposition had been open for a few days when the pavilion's staff were surprised to see Matsushita waiting in line outside. When they rushed out to usher the founder of their company indoors, he told them that he had stood in line to find out how long visitors had to wait before they were admitted. Later that day he ordered that the system be redesigned to speed up admission and that shade from the sun be provided for the people waiting outside.

From the 1970s onward Matsushita concentrated much of his time on developing and explaining his social and commercial philosophies, mainly in his 44 published books. His most popular title, *Developing a Road to Peace and Happiness through Prosperity*, sold over four million copies. He continued to teach his unique concept of management until his chronic lung problems claimed his life. He died of pneumonia on April 27, 1989. He was 94.

Context and Conclusions

Konosuke Matsushita founded one of Japan's greatest corporations, Matsushita Electric Industrial. Yet he is remembered for much more than the creation of an electrical goods empire. At MEI Matsushita implemented management practices that were far ahead of their time. He abandoned the conventional centralized management structure. He drew up a corporate creed and identified corporate values. He pioneered advertising in the press and competed both on price and quality.

The company grew to become one of the world's largest manufacturers of electric goods, contracting a stable of global brand names including Panasonics, Technics, and JVC.

Matsushita's philosophy can best be summed up by the "basic management objective" he formulated in 1929: "Recognizing our responsibilities as industrialists, we will devote ourselves to the progress and development of society and the well-being of people through our business activities, thereby enhancing the quality of life throughout the world." It was something Matsushita did to great effect.

For More Information

Books:

Gould, Rowland. *The Matsushita Phenomenon*. Tokyo: Diamond Sha, 1970.

Kotter, John P. *Matsushita: Leadership Lessons from the Life of the 20th Century's Most Remarkable Entrepreneur*. New York: Free Press, 1997.

Matsushita, Konosuke. *Quest for Prosperity—The Life of a Japanese Industrialist*. Tokyo: PHP Institute, 1988.

Web Site:

Panasonic USA: **www.panasonic.com**

"The mission of a manufacturer should be to overcome poverty, to relieve society as a whole from misery and bring it wealth."
(Konosuke Matsushita)

Louis B. Mayer

The real-life story of movie tycoon Louis B. Mayer (1885–1957) reads like a script from one of his movies. Mayer hauled himself up from his humble beginnings as the son of an immigrant scrap-metal dealer to become a Hollywood legend. Starting in 1907 with a small chain of movie theaters, by 1924 he was vice president of Metro Goldwyn Mayer, arguably the greatest studio in Hollywood history.

Over the following decades the studio with the famous lion emblem was a roaring success as Mayer exerted his despotic influence over every aspect of the moviemaking process. Like many dictators, benign or otherwise, Mayer was ousted from MGM in 1951 after a bitter power struggle.

MGM's classic symbol.

1885	Born.
1907	Buys rundown movie theater in Haverhill, Massachusetts.
1915	Shows D. W. Griffith's *Birth of a Nation* at his theaters.
1918	Starts movie production firm in Los Angeles—Louis B. Mayer Pictures.
1924	Louis B. Mayer Productions, the Samuel Goldwyn Company, and Metro merge to form Metro Goldwyn Mayer or MGM.
1926	*Ben Hur.*
1927	Formation of the Academy of Motion Pictures Arts and Sciences.
1932	*Grand Hotel.*
1936	Rival Irving Thalberg dies.
1951	Ousted from MGM after a power struggle with Dore Schary.
1957	Dies.

Background and Rise

Louis Burt Mayer was born Eliezar Mayer on July 4, 1885 in Minsk, Russia (now in Belarus). In 1888 Mayer emigrated with his family to New Brunswick, Canada. In Canada Mayer's father built a small junk-dealing business into a profitable scrap-metal organization. After elementary school Mayer joined his father's business, preferring the world of commerce to that of academia. Soon he had his own scrap business in Boston.

In 1907 Mayer took his first small step on the road to Hollywood. Relinquishing his position in the family business, he bought a small dilapidated movie theater in Haverhill, Massachusetts at a knockdown price.

In 1907 Mayer took his first small step on the road to Hollywood. Relinquishing his position in the family business, he bought a small dilapidated movie theater in Haverhill, Massachusetts at a knockdown price. In 1907 Mayer took his first small step on the road to Hollywood. Relinquishing his position in the family business, he bought a small dilapidated movie theater in Haverhill, Massachusetts at a knockdown price. He completely overhauled the theater and made a decision to show only quality movies. His gamble paid off. Soon he was the owner of the largest theater chain in New England. Film exhibitors fought to show new movies at Mayer's theaters. In 1915 he showed D.W Griffith's *Birth of a Nation*, one of the most popular movies of its time. The huge profit Mayer made from showing the movie helped finance his ensuing adventures in Hollywood.

Defining Moments

By 1918 Mayer was camped out in Los Angeles operating as a movie promoter through his company, Louis B. Mayer Pictures. It was the start of his personal main event. At first productions were funded from the proceeds of the theater chain business. He made a star of the actress Anita Stewart and, fired up by the acclaim received for his first production, *Virtuous Wives*, continued to use her as his main attraction for the following five years.

Hollywood was still in its infancy. For aspiring moguls there remained a once-in-a-lifetime opportunity to stake a claim in the city of celluloid. Mayer may have been wealthy because of his movie theater business, but his fortune was small change in an industry dominated by fabulously rich powerbrokers. And the mogul of all moguls was Marcus Loew. He commanded his fiefdom from the East Coast; three thousand miles away in his New York City office Loew pulled the strings that made Hollywood dance.

In 1924 Mayer hit the jackpot. Loew decided that he wanted his own studio, Metro, to merge with Louis B.

Mayer Pictures and the Samuel Goldwyn Company. What Loew wanted, he generally got, to the point that when Samuel Goldwyn backed out of the deal Loew retained the Goldwyn name, calling the newly formed company Metro Goldwyn Mayer (MGM). Mayer was appointed vice president. With his newly inherited stable of stars he was finally in a position to dominate Hollywood.

At MGM Mayer ostensibly shared his power with Irving Thalberg, hired in from Universal by Loew. In reality, Mayer ruled the roost, conducting a bitter battle behind the scenes with Thalberg that ended only with Thalberg's death in 1936.

By all accounts Mayer was an autocratic manipulative despot who ruled MGM using extreme cunning. He was described by Ephraim Katz, the late respected film scholar and author of the classic resource, *The Film Encyclopedia*, as "a ruthless, quick-tempered, paternalistically tyrannical executive." Mayer ruled MGM "as one big family, rewarding obedience, punishing insubordination, and regarding opposition as personal betrayal." His political acumen must truly have been brilliant to control the egos of movie stars such as Lon Chaney and Greta Garbo, as well as directors like King Vidor and Erich von Stroheim.

Unashamedly populist, Mayer was said to abhor intellectualism. Like many other media moguls he had an innate sense of what the masses wanted. He was also a hands-on operator. To the frequent annoyance of the studio employees who considered themselves the true auteurs, Mayer not only constantly intervened in moviemaking but also managed to take many of the plaudits.

Inexorably MGM's power grew and with it Mayer's. The studio churned out a movie a week and created its own town, Culver City, where thousands of studio employees participated in the American dream. Off screen, Mayer was as ruthless as ever. He was equally adept at cutting film or cutting staff. He used the rise of the talkies as an excuse for a purge of the studio stars. Names that Mayer had helped make he now discarded: Buster Keaton, Erich von Stroheim, even Greta Garbo, were swept off the lot as Mayer and MGM marched on through the 1930s and 1940s.

Mayer cleverly managed to thwart objections to MGM's increasing dominance of the movie industry by forming an alliance of sorts under the banner of the Academy of Motion Pictures Arts and Sciences. Mayer, along with Douglas Fairbanks Sr., was a prime mover behind the Academy's creation in 1927.

Like most dictatorial leaders, however, his ruthlessness eventually caught up with him. In the 1950s, lacking the energy of the emerging generation of would-be studio executives, he was finally ground down by the behind-the-scenes scheming. Outmaneuvered, he was ejected from MGM in 1951 to be replaced by Dore Schary. Grittily determined to the last, Mayer spent his final years failing to persuade the shareholders of MGM's parent company, Loew, to reinstate him and dump Schary. He died as a result of leukemia in 1957.

Context and Conclusions

In many ways Mayer's life was a drama in which he himself played the roles of both hero and villain. On his journey to moguldom he made countless enemies. It was said at the time of his death that the reason that half of Hollywood attended his funeral was to check that the great man was indeed dead. Mayer also earned the grudging respect of his competitors who harbored a sneaking admiration for his commercial acumen.

At MGM Mayer presided over a golden age of moviemaking. He was responsible for a host of hits like *Ben Hur* (1926) and *Dinner at Eight* (1933). At his zenith he commanded the highest salary in the world—over a million dollars a year. Bob Hope said of Mayer that he "came out west with twenty-eight dollars, a box camera, and an old lion. He built a monument to himself—the Bank of America."

Mayer ruled MGM "as one big family, rewarding obedience, punishing insubordination, and regarding opposition as personal betrayal."

Perhaps Mayer's most fitting epitaph is one of his own observations. Commenting on survival in the movie business, the combative son of a scrap dealer who became the most powerful man in Hollywood eloquently put it thus: "Look out for yourself or they'll pee on your grave."

For More Information

Books:

Altman, Diana. *Hollywood East: Louis B. Mayer and the Origins of the Studio System*. Secaucus, NJ: Carol Publishing Group, 1992.

Gabler, Neal. *An Empire of Their Own: How the Jews Invented Hollywood*. New York: Doubleday, 1988.

Schulberg, Budd. *Moving Pictures*. New York: Stein and Day, 1982.

Zierold, Norman. *The Moguls*. Los Angeles: Avon Books, 1972.

Web Site:

MGM: **www.mgm.com**

  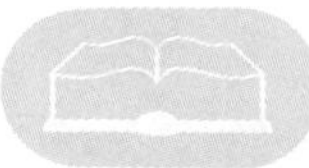    

J. P. Morgan

J. P. Morgan was one of the greatest financiers of his age. As a child he kept a close account of the receipt and expenditure of his allowance. As an adult he parlayed his attention to cash flow into a large fortune. He saw the Civil War as an opportunity to make money, and in 1862 he founded his own company, Dabrey, Morgan, and Co. By 1871 he had teamed up with the firm of Drexel to form Drexel, Morgan, and Co. He swiftly established himself as one of the leading financiers in New York. Industrialists and governments regularly turned to him for advice, and he helped avert a U.S. financial crisis in 1895. Morgan attempted to unify the railroad bosses in opposition to the U.S. government. A powerful influence in the formation of so-called industry "trusts," his business empire was eventually cut down to size by President Theodore Roosevelt.

J. P. Morgan—the man who bankrolled the United States.

1837	Born.
1857	Joins Duncan, Sherman, and Co.
1862	Founds Dabrey, Morgan, and Co.
1871	Teams up with the firm of Drexel to form Drexel, Morgan, and Co.
1879	Puts together stock offering of $18 million for the New York Central Railroad.
1887	U.S. government passes the Interstate Commerce Act.
1895	Helps avert U.S. financial crisis.
1907	Bails out U.S. government again.
1912	Appears before Pujo Committee.
1913	Dies.

Background and Rise

John Pierpont Morgan was born in Hartford, Connecticut, on April 17, 1837. In the year of his birth America was plunged into financial gloom. Morgan, however, was unaffected; his father was a rich commodity broker who managed to make the most of the financial downturn. While he was still a boy, his father moved the family to Boston where he became involved in the cotton trade.

Morgan was never a popular child at school. His aloof manner failed to impress his classmates, just as it would later alienate the U.S. public.

Morgan took an early interest in business. Spurning childhood games, he spent much of his time poring over his accounts (a habit he carried with him throughout his life), detailing the receipt and expenditure of his allowance. He had a bookish nature—partly a result of his interest in business and money, and partly a result of a sickly constitution. Morgan was never a popular child at school. His aloof manner failed to impress his classmates, just as it would later alienate the U.S. public. His habits, such as writing to Paris in fluent French to order a pair of $900 boots, only served to reinforce the impression of arrogance.

Morgan's education was in keeping with his privileged status. When his family moved to London, he was dispatched to a private school in Switzerland. He studied at the University of Göttingen and so impressed his tutors that he was asked to stay on as an assistant to one of the professors. The ambitious Morgan declined, insisting that he had to start out in business.

Defining Moments

Returning to America, in 1857 Morgan joined Duncan, Sherman, and Co., a firm with which his father had an association.

When the Civil War broke out in 1861, Morgan treated it not as a calamity but as an opportunity. He avoided enlistment through the accepted practice among the wealthy of paying a substitute to take his place. (The going rate was $300.) In 1862 he left Duncan Sherman and founded his own company, Dabrey, Morgan, and Co. While the war raged, Morgan piled up the profits. By 1864 he had amassed over $50,000. The war ended, but Morgan continued to go from strength to strength. By 1871 he had teamed up with the firm of Drexel based in Philadelphia to form Drexel, Morgan, & Co., based on the corner of Wall Street and Broad Street in New York.

Morgan swiftly established a reputation as one of the leading financiers in America. His salary was more than $500,000—an astronomical amount at the time. It was during the 1870s that his association with the railroads began. The financing of the railroads required significant private capital, something that Morgan was only too happy to arrange.

His importance in the railroad business grew to the extent that leading players would turn to him to resolve disputes and offer his opinion. In an industry where

"The first thing is character. . .before money or anything else. Money cannot buy it. . .because a man I do not trust could not get money from me on all the bonds in Christendom." (J. P. Morgan)

companies fought increasingly hostile battles to gain supremacy, Morgan found himself playing the role of mediator.

When the U.S. government passed the Interstate Commerce Act in 1887, banning price-fixing collusion among railroads, the railroad companies naturally turned to Morgan again to organize a response. Obtaining a lasting consensus among the distrustful company bosses proved a task beyond even his talents. The misguided effort suggests a man whose ego was beginning to run out of control. Not only did he fail to unite the railroads against the government, he succeeded in setting himself up as the head of a conspiracy and thus an obvious target for the U.S. government, which was aiming to cut powerful business interests down to size.

By the 1890s Morgan had turned into a figure of hate among the U.S. public. Yet, despite this perception, Morgan's greatest public service lay ahead of him. In 1893 the withdrawal of funds from the United States by British investors sparked a financial crisis. As banks failed and the stock market collapsed, the U.S. government resorted to shoring up the financial system with its gold reserves. Statute prohibited the value of the reserves from falling below a prescribed level. The magic figure was $100 million in gold. In January 1895 gold reserves collapsed to $58 million and the treasury secretary John Carlisle turned to Morgan to save the day. Morgan proposed a syndicate of investors who would sell gold coin to the U.S. Treasury, paid for with newly issued bonds. It was a brilliant solution, as it provided not only an economic way out but also a politically expedient one. Morgan went further and guaranteed the scheme to the then president, Grover Cleveland. The Morgan syndicate intervention succeeded in stopping the financial slide and made Morgan a considerable profit, estimated at anywhere between $250,000 and $16 million.

This episode merely reinforced Morgan's already legendary financial prowess. He followed his rescue of the U.S. financial system with a series of breathtaking deals such as the financing of United States Steel, the largest steel corporation in the world. From the 1900s onward he devoted his attention to consolidating the railroad companies through his concern the Northern Securities Corporation, and to building a shipping trust. Unfortunately for him, however, the incumbent president, Theodore Roosevelt, had decided that political advantage could be gained by cracking down on the so-called trusts. As the well-known figure of Morgan stood behind the Northern Securities Corporation, Roosevelt decided that it should be made an example of. This time Morgan had met his match. Apart from a brief respite in 1907, when a U.S. president again turned to him for salvation during a financial crisis, Morgan's power waned.

By then in his 70s, Morgan devoted more time to his hobby of collecting art and to his private life. He died in Rome at the age of 76.

Context and Conclusions

J. P. Morgan was a remarkable businessman. His success owed much to his self-belief and opportunism, and a little to his wealthy and well-connected father. He suffered ill health throughout his life, particularly the periodic embarrassment of a large red bulbous nose, a result of eczema, the appearance of which would inevitably send him into deep melancholia. Yet despite frequent periods of illness-induced rest and recuperation, Morgan managed to build a string of business interests in the fashionable industries of the day—railroads, shipping, and electricity. He also, on more than one occasion, financed the U.S. government out of a mess.

Obtaining a lasting consensus among the distrustful company bosses proved a task beyond even his talents. The misguided effort suggests a man whose ego was beginning to run out of control.

Although not as wealthy as the likes of Carnegie or the Vanderbilts, Morgan amassed a fortune worthy of Croesus. He also accumulated a fabulous hoard of art treasures—a who's who of the old masters, including works by Vermeer, Gainsborough, Rembrandt, and da Vinci—as well as one of the finest libraries in the world. His reputation as a proud, vain, arrogant, and greedy man is justified. But he could be generous when it interested him. To a woman who offered him one of a missing pair of porcelain figures, he gave a handsome sum of money and a cottage in Wales

CLOSE BUT NO CIGAR

Jay Gould

A U.S. financier born in 1836, Gould was the most despised and underhanded of the "robber barons." He started out as a mapmaker and publisher of local history, then inveigled his way into a tannery business. He gained full control when his partner committed suicide. In the 1860s he took to speculating on the railroads. There followed a period of unscrupulous dealings, bribery of officials, and dubious financial practices that would rival if not surpass the worst examples of modern times. Gould emerged from the 1860s/1870s with a fortune of some $25 million (many others lost the shirts from their backs). A neurotic man who suffered terribly from dyspepsia and took his personal chef with him wherever he traveled, Gould was the driving force behind the expansion of the railroads across vast tracts of the United States. He died from tuberculosis, aged 57.

For More Information

Books:

Wheeler, George. *Pierpont Morgan and Friends: The Anatomy of a Myth.* Upper Saddle River, NJ: Prentice Hall, 1973.

Winkler, John. *Morgan the Magnificent: Life of J.P. Morgan.* New York: The Vanguard Press, 1932.

Web Site:

JP Morgan: **www.jpmorgan.com**

"Morgan, Morgan, the Great Financial Gorgon!" (Popular song)

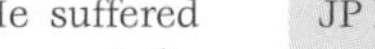

Akio Morita

Akio Morita passed up the opportunity to lead an easy and secure life at the helm of the family sake business. Instead he chose to pursue his love of electrical engineering and start his own business, with all the risks that entailed. Starting with a prototype for a humble rice cooker, Morita's small company TTK grew into the electronic products giant Sony. In a lifetime devoted to his company, Morita gave the world a stream of innovative technologies and gadgets, from the portable transistor radio to the Sony Playstation. He was also the man responsible for making music portable, introducing the word "Walkman" into the global lexicon. In later life Morita refused to take a comfortable retirement, choosing to remain at the helm of Sony until he was forced to step down because of ill health.

Sony—always ahead of the pack.

1921	Born.
1946	Cofounds Tokyo Tshushin Kyogu.
1953	Travels to United States to license transistor technology.
1958	Company changes name to Sony.
1960	World's first all-transistor television.
1961	First Japanese company to list on New York Stock Exchange.
1963	Moves with his family to United States to set up Sony America.
1980	Sony produces Sony Walkman.
1982	Sony produces first CD players.
1993	Suffers stroke while playing tennis.
1999	Dies.

Background and Rise

Akio Morita was born on January 26, 1921 in Nagoya, an industrial city in Japan. By Japanese standards his family was affluent middle class. Morita was heir to the family rice-wine brewing business, although he showed little interest in his father's company. Instead he preferred to tinker with electronics equipment. He soon became an avid amateur electronics enthusiast, neglecting his studies to build electronic gadgets, including a radio and a record player.

Morita's biggest breakthrough was the transistor radio, despite the fact that the transistor was a U.S., not a Japanese, invention.

Morita continued to pursue his interest in electronics in college by studying physics. He joined the Japanese army during World War II and rose to the rank of lieutenant.

After the war Morita passed up the easy career route of working in the family sake business. Instead, in 1946 he traveled to Tokyo, where he joined his future partner Masaru Ibuka. With a $530 loan, the two started a new company, Tokyo Tshushin Kyogu (TTK). It was housed in a bombed-out department store.

Defining Moments

Morita eventually built one of the world's largest electronics companies, famed for its sophisticated miniaturized products. His first product prototype was a little less glamorous—a specialized rice cooker. But radio components and radio upgrades followed, and in the 1950s Morita produced his first major product, the tape recorder. It was the first in Japan.

Morita's biggest breakthrough was the transistor radio, despite the fact that the transistor was a U.S., not a Japanese, invention. Nor was the miniature radio that Morita produced using transistor technology the first of its kind. Morita had traveled to the United States in 1953 to license the technology from Bell Laboratories, but it was a joint venture between Texas Instruments and Regency Electronics that produced the world's first commercial transistor radio, the Regency TR-1, in October 1954.

TTK's first model was the TR-55, a set for which serious transistor radio collectors today would happily trade their grandmothers. Made in August 1955 in limited numbers, its production was restricted to Japan. TTK's first radio for export was the TR-63, produced in 1957.

Morita's small TR-63 was extremely successful for two main reasons. First, it was a truly innovative design, sold in a presentation box complete with a soft leather case, antistatic cloth, and earphone.

The second factor was Morita's dogged persistence. Taking the product direct to the distributors, he trekked around New York convincing electronic store owners to stock the TTK radio. He even turned down one large order because the potential purchaser didn't want the TTK company name on the product. He returned to Japan with a full order book.

"All you need is the best product in the world, the most efficient production in the world, and global marketing." (Akio Morita)

  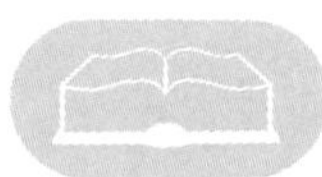    

In 1958 Morita pushed through a change of name for the company. A keen proponent of globalization, he was quick to realize that a name like Tokyo Tshushin Kyogu would prove an obstacle to capturing foreign markets. "We wanted a new name that could be recognized anywhere in the world, one that could be pronounced the same in any language," Morita said. He settled for Sony. This was a combination of the Latin word for sound—*sonus*—and the colloquial U.S. term "sonny." Morita's strategy clearly worked. When U.S. radio dealers were asked in a survey, "Have you ever handled Japanese radios?" they answered no. Asked whether they had ever dealt with Sony radios, they returned an unequivocal yes.

Over the years TTK/Sony produced a steady stream of innovative electronics products: the pocket radio in 1957, the world's first all-transistor television in 1960, and in 1968 the first home videotape recorder.

In 1963 Morita moved to the United States with his family and set up the Sony Corporation of America. It was a bold move for a man from a country whose businessmen were traditionally isolationist and protectionist in outlook. Morita pushed Sony's products in the United States, positioning the brand as premium quality. Soon the company's products were available nationwide.

When Morita noticed that young people liked listening to music wherever they went, he proposed that the company develop a portable tape cassette player. Morita's colleagues were unconvinced there was a market for a tape player of any size that lacked a recording facility. Morita stuck to his guns and persuaded his colleagues, and the Walkman was born in 1980. In a characteristically idiosyncratic move, there was no market research to back Morita's hunch. "The public does not know what is possible. We do," he said.

Interestingly, "Walkman" was not the product's universal name in the early days. Sony America thought the name poor English and changed it to "Soundabout" for the U.S. market. In Sweden it was known as "Freestyle" and in the United Kingdom, "Stowaway." Morita wasn't enthusiastic about this approach. As soon as he received a bad set of sales figures he used it as an excuse to change the name to Walkman throughout the world. The word has since become part of the global lexicon.

Another Sony innovation was video technology. Sony's Betamax technology lost out to VHS in the video standards war, but the company was instrumental in making home video recording a mainstream technology.

As the company's profits grew, Morita relentlessly pursued his vision of globalization. He used the expression "Think globally, act locally" to describe his philosophy of corporate values that transcended national boundaries. Management thinkers such as Theodore Levitt and later Kenichi Ohmae popularized the phrase and it became part of the business vernacular.

Having built Sony into a multibillion dollar company, Morita, by now a billionaire himself, refused to let up. Still brimming with energy, he spent time indulging in pastimes such as scuba diving, skiing, and tennis, all of which he started when he was past 50. He pursued a relentless schedule until he suffered a stroke while playing tennis. Ill health forced him to resign as president of Sony in 1993, and he died in October 1999.

As soon as he received a bad set of sales figures he used it as an excuse to change the name to Walkman throughout the world. The word has since become part of the global lexicon.

Context and Conclusions

Akio Morita, along with entrepreneurs like Eiji Toyoda and Soichiro Honda, ranks as one of Japan's greatest business executives. Blessed with extraordinary drive, Morita was a risk-taker who would doggedly pursue his instincts. Time and again he followed his intuition, beginning with his original rejection of the safe option of working in the family business in favor of starting an electronics company with virtually no experience. The scale of his ambition was apparent in his decision to take his business to the United States at a time when Japan was not yet celebrated for its manufacturing techniques or the quality of its products.

It was Morita who helped put Japanese innovation on the world map by pushing through his globalization agenda, and by backing his vision he established Sony as a truly global company. He is responsible for making Japanese electronics a byword for innovative design and function.

For More Information

Books:

Morita, Akio, with Edwin M. Reingold and Mitsuko Shimomura. *Made in Japan: Akio Morita and Sony.* New York: Dutton, 1989.

Nathan, John. *Sony: The Private Life.* Boston, MA: Houghton Mifflin, 2001.

Web Site:

Sony: **www.sony.com**

"Recession isn't the fault of the workers. If management takes the risk of hiring them, we have to take the responsibility for them."

(Akio Morita)

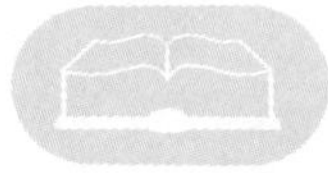

Rupert Murdoch

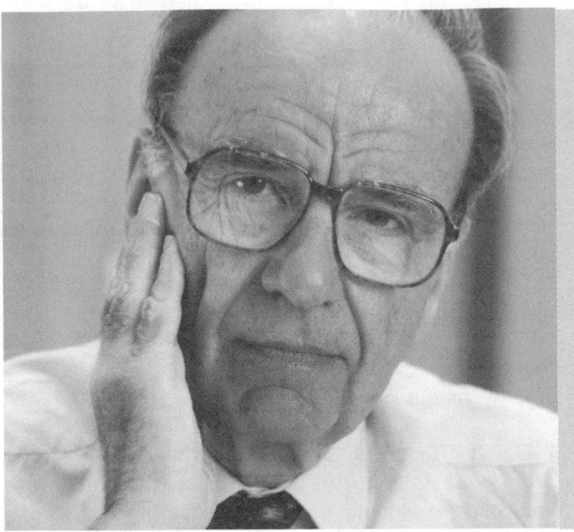

Rupert Murdoch (1931–) is one of the best known media barons of the modern age. After finishing his education at Oxford and a stint at the *Daily Express* newspaper, Murdoch returned to his native Australia to take over from his father at the helm of the *Adelaide News*.

He moved on to expand his media empire through a spate of acquisitions across the globe. In the 1980s he branched into movies and television, acquiring 20th Century Fox and Fox TV. In the United Kingdom he bought *The Times* and *The Sunday Times*, and emerged victorious from a bitter battle with the print unions. By the end of the 1980s the empire was mortgaged to the hilt, but after a major debt rescheduling exercise, Murdoch marched on into the 1990s, acquiring Star TV in Asia.

Rupert Murdoch—the man behind the headlines.

1931	Born.
1950	Attends Oxford University, England.
1952	Works in Fleet Street on the London *Daily Express*. Returns to Australia.
1960	Buys the *Sydney Daily Mirror*.
1964	Founds the *Australian*.
1969	Buys the *News of the World* and the *Sun* in the United Kingdom.
1976	Buys the *New York Post*.
1981	Buys *The Times* of London.
1986	The "battle of Wapping."
1990	Saves business empire by restructuring debt.
1993	Buys into Star TV in Asia.
2000	Attempts to merge Sky TV with GM's Direct TV.

Background and Rise

Now a U.S. citizen, Keith Rupert Murdoch was born in Melbourne, Australia, on March 11, 1931. His early education took place at Geelong Grammar school in Geelong, Victoria. He was not an impressive student—he admits he was "bone lazy" at school—other than in English, where his grades were above average. He also lacked sporting prowess. A restless child, he was more likely to be found cartwheeling across the outfield during play than participating in the school cricket match. His lack of interest on the athletic field led to him being disciplined on more than one occasion.

A restless child, he was more likely to be found cartwheeling across the outfield during play than participating in the school cricket match.

In 1950 he was sent to England to study economics at Worcester College, Oxford. While there, he stood unsuccessfully for president of the Labour Club—an interesting choice for a man whose political sympathies lay with the brand of right-wing ideology later embodied by Margaret Thatcher. His real education, however, took place on the *Daily Express* newspaper in Fleet Street, where he worked before returning home to Australia in 1952.

Back in Australia Murdoch, like the media baron William Randolph Hearst before him, was handed the opportunity to run a newspaper. On the death of his father, the Melbourne publisher Sir Keith Murdoch, he inherited the *Adelaide News*. It was the start of Murdoch's mercurial career as a news proprietor and media mogul.

Defining Moments

To begin with the board was reluctant to hand over complete control of the newspaper to the young tyro. But Murdoch wasn't a man to take no for an answer, even at this early stage in his career. He steered the newspaper in an avowedly populist direction. Headlines like the sensationalist "Queen eats a rat" boosted its circulation and gave it a new lease on life.

Murdoch's success with the *Adelaide News* spurred him on. He bought the *Daily Mirror* in Sydney and dabbled in television. His newspaper acquisitions were driven by opportunity rather than rationale at this point. "We tended to take the sick newspapers, the ones that weren't worth much, that people thought were about to fold up," he later observed. In 1964 he made his boldest move yet, founding the *Australian*—a national newspaper. The *Australian* gave Murdoch political clout and influence and made him a national figure, though commercially it was less successful.

Murdoch moved on from these early triumphs to expand his media empire through a spate of acquisitions across the globe. In the United Kingdom in 1969, he galloped in as an improbable white knight to save the *News of the World*, a downmarket and populist paper,

"I'm not going to claim that we fought the battle of Wapping because we wanted to bring a silver age to British journalism." (Rupert Murdoch)

from falling into enemy hands. The enemy in this case was Robert Maxwell, the Czech-born entrepreneur and budding media mogul. The owners of the paper, the Carrs, were reluctant sellers and strongly opposed a sale to a "foreigner." However when no home-grown business executive would come to their aid, they turned to the Australian Rupert Murdoch. It was the deal that gave Murdoch a toehold in the United Kingdom. Later that year he bought the newspaper the *Sun* for £500,000. In 1976 he added the *New York Post* to his growing empire. He subsequently lost, then regained, control of the newspaper. All the newspapers he acquired received the Murdoch treatment, adopting a right-wing, populist tone.

In 1981 Murdoch made an acquisition that was to have a long-lasting impact on newspapers in the United Kingdom. Fighting off fierce competition, he bought *The Times* of London. A serious newspaper, it seemed an unlikely target. Yet it was a clever purchase as it allowed him to reach a far broader cross-section of the British public. What followed was even more unexpected. Murdoch set himself on a collision course with the powerful U.K. print unions, challenging their inefficient working practices. He built a new printing plant at Wapping, away from Fleet Street, the traditional home of the London press, introduced computerization, and cut out the unions. The unions decided to make Wapping their Waterloo, and for most of 1986 the plant was under virtual siege, becoming the site for a pitched battle between the progressive Murdoch troops and the traditionalist unions. The outcome was a victory for Murdoch and his no-nonsense approach to business.

Wapping was a defining moment not only in union history in the United Kingdom but in the world's perception of Murdoch. He emerged from the episode as a tough, ruthless proprietor who would go to almost any lengths to achieve his aims. The truth was a little more prosaic. If Murdoch hadn't challenged the unions, someone else would have: Margaret Thatcher's Conservative government and the introduction of tough new antistrike legislation had provided a political context that was bound to result in such a battle. And there could be no resisting the march of technological progress—even in the printing industry.

The rest of the 1980s saw Murdoch branch into movies and television, acquiring Fox Studios in the United States in 1985, and seven Metromedia TV stations in 1986. By the end of the 1980s, however, Murdoch had overstretched himself, and a massive debt rescheduling exercise was required in 1990. This successfully shored up his empire. Murdoch then marched on through the 1990s, one deal coming hard on the heels of another. Today his business empire is a truly global one: in all, he has over 750 businesses in over 50 countries. At the end of 2000 his holding company, News Corporation, was worth some $38 billion, with sales of $14 billion. Companies in the News Corporation empire include HarperCollins Publishers, BSkyB, News International, the Los Angeles Dodgers, Fox TV, and Star TV.

Wapping was a defining moment not only in union history in the United Kingdom but in the world's perception of Murdoch.

Murdoch continues to work long days at a fast pace and shows little sign of slowing down. There is endless speculation in the media about who will eventually succeed him, his children—Lachlan, James, and Elisabeth Murdoch—being the main candidates. His third wife, Wendy Deng, is another possible. For now, though, as demonstrated by his recent attempts to merge GM-owned Direct TV with his own Sky TV, megabillionaire Murdoch retains an iron grip on his empire.

Context and Conclusions

Murdoch has more than his share of critics, many strident. He is accused of a variety of sins from wielding too much power to "dumbing down" his media vehicles. Perhaps the criticism is overdone. Murdoch has an innate sense of what the public wants, and he makes sure he provides it. He is an astute pragmatist and brilliant entrepreneur who has built the world's first global media empire through instinct, talent, and hard work.

For More Information

Books:

Crainer, Stuart. *Business the Rupert Murdoch Way*. New York: AMACOM, 1999.

Regan, Simon. *Rupert Murdoch: A Business Biography*. London: Angus & Robertson, 1976.

"Sometimes you have to pay a high price for an opportunity."

(Rupert Murdoch)

David Ogilvy

It was fortunate for the world of advertising that David Ogilvy eventually found his way to its door. But he took a circuitous route. After working in Paris, he returned to England and pursued a career as an Aga cooker salesman. Next he dallied with advertising at the agency Mather & Crowther, enjoying the bright lights of London before packing his bags and heading for America. A job as a pollster for Dr. George Gallup was followed by a stint as a tobacco farmer with the Amish community in Pennsylvania. Finally, in 1948 in his late thirties, Ogilvy started his own advertising agency. With a flair for copywriting, he was soon acknowledged by competitors and clients alike as one of the most brilliant advertising executives of his generation. He retired in 1975 after building Ogilvy & Mather into a business with annual billings of $800 million.

David Ogilvy was rarely lost for words.

1911	Born.
1938	Travels to the United States.
1948	Starts new advertising agency, Hewitt, Ogilvy, Benson, & Mather.
1960	Challenges the advertising industry practice of charging 15% commission.
1963	Publishes book *Confessions of an Advertising Man*.
1965	Merges firm with Mather & Crowther to form Ogilvy & Mather.
1975	Steps down from position as creative head.
1999	Dies.

Background and Rise

The son of a stockbroker, David Ogilvy was born on June 23, 1911. He was dispatched to Fettes School, a prestigious private school near Edinburgh, Scotland. What Ogilvy lacked in natural academic ability he made up for in scholarly application, securing a scholarship to study history at Christ Church College at Oxford University.

During World War II Ogilvy worked for British intelligence in Washington. When the war ended, he decided to try his hand at tobacco farming, acquiring several acres of land in the heart of the Amish community in Lancaster County, Pennsylvania.

When he left Oxford, the young Ogilvy sought adventure abroad. In France he worked in the kitchens of the Hotel Majestic. When Ogilvy had tired of *la vie parisienne*, he returned to England to sell a new type of stove, the Aga. As a salesman Ogilvy proved a great success, so much so that he was asked to write a manual for the Aga sales force on how to sell the stove. (30 years later, the editors of *Fortune* magazine announced that it was probably the best sales manual of all time.) Ogilvy sent his manuscript, "The Theory and Practice of Selling the Aga Cooker," to his brother, who was working at the London-based advertising agency Mather & Crowther. His winning way with words earned him a place as a trainee at the agency.

Defining Moments

Ogilvy enjoyed the London lifestyle, partying till dawn at every available opportunity. He combined his social life with hard work, showing a natural aptitude for his new vocation. Very early on he began to develop his own theories about advertising. "Concrete figures must be substituted for atmospheric claims; clichés must give way to facts, and empty exhortations to alluring offers," an enthusiastic Ogilvy wrote in a presentation to his colleagues in the early 1930s.

In 1938 he left his job and embarked on another adventure, this time to the United States. He enjoyed himself so much that he decided to stay, moving to Princeton, New Jersey, where he worked with Dr. George Gallup, the man behind the Gallup polls. The experience he gained working for Gallup was invaluable, if poorly paid, as it provided him with insights into U.S. consumer preferences and the way they were formed.

During World War II Ogilvy worked for British intelligence in Washington. When the war ended, he decided to try his hand at tobacco farming, acquiring several acres of land in the heart of the Amish community in Lancaster County, Pennsylvania. Exactly what possessed Ogilvy to pursue an agricultural career is unclear. What is certain is that he was most unsuited to it, and before long he was back in New York.

It is fair to say that, without the help of his brother Francis, Ogilvy might never have become one of the great advertising figures of the 20th century. Casting around for a job, the 37-year-old enlisted the help of his brother to set up his own advertising agency in America. His brother not only rounded up $45,000 to help finance the new

"When you have nothing to say, sing it." (David Ogilvy)

venture but also persuaded another British advertising agency, S. H. Benson, to invest a further $45,000 in return for a partnership. The newly created agency, Hewitt, Ogilvy, Benson, & Mather, opened for business in 1948. As an Englishman, Ogilvy struggled to win over U.S. clients, although the addition of ex-J. Walter Thompson employee Anderson Hewitt helped. It was Hewitt that saved the day when the business threatened to run out of capital after only a few months. Fortunately, Hewitt's uncle was the chairman of JPMorgan and he lent the agency $100,000 with no security. And it was Hewitt who brought in the first major account, Sun Oil, worth some $3 million.

Despite the agency's diminutive size, it was clear from the beginning that Ogilvy's advertising intuition set the company apart from its competitors. His style was evident in an early campaign for shirtmakers Hathaway. Ads featured a man with an eye patch, known as the man from Hathaway, who supported the small shirtmakers from Maine in their efforts to take on the giant shirtmaker Arrow. Ogilvy used photographs, then still a rarity in advertising, featuring a male model complete with eye patch performing a variety of unusual tasks. The Hathaway campaign made Ogilvy's reputation and was an early example of his approach to brand building and supporting brands through brand image. He followed the success of the Hathaway campaign with a campaign for Schweppes, the soft drink manufacturer. Putting to good use the knowledge he gained with Gallup, Ogilvy assuaged U.S. consumer sensibilities about class with Commander Edward Whitehead, the distinguished-looking gentleman who was boss of Schweppes at the time. Schweppes sales in the United States bubbled up by 500% over the following nine years.

Ogilvy's role at the agency was to be Jack of all trades, master of most. The exception was administration, for which he had little time. To his credit he realized that this weakness was hampering the firm and employed Esty Stowell, a Benson & Bowles executive, as vice president in 1957. Stowell took responsibility for managing the entire agency, with Ogilvy retaining control of the creative department only.

"At 60 miles an hour the loudest noise in this new Rolls-Royce comes from the electric clock." This was Ogilvy's slogan for his Rolls-Royce campaign. It exemplified his approach of putting the product center stage. "Make your product the hero of the commercial," he famously entreated. In 1960 he challenged one of the industry's prized but anachronistic practices—the 15% commission. As usual Ogilvy's stance was not merely ethical, but one guaranteed to attract publicity. It succeeded, bringing in new clients such as Shell who were only too happy to be rid of the 15% commission in exchange for a flat fee.

The 1960s was a big decade for Ogilvy. In 1963 he published his book *Confessions of an Advertising Man,* which sold well over half a million copies and cemented his position as an advertising guru. In 1965, the year after his brother's death, his firm merged with Mather & Crowther to form Ogilvy & Mather.

By 1975 Ogilvy & Mather was one of the top five advertising agencies in the world with a thousand clients, offices in 29 countries, and billings of some $800 million. In the same year Ogilvy stepped down from his position as creative head to spend more time at his home in the south of France. In 1989, following a wave of mergers in the industry, Ogilvy's remaining share in the business was acquired by the WPP group.

Context and Conclusions

David Ogilvy said the secret of success was simple: "First, make a reputation for being a creative genius. Second, surround yourself with partners who are better than you are. Third, leave them to get on with it." But the most important things that Ogilvy acquired in his time on Madison Avenue were the ability and creative flair needed to lead by example. "The most important ingredient in any agency is the ability of the top man to lead his troops," he said. He was a late starter in advertising at 39. Yet he still made it to the top of his profession—and made an indelible mark there too. Ogilvy died on July 21 1999.

Ogilvy's role at the agency was to be Jack of all trades, master of most. The exception was administration, for which he had little time.

CLOSE BUT NO CIGAR

Lord Saatchi/James Walter Thompson
Charles Saatchi built not one but two successful advertising agencies. First there was Saatchi & Saatchi, the U.K. agency that helped win a general election with its "Labour isn't Working" posters for the Conservative party. Then, when Charles and brother Maurice got a little overambitious and were kicked out of their own company after an ill-conceived bid for a well known bank, they started up another agency. The new agency was M&C Saatchi. They took a few prestigious clients with them. Soon Charles received a peerage, and M&C Saatchi overtook Saatchi & Saatchi in the billings rankings.

Thompson bought out William James Carlton, owner of advertising "broker" Carlton & Smith, for $500 in 1877. The furniture cost $800. In 1887 the JWT Company became the first agency to write advertisements for their clients rather than just sell them advertising space. By 1909 JWT had opened in London. It went on to become one of the world's most successful agencies.

For More Information

Books:

Ogilvy, David. *Blood, Brains and Beer.* New York: Atheneum, 1978.

Ogilvy, David. *Confessions of an Advertising Man.* New York: Atheneum, 1963.

Ogilvy, David. *Ogilvy on Advertising.* New York: Crown, 1983.

Web Site:

Ogilvy: **www.ogilvy.com**

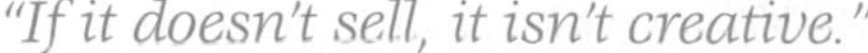

"If it doesn't sell, it isn't creative."

(David Ogilvy)

DAVID PACKARD

From a rented garage in Palo Alto, California, David Packard and Bill Hewlett founded one of Silicon Valley's most enduring IT companies—Hewlett-Packard. When Packard met Hewlett at Stanford University in the 1930s, Palo Alto was best known for its prunes. By the time he died, it had established itself as the epicenter of the most famous high-tech cluster in the world, and Hewlett-Packard had become one of the pillar companies of Silicon Valley.

Packard teamed up with Hewlett to start a rent-an-inventor company in a garage in Palo Alto. First-year profits were $1,539. By 1942, sales were $2 million. In the 1970s the company made a tactical switch to computing, and throughout the 1980s it was consistently among the top five IT companies.

David Packard, one half of the dynamic HP duo.

1912	Born.
1934	Meets friend and future partner Bill Hewlett at Stanford University, Palo Alto.
1938	After a stint at General Electric, teams up with Bill Hewlett once more.
1939	Starts Hewlett-Packard in a garage in Palo Alto with just $538 of capital.
1942	HP turnover is $2 million.
1970	The company declines to make wholesale layoffs when the U.S. economy hits a recession.
1972	HP introduces the handheld scientific calculator, the model 35.
1980s	HP consistently in top five computer manufacturers.
1990s	Back-to-basics drive revitalizes company fortunes.
1996	Dies.

BACKGROUND AND RISE

The company was founded in 1939 with just $538 of capital. The original location, a Palo Alto garage, was to become part of Silicon Valley folklore.

Born into a middle-class family on September 7, 1912, David Packard grew up in Pueblo, Colorado. At an early age he decided that he wanted to be an engineer. Unlike the millions of children whose ambitions to become an astronaut, firefighter, doctor, or nurse come to nothing, he was not be shaken from his goal.

Packard studied at Stanford University. It was there that he met his friend and partner-to-be, Bill Hewlett. When he graduated in 1934 America was still recovering from the Great Depression. Packard took one of the few jobs available to an electrical engineering student, working at General Electric. He also studied for a master's degree at the Massachusetts Institute of Technology. In 1938 Packard returned to Palo Alto and teamed up with Bill Hewlett. They decided to start their own company.

DEFINING MOMENTS

The company was founded in 1939 with just $538 of capital. The original location, a Palo Alto garage, was to become part of Silicon Valley folklore. It sent a message to all future entrepreneurs that great businesses could grow from small beginnings. A number of corporate giants were later to be hatched in the humble garage.

The original plan was for Packard to become a kind of rent-an-inventor. But his creativity soon ran riot, and he and Hewlett began developing their own gadgets together. The inventions were many and varied. Early designs included an electric shock machine to help people lose weight and an optical device to trigger automatic urinal flushing. But the first invention that made money was a piece of equipment designed to help sound engineers make better recordings. By the end of the first year of business, Hewlett and Packard had amassed a profit of $1,539. The garage was replaced with more substantial premises in 1940. The company, by now named Hewlett-Packard, prospered during World War II, even though Hewlett joined the Signal Corps and left Packard to run the business. By 1942 sales were $2 million. In the immediate postwar period, however, business dropped off alarmingly. Nevertheless, when Hewlett returned from the military, a number of talented staff were hired, and the business began to improve again.

In a division of duties Packard assumed the managerial role with Hewlett in charge of engineering and R&D. Although Packard had little theoretical knowledge of management—his only experience was growing the company—he proved a natural. He introduced a system of management that involved walking among the employees and maintaining a highly visible presence.

"We have a technique at Hewlett-Packard for helping managers and supervisors know their people and understand the work their people are doing. . .Management By Walking About." (David Packard)

This was in contrast to the idea, prevalent among companies at the time, that the management and the workforce were breeds apart and should have little to do with each other. That philosophy was perpetuated by corporate institutions such as the management dining room, where the great and the good tucked into a three--course culinary extravaganza while the workers huddled around their workstations eating baloney sandwiches.

Packard, however, spurned the trappings of executive status. He maintained a policy of openness, making himself available to speak to employees. His accessibility and the practice of Management By Walking About (MBWA for short) endeared him to the staff. Packard repaid their respect by empowering them in their daily work. "We figured that people will accomplish more," Packard said, "if they are given an opportunity to use their talents and abilities in the way they work best." While many managers have paid lip service to worker empowerment and enlightened management practice, these are often the first casualties in times of difficulty and economic downturn. Not in the case of Hewlett-Packard, however. In 1970, when the U.S. economy slipped into recession, Packard did not make wholesale layoffs. Instead, he agreed a new working pattern with the staff. Employees worked nine days in every two weeks instead of ten. In addition, management and workforce alike took a 10% pay cut.

Within a year, the U.S. economy was staging a recovery. Packard had avoided the unnecessary expense of layoffs followed by rehiring. Besides following forward-looking human resource policies, he took an innovative approach to organizational structure. "I've often thought that after you get organized you ought to throw the chart away", he opined. It wasn't that Packard didn't believe in organization, it was just that he believed in small agile units operating within the company. So, whenever a division grew cumbersome and unwieldy, Packard would break it up into small units. In 1972 Hewlett-Packard introduced a handheld scientific calculator, the model 35, and during the 1970s and 1980s the company moved into the computer business.

Throughout the 1980s, HP was one of the top five computer manufacturers in the United States. In the 1990s, however, it struggled as competitors began to out-innovate it. Packard's solution was a return to basics, back to Management By Walking About. Although both Packard and Hewlett were approaching 80, they took action to reinvigorate the company. The HP hierarchy had grown unwieldy, they decided, so they took a scalpel to the organization, cutting out unnecessary layers. The philosophy of small teams and less management was restored, as was Hewlett-Packard's competitiveness, and the company reclaimed its place among America's leading IT corporations.

David Packard died in 1996, knowing that his company was once more in shape to compete with the best. Today, HP's future looks less certain, but many of Packard's enlightened management principles remain etched in the company's culture.

Context and Conclusions

From a small engineering company founded in a garage, Dave Packard, with the help of his friend and fellow student Bill Hewlett, built a multinational technology company with over 100,000 employees and annual revenues in excess of $40 billion.

"We figured that people will accomplish more," Packard said, "if they are given an opportunity to use their talents and abilities in the way they work best."

Packard's key contribution to Hewlett-Packard and business, according to Bill Hewlett, his lifelong business partner and buddy, was "the HP Way," a set of values and management principles put together by Packard in 1957. In his book of the same name, he explains that one of the objectives of the company was "to maintain an organizational environment that fosters individual motivation, initiative, and creativity, and a wide latitude of freedom in working toward established objectives and goals." It is for this enlightened attitude to worker empowerment and the other forward-looking practices enshrined in *The HP Way* that Packard will probably be best remembered.

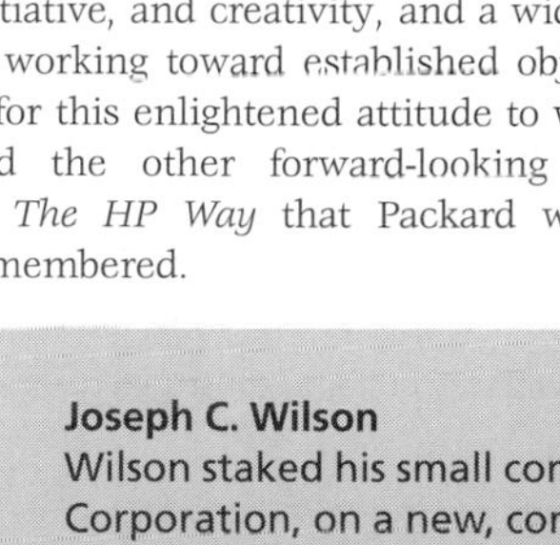

CLOSE BUT NO CIGAR

Joseph C. Wilson
Wilson staked his small company, Haloid Corporation, on a new, commercially untried technology developed by a physicist called Chester Carlson. The technology was xerography. The first copier, the 914, was shipped in March 1960. It was one of the most successful single products ever. In 1959 Haloid Corp. revenue was $2 million; in 1960 it was $4 million; in 1963 it was a staggering $422 million. The company went on to become the Xerox Corporation.

For More Information

Books:

Packard, David. *The HP Way: How Bill Hewlett and I Built Our Company*. New York: HarperBusiness, 1995.

Web Site:

Hewlett-Packard: **www.hp.com**

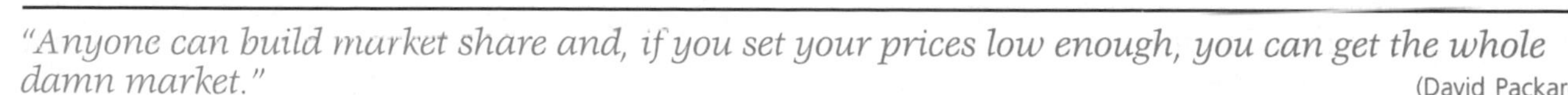

"Anyone can build market share and, if you set your prices low enough, you can get the whole damn market."
(David Packard)

  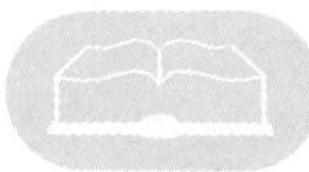    

JOHN H. PATTERSON

The seeds of John H. Patterson's (1844–1922) rise to fame were sown on his family's farm. If his father hadn't constantly asked him how much he charged customers for the farm produce, he might not have been interested in the invention of a local trader. Patterson took that invention, the automatic cash register, and turned it into a multimillion dollar business, National Cash Register. On his way to a personal fortune, Patterson redefined the art of salesmanship, introduced the idea of the corporate classroom, and saved a town from drowning. He was a pioneer in linking productivity to better working conditions.

John H. Patterson, the force behind NCR.

1844	Born.
1867	Graduates from Dartmouth College.
1884	Purchases National Manufacturing Company and renames it National Cash Register.
1887	Company holds first annual sales convention.
1893	New, modern factory building constructed.
1913	Dayton floods.
1915	Court of Appeals overturns Patterson's conviction on antitrust charges.
1922	Dies.

BACKGROUND AND RISE

Born near Dayton, Ohio, in 1844, John Henry Patterson spent his childhood working on the 2,000-acre family farm. One of eight children, Patterson would help out when he was growing up by selling his father's farm goods. The amounts charged for the produce would frequently go unrecorded, and Patterson would be interrogated by his father, day or night, about whom he had charged and how much they paid.

On his way to a personal fortune, Patterson redefined the art of salesmanship, introduced the idea of the corporate classroom, and saved a town from drowning. He was a pioneer in linking productivity to better working conditions.

Patterson attended local schools, followed by Miami University and Dartmouth College, graduating with a B.A. in 1867. In the meantime he fought in the Union army in the Civil War.

When Patterson left college he was determined to go into business for himself. He saved money from a job collecting tolls on the Miami & Erie Canal and set up as a coal retailer back in his hometown. From selling coal he moved into coal and iron ore mining with his brother Frank; then, again with his brother, he set up a mining supply store. At the store the stock sold well, but the profits failed to materialize. Since the brothers were applying a healthy markup, something else was clearly wrong. Patterson determined to track down the discrepancy. Hearing of a machine invented by local merchant that automatically recorded sales, he bought two.

DEFINING MOMENTS

Primitive though they were, when Patterson saw the machines he immediately appreciated the possibilities they offered. If he had a use for one, wouldn't every shopkeeper in the country? In 1884, moving swiftly, he bought out inventor Jacob Ritty's business for $6,500, changing the name from the National Manufacturing Company to National Cash Register. But when he looked over the books he discovered the business was losing money, and suffering a temporary loss of faith he offered $2,000 to get out of the contract. Luckily for him, the seller wasn't interested.

Patterson was forced to make a go of the cash register business. He acquired premises in a down-at-heel section of Dayton known as Slidertown and began manufacturing cash registers on a commercial scale. He was by no means an enlightened employer; he saw his work force only in terms of production. In return his employees, uninspired by their work and their boss, took advantage whenever they could. The result was poor quality—$50,000 worth of faulty machinery in one year—and poor performance.

Eventually it dawned on Patterson that if he were to treat his workers a little better, he might improve the quality of his products. He started in a small way by buying a property opposite the factory where the workers could get coffee. It was the first time any provision had been made for refreshments for them. He began buying other property in the neighborhood and gradually improving conditions in the surrounding area, where most of the work force lived. Turning his attention to the factory premises, he hired architects to design a new building that would be as comfortable for the work force as it was efficient for the work performed there. When the people of Dayton saw the new building—constructed predominantly from glass and steel—they laughed at Patterson, declaring that there wouldn't be an unbroken window in the building before a week was out. But Patterson had the last laugh. His modern building, with its built-in lecture rooms, air conditioning, showers, and movie theaters, instilled a sense of civic pride in Slidertown. Very few windows were broken. Patterson even opened up his private estate to the public, including his golf course and swimming pool.

Patterson's style of paternalistic leadership wasn't always successful. His insistence that workers use the baths provided by the company and attend various entertainments caused resentment. By the time he had backed down it was too late to stop a threatened strike. But in a masterly outflanking maneuver he gathered his employees together, reassured them that he understood the reasons for their dissatisfaction, and proclaimed that everyone needed a rest. At which point he promptly shut down the factory and went traveling. The stunned workers were triumphant at first, but as the weeks passed triumph quickly turned to concern and then to despair. The workers telegraphed Patterson, imploring him to reopen the factory. After two months he returned to a hero's welcome. His pointed comments about there being several offers on the table to relocate his factory elsewhere did not fall on deaf ears.

When Patterson returned he didn't hold a grudge against his employees, and they in turn put in extra effort. Patterson's innovative ideas on sales were beginning to reap rewards. NCR was one of the first companies in the United States to train a professional salesforce. Sales agents had to memorize a 16-page, 4500-word sales primer. Patterson would drop in on the agents and quiz them on the contents of the primer—anyone who failed was fired. By 1894 NCR was producing half a million copies of its sales newsletter, *Hustler*. Sales conventions were held annually after 1887.

Brilliant at promoting sales of NCR cash registers, Patterson was equally effective at stifling the sales of competitors' products. In fact he was sometimes too effective. Patterson called in a promising executive from the Rochester office to coordinate the company's response to the competition. The executive was a former piano salesman, Thomas J. Watson (who was later to found IBM). With Watson's help Patterson eliminated the competition by means of acquisitions and the vigorous defense of his cash register patents. So successful was his campaign that he attracted the unwelcome attention of the U.S. government. Against a backdrop of public antitrust sentiment, he and 28 other NCR executives each received a year's jail sentence and a $5,000 fine.

Patterson's reputation might have been permanently stained by the judgement were it not for the great Dayton floods. On the night of March 25–26, 1913, Dayton was submerged under 17 feet of water. Patterson personally took control of the situation. In the hours before the flood hit he organized safety and rescue plans and constructed hundreds of makeshift boats at the company's lumberyards, building rafts at the rate of one every seven minutes. For his role in the town's relief efforts he was dubbed "the Savior of Dayton." The townsfolk petitioned President Woodrow Wilson to pardon Patterson, a petition that would probably have been successful had the decision not been overturned in any case by the Court of Appeals in 1915.

> **Brilliant at promoting sales of NCR cash registers, Patterson was equally effective at stifling the sales of competitors' products.**

During World War I Patterson committed his company's resources to the war effort. He insisted on carrying out contracts on a fixed-fee instead of a cost-plus basis, refusing to profit from the war. He died on May 14, 1922.

Context and Conclusions

Patterson is the perfect example of a man with the right product at the right time. National Cash Register replaced the pencil behind the ear of the grocery store clerk with on-the-counter, state-of-the-art technology. In addition—after an early conversion—he turned out to be a model employer. An early exponent of classroom learning in the corporation, Patterson was one of the first of the great entrepreneurs of his time to make the connection between improved productivity and better working conditions. And unlike many of his contemporaries, his heroism was not just corporate: he was a real-life hero, too, organizing the rescue and relief of his hometown from dramatic floods.

For More Information

Books:

Marcosson, Isaac F. *Wherever Men Trade: The Romance of the Cash Register*. Manchester, NH: Ayer, 1972.

  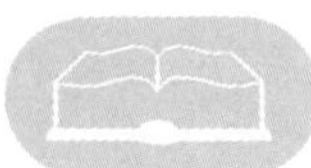    

Arthur Rock

Arthur Rock is the man credited with coining the term "venture capital." Without the venture capital industry, there probably would have been no new economy or information revolution. Without Rock, there might not be a venture capital industry. Rock was the first venture capitalist (VC) operating on the West Coast of the United States. He organized the funding that got the computer revolution under way when he helped eight researchers break out from William Shockley's laboratories to found Fairchild Semiconductors. Then, he rounded up financing for some of the biggest companies in Silicon Valley, including Intel and Apple. It wasn't just money that Rock supplied. He also provided sage advice from his seat on the board of directors. He was still passing on the benefit of his considerable experience well into his seventies.

Arthur Rock bestrides the venture capital industry.

1926	Born.
1948	Graduates from Syracuse University.
1951	Finishes MBA at Harvard Business School. Joins Hayden Stone.
1957	"Traitorous eight" leave Shockley labs.
1959	Fairchild Semiconductors formed.
1961	Founds the firm of Davis and Rock.
1968	Davis and Rock dissolved after a seven-year life. Backs Gordon Moore and Bob Noyce, who found Intel.
1970	Forms Arthur Rock & Associates; sets up on his own as Arthur Rock & Co.
1980	Invests in Apple Computing. Joins board of directors.
1993	Steps down from Apple board because of conflict of interests.
1994–1999	Director of Air Touch Communications.

Background and Rise

The son of a candy store owner, Arthur Rock was born in the United States in 1926. After graduating with an MBA from Harvard Business School in 1951, Rock went to work for Hayden Stone, a New York investment banking firm. Hayden Stone specialized in financing companies. At the time, the venture capital industry didn't exist in a formal sense: they tended to be private family organizations, such as the one run by the Rockefellers.

Rock's lucky break came when he was shown a letter sent to one of the firm's brokers by the son of a client. The writer of the letter was Eugene Kleiner, a scientist at William Shockley's laboratory in California. Shockley was a brilliant but erratic research scientist who pioneered research on the transistor. Unfortunately his man-management skills were negligible and he was verging on the paranoid, making the atmosphere at the labs extremely unpleasant. Revolution was in the air. Key employees decided that they could no longer work with Shockley, but, before the team was split up, Kleiner wrote a speculative letter to Hayden Stone asking if anyone knew of a place where they could continue to work together. Intrigued, Rock persuaded one of Hayden Stone's partners to fly out to the West Coast with him and meet Kleiner and his associates.

Defining Moments

Kleiner explained that the research team wanted to investigate the possibility of manufacturing transistors using silicon. If the process worked, it would revolutionize the computer industry. Rock was impressed with the young scientists and agreed that he would help Kleiner raise $1.5 m to set up a separate company. Rock contacted a long list of potential investors, but managed to raise nothing more than a few eyebrows. Luckily, at the last moment, he thought of Sherman Fairchild.

Sherman Fairchild was the largest stockholder in IBM; he had financed Tom Watson Sr. when he founded the predecessor company to IBM. He was also an inventor. Fairchild thought Rock's proposal was a good one and agreed to invest $1.5 m through Fairchild Camera and Instrument. Kleiner and his associates were given an option to buy all the stock for $3 m.

The new company was named Fairchild Semiconductors. It was the technology gene pool from which, eventually, the Silicon Valley high-tech phenomenon evolved. Rock's success with the Fairchild deal spurred him on to investigate other investment opportunities on the West Coast. He made friends with Tommy Davis. Davis was working for Kern County Land Company, advising the firm on using surplus cash to finance other companies. Davis left Kern County Land in 1961 to join up with Rock, and together they formed the investment partnership Rock & Davis.

Investment in Rock's first partnership fund came largely from private individuals on the East Coast who were his contacts. Institutional investors showed little enthusiasm. From an investment of roughly $3 m of the fund's capital, over $70 m was returned to the limited partners. Unlike some later VCs, Rock's approach was about much more than just investing money. He also sat on the boards of companies he invested in, working closely with them to increase their chances of success. In the case of Teledyne, one of the fund's first investments, Rock was on the board for 33 years. Another early investment was in Scientific Data Systems. The company was sold to Xerox in 1969 for some $990 m—in Rock's words, "a humongous deal in those days."

In 1970 Rock formed a new partnership, Arthur Rock & Associates. Fairchild Semiconductors was in a state of flux. Sherman Fairchild was dead and a new CEO, John Carter, was in charge of the Fairchild Group. Carter's ideas about business conflicted with the ideas of Bob Noyce and Gordon Moore, two of the key researchers at Fairchild. Disenchanted with life at Fairchild, Moore and Noyce approached Rock and explained that they wanted to start their own company to research and produce semiconductor memory. Rock raised $2.5 m from 25 investors to invest in the new company, including $300,000 of his own money. It took him two days. The new company was called Intel. The world's largest producer of microprocessors started with a modest $5.5 m of private funding, raised on the strength of a business plan written on one and a half pages. Rock remained on Intel's board for over 30 years.

The financing of two of the most important companies in the history of computing would have been enough to ensure Rock's place in the pantheon of venture capitalists, but Rock followed Intel with another seminal computing company, Apple Computers. Mike Markkula, ex-vice president of Intel, tipped Rock off about a small fledgling computer company called Apple. Rock was not immediately persuaded and decided to pay a visit to the San José Homebrew Computer Show to see for himself. When he arrived he was unable to get anywhere near the Apple stand because of the assembled crowds, desperate to get a glimpse of the mock-up computer the two young entrepreneurs, Steve Jobs and Steve Wozniak, were demonstrating. But despite the obvious interest, Rock invested only $57,000. As usual he assumed his position on the board, a position he relinquished years later only because of a conflict of interest.

A lot has changed in Rock's time as a venture capitalist. As Rock says, "It's just a different world. It's an order of magnitude different. The pace of venture capital has changed. You don't get much time to look at the company. Sometimes you have to make up your mind that day."

One of the questions Rock is asked most often is, "What makes a good VC?" Is it luck, or perhaps a technology background? Rock says neither. According to him, being a good VC is about the ability to listen, about having a diverse range of interests and, above all, about being able to read people. It's a talent that takes years to develop, and Rock has it in spades. In his seventies, Rock works in the industry he helped to create. Based in San Francisco, he is a director on a number of boards, both profit and nonprofit. And he still recalls the words of his Harvard professor: "If you're interested in building a business to make money, forget it. You won't. If you're interested in building a business to make a contribution to society, then let's talk."

The world's largest producer of microprocessors started with a modest $5.5 m of private funding, raised on the strength of a business plan written on one and a half pages.

Context and Conclusions

Arthur Rock is an important figure in postwar economic history. He lit the VC match that ignited the technology industry in Silicon Valley. Through his efforts, eight of the brightest researchers in their field were able to form Fairchild Semiconductors. Without him, the best research team in its field would have scattered across California, the United States, or even the world. Instead they worked together to give the world the silicon chip and then to found Intel, the powerhouse of the personal computer revolution. Rock also helped shape the nature of the PC by investing in Apple Computers. The fact that Eugene Kleiner, one of the original "Fairchildren," later went on to found the VC firm Kleiner Perkins means that Rock can also lay claim to having helped create the modern VC industry.

Rock lit the VC match that ignited the technology industry in Silicon Valley.

CLOSE BUT NO CIGAR

Tom Perkins

After a stellar career with tech companies like Spectra-Physics and Hewlett-Packard, Tom Perkins founded the venture capital firm Kleiner Perkins in 1972. Perkins's partner in the firm was Eugene Kleiner, the man who brought Arthur Rock out to the West Coast. Kleiner Perkins and its later partnership incarnation (Kleiner Perkins Caulfield & Byers) were at the heart of the IT revolution on Sand Hill Road in Menlo Park. The firm pioneered the concept of incubators and hatched companies such as Genentech, Tandem Computers, America Online and Amazon.

For More Information

Web Site:

Intel: **www.intel.com**

"Money is better than poverty, if only for financial reasons." (Woody Allen)

  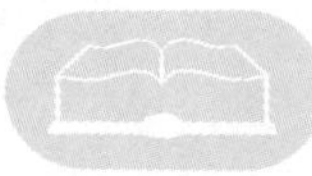    

JOHN D. ROCKEFELLER

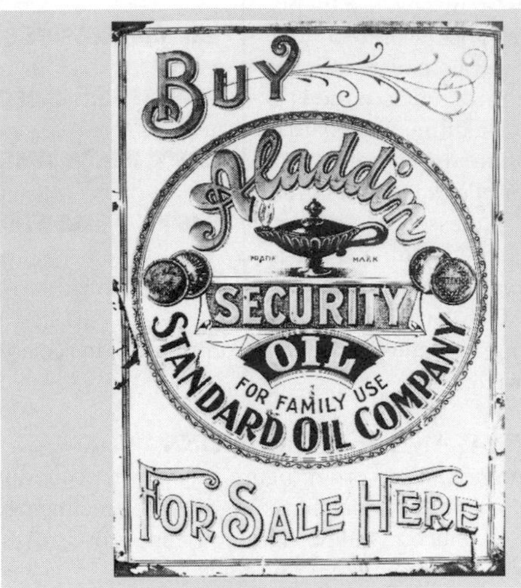

In the course of his long life, U.S. industrialist John D. Rockefeller (1839–1937), the son of a farmer, progressed from being an office boy earning $25 a month to being an oil tycoon worth over $900 million. Starting work at age 16, Rockefeller had his own firm within three years and by 1862 had moved into the oil business. After buying out most of the local competition, Rockefeller set his sights on building a national oil company with a national delivery network. He accomplished his vision with Standard Oil, which by 1879 controlled 90% of the oil refining in the United States. Rockefeller withdrew from active management of the company in 1897, remaining president until 1911, when the Standard Oil trust was finally dissolved by the U.S. government. Rockefeller's final years were devoted to giving away the bulk of his huge fortune.

Rockefeller's Standard Oil helped keep the United States on the move.

1839	Born.
1855	Starts work at Hewitt & Tuttle.
1869	Rockefeller, Andrews, & Flagler becomes the Standard Oil Company of Ohio.
1882	Standard Oil businesses brought under control of the Standard Oil Trust.
1890	Nationwide distribution system reaches most towns in the United States.
1892	Trust dissolved by Ohio government. Reconstitutes as Standard Oil Trust (New Jersey).
1900	Standard Oil controls over three-quarters of the U.S. petroleum industry.
1904	80% of U.S. towns served by Standard Oil carts.
1911	Resigns as president. Standard Oil Trust dissolved.
1913	Establishes Rockefeller Foundation.
1937	Dies.

BACKGROUND AND RISE

John Davison Rockefeller was born in 1839 in Richford, Tioga County, New York, the eldest son and second of six children. His parents were farmers, and Rockefeller, along with his brothers and sisters, was expected to help out on the farm.

Starting work at age 16, Rockefeller had his own firm within three years and by 1862 had moved into the oil business.

By the time Rockefeller was 14, his family had moved to Cleveland, Ohio. Here, in 1855, after a year at high school and a stint at Folsom Mercantile College, Rockefeller was offered employment as an office boy and assistant bookkeeper at the firm of Hewitt & Tuttle, forwarding and produce commission merchants. No salary was agreed at the outset, and Rockefeller received no payment for 14 weeks, at which point he was handed $50 and put on $25 per month.

Rockefeller stayed at Hewitt & Tuttle for three years, leaving when the firm declined to meet his wage demands of $800 a year. Having spent the previous three years paying particular attention to how a business is run, Rockefeller decided to start his own.

DEFINING MOMENTS

With his partner, Morris B. Clark, and $1000 borrowed from his father at 10%, Rockefeller started a produce business. He visited all the local farmers, charmed them, and left his card. The response was so good that, in its first year of business in 1859, the company's revenues were $500,000.

About this time oil was just beginning to make an impact in Ohio. Several refineries had been opened near Cleveland. Rockefeller, sensing the potential of the new fuel, wasted no time forming Andrews, Clark, and Co., oil refiners, in 1862. Later he sold his produce commission interests to Clark and bought out Clark's interest in Andrews, Clark, and Co., to form Rockefeller & Andrews.

By 1869 Rockefeller's firm had acquired a number of other similar small firms and was now called Rockefeller, Andrews, & Flagler. But the oil business generally was going through a tough time. With the proliferation of firms all trying to get in on the action, the price of oil became so severely depressed that many companies went bankrupt. Undeterred, Rockefeller chose to merge Rockefeller, Andrews, & Flagler into the Standard Oil Company of Ohio in 1869, with $1 million capital and himself as president.

He then proceeded to apply to Standard Oil's business the "combination" strategy that J.P. Morgan had so successfully applied to the steel industry. The best way to ensure survival, he figured, was to spread the risk of operating in such a volatile and risky industry. The

"I believe it is my duty to make money and still more money and to use the money I make for the good of my fellow man according to the dictates of my conscience." (John D. Rockefeller)

obvious way to achieve this was to buy up competitors, both locally and elsewhere in the United States. By 1872 Standard Oil had acquired all the refining firms in Cleveland. In 1882, after a prosperous decade, all the businesses belonging to Standard Oil were brought under the single umbrella of the Standard Oil Trust.

The dominance of the Standard Oil Trust soon gave rise to a barrage of criticism. In 1892 the Attorney General of Ohio won a suit to dissolve the Trust. During the court case, brought in 1890, Rockefeller was put under severe stress; he lost all his hair, including his eyebrows, and was reputed to have suffered a nervous breakdown. The effects of the court case on Standard Oil were less dramatic. The company simply reformed as the Standard Oil Company (New Jersey), because the laws of New Jersey permitted a parent company to own the stock of other companies. The Standard Oil Company (New Jersey) controlled three-quarters of the U.S. petroleum business.

Rockefeller remained president of Standard Oil until 1911. That was the year in which the U.S. Supreme Court finally ordered its dissolution, declaring the company to be in contravention of the country's antitrust laws. The 38 companies that made up the oil giant were split into separate entities.

During his lifetime Rockefeller came in for much criticism, as well as some odd mythologizing. It was claimed, for example, that he would eat only bread and milk. Another persistent story was of his phenomenal capacity for hard work and long hours, something that Rockefeller denied all knowledge of. "People persist in thinking that I was a tremendous worker, always at it, early and late, winter and summer," he said. "The real truth is that I was what would now be called a 'slacker' after I reached my middle thirties. . .I never, from the time I first entered an office, let business engross all my time and attention."

The latter years of Rockefeller's life were spent carrying out philanthropic work. He gave over $35 million to the University of Chicago, founded the Rockefeller Institute for Medical Research, the Rockefeller Foundation, and the Rockefeller Sanitary Commission, which eradicated hookworm in the southern areas of the United States. At its height Rockefeller's wealth was $900 million. When he died, aged 97, on May 23, 1937, at his home in Ormond Beach, he had given away all but $26,410,837.

Context and Conclusions

John D. Rockefeller created the modern oil industry. The impact of Rockefeller's business on the United States may have been less immediate than that of Edison's electric light or Ford's Model T automobile, but without the cheap gasoline that Standard Oil produced, it is unlikely that either the widescale electrification of the country or the mass-marketing of the car would have happened when they did.

During his lifetime Rockefeller came in for much criticism, as well as some odd mythologizing. It was claimed, for example, that he would eat only bread and milk.

One of Rockefeller's greatest attributes was his understanding of the importance of hiring brilliant people. "Men, not machinery or plant, make up an organization," was one of his sayings. He assembled a team of the brightest men in business and harnessed their collective abilities to drive Standard Oil's expansion. In later years he was vilified as the head of one of the hated "trusts" dominating industry in the United States. It should be remembered, however, that, despite its controlling influence, the establishment of the Standard Oil Trust saw the oil industry through some difficult times, and ensured its strength in the United States for the following decades.

For More Information

Books:

Chernow, Ron. *Titan: The Life of John D. Rockefeller, Sr.* New York: Random House, 1998.

Hawke, David Freeman. *John D.: The Founding Father of the Rockefellers.* New York: Harper & Row, 1980.

Anita Roddick

Anita Roddick (1942–), the British businesswoman and head of the cosmetics phenomenon The Body Shop, might never have started her business at all. It was an unusual combination of factors that led her to open her first store in 1976. But The Body Shop concept—based on environmentally friendly cosmetics and begun as a cottage industry—soon outgrew her small store in Brighton. If the company had expanded in the traditional manner, it might well have lost the small-business charm that made it so successful. Instead, Roddick expanded through franchises, a relatively new concept in the United Kingdom at the time, guaranteeing that the vibrancy and enthusiasm of the concept was maintained. By the year 2000 there were over 1,500 stores worldwide, and Roddick was spending much of her time and energy championing ethical causes close to her heart.

Anita Roddick—the ethical face of capitalism.

1942	Born.
1960	Attends Newton Park College of Education in Bath.
1962	Travels to Israel on a study scholarship.
1971	Opens bed and breakfast business in Littlehampton.
1976	The Body Shop opens in Brighton selling environmentally friendly cosmetics.
1976	Ian McGlinn's investment enables second store to be opened.
1978	First informal franchises open. First franchise outside the United Kingdom opens in Brussels.
1984	The Body Shop goes public.
1988	The Body Shop opens in the United States.
1989	Roddick commissions environmental audit of all company's practices.
1998	Steps down as C.E.O.

Background and Rise

Born in Sussex, England, in 1942, Roddick was the third of four children. Her parents ran an American-style diner in the sleepy English coastal town of Littlehampton. After secondary school, despite being offered a place at the prestigious Guildhall School of Music and Drama, Roddick attended the Newton Park College of Education in Bath.

After college Roddick flitted from one job to another. In Paris she worked for the *International Herald Tribune*; she taught in England; then she worked for the United Nations in Geneva.

After college Roddick flitted from one job to another. In Paris she worked for the *International Herald Tribune*; she taught in England; then she worked for the United Nations in Geneva. After the UN, Roddick followed what became known as the hippy trail to Africa, the Far East, and Australia, making her way around the globe. Her stay in South Africa was cut short when she was ejected for breaking the apartheid laws by attending a jazz club on "nonwhites" night. Her rebellious spirit may have earned her an early ticket out of Africa, but it was to stand her in good stead when she later launched The Body Shop.

Returning to Littlehampton, Roddick settled down, married, had children, and with her husband Gordon opened a hotel and then a restaurant. Running both businesses eventually became too demanding on family life. The restaurant was sold, and Roddick's husband declared that he was planning an ambitious expedition of his own—intending to ride a horse from South America to New York City.

Defining Moments

Unable to curb her entrepreneurial instincts, Roddick looked for another enterprise on which to concentrate, one that would also earn some money in her husband's absence. After some thought she came up with the idea of a cosmetics business with a difference: the use of natural ingredients. Her husband helped arrange a bank loan using the hotel as collateral, and Roddick bought premises next to a funeral parlor in the nearby town of Brighton.

On March 27, 1976, with her husband about to leave on his travels, Roddick opened for business, selling environmentally friendly cosmetics. The idea was not just to sell socially responsible products using natural ingredients, but to sell them in convenient small sizes that would tempt customers to try them out. Thus, many of The Body Shop's defining characteristics were decided upon at this early stage, though the decisions were often based on cost effectiveness rather than any grand strategic plan. The walls were painted green, not in anticipation of the Green movement, but to hide the damp patches. Product packaging was minimal and recyclable, and Roddick wrote the labels out by hand.

"If you think morality is a luxury business can't afford, try living in a world without it."

(Anita Roddick)

The Brighton store prospered, and she was soon planning another in nearby Chichester. When the bank refused to finance her, she turned to a local businessman, Ian McGlinn, who agreed to put up £4,000 for a half share of the business. Roddick agreed. For McGlinn, it proved to be the investment opportunity of his life. By the time Roddick's husband returned in 1977, The Body Shop concept was unstoppable. Her friends and family ran the first few stores, but requests to set up branches elsewhere in the country were flooding in. To cater to the demand for stores, Roddick and her husband began franchising the concept. Potential franchisees would finance the business and agree to buy their stock from Roddick, and, in return, would be licensed to use The Body Shop name. She interviewed many of the early franchisees herself. A high proportion of them were women, and she can justifiably claim to have helped change the traditional male-dominated image of entrepreneurs in the United Kingdom.

What she had started was not a conventional cosmetics business. Roddick had little time for the beauty industry, believing that it was in the business of selling unattainable dreams. The Body Shop was different. Roddick made no special claims for her products. In fact she didn't advertise, relying mainly on word of mouth to bring customers through the store doors.

"Making products that work—that aren't part of the cosmetic industry's lies to women—is all-important," Roddick has said. "Making sure we minimize our impact in our manufacturing processes, clean up our waste, put back into the community. . .we go where businesses never want to because they don't think it is the role of business to get involved."

Roddick espouses profits with principles. Through The Body Shop she has supported campaigns by Greenpeace, Friends of the Earth, and Amnesty International, among others. Messages on shopping bags and vehicles express The Body Shop's support for these causes.

In April 1984 the company became publicly listed. The share price shot up on the opening day, and Roddick, her husband, and Ian McGlinn all became paper millionaires overnight. From one small store next to a funeral parlor, The Body Shop network has expanded to over 1,800 stores worldwide, offering over 400 products. Roddick, now one of the richest women in England, has been showered with awards as a result of both her business endeavors and her social conscience. Besides the titles of London's Business Woman of the Year and Retailer of the Year, she has received the United Nations' "Global 500" environmental award and the Order of the British Empire.

In 1994 Roddick brought in external management help to refocus the business. Unsurprisingly she found the shift from her hands-on role difficult to adjust to. In 1998 she stepped down as C.E.O., and remained as co-chair with her husband Gordon until 2002, when she adopted a new role as creative consultant to the company. The fact that she now spends less time with The Body Shop allows her more scope to champion the causes she so passionately believes in.

Roddick had little time for the beauty industry, believing that it was in the business of selling unattainable dreams. The Body Shop was different.

Context and Conclusions

Displayed on the side of The Body Shop vehicles is the following: "If you think you are too small to have an impact, try going to bed with a mosquito." The phrase is one of Roddick's favorite quotations—not surprisingly, considering her achievements. She has taken on the big cosmetic companies and captured a large share of the market with her ethically driven approach to business. She has built a global company from a one-woman cottage industry, changed the attitude toward businesswomen through her franchise operation, and, in addition, found time to make her voice heard championing the rights of minorities and unsung causes—often through her company.

For More Information

Books:

Older, Jules. *Anita!: The Woman behind The Body Shop.* Watertown, MA: Charlesbridge Publishing, 1998.

Roddick, Anita. *Business As Unusual.* New York: HarperCollins Publishers, 2000.

Web Site:

The Body Shop: **www.thebodyshop.com**

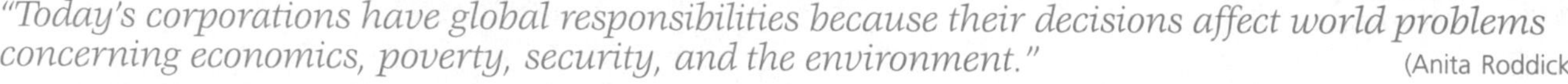

"Today's corporations have global responsibilities because their decisions affect world problems concerning economics, poverty, security, and the environment." (Anita Roddick)

  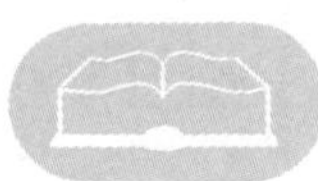    

Julius Rosenwald

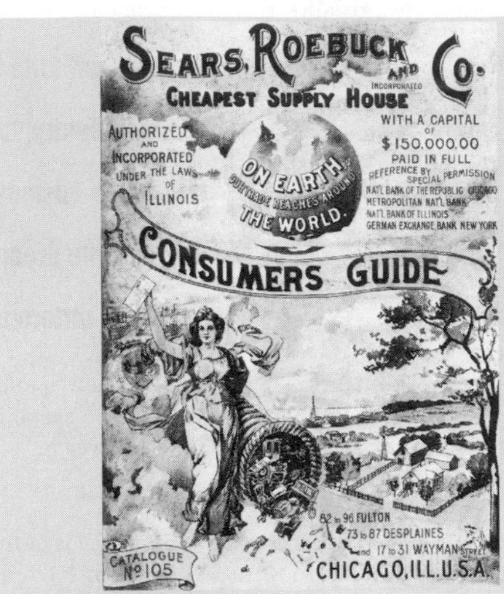

Julius Rosenwald started in the retail business at the tender age of 21, with his own clothes store in New York. He then showed an excellent nose for an opportunity, first by ditching his retail business to manufacture men's summer clothing, and then abandoning manufacturing to join Sears, Roebuck as vice president. His big break was choosing Chicago as the base for his manufacturing business. There he met the entrepreneur R. W. Sears, who made his fortune with a mail-order business. Sears needed the right person to take his business into the 20th century—he chose Rosenwald. By the time Rosenwald died in 1932, the company had revitalized its mail-order business, expanded its product range, introduced innovative work practices and opened hundreds of retail stores throughout America, leaving competitors like Montgomery Ward far behind.

Rosenwald racked up a catalog of success.

1862	Born.
1885	Moves to Chicago.
1885–1895	Manufactures men's summer clothing as Rosenwald & Weil.
1895	Takes share of Sears, Roebuck as sleeping partner.
1896	Becomes vice president of Sears.
1900–1906	Total sales increased from $11 million to over $50 million.
1908	Sears retires. Rosenwald becomes president.
1916	Over 40 m catalogs distributed.
1925	Opens first retail store. Becomes chairman. Personal holdings worth $150 million.
1932	Dies.

Background and Rise

Julius Rosenwald was born in Springfield, Illinois in 1862. As a child he would sell goods door to door in his hometown. During the summer vacation, he worked in a fancy goods store. He pumped the bellows on the church organ, peddled pamphlets and sold chromolithographs, the latest consumer craze.

Rosenwald pumped the bellows on the church organ, peddled pamphlets and sold chromolithographs, the latest consumer craze.

At age 16, Rosenwald left school to work for his uncle's wholesale clothing business in New York. By living frugally, he saved enough money so that at the age of 21 he could afford to buy a small retail clothing store on 4th Avenue.

One day Rosenwald was in idle conversation with the owner of a nearby business. The man, who manufactured summer clothing for men, revealed that he was struggling to keep pace with orders. Rosenwald turned the statement over and over in his mind until, in the middle of the night, he dramatically resolved to abandon his retail store. Chicago was the city that Rosenwald chose to start his new business. There, with partner Julius E. Weil, he formed Rosenwald & Weil, manufacturers and wholesalers of summer clothing.

Defining Moments

One of Rosenwald's best customers was Richard Warren Sears of Sears, Roebuck and Company. His one problem was that he needed more capital to expand. He asked if Rosenwald was interested in investing in the business. Rosenwald agreed, and took a quarter interest in Sears, Roebuck for $70,000.

To begin with, Rosenwald was a silent partner. However by 1896, Sears—who ran the company single-handed—asked Rosenwald to join him as vice president. Over the next 30 years, Rosenwald transformed Sears, Roebuck into one of the largest retailers in the United States.

Rosenwald first turned his attention to the Sears, Roebuck catalog. As Ingvar Kamprad of IKEA would find out over 50 years later, Rosenwald discovered that if mail-order companies were less than honest in the wording and illustration of their catalogs, it damaged the reputation of the entire industry. Even Sears, Roebuck was guilty of delivering products that didn't always correspond to the promises of the lavishly worded and sumptuously illustrated catalog.

Rosenwald insisted on a fastidiously precise correlation between the advertisements in the catalog and the goods supplied. First, he ensured that every illustration and description in the catalog was carefully compared with the relevant article. He set up laboratories and employed scientists to examine merchandise received from suppliers. Any defective goods were immediately rejected and returned. To increase consumer confidence, he introduced a novel concept—a "money back if not satisfied" guarantee, supported by an advertising campaign.

In this way Rosenwald removed the burden of risk from the consumer and placed it squarely on the shoulders of Sears, Roebuck.

Once consumer confidence was secure, Rosenwald set about broadening the range of products offered in a mail-order catalog. Soon everything from buttons to bungalows were sold by mail. Other innovations were introduced. To secure quality supplies, Rosenwald constructed factories employing over 20,000 workers. Technological innovations such as the conveyor belt were introduced (it was said that Henry Ford "borrowed" Rosenwald's idea for his assembly lines). The catalog was expanded, and special editions were introduced for seasonal goods and special events. New goods like shoes and books were featured in the catalog. Shoes, an unlikely candidate for mail order, earned revenues of $1 million a month. The sale of Encyclopedia Britannicas alone added an incredible $5 million in revenues to the annual balance sheet. Between 1900 and 1906, total sales increased from $11 million to over $50 million. By 1914 they had reached $100 m.

Rosenwald was also making changes to the way the company's employees were treated. He spurned the trappings of status, preferring to be seen as one of the workers. Asked what it felt like to have so many people working for him he replied, "I always think of them as just working with me." When he was presented with an oriental rug to cover the floor of his executive office, it remained rolled up in the corner. Rosenwald figured if linoleum was good enough for everybody else, it was good enough for him. "I have played only a very small part in the building up of Sears, Roebuck and Company," he modestly told his admirers. To improve the lot of his workers, Rosenwald introduced recreation facilities, as well as an innovative "employee savings and profit-sharing scheme." True, his management style was a little paternalistic. He was overprotective of his female employees, for example—familiarity between men and women was forbidden at social functions, and the sexes were segregated in the cafeteria.

Eternally cost-conscious in business, Rosenwald encouraged his workers to be equally parsimonious. Employees who earned below $1,500 received a bonus on the anniversary of their joining the company. The bonus was a percentage of the annual salary, equal to the number of years an employee had worked for the company. Starting in the fifth year, it rose to 10% in the tenth year, and remained at 10% thereafter. His employees, Rosenwald suggested, should save the bonus.

On Sears's retirement in 1908, Rosenwald became president and, in 1925, chairman. In the 1920s he took the company in a new direction. The mail-order catalog was still an essential element of the Sears, Roebuck retail strategy, but now Rosenwald expanded into retail stores. In 1925 Sears opened its first retail store in Chicago. By 1929 there were 324 stores with the name Sears, Roebuck above the doors.

In his final years, Rosenwald focused his attention on philanthropy. He established the Julius Rosenwald Fund, a charity for the economic, medical and cultural advancement of African Americans, with an endowment of $30 million. He gave money to aid the Jews in the Middle East and to help German children after World War I. He also endowed the University of Chicago and helped to establish the Museum of Science and Industry in Chicago. He died in 1932.

Context and Conclusions

Julius Rosenwald took a promising business and turned it into a great one. Without his intervention, it is arguable whether Sears, Roebuck would have become the retailing giant it did. At the time Rosenwald joined, the reputation of the mail-order industry was under a cloud because of the less-than-scrupulous practices of many of the companies involved. Through a variety of innovations, Rosenwald breathed new life into a tired format. Greater choice, better quality and a money-back guarantee were among the features that won the customers back. Internally, Rosenwald concentrated on ensuring a quality supply of merchandise and keeping the workforce happy. Finally, he moved to secure the future of the company by extending the brand and opening a chain of retail stores.

Rosenwald spurned the trappings of status, preferring to be seen as one of the workers.

CLOSE BUT NO CIGAR

Aaron Montgomery Ward
Montgomery Ward is said to have founded the first dry goods mail-order business in 1872. He also coined the phrase "satisfaction guaranteed or your money back." But by 1900, after Julius Rosenwald had injected new life into Sears, Roebuck, Montgomery Ward's eponymous company began to trail its main rival. Montgomery Ward died in 1913, 13 years before his company opened its first retail store. Had he been alive in 1930, he might have sanctioned a merger with Sears—proposed but declined by Ward's directors. Instead his company's fortunes subsided until, in 2001, it pulled down its shutters for the last time.

For More Information

Books:

Harris, Leon. *Merchant Princes*. New York: Harper & Row Publishers, 1979.
Sorenson, Lorin. *Sears, Roebuck and Co.: 100th Anniversary 1886–1996*. St. Helena, CA: Silverado Publishing Co, 1985.
Werner, M. R. *Julius Rosenwald: The Life of a Practical Humanitarian*. New York: Harper & Brothers, 1939.

  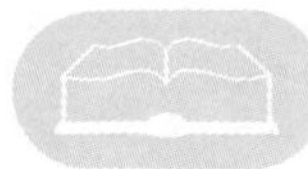    

DAVID SARNOFF

David Sarnoff (1891–1970) was a media pioneer. He was responsible for the introduction of radio and television in the United States as forms of mass media. Born in Russia, Sarnoff emigrated to the U.S. in 1900; by 1930 he was president of the Radio Corporation of America (RCA). He went on to develop FM radio on a commercial basis and bring color television to the American people. Behind Sarnoff's public success story with RCA, however, lay the personal saga of his long-running relationship with the inventor Edwin H. Armstrong. Originally based on friendship, the relationship descended into animosity and ended with Armstrong's suicide in 1954. Sarnoff was succeeded at RCA by his son, Robert, in 1965. The remaining years of his life were spent bitterly watching his son modernize the company that he had spent his life building.

David Sarnoff—RCA's biggest star.

1891	Born.
1916	Sarnoff states his vision for radio.
1919	Radio Corporation of America (RCA) incorporated.
1920	Cuts a deal with Armstrong to secure the latter's radio technology patents.
1921	RCA begins radio broadcasting.
1930	Aged 39, Sarnoff becomes president of RCA.
1933	Has new headquarters constructed for RCA. Armstrong invents FM.
1939	Introduces television to the United States just before World War II at the World's Fair.
1954	Introduces color television.
1965	His son Robert becomes president of the company; Sarnoff becomes chair.
1970	Dies.

BACKGROUND AND RISE

David Sarnoff was born in Uzlian in Russia. His father, Abraham, was a Jewish painter who traveled to the United States in 1896, determined to earn enough money to bring the rest of his family across the Atlantic to join him. It took him four years.

Like several other great business leaders of his generation, Sarnoff started out on the path to success in the employ of a telegraph company—in this case, American Marconi Wireless Telegraph.

When Sarnoff arrived in Manhattan on July 2, 1900, his father was renting a squalid apartment on the lower East Side. In the four years since Abraham had arrived in the sprawling metropolis, he had been struggling to make a living. Not only was he reduced to doing menial work for little pay, but his health had deteriorated to the point where he was unable to provide for his family. At the tender age of nine, therefore, Sarnoff became the family breadwinner.

He started by selling Yiddish newspapers on street corners, earning a quarter for every 50 papers sold. To supplement his income he delivered another paper in the morning and sang at the local synagogue for a small fee. Despite the long hours—he rose at 4:00 a.m. for the morning round—Sarnoff still managed to find time to study at a local school, the Educational Alliance. Within a year he could read the English newspapers. At 14 he opened his own newspaper stand, employing his father and brothers.

Like several other great business leaders of his generation, Sarnoff started out on the path to success in the employ of a telegraph company—in this case, American Marconi Wireless Telegraph. At that time Marconi's U.S. operation was a loss-making company, unlike its English parent. Sarnoff started at Marconi as an office boy, little realizing that he would spend the next 60 years at the company and its successor, the Radio Corporation of America, rising to become president before the age of 40.

DEFINING MOMENTS

Brashly, Sarnoff introduced himself in person to Marconi as the newest employee of the company. His impudence paid off, and he was promoted to junior wireless operator, and not long after to chief inspector.

It was as chief inspector that Sarnoff met the man who was to change his life. Edwin H. Armstrong was an inventor who had been working on an improved wireless receiver. At a demonstration of his invention in front of Sarnoff and three other Marconi engineers, Armstrong received radio signals from Clifden, Ireland, and a radio station in San Francisco. Sarnoff, immediately aware of the commercial potential of the machine, advised his bosses to explore the possibility of developing a similar device.

"Television thrives on unreason and unreason thrives on television." (Robin Day)

Unfortunately for Sarnoff, his superiors were not as impressed, preferring to stick with the existing point-to-point system that had served Marconi so well. In 1916 Sarnoff, with considerable foresight, wrote a memo to the board: "I have in mind a plan of development which would make radio a household utility in the same sense as the piano or the phonograph."

During World War I the U.S. Navy made significant technical advances in radio engineering. At the end of the war companies stood in line to purchase the new technology. The U.S. government was reluctant to hand over its know-how to a British company like Marconi, so a new company, Radio Corporation of America (RCA), was incorporated in 1919. The new company held the patents of GE and Marconi; its commercial manager and second-in-command was Sarnoff. Now in a better position to lobby for his vision of ubiquitous radio, Sarnoff sent a 28-page "blueprint for success" to the chairman. Sarnoff got his way, and RCA began to churn out radio sets. The ensuing radio craze assured RCA's success, despite competition from companies like Westinghouse.

Armstrong, meanwhile, was continuing to develop radio technology. In 1920, hearing that Armstrong had come up with yet another breakthrough, Sarnoff cut out the middlemen and went straight to him to secure the technology patents. After some tough bargaining, he got the technology and Armstrong received enough stock in RCA to make him the leading shareholder—plus some cash. Armstrong also agreed to give RCA first refusal on future innovations.

The Wall Street Crash of 1929 and ensuing financial chaos hit RCA badly. This was despite the company's domination of its market, the increasing popularity of radio as a form of entertainment, and the creation of the National Broadcasting Company. In January 1930 after a boardroom shuffle, Sarnoff, aged 39, became president of RCA.

In December 1933 Armstrong surfaced once more with yet another invention: Frequency Modulation (FM). This time, however, Sarnoff was less interested; his focus was directed toward television rather than radio. He introduced television in the United States just before the outbreak of World War II at the 1939 World's Fair.

After the war a private conflict broke out between Armstrong and Sarnoff over FM. Eventually, after years of banging his head against the giant RCA, Armstrong was forced to agree a settlement in the courts. In 1954, embittered by the outcome, Armstrong jumped to his death from a 13th-story window. Sarnoff's only comment on learning of the death of his one-time friend was, "I didn't kill Armstrong."

Sarnoff carried on business as usual. He introduced color television in 1954. To avoid damaging litigation, he placed all RCA's color television patents in the public domain and at the same time tripled spending on color programming. Any manufacturer could produce a color television set, but RCA had first mover advantage in color broadcasting.

Color television was Sarnoff's last throw of the dice. The protracted litigation with Armstrong may have taken more of a toll on him than he realized at the time. In 1965 his son, Robert, was made president of the company and Sarnoff became chair.

A change of name and logo for RCA, pushed through by his son, roused Sarnoff one last time, and he fought successfully to reinstate the old name. In reality it was a hollow victory. The RCA that Sarnoff had created metamorphosed into a conglomerate containing a disparate collection of companies including Hertz car rentals and Random House Publishing. After a lengthy illness David Sarnoff died in December 1970.

The RCA that Sarnoff had created metamorphosed into a conglomerate containing a disparate collection of companies including Hertz car rentals and Random House Publishing.

Context and Conclusions

Sarnoff was more than just a forerunner of modern media magnates such as Rupert Murdoch and Ted Turner. Sarnoff pioneered the mass-market entertainment industry of radio and television. Edwin Armstrong played a large part in creating the technology of commercial radio, but it was Sarnoff who had the vision to recognize the commercial potential of Armstrong's scientific inventions when others did not. Moreover, Sarnoff had the sense to tie up the technology patents in the case of radio and, more remarkably, to place all RCA's color television patents in the public domain. This last act alone is testimony to Sarnoff's genius and was a forerunner of the approach taken by Linus Torvald when developing the computer operating system Linux.

For More Information

Books:

Bilby, Kenneth M. *The General: David Sarnoff and the Rise of the Communications Industry*. New York: Harper & Row, 1986.

Dreher, Carl. *Sarnoff: An American Success*. New York: Quadrangle/New York Times Book Co., 1977.

Lyons, Eugene. *David Sarnoff: A Biography*. New York: Harper & Row, 1966.

Myers, Elisabeth P. *David Sarnoff: Radio and TV Boy*. Indianapolis, IN: Bobbs-Merrill Co., 1972.

Sobel, Robert. *RCA*. New York: Stein and Day, 1986.

Web Site:

RCA: **www.rca.com**

"Television contracts the imagination and radio expands it." (Terry Wogan)

ALFRED P. SLOAN, JR.

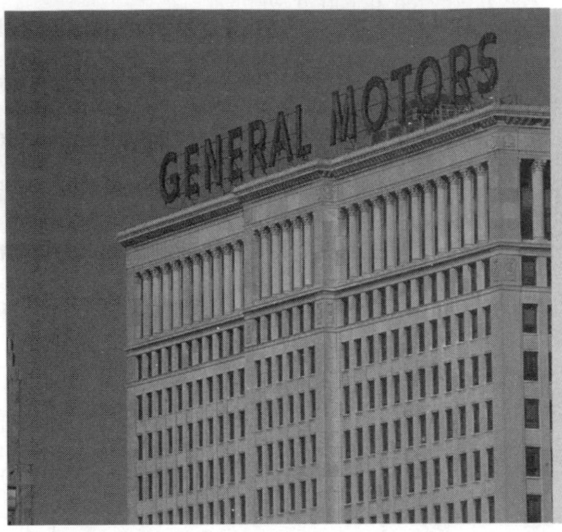

Alfred P. Sloan, Jr. (1875–1966) was both a brilliant engineer and a forward-thinking manager. After transforming the fortunes of Hyatt Roller Bearing Company, Sloan became president of United Motors Corporation, which soon merged with General Motors. Sloan succeeded Pierre du Pont as president of General Motors in 1923.

From this position Sloan created one of the most influential organizational designs of the 20th century. He restructured the company along divisional lines, with an executive committee sitting above the divisions. Sloan's design became the organizational blueprint for corporations for the next 50 years. Six years after Sloan took over the GM presidency, net sales were $1.5 billion and the stock price was up by 480%. During his tenure he consistently out-thought his main competitor, Ford, turning GM into the world's greatest automobile manufacturer.

Sloan rebuilt General Motors along his own lines.

1875	Born.
1889	Buys a controlling interest in Hyatt Roller Bearing Company.
1903	Hyatt makes profits of $60 million.
1916	Sloan becomes president of the United Motors Corporation.
1918	United Motors becomes part of General Motors.
1923	Sloan becomes president of General Motors.
1937	Steps down as president, but remains chairman and C.E.O.
1946	Steps down as C.E.O.
1956	Relinquishes position as chairman.
1966	Dies.

BACKGROUND AND RISE

Alfred Pritchard Sloan, Jr. was born in New Haven, Connecticut, on May 23, 1875, the first of five children in a prosperous family. His father, an engineer by training, was an importer of coffee and tea who later became a wholesale grocer.

At age ten Sloan moved with his family to Brooklyn, New York, where he attended public school and then Brooklyn Polytechnic Institute. Sloan wanted to go on to MIT. Told he was too young, he persisted with his application and eventually took his place there to study electrical engineering. The youngest member of his class, he graduated in 1895 after just three years.

Having displayed a talent for engineering, Sloan went to work at Hyatt Roller Bearing Company in Harrison, New Jersey. To his disappointment he was employed as a draftsman, salesperson, and general gofer. Sloan could see no future at the company, so he left to join a household refrigerator business. But he was not there long before he changed his mind and in 1889 returned to Hyatt. The firm was in financial difficulties, and with help from his father Sloan bought a controlling interest.

The ambitious young man soon brought his influence to bear on his new company. Aged 24, Sloan became president of Hyatt and proposed that the company manufacture a new antifriction bearing for automobiles. With this move to manufacturing products for the rapidly growing automobile market, Sloan forged a connection with the industry that would propel him to greatness.

DEFINING MOMENTS

Until Hyatt's production of the antifriction bearing, the automobile industry had been using a well-greased axle. Immediately the Olds Motors Company, followed by Ford and the other automobile manufacturers, turned to Sloan and signed contracts for the new bearing. By 1903 Hyatt was making profits of $60 million.

As part of the drive to keep Hyatt's customers happy, Sloan organized a big party once a year. Known as "frictionless feasts" in reference to the company's auto bearings, these events drew the greatest names in the automobile industry. Sloan would mingle with luminaries such as Henry Ford and the Dodge brothers as guests drank cocktails pumped from a 50-gallon container made to resemble a service station oil drum.

Sloan forged excellent contacts in the industry, particularly with Henry Leland, who became his mentor. Leland, one of the architects of manufacturing using interchangeable parts, had worked for Olds, Cadillac, and General Motors, and created the Lincoln. Leland's watchword was quality—a mantra that rubbed off on Sloan.

Despite Sloan's apparent success at Hyatt (people would comment on the constant emergence of new buildings as they passed the plant on the Pennsylvania Railroad), he was still concerned about the company's future prospects. Its two largest customers were Ford and GM, and either of these giants, Sloan knew, could easily build a plant to manufacture bearings.

"If you do it right 51 percent of the time you will end up a hero." (Alfred P. Sloan, Jr.)

  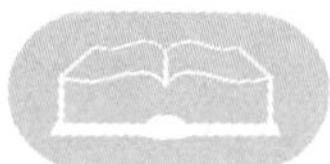    

In 1916 Sloan sealed his own and Hyatt's future by securing a deal in which William Crapo Durant, who had just regained control of GM, took a financial interest in Hyatt. Hyatt merged with several other companies to become United Motors Corporation and Sloan became president of the new company. United Motors was in turn subsumed into GM in 1918, with Sloan becoming vice president in charge of accessories and a member of GM's executive committee.

At GM Sloan worked closely with its founder, Durant. He admired Durant's tenacity while frequently disagreeing with his methods. By 1920 Sloan had risen to the position of vice president. In the same year Durant was forced by his bankers to relinquish his position in the company and was succeeded as president by Pierre S. du Pont. In 1923 du Pont was succeeded by Sloan.

As company president Sloan set about reorganizing GM. The organizational architecture he developed secured his place in business history. He structured the company into separate divisions. Under Durant's management GM cars had competed with each other in the market; Sloan ensured that each car and truck division had its own price and style categories. Each GM model was updated annually, offering greater choice to the consumer than Ford's mass-market Model T (famously available in any color—"as long as it's black").

Soon companies under the GM umbrella such as Buick, Cadillac, and Pontiac were semiautonomous, responsible for almost every aspect of their business. This mix of decentralization and coordinated policy control left Sloan and the senior executives free to worry about GM corporate strategy while the divisional managers ran their divisions as they saw fit—providing, of course, they made a profit.

And make a profit they did. When Sloan took over GM's presidency, net sales were $698 million. Just six years later, net sales were $1.5 billion and the stock price was up by 480%. With Sloan's new organizational structure came a new type of employee, the professional manager. Sloan took management—until then conducted largely in an amateurish, entrepreneurial way—and turned it into a serious professional discipline focusing on decision making based on facts, particularly financial facts.

Sloan remained president of GM for 14 years, from 1923 until 1937, continuing as chairman until 1956. He ran the company quietly from behind the scenes, known by his workers as "Silent Sloan" and preferring to trust in the ability of his managers. He also liked to get out of the office and visit his clients—he traveled the breadth of the country regularly.

Sloan forged excellent contacts in the industry, particularly with Henry Leland, who became his mentor.

Later in life Sloan made considerable philanthropic donations. He established the Alfred P. Sloan Foundation, to which he and his wife gave $305 million during his lifetime. Gifts from the foundation have benefited, among other institutions, the Sloan-Kettering Institute for Cancer Research in New York and Sloan's alma mater, MIT. Sloan died of a heart attack in 1966, aged 90.

Context and Conclusions

Alfred Sloan made his name by revolutionizing the structure of the corporation and, in doing so, making General Motors the greatest automobile company in the world. Unlike his contemporaries Henry Ford and William Crapo Durant, Sloan was as comfortable with his management role as he was in the workshop. A prudent man who took measured risks, Sloan restructured GM along divisional lines and introduced rigorous financial controls. At the same time he created a new type of business executive—the professional manager. Sloan may justifiably be remembered for his contribution to the U.S. automobile industry because of his work at General Motors. He should be remembered equally for his role in the evolution of management and corporate structure.

As company president Sloan set about reorganizing GM. The organizational architecture he developed secured his place in business history.

For More Information

Books:

Sloan, Alfred P., Jr., with Boyden Sparkes. *Adventures of a White-collar Man.* Manchester, NH: Ayer, 1977.

Sloan, Alfred P., Jr. *My Years with General Motors.* New York: Doubleday, 1990.

Web Site:

General Motors: **www.gm.com**

"I have never issued an order since I have been the operating head of the corporation."

(Alfred P. Sloan, Jr.)

Martha Stewart

A U.S. icon, Martha Stewart has fashioned a fortune from her lifestyle. She studied architectural history at college, and put the learning to good use renovating the country home that became the hub of her business empire. After careers in modeling and stockbroking, she turned to cooking, first in a small way, then in a multimillion-dollar way. Her catering business was lucrative, but it was her books that really launched her to stardom. Her first, *Entertaining*, was published in 1982. It was followed by TV shows, magazines, product endorsement, consultancy, and public speaking. In the 1990s everyone in the United States wanted a piece of Stewart's life. And she was only too happy to sell them her version. Her reign as the Queen of Homemaking has made her a billionaire.

Martha Stewart—The Queen of Homemaking.

1941	Born.
1964	Graduates from Barnard College.
1965	Gives up modeling.
1967	Obtains job as a stockbroker.
1972	Moves to Westport, Connecticut, and starts a catering business.
1982	Publishes her first book, *Entertaining*.
1987	Stewart signs up to a $5 million, five-year contract with Kmart.
1988	*Time* magazine refers to her as "the guru of good taste."
1990	Divorces Andy Stewart.
1991	Launches *Martha Stewart Living* magazine.
1997	Forms Martha Stewart Living Omnimedia. Becomes chair and C.E.O.
1998	*Fortune* magazine names her as one of America's "50 Most Powerful Women."
2000	Ranked in the Forbes Four Hundred list of billionaires.

Background and Rise

Martha Stewart was born Martha Kostyra in Jersey City, New Jersey, on August 3, 1941. When she was three, she moved with her family to Nutley, a New Jersey suburb of New York City. Stewart owes much of her later business success to her childhood. As a girl she would cook, bake, and sew with her mother, who was a schoolteacher by profession but stayed home to bring up six children. Her father, who was a pharmaceutical salesman, was a keen gardener and taught her about planting, garden design, and flower arranging.

Soon the house was completely renovated and the grounds boasted an orchard, vegetable garden, beehives, and a variety of livestock.

There was no clue to Stewart's eventual career, however, in her choice of subjects at college. She studied history and architectural history at Barnard College, Columbia University, on a partial scholarship. To pay for her tuition, she relied on modeling fees; she had modeled part time from the age of 13. While at college she married Yale law student Andy Stewart. She was 19.

It was to modeling that Stewart turned for full-time work when she left Barnard College in 1964. But she was forced to give it up in 1965 when she gave birth to her daughter. A complete change of direction followed when, in 1967, with the help of her father-in-law, she got a job as a stockbroker.

Stewart excelled at her new career, her salary soon reaching $100,000 plus. However, the timing was unfortunate. In the early 1970s the oil crisis brought about an economic slowdown in the United States. In 1973, with Wall Street in the grip of a recession, Stewart and her husband packed their bags and moved to Westport, Connecticut.

Defining Moments

Stewart readily adjusted to rural life. With her husband she set about restoring the farmhouse they had purchased, known locally as "the Westport Horror." While her husband commuted to New York City, Stewart redecorated the house and began to overhaul the garden. Soon the house was completely renovated and the grounds boasted an orchard, vegetable garden, beehives, and a variety of livestock. Stewart still lives in the house today, with her chow chow dogs and Himalayan cats. She uses it as a base for her business.

By 1976, with the house fixed up, Stewart had turned her attention to cooking. She gave herself a crash course in cookery and swiftly moved on to teach, first children and then adults, in her own home. She opened a small gourmet food business in Westport called Market Basket. When the business began to grow, she

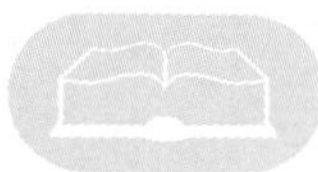

moved out of her shared premises and into her home. When requests for her services became too great for her to manage alone, she went into partnership with a friend, Norma Collier. But within a year the partnership was over. Collier said later that she didn't want to work a "128-hour week."

Stewart had no such qualms. She continued the business on her own, catering for celebrated Connecticut neighbors such as Paul Newman. She called her company Martha Stewart, Inc., and slowly raised her profile through teaching, catering, and writing articles for publications such as the *New York Times* and *Family Circle* magazine.

What started as cottage industry soon grew into a large business, and by 1986 was worth $1 million. She had, by this time, outgrown her house's kitchen and moved into a separate building next to the house. On the way to her first million, Stewart wrote one of America's most successful books of its type, *Entertaining*, published in 1982. A small library of books followed, each accompanied by promotional book signing tours and each garnering plaudits and more fans, so much so that by 1988 *Time* magazine was referring to her as "the guru of good taste (and taste buds) in American entertaining, looked to by millions of American women for guidance about everything from weddings to weeding."

Stewart was not without her detractors. After the publication of *Entertaining*, there were accusations of plagiarism. *Newsweek* reported similarities between her recipes for orange almond cake and cherry pound cake with raisins and recipes in *Mastering the Art of French Cooking, Vol III* by Simone Beck and Julia Child. But the allegations were never proved, and the controversy subsided. In her later books Stewart ensured that recipes were credited if necessary. But while her business life blossomed, her personal life suffered: she was divorced from her husband.

Business continued to grow at a phenomenal rate. In 1987 Stewart signed a $5 million, five-year contract as a consultant to Kmart department stores. She had her own lines of paint and linen, produced a series of commercials, and gave up the catering business to concentrate on writing.

The *Martha Stewart Living* magazine and television programs followed, as did lecturing, personal appearances, and a host of accolades. She was named among the "50 Most Powerful Women" by *Fortune* magazine in 1998, and received Emmy awards for her television shows. In 2000 she made the *Forbes* Four Hundred list of billionaires—a prime example of "the American dream" come true.

Context and Conclusions

Martha Stewart is a symbol of modern culture. She is a woman who has turned her life into a business, a woman who has, in the manner of the modern alchemist, transmuted cookies into cash. Many of us yearn for fame and riches; few of us achieve them. What better way to become both wealthy and famous than simply by living the life you would most wish to lead? As Stewart says, "My life is my work, my work is my life, and that it involves the home, the family, the gardens, everything else involved in living, is my luck... I can think about my work twenty-four hours a day and it's pleasant." But don't for one minute think it's easy. Underneath the glossy veneer of well-lit cuisine and perfectly painted interiors, beneath the public persona of the immaculately turned out, finely groomed ex-model, is a relentlessly driven, extremely hardworking, acutely savvy businesswoman.

Underneath the glossy veneer of well-lit cuisine and perfectly painted interiors, beneath the public persona of the immaculately turned out, finely groomed ex-model, is a relentlessly driven, extremely hardworking, acutely savvy businesswoman.

CLOSE BUT NO CIGAR

Delia Smith

The U.K. Martha Stewart equivalent, Smith has capitalized on her mildly mumsy image to cook up a small fortune. However, Smith will never quite make it to Stewart's exalted standing. Not that Smith lacks pep; she's always on the go, managing to combine her culinary empire with her directorship of Norwich City Football Club. But Smith has a different approach to the public/private mix. Her private persona is kept firmly under wraps; no holiday snaps or interior decor shots on her Web site! And, if the public don't have an admission ticket into her life, they're unlikely ever to aspire to be Delia Smith, or to connect with her as the U.S. public do with Martha Stewart.

For More Information

Books:

Byron, Christopher. *Martha Inc.: The Incredible Story of Martha Stewart Living Omnimedia*. New York: John Wiley, 2002.

Oppenheimer, Jerry. *Just Desserts: Martha Stewart, the Unauthorized Biography*. New York: Morrow, 1997.

Web Site:

Martha Stewart Living Omnimedia:
www.marthastewart.com

  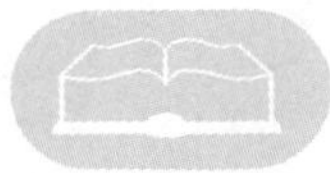    

EIJI TOYODA

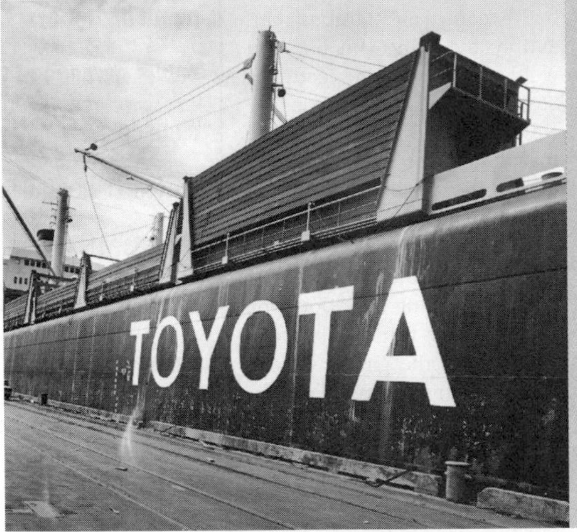

If Eiji Toyoda hadn't joined his family business, the Toyota name might have been associated with the textile industry instead of automobiles.

Toyoda helped to grow a thriving automobile business from a loom manufacturing company. He joined the company in 1936 and was responsible for recruiting the best research engineers and organizing production. Toyota's breakthrough came when Toyoda visited Ford's Rouge automobile plant in the 1950s. It was a revelation to him. He returned to Japan determined to combine the best of U.S. manufacturing processes with his own innovative approach to production. The result was the Toyota Production System. Successful models—from the Corolla to the introduction of the Lexus—paved the way for the company's global success.

Eiji Toyoda engineered Toyota's global success.

1913	Born.
1933	Cousin starts automobile production.
1936	Toyoda joins the firm, which is renamed Toyota.
1950	Toyoda visits Ford River Rouge plant in Dearborn, Michigan.
1955	Crown model successful in Japan but not in United States.
1967	Becomes president of Toyota.
1968	Successfully launches Corolla in United States.
1975	Toyota replaces Volkswagen as number one imported car in United States.
1989	Launches luxury Lexus model.
1994	Resigns from Toyota board.

BACKGROUND AND RISE

It is no surprise that Eiji Toyoda grew up to be an industrialist. Born on September 12, 1913, Toyoda spent much of his childhood in and around his father's textile mill near Nagoya. From his earliest years he was surrounded by both business and heavy machinery.

The driving force behind the textile business was Toyoda's uncle, Rashomon Sakichi Toyoda. Sakichi was a carpenter by trade and an inventor by nature.

The driving force behind the textile business was Toyoda's uncle, Rashomon Sakichi Toyoda. Sakichi was a carpenter by trade and an inventor by nature. In 1929 the British company Platt Brothers paid Sakichi £100,000 for the rights to a textile loom he had invented. Sakichi put the money to one side to invest in automobile production.

Given the nature of the family business, Eiji Toyoda's choice of an engineering degree was a natural one. He started his studies at Tokyo Imperial University in 1933. While Toyoda was taking his degree his cousin Kiichiro, Sakichi's eldest son, was setting up an automobile plant at the Toyoda Automatic Loom Works. In 1936, his degree completed, Toyoda joined his cousin at the plant. In that year the company changed its name from Toyoda Automatic Loom Works to Toyota.

DEFINING MOMENTS

Toyoda's first assignment was to organize the company's research facility, hiring talented scientists and engineers to work on research and development. Next he worked on the shop floor in production planning.

At that time Toyota was producing a car designed to be built with Chevrolet parts. Toyota's first cars rolled off the production line in 1936. The timing was unfortunate: the advent of World War II and Japan's entry into the war in December 1941 meant that Toyota's production expertise had to be redirected toward the manufacture of trucks for the war effort.

After the war Eiji Toyoda made plans to set up a chinaware business. Kiichiro Toyoda was diversifying the company, expecting the occupying forces to place limitations on the automobile business. Instead, as Japan underwent a period of reconstruction, the Toyota car plant was called upon to build vehicles to help get the country moving again.

Despite the boost in production, trading conditions were still extremely tough; Toyota was driven to the brink of bankruptcy. The company was saved only by dramatic cuts in the work force, which Toyoda had the painful task of enforcing. He also created a new company, Toyota Motor Sales, to help ease cash flow problems and satisfy his bankers' concerns.

It wasn't until the 1950s that Toyota firmly established itself as a major car manufacturer. The breakthrough came when Toyoda visited Ford's immense River Rouge plant in Dearborn, Michigan. Toyota had by then been in the car business for 13 years and had produced just over 2,500 automobiles. The River Rouge plant turned

"No other man-made device since the shields and lances of ancient knights fulfills a man's ego like an automobile."
(Rootes)

out a staggering 8,000 vehicles a day. Impressed with the scale of U.S. automobile production, Toyoda realized that if he could combine the best of U.S. and Japanese production methods, Toyota could be a world-beater.

With the help of his production guru Taichi Ohno, Toyoda established the Toyota Production System (TPS), also known as "lean production." It was a revolutionary approach to manufacturing comprising three main elements. The first is just-in-time production. There is no point in producing cars simply hoping that customers will buy them. Waste (Japanese *muda*) is bad; therefore production must be linked to the market's requirements. Second, responsibility for quality rests with everyone, and any quality defect needs to be rectified as soon as it is identified. The third element is the "value stream": instead of seeing the company as a series of unrelated products and processes, it should be seen as a continuous and uniform whole—a stream that includes suppliers as well as customers.

Toyota's first full scale production car, the Crown, proved a somewhat shaky start. Driven off the production line by Eiji Toyoda—dressed in a tuxedo—on New Year's Day, 1955, the Crown was a success in Japan, but it failed to make any impression on the U.S. market when it was introduced in 1957. Designed for Japanese roads, it was slow and prone to overheating—problems that made it ill-suited to U.S. highways.

Persistence eventually paid off and by the 1960s Toyota cars were a hit, with the Corona and Corolla both selling well. The success of the Corolla in 1968 enabled the company to make a big leap forward, and by 1975 Toyota had replaced Volkswagen as the number one imported car in the United States. In 1984 the company entered a joint venture with General Motors to build Toyota vehicles in the United States. Along the way Toyota established an unrivaled reputation for build quality. But it was the Toyota Lexus that finally secured the company's reputation in the United States.

The Lexus was a personal triumph for Toyoda. In August 1983 he had convened a top-secret meeting inside the company, asking those present, "Can we create a luxury car to challenge the very best?" The answer was a resounding yes.

In the luxury car market Toyota faced competition from a variety of established brands, including Mercedes and BMW. Undaunted by the scale of the task, Toyota created a new brand—the Lexus—to create psychological distance from the other Toyota value-for-money models. Toyoda neutralized any concerns over the reliability and quality of the Lexus by insisting that the company should out-engineer Mercedes and BMW. The eventual result was the Lexus LS400. It took seven years, $2 billion, 1,400 engineers, 2,300 technicians, and 450 prototypes—and generated 200 patents. The Lexus was tested in Japan on miles of carefully built highways that exactly imitated roads in the United States, Germany, and the United Kingdom. Toyota even reproduced foreign road signs.

Persistence eventually paid off and by the 1960s Toyota cars were a hit, with the Corona and Corolla both selling well.

Toyota is now the dominant car manufacturer in Japan and the third biggest carmaker in the world (behind General Motors and Ford). It now sells nearly 1.5 million cars in the United States every year. Toyoda stepped down as president in 1994.

Context and Conclusions

Eiji Toyoda didn't found the Toyota Motor Corporation, but he did help make it a world-beater.

After an inauspicious attempt to crack the U.S. market with the Crown, Toyoda was quick to admit that Toyota would need an extra competitive edge to compete with the likes of Ford and General Motors. It was no good trying to compete on price alone; instead Toyoda concentrated on efficiency and quality.

He employed the inventive Taichi Ohno to help develop a new production system that came to be known as the Toyota Production System. Through quality and reliability, Toyoda took on the great U.S. automobile manufacturers and emerged victorious. And if imitation is the sincerest form of flattery, the modest Toyoda must be embarrassed by the number of U.S. firms that have tried to adopt Toyota's production methods.

For More Information

Books:

Braddon, Russell. *The Other 100 Years War: Japan's Bid for Supremacy 1941–2041*. London: Collins, 1983.

Toyoda, Eiji. *Toyota: Fifty Years in Motion*. Tokyo: Kodansha International, 1987.

Web Site:

Toyota 2000: **www.toyota.com**

Robert Edward Turner III

Robert Edward Turner III (1938–) started in business in unfortunate circumstances after his father's suicide. Showing considerable resilience, he went on to improve on his father's business and, ultimately, to help create the biggest entertainment and media company in the world—AOL Time Warner. Turner became president and chief operating officer of the Turner Advertising Company in 1963 and set out on a trail of acquisitions and channel launches. A UHF station, professional sports teams, Headline News, TNT, The Cartoon Network, Turner Classic Movies, New Line Cinema: all these and many more came under Turner's control as he built his company—the Turner Broadcasting System—into a media giant. Turner is probably best known for the creation of the news station Cable News Network, CNN, in June 1980, and the part he played in the formation of AOL Time Warner in 2000/2001.

With CNN, Turner made news broadcasting 24/7.

1938	Born.
1970	Acquires the UHF station, WTCG.
1976	WTCG becomes WTBS and goes nationwide. Transmits across the United States via satellite. Buys the major-league baseball team, the Atlanta Braves.
1977	Wins America's Cup with his yacht *Courageous.*
1980	Cable News Network launched.
1986	Acquires MGM Entertainment Company.
1991	*Time Magazine's* "Man of the Year."
1994	Turner Broadcasting Systems merges with New Line Cinema.
1996	Turner Broadcasting Systems merges with Time Warner.
2001	Time Warner merger with AOL approved.

Background and Rise

Robert Edward Turner III was born in Cincinnati, Ohio, in 1938. His checkered school career was notable for eccentric and unconventional behavior rather than academic excellence. At McCallie, an exclusive school for boys in Chattanooga, Tennessee, he was an unruly pupil who showed a peculiar penchant for taxidermy and for catching squirrels in pillowcases. McCallie's method of punishing offenders was to issue demerits. Each demerit required the recipient to walk a quarter of a mile. Turner earned over 1,000 demerits in his first year, farther than any pupil could walk in the time available. The school was forced to reinvent its disciplinary methods especially for him.

At McCallie, an exclusive school for boys in Chattanooga, Tennessee, he was an unruly pupil who showed a peculiar penchant for taxidermy and for catching squirrels in pillowcases.

At Brown University Turner continued to challenge authority. Eventually, having been caught with a woman in his room, he was asked to leave but not before he had made a name for himself on the university sailing team. Sailing was to remain an abiding passion and he later won the America's Cup in 1977 with his yacht *Courageous*.

After college Turner returned home to work in his father's advertising billboard business. His father made him manager of the firm's operation in Macon, Georgia. Turner married and settled down to a tough schedule, working 15 hours per day for six and a half days each week. Like his father, he was a natural salesman making fast progress in the business.

Turner's often difficult relationship with his father came to a shocking end in March 1963 when he was just 24. His father, under severe pressure at work, took a silver .38 revolver and shot himself in the head. In these terrible circumstances Turner became president and C.E.O. of the Turner Advertising Company.

Defining Moments

Turner expanded the company into television with an audacious move to acquire the UHF station WTCG in 1970. At the time WTCG was the worst placed of the major television channels in Atlanta. Turner engineered a deal that involved taking Turner Advertising public, acquiring the assets of WTCG, and forming a new company, Turner Communications. Determined to lift the station's fortunes, he changed the programming schedule and fed the viewers a diet of reruns–classic shows and black and white movies. It worked. Bemused critics could only watch as the viewing figures shot up and the advertising revenue flooded in. In 1976 the station went nationwide as WTBS, transmitting to cable systems across the United States via satellite–it was the start of the "superstation concept."

Turner continued to diversify and expand, and not always into obvious areas. In 1976 he bought a major

"It's not how much you earn, it's how much you owe." (Ted Turner)

league baseball team, the Atlanta Braves, and in 1977 the Atlanta Hawks of the National Basketball Association. Once again he was ahead of the game. His instincts told him that televised sports would attract a big audience.

In 1980 Turner used the profits from Turner Broadcasting System to launch CNN (Cable News Network). The critics were scathing, predicting inevitable failure for the 24/7 all-news network. But once again Turner proved that, despite his often dogmatic approach, when it came to business he knew best. "I am the right man in the right place at the right time," he said. "Not me alone, but all the people who think the world can be brought together by telecommunications."

CNN was a hit. It brought news, like the Reagan assassination attempt, to viewers as events unfurled. It revolutionized the news industry. CNN cemented its reputation with its coverage of the Gulf War when, for the first time, a TV audience could watch a war in real time, from the comfort of their armchairs.

Turner continued to collect television stations: Headline News (1982), CNN International (1985), TNT (1988), SportsSouth (1990), The Cartoon Network (1992), Turner Classic Movies (1994), CNNfn (1995), and CNN SI (1997) were all added to the network. Shortly after Castle Rock Entertainment joined Turner Broadcasting in 1993, Turner merged TBS with New Line Cinema.

Not everything Turner touched turned to gold. Eager to purchase a film studio, he made a bid for CBS. The hostile takeover bid failed. Another Turner idea, the "Checkout Channel," providing in-store news and information, proved a disappointment. Turner also paid $1.6 billion for the MGM film library, a sum many commentators considered too generous.

In 1996 he completed the biggest deal of his career to date, when he merged TBS with Time Warner. Holding 10% of Time Warner, Turner had the largest single shareholding. It was an astute move, leaving him well positioned to profit from the development of a new communication phenomenon—the Internet. He assumed the role of vice chair in the new organization, taking responsibility for Time Warner's Cable Networks division, which included the assets of Turner Broadcasting System, Inc. (TBS, Inc.), Home Box Office, Cinemax, and Time Warner's interests in Comedy Central and Court TV. He was also responsible for New Line Cinema and the company's professional sports teams.

In 2001 Turner was involved in one of the biggest mergers of the postwar period when AOL merged with Time Warner to create the largest entertainment conglomerate in the world. Time Warner's shareholders received 45% of the new company to AOL's 55%. Turner became vice chair and senior adviser of AOL Time Warner.

CNN was a hit. It brought news, like the Reagan assassination attempt, to viewers as events unfurled. It revolutionized the news industry.

Context and Conclusions

Turner's career is distinguished by relentless drive, an uncanny ability to predict consumer demand, and a supreme confidence in his own vision. Competitiveness and drive are evident in his sailing achievements, too. He could have made a good living as an international yachtsman. Probably the best illustration of Turner's qualities, though, is the founding of CNN. Critics derided the idea of a nonstop news network. Turner thought differently and pursued his vision doggedly. He was right, the critics were wrong, and CNN's coverage of the Gulf War has become part of media folklore. Turner may make an occasional bad call, but more often than not his instincts have proved successful. It is this quality of vision, and having the guts to execute it, that has made him one of the world's great media magnates.

For More Information

Books:

Bibb, Porter. *It Ain't As Easy As It Looks: Ted Turner's Amazing Story*. New York: Crown Publishers, 1993.

Web Site:

CNN.com: **www.cnn.com**

"If I only had a little humility, I'd be perfect."

(Ted Turner)

Theodore Newton Vail

Most individuals would be happy with one successful career. The U.S. serial entrepreneur Theodore Newton Vail (1845–1921) enjoyed several. First Vail worked for the U.S. government reforming the postal delivery system. The next chapter of his working life was spent setting up and expanding the American Bell Telegraph Company. Vail exemplifies the truth that behind every successful great inventor is a business innovator capable of building an enterprise from scratch. Finally, after retiring to a tranquil life on his farm in Vermont, the 62-year-old Vail was persuaded to come out of retirement to save the American Telephone & Telegraph company.

Vail sent out the right signals to corporate America.

1845	Born.
1878	Joins Bell Telephone Co.
1882	Secures control of Western Electric Co.
1885	Incorporation of American Telephone & Telegraph Company.
1887	Resigns as president of AT&T, buys a 200-acre farm in Vermont.
1907	Recalled as president of AT&T.
1910	Buys control of Western Union Telegraph Company for $30 million.
1913	Forced by Justice Department to dispose of Western Union stock.
1919	Retires from AT&T.
1921	Dies.

Background and Rise

Theodore Newton Vail was born in 1845 in Carroll County, Ohio, where his father, who was from a Quaker family, and his Dutch mother had temporarily settled. Two years later the family returned to New Jersey. They remained there until 1866 when they moved to a farm in Iowa.

Unhappy with farming life and restless for adventure, the young Vail headed west, landing a job as an operator in a Union Pacific boxcar. Telegraphy was in the Vail genes. His uncle Alfred had helped finance F. S. B. Morse in the development of the telegraph.

Before long the restless Vail moved out of the boxcar and into the railroad mail delivery service. It was here that his talents began to shine. The railroad mail service was a shambles with no sorting system in the trains, no routing for letters other than to the major cities, and no systemized train connections. Vail set about sorting out the mess. He pored over railway timetables and train connections, calculating the quickest routes. The result was a railroad mail guide for the efficient transport of mail in the region.

Defining Moments

Eventually Vail's endeavors came to the attention of the U.S. government, and he was summoned to Washington. If he could reform local mail deliveries, the government figured, then why not the entire country's? Vail set about the task and swiftly rose from assistant superintendent of the mail service to general superintendent. It was a difficult task, not least because he was up against the vested interests of the railroad companies. Rescheduling the entire country's delivery service cut into the revenues of some of them. Vail, however, resisted their lobbying and carried the day.

It was his indomitable nature that brought him to the attention of Gardiner G. Hubbard, the father-in-law of Alexander Graham Bell, inventor of a contraption that had been exhibited at the Centennial Exposition in Philadelphia, much to the amusement of visitors. The invention was the telephone. When they proposed creating a commercial enterprise founded on the telephone, Bell and Hubbard were ridiculed. *The Times* of London called it "the latest American humbug." Hubbard needed a man with a forceful personality and uncompromising drive to build a viable company to exploit the telephone. Vail was that man. He had the vision to see how the telephone could revolutionize communications not only on a regional but also on a national level.

In 1878 Vail accepted the position of general manager at the newly founded American Bell Telephone Company. "I gave up a $3,500 salary for no salary," he remarked at the time. His salary at Bell was ostensibly $5,000, but he rarely collected it. Instead he devoted his entire energy and passion to rolling out the telephone nationwide. In 1882 he oversaw the purchase of the Western Electric Co. of Chicago, one of the premier manufacturers of telephone equipment. In 1885 the

group of companies Vail presided over was incorporated as AT&T (the American Telephone and Telegraph Company). Despite attempts from competitors Western Union to seduce him away from Bell, Vail stuck to his post. He stayed with Bell until it was sufficiently well established to secure enough capital to expand across the country, city by city. When in 1887 that moment arrived, he bought himself a 200-acre farm in Vermont.

Before retiring to his farm, the nomadic Vail toured South America, replaced the horse-drawn streetcars in Buenos Aires with electric ones, opened offices in London, spent time in France and Italy, and installed electric lighting and telephone systems in numerous other cities. Finally, his wanderlust apparently sated, he became a farmer. The farm was rapidly expanded to 6,000 acres as Vail set about farming with the same intensity that he applied to his earlier careers. No comfortable slippers and armchair for him.

Little did Vail realize that, though he was retired and past 60, some of his greatest achievements still lay ahead. In 1907 confidence in big business plummeted. Companies had overextended themselves. Banks withdrew credit, capital dried up, stocks withered, and new share issues failed. Amid the economic turmoil dark clouds were gathering over the AT&T. Its competitors had muddied the company's waters to the extent that the Federal Government was being urged to bust the "telephone trust." So, cap in hand, the directors of AT&T arrived at Vail's Lyndon ranch in Vermont and pleaded with him to help save the company. He said yes.

Using the considerable business acumen that he had acquired over the years, Vail swiftly raised $21 million of new capital followed by a quarter of a billion over the next six years. He attacked the critics of the "telephone trust" head on by buying up competitors and consolidating telephone networks under the AT&T umbrella. At the same time he campaigned under the slogan "One system, One policy, Universal Service" to persuade the public that a single telephone service was the best way. And to placate the government he acceded to regulatory supervision. It was a masterful performance. Vail saw off the financial crisis of October–November 1907 and AT&T emerged as the unquestioned dominant force in telephony. Vail also earned the loyalty of the workforce by increasing pension, sickness, and accident benefits.

A man of vision, Vail was still pursuing new ventures into his 70s. In 1910 he bought control of the Western Union Telegraph Company for $30 million. His intention was to bring people closer together with the "tel-letter"—mail delivered over the wire at a nominal cost. Unfortunately for Vail, the Department of Justice stepped in to break up the telegraph–telephone combine and Vail was forced to sell Western Union and agree that AT&T would not buy any more independents, thus scuttling his plans for the tel-letter.

In 1878 Vail accepted the position of general manager at the newly founded American Bell Telephone Company.

Context and Conclusions

Vail was one of a generation of entrepreneurs who helped change the face of the United States and the world at the turn of the 20th century. It was the era of the electrical revolution. The pioneering spirit of men such as Vail sparked the transformation from the steam age to the electrical age. A serial entrepreneur, the crowning glory of his achievements survives to this day: AT&T is one of the oldest companies quoted on the New York Stock Exchange.

Little did Vail realize that, though he was retired and past 60, some of his greatest achievements still lay ahead.

When asked how he managed to achieve so much in one lifetime Vail answered: "By never being unwilling when young to do another man's work, and then, when older, by never doing anything somebody else could do better for me."

For More Information

Books:

Boettinger, H. M. *The Telephone Book: Bell, Watson, Vail, and American Life, 1876–1976*. Newmarket, Ontario: Riverwood Publishers, 1977.

Paine, Albert Bigelow. *In One Man's Life: Being Chapters from the Personal & Business Career of Theodore N. Vail*. London: Harper & Brothers, 1921.

Web Site:

AT&T: **www.att.com**

"Communication, whether it be in the dance, or whether it be in the spoken word, is now the great need of the world."

(Martha Graham)

  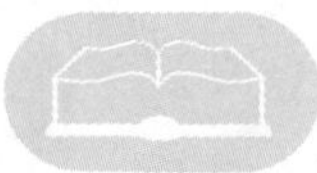    

CORNELIUS VANDERBILT

Cornelius "Commodore" Vanderbilt is one of America's greatest-ever businessmen. Applying the principles of economy, competition and innovation, Vanderbilt expanded from a small-time ferry operator to a shipping and railroad magnate. In his lifetime Vanderbilt amassed fabulous wealth—some $105 m. Yet he did so by genuinely improving the lot of people. Wherever Vanderbilt opened for business, the prices came down and the services improved. He risked arrest to bust state-subsidized monopolies by running competing services illegally. By eradicating state monopolies, Vanderbilt increased the incentive to invest in improving technology to provide a competitive advantage. It was a classic case of how capitalism and competition can deliver a better deal for the consumer, and benefit a nation's economy.

Vanderbilt revolutionized the U.S. transport industry.

1794	Born.
1810	Mother gives him $100 to clear and plant eight-acre field. He buys a boat with the proceeds.
1812	U.S. war with England.
1817	Robert Fulton and Robert R. Livingston introduce steamboats.
1829	Uses savings to start a steamboat business.
1851	Forms the Accessory Transit Company.
1863	Has amassed a fortune of $40 million. Switches focus to railroads.
1869	Merges the Hudson River Railroad with the New York Central system.
1877	Dies.

BACKGROUND AND RISE

Cornelius Vanderbilt was born on May 27, 1794 on Staten Island, New York. His father was a farmer who sold produce in the markets of New York, sailing across the harbor to get there.

Vanderbilt paid little attention to school, preferring the outdoor life. As a child he could barely read and write. He did, however, take a keen interest in business. In 1810, when he was 16, Vanderbilt's mother gave him $100 to clear and plant an eight-acre field. Instead of frittering the money away, the enterprising Vanderbilt used it to buy a small flat-bottom sailing boat. He then started a ferry business, taking passengers between Staten Island and New York City. The business was almost sunk in the first few weeks when the boat hit an obstacle, but both boat and business survived.

The ferry business taught Vanderbilt some important commercial lessons. Known locally as "Cornele, the boatman," he discovered that by taking any fare, no matter how rough the weather, he obtained a reputation for both reliability and a willingness to please the customer. This in turn brought him repeat business. He also learned the simple economics of low costs, high turnover, consistently undercutting his rivals, and filling his boat.

DEFINING MOMENTS

Like many other entrepreneurs, when war with England came in 1812 Vanderbilt saw the conflict as an opportunity to improve his business. As well as continuing to ply his normal routes, he was awarded an army contract and also made extra money ferrying food along the Hudson River to a blockaded New York City. With the profits, he bought an interest in two more boats.

By the age of 24, Vanderbilt had saved $9,000, expanded his business to ply the coastal routes between Chesapeake Bay and New York, and developed a retail business selling provisions to ships in the harbor. In addition, he owned interests in a number of boats. Things were going well for Vanderbilt when, in 1817, the steamboats arrived. Entrepreneurs Robert Fulton and Robert R. Livingston had brought their new technology to New York and were granted a monopoly on all steamboat traffic for a period of 30 years.

Realizing that sailboats were about to become obsolete, Vanderbilt sold up rather than persist with outdated technology. He went to work for a small steamboat operator, Thomas Gibbons, a wealthy attorney and plantation owner, and learned how to sail the steamboat. As soon as he was able, he began ferrying passengers from New Jersey to Manhattan in direct contravention of the monopoly. He persuaded passengers to use the service by undercutting Fulton and Livingston's $4 ticket price, charging only $1. The loss was made up on food and drink prices.

In 1824, the United States Supreme Court declared the Fulton and Livingston monopoly illegal. Now Vanderbilt could operate openly. With the monopoly broken, things changed quickly in the steamboat business. Prices came down, competitors entered the market and boat technology improved. In a competitive environment where innovation was rewarded, Vanderbilt thrived. In 1829 he used his savings to start his own steamboat business. He put together a connected service—steamboat, stagecoach, steamboat—from New York City to Philadelphia. And, in what became a classic Vanderbilt business strategy, he immediately slashed prices. The competition, fearing a price war, gathered enough money together to pay him to go away.

Vanderbilt had discovered a new way to make money. Keen to protect the market and unwilling to cut their profits to provide real value to the customer, the lazy established operators would rather pay Vanderbilt to stop operating. It was the same story in the Hudson River. Up against the Hudson River Steamboat Association, Vanderbilt cut fares savagely until he was carrying passengers for free and, as before, making the losses up on the food. It wasn't long before the Steamboat Association caved in. They gave Vanderbilt $100,000, as well as ten annual payments of $5,000, in return for him leaving the area.

Before long, Vanderbilt—now Commodore Vanderbilt—owned over 100 steamboats and was worth many millions of dollars. His next move was inspired by the discovery of gold in California in 1848. The ensuing gold rush created a demand for transport from East Coast to West. Initially clipper boats took passengers around Cape Horn—a journey that took 90 days. Next, an alternative route was organized that involved land travel across the Isthmus of Panama. It was at this point that the ever-innovative Vanderbilt entered the fray. Studying the maps he discovered a new route, which involved sailing inland along the San Juan River; on across Lake Nicaragua, and finally across the shortest 12-mile land gap to the Pacific Ocean. The critics said that the San Juan River couldn't be navigated. Vanderbilt proved them wrong, piloting a steamboat up the river himself.

Vanderbilt formed the Accessory Transit Company, struck a deal with the Nicaraguan government, constructed a port on the Pacific Coast and, in 1851, started sailing the new route. As usual his fares were cheaper—$400 compared to the competition's $600. And as usual, after some political wrangling and maneuvering, the competition offered Vanderbilt $672,000 not to operate a route to California. His first foray into the transatlantic and shipping routes was no less successful. Used to competing with government subsidized business by now, Vanderbilt cut fares, built volume and used the latest technology in shipping so that, when government subsidy was finally withdrawn from the competition, he was best-placed to take advantage.

By 1863 Vanderbilt, in his sixties, had amassed a fortune of $40 million. For most people this would have been enough. Not for him. Over the next 13 years, abandoning water for land, Vanderbilt switched from old technology—steamboats, to new technology—the railroads.

By 1869, Vanderbilt had taken control of the Hudson River Railroad and the New York Central system. He merged the two companies, gained control of railroad lines from New York to Chicago and created a consolidated railroad system between the two cities. Toward the end of his career, Vanderbilt continued to apply the principles of competitiveness, low costs and innovation to the business. He upgraded iron rails with steel imported from England, doubled tracks and built the Grand Central Depot in New York, the largest railroad terminal in the world.

In 1824, the United States Supreme Court declared the Fulton and Livingston monopoly illegal. Now Vanderbilt could operate openly.

By the time of his death on January 4, 1877, Vanderbilt commanded a railroad empire that extended over 740 miles of track and included 486 locomotives and 9,000 freight cars. Every year thousands of passengers were transported courtesy of Vanderbilt. When he died, he left a fortune of $105 million in his will.

Context and Conclusions

Cornelius Vanderbilt was simply the most brilliant businessman of his generation. He combined an innate understanding of the principles of economics with a consummate grasp of business strategy. Everything that Vanderbilt touched turned to gold. Only once was he ever bested. When he tried to corner the stock in the New York and Erie Railroad Company, notorious financiers Jay Gould and Jim Fisk merely kept on issuing new shares until finally Vanderbilt had to give up. But no one ever beat him fairly. Why? Because Vanderbilt understood that delivering a reasonable service, at a low cost, would always win out over a government-subsidized monopoly. Rather than fleece consumers by providing a substandard, outdated, expensive service, Vanderbilt gave his customers innovation and value for money. In doing so he helped drive economic growth on both the East and West Coast, and to fast-track technological innovation in transport. And, in the process, he became fabulously wealthy.

By 1869, Vanderbilt had taken control of the Hudson River Railroad and the New York Central system.

For More Information

Books:

Metzman, Gustav. *Commodore Vanderbilt (1794–1877): Forefather of the New York Central*. New York: The Newcomen Society of England, 1946.

Smith, Arthur D. Howden. *Commodore Vanderbilt: An Epic of American Achievement*. New York: Robert McBride, 1927.

"Successful entrepreneurs judge correctly the need for change, then do something about it."

(James Edward Hanson)

Samuel Walton

Samuel Moore Walton created a retail empire after the fashion of the great Frank Woolworth. A hard upbringing in the depression-ridden Midwest was followed by college and then commerce. Having sampled the retail business courtesy of JCPenney, Walton opened a Ben Franklin store with $25,000 borrowed from his father-in-law. When he lost the lease on his first store he simply opened another, and then another. Soon he had a small collection of retail outlets. To keep tight control of them, he would fly himself from one to the other. Walton opened the first Wal-Mart in 1962 and the second in 1964. By 1987 there were over 1,000. At the time of his death in 1992, Walton had made millions from his retail business and so had many of his shareholders. One hundred shares bought in 1970 for a mere $1,650 were, by 1992, worth a staggering $2.6 million.

Wal-Mart's appeal is undiminished.

1918	Born.
1945	Gets franchise for Ben Franklin store in Newport, Arkansas.
1953	Obtains pilot's license.
1962	Opens first Wal-Mart discount store in Rogers, Arkansas.
1964	Second Wal-Mart store in the town of Harrison, Arkansas.
1970	Raises $5 million on the stock market through a public offering of Wal-Mart stock.
1970s	Builds 452 new stores.
1974	Retires for two years.
1980s	Builds 1,237 new stores.
1985	Wal-Mart stock makes him wealthiest man in America.
1987	1,000th store opens.
1991	Wal-Mart overtakes Sears to become biggest retailer in the United States.
1992	Dies.

Background and Rise

Samuel Moore Walton was born in Oklahoma on March 29, 1918. His father was employed variously as a farm loan appraiser, a real estate salesman, and an insurance salesman. Walton and his family moved from small town to small town in Missouri as his father pursued work. When they finally settled in Columbia, Missouri in 1933, Walton helped bolster the family income by taking on several jobs.

Rather than place an order, Walton went to Little Rock and bought the distributor.

His work commitments did not prevent Walton from attending school. He was bright enough and hardworking enough to gain a place at the University of Missouri at Columbia, where he studied for a business degree, graduating in 1940. After college he decided to take a position as a management trainee in Des Moines, Iowa, at the retail store JCPenney. It was here that he learned many of the management techniques that he was to apply later—these included fostering a sense of inclusion by calling his employees "associates" and managing by walking about or, in Walton's case, by flying about.

Walton enlisted to fight in World War II. Unfit for full service because of a heart irregularity, he spent the war in the United States serving in the military police. He also married during the war, in 1943. It was a fortunate marriage. When Walton returned to civilian life at the end of the war, he decided to set up in business himself rather than return to JCPenney. He borrowed $20,000 from his father-in-law and bought a Ben Franklin store in Newport, Arkansas. It was September 1945, Walton was 27, and he was in the retail business.

Defining Moments

Walton proved tough competition for the nearby better established businesses. One such was the Sterling Variety store, where Bud Hewitt, who would become a great friend of his, worked. In 1947, however, they were in competition, and when Hewitt had a run on rayon underwear for women (he was cleaned out of stock), Walton was determined to outdo him. Rather than place an order, Walton went to Little Rock and bought the distributor. At a stroke he cut the competition out of the market and secured his own store's supply of lingerie.

In 1950, despite his success, Walton was unable to renew the lease on his Newport store and was forced to sell out. He didn't quit though; he merely moved to nearby Bentonville where he bought another Ben Franklin store, calling it "Walton's Five and Dime." Before long he had added to his burgeoning retail empire by acquiring a number of other stores in the region. They were spread out over a wide area and potentially difficult

"A computer can tell you down to the dime what you've sold, but it can never tell you how much you could have sold."
(Samuel Walton)

to keep in touch with and manage satisfactorily. He solved the problem imaginatively; he gained his pilot's license in 1953 and acquired a decrepit prewar airplane, in which he simply flew from one store to the next.

Walton then cast his eye further afield. He began by visiting a couple of Ben Franklin "self-service" stores in Minnesota. The idea of self-service was then a new one, and the fact that it enabled the owner to pass on cheaper prices to the customer appealed to him. Back in Bentonville he opened his own self-service store. One of Walton's greatest strengths was that he was always willing to embrace innovation, whether it was self-service or, as in the early 1960s, the discount store concept.

The first Wal-Mart opened in 1962. It owed a great deal to the Kmart store in Chicago, a shop that Walton had visited to observe its operations at first hand. It was tough going initially. It wasn't easy to stock a full range of goods, since suppliers were reluctant to be associated with mass merchandising. Walton spent much of his time over the next few years experimenting with different layouts and different mixes of stock to create the perfect discount store. All this time he continued to earn the bulk of his income from his chain of Ben Franklin stores. The second Wal-Mart opened in 1964 in Harrison, Arkansas. The first day was a disaster, primarily because of the inhospitable temperature of 115 degrees. The manure from the donkeys providing rides was trodden through the store. The watermelons outside popped in the heat. Local businessman David Glass uttered the legendary observation: "It was the worst retail store I've ever seen." Glass went on to become president of the Wal-Mart Corporation.

In 1970 Walton raised $5 million on the stock market through a public offering of Wal-Mart stock. The 1970 financing enabled Walton to construct six more stores as well as a distribution center. In fact, from the 1970s onward, the rate of construction of new Wal-Mart stores increased phenomenally; 452 were built during the 1970s and 1,237 in the 1980s.

As the Wal-Mart empire blossomed, Walton spent more and more time keeping his employees happy and up to scratch. He would still travel from store to store by plane and, where he found a store that didn't meet his high standards, he would close it on the spot and not reopen it until it was ready.

Somehow Walton managed to keep in touch with his thousands of employees. He wrote a monthly column in the company newspaper, *Wal-Mart World*, he personally replied to letters from staff raising questions or suggesting ideas, and he insisted on attending the opening of new stores whenever possible. His commitment to the staff in his business was illustrated in 1983 when he promised to dance down Wall Street in a grass skirt if the company posted profit targets. It did, and Wall Street was graced with the sight of Walton dancing the hula.

By 1987 Wal-Mart had opened its 1,000th store and was an early adopter of network technology linking all the stores through a satellite system, something that, sadly, obviated the need for Walton's airborne excursions, much to the relief of the shareholders. They profited greatly from his canny business sense. One hundred shares bought in 1970 for a mere $1,650 were, by the time of Walton's death, worth a staggering $2.6 million.

In 1968 Walton was diagnosed with bone marrow cancer. He died on April 6, 1992.

Context and Conclusions

Frank Woolworth pioneered the concept of the five and dime store. He was also one of the first mass-market retailers with thousands of stores across the world. Sam Walton was a retailer out of the same mold, the Frank Woolworth of his generation who steadily built up a network of mass-merchandise discount stores under the Wal-Mart name. Always keen to embrace innovation, he pioneered the self-service concept, was one of the first retailers to adopt network technology via satellite to link stores, and championed hypermarts. A stickler for high standards, he also was known to close down stores immediately if he felt they failed to come up to scratch. One of the greatest retailers of his generation, he died one of the richest men in the world, having built an empire of over 1,000 stores.

Local businessman David Glass uttered the legendary observation: "It was the worst retail store I've ever seen." Glass went on to become president of the Wal-Mart Corporation.

CLOSE BUT NO CIGAR

Sebastian Spering Kresge/
Richard Warren Sears

Kresge was a traveling tinware salesman who founded a chain of S.S. Kresge discount retail stores in 1912. All the goods were priced at less than a dime. World War I inflation pushed the price limit up to a dollar. Kresge opened his first Kmart store in 1962. He died in 1966, the same year company sales topped $1 billion.

Sears was station agent for the Minnesota and St. Louis Railroad in North Redwood when he became the beneficiary of an unwanted consignment of watches. He sold them to other station agents and started the R. W. Sears Watch Company in 1886. This became Sears, Roebuck, & Co. in 1893 with the addition of Alvah C. Roebuck, a watchmaker. Sears went on to build the biggest retail business in the United States through the use of the mail-order catalog.

For More Information

Web Site:
Wal-Mart: **www.walmart.com**

"Our best ideas come from clerks and schoolboys." (Samuel Walton)

THOMAS J. WATSON, SR.

Thomas J. Watson, Sr. is reported to have made the unfortunately inaccurate prediction, "I think that there may be a world market for possibly five computers." But his musjudgement didn't prevent him from building the industrial and technological titan IBM. He learned his trade under John Patterson, who taught him about commerce and social responsibility. When Watson was sacked by Patterson after an argument, he took with him progressive ideas about corporate culture and the working environment, and a small sign that said "THINK!" At Computing-Tabulating-Recording Co., the company that eventually became IBM, he engineered a corporate transformation, pumping money into research and development, nurturing exciting new technologies, and galvanizing the sales force.

Thomas J. Watson, Sr., champion of employee satisfaction.

1874	Born.
1893	Sells musical instruments.
1898	Joins the National Cash Register Company.
1914	Joins Computing-Tabulating-Recording Co. Revenues $4 million.
1924	Company's name changed to International Business Machines Corp.
1944	IBM builds world's first large-scale computer.
1946	IBM revenues $115 million.
1952	IBM manufactures world's first commercially available computer, the 701.
1956	Dies.

BACKGROUND AND RISE

Thomas John Watson, Sr. was born in Campbell, New York, on February 17, 1874. Son of an upstate New York farmer, Watson's upbringing was a traditional, rural 19th-century one. Life was shaped by a strong moral code. Dignity, respect for others, conscientious work, optimism, and loyalty were values ingrained in Watson throughout his childhood. Unlike many of his peers, he carried the values throughout his public and private life.

His first real job was as a bookkeeper at Clarence Risley's Market in Painted Post, NY.

His first real job was as a bookkeeper at Clarence Risley's Market in Painted Post, NY. Later, when he was 18, Watson drove a horse and buggy across northern New York State, hawking an unlikely combination of pianos and sewing machines to farmers. As farmers were often short of cash, he took all manner of goods in trade. Animals, farm equipment, and produce were all exchanged and then sold again by Watson. It was invaluable training. It taught him the value of goods and that if he kept his customers happy, more people would buy his goods on recommendation.

DEFINING MOMENTS

In 1898, Watson went to work for the National Cash Register Company, known universally as "the cash." NCR was run by John Patterson, an eccentric, charismatic businessman and a remarkable business pioneer, who introduced many enlightened liberal working practices. Watson joined as a salesman. His first few weeks were spent calling on various prospects, without success. His manager, after giving the dispirited Watson a talking to, promised to accompany him and show him how it should be done. He was true to his word; they traveled together, and Watson finally made a number of sales. The attitude of his manager made a great impression on Watson. Later at IBM, he made sure all managers were able to work with their staff and provide them with adequate training.

With his first few sales in the bag, Watson made swift progress. In 1899 he was promoted to manager of the company's Rochester branch and then to general sales manager—Patterson's right-hand man. While at NCR he came up with the slogan that would later become firmly associated with IBM—"THINK!" Not many people know that the motto was originally conceived, and used to good effect, to pep up a dispirited NCR salesforce.

After a number of disagreements with Patterson, Watson was fired from NCR. In 1914 he moved on to the Computing-Tabulating-Recording Company (CTR), an alliance of three small companies, as general manager. When he arrived, CTR was in poor shape. Worse still, as a newcomer brought into shake things up, Watson was resented by the staff who naturally feared for their jobs. But Watson did not fire a single member of staff. Instead he determined to make the existing workforce better at their jobs. This was the foundation of IBM's famous policy of job security. This policy was even adhered to during the great depression. Despite one quarter of the United States labor force being unemployed, IBM carried on expanding, producing excess inventory and stockpiling it, a gamble which ultimately paid off.

"Business is a game, the greatest game in the world if you know how to play it." (Thomas J. Watson, Sr.)

At CTR, Watson also took a lead from Patterson's liberal working practices and theories. He didn't have the resources to build a modern, forward-looking factory like NCR's in Dayton, but he did do everything in his power to create an enthusiastic atmosphere at the company. This included staging concerts, picnics, and other entertainment, as well as giving rousing speeches. This close and almost paternalistic relationship with his employees led to the "open door" policy, where Watson made himself available in person to see his employees whenever they wished and actively encouraged their visits. This policy was another key element of Watson's management strategy at IBM and only lapsed after his death, when the size of the company made it impracticable.

At IBM, Watson always went out of his way to keep his employees happy. In 1939, he took 10,000 people to IBM Day at the World's Fair, at the company's expense. The sales conventions became increasingly extravagant affairs. Waking delegates were greeted with newspapers recounting the previous day's events, and overseas visitors were provided with headphones through which they heard a translation of the proceedings. A visit by General Eisenhower in July 1948 was extended, after some persuasion by Watson, to allow Eisenhower to address workers at the IBM plant, who were all given time off work to attend.

Watson's obsession with excellent customer service is illustrated by an incident that occurred during World War II. On Good Friday in 1942, an official from the War Production Board telephoned Watson late in the afternoon. He placed an order for 150 machines and challenged Watson to deliver the equipment to Washington D.C. by the following Monday. Watson agreed. Saturday morning saw him, with his staff, phoning IBM offices across the country to organize the dispatch of 150 machines over the Easter holiday. To emphasize the effort he was making, he instructed his staff to let the War Production Board people know the minute each truck began its journey to Washington, no matter what time of day or night. Police and army officials were rounded up to escort trucks, which were driven through the night. A makeshift factory was also set up in Georgetown to deal with the reception and installation of the equipment. It was a remarkable effort, typical of Watson's attitude.

Between 1914 and 1946, IBM's profits grew 38 times, giving great weight to Watson's management strategy. And even though this growth was a magnificent achievement, it was nothing compared to what happened in the postwar period, as IBM grew its revenues from $115 m in 1946 to $1.7 billion by 1961, with employee numbers growing from 17,000 in the United States to 80,000 during the same period. One hundred shares bought in 1914 would have cost $2,740. By 1962, shortly after Watson's death, they were worth $5.45 m.

Much of this was due to the success of a new breed of computer. The Mach 1 was the world's first large-scale computer, built by IBM in collaboration with Dr. Howard Aiken and presented to Harvard University in 1944. This was followed with the first commercially available IBM computer, the 701, in 1952.

At IBM, Watson always went out of his way to keep his employees happy. In 1939, he took 10,000 people to IBM Day at the World's Fair, at the company's expense.

Thomas J. Watson, Sr. died on June 19, 1956. A month earlier, he passed over his control in the company to his eldest son, Thomas J. Watson, Jr.

Context and Conclusions

Thomas J. Watson, Sr. achieved great things at IBM. He managed the growth of a small company with a promising technology into a billion-dollar company with a technology that changed the world. The history of computing is not just about the scientists and inventors. It is also about the men who manage creativity and innovation, and who help turn the fantastic dreams of scientists into commercial reality. Watson was one such man. He cajoled, he improved, he inspired. Many of his methods he owed to his inspirational mentor, John Patterson at NCR. Watson took Patterson's ideals forward into the 20th century and, in doing so, created one of America's most enduring companies.

For More Information

Books:

Rodgers, F. G. Buck. *The IBM Way*. New York: Harper & Row Publishers, 1987.

Rodgers, William. *THINK. A Biography of the Watsons and IBM*. New York: Stein and Day, 1969.

Watson, Thomas J., Jr., with Peter Petre. *Father Son & Co: My Life at IBM and Beyond*. New York: Bantam, 1990.

(Thomas J. Watson, Sr.)

JACK WELCH

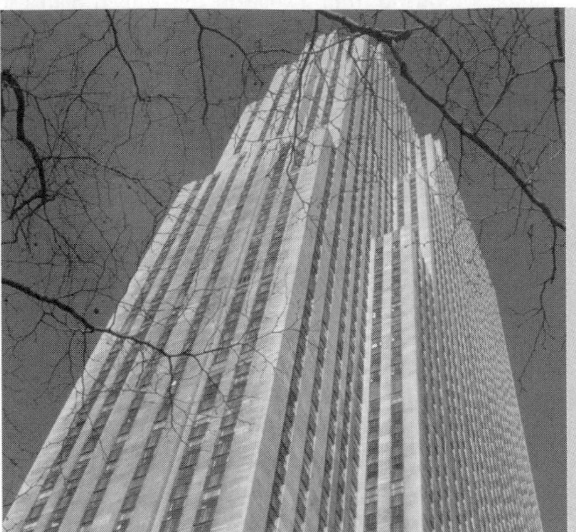

One of the most renowned corporate leaders of the 20th century, Jack Welch maintained General Electric's reputation as a world-beater throughout his 20-year reign as C.E.O. Under Welch the company moved into new business areas and reached new heights.

Jack Welch, named in 1999 as *Fortune*'s "manager of the century," started at General Electric as a trainee in 1960. At the age of 33 he became the youngest general manager in the company's history, and in 1981 became C.E.O. Over a 20-year period he oversaw revolution, reorganization, Six Sigma, tough targets, and a blaze of corporate acquisitions. The results were a 600% increase in profits, 100 consecutive quarters of increased earnings, and a status as one of the most profitable companies in the world. Welch stepped down as C.E.O. in September 2001.

The General Electric building, New York.

1935	Born.
1960	Starts at General Electric.
1961	Almost quits General Electric.
1963	Put in charge of chemical development.
1968	Becomes General Electric's youngest ever general manager.
1981	Becomes C.E.O.
1986	Buys RCA.
1995	Introduces Six Sigma.
2000	Postpones retirement to oversee Honeywell Bull deal.
2001	Steps down as C.E.O.

BACKGROUND AND RISE

Jack Francis Welch, Jr., one of most celebrated managers and leaders of the 20th century, was born on November 19, 1935 in Peabody, Massachusetts. He grew up in Salem, where his father worked as a railroad conductor. As a boy he suffered from a stutter that might have badly affected his confidence, had it not been for his mother's imaginative explanation. "She told me [it was] just that my brain worked too fast," Welch said.

On his employee evaluation form Welch was asked to state his long-term ambitions—to become C.E.O., he wrote. By 1979 he was vice chairman and executive officer.

At school he was a keen sportsman; he also was described by classmates as the "most talkative and noisiest boy" they knew. After high school he set off for the University of Massachusetts, where he studied chemistry. Then came the University of Illinois, where he obtained a Ph.D. in chemical engineering. From there he moved to Pittsfield, Massachusetts, to start his first real job at General Electric.

DEFINING MOMENTS

Welch's meteoric career at General Electric (GE) almost didn't happen. In 1961, sick of the cumbersome bureaucratic systems, Welch quit. Fortunately for GE, his boss at the time persuaded him to stay. In 1963 Welch was put in charge of chemical development, and in 1968, aged 33, he became GE's youngest general manager ever. By 1972 he had risen to the position of divisional vice president and set his sights on rising even higher. On his employee evaluation form Welch was asked to state his long-term ambitions–to become C.E.O., he wrote. By 1979 he was vice chairman and executive officer.

Along the way he built plastics into a formidable $2 billion business, turned around the medical diagnostics business, and began the development of GE Capital. In December 1980 Welch was announced as the new C.E.O. and chairman of GE, at 45 the youngest chief the company had ever appointed and only the eighth C.E.O. in 92 years.

At the time, GE was in reasonable shape. That year *Fortune* magazine voted it the best-managed company in America, and Reg Jones, the C.E.O. who Welch had replaced, was ranked number one among C.E.O.s. Yet GE's stock was performing poorly. Against the backdrop of a faltering world economy, the Japanese were posing a real threat to U.S. manufacturers with new production systems such as "lean manufacturing."

During the 1980s, recognizing that GE would have to change in order to compete successfully on the world stage, Welch declared that it was going become the world's most valuable company. This meant getting rid of all unprofitable areas. The focus was shifted to service industries, creating over 1000 new businesses, and resulting in the disposal of 70 existing businesses.

But that was only a start. Next Welch turned his attention to the organizational structure. He pared down the organization, devolving power to the individual business units in a massive push for decentralization. An

"People always overestimate how complex business is. This isn't rocket science; we've chosen one of the world's more simple professions." (Jack Welch)

elaborate management hierarchy was tossed onto the scrap heap. "Fight it. Hate it. Kick it. Break it," railed Welch in an antibureaucracy exhortation to the troops.

Nearly 200,000 GE employees left the company and over $6 billion was saved. The media dubbed Welch "Neutron Jack." But by the end of the 1980s, having proved that he could tear the company apart, Welch moved on to stage two: rebuilding a company fit for the 21st century. To encourage innovation and the communication of ideas, he vowed to create what he called a "boundaryless" organization. "Knock down the walls that separate us from each other on the inside and from our key constituents on the outside," was the way he put it. In the pre-Welch era, employees with a good idea would squirrel it away. Now they would be willing to share their ideas and would be encouraged to do so, and the culture would make sure that they received the praise they deserved.

To make sure that all employees were pulling in the same direction, Welch used corporate values as a reference to guide behavior. He famously carried a copy of them printed on a card.

In the mid-1990s, in a drive for quality, Welch adopted the concept of Six Sigma, developed by Motorola in 1985. A statistical term, Six Sigma refers to products with a 99.9998% perfection rate. Implementation relies on rigorous measurement and testing to deliver results. Welch made sure that the adoption of Six Sigma had 100% management backing, and attributed a 3% increase in profit margins between 1995 and 1999 to the roll out of Six Sigma at GE.

A stack of figures attest to the success of Jack Welch's reign: between March 31, 1981 and November 1999, for example, the GE stock price rose from just over $4 to $133 (allowing for four stock splits), an increase of 3,200%. From 1980 onward, the average total return on GE shares was about 27%, and the company has returned 100 consecutive quarters of increased earnings from continuing operations. To put the company's performance in context: if you had bought $10,000 worth of General Electric shares in March 1981 and reinvested the dividends, by the end of 1999 they would have been worth $640,000. Over the same period GE sales rose from $27.2 billion to $173.2 billion, while profits rose from $1.6 billion to $10.7 billion. By 1999 General Electric was the second most profitable company in the world.

The only slight tarnishing of Welch's luster came in 2001. Due to retire, Welch postponed his departure for one last hurrah: a mega deal with Honeywell Bull, snatched from under the noses of intended purchasers, United Technologies. Despite Welch's best efforts, however, this deal was scuppered by European Union regulators. In some ways it was an unfortunate end to a majestic career. Commenting on the affair, Welch was his characteristic self: "GE was a great company before I took a swing at it. It's a great company after. It would have been better if we had gotten it. But as far as regrets for doing it? No way. I'd do the same thing again tomorrow." He finally handed over the baton to his successor, Jeff Immelt, on September 7, 2001. His next job—to promote his autobiography, *Jack: Straight from the Gut.*

Context and Conclusions

The failed Honeywell takeover dominated press coverage of the end of Welch's rule at GE. The actions of the E.U. regulators briefly blotted out the achievements of an exceptional leader. But the three stages of development under Welch—destruction, creation, and quality—have reshaped GE and made Welch the C.E.O. role model of his generation. Inevitably, he also has his critics. They point to the size of corporate pay packets, GE's ecological record, high levels of layoffs, and the lack of loyalty throughout the organization. But there can be little disagreement that Welch has made a difference where it matters, from the investors' perspective at least. History will remember Welch as one of the most important corporate leaders of the 20th century.

A stack of figures attest to the success of Jack Welch's reign: between March 31, 1981 and November 1999, for example, the GE stock price rose from just over $4 to $133 (allowing for four stock splits), an increase of 3,200%.

CLOSE BUT NO CIGAR

John Marous
Concentrating on investor value worked for Welch, but it didn't work for Marous. A Westinghouse Electrical Company executive man and boy, Marous had been at the company for 40 years before he became C.E.O. in 1988. The similarities between Welch and Marous are many: both excelled at sports, were tough negotiators, and were results-driven in the extreme. "Don't just bring me bad news, bring me solutions," was a Marous motto. Under his leadership, some of Westinghouse's core businesses were sold off and Westinghouse Credit was given a free rein to lend, lend, lend. In 1990, the year Marous stepped down, the stock price was at its highest ever. But from there it was all downhill. After his departure the once great company drowned in the sea of bad debts left by its subsidiary Westinghouse Credit.

For More Information

Books:

Crainer, Stuart. *Business the Jack Welch Way*. New York: AMACOM, 1999.
Slater, Jack. *New GE: How Jack Welch Revived an American Institution*. Irwin: Business One, 1993.
Tichy, Noel M., and Sherman Stratford. *Control Your Destiny or Someone Else Will: How Jack Welch Is Making General Electric the World's Most Competitive Corporation*. New York: Currency Doubleday, 1993.

Web Site:
General Electric: **www.ge.com**

  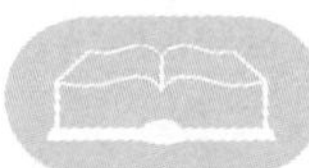    

Oprah Winfrey

The child of separated parents, the victim of childhood sexual abuse, teenage pregnancy, and juvenile delinquency, Oprah Winfrey (1954–) overcame a difficult start to become an American icon.

Her career in broadcasting began as a teenager reading the news on the radio. By the age of 30 she had become the talk-show queen of the United States, hosting the nation's number one talk show. In 1988 she became the third woman ever to own her own film studio, Harpo Productions. At a time when talk shows seemed to be descending into the gutter, she pulled them back out again with a move to "change your life" television. Winfrey's future seems assured: she has secured her talk-show contract until 2004, she publishes a number of magazines and produces other television programs, and she's becoming more involved with social issues in the United States.

Winfrey's informal style changed television radically.

1954	Born.
1963	Moves to live with mother.
1972	Wins Miss Black Tennessee pageant.
1976	Moves to Baltimore and lands job with WJZ-TV.
1984	Achieves first major television success with AM Chicago.
1985	Plays Sofia in movie *The Color Purple*.
1986	Goes nationwide with *The Oprah Winfrey Show*.
1987	Wins first daytime Emmy for *The Oprah Winfrey Show*.
1994	Repositions her show as "change your life television."
2000	Diversifies into publishing, brings out new magazine called *O*.

Background and Rise

Oprah Winfrey had a tough start in life. Born to unmarried teenagers on July 29, 1954, she grew up in poverty on her grandmother's farm in Mississippi. The first Winfrey's father knew of her existence was when he received an instruction to send some clothes for her. Brought up initially by her grandmother, at four she moved to Milwaukee to live with her mother. After a brief but happy interlude with her father, Vernon Winfrey, a businessman in Nashville, Tennessee, she again ended up with her mother in Milwaukee in 1963. During her time there she was raped, at the age of nine.

When she was initially offered a TV job, she turned it down until one of her professors persuaded her to change her mind.

Her mother attempted to send her to a home for juvenile delinquents, but she was unable to wait two weeks for a place to become available. Winfrey was despatched back to live with her father. Had it not been for her father, Winfrey's life might easily have been a tale of loss and waste. Luckily for her, her father was a strict disciplinarian, and with his help Winfrey began to turn her life around.

At 16 she got her first lucky break. As the first African American girl to win a national beauty contest, she was invited on a tour of a local radio station to pick up her prize. Her talent was spotted there and she was asked to read the radio news after school. She had her next big break at 19, landing a job as a reporter for the Nashville radio station WVOL. At the same time she enrolled at Tennessee State University to study performing arts.

When she was initially offered a TV job, she turned it down until one of her professors persuaded her to change her mind. Winfrey became a news anchor on WTVF-TV in Nashville, the first African American to do so. Her star quality was evident from the moment she was put in front of the camera. On television she was a natural. Her personality lit up the screen.

Defining Moments

In 1976 Winfrey moved to Baltimore, Maryland, and landed herself a job with WJZ-TV as a news co-anchor. The management wasn't impressed, criticizing her appearance and eventually demoting her to a morning spot. Luckily a station executive, Phil Baker, offered her an opportunity to co-host a chat show on the station. Reluctant at first, she accepted. It was a risk for the station to put an African American woman on as host of its principal talk show. And it was a risk for Winfrey, who thought her future lay in news. The show was called *People Are Talking*, and viewers were soon talking about Winfrey. They liked her down-to-earth style, and her Nielsen ratings began to rise. In 1984 she moved to Chicago to host WLS-TV's morning talk show, *AM Chicago*, going head-to-head with Phil Donahue, America's top-rated talk-show host. Her show ranked number one within a month. Winfrey was just 30 years old.

"You have to surround yourself with people you trust, and people that are good. But they also have to be people who will tell the emperor you have no clothes." (Oprah Winfrey)

Winfrey continued in her own inimitable style, being open and honest about her past and her emotions. It struck a chord with her audience. Viewers empathized with her. Her high profile began to pay dividends as she was asked to audition for the part of Sofia in Steven Spielberg's 1985 movie adaptation of Alice Walker's novel, *The Color Purple*. When she received a call telling her Steven Spielberg wanted her in his office in California the next day, she was at a health spa on one of her frequent attempts to lose weight. She was warned that if she lost as much as a pound it might jeopardize her chances of getting the part—she later joked that she stopped off at a Dairy Queen on the way to California. She got the part and was nominated for an Oscar for Best Supporting Actress.

The timing couldn't have been better for Winfrey. She was about to launch her nationally syndicated chat show, *The Oprah Winfrey Show*. It was 1986 and, despite one viewer in Iowa calling in to say he could get better ratings with a potato, Winfrey had hit the big time. Her style remained unaffected, and she soon racked up ten million viewers across the United States.

Astutely Winfrey took control of her own destiny in 1988 by forming Harpo Productions—her name spelled backward—acquiring the rights to her show from Capital Cities/ABC. She also spent $20 million on a production facility in Chicago, a step on the way to becoming only the third woman to own a major studio (following in the footsteps of Mary Pickford and Lucille Ball).

Winfrey's professional life was blooming, but her personal life was plagued by her struggle with her weight. Her repeated and very public attempts to reduce her weight varied from exercise to a radical, four-month-long liquid diet. Eventually she managed to come to terms with herself and her weight, an achievement that helped her self-esteem and her bank balance: her 1994 book *In the Kitchen with Rosie* (Rosie was her chef) became the fastest selling book in the country.

Winfrey's immense success spawned a host of imitators. Talk shows sprang up on every station, delving into the private lives of individuals, exposing the underbelly of human existence. Appealing to the lowest common denominator, such programs can at times seem little more than a license to televise sleaze. In 1994 Winfrey decided to distance herself from the excesses of the genre by repositioning herself in the marketplace. She vowed to concentrate on more uplifting and more highbrow issues, calling her concept "change your life" TV. She has succeeded in both redefining herself and differentiating her show in the talk-show marketplace. The shift of emphasis has secured another series run until 2004. The "Oprah Factor" has also begun to move beyond television in recent years. The appearance of "Oprah's Book Club" on U.S. screens in 1996 has had a dramatic effect on book sales in the United States, and any title recommended by Winfrey in the on-air book discussion group has gone on to massive success.

Context and Conclusions

Oprah Winfrey's story is one of triumph over adversity. It offers a message of hope to those from disadvantaged backgrounds: that it is possible to achieve success through talent, hard work, and a little good fortune. Overcoming a childhood marked by abuse and discrimination, Winfrey has become an American icon, an African American woman who has conquered television and found a place in the hearts of the American public. She has succeeded by being herself and today Winfrey is one of the most influential people in the United States. Her widely publicized comments about not eating beef, for example, were followed by a 10% drop in beef futures, an event that resulted in an unsuccessful attempt by the beef industry to sue her for millions of dollars in damages. With no sign of Winfrey's star fading, who knows what she will turn her hand to next? A growing interest in social issues suggests that her career could take on a more political direction.

Winfrey's immense success spawned a host of imitators. Talk shows sprang up on every station, delving into the private lives of individuals, exposing the underbelly of human existence.

For More Information

Book:

Mair, George. *Oprah Winfrey: The Real Story*. Rev. ed. New York: Carol, 1998.

Web Site:

Oprah®:com, **www.oprah.com**

"I don't invest in anything I don't understand—it makes more sense to buy TV stations than oil wells."

(Oprah Winfrey)

ROBERT WINSHIP WOODRUFF

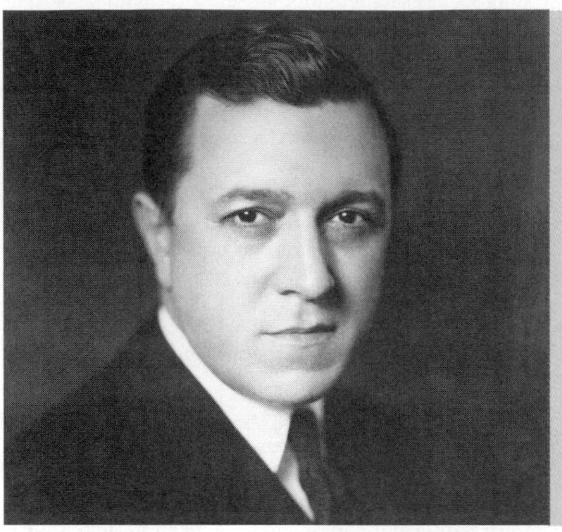

Robert Woodruff was the natural heir to the Coca-Cola empire. His father was behind the $25 million buyout of the Candler family interests in Coca-Cola in 1919. Yet to begin with his familial advantage did Woodruff no good at all. When he sought a job outside the family's beverage interests, his father attempted to restrict his career at every turn. Woodruff succeeded on his own terms as a sales representative for White Motor Company before bowing to the inevitable and joining Coca-Cola in 1923. For the next four decades until his official retirement in 1965, he ruled the company. He presided over a period of momentous growth that transformed Coca-Cola into a global corporation. By the time of his death in 1985 he had helped create one of the world's most valuable brands.

Robert Woodruff put the fizz back into Coca-Cola.

1889	Born.
1919	Father's syndicate buys Coca-Cola Company.
1923	Becomes president of Coca-Cola.
1926	Creates Coca-Cola's Foreign Department.
1928	Coca-Cola supplies beverages for Amsterdam Olympics.
1930	Foreign Department becomes Coca-Cola Export Corporation.
1933	Automatic Coca-Cola dispensers introduced at Chicago World's Fair.
1939	Steps down as president.
1965	Officially retires.
1985	Dies.

BACKGROUND AND RISE

Woodruff was born on December 6, 1889, in Columbus, Georgia. His father, Ernest Woodruff, was president of the Trust Company of Georgia, which was part of a syndicate that bought control of the Coca-Cola company. Ernest Woodruff became the company's president.

Woodruff's working life also got off to an inauspicious start. He was dismissed from a series of jobs for no obvious reason.

For the first stage of his education Woodruff was sent to the Georgia Military Academy. He proved a poor student. The school may have overlooked his disappointing grades, however, as the young Woodruff saved the academy from bankruptcy. Discovering that the Atlanta National Bank was about to foreclose on the school's mortgage, Woodruff paid a visit to the bank's vice president, and through a combination of bluffing and name-dropping he persuaded him to hold off.

Woodruff completed his education at Emory College, where he paid other students to complete his homework. When asked later in life about his tips for a being a successful manager, he replied, "If you can get someone to do something better than you can, it is always a good idea." Despite delegating his college work, he still failed to complete his degree.

Woodruff's working life also got off to an inauspicious start. He was dismissed from a series of jobs for no obvious reason. In fact he was not responsible for his appalling employment record: his father was. Ernest Woodruff had arranged for his son to be fired on each occasion to teach the young man that having a rich father was no guarantee of an easy life. Once, when Woodruff was refused a raise, he discovered that his father was interfering in his career and swore that he would never work for him again.

Instead he went to work as a truck sales representative at White Motor Company, but was swiftly promoted through the company, becoming vice president and then general manager.

DEFINING MOMENTS

While Woodruff was climbing the corporate ladder at White Motor Company, his father had been putting together an investment group that in 1919 paid $25 million for the Candler family's interest in the Coca-Cola Company. As part of the deal 500,000 shares of Coca-Cola common stock were sold on the stock market for $40 a share. Asked by his father if he wished to participate in the syndicate, Woodruff agreed—picking up a large holding of the company's stock at $5 a share.

In 1923, aged 33, Woodruff achieved a business reconciliation with his father by accepting the presidency of Coca-Cola. He must have wanted the position badly because he took a substantial pay cut and turned down an offer to be president of Standard Oil at a salary of $250,000. Woodruff later said that the reason he took the job was that it was the only way he could boost the value of his stock in the company.

Over the next six decades Woodruff oversaw the transformation of Coca-Cola from a promising U.S. soft-drink manufacturer into a global giant. His influence extended into every aspect of the company's operations and began with changing the company's marketing strategy. Only positive images were to be associated with the product: all negative connotations were banished, and Coca-Cola's medicinal roots were severed.

In production and distribution Woodruff set in motion a drive for quality. In 1928 soda fountains exceeded bottled sales, and Woodruff made sure the employees who serviced the fountains were highly trained and could pass their knowledge on to the storekeepers operating the fountains. A Fountain Training School was established where sales representatives could learn how to mix Coca-Cola properly. Woodruff also introduced a standard procedure manual. At the same time, realizing that the bottled drink was the future of the company, he introduced quality standards in the bottling plants. All employees were to wear uniforms, and hygiene and quality checks were introduced.

While all these changes were an essential part of Coca-Cola's success, Woodruff's most important contribution to the company was probably his move to open up international markets. As early as 1900 the Coca-Cola drink had been taken abroad by Asa Candler—the first international order was from England. Through the early 1900s the company built bottling plants in a number of countries from Cuba to the Philippines. But the expansion was disorganized, with no coordinated management of international product rollout.

In 1926 Woodruff changed that by creating the Foreign Department, which four years later became a full blown subsidiary, the Coca-Cola Export Corporation. Coca-Cola's march to global domination was inexorable under Woodruff. The company cleverly brokered a deal with the Olympics movement, with Coca-Cola being exported to Holland for sale at the 1928 Amsterdam Olympics. Woodruff secured Coca-Cola's beachheads abroad by investing in local economies, building bottling plants, and employing locals for the distribution. In this way the brand acquired goodwill in its export markets.

Although Woodruff resigned as president in 1939 he continued to play an active role in the company. As World War II approached he promised, "We'll see that every man in uniform gets a bottle of Coca-Cola for five cents, wherever he is and whatever it costs our company." The war helped proliferate Coca-Cola throughout the world.

In the postwar period Woodruff's efforts were increasingly concentrated on battling rival Pepsi-Cola. His influence at Coca-Cola persisted right up until and beyond his retirement in 1965. He remained a kingmaker, grooming potential C.E.O.s, including Roberto Goizueta, from behind the scenes. He died on March 7, 1985, aged 95.

Context and Conclusions

Robert Woodruff the private man was an enigma. He was not a cultured man: he didn't read, nor, unlike many other wealthy executives, was he interested in collecting art or antiques. He had a fear of being alone and would often call friends and colleagues to his home in the small hours to keep him company. Yet he was also an intensely private person who installed a private elevator to his office.

Woodruff "the Boss," however, was a different story. The force behind one of the biggest corporate success stories of the last century, he was a restless, driven, controlling figurehead. Unlike many entrepreneurs, Woodruff didn't invent the product his company sold. But he was responsible for aggressively marketing Coca-Cola to a thirsty world—and for taking a caramel-based soda drink and turning it into an American icon. Woodruff's personal creed was, "There is no limit to what a man can do or where he can go if he doesn't mind who gets the credit." Much of the credit for creating one of the world's most enduring products must go to him.

The force behind one of the biggest corporate success stories of the last century, he was a restless, driven, controlling figurehead.

For More Information

Book:

Pendergrast, Mark. *For God, Country, and Coca-Cola: The Definitive History of the Great American Soft Drink and the Company That Makes It*. 2nd ed. New York: Basic Books, 2000.

Web Site:

Coca-Cola: **www.cocacola.com**

"There is no limit to what a man can do or where he can go if he doesn't mind who gets the credit."

(Robert W. Woodruff)

FRANK WINFIELD WOOLWORTH

Frank Winfield Woolworth (1852–1919) was a pioneer of the chain store. He came from a humble background, and became one of the richest men in America, despite many early setbacks in his career. Emerging from a small town in New York State, the farmer's boy rolled out his "five and ten cents" concept first across America and then around the world. From a single store in 1879 to a thousand in 1918, the growth of F.W. Woolworth & Co. was phenomenal, changing the nature of retailing and bringing its founder riches and fame. Woolworths was the original price-driven retail chain. The secret of his success he put down to delegating well.

F. W. Woolworth changed the way the world shops.

1852	Born.
1858	Family move to 108-acre farm near Great Bend, New York.
1873	Woolworth goes to work at Augsbury & Moore's store.
1878	The five-cent table causes a stir in U.S. retailing.
1879	First Woolworth store opens in Utica, New York.
1895	28 stores and revenues of over $1 million.
1905	F.W. Woolworth & Co. incorporated.
1913	Company moves into the tallest skyscraper of its time, in New York City.
1918	In January the 1000th store opens on Fifth Avenue, New York City.
1919	Dies.

BACKGROUND AND RISE

Woolworth was born in Rodman, the eldest son of the family. In late 1858, when Woolworth was seven, the family moved to a 108-acre farm near Great Bend, New York. In a town with a population of only 125, Woolworth's opportunities for education were limited; there was only a one-room schoolhouse, which he attended along with his brother. Much of Woolworth's time, in fact, was taken up helping his father with the family's eight-cow dairy herd rather than studying.

At Augsbury & Moore Woolworth started at the bottom of the ladder. He swept floors, created window displays, delivered goods, and generally made himself useful.

When he was 16 Woolworth attended commercial college for a brief period before offering his services first to the stationmaster's small store, and then to Dan McNeil's general store in Great Bend as a clerk. On both occasions Woolworth worked for free. In return, Dan McNeil recommended Woolworth to William Moore, the owner of a leading dry goods store in Watertown, New York. In 1873 Moore agreed to take Woolworth on.

At Augsbury & Moore Woolworth started at the bottom of the ladder. He swept floors, created window displays, delivered goods, and generally made himself useful. The hours were long—six days a week, 7:00 a.m. to 9:00 p.m.—and the pay offered little compensation. The owners initially wanted Woolworth to work for a year with no salary, but after some discussion Woolworth persuaded them to let him work for three months for nothing, rising to $3.50 for the following three months.

Two years later Woolworth moved on to another store, Bushnall's Department Store, as a senior clerk. In 1876 he married Jennie Creighton, a Canadian, and purchased a four-acre farm. Unfortunately, the tough conditions and lack of support at work meant Woolworth suffered from fever and stress-related illness, which forced him to give up his position at Bushnall's and kept him at home for a year unable to work. As he was recovering, his old employer William Moore came knocking at his door requesting him to return to work at the now renamed Moore & Smith's. Woolworth accepted on a salary of $10 a week.

DEFINING MOMENTS

In 1878 Woolworth's daughter was born and his mother died. But it was also a year of radical change in the world of retailing. In stores in the Midwest a new tactic had made its debut—the five-cent table. Surplus merchandise was marked down to a nickel by retailers and displayed on a five-cent table. Customers snapped up the bargains and were then drawn into buying other goods at full price. Moore traveled to New York City and came home with $100 worth of five-cent goods for Moore & Smith. Woolworth arranged the counter, and they were sold out in a day.

With goods supplied by Moore, Woolworth opened his

"Retail has been described as selling things which don't come back to customers who do."

(Tom Farmer)

own store in Utica, New York, selling only on the five-cent principle. "The Great Five Cent Store" opened for business on a Saturday evening in February 1879 with $321 worth of five-cent goods. The first ever item sold was a fire shovel. However, the store was a failure and soon closed. Undaunted, Woolworth opened another in June of the same year in Lancaster, Pennsylvania. Now he sold goods for five and ten cents. The Lancaster store was a success. In November 1880 he opened a second store in Scranton, Pennsylvania. This too was a success, and Woolworth never looked back.

Woolworth brought in family members to help expand his empire. By 1895 he had 28 stores, including that of his ex-boss William Moore, and revenues of over $1 million. The growth continued at breakneck speed. In 1900 there were 35 stores; by 1908, 189; and by 1911, 600. In January 1918 the thousandth store opened on Fifth Avenue in New York City.

Woolworth's one-man retail business had burgeoned into a global enterprise. In 1905, bowing to commercial pressures, he incorporated F.W. Woolworth & Co. issuing 50,000 shares to executives and employees. Corporate offices were first located in the Stewart Building overlooking City Hall Park in New York City. Then, in April 1913, the company moved into the Woolworth Building, the tallest skyscraper of its time. Woolworth's office was situated on the 24th floor. Thirty feet square, its design was based on Napoleon's famous Empire Room and contained the clock and other articles from the original room.

In 1916 the F.W. Woolworth stores served over 700 million customers and had revenues of over $87 million. Every town in the United States with a population of over 8,000 had a Woolworth's.

By the time Woolworth was installed in the Woolworth Building he was approaching the end of his career. With his health failing, he began taking periods of rest in Europe. His wife, Jennie, was suffering from premature senility. Woolworth's own health continued to decline steadily, partly due to a refusal to care for his teeth. On April 4, 1919 he fell desperately ill, dying four days later.

Context and Conclusions

F.W. Woolworth & Co. was the pioneer of price-driven retail. Laying down a tradition of value for money that was later followed by companies such as Wal-Mart, Woolworth was one of the first merchants to build a retail empire founded on chain stores and volume retailing.

Working for very little or no money, enduring long periods of ill-health, and with three out of his first five stores failing, no one would have blamed Woolworth for giving up his business dreams. Instead, his persistence saw off all his five-and-ten-cents competitors and made him the most successful retailer of his time.

Woolworth's concept of a business based on bargain goods survived until the 1990s. In 1997, however, the Woolworth corporation announced that it was to close its last 400 F.W. Woolworth five-and-dime stores in the United States, finally retreating from the low-priced general merchandise business that had shaped its identity for 117 years.

In 1916 the F.W. Woolworth stores served over 700 million customers and had revenues of over $87 million.

What was Woolworth's secret? Delegation apparently: "So long as I was obsessed with the idea that I must attend personally to everything, large-scale success was impossible. A man must select able lieutenants and/or associates and give them power and responsibility."

For More Information

Books:

Baker, Nina Brown. *Nickels and Dimes: The Story of F.W. Woolworth*. New York: Harcourt, Brace & World, 1954.

Plunkett-Powell, Karen. *Remembering Woolworth's: A Nostalgic History of the World's Most Famous Five-and-Dime*. New York: St. Martin's Press, 1999.

Winkler, John Kennedy. *Five and Ten: The Fabulous Life of F.W. Woolworth*. Freeport, NY: Books for Libraries Press, 1970.

Dictionary

a-z DICTIONARY

Defining Business: The Most Up-to-Date Global Business English Dictionary
In a dynamic business environment, it is essential that managers keep up to date with the latest business terms and jargon.

The Dictionary provides clear definitions to more than 5,000 international business terms, abbreviations, and acronyms. It has been compiled by an international team of expert researchers and business information specialists, led by the Institute of Management in Europe. Extensive links with other sections in the work make it easier for you to explore interesting topics further.

Special features:

World Business English terms are included to reflect the globalization of the business world

Abbreviations, acronyms, and their expansions are shown in full and cross-referred for ease of use

Mini-essays explain more complex concepts and help you get to grips with ideas quickly

Expanded biographical entries detail the lives and careers of key business thinkers and leaders

Extensive listings of international stock exchanges and trade organizations

Business slang from around the world—some humorous, some serious, some baffling.

  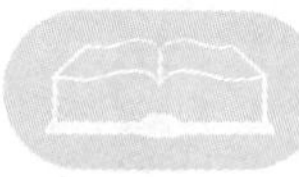    

AAA *abbr* E-COMMERCE authentication, authorization, and accounting, the software security verification procedures that acknowledge or validate an e-commerce user or message

AAMOF *abbr* GENERAL MANAGEMENT as a matter of fact (*slang*)

AASB FINANCE, BANKING, AND ACCOUNTING see ***Australian Accounting Standards Board***

AB *abbr* GENERAL MANAGEMENT used after the title of a Swedish business to identify it as a joint stock company

abandonment option FINANCE, BANKING, AND ACCOUNTING the option of terminating an investment before the time that it is scheduled to end

abandonment value FINANCE, BANKING, AND ACCOUNTING the value that an investment has if it is terminated at a particular time before it is scheduled to end

ABC FINANCE, BANKING, AND ACCOUNTING see ***activity based costing***

Abilene paradox GENERAL MANAGEMENT a theory stating that some decisions that seem to be based on consensus are in fact based on misperception and lead to courses of action that defeat original intentions. The Abilene paradox was proposed by Jerry Harvey in 1974 following a trip made by his family to the town of Abilene. One person suggested the visit as he felt the others needed entertainment, and the others agreed as they all believed that everyone else wanted to go. On their return, everyone admitted that they would rather have stayed at home. Harvey used this experience to illustrate the mismanagement of agreement, and of ***decision making*** in organizations when apparent consensus is actually founded on poor communication. The Abilene paradox shows similarities to the ***attribution theory of leadership***.

ability test HR & PERSONNEL see ***aptitude test***

ABN *abbr* FINANCE, BANKING, AND ACCOUNTING Australian Business Number, a numeric code that identifies an Australian business for the purpose of dealing with the Australian Tax Office and other government departments. ABNs are part of the new tax system that came into operation in Australia in 1998.

above-the-line MARKETING relating to marketing expenditure on advertising in media such as press, radio, television, cinema, and the World Wide Web, on which a commission is usually paid to an agency

ABS FINANCE, BANKING, AND ACCOUNTING see ***Australian Bureau of Statistics***

absenteeism HR & PERSONNEL the problem of employees taking short-term, unauthorized ***leave*** from work, resulting in lost ***productivity*** and increased costs. Absenteeism is usually sickness-related. Other causes may include a lack of ***motivation***, domestic difficulties, or poor management.

✔ MANAGING ABSENTEEISM (pp. 362–63)

absorbed account FINANCE, BANKING, AND ACCOUNTING an account that has lost its separate identity by being combined with related accounts in the preparation of a financial statement

absorbed business GENERAL MANAGEMENT a company that has been merged into another company

absorbed costs FINANCE, BANKING, AND ACCOUNTING the indirect costs associated with manufacturing, for example, insurance or property taxes

absorption costing FINANCE, BANKING, AND ACCOUNTING an accounting practice in which fixed and variable costs of production are absorbed by different cost centers

abusive tax shelter FINANCE, BANKING, AND ACCOUNTING a tax shelter that somebody claims illegally to avoid or minimize tax

ACA FINANCE, BANKING, AND ACCOUNTING see ***Australian Communications Authority***

ACCC *abbr* FINANCE, BANKING, AND ACCOUNTING Australian Competition and Consumer Commission, an independent statutory body responsible for monitoring trade practices in Australia. It was set up in November 1995 as a result of the merger of the Trade Practices Commission and the Prices Surveillance Authority.

accelerated cost recovery system FINANCE, BANKING, AND ACCOUNTING a system used for computing the depreciation of some assets acquired before 1986 in a way that reduces taxes. Abbr **ACRS**

accelerated depreciation ECONOMICS, FINANCE, BANKING, AND ACCOUNTING a system used for computing the depreciation of some assets in a way that assumes that they depreciate faster in the early years of their acquisition

acceptable quality level OPERATIONS & PRODUCTION the level at which an output of manufactured components is considered to be of satisfactory quality. Acceptable quality level is usually expressed with the number of defective items shown as a proportion of the total output. Today, owing to a general increase in competitive pressure, the only acceptable quality level is ***zero defects***, so the term is rarely used.

acceptance bonus HR & PERSONNEL a ***bonus*** paid to a new ***employee*** on acceptance of the job. An acceptance bonus can be a feature of a ***golden hello*** and is designed both to attract and to retain staff.

acceptance house (*U.K.*) ECONOMICS, FINANCE, BANKING, AND ACCOUNTING an institution that accepts financial instruments and agrees to honor them should the borrower default

acceptance region STATISTICS the set of values in a test statistic for which the null hypothesis can be accepted

acceptance sampling OPERATIONS & PRODUCTION a ***quality control*** decision-making technique used in a manufacturing environment, in which acceptance or rejection of a batch of parts is decided by testing a sample of the batch. The sample is checked against established standards and, if it meets those standards, the whole batch is deemed acceptable.

access bond (*S. Africa*) FINANCE, BANKING, AND ACCOUNTING a type of mortgage that permits borrowers to take out loans against extra capital paid into the account, home-loan interest rates being lower than interest rates on other forms of credit

ACCI FINANCE, BANKING, AND ACCOUNTING see ***Australian Chamber of Commerce and Industry***

account FINANCE, BANKING, AND ACCOUNTING a business arrangement involving the exchange of money or credit in which payment is deferred, or a record maintained by a financial institution itemizing its dealings with a particular customer

accountability GENERAL MANAGEMENT the allocation or acceptance of ***responsibility*** for actions

 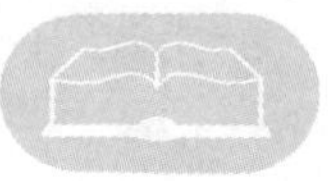    

accountant FINANCE, BANKING, AND ACCOUNTING a professional person who maintains and checks the business records of a person or organization and prepares forms and reports for financial purposes

accountant's letter FINANCE, BANKING, AND ACCOUNTING a written statement by an independent accountant that precedes a financial report, describing the scope of the report and giving an opinion on its validity

account day (*U.K.*) FINANCE, BANKING, AND ACCOUNTING the day on which an executed order is settled by the delivery of securities, payment to the seller, and payment by the buyer. This is the final day of the ***accounting period***.

account debtor FINANCE, BANKING, AND ACCOUNTING a person or organization responsible for paying for a product or service

account director MARKETING a senior person within an advertising agency responsible for overall policy on a client's advertising account

account executive MARKETING an employee of an organization such as a bank, public relations firm, or advertising agency who is responsible for the business of a particular client

accounting cost FINANCE, BANKING, AND ACCOUNTING the cost of maintaining and checking the business records of a person or organization and the preparation of forms and reports for financial purposes

accounting cycle FINANCE, BANKING, AND ACCOUNTING the regular process of formally updating a firm's financial position by recording, analyzing, and reporting its transactions during the accounting period

accounting equation FINANCE, BANKING, AND ACCOUNTING a formula in which a firm's assets must be equal to the sum of its liabilities and the owners' equity

accounting exposure ECONOMICS, FINANCE, BANKING, AND ACCOUNTING the risk that foreign currency held by a company may lose value because of exchange rate changes when it conducts overseas business

accounting insolvency ECONOMICS, FINANCE, BANKING, AND ACCOUNTING the condition that a company is in when its liabilities to its creditors exceed its assets

accounting period FINANCE, BANKING, AND ACCOUNTING an amount of time in which businesses may prepare internal accounts so as to monitor progress on a weekly, monthly, or quarterly basis. Accounts are generally prepared for external purposes on an annual basis.

accounting principles FINANCE, BANKING, AND ACCOUNTING the rules that apply to accounting practices and provide guidelines for dealing appropriately with complex transactions

accounting profit FINANCE, BANKING, AND ACCOUNTING the difference between total revenue and explicit costs

accounting rate of return FINANCE, BANKING, AND ACCOUNTING the ratio of profit before interest and taxation to the percentage of capital employed at the end of a period. Variations include using profit after interest and taxation, equity capital employed, and average capital for the period.

accounting ratio FINANCE, BANKING, AND ACCOUNTING an expression of accounting results as a ratio or percentage, for example, the ratio of ***current assets*** to ***current liabilities***

accounting system FINANCE, BANKING, AND ACCOUNTING the means, including staff and equipment, by which an organization produces its accounting information

accounting year (*U.K.*) FINANCE, BANKING, AND ACCOUNTING the annual ***accounting period***

account reconciliation FINANCE, BANKING, AND ACCOUNTING

1. a procedure for ensuring the reliability of accounting records by comparing balances of transactions

2. a procedure for comparing the register of a checkbook with an associated bank statement

accounts payable FINANCE, BANKING, AND ACCOUNTING the amount that a company owes for goods or services obtained on credit

accounts receivable FINANCE, BANKING, AND ACCOUNTING the money that is owed to a company by those who have bought its goods or services and have not yet paid for them

accounts receivable aging FINANCE, BANKING, AND ACCOUNTING a periodic report that classifies outstanding receivable balances according to customer and month of the invoice's original billing date

accounts receivable factoring FINANCE, BANKING, AND ACCOUNTING the buying of accounts receivable at a discount with the aim of making a profit from collecting them

accounts receivable financing ECONOMICS, FINANCE, BANKING, AND ACCOUNTING a form of borrowing in which a company uses money that it is owed as collateral for a loan it needs for business operations

accounts receivable turnover ECONOMICS, FINANCE, BANKING, AND ACCOUNTING a ratio that shows how long the customers of a business wait before paying what they owe. This can cause cash flow problems for small businesses.

accreditation of prior learning HR & PERSONNEL a process through which formal recognition for the achievements of past learning and experiences may be obtained. Accreditation of prior learning may be used to support the award of a vocational qualification.

accredited investor FINANCE, BANKING, AND ACCOUNTING an investor whose wealth or income is above a particular amount. It is illegal for an accredited investor to be a member of a private limited partnership.

accreted value FINANCE, BANKING, AND ACCOUNTING the value of a bond if interest rates do not change

accretion FINANCE, BANKING, AND ACCOUNTING the growth of a company through additions or purchases of plant or value-adding services

accretive FINANCE, BANKING, AND ACCOUNTING relating to company policies or strategies that involve accretion

accrual FINANCE, BANKING, AND ACCOUNTING a charge that has not been paid by the end of an accounting period but must be included in the accounting results for the period. If no invoice has been received for the charge, an estimate must be included in the accounting results.

accrual basis FINANCE, BANKING, AND ACCOUNTING = ***accrual method***

accrual concept FINANCE, BANKING, AND ACCOUNTING the idea that income and expense items must be included in financial statements as they are earned or incurred

accrual method FINANCE, BANKING, AND ACCOUNTING an accounting method that in-

  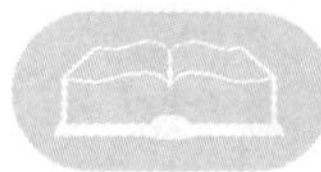    

cludes income and expense items as they are earned or incurred irrespective of when money is received or paid out. Also known as ***accrual basis***

accrual of discount FINANCE, BANKING, AND ACCOUNTING the annual gain in value of a bond owing to its having been bought originally for less than its par value

accrue FINANCE, BANKING, AND ACCOUNTING to include an income or expense item in the transaction records at the time it is earned or incurred

accrued expense FINANCE, BANKING, AND ACCOUNTING an expense that has been incurred but not yet paid

accrued income FINANCE, BANKING, AND ACCOUNTING income that has been earned but not yet received

accrued interest FINANCE, BANKING, AND ACCOUNTING the amount of interest earned by a bond or similar investment since the previous interest payment

accruing FINANCE, BANKING, AND ACCOUNTING added as a periodic gain, for example, as interest on money

accumulated depreciation FINANCE, BANKING, AND ACCOUNTING the cumulative annual depreciation of an asset that has been claimed as an expense since the asset was acquired

accumulated dividend FINANCE, BANKING, AND ACCOUNTING the amount of money in dividends earned by a stock or similar investment since the previous dividend payment

accumulated earnings tax *or* **accumulated profits tax** FINANCE, BANKING, AND ACCOUNTING the tax that a company must pay because it chose not to pay dividends that would subject its owners to higher taxes

accumulation unit (*U.K.*) FINANCE, BANKING, AND ACCOUNTING a share of a mutual fund that retains dividend income instead of distributing it to individual investors

accuracy STATISTICS the degree to which data conforms to a recognized standard value

ACH E-COMMERCE see ***automated clearing house***

acid test GENERAL MANAGEMENT a stringent test of the worth or reliability of something

Ackoff, **Russell Lincoln** (*b.* 1919) GENERAL MANAGEMENT U.S. academic. Pioneer of operations research, and systems thinking, whose publications include *Ackoff's Fables: Irreverent Reflections on Business and Bureaucracy* (1991).
✔ OPEN SYSTEMS THINKING (pp. 568–69)

ACM GENERAL MANAGEMENT see ***Australian Chamber of Manufactures***

acquiescence bias STATISTICS the bias produced when respondents in a survey give positive answers to two mutually conflicting questions

acquirer *or* **acquiring bank** E-COMMERCE a financial institution, commonly a bank, that processes a merchant's credit card authorizations and payments, forwarding the data to a credit card association, which in turn communicates with the issuer. Also known as ***clearing house***, ***processor***

acquisition GENERAL MANAGEMENT see ***merger***

acquisition accounting FINANCE, BANKING, AND ACCOUNTING the standard accounting procedures that must be followed when one company merges with another

acquisition rate GENERAL MANAGEMENT a measure of the ability of marketing programs to win new business

ACRS FINANCE, BANKING, AND ACCOUNTING see ***accelerated cost recovery system***

action-centered leadership GENERAL MANAGEMENT a ***leadership*** model developed by ***John Adair*** that focuses on what leaders actually have to do in order to be effective. The action-centered leadership model is illustrated by three overlapping circles representing the three key activities undertaken by leaders: achieving the task, building and maintaining the team, and developing the individual.
JOHN ADAIR (pp. 960–61)

action learning HR & PERSONNEL learning by sharing real problems with others, as opposed to theoretical classroom learning. Action learning was introduced in the mid-1940s by ***Reg Revans***, who expressed it as: Learning = Programmed knowledge + the ability to ask insightful Questions, or L = P + Q. The technique works best when people in small groups tackle real work-based problems with a view to solving them. Action learning differs from ***experiential learning***, which can apply to an individual alone.
REG REVANS (pp. 1042–43)

action research GENERAL MANAGEMENT research in which the researcher takes an involved role as a participant in planning and implementing change. Action research was originated by ***Kurt Lewin***, and it involves conducting experiments by making changes while simultaneously observing the results. Employees are encouraged to participate and to help in developing practical and practicable solutions to real problems.
KURT LEWIN (pp. 1014–15)

active asset FINANCE, BANKING, AND ACCOUNTING an asset that is used in the daily operations of a business

active fund management FINANCE, BANKING, AND ACCOUNTING the managing of a mutual fund by making judgments about market movements instead of relying on automatic adjustments such as indexation. See ***passive investment management***

active listening HR & PERSONNEL a technique for improving understanding of what is being said by taking into account how something is said and the nonverbal signs and ***body language*** that accompany it. This technique requires receptive awareness and response on the part of the listener. Six principles form the core of active listening: encourage people to express opinions; clarify perceptions of what is said; restate essential points and ideas; reflect the speaker's feeling and opinions; summarize the content of the message to check validity; and acknowledge the opinion and contribution of the speaker. It is used particularly in counseling.

active portfolio strategy FINANCE, BANKING, AND ACCOUNTING the managing of an investment portfolio by making judgments about market movements instead of relying on automatic adjustments

activist fiscal policy FINANCE, BANKING, AND ACCOUNTING the policy of a government or national bank that tries to affect the value of its country's money by such measures as changing interest rates for loans to banks and buying or selling foreign currencies

activity based budgeting FINANCE, BANKING, AND ACCOUNTING the allocation of resources to individual activities. Activity based budgeting involves determining which activities incur costs within an organization, establishing the relationships between them, and then deciding how much of the total ***budget*** should be allocated to each activity.

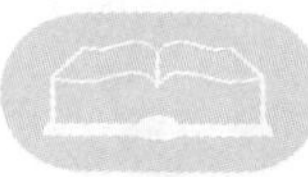

activity based costing FINANCE, BANKING, AND ACCOUNTING, GENERAL MANAGEMENT a method for calculating the cost of a business by focusing on the actual cost of activities, thereby producing an estimate of the cost of individual products or services. Activity based costing may be linked to ***activity based management***, which links with other techniques such as ***benchmarking***, ***performance management***, ***process management***, and reengineering. ABC analysis focuses directly on ***cost drivers*** rather than overheads per se.

activity based management GENERAL MANAGEMENT a management control technique that focuses on the resource costs of organizational activities and processes, and the improvement of quality, profitability, and customer value. This technique uses ***activity based costing*** information to identify strategies for removing resource waste from operating activities. Main tools employed include: ***strategic analysis***, ***value analysis***, cost analysis, ***lifecycle costing***, and ***activity based budgeting***.

activity driver GENERAL MANAGEMENT see ***cost driver***

activity indicator ECONOMICS a statistic used to measure labor productivity or manufacturing output in an economy

activity sampling OPERATIONS & PRODUCTION a ***work measurement*** technique used to analyze the activities of employees, machines, or business operations. Activity sampling requires random observations of the amount of time spent on a given activity to be recorded over a fixed period. The results are used to predict the total time spent on each activity and to highlight areas in need of quality, efficiency, or effectiveness improvement. Also known as ***work sampling***, ***ratio-delay study***, ***random observation method***

ACTU GENERAL MANAGEMENT Australian Council of Trade Unions, Australia's national labor union organization. It was founded in 1927 and is based in Melbourne.

actuals FINANCE, BANKING, AND ACCOUNTING earnings and expenses that have occurred rather than being only projected, or commodities that can be bought and used, as contrasted with commodities traded on a futures contract

actual to date FINANCE, BANKING, AND ACCOUNTING the cumulative value realized by something between an earlier date and the present

actual turnover FINANCE, BANKING, AND ACCOUNTING the number of times during a particular period that somebody spends the average amount of money that he or she has available to spend during that period

actuarial FINANCE, BANKING, AND ACCOUNTING relating to the work of actuaries

actuarial age FINANCE, BANKING, AND ACCOUNTING the statistically derived life expectancy for any given chronological age, used, for example, to calculate the periodic payments from an annuity

actuarial analysis FINANCE, BANKING, AND ACCOUNTING a life expectancy or risk calculation carried out by an actuary

actuarial science FINANCE, BANKING, AND ACCOUNTING, STATISTICS the branch of statistics used in calculating risk and life expectancy for the administration of pension funds and life insurance policies

actuary FINANCE, BANKING, AND ACCOUNTING, STATISTICS a statistician who calculates probable lengths of life so that the insurance premiums to be charged for various risks can be accurately determined

ACU FINANCE, BANKING, AND ACCOUNTING see ***Asian Currency Unit***

ad E-COMMERCE a banner, button, pop-up screen, or other on-screen device calling attention to an e-commerce product or business

Adair, John Eric (*b.* 1934) GENERAL MANAGEMENT British academic. Best known for his three-circle model of ***leadership***, which is based on overlapping circles representing the task, the team, and the individual. Adair's model, otherwise known as ***action-centered leadership***, is described in the book of the same name (1973). Like ***Warren Bennis***, Adair, who has a military background, believes that leadership can be taught.

Adams, Scott (*b.* 1957) GENERAL MANAGEMENT U.S. humorist. Creator of the ***Dilbert principle***, he satirizes the many absurdities of business life through his cartoons.

adaptive control OPERATIONS & PRODUCTION a system of automatic monitoring and adjustment, usually by computer, of an industrial process. Adaptive control allows operating parameters to be changed continuously in response to a changing environment in order to achieve optimum performance.

adaptive measure STATISTICS a means of choosing the most appropriate type of method for a statistical analysis

ad banner E-COMMERCE = ***banner***

ad click E-COMMERCE = ***click-through***

ad click rate E-COMMERCE = ***click-through rate***

added value
1. MARKETING an increase in the attractiveness to customers of a product or a service achieved by adding something to it
2. GENERAL MANAGEMENT see ***value added***

address book E-COMMERCE an e-mail software facility enabling people and businesses to store and manage e-mail addresses and contact information

address verification E-COMMERCE a procedure used by the processor of a credit card to verify that a customer's ordering address matches the address in the customer's record

ADF FINANCE, BANKING, AND ACCOUNTING see ***Approved Deposit Fund***

ad hoc research MARKETING a single, one-off piece of research designed for a particular purpose, as opposed to continuous, regularly repeated, or syndicated research

ad impression E-COMMERCE = ***ad view***

adjusted book value FINANCE, BANKING, AND ACCOUNTING the value of a company in terms of the current market values of its assets and liabilities. Also known as ***modified book value***

adjusted futures price FINANCE, BANKING, AND ACCOUNTING the current value of a futures contract to buy a commodity at a fixed future date

adjusted gross income FINANCE, BANKING, AND ACCOUNTING the amount of annual income that a person or company has after various adjustments for income or corporation tax purposes

adjusted present value FINANCE, BANKING, AND ACCOUNTING the value of a commodity when costs and advantages associated with taxes and borrowing are taken into consideration in addition to its market value

adminisphere GENERAL MANAGEMENT the part of an organization that deals with administrative matters, often perceived negatively by employees because of the apparently unnecessary nature of decisions taken by its members (*slang*)

administration GENERAL MANAGEMENT the management of the affairs of a business, especially the planning and control of its operations

administration school GENERAL MANAGEMENT see ***business administration***

administrivia E-COMMERCE the often tedious tasks associated with maintaining a Web site, mailing list, or any other form of Internet resource (*slang*)

admissibility STATISTICS the property of a procedure if and only if no other of its class exists that performs as well as it and better than it in at least one case

ADR *abbr* FINANCE, BANKING, AND ACCOUNTING American Depository Receipt, a document that indicates a U.S. investor's ownership of stock in a foreign corporation

Adshel™ MARKETING a type of bus shelter, specifically designed to carry advertising posters

ADSL *abbr* E-COMMERCE asymmetrical digital subscriber line, a system that provides high speed, high bandwidth connections to the Internet. ADSL is asymmetric because it has more capacity for data received by a computer than for data to be sent from it. This uneven upload/download balance means that downloaded text and graphics appear quickly and that audiovisual elements are of better quality than when sent via a normal telephone line. ADSL was initially developed by Bellcore Labs in New Jersey in 1993 as a means of bringing bandwidth to homes and small businesses.

adspend MARKETING see ***advertising expenditure***

ad transfer E-COMMERCE = ***click-through***

advance corporation tax FINANCE, BANKING, AND ACCOUNTING a tax paid by a company equal to a percentage of its dividends or other distributions of profit to its shareholders

advanced manufacturing technology GENERAL MANAGEMENT, OPERATIONS & PRODUCTION a high technology development in computing and microelectronics, designed to enhance manufacturing capabilities. Advanced manufacturing technology is used in all areas of manufacturing, including design, control, fabrication, and assembly. This family of technologies includes ***robotics***, ***computer-aided design*** (CAD), ***computer-aided engineering*** (CAE), ***MRP II***, automated ***materials handling*** systems, ***electronic data interchange*** (EDI), computer-integrated manufacturing (CIM) systems, ***flexible manufacturing systems***, and ***group technology***. Abbr **AMT**

advance payment FINANCE, BANKING, AND ACCOUNTING an amount paid before it is earned or incurred, for example, a prepayment by an importer to an exporter before goods are shipped, or a cash advance for travel expenses

adventure learning HR & PERSONNEL see ***adventure training***

adventure training HR & PERSONNEL activities undertaken out of doors and away from the everyday work environment with a view to developing the skills and abilities of participants. Adventure training often takes place at a residential outdoor activity center and may include physically challenging activities such as climbing and abseiling or group exercises and games. The activities are designed to promote ***experiential learning*** in areas such as ***interpersonal communication***, ***problem solving***, ***decision making***, and ***teamwork***, and to develop self-confidence and ***leadership*** skills. Adventure training has its origins in the work of Kurt Hahn, the founder of Gordonstoun School, who developed the Outward Bound program of outdoor activities during World War II. Adventure training programs for organizational personnel became popular during the late 1970s and 1980s, although some have doubted their value and effectiveness. Also known as ***outdoor training***, ***outward bound training***

advertisement MARKETING a public announcement by a company in a newspaper, on television or radio, or over the Internet, intended to attract buyers for a product or service

advertising MARKETING the promotion of goods, services, or ideas, through paid announcements. Advertising aims to persuade or inform the general public and can be used to induce purchase, increase ***brand awareness***, or enhance ***product differentiation***. An advertisement has two main components: the message and the medium by which it is transmitted. Advertising forms just one part of an organization's total marketing strategy.

advertising agency MARKETING an organization that, on behalf of clients, drafts and produces advertisements, places advertisements in the media, and plans ***advertising campaigns***. Advertising agencies may also perform other marketing functions, including ***market research*** and consultancy.

advertising campaign MARKETING a planned program using ***advertising*** aimed at a particular target market or audience over a defined period of time for the purpose of increasing sales or raising awareness of a product or service

advertising department MARKETING the department within an organization that is responsible for ***advertising*** its products or services. An advertising department is also the name given to the section of a publishing house that coordinates the placing of advertisements in its magazines, newspapers, or other publications. It is involved in the sale of advertising space to clients.

advertising expenditure MARKETING the amount spent by an organization on advertising, usually per year. Advertising expenditure is analyzed by breaking it down into the main advertising channels used by companies, such as newspapers, magazines, television, radio, movie theaters, and outdoor advertising. Expenditure can show the total spend nationally, by sector, by type and size of company, or may relate to one company's spend on advertising, including the proportion spent on its specific brands.

advertising manager MARKETING an employee of a business who is responsible for planning and controlling its advertising activities and budgets

advertising media MARKETING the communication channels used for advertising, including television, radio, the printed press, and outdoor advertising

advertising research MARKETING research carried out before or after advertising to ensure or test its effectiveness

advertorial MARKETING a combination of an ***advertisement*** and an article. The content of an advertorial is significantly influenced, and may even be entirely written, by the advertisers. Examples of advertorials include travel or leisure supplements in newspapers or magazines that are designed to attract advertisements from suppliers of relevant goods or services. A criticism of advertorials is that it is sometimes difficult to distinguish between an advertising article and ordinary journalistic articles, particularly when they appear in the same typeface as the other contents of the newspaper or magazine. To overcome this, some advertorials are headed "Advertisement." (*slang*)

advid MARKETING a video used to promote a product or service (*slang*)

ad view E-COMMERCE the number of times a banner or other ad is downloaded and presumably seen on a Web page. Also known as ***ad impression***, ***exposure***

AFAIK *abbr* GENERAL MANAGEMENT as far as I know (*slang*)

affiliate GENERAL MANAGEMENT a company that is controlled by another or is a member of a group, or either of two companies that owns a minority of the voting stock of the other

affiliate directory E-COMMERCE a directory that indexes sites belonging to affiliate schemes. Affiliate directories offer information for companies seeking to subscribe to a scheme, as well as for those wanting to set up affiliate schemes of their own.

affiliate marketing E-COMMERCE the use of ***affiliate programs***

affiliate partner MARKETING a company that markets a product or service on the Internet for another company

affiliate program E-COMMERCE an advertising program in which one merchant induces others to place his or her banners and buttons on their Web sites in return for a commission on purchases made by their customers. Also known as ***associate program***

affinity card MARKETING a credit or debit card for which the issuing bank makes a donation to a specified charity each time it is used

affirmative action HR & PERSONNEL preferential treatment, usually through a quota system, to prevent, or correct, discriminatory employment practices, particularly relating to recruitment and promotion. The term is widely used in the United States, whereas, in the United Kingdom, **positive discrimination** is the preferred term.

affluent society FINANCE, BANKING, AND ACCOUNTING a community in which material wealth is widely distributed

affluenza GENERAL MANAGEMENT feelings of unhappiness, stress, and guilt induced by the pursuit and possession of wealth (*slang*)

AFTA FINANCE, BANKING, AND ACCOUNTING see ***ASEAN Free Trade Area***

after-acquired collateral FINANCE, BANKING, AND ACCOUNTING collateral for a loan that a borrower obtains after making the contract for the loan

after-sales service MARKETING customer support following the purchase of a product or service. In some cases, after-sales service can be almost as important as the initial purchase. The manufacturer, retailer, or service provider determines what is included in any **warranty** (or guarantee) package. This will include the duration of the warranty—traditionally one year from the date of purchase, but increasingly two or more years—maintenance and/or replacement policy, items included/excluded, labor costs, and speed of response. In the case of a service provider, after-sales service might include additional top-up training or helpdesk availability. Of equal importance is the customer's perception of the degree of willingness with which a supplier deals with a query or complaint, speed of response, and action taken.

✔ SETTING UP A CUSTOMER SERVICE PROGRAM (pp. 478–79)

after-tax FINANCE, BANKING, AND ACCOUNTING relating to earnings or income from which tax has already been deducted

AG *abbr* FINANCE, BANKING, AND ACCOUNTING Aktiengesellschaft, used after the title of a German, Austrian, or Swiss business to identify it as a public limited company

against actuals FINANCE, BANKING, AND ACCOUNTING relating to a trade between owners of futures contracts that allows both to reduce their positions to cash instead of commodities

aged debt FINANCE, BANKING, AND ACCOUNTING a debt that is overdue by one or more given periods, usually increments of 30 days

aged debtor FINANCE, BANKING, AND ACCOUNTING a person or organization responsible for an overdue debt

age discrimination HR & PERSONNEL unfavorable treatment in employment based on prejudice in relation to a person's age. While age discrimination affects people at all stages of their working lives, difficulties experienced in selection, development, and promotion can be particularly acute at the two extremes of the age spectrum. Countries such as Australia have passed legislation to make it unlawful to discriminate on grounds of age.

ageism HR & PERSONNEL see ***age discrimination***

agency GENERAL MANAGEMENT a relationship between two people or organizations in which one is empowered to act on behalf of the other in dealings with a third party

agency commission MARKETING a percentage of advertising expenditure rebated to an advertising agency, media buyer, or client organization by a media owner

agency mark-up MARKETING a management fee charged by an advertising agency in addition to the cost of external services that it buys on behalf of a client

agenda GENERAL MANAGEMENT a list of topics to be discussed or business to be transacted during the course of a meeting, usually sent to those invited to attend prior to the meeting

agent GENERAL MANAGEMENT

1. a person or organization empowered to act on behalf of another when dealing with a third party

2. see ***executive***

agent bank (*ANZ*) FINANCE, BANKING, AND ACCOUNTING a bank that acts on behalf of a foreign bank, or a bank that participates in another bank's credit card program, acting as a depository for merchants

age pension (*ANZ*) FINANCE, BANKING, AND ACCOUNTING a sum of money paid regularly by the government to people who have reached the age of retirement, currently 65 for men and 60 for women

aggregate demand ECONOMICS the sum of all expenditures in an economy that makes up its ***GDP***, for example, consumers' expenditure on goods and services, investment in ***capital stocks***, and government spending

aggregate income FINANCE, BANKING, AND ACCOUNTING the total of all incomes in an economy without adjustments for inflation, taxation, or types of double counting

aggregate output ECONOMICS the total value of all goods and services produced in an economy

aggregate planning OPERATIONS & PRODUCTION medium-range ***capacity planning***, typically covering a period of 3 to 18 months. Aggregate planning is used in a manufacturing environment and determines not only the overall output levels planned but the appropriate resource input mix to be used for related

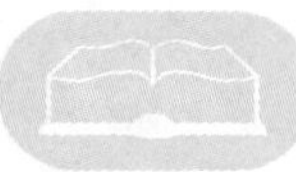

groups of products. Generally, planners focus on overall or aggregate capacity rather than on individual products or services. Aggregate planning can be used to influence demand as well as supply, in which case variables such as price, advertising, and the product mix are taken into account.

aggregate supply ECONOMICS the total of all goods and services produced in an economy

aggregator E-COMMERCE, MARKETING an organization that acts as an intermediary between producers and customers in an Internet business web. The aggregator selects products, sets prices, and ensures fulfillment of orders.

aggressive GENERAL MANAGEMENT relating to an investment strategy marked by willingness to accept high risk while trying to realize higher than average gains. Such a strategy involves investing in rapidly growing companies that promise capital appreciation but produce little or no income from dividends and de-emphasizes income-producing instruments such as bonds.

aggressive growth fund FINANCE, BANKING, AND ACCOUNTING a mutual fund that takes considerable risks in the hope of making large profits

agile manufacturing OPERATIONS & PRODUCTION a manufacturing philosophy that focuses on meeting the demands of customers by adopting flexible manufacturing practices. Agile manufacturing emerged as a reaction to ***lean production***. It differs by focusing on meeting the demands of customers without sacrificing quality or incurring added costs. Based on the idea of ***virtual organization***, agile manufacturing aims to develop flexible, often short-term, relationships with suppliers, as market opportunities arise. Stock control is considered less important than satisfying the customer, and so ***customer satisfaction*** measures become more important than output measures. Agile manufacturing requires an adaptable, innovative, and empowered work force.

agility GENERAL MANAGEMENT the organizational capability to be flexible, responsive, adaptive, and show initiative in times of change and uncertainty. Agility has origins in manufacturing and has been cited as a source of ***competitive advantage*** by many management gurus, including ***Rosabeth Moss Kanter*** and ***Tom Peters***. One writer who has explored the concept of agility in greater depth is ***Richard Pascale***, for whom the key to agility lies in what the organization is, as opposed to what it does. Agility grew as a reaction against the slowness of ***bureaucratic*** organizations to respond to changing market conditions. The ***virtual organization*** has been quoted as one extreme example of an agile organization.

ROSABETH MOSS KANTER (pp. 1008–09); RICHARD TANNER PASCALE (pp. 1034–35); TOM PETERS (pp. 1036–37)

AGM (*U.K.*) GENERAL MANAGEMENT = ***annual meeting***

agora E-COMMERCE a marketplace on the Internet. The term comes from an ancient Greek word for "market."

agreement of sale GENERAL MANAGEMENT a written contract specifying the terms under which the buyer agrees to buy particular real estate and the seller agrees to sell it

AHI (*S. Africa*) GENERAL MANAGEMENT Afrikaanse Handelsinstituut, the national chamber of commerce for Afrikaans businesses

aim GENERAL MANAGEMENT see ***objective***

AIM FINANCE, BANKING, AND ACCOUNTING Alternative Investment Market, the London market trading in shares of emerging or small companies not eligible for listing on the London Stock Exchange. It replaced the Unlisted Securities Market (USM) in 1995.

AIRC HR & PERSONNEL see ***Australian Industrial Relations Commission***

airtime MARKETING the amount of time given to an advertisement on television, radio, or in movie theaters

alignment GENERAL MANAGEMENT the process of building a corporate culture to achieve strategic goals

all equity rate FINANCE, BANKING, AND ACCOUNTING the interest rate that a lender charges because of the apparent risks of a project that are independent of the normal market risks of financing it

All Industrials Index FINANCE, BANKING, AND ACCOUNTING a subindex of the Australian All Ordinaries Index that includes all the companies from that index that are not involved in resources or mining

All Mining Index FINANCE, BANKING, AND ACCOUNTING a subindex of the Australian All Ordinaries Index that includes all the companies from that index that are involved in the mining industry

All Ordinaries Accumulation Index FINANCE, BANKING, AND ACCOUNTING a measure of the change in share prices on the Australian Stock Exchange, based on the All Ordinaries Index, but assuming that all dividends are reinvested

All Ordinaries Index FINANCE, BANKING, AND ACCOUNTING the major index of Australian stocks, comprising more than 300 of the most active Australian companies listed on the Australian Stock Exchange. Abbr **All Ords**

all-or-none underwriting (*ANZ*) FINANCE, BANKING, AND ACCOUNTING the option of canceling a public offering of stock if the underwriting is not fully subscribed

All Resources Index FINANCE, BANKING, AND ACCOUNTING a subindex of the Australian All Ordinaries Index that includes all the companies from that index that are involved in the resources industry

alphabet theories of management GENERAL MANAGEMENT management theories named along the lines of ***Douglas McGregor***'s ***Theory X*** and ***Theory Y***. Alphabet theories of management include ***Theory E***, ***Theory J***, ***Theory O***, ***Theory W***, and ***Theory Z***.

DOUGLAS MCGREGOR (pp. 1022–23)

alpha geek GENERAL MANAGEMENT the person who knows most about computer technology in a company or department (*slang*)

alpha test GENERAL MANAGEMENT a test of a new or upgraded piece of computer software or hardware carried out by the manufacturer before it is released to the public

alpha value FINANCE, BANKING, AND ACCOUNTING a sum paid to an employee when he or she leaves a company that can be transferred to a concessionally taxed investment account such as an ***Approved Deposit Fund***

alternate director FINANCE, BANKING, AND ACCOUNTING a person who is allowed to act for an absent named director of a company at a board meeting

alternative investment FINANCE, BANKING, AND ACCOUNTING an investment other than in bonds or shares of a large company or one listed on a stock exchange

Alternative Investment Market FINANCE, BANKING, AND ACCOUNTING see ***AIM***

alternative mortgage instrument FINANCE, BANKING, AND ACCOUNTING any form of mortgage other than a fixed-term amortizing loan

amalgamation GENERAL MANAGEMENT the process of two or more organizations joining together for mutual benefit, either through a ***merger*** or ***consolidation***

Amazon E-COMMERCE to claim a significant portion of the market from a traditional retail business that failed to develop an effective e-business strategy. The term stems from the seemingly overnight success of online bookseller Amazon.com™.

ambit claim *(ANZ)* GENERAL MANAGEMENT a claim made to an arbitration authority for higher pay or improved conditions that is deliberately exaggerated because the claimants know that they will subsequently have to compromise

American Depository Receipt FINANCE, BANKING, AND ACCOUNTING see ***ADR***

American option FINANCE, BANKING, AND ACCOUNTING an option contract that can be exercised at any time up to and including the expiration date. Most exchange-traded options are of this style. See ***European option***. Also known as ***American style option***

American Stock Exchange FINANCE, BANKING, AND ACCOUNTING see ***AMEX***

American style option FINANCE, BANKING, AND ACCOUNTING see ***American option***

AMEX FINANCE, BANKING, AND ACCOUNTING American Stock Exchange, a New York stock exchange listing smaller and less mature companies that those listed on the larger New York Stock Exchange (NYSE)

amortization FINANCE, BANKING, AND ACCOUNTING the gradual reduction of the value of an asset by systematically writing off its cost over a period of time, or the repayment of a debt in a series of regular installments or transfers

✔ HOW TO CONDUCT AMORTIZATION (p. 866)

amortize FINANCE, BANKING, AND ACCOUNTING to gradually reduce the value of an asset by systematically writing off its cost over a period of time, or to repay a debt in a series of regular installments or transfers

amortized value FINANCE, BANKING, AND ACCOUNTING the value at a particular time of a financial instrument that is being amortized

AMPS FINANCE, BANKING, AND ACCOUNTING see ***auction market preferred stock***

AMT OPERATIONS & PRODUCTION see ***advanced manufacturing technology***

analysis of variance STATISTICS the process of separating the statistical variance caused by a particular factor from that caused by other factors

analysis of variance table STATISTICS a table that shows the total variation in the observations in a statistical data set

angel investor E-COMMERCE an individual or group of individuals willing to invest in an unproven but well-researched e-business idea. Angel investors are typically the first port of call for Internet startups looking for financial backing, because they are more inclined to provide early funding than ***venture capital*** firms are. After investing in a company, angel investors take an advisory role without making demands.

angry fruit salad E-COMMERCE a garish and unattractive visual interface on a computer *(slang)*

angular histogram STATISTICS a histogram that represents data in a circular form

announcement FINANCE, BANKING, AND ACCOUNTING a statement that a company makes to provide information on its trading prospects that will be of interest to its existing and potential investors

annoyware E-COMMERCE a shareware program that repeatedly interrupts normal functioning to remind users they are using an unregistered copy and will have to pay in order to continue *(slang)*

annual general meeting *(U.K.)* GENERAL MANAGEMENT U.K. = ***annual meeting***

annual hours HR & PERSONNEL a ***flexible working hours*** practice in which working hours are averaged over a year. Employees are contracted to work a given number of hours per year rather than the traditional number of hours per week. Earnings are determined on a similar basis, but usually a fixed weekly or monthly salary is paid regardless of the number of hours worked. Hours are worked when demand dictates and therefore the need for ***overtime*** diminishes. Annual hours systems usually cover manual ***shiftworkers***, rather than other parts of the workforce.

annual meeting GENERAL MANAGEMENT a yearly meeting at which a company's management reports the year's results and stockholders have the opportunity to vote on company business, for example, the appointment of directors and auditors. Other business, for example, voting on dividend payments and board, and stockholder-sponsored resolutions, may also be transacted.

annual percentage rate *or* **annualized percentage rate** FINANCE, BANKING, AND ACCOUNTING see ***APR***

annual percentage yield FINANCE, BANKING, AND ACCOUNTING the effective or true annual rate of return on an investment, taking into account the effect of compounding. For example, an annual percentage rate of 6% compounded monthly translates into an annual percentage yield of 6.17%.

annual report GENERAL MANAGEMENT a document prepared each year to give a true and fair view of a company's state of affairs. Annual reports are issued to shareholders and filed at the Securities and Exchange Commission in accordance with the provisions of company legislation. Contents include a profit and loss account and ***balance sheet***, directors' report, auditors' report, and, where a company has subsidiaries, the company's group accounts.

✔ HOW TO READ AN ANNUAL REPORT (pp. 862–63)

annuity FINANCE, BANKING, AND ACCOUNTING a contract in which a person pays a lump-sum premium to an insurance company and in return receives periodic payments, usually yearly, often beginning on retirement

✔ HOW TO CALCULATE THE FUTURE VALUE OF AN ANNUITY (p. 836)

annuity in arrears FINANCE, BANKING, AND ACCOUNTING an annuity whose first payment is due at least one payment period after the start date of the annuity's contract

anorexic organization GENERAL MANAGEMENT an organization that has become so small that it has lost the strength and depth to compete effectively. An anorexic organization may have been through the process of extreme ***downsizing*** or ***delayering***, probably with accompanying ***redundancies***.

ANSI X.12 standard E-COMMERCE an American National Standards Institute-supported protocol for the electronic interchange of business transactions. Also known as ***X.12***

Ansoff, H. Igor *(b.* 1918) GENERAL MANAGEMENT Russian-born manager and academic. Established ***strategic planning*** (see ***planning***) as a management activity, developing a framework of tools and techniques by which strategic planning decisions could be made. He explained his approach in *Corporate Strategy* (1965). One of his most well-known models is the ***three Ss***. He later introduced the concept of ***strategic management***.

✔ STRATEGIC PLANNING (pp. 484–85)
IGOR ANSOFF (pp. 962–63)

anticipation note FINANCE, BANKING, AND ACCOUNTING a bond that a borrower intends to pay off with money from taxes due or money to be borrowed in a later and larger transaction

anticipatory hedging FINANCE, BANKING, AND ACCOUNTING hedging carried out before the transaction to which the hedge applies occurs

anticipointment GENERAL MANAGEMENT high public expectations of a new product, entertainment, or service that are subsequently disappointed (*slang*)

anti-dumping ECONOMICS intended to prevent the sale of goods on a foreign market at a price below their ***marginal cost***

anti-site E-COMMERCE a Web site devoted to attacking a company or organization. Typically, an anti-site is set up by an aggrieved customer who has been unable to contribute his or her opinion to the company's Web site. Anti-sites are often intended to parody or replicate the site they are targeting. In some instances, an anti-site can beat the official site in the search engine rankings by generating more site visits. Also known as ***hate site***

antitrust GENERAL MANAGEMENT relating to legislative initiatives aimed at protecting trade and commerce from monopolistic business practices that restrict or eliminate competition. Antitrust laws also attempt to curb trusts and cartels and to keep them from employing monopolistic practices to make unfair profits.

ANZCERTA FINANCE, BANKING, AND ACCOUNTING see ***Australia and New Zealand Closer Economic Relations Trade Agreement***

APEC FINANCE, BANKING, AND ACCOUNTING Asia-Pacific Economic Cooperation, a forum designed to promote trade and economic cooperation among countries bordering the Pacific Ocean. It was set up in 1989. Members include Australia, Indonesia, Thailand, the Philippines, Singapore, Brunei, and Japan.

applet E-COMMERCE a small application, usually written in ***Java***. Owing to their miniature size, applets can be set to download automatically when an Internet user visits a Web page.

application form HR & PERSONNEL a form used in the ***recruitment*** process to enable a job candidate to supply information about his or her qualifications, skills, and experience. Employers may ask a candidate to complete an application form instead of, or as well as, providing a ***résumé***. Application forms should be reviewed regularly to ensure that questions asked take account of current legislation, accepted good practice, and internal organizational developments. These questions should be job-related and avoid unjustifiable intrusion into a candidate's personal life.

application program interface GENERAL MANAGEMENT a computer program or piece of software designed to perform a function directly for a user, for example, a word processor, spell checker, or spreadsheet

application server E-COMMERCE an advanced type of server used to run programming languages that help Web sites to deliver dynamic information such as the latest news headlines, stock quotes, personalized information, or shopping carts

application service provider E-COMMERCE see ***ASP***

applied economics ECONOMICS the practical application of theoretical economic principles, especially in formulating national and international economic policies

appointment

1. GENERAL MANAGEMENT an engagement to meet at a particular place and time for a particular purpose
2. HR & PERSONNEL a position or job

appraisal HR & PERSONNEL see ***performance appraisal***

appropriation FINANCE, BANKING, AND ACCOUNTING a sum of money that has been allocated for a particular purpose

Approved Deposit Fund (*ANZ*) FINANCE, BANKING, AND ACCOUNTING a concessionally taxed fund managed by a financial institution into which Eligible Termination Payments can be transferred from a superannuation fund. Abbr **ADF**

APR *abbr* FINANCE, BANKING, AND ACCOUNTING Annual or Annualized Percentage Rate of interest, the interest rate that would exist if it were calculated as simple rather than compound interest. Also known as ***annual percentage rate***, ***effective annual interest rate***, ***nominal annual rate***

✔ HOW TO CALCULATE ANNUAL PERCENTAGE RATE (p. 822)

APRA FINANCE, BANKING, AND ACCOUNTING Australian Prudential Regulation Authority, a federal government body responsible for ensuring that financial institutions are able to meet their commitments

aptitude test HR & PERSONNEL a measure of a person's natural ability or potential to learn a skill or set of skills. Abilities that are typically measured by aptitude tests include abstract, verbal, and numerical reasoning, because these give a rounded view of a person's general ability in relation to the workplace. Aptitude tests are a form of ***psychometric test*** and are administered by trained users.

arb GENERAL MANAGEMENT, FINANCE, BANKING, AND ACCOUNTING an ***arbitrageur*** (*slang*)

arbitrage FINANCE, BANKING, AND ACCOUNTING the buying and selling of foreign currencies, products, or financial securities between two or more markets in order to make an immediate profit by exploiting differences in market prices quoted

arbitrage pricing theory FINANCE, BANKING, AND ACCOUNTING a model of financial instrument and portfolio behavior that provides a benchmark of return and risk for capital budgeting and securities analysis. It can be used to create portfolios that track a market index, estimate the risk of an asset allocation strategy, or estimate the response of a portfolio to economic developments.

arbitrageur FINANCE, BANKING, AND ACCOUNTING a firm or individual who purchases shares or financial securities to make a windfall profit

arbitration GENERAL MANAGEMENT, HR & PERSONNEL the settlement of a dispute by an independent third person, rather than by a court of law. Arbitration allows for claims or grievances to be settled quickly, cost-effectively, privately, and by somebody who is suitably qualified. A contract may include an arbitration clause to be invoked in the case of a dispute. ***Mediation*** is a related term.

arbitrator GENERAL MANAGEMENT an impartial person accepted by both parties in a dispute to hear both sides and make a judgment

area sampling STATISTICS a form of sampling in which a region is subdivided and some of the divisions are then selected at random for a complete survey

area under a curve STATISTICS a means of summarizing the information from a series of statistical measurements made over a period of time such as a month

Argyris, Christopher (*b.* 1923) GENERAL MANAGEMENT U.S. academic and consultant. Known for his work on ***training*** and ***organizational learning***, specifically ***T-Groups*** (see ***sensitivity training***), and single-loop and double-loop learning. Argyris's research is set out in *Organizational Learning* (1978), cowritten with ***Donald Schön***. Their work also produced the idea of a ***learning organization***, later developed by ***Peter Senge***.

CHRIS ARGYRIS (pp. 964–65); PETER SENGE (pp. 1046–47)

Arizmendietta, Jose Maria (1915–77) GENERAL MANAGEMENT Basque priest, more commonly known as Father Arizmendi. Cofounder of the ***Mondragon cooperative*** movement.

armchair economics GENERAL MANAGEMENT economic forecasting or theorizing based on insufficient data or knowledge of a subject (*slang*)

arm's-length price FINANCE, BANKING, AND ACCOUNTING a price at which an unrelated seller and buyer agree to transact on an asset or a product

ARPAnet E-COMMERCE the precursor to the Internet, an experimental network that linked scientists engaged in military research. It was developed by the U.S. Defense Department in the late 1960s, and was originally intended to link together different computers spread throughout the world.

arrow shooter GENERAL MANAGEMENT a person within an organization who produces visionary new ideas (*slang*)

art director MARKETING a person who is responsible for planning and designing the creative element for advertisements and other communications material

articles of incorporation FINANCE, BANKING, AND ACCOUNTING a legal document that creates a privately held company whose powers are governed by the general corporation laws of the state in which it was founded

artificial intelligence GENERAL MANAGEMENT a branch of computer science concerned with the development of computer systems capable of performing functions that normally require human intelligence, for example, reasoning, problem solving, learning from experience, and speech recognition. Artificial intelligence research combines elements of computer science and cognitive psychology. It is a controversial field because of the difficulty of defining its goals and disagreement over whether these goals are attainable. Much research has been done since World War II, beginning with the theoretical work of Alan Turing during the 1940s. The term became known with the publication in 1961 of the paper *Steps Towards Artificial Intelligence* by Marvin Minsky, cofounder with John McCarthy of the Artificial Intelligence Laboratory at Massachusetts Institute of Technology. Branches of artificial intelligence with applications in business and management include ***expert systems*** and ***robotics***.

ASAP *abbr* GENERAL MANAGEMENT as soon as possible (*slang*)

ASEAN Free Trade Area FINANCE, BANKING, AND ACCOUNTING a conceptual regional free trade agreement supported by Singapore to foster trade within the region. Abbr **AFTA**

A share (*U.K.*) FINANCE, BANKING, AND ACCOUNTING a nonvoting share of stock in a company issued to raise additional capital without diluting control of the company

Asian Currency Unit FINANCE, BANKING, AND ACCOUNTING a bookkeeping unit used for recording transactions made by approved financial institutions operating in the Asian Dollar market. Abbr **ACU**

ASIC FINANCE, BANKING, AND ACCOUNTING see ***Australian Securities and Investments Commission***

ask FINANCE, BANKING, AND ACCOUNTING the bid price at which a dealer in stocks and shares, commodities, or financial securities is prepared to buy the stocks and shares, commodities, or securities

asking price FINANCE, BANKING, AND ACCOUNTING the price that a seller puts on something before any negotiation

ASP FINANCE, BANKING, AND ACCOUNTING an application service provider, a hosting service that will operate, support, manage, and maintain a company's software applications for a fee

assembly OPERATIONS & PRODUCTION the joining together of components to make a complete product

assembly line OPERATIONS & PRODUCTION a line of production in which a number of assembly operations are performed in a set sequence. The speed of movement of an assembly line has to be matched with the skills and abilities of the ***workforce*** and the complexity of the assembly process to be performed. The assembly line emerged from the ideas of ***scientific management*** and was popularized by a number of entrepreneurs, including ***Henry Ford*** in the car production industry.

assembly plant OPERATIONS & PRODUCTION the building in which an ***assembly line*** is housed

assessed loss FINANCE, BANKING, AND ACCOUNTING the excess of tax-deductible expenses over taxable income as confirmed by the South African Revenue Service. It may be carried forward and deducted in determining the taxpayer's taxable income in subsequent years of assessment.

assessed value FINANCE, BANKING, AND ACCOUNTING a value for something that is calculated by a person such as an investment advisor

assessment center HR & PERSONNEL a process whereby a group of participants undertakes a series of job-related exercises under observation, so that skills, competencies, and character traits can be assessed. Specially trained assessors evaluate each participant against predetermined criteria. Various methods of assessment may be used, including interviews, ***psychometric tests***, group discussions, group problem solving exercises, individual job-simulated tasks, and role-plays. Assessment centers are used in selection for recruitment and promotion, and in training and development, and aim to provide an organization with an assessment process that is consistent, free of prejudice, and fair.

assessment of competence HR & PERSONNEL the measurement of an employee's performance against an agreed set of standards for work-based activities. In the United Kingdom, assessment of competence is generally made against indicators of the successful achievement of a particular job function. There are four dimensions to assessment: the knowledge and understanding required to

carry out a task; the ***performance indicators*** to be looked for; the scope or range of situations across which an employee is expected to perform; and any particular evidence requirements. ***Vocational qualifications*** for a wide range of jobs in the United Kingdom are based on a set of occupational standards that contain these elements. A wide variety of techniques or instruments exists to assess ***competence***. These include specific work-based ability and ***aptitude tests***, as well as traditional methods of ***performance appraisal*** and evaluation. Recent years have seen a dramatic rise in the use of direct observation at work by trained assessors, the collection of personal portfolios, and peer assessment techniques such as ***360 degree appraisal***. All require the careful review of work behavior against a set of indicators that have been clearly shown to be associated with successful performance.

asset FINANCE, BANKING, AND ACCOUNTING, GENERAL MANAGEMENT any tangible or intangible item to which a value can be assigned. Assets can be physical, such as machinery and consumer durables, or financial, such as cash and accounts receivable.

asset allocation *(ANZ)* FINANCE, BANKING, AND ACCOUNTING an investment strategy that distributes investments in a portfolio so as to achieve the highest investment return while minimizing risk. Such a strategy usually apportions investments among cash equivalents, stock in domestic and foreign companies, fixed-income investments, and real estate.

asset-backed security ECONOMICS, FINANCE, BANKING, AND ACCOUNTING a security for which the collateral is neither land nor land-based financial instruments

asset-based lending FINANCE, BANKING, AND ACCOUNTING the lending of money with the expectation that the proceeds from an asset or assets will allow the borrower to repay the loan

asset conversion loan FINANCE, BANKING, AND ACCOUNTING a loan that the borrower will repay with money raised by selling an asset

asset coverage FINANCE, BANKING, AND ACCOUNTING the ratio measuring a company's solvency and consisting of its net assets divided by its debt

asset demand ECONOMICS the amount of assets held as money, which will be low when interest rates are high and high when interest rates are low

asset financing FINANCE, BANKING, AND ACCOUNTING the borrowing of money by a company using its assets as collateral

asset for asset swap FINANCE, BANKING, AND ACCOUNTING an exchange of one bankrupt debtor's debt for that of another

asset management *(ANZ)* FINANCE, BANKING, AND ACCOUNTING an investment service offered by some financial institutions that combines banking and brokerage services

asset play FINANCE, BANKING, AND ACCOUNTING a purchase of a company's stock in the belief that it has assets that are not properly documented and therefore unknown to others

asset pricing model FINANCE, BANKING, AND ACCOUNTING a model used to determine the profit that an asset will yield

asset protection trust FINANCE, BANKING, AND ACCOUNTING a trust, often set up in a foreign country, used to make the trust's principal inaccessible to creditors

asset restructuring FINANCE, BANKING, AND ACCOUNTING the purchase or sale of assets worth more than 50% of a listed company's total or net assets

asset side FINANCE, BANKING, AND ACCOUNTING the side of a balance sheet that shows the economic resources a firm owns, for example, cash on hand or in bank deposits, products, or buildings and fixtures

assets requirements FINANCE, BANKING, AND ACCOUNTING the assets needed for a business to continue trading

asset-stripper FINANCE, BANKING, AND ACCOUNTING a company that acquires another company and sells its assets to make a profit without regard for the acquired company's future business success

asset-stripping FINANCE, BANKING, AND ACCOUNTING the purchase of a company whose market value is below its asset value, usually so that the buyer may sell the assets for immediate gain. The buyer usually has little or no concern for the purchased company's employees or other ***stakeholders***, so the practice is generally frowned on.

asset substitution FINANCE, BANKING, AND ACCOUNTING the purchase of assets that involve more risk than those a lender expected the borrower to buy

asset swap FINANCE, BANKING, AND ACCOUNTING an exchange of assets between companies so that they may divest parts no longer required and enter another product area

asset turnover FINANCE, BANKING, AND ACCOUNTING the ratio of a firm's sales revenue to its total assets, used as a measure of the firm's business efficiency

asset valuation FINANCE, BANKING, AND ACCOUNTING the aggregated value of the assets of a firm, usually the capital assets, as entered on its balance sheet

assign FINANCE, BANKING, AND ACCOUNTING to transfer ownership of an asset to another person or organization

assignable cause of variation OPERATIONS & PRODUCTION an evident reason for deviation from the norm. An assignable cause exists when variation within a process can be attributed to a particular cause that is a fundamental part of the process. Once identified, the assignable cause of the errors must be investigated and the process adjusted before other possible causes of variation are examined. Using the technique of ***statistical process control***, control charts can be used to distinguish causes that are assignable from those that are random.

assigned risk FINANCE, BANKING, AND ACCOUNTING a poor insurance risk that a company is required by law to insure against

associate *(ANZ)* FINANCE, BANKING, AND ACCOUNTING a member of a stock exchange who does not have a seat on the exchange

associate program E-COMMERCE = ***affiliate program***

assumable mortgage FINANCE, BANKING, AND ACCOUNTING a mortgage that the buyer of a property can take over from the seller

assumed bond FINANCE, BANKING, AND ACCOUNTING a bond for which a company other than the issuer takes over responsibility

assumption STATISTICS the conditions under which valid results can be obtained from a statistical technique

assured shorthold tenancy GENERAL MANAGEMENT a tenancy for a fixed period of at least six months during which the tenant cannot be evicted other than by court order. Any new tenancy without a written agreement is an assured shorthold tenancy.

assured tenancy FINANCE, BANKING, AND ACCOUNTING a tenancy for an indefinite period in which the tenant cannot be evicted other than by court order

ASX FINANCE, BANKING, AND ACCOUNTING see ***Australian Stock Exchange***

ASX 100 FINANCE, BANKING, AND ACCOUNTING a measure of the change in share prices on the ***Australian Stock Exchange*** based on changes in the stocks of the top 100 companies. Similar indexes include the ASX 20, ASX 50, ASX 200, and ASX 300.

asymmetrical digital subscriber line E-COMMERCE see ***ADSL***

asymmetrical distribution STATISTICS a frequency or probability distribution of statistical data that is not symmetrical about a central value in the data

asymmetric taxation FINANCE, BANKING, AND ACCOUNTING a difference in tax status between parties to a transaction, typically making the transaction attractive to both parties because of taxes that one or both can avoid

asynchronous transmission E-COMMERCE the transmission of data in which the end of the transmission of one unit denotes the start of the next, rather than transmission at fixed intervals

Athos, Anthony G. GENERAL MANAGEMENT U.S. academic. See ***Pascale, Richard Tanner***

ATM GENERAL MANAGEMENT see ***automated teller machine***

ATO FINANCE, BANKING, AND ACCOUNTING see ***Australian Taxation Office***

atom MARKETING any traditional nondigital means of delivering information such as a newspaper, book, or magazine

atomize GENERAL MANAGEMENT to split a large organization into smaller operating units

attachment E-COMMERCE a file that is attached to a standard text e-mail message

attendance HR & PERSONNEL presence at work, normally noted in an attendance register. The phenomenon of irregular attendance is referred to as ***absenteeism***. One method of improving attendance is by paying an ***attendance bonus***.

attendance bonus HR & PERSONNEL a financial or nonfinancial incentive offered to employees by an employer to arrive for work on time

attention management GENERAL MANAGEMENT a method of ensuring that employees are focused on their work and on organizational goals. Attention management is similar to ***time management***, as inattentiveness results in wasted time, and to ***information overload***. An important factor in winning and sustaining attention is tapping into people's emotions.

attitude GENERAL MANAGEMENT a mental position consisting of a feeling, emotion, or opinion evolved in response to an external situation. An attitude can be momentary or can develop into a habitual position that has a long-term influence on an individual's behavior. Attempts can be made to modify attitudes that have a negative effect in the workplace, for example, through education and training. The ***employee attitude survey*** is one tool used to assess prevalent attitudes in the workforce.

attitude research GENERAL MANAGEMENT an investigation into people's beliefs regarding an organization, its products or services, or its activities. Attitude research is used in marketing to ascertain opinions among consumers and the public in general. It is also used within organizations when ***employee attitude surveys*** are conducted.

attitude survey MARKETING a piece of research carried out to assess the feelings of a target audience toward a product, brand, or organization

attribute sampling OPERATIONS & PRODUCTION a random testing method for determining the quality of a finished product by inspecting a sample number of the items in each batch. The items selected are examined for a particular attribute, which is usually an abnormal or negative characteristic—for example, a sample of cars from one production run might be inspected for poor paintwork, and the number of sampled cars found with this attribute used to calculate the number of defective items in the whole batch.

attribution theory of leadership GENERAL MANAGEMENT a theory suggesting that leaders observe their followers' behavior, attribute it to particular causes, and as a result respond in a particular way. Attribution theory is rooted in psychology and proposes that people analyze events occurring around them to try to determine cause and effect relationships. It has been suggested that leaders utilize attribution to try to assess the behavior of their followers, in particular, their performance, and then to decide how to deal with good or poor performers.

auction E-COMMERCE, FINANCE, BANKING, AND ACCOUNTING a sale of goods or property by competitive bidding on the spot, by mail, telecommunications, or over the Internet

auction market preferred stock FINANCE, BANKING, AND ACCOUNTING stock in a company owned in the United Kingdom that pays dividends whose amounts track a money-market index. Abbr **AMPS**

AUD *abbr* FINANCE, BANKING, AND ACCOUNTING Australian dollar

audience MARKETING the total number of readers, viewers, or listeners who are exposed to an advertisement

audience research MARKETING research carried out to measure the size or composition of the target audience for a piece of advertising

audit FINANCE, BANKING, AND ACCOUNTING an accountant's formal examination and verification of the accuracy and completeness of financial records, especially those of a business. An ***internal audit*** is conducted by an employee of the business, and an ***external audit*** is performed by an independent outsider.

audit committee FINANCE, BANKING, AND ACCOUNTING a committee of a company's board of directors, from which the company's executives are excluded, that monitors the company's finances

audit of management GENERAL MANAGEMENT see ***operational audit***

Auditor-General FINANCE, BANKING, AND ACCOUNTING an officer of an Australian state or territory government who is responsible for ensuring that government expenditure is made in accordance with legislation

auditor's report FINANCE, BANKING, AND ACCOUNTING a certification by an auditor that a firm's financial records give a true and fair view of its profit and loss for the period

audit report GENERAL MANAGEMENT the summary submission made by auditors of the findings of an ***audit***. An audit report is usually of the financial records and accounts of a company and is a legal annual requirement in the United Kingdom. The report is filed with the Registrar of Companies along with the accounts. An auditor's report normally takes one of the forms approved by the accountancy professional organizations to cover all requirements imposed by law on the auditor. If reports do not support the company's records, they may be termed "qualified." A report is qualified if it contains any indication that the auditor has failed to satisfy himself or herself on any of the points that the law requires. The qualification may, for example, add a rider stating that the appointed auditor has had to rely on secondary information supplied by other auditors under circumstances in which it has been inappropriate to do otherwise. Qualifications may also refer to the inadequacy of information or explanations supplied, or to the fact that the auditor is not satisfied that proper books or other records are being kept.

audit trail GENERAL MANAGEMENT the records of all the sequential stages of a transaction. An audit trail may trace the process of a purchase, a sale, a customer complaint, or the supply of goods. Tracing what happened at each stage through the records can be a useful method of ***problem solving***. In financial markets, audit trails may be used to ensure fairness and accuracy on the part of the dealers.

aural signature MARKETING a musical theme that is part of a company or product's brand identity

Aussie Mac FINANCE, BANKING, AND ACCOUNTING an informal name for a mortgage-backed certificate issued in Australia by the National Mortgage Market Corporation. The corporation has been issuing such certificates since 1985.

Austrade FINANCE, BANKING, AND ACCOUNTING Australian Trade Commission, a federal government body responsible for promoting Australian products abroad and attracting business to Australia. It currently has 108 offices in 63 countries.

Australia and New Zealand Closer Economic Relations Trade Agreement FINANCE, BANKING, AND ACCOUNTING an accord between Australia and New Zealand designed to facilitate the exchange of goods between the two countries. It was signed on January 1, 1983. Abbr **ANZCERTA**

Australian Accounting Standards Board FINANCE, BANKING, AND ACCOUNTING a peak body that is responsible for setting and monitoring accounting standards in Australia. It was established under Corporations Law in 1988, replacing the Accounting Standards Review Board. Abbr **AASB**

Australian Bureau of Statistics STATISTICS an Australian federal government body responsible for compiling national statistics and conducting regular censuses. It was set up in 1906. Abbr **ABS**

Australian Chamber of Commerce and Industry FINANCE, BANKING, AND ACCOUNTING a national council of business organizations in Australia. It represents around 350,000 businesses and its members include state chambers of commerce as well as major national employer and industry associations. Abbr **ACCI**

Australian Chamber of Manufactures GENERAL MANAGEMENT a peak body representing Australian manufacturers, established in 1878. Abbr **ACM**

Australian Communications Authority FINANCE, BANKING, AND ACCOUNTING a government body responsible for regulating practices in the communications industries. It was set up in 1997 as a result of the merger of the Australian Telecommunications Authority and the Spectrum Management Agency. Abbr **ACA**

Australian Industrial Relations Commission HR & PERSONNEL an administrative tribunal responsible for settling industrial disputes by conciliation and for setting and modifying industrial awards. It was established in 1988 to replace the Arbitration Commission and other specialist tribunals. Abbr **AIRC**

Australian Prudential Regulation Authority FINANCE, BANKING, AND ACCOUNTING see ***APRA***

Australian Securities and Investments Commission FINANCE, BANKING, AND ACCOUNTING an Australian federal government body responsible for regulating Australian businesses and the provision of financial products and services to consumers. It was established in 1989, replacing the Australian Securities Commission. Abbr **ASIC**

Australian Stock Exchange FINANCE, BANKING, AND ACCOUNTING the principal market for trading shares and other securities in Australia. It was formed in 1987 as a result of the amalgamation of six state stock exchanges and has offices in most state capitals. Abbr **ASX**

Australian Taxation Office FINANCE, BANKING, AND ACCOUNTING a statutory body responsible for the administration of the Australian federal government's taxation system. It is based in Canberra and is also responsible for the country's superannuation system. Abbr **ATO**

authentication E-COMMERCE a software security verification procedure to acknowledge or validate an e-commerce message's source, uniqueness, and integrity to make sure data is not being tampered with. The verification is typically achieved through the use of an electronic signature in the form of a key or algorithm that is shared by the trading partners.

authority GENERAL MANAGEMENT the right to act or command. People willingly obey a person in authority, because they believe he or she has a legitimate entitlement to exercise power. ***Max Weber*** distinguishes three types of **legitimate authority**: rational-legal, derived from the office held; traditional, from custom, an ancient tradition of obedience; and charismatic, exerted by those whose exceptional abilities confer the right to lead. The third form is the basis for the ***charismatic authority*** leadership theory.

MAX WEBER (pp. 1060–61)

authority chart GENERAL MANAGEMENT a diagram showing the hierarchical lines of ***authority*** and reporting within an organization. ***Organization charts*** are similar.

authority-compliance management GENERAL MANAGEMENT see ***Managerial Grid***™

authorization FINANCE, BANKING, AND ACCOUNTING the process of assessing a financial transaction, confirming that it does not raise the account's debt above its limit, and allowing the transaction to proceed. This would be undertaken, for example, by a credit card issuer. A positive authorization results in an authorization code being generated and the relevant funds being set aside. The available credit limit is reduced by the amount authorized.

authorized capital FINANCE, BANKING, AND ACCOUNTING the money made by a company from the sale of authorized shares of ordinary and preferred stock. It is measured by multiplying the number of authorized shares by their par value.

authorized share FINANCE, BANKING, AND ACCOUNTING a share that a company is authorized to issue

authorized signatory (*ANZ*) FINANCE, BANKING, AND ACCOUNTING the most senior is-

suer of authorization certificates in an organization, recognized by a signatory authority and designated in a signatory certificate

automated clearing house E-COMMERCE a payment network available to POS or ATM systems for interbank clearing and settlement of financial transactions. The network is also used for electronic fund transfers from a checking or savings account.

automated handling OPERATIONS & PRODUCTION the use of computers to control the moving and positioning of materials in a warehouse or factory. Automated handling may involve the use of robots.

automated storage and retrieval systems OPERATIONS & PRODUCTION the use of computerized vehicles to store, select, and move pallets around a large warehouse

automated teller machine FINANCE, BANKING, AND ACCOUNTING an electronic machine from which bank customers can withdraw paper money using an encoded plastic card. Abbr **ATM**

automatic assembly OPERATIONS & PRODUCTION a computerized ***production control*** technique used in the production of manufactured goods to balance output of production with demand. All factors affecting production performance are input when setting the operating parameters of an automatic assembly system, including sales information and production ***capacity***.

automatic debit FINANCE, BANKING, AND ACCOUNTING an instruction given by an account holder to a bank to make regular payments on given dates to the same payee

automatic guided vehicle system OPERATIONS & PRODUCTION a transportation system consisting of driverless electric vehicles that follow a predetermined track, used for the distribution of materials around a plant

automation OPERATIONS & PRODUCTION the self-controlling operation of machinery that reduces or dispenses with human communication or control when used in normal conditions. Automation was first introduced in the late 1940s by the Ford Motor Company. Also known as ***mechanization***

autonomation OPERATIONS & PRODUCTION a production system in which workers are allowed, and machines are equipped with a mechanism, to stop production if a defect in a product is detected during the production process. Autonomation became known through the ***Toyota production system***. The concept evolved from braking devices on machines that automatically stop if a problem occurs. Within Toyota, the concept has been carried forward so that all machines are equipped with various safety devices to prevent defective products, and production workers are allowed to stop the production line if a problem occurs. The problem is then properly explored in order to find a solution and to ensure that everyone understands the underlying reasons for the problem. In the long term, this creates a more efficient production line.

autonomous work group HR & PERSONNEL a small group of people who are empowered to manage themselves and the work they do on a day-to-day basis. The members of an autonomous work group are usually responsible for a whole process, product, or service, and not only carry out the work but also design and manage it. Also known as ***self-directed team***, ***self-managed team***, ***self-managed work team***, ***self-managing team***

Auto Pact FINANCE, BANKING, AND ACCOUNTING the informal name for the Agreement Concerning Automotive Products between Canada and the United States, by which duties were reduced on imported cars for U.S. car makers assembling vehicles in Canada. Subsequent provisions of the North American Free Trade Agreement reduced its effect.

autoresponder E-COMMERCE an e-mail software application that enables Internet users to send automated e-mails when they are not able to respond to incoming e-mail. Some autoresponse software enables a degree of personalization, for example, by incorporating the recipient's name in the responding message.

availability float FINANCE, BANKING, AND ACCOUNTING money that is available to a company because checks that it has written have not yet been charged against its accounts

average STATISTICS the arithmetic mean of a sample of observations

average accounting return FINANCE, BANKING, AND ACCOUNTING the percentage return realized on an asset, as measured by its book value, after taxes and depreciation

average collection time FINANCE, BANKING, AND ACCOUNTING the mean time required for a firm to liquidate its accounts receivable, measured from the date each receivable is posted until the last payment is received

average cost of capital FINANCE, BANKING, AND ACCOUNTING the average of what a company is paying for the money it borrows or raises by selling stock

average deviation STATISTICS the spread of a sample of observations

average nominal maturity FINANCE, BANKING, AND ACCOUNTING the average length of time until a mutual fund's financial instruments mature

average option FINANCE, BANKING, AND ACCOUNTING an option whose value depends on the average price of a commodity during a particular period of time

Average Weekly Earnings STATISTICS a measure of wage levels in the Australian workforce that is calculated regularly by the ***Australian Bureau of Statistics***. The measure is considered one of Australia's key economic indicators. Abbr **AWE**

Average Weekly Ordinary Time Earnings STATISTICS a measure of wage levels in the Australian workforce that excludes overtime payments, published by the ***Australian Bureau of Statistics***. Abbr **AWOTE**

award HR & PERSONNEL
1. (*ANZ*) a decision handed down by a court of arbitration
2. the terms of employment set by an industrial court or tribunal for a particular occupation
Also known as ***industrial award***

award wage (*ANZ*) HR & PERSONNEL a rate of pay set by an industrial court or tribunal for a particular occupation

AWE STATISTICS see ***Average Weekly Earnings***

axis STATISTICS a reference line used in geometry to locate a point in space or in a plane

B2B *abbr* E-COMMERCE business-to-business, relating to an advertising or marketing program aimed at businesses doing business with other businesses as opposed to consumers. The term is most commonly used in reference to commerce or business that is conducted over the Internet between commercial enterprises.

B2B advertising MARKETING advertising that is aimed at buyers for organizations rather than domestic consumers

B2B agency MARKETING an advertising agency that specializes in planning, creating, and buying advertising aimed at buyers for organizations rather than domestic consumers

B2B auction E-COMMERCE a Web marketplace that provides a mechanism for negotiating prices and bidding for services. Web-based B2B auctions reverse the traditional auction formula in which the aim is to help the seller get the best price. B2B Web auctions involve suppliers competing with one another by bidding down the price of their service. This inevitably benefits the buyer, as instead of having to bid higher for a particular service or product he or she can wait until the suppliers have bid themselves down to a reasonable price. Typically, online auctions require companies to follow a registration process in order to take part. During this process, users have to provide their credit card information and shipping preferences as well as agree to the site's code of conduct. Some sites (for example, Business-Auctions.com) also manage secure auctions, which restrict potential bidders to specific firms or individuals.

B2B commerce E-COMMERCE the business conducted between companies, rather than between a company and individual consumers

B2B exchange GENERAL MANAGEMENT see *exchange*

B2B marketing
1. E-COMMERCE the planning, promotion, and distribution of goods or services for use by businesses rather than individual consumers
2. MARKETING marketing activities aimed at buyers for organizations rather than domestic consumers

B2B Web exchange E-COMMERCE see *exchange*

B2C *abbr* E-COMMERCE business-to-consumer, relating to an advertising or marketing program aimed at businesses doing business directly with consumers as opposed to other businesses. The term is most commonly used in reference to commerce or business that is conducted over the Internet between a commercial enterprise and a consumer.

B4N *abbr* GENERAL MANAGEMENT bye for now (*slang*)

backlink checking E-COMMERCE a means of finding out which Web pages are linking to a specific Web site. Many ***search engines*** enable users to conduct **backlink searches** by entering the name of a Web site into the search box preceded by a special command (for example, "link":). AltaVista and HotBot are two of the most popular search engines to offer this facility. The backlink checking process can be automated by using a service such as LinkPopularity.com, which enables users to search for linking sites at various search engines at once. Backlink checking enables e-business and Web site managers to keep track of their own and their competitors' online popularity.

backlog OPERATIONS & PRODUCTION the buildup of unfulfilled orders for a product, process, or production process that is behind schedule. A backlog can result from bad scheduling, production delays, an unanticipated demand for a product or process, or where the capacity of the process is not able to keep up with demand. Some large products, for example, aircraft and ships, have to be built to a backlog of orders and it is not feasible to supply them on demand.

back office FINANCE, BANKING, AND ACCOUNTING, GENERAL MANAGEMENT the administrative staff of a company who do not have face-to-face contact with the company's customers

back pay HR & PERSONNEL pay that is owed to an employee for work carried out before the current payment period and is either overdue or results from a backdated pay increase

back-to-back loan FINANCE, BANKING, AND ACCOUNTING an arrangement in which two companies in different countries borrow offsetting amounts in each other's currency and each repays it at a specified future date in its domestic currency. Such a loan, often between a company and its foreign subsidiary, eliminates the risk of loss from exchange rate fluctuations.

back-to-school sale GENERAL MANAGEMENT a store sale that is timed to coincide with the return of children to school after the summer vacation (*slang*)

backup FINANCE, BANKING, AND ACCOUNTING a period in which bond yields rise and prices fall, or a sudden reversal in a stock market trend

backup facility GENERAL MANAGEMENT a secondary system, record, or contract intended to take the place of another that fails

backward integration OPERATIONS & PRODUCTION the building of relationships with ***suppliers*** in order to secure the supply of ***raw materials***. Backward integration can involve taking control of supply companies and is a feature of Japanese ***keiretsu***. It is the opposite of ***forward integration***.

backward scheduling OPERATIONS & PRODUCTION a ***production scheduling*** (see ***production smoothing***) technique for planning work on the basis of when the completed work is due. By using backward scheduling, managers are able to assign work to particular workstations so that the overall task is completed exactly when it is due. The technique allows potential bottlenecks and idle time for particular workstations to be identified in advance.

bad debt FINANCE, BANKING, AND ACCOUNTING a debt that is unlikely to be repaid because a company or customer has become insolvent

bad debt reserve FINANCE, BANKING, AND ACCOUNTING an amount of money that a company sets aside to cover bad debts

bait and switch MARKETING a marketing practice whereby customers are encouraged to enter a store by an advertisement for one product and are then persuaded to buy another more expensive product (*slang*)

balance billing FINANCE, BANKING, AND ACCOUNTING the practice of requesting payment from a receiver of a service such as medical treatment for the part of the cost not covered by the person's insurance

balanced budget ECONOMICS a budget in which planned expenditure on goods and services and debt income can be met by current income from taxation and other central government receipts

balanced design STATISTICS an experimental design in which the same number of observations is used for each combination of the experimental factors

balanced fund FINANCE, BANKING, AND ACCOUNTING a mutual fund that invests in a variety of types of companies and financial instruments to reduce the risk of loss through poor performance of any one type

balanced investment strategy FINANCE, BANKING, AND ACCOUNTING a strategy of investing in a variety of types of companies and financial instruments to reduce the risk of

loss through poor performance of any one type

balanced line OPERATIONS & PRODUCTION an ***assembly line*** in which the cycle time for all the workstations is equal. A balanced line is achieved by allocating the right amount of work and the correct number of operators and machinery to produce a given flow of product over a set period, taking into account the fact that each workstation will have a different capacity and that each process involved has a different cycle time.

balanced quantity OPERATIONS & PRODUCTION an ***inventory*** measure of the quantity of materials and parts required by a workstation to achieve a planned level of output

balanced scorecard GENERAL MANAGEMENT a system that measures and manages an organization's progress toward strategic objectives. Introduced by ***Robert Kaplan*** and ***David Norton*** in 1992, the balanced scorecard incorporates not only financial indicators but also three other perspectives: customer, internal business, and learning/innovation. The scorecard shows how these measures are interlinked and affect each other, enabling an organization's past, present, and potential performance to be tracked and managed.

✔ IMPLEMENTING THE BALANCED SCORECARD (pp. 510–11)
ROBERT S. KAPLAN (pp. 1010–11)

balance of payments ECONOMICS a list of a country's credit and debit transactions with international financial institutions and foreign countries in a specific period

balance of payments on capital account FINANCE, BANKING, AND ACCOUNTING a system of recording a country's imports and exports of goods and services during a period, usually one year

balance of payments on current account FINANCE, BANKING, AND ACCOUNTING a system of recording a country's investment transactions with the rest of the world during a given period, usually one year. Among the included transactions are the purchase of physical and financial assets, intergovernmental transfers, and the provision of economic aid to developing nations.

balance of trade ECONOMICS the difference between a country's exports and imports of goods and services

balance sheet FINANCE, BANKING, AND ACCOUNTING a financial report stating the total assets, liabilities, and owner's equity of an organization at a given date, usually the last day of the accounting period. The debit, or left, side of the balance sheet states assets, while the credit, or right, side states liability and equity, and the two sides must be equal, or balance.

✔ HOW TO CREATE A BALANCE SHEET (p. 848); HOW TO READ A BALANCE SHEET (pp. 851–52)

ball

carry the ball GENERAL MANAGEMENT to have responsibility for a project (*slang*)

drop the ball GENERAL MANAGEMENT to avoid your responsibilities (*slang*)

take the ball and run with it GENERAL MANAGEMENT to take an idea and implement it (*slang*)

balloon loan FINANCE, BANKING, AND ACCOUNTING a loan repaid in regular installments with a single larger final payment

balloon payment FINANCE, BANKING, AND ACCOUNTING the final larger payment on a balloon loan

ballpark GENERAL MANAGEMENT an informal term for a rough, estimated figure. The term was derived from the approximate assessment of the number of spectators that might be made on the basis of a glance around at a sporting event.

banded pack MARKETING a product pack that has an additional product or promotional offer attached to it

bang for the buck GENERAL MANAGEMENT a return on investment (*slang*)

bangtail MARKETING an order form for a new product that is attached by a perforated join to an envelope flap (*slang*)

bank FINANCE, BANKING, AND ACCOUNTING a commercial institution that keeps money in accounts for individuals or organizations, makes loans, exchanges currencies, provides credit to businesses, and offers other financial services

bank bill FINANCE, BANKING, AND ACCOUNTING

1. a banknote

2. (*U.K.*) a bill of exchange issued or accepted by a bank

bank card FINANCE, BANKING, AND ACCOUNTING a plastic card issued by a bank and accepted by merchants in payment for transactions. The most common types are ***credit cards*** and ***debit cards***, although ***smart cards*** have been introduced. Bank cards are governed by an internationally recognized set of rules for the authorization of their use and the clearing and settlement of transactions.

bank credit FINANCE, BANKING, AND ACCOUNTING the maximum credit available to an individual from a particular bank

bank discount FINANCE, BANKING, AND ACCOUNTING the charge made by a bank to a company or customer who pays a note before it is due

bank discount basis FINANCE, BANKING, AND ACCOUNTING the expression of yield that is used for treasury bills, based on a 360-day year

bank-eligible issue FINANCE, BANKING, AND ACCOUNTING U.S. Treasury obligations that commercial banks may buy

banker FINANCE, BANKING, AND ACCOUNTING somebody who owns or is a senior executive of a bank

banker's credit *or* **banker's acceptance** FINANCE, BANKING, AND ACCOUNTING a financial instrument, typically issued by an exporter or importer for a short term, that a bank guarantees

banker's draft FINANCE, BANKING, AND ACCOUNTING a bill of exchange payable on demand and drawn by one bank on another. Regarded as being equivalent to cash, the draft cannot be returned unpaid.

bankers' hours FINANCE, BANKING, AND ACCOUNTING short hours of work. The term refers to the relatively short time that a bank is open, specifically the hours from nine in the morning to three in the afternoon. (*slang*)

bank fee FINANCE, BANKING, AND ACCOUNTING a charge included in most lease transactions that is either paid in advance or is included in the gross capitalized cost. The fee usually covers administrative costs such as the costs of obtaining a credit report, verifying insurance coverage, and checking the lease documentation.

Bank for International Settlements FINANCE, BANKING, AND ACCOUNTING see ***BIS***

bank guarantee FINANCE, BANKING, AND ACCOUNTING a commitment made by a bank to a foreign buyer that the bank will pay an exporter for goods shipped if the buyer defaults

  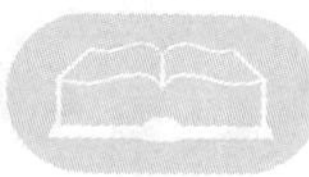    

bank holding company FINANCE, BANKING, AND ACCOUNTING a company that owns one or more banks as part of its assets

banking insurance fund FINANCE, BANKING, AND ACCOUNTING a fund maintained by the Federal Deposit Insurance Corporation to provide deposit insurance for banks other than savings and savings and loan banks

Banking Ombudsman FINANCE, BANKING, AND ACCOUNTING an official of the Australian or New Zealand government responsible for dealing with complaints relating to banking practices

banking passport FINANCE, BANKING, AND ACCOUNTING a document used to provide somebody with a false identity for banking transactions in another country

banking syndicate FINANCE, BANKING, AND ACCOUNTING a group of investment banks that jointly underwrite and distribute a new security offering

banking system FINANCE, BANKING, AND ACCOUNTING a network of commercial, savings, and specialized banks that provide financial services including accepting deposits, loans and credit, and providing money transmission and investment facilities

bank investment contract FINANCE, BANKING, AND ACCOUNTING a contract that specifies what a bank will pay its investors

bankmail FINANCE, BANKING, AND ACCOUNTING an agreement by a bank not to finance any rival's attempt to take over the same company that a particular customer is trying to buy

bank reserve ratio FINANCE, BANKING, AND ACCOUNTING a standard established by a central bank governing the relationship between the amount of money that other banks must keep on hand and the amount that they can loan out. By raising and lowering the ratio, the central bank can decrease or increase the money supply.

bank reserves FINANCE, BANKING, AND ACCOUNTING the money that a bank has available to meet the demands of its depositors

bankroll FINANCE, BANKING, AND ACCOUNTING the money used as finance for a project

bankruptcy FINANCE, BANKING, AND ACCOUNTING the condition of being unable to pay debts, with liabilities greater than assets

bank term loan FINANCE, BANKING, AND ACCOUNTING a loan from a bank that has a term of at least one year

banner *or* **banner ad** E-COMMERCE an online interactive ad, often using graphic images and sound as well as text, placed on a Web page that is linked to an external advertiser's Web site. The banner typically is sized so as to appear at the top or bottom of the Web page. Also known as ***ad banner***

banner advertising MARKETING the use of rectangular advertisements or logos across the width of a page on a Web site

banner exchange E-COMMERCE an advertising program in which one merchant induces others to place his or her banners and buttons on their Web sites in return for similarly displaying theirs

bar *(U.K.)* FINANCE, BANKING, AND ACCOUNTING one million pounds sterling *(slang)*

bar chart GENERAL MANAGEMENT the presentation of data in the form of a graph, using blocks or bars of color or shading. A bar chart is especially useful for showing the impact of one factor against another, for example, income over time or customer calls against sales.

bar coding OPERATIONS & PRODUCTION the process of attaching a machine-readable code to a product, package, container, or subassembly, and using a scanner to relate its location to the product characteristics. Bar codes have uses in stock control and order picking and are used to validate every single transaction from packaging through to customer delivery.

barefoot pilgrim FINANCE, BANKING, AND ACCOUNTING an unsophisticated investor who has lost everything trading in securities *(slang)*

bargain FINANCE, BANKING, AND ACCOUNTING a transaction on a stock market *(slang)*

bargaining chip FINANCE, BANKING, AND ACCOUNTING something that can be used as a concession or inducement in negotiation

bargain tax date FINANCE, BANKING, AND ACCOUNTING the date of a transaction on a stock market

Barnard, **Chester** (1886–1961) GENERAL MANAGEMENT U.S. business executive. President of the New Jersey Bell Telephone Company, whose book, *The Functions of the Executive* (1938), looked at the relationship of the individual to the organization and at ***organization structure***. Barnard's observations also covered the topics of ***communication***, ***authority***, and organizational ***core values***.

Barnevik, **Percy** (*b.* 1941) GENERAL MANAGEMENT Swedish business executive. Formerly chief executive, and now chairman, of Asea Brown Boveri, where he reduced ***bureaucracy***, decentralized resources and ***authority***, introduced a ***matrix management*** structure, and ran a global expansion strategy.

barren money FINANCE, BANKING, AND ACCOUNTING money that is unproductive because it is not invested

barrier option FINANCE, BANKING, AND ACCOUNTING an option that includes automatic trading in other options when a commodity reaches a specified price

barrier to entry GENERAL MANAGEMENT a factor preventing a company from entering a market. A barrier to entry may be created, for example, by the fact that current companies in that market have patents so that goods cannot be copied, or by the high cost of advertising needed to gain any ***market share***. There may be strong ***brand loyalty*** to an existing product, or a large company may be able to produce goods very cheaply, whereas a small newcomer would have to charge higher prices. If too many barriers to entry exist, then competition within that market will be limited.

barrier to exit GENERAL MANAGEMENT a factor preventing a company from leaving a market in which it is currently doing business. A barrier to exit makes it difficult for a company to abandon an unprofitable product or service because of factors such as possession of specialist equipment only suited to the manufacture of one product, high costs of retraining the workforce in different skills, or the detrimental effect of withdrawing one product from a range on the rest of the product family. There may also be legal considerations or labor union agreements that prevent closure of a factory or redundancies.

Bartlett, **Christopher A.** (*b.* 1943) GENERAL MANAGEMENT Australian-born academic. Professor at Harvard Business School, and coauthor with ***Sumantra Ghoshal*** of *Managing Across Borders* (1989).

BAS GENERAL MANAGEMENT see ***Business Activity Statement***

  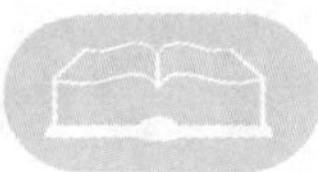    

base currency FINANCE, BANKING, AND ACCOUNTING the currency used for measuring the return on an investment

base date ECONOMICS the reference date from which an index number such as the ***retail price index*** is calculated

base interest rate FINANCE, BANKING, AND ACCOUNTING the minimum interest rate that investors will expect for investing in a non-Treasury security

base pay HR & PERSONNEL a guaranteed sum of money given to an employee in payment for work, disregarding any fringe benefits, allowances, or extra rewards from an ***incentive scheme***

base rate FINANCE, BANKING, AND ACCOUNTING the interest rate set by the Federal Reserve that dictates the rate at which money is lent to other banks and which they in turn charge their customers

base rate tracker mortgage FINANCE, BANKING, AND ACCOUNTING a mortgage whose interest rate varies periodically, usually annually, so as to remain a specified amount above a particular standard rate

base year ECONOMICS the year from which an index is calculated, for example, 1990 = 100

basic pay *(U.K.)* HR & PERSONNEL = ***base pay***

basic wage HR & PERSONNEL the minimum rate of pay set by an industrial court or tribunal for a particular occupation

basis risk FINANCE, BANKING, AND ACCOUNTING the risk that price variations in the cash or futures market will diminish revenue when a futures contract is liquidated, or the risk that changes in interest rates will affect repricing interest-bearing liabilities

basket case FINANCE, BANKING, AND ACCOUNTING a company or individual considered to be in such dire circumstances as to be beyond help *(slang)*

basket of currencies FINANCE, BANKING, AND ACCOUNTING a group of selected currencies used in establishing a standard of value for another unit of currency

batch E-COMMERCE a collection of credit card transactions including authorizations, payments, and credits saved for electronic submission to an ***acquirer*** for settlement. The merchant is encouraged to submit one large batch rather than several small ones by being charged a fee for each batch submitted.

batch costing OPERATIONS & PRODUCTION see ***operating costing***

batch production OPERATIONS & PRODUCTION a production system in which a process is broken down into distinct operations that are completed on a batch or group of products before moving to the next production stage. Batch production has similarities with ***job production***. As batch sizes can vary from very small to extremely large quantities, batch production offers greater flexibility than other production systems.

bath
take a bath FINANCE, BANKING, AND ACCOUNTING to suffer a serious financial loss *(slang)*

baud FINANCE, BANKING, AND ACCOUNTING a unit used to measure speed of data transmission, equal to one data unit per second

Bayesian theory STATISTICS a statistical theory and method for drawing conclusions about the future occurrence of a given parameter of a statistical distribution by calculating from prior data on its frequency of occurrence. The theory is useful in the solution of theoretical and applied problems in science, industry, and government, for example, in econometrics and finance.

Bayes' theorem STATISTICS a probability theorem that allows statisticians continually to revise the probability of an event according to new evidence

BBS *abbr* E-COMMERCE bulletin board system, a system enabling Internet users to read and post messages in newsgroups

BCA GENERAL MANAGEMENT see ***Business Council of Australia***

bcc *abbr* E-COMMERCE blind carbon copy, a function that enables a user to send an e-mail message to any number of e-mail addresses while concealing each recipient's e-mail address. The bcc box is widely used for distributing press releases, newsletters, and other mass mailings via e-mail. If there is no desire to conceal names, the ***cc*** address line can be used.

BCCS FINANCE, BANKING, AND ACCOUNTING see ***Board of Currency Commissioners***

BCNU *abbr* GENERAL MANAGEMENT be seeing you *(slang)*

bean counter GENERAL MANAGEMENT a person of low rank within an organization who has no real influence on the decision-making process *(slang)*

bear FINANCE, BANKING, AND ACCOUNTING somebody who anticipates unfavorable business conditions, especially somebody who sells stocks or commodities expecting their prices to fall, often with the intention of buying them back cheaply later. See ***bull***

bearer bond FINANCE, BANKING, AND ACCOUNTING a bond that is not registered on the books of the issuer and is therefore payable only to the party that presents it for payment

bearer instrument FINANCE, BANKING, AND ACCOUNTING a financial instrument such as a check or bill of exchange that entitles the person who presents it to receive payment

bear hug GENERAL MANAGEMENT an attempt to get the board of a company that is a target acquisition to recommend an offer to its shareholders. A bear hug may include the acquiring company offering to buy shares in the target at a premium. In a **reverse bear hug**, the board of the company to be acquired demonstrates its willingness to recommend an offer, usually on particular conditions. *(slang)*

bearish FINANCE, BANKING, AND ACCOUNTING relating to unfavorable business conditions or selling activity in anticipation of falling prices. See ***bullish***

bear market FINANCE, BANKING, AND ACCOUNTING a market in which prices are falling and in which a dealer is more likely to sell securities than to buy them. See ***bull market***

bear raid FINANCE, BANKING, AND ACCOUNTING = ***raid***

bear spread FINANCE, BANKING, AND ACCOUNTING a combination of purchases and sales of options for the same commodity or stock with the intention of making a profit when the price falls. See ***bull spread***

bear tack FINANCE, BANKING, AND ACCOUNTING a downward movement in the value of a stock, part of the market, or the market as a whole

bed
get into bed with somebody HR & PERSONNEL to begin a business association with an individual or organization *(slang)*

put something to bed GENERAL MANAGEMENT to dismiss an idea or put an end to a project (*slang*)

bed and breakfast deal FINANCE, BANKING, AND ACCOUNTING a transaction in which somebody sells shares at the end of one trading day and repurchases them at the beginning of the next. This is usually done to establish formally the profit or loss accrued to these shares for tax or reporting purposes.

beepilepsy GENERAL MANAGEMENT the sudden jerk of surprise given by a person when his or her beeper goes off (*slang*)

Beer, Stafford (*b.* 1926) GENERAL MANAGEMENT British industrialist and writer. Organization systems thinker, associated with cybernetics. His approach was first laid out in *Cybernetics and Management* (1959).

before-tax profit margin FINANCE, BANKING, AND ACCOUNTING the amount by which net income before tax exceeds expenditure

behavioral interview HR & PERSONNEL see ***interviewing***

behavioral modeling HR & PERSONNEL

1. a process of capturing and encoding unconscious human expertise to make it transferable to others

2. a skills training technique that seeks to imitate models and maintain learned behaviors

behavioral science HR & PERSONNEL academic disciplines such as sociology and psychology that relate to the study of the way in which humans conduct themselves. In the field of management, the behavioral sciences are used to study ***organization behavior***.

behaviorist theories GENERAL MANAGEMENT a school of thought that defines ***leadership*** by leaders' actions, rather than by their personality characteristics or their sources of ***power***. Behaviorist theories were developed in the 1970s as disillusionment with situational theory grew. There are many different behaviorist theories, and some are contradictory. One of the most prominent—the ***Managerial Grid***™—was developed by ***Robert Blake*** and ***Jane Mouton*** as a tool to enable leaders to understand their own behavior patterns. ***Rensis Likert*** also conducted research in this area, focusing on how behavior adapts to take account of people and situations.

Behn, Hernand (1880–1933) GENERAL MANAGEMENT U.S. industrialist. Founder, with his brother ***Sosthenes Behn***, of the conglomerate International Telephone and Telegraph (ITT) in 1920.

Behn, Sosthenes (1882–1957) GENERAL MANAGEMENT U.S. industrialist. Founder, with his brother ***Hernand Behn***, of the conglomerate International Telephone and Telegraph (ITT) in 1920. Under Behn's leadership, ITT expanded from the United States into Europe and South America. When Behn retired from ITT in 1956, most of its turnover came from its overseas interests. Under the leadership of ***Harold Geneen***, ITT then developed into a massive diverse multinational incorporating hotels, car rental, frozen foods, potato chips, and candy. The history of ITT is detailed in *Sovereign State—the Secret History of ITT* (1973).

Belbin, R. Meredith (*b.* 1926) GENERAL MANAGEMENT British academic and consultant. Acknowledged as the father of team-role theory, which identifies nine useful roles necessary for a successful team of managers. Belbin's approach to teambuilding and ***teamwork*** was described in *Management Teams: Why They Succeed or Fail* (1981). Other models of team relationships include the Team Management System, developed by ***Charles Margerison*** and ***Dick McCann***.

R. MEREDITH BELBIN (pp. 966–67)

bell cow FINANCE, BANKING, AND ACCOUNTING a product that sells well and makes a reasonable profit (*slang*)

bells and whistles (*slang*)

1. MARKETING unnecessary but desirable peripheral features of a product

2. FINANCE, BANKING, AND ACCOUNTING special features attached to a derivatives instrument or securities issue that are intended to attract investors or reduce issue costs

bellwether FINANCE, BANKING, AND ACCOUNTING a security whose price is viewed by investors as an indicator of future developments or trends

belly

go belly up FINANCE, BANKING, AND ACCOUNTING to fail financially or go bankrupt (*slang*)

below-the-line MARKETING relating to the proportion of marketing expenditure allocated to nonadvertising activities such as public relations, sales promotion, printing, presentations, sponsorship, and sales force support

benchmark GENERAL MANAGEMENT a point of reference or standard against which to measure performance. Originally used for a set of computer programs to measure the performance of a computer against similar models, benchmark is now used more generally to describe a measure identified in the context of a ***benchmarking*** program against which to evaluate an organization's performance in a specific area.

benchmarking MARKETING a systematic process of comparing the activities and work processes of an organization or department with those of outstanding organizations or departments in order to identify ways to improve performance. Benchmarking was first developed by the Xerox Corporation in the late 1970s in order to learn from the achievements of Japanese competitors and was described by a Xerox manager, Robert C. Camp, in his book *Benchmarking: The Search for Industry Best Practices that Lead to Superior Performance* (1989).The use of benchmarking has become widespread and individual organizations have developed distinct approaches toward it. Benchmarking programs commonly include the following stages: identifying the area requiring benchmarking and the process to use, collecting and analyzing the data, implementing changes, and monitoring and reviewing improvements. Benchmarking is used in business appraisal, often as part of a ***total quality management*** or ***business process reengineering*** program

✔ A PROGRAM FOR BENCHMARKING (pp. 488–89)

benchmark interest rate FINANCE, BANKING, AND ACCOUNTING the lowest interest rate that U.S. investors will accept on securities other than Treasury bills

beneficial owner FINANCE, BANKING, AND ACCOUNTING somebody who receives all the benefits of a stock such as dividends, rights, and proceeds of any sale but is not the registered owner of the stock

beneficiary bank FINANCE, BANKING, AND ACCOUNTING a bank that handles a gift such as a bequest

benefit FINANCE, BANKING, AND ACCOUNTING something that improves the profitability or efficiency of an organization or reduces its risk, or any nonmonetary reward given to employees, for example, paid vacations or employer contributions to pensions

benefit in kind (*U.K.*) HR & PERSONNEL a ***benefit*** other than cash received by employees as part of their total ***compensation package***

benefits plan HR & PERSONNEL a government program for the employment of Canadians and for providing Canadian manufacturers, consultants, contractors, and service companies with opportunities to compete for projects

Bennis, Warren G. (*b.* 1925) GENERAL MANAGEMENT U.S. academic. Guru of ***leadership*** theory, who has also carried out work in the areas of small ***group dynamics***, change in social systems, and ***T-Groups*** (see ***sensitivity training***). Bennis wrote his first article on leadership in 1959, and subsequently carried out extensive research in the United States into common leadership factors. His findings are reported in *Leaders: the Strategies for Taking Charge* (1985). He was influenced by the theories of ***Douglas McGregor***.

✔ LEADING FROM THE MIDDLE (pp. 360–61)
WARREN BENNIS (pp. 968–69); DOUGLAS MCGREGOR (pp. 1022–23)

Berhad FINANCE, BANKING, AND ACCOUNTING a Malay term for "private." Companies can use "sendiran berhad" or "Sdn Bhd" in their name instead of "plc." Abbr **Bhd**

Berners-Lee, Tim (*b.* 1955) GENERAL MANAGEMENT British computer scientist. Creator of the World Wide Web and director of the World Wide Web Consortium, the world coordinating body for developing the Web. Berners-Lee is concerned that the growth of the Web should benefit all, rather than make money for the few. His experiences and thoughts are recorded in *Weaving the Web: The Original Design and Ultimate Destiny of the World Wide Web* (1999).

best-in-class GENERAL MANAGEMENT leading a market or industrial sector in efficiency. An organization that is best in its class exhibits exemplary ***best practice***. Such an organization is clearly singled out from the pack and is recognized as a leader for its procedures for dealing with the acquisition and processing of materials, and the delivery of end products or services to its customers. The concept of best in class is closely allied with ***total quality management***, and one tool that can help in achieving this status is ***benchmarking***.

best practice GENERAL MANAGEMENT the most effective and efficient method of achieving any objective or task. What constitutes best practice can be determined through a process of ***benchmarking***. An organization can move toward achieving best practice, either across the whole organization or in a specific area, through ***continuous improvement***. In production-based organizations, ***world class manufacturing*** is a related concept. More generally, a market or sector leader may be described as ***best-in-class***.

best value GENERAL MANAGEMENT a U.K. government initiative intended to ensure cost efficiency and effectiveness in the delivery of public services by local authorities. The best value initiative was announced in early 1997 to replace **compulsory competitive tendering (CCT)**, and pilot schemes in selected local authorities began in April 1998. The Local Government Act 1999 requires councils, as part of the best value process, to review all services over a five-year period, setting standards and performance indicators for each service, comparing performance with that of other bodies, and undertaking consultation with local taxpayers and service users.

beta FINANCE, BANKING, AND ACCOUNTING a numerical measure of the change in value of something such as a stock. One is the average beta of an instrument of the same type.

beta software E-COMMERCE a version of a software product that is almost ready for release but needs more testing. It is possible to download beta software on the Internet free, as software companies like to test their products on members of the public before they are put on the market.

beta test E-COMMERCE a test of a new or upgraded piece of computer software or hardware carried out by a few chosen customers before it is released to the public

Bhd FINANCE, BANKING, AND ACCOUNTING see ***Berhad***

BHP *abbr* GENERAL MANAGEMENT Broken Hill Proprietary Company Ltd., Australia's largest manufacturing company. Also known as Big Australian.

bias STATISTICS inaccuracy or deviation in inferences, results, or a statistical method

bid FINANCE, BANKING, AND ACCOUNTING an offer to buy all or a majority of the capital shares of a company in an attempted takeover, or the highest price a prospective bidder is prepared to pay

bid-ask quote FINANCE, BANKING, AND ACCOUNTING a statement of the prices that are being offered and asked for a security or option contract

bid bond FINANCE, BANKING, AND ACCOUNTING a guarantee by a financial institution of the fulfillment of an international tender offer

bidding war FINANCE, BANKING, AND ACCOUNTING a competition between prospective buyers who successively offer more than each other for the same stock or security

bid form FINANCE, BANKING, AND ACCOUNTING a form containing details of an offer to underwrite municipal bonds

bid market FINANCE, BANKING, AND ACCOUNTING a market for bids (the price at which a dealer will buy shares)

bid-offer spread FINANCE, BANKING, AND ACCOUNTING the difference between the highest price that a buyer is prepared to offer and the lowest price that a seller is prepared to accept

bid price FINANCE, BANKING, AND ACCOUNTING the price a stock exchange dealer will pay for a security or option contract

bid-to-cover ratio FINANCE, BANKING, AND ACCOUNTING a number that shows how many more people wanted to buy Treasury bills than actually did buy them

bid up FINANCE, BANKING, AND ACCOUNTING to bid for something merely to increase its price, or to make successive increases to the bid price for a security so that unopened orders do not remain unexecuted

Big Australian (*ANZ*) GENERAL MANAGEMENT see ***BHP***

big business GENERAL MANAGEMENT powerful business interests or companies in general. The term is particularly used when referring to ***large-sized businesses*** or ***multinational businesses***.

Big Four (*ANZ*) FINANCE, BANKING, AND ACCOUNTING Australia's four largest banks: the Commonwealth Bank of Australia, Westpac Banking Corporation, National Australia Bank, and ANZ Bank

big picture GENERAL MANAGEMENT an informal term for a broad perspective on an issue that encompasses its surrounding context and long-term implications

big swinging dick FINANCE, BANKING, AND ACCOUNTING a very successful financial trader (*slang*)

bilateral facility FINANCE, BANKING, AND ACCOUNTING a loan by one bank to one borrower

  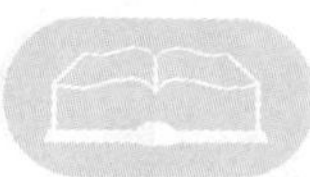  

bilateral monopoly ECONOMICS a market in which there is a single seller and a single buyer

bilateral trade ECONOMICS trade between two countries who give each other specific privileges such as favorable import quotas that are denied to other trading partners

bill broker FINANCE, BANKING, AND ACCOUNTING somebody who buys and sells promissory notes and bills of exchange

bill discount FINANCE, BANKING, AND ACCOUNTING the interest rate that the Federal Reserve charges banks for short-term loans. This establishes a de facto floor for the interest rate that banks charge their customers, usually a fraction above the discount rate.

bill discounting rate FINANCE, BANKING, AND ACCOUNTING the amount by which the price of a Treasury bill is reduced to reflect expected changes in interest rates

billing cycle FINANCE, BANKING, AND ACCOUNTING a period of time, often one month, between successive requests for payment

bill of entry FINANCE, BANKING, AND ACCOUNTING a statement of the nature and value of goods to be imported or exported, prepared by the shipper and presented to a customhouse

bill of exchange FINANCE, BANKING, AND ACCOUNTING a document containing instructions to pay a specified person a particular amount on a specified date or on request

bill of goods (*ANZ*) FINANCE, BANKING, AND ACCOUNTING a consignment of goods, or a statement of their nature and value

bill of lading FINANCE, BANKING, AND ACCOUNTING a statement of the nature and value of goods being transported, especially by ship, along with the conditions applying to their transportation. Drawn up by the carrier, this document serves as a contract between the owner of the goods and the carrier.

binary thinker GENERAL MANAGEMENT somebody who thinks only in absolute, black-and-white terms (*slang*)

bingo card MARKETING a postcard advertisement for a product that is bound into a publication and can be returned to the manufacturer for additional information on the product (*slang*)

biodata HR & PERSONNEL

1. information taken from an ***application form***, ***résumé***, or questionnaire concerning an employee's or potential employee's background and experience that is objectively scored by recruiters to predict job performance

2. a canned biography placed in a periodical article or conference paper

biometrics E-COMMERCE the study of measurable biological characteristics, or in computer security, authentication techniques that use characteristics such as speech, fingerprints, or scans of the human eye

biomimicry GENERAL MANAGEMENT the use in business of processes that imitate natural ones to reduce waste and limit impact on the environment

biorhythm HR & PERSONNEL any recurring biological cycle thought to affect the physical or mental state of a person, particularly patterns of digestion, sleep, and fatigue

birth-death ratio STATISTICS the ratio of the number of births to the number of deaths in a population over a period of time such as 10 years

BIS FINANCE, BANKING, AND ACCOUNTING Bank for International Settlements, a bank that promotes cooperation between central banks, provides facilities for international financial operations, and acts as agent or trustee in international financial settlements. The 17-member board of directors consists of the governors of the central banks of Belgium, Canada, France, Germany, Italy, Japan, the Netherlands, Sweden, Switzerland, the United Kingdom, and the United States.

bit E-COMMERCE

1. a binary digit number (0 or 1), the smallest unit of computerized data

2. an item of information or knowledge

bivariate data STATISTICS data in which two variables are involved in each subject

bivariate distribution STATISTICS a form of distribution involving two random variables

black

in the black FINANCE, BANKING, AND ACCOUNTING making profit, or having more assets than debt (*slang*)

blackbox engineering OPERATIONS & PRODUCTION the manufacturing of a component in which the supplier has total control over the design and content of the component and the purchaser knows only its external and physical specifications. The term blackbox engineering is derived from the fact that the component in question appears as a black box on the design drawings for the purchaser.

black chip (*S. Africa*) GENERAL MANAGEMENT a company that is owned or managed by black people, or is controlled by black shareholders

black economic empowerment (*S. Africa*) GENERAL MANAGEMENT the promotion of black ownership and control of South Africa's economic assets

black economy ECONOMICS economic activity that is not declared for tax purposes and is usually carried out in exchange for cash

Black Friday FINANCE, BANKING, AND ACCOUNTING any precipitous one-day drop in a financial market, originally September 24, 1869, when prospectors attempting to corner the gold market caused a business panic followed by a depression

black hole GENERAL MANAGEMENT a project that consumes unlimited amounts of resources without yielding any profit (*slang*)

black knight GENERAL MANAGEMENT see ***knight***

black market GENERAL MANAGEMENT an illegal ***market***, usually for goods that are in short supply. Black market trading breaks government regulations or legislation and is particularly prevalent during times of shortage, such as rationing, or in industries that are very highly regulated, such as pharmaceuticals or armaments. Also known as ***shadow market***

black market economy FINANCE, BANKING, AND ACCOUNTING a system of illegal trading in officially controlled goods, or an illicit secondary currency market that has rates markedly different from those in the official market

Black Monday FINANCE, BANKING, AND ACCOUNTING either of two Mondays, October 28, 1929 or October 19, 1987, that were marked by the largest stock market declines of the 20th century. Although both market crashes originated in the United States, they were immediately followed by similar market crashes around the world.

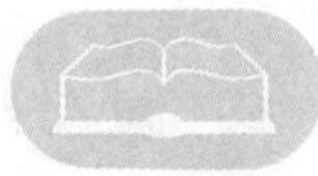

black money ECONOMICS money circulating in the ***black economy*** in payment for goods and services

Black Tuesday FINANCE, BANKING, AND ACCOUNTING October 29, 1929, when values of stocks fell precipitously

Blake, Robert R. (*b.* 1918) GENERAL MANAGEMENT U.S. psychologist. Collaborated with ***Jane Mouton*** on the development of *The **Managerial Grid*** (1964), a framework for understanding managerial behavior.

blamestorming GENERAL MANAGEMENT group discussion as to the reasons why a project has failed or is late and who is to blame for it. The term is modeled on "brainstorming." (*slang*)

blame-time GENERAL MANAGEMENT the moment in an organization when blame for the failure of a project or task is publicly allocated (*slang*)

Blanchard, Kenneth (*b.* 1939) GENERAL MANAGEMENT U.S. academic. Best known for his concept of one-minute management. *The One Minute Manager* (1982), cowritten with ***Spencer Johnson***, was a bestseller in the tradition of management self-help books alongside those by ***Dale Carnegie*** and ***Stephen Covey***.
KENNETH BLANCHARD (pp. 970–71)

blanket bond FINANCE, BANKING, AND ACCOUNTING an insurance policy that covers a financial institution for losses caused by the actions of its employees

bleed MARKETING an area of a piece of printed material that extends beyond given margins or its edges

blended rate FINANCE, BANKING, AND ACCOUNTING an interest rate charged by a lender that is between an old rate and a new one

blind carbon copy GENERAL MANAGEMENT see ***bcc***

blind certificate E-COMMERCE a ***cookie*** from which the user's name is omitted so as to protect his or her privacy while making collected data available for marketing studies

blind entry FINANCE, BANKING, AND ACCOUNTING

1. a document issued by a supplier that stipulates the amount charged for goods or services as well as the amount of GST payable
2. a bookkeeping entry that records a debit or credit but fails to show other essential information

blind offer MARKETING an inconspicuous offer buried in the body copy of a print advertisement, often used to determine the degree of reader attention to the advertisement

blind pool FINANCE, BANKING, AND ACCOUNTING a limited partnership in which the investment opportunities the general partner plans to pursue are not specified

blindside MARKETING to attack somebody in a way that he or she cannot anticipate (*slang*)

blind trust FINANCE, BANKING, AND ACCOUNTING a trust that manages somebody's business interests, with contents that are unknown to the beneficiary. People assuming public office use such trusts to avoid conflicts of interest.

block diagram STATISTICS a diagram that represents statistical data by rectangular blocks

blocked account FINANCE, BANKING, AND ACCOUNTING a bank account from which funds cannot be withdrawn for any of a number of reasons, for example, bankruptcy proceedings, liquidation of a company, or government order when freezing foreign assets

blocked currency FINANCE, BANKING, AND ACCOUNTING a currency that people cannot easily trade for other currencies because of foreign exchange control

block grant FINANCE, BANKING, AND ACCOUNTING money that the federal government gives to a local government to spend in ways that the recipient determines

blockholder FINANCE, BANKING, AND ACCOUNTING an individual or institutional investor who holds a large number of shares of stock or a large dollar amount of bonds in a given company

block investment (*ANZ*) FINANCE, BANKING, AND ACCOUNTING the purchase or holding of a large number of shares of stock or a large dollar amount of bonds in a given company

block release HR & PERSONNEL an arrangement whereby an employer permits an employee to be away from work to attend an educational institution for a period of time, usually several weeks

block trade FINANCE, BANKING, AND ACCOUNTING a sale of a large round number of stocks or amount of bonds

blow-in MARKETING advertising in the form of cards bound inside magazines or newspapers (*slang*)

blow-off top FINANCE, BANKING, AND ACCOUNTING a rapid increase in the price of a financial stock followed by an equally rapid drop in price (*slang*)

bludge (*ANZ*) GENERAL MANAGEMENT to shirk work or responsibility, or live off the earnings of others

blue chip GENERAL MANAGEMENT relating to the highest-quality and lowest-risk ordinary equity shares or to high-quality established stable companies. The term is derived from the game of poker, in which blue is the highest value chip.

blue-chip stocks FINANCE, BANKING, AND ACCOUNTING common shares of stock in a company that is considered to be well established, highly successful, and reliable, and is traded on a stock market

blue-collar job HR & PERSONNEL a position that principally or exclusively involves physical labor. With the decline in manufacturing and an increase in harmonization agreements, the term blue collar is now rarely used. Blue collar refers to the blue overalls traditionally worn in factories in contrast to the white shirt and tie supposedly worn by an office worker, known as a ***white-collar worker***.

blue-collar worker HR & PERSONNEL see ***blue-collar job***

blue hair MARKETING used in advertising and marketing to refer to women customers of advanced years (*slang*)

blueshirt GENERAL MANAGEMENT an employee of the computer company IBM (*slang*)

blue-sky ideas GENERAL MANAGEMENT extremely ambitious, idealistic, or unrealistic proposals, apparently unconfined by conventional thinking (*slang*)

blue-sky law FINANCE, BANKING, AND ACCOUNTING a state law that regulates investments to prevent investors from being defrauded

blue-sky securities FINANCE, BANKING, AND ACCOUNTING stocks and bonds that have no value, being worth the same as a piece of "blue sky" (*slang*)

blur GENERAL MANAGEMENT a period of transition for a business in which changes occur at great speed and on a large scale

board GENERAL MANAGEMENT a body of individuals chosen by the stockholders to make executive or managerial decisions for a company

board dismissal GENERAL MANAGEMENT the dismissal and removal from power of an entire ***board*** or ***board of directors***

Board of Currency Commissioners FINANCE, BANKING, AND ACCOUNTING the sole currency issuing authority in Singapore, established in 1967. Abbr **BCCS**

board of directors GENERAL MANAGEMENT the people selected to sit on an authoritative standing committee or governing body, taking responsibility for the management of an organization. Members of the board of directors are officially chosen by shareholders, but in practice they are usually selected on the basis of the current board's recommendations. The board usually includes major shareholders as well as directors of the company.

board of trustees GENERAL MANAGEMENT a committee or governing body that takes responsibility for managing, and holds in trust, funds, assets, or property belonging to others, for example, charitable or pension funds or assets

boardroom GENERAL MANAGEMENT a room in which board meetings are held. A boardroom may be a room used only for board meetings or can be a multiuse room that becomes a boardroom for the duration of a board meeting.

boardroom battle GENERAL MANAGEMENT a conflict or power struggle between individual board members or between groups of board members

board seat GENERAL MANAGEMENT a position of membership of a board, especially a ***board of directors***

board secretary GENERAL MANAGEMENT see ***company secretary***

body language HR & PERSONNEL the combination of often subconscious gestures, postures, and facial expressions that send out messages about a person's feelings and emotions. Body language is an important aspect of ***nonverbal communication***.

body of creditors FINANCE, BANKING, AND ACCOUNTING the creditors of a company or individual treated as a single creditor in dealing with the debtor

body of shareholders FINANCE, BANKING, AND ACCOUNTING the shareholders of a company treated as a single shareholder in dealing with the company

BOGOF MARKETING buy one get one free, a sales promotion technique, consumers are offered two products for the price of one

bogus degree HR & PERSONNEL a qualification awarded by an organization of questionable or unrecognized standing, usually capitalizing on the naiveté of overseas students and the reputation of the education system of the host country. A bogus degree is normally offered by an organization with a similar sounding name to a university of good standing.

boilerplate GENERAL MANAGEMENT a standard version of a contract that can be used interchangeably from contract to contract (*slang*)

bond FINANCE, BANKING, AND ACCOUNTING
1. a promise to repay with interest on specified dates money that an investor lends a company or government
2. a certificate issued by a company or government that promises repayment of borrowed money at a set rate of interest on a particular date
3. (*ANZ*) a sum of money paid as a deposit, especially on rented premises
4. (*S. Africa*) a mortgage bond

bond anticipation note FINANCE, BANKING, AND ACCOUNTING a loan that a government agency receives to provide capital that will be repaid from the proceeds of bonds that the agency will issue later

bonded warehouse FINANCE, BANKING, AND ACCOUNTING a warehouse that holds goods awaiting duty or tax to be paid on them

bond equivalent yield FINANCE, BANKING, AND ACCOUNTING the interest rate that an investor would have to receive on a bond to profit as much as from a particular investment in another type of security. Also known as ***equivalent bond yield***

bond fund FINANCE, BANKING, AND ACCOUNTING a mutual fund that invests in bonds

bondholder FINANCE, BANKING, AND ACCOUNTING an individual or institution owning bonds issued by a government or company and entitled to payments of the interest as due and return of the principal when the bond matures

bond indenture FINANCE, BANKING, AND ACCOUNTING a document that specifies the terms of a bond

bond indexing FINANCE, BANKING, AND ACCOUNTING the practice of investing in bonds in such a way as to match the yield of a designated index

bond issue FINANCE, BANKING, AND ACCOUNTING additional shares of stock in a company given by the company to existing shareholders in proportion to their prior holding

bond quote FINANCE, BANKING, AND ACCOUNTING a statement of the current market price of a bond

bond swap FINANCE, BANKING, AND ACCOUNTING an exchange of some bonds for others, usually to gain tax advantage or to diversify a portfolio

bond value FINANCE, BANKING, AND ACCOUNTING the value of an asset or liability recorded in the accounts of an entity

bond-washing FINANCE, BANKING, AND ACCOUNTING the practice of selling a bond before its dividend is due and buying it back later in order to avoid paying tax

bonus HR & PERSONNEL a financial incentive given to employees in addition to their ***base pay*** in the form of a one-off payment or as part of a ***bonus scheme***

bonus issue (*U.K.*) FINANCE, BANKING, AND ACCOUNTING additional shares of stock in a company given by the company to existing shareholders in proportion to their prior holding

bonus offer MARKETING a sales promotion technique offering consumers an additional amount of product for the basic price

bonus scheme HR & PERSONNEL a form of ***incentive scheme*** under which a ***bonus*** is paid to employees in accordance with rules concerning eligibility, performance targets, time period, and size and form of payments. A bonus scheme may apply to some or all employees and may be determined on organization, business unit, or individual performance, or on a combination of these. A bonus payment may be expressed as a percentage of salary or as a flat-rate sum.

book-building FINANCE, BANKING, AND ACCOUNTING the research done among potential institutional investors to determine the optimum offering price for a new issue of stock

book cost FINANCE, BANKING, AND ACCOUNTING the price paid for a stock, including any commissions

book-entry FINANCE, BANKING, AND ACCOUNTING an accounting entry indicated in a record somewhere but not represented by any document

book inventory FINANCE, BANKING, AND ACCOUNTING the number of items in stock according to accounting records. This number can be validated only by a physical count of the items.

bookkeeping FINANCE, BANKING, AND ACCOUNTING the activity or profession of recording the money received and spent by an individual, business, or organization

bookmark[1] E-COMMERCE a Web browser software tool that enables users to select and store pages they are likely to return to, so that they can be accessed quickly and conveniently. On Microsoft Internet Explorer (the most popular Web browser) this function is referred to as "Favorites."

bookmark[2] GENERAL MANAGEMENT to make a mental note to remember somebody or something for future reference (*slang*)

book of account FINANCE, BANKING, AND ACCOUNTING the ledgers and journals used in the preparation of financial statements

book-to-bill ratio FINANCE, BANKING, AND ACCOUNTING a ratio of the value of orders that a company has received to the amount for which it has billed its customers

book transfer FINANCE, BANKING, AND ACCOUNTING a transfer of ownership of a security without physical transfer of any document that represents the instrument

book value FINANCE, BANKING, AND ACCOUNTING the value of a company's stock according to the company itself, which may differ considerably from the market value

✔ HOW TO CALCULATE BOOK VALUE (p. 824)

book value per share FINANCE, BANKING, AND ACCOUNTING the value of one share of a stock according to the company itself, which may differ considerably from the market value

Boolean search E-COMMERCE a search allowing the inclusion or exclusion of documents containing certain words through the use of operators such as AND, NOT, and OR

boomerang worker HR & PERSONNEL an employee who returns to work for a previous employer (*slang*)

boot camp HR & PERSONNEL an ***induction*** or orientation program for new employees, designed to push recruits to their limits. Boot camps are modeled on the basic training of the U.S. Marine Corps and aim to immerse new employees in the ***corporate culture*** of the employer, as well as transferring knowledge about technical skills.

bootstrapping GENERAL MANAGEMENT the early stages of setting up a new business, when a lot of effort is required (*slang*)

border crosser HR & PERSONNEL a multi-skilled employee who is able to move from job to job within a company (*slang*)

borderless world E-COMMERCE the global economy considered as having had barriers to international trade removed by use of the Internet

border tax adjustment FINANCE, BANKING, AND ACCOUNTING the application of a domestic tax on imported goods while exempting exported goods from the tax in an effort to make the exported goods' price competitive both nationally and internationally

bosberaad GENERAL MANAGEMENT
1. (*S. Africa*) a ***think tank***, ***strategy***, or long-term planning meeting. Also known as ***lekgotla***
2. a meeting of leaders at a remote place to avoid distractions. The word means literally "bush summit."

boss GENERAL MANAGEMENT the person in charge of a job, process, department, or organization, more formally known as a ***manager*** or ***supervisor***

Boston Box GENERAL MANAGEMENT a model used for analyzing a company's potential by plotting ***market share*** against growth rate. The Boston Box was conceived by the Boston Consulting Group in the 1970s to help in the process of assessing in which businesses a company should invest and of which it should divest itself. A business with a high market share and high growth rate is a **star**, and one with a low market share and low growth rate is a **dog**. A high market share with low growth rate is characteristic of a ***cash cow***, which could yield significant but short-term gain, and a low market share coupled with high growth rate produces a **question mark company**, which offers a doubtful return on investment. To be useful, this model requires accurate assessment of a business's strengths and weaknesses, which may be difficult to obtain.

Boston matrix MARKETING a management technique developed by the Boston Consulting Group for assessing the long-term viability or profitability of products and market sectors. Categories include ***cash cows***, dogs, stars, and ***question mark company*** (see ***Boston Box***).

bottleneck OPERATIONS & PRODUCTION a limiting factor on the rate of an operation. A workstation operating at its maximum ***capacity*** becomes a bottleneck if the rate of production elsewhere in the plant increases, but throughput at that workstation cannot be increased to meet demand. An understanding of bottlenecks is important if the efficiency and capacity of an ***assembly line*** are to be increased. The techniques of ***fishbone charts***, ***Pareto charts***, and ***flow charts*** can be used to identify where and why bottlenecks occur.

bottom fisher FINANCE, BANKING, AND ACCOUNTING an investor who searches for bargains among stocks that have recently dropped in price (*slang*)

bottom line
1. FINANCE, BANKING, AND ACCOUNTING the net profit or loss that a company makes at the end of a given period of time, used in the calculation of the earnings-per-share business ratio
2. GENERAL MANAGEMENT work that produces net gain for an organization

bottom-of-the-harbor scheme (*ANZ*) FINANCE, BANKING, AND ACCOUNTING a tax avoidance strategy that involves stripping a company of assets then selling it a number of times so that it is hard to trace

bottom out FINANCE, BANKING, AND ACCOUNTING to reach the lowest level in the downward trend of the market price of securities or commodities before the price begins an upward trend again

bottom-up FINANCE, BANKING, AND ACCOUNTING relating to an approach to investing that seeks to identify individual companies that are fundamentally sound and whose stock will perform well regardless of general economic or industry-group trends

bottom-up approach GENERAL MANAGEMENT a consultative ***leadership*** style that promotes ***employee participation*** at all levels in ***decision making*** and ***problem solving***. A bottom-up approach to leadership is associated with ***flat organizations*** and the ***empowerment*** of employees. It can encourage ***creativity*** and flexibility and is the opposite of a ***top-down approach***.

bought-in goods OPERATIONS & PRODUCTION components and subassemblies that are purchased from an outside supplier instead of being made within the organization

bounce FINANCE, BANKING, AND ACCOUNTING to refuse payment of a check because the account for which it is written holds insufficient money (*slang*) Also known as ***dishonor***

bounced
get bounced HR & PERSONNEL to be dismissed from employment (*slang*)

bounced check FINANCE, BANKING, AND ACCOUNTING a draft on an account that a bank will not honor, usually because there are insufficient funds in the account

bounce off GENERAL MANAGEMENT to discuss a new idea with somebody in order to find out what his or her reaction to it is (*slang*)

bourse FINANCE, BANKING, AND ACCOUNTING a European stock exchange, especially the one in Paris

boutique investment house FINANCE, BANKING, AND ACCOUNTING a brokerage that deals in securities of only one particular industry

box
think outside the box GENERAL MANAGEMENT to think imaginatively about a problem (*slang*)

box spread FINANCE, BANKING, AND ACCOUNTING an arbitrage strategy that eliminates risk by buying and selling the same thing

Boyatzis, **Richard Eleftherios** (*b*. 1946) GENERAL MANAGEMENT U.S. academic. One of the key movers of the ***competence*** movement. His book, *The Competent Manager* (1982), acknowledged ***David McClelland***'s earlier work.

BPR GENERAL MANAGEMENT see ***business process reengineering***

bracket creep FINANCE, BANKING, AND ACCOUNTING the way in which a gradual increase in income moves somebody into a higher tax bracket

Brady bond FINANCE, BANKING, AND ACCOUNTING a bond issued by an emerging nation that has U.S. Treasury bonds as collateral

braindrain GENERAL MANAGEMENT the overseas migration of specialists, usually highly qualified scientists, engineers, or technical experts, in pursuit of higher salaries, better research funding, and a perceived higher quality of working life

brainiac HR & PERSONNEL a highly intelligent and creative employee who is also unpredictable and eccentric (*slang*)

brainstorming GENERAL MANAGEMENT a technique for generating ideas, developing ***creativity***, or ***problem solving*** in small groups, through the free-flowing contributions of participants. The concept of brainstorming was originated by A. F. Osborn and described in his book *Applied Imagination: Principles and Practices of Creative Thinking* (1957). To encourage the free flow of ideas, brainstorming sessions operate according to a set of guidelines, and the production and evaluation of ideas are kept separate. Several variations of brainstorming and related techniques have emerged such as **brainwriting**, where ideas are written down by individuals, **nominal group technique**, **electronic brainstorming**, and ***buzz groups***.
✔ BRAINSTORMING (pp. 542–43)

brainwriting GENERAL MANAGEMENT see ***brainstorming***

branch office FINANCE, BANKING, AND ACCOUNTING a bank or other financial institution that is part of a larger group and is located in a different part of a geographic area from the parent organization

branch tax FINANCE, BANKING, AND ACCOUNTING a South African tax imposed on nonresident companies that register a branch rather than a separate company

brand MARKETING the distinguishing proprietary name, symbol, or ***trademark*** that differentiates a particular product, or service, from others of a similar nature

brand awareness MARKETING the level of ***brand recognition*** that consumers have of a particular brand and its specific product category. Brand awareness examines three levels of recognition: whether the brand name is the first to come to mind when a consumer is questioned about a particular product category; whether the brand name is one of several that come to mind when a consumer is questioned about a particular product category; and whether or not a consumer has heard of a particular brand name.

brand building MARKETING the establishment and improvement of a brand's identity, including giving the brand a set of values that the consumer wants, recognizes, identifies with, and trusts. Values developed in the process of brand building include psychological, physical, and functional properties that consumers desire and should always identify a property that is unique to that brand.

brand champion MARKETING an employee of an organization who is responsible for the development, performance, and communication of a particular brand

brand equity MARKETING a financial measure relating to the estimated value of a ***brand***

brand extension MARKETING the exploitation, diversification, or stretching of a brand to revive or reinvigorate it in the marketplace. Products developed in the brand extension process may be directly recognizable derivatives or may look and feel completely different.

brand image MARKETING the perception that consumers have of a brand. Brand image is usually carefully developed by the brand owner through marketing campaigns or product positioning. Occasionally, the image of a brand may develop spontaneously through customer responses to a product. The image of a brand can be seriously tarnished through inappropriate advertising or association with somebody or something that has fallen from public favor.

branding MARKETING a means of distinguishing one firm's products or services from another's and of creating and maintaining an image that encourages confidence in the quality and performance of that firm's products or services

brand leader MARKETING the brand with the largest ***market share***

brand life cycle MARKETING the three phases through which brands pass as they are introduced, grow, and then decline. The three stages of the brand life cycle are: the introductory period, during which the brand is developed and is introduced to the market; the growth period, when the brand faces competition from other products of a similar nature; and, finally, the maturity period in which the brand either extends to other products or its image is constantly updated. Without careful *brand management*, the maturity period can lead to decline and result in the brand being withdrawn. Similar stages can be observed in the *product life cycle*.

brand loyalty MARKETING a long-term customer preference for a particular product or service. Brand loyalty can be produced by factors such as customer satisfaction with the performance or price of a specific product or service, or through identifying with a *brand image*. It can be encouraged by *advertising*.

brand management MARKETING the marketing of one or more proprietary products. *Brand managers* (see *product management*) have responsibility for the promotion and marketing of one or more commercial brands. This includes setting targets, advertising, and retailing, and coordinating all related activities to achieve those targets. In the case of multiple brand management, consideration needs be given to questions relating to the treatment of the brands as equal or as having some differentiating value. This may affect the amount of resources committed to each brand.

brand manager MARKETING see *brand management*

brand positioning MARKETING the development of a brand's position in the market by heightening customer perception of the brand's superiority over other brands of a similar nature. Brand positioning relies on the identification of a real strength or value that has a clear advantage over the nearest competitor and is easily communicated to the consumer.

brand recognition MARKETING a measurement of the ability of consumers to recall their experience or knowledge of a particular brand. Brand recognition forms part of *brand awareness*.

brand value MARKETING the amount that a brand is worth in terms of income, potential income, reputation, prestige, and market value. Brands with a high value are regarded as considerable assets to a company, so that when a company is sold, a brand with high value may be worth more than any other consideration.

brand wagon MARKETING the trend toward using branding in marketing concepts and techniques (*slang*)

brandwidth MARKETING the degree to which a brand of product or service is recognized (*slang*)

Branson, Sir Richard (*b.* 1950) GENERAL MANAGEMENT British entrepreneur. Chairman of the Virgin Group, whose dominant *corporate strategy* has been to enter a variety of industries and challenge the existing leaders, using his flair for publicity. This *diversification* strategy is balanced by that of limiting *risk*. Branson's approach is explained in *Losing My Virginity: the Autobiography* (1998).

BRB *abbr* GENERAL MANAGEMENT be right back (*slang*)

breach of contract GENERAL MANAGEMENT a refusal or failure to carry out an obligation imposed by a *contract*

breadth-of-market theory FINANCE, BANKING, AND ACCOUNTING the theory that the health of a market is measured by the relative volume of items traded that are going up or down in price

break-even MARKETING the point at which revenue equals costs

break-even analysis GENERAL MANAGEMENT a method for determining the point at which fixed and variable production costs are equaled by sales revenue and where neither a profit nor a loss is made. Usually illustrated graphically through the use of a *break-even chart*, break-even analysis can be used to aid *decision making*, set product prices, and determine the effects of changes in production or sales volume on costs and profits.

break-even chart GENERAL MANAGEMENT a management aid used in conjunction with *break-even analysis* to calculate the point at which fixed and variable production costs are met by incoming revenue. Lines are plotted to indicate expected sales revenue and production costs. The point at which lines intersect marks the break-even point where no profit or loss is made.

break-even point FINANCE, BANKING, AND ACCOUNTING the point or level of financial activity at which expenditure equals income, or the value of an investment equals its cost so that the result is neither a profit nor a loss

breakout
1. GENERAL MANAGEMENT a summary or breakdown of data that has been collected
2. FINANCE, BANKING, AND ACCOUNTING a rise in a security's price above its previous highest price, or a drop below its former lowest price, taken by technical analysts to signal a continuing move in that direction

breakthrough strategy GENERAL MANAGEMENT a strategy that achieves significant new results

break-up value FINANCE, BANKING, AND ACCOUNTING the combined market value of a firm's assets if each were sold separately as contrasted with selling the firm as an ongoing business. Analysts look for companies with a large break-up value relative to their market value to identify potential takeover targets.

Brech, Edward Francis Leopold (*b.* 1909) GENERAL MANAGEMENT British manager, writer, and historian. A publicizer and developer of the theories of *Henri Fayol* and *Frederick Winslow Taylor*, in common with *Lyndall Urwick*. Brech's *Principles and Practice of Management* (1953), sets down a structural and functional approach to management. In the 1990s, Brech completed a history of British management.

HENRI FAYOL (pp. 986–87); FREDERICK WINSLOW TAYLOR (pp. 1054–55)

Bretton Woods ECONOMICS an agreement signed at a conference at Bretton Woods in July 1944 that set up the *IMF* and the *IBRD*

bribery HR & PERSONNEL the act of persuading somebody to exercise his or her business judgment in one's favor by offering cash or a gift and thereby gaining an unfair advantage. Many organizations have *codes of conduct* that expressly forbid the soliciting or payment of bribes.

brick
hit the bricks GENERAL MANAGEMENT to go out on strike (*slang*)

bricks-and-mortar E-COMMERCE relating to a traditional business not involved in e-commerce and incurring the cost of physical structures such as warehouses

bricolage E-COMMERCE the opportunistic way in which the Web is put together, with Web designers being able to take *GIFs*, formats, and links from elsewhere on the Web to create new pages

bridge financing FINANCE, BANKING, AND ACCOUNTING borrowing that the borrower expects to repay with the proceeds of later larger loans. See *takeout financing*

bridge loan FINANCE, BANKING, AND ACCOUNTING a temporary loan providing funds until further money is received, for example, for buying one property while trying to sell another. U.K. term bridging loan.

bridging FINANCE, BANKING, AND ACCOUNTING the obtaining of a short-term loan to provide a continuing source of financing in anticipation of receiving an intermediate- or long-term loan. Bridging is routinely employed to finance the purchase or construction of a new building or property until an old one is sold.

bridging loan FINANCE, BANKING, AND ACCOUNTING = ***bridge loan***

brief MARKETING a document or set of instructions issued to somebody as guidance in developing a marketing or advertising proposal

briefing group HR & PERSONNEL see ***team briefing***

Briggs, **Katherine Cook** (1875–1968) GENERAL MANAGEMENT U.S. researcher. Inventor, together with her daughter, ***Isabel Briggs-Myers***, of the ***Myers-Briggs type indicator***.

Briggs-Myers, **Isabel** (1897–1980) GENERAL MANAGEMENT U.S. researcher. Inventor, together with her mother, ***Katherine Cook Briggs***, of the ***Myers-Briggs type indicator***.

brightsizing HR & PERSONNEL the reduction of staff within a company by letting go the mostly recently hired employees, an unintentional byproduct of which being that often the most highly capable or qualified employees are lost *(slang)*

bring forward FINANCE, BANKING, AND ACCOUNTING to carry a sum from one column or page to the next

Brisch system OPERATIONS & PRODUCTION a coding system developed for the engineering industry by E. G. Brisch and Partners in which a code is assigned to every item of resources, including materials, labor, and equipment.

broadband E-COMMERCE a class of transmission system that allows large amounts of data to be transferred at high speed

broadbanding HR & PERSONNEL the reworking of the pay hierarchy into fewer, wider ***pay scales***. Broadbanding provides a more flexible reward structure that is more in tune with the ***flat organization***. Pioneered by GEC in the United States, the introduction of broadbanding can provide a method for pay increases and ***career development*** even without a formal career ladder, and consequently can help improve ***motivation***.

brochure FINANCE, BANKING, AND ACCOUNTING a booklet or pamphlet that contains descriptive information or advertising, for example, in relation to a product or real estate for sale, or an available service

brochureware E-COMMERCE a Web site that is the online equivalent of a printed brochure providing information about products and services. The term is most often used derogatorily in reference to electronic advertising for planned but nonexistent products.

broker GENERAL MANAGEMENT to act as an agent in arranging a deal, sale, or contract

brokerage FINANCE, BANKING, AND ACCOUNTING

1. a company whose business is buying and selling stocks and bonds for its clients
2. the business of being a broker
3. a fee paid to somebody who acts as a financial agent for somebody else

brokered market FINANCE, BANKING, AND ACCOUNTING a market in which brokers bring buyers and sellers together

broker loan rate FINANCE, BANKING, AND ACCOUNTING the interest rate that banks charge brokers on money that they lend for purchases on margin

Brown, **Wilfred** (1908–85) GENERAL MANAGEMENT British business executive. Chairman and managing director of the Glacier Metal Company who introduced works councils as an attempt at ***industrial democracy***. During Brown's leadership, the Glacier Metal Company was used as the basis for the ***Glacier studies***, carried out by ***Elliot Jaques*** of the Tavistock Institute of Human Relations.

brownfield site GENERAL MANAGEMENT an industrial site, usually located in an urban area, that is abandoned, inactive, or underutilized because of real or perceived environmental contamination

brown goods MARKETING electrical consumer goods used primarily for home entertainment, for example, televisions, radios, and hi-fis

browser E-COMMERCE a piece of software that allows people to access the Internet and World Wide Web. Internet Explorer and Netscape Navigator are the most commonly used browsers.

B share *(ANZ)* FINANCE, BANKING, AND ACCOUNTING a share in a mutual fund that has no front-end sales charge but carries a redemption fee, or back-end load, payable only if the share is redeemed. This load, called a CDSC or contingent deferred sales charge, declines every year until it disappears, usually after six years.

BTI FINANCE, BANKING, AND ACCOUNTING see ***Business Times Industrial index***

BTW *abbr* GENERAL MANAGEMENT by the way *(slang)*

bubble economy ECONOMICS an unstable boom based on speculation in shares, often followed by a financial crash. This happened, for example, in the 1630s in the Netherlands and the 1720s in England.

bucket shop *(U.K.)* FINANCE, BANKING, AND ACCOUNTING a firm of brokers or dealers that sells shares of questionable value

bucket trading FINANCE, BANKING, AND ACCOUNTING an illegal practice in which a stockbroker accepts a customer's order but does not execute the transaction until it is financially advantageous to the broker but at the customer's expense

budget FINANCE, BANKING, AND ACCOUNTING a plan specifying how a company's or department's resources will be spent or allocated during a particular period

budget account *(U.K.)* FINANCE, BANKING, AND ACCOUNTING a bank account set up to control a person's regular expenditures, for example, the payment of insurance premiums, mortgage, utilities, or telephone bills. The annual expenditure for each item is paid into the account in equal monthly installments, bills being paid from the budget account as they become due.

budgetary FINANCE, BANKING, AND ACCOUNTING relating to a detailed plan of financial operations, with estimates of both revenue and expenditures for a specific future period

budget deficit FINANCE, BANKING, AND ACCOUNTING the extent by which expenditure exceeds revenue. Also known as ***deficit***

budget management FINANCE, BANKING, AND ACCOUNTING the comparison of actual financial results with the estimated expenditures and revenues for the given time period of a budget and the taking of corrective action as necessary

budget surplus FINANCE, BANKING, AND

ACCOUNTING the extent by which revenue exceeds expenditure. Also known as ***surplus***

buffer inventory OPERATIONS & PRODUCTION the products or supplies of an organization maintained on hand or in transit to stabilize variations in supply, demand, production, or lead time

buffer stock OPERATIONS & PRODUCTION an accumulation of stock, usually ***raw materials***, for use in case of supply problems or cash flow difficulties that prevent purchase of new stock. A buffer stock, or **safety stock**, is an insurance against unexpected problems, but excessive hoarding ties up assets and limits supplies of the resource to other companies. The use of ***just-in-time*** techniques has reduced the requirement for buffer stock.

Buffet, Warren (*b.* 1930) GENERAL MANAGEMENT U.S. investment banker. Chairman and C.E.O. of Berkshire Hathaway, a vehicle for investing his vast wealth realized from a unique and successful share-purchase strategy. Buffet, dubbed the "sage of Omaha," is much admired by ***Bill Gates***.

building society FINANCE, BANKING, AND ACCOUNTING in the United Kingdom, a financial institution that offers interest-bearing savings accounts, the deposits being reinvested by the society in long-term loans, primarily mortgage loans for the purchase of real estate

bulk handling FINANCE, BANKING, AND ACCOUNTING the financing of receivables in bulk to reduce processing costs

bull FINANCE, BANKING, AND ACCOUNTING
1. somebody who anticipates favorable business conditions
2. somebody who buys particular stocks or commodities in anticipation that their prices will rise, often with the expectation of selling them at a large profit at a later time. See ***bear***

bulldog GENERAL MANAGEMENT to attack a problem relentlessly (*slang*)

bulletin board E-COMMERCE a computer-based forum used by an interest group to allow members to exchange e-mails, chat online, and access software

bulletin board system E-COMMERCE see ***BBS***

bullet loan FINANCE, BANKING, AND ACCOUNTING a loan that involves specified payments of interest until maturity, when the principal is repaid

bullish
1. GENERAL MANAGEMENT anticipating favorable business conditions
2. FINANCE, BANKING, AND ACCOUNTING conducive to or characterized by buying stocks or commodities in anticipation of rising prices. See ***bearish***

bull market FINANCE, BANKING, AND ACCOUNTING a market in which prices are rising and in which a dealer is more likely to be a buyer than a seller. See ***bear market***

bullshit bingo GENERAL MANAGEMENT a game that involves counting how frequently words of incomprehensible jargon are used (*slang*)

bull spread FINANCE, BANKING, AND ACCOUNTING a combination of purchases and sales of options for the same commodity or stock intended to produce a profit when the price rises. See ***bear spread***

bullying HR & PERSONNEL see ***workplace bullying***

bump up GENERAL MANAGEMENT to upgrade somebody to a higher class of service than has been paid for, for example, in an airplane or hotel (*slang*)

bundle MARKETING to group together two or more products or services into a single package that is then offered to the consumer at one price, for example, by providing software with a personal computer

bundling MARKETING the practice of grouping together two or more products or services into a single package that is then offered to the consumer at one price

Bundy (*ANZ*) HR & PERSONNEL a timing system that records the arrival and departure of employees at their place of work

Bundy off (*ANZ*) HR & PERSONNEL to clock off from work

Bundy on (*ANZ*) HR & PERSONNEL to clock on for work

bureaucracy GENERAL MANAGEMENT an ***organization structure*** with a rigid hierarchy of ***personnel***, regulated by set rules and procedures. ***Max Weber*** believed that a bureaucracy was technically the most efficient form of organization. He described a bureaucracy as an organization structured around official functions that are bound by rules, each function having its own specified competence. The functions are structured into offices, which are organized into a hierarchy that follows technical rules and norms. Managers in a bureaucracy possess a rational-legal type of ***authority*** derived from the office they hold. Bureaucracies have been criticized for eradicating inspiration and ***creativity*** in favor of impersonality and the mundanity and regularity of corporate life. This was best described in ***William H. Whyte***'s *The Organization Man,* published in 1956, in which the individual was taken over by the bureaucratic machine in the name of efficiency. A more recent and humorous interpretation of life in a bureaucracy has been depicted by ***Scott Adams*** in *The Dilbert Principle* (1996). The term bureaucracy has gradually become a pejorative synonym for excessive and time-consuming paperwork and administration. Bureaucracies fell subject to ***delayering*** and ***downsizing*** from the 1980s onward, as the flatter organization became the target structure to ensure swifter market response and organizational flexibility.

Burns, James MacGregor (*b.* 1918) GENERAL MANAGEMENT U.S. political scientist. Noted in the business sphere for identifying two approaches to leadership, the ***transactional theory of leadership*** and the ***transformational theory of leadership***, described in his book *Leadership* (1978), which has an historical, social, and political perspective.

bush telegraph GENERAL MANAGEMENT a method of communicating information or rumors swiftly and unofficially by word of mouth or other means

Business Activity Statement FINANCE, BANKING, AND ACCOUNTING a standard document used in Australia to report the amount of GST and other taxes paid and collected by a business. Abbr **BAS**

business administration GENERAL MANAGEMENT
1. a form of ***management***. Business administration is used as a synonym for management, notably in government or the public sector. This use has developed from the **administration school** of thought established by ***Henri Fayol***, which defines management activities as a set of processes. He argued that to manage was to plan, organize, coordinate, command, and control. These principles were put into exemplary practice by ***Alfred P. Sloan, Jr.*** at General Motors and are often seen as characteristic of large ***bureaucracies***.
2. the establishment and maintenance of ***procedures***, records, and regulations in the pursuit of a commercial activity. Business administra-

tion involves the conduct of activities leading to, and resulting from, the delivery of a product or service to the customer. Administration is often seen as paperwork and form-filling, but it reaches wider than that to encompass the co-ordination of all the procedures that enable a product or service to be delivered, together with the keeping of records that can be checked to identify errors or opportunities for improvement.

business card FINANCE, BANKING, AND ACCOUNTING a small card printed with somebody's name, job title, business address, and contact numbers or e-mail address

business case (*U.K.*) GENERAL MANAGEMENT the essential value to the organization of a proposal. A business case is made through the preparation and presentation of a business plan and is used to prevent ***blue-sky ideas*** taking root without justifiable or provable value to an organization.

business cluster GENERAL MANAGEMENT a group of small firms from similar industries that team up and act as one body. Creating a business cluster enables firms to enjoy economies of scale usually only available to bigger competitors. Marketing costs can be shared and goods can be bought more cheaply. There are also networking advantages, in which small firms can share experiences and discuss business strategies.

business continuity GENERAL MANAGEMENT the uninterrupted maintenance of business activities. Ensuring business continuity requires a proactive process of identifying essential business functions within an organization and threats to those functions. Plans and procedures may then be put in place to ensure that key functions can continue whatever the circumstances. Plans may be drawn up, for example, for ***contingency***, ***disaster***, and ***risk management***, or for ***total loss control***.

Business Council of Australia GENERAL MANAGEMENT a national association of chief executives, designed as a forum for the discussion of matters pertaining to business leadership in Australia. Abbr **BCA**

business cycle ECONOMICS a regular pattern of fluctuation in national income, moving from upturn to downturn in about five years

business efficiency GENERAL MANAGEMENT a situation in which an organization maximizes benefit and profit, while minimizing effort and expenditure. Maximization of business efficiency is a balance between two extremes. Managed correctly, it results in reduced costs, waste, and duplication. ***Max Weber***, who developed the concept of the ***bureaucracy***, believed that efficiency was the goal of all bureaucratic organizations, which were designed to run like smooth machines. The greater the efficiency, the more impersonal, rational, and emotionally detached a bureaucracy becomes. The flatter organizations more prevalent today attempt to be more customer-responsive than efficient in this sense, and the notion of such an ordered and impersonal efficiency has lost favor in an era when ***creativity*** and ***innovation*** are valued as a ***competitive advantage***.

business ethics GENERAL MANAGEMENT a system of moral principles applied in the commercial world. Business ethics provide guidelines for acceptable behavior by organizations in both their strategy formulation and day-to-day operations. An ethical approach is becoming necessary both for corporate success and a positive ***corporate image***. Following pressure from consumers for more ethical and responsible business practices, many organizations are choosing to make a public commitment to ethical business by formulating ***codes of conduct*** and operating principles. In doing so, they must translate into action the concepts of personal and corporate accountability, ***corporate giving***, corporate governance, and ***whistleblowing***. Also known as ***morality in business***

business excellence GENERAL MANAGEMENT see ***excellence***

business excellence model GENERAL MANAGEMENT see ***EFQM Excellence Model***

business failure GENERAL MANAGEMENT an organization that has gone bankrupt. A business that is at risk of failure may be saved by ***turnaround management***, which identifies and deals with the reasons for decline. Also known as ***failure***

business game GENERAL MANAGEMENT a type of ***simulation game*** in which a copy or replica of a business situation is explored competitively for the purpose of learning

business gift MARKETING a present, usually from a supplier to a customer, often used to maintain good relations. Business gifts may range from a pen to a hamper and are often a form of ***merchandising***. The acceptance of a business gift is often governed by an organization's ***code of conduct*** and is often forbidden on the grounds that business gifts, particularly high value ones, may be seen as an attempt to bribe.

business intelligence GENERAL MANAGEMENT any information that can be of strategic use to a business

business interruption insurance FINANCE, BANKING, AND ACCOUNTING a policy indemnifying an organization for loss of profits and continuing fixed expenses when some insurable disaster, for example, a fire, causes the organization to stop or reduce its activities

business objective GENERAL MANAGEMENT a goal that an organization sets for itself, for example, profitability, sales growth, or return on investment. These goals are the foundation upon which the strategic and operational policies adopted by the organization are based.

business park GENERAL MANAGEMENT see ***science park***

business plan GENERAL MANAGEMENT a document describing the current activities of a business, setting out its aims and objectives and how they are to be achieved over a set period of time. A business plan may cover the activities of an organization or a group of companies, or it may deal with a single department within the organization. In the former case, it is sometimes referred to as a **corporate plan**. The sections of a business plan usually include a market analysis describing the target market, customers, and competitors, an operations plan describing how products and services will be developed and produced, and a financial section providing profit, budget, and cash flow forecasts, annual accounts, and financial requirements. Businesses may use a business plan internally as a framework for implementing strategy and improving performance or externally to attract investment or raise capital for development plans. A business plan may form part of the overall planning process, or ***corporate planning***, within an organization and be used for the implementation of corporate strategy.

✔ WRITING A BUSINESS PLAN (pp. 486–87)

business process reengineering GENERAL MANAGEMENT, OPERATIONS & PRODUCTION the initiation and control of the change of ***processes*** within an organization, in order to derive ***competitive advantage*** from improvement in the quality of products. Business process reengineering was popularized by ***Michael Hammer***. It requires a review and imaginative analysis of the processes currently used by the

  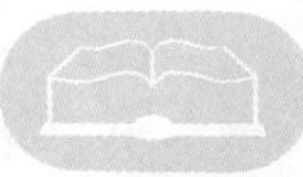    

organization. BPR, therefore, has similarities to ***benchmarking***, as this review of processes can reveal critical points where significant improvements in ***quality*** can be made. Business process reengineering was at the height of its popularity in the early- to mid-1990s. It has been criticized as one of the root causes of the bouts of ***downsizing*** and ***delayering*** that have affected many parts of industry. It has also received a negative press because few BPR projects have delivered the benefits expected of them. Abbr **BPR**

business risk FINANCE, BANKING, AND ACCOUNTING the uncertainty associated with the unique circumstances of a particular company, for example, the introduction of a superior technology which might affect the price of that company's securities

business school GENERAL MANAGEMENT a higher education institution that offers undergraduate and postgraduate courses in business-related subjects. Business schools provide courses of varying length and level, up to the ***Master of Business Administration***. They cater for full-time students, but also offer part-time and ***distance learning*** to those already in employment. Subject coverage is broad, and courses cover all areas of business administration, management, technology, finance, and interpersonal skills.

business strategy FINANCE, BANKING, AND ACCOUNTING a long-term approach to implementing a firm's business plans to achieve its business objectives

business theory GENERAL MANAGEMENT see ***organization theory***

Business Times Industrial index FINANCE, BANKING, AND ACCOUNTING an index of 40 Singapore and Malaysian shares. Abbr **BTI**

business-to-business E-COMMERCE see ***B2B***

business-to-consumer E-COMMERCE see ***B2C***

business transfer relief FINANCE, BANKING, AND ACCOUNTING the U.K. tax advantage gained when selling a business for shares in stock of the company that buys it

business unit GENERAL MANAGEMENT a part of an organization that operates as a distinct function, department, division, or stand-alone business. Business units are usually treated as a separate ***profit center*** within the overall, owning business.

business web E-COMMERCE see ***b-web***

bust-up proxy proposal FINANCE, BANKING, AND ACCOUNTING an overture to a company's stockholders for a ***leveraged buyout*** in which the acquirer sells some of the company's assets in order to repay the debt used to finance the takeover

busymeet GENERAL MANAGEMENT a business meeting (*slang*)

butterfly spread FINANCE, BANKING, AND ACCOUNTING a complex option strategy based on simultaneously purchasing and selling calls at different exercise prices and maturity dates, the profit being the premium collected when the options are sold. Such a strategy is most profitable when the price of the underlying security is relatively stable.

button E-COMMERCE an online interactive ad, smaller than the traditional ***banner***, placed on a Web page and linked to an external advertiser's site. Buttons are usually square in shape, represented to look like a push button, and located down the left or right edge of the page.

buy and hold FINANCE, BANKING, AND ACCOUNTING an investment strategy based on retaining securities for a long time

buy and write FINANCE, BANKING, AND ACCOUNTING an investment strategy involving buying stock and selling options to eliminate the possibility of loss if the value of the stock goes down

buy-back FINANCE, BANKING, AND ACCOUNTING the repurchase of bonds or shares, as agreed by contract

buydown FINANCE, BANKING, AND ACCOUNTING the payment of principal amounts that reduce the monthly payments due on a mortgage

buyer FINANCE, BANKING, AND ACCOUNTING
1. somebody who is in the process of buying something or who intends to buy something
2. somebody whose job is to choose and buy goods, merchandise, services, or media time or space for a company, factory, store, or advertiser

buyer expectation GENERAL MANAGEMENT see ***customer expectation***

buyer's guide MARKETING a document that offers information on a range of related products, usually from a number of different organizations

buyer's market FINANCE, BANKING, AND ACCOUNTING a situation in which supply exceeds demand, prices are relatively low, and buyers therefore have an advantage

buy in FINANCE, BANKING, AND ACCOUNTING to buy stock in a company so as to have a controlling interest. This is often done by or for executives from outside the company.

buying economies of scale FINANCE, BANKING, AND ACCOUNTING a reduction in the cost of purchasing raw materials and components or of borrowing money due to the increased size of the purchase

buying manager OPERATIONS & PRODUCTION see ***purchasing manager***

buy on close FINANCE, BANKING, AND ACCOUNTING a purchase at the end of the trading day

buy one get one free MARKETING see ***BOGOF***

buy on opening FINANCE, BANKING, AND ACCOUNTING a purchase at the beginning of the trading day

buy or make OPERATIONS & PRODUCTION see ***purchasing versus production***

buy out GENERAL MANAGEMENT
1. to purchase the entire stock of, or controlling financial interest in, a company
2. to pay somebody to relinquish his or her interest in a property or other enterprise

buyout
1. GENERAL MANAGEMENT the purchase and ***takeover*** of an ongoing business. It is more formally known as an ***acquisition*** (see ***merger***). If a business is purchased by managers or staff, it is known as a ***management buy-out***.
2. GENERAL MANAGEMENT the purchase of somebody else's entire stock ownership in a firm. It is more formally known as an ***acquisition*** (see ***merger***).
3. HR & PERSONNEL an option to transfer benefits of an occupational pension scheme on leaving a company

buy stop order FINANCE, BANKING, AND ACCOUNTING an order to buy stock when its price reaches a specified level

Buzan, Tony (*b.* 1942) GENERAL MANAGEMENT British writer. Originator of the ***mind map***™, a technique he explained in *Use Your Head* (1974).

buzz group GENERAL MANAGEMENT a small discussion group formed for a specific task such as generating ideas, solving problems, or reaching a common viewpoint on a topic within a specific period of time. The use of buzz groups was first associated with J. D. Phillips and is sometimes known as the Phillips 66 technique. Large groups may be divided into buzz groups after an initial presentation in order to cover different aspects of a topic or maximize participation. Each group appoints a spokesperson to report the results of the discussion to the larger group. Buzz groups are a form of ***brainstorming***.

buzzword-compliant E-COMMERCE familiar with the latest Internet jargon (*slang*)

BV *abbr* FINANCE, BANKING, AND ACCOUNTING the Dutch term for a limited liability company

b-web E-COMMERCE a business web, a group of complementary businesses that come together over the Internet. While each company retains its autonomous identity, the businesses work in unison to generate more income than they could individually. Characteristics of b-webs include ***extranets***, ***viral marketing***, online marketplaces, and affiliate schemes. The term was originally used by Don Tapscott, David Ticoll, and Alex Lowry in an article published by *eCompany Now* magazine.

by-bidder FINANCE, BANKING, AND ACCOUNTING somebody who bids at an auction solely to raise the price for the seller

Byham, **William C.** GENERAL MANAGEMENT U.S. consultant and writer. Coauthor of *Zapp! The Lightning of Empowerment* (1987), a modern fable in an industrial setting that popularized the benefits that ***empowerment*** can bring to the workplace.

bypass trust FINANCE, BANKING, AND ACCOUNTING a trust that leaves money in a will in trust to people other than the prime beneficiary in order to gain tax advantage

byte E-COMMERCE a unit of computer memory equal to that needed to store a single character, now commonly a group of eight adjacent bits

cache E-COMMERCE a small memory bank inside a computer that stores all the images and text from every Web site visited. This speeds up the download time when an Internet user revisits a site.

CAD OPERATIONS & PRODUCTION see ***computer-aided design***

Cadbury, **Sir George Adrian Hayhurst** (*b.* 1929) GENERAL MANAGEMENT British business executive. Former chairman of Cadbury Schweppes and, in the 1990s, chairman of the Committee on the Financial Aspects of ***Corporate Governance***.

Cadbury, **Sir Nicholas Dominic** (*b.* 1940) GENERAL MANAGEMENT British industrialist. Chair of the Wellcome Trust, and past chair of Cadbury Schweppes. Sir Dominic Cadbury is celebrated for his oft-quoted dictum "There is no such thing as a career path; it is crazy-paving and you have to lay it yourself."

CAD/CAM GENERAL MANAGEMENT the integration of data and technologies from ***computer-aided design*** and ***computer-aided manufacturing*** into the entire design-to-manufacture cycle. Data from a combined CAD/CAM database can be used for the control of a totally automated computer-integrated manufacturing system.

CAE OPERATIONS & PRODUCTION see ***computer-aided engineering***

call FINANCE, BANKING, AND ACCOUNTING an option to buy stock. Also known as ***call option***

callable FINANCE, BANKING, AND ACCOUNTING a financial instrument with a call provision in its indenture

call bond FINANCE, BANKING, AND ACCOUNTING a bond that the issuer may call

call center GENERAL MANAGEMENT a department or business wholly focused on telephone inquiries. Call centers usually provide a centralized point of contact for an organization and support ***telephone selling***, ***after-sales service***, telephone helplines, or information services either for a parent organization or on a contract basis for other businesses.

calling line identification GENERAL MANAGEMENT see ***computer telephony integration***

call money FINANCE, BANKING, AND ACCOUNTING money that brokers use for their own purchases or to help their customers buy on margin

call option FINANCE, BANKING, AND ACCOUNTING = ***call***

call payment FINANCE, BANKING, AND ACCOUNTING an amount that a company demands in partial payment for stock such as a rights issue that is not paid for at one time

call provision FINANCE, BANKING, AND ACCOUNTING a clause in an indenture that lets the issuer of a bond redeem it before the date of its maturity

CAM OPERATIONS & PRODUCTION see ***computer-aided manufacturing***

campaign MARKETING a program of advertising and marketing activities with a specific objective

camp on the line GENERAL MANAGEMENT to wait on hold for a long time on the telephone (*slang*)

can HR & PERSONNEL to dismiss somebody from employment (*slang*)

cap FINANCE, BANKING, AND ACCOUNTING an upper limit such as on a rate of interest for a loan

capacity OPERATIONS & PRODUCTION the measure of the capability of a workstation or a plant to produce output. Capacity measures can focus on a variety of factors, which typically include: quantity, for example, the number of items produced over a given period; and scope, for example, the range of items produced by type or size.

capacity planning OPERATIONS & PRODUCTION the process of measuring the amount of work that can be completed within a given time and determining the necessary physical and human resources needed to accomplish it. Capacity planning uses ***capacity utilization*** to ensure that the maximum amount of product possible is made and sold. The planning process involves a regulation process that identifies deviations from the plan, allowing corrective action to be taken. A ***capacity requirements planning*** program can aid in the process of capacity planning.

capacity requirements planning OPERATIONS & PRODUCTION, GENERAL MANAGEMENT a computerized tracking process that translates production requirements into practical implications for manufacturing resources. Capacity requirements planning is part of manufacturing resource planning and is carried out after a manufacturing resource planning program has been run. This produces an **infinite capacity plan**, as it does not take account of the capacity constraints of each workstation. Where the process is extended to cover capacity requirements, a **finite capacity plan** is produced. This enables ***loading*** at each workstation to be smoothed and determines the need for additional resources.

capacity utilization
1. ECONOMICS the output of an economy, firm, or plant divided by its output when working at full capacity
2. OPERATIONS & PRODUCTION, GENERAL MANAGEMENT a measure of the plant and equipment of a company or industry that is actually being used to produce goods or services. Capacity utilization usually is the measure of output over a specific period, for example, the average output for a month, or at a given point in time, for example, on a given date. It can be expressed as a ratio, where utilization = actual output/design capacity. This measure is used in both ***capacity planning*** and ***capacity requirements planning*** processes.

capital FINANCE, BANKING, AND ACCOUNTING money that can be invested by an individual or organization in order to make a profit

capital account FINANCE, BANKING, AND ACCOUNTING the sum of a company's capital at a particular time

capital allowance FINANCE, BANKING, AND ACCOUNTING the tax advantage that a company is granted for money that it spends on fixed assets

capital appreciation FINANCE, BANKING, AND ACCOUNTING the increase in a company's or individual's wealth

capital appreciation fund FINANCE, BANKING, AND ACCOUNTING a mutual fund that aims to increase the value of its holdings without regard to the provision of income to its owners

capital asset FINANCE, BANKING, AND ACCOUNTING an asset that is difficult to sell quickly, for example, real estate

capital asset pricing model ECONOMICS a model of the market used to assess the cost of capital for a company based on the rate of return on its assets

capital budget FINANCE, BANKING, AND ACCOUNTING a budget for the use of a company's money

capital controls ECONOMICS regulations placed by a government on the amount of capital residents may hold

capital cost allowance FINANCE, BANKING, AND ACCOUNTING a tax advantage in Canada for the depreciation in value of capital assets

capital deepening ECONOMICS more capital-intensive production that results when a country's ***capital stock*** increases but the numbers employed fall or remain constant

capital expenditure FINANCE, BANKING, AND ACCOUNTING an outlay of money, especially on fixed assets

capital formation ECONOMICS addition to the stock of a country's ***real capital*** by investment in fixed assets

capital gain FINANCE, BANKING, AND ACCOUNTING the financial gain made upon the disposal of an asset. The gain is the difference between the cost of its acquisition and net proceeds upon its sale.

capital gains distribution FINANCE, BANKING, AND ACCOUNTING a sum of money that, for example, a mutual fund pays to its owners in proportion to the owners' share of the organization's capital gains for the year

capital gains reserve FINANCE, BANKING, AND ACCOUNTING a tax advantage in Canada for money not yet received in payment for something that has been sold

capital gearing FINANCE, BANKING, AND ACCOUNTING the amount of fixed-cost debt that a company has for each share of its common stock

capital goods ECONOMICS stocks of physical or financial assets that are capable of generating income

capital inflow ECONOMICS the amount of capital that flows into an economy from services rendered abroad

capital-intensive FINANCE, BANKING, AND ACCOUNTING using a greater proportion of capital as opposed to labor

capitalism ECONOMICS an economic and social system in which individuals can maximize profits because they own the means of production

capitalist FINANCE, BANKING, AND ACCOUNTING an investor of capital in a business

capitalization FINANCE, BANKING, AND ACCOUNTING the amount of money invested in a company or the worth of the bonds and stocks of a company

capitalization issue (*U.K.*) FINANCE, BANKING, AND ACCOUNTING = ***stock split***

capitalization rate FINANCE, BANKING, AND ACCOUNTING the rate at which a company's ***reserves*** are converted into capital by way of a ***stock split***

capitalization ratio FINANCE, BANKING, AND ACCOUNTING the proportion of a company's value represented by debt, stock, assets, and other items

capitalize FINANCE, BANKING, AND ACCOUNTING to finance the vehicles, plant, etc. of a business.

capital levy FINANCE, BANKING, AND ACCOUNTING a tax on fixed assets or property

capital loss FINANCE, BANKING, AND ACCOUNTING a loss made through selling an asset for less than its cost

capital market FINANCE, BANKING, AND ACCOUNTING a financial market dealing with securities that have a life of more than one year

capital project OPERATIONS & PRODUCTION see ***capital project management***

capital project management GENERAL MANAGEMENT control of a ***project*** that involves expenditure of an organization's monetary resources for the purpose of creating ***capacity*** for ***production***. Capital project management often involves the organization of major construction or engineering work. **Capital projects** are usually large scale, complex, need to be completed quickly, and involve capital investment. Different techniques have evolved for capital project management from those used for normal ***project management***, including methods for managing the complexity of such projects, and for analyzing return on investment afterward.

capital property FINANCE, BANKING, AND ACCOUNTING under Canadian tax law, assets that can depreciate in value or be sold for a capital gain or loss

capital ratio FINANCE, BANKING, AND ACCOUNTING a company's income expressed as a fraction of its tangible assets

capital rationing FINANCE, BANKING, AND ACCOUNTING the restriction of new investment by a company

capital stock FINANCE, BANKING, AND ACCOUNTING the stock authorized by a company's charter, representing no ownership rights

capital structure FINANCE, BANKING, AND ACCOUNTING the proportions of a company's assets and liabilities of various sorts, especially long-term debt

capital sum FINANCE, BANKING, AND ACCOUNTING a lump sum of money that an insurer pays, for example, on the death of the insured person

capital surplus FINANCE, BANKING, AND ACCOUNTING the value of all of the stock in a company that exceeds the par value of the stock

capital turnover FINANCE, BANKING, AND ACCOUNTING the value of annual sales as a multiple of the value of the company's stock

capital widening ECONOMICS less capital-intensive production that results when both a country's ***capital stock*** and the numbers employed increase

CAPM OPERATIONS & PRODUCTION see ***computer-aided production management***

capture E-COMMERCE the submission of a credit card transaction for processing and settlement. Capture initiates the process of moving funds from the ***issuer*** to the ***acquirer*** to the merchant's account.

carbon copy E-COMMERCE see ***cc***

cardholder E-COMMERCE an individual or company that has an active credit card account with an ***issuer*** with which transactions can be initiated

card-issuing bank E-COMMERCE = ***issuer***

card-not-present merchant account E-COMMERCE an account that permits e-merchants to process credit card transactions without the purchaser being physically present for the transaction

career anchor HR & PERSONNEL a guiding force that influences people's career choices, based on self-perception of their own skills, ***motivation***, and values. The term was coined by ***Edgar Schein*** in *Career Anchors: Discovering Your Real Values*, published in 1985. He believed that people develop one underlying anchor, perhaps subconsciously, that they are unwilling to give up when faced with different pressures. Schein distinguishes several career anchor groups such as technical/functional competence, managerial ***competence***, ***creativity***, security or stability, and autonomy.

EDGAR SCHEIN (pp. 1044–45)

career break HR & PERSONNEL

1. a planned interruption to working life, supported by an employer, usually for a predetermined period of time. A career break is usually designed either to aid ***career development*** or to enable somebody to balance work and family life. It may take the form of parental leave, or a ***sabbatical*** for study, research, or exploring alternative activities. A career break may be sanctioned by an employer in order to keep a valued member of staff from leaving the organization.

2. a withdrawal from employment, either to meet caring responsibilities or to undertake a course of study, without the support of an employer

career change HR & PERSONNEL a switch in profession or in type of job, often to a different employer. Career change may be planned as part of the ***CPD*** or ***career development*** processes, or it may be forced on an employee by ***redundancy***, ill-health, or a change in personal circumstance.

career development HR & PERSONNEL progression through a sequence of jobs, involving continually more advanced or diverse activities and resulting in wider or improved skills, greater responsibility and prestige, and higher income. Formerly, career development was seen as the responsibility of the employer, and many organizations had formal career development programs that marked an employee's advancement through the levels of management. It is now more usually held to be the responsibility of the employees, sometimes as part of the ***CPD*** process.

career ladder HR & PERSONNEL a sequence of posts from most junior to most senior within an organization or department. A career ladder provides a structured path for an employee to climb up through an organization. It is most typical of ***bureaucracies***, as ***flat organization*** structures tend not to be hierarchical to the same extent.

career-limiting move HR & PERSONNEL see ***CLM***

career path HR & PERSONNEL a planned, logical progression of jobs within one or more professions throughout working life. A career path can be planned with greater assurance in market conditions of stability and little change. In times of great change and uncertainty, some people, such as ***Dominic Cadbury***, have argued that there is no longer such a thing as a planned career path and instead place greater emphasis on the importance of ***CPD*** in order to maintain ***employability***.

career pattern HR & PERSONNEL the sequence of jobs undertaken by somebody during his or her working life. A career pattern can be structured in advance as part of ***career development*** planning, and may allow for ***career breaks*** or ***career changes***. Career patterns can also be discerned more generally as trends in employee development within particular sectors of the ***labor force***.

careline MARKETING a telephone service allowing customers to obtain information, advice, or assistance from retailers

caring economy ECONOMICS an economy based on amicable and helpful relationships between businesses and people

Carnegie, Dale Breckinridge (1888–1955) GENERAL MANAGEMENT U.S. writer and trainer. Best known for his advice on self-improvement, which focused on ***interpersonal*** and effective ***communication skills***, including public speaking. Carnegie's best-seller, *How to Win Friends and Influence People* (1936), included guidance on never criticizing, complaining about, or condemning another person, giving sincere appreciation to others, and stimulating in others a specific desire in order to motivate them.

carpet

be called on the carpet GENERAL MANAGEMENT to be rebuked by your boss for a wrongdoing (*slang*)

carrier GENERAL MANAGEMENT a telecommunications company that provides network infrastructure services and charges customers for carrying their communications over the network. Carriers do not necessarily own their own network, but may rent time on a number of networks.

cartel FINANCE, BANKING, AND ACCOUNTING an alliance of business companies formed to control production, competition, and prices

cartogram STATISTICS a diagrammatic map on which statistical information is represented by shading and symbols

cash account FINANCE, BANKING, AND ACCOUNTING a brokerage account that permits no buying on margin

cash advance FINANCE, BANKING, AND ACCOUNTING a loan on a credit card account

cash and carry GENERAL MANAGEMENT see ***wholesaler***

cash available to invest FINANCE, BANKING, AND ACCOUNTING the amount, including cash on account and balances due soon for outstanding transactions, that a client has available for investment with a broker

cashback MARKETING a sales promotion technique offering customers a cash refund after they buy a product

cash basis FINANCE, BANKING, AND ACCOUNTING the bookkeeping practice of accounting for money only when it is actually received or spent

cash bonus FINANCE, BANKING, AND ACCOUNTING an unscheduled dividend that a company declares because of unexpected income

cash contract FINANCE, BANKING, AND ACCOUNTING a contract for actual delivery of a commodity

cash conversion cycle FINANCE, BANKING, AND ACCOUNTING the time between the acquisition of a raw material and the receipt of payment for the finished product. Also called ***cash cycle***

cash cow
1. MARKETING a product that sells well and makes a substantial profit without requiring much advertising or investment (*slang*)
2. GENERAL MANAGEMENT see ***Boston Box***

cash crop ECONOMICS a crop, for example, tobacco, that can be sold for cash, usually by a developing country

cash cycle FINANCE, BANKING, AND ACCOUNTING see ***cash conversion cycle***

cash deficiency agreement FINANCE, BANKING, AND ACCOUNTING a commitment to supply whatever additional cash is needed to complete the financing of a project

cash flow FINANCE, BANKING, AND ACCOUNTING the movement of money through an organization that is generated by its own operations as opposed to borrowing. It is the money that a business actually receives from sales (the cash inflow) and the money that it pays out (the cash outflow).

cash flow coverage ratio FINANCE, BANKING, AND ACCOUNTING the ratio of income to cash obligations

cash flow life HR & PERSONNEL a lifestyle characterized by working for individual project fees rather than a regular salary

cash flow per common share FINANCE, BANKING, AND ACCOUNTING the amount of cash that a company has for each share of its common stock

cashless pay HR & PERSONNEL the payment of a weekly or monthly wage through the electronic transfer of funds directly into the bank account of an ***employee***

cashless society ECONOMICS a society in which all bills and debits are paid by electronic money media, for example, bank and credit cards, direct debits, and online payments

cash loan company (*S. Africa*) FINANCE, BANKING, AND ACCOUNTING a microlending business that provides short-term loans without collateral, usually at high interest rates

cash offer FINANCE, BANKING, AND ACCOUNTING an offer to buy a company for cash rather than for stock

cash ratio FINANCE, BANKING, AND ACCOUNTING the ratio of a company's liquid assets such as cash and securities divided by total liabilities. Also known as ***liquidity ratio***

cash settlement FINANCE, BANKING, AND ACCOUNTING
1. **cash settlement** *or* **cash sale** an immediate payment on an options contract without waiting for expiration of the normal, usually five-day, settlement period
2. the completion of a transaction by paying for securities

cash surrender value FINANCE, BANKING, AND ACCOUNTING the amount of money that an insurance company will pay to terminate a policy at a particular time if the policy does not continue until its normal expiration date

casual worker HR & PERSONNEL somebody who provides labor or services under an irregular or informal working arrangement. A casual worker is usually considered as an independent contractor rather than an ***employee***. Consequently, there is no obligation on the part of an employer to provide work, and there is no obligation on the part of the casual worker to accept all offers of work made by an employer.

category management MARKETING the process of manufacturers and retailers working together to maximize profits and enhance customer value in any given product category. Category management has developed from ***brand management*** and the techniques of efficient consumer response, and is most prevalent in the fast moving consumer goods sector. It is founded on the assumption that consumer purchase decisions are made from a range of products within a category and not merely by ***brand*** and has gained in prominence, as it is believed to meet customer needs better than standard brand management. Abbr **CM**

causality STATISTICS the relation of events to the effects they produce

cause and effect diagram GENERAL MANAGEMENT see ***fishbone chart***

CBD *abbr* GENERAL MANAGEMENT central business district, the area of a city where most of its company offices are located

cc *abbr* E-COMMERCE carbon copy, a function included on most e-mail programs that enables Internet users to send a copy of the same message to as many people as they choose. All they need to do is place the e-mail addresses of intended recipients in the cc address line. Recipients see all other names. To conceal names, the ***bcc*** address line can be used.

CC *abbr* (*S. Africa*) FINANCE, BANKING, AND ACCOUNTING close corporation

ceiling effect STATISTICS the occurrence of clusters of scores near the upper limit of the data in a statistical study

cellular manufacturing OPERATIONS & PRODUCTION = ***group technology***

cellular organization OPERATIONS & PRODUCTION a form of organization consisting of a collection of self-managing firms or cells held together by mutual interest. A cellular organization is built on the principles of self-organization, member ownership, and entrepreneurship. Each cell within the organization shares common features and purposes with its sister cells but is also able to function independently. The idea is an extension of the principles of ***group technology***, or cellular manufacturing.

cellular production OPERATIONS & PRODUCTION = ***group technology***

census STATISTICS a study in which every member of a population is observed

central bank ECONOMICS the bank of a country that controls its credit system and its money supply

central business district GENERAL MANAGEMENT see ***CBD***

centralization GENERAL MANAGEMENT the gathering together, at a corporate headquarters, of specialist functions such as finance, personnel, and information technology. Centralization is usually undertaken in order to effect economies of scale and to standardize operating procedures throughout the organization. Centralized management can become cumbersome and inefficient and may produce communication problems. Some organizations have shifted toward ***decentralization*** to try to avoid this.

centralized purchasing OPERATIONS & PRODUCTION the control by a central department of all the purchasing undertaken within an organization. In a large organization centralized purchasing is often located within the headquarters. Centralization has the advantages of reducing duplication of effort, pooling volume purchases for discounts, enabling more effective inventory control, consolidating transport loads to achieve lower costs, increasing skills development in purchasing personnel, and enhancing relationships with ***suppliers***.

Central Provident Fund HR & PERSONNEL a retirement benefit scheme for Singaporeans. All employees and employers make compulsory contributions each month. Abbr **CPF**

Centrelink GENERAL MANAGEMENT an Australian government authority responsible for providing access to government services, including social security allowances and employment schemes. Established in 1997, it maintains a network of around 1,000 outlets.

C.E.O. GENERAL MANAGEMENT see ***chief executive officer***

C.E.O. churning GENERAL MANAGEMENT the rapid rate at which chief executive officers are often removed from their posts (*slang*)

CER GENERAL MANAGEMENT see ***Australia and New Zealand Closer Economic Relations Trade Agreement***

certificate FINANCE, BANKING, AND ACCOUNTING a document representing partial ownership of a company that states the number of shares that the document is worth and the names of the company and the owner of the shares

certificate authority E-COMMERCE an independent organization that verifies the identity of a purchaser or merchant and issues a ***digital certificate*** attesting to this for use in e-commerce transactions

C.F.O. GENERAL MANAGEMENT see ***chief financial officer***

CFR E-COMMERCE see ***cost and freight***

CGI Joe HR & PERSONNEL a computer programmer who lacks social skills and charisma. The term is modeled on "GI Joe," a word for a U.S. soldier that dates from World War II; its first part is an abbreviation of "computer generated imagery." (*slang*)

chaebol GENERAL MANAGEMENT see ***keiretsu***

chain of command HR & PERSONNEL the line of authority in a hierarchical organization through which instructions pass. The chain of command usually runs from the most senior personnel, through all reporting links in an organization's or department's structure, to a targeted person or to front-line employees. ***Line management*** relies on the chain of command in order for instructions to pass throughout an organization.

chainsaw consultant HR & PERSONNEL an outside expert brought into a company to reduce staff levels (*slang*)

chair GENERAL MANAGEMENT the most senior executive in an organization. The chair of an organization is responsible for running the ***annual meeting***, and meetings of the ***board of directors***. He or she may be a figurehead, appointed for prestige or power, and may have no role in the day-to-day running of the organization. Sometimes the roles of chair and ***chief executive*** are combined, and the chair then has more control over daily operations; sometimes the chair is a retired chief executive. In the United States, the person who performs this function is often called a **president**. Historically, the term **chairman** was more common. The terms **chairwoman** or **chairperson** are later developments, although chair is now the most generally acceptable. Chairman, however, remains in common use, especially in the corporate sector

chairman GENERAL MANAGEMENT see ***chair***

chairperson GENERAL MANAGEMENT see ***chair***

chairwoman GENERAL MANAGEMENT see ***chair***

Champy, James (*b.* 1942) GENERAL MANAGEMENT U.S. consultant. See ***Hammer, Michael***

Chandler, Alfred D. (*b.* 1918) GENERAL MANAGEMENT U.S. academic. Pioneer of business history who established a framework and rationale for the subject and suggested that the main function of an organization is to implement ***strategy***. In *Strategy and Structure* (1962), he argued that the optimum use of resources stemmed not merely from the way they were organized but, more importantly, from the organization's strategic goals.
ALFRED D. CHANDLER, JR. (pp. 974–75)

change agent GENERAL MANAGEMENT see ***change management***

change management GENERAL MANAGEMENT the coordination of a structured period of transition from situation A to situation B in order to achieve lasting change within an organization. Change management can be of varying scope, from ***continuous improvement***, which involves small ongoing changes to existing processes, to radical and substantial change involving organizational strategy. Change management can be reactive or proactive. It can be instigated in reaction to something in an organization's external environment, for example, in the realms of economics, politics, legislation, or competition, or in reaction to something within the processes, structures, people, and events of the organization's internal environment. It may also be instigated as a proactive measure, for example, in anticipation of unfavorable economic conditions in the future. Change management usually follows five steps: recognition of a trigger indicating that change is needed; clarification of the end point, or "where we want to be"; planning how to achieve the change; accomplishment of the transition; and maintenance to ensure the change is lasting. Effective change management involves alterations on a personal level, for example, a shift in attitudes or work routines, and thus personnel management skills such as ***motivation*** are vital to successful change. Other important influences on the success of change management include leadership style, communication, and a unified positive attitude to the change among the workforce. ***Business process reengineering*** is one type of change management, involving the redesign of processes within an organization to raise performance. **Change agents** are those people within an organization who are leaders and champions of the change process. With the accelerating pace of change in the business environment in the 1990s and 2000s, change has become accepted as a fact of business life and is the subject of books on management.

✔ IMPLEMENTING AN EFFECTIVE CHANGE PROGRAM (pp. 504–05); MOTIVATING YOUR STAFF IN A TIME OF CHANGE (pp. 372–73)

channel MARKETING a method of selling and distributing products to customers, directly or through intermediaries. Channels include direct sales, retail outlets, the Internet, and wholesalers.

channel communications MARKETING communications aimed at organizations that sell and distribute products to customers, for example, retailers, sales teams, or wholesalers

channel management MARKETING the organization of the ways in which companies reach and satisfy their customers. Channel management involves more than just ***distribution*** and has been described as management of how and where a product is used and of how the customer and the product interact. Channel management covers processes for identifying key customers, communicating with them, and continuing to create value after the first contact.

channel strategy MARKETING a management technique for determining the most effective method of selling and distributing products to customers

channel stuffing FINANCE, BANKING, AND ACCOUNTING the artificial boosting of sales at the end of a financial year by offering distributors and dealers incentives to buy a greater quantity of goods than they actually need (*slang*)

channel support MARKETING marketing or financial support aimed at improving the performance of organizations that sell and distribute products to customers, for example, retailers, sales teams, or wholesalers

chaos

1. STATISTICS a situation in which a deterministic model displays behavior that appears to be random
2. GENERAL MANAGEMENT a situation of unpredictability and rapid change. **Chaos theory** emerged in the 1970s as a mathematical concept that defied the theory of cause and effect to assert that behavior is essentially random. Such writers as ***Tom Peters***, who wrote *Thriving on Chaos* in 1987, have applied the theory to management, arguing that attempts to plan and control management processes are fundamentally doomed to failure and that, instead, managers should embrace change and flexibility in order to cope with an environment that is altering at an ever-increasing rate.

chaos theory GENERAL MANAGEMENT see *chaos*

charismatic authority GENERAL MANAGEMENT a style of ***leadership*** based on the leader's exceptional personal qualities. Charismatic authority is one of ***Max Weber***'s three types of legitimate ***authority***. A charismatic leader is set apart from others by special qualities that inspire employees to follow and obey of their own free will. This is similar to the ***great man theory*** of leadership.

MAX WEBER (pp. 1060–61)

chase demand plan OPERATIONS & PRODUCTION a ***production control*** plan that attempts to match ***capacity*** to the varying levels of forecast demand. Chase demand plans require ***flexible working*** practices and place varying demands on equipment requirements. Pure chase demand plans are difficult to achieve and are most commonly found in operations where output cannot be stored or where the organization is seeking to eliminate stores of finished goods.

chat system E-COMMERCE a system that enables Internet users to communicate in real time. Messages posted via a chat system will be seen by every member of the participating group.

checking account ECONOMICS a bank account in which deposits can be withdrawn at any time, but do not usually earn interest, except in the case of some online accounts. It is the most common type of bank account.

cherry picking GENERAL MANAGEMENT the selection of what is perceived to be the best or most valuable from a series of ideas or options

CHESS GENERAL MANAGEMENT Clearing House Electronic Subregister System, a centralized electronic share transfer and settlement system operated by the Australian Stock Exchange. It issues shareholders with regular holding statements.

chief executive GENERAL MANAGEMENT the person with overall responsibility for ensuring that the daily operations of an organization run efficiently and for carrying out strategic plans. The chief executive of an organization normally sits on the ***board of directors***. In a limited company, the chief executive is usually known as a ***managing director***.

chief executive officer GENERAL MANAGEMENT the highest ranking executive officer within a company or corporation, who has responsibility for overall management of its day-to-day affairs under the supervision of the board of directors. Abbr **C.E.O.**

chief financial officer GENERAL MANAGEMENT the officer in an organization responsible for handling funds, signing checks, the keeping of financial records, and financial planning for the company. Abbr **C.F.O.**

chief information officer GENERAL MANAGEMENT the officer in an organization responsible for its internal information systems and sometimes for its e-business infrastructure. Abbr **C.I.O.**

chief operating officer GENERAL MANAGEMENT the officer in a corporation responsible for the day-to-day management of a company and usually reporting to the chief executive officer. Abbr **C.O.O.**

chief technology officer *or* **chief technical officer** GENERAL MANAGEMENT the officer in an organization responsible for research and development and possibly for new product plans. Abbr **C.T.O.**

childcare provision HR & PERSONNEL a ***personnel policy*** to supply or to help toward the cost of care for the children of employees during working hours. The aim of childcare provision is to enable primary carers to return to work despite childcare responsibilities. It may apply to children of all ages and can be implemented in a single scheme or as a combination of options, for example, by setting up a workplace nursery or giving childcare vouchers or allowances. To comply with ***equal opportunities*** legislation, childcare provision has to be made available to both male and female employees.

Chinese wall GENERAL MANAGEMENT the procedures enforced within a securities firm to prevent the exchange of confidential information between the firm's departments so as to avoid the illegal use of inside information

  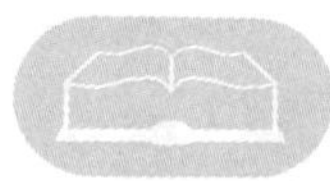    

chit
call in chits GENERAL MANAGEMENT to ask favors from people indebted to you (*slang*)

churn
1. FINANCE, BANKING, AND ACCOUNTING to encourage an investor to change stock frequently because the broker is paid every time there is a change in the investor's portfolio (*slang*)
2. GENERAL MANAGEMENT to suffer a high labor turnover rate, especially in areas such as call centers or at chief executive level in large companies
3. GENERAL MANAGEMENT to purchase a quick succession of products or services without displaying loyalty to any of them, often as a result of competitive marketing strategies that continually undercut rival prices, thus encouraging customers to switch brands constantly in order to take advantage of the cheapest or most attractive offers

churn rate
1. FINANCE, BANKING, AND ACCOUNTING a measure of the frequency and volume of trading of stocks and bonds in a brokerage account
2. GENERAL MANAGEMENT the rate at which new customers try a product or service and then stop using it

chute
right out of the chute HR & PERSONNEL extremely inexperienced (*slang*)

CIF E-COMMERCE see ***cost, insurance, and freight***

cigar
close, but no cigar GENERAL MANAGEMENT almost correct, but not quite. The term refers to the fact that cigar smoking is seen by many businesspeople as a symbol of the celebration of a success. (*slang*)

C.I.O. GENERAL MANAGEMENT see ***chief information officer***

circle the drain GENERAL MANAGEMENT to be on the brink of complete failure (*slang*)

circuit breaker FINANCE, BANKING, AND ACCOUNTING a rule created by the major U.S. stock exchanges and the ***Securities and Exchange Commission*** by which trading is halted during times of extreme price fluctuations (*slang*)

circular file GENERAL MANAGEMENT a wastebasket in an office (*slang*)

circular flow of income ECONOMICS a model of a country's economy showing the flow of resources when consumers' wages and salaries are used to buy goods and so generate income for manufacturing firms

circular merger GENERAL MANAGEMENT see ***merger***

circulation MARKETING the number of copies sold or distributed of a single issue of a newspaper or magazine

claims adjuster FINANCE, BANKING, AND ACCOUNTING somebody who determines the value of a claim made under an insurance policy

classical economics ECONOMICS a theory focusing on the functioning of a market economy and providing a rudimentary explanation of consumer and producer behavior in particular markets. The theory postulates that, over time, the economy would tend to operate at full employment because increases in supply would create corresponding increases in demand.

classified advertising MARKETING advertising placed in newspapers or magazines under specific categories, for example, motoring or real estate

classified stock FINANCE, BANKING, AND ACCOUNTING a company's common stock divided into classes such as Class A and Class B

class interval STATISTICS any of the intervals of the frequency distribution in a set of statistical observations

clean float ECONOMICS a floating exchange rate that is allowed to vary without any intervention from the country's monetary authorities

clearing bank FINANCE, BANKING, AND ACCOUNTING a bank that deals with other banks through a clearing house in the United Kingdom

clearing house
1. E-COMMERCE = ***acquirer***
2. FINANCE, BANKING, AND ACCOUNTING an institution that settles accounts between banks

clearing system FINANCE, BANKING, AND ACCOUNTING the system of settling accounts among banks

clear title FINANCE, BANKING, AND ACCOUNTING = ***good title***

clerical work improvement program GENERAL MANAGEMENT a ***clerical work measurement*** technique that applies ***standard time*** data to clerical and administrative jobs, the aim of which is to ensure higher productivity and greater efficiency

clerical work measurement GENERAL MANAGEMENT an umbrella term for a collection of methods for measuring administrative and clerical work activities. Clerical work measurement is a variation on conventional ***work measurement*** practices. The main clerical work measurement techniques include ***clerical work improvement programs*** and ***group capacity assessment***.

CLI *abbr* GENERAL MANAGEMENT calling line identification

clickable corporation E-COMMERCE a company that operates on the Internet

click rate E-COMMERCE = ***click-through rate***

clicks and bricks GENERAL MANAGEMENT a business strategy that involves combining traditional retail outlets with online commerce (*slang*)

clicks-and-mortar E-COMMERCE combining a traditional bricks-and-mortar organization with the click technology of the Internet. A clicks-and-mortar organization has both a virtual and a physical presence. Examples include retailers with physical shops on the high street and also Web sites where their goods can be bought online.

clicks-and-mortar business E-COMMERCE a hybrid business involved in e-commerce and also in marketing its products through a traditional store or otherwise incurring the cost of physical structures such as warehouses

clickstream E-COMMERCE the virtual trail that a user leaves behind while surfing the Internet. A clickstream is a record of a user's activity on the Internet, including every Web page visited, how long each page is visited for, and the order in which the pages are visited. Both ***ISPs*** and individual Web sites are able to track an Internet user's clickstream.

click-through E-COMMERCE the selection of an ad by clicking on the banner or other on-screen device to take the user to the advertiser's Web site. The number of times users click on an ad can be counted, the total number of click-throughs being a measure of the

success of the ad. Also known as ***ad click***, ***ad transfer***

click-through rate E-COMMERCE the percentage of ad views that result in a click-through, a measure of the success of the ad in enticing users to the advertiser's Web site. Also known as ***ad click rate***, ***click rate***

click wrap agreement *or* **click wrap license** E-COMMERCE a contract presented entirely over the Internet, the purchaser indicating assent to be bound by the terms of the contract by clicking on an "I agree" button. The term stems from "shrink wrap" agreements, licenses that become enforceable when the user removes designated packaging containing a copy of the agreement. Also known as ***point and click agreement***

client
1. MARKETING a person or organization that employs the services of a professional person or organization
2. E-COMMERCE see ***server***

client base MARKETING the regular ***clients*** of an organization or professional person

clinical trial STATISTICS a statistical study of human subjects to determine the effectiveness of a medical treatment

Clintonomics ECONOMICS the policy of former President Clinton's Council of Economic Advisors to intervene in the economy to correct market failures and redistribute income

CLM *abbr* HR & PERSONNEL a career-limiting move, an action that could endanger your career prospects, for example, criticizing your boss publicly (*slang*)

CLOB International FINANCE, BANKING, AND ACCOUNTING a mechanism for buying and selling foreign shares, especially Malaysian shares, in Singapore

clock in
1. HR & PERSONNEL to register your arrival for work by inserting a card into a machine to record the time. Clocking in is a method of officially monitoring employees' ***time keeping***.
2. GENERAL MANAGEMENT to register arrival at work without actually inserting a card into a time clock (*slang*)

close company *or* **closed company** (*U.K.*) GENERAL MANAGEMENT a company in which five or fewer people control more than half the voting shares or in which such control is exercised by any number of people who are also directors

close corporation *or* **closed corporation**
1. GENERAL MANAGEMENT a public corporation in which all of the voting stock is held by a few shareholders, for example, management or family members. Although it is a public company, shares would not normally be available for trading because of a lack of liquidity.
2. (*S. Africa*) FINANCE, BANKING, AND ACCOUNTING a business registered in terms of the Close Corporations Act of 1984, consisting of not more than 10 members who share its ownership and management. Abbr **CC**

closed-door policy GENERAL MANAGEMENT see ***open-door policy***

closed economy ECONOMICS an economic system in which little or no external trade takes place

closed-end credit GENERAL MANAGEMENT a loan, plus any interest and finance charges, that is to be repaid in full by a specified future date. Loans that have real estate or motor vehicles as collateral are usually closed-end. See ***open-end credit***

closed-end fund *or* **closed-end investment company** FINANCE, BANKING, AND ACCOUNTING a mutual fund that has a fixed number of shares. See ***open-end fund***

closed-end mortgage FINANCE, BANKING, AND ACCOUNTING a mortgage in which no prepayment is allowed. See ***open-end mortgage***. Also known as ***closed mortgage***

closed-loop production system OPERATIONS & PRODUCTION an environmentally friendly production system in which any industrial output is capable of being recycled to create another product

closed mortgage FINANCE, BANKING, AND ACCOUNTING = ***closed-end mortgage***

closed shop HR & PERSONNEL an agreement requiring members of a particular group of employees to be or to become members of a specified ***labor union***

closely held shares FINANCE, BANKING, AND ACCOUNTING shares that are publicly traded but held by very few people

Closer Economic Relations agreement FINANCE, BANKING, AND ACCOUNTING see ***Australia and New Zealand Closer Economic Relations Trade Agreement***

closing bell FINANCE, BANKING, AND ACCOUNTING the end of a trading session at a stock or commodities exchange

closing price FINANCE, BANKING, AND ACCOUNTING the price of the last transaction for a particular security or commodity at the end of a trading session

closing quote FINANCE, BANKING, AND ACCOUNTING the last bid and offer prices recorded at the close of a trading session

closing sale FINANCE, BANKING, AND ACCOUNTING a sale that reduces the risk that the seller has through holding a greater number of shares or a longer term contract

club culture GENERAL MANAGEMENT a ***corporate culture*** in which all lines of communication lead formally or informally to the leader. Club culture was identified by ***Charles Handy***.
CHARLES HANDY (pp. 1000–01)

cluster analysis MANAGEMENT a statistical method used to analyze complex data and identify groupings that share common features. Cluster analysis is a form of ***multivariate analysis*** that attempts to explain variability in a set of data. It involves finding unifying elements that enable identification of groups or clusters displaying common characteristics. It could be used, for example, to analyze results of ***attitude research*** and delineate groups of respondents that share certain attitudes.

clustered data STATISTICS data in which sampling units in a study are grouped into clusters sharing a common feature, or longitudinal data in which clusters are defined by repeated measures on the unit

cluster sampling OPERATIONS & PRODUCTION see ***random sampling***

Clutterbuck, David (*b.* 1947) GENERAL MANAGEMENT British academic. Best known for his work on ***mentoring***, and his research, with Walter Goldsmith, on consistently high-performing companies. Their findings were published in *The Winning Streak* (1984), which was viewed as the British equivalent of ***Tom Peters***'s and ***Robert Waterman***'s *In Search of Excellence* (1982).

CM GENERAL MANAGEMENT see ***category management***

coaching HR & PERSONNEL the development of somebody's skills and knowledge through one-to-one ***training***. Coaching is usually conducted by a more senior and experienced col-

league. It involves planned training activities that have measurable outcomes and is designed to facilitate learning by providing guidance and support as well as tutoring. ***Executive coaching*** is a form of coaching used with senior managers.

COAG GENERAL MANAGEMENT see ***Council of Australian Governments***

cobweb site E-COMMERCE an Internet site that has not been updated for a long time (*slang*)

code of conduct GENERAL MANAGEMENT a statement and description of required behaviors, responsibilities, and actions expected of employees of an organization or of members of a professional body. A code of conduct usually focuses on ethical and socially responsible issues and applies to individuals, providing guidance on how to act in cases of doubt or confusion. Related concepts are a code of ethics and a ***code of practice***.

code of practice GENERAL MANAGEMENT a policy statement and description of preferred methods for organizational ***procedures***. Codes of practice may govern procedures for industrial relations, health and safety, and, more recently, customer service and professional development. An agreed code of practice enables activities to be carried out to a required organizational standard and provides a basis for dispute resolution. A ***code of conduct*** is a related concept.

coefficient of variation STATISTICS a measure of the spread of a set of statistical data, calculated as the mean or standard deviation of the data multiplied by 100

co-financing FINANCE, BANKING, AND ACCOUNTING the joint provision of money for a project by two or more parties

coherence STATISTICS a measure of the strength of association between two time series

cohesion fund GENERAL MANAGEMENT the main financial instrument for reducing economic and social disparities within the European Union by providing financial help for projects in the fields of environment and transport infrastructure

cohort STATISTICS a group of individuals in a statistical study that have a common characteristic

cohort study STATISTICS a study in which a group of individuals such as children with the same birth date are observed over several years

coincidence STATISTICS the occurrence of events that are related but have no apparent common cause

cold calling MARKETING the practice of making unsolicited calls to customers or consumers in an attempt to sell products or services. Cold calling is disliked, particularly by individual consumers, and is an inefficient way of selling as the take-up rate is very low.

cold transfer GENERAL MANAGEMENT an incoming phone call that is transferred by an operator without giving any notice or explanation to the caller or to the recipient of the call (*slang*)

collaborative working HR & PERSONNEL a method of working in which people at different locations or from different organizations work together electronically using videoconferencing, e-mail, networks, and other communication tools

collateral FINANCE, BANKING, AND ACCOUNTING property or goods used as security against a loan and forfeited to the lender if the borrower defaults

collateral trust certificate FINANCE, BANKING, AND ACCOUNTING a bond for which shares in another company, usually a subsidiary, are used as collateral

collective agreement HR & PERSONNEL a contract between a ***labor union*** and an employer, resulting from ***collective bargaining*** and covering ***conditions of employment*** and procedural arrangements for resolving disputes. In the United Kingdom, a collective agreement is not legally binding unless it is in writing and specifically states the parties' intention to be bound. An agreement can become legally binding by being incorporated into an employee's personal ***contract of employment***. Agreements may be concluded at organization or industry level.

collective bargaining HR & PERSONNEL negotiations about ***conditions of employment*** between an employer, a group of employers or their representatives, and employees' representatives such as ***labor unions*** with a view to reaching a ***collective agreement***

combination bond FINANCE, BANKING, AND ACCOUNTING a government bond for which the collateral is both revenue from the financed project and the government's credit

combined financial statement FINANCE, BANKING, AND ACCOUNTING a written record covering the assets, liabilities, net worth, and operating statement of two or more related or affiliated companies

COMEX FINANCE, BANKING, AND ACCOUNTING see ***commodity exchange***

command and control approach GENERAL MANAGEMENT a style of leadership that uses standards, ***procedures***, and output statistics to regulate the organization. A command and control approach to leadership is authoritative in nature and uses a ***top-down approach***, which fits well in ***bureaucratic*** organizations in which privilege and power are vested in ***senior management***. It is founded on, and emphasizes a distinction between, executives on the one hand and workers on the other. It stems from the principles of ***Frederick Winslow Taylor***, and the applications of ***Henry Ford*** and ***Alfred P. Sloan, Jr.*** As more ***empowered***, ***flat organizations*** have come to the fore, command and control leaders have been increasingly criticized for stifling creativity and limiting flexibility.

ALFRED P. SLOAN, JR. (pp. 1140–41)
FREDERICK WINSLOW TAYLOR (pp. 1054–55)

command economy ECONOMICS an economy in which all economic activity is regulated by the government, as in the former Soviet Union or China

commerce FINANCE, BANKING, AND ACCOUNTING the large-scale buying and selling of goods and services, usually applied to trading between different states or countries

commerce integration FINANCE, BANKING, AND ACCOUNTING the blending of Internet-based commerce capabilities with the ***legacy systems*** of a traditional business to create a seamless transparent process

commerce server E-COMMERCE
1. a computer in a network that maintains all transactional and backend data for an e-commerce Web site
2. a networked computer that contains the programs required to process transactions via the Internet, including dynamic inventory databases, shopping cart software, and online payment systems

commerce service provider E-COMMERCE an organization or company that provides a service to a company to facilitate some aspect of electronic commerce, for example, by functioning as an Internet ***payment gateway***. Abbr **CSP**

commercial[1] FINANCE, BANKING, AND ACCOUNTING relating to the buying and selling of goods and services

commercial[2] MARKETING an advertising message that is broadcast on television or radio

commercial bank FINANCE, BANKING, AND ACCOUNTING a bank that holds deposits, makes loans, and provides related services. See ***investment bank***

commercial exposure potential MARKETING the estimated number of possible recipients of a commercial message

commercial hedger FINANCE, BANKING, AND ACCOUNTING a company that holds options in the commodities it produces

commercialization FINANCE, BANKING, AND ACCOUNTING the application of business principles to something in order to run it as a business

commercial law GENERAL MANAGEMENT the body of law that deals with the rules and institutions of commercial transactions, including banking, commerce, contracts, copyrights, insolvency, insurance, patents, trademarks, shipping, storage, transportation, and warehousing

commercial loan FINANCE, BANKING, AND ACCOUNTING a short-term renewable loan or line of credit used to finance the seasonal or cyclical working capital needs of a company

commercial paper FINANCE, BANKING, AND ACCOUNTING uncollateralized loans obtained by companies, usually on a short-term basis. Also known as ***mercantile paper***

commercial report FINANCE, BANKING, AND ACCOUNTING an investigative report made by an organization such as a credit bureau that specializes in obtaining information regarding a person or organization applying for something such as credit or employment

commercial time MARKETING an interval of time, usually measured in multiples of 15 seconds, during a radio or television broadcast available for purchase by an advertiser to broadcast its commercial message

commercial version GENERAL MANAGEMENT a version of a software program that is released for sale to customers. Earlier versions, called test versions or beta versions, are used to develop and test the software.

commercial year FINANCE, BANKING, AND ACCOUNTING an artificial year treated as having 12 months of 30 days each, used for calculating such things as monthly sales data and inventory levels

commission HR & PERSONNEL a payment made to an intermediary, often calculated as a percentage of the value of goods or services provided. Commission is most often paid to sales staff, brokers, or agents.

commitment document FINANCE, BANKING, AND ACCOUNTING a contract, change order, purchase order, or letter of intent pertaining to the supply of goods and services that commits an organization to legal, financial, and other obligations

commitment fee FINANCE, BANKING, AND ACCOUNTING a fee that a lender charges to guarantee a rate of interest on a loan a borrower is soon to make

commitment letter FINANCE, BANKING, AND ACCOUNTING an official notice from a lender to a borrower that the borrower's application has been approved and confirming the terms and conditions of the loan

committee GENERAL MANAGEMENT a group of people appointed and authorized to study, investigate, or make recommendations on a particular matter

commodities exchange FINANCE, BANKING, AND ACCOUNTING a market in which raw materials are bought and sold in large quantities as ***actuals*** or ***futures***

commodity ECONOMICS a good or service, for example, cotton, wool, or a laptop computer, resulting from the process of ***production***

commodity-backed bond FINANCE, BANKING, AND ACCOUNTING a bond tied to the price of an underlying commodity, for example, gold or silver, often used as a hedge against inflation

commodity exchange FINANCE, BANKING, AND ACCOUNTING an exchange where futures are traded, for example, the commodity exchange for metals. Abbr **COMEX**

commodity future FINANCE, BANKING, AND ACCOUNTING a contract to buy or sell a commodity at a predetermined price and on a particular delivery date

commodity paper FINANCE, BANKING, AND ACCOUNTING loans for which commodities are collateral

commodity pool FINANCE, BANKING, AND ACCOUNTING a group of people who join together to trade in options

commodity-product spread FINANCE, BANKING, AND ACCOUNTING coordinated trades in both a commodity and a product made from it

common market ECONOMICS an economic association, typically between nations, with the goal of removing or reducing trade barriers

common stock FINANCE, BANKING, AND ACCOUNTING a stock that pays a dividend after dividends for preferred stock have been paid

common stock ratio FINANCE, BANKING, AND ACCOUNTING a measure of the interest each stockholder has in the company's capital

Commonwealth GENERAL MANAGEMENT Australia, or its federal government, as distinct from its individual state and territory governments

Commonwealth of Australia GENERAL MANAGEMENT the full, official name of the country of Australia

Commonwealth of Australia Gazette GENERAL MANAGEMENT a journal that reports the actions and decisions of the Australian federal government. It has been published since 1901.

Commonwealth Scientific and Industrial Research Organization *(ANZ)* GENERAL MANAGEMENT see ***CSIRO***

communication GENERAL MANAGEMENT the exchange of messages conveying information, ideas, attitudes, emotions, opinions, or instructions between individuals or groups with the aim of creating, understanding, or coordinating activities. Communication is essential to the effective operation of an organization. It may be conducted informally through a ***grapevine*** or formally by means of letters, reports, briefings, and ***meetings***. Communication may be verbal or ***nonverbal communication*** and includes spoken, written, and visual elements.

communications GENERAL MANAGEMENT **1.** systems or technologies used for the communication of messages, such as postal and

telephone networks, or for communicating within an organization
2. messages exchanged in the process of ***communication***

communications channel GENERAL MANAGEMENT a medium through which a message is passed in the process of ***communication***. Communications channels include the spoken, written, and printed word, and electronic or computer-based media such as radio and television, telephones, video-conferencing, and electronic mail. The most effective channel for a specific message depends on the nature of the message and the audience to be reached, as well as the context in which the message is to be transmitted.

communications envelope E-COMMERCE = ***electronic envelope***

communication skills HR & PERSONNEL skills that enable people to communicate effectively with one another. Effective communication involves the choice of the best ***communications channel*** for a specific purpose, the technical knowledge to use the channel appropriately, the presentation of information in an appropriate manner for the target audience, and the ability to understand messages and responses received from others. The ability to establish and develop mutual understanding, trust, and cooperation is also important. More specifically, communication skills include the ability to speak in public, make presentations, write letters and reports, chair committees and meetings, and conduct negotiations.

communications management MARKETING the management, measurement, and control activities undertaken to ensure the effectiveness of marketing communications

communications strategy MARKETING a management technique for determining the most effective method of communicating with the marketplace

communication technology GENERAL MANAGEMENT electronic systems used for communication between individuals or groups. Communication technology facilitates communication between individuals or groups who are not physically present at the same location. Systems such as telephones, telex, fax, radio, television, and video are included, as well as more recent computer-based technologies, including ***electronic data interchange*** and ***e-mail***.

Communism ECONOMICS a classless society where private ownership of goods is abolished and the means of production belong to the community

community E-COMMERCE
1. a group of Internet users with a shared interest or concept who interact with each other in newsgroups, mailing-list discussion groups, and other online interactive forums
2. a business-to-business marketplace

community initiative GENERAL MANAGEMENT see ***community involvement***

community involvement GENERAL MANAGEMENT programs through which organizations aim to make a positive contribution to the local community by identifying problems and initiating practical action in order to adress them in partnership with local people. Community involvement programs developed through the growing emphasis on the social responsibility of business in the 1960s and 1970s. Such **community initiatives** often seek to promote economic and social regeneration in urban or rural areas and include activities such as the ***secondment*** of employees with appropriate skills, educational and training initiatives, ***sponsorship*** of arts and sports programs, and ***corporate giving*** programs.

companion bond FINANCE, BANKING, AND ACCOUNTING a class of a collateralized mortgage obligation that is paid off first when interest rates fall leading to the underlying mortgages being prepaid. Conversely, the principal on these bonds will be repaid more slowly when interest rates rise and fewer mortgages are prepaid.

company GENERAL MANAGEMENT an association of people formed into a legal entity for the purpose of doing business

company law GENERAL MANAGEMENT the body of legislation that relates to the formation, status, conduct, and ***corporate governance*** of companies as legal entities

company policy GENERAL MANAGEMENT a statement of desired standards of behavior or procedure applicable across an organization. Company policy defines ways of acting for staff in areas where there appears to be latitude in deciding how best to operate. This may concern areas such as time off for special circumstances, drug or alcohol abuse, ***workplace bullying***, personal use of ***Internet*** facilities, or business travel. Company policy may also apply to customers, for example, policy on ***complaints***, ***customer retention***, or ***disclosure of information***. Sometimes a company policy may develop into a ***code of practice***.

company report GENERAL MANAGEMENT a document giving details of the activities and performance of a company. Companies are legally required to produce particular reports and submit them to the competent authorities in the country of their registration. These include ***annual reports*** and financial reports. Other reports may cover specific aspects of an organization's activities, for example, environmental or social impact.

company secretary (*U.K.*) HR & PERSONNEL a senior employee in an organization with director status and administrative and legal authority. A company secretary is a legal requirement for all limited companies. A company secretary can also be a **board secretary** with appropriate qualifications.

comparative advantage GENERAL MANAGEMENT an instance of higher, more efficient production in a particular area. A country that produces far more cars than another, for example, is said to have the comparative advantage in car production. ***David Ricardo*** originally argued that specialization in activities in which individuals or groups have a comparative advantage will result in gains in trade.

comparative advertising MARKETING a form of advertising that gives carefully selected details of competitor products for comparison with a company's own product, usually to the detriment of competitors. Comparative advertising is frequently used to advertise cars, where the availability of features such as a sun roof, air conditioning, advanced braking systems, fuel efficiency, safety features, and warranty terms in similarly priced cars are given.

comparative balance sheet FINANCE, BANKING, AND ACCOUNTING one of two or more financial statements prepared on different dates that lend themselves to a comparative analysis of the financial condition of an organization

comparative credit analysis FINANCE, BANKING, AND ACCOUNTING an analysis of the risk associated with lending to different companies

comparative management GENERAL MANAGEMENT the simultaneous study of management or business practice in two or more different cultures, countries, companies, or departments

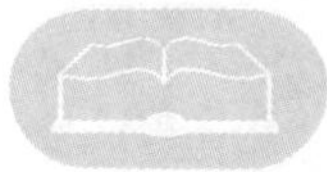

compassionate leave HR & PERSONNEL exceptional leave that may be granted to an employee on the death or serious illness of a close relative

compensating balance FINANCE, BANKING, AND ACCOUNTING

1. the amount of money a bank requires a customer to maintain in a non-interest-bearing account, in exchange for which the bank provides free services

2. the amount of money a bank requires a customer to maintain in an account in return for holding credit available, thereby increasing the true rate of interest on the loan

compensation HR & PERSONNEL

1. ***pay*** given in recompense for work performed

2. money paid by an employer on the order of an employment tribunal to an employee who has been unfairly dismissed

compensation package HR & PERSONNEL a bundle of rewards including ***pay***, financial incentives, and fringe benefits offered to, or negotiated by, an employee

competence GENERAL MANAGEMENT, HR & PERSONNEL an acquired personal skill that is demonstrated in an employee's ability to provide a consistently adequate or high level of performance in a specific job function. Competence should be distinguished from ***competency***, although in general usage the terms are used interchangeably. Early attempts to define the qualities of effective managers were based on lists of the personality traits and skills of the ideal manager. This is an input model approach, focusing on the skills that are needed to do the job. These skills are competencies and reflect potential ability to do something. With the advent of scientific management, people turned their attention more to the behavior of effective managers and to the outcomes of successful management. This approach is an output model, in which a manager's effectiveness is defined in terms of actual achievement. This achievement manifests itself in competences, which demonstrate that somebody has learned to do something well. There tends to be a focus in the United Kingdom on competence, whereas in the United States, the concept of competency is more popular. Competences are used in the workplace in a variety of ways. Training is often competence based, and the U.K. National Vocational Qualification system is based on competence standards. Competences also are used in reward management, for example, in competence-based pay. The ***assessment of competence*** is a necessary process for underpinning these initiatives by determining what competences an employee shows. At an organizational level, the idea of ***core competence*** is gaining popularity.

competency GENERAL MANAGEMENT, HR & PERSONNEL an innate personal skill or ability. See ***competence***

competition GENERAL MANAGEMENT rivalry between companies to achieve greater ***market share***. Competition between companies for customers will lead to product ***innovation*** and improvement, and ultimately lower prices. The opposite of market competition is either a ***monopoly*** or a **controlled economy**, where production is governed by quotas. A company that is leading the market is said to have achieved ***competitive advantage*** and business ***excellence***.

competitive advantage GENERAL MANAGEMENT a factor giving an advantage to a nation, company, group, or individual in competitive terms. Used by ***Michael Porter*** for the title of his classic text on international corporate strategy, *The Competitive Advantage of Nations* (1990), the concept of competitive advantage derives from the ideas on ***comparative advantage*** of the 19th-century economist ***David Ricardo***.

MICHAEL PORTER (pp. 1038–39)

competitive analysis GENERAL MANAGEMENT analysis carried out for marketing purposes that can include industry, customer, and ***competitor analysis***. A thorough competitive analysis done within a strategic framework can provide in-depth evaluation of the capabilities of key competitors. Also known as ***competitor profiling***

competitive equilibrium price ECONOMICS the price at which the number of buyers willing to buy a good equals the number of sellers prepared to sell it

competitive forces GENERAL MANAGEMENT the external business and economic factors that compel an organization to improve its competitiveness

competitive intelligence GENERAL MANAGEMENT data gathered to improve an organization's competitive capacity. Competitive intelligence may include, for example, information about competitors' plans, activities, or products, and may sometimes be gained through ***industrial espionage***.

competitiveness index GENERAL MANAGEMENT an international ranking of states using economic and other information to list countries in order of their competitive performance. A competitiveness index can show which countries have overall or industry sector ***competitive advantage***.

competitor analysis GENERAL MANAGEMENT the gathering and analysis of information about competitors, especially in a corporate context, for ***competitive intelligence*** purposes

competitor profiling GENERAL MANAGEMENT see ***competitor analysis***

complaint GENERAL MANAGEMENT an expression of dissatisfaction with a product or service, either orally or in writing, from an internal or external customer. A customer may have a genuine cause for complaint, although some complaints may be made as a result of a misunderstanding or an unreasonable expectation of a product or service. How a complaint is handled will affect the overall level of ***customer satisfaction*** and may affect long-term customer loyalty. It is important for providers to have clear procedures for dealing rapidly with any complaints, to come to a fair conclusion, and to explain the reasons for what may be perceived by the customer as a negative response. Also known as ***customer complaint***

✔ HANDLING COMPLAINTS (pp. 464–65)

complaints management MARKETING a management technique for assessing, analyzing, and responding to customer complaints

complementary goods MARKETING goods sold separately, but dependent on each other for sales. Examples of complementary goods include toothbrushes and toothpaste or computers and computer desks.

complementor GENERAL MANAGEMENT a company that supplies a product that complements a product supplied by another company, for example, computers and software

complex adaptive system GENERAL MANAGEMENT a system that overrides conventional human controls because those controls will subdue inevitable change and development within that system. Complex adaptive systems are a product of the application of ***chaos theory*** (see ***chaos***) and ***complexity theory*** to the world of organizations. According to writers such as ***Richard Pascale***, organizations that are subject to too much control are at risk of failure. The ***bureaucracy*** has been cited as an example of extreme control and the ***top down approach*** to management. However, if a bureaucracy is left to adapt naturally, it could

  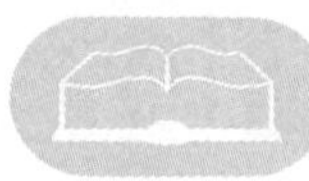    

become capable of self-organization and of creating new methods of operating.

complexity theory GENERAL MANAGEMENT the theory that random events, if left to happen without interference, will settle into a complicated pattern rather than a simple one. Complexity theory is a development of ***chaos theory*** (see ***chaos***). In a business context, it suggests that events within organizations and in the wider economic and social spheres cannot be predicted by simple models but will develop in a seemingly random and complex manner.

compliance documentation FINANCE, BANKING, AND ACCOUNTING documents that a share-issuing company publishes in line with regulations on share issues

compliance officer FINANCE, BANKING, AND ACCOUNTING an employee of a financial organization who ensures that regulations governing its business are observed

compounding FINANCE, BANKING, AND ACCOUNTING the calculation, payment, or receipt of ***compound interest***

compound interest FINANCE, BANKING, AND ACCOUNTING interest calculated on the sum of the original borrowed amount and the accrued interest. See ***simple interest***

compressed workweek HR & PERSONNEL a standard number of working hours squeezed into fewer than five days. Common models of the compressed workweek include four ten-hour days or three twelve-hour days each week. An alternative variation is to lengthen the normal workday to a lesser extent, for example, by 45 minutes, to allow an extra day off every two or three weeks. The minimum modification is to work a slightly longer day for four days in return for a shorter Friday. A compressed workweek is often introduced as an employee benefit to provide an extended weekend through shorter Friday working.

compulsory acquisition FINANCE, BANKING, AND ACCOUNTING the purchase, by right, of the last 10% of shares in an issue in the United Kingdom by a bidder at the offer price

computer-aided design OPERATIONS & PRODUCTION the use of a computer to assist with the design of a product. Computer graphics, modeling, and simulation are used to represent a product on screen, so that designers can produce more accurate drawings than is possible on paper alone and to perform calculations easily, thereby optimizing designs for production. Abbr **CAD**. Also known as ***computer-assisted design***

computer-aided diagnosis STATISTICS the use of a computer program that presents a patient with a series of diagnostic questions designed to produce a diagnosis of a health problem

computer-aided engineering OPERATIONS & PRODUCTION the application of computers to the generation of the engineering specifications of a product. Computer-aided engineering fits into the production process between ***computer-aided design*** and ***computer-aided manufacturing***. It is similar to ***CAD/CAM*** software, but with a focus on the engineering processes required for converting a design to a manufacturable product. The software package can include aspects of design, analysis, process planning, numerical control, mold and tool design, and ***quality control***. Abbr **CAE**

computer-aided manufacturing OPERATIONS & PRODUCTION a system in which the manufacture and assembly of a product are directed by a computer. Computer-aided manufacturing can be integrated with ***computer-aided design*** to create a ***CAD/CAM*** system. Abbr **CAM**. Also known as ***computer-assisted manufacturing***

computer-aided production management OPERATIONS & PRODUCTION a system that enables all functions within an organization that are associated with production management to be directed by computer. ***MRP II*** is a well-known form of computer-aided production management. Abbr **CAPM**

computer-assisted design OPERATIONS & PRODUCTION see ***computer-aided design***

computer-assisted interview STATISTICS an interview in which the interviewee keys in answers to questions displayed on screen by a computer program

computer-assisted manufacturing OPERATIONS & PRODUCTION see ***computer-aided manufacturing***

computer-based training HR & PERSONNEL training carried out via a stand-alone or networked computer. Programs are usually interactive, so that students can select from multiple-choice options or key in their own answers. A popular medium for computer-based training is CD-ROM, although there is a growing trend toward **online training**, where computer-based training is delivered over the Internet or through company intranets. Computer-based training is one form of ***e-learning***.

computer telephony integration GENERAL MANAGEMENT the combining of computer and telephone technology to allow a computer to dial telephone numbers, route calls, and send and receive messages. One product of computer telephony integration is the process of **calling line identification**, or CLI. CLI identifies the telephone number a customer is calling from, searches the customer database to identify the caller, and pops up the customer account on the receiver's computer screen, using the facility known as **screen popping**, before the call is answered. Abbr **CTI**

concentration services FINANCE, BANKING, AND ACCOUNTING the placing of money from various accounts into a single account

concept board MARKETING a board used for presenting creative advertising ideas

concept search E-COMMERCE an online search for documents related conceptually to a word, rather than specifically containing the word itself

concept testing MARKETING research carried out to test the effectiveness of a creative advertising idea

concession GENERAL MANAGEMENT

1. a compromise in opinion or action by a party to a dispute

2. a reduction in price for a particular group of people

3. the right of a retail outlet to set up and sell goods within another establishment

4. an agreement to ignore the failure of a product or service to conform to its specification, with a possible resultant deterioration in the quality of the product or service

conciliation HR & PERSONNEL action taken by an independent negotiator to bring disputing sides together with the aim of restoring trust or goodwill and reaching an agreement or bringing about a reconciliation

concurrent engineering OPERATIONS & PRODUCTION a team-based cooperative approach to product design and development, in which all parties are involved in ***new product development*** work in parallel. Concurrent engineering reduces or removes the timelag between the different stages of a product's development, and earlier entry into a market is

  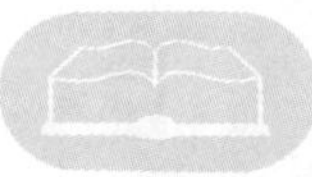    

therefore possible. Product quality is improved, development and product costs are minimized, and competitiveness is increased. Also known as ***parallel engineering***, ***simultaneous engineering***

conditional distribution STATISTICS the probability distribution of a random variable while the values of one or more random variables are fixed

conditions of employment GENERAL MANAGEMENT, HR & PERSONNEL terms agreed between an employer and employee that are legally enforceable through a ***contract of employment***. Conditions of employment include conditions that may be unique to the individual, for example, ***notice periods***, remuneration, fringe benefits, and ***hours of work***, as well as those that form organization-wide policies, for example, discipline and ***grievance procedures***, and those dictated by legislation.

✔ DRAWING UP A CONTRACT OF EMPLOYMENT (pp. 530–31)

conference GENERAL MANAGEMENT a type of ***meeting*** held between members of often disparate organizations to discuss matters of mutual interest. Conferences are held for a variety of reasons, including resolving problems, taking decisions, developing cooperation, and publicizing ideas, products, and services. They may take place within an organization but often draw people together regionally, nationally, or internationally, and involve a large number of speakers and delegates. Many conferences are organized for commercial profit.

conference call GENERAL MANAGEMENT a telephone call that connects three or more lines so that people in different locations can communicate and exchange information by voice. Conference calls reduce the cost of ***meetings*** by eliminating travel time and expenditure. Public switched telephone networks or dedicated private networks and a centrally located device called a bridge are used to connect the participants. Microphones and loudspeakers may also be used to make group-to-group communication possible. Conference calls are a type of ***teleconferencing***.

confidence indicator FINANCE, BANKING, AND ACCOUNTING a number that gives an indication of how well a market or an economy will fare

confidence interval STATISTICS the range of values of sample observations in a statistical study that contain the true parameter value within a given probability

confidentiality agreement GENERAL MANAGEMENT an agreement whereby an organization that has access to information about the affairs of another organization makes an undertaking to treat the information as private and confidential. A potential buyer of a company who requires further information in the process of due diligence may be asked to sign a confidentiality agreement stating that the information will only be used for the purpose of deciding whether to go ahead with the deal and will only be disclosed to employees involved in the negotiations. Such agreements are also used where information is shared in the context of a partnership or ***benchmarking*** program.

conflict management GENERAL MANAGEMENT, HR & PERSONNEL the identification and control of conflict within an organization. There are three main philosophies of conflict management: all conflict is bad and potentially destructive; conflict is inevitable and managers should attempt to harness it positively; conflict is essential to the survival of an organization and should be encouraged.

✔ HANDLING CONFLICT SITUATIONS (pp. 356–57)

conflict of interests GENERAL MANAGEMENT a situation in which a person or institution is caught between opposing concerns, loyalties, or objectives that prejudice impartiality. A conflict of interests may be between self-advantage and the benefit of an organization for which somebody works, or it could arise when somebody is connected with two or more companies that are competing. The correct course of action in such cases is for the person concerned to declare any interests, to make known the way in which those interests conflict, and to abstain from participating in the decision-making process involving those interests. A conflict of interests may also arise when an institution acts for parties on both sides of a transaction and could derive an advantage from a particular outcome.

confusion matrix GENERAL MANAGEMENT see ***discriminant analysis***

conglomerate company GENERAL MANAGEMENT an organization that owns a diverse range of companies in different industries. Conglomerates are usually ***holding companies*** with subsidiaries in wide-ranging business areas, often built up through mergers and takeovers and operating on an international scale.

conglomerate diversification GENERAL MANAGEMENT the ***diversification*** of a ***conglomerate company*** through the setting up of ***subsidiary companies*** with activities in various areas

conjoint analysis GENERAL MANAGEMENT a research method aimed at discovering the most attractive combination of attributes, including price, package style, and size, for a product or service. In conjoint analysis, respondents express their preferences by filling in a questionnaire and ranking a number of contrasting combinations of attributes from the most to the least preferred. This enables values to be assigned to the range of features that customers consider when making a decision to purchase. Conjoint analysis is also known as **trade off analysis**.

connectivity GENERAL MANAGEMENT the ability of electronic products to connect with others, or of individuals, companies, and countries to be connected with one another electronically

connexity GENERAL MANAGEMENT the condition of being closely and intricately connected by worldwide communications networks

consolidated balance sheet FINANCE, BANKING, AND ACCOUNTING a listing of the most significant details of a company's finances

consolidated debt FINANCE, BANKING, AND ACCOUNTING the use of a large loan to eliminate smaller ones

consolidated financial statement FINANCE, BANKING, AND ACCOUNTING a listing of the most significant details of the finances of a company and of all its subsidiaries

consolidated fund FINANCE, BANKING, AND ACCOUNTING a fund of public money, especially from taxes, used by the government to make interest payments on the national debt and other regular payments

consolidated invoice FINANCE, BANKING, AND ACCOUNTING an invoice that covers all items shipped by one seller to one buyer during a particular period

consolidated loan FINANCE, BANKING, AND ACCOUNTING a large loan, the proceeds of which are used to eliminate smaller ones

consolidated tape FINANCE, BANKING, AND ACCOUNTING a ticker tape that lists all transactions of the New York and other U.S. stock exchanges

consolidated tax return FINANCE, BANKING, AND ACCOUNTING a tax return that covers several companies, typically a parent company and all of its subsidiaries

consolidation FINANCE, BANKING, AND ACCOUNTING
1. the uniting of two or more businesses into one company
2. the combination of several lower-priced shares into one higher-priced one

consortium GENERAL MANAGEMENT a group of independent organizations that join forces to achieve a particular goal, for example, to bid for a project or to carry out cooperative purchasing. A consortium goes on to complete the project if its bid is successful and is often dissolved on completion. This form of temporary alliance allows diverse skills, capabilities, and knowledge to be brought together.

Constable, **John** (*b.* 1936) GENERAL MANAGEMENT British educator and consultant. Best known for the report *The Making of British Managers* (1987), with ***Roger McCormick***, which led to major changes in the structure of ***management development*** in the United Kingdom. The publication of the report coincided with the equally influential *The Making of Managers: A Report on Management Education, Training, and Development in the USA, West Germany, France, Japan, and the U.K.* (1987) by ***Charles Handy*** and others.
CHARLES HANDY (pp. 1000–01)

constitutional strike HR & PERSONNEL a form of ***industrial action*** that takes place after all dispute procedures or other provisions for the avoidance of strikes agreed between labor union and employer representatives have been exhausted. A ***no-strike agreement*** effectively precludes constitutional strikes because it generally provides for automatic ***arbitration***.

constructive dismissal (*U.K.*) HR & PERSONNEL a form of ***dismissal*** that occurs when an employee leaves a job and his or her claim of ***breach of contract*** or overbearing conduct by the employer is proven

consultant GENERAL MANAGEMENT an expert in a specialized field brought in to provide independent professional advice to an organization on some aspect of its activities. A consultant may advise on the overall management of an organization or on a specific project such as the introduction of a new computer system. Consultants are usually retained by a client for a set period of time during which they will investigate the matter in hand and produce a report detailing their recommendations. Consultants may set up in business independently or be employed by a large consulting firm. Specific types of consultants include ***management consultants*** and ***internal consultants***.

consultative committee HR & PERSONNEL a meeting of representatives of management and staff, convened for the purposes of joint consultation

consultative management GENERAL MANAGEMENT a style of management that takes employees' views into account for decision-making purposes

consumer MARKETING the user of a product or service. A consumer may not be the purchaser of a product or service and should be distinguished from a ***customer***, who is the person or organization that purchased the product or service. Also known as ***end consumer***

consumer advertising MARKETING advertising aimed at individuals and the domestic and family market as opposed to ***industrial advertising***, which is aimed at businesses

consumer behavior MARKETING see ***consumer demand***

consumer demand MARKETING the patterns of **consumer behavior** that affect buying decisions. Consumer demand is influenced in various ways. Psychologists and marketers have identified three important factors affecting buying decisions: needs, which are things we must have, such as food; wants, which are nice to have but not essential, such as a new car; and motives, such as keeping up appearances. These factors form part of a psychological and physiological profile that includes motivations, personality, perceptions, cognition, attitudes, and values. Other factors that influence demand include gender, age, social grouping, education, location, income, culture, and the seasons. Consumers can therefore be divided into discrete segments, each of which has a particular pattern of buying behavior. Products and services can then be targeted at specific segments of the market.

consumer goods marketing MARKETING the promotion of products to members of the public. Consumer goods marketing is aimed at individuals rather than organizations and promotes products directly to the end user rather than to intermediaries. Marketing strategies will be different from those used in ***industrial goods marketing***.

consumerism MARKETING the influence of the general public, as end users of products and services, on the way companies manufacture and sell their goods. Consumers exert considerable power over companies as organizations become more customer-focused. Demand is rising for products that are high quality, ethically produced, well priced, and safe, and consumerism pressurizes companies to operate and produce goods and services in accordance with the public's wishes. In fact, the aims of consumerism are not at odds with those of ***marketing*** (see ***marketing management***), as both have the end goal of pleasing the consumer. In practice, however, marketing does not always succeed, and there is still a need for legislation to back up the right of consumers to demand products that are of good quality and for consumer protection bodies that influence the commercial world on consumers' behalf. A particular form of consumer pressure, motivated by environmental concerns, is **green consumerism**, which campaigns for environmentally friendly goods, services, and means of production.

consumer market research MARKETING ***market research*** that focuses on gathering and analyzing data on individual or domestic consumers, as opposed to industrial or business customers. Also known as ***consumer research***

consumer panel MARKETING a carefully selected group of people whose purchasing habits are regularly monitored. A consumer panel usually consists of a large cross-section of the population so as to provide meaningful data. There are two types of panel: **diary panels**, where members fill in a regular detailed diary of purchases, and, less commonly, **home audit panels**, where visits are made to the homes of members to check purchases, packaging, and used cartons. These panels run over a period of time to gain a broad overview of purchasing habits. A ***focus group*** is similar to a consumer panel, but is usually used to determine customers' views of a specific product or range of products. Members of a group meet together under the guidance of a facilitator to discuss their opinions on a face-to-face basis.

consumer price index (*ANZ*) ECONOMICS an index of the prices of goods and services that consumers purchase, used to measure the cost of living or the rate of inflation in an economy. Abbr **CPI**

consumer profile MARKETING a detailed analysis of a group of like ***consumers***, covering influences on their purchasing habits such as age, gender, education, occupation, income, and personal and psychological characteristics. Consumer profiles are built up from extensive ***market research*** and are used for market segmentation purposes.

consumer protection MARKETING the safeguarding of ***consumer*** interests in terms of quality, price, and safety, usually within a statutory framework. The growing purchasing power of consumers and the rise in ***consumerism*** from the late 1950s onward led to increased demands for protection against unsafe goods and services and unscrupulous trading practices.

consumer research MARKETING see ***consumer market research***

consumer services marketing MARKETING the marketing of services to domestic consumers. Consumer services marketing may promote such services as banking, insurance, travel and tourism, leisure, telecommunications, and services provided by local authorities. Strategies to market these services to business constitute ***industrial services marketing***.

consumer spending MARKETING the total value of household and personal expenditure measured at macro and micro levels. At the macro level, consumer confidence can be measured by the overall levels of consumer spending and from a demonstration that earnings have increased at a faster rate than prices, which indicates that spending power, or disposable income, has increased. At a micro level, there are innumerable market reports on the value of actual and predicted spend on a vast range of consumer goods, including food, pharmaceuticals, clothing, cars, and vacations. ***Consumer demand*** is a related concept.

consumer-to-consumer commerce E-COMMERCE e-business transactions conducted between two individuals

consumption ECONOMICS the quantity of resources that consumers use to satisfy their current needs and wants, measured by the sum of the current expenditure of the government and individual consumers

contact card E-COMMERCE a ***smart card*** in which the microprocessor chip is visible and can make physical contact with the reading device

contactless card E-COMMERCE a ***smart card*** in which the microprocessor chip is not visible and is accessed by the reading device by radio signals rather than by physical contact. An increasingly common use of this technology is in such applications as toll collection where the card is accessed as the motorist displays it to the reading device in passing.

content E-COMMERCE the textual, graphical, and multimedia material that constitutes a Web page or Web site

content management E-COMMERCE the means and methods of managing the textual and graphical content of a Web site. For large sites with thousands of pages and many interchangeable words and images, it pays to invest in a content management application system that facilitates the creation and organization of Web content. Some content management systems also offer server caching (where a server stores frequently requested information) and analysis of site traffic.

contestable market ECONOMICS a market in which there are no barriers to entry, as in ***perfect competition***

context E-COMMERCE information about a product made available on an Internet site that is seen as adding value for the consumer, for example, book reviews on a book site

contingency allowance GENERAL MANAGEMENT see ***standard time***

contingency management GENERAL MANAGEMENT the capacity for flexibility in varying responses and attitudes to meet the needs of different situations. Contingency management may be practiced by both individuals and organizations. Within the latter, it may be formalized through a ***contingency plan*** linked to ***risk*** or ***crisis management*** strategies, or be derived from the results of ***scenario planning***.

contingency plan GENERAL MANAGEMENT a plan, drawn up in advance, to ensure a positive and rapid response to a changing situation. A contingency plan often results from ***scenario planning*** and may form part of an organization's ***disaster management*** strategy.

contingency planning GENERAL MANAGEMENT see ***FMEA***

contingency table STATISTICS a table in which observations on several categorical variables are cross-classified

contingency tax ECONOMICS a one-off tax levied by a government to deal with a particular economic problem, for example, too high a level of imports coming into the country

contingency theory GENERAL MANAGEMENT

1. in management, the theory that there is no single best way to organize or manage and each firm should be organized and structured to suit the technology used and the environment around it. Contingency theory is particularly attributed to ***Joan Woodward***, whose extensive company research during the 1950s found that different types of production processes were linked to different structures and spans of control. During the 1960s, contingency theory was further extended, especially by Tom Burns.

2. in leadership, the theory that different ***management styles*** will be more effective in different situations. In this context, contingency theory developed from situational leadership theory and is usually linked to the 1970s' work of Fred Fiedler.

continuing professional development HR & PERSONNEL see ***CPD***

continuous disclosure FINANCE, BANKING, AND ACCOUNTING in Canada, the practice of ensuring that complete, timely, accurate, and balanced information about a public company is made available to stockholders

continuous improvement OPERATIONS & PRODUCTION, GENERAL MANAGEMENT the seeking of small improvements in processes and products, with the aim of increasing quality and reducing waste. Continuous improvement is one of the tools that underpin the philosophies of ***total quality management*** and ***lean production***. Through constant study and revision of processes, a better product can result at reduced cost. ***Kaizen*** has become a foundation for many continuous improvement strategies, and for many employees it is synonymous with continuous improvement.

continuous relationship marketing GENERAL MANAGEMENT see ***pyramid selling***

continuous service HR & PERSONNEL a period of employment with one ***employer***, which begins with the day on which the ***employee*** starts work and ends with the date of ***resignation*** or ***dismissal***. All service, regardless of hours worked, counts toward calculating continuous service. The length of continuous service may affect the length of ***notice period*** and is taken into account when calculating redundancy pay.

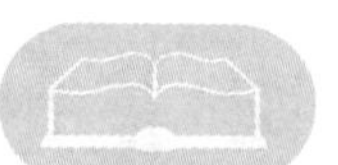     

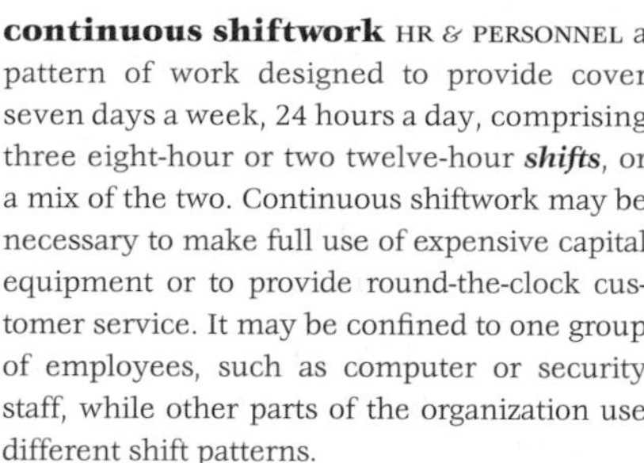

continuous shiftwork HR & PERSONNEL a pattern of work designed to provide cover seven days a week, 24 hours a day, comprising three eight-hour or two twelve-hour ***shifts***, or a mix of the two. Continuous shiftwork may be necessary to make full use of expensive capital equipment or to provide round-the-clock customer service. It may be confined to one group of employees, such as computer or security staff, while other parts of the organization use different shift patterns.

contour plot STATISTICS a graphical representation of data in which three variables are plotted on a topographical map

contract GENERAL MANAGEMENT a legally binding agreement between two or more parties. A contract is made as a result of an offer by one party and acceptance on the part of the other. It normally involves an undertaking made by one party in consideration of an undertaking made by the other party or parties. Contracts are generally in writing but may be oral. Contract law may lay down additional conditions for the creation of valid contracts in some cases. Types of contract include contracts for the supply of goods or services and ***contracts of employment***.

contract broker FINANCE, BANKING, AND ACCOUNTING a broker who fills an order placed by somebody else

contract distribution GENERAL MANAGEMENT the ***outsourcing*** of a company's distribution requirement to a third party under contract. Contract distribution can help a company drive down costs, reduce stockholdings, and achieve increased flexibility of delivery.

contract hire GENERAL MANAGEMENT an arrangement whereby an organization enters into a ***contract*** for the use of assets owned by another organization, as an alternative to purchasing the assets itself. Contract hire agreements normally cover a period shorter that the useful economic life of the assets concerned and often include arrangements for maintenance and replacement. Organizations frequently use contract hire arrangements for the provision of company cars or office equipment. A contract hire arrangement is sometimes referred to as an **operating lease**.

contracting GENERAL MANAGEMENT the process of making an agreement governed by a ***contract*** for the provision of goods or services to an organization

contracting out

1. GENERAL MANAGEMENT = ***outsourcing***

2. (*U.K.*) HR & PERSONNEL the withdrawal of employees by an employer from the State Earnings-Related Pension Scheme and their enrollment in an occupational pension scheme that meets specified standards

3. (*U.K.*) HR & PERSONNEL the withdrawal by an employee from the State Earnings-Related Pension Scheme and the purchase by the employee of an appropriate ***personal pension***

contract manufacturing OPERATIONS & PRODUCTION the ***outsourcing*** of a requirement to manufacture a particular product or component to a third-party company. Contract manufacturing enables companies to reduce the level of investment in their own capabilities to manufacture, while retaining a product produced to a high quality, at a reasonable price, and delivered to a flexible schedule.

contract month FINANCE, BANKING, AND ACCOUNTING the month in which an option expires and goods covered by it must be delivered. Also known as ***delivery month***

contract note FINANCE, BANKING, AND ACCOUNTING a document with the complete description of a stock transaction

contract of employment HR & PERSONNEL, GENERAL MANAGEMENT a legally enforceable agreement, either oral or written, between an employer and employee that defines terms and ***conditions of employment*** to which both parties must adhere. Express terms of the contract are agreed between the two parties and include the organization's normal terms and conditions in addition to those that relate specifically to the individual. These terms can only be changed by employee agreement, if the contract itself allows for variation, or by terminating the contract. Terms are also implied in the contract by custom and practice or by common law.

contract purchasing OPERATIONS & PRODUCTION a mechanism for buying leased goods. In contract purchasing, a purchaser agrees to buy goods or equipment to be paid for in a series of installments, each comprising a proportion of the capital and an interest element. After a final payment, legal ownership passes to the user.

contractual obligation HR & PERSONNEL the legal duty to take a stated course of action, as imposed by a commercial ***contract*** or a ***contract of employment***

contributed surplus FINANCE, BANKING, AND ACCOUNTING the portion of shareholders' equity that comes from sources other than earnings, for example, from the initial sale of stock above its par value

contributions holiday FINANCE, BANKING, AND ACCOUNTING a period during which a company stops making contributions to its pension plan because the plan is sufficiently well funded

control GENERAL MANAGEMENT the effective monitoring, regulation, and direction of operations and budgets by senior managers. Control is often considered to be the primary task of management and has traditionally been strongly linked to accounting, stock control, ***production*** or ***operations management***, and ***quality control***. It is usually linked to ***management control systems*** such as performance measurement and ***performance indicators***, procedures, and inspections.

controlled circulation MARKETING the number of copies of a newspaper or magazine distributed, usually free of charge, to an approved target audience

controlled disbursement FINANCE, BANKING, AND ACCOUNTING the presentation of checks only once each day

controlled economy GENERAL MANAGEMENT see ***competition***

conversion FINANCE, BANKING, AND ACCOUNTING

1. a trade of one convertible financial instrument for another, for example, a bond for shares

2. a trade of shares of one mutual fund for shares of another in the same family

conversion rate

1. MARKETING in marketing terms, the percentage of inquiries or sales calls resulting in sales

2. E-COMMERCE the percentage of potential customers at an e-commerce site who actually make a purchase

conversion ratio FINANCE, BANKING, AND ACCOUNTING an expression of the quantity of one security that can be obtained for another, for example, shares for a convertible bond

conversion value FINANCE, BANKING, AND ACCOUNTING the value a security would have if converted into shares

convertible ARM FINANCE, BANKING, AND ACCOUNTING an adjustable-rate mortgage that the borrower can convert into a fixed-rate mortgage under specified terms

convertible bond FINANCE, BANKING, AND ACCOUNTING a bond that the owner can convert into another asset, especially common stock

convertible security FINANCE, BANKING, AND ACCOUNTING a convertible bond, warrant, or share of preferred stock

convertible term insurance FINANCE, BANKING, AND ACCOUNTING term insurance that the policyholder can convert to fixed life insurance under particular conditions

C.O.O. GENERAL MANAGEMENT see ***chief operating officer***

cookie E-COMMERCE a file written to a computer's hard disk by an Internet application to store small amounts of information that can be accessed to identify users and customize interactions with them. Cookies contain such data as registration or login information, user preferences, shopping cart items, and credit card numbers and expiration dates. The name is derived from UNIX objects called "magic cookies."

cooling-off period HR & PERSONNEL an agreed pause in a dispute, especially a labor dispute, to allow the tempers of the negotiating parties to cool before the resumption of negotiations

Cooper, **Cary L.** (*b.* 1940) GENERAL MANAGEMENT U.S.-born academic. Based at the School of Management, University of Manchester Institute of Science & Technology, United Kingdom, Cooper focuses on ***occupational psychology***, particularly ***stress*** management issues. His biggest-selling book is *Living with Stress* (1988, coauthor).

✔ STRESS MANAGEMENT: SELF FIRST (pp. 412–13)

cooperative MARKETING a business that is jointly owned by the people who operate it, with all profits shared equally

cooperative advertising MARKETING a joint advertising campaign between groups with a shared objective, for example, retailer groups or manufacturer and retailer

cooperative movement GENERAL MANAGEMENT a movement that aims to share profits and benefits from jointly owned commercial enterprises among members. The movement was begun in Rochdale, Lancashire, England, in 1844 by 28 weavers and developed to include manufacturing and wholesale businesses as well as insurance and financial services. The Co-op in the United Kingdom and the ***Mondragon cooperative*** in Spain are two of the best known examples.

coopetition GENERAL MANAGEMENT cooperation between competing companies (*slang*)

copyright MARKETING the legal protection for creative ideas, trademarks, and other brand-related material

copy testing MARKETING research carried out to test the effectiveness of creative advertising copy

copywriter MARKETING somebody who devises the wording of an advertisement or promotional material. A copywriter may be employed by an advertising agency or, in scientific or technical areas, directly by a manufacturing or distribution company. Many copywriters also work ***freelance***.

core business GENERAL MANAGEMENT the central, and usually the original, focus of an organization's activities that differentiates it from others and makes a vital contribution to its success. The concept of core business became prominent in the 1980s when ***diversification*** by large companies failed to generate the anticipated degree of commercial success. In 1982, ***Tom Peters's*** and ***Robert Waterman***'s book *In Search of Excellence* suggested that organizations should ***stick to the knitting*** and avoid diversifying into areas beyond their field of expertise. An organization's core business should be defined by the ***core competences*** of the organization.

core capability GENERAL MANAGEMENT see ***core competence***

core competence GENERAL MANAGEMENT, HR & PERSONNEL a key ability or strength that an organization has acquired that differentiates it from others, gives it ***competitive advantage***, and contributes to its long-term success. The concept of core competence is most closely associated with the work of ***Gary Hamel*** and ***C. K. Prahalad***, notably in their book *Competing for the Future* (1994). They describe core competences as bundles of skills and technologies resulting from organizational learning. These provide access to markets, contribute to customer value, and are difficult for competitors to imitate. Core competence is a resource-based approach to ***corporate strategy***. The terms core competence and **core capability** are often used interchangeably, but some writers make varying distinctions between the two concepts.

💡 C. K. PRAHALAD (pp. 1040–41)

core values

1. GENERAL MANAGEMENT the guiding principles of an organization, espoused by senior management, and accepted by employees, often reflected in the ***mission statement*** of the organization. Core values often influence the ***culture*** of an organization and are normally long-standing beliefs. As **shared values**, they are included in the ***McKinsey 7-S framework***, and are reported in ***Richard Pascale***'s and ***Anthony Athos***'s *The Art of Japanese Management* in their analysis of the rise of ***Konosuke Matsushita***.

💡 KONOSUKE MATSUSHITA (pp. 1112–13)

💡 RICHARD TANNER PASCALE (pp. 1034–35)

2. HR & PERSONNEL a small set of key concepts and ideals that guide a person's life and help him or her to make important decisions

corpocracy GENERAL MANAGEMENT excessive or unwieldy corporate management resulting from the merger of several companies (*slang*)

corporate action FINANCE, BANKING, AND ACCOUNTING a measure that a company takes that has an effect on the number of shares outstanding or the rights that apply to shares

corporate amnesia GENERAL MANAGEMENT loss of organizational history and memory. Corporate amnesia occurs when senior or long-standing members of staff leave and their personal knowledge, built up from years of experience in the company, goes with them. This is occurring more frequently with the rise in ***downsizing*** and ***delayering***, and the phenomenon goes hand in hand with the ***anorexic organization***. Amnesia can be a significant disadvantage to an organization, causing it to forget the lessons it has learned and to waste time and effort in doing things again.

corporate anorexia GENERAL MANAGEMENT see ***anorexic organization***

corporate bond FINANCE, BANKING, AND ACCOUNTING a long-term bond with fixed interest issued by a corporation

corporate brand GENERAL MANAGEMENT the coherent outward expression projected by an organization. A corporate brand is a product of an organization's ***corporate strategy***, ***mission***, ***image***, and activities. Corporate brands distinguish organizations from their competitors, orient the organization in the minds of customers and employees, and create a perception of what an organization stands for. There is much debate about the precise nature of corporate brands, and about their depth.

Corporate branding has been seen as a superficial quick fix to restore a company's tarnished image or revitalize an ailing company. It requires board level coordination, however, and rather than being arbitrarily imposed on an organization, it is actually a product of the sum of its activities. Changing a corporate brand, or rebranding a company, can only be accomplished by changing strategy and activity within the company.

corporate climate GENERAL MANAGEMENT the environment created by the managerial style and attitudes that pervade an organization. Corporate climate is strongly linked to ***corporate culture*** in creating the general feeling and atmosphere of an organization. The climate within an organization can affect aspects such as ***productivity***, ***creativity***, and ***customer focus***, and each organization needs to create a climate that will facilitate organizational success.

corporate communication GENERAL MANAGEMENT the activities undertaken by an organization to communicate both internally with employees and externally with existing and prospective customers and the wider public. Corporate communication is sometimes used to refer principally to external communication and sometimes to internal communication, but strictly speaking covers both. The term implies an emphasis on promoting a sense of ***corporate identity*** and presenting a consistent and coherent ***corporate image***.

corporate concierge GENERAL MANAGEMENT an employee whose job involves doing personal tasks such as booking hotels or collecting shopping on behalf of other employees who have no time for such things (*slang*)

corporate culture GENERAL MANAGEMENT the combined beliefs, values, ethics, procedures, and atmosphere of an organization. The culture of an organization is often expressed as "the way we do things around here" and consists of largely unspoken values, norms, and behaviors that become the natural way of doing things. An organization's culture may be more apparent to an external observer than an internal practitioner. The first person to attempt a definition of corporate culture was ***Edgar Schein***, who said that it consisted of rules, procedures, and processes that governed how things were done, as well as the philosophy that guides the attitude of senior management toward staff and customers. The difficulty in identifying the traits of culture and changing them is borne out by the fact that culture is not merely climate, power, and politics, but all those things and more. There can be several subcultures within an organization, for example, defined by hierarchy—shop floor or executive—or by function—sales, design, or production. Changing or renewing corporate culture in order to achieve the organization's strategy is considered one of the major tasks of organization ***leadership***, as it is recognized that such a change is hard to achieve without the will of the leader. Also known as ***organizational culture***

CHARLES HANDY (pp. 1000–01)

corporate evolution GENERAL MANAGEMENT the way in which organizations are transformed through the use of information technology

corporate giving GENERAL MANAGEMENT monetary or in-kind donations by organizations as part of the process of ***community involvement***

corporate governance GENERAL MANAGEMENT the managerial and directorial control of an incorporated organization, which, when well-practiced, can reduce the risk of fraud, improve company performance and leadership, and demonstrate ***social responsibility***

corporate hospitality GENERAL MANAGEMENT entertainment provided by an organization. Corporate hospitality was originally designed to help sales people build relationships with customers, but it is now increasingly used as a staff ***incentive*** and in employee teambuilding and training exercises.

corporate identity GENERAL MANAGEMENT the distinctive characteristics or personality of an organization, including ***corporate culture***, values, and philosophy as perceived by those within the organization and presented to those outside. Corporate identity is expressed through the name, symbols, and logos used by the organization, and the design of communication materials, and is a factor influencing the ***corporate image*** of an organization. The creation of a strong corporate identity also involves consistency in the organization's actions, behavior, products, and brands, and often reflects the ***mission statement*** of an organization. A positive corporate identity can promote a sense of purpose and belonging within the organization and encourage ***employee commitment*** and involvement.

corporate image GENERAL MANAGEMENT the perceptions and impressions of an organization by the public as a result of interaction with the organization and the way the organization presents itself. Organizations have traditionally focused on the design of communication and advertising materials, using logos, symbols, text, and color to create a favorable impression on target groups, but a range of additional activities contribute to a positive corporate image. These include ***PR*** programs such as ***community involvement***, ***sponsorship***, and environmental projects, participation in quality improvement schemes, and good practice in industrial relations.

corporate planning GENERAL MANAGEMENT the process of drawing up detailed action plans to achieve an organization's aims and objectives, taking into account the resources of the organization and the environment within which it operates. Corporate planning represents a formal, structured approach to achieving objectives and to implementing the ***corporate strategy*** of an organization. It has traditionally been seen as the responsibility of senior management. The use of the term became predominant during the 1960s but has now been largely superseded by the concept of ***strategic management***.

corporate portal GENERAL MANAGEMENT a single gateway to information and software applications held within an organization that also allows links to information outside the organization. A corporate portal is a development of ***intranet*** technology. Ideally, it should allow users to access groupware, e-mail, and desktop applications, and to customize both the way information is presented and the way it is used. It should also provide dynamic access to data held within an ***MIS***, ***decision support system***, or other corporate database, and enable ***virtual team*** working across an organization. Like many purely technological solutions, a corporate portal still relies on good ***internal communication*** and a ***corporate culture*** that embraces openness and information sharing.

corporate restructuring GENERAL MANAGEMENT a fundamental change in direction and strategy for an organization that affects the way in which the organization is structured. Corporate restructuring may involve increasing or decreasing the layers of personnel between the top and the bottom of an organization, or reassigning roles and responsibilities. Invariably, corporate restructuring has come to mean reorganizing after a period of unsatisfactory performance and poor results, and is often manifested in the ***divestment*** or closure of parts of the business and the ***outplacement***, or shedding, of personnel. In this case, corporate restructuring is used as a euphemism for ***delayering***, ***rationalization***, ***downsizing***, or ***rightsizing***.

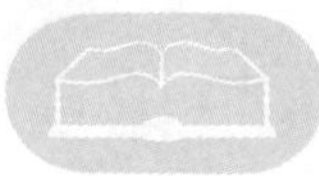

corporate strategy GENERAL MANAGEMENT the direction an organization takes with the aim of achieving business success in the long term. A number of models such as ***Michael Porter***'s Five Forces model and ***Gary Hamel***'s and ***C. K. Prahalad***'s model of ***core competencies*** have been used to develop corporate strategy. More recent approaches have focused on the need for companies to adapt to and anticipate changes in the business environment. The formulation of corporate strategy involves establishing the purpose and scope of the organization's activities and the nature of the business it is in, taking the environment in which it operates, its position in the marketplace, and the competition it faces into consideration. ***Corporate planning*** and ***business plans*** are used to implement corporate strategy.

corporate university HR & PERSONNEL a centralized training and education facility within an organization, offering ***training*** and development only to employees of that organization. Traditionally, corporate universities only offered internal qualifications and were used as a means of channeling ***employee development*** toward meeting corporate goals, sharing corporate information or knowledge, and disseminating ***corporate culture***. More recently, some corporate universities have established links with academic institutions in order to offer formal qualifications.

corporate veil GENERAL MANAGEMENT immunity granted to stockholders to protect them from legal action in the event of the failure of a business

corporate venturing GENERAL MANAGEMENT the undertaking of an investment initiative by a commercial organization to gain experience of a new technology or an unfamiliar market

corporate vision GENERAL MANAGEMENT the overall goal of an organization that all business activities and processes should contribute toward achieving. Ideally, the workforce should be committed to, and driven by, the vision, because it is they who make it happen. As the vision nears achievement, a new corporate vision or an evolution of the existing one should be established. Corporate vision is usually summed up in a formal ***vision statement***.

corporation FINANCE, BANKING, AND ACCOUNTING an organization in which a number of people provide finance in return for shares. The principle of limited liability limits the maximum loss a shareholder can make if the company fails.

correlation STATISTICS the interdependence between pairs of variables in data

correlation coefficient STATISTICS an index of the linear relationship between two variables in data

cosmeceuticals GENERAL MANAGEMENT pharmaceuticals such as anti-aging creams that have a cosmetic rather than a health-related purpose *(slang)*

cost, insurance, and freight E-COMMERCE indicates that a quoted price includes the costs of the merchandise, transportation, and insurance. Abbr **CIF**

cost accounting GENERAL MANAGEMENT the maintaining and checking of detailed records of the costs involved in manufacturing a product or providing a service in order to provide the information required for ***costing*** purposes. Cost accounting tries to identify the costs of outputs. This information is useful for pricing, budgeting, control of manufacturing or service processes, and planning materials and labor.

cost and freight E-COMMERCE indicates that a quoted price includes the costs of the merchandise and the transportation but not the cost of insurance. Abbr **CFR**

cost-benefit analysis GENERAL MANAGEMENT a technique for comparing the tangible and intangible costs of a project with the resulting benefits. Cost-benefit analysis assigns monetary value to the costs and benefits (social, environmental, and monetary) associated with a project for the purpose of evaluating and selecting investment project opportunities.

cost center GENERAL MANAGEMENT a department, function, section, or individual whose cost, overall or in part, is an accepted overhead of a business in return for services provided to other parts of the organization. A cost center is usually an ***indirect cost*** of an organization's products or services.

cost-cutting GENERAL MANAGEMENT the reducing of the amount of money spent on the operations of an organization or on the provision of products and services. Cost-cutting measures such as budget reductions, salary freezes, and staff redundancies may be taken by an organization at a time of ***recession*** or financial difficulty or in situations where inefficiency has been identified. Alternative approaches to cost-cutting include modifying organizational structures and redesigning organizational processes for greater efficiency. Excessive cost-cutting may affect ***productivity*** and quality or the organization's ability to add value.

cost driver GENERAL MANAGEMENT a factor that determines the cost of an activity. Cost drivers are analyzed as part of ***activity based costing*** and can be used in ***continuous improvement*** programs. They are usually assessed together as multiple drivers rather than singly. There are two main types of cost driver: the first is a **resource driver**, which refers to the contribution of the quantity of resources used to the cost of an activity; the second is an **activity driver**, which refers to the costs incurred by the activities required to complete a particular task or project.

cost-effective GENERAL MANAGEMENT offering the maximum benefit for a given level of expenditure. When limited resources are available to meet specific objectives, the cost-effective solution is the best that can be achieved for that level of expenditure and the one that provides good value for money. The term is also used to refer to a level of expenditure that is perceived to be commercially viable.

cost-effectiveness analysis GENERAL MANAGEMENT a method for measuring the benefits and effectiveness of a particular item of expenditure. Cost-effectiveness analysis requires an examination of expenditure to determine whether the money spent could have been used more effectively or whether the resulting benefits could have been attained through less financial outlay.

cost function ECONOMICS a mathematical function relating a firm's or an industry's total cost to its output and factor costs

costing GENERAL MANAGEMENT the determination of the total cost of a product, from the purchase of ***raw materials*** to delivery to the consumer. There are a large number of costing techniques, including ***life-cycle costing***, ***activity based costing***, and ***operating costing***.

cost of entry MARKETING the cost of introducing a new product to the market. Cost of entry calculations include the cost of all research, development, production, testing, marketing, advertising, and distribution of a product.

cost per action E-COMMERCE see ***CPA***

cost-plus pricing MARKETING a standard ***markup*** added to the cost of a product or ser-

vice to establish a selling price. Many companies simply add a percentage of production costs to arrive at a selling price. The degree of markup depends on the level of anticipated sales. Low volume luxury goods may have a high markup; high volume goods may have a relatively lower markup.

Council of Australian Governments GENERAL MANAGEMENT a body consisting of the heads of the Australian federal, state, and territory governments that meets to discuss matters of national importance. Abbr **COAG**

Council of Trade Unions *(ANZ)* GENERAL MANAGEMENT see ***CTU***

counseling HR & PERSONNEL the provision of help by a trained person to permit somebody to clarify concerns, come to terms with feelings, and take responsibility for and begin to resolve difficulties. Counseling is a technique inherent to the ***mentoring*** process.

counterfactual GENERAL MANAGEMENT untrue *(slang)*

counterfeit GENERAL MANAGEMENT to produce forged or imitation goods or money intended to deceive or defraud. Counterfeited goods of inferior quality are often sold at substantially lower prices than genuine products and may bear the ***brand*** or ***trade name*** of the company. Counterfeiting violates ***trademark*** and ***intellectual property*** rights and may damage the reputation of producers of authentic goods. National and international legislation provides some recourse to companies against counterfeiters, but strategies such as consumer warnings and labeling methods are also used to minimize the impact of counterfeiting. Efforts to eliminate counterfeiting are coordinated by the International Anti-Counterfeiting Coalition.

counterparty FINANCE, BANKING, AND ACCOUNTING a person with whom somebody is entering into a contract

counterpurchase ECONOMICS see ***countertrade***

countertrade ECONOMICS a range of reciprocal trading practices. This umbrella term encompasses the direct exchange of goods for goods (or **barter**) where no cash changes hands to more complex variations; **counterpurchase**, which involves a traditional export transaction plus the commitment of the exporter to buy additional goods or services from that country; and ***buy-back***, in which the supplier of plant or equipment is paid from the future proceeds resulting from the use of the plant. Countertrade conditions vary widely from country to country and can be costly and administratively cumbersome.

country club management GENERAL MANAGEMENT see ***Managerial Grid***™

country risk ECONOMICS the level of bad debt held by an economy, which determines its credit rating in the eyes of financial institutions such as the ***IMF***

coupon FINANCE, BANKING, AND ACCOUNTING
1. a piece of paper that a bondholder presents to request payment
2. the rate of interest on a bond
3. an interest payment made to a bondholder

clip coupons FINANCE, BANKING, AND ACCOUNTING to collect periodic interest on a bond *(slang)*

covariance STATISTICS the value that is predicted from the product of the deviations of two variables from each of their means

covariate STATISTICS a variable that is not crucial in an investigation but may affect the crucial variables from which a model is being built

coverage MARKETING the percentage of a target audience reached by different media

Coverdale training HR & PERSONNEL a system of training that concentrates on improving ***teamwork*** and methods of getting a job done. Coverdale training is concerned with management behavior, including setting ***objectives***, briefing subordinates, and tackling a job. Groups of people are put into ***scenarios*** reproducing everyday situations and encouraged to experiment and build up successful working practices.

covered option FINANCE, BANKING, AND ACCOUNTING an option whose owner has the shares for the option

covered warrant FINANCE, BANKING, AND ACCOUNTING a futures contract for shares in a company

cover note FINANCE, BANKING, AND ACCOUNTING a document that an insurance company issues to a customer to serve as a temporary insurance certificate until the issue of the policy itself

Covey, Stephen R. *(b.* 1932) GENERAL MANAGEMENT U.S. writer and consultant. Offers a holistic approach to life and work, based on Mormon principles, the self-drive philosophy of ***Dale Carnegie***, and the self-help advice of Samuel Smiles. His message is enshrined in *The Seven Habits of Highly Effective People* (1989), which calls for a rethink of many fundamental assumptions and attitudes.
STEPHEN R. COVEY (pp. 976–77)

CPA *abbr* E-COMMERCE cost per action, a pricing model for online advertising based on the number of times an Internet user clicks on a banner ad that is linked to a particular Web site

CPD *abbr* HR & PERSONNEL continuing professional development, ongoing training and education throughout a career to improve the skills and knowledge used to perform a job or succession of jobs. CPD should be a planned, structured process, involving the assessment of development needs and the tailoring of training to meet those needs. CPD is founded on the belief that the development of professionals should not finish after initial qualification, especially in a fast changing business environment in which skills are likely to obsolesce quickly. CPD requires commitment and resources from the employee, the employer, and supportive agencies such as professional bodies. Advocates of CPD argue that it can enhance ***employability*** and ***career development*** by keeping skills up to date and broadening a person's skill base. ***Dominic Cadbury*** has said that CPD should be centered on the individual, who must take responsibility for the continuing assessment and satisfaction of his or her own development needs. Much can be found in support of the principle of CPD in the concepts of ***David Kolb***'s ***experiential learning*** cycle, ***Peter Honey***'s and ***Alan Mumford***'s learning types, the ***personal development*** cycle, and ***lifelong learning***.

CPF see ***Central Provident Fund***

CPI ECONOMICS see ***consumer price index***

CPIX *abbr (ANZ)* ECONOMICS the ***consumer price index*** excluding interest costs, on the basis that these are a direct outcome of monetary policy

CPM *abbr* E-COMMERCE cost per thousand impressions, a pricing model for online advertising. The M represents the Roman numeral for 1,000.

crash
1. FINANCE, BANKING, AND ACCOUNTING a precipitous drop in value, especially of the stocks traded in a market
2. E-COMMERCE a hardware failure or program error that stops a computer working. If data has not been backed up it can be lost as a result of a crash.

3. ECONOMICS a sudden and catastrophic downturn in an economy. The crash in the United States in 1929 is one of the most famous.

creative accounting FINANCE, BANKING, AND ACCOUNTING the use of accounting methods to hide aspects of a company's financial dealings in order to make the company appear less or more successful than it is in reality (*slang*)

creative consultancy MARKETING an organization that plans and creates advertising on behalf of a client

creative director MARKETING an employee of an advertising agency who is responsible for planning and managing the creative work of a campaign

creative strategy MARKETING a technique for determining the most effective creative approach to reach a target audience

creative thinking GENERAL MANAGEMENT see ***creativity***

creativity GENERAL MANAGEMENT the generation of new ideas by approaching problems or existing practices in innovative or imaginative ways. Psychologists have disagreed on the nature of creativity. Until about 1980, research concentrated on identifying the personality traits of creative people, but more recently psychologists have focused on the mental processes involved. Creativity involves reexamining assumptions and reinterpreting facts, ideas, and past experience. A growing interest in creativity as a source of ***competitive advantage*** has developed in recent years, and creativity is considered important, not just for the development of new products and services, but also for its role in organizational ***decision making*** and ***problem solving***. Many organizations actively seek a ***corporate culture*** that encourages creativity. There are a number of techniques used to foster **creative thinking**, including ***brainstorming*** and ***lateral thinking***. Creativity is linked to ***innovation***, which is the process of taking a new idea and turning it into a market offering.
☆ CREATING CORPORATE CREATIVITY (pp. 271–72)

credit FINANCE, BANKING, AND ACCOUNTING the trust that people have in somebody's ability to repay a loan, or a loan itself

credit account FINANCE, BANKING, AND ACCOUNTING an account that allows the holder to buy goods or services without having to pay until a later date

credit availability FINANCE, BANKING, AND ACCOUNTING money that can be borrowed

credit available FINANCE, BANKING, AND ACCOUNTING the amount of money that somebody can borrow at a given time

credit balance FINANCE, BANKING, AND ACCOUNTING the amount of money that somebody owes on a credit account

credit bureau FINANCE, BANKING, AND ACCOUNTING a company that assesses the creditworthiness of people for businesses or banks. See ***mercantile agency***

credit capacity FINANCE, BANKING, AND ACCOUNTING the amount of money that somebody can borrow and be expected to repay

credit card E-COMMERCE, FINANCE, BANKING, AND ACCOUNTING a card issued by a bank or financial institution and accepted by a merchant in payment for a transaction for which the cardholder must subsequently reimburse the issuer

credit ceiling FINANCE, BANKING, AND ACCOUNTING the largest amount that a lender will permit somebody to borrow, for example, on a credit card

credit committee FINANCE, BANKING, AND ACCOUNTING a committee that evaluates a potential borrower's creditworthiness

credit company FINANCE, BANKING, AND ACCOUNTING a company that extends credit to people

credit cooperative FINANCE, BANKING, AND ACCOUNTING an organization of people who join together to gain advantage in borrowing

credit creation FINANCE, BANKING, AND ACCOUNTING the collective ability of lenders to make money available to borrowers

credit crunch FINANCE, BANKING, AND ACCOUNTING a situation in which money for borrowing is unavailable

credit deposit E-COMMERCE the value of the credit card purchases deposited in a merchant's bank account after the acquirer's fees are deducted

credit derivative FINANCE, BANKING, AND ACCOUNTING a financial instrument that transfers a lender's risk to a third party

credit entity FINANCE, BANKING, AND ACCOUNTING a borrower or lender

credit entry FINANCE, BANKING, AND ACCOUNTING an item on the asset side of a financial statement

credit exposure FINANCE, BANKING, AND ACCOUNTING the risk to a lender of a borrower defaulting

credit granter FINANCE, BANKING, AND ACCOUNTING a person or organization that lends money

credit history FINANCE, BANKING, AND ACCOUNTING a potential borrower's record of debt repayment

crediting rate FINANCE, BANKING, AND ACCOUNTING the interest rate paid on an insurance policy that is an investment

credit limit FINANCE, BANKING, AND ACCOUNTING the highest amount that a lender will allow somebody to borrow, for example, on a credit card

credit line FINANCE, BANKING, AND ACCOUNTING = ***line of credit***

credit note FINANCE, BANKING, AND ACCOUNTING a document stating that a store owes somebody an amount of money and entitling the person to goods to the specified value

creditor FINANCE, BANKING, AND ACCOUNTING a person or organization that is owed money

creditor nation ECONOMICS a country that has a balance of payments surplus

creditors' committee FINANCE, BANKING, AND ACCOUNTING a group that directs the efforts of creditors to receive partial repayment from a bankrupt person or organization. Also known as ***creditors' steering committee***

creditors' meeting FINANCE, BANKING, AND ACCOUNTING a meeting of those to whom a bankrupt person or organization owes money

creditors' settlement FINANCE, BANKING, AND ACCOUNTING an agreement on partial repayment to those to whom a bankrupt person or organization owes money

creditors' steering committee FINANCE, BANKING, AND ACCOUNTING = ***creditors' committee***

credit rating *or* **credit ranking** FINANCE, BANKING, AND ACCOUNTING
1. an assessment of somebody's creditworthiness
2. the process of assessing somebody's creditworthiness

credit rating agency FINANCE, BANKING, AND ACCOUNTING a company that assesses the creditworthiness of people on behalf of businesses or banks. U.K. term credit reference agency.

credit rationing FINANCE, BANKING, AND ACCOUNTING the process of making credit less easily available or subject to high interest rates

credit-reference agency (*U.K.*) FINANCE, BANKING, AND ACCOUNTING = ***credit rating agency***

credit risk FINANCE, BANKING, AND ACCOUNTING
1. the chance that a borrower will default on a loan
2. a borrower who may default on a loan

credit sale FINANCE, BANKING, AND ACCOUNTING a sale for which the buyer need not pay immediately

credit scoring FINANCE, BANKING, AND ACCOUNTING a calculation done in the process of credit rating

credit side FINANCE, BANKING, AND ACCOUNTING the part of a financial statement that lists assets

credit squeeze FINANCE, BANKING, AND ACCOUNTING a situation in which credit is not easily available or is subject to high interest rates

credit standing FINANCE, BANKING, AND ACCOUNTING the reputation that somebody has with regard to meeting financial obligations

credit system FINANCE, BANKING, AND ACCOUNTING a set of rules and organizations involved in making loans

credit union FINANCE, BANKING, AND ACCOUNTING a cooperative savings association that lends money to members at low rates of interest

creditworthy FINANCE, BANKING, AND ACCOUNTING regarded as being reliable in terms of meeting financial obligations

creeping takeover FINANCE, BANKING, AND ACCOUNTING a takeover achieved by the gradual acquisition of small amounts of stock over an extended period of time (*slang*)

creeping tender offer FINANCE, BANKING, AND ACCOUNTING an acquisition of many shares in a company by purchase, especially to avoid restrictions on tender offers

CREST FINANCE, BANKING, AND ACCOUNTING the paperless system used for settling stock transactions electronically in the United Kingdom

crisis management MARKETING actions taken by an organization in response to unexpected events or situations with potentially negative effects that threaten resources and people or the success and continued operation of the organization. Crisis management includes the development of plans to reduce the risk of a crisis occurring and to deal with any crises that do arise, and the implementation of these plans so as to minimize the impact of crises and assist the organization to recover from them. Crisis situations may occur as a result of external factors such as the development of a new product by a competitor or changes in legislation, or internal factors such as a product failure or faulty ***decision making***, and often involve the need to make quick decisions on the basis of uncertain or incomplete information. See also ***risk management***, ***disaster management***

critical mass GENERAL MANAGEMENT the point at which an organization or ***project*** has gained sufficient momentum or ***market share*** to be either self-sustaining or worth the input of extra investment or resources

critical-path analysis GENERAL MANAGEMENT, OPERATIONS & PRODUCTION see ***critical-path method***

critical-path method GENERAL MANAGEMENT, OPERATIONS & PRODUCTION a ***network analysis*** planning technique used especially in ***project management*** to identify the activities within a project that are critical for its success. In critical-path method, individual activities within a project and their duration are recorded in a diagram or flow chart. A critical path is plotted through the diagram, showing the sequence in which activities must be completed in order to complete the project in the shortest amount of time, incurring the least cost. The technique is sometimes called **critical-path analysis**, but the two terms are not synonymous.

critical-ratio analysis GENERAL MANAGEMENT a technique used in inventory control to calculate comparative priorities for the reordering of stock. Critical-ratio analysis requires the division of remaining stock items by the likely daily demand for them. This figure is then divided by the time taken to process an order to derive the critical ratio. The smaller the ratio, the greater the reorder priority. A ratio of less than 1 indicates an imminent shortage. Critical ratios are also used in conjunction with ***MRP II*** systems to determine the sequence in which orders should be processed. In this case, a ratio of less than 1 indicates that the order is behind schedule.

critical region STATISTICS the range of values of a test statistic that lead a researcher to reject the null hypothesis

critical restructuring GENERAL MANAGEMENT major economic or social changes that fundamentally reshape traditional patterns of organization

critical success factors GENERAL MANAGEMENT the aspects of a business that are identified as vital for successful targets to be reached and maintained. Critical success factors are normally identified within such areas as production processes, employee and organization skills, functions, techniques, and technologies. The identification and strengthening of such factors may be similar to identifying ***core competences***, and is considered an essential element in achieving and maintaining ***competitive advantage***.

critical value STATISTICS the value with which a researcher compares a statistic from sample data in order to determine whether or not the null hypothesis should be rejected

CRM MARKETING see ***customer relationship management***

crony capitalism ECONOMICS a form of capitalism in which business contracts are awarded to the family and friends of the government in power rather than by open-market tender

Crosby, **Philip B.** (1926–2001) GENERAL MANAGEMENT U.S. business executive and consultant ***Quality*** guru who introduced and popularized catchphrases such as "zero defects," "get it right first time," and "quality is free." Crosby summarized his approach toward quality improvement as the Fourteen Steps, set down in *Quality is Free* (1979).
PHILIP CROSBY (pp. 978–79)

cross FINANCE, BANKING, AND ACCOUNTING a transaction in securities in which one broker acts for both parties

cross-border trade ECONOMICS trade between two countries that have a common frontier

cross-hedging FINANCE, BANKING, AND ACCOUNTING a form of hedging using an option on a different but related commodity, especially a currency

cross listing FINANCE, BANKING, AND ACCOUNTING the practice of offering the same item for sale in more than one place

crossposting E-COMMERCE the act of posting the same Internet messages into several different news or discussion groups at the same time

cross-rate ECONOMICS the rate of exchange between two currencies in terms of the rate of exchange between them and a third currency, for example, sterling and the peso in relation to the dollar

cross-sectional study STATISTICS a statistical study in which a range of information is collected at the same time, for example, in a single telephone call

cross sell MARKETING to sell existing customers different products from the company's range

crowding out FINANCE, BANKING, AND ACCOUNTING the effect on markets of credit produced by extraordinarily large borrowing by a national government

crude annual death rate STATISTICS the total number of deaths in a population in one year divided by the total population at the midpoint of the year

CSIRO *abbr* (*ANZ*) GENERAL MANAGEMENT Commonwealth Scientific and Industrial Research Organization, an Australian federal government body in charge of scientific research, established in 1949

CSP E-COMMERCE see ***commerce service provider***

CTU *abbr* GENERAL MANAGEMENT Council of Trade Unions, New Zealand's national labor union organization. It has 19 affiliated unions and represents approximately 200,000 workers.

cube farm GENERAL MANAGEMENT an office that is divided into cubicles (*slang*)

cue GENERAL MANAGEMENT a factor that differentiates a high-value product from an ordinary commodity

CUL *abbr* GENERAL MANAGEMENT see you later (*slang*)

cultural creative HR & PERSONNEL somebody who values personal and spiritual development, enjoys change, likes learning about new cultures, and typically desires to live a simpler way of life

✔ DOWNSHIFTING: WORKING LESS AND ENJOYING IT MORE (pp. 812–13)

cultural synergy GENERAL MANAGEMENT the harmonization of the direction and operation of separate organizations into a whole. Whether cultural synergy can be achieved lies in the degree to which there is congruence of ***vision***, mission, values, strategy, and operational processes in the different organizations. The lack of cultural and ***strategic fit*** is the main cause of failure of ***mergers***, sometimes because of the major partner imposing its own ***corporate culture***, rather than developing a shared culture. Cultural integration, therefore, needs to be carefully analyzed, planned, and implemented.

culture shock GENERAL MANAGEMENT the effects on an employee or organization when faced with new, unfamiliar, or rapidly changing circumstances. Symptoms of culture shock include uncertainty, ***stress***, confusion, disorientation, or simply not knowing how to act in the circumstances. Culture shock can occur in a number of scenarios, for example, when new staff are thrown into the deep end of a busy department, when two organizations merge with poor strategic, operational, or ***cultural synergy***, or when public sector organizations adopt private sector practices. The degree of shock can be reduced through careful analysis, planning, training, and consequent preparedness.

cum FINANCE, BANKING, AND ACCOUNTING with

cum rights FINANCE, BANKING, AND ACCOUNTING an indication that the buyer of the shares is entitled to participate in a forthcoming rights issue

cumulative method FINANCE, BANKING, AND ACCOUNTING a system in which items are added together

cumulative preferred stock FINANCE, BANKING, AND ACCOUNTING preferred stock for which dividends accrue even if they are not paid when due

currency FINANCE, BANKING, AND ACCOUNTING the money in circulation in a particular country

currency future FINANCE, BANKING, AND ACCOUNTING an option on currency

currency note FINANCE, BANKING, AND ACCOUNTING a banknote

currency risk FINANCE, BANKING, AND ACCOUNTING the risk that a currency used for a transaction may lose value

currency unit ECONOMICS each of the notes and coins that are the medium of exchange in a country

current account (*U.K.*) FINANCE, BANKING, AND ACCOUNTING = ***checking account***

current account equilibrium ECONOMICS a country's economic circumstances when its expenditure equals its income from trade and invisible earnings

current assets FINANCE, BANKING, AND ACCOUNTING cash or assets that are readily convertible to cash

current assets financing FINANCE, BANKING, AND ACCOUNTING the use of current assets as collateral for a loan

current cash balance FINANCE, BANKING, AND ACCOUNTING the amount, which excludes balances due soon for outstanding transactions, that a client has available for investment with a broker

current-cost accounting FINANCE, BANKING, AND ACCOUNTING accounting based on the cost of items at the time of the financial statement

current earnings FINANCE, BANKING, AND ACCOUNTING the annual earnings most recently reported by a company

current liabilities FINANCE, BANKING, AND ACCOUNTING business liabilities that are to be cleared within the financial year

current principal factor FINANCE, BANKING, AND ACCOUNTING the portion of the initial amount of a loan that remains to be paid

current ratio FINANCE, BANKING, AND ACCOUNTING a ratio of ***current assets*** to ***current liabilities***

✔ HOW TO MEASURE CURRENT RATIO (p. 842)

current stock value FINANCE, BANKING, AND ACCOUNTING the value of all stock in a portfolio, including stock in transactions that have not yet been settled

current value FINANCE, BANKING, AND AC-

COUNTING a ratio indicating the amount by which ***current assets*** exceed ***current liabilities***

current yield FINANCE, BANKING, AND ACCOUNTING the interest being paid on a bond divided by its current market price, expressed as a percentage

curriculum vitae *(U.K.)* HR & PERSONNEL = ***résumé***

cushion bond FINANCE, BANKING, AND ACCOUNTING a bond that pays a high rate of interest but sells at a low premium because of the risk of its being called soon

customer MARKETING a purchaser of a product or service. A customer is a person or organization that purchases or obtains goods or services from other organizations such as manufacturers, retailers, wholesalers, or service providers. A customer is not necessarily the same person as the ***consumer***, as a product or service can be paid for by one party, the customer, and used by another, the consumer.

customer capital GENERAL MANAGEMENT the value of an organization's relationships with its customers, which involves factors such as market share, customer retention rates, and profitability of customers

customer care MARKETING see ***customer relations***

customer-centric model GENERAL MANAGEMENT a business model organized around the needs of the customer

customer complaint GENERAL MANAGEMENT see ***complaint***

customer expectation GENERAL MANAGEMENT the needs, wants, and preconceived ideas of a customer about a product or service. Customer expectation will be influenced by a customer's perception of the product or service and can be created by previous experience, advertising, hearsay, awareness of competitors, and ***brand image***. The level of ***customer service*** is also a factor, and a customer might expect to encounter efficiency, helpfulness, reliability, confidence in the staff, and a personal interest in his or her custom. If customer expectations are met, then ***customer satisfaction*** results. Also known as ***buyer expectation***

customer flow MARKETING the number and pattern of customers coming into a store or passing through a railway or bus station, airport, or other large service, retail, or leisure area. Customer flow can be monitored by observation, time lapse or normal closed circuit television, or, less satisfactorily, by analysis of purchase data. This provides useful information about the number of customers, flow patterns, bottlenecks, areas not visited, and other aspects of ***consumer behavior*** (see ***consumer demand***).

customer focus MARKETING an organizational orientation toward satisfying the needs of potential and actual ***customers***. Customer focus is considered to be one of the keys to business success. Achieving customer focus involves ensuring that the whole organization, and not just frontline service staff, puts its customers first. All activities, from the planning of a new product to its production, marketing, and after-sales care, should be built around the customer. Every department and every employee should share the same customer-focused vision. This can be aided by practicing good ***customer relationship management*** and maintaining a ***customer relations*** program.

customer profitability MARKETING the degree to which a ***customer*** or segment of customers contributes toward organization profits. Customer profitability has been shown to be produced primarily by a small proportion of customers, perhaps 10% to 20%, who generate up to 80% of a company's profits. Up to 40% of customers may generate only moderate profits, and the other 40% may be loss making. Such data enables companies to focus efforts on the most profitable segments.

customer recovery MARKETING activities intended to win back customers who no longer buy from an organization

customer relations MARKETING the approach of an organization to winning and retaining customers. The most critical activity of any organization wishing to stay in business is its approach to dealing with its customers. Putting customers at the center of all activities is seen by many as an integral part of quality, pricing, and product differentiation. On one level, customer relations means keeping customers fully informed, turning complaints into opportunities, and genuinely listening to customers. On another level, being a customer-focused organization means ensuring that all activities relating to trading—for example, planning, design, production, marketing, and after-sales of a product or service—are built around the customer, and that every department and individual employee understands and shares the same vision. Only then can a company deliver continuous ***customer satisfaction*** and experience good customer relations.

customer relationship management MARKETING the cultivation of meaningful relationships with actual or potential purchasers of goods or services. Customer relationship management aims to increase an organization's sales by promoting ***customer satisfaction*** and can be achieved using tools such as relationship marketing. Abbr **CRM**

customer retention MARKETING the maintenance of the custom of people who have purchased a company's goods or services once and the gaining of repeat purchases. Customer retention occurs when a customer is loyal to a company, ***brand***, or to a specific product or service, expressing long-term commitment and refusing to purchase from competitors. A company can adopt a number of strategies to retain its customers. Of critical importance to such strategies are the wider concepts of ***customer service***, ***customer relations***, and relationship marketing. Companies can build loyalty and retention through the use of a number of techniques, including ***database marketing***, the issue of loyalty cards, redeemable against a range of goods or services, preferential ***discounts***, free gifts, special promotions, newsletters or magazines, members' clubs, or customized products in limited editions. It has been argued that customer retention is linked to employee loyalty, since loyal employees build up long-term relationships with customers.

customer satisfaction MARKETING the degree to which customer expectations of a product or service are met or exceeded. Corporate and individual customers may have widely differing reasons for purchasing a product or service and therefore any measurement of satisfaction will need to be able to measure such differences. The quality of ***after-sales service*** can also be a crucial factor in influencing any purchasing decision. More and more companies are striving, not just for customer satisfaction, but for customer delight, that extra bit of added value that may lead to increased customer loyalty. Any extra added value, however, will need to be carefully costed.

customer service MARKETING the way in which an organization deals with its ***customers***. Customer service is most evident in sales and ***after-sales service***, but should infuse all the processes in the ***value chain***. Good customer service is the result of adopting ***customer focus***. Poor customer service can be a product of poor ***customer relations***.

customization GENERAL MANAGEMENT the process of modifying products or services to

meet the requirements of individual customers

customized service GENERAL MANAGEMENT a service tailored to the requirements of an individual customer

cutthroat MARKETING aggressively ruthless, especially in dealing with competitors

cutting-edge GENERAL MANAGEMENT at the forefront of new technologies or markets

cyberbole E-COMMERCE hype about the Internet and the online world (*slang*)

cybercrud E-COMMERCE confusing and useless computer jargon (*slang*)

cyber mall E-COMMERCE a Web site shared by two or more commercial organizations, usually with some similarity in appearance, function, product, or service. Also known as ***e-commerce mall***, ***electronic mall***, ***online shopping mall***

cybermarketing E-COMMERCE the use of Internet-based promotions of any kind. This may involve targeted e-mail, bulletin boards, Web sites, or sites from which the customer can download files.

cybersales FINANCE, BANKING, AND ACCOUNTING sales made electronically through computers and information systems

cyberslacker GENERAL MANAGEMENT somebody who spends time surfing the Internet for personal purposes during office hours (*slang*)

cyberspace E-COMMERCE the online world and its communication networks

cycle plot STATISTICS a graphical representation of the behavior of seasonal time series

cycle time OPERATIONS & PRODUCTION see ***lead time***

cyclical stock FINANCE, BANKING, AND ACCOUNTING a stock whose value rises and falls periodically, for example, according to the seasons of the year or economic cycles

cyclical unemployment ECONOMICS unemployment, usually temporary, caused by a lack of ***aggregate demand***, for example, during a downswing in the business cycle

cyclic variation STATISTICS the repeatable systematic variation of a variable over time

D

daily price limit FINANCE, BANKING, AND ACCOUNTING the amount by which the price of an option can rise or fall within one trading day

daisy chaining FINANCE, BANKING, AND ACCOUNTING an illegal financial practice whereby traders create artificial transactions in order to make a particular security appear more active than it is in reality (*slang*)

dancing frog E-COMMERCE a problem or image on somebody's computer screen that disappears when shown to somebody else (*slang*)

Darwin Trade Development Zone GENERAL MANAGEMENT a free trade zone in the city of Darwin in the Northern Territory of Australia. Companies operating within the zone, which is intended to facilitate trade with Asia, are exempt from certain state taxes and customs duties. Abbr **DTDZ**

data STATISTICS the measurements and observations collected during a statistical investigation

database GENERAL MANAGEMENT a structured collection of related information held in any form, especially on a computer. The creation of a database assists organizations in keeping records and facilitates the retrieval of specific facts or different categories of information as and when required. Databases of various kinds may form part of an organization's ***MIS***.

database management system STATISTICS a dedicated computer program designed to manipulate a collection of information

database marketing FINANCE, BANKING, AND ACCOUNTING the collection and analysis of information about customers and their buying habits, lifestyles, and other such data. Database marketing is used to build profiles of individual customers, who are then targeted with customized mailings, special offers, and other incentives to encourage spending. Database marketing is a form of relationship marketing.

data capture MARKETING the acquisition of information through advertisement coupons, inquiry forms, or other response mechanisms

data cleansing MARKETING the process of ensuring that data is up-to-date and free of duplication or error

data dredging STATISTICS the process of making comparisons and drawing conclusions from data that was not part of the original brief for a study

data editing STATISTICS the removal of keying or format errors from data

Data Encryption Standard E-COMMERCE see ***DES***

dataholic GENERAL MANAGEMENT somebody who is obsessed with obtaining information, especially on the Internet (*slang*)

data mining

1. E-COMMERCE the process of using sophisticated software to identify commercially useful statistical patterns or relationships in online databases

2. MARKETING the extraction of information from a ***data warehouse*** to assist managerial ***decision making***. The information obtained in this way helps organizations gain a better understanding of their customers and can be used to improve customer support and marketing activities.

data protection MARKETING the safeguards that govern the storage and use of personal data held on computer systems and in paper-based filing systems. The growing use of computers to store information about individuals has led to the enactment of legislation in many countries designed to protect the privacy of individuals and prevent the disclosure of information to unauthorized persons.

data reduction STATISTICS the process of summarizing large data sets into histograms or frequency distributions so that calculations such as means can be made

data screening STATISTICS the process of assessing a set of observations to detect significant deviations such as outliers

data set STATISTICS all of the measurements or observations collected in a statistical investigation

data smoothing algorithm STATISTICS a procedure for removing meaningless data from a sequence of observations so that a pattern can be detected

data warehouse GENERAL MANAGEMENT a collection of subject-orientated data collected over a period of time and stored on a computer to provide information in support of managerial ***decision making***. A data warehouse contains a large volume of information selected from different sources, including operational systems and organizational databases, and brought together in a standard format to facilitate retrieval and analysis. Like ***EISs***, data warehouses can be used to support decision making, but the ways in which they can be searched are not predetermined. Organizations often use data warehouses for marketing purposes, for example, the analysis of customer information, or for market segmentation. ***Data mining*** techniques are used to access the information in a data warehouse.

DAX FINANCE, BANKING, AND ACCOUNTING the principal German stock exchange, in Frankfurt. Abbr of ***Deutscher Aktienindex***

day in the sun GENERAL MANAGEMENT the period of time during which a product is successful in the marketplace

day order FINANCE, BANKING, AND ACCOUNTING an order that is valid only during one trading day

day release (*U.K.*) HR & PERSONNEL the discharge of an employee from normal work to take part in education or training. Day release is normally for one day each week, fortnight, or month, and it enables an employee to study for further education or ***vocational qualifications*** on a part-time basis.

day trader FINANCE, BANKING, AND ACCOUNTING somebody who makes trades with very close dates of maturity

day trading FINANCE, BANKING, AND ACCOUNTING the making of trades that have very close dates of maturity

DCM (*S. Africa*) FINANCE, BANKING, AND ACCOUNTING see ***Development Capital Market***

dead cat bounce FINANCE, BANKING, AND ACCOUNTING a short-term increase in the value of a stock following a precipitous drop in value (*slang*)

dead tree edition E-COMMERCE the print version of a publication that is also available in electronic form (*slang*)

dead wood HR & PERSONNEL employees who are no longer considered to be useful to a company (*slang*)

deal

cut somebody a deal GENERAL MANAGEMENT to agree on terms for a business arrangement with somebody (*slang*)

dealership MARKETING a retail outlet distributing, selling, and servicing products such as cars or construction plant on behalf of a manufacturer

death by committee GENERAL MANAGEMENT the prevention of serious consideration of a proposal by assigning a committee to look at it

Death Valley curve GENERAL MANAGEMENT a point in the development of a new business when losses begin to erode the company's equity base, so that it becomes difficult to raise new equity (*slang*)

debenture FINANCE, BANKING, AND ACCOUNTING

1. an unsecured bond backed only by the issuer's credit standing

2. a bond, usually repayable at a fixed date

debit card FINANCE, BANKING, AND ACCOUNTING a card issued by a bank or financial institution and accepted by a merchant in payment for a transaction. Unlike the procedure with a ***credit card***, purchases are deducted from the cardholder's account, as with a check, when the transaction takes place.

de Bono, Edward (*b.* 1933) GENERAL MANAGEMENT Maltese-born academic and consultant. Creator of the concept of ***lateral thinking***, which was introduced in *Lateral Thinking: a Textbook of Creativity* (1970).

debt FINANCE, BANKING, AND ACCOUNTING an amount of money owed to a person or organization

debt/equity ratio FINANCE, BANKING, AND ACCOUNTING the ratio of what a company owes to the value of all of its outstanding shares

debt instrument FINANCE, BANKING, AND ACCOUNTING any document used or issued for raising money, for example, a bill of exchange, bond, or promissory note

debtor FINANCE, BANKING, AND ACCOUNTING a person or organization that owes money

debt rescheduling GENERAL MANAGEMENT the renegotiation of debt repayments. Debt rescheduling is necessary when a company can no longer meet its debt payments. It can involve deferring debt payments, deferring payment of interest, or negotiating a new loan. It is usually undertaken as part of ***turnaround management*** to avoid ***business failure***. Debt rescheduling is also undertaken in less developed countries that encounter national debt difficulties. Such arrangements are usually overseen by the International Monetary Fund.

debt/service ratio ECONOMICS the ratio of a country's or company's borrowing to its equity or ***venture capital***

debugging STATISTICS the identification and removal of errors in a computer program or system

decentralization GENERAL MANAGEMENT the dispersal of decision-making control. Decentralization involves moving power, authority, and decision-making control within an organization from a central headquarters or from high managerial levels to subsidiaries, branches, divisions, or departments. As an organizational concept, decentralization implies a ***delegation*** both of power and responsibility by top management in order to promote flexibility through faster decision making and improved response times. Decentralization is, therefore, strongly related to the concept of ***empowerment***, though the latter is perhaps more focused on direct working front-line staff.

decision lozenge GENERAL MANAGEMENT see ***flow chart***

decision-maker GENERAL MANAGEMENT somebody with the responsibility and authority to make decisions within an organization, especially those that determine future direction and strategy. ***Decision theory*** is used to assist decision-makers in the process of decision making.

decision making GENERAL MANAGEMENT the process of choosing between alternative courses of action. Decision making may take place at an individual or organizational level. The process may involve establishing objectives, gathering relevant information, identifying alternatives, setting criteria for the decision, and selecting the best option. The nature of the decision-making process within an organization is influenced by its culture and structure, and a number of theoretical models have been developed. One well-known method for individual decision making was developed by ***Charles Kepner*** and ***Benjamin Tregoe*** in their book *The New Rational Manager* (1981). ***Decision theory*** can be used to assist in the process of decision making. Specific techniques used in decision making include ***heuristics*** and ***decision trees***. Computer systems designed to assist managerial decision making are known as ***decision support systems***.

decision-making unit MARKETING a group of people who directly or indirectly influence the purchase of a product or service

decision support system GENERAL MANAGEMENT a computer system designed to collect, store, process, and provide access to information to support managerial ***decision making***. Decision support systems were developed in the 1970s to facilitate unstructured and one-off decision making, as the standard reporting capabilities of ***MISs*** were perceived to be more suitable for routine day-to-day decisions. Data on an organization's external operating environment, as well as internal operational information, is included and an interactive interface allows managers to retrieve and manipulate data. Modeling techniques are used to examine the results of alternative courses of action.

decision theory *or* **decision analysis** GENERAL MANAGEMENT a body of knowledge that attempts to describe, analyze, and model the process of ***decision making*** and the factors influencing it. Decision theory encompasses both formal mathematical and statistical approaches to solving decision problems, using quantitative techniques such as probability and ***game theory***, and more informal behavioral approaches. It is used to inform and assist decision making in organizations.

decision tree GENERAL MANAGEMENT a diagram designed to help decision-makers by representing available options and possible outcomes as branches of a tree. Decision trees provide an overview of multiple-stage ***decision making*** by showing successive decision points arising from previous choices. Values representing the relative probability of individual outcomes may be assigned to each branch of the tree in order to compare strategies and select the most favorable.

deconstruction GENERAL MANAGEMENT the breaking up of traditional business structures to meet the requirements of the modern economy

de-diversify GENERAL MANAGEMENT to sell off parts of a company or companies that are not considered directly relevant to a corporation's main area of interest

deep-in-the-money call option FINANCE, BANKING, AND ACCOUNTING a call option that has become very profitable and is likely to remain so

deep-in-the-money put option FINANCE, BANKING, AND ACCOUNTING a put option that has become very profitable and is likely to remain so

de facto standard GENERAL MANAGEMENT a standard set in a given market by a highly successful product or service

defensive stock FINANCE, BANKING, AND ACCOUNTING stock that prospers predictably regardless of external circumstances such as an economic slowdown, for example, the stock of a company that markets a product everyone must have

deferred coupon FINANCE, BANKING, AND ACCOUNTING a coupon that pays no interest at first, but pays relatively high interest after a specified date

deferred month FINANCE, BANKING, AND ACCOUNTING a month relatively late in the term of an option

deficit FINANCE, BANKING, AND ACCOUNTING = ***budget deficit***

deficit financing FINANCE, BANKING, AND ACCOUNTING the borrowing of money because expenditures will exceed receipts

deficit spending FINANCE, BANKING, AND ACCOUNTING government spending financed through borrowing rather than taxation

deflation ECONOMICS a reduction in the general level of prices sustained over several months, usually accompanied by declining employment and output

deflationary fiscal policy ECONOMICS a government policy that raises taxes and reduces public expenditure in order to reduce the level of ***aggregate demand*** in the economy

deflationary gap ECONOMICS a gap between ***GDP*** and the potential output of the economy

de Geus, Arie P. (*b.* 1930) GENERAL MANAGEMENT Dutch business executive, adviser, and consultant. Former strategist for Royal Dutch Shell who, in *The Living Company* (1997), identified the characteristics of long-lived companies: financial conservatism, sensitivity to their environment, cohesiveness, and tolerance of unconventional thinking.

degree mill HR & PERSONNEL an establishment that offers to award a qualification for little or no work, often on payment of a large sum of money. Degree mills mostly operate on the edge of the law, often being uncredited or unregistered as educational institutions. Most degree mills fail to offer any worthwhile education, and those that do lack the appropriate accreditation that makes qualifications acceptable by employers, with the result that they award ***bogus degree*** certificates.

delayed settlement processing E-COMMERCE a procedure for storing authorized transaction settlements online until after the merchant has shipped the hard goods to the purchaser

delayering GENERAL MANAGEMENT the removal of supposedly unproductive layers of middle management to make organizations more efficient and customer responsive. The term came into vogue during the 1980s. When taken to extremes, delayering can lead to an ***anorexic organization***.

delegation HR & PERSONNEL the process of entrusting somebody else with the appropriate responsibility and authority for the accomplishment of a particular activity. Delegation involves briefing somebody else to carry out a task for which the delegator holds individual responsibility, but which need not be executed by him or her. It does not involve the delegate doing something he or she is already paid to do as part of his or her job. There are various degrees of delegation: for example, a manager may delegate responsibility, but not necessarily full authority, and continue to supervise the activity. Delegation should be a positive activity, for example, as an aid to ***employee development***, rather than a negative one, for example, passing on an unpopular task. It should be accompanied by support and encouragement from the delegator to the delegate. An extension of delegation is ***empowerment***, in which complete authority for a task is passed to somebody else, who takes full responsibility for its objectives, execution, and results.

delist FINANCE, BANKING, AND ACCOUNTING to remove a company from the list of companies whose stocks are traded on an exchange

delivery month FINANCE, BANKING, AND ACCOUNTING = ***contract month***

Dell, Michael S. (*b.* 1965) GENERAL MANAGEMENT U.S. business executive. Founder of Dell Computer Corporation and youngest

C.E.O. to run a ***Fortune 500*** company, whose business achieved success through building to order, ***direct selling***, minimizing ***inventory***, and using ***Internet*** technology.

Delphi technique GENERAL MANAGEMENT a qualitative ***forecasting*** method in which a panel of experts respond individually to a questionnaire or series of questionnaires, before reaching a consensus. The Delphi technique requires individual submission of, and response to, the questionnaire on the topic under investigation, in order to avoid the effect of a dominant personality influencing a group discussion. A summary of the written replies is then distributed so that responses can be revised in the light of the views expressed. This cycle is repeated until the coordinator of the group is satisfied that the best possible consensus has been reached. The Delphi technique was developed at the Rand Corporation during the late 1940s and 1950s and owes its name to the Greek oracle at Delphi, which was believed to make predictions about the future.

demand forecasting GENERAL MANAGEMENT the activity of estimating the quantity of a product or service that consumers will purchase. Demand forecasting involves techniques including both informal methods, such as educated guesses, and quantitative methods, such as the use of historical sales data or current data from test markets. Demand forecasting may be used in making pricing decisions, in assessing future capacity requirements, or in making decisions on whether to enter a new market.

demarcation dispute HR & PERSONNEL an industrial ***dispute*** between ***labor unions*** or between members of the same union regarding the allocation of work between different types of workers. Demarcation disputes are much less prevalent than in the past because of ***multiskilling*** agreements between employers and unions and the greater use of ***teamwork***.

demassifying GENERAL MANAGEMENT the process of changing a mass medium to a medium that is customized to meet the requirements of individual consumers

Deming, **W. Edwards** (1900–93) GENERAL MANAGEMENT U.S. academic and statistician. A leading champion of the ***quality*** movement and the most influential catalyst for the economic resurgence of postwar Japan. Deming's approach is summarized in his 14 points, which form the central thesis to his book *Out of the Crisis* (1986).

W. EDWARDS DEMING (pp. 980–81)

Deming Prize GENERAL MANAGEMENT an annual award to a company that has achieved significant performance improvement through the successful application of company-wide ***quality control***. The Deming Prize was set up in recognition of the work carried out by ***W. Edwards Deming*** in postwar Japan to improve manufacturing quality by reducing the potential for error. The Deming Prize has been awarded annually since 1951 by the Union of Japanese Scientists and Engineers. Contenders have to be able to demonstrate that, by applying the disciplines outlined by the assessment components, the productivity, growth, and financial performance of the organization have been improved. Entrants require a substantial resource in order to be able to submit their entry, which can take years to prepare. The focus of the Deming Prize reflects a rigor for the identification and elimination of defects through teamwork. The prize was also the first to apply the process of self-assessment, which has been adopted by other models such as the ***Malcolm Baldrige National Quality Award*** and the ***EFQM Excellence Model***.

W. EDWARDS DEMING (pp. 980–81)

democracy GENERAL MANAGEMENT a form of government in which people govern themselves, usually by electing representatives from their own number who are charged with governing in the best interests of the people. Democracy enables participation by the electorate in ***decision making*** and thus encourages ***empowerment***. In an organizational context, it is known as ***industrial democracy***.

demographics STATISTICS the characteristics of the size and structure of a human population

demography STATISTICS the study of the size and structural characteristics of human populations

department GENERAL MANAGEMENT a section of an organization, usually centered on a specialized function, under the responsibility of a head of department or team leader

departmentalization GENERAL MANAGEMENT the division of an organization into sections. Departmentalization is usually based on operating function, and organizations will commonly have departments for, for example, finance, personnel, or marketing. Such organizational structure is typical of a ***bureaucracy***. It may be used in ***centralization***, when a particular activity is undertaken by one department in one location on behalf of the whole organization, but may equally be a feature of a ***decentralized*** organization, in which departments are used as individual operating units responsible for their own management.

deposit protection FINANCE, BANKING, AND ACCOUNTING insurance that depositors have against loss. In the United States, the Federal Deposit Insurance Corporation (FDIC) provides this.

depression ECONOMICS a high level of unemployment during a downturn in the business cycle, sustained for months or years. The depression in the United States in the early 1930s is one of the best known.

deregulation GENERAL MANAGEMENT the process of removing government regulations from an industry

derivative FINANCE, BANKING, AND ACCOUNTING a security, such as an option, the price of which has a strong correlation with an underlying financial instrument

Derivative Trading Facility FINANCE, BANKING, AND ACCOUNTING a computer system and associated network operated by the Australian Stock Exchange to facilitate the purchase and sale of exchange-traded options. Abbr **DTF**

DES E-COMMERCE Data Encryption Standard, the most widely used standard for encrypting sensitive business information

design audit MARKETING an examination of the branding, style, and design of an organization's marketing material. A design agency may carry out a design audit free of charge in the hope that an organization will accept their recommendations and place design of material with them.

design consultancy MARKETING an organization that plans and carries out design work for clients, including packaging, corporate identity, products, and publication graphics

design for manufacturability, **design for assembly**, *or* **design for production** GENERAL MANAGEMENT the process of designing a product for best-fit with the manufacturing system of an organization in order to reduce the problems of bringing a product to market. Design for manufacturability is a team approach to manufacturing that pairs those responsible for the design of a product with those who build it. The manufacturing issues that need to be taken into account in the design process may include using the minimum number of parts, selecting appropriate materials, ease of assembly, and minimizing the number of machine set-ups. Design for manufacturability is one of the elements of ***concurrent engineering*** and is sometimes used as a synonym for it. Also known as ***engineering for excellence***, ***manufacturing for excellence***, ***producibility engineering***

design protection MARKETING see ***copyright***

deskfast GENERAL MANAGEMENT breakfast eaten in the office at a desk (*slang*)

de-skilling HR & PERSONNEL the removal of the need for skill or judgment in the performance of a task, often because of new technologies. While it can be argued that de-skilling has adversely affected some ***manual workers*** in traditional manufacturing industries, the technologies used in modern production systems require a wider range and higher level of skill among the workforce as a whole.

desk jockey GENERAL MANAGEMENT somebody who works at a desk (*slang*)

desk research MARKETING research carried out using documents, telephone interviews, or the Internet

Deutscher Aktienindex FINANCE, BANKING, AND ACCOUNTING see ***DAX***

devaluation ECONOMICS a reduction in the official fixed rate at which one currency exchanges for another under a fixed-rate regime, usually to correct a balance of payments deficit

developing country ECONOMICS a country, often a producer of primary goods like cotton or rubber, that cannot generate investment income to stimulate growth and possesses a national income that is vulnerable to change in commodity prices

development capital GENERAL MANAGEMENT finance for the expansion of an established business

Development Capital Market (*S. Africa*) FINANCE, BANKING, AND ACCOUNTING a sector on the JSE Securities Exchange for listing smaller developing companies. Criteria for listing in the Development Capital Market sector are less stringent than for the main board listing. Abbr **DCM**

development cycle MARKETING see ***new product development***

Diagonal Street (*S. Africa*) FINANCE, BANKING, AND ACCOUNTING an informal term for the financial center of Johannesburg or, by extension, South Africa

dial and smile MARKETING to cold call potential customers of a product or service (*slang*)

dicing and slicing MARKETING the analysis of raw data to extract information under different categories

differential pricing MARKETING a method of pricing that offers the same product at different prices, for example, in different markets, countries, or retail outlets

differentiation MARKETING see ***product differentiation***

digerati E-COMMERCE people who have or claim to have a sophisticated understanding of Internet or computer technology (*slang*)

digital cash E-COMMERCE an anonymous form of ***digital money*** that can be linked directly to a bank account or exchanged for physical money. As with physical cash, there is no way to obtain information about the buyer from it, and it can be transferred by the seller to pay for subsequent purchases. Also known as ***e-cash***, ***electronic cash***

digital certificate E-COMMERCE an electronic document issued by a recognized authority that validates a purchaser. It is used much as a driver's license or passport is used for identification in a traditional business transaction.

digital coins E-COMMERCE a form of electronic payment authorized for instant transactions that facilitates the purchase of items priced in small denominations of ***digital cash***. Digital coins are transferred from customer to merchant for a transaction such as the purchase of a newspaper using a ***smart card*** for payment.

digital coupon E-COMMERCE a voucher or similar form that exists electronically, for example, on a Web site, and can be used to reduce the price of goods or services

digital Darwinism E-COMMERCE the idea that the development of Internet companies is governed by rules similar to Darwin's theory of evolution and that those that adapt best to their environment will be the most successful

digital economy ECONOMICS an economy in which the main productive functions are in electronic commerce, for example, trade on the Internet

digital goods E-COMMERCE merchandise that is sold and delivered electronically, for example, over the Internet

digital hygienist GENERAL MANAGEMENT somebody within a company who is responsible for checking employees' e-mails and surfing habits for non-work-related activity (*slang*)

digital money E-COMMERCE a series of numbers with an intrinsic value in some physical currency. Online digital money requires electronic interaction with a bank to conduct a transaction; offline digital money does not. Anonymous digital money is synonymous with ***digital cash***. Identified digital money carries with it information revealing the identities of those involved in the transaction. Also known as ***e-money***, ***electronic money***

digital nervous system GENERAL MANAGEMENT an information system that allows an organization to respond to external events through the accumulation, management, and distribution of knowledge

digital strategy GENERAL MANAGEMENT a business strategy that is based on the use of information technology

digital wallet
1. E-COMMERCE software on the hard drive of an online shopper from which the purchaser can pay for the transaction electronically. The wallet can hold in encrypted form such items as credit card information, digital cash or coins, a digital certificate to identify the user, and standardized shipping information. Also called ***electronic wallet***
2. FINANCE, BANKING, AND ACCOUNTING a collection of digital cash

digithead GENERAL MANAGEMENT somebody who is very knowledgeable about technology and mathematics but has poor social skills (*slang*)

digitizable E-COMMERCE capable of being converted to digital form for distribution via the Internet or other networks

dilberted HR & PERSONNEL badly treated by your boss. The term derives from the same fictional character who gave his name to the Dilbert principle. (*slang*)

  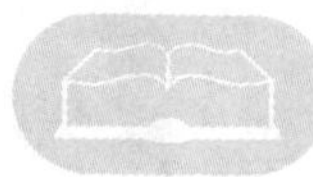    

Dilbert principle HR & PERSONNEL the principle that the most inefficient employees are moved to the place where they can do the least damage. Dilbert is the main character in a comic strip and cartoon series by Scott Adams that satirizes office and corporate life. (*slang*)

DINKY GENERAL MANAGEMENT Dual Income, No Kids (*slang*)

direct action marketing MARKETING see ***direct response marketing***

direct channel MARKETING a method of selling and distributing products direct to customers. Direct channels include direct sales, sales force, mail order, and the Internet.

direct connection E-COMMERCE a permanent connection between a computer system and the Internet

direct cost GENERAL MANAGEMENT, OPERATIONS & PRODUCTION a variable cost directly attributable to production. Items that are classed as direct costs include materials used, labor deployed, and marketing budget, and amounts spent will vary with output. See ***indirect cost***

direct labor HR & PERSONNEL personnel directly involved in the manufacturing of products or the provision of services. Direct labor includes blue-collar workers.

direct mail MARKETING the sending by mail, fax, or e-mail of ***advertising*** communications addressed to specific prospective customers. Direct mail is one tool that can be used as part of a marketing strategy. The use of direct mail is often administered by third-party companies that own databases containing not only names and addresses, but also social, economic, and lifestyle information. It is sometimes seen as an invasion of personal privacy, and there is some public resentment of this form of advertising. This is particularly true of e-mailed direct mail, known derogatively as ***spam***. By enabling advertisers to target a specific type of potential customer, however, direct mail can be more cost-efficient than other ***advertising media***. It is frequently used as part of a relationship marketing strategy.

direct mail preference scheme MARKETING an arrangement that allows individuals and organizations to refuse direct mail by having participating organizations remove them from their mailing lists

direct marketing MARKETING see ***direct response marketing***

directorate GENERAL MANAGEMENT the governing or controlling body of an organization responsible for the organization's ***corporate strategy*** and accountable to its ***stakeholders*** for business results. A directorate may also be known as a ***board of directors*** or council, or at an inner level, the executive or management committee.

director's dealing FINANCE, BANKING, AND ACCOUNTING the purchase or sale of a company's stock by one of its directors

direct response marketing *or* **direct response advertising** MARKETING the use of direct forms of ***advertising*** to elicit inquiries or sales from potential customers, directly to the producers or service providers. Direct response marketing aims to bypass intermediaries such as retailers or wholesalers and contact the general public directly. Forms of communication used include ***direct mail***, home shopping channels, and television and press advertisements. Potential ***customers*** are encouraged to contact the producers directly, for example, using a free phone telephone number, to inquire about a product or to order goods. Also known as ***direct action marketing***, ***direct marketing***

direct selling MARKETING the selling of products or services directly to customers without the use of intermediaries such as wholesalers, retailers, or brokers. Direct selling offers many advantages to the customer, including lower prices and shopping from home. Potential disadvantages include lack of ***after-sales service***, an inability to inspect products prior to purchase, lack of specialist advice, and difficulties in returning or exchanging goods. Methods of direct selling include mail order catalogs and door-to-door and telephone sales, and direct selling has increased with the growth of the Internet, which enables producers to make direct contact with potential customers.

direct tax FINANCE, BANKING, AND ACCOUNTING a tax on income or capital that is paid directly rather than in buying goods or services

dirty float ECONOMICS a floating exchange rate that cannot float freely because a country's central bank intervenes on foreign exchange markets to alter its level

dirty price FINANCE, BANKING, AND ACCOUNTING the price of a debt instrument that includes the amount of accrued interest that has not yet been paid

disaggregation GENERAL MANAGEMENT the breaking apart of an alliance of companies to review their strengths and contributions as a basis for rebuilding an effective business web

disaster management GENERAL MANAGEMENT the actions taken by an organization in response to unexpected events that are adversely affecting people or resources and threatening the continued operation of the organization. Disaster management includes the development of **disaster recovery plans** for minimizing the risk of disasters and for handling them when they do occur, and the implementation of such plans. Disaster management usually refers to the management of natural catastrophes such as fire, flooding, or earthquakes. Related techniques include ***crisis management***, ***contingency management***, and ***risk management***.

disaster recovery plan GENERAL MANAGEMENT see ***disaster management***

disciplinary procedure HR & PERSONNEL see ***discipline***

discipline HR & PERSONNEL standards of required behavior or performance. Good practice requires an organization to establish a **disciplinary procedure** in order to ensure just decisions. A disciplinary procedure should consist of a formal system of documented warnings and hearings, with rights of representation and appeal at each stage.

disclosure of information GENERAL MANAGEMENT the release of information that may be considered confidential to a third party or parties. The disclosure of information in the public interest may be prohibited, permitted, or required, by legislation in a variety of contexts. For example: ***data protection*** legislation restricts the disclosure of personal data held by organizations; ***company law*** requires the publication of certain financial and company data; and ***whistleblowing*** legislation entitles employees to divulge information relating to unethical or illegal conduct in the workplace. Restrictive covenants and ***confidentiality agreements*** also regulate the information that may be disclosed to third parties.

discount GENERAL MANAGEMENT, FINANCE, BANKING, AND ACCOUNTING a reduction in the price of goods or services in relation to the standard price. A discount is a selling technique to encourage customers to buy and is offered for a variety of reasons: for buying in quantity or for repeat buying; as a special

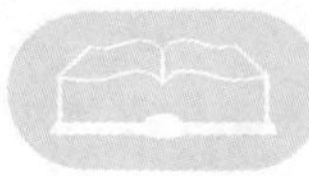

offer to move a slow-moving line; as a loss leader; or for payment by cash or direct debit. The greater the purchasing power of the buyer, the greater the discounts that can be negotiated. Some companies inflate original list prices to give the impression that discounts offer value for money; conversely too many genuine discounts may harm profitability.

discount broker FINANCE, BANKING, AND ACCOUNTING a broker who charges relatively low fees because he or she provides restricted services

discounted bond FINANCE, BANKING, AND ACCOUNTING a bond that is sold for less than its face value because its yield is not as high as that of other bonds

discounted dividend model FINANCE, BANKING, AND ACCOUNTING a method of calculating a stock's value by reducing future dividends to the present value. Also known as ***dividend discount model***

discount loan FINANCE, BANKING, AND ACCOUNTING a loan that amounts to less than its face value because payment of interest has been subtracted

discount rate E-COMMERCE a percentage fee that an e-commerce merchant pays to an account provider or independent sales organization for settling an electronic transaction

discount security FINANCE, BANKING, AND ACCOUNTING a security that is sold for less than its face value in lieu of bearing interest

discrete variable STATISTICS a variable in a statistical study that has only a whole number value, such as the number of deaths in a population

discretionary account FINANCE, BANKING, AND ACCOUNTING a securities account in which the broker has the authority to make decisions about buying and selling without the customer's prior permission

discretionary order FINANCE, BANKING, AND ACCOUNTING a security transaction in which a broker controls the details, such as the time of execution

discriminant analysis GENERAL MANAGEMENT a statistical technique designed to predict the groups or categories into which individual cases will fall on the basis of a number of independent variables. Discriminant analysis attempts to identify which variables or combinations of variables accurately discriminate between groups or categories by means of a scatter diagram or classification table called a **confusion matrix**. Discriminant analysis has applications in finance, for example, credit risk analysis, or in the prediction of company failure, and in the field of marketing, for market segmentation purposes.

discriminating monopoly ECONOMICS a company able to charge different prices for its output in different markets because it has some level of market power to influence prices for its goods

discrimination HR & PERSONNEL unfavorable treatment in employment based on prejudice. Major forms of outlawed discrimination include sex discrimination, ***racial discrimination***, disability discrimination, and, in some countries, ***age discrimination***. Discrimination may also be practiced through ***indirect discrimination***.

discussion list E-COMMERCE an arrangement for sending e-mail messages to a number of people that also allows recipients to respond and everyone else on the list to see these responses. A discussion list is similar to a distribution list except that it is based on a two-way model. Discussion lists can be moderated or unmoderated. In a moderated list, all mail is screened by an intermediary, typically the individual or organization that set up the list. Unmoderated lists involve no editorial process, and so any subscriber can contribute anything he or she wants to the e-mail discussion. Unlike newsgroups, discussion lists do not provide a consolidated record of responses.

disequilibrium price ECONOMICS the price of a good set at a level at which demand and supply are not in balance

dishonor FINANCE, BANKING, AND ACCOUNTING to refuse payment of a check because the account for which it is written holds insufficient money. Also known as ***bounce***

disinflation ECONOMICS the elimination or reduction of inflation or inflationary pressures in an economy by fiscal or monetary policies

disintermediation E-COMMERCE the elimination of intermediaries, for example, the wholesalers found in traditional retail channels, in favor of direct selling to the consumer. See ***reintermediation***

dismissal HR & PERSONNEL the termination of an ***employee's*** employment by his or her ***employer***

dismissal pay HR & PERSONNEL see ***severance pay***

dispersion STATISTICS the amount by which a set of observations deviates from its mean

display advertising MARKETING newspaper or magazine advertisements that use eyecatching typography and graphic images

disposable income FINANCE, BANKING, AND ACCOUNTING income that is left for spending after tax and other deductions

dispute HR & PERSONNEL a disagreement or argument. An **industrial dispute** is a disagreement between an ***employer*** and an employees' representative, usually a ***labor union***, over pay and conditions and can result in ***industrial action***. A **commercial dispute** is a disagreement between two businesses, usually over a contract. There are three main types of dispute resolution: litigation, ***arbitration***, and alternative dispute resolution.

distance learning GENERAL MANAGEMENT a course of study that involves minimal or no attendance at an academic institution, but relies instead on personal study, using books, audiovisual materials, and computer-based materials. Tutorial support may be available via the telephone or Internet, and attendance at weekend or summer schools may be required. Distance learning is similar to ***open learning***.

distance sampling STATISTICS a method of sampling in ecological statistics used to determine the number of animals that feed or plants that grow in a particular habitat

distribution center OPERATIONS & PRODUCTION a warehouse or storage facility where the emphasis is on processing and moving goods on to wholesalers, retailers, or consumers rather than on storage

distribution channel OPERATIONS & PRODUCTION the route by which a product or service is moved from a producer or supplier to customers. A distribution channel usually consists of a chain of intermediaries, including ***wholesalers***, ***retailers***, and distributors, that is designed to transport goods from the point of production to the point of consumption in the most efficient way.

distribution list E-COMMERCE a list of e-mail addresses given one collective name. Internet users can send a message to all the addresses on the list simultaneously by referring to the list name.

distribution management OPERATIONS & PRODUCTION the management of the efficient transfer of goods from the place of manufacture to the point of sale or consumption. Distribution management encompasses such activities as ***warehousing***, ***materials handling***, packaging, stock control, order processing, and transportation.

distribution resource planning OPERATIONS & PRODUCTION a computerized system that integrates distribution with manufacturing by identifying requirements for finished goods and producing schedules for ***inventory*** and its movement within the distribution. Distribution resource planning systems receive data on sales forecasts, customer order and delivery requirements, available inventory, ***logistics***, and manufacturing and purchasing ***lead times***. This data is analyzed to produce a time-phased schedule of resource requirements that is matched against existing supply sources and production schedules to identify the actions that must be taken to synchronize supply and demand. The effective integration of material requirements planning and distribution resource planning systems leads to the more effective and timely delivery of finished goods to the customer and to reduced inventory levels and lower material costs. Abbr **DRP**

distributive network E-COMMERCE a system or infrastructure that enables products and services to move around. Offline distributive networks include roads, telephone companies, electrical power grids, and the mail service. In the new economy, distributive networks include online banks and Web-enabled mobile telephones.

distributor MARKETING an organization that distributes products to retailers on behalf of a manufacturer

distributor support MARKETING marketing or financial support by manufacturers aimed at improving the performance of organizations that distribute their products

diversification GENERAL MANAGEMENT a strategy to increase the variety of business, service, or product types within an organization. Diversification can be a growth strategy, taking advantage of market opportunities, or it may be aimed at reducing risk by spreading interests over different areas. It can be achieved through ***acquisition*** or through internal research and development, and it can involve managing two, a few, or many different areas of interest. Diversification can also be a ***corporate strategy*** of investment in acquisitions within a broad portfolio range by a large ***holding company***. One distinct type is **horizontal diversification**, which involves expansion into a similar product area, for example, a domestic furniture manufacturer producing office furniture. Another is **vertical diversification**, in which a company moves into a different level of the ***supply chain***, for example, a manufacturing company becoming a retailer. A well-known example of diversification is the move of Bic, the ballpoint pen manufacturer, into the production of disposable razors.

diversified investment company FINANCE, BANKING, AND ACCOUNTING a mutual fund with a variety of types of investments

diversity GENERAL MANAGEMENT difference between people, for example, in race, age, gender, disability, geographic origin, family status, education, or personality, that can affect workplace relationships and achievement. Diversity management aims to value these differences and encourage each person to fulfill his or her potential in terms of organizational objectives. The approach goes beyond ***equal opportunities***, which stresses the rights of particular disadvantaged groups rather than those of the individual.

divestment GENERAL MANAGEMENT the sale or closure of several businesses, a business, or parts of a business. Divestment often takes place as part of a ***rationalization*** effort to cut costs or to enable an organization to concentrate on core business or competences, and may take the form of a ***management buy-out***.

dividend clawback FINANCE, BANKING, AND ACCOUNTING an agreement that dividends will be reinvested as part of the financing of a project

dividend discount model FINANCE, BANKING, AND ACCOUNTING = ***discounted dividend model***

dividend limitation FINANCE, BANKING, AND ACCOUNTING a provision in a bond limiting the dividends that may be paid

dividend reinvestment plan FINANCE, BANKING, AND ACCOUNTING a plan that provides for the reinvestment of dividends in the shares of the company paying the dividends. Abbr **DRIP**

dividend rights FINANCE, BANKING, AND ACCOUNTING rights to receive dividends

dividends-received deduction FINANCE, BANKING, AND ACCOUNTING a tax advantage on dividends that a company receives from a company it owns

dividend yield FINANCE, BANKING, AND ACCOUNTING dividends expressed as a percentage of a stock's price

division of labor OPERATIONS & PRODUCTION the allocation of each task in a process to a different worker. Division of labor is a concept originated by ***Adam Smith*** in order to increase output. It enables workers to become highly skilled at one job, but they may lack transferable skills and find their work monotonous. To a certain extent, division of labor has been superseded by ***multiskilling***.

ADAM SMITH (pp. 1048–49)

document E-COMMERCE a file containing text, graphics, multimedia, or hyperlinks

dog GENERAL MANAGEMENT see ***Boston Box***

that dog won't hunt GENERAL MANAGEMENT that idea will not work *(slang)*

dog and pony show GENERAL MANAGEMENT a national tour by the top staff of a company aimed at persuading investors to invest in the company *(slang)*

dog-eat-dog MARKETING ruthless, especially in the marketplace *(slang)*

dogfood E-COMMERCE temporary software used by an organization for testing purposes

dogs of the Dow FINANCE, BANKING, AND ACCOUNTING the stocks in the Dow-Jones Industrial Average that pay the smallest dividends as a percentage of their prices *(slang)*

dole bludger *(ANZ)* GENERAL MANAGEMENT somebody who lives off social security payments and makes no attempt to find work *(slang)*

dollar cost averaging FINANCE, BANKING, AND ACCOUNTING the regular periodic purchase of the same amount in dollars of the same security regardless of its price

dollar roll FINANCE, BANKING, AND ACCOUNTING an agreement to sell a stock and buy it later for a specified price

dollars-and-cents FINANCE, BANKING, AND ACCOUNTING considering money as the determining factor

domain name E-COMMERCE the officially registered Web site address of a Web site. Domain names typically contain two or more parts separated from each other by a dot, for example, www.yahoo.com. The domain name suffix (following the final dot) is intended to indicate either the nature or location of the Web site, for example, com for a commercial Web site and co.uk for a British Web site.

domicilium citandi et executandi *(S. Africa)* FINANCE, BANKING, AND ACCOUNTING the address where a summons or other official notice should be served when or if necessary, which must be supplied by somebody applying for credit or entering into a contract

donut MARKETING the middle section of a commercial where the product information is usually placed *(slang)*

dot bam E-COMMERCE a real-world business with a strong Web presence. The "bam" stands for "bricks and mortar."

dot.bomb *or* **dot-bomb** E-COMMERCE an e-commerce enterprise that has gone out of business *(slang)*

dot-com *or* **dot.com** E-COMMERCE an e-commerce enterprise that markets its products through the Internet, rather than through traditional channels

dotted-line relationships HR & PERSONNEL the links, as shown on an organizational chart, that exist between managers and staff whom they oversee indirectly rather than on a day-to-day basis *(slang)*

double-blind STATISTICS relating to an experiment, usually a medical one, in which neither the experimenter nor the subject knows whether the treatment being administered is genuine or a control procedure

double dipping GENERAL MANAGEMENT the practice of receiving income from a government pension as well as social security payments

double indemnity FINANCE, BANKING, AND ACCOUNTING a provision in an insurance policy that guarantees payment of double its face value on the accidental death of the holder

double taxation FINANCE, BANKING, AND ACCOUNTING the taxing of something twice, usually the combination of corporation tax and tax on the dividends that shareholders earn

doughnut principle GENERAL MANAGEMENT a concept that likens an organization to an **inverted doughnut** with a center of dough—the core activities—surrounded by a hole—a flexible area containing the organization's partners. The doughnut principle was originated by ***Charles Handy*** in *The Empty Raincoat* (1994). He saw organizations as having an essential core of jobs and people, surrounded by a space filled with flexible workers and flexible supply contracts. He maintained that organizations often neglect the core, developing the surrounding hole instead. The doughnut analogy is a way of helping a balance to be achieved between what has to be done and what could be done, by analyzing the dough and the hole of a particular organization. The principle has also been applied to personal life.

CHARLES HANDY (pp. 1000–01)

Dow Jones Averages FINANCE, BANKING, AND ACCOUNTING an index of the prices of selected stocks on the New York Stock Exchange compiled by Dow Jones & Company, Inc

downshifting GENERAL MANAGEMENT the concept of giving up all or part of your work commitment and income in exchange for a greater quality of life. The term was coined by ***Charles Handy***. Downshifting has increased in popularity because of rising ***stress*** in the workplace caused partly by the ***downsizing*** trend of the late 20th century, and may be contrasted with the concept of the ***organization man***. Downshifting is integral to the idea of ***portfolio working***, in which individuals opt out of a formal employee relationship to sell their services at a pace and at a price to suit themselves.

CHARLES HANDY (pp. 1000–01)

downsize HR & PERSONNEL to reduce the size of a business, especially by reducing the number of its employees

downsizing HR & PERSONNEL the reduction of the size of a business, especially by reducing the number of its employees by making staff redundant. Downsizing may be part of a ***rationalization*** process, or ***corporate restructuring***, with the removal of hierarchies or the closure of departments or functions either after a period of unsatisfactory results or as a consequence of strategic review. The terms **upsizing** and **resizing** are applied when an organization increases the number of staff employed again.

downstream OPERATIONS & PRODUCTION later in the production process

downstream progress GENERAL MANAGEMENT movement by a company toward achieving its objectives that is easy to achieve because it involves riding a wave or trend and benefiting from favorable conditions. See ***upstream progress***

downtime OPERATIONS & PRODUCTION a period of time during which a machine is not available for use because of maintenance or a breakdown

Dow Theory FINANCE, BANKING, AND ACCOUNTING the theory that stock market prices can be forecast on the basis of the movements of selected industrial and transportation stocks

Doz, Yves L. (*b.* 1947) GENERAL MANAGEMENT French academic. Collaborator with ***C. K. Prahalad*** and ***Gary Hamel*** in researching ***strategic models*** to tackle the complexities and ***globalization*** of markets. His *Alliance Advantage* (1998, coauthor), focuses on ***strategic partnering***.

GARY HAMEL (pp. 998–99); C. K. PRAHALAD (pp. 1040–41)
✔ STRATEGIC PARTNERING (pp. 482–83)

drawing account FINANCE, BANKING, AND ACCOUNTING an account that permits the tracking of withdrawals

dress-down day HR & PERSONNEL a day on which employees are allowed to wear informal clothes to work *(slang)*

drilling down MARKETING a technique for managing data by arranging it in hierarchies that provide increasing levels of detail

DRIP FINANCE, BANKING, AND ACCOUNTING see ***dividend reinvestment plan***

drip method MARKETING a marketing method that involves calling potential customers at regular intervals until they agree to make a purchase *(slang)*

drive time MARKETING the time of the day when most people are likely to be in their cars, usually early in the morning or late in the afternoon, considered to be the optimum time to broadcast a radio commercial *(slang)*

drop a bundle FINANCE, BANKING, AND ACCOUNTING to spend or lose a lot of money, especially on the stock market *(slang)*

drop lock FINANCE, BANKING, AND ACCOUNTING the automatic conversion of a debt instrument with a floating rate to one with a fixed rate when interest rates fall to an agreed percentage

drownloading E-COMMERCE the act of simultaneously downloading so many files that a computer crashes

DRP OPERATIONS & PRODUCTION see ***distribution resource planning***

Drucker, **Peter F.** (*b.* 1909) GENERAL MANAGEMENT U.S. academic. Recognized as the father of management thinking. His earlier works studied management practice, while later he tackled the complexities and the management implications of the postindustrial world. *The Practice of Management* (1954), best known perhaps for the introduction of ***management by objectives***, remains a classic. He also foreshadowed other management themes such as the importance of ***marketing*** (see ***marketing management***) and the rise of the ***knowledge worker***.
PETER F. DRUCKER (pp. 982–85)

DTF (*ANZ*) FINANCE, BANKING, AND ACCOUNTING see ***Derivative Trading Facility***

dual currency bond FINANCE, BANKING, AND ACCOUNTING a bond that pays interest in a currency other than the one used to buy it

dual economy ECONOMICS an economy in which the manufacturing and service sectors are growing at different rates

dual trading FINANCE, BANKING, AND ACCOUNTING the practice of acting as agent for both a broker's own firm and customers

duck
get your ducks in a row/line up your ducks GENERAL MANAGEMENT (*slang*)
1. to get everything properly organized
2. to get all concerned parties to agree to a plan of action

due-on-sale clause FINANCE, BANKING, AND ACCOUNTING a provision requiring a homeowner to pay off a mortgage upon sale of the property

dumbsizing HR & PERSONNEL the process of reducing the size of a company to such an extent that it is no longer profitable or efficient (*slang*)

DUMP GENERAL MANAGEMENT Destitute Unemployed Mature Professional (*slang*)

dumping ECONOMICS the selling of a commodity on a foreign market at a price below its ***marginal cost***, either to dispose of a temporary surplus or to achieve a monopoly by eliminating competition

Dunlap, **Albert J.** (*b.* 1937) GENERAL MANAGEMENT U.S. business executive. Noted for his ***turnaround management*** capabilities, based on ***downsizing*** and ***cost-cutting***, which earned him the nickname "Chainsaw Al" and which are described in his book *Mean Business* (1996).

duopoly ECONOMICS a market in which only two sellers of a good exist. If one decides to alter the price, the other will respond and influence the market's response to the first decision.

duvet day GENERAL MANAGEMENT a day sanctioned by an employing organization as a day when an employee may call in and say that they will not attend work that day because they do not feel like it. A duvet day does not form part of an employee's ***leave*** entitlement, but will be recorded as a sanctioned absence. Duvet days are more popular in the United States than in the United Kingdom, and those organizations that allow them do not usually make them part of written policy, limit them to two or three per year, and sometimes only offer them to key employees.

dynamic pricing GENERAL MANAGEMENT pricing that changes in line with patterns of demand

dynamic programming GENERAL MANAGEMENT a mathematical technique used in ***management science*** to solve complex problems in the fields of production planning and inventory control. Dynamic programming divides the problem into subproblems or decision stages that can be addressed sequentially, normally by working backward from the last stage. Applications of the technique include maintenance and replacement of equipment, resource allocation, and process design and control. The term comes from the work of Richard Bellman published in the late 1950s and early 1960s.

E

E2E E-COMMERCE see ***exchange***

EAI E-COMMERCE see ***enterprise application integration***

EAP HR & PERSONNEL see ***employee assistance program***

ear candy HR & PERSONNEL pleasant but meaningless noise or talk (*slang*)

early adopter GENERAL MANAGEMENT an individual or organization that is among the first to make use of a new technology

early retirement HR & PERSONNEL ***retirement*** from work before the statutory retirement age or before the normal retirement age set by an employer. Early retirement may be taken because of ill health or at the request of the employee or employer. An employer may offer opportunities for early retirement on advantageous financial terms as a way of reducing staff numbers without ***redundancies***. Also known as ***premature retirement***

earnings
1. HR & PERSONNEL a sum of money gained from paid employment, usually quoted before tax, including any extra rewards such as ***fringe benefits***, allowances, or incentives. Also known as ***pay***
2. FINANCE, BANKING, AND ACCOUNTING income or profit from a business, quoted gross or net of tax, which may be retained and distributed in part to the shareholders

earnings before interest and taxes OPERATIONS & PRODUCTION = ***operating income***

earnings per share FINANCE, BANKING, AND ACCOUNTING a financial ratio that measures the portion of a company's profit allocated to each outstanding share of common stock

earnings surprise FINANCE, BANKING, AND ACCOUNTING a report by a company that its earnings vary considerably from expectations

earnings yield FINANCE, BANKING, AND ACCOUNTING money earned by a company during a year, expressed as a percentage of the price of one of its shares

EASDAQ FINANCE, BANKING, AND ACCOUNTING European Association of Securities Dealers Automated Quotations, a stock exchange for technology and growth companies based in Europe and modeled on ***NASDAQ*** in the United States

EBIT OPERATIONS & PRODUCTION earnings before interest and taxes

EBQ *abbr* OPERATIONS & PRODUCTION economic batch quantity, the optimum batch size for the manufacture of an item or component, at the lowest cost. The batch size is a tradeoff between unit costs that increase with batch size and those that decrease. The point of lowest combined or total cost indicates the

most economic batch size for production. Also known as ***economic lot quantity***. See ***economic order quantity***

EBRD *abbr* FINANCE, BANKING, AND ACCOUNTING European Bank for Reconstruction and Development. Established in 1991, the bank developed programs for the creation and strengthening of infrastructure; for privatization; for reform of the financial sector, including the development of capital markets and the privatization of commercial banks; for the development of productive competitive private sectors of small and medium-sized enterprises in industry, agriculture, and services; for restructuring industrial sectors to put them on a competitive basis; and for encouraging foreign investment and cleaning up the environment. The EBRD had 41 original members: the European Commission, the European Investment Bank, all the EEC countries, and all the countries of Eastern Europe except Albania, which finally became a member in October 1991, followed by all the republics of the former USSR in March 1992.

e-business E-COMMERCE
1. the conduct of business on the Internet, including the electronic purchasing and selling of goods and services, servicing customers, and communications with business partners. Also called ***electronic business***
2. a company that conducts business on the Internet

e-cash E-COMMERCE = ***digital cash***

ECB *abbr* FINANCE, BANKING, AND ACCOUNTING European Central Bank, which in 1998 replaced the European Monetary Institute (EMI) and is responsible for carrying out EU monetary policy and administering the Euro

ECML E-COMMERCE see ***electronic commerce modeling language***

ecoconsumer GENERAL MANAGEMENT a customer who will only select from, or subscribe to, goods that meet environmentally sound considerations

ecolabel GENERAL MANAGEMENT a label used to characterize products that satisfy particular total ***environmental management*** considerations with regard to their production, usage, or disposal

ecological priority GENERAL MANAGEMENT the priority for organizations and governments to put as much emphasis on environmental protection as economic performance

ecological statistics STATISTICS statistical studies in the field of ecology using such techniques as ***distance sampling***

ECO-Management Audit Scheme GENERAL MANAGEMENT see ***environmental management***

e-commerce E-COMMERCE the exchange of goods, information products, or services via an electronic medium such as the Internet. E-commerce includes both electronic shopping and electronic purchasing. Originally limited to buying and selling, it has evolved to include such functions as customer service, marketing, and advertising. Also known as ***electronic commerce***, ***web commerce***

e-commerce mall E-COMMERCE = ***cyber mall***

e-commerce processes E-COMMERCE the flow of information through planning, design, manufacture, sales, order processing, distribution, and quality in an e-business

e-company E-COMMERCE an e-commerce enterprise. Also known as ***dot.com***

econometric model ECONOMICS a way of representing the relationship between economic variables as an equation or set of equations with statistically precise parameters linking the variables

econometrics ECONOMICS the setting up of mathematical models to describe the relationships in an economy, for example, between wage rates and levels of employment

Economic and Monetary Union FINANCE, BANKING, AND ACCOUNTING see ***EMU***

economic assumption ECONOMICS an assumption built into an economic model, for example, that output will grow at 2.5% in the next tax year

economic batch quantity OPERATIONS & PRODUCTION see ***EBQ***

Economic Development Board FINANCE, BANKING, AND ACCOUNTING an organization established in 1961 that aims to promote investment in Singapore by providing various services and assistance schemes to foreign and local companies. Abbr **EDB**

economic goods ECONOMICS services or physical objects that can command a price in the market

economic growth ECONOMICS an increase in the national income of a country created by the long-term productive potential of its economy

economic indicator ECONOMICS a statistic, for example, rising prices at the factory gate or falling exports, that may be important for a country's long-term economic health

economic life ECONOMICS the conditions of trade and manufacture in a country that contribute to its prosperity or poverty

economic lot quantity GENERAL MANAGEMENT see ***EBQ***

economic miracle ECONOMICS the rapid growth after 1945 in countries such as Germany and Japan, where in ten years economies shattered by World War II had been regenerated

economic order quantity GENERAL MANAGEMENT a reorder method that attempts to estimate the best order quantity by balancing the conflicting costs of holding stock and of placing replenishment orders. For large orders, the unit cost may be lower, but storage costs will be higher, because the average storage time will increase. For small orders, the cost of order processing and unit cost may be higher, but storage costs will be lower, because the average storage time is less.

economic paradigm ECONOMICS a basic unchanging economic principle

Economic Planning and Advisory Council FINANCE, BANKING, AND ACCOUNTING a committee of business people and politicians appointed to advise the Australian government on economic issues. Abbr **EPAC**

economic pressure ECONOMICS a condition in a country's economy in which economic indicators are unfavorable

economics ECONOMICS the study of the consumption, distribution, and production of wealth in a society

economic surplus ECONOMICS the difference between an economy's output and the cost of producing it, for example, in wages, raw material costs, and depreciation

economic theory of the firm GENERAL MANAGEMENT a theory that states that the only duty that a company has to those external to it is financial. The economic theory of the firm holds that shareholders should be the prime beneficiaries of an organization's activities.

  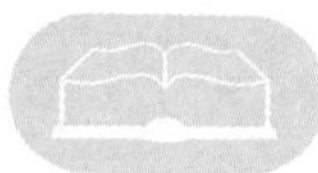    

The theory is associated with ***top-down leadership***, and ***cost-cutting*** through ***rationalization*** and ***downsizing***. With immediate share price dominating management activities, economic theory has been criticized as being too short term, as opposed to the longer-term thinking behind ***stakeholder theory***.

economic welfare ECONOMICS the level of prosperity in an economy, as measured by employment and wage levels

economist ECONOMICS somebody who studies the consumption, distribution, and production of wealth in a society

economy ECONOMICS the distribution of wealth in a society and the means by which that wealth is produced and consumed

economy efficiency principle ECONOMICS the principle that if an economy is efficient, no one can be made better off without somebody else being made worse off

ecopreneur GENERAL MANAGEMENT an entrepreneur who is concerned with environmental issues

EDB FINANCE, BANKING, AND ACCOUNTING see ***Economic Development Board***

EDC E-COMMERCE see ***electronic data capture***

EDI E-COMMERCE see ***electronic data interchange***

EDI envelope E-COMMERCE = ***electronic envelope***

EDIFACT E-COMMERCE see ***UN/EDIFACT***

EDI For Administration, Commerce, and Trade E-COMMERCE see ***UN/EDIFACT***

educational leave HR & PERSONNEL ***special leave*** granted to assist those undertaking a course of study

Edwardes, Sir Michael (*b.* 1930) GENERAL MANAGEMENT South African-born business executive. Chairman of British Leyland from 1977 to 1982, who was appointed to rescue the company from financial difficulties and industrial disruption. His reassertion of the manager's right to manage led to the coining of the term ***macho management***. He recorded his experiences in *Back from the Brink* (1983).

e-economy ECONOMICS an economy that is characterized by extensive use of the Internet and information technology

effect STATISTICS the change in a response that is created by a change in one or more of the explanatory ***variables*** in a statistical study

effective annual interest rate FINANCE, BANKING, AND ACCOUNTING = ***APR***

effective capacity OPERATIONS & PRODUCTION the volume that a workstation or process can produce in a given period under normal operating conditions. Effective capacity can be influenced by the age and condition of the machine, the skills, training, and flexibility of the workforce, and the availability of ***raw materials***.

effective date FINANCE, BANKING, AND ACCOUNTING the date when an action, such as an issuance of new stock, is effective

effective sample size STATISTICS the remaining size of a sample after irrelevant or excluded factors have been removed

effective spread FINANCE, BANKING, AND ACCOUNTING the difference between the price of a newly issued share and what the underwriter pays, adjusted for the effect of the announcement of the offering

effective strike price FINANCE, BANKING, AND ACCOUNTING the price of an option at a specified time, adjusted for fluctuation since the initial offering

efficiency GENERAL MANAGEMENT the achievement of goals in an economic way. Efficiency involves seeking a good balance between economy in terms of resources such as time, money, space, or materials, and the achievement of an organization's aims and objectives. A distinction is often made between technical and economic efficiency. **Technical efficiency** means producing maximum output with a minimum input, while **economic efficiency** means the production and distribution of goods at the lowest possible cost. In management, a further distinction is often made between efficiency and effectiveness, with the latter denoting performance in terms of achieving objectives. Achieving efficient performance is one of the key drivers behind ***scientific management***.

efficient capital market GENERAL MANAGEMENT a market in which share prices reflect all the information available to the market about future economic trends and company profitability

EFQM European Excellence Award GENERAL MANAGEMENT see ***EFQM Excellence Model***

EFQM Excellence Model *or* **EFQM European Excellence Model** GENERAL MANAGEMENT a framework that can be used to assess a company's achievement of business ***excellence***. The European Foundation for Quality Management (EFQM) was founded in the late 1980s by leading companies in Western Europe that saw a need for the implementation of a ***quality award*** in Europe. EFQM launched the **European Quality Award** in 1991. In the United Kingdom, the British Quality Foundation promoted the model, now often referred to as the **Business Excellence Model**. The model was revised in 1999 and renamed the EFQM European Excellence Model. The model focuses on all the key elements that sustain business success, and incorporates nine criteria that cover all aspects of business.

EFT E-COMMERCE see ***electronic funds transfer***

EGM GENERAL MANAGEMENT see ***extraordinary general meeting***

egosurfing GENERAL MANAGEMENT the practice of surfing the Internet in search of references to yourself (*slang*)

EIB FINANCE, BANKING, AND ACCOUNTING European Investment Bank, a financial institution whose main task is to further regional development within the EU by financing capital projects, modernizing or converting undertakings, or developing new activities

86 GENERAL MANAGEMENT to discard something such as a proposal or a document (*slang*)

eighty-twenty rule GENERAL MANAGEMENT the principle that explores the natural balance between the causes and effects of business activities and that holds that all business activities display an 80%/20% split. Developed by ***Vilfredo Pareto***, the eighty-twenty rule can be used to concentrate management control and identify problem areas. Examples of the eighty-twenty rule in practice might include: 20% of the workforce accounting for 80% of the salary bill; 80% of a company's profits coming from 20% of its products; 80% of the stock value being tied up in 20% of the inventory. The rule can be represented graphically in the form of a ***Pareto chart***, which is a bar chart identifying the relationships between causes and effects of activities. Also known as ***Pareto's analysis***, ***Pareto's principle***. See ***Pareto's Law***

EIS *abbr* GENERAL MANAGEMENT
1. see ***Environmental Impact Statement***

2. see ***Environmental Impact Study***
3. executive information system, a computer system designed to collect, store, process, and provide access to information appropriate to the needs of senior management. Executive information systems combine internal organizational information with data from external sources. The emphasis of executive information systems is on supporting strategic ***decision making*** by presenting information in accessible formats and enabling users to get an overview of trends often through the use of advanced graphical capabilities. Decision making at managerial levels is supported by ***decision support systems***.

Eisner, **Michael** (*b.* 1942) GENERAL MANAGEMENT U.S. business executive. C.E.O. and chairman of Disney who ***turned around*** the company, by encouraging ***creativity*** while maintaining financial control and discipline. His autobiography *Work in Progress* (1998) explains his ***leadership*** philosophy.

either-way market FINANCE, BANKING, AND ACCOUNTING a currency market with identical prices for buying and selling, especially for the Euro

e-lance GENERAL MANAGEMENT a type of ***freelance*** work that makes use of the ***Internet***. It enables a freelancer to take up work opportunities anywhere in the world.

eldercare GENERAL MANAGEMENT an organization's approach toward care for employees' elderly relatives in the form of an ***employee assistance program***

e-learning HR & PERSONNEL the facilitation of learning through the ***Internet*** or an ***intranet***. E-learning is a development from ***computer-based training*** and consists of self-contained learning materials and resources that can be used at the pace and convenience of the learner. An e-learning package normally incorporates some form of test that can demonstrate how much an e-learner has assimilated from a course, as well as some form of monitoring to enable managers to check the use of the system of e-learning. Successful e-learning depends largely on the self-motivation of individuals to study effectively. Because it is Internet-based, it has the potential to respond to a company's rapidly changing needs and offer new learning opportunities relevant to a company's new position very quickly. Also known as ***electronic learning***

elected officers HR & PERSONNEL officials such as directors or union representatives chosen by a vote of the members or shareholders of an organization, who hold a ***decision making*** position on a committee or board

electronic brainstorming GENERAL MANAGEMENT see ***brainstorming***

electronic business E-COMMERCE = ***e-business***

electronic cash E-COMMERCE = ***digital cash***

electronic catalog E-COMMERCE a listing of available products that can be viewed in an electronic format, for example, on a Web site, and can include information such as illustrations, prices, and product descriptions

electronic check E-COMMERCE a payment system in which fund transfers are made electronically from the buyer's checking account to the seller's bank account

electronic commerce E-COMMERCE = ***e-commerce***

electronic commerce modeling language E-COMMERCE a standardization of field names to streamline the process by which e-merchants electronically collect information from consumers about order shipping, billing, and payment. Abbr **ECML**

electronic data capture E-COMMERCE the use of a point-of-sale terminal or other data-processing equipment to validate and submit credit or debit card transactions. Abbr **EDC**

electronic data interchange E-COMMERCE a standard for exchanging business documents such as invoices and purchase orders in a standard form between computers through the use of electronic networks such as the Internet. Abbr **EDI**

electronic envelope E-COMMERCE the header and trailer information that precedes and follows the data in an electronic transmission to provide routing information and security. Also known as ***communications envelope***, ***EDI envelope***, ***envelope***

electronic funds transfer E-COMMERCE a payment system that processes financial transactions between two or more parties or institutions. Abbr **EFT**

electronic learning HR & PERSONNEL see ***e-learning***

electronic mail GENERAL MANAGEMENT see ***e-mail***

electronic mall E-COMMERCE = ***cyber mall***

electronic money E-COMMERCE = ***digital money***

electronic office GENERAL MANAGEMENT see ***paperless office***

electronic payment system E-COMMERCE a means of being reimbursed in a transaction over an electronic network such as the Internet

electronic procurement E-COMMERCE = ***e-procurement***

electronic retailer E-COMMERCE = ***e-retailer***

electronic shopping E-COMMERCE the process of selecting, ordering, and paying for goods or services over an electronic network such as the Internet. Also known as ***online shopping***

electronic software distribution E-COMMERCE a form of electronic shopping in which computer programs can be purchased and downloaded directly from the Internet

electronic store E-COMMERCE a Web site that is designed specifically to provide product information and handle transactions, including accepting payments

electronic trading FINANCE, BANKING, AND ACCOUNTING the buying and selling of investment instruments using computers

electronic wallet E-COMMERCE = ***digital wallet***

elephant GENERAL MANAGEMENT a large corporate institution (*slang*)

elevator pitch E-COMMERCE the practice of pitching dot-com business plans to investors in a short space of time

Eligible Service Period GENERAL MANAGEMENT the amount of time an employee works for one employer or contributes to a particular superannuation scheme. Abbr **ESP**

Eligible Termination Payment FINANCE, BANKING, AND ACCOUNTING a sum paid to an employee when he or she leaves a company, that can be transferred to a concessionally taxed investment account, such as an Approved Deposit Fund. Abbr **ETP**

Elvis year GENERAL MANAGEMENT the year in which the popularity of a product, service, or individual is at its peak (*slang*)

  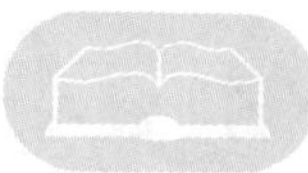    

e-mail E-COMMERCE electronic mail, a message sent across the Internet, or a system for transferring messages between computers, mobile phones, or other communications attached to the Internet

e-mail address E-COMMERCE somebody's electronic address on the Internet or an intranet. An e-mail address is commonly formed by joining the user name and the mail server name, separating the two by an @ symbol.

e-mail system E-COMMERCE the collective e-mail software that allows somebody to create, send, receive, and store e-mail messages

EMAS *abbr* GENERAL MANAGEMENT ECO-Management Audit Scheme

emerging market FINANCE, BANKING, AND ACCOUNTING a country that is becoming industrialized

Emery, **Frederick Edmund** (1928–97) GENERAL MANAGEMENT Australian psychologist and sociologist. Contributor to the development of theories of ***industrial democracy*** in collaboration with ***Einar Thorsrud*** at the Tavistock Institute of Human Relations.

e-money E-COMMERCE – ***digital money***

emotag E-COMMERCE a tag such as <smile> or <growl> used in an e-mail instead of an emoticon (*slang*)

emoticon E-COMMERCE a symbol commonly used in e-mail and newsgroup messages to denote a particular emotion by representing a face on its side. For example,:-) indicates happiness by representing a smiley face. The word is a combination of "emotion" with "icon."

emotional capital GENERAL MANAGEMENT the intangible organizational asset created by employees' cumulative emotional experiences, which give them the ability to successfully communicate and form interpersonal relationships. The emotional capital is increasingly being seen as an important factor in company performance. Low emotional capital can result in conflict between staff, poor ***teamwork***, and poor ***customer relations***. By contrast, high emotional capital is evidence of ***emotional intelligence*** and an ability to think and feel in a positive way that results in good ***interpersonal communication*** and self-motivation. Related concepts are ***intellectual capital*** and ***social capital***.

emotional intelligence HR & PERSONNEL the ability to perceive and understand personal feelings and those of others. Emotional intelligence means recognizing emotions and acting on them in a reflective and rational manner. A person employing emotional intelligence needs to have self-awareness and empathy for other people, together with self-restraint so that reactions are shaped by thought and not feeling. In the workplace, this ability can greatly enhance ***interpersonal communication*** and people skills. Emotional intelligence was first broadly discussed by ***Daniel Goleman***.

DANIEL GOLEMAN (pp. 996–97)

employability HR & PERSONNEL the potential for obtaining and keeping fulfilling work through the development of skills that are transferable from one employer to another. Employability is affected by market demand for a particular set of skills and by personal circumstances. Employees may take responsibility for developing their own employability through learning and training, but as part of the ***psychological contract*** employers may assist their employees in enhancing their employability. An important factor in employability is the concept of ***lifelong learning***.

employee HR & PERSONNEL someone hired by an employer under a ***contract of employment*** to carry out work on a regular basis at the employer's behest. An employee works either at the employer's premises or at a place otherwise agreed, is paid regularly, and enjoys ***fringe benefits*** and ***employment protection***.

employee assistance program HR & PERSONNEL a structured and integrated support service that identifies and resolves the concerns of employees that may affect performance. Employee assistance programs can range from support for staff during periods of intensive change, ***counseling*** to tackle the problem of ***stress***, return-to-work, and ***eldercare*** initiatives, to defined organizational policies on substance abuse and bullying. Employee assistance programs are set up by employers who recognize that providing professional support for their staff makes good business sense. Some organizations find it cost-effective to ***outsource*** the program depending on the nature of the problem and on the size of the organization. Abbr **EAP**

employee association (*U.K.*) HR & PERSONNEL a professional or social body of employees who work for the same organization

employee attitude survey HR & PERSONNEL a systematic investigation of the views and opinions of those employed by an organization on issues relating to the work of that organization or their role within it. Employee attitude surveys may be conducted by means of questionnaires or interviews. They may be undertaken occasionally or at regular intervals and may be used to make a general assessment of employee morale or focus on a specific issue such as the introduction of a new policy. Aims may be to identify or gain an understanding of problems so that action to resolve them can be taken, to encourage employee involvement and commitment, or to assist in planning, implementing, and evaluating new initiatives.

employee commitment HR & PERSONNEL the psychological bond of an employee to an organization, the strength of which depends on the degree of ***employee involvement***, employee loyalty, and belief in the values of the organization. Employee commitment was badly damaged in the late 20th century during corporate reorganizations and ***downsizing***, which undermined job security and resulted in fewer ***promotion*** opportunities. This led to the renegotiation of the ***psychological contract*** and the need to develop strategies for increasing commitment. These included ***flexible working*** and ***work-life balance*** policies, ***teamwork***, ***training*** and development, ***employee participation***, and ***empowerment***.

employee development HR & PERSONNEL the enhancement of the skills, knowledge, and experience of employees with the purpose of improving performance. Employee development, unlike ***personal development***, is usually coordinated by the employing organization. It can use a range of ***training*** methods, and is usually conducted on a planned basis, perhaps as a result of a ***performance appraisal***.

employee discount HR & PERSONNEL a reduction in the price of company goods or services offered to employees as one of their ***fringe benefits***

employee handbook HR & PERSONNEL a reference document containing information on what an employee should know about his or her organization or employment. Employee handbooks typically include information on terms and ***conditions of employment***, organizational policies and procedures, and ***fringe benefits***.

employee involvement HR & PERSONNEL a range of management practices centered on ***empowerment*** and trust that are designed to increase ***employee commitment*** to organizational objectives and performance improve-

  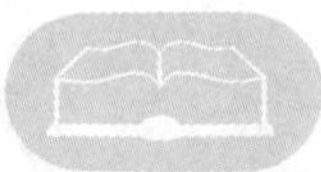    

ment. The term employee involvement is often used interchangeably with ***employee participation***, but employee involvement practices tend to take place at individual or workgroup level, rather than at higher ***decision making*** levels. Employee involvement can take many forms, including single status, ***flexible working***, and communication methods such as ***team briefing*** and ***quality circles***.

employee ownership HR & PERSONNEL the possession of shares in a company, in whole or in part, by the workers. There are various forms of employee ownership that give employees a greater or lesser stake in the business. These include: ***employee stock ownership plans***, employee buy-outs, cooperatives, and employee trusts. Ownership does not necessarily lead to greater ***employee participation*** in decision making, although the evidence suggests that, where employees are involved in this, the company is more successful.

employee participation HR & PERSONNEL the involvement of workers in ***decision making***. Employee participation can take either a representational or direct form. Representation takes place through bodies such as consultative committees. Direct participation can be achieved through communication methods such as newsletters, ***employee attitude surveys***, ***team briefing***, and ***open book management***, or through involvement initiatives such as self-managed teams, ***suggestion schemes***, and ***quality circles***. Employee participation is sometimes linked to ***employee ownership***.

employee referral program HR & PERSONNEL a policy, popular in the United States, for encouraging employees, usually through cash incentives, to nominate potential job candidates as part of the recruiting process. Employee referral programs have been developed in an attempt to address the recruitment difficulties experienced by organizations in times of full employment. Although they can be very successful, there is a danger that if a referral program is relied on too heavily, only limited sectors of the potential labor force will be available for recruitment, which might lead to a reduction in the ***diversity*** of the workforce.

employee stock fund FINANCE, BANKING, AND ACCOUNTING a fund from which money is taken to buy shares of a company's stock for its employees

employee stock ownership plan HR & PERSONNEL a scheme sponsored by a company by which a trust holds shares in the company on behalf of ***employees*** and distributes those shares to employees. In the United States, shares can only be sold when an employee leaves the organization, and are thus thought of as a form of pension provision. In the United Kingdom, shares can be disposed of at any time. There are two types of employee stock ownership plan in the United Kingdom: the case-law employee stock ownership plan, which can benefit all or some employees but may not qualify for tax benefits; and the employee share ownership trust. Abbr **ESOP**

employer HR & PERSONNEL a person or organization that pays people to carry out specified activities. An employer usually contracts an ***employee*** to fill a permanent or temporary position to carry out work on a regularly paid basis within the relevant legal framework of the country of residence.

employers' association (*U.K.*) HR & PERSONNEL a body that regulates relations between employers and employees, represents members' views on public policy issues affecting their business to national and international policy makers, and supplies support and advice. An employers' association represents companies within one or many sectors at regional, national, or international level and is usually a nonprofit, nonparty political organization, funded by subscriptions paid by its members.

Employment Court HR & PERSONNEL a higher court in New Zealand responsible for arbitrating in industrial relations disputes. It hears cases relating to disputes between employers and employees or unions as well as appeals referred to the court by ***Employment Tribunals***.

employment equity (*S. Africa*) HR & PERSONNEL the policy of giving preference in employment opportunities to qualified people from sectors of society that were previously discriminated against, for example, black people, women, and physically challenged people

employment law HR & PERSONNEL the collection of statutes, common law rules, and decisions in court or employment tribunal cases that govern the rights and duties of employers and employees. The ***contract of employment*** forms the cornerstone of employment law, which also embraces ***discrimination*** and ***redundancy*** rights, ***collective bargaining***, health and safety, union membership, and ***industrial action***.

employment pass (*S. Africa*) GENERAL MANAGEMENT a visa issued to a foreign national who is a professional earning in excess of S$1,500 per month

employment protection HR & PERSONNEL the legal framework for establishing and defending the rights of employees

Employment Tribunal HR & PERSONNEL a government body responsible for hearing and adjudicating in disputes between employees and employers

empowerment GENERAL MANAGEMENT the redistribution of ***power*** and ***decision making*** responsibilities, usually to ***employees***, where such ***authority*** was previously a management prerogative. Empowerment is based on the recognition that employee abilities are frequently underused, and that, given the chance, most employees can contribute more. Empowered workplaces are characterized by managers who focus on the energizing, supporting, and ***coaching*** of their staff in a blame-free environment of trust.

ROSABETH MOSS KANTER (pp. 1008–09); DOUGLAS MCGREGOR (pp. 1022–23)

empty suit GENERAL MANAGEMENT a corporate executive who dresses very smartly and follows all procedures exactly without actually contributing anything of significance to the company (*slang*)

EMS *abbr*

1. GENERAL MANAGEMENT see ***environmental management system***
2. FINANCE, BANKING, AND ACCOUNTING European Monetary System, the first stage of economic and monetary union of the EU, which came into force in March 1979, giving stable, but adjustable, exchange rates

EMU FINANCE, BANKING, AND ACCOUNTING Economic and Monetary Union, or European Monetary Union, the timetable for achieving which within the European Union was outlined in the Maastricht Treaty in 1991. The criteria were that national debt must not exceed 60% of GDP; budget deficit should be 3% or less of GDP; inflation should be no more than 1.5% above the average rate of the three best performing economies of the EU in the previous 12 months; and applicants must have been members of the ***ERM*** for two years without having realigned or devalued their currency.

encryption E-COMMERCE a means of encoding information, especially financial data, so that it can be transmitted over the Internet without being read by unauthorized parties

encryption key E-COMMERCE a sequence of characters known to both or all parties to a communication, used to initiate the ***encryption*** process

end-around GENERAL MANAGEMENT an approach to a problem that does not attack it directly but rather tries to avoid it

end consumer MARKETING = ***consumer***

endogenous variable STATISTICS the dependent variable in an econometric study

endorsement GENERAL MANAGEMENT the public approval of a product or technology by a person or organization. The endorsement can be used to promote the product to other organizations that may be more cautious in their approach to adopting new products.

endowment fund FINANCE, BANKING, AND ACCOUNTING a mutual fund that supports a nonprofit institution

endowment policy FINANCE, BANKING, AND ACCOUNTING an insurance policy of a type popular in the United Kingdom that pays a set amount to the policyholder when the policy matures, or to a beneficiary if the policyholder dies before it matures

endpoint STATISTICS a point at which a definable event in a study takes place, for example, the recovery of a patient in a medical study

energy audit GENERAL MANAGEMENT a review, inspection, and evaluation of sources and uses of energy within an organization to ensure efficiency and lack of waste

energy conservation GENERAL MANAGEMENT the minimization of fuel consumption. Energy conservation, through the monitoring and control of the amounts of electricity, gas, and other fuels used in the workplace, can help reduce costs and damage to the environment. An energy management scheme provides a systematic method of assessing, evaluating, and improving an organization's energy usage. This forms part of an organization's approach to ***environmental management***.

engineering for excellence OPERATIONS & PRODUCTION = ***design for manufacturability***

English disease GENERAL MANAGEMENT the supposed predilection of British workforces to opt for ***strike*** action. In the United Kingdom in the 1960s and 1970s, strikes were commonly used by workers for ***dispute*** resolution. Government legislation in the 1980s, however, made striking more difficult for workers.

enterprise GENERAL MANAGEMENT a venture characterized by ***innovation***, ***creativity***, dynamism, and risk. An enterprise can consist of one project, or may refer to an entire organization. It usually requires several of the following attributes: flexibility, initiative, ***problem solving*** ability, independence or autonomy, and imagination. Enterprises flourish in the environment of ***delayered***, nonhierarchical organizations but can be stifled by ***bureaucracy***. Enterprises are often created by ***entrepreneurs***.

enterprise application integration E-COMMERCE the unrestricted sharing of data and business processes via integrated and compatible software programs. As businesses expand and recognize the need for their information and applications to be shared between systems, they are investing in enterprise application integration in order to streamline processes and keep all the elements of their organizations, for example, human resources and inventory control connected. Abbr **EAI**

enterprise culture GENERAL MANAGEMENT an organizational or social environment that encourages and makes possible initiative and ***innovation***. An organization with an enterprise culture is usually more competitive and more profitable than a ***bureaucracy***. Such an organization is believed to be more rewarding and stimulating to work in. A society with an enterprise culture facilitates individuality and requires people to take responsibility for their own welfare. Conservative governments in the United Kingdom during the 1980s and 1990s promoted an enterprise culture by introducing market principles into all areas of economic and social life. These included policies of deregulation of financial services, ***privatization*** of utilities and national monopolies, and commercialization of the public sector.

enterprise resource planning GENERAL MANAGEMENT see ***ERP***

entertainment expenses HR & PERSONNEL costs, reimbursable by the ***employer***, that are incurred by an ***employee*** in hosting social events for clients or suppliers in order to obtain or maintain their custom or goodwill

entitlement GENERAL MANAGEMENT the expectation that an organization or individual will make large profits regardless of their contribution to the economy

entitlement offer FINANCE, BANKING, AND ACCOUNTING an offer that cannot be transferred to anyone else

entreprenerd GENERAL MANAGEMENT an entrepreneur with computing skills, especially one who starts up an Internet business (*slang*)

entrepreneur GENERAL MANAGEMENT somebody who sets up a business or ***enterprise***. An entrepreneur typically demonstrates effective application of a number of enterprising attributes such as creativity, initiative, risk taking, problem solving ability, and autonomy, and will often risk his or her own capital to set up a business. See ***intrapreneur***

entropy STATISTICS a measure of the rate of transfer of the information that a system such as a computer program or factory machine receives or outputs

entry barrier MARKETING a perceived or real obstacle preventing a competitor from entering a market

envelope E-COMMERCE = ***electronic envelope***

environmental analysis GENERAL MANAGEMENT = ***environmental scanning***

environmental audit GENERAL MANAGEMENT the regular systematic gathering of information to monitor the effectiveness of environmental policies. An environmental audit now often forms part of an organization's ***environmental management*** systems, and therefore is concerned with checking conformity with legislative requirements and environmental standards such as ***ISO 14001*** (see ***ISO 14000***), as well as with company policy. The audit may also cover potential improvements in environmental performance and systems.

Environmental Impact Statement GENERAL MANAGEMENT a report on the results of an Environmental Impact Study. Abbr **EIS**

Environmental Impact Study GENERAL MANAGEMENT an analysis of the potential effects of a building development or a similar project on the natural environment. Abbr **EIS**

environmental management GENERAL MANAGEMENT a systematic approach to minimizing the damage created by an organization to the environment in which it operates. Environmental management has become an issue in organizations in that consumers now expect them to be environmentally aware, if not environmentally friendly. Senior managers and directors are increasingly being held liable for their organizations' environmental performance, and the onus is on them to adopt a ***corporate strategy*** that balances economic growth with environmental protection. Environmental management involves reducing pollution, waste, and the consumption of natural resources by implementing an environmental action plan. This plan brings together the key elements of environmental management, including an organization's ***environmental policy*** statement, an ***environmental audit***, ***environmental management system***, and standards such as the EC **ECO-Management Audit Scheme** and ***ISO 14000***.

✔ TAKING ACTION ON THE ENVIRONMENT (pp. 520–21)

environmental management system GENERAL MANAGEMENT a procedure to manage and control an organization's impact on the environment. An environmental management system is part of an organization's ***environmental management*** practice. It includes creation of an ***environmental policy***, which sets objectives and targets a program of implementation, effectiveness monitoring, problem correction, and system review. An environmental management system should also identify key resources and holders of responsibility for determining and implementing environmental policy. Systems for environmental management have been formalized in the ***ISO 14000*** quality standards. Abbr **EMS**

environmental policy GENERAL MANAGEMENT a statement of organizational intentions regarding the safeguarding of the environment. Clause 4.2 of the ***ISO 14001*** (see ***ISO 14000***) series of environmental management standards, which many organizations now either apply in full or make use of for guidance on environmental management, focuses on environmental policy and states the necessary themes and commitments for an environmental policy that conforms to ISO 14001 requirements.

✔ TAKING ACTION ON THE ENVIRONMENT (pp. 520–21)

environmental scanning GENERAL MANAGEMENT the monitoring of changes in the external environment in which an organization operates in order to identify threats and opportunities for the future and maintain ***competitive advantage***. The process of environmental scanning includes gathering information on an organization's task environment of competitors, markets, customers, and suppliers, carrying out a ***PEST analysis*** of social, economic, technological, and political factors that may affect the organization, and analyzing the implications of this research. Environmental scanning may be undertaken systematically by a dedicated department or unit within an organization or more informally by project groups and may be used in the planning and development of ***corporate strategy***. Also known as ***environmental analysis***

environmental statistics STATISTICS statistical studies concerning environmental matters such as pollution

epidemiology STATISTICS the statistical study of the incidence of a particular disease in a given population

e-procurement E-COMMERCE the business-to-business sale and purchase of goods and services over an electronic network such as the Internet. Also known as ***electronic procurement***

equal opportunities HR & PERSONNEL the granting of equal rights, privileges, and status regardless of gender, age, race, religion, disability, or sexual orientation. Equality in employment is regulated by law in most Western countries. An organizational equal opportunities policy aims to go further than the regulatory framework demands. Such a policy should focus on preventing discriminatory or harassing behavior in the workplace and achieving equal access to training, job, and promotion opportunities. ***Affirmative action***, which is referred to as positive discrimination in the United Kingdom, is a controversial approach to encouraging the advancement of minorities. ***Diversity*** management builds on and goes beyond equal opportunities by looking at the rights of individuals rather than groups.

equal pay HR & PERSONNEL the principle and practice of paying men and women in the same organization at the same rate for like work or work that is rated as of equal value. Work is assessed either through an organization's ***job evaluation*** scheme or the judgment of an independent expert appointed by an industrial tribunal. Although many countries have legislation on equal pay, a gap still exists between men's pay and women's pay and is attributed to sexual discrimination in job evaluation and payment systems.

equal treatment HR & PERSONNEL a principle of the European Union that requires that member states should ensure that there is no ***discrimination*** with regard to employment, vocational training, and working conditions. The principle of equal treatment is applied through Europe-wide directives and national legislation of the member states.

equilibrium price ECONOMICS the price that regulates supply and demand. Suppliers will increase prices when demand is high and reduce prices when demand is low.

equilibrium quantity ECONOMICS the quantity that regulates supply and demand. Suppliers will increase quantity when demand is high and reduce quantity when demand is low.

equilibrium rate of interest ECONOMICS the rate at which the expected interest rate in a market equals the actual rate prevailing

equipment trust certificate FINANCE, BANKING, AND ACCOUNTING a bond in the United Kingdom sold for a 20% down payment and collateralized by the equipment purchased with its proceeds

equity claim FINANCE, BANKING, AND ACCOUNTING a claim on earnings that remain after debts are satisfied

equity contribution agreement FINANCE, BANKING, AND ACCOUNTING an agreement to provide equity under specified circumstances

equity floor FINANCE, BANKING, AND ACCOUNTING an agreement to pay whenever some indicator of a stock market's value falls below a specified limit

equity multiplier FINANCE, BANKING, AND ACCOUNTING a measure of a company's worth expressed as a multiple of each dollar of its stock's price

equivalent annual cash flow FINANCE, BANKING, AND ACCOUNTING the value of an annuity required to provide an investor with the same return as some other form of investment

equivalent bond yield FINANCE, BANKING, AND ACCOUNTING = ***bond equivalent yield***

equivalent taxable yield FINANCE, BANKING, AND ACCOUNTING the value of a taxable investment required to provide an investor with the same return as some other form of investment

e-retailer E-COMMERCE a business that uses an electronic network such as the Internet to sell its goods or services. Also known as ***electronic retailer***, ***e-tailer***

erf (*S. Africa*) FINANCE, BANKING, AND ACCOUNTING a plot of rural or urban land, usually no larger than a smallholding

ergonomics HR & PERSONNEL, GENERAL MANAGEMENT the study of workplace design and the physical and psychological impact it has on workers. Ergonomics is about the fit between people, their work activities, equipment, work systems, and environment to ensure that workplaces are safe, comfortable, efficient, and that ***productivity*** is not compromised. Ergonomics may examine the design and layout of buildings, machines, and equipment, as well as aspects such as lighting, temperature, ventilation, noise, color, and texture. Ergonomic principles also apply to working methods such as systems and ***procedures***, and the allocation and scheduling of work.

ERM *abbr* FINANCE, BANKING, AND ACCOUNTING Exchange Rate Mechanism, formerly a system for coordinating the currencies of the European Union member states to maintain exchange rate stability. Central banks were not allowed to let their currencies fluctuate more than a specified percentage above (ceiling rate) or below (minimum rate) a central rate established by comparing all the currencies in the ERM and the ecu.

ERP *abbr* GENERAL MANAGEMENT enterprise resource planning, a software system that coordinates every important aspect of an organization's production into one seamless process so that maximum efficiency can be achieved

error account FINANCE, BANKING, AND ACCOUNTING an account for the temporary placement of funds involved in a financial transaction known to have been executed in error

ESC *abbr* FINANCE, BANKING, AND ACCOUNTING European Social Charter, a charter adopted by the European Council of the EU in 1989. The 12 rights it contains are: freedom of movement, employment, and remuneration; social protection; improvement of living and working conditions; freedom of association and collective bargaining; worker information; consultation and participation; vocational training; equal treatment of men and women; health and safety protection in the workplace; pension rights; integration of those with disabilities; protection of young people.

e-shock E-COMMERCE the forward momentum of electronic commerce, considered as irresistible

ESOP FINANCE, BANKING, AND ACCOUNTING see ***employee stock ownership plan***

ESP GENERAL MANAGEMENT see ***Eligible Service Period***

estimate GENERAL MANAGEMENT an approximate calculation of an uncertain value. An estimate may be a reasonable guess based on knowledge and experience or it may be calculated using more sophisticated techniques designed to forecast projected costs, profits, losses, or value. The term also is used to refer to an approximate price quoted for work to be undertaken by an organization.

estimation STATISTICS the provision of a numerical value for a parameter of a population that has been sampled

e-tailer E-COMMERCE = ***e-retailer***

e-tailing E-COMMERCE the practice of doing business over an electronic network such as the Internet

ethical investment FINANCE, BANKING, AND ACCOUNTING investment only in companies whose policies meet the ethical criteria of the investor. Also known as ***socially conscious investing***

ethnic monitoring HR & PERSONNEL the recording and evaluation of the racial origins of employees or customers with the aim of ensuring that all parts of the population are represented. When ethnic monitoring is carried out as a part of the ***recruitment*** process, candidates are asked to indicate their ethnic origin on an anonymous basis. Information thus supplied is removed from the application as soon as it is received by the prospective employer.

ETP FINANCE, BANKING, AND ACCOUNTING see ***Eligible Termination Payment***

EU *abbr* FINANCE, BANKING, AND ACCOUNTING European Union. A social, economic, and political organization of European countries whose aim is integration for all member nations. So called since November 1993 under the Maastricht Treaty, before which it was known as the European Community (EC) and before that as the European Economic Community.

EUREX FINANCE, BANKING, AND ACCOUNTING Eureka Research Expert System, established by Eureka (European Research and Coordination Agency) in 1985 on a French initiative for nonmilitary industrial research in advanced technologies in Europe

Euro FINANCE, BANKING, AND ACCOUNTING the currency of 12 member nations of the European Union. The Euro was introduced in 1999, when the first 11 countries to adopt it joined together in an Economic and Monetary Union and fixed their currencies' exchange rate to the Euro. Notes and coins were brought into general circulation in January 2002, although banks and other financial institutions had before that time carried out transactions in Euros.

Eurobank FINANCE, BANKING, AND ACCOUNTING a bank that handles transactions in foreign currencies

Eurobond FINANCE, BANKING, AND ACCOUNTING a bond specified in the currency of one country and sold to investors from another country. Also known as ***global bond***

Euro-commercial paper FINANCE, BANKING, AND ACCOUNTING short-term uncollateralized loans obtained by companies in foreign countries

Eurocredit FINANCE, BANKING, AND ACCOUNTING intermediate-term notes used by banks to lend money to governments and companies

Eurocurrency FINANCE, BANKING, AND ACCOUNTING money deposited in one country but denominated in the currency of another country

Eurodeposit FINANCE, BANKING, AND ACCOUNTING a short-term deposit of Eurocurrency

Eurodollar FINANCE, BANKING, AND ACCOUNTING a dollar deposited in a European bank or other bank outside the United States

Euroequity issue FINANCE, BANKING, AND ACCOUNTING a note issued by banks in several countries

Euro-note FINANCE, BANKING, AND ACCOUNTING a note in the Eurocurrency market

European Association of Securities Dealers Automated Quotations FINANCE, BANKING, AND ACCOUNTING see ***EASDAQ***

European Bank for Reconstruction and Development FINANCE, BANKING, AND ACCOUNTING see ***EBRD***

  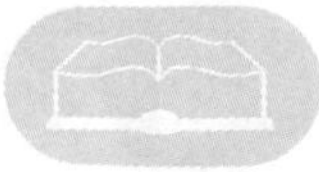  

European Central Bank FINANCE, BANKING, AND ACCOUNTING see ***ECB***

European Economic Community *or* **European Community** FINANCE, BANKING, AND ACCOUNTING see ***EU***

European Investment Bank FINANCE, BANKING, AND ACCOUNTING see ***EIB***

European Monetary System FINANCE, BANKING, AND ACCOUNTING see ***EMS***

European Monetary Union FINANCE, BANKING, AND ACCOUNTING see ***EMU***

European option FINANCE, BANKING, AND ACCOUNTING an option that the buyer can exercise only on the day that it expires. See ***American option***

European Quality Award GENERAL MANAGEMENT see ***EFQM Excellence Model***

European Social Charter FINANCE, BANKING, AND ACCOUNTING see ***ESC***

European Union FINANCE, BANKING, AND ACCOUNTING see ***EU***

Euroyen bond FINANCE, BANKING, AND ACCOUNTING a Eurobond denominated in yen

evaluation of training HR & PERSONNEL a continuous cycle consisting of defining training objectives, carrying out ***training needs analysis***, delivering training, assessing reactions to, and analyzing the transfer of, training, and measuring the bottom-line effects of training

event marketing MARKETING the promotion and marketing of a specific event such as a conference, seminar, exhibition, or trade fair. Event marketing may encompass ***corporate hospitality*** activities, business or charity functions, or sporting occasions. The planning, marketing, and managing of the function on the day are sometimes entirely ***outsourced*** to companies specializing in event management.

evergreen loan (*U.K.*) FINANCE, BANKING, AND ACCOUNTING a series of loans providing a continuing stream of capital for a project

ex-all (*U.K.*) FINANCE, BANKING, AND ACCOUNTING having no right in any transaction that is pending with respect to shares, such as a split or the issuance of dividends

excellence GENERAL MANAGEMENT, OPERATIONS & PRODUCTION a state of organizational performance achieved through the successful integration of a variety of operational and strategic elements that enables an organization to become one of the best in its field. Excellence is initially evident when an organization rises above its competitors, and it is usually measured by the ability to sustain a leading or significant market share. The strategic and operational elements contributing to excellence include the organization's approach to ***total quality management***, ***quality assurance***, ***quality awards*** and ***quality standards***, core competency, ***benchmarking***, ***customer service***, the ***balanced scorecard***, and ***leadership***. Taken altogether, these components should produce an organizational approach to the generation, development, and delivery of products and services that is better, cheaper, and smarter than that of the competition. Attempts at becoming an excellent organization have spawned terms such as ***best practice***, ***best-in-class***, and ***world class manufacturing*** and are usually associated with a holistic approach to ***competitive advantage***.

W. EDWARDS DEMING (pp. 980–81); TOM PETERS (pp. 1036–37)

exception reporting GENERAL MANAGEMENT the passing on of information only when it breaches or transcends agreed norms. Exception reporting is intended to reduce ***information overload*** by minimizing the circulation of repetitive or old information. Under this system, only information that is new and out of the ordinary will be transmitted. It has similarities to ***management by exception***.

excess profits tax FINANCE, BANKING, AND ACCOUNTING a tax levied by a government on a company that makes extraordinarily large profits in times of unusual circumstances, for example, during a war. An excess profits tax was imposed in both the United States and the United Kingdom during World War II.

exchange E-COMMERCE the main type of business-to-business marketplace. The **B2B exchange** enables suppliers, buyers, and intermediaries to come together and offer products to each other according to a set of criteria. **B2B Web exchanges** provide constant price adjustments in line with fluctuations of supply and demand. In E2E or "exchange-to-exchange" e-commerce, buyers and sellers conduct transactions not only within exchanges but also between them.

exchange controls ECONOMICS the regulations by which a country's banking system controls its residents' or resident companies' dealings in foreign currencies and gold

exchange equalization account ECONOMICS the Bank of England account that sells and buys sterling for gold and foreign currencies to smooth out fluctuations in the exchange rate of the British pound

exchange offer FINANCE, BANKING, AND ACCOUNTING an offer to trade one security for another

exchange rate FINANCE, BANKING, AND ACCOUNTING the rate at which one country's currency can be exchanged for that of another

Exchange Rate Mechanism FINANCE, BANKING, AND ACCOUNTING see ***ERM***

exchange rate parities FINANCE, BANKING, AND ACCOUNTING relationships between the values of various currencies

exchange rate risk FINANCE, BANKING, AND ACCOUNTING the risk of suffering loss on converting another currency to the currency of a company's own country

excise duty FINANCE, BANKING, AND ACCOUNTING a tax on goods such as alcohol or tobacco produced and sold within a particular country

exclusive economic zone ECONOMICS a zone in a country in which particular economic conditions apply. The Special Economic Zone (SEZ) in China, where trade is conducted free of state control, is an example.

executive GENERAL MANAGEMENT an employee in a position of senior responsibility in an organization. An executive is involved in planning, strategy, policy making, and ***line management***. The term executive can also be used as an alternative to ***manager***, ***consultant***, **officer**, **agent**, or **operative**.

executive chairman GENERAL MANAGEMENT see ***chair***

executive coaching HR & PERSONNEL regular one-to-one ***coaching*** for leaders, designed as part of a ***management development*** program to provide knowledge and skills in a particular area. Executive coaching involves giving ***feedback*** to a leader and assisting in the creation of a development plan, often using ***360 degree appraisal***. It can include in-depth development coaching conducted by colleagues, superiors, or specialist trainers, lasting perhaps six to twelve months.

executive director GENERAL MANAGEMENT a senior employee of an organization, usually with line responsibility for a particular func-

  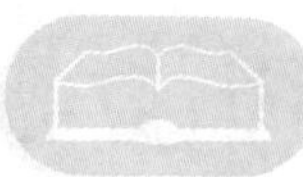    

tion and usually, but not always, a member of the ***board of directors***

executive information system GENERAL MANAGEMENT see ***EIS***

executive officer GENERAL MANAGEMENT see ***executive***

executive search HR & PERSONNEL the identification of suitable external candidates for senior positions on behalf of an organization by recruitment agents or consultants, often using ***headhunting*** techniques. Executive search consultants work from personal recommendation and lists of their own contacts, and monitor rising stars or key personnel in particular organizations or professions. The number of potential candidates is usually limited because of the specialty or seniority of the post, so that the search takes place within upper salary ranges. Executive search consultants rarely advertise because the publicity may be unfruitful or detrimental to the organization for which they are working and they do not find posts for individual job hunters.

exempt gift FINANCE, BANKING, AND ACCOUNTING a gift that is not subject to the gift tax

exemption FINANCE, BANKING, AND ACCOUNTING an amount per family member that an individual can subtract when reporting income to be taxed

exempt purchaser FINANCE, BANKING, AND ACCOUNTING an institutional investor who may buy newly issued securities without filing a prospectus with a securities commission

exempt securities FINANCE, BANKING, AND ACCOUNTING securities that are not subject to a provision of law such as margin or registration requirements

exercise notice FINANCE, BANKING, AND ACCOUNTING an option holder's notification to the option's writer of his or her desire to exercise the option

exercise of warrants FINANCE, BANKING, AND ACCOUNTING the use of a warrant to purchase stock

exercise value FINANCE, BANKING, AND ACCOUNTING the amount of profit that can be realized by cashing in an option

ex-gratia payment HR & PERSONNEL a one-off extra payment in addition to normal ***pay***, made out of gratitude, courtesy, or in recognition of a special contribution

exhibition MARKETING an event organized to bring together buyers and sellers at a single venue

Eximbank FINANCE, BANKING, AND ACCOUNTING Export-Import Bank, a bank founded in 1934 that provides loans direct to foreign importers of U.S. goods and services

existential culture GENERAL MANAGEMENT a form of ***corporate culture*** in which the organization exists to serve the individual, rather than individuals being servants of the organization. Existential culture was identified by ***Charles Handy***. It typically consists of a group of professionals who work together, but have no leader as such.

CHARLES HANDY (pp. 1000–01)

exit interview HR & PERSONNEL a meeting between an employee and a management representative on the employee's departure from an organization. An exit interview is conducted in order to ascertain why an employee is leaving, either because of pull factors such as better pay and conditions or push factors such as poor training or management. Another purpose of the exit interview is to capture information relating to the departing employee's knowledge and experience.

exit PE ratio FINANCE, BANKING, AND ACCOUNTING the price-earnings ratio when a company changes hands

exogenous variable STATISTICS any variable in an econometric study that has an impact on it from outside

expatriate HR & PERSONNEL somebody who has left his or her home country to live or work abroad, either for a long period of time or permanently

expectancy theory HR & PERSONNEL a view that people will be motivated to behave in particular ways if they believe that doing so will bring them rewards they both seek and value. Expectancy theory was first applied in the context of the workplace by ***Victor Vroom*** in the 1960s. He defined the concepts of valence and expectancy to explain how people will decide to act. Valence refers to somebody's perception of the value of the reward or outcome that might be obtained if he or she performs a task successfully. Expectancy refers to how likely an outcome is perceived to be.

expected return FINANCE, BANKING, AND ACCOUNTING the average profit that can be expected from a risky investment, expressed as a percentage

expenditure switching ECONOMICS government action to improve the attractiveness of home-produced goods at the expense of imports or to make domestic spending switch from imports to home-produced goods

expense FINANCE, BANKING, AND ACCOUNTING

1. a cost incurred in buying goods or services
2. a charge against a company's profit

expense account HR & PERSONNEL an amount of money that an employee or group of employees can draw on to reclaim personal ***expenses*** incurred in carrying out activities for an organization

expenses HR & PERSONNEL personal costs incurred by an employee in carrying out activities for an organization that are reimbursed by the employer

experience curve GENERAL MANAGEMENT see ***learning curve***

experience economy GENERAL MANAGEMENT an economy in which products are differentiated through the quality of the "consumer experience" or level of added value (*slang*)

experiential learning HR & PERSONNEL a model that views learning as a cyclical process in four stages: concrete experience, reflective observation, abstract conceptualization, and active experimentation. Experiential learning relates to participants' activities and reactions to a training event, in contrast to passive learning. Proposed by ***David Kolb*** in 1971, the model was later expanded by other practitioners including ***Peter Honey*** and ***Alan Mumford***. Experiential learning differs from ***action learning*** in that it can apply to an individual working alone while action learning is seen essentially as a group activity.

experimental design STATISTICS the planning of the procedures to be used in an experimental study

experimental study STATISTICS a statistical investigation in which the researcher can influence events in the study

expert system GENERAL MANAGEMENT a computer program that emulates the reasoning and ***decision making*** of a human expert in a particular field. The main components of an expert system are the knowledge base, which consists of facts and rules about appropriate courses of action based on the knowledge and experience of human experts, the inference engine, which simulates the inductive reasoning of a human expert, and the user interface, which enables users to interact with the system. Expert systems may be used by nonexperts to solve well-defined problems when human expertise is unavailable or expensive, or by experts seeking to find solutions to complex questions. They are used for a wide variety of tasks including medical diagnostics and financial decision making, and are an application of ***artificial intelligence***.

explicit knowledge GENERAL MANAGEMENT see ***knowledge***

exploding bonus HR & PERSONNEL a bonus offered to recent graduates that encourages them to sign for a job as quickly as possible as it reduces in value with every day of delay (*slang*)

exponential smoothing GENERAL MANAGEMENT a statistical technique used in quantitative ***forecasting***, particularly in the areas of inventory control and ***sales forecasting***, that adjusts data to give a clearer view of trends in the long term. In exponential smoothing, values are calculated using a formula that takes all previous values into account but assigns greatest weight to the most recent data.

exponential trend STATISTICS a statistical trend that is revealed in a ***time series***

export agent GENERAL MANAGEMENT an intermediary who acts on behalf of a company to open up or develop a market in a foreign country. Export agents are often paid a commission on all sales and may have exclusive rights in a particular geographic area. A good agent will know or get to know local market conditions and will have other valuable information that can be used to mutual benefit.

Export-Import Bank FINANCE, BANKING, AND ACCOUNTING see ***Eximbank***

exporting MARKETING the process of selling goods to other countries. Exporting provides access to nondomestic markets and can be coordinated by an **export manager**. As with all business activities, careful ***market research*** needs to be undertaken. This can be carried out by the company itself or through an experienced ***export agent***. Many companies produce goods almost entirely for export. Services also can be exported, but require different delivery mechanisms through subsidiary offices or local ***franchise***, or ***licensing agreements***.

export-led growth ECONOMICS growth in which a country's main source of income is from its export trade

export manager MARKETING see ***exporting***

exposure E-COMMERCE = ***ad view***

ex-rights FINANCE, BANKING, AND ACCOUNTING for sale without rights, for example, voting or conversion rights. The term can be applied to transactions such as the purchase of new shares.

ex-rights date FINANCE, BANKING, AND ACCOUNTING the date when a stock first trades ex-rights

extendable bond FINANCE, BANKING, AND ACCOUNTING a bond whose maturity can be delayed by either the issuer or the holder

extendable note FINANCE, BANKING, AND ACCOUNTING a note whose maturity can be delayed by either the issuer or the holder

extended fund facility ECONOMICS a credit facility of the ***IMF*** that allows a country up to eight years to repay the funds it has borrowed from the Fund

external audit FINANCE, BANKING, AND ACCOUNTING an audit of a company done by people who are external to, and independent of, the organization. See ***internal audit***

external communication GENERAL MANAGEMENT the exchange of information and messages between an organization and other organizations, groups, or individuals outside the formal structure of the organization. The aims of external communication are to facilitate cooperation with groups such as suppliers, investors, and shareholders, and to present a favorable image of an organization and its products or services to potential and actual customers and to society at large. A variety of channels may be used for external communication including face-to-face meetings, print or broadcast media, electronic and computer-based communication technologies such as the Internet. External communication includes the fields of ***PR***, media relations, ***advertising***, and ***marketing management***.

external debt ECONOMICS the part of a country's debt that is owed to creditors who are not residents of the country

external finance FINANCE, BANKING, AND ACCOUNTING money that a company obtains from investors, for example, by loans or by issuing stock

extranet E-COMMERCE a closed network of Web sites and e-mail systems that is open to people outside as well as inside an organization. An extranet enables third-party access to internal applications or information. This is useful for organizations that need to share internal systems and information with potential partners. As with ***intranets***, extranets provide all the benefits of Internet technology with the added benefit of security. They use the same Internet technology (browsers, Web servers, HTML, etc.) and are confined to an isolated network.

extraordinary general meeting GENERAL MANAGEMENT any general meeting of an organization other than the ***annual meeting***. Directors can usually call an extraordinary general meeting at their discretion, as can company members who either hold not less than 10% of the paid-up voting shares, or who represent not less than 10% of the voting rights. Directors are obliged to call an EGM if there is a substantial loss of capital. Fourteen days' written notice must be given, or 21 days' written notice if a special resolution is to be proposed. Only special business can be transacted at the meeting, the general nature of which must be specified in the convening notice.

extrapolate STATISTICS to estimate from a data set values that lie beyond the range of the data collected

extreme value STATISTICS either of the smallest or largest variate values in a sample of observations from a statistical study

eyeballing STATISTICS the process of informally inspecting statistical data by simply looking at it to assess results

eyeballs E-COMMERCE a measure of the number of visits made to a Web site (*slang*)

eyebrow management GENERAL MANAGEMENT a management style whereby a manager or top executive can change a course of action simply by implying his or her disapproval (*slang*)

eye candy GENERAL MANAGEMENT visually attractive material (*slang*)

eye service HR & PERSONNEL the practice of working only when a supervisor is present and able to see you (*slang*)

e-zine E-COMMERCE a regular publication on a particular topic distributed in digital form, mainly via the Web but also by e-mail or floppy disk

  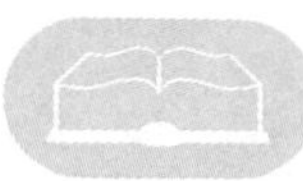    

F2F *abbr* GENERAL MANAGEMENT face-to-face (*slang*)

face time HR & PERSONNEL time spent in face-to-face communication as opposed to time spent communicating electronically (*slang*)

facilitation HR & PERSONNEL the process of helping groups, or individuals, to learn, find a solution, or reach a consensus, without imposing or dictating an outcome. Facilitation aims to ***empower*** individuals or groups to learn for themselves or find their own answers to problems without control or manipulation. Facilitators need good ***communication skills***, including listening, questioning, and reflecting. Facilitation is used in a range of contexts including ***training***, ***experiential learning***, conflict resolution, and ***negotiation***.

facilities management GENERAL MANAGEMENT
1. the management of an organization's property
2. the provision of information technology, systems, and electronic data services to an organization by an agent company
3. the provision of equipment or services to an organization by an agent or company. Also known as ***outsourcing***

facing matter MARKETING advertisements printed opposite editorial material in newspapers or magazines

factor STATISTICS a variable investigated in a statistical study

factor analysis STATISTICS the examination of the covariances, correlations, or relationships between the variables observed in a statistical study

factor four OPERATIONS & PRODUCTION a concept of environmentally friendly production based on increasing the productivity of resources by a factor of four to reduce waste

factor market ECONOMICS a market in which factors of production are bought and sold, for example, the capital market or the labor market

factory GENERAL MANAGEMENT a building or set of buildings housing workers and equipment for the sole purpose of manufacturing goods, often on a large scale

factory gate price OPERATIONS & PRODUCTION the actual cost of manufacturing goods before any ***markup*** is added to give profit. The factory gate price includes direct costs such as labor, ***raw materials***, and energy, and indirect costs such as interest on loans, plant maintenance, or rent.

failure GENERAL MANAGEMENT = ***business failure***

failure mode effects analysis GENERAL MANAGEMENT see ***FMEA***

fallen angel FINANCE, BANKING, AND ACCOUNTING a stock that was once very desirable but has now dropped in value (*slang*)

family business GENERAL MANAGEMENT a ***small*** or ***medium-sized business***, run by a family owner, often with the help of other family members, and passed on within the family. If a family business grows, it may be run as an unregistered partnership or, more commonly, registered as a limited company, although in both cases the partners or the directors will be appointed from within the family to retain family control. In the case of larger, ***public limited*** family businesses, family members are usually majority shareholders and retain control of the ***board of directors***, although nonfamily directors and shareholders will have an influence on the way the company is run. The most common cause of ***business failure*** in family-owned businesses is poor ***succession planning***.

family friendly policy HR & PERSONNEL a range of working practices designed to enable employees to achieve a satisfactory ***work-life balance***. A family friendly policy is often introduced by an organization to facilitate the reintroduction of women with children into the workplace. ***Equal opportunities*** legislation and corporate good practice, however, require that such a policy is open to all employees. Typically, a family friendly policy will allow for a range of ***flexible working*** practices and may go further by providing childcare or eldercare facilities, or paid time off for participation in community activities as part of a ***community involvement*** program. Although the introduction of a family friendly policy may initially be expensive, benefits to the organization, including improved employee retention and higher ***motivation*** and ***job satisfaction*** levels, are believed to offset these costs.

Fannie Mae FINANCE, BANKING, AND ACCOUNTING see ***FNMA***

FAO *abbr* GENERAL MANAGEMENT Food and Agriculture Organization of the United Nations, whose priority objectives include encouraging sustainable agriculture and rural development and ensuring the availability of adequate food supplies

FAQ *abbr* E-COMMERCE a frequently asked question or frequently asked questions. FAQ pages are often included on Web sites to provide first-time visitors with answers to the most likely questions they may have. FAQ pages are also used in newsgroups and software applications.

far month FINANCE, BANKING, AND ACCOUNTING the latest month for which there is a futures contract for a particular commodity. See ***nearby month***

FASB *abbr* FINANCE, BANKING, AND ACCOUNTING Financial Accounting Standards Board, a body that frames the rules of accounting for companies. The task is left to the FASB although the Securities and Exchange Commission (SEC) is the legal body for setting the rules.

FASTER FINANCE, BANKING, AND ACCOUNTING Fully Automated Screen Trading and Electronic Registration, a computer-based clearing, settlement, registration, and information system operated by the New Zealand Stock Exchange

fast track GENERAL MANAGEMENT a rapid route to success or advancement. The fast track involves competition and a race to get ahead, and is associated with high ambition and great activity. An employee can be on a fast track, for example, to ***promotion***, but an activity also can be said to take the fast track, for example, to rapid ***product development***. The ***horizontal fast track*** is a variation on the idea of the fast track in which advancement is not upward but sideways. Also known as ***fast lane***

fat
trim the fat GENERAL MANAGEMENT to lay off unnecessary staff in an organization during a time of economic difficulty (*slang*)

faxback MARKETING a method of distributing information in which customers dial a dedicated fax machine that automatically sends information back to the customer's fax machine

Fayol, Henri Louis (1841–1925) GENERAL MANAGEMENT French engineer and industrialist. First European to define ***management*** as a process, consisting, he argued, of five activities—planning, organizing, coordinating,

commanding, and controlling— with further detail contained in 14 general principles. Fayol's ideas were published in *Administration Industrielle et Générale* (1916), and were practiced by others, notably ***Alfred P. Sloan, Jr.***
HENRI FAYOL (pp. 986–87)
ALFRED P. SLOAN, JR. (pp. 1140–41)

FCM *abbr* FINANCE, BANKING, AND ACCOUNTING futures commission merchant

FCOL *abbr* GENERAL MANAGEMENT for crying out loud *(slang)*

feasibility study GENERAL MANAGEMENT an investigation into a proposed plan or project to determine whether and how it can be successfully and profitably carried out. Frequently used in ***project management***, a feasibility study may examine alternative methods of reaching objectives or be used to define or redefine the proposed project. The information gathered must be sufficient to make a decision on whether to go ahead with the project or to enable an investor to decide whether to commit finances to it. This will normally require analysis of technical, financial, and market issues, including an estimate of resources required in terms of materials, time, personnel, and finance, and the expected return on investment.

Federal Funds FINANCE, BANKING, AND ACCOUNTING deposits held in reserve by the Federal Reserve System

federal government *(ANZ)* GENERAL MANAGEMENT Australia's national government as opposed to its state and territory governments

federal organization GENERAL MANAGEMENT a form of ***organization structure***, identified by ***Charles Handy***, in which subsidiaries federate to gain benefits of scale. In a federal organization, the leader provides coordination and vision, and initiatives are generated from the component subsidiary organizations. Federal organization is one of the many ways in which organizations ***restructure*** in order to deal with the dilemmas of power and control. According to Handy, federal organization offers an enabling framework for autonomy to release corporate energy for people to do things in their own way, provided that it is in the common interest, and for people to be well informed so as to be able to interpret that common interest. Handy cites Royal Dutch Shell, Unilever, and ABB as exemplars of federalism.

Federal Reserve Bank FINANCE, BANKING, AND ACCOUNTING a bank that is a member of the Federal Reserve System

Federal Reserve Board FINANCE, BANKING, AND ACCOUNTING a body of seven governors appointed by Congress on the nomination of the President, that supervises the U.S. Federal Reserve System. Appointees serve for 14 years. Abbr **FRB**

Federal Reserve note FINANCE, BANKING, AND ACCOUNTING a note issued by the Federal Reserve System to increase the availability of money temporarily

Federal Reserve System FINANCE, BANKING, AND ACCOUNTING the central banking system of the United States, founded in 1913 by an Act of Congress. The board of governors, made up of seven members, is based in Washington, D.C. and 12 Reserve Banks can be found in major cities across the United States.

Fed pass FINANCE, BANKING, AND ACCOUNTING the Federal Reserve's addition of reserves to the Federal Reserve System to increase credit availability

FEDUSA *abbr* GENERAL MANAGEMENT Federation of Unions of South Africa

Fedwire FINANCE, BANKING, AND ACCOUNTING the U.S. Federal Reserve System's electronic system for transferring funds

feedback GENERAL MANAGEMENT the communication of responses and reactions to proposals and changes or of the findings of ***performance appraisals*** with the aim of enabling improvements to be made. Feedback can be either positive or negative. In the context of performance evaluation or ***performance appraisal***, positive feedback should be delivered to reinforce good performance, whereas negative feedback should be intended to correct or improve poor performance. Feedback that is delivered inappropriately can be very demotivating, so good communication skills are a prerequisite.

feeding frenzy FINANCE, BANKING, AND ACCOUNTING a period of frantic buyer activity in a market *(slang)*

feet
get your feet wet GENERAL MANAGEMENT to begin a new project or activity *(slang)*

fee work GENERAL MANAGEMENT work on a project carried out by independent workers or contractors, rather than employees of an organization

Feigenbaum, Armand Vallin *(b.* 1920) GENERAL MANAGEMENT U.S. manager and author. Originator of the concept of total ***quality control***, the forerunner of ***total quality management***. In *Quality Control* (1951), Feigenbaum argued that quality should be a companywide process.
✔ TOTAL QUALITY: MAPPING A TQM STRATEGY (pp. 524–25)

Ferguson, Sir Alex *(b.* 1941) GENERAL MANAGEMENT British football manager. Considered to be one of the most successful club managers of all time, whose management methods, particularly in the area of ***motivation***, are studied by other business leaders. His approach is set out in *Managing My Life: My Autobiography* (1999).
✔ MOTIVATING YOUR STAFF IN A TIME OF CHANGE (pp. 372–73)

FID *abbr (ANZ)* FINANCE, BANKING, AND ACCOUNTING Financial Institutions Duty

field a call GENERAL MANAGEMENT to take a difficult phone call from somebody *(slang)*

field plot STATISTICS a statistical study, usually in agriculture, of the results of an operation such as planting GM crops in a particular field

field research MARKETING the collection of data directly from contact with customers and potential customers through surveys, interviews, and other forms of ***market research***

field staff HR & PERSONNEL sales staff who cover a specific geographic region and who travel regularly to meet customers. The term field staff may also be applied to professional and technical staff who operate mainly on site such as conservationists and archeologists. It excludes staff located permanently in their own offices or shops.

field trial MARKETING a limited pilot test of a product under real conditions. A field trial is undertaken to test the physical or engineering properties of a product in order to identify and iron out any technical shortcomings prior to marketing. Customers may be involved in some trials, for example, in testing a new washing powder. Field trials should not be confused with ***test marketing***, which is used to determine the likely market for, and likely consumer response to, a new product or service.

field work MARKETING practical work, study, or research carried out in the real world away from the desk. In a marketing context, field work forms primary ***market research*** and

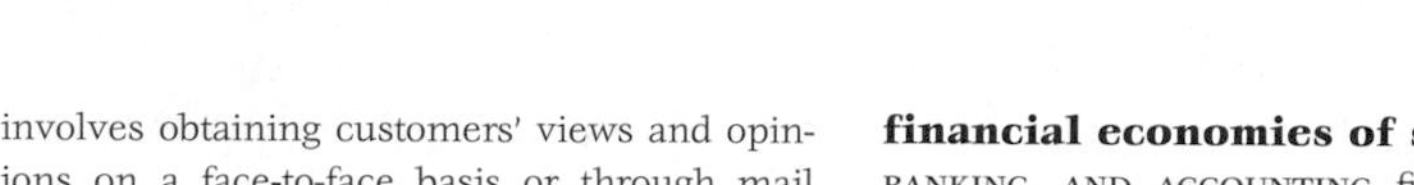

involves obtaining customers' views and opinions on a face-to-face basis or through mail questionnaires or telephone surveys.

FIFO OPERATIONS & PRODUCTION first in first out, a method of inventory control where the stock of a given product first placed in store is used before more recently produced or acquired goods or materials

FIF Tax (*ANZ*) GENERAL MANAGEMENT see ***Foreign Investment Funds Tax***

file server E-COMMERCE a computer that stores and makes software programs and data available to other computers on a network

File Transfer Protocol E-COMMERCE see ***FTP***

filter GENERAL MANAGEMENT a process for analyzing large amounts of incoming information to identify any material that might be of interest to an organization

Filthy Five GENERAL MANAGEMENT a list of companies with a poor environmental record, compiled annually by *Mother Jones Magazine*

finance FINANCE, BANKING, AND ACCOUNTING the money needed by an individual or company to pay for something, for example, a project or stocks

finance bill (*U.K.*) FINANCE, BANKING, AND ACCOUNTING an act passed by a legislature to provide money for public spending

finance company FINANCE, BANKING, AND ACCOUNTING a business that lends money to people or companies against collateral

finance house (*U.K.*) FINANCE, BANKING, AND ACCOUNTING a financial institution

financial FINANCE, BANKING, AND ACCOUNTING relating to finance

Financial Accounting Standards Board FINANCE, BANKING, AND ACCOUNTING see ***FASB***

financial adviser FINANCE, BANKING, AND ACCOUNTING somebody whose job is to give advice about investments

financial analyst FINANCE, BANKING, AND ACCOUNTING = ***investment analyst***

financial distress FINANCE, BANKING, AND ACCOUNTING the condition of being in severe difficulties over money, especially being close to bankruptcy

financial economies of scale FINANCE, BANKING, AND ACCOUNTING financial advantages gained by being able to do things on a large scale

financial engineering FINANCE, BANKING, AND ACCOUNTING the conversion of one form of financial instrument into another, such as the swap of a fixed-rate instrument for a floating-rate one

financial incentive scheme GENERAL MANAGEMENT see ***incentive scheme***

Financial Institutions Duty FINANCE, BANKING, AND ACCOUNTING a tax on monies paid into financial institutions imposed by all state governments in Australia except for Queensland. Financial institutions usually pass the tax on to customers. Abbr **FID**

financial instrument FINANCE, BANKING, AND ACCOUNTING a document that has a cash face value or represents a financial transaction

Financial Planning Association of Australia FINANCE, BANKING, AND ACCOUNTING a national organization representing companies and individuals working in the Australian financial planning industry. Established in 1992, the association is responsible for monitoring standards among its 10,000 or so members. Abbr **FPA**

Financial Reporting Standards Board FINANCE, BANKING, AND ACCOUNTING a peak body that is responsible for setting and monitoring accounting standards in New Zealand. Abbr **FRSB**

financial risk FINANCE, BANKING, AND ACCOUNTING the possibility of loss in an investment or speculation

financier FINANCE, BANKING, AND ACCOUNTING somebody who provides financing

financing gap ECONOMICS the gap in funding for institutions such as the ***IMF*** caused by canceling the debts of poorer countries such as those in West Africa

find time MARKETING the time it takes a consumer to locate a company's product among other products on the shelf (*slang*)

finished goods OPERATIONS & PRODUCTION completed goods that are available for sale to customers

finite capacity plan OPERATIONS & PRODUCTION see ***capacity requirements planning***

finite loading OPERATIONS & PRODUCTION the scheduling or ***loading*** of jobs onto a workstation so that the number of jobs matches the ***effective capacity*** of that station over a given time period. Finite loading is often used in a computerized operation of ***loading***. See ***infinite loading***

finite population STATISTICS a statistical population that has a limited size

FIRB (*ANZ*) FINANCE, BANKING, AND ACCOUNTING see ***Foreign Investment Review Board***

firewall E-COMMERCE a combination of hardware, software, and procedures that controls access to an intranet. Firewalls help to control the information that passes between an intranet and the Internet. A firewall can be simple or complex depending on how an organization decides to control its Internet traffic. It may, for example, be set up to limit Internet access to e-mail only, so that no other types of information can pass between the intranet and the Internet.

firm GENERAL MANAGEMENT a ***partnership*** business. A firm is strictly the name for a business run by partners, but it is often used more generally as a synonym for a ***company***, or ***organization***, usually in the ***private sector***.

first in first out OPERATIONS & PRODUCTION see ***FIFO***

first-line management HR & PERSONNEL see ***supervisory management***

first mover MARKETING the company that first introduces a new type of product or service to a market. Those organizations that follow a first mover to market are known as **followers** or **laggards**—terms that also describe companies that are not the recognized leaders in a sector.

first mover advantage GENERAL MANAGEMENT the benefit produced by being the first to enter a market with a new product or service. First mover advantages include becoming a ***market leader*** in a new area establishing a new leading ***brand***, being able to charge a premium until competitor products appear, enhanced reputation, design, and copyright protection, and possibly setting an industry standard to which other competitors may have to aspire. Disadvantages include: cheaper, and possibly better, **follower** products; the possibility of having to reduce prices or continuously having to add value to stay ahead; first mover development costs; a possible shift in consumer tastes away from the product; obso-

  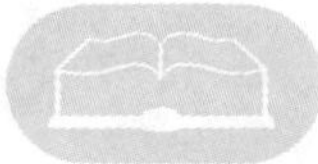    

lescence; and a follower product being accepted as the industry standard.

first-round financing FINANCE, BANKING, AND ACCOUNTING the first infusion of capital into a project

fiscal FINANCE, BANKING, AND ACCOUNTING relating to financial matters, especially in respect of governmental collection, use, and regulation of money through taxation

fiscal balance ECONOMICS a taxation policy that keeps a country's employment and taxation levels in balance

fiscal drag (*U.K.*) FINANCE, BANKING, AND ACCOUNTING the effect that inflation has on taxation in that it raises the amount of tax collected as earnings rise without increasing tax rates

fiscal policy ECONOMICS the central government's policy on lowering or raising taxation or increasing or decreasing public expenditure in order to stimulate or depress ***aggregate demand***

fishbone chart GENERAL MANAGEMENT a diagram resembling the skeleton of a fish that is used to identify and categorize the possible causes of problems. Within a fishbone chart, the topic or problem to be discussed is placed in a box at the right-hand side that corresponds to the fish's head, and the major elements to be investigated are shown as branches at an angle to the horizontal spine. Questions are asked to identify possible causes of problems in each area and the results are added to the diagram as additional layers of branches. This ensures that all aspects of the problem are considered systematically. The fishbone chart is also known as a **cause and effect diagram** or an **Ishikawa diagram** after the originator, Professor ***Kaoru Ishikawa*** of Tokyo University, and is frequently used in ***brainstorming*** and ***problem solving***.

5-S concept OPERATIONS & PRODUCTION a technique that evolved in Japan to establish and maintain a quality culture environment within an organization. The 5-S concept has been associated with ***total productive maintenance*** and ***industrial housekeeping*** in both manufacturing and services. It is seen as being fundamental to quality and productivity. The 5-S's relate to Japanese words that have been variously translated into English. The words are: Seiri, for sort; Seiton, for simplify or straighten; Seiso, for shine or sweep; Seiketsu, for standardize; and Shitsuke, for sustain or self-discipline. The application of these ideas can reduce waste, and increase efficiency, productivity, and quality.

fixed asset FINANCE, BANKING, AND ACCOUNTING a long-term asset of a business such as a machine or building that will not usually be traded

fixed cost FINANCE, BANKING, AND ACCOUNTING a business expense that is constant regardless of the amount of business being done

fixed exchange rate system FINANCE, BANKING, AND ACCOUNTING a system of currency exchange in which there is no change of rate

fixed-interest loan FINANCE, BANKING, AND ACCOUNTING a loan whose rate of interest does not change

fixed interval re-order system OPERATIONS & PRODUCTION = ***periodic inventory review system***

fixed rate GENERAL MANAGEMENT an interest rate for loans that does not change with fluctuating conditions in the market

flagpole

let's run it up a flagpole and see who salutes GENERAL MANAGEMENT let's try this idea and see what level of support or popularity it commands (*slang*)

flame E-COMMERCE a hostile or aggressive message sent via e-mail or posted into an online newsgroup. Typically, flame messages are sent in response to ***spam*** or unsolicited commercial e-mail. If a flame message is responded to in a similarly hostile manner, it can lead to a **flame war**.

flat organization GENERAL MANAGEMENT, HR & PERSONNEL a slimmed-down ***organization structure***, with fewer levels between top and bottom than a traditional ***bureaucracy*** that is supposedly more responsive and better able to cope with fast-moving change. A flat organization can be the result of ***delayering***. Also known as ***horizontal organization***

flat yield curve FINANCE, BANKING, AND ACCOUNTING a ***yield curve*** with the same interest rates for long-term bonds as for short-term bonds

flexecutive HR & PERSONNEL a multiskilled executive able to switch jobs or tasks easily (*slang*)

flexible benefit GENERAL MANAGEMENT see ***fringe benefits***

flexible exchange rate system FINANCE, BANKING, AND ACCOUNTING a system of currency exchange in which rates change from time to time

flexible manufacturing system OPERATIONS & PRODUCTION an integrated system of computer-controlled machine tools and transport and handling systems under the control of a larger computer. Within a flexible manufacturing system, flexibility is achieved by having an overall method of control that coordinates the functions of both the machine tools and the handling systems. A flexible manufacturing system is a type of ***advanced manufacturing technology***. Abbr **FMS**

flexible working HR & PERSONNEL a generic term for employment practices that differ from the traditional norm in terms of the hours worked, the length of contract, or the place of work. Flexible working practices can be divided into three categories: those that give flexibility in the management of time through ***flexible working hours*** schemes such as ***flexitime*** or ***shiftwork***; those that allow employers to cater for peaks or troughs in demand through numerical flexibility, for example, by employing temporary staff; and those that give flexibility regarding the place of work, for example, teleworking.

flexible working hours HR & PERSONNEL flexibility in the management of working time. Flexible working hours are achieved through systems such as ***annual hours***, ***part-time work***, ***flexitime***, or job sharing that are arranged to meet organizational requirements or to help employees reconcile the demands of work and personal circumstances.

flexilagger HR & PERSONNEL a company or organization considered to put too little emphasis on flexibility in its employment practices (*slang*)

flexileader HR & PERSONNEL a company or organization considered to put a great deal of emphasis on flexibility in its employment practices (*slang*)

flexitime HR & PERSONNEL a system of ***flexible working hours*** based on a set number of hours to be worked per week. Employees are able to determine their precise hours of work, provided business demands are met and attendance at work during core periods is

achieved. A debit or credit of hours can be carried forward into the next accounting period.

flight risk HR & PERSONNEL an employee who may be planning to leave a company in the near future (*slang*)

flip GENERAL MANAGEMENT a startup company that aims to build market share quickly and generate short-term personal wealth for its founders through flotation or sell-off

float[1] FINANCE, BANKING, AND ACCOUNTING to sell shares or bonds, for example, to finance a project

float[2] FINANCE, BANKING, AND ACCOUNTING
1. the period between the presentation of a check as payment and the actual payment to the payee
2. the financial advantage provided by a float to the drawer of a check

floating debt FINANCE, BANKING, AND ACCOUNTING a short-term borrowing that is repeatedly refinanced

floating rate FINANCE, BANKING, AND ACCOUNTING an interest rate that is not fixed and which changes according to fluctuations in the market

floor FINANCE, BANKING, AND ACCOUNTING a lower limit on an interest rate, price, or the value of an asset

floor effect STATISTICS the occurrence of clusters of scores near the lower limit of the data in a statistical study

flow chart *or* **flow diagram** GENERAL MANAGEMENT a graphic representation of the stages in a process or system or of the steps required to solve a problem. A flow chart is commonly used to represent the sequence of functions in a computer program or to model the movement of materials, money, or people in a complex process. Two primary symbols used in flow charts are the **process box**, indicating a process or action taking place, and the **decision lozenge**, indicating the need for a decision.

flow line production *or* **flow lines** OPERATIONS & PRODUCTION see ***flow production***

flow on GENERAL MANAGEMENT a pay increase awarded to one group of workers as a result of a pay rise awarded to another group working in the same field

flow production OPERATIONS & PRODUCTION a production method in which successive operations are carried out on a product in such a way that it moves through the factory in a single direction. Flow production is most widely used in ***mass production*** on production lines. More recently, it has been linked with ***batch production***. Under flow production, inventory is often kept to the minimum necessary to ensure continued activity. Stoppages and interruptions to the flow indicate a fault, and corrective action can be taken. ***Assembly line*** production is an extreme version of flow production. Also known as ***flow line production***, ***flow lines***

flow theory GENERAL MANAGEMENT a theory of the way in which people become engaged with, or disengaged from, change. Flow theory suggests that people harmonize in change situations, and open, honest, trusting relationships emerge. The theory recognizes the unpredictability and rigidity of human nature when faced with change. See also ***change management***

fluff it and fly it MARKETING to make a product look good and then sell it (*slang*)

FMCG *abbr* GENERAL MANAGEMENT fast moving consumer goods

FMEA *abbr* GENERAL MANAGEMENT failure mode effects analysis, a technique for analyzing the causes, risks, and effects of potential systems or component failures that is used as a basis for prevention and **contingency planning**. FMEA was developed by engineers primarily to prevent defects in electrical and mechanical systems. All possible failures and their potential effects are listed and ranked according to severity of impact and probability of occurrence so that prevention efforts can be focused on the most critical issues.

FMS OPERATIONS & PRODUCTION see ***flexible manufacturing system***

FNMA *abbr* FINANCE, BANKING, AND ACCOUNTING Federal National Mortgage Association. Also known as ***Fannie Mae***

focus group MARKETING a carefully selected representative range of consumers or employees used for the purposes of providing feedback on consumer preferences and responses to a selected range of products or marketing issues. A focus group usually operates with a ***facilitator*** to guide discussion. Although primarily used for marketing purposes, focus groups are also being more widely used to obtain employee feedback on a wide range of employment and other issues within an organization.

followback survey STATISTICS a further survey of a statistical population carried out a period of years after an original survey

follower MARKETING see ***first mover***

Fong Kong (*S. Africa*) GENERAL MANAGEMENT a product with a fake designer label, especially sports shoes (*slang*)

Food and Agriculture Organization GENERAL MANAGEMENT see ***FAO***

footfall MARKETING a measure of the number of people who walk past a store (*slang*)

Forbes 500 FINANCE, BANKING, AND ACCOUNTING a list of the 500 largest public companies in the United States, ranked according to various criteria by *Forbes* magazine

force field analysis GENERAL MANAGEMENT a technique for promoting change by identifying positive and negative factors and by working to lessen the negative forces while developing the positive ones. Force field analysis was developed by ***Kurt Lewin*** as an aid to ***decision making***, ***problem solving***, and conflict prevention.

Ford, Henry (1863–1947) GENERAL MANAGEMENT U.S. industrialist. Founder of the Ford Motor Company, who organized the ***assembly line*** along the scientific management principles of ***Frederick Winslow Taylor*** and recorded his philosophy in *My Life and Work* (1922).
FREDERICK WINSLOW TAYLOR (pp. 1054–55)

forecast STATISTICS a prediction of the value of a variable in a statistical study

forecasting GENERAL MANAGEMENT the prediction of outcomes, trends, or expected future behavior of a business, industry sector, or the economy through the use of statistics. Forecasting is an ***operational research*** technique used as a basis for management planning and decision making. Common types of forecasting include trend analysis, ***regression analysis***, ***Delphi technique***, time series analysis, ***correlation***, ***exponential smoothing***, and input-output analysis.

foreign bill FINANCE, BANKING, AND ACCOUNTING a bill of exchange that is not payable in the country where it is issued

foreign currency ECONOMICS the currency or interest-bearing bonds of a foreign country

foreign debt FINANCE, BANKING, AND ACCOUNTING hard-currency debt owed to a foreign country in payment for goods and services

foreign dividend FINANCE, BANKING, AND ACCOUNTING a dividend paid by a country other than the United Kingdom, possibly subject to special rules under U.K. tax codes

foreign draft FINANCE, BANKING, AND ACCOUNTING a check that is not both drawn and payable in a country

foreign equity market FINANCE, BANKING, AND ACCOUNTING the market in one country for equities of companies in other countries

foreign exchange FINANCE, BANKING, AND ACCOUNTING the currencies of other countries, or dealings in these

foreign income dividend FINANCE, BANKING, AND ACCOUNTING a dividend paid from earnings in other countries

Foreign Investment Funds Tax FINANCE, BANKING, AND ACCOUNTING a tax imposed by the Australian government on unrealized gains made by Australian residents from offshore investments. It was introduced in 1992 to prevent overseas earnings being taxed at low rates and never brought to Australia. Abbr **FIF Tax**

Foreign Investment Review Board FINANCE, BANKING, AND ACCOUNTING a nonstatutory body that regulates and advises the federal government on foreign investment in Australia. It was set up in 1976. Abbr **FIRB**

foreign reserve FINANCE, BANKING, AND ACCOUNTING the currency of other countries held by an organization, especially a country's central bank

foreign subsidiary company GENERAL MANAGEMENT see ***subsidiary company***

foreign tax credit FINANCE, BANKING, AND ACCOUNTING a tax advantage for taxes paid to or in another country

formica parachute HR & PERSONNEL unemployment insurance (*slang*)

Fortune 500 FINANCE, BANKING, AND ACCOUNTING a list of the 500 largest industrial companies in the United States, compiled annually by *Fortune* magazine

forum E-COMMERCE a newsgroup, mailing-list discussion group, chat room, or other online area that enables Internet users to read, post, and respond to messages

forward contract FINANCE, BANKING, AND ACCOUNTING a private futures contract for delivery of a commodity

forward cover FINANCE, BANKING, AND ACCOUNTING the purchase for cash of the quantity of a commodity needed to fulfill a futures contract

forward integration OPERATIONS & PRODUCTION a means of guaranteeing ***distribution channels*** for products and services by building relationships with, or taking control of, ***distributors***. Forward integration can free the supplier from the threat or influence of major buyers and can also provide a barrier to market entry by potential rivals. ***Backward integration*** can provide similar guarantees on the supply side. Forward integration is a feature of Japanese ***keiretsu***.

forward interest rate FINANCE, BANKING, AND ACCOUNTING an interest rate specified for a loan to be made at a future date

forward-looking study STATISTICS a survey of a statistical population carried out for a period such as a year after an original survey

forward pricing FINANCE, BANKING, AND ACCOUNTING the establishment of the price of a share in a mutual fund based on the next asset valuation

forward rate FINANCE, BANKING, AND ACCOUNTING an estimate of what an interest rate will be at a specified future time

forward scheduling OPERATIONS & PRODUCTION a method for determining the start times for the various operations involved in a particular ***job***. Forward scheduling is most often used when the operations department sets the delivery date for a job, rather than the sales or marketing departments. Jobs are scheduled for the various operations as the workstations are expected to become available. The customer can then be informed of the projected delivery date. See ***backward scheduling***

fourth level of service GENERAL MANAGEMENT a very high rating in a system of measuring the added value in a product or service

fourth market FINANCE, BANKING, AND ACCOUNTING trading carried out directly without brokers, usually by large institutions

FPA GENERAL MANAGEMENT see ***Financial Planning Association of Australia***

fractional currency FINANCE, BANKING, AND ACCOUNTING the paper money that is in denominations smaller than one unit of a standard national currency

frames E-COMMERCE a feature of ***HTML*** that allows different Web pages to be displayed in one window simultaneously. Frames enable Web sites to keep a standard navigation bar on the screen regardless of the Web page a visitor decides to access. However, there are a number of problems with frames. For instance, pages can be more difficult to print and bookmark because browsers can often only recognize one frame at a time.

franchise MARKETING an agreement enabling a third party to sell or provide products or services owned by a manufacturer or supplier. A franchise is granted by the manufacturer, or **franchisor**, to a **franchisee**, who then retails the product. The franchise is regulated by a **franchise contract**, or **franchise agreement**, that specifies the terms and conditions of the franchise. These may include an obligation for the franchisor to provide national advertising or training for sales staff in return for the meeting of agreed sales targets by the franchisee. The franchisee normally retains a percentage of sales income. In other cases, a franchise may involve the ***licensing*** of a franchisee to manufacture a product to the franchisor's specification, and the sale of this product to retailers. Franchises can also be organized by issue of a ***master franchise***.

franchise agreement MARKETING see ***franchise***

franchise chain MARKETING a number of retail outlets operating the same ***franchise***. A franchise chain may vary in size from a few to many thousands of outlets and in coverage from a small local area to worldwide.

franchise contract MARKETING see ***franchise***

franchisee MARKETING see ***franchise***

franchisor MARKETING see ***franchise***

fraud GENERAL MANAGEMENT the use of dishonesty, deception, or false representation in order to gain a material advantage or to injure the interests of others. Types of fraud include false accounting, theft, third party or investment fraud, employee collusion, and computer fraud.

FRB FINANCE, BANKING, AND ACCOUNTING see ***Federal Reserve Board***

free agent HR & PERSONNEL a worker who operates on a ***freelance*** or ***e-lance*** basis, offering skills and expertise to companies anywhere in the world. A free agent works independently and may follow a pattern of ***portfolio working***.

freebie MARKETING a product or service that is given away, often as a business promotion

free coinage FINANCE, BANKING, AND ACCOUNTING a government's minting of coins from precious metals provided by citizens

free enterprise ECONOMICS the trade carried on in a free-market economy, where resources are allocated on the basis of supply and demand

free gold FINANCE, BANKING, AND ACCOUNTING gold held by a government but not pledged as a reserve for the government's currency

freelance GENERAL MANAGEMENT work undertaken by somebody who is usually self-employed and who may work for several employers at the same time, perhaps on a temporary basis. Freelance workers have been described by ***Charles Handy*** as ideally suited to ***portfolio working***.
CHARLES HANDY (pp. 1000–01)

free market ECONOMICS a market in which supply and demand are unregulated except by the country's competition policy, and rights in physical and intellectual property are upheld

freephone (*U.K.*) MARKETING a telephone service in which the cost of calls to an organization is borne by the organization rather than the caller

freepost (*U.K.*) MARKETING a postal service in which the cost of postage to an organization is borne by the organization rather than the sender

freeware E-COMMERCE free software programs

free worker HR & PERSONNEL somebody who frequently moves from one job or project to another, transferring skills and ideas. The term free worker was coined by the Industrial Society in the United Kingdom in 2000. Free workers have knowledge or skills that organizations value. They do not subscribe to the idea of a job for life or long-term loyalty to any one organization but instead work on short-term ***personal contracts***. They depend largely on networking to find new assignments. They may be ***freelance*** or ***e-lance*** workers and may follow a pattern of ***portfolio working***.

freeze-out GENERAL MANAGEMENT the exclusion of minority ***shareholders*** in a company that has been taken over. A freeze-out provision may exist in a ***takeover*** agreement, which permits the acquiring organization to buy the noncontrolling shares held by small shareholders. A fair price is usually set, and the freeze-out may take place at a specified time, perhaps two to five years after the takeover. A freeze-out can still take place, even if provision for it is not made in a corporate charter, by applying pressure to minority shareholders to sell their shares to the acquiring company.

freight OPERATIONS & PRODUCTION goods loaded for onward transport, most often by sea or by air

freight forwarder OPERATIONS & PRODUCTION an organization that collects shipments from a number of businesses and consolidates them into larger shipments for economies of scale. A freight forwarder often also deals with route selection, price negotiation, and documentation of distribution, and can act as a distribution agent for a business. By consolidating loads, a freight forwarder can negotiate cheaper rates of transportation than the individual businesses and can prebook space to ensure a more rapid delivery schedule.

frequency analysis MARKETING a technique for comparing the number of opportunities to reach the same target audience in different media

frequency distribution STATISTICS the process of dividing a sample of observations in a statistical study into classes and listing the number of observations in each class

frequency polygon STATISTICS a diagrammatic representation showing the values in a ***frequency distribution***

frequently asked question E-COMMERCE see ***FAQ***

frictional unemployment ECONOMICS a situation in which people are temporarily out of the labor market. They could be seeking a new job, incurring search delays as they apply, attending interviews, and relocating.

friction-free market GENERAL MANAGEMENT a market in which there is little differentiation between competing products, so that the customer has exceptional choice

fringe benefits HR & PERSONNEL rewards given or offered to employees in addition to their wages or salaries and included in the ***contract of employment***. Fringe benefits range from share options, company cars, expense accounts, cheap loans, medical insurance, and other types of ***incentive scheme*** to discounts on company products, subsidized meals, and membership of social and health clubs. Many of these benefits are liable for tax. A **cafeteria benefits** scheme permits employees to select from a variety of such benefits, although usually some are deemed to be core and not exchangeable for others. Minor benefits, sometimes appropriated rather than given, are known as **perks**.

front end GENERAL MANAGEMENT the part of an organization that deals with customers on a face-to-face basis

FRSB (*ANZ*) GENERAL MANAGEMENT see ***Financial Reporting Standards Board***

FTP *abbr* E-COMMERCE file transfer protocol, a set of communication rules that allow data or files to be transferred between computers over a network

fulfillment MARKETING the process of responding to customer inquiries, orders, or sales promotion offers

fulfillment house MARKETING an organization that specializes in responding to inquiries, orders, or sales promotion offers on behalf of a client

full bank FINANCE, BANKING, AND ACCOUNTING a local or foreign bank permitted to engage in the full range of domestic and international services

full coupon bond FINANCE, BANKING, AND ACCOUNTING a bond whose interest rate is competitive in the current market

full nine yards
go the full nine yards to follow something through completely or do something to its greatest extent (*slang*)

full-text index E-COMMERCE an index consisting of every single word of every document cataloged

  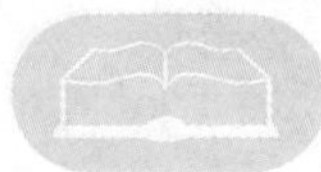    

full-time HR & PERSONNEL standard hours of ***attendance*** in an organization, on the basis of a permanent ***contract of employment***, for example, 9a.m.–5p.m., five days a week

Fully Automated Screen Trading and Electronic Registration (*ANZ*) GENERAL MANAGEMENT see ***FASTER***

fully connected world GENERAL MANAGEMENT a world in which most people and organizations are linked by networks such as the Internet

fully distributed issue FINANCE, BANKING, AND ACCOUNTING an issue of shares sold entirely to investors rather than held by dealers

functional relationship STATISTICS the relationship between the variables in a study, in which there is no bias or any other distorting factor

fund manager FINANCE, BANKING, AND ACCOUNTING somebody who manages the investments of a mutual fund or large financial institution

fund of funds (*S. Africa*) FINANCE, BANKING, AND ACCOUNTING a registered mutual fund that invests in a range of underlying mutual funds and in which subscribers own units in the fund of funds, not in the underlying mutual funds

fungible FINANCE, BANKING, AND ACCOUNTING interchangeable and indistinguishable for business purposes from other items of the same type

funny money FINANCE, BANKING, AND ACCOUNTING an unusual type of financial instrument created by a company

future FINANCE, BANKING, AND ACCOUNTING a contract to deliver a commodity at a future date. Also known as ***futures contract***

future option FINANCE, BANKING, AND ACCOUNTING a contract in which somebody agrees to buy or sell a commodity, currency, or security at an agreed price for delivery in the future

futures commission merchant FINANCE, BANKING, AND ACCOUNTING somebody who acts as a broker for futures contracts. Abbr **FCM**

futures contract FINANCE, BANKING, AND ACCOUNTING = ***future***

futures exchange FINANCE, BANKING, AND ACCOUNTING an exchange on which futures contracts are traded

futures market FINANCE, BANKING, AND ACCOUNTING a market for buying and selling securities, commodities, or currencies that tend to fluctuate in price over a period of time. The market's aim is to reduce the risk of uncertainty about future prices.

futures option FINANCE, BANKING, AND ACCOUNTING a contract in which somebody agrees to buy or sell a commodity, currency, or security at an agreed price for delivery at a future date

futures research GENERAL MANAGEMENT the identification of possible future ***scenarios*** with the aim of anticipating and perhaps influencing what the future holds. Futures research is important to the process of ***issues management***. It normally identifies several possible scenarios for any particular set of circumstances. This enables an informed decision to be made, so that action can be taken to ensure that it is the best scenario that actually comes to pass.

futurize GENERAL MANAGEMENT to ensure that an organization is taking full advantage of the latest technologies

fuzzword GENERAL MANAGEMENT a piece of jargon that is obscure or difficult to understand (*slang*)

FWIW *abbr* GENERAL MANAGEMENT for what it's worth (*slang*)

FYI *abbr* GENERAL MANAGEMENT for your information (*slang*)

G

G7 FINANCE, BANKING, AND ACCOUNTING the group of seven major industrial nations established in 1985 to discuss the world economy, consisting of the United States, Canada, the United Kingdom, France, Germany, Italy, and Japan

G8 FINANCE, BANKING, AND ACCOUNTING the group of eight major industrial nations consisting of ***G7*** plus Russia

gain sharing HR & PERSONNEL a group-based ***bonus scheme*** to share profits from improvements in production efficiency between the employees and the company. There are many variants of gain sharing, the ***Rucker*** and ***Scanlon plans*** being the best known.

game plan GENERAL MANAGEMENT a strategy worked out in advance. The term game plan derives from sporting terminology.

game theory GENERAL MANAGEMENT a mathematical technique used in ***operational research*** to analyze and predict the outcomes of games of strategy and conflicts of interest. Game theory is used to represent conflicts and problems involved in formulating marketing and organizational strategy, with the aim of identifying and implementing optimal strategies. It involves assessing likely strategies to be adopted by players in a given situation under a particular set of rules. It was initially developed by John Von Neumann, who later developed the theory further with Oskar Morgenstern to apply it to economics.

Gantt, Henry Laurence (1861–1919) GENERAL MANAGEMENT U.S. mechanical engineer and consultant. Originated the ***Gantt chart***, which was popularized by Wallace Clark in *The Gantt Chart: a Working Tool of Management* (1952).

✔ MANAGING PROJECTS (pp. 512–13)

Gantt chart GENERAL MANAGEMENT a graphic tool widely used in ***project management*** for planning and scheduling work, setting out tasks and the time periods within which they should be completed. The Gantt chart looks like a lateral bar chart and was initially developed by ***Henry Gantt*** during the 1900s. It is still used both in its traditional form and in the evolved form of program evaluation and review technique.

gap analysis MARKETING a marketing technique used to identify gaps in market or product coverage. In gap analysis, consumer information or requirements are tabulated and matched to product categories in order to identify product or service opportunities or gaps in product planning.

garbatrage FINANCE, BANKING, AND ACCOUNTING stocks that rise because of a takeover but are not connected to the target company (*slang*)

garden leave GENERAL MANAGEMENT a clause in a ***contract of employment*** that allows the employer to send an employee home on full pay, but not require him or her to work, during the employee's contractual ***notice period***. Garden leave thereby prevents the employee from working in competition with the employer until the notice period has expired, by which time any confidential information the employee holds is likely to have become commercially out of date and links with customers will have been broken. Such a clause may be unenforceable if judged by the courts to be in restraint of trade.

gatekeeper GENERAL MANAGEMENT somebody within an organization who controls the flow of information and therefore influences policy

Gates, Bill (*b.* 1955) GENERAL MANAGEMENT U.S. entrepreneur. Founder of the Microsoft™ Corporation, which led the information technology revolution and still dominates the world software market through the Windows™ operating system and the Web browser Internet Explorer. Microsoft has made Gates one of the richest men in the world, although antitrust proceedings have forced him to step down as C.E.O.. His book *Business@the Speed of Thought* (1999) focuses on the impact of technology on business.

gateway E-COMMERCE a point where two or more computer networks meet and can exchange data

gateway page E-COMMERCE a Web page customized to each search engine with specific meta-tags and keywords. These pages are intended to appeal to search engine robots and are not always visible to customers who visit the Web site.

gazelle GENERAL MANAGEMENT a fast-growing and volatile new company (*slang*)

GBE (*ANZ*) GENERAL MANAGEMENT see ***Government Business Enterprise***

GDP *abbr* ECONOMICS gross domestic product, the total flow of services and goods produced by an economy over a quarter or a year, measured by the aggregate value of services and goods at market prices

GDP per capita ECONOMICS *GDP* divided by the country's population so as to achieve a figure per head of population

GEAR FINANCE, BANKING, AND ACCOUNTING Growth, Employment, And Redistribution, the macro-economic reform program of the South African government, intended to foster economic growth, create employment, and redistribute income and opportunities in favor of the poor

Geneen, Harold (1910–97) GENERAL MANAGEMENT British-born business executive. C.E.O. of International Telephone and Telegraph (ITT) in the 1960s and 1970s, who turned a moderately successful U.S. company into a massive, international conglomerate. Geneen built a business machine that was almost without parallel in terms of its systematic efficiency. He explained his approach in *Managing* (1985). ITT was broken up following antitrust proceedings during the 1980s and ***taken over*** in 1997.

HAROLD GENEEN (pp. 1084–85)

general ledger FINANCE, BANKING, AND ACCOUNTING a book that lists all of the financial transactions of a company

general manager GENERAL MANAGEMENT, HR & PERSONNEL a ***manager*** whose work encompasses all areas of an organization. A general manager is traditionally nonspecialist, has a working knowledge of all aspects of an organization's activities, and oversees all operating functions. In large companies and the public sector, specialist managers with expert knowledge may control departments, while a general manager provides unifying ***leadership*** from the top.

Generation X GENERAL MANAGEMENT, HR & PERSONNEL the generation of people born between 1963 and 1981 who entered the workplace from the 1980s onward, bringing new attitudes to working life that run contrary to traditional corporate expectations. The term was popularized by the writing of Douglas Coupland and also by ***Bruce Tulgan*** in *Managing Generation X* (1995). Those who belong to Generation X are said to be not solely motivated by money, but they look to a ***work-life balance***, favor ***flexible working***, embrace the concept of ***employability***, and value opportunities for learning, self-advancement, and new challenges. Human resource management practices are increasingly being adapted to accommodate the favored new ways of working.

generic strategy GENERAL MANAGEMENT a strategy for marketing products or services. Generic strategy is a term introduced by ***Michael Porter***. He suggested there are three generic strategies for marketing products or services: cost leadership, differentiation, and focus. The first implies the supply of products in a more cost-effective way than competitors; the second refers to adding value to products or services; and the third focuses on a specific product market segment with the aim of establishing a ***monopoly***.

MICHAEL PORTER (pp. 1038–39)

geographical information systems MARKETING technology used to integrate maps and data to provide multidimensional marketing information. Abbr **GIS**

Ghoshal, Sumantra (*b.* 1946) GENERAL MANAGEMENT Indian-born academic. Author of work that has shifted its focus from international ***strategy*** to the importance of people and ***creativity***. Ghoshal put forward a new model of transnational enterprise to cope with the complexities of ***competition*** and the growing global marketplace. He also suggested the **three Ps** of Purpose, Process, and People to replace the old model of Strategy, Structure, and Systems and proposed a new moral contract. He first came to prominence with *Managing Across Borders* (1989), coauthored with ***Christopher Bartlett***.

ghost rider GENERAL MANAGEMENT somebody who claims to have been in a vehicle that was involved in an accident in order to claim compensation (*slang*)

GIF E-COMMERCE graphics interchange format, a file used to compress and store images for transfer via the Internet. GIF files are more suited to images without much detail. Photographic images can be compressed using ***JPEG*** files.

gift-leaseback FINANCE, BANKING, AND ACCOUNTING the practice of giving somebody a property and then leasing it back, usually for tax advantage or charitable purposes

gig GENERAL MANAGEMENT an individual project or assignment, typical of a working pattern made up of a series of one-off projects rather than a career with a single employer

gigabyte GENERAL MANAGEMENT a measure of the memory capacity of a computer. One gigabyte equals 1024 megabytes.

Gilbreth, Frank (1868–1924) GENERAL MANAGEMENT U.S. consulting engineer. Formed a husband-and-wife team with ***Lillian Gilbreth*** and pioneered the principles of ***motion study***, which embraced ***work simplification***, and took a strong interest in ***occupational psychology***. Their work, which straddled the ***scientific management*** and ***human relations*** schools of management, is recorded in *Writings of the Gilbreths* (1953), edited by William R. Spriegel and Clark E. Myers.

Gilbreth, Lillian (1878–1972) GENERAL MANAGEMENT U.S. consulting engineer. See ***Gilbreth, Frank***

Ginnie Mae FINANCE, BANKING, AND ACCOUNTING see ***GNMA***

GIS MARKETING see ***geographical information systems***

Glacier studies GENERAL MANAGEMENT research experiments conducted at the Glacier Metal Company in London from 1948 to 1965 to investigate the development of group relations, the effects of ***change***, and employee roles and responsibilities. The Glacier studies were conducted by the Tavistock Institute of Human Relations with the research being headed by ***Elliot Jaques*** and ***Fred Emery***. Findings from the initial study came from a methodology called "working-through," which examined possible social and personal factors at play in any potential dispute. From this arose an early form of works council where employees could ***participate*** in setting policy for their department. It was also discovered that employees felt the need to have their role and status defined in a way acceptable to both themselves and their colleagues. This research into job roles led Jaques to come up with the notion of the ***time span of discretion***, according to which all jobs, no matter how strictly defined, have some level of content that requires judgment and therefore discretion by the jobholder. Jaques then examined this phenomenon in bureaucratic organizations. In defining a ***bureaucracy*** as a hierarchical system in which employees are accountable to their bosses for the work they do, he took a different stance from ***Max Weber***. Much like the ***Hawthorne experiments***, the Glacier studies had far-reaching implications for the way organizations were managed. The initial findings were written up by Jaques in *The Changing Culture of a Factory* (1951). In 1965, Jaques published the *Glacier Project Papers* with ***Wilfred Brown***, the managing director of Glacier.

MAX WEBER (pp. 1060–61)

glad-hand GENERAL MANAGEMENT to shake hands with and greet people at a business party or meeting (*slang*)

glass ceiling GENERAL MANAGEMENT the level in an organization beyond which women are supposedly unable to gain ***promotion***. A glass ceiling often exists at ***senior management*** level and is perceived as an invisible barrier to career progression for women. ***Equal opportunities*** policies and legislation aim to break such ceilings to make equal career advancement opportunities available to both men and women.

Glass-Steagall Act FINANCE, BANKING, AND ACCOUNTING a law that enforces the separation of the banking and brokerage industries

glaze GENERAL MANAGEMENT to doze or sleep with the eyes open during a business meeting (*slang*)

global bond FINANCE, BANKING, AND ACCOUNTING = ***Eurobond***

global brand MARKETING the brand name of a product that has worldwide recognition. A global brand has the advantage of economies of scale in terms of production, recognition, and packaging. While the product or brand itself remains the same, the marketing must take into account the local market conditions and the resulting marketing campaign must be tailored accordingly. Care must also be taken to ensure that there is nothing offensive in terms of the name or packaging in the various cultures and languages. A problem with global branding is that if problems are experienced in one country, there could be worldwide repercussions for the brand. Also known as ***global product***

global hedge FINANCE, BANKING, AND ACCOUNTING = ***macrohedge***

globalization GENERAL MANAGEMENT the creation of international strategies by organizations for overseas expansion and operation on a worldwide level. The process of globalization has been precipitated by a number of factors including rapid technology developments that make global communications possible, political developments such as the fall of communism, and transport developments that make traveling faster and more frequent. These produce greater development opportunities for companies with the opening up of additional markets, allow greater customer harmonization as a result of the increase in shared cultural values, and provide a superior competitive position with lower operating costs in other countries and access to new raw materials, resources, and investment opportunities.

global marketing MARKETING a marketing strategy used mainly by multinational companies to sell goods or services internationally. Global marketing requires that there is harmonization between the marketing policies for different countries and that the ***marketing mix*** for the different countries can be adapted to the local market conditions. Global marketing is sometimes used to refer to overseas expansion efforts through ***licensing***, ***franchises***, and ***joint ventures***.

global pricing contract OPERATIONS & PRODUCTION a contract between a customer and a supplier whereby the supplier agrees to charge the customer the same price for the delivery of parts or services anywhere in the world. As ***globalization*** increases, more customers are likely to press their suppliers for global pricing contracts. Through such contracts suppliers can benefit by gaining access to new markets and growing their business, achieving economies of scale, developing strong relationships with customers, and thereby gaining a ***competitive advantage*** that is difficult for competitors to break. There are risks involved, too, for example, being in the middle of a conflict between a customer's head office and its local business units, or being tied to one customer when there are more attractive customers to serve.

global product MARKETING see ***global brand***

glocalization GENERAL MANAGEMENT the process of tailoring products or services to different local markets around the world. Glocalization is a combination of globalization and localization. Improved communication and the advancements in technology have made worldwide markets accessible to even small companies but, rather than being homogenous, the global market is in fact made up of many different localities. Success in a globalized environment is more likely if products are not globalized or ***mass marketed***, but glocalized and customized for individual local communities that have different needs and different cultural approaches.

glue GENERAL MANAGEMENT something such as information that unifies organizations, supply chains, and other commercial groups

GmbH GENERAL MANAGEMENT Gesellschaft mit beschränkter Haftung, the German equivalent of a corporation

GNMA *abbr* FINANCE, BANKING, AND ACCOUNTING Government National Mortgage Association, a U.S.-owned corporation that issues mortgage-backed bonds. Also known as ***Ginnie Mae***

GNP *abbr* ECONOMICS gross national product, GDP plus domestic residents' income from investment abroad less income earned in the domestic market accruing to noncitizens abroad

GNP per capita ECONOMICS ***GNP*** divided by the country's population so as to achieve a figure per head of population

goal GENERAL MANAGEMENT see ***objective***

gofer GENERAL MANAGEMENT an employee who carries out menial duties for a manager or another employee (*slang*)

go-go fund FINANCE, BANKING, AND ACCOUNTING a mutual fund that trades heavily and predominantly in high-return, high-risk investments

gold bond FINANCE, BANKING, AND ACCOUNTING a bond for which gold is collateral, often issued by mining companies

goldbricker *or* **gold brick** HR & PERSONNEL a lazy employee who attempts to get away with doing the least possible amount of work (*slang*)

gold certificate FINANCE, BANKING, AND ACCOUNTING a document that shows ownership of gold

golden handshake *or* **golden goodbye** HR & PERSONNEL a sum of money given to a senior executive on his or her involuntary departure from an employing organization as a form of ***severance pay***. A golden handshake can be offered when an executive is required to leave before the expiration of his or her contract, for example, because of a ***merger*** or ***corporate restructuring***. It is intended as compensation for loss of office. It can be a very large sum of money, but often it is not related to the perceived performance of the executive concerned. A golden handshake is sometimes known as a **golden goodbye**. (*slang*)

golden hello HR & PERSONNEL a welcome package for a new ***employee*** that may include a ***bonus*** and share options. A golden hello is designed as an incentive to attract employees. Some of the contents of the welcome package may be contingent on the performance of the employee.

golden parachute HR & PERSONNEL a clause inserted in the ***contract of employment*** of a senior employee that details a financial package payable if the employee is dismissed. A golden parachute provides an executive with a measure of financial security and may be payable if the employee leaves the organization following a ***takeover*** or ***merger***, or is dismissed as a result of poor performance. Also known as ***golden umbrella***

golden rolodex GENERAL MANAGEMENT the small group of experts who are most frequently quoted in news stories or asked to appear on television to give an opinion. "Rolodex" is a trademark for a desktop card index. (*slang*)

golden share FINANCE, BANKING, AND ACCOUNTING a controlling shareholding retained by a government in a company that has been privatized after having been in public ownership

golden umbrella HR & PERSONNEL see ***golden parachute***

Goldratt, Eliyahu M. (*b.* 1948) GENERAL MANAGEMENT Israeli author and educator. Disseminator of theories, through the medium of novels, on optimizing ***production*** methods and ***project management***. Goldratt explained the technique of ***optimized production technology*** in *The Goal* (1993, co-authored), and his theory later broadened into the ***Theory of Constraints*** (see ***optimized production technology***). His third novel applies the concept of the theory of constraints to ***project management***.

gold reserve FINANCE, BANKING, AND ACCOUNTING gold coins or bullion held by a central bank to support a paper currency and provide security for borrowing

gold standard FINANCE, BANKING, AND ACCOUNTING a system in which a currency unit is defined in terms of its value in gold

Goleman, Daniel (*b.* 1946) GENERAL MANAGEMENT U.S. psychologist and journalist. Developer of the concept of ***emotional intelligence***, who is credited with making it generally accessible, initially through the book of the same name (1995). He was influenced by ***Richard E. Boyatzis***.

DANIEL GOLEMAN (pp. 996–97)

Goods and Services Tax

1. FINANCE, BANKING, AND ACCOUNTING a 3% tax payable on all purchase transactions. Abbr **GST**

2. GENERAL MANAGEMENT a government-imposed consumption tax, currently of 10%, added to the retail cost of goods and services in Australia

3. GENERAL MANAGEMENT a Canadian tax on goods and services. It was a value-added tax and was replaced by the ***harmonized sales tax***. Abbr **GST**

good 'til cancel FINANCE, BANKING, AND ACCOUNTING relating to an order to buy or sell a security that is effective until an investor cancels it, up to a maximum of 60 days

good title FINANCE, BANKING, AND ACCOUNTING the legally unquestionable title to property. Also known as ***clear title***

goodwill GENERAL MANAGEMENT an intangible asset of a company that includes factors such as reputation, contacts, and expertise, for which a buyer of the company may have to pay a premium

✔ HOW TO CALCULATE THE VALUE OF GOODWILL AND PATENTS (p. 860)

gopher an employee who carries out menial duties for a manager or another employee (*slang*)

go plural GENERAL MANAGEMENT to engage in a form of ***downshifting*** by leaving full-time employment in order to undertake ***part-time work*** or ***portfolio working*** (*slang*)

go public GENERAL MANAGEMENT to float the shares of a ***company*** on a stock exchange, thereby changing the company status to that of a ***public limited company*** (*slang*)

go-slow HR & PERSONNEL a protest in which employees demonstrate their dissatisfaction by carrying out their work slowly. A go-slow is a form of ***industrial action*** designed to inconvenience an employer without the more serious effects of an all-out ***strike***.

Government Business Enterprise GENERAL MANAGEMENT an Australian business that is fully or partly owned by the state. Abbr **GBE**

government gazette (*ANZ*) GENERAL MANAGEMENT a journal published by the Australian federal government or a state or territory government that reports all actions and decisions made by that body

Government National Mortgage Association FINANCE, BANKING, AND ACCOUNTING see ***GNMA***

gradual retirement HR & PERSONNEL see ***phased retirement***

grapevine GENERAL MANAGEMENT an informal communication network within an organization that conveys information through unofficial channels independent of management control. Information travels much more quickly through the grapevine than through formal channels and may become distorted. A grapevine may reinterpret official corporate messages or spread gossip and rumor in the absence of effective organization channels. It can, however, also complement official communication, provide feedback, and strengthen social relationships within the organization.

graph GENERAL MANAGEMENT a diagram depicting the relationship between dependent and independent variables through the use of lines, curves, or figures on horizontal and vertical axes. Time is the most common independent variable, showing how the dependent variable has altered over a defined period.

graphical user interface E-COMMERCE an easy-to-use interface or operating system that allows a user to give a computer instructions by using icons, menus, and windows

Graphics Interchange Format E-COMMERCE see ***GIF***

graphology HR & PERSONNEL the study of handwriting styles in an attempt to identify personality traits and to predict how somebody may react in particular situations. Graphology is sometimes used as part of the ***recruitment*** process. Because it cannot be substantiated, it is not recommended as a formal test and tends to be used informally.

grass ceiling GENERAL MANAGEMENT the set of social and cultural factors that discourage or prevent women from using golf to conduct business (*slang*)

graybar-land GENERAL MANAGEMENT a state of vagueness induced by staring at the gray bar that appears on a computer screen when the computer is processing something (*slang*)

gray knight GENERAL MANAGEMENT see ***knight***

gray market MARKETING

1. a ***market*** in which goods are sold that have been manufactured abroad and imported. A gray market product is one that has been imported legally, in contrast to one on the ***black market***, which is illegal. Such markets arise when there is a supply shortage, usually for exclusive goods, and offer goods for sale at lower prices than the equivalent goods manufactured in the home country.

2. the market segment occupied by older members of a population

3. the unofficial trading of securities that have not yet been formally issued

gray marketing MARKETING marketing aimed at older age groups

gray matter GENERAL MANAGEMENT older and more experienced business experts who are hired by young companies to give an impression of seriousness and reliability (*slang*)

greater fool theory FINANCE, BANKING, AND ACCOUNTING the investing strategy that assumes it is wise to buy a stock that is not worth its current price. The assumption is that somebody will buy it from you later for an even greater price.

great man theory GENERAL MANAGEMENT the idea that ***leaders*** possess innately superior qualities that distinguish them from other people, including the ability to capture the imagination and loyalty of the masses

green ban (*ANZ*) GENERAL MANAGEMENT a ban imposed by unions on work that is perceived to pose a threat to the natural environment or an area of historical significance

green issues GENERAL MANAGEMENT see ***environmental management***

greenmail GENERAL MANAGEMENT, FINANCE, BANKING, AND ACCOUNTING the purchase of enough of a company's shares to threaten it with takeover, so that the company is forced to buy back the shares at a higher price to avoid the takeover (*slang*)

green marketing MARKETING marketing that highlights an organization's environmentally friendly policies or achievements

green pound ECONOMICS the fixed European Currency Unit (ECU) in which prices of agricultural goods in the European Union are set

green taxes FINANCE, BANKING, AND ACCOUNTING taxes levied to discourage behavior that will be harmful to the environment

greenwash GENERAL MANAGEMENT information produced by an organization to present an environmentally responsible public image (*slang*)

grievance procedure HR & PERSONNEL a process for settling or redressing employee complaints. A grievance procedure is part of an organization's ***personnel policy*** and sets out how an employee with a work-related grievance can bring up the issue and how it may be addressed and resolved. Such a procedure should focus on settling the matter as soon as possible, so as to promote employee satisfaction and prevent the issue escalating into a ***dispute***.

✔ SETTING UP A GRIEVANCE PROCEDURE (pp. 452–53)

gross FINANCE, BANKING, AND ACCOUNTING total, before consideration of taxes

gross domestic fixed capital formation ECONOMICS investment in the fixed asset in an economy, including depreciation

gross domestic product ECONOMICS see ***GDP***

gross lease FINANCE, BANKING, AND ACCOUNTING a lease that does not require the lessee to pay for things the owner usually pays for. See ***net lease***

gross misconduct HR & PERSONNEL behavior in the workplace that may lead to a warning or to dismissal in extreme cases. Most contracts of employment provide guidelines on the type of behavior that constitutes gross misconduct.

gross national product ECONOMICS see ***GNP***

gross negligence GENERAL MANAGEMENT see ***negligence***

gross profit GENERAL MANAGEMENT sales revenue less the cost of goods sold

gross profit margin GENERAL MANAGEMENT see ***profit margin***

group capacity assessment GENERAL MANAGEMENT the application of ***work measurement*** techniques such as ***activity sampling*** and ***standard time*** data to clerical, administrative, and indirect staff to measure group effort and establish optimum performance levels. Group capacity assessment is used to plan and control payroll costs for groups of clerical and administrative workers.

group certificate (*ANZ*) HR & PERSONNEL a document provided by an employer that records an employee's income, income tax payments, and superannuation contributions during the previous financial year

group discussion MARKETING a research technique in which groups of people discuss attitudes to a product or organization

group dynamics HR & PERSONNEL the interaction and interpersonal relationships between members of a group and the ways in which groups form, function, and dissolve. Group dynamics is an important aspect of successful ***teamwork*** and is a factor influencing the outcome of any form of group activity, including ***training*** courses. Issues of power, influence, and interpersonal conflict all affect dynamics and group performance. One means of helping people to create positive group dynamics is ***sensitivity training***.

group incentive scheme HR & PERSONNEL a reward system giving ***bonuses*** to workers in a team. A group incentive scheme is designed

to promote effective ***teamwork***, as the bonus is dependent on the performance and output of the team as a whole.

group interview HR & PERSONNEL see ***group selection***

group investment FINANCE, BANKING, AND ACCOUNTING an investment made by more than one person

group selection HR & PERSONNEL a method of ***recruitment*** in which candidates are assessed in groups rather than individually. Group selection can take place in an ***assessment center***. It should not be confused with a ***panel interview***, which involves one candidate but several interviewers. Also known as ***group interview***

group technology OPERATIONS & PRODUCTION the practice of gathering operations and resources for the manufacture of specific components or products into groups or cells with the aim of simplifying manufacturing operations. Group technology is an attempt to take advantage of the benefits of both ***batch production*** and ***flow production***. Similar tasks or products are identified and are grouped into families. This requires a robust coding or classification scheme. The manufacturing resources, including workers, for each family are then grouped together into cells. The sense of ownership encouraged by such organization has resulted in benefits including improved quality, ***productivity***, and ***motivation*** of employees, as well as reductions in work in progress, inventory, and materials movement. Also known as ***cellular manufacturing***, ***cellular production***

groupthink GENERAL MANAGEMENT a phenomenon that occurs during ***decision making*** or ***problem solving*** when a team's desire to reach an agreement overrides its ability to appraise the problem properly. It is similar to the ***Abilene paradox*** in that it is based on people's desire to conform and please others.

group tool GENERAL MANAGEMENT an electronic tool such as videoconferencing, networking, or electronic mail that allows people in different locations to collaborate on a project

groupware GENERAL MANAGEMENT software that enables a group whose members are based in different locations to work together and share information. Groupware enables collective working by providing communal diaries, address books, work planners, bulletin boards, newsletters, and so on, in electronic format on a closed network. This network may take the form of an ***intranet***. Groupware can be used to facilitate collaborative ***project management*** or to coordinate any kind of work involving input from more than one person, and is particularly useful to those working in a ***virtual team***.

Grove, Andrew S. (*b.* 1936) GENERAL MANAGEMENT U.S. business executive. Chairman of Intel Corporation, which became the world's largest semiconductor manufacturer. He coined the term ***strategic inflection point***, which he discusses in *Only the Paranoid Survive* (1996).

Growth, Employment, And Redistribution FINANCE, BANKING, AND ACCOUNTING see ***GEAR***

growth and income fund FINANCE, BANKING, AND ACCOUNTING a mutual fund that tries to maximize growth of capital while paying significant dividends

growth capital FINANCE, BANKING, AND ACCOUNTING funding that allows a company to accelerate its growth. For new startup companies, growth capital is the second stage of funding after ***seed money***.

growth company ECONOMICS a company whose contribution to the economy is growing because it is increasing its workforce or earning increased foreign exchange for its exported goods

growth curve STATISTICS a line plotted on a graph that shows statistically an increase over a period of time

growth fund FINANCE, BANKING, AND ACCOUNTING a mutual fund that tries to maximize growth of capital without regard to dividends

growth rate ECONOMICS the rate of an economy's growth as measured by its technical progress, the growth of its labor, and the increase in its ***capital stock***

growth share

1. FINANCE, BANKING, AND ACCOUNTING a stock or share that offers investors the prospect of longer-term earnings, rather than a quick return

2. GENERAL MANAGEMENT a share that has been rising greatly in value, relative to its industry or to the market as a whole

growth stock FINANCE, BANKING, AND ACCOUNTING stock that offers investors the prospect of longer-term earnings, rather than a quick return

grupo GENERAL MANAGEMENT a group of companies in Mexico, based on a parent company or central family. Grupos may be involved in a cross-section of industries, much like a ***conglomerate company***. Some grupos are integrated financially, legally, and administratively, while others have a looser structure with stockholding interests and interrelated directorates.

GST FINANCE, BANKING, AND ACCOUNTING see ***goods and services tax***

guan xi GENERAL MANAGEMENT a Mandarin term for "connections," used to describe the level of personal trust required between business partners

guaranteed employment HR & PERSONNEL an arrangement to protect employees in the event of a shortage of work. Guaranteed employment requires the payment of a minimum wage for a maximum number of workless days or hours. In some cases, a worker may qualify for a legal right to a guaranteed payment. An employer cannot lay off workers without a term in the individual ***contract of employment***. The right to do so usually lies in a ***collective agreement*** incorporated into the contract of employment. Also known as ***guaranteed wage***, ***guaranteed week***

guaranteed investment contract FINANCE, BANKING, AND ACCOUNTING an investment instrument issued by an insurance company that guarantees interest but not principal. Also called ***guaranteed interest contract***

guaranteed wage HR & PERSONNEL see ***guaranteed employment***

guaranteed week HR & PERSONNEL see ***guaranteed employment***

guarantor FINANCE, BANKING, AND ACCOUNTING a person or organization that guarantees repayment of a loan if the borrower defaults or is unable to pay

guard book MARKETING a book or folder for storing copies of published advertisements

guerilla marketing MARKETING a marketing technique, the aim of which is to damage the market share of competitors

GUI GENERAL MANAGEMENT see ***graphical user interface***

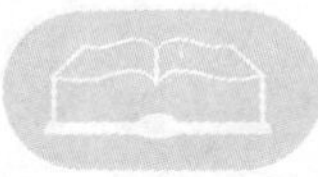

Gulick, **Luther** (1892–1993) GENERAL MANAGEMENT U.S. academic. Member of President Roosevelt's Committee on Administrative Management (1936–38), who, following the earlier work of ***Henri Fayol***, coined the acronym ***POSDCORB*** to describe the functions of management.

GW *abbr* E-COMMERCE payment gateway

gweeping GENERAL MANAGEMENT the activity of spending many hours at a time surfing the Internet *(slang)*

H

hacker E-COMMERCE somebody who gains unauthorized access to computer systems, often to corrupt or steal stored data

haggle FINANCE, BANKING, AND ACCOUNTING to negotiate a price with a buyer or seller by the gradual raising of offers and lowering of asking prices until a mutually agreeable price is reached

half-normal plot STATISTICS a plot of statistical data used to check for the presence of ***outliers*** in the data

Hamel, **Gary** (*b.* 1954) GENERAL MANAGEMENT U.S. academic. With ***C. K. Prahalad***, introduced the concept of ***core competences*** and argued for an innovative approach to ***corporate strategy*** creation, based on emotion as well as analysis. They coauthored *Competing for the Future* (1994), which set out their revolutionary but well-respected view of strategy.
C. K. PRAHALAD (pp. 1040–41)

Hammer, **Michael** (*b.* 1948) GENERAL MANAGEMENT U.S. academic and consultant. Advocate of reengineering, a concept he explained in the book *Reengineering the Corporation* (1993), coauthored with ***James Champy***.
✔ IMPLEMENTING BUSINESS PROCESS REENGINEERING (pp. 506–07)

Hampel, **Sir Ronald Claus** (*b.* 1932) GENERAL MANAGEMENT British business executive. Former chairman of ICI and chairman of the Committee on ***Corporate Governance*** 1995–98.

hand-hold HR & PERSONNEL to reassure a nervous client or colleague *(slang)*

hand off *(U.S.)* *(& Canada)* GENERAL MANAGEMENT to transfer responsibility for a project

hands-off GENERAL MANAGEMENT without continuing management attention

hands-on GENERAL MANAGEMENT favoring firsthand personal involvement in a task

Handy, **Charles** (*b.* 1932) GENERAL MANAGEMENT Irish-born academic, writer, and social commentator. Known for his work on ***organization structures***, the future of work, and the implications of change for people. Since his landmark book *Understanding Organizations* (1976), he has originated concepts such as the ***shamrock organization***, the ***federal organization***, the ***doughnut principle***, and ***portfolio working***.
CHARLES HANDY (pp. 1000–01)

hang out loan FINANCE, BANKING, AND ACCOUNTING the amount of a loan that is still outstanding after the termination of the loan

Hang Seng index FINANCE, BANKING, AND ACCOUNTING an index of the prices of selected shares on the Hong Kong Stock Exchange

happy camper GENERAL MANAGEMENT somebody who has no grievances against his or her employer *(slang)*

hard currency ECONOMICS a currency that is traded in a foreign exchange market and for which demand is persistently high relative to its supply

hard disk E-COMMERCE a thin rigid magnetized disk inside a computer, used for storing data and programs

hard landing ECONOMICS a sustained period of growth that ends with the economy moving rapidly into recession and business stagnation

hard sell MARKETING a heavily persuasive and highly pressured approach used to sell a product or service. In a hard sell situation, salespeople may use incentives such as a limited special offer or a discount to encourage people to buy, or to sign an agreement to buy on the spot.

hard systems GENERAL MANAGEMENT see ***systems method***

hardware E-COMMERCE the physical components of a computer system such as the processor, keyboard, and monitor. **Software** is the name given to operating systems and applications.

harmonization GENERAL MANAGEMENT
1. the resolution of inequalities in the ***pay*** and ***conditions of employment*** between manual and ***white-collar workers***
2. the alignment of the systems of pay and benefits of two companies on ***merger***, acquisition, or takeover
3. the removal of discrimination between full- and part-time workers
4. the convergence of social regulation in the European Union

harmonized sales tax FINANCE, BANKING, AND ACCOUNTING a Canadian tax on goods and services. It is a value-added tax that replaced the Goods and Services Tax. Abbr **HST**

Harrigan, **Kathryn Mary Rudie** (*b.* 1951) GENERAL MANAGEMENT U.S. academic. Known for her work on mature and declining industries, rather than growth industries, and on ***strategic alliances***.

Harvey-Jones, **Sir John** (*b.* 1924) GENERAL MANAGEMENT British business executive. Chairman of ICI 1982–87, who recorded his reflections on leadership in *Making it Happen* (1987). After his retirement, he advised ailing British companies in a television series, "Troubleshooter."

hate site GENERAL MANAGEMENT = ***anti-site***

Hawthorne effect GENERAL MANAGEMENT see ***Hawthorne experiments***

Hawthorne experiments GENERAL MANAGEMENT a series of studies undertaken at the Hawthorne plant of Western Electric in the United States from which ***Elton Mayo*** concluded that an approach emphasizing ***employee participation*** can improve ***productivity***. The Hawthorne experiments began in 1924 as a study conducted by the National Research Council into the relationship between workplace lighting and employee efficiency, and was then extended to include ***wage incentives*** and ***rest periods***. It was found that whatever variations were applied upward or downward, output rose, and this was termed the **Hawthorne effect**. The increased productivity was attributed to several causes, including small group size, earnings, the novelty of being part of an experiment, and the increased attention given to the employees being studied. The style of the supervisor, which was relaxed and friendly, in contrast to the then standard practice, was found to be particularly important. In a second group of employees, however, it was observed that, as the experiments progressed, output was restricted, and that whatever the incentive, the group showed a resistance to it. In 1929, and 1930, Elton Mayo visited Hawthorne. He

linked supervisory style and levels of morale with productivity. High productivity resulted from an engaged supervisory style that encouraged participation. Low productivity resulted when a supervisor remained remote and retained a traditional supervisory role. The Hawthorne experiments established the importance of management style and interpersonal skills to organizational success.
ELTON MAYO (pp. 1020–21)

Hayes, **Robert H.** (*b.* 1936) GENERAL MANAGEMENT U.S. academic. Harvard professor who came to prominence following the publication in 1981 of his coauthored *Harvard Business Review* article, "Managing our way to economic decline." Hayes argued that U.S. manufacturing companies were at a competitive disadvantage as a result of a too heavy reliance on detached, precisely structured analysis. A more positive future was foreseen by Hayes in the cowritten *Restoring our Competitive Edge* (1984), which examines the structural changes required of manufacturing in order to succeed and provides some guidance on how management practices need to change.

hazardous substance GENERAL MANAGEMENT a substance that creates a potential danger to people in the workplace. Employers have a duty to assess the risks from hazardous substances to personnel and customers, and to ensure that no one is endangered. Substances classed as hazards could be raw materials used in production, fumes, or other byproducts resulting from workplace activities. They may also be substances linked to seemingly innocuous activities, for example, cleaning fluids and toner for photocopiers. ***Health and safety*** policies must cover this area, and ***risk assessments*** must be carried out to ascertain the potential dangers.

head
be in over your head GENERAL MANAGEMENT to be attempting more or more difficult work than you can really do (*slang*)

headcount HR & PERSONNEL the total number of ***employees*** in an organization

headhunting HR & PERSONNEL the practice of approaching people already working for one company with an offer of a job at another. Headhunting is usually carried out by a recruiter—either an employee within a company or an employment agency—who keeps an eye on the performance of targeted personnel. The recruiter then matches high-performing personnel with job vacancies, contacting individuals directly, without the knowledge of the employer, with a job offer. Headhunters most often perform ***executive searches***, but they may also work at lower levels with the intention of picking out those with management potential. Headhunting is often seen as poaching, and it can create employee retention problems, since a company's best staff can be tempted to leave by better job offers.

headline rate of inflation ECONOMICS a measure of inflation that takes account of home owners' mortgage costs

heads of agreement GENERAL MANAGEMENT the most important elements of a commercial agreement

health and safety HR & PERSONNEL, GENERAL MANAGEMENT the area of policy and legislation covering employee well-being. Health and safety within an organization is often coordinated by a particular person, but it is the responsibility of all employees. Maintaining a safe working environment and safe working practices and ensuring that employees' health is not detrimentally affected by their work is a statutory duty of organizations.

health screening HR & PERSONNEL the checking of employees' health to ensure they are fit for work. Health screening can take the form of **preemployment screening**, which takes place after a new employee has been appointed, but before employment commences. It also is a feature of ***occupational health*** schemes and involves the monitoring of employee health at work. This is particularly important if the work involves hazardous substances or strenuous physical conditions. Health screening can also be used, for example, to detect substance abuse or to carry out eyesight tests for users of VDUs.

heatseeker E-COMMERCE somebody who always buys the latest version of a software product as soon as it comes on the market (*slang*)

heavy hitter GENERAL MANAGEMENT an executive or company that performs extremely well (*slang*)

heavy site E-COMMERCE see ***sticky site*** (*slang*)

hedge fund FINANCE, BANKING, AND ACCOUNTING a mutual fund that takes considerable risks, including heavy investment in unconventional instruments, in the hope of generating great profits

held order FINANCE, BANKING, AND ACCOUNTING an order that a dealer does not process immediately, often because of its great size

Helgeson, **Sally** (*b.* 1948) GENERAL MANAGEMENT U.S. consultant and author. Researcher on the effects of changing technology, demographics, and the knowledge economy on organizations and ***leadership***. Her book *The Female Advantage* (1990) considers women's ***management styles***.

helicopter view GENERAL MANAGEMENT an overview of a problem (*slang*)

helpline MARKETING a telephone service operated by a company that offers customers product information, advice, or technical support

Henderson, **Bruce** (1915–92) GENERAL MANAGEMENT Australian engineer and consultant. Founder of the Boston Consulting Group (1963), a firm that has specialized in ***corporate strategy*** and conceived the ***experience curve*** and the ***Boston Box***.

Herzberg, **Frederick** (*b.* 1923) GENERAL MANAGEMENT U.S. psychologist and academic. Took a particular interest in ***motivation*** and put forward the "hygiene-motivation theory" of ***job satisfaction***. Herzberg was a coauthor of *The Motivation to Work* (1959) and the author of "One More Time: How do You Motivate Employees?" (1968), one of the most requested reprints of all time from *Harvard Business Review*.
FREDERICK HERZBERG (pp. 1002–03)
✔ MOTIVATING YOUR STAFF IN A TIME OF CHANGE (pp. 372–73)

heuristics GENERAL MANAGEMENT a method for ***problem solving*** or ***decision making*** that arrives at solutions through exploratory means such as experimentation, trial and error, or evaluation

HHOK *abbr* GENERAL MANAGEMENT ha ha only kidding (*slang*)

high concept GENERAL MANAGEMENT a compelling idea expressed clearly and economically

highdome GENERAL MANAGEMENT a scientist. This term stems from the stereotype of scientists, who are often depicted as having high foreheads that are supposed to be a sign of intelligence. (*slang*)

high-end GENERAL MANAGEMENT relating to the most expensive, most advanced, or most powerful in a range of things, for example, computers

high-powered GENERAL MANAGEMENT having great dynamism and ability

high-premium convertible debenture FINANCE, BANKING, AND ACCOUNTING a convertible bond sold at a high premium that offers a competitive rate of interest and has a long term

high-pressure MARKETING a selling technique in which the sales representative attempts to persuade a buyer very forcefully and persistently

high-risk company GENERAL MANAGEMENT a company that is exposed to high levels of business risk

high street *(U.K.)* GENERAL MANAGEMENT a main street considered as an important retail area

hip shooter GENERAL MANAGEMENT an executive who follows his or her immediate instinct when responding to a question or problem rather than considering it rationally *(slang)*

hired gun *(slang)*
1. HR & PERSONNEL somebody who works for whoever will contract for his or her services for as long as he or she is needed for a particular project
2. GENERAL MANAGEMENT an advisor, lawyer, or accountant brought into a company during a takeover battle

hire purchase *(U.K.)* FINANCE, BANKING, AND ACCOUNTING = ***installment plan***

historic pricing FINANCE, BANKING, AND ACCOUNTING the establishment of the price of a share in a mutual fund on the basis of the most recent values of its holdings

hit E-COMMERCE a measure of the number of files or images that are sent to a browser from a Web site in response to a single request. Because Web sites typically contain more than one file or image, the number of hits is usually greater than the number of requestors.

hit squad GENERAL MANAGEMENT a company's acquisitions team *(slang)*

hockey stick FINANCE, BANKING, AND ACCOUNTING a performance curve typical of businesses in their early stages that descends then rises sharply in a straight line, creating a shape similar to that of a hockey stick *(slang)*

Hofstede, Geert H. *(b.* 1928) GENERAL MANAGEMENT Dutch academic and business executive. Identified four work-related dimensions of national culture, thus providing a framework for understanding cultural differences within business. His work, first published in *Culture's Consequences* (1980), has been extended by ***Fons Trompenaars***.
GEERT HOFSTEDE (pp. 1004–05)

holdback E-COMMERCE funds from a merchant's credit card transactions held in reserve for a predetermined time by the merchant account provider to cover possible disputed charges. Also known as ***reserve account***

holding company GENERAL MANAGEMENT a parent organization that owns and controls other companies. In the United Kingdom, a holding company has to own over half of the nominal share capital in companies that are then deemed to be its subsidiaries. A holding company may have no other business than the holding of shares of other companies.

holiday *(U.K.)* HR & PERSONNEL = ***vacation***

home loan *(ANZ)* FINANCE, BANKING, AND ACCOUNTING a mortgage

homepage E-COMMERCE the first and/or main page on a Web site

home run
1. GENERAL MANAGEMENT, FINANCE, BANKING, AND ACCOUNTING a very great achievement
2. GENERAL MANAGEMENT, FINANCE, BANKING, AND ACCOUNTING an investment that produces a high rate of return in a short time
3. GENERAL MANAGEMENT the journey home at the end of the working day *(slang)*

home shopping MARKETING the ordering of goods from home by telephone, Internet, mail order, or direct-response television

homeworker HR & PERSONNEL somebody who carries out paid work in his or her home for one or more businesses, but who is not ***self-employed***. The method of working can be a permanent or occasional arrangement, or may involve a split of work between an employer's premises and home. See ***teleworker***

homogenization GENERAL MANAGEMENT the removal of characteristic differences between separate markets and cultures. Globalization is frequently blamed for homogenization.

Honey, Peter GENERAL MANAGEMENT British psychologist and consultant. With ***Alan Mumford***, identified four types of ***learning style*** and devised an instrument to determine somebody's predominant style in their book, *The Manual of Learning Styles* (1982).

honorarium HR & PERSONNEL a token sum given in recognition of the recipient's performance of specific, nononerous duties. An honorarium may take the form of an annual retainer.

hook
by hook or by crook GENERAL MANAGEMENT in any way possible, whether or not moral, honest, or legal *(slang)*

HOPEFUL GENERAL MANAGEMENT Hard-up Older Person Expecting Full Useful Life *(slang)*

HOQ OPERATIONS & PRODUCTION see ***house of quality***

horizontal diversification GENERAL MANAGEMENT see ***diversification***

horizontal fast track GENERAL MANAGEMENT a variation of ***fast track*** developed by ***Charles Handy*** in which talented people are moved around from task to task to test and develop their capability in different working situations
CHARLES HANDY (pp. 1000–01)

horizontal integration GENERAL MANAGEMENT the merging of functions or organizations that operate on a similar level. Horizontal integration involves the union of companies producing the same kinds of goods or operating at the same stage of the ***supply chain***. It may also describe the merging of departments within an organization that carry out similar tasks. See ***vertical integration***

horizontal keiretsu GENERAL MANAGEMENT see ***keiretsu***

horizontal merger GENERAL MANAGEMENT see ***merger***

horizontal organization GENERAL MANAGEMENT see ***flat organization***

horizontal spread FINANCE, BANKING, AND ACCOUNTING a purchase of two options that are identical except for their dates of maturity

hostile takeover GENERAL MANAGEMENT see ***takeover***

hot button MARKETING a sales or marketing offer that particularly appeals to a buyer *(slang)*

hot-desking GENERAL MANAGEMENT a flexible working practice enabling employees to occupy any vacant workspace instead of sitting at a permanent personalized desk. Organizations using a hot-desking system may have a set of standardized workspaces equipped with ***information and communications technologies***, and employees may sit at a different desk each day. Alternatively, the majority of employees may have their own desks, but some employees, such as consultants or part-time workers, may sit at any desk that happens to be free that day. Most conventional offices are only full for a fraction of the time they are open because of sickness, vacations, or ***teleworking*** and this results in empty desks and wasted resources. Hot-desking enables expensive office space to be fully utilized and forms part of the concept of the ***virtual office***. Although employees practicing hot-desking may have limited storage space in the form of a filing cabinet or locker, most of their work and information will be stored electronically. *(slang)*

hoteling GENERAL MANAGEMENT the practice of occupying a desk or workspace in another employer's premises. Hoteling is normally carried out by employees such as consultants or sales people, who spend more time with customers than at their employer's offices and rely on their clients to provide desk space. Hoteling has developed through improved ***information and communications technologies*** and is an extension of the ***virtual office***.

hours of work
1. HR & PERSONNEL the hours agreed between an employer and employee for which the employee is paid
2. GENERAL MANAGEMENT the actual hours worked by an employee, often well in excess of those stated in the ***contract of employment*** and sometimes without the payment of ***overtime***

house journal GENERAL MANAGEMENT see ***newsletter***

house of quality OPERATIONS & PRODUCTION a ***decision making*** and planning tool that brings the customer and the engineer together in the product design process. House of quality is one of the four houses or phases of ***quality function deployment***. House of quality provides a structure for the design and development cycle. The name is derived from the use of matrices that explore the relationship between customer needs and design attributes. The matrices used in the analysis fit together to form a houselike structure. Abbr **HOQ**. Also known as ***quality table***

HR HR & PERSONNEL see ***human resources***

HREOC *(ANZ)* GENERAL MANAGEMENT see ***Human Rights and Equal Opportunities Commission***

HRIS HR & PERSONNEL see ***human resource information system***

HRM HR & PERSONNEL **human resource management**, a model of ***personnel management*** that focuses on the individual rather than taking a collective approach. Responsibility for human resource management is often devolved to ***line management***. It is characterized by an emphasis on strategic integration, ***employee commitment***, workforce flexibility, and quality of goods and services.

HR service center HR & PERSONNEL a ***centralized*** office that handles routine administration and answers inquiries from managers and staff throughout an organization on ***human resources***-related matters

HST FINANCE, BANKING, AND ACCOUNTING see ***harmonized sales tax***

HTH *abbr* GENERAL MANAGEMENT hope this helps *(slang)*

HTML E-COMMERCE hypertext markup language, a computer code used to build and develop Web pages. It is used to format the text of a document and indicate ***hyperlinks*** to other Web pages and describes the layout of the Web page.

HTTP E-COMMERCE hypertext transport (or transfer) protocol, the communications mechanism used to exchange information on the Internet

hub and spoke GENERAL MANAGEMENT any arrangement of component parts resembling a wheel, with a central hub and a series of spokes radiating outward. The metaphor of the hub and spoke arrangement can be applied to any area. Examples include ***organization structure***, computer network design, work processes, service delivery methods, and transport systems.

humanagement GENERAL MANAGEMENT a style of management that emphasizes the ***empowerment*** of people

human asset accounting HR & PERSONNEL see ***human capital accounting***

human capital HR & PERSONNEL the ***employees*** of an organization. The term builds on the concept of capital as an asset of an organization, implying recognition of the importance and monetary worth of the skills and experience of its employees. It is measured through ***human capital accounting***.

human capital accounting HR & PERSONNEL an attempt to place a financial figure on the knowledge and skills of an organization's ***employees*** or ***human capital***. Also known as ***human asset accounting***, ***human resource accounting***

human factors engineering GENERAL MANAGEMENT the analysis of human needs and abilities in the design of workplace activities, facilities, and systems in order to optimize employee performance. Human factors engineering uses, for example, ***ergonomics*** in the design of the workplace and aims to offer a better choice of computer software by striving to obtain a fit between human operators and the equipment or technology that they are using. In this way, human factors engineering tries to reduce risk by raising safety levels and to produce cost savings by improving performance.

human relations HR & PERSONNEL an interdisciplinary study of social relations in the workplace that embraces sociology, social anthropology, and social psychology. The human relations movement presents a counterpoint to the scientific management view that focuses on maximizing the productivity and income of individual manual workers and on the separation of mental and physical work between management and workers. In contrast, supporters of the human relations movement believe that workers want to feel part of a team with socially supportive relationships and to grow and develop. ***Motivation***, communication, ***employee participation***, and ***leadership*** are significant issues.
MARY PARKER FOLLETT (pp. 988–89)

human resource accounting GENERAL MANAGEMENT see ***human capital accounting***

human resource information system HR & PERSONNEL a data ***MIS***, usually computerized, that facilitates strategic and operational ***decision making*** for ***human resource management*** (see ***HRM***). Abbr **HRIS**

human resource management GENERAL MANAGEMENT see ***HRM***

  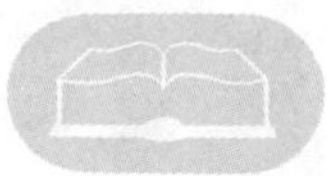    

human resource planning HR & PERSONNEL the development of strategies for matching the size and skills of the workforce to organizational needs. Human resource planning assists organizations to recruit, retain, and optimize the deployment of the personnel needed to meet business objectives and to respond to changes in the external environment. The process involves carrying out a ***skills analysis*** of the existing workforce, carrying out ***manpower forecasting***, and taking action to ensure that supply meets demand. This may include the development of training and retraining strategies. Also known as ***manpower planning***

human resources HR & PERSONNEL
1. the discipline of managing people in an organization. Abbr **HR**
2. the employees of an organization

Human Rights and Equal Opportunities Commission HR & PERSONNEL an Australian federal government body that administers legislation relating to human rights, antidiscrimination, privacy, and social justice. It was set up in 1986, replacing the Human Rights Commission. Abbr **HREOC**

Humble, **John William** (*b.* 1925) GENERAL MANAGEMENT British consultant. Popularized ***Peter Drucker***'s concept of ***management by objectives***, which he explained in *Improving Business Results* (1967).
PETER DRUCKER (pp. 982–85)

hunch marketing MARKETING marketing based on instinct rather than research (*slang*)

hurry sickness GENERAL MANAGEMENT a state of anxiety caused by the feeling of not having enough time in the day to achieve everything that is required (*slang*)

hybrid financial instrument FINANCE, BANKING, AND ACCOUNTING a financial instrument such as a convertible bond that has characteristics of multiple types of instruments, often convertible from one to another

hygiene factors GENERAL MANAGEMENT see ***job satisfaction***

hymn sheet
sing from the same hymn sheet HR & PERSONNEL to be in agreement about something with another person or group of people (*slang*)

hyperinflation ECONOMICS very rapid growth in the rate of inflation so that money loses value and physical goods replace currency as a medium of exchange. This happened in Latin America in the early 1990s, for example.

hyperlink E-COMMERCE an image or piece of text that enables the user, by clicking on it, to move directly to other Web pages. Hyperlinks are most commonly found on Web pages, and can be used to connect Web pages within the same site, as well as to link to other Web sites. Hyperlinks can be added to Web pages by using simple ***HTML*** commands. They can also be used in e-mail messages, for example, to include the address of a company's Web site. Also known as ***hypertext link***

hyperpartnering E-COMMERCE a form of commerce in which companies use Internet technology to form partnerships and execute transactions at high speed and low cost in order to take advantage of business opportunities as soon as they appear

hypertext link E-COMMERCE = ***hyperlink***

hypertext markup language E-COMMERCE see ***HTML***

hypertext transport protocol *or* **hypertext transfer protocol** E-COMMERCE see ***HTTP***

hyper time E-COMMERCE the apparent fast pace and decentralized nature of Internet time

hypothecate FINANCE, BANKING, AND ACCOUNTING to use a property as collateral for a loan

hypothesis testing STATISTICS the process of testing sample data from a statistical study to determine whether it is consistent with what is known about the sample population

I

Iacocca, **Lee A.** (*b.* 1924) GENERAL MANAGEMENT U.S. business executive. President of the Ford Motor Company and subsequently Chairman and Chief Executive of the Chrysler Corporation. His experiences are described in *Iacocca: an Autobiography* (1985).

IANAL *abbr* GENERAL MANAGEMENT I am not a lawyer (*slang*)

IAP *abbr* E-COMMERCE Internet access provider

IAS (*ANZ*) GENERAL MANAGEMENT see ***Instalment Activity Statement***

IASC *abbr* FINANCE, BANKING, AND ACCOUNTING International Accounting Standards Committee, an organization based in London that works toward achieving global agreement on accounting standards

IBRD *abbr* FINANCE, BANKING, AND ACCOUNTING International Bank for Reconstruction and Development, a United Nations organization that provides funds, policy guidance, and technical assistance to facilitate economic development in its poorer member countries

ICA GENERAL MANAGEMENT see ***Insurance Council of Australia***

ICC FINANCE, BANKING, AND ACCOUNTING International Chamber of Commerce, an organization that represents business interests to governments, aiming to improve trading conditions and foster private enterprise

iceing GENERAL MANAGEMENT dismissal from employment. The first part of the word is an acronym from "involuntary career event." (*slang*)

ICT GENERAL MANAGEMENT see ***information and communications technologies***

IDA *abbr*
1. FINANCE, BANKING, AND ACCOUNTING International Development Association, an agency administered by the IBRD to provide assistance on concessional terms to the poorest developing countries. Its resources consist of subscriptions and general replenishments from its more industrialized and developed members, special contributions, and transfers from the net earnings of the IBRD.
2. GENERAL MANAGEMENT see ***Infocomm Development Authority***

idea
let's put some ideas on the ground and see if any of them walk GENERAL MANAGEMENT let's try some of these ideas and see whether any of them is successful (*slang*)

idea hamster GENERAL MANAGEMENT somebody who appears to have an endless source of new ideas (*slang*)

Identrus E-COMMERCE a consortium of financial institutions engaged in developing a standard for a network over which business-to-business e-commerce can be conducted securely

idle time GENERAL MANAGEMENT time spent waiting to continue working on a task while there is a delay (*slang*)

IEA *abbr* FINANCE, BANKING, AND ACCOUNTING International Energy Agency, an autonomous agency within the OECD whose objectives include improving global energy cooperation, developing alternative energy sources, and promoting relations between oil-producing and oil-consuming countries

IFC *abbr* FINANCE, BANKING, AND ACCOUNTING International Finance Corporation, a United Nations organization promoting private sector investment in developing countries to reduce poverty and improve the quality of people's lives. It finances private sector projects that are profit-oriented and environmentally and socially sound, and helps to foster development. IFC has a staff of 2,000 professionals around the world who seek profitable and creative solutions to complex business issues.

illegal parking FINANCE, BANKING, AND ACCOUNTING a stock market practice that involves a broker or company purchasing securities in another company's name though they are guaranteed by the real investor (*slang*)

IMA (*ANZ*) GENERAL MANAGEMENT see ***Investment Management Agreement***

image advertising MARKETING a form of advertising that attempts to create a positive attitude to a product, brand, or company

imaginization GENERAL MANAGEMENT an approach to ***creativity*** originated by ***Gareth Morgan*** in 1993. Imaginization is concerned with improving our ability to see and understand situations in new ways, with finding new ways of organizing, with creating shared understanding and personal ***empowerment***, and with developing a capability for continuing self-organization.

IMAP E-COMMERCE Internet message access protocol, a protocol that enables e-mails to be received from any computer

IMF *abbr* FINANCE, BANKING, AND ACCOUNTING International Monetary Fund, the organization that industrialized nations have established to reduce trade barriers and stabilize currencies, especially those of less industrialized nations

IMHO *abbr* GENERAL MANAGEMENT in my humble opinion (*slang*)

IMNSHO *abbr* GENERAL MANAGEMENT in my not so humble opinion (*slang*)

IMO *abbr* GENERAL MANAGEMENT in my opinion (*slang*)

impaired capital FINANCE, BANKING, AND ACCOUNTING a company's capital that is worth less than the par value of its stock

impairment of capital FINANCE, BANKING, AND ACCOUNTING the extent to which the value of a company is less than the par value of its stock

imperfect competition FINANCE, BANKING, AND ACCOUNTING a situation that exists in a market when there are strong barriers to the entry of new competitors

implicit knowledge GENERAL MANAGEMENT see ***knowledge***

import MARKETING a product or service brought into another country from its country of origin either for sale or for use in manufacturing

import penetration ECONOMICS a situation in which one country's imports dominate the market share of those from other industrialized countries. This is the case, for example, with high-tech imports to the United States from Japan.

impression E-COMMERCE a measure of the number of times an online advertisement is viewed. One impression is equal to one ***click-through***.

improvement curve GENERAL MANAGEMENT see ***learning curve***

imputation system FINANCE, BANKING, AND ACCOUNTING a system in which recipients of dividends gain tax advantage for taxes paid by the company that paid the dividends

in box GENERAL MANAGEMENT a receptacle for documents and other items requiring the attention of an individual. An in box is normally placed on the desk or in the office of the person responsible for dealing with the contents. The phrase "in the in box" is also used figuratively to describe items that have not yet been dealt with.

inc *abbr* GENERAL MANAGEMENT incorporated

incentive program MARKETING an award or reward scheme designed to improve sales force or retail performance

incentive scheme HR & PERSONNEL a program set up to give benefits to employees to reward them for improved commitment and performance and as a means of motivation. An incentive scheme is designed to supplement ***base pay*** and ***fringe benefits***. A **financial incentive scheme** may offer share options or a cash bonus, whereas a **nonfinancial incentive scheme** offers benefits such as additional paid vacations. Awards from incentive schemes may be made on an individual or team basis.

income FINANCE, BANKING, AND ACCOUNTING money received by a company or individual

income bond FINANCE, BANKING, AND ACCOUNTING a bond that a company repays only from its profits

income-linked gilt FINANCE, BANKING, AND ACCOUNTING a bond whose principal and interest track the retail price index

income redistribution ECONOMICS a government policy to redirect income to a targeted sector of a country's population, for example, by lowering the rate of tax paid by low-income earners

incomes policy (*U.K.*) ECONOMICS a government policy that seeks to restrain increases in wages or prices by regulating the permitted level of increase

income stream FINANCE, BANKING, AND ACCOUNTING the income received by a company from a particular product or activity

income tax FINANCE, BANKING, AND ACCOUNTING a tax levied directly on the income of a person or a company and paid to the local, state, or federal government

income tax return FINANCE, BANKING, AND ACCOUNTING a form used for reporting income and computing the tax due on it

income unit FINANCE, BANKING, AND ACCOUNTING a share in a mutual fund that makes regular payments to its shareholders

in-company training HR & PERSONNEL programs of ***employee development*** that are delivered within an organization by external training providers. In-company training allows programs to be tailored to a company's specific needs. It is the opposite of **public training programs**, which have a set syllabus and are open to employees of any organization.

incrementalism GENERAL MANAGEMENT a collective term for the many initiatives of the 1980s and 1990s that took a small step approach to improving quality and productivity and reducing costs. Incrementalism encompasses initiatives such as ***total quality management***, ***continuous improvement***, and ***benchmarking***. Although incrementalism originally provided a source of ***competitive advantage***, it is generally recognized today that a more radical approach is required.

indaba (*S. Africa*) GENERAL MANAGEMENT a meeting or conference

independent service organization E-COMMERCE see ***ISO***

index FINANCE, BANKING, AND ACCOUNTING
1. a standard that represents the value of stocks in a market, particularly a figure such as the Hang Seng, Dow Jones, or Nikkei average
2. an amount calculated to represent the relative value of a group of things

indexation FINANCE, BANKING, AND ACCOUNTING the linking of a rate to a standard index of prices, interest rates, share prices, or similar items

index fund FINANCE, BANKING, AND ACCOUNTING a mutual fund composed of companies listed in an important stock market index in order to match the market's overall performance. See ***managed fund***. Also known as ***index-tracker***, ***tracker fund***

index number ECONOMICS a weighted average of a number of observations of an economic attribute such as retail prices expressed as a percentage of a similar weighted average calculated at an earlier period

index-tracker FINANCE, BANKING, AND ACCOUNTING = ***index fund***

indicated dividend FINANCE, BANKING, AND ACCOUNTING the forecast total of all dividends in a year if the amount of each dividend remains as it is

indicated yield FINANCE, BANKING, AND ACCOUNTING the yield that an indicated dividend represents

indirect channel MARKETING the selling and distribution of products to customers through intermediaries such as wholesalers, distributors, agents, dealers, or retailers

indirect cost GENERAL MANAGEMENT a fixed or overhead cost that cannot be attributed directly to the production of a particular item and is incurred even when there is no output. Indirect costs may include the ***cost center*** functions of finance and accounting, information technology, administration, and personnel. See ***direct cost***

indirect discrimination HR & PERSONNEL apparently ***equal treatment*** that in fact ***discriminates*** because the employment requirement can only be met by a proportion of those in the relevant group and cannot be justified on nondiscriminatory grounds

indirect labor HR & PERSONNEL personnel not directly engaged in the manufacturing of products or the provision of services. Indirect labor includes ***white-collar workers*** and office and support staff.

individual savings account FINANCE, BANKING, AND ACCOUNTING an equivalent in the United Kingdom of a Roth Individual Retirement Account in the United States

induction HR & PERSONNEL a process through which a new employee is integrated into an organization, learning about its ***corporate culture***, policies and ***procedures***, and the specific practicalities of his or her job. An induction program should not consist of a one-day introduction, but should be planned and paced over a few days or weeks. There is a growing use of ***boot camps***, which aim to assimilate a new employee rapidly into the culture of the employing organization.

industrial action HR & PERSONNEL concerted action taken by employees to pressurize an employer to accede to a demand, usually work-related, but sometimes of a political or social nature. Examples of industrial action include ***strikes***, overtime bans, ***go-slows***, and extended coffee breaks.

industrial advertising MARKETING the advertising of technical products and services to the industrial or business sectors

industrial award GENERAL MANAGEMENT see ***award***

industrial cooperative GENERAL MANAGEMENT a group of individuals who together produce goods or provide services and share any profits that are made. Industrial cooperatives are an extension of the ***cooperative movement*** that developed during the 1800s.

industrial court HR & PERSONNEL a state body in Australia responsible for arbitrating in industrial disputes and setting wage awards

industrial democracy (*U.K.*) HR & PERSONNEL a way of running an organization that involves employees in strategy and ***decision making***. Industrial democracy involves ***employee participation*** in management, which empowers employees and aids ***motivation***. It can be facilitated by such setups as consultation committees. In an industrial democracy, workers should not only share in inputs to the running of the organization but also in its outputs, for example, by taking part in a profit-sharing scheme.

industrial dispute GENERAL MANAGEMENT see ***dispute***

industrial engineering GENERAL MANAGEMENT an applied science discipline concerned with the prediction, planning, evaluation, and improvement of company effectiveness. The purpose of industrial engineering is to maximize efficiency, quality, and production through the best use of personnel, materials, facilities, and equipment.

industrial espionage GENERAL MANAGEMENT the practice of spying on a business competitor in order to obtain their trade or commercial secrets. Information sought through industrial espionage will often refer to new products, designs, formulas, manufacturing processes, marketing surveys, research, or future plans. The aim of industrial espionage is either to injure the business prospects or market share of the target company or to use the secrets discovered for another organization's commercial benefit.

industrial goods OPERATIONS & PRODUCTION goods produced for industry, which include processed or ***raw materials***, goods used to produce other goods, machinery, components, and equipment

industrial goods marketing MARKETING the ***industrial marketing*** of products. Industrial goods marketing is different from the marketing of consumer goods in that it is directed at organizations, businesses, and other institutions, rather than at the individual end user of a product. It may require different marketing strategies from those used in ***consumer goods marketing*** to be effective.

industrial housekeeping GENERAL MANAGEMENT the process of ensuring that the workplace is kept clean and tidy. Industrial housekeeping forms part of the general responsibility of managers. It includes the provision of adequate workspace, adequate storage arrangements, both around the workstation and within the unit, and the development of effective administration and procedures to ensure a culture of tidiness and cleanliness within the workforce. A lack of concern with housekeeping can result in an increase in accidents and machine failure and in a reduction in the overall efficiency of the unit. The introduction of the Japanese 5-S concept into Western companies has renewed management interest in industrial housekeeping.

industrialization GENERAL MANAGEMENT the change from a society based on agriculture to one based on manufacturing. Industrialization is the process undergone in much of the developed world during the Industrial Revolution. Features of the process include ***automation***, scientific development, the introduction of factories, the ***division of labor***, the replacement of barter with a money-based economy, a more mobile workforce, and the growth of urban centers. The phase of development following industrialization is the ***postindustrial society***.

industrial marketing MARKETING the marketing of goods or services to companies, as opposed to individual consumers. Industrial marketing involves a number of key differences from selling to consumers. These include a smaller customer base with higher value or larger unit purchases, more technically complex or specially tailored products, professionally qualified purchasers, closer buyer-seller relationships, and possible group purchasing decision making. Also known as ***B2B***, ***business-to-business marketing***

industrial market research MARKETING ***market research*** into the ***marketing*** of services and goods to industry, businesses, and other institutions. Industrial market research is used as an aid to ***decision making*** and concerns the manufacture, selling, and distribution of products with the aim of reducing costs and increasing profits. It considers factors such as the available labor force, location of the firm, export market potential, and use of resources.

industrial production ECONOMICS the output of a country's productive industries. Until the 1960s, this was commonly iron and steel or coal, but since then lighter engineering in motor car or robotics manufacture has taken over.

industrial psychology HR & PERSONNEL = ***occupational psychology***

Industrial Relations Commission GENERAL MANAGEMENT see ***Australian Industrial Relations Commission***

Industrial Relations Court of Australia HR & PERSONNEL an Australian superior court responsible for enforcing industrial awards, hearing and ruling on claims for unfair dismissal, and ruling on points of industrial law. Abbr **IRCA**

industrial revenue bond FINANCE, BANKING, AND ACCOUNTING a bond that a private company uses to finance construction

industrial-sector cycle ECONOMICS a business cycle that reflects patterns of an old economy rather than the new electronic economy

industrial services marketing MARKETING the ***industrial marketing*** of services. Industrial services marketing may promote to industry, businesses, and other institutions, services such as maintenance contracts, insurance and other financial services, professional services such as training, transportation, office cleaning, and advertising. Many services offered to industry are also offered to the consumer, but promoting them to consumers requires strategies derived from ***consumer services marketing***.

industry rules GENERAL MANAGEMENT the unwritten conventions that are considered to govern the interactions of organizations within an industry

inertia selling *(U.K.)* MARKETING a method of selling that involves the sending of unsolicited goods on a sale or return policy. Inertia selling relies on the passive reaction of a potential purchaser to choose to pay for the goods received rather than undertake the effort to send them back. The receiver of the goods is not bound by law to pay for them but must keep them in good condition until they are collected or returned. Regarded by some as unethical, inertia selling is the principle by which many mail-order book, record, and video clubs operate.

inference STATISTICS a conclusion drawn by a researcher about a statistical population after observing individuals in the population

infinite capacity plan OPERATIONS & PRODUCTION see ***capacity requirements planning***

infinite loading OPERATIONS & PRODUCTION the scheduling or loading of jobs onto a workstation as if it had a limitless capacity to handle them. See ***finite loading***

inflation ECONOMICS a sustained increase in a country's general level of prices that devalues its currency, often caused by excess demand in the economy

inflation accounting FINANCE, BANKING, AND ACCOUNTING the adjustment of a company's accounts to reflect the effect of inflation and provide a more realistic view of the company's position

inflationary ECONOMICS characterized by excess demand or high costs creating an excessive increase in the country's money supply

inflationary gap ECONOMICS a gap that exists when an economy's resources are utilized and ***aggregate demand*** is more than the full-employment level of output. Prices will rise to remove the excess demand.

inflationary spiral ECONOMICS the vicious circle in which, in inflationary conditions, excess demand causes producers to raise prices and workers to demand wage rises to sustain their living standards

inflation rate ECONOMICS the rate at which general price levels increase over a period of time

inflation tax ECONOMICS an incomes policy that taxes companies that grant pay rises above a particular level

Infocomm Development Authority GENERAL MANAGEMENT a statutory board responsible for developing the information and communications sector in Singapore. It was formed in 1999 as a result of the merger of the Telecommunications Authority of Singapore and the National Computer Board. Abbr **IDA**

infoholic GENERAL MANAGEMENT somebody who is obsessed with obtaining information, especially on the Internet (*slang*)

infomatics GENERAL MANAGEMENT the process of automation using information systems

infomediary E-COMMERCE a Web site that provides and aggregates relevant customer or industry information for other companies

infomercial MARKETING a television or cinema commercial that includes helpful information about a product as well as advertising content

informal economy ECONOMICS the economy that runs in parallel to the formal economy but outside the reach of the tax system, most transactions being paid for in cash or goods

information and communications technologies GENERAL MANAGEMENT computer and telecommunications technologies considered collectively. Information and communications technology convergence has given rise to technologies such as the ***Internet***, ***videoconferencing***, ***groupware***, ***intranets***, and third-generation mobile phones. Information and communications technologies enable

organizations to be more flexible in the way they are structured and in the way they work, and this has given rise to both the ***virtual organization*** and the ***virtual office***. Abbr **ICT**

information architecture E-COMMERCE the means and methods of designing metadata, navigation, search, and content layout for a Web site

information management GENERAL MANAGEMENT the acquisition, recording, organizing, storage, dissemination, and retrieval of information. Good information management has been described as getting the right information to the right person in the right format at the right time.

information overload E-COMMERCE the problem caused by the excessive quantity of Web and e-mail-based information and the Internet's inability to discriminate between useful and useless material. In 1997, the problem of information overload was identified in an influential report from the British MCA (Marketing and Communication Agency). The report concluded that "information overload is not simply the problem of too much information. It is the problem of too much *irrelevant* information caused by the heavy reliance on one medium (the Internet) to distribute information."

information space E-COMMERCE the abstract concept of all the knowledge, expertise, and information accessible on the Web

infrastructure GENERAL MANAGEMENT the basic elements that together support something, for example, the network and systems that support computing or the public services and facilities that support business activity

in-house newsletter GENERAL MANAGEMENT see ***newsletter***

initial offer FINANCE, BANKING, AND ACCOUNTING the first offer that a company makes to buy the shares of another company in the United Kingdom

initial public offering FINANCE, BANKING, AND ACCOUNTING the first instance of making particular shares available for sale to the public

Inland Revenue Department FINANCE, BANKING, AND ACCOUNTING the New Zealand government body responsible for the administration of the national taxation system. Abbr **IRD**

innovation GENERAL MANAGEMENT the creation, development, and implementation of a new product, process, or service, with the aim of improving efficiency, effectiveness, or ***competitive advantage***. Innovation may apply to products, services, manufacturing processes, managerial processes, or the design of an organization. It is most often viewed at a product, or process level, where product innovation satisfies a customer's needs, and process innovation improves efficiency and effectiveness. Innovation is linked with ***creativity*** and the creation of new ideas, and involves taking those new ideas and turning them into reality through invention, research, and ***new product development***.

input tax credit (*ANZ*) FINANCE, BANKING, AND ACCOUNTING an amount paid as ***Goods and Services Tax*** on supplies purchased for business purposes, which can be offset against Goods and Services Tax collected

insert MARKETING a loose piece of advertising material, for example, a card or brochure, placed inside a newspaper or magazine

insertion rate MARKETING the cost of a single appearance of an advertisement

inside information FINANCE, BANKING, AND ACCOUNTING information that is of advantage to investors but is only available to people who have personal contact with a company

inside quote FINANCE, BANKING, AND ACCOUNTING a range of prices for a security, from the highest offer to buy to the lowest offer to sell

insider
1. FINANCE, BANKING, AND ACCOUNTING somebody intending to buy shares using access to privileged or confidential information that is not available to general investors
2. GENERAL MANAGEMENT somebody who has access to information that is privileged and unavailable to most members of the public

insider trading *or* **insider dealing** FINANCE, BANKING, AND ACCOUNTING profitable, usually illegal, trading in securities carried out using privileged information

insolvency FINANCE, BANKING, AND ACCOUNTING, GENERAL MANAGEMENT the inability to pay debts when they become due. Insolvency will apply even if total assets exceed total liabilities, if those assets cannot be readily converted into cash to meet debts as they mature. Even then, insolvency may not necessarily mean ***business failure***. ***Bankruptcy*** may be avoided through ***debt rescheduling*** or ***turnaround management***.

insourcing GENERAL MANAGEMENT the use of in-house personnel or an internal department to meet an organization's need for specific services. Insourcing is seen as a reaction to the growing popularity of ***outsourcing*** that has not always met expectations. An insourcing strategy is chosen where it appears that a better service can be provided from internal resources than from an external supplier. In some cases, organizations opt for a combination of outsourcing and insourcing in which external service providers work in cooperation with in-house personnel.

installment plan FINANCE, BANKING, AND ACCOUNTING a method of buying something by paying for it in regular equal amounts over a period of time

installment purchase FINANCE, BANKING, AND ACCOUNTING a financing arrangement in which the buyer pays by a series of installments over a period of time

Instalment Activity Statement FINANCE, BANKING, AND ACCOUNTING a standard form used in Australia to report ***Pay-As-You-Go*** installment payments on investment income. Abbr **IAS**

institutional investor FINANCE, BANKING, AND ACCOUNTING an institution that makes investments

institutional survey STATISTICS a statistical investigation in which an institution such as a company is the unit of analysis

instrument HR & PERSONNEL = ***psychometric test***

insurance GENERAL MANAGEMENT an arrangement in which individuals or companies pay another company to guarantee them compensation if they suffer loss resulting from risks such as fire, theft, or accidental damage

Insurance and Superannuation Commission GENERAL MANAGEMENT an Australian federal government body responsible for regulating the superannuation and insurance industries. Abbr **ISC**

insurance broker GENERAL MANAGEMENT a person or company that acts as an intermediary between companies providing insurance and individuals or companies who need insurance

Insurance Council of Australia GENERAL MANAGEMENT an independent body rep-

resenting the interests of businesses involved in the insurance industry. It was set up in 1975 and currently represents around 110 companies. Abbr **ICA**

insurance policy GENERAL MANAGEMENT a document that sets out the terms and conditions for providing insurance cover against specified risks

intangible asset FINANCE, BANKING, AND ACCOUNTING an asset such as intellectual property or goodwill that is not physical

integrated implementation model GENERAL MANAGEMENT see ***new product development***

Integrated Services Digital Network GENERAL MANAGEMENT see ***ISDN***

intellectual assets GENERAL MANAGEMENT the knowledge, experience, and skills of its staff that an organization can make use of

intellectual capital GENERAL MANAGEMENT the combined intangible assets owned or controlled by a company or organization that provide ***competitive advantage***. Intellectual capital assets can include the knowledge and expertise of employees, brands, customer information and relationships, contracts, ***intellectual property*** such as patents and copyright, and organizational technologies, processes, and methods. Intellectual capital can be implicit and intangible—stored in people's heads—or explicit and documented in written or electronic format.

intellectual property GENERAL MANAGEMENT the ownership of rights to ideas, designs, and inventions, including ***copyrights***, ***patents***, and ***trademarks***. Intellectual property is protected by law in most countries, and the World Intellectual Property Organization is responsible for harmonizing the law across different countries and promoting the protection of intellectual property rights.

intelligence test HR & PERSONNEL see ***aptitude test***

intelligent e-mail E-COMMERCE an automated e-mail system that is able to analyze incoming messages without the need for criteria preset by each user

interactive E-COMMERCE relating to a facility of an online service or software program that allows the user to enter data or issue commands

interactive planning GENERAL MANAGEMENT a process that promotes participation in both the design of a desirable future and the developments that enable this future to be achieved rather than waiting for it to happen. Interactive planning is associated with ***Russell Ackoff***, and was outlined in *Creating the Corporate Future* (1981).

interchange E-COMMERCE a transaction between the acquiring bank and the issuing bank

interchangeable bond FINANCE, BANKING, AND ACCOUNTING a bond whose owner can change it at will between bearer and book-entry form

interchange fee E-COMMERCE the charge on a transaction between the acquiring bank and the issuing bank, paid by the acquirer to the issuer

intercommodity spread FINANCE, BANKING, AND ACCOUNTING a combination of purchase and sale of options for related commodities with the same delivery date

intercompany pricing GENERAL MANAGEMENT the setting of prices by companies within a group to sell products or services to each other, rather than to external customers

interest FINANCE, BANKING, AND ACCOUNTING the rate that a lender charges for the use of money that is a loan

interest assumption FINANCE, BANKING, AND ACCOUNTING the expected rate of return on a portfolio

interest-elastic investment FINANCE, BANKING, AND ACCOUNTING an investment with a rate of return that varies with interest rates

interest-inelastic investment FINANCE, BANKING, AND ACCOUNTING an investment with a rate of return that does not vary with interest rates

interest rate FINANCE, BANKING, AND ACCOUNTING the amount of interest charged for borrowing a particular sum of money over a specified period of time

interest rate cap FINANCE, BANKING, AND ACCOUNTING an upper limit on a rate of interest, for example, in an adjustable-rate mortgage

interest rate effect ECONOMICS the mechanism by which interest rates adjust so that investment is equal to savings in an economy

interest rate floor FINANCE, BANKING, AND ACCOUNTING a lower limit on a rate of interest, for example, in an adjustable-rate mortgage

interest rate swap FINANCE, BANKING, AND ACCOUNTING an exchange of two debt instruments with different rates of interest, made to tailor cash flows to the participants' different requirements

interface GENERAL MANAGEMENT

1. the point of contact between two or more things, for example, between a computer and user, or customer and seller

2. a face-to-face meeting (*slang*)

interfirm cooperation GENERAL MANAGEMENT a formal or informal agreement between organizations to collaborate in achieving common or new aims more efficiently or effectively. Interfirm cooperation usually takes the form of a ***joint venture***, ***strategic alliance***, or ***strategic partnering*** arrangement.

interim certificate FINANCE, BANKING, AND ACCOUNTING a document certifying partial ownership of stock that is not totally paid for at one time

interim dividend FINANCE, BANKING, AND ACCOUNTING a dividend whose value is determined on the basis of a period of time of less than a full fiscal year

interim financing FINANCE, BANKING, AND ACCOUNTING financing by means of bridge loans

interim management (*U.K.*) GENERAL MANAGEMENT the temporary employment of an experienced manager by an organization seeking to fill a temporary vacancy or coordinate a particular project. Interim managers are generally used to bring in skills not already present in an organization. Sometimes they are employed when an organization is facing ***business failure***, but increasingly they are used as a strategic resource as and when required. **Interim managers** work on a ***freelance*** or ***portfolio working*** basis.

interim manager GENERAL MANAGEMENT see ***interim management***

interim statement FINANCE, BANKING, AND ACCOUNTING a financial statement relating to a period of time of less than a full fiscal year

intermarket spread FINANCE, BANKING, AND ACCOUNTING a combination of purchase and sale of options for the same commodity with the same delivery date on different markets

intermediary FINANCE, BANKING, AND ACCOUNTING somebody who makes investments for others

intermediate goods OPERATIONS & PRODUCTION goods bought for use in the production of other products

intern HR & PERSONNEL a trainee working in a low-ranking position in a company

internal audit FINANCE, BANKING, AND ACCOUNTING an audit of a company undertaken by its employees. See ***external audit***

internal communication GENERAL MANAGEMENT communication between employees or departments across all levels or divisions of an organization. Internal communication is a form of ***corporate communication*** and can be formal or informal, upward, downward, or horizontal. It can take various forms such as ***team briefing***, ***interviewing***, employee or works councils, ***meetings***, ***memos***, an ***intranet***, ***newsletters***, ***suggestion schemes***, the ***grapevine***, and reports.

internal consultant GENERAL MANAGEMENT an employee who uses knowledge and expertise to offer advice or business solutions to another department or business unit within an organization. **Internal consulting** is one aspect of work carried out by a ***management services*** department.

internal consulting GENERAL MANAGEMENT see ***internal consultant***

internal cost analysis GENERAL MANAGEMENT an examination of an organization's value-creating activities to determine sources of profitability and to identify the relative costs of different processes. Internal cost analysis is a tool for analyzing the ***value chain***. Principle steps include identifying those processes that create value for the organization, calculating the cost of each value-creating process against the overall cost of the product or service, identifying the cost components for each process, establishing the links between the processes, and working out the opportunities for achieving relative cost advantage.

internal differentiation analysis GENERAL MANAGEMENT an examination of processes in the ***value chain*** to determine which of them create differentiation of the product or service in the customer's eyes, and thus enhance its value. Internal differentiation analysis enables an organization to focus on improving the identified processes to maximize ***competitive advantage***. Steps involve identification of value-creating activities; evaluation of strategies that can enhance value for the customer; and assessment of which differentiation strategies are the most sustainable.

internal marketing MARKETING the application of the principles of marketing within an organization. Internal marketing involves the creation of an internal market by dividing departments into ***business units***, with control over their own operations and expenditure, with attendant impacts on ***corporate culture***, politics, and power. Internal marketing also involves treating employees as internal customers with the aim of increasing employees' motivation and ***customer focus***.

internal recruitment HR & PERSONNEL ***recruitment*** carried out within the existing workforce. Internal recruitment allows employees to have ***promotion*** opportunities and to develop new skills.

internal versus external sourcing GENERAL MANAGEMENT see ***purchasing versus production***

International Accounting Standards Committee FINANCE, BANKING, AND ACCOUNTING see ***IASC***

International Bank for Reconstruction and Development FINANCE, BANKING, AND ACCOUNTING see ***IBRD***

International Chamber of Commerce FINANCE, BANKING, AND ACCOUNTING see ***ICC***

International Development Association FINANCE, BANKING, AND ACCOUNTING see ***IDA***

International Energy Authority FINANCE, BANKING, AND ACCOUNTING see ***IEA***

International Finance Corporation FINANCE, BANKING, AND ACCOUNTING see ***IFC***

international fund FINANCE, BANKING, AND ACCOUNTING a mutual fund that invests in securities both inside and outside the country

international management GENERAL MANAGEMENT

1. the maintaining and developing of an organization's ***production*** or market interests across national borders with either local or ***expatriate*** staff

2. the process of running a ***multinational business***, made up of formerly independent organizations

3. the body of skills, knowledge, and understanding required to manage cross-cultural operations

International Monetary Fund FINANCE, BANKING, AND ACCOUNTING see ***IMF***

Internesia E-COMMERCE the tendency to find interesting Web sites on the Internet and then forget how to locate them again (*slang*)

Internet E-COMMERCE the global network of computers accessed with the aid of a modem. The Internet includes Web sites, e-mail, newsgroups, and other forums. It is a public network, although many of the computers connected to it are also part of ***Intranets***. It uses the **Internet Protocol** (IP) as a communication standard.

Internet access provider E-COMMERCE a company or organization that provides its customers with an entry point to the Internet via a dial-up connection, cable modem, or wireless application. Abbr **IAP**

Internet commerce E-COMMERCE the part of ***e-commerce***, which includes all electronic commercial activities, that consists of commercial transactions conducted over the Internet

Internet merchant E-COMMERCE a businessperson who sells a product or service over the Internet

Internet Message Access Protocol E-COMMERCE see ***IMAP***

Internet payment system E-COMMERCE any mechanism for fund transfer from customer to merchant or business to business, ranging from traditional credit card processing to direct electronic funds transfer

Internet Protocol E-COMMERCE see ***Internet***

Internet service provider E-COMMERCE see ***ISP***

interoperability GENERAL MANAGEMENT the ability of products from different manufacturers to be used in conjunction with each other

interpersonal communication HR & PERSONNEL all aspects of personal interaction, contact, and communication between individuals or members of a group. Effective interpersonal communication depends on a range of **interpersonal skills** including listening, asserting, influencing, persuading,

empathizing, sensitivity, and diplomacy. Important aspects of communication between people include ***body language*** and other forms of ***nonverbal communication***.

interpersonal skills HR & PERSONNEL see ***interpersonal communication***

interquartile range STATISTICS the difference between the first and third quartiles of a statistical sample, used to measure the spread of variables in the data

interstate commerce FINANCE, BANKING, AND ACCOUNTING commerce that involves more than one state and is therefore subject to regulation by Congress. See ***intrastate commerce***

interstitial E-COMMERCE a Web advertisement that appears on its own page, sandwiched between content pages on a Web site, in a similar way to that used in traditional magazine advertising

intervention ECONOMICS government action to intervene in the market, manipulating market forces for political or economic purposes

interviewer bias STATISTICS distortion in the results of a statistical survey caused by actions of the interviewer such as cues given to the interviewee

interviewing HR & PERSONNEL the practice of asking questions of another person in order to gain information and make an assessment. Interviewing is a selection tool used in recruitment to assess somebody's suitability for a job. A **structured interview** relies on asking the same job-related questions of all candidates and systematically evaluating their responses. There are two principal models: the **behavioral interview**, which aims to find out how applicants have behaved in the past in similar situations; and the **situational interview**, in which they are asked hypothetical questions to determine how they might act in the future. Interviewing is a technique also used in ***counseling***, ***performance appraisal***, and as part of a ***disciplinary procedure*** (see ***discipline***). See ***discipline***

in the loop GENERAL MANAGEMENT up to date with what is happening currently (*slang*)

intranet E-COMMERCE a corporate network of computers utilizing ***Internet*** tools and technology for the purpose of communication and information sharing. Intranets have been introduced by many organizations as an aid to ***internal communication***. Where an intranet is extended beyond the employees of an organization, perhaps to suppliers, customers, or distributors, it is called an ***extranet***.

intrapreneur GENERAL MANAGEMENT an ***employee*** who uses the approach of an ***entrepreneur*** within an organizational setting. An intrapreneur must have freedom of action to explore and implement ideas, although the outcome of such work will be owned by the organization rather than the intrapreneur, and it is the organization that will take the associated risk. Managers of organizations in which intrapreneurs are allowed to operate subscribe to the view that ***innovation*** can be achieved by encouraging ***creative*** and exploratory activity in semiautonomous units.

intrastate commerce GENERAL MANAGEMENT commerce that occurs within a single state. See ***interstate commerce***

in tray GENERAL MANAGEMENT, HR & PERSONNEL = ***in box***

in-tray learning HR & PERSONNEL a training exercise in which the trainee plays the role of a manager dealing with the contents of an ***in box*** within a set period of time. In-tray training is a form of ***simulation*** used to develop the ***decision making***, prioritizing, and ***time management*** skills of managers and supervisors in the context of the normal working day. Also known as ***in-basket training***

intrinsic value FINANCE, BANKING, AND ACCOUNTING the extent to which an option is in the money

introducing broker FINANCE, BANKING, AND ACCOUNTING a broker who cannot accept payment from customers

intuitive management GENERAL MANAGEMENT a ***management style*** that relies on gut feeling or a sixth sense, rather than on analytical or objective reasoning. Intuitive management exploits the holistic, imaginative, spiritual skills of the right side of the brain, whereas the conventional school of management favors the left side of the brain skills, which are logical, rational, linear, and mathematical in nature. Intuitive management is closely linked to a style of ***decision making*** that encourages ***creativity*** and ***innovation***. Because this style of decision making has no rational basis, however, it can be difficult to justify decisions that turn out to be wrong.

inventory

1. GENERAL MANAGEMENT the stock of finished goods, raw materials, and work in progress held by a company

2. FINANCE, BANKING, AND ACCOUNTING the total of an organization's commercial assets

inventory record OPERATIONS & PRODUCTION a record of the ***inventory*** held by an organization. An inventory record forms an important part of material requirements planning systems. Such records usually make use of some form of part numbering or classification system, and include a description of the part, the quantity held, and the location of all the holdings. A **transaction file** keeps track of inventory use and replenishment.

inventory turnover OPERATIONS & PRODUCTION an accounting ratio of the number of times ***inventory*** is replaced during a given period. The ratio is calculated by dividing net sales by average inventory over a given period. Values are expressed as times per period, most often a year, and a higher figure indicates a more efficient manufacturing operation. Also known as ***stock turnover***, ***stock turns***

inverse floating rate note FINANCE, BANKING, AND ACCOUNTING a note whose interest rate varies inversely with a ***benchmark interest rate***

inverted doughnut GENERAL MANAGEMENT see ***doughnut principle***

inverted market FINANCE, BANKING, AND ACCOUNTING a situation in which near-term futures cost more than long-term futures for the same commodity

inverted yield curve FINANCE, BANKING, AND ACCOUNTING a yield curve with lower interest rates for long-term bonds than for short-term bonds. See ***yield curve***

investment GENERAL MANAGEMENT the spending of money on stocks, shares, and other securities, or on assets such as plant and machinery

investment analyst FINANCE, BANKING, AND ACCOUNTING an employee of a stock exchange company who researches other companies and identifies investment opportunities for clients. Also known as ***financial analyst***

investment bank FINANCE, BANKING, AND ACCOUNTING

1. a bank that specializes in providing funds to corporate borrowers for start-up or expansion

2. a bank that does not accept deposits but provides services to those who offer securities to investors, and to those investors. See ***commercial bank***

  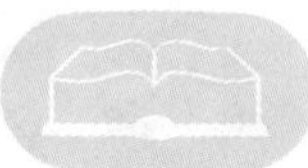    

investment bill FINANCE, BANKING, AND ACCOUNTING a bill of exchange that is an investment

investment borrowing ECONOMICS funds borrowed to encourage a country's economic growth or to support the development of particular industries or regions by adding to physical or human capital

investment club FINANCE, BANKING, AND ACCOUNTING a group of people who join together to make investments in securities

investment committee FINANCE, BANKING, AND ACCOUNTING a group of employees of an investment bank who evaluate investment proposals

investment company FINANCE, BANKING, AND ACCOUNTING a company that pools for investment the money of several investors by means of mutual funds

investment dealer *(Can)* FINANCE, BANKING, AND ACCOUNTING a securities broker

investment fund FINANCE, BANKING, AND ACCOUNTING a savings scheme that invests its clients' funds in corporate start-up or expansion projects

Investment Management Agreement *(ANZ)* FINANCE, BANKING, AND ACCOUNTING a contract between an investor and an investment manager required under SIS legislation. Abbr **IMA**

investment tax credit FINANCE, BANKING, AND ACCOUNTING a tax advantage for investment, available until 1986

investment trust FINANCE, BANKING, AND ACCOUNTING an association of investors that invests in securities

investomer FINANCE, BANKING, AND ACCOUNTING a customer of a business who is also an investor *(slang)*

investor FINANCE, BANKING, AND ACCOUNTING a person or organization that invests money in something, especially in shares of publicly owned corporations

investor relations research MARKETING research carried out on behalf of an organization in order to gain an understanding of how financial markets regard the organization, its shares, and its sector

invisible exports ECONOMICS the profits, dividends, interest, and royalties received from selling a country's services abroad

invisible imports ECONOMICS the profits, dividends, interest, and royalties paid to foreign service companies based in a country

invisibles ECONOMICS items such as financial and leisure services, as opposed to physical goods, that are traded by a country

invisible trade ECONOMICS trade in items such as financial and other services that are listed in the current account of the balance of payments

invitation to tender GENERAL MANAGEMENT a formal statement of requirements sent to shortlisted suppliers, inviting the submission of a formal proposal for completing a particular piece of work. An invitation to tender should provide background information on the organization and identify the key areas that suppliers need to address such as functionality and operating requirements. A timetable for the tendering process should also be included.

invoice FINANCE, BANKING, AND ACCOUNTING a document that a supplier sends to a customer detailing the cost of products or services supplied and requesting payment

invoice date FINANCE, BANKING, AND ACCOUNTING the date on which an invoice is issued. The invoice date may be different from the delivery date.

invoice discounting FINANCE, BANKING, AND ACCOUNTING the selling of invoices at a discount for collection by the buyer

invoicing FINANCE, BANKING, AND ACCOUNTING the process of issuing invoices

involuntary liquidation preference FINANCE, BANKING, AND ACCOUNTING a payment that a company must make to holders of its preferred stock if it is forced to sell its assets when facing bankruptcy

inward investment FINANCE, BANKING, AND ACCOUNTING investment by a government or company in its own country or region, often to stimulate employment or develop a business infrastructure

IOW *abbr* GENERAL MANAGEMENT in other words *(slang)*

IP E-COMMERCE see ***Internet***

IP address E-COMMERCE Internet protocol address, an identifier for a computer or other Internet-enabled device on the Internet and other ***TCP/IP*** networks. The format of an IP address is a numeric address written as four groups of numbers separated by dots. For example, 1.542.20.350 could be an IP address.

IRCA GENERAL MANAGEMENT see ***Industrial Relations Court of Australia***

IRD *(ANZ)* FINANCE, BANKING, AND ACCOUNTING see ***Inland Revenue Department***

IRD number FINANCE, BANKING, AND ACCOUNTING a numeric code assigned to all members of the New Zealand workforce for the purpose of paying income tax

IRL *abbr* GENERAL MANAGEMENT in real life *(slang)*

irritainment GENERAL MANAGEMENT television programs or other forms of entertainment that are irritating but nevertheless compulsive viewing *(slang)*

ISC *(ANZ)* GENERAL MANAGEMENT see ***Insurance and Superannuation Commission***

ISDN *abbr* E-COMMERCE Integrated Services Digital Network, a digital telephone network supporting advanced communications services and used for high-speed data transmission

ISDN line E-COMMERCE a digital telephone line supporting advanced communications services and used for high-speed data transmission

Ishikawa, Kaoru (1915–89) GENERAL MANAGEMENT Japanese academic. Originator of ***fishbone charts*** and champion of other ***quality control*** tools such as ***Pareto charts***, as explained in *Guide to Quality Control* (1976).

Ishikawa diagram GENERAL MANAGEMENT see ***fishbone chart***

ISO *abbr*
1. E-COMMERCE independent service organization, a company that processes online credit card transactions for small businesses, usually in exchange for a fee or percentage of sales
2. GENERAL MANAGEMENT International Standards Organization, an organization responsible for determining and managing common standards for products and for business and manufacturing processes

ISO 14000 GENERAL MANAGEMENT a series of internationally recognized ***quality standards*** providing a framework that organizations can use to regulate the environmental impact of their activities. ISO 14000 is a management system standard rather than a performance standard and can be applied to organizations of all shapes and sizes, wherever they may be located. The standard does not identify specific goals but presents a framework for carrying out environmental management. **ISO 14001** is the part of the standard that specifies the requirements that organizations must meet if they are to obtain certification. ISO 14001 gives a framework for identifying operations, processes, and products that impact on the environment, for evaluating these impacts, for setting objectives and targets for reducing any negative impacts that have been identified, and for implementing activities to achieve targets. ISO 14000 provides a certified standard that can be seen as a reflection of an organization's ethical achievements. It pays no attention, however, to cultural or human dimensions and disregards the fact that organizations will need to perceive bottom-line cost benefits if they are to implement the standard.

ISO 14001 GENERAL MANAGEMENT see ***ISO 14000***

ISO 9000 GENERAL MANAGEMENT a series of international quality management system ***standards***. ISO 9000 provides a framework that can be used by any size or type of organization to develop a quality system. It lays down a general set of principles about good management practice, which identify the basic disciplines and specify criteria to ensure that products and services meet customers' requirements. The framework enables the measurement of consistency of an organization's systems for dealing with customer orders, purchasing, stock control, service provision, and service delivery. Requirements for certification include written quality procedures, regular management reviews, control of documentation, traceability, internal auditing, and the provision of training.

ISP *abbr* E-COMMERCE Internet service provider, a company or organization that not only provides an entry point to the Internet, like an ***Internet access provider***, but also additional services such as Web site hosting and Web page development

issue FINANCE, BANKING, AND ACCOUNTING a set of stocks or bonds that a company offers for sale at one time

Issue Department FINANCE, BANKING, AND ACCOUNTING the department of the Bank of England that is responsible for issuing currency

issue price FINANCE, BANKING, AND ACCOUNTING the price at which securities are first offered for sale

issuer E-COMMERCE a financial institution that issues payment cards such as credit or debit cards, pays out to the merchant's account, and bills the customer or debits the customer's account. The issuer guarantees payment for authorized transactions using the payment card. Also called ***card-issuing bank***, ***issuing bank***

issuer bid FINANCE, BANKING, AND ACCOUNTING an offer that an issuer that is disappointed by the offers of others makes for its own securities

issues management GENERAL MANAGEMENT the anticipation and assessment of key trends and themes of the next decade, and the relation of these to the organization. Issues management is informed by ***futures research*** in order to formulate strategic plans and actions.

issuing bank E-COMMERCE = ***issuer***

itchy finger syndrome E-COMMERCE the Internet user's need for interactivity. Sites can combat this by adding interactive elements such as ***hyperlinks*** and online ***forums***.

item non-response STATISTICS a refusal to respond to a question in a statistical survey or a response that cannot be fitted into the given response design

J

jack in GENERAL MANAGEMENT to connect to something electronically, especially to a network via a modem or other communication device

Japanese management GENERAL MANAGEMENT, HR & PERSONNEL a ***management style*** with particular emphasis on employees and manufacturing techniques, to which the Japanese economic miracle that began in the 1960s is attributed. Japanese management practices have been studied in the rest of the world in the hope that the economic success they brought to Japan can be recreated elsewhere. These practices include forming collaborations, particularly in times of uncertainty, on human resources, on closer superior-subordinate relationships, and on consensus as a means of facilitating implementation. ***Richard Pascale*** and ***Anthony Athos*** suggested that the Japanese ***competitive advantage*** stemmed from skills, staff, and superordinate goals, the softer features identified by the ***McKinsey 7-S framework***. Other dominant characteristics include people-centered management, loyalty to employees, ***just-in-time***, ***kaizen***, ***continuous improvement***, ***quality control***, ***total quality management***, and the ideas of ***W. Edwards Deming***. ***William Ouchi*** expounded ***Theory J*** and ***Theory Z***, which demonstrated the differences between U.S. and Japanese styles of management. With the downturn in the Japanese economy in the 1990s, management practices were reappraised, and there emerged a focus on radical change as opposed to incremental improvement. Customers were offered less variety, there was a shift toward simplicity, and an alternative to consensus-based decision making was adopted, with individuals making decisions based on high-tech information systems.

W. EDWARDS DEMING (pp. 980–81); RICHARD TANNER PASCALE (pp. 1034–35)

Japanese payment option E-COMMERCE a series of extensions to the ***SET*** protocol to facilitate handling features unique to the Japanese market. Abbr **JPO**

Jaques, Elliot (*b.* 1917) GENERAL MANAGEMENT Canadian psychologist and writer. Best known for his participation in the ***Glacier studies***, and for originating the ***time span of discretion*** theory.

Java E-COMMERCE a programming language developed in the mid-1990s to enhance the visual appearance and interactive elements of Web documents. Java is automatically translated using a Java-compatible Web browser. For example, an Internet user can connect to a Java ***applet*** on the Web, download it, and run it, all at the click of a mouse.

JEPI E-COMMERCE see ***joint electronic payment initiative***

JIT OPERATIONS & PRODUCTION see ***just-in-time***

job

1. HR & PERSONNEL a position of employment
2. OPERATIONS & PRODUCTION a batch of work that undergoes a specific action through a workstation or workshop

jobbing OPERATIONS & PRODUCTION = ***job production***

job classification HR & PERSONNEL the listing of jobs in groups according to areas of similarity. The term job classification normally applies to a broad classification of work such as the schemes produced by the Office for National Statistics in the United Kingdom or the International Labor Office in Geneva. At an organizational level, job classification is more usually referred to as **job grading** and is used for ***job evaluation*** purposes.

job design HR & PERSONNEL the process of putting together various elements to form a job, bearing in mind organizational and individual worker requirements, as well as considerations of health, safety, and ***ergonomics***. The ***scientific management*** approach of ***Frederick Winslow Taylor*** viewed job design as purely mechanistic, but the later ***human relations*** movement rediscovered the importance of workers' relationship to their work and stressed the importance of ***job satisfaction***.

job enlargement HR & PERSONNEL the addition of extra similar tasks to a job. In job enlargement, the job itself remains essentially unchanged, the employee rarely needs to acquire new skills to carry out the additional task, and the motivational benefits of job enrichment are not experienced. Job enlargement is sometimes viewed by employees as a requirement to carry out more work for the same amount of pay.

job evaluation HR & PERSONNEL a technique that aims to provide a systematic, rational, and consistent approach to defining the relative worth of jobs within an organization. Job evaluation is a system for analyzing and comparing different jobs and placing them in a ranking order according to the overall demands of each one. It is not concerned with the volume of work or with the person doing it or with determining pay. It is used in order to provide the basis for an equitable and defensible pay structure, particularly in determining ***equal pay*** for equal value. Job evaluation schemes can be divided into two main categories: nonanalytical and analytical. In nonanalytical schemes a job is compared with others as a whole, but such schemes have a limited use, because they are unlikely to succeed as a defense against an equal value claim. In an analytical scheme, a job is split up into a number of different aspects and each factor is measured separately. The main types of analytical schemes are factor comparison, point-factor rating, competency-based schemes, and the ***profile method***.

job family HR & PERSONNEL a category of jobs in a similar area. Examples of job families might be engineering, agriculture, health, and sport and leisure. Job families are also found within an organization, for example, clerical, sales, information technology, etc. Such families are sometimes used when determining ***pay scales*** or for statistical analysis of the ***workforce***.

job grading HR & PERSONNEL see ***job classification***

job lock GENERAL MANAGEMENT the inability to leave a job because of a fear of losing the benefits associated with it (*slang*)

job process system OPERATIONS & PRODUCTION see ***job production***

job production OPERATIONS & PRODUCTION the manufacture of different products in unit quantities or in very small numbers. In job production, a complete task may be handled by one worker and is often carried out in a ***job shop***. A company may operate under a **job process system**, producing small batches of sometimes unique products and so becoming a job shop in itself. Job production is characterized by a functional grouping of equipment and staff and by the considerable variation in the time it takes to complete a given job. Also known as ***jobbing***

job rotation HR & PERSONNEL the movement of employees through a range of jobs in order to increase interest and ***motivation***. Job rotation can improve ***multiskilling*** but involves the need for greater ***training***.

job satisfaction HR & PERSONNEL the sense of fulfillment and pride felt by people who enjoy their work and do it well. Various factors influence job satisfaction, and our understanding of the significance of these stems in part from ***Frederick Herzberg***. He called elements such as remuneration, working relationships, status, and job security " **hygiene factors**" because they concern the context in which somebody works. Hygiene factors do not in themselves promote job satisfaction, but serve primarily to prevent job dissatisfaction. **Motivators** contribute to job satisfaction and include achievement, recognition, the work itself, responsibility, advancement, and growth. An absence of job satisfaction can lead to poor ***motivation***, ***stress***, ***absenteeism***, and high labor turnover.

job-share HR & PERSONNEL a form of employment in which two or more people occupy a single job. Each person works on a part-time basis and is paid pro-rata for the number of hours they work in the job.

job shop OPERATIONS & PRODUCTION a manufacturing facility designed to work on a ***job production*** basis, producing small quantities of what are often specialized or expensive items. A job shop can be a special facility within a factory, or a whole company can be run as a job shop. Job shops often have the ability to produce a wide variety of products.

job vacuum GENERAL MANAGEMENT an employee who voluntarily takes on extra duties (*slang*)

Johari window HR & PERSONNEL a ***communication*** model that facilitates analysis of both how someone gives and receives information and the dynamics of ***interpersonal communication***. The Johari window was developed by Joseph Luft and Henry Ingram. It is normally represented in the form of a grid divided into four sections, each of which represents a type of communication exchange. First, there is the open self: you have awareness of the impact you have on the other and the impact they have on you, so that the risk of interpersonal conflict is minimized. The second sector covers the hidden self: you have awareness of your impact on others, but not of their impact on you. This leads to defensive behavior in which you seek to hide what you want and increases the possibility of interpersonal conflict. In the third sector, or blind self, you have awareness of what the other wants, but you lack self-awareness of the impact of your communication or actions. Finally, there is the undiscovered self: you lack self-awareness and are either unaware of or cannot understand the other. Although the Johari window can be used in a number of situations, it is most frequently used as a tool for ***training*** or ***coaching*** purposes, in order to provide feedback on communication skills.

Johnson, Spencer GENERAL MANAGEMENT U.S. writer and consultant. Collaborated with ***Kenneth Blanchard*** on the concept of one minute management, but is also known for *Who Moved My Cheese?* (1998), a parable on ***change management***.

KENNETH BLANCHARD (pp. 970–71)

joined-up (*U.K.*) GENERAL MANAGEMENT relating to an idea or initiative that involves both the community and government in an effort to improve the quality of life for everyone (*slang*)

joint account FINANCE, BANKING, AND ACCOUNTING an account, for example, one held at a bank or by a broker, that two or more people own in common and have access to

joint electronic payment initiative E-COMMERCE a proposed industry standard protocol for electronic payment in e-commerce transactions. Abbr **JEPI**

joint float ECONOMICS a situation in which a group of currencies maintains a fixed relationship relative to each other but moves jointly relative to another currency

joint ownership GENERAL MANAGEMENT ownership by more than one party, each with equal rights in the item owned. Joint ownership is often applied to property or other assets.

Joint Photographics Experts Group E-COMMERCE see ***JPEG***

joint return FINANCE, BANKING, AND ACCOUNTING a tax return filed jointly by a husband and a wife

joint venture FINANCE, BANKING, AND ACCOUNTING a business project in which two or more independent companies collaborate and share the risks and rewards

JPEG E-COMMERCE Joint Photographics Experts Group, a file format used to compress and store photographic images for transfer over the Internet. See ***GIF***

JPO E-COMMERCE see ***Japanese payment option***

JSE *abbr* FINANCE, BANKING, AND ACCOUNTING Johannesburg Stock Exchange, now officially the JSE Securities Exchange

jumbo mortgage FINANCE, BANKING, AND ACCOUNTING a mortgage that is too large to qualify for favorable treatment by a government agency

junior debt FINANCE, BANKING, AND ACCOUNTING a debt that has no claim on a debtor's assets or less claim than another debt. See ***senior debt***. Also known as ***subordinated debt***

junior mortgage FINANCE, BANKING, AND ACCOUNTING a mortgage whose holder has less claim on a debtor's assets than the holder of another mortgage. See ***senior mortgage***

junk bond FINANCE, BANKING, AND ACCOUNTING a bond with high return and high risk

Juran, Joseph Moses (*b.* 1904) GENERAL MANAGEMENT Romanian-born engineer and consultant. Introduced ideas on ***total quality management*** to Japan and later, like ***W. Edwards Deming***, to the West. Juran's methods, first published in *Quality Control Handbook* (1951), center on building a customer-focused organization through planning, control and improvement, and good people management.

✔ TOTAL QUALITY: MAPPING A TQM STRATEGY (pp. 524–25); TOTAL QUALITY: GETTING TQM TO WORK (pp. 522–23)
W. EDWARDS DEMING (pp. 980–81)

just-in-time OPERATIONS & PRODUCTION, GENERAL MANAGEMENT a manufacturing philosophy involving the total elimination of waste. Just-in-time is a system of supplying to each process what is needed, at the time it is needed, and in the quantity it is needed. Production ***lead time*** is minimized and significant savings can be made from reduced ***inventory***. Just-in-time requires all activities in the production process to be geared to adding value for the customer. Critical components of the system include ***total quality management*** and ***employee involvement***. The concept was invented by Kiichiro Toyoda and developed further by ***Taiichi Ohno*** at the Toyota Motor Company following World War II. ***Kanban*** is part of this system but is aimed solely at the elimination of waste. Abbr **JIT**

K

kaizen OPERATIONS & PRODUCTION, GENERAL MANAGEMENT the Japanese term for the ***continuous improvement*** of current processes. Kaizen is derived from the words "kai," meaning "change," and "zen," meaning "good" or "for the better." It is a philosophy that can be applied to any area of life, but its application has been most famously developed at the Toyota Motor Company, and it underlies the philosophy of ***total quality management***. Under kaizen, continuous improvement can mean waste elimination, innovation, or working to new standards. The kaizen process makes use of a range of techniques, including small-group ***problem solving***, ***suggestion schemes***, statistical techniques, ***brainstorming***, and ***work study***. Although kaizen forms only part of a strategy of continuous improvement, for many employees it is the element that most closely affects them and is therefore synonymous with continuous improvement.

kanban OPERATIONS & PRODUCTION a Japanese production management technique that uses cards attached to components to monitor and control workflow in a factory. The kanban system was first developed by the car manufacturer Toyota.

kanbrain GENERAL MANAGEMENT relating to the technology that is used in the transmission of knowledge (*slang*)

Kanter, Rosabeth Moss (*b.* 1943) GENERAL MANAGEMENT U.S. academic. Known for her interest in new ***organization structures***, with a focus on harnessing ***change***, encouraging ***innovation***, and increasing ***empowerment*** among employees. Her research has also embraced ***globalization***. Among her many books is *The Change Masters* (1988).

ROSABETH MOSS KANTER (pp. 1008–09)

Kaplan, Robert S. GENERAL MANAGEMENT U.S. academic. Codeveloper, with ***David P. Norton***, of the ***balanced scorecard***, which looks at intangible assets such as ***customer satisfaction*** alongside traditional financial measures. This concept, introduced in a *Harvard Business Review* article of 1992 with the saying "What you measure is what you get," was explained in *The Balanced Scorecard* (1996).

✔ IMPLEMENTING THE BALANCED SCORECARD (pp. 510–11)
ROBERT S. KAPLAN (pp. 1010–11)

KBG GENERAL MANAGEMENT see ***keiretsu***

keiretsu *or* **keiretsu business group** GENERAL MANAGEMENT, OPERATIONS & PRODUCTION a Japanese loose ***conglomerate company*** that promotes interdependencies between firms with interlocking interests in each other and is characterized by close internal control, policy coordination and cohesiveness. Keiretsu business groups are alliances between firms that share close buyer-supplier relationships. The issue of interlocking shares by group affiliated companies to member companies of the group keeps ownership in friendly hands, helps prevent foreign ***takeovers***, and aids a company's long-term survival and growth. There are two sorts of keiretsu operation: **horizontal keiretsu**, in which member firms are involved in different industries: and **vertical keiretsu**, in which member firms in one industry form themselves into a hierarchy with a lead company. Vertical KBGs consist largely of manufacturing companies and their subcontractors. Some keiretsu are 350 years old, but most developed from the prewar ***zaibatsu***. The Korean equivalent of the keiretsu is the **chaebol**, and a Mexican equivalent is the ***grupo***. Abbr **KBG**

Keough Plan FINANCE, BANKING, AND ACCOUNTING a pension subject to tax advantage for somebody who is self-employed or has an interest in a small company. See ***stakeholder pension***

Kepner, Charles Higgins (*b.* 1922) GENERAL MANAGEMENT U.S. manager and consultant. Originator with ***Benjamin Tregoe*** of a methodological approach to ***decision making*** based on information gathering, organization, and analysis, which was first explained in the *Rational Manager* (1965).

kerb market (*U.K.*) FINANCE, BANKING, AND ACCOUNTING a stock market that exists outside the stock exchange. The term originates from markets held in the street.

Kets de Vries, **Manfred Florian Robert** (*b.* 1942) GENERAL MANAGEMENT Dutch psychoanalyst and academic. His principal academic interests focus on the interface between psychoanalysis/dynamic psychiatry and ***management***, ***leadership***, ***entrepreneurship***, and ***family business***.

key account management MARKETING the management of the customer relationships that are most important to a company. Key accounts are those held by customers who produce most ***profit*** for a company or have the potential to do so, or those who are of strategic importance. Development of these ***customer relations*** and ***customer retention*** is important to business success. Particular emphasis is placed on analyzing which accounts are key to a company at any one time, determining the needs of these particular customers, and implementing procedures to ensure that they receive premium ***customer service*** and to increase ***customer satisfaction***.

keyboard plaque GENERAL MANAGEMENT the buildup of dirt that becomes ingrained in computer keyboards (*slang*)

key-man insurance GENERAL MANAGEMENT see ***key-person insurance***

Keynesian economics ECONOMICS the economic teachings and doctrines associated with John Maynard Keynes

key-person insurance GENERAL MANAGEMENT an insurance policy taken out to cover the costs of replacing a key ***employee***. Key person insurance comes into play in the case of an employee's death or medium- to long-term sickness or death. Also known as ***key-man insurance***

keyword E-COMMERCE a word used by a search engine to help locate and register a Web site. Companies need to think very carefully about the keywords they place in their ***meta-tags*** and in Web pages in order to attract relevant search-engine traffic.

keyword search E-COMMERCE a search for documents containing one or more words that are specified by a search-engine user

kiasu GENERAL MANAGEMENT a Hokkien word, used to describe the "must win, never lose" mentality of Singaporeans

killer app E-COMMERCE a computer application that is extremely effective or commercially successful

killerbee FINANCE, BANKING, AND ACCOUNTING somebody, especially a banker, who helps a company avoid being taken over

killfile E-COMMERCE a list on an Internet newsreader of undesirable authors or threads that can be filtered out by the user (*slang*)

Kim, **W. Chan** GENERAL MANAGEMENT Korean-born academic. INSEAD Professor, Fellow of the World Economic Forum, writer on the knowledge economy and collaborator with ***Renée Mauborgne*** on research into ***corporate strategy*** and ***value innovation***.

kimono

open the kimono GENERAL MANAGEMENT to inspect something that has not been open for examination before, especially a company's accounts (*slang*)

KISS *abbr* GENERAL MANAGEMENT keep it simple stupid (*slang*)

kiss up to sb GENERAL MANAGEMENT to attempt to ingratiate yourself with somebody who is in a position of power (*slang*)

knight GENERAL MANAGEMENT a term borrowed from chess strategy to describe a company involved in the politics of a ***takeover*** bid. There are three main types of knight. A **white knight** is a company that is friendly to the board of the company to be acquired. If the white knight gains control, it may retain the existing ***board of directors***. A **black knight** is a former white knight that has disagreed with the board of the company to be acquired and has set up its own hostile bid. A **gray knight** is a white knight that does not have the confidence of the company to be acquired.

Knight, **Phil** (*b.* 1938) GENERAL MANAGEMENT U.S. entrepreneur. Founder of Nike Inc., whose company's worldwide success is based on strong ***brand building***, aggressive marketing, and the ***outsourcing*** of production to Asia.

knocking copy GENERAL MANAGEMENT advertising copy that consists of criticism of a competitor's product or company

knockout option FINANCE, BANKING, AND ACCOUNTING an option to which a condition relating to the underlying security or commodity's present price is attached so that it effectively expires when it goes out of the money

know-how GENERAL MANAGEMENT practical knowledge and experience of a particular product, market, or technology

knowledge GENERAL MANAGEMENT information acquired by the interpretation of experience. Knowledge is built up from interaction with the world and organized and stored in each individual's mind. It is also stored on an organizational level within the minds of employees and in paper and electronic records. Two forms of knowledge can be distinguished: **tacit knowledge** or **implicit knowledge**, which is held in a person's mind and is instinctively known without being formulated into words; and **explicit knowledge**, which has been communicated to others and is contained in written documents and procedures. Organizations are increasingly recognizing the value of knowledge, and many employees are now recognized as ***knowledge workers***. A major writer in this area is ***Ikujiro Nonaka***, author of *The Knowledge-Creating Company (1995)*, who asserted that knowledge is the greatest ***core capability*** (see ***core competence***) that an organization can have.

knowledge capital GENERAL MANAGEMENT knowledge that a company possesses and can put to profitable use

knowledge management GENERAL MANAGEMENT

1. the process of acquiring, storing, distributing, and using information within a company. The information is generally held on a powerful database and distributed via a communications network.

2. the coordination and exploitation of an organization's ***knowledge*** resources, in order to create benefit and ***competitive advantage***

PETER DRUCKER (pp. 982–85)

knowledge worker GENERAL MANAGEMENT an ***employee*** who deals in information, ideas, and expertise. Knowledge workers are products of the so-called information age, in which the onus is on ***creativity*** and ***innovation*** rather than on maintaining the status quo. According to ***Peter Drucker***, in the new economy every employee is becoming a knowledge worker.

Kolb, **David A.** (*b.* 1939) GENERAL MANAGEMENT U.S. academic. Originator of the concept of ***experiential learning***, a model describing how adults learn, which he explained in the book of the same name (1984).

Kotler, **Philip** (*b.* 1931) GENERAL MANAGEMENT U.S. academic. Acknowledged as an ex-

  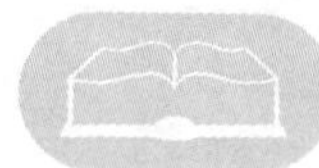    

pert in ***marketing*** theory, which he has made a major business function and academic discipline and which he explained in *Marketing Management* (first published 1980).

Krugerrand FINANCE, BANKING, AND ACCOUNTING a South African coin consisting of one ounce of gold, first minted in 1967, bearing the portrait of Paul Kruger on the obverse

L

laboratory training GENERAL MANAGEMENT = ***sensitivity training***

labor dispute HR & PERSONNEL
1. a disagreement or conflict between an ***employer*** and ***employees*** or between the ***employers' association*** and ***labor union*** that represent them
2. = ***strike***

labor force HR & PERSONNEL people of working age who are available for paid employment, including the unemployed looking for work, but excluding categories such as full-time students, carers, and the long-term sick and disabled

labor-intensive FINANCE, BANKING, AND ACCOUNTING involving large numbers of workers or high labor costs

labor market HR & PERSONNEL a market that brings together employers and people who are looking for employment

labor shortage HR & PERSONNEL
1. a lack of workers or potential workers to fill the jobs available
2. a lack of suitably qualified and skilled workers to fill particular vacancies. This is more correctly described as a ***skills shortage***.

labor tourist HR & PERSONNEL somebody who lives in one country but works in another (*slang*)

labor union HR & PERSONNEL, GENERAL MANAGEMENT an organization of ***employees*** within a trade or profession that has the objective of representing its members' interests, primarily through improving pay and conditions, and provides a variety of services

Lady Macbeth strategy GENERAL MANAGEMENT a change of approach on the part of a presumed white ***knight***, in which it becomes a black knight. A Lady Macbeth strategy is usually associated with ***takeover*** battles and has connotations of treachery.

laggard MARKETING see ***first mover***

lagging indicator ECONOMICS a measurable economic factor, for example, corporate profits or unemployment, that changes after the economy has already moved to a new trend, which it can confirm but not predict

LAN E-COMMERCE see ***network***

land tax FINANCE, BANKING, AND ACCOUNTING a form of wealth tax imposed in Australia on the value of residential land. The level and conditions of the tax vary from state to state.

lapse FINANCE, BANKING, AND ACCOUNTING the termination of an option without trade in the underlying security or commodity

lapse rights FINANCE, BANKING, AND ACCOUNTING the rights, such as those to a specified premium, owned by the person who allows an offer to lapse

laptop GENERAL MANAGEMENT a compact portable computer

large-sized business GENERAL MANAGEMENT an organization that has grown beyond the limits of a ***medium-sized business*** and has 500 or more employees. It is usually from the ranks of large-sized businesses that ***multinational businesses*** arise.

last-in, first-out HR & PERSONNEL see ***LIFO***

latent market MARKETING a group of people who have been identified as potential consumers of a product that does not yet exist

lateral thinking GENERAL MANAGEMENT a creative method of problem solving that ignores traditional logic and approaches problems from unorthodox perspectives. Lateral thinking was developed by ***Edward de Bono***, who distinguished two forms of thinking: vertical thinking, which is based on logic; and lateral thinking, which disregards apparently rational trains of thought and branches out at tangents. Lateral thinking involves the examination of a problem and its possible solutions from all angles. Seemingly intractable problems often can be solved in this manner, and it is a technique used in ***brainstorming*** or to help generate ***creativity*** and ***innovation*** within organizations.

launch MARKETING the process of introducing a new product to the market

laundering FINANCE, BANKING, AND ACCOUNTING the process of making money obtained illegally appear legitimate by passing it through banks or businesses

law of diminishing returns GENERAL MANAGEMENT a rule stating that as one factor of production is increased, while others remain constant, the extra output generated by the additional input will eventually fall. The law of diminishing returns therefore means that extra workers, extra capital, extra machinery, or extra land may not necessarily raise output as much as expected. For example, increasing the supply of raw materials to a production line may allow additional output to be produced by using any spare capacity workers have. Once this capacity is fully used, however, continually increasing the amount of raw material without a corresponding increase in the number of workers will not result in an increase of output.

law of supply and demand GENERAL MANAGEMENT see ***supply and demand***

lay-by (*ANZ*) GENERAL MANAGEMENT the reservation of an article for purchase by the payment of an initial deposit followed by regular interest-free installments, on completion of which the article is claimed by the buyer

lay off HR & PERSONNEL
1. to dismiss workers permanently
2. to suspend workers temporarily because of lack of work

layout by function OPERATIONS & PRODUCTION = ***process layout***

LBO FINANCE, BANKING, AND ACCOUNTING see ***leveraged buyout***

LDC ECONOMICS see ***less developed country***

leader
1. GENERAL MANAGEMENT, HR & PERSONNEL a business executive who possesses exceptional leadership qualities as well as management skills
2. MARKETING the most successful product or company in a marketplace

leadership GENERAL MANAGEMENT, HR & PERSONNEL the capacity to establish direction and to influence and align others toward a common aim, motivating and committing them to action and making them responsible for their performance. Leadership theory is one of the most discussed areas of management, and many different approaches are taken to the topic. Some notions of leadership are related to types of ***authority*** delineated by ***Max Weber***. These imply involuntary or forced obedience to orders by those receiving them and envision an inspiring or dictatorial leader. It is often suggested that leaders possess innate personal qualities that distinguish them from others, and ***great man theory*** and ***trait theory*** express this idea. Other theories suggest, however, that leadership is defined by action and behavior, rather than by personality characteristics. ***Behaviorist theories*** of leadership show research in this direction. A related idea is that leadership style is not fixed but should be adapted to different situations, and this is explored in ***contingency theory*** and situational theory. A further branch of research that examines relationships between leaders and followers is found in ***transactional***, ***transformational***, ***attribution***, and ***power and influence theories of leadership***. Perhaps the most simple model of leadership is ***action-centered leadership***, which focuses on what an effective leader actually does. These many approaches and differences of opinion illustrate the complexity of the leadership role and the intangibility of the essence of good leadership.

MAX WEBER (pp. 1060–61)

leading economic indicator ECONOMICS a factor such as private-sector wages that is used as a reference for public-sector wage claims

leading edge GENERAL MANAGEMENT situated at the forefront of ***innovation***. A leading edge company is ahead of others in such areas as inventing or implementing new technologies, and in entering new markets.

lead partner GENERAL MANAGEMENT the organization that takes the lead role in an alliance

lead time OPERATIONS & PRODUCTION

1. in inventory control, the time between placing an order and its arrival on site. Lead time differs from delivery time in that it also includes the time required to place an order and the time it takes inspecting the goods and receiving them into the appropriate store. Inventory levels can afford to be lower and orders smaller when purchasing lead times are short.

2. in ***new product development*** and manufacturing, the time required to develop a product from concept to market delivery. Lead time increases as a result of the poor sequencing of dependent activities, the lack of availability of resources, poor quality in the component parts, and poor plant layout. The technique of ***concurrent engineering*** focuses on the entire concept-to-customer process with the aim of reducing lead time. Companies can gain a ***competitive advantage*** by achieving a lead time reduction and so getting products to market faster. Also known as ***cycle time***

leaky reply E-COMMERCE an e-mail response that is accidentally sent to the wrong recipient and causes embarrassment to the sender (*slang*)

lean enterprise OPERATIONS & PRODUCTION an organizational model that strategically applies the key ideas behind ***lean production***. The concept of the lean enterprise was proposed by J. P. Womack and D. T. Jones in their 1994 *Harvard Business Review* article "From lean production to the lean enterprise." They view the lean enterprise as a group of separate individuals, functions, or organizations that operate as one entity. The aim is to apply lean techniques that create individual breakthroughs in companies and to link these up and down the ***supply chain*** to form a continuous value stream to raise the whole chain to a higher level.

lean manufacturing OPERATIONS & PRODUCTION see ***lean production***

lean operation OPERATIONS & PRODUCTION see ***lean production***

lean production OPERATIONS & PRODUCTION a methodology aimed at reducing waste in the form of overproduction, excessive ***lead time***, or product defects in order to make a business more effective and more competitive. Lean production originates in the production systems established by Toyota in Japan in the 1950s. In the early 1980s there was a significant increase in the application of lean production in Western companies. Lean production is characterized by **lean operations** with low ***inventories***, ***quality management*** through prevention of errors, small batch runs, ***just-in-time*** production, high commitment human resource policies, team-based working, and close relations with suppliers. The term lean production was popularized by researchers on the International Motor Vehicle Program of the Massachusetts Institute of Technology in their book *The Machine that Changed the World*. Concepts that can help an organization move toward lean production include ***continuous improvement*** and ***world class manufacturing***.

☆ LEAN MANUFACTURING (pp. 183–84)

LEAPS FINANCE, BANKING, AND ACCOUNTING long-term equity anticipation securities, options that expire between one and three years in the future

learning by doing GENERAL MANAGEMENT the acquisition of knowledge or skills through direct experience of carrying out a task. Learning by doing often happens under supervision, as part of a training or ***induction*** process, and is closely associated with the practical experience picked up by " **sitting with Nellie**." It is an outcome of the research into learning of ***David Kolb*** and ***Reg Revans***. A more formalized approach to learning by doing is ***experiential learning***.

REG REVANS (pp. 1042–43)

learning curve GENERAL MANAGEMENT

1. a graphic representation of the acquisition of knowledge or experience over time. A steep learning curve reflects a substantial amount of learning in a short time, and a shallow curve reflects a slower learning process. The curve eventually levels out to a plateau, during which time the knowledge gained is being consolidated.

2. the proportional decrease in effort when production is doubled. The learning curve has its origin in ***productivity*** research in the airplane industry of the 1930s, when ***T. P. Wright*** discovered that in assembling an aircraft, the time and effort decreased by 20% each time the cumulative number of planes produced doubled. ***Bruce Henderson*** of the Boston Consulting Group formulated the learning curve as a strategic planning device in the 1960s by plotting product costs against cumulative volume.

learning organization GENERAL MANAGEMENT an organizational model characterized by a ***flat*** structure and ***customer-focused*** teams that engenders the collective ability to develop shared visions by capturing and exploiting employees' willingness, commitment, and curiosity. The concept of the learning organization was proposed by ***Chris Argyris*** and ***Donald Schon*** as part of their work on ***organizational learning***, but was brought back to public attention in the 1990s by ***Peter Senge***. For Senge, a learning organization is one with the capacity to shift away from views inherent to a traditional hierarchical, organization, toward the ability of all employees to challenge prevailing thinking and gain a balanced perspective. Senge believes the five major elements of a learning organization are mental models, personal mastery, ***systems thinking***, shared vision, and team learning. Because of the requirement for an open risk-tolerant culture, which is the opposite of the ***corporate culture*** of most organizations today, the learning organization remains, for many, an unattainable ideal.

CHRIS ARGYRIS (pp. 964–65); PETER SENGE (pp. 1046–47)

learning relationship GENERAL MANAGEMENT a relationship between a supplier and a customer in which the supplier modifies or customizes a product as it learns more about the customer's requirements

learning style GENERAL MANAGEMENT the way in which somebody approaches the acquisition of knowledge and skills. Learning styles have been divided into four main types by ***Peter Honey*** and ***Alan Mumford***, in their *Manual of Learning Styles* (1982). The types of learner are: the activist, who likes to get involved in new experiences and enjoys the challenges of change; the theorist, who likes to question assumptions and methodologies and learns best when there is time to explore links between ideas and situations; the pragmatist, who prefers practicality and learns best when there is a link between the subject matter and the job in hand and when he or she can try out what he or she has learned; and the reflector, who likes to take his or her time and think things through, and who learns best from activities where he or she can observe and carry out research. One person can demonstrate more than one learning style, and the category or categories that best describe somebody can be determined through use of a learning styles questionnaire.

leave HR & PERSONNEL work time when an employee is paid, but is not required to be at work. Leave takes several forms. It includes ***vacation*** entitlement. The number of days of vacation is agreed in the ***contract of employment*** and may be dependent on the employee's length of service. It may also take the form of ***sick leave***, ***compassionate leave***, ***garden leave***, ***educational leave***, or ***maternity*** or ***paternity leave***.

Leavitt, **Harold J.** (*b.* 1922) GENERAL MANAGEMENT U.S. psychologist and academic. Researcher with an interest in ***organization behavior*** and psychology, and originator of ***Leavitt's Diamond***. See *Managerial Psychology*(first published 1958).

Leavitt's Diamond GENERAL MANAGEMENT a model for analyzing management change, developed by ***Harold J. Leavitt***. Leavitt's Diamond is based on the idea that it is rare for any change to occur in isolation. Leavitt sees technology, tasks, people, and the organizational structure in which they function as four interdependent variables, visualized as the four points of a diamond. Change at any one point of the diamond will impact on some or all of the others. Thus, a changed task will necessarily affect the people involved in it, the structure in which they work, and the technology that they use. Failure to manage these interdependencies at critical times of change can create problems. See also ***change management***

legacy system E-COMMERCE an existing computer system that provides a strategic function for a specific part of a business. Inventory management systems, for example, are legacy systems.

legal loophole GENERAL MANAGEMENT an area in the law that is insufficiently explicit or comprehensive and allows the law to be circumvented

legs GENERAL MANAGEMENT a longer-than-usual life for an advertising campaign, movie, book, or other short-lived product (*slang*)

lekgotla (*S. Africa*) GENERAL MANAGEMENT = ***bosberaad***

lemon GENERAL MANAGEMENT a product, especially a car, that is defective in some way (*slang*)

lender of last resort FINANCE, BANKING, AND ACCOUNTING a central bank, which lends money to banks that cannot borrow it elsewhere

length of service HR & PERSONNEL the period in which a person has been continually employed within an organization, without breaks in the ***contract of employment***. Length of service may determine entitlement to employment rights or ***fringe benefits***, for example, the amount of annual leave allocated.

less developed country ECONOMICS a country whose economic development is held back by the lack of natural resources to produce goods demanded on world markets. Abbr **LDC**

letter of agreement GENERAL MANAGEMENT a document that constitutes a simple form of contract

letter of allotment FINANCE, BANKING, AND ACCOUNTING a document that says how many shares have been allotted to a shareholder

letter of credit FINANCE, BANKING, AND ACCOUNTING a letter issued by a bank that can be presented to another bank to authorize the issue of credit or money

letter of indemnity FINANCE, BANKING, AND ACCOUNTING a statement that a stock certificate has been lost, destroyed, or stolen and that the shareholder will indemnify the company for any loss that might result from its reappearance after the company has issued a replacement to the shareholder

letter of renunciation FINANCE, BANKING, AND ACCOUNTING a form used to transfer an allotment

level playing field GENERAL MANAGEMENT a situation in which all competitors are in a position of equal strength or weakness (*slang*)

level production GENERAL MANAGEMENT see ***production smoothing***

leverage FINANCE, BANKING, AND ACCOUNTING a method of corporate funding in which a higher proportion of funds is raised through borrowing than share issue

leveraged bid FINANCE, BANKING, AND ACCOUNTING a takeover bid financed by borrowed money, rather than by an issue of shares

leveraged buyout FINANCE, BANKING, AND ACCOUNTING a takeover using borrowed money, with the purchased company's assets as collateral. Abbr **LBO**

leveraged required return FINANCE, BANKING, AND ACCOUNTING the rate of return from an investment of borrowed money needed to make the investment worthwhile

Levitt, **Theodore** (*b.* 1925) GENERAL MANAGEMENT German-born academic. Harvard professor, who wrote the landmark article "Marketing Myopia," *Harvard Business Review* (1960).

THEODORE LEVITT (pp. 1012–13)

Lewin, **Kurt** (1890–1947) GENERAL MANAGEMENT German-born social psychologist. Known for studies of ***leadership*** styles and group ***decision making***, developer of ***force field analysis*** with a linked ***change management*** model, pioneer of ***action research*** and the ***T-Group*** (see ***sensitivity training***) approach.

KURT LEWIN (pp. 1014–15)

liability FINANCE, BANKING, AND ACCOUNTING a debt that has no claim on a debtor's assets, or less claim than another debt

liability insurance FINANCE, BANKING, AND ACCOUNTING insurance against legal liability that the insured might incur, for example, from causing an accident

license GENERAL MANAGEMENT a contractual arrangement, or a document representing this, in which one organization gives another the rights to produce, sell, or use something in return for payment

licensing MARKETING the transfer of rights to manufacture or market a particular product to another individual or organization through a legal arrangement or contract. Licensing usually requires that a fee, commission, or royalty is paid to the licensor. See ***franchise***

licensing agreement MARKETING an agreement permitting a company to market or produce a product or service owned by another company. A licensing agreement grants a license in return for a fee or royalty payment. Items licensed for use can include patents, trademarks, techniques, designs, and expertise. This kind of agreement is one way for a company to penetrate overseas markets in that it provides a middle path between direct export and investment overseas.

life annuity FINANCE, BANKING, AND ACCOUNTING an annuity that pays a fixed amount per month until the holder's death

life assurance (*U.K.*) FINANCE, BANKING, AND ACCOUNTING = ***life insurance***

lifeboat (*S. Africa*) FINANCE, BANKING, AND ACCOUNTING a low-interest emergency loan made by a central bank to rescue a commercial bank in danger of becoming insolvent

life cycle GENERAL MANAGEMENT the sales pattern of a product or service over a period of time. Typically, a life cycle falls into four stages: introduction, growth, maturity, and decline.

life-cycle costing OPERATIONS & PRODUCTION a method of calculating the total cost of a physical asset throughout its life. Life-cycle costing is concerned with all costs of ownership, and takes account of the costs incurred by an asset from its acquisition to its disposal, including design, installation, operating, and maintenance costs.

life-cycle savings motive ECONOMICS the reasons that a household or individual has for saving or spending in the course of life. These can include spending when starting a family or saving when near retirement.

life expectancy STATISTICS the number of years that somebody of a given age is expected to live

life insurance FINANCE, BANKING, AND ACCOUNTING insurance that pays a specified sum to the insured person's beneficiaries after the person's death

lifelong learning GENERAL MANAGEMENT the continual acquisition of knowledge and skills throughout somebody's life. Lifelong learning occurs in preparation for, and in response to, the different roles, situations, and environments that somebody will encounter in the course of a lifetime. It is supported by formal and informal education systems, both within and outside the workplace, through which somebody can both learn and receive guidance and encouragement. The adoption of lifelong learning is seen as a key element in ***CPD***, and as an important tool in maintaining ***employability***.

life table STATISTICS a table that shows the probabilities of death, survival, and remaining years of life for people of given ages

lifetime customer value MARKETING a measure or forecast of a customer's total expenditure on an organization's products over a period of time

lifetime value GENERAL MANAGEMENT a measure of the total value to a supplier of a customer's business over the duration of their transactions

LIFO HR & PERSONNEL last in first out, a technique used when selecting employees for ***redundancy***, where the most recent recruits are the first to be made redundant. The LIFO technique has the benefits of reducing redundancy costs and of being seen as fair by some employees. Its disadvantages, however, are increasingly being recognized. It can result in a serious imbalance in the age profile of the workforce and can remove recently acquired skills. It also may be discriminatory, as men are more likely to have built up periods of ***continuous service*** than women.

lift

let's put it in a lift and see what floor it stops at (*U.K.*) GENERAL MANAGEMENT let's try this idea and see what happens (*slang*)

lightning strike (*U.K.*) HR & PERSONNEL a ***strike*** that occurs at very short notice. It may be of short duration and may not be sanctioned by a ***labor union***.

Likert, Rensis (1903–81) GENERAL MANAGEMENT U.S. psychologist and academic. Known for situational leadership research and in particular for establishing four systems of management to interpret the way managers behave toward others. In *New Patterns of Management* (1961), Likert described these systems as exploitive/authoritative, benevolent/authoritative, consultative, and participative. He later suggested a system 5 in which the authority of hierarchy disappears.

limit FINANCE, BANKING, AND ACCOUNTING an amount above or below which a broker is not to conclude the purchase or sale of a security for the client who specifies it

limit down FINANCE, BANKING, AND ACCOUNTING the most that the price of an option may fall in one day on a particular market

limited company GENERAL MANAGEMENT, HR & PERSONNEL see ***private company***, ***public limited company***

limited liability FINANCE, BANKING, AND ACCOUNTING the restriction of an owner's loss in a business to the amount of capital he or she has invested in it

limited liability company (*U.K.*) FINANCE, BANKING, AND ACCOUNTING a company in which a number of people provide finance in return for shares. The principle of limited liability limits the maximum loss a shareholder can make if the company fails. Abbr **ltd.** = ***corporation***

limit up FINANCE, BANKING, AND ACCOUNTING the most that the price of an option may rise in one day on a particular market

linear programming GENERAL MANAGEMENT a mathematical technique used to identify an optimal solution for the deployment of resources to meet organizational objectives. Linear programming uses graphic and algebraic means to calculate which combination of resources, subject to predicted constraints, is most likely to fulfill a given objective. It was developed during the 1940s for use in military planning.

line management (*U.K.*) HR & PERSONNEL, GENERAL MANAGEMENT a hierarchical ***chain of command*** from executive to front-line level. Line management is the oldest and least complex management structure, in which top management have total and direct authority and employees report to only one ***supervisor***. Managers in this type of ***organization structure*** have direct responsibility for, and are authorized to give, orders to their subordinates. They are usually organized along functional lines, although they increasingly undertake cross-functional duties such as ***employee develop-***

  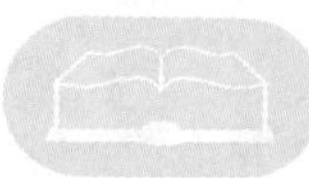  

ment or strategic direction. The lowest managerial level in an organization following a line management structure is ***supervisory management***.

line manager (*U.K.*) HR & PERSONNEL an employee's immediate superior, who oversees and has responsibility for the employee's work. A line manager at the lowest level of a large organization is a ***supervisor***, but a manager at any level with direct responsibility for employees' work can be described as a line manager.

line of credit FINANCE, BANKING, AND ACCOUNTING an agreed finance facility that allows a company or individual to borrow money. Also known as ***credit line***

line organization GENERAL MANAGEMENT an ***organization structure*** based on ***line management***

liquid asset ratio FINANCE, BANKING, AND ACCOUNTING the ratio of liquid assets to total assets

liquid assets FINANCE, BANKING, AND ACCOUNTING financial assets that can be quickly converted to cash

liquidated damages FINANCE, BANKING, AND ACCOUNTING an amount of money somebody pays for breaching a contract

liquidation FINANCE, BANKING, AND ACCOUNTING a process in which a company ceases to be a legal entity, usually because it is insolvent. The company's assets are then sold by a ***liquidator*** to discharge debts.

liquidation value FINANCE, BANKING, AND ACCOUNTING the amount of money that a quick sale of all of a company's assets would yield

liquidator FINANCE, BANKING, AND ACCOUNTING the person appointed by a company, its creditors, or its shareholders to sell the assets of an insolvent company. The proceeds of the sale are used to discharge debts to creditors, with any surplus distributed to shareholders.

liquidity FINANCE, BANKING, AND ACCOUNTING the ability to convert an asset to cash quickly at its market value

liquidity agreement FINANCE, BANKING, AND ACCOUNTING an agreement to allow conversion of an asset into cash

liquidity preference ECONOMICS a choice made by people to hold their wealth in the form of liquid cash rather than bonds or stocks

liquidity ratio FINANCE, BANKING, AND ACCOUNTING = ***cash ratio***

liquidity trap FINANCE, BANKING, AND ACCOUNTING a central bank's inability to lower interest rates once investors believe rates can go no lower

liquid market FINANCE, BANKING, AND ACCOUNTING a market in which an ample number of shares is being traded

list broker GENERAL MANAGEMENT, FINANCE, BANKING, AND ACCOUNTING a person or organization that makes the arrangements for one company to use another company's direct mail list

listed company FINANCE, BANKING, AND ACCOUNTING a company whose shares trade on an exchange

listed security FINANCE, BANKING, AND ACCOUNTING a security listed on an exchange

list price OPERATIONS & PRODUCTION the price of goods or services published by a supplier. The list price of an item may be discounted to regular customers, or to ensure ***repeat business***, or for bulk purchases.

list renting GENERAL MANAGEMENT an arrangement in which a company that owns a direct mail list lets another company use it for a fee

litigation GENERAL MANAGEMENT the process of bringing a lawsuit against an individual or organization

livery MARKETING a mark of corporate identity used on a company vehicle

load fund FINANCE, BANKING, AND ACCOUNTING a unit trust that charges a fee for the purchase or sale of shares. See ***no-load fund***

loading
1. OPERATIONS & PRODUCTION the assignment of tasks or jobs to a workstation. The loading of jobs is worked out through the use of ***master production scheduling***. Workstations may be loaded to ***finite*** or ***infinite loading*** levels.
2. (*ANZ*) HR & PERSONNEL a payment made to workers over and above the basic wage in recognition of special skills or unfavorable conditions, for example, for overtime or shiftwork

loanable funds theory FINANCE, BANKING, AND ACCOUNTING the theory that interest rates are determined solely by supply and demand

loanback FINANCE, BANKING, AND ACCOUNTING the return to somebody as a loan money that has been given, often as a way of illegally masking the money's true owner

loan constant ratio FINANCE, BANKING, AND ACCOUNTING the total of annual payments due on a loan as a fraction of the amount of the principal

Loan Council FINANCE, BANKING, AND ACCOUNTING an Australian federal body made up of treasurers from the states and the Commonwealth of Australia that monitors borrowing by state governments

loan loss reserves FINANCE, BANKING, AND ACCOUNTING the money a bank holds to cover losses through defaults on loans that it makes

loan production cycle FINANCE, BANKING, AND ACCOUNTING the period that begins with an application for a loan and ends with the lending of the money

loan schedule FINANCE, BANKING, AND ACCOUNTING a list of the payments due on a loan and the balance outstanding after each has been made

loan shark FINANCE, BANKING, AND ACCOUNTING somebody who lends money at excessively, and often illegally, high rates of interest

loan to value ratio FINANCE, BANKING, AND ACCOUNTING the ratio of the amount of a loan to the value of the collateral for it

loan value FINANCE, BANKING, AND ACCOUNTING the amount that a lender is willing to lend a borrower

lobby GENERAL MANAGEMENT a pressure group that seeks to influence government or legislators on behalf of a particular cause or interest

lock-out HR & PERSONNEL a form of industrial action taken by an employer during a dispute in which employees are prevented from entering the business premises

logistics OPERATIONS & PRODUCTION the management of the movement, storage, and processing of materials and information in the ***supply chain***. Logistics encompasses the acquisition of raw materials and components, manufacturing or processing, and the distribu-

  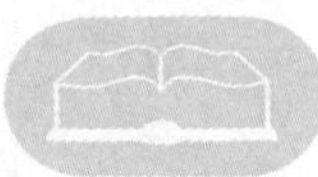    

tion of finished products to the end user. Each organization focuses on a different aspect of logistics, depending on its area of interest. For example, one might apply logistics to find a way of linking ***physical distribution management*** with earlier events in the supply chain, another to plan its acquisition and storage, while a third might use logistics as a support operation.

logistics management OPERATIONS & PRODUCTION the management of the distribution of products to the market

logo GENERAL MANAGEMENT a graphic device or symbol used by an organization as part of its corporate identity. A logo is used to facilitate instant recognition of an organization and to reinforce ***brand*** expectations and public image.

log of claims (*ANZ*) HR & PERSONNEL a document listing the demands made by employees on an employer or vice versa, often submitted during industrial negotiations

LOL *abbr* GENERAL MANAGEMENT laughing out loud (*slang*)

long FINANCE, BANKING, AND ACCOUNTING having more shares than are promised for sale

long-dated bond FINANCE, BANKING, AND ACCOUNTING a bond issued by the United Kingdom with a maturity at least 15 years in the future

longitudinal study STATISTICS a statistical study that produces data gathered over a period of time

long-service award HR & PERSONNEL a gift to recognize the ***length of service*** of an employee within an organization. A long-service award may be cash or may take the form of something an employee will value. The tradition of a clock or watch for 25 or 40 years of service is being replaced by awards recognizing shorter durations of employment and the greater mobility of employees.

long-service leave (*ANZ*) HR & PERSONNEL a period of paid leave awarded by some employers to staff who have completed several years of service

long-term GENERAL MANAGEMENT involving a long period of time, for example, years rather than weeks or months

long-term debt FINANCE, BANKING, AND ACCOUNTING loans that are due more than one year from the current date

long-term equity anticipation securities FINANCE, BANKING, AND ACCOUNTING see ***LEAPS***

long-term financing FINANCE, BANKING, AND ACCOUNTING forms of funding such as loans or stock issue that do not have to be repaid immediately

long-term lease FINANCE, BANKING, AND ACCOUNTING a lease of at least ten years

long-term liabilities FINANCE, BANKING, AND ACCOUNTING forms of debt such as loans that do not have to be repaid immediately

lookback option FINANCE, BANKING, AND ACCOUNTING an option whose price the buyer chooses from all of the prices that have existed during the option's life

loss FINANCE, BANKING, AND ACCOUNTING a financial position in which costs exceed income

loss adjuster GENERAL MANAGEMENT, FINANCE, BANKING, AND ACCOUNTING a professional person acting on behalf of an insurance company to assess the value of an insurance claim. Also known as ***claims adjuster***

loss control GENERAL MANAGEMENT see ***total loss control***

lossmaker GENERAL MANAGEMENT a product or company that fails to make a profit or break even

lowball GENERAL MANAGEMENT to begin a sales negotiation by quoting low prices, and then raise them once a buyer appears interested (*slang*)

lower level domain E-COMMERCE the main part of a domain name. For most e-business sites this is usually the company or brand name.

low-hanging fruit (*slang*)
1. MARKETING people who are easy marketing targets because they are already thinking about buying a product or signing up for a service
2. GENERAL MANAGEMENT something that is easy to obtain. Low-hanging fruit is highly visible, easily obtained, and provides good short-term opportunities for profit. Such fruit must be taken advantage of quickly, because it is accessible to anyone and there might be considerable competition. Picking low-hanging fruit may involve, for example, taking over a company or choosing the easiest tasks to do first, in order to achieve a quick result.

loyalty scheme MARKETING a sales promotion technique to encourage customers to continue buying a product or using an organization's services. Examples include a shopper card that gives discounts on purchases over a period of time.

Ltd. (*U.K.*) FINANCE, BANKING, AND ACCOUNTING see ***limited liability company***

lunch
do lunch GENERAL MANAGEMENT to have a lunch meeting with somebody (*slang*)

lurk E-COMMERCE to visit an Internet newsgroup without taking part. People wishing to promote their company's products or services within a newsgroup lurk to see whether the group accepts commercial messages or whether there are any questions they could answer. Lurking is important because inappropriate messages are likely to receive a hostile response from newsgroup members and may even be considered as ***spam***. Lurking in relevant newsgroups can also be an effective means of online market research.

M

M1 ECONOMICS the narrowest definition of the amount of money in the U.K. economy, including notes and coins in public circulation and sterling demand deposits held in the private sector

Ma and Pa shop GENERAL MANAGEMENT a small family-run business (*slang*)

Machiavelli, **Niccolò** (1469–1527) GENERAL MANAGEMENT Italian politician. Machiavelli's *The Prince* (1532) is one of the earliest works on political theory, embracing the concepts of ***power***, ***authority***, and ***leadership***. In *Management and Machiavelli* (1967), Antony Jay sought to show the relevance of Machiavelli's philosophy to modern society.
NICCOLò MACHIAVELLI (pp. 1016–17)

machine code E-COMMERCE a set of instructions to a computer in the form of a binary code

macho management GENERAL MANAGEMENT an authoritarian management style that asserts a manager's right to manage. Macho management is a term coined by ***Michael Edwardes***, and it was adopted by the media in the 1980s. Macho managers tend to take a tough approach to improving ***productivity*** and efficiency, and are unsympathetic to ***labor unions***.

macroeconomics ECONOMICS the branch of economics that studies national income and the economic systems of national economies

macroeconomy ECONOMICS those broad sectors of a country's economic activity, for example, the financial or industrial sector, that are aggregated to form its economic system as a whole

macrohedge FINANCE, BANKING, AND ACCOUNTING a hedge that pertains to an entire portfolio. See ***microhedge***. Also known as ***global hedge***

mail form E-COMMERCE a Web page that requires the user to input data, for example, name, address, or order or shipping information, that is transmitted to an e-merchant via e-mail

mailing house MARKETING an organization that specializes in planning, creating, and implementing direct mail campaigns for clients

mailing list MARKETING the names and addresses of a particular group of people compiled for marketing purposes. A mailing list may be compiled internally or bought or rented from an outside agency, and can be used for advertising, fundraising, news releases, or for ***direct mail*** or a ***mailshot***. A mailing list is usually compiled for a selected group using one or more criteria, such as men between the ages of 15 and 20.

✔ BUILDING A MAILING LIST (pp. 682–83)

mail order MARKETING a form of retailing in which consumers order products from a catalog for delivery to their home

mail-out GENERAL MANAGEMENT a single instance of using direct mail

mail server E-COMMERCE a remote computer enabling people and organizations to send and receive e-mail

mailshot MARKETING the speculative targeting of a particular or specified group of people by mail. A mailshot normally contains ***advertising***, fundraising requests, or ***press releases***.

mailsort MARKETING a sorting service offered to organizations by the Post Office, intended to reduce the cost and time spent on direct mail

mainframe E-COMMERCE a powerful computer capable of supporting hundreds of thousands of users simultaneously

mainstream corporation tax FINANCE, BANKING, AND ACCOUNTING the principal U.K. tax on corporations

maintenance OPERATIONS & PRODUCTION the process of keeping physical assets in working order to ensure their availability and to reduce the chance of failure. An effective maintenance program can enhance safety, increase reliability, reduce quality errors, lower operating costs, and increase the life span of assets. There are different maintenance approaches, including ***reactive maintenance***, ***predictive maintenance***, and ***preventive maintenance***. ***Reliability centered maintenance*** and ***total productive maintenance*** are two strategies that have more recently become prominent.

maintenance bond FINANCE, BANKING, AND ACCOUNTING a bond that provides a guarantee against defects for some time after a contract has been fulfilled

make or buy GENERAL MANAGEMENT see ***purchasing versus production***

make-to-order OPERATIONS & PRODUCTION the production of goods or components to meet an existing order. Make-to-order products are made to the customer's specification, and are often processed in small batches.

Malcolm Baldrige National Quality Award GENERAL MANAGEMENT an award recognizing achievements in quality and business performance. The Malcolm Baldrige National Quality Award was launched by the U.S. government in 1987 to encourage American companies to publicize successful quality and improvement strategies, to adopt ***total quality management***, and to encourage competitiveness. In assessing companies for the award, examiners allocate points in seven major areas: 1. Leadership 2. Information and analysis 3. Strategic planning 4. Human resource development 5. Process management 6. Customer focus and satisfaction 7. Business results. The Award also involves evaluation of companies according to three main factors: 1. What is the organization's approach to achieving its goals: how does it attempt to achieve top-class performance? 2. How is this approach put into practice in the organization, what resources are being brought to bear, and how widespread is this action throughout the organization? 3. What evidence is there to demonstrate that improvements are really taking place?

managed currency fund FINANCE, BANKING, AND ACCOUNTING a mutual fund that makes considered investments in currencies

managed economy FINANCE, BANKING, AND ACCOUNTING an economy directed by a government rather than the free market

managed float ECONOMICS the position when the exchange rate of a country's currency is influenced by government action in the foreign exchange market

managed fund FINANCE, BANKING, AND ACCOUNTING a mutual fund that makes considered investments. See ***index fund***

management GENERAL MANAGEMENT, HR & PERSONNEL the use of professional skills for identifying and achieving organizational objectives through the deployment of appropriate resources. Management involves identifying what needs to be done, and organizing and supporting others to perform the necessary tasks. A manager has complex and ever-changing responsibilities, the focus of which shifts to reflect the issues, trends, and preoccupations of the time. At the beginning of the 20th century, the emphasis was both on supporting the organization's administration and managing ***productivity*** through increased efficiency. Organizations following ***Henri Fayol***'s and ***Max Weber***'s models built the functional divisions of personnel management, production management, marketing management, operations management, and financial management. At the beginning of the 21st century, those original drivers are still much in evidence, although the emphasis has moved to the key areas of ***competence*** such as people management. Although management is a profession in its own right, its skill-set often applies to professionals of other disciplines.

HENRI FAYOL (pp. 986–87); MAX WEBER (pp. 1060–61)

management accounting FINANCE, BANKING, AND ACCOUNTING the preparation and use of financial information to support management decisions

management audit GENERAL MANAGEMENT see ***operational audit***

management buy-in GENERAL MANAGEMENT the purchase of an existing business by an individual manager or management group outside that business. In the United Kingdom, the unique company 3i is often involved in supporting management buy-ins. 3i has also promoted a hybrid form of management buy-in and ***management buy-out***, given the acronym **BIMBO**, which involves an incoming chief executive sharing his or her investment with the company's existing management team. Abbr **MBI**

management buy-out GENERAL MANAGEMENT the purchase of an existing business by an individual manager or management group from within that business. Abbr **MBO**

management by exception GENERAL MANAGEMENT a system of management in which only deviations from the plan or the norm are to be reported to the manager, ensuring management attention is only given when necessary

management by objectives GENERAL MANAGEMENT a method of managing an organization by setting a series of ***objectives*** that contribute toward the achievement of its goals. Abbr **MBO**

PETER DRUCKER (pp. 982–85)

management by results GENERAL MANAGEMENT see ***management by objectives***

management company GENERAL MANAGEMENT

1. a company that takes over responsibility from internal staff for managing facilities such as computer systems, telecommunications, or maintenance. The process is known as ***outsourcing***.

2. a hands-on style of management based on regularly walking around to speak, question, and listen to the suggestions or problems of employees, and to learn more about work processes

management consultancy GENERAL MANAGEMENT

1. the activity of advising on management techniques and practices. Management consultancy usually involves the identification of a problem, or the analysis of a specific area of one organization, and the reporting of any resulting findings. The consultancy process can sometimes be extended to help put into effect the recommendations made.

2. a firm of ***management consultants***

management consultant GENERAL MANAGEMENT a person professionally engaged in advising on, and providing, a detached, external view about a company's management techniques and practices. A management consultant may be self-employed, a partner, or employed within a ***management consultancy***. Consultants can be called in for many reasons, but are employed particularly for projects involving business improvement, ***change management***, information technology, and long-term planning.

management control systems GENERAL MANAGEMENT measures, procedures, ***performance indicators***, and other instruments used to systematically check and regulate operations. Management control systems are set up to maintain management ***control*** on a routine basis, and can include ***budgets*** and budgetary controls, credit control, working procedures, inventory control, production processes, and quality measures or controls.

management development HR & PERSONNEL the process of creating, and enhancing, the ***competences*** of ***managers*** and potential managers. Management development is usually thought of as a planned process, focusing on a long-term development program to increase managerial effectiveness, but it also incorporates informal and unplanned elements such as learning from day-to-day experience. Management development programs within an organization aim to identify and recruit potential managers, and develop their knowledge and skills to meet organizational needs. They also equip managers for more senior posts. Management development activities include short courses, ***management education*** programs, ***management training***, ***coaching***, and ***mentoring***.

management education HR & PERSONNEL formal instruction in the principles and techniques of ***management***, and in related subjects, leading to a qualification. Management education aims to develop management knowledge, understanding, and ***competence*** through classroom or distance-based methods. Management education is a main component of ***management development***, and differs from ***management training*** in that the latter may exploit any one of a variety of formal or informal methods, tends to be focused on a specific skill, and does not result directly in a formal qualification.

management guru GENERAL MANAGEMENT an informal term for a ***management theorist***

management information system GENERAL MANAGEMENT see ***MIS***

management science GENERAL MANAGEMENT the application of scientific methods and principles to management ***decision making*** and ***problem solving***. Management science encompasses the use of quantitative, mathematical, and statistical techniques. The term can be used to denote scientific management, which has origins in the work of ***Frederick Winslow Taylor***, ***Henry Gantt***, and ***Frank*** and ***Lillian Gilbreth***. Management science lies at the opposite end of the spectrum to the ***human relations*** school.

HENRY LAURENCE GANTT (pp. 990–91); FREDERICK WINSLOW TAYLOR (pp. 1054–55)

management services GENERAL MANAGEMENT a department or team of internally employed technical and professional specialists offering services or advice to management. Management services can cover areas such as work study, legal, computer, information, economic intelligence, and similar specialist support services.

management standards GENERAL MANAGEMENT published guidelines to best practice, outlining the knowledge, understanding, and personal ***competences*** that managers need to develop and demonstrate if they are to be effective

management style GENERAL MANAGEMENT the general manner, outlook, attitude, and behavior of a manager in his or her dealings with subordinates. Organizations may have, or seek to have, distinctive management styles, and sometimes train employees to try to ensure that a preferred style, fitting in with the desired ***corporate culture***, is always used. Management styles can vary widely between extremes of control and consultation. The latter are generally thought to encourage degrees of ***employee participation*** in management with consequently improved ***employee commitment***, ***employee involvement***, and ***empowerment***. More participatory styles are also usually related to more open organizational cultures and flatter organizational structures. One well-known instrument for distinguishing individual management styles is ***Robert Blake's*** and ***Jane Mouton***'s ***Managerial Grid***™.

management succession GENERAL MANAGEMENT see ***succession planning***

management team GENERAL MANAGEMENT see ***senior management***

management theorist GENERAL MANAGEMENT somebody who puts forward original ideas and theories about management. The work of a management theorist is usually presented through books or articles, and often has its base in practical or academic research, and consultancy or practical work experience.

management threshold GENERAL MANAGEMENT an outmoded term for a level of seniority in an organization which somebody cannot surmount. The management threshold is reached by an ***employee*** who has risen to a certain level in an organization and seems unable to rise any farther. It can lead to plateauing, where an employee is unable to gain ***promotion*** and stays in the same role for many years. Failure to surmount the management threshold can be caused by lack of opportunities for advancement, lack of ambition, or lack of skills or ability.

management trainee HR & PERSONNEL an employee who holds a low-level management position while undergoing formal training in management techniques

management training HR & PERSONNEL planned activities for ***management development***. Management training methods include public or ***in-company training*** courses and ***on-the-job training*** designed to improve managerial ***competences***. Management training tends to be practical and to focus on specific management techniques. Unlike ***management education***, it does not result in a formal qualification.

manager GENERAL MANAGEMENT a person who identifies and achieves organizational objectives through the deployment of appropriate resources. A manager can have responsibilities in one or more of five key areas: managing activities; managing resources; managing information; managing people; and managing him- or herself at the same time as working within the context of the organizational, political, and economic business environments. There are managers in all disciplines and activities, although some may not bear the title of manager. Some specialize in areas such as personnel, marketing, production, finance, or project management, while others are ***general managers***, applying ***management*** skills across all business areas. Very few jobs are entirely managerial, and very few exist without any management responsibilities. It is the capability to harness resources that largely distinguishes a manager from a non-manager.

Managerial Grid™ GENERAL MANAGEMENT a tool to measure and understand managerial behavior which places concern for task and concern for people on two matrices against which a manager's style can be plotted. The Managerial Grid™ grades each matrix 1 to 9, and identifies five different managerial behavior patterns: 1–1, or **impoverished management**, in which a minimum of concern for either people or task is displayed; 9–1, or **authority-compliance management**, in which a preoccupation with task is displayed; 5–5, or **middle of the road management**, in which a balance between task and people is striven for; 1–9, **country club management**, which is concerned with human relations to the detriment of output; and 9–9, **team management**, the ideal, in which production and human requirements are integrated in a team approach to achieving results.

managerialism GENERAL MANAGEMENT emphasis on efficient management, and the use of systems, planning, and management practice. Managerialism often is used in a critical sense, especially from the perspective of the public sector, to imply overenthusiasm for efficiency, or private sector management techniques, and systems, possibly at the expense of service, or quality considerations. The term also is used to describe confrontational attitudes, or actions, displayed by management toward labor unions.

managing director GENERAL MANAGEMENT a director of a company who has overall responsibility for its day-to-day operations

mandarin GENERAL MANAGEMENT a high-ranking and influential adviser, especially in government circles

mandatory quote period (*U.K.*) FINANCE, BANKING, AND ACCOUNTING a period of time during which prices of securities must be displayed in a market

manpower forecasting GENERAL MANAGEMENT the prediction of future levels of demand for, and supply of, workers and skills at organizational, regional, or national level. A range of techniques are used in manpower forecasting, including the statistical analysis of current trends and the use of mathematical models. At national level, these include the analysis of census statistics; at organizational level, projections of future requirements may be made from sales and production figures. Manpower forecasting forms part of the ***manpower planning*** process.

manpower planning GENERAL MANAGEMENT the development of strategies to match the supply of workers to the availability of jobs at organizational, regional, or national level. Manpower planning involves reviewing current manpower resources, forecasting future requirements and availability, and taking steps to ensure that the supply of people and skills meets demand. At a national level, this may be carried out by government or industry bodies, and at an organizational level, by human resource managers. A more current term for manpower planning at organizational level is ***human resource planning***.

manual worker HR & PERSONNEL an employee who carries out physical work, especially in a factory or outdoors. Traditionally, a manual worker is somebody who works with his or her hands. Also known as ***blue-collar worker***

manufacture OPERATIONS & PRODUCTION the large-scale production of goods from raw materials or constituent parts

manufacturer OPERATIONS & PRODUCTION a person or organization involved in ***production***

manufacturer's agent OPERATIONS & PRODUCTION a person or organization with authority to act for a ***manufacturer*** in obtaining a ***contract*** with a third party

manufacturing GENERAL MANAGEMENT see ***production***

manufacturing cost OPERATIONS & PRODUCTION the expenditure incurred in carrying out the ***production*** processes of an organization. The manufacturing cost includes ***direct costs***, for example, labor, materials, and expenses, and indirect costs, for example, ***subcontracting*** and overheads.

manufacturing for excellence GENERAL MANAGEMENT see ***design for manufacturability***

manufacturing information system OPERATIONS & PRODUCTION an ***MIS*** designed specifically for use in a ***production*** environment

manufacturing management GENERAL MANAGEMENT see ***production management***

manufacturing resource planning OPERATIONS & PRODUCTION see ***MRP II***

manufacturing system OPERATIONS & PRODUCTION a method of organizing ***production***. Manufacturing systems include assembly and ***batch production***, ***flexible manufacturing systems***, ***lean production***, ***group technology***, ***job production***, ***kanban***, and ***mass production***.

manufacturing to order OPERATIONS & PRODUCTION a production management technique in which goods are produced to meet firm orders, rather than being produced for stock

MAPS E-COMMERCE Mail Abuse Prevention System, the leading organization campaigning against unsolicited commercial e-mail messages, or "spam"

Margerison, Charles J. (*b.* 1940) GENERAL MANAGEMENT British business researcher and writer. See ***McCann, Dick***

margin
1. GENERAL MANAGEMENT, FINANCE, BANKING, AND ACCOUNTING the difference between the cost and the selling price of a product or service
2. (*ANZ*) HR & PERSONNEL a payment made to workers over and above the basic wage in recognition of special skills

margin account FINANCE, BANKING, AND ACCOUNTING an account with a broker who lends money for investments

marginal analysis ECONOMICS the study of how small changes in an economic variable will affect an economy

marginal cost ECONOMICS the amount by which the costs of a firm will be increased if its output is increased by one more unit
✔ HOW TO CALCULATE MARGINAL COST (p. 831)

marginal costs and benefits ECONOMICS the amount by which an individual or household will lose or benefit from a small change in a variable, for example, food consumption or income received

marginalization GENERAL MANAGEMENT the process by which countries lose importance and status because they are unable to participate in mainstream activities such as industrialization or the Internet economy

marginal lender FINANCE, BANKING, AND ACCOUNTING a lender who will make a loan only at or above a particular rate of interest

marginal private cost ECONOMICS the cost to an individual of a small change in the price of a variable, for example, gas

marginal revenue GENERAL MANAGEMENT the revenue generated by additional units of production

marginal tax rate FINANCE, BANKING, AND ACCOUNTING the rate of tax payable on a person's income after business expenses have been deducted

margin of error OPERATIONS & PRODUCTION an allowance made for the possibility of miscalculation

margin of safety OPERATIONS & PRODUCTION the difference between the level of activity at which an organization breaks even and the level of activity greater than this point. For example, a margin of safety of $300,000 is achieved when the breakeven point is $900,000 and sales reach $1,200,000. This measure can be expressed as a proportion of sales value, as a number of units sold, or as a percentage of ***capacity***.

marked price GENERAL MANAGEMENT the original displayed price of a product in a shop. In a sale, consumers may be offered a saving on the marked price.

market
1. GENERAL MANAGEMENT a grouping of people or organizations unified by a common need
2. GENERAL MANAGEMENT a gathering of sellers and purchasers to exchange commodities
3. FINANCE, BANKING, AND ACCOUNTING the rate at which financial commodities or securities are being sold

marketable MARKETING possessing the potential to be commercially viable. To determine whether a new product or service is marketable, an assessment needs to be carried out to see if it is likely to make a profit. The assessment is often based on detailed ***market research*** analyzing the potential market, and the projected financial returns and any other benefits for the company.

market analysis MARKETING the study of a market to identify and quantify business opportunities

market area MARKETING the geographic location of a market

market bubble FINANCE, BANKING, AND ACCOUNTING a stock market phenomenon in which values in a particular sector become inflated for a short period. If the bubble bursts, share prices in that sector collapse.

market coverage GENERAL MANAGEMENT the degree to which a product or service meets the needs of a market

market development MARKETING marketing activities designed to increase the overall size of a market through education and awareness

market driven MARKETING using market knowledge to determine the ***corporate strategy*** of an organization. A market driven organization has a ***customer focus***, together with awareness of competitors and an understanding of the ***market***.

market economy ECONOMICS an economy in which a ***free market*** in goods and services operates

marketer MARKETING somebody who is responsible for developing and implementing marketing policy

marketface GENERAL MANAGEMENT the interface between suppliers and customers

market-facing enterprise GENERAL MANAGEMENT an organization that aligns itself with its markets and customers

market-focused organization MARKETING an organization whose strategies are determined by market requirements rather than organizational demands

market fragmentation MARKETING a situation in which the buyers or sellers in a market consist of a large number of small organizations

market gap MARKETING an opportunity in a market where no supplier provides a product or service that buyers need

market if touched FINANCE, BANKING, AND ACCOUNTING an order to trade a security if it reaches a specified price. Abbr **MIT**

marketing MARKETING see ***marketing management***
4 Ps of marketing GENERAL MANAGEMENT see ***marketing mix***

marketing audit MARKETING an analysis of either the external marketing environment or a company's internal marketing aims, objectives, operations, and efficiency. An external marketing audit covers issues such as economic, political, infrastructure, technological, and consumer perspectives; ***market size*** and ***structure***; and competitors, suppliers, and distributors. An internal marketing audit covers aspects such as the company's ***mission statement***, aims, and objectives; its structure, corporate culture, systems, operations, and processes; ***product development*** and pricing; profitability and efficiency; ***advertising***; and deployment of the ***sales force***.

marketing consultancy MARKETING an organization that plans and develops marketing strategies and programs on behalf of clients

marketing information system MARKETING an information system concerned with the collection, storage, and analysis of information and data for marketing ***decision making*** purposes. Information for use in marketing information systems is gathered from customers, competitors and their products, and from the market itself.

  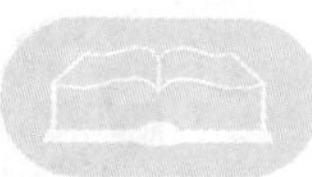  

marketing management MARKETING one of the main management disciplines, encompassing all the strategic planning, operations, activities, and processes involved in achieving organizational objectives by delivering value to customers. Marketing management focuses on satisfying customer requirements by identifying needs and wants, and developing products and services to meet them. In seeking to satisfy customer requirements, **marketing** aims to build long-term relationships with customers and with other interested parties and to provide value to them. This begins with ***market research***, which analyzes needs and wants in society, and continues with attracting customers and the cultivation of mutually beneficial exchange processes with them. Tools used in this process are diverse and include market segmentation, ***brand management***, ***PR***, ***logistics***, and ***direct response marketing***, ***sales promotion***, and ***advertising***.

marketing manager MARKETING an employee of a client organization who is responsible for planning and controlling its marketing activities and budgets

marketing mix MARKETING the range of integrated decisions taken by a marketing manager to ensure successful marketing. These decisions are taken in four key areas known as the **4 Ps of marketing**—product, price, place, and promotion—and cover issues such as the type of product to be marketed, brand name, pricing, advertising, publicity, geographic coverage, retailing, and distribution.

marketing myopia MARKETING the name given to the theory that challenged the assumption that organizations should be production-oriented by suggesting that to be successful, the wants of customers must be their central consideration. First promoted by ***Theodore Levitt*** in "Marketing myopia," published in the *Harvard Business Review* during 1960, the theory has gained such widespread acceptance that it now appears commonplace.

marketing plan MARKETING overall marketing objectives and the strategies and programs of action designed to achieve those objectives

marketing planning MARKETING the process of producing a ***marketing plan***. Marketing planning requires a careful examination of all strategic issues, including the business environment, the markets themselves, competitors, the corporate ***mission statement***, and organizational capabilities. The resulting marketing plan should be communicated to appropriate staff through an oral briefing to ensure it is fully understood.

market intelligence MARKETING a collection of internal and external data on a given market. Market intelligence focuses particularly on competitors, customers, consumer spending, market trends, and suppliers.

market leader MARKETING an organization that has the largest share in a particular market

market logic FINANCE, BANKING, AND ACCOUNTING the prevailing forces or attitudes that determine a company's success or failure on the stock market

market maker FINANCE, BANKING, AND ACCOUNTING

1. (*U.K.*) somebody who works in a stock exchange to facilitate trades in one particular company. Also known as ***specialist***

2. a broker or bank that maintains a market for a security that does not trade on any exchange

market order FINANCE, BANKING, AND ACCOUNTING an order to trade a security at the best price the broker can obtain

market penetration HR & PERSONNEL a measure of the percentage or potential percentage of the market that a product or company is able to capture, expressed in terms of total sales or turnover. Market penetration is often used to measure the level of success a new product or service has achieved.

market penetration pricing MARKETING the policy of pricing a product or service very competitively, and sometimes at a loss to the producer, in order to increase its ***market share***

market position MARKETING the place held by a product or service in a ***market***, usually determined by its percentage of total sales. An ideal market position is often predefined for a product or service. Analysis of potential customers and competing products can be used with product differentiation techniques to formulate a product to fill the desired market position.

market potential MARKETING a forecast of the size of a market in terms of revenue, numbers of buyers, or other factors

market power MARKETING the dominance of a market either by customers, who create a buyer's market, or by a particular company, which creates a seller's market. Individuals or companies retain control of the market by fixing the pricing and number of products available.

market price ECONOMICS in economics, the theoretical price at which supply equals demand

market research MARKETING research carried out to assess the size and nature of a market

market sector MARKETING a subdivision of a ***market***. Market sectors are usually determined by market segmentation, which divides a market into different categories. Car buyers, for example, could be put into sectors such as car fleet buyers, private buyers, buyers under 20 years old, and so on. The smaller the sector, the more its members will have in common.

market segment MARKETING a part of a market that has distinctive characteristics. Sellers may decide to compete in the whole market or only in segments that are attractive to them or where they have an advantage.

market share MARKETING the proportion of the total market value of a product or group of products or services that a company, service, or product holds. Market share is shown as a percentage of the total value or output of a market, usually expressed in sterling or U.S. dollars, by weight (tons or tonnes), or as individual units, depending on the commodity. The product, service, or company with a dominant market share is referred to as the **market leader**.

market site E-COMMERCE a Web site shared by multiple e-commerce vendors, each having a different specialty, to conduct business over the Internet

market size FINANCE, BANKING, AND ACCOUNTING the largest number of shares that a market will handle in one trade of a particular security

market structure MARKETING the makeup of a particular ***market***. Market structure can be described with reference to different characteristics of a market, including its size and value, the number of providers and their ***market share***, consumer and business purchasing behavior, and growth forecasts. The description may also include a demographic and regional breakdown of providers and customers and an analysis of pricing structures, likely technological impacts, and domestic and overseas sales.

market targeting MARKETING the selection of a particular market segment toward which all marketing effort is directed. Market targeting enables the characteristics of the chosen segment to be taken into account when formulating a product or service and its advertising.

market value FINANCE, BANKING, AND ACCOUNTING the price that buyers are willing to pay for a good or service

markup GENERAL MANAGEMENT the difference between the cost of a product or service and its selling price. Markup is often calculated as a percentage of the production and overhead costs, and represents the profit made on the product or service.

Marxism ECONOMICS a view of social development found in the writings of Karl Marx, stating that a country's culture is determined by how its goods and services are produced

marzipan HR & PERSONNEL belonging to the level of management immediately below the top executives (*slang*)

Maslow, **Abraham** (1908–70) GENERAL MANAGEMENT U.S. psychologist and behavioral scientist. Known for his work on ***motivation***, principally the hierarchy of needs, which was set out in his book *Motivation and Personality* (1954). Maslow's concepts were originally offered as general explanations of human behavior but are now seen as a significant contribution to workplace motivation theory. He is often mentioned in connection with his contemporaries ***Douglas McGregor*** and ***Frederick Herzberg***, all part of the ***human relations*** movement in management.

✔ MOTIVATING YOUR STAFF IN A TIME OF CHANGE (pp. 372–73)

FREDERICK HERZBERG (pp. 1002–03); DOUGLAS MCGREGOR (pp. 1022–23); ABRAHAM MASLOW (pp. 1018–19)

massaging FINANCE, BANKING, AND ACCOUNTING the adjustment of financial figures to create the impression of better performance

mass customization OPERATIONS & PRODUCTION a process that allows a standard, mass-produced item, for example, a bicycle, to be individually tailored to specific customer requirements

mass market MARKETING a market that covers substantial numbers of the population. A mass market may consist of a whole population or just a segment of that population. ***Mass customization*** of products has allowed a greater number of single products to satisfy a mass market.

mass medium MARKETING an advertising medium such as television or national newspapers which reaches a very large audience

mass meeting HR & PERSONNEL the assembling of most or all of the members of a ***labor union*** in order to reach a decision on workforce policy. Mass meetings were frequently called during the 1960s and 1970s to determine whether or not ***industrial action*** would take place. In the United Kingdom, the most memorable examples occurred at British Leyland.

mass production OPERATIONS & PRODUCTION large-scale manufacturing, often designed to meet the demand for a particular product. Mass production methods were developed by ***Henry Ford***, founder of the Ford Motor Company. Mass production involves using a moving production or assembly line on which the product moves while operators remain at their stations carrying out their work on each passing product. Mass production is now challenged by methods including ***just-in-time*** and ***lean production***.

master franchise MARKETING a license issued by the owner of a product or service to another party or master franchisee allowing them to issue further ***franchise*** licenses. A master franchise can benefit the original franchisor, as the master franchisee effectively develops the ***franchise chain*** on their behalf. A master franchise usually grants further licenses within a defined geographic area, and several master franchises may cover a country.

master limited partnership FINANCE, BANKING, AND ACCOUNTING a partnership of a type that combines tax advantages and advantages of liquidity

Master of Business Administration GENERAL MANAGEMENT a postgraduate qualification awarded after a period of study of topics relating to the strategic management of businesses. A Master of Business Administration course can be followed at a ***business school*** or university, and covers areas such as finance, personnel, and resource management, as well as the wider business environment and skills such as information technology use. The course is mostly taken by people with experience of managerial work, and is offered by universities worldwide. Part-time or distance learning MBAs are available, so that students can study while still working. There are an increasing number of MBA graduates, as an MBA is seen as a passport to a better job and higher salary. For many positions at a higher level within organizations, an MBA is now a prerequisite.

master production scheduling OPERATIONS & PRODUCTION a technique used in material requirements planning systems to develop a detailed plan for product manufacturing. The master production schedule, compiled by a master scheduler, takes account of the requirements of various departments, including sales (delivery dates), finance (inventory minimization), and manufacturing (minimization of setup times) and schedules production, and the purchasing of materials within the capacity of and resources available to the production system.

material cost OPERATIONS & PRODUCTION the cost of the raw materials that go into a product. The material cost of a product excludes any ***indirect costs***, for example, overheads or wages, associated with producing the item.

materials handling OPERATIONS & PRODUCTION the techniques employed to move, transport, store, and distribute materials, with or without the aid of mechanical equipment

materials management OPERATIONS & PRODUCTION an approach for planning, organizing, and controlling all those activities principally concerned with the flow of materials into an organization. The scope of materials management varies greatly from company to company and may include material planning and control, ***production planning***, ***purchasing***, inventory control and stores, in-plant materials movement, and ***waste management***.

materials testing OPERATIONS & PRODUCTION the process of analyzing the physical and chemical characteristics of materials against a specification

maternity leave HR & PERSONNEL time off work because of pregnancy and childbirth. All female ***employees***, regardless of ***length of service*** and ***hours of work***, are legally entitled to statutory maternity leave and to statutory ***maternity pay***. Many ***employers*** offer improved maternity arrangements but these vary from organization to organization and often depend on length of service.

maternity pay HR & PERSONNEL earnings paid by an ***employer*** to ***employees*** who take ***maternity leave***, or leave employment because of pregnancy, and who satisfy certain qualifying conditions

  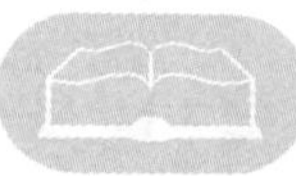    

matrix management GENERAL MANAGEMENT management based on two or more reporting systems linked to the vertical organization hierarchy, and to horizontal relationships based on geographic, product, or project requirements

matrix organization GENERAL MANAGEMENT organization by both vertical administrative functions, and horizontal tasks, areas, processes, or projects. Matrix organization originated in the 1960s and 1970s, particularly within the U.S. aerospace industry, when ***organization charts*** showing how the management of a given ***project*** would relate to ***senior management*** were often required to win government contracts. A two-dimensional **matrix** chart best illustrates the dual horizontal, and vertical, reporting relationships. Matrix organization is closely linked to ***matrix management***.

matrix structure GENERAL MANAGEMENT a form of ***organization structure*** based on horizontal and vertical relationships. The matrix structure is linked closely to ***matrix management***, and is related to ***project management***. It emerged on an improvised rather than planned basis as a way of showing how people work with or report to others in their organization, project, geographic region, process, or team.

Matsushita, **Konosuke** (1894–1989) GENERAL MANAGEMENT Japanese entrepreneur, business executive, and philanthropist. Founder of Matsushita Electric, and owner of the Panasonic brand, noted for his humanistic approach to business, which was described by John P. Kotter in *Matsushita Leadership* (1997).
KONOSUKE MATSUSHITA (pp. 1112–13)

mature economy FINANCE, BANKING, AND ACCOUNTING an economy that is no longer developing or growing rapidly

maturity GENERAL MANAGEMENT the stage at which a financial instrument, such as a bond, is due for repayment

maturity date FINANCE, BANKING, AND ACCOUNTING the date when an ***option*** expires

Mauborgne, **Renée** GENERAL MANAGEMENT French academic. INSEAD Professor, Fellow of the World Economic Forum, and collaborator of ***W. Chan Kim*** on research into ***corporate strategy*** and ***value innovation***.

Mayo, **Elton** (1880–1949) GENERAL MANAGEMENT Australian psychologist and academic. Responsible for finding, through the ***Hawthorne experiments***, that ***job satisfaction*** increases through employee participation in decision making, rather than through short-term incentives. The results of the Hawthorne studies were published in Mayo's *The Human Problems of an Industrial Civilization* (1933), and were further publicized by one of his collaborators, ***Fritz Jules Roethlisberger***. Mayo is recognized as the founder of the ***human relations*** school of management.
ELTON MAYO (pp. 1020–21)

MBA GENERAL MANAGEMENT see ***Master of Business Administration***

MBI GENERAL MANAGEMENT see ***management buy-in***

MBIA *abbr* FINANCE, BANKING, AND ACCOUNTING Munipical Bond Insurance Association, a group of insurance companies that insure high-rated municipal bonds

MBO GENERAL MANAGEMENT see ***management buy-out***, ***management by objectives***

McCann, **Dick** (*b.* 1943) GENERAL MANAGEMENT Australian business researcher and writer. Developer, with ***Charles Margerison***, of the ***Team Management Wheel***™, and the team management index/questionnaire, as originally reported in *How to Lead a Winning Team* (1985). Their work on team roles and work preferences compares with that of Carl Jung and ***R. Meredith Belbin***.
R. MEREDITH BELBIN (pp. 966–67)

McClelland, **David Clarence** (1917–98) GENERAL MANAGEMENT U.S. academic. Initiator of research into the use of ***competences*** to predict effective job performance, later developed by ***Richard Boyatzis***. See *American Psychologist*, "Testing for competence rather than for intelligence," (1973).

McCormick, **Roger** GENERAL MANAGEMENT U.K. business executive

McGregor, **Douglas** (1906–64) GENERAL MANAGEMENT U.S. social psychologist and academic. Developer of ***Theory X*** and ***Theory Y***, which describe two views of people at work and two opposing ***management styles***. McGregor's writings on ***motivation*** and ***leadership***, first published in *The Human Side of Enterprise* (1960), have been very influential. ***William G. Ouchi*** later developed the idea of ***Theory Z***.
✔ MOTIVATING YOUR STAFF IN A TIME OF CHANGE (pp. 372–73)
DOUGLAS MCGREGOR (pp. 1022–23)

McKinsey 7-S framework GENERAL MANAGEMENT a model for identifying and exploiting an organization's ***human resources*** in order to create ***competitive advantage***. The McKinsey 7-S framework was developed by McKinsey consultants, including ***Tom Peters***, and ***Robert H. Waterman***, with the academic partnership of ***Richard Pascale*** and ***Anthony G. Athos*** in the early 1980s. It sought to present an emphasis on human resources, rather than the traditional mass production tangibles of capital, infrastructure, and equipment. The 7-Ss are: Structure, Strategy, Skills, Staff, Style, Systems, ***Shared values*** (see ***core values***).

m-commerce E-COMMERCE electronic transactions between buyers and sellers using mobile communications devices such as mobile phones, personal digital assistants (PDAs), or portable laptop computers

MD GENERAL MANAGEMENT see ***chief executive***

mean STATISTICS a central value or location for a continuous variable in a statistical study

mean reversion FINANCE, BANKING, AND ACCOUNTING the tendency of a variable such as price to return toward its average value after approaching an extreme position

measurement error STATISTICS an error in the recording, calculating, or reading of a numerical value in a statistical study

mechanical handling OPERATIONS & PRODUCTION the use of machines for moving and positioning materials in a warehouse or factory

mechanization GENERAL MANAGEMENT see ***automation***

medallion E-COMMERCE the microprocessor chip in a ***smart card***

media independent MARKETING an organization that specializes in planning and buying advertising for clients or advertising agencies

median STATISTICS the value that divides a set of ranked observations into two parts of equal size

media plan MARKETING an assessment and outline of the various ***advertising media*** to be used for a campaign

  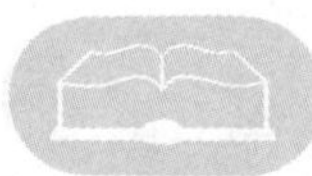    

media planner MARKETING an employee of an advertising agency or media independent who chooses the media, timing, and frequency of advertising

media schedule MARKETING a document that sets out the choice of media, timing, and frequency for advertising

mediation HR & PERSONNEL intervention by a third party in a dispute in order to try to reach agreement between the disputing parties. Mediation is also known as ***conciliation***. Where a commitment or award is imposed on either party the process is known as ***arbitration***.

Medicare
1. FINANCE, BANKING, AND ACCOUNTING a health insurance program in which the government pays part of the cost of medical care and hospital treatment for people over 65
2. GENERAL MANAGEMENT the Australian public health insurance system. It was created in 1983 and is funded by a levy on income.

medium-sized business GENERAL MANAGEMENT an organization with between 100 and 500 employees. See ***small business***, ***large-sized business***

meeting GENERAL MANAGEMENT a gathering of two or more people for a particular purpose. Meetings are convened for a variety of purposes, including planning, ***decision making***, ***problem solving***, communication, and the exchange of information. They may be informal, for example, a few people getting together to discuss ideas, or they may be formal, following strict procedures. Formal meetings are conducted by a ***chairperson*** (see ***chair***) according to an ***agenda*** set in advance, and the proceedings are recorded in ***minutes***. Some meetings, such as company board meetings and ***annual meetings***, are a legal requirement and take place on a regular basis.

megacity GENERAL MANAGEMENT a very large city in which media and political power is concentrated because of its key role in global information networks

megacorporation *or* **megacorp** GENERAL MANAGEMENT an extremely large and powerful business organization (*slang*)

megatrend GENERAL MANAGEMENT a general shift in thinking or approach affecting countries, industries, and organizations. The term was made popular by ***John Naisbitt*** in his bestseller *Megatrends* (1982).

MEGO GENERAL MANAGEMENT my eyes glaze over, an often sarcastic exclamation of wonder at the complexity of what a person has just said (*slang*)

member bank FINANCE, BANKING, AND ACCOUNTING a bank that is a member of the Federal Reserve System

memo GENERAL MANAGEMENT a documented note that acts as a reminder and is used for conveying and recording information. The memo has to some extent been displaced by e-mail, although it is still sometimes used for important communications.

memory E-COMMERCE the facility that enables a computer to store data and programs

mentoring HR & PERSONNEL a form of ***employee development*** whereby a trusted and respected person—the mentor—uses their experience to offer guidance, encouragement, and support to another person—the mentee. The aim of mentoring is to facilitate the mentee's learning and development and to enable them to discover more about their potential. Mentoring can occur informally or it can be arranged by means of an organizational scheme.
✔ MENTORING IN PRACTICE (pp. 368–69)

mercantile ECONOMICS relating to trading or commercial activity

mercantile agency FINANCE, BANKING, AND ACCOUNTING a company that evaluates the creditworthiness of potential corporate borrowers. See ***credit bureau***

mercantile paper FINANCE, BANKING, AND ACCOUNTING = ***commercial paper***

mercantilism ECONOMICS the body of economic thought developed between the 1650s and 1750s, stating that a country's wealth depended on the strength of its foreign trade

merchandising MARKETING
1. the process of increasing the market share of a product in retail outlets using display, stocking, and sales promotion techniques
2. the promotion of goods associated with a particular ***brand***, movie, or celebrity. Merchandising based on a specific movie, for example, may significantly add to its total revenues through appropriate ***licensing*** opportunities. Merchandising may include clothing, toys, food products, or music and often extends well beyond the ***core business*** of the producer of the original product.

merchant bank
1. E-COMMERCE a financial institution at which an e-merchant has opened a **merchant account** into which the proceeds of credit card transactions are credited after the institution has subtracted its fee
2. (*U.K.*) FINANCE, BANKING, AND ACCOUNTING a bank that does not accept deposits but only provides services to those who offer securities to investors and to those investors. = ***investment bank***

merger GENERAL MANAGEMENT the union of two or more organizations under single ownership, through the direct **acquisition** by one organization of the net assets or liabilities of the other. A merger can be the result of a friendly ***takeover***, which results in the combining of companies on an equal footing. After a merger, the legal existence of the acquired organization is terminated. There is no standard definition of a merger, as each union is different, depending on what is expected from the merger, and on the negotiations, strategy, stock and assets, human resources, and shareholders of the players. Four broad types of merger are recognized. A **horizontal merger** involves firms from the same industry, while a **vertical merger** involves firms from the same supply chain. A **circular merger** involves firms with different products but similar distribution channels. A ***conglomerate company*** is produced by the union of firms with few or no similarities in production or marketing but that come together to create a larger economic base and greater profit potential. Also known as ***acquisition***, ***one-to-one merger***. See ***consolidation***, ***joint venture***, ***partnership***

merit rating *or* **merit pay** HR & PERSONNEL a payment system in which the personal qualities of an employee are rated according to organizational requirements, and a pay increase or bonus is made against the results of this rating. Merit rating has been in use since the 1950s. Unlike new ***performance-related pay*** systems, which focus rewards on the output of an employee, merit rating examines an employee's input to the organization—for example, their attendance, adaptability, or aptitude—as well as the quality or quantity of work produced. In merit rating schemes, these factors may be weighted to reflect their relative importance and the resultant points score determines whether the employee earns a bonus or pay increase.

meta-tag E-COMMERCE any of the keyword and description commands used in a Web page code that are used to help search engines index the Web site

Metcalfe's law E-COMMERCE the proposition that networks dramatically increase in value with each additional user. Metcalfe's law was formulated by Robert Metcalfe, founder of 3Com, and has been instrumental in developing the concept of ***viral marketing***.

methods-time measurement GENERAL MANAGEMENT a system of ***standard times*** for movements made by people in the performance of work tasks. Methods-time measurement was developed in the 1940s and is the most widely used of ***predetermined motion-time systems*** of ***work measurement*** designed to increase efficiency and consistency in work operations. Work operations are broken down into a set of basic motions such as reach, grasp, position, and release and standard times for each motion are calculated by analyzing films of industrial operations. Simplified versions of the system called **MTM2** and **MTM3**, approved in 1965 and 1970 respectively, use combinations of the basic motions such as get and put. Abbr **MTM**

method study GENERAL MANAGEMENT the systematic recording, examination, and analysis of existing and proposed ways of carrying out work tasks in order to discover the most efficient and economical methods of performing them. The basic procedure followed in method study is as follows: select the area to be studied; record the data; examine the data; develop alternative approaches; install the new method; maintain the new method. Method study forms part of ***work study*** and is normally carried out prior to ***work measurement***. The technique was initially developed to evaluate manufacturing processes but has been used more widely to evaluate alternative courses of action. It is based on research into ***motion study*** carried out by ***Frank*** and ***Lillian Gilbreth*** during the 1920s and 1930s.

Mickey Mouse GENERAL MANAGEMENT so simple as to appear silly or trivial *(slang)*

microbusiness GENERAL MANAGEMENT a very ***small business*** with fewer than ten employees

microcash E-COMMERCE a form of electronic money with no denominations, permitting sub-denomination transactions of a fraction of a cent or penny

microeconomic incentive ECONOMICS a tax benefit or subsidy given to a business to achieve a particular objective such as increased sales overseas

microeconomics ECONOMICS the branch of economics that studies the contribution of groups of consumers or firms, or of individual consumers, to a country's economy

microeconomy ECONOMICS those narrow sectors of a country's economic activity that influence the behavior of the economy as a whole, for example, consumer choices

microhedge FINANCE, BANKING, AND ACCOUNTING a hedge that relates to a single asset or liability. See ***macrohedge***

micromarketing MARKETING marketing to individuals or very small groups. Micromarketing contrasts with mass marketing and targets the specific interests and needs of individuals by offering customized products or services. It is similar to ***niche marketing***, but rather than targeting one large niche, a micromarketing company targets a large number of very small niches.

micromerchant E-COMMERCE a provider of goods or services on the Internet in exchange for electronic money

micropayment E-COMMERCE, FINANCE, BANKING, AND ACCOUNTING a payment protocol for small amounts of electronic money, ranging from a fraction of a cent or penny to no more than ten U.S. dollars or Euros

middleman GENERAL MANAGEMENT an intermediary in a transaction. With direct sales models, manufacturers cut out the middleman by dealing directly with end customers.

middle management HR & PERSONNEL the position held by managers who are considered neither senior nor junior in an organization. Middle managers were subject to ***delayering*** and ***downsizing*** in the 1980s as organizations sought to reduce costs by removing the layer of managers between those who had direct interface with customers and senior decision makers.

mid-range STATISTICS the mean of the largest and smallest values in a statistical sample

migrate GENERAL MANAGEMENT to transfer data and applications from an existing computer system to a new one

milking GENERAL MANAGEMENT taking profit from a product or service which is in the declining stage of its life cycle *(slang)*

millennium bug GENERAL MANAGEMENT the inability of some computer systems to recognize the year 2000 as a date. The millennium bug arose from the computer programming practice of using two digits to represent a year. It was thought that this could cause great problems when digital clocks turned from 1999 to 2000, because computers would read 00 and cease to function. The millennium bug was thought to affect any business system that used electronically generated date information. Speculation on what would happen sparked fears of global disaster. Much work was carried out in the late 1990s in order to correct the problem and systems that did not have the bug were referred to as **Y2K-compliant**, Y2K being shorthand for Year 2000. In the event, the anticipated disaster did not occur.

millionerd E-COMMERCE somebody who has become a millionaire through working in a high-tech business *(slang)*

MIME E-COMMERCE multipurpose Internet mail extension, a standard Internet protocol enabling users to send binary files as e-mail attachments

Mind Map™ GENERAL MANAGEMENT a graphic tool that can be used to visualize and clarify thoughts or ideas. In a Mind Map, the central image or idea is drawn in the middle of a piece of paper with major branches radiating from it to denote related themes. Second and third levels of thought are connected by thinner branches. Mind Maps can include the use of color or pictures. Developed by ***Tony Buzan***, the Mind Mapping technique can be used to introduce order and rationality to thought processes, and develop the creative, artistic, logical, and mathematical elements of the brain.

mindshare MARKETING the process of fostering favorable attitudes toward a product or organization

minimum lending rate FINANCE, BANKING, AND ACCOUNTING an interest rate charged by a central bank, which serves as a floor for loans in a country

minimum quote size FINANCE, BANKING, AND ACCOUNTING the smallest number of shares that a market must handle in one trade of a particular security

minimum salary HR & PERSONNEL the lowest amount of money that an employee is guaranteed to earn. A minimum salary is ***base pay***, which may be increased if an employee qualifies for a ***bonus*** by performing well. ***Payment by results***, ***performance-related pay***,

and sales ***commission*** are paid on top of a minimum salary.

minimum wage HR & PERSONNEL an hourly rate of pay, usually set by government, to which all ***employees*** are legally entitled

Mintzberg, **Henry** (*b.* 1939) GENERAL MANAGEMENT Canadian academic. Known for his views on ***strategic management*** and ***strategic planning*** (see ***planning***), and for analyzing managerial work. In *The Nature of Managerial Work* (1973), he showed that the work done by managers was substantially different from the way it was described in business theory.
✔ STRATEGIC PLANNING (pp. 484–85)
HENRY MINTZBERG (pp. 1024–25)

minutes GENERAL MANAGEMENT an official written record of the proceedings of a ***meeting***. Minutes normally record points for action, and indicate who is responsible for implementing decisions. Good practice requires that the minutes of a meeting be circulated well in advance of the next meeting, and that those attending that meeting read the minutes in advance. Registered companies are required to keep minutes of meetings and make them available at their registered offices for inspection by company members and shareholders.

mirror E-COMMERCE a copy of a Web site held on a different server and therefore available at a different location. Mirror sites can be used to accelerate download times by alleviating Web site congestion. Sites offering software downloads are the most common form of mirror site.

MIS *abbr* GENERAL MANAGEMENT management information system, a computer-based system for collecting, storing, processing, and providing access to information used in the management of an organization. Management information systems evolved from early electronic data processing systems. They support managerial ***decision making*** by providing regular structured reports on organizational operations. Management information systems may support the functional areas of an organization such as finance, marketing, or production. ***Decision support systems*** and ***EISs*** are types of MIS developed for more specific purposes.

mismanagement GENERAL MANAGEMENT functional or ethical dereliction of duty due to ignorance, negligence, incompetence, avoidance, or criminality

missing value STATISTICS an observation that is absent from a set of statistical data, for example, because a member of a population to be sampled was not at home when the researcher called

missing values STATISTICS observations that are absent from a data set

mission statement GENERAL MANAGEMENT a short memorable statement of the reasons for the existence of an organization. See ***vision statement***

MIT FINANCE, BANKING, AND ACCOUNTING see ***market if touched***

Mittelstand GENERAL MANAGEMENT a German term for ***medium-sized business***, which incorporates the meaning of ***small and medium-sized enterprises***

mixed economy ECONOMICS an economy in which both public and private enterprises participate in the production and supply of goods and services

mobile office GENERAL MANAGEMENT the practice of working on the move. Mobile office equipment would typically include a mobile phone, laptop computer, and a modem to link the computer to the Internet or a company's main office.

mobile worker HR & PERSONNEL an employee who does not have one fixed place of work. Mobile workers are linked to a central base by telephone and sometimes by computer technology. A ***teleworker*** is a form of mobile worker.

mode STATISTICS the most frequently occurring value in a set of ranked observations

model building STATISTICS the process of providing an adequate fit to the data in a set of observations in a statistical study

modem E-COMMERCE a device that transforms computer data into signals that can be sent over telephone lines. The modem enables computers to transmit and receive data. The speed at which it can send and receive data is measured in BPS (bits per second).

moderator E-COMMERCE somebody in charge of a newsgroup, mailing list discussion group, or similar forum

modernization GENERAL MANAGEMENT investing in new equipment or upgrading existing equipment to bring resources up to date or improve efficiency

modified ACRS FINANCE, BANKING, AND ACCOUNTING a system used for computing the depreciation of some assets acquired after 1985 in a way that reduces taxes. The ACRS applies to older assets. See ***accelerated cost recovery system***

modified book value FINANCE, BANKING, AND ACCOUNTING = ***adjusted book value***

modified cash basis FINANCE, BANKING, AND ACCOUNTING the bookkeeping practice of accounting for short-term assets on a cash basis and for long-term assets on an accrual basis

Moller, **Claus** (*b.* 1942) GENERAL MANAGEMENT Danish consultant. Founder of Time Manager International™ (1975), advocate of the theory that effective ***customer service*** is achieved through employees' personal development, he is the originator of the concepts "Time Manager" and "Putting People First."

mom-and-pop operation (*U.S. & Canada*) GENERAL MANAGEMENT a business owned and run by a couple (*slang*)

moment of conception GENERAL MANAGEMENT the point at which a new organization takes shape in the mind of its founder

Monday-morning quarterback (*U.S. & Canada*) GENERAL MANAGEMENT somebody who criticizes a decision only when it is too late to change it (*slang*)

Mondex E-COMMERCE an electronic cash system that uses a smart card for both traditional shopping and e-commerce transactions

Mondragon cooperative GENERAL MANAGEMENT a large, worker-ownership movement based in the town of Mondragon, in the Basque region of northwest Spain. The Mondragon cooperative movement started in 1956, and was founded on the teachings of ***Jose Maria Arizmendietta***. It consists of worker-owned businesses, supported by a savings bank that raises money for the cooperative enterprises. Mondragon is not part of the traditional ***cooperative movement***, and is instead based on ten principles: equality of opportunity; the democratic election of managers; sovereignty of labor; a requirement for capital to be used by labor rather than labor used by capital; participative management; low pay differentials; cooperation with other cooperative movements; social change; solidarity with those working for peace, justice, and development; and education.

monetarism ECONOMICS an economic theory that states that inflation is caused by increases in a country's money supply

monetary FINANCE, BANKING, AND ACCOUNTING relating to or involving money, cash, or assets

monetary base ECONOMICS the stock of a country's coins, notes, and bank deposits with the central bank

monetary base control ECONOMICS government measures to restrict the amount of stocks of ***liquid assets*** in an economy

monetary policy ECONOMICS, FINANCE, BANKING, AND ACCOUNTING government economic policy concerning a country's rate of interest, its exchange rate, and the amount of money in the economy

monetary reserve FINANCE, BANKING, AND ACCOUNTING the foreign currency and precious metals that a country holds, usually in a central bank

monetary system ECONOMICS the set of government regulations concerning a country's monetary reserves and its holdings of notes and coins

monetary unit FINANCE, BANKING, AND ACCOUNTING the standard unit of a country's currency

monetize ECONOMICS to establish a currency as a country's legal tender

money ECONOMICS a medium of exchange that is accepted throughout a country as payment for services and goods and as a means of settling debts

moneyer FINANCE, BANKING, AND ACCOUNTING somebody who is authorized to coin money

money illusion ECONOMICS the tendency of consumers to react to prices in monetary terms rather than taking account of factors such as inflation

money laundering FINANCE, BANKING, AND ACCOUNTING the process of making money obtained illegally appear legitimate by passing it through banks or businesses

moneylender FINANCE, BANKING, AND ACCOUNTING a person who lends money for interest

moneyman FINANCE, BANKING, AND ACCOUNTING a financier or somebody in a company with responsibility for finance

money market ECONOMICS a country's financial center, where foreign currency and domestic and foreign bills are bought and sold

money market fund FINANCE, BANKING, AND ACCOUNTING a mutual fund that invests in short-term debt securities

money national income ECONOMICS GDP measured using money value, not adjusted for the effect of inflation

money of account FINANCE, BANKING, AND ACCOUNTING a monetary unit that is used in keeping accounts but is not necessarily an actual currency unit

money order FINANCE, BANKING, AND ACCOUNTING a written order to pay somebody a sum of money, issued by a bank or post office

money purchase pension HR & PERSONNEL a pension plan to which both employer and employee make contributions

money substitute ECONOMICS the use of goods as a medium of exchange because of the degree of devaluation of a country's currency

money supply ECONOMICS the stock of ***liquid assets*** in a country's economy that can be given in exchange for services or goods

money wages (*U.K.*) ECONOMICS see ***nominal wages***

monopoly

1. ECONOMICS a ***market*** in which there is only one supplier
2. GENERAL MANAGEMENT a ***market*** in which there is only one producer or one seller. A company establishes a monopoly by entering a new market or eliminating all competitors from an existing market. A company that holds a monopoly has control of a market and the ability to fix prices. For this reason, governments usually try to avoid monopoly situations. Some monopolies, however, such as government-owned utilities, are seen as beneficial to ***consumers***.

Monte Carlo method GENERAL MANAGEMENT a statistical technique used in business ***decision making*** that involves a number of uncertain variables, such as capital investment and resource allocation. The name of the Monte Carlo method derives from the use of random numbers as generated by a roulette wheel. The numbers are used in repeated simulations, often performed by spreadsheet programs on computers, to calculate a range of possible outcomes. The technique was developed by mathematicians in the early 1960s for use in nuclear physics and ***operational research*** but has since been used more widely.

moonlighting HR & PERSONNEL undertaking a second job, often for cash and in the evenings, in addition to a full-time permanent job

Moore's law E-COMMERCE the proposition that every 18 months computer chip density (and hence computer power) will double while costs remain constant, creating ever more powerful computers without raising their price. Moore's law was formulated by Intel founder Gordon Moore in the 1960s. IBM and Intel research published in 1997 corroborates it.

moral hazard FINANCE, BANKING, AND ACCOUNTING a risk that somebody will behave immorally because insurance, the law, or some other agency protects them against loss that the immoral behavior might otherwise cause

moratorium FINANCE, BANKING, AND ACCOUNTING a period of delay, for example, additional time agreed by a creditor and a debtor for recovery of a debt

more bang for your buck FINANCE, BANKING, AND ACCOUNTING a better return on your investment (*slang*)

Morgan, **Gareth** (*b.* 1943) GENERAL MANAGEMENT Canadian academic. Originator of the term ***imaginization***, which he described in the book of the same name (1993).

Morita, **Akio** (1921–99) GENERAL MANAGEMENT Japanese business executive. Cofounder and chairman of the electronics company Sony, whose global success has been based on product innovation, most famously the Walkman. The phrase "Think global, act local" has been attributed to Morita. His experiences are recorded in his autobiography *Made in Japan* (1986).

mortgage FINANCE, BANKING, AND ACCOUNTING a financial lending arrangement whereby an individual borrows money from a bank, or another lending institution, in order to buy property or land. The original amount borrowed, the **principal**, is then repaid with interest to the lender over a fixed number of years.

  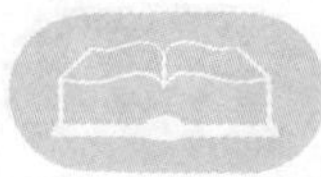    

mortgage-backed security FINANCE, BANKING, AND ACCOUNTING a security for which a mortgage is collateral

mortgage bank FINANCE, BANKING, AND ACCOUNTING a bank that trades in mortgages

mortgage broker FINANCE, BANKING, AND ACCOUNTING a person or company that acts as an agent between people seeking mortgages and organizations that offer them

mortgagee FINANCE, BANKING, AND ACCOUNTING a person or organization that lends money to a borrower under a mortgage agreement. See ***mortgagor***

mortgage equity analysis FINANCE, BANKING, AND ACCOUNTING a computation of the difference between the value of a property and the amount owed on it in the form of mortgages

mortgage insurance FINANCE, BANKING, AND ACCOUNTING insurance that provides somebody holding a mortgage with protection against default

mortgage lien FINANCE, BANKING, AND ACCOUNTING a claim against a property that is mortgaged

mortgage note FINANCE, BANKING, AND ACCOUNTING a note that documents the existence and terms of a mortgage

mortgage pool FINANCE, BANKING, AND ACCOUNTING a group of mortgages with similar characteristics packaged together for sale

mortgage portfolio FINANCE, BANKING, AND ACCOUNTING a group of mortgages held by a mortgage banker

mortgage rate FINANCE, BANKING, AND ACCOUNTING the interest rate charged on a mortgage by a lender

mortgage tax FINANCE, BANKING, AND ACCOUNTING a tax on mortgages

mortgagor FINANCE, BANKING, AND ACCOUNTING somebody who has taken out a mortgage to borrow money. See ***mortgagee***

Mosaic E-COMMERCE the first Web browser made available for Macintosh and Windows. It was developed by Netscape founder Marc Andreesen.

most distant futures contract FINANCE, BANKING, AND ACCOUNTING a futures option with the latest delivery date. See ***nearby futures contract***

MOTAS GENERAL MANAGEMENT member of the appropriate sex (*slang*)

motion study GENERAL MANAGEMENT the observation of physical movements involved in the performance of work and investigation of how these can be made more effective and cost efficient. Motion study was originally developed by ***Frank*** and ***Lillian Gilbreth***, and is now often grouped with ***time study***, to form ***time and motion study***.

motion-time analysis GENERAL MANAGEMENT see ***predetermined motion-time system***

motivate (*S. Africa*) GENERAL MANAGEMENT to argue for a position or request, especially in a proposal

motivation GENERAL MANAGEMENT

1. the creation of stimuli, incentives, and working environments which enable people to perform to the best of their ability in pursuit of organizational success. Motivation is commonly viewed as the magic driver that enables managers to get others to achieve their targets. In the 20th century, there was a shift, at least in theory, away from motivation by dictation and discipline, exemplified by ***Frederick Winslow Taylor***'s scientific management, toward motivation by creating an appropriate corporate climate and addressing the needs of individual employees. Although it is widely agreed to be one of the key management tasks, it has frequently been argued that one person cannot motivate others but can only create conditions for others to self-motivate. Many ***management theorists*** have provided insights into motivation. ***Elton Mayo***'s ***Hawthorne experiments*** identify some root causes of self-motivation, and ***Abraham Maslow***'s hierarchy of needs provides insight into personal behavior patterns. Other influential research has been carried out by ***Frederick Herzberg***, who looked at ***job satisfaction***, and ***Douglas McGregor*** whose ***Theory X*** and ***Theory Y*** suggest management styles that motivate and demotivate employees.

✔ MOTIVATING YOUR STAFF IN A TIME OF CHANGE (pp. 372–73)
💡 ELTON MAYO (pp. 1020–21); DOUGLAS MCGREGOR (pp. 1022–23)

2. (*S. Africa*) a formal written proposal

motivators GENERAL MANAGEMENT see ***job satisfaction***

MOTOS *abbr* GENERAL MANAGEMENT member of the opposite sex (*slang*)

MOTSS *abbr* GENERAL MANAGEMENT member of the same sex (*slang*)

mouse milk GENERAL MANAGEMENT to do a disproportionately large amount of work on a project that yields very little return (*slang*)

mouse potato E-COMMERCE a person who spends an excessive amount of time using a computer (*slang*)

mousetrap
build a better mousetrap MARKETING to create a new or better product (*slang*)

Mouton, Jane S. (1930–87) GENERAL MANAGEMENT U.S. psychologist. See ***Blake, Robert R.***

mover and shaker GENERAL MANAGEMENT an influential and dynamic person within an organization or group of people (*slang*)

MRP II OPERATIONS & PRODUCTION manufacturing resource planning, a computer-based manufacturing, inventory planning and control system that broadens the scope of production planning by involving other functional areas that impact on production decisions. Manufacturing resource planning evolved from material requirements planning to integrate other functions in the planning process. These functions may include engineering, marketing, purchasing, production scheduling, business planning, and finance.

MTM GENERAL MANAGEMENT see ***methods-time measurement***

multichannel E-COMMERCE using a combination of online and offline communication methods to conduct business

multicurrency FINANCE, BANKING, AND ACCOUNTING relating to a loan that gives the borrower a choice of currencies

multiemployer bargaining HR & PERSONNEL the centralization of ***pay*** negotiations at industry level, either nationally or regionally, usually conducted by ***employers' associations*** and ***labor unions***. Multiemployer bargaining is a form of ***collective bargaining*** that declined in the United Kingdom in the 1980s. Seen as having a moderating influence on pay rises, it hinders flexibility to link pay awards to company or individual employee performance.

multilevel marketing GENERAL MANAGEMENT = ***network marketing***

multimedia GENERAL MANAGEMENT a method of presenting information on a computer, CD-ROM, television, or games console. The presentation combines different media such as sound, graphics, video, and text.

multimedia document GENERAL MANAGEMENT an electronic document that incorporates interactive material from a range of different media such as text, video, sound, graphics, and animation. Such documents can be viewed on a multimedia computer or transmitted via the Internet.

multinational business *or* **multinational company** GENERAL MANAGEMENT a company, or corporation, that operates internationally, usually with subsidiaries, offices, or production facilities in more than one country

multiparty auction E-COMMERCE a method of buying and selling on the Internet in which prospective buyers make electronic bids

multiple regression analysis GENERAL MANAGEMENT see ***regression analysis***

multiple sourcing OPERATIONS & PRODUCTION a ***purchasing*** policy of using two or more suppliers for products or services. Multiple sourcing prevents reliance on any one supplier, as is the case in ***single sourcing***. It encourages competition between suppliers, and ensures access to a wide range of goods or services. Dealing with more than one supplier can improve access to market information but can also entail more administration.

multiple time series STATISTICS two or more ***time series*** that are observed simultaneously

multiskilling HR & PERSONNEL, OPERATIONS & PRODUCTION a process by which employees acquire new skills. Multiskilling is a form of ***flexible working*** in which employees are available to undertake a number of different jobs. It has led to a reduction in ***demarcation disputes*** and greater ***employability*** for employees.

multitasking E-COMMERCE the ability to execute more than one task at a time. In a computing context, a task is a program that is running on a computer.

multivariate analysis GENERAL MANAGEMENT any of a number of statistical techniques used in ***operational research*** to examine the characteristics and relationships between multiple variables. Multivariate analysis techniques include ***cluster analysis***, ***discriminant analysis***, and multiple ***regression analysis***.

multivariate data STATISTICS data for which each observation involves values for more than one random variable

mum and dad investors (*ANZ*) GENERAL MANAGEMENT people who hold or wish to purchase shares but have little experience or knowledge of the stock market (*slang*)

Mumford, Alan GENERAL MANAGEMENT British academic. See ***Honey, Peter***

Mumford, Enid (*b.* 1924) GENERAL MANAGEMENT British academic. She adopted the sociotechnical approach of the Tavistock Institute of Human Relations, applying it to the design and implementation of information technology. Mumford termed her method ETHICS (Effective Technical and Human Implementation of Computer-based Systems), which is explained in *Effective Systems Design and Requirements Analysis: The ETHICS Approach* (1995).

mushroom job GENERAL MANAGEMENT a job that is unpleasant (*slang*)

mutual company FINANCE, BANKING, AND ACCOUNTING a company that is owned by its customers who share in the profits

mutual fund FINANCE, BANKING, AND ACCOUNTING an investment company that sells shares to investors and invests for their benefit

mutual insurance FINANCE, BANKING, AND ACCOUNTING an insurance company that is owned by its policy holders who share the profits and cover claims with their pooled premiums

mutual savings bank FINANCE, BANKING, AND ACCOUNTING a savings bank that has no shareholders but is a mutual company run by its customers

Myers-Briggs type indicator HR & PERSONNEL a ***psychometric test*** that identifies four basic preferences in people's behavior. The indicator was created in the 1940s by ***Katherine Cook Briggs*** and her daughter ***Isabel Briggs-Myers***. It is based largely on the Jungian theory of personality types. The four preferences identified are made up of pairs of opposites: extraversion and introversion; sensing and intuition; thinking and feeling; and judgment and perception. The indicator provides a framework allowing people to understand themselves and others more fully, as well as encouraging the appreciation of different styles and perceptions. It is often used in teambuilding and in the ***recruitment*** process.

MYOB *abbr* GENERAL MANAGEMENT mind your own business (*slang*)

mystery shopping MARKETING the use of employees or agents to visit a store or use a service anonymously and assess its quality. Mystery shopping is used to assess such factors as the quality of customer service, including general and technical efficiency, and friendliness of staff, layout and appearance of the premises, and quality and range of goods or services on offer. Mystery shoppers fill in a questionnaire based on their impressions and this information is then used to identify possible areas for business or service improvement.

N

Naisbitt, John (*b.* 1930) GENERAL MANAGEMENT U.S. business executive and forecaster. Known for the publication of *Megatrends* (1982) in which he predicted ten main patterns of change that would shape the world.

naked option FINANCE, BANKING, AND ACCOUNTING an option in which the underlying asset is not owned by the seller, who risks considerable loss if the price of the asset falls

naked writer FINANCE, BANKING, AND ACCOUNTING a writer of an option who does not own the underlying shares

Napsterize E-COMMERCE

1. to distribute without charge something that somebody else owns. The term stems from the peer-to-peer business model pioneered by Napster, a software package for electronically distributing copies of copyrighted music without charge or payment of royalties. (*slang*)

2. to legally prevent somebody from giving away without charge something that is owned by somebody else

narrowcasting E-COMMERCE targeting information to a niche audience. Owing to its ability to personalize information to the requirements of individual users, the Internet is generally viewed as a narrowcast (rather than broadcast) medium.

NASDAQ FINANCE, BANKING, AND ACCOUNTING National Association of Security Dealers Automated Quotation system, a screen-based quotation system supporting market making in registered equities. NASDAQ International has operated from London since 1992.

  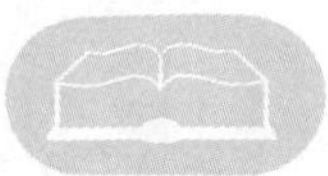    

NASDAQ Composite Index FINANCE, BANKING, AND ACCOUNTING a specialist U.S. share price index covering shares of high-technology companies

National Association of Investors Corporation FINANCE, BANKING, AND ACCOUNTING an organization that fosters investment clubs

national bank FINANCE, BANKING, AND ACCOUNTING
1. a bank that operates under federal charter and is legally required to be a member of the Federal Reserve System
2. a bank owned or controlled by the state that acts as a bank for the government and implements its monetary policies

national debt ECONOMICS, FINANCE, BANKING, AND ACCOUNTING the total borrowing of a country's central government that is unpaid

national demand ECONOMICS the total demand of consumers in an economy

National Guarantee Fund FINANCE, BANKING, AND ACCOUNTING a supply of money held by the Australian Stock Exchange which is used to compensate investors for losses incurred when an exchange member fails to meet its obligations

national income ECONOMICS the total earnings from a country's production of services and goods in a particular year

nationalization GENERAL MANAGEMENT the taking over of privately owned companies by government. Nationalization has strong political connotations. Recent global political trends have moved away from nationalization by introducing more competition and liberalization into markets. See ***privatization***

National Occupational Health and Safety Commission GENERAL MANAGEMENT an Australian statutory body responsible for coordinating efforts to prevent injury, disease, and deaths occurring in the workplace. Abbr **NOHSC**. Also known as ***Worksafe Australia***

natural capitalism GENERAL MANAGEMENT an approach to capitalism in which protection of the earth's resources is a strategic priority

NAV FINANCE, BANKING, AND ACCOUNTING see ***net asset value***

navigate E-COMMERCE to find your way around the Internet, a Web site, or an HTML document

NBFI *abbr (ANZ)* FINANCE, BANKING, AND ACCOUNTING nonbank financial institution

NDA GENERAL MANAGEMENT see ***nondisclosure agreement***

nearby futures contract FINANCE, BANKING, AND ACCOUNTING a futures option with the earliest delivery date. See ***most distant futures contract***

nearby month FINANCE, BANKING, AND ACCOUNTING the earliest month for which there is a futures contract for a particular commodity. Also known as ***spot month***. See ***far month***

near money FINANCE, BANKING, AND ACCOUNTING assets that can quickly be turned into cash

negative amortization FINANCE, BANKING, AND ACCOUNTING an increase in the ***principal*** (see ***mortgage***) of a loan due to the inadequacy of payments to cover the interest

negative carry FINANCE, BANKING, AND ACCOUNTING interest that is so high that the borrowed money does not return enough profit to cover the cost of borrowing

negative equity FINANCE, BANKING, AND ACCOUNTING a situation in which a fall in prices leads to a property being worth less than was paid for it

negative gearing FINANCE, BANKING, AND ACCOUNTING the practice of borrowing money to invest in property or shares and claiming a tax deduction on the difference between the income and the interest repayments

negative income tax ECONOMICS payments such as tax credits made to households or individuals to make their income up to a guaranteed minimum level

negative pledge clause FINANCE, BANKING, AND ACCOUNTING a provision in a bond that prohibits the issuer from doing something that would give an advantage to holders of other bonds

negative yield curve FINANCE, BANKING, AND ACCOUNTING a representation of interest rates that are higher for short-term bonds than they are for long-term bonds

negligence GENERAL MANAGEMENT the breach of a duty of care, resulting in harm to one or more people. Negligence occurs when an organization commits harm or injury through carelessness or inattention to the needs of the groups to which it owes a duty of care. These can include its customers, consumers of its product or service, shareholders, or the local community. Victims of negligence are entitled to claim compensation. Negligence is considered to be **gross negligence** if it is the result of excessively careless behavior.

negotiable certificate of deposit FINANCE, BANKING, AND ACCOUNTING a certificate of deposit with a very high value that can be freely traded

negotiable order of withdrawal FINANCE, BANKING, AND ACCOUNTING a check drawn on an account that bears interest

negotiable security FINANCE, BANKING, AND ACCOUNTING a security that can be freely traded

negotiated commissions FINANCE, BANKING, AND ACCOUNTING commissions that result from bargaining between brokers and their customers, typically large institutions

negotiated issue FINANCE, BANKING, AND ACCOUNTING = ***negotiated offering***

negotiated market FINANCE, BANKING, AND ACCOUNTING a market in which each transaction results from negotiation between a buyer and a seller

negotiated offering FINANCE, BANKING, AND ACCOUNTING a public offering, the price of which is determined by negotiations between the issuer and a syndicate of underwriters. Also known as ***negotiated issue***

negotiated sale FINANCE, BANKING, AND ACCOUNTING a public offering, the price of which is determined by negotiations between the issuer and a single underwriter

negotiation GENERAL MANAGEMENT a discussion with the aim of resolving a difference of opinion, or dispute, or to settle the terms of an agreement or transaction

Nellie
sitting with Nellie HR & PERSONNEL see ***on-the-job training*** *(slang)*

nester MARKETING in advertising or marketing, a consumer who is not influenced by advertising hype but prefers value for money and traditional products *(slang)*

net advantage of refunding FINANCE, BANKING, AND ACCOUNTING the amount realized by refunding debt

net advantage to leasing FINANCE, BANKING, AND ACCOUNTING the amount by which leasing something is financially better than borrowing money and purchasing it

net advantage to merging FINANCE, BANKING, AND ACCOUNTING the amount by which the value of a merged enterprise exceeds the value of the preexisting companies, minus the cost of the merger

net assets FINANCE, BANKING, AND ACCOUNTING the amount by which the value of a company's assets exceeds its liabilities

net asset value FINANCE, BANKING, AND ACCOUNTING a sum of the values of all that a mutual fund owns at the end of a trading day. Abbr **NAV**

NetBill E-COMMERCE a micropayment system developed at Carnegie Mellon University for purchasing digital goods over the Internet. After the goods are delivered in encrypted form to the purchaser's computer, the money is debited from the purchaser's prefunded account and the goods are decrypted for the purchaser's use.

net capital FINANCE, BANKING, AND ACCOUNTING the amount by which net assets exceed the value of assets not easily converted to cash

net cash balance FINANCE, BANKING, AND ACCOUNTING the amount of cash that is on hand

NetCheque E-COMMERCE a trademark for an electronic payment system developed at the University of Southern California to allow users to write electronic checks to one another

net current assets FINANCE, BANKING, AND ACCOUNTING the amount by which the value of a company's current assets exceeds its current liabilities

net dividend FINANCE, BANKING, AND ACCOUNTING the value of a dividend after the recipient has paid tax on it

net domestic product ECONOMICS the figure produced after factors such as depreciation have been deducted from ***GDP***

net errors and omissions FINANCE, BANKING, AND ACCOUNTING the net amount of the discrepancies that arise in calculations of balances of payments

net fixed assets FINANCE, BANKING, AND ACCOUNTING the value of fixed assets after depreciation

net foreign factor income FINANCE, BANKING, AND ACCOUNTING income from outside a country, constituting the amount by which a country's gross national product exceeds its gross domestic product

nethead E-COMMERCE somebody who is obsessed with the Internet (*slang*)

Net imperative E-COMMERCE the idea that Internet business processes must be adopted by organizations for future success

netiquette E-COMMERCE the etiquette of the Internet. The tern is used mainly in the context of e-mail and newsgroup communication.

netizen E-COMMERCE a regular user of the Internet

net lease FINANCE, BANKING, AND ACCOUNTING a lease that requires the lessee to pay for things that the owner usually pays for. See ***gross lease***

net margin FINANCE, BANKING, AND ACCOUNTING the percentage of revenues that is profit

net operating income FINANCE, BANKING, AND ACCOUNTING the amount by which income exceeds expenses, before considering taxes and interest

net operating margin FINANCE, BANKING, AND ACCOUNTING net operating income as a percentage of revenues

net pay HR & PERSONNEL = ***take-home pay***

net position FINANCE, BANKING, AND ACCOUNTING the difference between an investor's long and short positions in the same security

net present value FINANCE, BANKING, AND ACCOUNTING the value of an investment calculated as the sum of its initial cost and the ***present value*** of expected future cash flows

✔ HOW TO CALCULATE NET PRESENT VALUE (p. 831)

net proceeds FINANCE, BANKING, AND ACCOUNTING the amount realized from a transaction minus the cost of making it

net profit FINANCE, BANKING, AND ACCOUNTING gross profit minus costs

net profit margin GENERAL MANAGEMENT see ***profit margin***

net realizable value FINANCE, BANKING, AND ACCOUNTING the value of an asset if sold, allowing for costs

net return FINANCE, BANKING, AND ACCOUNTING the amount realized on an investment, taking taxes and transaction costs into account

net salvage value FINANCE, BANKING, AND ACCOUNTING the amount expected to result from terminating a project, taking tax consequences into consideration

network

1. HR & PERSONNEL to build up and maintain relationships with people whose interests are similar or whose friendship could bring advantages such as job or business opportunities

✔ HOW TO NETWORK AND MARKET YOURSELF (pp. 758–59)

2. E-COMMERCE a group of computers that are able to communicate with each other. There are two types of computer networks: LAN (a local area network) and **WAN** (a wide area network). LANs are typically used by organizations that have a large number of computers based in one location and connected to a single computer server. They are often used as the basis for private networks such as ***Intranets***. WANs are slower than LANs because they use telephone cables as well as computer servers. The Internet is the main WAN in existence.

network analysis GENERAL MANAGEMENT, OPERATIONS & PRODUCTION any of a set of techniques developed to aid the planning, monitoring, and controlling of complex ***projects*** and project resources. Network analysis is a tool of ***project management*** that involves breaking down a project into component parts or individual activities and recording them on a network diagram or ***flow chart***. The resulting chart shows the interaction and interrelations between activities and can be used to determine project duration, time and resource limitations, and cost estimates. Constituent techniques include the ***critical-path method*** and the program evaluation and review technique. Also known as ***network planning***, ***network flow analysis***

network culture GENERAL MANAGEMENT forms of culture that are heavily influenced by communication using global networks

network flow analysis GENERAL MANAGEMENT see ***network analysis***

network management GENERAL MANAGEMENT the coordinated control of computer systems and programs to allow access to and delivery of information to a number of users. Network management enables users to connect by means of cabling within a local area network or via telecommunications lines in a wide area network.

network marketing MARKETING the selling of goods or services through a network of self-employed agents or representatives. Network marketing usually involves several levels of agents, each level on a different commission rate. Each agent is encouraged to recruit other agents. In genuine network marketing, in contrast to ***pyramid selling***, there is an end product or service sold on to customers. Another version of network marketing is the loose cooperative relationship between a company, its competitors, collaborators, suppliers, and other organizations affecting the overall marketing function. Also known as ***multilevel marketing***

network organization GENERAL MANAGEMENT a company or group of companies that has a minimum of formal structures and relies instead on the formation and dissolution of teams to meet specific objectives. A network organization utilizes ***information and communications technologies*** extensively, and makes use of know-how across and within companies along the ***value chain***. See ***virtual organization***

network revolution GENERAL MANAGEMENT the fundamental change in business practices triggered by the growth of global networks

network society GENERAL MANAGEMENT a society in which patterns of work, communication, and government are characterized by the use of global networks

net worth FINANCE, BANKING, AND ACCOUNTING the difference between the assets and liabilities of a person or company

net yield FINANCE, BANKING, AND ACCOUNTING the rate of return on an investment after considering all costs and taxes

neural network STATISTICS a computer system designed to mimic the neural patterns of the human brain

neurolinguistic programming GENERAL MANAGEMENT an approach to recognizing, applying, developing, and reproducing behavior, thought processes, and ways of communicating that contribute to success. Neurolinguistic programming was developed by Richard Bandler and John Grinder through their observations of how therapists achieved excellent results with clients. It is popular in the business environment, where its influencing techniques can help firms implement change initiatives, improve communication and management skills, and develop training techniques. Abbr **NLP**

new economy ECONOMICS firms in the e-commerce sector and in the ***digital economy*** that often trade online rather than in the bricks and mortar of physical premises in the main

new entrants MARKETING organizations or products that have recently come into a market or sector

newly industrialized economy ECONOMICS a country whose industrialization has reached a level beyond that of a developing country. Mexico and Malaysia are examples of newly industrialized economies.

new product development MARKETING the processes involved in getting a new product or service to market. The traditional **product development cycle**, the **stage-gate model**, embraces the conception, generation, analysis, development, testing, marketing, and commercialization of new products or services. Alternative models of new product development fall into two broad categories: **accelerating time to market models** and **integrated implementation models**. These aim to achieve both flexibility and acceleration of development. All activities such as design, production planning, and test marketing are carried out in parallel rather than going through a sequential linear progression. Abbr **NPD**

newsletter GENERAL MANAGEMENT an informal publication, issued periodically by an organization or agency to provide information to a particular audience. A newsletter may be issued externally or it may take the form of an **in-house newsletter**, or **house journal**, used to aid the ***internal communication*** process. It is becoming more common for newsletters to be issued in electronic format.

newsreader E-COMMERCE a program that enables Internet users to send and access newsgroup messages. Newsreader programs are contained within e-mail software available as independent programs.

New Zealand Stock Exchange FINANCE, BANKING, AND ACCOUNTING the principal market in New Zealand for trading in securities. It was established in 1981, replacing the Stock Exchange Association of New Zealand and a number of regional trading floors. Abbr **NZSE**

New Zealand Trade Development Board FINANCE, BANKING, AND ACCOUNTING a government body responsible for promoting New Zealand exports and facilitating foreign investment in New Zealand. Also known as ***TRADENZ***

next futures contract FINANCE, BANKING, AND ACCOUNTING an option for the month after the current month

nice guys finish last GENERAL MANAGEMENT an axiom used in business to suggest that people should think about themselves first (*slang*)

nice-to-haves HR & PERSONNEL benefits of a job, such as free parking or subsidized meals, that are good to have but not essential (*slang*)

niche market MARKETING a very specific market segment within a broader segment. A niche market involves specialist goods or services with relatively few or no competitors. Niche consumers often look for exclusiveness or some other differentiating factor such as high status. Alternatively, they may have a specific requirement not satisfied by standard products. Allergy sufferers, for example, may require specially formulated soaps and detergents. Niche markets are often targeted by small companies that produce specialized goods and services. See ***micromarketing***

nifty fifty FINANCE, BANKING, AND ACCOUNTING on Wall Street, the fifty most popular stocks among institutional investors (*slang*)

night shift HR & PERSONNEL a ***shift*** within a ***shiftwork*** pattern that takes place during the evening and overnight. Night shifts involve particular health and social issues, and the antisocial hours usually incur a pay premium.

NIH syndrome GENERAL MANAGEMENT a problem afflicting large old-fashioned companies which reject ideas that come from outside the company simply because they were "not invented here" (*slang*)

Nikkei 225 FINANCE, BANKING, AND ACCOUNTING the Japanese share price index

nil paid (*U.K.*) FINANCE, BANKING, AND ACCOUNTING with no money yet paid. This term is used in reference to the purchase of newly issued shares, or to the shares themselves, when the shareholder entitled to buy new shares has not yet made a commitment to do so and may sell the rights instead.

NIMBY GENERAL MANAGEMENT Not In My Back Yard (*slang*)

NLP GENERAL MANAGEMENT see ***neurolinguistic programming***

node E-COMMERCE any single computer connected to a network

NOHSC GENERAL MANAGEMENT see ***National Occupational Health and Safety Commission***

Nolan, Lord Michael Patrick, Baron of Brasted (*b.* 1928) GENERAL MANAGEMENT British lawyer. Chairman of the Committee on Standards in Public Life 1994–97.

no-load fund FINANCE, BANKING, AND ACCOUNTING a mutual fund that does not charge a fee for purchase or sale of shares. See ***load fund***

nomadic worker HR & PERSONNEL see ***mobile worker***

nominal annual rate FINANCE, BANKING, AND ACCOUNTING see ***APR***

nominal capital FINANCE, BANKING, AND ACCOUNTING the total value of all of a corporation's stock

nominal cash flow FINANCE, BANKING, AND ACCOUNTING cash flow in terms of currency unadjusted for inflation

nominal exchange rate FINANCE, BANKING, AND ACCOUNTING the exchange rate as specified, without adjustment for transaction costs or differences in purchasing power

nominal group technique GENERAL MANAGEMENT see ***brainstorming***

nominal interest rate FINANCE, BANKING, AND ACCOUNTING the interest rate as specified, without adjustment for compounding or inflation

nominal ledger FINANCE, BANKING, AND ACCOUNTING in the United Kingdom, a ledger listing revenue, operating expenses, assets, and capital

nominal value FINANCE, BANKING, AND ACCOUNTING the value of a newly issued share

nominal wages ECONOMICS wages that are expressed in terms of money units and are not adjusted for changes in price

Nonaka, Ikujiro (*b.* 1935) GENERAL MANAGEMENT Japanese academic. Focuses on the creation of organizational ***knowledge***, believing this to be the most meaningful ***core competence*** for a company, particularly because it leads to ***innovation*** and ***competitive advantage***. His ideas on knowledge management, published in *The Knowledge Creating Company* (1995, coauthored by Hirotaka Takeuchi) draw on ***Peter Drucker***'s earlier ideas of the ***knowledge worker*** and the knowledge society.

nonbranded goods MARKETING generic goods that are not linked to a particular ***brand*** name, manufacturer, or producer, such as food produce, pharmaceuticals, floor coverings, furniture, computer keyboards, or hand tools. Nonbranded goods are often widely available in street markets or by mail order and like ***private labels*** are often perceived to be of low quality.

nonconformance costs GENERAL MANAGEMENT = ***quality costs***

nonconforming loan FINANCE, BANKING, AND ACCOUNTING a loan that does not conform to the lender's standards, especially those of a U.S. government agency

noncontributory pension plan FINANCE, BANKING, AND ACCOUNTING a pension plan to which the employee makes no contribution

non-contributory pension scheme (*U.K.*) FINANCE, BANKING, AND ACCOUNTING = ***noncontributory pension plan***

nondeductible FINANCE, BANKING, AND ACCOUNTING not allowed to be deducted, especially as an allowance against income taxes

nondisclosure agreement HR & PERSONNEL a legally enforceable agreement preventing present or past ***employees*** from disclosing commercially sensitive information belonging to the employer to any other party. A nondisclosure agreement can remain in force for several years after an employee leaves a company. In the event of a dispute, a company may be required to prove that the information in question belongs to the company itself, is not in the public domain, or cannot be obtained elsewhere. Abbr **NDA**

nondisparagement agreement HR & PERSONNEL an agreement that prevents present or past ***employees*** from criticizing an employing organization in public. Nondisparagement agreements are a relatively new type of agreement and have arisen primarily to prevent employees putting comments about their employing organization onto the Internet. Case law has yet to determine whether such agreements are legally binding. Abbr **NDA**

nonexecutive director GENERAL MANAGEMENT a part-time, nonsalaried member of the ***board of directors***, involved in the planning, strategy, and policy making of an organization but not in its day-to-day operations. The appointment of a nonexecutive director to a board is normally made in order to provide independence and balance to that board, and to ensure that good ***corporate governance*** is practiced. A nonexecutive director may be selected for the prestige they bring or for their experience, contacts, or specialist knowledge. Also known as ***part-time director***, ***outside director***

nonfinancial asset FINANCE, BANKING, AND ACCOUNTING an asset that is neither money nor a financial instrument, for example, real or personal property

nonfinancial incentive scheme HR & PERSONNEL see ***incentive scheme***

noninterest-bearing bond FINANCE, BANKING, AND ACCOUNTING a bond that is sold at a discount instead of with a promise to pay interest

nonjudicial foreclosure FINANCE, BANKING, AND ACCOUNTING a foreclosure on property without recourse to a court

nonnegotiable instrument FINANCE, BANKING, AND ACCOUNTING a financial instrument that cannot be signed over to anyone else

nonoperational balances FINANCE, BANKING, AND ACCOUNTING accounts that banks maintain at the Bank of England without the power of withdrawal

nonoptional FINANCE, BANKING, AND ACCOUNTING not subject to approval by shareholders

nonperforming asset FINANCE, BANKING, AND ACCOUNTING an asset that is not producing income

nonprofit organization GENERAL MANAGEMENT, HR & PERSONNEL an ***organization***

that does not have financial profit as a main strategic objective. Nonprofit organizations include charities, professional associations, labor unions, and religious, arts, community, research, and campaigning bodies. These organizations are not situated in either the ***public*** or ***private sectors***, but in what has been called the **third sector**. Many have paid staff and working capital but, according to ***Peter Drucker***, their fundamental purpose is not to provide a product or service, but to change people. They are led by values rather than financial commitments to shareholders.

nonrandom sampling OPERATIONS & PRODUCTION a ***sampling*** technique which is used when it cannot be ensured that each item has an equal chance of being selected, or when selection is based on expert knowledge of the population. See ***random sampling***

nonrecourse debt FINANCE, BANKING, AND ACCOUNTING a debt for which the borrower has no personal responsibility, typically a debt of a limited partnership

nonrecoverable FINANCE, BANKING, AND ACCOUNTING relating to a debt that will never be paid, for example, because of the borrower's bankruptcy

nonrecurring charge FINANCE, BANKING, AND ACCOUNTING a charge that is made only once

Non-Resident Withholding Tax FINANCE, BANKING, AND ACCOUNTING a duty imposed by the New Zealand government on interest and dividends earned by a nonresident from investments. Abbr **NRWT**

nonstore retailing E-COMMERCE the selling of goods and services electronically without setting up a physical store

nontariff barrier ECONOMICS see ***NTB***

nontaxable FINANCE, BANKING, AND ACCOUNTING not subject to tax

nonverbal communication GENERAL MANAGEMENT any form of ***communication*** that is not expressed in words. Nonverbal communication is estimated to make up 65–90% of all communication, and understanding, interpreting, and using it are essential skills. Forms of nonverbal communication include actions and behavior such as silence, failure or slowness to respond to a message, and lateness in arriving for a meeting. ***Body language*** is also an important part of nonverbal communication. Nonverbal elements of communication may reinforce or contradict a verbal message.

Nordstrom, **Kjell** (*b.* 1958) GENERAL MANAGEMENT Swedish academic. Known for a focus on ***globalization***, ***innovation***, ***agility***, and ***product differentiation***. Coauthor of *Funky Business* (2000), with Jonas Ridderstrale.

norm STATISTICS a range of statistics that are normal for a population

normal distribution STATISTICS the probability distribution of a random variable

normal profit ECONOMICS the minimum level of profit that will attract an entrepreneur to begin a business or remain trading

normal yield curve FINANCE, BANKING, AND ACCOUNTING a yield curve with higher interest rates for long-term bonds than for short-term bonds. See ***yield curve***

Norton, **David P.** (*b.* 1941) GENERAL MANAGEMENT U.S. consultant. See ***Kaplan, Robert S.***

no-strike agreement HR & PERSONNEL a formal understanding between an ***employer*** and a ***labor union*** that the union will not call its members out on ***strike***. A no-strike agreement is usually won by the employer in exchange for improved terms and ***conditions of employment***, including pay, and sometimes ***guaranteed employment***.

notch (*S. Africa*) HR & PERSONNEL an increment on a salary scale

notes to the accounts FINANCE, BANKING, AND ACCOUNTING explanation of particular items in a set of accounts

notes to the financial statements FINANCE, BANKING, AND ACCOUNTING explanation of particular items in a set of financial statements

notice period HR & PERSONNEL the amount of time specified in the terms and ***conditions of employment*** that an ***employee*** must work between resigning from an organization and leaving the employment of that organization. Part of a notice period may sometimes be waived while in other circumstances employees may be required to take ***garden leave***.

notional principal amount FINANCE, BANKING, AND ACCOUNTING the value used to represent a loan in calculating ***interest rate swaps***

NPD MARKETING see ***new product development***

NRWT GENERAL MANAGEMENT see ***Non-Resident Withholding Tax***

NTB *abbr* ECONOMICS nontariff barrier, a country's economic regulation on something such as safety standards that impedes imports, often from developing countries

nuisance parameter STATISTICS a parameter in a statistical model that is insignificant in itself but whose unknown value is needed to make inferences about significant variables in a study

numbered account FINANCE, BANKING, AND ACCOUNTING a bank account identified by a number to allow the holder to remain anonymous

numerical control OPERATIONS & PRODUCTION the use of numerical data to influence the operation of equipment. Numerical control allows the operation of machinery to be automated and usually involves the use of computer systems. Data is generated, stored, manipulated, and retrieved while a process is in operation.

NYMEX FINANCE, BANKING, AND ACCOUNTING New York Mercantile Exchange, a commodity market that deals in futures of crude and heating oil, gasoline, platinum, and palladium

NYSE *abbr* FINANCE, BANKING, AND ACCOUNTING New York Stock Exchange, the leading stock exchange in New York which is self-regulatory but has to comply with the regulations of the U.S. Securities and Exchange Commission

NZSE *abbr* FINANCE, BANKING, AND ACCOUNTING New Zealand Stock Exchange

NZSE10 Index FINANCE, BANKING, AND ACCOUNTING a measure of changes in share prices on the New Zealand Stock Exchange, based on the change in value of the stocks of the 10 largest companies

NZSE30 Selection Index FINANCE, BANKING, AND ACCOUNTING a measure of changes in share prices on the New Zealand Stock Exchange, based on the change in value of the stocks of the 30 largest companies. Abbr **NZSE30**

NZSE40 FINANCE, BANKING, AND ACCOUNTING the principal measure of changes in stock prices on the New Zealand Stock Exchange, based on the change in value of the stocks of the 40 largest companies. The makeup of the index is reviewed every three months.

Obeng, **Eddie** (*b.* 1959) GENERAL MANAGEMENT Ghanaian-born academic and consultant. Pioneer of the first virtual business school. Obeng founded the school, named Pentacle, in 1994, to assist managers and organizations facing the pressures and challenges of the global economy, a situation described in his book *New Rules for the New World* (1997).

OBI E-COMMERCE see ***open buying on the Internet***

object and task technique GENERAL MANAGEMENT a method of budgeting that involves assessing a project's objectives, determining the tasks required for their accomplishment, and then estimating the cost of each task

objective GENERAL MANAGEMENT, HR & PERSONNEL an end toward which effort is directed and on which resources are focused, usually to achieve an organization's ***strategy***. There is endless discussion on whether objective, **goal**, **target**, and **aim** are the same. In general usage, the terms are often used interchangeably, so it is important that if an organization has a particular meaning for one of these terms it must define it in its documentation. Sometimes an objective is seen as the desired final end result, while a goal is a smaller step on the road to it. Objective setting is given a practical application in ***management by objectives***.

obscuranto GENERAL MANAGEMENT incomprehensible jargon used by large international organizations such as the European Commission (*slang*)

obsolescence MARKETING the decline of products in a market due to the introduction of better competitor products or rapid technology developments. Obsolescence of products can be a planned process, controlled by introducing deliberate minor cosmetic changes to a product every few years to encourage new purchases. It can also be unplanned, however, and in some sectors the pace of technological change is so rapid that the rate of obsolescence is high. This is the case particularly in consumer and industrial electronics, affecting computers, Internet-related products, telecommunications, and television, audio, and car technology. Obsolescence is part of the product ***life cycle***, and if a product cannot be turned around, it may lead to ***product abandonment***.

occupational health HR & PERSONNEL the well-being of ***employees*** at work. An occupational health service is concerned with reacting to and preventing work-related illness and injury, and with maintaining and improving employees' health. Occupational health may involve some or all of these elements: health screening, including ***preemployment screening*** (see ***health screening***); monitoring compliance with health and safety legislation; health promotion activities; and initiating and maintaining health-related policies. There may be some overlap with ***employee assistance programs***. An occupational health service aims to reduce ***absenteeism*** and improve employee morale and performance.

occupational illness HR & PERSONNEL an illness associated with a particular job. Occupational illnesses include lung disease, which can affect miners, ***repetitive strain injury***, which can be suffered by keyboard users, and asbestosis, caused by working with asbestos. ***Occupational health*** policies must take all hazards into account and minimize the potential for these diseases to develop. Government benefits are sometimes available to sufferers who are disadvantaged because of occupational illness.

occupational psychology HR & PERSONNEL the branch of psychology concerned with the assessment of the well-being of ***employees*** within their work environment in order to improve performance and efficiency, ***job satisfaction***, and ***occupational health***. Eight main areas of occupational psychology exist: human-machine interaction; design of working environment and ***health and safety***; personnel ***recruitment*** and assessment; ***performance appraisal*** and career development; ***counseling*** and ***personal development***; ***training***; ***motivation*** and industrial relations; and organization change and development. Also known as ***industrial psychology***

OCR FINANCE, BANKING, AND ACCOUNTING see ***official cash rate***

Odiorne, **George Stanley** GENERAL MANAGEMENT U.S. academic. Known for his popularization in the United States of ***Peter Drucker***'s ***Management by Objectives***. Odiorne is said to have coined the saying "If you can't measure it, you can't manage it."

OEM OPERATIONS & PRODUCTION see ***original equipment manufacturer***

off-balance-sheet financing FINANCE, BANKING, AND ACCOUNTING financing obtained by means other than debt and equity instruments, for example, partnerships, joint ventures, and leases

offer document FINANCE, BANKING, AND ACCOUNTING a description of the loan a lender is offering to provide

offering memorandum FINANCE, BANKING, AND ACCOUNTING a description of an offer to sell securities privately

offering price FINANCE, BANKING, AND ACCOUNTING the price at which somebody offers a share of a stock for sale. Also called ***offer price***

offeror FINANCE, BANKING, AND ACCOUNTING somebody who makes a bid

offer price FINANCE, BANKING, AND ACCOUNTING see ***offering price***

office design GENERAL MANAGEMENT the arrangement of workspace so that work can be carried out in the most efficient way. Office design incorporates both ***ergonomics*** and **work flow**, which examine the way in which work is performed in order to optimize layout. Office design is an important factor in ***job satisfaction***. It affects the way in which employees work, and many organizations have implemented open-plan offices to encourage ***teamwork***. The development of ***information and communications technologies*** has led to changes in traditional layouts and some offices are designed to facilitate ***hot-desking*** or ***hoteling***. The design of workspaces must conform to health and safety legislation.

office-free HR & PERSONNEL used to refer to employees whose jobs do not require them to work in an office (*slang*)

office junior FINANCE, BANKING, AND ACCOUNTING an employee with no responsibilities who carries out mundane or routine tasks in an office

office politics GENERAL MANAGEMENT interpersonal dynamics within a workplace. Office politics involves the complex network of power and status that exists within any group of people.

officer GENERAL MANAGEMENT see ***executive***

official banks FINANCE, BANKING, AND ACCOUNTING banks that have charters from governments

official books of account FINANCE, BANKING, AND ACCOUNTING the official financial records of an institution

official cash rate FINANCE, BANKING, AND ACCOUNTING the current interest rate as set by a central bank. Abbr **OCR**

official development assistance FINANCE, BANKING, AND ACCOUNTING money that the Organization for Economic Cooperation and Development's Development Assistance Committee gives or lends to a developing country

official exchange rate list FINANCE, BANKING, AND ACCOUNTING the list of official exchange rates

official receiver GENERAL MANAGEMENT an officer of the court who is appointed to wind up the affairs of an organization that goes bankrupt. In the United Kingdom, an official receiver is appointed by the Department of Trade and Industry and often acts as a ***liquidator***. The job involves realizing any assets that remain to repay debts, for example, by selling property.

off-line transaction processing E-COMMERCE the receipt and storage of order and credit or debit card information through a computer network or point-of-sale terminal for subsequent authorization and processing

offset FINANCE, BANKING, AND ACCOUNTING a transaction that balances all or part of an earlier transaction in the same security

offset clause FINANCE, BANKING, AND ACCOUNTING a provision in an insurance policy that permits the balancing of credits against debits so that, for example, a party can reduce or omit payments to another party that owes it money and is bankrupt

offshore bank FINANCE, BANKING, AND ACCOUNTING a bank that offers only limited wholesale banking services to nonresidents

offshore finance subsidiary *(U.K.)* FINANCE, BANKING, AND ACCOUNTING = ***offshore financial subsidiary***

offshore financial center FINANCE, BANKING, AND ACCOUNTING a country or other political unit that has banking laws intended to attract business from industrialized nations

offshore financial subsidiary FINANCE, BANKING, AND ACCOUNTING a company created in another country to handle financial transactions, giving the owning company certain tax and legal advantages in its home country

offshore holding company FINANCE, BANKING, AND ACCOUNTING a company created in another country to own other companies, giving the owning company certain legal advantages in its home country

offshore production OPERATIONS & PRODUCTION the manufacture of goods abroad for import to the domestic market

offshore trading company FINANCE, BANKING, AND ACCOUNTING a company created in another country to handle commercial transactions, giving the owning company certain legal advantages in its home country

off-topic GENERAL MANAGEMENT irrelevant or off the subject *(slang)*

Ohmae, Kenichi *(b.* 1943) GENERAL MANAGEMENT Japanese consultant, writer, and politician. Herald of Japanese management techniques in the West, arguing that the success of Japanese companies could be attributed to Japanese strategic thinking based on ***creativity*** and ***innovation***. In *The Mind of the Strategist* (1982), Ohmae identified key differences between the strategies adopted by Japanese managers and their Western counterparts. He later challenged all companies to take account of ***globalization*** in their ***strategic planning*** (see ***planning***) and to focus on the relationship between business and the nation state. His recent work examines the relationship between old economy and ***new economy*** companies and identifies the basic forces influencing the new economy.
KENICHI OHMAE (pp. 1028–29)

Ohno, Taiichi *(b.* 1912) GENERAL MANAGEMENT Japanese business executive. Responsible for much of the background work and thinking that created the ***Toyota production system***, explained in the book of the same name (1988).

ohnosecond GENERAL MANAGEMENT the short time required to realize that you have made a serious mistake *(slang)*

oil
the good oil *(ANZ)* GENERAL MANAGEMENT accurate and useful information *(slang)*

OINK GENERAL MANAGEMENT One Income, No Kids *(slang)*

older worker HR & PERSONNEL generally considered to mean an employee aged 50 or over but in some industries, such as IT, an older worker is somebody over 30. Older workers can be subject to ***age discrimination***.

old old MARKETING the oldest age group, consisting of people over the age of 75

oligarchy GENERAL MANAGEMENT an organization in which a small group of managers exercises control. Within an oligarchy, the controlling group often directs the organization for its own purposes, or for purposes other than the best interests of the organization.

oligopoly ECONOMICS a market in which there are only a few, very large, suppliers

omitted dividend FINANCE, BANKING, AND ACCOUNTING a regularly scheduled dividend that a company does not pay

omnibus account FINANCE, BANKING, AND ACCOUNTING an account of one broker with another that combines the transactions of multiple investors for the convenience of the brokers

omnibus survey MARKETING a survey covering a number of topics usually undertaken on behalf of several clients who share the cost of conducting the survey

on account FINANCE, BANKING, AND ACCOUNTING paid in advance against all or part of money due in the future

one-to-one marketing MARKETING a marketing technique using detailed data, personalized communications, and customized products or services to match the requirements of individual customers

one-to-one merger GENERAL MANAGEMENT see ***merger***

on-hold advertising MARKETING telephone advertising aimed at consumers who are being kept on hold while waiting to speak to somebody *(slang)*

online capture E-COMMERCE a payment transaction generated after goods have been shipped, in which funds are transferred from issuer to acquirer to merchant account

online catalog E-COMMERCE a business-to-business marketplace that collects the catalog data of every supplier in a particular industry and places it on one central Web resource. Catalogs are important to companies for marketing purposes because they are one of the main ways to distribute product information to public marketplaces and private exchanges. Also known as ***procurement portal***

online shopping E-COMMERCE = ***electronic shopping***

online shopping mall E-COMMERCE = ***cyber mall***

online training HR & PERSONNEL see ***computer-based training***

on-pack offer MARKETING a sales promotion technique in which customers are offered a premium on the pack

on target earnings HR & PERSONNEL the amount earned by a person working on ***commission*** who has achieved the targets set. Abbr **OTE**

on-the-job training HR & PERSONNEL ***training*** given to employees in the workplace as they perform everyday work activities. On-the-job training is based on the principle of ***learning by doing*** and includes demonstration and explanation by a more experienced employee, supervisor, or manager; performance of tasks under supervision; and the provision of appropriate ***feedback***. On-the-job training is sometimes informally referred to as **sitting with Nellie**. Types of on-the-job training include ***coaching***, ***delegation***, ***job rotation***, ***secondment***, and participation in special projects.

open book management GENERAL MANAGEMENT a ***management style*** in which everything is revealed to employees and there are no secrets. Open book management involves not only revealing a company's full financial information to its employees but also making transparent all of the workings of the company. Open book management has been viewed as enabling the ***empowerment*** and ***involvement*** of the workforce, increasing employee ***motivation*** and organizational efficiency.

open buying on the Internet E-COMMERCE, FINANCE, BANKING, AND ACCOUNTING a standard built around a common set of business requirements for electronic communication between buyers and sellers that, when implemented, allows different e-commerce systems to talk to one another. Abbr **OBI**. See ***open trading protocol***

open-collar worker HR & PERSONNEL a person who works from home (*slang*)

open communication GENERAL MANAGEMENT a communications policy intended to ensure that employees have full information about their organization

open-door policy GENERAL MANAGEMENT a receptive, listening approach to management characterized by a ready, informal availability on the part of the manager toward employees. Open-door management removes the need to make appointments or to show the deference traditionally associated with relationships between superiors and subordinates in hierarchies. The opposite management style is a **closed-door policy**, which is more formal. Open- and closed-door policies can reflect different kinds of ***corporate culture***.

open economy ECONOMICS an economy that places no restrictions on the movement of capital and labor, foreign trade, and payments into and out of the country

open-end credit FINANCE, BANKING, AND ACCOUNTING a form of credit that does not have an upper limit on the amount that can be borrowed or a time limit before repayment is due

open-ended credit (*U.K.*) FINANCE, BANKING, AND ACCOUNTING = ***open-end credit***

open-ended fund (*U.K.*) FINANCE, BANKING, AND ACCOUNTING = ***open-end fund***

open-ended investment company (*U.K.*) FINANCE, BANKING, AND ACCOUNTING = ***open-end investment company***

open-ended management company (*U.K.*) FINANCE, BANKING, AND ACCOUNTING = ***open-end management company***

open-ended mortgage (*U.K.*) FINANCE, BANKING, AND ACCOUNTING = ***open-end mortgage***

open-end fund FINANCE, BANKING, AND ACCOUNTING a mutual fund that has a variable number of shares

open-end investment company FINANCE, BANKING, AND ACCOUNTING a mutual fund, as distinguished from an investment trust, or closed-end fund. See ***open-end fund***

open-end management company FINANCE, BANKING, AND ACCOUNTING a company that sells mutual funds

open-end mortgage FINANCE, BANKING, AND ACCOUNTING a mortgage in which prepayment is allowed

opening balance FINANCE, BANKING, AND ACCOUNTING the value of a financial quantity at the beginning of a period of time, such as a day or a year

opening balance sheet FINANCE, BANKING, AND ACCOUNTING an account showing an organization's opening balances

opening bell FINANCE, BANKING, AND ACCOUNTING the beginning of a day of trading on a market

opening price FINANCE, BANKING, AND ACCOUNTING a price for a security at the beginning of a day of trading on a market

opening purchase FINANCE, BANKING, AND ACCOUNTING a first purchase of a series to be made in options of a particular type for a particular commodity or security

open interest FINANCE, BANKING, AND ACCOUNTING options that have not yet been closed

open learning HR & PERSONNEL a flexible approach to a course of study that allows individuals to learn at a time, place, and pace to suit their needs. A typical open learning program might offer the student a range of delivery methods, including tutorials, workshops, formal lectures, and the Internet, supported by a variety of learning materials such as textbooks, workbooks, and video, audio, and computer-based materials. See ***distance learning***

open market FINANCE, BANKING, AND ACCOUNTING a market that is widely available

open market operation FINANCE, BANKING, AND ACCOUNTING a transaction by a central bank in a public market

open standard GENERAL MANAGEMENT a standard for computers and related products that allows pieces of equipment from different manufacturers to operate with each other

open system FINANCE, BANKING, AND ACCOUNTING an operating system whose developer encourages the development of applications that use it

open systems thinking GENERAL MANAGEMENT a learning and ***problem solving*** approach that involves describing the behavior of a system, then exploring possibilities for improving it. Open systems thinking encourages ***creativity*** and is used by ***learning organizations***.

open trading protocol E-COMMERCE a standard designed to support Internet-based retail transactions, that, when implemented, allows different systems to communicate with each other for a variety of payment-related activities. The ***open buying on the Internet*** protocol is a competing standard. Abbr **OTP**. See ***open buying on the Internet***

operating cash flow FINANCE, BANKING, AND ACCOUNTING the amount used to represent the money moving through a company as a result of its operations, as distinct from its purely financial transactions

operating costing OPERATIONS & PRODUCTION a costing system that is applied to continuous operations in mass production or in the service industries. In the simplest form of operating costing, the costing period is set at a specific length of time, usually a calendar month or four weeks. The costs incurred over the period are related to the number of units produced, and the division of the first by the second gives the average unit cost for the period. Also known as ***batch costing***

operating cycle OPERATIONS & PRODUCTION the cycle of business activity in which cash is used to buy resources which are converted into products or services and then sold for cash

operating income OPERATIONS & PRODUCTION revenue minus the cost of goods sold and normal operating expenses. Also known as ***earnings before income and taxes***

operating margin GENERAL MANAGEMENT see ***profit margin***

operating system FINANCE, BANKING, AND ACCOUNTING a program that controls the basic operation of a computer and its communication with devices such as the keyboard, printer, and mouse

operational audit GENERAL MANAGEMENT a structured review of the systems and procedures of an organization in order to evaluate whether they are being carried out efficiently and effectively. An operational audit involves: establishing performance ***objectives***, agreeing the standards and criteria for assessment, and evaluating actual performance against targeted performance. Also known as ***management audit***

operational gearing FINANCE, BANKING, AND ACCOUNTING the ongoing financial operations of a company

operational research GENERAL MANAGEMENT the application of scientific methods to the solution of managerial and administrative problems, involving complex systems or processes. Operational research aims to find the optimum plan for the control and operation of a system or process. It was originally used during World War II as a means of solving logistical problems. It has since developed into a planning, scheduling, and ***problem solving*** technique applied across the industrial, commercial, and public sectors.

operation planning OPERATIONS & PRODUCTION see ***planning***

operations OPERATIONS & PRODUCTION see ***operations management***

operations audit GENERAL MANAGEMENT see ***operational audit***

operations management OPERATIONS & PRODUCTION the maintenance, control, and improvement of organizational activities that are required to produce goods or services for consumers. Operations management has traditionally been associated with manufacturing activities but can also be applied to the service sector. The measurement and evaluation of operations is usually undertaken through a process of business appraisal. Efficiency and effectiveness may be monitored by the application of ***ISO*** 9001 quality systems, or ***total quality management*** techniques.

opinion leader MARKETING a high-profile person or organization that can significantly influence public opinion. An opinion leader can be a politician, religious, business or community leader, journalist, or educationalist. Show business and sports personalities can exert a great deal of influence on young people's leisure lifestyles and buying habits and are consequently frequently used in ***advertising campaigns***.

opinion leader research MARKETING the investigation of the perceptions of ***corporate image*** and reputation among the people at the top of a company, industry, or profession

opinion shopping GENERAL MANAGEMENT the practice of searching for an auditor whose views are in line with those of a company being audited. Opinion shopping can take place when a company is about to be audited and has recently undertaken questionable dealings. Auditors are sought whose interpretation of the law matches the company's own, and who will approve the company's financial statements.

opinion survey STATISTICS a survey carried out to determine what members of a population think about a given topic

opportunity cost GENERAL MANAGEMENT, FINANCE, BANKING, AND ACCOUNTING an amount of money lost as a result of choosing one investment rather than another

OPT OPERATIONS & PRODUCTION see ***optimized production technology***

optimal portfolio FINANCE, BANKING, AND ACCOUNTING a theoretical set of investments that would be most profitable for an investor

optimal redemption provision FINANCE, BANKING, AND ACCOUNTING a provision that specifies when an issuer can call a bond

optimize FINANCE, BANKING, AND ACCOUNTING to allocate such things as resources or capital as efficiently as possible

optimized production technology OPERATIONS & PRODUCTION a sophisticated ***production planning*** and ***control*** system, based on ***finite loading*** procedures, that concentrates on reducing ***bottlenecks*** in the system in order to improve efficiency. The key task of OPT is to increase total systems throughput by realizing existing capacity in other parts of the system. OPT is a practical application of the **theory of constraints**. Abbr **OPT**

optimum capacity OPERATIONS & PRODUCTION the level of output at which the minimum cost per unit is incurred

option FINANCE, BANKING, AND ACCOUNTING a contract for the right to buy or sell an asset, typically a commodity, under certain terms. Also known as ***option contract***

option account FINANCE, BANKING, AND ACCOUNTING a brokerage account used for trading in options

optionaire FINANCE, BANKING, AND ACCOUNTING a millionaire whose wealth consists of stock options (*slang*)

option buyer FINANCE, BANKING, AND ACCOUNTING an investor who buys an option

option class FINANCE, BANKING, AND ACCOUNTING a set of options that are identical with respect to type and underlying asset

option contract FINANCE, BANKING, AND ACCOUNTING = ***option***

option elasticity FINANCE, BANKING, AND ACCOUNTING the relative change in the value of an option as a function of a change in the value of the underlying asset

option income fund FINANCE, BANKING, AND ACCOUNTING a mutual fund that invests in options

option premium FINANCE, BANKING, AND ACCOUNTING the amount per share that a buyer pays for an option

option price FINANCE, BANKING, AND ACCOUNTING the price of an option

option pricing model FINANCE, BANKING, AND ACCOUNTING a model that is used to determine the fair value of options

options clearing corporation FINANCE, BANKING, AND ACCOUNTING the organization that is responsible for the listing of options and clearing trades in them

option seller FINANCE, BANKING, AND ACCOUNTING = ***option writer***

option series FINANCE, BANKING, AND ACCOUNTING a collection of options that are identical in terms of what they represent

options market FINANCE, BANKING, AND ACCOUNTING the trading in options, or a place where options trading occurs

options on physicals FINANCE, BANKING, AND ACCOUNTING options on securities with fixed interest rates

option writer FINANCE, BANKING, AND ACCOUNTING a person or institution who sells an option. Also known as ***option seller***

order

1. OPERATIONS & PRODUCTION a ***contract*** made between a customer and a supplier for the supply of a range of goods or services in a determined quantity and quality, at an agreed price, and for delivery at or by a specified time

2. FINANCE, BANKING, AND ACCOUNTING an occasion when a broker is told to buy or sell something for an investor's own account

order book OPERATIONS & PRODUCTION a record of the outstanding orders that an organization has received. An order book may be physical, with the specifications and delivery times of orders recorded in it, or the term may be used generally to describe the health of a company. A full order book implies a successful company, while an empty order book can indicate an organization at risk of ***business failure***.

order confirmation E-COMMERCE an e-mail message informing a purchaser that an order has been received

order picking OPERATIONS & PRODUCTION selecting and withdrawing goods or components from a store or warehouse to meet production requirements or to satisfy customer orders

order point FINANCE, BANKING, AND ACCOUNTING the quantity of an item that is on hand when more units of the item are to be ordered

order processing OPERATIONS & PRODUCTION the tracking of ***orders*** with suppliers and from customers

orders pending FINANCE, BANKING, AND ACCOUNTING orders that have not yet resulted in transactions

ordinary interest FINANCE, BANKING, AND ACCOUNTING interest calculated on the basis of a year having only 360 days

ordinary shares FINANCE, BANKING, AND ACCOUNTING shares bought by investors in the United States in foreign companies that are traded on their home markets, as opposed to shares that trade in the United States

organigram FINANCE, BANKING, AND ACCOUNTING a chart that represents the detail of an organization or process. See ***organization chart***

organization GENERAL MANAGEMENT an arrangement of people and resources working in a planned manner toward specified strategic goals. An organization can be any structured body such as a business, company, or firm in the private, or public sector, or a nonprofit association. See ***organization structure***, ***organization theory***

organizational analysis GENERAL MANAGEMENT a type of internal business appraisal aimed at identifying areas of inefficiency and opportunities for streamlining and reorganization

organizational change GENERAL MANAGEMENT see ***change management***

organizational chart GENERAL MANAGEMENT = ***organization chart***

organizational commitment GENERAL MANAGEMENT

1. the commitment of an organization to given aims and objectives, as demonstrated through its stated aims and policies and its actions, and allocation of resources

2. the degree of ***employee commitment*** within an organizational workforce

organizational culture GENERAL MANAGEMENT = ***corporate culture***

organizational design GENERAL MANAGEMENT see ***organization structure***

organizational development GENERAL MANAGEMENT a planned approach to far-reaching, organization-wide change designed to enable an organization to respond and adapt to changing market conditions and to set a new agenda. Organizational development is frequently linked to ***organization structure***, which can act either as an enabling or restrictive mechanism for change. For organizational development to succeed, any policies or strategies introduced must fit with the ***corporate culture***.

organizational federalism GENERAL MANAGEMENT see ***federal organization***

organizational learning GENERAL MANAGEMENT a culture of change and improvement within an organization, characterized by employee enthusiasm, energy, and high levels of ***creativity*** and ***innovation***. In their book *Organizational Learning* (1978), ***Chris Argyris***, and ***Donald Schön*** suggest that if a number of employee development activities are in progress within an organization, a sense of organizational movement and development can be achieved, and that with the right encouragement, support, and reward, this can become self-perpetuating. The concept of organizational learning was further developed by ***Peter Senge***, and repopularized as the ***learning organization***.

CHRIS ARGYRIS (pp. 964–65); PETER SENGE (pp. 1046–47)

organization behavior GENERAL MANAGEMENT the study of human and group behavior within organizational settings. The study of organization behavior involves looking at the attitudes, interpersonal relationships, performance, ***productivity***, ***job satisfaction***, and commitment of employees, as well as levels of ***organizational commitment*** and industrial relations. Organization behavior can be affected by ***corporate culture***, ***leadership***, and ***management style***. Organization behavior emerged as a distinct specialism from ***organization theory*** in the late 1950s and early 1960s through attempts to integrate different perspectives on human and management problems and develop an understanding of

behavioral dynamics within organizations.
CHRIS ARGYRIS (pp. 964–65); DOUGLAS MCGREGOR (pp. 1022–23)

organization chart GENERAL MANAGEMENT a graphic illustration of an ***organization's structure***, showing hierarchical authority and relationships between departments and jobs. The horizontal dimension of an organization chart shows the nature of job function and responsibility and the vertical dimension shows how jobs are coordinated in reporting or authority relationships. Some charts include managers' names, others only job titles. Organization charts are widely used to bring order and clarity to the way the organization is structured. Despite this, they reflect little of the way organizations actually work and can appear complex, especially in highly ***bureaucratic*** organizations. The first recorded organization chart was produced in the United States by David C. McCallum for the New York and Erie Railroad. Also known as ***organizational chart***, ***organigram***

organization hierarchy GENERAL MANAGEMENT the vertical layers of ranks of personnel within an organization, each layer subordinate to the one above it. Organization hierarchy is often shown in the form of an ***organization chart***. An extended hierarchy is typical of a ***bureaucracy***, but during the later 20th and early 21st centuries the layers of hierarchical positions within large organizations have often been reduced as part of ***downsizing*** exercises. These result in the shallow or nonexistent hierarchies of flexible, ***flat organizations*** within which there is greater employee ***empowerment*** and autonomy.

organization man GENERAL MANAGEMENT somebody who fully accepts and may be absorbed by organizational objectives and values. *The Organization Man*, a bestselling novel by ***William Whyte***, is the source of the phrase.

organization structure GENERAL MANAGEMENT the form of an organization that is evident in the way divisions, departments, functions, and people link together and interact. Organization structure reveals vertical operational responsibilities, and horizontal linkages, and may be represented by an ***organization chart***. The complexity of an organization's structure is often proportional to its size and its geographic dispersal. The traditional organization structure for many businesses in the 20th century was the ***bureaucracy***, originally defined by ***Max Weber***. More recent forms include the ***flat***, ***network***, ***matrix*** (see ***matrix organization***), and ***virtual*** organizations. These forms have become more prevalent during the last decades of the 20th century as a result of the trend toward restructuring and downsizing and developments in telecommunications technology. According to ***Harold J. Leavitt***, organization structure is inextricably linked to the technology and people who carry out the tasks. ***Charles Handy*** has shown that it is also directly linked to ***corporate culture***.
CHARLES HANDY (pp. 1000–01); MAX WEBER (pp. 1060–61)

organization theory GENERAL MANAGEMENT the body of research and knowledge concerning organizations. Organization theory originally focused primarily on the organization as a unit, as opposed to ***organization behavior***, which explored individual and group behavior within the organization. Organization behavior emerged as a separate discipline in the late 1950s and early 1960s but there remains a large amount of overlap between the two. Organization theory covers a range of areas including ***organization structure*** and organizational psychology.
CHARLES HANDY (pp. 1000–01); HENRY MINTZBERG (pp. 1024–25)

organized labor HR & PERSONNEL
1. all labor unions considered collectively
2. employees belonging to labor unions

org chart GENERAL MANAGEMENT an informal term for an organization chart

original equipment manufacturer
1. OPERATIONS & PRODUCTION a company that assembles components from other suppliers or subcontractors to produce a complete product such as a car or aircraft. Abbr **OEM**
2. FINANCE, BANKING, AND ACCOUNTING a company that makes a product that works with a basic and common product, for example, a computer

original face value FINANCE, BANKING, AND ACCOUNTING the amount of the principal of a mortgage on the day it is created

original issue discount FINANCE, BANKING, AND ACCOUNTING the discount offered on the day of sale of a debt instrument

original maturity FINANCE, BANKING, AND ACCOUNTING a date on which a debt instrument is due to mature

origination fee FINANCE, BANKING, AND ACCOUNTING a fee charged by a lender for providing a mortgage, usually expressed as a percentage of the principal

orthogonal STATISTICS statistically independent

OTE HR & PERSONNEL see ***on target earnings***

other capital FINANCE, BANKING, AND ACCOUNTING capital that is not listed in other, more specific, categories

other current assets FINANCE, BANKING, AND ACCOUNTING assets that are not cash and are due to mature within a year

other long-term capital FINANCE, BANKING, AND ACCOUNTING long-term capital that is not listed in other, more specific, categories

other prices FINANCE, BANKING, AND ACCOUNTING prices that are not listed in a catalog

other short-term capital FINANCE, BANKING, AND ACCOUNTING short-term capital that is not listed in other, more specific, categories

OTOH *abbr* GENERAL MANAGEMENT on the other hand (*slang*)

OTP E-COMMERCE see ***open trading protocol***

Ouchi, **William G.** (*b.* 1943) GENERAL MANAGEMENT Japanese-U.S. academic. Best known for ***Theory Z*** (1981) which developed the work of ***Douglas McGregor***.
DOUGLAS MCGREGOR (pp. 1022–23)

outdoor advertising MARKETING the use of outdoor advertising media in venues such as airports, shopping malls, bus shelters, and railway stations

outdoor training HR & PERSONNEL = ***adventure training***

outlier STATISTICS a statistical observation that deviates significantly from other members of a sample

out of the loop GENERAL MANAGEMENT excluded from communication within a group. Somebody who is out of the loop may have been deliberately or inadvertently excluded from the decision making process or the information flow around an organization. That person is likely to feel isolated and will be unable to contribute fully to the organization. Effective networking may help to prevent this from happening. (*slang*)

outplacement HR & PERSONNEL a program of resources, information, and advice provided by an employing organization for employees who are about to be made redundant. Outplacement agencies typically help by

  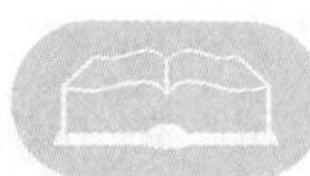    

drafting résumés, offering career guidance, providing practice interviews, and placing redundant employees in new jobs. Outplacement programs are often put into place well before the redundant employees leave the employer and, in the case of large-scale redundancy programs, may remain in place for several years.

output FINANCE, BANKING, AND ACCOUNTING anything produced by a company, usually physical products

output gap ECONOMICS the difference between the amount of activity that is sustainable in an economy and the amount of activity actually taking place

output method ECONOMICS an accounting system that classifies costs according to the ***outputs*** for which they are incurred, not the inputs they have bought

output tax (*ANZ*) FINANCE, BANKING, AND ACCOUNTING the amount of GST (goods and services tax) paid to the tax office after the deduction of ***input tax credits***

outside director GENERAL MANAGEMENT a member of a company's ***board of directors*** neither currently, or formerly, in the company's employment. An outside director is sometimes described as being synonymous with a ***nonexecutive director***, and as usually being employed by a holding or associated company. The U.S. view suggests that an outside director is somebody who has no relationships at all to a company. In U.S. public companies, compensation and audit committees are generally made up of outside directors, and use of outside directors to select board directors is becoming more common.

outsourcing GENERAL MANAGEMENT the transfer of the provision of services previously carried out by in-house personnel to an external organization, usually under a ***contract*** with agreed standards, costs, and conditions. Areas traditionally outsourced include legal services, transport, catering, and security. An increasing range of activities, including IT services, training, and public relations are now being outsourced. Outsourcing, or **contracting out**, is often introduced with the aim of increasing efficiency and reducing costs, or to enable the organization to develop greater flexibility or to concentrate on ***core business*** activities. The term ***subcontracting*** is sometimes used to refer to outsourcing.

outstanding share FINANCE, BANKING, AND ACCOUNTING a share that a company has issued and somebody has bought

outstanding share capital FINANCE, BANKING, AND ACCOUNTING the value of all of the stock of a company minus the value of retained shares

out-tray GENERAL MANAGEMENT a receptacle for documents and other items that have been dealt with. An out-tray is normally placed in the office or on the desk of the person responsible for dealing with the contents. Items are placed in the out-tray before being filed or delivered to another person.

outward bound training HR & PERSONNEL = ***adventure training***

outwork FINANCE, BANKING, AND ACCOUNTING, GENERAL MANAGEMENT work carried out for a company away from its premises, for example, by subcontractors or employees working from home

outworker FINANCE, BANKING, AND ACCOUNTING, GENERAL MANAGEMENT a subcontractor or employee carrying out work for a company away from its premises

overall capitalization rate FINANCE, BANKING, AND ACCOUNTING net operating income other than debt service divided by value

overall market capacity ECONOMICS the amount of a service or good that can be absorbed in a market without affecting the price

overall rate of return FINANCE, BANKING, AND ACCOUNTING the yield of a bond held to maturity, expressed as a percentage

overbid FINANCE, BANKING, AND ACCOUNTING
1. to bid more than necessary
2. an amount that is bid that is unnecessarily high

overcapacity OPERATIONS & PRODUCTION an excess of capability to produce goods or provide a service over the level of demand

overcapitalize FINANCE, BANKING, AND ACCOUNTING to supply a company with more capital than it needs or should have with the result that it is liable for unnecessary interest charges or dividend payments

overdraft FINANCE, BANKING, AND ACCOUNTING the amount by which the money withdrawn from a bank account exceeds the balance in the account

overdraft facility FINANCE, BANKING, AND ACCOUNTING a credit arrangement with a bank, allowing a person or company with an account to use borrowed money up to an agreed limit when nothing is left in the account

overdraft line FINANCE, BANKING, AND ACCOUNTING an amount in excess of the balance in an account that a bank agrees to pay in honoring checks on the account

overdraft protection FINANCE, BANKING, AND ACCOUNTING the bank service, amounting to a line of credit, that assures that the bank will honor overdrafts, up to a limit and for a fee

overdraw FINANCE, BANKING, AND ACCOUNTING to withdraw more money from a bank account than it contains, thereby exceeding an agreed credit limit

overdrawn FINANCE, BANKING, AND ACCOUNTING in debt to a bank because the amount withdrawn from an account exceeds its balance

overdue FINANCE, BANKING, AND ACCOUNTING an amount still owed after the date due

overdue account
1. GENERAL MANAGEMENT a record of transactions between a supplier and customer, showing the customer's late payment
2. FINANCE, BANKING, AND ACCOUNTING an account whose holder owes money that should have been paid earlier

overhead cost GENERAL MANAGEMENT the indirect recurring costs of running a business

overnight GENERAL MANAGEMENT to send something by overnight courier or mail (*slang*)

overnight position FINANCE, BANKING, AND ACCOUNTING a trader's position in a security or option at the end of a trading day

overprice MARKETING to set the price of a product or service too high, with the result that it is unacceptable to the market

Overseas Investment Commission FINANCE, BANKING, AND ACCOUNTING an independent body reporting to the New Zealand government that regulates foreign investment in New Zealand. It was set up in 1973 and is funded by the Reserve Bank of New Zealand.

over-the-counter market FINANCE, BANKING, AND ACCOUNTING a market that is not one of the major exchanges

overtime HR & PERSONNEL extra time worked beyond normal ***hours of work***. Overtime is a traditional form of ***flexible working***, often used by employers to cover periods of peak demand without incurring a permanent increase in costs. Some workers are entitled to a higher rate of ***overtime pay*** for the extra hours, but salaried workers in particular can be expected to work overtime with no additional reward.

overtime pay HR & PERSONNEL remuneration for ***overtime*** worked. Overtime pay often comes at a premium rate but in some occupations overtime is paid at a lower rate than the standard rate of pay.

Owen, **Robert** (1771–1858) GENERAL MANAGEMENT British industrialist, and social reformer. Owner of a factory at New Lanark that he ran on model lines, pioneering improved working and living conditions for his employees. Author of *A New View of Society* (1813).

ROBERT OWEN (pp. 1032–33)

own brand MARKETING = ***private label***

owner GENERAL MANAGEMENT

1. a person or organization that has legal title to products or services

2. the person who controls a private company

owner-operator GENERAL MANAGEMENT = ***sole proprietor***

ownership of companies GENERAL MANAGEMENT the possession of shares in companies. Company ownership structures can differ widely. Owners of public companies may be institutions, or individuals, or a mixture of both. Directors are often offered company shares as incentives and more participative companies may offer shares to employees through ***employee ownership*** schemes. Private companies are usually owned by individuals, families, or groups of individual shareholders. Nationalized industries are publicly owned. Cooperatives are wholly owned by employees. A separation between the ownership and control of companies became a widely discussed issue during the 20th century, especially in the United States and the United Kingdom where shareholders have tended to be more passive. Managers were viewed as having come to occupy controlling positions as the scale of industry grew. From the 1980s, this position changed to some extent as ***privatization***, ***management buy-outs***, restructuring, and ***share incentive schemes*** led to greater share ownership among managers and produced less passive shareholders.

own-label MARKETING = ***private label***

P

P2P *abbr* E-COMMERCE peer-to-peer, a type of e-commerce in which trading is accomplished directly from one computer to another without passing through a central server. This allows any individual or enterprise to transfer digital goods or conduct business with any other individual or enterprise without anyone else being aware of the transaction.

paced line OPERATIONS & PRODUCTION a production line that moves at a constant speed. A paced line, such as a car ***assembly line***, moves partly finished products past a ***workstation*** or zone at a constant speed. Work is carried out on the product within each work zone as the line continues to move. The speed of movement of the line is set to match worker proficiency or machine processing speed.

packaging

1. OPERATIONS & PRODUCTION materials used for containing, protecting, and presenting of goods during the delivery process from the producer to the consumer. Packaging has evolved from the basic function of protection to become an important marketing tool for communicating brand values. See ***bundling***

2. FINANCE, BANKING, AND ACCOUNTING the practice of combining securities in a single trade

Packard, **David** (1912–96) GENERAL MANAGEMENT U.S. entrepreneur and business executive. Co-founder of Hewlett-Packard. Hewlett-Packard was noted for its ***corporate culture*** and ***management style*** based on openness, and respect for its employees. See Packard's book *The HP Way* (1995).

Pac Man defense FINANCE, BANKING, AND ACCOUNTING avoiding purchase by making an offer to buy the prospective buyer

page counter E-COMMERCE a utility program that registers the number of times a Web page is visited, for example, by means of a ***click-through***

page impressions E-COMMERCE the number of customers who land on a Web page, as in an ***ad view***

page views E-COMMERCE a measure of the frequency with which a given Web page has been visited

paid circulation MARKETING the number of copies of a newspaper or magazine that are actually bought

painting the tape FINANCE, BANKING, AND ACCOUNTING an illegal practice in which traders break large orders into smaller units in order to give the illusion of heavy buying activity. This encourages investors to buy and the traders then sell as the price of the stock goes up. (*slang*)

palmtop GENERAL MANAGEMENT a very small portable computer. Compared to a personal computer or laptop, the functionality of a palmtop is currently limited but it is increasing.

P & L FINANCE, BANKING, AND ACCOUNTING see ***profit and loss statement***

panel interview HR & PERSONNEL an interview that takes place before two or more interviewers who may be from different parts of the interviewing organization or external to it

panel study STATISTICS a study that surveys a selected group of people over a period of time

panic buying FINANCE, BANKING, AND ACCOUNTING an abnormal level of buying caused by fear or rumors of product shortages or by severe price rises

PANSE GENERAL MANAGEMENT Politically Active and Not Seeking Employment (*slang*)

pants

drop your pants MARKETING to lower the price of a product in order to sell it (*slang*)

put some pants on something GENERAL MANAGEMENT to supply the missing details of a plan or idea (*slang*)

paper architecture GENERAL MANAGEMENT an ambitious business project that never gets beyond the planning stage because of lack of funding or because it is not feasible (*slang*)

paper company GENERAL MANAGEMENT, FINANCE, BANKING, AND ACCOUNTING a company that only exists on paper and has no physical assets

paperless office GENERAL MANAGEMENT a workplace in which as much communication and as many procedures as possible have been computerized. The paperless office was predicted in the 1960s. The recent widespread availability of ***e-mail***, the ***Internet***, and word processing, file transfer, and ***intranet*** systems means that it is beginning to become achievable for those organizations that wish to pursue it. In a truly paperless office, document storage is on computer rather than in filing cabinets and written communication is not circulated in hard copy but e-mailed. This is largely unattainable, as most people still prefer paper to electronic copy, especially when faced with reading more than one page. Encouraging employees to cut down on paper usage can help achieve ***environmental management*** targets, and storing information electronically can lead to greater communication efficiency which may result in ***competitive advantage***.

paper trail GENERAL MANAGEMENT all of the documentation of an event, especially a decision (*slang*)

PAR FINANCE, BANKING, AND ACCOUNTING see ***prime assets ratio***

paradigm shift GENERAL MANAGEMENT a change in an accepted pattern of thought or behavior

parallel engineering OPERATIONS & PRODUCTION = ***concurrent engineering***

parallel pricing FINANCE, BANKING, AND ACCOUNTING the practice of varying prices in a similar way and at the same time as competitors, which may be done by agreement with them

paralysis by analysis GENERAL MANAGEMENT the inability of managers to make decisions as a result of a preoccupation with attending meetings, writing reports, and collecting statistics and analyses. Paralysis of effective ***decision making*** in organizations can occur in situations where there is horizontal conflict, disagreement between different hierarchical levels, or unclear objectives.

parameter STATISTICS a quantity that is numerically characteristic of a whole model or population

parameter design STATISTICS a process aimed at reducing variation in processes or products

parent company GENERAL MANAGEMENT, FINANCE, BANKING, AND ACCOUNTING a company that owns or controls a number of other companies

Pareto, Vilfredo Frederico Damaso (1848–1923) GENERAL MANAGEMENT Italian economist, mathematician, and sociologist. Originator of the ***eighty-twenty rule***, and of the law of income distribution known as ***Pareto's Law***, which he explained in *Cours d'Économie Politique* (1896–97).

Pareto analysis GENERAL MANAGEMENT = ***eighty-twenty rule***

Pareto chart GENERAL MANAGEMENT a graphical representation of the ***eighty-twenty rule***. This is usually in the form of a ***bar chart*** identifying the relationships between the causes and effects of activities.

Pareto's Law GENERAL MANAGEMENT a theory of income distribution. Developed by ***Vilfredo Pareto***, Pareto's Law states that regardless of political or taxation conditions, income will be distributed in the same way across all countries.

Pareto's principle GENERAL MANAGEMENT = ***eighty-twenty rule***

pari passu FINANCE, BANKING, AND ACCOUNTING ranking equally

parity bit E-COMMERCE an odd or even digit used to check binary computer data for errors

parity value FINANCE, BANKING, AND ACCOUNTING = ***conversion value***

park FINANCE, BANKING, AND ACCOUNTING to place owned shares with third parties to disguise their ownership, usually illegally

Parker Follet, Mary (1868–1933) GENERAL MANAGEMENT U.S. academic. Applied psychological and social science insights to the study of industrial organization at a time when the ***scientific management*** methods of ***Frederick Winslow Taylor*** were predominant. Recent interest in her work owes much to Pauline Graham's writings, for example, *Mary Parker Follett: Prophet of Management* (1995).

MARY PARKER FOLLETT (pp. 988–89); FREDERICK WINSLOW TAYLOR (pp. 1054–55)

Parkinson, C. Northcote (1909–93) GENERAL MANAGEMENT British academic. Known for ***Parkinson's Law*** (1957).

Parkinson's Law HR & PERSONNEL the facetious assertion that work will expand to fill the time available

partial retirement HR & PERSONNEL see ***phased retirement***

participating bond FINANCE, BANKING, AND ACCOUNTING a bond that pays the dividends that stockholders receive as well as interest

participating insurance FINANCE, BANKING, AND ACCOUNTING insurance in which policy holders receive a dividend from the insurer's profits

partnering GENERAL MANAGEMENT see ***strategic partnering***

partnership GENERAL MANAGEMENT a contractual relationship between two or more people who agree to share in the profits and losses of a business. A partnership is not an incorporated company and the individual partners are responsible for decisions and debts. A partnership at organizational level is known as a ***joint venture*** or ***strategic alliance***.

part-time director GENERAL MANAGEMENT = ***nonexecutive director***

part-time work GENERAL MANAGEMENT work that occupies fewer hours than ***full-time*** work. Traditionally, working part-time simply meant working fewer hours a day, or fewer days a week, than a full-time employee, but part-time working is now seen as one of several ***flexible working hours*** alternatives to the 9–5 working day.

party plan MARKETING a sales technique in which local agents host parties to demonstrate or sell products to customers

Pascale, Richard Tanner (*b*. 1938) GENERAL MANAGEMENT U.S. academic and consultant. Co-developer of the ***McKinsey 7-S framework*** of corporate success, and coauthor, with ***Anthony Athos***, of *The Art of Japanese Management* (1981). Pascale also originated the concept of organizational ***agility***. Pascale and Athos collaborated with ***Tom Peters*** and ***Bob Waterman*** on the 7-S model at the management consultancy company McKinsey. Peters and Waterman cited U.S. examples of success in *In Search of Excellence*, but it was Pascale and Athos who explored the model in greater depth, tracing many of its origins to working practice in Japanese organizations.

RICHARD TANNER PASCALE (pp. 1034–35); TOM PETERS (pp. 1036–37)

passing off FINANCE, BANKING, AND ACCOUNTING a form of fraud in which a company tries to sell its own product by deceiving buyers into thinking it is another product

passive investment management FINANCE, BANKING, AND ACCOUNTING the managing of a mutual fund or other investment portfolio by relying on automatic adjustments such as indexation instead of making personal judgments. See ***active fund management***

passive portfolio strategy FINANCE, BANKING, AND ACCOUNTING the managing of an investment portfolio by relying on automatic adjustments or tracking an index

password E-COMMERCE a series of characters that enables a user to access a private file, Web site, computer, or application

patent MARKETING a type of ***copyright*** granted as a fixed-term monopoly to an inventor by the state to prevent others copying an invention, or improvement of a product or process. The granting of a patent requires the publication of full details of the invention or improvement but the use of the patented information is restricted to the patent holder or any organizations licensed by them.

patent attorney GENERAL MANAGEMENT a lawyer who specializes in the type of intellectual property called a patent

paternity leave HR & PERSONNEL time off work given to a new father on the birth of his child. Paternity leave is a form of ***special leave***, and is granted at an organization's discretion. It may be paid, or unpaid. Paternity leave forms an important part of an organization's ***family friendly policies***.

path analysis STATISTICS a means of showing the correlation between variables in a statistical study

path diagram STATISTICS a diagram that shows the correlation between variables in a statistical study

pay HR & PERSONNEL a sum of money given in return for work done or services provided. Pay, in the form of ***salary*** or ***wages***, is generally provided in weekly or monthly fixed amounts, and is usually expressed in terms of the total sum earned per year. It may also be allocated using a ***piece-rate system***, where workers are paid for each unit of work they carry out.

Pay As You Earn HR & PERSONNEL in the United Kingdom, a system for collecting direct taxes that requires employers to deduct taxes from employees' ***pay*** before payment is made. Abbr **PAYE**

pay-as-you-go (*Can*) HR & PERSONNEL a means of financing a pension system whereby benefits of current retirees are financed by current workers

Pay-As-You-Go (*ANZ*) FINANCE, BANKING, AND ACCOUNTING Pay as You Go, a system used in Australia for paying income tax installments on business and investment income. PAYG is part of the new tax system introduced by the Australian government on July 1, 2000. Abbr **PAYG**

PAYE HR & PERSONNEL see ***Pay As You Earn***

PAYG (*ANZ*) FINANCE, BANKING, AND ACCOUNTING see ***Pay-As-You-Go***

payload FINANCE, BANKING, AND ACCOUNTING the amount of cargo that a vessel can carry

paymaster FINANCE, BANKING, AND ACCOUNTING the person responsible for paying an organization's employees

payment by results HR & PERSONNEL a system of ***pay*** that directly links an employee's ***compensation*** to their work output. The system is based on the view put forward by ***Frederick Winslow Taylor*** that payment by results will increase workers' productivity by appealing to their materialism. The concept is closely related to ***performance-related pay*** which rewards employees for behavior and skills rather than quantifiable productivity measures.
FREDERICK WINSLOW TAYLOR (pp. 1054–55)

payment gateway E-COMMERCE a company or organization that provides an interface between a merchant's point-of-sale system, ***acquirer*** payment systems, and ***issuer*** payment systems. Abbr **GW**

payment-in-kind HR & PERSONNEL an alternative form of ***pay*** given to employees in place of monetary reward but considered to be of equivalent value. A payment in kind may take the form of use of a car, purchase of goods at cost price, or other nonfinancial exchange that benefits the employee. It forms part of the total pay package rather than being an extra benefit.

payment-in-lieu HR & PERSONNEL payment that is given in place of an entitlement

payout ratio FINANCE, BANKING, AND ACCOUNTING an expression of the percentage of a company's earnings that it pays in the form of dividends

Pay Pal E-COMMERCE a Web-based service that enables Internet users to send and receive payments electronically. To open a Pay Pal account, users register and provide their credit card details. When they decide to make a transaction via Pay Pal, their card is charged for the transfer.

pay-per-click E-COMMERCE a Web site that charges a ***micropayment*** to see digital information, for example, an e-book or e-magazine, or an event such as a prize

pay-per-play E-COMMERCE a Web site that charges a ***micropayment*** to play an interactive game over the Internet

pay-per-view FINANCE, BANKING, AND ACCOUNTING a method of collecting revenue from television viewers. The viewer pays a fee for watching an individual program, typically a sports or entertainment event.

payroll HR & PERSONNEL the organizational function that organizes the payment of employees. Payroll also can refer to the list of employees and their ***pay*** details, or to the total cost of pay to an organization.

pay scale HR & PERSONNEL a framework that groups together jobs of broadly equivalent worth into job grades, based on ***job evaluation***, with a ***pay*** range given to each grade. Although pay scales are still widely used, other pay structures such as ***broadbanding*** are replacing the traditional approach. Some organizations do not have a formal structure and instead rely on ***personal contracts***. Also known as ***salary scale***, ***wage scale***. See ***job family***

payslip HR & PERSONNEL a document given to employees when they are paid, providing a statement of ***pay*** for that period. A payslip includes details of deductions such as ***income tax***, social security contributions, pension contributions, and labor union dues.

PDA *abbr* E-COMMERCE personal digital assistant, a handheld mobile device that can access the Internet and act as a personal organizer

PDF GENERAL MANAGEMENT, MARKETING see ***portable document format***

penalty rate (*ANZ*) HR & PERSONNEL a higher than normal rate of pay awarded for work performed outside normal working hours

pencil-whip GENERAL MANAGEMENT to criticize somebody in writing (*slang*)

penetrated market MARKETING the existing customers within a market

penetration pricing FINANCE, BANKING, AND ACCOUNTING setting prices low, especially for new products, in order to maximize market penetration

penny stock FINANCE, BANKING, AND ACCOUNTING very low-priced stock, typically under one dollar, that is a speculative investment

  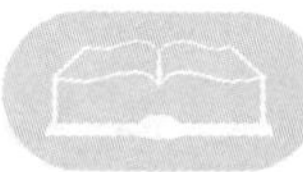    

pension FINANCE, BANKING, AND ACCOUNTING money received regularly after ***retirement***, from a ***personal*** or state pension scheme. Also known as ***retirement pension***

people churner HR & PERSONNEL a bad boss with a reputation for losing talented staff (*slang*)

P/E ratio FINANCE, BANKING, AND ACCOUNTING the price/earnings ratio is an important financial ratio. It is calculated by dividing a company's share price by its earnings per share.

per capita income ECONOMICS the average income of each of a particular group of people, for example, citizens of a country

percussive maintenance GENERAL MANAGEMENT the practice of hitting or shaking an electronic device in order to make it work (*slang*)

per diem HR & PERSONNEL a rate paid per day, for example, for expenses when an employee is working away from the office

perfect capital market ECONOMICS a capital market in which the decisions of buyers and sellers have no effect on market price

perfect competition ECONOMICS a market in which no buyer or seller can influence prices. In practice, perfect markets are characterized by few or no barriers to entry and by many buyers and sellers.

perfect hedge FINANCE, BANKING, AND ACCOUNTING a hedge that exactly balances the risk of another investment

performance appraisal HR & PERSONNEL a face-to-face discussion in which one employee's work is discussed, reviewed, and appraised by another, using an agreed and understood framework. Usually, line managers conduct the appraisals of their staff, although peers can appraise each other, and line managers can themselves be appraised by their staff through ***360 degree appraisal***. The appraisal process focuses on behaviors and outcomes, and aims to improve ***motivation***, growth, and performance of the appraisee. Performance appraisals should be carried out at least once per year. Also known as ***performance evaluation***

performance criteria FINANCE, BANKING, AND ACCOUNTING the standards used to evaluate a product, service, or employee

performance evaluation HR & PERSONNEL = ***performance appraisal***

performance indicator HR & PERSONNEL a key measure designed to assess an aspect of the qualitative or quantitative performance of a company. Performance indicators can relate to operational, strategic, confidence, behavioral, and ethical aspects of a company's operation and can help to pinpoint its strengths and weaknesses. They are periodically monitored to ensure the company's long-term success.

performance management GENERAL MANAGEMENT the facilitation of high achievement by employees. Performance management involves enabling people to carry out their work to the best of their ability, meeting and perhaps exceeding targets and standards. Performance management can be coordinated by an interrelated framework between manager and employee. Key areas of the framework to be agreed are ***objectives***, ***human resource management*** (see ***HRM***), standards and ***performance indicators***, and means of reward. For successful performance management to flourish, a culture of collective and individual responsibility for the continuing improvement of business processes needs to be established, and individual skills and contributions need to be encouraged and nurtured. One tool for monitoring performance management is ***performance appraisal***. For organizations, performance management is usually known as company performance and is monitored through business appraisal.

performance-related pay HR & PERSONNEL a ***compensation*** system in which the level of ***pay*** is dependent on the employee's performance. Performance-related pay can be entirely dependent or only partly dependent on performance. There are usually three stages to a performance-related pay system: determining the criteria by which the employee is assessed, establishing whether the employee has met the criteria, and linking the employee's achievements to the pay structure. Performance measures can incorporate skills, knowledge, and behavioral indicators. The system can be compared to ***payment by results***, which is based solely on quantitative productivity measures.

periodic inventory review system OPERATIONS & PRODUCTION a system for placing orders of varying sizes at regular intervals to replenish ***inventory*** up to a specified or target inventory level. A periodic inventory review system fixes a specific reorder period, but the reorder quantity can vary according to need. The quantity reordered is calculated by subtracting existing inventory and on-order inventory from the target inventory level. Also known as ***fixed interval reorder system***

perk HR & PERSONNEL see ***fringe benefits***

permalancer HR & PERSONNEL a freelance worker who has worked in one company for so long that he or she is virtually a permanent member of staff (*slang*)

permanent interest-bearing shares FINANCE, BANKING, AND ACCOUNTING shares issued by the U.K. equivalent of a credit union to raise capital because the law prohibits it from raising capital in more conventional ways. Abbr **PIBS**

permission marketing E-COMMERCE any form of online direct marketing that involves gaining each recipient's permission. This type of marketing typically involves sending promotional material via e-mail to an opt-in list of subscribers. The term was popularized by business author Seth Godin, who has written a book on the subject, *Permission Marketing* (1999).

Perot GENERAL MANAGEMENT to leave, fail, or give up something unexpectedly. The term comes from the sudden withdrawal from the presidential race of candidate Ross Perot in the 1990s. (*slang*)

perpetual bond FINANCE, BANKING, AND ACCOUNTING a bond that has no date of maturity

perpetual debenture FINANCE, BANKING, AND ACCOUNTING a debenture that pays interest in perpetuity, having no date of maturity

perpetual inventory FINANCE, BANKING, AND ACCOUNTING the daily tracking of inventory

personal contract HR & PERSONNEL a ***contract of employment*** that is negotiated on an employee by employee basis, rather than using a traditional structured system that gives identical contracts to groups of workers

personal development HR & PERSONNEL the acquisition of knowledge, skills, and experience for the purpose of enhancing individual performance and self-perception. Personal development is usually led by the individual, in contrast to ***employee development***, which is initiated by an employing organization. To be effective, it should follow a personal development cycle: 1. Establish the purpose, or the reason for development 2. Identify the skills, or knowledge areas, that need developing 3. Look at development opportunities 4. Formulate an action plan 5. Undertake the development 6. Record the outcomes of the development activity 7. Review and evaluate the outputs and benefits. Personal development is an important aspect of ***CPD***. Also known as ***self-development***

✔ PERSONAL DEVELOPMENT PLANNING (pp. 400–01)

personal digital assistant GENERAL MANAGEMENT see ***PDA***

personality test HR & PERSONNEL see ***psychometric test***

personal pension HR & PERSONNEL a pension taken out by an individual with a private sector insurance company or bank. A personal pension usually takes the form of a scheme in which an individual regularly contributes money to a pension provider who invests it in a pension fund. On retirement, a lump sum is available for the purchase of an annuity that provides weekly or monthly payments.

personnel HR & PERSONNEL
1. the people employed in an organization, considered collectively
2. the department of an organization that deals with the employment of staff and staffing issues

personnel management HR & PERSONNEL the part of management that is concerned with people and their relationships at work. Personnel management is the responsibility of all those who manage people, as well as a description of the work of specialists. ***Personnel managers*** advise on, formulate, and implement ***personnel policies*** such as ***recruitment***, ***conditions of employment***, ***performance appraisal***, ***training***, industrial relations, and ***health and safety***. There are various models of personnel management, of which ***human resource management*** (see ***HRM***) is the most recent.

personnel manager HR & PERSONNEL a professional specialist and manager responsible for advising on, formulating, and implementing personnel or human resources strategy, and personnel policies. The nature of the personnel manager's job is dependent on the size of the organization and the extent to which personnel responsibilities are devolved to ***line managers***.

personnel planning HR & PERSONNEL see ***human resource planning***

personnel policy HR & PERSONNEL a set of rules that define the manner in which an organization deals with a ***human resources*** or ***personnel***-related matter. A personnel policy should reflect good practice, be written down, be communicated across the organization, and should adapt to changing circumstances.

PEST analysis MANAGEMENT a management technique that enables an analysis of four external factors that may impact the performance of the organization. These factors are: Political; Economic; Social; and Technological. PEST analysis is often carried out using ***brainstorming*** techniques. It offers an environment-to-organization perspective as opposed to the organization-to-environment perspective offered by ***SWOT analysis***.

Peter, Laurence J. (1919–90) GENERAL MANAGEMENT Canadian academic. Founder of the ***Peter Principle***, described in the book of the same name (coauthored with Raymond Hull, 1970).

Peter Principle HR & PERSONNEL a tenet holding that all employees tend to rise to their level of incompetence within an organization, at which point it is too late to move them down or sideways

Peters, Tom (*b.* 1942) GENERAL MANAGEMENT U.S. consultant, writer, and lecturer. Codeveloper of the ***McKinsey 7-S framework*** of corporate success, and coauthor, with ***Bob Waterman***, of *In Search of Excellence* (1982), which identified eight characteristics of successful companies. Peters moved the discussion of ***management*** away from the established structure of ***bureaucracy*** toward a more innovative, intuitive, and people-centered approach in which change is to be embraced, not resisted. *In Search of Excellence* was one of the first books to make management ideas generally accessible and his seminar presentations have earned Peters a reputation as an energetic, entertaining performer.

petites et moyennes entreprises GENERAL MANAGEMENT French for small and medium-sized businesses. Abbr **PME**

petty cash FINANCE, BANKING, AND ACCOUNTING a small store of cash used for minor business expenses

PFI FINANCE, BANKING, AND ACCOUNTING see ***Private Finance Initiative***

phantom bid FINANCE, BANKING, AND ACCOUNTING a reported but nonexistent attempt to buy a company

phantom income FINANCE, BANKING, AND ACCOUNTING income that is subject to tax even though the recipient never actually gets control of it, for example, income from a limited partnership

phased retirement HR & PERSONNEL a gradual reduction in the hours of work, typically through working a three- or four-day week in the last six months leading up to ***retirement***. Phased retirement is a ***personnel policy*** introduced by organizations to try to ease the transition between employment and retirement which for many employees can prove to be a traumatic change. Also known as ***gradual retirement***

Phillips curve STATISTICS a graphical representation of the relationship between unemployment and the rate of inflation

phone lag GENERAL MANAGEMENT tiredness caused by having to conduct business on the telephone with people who are based in different time zones (*slang*)

physical asset FINANCE, BANKING, AND ACCOUNTING an asset that has a physical embodiment as opposed to cash or securities

physical distribution management OPERATIONS & PRODUCTION the planning, monitoring, and control of the distribution and delivery of manufactured goods

physical market FINANCE, BANKING, AND ACCOUNTING a market in futures that involves physical delivery of the commodities involved instead of simple cash transactions

physical retail shopping GENERAL MANAGEMENT shopping carried out by visiting high-street shops rather than buying online

physical working conditions HR & PERSONNEL the surroundings within which somebody works, taking into account aspects such as temperature, air quality, lighting, safety, cleanliness, and noise

PIBS FINANCE, BANKING, AND ACCOUNTING see ***permanent interest-bearing shares***

pick and shovel work GENERAL MANAGEMENT boring and detailed work such as the examination of documents for mistakes (*slang*)

piece-rate system *or* **piece work** HR & PERSONNEL a system of payment through which an employee is paid a predetermined amount for each unit of output. The rate of ***pay***, or piece rate, is usually fixed subjectively, rather than by a more objective technique such as ***work study***. Rates are said to be tight when it is difficult for an employee to earn a bonus and loose when bonuses are easily earned. Piece-rate systems, or **piece work**, are a form of ***payment by results*** or ***performance-related pay***.

pie chart STATISTICS a chart drawn as a circle divided into proportional sections like portions of a pie

piggyback advertising MARKETING an offer or promotion that runs in parallel with another campaign and incurs no costs

piggyback loan FINANCE, BANKING, AND ACCOUNTING a loan that is raised against the same security as an existing loan

piggyback rights FINANCE, BANKING, AND ACCOUNTING the permission to sell existing shares in conjunction with the sale of like shares in a new offering

pig in a python GENERAL MANAGEMENT the large increase in the birthrate between 1946 and 1964 *(slang)*

pilot fish HR & PERSONNEL a junior executive who follows close behind a more senior executive *(slang)*

pilot survey MARKETING a preliminary piece of research carried out before a complete survey to test the effectiveness of the research methodology

pin-drop syndrome HR & PERSONNEL stress induced by extreme quietness in a working environment *(slang)*

pink advertising MARKETING advertising aimed at the gay and lesbian community

pink-collar job HR & PERSONNEL a sexist term for a position normally held by a woman, especially a young one *(slang)*

pink dollar FINANCE, BANKING, AND ACCOUNTING money spent by gays and lesbians

pink pound *(U.K.)* FINANCE, BANKING, AND ACCOUNTING = ***pink dollar***

pink slip
get your pink slip HR & PERSONNEL to be dismissed from employment *(slang)*

pink slipper HR & PERSONNEL a person who has been dismissed from employment *(slang)*

piracy GENERAL MANAGEMENT illegal copying of a product such as software or music

pitch GENERAL MANAGEMENT an attempt to win business from a customer, especially a ***sales presentation***

placement fee FINANCE, BANKING, AND ACCOUNTING a fee that a stockbroker receives for a sale of shares

plank
make somebody walk the plank HR & PERSONNEL to dismiss somebody from employment *(slang)*

planned maintenance OPERATIONS & PRODUCTION = ***preventive maintenance***

planned obsolescence OPERATIONS & PRODUCTION a policy of designing products to have a limited life span so that customers will have to buy replacements

planning GENERAL MANAGEMENT the process of setting ***objectives***, or ***goals*** (see ***objective***), and formulating policies, strategies, and procedures to meet them. Planning can refer to both long-term or **strategic planning**, and short-term or **operation planning**. It can be documented in the form of a ***business plan***.

plant OPERATIONS & PRODUCTION the capital assets used to produce goods, typically factories, production lines, and large equipment

plant layout OPERATIONS & PRODUCTION the grouping of equipment and operations in a factory for the greatest degree of efficiency. See ***process layout***, ***product layout***

plateauing HR & PERSONNEL the process of reaching a phase where performance is stable. Plateauing may be experienced by an employee due to a lack of ambition or ability or a lack of opportunity for ***promotion*** within the organizational hierarchy. One form of plateau is the ***management threshold***.

platform GENERAL MANAGEMENT a product used as a basis for building more complex products or delivering services. For example, a communications network is a platform for delivering knowledge or data.

plc *or* **PLC** FINANCE, BANKING, AND ACCOUNTING see ***public limited company***

plentitude ECONOMICS a hypothetical condition of an economy in which manufacturing technology has been perfected and scarcity is replaced by an abundance of products

plug and play GENERAL MANAGEMENT relating to an electronic device such as a printer that can be plugged in and used immediately after purchase *(slang)*

plug-in E-COMMERCE a software application that can be added to a Web browser to enable added functionality, for example, the receipt of audio or multimedia files

PME GENERAL MANAGEMENT see ***petites et moyennes entreprises***

PMTS GENERAL MANAGEMENT see ***predetermined motion-time system***

poaching HR & PERSONNEL the practice of recruiting people from other companies by offering inducements

point FINANCE, BANKING, AND ACCOUNTING a unit used for calculation of a value, such as a hundredth of a percentage point for interest rates

point and click agreement E-COMMERCE = ***click wrap agreement***

point-factor system HR & PERSONNEL = ***points plan***

point of presence GENERAL MANAGEMENT an access point to the ***Internet***. A point of presence is usually controlled by an Internet service provider. Subscribers can use this to gain access to the Internet, normally by dialing a local number, and thereby saving the cost of a national phone call. A point of presence has a unique ***IP address***. Abbr **POP**

point of purchase GENERAL MANAGEMENT see ***point of sale***

point-of-purchase display GENERAL MANAGEMENT the physical arrangement of products and marketing material at the place where an item is bought. A point-of-purchase display is designed to encourage sales. It can include posters, showcards, leaflets, and dispensers to attract customers.

point of sale GENERAL MANAGEMENT the place at which a product is purchased by the customer. The point of sale can be a retail outlet, a display case, or even a particular shelf. Retailers refer to both point of sale and to **point of purchase**. The distinction is a fine one, but a sale and a purchase do not always take place at the same time. The difference becomes relevant where they are clearly separate, for example, with ***mail order*** and ***Internet*** shopping. Abbr **POS**

points plan HR & PERSONNEL a method of ***job evaluation*** that uses a points scale for rating different criteria. Also known as ***point-factor system***

poison pill FINANCE, BANKING, AND ACCOUNTING a measure taken by a company to avoid a hostile takeover, for example, the purchase of a business interest that will make the company unattractive to the potential buyer (*slang*)

political economy ECONOMICS a country's economic organization

political price GENERAL MANAGEMENT the negative impact on a government of a business or economic decision such as raising interest rates

political risk GENERAL MANAGEMENT the potential negative impact on a government of a business or economic decision

politics GENERAL MANAGEMENT the theory of government, the making of policy, or the power struggles within an organization

POP E-COMMERCE Post Office protocol, the most common Internet standard for e-mail. Once POP is in use, all new incoming messages are downloaded from the server as soon as the e-mail account is accessed. All POP e-mails are stored on the server until the user removes them.

population STATISTICS the entire collection of units such as events or people from which a sample may be observed in a statistical study

population pyramid STATISTICS a graphical presentation of data in the form of two histograms with a common base, showing a comparison of a human population in terms of sex and age

portable document format GENERAL MANAGEMENT, MARKETING an electronic document format that allows all elements of a document, including page layout, text, photographs, and colors to be viewed on different computers or systems. Abbr **PDF**

portal E-COMMERCE a Web site that provides access and links to other sites and pages on the Web. ***Search engines*** and directories are the most common portal sites.

Porter, **Michael E.** (*b.* 1947) GENERAL MANAGEMENT U.S. academic and consultant. Known for his theories such as the ***value chain*** designed to help businesses examine their competitive capabilities. In *Competitive Strategy* (1980), Porter argued that to gain ***competitive advantage***, an organization needs to perform the activities in the value chain more cheaply or in a better way than its competitors. More recently, in response to thinkers such as ***Gary Hamel***, he advised on using the value chain to achieve differentiation from other players in a market.

portfolio FINANCE, BANKING, AND ACCOUNTING the range of investments, such as stocks and shares, owned by an individual or an organization

portfolio career HR & PERSONNEL a career based on a series of varied shorter-term jobs as opposed to one based on a progression up the ranks of a particular profession
CHARLES HANDY (pp. 1000–01)

portfolio immunization FINANCE, BANKING, AND ACCOUNTING measures taken by traders to protect their share portfolios (*slang*)

portfolio insurance FINANCE, BANKING, AND ACCOUNTING options that provide hedges against stock in a portfolio

portfolio investment FINANCE, BANKING, AND ACCOUNTING a form of investment that aims for a mixture of income and capital growth

portfolio manager FINANCE, BANKING, AND ACCOUNTING a person or company that specializes in managing an investment portfolio on behalf of investors

portfolio working GENERAL MANAGEMENT, HR & PERSONNEL the working pattern of following several simultaneous career pursuits at any one time. Portfolio working was coined by ***Charles Handy*** to describe a style of working life which no longer involves working full-time for one employer. See ***downshifting***
CHARLES HANDY (pp. 1000–01)

POS GENERAL MANAGEMENT see ***point of sale***

POSDCORB GENERAL MANAGEMENT Planning, Organizing, Staffing, Directing, Coordinating, Reporting, and Budgeting. POSDCORB was coined in 1935 by ***Luther Gulick*** to describe the functional elements of the work of a ***chief executive***. It is based on the functional analysis of management of ***Henri Fayol***.
HENRI FAYOL (pp. 986–87)

position FINANCE, BANKING, AND ACCOUNTING the number of shares of a security that are owned

position limit FINANCE, BANKING, AND ACCOUNTING the largest amount of a security that any group or individual may own

positive economics ECONOMICS the study of economic propositions that are capable of being verified by observing economic events in the real economy

possessor in bad faith FINANCE, BANKING, AND ACCOUNTING somebody who occupies land even though they do not believe they have a legal right to do so

possessor in good faith FINANCE, BANKING, AND ACCOUNTING somebody who occupies land believing they have a legal right to do so

possessory action FINANCE, BANKING, AND ACCOUNTING a lawsuit over the right to own land

post a credit FINANCE, BANKING, AND ACCOUNTING to enter a credit item in a ledger

postal survey MARKETING a research technique in which questionnaires are sent and returned by mail

postdate FINANCE, BANKING, AND ACCOUNTING to put a later date on a document or check than the date when it is signed, with the effect that it is not valid until the later date

postindustrial society GENERAL MANAGEMENT a society in which the resources of labor and capital are replaced by those of knowledge and information as the main sources of wealth creation. The postindustrial society involves a shift in focus from manufacturing industries to service industries and is enabled by technological advances. The idea is associated with sociologist Daniel Bell, who wrote *The Coming of Post-Industrial Society: A Venture in Social Forecasting* in 1973.

potential GDP ECONOMICS a measure of the real value of the services and goods that can be produced when a country's factors of production are fully employed

pot trust FINANCE, BANKING, AND ACCOUNTING a trust, typically created in a will, for a group of beneficiaries

pound cost averaging (*U.K.*) FINANCE, BANKING, AND ACCOUNTING = ***dollar cost averaging***

power GENERAL MANAGEMENT the ability to compel others to obey. Power refers to an authority or influence over others which, in an organizational context, may be derived from the holder's rank or status, or from their personality. According to ***Max Weber***, power describes the probability of carrying out one's own will despite resistance. It is closely linked to, but not the same as, ***leadership***, ***authority***, and ***responsibility***. Organizational power is linked to ***organization structure*** and is an inherent part of any hierarchy or ***bureaucracy***.

  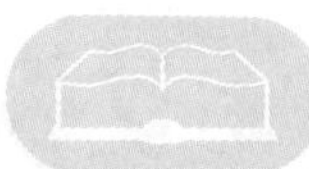    

power and influence theory of leadership GENERAL MANAGEMENT the idea that ***leadership*** is based on the form of relationships between people rather than on the abilities of a single person. The power and influence theory of leadership sees a network of interaction between people, shaped by the power and influence emanating from the leader. Leadership and followership are products of the flow of power between individuals.

power center GENERAL MANAGEMENT the part of an organization that has the strongest influence on policy

power lunch HR & PERSONNEL see ***working lunch***

power structure GENERAL MANAGEMENT the way in which power is distributed among different groups or individuals in an organization

PPP ECONOMICS see ***purchasing power parity***

PR *abbr* MARKETING public relations, the presentation of an organization and its activities to target audiences with the aim of gaining awareness and understanding, influencing public opinion, generating support, and developing trust and cooperation. Public relations programs aim to create and maintain a positive ***corporate image*** and enhance an organization's reputation. The work of a public relations department includes research into current perceptions of the organization, the production of publicity material, the organization of events and ***sponsorship*** programs, and the evaluation of responses to these activities. Target audiences include the media, government bodies, customers and suppliers, investors, the wider community, or an organization's own employees. Public relations practice originated in the United States in the mid-19th century. Public relations forms part of an organization's overall ***external communication*** strategy.

Prahalad, C. K. (*b.* 1941) GENERAL MANAGEMENT Indian-born academic. Developer with ***Gary Hamel*** of a new view of competitiveness, of ***strategy***, and of ***organizations*** in reaction to traditional strategic thinking. Prahalad and Hamel originated the ideas of strategic intent, ***core competences***, and strategy as stretch, and published them in *Competing for the Future* (1994).
C. K. PRAHALAD (pp. 1040–41)

prairie dogging GENERAL MANAGEMENT in an office that is divided into cubicles, the sudden appearance of people's heads over the top of the cubicle walls when something interesting or noisy happens (*slang*)

preauthorized electronic debit FINANCE, BANKING, AND ACCOUNTING a scheme in which a payer agrees to let a bank make payments from an account to somebody else's account

prebilling FINANCE, BANKING, AND ACCOUNTING the practice of submitting a bill for a product or service before it has actually been delivered

predatory pricing FINANCE, BANKING, AND ACCOUNTING the practice of setting prices for products that are designed to win business from competitors

predetermined motion-time system GENERAL MANAGEMENT a ***work measurement*** technique that uses a set of established times for basic human motions to build up ***standard times*** for jobs and processes at a specific level of performance. The predetermined motion-time system is based on the idea, first conceived by ***Frederick Winslow Taylor*** and later developed by ***Frank*** and ***Lillian Gilbreth***, that the same length of time is required for basic human motions in whatever context they are performed. These standard times are established using ***time study*** techniques and can then be combined to provide a standard time for specific work tasks. The first PMTS, called **motion time analysis**, was developed in 1927, and others appeared in the United States during the 1930s. Interest in the use of PMTS increased during and after World War II. The most widely used system is ***methods-time measurement***. Abbr **PMTS**

predictive maintenance OPERATIONS & PRODUCTION a set of techniques used to manage the ***maintenance*** of high-cost equipment that experiences extremely low failure rates. Statistical techniques for predicting service before failure are not effective for equipment with extremely low failure rates. Predictive maintenance uses the techniques of surveillance, diagnosis, and remedy to manage the maintenance of such equipment. It is based on the premise that most equipment will give indications of impending failure well in advance of it actually happening.

preemployment screening HR & PERSONNEL see ***health screening***

pre-emptive right FINANCE, BANKING, AND ACCOUNTING the right of a stockholder to maintain proportional ownership in a corporation by purchasing newly issued stock

preference option FINANCE, BANKING, AND ACCOUNTING an option for preferred stock

preference shares (*U.K.*) FINANCE, BANKING, AND ACCOUNTING = ***preferred stock***

preferential creditor FINANCE, BANKING, AND ACCOUNTING a creditor who is entitled to payment, especially from a bankrupt, before other creditors

preferential issue FINANCE, BANKING, AND ACCOUNTING an issue of stock available only to designated buyers

preferred ordinary shares FINANCE, BANKING, AND ACCOUNTING ordinary shares of ***preferred stock***

preferred position FINANCE, BANKING, AND ACCOUNTING the particular position in which an advertiser wants an advertisement to appear, for example, in a publication or on a Web site

preferred risk FINANCE, BANKING, AND ACCOUNTING somebody considered by an insurance company to be less likely to collect on a policy than the average person, for example, a nonsmoker

preferred stock FINANCE, BANKING, AND ACCOUNTING stock that entitles the owner to preference in the distribution of dividends and the proceeds of liquidation in the event of bankruptcy

pre-financing FINANCE, BANKING, AND ACCOUNTING the practice of arranging funding for a project before the project begins

prelaunch MARKETING the activities that precede the launch of a new product

preliminary prospectus FINANCE, BANKING, AND ACCOUNTING a document issued prior to a share issue that gives details of the shares available

premature retirement HR & PERSONNEL = ***early retirement***

Premiers' Conference GENERAL MANAGEMENT an annual meeting at which the premiers of the states and territories of Australia meet with the federal government to discuss their funding allocations

premium
1. GENERAL MANAGEMENT a higher price paid for a scarce product or service
2. GENERAL MANAGEMENT, MARKETING a pricing method that uses high price to indicate high quality

premium offer MARKETING a sales promotion technique in which customers are offered a free gift

premium pricing MARKETING the deliberate setting of high prices for a product or service to emphasize its quality or exclusiveness. Also known as ***prestige pricing***

prepackaged choice GENERAL MANAGEMENT a package of multimedia computer material that cannot be customized by the user

prepaid interest FINANCE, BANKING, AND ACCOUNTING interest paid in advance of its due date

prepayment FINANCE, BANKING, AND ACCOUNTING the payment of a debt, for example, a payment on a mortgage or other loan, before it is due to be paid

prepayment penalty FINANCE, BANKING, AND ACCOUNTING a charge that may be levied against somebody who makes a payment before its due date. The penalty compensates the lender or seller for potential lost interest.

prepayment privilege FINANCE, BANKING, AND ACCOUNTING the right to make a prepayment, for example, on a loan or mortgage, without penalty

prepayment risk FINANCE, BANKING, AND ACCOUNTING the risk that a debtor will avoid interest charges by making partial or total prepayments, especially when interest rates fall

prequalification MARKETING a sales technique in which the potential value of a prospect is carefully evaluated through research

prescribed payments system FINANCE, BANKING, AND ACCOUNTING a system under which employers are obliged to deduct a certain amount of tax from cash payments made to casual workers. The system was introduced in Australia in 1983.

presentation GENERAL MANAGEMENT an event at which preplanned material is shown to an audience for a specific purpose. Although a presentation is a verbal form of communication, it is often supported by other media, such as computer software, slides, printed handouts, and so on and to be successful, appropriate ***body language*** and good ***interpersonal communication*** skills are required. A presentation is normally intended to either introduce something new to the audience, to persuade them of a viewpoint, or to inform them. ***Sales representatives*** use presentations when introducing a product to a potential customer. Presentations are also used in ***team briefing*** and other business contexts.

presenteeism HR & PERSONNEL an employee or organization subscribing to the view that the hours spent at work have more value than ***productivity*** or results. Presenteeism is often displayed by ***workaholics***. At its most extreme, presenteeism can be seen in a worker who reports for work even when sick, for fear of letting the company down or of losing their job. (*slang*) See ***absenteeism***

present value FINANCE, BANKING, AND ACCOUNTING
1. the amount that a future interest in a financial asset is currently worth, discounted for inflation
2. the value now of an amount of money that somebody expects to receive at a future date, calculated by subtracting any interest that will accrue in the interim

preservation of capital FINANCE, BANKING, AND ACCOUNTING an approach to financial management that protects a person's or company's capital by arranging additional forms of finance

press advertising MARKETING advertising in newspapers or magazines

press clipping GENERAL MANAGEMENT a copy of a news item kept by a company because it contains important business information or is a record of news published about the company

press communications MARKETING communications activities designed to improve press awareness and attitudes to a product or an organization

press conference MARKETING a meeting to which journalists are invited to hear about a new product or other news about an organization

press cutting (*U.K.*) GENERAL MANAGEMENT = ***press clipping***

press date MARKETING the date on which a newspaper or magazine is printed

press release MARKETING an item of news about an organization, its staff, products, or services that is sent to selected members of the press

press the flesh GENERAL MANAGEMENT to shake hands with people at a business function (*slang*)

pressure group GENERAL MANAGEMENT a body of people who have banded together to campaign on one or more issues of importance to them. A pressure group usually has a formal constitution and coordinates its activities to influence the attitudes or activities of business or government. One area in which pressure groups operate is the environment and some large companies that have failed to practice good ***environmental management*** have been targeted by campaigners. Pressure groups often represent widespread views, so it is important for a company to maintain good relations with them.

prestige pricing MARKETING = ***premium pricing***

pre-syndicate bid FINANCE, BANKING, AND ACCOUNTING a bid made before a group of buyers can offer blocks of shares in an offering to the public

pretax FINANCE, BANKING, AND ACCOUNTING before tax is considered or paid

pretax profit FINANCE, BANKING, AND ACCOUNTING the amount of profit a company makes before taxes are deducted

pretax profit margin FINANCE, BANKING, AND ACCOUNTING the profit made by a company, calculated as a percentage of sales, before taxes are considered

pretesting MARKETING the practice of assessing the effectiveness of an advertising campaign or marketing activity in a small sector or single region before running the full campaign

prevalence STATISTICS a measure of the number of people with a particular quality in a statistical population

preventive maintenance *or* **preventative maintenance** OPERATIONS & PRODUCTION the scheduling of a program of planned ***maintenance*** services or equipment overhauls. The aim of preventive maintenance is to reduce equipment failure and the need for corrective maintenance. It can be carried out at regular time intervals, after a specified amount of equipment use, when the opportunity arises, for example, at a factory's annual shutdown, or when certain preset conditions occur to trigger the need for action. Also known as ***planned maintenance***. See ***reactive maintenance***

price FINANCE, BANKING, AND ACCOUNTING an amount of money that somebody charges for a good or service

price-book ratio FINANCE, BANKING, AND ACCOUNTING = ***price-to-book ratio***

price ceiling FINANCE, BANKING, AND ACCOUNTING the highest price that a buyer is willing to pay

price competition GENERAL MANAGEMENT a form of competition based on price rather than factors such as quality or design

price control ECONOMICS government regulations that set maximum prices for commodities or control price levels by credit controls

price differentiation GENERAL MANAGEMENT a pricing strategy in which a company sells the same product at different prices in different markets

price discovery FINANCE, BANKING, AND ACCOUNTING the process by which price is determined by negotiation in a free market

price discrimination ECONOMICS the practice of selling of the same product to different buyers at different prices

price-dividend ratio FINANCE, BANKING, AND ACCOUNTING the price of a stock divided by the annual dividend paid on a share

price-earnings ratio FINANCE, BANKING, AND ACCOUNTING the price of a stock divided by the company's earnings per share

price effect ECONOMICS the impact of price changes on a market or economy

price elasticity of demand ECONOMICS the percentage change in demand divided by the percentage change in price of a good

price elasticity of supply ECONOMICS the percentage change in supply divided by the percentage change in price of a good

price escalation clause GENERAL MANAGEMENT a contract provision that permits the seller to raise prices in response to increased costs

price fixing FINANCE, BANKING, AND ACCOUNTING an often illegal agreement between producers of a good or service in order to maintain prices at a particular level

price floor FINANCE, BANKING, AND ACCOUNTING the lowest price at which a seller is prepared to do business

price index FINANCE, BANKING, AND ACCOUNTING an index, such as the consumer price index, that measures inflation

price indicator ECONOMICS a price that is a measurable variable and can be used, for example, as an index of the cost of living

price-insensitive FINANCE, BANKING, AND ACCOUNTING used of a good or service for which sales remain constant no matter what its price, for example, because it is essential to buyers

price instability ECONOMICS a situation in which the prices of goods alter daily or even hourly

price leadership MARKETING the establishment of price levels in a market by a dominant company or brand

price list GENERAL MANAGEMENT a document that sets out the prices of different products or services

price range GENERAL MANAGEMENT the variety of prices at which competitive products or services are available in the market

price ring FINANCE, BANKING, AND ACCOUNTING a group of traders who make an agreement, often illegally, to maintain prices at a particular level

prices and incomes policy ECONOMICS a policy of using government regulations to limit price or wage increases

price-sensitive FINANCE, BANKING, AND ACCOUNTING changing in line with prices

price stability FINANCE, BANKING, AND ACCOUNTING a situation in which there is little change in the price of goods or services

price support ECONOMICS the use of government regulations to keep market prices from falling below a minimum level

price tag GENERAL MANAGEMENT
1. a label attached to an item being sold that shows its price
2. the value of a person or thing

price-to-book ratio FINANCE, BANKING, AND ACCOUNTING the ratio of the value of all of a company's stock to its ***book value***. Also known as ***price-book ratio***

price-to-cash-flow ratio FINANCE, BANKING, AND ACCOUNTING the ratio of the value of all of a company's stock to its cash flow for the most recent complete fiscal year

price-to-sales ratio FINANCE, BANKING, AND ACCOUNTING the ratio of the value of all of a company's stock to its sales for the previous twelve months

price war MARKETING a situation in which two or more companies each try to increase their own share of the market by lowering prices. A price war involves companies undercutting each other in an attempt to encourage more customers to buy their goods or services. In the long term, this can devalue a market and lead to loss of profits, but it can sometimes have short-term success.

price-weighted index FINANCE, BANKING, AND ACCOUNTING an index of production or market value that is adjusted for price changes

pricing policy MARKETING the method of ***decision making*** used for setting the prices for a company's products or services. A pricing policy is usually based on the costs of production or provision with a margin for profit, such as, for example, ***cost-plus pricing***.

primary account number FINANCE, BANKING, AND ACCOUNTING an identifier for a credit card used in secure electronic transactions

primary data *or* **primary information** MARKETING original data derived from a new research study and collected at source as opposed to previously published material

primary liability FINANCE, BANKING, AND ACCOUNTING responsibility to pay before anyone else, for example, for damages covered by insurance

primary market FINANCE, BANKING, AND ACCOUNTING a market for a new offering. See ***secondary market***

primary sector ECONOMICS the firms and corporations of the productive sector of a country's economy

  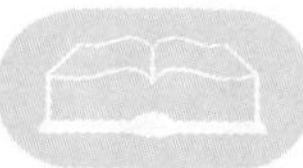    

prime assets ratio FINANCE, BANKING, AND ACCOUNTING the proportion of total liabilities which Australian banks are obliged by the Reserve Bank to hold in secure assets such as cash and government securities. Abbr **PAR**

prime rate *or* **prime interest rate** FINANCE, BANKING, AND ACCOUNTING the lowest interest rate that commercial banks offer on loans

principal FINANCE, BANKING, AND ACCOUNTING see ***mortgage***

principal shareholders FINANCE, BANKING, AND ACCOUNTING the shareholders who own the largest percentage of shares in an organization

print farming MARKETING the management of an organization's print requirements, including choosing printers and overseeing production

prior lien bond FINANCE, BANKING, AND ACCOUNTING a bond whose holder has more claim on a debtor's assets than holders of other types of bonds

private bank FINANCE, BANKING, AND ACCOUNTING a bank that is owned by a single person or a limited number of private shareholders

private company (*U.K.*) GENERAL MANAGEMENT a ***registered company*** whose shares are not offered for sale to the public

private cost ECONOMICS the cost incurred by individuals when they use scarce resources such as gas

private debt FINANCE, BANKING, AND ACCOUNTING money owed by individuals and organizations other than governments

private enterprise ECONOMICS the parts of an economy that are controlled by companies or individuals rather than the government

Private Finance Initiative FINANCE, BANKING, AND ACCOUNTING the program in the United Kingdom under which the government contracts with private companies for buildings and services instead of providing them directly. Abbr **PFI**

private label MARKETING a product or range of products offered by a retailer under their own name in competition with branded goods. Private label products, like ***non-branded goods***, are normally cheaper than branded items but are often perceived to be of lower quality. Also known as ***own-label***

private placement FINANCE, BANKING, AND ACCOUNTING the sale of securities directly to institutions for investment rather than resale

private sector ECONOMICS the organizations in the section of the economy that is financed and controlled by individuals or private institutions, such as companies, shareholders, or investment groups. See ***public sector***

private sector investment ECONOMICS investment by the private enterprise sector of the economy

private treaty FINANCE, BANKING, AND ACCOUNTING the sale of land without an auction

privatization FINANCE, BANKING, AND ACCOUNTING the transfer of a company from ownership by either a government or a few individuals to the public via the issuance of stock

probability STATISTICS the quantitative measure of the likelihood that a given event will occur

probability distribution STATISTICS a mathematical formula showing the probability for each value of a variable in a statistical study

probability plot STATISTICS a graphic plot of data that compares two probability distributions

probability sample STATISTICS a sample in which every individual in a finite statistical ***population*** has a known chance, but not necessarily an equal chance, of being included

probability sampling STATISTICS sampling in which every individual in a finite ***population*** has a known but not necessarily equal chance of being included in the sample

probation HR & PERSONNEL a trial period in the first months of employment when the employer checks the suitability and capability of a person in a certain role, and takes any necessary corrective action. An employee's performance during a probation period may be evaluated informally, for example, by means of conversations with a supervisor. If a probationary period is included in a ***contract of employment***, formal documented assessment is required.

problem child FINANCE, BANKING, AND ACCOUNTING a ***subsidiary company*** that is not performing well or is damaging the ***parent company*** in some way

problem solving GENERAL MANAGEMENT a systematic approach to overcoming obstacles or problems in the management process. Problems occur when something is not behaving as it should, when something deviates from the norm, or when something goes wrong. A number of problem solving methodologies exist, but the most widely used is that proposed by ***Charles H. Kepner*** and ***Benjamin B. Tregoe***. Steps in their problem solving process include: recognizing a problem exists and defining it; generating a range of solutions; evaluating the possible solutions and choosing the best one; implementing the solution and evaluating its effectiveness in solving the problem. Various techniques can aid problem solving, such as ***brainstorming***, ***fishbone charts***, and ***Pareto charts***.

procedure GENERAL MANAGEMENT a set of step-by-step instructions designed to ensure that a task is efficiently and consistently carried out. Procedures regulate the conduct of an organization's activities and ensure that ***decision making*** is undertaken fairly and with due consideration, as, for example, in the case of disciplinary and complaints procedures. In the context of formal quality management systems, procedures are used to control and monitor work processes and to ensure that standards are met.

procedure manual GENERAL MANAGEMENT a document containing written rules and regulations that govern the conduct of ***procedures*** within an organization. Procedure manuals are often used in the induction and training of new recruits.

proceeds FINANCE, BANKING, AND ACCOUNTING the income from a transaction

process GENERAL MANAGEMENT a structured and managed set of work activities designed to produce a particular output

process box GENERAL MANAGEMENT see ***flow chart***

process chart GENERAL MANAGEMENT a diagrammatic representation of the sequence of work and the nature of events in a ***process***. A process chart provides the basis for visualizing the different stages for evaluation and possible improvement.

process control OPERATIONS & PRODUCTION the inspection of work-in-progress to provide feedback on, and correct, a production process. First developed as a mechanical feedback mechanism, process control is now widely used to monitor and maintain the quality of output. See ***statistical process control***

process layout OPERATIONS & PRODUCTION a type of office or ***plant layout*** that groups together workstations or equipment that undertake similar processes. Within a process layout organization, the partly finished product moves from process to process and each batch may follow a different route. Also known as ***process-oriented layout, layout by function***. See ***product layout***

process management OPERATIONS & PRODUCTION the operation, ***control***, evaluation, and improvement of interconnected tasks, with the aim of maximizing effectiveness and efficiency

processor E-COMMERCE = ***acquirer***

process-oriented layout OPERATIONS & PRODUCTION = ***process layout***

process production OPERATIONS & PRODUCTION the continuous production of a product in bulk, often by a chemical rather than mechanical ***process***

procurement GENERAL MANAGEMENT see ***purchasing***

procurement exchange E-COMMERCE a group of companies that act together to buy products or services they need at lower prices

procurement manager GENERAL MANAGEMENT see ***purchasing manager***

procurement portal GENERAL MANAGEMENT see ***online catalog***

producer price index ECONOMICS a statistical measure, the weighted average of the prices of commodities that firms buy from other firms

producibility engineering OPERATIONS & PRODUCTION see ***design for manufacturability***

product MARKETING anything that is offered to a market that customers can acquire, use, interact with, experience, or consume, to satisfy a want or need. Early ***marketing*** tended to focus on tangible physical goods and these were distinguished from ***services***. More recently, however, the distinction between products and services has blurred, and the concept of the product has been expanded so that in its widest sense it can now be said to cover any tangible or intangible thing that satisfies the consumer. Products that are marketed can include services, people, places, and ideas.

product abandonment MARKETING the ending of the manufacture and sale of a product. Products are abandoned for many reasons. The market may be saturated or declining, the product may be superseded by another, costs of production may become too high, or a product may simply become unprofitable. Product abandonment usually occurs during the decline phase of the ***product life cycle***.

product assortment MARKETING = ***product mix***

product churning GENERAL MANAGEMENT the flooding of a market with new products in the hope that one of them will become successful. Product churning is especially prevalent in Japan, where prelaunch ***test marketing*** is often replaced by multiple product launches. Most of these products will decline and disappear, but one or more of the new products churned out may become profitable.

product development MARKETING the revitalization of a product through the introduction of a new concept or consumer benefit. Product development is part of the ***product life cycle***. The concepts or benefits that can be implemented range from modification of the product to simply introducing new packaging

product development cycle MARKETING see ***new product development***

product differentiation MARKETING a marketing technique that promotes and emphasizes a product's difference from other products of a similar nature. Product differentiation is one of the aspects of ***Michael Porter***'s ***generic strategy*** theory and it has been described by ***Anita Roddick*** as being the key to the success of the Body Shop. Also known as ***differentiation***

✔ BETTER COMMUNICATION WITH RESELLERS (pp. 650–51)

product family MARKETING a group of products or services that meet a similar need in the market

production OPERATIONS & PRODUCTION the processes and techniques used in making a product. Also known as ***manufacturing***

production control OPERATIONS & PRODUCTION the control of all aspects of ***production***, according to a predetermined production plan. ***Production planning*** and production control are closely linked, and sometimes the terms are used interchangeably. Nevertheless, they differ in focus: production planning focuses on the scheduling of the production process; production control focuses on the application of the plan which results from the production planning. Computerized techniques, such as material requirements planning and ***optimized production technology*** combine elements of planning and control.

production leveling OPERATIONS & PRODUCTION = ***production smoothing***

production management OPERATIONS & PRODUCTION the management of those resources and activities of a business that are required to produce goods for sale to consumers or to other organizations. Production management is concerned with the manufacturing industry. The growing interest in the production management task in service industries has led to the use of ***operations management*** as a more general term. Also known as ***manufacturing management***

production planning *or* **production scheduling** OPERATIONS & PRODUCTION the process of producing a specification or chart of the manufacturing operations to be carried out by different functions and workstations over a particular time period. Production scheduling takes account of factors such as the availability of plant and materials, customer delivery requirements, and maintenance schedules.

production smoothing OPERATIONS & PRODUCTION the smoothing, or leveling, of **production scheduling** so that mix and volume are even over time. Production smoothing is an important condition for production by ***kanban***, and is key to the ***Toyota production system***. The aim is to minimize idle time. Also known as ***production leveling***

production versus purchasing OPERATIONS & PRODUCTION see ***purchasing versus production***

productive capacity OPERATIONS & PRODUCTION the maximum amount of output that an organization or company can generate at any one time

productivity GENERAL MANAGEMENT, OPERATIONS & PRODUCTION a measurement of the efficiency of production, taking the form of a ratio of the output of goods and services to the input of factors of production. **Labor productivity** takes account of inputs of employee hours worked; **capital productivity** takes account of inputs of machines or land; and **marginal productivity** measures the additional output gained from an additional unit of input. Techniques to improve productivity

  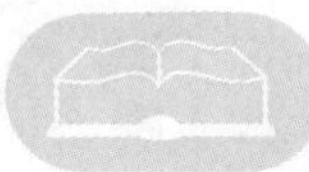  

include greater use of new technology, altered working practices, and improved training of the workforce.

productivity agreement HR & PERSONNEL see ***productivity bargaining***

productivity bargaining HR & PERSONNEL a form of ***collective bargaining*** leading to a **productivity agreement** in which management offers a pay rise in exchange for alterations to employee working practices designed to increase ***productivity***

productivity measurement HR & PERSONNEL see ***productivity***

product launch MARKETING the introduction of a new product to a market

product layout OPERATIONS & PRODUCTION the organization of a factory or office so that the position of the ***workstations*** is optimized to suit the product. Product layout ensures that products follow an ***assembly line*** where the different operations are undertaken in a logical sequence. Also known as ***product-oriented layout***. See ***process layout***

product leader MARKETING see ***brand leader***

product liability MARKETING a manufacturer's, producer's, or service provider's obligation to accept responsibility for defects in their products or services. Faulty products may result in personal injury or damage to property, in which case product liability may result in the payment of compensation to the purchaser.

product life cycle MARKETING the life span of a product from development, through testing, promotion, growth, and maturity, to decline and perhaps regeneration. A new product is first developed and then introduced to the market. Once the introduction is successful, a growth period follows with wider awareness of the product and increasing sales. The product enters maturity when sales stop growing and demand stabilizes. Eventually, sales may decline until the product is finally withdrawn from the market or redeveloped.

product line MARKETING a family of related products. Products within a line may be the same type of product, they may be sold to the same type of customer, or through similar outlets, or they may all be within a certain price range.

product management MARKETING a system for the coordination of all the stages through which a product passes during its life cycle. Product management involves control of a product from its innovation and development to its decline. The process is coordinated by a **product manager** who focuses on the marketing of the product but may also be responsible for pricing, packaging, branding, research and development, production, distribution, sales targets, and product performance appraisal. This cross-departmental approach is based on the theory that a dedicated product management system will lead to tighter control over the product, and thus higher sales and profits. A **brand manager** fulfills a similar function to a product manager, concentrating on products within one brand.

product market MARKETING the ***market*** in which products are sold, usually to organizations rather than consumers. The product market is concerned with ***purchasing*** by organizations for their own use, and includes such items as raw materials, machinery, and equipment which may in turn be used to manufacture items for the consumer market.

product mix MARKETING the range of product lines that a company produces, or that a retailer stocks. Product mix usually refers to the length (the number of products in the product line), breadth (the number of product lines that a company offers), depth (the different varieties of product in the product line), and consistency (relation of the products in their final destination) of product lines. Product mix is sometimes called **product assortment**.

product-oriented layout OPERATIONS & PRODUCTION = ***product layout***

product placement MARKETING a form of advertising in which an identifiable branded product is seen by the audience during a movie or television program

product portfolio MARKETING the range of products manufactured or supplied by an organization

product positioning MARKETING see ***brand positioning***

product range MARKETING all of the types of product made by one company

product recall OPERATIONS & PRODUCTION the removal from sale of products that may constitute a risk to consumers because of contamination, ***sabotage***, or faults in the production process. A product recall usually originates from the product manufacturer but retailers may act autonomously, especially if they believe their outlets are at particular risk. See ***brand positioning***

profession HR & PERSONNEL an occupational group characterized by extensive education and specialized training, the use of skills based on theoretical knowledge, a ***code of conduct***, and an association that organizes its members. Members of a profession are normally well paid and derive social status and prestige from their occupation. They have substantial autonomy and tend to be highly resistant to control or interference in their affairs by outside groups. As many professionals now work within organizations rather than independently, there may be a conflict of interests between professional and corporate values, and between professional autonomy and bureaucratic direction.

professional
1. HR & PERSONNEL a member of a particular ***profession***
2. HR & PERSONNEL somebody paid to do a job, rather than working as a volunteer or pursuing a hobby
3. GENERAL MANAGEMENT somebody who shows a high level of skill or ***competence***
4. GENERAL MANAGEMENT somebody who habitually indulges in a particular activity, fanatically and annoyingly (*slang*)

professional body GENERAL MANAGEMENT an organization that sets and monitors standards for a profession such as law, marketing, or public relations

professionalism HR & PERSONNEL the skill, ***competence***, or standards expected of a member of a ***profession***

profile FINANCE, BANKING, AND ACCOUNTING a description of a company, including its products and finances

profile method HR & PERSONNEL an analytical form of ***job evaluation*** used by management consultants. The most well-known version of the profile method is the "Hay Guide Chart and Profile Methodology."

profitability index FINANCE, BANKING, AND ACCOUNTING the present value of the money an investment will earn divided by the amount of the investment

profitability threshold FINANCE, BANKING, AND ACCOUNTING the point at which a business begins to make profits

profitable FINANCE, BANKING, AND ACCOUNTING making money

profit and loss FINANCE, BANKING, AND ACCOUNTING the difference between a company's income and its costs

profit and loss statement FINANCE, BANKING, AND ACCOUNTING the summary record of a company's external financial transactions, typically for a year or a quarter Abbr **P & L**

✔ HOW TO READ A PROFIT AND LOSS ACCOUNT (pp. 853–54)

profit before tax FINANCE, BANKING, AND ACCOUNTING the amount that a company or investor has made, without taking taxes into account

profit center GENERAL MANAGEMENT a person, unit, or department within an organization that is considered separately when calculating profit. Profit centers are used as part of ***management control systems***. They operate with a degree of autonomy with regard to marketing and pricing, and have responsibility for their own costs, revenues, and profits.

profit distribution FINANCE, BANKING, AND ACCOUNTING the allocation of profits to different recipients such as shareholders and owners, or for different purposes such as research or investment

profit from ordinary activities FINANCE, BANKING, AND ACCOUNTING profits earned in the normal course of business, as opposed to profits from extraordinary sources such as windfall payments

profit margin GENERAL MANAGEMENT the amount by which income exceeds expenditure. The profit margin of an individual product is the sale price minus the cost of production and associated costs such as ***distribution*** and ***advertising***. On a larger scale, the profit margin is an accounting ratio of company income compared with sales. The profit margin ratio can be used to compare the efficiency and profitability of a company over a number of years, or to compare different companies. The **gross profit margin** or **operating margin** of a company is its operating, or gross, profit divided by total sales. The **net profit margin** or **return on sales** is net income after taxes, divided by total sales.

profit motive FINANCE, BANKING, AND ACCOUNTING the desire of a business or service provider to make profit

profit-related pay (*U.K.*) HR & PERSONNEL a ***profit sharing*** scheme, approved by the Inland Revenue, in which employees received tax-free payments in addition to their basic salary. Profit-related pay was phased out during 2000.

profit sharing HR & PERSONNEL a scheme giving ***employees*** a payment that is conditional on the company's profits. Profit sharing takes the form of a ***share incentive scheme***, or a pay ***bonus***. The purpose of relating payment to company performance is to increase ***employee commitment*** and ***motivation***.

profit-sharing debenture FINANCE, BANKING, AND ACCOUNTING a debenture, held by an employee, whose payouts depend on the company's financial success

profit warning FINANCE, BANKING, AND ACCOUNTING a statement by a company's executives that the company may realize less profit in a coming quarter than investors expect

pro-forma GENERAL MANAGEMENT a document issued before all relevant details are known, usually followed by a final version

pro-forma invoice FINANCE, BANKING, AND ACCOUNTING an invoice that does not include all the details of a transaction, often sent before goods are supplied and followed by a final detailed invoice

program E-COMMERCE a set of instructions for a computer to act upon

program trading FINANCE, BANKING, AND ACCOUNTING the trading of securities electronically, by sending messages from the investor's computer to a market

progressive tax FINANCE, BANKING, AND ACCOUNTING a tax with a rate that increases proportionately with the taxable income. See ***proportional tax***, ***regressive tax***

project GENERAL MANAGEMENT a set of activities designed to achieve a specified goal, within a given period of time. Projects focus on activities outside the routine operations of an organization. They vary immensely in size, scope, and complexity and often involve drawing together resources from different parts of an organization for the duration of the project. The process of planning and completing projects is known as ***project management***.

project management GENERAL MANAGEMENT the coordination of resources to ensure the achievement of a ***project***. Project management includes the planning and allocation of financial, material, and human resources and the organization of the work needed to complete a project. Formal, structured approaches to project management began to emerge in the late 1950s in the construction and military industries, where methods such as **PRINCE**—PRojects IN Controlled Environments—developed to facilitate the process.

promissory note FINANCE, BANKING, AND ACCOUNTING a contract to pay money

promotion
1. HR & PERSONNEL, GENERAL MANAGEMENT the award to an employee of a job at a higher grade, usually offering greater responsibility and more money
2. MARKETING = ***sales promotion***

proof-of-purchase MARKETING a token or coupon cut from a package or publication and exchanged in a promotional offer

property FINANCE, BANKING, AND ACCOUNTING assets, such as land or goods, that somebody owns

property bond FINANCE, BANKING, AND ACCOUNTING a bond, especially a bail bond, for which a property is collateral

property damage insurance FINANCE, BANKING, AND ACCOUNTING insurance against the risk of damage to property

proportional tax FINANCE, BANKING, AND ACCOUNTING a tax whose amount is strictly proportional to the value of the item being taxed, especially income. See ***progressive tax***, ***regressive tax***

proprietary ordering system E-COMMERCE a family of computer programs, usually interactive and online, that is developed and owned by a supplier and made available to its customers to facilitate ordering

ProShare FINANCE, BANKING, AND ACCOUNTING a group that acts in the interests of private investors in securities of the London Stock Exchange

prospect MARKETING a person or organization considered likely to buy a product or service

prospecting MARKETING the process of identifying people or organizations that are likely to buy a product or service

prospectus FINANCE, BANKING, AND ACCOUNTING a document that sets out corporate and financial information for prospective shareholders. A prospectus is usually issued when a company is offering new shares to the market.

prosuming GENERAL MANAGEMENT acting both as producer and consumer, as, for example, when a person plays an interactive computer game (*slang*)

protected class HR & PERSONNEL an employee with skills that are currently in short supply (*slang*)

protectionism ECONOMICS a government economic policy of restricting the level of imports by using measures such as tariffs and ***NTBs***

protective put buying FINANCE, BANKING, AND ACCOUNTING the purchase of ***puts*** for stocks already owned

protective tariff ECONOMICS a tariff imposed to restrict imports into a country

protocol FINANCE, BANKING, AND ACCOUNTING a set of rules that govern and regulate a process

prototype GENERAL MANAGEMENT an initial version or working model of a new product or invention. A prototype is constructed and tested in order to evaluate the feasibility of a design and to identify problems that need to be corrected. Building a prototype is a key stage in ***new product development***.

provisional tax FINANCE, BANKING, AND ACCOUNTING tax paid in advance on the following year's income, the amount being based on the actual income from the preceding year

proxy GENERAL MANAGEMENT somebody who votes on behalf of another person at a company meeting

proxy fight FINANCE, BANKING, AND ACCOUNTING the use of proxy votes to settle a contentious issue at a company meeting

proxy server E-COMMERCE a program added to an intranet to provide one-way (outward) access to the Internet. In addition to providing Internet access for those within the intranet, the proxy server creates a ***firewall*** to prevent external users from accessing the private network.

proxy statement FINANCE, BANKING, AND ACCOUNTING a notice that a company sends to stockholders allowing them to vote and giving them all the information they need to vote in an informed way

psychic income HR & PERSONNEL the level of satisfaction derived from a job rather than the salary earned doing it (*slang*)

psychological contract HR & PERSONNEL the set of unwritten expectations concerning the relationship between an ***employee*** and an ***employer***. The psychological contract addresses factors that are not defined in a written ***contract of employment*** such as levels of ***employee commitment***, ***productivity***, ***quality of working life***, ***job satisfaction***, attitudes to ***flexible working***, and the provision and take-up of suitable training. Expectations from both employer and employee can change, so the psychological contract must be reevaluated at intervals to minimize misunderstandings.

psychological test HR & PERSONNEL see ***psychometric test***

psychometric test HR & PERSONNEL a series of questions, problems, or practical tasks that provide a measurement of aspects of somebody's personality, knowledge, ability, or experience. There are two main categories of psychometric test: ability or ***aptitude tests*** and **personality tests**. A test should be both valid—it should measure what it says it measures—and reliable—it should give consistent scores. Tests are used in ***recruitment*** and ***employee development*** and their administration and interpretation must be carried out by qualified people. Tests are increasingly taken, scored, and interpreted with the aid of computer-based systems. A test may also be referred to as an **instrument**, and tests can be grouped into a **test battery**.

Pty *abbr* (*S. Africa*) FINANCE, BANKING, AND ACCOUNTING used in company names to indicate a private limited liability company

public debt FINANCE, BANKING, AND ACCOUNTING the money that a government or a set of governments owes

public expenditure ECONOMICS spending by the government of a country on things such as pension provision and infrastructure enhancement

public finance law FINANCE, BANKING, AND ACCOUNTING legislation relating to the financial activities of government or public sector organizations

public-liability insurance FINANCE, BANKING, AND ACCOUNTING insurance against the risk of being held financially liable for injury to somebody

public limited company GENERAL MANAGEMENT a company in the United Kingdom that is required to have a minimum authorized capital of £50,000 and to offer its shares to the public. A public limited company has the letters "plc" after its name. In the United Kingdom, only public limited companies can be listed on the London Stock Exchange. = ***publicly held corporation***

publicly held corporation GENERAL MANAGEMENT an organization with common stock listed on a stock exchange

public monopoly GENERAL MANAGEMENT a situation of limited competition in the public sector, usually relating to nationalized industries

public offering FINANCE, BANKING, AND ACCOUNTING a method of raising money used by a company in which it invites the public to apply for shares

public relations MARKETING see ***PR***

public relations consultancy MARKETING an organization specializing in planning and implementing public relations strategies

public sector
1. GENERAL MANAGEMENT the organizations in the section of the economy that is financed and controlled by central government, local authorities, and publicly funded corporations
2. ECONOMICS see ***private sector***

public servant GENERAL MANAGEMENT a person employed by a government department or agency

public service GENERAL MANAGEMENT the various departments and agencies that carry out government policies and provide government-funded services

public spending ECONOMICS spending by the government of a country on publicly provided goods and services

public training program HR & PERSONNEL see ***in-company training***

puff FINANCE, BANKING, AND ACCOUNTING to overstate the virtues of a product, especially a stock (*slang*)

puffery MARKETING exaggerated claims made for a product or service. In general, puffery does not constitute false advertising under law. (*slang*)

puff piece MARKETING an article in a newspaper or magazine promoting a product, person, or service (*slang*)

pull strategy MARKETING see ***push and pull strategies***

pull system OPERATIONS & PRODUCTION a production planning and control system in which the specification and pace of output of a delivery, or supplier, workstation is set by the receiving, or customer, ***workstation***. In pull systems, the customer acts as the only trigger for movement. The supplier workstation can only produce output on the instructions of the customer for delivery when the customer is ready to receive it. Demand is therefore transferred down through the stages of production from the order placed by an end customer. Pull systems are far less likely to result in work-in-progress inventory, and are favored by just-in-time or ***lean production*** systems. See ***push system***

pull technology E-COMMERCE technology that enables users to seek out and then pull in information, rather than having it pushed in their way. Understanding the "pull" nature of the Internet is often considered to be one of the key factors in determining a Web site's success. The Internet is essentially a pull technology, though direct outbound e-mail can be classified as a **push technology**.

pull the plug on something GENERAL MANAGEMENT to bring something such as a business project to an end, especially by cutting off its financial support (*slang*)

pump priming GENERAL MANAGEMENT the injection of further investment in order to revitalize a company in stagnation, or to help a ***startup*** over a critical period. Pump priming has a similar effect to the provision of ***seed money***.

punt GENERAL MANAGEMENT to stop trying to accomplish something and just try to avoid losing any more resources (*slang*)

purchase contract FINANCE, BANKING, AND ACCOUNTING a form of agreement to buy specified products at an agreed price

purchase history MARKETING a record of a customer's transactions with an organization

purchase ledger GENERAL MANAGEMENT a record of all purchases made by an organization

purchase money mortgage FINANCE, BANKING, AND ACCOUNTING a mortgage whose proceeds the borrower uses to buy the property that is collateral for the loan

purchase order GENERAL MANAGEMENT a document that authorizes a person or an organization to deliver goods or perform a service and that guarantees payment

purchase price FINANCE, BANKING, AND ACCOUNTING the price that somebody pays to buy a good or service

purchasing OPERATIONS & PRODUCTION the acquisition of goods and services needed to support the various activities of an organization, at the optimum cost and from reliable suppliers. Purchasing involves defining the need for goods and services; identifying and comparing available supplies and suppliers; negotiating terms for price, quantity, and delivery; agreeing contracts and placing orders; receiving and accepting delivery; and authorizing the payment for goods and services. Also known as ***procurement***

purchasing by contract OPERATIONS & PRODUCTION see ***contract purchasing***

purchasing manager OPERATIONS & PRODUCTION an individual with responsibility for all activities concerned with ***purchasing***. The responsibilities of a purchasing manager can include ordering, commercial negotiations, and delivery chasing. A purchasing manager is sometimes called a **buying manager**, or **procurement manager**.

purchasing power OPERATIONS & PRODUCTION a measure of the ability of a person, organization, or sector to buy goods and services

purchasing power parity ECONOMICS an exchange rate between two countries that makes the price of a good the same when converted at that rate. Abbr **PPP**

purchasing versus production OPERATIONS & PRODUCTION a decision on whether to produce goods internally or to buy them in from outside the organization. The aim of purchasing versus production is to secure needed items at the best possible cost, while making optimum use of the resources of the organization. Factors influencing the decision may include: cost, spare ***capacity*** within the organization, the need for tight quality and scheduling control, flexibility, the enhancement of skills that can then be used in other ways, volume and economies of scale, utilization of existing personnel, the need for secrecy, capital and financing requirements, and the potential reliability of supply. Also known as ***buy or make***, ***make or buy***, ***internal versus external sourcing***

pure competition FINANCE, BANKING, AND ACCOUNTING a situation in which there are many sellers in a market and there is free flow of information

pure endowment FINANCE, BANKING, AND ACCOUNTING a gift whose use is fully prescribed by the donor

pure play E-COMMERCE a company that conducts business only over the Internet, provides only Internet services, or sells only to other Internet companies (*slang*)

purpose credit FINANCE, BANKING, AND ACCOUNTING credit used for trade in securities

push and pull strategies MARKETING approaches used as part of a marketing strategy to encourage customers to purchase a product or service. Push and pull strategies are contrasting approaches and tend to target different types of consumer. A **pull strategy** targets the end consumer, using ***advertising***, ***sales promotions***, and ***direct response marketing*** to pull the customer in. This approach is common in consumer markets. A **push strategy** targets members of the ***distribution channel***, such as ***wholesalers*** and ***retailers***, to push the promotion up through the channel to the consumers. This approach is more common in industrial markets.

push system OPERATIONS & PRODUCTION a ***production control*** and planning system in which demand is predicted centrally and each ***workstation*** pushes work out without considering if the next station is ready for it. While the central control aspect of a push system can achieve a balance across workstations, in practice a particular station can suffer from any one of a number of problems that delays work flow, so affecting the whole system. Push systems are characterized by work-in-progress inventory, lines, and idle time. See ***pull system***

push technology E-COMMERCE see ***pull technology***

push the envelope GENERAL MANAGEMENT to exceed normal limits. Pushing the envelope is a term adapted from aviation. The term implies a sense of risk at transcending normal safe limits of operation.

put *or* **put option** FINANCE, BANKING, AND ACCOUNTING an option to sell stock within a specified time at a specified price

pyramid selling MARKETING the sale of the right to sell products or services to distributors who in turn recruit other distributors. Sometimes ending with no final buyer, pyramid selling is a form of multilevel marketing, and often involves a system of franchises. It is similar to ***network marketing***, but in many cases no end products are actually sold. Unscrupulous instigators of a pyramid marketing scheme profit from the initial fees paid to them by distributors in advance of promised sales income.

QFD OPERATIONS & PRODUCTION see ***quality function deployment***

qualification payment GENERAL MANAGEMENT an additional payment sometimes made to employees of New Zealand companies, who have gained an academic qualification relevant to their job

qualified domestic trust FINANCE, BANKING, AND ACCOUNTING a trust for the noncitizen spouse of an American, affording tax advantages at the time of the citizen's death

qualified lead FINANCE, BANKING, AND ACCOUNTING a sales prospect whose potential value has been carefully evaluated through research

qualified listed security FINANCE, BANKING, AND ACCOUNTING a security that is eligible for purchase by a regulated entity such as a trust

qualitative lending guideline FINANCE, BANKING, AND ACCOUNTING a rule for evaluating creditworthiness that is not objective

qualitative research MARKETING research that focuses on "soft" data, for example, attitude research or focus groups. See ***quantitative research***

quality GENERAL MANAGEMENT all the features and characteristics of a product or service that affect its ability to meet stated or implied needs. Quality can be assessed in terms of conforming to specification, being fit for purpose, having zero defects, and producing ***customer satisfaction***. Quality can be managed through ***total quality management***, ***quality standards***, and ***performance indicators***.

quality assurance GENERAL MANAGEMENT all the methods used to ensure compliance with a ***quality standard***. Quality assurance is recognized by the international standard ***ISO 9000***.

quality audit GENERAL MANAGEMENT an independent and systematic examination to establish whether quality activities and related results comply with planned arrangements. A quality audit is a form of internal ***audit*** useful in the maintenance of ***quality control***. A quality audit needs to look at effective implementation of quality arrangements and whether they are suitable for the achievement of objectives. It is an integral part of working toward a ***quality standard*** or a ***quality award***.

quality award GENERAL MANAGEMENT a formal recognition of quality and business ***excellence***. The best known quality awards include the ***Malcolm Baldrige National Quality Award***, the ***Deming Prize***, and the ***EFQM Excellence Model***.

quality circle GENERAL MANAGEMENT, HR & PERSONNEL a group of employees who meet voluntarily and on a regular basis to discuss performance and problems evident in their working environment. A quality circle is usually made up of employees from the shop floor, led by a supervisor. The group has responsibility for implementing solutions to identified problems. Participants are trained in the necessary leadership, ***problem solving***, and ***decision making*** skills to enable them to contribute fully to the group. The quality circle is a form of ***employee involvement*** derived from a Japanese idea.

quality control GENERAL MANAGEMENT an inspection system for ensuring that predetermined ***quality standards*** are being met. Quality control measures the progress of an activity by means of a quality inspection checking for and identifying non-conformance.
PHILIP CROSBY (pp. 978–79)

quality control plan OPERATIONS & PRODUCTION a means of setting out practices, resources, and sequences of activities relevant to the ***quality control*** of a particular product, service, contract, or project

quality costs GENERAL MANAGEMENT costs associated with the failure to achieve conformance to requirements. Quality costs accrue when organizations waste large sums of money because of carrying out the wrong tasks, or failing to carry out the right tasks ***right first time***. Also known as ***nonconformance costs***

quality function deployment OPERATIONS & PRODUCTION a ***quality*** technique used to design services or products based on customer expectations. Quality function deployment is an approach that sees quality as something that can be designed into a product or service at an early stage. It involves converting customers' demands into quality characteristics of the finished product. The four phases of the approach are design or ***house of quality***, detail, process, and production. Each phase helps to steer a design team toward ***customer satisfaction***. Quality function deployment is based on methods developed by ***Genichi Taguchi***. Abbr **QFD**

quality inspection GENERAL MANAGEMENT see ***quality control***

quality loss OPERATIONS & PRODUCTION see ***Taguchi methods***

quality management GENERAL MANAGEMENT the use of a program to ensure the production of high-quality products

quality manual GENERAL MANAGEMENT a document containing the quality policy, quality objectives, structure chart, and description of the quality system of an organization. A quality manual often explains how the requirements of a ***quality standard*** are to be met and identifies the person responsible for ***quality management*** functions.

quality of design OPERATIONS & PRODUCTION the degree to which the design of a product or service meets its purpose. Quality of design is an important factor in ***customer satisfaction***.

quality of life HR & PERSONNEL

1. at a personal level, the degree of enjoyment and satisfaction experienced in everyday life, embracing health, personal relationships, the environment, ***quality of working life***, social life, and leisure time

2. at community level, a set of social indicators such as nutrition, air quality, incidence of disease, crime rates, health care, educational services, and divorce rates

quality of working life HR & PERSONNEL the degree of personal satisfaction experienced at work. Quality of working life is dependent on the extent to which an employee feels valued, rewarded, motivated, consulted, and empowered. It is also influenced by factors such as job security, opportunities for ***career development***, work patterns, and ***work-life balance***.

quality standard GENERAL MANAGEMENT a framework for achieving a recognized level of ***quality*** within an organization. Achievement of a quality standard demonstrates that an organization has met the requirements laid out by a certifying body. Quality standards recognized on an international basis include ***ISO 9000*** and ***ISO 14000***.

quality table OPERATIONS & PRODUCTION = ***house of quality***

quality time GENERAL MANAGEMENT time that is set aside for activities which you consider important, for example, time spent with your family (*slang*)

quantitative research FINANCE, BANKING, AND ACCOUNTING the gathering and analysis of data that can be expressed in numerical form. Quantitative research involves data that is measurable and can include statistical results, financial data, or demographic data. See ***qualitative research***

quarterback GENERAL MANAGEMENT to give directions on a project (*slang*)

quartile STATISTICS any of the values in a frequency or probability distribution that divide it into four equal parts

quasi-public corporation GENERAL MANAGEMENT an organization that is owned partly by private or public shareholders and partly by the government

quasi-rent ECONOMICS the short-run excess earnings made by a firm, the difference between production cost (the cost of labor and materials) and selling cost

question mark company GENERAL MANAGEMENT see ***Boston Box***

questionnaire GENERAL MANAGEMENT a collection of structured questions designed to elicit information for a specific purpose. Questionnaires are commonly used in ***market research*** and make use of two types of question: multiple choice questions, which are designed to produce a limited response, and open questions, which allow respondents the opportunity to air their views freely.

queuing theory GENERAL MANAGEMENT techniques developed by the study of people standing in line to determine the optimum level of service provision. In queuing theory, mathematical formulae, or ***simulations***, are used to calculate variables such as length of time spent standing in line and average service time, which depend on the frequency and number of arrivals and the facilities available. The results enable decisions to be made on the most cost-effective level of facilities and the most efficient organization of the process. Early developments in queuing theory were applied to the provision of telephone switching equipment but the techniques are now used in a wide variety of contexts, including machine maintenance, production lines, and air transportation.

quick ratio FINANCE, BANKING, AND ACCOUNTING

1. a measure of the amount of cash a potential borrower can acquire in a short time, used in evaluating creditworthiness

2. the ratio of liquid assets to current debts

quote FINANCE, BANKING, AND ACCOUNTING a statement of what a person is willing to accept when selling or to pay when buying

quoted company FINANCE, BANKING, AND ACCOUNTING a company whose shares are listed on a stock exchange

quoted securities FINANCE, BANKING, AND ACCOUNTING securities or shares that are listed on a stock exchange

R

R150 Bond FINANCE, BANKING, AND ACCOUNTING the benchmark South African government bond which has a fixed interest rate of 12% and matures in 2005

racial discrimination HR & PERSONNEL the practice of making unfavorable distinctions between the members of different groups of people on the grounds of color, race, nationality, or ethnic origin. See ***indirect discrimination***

radio button GENERAL MANAGEMENT a device on a computer screen that can be used to select an option from a list

raid FINANCE, BANKING, AND ACCOUNTING the illegal practice of selling shares short to drive the price down. Also known as ***bear raid***

raider FINANCE, BANKING, AND ACCOUNTING a person or company that makes hostile takeover bids

rainmaker HR & PERSONNEL somebody, especially a lawyer, who procures clients who spend a lot of money on their firm's business

rally FINANCE, BANKING, AND ACCOUNTING a rise in share prices after a fall

rand FINANCE, BANKING, AND ACCOUNTING the South African unit of currency, equal to 100 cents

R & D OPERATIONS & PRODUCTION see ***research and development***

Randlord FINANCE, BANKING, AND ACCOUNTING originally a Johannesburg-based mining magnate or tycoon of the late 19th or early 20th centuries, now used informally for any wealthy or powerful Johannesburg businessman

random STATISTICS not part of a pattern but governed by chance

random observation method GENERAL MANAGEMENT = ***activity sampling***

random sampling OPERATIONS & PRODUCTION an unbiased ***sampling*** technique in which every member of the population has an equal chance of being included in the sample. Based on probability theory, random sampling is the process of selecting and canvassing a representative group of individuals from a particular population in order to identify the attributes or attitudes of the population as a whole. Related sampling techniques include: **stratified sampling**, in which the population is divided into classes, and random samples are taken from each class; **cluster sampling**, in which a unit of the sample is a group such as a household; and **systematic sampling**, which refers to samples chosen by any system other than random selection. See ***nonrandom sampling***

range STATISTICS the difference between the smallest and the largest observations in a data set

ranking STATISTICS the ordered arrangement of a set of variable values

ratable value FINANCE, BANKING, AND ACCOUNTING the value of something as calculated with reference to a rule

ratchet effect ECONOMICS the result when households adjust more easily to rising incomes than to falling incomes, as, for example, when their consumption drops by less than their income in a recession

rate of exchange FINANCE, BANKING, AND ACCOUNTING = ***exchange rate***

rate of interest FINANCE, BANKING, AND ACCOUNTING a percentage charged on a loan or paid on an investment for the use of the money

rate of return FINANCE, BANKING, AND ACCOUNTING an accounting ratio of the income

from an investment to the amount of the investment, used to measure financial performance. Also known as ***return***

✔ How to Calculate Expected Rate of Return (p. 829)

ratings MARKETING the proportion of a target audience who are exposed to a television or radio commercial

ratio analysis FINANCE, BANKING, AND ACCOUNTING the use of ratios to measure financial performance

ratio-delay study GENERAL MANAGEMENT = ***activity sampling***

rationalization GENERAL MANAGEMENT the application of efficiency or effectiveness measures to an organization. Rationalization can occur at the onset of a downturn in an organization's performance or results. It usually takes the form of cutbacks aimed to bring the organization back to profitability and may involve ***redundancies***, plant closures, and cutbacks in supplies and resources. It often involves changes in ***organization structure***, particularly in the form of ***downsizing***. The term is also used in a cynical way as a euphemism for mass redundancies.

raw materials OPERATIONS & PRODUCTION items bought for use in the manufacturing or development processes of an organization. While most often referring to bulk materials, raw materials can also include components, subassemblies, and complete products.

RBA FINANCE, BANKING, AND ACCOUNTING see ***Reserve Bank of Australia***

RBNZ FINANCE, BANKING, AND ACCOUNTING see ***Reserve Bank of New Zealand***

RDO *abbr* (*ANZ*) HR & PERSONNEL rostered day off, a day of leave allocated under certain employment agreements to staff in lieu of accumulated overtime

RDP FINANCE, BANKING, AND ACCOUNTING Reconstruction and Development Program, a policy framework by means of which the South African government intends to correct the socioeconomic imbalances caused by apartheid

reactive maintenance OPERATIONS & PRODUCTION a form of ***maintenance*** in which equipment and facilities are repaired only in response to a breakdown or a fault. Because of the potential for loss of production, reactive maintenance is at odds with ***just-in-time***. See ***preventive maintenance***

readership MARKETING a detailed profile of the readers of a newspaper or magazine

Reaganomics ECONOMICS the policy of former U.S. President Reagan in the 1980s, who reduced taxes and social security support and increased the national budget deficit to an unprecedented level

real FINANCE, BANKING, AND ACCOUNTING after the effects of inflation are taken into consideration

real asset FINANCE, BANKING, AND ACCOUNTING a nonmovable asset such as land or a building

real balance effect ECONOMICS the effect on income and employment when prices fall and consumption increases

real capital FINANCE, BANKING, AND ACCOUNTING assets that can be assigned a monetary value

real estate GENERAL MANAGEMENT property consisting of land or buildings

real estate developer GENERAL MANAGEMENT a person or company that develops land or buildings to increase their value

real exchange rate FINANCE, BANKING, AND ACCOUNTING an exchange rate that has been adjusted for inflation

real GDP ECONOMICS ***GDP*** adjusted for changes in prices

real growth ECONOMICS the growth of a country or a household adjusted for changes in prices

reality check GENERAL MANAGEMENT a consideration of limiting factors such as cost when discussing or contemplating an ambitious project (*slang*)

real purchasing power ECONOMICS the purchasing power of a country or a household adjusted for changes in prices

real time company GENERAL MANAGEMENT a company that uses the Internet and other technologies to respond immediately to customer demands

real time credit card processing E-COMMERCE the online authorization of a credit card indicating that the credit card has been approved or rejected during the transaction

real time data FINANCE, BANKING, AND ACCOUNTING information received very soon after a company comes into existence

real time EDI E-COMMERCE online electronic data interchange, the online transfer and processing of business data, for example, purchase orders, customer invoices, and payment receipts, between suppliers and their customers

real time manager GENERAL MANAGEMENT a manager who is responsible for delivering the immediate service that customers expect using the Internet and other technologies

real time transaction E-COMMERCE an Internet payment transaction that is approved or rejected immediately when the customer completes the online order form

rebadge FINANCE, BANKING, AND ACCOUNTING to buy a product or service from another company and sell it as part of your own product range

rebating MARKETING a sales promotion technique in which the customer is offered a rebate for reaching volume targets

receiver FINANCE, BANKING, AND ACCOUNTING the person appointed to sell the assets of a company that is insolvent. The proceeds of the sale are used to discharge debts to creditors, with any surplus distributed to shareholders.

Receiver of Revenue FINANCE, BANKING, AND ACCOUNTING
1. a local office of the South African Revenue Service
2. an informal term for the South African Revenue Service as a whole

recession GENERAL MANAGEMENT a stage of the ***business cycle*** in which economic activity is in slow decline. Recession usually follows a boom, and precedes a ***depression***. It is characterized by rising unemployment and falling levels of output and investment.

recessionary gap ECONOMICS the shortfall in the amount of ***aggregate demand*** in an economy needed to create full employment

reconciliation FINANCE, BANKING, AND ACCOUNTING adjustment of an account, such as an individual's own record of a bank account, to match more authoritative information

record date GENERAL MANAGEMENT the date when a computer data entry or record is made

recovery ECONOMICS the return of a country to economic health after a crash or a depression

recruitment HR & PERSONNEL the activity of employing workers to fill vacancies or enrolling new members. Employment recruitment is composed of several stages: verifying that a vacancy exists; drawing up a job specification; finding candidates; selecting them by ***interviewing*** and other means such as carrying out a ***psychometric test***; and making a job offer. Effective recruitment is important in achieving high organizational performance and minimizing labor turnover. Employees may be recruited either externally or internally.

recurring billing transaction E-COMMERCE an electronic payment facility based on the automatic charging of a customer's credit card in each payment period

recurring payments E-COMMERCE an electronic payment facility that permits a merchant to process multiple authorizations by the same customer either as multiple payments for a fixed amount or recurring billings for varying amounts

red
in the red FINANCE, BANKING, AND ACCOUNTING in debt, or losing money (*slang*)

Reddin, William James (*b.* 1930) GENERAL MANAGEMENT British-born Canadian academic. Best known for his research on ***three-dimensional management***, a development of the work of ***Robert Blake*** and ***Jane Mouton*** explained in *Managerial Effectiveness* (1970)

redemption FINANCE, BANKING, AND ACCOUNTING the purchase by a company of its own shares from shareholders

redeployment HR & PERSONNEL the movement of employees by their employer from one location or task to another. Redeployment is often used to minimize redundancies, ensure the fulfillment of a specific order, or ensure the most cost-effective use of employees.

red herring FINANCE, BANKING, AND ACCOUNTING a statement or action intended to mislead

redistributive effect FINANCE, BANKING, AND ACCOUNTING an effect of a progressive tax or benefit that tends to equalize people's wealth

redundancy HR & PERSONNEL dismissal from work because a job ceases to exist. Redundancy occurs most frequently when an employer goes out of business, suffers a drop in business necessitating a cutback in the workforce, or relocates part, or all, of the company. Redundancy may also be due to a reduced requirement for employees to carry out work of a particular kind. Employees who are made redundant may qualify for a ***redundancy payment***. If the redundancy process is handled incorrectly, the employer may be faced with claims for unfair dismissal.

redundancy package FINANCE, BANKING, AND ACCOUNTING a package of benefits that an employer gives to somebody who is made redundant

redundancy payment HR & PERSONNEL a one-off payment given to a worker who has been made ***redundant***, usually calculated with reference to age, length of service, and weekly rate of pay

redundant capacity OPERATIONS & PRODUCTION = ***surplus capacity***

reengineering GENERAL MANAGEMENT see ***business process reengineering***

reference HR & PERSONNEL a statement of facts and opinions concerning the qualifications, skills, capabilities, personal qualities, conduct, and attitudes of a person, usually a job applicant. Employers supplying references have a legal obligation to take reasonable care that the information provided is accurate.

reference population STATISTICS a standard against which a statistical population under study can be compared

reference site E-COMMERCE a customer site where a new technology is being used successfully

referred share FINANCE, BANKING, AND ACCOUNTING a share that is ex dividend

refinance FINANCE, BANKING, AND ACCOUNTING to replace one loan with another, especially at a lower rate of interest

refinancing FINANCE, BANKING, AND ACCOUNTING the process of taking out a loan to pay off other loans, or loans taken out for that purpose

reflation ECONOMICS a government policy of reducing unemployment by increasing an economy's ***aggregate demand***

refugee capital FINANCE, BANKING, AND ACCOUNTING people and resources that come into a country because they have been forced to leave their own country for economic or political reasons

refund MARKETING the reimbursement of the purchase price of a good or service, for reasons such as faults in manufacturing or dissatisfaction with the service provided

regeneration GENERAL MANAGEMENT the redevelopment of industrial or business areas that have suffered decline, in order to increase employment and business activity

regional fund FINANCE, BANKING, AND ACCOUNTING a mutual fund that invests in the markets of a geographic region

registered bond FINANCE, BANKING, AND ACCOUNTING a bond whose ownership is recorded on the books of the issuer

registered broker FINANCE, BANKING, AND ACCOUNTING a broker registered on a particular exchange

registered company GENERAL MANAGEMENT a company that has lodged official documents with the ***Registrar of Companies*** at Companies House. A registered company is obliged to conduct itself in accordance with company law. All organizations must register in order to become companies.

registered share FINANCE, BANKING, AND ACCOUNTING a share the ownership of which is recorded on the books of the issuer

registered trademark GENERAL MANAGEMENT see ***trademark***

Registrar of Companies (*U.K.*) GENERAL MANAGEMENT the official charged with the duty of holding and registering the official startup and constitutional documents of all ***registered companies*** in the United Kingdom

registration sticker FINANCE, BANKING, AND ACCOUNTING a prominent sticker displayed inside the window of a motor vehicle to prove that the owner has paid road tax on it

regression analysis GENERAL MANAGEMENT a ***forecasting*** technique used to establish the relationship between quantifiable variables. In regression analysis, data on dependent and independent variables is plotted on a scatter graph or diagram and trends are indicated through a line of best fit. The use of a single independent variable is known as **simple re-**

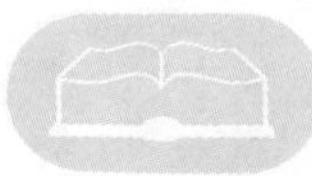

gression analysis, while the use of two or more independent variables is called **multiple regression analysis**.

regressive tax FINANCE, BANKING, AND ACCOUNTING a tax whose percentage falls as the value of the item being taxed, especially income, rises. U.S. social security taxes are regressive. See ***progressive tax***, ***proportional tax***

regulated superannuation fund FINANCE, BANKING, AND ACCOUNTING an Australian superannuation fund that is regulated by legislation and therefore qualifies for tax concessions. To attain this status, a fund must show that its main function is the provision of pensions or adopt a corporate trustee structure.

regulator GENERAL MANAGEMENT an official or body that monitors the behavior of companies and the level of competition in particular markets such as telecommunications or energy

regulatory body FINANCE, BANKING, AND ACCOUNTING, GENERAL MANAGEMENT an independent organization, usually set up by government, that regulates the activities of companies in an industry

regulatory pricing risk FINANCE, BANKING, AND ACCOUNTING the risk an insurance company faces that a government will regulate the prices it can charge

reinsurance FINANCE, BANKING, AND ACCOUNTING a method of reducing risk by transferring all or part of an insurance policy to another insurer

reintermediation E-COMMERCE the reintroduction of intermediaries found in traditional retail channels. See ***disintermediation***

reinvestment risk FINANCE, BANKING, AND ACCOUNTING the risk that it will not be possible to invest the proceeds of an investment at as high a rate as they earned

reinvestment unit trust FINANCE, BANKING, AND ACCOUNTING a mutual fund in the United Kingdom that uses dividends to buy more shares in the company issuing them

relational database GENERAL MANAGEMENT a computer database in which different types of data are linked for analysis

relationship management MARKETING the process of fostering good relations with customers to build loyalty and increase sales

relationship marketing MARKETING see ***pyramid selling***

relative income hypothesis ECONOMICS the theory that consumers are concerned less with their absolute living standards than with consumption relative to other consumers

relaxation allowance GENERAL MANAGEMENT see ***standard time***

release E-COMMERCE a version of a software program that has been modified. Release 1.0 would be followed by release 1.1 after minor modification, or release 2.0 after major changes to the program.

relevant interest (*ANZ*) FINANCE, BANKING, AND ACCOUNTING the legal status held by share investors who can legally dispose of or influence the disposal of shares

reliability GENERAL MANAGEMENT the quality of being fit for an intended purpose over a continued period of time

reliability centered maintenance OPERATIONS & PRODUCTION a ***maintenance*** system that focuses on ensuring equipment is always functioning reliably. Reliability centered maintenance involves assessing each piece of equipment or other asset individually and in the context of how it is being used, for example, frequency of use and volume of output. Analysis is made of its weak points and a ***preventive maintenance*** schedule is drawn up taking them into account.

relocation GENERAL MANAGEMENT the transfer of a business from one location to another. Relocation occurs for a variety of reasons, including the need for more space, the desire to centralize operations, or to be nearer to suppliers, customers, or raw materials.

remuneration HR & PERSONNEL see ***earnings***

remuneration package HR & PERSONNEL the salary, pension contributions, bonuses, and other forms of payment or benefit that make up an employee's remuneration

repeat business MARKETING the placing of order after order with the same supplier. Repeat business can be implemented by an agreement between the customer and supplier for purchase on a regular basis. It is often used where there are small numbers of customers, or high volumes per product and low product variety. There is only market competition for the first order, and customization is usually only available for the initial purchase. Sales and marketing have a diminished role once the business has been gained.

repertory grid GENERAL MANAGEMENT a technique for gathering information on an individual's personal constructs or perceptions of their environment through mapping interview responses to a matrix. The repertory grid was initially used and developed by clinical psychologists in the 1930s. It has business applications in job analysis, performance measurement, ***evaluation of training***, questionnaire design, and ***market research***.

repetitive strain injury GENERAL MANAGEMENT damage caused to muscles or tendons as the result of prolonged repetitive movements or actions. Repetitive strain injury is most commonly associated with injury to the wrist or arms through the use of computer keyboards. Abbr **RSI**

replacement cost FINANCE, BANKING, AND ACCOUNTING the cost of replacing an asset or service with its current equivalent

replacement cost accounting FINANCE, BANKING, AND ACCOUNTING a method of valuing company assets based on their replacement cost

replacement ratio ECONOMICS the ratio of the total resources received when unemployed to those received when in employment

replenishment system OPERATIONS & PRODUCTION an inventory control system that relies on accurate estimates of usage rates and delivery lead times to allow orders to be completed and to ensure stock does not run out. The timing of a replenishment order is crucial, as ***buffer stock*** should not be allowed to run out during the time it takes for a delivery to arrive.

repositioning MARKETING a marketing strategy that changes aspects of a product or brand in order to change ***market position*** and alter consumer perceptions

request form E-COMMERCE an interactive Web page that accepts user-provided data, for example, name, address, or shipping information, that can be saved for recurring use or sent by e-mail to the page owner

requisition FINANCE, BANKING, AND ACCOUNTING an official order form used by companies when purchasing a product or service

resale price maintenance *(U.K.)* MARKETING an agreement between suppliers or manufacturers and retailers, restricting the price that retailers can ask for a product or service. Resale price maintenance was designed to enable all retailers to make a profit. The Resale Prices Act now prevents this practice on the grounds that it is uncompetitive. Now, unless they can prove that resale price maintenance is in the public interest, manufacturers can only recommend a retail price.

research and development OPERATIONS & PRODUCTION the pursuit of new knowledge and ideas and the application of that knowledge to exploit new opportunities to the commercial advantage of a business. The research and development functions are often grouped together to form a division or department within an organization. Abbr **R & D**

reserve account E-COMMERCE = ***holdback***

reserve bank FINANCE, BANKING, AND ACCOUNTING a bank such as a Federal Reserve Bank that holds the reserves of other banks

Reserve Bank of Australia FINANCE, BANKING, AND ACCOUNTING Australia's central bank, which is responsible for managing the Commonwealth's monetary policy, ensuring financial stability, and printing and distributing currency. Abbr **RBA**

Reserve Bank of New Zealand FINANCE, BANKING, AND ACCOUNTING New Zealand's central bank, which is responsible for managing the government's monetary policy, ensuring financial stability, and printing and distributing currency. Abbr **RBNZ**

reserve currency FINANCE, BANKING, AND ACCOUNTING foreign currency that a central bank holds for use in international trade

reserve for fluctuations FINANCE, BANKING, AND ACCOUNTING money set aside to allow for changes in the values of currencies

reserve requirements FINANCE, BANKING, AND ACCOUNTING the requirements an agency levies on a nation's banks to hold reserves

reserves FINANCE, BANKING, AND ACCOUNTING the money that a bank holds to ensure that it can satisfy its depositors' demands for withdrawals

resignation HR & PERSONNEL the act of voluntarily leaving a job. Resignation is normally signaled by a formal letter of resignation. On acceptance, a ***notice period*** is usually served before the employee can leave.

resizing HR & PERSONNEL see ***downsizing***

resource allocation OPERATIONS & PRODUCTION the process of assigning human and material resources to projects to ensure that they are used in the optimum way. Resource allocation is used in conjunction with ***network analysis*** techniques such as ***critical-path analysis*** (see ***critical-path method***). Basic data assembled for a project is displayed as a ***bar chart*** with start and finish times and resources required for each day of the project being easily identifiable. If there is a mismatch between planned resources and those available, resources can be reallocated or smoothed by manipulating start and finish times, or changing activities around. Resource allocation is usually computerized.

resource driver GENERAL MANAGEMENT see ***cost driver***

resource productivity GENERAL MANAGEMENT an environmentally friendly approach to production based on increasing the productivity of resources to reduce waste

resources OPERATIONS & PRODUCTION anything that is available to an organization to help it achieve its purpose. Resources are often categorized into finance, property, premises, equipment, people, and raw materials.

response bias STATISTICS the disparity between information that a survey respondent provides and data analysis, for example, a person claiming to watch little television but giving answers showing 30 hours' weekly viewing

response level MARKETING a measurement of response to an advertising or marketing campaign

response marketing E-COMMERCE in e-marketing, the process of managing responses or leads from the time they are received through to conversion to sale

response mechanism MARKETING a means of reply such as a coupon or reply card in an advertisement or mail shot by which customers can request further information

response rate STATISTICS the proportion of subjects in a statistical study who respond to a researcher's questionnaire

response surface methodology STATISTICS mathematical and statistical techniques that are used to improve product design systems

responsibility GENERAL MANAGEMENT the duty to carry out certain activities and be accountable for them to others

responsibility accounting FINANCE, BANKING, AND ACCOUNTING keeping financial records with an emphasis on who is responsible for each item

restated balance sheet FINANCE, BANKING, AND ACCOUNTING a balance sheet reframed to serve a particular purpose, such as highlighting depreciation on assets

rest break HR & PERSONNEL a period of time during the working day when an employee is allowed to be away from their workstation for a rest or meal break. Many countries have statutory regulations governing the frequency and length of rest breaks related to the hours worked in a day. Regulations also may cover the requirement for a ***rest period*** over a working week or month.

rest period HR & PERSONNEL the length of time between periods of work that an employee is entitled to have for rest. Many countries have statutory regulations governing the rights of employees to periods of rest over daily, weekly, and, sometimes, monthly timescales. Different allowances may be given to younger workers. In addition, employees may be entitled to ***rest breaks*** during the working day.

restraint of trade GENERAL MANAGEMENT, HR & PERSONNEL a term in a contract of employment that restricts a person from carrying on their trade or profession if they leave an organization. Generally illegal, it is usually intended to prevent key employees from leaving an organization to set up in competition.

restricted tender FINANCE, BANKING, AND ACCOUNTING an offer to buy shares only under specified conditions

restructuring GENERAL MANAGEMENT see ***corporate restructuring***

result-driven GENERAL MANAGEMENT relating to a form of ***corporate strategy*** focused on outcomes and achievements. A result-driven organization concentrates on meeting objectives, delivering to the required time, cost, and quality, and holds performance to be more important than ***procedures***.

résumé HR & PERSONNEL a document that provides a summary of personal career history, skills, and experience. A résumé is usually prepared to aid in a job application. A job advertisement may ask either for a résumé or instead may require a candidate to complete an ***application form***.

retail cooperative GENERAL MANAGEMENT a concern for the collective purchase and sale of goods by a group who share profits or benefits. Retail cooperatives were the first offshoot of the ***cooperative movement*** and profits were originally shared among members through dividend payments proportionate to a member's purchases.

retailer MARKETING, OPERATIONS & PRODUCTION an outlet through which products or services are sold to customers. Retailers can be put into three broad groups: independent traders, multiple stores, or ***retail cooperatives***.

retail investor FINANCE, BANKING, AND ACCOUNTING an investor who buys and sells shares in retail organizations

retail management MARKETING marketing or financial support aimed at improving the performance of retail outlets

retail price MARKETING a price charged to customers who buy in limited quantities

retail price index MARKETING a listing of the average levels of prices charged by retailers for goods or services. The retail price index is calculated on a set range of items, and usually excludes luxury goods. It is updated monthly, and provides a running indicator of changing costs. It provides a similar but narrower measure to the cost of living. Abbr **RPI**

retained earnings FINANCE, BANKING, AND ACCOUNTING see ***retained profits***

retained profits FINANCE, BANKING, AND ACCOUNTING the amount of profit remaining after tax and distribution to shareholders that is retained in a business and used as a reserve or to finance expansion or investment

retirement HR & PERSONNEL the voluntary or forced termination of employment because of age, illness, or disability. **Retirement age** is often stipulated in the ***contract of employment***. Differences between the retirement ages of men and women are no longer allowed in many countries. Employees may take ***early retirement*** from their employer, or may, with the agreement of their employer, take gradual, or ***phased retirement***. A ***pension*** may be drawn on reaching retirement age.

retirement age HR & PERSONNEL see ***retirement***

retirement pension FINANCE, BANKING, AND ACCOUNTING = ***pension***

retraining HR & PERSONNEL ***training*** designed to enable employees to perform a job that their previous training has not equipped them for or to adapt to changes in the workplace. Retraining may be needed when new methods or equipment are introduced or when jobs for which employees have trained are phased out. It may also be provided by employers or governments for employees who have been made ***redundant*** and are no longer able to find employment using the skills they already possess. The need for retraining may arise because of a decline in a particular industry sector or because of rapid technological change.

retrenchment FINANCE, BANKING, AND ACCOUNTING the reduction of costs in order to improve profitability

retrospective study STATISTICS a study that examines data collected before it began, for example, to measure the risk factors that predispose people to disease

return FINANCE, BANKING, AND ACCOUNTING
1. = ***rate of return***
2. = ***tax return***
3. the income derived from an activity

return on assets FINANCE, BANKING, AND ACCOUNTING a measure of profitability calculated by expressing a company's net income as a percentage of total assets

return on capital FINANCE, BANKING, AND ACCOUNTING a ratio of the profit made in a financial year as a percentage of the capital employed

return on capital employed FINANCE, BANKING, AND ACCOUNTING in the United Kingdom, the profitability of a corporation expressed as a percentage of its capital in a formulation similar to that of ROE

return on equity FINANCE, BANKING, AND ACCOUNTING the ratio of a company's net income as a percentage of book value

return on investment FINANCE, BANKING, AND ACCOUNTING a ratio of the profit made in a financial year as a percentage of an investment

return on net assets FINANCE, BANKING, AND ACCOUNTING a ratio of the profit made in a financial year as a percentage of the assets of a company

return on sales FINANCE, BANKING, AND ACCOUNTING see ***profit margin***

returns to scale ECONOMICS the proportionate increase in a country's or firm's output as a result of proportionate increases in all its inputs

revaluation ECONOMICS the restoration of the value of a country's depreciated currency, for example, by encouraging exports to increase foreign exchange

revaluation of assets FINANCE, BANKING, AND ACCOUNTING revaluation of a company's assets to take account of inflation or changes in value since the assets were acquired

revaluation reserve FINANCE, BANKING, AND ACCOUNTING money set aside to account for the fact that the values of assets may vary due to accounting in different currencies

revalue FINANCE, BANKING, AND ACCOUNTING to change the exchange rate of a currency

Revans, Reginald William (*b.* 1907) GENERAL MANAGEMENT British educator and academic. Originator of ***action learning***, explained in the book of the same name (1980), which rejected the traditional approach to ***management education*** in favor of learning from sharing problems with others.
REG REVANS (pp. 1042–43)

revenue GENERAL MANAGEMENT the income generated by a product or service over a period of time

revenue anticipation note FINANCE, BANKING, AND ACCOUNTING a government-issued debt instrument for which expected income from taxation is collateral

revenue bond FINANCE, BANKING, AND ACCOUNTING a bond that a government issues, to be repaid from the money made from the project financed with it

revenue ledger FINANCE, BANKING, AND ACCOUNTING a record of all income received by an organization

revenue sharing FINANCE, BANKING, AND ACCOUNTING
1. distribution to states by the federal government of money that it collects in taxes
2. the distribution of income within limited partnerships

revenue stamp FINANCE, BANKING, AND ACCOUNTING a stamp that a government issues to certify that somebody has paid a tax

revenue tariff FINANCE, BANKING, AND ACCOUNTING a tax levied on imports or exports to raise revenue for a national government

reversal stop FINANCE, BANKING, AND ACCOUNTING a price at which a trader stops buying and starts selling a security, or vice versa

reverse bear hug GENERAL MANAGEMENT see ***bear hug***

reverse commuter GENERAL MANAGEMENT a commuter who travels to work in the opposite direction to the majority of people (*slang*)

reverse engineering OPERATIONS & PRODUCTION the taking apart of a product to establish how it was put together. Reverse engineering enables a company to redesign a product. It also enables competitors to analyze the composition, technology, and development of rival products. Also known as ***decompilation***

reverse leverage FINANCE, BANKING, AND ACCOUNTING the negative flow of cash, or borrowing money at a rate of interest higher than the expected rate of return on investing the money borrowed

reverse mortgage FINANCE, BANKING, AND ACCOUNTING a financial arrangement in which a lender such as a bank takes over a mortgage then pays an annuity to the homeowner

reverse split FINANCE, BANKING, AND ACCOUNTING the issuing to shareholders of a fraction of one share for every share that they own. See ***split***

reverse takeover GENERAL MANAGEMENT the ***takeover*** of a large company by a smaller one, or the takeover of a public company by a private one

revolving charge account FINANCE, BANKING, AND ACCOUNTING a charge account with a company for use in buying that company's goods with ***revolving credit***

revolving credit FINANCE, BANKING, AND ACCOUNTING credit given to a person up to a certain amount, with each repayment of the sum making the same amount of credit available again

revolving fund FINANCE, BANKING, AND ACCOUNTING a fund the resources of which are replenished from the revenue of the projects that it finances

reward management HR & PERSONNEL the setting up, maintenance, and development of a system that rewards the work done by employees. Reward management involves offering not only ***base pay***, but also an ***incentive scheme*** and ***fringe benefits***. Levels of reward may be based on different criteria. Some involve ***performance appraisal*** to determine whether an employee merits a certain reward, while others may be dependent on length of service, type of job, or team or company performance. The notion of a reward system is gradually replacing the traditional idea of a standard pay system, as it incorporates all aspects of employee compensation into one package.

Ricardo, **David** (1772–1823) GENERAL MANAGEMENT British economist. Developer of the concept of ***comparative advantage***, as explained in his book *Principles of Political Economy* (1820).

rich media E-COMMERCE technology that can integrate audio, video, and high-resolution graphics

Ridderstråle, **Jonas** (*b.* 1966) GENERAL MANAGEMENT Swedish academic. See ***Nordstrom, Kjell***

ride the curve E-COMMERCE to take advantage of rapid growth in demand for a new technology as it becomes widely adopted (*slang*)

right first time OPERATIONS & PRODUCTION a concept integral to ***total quality management*** where there is a commitment to customers not to make mistakes. The approach requires employees at all levels to commit to, and take responsibility for, achieving this goal. ***Quality circles*** are sometimes used as a method to help in this process.

rights issue FINANCE, BANKING, AND ACCOUNTING an issue of new shares to existing holders who have the right to buy them at a discount

rightsizing GENERAL MANAGEMENT ***corporate restructuring***, or ***rationalization***, with the aim of reducing costs, and improving efficiency and effectiveness. Rightsizing is often used as a euphemism for ***downsizing***, or ***delayering***, with the suggestion that it is not as far-reaching. Rightsizing can also be used to describe increasing the size of an organization, perhaps as an attempt to correct a previous downsizing, or delayering, exercise.

rights offering FINANCE, BANKING, AND ACCOUNTING an offering for sale of a ***rights issue***

risk GENERAL MANAGEMENT the possibility of suffering damage or loss in the face of uncertainty about the outcome of actions, future events, or circumstances. Organizations are exposed to various types of risk including damage to property, injury to personnel, financial loss, and legal liability. These may affect profitability, hinder the achievement of objectives, or lead to business interruption or failure. Risk may be deemed high or low depending on the probability of an adverse outcome. Risks that can be quantified on the basis of past experience are insurable and those that cannot be calculated are uninsurable.

risk adjusted return on capital FINANCE, BANKING, AND ACCOUNTING return on capital calculated in a way that takes into account the risks associated with income

risk analysis GENERAL MANAGEMENT the identification of risks to which an organization is exposed and the assessment of the potential impact of those risks on the organization. The aim of risk analysis is to identify and measure the risks associated with different courses of action in order to inform the ***decision making*** process. In the context of business decision making, risk analysis is especially used in investment decisions and capital investment appraisal. Techniques used in risk analysis include sensitivity analysis, probability analysis, ***simulation***, and modeling. Risk analysis may be used to develop an organizational ***risk profile***, and also may be the first stage in a ***risk management*** program.

risk arbitrage FINANCE, BANKING, AND ACCOUNTING ***arbitrage*** without certainty of profit

risk assessment GENERAL MANAGEMENT the determination of the level of risk in a particular course of action. Risk assessments are an important tool in areas such as ***health and safety*** management and ***environmental management***. Results of a risk assessment can be used to identify areas in which safety can be improved. Risk assessment can also be used to determine more intangible forms of risk, including economic and social risk, and can inform the ***scenario planning*** process. The amount of risk involved in a particular course of action is compared to its expected benefits to provide evidence for decision making.

risk-bearing economy of scale FINANCE, BANKING, AND ACCOUNTING conducting business on such a large scale that the risk of loss is reduced because it is spread over so many independent events, as in the issuance of insurance policies

risk capital FINANCE, BANKING, AND ACCOUNTING = ***venture capital***

risk factor GENERAL MANAGEMENT the degree of risk in a project or other business activity

risk-free return FINANCE, BANKING, AND ACCOUNTING the profit made from an investment that involves no risk

risk management GENERAL MANAGEMENT the range of activities undertaken by an organization to control and minimize threats to the continuing efficiency, profitability, and success of its operations. The process of risk management includes the identification and analysis of risks to which the organization is exposed, the assessment of potential impacts on the business, and deciding what action can be taken to eliminate or reduce risk and deal with the impact of unpredictable events causing loss or damage. Risk management strategies include taking out insurance against financial loss or legal liability and introducing safety or security measures.

risk profile GENERAL MANAGEMENT
1. an outline of the risks to which an organization is exposed. An organizational risk profile may be developed in the course of ***risk analysis*** and used for ***risk management***. It examines the nature of the threats faced by an organization, the likelihood of adverse effects occurring, and the level of disruption and costs associated with each type of risk.
2. an analysis of the willingness of individuals or organizations to take risks. A risk profile describes the level of risk considered acceptable by an individual, or by the leaders of an organization, and considers how this will affect ***decision making*** and ***corporate strategy***.

robot OPERATIONS & PRODUCTION a programmable machine equipped with sensing capabilities used in ***production*** environments. Robots are used in automatic assembly and ***automated handling*** situations.

robotics GENERAL MANAGEMENT the industrial use of robots to perform repetitive tasks. Robotics is an application of artificial intelligence.

Roddick, **Anita Lucia** (*b.* 1942) GENERAL MANAGEMENT British business executive. Founder of the Body Shop, whose principles, reflected in the company's ***core values*** of ***social responsibility*** and care for the environment, are explained in her autobiography *Business as Unusual* (2000).

Roethlisberger, **Fritz Jules** (1898–1974) GENERAL MANAGEMENT U.S. academic. Collaborated with ***Elton Mayo*** in the ***Hawthorne experiments***, leading the research and data analysis and publicizing the findings in *Management and the Worker* (1939).
ELTON MAYO (pp. 1020–21)

rogue trader FINANCE, BANKING, AND ACCOUNTING a dealer in stocks and shares who uses illegal methods to make profits

role ambiguity GENERAL MANAGEMENT a lack of clarity on the part of an employee about the expectations of colleagues concerning his or her role within an organization. Role ambiguity may occur in newly created posts or in positions that are undergoing change. When role ambiguity extends to responsibilities or priorities it can lead to ***role conflict***.

role conflict GENERAL MANAGEMENT a situation in which two or more job requirements are incompatible. Role conflict can arise from others' misperceptions of what the priorities of a role holder should be. It may also be caused by a division of loyalties between departmental peers and the organization or between personal professional ethics and those of the organization.

role culture GENERAL MANAGEMENT a style of ***corporate culture***, identified by ***Charles Handy***, which assumes that employees are rational and that roles can be defined and discharged within clearly defined procedures. An organization with a role culture is believed to be generally very stable but poor at implementing ***change management***.
CHARLES HANDY (pp. 1000–01)

role playing HR & PERSONNEL performing either as oneself in a contrived situation, in order to analyze how one reacts in such a setting, or in the manner expected of another person. The role playing technique is a useful tool in ***training***, as it enables trainees to gain a better understanding of themselves, of other people, new situations, and different jobs.

roll-out MARKETING the full-scale implementation of an advertising campaign or marketing program

roll up FINANCE, BANKING, AND ACCOUNTING the addition of interest amounts to principal in loan repayments

root cause analysis GENERAL MANAGEMENT a technique used in ***problem solving*** to identify the underlying reason why something has gone wrong or why a difficulty has arisen. The root cause of a problem may be identified by repeatedly asking the question "Why?", by examining relationships of cause and effect, or by defining the distinctive features of the problem and developing a number of hypotheses that can be tested. Root cause analysis has been criticized on the grounds that it presupposes a single source for a problem, while in reality the situation may be more complex.

rootless capitalism GENERAL MANAGEMENT a form of capitalism that is not tied to a specific country or economy

rort (*ANZ*) GENERAL MANAGEMENT
1. an illegal or underhand strategy
2. to manipulate or break the rules of a system for personal gain

RosettaNet E-COMMERCE a consortium focusing on the development of e-business interfaces and a common global business language that would permit sharing of efficient e-business processes, for example, manufacturing, distribution, and sales

ROTFL *abbr* GENERAL MANAGEMENT rolling on the floor laughing (*slang*)

round figures FINANCE, BANKING, AND ACCOUNTING figures that have been adjusted up or down to the nearest 10, 100, 1,000, and so on

rounding STATISTICS the practice of reducing the number of significant digits in a number, for example, expressing a figure that has four decimal places with only two decimal places

router GENERAL MANAGEMENT a telecommunications device used to transfer calls to an alternative network that may offer cheaper rates

routing number FINANCE, BANKING, AND ACCOUNTING a combination of numbers that identifies a bank branch on official documentation, such as bank statements and checks

royalties FINANCE, BANKING, AND ACCOUNTING a proportion of the income from the sale of a product paid to its creator, for example, an inventor, author, or composer

RPI ECONOMICS see ***retail price index***

RRP MARKETING see ***resale price maintenance***

RSI GENERAL MANAGEMENT see ***repetitive strain injury***

RTM *abbr* GENERAL MANAGEMENT read the manual (*slang*)

RTSC *abbr* GENERAL MANAGEMENT read the source code (*slang*)

RUBBY MARKETING Rich Urban Biker (*slang*)

Rucker plan OPERATIONS & PRODUCTION, HR & PERSONNEL a type of ***gain sharing*** scheme that is concerned with the value added by labor. The Rucker plan was developed in the 1950s by Allen W. Rucker. A typical Rucker plan includes a ***suggestion scheme***, a committee system, and a ***bonus*** formula, based on ***value added***. It as-

  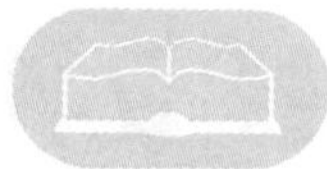    

sesses the relationship between the value added to goods as they pass through the manufacturing process, and the total labor costs. Bonuses are earned when the current ratio is better than the base ratio over a given time period. A Rucker plan usually has a far less elaborate structure than the similar ***Scanlon plan***.

rumortrage FINANCE, BANKING, AND ACCOUNTING speculation in securities issued by companies that are rumored to be the target of an imminent takeover attempt (*slang*)

run STATISTICS an uninterrupted sequence of the same value in a statistical series

run with something GENERAL MANAGEMENT to pursue an idea or project (*slang*)

rust belt GENERAL MANAGEMENT the manufacturing areas in the Midwest that have experienced severe decline following the move away from manufacturing to service industries (*slang*)

SA FINANCE, BANKING, AND ACCOUNTING see ***Société Anonyme, Sociedad Anónima***

sabbatical HR & PERSONNEL a period of ***special leave***, traditionally a year, granted to an employee for the purpose of study, work experience, or travel

sabotage GENERAL MANAGEMENT a deliberate action to damage property or equipment. In an industrial context sabotage may be undertaken by employees who have a grievance against an employer in order to halt production or undermine the efficiency of an organization. Sabotage of this type may include time wasting or other measures designed to reduce ***productivity***. Sabotage against organizations is also undertaken by terrorist or political groups in protest against their actions or policies. Security measures may be necessary to prevent sabotage.

SADC *abbr* FINANCE, BANKING, AND ACCOUNTING Southern African Development Community, an organization that aims to harmonize economic development in countries of Southern Africa. Member countries are Angola, Botswana, Democratic Republic of Congo, Lesotho, Malawi, Mauritius, Mozambique, Namibia, South Africa, Seychelles, Swaziland, Tanzania, Zambia, Zimbabwe.

salad
let's toss it around and see if it makes a salad GENERAL MANAGEMENT let's try this idea and see if it is successful (*slang*)

salary HR & PERSONNEL a form of ***pay*** given to employees at regular intervals in exchange for the work they have done. Traditionally, a salary is a form of remuneration given to professional employees on a monthly basis. In modern usage, the word refers to any form of pay that employees receive on a regular basis, and it is often used interchangeably with the term ***wages***. A salary is normally paid straight into an employee's account.

salary ceiling HR & PERSONNEL
1. the highest level on a ***pay scale*** that a particular employee can achieve under their contract
2. an upper limit on ***pay*** imposed by government or according to ***labor union*** and employer agreements

salary review HR & PERSONNEL a reassessment of an individual employee's rate of ***pay***, usually carried out on an annual basis

salary scale HR & PERSONNEL = ***pay scale***

sales MARKETING the activity of selling a company's products or services, the income generated by this, or the department that deals with selling

sales channel GENERAL MANAGEMENT a means of distributing products to the marketplace, either directly to the end customer, or indirectly through intermediaries such as retailers or dealers

sales conference MARKETING a conference at which the members of a sales team are brought together for a review or a significant announcement such as a product launch

sales contest MARKETING a prize competition for salespeople, often part of an ***incentive scheme***, designed to increase sales. A sales contest winner is usually the person who has achieved the most sales for a particular time period.

sales force MARKETING a group of salespeople or sales representatives responsible for the sales of either a single product or the entire range of an organization's products. A sales force normally reports to a ***sales manager***. Also known as ***sales team***

sales force communications MARKETING communications aimed at improving the performance and market awareness of a sales force

sales forecast MARKETING a prediction of future sales, based mainly on past sales performance. Sales forecasting takes into account the economic climate, current sales trends, company capacity for production, ***company policy***, and ***market research***. A sales forecast can be a good indicator of future sales in stable market conditions, but may be less reliable in times of rapid market change.

sales manager MARKETING the manager directly responsible for the planning, organization, and performance of the ***sales force***

sales network MARKETING the distribution network by which goods and services are sold. A sales network will include both independent agents and retailers.

sales office MARKETING the department responsible for selling a company's products or services, or the office in the company's premises that this department occupies

sales outlet MARKETING a company's office that deals with customers in a particular region or country

sales plan GENERAL MANAGEMENT the development of the future objectives of a sales department in order to improve performance and increase sales. A sales plan is a form of ***business plan*** that sets out the short- and long-term opportunities for the sales department, concentrating on building on the department's strengths and analyzing and avoiding weaknesses. It also includes the setting of future sales objectives, based on realistic projections, looking at future costs, and taking into account the objectives of other departments.

sales presentation MARKETING a structured product presentation using a binder, flipchart, or laptop computer

sales promotion MARKETING activities, usually short-term, designed to attract attention to a particular product and to increase its sales using ***advertising*** and publicity. Sales promotion usually runs in conjunction with an advertising campaign that offers free samples or money-off coupons. During the period of a sales promotion, the product may be offered at a reduced price and the campaign may be supported by additional telephone or door-to-door selling or by competitions. Also known as ***promotion***

sales promotion agency MARKETING an organization that specializes in planning, creating, and implementing sales promotion activities

sales quota GENERAL MANAGEMENT a target set for the ***sales force*** stating the number and range of products or services that should be sold

sales representative MARKETING a salesperson selling the products or services of a particular organization or manufacturer. Sales representatives are sometimes employed directly by a company as part of the ***sales force***, or they may work independently and be employed by contract. Sales representatives are often paid by commission.

sales resistance MARKETING a potential customer's refusal to allow a ***sales representative's*** sales pitch to persuade them to buy. Sales resistance may be caused, for example, by lack of interest in, or determined dislike of, the product or service offered.

sales statistics MARKETING data relating to the sales of a particular ***product***, service, or ***brand***. Sales statistics include numbers and types of products sold, areas where they are sold, calls and visits made, contacts established, categories of customers, costs and time spent on sales activities, and administration. These statistics are often used in conjunction with the ***sales plan*** and for sales forecasting. They can also be used to identify areas of weakness in sales support staff and to identify areas for training. Statistics can also contribute to the identification of profitable product lines or products to ***abandon***.

sales team MARKETING see ***sales force***

sales territory MARKETING a defined area within which a designated salesperson is responsible for selling a product or service. A sales territory is usually organized along geographic lines, for example, counties or regions, but it can also be defined by ***market sector*** or by product group.

sales turnover MARKETING the total amount sold within a specified time period, usually a year. Sales turnover is often expressed in monetary terms but can also be expressed in terms of the total amount of stock or products sold.

salmon day GENERAL MANAGEMENT a day spent making a great deal of effort to achieve something but getting nowhere (*slang*)

sample STATISTICS a subset of a population in a statistical study chosen so that selected properties of the overall population can be investigated

sample size STATISTICS the number of individuals included in a statistical survey

sample survey STATISTICS a statistical study of a sample of individuals designed to collect information on specific subjects such as buying habits or voting behavior

sampling
1. MARKETING a sales promotion technique in which customers and prospects are offered a free sample of a product
2. OPERATIONS & PRODUCTION the selection of a small proportion of a set of items being studied, from which valid inferences about the whole set or population can be made. Sampling makes it possible to obtain valid research results when it is impracticable to survey the whole population. The size of the sample needed for valid results depends on a number of factors, including the uniformity of the population being studied and the level of accuracy required. The technique is based on the laws of probability, and a number of different sampling methods can be used, including ***random sampling*** and ***nonrandom sampling***. Specialized applications of sampling include ***activity sampling***, ***acceptance sampling***, and ***attribute sampling***.

sampling design STATISTICS the procedure by which a particular sample is chosen from a population

sampling error STATISTICS the difference between the population characteristic being estimated in a statistical study and the result produced by the sample investigated

sampling units STATISTICS the elements chosen to be sampled by a sampling design

sampling variation STATISTICS variation between different samples of the same size taken from the same population

sanity check GENERAL MANAGEMENT a check to verify that no obvious mistakes have been made (*slang*)

SARS *abbr* FINANCE, BANKING, AND ACCOUNTING South African Revenue Service

satellite center GENERAL MANAGEMENT a ***telecenter*** that houses employees from a single organization

savings and loan association FINANCE, BANKING, AND ACCOUNTING a chartered bank that offers savings accounts, pays dividends, and invests in new mortgages. See ***thrift institution***

savings bank FINANCE, BANKING, AND ACCOUNTING a bank that specializes in managing small investments. See ***thrift institution***

savings bond FINANCE, BANKING, AND ACCOUNTING a U.S. bond that an individual buys from the federal government

savings function FINANCE, BANKING, AND ACCOUNTING an expression of the extent to which people save money instead of spending it

savings ratio ECONOMICS the proportion of the income of a country or household that is saved in a particular period

SC FINANCE, BANKING, AND ACCOUNTING see ***Securities Commission***

scaleability E-COMMERCE the capability of the hardware and software that support an e-business to grow in capacity as transaction demand increases

Scanlon plan HR & PERSONNEL a type of ***gain sharing*** plan that pays a ***bonus*** to employees for incremental improvements. The Scanlon plan was developed by Joseph N. Scanlon in the 1930s. A typical Scanlon plan includes an employee ***suggestion scheme***, a committee system, and a formula-based bonus system. The simplest formula is: base ratio = HR payroll costs divided by net sales or production value. A Scanlon organization is characterized by ***teamwork*** and ***employee participation***. A bonus is paid when the current ratio is better than that of the base period. A Scanlon plan focuses attention on the variables over which the organization and its employees have some control. See ***Rucker plan***

scatter STATISTICS the amount by which a set of observations deviates from its mean

scatter chart *or* **scatter diagram** STATISTICS a chart or diagram that plots a sample of bivariate observations in two dimensions

scatter diagram STATISTICS a diagram or graphic representation that plots a sample of bivariate observations in two dimensions

scenario GENERAL MANAGEMENT a possible future state of affairs or sequence of events. Scenarios are imagined or projected on the basis of current circumstances and trends and expectations of change in the future.

scenario planning GENERAL MANAGEMENT a technique that requires the use of a scenario in the process of ***strategic planning*** (see ***planning***) to aid the development of ***corporate strategy*** in the face of uncertainty about the future. Scenario planning was developed in a military context during the 1940s. Its use in a business context was pioneered at Royal Dutch

  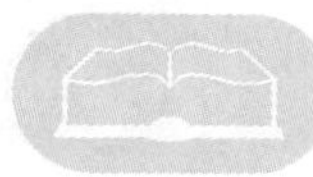    

Shell during the 1960s and increased after the 1972 oil crisis. The process of identifying alternative scenarios of the future, based on a range of differing assumptions, can help managers anticipate changes in the business environment and raise awareness of the frame of reference within which they are operating. The scenarios are then used to assist in both the development of strategies for dealing with unexpected events and the choice between alternative strategic options.

Schein, Edgar H. (*b.* 1928) GENERAL MANAGEMENT U.S. academic. The first to define ***corporate culture*** in *Organizational Culture and Leadership* (1985), and the developer of the notion of the ***psychological contract***, originated by ***Chris Argyris***.

CHRIS ARGYRIS (pp. 964–65); EDGAR SCHEIN (pp. 1044–45)

schmooze GENERAL MANAGEMENT to behave flatteringly during a social event toward somebody who might be in a position to benefit your career (*slang*)

Schön, Donald A. (1931–97) GENERAL MANAGEMENT U.S. academic.

CHRIS ARGYRIS (pp. 964–65)

Schonberger, Richard J. (*b.* 1937) GENERAL MANAGEMENT U.S. industrial engineer and writer. Known for showing how techniques such as ***total quality management*** and ***just-in-time*** can be used to achieve ***world class manufacturing***. Author of *World Class Manufacturing* (1986).

✔ DEVELOPING A STRATEGY FOR WORLD-CLASS BUSINESS (pp. 460–61)

Schumacher, Ernst Friedrich (1911–77) GENERAL MANAGEMENT German economist. Author of *Small is Beautiful* (1973), a counterblast to the dominance of big companies. Schumacher developed his people-centered approach to life and business working alongside ***Reg Revans***.

science park GENERAL MANAGEMENT an area developed as a location for high-tech or research-based companies. Usually developed by a university or local authority, a science park is often in the same locality as a higher education establishment.

scientific management GENERAL MANAGEMENT, HR & PERSONNEL an analytical approach to managing activities by optimizing efficiency and ***productivity*** through measurement and control. Scientific management theories, attributed to ***Frederick Winslow Taylor***, dominated the 20th century, and many management techniques such as ***benchmarking***, ***total quality management***, and ***business process reengineering*** result from a scientific management approach. Other figures such as ***Henry Gantt*** and ***Frank*** and ***Lillian Gilbreth*** were firmly in the scientific school and furthered its influence, particularly through the ***time and motion study***. Such was the dominance of Taylor's influence that scientific management is also known as Taylorism. The main criticism of Taylorism is that it degenerated into an inhumane and mechanistic approach to working, treating people like machines.

screen-based activity GENERAL MANAGEMENT a task that requires access to a computer

screening study STATISTICS a medical statistical study of a population carried out to investigate the prevalence of a disease

screen popping GENERAL MANAGEMENT see ***computer telephony integration*** (*slang*)

screensaver GENERAL MANAGEMENT a program designed to prevent a static image being burned into the phosphor monitor screen when a computer is idle by displaying a series of moving images

scrip dividend FINANCE, BANKING, AND ACCOUNTING a dividend that shareholders can accept in the form of possibly fractional shares of the company instead of cash

scrip issue FINANCE, BANKING, AND ACCOUNTING = ***stock split***

scripophily FINANCE, BANKING, AND ACCOUNTING the collection of valueless share or bond certificates

scroll bar E-COMMERCE a bar at the right-hand side and/or bottom of a window that enables users to view more information on a Web page

SCUM GENERAL MANAGEMENT Self-Centered Urban Male (*slang*)

Sdn FINANCE, BANKING, AND ACCOUNTING see ***Sendirian***

seagull manager HR & PERSONNEL a manager who is brought in to deal with a project, makes a lot of fuss, achieves nothing, and then leaves (*slang*)

search engine E-COMMERCE
1. a Web site that enables users to conduct ***keyword*** searches of indexed information on its database
2. the software used in this process

seasonal adjustment FINANCE, BANKING, AND ACCOUNTING an adjustment made to accounts to allow for any short-term seasonal factors, such as Christmas sales, that may distort the figures

seasonal business FINANCE, BANKING, AND ACCOUNTING trade that is affected by seasonal factors, for example, trade in goods such as suntan products or Christmas trees

seasonal products MARKETING products that are only marketed at particular times of the year, for example, Christmas trees or fireworks

seasonal variation STATISTICS the variation of data according to particular times of the year such as winter months or a tourist season

seasoned equity FINANCE, BANKING, AND ACCOUNTING shares that have traded long enough to have a well-established value

seasoned issue FINANCE, BANKING, AND ACCOUNTING an issue for which there is a preexisting market. See ***unseasoned issue***

SEATS FINANCE, BANKING, AND ACCOUNTING Stock Exchange Automatic Trading System, the electronic screen-trading system operated by the Australian Stock Exchange.It was introduced in 1987.

SEC FINANCE, BANKING, AND ACCOUNTING see ***Securities and Exchange Commission***

secondary issue FINANCE, BANKING, AND ACCOUNTING an offer of listed shares that have not previously been publicly traded

secondary market FINANCE, BANKING, AND ACCOUNTING a market that trades in existing shares rather than new share issues, for example, a stock exchange

secondary offering FINANCE, BANKING, AND ACCOUNTING an offering of securities of a kind that is already on the market

secondary sector ECONOMICS the sector of the labor force with employment options other than the wage earned in the market, consisting of married women, the semi-retired, and young people

secondment HR & PERSONNEL the temporary transfer of a member of staff to another organization for a defined length of time, usually for a specific purpose. Secondment has grown in popularity in recent years, primarily for ***career development*** purposes. Secondments have been carried out between the public and private sectors as a mechanism to share management techniques and to disseminate ***best practice***.

secretary of the board GENERAL MANAGEMENT see ***company secretary***

Section 21 Company (*S. Africa*) FINANCE, BANKING, AND ACCOUNTING a company established as a nonprofit organization

sector index FINANCE, BANKING, AND ACCOUNTING an index of companies in particular parts of a market whose shares are listed on a general or specialist stock exchange

secular trend STATISTICS the underlying smooth movement of a ***time series*** over a time period of several years

secured bond FINANCE, BANKING, AND ACCOUNTING a collateralized bond

secure electronic transaction protocol E-COMMERCE = ***SET***

secure server E-COMMERCE a combination of hardware and software that secures e-commerce credit card transactions so that there is no risk of unauthorized people gaining access to credit card details online

secure sockets layer E-COMMERCE = ***SSL***

securities account FINANCE, BANKING, AND ACCOUNTING an account that shows the value of financial assets held by a person or organization

securities analyst FINANCE, BANKING, AND ACCOUNTING a professional person who studies the performance of securities and the companies that issue them

Securities and Exchange Commission FINANCE, BANKING, AND ACCOUNTING the government agency that regulates the securities industry. Abbr **SEC**

Securities and Investment Board FINANCE, BANKING, AND ACCOUNTING the agency that regulates the securities industry in the United Kingdom

Securities Commission FINANCE, BANKING, AND ACCOUNTING a statutory body responsible for monitoring standards in the New Zealand securities markets and for promoting investment in New Zealand. Abbr **SC**

securities deposit account FINANCE, BANKING, AND ACCOUNTING a brokerage account into which securities are deposited electronically

Securities Institute of Australia FINANCE, BANKING, AND ACCOUNTING a national professional body that represents people involved in the Australian securities and financial services industry. Abbr **SIA**

security deposit FINANCE, BANKING, AND ACCOUNTING an amount of money paid before a transaction occurs to provide the seller with recourse in the event that the transaction is not concluded and this is the buyer's fault

security investment company FINANCE, BANKING, AND ACCOUNTING a financial institution that specializes in the analysis and trading of securities

seed capital (*U.K.*) GENERAL MANAGEMENT = ***seed money***

seed money GENERAL MANAGEMENT a usually modest amount of money used to convert an idea into a viable business. Seed money is a form of ***venture capital***.

segmentation STATISTICS the division of the data in a study into regions

selection bias STATISTICS the effect on a statistical or clinical trial of unmeasured variables that are unknown to the researcher

selection board HR & PERSONNEL see ***panel interview***

selection instrument HR & PERSONNEL see ***psychometric test***

selection interviewing HR & PERSONNEL see ***interviewing***

selection of personnel HR & PERSONNEL see ***recruitment***

selection test HR & PERSONNEL see ***psychometric test***

self actualization HR & PERSONNEL the maximization of your skills and talents. Self actualization was considered by ***Abraham Maslow*** as the pinnacle of his hierarchy of needs. Also known as ***self-fulfillment***

self-appraisal HR & PERSONNEL an assessment carried out by an individual on his or her own ability or understanding. Self-appraisal is sometimes part of the ***performance appraisal*** process but is also carried out as part of ***continuing professional development*** or ***career development***.

self-assessment OPERATIONS & PRODUCTION a systematic and regular review of the activities of an organization and the referencing of the results against a model of ***excellence*** that is carried out by the organization itself. Self assessment allows an organization to identify its strengths and weaknesses and to plan improvement activities. The technique came to prominence with the spread of the ***EFQM Excellence Model***.

self-certification HR & PERSONNEL the notification and recording of the first seven days of an employee's ***sick leave***. Self-certification requires the completion of a form by the employee on their return to work, indicating the nature and duration of their illness and countersigned by a manager.

self-development HR & PERSONNEL = ***personal development***

self-directed team HR & PERSONNEL see ***autonomous work group***

self-employment HR & PERSONNEL being in business on one's own account, either on a ***freelance*** basis, or by reason of owning a business, and not being engaged as an ***employee*** under a ***contract of employment***. The distinction between the self-employed and the employed is not always clear in law, but has a crucial bearing on matters such as the tax treatment of pay and the applicability of ***employment protection***. A self-employed person may be an ***employer*** of others.

self-fulfillment HR & PERSONNEL = ***self actualization***

self-insurance FINANCE, BANKING, AND ACCOUNTING the practice of saving money to pay for a possible loss rather than taking out an insurance policy against it

self-liquidating FINANCE, BANKING, AND ACCOUNTING providing enough income to pay off the amount borrowed for financing

self-liquidating premium MARKETING a sales promotion technique that pays for itself, in which customers send money and vouchers or proof of purchase to obtain a premium gift

self-liquidating promotion MARKETING a sales promotion in which the cost of the campaign is covered by the incremental revenue generated by the promotion

self-managed team HR & PERSONNEL = ***autonomous work group***

self-managed work team HR & PERSONNEL = ***autonomous work group***

self-managing team HR & PERSONNEL = ***autonomous work group***

self-regulatory organization GENERAL MANAGEMENT an organization that polices its members, for example, an exchange

sell and build GENERAL MANAGEMENT an approach to manufacturing in which the producer builds only when a customer has placed an order and paid for it, rather than building products for stock

seller's market FINANCE, BANKING, AND ACCOUNTING a market in which sellers can dictate prices, typically because demand is high or there is a product shortage

selling season FINANCE, BANKING, AND ACCOUNTING a period in which market conditions are favorable to sellers

seminar GENERAL MANAGEMENT a small business meeting at which participants present information or exchange ideas

Semler, **Ricardo** (*b.* 1957) GENERAL MANAGEMENT Brazilian business executive. Owner of Semco, which he ***turned around***, using three main strategies: ***employee democracy***, ***open book management***, and self-setting salaries. His methods were written up in *Maverick!* (1993).

Sendirian GENERAL MANAGEMENT Malay term for "limited." Companies can use "sendirian berhad" or "Sdn Bhd" in their name instead of "Pte Ltd." Abbr **Sdn**

Senge, **Peter** (*b.* 1947) GENERAL MANAGEMENT U.S. academic. Popularized the theory of the ***learning organization***, first suggested by ***Chris Argyris*** and ***Donald Schön***. Senge studied how organizations develop adaptive capabilities in a world of increasing complexity and change. His work culminated in the publication of *The Fifth Discipline: the Art and Practice of the Learning Organization* (1990).

CHRIS ARGYRIS (pp. 964–65); PETER SENGE (pp. 1046–47)

senior debt FINANCE, BANKING, AND ACCOUNTING a debt whose holder has more claim on the debtor's assets than the holder of another debt. See ***junior debt***

senior management GENERAL MANAGEMENT the managers and executives at the highest level of an organization. Senior management includes the ***board of directors***. Senior management has responsibility for ***corporate governance***, ***corporate strategy***, and the interests of all the organization's ***stakeholders***. Also known as ***management team***

senior mortgage FINANCE, BANKING, AND ACCOUNTING a mortgage whose holder has more claim on the debtor's assets than the holder of another mortgage. See ***junior mortgage***

sensitivity training HR & PERSONNEL group-based training designed to help participants develop ***interpersonal skills*** (see ***interpersonal communication***). Sensitivity training is a form of human relations training, and was developed by ***Kurt Lewin***, and others at the National Training Laboratory in the United States during the 1940s. The format most commonly used is a **training group**, or **T-Group**, consisting of between 7 and 12 people who meet together over a period of about two weeks, normally at a residential training center. The aims are to develop sensitivity and awareness of participants' own feelings and reactions, to increase their understanding of ***group dynamics***, and to help them learn to adapt their behavior in appropriate ways. Group activities may include discussion, games, and exercises but may also be relatively unstructured. The provision of ***feedback*** is a key feature. This type of training has been controversial, as the group interactions can be confrontational, and some have suggested that participants could suffer emotional harm. The popularity of T-Groups has declined since the 1960s and 1970s. Sensitivity training is also known as **laboratory training**. This term emphasizes the way participants are placed in an environment in which different ways of interacting can be tried out. Lewin's early work in this field was developed at the National Training Laboratories, founded in 1947, in the United States.

KURT LEWIN (pp. 1014–15)

separation HR & PERSONNEL a term used to refer to ***termination of service*** or ***resignation***

separation pay HR & PERSONNEL = ***severance pay***

serial entrepreneur GENERAL MANAGEMENT an ***entrepreneur*** who sets up a string of new ventures, one after the other

seriation STATISTICS the process of arranging a set of objects in a series on the basis of similarities or dissimilarities

server E-COMMERCE a computer that provides services to another computer. Typically, a server stores data to be shared over a computer network. The computers receiving services are called **clients**.

server farm E-COMMERCE a place where a number of server computers are located, usually providing server functions for a number of different organizations

service MARKETING any activity with a mix of tangible and intangible outcomes that is offered to a market with the aim of satisfying a customer's need or desire. Early ***marketing*** tended to distinguish a service from a physical good, but more recently these two have been seen as interrelated because service delivery frequently has physical aspects. For example, in a restaurant, service is provided by a waiter but physical goods, such as the food and the dining room, are also involved. In modern marketing, all forms of services and goods can be seen as ***products***.

service charge

1. MARKETING a gratuity usually paid in restaurants and hotels. A service charge may be voluntary or may be added as a percentage to the bill.

2. FINANCE, BANKING, AND ACCOUNTING a fee for any service provided, or additional fee for any enhancements to an existing service. For example, banks may charge a fee for obtaining foreign currency for customers. Residents in apartment buildings may pay an annual maintenance fee that is also referred to as a service charge.

service contract HR & PERSONNEL a ***contract of employment*** for ***executive directors*** which lays down the ***conditions of employment*** and details of any ***bonus*** which may be paid, and outlines the procedure for ***termination of service***

service level agreement MARKETING an agreement drawn up between a customer or client and the provider of a service or product. A service level agreement can cover a straightforward provision of a service, for example, office cleaning, or the provision of a complete function such as the ***outsourcing*** of the administration of a payroll or maintenance of plant and equipment for a large company. The agreement lays down the detailed specification for the level and quality of the service to be provided. The agreement is essentially a legally binding contract.

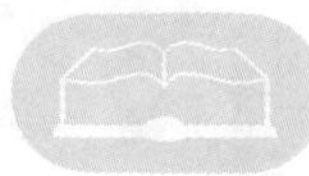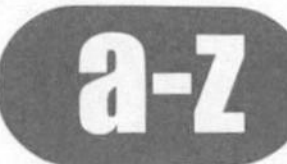

SET E-COMMERCE secure electronic transaction, a payment protocol that permits secure credit card transactions over open networks such as the Internet, developed by Visa and MasterCard

set-off FINANCE, BANKING, AND ACCOUNTING an agreement between two parties to balance one debt against another or a loss against a gain

set the bar HR & PERSONNEL to motivate staff by setting targets that are above their current level of achievement

settlement
1. E-COMMERCE the portion of an electronic transaction during which the customer's credit card is charged for the transaction and the proceeds are deposited into the merchant account by the acquirer
2. FINANCE, BANKING, AND ACCOUNTING the payment of a debt or charge

settlement date FINANCE, BANKING, AND ACCOUNTING the date on which an outstanding debt or charge is due to be paid

setup costs GENERAL MANAGEMENT the costs associated with making a workstation or equipment available for use. Setup costs include the personnel needed to set up the equipment, the cost of down time during a new setup, and the resources and time needed to test the new setup to achieve the specification of the parts or materials produced.

setup fees E-COMMERCE the costs associated with establishing a ***merchant account*** (see ***merchant bank***), for example, application and software licensing fees and point-of-sale equipment purchases

setup time OPERATIONS & PRODUCTION the time it takes to prepare, calibrate, and test a piece of equipment to produce a required output

setup time reduction OPERATIONS & PRODUCTION see ***single minute exchange of dies***

severance pay HR & PERSONNEL a lump-sum payment made by an employer to an employee at the point at which the employee leaves the organization. Redundancy pay is similar, but is regulated by legislation. Also known as ***dismissal pay***, ***separation pay***, ***termination pay***

sexual discrimination HR & PERSONNEL unfavorable treatment, or ***discrimination***, especially in employment, based on prejudice against a person's sex. Legislation against sexual discrimination is in place in many countries and many organizations have specific ***personnel policies*** to prevent sex discrimination in the workplace.

sexual harassment HR & PERSONNEL a form of ***discrimination*** through the unwelcome and unwanted sexual conduct of one employee toward another. Most of the victims of sexual harassment are women, and the most common forms are physical, verbal, suggestive gesturing, written messages, graphic or pictorial displays, or the emotional isolation of an individual. The effective promotion of a policy to protect employees and customers from such harassment is good organizational practice.

SFE FINANCE, BANKING, AND ACCOUNTING see ***Sydney Futures Exchange***

shadow market GENERAL MANAGEMENT = ***black market***

shadow price ECONOMICS the ***opportunity cost*** to an individual or economy of engaging in an economic activity

shakeout FINANCE, BANKING, AND ACCOUNTING the elimination of weak or cautious investors during a crisis in the financial market (*slang*)

shamrock organization GENERAL MANAGEMENT a form of ***organization structure*** with three bases on which people can be employed and on which organizations can be linked to each other. The shamrock organization was identified by ***Charles Handy***. The three bases or groups are professional managers, contracted specialists such as advertising, computing, or catering personnel, and a flexible labor force discharging part-time, temporary, or seasonal roles.

shape up or ship out HR & PERSONNEL an order to improve your performance at work or else be fired (*slang*)

share FINANCE, BANKING, AND ACCOUNTING any of the equal parts into which a company's capital stock is divided, whose owners are entitled to a proportionate share of the company's profits

share capital FINANCE, BANKING, AND ACCOUNTING the amount of capital that a company raises by issuing shares

share certificate (*U.K.*) FINANCE, BANKING, AND ACCOUNTING = ***stock certificate***

shared drop MARKETING a sales promotion technique in which a number of promotional offers are delivered by hand to ***prospects*** at the same time

shared values GENERAL MANAGEMENT see ***core values***

shareholder GENERAL MANAGEMENT, FINANCE, BANKING, AND ACCOUNTING a person or organization that owns shares in a limited company or partnership. A shareholder has a stake in the company and becomes a member of it, with rights to attend the ***annual meeting***. Since shareholders have invested money in a company, they have a vested interest in its performance, can be a powerful influence on company policy, and should consequently be considered ***stakeholders*** as well as shareholders. Some ***pressure groups*** have sought to exploit this by becoming shareholders in order to get a particular viewpoint or message across. At the same time, managers must, in order to maintain or increase the company's market value, consider their responsibility to shareholders when formulating strategy. It has been argued that on some occasions the desire to make profits to raise returns for shareholders has damaged companies because it has limited the amount of money spent in other areas, such as the development of facilities or health and safety.

shareholder value analysis GENERAL MANAGEMENT a calculation of the value of a company by looking at the returns it gives to its shareholders. Shareholder value analysis, like the ***economic theory of the firm***, assumes that the objective of a company director is to maximize the wealth of the company's shareholders. It is based on the premise that discounted cash flow principles can be applied to the business as a whole. SVA is calculated by estimating the total net value of a company and dividing this figure by the value of shares. Shareholder value analysis can be applied to assess the contribution of a business unit or to evaluate individual projects. Abbr **SVA**

share incentive scheme HR & PERSONNEL a type of financial ***incentive scheme*** in which employees can acquire shares in the company in which they work and so have an interest in its financial performance. A share incentive scheme is a type of ***employee stock ownership plan***, in which employees may be given shares by their employer, or shares may be offered for purchase at an advantageous price, as a reward for personal or group performance. A ***share option*** is a type of share incentive scheme.

  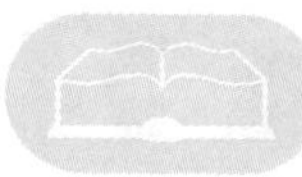    

share index (*U.K.*) FINANCE, BANKING, AND ACCOUNTING = ***index***

share issue FINANCE, BANKING, AND ACCOUNTING an occasion when shares in a business are offered for sale. The ***capital*** derived from share issues can be used for investment in the core business or for expansion into new commercial ventures.

share of voice MARKETING an individual company's proportion of the total advertising expenditure in a sector

share option FINANCE, BANKING, AND ACCOUNTING, HR & PERSONNEL a type of ***share incentive scheme*** in which an employee is given the option to buy a specified number of shares at a future date, at a price agreed at the present time. Share options provide a financial benefit to the recipient only if the share price rises over the period the option is available. If the share price falls over the period, the employee is under no obligation to buy the shares. There may be a tax advantage to the employees who participate in such a scheme. Share options may be available to all employees or operated on a discretionary basis.

shareowner FINANCE, BANKING, AND ACCOUNTING somebody who owns a share of stock

share premium FINANCE, BANKING, AND ACCOUNTING the amount by which the price at which a company sells a share exceeds its par value

share register FINANCE, BANKING, AND ACCOUNTING a list of the shareholders in a particular company

shareware E-COMMERCE software distributed free of charge, but usually with a request that users pay a small fee if they like the program

shark repellent GENERAL MANAGEMENT provisions in a company's bylaws that make it more difficult for a proposition such as a change of status or the acceptance of a hostile ***takeover*** bid to succeed. Elements of shark repellent may include: requiring a vote that is substantially higher than that required by law; creating different voting rights attached to different stocks; very long notice for special business meetings; or requiring certain shareholders to waive rights to any capital gains resulting from a takeover. (*slang*)

shelfspace MARKETING the amount of space allocated to a product in a retail outlet

shell company FINANCE, BANKING, AND ACCOUNTING a company that has ceased to trade but is still registered, especially one sold to enable the buyer to begin trading without having to set up a new company

Shewhart, **Walter Andrew** (1891–1967) GENERAL MANAGEMENT U.S. statistician. Pioneer of the development and application of statistical techniques for the control of variation in industrial production, in particular ***statistical process control***. Mentor of ***W. Edwards Deming***.

W. EDWARDS DEMING (pp. 980–81)

shift HR & PERSONNEL

1. a designated period during a working day when a group of employees work continuously. Shifts are arranged in a variety of different patterns during a day or over a week or month, to enable a business to make more effective use of its equipment, and to enable a greater level of output to be achieved.

2. the groups of employees working for a designated period during a working day. Where a shift pattern changes, the hours of work for the whole group of employees alters.

shift differential HR & PERSONNEL a payment made to employees over and above their basic rate to compensate them for the inconvenience of the pattern of ***shiftwork***. A shift differential usually takes account of the time of day when the shift is worked, the duration of the shift, the extent to which weekend working is involved, and the speed of rotation within the shift. Also known as ***shift allowance***, ***shift bonus***, ***shift premium***

shiftwork HR & PERSONNEL an arrangement whereby the working day is divided into a number of ***shifts***, and a separate group of employees works for each period

shingle

hang out your shingle GENERAL MANAGEMENT to start a business or announce the startup of a new business (*slang*)

Shingo, **Shigeo** (1909–90) GENERAL MANAGEMENT Japanese researcher and consultant. Inventor of the ***single minute exchange of dies*** and a developer of the ***Toyota production system***. Methods to achieve ***zero defects*** were explained in *Zero Quality Control* (1985).

shopbot E-COMMERCE an automated means of searching the Internet for particular products or services, allowing the user to compare prices or specifications

shopping basket E-COMMERCE = ***shopping cart***

shopping cart *or* **shopping basket** E-COMMERCE a software package that collects and records items selected for purchase along with associated data, for example, item price and quantity desired, during shopping at an electronic store. Also known as ***shopping trolley***

shopping experience E-COMMERCE the virtual environment in which a customer visits an e-merchant's Web site, selects items and places them in an electronic ***shopping cart***, and notifies the merchant of the order. The experience does not include a payment transaction, which is initiated by a message generated to the point-of-sale program when the customer signals the experience is completed.

shopping trolley E-COMMERCE = ***shopping cart***

shop steward (*U.K.*) HR & PERSONNEL a representative elected by ***labor union*** members within an office or factory to represent their feelings, wishes, and grievances to management. A shop steward is often the first point of contact for supervisors and personnel officers in their industrial relations dealings with an outside labor union.

shorthand FINANCE, BANKING, AND ACCOUNTING a system of rapid note-taking, using abbreviations and symbols to represent words and phrases

short-interval scheduling OPERATIONS & PRODUCTION a technique for assigning a planned quantity of work to a workstation, to be completed in a specific time. Short-interval scheduling was pioneered during the 1930s by large mail-order houses in the United States and was widely used in the 1950s to provide greater control of routine and semiroutine processes through regular checks of individual performance over short spans of time. Short-interval scheduling enables ***productivity*** to be improved, as all delays can be identified and corrected at an early stage.

short-run production OPERATIONS & PRODUCTION a production system designed to produce unique or small batches of a product

short-term debt FINANCE, BANKING, AND ACCOUNTING debt with a term of one year or less

short-term economic policy FINANCE, BANKING, AND ACCOUNTING an economic policy with objectives that can be met within a period of months or a few years

short-termism GENERAL MANAGEMENT an approach to business that concentrates on short-term results rather than long-term objectives

shovelware E-COMMERCE a derogatory term for the materials produced by converting existing materials from a traditional medium, for example, a catalog, without taking advantage of the digital medium's audiovisual and linking possibilities (*slang*)

shutdown of production OPERATIONS & PRODUCTION the action of stopping production due to a lack of resources or components, as a result of equipment failure or installation, or as a result of ***industrial action*** by workers. Shutdown of production may also be instigated by management to reduce output or it may be used for the maintenance of equipment. A shutdown can be a temporary measure, for example, in holiday periods, but it can also be permanent, for example, when a manufacturing company closes down after ***business failure***.

SIA FINANCE, BANKING, AND ACCOUNTING see ***Securities Institute of Australia***

sickie (*U.K.*) (*ANZ*) HR & PERSONNEL a day of sick leave, often implying that the sickness is not genuine (*slang*)

sick leave *or* **sickness absence** HR & PERSONNEL absence from work caused by illness

sickout HR & PERSONNEL a form of protest by a group of employees who attempt to achieve their demands by absenting themselves from work on the grounds of ill-health (*slang*)

sight bill FINANCE, BANKING, AND ACCOUNTING a bill of exchange payable on sight

sight deposit FINANCE, BANKING, AND ACCOUNTING a bank deposit against which the depositor can immediately draw

sight draft FINANCE, BANKING, AND ACCOUNTING a draft payable on sight

signature E-COMMERCE the name, position, and full contact details of the sender of an e-mail, added to the end of a business message. Some e-mail programs enable users to automatically add a signature to all sent messages.

signature guarantee FINANCE, BANKING, AND ACCOUNTING a stamp or seal, usually from a bank or a broker, that vouches for the authenticity of a signature

signature loan FINANCE, BANKING, AND ACCOUNTING = ***unsecured loan***

silent partner FINANCE, BANKING, AND ACCOUNTING a person or organization that invests money in a company but takes no active part in the management of the business. Although a silent partner is inactive in the operation of the business, they have legal obligations and benefits of ownership, and are therefore fully liable for any debts.

silversurfer E-COMMERCE an Internet user aged between 45 and 65 (*slang*)

silvertail (*ANZ*) GENERAL MANAGEMENT a wealthy person of high social standing (*slang*)

Simon, Herbert A. (1916–2001) GENERAL MANAGEMENT U.S. economist, and political and social scientist. Respected for his work on ***problem solving***, ***decision making***, and ***artificial intelligence***. He began developing his ideas in *Administrative Behavior* (1946).

simple interest FINANCE, BANKING, AND ACCOUNTING interest charged simply as a constant percentage of principal and not compounded. See ***compound interest***

simple moving average STATISTICS the selection of units from a population in such a way that every possible combination of selected units is equally likely to be in the sample chosen

simple regression analysis GENERAL MANAGEMENT see ***regression analysis***

simulation GENERAL MANAGEMENT the construction of a mathematical model to imitate the behavior of a real-world situation or system in order to test the outcomes of alternative courses of action. Simulation was used in a military context by the Chinese as many as 5,000 years ago and has applications in the fields of science, research and development, economics, and business systems. The use of simulation has become more widespread since the development of computers in the 1950s, which facilitated the manipulation of large quantities of data and made it possible to model more complex systems. Simulation techniques are used in situations where real-life experimentation would be impossible, costly, or dangerous, and for training purposes.

simulation game GENERAL MANAGEMENT an interactive game based on a simulation of a real-life situation, where participants role-play, make decisions, and receive ***feedback*** on the results of their actions. A simulation game is used for training purposes and enables trainees to put theory into practice in a risk-free environment. Simulation games are used to increase business awareness and develop management skills such as ***decision making***, ***problem solving***, and team working. An element of competition between individuals or teams of players is normally involved. Formats used include board games and computer-based simulations of the running of a business.

simulation model GENERAL MANAGEMENT a mathematical representation of the essential characteristics of a real-world system or situation, which can be used to predict future behavior under a variety of different conditions. The process of developing a simulation model involves defining the situation or system to be analyzed, identifying the associated variables, and describing the relationships between them as accurately as possible.

simultaneous engineering OPERATIONS & PRODUCTION = ***concurrent engineering***

simultaneous management GENERAL MANAGEMENT a ***management style*** in which managers organize competing demands in an integrated way, rather than sequentially. Simultaneous management reflects the increasingly rapid changes of the business environment, which create conflicting demands on a manager's attention. It involves integrating tasks, people, and procedures and handling them in an interactive way, rather than tackling problems individually and one at a time.

SINBAD MARKETING Single Income, No Boyfriend, And Absolutely Desperate, one of many humorous acronyms used in U.K. advertising to help define the market of a product or service (*slang*)

Singapore dollar FINANCE, BANKING, AND ACCOUNTING Singapore's unit of currency, whose exchange rate is quoted as S$ per U.S.$

Singapore Exchange FINANCE, BANKING, AND ACCOUNTING a merger of the Stock Exchange of Singapore and the Singapore International Monetary Exchange, established in 1999. It provides securities and derivatives trading, securities clearing and depository, and derivatives clearing services. Abbr **SGX**

Singapore Immigration and Registration GENERAL MANAGEMENT the department responsible for all entry and immigration issues relating to Singapore. Abbr **SIR**

  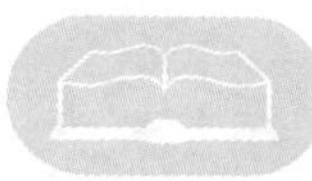  

single currency FINANCE, BANKING, AND ACCOUNTING denominated entirely in one currency

single customs document FINANCE, BANKING, AND ACCOUNTING a standard universally used form for the passage of goods through customs

single-employer bargaining HR & PERSONNEL see ***collective bargaining***

single entry FINANCE, BANKING, AND ACCOUNTING a type of bookkeeping where only one entry, reflecting both a credit to one account and a debit to another, is made for each transaction

single minute exchange of dies OPERATIONS & PRODUCTION a technique for reducing the ***setup times*** of equipment. Single minute exchange of dies was developed by ***Shigeo Shingo*** to improve setup times in the ***Toyota production system***. It is a simple technique that divides the elements of a setup task into internal activities (those that can only be carried out when the machine is stopped) and external activities (those that can be carried out in advance). Single minute refers to making the changes in less than ten minutes, while exchange of dies comes from the steel presses that were the focus of Shingo's attention. By converting as many internal activities to external activities as possible, Shingo was able to reduce a four-hour setup time on a large press to less than ten minutes. Abbr **SMED**

single-payment bond FINANCE, BANKING, AND ACCOUNTING a bond redeemed with a single payment combining principal and interest at maturity

single premium deferred annuity FINANCE, BANKING, AND ACCOUNTING an annuity that gives tax advantage, paid for with a single payment at inception, and paying returns regularly after a set date

single sourcing OPERATIONS & PRODUCTION the ***purchasing*** policy of using one supplier for a particular component or service. Single sourcing can result in higher quality and a greater level of cooperation in ***product development*** than the traditional Western approach of ***multiple sourcing***. Single sourcing has risen in prominence in the West following the introduction of Japanese production techniques, particularly ***just-in-time***, which encourage manufacturers to establish closer relationships with a smaller number of suppliers.

single tax FINANCE, BANKING, AND ACCOUNTING a tax that supplies all revenue, especially on land

SINK MARKETING Single, Independent, No Kids (*slang*)

SIR GENERAL MANAGEMENT see ***Singapore Immigration and Registration***

SIS GENERAL MANAGEMENT see ***strategic information systems***

site analysis E-COMMERCE analysis of information about a Web site stored on Web servers. Typically, this information details how many page views they serve, as well as more specific data about the site's performance such as how long visitors stayed on the site and which pages they looked at when they were there.

situational interview HR & PERSONNEL see ***interviewing***

Six Sigma OPERATIONS & PRODUCTION a data-driven method for achieving near perfect quality. Sigma is the Greek letter used to denote ***standard deviation***, or measure of variation from the mean, which in production terms is used to imply defect. The greater the number of sigmas, the fewer the defects. In true Six Sigma environments, companies operate at a quality level of six standard deviations from the mean, or at a defect level of 3.4 per million. Six Sigma analysis can be focused upon any part of production or service activities, and has a strong emphasis on statistical analysis in design, manufacturing, and customer-oriented activities. It is based on the statistical tools and techniques of quality management developed by ***Joseph Juran***.

size of firm GENERAL MANAGEMENT a method of categorizing companies according to size for the purposes of government statistics. Divisions are typically ***microbusiness***, ***small business***, ***medium-sized business***, and ***large-sized business***.

skeleton staff HR & PERSONNEL the minimum number of employees needed to keep a business running, for example, during a holiday period

skewness STATISTICS a lack of symmetry in a probability distribution

skill HR & PERSONNEL the ability to do something well, gained through training and experience. See ***competence***

skills analysis HR & PERSONNEL the process of obtaining information on employees' technical and behavioral ***skills***. Skills analysis is used to define the skills or ***competencies*** required in a particular job. It is also used to identify those skills that are not being deployed at all or could be utilized by another part of the organization. Also known as ***skills mapping***

skills mapping HR & PERSONNEL = ***skills analysis***

skills shortage HR & PERSONNEL a shortfall in the number of workers with the ***skills*** needed to fill the jobs currently available. A skills shortage may be caused by a lack of education and ***vocational training***, or by wider social and economic factors such as new technological developments. A skills shortage may affect a region, an industry, or a whole country. Skills shortages of this type need to be addressed at national level through effective ***manpower planning*** and the development of strategies for adult education and vocational training. An organization may suffer from a skills shortage as a result of poor ***recruitment*** and retention of employee policies, or through inadequate provision of training and employee development opportunities.

skimming FINANCE, BANKING, AND ACCOUNTING the practice of taking small amounts of money from accounts, usually illegally or at least unethically

skunkworks GENERAL MANAGEMENT a fast-moving group, working at the edge of the ***organization structure***, which aims to accelerate the ***innovation*** process without the restrictions of organizational policies and procedures. Skunkworks can operate unknown to an organization, or with its tacit acceptance. With the organization's acceptance, skunkworks are an extreme form of ***intrapreneurialism***. The term skunkworks was popularized by ***Tom Peters*** and Bob Waterman in *A Passion for Excellence* (1984).

sleeping partner (*U.K.*) GENERAL MANAGEMENT = ***silent partner***

Sloan, Alfred Pritchard (1875–1966) GENERAL MANAGEMENT U.S. industrialist. Chairman and C.E.O. of General Motors, which he built into the largest company in the world by adopting a ***decentralized organization structure*** and the theories of ***Henri Fayol***. Sloan's divisional structure, which became the model for organizing large business, is described in *My years with General Motors* (1963).
ALFRED P. SLOAN, JR. (pp. 1140–41)

slowdown ECONOMICS a fall in demand that causes a lowering of economic activity, less severe than a ***recession*** or ***slump***

  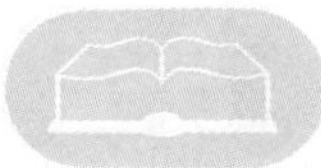    

slump ECONOMICS a severe downturn phase in the business cycle

slumpflation ECONOMICS a collapse in all economic activity accompanied by wage and price inflation. This happened, for example, in the United States and Europe in 1929. (*slang*)

slush fund FINANCE, BANKING, AND ACCOUNTING a fund used by a company for illegal purposes such as bribing officials to obtain preferential treatment for planned work or expansion

small and medium-sized enterprises GENERAL MANAGEMENT organizations that are in the ***startup*** or growth phase of development and have between 10 and 500 employees. This definition of small and medium-sized enterprises is the one adopted by the United Kingdom's Department of Trade and Industry for statistical purposes. ***Small businesses*** are usually in the startup phase, and in the growth phase they usually become ***medium-sized businesses***. Abbr **SME**

small business GENERAL MANAGEMENT an organization that is small in relation to the potential market size, managed by its owners, and not part of a larger organization. There is no single official definition of what constitutes a small business. A standard definition for the size of small business, adopted by the United Kingdom's Department of Trade and Industry for purposes of examining trends and for distinguishing from ***microbusiness***, ***medium-sized business***, and ***large-sized business***, is an organization of between 10 and 99 employees.

small print GENERAL MANAGEMENT details in an official document such as a contract that are usually printed in a smaller size than the rest of the text and, while often important, may be overlooked. Items often referred to as "small print" can include terms and conditions or penalty clauses.

smart card E-COMMERCE a small plastic card containing a microprocessor that can store and process transactions and maintain a bank balance, thus providing a secure, portable medium for electronic money. Financial details and personal data stored on the card can be updated each time the card is used.

smart market E-COMMERCE a market in which all transactions are carried out electronically using network communications

smartsizing HR & PERSONNEL the process of reducing the size of a company by laying off employees on the basis of incompetence and inefficiency (*slang*)

SME GENERAL MANAGEMENT see ***small and medium-sized enterprises***

SMED OPERATIONS & PRODUCTION see ***single minute exchange of dies***

Smith, **Adam** (1723–90) GENERAL MANAGEMENT Scottish political economist and philosopher. Author of *The Wealth of Nations* (1776), one of the most influential books written on political economy, Smith did much to promulgate the theory of free trade in a society based on ***mercantilism***. He is recognized for his use of the expression, "the invisible hand" which he used to describe the important role of self-interest in a free market.

smoking memo GENERAL MANAGEMENT a memo, letter, or e-mail message containing evidence of a corporate crime (*slang*)

smoko (*ANZ*) GENERAL MANAGEMENT a break taken by employees during working hours, traditionally to smoke cigarettes but often to take tea or other refreshments (*slang*)

smoothing methods STATISTICS procedures used in fitting a model to a set of statistical observations in a study, often by graphing the data to highlight its characteristics

SMS *abbr* E-COMMERCE short messaging service, the system used to send text messages via mobile phone networks

SMTP *abbr* E-COMMERCE simple mail transfer protocol, an e-mail protocol used to help pass messages along their route. SMTP is understood by e-mail software and by the server computers each e-mail message passes.

snail mail E-COMMERCE a derogatory term for the mail service, viewed as slow in comparison to e-mail

snowball sampling STATISTICS a form of sampling in which existing sample members suggest potential new sample members, for example, personal acquaintances

snowflake STATISTICS a graph that shows ***multivariate data***

SO *abbr* GENERAL MANAGEMENT significant other (*slang*)

social audit GENERAL MANAGEMENT a process for evaluating, reporting on, and improving an organization's performance and behavior, and for measuring its effects on society. The social audit can be used to produce a measure of the ***social responsibility*** of an organization. It takes into account any internal ***code of conduct*** as well as the views of all ***stakeholders*** and draws on ***best practice*** factors of ***total quality management*** and human resource development. Like ***internal auditing***, social auditing requires an organization to identify what it is seeking to achieve, who the stakeholders are, and how it wants to measure performance.

social capital GENERAL MANAGEMENT the asset to an organization produced by the cumulative social skills of its employees. Social capital, like ***intellectual*** and ***emotional capital***, is intangible and resides in the employees of the organization. It is a form of capital produced by good ***interpersonal skills*** (see ***interpersonal communication***), which can be considered an asset as they are an important factor in organizational success. Key components of social capital include: trust; a sense of community and belonging; unrestricted and participative communication; democratic decision making; and a sense of collective responsibility. Evidence of social capital can be seen, for example, in trust relationships, in the establishment of effective personal networks, in efficient ***teamwork***, and in an organization's exercise of ***social responsibility***.

socialism ECONOMICS a way of organizing society in which the use and production of goods are in collective (usually government) ownership

socially conscious investing FINANCE, BANKING, AND ACCOUNTING investment only in companies whose policies meet the ethical criteria of the investor

social marginal cost ECONOMICS the additional cost to a society of a change in an economic variable, for example, the price of gas or bread

social responsibility GENERAL MANAGEMENT the approach of an organization to managing the impact it has on society. Social responsibility involves behaving within certain socially acceptable limits. These limits may not always take the form of written laws or regulations but they amount to an accepted organization-wide moral or ethical code. Organizations that transgress this code are viewed as irresponsible. In order to determine levels of social responsibility, organizations may choose to undertake a ***social audit*** or more specifically an ***environmental audit***. Social responsibility, along with ***business ethics***, has grown as a strategic issue as ***empowerment***

and the ***flat organization*** have pushed decision making down to a wider range of employees at the same time as green or caring consumers are becoming a more powerful market segment.

Sociedad Anónima FINANCE, BANKING, AND ACCOUNTING the Spanish equivalent of a private limited company. Abbr **SA**

Société Anonyme FINANCE, BANKING, AND ACCOUNTING the French equivalent of a private limited company. Abbr **SA**

sociocultural research MARKETING exploration of social and cultural trends which identifies how they are likely to impact on different ***market sectors***

socioeconomic ECONOMICS involving both social and economic factors. Structural unemployment, for example, has socioeconomic causes.

socioeconomic environment GENERAL MANAGEMENT the combination of external social and economic conditions that influence the operation and performance of an organization. The socioeconomic environment is part of the overall business environment.

socioeconomic segmentation MARKETING the division of a market by socioeconomic categories

soft benefits HR & PERSONNEL nonmonetary benefits offered to employees (*slang*)

soft commissions FINANCE, BANKING, AND ACCOUNTING brokerage commissions that are rebated to an institutional customer in the form of, or to pay for, research or other services

soft-core radicalism MARKETING a marketing technique that plays on people's concerns about environmental and ethical issues in order to sell them a product (*slang*)

soft landing ECONOMICS a situation in which a country's economic activity slows down but demand does not fall far or rapidly enough to cause a recession

soft loan FINANCE, BANKING, AND ACCOUNTING a loan on exceptionally favorable terms, for example, for a project that a government considers worthy

soft systems GENERAL MANAGEMENT see ***systems method***

sole proprietor GENERAL MANAGEMENT somebody who owns and runs an unincorporated business by themselves. In the United Kingdom, a sole proprietor does not have to register the company or publish annual accounts and is taxed as an individual. They are personally liable, however, for all business losses or debts and in the event of ***bankruptcy*** personal possessions may be forfeited. Also known as ***sole trader***

sole trader (*U.K.*) (*ANZ*) GENERAL MANAGEMENT = ***sole proprietor***

solus position MARKETING the condition of being the only advertisement to appear on a page

solution brand GENERAL MANAGEMENT a combination of products and related services, for example, a computer system with presales consultancy, installation, and maintenance, that meets a customer's needs more effectively than a product alone

solvency ratio FINANCE, BANKING, AND ACCOUNTING a ratio of assets to liabilities, used to measure a company's ability to meet its debts

solvent FINANCE, BANKING, AND ACCOUNTING a company or individual able to pay off all debts

sort code (*U.K.*) FINANCE, BANKING, AND ACCOUNTING = ***routing number***

sort field GENERAL MANAGEMENT a computer field used to identify data in such a way that it can be easily categorized and arranged in sequence

spam

1. E-COMMERCE unsolicited bulk e-mail, usually sent for commercial purposes. Spam is used by some companies as a cheap form of advertising, although it is generally considered offensive and unwelcome by the Internet community. Sending spam is regarded as unethical because the cost is paid by the recipient's site or server, not the sender's. Various Internet bodies campaign against spam and those individuals or organizations accused of spamming. The term may originate from a sketch in the U.K. comedy program *Monty Python* in which customers at a "greasy spoon" café are served the tinned meat Spam with everything, or may simply derive from the preexisting use of the word to represent something, like the rations available to soldiers in World War II, that is plentiful and unappetizing.

2. MARKETING see ***direct mail***

spamkiller software E-COMMERCE software that can block e-mail messages from companies sending unsolicited commercial e-mail

span of control GENERAL MANAGEMENT the number and range of subordinates for whom a manager is responsible. The span of control can be calculated by various methods which take into account such factors as whether those supervised are doing the same or different jobs and their levels of seniority, ***empowerment***, experience, and qualification.

spare parts OPERATIONS & PRODUCTION a stock of components of machinery or plant held in store in case of breakdown

spatial data STATISTICS variables that are measured at different locations to illustrate the spatial organization of data

SPC OPERATIONS & PRODUCTION see ***statistical process control***

speako GENERAL MANAGEMENT a mistake made by a computer while using a speech-recognition program (*slang*)

spear carrier HR & PERSONNEL somebody who is in the second tier of command in an organization and is responsible for carrying out the commands and communicating the messages of the top-level executives (*slang*)

special deposit FINANCE, BANKING, AND ACCOUNTING an amount of money set aside for the rehabilitation of a mortgaged house

special leave HR & PERSONNEL exceptional ***leave*** that may be granted to an ***employee***. Special leave includes ***sabbatical***s, leave granted for study (also known as ***educational leave***), leave for jury service, for volunteer forces training, leave granted to candidates for local or national elections, or for labor union duties and activities, and for ***community involvement*** purposes. Special leave can also refer to ***maternity leave*** and ***paternity leave***.

special purpose bond FINANCE, BANKING, AND ACCOUNTING a bond for one particular project, financed by levies on the people who benefit from the project

specification OPERATIONS & PRODUCTION documentation relating to the required quantity and quality of materials, and the order of the work to be carried out to complete a task

speculation FINANCE, BANKING, AND ACCOUNTING a purchase made solely to make a profit when the price or value increases

speech GENERAL MANAGEMENT a formal spoken address made to an audience by a

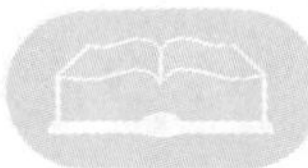

speaker. Speeches are made in the context of a meeting or conference or on other occasions such as after a business dinner. The aim of a speech may be to motivate, inspire, or entertain as well as to inform. In contrast to ***presentations***, speeches are a form of public speaking normally made without the assistance of audiovisual aids, and may be wide ranging rather than focusing on a well-defined topic or proposal. Jokes, humorous anecdotes, and quotations are frequently used in speeches. To give a speech successfully requires good ***communication skills***.

spider food E-COMMERCE words that are embedded in a Web page to attract search engines (*slang*)

spiffs MARKETING gifts or money offered to store managers in exchange for promoting a product (*slang*)

spin-off GENERAL MANAGEMENT a company or subsidiary formed by splitting away from a parent company. A spin-off company can, for example, be created when research and development yields a new product that does not fit into the company's current portfolio, or when a company wants to explore a new venture related to its current activities. It also can be formed from a demerger, in which acquired companies or parts of a business are separated in order to create a more streamlined parent organization. A spin-off is often entrepreneurial in spirit, but the backing of the parent company can provide financial stability.

split FINANCE, BANKING, AND ACCOUNTING an issuance to shareholders of more than one share for every share owned. See ***reverse split***. Also known as ***stock split***

split commission FINANCE, BANKING, AND ACCOUNTING ***commission*** that is divided between two or more parties in a transaction

split coupon bond FINANCE, BANKING, AND ACCOUNTING = ***zero coupon bond***

sponsorship MARKETING a form of advertising in which an organization provides funds for something such as a television program or sports event in return for exposure to a target audience

Spoornet GENERAL MANAGEMENT the rail division of the state-owned South African transport company, Transnet Ltd

spot MARKETING a TV or radio commercial (*slang*)

spot color MARKETING a single color overprinted on a black-and-white advertisement

spot exchange rate FINANCE, BANKING, AND ACCOUNTING the exchange rate used for immediate currency transactions

spot interest rate FINANCE, BANKING, AND ACCOUNTING an interest rate that is determined when a loan is made

spot market FINANCE, BANKING, AND ACCOUNTING a market that deals in commodities or foreign exchange for immediate rather than future delivery

spot month FINANCE, BANKING, AND ACCOUNTING = ***nearby month***

spot price FINANCE, BANKING, AND ACCOUNTING the price for immediate delivery of commodities or foreign exchange

spot transaction FINANCE, BANKING, AND ACCOUNTING a transaction in commodities or foreign exchange for immediate delivery

spread FINANCE, BANKING, AND ACCOUNTING
1. the difference between the buying and selling price of a share on a stock exchange
2. the range of investments in a portfolio

spreadsheet FINANCE, BANKING, AND ACCOUNTING a computer program that provides a series of ruled columns in which data can be entered and analyzed

sprinkling trust FINANCE, BANKING, AND ACCOUNTING a trust with multiple beneficiaries whose distributions occur at the trustee's total discretion

spruik (*ANZ*) GENERAL MANAGEMENT to publicize goods or services, typically by standing at the door of a shop and addressing passersby using a microphone (*slang*)

squatter (*ANZ*) GENERAL MANAGEMENT a wealthy landowner (*slang*)

squattocracy (*ANZ*) GENERAL MANAGEMENT a derogatory term for wealthy landowners, who are considered as a powerful social class (*slang*)

squeaky wheel GENERAL MANAGEMENT somebody who gets good results by being extremely assertive in their dealings with other people (*slang*)

squeeze ECONOMICS a government policy of restriction, commonly affecting the availability of credit in an economy

squirt the bird GENERAL MANAGEMENT to transmit a signal to a satellite (*slang*)

SSADM GENERAL MANAGEMENT see ***structured systems analysis and design method***

SSL *abbr* E-COMMERCE secure sockets layer, a widely used protocol for encrypting data that permits the transmission of credit card transactions in a secure fashion

stabilization fund ECONOMICS a fund created by a government as an emergency savings account for international financial support

staffing level HR & PERSONNEL the number and type of personnel employed by an organization for the performance of a given workload. The ideal staffing level for an organization depends on the amount of work to be done and the skills required to do it. If the number and quality of staff employed are greater than necessary for the workload, an organization may be deemed to be overstaffed; if the number of staff is insufficient for the workload, an organization is deemed to be understaffed. Effective ***human resource planning*** will determine the appropriate staffing level for an organization at any given point in time.

stage-gate model MARKETING see ***new product development***

stagflation ECONOMICS the result when both inflation and unemployment exist at the same time in an economy. There was stagflation in the United Kingdom in the 1970s, for example.

stakeholder GENERAL MANAGEMENT a person or organization with a vested interest in the successful operation of a company or organization. A stakeholder may be an employee, customer, supplier, partner, or even the local community within which an organization operates.

stakeholder pension (*U.K.*) FINANCE, BANKING, AND ACCOUNTING, HR & PERSONNEL a pension, bought from a private company, in which the retirement income depends on the level of contributions made during a person's working life. Stakeholder pensions are designed for people without access to an occupational pension scheme, and are intended to provide a low-cost supplement to the state earnings related pension scheme. A stakeholder pension scheme can either be trust-based, like an occupational pension scheme, or contract-based, similar to a personal pension. Subject to certain exceptions, employers must provide access to a stakeholder pension scheme for employees, although they are not required to establish a stakeholder pension scheme themselves. Membership of a stakeholder pension scheme is voluntary. See ***Keough Plan***

stakeholder theory GENERAL MANAGEMENT the theory that an organization can enhance the interests of its shareholders without damaging the interests of its wider ***stakeholders***. Stakeholder theory grew in response to the ***economic theory of the firm***, and contrasts with ***Theory E***. One of the difficulties of stakeholder theory is allocating importance to the values of different groups of stakeholders, and a solution to this is proposed by ***stakeholder value analysis***.

stakeholder value analysis GENERAL MANAGEMENT a method of determining the values of all ***stakeholders*** within an organization for purposes of strategic and operational decisions. Stakeholder value analysis is one method of justifying an approach based on ***stakeholder theory*** rather than the ***economic theory of the firm***. It involves identifying groups of stakeholders and eliciting their views on particular issues in order that these views may be taken into account when making decisions.

stamp duty FINANCE, BANKING, AND ACCOUNTING a duty that is payable on some legal documents and is shown to have been paid by a stamp being fixed to the document

Standard 8 FINANCE, BANKING, AND ACCOUNTING a standard used in Internet commerce

Standard & Poor's 500 FINANCE, BANKING, AND ACCOUNTING a U.S. index of 500 general share prices selected by the Standard & Poor agency

Standard & Poor's rating FINANCE, BANKING, AND ACCOUNTING a share rating service provided by the U.S. agency Standard & Poor

standard business transaction E-COMMERCE any business procedure conducted between trading partners, characterized by a paper document or its equivalent EDI transaction set or message

standard deviation OPERATIONS & PRODUCTION a measure of how dispersed a set of numbers are, around their mean

standard of living GENERAL MANAGEMENT a measure of economic well-being based on the ability of people to buy the goods and services they desire

standard time GENERAL MANAGEMENT
1. the length of time taken by a worker to complete a particular motion, such as reaching or grasping
2. the total time required to complete a specific task for an employee working at the expected rate. The standard time for any particular task is derived through ***work measurement*** and ***time study*** techniques, and takes into account **relaxation allowances**, which allow employees time to recover from the psychological or physiological effects of carrying out a task, and **contingency allowances**, which recognize that there may be legitimate causes of delay before a task can be completed. ***Predetermined motion-time systems*** may be used to help determine a standard time.

standby credit ECONOMICS credit drawing rights given to a developing country by an international financial institution, to fund industrialization or other growth policies

standby loan ECONOMICS a loan given to a developing country by an international financial institution, to fund technology hardware purchase or other growth policies

stand down *(ANZ)* HR & PERSONNEL to suspend an employee without pay *(slang)*

standing order *(U.K.)* FINANCE, BANKING, AND ACCOUNTING = ***automatic debit***

standing room only MARKETING a sales technique whereby customers are given the impression that there are many other people waiting to buy the same product at the same time *(slang)*

star GENERAL MANAGEMENT see ***Boston Box***

startup GENERAL MANAGEMENT a relatively new, usually small business, particularly one supported by venture capital and within those sectors closely linked to new technologies

startup model GENERAL MANAGEMENT a business model based on rapid short-term success. Typically, the aim is to acquire venture capital, grow rapidly, and float or sell off quickly, generating profit for the founders but not necessarily for the business.

state bank FINANCE, BANKING, AND ACCOUNTING a bank chartered by a state

state capitalism ECONOMICS a way of organizing society in which the state controls most of a country's means of production and capital

state enterprise GENERAL MANAGEMENT an organization in which the government or state has a controlling interest

statement of account FINANCE, BANKING, AND ACCOUNTING a summary of recent transactions between two parties

statement of cash flows FINANCE, BANKING, AND ACCOUNTING a statement that documents actual receipts and expenditures of cash

statement-of-cash-flows method FINANCE, BANKING, AND ACCOUNTING a method of accounting that is based on flows of cash rather than balances on accounts

statement of changes in financial position FINANCE, BANKING, AND ACCOUNTING a financial report of a company's incomes and outflows during a period, usually a year or a quarter

state of balance GENERAL MANAGEMENT an approach to capitalism that balances ecological and economic priorities

state planning ECONOMICS the regulation of a sector of an economy by administrators rather than by the price system

statistic FINANCE, BANKING, AND ACCOUNTING a piece of information in numerical form

statistical expert system STATISTICS a computer program used to conduct a statistical analysis of a set of data

statistical model STATISTICS the particular methods used to investigate the data in a statistical study

statistical process control OPERATIONS & PRODUCTION a means of monitoring a ***process*** to assist in identifying causes of variation with the aim of improving process performance. Statistical process control consists of three elements: data gathering; determining control limits; and variation reduction. The tools used include process ***flow charts***, tally charts, histograms, graphs, ***fishbone charts***, and control charts. The thinking behind SPC has been attributed to ***Walter Shewhart*** in the 1920s. Abbr **SPC**

statistical quality control STATISTICS the process of inspecting samples of a product to check for consistent quality according to given parameters

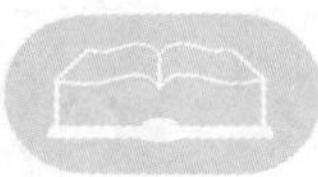

statistical significance FINANCE, BANKING, AND ACCOUNTING the level of importance at which an event influences a set of ***statistics***

statistics FINANCE, BANKING, AND ACCOUNTING information in numerical form and its collection, analysis, and presentation

statutory auditor (*U.K.*) FINANCE, BANKING, AND ACCOUNTING a professional person qualified to carry out an audit required by the U.K. Companies Act

STC *abbr* (*S. Africa*) FINANCE, BANKING, AND ACCOUNTING Secondary Tax on Companies, a secondary tax levied on corporate dividends

STEP analysis GENERAL MANAGEMENT see ***PEST analysis***

Stewart, Rosemary Gordon GENERAL MANAGEMENT British academic. Respected for her research on managerial work and behavior, including the essential aspects of becoming an effective manager, published in *The Reality of Management* (1963).

Stewart, Thomas A. (*b.* 1948) GENERAL MANAGEMENT U.S. publisher and writer. A leader in the ***knowledge management*** debate who, in *Intellectual Capital: the New Wealth of Organizations* (1997), encouraged organizations to exploit their untapped knowledge.

stickiness E-COMMERCE a Web site's ability to hold visitors and to keep them coming back

stick to the knitting GENERAL MANAGEMENT an exhortation to organizations to concentrate on the activities, products, and services that are key to their ***core business*** and consequently to their success. Stick to the knitting was popularized by ***Tom Peters*** and ***Bob Waterman*** in their book *In Search of Excellence* (1984).

sticky site E-COMMERCE a Web site that holds the interest of visitors for a substantial amount of time and is therefore effective as a marketing vehicle (*slang*) Also known as ***heavy site***

stipend HR & PERSONNEL a regular remuneration or allowance paid to an individual holding a particular office

stock FINANCE, BANKING, AND ACCOUNTING
1. a form of security that offers fixed interest
2. (*U.K.*) the ***capital*** made available to an organization after a ***share issue***

stockbroker FINANCE, BANKING, AND ACCOUNTING somebody who arranges the sale and purchase of stocks

stock certificate FINANCE, BANKING, AND ACCOUNTING a document that certifies ownership of a share in a company

stock control FINANCE, BANKING, AND ACCOUNTING see ***inventory***

stockcount FINANCE, BANKING, AND ACCOUNTING profit gained from ownership of a stock or share

stock exchange FINANCE, BANKING, AND ACCOUNTING an organization that maintains a market for the trading of stock

stockjobber (*S Asia*) FINANCE, BANKING, AND ACCOUNTING see ***market maker***

stock market FINANCE, BANKING, AND ACCOUNTING the trading of stocks, or a place where this occurs

stockout OPERATIONS & PRODUCTION the situation where the stock of a particular component or part has been used up and has not yet been replenished. Stockouts result from poor inventory control or the failure of a ***just-in-time*** supply system. They can result in delays in the delivery of customer orders and can damage the reputation of the business.

stock split FINANCE, BANKING, AND ACCOUNTING a proportional issue of free shares to existing owners of a company's stock. Also known as ***scrip issue***

stocktaking OPERATIONS & PRODUCTION the process of measuring the quantities of stock held by an organization. Stock, or ***inventory***, can be held both in stores and within the processes of the operation. Better ***materials management*** and inventory systems have made annual stocktaking less important.

stock turns *or* **stock turnover** OPERATIONS & PRODUCTION = ***inventory turnover***

stokvel (*S. Africa*) FINANCE, BANKING, AND ACCOUNTING an informal, widely used cooperative savings scheme that provides small-scale loans

stop-go ECONOMICS the alternate tightening and loosening of fiscal and monetary policies. This characterized the U.K. economy in the 1960s and 1970s.

stop limit order FINANCE, BANKING, AND ACCOUNTING an order to trade only if and when a security reaches a specified price

stop loss FINANCE, BANKING, AND ACCOUNTING an order to trade only if and when a security falls to a specified price

stop order FINANCE, BANKING, AND ACCOUNTING an order to trade only if and when a security rises above or falls below its current price

stop-work meeting (*ANZ*) HR & PERSONNEL a meeting held by employees during working hours to discuss issues such as wage claims and working conditions with union representatives or management

story stock FINANCE, BANKING, AND ACCOUNTING a stock that is the subject of a press or financial community story that may affect its price

straight-line depreciation FINANCE, BANKING, AND ACCOUNTING a form of depreciation in which the cost of a fixed asset is spread equally over each year of its anticipated lifetime

Straits Times Industrial Index FINANCE, BANKING, AND ACCOUNTING an index of 30 Singapore stocks and the most commonly quoted indicator of stock market activity in Singapore

strata title (*ANZ*) GENERAL MANAGEMENT a system for registering ownership of space within a multilevel building, under which a title applies to the space and a proportion of the common property

strata unit (*ANZ*) GENERAL MANAGEMENT an apartment or office within a multilevel building that has been registered under the ***strata title*** system

STRATE (*S. Africa*) FINANCE, BANKING, AND ACCOUNTING Share Transactions Totally Electronic, the electronic share transactions system of the Johannesburg Stock Exchange

strategic alignment GENERAL MANAGEMENT = ***strategic fit***

strategic alliance GENERAL MANAGEMENT an agreement between two or more organizations to cooperate in a specific business activity, so that each benefits from the strengths of the other, and gains ***competitive advantage***. The formation of strategic alliances has been seen as a response to ***globalization*** and increasing uncertainty and complexity in the business environment. Strategic alliances involve the sharing of knowledge and expertise between partners as well as the reduction of risk and costs in areas such as relationships with suppliers and the development of new products and technologies. A strategic alliance is sometimes equated with a ***joint venture***, but an alliance may involve competitors, and gen-

  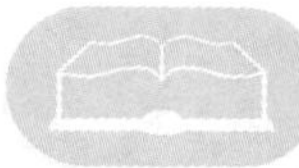    

erally has a shorter life span. ***Strategic partnering*** is a closely related concept.

strategic analysis GENERAL MANAGEMENT the process of researching and reflecting on the business environment within which an organization operates, competitors of the organization, and the organization itself, in order to formulate ***strategy***. A number of tools are used in the process of strategic analysis, including ***PEST***, ***SWOT analysis***, and ***Michael Porter***'s five forces model.

strategic business unit GENERAL MANAGEMENT a division within a large organization that shares the organization's market and customer focus but has responsibility for the development of its own marketing strategy. The establishment of a structure based on a strategic business unit recognizes that a single strategic approach is often inappropriate in large diversified organizations or multinational companies.

strategic fit GENERAL MANAGEMENT the extent to which the activities of a single organization or of organizations working in partnership complement each other in such a way as to contribute to ***competitive advantage***. The benefits of good strategic fit include cost reduction, due to economies of scale, and the transfer of knowledge and skills. The success of a ***merger***, ***joint venture***, or ***strategic alliance*** may be affected by the degree of strategic fit between the organizations involved. Similarly, the strategic fit of one organization with another is often a factor in decisions about acquisitions, mergers, ***diversification***, or ***divestment***. Also known as ***strategic alignment***

strategic goal GENERAL MANAGEMENT the overall aim of an organization in terms of its market position in the medium or long-term. A strategic goal forms part of an organization's ***corporate strategy*** and should act as a motivating force as well as a measure of performance and achievement for those working in an organization.

strategic inflection point GENERAL MANAGEMENT the time at which an organization takes a decision to change its ***corporate strategy*** to pursue a different direction and avoid the risk of decline. The term was coined by ***Andy Grove*** of Intel to describe the period of change that affects an organization's competitive position. It also concerns the ability of organizations to recognize and adapt to change factors of major significance.

strategic information systems GENERAL MANAGEMENT an information system established with the aim of creating ***competitive advantage*** and improving the competitive position of an organization. A strategic information system supports and shapes the ***corporate strategy*** of an organization, often leading to innovation in the way the organization conducts its business, the creation of new business opportunities, or the development of products and services based on information technology. Strategic information systems represent a development in organizational use of information systems following in the wake of ***MISs***, ***EISs***, and ***decision support systems***.

strategic management GENERAL MANAGEMENT the development of ***corporate strategy***, and the management of an organization according to that strategy. Strategic management focuses on achieving and maintaining a strong ***competitive advantage***. It involves the application of corporate strategy to all aspects of the organization, and especially to ***decision making***. As a discipline, strategic management developed in the 1970s, but it has evolved in response to changes in ***organization structure*** and ***corporate culture***. With greater ***empowerment***, strategy has become the concern not just of directors but also of employees at all levels of the organization.

strategic marketing MARKETING a method of selling products directly to customers, bypassing traditional retailers or distributors

strategic partnering GENERAL MANAGEMENT structured collaboration between organizations to take joint advantage of market opportunities, or to respond to customers more effectively than could be achieved in isolation. Strategic partnering occurs both in and between the public and private sectors. Besides allowing information, skills, and resources to be shared, a strategic partnership also permits the partners to share risk. See ***strategic alliance***

strategic planning GENERAL MANAGEMENT see ***planning***

strategy GENERAL MANAGEMENT, HR & PERSONNEL a planned course of action undertaken to achieve the aims and objectives of an organization. The term was originally used in the context of warfare to describe the overall planning of a campaign as opposed to tactics, which enable the achievement of specific short-term objectives. The overall strategy of an organization is known as ***corporate strategy***, but strategy may also be developed for any aspect of an organization's activities such as ***environmental management*** or manufacturing strategy.

stratified random sampling STATISTICS sampling carried out at random from each stratum of a stratified population

stratified sampling OPERATIONS & PRODUCTION see ***random sampling***

straw man GENERAL MANAGEMENT a first proposal for a solution to a problem, offered more as a place to start looking for a solution than as a serious suggestion for final action

stress HR & PERSONNEL the psychological and physical state that results when perceived demands exceed an individual's ability to cope with them

stress puppy HR & PERSONNEL somebody who complains a lot and seems to enjoy being stressed (*slang*)

strike HR & PERSONNEL a concerted refusal to work by employees, with the aim of improving wages or employment conditions, voicing a grievance, making a protest, or supporting other workers in such an endeavor. A strike is a form of ***industrial action***.

strike pay *or* **strike benefit** HR & PERSONNEL a benefit or allowance paid by a ***labor union*** to its members during the course of official ***strike*** action to help offset loss of earnings, albeit a much reduced ***benefit***. Also known as ***dispute benefit***

strike price FINANCE, BANKING, AND ACCOUNTING the price for a security or commodity that underlies an option

stripped bond FINANCE, BANKING, AND ACCOUNTING a bond that can be divided into separate zero-coupon bonds to represent its principal repayment and its interest

stripped stock FINANCE, BANKING, AND ACCOUNTING stock whose rights to dividends have been separated and sold

strips FINANCE, BANKING, AND ACCOUNTING the parts of a bond that entitle the owner only to interest payments or only to the repayment of principal

structural adjustment ECONOMICS a change in the output composition of an economy that creates the need to reallocate its resources

structural change ECONOMICS a change in the composition of output in an economy that means that resources have to be reallocated

structural fund FINANCE, BANKING, AND ACCOUNTING a mutual fund that invests in projects that contribute to the economic development of poorer nations in the European Union

structural inflation FINANCE, BANKING, AND ACCOUNTING inflation that naturally occurs in an economy, without any particular triggering event

structural unemployment ECONOMICS the situation where demand or technology changes so that there is too much labor in particular locations or with particular skills

structured interview HR & PERSONNEL see ***interviewing***

structured systems analysis and design method GENERAL MANAGEMENT a technique for the analysis and design of computer systems. The structured systems analysis and design method was developed by the Central Computer and Telecommunications Agency in the United Kingdom in the early 1980s. The technique adopts a structured methodology toward systems development through the use of data flow, logical data, and entity event modeling. Core development stages include: ***feasibility study***; requirements analysis; requirements specification; logical system specification; and physical design. All the steps and tasks within each stage must be complete before subsequent stages can begin. Abbr **SSADM**

stub equity FINANCE, BANKING, AND ACCOUNTING the money raised through the sale of high risk bonds in large amounts or quantities, as in a leveraged takeover or a leveraged buyout

subcontract GENERAL MANAGEMENT a ***contract*** under which all, or part, of the work specified in an existing contract is delegated to another person or organization

subcontracting GENERAL MANAGEMENT, OPERATIONS & PRODUCTION the delegation to a third party of some, or all, of the work that one has ***contracted*** to do. Subcontracting usually occurs where the contracted work, for example, the construction of a building, requires a variety of skills. Responsibility for the fulfillment of the original ***contract*** remains with the original contracting party. Where the fulfillment of a contract depends on the skills of the person who has entered into the contract, for example, in the painting of a portrait, then the work cannot be subcontracted to a third party. The term subcontracting is sometimes used to describe ***outsourcing*** arrangements.

subject to collection FINANCE, BANKING, AND ACCOUNTING dependent upon the ability to collect the amount owed

subliminal advertising MARKETING advertising intended to influence an audience subconsciously, especially through images shown very briefly on a movie or television screen

subordinated debt FINANCE, BANKING, AND ACCOUNTING = ***junior debt***

subsidiary account FINANCE, BANKING, AND ACCOUNTING an account for one of the individual people or organizations that jointly hold another account

subsidiary company GENERAL MANAGEMENT a company that is controlled by another. A subsidiary company operates under the control of a parent or ***holding company***, which may have a majority on the subsidiary's ***board of directors***, or a majority shareholding in the subsidiary, giving it majority voting rights, or it may be named in a contract as having control of the subsidiary. If all of the stock in a company is owned by its parent, it is known as a ***wholly-owned subsidiary***. A subsidiary that is located in a different country to the parent is a **foreign subsidiary company**.

subsidiary right FINANCE, BANKING, AND ACCOUNTING a right that is included in another right

subsistence allowance HR & PERSONNEL ***expenses*** paid by an ***employer***, usually within preset limits, to cover the cost of accommodation, meals, and incidental expenses incurred by ***employees*** when away on business

subtreasury FINANCE, BANKING, AND ACCOUNTING a place where some of a nation's money is held

succession planning GENERAL MANAGEMENT the preparation for the replacement of one postholder by another, usually prompted by ***retirement*** or ***resignation***. Succession planning involves preparing the new postholder before the old one leaves, possibly with training or through work shadowing. At a senior level, **management succession** should be accomplished as smoothly as possible in order to avoid organizational crises caused by absent or inadequate top management. General Electric is held to be an exemplar of succession planning for its preparation for the retirement of ***Jack Welch***.

suggestion scheme HR & PERSONNEL a policy designed to encourage employees to generate ideas or proposals that improve work processes, for which they receive a gift or cash reward. The objective of a suggestion scheme is to promote ***employee involvement***, creative thinking, and continuous improvement. Its success can be evaluated in terms of the participation rate, or by the level of cost savings, but there may be an incalculable beneficial effect on sales, customer loyalty, retention of employees, and ***motivation***.

suit GENERAL MANAGEMENT somebody who works for a large corporation and is required to wear a suit for work (*slang*)

sum FINANCE, BANKING, AND ACCOUNTING an amount or total of any given item, such as money, stocks, or securities

sum at risk FINANCE, BANKING, AND ACCOUNTING an amount of any given item, such as money, stocks, or securities that an investor may lose

sum-of-the-year's-digits depreciation FINANCE, BANKING, AND ACCOUNTING accelerated depreciation, conferring tax advantage by assuming more rapid depreciation when an asset is new

Sunday night syndrome GENERAL MANAGEMENT feelings of depression experienced by employees when they consider their return to work on Monday morning

sunshine law FINANCE, BANKING, AND ACCOUNTING a law that requires public disclosure of a government act

super (*ANZ*) FINANCE, BANKING, AND ACCOUNTING an informal abbreviation of superannuation (*slang*)

superannuation plan HR & PERSONNEL a pension plan in Australia

superannuation scheme HR & PERSONNEL a pension plan in New Zealand

superindustrial society GENERAL MANAGEMENT a society in which technology dominates both the personal and working lives of its members

superstitial E-COMMERCE a form of Web-based advertisement that is run while new

Web pages are loading onto a user's computer. Unlike ***interstitials***, superstitials are loaded onto the computer using a "cache-and-play" delivery system that works while the Internet user is browsing the Web. Superstitials are mainly used during business-to-consumer advertising campaigns.

supervisor GENERAL MANAGEMENT, HR & PERSONNEL an employee who is given authority and responsibility for planning and controlling the work of a group through close contact. A supervisor is the first level of management in an organization. The subordinates he or she controls are usually at a nonmanagerial level and the supervisor is wholly responsible for their work. Supervisors are often ***delegated*** the responsibility for the human resource issues of ***recruitment***, handling grievances, discipline, and dismissal of staff within their group, and the production issues of quantity and quality of output.

supervisory management GENERAL MANAGEMENT, HR & PERSONNEL the most junior level of management within an organization. Supervisory management is carried out by ***supervisors*** who have direct responsibility for the day-to-day activities of a group of employees. Supervisory management activities include staff ***recruitment***, handling day-to-day grievances and staff discipline, and ensuring that quality and production targets are met. Also known as ***first-line management***

supplier OPERATIONS & PRODUCTION, HR & PERSONNEL an organization that delivers materials, components, goods, or services to another organization

supplier appraisal OPERATIONS & PRODUCTION see ***vendor rating***

supplier development HR & PERSONNEL the development of close and long-term relationships between a customer and a ***supplier***. Supplier development tends to be associated with ***Japanese management*** practices and has only recently been introduced to the West. Various approaches to customer-supplier relations have emerged, including comakership, partnership sourcing, collaborative sourcing, and cooperative sourcing. All these forms of supplier development are characterized by a long-term commitment, an integration of key functions and activities, a structured framework for determining price and sharing cost and profit, a proactive approach to ***problem solving***, and the adoption of both a win-win philosophy and a culture of continuous improvement.

supplier evaluation OPERATIONS & PRODUCTION the process of screening and evaluating potential suppliers of materials, goods, or services. Supplier evaluation involves establishing a set of requirements, which may include basic business robustness, performance elements specific to the product or service, and the key order winning criteria for final selection. Existing and potential suppliers are screened against these criteria, prior to placing a new order. When this process is undertaken after the fulfillment of an order, it is known as ***vendor rating***.

supplier rating OPERATIONS & PRODUCTION see ***vendor rating***

supply and demand OPERATIONS & PRODUCTION, GENERAL MANAGEMENT the quantity of goods available for sale at a given price, and the level of consumer need for those goods at a given price. The balance of supply and demand fluctuates as external economic factors such as the cost of materials and the level of competition in the marketplace influence the level of demand from consumers and the desire and ability of producers to supply the goods. Supply and demand is recognized as an economic principle, and is often referred to as the **law of supply and demand**.

supply chain OPERATIONS & PRODUCTION, GENERAL MANAGEMENT the network of ***manufacturers***, ***wholesalers***, distributors, and ***retailers***, who turn ***raw materials*** into ***finished goods*** and services and deliver them to ***consumers***. Supply chains are increasingly being seen as integrated entities, and closer relationships between the organizations throughout the chain can bring ***competitive advantage***, reduce costs, and help to maintain a loyal customer base.

supply chain management OPERATIONS & PRODUCTION the management of the movement of goods and flow of information between an organization and its ***suppliers*** and ***customers***, to achieve strategic advantage. Supply chain management covers the processes of ***materials management***, ***logistics***, ***physical distribution management***, ***purchasing***, and ***information management***.

supply-side economics ECONOMICS the study of how economic agents behave when supply is affected by changing price

support MARKETING help, advice, and services offered to customers by a seller after a sale

support price ECONOMICS the price of a product that is fixed or stabilized by a government so that it cannot fall below a certain level

surplus FINANCE, BANKING, AND ACCOUNTING see ***budget surplus***

surplus capacity OPERATIONS & PRODUCTION the capability of a factory or workstation to produce output over and above the level required by consumers or subsequent processes. Surplus capacity is a product of materials, personnel, and equipment that are superfluous, or not working to maximum ***capacity***. Some surplus capacity is required in any production system to deal with fluctuations in demand, and as a backup in case of failure. Excessive surplus capacity, however, adds to the cost of the production process as work-in-process inventory or finished-goods storage increases, and can result in ***overcapacity***. If a workstation has no surplus capacity its workloads cannot be increased, so it is at risk of becoming a ***bottleneck***. Also known as ***redundant capacity***

surrender value FINANCE, BANKING, AND ACCOUNTING the sum of money offered by an insurance company to somebody who cancels a policy before it has completed its full term

surtax FINANCE, BANKING, AND ACCOUNTING a tax paid in addition to another tax, typically levied on an a corporation with very high income

survey GENERAL MANAGEMENT the collection of data from a given population for the purpose of analysis of a particular issue. Data is often collected only from a sample of a population, and this is known as a ***sample survey***. Surveys are used widely in research, especially in ***market research***.

survivalist enterprise (*S. Africa*) GENERAL MANAGEMENT a business that has no paid employees, generates income below the poverty line, and is considered the lowest level of microenterprise

sustainable advantage GENERAL MANAGEMENT a competitive advantage that can be maintained over the long term, as opposed to one resulting from a short-term tactical promotion

sustainable development GENERAL MANAGEMENT development that meets the needs of the present without compromising the ability of future generations to meet their own needs. The concept of sustainable development was introduced by the Brundtland Report, the first report of the World Commission on Environment and Development, set up by the United Nations in 1983. It advocates the integration of social, economic, and en-

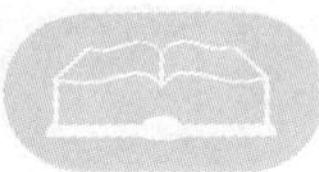

vironmental considerations into policy decisions by business and government. Particular emphasis is given to social, cultural, and ethical implications of development. Sustainable development can be achieved through ***environmental management*** and is a feature of a socially responsible business.

SVA GENERAL MANAGEMENT see ***shareholder value analysis***

swap FINANCE, BANKING, AND ACCOUNTING an exchange of credits or liabilities. See ***interest rate swap***, ***bond swap***, ***asset swap***

swap book FINANCE, BANKING, AND ACCOUNTING a broker's list of stocks or securities that clients wish to swap

swaption FINANCE, BANKING, AND ACCOUNTING an option to enter into a ***swap*** contract

sweat equity GENERAL MANAGEMENT an investment of labor rather than cash in a business enterprise (*slang*)

sweetener GENERAL MANAGEMENT an incentive offered to somebody to take a particular course of action

sweetheart agreement (*ANZ*) HR & PERSONNEL an agreement reached between employees and their employer without recourse to arbitration

SWELL (*U.K.*) MARKETING Single Woman Earning Lots in London (*slang*)

swing trading FINANCE, BANKING, AND ACCOUNTING the trading of stock by individuals that takes advantage of sudden price movements that occur especially when large numbers of traders have to cover short sales

swipe box E-COMMERCE an electronic device used for reading the magnetic data on a credit card during a card-present transaction

SWOT analysis GENERAL MANAGEMENT an assessment of Strengths, Weaknesses, Opportunities, and Threats. SWOT analysis is used within organizations in the early stages of strategic and ***marketing planning***. It is also used in ***problem solving***, ***decision making***, or for making staff aware of the need for change. It can be used at a personal level when examining your ***career path*** or determining possible ***career development***.

Sydney Futures Exchange FINANCE, BANKING, AND ACCOUNTING the principal market in Australia for trading financial and commodity futures. It was set up in 1962 as a wool futures market, the Sydney Greasy Wool Futures Exchange, but adopted its current name in 1972 to reflect its widening role. Abbr **SFE**

symmetrical distribution STATISTICS a distribution of statistical data that is symmetrical about a central value

syndicated research MARKETING trend data supplied by research agencies from their regularly operated retail audits or consumer panels

sysop E-COMMERCE systems operator, somebody who manages a Web site or bulletin board (*slang*)

systematic sampling OPERATIONS & PRODUCTION see ***random sampling***

system attack E-COMMERCE a deliberate attack on an e-mail system, usually in the form of a barrage of messages sent to one address simultaneously

systems administrator E-COMMERCE the person responsible for the management of an e-mail system

systems analysis GENERAL MANAGEMENT the examination and evaluation of an operation or task in order to identify and implement more efficient methods, usually through the use of computers. Systems analysis can be broken down into three main areas: the production of a statement of objectives; determination of the methods of best achieving these objectives in a cost-effective and efficient way; and the preparation of a ***feasibility study***. Also known as ***systems planning***

systems approach GENERAL MANAGEMENT a technique employed for organizational ***decision making*** and ***problem solving*** involving the use of computer systems. The systems approach uses ***systems analysis*** to examine the interdependency, interconnections, and interrelations of a system's components. When working in synergy, these components produce an effect greater than the sum effects of the parts. System components might comprise departments or functions of an organization or business which work together for an overall objective.

systems audit GENERAL MANAGEMENT an approach to ***auditing*** which utilizes the ***systems method***. By using a systems audit to assess the internal control system of an organization, it is possible to assess the quality of the accounting system and the level of testing required from the financial statements. One shortcoming of systems audit is that it does not consider audit ***risk***. Consequently, risk-based audit is now considered more effective.

systems design GENERAL MANAGEMENT the creation of a computer program to meet predetermined functional, operational, and personnel specifications. The systems design process involves the use of ***systems analysis*** and flow-charting of organizational functions and operations. It can be split into four stages: definition of the system's goals; preparation of a conceptual model of how these goals will be achieved; development of a physical design; and preparation of a system specification.

systems dynamics GENERAL MANAGEMENT a computer-based tool, developed at the Massachusetts Institute of Technology, designed to model the behavior of constantly changing systems. Systems dynamics investigates the combined effects of individual changes made at different points in a system, and uses ***simulation*** to design information feedback structures.

systems engineering GENERAL MANAGEMENT the process of planning, designing, creating, testing, and operating complex systems. Systems engineering can be viewed as a continuous cycle, aimed at developing alternative strategies for effective systems utilization. It is concerned with the definition, planning, and deployment of future systems.

systems method GENERAL MANAGEMENT a widely used group of methodologies which explore the nature of complex business situations by mapping activities in a model. The systems method can be applied to systems that are either **hard systems**, where precise objectives are expressed in mathematical terms, or **soft systems**, where a human factor is involved and situations often do not involve such precise objectives. A range of ***systems approaches*** are available including ***operational research***, ***systems analysis***, and ***systems dynamics***.

systems planning GENERAL MANAGEMENT see ***systems analysis***

T+ FINANCE, BANKING, AND ACCOUNTING an expression of the number of days allowed for settlement of a transaction

TA GENERAL MANAGEMENT see ***transactional analysis***

tacit knowledge GENERAL MANAGEMENT see ***knowledge***

tactical campaign MARKETING a series of marketing activities designed to achieve short-term targets

TAFN *abbr* GENERAL MANAGEMENT that's all for now (*slang*)

Taguchi, Genichi (*b.* 1924) GENERAL MANAGEMENT Japanese academic and consultant. Known for his contribution to quality engineering and founder of the ***Taguchi method*** which seeks to integrate ***quality control*** into product design, using experiment and statistical analysis. His concepts, including ***quality loss*** (see ***Taguchi methods***), are explained in publications such as *Introduction to Quality Engineering* (1986).

Taguchi methods OPERATIONS & PRODUCTION the pioneering techniques of ***quality control*** developed by ***Genichi Taguchi***, which focus on improving the quality of a product or process at the design stage rather than after manufacture or delivery. Taguchi's philosophy is that a quality approach that focuses on the parameters or factors of design produces a design that is more robust and is capable of withstanding variations from unwanted sources in the production or delivery process. He developed methods for both offline—design—and online—production—quality control. He developed the concepts of **quality loss** and the signal to noise ratio and a product design improvement process based on three steps: system design, parameter design, and tolerance design.

tailormade promotion MARKETING a promotional campaign that is customized for a particular customer

takeaway GENERAL MANAGEMENT the impressions that a consumer forms about a product or service

take-home pay HR & PERSONNEL the amount of ***pay*** an employee receives after all deductions, such as income tax, social security, or pension contributions. Also known as ***net pay***

takeout financing FINANCE, BANKING, AND ACCOUNTING loans used to replace bridge financing

takeover GENERAL MANAGEMENT, HR & PERSONNEL one company's acquisition of control over another. The target company that is taken over is usually smaller than the acquiring company. Acquisition is normally by means of buying shares in the company, with or without the approval of management or shareholders. If there is resistance the takeover is described as a **hostile takeover**. If the takeover is welcome it results in a ***merger***.

takeover bid MARKETING an attempt by one company to acquire another. A takeover bid can be made either by a person or an organization, and usually takes the form of an approach to ***shareholders*** with an offer to purchase. The bidding stage is often difficult and fraught with politics, and various forms of ***knight*** may be involved.

talent HR & PERSONNEL people with exceptional abilities, especially a company's most valued employees (*slang*)

talk offline GENERAL MANAGEMENT

1. to continue a particular line of discussion outside the original context. A person may wish to talk offline about an issue tangential to the current discussion, or may carry on that branch of the conversation at a later time, using different media. (*slang*)

2. to express an opinion in opposition to an employing organization's official position

tall organization GENERAL MANAGEMENT an ***organization structure*** with many levels of management. A tall organization contrasts with a ***flat organization***, since it has an extended vertical structure with well-defined but long reporting lines. The number of different levels may cause ***communication*** problems and slow ***decision making***. It is for this reason that many companies are converting to flatter structures more suited to the fast responses needed in a rapidly changing business environment.

tall poppy (*ANZ*) GENERAL MANAGEMENT a prominent member of society (*slang*)

tall poppy syndrome (*ANZ*) GENERAL MANAGEMENT an inclination in the media and among the general public to belittle the achievements of prominent people (*slang*)

tank FINANCE, BANKING, AND ACCOUNTING to fall precipitously. This term is used especially in reference to stock prices. (*slang*)

tape

don't fight the tape FINANCE, BANKING, AND ACCOUNTING don't go against the direction of the market (*slang*)

target GENERAL MANAGEMENT see ***objective***

target audience MARKETING a group of people considered likely to buy a product or service

target cash balance FINANCE, BANKING, AND ACCOUNTING the amount of cash that a company would like to have in hand

targeted repurchase FINANCE, BANKING, AND ACCOUNTING a company's purchase of its own shares from somebody attempting to buy the company

target population STATISTICS the collection of individuals or regions that are to be investigated in a statistical study

target savings motive ECONOMICS the motive that people have not to save when their families are growing up but to save when they are in middle age and trying to build up a pension

target stock level OPERATIONS & PRODUCTION the level of ***inventory*** that is needed to satisfy all demand for a product or component over a specified period

tariff ECONOMICS a government duty imposed on imports or exports to stimulate or dampen economic activity

Tariff Concession Scheme FINANCE, BANKING, AND ACCOUNTING a system operated by the Australian government in which imported goods that have no locally produced equivalent attract reduced duties. Abbr **TCS**

tariff office FINANCE, BANKING, AND ACCOUNTING an insurance company whose premiums are determined according to a scale set collectively by several companies

task analysis HR & PERSONNEL a methodology for identifying and examining the jobs performed by users when interacting with computerized, or noncomputerized, systems. Task analysis employs a range of techniques to help analysts collect information, organize it, and use it to integrate the human element in systems. It assists in the achievement of higher safety, ***productivity***, and maintenance standards.

task culture GENERAL MANAGEMENT a form of ***corporate culture*** based on individual projects carried out by small teams. Task culture was identified by ***Charles Handy***. It draws resources from different parts of the organization to form study groups, working parties, and ad hoc committees to take on problems, projects, and initiatives as they arise.

CHARLES HANDY (pp. 1000–01)

  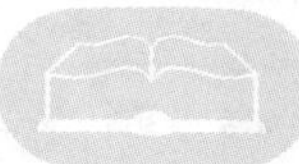  

task group HR & PERSONNEL a group of employees temporarily brought together to complete a specific project or task. A task group can take the form of an ***autonomous work group*** if it is responsible for its own management.

taste space MARKETING a community of consumers identified as sharing similar tastes or interests, for example, in music or books, enabling companies to recommend purchases or target advertising at them (*slang*)

tax FINANCE, BANKING, AND ACCOUNTING a governmental charge that is not a price for a good or service

taxability FINANCE, BANKING, AND ACCOUNTING the extent to which a good or individual is subject to a tax

taxable FINANCE, BANKING, AND ACCOUNTING subject to a tax

taxable base FINANCE, BANKING, AND ACCOUNTING the amount subject to taxation

taxable income FINANCE, BANKING, AND ACCOUNTING income that is subject to taxes

taxable matters FINANCE, BANKING, AND ACCOUNTING goods or services that can be taxed

tax adviser FINANCE, BANKING, AND ACCOUNTING somebody who gives people advice about taxes

tax and price index (*U.K.*) ECONOMICS an index number measuring the percentage change in gross income that taxpayers need if they are to maintain their real disposable income

tax auditor FINANCE, BANKING, AND ACCOUNTING a government employee who investigates taxpayers' declarations

tax avoidance FINANCE, BANKING, AND ACCOUNTING strategies to ensure the payment of as little in taxes as is legally possible. See ***tax evasion***

tax bracket FINANCE, BANKING, AND ACCOUNTING a range of income levels subject to marginal tax at the same rate

tax-deductible FINANCE, BANKING, AND ACCOUNTING able to be subtracted from taxable income before tax is paid

tax-deductible public debt FINANCE, BANKING, AND ACCOUNTING debt instruments exempt from federal income tax

tax-deferred FINANCE, BANKING, AND ACCOUNTING not to be taxed until a later time

tax domicile FINANCE, BANKING, AND ACCOUNTING a place that a government levying a tax considers to be a person's home

tax-efficient FINANCE, BANKING, AND ACCOUNTING financially advantageous by leading to a reduction of taxes to be paid

tax evasion FINANCE, BANKING, AND ACCOUNTING the illegal practice of paying less money in taxes than is due. See ***tax avoidance***

tax evasion amnesty FINANCE, BANKING, AND ACCOUNTING a governmental measure that affords those who have evaded a tax in some specified way freedom from punishment for their violation of the tax law

tax-exempt FINANCE, BANKING, AND ACCOUNTING not subject to tax

tax exemption cutoff FINANCE, BANKING, AND ACCOUNTING a limit on tax exemption because of high income

tax exile FINANCE, BANKING, AND ACCOUNTING a person or business that leaves a country to avoid paying taxes, or the condition of having done this

tax-favored asset FINANCE, BANKING, AND ACCOUNTING an asset that receives more favorable tax treatment than some other asset

tax file number FINANCE, BANKING, AND ACCOUNTING an identification number assigned to each taxpayer in Australia. Abbr **TFN**

tax-free FINANCE, BANKING, AND ACCOUNTING not subject to tax

tax harmonization FINANCE, BANKING, AND ACCOUNTING the enactment of taxation laws in different jurisdictions, such as neighboring countries, provinces, or states of the United States, that are consistent with one another

tax haven FINANCE, BANKING, AND ACCOUNTING a country that has generous tax laws, especially one that encourages noncitizens to base operations in the country to avoid higher taxes in their home countries

tax holiday (*U.K.*) FINANCE, BANKING, AND ACCOUNTING an exemption from tax granted for a specified period of time

taxi industry FINANCE, BANKING, AND ACCOUNTING the privately owned minibus taxi services, which constitute the largest sector of public transport in South Africa

tax incentive FINANCE, BANKING, AND ACCOUNTING a tax reduction afforded to people for particular purposes, for example, sending their children to college

tax inspector FINANCE, BANKING, AND ACCOUNTING a government employee who investigates taxpayers' declarations

tax invoice (*ANZ*) FINANCE, BANKING, AND ACCOUNTING a document issued by a supplier which stipulates the amount charged for goods or services as well as the amount of GST payable

tax law FINANCE, BANKING, AND ACCOUNTING the body of all laws on taxation, or one such law

tax loophole FINANCE, BANKING, AND ACCOUNTING a provision in a tax law that permits some individuals and companies to avoid or reduce taxes

tax loss FINANCE, BANKING, AND ACCOUNTING a loss of money that can serve to reduce tax liabilities

tax loss carry back FINANCE, BANKING, AND ACCOUNTING the reduction of taxes in a previous year by subtraction from income for that year of losses suffered in the current year

tax loss carry forward FINANCE, BANKING, AND ACCOUNTING the reduction of taxes in a future year by subtraction from income for that year of losses suffered in the current year

tax obligation FINANCE, BANKING, AND ACCOUNTING the amount of tax a person or company owes

tax on capital income FINANCE, BANKING, AND ACCOUNTING a tax on the income from sales of capital assets

tax payable FINANCE, BANKING, AND ACCOUNTING the amount of tax a person or company has to pay

taxpayer FINANCE, BANKING, AND ACCOUNTING an individual or corporation who pays a tax

tax rate FINANCE, BANKING, AND ACCOUNTING a percentage of a taxable amount that is due to be paid in taxes

tax refund FINANCE, BANKING, AND ACCOUNTING an amount that a government gives back to a taxpayer who has paid more taxes than were due

tax relief (*U.K.*) FINANCE, BANKING, AND ACCOUNTING the reduction in the amount of taxes payable, for example, on capital goods a company has purchased

tax return FINANCE, BANKING, AND ACCOUNTING an official form on which a company or individual enters details of income and expenses, used to assess tax liability. Also known as ***return***

tax revenue FINANCE, BANKING, AND ACCOUNTING money that a government receives in taxes

tax sale FINANCE, BANKING, AND ACCOUNTING a sale of an item by a government to recover overdue taxes on a taxable item

tax shelter FINANCE, BANKING, AND ACCOUNTING a financial arrangement designed to reduce tax liability. See ***abusive tax shelter***

tax subsidy FINANCE, BANKING, AND ACCOUNTING a tax reduction that a government gives a business for a particular purpose, usually to create jobs

tax system FINANCE, BANKING, AND ACCOUNTING the system of taxation adopted by a country

tax treaty FINANCE, BANKING, AND ACCOUNTING an international treaty that deals with taxes, especially taxes by multiple countries on the same individuals

tax year FINANCE, BANKING, AND ACCOUNTING a period covered by a statement about taxes

Taylor, Frederick Winslow (1856–1917) GENERAL MANAGEMENT U.S. engineer. Acknowledged as the father of ***scientific management***, which is sometimes referred to as "Taylorism." Taylor's methods, recorded in *The Principles of Scientific Management* (1911), have been criticized as too mechanistic, treating people like machines rather than human beings to be motivated. They were later counterbalanced by the ***human relations*** school of management.

FREDERICK WINSLOW TAYLOR (pp. 1054–55)

T-bill FINANCE, BANKING, AND ACCOUNTING a debt instrument of the U.S. government. See ***Treasury bill***

TCO GENERAL MANAGEMENT see ***total cost of ownership***

T-commerce E-COMMERCE business that is conducted by means of interactive television (*slang*)

TCP/IP E-COMMERCE transmission control protocol/Internet protocol, the combination of protocols that enables the Internet to function. **TCP** deals with the process of sending packets of information from one computer to another. **IP** is the process of passing each packet between computers until it reaches its intended destination.

TCS FINANCE, BANKING, AND ACCOUNTING see ***Tariff Concession Scheme***

TDB FINANCE, BANKING, AND ACCOUNTING see ***Trade Development Board***

team briefing HR & PERSONNEL a regular meeting between managers or supervisors and their teams to exchange information and ideas. The idea of team briefing evolved from the concept of **briefing groups** which was developed in the United Kingdom in the 1960s and promoted by the Industrial Society as a means of communicating systematically with managers and employees throughout an organization. The aim was to reduce misunderstandings and rumors and increase cooperation, ***employee commitment***, and ***team building***. Team briefings are characterized as being regular face-to-face meetings of small teams which are led by a team leader and are relevant to the work of the group, providing an opportunity for questions.

team building GENERAL MANAGEMENT, HR & PERSONNEL the selection and grouping of a mix of people and the development of skills required within the group to achieve agreed objectives. Effective team building can be achieved through a number of models, one of the most established of which was created by ***R. Meredith Belbin***.

team management GENERAL MANAGEMENT see ***Managerial Grid™***

Team Management Wheel™ GENERAL MANAGEMENT a visual aid for the efficient coordination of ***teamwork***, which can be used to analyze how teams work together, assist in ***team building***, and aid self-development and training. The Team Management Wheel outlines eight main team roles. Team members can determine the main functions of their jobs, that is, what they have to do, by using the "Types of Work Index," and can determine their own work preferences, that is, what they want to do, using the "Team Management Index." They are then assigned one major role and two minor roles on the Team Management Wheel. At the center of the Wheel are the linking skills common to all team members. The Team Management Wheel was developed by ***Charles Margerison*** and ***Dick McCann*** in 1984.

team player GENERAL MANAGEMENT somebody who works well within a team (*slang*)

teamwork GENERAL MANAGEMENT, HR & PERSONNEL, OPERATIONS & PRODUCTION collaboration by a group of people to achieve a common purpose. Teamwork is often a feature of day-to-day working, and is increasingly used to accomplish specific projects, in which case it may bring together people from different functions, departments, or disciplines. A team should ideally consist of people with complementary skills, and ***R. Meredith Belbin*** has established nine personality types that are needed in every team. One tool aimed at effective ***team building*** is the ***Team Management Wheel™***. There are various types of teamworking, including the ***autonomous work group*** and the ***virtual team***.

technocracy GENERAL MANAGEMENT an organization controlled by technical experts. See ***bureaucracy***

techno-determinist GENERAL MANAGEMENT somebody who believes that technological progress is inevitable

technographics GENERAL MANAGEMENT a research process that evaluates the attitudes of consumers toward technology. The process was introduced by Forrester Research.

technology adoption life cycle GENERAL MANAGEMENT a model used to describe the adoption of new technologies, typically including the stages of innovators, early adopters, early majority, late majority, and ***technology laggards***

technology laggard GENERAL MANAGEMENT an organization that is very slow or reluctant to adopt new technology

technology stock FINANCE, BANKING, AND ACCOUNTING stock issued by a company that is involved in new technology

telcos (*ANZ*) GENERAL MANAGEMENT an informal abbreviation of telecommunications companies (*slang*)

telebanking FINANCE, BANKING, AND ACCOUNTING electronic banking carried out by using a telephone line to communicate with a bank

telecenter GENERAL MANAGEMENT a building offering office space and facilities outside the home but away from the main workplace to enable remote working. A telecenter may be owned by one employer—in which case it is known as a ***satellite center***—or may be independently run on behalf of a number of organizations. Employees avoid long commuting times but work in an office rather than at home; employers avoid having to equip several homes with expensive office equipment. Also known as ***telecottage***

telecommute GENERAL MANAGEMENT to work without leaving your home by using telephone lines to carry data between your home and your employer's place of business

telecommuter GENERAL MANAGEMENT = ***teleworker***

telecommuting GENERAL MANAGEMENT a geographically dispersed work environment where workers can work at home on a computer and transmit data and documents to a central office via telephone lines. The term was first used by Jack Nilles in 1972. Also known as ***teleworking***

teleconferencing GENERAL MANAGEMENT the use of telephone or television channels to connect people in different locations in order to conduct group discussions, meetings, conferences, or courses

telecottage GENERAL MANAGEMENT see ***telecenter***

telemarketing MARKETING = ***telephone selling***

telephone interview survey STATISTICS a method of sampling a population by telephoning its members

telephone number salary HR & PERSONNEL a six- or seven-figure salary (*slang*)

telephone selling MARKETING the sale of products or services to customers over the telephone. Telephone selling may be used as an alternative, cheaper, method than door-to-door selling, or may be used to obtain an initial appointment for a salesperson to visit a potential customer. Also known as ***telemarketing***, ***telesales***

telephone survey MARKETING a research technique in which members of the public are asked a series of questions on the telephone

telephone switching FINANCE, BANKING, AND ACCOUNTING the process of connecting telephones to one another

telephone tag GENERAL MANAGEMENT the reciprocal calling and leaving of messages by two people who wish to speak to each other but are never available to speak on their telephones when the other calls (*slang*)

telesales GENERAL MANAGEMENT see ***telephone selling***

television audience measurement MARKETING the recording of the viewing patterns of a sample of the population, used as the basis for estimating national viewing figures for individual programs

teleworker GENERAL MANAGEMENT an employee who spends a substantial amount of working time away from the employer's main premises and communicates with the organization through the use of computing and telecommunications equipment. A teleworker may be based at home, in which case the worker is known as a ***homeworker***, or in a ***telecenter***, or on a variety of sites, in which case he or she may be known as a ***mobile worker***. Also known as ***telecommuter***

teleworking (*U.K.*) GENERAL MANAGEMENT a geographically dispersed work environment where workers can work at home on a computer and transmit data and documents to a central office via telephone lines. As people become accustomed to working via e-mail and the Web, teleworking is proving ever more popular. Also known as ***telecommuting***

tender GENERAL MANAGEMENT to make or submit a bid to undertake work or supply goods at a stated price. A tender is usually submitted in response to an invitation to bid for a work contract in competition with other suppliers.

terminal identification number E-COMMERCE = ***TIN***

termination interview HR & PERSONNEL a meeting between an employee and a management representative in order to ***dismiss*** the employee. A termination interview should be brief, explaining the reasons for the dismissal, and giving details of whether a ***notice period*** should be worked, and whether, especially in the case of ***redundancy***, additional assistance will be forthcoming from the employer.

termination of service HR & PERSONNEL the ending of an employee's ***contract of employment*** for a reason such as ***redundancy***, employer ***insolvency***, or ***dismissal***

termination pay HR & PERSONNEL see ***severance pay***

term insurance FINANCE, BANKING, AND ACCOUNTING insurance, especially life insurance, that is in effect for a specified period of time

terms of trade ECONOMICS a ratio to determine whether the conditions under which a country conducts its trade are favorable or unfavorable

terotechnology OPERATIONS & PRODUCTION a multidisciplinary technique that combines the areas of management, finance, and engineering with the aim of optimizing life-cycle costs for physical assets and technologies. Terotechnology is concerned with acquiring and caring for physical assets. It covers the specification and design for the reliability and maintainability of plant, machinery, equipment, buildings, and structures, including the installation, commissioning, maintenance, and replacement of this plant, and also incorporates the feedback of information on design, performance, and costs.

tertiary sector ECONOMICS the part of the economy made up of nonprofit organizations such as consumer associations and self-help groups

test battery HR & PERSONNEL see ***psychometric test***

testimonial advertising MARKETING advertising in which customers or celebrities recommend the product

test marketing MARKETING the use of a small-scale version of a ***marketing plan***, usually in a restricted area or with a small group, to test the marketing strategy for a new product. Test marketing gauges both the success of the marketing strategy and the reactions of consumers to a new product by giving an indication of the potential response to a product nationwide. Test marketing avoids the costs of a full-scale launch of an untested product, but a drawback is that both the product and marketing plan are exposed to competitors.

TFN FINANCE, BANKING, AND ACCOUNTING see ***tax file number***

TFN Withholding Tax (*ANZ*) FINANCE, BANKING, AND ACCOUNTING Tax File Number Withholding Tax, a levy imposed on financial transactions involving an individual who has not disclosed his or her tax file number

TGIF *abbr* GENERAL MANAGEMENT thank God it's Friday (*slang*)

T-Group GENERAL MANAGEMENT see ***sensitivity training***

Theory E GENERAL MANAGEMENT a mechanism for bringing about change in an organization through the creation of economic value and improved profits for the shareholders. Theory E has the single goal of satisfying the financial markets with a ***top-down approach*** style of ***leadership*** from the ***chief executive***. Theory E contrasts with ***Theory O***, which involves employee ***empowerment*** and ***employee participation*** in leadership. See ***alphabet theories of management***

Theory J GENERAL MANAGEMENT the ***Japanese*** form of management. Theory J is closely related to ***Theory Z***, and was expounded by ***William Ouchi***. See also ***alphabet theories of management***

Theory O GENERAL MANAGEMENT a mechanism for organizational **change** based on developing ***corporate culture*** and human capability through personal and ***organizational learning***. Theory O involves fostering a culture that encourages employees to find their own solutions to problems through ***empowerment*** and participative ***leadership***. Theory O contrasts with ***Theory E***, which involves a ***top-down approach*** style of leadership rather than ***employee participation***.

theory of constraints OPERATIONS & PRODUCTION see ***optimized production technology***

theory of the horizontal fast track GENERAL MANAGEMENT a variation of ***fast track*** coined by ***Charles Handy***. The theory of the horizontal fast track describes the development of talented people who are moved around from task to task to test and develop their capability in different working situations.
CHARLES HANDY (pp. 1000–01)

Theory W GENERAL MANAGEMENT an extreme extension of ***Douglas McGregor***'s ***Theory X***, which proposes that not only should employees be coerced into action but that force is often required. Theory W is a humorous contribution to the ***alphabet theories of management***. Theory W stands for Theory Whiplash.

Theory X GENERAL MANAGEMENT a management theory based on the assumption that most people are naturally reluctant to work and need discipline, direction, and close control if they are to meet work requirements. Theory X was coined by ***Douglas McGregor*** in *The Human Side of Enterprise*, and it was considered by him to be an implicit basis for traditional hierarchical management. See also ***alphabet theories of management***
DOUGLAS MCGREGOR (pp. 1022–23)

Theory Y GENERAL MANAGEMENT a management theory based on the assumption that employees want to work, achieve, and take responsibility for meeting their work requirements. Theory Y was coined by ***Douglas McGregor*** in *The Human Side of Enterprise*. Although he recognized that Theory Y could not solve all ***human resource management*** (see ***HRM***) problems, McGregor favored it over his ***Theory X***, which required an autocratic management style. See also ***alphabet theories of management***
DOUGLAS MCGREGOR (pp. 1022–23)

Theory Z GENERAL MANAGEMENT a management theory based on the assumption that greater employee involvement leads to greater productivity. Theory Z was proposed by ***Douglas McGregor*** shortly before his death in an attempt to address the criticisms of his ***Theory X*** and ***Theory Y***. McGregor's ideas were expanded by ***William Ouchi*** in his book *Theory Z*, reflecting the Japanese approach to ***human resource management*** (see ***HRM***). Theory Z advocates greater ***employee participation*** in management, greater recognition of employees' contributions, better career prospects and security of employment, and greater mutual respect between employees and managers. See also ***alphabet theories of management***
DOUGLAS MCGREGOR (pp. 1022–23)

think tank GENERAL MANAGEMENT an organization or group of experts researching and advising on issues of society, science, technology, industry, or business

third market FINANCE, BANKING, AND ACCOUNTING a market other than the main stock exchange in which stocks are traded

third-party network *or* **third-party service provider** E-COMMERCE = ***value-added network***

third sector HR & PERSONNEL see ***nonprofit organization***

Thorsrud, Einar (1923–85) GENERAL MANAGEMENT Norwegian academic. Researcher at the Tavistock Institute of Human Relations and collaborator with ***Fred Emery***. Thorsrud set up an institute in Oslo which became the center of Scandinavian exploration of the concept of ***industrial democracy***.

three-dimensional management *or* **3-D management** GENERAL MANAGEMENT a theory outlining eight ***management styles*** that differ in effectiveness. Three-dimensional management was coined by ***Bill Reddin*** and was a development of the work of ***Robert Blake*** and ***Jane Mouton***. Reddin described four managerial styles that he considered more effective, and four that he considered less effective. These can be plotted in grids, showing how each style approaches relationships and tasks. The least effective type of manager is called the Deserter, the most effective is the Executive. Reddin believed that different styles are used in different types of work settings and that managers modify their style to suit different circumstances.

three martini lunch GENERAL MANAGEMENT a business lunch involving a lot of alcohol to relax the client (*slang*)

three Ps GENERAL MANAGEMENT a model proposed by ***Sumantra Ghoshal*** to succeed the ***three Ss***, which refers to the three foundations of today's leading companies: purpose, process, and people

360 degree appraisal HR & PERSONNEL the ***management style*** adopted depending on the location of a manager on the ***Managerial Grid™***, indicating a preference for focusing on the task or people side of management

360 degree branding MARKETING taking an inclusive approach in branding a product by bringing the brand to all points of consumer contact

three Ss GENERAL MANAGEMENT a classification of ***decision making*** relating to strategy, structure, and systems. ***Sumantra Ghoshal*** has suggested replacing the three Ss model with the ***three Ps***.

three steps and a stumble FINANCE, BANKING, AND ACCOUNTING a rule of thumb used on the stock market that if the Federal Reserve increases interest rates three times consecutively, stock market prices will go down (*slang*)

threshold company GENERAL MANAGEMENT a company that is on the verge of becoming well established in the business world (*slang*)

thrift institution FINANCE, BANKING, AND ACCOUNTING a bank that offers savings accounts. See ***savings and loan association***, ***savings bank***

THRIP (*S. Africa*) FINANCE, BANKING, AND ACCOUNTING Technology and Human Resources for Industry Programme, a collabora-

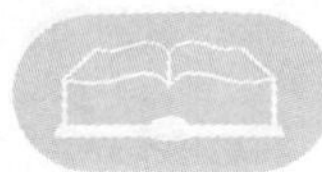

tive program involving industry, government, and educational and research institutions that supports research and development in technology, science, and engineering

throw somebody a curve ball GENERAL MANAGEMENT to do or say something unexpected, for example, during a meeting or a project *(slang)*

Tichy, **Noel M.** GENERAL MANAGEMENT U.S. academic. Known for his research on the ***transformational theory of leadership***, which developed the work of ***James Burns***. See *The Transformational Leader*, (1986 coauthor).

tick FINANCE, BANKING, AND ACCOUNTING the least amount by which a value such as the price of a stock or a rate of interest can rise or fall. This could be, for example, an eighth of a dollar or a hundredth of a percentage point.
have ticks in all the right boxes GENERAL MANAGEMENT to be on course to meet a series of objectives *(slang)*

tie-in MARKETING an advertising campaign in which two or more companies share the costs by combining their products or services *(slang)*

tight money ECONOMICS a situation where it is expensive to borrow because of restrictive government policy or high demand

time and motion study HR & PERSONNEL the measurement and analysis of the motions or steps involved in a particular task and the time taken to complete each one. Time and motion study can be broken down into two distinct techniques: ***method study***, the analysis of how people work and how jobs are performed, and ***work measurement***, the time taken to complete each job. It can be used to set job standards, simplify work, and check and improve the efficiency of workers. Time and motion study is similar to the broader concept of ***work study***.

time keeping HR & PERSONNEL the activity of recording the amount of time an employee works. Time keeping may involve a formal ***clock in*** system or it may be an informal arrangement based on trust.

time management GENERAL MANAGEMENT conscious control of the amount of time spent on work activities, in order to maximize personal efficiency. Time management involves analyzing how time is spent, and then prioritizing different work tasks. Activities can be reorganized to concentrate on those that are most important. Various techniques can be of help in carrying out tasks more quickly, and efficiently, such as information handling skills; verbal, and written, communication skills; ***delegation***; and daily time planning. Time management is an important tool in avoiding ***information overload***.

time off in lieu HR & PERSONNEL ***leave*** given to compensate an employee for additional hours worked. Time off in lieu is often given instead of a payment for ***overtime***. Abbr **TOIL**

timeous (*S. Africa*) GENERAL MANAGEMENT done or happening in good time

time series GENERAL MANAGEMENT a series of measurements, observations, and recordings of a set of variables at successive points in time. The time series forecasting technique is commonly used to track long-term trends and seasonal fluctuations and variations in data or statistics. It can be applied in an economic context in the review of sales, production, and investment performance, or in a sociological context in the compilation of census or panel study statistics. It can include the use of input-output analysis and ***exponential smoothing***.

time sovereignty GENERAL MANAGEMENT control over the way you spend your time. Time sovereignty gives employees the ability to arrange their working lives to suit their own situations. It involves handing decisions on working hours to employees, enabling them to ***work flexibly***, so that they can better juggle the ***work-life balance***. Time sovereignty is more than just good ***time management***, as it gives people control over the way they arrange their lives, rather than having to manage time within the decreed hours. It has been argued that rather than viewing work and home as separate lives, employees should see that they are living just one life that integrates both parts. Time sovereignty gives mastery over managing life as a whole.

time span of discretion HR & PERSONNEL the time between starting and completing the longest task within a job, used as a measure of the level of a job within an organization. The time span of discretion was originated by ***Elliot Jaques*** as part of the ***Glacier studies***. He saw two components to any job: prescribed and discretionary. The time span of the discretionary component refers to the longest span of time that employees spend working on a task on their own initiative, and often unsupervised. This reflects the amount of responsibility an individual has, and Jaques found that the time span of discretion rises steadily with the position of an employee in the company hierarchy. An hourly worker may have a one-hour time span of discretion, a middle manager may have one year, and a chief executive of a large company may have 20 years.

time spread FINANCE, BANKING, AND ACCOUNTING the purchase and sale of options in the same commodity or security with the same price and different maturities

time study GENERAL MANAGEMENT a ***work measurement*** technique designed to establish the time taken to complete work tasks in order to set a ***standard time*** for each task

time value FINANCE, BANKING, AND ACCOUNTING the premium at which an option is trading relative to its ***intrinsic value***

TIN *abbr* E-COMMERCE terminal identification number, a bank-provided identification number that uniquely identifies a merchant for point-of-sale transactions

tire kicker MARKETING a prospective customer who asks for a lot of information and requires a lot of attention but does not actually buy anything *(slang)*

title inflation HR & PERSONNEL the practice of giving an employee a job title that implies status and importance. Title inflation renames an employee's job with a title that sounds more elevated or grand than the old one even though the nature of the job has not changed. This is sometimes used as a form of ***motivation*** or incentive to make employees feel rewarded and more valued.

TLS *abbr* E-COMMERCE transaction layer security, a payment protocol based on ***SSL*** that offers improved security for credit card transactions

TNA HR & PERSONNEL see ***training needs analysis***

Toffler, **Alvin** (*b.* 1928) GENERAL MANAGEMENT U.S. futurist and social commentator. Known for his analyses of the future which embraced the impact of the Information Society and the wired age, and the knowledge economy. His first book was *Future Shock* (1970).

TOIL HR & PERSONNEL see ***time off in lieu***

top-down approach GENERAL MANAGEMENT an autocratic style of ***leadership*** in which strategies and solutions are identified by ***senior management*** and then cascaded down through the organization. The top-down approach can be considered a feature of large ***bureaucracies*** and is associated with a ***command and control approach*** to management. A number of management gurus, particularly ***Gary Hamel***, have criticized it as an out-of-date style that leads to stagnation and ***business failure***. It is the opposite of a ***bottom-up approach***.

top level domain E-COMMERCE the concluding part of a domain name, for example, the .com,.net, or .co.uk suffixes.

top management HR & PERSONNEL an informal term for ***senior management*** or a ***board of directors***

total cost of ownership GENERAL MANAGEMENT a structured approach to calculating the ***costs*** associated with buying and using a product or service. Total cost of ownership takes the purchase cost of an item into account but also considers related costs such as ordering, delivery, subsequent usage and maintenance, supplier costs, and after-delivery costs. Originally designed as a process for measuring IT expense after implementation, total cost of ownership considers only financial expenses and excludes any ***cost-benefit analysis***. Abbr **TCO**

total-debt-to-total-assets FINANCE, BANKING, AND ACCOUNTING the premium at which an option is trading relative to its ***intrinsic value***

total environmental management GENERAL MANAGEMENT see ***environmental management***

total loss control GENERAL MANAGEMENT the implementation of safety procedures to prevent or limit the impact of a complete or partial loss of an organization's physical assets. Total loss control is based on safety audit and prevention techniques. It is concerned with reduction or elimination of losses caused by accidents and occupational ill health. The extent to which it is implemented is usually decided by calculating the total organizational asset cost and weighing this against the likelihood of failure and its worst possible effects on the organization. Total loss control was developed in the 1960s as an approach to ***risk management***.

total productive maintenance OPERATIONS & PRODUCTION a Japanese approach to maximizing the effectiveness of the facilities used within a business. Total productive maintenance, or TPM, aims to improve the condition and performance of particular facilities through simple, repetitive maintenance activities. Based on a culture of teamworking and consensus, TPM teams are encouraged to take a proactive approach to maintenance. A team is made up of operators and those involved in the setting up and the maintenance of the facilities. TPM can be compared to ***reliability centered maintenance***.

total quality management GENERAL MANAGEMENT a philosophy and style of management that gives everyone in an organization responsibility for delivering quality to the customer. Total quality management views each task in the organization as a process that is in a customer/supplier relationship with the next process. The aim at each stage is to define and meet the customer's requirements in order to maximize the satisfaction of the final consumer at the lowest possible cost. Total quality management constitutes a challenge to organizations that have to manage the conflict between ***cost-cutting*** and the commitment of employees to ***continuous improvement***. Achievement of quality can be assessed by ***quality awards*** and ***quality standards***. Abbr **TQM**

PHILIP CROSBY (pp. 978–79); W. EDWARDS DEMING (pp. 980–81)

touchdown center GENERAL MANAGEMENT a center where businesspeople can make calls and use computers and the Internet whilst traveling (*slang*)

tourist HR & PERSONNEL somebody who takes a training course in order to get away from his or her job (*slang*)

Townsend, Robert (*b.* 1920) GENERAL MANAGEMENT U.S. business executive. One time chairman of Avis Rent-a-car, who built up the company into an international organization. Best known for his book *Up the Organization* (1970), a humorous A-Z of management practices.

toxic employee HR & PERSONNEL a disgruntled and resentful employee who spreads discontent within a company or department (*slang*)

Toyota production system OPERATIONS & PRODUCTION a ***manufacturing system***, developed by Toyota in Japan after World War II, which aims to increase production efficiency by the elimination of waste in all its forms. The Toyota production system was invented, and made to work, by ***Taiichi Ohno***. Japan's fledgling car-making industry was suffering from poor ***productivity***, and Ohno was brought into Toyota with an initial assignment of catching up with the productivity levels of Ford's car plants. In analyzing the problem, he decided that although Japanese workers must be working at the same rate as their American counterparts, waste and inefficiency were the main causes of their different productivity levels. Ohno identified waste in a number of forms, including overproduction, waiting time, transportation problems, inefficient processing, ***inventory***, and defective products. The philosophy of TPS is to remove or minimize the influence of all these elements. In order to achieve this, TPS evolved to operate under ***lean production*** conditions. It is made up of soft, or cultural aspects, such as automation with the human touch—***autonomation***—and hard, or technical, aspects, which include ***just-in-time***, ***kanban***, and ***production smoothing***. Each aspect is equally important and complementary. TPS has proven itself as one of the most efficient manufacturing systems in the world but although leading companies have adopted it in one form or another, few have been able to replicate the success of Toyota. Abbr **TPS**

TPM OPERATIONS & PRODUCTION see ***total productive maintenance***

TPS OPERATIONS & PRODUCTION see ***Toyota production system***

TQM GENERAL MANAGEMENT see ***total quality management***

tracker fund FINANCE, BANKING, AND ACCOUNTING = ***index fund***

tracking MARKETING research designed to monitor changes in the public perception of a product or organization over a period of time

tracking stock FINANCE, BANKING, AND ACCOUNTING a stock whose dividends are tied to the performance of a subsidiary of the corporation that owns it

trade barrier ECONOMICS a condition imposed by a government to limit free exchange of goods internationally. ***NTBs***, safety standards, and tariffs are typical trade barriers.

trade delegation MARKETING a group of manufacturers or suppliers who visit another country to increase export business

Trade Development Board FINANCE, BANKING, AND ACCOUNTING a government agency that was established in 1983 to promote trade and explore new markets for Singapore products and offers various schemes of assistance to companies. Abbr **TDB**

traded option FINANCE, BANKING, AND ACCOUNTING an option that is bought and sold on an exchange

  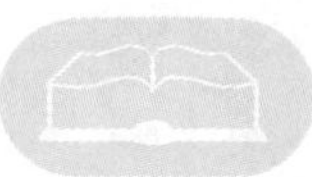    

tradefair MARKETING a commercial exhibition designed to bring together buyers and sellers from a particular market sector. For the publishing industry, for example, the annual Frankfurt Book Fair is a key trade fair.

trademark GENERAL MANAGEMENT an identifiable mark on a product that may be a symbol, words, or both, that connects the product to the trader or producer of that product. In the United Kingdom, a trademark can be registered at the Register of Trademarks, giving the producer or trader protection from fraudulent use. Any use of the trademark without permission gives the owner the right to sue for damages.

trade name MARKETING the proprietary name given by the producer or manufacturer to a product or service. A trade name occasionally becomes the generic name for products of a similar nature, for example, "Thermos" is often applied to all insulated flasks, and "Kleenex" to all tissues.

Tradenet GENERAL MANAGEMENT an electronic system for applying for import or export licenses from ***Trade Development Boards***

TRADENZ FINANCE, BANKING, AND ACCOUNTING see ***New Zealand Trade Development Board***

trade off analysis GENERAL MANAGEMENT see ***conjoint analysis***

trade point FINANCE, BANKING, AND ACCOUNTING a stock exchange that is less formal than the major exchanges

trade press MARKETING specialist publications aimed at people in particular industries or business sectors

trades and labour council (*ANZ*) HR & PERSONNEL a collective organization that represents unions at a particular level such as that of a state or territory

trade union (*U.K.*) HR & PERSONNEL, GENERAL MANAGEMENT = ***labor union***

trade war ECONOMICS competition between two or more countries for a share of international or domestic trade

trade-weighted index ECONOMICS an index that measures the value of a country's currency in relation to the currencies of its trading partners

trading halt FINANCE, BANKING, AND ACCOUNTING a stoppage of trading in a stock on an exchange, usually in response to information about a company, or concern about rapid movement of the share price

trading partner E-COMMERCE the merchant, customer, or financial institution with whom an EDI (***electronic data interchange***) transaction takes place. Transactions can be either between senders and receivers of EDI messages or within distribution channels in an industry, for example, financial institutions or wholesalers.

traffic E-COMMERCE the number of visitors to a Web site measured in any of several ways, for example, ***click-throughs***, hits, or page views

traffic builder MARKETING a marketing promotion that is designed to generate an increase in customers (*slang*)

training HR & PERSONNEL activities designed to facilitate the learning and development of new and existing skills, and to improve the performance of specific tasks or roles. Training may involve structured programs or more informal and interactive activities, such as group discussion or ***role playing***, which promote ***experiential learning***. A wide range of activities, including classroom-based courses, ***on-the-job training***, and business or ***simulation games***, are used for training. Audio-visual and multimedia aids such as videos and CD-ROMs may also be employed. Training may be carried out by an internal training officer or department, or by external training organizations. The effectiveness of training can be maximized by conducting a ***training needs analysis*** beforehand, and following up with ***evaluation of training***. Training should result in individual learning and enhanced organizational performance.

training group HR & PERSONNEL see ***sensitivity training***

training needs HR & PERSONNEL a shortage of skills or abilities which could be reduced or eliminated by means of training and development. Training needs hinder employees in the fulfillment of their job responsibilities and prevent an organization from achieving its objectives. They may be caused by a lack of skills, knowledge, or understanding, or arise from changes in the workplace. Training needs are identified through ***training needs analysis***.

training needs analysis HR & PERSONNEL the identification of ***training needs*** at employee, departmental, or organizational level, in order for the organization to perform effectively. The aim of training needs analysis is to ensure that training addresses existing problems, is tailored to organizational objectives, and is delivered in an effective and cost-efficient manner. Training needs analysis involves: monitoring current performance using techniques such as observation, interviews, and questionnaires; anticipating future shortfalls or problems; identifying the type and level of training required; and analyzing how this can best be provided. Abbr **TNA**

trait theory GENERAL MANAGEMENT the belief that all leaders display the same key personality traits. Trait theory developed from the ***great man theory*** of leadership as researchers attempted to identify universally applicable characteristics that distinguish leaders from other people. During the 1920s and 1930s, theorists compiled lists of traits, but these were often contradictory and no single trait was consistently identified with good leadership.

transaction FINANCE, BANKING, AND ACCOUNTING a trade of a security

transactional analysis GENERAL MANAGEMENT a theory that describes sets of feelings, thoughts, and behavior or ego states that influence how individuals interact, communicate, and relate with each other. The theories of transactional analysis were developed between the 1950s and 1970s by Eric Berne, a U.S. psychiatrist who studied the behavior patterns of his patients. Berne identified three ego states, parent, adult, and child, and examined how these affected interactions or transactions between individuals. Transactional analysis is used in psychotherapy but also has applications in education and training. In ***human relations*** training, transactional analysis is used to help people understand and adapt their behavior and develop more effective ways of communicating. Abbr **TA**

transactional theory of leadership GENERAL MANAGEMENT the idea that effective ***leadership*** is based on a reciprocal exchange between leaders and followers. Transactional leadership involves giving employees something in return for their compliance and acceptance of authority, usually in the form of incentives such as pay raises or an increase in status. The theory was propounded by ***James MacGregor Burns***, and is closely linked with his ***transformational theory of leadership***, which involves moral, rather than tangible, rewards for compliance.

transaction e-commerce E-COMMERCE the electronic sale of goods and services, either business-to-business or business-to-customer

transaction file OPERATIONS & PRODUCTION see ***inventory record***

transaction history FINANCE, BANKING, AND ACCOUNTING a record of all of an investor's transactions with a broker

transaction layer security E-COMMERCE = ***TLS***

transaction message *or* **transaction set** E-COMMERCE the EDI (***electronic data interchange***) equivalent of a paper document, exchanged as part of an e-commerce transaction, comprising at least one data segment representing the document sandwiched between a header and a trailer. It is called a transaction message within the ***UN/EDIFACT*** protocol and a transaction set within the ANSI X.12 protocol.

transactions motive ECONOMICS the motive that consumers have to hold money for their likely purchases in the immediate future

transferable skill HR & PERSONNEL a skill typically considered as not specifically related to a particular job or task. Transferable skills are usually those related to relationship, leadership, communication, critical thinking, analysis, and organization.

✔ STAYING MARKETABLE: IDENTIFYING YOUR TRANSFERABLE SKILLS (pp. 786–87)

transfer of training HR & PERSONNEL the appropriate and continued application of skills learned during a training course to the working environment. A measure of the transfer of training should form part of any ***evaluation of training*** carried out, as it can help demonstrate the cost-effectiveness of a training program. It is normally measured between three to six months after the training course in order to allow trainees to apply their newly learned skills in the workplace.

transfer out fee FINANCE, BANKING, AND ACCOUNTING a fee for closing an account with a broker

transfer pricing MARKETING a pricing method used when supplying products or services from one part of an organization to another. The transfer pricing method can be used to supply goods either at cost or at profit if profit targets are to be achieved. This can cause difficulties if an internal customer can buy more cheaply outside the organization. Multinational businesses have been known to take advantage of this pricing policy by transferring products from one country to another in order for profits to be higher in the country where corporation tax is lower.

transformational theory of leadership GENERAL MANAGEMENT the idea that effective ***leadership*** is based on inspiring and enthusing subordinates with a ***corporate vision*** in order to gain their commitment. Transformational leadership theory was developed by ***James MacGregor Burns***, and is similar to his ***transactional theory of leadership***. Both involve an exchange between leaders and followers, but while the transactional leader offers tangible rewards for compliance, the transformational leader offers moral rewards.

transformative potential GENERAL MANAGEMENT the ability of a force such as information technology to transform the economy, society, and business

transmission E-COMMERCE digital data sent electronically from one trading partner to another or from a trading partner to a ***value-added network***

transmission control standards E-COMMERCE the defined format by which to address the ***electronic envelopes*** used by trading partners to exchange business data

Transnet GENERAL MANAGEMENT a state-owned holding company that controls the main South African transport networks

treasurer FINANCE, BANKING, AND ACCOUNTING somebody who is responsible for an organization's funds

Treasurer (*ANZ*) FINANCE, BANKING, AND ACCOUNTING the minister responsible for financial and economic matters in a national, state, or territory government

Treasury bill FINANCE, BANKING, AND ACCOUNTING a short-term security issued by the government. Also known as ***T-bill***

Treasury bond FINANCE, BANKING, AND ACCOUNTING a long-term bond issued by the U.S. government that bears interest

treasury management GENERAL MANAGEMENT the management functions responsible for the custody and investment of money, cashflow forecasting, capital provision, credit management, ***risk management***, and the collection of accounts. Treasury management has a strategic role in the management of an organization's finances.

Treasury note FINANCE, BANKING, AND ACCOUNTING

1. a note issued by the U.S. government

2. a short-term debt instrument issued by the Australian federal government. Treasury notes are issued on a tender basis for periods of 13 and 26 weeks.

tree

like nailing jelly to a tree GENERAL MANAGEMENT used for describing a task that is considered impossible, especially when the difficulty arises from poor or sloppy specifications (*slang*)

Tregoe, Benjamin Bainbridge (*b.* 1927) GENERAL MANAGEMENT U.S. manager and consultant. See ***Kepner, Charles Higgins***

trend STATISTICS the movement in a particular direction of the values of a variable in a statistical study over a period of time

trendline STATISTICS the tendency to move in a particular direction shown by data variables over a period of time such as a month or year

trickle-down theory ECONOMICS the theory that if markets are open and programs exist to improve basic health and education, growth will extend from successful parts of a developing country economy to the rest

triple I organization GENERAL MANAGEMENT a type of ***corporate culture*** identified by ***Charles Handy*** in which the focus is on three areas: Information, Intelligence, and Ideas. The triple I organization recognizes the value of information and learning. It minimizes the distinction between managers and workers, concentrating instead on people and the need to pursue learning, both personal, ***lifelong learning***, and ***organizational learning***, in order to keep up with the pace of change.

triple tax exempt FINANCE, BANKING, AND ACCOUNTING exempt from federal, state, and local income taxes

Trist, Eric Lansdown (1909–93) GENERAL MANAGEMENT British social psychologist. Known for research into sociotechnical systems, particularly in the U.K. coal-mining industry, with associates such as ***Fred Emery***, at the Tavistock Institute of Human Relations.

trolling MARKETING making cold calls in an effort to solicit new business (*slang*)

Trompenaars, Fons (*b.* 1952) GENERAL MANAGEMENT Dutch academic. Known for his research into how national cultures influence ***corporate cultures***. His work owes much to that of ***Geert Hofstede***, and is published in *Riding the Waves of Culture* (1993).

GEERT HOFSTEDE (pp. 1004–05)

trophy wife GENERAL MANAGEMENT the young wife of an older executive (*slang*)

true interest cost FINANCE, BANKING, AND ACCOUNTING the effective rate of interest paid by the issuer on a debt security that is sold at a discount

trump MARKETING to make something such as an opponent's product appear useless because what you have is so much better (*slang*)

trust
1. FINANCE, BANKING, AND ACCOUNTING a collection of assets held by somebody for another person's benefit
2. ECONOMICS a company that has a ***monopoly***

trust account FINANCE, BANKING, AND ACCOUNTING a bank account that is held in trust for somebody else

trust company FINANCE, BANKING, AND ACCOUNTING a company whose business is administering trusts

trustee FINANCE, BANKING, AND ACCOUNTING somebody who holds assets in trust

trustee in bankruptcy FINANCE, BANKING, AND ACCOUNTING somebody appointed by a court to manage the finances of a bankrupt person or company

trusteeship FINANCE, BANKING, AND ACCOUNTING the holding of a trust, or the term of such a holding

trust fund FINANCE, BANKING, AND ACCOUNTING assets held in trust by a trustee for the trust's beneficiaries

trust officer FINANCE, BANKING, AND ACCOUNTING somebody who manages the assets of a trust, especially for a bank that is acting as a trustee

tshayile time (*S. Africa*) GENERAL MANAGEMENT an informal term for the end of the working day (*slang*)

TTFN *abbr* GENERAL MANAGEMENT ta ta for now (*slang*)

TTP *abbr* E-COMMERCE Trusted Third Party, an independent, trustworthy organization that verifies individuals, companies, and organizations over the Internet

Tulgan, Bruce Lorin (*b.* 1967) GENERAL MANAGEMENT U.S. lawyer, writer, and consultant. Pioneer of the concept that young people have a different attitude to work than their forebears and need to be managed differently. He explores this in *Managing Generation X* (1995).

turkey trot HR & PERSONNEL the practice of transferring a difficult, incompetent, or nonessential employee from one department to another (*slang*)

turn a profit GENERAL MANAGEMENT to make a profit (*slang*)

turnaround management GENERAL MANAGEMENT the implementation of a set of actions required to save an organization from ***business failure*** and return it to operational normality and financial solvency. Turnaround management usually requires strong ***leadership*** and can include ***corporate restructuring*** and ***redundancies***, an investigation of the root causes of failure, and long-term programs to revitalize the organization.

turnkey contract GENERAL MANAGEMENT an agreement in which a contractor designs, constructs, and manages a ***project*** until it is ready to be handed over to the client and operation can begin immediately

24 E-COMMERCE the American National Standards Institute accepted protocol for the electronic interchange of business transactions

24/7 GENERAL MANAGEMENT twenty-four hours a day, seven days a week. Businesses often advertise themselves as being "open 24/7." (*slang*)

2L8 *abbr* GENERAL MANAGEMENT too late (*slang*)

type I error STATISTICS an error arising from incorrectly rejecting the null hypothesis in a statistical study

type II error STATISTICS an error arising from incorrectly accepting the null hypothesis in a statistical study

Tzu, Sun (*b.* uncertain) GENERAL MANAGEMENT Chinese general. Although he lived over 2,400 years ago, he is said to influence modern business thinking, based on his thoughts on ***strategy*** recorded in *The Art of War* (various translations).

 SUN TZU (pp. 1050–51)

U

UCE *abbr* E-COMMERCE unsolicited commercial e-mail, the official term for ***spam***

UIF *abbr* (*S. Africa*) FINANCE, BANKING, AND ACCOUNTING Unemployment Insurance Fund, a system administered through payroll deductions that insures employees against loss of earnings through being made unemployed by such causes as retrenchment, illness, or maternity

ultra vires activity FINANCE, BANKING, AND ACCOUNTING an act that is not permitted by applicable rules, such as a corporate charter

unbalanced growth ECONOMICS the result when not all sectors of an economy can grow at the same rate

unbundling FINANCE, BANKING, AND ACCOUNTING dividing a company into separate constituent companies, often to sell all or some of them after a takeover

uncertainty analysis STATISTICS a study designed to assess the extent to which the variability in an outcome variable is caused by uncertainty at the time of estimating the input parameters of the study

uncollected funds FINANCE, BANKING, AND ACCOUNTING money deriving from the deposit of an instrument that a bank has not been able to negotiate

uncollected trade bill FINANCE, BANKING, AND ACCOUNTING an account with an outstanding balance for purchases made from the company that holds it

unconditional bid FINANCE, BANKING, AND ACCOUNTING in a takeover battle, an occasion in which a bidder will pay the offered price irrespective of how many shares are acquired

unconsolidated FINANCE, BANKING, AND ACCOUNTING not grouped together, as of shares or holdings

uncontested bid FINANCE, BANKING, AND ACCOUNTING an offering of a contract by a government or other organization to one bidder only, without competition

UNCTAD *abbr* FINANCE, BANKING, AND ACCOUNTING United Nations Conference on Trade and Development, the focal point within the UN system for the integrated treatment of development and interrelated issues in trade, finance, technology, and investment

underbanked FINANCE, BANKING, AND ACCOUNTING without enough brokers to sell a new issue

underlying asset FINANCE, BANKING, AND ACCOUNTING an asset that is the subject of an option

underlying inflation FINANCE, BANKING, AND ACCOUNTING the rate of inflation that does not take mortgage costs into account

underlying security FINANCE, BANKING, AND ACCOUNTING a security that is the subject of an option

undermargined account FINANCE, BANKING, AND ACCOUNTING an account that does not have enough money to cover its margin requirements, resulting in a margin call

undervalued FINANCE, BANKING, AND ACCOUNTING used to describe an asset that is available for purchase at a price lower than its worth

undervalued currency FINANCE, BANKING, AND ACCOUNTING a currency that costs less to buy with another currency than its worth in goods

underwrite FINANCE, BANKING, AND ACCOUNTING to assume risk, especially for a new issue or an insurance policy

underwriter FINANCE, BANKING, AND ACCOUNTING a person or organization that buys an issue from a corporation and sells it to investors

underwriters' syndicate FINANCE, BANKING, AND ACCOUNTING a group of organizations that buys an issue from a corporation and sells it to investors

underwriting FINANCE, BANKING, AND ACCOUNTING the buying of an issue from a corporation for the purpose of selling it to investors

underwriting income FINANCE, BANKING, AND ACCOUNTING the money that an insurance company makes because the premiums it collects exceed the claims it pays out

underwriting spread FINANCE, BANKING, AND ACCOUNTING an amount that is the difference between what an organization pays for an issue and what it receives when it sells the issue to investors

UNDP *abbr* FINANCE, BANKING, AND ACCOUNTING United Nations Development Program, the world's largest source of grants for sustainable human development. Its aims include the elimination of poverty, environmental regeneration, job creation, and advancement of women.

unearned income FINANCE, BANKING, AND ACCOUNTING income received from sources other than employment

unearned increment FINANCE, BANKING, AND ACCOUNTING an increase in the value of a property that arises from causes other than the owner's improvements or expenditure

unearned premium FINANCE, BANKING, AND ACCOUNTING the amount of premiums paid on a policy that an insurance company refunds when the policy is terminated

uneconomic ECONOMICS not profitable for a country, firm, or investor in the short or long run

UN/EDIFACT E-COMMERCE a standard for ***electronic data interchange*** widely used in Western Europe and very similar to the ***ANSI X.12 standard***. Also known as ***EDIFACT***, ***EDI For Administration, Commerce, and Trade***

unemployment ECONOMICS the situation when some members of a country's labor force are willing to work but cannot find employment

uneven playing field MARKETING a situation in which some competitors have an unfair advantage over others (*slang*)

ungluing GENERAL MANAGEMENT the process of breaking up traditional supply chains or groups of cooperating organizations by taking control of the element of mutual interest that holds the partners together

unhappy camper HR & PERSONNEL somebody who has grievances against his or her employer (*slang*)

unimodal STATISTICS describes a frequency or probability distribution that has only one mode

uninstalled HR & PERSONNEL dismissed from employment (*slang*)

uninsurable FINANCE, BANKING, AND ACCOUNTING considered unsuitable for insurance, especially because of being a poor risk

unique selling point MARKETING, OPERATIONS & PRODUCTION a specific feature that differentiates a product from similar products. Also known as a **unique selling proposition**. Abbr **USP**

unique visitor E-COMMERCE somebody who visits a Web site more than once within a specified period of time. Tracking software that monitors site traffic can distinguish between visitors who only visit the site once and unique visitors who return to the site. Unique visitor statistics are considered to be the most accurate measurement of a Web site's popularity because they reflect the number of people who want to be there rather than those who have arrived there by accident. Furthermore, unlike hits (which are measured by the number of files that are requested from a site) unique visitors are measured according to their unique ***IP addresses***. This means that no matter how many times they visit the site, they are only counted once.

unissued stock FINANCE, BANKING, AND ACCOUNTING stock that is authorized but has not been issued

unit FINANCE, BANKING, AND ACCOUNTING a collection of securities traded together as one item

unit cost FINANCE, BANKING, AND ACCOUNTING the cost to a company of producing one item that it markets

unit of account ECONOMICS a unit of a country's currency that can be used in payment for goods or in a firm's accounting

unit of trade FINANCE, BANKING, AND ACCOUNTING the smallest amount that can be bought or sold of a share of stock, or a contract included in an option

unit trust (*U.K.*) FINANCE, BANKING, AND ACCOUNTING = ***mutual fund***

universe MARKETING the total market for a product or service

UNIX E-COMMERCE a computer operating system enabling many people to connect to the same resources at any given time and limiting the risk of a crash

unlimited liability FINANCE, BANKING, AND ACCOUNTING full responsibility for the obligations of a general partnership

unlisted FINANCE, BANKING, AND ACCOUNTING not traded on an exchange

unlisted securities market FINANCE, BANKING, AND ACCOUNTING the market for stocks that are not listed on an exchange

unlisted security FINANCE, BANKING, AND ACCOUNTING a security that is not traded on an exchange

unofficial strike HR & PERSONNEL a ***strike*** that is called without the approval or recognition of a labor union. An unofficial strike, also described as a **wildcat strike**, is a form of ***industrial action*** often associated with the activities of shop stewards. Any workers involved do not receive ***strike pay***.

unquoted FINANCE, BANKING, AND ACCOUNTING having no publicly stated price, usually referring to an unlisted security

unrealized capital gain FINANCE, BANKING, AND ACCOUNTING a profit from the holding of an asset worth more than its purchase price, but not yet sold

unrealized profit/loss FINANCE, BANKING, AND ACCOUNTING a profit/loss that need not be reported as income, for example, deriving from the holding of an asset worth more/less than its purchase price, but not yet sold

unreason GENERAL MANAGEMENT the process of thinking the unlikely and doing the unreasonable that can be a means by which an organization or individual achieves success

unremittable gain (*U.K.*) FINANCE, BANKING, AND ACCOUNTING in the United Kingdom, a capital gain that cannot be imported into the taxpayer's country, especially because of currency restrictions

unseasoned issue FINANCE, BANKING, AND ACCOUNTING an issue of shares or bonds for which there is no existing market. See ***seasoned issue***

unsecured FINANCE, BANKING, AND ACCOUNTING without collateral

unsecured debt FINANCE, BANKING, AND ACCOUNTING money borrowed without supplying collateral

unsecured loan FINANCE, BANKING, AND ACCOUNTING a loan made with no collateral. Also known as ***signature loan***

unsocial hours HR & PERSONNEL the working hours of an employee outside the socially recognized working day, for which an additional payment is sometimes made

unstable equilibrium ECONOMICS a market situation in which if there is a movement (of price or quantity) away from the equilibrium, existing forces will push the price even further away

upsell MARKETING to sell customers a higher-priced version of a product they have bought previously

upsizing HR & PERSONNEL see ***downsizing***

upstairs market FINANCE, BANKING, AND ACCOUNTING the place where traders for major brokerages and institutions do business at an exchange

upstream progress GENERAL MANAGEMENT advancement against opposition or in difficult conditions. A company or project can make upstream progress if it moves toward achieving its objectives despite impediments. See ***downstream progress***

URL *abbr* E-COMMERCE uniform resource locator, a full Web address, for example, http://www.yahoo.com.

Urwick, Lyndall Fownes (1891–1983) GENERAL MANAGEMENT British educator and consultant. Promulgator of the theories of ***Frederick Winslow Taylor*** and ***Henri Fayol***, which he developed in *Elements of Administration* (1944). Urwick was a founder of the British Institute of Management (1947), and of the management consultancy firm, Urwick Orr (1934).

HENRI FAYOL (pp. 986–87); FREDERICK WINSLOW TAYLOR (pp. 1054–55)

usability E-COMMERCE the suitability of a Web site design from the user's perspective. The term has been popularized by Web design guru Jakob Nielsen who has stressed that a Web site must be simple to use. One of the main points of usability relates to download times. For Nielsen, "fast response times are the most important criterion for Web pages." Nielsen also believes usability involves a human approach. He states that "what constitutes a good site relates to the core basis of human nature and not to technology."

used credit FINANCE, BANKING, AND ACCOUNTING the portion of a line of credit that is no longer available

usenet E-COMMERCE the vast information space encompassed by the thousands of publicly available newsgroups

USP MARKETING, OPERATIONS & PRODUCTION see ***unique selling point***

utopian socialism ECONOMICS a form of socialism in which the use and production of all services and goods are held collectively by the group or community, rather than by a central government

V

vacation HR & PERSONNEL a day of work on which an employee is not required to be at work but is paid by the employer. The number of days of vacation is agreed in the ***contract of employment*** and may be dependent on the employee's length of service.

valence HR & PERSONNEL see ***expectancy theory***

value added GENERAL MANAGEMENT
1. originally, the difference between the cost of bought-in materials and the eventual selling price of the finished product
2. loosely, the features that differentiate one product or service from another and thus create value for the customer. Value added is a customer perception of what makes a product or service desirable over others and worth a higher price. Value added is more difficult to measure without a physical end product, but value can be added to services as well as physical goods, through the process of ***value engineering***. Also known as ***added value***

value-added network E-COMMERCE an organization that provides messaging-related functions and EDI communications services, for example, protocol matching and line-speed conversion, between trading partners. Abbr **VAN**. Also known as ***third-party network***, ***third-party service provider***

value-added reseller FINANCE, BANKING, AND ACCOUNTING a merchant who buys products at retail and packages them with additional items for sale to customers. Abbr **VAR**

value-added services MARKETING services that enhance a basic product, such as the design in engineering components or technical support for software

value-added tax FINANCE, BANKING, AND ACCOUNTING a tax added at each stage in the manufacture of a product. It acts as a replacement for a sales tax in almost every industrialized country outside North America. It is levied on selected goods and services, paid by organizations on items they buy and then charged to customers of what they produce or provide. Abbr **VAT**

value-adding intermediary GENERAL MANAGEMENT a distributor who adds value to a product before selling it to a customer, for example, by installing software or a modem in a computer

value analysis OPERATIONS & PRODUCTION a cost reduction and ***problem solving*** technique that analyzes an existing product or service in order to reduce or eliminate any costs that do not contribute to value or performance. Value analysis usually focuses on design issues relating to the function of a product or service, looking at the properties that make it work, or which are ***unique selling points***.

value chain
1. HR & PERSONNEL the most traditional approach to exploring one's career prospects, which involves identifying the next, most obvious, move in a career path. The next step is usually assumed to be the role occupied by a manager.
2. GENERAL MANAGEMENT the sequence of activities a company performs in order to design, produce, market, deliver, and support its product or service. The concept of the value chain was first suggested by ***Michael Porter*** in 1985, to demonstrate how value for the customer accumulates along the chain of organizational activities that make up the final customer product or service. Porter describes two different types of business activity: primary and secondary. Primary activities are concerned principally with transforming inputs, such as raw materials, into outputs, in the form of products or services and in delivery and after-sales support. Secondary activities support the primary activities and include procurement, technology development, and human resource management. All of these activities form part of the value chain and can be analyzed to assess where opportunities for ***competitive advantage*** may lie. To survive competition and supply what customers want to buy the firm has to ensure that all value chain activities link together and fit, even if some of the activities take place outside the organization. Techniques for **value chain analysis** include ***internal cost analysis***, ***internal differentiation analysis***, and ***vertical linkage analysis***.

value chain analysis GENERAL MANAGEMENT see ***value chain***

value engineering OPERATIONS & PRODUCTION the practice of designing a product or service so that it gives as much value as possible to the consumer. Value engineering analyses a developing product so that the focus is on those attributes that make the product appeal to the consumer over competing items and produce ***customer satisfaction***. Value engineering also concentrates on eliminating costs that do not contribute to the creation of customer value.

value for customs purposes only FINANCE, BANKING, AND ACCOUNTING what somebody importing something into the United States declares that it is worth

value innovation GENERAL MANAGEMENT a strategic approach to business growth, involving a shift away from a focus on the existing competition to one of trying to create entirely new markets. Value innovation can be achieved by implementing a focus on ***innovation*** and creation of new marketspace. The term was coined by ***W. Chan Kim*** and ***Renée Mauborgne*** in 1997.

value investing FINANCE, BANKING, AND ACCOUNTING the preferential buying of securities that appear to be worth far more than their prices

value map GENERAL MANAGEMENT the level of value that the market recognizes in a product or service and that helps to differentiate it from competitors

value mesh HR & PERSONNEL an expanded look at the positioning of a job in the overall marketplace. Seen as a way of helping employees identify their next move, a value mesh encourages them to consider all opportunities within their organization and others.

value proposition
1. MARKETING a statement by an organization of the way in which it can provide value for a prospective customer. A value proposition is a marketing tool that explains why customers can benefit from a company's products or services. It can also be created for ***recruitment*** purposes, to show applicants the value of becoming an employee of the company.
2. GENERAL MANAGEMENT a proposed scheme for making a profit (*slang*)

VAN E-COMMERCE see ***value-added network***

VAR FINANCE, BANKING, AND ACCOUNTING see ***value-added reseller***

variable STATISTICS an element of data whose changes are the object of a statistical study

variable annuity FINANCE, BANKING, AND ACCOUNTING an annuity whose payments depend either on the success of investments that underlie it, or on the value of an index

variable cost FINANCE, BANKING, AND ACCOUNTING a cost of production that is directly proportional to the number of units produced

variable interest rate FINANCE, BANKING, AND ACCOUNTING an interest rate that changes, usually in relation to a standard index, during the period of a loan

variable rate note FINANCE, BANKING, AND ACCOUNTING a note the interest rate of which is tied to an index, such as the prime rate in the United States or the London InterBank Offering Rate (LIBOR) in the United Kingdom. Abbr **VRN**

variance OPERATIONS & PRODUCTION
1. the square of a standard deviation
2. a measure of the difference between actual performance and forecast, or standard, performance. Variance is a key measure in ***statistical process control***.

variance analysis GENERAL MANAGEMENT a standard costing technique involving the comparison, calculation, and explanation of ***variances*** between actual and standard costs. Variance analysis is used to evaluate success in conforming to plans and budgets.

variance components STATISTICS the changes in random effect terms such as error terms in a linear statistical model

variety reduction OPERATIONS & PRODUCTION the process of controlling and minimizing the range of new parts, equipment, materials, methods, and procedures that are used to produce goods or services. Variety reduction aims to minimize the variety of all elements in the production or service delivery process. Variety adds costs to any organization and variety management and reduction can immediately benefit profitability. The main techniques of variety reduction are simplification, standardization, and specialization.

VAT FINANCE, BANKING, AND ACCOUNTING see ***value-added tax***

VAT collected FINANCE, BANKING, AND ACCOUNTING with the VAT already collected by a taxing authority

VAT paid FINANCE, BANKING, AND ACCOUNTING with the VAT already paid

VAT receivable FINANCE, BANKING, AND ACCOUNTING with the VAT for an item not yet collected by a taxing authority

VAT registration FINANCE, BANKING, AND ACCOUNTING listing with a European government as a company eligible for return of VAT in certain cases

VCM FINANCE, BANKING, AND ACCOUNTING see *Venture Capital Market*

velocity of circulation of money FINANCE, BANKING, AND ACCOUNTING the rate at which money circulates in an economy

vendor rating OPERATIONS & PRODUCTION a system for recording and ranking the performance of a supplier in terms of a range of issues, which may include delivery performance and the quality of the items. A process of vendor rating is essential to effective ***purchasing***. When carried out before an order is placed, it is known as ***supplier evaluation***. When undertaken after the fulfillment of an order, it is called **supplier rating**, or **supplier appraisal**.

Venn diagram STATISTICS a diagram in which overlapping circles are used to show how two or more items in a statistical study are mutually inclusive or exclusive

venture capital FINANCE, BANKING, AND ACCOUNTING

1. money used to finance new companies or projects, especially those with high earning potential and high risk. Also known as ***risk capital***

2. the money invested in a new company or business venture

Venture Capital Market FINANCE, BANKING, AND ACCOUNTING a sector on the ***JSE*** Securities Exchange for listing smaller developing companies. Criteria for listing in the VCM sector are less stringent than for the DCM (***Development Capital Market***) sector. See ***Development Capital Market***. Abbr **VCM**

venture funding FINANCE, BANKING, AND ACCOUNTING the round of funding for a new company that follows seed funding, provided by venture capitalists

venture management GENERAL MANAGEMENT the collaboration of various sections within an organization to encourage an ***entrepreneurial*** spirit, increase ***innovation***, and produce successful ***new products*** more quickly. Venture management is used within large organizations to create a small-firm, entrepreneurial atmosphere, releasing innovation and talent from promising employees. It cuts out ***bureaucracy*** and bypasses traditional management systems. The collaboration is generally between research and development, corporate planning, marketing, finance, and purchasing functions.

verbal contract GENERAL MANAGEMENT an agreement that is oral and not written down. It remains legally enforceable by the parties who have agreed to it.

versioning MARKETING the practice of offering information to customers in different versions to suit particular customer groups (*slang*)

vertical diversification GENERAL MANAGEMENT see ***diversification***

vertical integration GENERAL MANAGEMENT the practice of combining some or all of the sequential operations of the ***supply chain*** between the sourcing of ***raw materials*** and sale of the final product. Vertical integration can be pursued as a strategy through the acquisition of ***suppliers***, ***wholesalers***, and ***retailers*** to increase control and reliability. It also can be achieved when a company gains strong control over suppliers or distributors, usually by exercising purchasing power.

vertical keiretsu GENERAL MANAGEMENT see ***keiretsu***

vertical linkage analysis GENERAL MANAGEMENT a tool that enables analysis of the ***value chain*** in order to determine where opportunities for enhancing ***competitive advantage*** may lie. Vertical linkage analysis extends the value chain beyond the organization to incorporate the suppliers and users who are at either end of the chain. This maximizes the number of locations where value can be created for customers. Vertical linkage analysis incorporates three steps: working out the value chain for the industry and costing value-creating activities; determining cost drivers for each of these activities; and evaluating opportunities for competitive advantage.

vertical market E-COMMERCE a market that is oriented to one particular specialty, for example, plastics manufacturing or transportation engineering

vertical merger GENERAL MANAGEMENT see ***merger***

vertical thinking GENERAL MANAGEMENT see ***lateral thinking***

vested rights FINANCE, BANKING, AND ACCOUNTING the value of somebody's rights in a pension if he or she leaves a job

v-form FINANCE, BANKING, AND ACCOUNTING a graphic representation that something had been falling in value and is now rising

videoconferencing GENERAL MANAGEMENT the use of a live video link to connect people in different locations so that they can see and hear one another and conduct real-time ***meetings***. Videoconferencing is a useful tool for managing ***communication*** with remote workers, between staff at geographically dispersed offices, including those who form a ***virtual team***, or with clients at remote locations. It is also used in ***distance learning*** courses.

viewing figures MARKETING the number of people who watch a particular television program or channel

viewtime E-COMMERCE the length of time an advertising banner is visible on a Web page

viral marketing MARKETING the rapid spread of a message about a new product or service in a similar way to the spread of a virus. Viral marketing can be by word of mouth but it is particularly common on the Internet, where messages can be spread easily and quickly to reach millions of people. Products can become household names in this way with very little advertising expenditure.

virtualization GENERAL MANAGEMENT the creation of a product, service, or organization that has an electronic rather than a physical existence

virtual office GENERAL MANAGEMENT a workplace that is not based in one physical location but consists of employees working remotely by using ***information and communications technologies***. A virtual office is characterized by the use of ***teleworkers***, ***telecenters***, ***mobile workers***, ***hot-desking***, and ***hoteling***, and promotes the use of ***virtual teams***. A virtual office can increase an organization's flexibility, cost effectiveness, and efficiency.

virtual organization OPERATIONS & PRODUCTION a temporary network of companies, suppliers, customers, or employees, linked by ***information and communications technologies***, with the purpose of delivering a service or product. A virtual organization can bring together companies in ***strategic partnering*** or ***outsourcing*** arrangements, enabling them to share expertise, resources, and cost savings until objectives are met and the network is dissolved. Such organizations are virtual not only in the sense that they exist largely in cyberspace, but also that they employ various forms of flexibility unconstrained by the traditional barriers of time and place, such as ***virtual teams***. A greater level of trust is required between employer and employee or coworkers,

or partner organizations, because they will be working out of one another's sight for the majority of the time. A virtual organization has similarities to a ***network organization***.

virtual team GENERAL MANAGEMENT a group of employees using ***information and communications technologies*** to collaborate from different work bases. Members of a virtual team may work in different parts of the same building or may be scattered across a country or around the world. The team can be connected by technology such as ***groupware***, e-mail, an ***intranet***, or by ***videoconferencing*** and can be said to inhabit a ***virtual office***. Although virtual teams can work efficiently, occasional face-to-face meetings can be important to avoid feelings of isolation and to enable teambuilding.

virus E-COMMERCE a computer program designed to damage or destroy computer systems and the information contained within them. The fact that extremely destructive viruses can be attached to, and even embedded within, e-mail messages means that anyone with an e-mail account is a potential target. Although there is no single foolproof way to eradicate the risk of viruses, the threat they pose can be reduced in a number of ways. The main precaution that should be taken is to invest in antivirus software that can check e-mail messages and attachments automatically.

visible trade ECONOMICS trade in physical goods and merchandise

vision statement GENERAL MANAGEMENT a statement giving a broad, aspirational image of the future that an organization is aiming to achieve. Vision statements express ***corporate vision***. They are related to ***mission statements***.

visit E-COMMERCE the first entry in a given time period into a Web site by a Web user as identified by a unique Web address. A visit is considered to be concluded when the user has not viewed any page at the Web site in a given time period.

vocational qualification HR & PERSONNEL a qualification awarded after a period of ***vocational training*** has been successfully completed. Vocational qualifications provide the knowledge and skills for a particular trade or profession and may lead to full membership of a professional body.

vocational training HR & PERSONNEL ***training*** that equips somebody for a specific trade or profession. Vocational training may lead to a recognized ***vocational qualification***, or it may form part of in-company ***employee development***. It might take the form of a short course, practical training, or part-time or full-time study at a college or university.

voetstoots (*S. Africa*) FINANCE, BANKING, AND ACCOUNTING purchased at the buyer's risk or without warranty

volume of retail sales ECONOMICS the amount of trade in goods carried out in the retail sector of an economy in a particular period

voluntary arrangement FINANCE, BANKING, AND ACCOUNTING an agreement the terms of which are not legally binding on the parties

voluntary bankruptcy GENERAL MANAGEMENT see ***bankruptcy***

vortal E-COMMERCE a portal Web site devoted to one specific industry. These sites enable business-to-business e-commerce transactions by bringing businesses at different points of the supply chain together. Vortal is formed from "vertical portal."

voting rights FINANCE, BANKING, AND ACCOUNTING the rights that shareholders have to vote on matters affecting a corporation

voting stock FINANCE, BANKING, AND ACCOUNTING shares whose owners have voting rights

voting trust FINANCE, BANKING, AND ACCOUNTING a group of individuals who have collectively received voting rights from shareholders

Vroom, Victor Harold (*b.* 1932) GENERAL MANAGEMENT Canadian academic. An authority on the psychological analysis of behavior in organizations, whose work includes contributions on ***motivation***, ***leadership*** styles and ***decision making***. He described his ***expectancy theory*** in *Work and Motivation* (1964).

vulture capitalist FINANCE, BANKING, AND ACCOUNTING a venture capitalist who structures deals on behalf of an entrepreneur in such a way that the investors benefit rather than the entrepreneur (*slang*)

W

wage incentive HR & PERSONNEL a monetary benefit offered as a reward to those employees who perform well in a specified area

wages HR & PERSONNEL a form of ***pay*** given to employees in exchange for the work they have done. Traditionally, the term wages applied to the weekly pay of manual, or nonprofessional workers. In modern usage, the term is often used interchangeably with ***salary***.

wage scale HR & PERSONNEL = ***pay scale***

waiver of premium FINANCE, BANKING, AND ACCOUNTING a provision of an insurance policy that suspends payment of premiums, for example, if the insured suffers disabling injury

walk GENERAL MANAGEMENT to resign from a job (*slang*)

walking papers
handed your walking papers HR & PERSONNEL given the sack (*slang*)

wall
let's throw it at the wall and see if it sticks GENERAL MANAGEMENT let's try this idea and see if it is successful (*slang*)

walled garden E-COMMERCE an environment on the Internet in which customers can access only e-merchants selected by the owner of the environment (*slang*)

wallet technology E-COMMERCE a software package providing ***digital wallets*** or purses on the computers of merchants and customers to facilitate payment by digital cash

Wall Street FINANCE, BANKING, AND ACCOUNTING the U.S. financial industry, or the area of New York City where much of its business is done

WAN E-COMMERCE see ***network***

WAP E-COMMERCE wireless application protocol, the mobile equivalent of ***HTML***, enabling Web sites to be accessed via mobile devices

warehousing OPERATIONS & PRODUCTION the storage and protection of ***raw materials*** and ***finished goods*** in a dedicated building or room

war for talent GENERAL MANAGEMENT competition between organizations to attract and retain the most able employees

warrants risk warning notice FINANCE, BANKING, AND ACCOUNTING a statement that a broker in the United Kingdom gives to clients to alert them to the risks inherent in trading in options

waste management *or* **waste control** GENERAL MANAGEMENT a sustainable process for reducing the environmental impact of the disposal of all types of materials used by businesses. Waste management aims to avoid excessive use of resources and damage to the environment and may be carried out through processes such as recycling. It focuses on efficiency in the use of materials and on disposing of rubbish in the least harmful way. Waste management also involves compliance with the legislation and regulations covering this area.

wasting asset FINANCE, BANKING, AND ACCOUNTING an asset that will cease to have any value at all at a date in the future, such as an option or a short-term lease

water
let's put it in the water and see if it floats GENERAL MANAGEMENT let's try this idea and see if it is successful (*slang*)

Waterman, **Robert H.** (*b.* 1936) GENERAL MANAGEMENT U.S. consultant. Former McKinsey consultant, who, with ***Tom Peters***, wrote the best-selling *In Search of Excellence* (1984).

Watson, Jr., **Thomas J.** (1914–93) GENERAL MANAGEMENT U.S. industrialist. C.E.O. of IBM, 1956–70, who gave the company a strong core philosophy and led it through a period of complete domination of the computer industry. His beliefs, which centered on consideration for the employee, care for the customer, and taking time to get things right, are described in *A Business and its Beliefs: the Ideas that Helped Build IBM* (1963).

wealth ECONOMICS physical assets such as a house or financial assets such as stocks and shares that can yield an income for their holder

wealth tax FINANCE, BANKING, AND ACCOUNTING a tax on somebody's accumulated wealth, as opposed to their income

wear a hat GENERAL MANAGEMENT to fulfill a specified role at a particular moment in time. Somebody may be required to wear several hats within the same company. (*slang*)

Web cast E-COMMERCE use of the Web to broadcast information. A Web cast event is intended to be viewed simultaneously by numerous people connecting to the same Web site. Web cast events often use ***rich media*** technology.

web commerce E-COMMERCE = ***e-commerce***

Weber, **Max** (1864–1920) GENERAL MANAGEMENT German sociologist. Remembered for his work on ***power*** and ***authority***, published in *Theory of Social and Economic Organization* (1924), where he proposed ***bureaucracy*** as the most efficient form of ***organization***.

Web marketing E-COMMERCE the process of creating, developing, and enhancing a Web site in order to increase the number of visits by potential customers

Web marketplace E-COMMERCE a business-to-business Web community that brings business buyers and sellers together. Although their exact nature can vary considerably, there are essentially three types of Web-based B2B marketplace: ***online catalogs***, ***auctions***, and ***exchanges***.

Web master E-COMMERCE the person responsible for managing the content of a Web site and monitoring traffic through the site. The role of Web master may be shared between numerous individuals within an organization.

Web server E-COMMERCE
1. the physical computer that supports a Web site
2. the software that runs on Web servers. Web-server software delivers Web pages to browsers on Internet-based computers.

weighted average STATISTICS an average of quantities that have been adjusted by the addition of a statistical value to allow for their relative importance in a data set

weighted average cost price FINANCE, BANKING, AND ACCOUNTING a value for the cost of each item of a specific type in an inventory, taking into account what quantities were bought at what prices

weighting STATISTICS the assigning of greater importance to particular items in a data set

weightlessness GENERAL MANAGEMENT a quality considered to characterize an economy that is based on knowledge or other intangibles rather than on physical assets

Welch, **Jack** (*b.* 1935) GENERAL MANAGEMENT U.S. business executive ***Turned around*** General Electric in the 1980s by making ***redundancies***, ***divesting*** and ***acquiring*** (see ***merger***) businesses, and introducing "Work-Out," a program centered on ***communication*** and ***innovation***

welfare HR & PERSONNEL the physical and mental well-being of employees, and the provision of help for those in need of assistance. Welfare embraces: 1. ***physical working conditions***, such as hygiene, sanitation, temperature, humidity, ventilation, lighting, physical comfort, and refreshments; 2. ***occupational health*** or wellness promotion; 3. ***counseling*** and advice on personal problems, such as bereavement, drug abuse, or ***stress***; 4. working time, covering matters such as ***hours of work***, rest periods, paid vacation, and ***shiftwork***. ***Employee assistance programs*** are a modern form of welfare policy, although not common outside the United States.

well
let's drop it down the well and see what kind of splash it makes GENERAL MANAGEMENT let's try this idea and see if it is successful (*slang*)

wellness program HR & PERSONNEL a company program offering benefits, activities, or training, to improve and promote employees' health and fitness. A wellness program can include **wellness benefits** such as fitness training, company sponsored athletics and sports teams, health education, and life improvement classes. It also includes prevention of mental health problems by ***stress*** management.

wet signature GENERAL MANAGEMENT a signature on paper rather than a faxed or e-mailed copy (*slang*)

wharfie (*ANZ*) GENERAL MANAGEMENT a docker (*slang*)

whisper number FINANCE, BANKING, AND ACCOUNTING an estimate of a company's earnings that is based on rumors

whisper stock FINANCE, BANKING, AND ACCOUNTING a stock about which there is talk of a likely change in value, usually upward and often related to a takeover

whistle
blow the whistle on somebody or something GENERAL MANAGEMENT to speak out publicly about malpractice or incompetence within an organization (*slang*)

whistleblowing GENERAL MANAGEMENT speaking out to the media or the public on malpractice, misconduct, corruption, or mismanagement witnessed in an organization.

Whistleblowing is usually undertaken on the grounds of morality or conscience or because of a failure of ***business ethics*** on the part of the organization being reported.

white coat rule MARKETING a Federal Trade Commission rule prohibiting the use of actors dressed as doctors to promote a product in TV commercials (*slang*)

white-collar crime GENERAL MANAGEMENT a crime committed by somebody with a white-collar job

white-collar job HR & PERSONNEL a position that does not involve physical labor. See ***blue-collar job***

white-collar worker HR & PERSONNEL an office worker who traditionally wore a white shirt and a tie

white goods MARKETING large household electrical appliances such as ranges, refrigerators, and freezers

white knight FINANCE, BANKING, AND ACCOUNTING see ***knight***

white squire GENERAL MANAGEMENT a ***shareholder*** who purchases a significant, but not controlling, number of shares in order to prevent a ***takeover bid*** from succeeding. A white squire is often invited to purchase the shares by the company to be acquired, and may be required to sign an agreement to prevent them from later becoming a black ***knight***.

whizz kid FINANCE, BANKING, AND ACCOUNTING a young, exceptionally successful person, especially one who makes a lot of money in large financial transactions, including takeovers

wholesale price FINANCE, BANKING, AND ACCOUNTING a price charged to customers who buy large quantities of an item for resale in smaller quantities to others

wholesale price index FINANCE, BANKING, AND ACCOUNTING a government-calculated index, indicative of inflation in an economy, of wholesale prices

wholesaler MARKETING, OPERATIONS & PRODUCTION an intermediary who buys in bulk from manufacturers for resale to ***retailers*** or other traders. Some wholesalers sell directly to the public. One type of wholesaler is a **cash and carry**, which offers discounted prices for bulk purchases that are paid for and taken away at the time of sale. Cash and carries traditionally serve the business community, but many now allow the general public to buy from them.

wholesale trade FINANCE, BANKING, AND ACCOUNTING trade at wholesale prices

wholly-owned subsidiary GENERAL MANAGEMENT a company that is completely owned by another company. A wholly-owned subsidiary is a ***registered company*** with board members who all represent one ***holding company*** or corporation. Board members may be directly from the holding company or acting as its nominees, or they may be from other wholly-owned subsidiaries of the holding company.

Whyte, William Hollingsworth (1917–99) GENERAL MANAGEMENT U.S. urban theorist. Author of *The Organization Man* (1956), a study of the impact of the power of ***corporate culture*** on individuals from the suburban middle class.

Wickens, Peter D. (*b.* 1938) GENERAL MANAGEMENT British business executive. Personnel director at Nissan U.K., where he helped to introduce Japanese working practices, such as ***continuous improvement***, into the U.K. car industry. Wickens's employee relations philosophy at Nissan was based on job flexibility, ***single status***, and a single union deal. His book, *The Ascendant Organisation* (1995), brings together his experience and knowledge of ***best practice***.

widow-and-orphan stock FINANCE, BANKING, AND ACCOUNTING a stock considered extremely safe as an investment

wiggle room GENERAL MANAGEMENT flexibility in matters relating to contracts or deadlines (*slang*)

Willie Sutton rule GENERAL MANAGEMENT the maxim that it is most logical to concentrate on areas that yield most profit. The Willie Sutton rule is based on an alleged remark made by bank robber Willie Sutton. He was reputedly asked why he robbed banks and replied "Because that's where the money is." A person or organization following this rule will focus their effort on those activities that give the greatest return.

windfall profit FINANCE, BANKING, AND ACCOUNTING a sudden large profit, subject to extra tax

windfall tax FINANCE, BANKING, AND ACCOUNTING excess profits tax

win win situation GENERAL MANAGEMENT a business situation in which all parties stand to gain something (*slang*)

wire

down to the wire GENERAL MANAGEMENT approaching the moment when something is due (*slang*)

wired company GENERAL MANAGEMENT a company that makes full use of information technology to run its business (*slang*)

witching hour FINANCE, BANKING, AND ACCOUNTING the time when a type of derivative financial instrument such as a ***put***, a ***call***, or a contract for advance sale becomes due (*slang*)

withdrawal FINANCE, BANKING, AND ACCOUNTING regular disbursements of dividend or capital gain income from an open-end mutual fund

withholding tax FINANCE, BANKING, AND ACCOUNTING the money that an employer pays directly to the U.S. government as a payment of the income tax on the employee

WOMBAT GENERAL MANAGEMENT waste of money, brains, and time, used to refer to problems that are unlikely to produce any beneficial result even when solved (*slang*)

wood

put wood behind the arrow GENERAL MANAGEMENT to provide resources or money for a project or enterprise (*slang*)

Woodward, Joan (1916–71) GENERAL MANAGEMENT British academic. Originator of what subsequently became known as the ***contingency theory*** of organizations, based on research inspired by ***Elton Mayo*** and which was written up in *Industrial Organization* (1965).

ELTON MAYO (pp. 1020–21)

word of mouse E-COMMERCE word-of-mouth publicity on the Internet. Owing to the fast-paced and interactive nature of online markets, word of mouse can spread much faster than its offline counterpart. (*slang*)

work GENERAL MANAGEMENT the expenditure of physical or mental energy to achieve a purposeful task. Work is usually performed by ***employees*** within organizations, where it involves completion of a particular activity that contributes to the achievement of organizational goals.

workaholic HR & PERSONNEL somebody who is addicted to working. A workaholic spends long hours in the workplace and probably suffers from ***presenteeism***. While workaholics may be very productive, workaholism is sometimes a sign of ***stress*** or personal problems. The term was coined in the 1960s.

worker control GENERAL MANAGEMENT participation by employees in the management of an organization. Worker control can involve ***worker directors*** or a management buyout.

worker director HR & PERSONNEL an ***employee*** raised to executive status within an organization, usually as part of a structured program of ***employee participation*** in management. A worker director usually represents the views of staff at board level.

workers' cooperative GENERAL MANAGEMENT see ***industrial cooperative***

work ethic GENERAL MANAGEMENT the belief that ***work*** itself is as important and fulfilling as the end result. The work ethic originated among Protestants and was central to the views of Martin Luther and John Calvin. It played an important role in the achievements of the Industrial Revolution.

work experience HR & PERSONNEL the temporary placement of young people in organizations to give them a taste of the work environment. Successful work experience programs require adequate preparation by schools and employing organizations, together with follow-up activities to monitor the outcomes of a placement.

work flow GENERAL MANAGEMENT see ***office design***

workforce HR & PERSONNEL the whole body of employees either in an organization or across an industry

working hours HR & PERSONNEL see ***hours of work***

working lunch GENERAL MANAGEMENT a lunchtime meal during which business is transacted. A working lunch can occur either when an employee continues to work through their lunch hour, or when clients or colleagues are entertained and business is conducted at the same time, when it is also known as a **power lunch**.

work-life balance HR & PERSONNEL the equilibrium between the amount of time and effort somebody devotes to work and that given to other aspects of life. Work-life balance is the subject of widespread public debate on how to allow ***employees*** more control over their working arrangements in order to better accommodate other aspects of their lives, while still benefiting their organizations. The agenda consists primarily of ***flexible working*** practices and ***family friendly policies***, although good practice demonstrates that flexibility should be open to all, including those without caring responsibilities. The work-life balance debate has arisen through social and economic changes, such as greater numbers of women in the workforce, the expectations of the younger ***Generation X***, a growing reluctance to accept the longer hours culture, the rise of the 24/7 society, and technological advancements. It has been supported by government and by organizations which see it as a means of aiding ***recruitment*** and employee retention.

work measurement GENERAL MANAGEMENT the establishment of ***standard times*** for the completion of particular work tasks to a particular level of performance. In work measurement, tasks are broken down into elements. The time required for each is established and an assessment of relaxation and contingency allowances is made. Work measurement forms part of ***work study*** and is normally carried out subsequent to ***method study*** with the aim of increasing efficiency and ***productivity***. Work measurement was developed in the context of industrial ***production management*** but has recently become more widely used. ***Time study*** and ***predetermined motion-time systems*** are used in work measurement.

work permit HR & PERSONNEL a license granted to a foreign national in order that they may perform a specific job for a limited period. A work permit scheme is intended to safeguard the interests of the resident labor force while enabling employers to recruit or transfer skilled workers from abroad. It is the responsibility of the employing organization to obtain permits from its national government.

workplace bullying HR & PERSONNEL persistent intimidation or harassment at work which demoralizes and humiliates a person or group. There are no universally agreed definitions of what constitutes workplace bullying, as there are many ways in which bullying can occur, and many kinds of bullying behaviors or tactics. As a general guideline to distinguish between workplace bullying and legitimate criticism, comments should follow the principles for offering ***feedback***: it should be properly conducted, nonpersonal, and constructive, and should not be abusive, aiming to help people to improve their behavior or performance rather than cause them anxiety or distress.

work profiling HR & PERSONNEL see ***profile method***

work rage GENERAL MANAGEMENT an expression of irrational anger felt by an employee in the workplace (*slang*)

work sampling GENERAL MANAGEMENT = ***activity sampling***

work shadow HR & PERSONNEL somebody who observes a jobholder in action with the aim of learning something about how that role is performed. Work shadowing has traditionally been seen as a way of giving ***work experience*** to school students or graduates but it is also a means of offering employees the opportunity to find out more about other jobs within their own or other organizations. It can be used, for example, as a form of ***secondment***, or as a preliminary to a sideways move for somebody experiencing ***plateauing***.

work simplification GENERAL MANAGEMENT an idea pioneered by ***Frank*** and ***Lillian Gilbreth*** and favored by practitioners of ***scientific management***. Any work that does not add value to an idea or process is seen as reducible waste. Tasks in a procedure are analyzed to see if unnecessary steps can be eliminated, thereby reducing complexity as much as possible. This should enable workers to complete tasks more quickly. Work simplification is most suited to manufacturing processes and low-skilled jobs. It can lead to cost savings and better use of resources but it has been criticized for resulting in workers specializing in only one task and for making work repetitive and monotonous.

works manager HR & PERSONNEL the person in charge of a factory, plant, or area of operations in a manufacturing company. A works manager is usually a ***general manager***, with responsibility not just for the manufacturing operation but also for personnel, finance, marketing, etc.

workstation

1. E-COMMERCE a powerful, single-user computer. A workstation is like a personal computer, but it has a more powerful microprocessor and a higher-quality monitor.

2. GENERAL MANAGEMENT the place where a person or small group carries out their particular work tasks. A workstation might take the form of an individual unit where a stage of the manufacturing process is carried out. A factory may contain many workstations, organized to optimize the production process. In an office environment, a workstation may refer to a desk with a computer, telephone, and other equipment at which one person sits.

work structuring HR & PERSONNEL the design of work processes. Work structuring involves arranging the factors that make up employees' jobs in the most efficient way. Factors to be engineered include ***hours of work***, duties performed, and level of ***empowerment***. Work structuring can make use of practices such as ***flexible working***, ***teamwork***, job enrichment, ***job enlargement***, and ***job rotation***. It is similar to ***job design***.

work study GENERAL MANAGEMENT, HR & PERSONNEL, OPERATIONS & PRODUCTION the analysis of activities of employees within an organizational context. Work study comprises a set of techniques that are used to examine a work process and determine where improvements can be made. It usually involves ***method study*** followed by ***work measurement***, and is an important tool in ***total quality management***. It is similar to ***time and motion study***.

work-to-rule HR & PERSONNEL a form of ***industrial action*** in which employees work strictly according to the terms of their ***contract of employment***. A work-to-rule usually involves refusal to do any extra tasks and an overtime ban, causing production to slow down.

world class manufacturing OPERATIONS & PRODUCTION the capability of a manufacturer to compete with any other manufacturing organization in a chosen market, with the aspiration of achieving world-beating standards in all organizational aspects. World class manufacturing encompasses the practices of ***total quality management***, ***continuous improvement***, international ***benchmarking***, and ***flexible working***.

world economy ECONOMICS the global marketplace that has grown up since the 1970s in which goods can be produced wherever production cost is cheapest

wrap fund (*S. Africa*) FINANCE, BANKING, AND ACCOUNTING a registered fund, not itself a unit trust but with similar status to that of a stockbroker's portfolio, which invests in a range of underlying unit trusts, each of which is treated as a discrete holding

WRF *abbr* E-COMMERCE Web response form, a Web-based form designed to collect site-visitor contact and other information. A WRF often forms part of a landing page or termination point of a Web site address intended to funnel response not just from a Web site but also from traditional direct marketing material.

Wright, T. P. GENERAL MANAGEMENT originator of a mathematical model describing a ***learning curve***, introduced in an article entitled "Factors Affecting the Cost of Airplanes" in the *Journal of Aeronautical Science* (February 1936)

WRT *abbr* GENERAL MANAGEMENT with respect to (*slang*)

WYSIWYG E-COMMERCE What you see is what you get, refers to Web creation software that enables users to design content on their computer that will look exactly the same when transferred to the Web

XML E-COMMERCE a metalanguage that describes rules for defining tagged markup languages. XML is similar to ***HTML*** except that it is intended to deliver data to a variety of applications and is designed to be read by the application run by a system, whereas HTML is designed to be read from a Web browser by a person.

Y2K-compliant GENERAL MANAGEMENT see ***millennium bug***

yakka (*ANZ*) HR & PERSONNEL an informal term for work

YAPPY MARKETING Young Affluent Parent (*slang*)

year-end FINANCE, BANKING, AND ACCOUNTING relating to the end of a financial or fiscal (tax) year

year-end closing FINANCE, BANKING, AND ACCOUNTING the financial statements issued at the end of a company's fiscal (tax) year

yield FINANCE, BANKING, AND ACCOUNTING a percentage of the amount invested that is the annual income from an investment

yield curve FINANCE, BANKING, AND ACCOUNTING a representation of relative interest rates of short- and long-term bonds. It may be normal, flat, or inverted.

yield gap FINANCE, BANKING, AND ACCOUNTING an amount representing the difference between the yield on a very safe investment and the yield on a riskier one

yield to call FINANCE, BANKING, AND ACCOUNTING the yield on a bond at a date when the bond can be called

yield to maturity FINANCE, BANKING, AND ACCOUNTING the yield on a bond if it is held to maturity

young old MARKETING the group of people aged between 55 and 75

YUPPY GENERAL MANAGEMENT Young Urban Professional (*slang*)

zaibatsu GENERAL MANAGEMENT Japanese mining-to-manufacture conglomerates dating from before World War II. At the end of World War II, zaibatsu were disbanded because of their involvement in the war effort. When postwar restrictions were relaxed, these groups of companies reformed as ***keiretsu***.

Zaleznik, Abraham (*b.* 1924) GENERAL MANAGEMENT U.S. academic. Author of the landmark article *Managers and Leaders: Are They Different?* published in the "Harvard Business Review" (1977), which influenced the ideas of ***Warren Bennis*** on the key elements found in effective ***leaders***.

Z bond FINANCE, BANKING, AND ACCOUNTING a bond whose holder receives no accrued interest until all of the holders of other bonds in the same series have received theirs

zero-balance account FINANCE, BANKING, AND ACCOUNTING a bank account that does not hold funds continuously, but has money automatically transferred into it from another account when claims arise against it

zero-coupon FINANCE, BANKING, AND ACCOUNTING returning principal and a premium over the purchase price at maturity, but no interest

zero coupon bond FINANCE, BANKING, AND ACCOUNTING a bond that pays no interest and is sold at a large discount

zero defects OPERATIONS & PRODUCTION a ***quality*** philosophy according to which organizations aim to produce goods that are 100%

perfect. Zero defects was developed during the early 1960s in the United States by ***Philip Crosby*** while he was working for the Martin-Marietta Corporation. The aim is to eliminate the smallest defects at each process stage. It requires a high level of ***employee participation***, and when introduced in Japan it merged with ***quality circle*** concepts.

zero-fund GENERAL MANAGEMENT to assign no money to a business project without actually canceling it (*slang*)

zero growth ECONOMICS a fall in output for two successive quarters

zero out GENERAL MANAGEMENT to dial zero when using an automated call system in the hope of finding a live person to speak to (*slang*)

World Business Almanac

  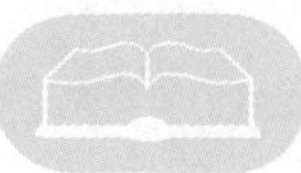    

WORLD BUSINESS ALMANAC

Making Sense of the Wealth of Information about the World's Economy

The World Business Almanac provides you with a one-stop source for statistics, facts, and figures on the global economy and business. It is meant to complement rather than compete with the more specialized, more frequently published, and more speculative information that is to be found in the press, in periodicals, and in information services, which are referenced throughout.

The Almanac includes up-to-date profiles of over 150 countries, all 50 U.S. states, and 24 industry sectors.

A key part of the Almanac is the **World Economy** section, which provides graphics illustrating a wide assortment of business and market statistics and demographic and economic information in an engaging and accessible format.

Whether you are looking for accurate informative data about a country or industry, the World Business Almanac should be your starting point.

Richard Green, Editor

Key Facts

GNI pc: gross national income per capita.
Head of state and head of government: titles only are given; names of current incumbents will be on the BUSINESS Web site at www.ultimatebusinessresource.com.
Currency: principal currency unit, followed by the usual symbol in parentheses.
Language: most commonly spoken language/s.
Best buy: the best things to buy for visiting business people.

Definitions

Growth throughout this section is real growth unless otherwise stated, for example GDP growth is at constant prices, and growth in output is in volume rather than value terms. Annual growth over a number of years is average growth, except when it is said to be compound.

Gross national income—as defined by the World Bank—is the sum of gross value added by resident producers (plus taxes less subsidies) and net primary income from non-resident sources (previously referred to as gross national product).

Gross registered tonnage—a measure of ship size—is actually a measure of ships' volume: 1 grt = 100 cubic feet.

Abbreviations

The abbreviations listed below are used frequently in the World Business Almanac.

ASEAN	Association of Southeast Asian Nations
ATM	automated teller machine
BOOT	build, own, operate, transfer
CEFTA	Central European Free Trade Agreement
DOM-TOM	Les Départements et Territoires d'Outre-Mer (overseas departments of France)
EEA	European Economic Area
EBRD	European Bank for Reconstruction and Development
FDI	foreign direct investment
FSU	former Soviet Union
GNI	gross national income (see *Definitions* above)
grt	gross registered tonnage (see *Definitions* above)
GSP	gross social product
HIPC	highly-indebted poor countries
ICT	information and communications technology
ILO	International Labour Organisation
IMD	International Institute for Management Development
LNG	liquefied natural gas
PJ	petajoules
ro-ro	roll-on roll-off
teus	twenty-foot equivalent units (measure of shipping volume)
TWh	terawatt hour
UMTS	Universal Mobile Telecommunications System
WAP	wireless application protocol
WTO	World Trade Organisation

Maps

All world maps in the World Business Almamac © Myriad Editions Ltd
www.myriadeditions.com
All country maps in the World Business Almamac © Digital Wisdom
www.digiwis.com

Contents

 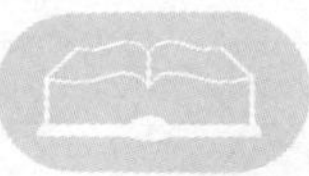    

ICELAND
GREENLAND
NORWAY
FINLAND
SWEDEN
ESTONIA
LATVIA
DENMARK
LITHUANIA
IRELAND
UNITED KINGDOM
CANADA
NETHERLANDS
GERMANY
POLAND
BELARUS
BELGIUM
LUXEMBURG
CZECH REPUBLIC
SLOVAKIA
UKRAINE
MOLDOVA
FRANCE
SWITZERLAND
AUSTRIA
SLOVENIA
HUNGARY
ROMANIA
ANDORRA
MONACO
CROATIA
BOSNIA-HERCEGOVINA
SAN MARINO
YUGOSLAVIA
BULGARIA
MACEDONIA
PORTUGAL
SPAIN
VATICAN
ALBANIA
ITALY
GREECE
UNITED STATES OF AMERICA
TUNISIA
MALTA
TURKEY
CYPRUS
SYRIA
LEBANON
ISRAEL
JORDAN
BERMUDA
MOROCCO
BAHAMAS
ALGERIA
LIBYA
MEXICO
TURKS & CAICOS
WESTERN SAHARA
EGYPT
CUBA
DOMINICAN REPUBLIC
JAMAICA
HAITI
ANGUILLA
BELIZE
ST KITTS & NEVIS
ANTIGUA & BARBUDA
GUATEMALA
HONDURAS
GUADELOUPE
MAURITANIA
DOMINICA
MALI
NIGER
MARTINIQUE
CAPE VERDE
EL SALVADOR
ST LUCIA
SENEGAL
NICARAGUA
ST VINCENT & GRENAD.
GRENADA
BARBADOS
GAMBIA
CHAD
SUDAN
BURKINA FASO
GUINEA-BISSAU
COSTA RICA
TRINIDAD & TOBAGO
VENEZUELA
GUINEA
NIGERIA
PANAMA
GUYANA
CÔTE D'IVOIRE
GHANA
TOGO
BENIN
SIERRA LEONE
SURINAME
FRENCH GUIANA (Fr)
CAR
COLOMBIA
LIBERIA
CAMEROON
EQUATORIAL GUINEA
UGANDA
ECUADOR
SAO TOME & PRINCIPE
GABON
DEM REP CONGO
RWANDA
CONGO
BURUNDI
TANZANIA
BRAZIL
ANGOLA
PERU
ZAMBIA
MALAWI
BOLIVIA
ZIMBABWE
NAMIBIA
BOTSWANA
CHILE
PARAGUAY
MOZAMBIQUE
SWAZILAND
SOUTH AFRICA
LESOTHO
URUGUAY
ARGENTINA

RUSSIA
KAZAKHSTAN
MONGOLIA
UZBEKISTAN
KYRGYZSTAN
GEORGIA
AZERBAIJAN
ARMENIA
TURKMEN
TAJIKISTAN
CHINA
NORTH KOREA
JAPAN
SOUTH KOREA
AFGHANISTAN
IRAQ
IRAN
KUWAIT
PAKISTAN
NEPAL
BHUTAN
BAHRAIN
QATAR
UNITED ARAB EMIRATES
INDIA
Macao
Hong Kong
TAIWAN
BANGLADESH
MYANMAR
LAOS
VIETNAM
SAUDI ARABIA
OMAN
THAILAND
ERITREA
YEMEN
CAMBODIA
PHILIPPINES
DJIBOUTI
ETHIOPIA
SOMALIA
MALDIVES
SRI LANKA
PALAU
MARSHALL ISLANDS
MICRONESIA
BRUNEI
MALAYSIA
SINGAPORE
KENYA
SEYCHELLES
KIRIBATI
NAURU
INDONESIA
PAPUA NEW GUINEA
COMOROS
TUVALU
SAMOA
FRENCH POLYNESIA
MADAGASCAR
MAURITIUS
VANUATU
FIJI
NIUE
COOK IS.
TONGA
AUSTRALIA
NEW CALEDONIA
NEW ZEALAND

National Prosperity

GREENLAND
ICELAND
FAEROE ISLANDS
NORWAY
SWEDEN
FINLAND
ESTONIA
LATVIA
LITHUANIA
$1,404bn UNITED KINGDOM
IRELAND
DENMARK
$397bn NETH.
$2,104bn GERMANY
POLAND
BELARUS
$252bn BELGIUM
CZECH REPUBLIC
SLOVAKIA
UKRAINE
FRANCE
LUX.
LIECH.
AUSTRIA
HUNGARY
SWITZ.
SLOVENIA
ROMANIA
CROATIA
$1,453bn
MONACO
ITALY
BULGARIA
$274bn
PORTUGAL
$583bn SPAIN
$1,163bn
GREECE
TUNISIA
MALTA
TURKEY
CYPRUS
SYRIA
LEB
ISRAEL
JOR
MOROCCO
ALGERIA
LIBYA
EGYPT
SUDAN

$614bn
CANADA
UNITED STATES OF AMERICA
$8,880bn
BERMUDA
BAHAMAS
$429bn
MEXICO
CAYMAN ISLANDS
DOMINICAN REPUBLIC
BELIZE
JAMAICA
ST KITTS & NEVIS
ANTIGUA & BARBUDA
GUATEMALA
EL SALVADOR
DOMINICA
ST LUCIA
ARUBA
GRENADA
BARBADOS
COSTA RICA
TRINIDAD & TOBAGO
VENEZUELA
PANAMA
COLOMBIA
ECUADOR
$730bn
BRAZIL
PERU
BOLIVIA
PARAGUAY
CHILE
$276bn
ARGENTINA
URUGUAY

CÔTE D'IVOIRE
GHANA
NIGERIA
CAMEROON
UGANDA
GABON
TANZANIA
ANGOLA
ZAMBIA
ZIMBABWE
NAMIBIA
BOTSWANA
SOUTH AFRICA

GDP Growth

Countries with average annual growth of 5% and over (1990–99)

10.7% China

8.2% Sudan
8.1% Vietnam
8.0% Singapore
7.7% Lebanon

7.3% Malaysia
7.2% Chile
7.2% Uganda
6.9% Ireland

6.2% Mozambique
6.0% India
5.9% Oman
5.8% Dominican Rep.
5.7% South Korea
5.7% Syria

5.3% Jordan
5.3% Sri Lanka
5.2% Israel
5.1% Costa Rica
5.1% Mauritius
5.0% El Salvador
5.0% Peru

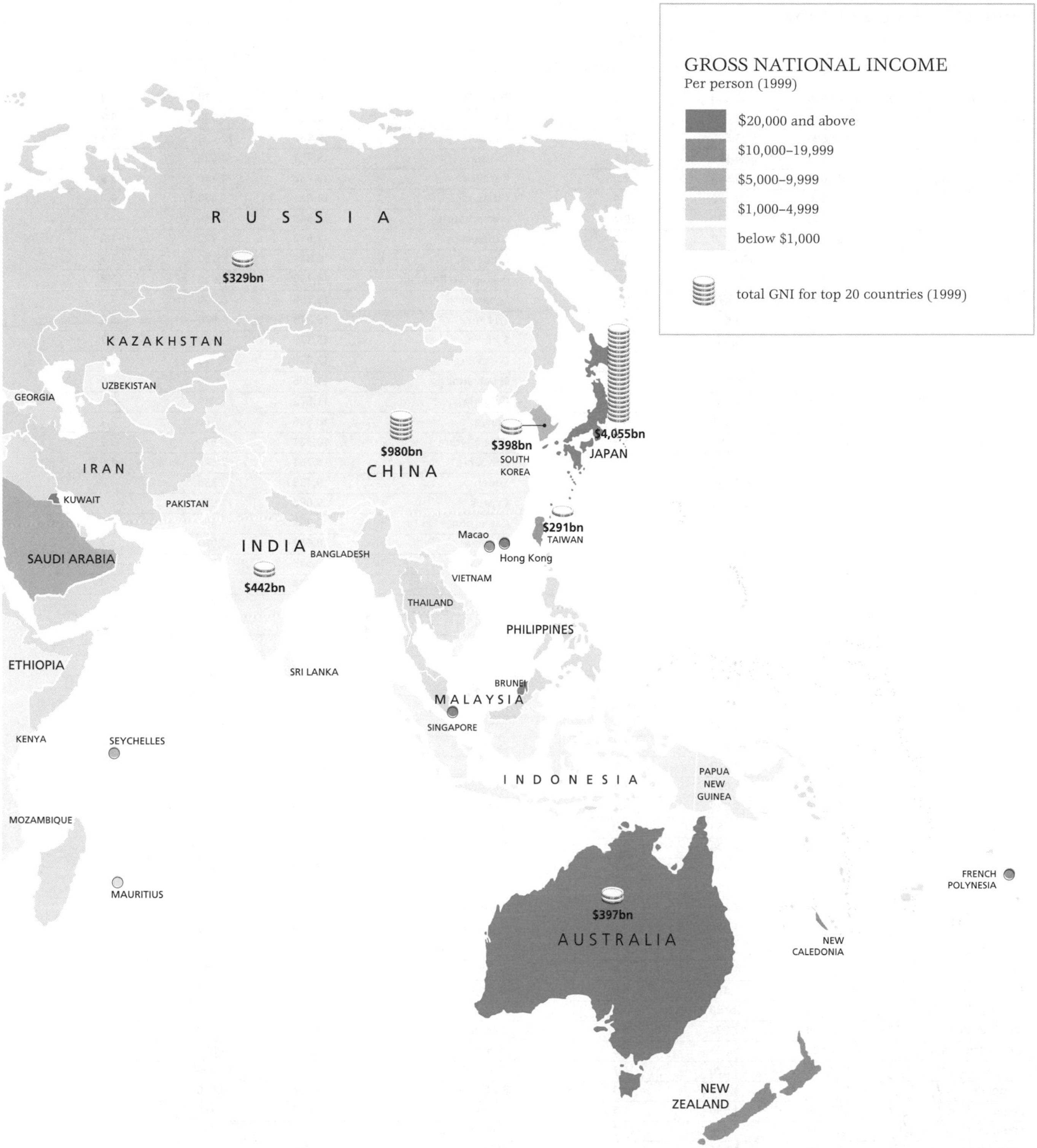

GROSS NATIONAL INCOME

Per person (1999)

- $20,000 and above
- $10,000–19,999
- $5,000–9,999
- $1,000–4,999
- below $1,000

total GNI for top 20 countries (1999)

RUSSIA
$329bn
KAZAKHSTAN
GEORGIA
UZBEKISTAN
IRAN
KUWAIT
PAKISTAN
SAUDI ARABIA
$980bn
CHINA
$398bn
SOUTH KOREA
$4,055bn
JAPAN
$291bn
TAIWAN
Macao
Hong Kong
INDIA
BANGLADESH
$442bn
VIETNAM
THAILAND
PHILIPPINES
ETHIOPIA
SRI LANKA
BRUNEI
MALAYSIA
SINGAPORE
KENYA
SEYCHELLES
INDONESIA
PAPUA NEW GUINEA
MOZAMBIQUE
MAURITIUS
FRENCH POLYNESIA
$397bn
AUSTRALIA
NEW CALEDONIA
NEW ZEALAND

National Income and Growth

	GNI ($ million) 1999	GNI per capita ($) 1999	GDP growth (% p.a.) 1990–99
United States	8,879,500	31,910	3.3
Japan	4,054,545	32,030	1.3
Germany	2,103,804	25,620	1.3
France	1,453,211	24,170	1.5
United Kingdom	1,403,843	23,590	2.5
Italy	1,162,910	20,170	1.4
China	979,894	780	10.7
Brazil	730,424	4,350	3.0
Canada	614,003	20,140	2.7
Spain	583,082	14,800	2.2
India	441,834	440	6.0
Mexico	428,877	4,440	2.7
South Korea	397,910	8,490	5.7
Netherlands	397,384	25,140	2.7
Australia	397,345	20,950	4.1
Russia	328,995	2,250	–6.1
Taiwan	290,500	13,235	–
Argentina	276,097	7,550	4.9
Switzerland	273,856	38,380	0.6
Belgium	252,051	24,650	1.7
Sweden	236,940	26,750	1.6
Austria	205,743	25,430	1.9
Turkey	186,490	2,900	3.8
Denmark	170,685	32,050	2.4
Hong Kong	165,122	24,570	3.9
Poland	157,429	4,070	4.5
Norway	149,280	33,470	3.8
Saudi Arabia	139,365	6,900	1.6
South Africa	133,569	3,170	1.9
Finland	127,764	24,730	2.4
Greece	127,648	12,110	2.2
Indonesia	125,043	600	4.7
Thailand	121,051	2,010	4.7
Iran	113,729	1,810	3.6
Portugal	110,175	11,030	2.5
Israel	99,574	16,310	5.2
Singapore	95,429	24,150	8.0
Colombia	90,007	2,170	3.3
Venezuela	87,313	3,680	1.7
Egypt	86,544	1,380	4.4
Ireland	80,559	21,470	6.9
Philippines	77,967	1,050	3.2
Malaysia	76,944	3,390	7.3
Chile	69,602	4,630	7.2
Pakistan	62,915	470	3.8
Peru	53,705	2,130	5.0
New Zealand	53,299	13,990	3.1
Czech Republic	51,623	5,020	0.8
Bangladesh	47,071	370	4.7
Hungary	46,751	4,640	1.0
Algeria	46,548	1,550	1.6
Ukraine	41,991	840	–10.7
Morocco	33,715	1,190	2.3
Romania	33,034	1,470	–0.8
Nigeria	31,600	260	2.4
Vietnam	28,733	370	8.1
Belarus	26,299	2,620	–3.0
Uruguay	20,604	6,220	3.8
Slovakia	20,318	3,770	1.8
Croatia	20,222	4,530	0.2
Slovenia	19,862	10,000	2.4
Tunisia	19,757	2,090	4.6
Kazakhstan	18,732	1,250	–5.9
Guatemala	18,625	1,680	4.2
Luxembourg	18,545	42,930	–
Uzbekistan	17,613	720	–1.2
Ecuador	16,841	1,360	2.2
Dominican Republic	16,130	1,920	5.8
Lebanon	15,796	3,700	7.7
Sri Lanka	15,578	820	5.3
Syria	15,172	970	5.7
Costa Rica	12,828	3,570	5.1
El Salvador	11,806	1,920	5.0
Bulgaria	11,572	1,410	–2.7
Kenya	10,696	360	2.2
Côte d'Ivoire	10,387	670	3.7
Lithuania	9,751	2,640	–4.0
Sudan	9,435	330	8.2
Cyprus	9,086	11,950	–
Cameroon	8,798	600	1.3
Panama	8,657	3,080	4.2
Tanzania	8,515	260	2.8
Paraguay	8,374	1,560	2.4
Iceland	8,197	29,540	–
Bolivia	8,092	990	4.2
Jordan	7,717	1,630	5.3
Ghana	7,451	400	4.3
Uganda	6,794	320	7.2
Ethiopia	6,524	100	4.6
Jamaica	6,311	2,430	0.3
Zimbabwe	6,302	530	2.8
Macao	6,161	14,200	–
Trinidad and Tobago	6,142	4,750	2.7
Latvia	5,913	2,430	–4.8
Botswana	5,139	3,240	4.3
Estonia	4,906	3,400	–1.3
Mauritius	4,157	3,540	5.1
Gabon	3,987	3,300	3.2
French Polynesia	3,908	16,930	–
Papua New Guinea	3,834	810	4.7
Mozambique	3,804	220	6.2
Malta	3,492	9,210	–
Georgia	3,362	620	–
Angola	3,276	270	0.4
Zambia	3,222	330	0.2
Namibia	3,211	1,890	3.4
New Caledonia	3,169	15,160	–
Barbados	2,294	8,600	–
Belize	673	2,730	–
Antigua and Barbuda	606	8,990	–
St Lucia	590	3,820	–
Seychelles	520	6,500	–
Grenada	334	3,440	–
St Kitts and Nevis	259	6,330	–
Dominica	238	3,260	–

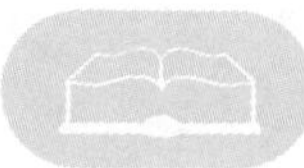

Highest GNI Per Capita

	GNI per capita ($) 1999
Luxembourg	42,930
Switzerland	38,380
Norway	33,470
Denmark	32,050
Japan	32,030
United States	31,910
Iceland	29,540
Sweden	26,750
Germany	25,620
Austria	25,430
Netherlands	25,140
Finland	24,730
Belgium	24,650
Hong Kong	24,570
France	24,170
Singapore	24,150
United Kingdom	23,590
Ireland	21,470
Australia	20,950
Italy	20,170
Canada	20,140
French Polynesia	16,930
Israel	16,310
New Caledonia	15,160
Spain	14,800
Macao	14,200
New Zealand	13,990
Taiwan	13,235
Greece	12,110
Cyprus	11,950
Portugal	11,030
Slovenia	10,000
Malta	9,210
Antigua and Barbuda	8,990
Barbados	8,600
South Korea	8,490
Argentina	7,550
Saudi Arabia	6,900
Seychelles	6,500
St Kitts and Nevis	6,330
Uruguay	6,220
Czech Republic	5,020
Trinidad and Tobago	4,750
Hungary	4,640
Chile	4,630
Croatia	4,530
Mexico	4,440
Brazil	4,350
Poland	4,070
St Lucia	3,820
Slovakia	3,770
Lebanon	3,700
Venezuela	3,680
Costa Rica	3,570
Mauritius	3,540
Grenada	3,440
Estonia	3,400
Malaysia	3,390
Gabon	3,300
Dominica	3,260
Botswana	3,240
South Africa	3,170
Panama	3,080
Turkey	2,900
Belize	2,730
Lithuania	2,640
Belarus	2,620
Jamaica	2,430
Latvia	2,430
Russia	2,250
Colombia	2,170
Peru	2,130
Tunisia	2,090
Thailand	2,010
Dominican Republic	1,920
El Salvador	1,920
Namibia	1,890
Iran	1,810
Guatemala	1,680
Jordan	1,630
Paraguay	1,560
Algeria	1,550
Romania	1,470
Bulgaria	1,410
Egypt	1,380
Ecuador	1,360
Kazakhstan	1,250
Morocco	1,190
Philippines	1,050
Bolivia	990
Syria	970
Ukraine	840
Sri Lanka	820
Papua New Guinea	810
China	780
Uzbekistan	720
Côte d'Ivoire	670
Georgia	620
Indonesia	600
Cameroon	600
Zimbabwe	530
Pakistan	470
India	440
Ghana	400
Bangladesh	370
Vietnam	370
Kenya	360
Sudan	330
Zambia	330
Uganda	320
Angola	270
Nigeria	260
Tanzania	260
Mozambique	220
Ethiopia	100

Lowest GNI Per Capita

	GNI per capita ($) 1999
Ethiopia	100
Mozambique	220
Nigeria	260
Tanzania	260
Angola	270
Uganda	320
Sudan	330
Zambia	330
Kenya	360
Bangladesh	370
Vietnam	370
Ghana	400
India	440
Pakistan	470
Zimbabwe	530
Indonesia	600
Cameroon	600
Georgia	620
Côte d'Ivoire	670
Uzbekistan	720
China	780
Papua New Guinea	810
Sri Lanka	820
Ukraine	840
Syria	970
Bolivia	990
Philippines	1,050
Morocco	1,190
Kazakhstan	1,250
Ecuador	1,360
Egypt	1,380
Bulgaria	1,410
Romania	1,470
Algeria	1,550
Paraguay	1,560
Jordan	1,630
Guatemala	1,680
Iran	1,810
Namibia	1,890
Dominican Republic	1,920
El Salvador	1,920
Thailand	2,010
Tunisia	2,090
Peru	2,130
Colombia	2,170
Russia	2,250
Jamaica	2,430
Latvia	2,430
Belarus	2,620
Lithuania	2,640
Belize	2,730
Turkey	2,900
Panama	3,080
South Africa	3,170
Botswana	3,240
Dominica	3,260
Gabon	3,300
Malaysia	3,390
Estonia	3,400
Grenada	3,440
Mauritius	3,540
Costa Rica	3,570
Venezuela	3,680
Lebanon	3,700
Slovakia	3,770
St Lucia	3,820
Poland	4,070
Brazil	4,350
Mexico	4,440
Croatia	4,530
Chile	4,630
Hungary	4,640
Trinidad and Tobago	4,750
Czech Republic	5,020
Uruguay	6,220
St Kitts and Nevis	6,330
Seychelles	6,500
Saudi Arabia	6,900
Argentina	7,550
South Korea	8,490
Barbados	8,600
Antigua and Barbuda	8,990
Malta	9,210
Slovenia	10,000
Portugal	11,030
Cyprus	11,950
Greece	12,110
Taiwan	13,235
New Zealand	13,990
Macao	14,200
Spain	14,800
New Caledonia	15,160
Israel	16,310
French Polynesia	16,930
Canada	20,140
Italy	20,170
Australia	20,950
Ireland	21,470
United Kingdom	23,590
Singapore	24,150
France	24,170
Hong Kong	24,570
Belgium	24,650
Finland	24,730
Netherlands	25,140
Austria	25,430
Germany	25,620
Sweden	26,750
Iceland	29,540
United States	31,910
Japan	32,030
Denmark	32,050
Norway	33,470
Switzerland	38,380
Luxembourg	42,930

  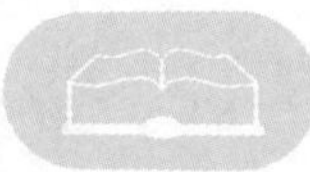  

Highest GDP Growth 1990–99

	GDP growth (% p.a.)1990–99
China	10.7
Sudan	8.2
Vietnam	8.1
Singapore	8.0
Lebanon	7.7
Malaysia	7.3
Chile	7.2
Uganda	7.2
Ireland	6.9
Mozambique	6.2
India	6.0
Oman	5.9
Dominican Republic	5.8
South Korea	5.7
Syria	5.7
Jordan	5.3
Sri Lanka	5.3
Israel	5.2
Costa Rica	5.1
Mauritius	5.1
Peru	5.0
El Salvador	5.0
Argentina	4.9
Thailand	4.7
Papua New Guinea	4.7
Indonesia	4.7
Bangladesh	4.7
Tunisia	4.6
Ethiopia	4.6
Poland	4.5
Egypt	4.4
Botswana	4.3
Ghana	4.3
Panama	4.2
Guatemala	4.2
Bolivia	4.2
Australia	4.1
Hong Kong	3.9
Norway	3.8
Uruguay	3.8
Turkey	3.8
Pakistan	3.8
Côte d'Ivoire	3.7
Iran	3.6
Namibia	3.4
United States	3.3
Colombia	3.3
Gabon	3.2
Philippines	3.2
New Zealand	3.1
Puerto Rico	3.1
Brazil	3.0
United Arab Emirates	2.9

	GDP growth (% p.a.)1990–99
Zimbabwe	2.8
Tanzania	2.8
Netherlands	2.7
Canada	2.7
Trinidad and Tobago	2.7
Mexico	2.7
United Kingdom	2.5
Portugal	2.5
Denmark	2.4
Finland	2.4
Slovenia	2.4
Paraguay	2.4
Nigeria	2.4
Morocco	2.3
Spain	2.2
Greece	2.2
Ecuador	2.2
Kenya	2.2
Austria	1.9
South Africa	1.9
Slovakia	1.8
Belgium	1.7
Venezuela	1.7
Sweden	1.6
Saudi Arabia	1.6
Algeria	1.6
France	1.5
Italy	1.4
Japan	1.3
Germany	1.3
Cameroon	1.3
Hungary	1.0
Czech Republic	0.8
Switzerland	0.6
Angola	0.4
Jamaica	0.3
Croatia	0.2
Zambia	0.2
Romania	–0.8
Uzbekistan	–1.2
Estonia	–1.3
Bulgaria	–2.7
Belarus	–3.0
Lithuania	–4.0
Latvia	–4.8
Kazakhstan	–5.9
Russia	–6.1
Ukraine	–10.7

Lowest GDP Growth 1990–99

	GDP growth (% p.a.)1990–99
Ukraine	–10.7
Russia	–6.1
Kazakhstan	–5.9
Latvia	–4.8
Lithuania	–4.0
Belarus	–3.0
Bulgaria	–2.7
Estonia	–1.3
Uzbekistan	–1.2
Romania	–0.8
Croatia	0.2
Zambia	0.2
Jamaica	0.3
Angola	0.4
Switzerland	0.6
Czech Republic	0.8
Hungary	1.0
Japan	1.3
Germany	1.3
Cameroon	1.3
Italy	1.4
France	1.5
Sweden	1.6
Saudi Arabia	1.6
Algeria	1.6
Belgium	1.7
Venezuela	1.7
Slovakia	1.8
Austria	1.9
South Africa	1.9
Spain	2.2
Greece	2.2
Ecuador	2.2
Kenya	2.2
Morocco	2.3
Denmark	2.4
Finland	2.4
Slovenia	2.4
Paraguay	2.4
Nigeria	2.4
United Kingdom	2.5
Portugal	2.5
Netherlands	2.7
Canada	2.7
Trinidad and Tobago	2.7
Mexico	2.7
Zimbabwe	2.8
Tanzania	2.8
United Arab Emirates	2.9
Brazil	3.0
New Zealand	3.1
Puerto Rico	3.1
Gabon	3.2

	GDP growth (% p.a.)1990–99
Philippines	3.2
United States	3.3
Colombia	3.3
Namibia	3.4
Iran	3.6
Côte d'Ivoire	3.7
Norway	3.8
Uruguay	3.8
Turkey	3.8
Pakistan	3.8
Hong Kong	3.9
Australia	4.1
Panama	4.2
Guatemala	4.2
Bolivia	4.2
Botswana	4.3
Ghana	4.3
Egypt	4.4
Poland	4.5
Tunisia	4.6
Ethiopia	4.6
Thailand	4.7
Papua New Guinea	4.7
Indonesia	4.7
Bangladesh	4.7
Argentina	4.9
Peru	5.0
El Salvador	5.0
Costa Rica	5.1
Mauritius	5.1
Israel	5.2
Jordan	5.3
Sri Lanka	5.3
South Korea	5.7
Syria	5.7
Dominican Republic	5.8
Oman	5.9
India	6.0
Mozambique	6.2
Ireland	6.9
Chile	7.2
Uganda	7.2
Malaysia	7.3
Lebanon	7.7
Singapore	8.0
Vietnam	8.1
Sudan	8.2
China	10.7

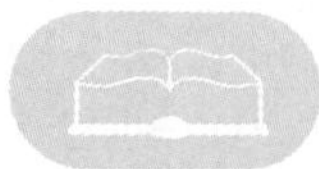

Growth of Output 1990–99

	Services (% p.a.) 1990–99	Industry (% p.a.) 1990–99	Agriculture (% p.a.)1990–99	Manufacturing (% p.a.)1990–99
Algeria	2.7	1.0	–5.7	3.0
Angola	–2.4	2.7	–1.4	–3.0
Argentina	5.0	4.6	3.5	3.8
Australia	4.4	3.0	2.0	3.0
Austria	2.0	1.9	1.5	0.4
Bangladesh	4.4	7.4	7.5	2.5
Belarus	–1.3	–3.8	–2.6	–5.4
Belgium	1.8	1.5	1.4	1.2
Bolivia	4.5	4.5	4.5	3.2
Botswana	6.3	2.8	3.9	0.3
Brazil	3	2.7	2.1	3.3
Bulgaria	–1.8	–4.7	–	0.3
Cameroon	0.1	–2	0.1	5.3
Canada	2.5	2.6	3.8	1.0
Chile	7.6	6.2	5.0	1.1
China	9.2	14.4	13.9	4.3
Colombia	5.2	1.4	–2.9	–2.0
Costa Rica	4.7	6.0	6.4	4.3
Côte d'Ivoire	2.8	6.4	5.1	3.1
Croatia	1.9	–3.6	–4.9	–2.5
Czech Republic	1.0	–0.1	–	2.7
Denmark	2.6	1.6	1.2	3.2
Dominican Republic	5.7	6.9	4.8	3.6
Ecuador	1.6	3	2.4	2.3
Egypt	4.8	3.9	6.0	3.1
El Salvador	5.8	5.4	5.3	1.1
Estonia	1.1	–4.2	–	–3.7
Ethiopia	6.8	5.7	5.8	2.3
Finland	1.8	4.2	5.8	1.1
France	1.5	0.9	–	1.9
Gabon	4.5	2.6	0.6	–1.9
Germany	1.9	0.3	–0.3	2.2
Ghana	5.8	2.4	–4.5	3.4
Greece	2.4	1.1	0.5	0.4
Guatemala	4.7	4.4	2.8	2.8
Hungary	0.8	2.3	7.2	–3.1
India	7.8	6.7	7.5	3.4
Indonesia	4.0	6.5	7.6	2.3
Iran	4.7	2.8	4.8	4.2
Italy	1.5	1.1	1.5	1.7
Jamaica	0.6	–0.5	–1.9	2.2
Japan	2.2	0.8	1.2	–1.6
Jordan	5.1	5.6	5.9	–1.9
Kazakhstan	2.2	–10.1	–	–13.4
Kenya	3.5	1.9	2.4	1.4
Latvia	1.9	–10.5	–9.8	–8.2
Lithuania	–0.1	–8.1	–10.3	–1.1
Malaysia	8.0	8.8	9.7	0.2
Mauritius	6.3	5.4	5.4	–0.7
Mexico	2.5	3.5	4	1.6
Morocco	2.6	3.1	2.6	–0.4
Mozambique	2.7	12.6	17.6	5.5
Namibia	3.4	2.5	4.3	3.8
Netherlands	3.1	1.7	2.2	2.1
New Zealand	3.7	2.4	–	2.7
Nigeria	2.8	1.7	2.0	2.9
Norway	3.6	4.2	–	2.6
Pakistan	4.4	4.0	3.7	4.4
Panama	4.1	5.9	3.5	2.1
Papua New Guinea	3.3	6.7	6.3	4.4
Paraguay	1.9	3.0	0.5	2.8
Peru	4.2	6.2	4.2	5.6
Philippines	4.0	3.2	2.9	1.4
Poland	4.1	3.8	–	–0.1
Portugal	2.4	2.7	–	0.4
Romania	–0.8	–0.8	–	0.1
Russia	–2.2	–9.6	–	–7.9
Saudi Arabia	2.2	1.5	2.7	0.7
Singapore	8	7.9	6.7	0.4
Slovakia	6.8	–3.5	–	0.7
Slovenia	3.8	2.5	3.8	0.2
South Africa	2.4	0.9	1.1	1.0
South Korea	5.8	6.2	7.1	2.1
Sri Lanka	6.1	7.0	8.2	1.8
Sudan	3.3	5.6	2.8	14.3
Sweden	1.2	3.0	–	0.0
Tanzania	2.4	2.5	2.3	3.2
Thailand	4.4	5.7	6.7	2.5
Trinidad and Tobago	2.6	2.8	4.0	1.8
Tunisia	5.3	4.5	5.4	2.1
Turkey	3.9	4.3	5.1	1.4
Uganda	8.1	12.7	14.2	3.7
Ukraine	–3.1	–13.5	–13.4	–6.3
United Kingdom	3.1	1.3	–	–0.2
Uruguay	5.0	1.3	0.1	3.7
Uzbekistan	–0.4	–4.0	–	–0.4
Venezuela	0.2	3.3	1.3	1.5
Vietnam	8.1	12.5	–	4.9
Zambia	0.3	–3.9	0.7	9.4
Zimbabwe	3.5	0.7	0.7	4.6

TRADE

NORWAY
FINLAND
SWEDEN
30.5%
ESTONIA
UNITED KINGDOM
15.1%
LATVIA
14.0%
IRELAND
DENMARK
15.9%
LITHUANIA
BELARUS
NETH.
GERMANY
10.7%
POLAND
21.7%
BELGIUM
CZECH REP.
12.2%
SLOVAKIA
12.2%
10.9%
UKRAINE
FRANCE
AUSTRIA
HUNGARY
SWITZ.
SLOVENIA
ROMANIA
CROATIA
10.9%
10.5%
BULGARIA
ITALY
PORTUGAL
10.0%
SPAIN
GREECE
10.5%
TURKEY
TUNISIA
SYRIA
LEB
ISRAEL
11.2%
JOR
MOROCCO
ALGERIA
LIBYA
EGYPT

CANADA
UNITED STATES OF AMERICA
16.1%
MEXICO
DOMINICAN REPUBLIC
11.6%
JAMAICA
GUATEMALA
12.4%
EL SALVADOR
COSTA RICA
TRINIDAD & TOBAGO
18.7%
VENEZUELA
10.5%
PANAMA
COLOMBIA
ECUADOR
10.5%
BRAZIL
PERU
BOLIVIA
CHILE
PARAGUAY
12.8%
URUGUAY
ARGENTINA

11.8%
CÔTE D'IVOIRE
GHANA
NIGERIA
CAMEROON
21.6%
UGANDA
GABON
10.2%
TANZANIA
ANGOLA
ZAMBIA
ZIMBABWE
NAMIBIA
BOTSWANA
MOZAMBIQUE
SOUTH AFRICA

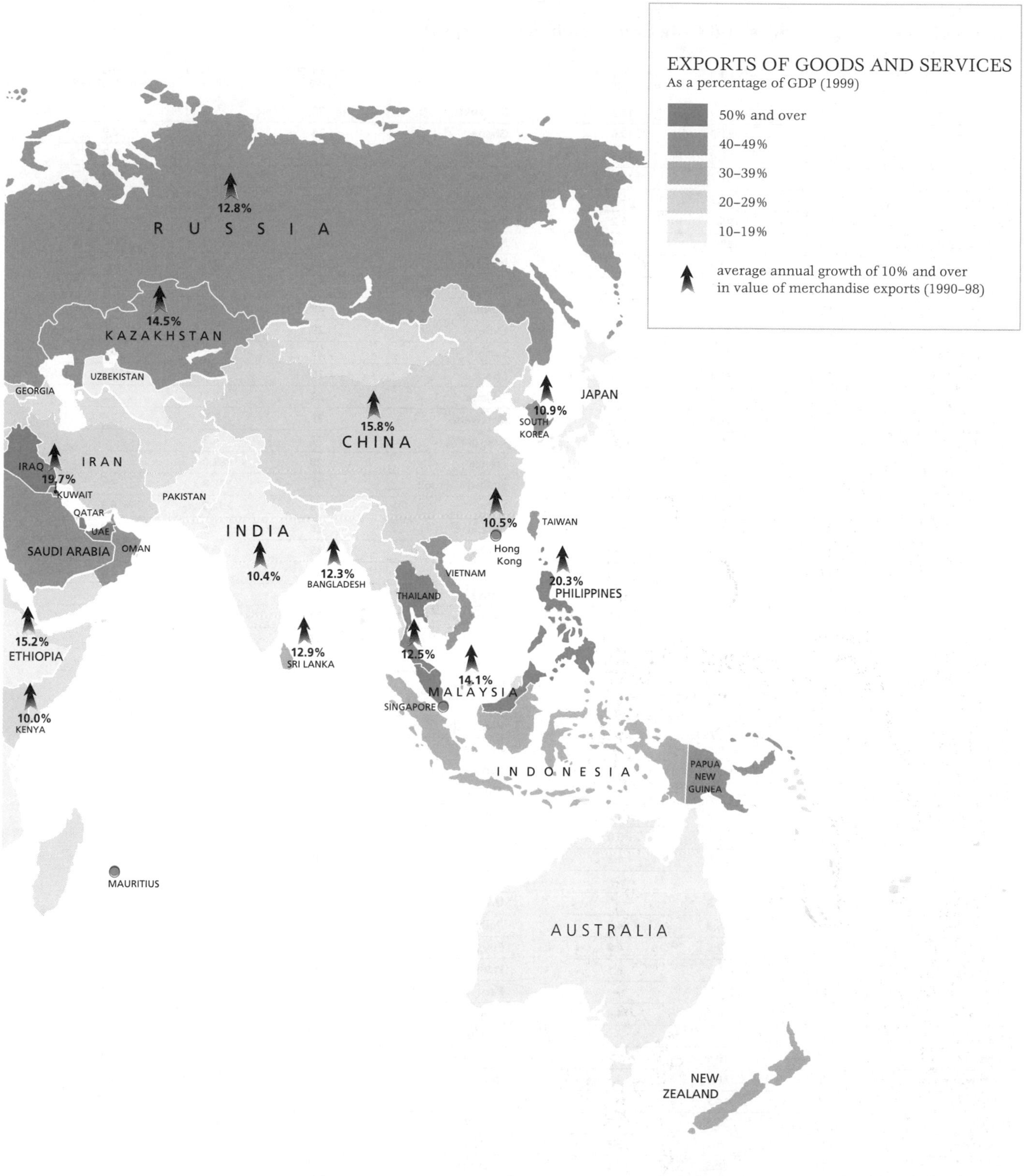

EXPORTS OF GOODS AND SERVICES

As a percentage of GDP (1999)

- 50% and over
- 40–49%
- 30–39%
- 20–29%
- 10–19%

▲ average annual growth of 10% and over in value of merchandise exports (1990–98)

RUSSIA 12.8%
KAZAKHSTAN 14.5%
UZBEKISTAN
GEORGIA
CHINA 15.8%
SOUTH KOREA 10.9%
JAPAN
IRAQ 19.7%
IRAN
KUWAIT
QATAR
UAE
SAUDI ARABIA
OMAN
PAKISTAN
INDIA 10.4%
BANGLADESH 12.3%
SRI LANKA 12.9%
Hong Kong 10.5%
TAIWAN
VIETNAM
THAILAND
PHILIPPINES 20.3%
12.5%
MALAYSIA 14.1%
SINGAPORE
INDONESIA
PAPUA NEW GUINEA
ETHIOPIA 15.2%
KENYA 10.0%
MAURITIUS
AUSTRALIA
NEW ZEALAND

  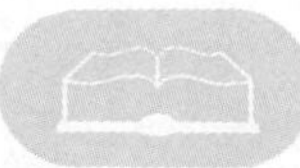    

Exports of Goods and Services and Growth in Merchandise Exports

	Exports (% GDP) 1999	Exports ($ billion) 1999	Volume growth (% p.a.) 1990–98
Singapore	164	139.3	16.2
Hong Kong	133	211.8	10.0
Malaysia	122	96.0	15.5
Ireland	88	81.7	14.2
Estonia	77	3.9	–
Belgium	76	194.2	6.2
United Arab Emirates	76	39.9	9.9
Czech Republic	64	33.2	–
Mauritius	64	2.7	4.5
Slovakia	62	12.1	–
Belarus	62	6.7	–
Netherlands	61	248.7	6.9
Thailand	57	71.4	5.1
Angola	57	5.4	4.5
Iraq	54	12.8	10.7
Costa Rica	54	8.2	13.7
Hungary	53	27.5	6.0
Ukraine	53	17.1	–
Slovenia	53	10.5	–
Namibia	53	1.6	–
Philippines	51	39.0	18.6
Qatar	50	6.1	–
Trinidad and Tobago	50	3.4	2.7
Jamaica	49	3.4	5.1
Oman	48	7.2	4.6
Kuwait	47	14.0	19.2
Latvia	47	2.9	6.2
Russia	46	84.9	–
Austria	45	94.9	–
Kazakhstan	45	6.9	–
Gabon	45	2.8	5.5
Zimbabwe	45	2.5	8.4
Papua New Guinea	45	2.2	–5.3
Canada	44	277.7	9.0
Sweden	44	107.5	1.2
Vietnam	44	14.2	–
Bulgaria	44	5.8	–
Côte d'Ivoire	44	5.3	4.7
Jordan	44	3.5	4.0
South Korea	42	171.7	9.1
Taiwan	42	121.6	–
Tunisia	42	8.8	4.8
Croatia	41	8.1	–
Switzerland	40	119.0	–
Saudi Arabia	40	56.1	4.3
Lithuania	40	4.2	–
Norway	39	54.8	7.6
Denmark	37	65.7	5.3
Finland	37	48.5	9.3
Nigeria	37	13.9	5.5
Ecuador	37	5.3	8.7
Israel	36	35.9	9.6
Indonesia	35	55.8	9.0
Sri Lanka	35	5.6	1.5
Ghana	34	2.6	12.9
Panama	33	6.9	6.2
Mexico	31	148.1	15.3
Portugal	31	34.0	–
New Zealand	31	16.9	5.0
Morocco	30	10.6	10.2
Romania	30	9.9	–
Dominican Republic	30	8.0	1.8
Germany	29	626.0	5.6
Chile	29	19.4	9.9
Syria	29	5.5	0.4
Spain	28	164.4	12.1
Algeria	28	12.9	1.2
Botswana	28	3.0	5.5
Georgia	27	0.7	–
France	26	382.0	5.8
United Kingdom	26	373.8	6.4
Italy	26	292.3	6.3
Poland	26	38.5	8.4
South Africa	25	33.3	7.4
El Salvador	25	3.1	2.8
Kenya	24	2.7	6.0
Cameroon	24	2.2	–1.3
Turkey	23	45.7	10.3
Libya	23	7.3	–5.3
Paraguay	23	3.3	0.0
China	22	218.5	10.7
Venezuela	22	22.1	6.1
Zambia	22	0.9	3.2
Iran	21	20.2	–1.7
Australia	19	73.4	7.7
Greece	19	14.9	8.9
Guatemala	19	3.5	7.0
Uzbekistan	19	3.2	–
Colombia	18	13.9	5.2
Uruguay	18	3.6	7.4
Bolivia	17	1.3	2.7
Egypt	16	13.5	1.9
Pakistan	15	8.8	–3.7
Peru	15	7.6	8.6
Ethiopia	14	0.9	8.8
Bangladesh	13	6.0	13.3
Tanzania	13	1.2	6.6
India	12	54.0	2.7
Mozambique	12	0.6	10.8
United States	11	956.2	6.8
Brazil	11	55.7	4.4
Lebanon	11	1.8	3.9
Uganda	11	0.7	19.5
Japan	10	464.7	1.9
Argentina	10	27.7	10.3
Sudan	9	0.8	14.3

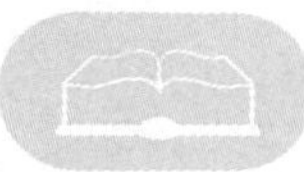

Largest Exporters of Goods and Services

	Exports ($ billion) 1999
United States	956.2
Germany	626.0
Japan	464.7
France	382.0
United Kingdom	373.8
Italy	292.3
Canada	277.7
Netherlands	248.7
China	218.5
Hong Kong	211.8
Belgium	194.2
South Korea	171.7
Spain	164.4
Mexico	148.1
Singapore	139.3
Taiwan	121.6
Switzerland	119.0
Sweden	107.5
Malaysia	96.0
Austria	94.9
Russia	84.9
Ireland	81.7
Australia	73.4
Thailand	71.4
Denmark	65.7
Saudi Arabia	56.1
Indonesia	55.8
Brazil	55.7
Norway	54.8
India	54.0
Finland	48.5
Turkey	45.7
United Arab Emirates	39.9
Philippines	39.0
Poland	38.5
Israel	35.9
Portugal	34.0
South Africa	33.3
Czech Republic	33.2
Argentina	27.7
Hungary	27.5
Venezuela	22.1
Iran	20.2
Chile	19.4
Ukraine	17.1
New Zealand	16.9
Greece	14.9
Vietnam	14.2
Kuwait	14.0
Nigeria	13.9
Colombia	13.9
Egypt	13.5
Algeria	12.9

	Exports ($ billion) 1999
Iraq	12.8
Slovakia	12.1
Morocco	10.6
Slovenia	10.5
Romania	9.9
Tunisia	8.8
Pakistan	8.8
Costa Rica	8.2
Croatia	8.1
Dominican Republic	8.0
Peru	7.6
Libya	7.3
Oman	7.2
Kazakhstan	6.9
Panama	6.9
Belarus	6.7
Qatar	6.1
Bangladesh	6.0
Bulgaria	5.8
Sri Lanka	5.6
Syria	5.5
Angola	5.4
Côte d'Ivoire	5.3
Ecuador	5.3
Lithuania	4.2
Estonia	3.9
Uruguay	3.6
Jordan	3.5
Guatemala	3.5
Trinidad and Tobago	3.4
Jamaica	3.4
Paraguay	3.3
Uzbekistan	3.2
El Salvador	3.1
Botswana	3.0
Latvia	2.9
Gabon	2.8
Mauritius	2.7
Kenya	2.7
Ghana	2.6
Zimbabwe	2.5
Papua New Guinea	2.2
Cameroon	2.2
Lebanon	1.8
Namibia	1.6
Bolivia	1.3
Tanzania	1.2
Zambia	0.9
Ethiopia	0.9
Sudan	0.8
Georgia	0.7
Uganda	0.7
Mozambique	0.6

Fastest Growth in Merchandise Exports 1990–98

	Volume growth (% p.a.) 1990–98
Uganda	19.5
Kuwait	19.2
Philippines	18.6
Singapore	16.2
Malaysia	15.5
Mexico	15.3
Sudan	14.3
Ireland	14.2
Costa Rica	13.7
Bangladesh	13.3
Ghana	12.9
Spain	12.1
Mozambique	10.8
China	10.7
Iraq	10.7
Turkey	10.3
Argentina	10.3
Morocco	10.2
Hong Kong	10.0
United Arab Emirates	9.9
Chile	9.9
Israel	9.6
Finland	9.3
South Korea	9.1
Canada	9.0
Indonesia	9.0
Greece	8.9
Ethiopia	8.8
Ecuador	8.7
Peru	8.6
Poland	8.4
Zimbabwe	8.4
Australia	7.7
Norway	7.6
South Africa	7.4
Uruguay	7.4
Guatemala	7.0
Netherlands	6.9
United States	6.8
Tanzania	6.6
United Kingdom	6.4
Italy	6.3
Belgium	6.2
Panama	6.2
Latvia	6.2
Venezuela	6.1
Hungary	6.0
Kenya	6.0
France	5.8
Germany	5.6
Nigeria	5.5
Botswana	5.5
Gabon	5.5

	Volume growth (% p.a.) 1990–98
Denmark	5.3
Colombia	5.2
Thailand	5.1
Jamaica	5.1
New Zealand	5.0
Tunisia	4.8
Côte d'Ivoire	4.7
Oman	4.6
Angola	4.5
Mauritius	4.5
Brazil	4.4
Saudi Arabia	4.3
Jordan	4.0
Lebanon	3.9
Zambia	3.2
El Salvador	2.8
India	2.7
Trinidad and Tobago	2.7
Bolivia	2.7
Japan	1.9
Egypt	1.9
Dominican Republic	1.8
Sri Lanka	1.5
Sweden	1.2
Algeria	1.2
Syria	0.4
Paraguay	0.0
Cameroon	–1.3
Iran	–1.7
Pakistan	–3.7
Libya	–5.3
Papua New Guinea	–5.3

DEBT

ESTONIA
LATVIA
LITHUANIA
$54.3bn
POLAND
BELARUS
$22.6bn
CZECH REPUBLIC
SLOVAKIA
UKRAINE
HUNGARY
SLOVENIA
CROATIA
ROMANIA
$29bn
BULGARIA
$22.4bn
$101.8bn
TURKEY
TUNISIA
CYPRUS
SYRIA
ISRAEL
LEB
JOR
MOROCCO
$40.7bn
$28bn
ALGERIA
$30.4bn
EGYPT
$167bn
MEXICO
CUBA
BAHAMAS
DOMINICAN REPUBLIC
JAMAICA
GUATEMALA
EL SALVADOR
ST LUCIA
BARBADOS
TRINIDAD & TOBAGO
$35.9bn
VENEZUELA
COSTA RICA
PANAMA
$34.5bn
COLOMBIA
ECUADOR
SUDAN
CÔTE D'IVOIRE
GHANA
$29.4bn
NIGERIA
CAMEROON
GABON
UGANDA
TANZANIA
$244.7bn
BRAZIL
$32.3bn
PERU
BOLIVIA
PARAGUAY
ANGOLA
ZAMBIA
ZIMBABWE
NAMIBIA
BOTSWANA
MOZAMBIQUE
$37.8bn
CHILE
$147.9bn
ARGENTINA
URUGUAY
$24.2bn
SOUTH AFRICA

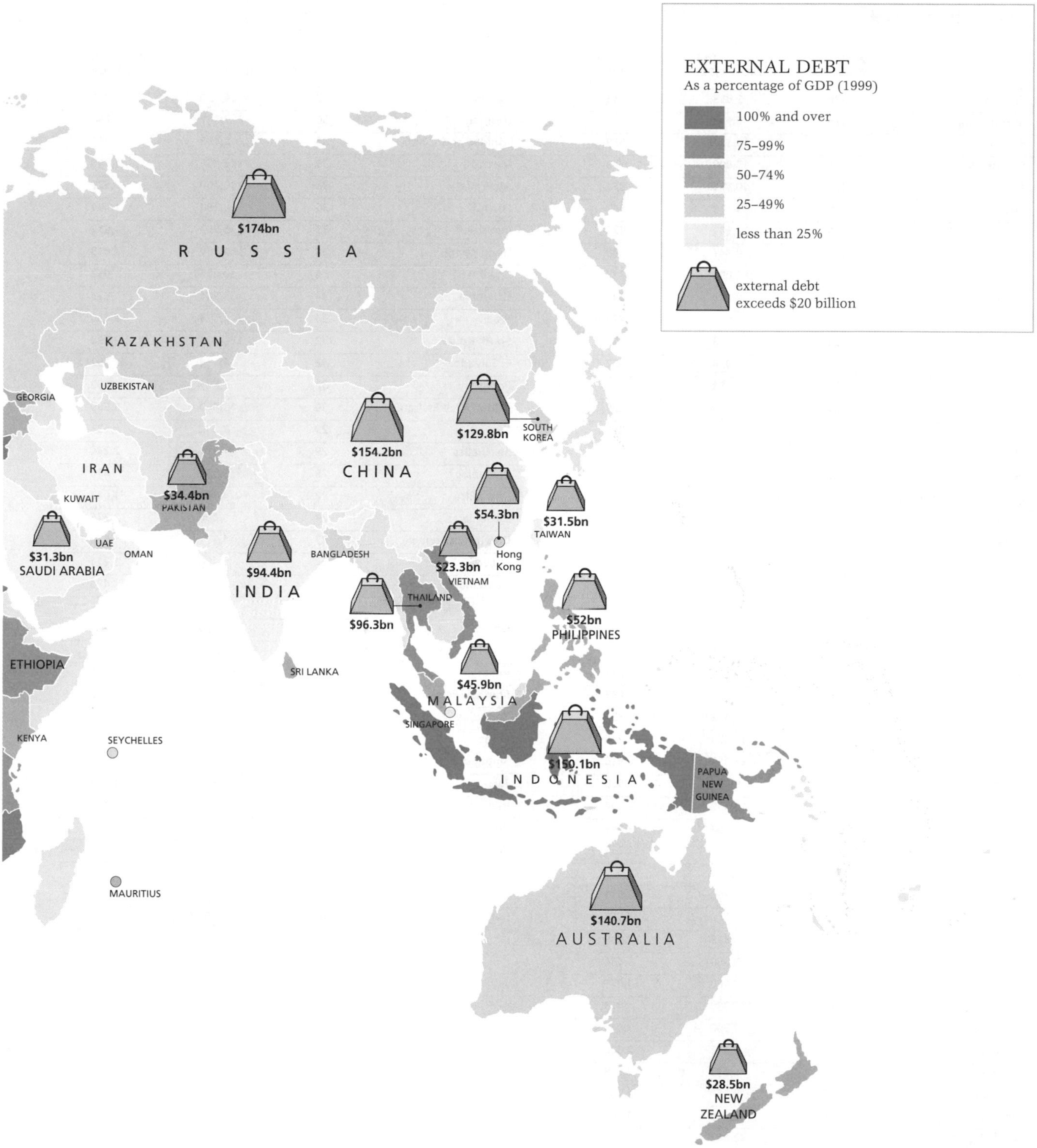

EXTERNAL DEBT

As a percentage of GDP (1999)

- 100% and over
- 75–99%
- 50–74%
- 25–49%
- less than 25%

external debt exceeds $20 billion

$174bn
RUSSIA
KAZAKHSTAN
UZBEKISTAN
GEORGIA
IRAN
$34.4bn
PAKISTAN
KUWAIT
$31.3bn
SAUDI ARABIA
UAE
OMAN
$94.4bn
INDIA
BANGLADESH
SRI LANKA
$154.2bn
CHINA
$129.8bn
SOUTH KOREA
$54.3bn
Hong Kong
$31.5bn
TAIWAN
$23.3bn
VIETNAM
$96.3bn
THAILAND
$52bn
PHILIPPINES
$45.9bn
MALAYSIA
SINGAPORE
$150.1bn
INDONESIA
PAPUA NEW GUINEA
$140.7bn
AUSTRALIA
$28.5bn
NEW ZEALAND
ETHIOPIA
KENYA
SEYCHELLES
MAURITIUS

Total External Debt

	Total external debt (% GDP) 1999	Total external debt ($ million) 1999	Dept per capita ($) 1999
Zambia	186	5,853	652
Mozambique	176	6,959	361
Sudan	166	16,132	559
Cyprus	153	13,800	17,738
Angola	127	10,871	871
Côte d'Ivoire	118	13,170	907
Syria	115	22,369	1,423
Jordan	111	8,947	1,380
Indonesia	105	150,096	717
Cameroon	103	9,443	643
Tanzania	91	7,967	243
Gabon	91	3,978	3,323
Ghana	89	6,928	352
Ethiopia	86	5,551	91
Nigeria	84	29,358	269
Vietnam	81	23,260	296
Zimbabwe	81	4,566	396
Bulgaria	80	9,872	1,192
Papua New Guinea	79	2,847	605
Thailand	77	96,335	1,583
Panama	77	7,313	2,601
Ecuador	76	14,506	1,169
Bolivia	74	6,157	756
Philippines	68	52,022	699
Uganda	64	4,077	193
Peru	62	32,284	1,280
Kenya	62	6,562	222
Hungary	60	29,042	2,882
Georgia	60	1,652	330
Pakistan	59	34,423	226
Algeria	59	28,015	910
Sri Lanka	59	9,472	508
Malaysia	58	45,939	2,104
Mauritius	58	2,464	2,143
Tunisia	57	11,872	1,255
Jamaica	57	3,913	1,529
Chile	56	37,762	2,514
Turkey	55	101,796	1,553
Estonia	55	2,879	2,039
Morocco	54	19,060	684
Cuba	54	12,000	1,075
Argentina	52	147,880	4,043
New Zealand	52	28,500	7,445
Lebanon	49	8,441	2,608
Croatia	46	9,443	2,109
Slovakia	46	9,150	1,700
Russia	43	173,940	1,182
Czech Republic	43	22,582	2,201
Latvia	42	2,657	1,112
Israel	40	40,700	6,671
Colombia	40	34,538	831
Kazakhstan	39	6,182	380
Bangladesh	38	17,534	138
Ukraine	37	14,136	279
Uruguay	36	7,447	2,248
Trinidad and Tobago	36	2,462	1,910
Mexico	35	166,960	1,715
Australia	35	140,700	7,522
Poland	35	54,268	1,401
Venezuela	35	35,852	1,512
Hong Kong	34	54,300	7,813
Egypt	34	30,404	452
Lithuania	34	3,584	973
Brazil	33	244,673	1,456
South Korea	32	129,784	2,792
El Salvador	32	4,014	652
Paraguay	32	2,514	469
United Arab Emirates	30	15,800	6,589
Kuwait	29	8,600	4,533
Seychelles	29	172	2,234
Romania	28	9,367	418
Costa Rica	28	4,182	1,063
Slovenia	27	5,400	2,715
Dominican Republic	27	4,771	570
St Lucia	27	184	1,211
Guatemala	26	4,660	420
Uzbekistan	24	4,163	174
Oman	24	3,603	1,465
Saudi Arabia	22	31,300	1,498
India	21	94,393	95
South Africa	18	24,158	605
Barbados	17	430	1,599
China	16	154,223	122
Singapore	13	10,700	3,038
Taiwan	11	31,500	1,401
Iran	9	10,357	155
Bahamas	9	390	1,297
Botswana	8	462	289
Namibia	5	148	87
Belarus	4	1,136	111
Italy	0.05	600	10

Largest Debtors

	Total external debt ($ billion) 1999
Brazil	244.7
Russia	173.9
Mexico	167.0
China	154.2
Indonesia	150.1
Argentina	147.9
Australia	140.7
South Korea	129.8
Turkey	101.8
Thailand	96.3
India	94.4
Hong Kong	54.3
Poland	54.3
Philippines	52.0
Malaysia	45.9
Israel	40.7
Chile	37.8
Venezuela	35.9
Colombia	34.5
Pakistan	34.4
Peru	32.3
Taiwan	31.5
Saudi Arabia	31.3
Egypt	30.4
Nigeria	29.4
Hungary	29.0
New Zealand	28.5
Algeria	28.0
South Africa	24.2
Vietnam	23.3
Czech Republic	22.6
Syria	22.4
Morocco	19.1
Bangladesh	17.5
Sudan	16.1
United Arab Emirates	15.8
Ecuador	14.5
Ukraine	14.1
Cyprus	13.8
Côte d'Ivoire	13.2
Cuba	12.0
Tunisia	11.9
Angola	10.9
Singapore	10.7
Iran	10.4
Bulgaria	9.9
Sri Lanka	9.5
Cameroon	9.4
Croatia	9.4
Romania	9.4
Slovakia	9.2
Jordan	8.9
Kuwait	8.6

	Total external debt ($ billion) 1999
Lebanon	8.4
Tanzania	8.0
Uruguay	7.4
Panama	7.3
Mozambique	7.0
Ghana	6.9
Kenya	6.6
Kazakhstan	6.2
Bolivia	6.2
Zambia	5.9
Ethiopia	5.6
Slovenia	5.4
Dominican Republic	4.8
Guatemala	4.7
Zimbabwe	4.6
Costa Rica	4.2
Uzbekistan	4.2
Uganda	4.1
El Salvador	4.0
Gabon	4.0
Jamaica	3.9
Oman	3.6
Lithuania	3.6
Estonia	2.9
Papua New Guinea	2.8
Latvia	2.7
Paraguay	2.5
Mauritius	2.5
Trinidad and Tobago	2.5
Georgia	1.7
Belarus	1.1
Italy	0.6
Botswana	0.5
Barbados	0.4
Bahamas	0.4
St Lucia	0.2
Seychelles	0.2
Namibia	0.1

Largest Per Capita External Debt

	Debt per capita ($) 1999
Cyprus	17,738
Hong Kong	7,813
Australia	7,522
New Zealand	7,445
Israel	6,671
United Arab Emirates	6,589
Kuwait	4,533
Argentina	4,043
Gabon	3,323
Singapore	3,038
Hungary	2,882
South Korea	2,792
Slovenia	2,715
Lebanon	2,608
Panama	2,601
Chile	2,514
Uruguay	2,248
Seychelles	2,234
Czech Republic	2,201
Mauritius	2,143
Croatia	2,109
Malaysia	2,104
Estonia	2,039
Trinidad and Tobago	1,910
Mexico	1,715
Slovakia	1,700
Barbados	1,599
Thailand	1,583
Turkey	1,553
Jamaica	1,529
Venezuela	1,512
Saudi Arabia	1,498
Oman	1,465
Brazil	1,456
Syria	1,423
Poland	1,401
Taiwan	1,401
Jordan	1,380
Bahamas	1,297
Peru	1,280
Tunisia	1,255
St Lucia	1,211
Bulgaria	1,192
Russia	1,182
Ecuador	1,169
Latvia	1,112
Cuba	1,075
Costa Rica	1,063
Lithuania	973
Algeria	910
Côte d'Ivoire	907
Angola	871
Colombia	831

	Debt per capita ($) 1999
Bolivia	756
Indonesia	717
Philippines	699
Morocco	684
Zambia	652
El Salvador	652
Cameroon	643
South Africa	605
Papua New Guinea	605
Dominican Republic	570
Sudan	559
Sri Lanka	508
Paraguay	469
Egypt	452
Guatemala	420
Romania	418
Zimbabwe	396
Kazakhstan	380
Mozambique	361
Ghana	352
Georgia	330
Vietnam	296
Botswana	289
Ukraine	279
Nigeria	269
Tanzania	243
Pakistan	226
Kenya	222
Uganda	193
Uzbekistan	174
Iran	155
Bangladesh	138
China	122
Belarus	111
India	95
Ethiopia	91
Namibia	87
Italy	10

 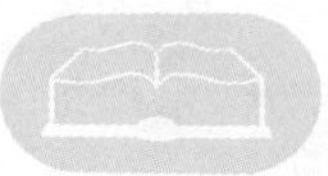    

ENTERPRISE AND OPPORTUNITY

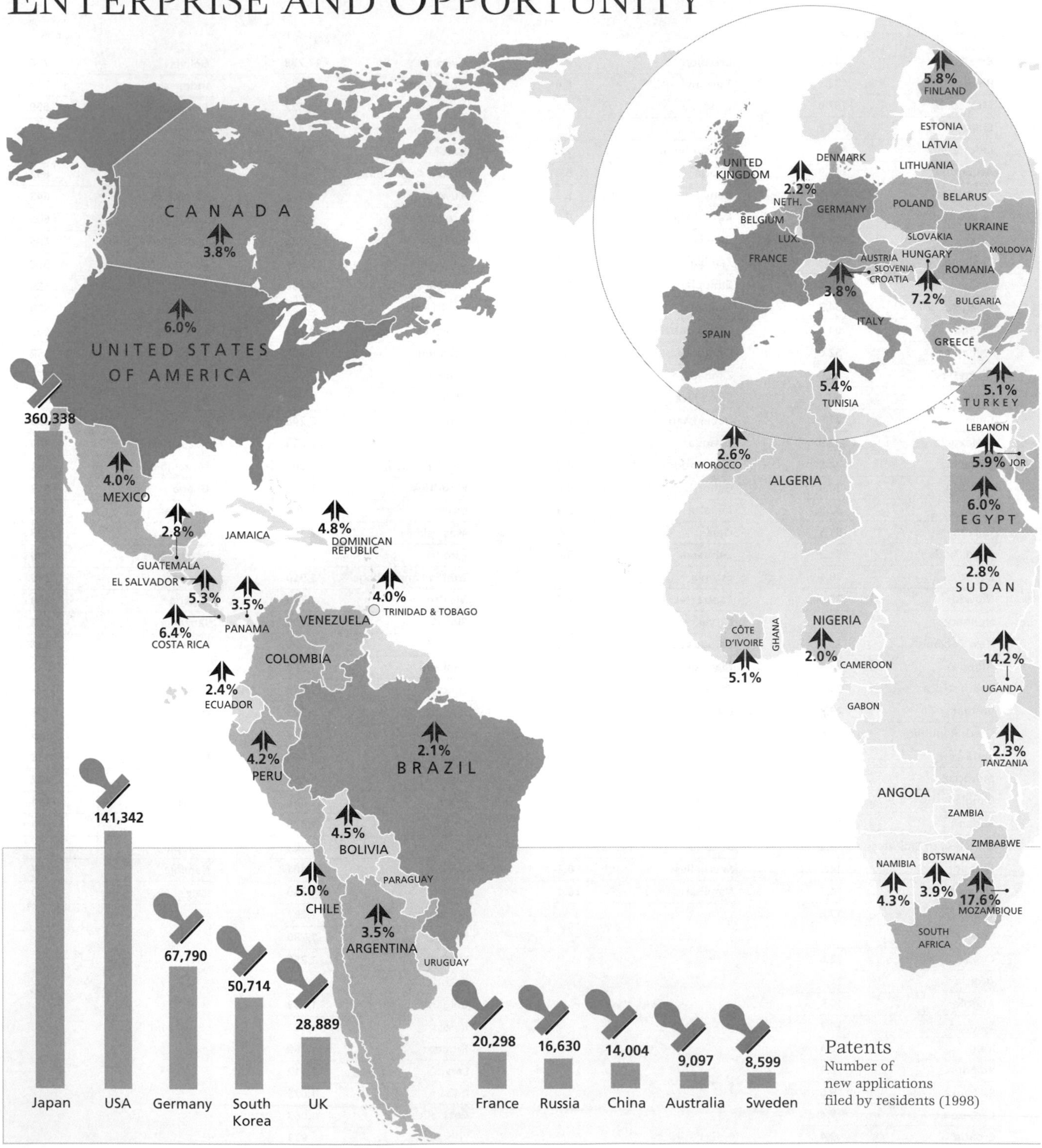

CANADA 3.8%
UNITED STATES OF AMERICA 6.0%
MEXICO 4.0%
GUATEMALA 2.8%
EL SALVADOR 5.3%
COSTA RICA 6.4%
PANAMA 3.5%
JAMAICA
DOMINICAN REPUBLIC 4.8%
TRINIDAD & TOBAGO 4.0%
VENEZUELA
COLOMBIA
ECUADOR 2.4%
PERU 4.2%
BRAZIL 2.1%
BOLIVIA 4.5%
PARAGUAY
CHILE 5.0%
ARGENTINA 3.5%
URUGUAY
FINLAND 5.8%
ESTONIA
LATVIA
LITHUANIA
DENMARK
UNITED KINGDOM
NETH. 2.2%
BELGIUM
LUX.
GERMANY
POLAND
BELARUS
UKRAINE
SLOVAKIA
MOLDOVA
FRANCE
AUSTRIA
HUNGARY 7.2%
SLOVENIA
CROATIA
ROMANIA
ITALY 3.8%
BULGARIA
SPAIN
GREECE
TUNISIA 5.4%
TURKEY 5.1%
LEBANON
JOR 5.9%
MOROCCO 2.6%
ALGERIA
EGYPT 6.0%
SUDAN 2.8%
CÔTE D'IVOIRE 5.1%
GHANA
NIGERIA 2.0%
CAMEROON
GABON
UGANDA 14.2%
TANZANIA 2.3%
ANGOLA
ZAMBIA
ZIMBABWE
NAMIBIA 4.3%
BOTSWANA 3.9%
MOZAMBIQUE 17.6%
SOUTH AFRICA

Patents
Number of new applications filed by residents (1998)

Japan	USA	Germany	South Korea	UK	France	Russia	China	Australia	Sweden
360,338	141,342	67,790	50,714	28,889	20,298	16,630	14,004	9,097	8,599

 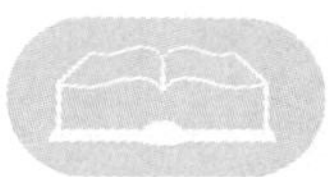    

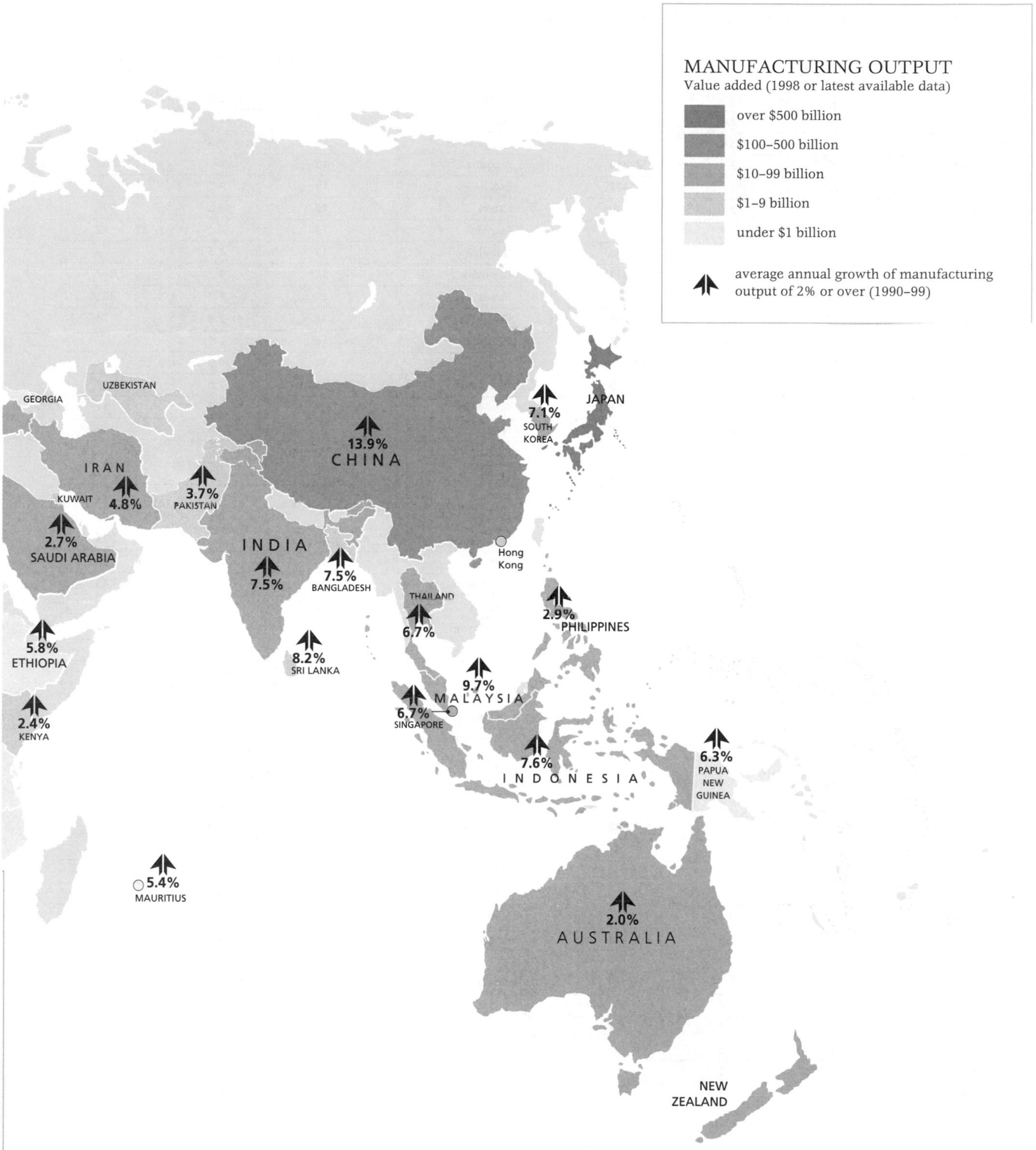

MANUFACTURING OUTPUT

Value added (1998 or latest available data)

- over $500 billion
- $100–500 billion
- $10–99 billion
- $1–9 billion
- under $1 billion

average annual growth of manufacturing output of 2% or over (1990–99)

GEORGIA
UZBEKISTAN
IRAN 4.8%
KUWAIT
2.7% SAUDI ARABIA
3.7% PAKISTAN
13.9% CHINA
7.1% SOUTH KOREA
JAPAN
INDIA 7.5%
7.5% BANGLADESH
Hong Kong
THAILAND 6.7%
2.9% PHILIPPINES
5.8% ETHIOPIA
8.2% SRI LANKA
9.7% MALAYSIA
6.7% SINGAPORE
2.4% KENYA
7.6% INDONESIA
6.3% PAPUA NEW GUINEA
5.4% MAURITIUS
2.0% AUSTRALIA
NEW ZEALAND

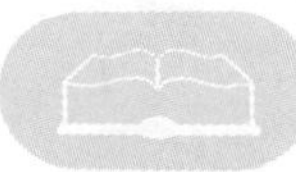

Manufacturing Output and New Patent Applications

	Manufacturing output (% GDP)1998–99	Growth of output (% p.a.) 1990–99	New patent applications 1998
China	38	13.9	14,004
Belarus	35	–2.6	919
Ukraine	33	–13.4	5,327
South Korea	32	7.1	50,714
Thailand	32	6.7	477
Malaysia	32	9.7	179
Costa Rica	30	6.4	–
Slovenia	28	3.8	296
Singapore	26	6.7	311
Indonesia	25	7.6	0
Hungary	25	7.2	751
Mauritius	25	5.4	3
Japan	24	1.2	360,338
Portugal	24	0.2	119
Peru	24	4.2	48
Brazil	23	2.1	2,535
El Salvador	23	5.3	–
Romania	22	–	1,308
Slovakia	22	–	224
Germany	21	–0.3	67,790
Mexico	21	4.0	472
Finland	21	5.8	4,796
Philippines	21	2.9	163
New Zealand	21	–	1,353
Ecuador	21	2.4	8
Côte d'Ivoire	21	5.1	–
Egypt	20	6.0	494
Croatia	20	–4.9	273
France	19	1.2	20,298
Italy	19	1.5	3,167
Spain	19	–0.7	3,119
Austria	19	1.5	3,023
South Africa	19	1.1	–
United States	18	6.0	141,342
Argentina	18	3.5	861
Belgium	18	1.4	1,899
Poland	18	–	2,410
Tunisia	18	5.4	46
Lithuania	18	–10.3	135
Vietnam	18	–	30
United Kingdom	17	–	28,889
Canada	17	3.8	4,841
Iran	17	4.8	337
Morocco	17	2.6	90
Uruguay	17	0.1	27
Dominican Republic	17	4.8	–
Lebanon	17	–	–
Zimbabwe	17	0.7	8
Netherlands	16	2.2	5,751
India	16	7.5	2,111
Chile	16	5.0	189
Pakistan	16	3.7	16
Sri Lanka	16	8.2	81
Jordan	16	5.9	0
Turkey	15	5.1	231
Bangladesh	15	7.5	32
Bulgaria	15	–	281
Bolivia	15	4.5	–
Latvia	15	–9.8	195
Estonia	15	–	22
Namibia	15	4.3	–
Denmark	14	1.2	2,897
Venezuela	14	1.3	201
Colombia	14	–2.9	74
Paraguay	14	0.5	–
Jamaica	14	–1.9	–
Australia	13	2.0	9,097
Guatemala	13	2.8	11
Mozambique	13	17.6	–
Kuwait	12	–	–
Zambia	12	0.7	7
Norway	11	2.3	1,642
Greece	11	0.5	68
Uzbekistan	11	–	723
Kenya	11	2.4	33
Saudi Arabia	10	2.7	45
Algeria	10	–5.7	42
Cameroon	10	0.1	–
Sudan	9	2.8	6
Ghana	9	–4.5	6
Uganda	9	14.2	7
Panama	8	3.5	31
Trinidad and Tobago	8	4.0	17
Papua New Guinea	8	6.3	–
Georgia	8	–	280
Tanzania	7	2.3	–
Ethiopia	7	5.8	4
Hong Kong	6	–	128
Nigeria	5	2.0	–
Botswana	5	3.9	7
Gabon	5	0.6	–
Angola	4	–1.4	–

Source (new patent applications): World Intellectual Property Organization

Fastest Growth of Manufacturing Output 1990–99

	Growth of output (% p.a.) 1990–99
Mozambique	17.6
Uganda	14.2
China	13.9
Malaysia	9.7
Sri Lanka	8.2
Indonesia	7.6
Bangladesh	7.5
India	7.5
Hungary	7.2
South Korea	7.1
Thailand	6.7
Singapore	6.7
Costa Rica	6.4
Papua New Guinea	6.3
United States	6.0
Egypt	6.0
Jordan	5.9
Finland	5.8
Ethiopia	5.8
Mauritius	5.4
Tunisia	5.4
El Salvador	5.3
Côte d'Ivoire	5.1
Turkey	5.1
Chile	5.0
Iran	4.8
Dominican Republic	4.8
Bolivia	4.5
Namibia	4.3
Peru	4.2
Mexico	4.0
Trinidad and Tobago	4.0
Botswana	3.9
Slovenia	3.8
Canada	3.8
Pakistan	3.7
Argentina	3.5
Panama	3.5
Philippines	2.9
Guatemala	2.8
Sudan	2.8
Saudi Arabia	2.7
Morocco	2.6
Ecuador	2.4
Kenya	2.4
Norway	2.3
Tanzania	2.3
Netherlands	2.2
Brazil	2.1
Australia	2.0
Nigeria	2.0
Italy	1.5
Austria	1.5
Belgium	1.4
Venezuela	1.3
Japan	1.2
France	1.2
Denmark	1.2
South Africa	1.1
Zimbabwe	0.7
Zambia	0.7
Gabon	0.6
Paraguay	0.5
Greece	0.5
Portugal	0.2
Uruguay	0.1
Cameroon	0.1
Germany	–0.3
Spain	–0.7
Angola	–1.4
Jamaica	–1.9
Belarus	–2.6
Colombia	–2.9
Ghana	–4.5
Croatia	–4.9
Algeria	–5.7
Latvia	–9.8
Lithuania	–10.3
Ukraine	–13.4

Most New Patent Applications Filed by Residents

	New patent applications 1998
Japan	360,338
United States	141,342
Germany	67,790
South Korea	50,714
United Kingdom	28,889
France	20,298
China	14,004
Australia	9,097
Netherlands	5,751
Ukraine	5,327
Canada	4,841
Finland	4,796
Italy	3,167
Spain	3,119
Austria	3,023
Denmark	2,897
Brazil	2,535
Poland	2,410
India	2,111
Belgium	1,899
Norway	1,642
New Zealand	1,353
Romania	1,308
Belarus	919
Argentina	861
Hungary	751
Uzbekistan	723
Egypt	494
Thailand	477
Mexico	472
Iran	337
Singapore	311
Slovenia	296
Bulgaria	281
Georgia	280
Croatia	273
Turkey	231
Slovakia	224
Venezuela	201
Latvia	195
Chile	189
Malaysia	179
Philippines	163
Lithuania	135
Hong Kong	128
Portugal	119
Morocco	90
Sri Lanka	81
Colombia	74
Greece	68
Peru	48
Tunisia	46
Saudi Arabia	45
Algeria	42
Kenya	33
Bangladesh	32
Panama	31
Uruguay	27
Estonia	22
Trinidad and Tobago	17
Pakistan	16
Guatemala	11
Ecuador	8
Zimbabwe	8
Uganda	7
Botswana	7
Zambia	7
Sudan	6
Ghana	6
Ethiopia	4
Mauritius	3
Indonesia	0
Jordan	0

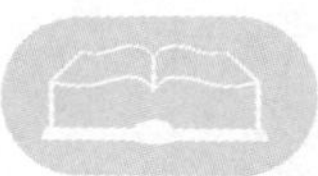

SERVICES

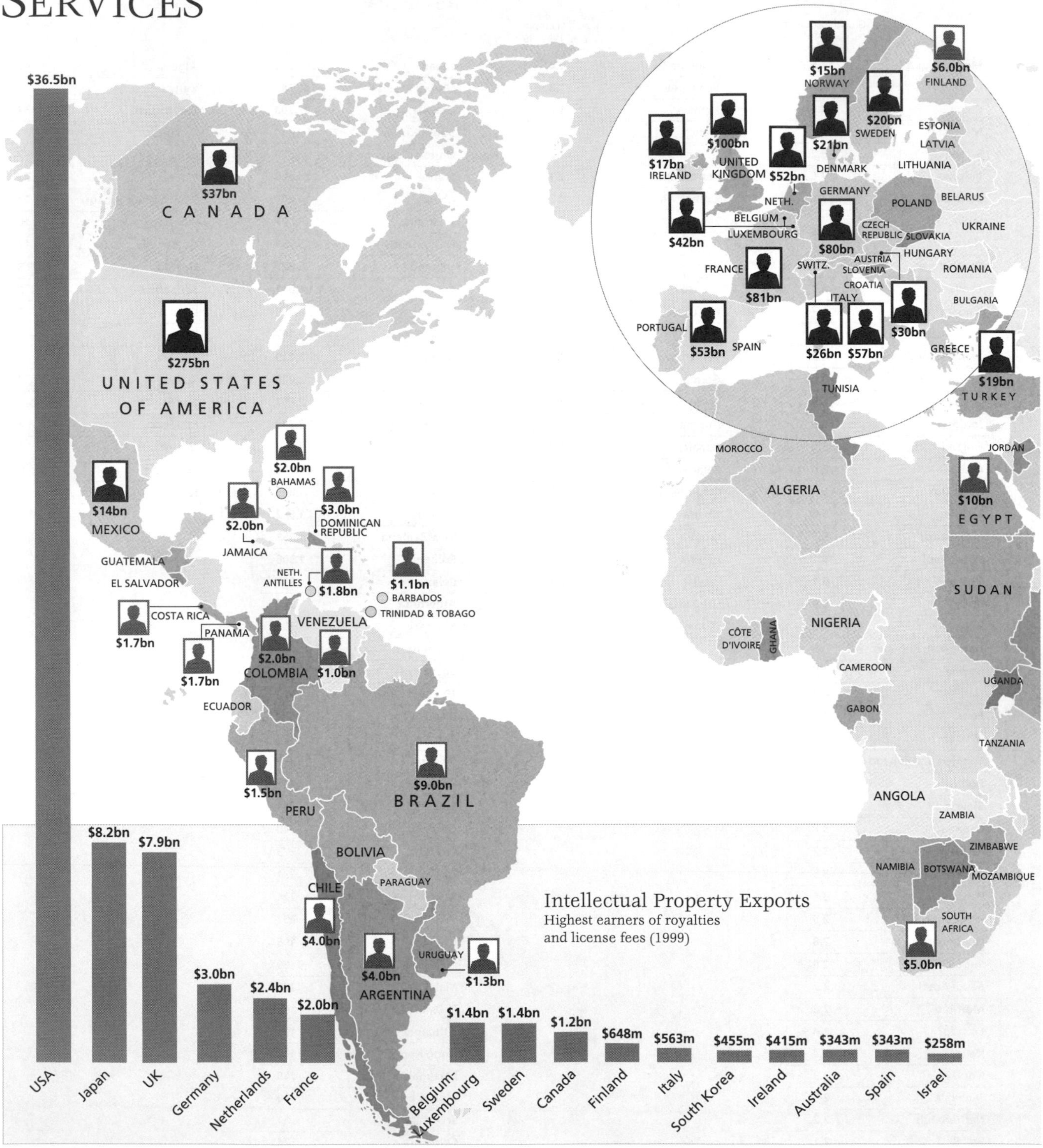

$37bn CANADA
$275bn UNITED STATES OF AMERICA
$14bn MEXICO
$2.0bn BAHAMAS
$2.0bn JAMAICA
$3.0bn DOMINICAN REPUBLIC
GUATEMALA
EL SALVADOR
NETH. ANTILLES $1.8bn
$1.1bn BARBADOS
TRINIDAD & TOBAGO
$1.7bn COSTA RICA
$1.7bn PANAMA
VENEZUELA
$2.0bn COLOMBIA
$1.0bn
ECUADOR
$1.5bn PERU
$9.0bn BRAZIL
BOLIVIA
PARAGUAY
CHILE $4.0bn
$4.0bn ARGENTINA
URUGUAY $1.3bn

$15bn NORWAY
$6.0bn FINLAND
$20bn SWEDEN
ESTONIA
LATVIA
LITHUANIA
$17bn IRELAND
$100bn UNITED KINGDOM
$21bn DENMARK
$52bn NETH.
GERMANY
POLAND
BELARUS
$42bn BELGIUM LUXEMBOURG
CZECH REPUBLIC
SLOVAKIA
UKRAINE
$80bn
AUSTRIA
HUNGARY
SLOVENIA
ROMANIA
FRANCE $81bn
SWITZ.
CROATIA
ITALY
BULGARIA
PORTUGAL
$53bn SPAIN
$26bn $57bn
$30bn
GREECE
$19bn TURKEY
TUNISIA
MOROCCO
ALGERIA
JORDAN
$10bn EGYPT
SUDAN
CÔTE D'IVOIRE
GHANA
NIGERIA
CAMEROON
UGANDA
GABON
TANZANIA
ANGOLA
ZAMBIA
ZIMBABWE
NAMIBIA
BOTSWANA
MOZAMBIQUE
SOUTH AFRICA
$5.0bn

Intellectual Property Exports

Highest earners of royalties and license fees (1999)

USA	$36.5bn
Japan	$8.2bn
UK	$7.9bn
Germany	$3.0bn
Netherlands	$2.4bn
France	$2.0bn
Belgium-Luxembourg	$1.4bn
Sweden	$1.4bn
Canada	$1.2bn
Finland	$648m
Italy	$563m
South Korea	$455m
Ireland	$415m
Australia	$343m
Spain	$343m
Israel	$258m

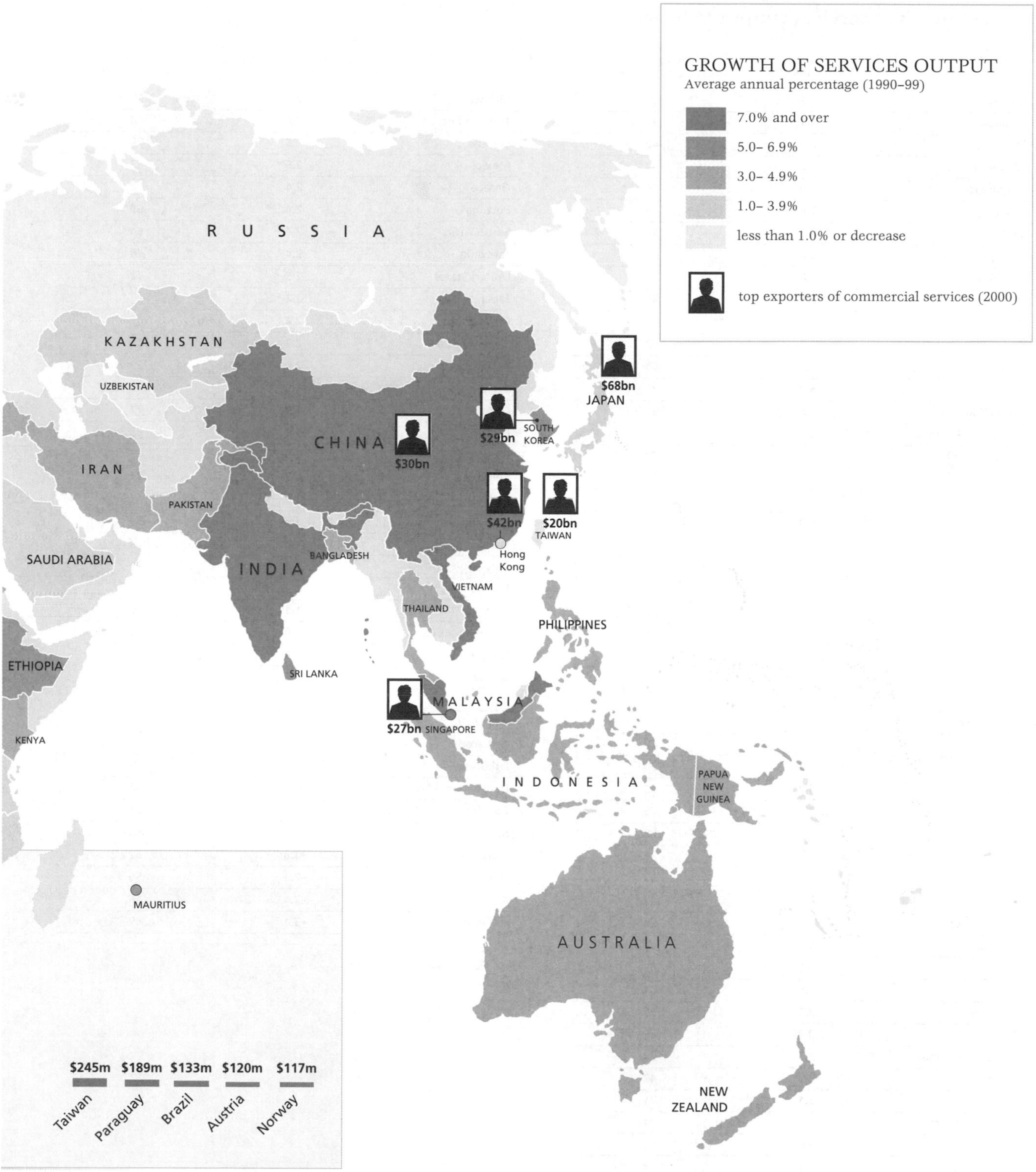

GROWTH OF SERVICES OUTPUT

Average annual percentage (1990–99)

- 7.0% and over
- 5.0– 6.9%
- 3.0– 4.9%
- 1.0– 3.9%
- less than 1.0% or decrease
- top exporters of commercial services (2000)

RUSSIA
KAZAKHSTAN
UZBEKISTAN
CHINA
$30bn
$29bn
SOUTH KOREA
$68bn
JAPAN
IRAN
PAKISTAN
$42bn
$20bn
TAIWAN
Hong Kong
SAUDI ARABIA
BANGLADESH
INDIA
VIETNAM
THAILAND
PHILIPPINES
ETHIOPIA
SRI LANKA
MALAYSIA
$27bn
SINGAPORE
KENYA
INDONESIA
PAPUA NEW GUINEA
MAURITIUS
AUSTRALIA
NEW ZEALAND

$245m	$189m	$133m	$120m	$117m
Taiwan	Paraguay	Brazil	Austria	Norway

Fastest Growth of Services Output 1990–99

	Growth of services output (% p.a.)1990–99	Services output (% of GDP) 1999
China	9.2	33
Uganda	8.1	38
Vietnam	8.1	40
Malaysia	8.0	43
Singapore	8.0	64
India	7.8	46
Chile	7.6	57
Ethiopia	6.8	37
Slovakia	6.8	64
Botswana	6.3	51
Mauritius	6.3	61
Sri Lanka	6.1	52
El Salvador	5.8	60
Ghana	5.8	39
South Korea	5.8	51
Dominican Republic	5.7	54
Tunisia	5.3	59
Colombia	5.2	61
Jordan	5.1	72
Argentina	5.0	67
Uruguay	5.0	67
Egypt	4.8	51
Costa Rica	4.7	53
Guatemala	4.7	57
Iran	4.7	48
Bolivia	4.5	64
Gabon	4.5	51
Australia	4.4	72
Bangladesh	4.4	50
Pakistan	4.4	49
Thailand	4.4	50
Peru	4.2	55
Panama	4.1	76
Poland	4.1	65
Indonesia	4.0	37
Philippines	4.0	52
Turkey	3.9	60
Slovenia	3.8	58
New Zealand	3.7	–
Norway	3.6	67
Kenya	3.5	61
Zimbabwe	3.5	55
Namibia	3.4	55
Papua New Guinea	3.3	24
Sudan	3.3	42
Netherlands	3.1	74
United Kingdom	3.1	74
Brazil	3.0	61
Côte d'Ivoire	2.8	48
Nigeria	2.8	28
Algeria	2.7	38
Mozambique	2.7	42
Denmark	2.6	76
Morocco	2.6	53
Trinidad and Tobago	2.6	58
Canada	2.5	73
Mexico	2.5	67
Greece	2.4	72
Portugal	2.4	69
South Africa	2.4	64
Tanzania	2.4	40
United States	2.3	72
Japan	2.2	62
Kazakhstan	2.2	57
Saudi Arabia	2.2	45
Austria	2.0	69
Croatia	1.9	59
Germany	1.9	71
Latvia	1.9	68
Paraguay	1.9	45
Belgium	1.8	73
Finland	1.8	68
Ecuador	1.6	50
France	1.5	74
Italy	1.5	71
Sweden	1.2	–
Estonia	1.1	69
Czech Republic	1.0	53
Hungary	0.8	61
Jamaica	0.6	61
Zambia	0.3	51
Venezuela	0.2	59
Cameroon	0.1	38
Lithuania	–0.1	59
Uzbekistan	–0.4	43
Romania	–0.8	53
Belarus	–1.3	45
Bulgaria	–1.8	62
Russia	–2.2	56
Angola	–2.4	16
Ukraine	–3.1	49

United States: growth rate is for 1990–97

  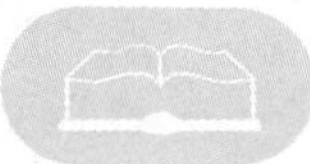  

Largest Exporters of Commercial Services

	Exports of commercial services ($ billion) 2000	Imports of commercial services ($ billion) 2000
United States	274.6	198.9
United Kingdom	99.9	82.1
France	81.2	61.5
Germany	80.0	132.3
Japan	68.3	115.7
Italy	56.7	55.7
Spain	53.0	30.8
Netherlands	52.3	51.1
Belgium-Luxembourg	42.0	38.3
Hong Kong	42.0	26.0
Canada	37.2	41.9
Austria	30.0	29.1
China	30.0	36.0
South Korea	29.0	33.0
Singapore	27.0	21.0
Switzerland	26.4	15.5
Denmark	20.6	18.3
Sweden	20.0	23.4
Taiwan	20.0	26.0
Turkey	19.2	7.6
Ireland	16.6	28.7
Norway	15.0	14.5
Mexico	13.6	16.8
Greece	10.2	–
Egypt	10.0	7.0
Brazil	8.8	15.9
South Africa	5.0	5.0
Argentina	4.4	8.6
Chile	3.8	4.3
Cuba	3.1	–
Dominican Republic	3.1	1.3
Bahamas	2.0	0.9
Colombia	2.0	3.2
Jamaica	2.0	1.3
Netherlands Antilles	1.8	1.0
Costa Rica	1.7	1.3
Panama	1.7	1.0
Peru	1.5	2.2
Uruguay	1.3	–
Barbados	1.1	–

Source: World Trade Organization

Largest Exporters of Intellectual Property

	Receipts of royalties and fees ($ million) 1999	Royalties and fees paid ($ million) 1999
United States	36,467	13,275
Japan	8,190	9,855
United Kingdom	7,942	6,301
Germany	3,017	4,405
Netherlands	2,391	3,448
France	1,983	2,297
Belgium-Luxembourg	1,399	2,159
Sweden	1,386	1,147
Canada	1,178	2,602
Finland	648	375
Italy	563	1,382
South Korea	455	2,661
Ireland	415	6,943
Australia	343	1,132
Spain	343	1,864
Israel	258	263
Taiwan	245	1,637
Paraguay	189	3
Brazil	133	1,283
Austria	120	623
Norway	117	296
Chile	99	51
China	75	792
South Africa	71	162
Hungary	62	307
New Zealand	49	317
Egypt	47	329
Russia	43	8
Czech Republic	43	137
Mexico	42	554

Source: World Trade Organization

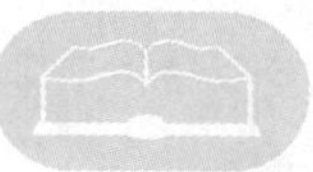

Markets

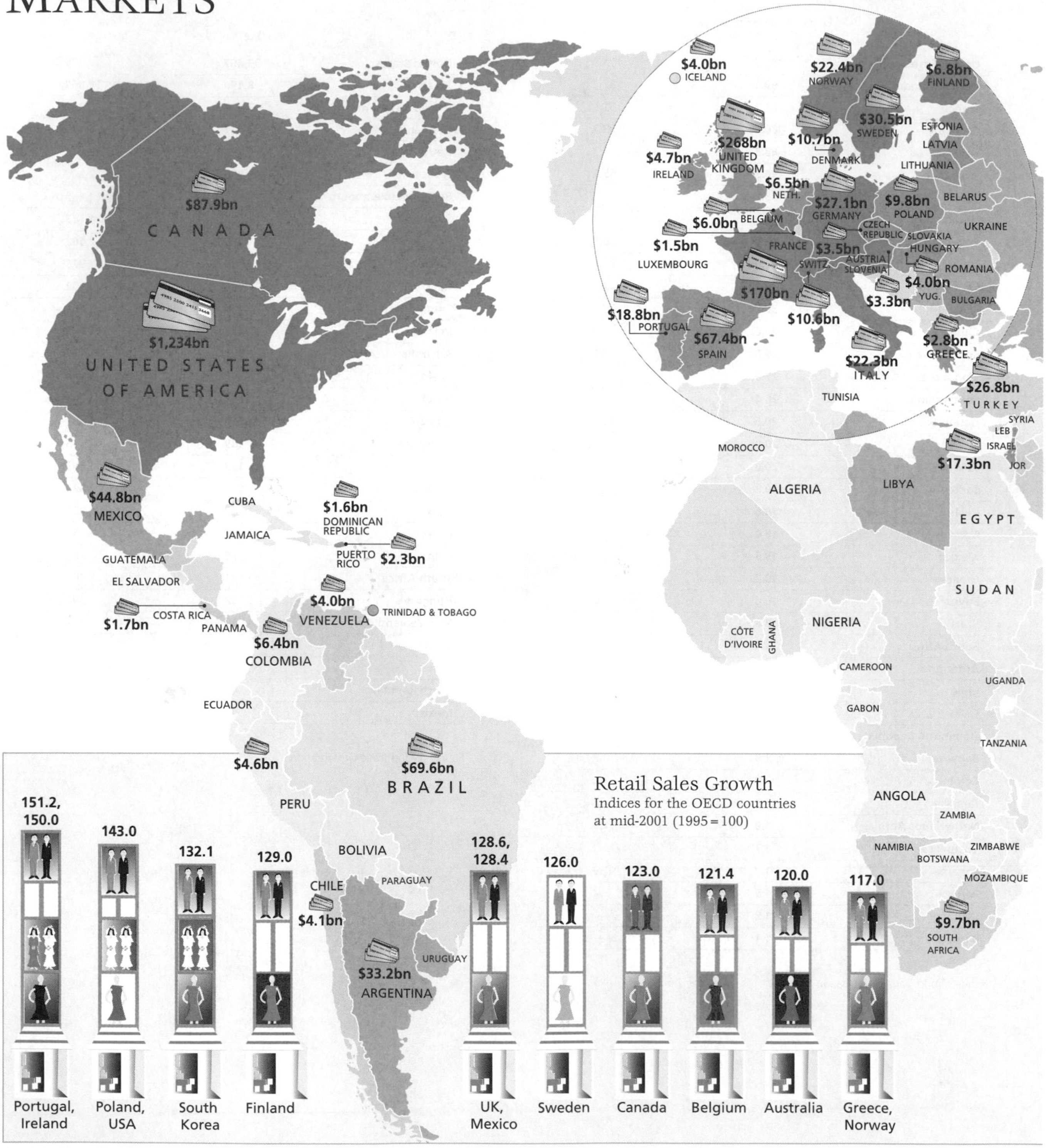

$4.0bn ICELAND
$22.4bn NORWAY
$6.8bn FINLAND
$30.5bn SWEDEN
ESTONIA
LATVIA
LITHUANIA
$268bn UNITED KINGDOM
$10.7bn DENMARK
$4.7bn IRELAND
$6.5bn NETH.
$27.1bn GERMANY
$9.8bn POLAND
BELARUS
UKRAINE
$6.0bn BELGIUM
$1.5bn LUXEMBOURG
CZECH REPUBLIC
SLOVAKIA
HUNGARY
FRANCE
$3.5bn SWITZ.
AUSTRIA
SLOVENIA
ROMANIA
$4.0bn
$170bn
$3.3bn YUG.
BULGARIA
$18.8bn PORTUGAL
$10.6bn
$67.4bn SPAIN
$2.8bn GREECE
$22.3bn ITALY
$26.8bn TURKEY
TUNISIA
SYRIA
LEB
ISRAEL
$17.3bn
JOR
MOROCCO
ALGERIA
LIBYA
EGYPT
SUDAN
$87.9bn CANADA
$1,234bn UNITED STATES OF AMERICA
$44.8bn MEXICO
CUBA
JAMAICA
$1.6bn DOMINICAN REPUBLIC
PUERTO RICO $2.3bn
GUATEMALA
EL SALVADOR
$4.0bn VENEZUELA
TRINIDAD & TOBAGO
$1.7bn COSTA RICA
PANAMA
$6.4bn COLOMBIA
ECUADOR
$4.6bn
PERU
$69.6bn BRAZIL
BOLIVIA
CHILE
$4.1bn
PARAGUAY
URUGUAY
$33.2bn ARGENTINA
CÔTE D'IVOIRE
GHANA
NIGERIA
CAMEROON
GABON
UGANDA
TANZANIA
ANGOLA
ZAMBIA
NAMIBIA
BOTSWANA
ZIMBABWE
MOZAMBIQUE
$9.7bn SOUTH AFRICA

Retail Sales Growth

Indices for the OECD countries at mid-2001 (1995 = 100)

Portugal, Ireland	151.2, 150.0
Poland, USA	143.0
South Korea	132.1
Finland	129.0
UK, Mexico	128.6, 128.4
Sweden	126.0
Canada	123.0
Belgium	121.4
Australia	120.0
Greece, Norway	117.0

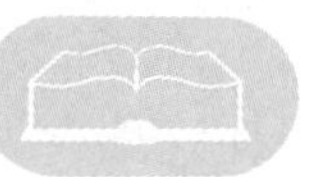

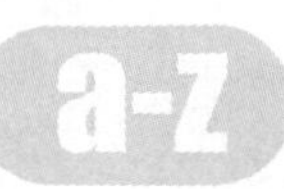

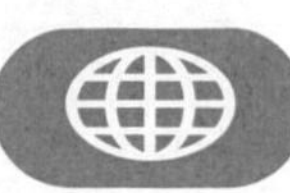

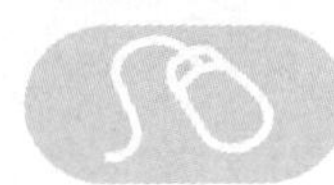

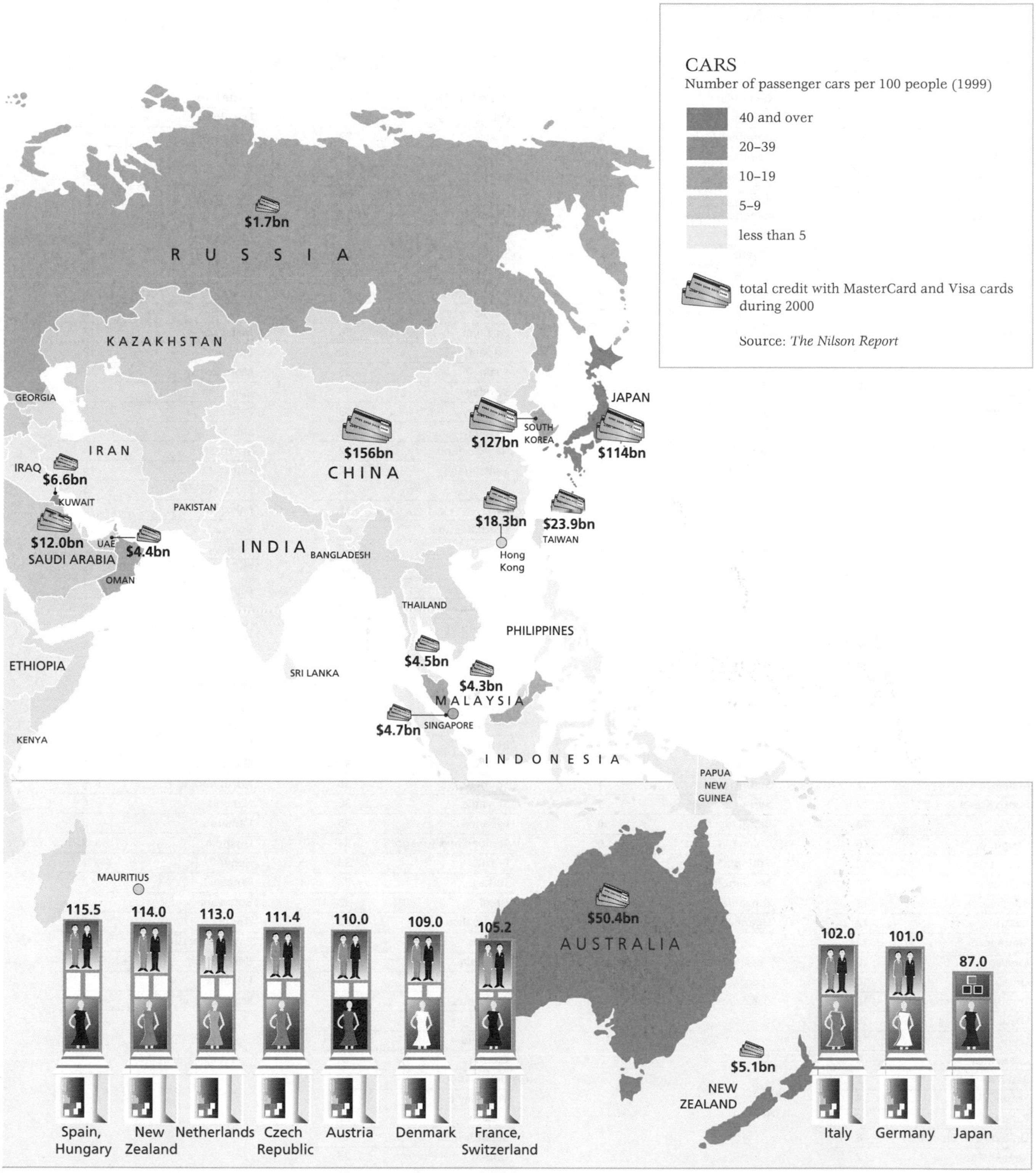

CARS
Number of passenger cars per 100 people (1999)
40 and over
20–39
10–19
5–9
less than 5
total credit with MasterCard and Visa cards during 2000
Source: The Nilson Report
$1.7bn
RUSSIA
KAZAKHSTAN
GEORGIA
IRAN
IRAQ
$6.6bn
KUWAIT
$12.0bn
SAUDI ARABIA
UAE
$4.4bn
OMAN
PAKISTAN
INDIA
BANGLADESH
$156bn
CHINA
$127bn
SOUTH KOREA
JAPAN
$114bn
$18.3bn
Hong Kong
$23.9bn
TAIWAN
THAILAND
PHILIPPINES
$4.5bn
$4.3bn
MALAYSIA
$4.7bn
SINGAPORE
SRI LANKA
ETHIOPIA
KENYA
INDONESIA
PAPUA NEW GUINEA
MAURITIUS
$50.4bn
AUSTRALIA
$5.1bn
NEW ZEALAND
115.5
Spain, Hungary
114.0
New Zealand
113.0
Netherlands
111.4
Czech Republic
110.0
Austria
109.0
Denmark
105.2
France, Switzerland
102.0
Italy
101.0
Germany
87.0
Japan

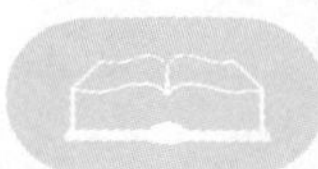

Automobile and TV Ownership

	Automobiles per 100 people, 1999
Italy	54
Germany	51
Austria	50
Australia	49
Switzerland	49
New Zealand	48
United States	48
France	47
Canada	46
Belgium	45
Sweden	44
Slovenia	42
Norway	41
Finland	40
Japan	40
Spain	39
Netherlands	38
United Kingdom	37
Denmark	35
Czech Republic	34
Estonia	32
Kuwait	32
Lebanon	31
Portugal	31
Lithuania	29
Ireland	27
Greece	25
Hungary	24
Poland	24
Bulgaria	23
Puerto Rico	23
Slovakia	23
Israel	22
Latvia	22
Yugoslavia	18
Malaysia	17
South Korea	17
Libya	16
Uruguay	16
Argentina	14
Belarus	14
Romania	13
Russia	12
Singapore	12
Mexico	10
Oman	10
Trinidad and Tobago	10
Ukraine	10
Chile	9
Costa Rica	9
Saudi Arabia	9
South Africa	9
Panama	8
United Arab Emirates	8
Kazakhstan	7
Mauritius	7
Venezuela	7
Hong Kong	6
Turkey	6
Georgia	5
Guatemala	5
Jordan	5
Namibia	5
Colombia	4
Ecuador	4
Iraq	4
Jamaica	4
Morocco	4
Algeria	3
Bolivia	3
Botswana	3
Dominican Republic	3
El Salvador	3
Iran	3
Peru	3
Thailand	3
Tunisia	3
Zimbabwe	3
Angola	2
Côte d'Ivoire	2
Cuba	2
Egypt	2
Gabon	2
Sri Lanka	2
Zambia	2
Cameroon	1
Ghana	1
India	1
Indonesia	1
Kenya	1
Nigeria	1
Pakistan	1
Papua New Guinea	1
Paraguay	1
Philippines	1
Sudan	1
Syria	1
Bangladesh*	0
China*	0
Ethiopia*	0
Mozambique*	0
Tanzania*	0
Uganda*	0

* less than 0.5 automobiles per 100 people

Source: International Road Federation

	TV sets per 100 people, 1999
United States	84
Latvia	74
Japan	72
Canada	72
Australia	71
United Kingdom	65
Norway	65
Finland	64
France	62
Denmark	62
Netherlands	60
Germany	58
Portugal	56
Estonia	56
Spain	55
Sweden	53
Uruguay	53
Belgium	52
New Zealand	52
Switzerland	52
Austria	52
Italy	49
Czech Republic	49
Greece	48
Kuwait	48
Georgia	47
Hungary	45
Hong Kong	43
Russia	42
Lithuania	42
Slovakia	42
Ukraine	41
Bulgaria	41
Ireland	41
Poland	39
South Korea	36
Slovenia	36
Lebanon	35
Trinidad and Tobago	34
Brazil	33
Turkey	33
Israel	33
Puerto Rico	32
Belarus	32
Romania	31
Singapore	31
Argentina	29
China	29
Thailand	29
Croatia	28
Uzbekistan	28
Yugoslavia	27
Mexico	27
Saudi Arabia	26
United Arab Emirates	25
Gabon	25
Cuba	25
Chile	24
Kazakhstan	24
Mauritius	23
Costa Rica	23
Ecuador	21
Paraguay	21
Colombia	20
Panama	19
El Salvador	19
Tunisia	19
Jamaica	19
Venezuela	19
Vietnam	18
Egypt	18
Zimbabwe	18
Malaysia	17
Sudan	17
Morocco	17
Iran	16
Peru	15
Zambia	15
Indonesia	14
Libya	14
South Africa	13
Pakistan	12
Bolivia	12
Ghana	12
Philippines	11
Algeria	11
Sri Lanka	10
Dominican Republic	10
Iraq	8
Jordan	8
India	8
Côte d'Ivoire	7
Nigeria	7
Syria	7
Guatemala	6
North Korea	6
Namibia	4
Cameroon	3
Uganda	3
Kenya	2
Tanzania	2
Botswana	2
Angola	2
Papua New Guinea	1
Bangladesh	1
Ethiopia	1
Mozambique	1

Source: International Telecommunication Union

Total Credit with MasterCard and Visa

	Credit card transactions ($ million) 2000
United States	1,233,500
United Kingdom	267,950
France	169,700
China	156,270
South Korea	127,270
Japan	114,340
Canada	87,940
Brazil	69,630
Spain	67,380
Australia	50,390
Mexico	44,840
Argentina	33,160
Sweden	30,450
Germany	27,140
Turkey	26,810
Taiwan	23,890
Norway	22,400
Italy	22,340
Portugal	18,780
Hong Kong	18,310
Israel	17,270
Saudi Arabia	11,990
Denmark	10,650
Switzerland	10,560
Poland	9,810
South Africa	9,670
Finland	6,780
Kuwait	6,560
Netherlands	6,540
Colombia	6,380
Belgium	5,950
New Zealand	5,050
Singapore	4,740
Ireland	4,720
Peru	4,620
Thailand	4,500
United Arab Emirates	4,390
Malaysia	4,340
Chile	4,120
Venezuela	4,010
Iceland	3,990
Hungary	3,960
Czech Republic	3,490
Austria	3,250
Greece	2,840
Puerto Rico	2,290
Costa Rica	1,740
Russia	1,670
Dominican Republic	1,560
Luxembourg	1,530

Source: The Nilson Report (www.nilsonreport.com)

Retail Sales Growth for OECD Countries 1995–2001

	Indices at mid- 2001 (1995=100)
Portugal	151.2
Ireland	150.0
Poland	143.0
United States	143.0
South Korea	132.1
Finland	129.0
United Kingdom	128.6
Mexico	128.4
Sweden	126.0
Canada	123.0
Belgium	121.4
Australia	120.0
Greece	117.0
Norway	117.0
Spain	115.6
Hungary	115.5
New Zealand	114.0
Netherlands	113.0
Czech Republic	111.4
Austria	110.0
Denmark	109.0
France	105.3
Switzerland	105.0
Italy	102.0
Germany	101.0
Japan	87.0

Source: OECD

Billion-dollar Brands

Brand	Product description/sector	Global sales for 12 months ending Q1 2001 ($ billion)
Coca-Cola	Carbonated drink	15+
Marlboro	Tobacco	15+
Pepsi	Carbonated drink	5–15
Budweiser	Beer	3–5
Campbell's	Soups	3–6
Kellogg's	Cereals	3–7
Pampers	Diapers/nappies	3–8
Benson & Hedges	Tobacco	2–3
Camel	Tobacco	2–3
Danone	Yogurt	2–3
Fanta	Carbonated drinks	2–3
Friskies	Petfood	2–3
Gillette	Blades and razors	2–3
Huggies	Diapers/nappies	2–3
Nescafe	Coffee	2–3
Sprite	Carbonated drink	2–3
Tide	Detergent	2–3
Tropicana	Still drinks	2–3
Wrigley's	Chewing gum	2–3
Colgate	Toothpaste	1.5–2.0
Duracell	Batteries	1.5–2.0
Heineken	Beer	1.5–2.0
Kodak	Photography	1.5–2.0
L&M	Tobacco	1.5–2.0
Lay's	Snacks	1.5–2.0
Pedigree	Pet food	1.5–2.0
Always	Sanitary protection	1.0–1.5
Doritos	Snacks	1.0–1.5
Energizer	Batteries	1.0–1.5
Gatorade	Sports drinks	1.0–1.5
Guinness	Beer	1.0–1.5
Kinder	Chocolate	1.0–1.5
Kleenex	Tissues	1.0–1.5
L'Oréal	Beauty	1.0–1.5
Maxwell House	Coffee	1.0–1.5
Minute Maid	Still drinks	1.0–1.5
Nivea	Beauty	1.0–1.5
Pantene	Shampoo	1.0–1.5
Philadelphia	Cheese	1.0–1.5
Pringles	Snacks	1.0–1.5
Seven-Up	Carbonated drink	1.0–1.5
Tylenol	Pain remedies	1.0–1.5
Whiskas	Petfood	1.0–1.5

Source: ACNielsen

TOURISM

CANADA 19,557
UNITED STATES OF AMERICA 48,491
MEXICO 19,043
BAHAMAS
DOMINICAN REP.
PUERTO RICO
JAMAICA
BELIZE
ST KITTS & NEVIS
ANTIGUA & BARBUDA
GUATEMALA
DOMINICA
EL SALVADOR
ST LUCIA
BARBADOS
GRENADA
TRINIDAD & TOBAGO
COSTA RICA
PANAMA
VENEZUELA
COLOMBIA
ECUADOR
BRAZIL 5,107
PERU
BOLIVIA
CHILE
PARAGUAY
URUGUAY
ARGENTINA

NORWAY
SWEDEN
FINLAND
ESTONIA
LATVIA
LITHUANIA
UNITED KINGDOM 25,740
IRELAND 6,511
DENMARK 16,031
NETH. 9,881
BELGIUM 6,369
GERMANY 17,116
POLAND 17,950
BELARUS
UKRAINE 7,500
CZECH REPUBLIC
SLOVAKIA
FRANCE 73,042
SWITZ. 10,800
AUSTRIA 17,467
SLOVENIA
HUNGARY
CROATIA
ROMANIA 12,930
BULGARIA
ITALY 36,097
SPAIN 51,772
PORTUGAL 11,600
GREECE 12,000
TURKEY 6,893
TUNISIA
MALTA
CYPRUS
SYRIA
LEB.
ISRAEL
JOR.
MOROCCO
ALGERIA
EGYPT
SUDAN
CÔTE D'IVOIRE
GHANA
NIGERIA
CAMEROON
GABON
UGANDA
TANZANIA
ANGOLA
ZAMBIA
ZIMBABWE
NAMIBIA
BOTSWANA
SOUTH AFRICA 6,253

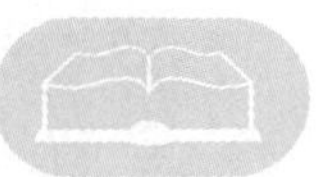

TOURISM EARNINGS
As a percentage of GDP (1999)

- 10% and over
- 5.0–9.9%
- 2.0–4.9%
- 1.0–1.9%
- less than 1.0%

over 5 million tourist arrivals in 1999 (figures in thousands)

RUSSIA
18,496
KAZAKHSTAN
UZBEKISTAN
GEORGIA
CHINA
27,047
JAPAN
SOUTH KOREA
IRAN
KUWAIT
PAKISTAN
5,050
11,328
Macao
Hong Kong
TAIWAN
INDIA
BANGLADESH
UAE
SAUDI ARABIA
OMAN
VIETNAM
8,651
THAILAND
PHILIPPINES
ETHIOPIA
SRI LANKA
7,931
BRUNEI
MALAYSIA
6,258
SINGAPORE
KENYA
SEYCHELLES
INDONESIA
PAPUA NEW GUINEA
MAURITIUS
AUSTRALIA
NEW ZEALAND

Most Popular Tourism Destinations

	Tourist arrivals (thousands) 1999	Contribution to GDP (%) 1999
France	73,042	2.2
Spain	51,772	5.5
United States	48,491	0.8
Italy	36,097	2.4
China	27,047	1.4
United Kingdom	25,740	1.5
Canada	19,557	1.6
Mexico	19,043	1.5
Russia	18,496	1.9
Poland	17,950	3.9
Austria	17,467	5.3
Germany	17,116	0.8
Czech Republic	16,031	5.7
Hungary	12,930	7.0
Greece	12,000	7.0
Portugal	11,600	4.5
Hong Kong	11,328	4.5
Switzerland	10,800	2.8
Netherlands	9,881	1.8
Thailand	8,651	5.4
Malaysia	7,931	3.6
Ukraine	7,500	14.0
Turkey	6,893	2.8
Ireland	6,511	3.5
Belgium	6,369	2.2
Singapore	6,258	7.0
South Africa	6,253	2.1
Brazil	5,107	0.5
Macao	5,050	–
Tunisia	4,832	7.4
Indonesia	4,700	2.8
South Korea	4,660	1.7
Egypt	4,489	4.4
Norway	4,481	1.5
Australia	4,459	1.9
Japan	4,438	0.1
Morocco	3,824	5.6
Saudi Arabia	3,700	1.0
Croatia	3,443	12.2
Romania	3,209	0.7
Puerto Rico	3,024	4.5
Argentina	2,898	1.0
Finland	2,700	1.1
Dominican Republic	2,649	14.5
Sweden	2,595	1.6
India	2,482	0.7
United Arab Emirates	2,481	1.3
Bulgaria	2,472	7.5
Cyprus	2,434	21.0
Andorra	2,347	–
Zimbabwe	2,328	2.6
Israel	2,275	3.0
Philippines	2,171	3.3
Uruguay	2,139	3.1
Denmark	2,023	2.1
Bahrain	1,991	–
Vietnam	1,782	0.3
Chile	1,626	1.6
New Zealand	1,607	3.8
Cuba	1,561	–
Bahamas	1,540	30.9
Lithuania	1,422	5.2
Syria	1,386	7.0
Jordan	1,358	9.8
Jamaica	1,248	17.9
Malta	1,214	20.4
Iran	1,174	0.6
Guam	1,162	–
Costa Rica	1,027	6.6
Slovakia	975	2.3
Brunei	964	0.8
Estonia	950	10.7
Peru	944	1.8
Kenya	943	2.4
Slovenia	884	5.0
Colombia	841	1.1
Guatemala	823	3.1
Luxembourg	789	–
Algeria	755	0.1
Botswana	740	2.9
Nigeria	739	0.4
Aruba	683	–
Lebanon	673	4.7
El Salvador	658	1.7
Venezuela	587	0.6
Mauritius	578	12.8
Namibia	560	9.4
Barbados	512	28.2
Ecuador	509	1.8
Oman	502	0.7
Latvia	489	1.8
US Virgin Islands	485	–
Northern Marianas	481	–
Zambia	456	2.7
Qatar	451	–
Tanzania	450	8.4
Sri Lanka	436	1.7
Panama	431	4.0
Pakistan	429	0.1
Bolivia	410	2.0
Cayman Islands	395	–
Georgia	384	14.6
Ghana	373	3.7
Belarus	355	0.1
Bermuda	354	–
Trinidad and Tobago	336	2.9
Côte d'Ivoire	301	1.0
Monaco	278	–
Paraguay	272	7.7
Uzbekistan	272	0.1
Iceland	263	–
St Lucia	261	42.8
Uganda	238	2.2
Antigua and Barbuda	226	38.8
French Polynesia	211	–
Gabon	194	0.3
Bangladesh	173	0.1
Belize	157	14.1
Yugoslavia	152	–
Cameroon	135	0.4
North Korea	130	–
Grenada	125	17.5
Seychelles	125	18.8
New Caledonia	100	–
Ethiopia	91	0.2
St Kitts and Nevis	85	21.6
Kuwait	77	0.7
Papua New Guinea	70	2.9
Dominica	66	14.6
Liechtenstein	60	–
Palau	55	–
Iraq	51	–
Angola	45	0.2
Libya	40	–
Sudan	39	0.1
American Samoa	21	–

Source: World Tourism Organization

Largest Tourism Earnings

	Tourism earnings ($ million) 1999
United States	74,448
Spain	32,913
France	31,699
Italy	28,357
United Kingdom	20,972
Germany	16,828
China	14,098
Austria	11,088
Canada	10,025
Greece	8,765
Russia	7,771
Australia	7,525
Switzerland	7,355
Mexico	7,223
Hong Kong	7,210
Netherlands	7,092
South Korea	6,802
Thailand	6,695
Poland	6,100
Singapore	5,974
Belgium	5,437
Ukraine	5,407
Turkey	5,203
Portugal	5,169
Indonesia	4,045
Brazil	3,994
Egypt	3,903
Sweden	3,894
Denmark	3,682
Japan	3,428
Hungary	3,394
Ireland	3,306
Israel	3,050
India	3,036
Czech Republic	3,035
Malaysia	2,822
Argentina	2,812
South Africa	2,738
Philippines	2,534
Dominican Republic	2,524
Croatia	2,502
Norway	2,229
Puerto Rico	2,138
New Zealand	2,083
Morocco	1,960
Cyprus	1,894
Tunisia	1,560
Saudi Arabia	1,462
Finland	1,460
Bahamas	1,408
Syria	1,360
Jamaica	1,233
Chile	1,062
Slovenia	1,005
Costa Rica	1,002
Colombia	939
Bulgaria	930

	Tourism earnings ($ million) 1999
Peru	913
Lebanon	807
Jordan	795
Tanzania	733
Barbados	703
Malta	675
Iran	662
Venezuela	656
Uruguay	653
United Arab Emirates	607
Paraguay	595
Guatemala	570
Estonia	560
Lithuania	550
Mauritius	545
Slovakia	461
Georgia	400
Panama	379
Ecuador	343
St Lucia	291
Namibia	288
Ghana	284
Sri Lanka	275
Kenya	256
Antigua and Barbuda	256
Romania	254
El Salvador	211
Kuwait	207
Trinidad and Tobago	201
Botswana	175
Bolivia	170
Zimbabwe	145
Nigeria	142
Uganda	142
Latvia	111
Seychelles	111
Côte d'Ivoire	108
Oman	104
Papua New Guinea	104
Belize	99
Vietnam	86
Zambia	85
Pakistan	76
St Kitts and Nevis	66
Grenada	63
Bangladesh	50
Cameroon	40
Dominica	38
Brunei	37
Algeria	24
Belarus	22
Uzbekistan	21
Angola	13
Gabon	11
Ethiopia	11
Sudan	8

Source: World Tourism Organization

Largest Contributions to GDP

	Contribution to GDP (%) 1999
St Lucia	42.8
Antigua and Barbuda	38.8
Bahamas	30.9
Barbados	28.2
St Kitts and Nevis	21.6
Cyprus	21.0
Malta	20.4
Seychelles	18.8
Jamaica	17.9
Grenada	17.5
Georgia	14.6
Dominica	14.6
Dominican Republic	14.5
Belize	14.1
Ukraine	14.0
Mauritius	12.8
Croatia	12.2
Estonia	10.7
Jordan	9.8
Namibia	9.4
Tanzania	8.4
Paraguay	7.7
Bulgaria	7.5
Tunisia	7.4
Hungary	7.0
Greece	7.0
Singapore	7.0
Syria	7.0
Costa Rica	6.6
Czech Republic	5.7
Morocco	5.6
Spain	5.5
Thailand	5.4
Austria	5.3
Lithuania	5.2
Slovenia	5.0
Lebanon	4.7
Portugal	4.5
Hong Kong	4.5
Puerto Rico	4.5
Egypt	4.4
Panama	4.0
Poland	3.9
New Zealand	3.8
Ghana	3.7
Malaysia	3.6
Ireland	3.5
Philippines	3.3
Uruguay	3.1
Guatemala	3.1
Israel	3.0
Botswana	2.9
Trinidad and Tobago	2.9
Papua New Guinea	2.9
Switzerland	2.8
Turkey	2.8
Indonesia	2.8

	Contribution to GDP (%) 1999
Zambia	2.7
Zimbabwe	2.6
Italy	2.4
Kenya	2.4
Slovakia	2.3
France	2.2
Belgium	2.2
Uganda	2.2
South Africa	2.1
Denmark	2.1
Bolivia	2.0
Russia	1.9
Australia	1.9
Netherlands	1.8
Peru	1.8
Ecuador	1.8
Latvia	1.8
South Korea	1.7
El Salvador	1.7
Sri Lanka	1.7
Canada	1.6
Sweden	1.6
Chile	1.6
United Kingdom	1.5
Mexico	1.5
Norway	1.5
China	1.4
United Arab Emirates	1.3
Finland	1.1
Colombia	1.1
Saudi Arabia	1.0
Argentina	1.0
Côte d'Ivoire	1.0
United States	0.8
Germany	0.8
Brunei	0.8
Romania	0.7
India	0.7
Oman	0.7
Kuwait	0.7
Iran	0.6
Venezuela	0.6
Brazil	0.5
Nigeria	0.4
Cameroon	0.4
Vietnam	0.3
Gabon	0.3
Ethiopia	0.2
Angola	0.2
Japan	0.1
Algeria	0.1
Pakistan	0.1
Belarus	0.1
Uzbekistan	0.1
Bangladesh	0.1
Sudan	0.1

Source: World Tourism Organization

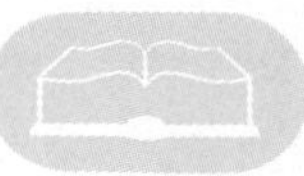

Population

GREENLAND
ICELAND
FAEROE ISLANDS
NORWAY
FINLAND
UNITED KINGDOM
London 7,341,400
SWEDEN
ESTONIA
LATVIA
DENMARK
LITHUANIA
IRELAND
NETH.
BELARUS
Moscow 8,383,000
BELGIUM
GERMANY
POLAND
CZECH REPUBLIC
SLOVAKIA
UKRAINE
LUX.
LIECHTENSTEIN
AUSTRIA
HUNGARY
FRANCE
SWITZ.
SLOVENIA
CROATIA
ROMANIA
MONACO
ITALY
YUGOSLAVIA
BULGARIA
ANDORRA
PORTUGAL
SPAIN
GREECE
GIBRALTAR
TUNISIA
MALTA
Istanbul 9,018,500
TURKEY
CYPRUS
SYRIA
LEB
ISRAEL
JOR
CANADA
UNITED STATES OF AMERICA
New York 8,056,200
BERMUDA
MEXICO
Mexico City 8,578,300
BAHAMAS
CUBA
TURKS & CAICOS
CAYMAN ISLANDS
DOMINICAN REP.
PUERTO RICO
VIRGIN ISLANDS (UK)
BELIZE
JAMAICA
VIRGIN ISLANDS (US)
ANTIGUA & BARBUDA
ST KITTS & NEVIS
GUADELOUPE
DOMINICA
GUATEMALA
EL SALVADOR
ARUBA
NETH. ANTILLES
MARTINIQUE
ST LUCIA
BARBADOS
GRENADA
TRINIDAD & TOBAGO
COSTA RICA
PANAMA
VENEZUELA
COLOMBIA
FRENCH GUIANA
ECUADOR
Lima 7,451,900
BRAZIL
PERU
São Paulo 9,921,200
BOLIVIA
CHILE
PARAGUAY
URUGUAY
Buenos Aires 11,624,000
ARGENTINA
MOROCCO
ALGERIA
LIBYA
Cairo 7,594,800
EGYPT
SUDAN
CÔTE D'IVOIRE
GHANA
NIGERIA
Lagos 7,720,200
CAMEROON
GABON
UGANDA
TANZANIA
ANGOLA
ZAMBIA
ZIMBABWE
NAMIBIA
BOTSWANA
MOZAMBIQUE
SOUTH AFRICA

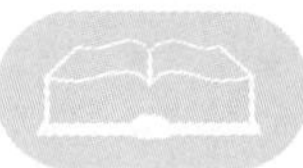

POPULATION
(1999)

- over 500 million
- 100–499 million
- 50–99 million
- 10–49 million
- under 10 million

20 largest city populations (2001)

Source: The World Gazetteer (www.gazetteer.de)

RUSSIA
KAZAKHSTAN
UZBEKISTAN
GEORGIA
Tehran 7,555,000
IRAQ
IRAN
KUWAIT
BAHRAIN
QATAR
UAE
SAUDI ARABIA
OMAN
PAKISTAN
Karachi 10,013,400
Delhi 10,095,200
INDIA
Mumbai 12,916,600
CHINA
BANGLADESH
Dhaka 8,154,100
NORTH KOREA
SOUTH KOREA
Seoul 11,019,900
JAPAN
Tokyo 8,021,500
Shanghai 8,914,500
TAIWAN
Macao
Hong Kong
VIETNAM
THAILAND
Manila 10,032,900
PHILIPPINES
NORTHERN MARIANAS
GUAM
PALAU
SRI LANKA
BRUNEI
MALAYSIA
SINGAPORE
ETHIOPIA
KENYA
SEYCHELLES
INDONESIA
Jakarta 10,226,200
PAPUA NEW GUINEA
AMERICAN SAMOA
FRENCH POLYNESIA
NEW CALEDONIA
MAURITIUS
REUNION
AUSTRALIA
NEW ZEALAND

Population and Land Area

	Total population (thousands) 1999	Land area (km²)	Population per km² 1999
Algeria	30,774	2,381,700	13
American Samoa	64	197	324
Andorra	75	464	162
Angola	12,479	1,246,700	10
Antigua and Barbuda	67	443	151
Argentina	36,577	2,736,700	13
Aruba	69	193	356
Australia	18,705	7,682,300	2
Austria	8,177	82,700	99
Bahamas	301	13,939	22
Bahrain	606	694	873
Bangladesh	126,947	130,200	975
Barbados	269	431	624
Belarus	10,274	207,500	50
Belgium	10,152	33,000	308
Belize	235	22,800	10
Bermuda	63	52	1,202
Bolivia	8,142	1,084,400	8
Botswana	1,597	566,700	3
Brazil	167,988	8,456,500	20
British Virgin Islands	19	153	125
Brunei	322	5,300	61
Bulgaria	8,279	110,600	75
Cameroon	14,693	465,400	32
Canada	30,857	9,221,000	3
Cayman Islands	39	259	152
Chile	15,019	748,800	20
China	1,266,838	9,327,400	136
Colombia	41,564	1,038,700	40
Costa Rica	3,933	51,100	77
Côte d'Ivoire	14,526	318,000	46
Croatia	4,477	55,900	80
Cuba	11,160	109,800	102
Cyprus	778	9,200	85
Czech Republic	10,262	77,300	133
Denmark	5,282	42,400	125
Dominica	71	750	95
Dominican Republic	8,364	48,400	173
Ecuador	12,411	276,800	45
Egypt	67,226	995,500	68
El Salvador	6,154	20,700	297
Estonia	1,412	42,300	33
Ethiopia	61,095	1,127,130	54
Faeroe Islands	45	1,414	32
Finland	5,165	304,600	17
France	58,886	550,100	107
French Guiana	168	83,534	2
French Polynesia	233	3,887	60
Gabon	1,197	257,700	5
Georgia	5,006	69,700	72
Germany	82,178	349,300	235
Ghana	19,678	227,500	86
Gibraltar	29	7	4,462

	Total population (thousands) 1999	Land area (km²)	Population per km² 1999
Greece	10,626	128,900	82
Greenland	60	2,175,600	0
Grenada	93	345	270
Guadeloupe	428	1,780	240
Guam	152	545	278
Guatemala	11,090	108,400	102
Hong Kong	6,850	1,092	6,273
Hungary	10,076	92,300	109
Iceland	279	100,300	3
India	998,056	2,973,200	336
Indonesia	209,255	1,811,600	116
Iran	66,796	1,622,000	41
Iraq	22,450	437,400	51
Ireland	3,705	68,900	54
Isle of Man	74	572	130
Israel	6,101	20,600	296
Italy	57,343	294,100	195
Jamaica	2,560	10,800	237
Japan	126,505	376,500	336
Jordan	6,482	88,900	73
Kazakhstan	16,269	2,670,700	6
Kenya	29,549	569,100	52
Kuwait	1,897	17,800	107
Latvia	2,389	62,100	38
Lebanon	3,236	10,200	317
Libya	5,471	1,759,500	3
Liechtenstein	32	160	200
Lithuania	3,682	64,800	57
Luxembourg	426	2,586	165
Macao	437	24	18,530
Malaysia	21,830	328,600	66
Malta	386	316	1,222
Martinique	381	1,128	338
Mauritius	1,150	1,864	617
Mexico	97,365	1,908,700	51
Monaco	33	2	16,923
Morocco	27,867	446,300	62
Mozambique	19,286	784,100	25
Namibia	1,695	823,300	2
Netherlands	15,735	33,900	464
Netherlands Antilles	248	800	310
New Caledonia	215	18,736	11
New Zealand	3,828	268,000	14
Nigeria	108,945	910,800	120
North Korea	23,702	120,400	197
Northern Marianas	75	477	158
Norway	4,442	306,800	14
Oman	2,460	212,500	12
Pakistan	152,331	770,900	198
Palau	19	458	41
Panama	2,812	74,400	38
Papua New Guinea	4,702	452,900	10
Paraguay	5,358	397,300	13

Population and Land Area (continued)

	Total population (thousands) 1999	Land area (km²)	Population per km² 1999
Peru	25,230	1,280,000	20
Philippines	74,454	298,200	250
Poland	38,740	304,400	127
Portugal	9,873	91,500	108
Puerto Rico	3,884	9,104	427
Qatar	589	11,000	54
Reunion	718	2,547	282
Romania	22,402	230,300	97
Russia	147,196	16,888,500	9
St Kitts and Nevis	39	262	149
St Lucia	152	616	247
Saudi Arabia	20,899	2,149,700	10
Seychelles	77	455	169
Singapore	3,522	648	5,435
Slovakia	5,382	48,100	112
Slovenia	1,989	20,100	99
South Africa	39,900	1,221,000	33
South Korea	46,480	98,700	471
Spain	39,634	499,400	79
Sri Lanka	18,639	64,600	289
Sudan	28,883	2,376,000	12
Sweden	8,892	411,600	22
Switzerland	7,344	39,600	185
Syria	15,725	183,800	86
Taiwan	22,113	36,175	611
Tanzania	32,793	883,600	37
Thailand	60,856	510,900	119
Trinidad and Tobago	1,289	5,100	253
Tunisia	9,460	155,400	61
Turkey	65,546	769,600	85
Turks and Caicos Islands	17	497	34
Uganda	21,143	199,700	106
Ukraine	50,658	579,400	87
United Arab Emirates	2,398	83,600	29
United Kingdom	58,744	241,600	243
United States	276,218	9,159,100	30
Uruguay	3,313	174,800	19
US Virgin Islands	120	363	330
Uzbekistan	23,942	414,200	58
Venezuela	23,706	882,100	27
Vietnam	78,705	325,500	242
Yugoslavia	10,637	102,100	104
Zambia	8,976	743,400	12
Zimbabwe	11,529	386,900	30

Largest Populations

	Total population (thousands) 1999
China	1,266,838
India	998,056
United States	276,218
Indonesia	209,255
Brazil	167,988
Pakistan	152,331
Russia	147,196
Bangladesh	126,947
Japan	126,505
Nigeria	108,945
Mexico	97,365
Germany	82,178
Vietnam	78,705
Philippines	74,454
Egypt	67,226
Iran	66,796
Turkey	65,546
Ethiopia	61,095
Thailand	60,856
France	58,886
United Kingdom	58,744
Italy	57,343
Ukraine	50,658
South Korea	46,480
Colombia	41,564
South Africa	39,900
Spain	39,634
Poland	38,740
Argentina	36,577
Tanzania	32,793
Canada	30,857
Algeria	30,774
Kenya	29,549
Sudan	28,883
Morocco	27,867
Peru	25,230
Uzbekistan	23,942
Venezuela	23,706
North Korea	23,702
Iraq	22,450
Romania	22,402
Taiwan	22,113
Malaysia	21,830
Uganda	21,143
Saudi Arabia	20,899
Ghana	19,678
Mozambique	19,286
Australia	18,705
Sri Lanka	18,639
Kazakhstan	16,269
Netherlands	15,735
Syria	15,725
Chile	15,019

	Total population (thousands) 1999
Cameroon	14,693
Côte d'Ivoire	14,526
Angola	12,479
Ecuador	12,411
Zimbabwe	11,529
Cuba	11,160
Guatemala	11,090
Yugoslavia	10,637
Greece	10,626
Belarus	10,274
Czech Republic	10,262
Belgium	10,152
Hungary	10,076
Portugal	9,873
Tunisia	9,460
Zambia	8,976
Sweden	8,892
Dominican Republic	8,364
Bulgaria	8,279
Austria	8,177
Bolivia	8,142
Switzerland	7,344
Hong Kong	6,850
Jordan	6,482
El Salvador	6,154
Israel	6,101
Libya	5,471
Slovakia	5,382
Paraguay	5,358
Denmark	5,282
Finland	5,165
Georgia	5,006
Papua New Guinea	4,702
Croatia	4,477
Norway	4,442
Costa Rica	3,933
Puerto Rico	3,884
New Zealand	3,828
Ireland	3,705
Lithuania	3,682
Singapore	3,522
Uruguay	3,313
Lebanon	3,236
Panama	2,812
Jamaica	2,560
Oman	2,460
United Arab Emirates	2,398
Latvia	2,389
Slovenia	1,989
Kuwait	1,897
Namibia	1,695
Botswana	1,597
Estonia	1,412

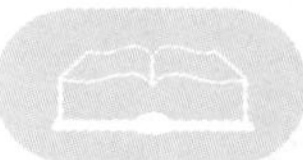

Largest Land Area

	Land area (km²)
Russia	16,888,500
China	9,327,400
Canada	9,221,000
United States	9,159,100
Brazil	8,456,500
Australia	7,682,300
India	2,973,200
Argentina	2,736,700
Kazakhstan	2,670,700
Algeria	2,381,700
Sudan	2,376,000
Greenland	2,175,600
Saudi Arabia	2,149,700
Mexico	1,908,700
Indonesia	1,811,600
Libya	1,759,500
Iran	1,622,000
Peru	1,280,000
Angola	1,246,700
South Africa	1,221,000
Ethiopia	1,127,130
Bolivia	1,084,400
Colombia	1,038,700
Egypt	995,500
Nigeria	910,800
Tanzania	883,600
Venezuela	882,100
Namibia	823,300
Mozambique	784,100
Pakistan	770,900
Turkey	769,600
Chile	748,800
Zambia	743,400
Ukraine	579,400
Kenya	569,100
Botswana	566,700
France	550,100
Thailand	510,900
Spain	499,400
Cameroon	465,400
Papua New Guinea	452,900
Morocco	446,300
Iraq	437,400
Uzbekistan	414,200
Sweden	411,600
Paraguay	397,300
Zimbabwe	386,900
Japan	376,500
Germany	349,300
Malaysia	328,600
Vietnam	325,500
Côte d'Ivoire	318,000
Norway	306,800

Smallest Land Area

	Land area (km²)
Monaco	2
Gibraltar	7
Macao	24
Bermuda	52
British Virgin Islands	153
Liechtenstein	160
Aruba	193
American Samoa	197
Cayman Islands	259
St Kitts and Nevis	262
Malta	316
Grenada	345
US Virgin Islands	363
Barbados	431
Antigua and Barbuda	443
Seychelles	455
Palau	458
Andorra	464
Northern Marianas	477
Turks and Caicos Islands	497
Guam	545
Isle of Man	572
St Lucia	616
Singapore	648
Bahrain	694
Dominica	750
Netherlands Antilles	800
Hong Kong	1,092
Martinique	1,128
Faeroe Islands	1,414
Guadeloupe	1,780
Mauritius	1,864
Reunion	2,547
Luxembourg	2,586
French Polynesia	3,887
Trinidad and Tobago	5,100
Brunei	5,300
Puerto Rico	9,104
Cyprus	9,200
Lebanon	10,200
Jamaica	10,800
Qatar	11,000
Bahamas	13,939
Kuwait	17,800
New Caledonia	18,736
Slovenia	20,100
Israel	20,600
El Salvador	20,700
Belize	22,800
Belgium	33,000
Netherlands	33,900
Taiwan	36,175
Switzerland	39,600

Most Densely Populated

	Population per km² 1999
Macao	18,530
Monaco	16,923
Hong Kong	6,273
Singapore	5,435
Gibraltar	4,462
Malta	1,222
Bermuda	1,202
Bangladesh	975
Bahrain	873
Barbados	624
Mauritius	617
Taiwan	611
South Korea	471
Netherlands	464
Puerto Rico	427
Aruba	356
Martinique	338
India	336
Japan	336
US Virgin Islands	330
American Samoa	324
Lebanon	317
Netherlands Antilles	310
Belgium	308
El Salvador	297
Israel	296
Sri Lanka	289
Reunion	282
Guam	278
Grenada	270
Trinidad and Tobago	253
Philippines	250
St Lucia	247
United Kingdom	243
Vietnam	242
Guadeloupe	240
Jamaica	237
Germany	235
Liechtenstein	200
Pakistan	198
North Korea	197
Italy	195
Switzerland	185
Dominican Republic	173
Seychelles	169
Luxembourg	165
Andorra	162
Northern Marianas	158
Cayman Islands	152
Antigua and Barbuda	151
St Kitts and Nevis	149
China	136
Czech Republic	133

Least Densely Populated

	Population per km² 1999
Greenland	0.03
Australia	2
French Guiana	2
Namibia	2
Botswana	3
Canada	3
Iceland	3
Libya	3
Gabon	5
Kazakhstan	6
Bolivia	8
Russia	9
Angola	10
Belize	10
Papua New Guinea	10
Saudi Arabia	10
New Caledonia	11
Oman	12
Sudan	12
Zambia	12
Algeria	13
Argentina	13
Paraguay	13
New Zealand	14
Norway	14
Finland	17
Uruguay	19
Brazil	20
Chile	20
Peru	20
Bahamas	22
Sweden	22
Mozambique	25
Venezuela	27
United Arab Emirates	29
United States	30
Zimbabwe	30
Cameroon	32
Faeroe Islands	32
Estonia	33
South Africa	33
Turks and Caicos Islands	34
Tanzania	37
Latvia	38
Panama	38
Colombia	40
Iran	41
Palau	41
Ecuador	45
Côte d'Ivoire	46
Belarus	50
Iraq	51
Mexico	51

Most Urbanized Populations

	Urban population (%) 1999
Monaco	100
Singapore	100
Kuwait	98
Belgium	97
Andorra	94
Bahrain	92
Iceland	92
Qatar	92
Israel	91
Luxembourg	91
Uruguay	91
Argentina	90
Malta	90
Lebanon	89
Netherlands	89
United Kingdom	89
Bahamas	88
Germany	87
Libya	87
Venezuela	87
New Zealand	86
Australia	85
Chile	85
Denmark	85
Saudi Arabia	85
United Arab Emirates	85
Oman	83
Sweden	83

	Urban population (%) 1999
Brazil	81
South Korea	81
Gabon	80
Japan	79
Canada	77
Iraq	77
Russia	77
Spain	77
United States	77
Cuba	75
Czech Republic	75
France	75
Norway	75
Colombia	74
Jordan	74
Mexico	74
Trinidad and Tobago	74
Turkey	74
Brunei	72
Palau	72
Peru	72
Belarus	71
Dominica	70
Bulgaria	69
Estonia	69
Latvia	69
Lithuania	68
Switzerland	68

	Urban population (%) 1999
Ukraine	68
Finland	67
Italy	67
Austria	65
Poland	65
Tunisia	65
Dominican Republic	64
Ecuador	64
Hungary	64
Portugal	63
Bolivia	62
Seychelles	62
Iran	61
Algeria	60
Georgia	60
Greece	60
North Korea	60
Ireland	59
Philippines	58
Croatia	57
Malaysia	57
Slovakia	57
Cyprus	56
Jamaica	56
Kazakhstan	56
Panama	56
Romania	56
Morocco	55

	Urban population (%) 1999
Paraguay	55
Belize	54
Syria	54
Yugoslavia	52
Botswana	50
Slovenia	50
South Africa	50
Barbados	49
Cameroon	48
Costa Rica	48
Côte d'Ivoire	46
El Salvador	46
Egypt	45
Nigeria	43
Mauritius	41
Guatemala	40
Indonesia	40
Zambia	40
Mozambique	39
Ghana	38
Grenada	38
St Lucia	38
Antigua and Barbuda	37
Pakistan	37
Uzbekistan	37
Sudan	35
Zimbabwe	35
Angola	34

Most Populous Cities

City	Country	Population 2001
Mumbai	India	12,916,600
Buenos Aires	Argentina	11,624,000
Seoul	South Korea	11,019,900
Jakarta	Indonesia	10,226,200
Delhi	India	10,095,200
Manila	Philippines	10,032,900
Karachi	Pakistan	10,013,400
São Paulo	Brazil	9,921,200
Istanbul	Turkey	9,018,500
Shanghai	China	8,914,500
Mexico City	Mexico	8,578,300
Moscow	Russia	8,383,000
Dhaka	Bangladesh	8,154,100
New York	United States	8,056,200
Tokyo	Japan	8,021,500
Lagos	Nigeria	7,720,200
Cairo	Egypt	7,594,800
Tehran	Iran	7,555,000
Lima	Peru	7,451,900
London	United Kingdom	7,341,400

Most Populous Urban Agglomerations

Urban agglomeration	Country	Population 2001
Tokyo	Japan	30,988,100
New York–Philadelphia	United States	29,551,300
Mexico City	Mexico	20,750,500
Seoul	South Korea	19,624,500
São Paulo	Brazil	18,167,200
Mumbai	India	17,742,800
Osaka-Kobe-Kyoto	Japan	17,734,500
Jakarta	Indonesia	17,094,000
Los Angeles	United States	16,401,600
Delhi	India	16,200,000
Cairo	Egypt	15,206,000
Manila	Philippines	13,220,300
Kolkata	India	12,900,000
Buenos Aires	Argentina	12,761,500
Moscow	Russia	12,230,000
Shanghai	China	11,826,700
Rhein-Ruhr	Germany	11,308,700
Paris	France	11,254,700
London	United Kingdom	11,216,000
Rio de Janeiro	Brazil	11,058,300

Source: The World Gazetteer (www.gazetteer.de)

EDUCATION

CANADA
UNITED STATES OF AMERICA
22
27
BERMUDA
MEXICO
26
CAYMAN ISLANDS
CUBA
JAMAICA
DOMINICAN REP.
PUERTO RICO
44
VIRGIN ISLANDS (US)
GUATEMALA
EL SALVADOR
85
33
ARUBA
NETH. ANTILLES
BARBADOS
TRINIDAD & TOBAGO
COSTA RICA
PANAMA
VENEZUELA
21
COLOMBIA
ECUADOR
BRAZIL
PERU
BOLIVIA
CHILE
PARAGUAY
29
URUGUAY
ARGENTINA
54
ICELAND
59
NORWAY
46
SWEDEN
FINLAND
45
33
31
ESTONIA
25
LATVIA
DENMARK
LITHUANIA
IRELAND
UNITED KINGDOM
31
NETH.
31
25
BELARUS
33
BELGIUM
GERMANY
CZECH REPUBLIC
POLAND
UKRAINE
LUXEMBOURG
22
FRANCE
SLOVAKIA
30
SWITZ.
AUSTRIA
HUNGARY
SLOVENIA
CROATIA
ROMANIA
34
30
26
25
YUGOSLAVIA
BULGARIA
PORTUGAL
SPAIN
MONACO
60
ITALY
GREECE
23
LIECHTENSTEIN
GIBRALTAR
TUNISIA
MALTA
TURKEY
CYPRUS
SYRIA
LEB
ISRAEL
29
JOR
MOROCCO
ALGERIA
LIBYA
EGYPT
SUDAN
CÔTE D'IVOIRE
GHANA
NIGERIA
CAMEROON
GABON
UGANDA
TANZANIA
ANGOLA
ZAMBIA
ZIMBABWE
NAMIBIA
BOTSWANA
MOZAMBIQUE
SOUTH AFRICA

TERTIARY EDUCATION

Percentage of age group enrolled
(1997 or latest available data)

- 50% and over
- 40–49%
- 30–39%
- 20–29%
- 10–19%
- under 10%

NEWSPAPER CIRCULATION

daily newspaper circulation of more than 20 per 100 people (1996)

RUSSIA
KAZAKHSTAN
UZBEKISTAN
GEORGIA
IRAN
IRAQ
37
KUWAIT
BAHRAIN
QATAR
UAE
SAUDI ARABIA
OMAN
PAKISTAN
INDIA
BANGLADESH
CHINA
39
SOUTH KOREA
JAPAN
58
79
Macao
Hong Kong
46
THAILAND
VIETNAM
PHILIPPINES
SRI LANKA
BRUNEI
36
MALAYSIA
SINGAPORE
INDONESIA
PAPUA NEW GUINEA
ETHIOPIA
KENYA
MAURITIUS
29
AUSTRALIA
22
NEW ZEALAND

Tertiary Education, Newspaper Circulation, and Youth Literacy

	Enrolment (% of age group) 1996–97	Newspaper circulation (per 100 people) 1996	Youth literacy (% of males) 1999	Youth literacy (% of females) 1999
Algeria	12	3.8	92	84
Angola	1	1.1	–	–
Argentina	42	12.3	98	99
Australia	80	29.3	–	–
Austria	48	29.6	–	–
Bahrain	19	11.7	–	–
Bangladesh	6	0.9	60	39
Barbados	29	19.9	–	–
Belarus	44	17.4	100	100
Belgium	56	16.0	–	–
Bolivia	24	5.5	98	93
Botswana	6	2.7	84	92
Brazil	15	4.0	90	94
Brunei	7	6.9	–	–
Bulgaria	41	25.7	100	99
Cameroon	4	0.7	94	93
Canada	88	15.9	–	–
Chile	32	9.8	98	99
China	6		99	96
Colombia	17	4.6	96	97
Costa Rica	30	9.4	98	99
Côte d'Ivoire	6	1.7	69	58
Croatia	28	11.5	100	100
Cuba	12	11.8	100	100
Cyprus	23	11.1	–	–
Czech Republic	24	25.4	–	–
Denmark	48	30.9	–	–
Dominican Republic	23	5.2	90	91
Ecuador	26	7.0	97	96
Egypt	20	4.0	76	62
El Salvador	18	4.8	89	87
Estonia	42	17.4	–	–
Ethiopia	1	0.2	54	52
Finland	74	45.5	–	–
France	51	21.8	–	–
Gabon	8	2.9	–	–
Georgia	42	–	–	–
Germany	47	31.1	–	–
Ghana	1	1.4	93	87
Greece	47	15.3	100	100
Guatemala	9	3.3	85	72
Hungary	24	18.6	100	100
Iceland	37	53.5	–	–
India	7	–	79	64
Indonesia	11	2.4	98	97
Iran	18	2.8	96	91
Iraq	11	1.9	77	66
Ireland	41	15.0	–	–
Israel	41	29.0	100	100
Italy	47	10.4	100	100
Jamaica	8	6.2	90	97
Japan	41	57.8	–	–
Jordan	18	5.8	99	100
Kazakhstan	33	–	–	–
Kenya	2	0.9	96	94
Kuwait	19	37.4	91	93
Latvia	33	24.7	100	100
Lebanon	27	10.7	97	93
Libya	20	1.4	100	93
Lithuania	31	9.3	100	100
Luxembourg	10	32.8	–	–
Macao	28	45.5	–	–
Malaysia	12	15.8	97	97
Malta	29	12.7	–	–
Mauritius	6	7.5	93	94
Mexico	16	9.7	97	96
Morocco	11	2.6	76	57
Mozambique	1	0.3	74	45
Namibia	8	1.9	90	93
Netherlands	47	30.6	–	–
New Zealand	63	21.6	–	–
Nigeria	4	2.4	89	82
Norway	62	58.8	–	–
Oman	8	2.9	99	95
Pakistan	4	2.3	76	48
Panama	32	6.2	97	96
Papua New Guinea	3	1.5	80	70
Paraguay	10	4.3	97	97
Peru	26	8.4	98	95
Philippines	29	7.9	98	99
Poland	25	11.3	100	100
Portugal	39	7.5	100	100
Puerto Rico	42	12.6	97	98
Qatar	27	16.1	–	–
Romania	23	30.0	99	100
Russia	43	10.5	100	100
Saudi Arabia	16	5.7	95	90
Singapore	39	36.0	100	100
Slovakia	22	18.5	–	–
Slovenia	36	19.9	100	100
South Africa	19	3.2	91	91
South Korea	68	39.3	100	100
Spain	51	10.0	100	100
Sri Lanka	5	2.9	97	96
Sudan	4	2.7	82	70
Sweden	50	44.5	–	–
Switzerland	33	33.7	–	–
Syria	16	2.0	95	78
Tanzania	1	0.4	93	88
Thailand	22	6.3	99	98
Trinidad and Tobago	8	12.3	98	97
Tunisia	14	3.1	97	88
Turkey	21	11.1	99	94
Uganda	2	0.2	85	71
Ukraine	42	5.4	100	100
United Arab Emirates	12	15.6	85	94
United Kingdom	52	32.9	–	–
United States	81	21.5	–	–
Uruguay	30	29.3	99	100
Uzbekistan	36	0.3	98	95
Venezuela	25	20.6	97	98
Vietnam	7	0.4	97	97
Yugoslavia	22	10.7	–	–
Zambia	3	1.2	90	85
Zimbabwe	7	1.9	98	95

Source: UNESCO

Best Access to Tertiary Education

	Enrolment (% of age group) 1996–97
Canada	88
United States	81
Australia	80
Finland	74
South Korea	68
New Zealand	63
Norway	62
Belgium	56
United Kingdom	52
France	51
Spain	51
Sweden	50
Denmark	48
Austria	48
Germany	47
Netherlands	47
Greece	47
Italy	47
Belarus	44
Russia	43
Estonia	42
Puerto Rico	42
Argentina	42
Ukraine	42
Japan	41
Israel	41
Bulgaria	41
Ireland	41
Singapore	39
Portugal	39
Iceland	37
Slovenia	36
Uzbekistan	36
Switzerland	33
Latvia	33
Chile	32
Panama	32
Lithuania	31
Uruguay	30
Costa Rica	30
Barbados	29
Malta	29
Philippines	29
Macao	28
Croatia	28
Qatar	27
Lebanon	27
Peru	26
Ecuador	26
Venezuela	25
Poland	25
Czech Republic	24
Hungary	24
Bolivia	24
Romania	23
Cyprus	23
Dominican Republic	23
Slovakia	22
Yugoslavia	22
Thailand	22
Turkey	21
Egypt	20
Libya	20
Kuwait	19
Bahrain	19
South Africa	19
Jordan	18
El Salvador	18
Iran	18
Colombia	17
Mexico	16
Saudi Arabia	16
Syria	16
Brazil	15
Tunisia	14
Malaysia	12
United Arab Emirates	12
Cuba	12
Algeria	12
Morocco	11
Indonesia	11
Iraq	11
Luxembourg	10
Paraguay	10
Guatemala	9
Trinidad and Tobago	8
Jamaica	8
Gabon	8
Oman	8
Namibia	8
Brunei	7
Zimbabwe	7
Vietnam	7
Mauritius	6
Botswana	6
Côte d'Ivoire	6
Bangladesh	6
Sri Lanka	5
Sudan	4
Nigeria	4
Pakistan	4
Cameroon	4
Papua New Guinea	3
Zambia	3
Kenya	2
Uganda	2
Ghana	1
Angola	1
Tanzania	1
Mozambique	1
Ethiopia	1

Source: UNESCO

Largest Newspaper Circulation

	Newspaper circulation (per 100 people) 1996
Aruba	85.2
Hong Kong	79.2
Liechtenstein	60.2
Norway	58.8
Japan	57.8
Iceland	53.5
Finland	45.5
Macao	45.5
Sweden	44.5
US Virgin Islands	43.7
South Korea	39.3
Kuwait	37.4
Singapore	36.0
Switzerland	33.7
Netherlands Antilles	33.4
United Kingdom	32.9
Luxembourg	32.8
Germany	31.1
Denmark	30.9
Netherlands	30.6
Romania	30.0
Austria	29.6
Australia	29.3
Uruguay	29.3
Israel	29.0
Bermuda	27.2
Bulgaria	25.7
Cayman Islands	25.6
Czech Republic	25.4
Monaco	25.1
Latvia	24.7
Gibraltar	23.3
France	21.8
New Zealand	21.6
United States	21.5
Venezuela	20.6
Slovenia	19.9
Barbados	19.9
North Korea	19.9
Hungary	18.6
Slovakia	18.5
Guam	17.8
Belarus	17.4
Estonia	17.4
Qatar	16.1
Belgium	16.0
Canada	15.9
Malaysia	15.8
United Arab Emirates	15.6
Greece	15.3
Ireland	15.0
Faeroe Islands	14.5
Malta	12.7
Puerto Rico	12.6
Argentina	12.3
Trinidad and Tobago	12.3
New Caledonia	12.1
Cuba	11.8
Bahrain	11.7
Croatia	11.5
Poland	11.3
Cyprus	11.1
Turkey	11.1
French Polynesia	11.0
Lebanon	10.7
Yugoslavia	10.7
Russia	10.5
Italy	10.4
Spain	10.0
Bahamas	9.9
Chile	9.8
Mexico	9.7
Costa Rica	9.4
Lithuania	9.3
Antigua and Barbuda	9.1
American Samoa	8.5
Peru	8.4
Reunion	8.3
Guadeloupe	8.1
Philippines	7.9
Martinique	7.8
Portugal	7.5
Mauritius	7.5
Ecuador	7.0
Brunei	6.9
Thailand	6.3
Panama	6.2
Jamaica	6.2
Andorra	6.0
Jordan	5.8
Saudi Arabia	5.7
Bolivia	5.5
Ukraine	5.4
Dominican Republic	5.2
El Salvador	4.8
Colombia	4.6
Seychelles	4.6
Paraguay	4.3
Egypt	4.0
Brazil	4.0
Algeria	3.8
Guatemala	3.3
South Africa	3.2
Tunisia	3.1
Gabon	2.9
Oman	2.9
Sri Lanka	2.9
Iran	2.8
Botswana	2.7
Sudan	2.7
Morocco	2.6

Source: UNESCO

Financial Times MBA Rankings

2002 Rank	2001 Rank	2000 Rank	Business School	Location	Salary ($)	Salary increase (%)	Women students (%)	International students (%)
1	1	2	University of Pennsylvania: Wharton	United States	165,277	228	32	42
2	2	1	Harvard Business School	United States	175,562	194	36	37
3	5	5	Columbia University GSB	United States	153,290	247	34	30
3	3	3	Stanford University GSB	United States	178,576	178	38	23
3	4	6	University of Chicago GSB	United States	157,790	252	22	40
6	7	9	Insead	France	136,817	148	24	91
6	6	4	MIT: Sloan	United States	161,024	191	27	34
8	10	13	New York University: Stern	United States	127,320	233	34	30
9	8	8	London Business School	United Kingdom	124,538	171	33	85
10	9	7	Northwestern University: Kellogg	United States	151,179	192	28	29
11	13	15	Dartmouth College: Tuck	United States	154,817	207	32	34
12	20	18	Yale School of Management	United States	128,164	223	26	43
13	15	10	Cornell University: Johnson	United States	140,109	200	28	33
14	11	11	IMD	Switzerland	134,544	112	19	94
15	14	12	University of California at Berkeley: Haas	United States	129,065	166	29	33
16	12	14	University of California at Los Angeles: Anderson	United States	133,526	170	30	25
16	22	19	University of Virginia: Darden	United States	134,661	192	30	29
18	19	19	University of Western Ontario: Ivey	Canada	106,334	193	25	40
19	18	17	Duke University: Fuqua	United States	128,885	179	30	34
20	21	23	University of North Carolina: Kenan-Flagler	United States	112,335	178	29	32
21	17	21	Carnegie Mellon University	United States	115,957	182	25	36
22	new	new	University of Cambridge: Judge	United Kingdom	123,717	122	23	77
23	16	16	University of Michigan Business School	United States	123,651	158	28	32
24	25	27	Vanderbilt University: Owen	United States	122,232	187	24	30
25	29	28	Georgetown University: McDonough	United States	122,566	195	25	35
25	24	25	Iese Business School	Spain	96,138	211	20	54
27	27	29	Rotterdam School of Management	Netherlands	94,173	142	27	95
28	34	new	University of Oxford: Said	United Kingdom	124,612	164	20	82
29	23	31	University of Maryland: Smith	United States	93,335	177	27	42
30	32	new	University of Southern California: Marshall	United States	111,883	169	30	29
31	28	35	Emory University: Goizueta	United States	109,509	170	20	36
31	39	48	SDA Bocconi	Italy	105,181	158	28	41
31	46	41	University of Toronto: Rotman	Canada	93,160	185	31	36
31	35	45	York University: Schulich	Canada	88,477	170	42	59
35	31	24	Instituto de Empresa	Spain	91,948	135	41	71
36	37	49	McGill University	Canada	80,085	162	36	51
36	40	59	Warwick Business School	United Kingdom	101,626	121	38	68
38	55	40	Rice University: Jones	United States	108,873	188	38	30
38	45	34	University of South Carolina: Moore	United States	90,148	181	30	32
40	24	32	University of Texas at Austin	United States	104,801	157	23	28
41	33	26	Washington University: Olin	United States	98,004	183	25	32
42	29	33	University of Rochester: Simon	United States	96,120	177	24	55
43	42	38	Purdue University: Krannert	United States	96,757	157	26	39
44	41	35	Cranfield School of Management	United Kingdom	117,446	118	20	52
45	42	29	Indiana University: Kelley	United States	110,086	147	22	31
46	87	new	Queen's School of Business	Canada	94,185	165	21	22
47	48	70	Hong Kong University of Science and Technology	China	63,361	99	66	55

Salary is the average salary three years after graduation, adjusted for variation between industry sectors. Salary increase is the average percentage rise in salary from start of the MBA to three years after graduation. Both figures are weighted averages from three surveys: 2000, 2001 and 2002.

2002 Rank	2001 Rank	2000 Rank	Business School	Location	Salary ($)	Salary increase (%)	Women students (%)	International students (%)
48	36	43	Manchester Business School	United Kingdom	91,334	146	24	78
49	47	47	Southern Methodist University: Cox	United States	98,688	180	28	24
49	84	67	College of William & Mary	United States	93,790	183	40	43
49	57	62	University of Iowa: Tippie	United States	75,833	171	29	45
52	51	43	Arizona State University	United States	95,949	141	24	23
53	53	52	Babson College: Olin	United States	101,714	160	32	38
53	72	69	University of Pittsburgh: Katz	United States	76,761	135	44	42
55	---	59	Ohio State University: Fisher	United States	90,854	135	40	35
55	77	39	Pennsylvania State University: Smeal	United States	87,706	162	24	32
57	55	45	Thunderbird	United States	87,673	145	27	63
57	66	new	Tulane University:Freeman	United States	92,492	158	23	39
57	48	new	University of Illinois at Urbana-Champaign	United States	77,812	131	27	51
60	59	new	University of British Columbia	Canada	71,329	122	41	48
60	63	50	University of Wisconsin-Madison	United States	86,873	153	28	42
60	new	new	Virginia Tech: Pamplin	United States	80,096	182	31	35
63	75	71	Brigham Young University: Marriott	United States	85,548	190	15	13
63	38	22	University of California at Irvine GSB	United States	89,667	139	32	26
65	73	64	University of Notre Dame: Mendoza	United States	97,351	148	28	25
65	55	56	Wake Forest University: Babcock	United States	90,938	177	23	33
67	42	65	Australian Graduate School of Management	Australia	93,605	112	24	52
67	new	new	Chinese University of Hong Kong	China	58,548	155	62	41
67	52	50	HEC	France	97,623	109	26	70
70	79	new	University of Arizona: Eller	United States	80,519	138	26	39
71	77	55	Michigan State University: Broad	United States	79,612	138	24	41
71	61	new	University of Minnesota: Carlson	United States	88,105	122	26	22
73	70	59	University of Georgia: Terry	United States	89,081	152	33	28
74	new	new	Boston University	United States	110,981	122	33	44
74	60	41	University College Dublin: Smurfit	Ireland	94,761	133	27	48
76	97	new	Trinity College Dublin	Ireland	86,115	102	38	76
77	76	56	Case Western Reserve: Weatherhead	United States	81,864	138	29	47
77	50	37	Edinburgh University Management School	United Kingdom	91,054	129	28	73
79	64	74	Esade	Spain	70,470	118	30	65
79	82	75	Tec de Monterrey Egade	Mexico	81,951	139	24	67
81	73	66	City University Business School	United Kingdom	79,403	118	40	70
82	67	new	Texas A & M University: Mays	United States	81,452	160	12	11
83	new	new	University of Calgary	Canada	73,976	114	43	35
84	58	56	Melbourne Business School	Australia	94,472	104	29	47
85	new	new	Georgia Institute of Technology: DuPree	United States	89,833	128	25	38
85	64	54	Imperial College Management School	United Kingdom	85,701	99	26	61
87	70	73	Universiteit Nyenrode	Netherlands	81,384	112	23	53
88	80	new	McMaster University: DeGroote	Canada	69,783	152	43	16
89	85	new	Strathclyde Graduate School of Business	United Kingdom	73,915	94	33	61
89	96	new	University of Bath School of Management	United Kingdom	76,185	94	43	65
89	new	new	University of Durham Business School	United Kingdom	75,926	120	36	70
92	new	new	Ceibs	China	35,048	160	39	2
92	91	new	ENPC School of International Management	France	70,012	99	29	74
92	new	new	University of California, Davis	United States	97,440	85	36	21
95	99	new	Coppead	Brazil	73,063	134	36	2
96	94	new	Ipade	Mexico	82,831	179	30	17
97	81	52	Ashridge Management College	United Kingdom	115,435	121	27	50
98	67	new	IEP	France	81,358	80	33	57
99	61	68	ESCP-EAP	France	75,611	64	48	83
99	89	new	National University of Singapore	Singapore	62,656	97	34	81

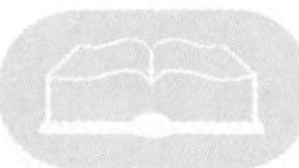

HEALTH

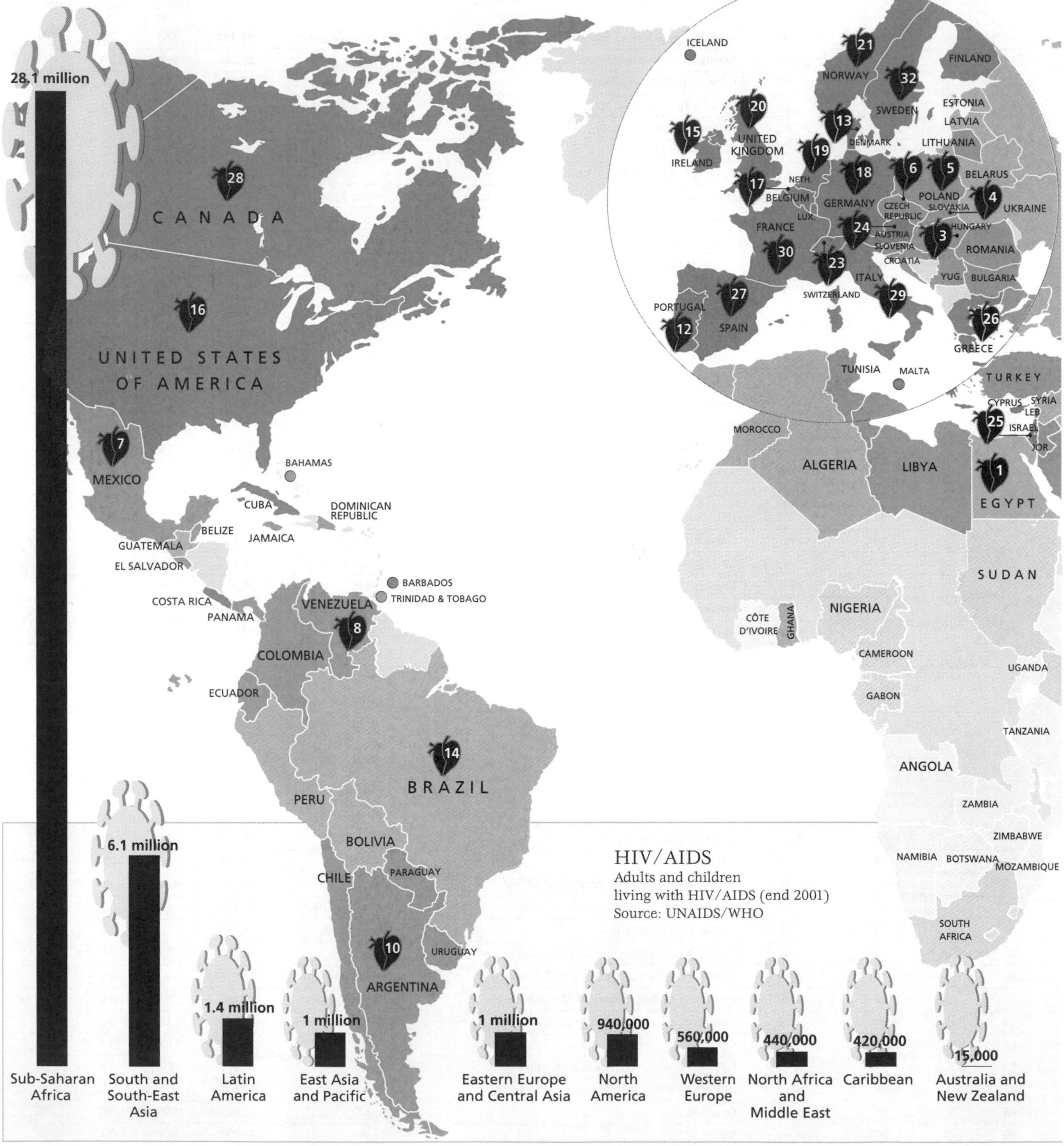

HIV/AIDS

Adults and children living with HIV/AIDS (end 2001)
Source: UNAIDS/WHO

	Adults and children living with HIV/AIDS
Sub-Saharan Africa	28.1 million
South and South-East Asia	6.1 million
Latin America	1.4 million
East Asia and Pacific	1 million
Eastern Europe and Central Asia	1 million
North America	940,000
Western Europe	560,000
North Africa and Middle East	440,000
Caribbean	420,000
Australia and New Zealand	15,000

ICELAND
21 NORWAY
FINLAND
32 SWEDEN
ESTONIA
LATVIA
20 UNITED KINGDOM
15 IRELAND
13 DENMARK
LITHUANIA
19 NETH.
28 CANADA
18 GERMANY
6 POLAND
5 BELARUS
17 BELGIUM
LUX.
CZECH REPUBLIC
SLOVAKIA
4 UKRAINE
FRANCE
24 AUSTRIA
HUNGARY
3 ROMANIA
30
SLOVENIA
CROATIA
23 SWITZERLAND
ITALY
YUG.
BULGARIA
27 SPAIN
12 PORTUGAL
29
26 GREECE
16 UNITED STATES OF AMERICA
TUNISIA
MALTA
TURKEY
CYPRUS
SYRIA
LEB
25 ISRAEL
JOR
7 MEXICO
MOROCCO
ALGERIA
LIBYA
1 EGYPT
BAHAMAS
CUBA
DOMINICAN REPUBLIC
BELIZE
JAMAICA
GUATEMALA
EL SALVADOR
SUDAN
BARBADOS
TRINIDAD & TOBAGO
COSTA RICA
PANAMA
8 VENEZUELA
NIGERIA
CÔTE D'IVOIRE
GHANA
COLOMBIA
CAMEROON
UGANDA
GABON
ECUADOR
TANZANIA
14 BRAZIL
ANGOLA
PERU
ZAMBIA
BOLIVIA
ZIMBABWE
NAMIBIA
BOTSWANA
MOZAMBIQUE
CHILE
PARAGUAY
SOUTH AFRICA
URUGUAY
10 ARGENTINA

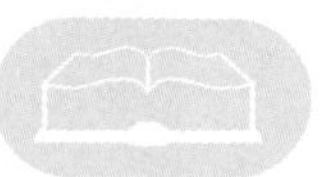

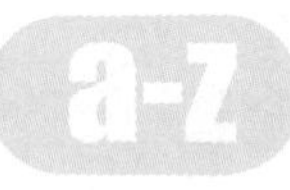

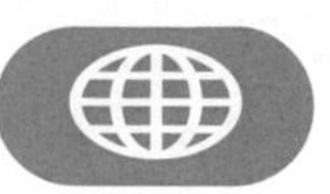

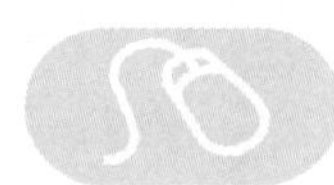

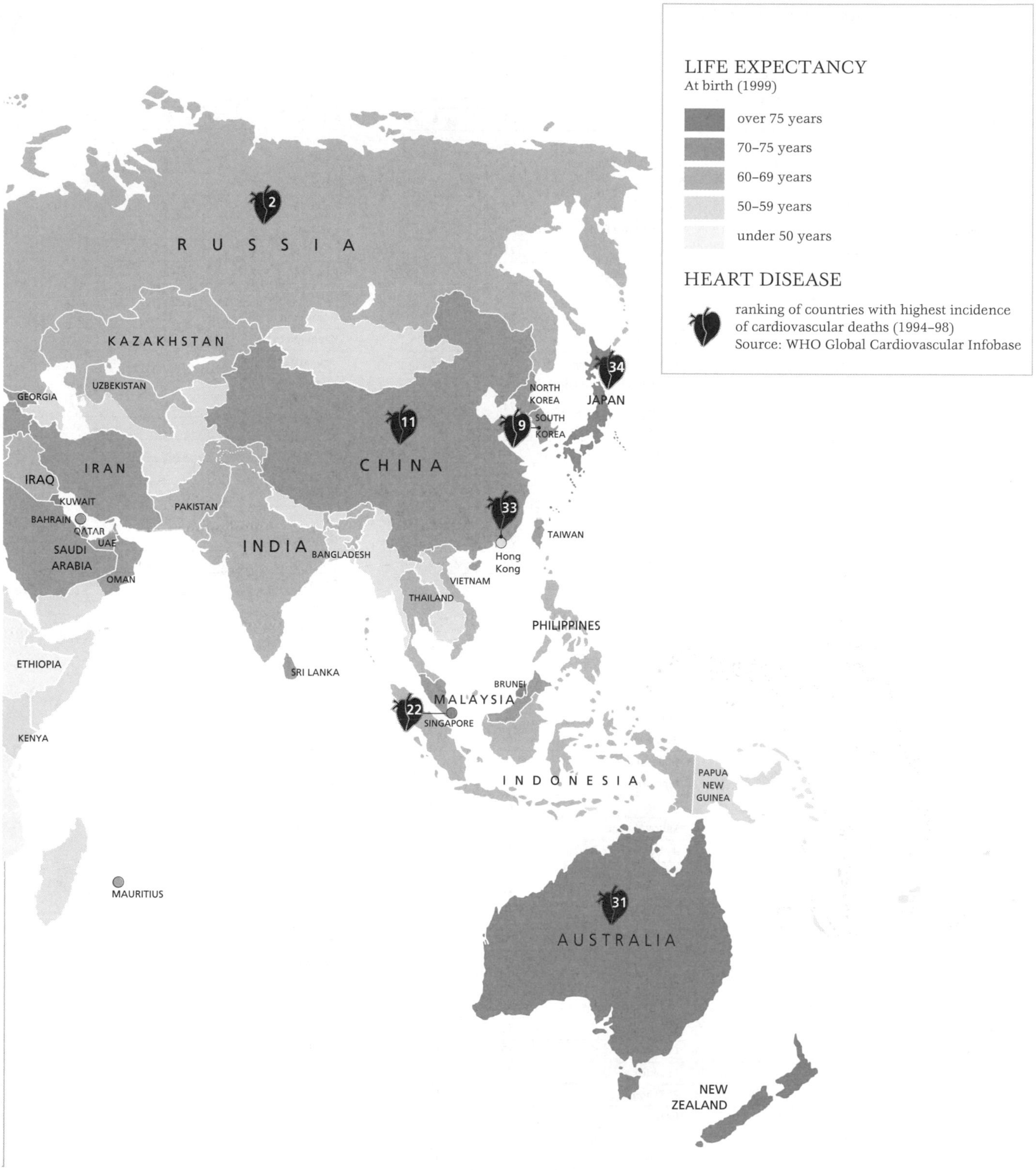

LIFE EXPECTANCY
At birth (1999)
over 75 years
70–75 years
60–69 years
50–59 years
under 50 years
HEART DISEASE
ranking of countries with highest incidence of cardiovascular deaths (1994–98)
Source: WHO Global Cardiovascular Infobase
RUSSIA
2
KAZAKHSTAN
UZBEKISTAN
GEORGIA
IRAN
IRAQ
KUWAIT
BAHRAIN
QATAR
UAE
SAUDI ARABIA
OMAN
PAKISTAN
INDIA
BANGLADESH
CHINA
11
NORTH KOREA
SOUTH KOREA
9
JAPAN
34
33
Hong Kong
TAIWAN
VIETNAM
THAILAND
PHILIPPINES
SRI LANKA
BRUNEI
MALAYSIA
22
SINGAPORE
INDONESIA
PAPUA NEW GUINEA
ETHIOPIA
KENYA
MAURITIUS
AUSTRALIA
31
NEW ZEALAND

Life Expectancy and Infant Mortality

	Life expectancy at birth (years) 1999	Infant mortality (per 1,000 live births) 1999
Andorra	83	6
Macao	82	4
Hong Kong	80	6
Japan	80	4
Aruba	79	6
Canada	79	6
Cayman Islands	79	10
Faeroe Islands	79	7
Gibraltar	79	5
Iceland	79	5
Liechtenstein	79	10
Monaco	79	5
Sweden	79	3
Switzerland	79	3
Australia	78	5
Cyprus	78	7
France	78	5
Greece	78	6
Guam	78	7
Isle of Man	78	6
Israel	78	6
Italy	78	6
Malta	78	6
Martinique	78	8
Netherlands	78	5
Norway	78	4
Singapore	78	4
Spain	78	6
United Kingdom	78	6
US Virgin Islands	78	9
Austria	77	4
Barbados	77	14
Belgium	77	6
Bermuda	77	10
Finland	77	4
Germany	77	5
Guadeloupe	77	10
Ireland	77	6
Luxembourg	77	5
New Zealand	77	6
United States	77	7
British Virgin Islands	76	20
Brunei	76	8
Costa Rica	76	13
Cuba	76	6
Denmark	76	4
French Guiana	76	14
Kuwait	76	11
Northern Marianas	76	6
Portugal	76	5
Puerto Rico	76	11
American Samoa	75	10
Belize	75	35

	Life expectancy at birth (years) 1999	Infant mortality (per 1,000 live births) 1999
Chile	75	11
French Polynesia	75	9
Jamaica	75	10
Netherlands Antilles	75	11
Slovenia	75	5
Taiwan	75	6
United Arab Emirates	75	8
Bahamas	74	18
Czech Republic	74	5
Dominica	74	16
Panama	74	21
Sri Lanka	74	17
Trinidad and Tobago	74	17
Turks and Caicos Islands	74	18
Uruguay	74	15
Argentina	73	19
Bahrain	73	13
Croatia	73	8
Georgia	73	19
Mexico	73	27
New Caledonia	73	8
North Korea	73	23
Poland	73	9
Reunion	73	8
St Lucia	73	17
Slovakia	73	9
South Korea	73	5
Venezuela	73	20
Yugoslavia	73	20
Bulgaria	72	14
Malaysia	72	8
Mauritius	72	19
Qatar	72	12
Saudi Arabia	72	20
Antigua and Barbuda	71	17
Colombia	71	26
Dominican Republic	71	43
Hungary	71	9
Jordan	71	29
Lithuania	71	18
Oman	71	14
St Kitts and Nevis	71	24
Seychelles	71	13
China	70	33
Ecuador	70	27
El Salvador	70	35
Iran	70	37
Lebanon	70	28
Libya	70	19
Paraguay	70	27
Romania	70	21
Tunisia	70	24
Turkey	70	40

	Life expectancy at birth (years) 1999	Infant mortality (per 1,000 live births) 1999
Algeria	69	36
Estonia	69	17
Latvia	69	17
Palau	69	17
Peru	69	42
Philippines	69	31
Syria	69	25
Thailand	69	26
Ukraine	69	17
Belarus	68	23
Greenland	68	18
Kazakhstan	68	35
Uzbekistan	68	45
Vietnam	68	31
Brazil	67	34
Egypt	67	41
Morocco	67	45
Russia	67	18
Indonesia	66	38
Grenada	65	22
Guatemala	65	45
Iraq	65	104
Pakistan	65	84
India	63	70
Bolivia	62	64
Ghana	61	63
Bangladesh	59	58
Papua New Guinea	59	79
Sudan	56	67
Cameroon	54	95
Gabon	52	85
South Africa	52	54
Kenya	51	76
Nigeria	50	112
Angola	48	172
Namibia	48	56
Tanzania	48	90
Côte d'Ivoire	47	102
Botswana	45	46
Ethiopia	44	118
Zimbabwe	43	60
Mozambique	42	127
Uganda	42	83
Zambia	41	112

Highest Prevalence of Heart Disease

	Cardiovascular deaths (per 100,000) 1994–98	Cardiovascular deaths, males (per 100,000) 1994–98	Cardiovascular deaths, females (per 100,000) 1994–98	Cancer deaths (per 100,000) 2000
Egypt	2,891	1,511	1,380	145
Russia	1,961	1,322	639	312
Hungary	1,725	1,136	589	420
Slovakia	1,464	941	523	327
Poland	1,442	941	502	317
Czech Republic	1,392	874	517	350
Mexico	1,354	798	556	219
Venezuela	1,327	792	536	196
South Korea	1,317	865	451	261
Argentina	1,308	837	470	252
China	1,243	724	519	220
Portugal	1,158	745	413	246
Denmark	1,150	684	466	329
Brazil	1,109	660	450	232
Ireland	1,109	689	420	298
United States	1,010	618	392	278
Belgium	1,001	645	356	312
Germany	987	626	361	294
Netherlands	979	617	363	302
United Kingdom	958	581	377	299
Norway	933	592	341	269
Singapore	915	556	360	272
Switzerland	905	576	329	274
Austria	900	565	335	282
Israel	875	513	363	246
Greece	873	533	341	231
Spain	860	563	297	261
Canada	859	532	327	277
Italy	837	532	305	275
France	831	552	279	300
Australia	829	513	315	254
Sweden	823	507	315	242
Hong Kong	756	478	278	269
Japan	749	481	268	243

Deaths per 100,000 people at risk and age-adjusted to world standard.

Source: WHO Global Cardiovascular Infobase

Highest Prevalence of Cancer

	Cancer deaths (per 100,000) 2000
Hungary	420
Czech Republic	350
Croatia	335
Denmark	329
Slovakia	327
Uruguay	324
Slovenia	319
Poland	317
Russia	312
Belgium	312
Estonia	306
Kazakhstan	304
Netherlands	302
Luxembourg	300
France	300
Latvia	299
United Kingdom	299
New Zealand	298
Ireland	298
Germany	294
Lithuania	293
Austria	282
Belarus	280
Zimbabwe	279
Ukraine	278
United States	278
Canada	277
Italy	275
Switzerland	274
Singapore	272
Hong Kong	269
Norway	269
Malta	267
Barbados	265
Spain	261
North Korea	261
South Korea	261
South Africa	260
Iceland	260
Philippines	259
Australia	254
Argentina	252
Chile	250
Jamaica	250
Israel	246
Portugal	246
Cuba	245
Japan	243
Sweden	242
Costa Rica	242
Romania	240
Bulgaria	240
Finland	238
Zambia	234
Kenya	233
Malaysia	232
Brazil	232
Bahamas	232
Cyprus	231
Greece	231
Mozambique	230

	Cancer deaths (per 100,000) 2000
Papua New Guinea	230
Tanzania	230
Bolivia	226
Ethiopia	225
Botswana	224
Yugoslavia	223
Guam	223
Colombia	223
China	220
Mexico	219
Belize	218
Guatemala	218
Ecuador	209
Trinidad and Tobago	205
Panama	204
Namibia	199
Venezuela	196
Uganda	195
Puerto Rico	191
Thailand	191
El Salvador	188
Lebanon	187
Syria	187
Peru	187
Pakistan	183
Vietnam	182
Georgia	180
Cameroon	179
Brunei	176
Gabon	173
Angola	172
Turkey	167
Algeria	165
Uzbekistan	165
Dominican Republic	164
Saudi Arabia	161
Bahrain	158
Qatar	158
United Arab Emirates	158
Iran	158
Jordan	155
Paraguay	154
Iraq	154
Morocco	154
Libya	152
Mauritius	146
Egypt	145
Sudan	144
Kuwait	142
India	138
Indonesia	137
Bangladesh	134
Sri Lanka	128
Tunisia	126
Oman	119
Ghana	116
Nigeria	114
Côte d'Ivoire	110

Deaths per 100,000 people at risk and age-adjusted to world standard. Source: International Agency for Research on Cancer

46%
CANADA
46%
UNITED STATES OF AMERICA
MEXICO
CUBA
DOMINICAN REPUBLIC
PUERTO RICO
46%
JAMAICA
GUATEMALA
EL SALVADOR
COSTA RICA
PANAMA
TRINIDAD & TOBAGO
VENEZUELA
COLOMBIA
ECUADOR
PERU
BRAZIL
BOLIVIA
CHILE
PARAGUAY
42%
URUGUAY
ARGENTINA
46%
NORWAY
48%
FINLAND
48%
SWEDEN
ESTONIA
49%
LATVIA
50%
48%
LITHUANIA
44%
UNITED KINGDOM
IRELAND
46%
DENMARK
NETH.
49%
BELARUS
42%
GERMANY
46%
POLAND
41%
BELGIUM
47%
CZECH REPUBLIC
48%
SLOVAKIA
UKRAINE
49%
45%
FRANCE
SWITZ.
47%
AUSTRIA
HUN.
SLOVENIA
CROATIA
45%
45%
ROMANIA
ITALY
BULGARIA
48%
44%
PORTUGAL
SPAIN
44%
43%
YUGOSLAVIA
GREECE
TUNISIA
TURKEY
LEB
ISRAEL
41%
JOR
MOROCCO
ALGERIA
LIBYA
EGYPT
SUDAN
51%
CÔTE D'IVOIRE
GHANA
NIGERIA
48%
UGANDA
CAMEROON
GABON
45%
TANZANIA
49%
46%
ANGOLA
45%
ZAMBIA
45%
ZIMBABWE
45%
BOTSWANA
41%
NAMIBIA
48%
MOZAMBIQUE
SOUTH AFRICA

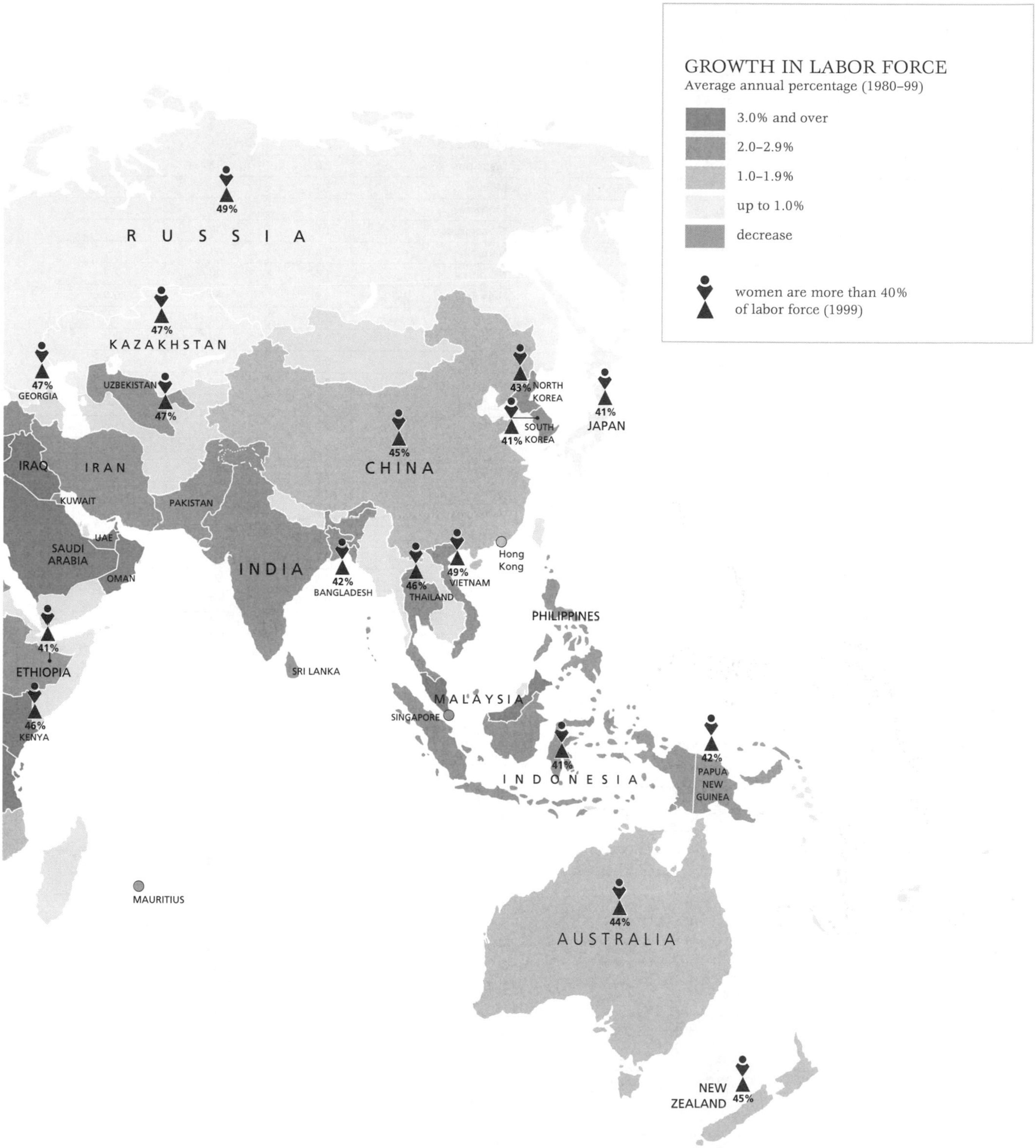

GROWTH IN LABOR FORCE

Average annual percentage (1980–99)

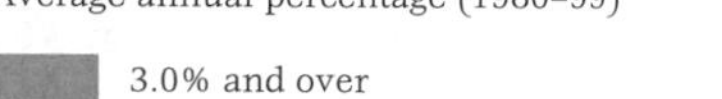

3.0% and over
2.0–2.9%
1.0–1.9%
up to 1.0%
decrease

women are more than 40% of labor force (1999)

RUSSIA 49%
KAZAKHSTAN 47%
GEORGIA 47%
UZBEKISTAN 47%
NORTH KOREA 43%
SOUTH KOREA 41%
JAPAN 41%
CHINA 45%
IRAQ
IRAN
KUWAIT
PAKISTAN
UAE
SAUDI ARABIA
OMAN
INDIA
BANGLADESH 42%
THAILAND 46%
VIETNAM 49%
Hong Kong
PHILIPPINES
ETHIOPIA 41%
SRI LANKA
MALAYSIA
SINGAPORE
KENYA 46%
INDONESIA 41%
PAPUA NEW GUINEA 42%
MAURITIUS
AUSTRALIA 44%
NEW ZEALAND 45%

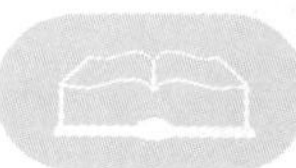

Labor Force

	Growth of labor force (% p.a.) 1980–99	Women (% of labor force) 1999	Unemployment (%) 2000
Algeria	3.8	27	–
Angola	2.6	46	–
Argentina	1.7	33	14.7
Australia	1.9	44	6.3
Austria	0.6	40	3.7
Bangladesh	2.6	42	–
Belarus	0.2	49	–
Belgium	0.4	41	7.0
Bolivia	2.6	38	–
Botswana	3.0	45	–
Brazil	2.6	35	7.1
Bulgaria	-0.5	48	–
Cameroon	2.6	38	–
Canada	1.5	46	6.8
Chile	2.5	33	8.3
China	1.7	45	–
Colombia	3.4	38	–
Costa Rica	3.1	31	–
Côte d'Ivoire	3.4	33	–
Croatia	–0.2	44	–
Cuba	2.1	39	–
Czech Republic	0.4	47	8.9
Denmark	0.4	46	4.7
Dominican Republic	2.9	30	–
Ecuador	3.3	28	–
Egypt	2.7	30	–
El Salvador	2.8	36	–
Estonia	–0.1	49	–
Ethiopia	2.5	41	–
Finland	0.4	48	9.7
France	0.6	45	9.5
Gabon	2.2	45	–
Georgia	0.3	47	–
Germany	0.5	42	7.9
Ghana	2.9	51	–
Greece	1.0	38	–
Guatemala	2.9	28	–
Hong Kong	1.9	37	–
Hungary	-0.3	45	6.5
India	2.0	32	–
Indonesia	2.8	41	–
Iran	2.6	27	–
Iraq	3.0	19	–
Ireland	1.2	34	4.2
Israel	3.1	41	–
Italy	0.7	38	10.5
Jamaica	1.8	46	–
Japan	0.9	41	4.7
Jordan	5.2	24	–
Kazakhstan	0.2	47	–
Kenya	3.4	46	–
Kuwait	2.3	31	–
Latvia	-0.4	50	–
Lebanon	2.9	29	–
Libya	2.6	23	–
Lithuania	0.3	48	–
Malaysia	3.0	38	–
Mauritius	2.0	32	–
Mexico	3.1	33	–
Morocco	2.5	35	–
Mozambique	1.5	48	–
Namibia	2.4	41	–
Netherlands	1.4	40	2.9
New Zealand	1.9	45	6.0
Nigeria	2.7	36	–
North Korea	2.5	43	–
Norway	0.9	46	3.5
Oman	3.4	16	–
Pakistan	2.8	28	–
Panama	2.9	35	–
Papua New Guinea	2.2	42	–
Paraguay	2.9	30	–
Peru	2.9	31	–
Philippines	2.6	38	–
Poland	0.3	46	16.1
Portugal	0.5	44	4.1
Puerto Rico	1.9	37	–
Romania	-0.1	45	–
Russia	0.1	49	10.4
Saudi Arabia	4.6	16	–
Singapore	2.9	39	–
Slovakia	0.9	48	–
Slovenia	0.3	47	–
South Africa	2.5	38	–
South Korea	2.2	41	–
Spain	1.1	37	14.1
Sri Lanka	2.2	36	–
Sudan	2.7	29	–
Sweden	0.7	48	5.9
Switzerland	1.2	40	2.0
Syria	3.6	27	–
Tanzania	3.0	49	–
Thailand	2.1	46	–
Trinidad and Tobago	1.6	34	–
Tunisia	2.8	31	–
Turkey	2.6	37	–
Uganda	2.5	48	–
Ukraine	–0.2	49	–
United Arab Emirates	4.8	15	–
United Kingdom	0.5	44	5.5
United States	1.4	46	4.0
Uruguay	1.4	42	–
Uzbekistan	2.4	47	–
Venezuela	3.3	35	–
Vietnam	2.3	49	–
Yugoslavia	0.6	43	–
Zambia	2.9	45	–
Zimbabwe	2.9	45	–

Fastest Growth of Labor Force

	Growth of labor force (% p.a.) 1980–99
Jordan	5.2
United Arab Emirates	4.8
Saudi Arabia	4.6
Algeria	3.8
Syria	3.6
Colombia	3.4
Côte d'Ivoire	3.4
Kenya	3.4
Oman	3.4
Ecuador	3.3
Venezuela	3.3
Costa Rica	3.1
Israel	3.1
Mexico	3.1
Botswana	3.0
Iraq	3.0
Malaysia	3.0
Tanzania	3.0
Dominican Republic	2.9
Ghana	2.9
Guatemala	2.9
Lebanon	2.9
Panama	2.9
Paraguay	2.9
Peru	2.9
Singapore	2.9
Zambia	2.9
Zimbabwe	2.9
El Salvador	2.8
Indonesia	2.8
Pakistan	2.8
Tunisia	2.8
Egypt	2.7
Nigeria	2.7
Sudan	2.7
Angola	2.6
Bangladesh	2.6
Bolivia	2.6
Brazil	2.6
Cameroon	2.6
Iran	2.6
Libya	2.6
Philippines	2.6
Turkey	2.6
Chile	2.5
Ethiopia	2.5
Morocco	2.5
North Korea	2.5
South Africa	2.5
Uganda	2.5
Namibia	2.4
Uzbekistan	2.4
Kuwait	2.3
Vietnam	2.3

	Growth of labor force (% p.a.) 1980–99
Gabon	2.2
Papua New Guinea	2.2
South Korea	2.2
Sri Lanka	2.2
Cuba	2.1
Thailand	2.1
India	2.0
Mauritius	2.0
Australia	1.9
Hong Kong	1.9
New Zealand	1.9
Puerto Rico	1.9
Jamaica	1.8
Argentina	1.7
China	1.7
Trinidad and Tobago	1.6
Canada	1.5
Mozambique	1.5
Netherlands	1.4
United States	1.4
Uruguay	1.4
Ireland	1.2
Switzerland	1.2
Spain	1.1
Greece	1.0
Japan	0.9
Norway	0.9
Slovakia	0.9
Italy	0.7
Sweden	0.7
Austria	0.6
France	0.6
Yugoslavia	0.6
Germany	0.5
Portugal	0.5
United Kingdom	0.5
Belgium	0.4
Czech Republic	0.4
Denmark	0.4
Finland	0.4
Georgia	0.3
Lithuania	0.3
Poland	0.3
Slovenia	0.3
Belarus	0.2
Kazakhstan	0.2
Russia	0.1
Estonia	–0.1
Romania	–0.1
Croatia	–0.2
Ukraine	–0.2
Hungary	–0.3
Latvia	–0.4
Bulgaria	–0.5

Highest Proportion of Women in Labor Force

	Women (% of labor force) 1999
Ghana	51
Latvia	50
Tanzania	49
Vietnam	49
Russia	49
Estonia	49
Belarus	49
Ukraine	49
Mozambique	48
Bulgaria	48
Sweden	48
Finland	48
Lithuania	48
Slovakia	48
Uganda	48
Czech Republic	47
Kazakhstan	47
Uzbekistan	47
Georgia	47
Slovenia	47
Denmark	46
Angola	46
Thailand	46
Norway	46
Poland	46
Jamaica	46
Kenya	46
United States	46
Canada	46
Botswana	45
China	45
Zambia	45
France	45
New Zealand	45
Hungary	45
Gabon	45
Zimbabwe	45
Romania	45
Croatia	44
Portugal	44
United Kingdom	44
Australia	44
North Korea	43
Yugoslavia	43
Bangladesh	42
Germany	42
Papua New Guinea	42
Uruguay	42
Japan	41
South Korea	41
Israel	41
Ethiopia	41
Namibia	41
Belgium	41

	Women (% of labor force) 1999
Indonesia	41
Netherlands	40
Switzerland	40
Austria	40
Cuba	39
Singapore	39
Colombia	38
Italy	38
Cameroon	38
Malaysia	38
Bolivia	38
Philippines	38
South Africa	38
Greece	38
Turkey	37
Hong Kong	37
Spain	37
Puerto Rico	37
Nigeria	36
Sri Lanka	36
El Salvador	36

Lowest Unemployment

	Unemployment (%) 2000
Switzerland	2.0
Luxembourg	2.4
Netherlands	2.9
Norway	3.5
Austria	3.7
United States	4.0
Portugal	4.1
Ireland	4.2
Japan	4.7
Denmark	4.7
United Kingdom	5.5
Sweden	5.9
New Zealand	6.0
Australia	6.3
Hungary	6.5
Canada	6.8
Belgium	7.0
Brazil	7.1
Germany	7.9
Chile	8.3
Czech Republic	8.9
France	9.5
Finland	9.7
Russia	10.4
Italy	10.5
Spain	14.1
Argentina	14.7
Poland	16.1

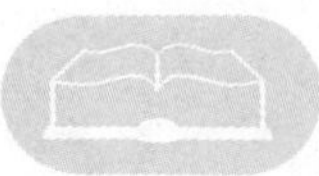

INFLATION

11
ICELAND
8
NORWAY
FINLAND
SWEDEN
ESTONIA
LATVIA
DENMARK
LITHUANIA
IRELAND
UNITED KINGDOM
NETH.
19
POLAND
BELARUS
BELGIUM
GERMANY
8
CZECH REPUBLIC
SLOVAKIA
UKRAINE
LUX.
FRANCE
AUSTRIA
HUNGARY
7
SLOVENIA
17
12
ROMANIA
16
CROATIA
20
BULGARIA
ITALY
YUGOSLAVIA
PORTUGAL
SPAIN
SWITZERLAND
GREECE
13
TUNISIA
MALTA
TURKEY
CYPRUS
SYRIA
LEB
20
ISRAEL
JOR
MOROCCO
ALGERIA
EGYPT
CANADA
UNITED STATES OF AMERICA
2
BERMUDA
16
BAHAMAS
CAYMAN ISLANDS
4
MEXICO
BELIZE
JAMAICA
DOMINICAN REPUBLIC
PUERTO RICO
ST KITTS & NEVIS
ANTIGUA & BARBUDA
15
DOMINICA
ST LUCIA
BARBADOS
GUATEMALA
EL SALVADOR
GRENADA
TRINIDAD & TOBAGO
COSTA RICA
PANAMA
VENEZUELA
12
FRENCH GUIANA
COLOMBIA
ECUADOR
11
BRAZIL
PERU
BOLIVIA
CHILE
15
PARAGUAY
18
URUGUAY
ARGENTINA
CÔTE D'IVOIRE
GHANA
NIGERIA
CAMEROON
GABON
UGANDA
TANZANIA
5
ANGOLA
10
ZAMBIA
ZIMBABWE
NAMIBIA
BOTSWANA
3
4
9
MOZAMBIQUE
1
SOUTH AFRICA

MARKET CAPITALIZATION

Average annual percentage (1990–99)

- less than 2.0%
- 2.0–3.9%
- 4.0–9.9%
- 10–30%
- over 30%

COST OF LIVING

- most expensive countries ranked 1 to 20
- least expensive countries ranked 1 to 20

Source: rankings based on ECA International's indices

RUSSIA 6
KAZAKHSTAN
UZBEKISTAN 3
CHINA
JAPAN 1
SOUTH KOREA 19
IRAN
PAKISTAN 2
BAHRAIN
UAE
SAUDI ARABIA
OMAN
INDIA 5
BANGLADESH 10
Hong Kong 18
VIETNAM
THAILAND 17
PHILIPPINES 14
GUAM 9
PALAU
SRI LANKA 6
ETHIOPIA
KENYA
SEYCHELLES 14
BRUNEI
MALAYSIA
SINGAPORE
INDONESIA
PAPUA NEW GUINEA
MAURITIUS
AUSTRALIA
NEW CALEDONIA 13
FRENCH POLYNESIA 7
NEW ZEALAND

Consumer Price Inflation

	Inflation (% p.a.) 1990–99	Inflation (%) 2000
Algeria	19.1	0.3
Angola	813.7	344.0
Antigua and Barbuda*	2.5	1.6
Argentina	6.2	–0.9
Australia	1.3	4.5
Austria	2.2	2.4
Bahamas	2.6	1.6
Bahrain	–0.2	2.0
Bangladesh	4.1	2.3
Barbados	3.1	2.4
Belarus	393.5	169.0
Belgium	2.2	2.5
Belize	2.9	0.6
Bermuda	3.5	2.7
Bolivia	9.1	4.6
Botswana	10.0	8.7
Brazil	263.9	7.0
Brunei*	1.1	1.0
Bulgaria	112.0	10.0
Cameroon	5.5	1.0
Canada	1.4	2.7
Chile	8.0	3.8
China	8.2	0.4
Colombia	22.7	9.2
Costa Rica	16.7	11.0
Côte d'Ivoire	8.2	2.4
Croatia	104.9	6.2
Cyprus	3.5	4.1
Czech Republic	12.4	3.9
Denmark	2.0	2.9
Dominica	3.2	2.5
Dominican Republic	9.9	7.7
Ecuador	33.8	96.1
Egypt	8.8	2.7
El Salvador	8.1	2.2
Estonia	62.7	0.3
Ethiopia	7.6	5.0
Finland	2.0	3.4
France	1.6	1.7
Gabon	5.8	0.4
Germany	1.9	1.9
Ghana	27.4	25.2
Greece	9.5	3.1
Grenada	2.6	2.5
Guatemala	10.9	6.0
Hong Kong	5.2	–3.8
Hungary	20.6	9.8
Iceland	3.3	5.1
India	8.5	4.0
Indonesia	14.7	3.7
Iran	27.0	14.5
Ireland	3.4	5.6
Israel	10.7	1.1
Italy	4.0	2.5
Jamaica	27.6	8.2
Japan	0.1	–0.7
Jordan	3.5	0.7
Kazakhstan	255.9	13.2
Kenya	14.9	5.8
Latvia	57.9	2.6
Lebanon	24.0	–1.0
Lithuania	90.7	1.4
Luxembourg	2.4	3.8
Malaysia	3.9	1.5
Malta	2.9	2.4
Mauritius	6.3	4.2
Mexico	19.5	9.5
Morocco	3.2	1.9
Mozambique	36.4	11.4
Namibia	9.8	9.2
Netherlands	1.9	2.5
New Zealand	1.4	2.7
Nigeria	31.6	6.9
Norway	2.1	3.1
Oman	–2.9	–0.8
Pakistan	10.6	4.4
Palau	6.4	3.4
Panama	2.1	1.4
Papua New Guinea	7.1	15.6
Paraguay	13.4	8.9
Peru	31.0	3.8
Philippines	8.6	4.4
Poland	25.0	10.1
Portugal	5.6	2.9
Puerto Rico	3.7	5.7
Romania	105.6	45.6
Russia	190.4	20.8
St Kitts and Nevis	3.1	2.1
St Lucia	2.7	2.0
Saudi Arabia	1.2	–0.8
Seychelles	1.5	6.3
Singapore	1.6	1.4
Slovakia	11.4	12.0
Slovenia	23.3	8.9
South Africa	10.2	5.3
South Korea	5.8	2.3
Spain	4.1	3.4
Sri Lanka	9.4	6.2
Sweden	2.2	1.0
Switzerland	1.4	1.5
Syria	8.7	–0.4
Tanzania	23.1	5.9
Thailand	4.6	1.6
Trinidad and Tobago	5.8	3.5
Tunisia	4.6	2.9
Turkey	78.3	54.9
Uganda	13.8	6.3
Ukraine	339.1	28.2
United Arab Emirates	2.4	2.5
United Kingdom	3.0	0.8
United States	2.1	3.4
Uruguay	35.2	4.8
Uzbekistan	293.0	24.9
Venezuela	47.5	16.2
Vietnam	16.8	–1.7
Zambia	57.4	26.0
Zimbabwe	23.6	55.7

* 1999 data

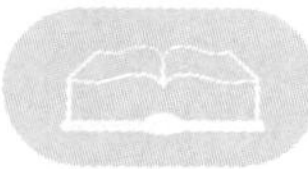

Lowest Inflation 1990–99

	Inflation (% p.a.) 1990–99
Oman	–2.9
Bahrain	–0.2
Japan	0.1
Brunei	1.1
Saudi Arabia	1.2
Australia	1.3
Canada	1.4
New Zealand	1.4
Switzerland	1.4
Seychelles	1.5
France	1.6
Singapore	1.6
Germany	1.9
Netherlands	1.9
Denmark	2.0
Finland	2.0
Norway	2.1
Panama	2.1
United States	2.1
Austria	2.2
Belgium	2.2
Sweden	2.2
Luxembourg	2.4
United Arab Emirates	2.4
Antigua and Barbuda*	2.5
Bahamas	2.6
Grenada	2.6
St Lucia	2.7
Belize	2.9
Malta	2.9
United Kingdom	3.0
Barbados	3.1
St Kitts and Nevis	3.1
Dominica	3.2
Morocco	3.2
Iceland	3.3
Ireland	3.4
Bermuda	3.5
Cyprus	3.5
Jordan	3.5
Puerto Rico	3.7
Malaysia	3.9
Italy	4.0
Bangladesh	4.1
Spain	4.1
Thailand	4.6
Tunisia	4.6
Hong Kong	5.2
Cameroon	5.5
Portugal	5.6
Gabon	5.8
South Korea	5.8
Trinidad and Tobago	5.8
Argentina	6.2
Mauritius	6.3
Palau	6.4
Papua New Guinea	7.1
Ethiopia	7.6
Chile	8.0
El Salvador	8.1
China	8.2
Côte d'Ivoire	8.2
India	8.5
Philippines	8.6
Syria	8.7
Egypt	8.8
Bolivia	9.1
Sri Lanka	9.4
Greece	9.5
Namibia	9.8
Dominican Republic	9.9
Botswana	10.0
South Africa	10.2
Pakistan	10.6
Israel	10.7
Guatemala	10.9
Slovakia	11.4
Czech Republic	12.4
Paraguay	13.4
Uganda	13.8
Indonesia	14.7
Kenya	14.9
Costa Rica	16.7
Vietnam	16.8
Algeria	19.1
Mexico	19.5
Hungary	20.6
Colombia	22.7
Tanzania	23.1
Slovenia	23.3
Zimbabwe	23.6
Lebanon	24.0
Poland	25.0
Iran	27.0
Ghana	27.4
Jamaica	27.6
Peru	31.0
Nigeria	31.6
Ecuador	33.8
Uruguay	35.2
Mozambique	36.4
Venezuela	47.5
Zambia	57.4
Latvia	57.9
Estonia	62.7
Turkey	78.3
Lithuania	90.7
Croatia	104.9
Romania	105.6
Bulgaria	112.0
Russia	190.4
Kazakhstan	255.9
Brazil	263.9
Uzbekistan	293.0
Ukraine	339.1
Belarus	393.5
Angola	813.7

Highest Inflation 1990–99

	Inflation (% p.a.) 1990–99
Angola	813.7
Belarus	393.5
Ukraine	339.1
Uzbekistan	293.0
Brazil	263.9
Kazakhstan	255.9
Russia	190.4
Bulgaria	112.0
Romania	105.6
Croatia	104.9
Lithuania	90.7
Turkey	78.3
Estonia	62.7
Latvia	57.9
Zambia	57.4
Venezuela	47.5
Mozambique	36.4
Uruguay	35.2
Ecuador	33.8
Nigeria	31.6
Peru	31.0
Jamaica	27.6
Ghana	27.4
Iran	27.0
Poland	25.0
Lebanon	24.0
Zimbabwe	23.6
Slovenia	23.3
Tanzania	23.1
Colombia	22.7
Hungary	20.6
Mexico	19.5
Algeria	19.1
Vietnam	16.8
Costa Rica	16.7
Kenya	14.9
Indonesia	14.7
Uganda	13.8
Paraguay	13.4
Czech Republic	12.4
Slovakia	11.4
Guatemala	10.9
Israel	10.7
Pakistan	10.6
South Africa	10.2
Botswana	10.0
Dominican Republic	9.9
Namibia	9.8
Greece	9.5
Sri Lanka	9.4
Bolivia	9.1
Egypt	8.8
Syria	8.7
Philippines	8.6
India	8.5
China	8.2
Côte d'Ivoire	8.2
El Salvador	8.1
Chile	8.0
Ethiopia	7.6
Papua New Guinea	7.1
Palau	6.4
Mauritius	6.3
Argentina	6.2
Gabon	5.8
South Korea	5.8
Trinidad and Tobago	5.8
Portugal	5.6
Cameroon	5.5
Hong Kong	5.2
Thailand	4.6
Tunisia	4.6
Bangladesh	4.1
Spain	4.1
Italy	4.0
Malaysia	3.9
Puerto Rico	3.7
Bermuda	3.5
Cyprus	3.5
Jordan	3.5
Ireland	3.4
Iceland	3.3
Dominica	3.2
Morocco	3.2
Barbados	3.1
St Kitts and Nevis	3.1
United Kingdom	3.0
Belize	2.9
Malta	2.9
St Lucia	2.7
Bahamas	2.6
Grenada	2.6
Antigua and Barbuda*	2.5
Luxembourg	2.4
United Arab Emirates	2.4
Austria	2.2
Belgium	2.2
Sweden	2.2
Norway	2.1
Panama	2.1
United States	2.1
Denmark	2.0
Finland	2.0
Germany	1.9
Netherlands	1.9
France	1.6
Singapore	1.6
Seychelles	1.5
Canada	1.4
New Zealand	1.4
Switzerland	1.4
Australia	1.3
Saudi Arabia	1.2
Brunei	1.1
Japan	0.1
Bahrain	–0.2
Oman	–2.9

ECA International Cost of Living Ranking, December 2001

Most Expensive Countries for Expatriates

Rank	
2	Japan
4	Bermuda
5	Uzbekistan
6	Cayman Islands
7	Angola
9	Russia
10	French Polynesia
11	Norway
12	Guam
13	Zimbabwe
14	Iceland
15	French Guiana
16	New Caledonia
17	Seychelles
18	Barbados
19	Bahamas
20	Switzerland
21	Hong Kong
22	South Korea
23	Israel
24	Martinique
25	Sudan
26	British Virgin Islands
27	Antigua and Barbuda
28	Cuba
30	Lebanon
31	Denmark
32	Taiwan
33	St Lucia
34	Libya
36	Netherlands Antilles
37	Argentina
38	Côte d'ivoire
39	Finland
40	China
41	Dominican Republic
42	Palau
46	Puerto Rico
48	Venezuela
49	Ukraine
51	Nigeria
52	Monaco
53	Mexico
56	Trinidad and Tobago
57	Jordan
58	Oman
59	United Kingdom
60	Austria
62	Kuwait
63	Belize
66	Singapore
67	United Arab Emirates
68	Uruguay
69	Sweden
70	Luxembourg
71	El Salvador
72	Guatemala
77	France
78	Germany
80	Costa Rica
81	Bahrain
82	Qatar
84	Belgium
85	Panama
86	Ireland
87	Syria
88	Indonesia
89	Gibraltar
90	Italy
92	Netherlands
94	Brunei
95	Tanzania
96	Peru
98	Georgia
99	Colombia
100	Canada
101	Morocco
102	Greece
104	Croatia
105	Ecuador
108	Iran
109	Latvia
111	Cameroon
112	Saudi Arabia
114	Lithuania
115	Ghana
119	Malta
120	Spain
121	Kenya
123	Cyprus
124	Tunisia
125	Uganda
127	Estonia
128	Portugal
129	Ethiopia
131	Australia
132	Poland
134	Slovenia
135	Egypt
136	Malaysia
138	Bolivia
139	Papua New Guinea
140	Mauritius
141	Vietnam
142	New Zealand
146	Zambia
148	Serbia
149	Czech Republic
150	Paraguay
151	Thailand
152	Bulgaria
153	Chile
155	Philippines
156	Turkey
157	Hungary
158	Brazil
159	Bangladesh
161	Mozambique
162	Slovakia
163	Romania
165	Sri Lanka
166	India
167	Botswana
168	Namibia
169	Pakistan
172	South Africa

Least Expensive Countries for Expatriates

Rank	
172	South Africa
169	Pakistan
168	Namibia
167	Botswana
166	India
165	Sri Lanka
163	Romania
162	Slovakia
161	Mozambique
159	Bangladesh
158	Brazil
157	Hungary
156	Turkey
155	Philippines
153	Chile
152	Bulgaria
151	Thailand
150	Paraguay
149	Czech Republic
148	Serbia
146	Zambia
142	New Zealand
141	Vietnam
140	Mauritius
139	Papua New Guinea
138	Bolivia
136	Malaysia
135	Egypt
134	Slovenia
132	Poland
131	Australia
129	Ethiopia
128	Portugal
127	Estonia
125	Uganda
124	Tunisia
123	Cyprus
121	Kenya
120	Spain
119	Malta
115	Ghana
114	Lithuania
112	Saudi Arabia
111	Cameroon
109	Latvia
108	Iran
105	Ecuador
104	Croatia
102	Greece
101	Morocco
100	Canada
99	Colombia
98	Georgia
96	Peru
95	Tanzania
94	Brunei
92	Netherlands
90	Italy
89	Gibraltar
88	Indonesia
87	Syria
86	Ireland
85	Panama
84	Belgium
82	Qatar
81	Bahrain
80	Costa Rica
78	Germany
77	France
72	Guatemala
71	El Salvador
70	Luxembourg
69	Sweden
68	Uruguay
67	United Arab Emirates
66	Singapore
63	Belize
62	Kuwait
60	Austria
59	United Kingdom
58	Oman
57	Jordan
56	Trinidad and Tobago
53	Mexico
52	Monaco
51	Nigeria
49	Ukraine
48	Venezuela
46	Puerto Rico
42	Palau
41	Dominican Republic
40	China
39	Finland
38	Côte d'ivoire
37	Argentina
36	Netherlands Antilles
34	Libya
33	St Lucia
32	Taiwan
31	Denmark
30	Lebanon
28	Cuba
27	Antigua and Barbuda
26	British Virgin Islands
25	Sudan
24	Martinique
23	Israel
22	South Korea
21	Hong Kong
20	Switzerland
19	Bahamas
18	Barbados
17	Seychelles
16	New Caledonia
15	French Guiana
14	Iceland
13	Zimbabwe
12	Guam
11	Norway
10	French Polynesia
9	Russia
7	Angola
6	Cayman Islands
5	Uzbekistan
4	Bermuda
2	Japan

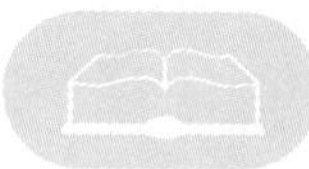

ECA International Expatriate Accommodation Cost Ranking 2001

Accommodation costs are one of the largest expenditures a company may face when sending an expatriate abroad. When costing an assignment, accommodation accounts for as much as 26% of expenditure and in some cases, the cost of accommodation may exceed the expatriate's salary.

Highest Monthly Rent

City	Country	Monthly rent ($) 2001
Hong Kong	Hong Kong	7,627
Tokyo	Japan	7,601
New York	USA	5,653
Seoul	South Korea	4,756
Moscow	Russia	4,346
London	UK	4,296
Beijing	China	4,081
Shanghai	China	3,993
Singapore	Singapore	3,522
Mumbai	India	3,323

Lowest Monthly Rent

City	Country	Monthly rent ($) 2001
Karachi	Pakistan	487
Nairobi	Kenya	843
Doha	Qatar	911
Muscat	Oman	940
Johannesburg	South Africa	951
Montreal	Canada	1,036
Melbourne	Australia	1,175
Helsinki	Finland	1,225
Frankfurt	Germany	1,225
Hamburg	Germany	1,254

The Economist Big Mac Index, December 2001

'Burgernomics' is based on the theory of purchasing-power parity (PPP), the notion that a dollar should buy the same amount in all countries. Thus in the long run, the exchange rate between two countries should move towards the rate that equalises the prices of an identical basket of goods and services in each country. Our 'basket' is a McDonald's Big Mac, which is produced in about 120 countries. The Big Mac PPP is the exchange rate that would mean hamburgers cost the same in the US as abroad. Comparing actual exchange rates with PPPs indicates whether a currency is under- or overvalued.

	Big Mac price ($)	Local currency valuation against $
United Kingdom	2.89	11.6
Peru	2.89	11.6
Israel	2.82	8.9
United States	2.59	0.0
Argentina	2.50	-3.5
Euro area	2.42	-6.6
Mexico	2.42	-6.6
South Korea	2.41	-6.9
Saudi Arabia	2.40	-7.3
Colombia	2.33	-10.0
Japan	2.31	-10.8
Turkey	2.04	-21.2
Taiwan	2.03	-21.6
Chile	2.01	-22.4
Singapore	1.80	-30.5
Hungary	1.68	-35.1
Czech Republic	1.55	-40.2
Indonesia	1.55	-40.2
Brazil	1.51	-41.7
Poland	1.47	-43.2
Hong Kong	1.44	-44.4
Thailand	1.26	-51.4
Russia	1.25	-51.7
China	1.21	-53.3
Malaysia	1.19	-54.1
Philippines	1.13	-56.4
South Africa	0.82	-68.3

INVESTMENT

$801bn
CANADA
$16,635bn
UNITED STATES OF AMERICA
MEXICO
GUATEMALA
EL SALVADOR
JAMAICA
1,486%
DOMINICAN REPUBLIC
522%
TRINIDAD & TOBAGO
COSTA RICA
PANAMA
575%
COLOMBIA
VENEZUELA
ECUADOR
1,201%
PERU
$226bn 1,283%
BRAZIL
BOLIVIA
CHILE
PARAGUAY
URUGUAY
$166bn
ARGENTINA
4,982 %

NETHERLANDS
480%
NORWAY
$373bn
SWEDEN
$349bn
FINLAND
1,438%
$2,933bn
UNITED KINGDOM
IRELAND
$695bn
DENMARK
ESTONIA
LATVIA
LITHUANIA
BELARUS
$185bn
BELGIUM
FRANCE
GERMANY
$1,432bn
21,622%
POLAND
CZECH REPUBLIC
SLOVAKIA
HUNGARY
UKRAINE
AUSTRIA
SLOVENIA
CROATIA
ROMANIA
SWITZ.
$1,475bn
2,280%
623%
PORTUGAL
SPAIN
$432bn
$693bn
ITALY
$728bn
BULGARIA
GREECE
628%
TUNISIA
TURKEY
SYRIA
LEB
ISRAEL
JOR
MOROCCO
1,028%
1,828%
ALGERIA
1,528%
EGYPT
SUDAN
NIGERIA
CÔTE D'IVOIRE
GHANA
CAMEROON
GABON
UGANDA
TANZANIA
ANGOLA
ZAMBIA
ZIMBABWE
NAMIBIA
BOTSWANA
MOZAMBIQUE
SOUTH AFRICA
$205bn

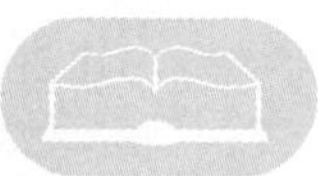

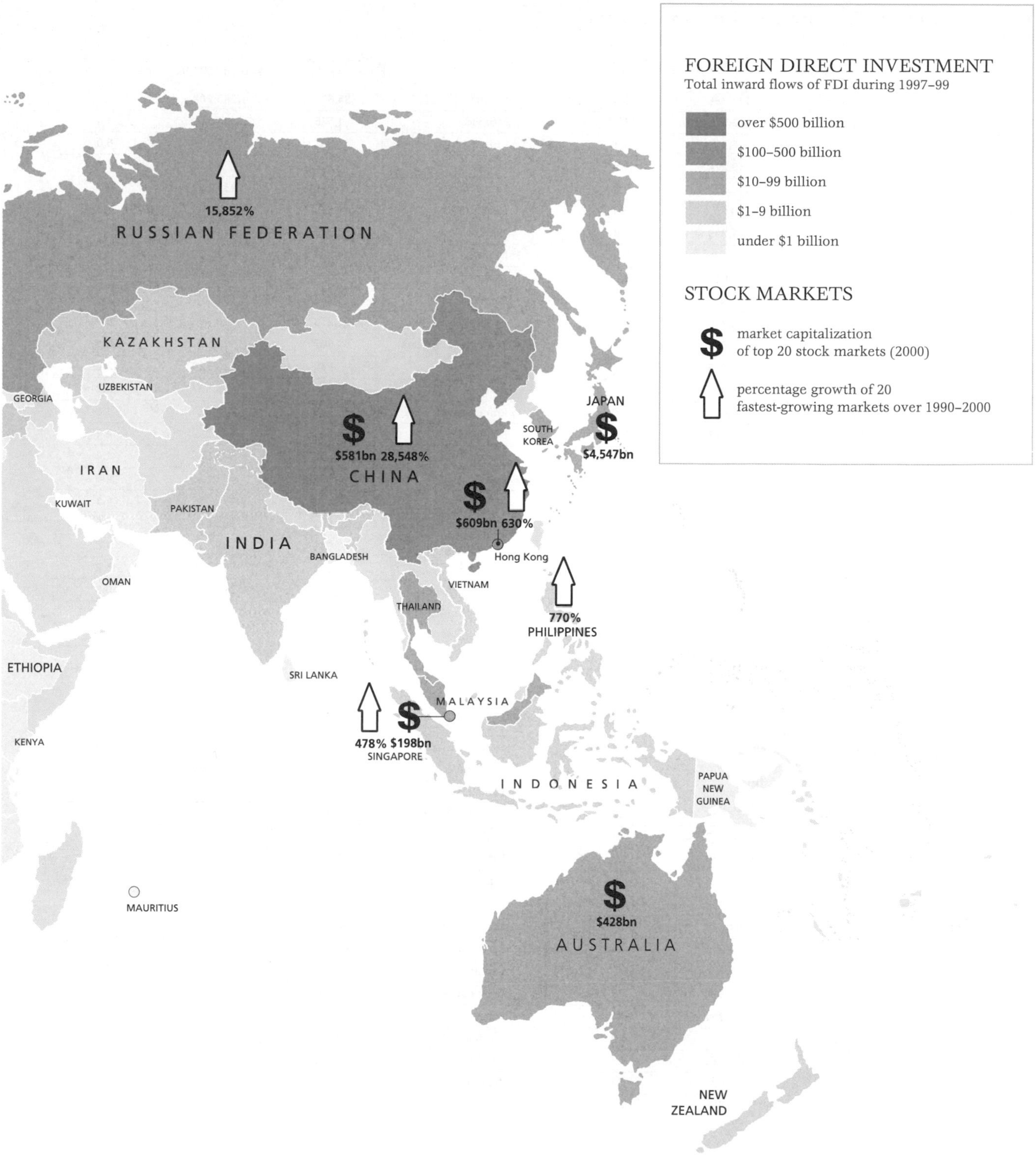

FOREIGN DIRECT INVESTMENT

Total inward flows of FDI during 1997–99

- over $500 billion
- $100–500 billion
- $10–99 billion
- $1–9 billion
- under $1 billion

STOCK MARKETS

- $ market capitalization of top 20 stock markets (2000)
- percentage growth of 20 fastest-growing markets over 1990–2000

15,852%
RUSSIAN FEDERATION
KAZAKHSTAN
UZBEKISTAN
GEORGIA
$581bn 28,548%
CHINA
SOUTH KOREA
JAPAN
$4,547bn
IRAN
KUWAIT
PAKISTAN
$609bn 630%
Hong Kong
INDIA
BANGLADESH
OMAN
VIETNAM
THAILAND
770%
PHILIPPINES
ETHIOPIA
SRI LANKA
MALAYSIA
478% $198bn
SINGAPORE
KENYA
INDONESIA
PAPUA NEW GUINEA
MAURITIUS
$428bn
AUSTRALIA
NEW ZEALAND

Total Inward Flows of Foreign Direct Investment 1997–99

	Total inward flows of FDI ($ million) 1997–99	Total GDP ($ million) 1997–99	Inward flows of FDI (% GDP) 1997–99
Algeria	19	142,291	0.0
Angola	3,181	23,679	13.4
Argentina	36,724	906,309	4.1
Australia	20,966	1,159,274	1.8
Austria	11,334	626,263	1.8
Bangladesh	622	130,082	0.5
Belarus	574	71,999	0.8
Bolivia	2,489	24,886	10.0
Botswana	232	15,942	1.5
Brazil	84,224	2,350,095	3.6
Bulgaria	1,705	34,746	4.9
Cameroon	135	27,003	0.5
Canada	48,775	1,823,265	2.7
Chile	19,276	223,289	8.6
China	126,740	2,850,476	4.5
Colombia	10,129	285,246	3.6
Costa Rica	1,285	35,148	3.7
Côte d'Ivoire	1,112	32,462	3.4
Croatia	2,669	61,259	4.4
Czech Republic	8,933	161,525	5.5
Denmark	17,647	519,187	3.4
Dominican Republic	2,434	48,290	5.0
Ecuador	2,098	57,119	3.7
Egypt	3,032	247,463	1.2
El Salvador	254	35,601	0.7
Estonia	1,152	15,117	7.6
Ethiopia	99	19,364	0.5
Finland	18,911	372,997	5.1
France	89,871	4,251,791	2.1
Gabon	50	15,023	0.3
Georgia	182	13,110	1.4
Germany	70,600	6,338,465	1.1
Ghana	203	22,159	0.9
Greece	1,968	368,758	0.5
Guatemala	918	54,929	1.7
Hungary	5,965	141,968	4.2
India	8,155	1,258,882	0.7
Indonesia	1,576	451,662	0.4
Iran	159	313,910	0.1
Ireland	24,738	250,389	9.9
Israel	6,919	299,446	2.3
Italy	13,118	3,488,396	0.4
Jamaica	1,030	17,442	5.9
Japan	18,776	12,320,119	0.2
Jordan	490	22,481	2.2
Kazakhstan	4,066	59,986	6.8
Kenya	45	32,457	0.1
Kuwait	147	85,116	0.2
Latvia	1,226	18,183	6.7
Lebanon	600	49,420	1.2
Lithuania	1,768	30,955	5.7
Malaysia	11,659	250,001	4.7
Mauritius	114	12,841	0.9
Mexico	34,501	1,280,208	2.7
Morocco	1,525	104,058	1.5
Mozambique	632	10,603	6.0
Namibia	187	9,872	1.9
Netherlands	76,225	1,135,789	6.7
New Zealand	1,678	172,068	1.0
Nigeria	3,595	116,254	3.1
Norway	10,739	452,198	2.4
Oman	256	42,026	0.6
Pakistan	1,743	183,190	1.0
Panama	2,258	26,945	8.4
Papua New Guinea	607	11,971	5.1
Paraguay	578	26,529	2.2
Peru	5,929	178,527	3.3
Philippines	3,508	223,823	1.6
Poland	18,543	449,399	4.1
Portugal	4,608	322,546	1.4
Romania	4,287	107,028	4.0
Russia	12,314	1,125,035	1.1
Singapore	22,833	265,643	8.6
Slovakia	1,081	59,535	1.8
Slovenia	667	57,736	1.2
South Africa	3,651	393,682	0.9
South Korea	17,592	1,170,231	1.5
Spain	26,269	1,681,191	1.6
Sri Lanka	800	46,758	1.7
Sudan	742	30,308	2.5
Sweden	88,666	692,813	12.8
Switzerland	15,432	777,445	2.0
Syria	251	54,691	0.5
Tanzania	513	23,696	2.2
Thailand	16,899	389,605	4.3
Trinidad and Tobago	1,703	19,143	8.9
Tunisia	1,316	59,837	2.2
Turkey	2,528	574,413	0.4
Uganda	602	19,768	3.1
Ukraine	1,862	131,945	1.4
United Kingdom	190,374	4,085,472	4.7
United States	562,356	25,216,531	2.2
Uruguay	553	61,354	0.9
Uzbekistan	598	63,136	1.0
Venezuela	12,709	284,725	4.5
Vietnam	4,609	80,714	5.7
Zambia	305	10,367	2.9
Zimbabwe	205	20,852	1.0

Largest Inward Flows of FDI 1997–99

	Total inward flows of FDI ($ million) 1997–99
United States	562,356
United Kingdom	190,374
China	126,740
France	89,871
Sweden	88,666
Brazil	84,224
Netherlands	76,225
Germany	70,600
Canada	48,775
Argentina	36,724
Mexico	34,501
Spain	26,269
Ireland	24,738
Singapore	22,833
Australia	20,966
Chile	19,276
Finland	18,911
Japan	18,776
Poland	18,543
Denmark	17,647
South Korea	17,592
Thailand	16,899
Switzerland	15,432
Italy	13,118
Venezuela	12,709
Russia	12,314
Malaysia	11,659
Austria	11,334
Norway	10,739
Colombia	10,129
Czech Republic	8,933
India	8,155
Israel	6,919
Hungary	5,965
Peru	5,929
Vietnam	4,609
Portugal	4,608
Romania	4,287
Kazakhstan	4,066
South Africa	3,651
Nigeria	3,595
Philippines	3,508
Angola	3,181
Egypt	3,032
Croatia	2,669
Turkey	2,528
Bolivia	2,489
Dominican Republic	2,434
Panama	2,258
Ecuador	2,098
Greece	1,968
Ukraine	1,862
Lithuania	1,768
Pakistan	1,743
Bulgaria	1,705
Trinidad and Tobago	1,703
New Zealand	1,678
Indonesia	1,576
Morocco	1,525
Tunisia	1,316
Costa Rica	1,285
Latvia	1,226
Estonia	1,152
Côte d'Ivoire	1,112
Slovakia	1,081
Jamaica	1,030
Guatemala	918
Sri Lanka	800
Sudan	742
Slovenia	667
Mozambique	632
Bangladesh	622
Papua New Guinea	607
Uganda	602
Lebanon	600
Uzbekistan	598
Paraguay	578
Belarus	574
Uruguay	553
Tanzania	513
Jordan	490
Zambia	305
Oman	256
El Salvador	254
Syria	251
Botswana	232
Zimbabwe	205
Ghana	203
Namibia	187
Georgia	182
Iran	159
Kuwait	147
Cameroon	135
Mauritius	114
Ethiopia	99
Gabon	50
Kenya	45
Algeria	19

Largest Inward Flows of FDI 1997–99 as a Share of GDP

	Inward flows of FDI (% GDP) 1997–99
Angola	13.4
Sweden	12.8
Bolivia	10.0
Ireland	9.9
Trinidad and Tobago	8.9
Chile	8.6
Singapore	8.6
Panama	8.4
Estonia	7.6
Kazakhstan	6.8
Latvia	6.7
Netherlands	6.7
Mozambique	6.0
Jamaica	5.9
Lithuania	5.7
Vietnam	5.7
Czech Republic	5.5
Papua New Guinea	5.1
Finland	5.1
Dominican Republic	5.0
Bulgaria	4.9
Malaysia	4.7
United Kingdom	4.7
Venezuela	4.5
China	4.5
Croatia	4.4
Thailand	4.3
Hungary	4.2
Poland	4.1
Argentina	4.1
Romania	4.0
Ecuador	3.7
Costa Rica	3.7
Brazil	3.6
Colombia	3.6
Côte d'Ivoire	3.4
Denmark	3.4
Peru	3.3
Nigeria	3.1
Uganda	3.1
Zambia	2.9
Mexico	2.7
Canada	2.7
Sudan	2.5
Norway	2.4
Israel	2.3
United States	2.2
Tunisia	2.2
Jordan	2.2
Paraguay	2.2
Tanzania	2.2
France	2.1
Switzerland	2.0
Namibia	1.9
Slovakia	1.8
Austria	1.8
Australia	1.8
Sri Lanka	1.7
Guatemala	1.7
Philippines	1.6
Spain	1.6
South Korea	1.5
Morocco	1.5
Botswana	1.5
Portugal	1.4
Ukraine	1.4
Georgia	1.4
Egypt	1.2
Lebanon	1.2
Slovenia	1.2
Germany	1.1
Russia	1.1
Zimbabwe	1.0
New Zealand	1.0
Pakistan	1.0
Uzbekistan	1.0
South Africa	0.9
Ghana	0.9
Uruguay	0.9
Mauritius	0.9
Belarus	0.8
El Salvador	0.7
India	0.7
Oman	0.6
Greece	0.5
Ethiopia	0.5
Cameroon	0.5
Bangladesh	0.5
Syria	0.5
Turkey	0.4
Italy	0.4
Indonesia	0.4
Gabon	0.3
Kuwait	0.2
Japan	0.2
Kenya	0.1
Iran	0.1
Algeria	0.0

Market Capitalization of Stock Markets 1990 and 2000

	Market capitalization ($ million) 1990	Market capitalization ($ million) 2000	Growth in market capitalization (%) 1990–2000
Argentina	3,268	166,068	4,982
Australia	108,879	427,683	293
Austria	11,476	33,025	188
Bangladesh	321	1,186	269
Belgium	65,449	184,942	183
Bolivia	–	116	–
Botswana	261	978	275
Brazil	16,354	226,152	1,283
Bulgaria	–	617	–
Canada	241,920	800,914	231
Chile	13,645	60,401	343
China	2,028	580,991	28,548
Colombia	1,416	9,560	575
Costa Rica	475	2,303	385
Côte d'Ivoire	549	1,185	116
Croatia	–	2,742	–
Czech Republic	–	11,002	–
Denmark	39,063	105,293	170
Dominican Republic	–	141	–
Ecuador	69	704	920
Egypt	1,765	28,741	1,528
El Salvador	–	2,141	–
Estonia	–	1,846	–
Finland	22,721	349,409	1,438
France	314,384	1,475,457	369
Germany	355,073	1,432,190	303
Ghana	76	502	561
Greece	15,228	110,839	628
Guatemala	–	215	–
Hong Kong	83,397	609,090	630
Hungary	505	12,021	2,280
India	38,567	148,064	284
Indonesia	8,081	26,834	232
Iran	34,282	21,830	–36
Ireland	–	42,458	–
Israel	3,324	64,081	1,828
Italy	148,766	728,273	390
Jamaica	911	3,582	293
Japan	2,917,679	4,546,937	56
Jordan	2,001	4,943	147
Kazakhstan	–	2,260	–
Kenya	453	1,283	183
Kuwait	–	18,814	–
Latvia	–	563	–
Lebanon	–	1,583	–
Lithuania	–	1,588	–
Malaysia	48,611	116,935	141
Mauritius	268	1,331	397
Mexico	32,725	125,204	283
Morocco	966	10,899	1,028
Namibia	21	311	1,381
Netherlands	119,825	695,209	480
New Zealand	8,835	28,352	221
Nigeria	1,372	4,237	209
Norway	26,130	63,696	144
Oman	1,061	3,463	226
Pakistan	2,850	6,581	131
Panama	226	3,584	1,486
Paraguay	–	423	–
Peru	812	10,562	1,201
Philippines	5,927	51,554	770
Poland	144	31,279	21,622
Portugal	9,201	66,488	623
Romania	–	1,069	–
Russia	244	38,922	15,852
Saudi Arabia	48,213	67,171	39
Singapore	34,308	198,407	478
Slovakia	–	742	–
Slovenia	–	2,547	–
South Africa	137,540	204,952	49
South Korea	110,594	148,649	34
Spain	111,404	431,668	287
Sri Lanka	917	1,074	17
Sweden	97,929	373,278	281
Switzerland	160,044	693,127	333
Tanzania	–	181	–
Thailand	23,896	29,489	23
Trinidad and Tobago	696	4,330	522
Tunisia	533	2,828	431
Turkey	19,065	69,659	265
Ukraine	–	1,881	–
United Arab Emirates	–	28,211	–
United Kingdom	848,866	2,933,280	246
United States	3,059,434	16,635,114	444
Uruguay	–	168	–
Uzbekistan	–	119	–
Venezuela	8,361	8,128	–3
Yugoslavia	–	10,817	–
Zambia	–	291	–
Zimbabwe	2,395	2,432	2

Source: Standard & Poor's

Largest Market Capitalization in 2000

	Market capitalization ($ million) 2000
United States	16,635,114
Japan	4,546,937
United Kingdom	2,933,280
France	1,475,457
Germany	1,432,190
Canada	800,914
Italy	728,273
Netherlands	695,209
Switzerland	693,127
Hong Kong	609,090
China	580,991
Spain	431,668
Australia	427,683
Sweden	373,278
Finland	349,409
Brazil	226,152
South Africa	204,952
Singapore	198,407
Belgium	184,942
Argentina	166,068
South Korea	148,649
India	148,064
Mexico	125,204
Malaysia	116,935
Greece	110,839
Denmark	105,293
Turkey	69,659
Saudi Arabia	67,171
Portugal	66,488
Israel	64,081
Norway	63,696
Chile	60,401
Philippines	51,554
Ireland	42,458
Russia	38,922
Austria	33,025
Poland	31,279
Thailand	29,489
Egypt	28,741
New Zealand	28,352
United Arab Emirates	28,211
Indonesia	26,834
Iran	21,830
Kuwait	18,814
Hungary	12,021
Czech Republic	11,002
Morocco	10,899
Yugoslavia	10,817
Peru	10,562
Colombia	9,560
Venezuela	8,128
Pakistan	6,581
Jordan	4,943
Trinidad and Tobago	4,330
Nigeria	4,237
Panama	3,584
Jamaica	3,582
Oman	3,463
Tunisia	2,828
Croatia	2,742
Slovenia	2,547
Zimbabwe	2,432
Costa Rica	2,303
Kazakhstan	2,260
El Salvador	2,141
Ukraine	1,881
Estonia	1,846
Lithuania	1,588
Lebanon	1,583
Mauritius	1,331
Kenya	1,283
Bangladesh	1,186
Côte d'Ivoire	1,185
Sri Lanka	1,074
Romania	1,069
Botswana	978
Slovakia	742
Ecuador	704
Bulgaria	617
Latvia	563
Ghana	502
Paraguay	423
Namibia	311
Zambia	291
Guatemala	215
Tanzania	181
Uruguay	168
Dominican Republic	141
Uzbekistan	119
Bolivia	116

Fastest Stock Market Growth 1990–2000

	Growth in market capitalization (%) 1990–2000
China	28,548
Poland	21,622
Russia	15,852
Argentina	4,982
Hungary	2,280
Israel	1,828
Egypt	1,528
Panama	1,486
Finland	1,438
Namibia	1,381
Brazil	1,283
Peru	1,201
Morocco	1,028
Ecuador	920
Philippines	770
Hong Kong	630
Greece	628
Portugal	623
Colombia	575
Ghana	561
Trinidad and Tobago	522
Netherlands	480
Singapore	478
United States	444
Tunisia	431
Mauritius	397
Italy	390
Costa Rica	385
France	369
Chile	343
Switzerland	333
Germany	303
Jamaica	293
Australia	293
Spain	287
India	284
Mexico	283
Sweden	281
Botswana	275
Bangladesh	269
Turkey	265
United Kingdom	246
Indonesia	232
Canada	231
Oman	226
New Zealand	221
Nigeria	209
Austria	188
Kenya	183
Belgium	183
Denmark	170
Jordan	147
Norway	144
Malaysia	141
Pakistan	131
Côte d'Ivoire	116
Japan	56
South Africa	49
Saudi Arabia	39
South Korea	34
Thailand	23
Sri Lanka	17
Zimbabwe	2
Venezuela	–3
Iran	–36

COMMUNICATIONS

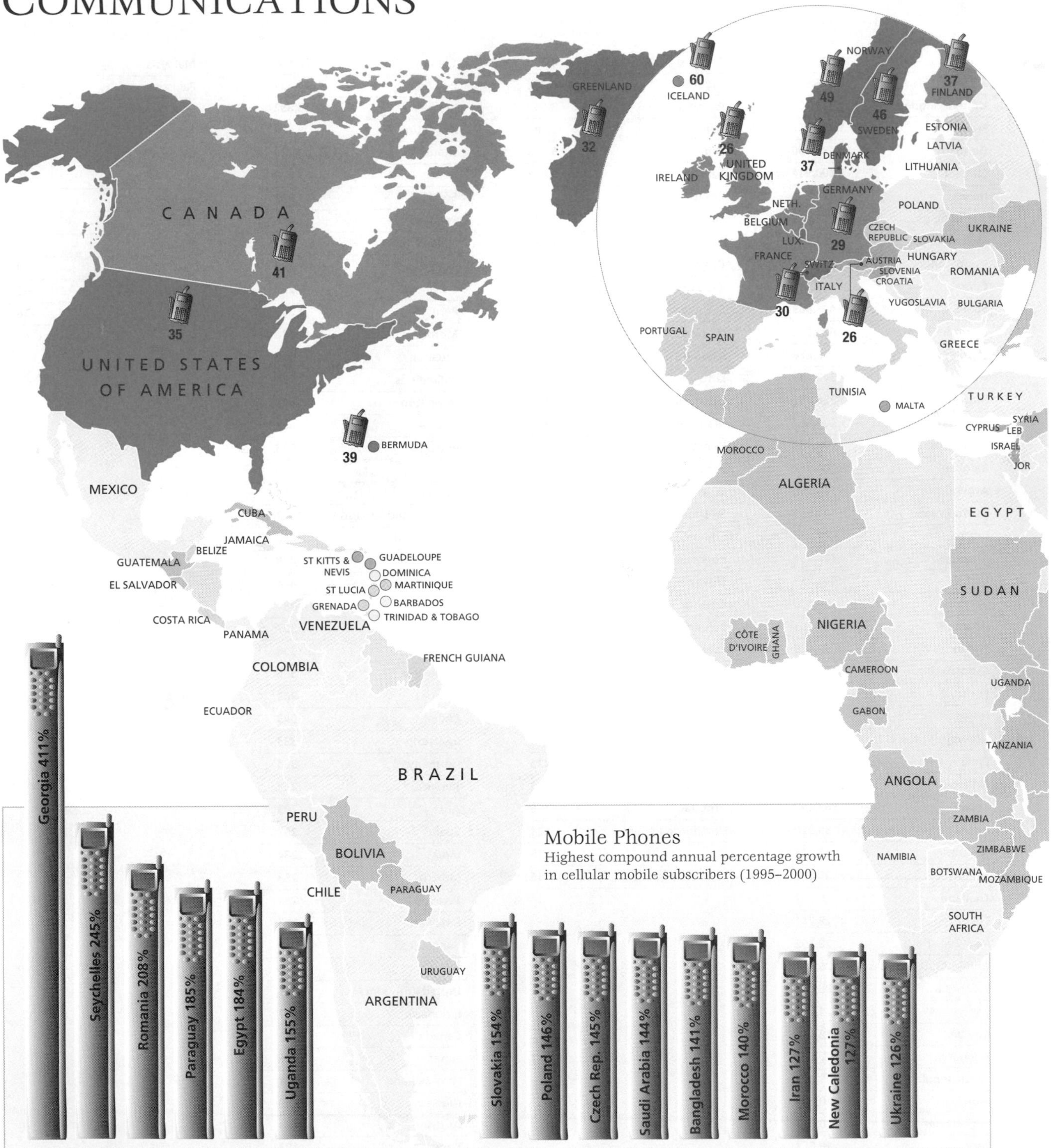

Mobile Phones

Highest compound annual percentage growth in cellular mobile subscribers (1995–2000)

- Georgia 411%
- Seychelles 245%
- Romania 208%
- Paraguay 185%
- Egypt 184%
- Uganda 155%
- Slovakia 154%
- Poland 146%
- Czech Rep. 145%
- Saudi Arabia 144%
- Bangladesh 141%
- Morocco 140%
- Iran 127%
- New Caledonia 127%
- Ukraine 126%

 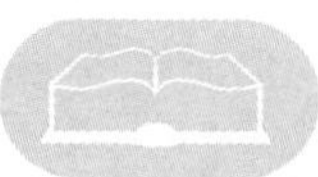    

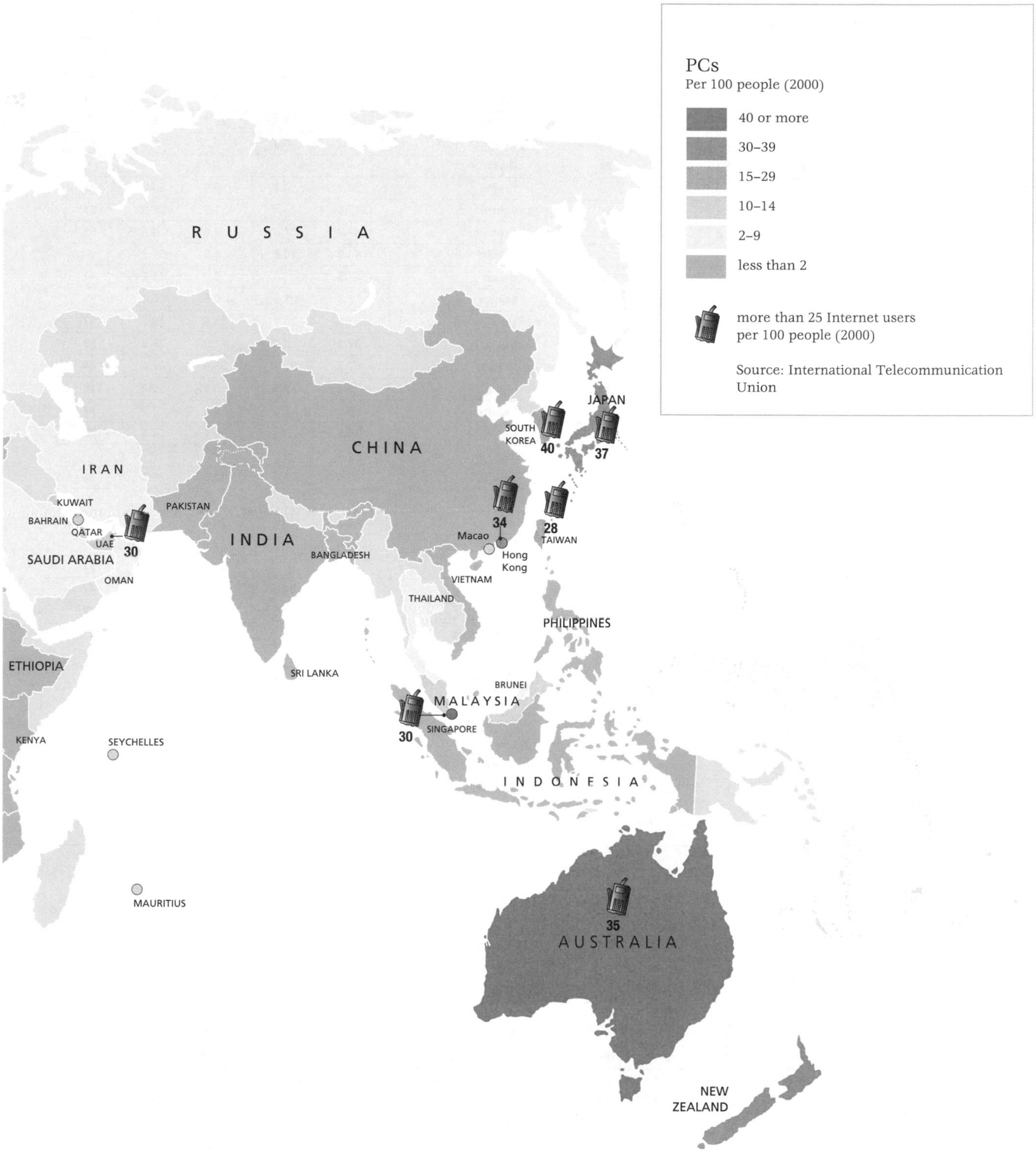

PCs
Per 100 people (2000)

- 40 or more
- 30–39
- 15–29
- 10–14
- 2–9
- less than 2

more than 25 Internet users per 100 people (2000)

Source: International Telecommunication Union

RUSSIA
CHINA
JAPAN
SOUTH KOREA
40
37
IRAN
KUWAIT
BAHRAIN
QATAR
UAE
30
SAUDI ARABIA
OMAN
PAKISTAN
INDIA
BANGLADESH
34
Macao
Hong Kong
28
TAIWAN
VIETNAM
THAILAND
PHILIPPINES
ETHIOPIA
SRI LANKA
BRUNEI
MALAYSIA
SINGAPORE
30
KENYA
SEYCHELLES
INDONESIA
MAURITIUS
35
AUSTRALIA
NEW ZEALAND

Information and Communications Technology

	Main telephone lines (per 100 people) 2000	PCs (per 100 people) 2000	Internet users (per 100 people) 2000	Cellular mobile subscribers (per 100 people) 2000	Growth in mobile subscribers (% p.a.) 1995–2000
Algeria	5.7	0.7	0.2	0.3	79
American Samoa	–	–	–	–	–
Andorra	43.9	–	6.7	30.2	53
Angola	0.5	0.1	0.2	0.2	67
Antigua and Barbuda	50.0	–	6.5	28.7	–
Argentina	21.3	5.1	6.8	16.3	78
Aruba	37.2	–	4.1	14.6	54
Australia	52.4	46.5	35.0	44.6	31
Austria	47.4	27.7	25.6	78.6	76
Bahamas	37.6	–	4.3	10.4	50
Bahrain	25.0	14.0	5.8	30.1	49
Bangladesh	0.3	0.1	0.0	0.2	141
Barbados	43.7	7.8	2.2	11.1	60
Belarus	26.9	–	1.8	0.5	53
Belgium	49.9	34.5	19.7	54.9	88
Belize	15.0	10.6	6.2	3.0	36
Bermuda	87.0	43.7	39.0	19.6	26
Bolivia	6.1	1.2	1.4	7.0	125
Botswana	9.3	3.7	0.9	12.3	–
Brazil	18.2	4.4	2.9	13.6	78
British Virgin Islands	–	–	–	–	–
Brunei	24.5	7.0	9.1	28.9	22
Bulgaria	35.0	2.7	5.2	9.0	104
Cameroon	0.6	0.3	0.1	1.0	121
Canada	67.7	39.0	41.3	28.5	28
Cayman Islands	–	–	–	–	–
Channel Islands	–	–	–	–	–
Chile	22.1	8.6	11.6	22.4	77
China	11.1	1.6	1.7	6.6	88
Colombia	16.9	3.4	2.1	5.3	52
Costa Rica	24.9	10.2	6.2	5.2	62
Côte d'Ivoire	1.8	0.6	0.3	3.0	–
Croatia	36.5	8.1	4.5	23.1	98
Cuba	4.4	1.0	0.5	0.1	28
Cyprus	64.7	19.3	17.7	32.1	38
Czech Republic	37.8	12.2	9.8	42.4	145
Denmark	75.3	43.2	36.6	61.0	32
Dominica	29.4	6.5	2.6	0.9	–
Dominican Republic	10.5	–	0.6	8.3	66
Ecuador	10.0	2.0	1.4	3.8	55
Egypt	8.6	2.2	0.7	2.1	184
El Salvador	9.1	1.6	0.7	11.3	121
Estonia	36.3	13.5	25.5	38.7	79
Ethiopia	0.4	0.1	0.0	0.0	–
Faeroe Islands	55.5	–	6.7	37.7	46
Finland	54.7	39.6	37.2	72.6	29
France	58.0	30.5	14.5	49.4	86
French Guiana	28.3	13.2	1.2	22.0	–
French Polynesia	22.1	–	2.2	9.5	109
Gabon	3.2	0.8	1.2	9.8	97
Georgia	12.3	–	0.4	1.9	411
Germany	60.1	33.6	29.2	58.6	67
Ghana	1.2	0.3	0.2	0.6	84
Gibraltar	–	–	–	–	–
Greece	53.2	7.1	9.4	55.9	85
Greenland	46.8	–	31.9	28.5	51
Grenada	33.2	11.8	4.4	4.6	61
Guadeloupe	44.9	18.9	1.8	37.3	–
Guam	47.8	–	3.0	16.2	41
Guatemala	5.7	1.0	0.6	6.1	88
Hong Kong	57.8	34.7	33.6	80.2	47
Hungary	37.1	8.5	7.0	29.3	63
Iceland	67.7	39.2	59.8	67.0	44
India	3.2	0.5	0.5	0.4	116
Indonesia	3.1	1.0	0.9	1.7	77
Iran	14.9	5.6	0.4	1.5	127
Iraq	2.9	–	–	–	–
Ireland	42.6	36.5	21.0	66.8	74
Isle of Man	–	–	–	–	–
Israel	48.2	25.4	20.3	70.2	58
Italy	47.4	13.9	23.0	73.7	61
Jamaica	19.9	4.3	2.3	14.2	52
Japan	58.5	31.5	37.1	52.6	42
Jordan	9.3	2.3	1.9	5.8	99
Kazakhstan	10.8	–	0.4	0.3	81
Kenya	1.1	0.5	0.7	0.4	124
Kuwait	24.4	12.1	7.8	24.9	32
Latvia	31.2	8.2	6.3	16.9	93
Lebanon	19.5	4.6	8.6	21.3	44
Libya	10.8	–	0.2	0.7	–
Liechtenstein	–	–	–	–	–
Lithuania	32.1	6.0	6.1	14.2	104
Luxembourg	76.0	45.9	23.0	87.2	70
Macao	–	13.7	13.6	–	27
Malaysia	19.9	10.3	15.9	21.3	38
Malta	52.5	20.6	10.3	29.4	60
Martinique	43.4	11.5	1.3	41.0	–
Mauritius	23.5	10.1	7.3	15.1	73
Mexico	12.5	5.1	2.7	14.2	83
Monaco	–	–	–	–	–
Morocco	5.0	1.2	0.4	8.3	140
Mozambique	0.4	0.3	0.2	0.1	–
Namibia	5.9	3.4	1.7	4.7	88
Netherlands	61.9	39.5	23.8	67.1	82
Netherlands Antilles	37.2	–	0.9	7.5	11
New Caledonia	23.7	–	11.2	23.2	127
New Zealand	50.0	36.0	21.7	56.3	43
Nigeria	0.4	0.7	0.2	0.0	18
North Korea	4.6	–	–	–	–
Northern Marianas	50.6	–	–	5.6	25
Norway	72.9	49.1	49.1	70.3	26
Oman	8.9	2.6	3.6	6.5	83
Pakistan	2.3	0.4	0.1	0.3	54

	Main telephone lines (per 100 people) 2000	PCs (per 100 people) 2000	Internet users (per 100 people) 2000	Cellular mobile subscribers (per 100 people) 2000	Growth in mobile subscribers (% p.a.) 1995–2000
Palau	–	–	–	–	–
Panama	16.4	3.2	1.6	8.3	–
Papua New Guinea	1.4	–	2.8	0.2	–
Paraguay	5.0	1.1	0.4	19.6	185
Peru	6.4	3.6	9.7	4.8	75
Philippines	4.0	1.9	2.6	8.4	67
Poland	28.2	6.9	7.2	17.4	146
Portugal	43.1	10.5	25.0	66.5	81
Puerto Rico	33.2	–	5.1	23.7	26
Qatar	26.8	13.6	5.0	20.0	45
Reunion	38.9	–	–	39.5	119
Romania	17.5	3.2	3.6	11.2	208
Russia	21.8	4.3	2.1	2.2	106
St Kitts and Nevis	56.9	15.5	5.2	1.8	–
St Lucia	31.4	13.7	2.0	1.3	24
Saudi Arabia	13.7	5.7	0.9	6.4	144
Seychelles	25.4	13.5	7.4	30.1	245
Singapore	48.5	48.3	29.9	68.4	55
Slovakia	31.4	10.9	12.0	23.9	154
Slovenia	37.8	27.6	15.1	54.7	109
South Africa	11.4	6.2	5.5	19.0	73
South Korea	46.4	19.0	40.3	56.7	75
Spain	42.1	14.3	13.3	60.9	92
Sri Lanka	4.1	0.6	0.6	2.4	55
Sudan	1.2	0.3	0.1	0.1	–
Sweden	68.2	50.7	45.6	71.4	26
Switzerland	72.0	50.3	29.8	64.5	60
Syria	10.4	1.4	0.2	0.2	–
Taiwan	56.8	22.5	28.1	80.3	88
Tanzania	0.5	0.3	0.3	0.5	120
Thailand	8.7	2.4	3.8	5.0	19
Trinidad and Tobago	23.1	5.4	7.7	10.3	84
Tunisia	9.0	2.3	1.0	0.6	104
Turkey	28.0	3.8	3.0	24.6	106
Turks and Caicos Islands	–	–	–	–	–
Uganda	0.3	0.3	0.2	0.9	155
Ukraine	19.9	1.6	0.4	1.6	126
United Arab Emirates	41.8	12.5	30.1	58.5	62
United Kingdom	58.9	33.8	25.8	72.7	50
United States	70.0	58.5	34.7	39.8	27
Uruguay	27.8	10.0	11.1	13.2	62
US Virgin Islands	57.0	–	10.0	21.1	–
Uzbekistan	6.6	–	0.0	0.2	70
Venezuela	10.8	4.6	3.9	21.8	67
Vietnam	3.2	0.9	0.3	1.0	102
Yugoslavia	22.6	2.1	3.8	12.3	–
Zambia	0.9	0.7	0.2	0.5	100
Zimbabwe	1.9	1.3	0.2	2.5	–

Source: International Telecommunication Union

Highest Density of Landlines

	Main telephone lines (per 100 people) 2000	Cellular mobile subscribers (per 100 people) 2000	Growth in mobile subscribers (% p.a.) 1995–2000
Bermuda	87.0	19.6	26
Luxembourg	76.0	87.2	70
Denmark	75.3	61.0	32
Norway	72.9	70.3	26
Switzerland	72.0	64.5	60
United States	70.0	39.8	27
Sweden	68.2	71.4	26
Iceland	67.7	67.0	44
Canada	67.7	28.5	28
Cyprus	64.7	32.1	38
Netherlands	61.9	67.1	82
Germany	60.1	58.6	67
United Kingdom	58.9	72.7	50
Japan	58.5	52.6	42
France	58.0	49.4	86
Hong Kong	57.8	80.2	47
US Virgin Islands	57.0	21.1	–
St Kitts and Nevis	56.9	1.8	–
Taiwan	56.8	80.3	88
Faeroe Islands	55.5	37.7	46
Finland	54.7	72.6	29
Greece	53.2	55.9	85
Malta	52.5	29.4	60
Australia	52.4	44.6	31
Northern Marianas	50.6	5.6	25
New Zealand	50.0	56.3	43
Antigua and Barbuda	50.0	28.7	–
Belgium	49.9	54.9	88
Singapore	48.5	68.4	55
Israel	48.2	70.2	58
Guam	47.8	16.2	41
Italy	47.4	73.7	61
Austria	47.4	78.6	76
Greenland	46.8	28.5	51
South Korea	46.4	56.7	75
Guadeloupe	44.9	37.3	–
Andorra	43.9	30.2	53
Barbados	43.7	11.1	60
Martinique	43.4	41.0	–
Portugal	43.1	66.5	81
Ireland	42.6	66.8	74
Spain	42.1	60.9	92
United Arab Emirates	41.8	58.5	62
Reunion	38.9	39.5	119
Slovenia	37.8	54.7	109
Czech Republic	37.8	42.4	145
Bahamas	37.6	10.4	50
Aruba	37.2	14.6	54
Netherlands Antilles	37.2	7.5	11
Hungary	37.1	29.3	63
Croatia	36.5	23.1	98
Estonia	36.3	38.7	79
Bulgaria	35.0	9.0	104
Grenada	33.2	4.6	61
Puerto Rico	33.2	23.7	26
Lithuania	32.1	14.2	104
Slovakia	31.4	23.9	154
St Lucia	31.4	1.3	24
Latvia	31.2	16.9	93
Dominica	29.4	0.9	–

Highest Density of PCs

	PCs (per 100 people) 2000
United States	58.5
Sweden	50.7
Switzerland	50.3
Norway	49.1
Singapore	48.3
Australia	46.5
Luxembourg	45.9
Bermuda	43.7
Denmark	43.2
Finland	39.6
Netherlands	39.5
Iceland	39.2
Canada	39.0
Ireland	36.5
New Zealand	36.0
Hong Kong	34.7
Belgium	34.5
United Kingdom	33.8
Germany	33.6
Japan	31.5
France	30.5
Austria	27.7
Slovenia	27.6
Israel	25.4
Taiwan	22.5
Malta	20.6
Cyprus	19.3
South Korea	19.0
Guadeloupe	18.9
St Kitts and Nevis	15.5
Spain	14.3
Bahrain	14.0
Italy	13.9
Macao	13.7
St Lucia	13.7
Qatar	13.6
Estonia	13.5
Seychelles	13.5
French Guiana	13.2
United Arab Emirates	12.5
Czech Republic	12.2
Kuwait	12.1
Grenada	11.8
Martinique	11.5
Slovakia	10.9
Belize	10.6
Portugal	10.5
Malaysia	10.3
Costa Rica	10.2
Mauritius	10.1
Uruguay	10.0
Chile	8.6
Hungary	8.5
Latvia	8.2
Croatia	8.1
Barbados	7.8
Greece	7.1
Brunei	7.0
Poland	6.9

	PCs (per 100 people) 2000
Dominica	6.5
South Africa	6.2
Lithuania	6.0
Saudi Arabia	5.7
Iran	5.6
Trinidad and Tobago	5.4
Argentina	5.1
Mexico	5.1
Lebanon	4.6
Venezuela	4.6
Brazil	4.4
Jamaica	4.3
Russia	4.3
Turkey	3.8
Botswana	3.7
Peru	3.6
Namibia	3.4
Colombia	3.4
Panama	3.2
Romania	3.2
Bulgaria	2.7
Oman	2.6
Thailand	2.4
Tunisia	2.3
Jordan	2.3
Egypt	2.2
Yugoslavia	2.1
Ecuador	2.0
Philippines	1.9
El Salvador	1.6
China	1.6
Ukraine	1.6
Syria	1.4
Zimbabwe	1.3
Bolivia	1.2
Morocco	1.2
Paraguay	1.1
Cuba	1.0
Guatemala	1.0
Indonesia	1.0
Vietnam	0.9
Gabon	0.8
Zambia	0.7
Nigeria	0.7
Algeria	0.7
Côte d'Ivoire	0.6
Sri Lanka	0.6
Kenya	0.5
India	0.5
Pakistan	0.4
Cameroon	0.3
Sudan	0.3
Ghana	0.3
Mozambique	0.3
Tanzania	0.3
Uganda	0.3
Angola	0.1
Bangladesh	0.1
Ethiopia	0.1

Greatest Use of Internet

	Internet users (per 100 people) 2000
Iceland	59.8
Norway	49.1
Sweden	45.6
Canada	41.3
South Korea	40.3
Bermuda	39.0
Finland	37.2
Japan	37.1
Denmark	36.6
Australia	35.0
United States	34.7
Hong Kong	33.6
Greenland	31.9
United Arab Emirates	30.1
Singapore	29.9
Switzerland	29.8
Germany	29.2
Taiwan	28.1
United Kingdom	25.8
Austria	25.6
Estonia	25.5
Portugal	25.0
Netherlands	23.8
Italy	23.0
Luxembourg	23.0
New Zealand	21.7
Ireland	21.0
Israel	20.3
Belgium	19.7
Cyprus	17.7
Malaysia	15.9
Slovenia	15.1
France	14.5
Macao	13.6
Spain	13.3
Slovakia	12.0
Chile	11.6
New Caledonia	11.2
Uruguay	11.1
Malta	10.3
US Virgin Islands	10.0
Czech Republic	9.8
Peru	9.7
Greece	9.4
Brunei	9.1
Lebanon	8.6
Kuwait	7.8
Trinidad and Tobago	7.7
Seychelles	7.4
Mauritius	7.3
Poland	7.2
Hungary	7.0
Argentina	6.8
Faeroe Islands	6.7
Andorra	6.7
Antigua and Barbuda	6.5
Latvia	6.3
Belize	6.2
Costa Rica	6.2

	Internet users (per 100 people) 2000
Lithuania	6.1
Bahrain	5.8
South Africa	5.5
Bulgaria	5.2
St Kitts and Nevis	5.2
Puerto Rico	5.1
Qatar	5.0
Croatia	4.5
Grenada	4.4
Bahamas	4.3
Aruba	4.1
Venezuela	3.9
Thailand	3.8
Yugoslavia	3.8
Romania	3.6
Oman	3.6
Guam	3.0
Turkey	3.0
Brazil	2.9
Papua New Guinea	2.8
Mexico	2.7
Dominica	2.6
Philippines	2.6
Jamaica	2.3
Barbados	2.2
French Polynesia	2.2
Russia	2.1
Colombia	2.1
St Lucia	2.0
Jordan	1.9
Belarus	1.8
Guadeloupe	1.8
China	1.7
Namibia	1.7
Panama	1.6
Bolivia	1.4
Ecuador	1.4
Martinique	1.3
Gabon	1.2
French Guiana	1.2
Tunisia	1.0
Indonesia	0.9
Netherlands Antilles	0.9
Saudi Arabia	0.9
Botswana	0.9
Egypt	0.7
El Salvador	0.7
Kenya	0.7
Sri Lanka	0.6
Dominican Republic	0.6
Guatemala	0.6
Cuba	0.5
India	0.5
Kazakhstan	0.4
Iran	0.4
Ukraine	0.4
Georgia	0.4
Paraguay	0.4
Morocco	0.4

Greatest Use of Cellular Phones

	Cellular mobile subscribers (per 100 people) 2000	Growth in mobile subscribers (% p.a.) 1995–2000
Luxembourg	87.2	70
Taiwan	80.3	88
Hong Kong	80.2	47
Austria	78.6	76
Italy	73.7	61
United Kingdom	72.7	50
Finland	72.6	29
Sweden	71.4	26
Norway	70.3	26
Israel	70.2	58
Singapore	68.4	55
Netherlands	67.1	82
Iceland	67.0	44
Ireland	66.8	74
Portugal	66.5	81
Switzerland	64.5	60
Denmark	61.0	32
Spain	60.9	92
Germany	58.6	67
United Arab Emirates	58.5	62
South Korea	56.7	75
New Zealand	56.3	43
Greece	55.9	85
Belgium	54.9	88
Slovenia	54.7	109
Japan	52.6	42
France	49.4	86
Australia	44.6	31
Czech Republic	42.4	145
Martinique	41.0	–
United States	39.8	27
Reunion	39.5	119
Estonia	38.7	79
Faeroe Islands	37.7	46
Guadeloupe	37.3	–
Cyprus	32.1	38
Andorra	30.2	53
Seychelles	30.1	245
Bahrain	30.1	49
Malta	29.4	60
Hungary	29.3	63
Brunei	28.9	22
Antigua and Barbuda	28.7	–
Greenland	28.5	51
Canada	28.5	28
Kuwait	24.9	32
Turkey	24.6	106
Slovakia	23.9	154
Puerto Rico	23.7	26
New Caledonia	23.2	127
Croatia	23.1	98
Chile	22.4	77
French Guiana	22.0	–
Venezuela	21.8	67
Malaysia	21.3	38
Lebanon	21.3	44
US Virgin Islands	21.1	–
Qatar	20.0	45
Bermuda	19.6	26
Paraguay	19.6	185
South Africa	19.0	73
Poland	17.4	146
Latvia	16.9	93
Argentina	16.3	78
Guam	16.2	41
Mauritius	15.1	73
Aruba	14.6	54
Jamaica	14.2	52
Mexico	14.2	83
Lithuania	14.2	104
Brazil	13.6	78
Uruguay	13.2	62
Botswana	12.3	–
Yugoslavia	12.3	–
El Salvador	11.3	121
Romania	11.2	208
Barbados	11.1	60
Bahamas	10.4	50
Trinidad and Tobago	10.3	84
Gabon	9.8	97
French Polynesia	9.5	109
Bulgaria	9.0	104
Philippines	8.4	67
Panama	8.3	–
Morocco	8.3	140
Dominican Republic	8.3	66
Netherlands Antilles	7.5	11
Bolivia	7.0	125
China	6.6	88
Oman	6.5	83
Saudi Arabia	6.4	144
Guatemala	6.1	88
Jordan	5.8	99
Northern Marianas	5.6	25
Colombia	5.3	52
Costa Rica	5.2	62
Thailand	5.0	19
Peru	4.8	75
Namibia	4.7	88
Grenada	4.6	61
Ecuador	3.8	55
Côte d'Ivoire	3.0	–
Belize	3.0	36
Zimbabwe	2.5	–
Sri Lanka	2.4	55
Russia	2.2	106
Egypt	2.1	184
Georgia	1.9	411
St Kitts and Nevis	1.8	–
Indonesia	1.7	77
Ukraine	1.6	126
Iran	1.5	127
St Lucia	1.3	24
Vietnam	1.0	102
Cameroon	1.0	121
Dominica	0.9	–
Uganda	0.9	155
Libya	0.7	–
Ghana	0.6	84
Tunisia	0.6	104

Highest Growth of Cellular Phone Use

	Compound growth in mobile subscribers (% p.a.) 1995–2000
Georgia	411
Seychelles	245
Romania	208
Paraguay	185
Egypt	184
Uganda	155
Slovakia	154
Poland	146
Czech Republic	145
Saudi Arabia	144
Bangladesh	141
Morocco	140
Iran	127
New Caledonia	127
Ukraine	126
Bolivia	125
Kenya	124
Cameroon	121
El Salvador	121
Tanzania	120
Reunion	119
India	116
French Polynesia	109
Slovenia	109
Turkey	106
Russia	106
Lithuania	104
Tunisia	104
Bulgaria	104
Vietnam	102
Zambia	100
Jordan	99
Croatia	98
Gabon	97
Latvia	93
Spain	92
Belgium	88
China	88
Namibia	88
Guatemala	88
Taiwan	88
France	86
Greece	85
Ghana	84
Trinidad and Tobago	84
Mexico	83
Oman	83
Netherlands	82
Portugal	81
Kazakhstan	81
Algeria	79
Estonia	79
Brazil	78
Argentina	78
Indonesia	77
Chile	77
Austria	76
Peru	75
South Korea	75
Ireland	74

MEDIA

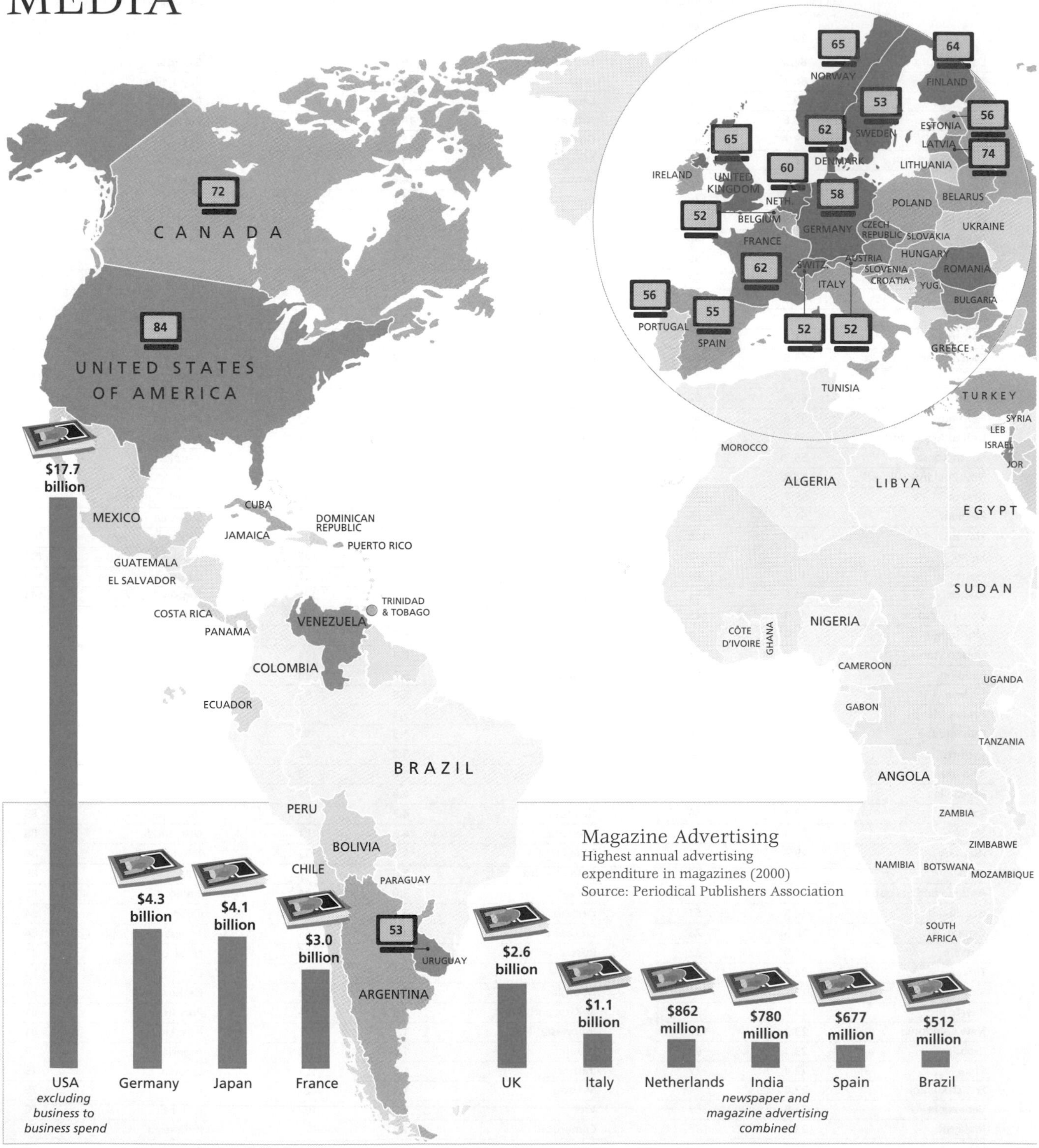

CANADA 72

UNITED STATES OF AMERICA 84

MEXICO

CUBA

JAMAICA

DOMINICAN REPUBLIC

PUERTO RICO

GUATEMALA

EL SALVADOR

COSTA RICA

PANAMA

VENEZUELA

TRINIDAD & TOBAGO

COLOMBIA

ECUADOR

BRAZIL

PERU

BOLIVIA

CHILE

PARAGUAY

URUGUAY 53

ARGENTINA

NORWAY 65

FINLAND 64

SWEDEN 53

ESTONIA 56

DENMARK 62

LATVIA

LITHUANIA 74

IRELAND

UNITED KINGDOM 65

NETH. 60

GERMANY 58

BELGIUM 52

POLAND

BELARUS

UKRAINE

FRANCE 62

CZECH REPUBLIC

SLOVAKIA

AUSTRIA

HUNGARY

SWITZ.

SLOVENIA

CROATIA

ROMANIA

YUG.

ITALY 52

BULGARIA

PORTUGAL 56

SPAIN 55

GREECE

52

TUNISIA

TURKEY

SYRIA

LEB

ISRAEL

JOR

MOROCCO

ALGERIA

LIBYA

EGYPT

SUDAN

NIGERIA

CÔTE D'IVOIRE

GHANA

CAMEROON

GABON

UGANDA

TANZANIA

ANGOLA

ZAMBIA

ZIMBABWE

NAMIBIA

BOTSWANA

MOZAMBIQUE

SOUTH AFRICA

Magazine Advertising

Highest annual advertising expenditure in magazines (2000)

Source: Periodical Publishers Association

USA *excluding business to business spend*	$17.7 billion
Germany	$4.3 billion
Japan	$4.1 billion
France	$3.0 billion
UK	$2.6 billion
Italy	$1.1 billion
Netherlands	$862 million
India *newspaper and magazine advertising combined*	$780 million
Spain	$677 million
Brazil	$512 million

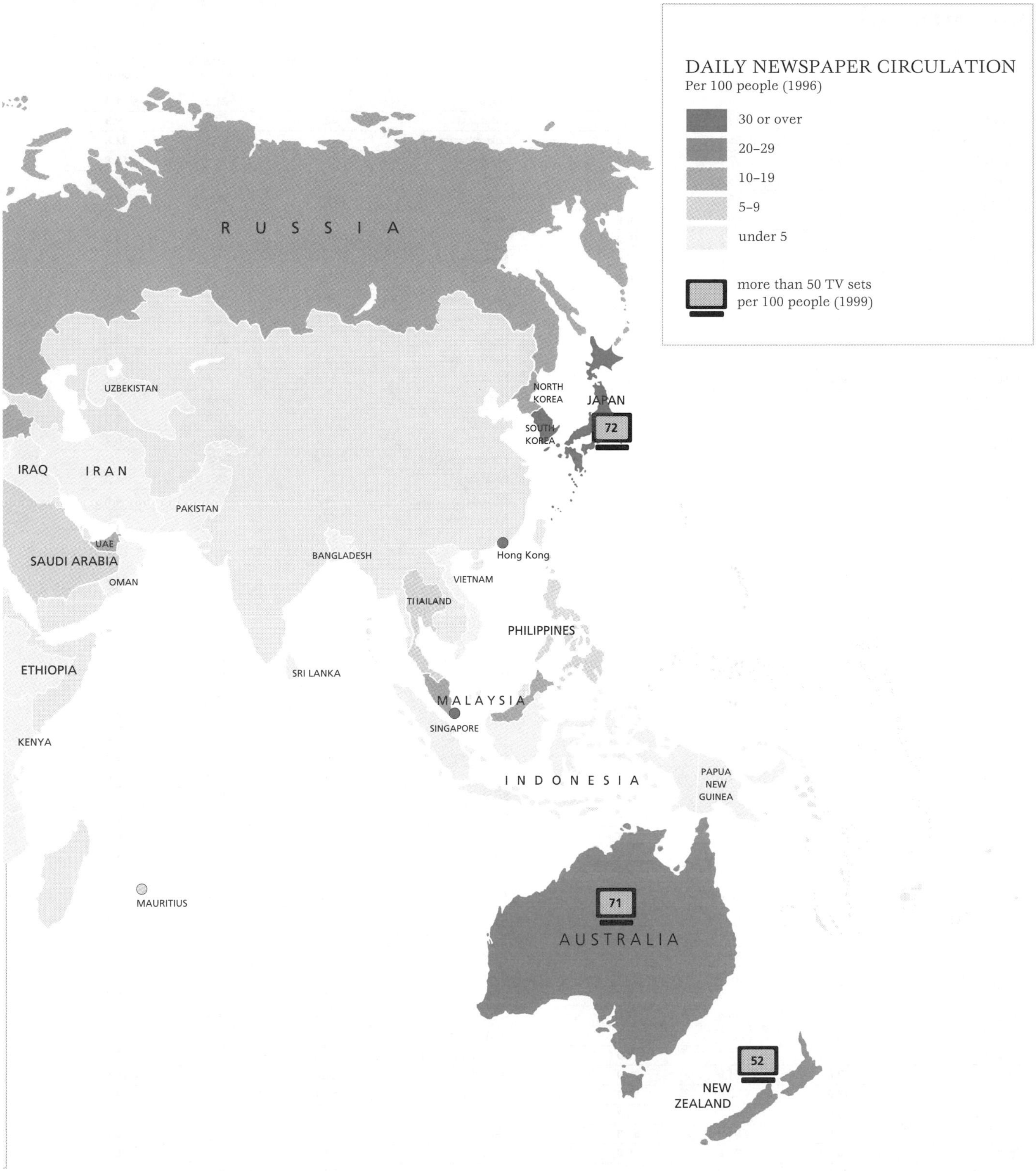

DAILY NEWSPAPER CIRCULATION

Per 100 people (1996)

- 30 or over
- 20–29
- 10–19
- 5–9
- under 5

- more than 50 TV sets per 100 people (1999)

RUSSIA
UZBEKISTAN
NORTH KOREA
JAPAN
72
SOUTH KOREA
IRAQ
IRAN
PAKISTAN
UAE
SAUDI ARABIA
OMAN
BANGLADESH
Hong Kong
VIETNAM
THAILAND
PHILIPPINES
ETHIOPIA
SRI LANKA
MALAYSIA
SINGAPORE
KENYA
INDONESIA
PAPUA NEW GUINEA
MAURITIUS
71
AUSTRALIA
52
NEW ZEALAND

Access to the Media

	TV sets (per 100 people) 1999	Radios (per 100 people) 1997–99	Daily newspaper circulation (per 100 people) 1996
Algeria	10.7	24.1	3.8
Angola	1.5	6.2	1.1
Argentina	29.3	68.1	12.3
Australia	70.6	137.8	29.3
Austria	51.6	75.3	29.6
Bahrain	–	58.0	11.7
Bangladesh	0.7	5.0	0.9
Barbados	–	88.8	19.9
Belarus	32.2	29.6	17.4
Belgium	52.3	79.2	16.0
Bolivia	11.8	67.6	5.5
Botswana	2.0	15.6	2.7
Brazil	33.3	44.4	4.0
Brunei	–	30.2	6.9
Bulgaria	40.8	54.3	25.7
Cameroon	3.4	16.3	0.7
Canada	71.5	104.7	15.9
Chile	24.0	35.5	9.8
China	29.2	33.4	–
Colombia	19.9	56.0	4.6
Costa Rica	22.9	77.6	9.4
Côte d'Ivoire	7.0	16.4	1.7
Croatia	27.9	33.6	11.5
Cuba	24.6	35.5	11.8
Cyprus	–	40.6	11.1
Czech Republic	48.7	80.3	25.4
Denmark	62.1	131.8	30.9
Dominican Republic	9.6	17.8	5.2
Ecuador	20.5	42.0	7.0
Egypt	18.3	32.4	4.0
El Salvador	19.1	47.8	4.8
Estonia	55.5	96.6	17.4
Ethiopia	0.6	19.6	0.2
Finland	64.3	156.3	45.5
France	62.3	93.7	21.8
Gabon	25.1	50.0	2.9
Georgia	47.4	55.5	–
Germany	58.0	94.8	31.1
Ghana	11.5	68.0	1.4
Greece	48.0	47.8	15.3
Guatemala	6.1	8.0	3.3
Hong Kong	43.4	67.8	79.2
Hungary	44.8	68.7	18.6
Iceland	–	95.0	53.5
India	7.5	12.1	–
Indonesia	14.3	15.7	2.4
Iran	15.7	26.4	2.8
Iraq	8.3	22.9	1.9
Ireland	40.6	69.9	15.0
Israel	32.8	51.9	29.0
Italy	48.8	88.0	10.4
Jamaica	18.9	79.5	6.2
Japan	71.9	96.0	57.8
Jordan	8.3	28.8	5.8
Kazakhstan	23.8	39.5	–
Kenya	2.2	10.4	0.9
Kuwait	48.0	63.2	37.4
Latvia	74.1	68.4	24.7
Lebanon	35.1	90.8	10.7
Libya	13.6	24.3	1.4
Lithuania	42.0	50.0	9.3
Luxembourg	–	68.3	32.8
Malaysia	17.4	41.9	15.8
Malta	–	66.9	12.7
Mauritius	23.0	36.8	7.5
Mexico	26.7	32.5	9.7
Morocco	16.5	24.1	2.6
Mozambique	0.5	4.0	0.3
Namibia	3.8	14.4	1.9
Netherlands	60.0	98.1	30.6
New Zealand	51.8	98.9	21.6
Nigeria	6.8	22.4	2.4
North Korea	5.5	14.7	19.9
Norway	64.8	91.6	58.8
Oman	–	59.8	2.9
Pakistan	11.9	10.4	2.3
Panama	19.2	30.0	6.2
Papua New Guinea	1.3	9.5	1.5
Paraguay	20.5	18.2	4.3
Peru	14.7	27.3	8.4
Philippines	11.0	15.9	7.9
Poland	38.7	52.2	11.3
Portugal	56.0	30.4	7.5
Puerto Rico	32.4	74.2	12.6
Qatar	–	45.0	16.1
Romania	31.2	33.5	30.0
Russia	42.1	41.8	10.5
Saudi Arabia	26.3	32.1	5.7
Singapore	30.8	68.2	36.0
Slovakia	41.7	96.7	18.5
Slovenia	35.6	40.7	19.9
South Africa	12.9	33.3	3.2
South Korea	36.1	103.3	39.3
Spain	54.7	33.3	10.0
Sri Lanka	10.2	20.9	2.9
Sudan	17.3	27.1	2.7
Sweden	53.1	93.2	44.5
Switzerland	51.8	100.0	33.7
Syria	6.6	27.7	2.0
Tanzania	2.1	27.9	0.4
Thailand	28.9	23.3	6.3
Trinidad and Tobago	33.7	53.5	12.3
Tunisia	19.0	15.8	3.1
Turkey	33.2	18.0	11.1
Uganda	2.8	12.7	0.2
Ukraine	41.3	88.4	5.4
United Arab Emirates	25.2	34.5	15.6
United Kingdom	65.2	143.5	32.9
United States	84.4	214.6	21.5
Uruguay	53.1	60.6	29.3
Uzbekistan	27.6	45.8	0.3
Venezuela	18.5	47.0	20.6
Vietnam	18.4	10.7	0.4
Yugoslavia	27.3	29.7	10.7
Zambia	14.5	16.0	1.2
Zimbabwe	18.0	39.0	1.9

Sources: International Telecommunication Union, UNESCO

Greatest Access to TV

	TV sets (per 100 people) 1999
United States	84.4
Latvia	74.1
Japan	71.9
Canada	71.5
Australia	70.6
United Kingdom	65.2
Norway	64.8
Finland	64.3
France	62.3
Denmark	62.1
Netherlands	60.0
Germany	58.0
Portugal	56.0
Estonia	55.5
Spain	54.7
Sweden	53.1
Uruguay	53.1
Belgium	52.3
New Zealand	51.8
Switzerland	51.8
Austria	51.6
Italy	48.8
Czech Republic	48.7
Greece	48.0
Kuwait	48.0
Georgia	47.4
Hungary	44.8
Hong Kong	43.4
Russia	42.1
Lithuania	42.0
Slovakia	41.7
Ukraine	41.3
Bulgaria	40.8
Ireland	40.6
Poland	38.7
South Korea	36.1
Slovenia	35.6
Lebanon	35.1
Trinidad and Tobago	33.7
Brazil	33.3
Turkey	33.2
Israel	32.8
Puerto Rico	32.4
Belarus	32.2
Romania	31.2
Singapore	30.8
Argentina	29.3
China	29.2
Thailand	28.9
Croatia	27.9
Uzbekistan	27.6
Yugoslavia	27.3
Mexico	26.7
Saudi Arabia	26.3
United Arab Emirates	25.2
Gabon	25.1
Cuba	24.6
Chile	24.0
Kazakhstan	23.8
Mauritius	23.0

Most Radios

	Radios (per 100 people) 1997–99
United States	214.6
Finland	156.3
United Kingdom	143.5
Australia	137.8
Denmark	131.8
Canada	104.7
South Korea	103.3
Switzerland	100.0
New Zealand	98.9
Netherlands	98.1
Slovakia	96.7
Estonia	96.6
Japan	96.0
Iceland	95.0
Germany	94.8
France	93.7
Sweden	93.2
Norway	91.6
Lebanon	90.8
Barbados	88.8
Ukraine	88.4
Italy	88.0
Czech Republic	80.3
Jamaica	79.5
Belgium	79.2
Costa Rica	77.6
Austria	75.3
Puerto Rico	74.2
Ireland	69.9
Hungary	68.7
Latvia	68.4
Luxembourg	68.3
Singapore	68.2
Argentina	68.1
Ghana	68.0
Hong Kong	67.8
Bolivia	67.6
Malta	66.9
Kuwait	63.2
Uruguay	60.6
Oman	59.8
Bahrain	58.0
Colombia	56.0
Georgia	55.5
Bulgaria	54.3
Trinidad and Tobago	53.5
Poland	52.2
Israel	51.9
Gabon	50.0
Lithuania	50.0
El Salvador	47.8
Greece	47.8
Venezuela	47.0
Uzbekistan	45.8
Qatar	45.0
Brazil	44.4
Ecuador	42.0
Malaysia	41.9
Russia	41.8
Slovenia	40.7
Cyprus	40.6
Kazakhstan	39.5
Zimbabwe	39.0
Mauritius	36.8
Chile	35.5
Cuba	35.5
United Arab Emirates	34.5
Croatia	33.6
Romania	33.5
China	33.4
South Africa	33.3
Spain	33.3
Mexico	32.5
Egypt	32.4
Saudi Arabia	32.1
Portugal	30.4
Brunei	30.2
Panama	30.0
Yugoslavia	29.7
Belarus	29.6
Jordan	28.8
Tanzania	27.9
Syria	27.7
Peru	27.3
Sudan	27.1
Iran	26.4
Libya	24.3
Algeria	24.1
Morocco	24.1
Thailand	23.3
Iraq	22.9
Nigeria	22.4
Sri Lanka	20.9
Ethiopia	19.6
Paraguay	18.2
Turkey	18.0
Dominican Republic	17.8
Côte d'Ivoire	16.4
Cameroon	16.3
Zambia	16.0
Philippines	15.9
Tunisia	15.8
Indonesia	15.7
Botswana	15.6
North Korea	14.7
Namibia	14.4
Uganda	12.7
India	12.1
Vietnam	10.7
Kenya	10.4
Pakistan	10.4
Papua New Guinea	9.5
Guatemala	8.0
Angola	6.2
Bangladesh	5.0
Mozambique	4.0

Greatest Daily Newspaper Circulation

	Daily newspaper circulation (per 100 people) 1996
Hong Kong	79.2
Norway	58.8
Japan	57.8
Iceland	53.5
Finland	45.5
Sweden	44.5
South Korea	39.3
Kuwait	37.4
Singapore	36.0
Switzerland	33.7
United Kingdom	32.9
Luxembourg	32.8
Germany	31.1
Denmark	30.9
Netherlands	30.6
Romania	30.0
Austria	29.6
Australia	29.3
Uruguay	29.3
Israel	29.0
Bulgaria	25.7
Czech Republic	25.4
Latvia	24.7
France	21.8
New Zealand	21.6
United States	21.5
Venezuela	20.6
Barbados	19.9
North Korea	19.9
Slovenia	19.9
Hungary	18.6
Slovakia	18.5
Belarus	17.4
Estonia	17.4
Qatar	16.1
Belgium	16.0
Canada	15.9
Malaysia	15.8
United Arab Emirates	15.6
Greece	15.3
Ireland	15.0
Malta	12.7
Puerto Rico	12.6
Argentina	12.3
Trinidad and Tobago	12.3
Cuba	11.8
Bahrain	11.7
Croatia	11.5
Poland	11.3
Cyprus	11.1
Turkey	11.1
Lebanon	10.7
Yugoslavia	10.7
Russia	10.5
Italy	10.4
Spain	10.0
Chile	9.8
Mexico	9.7
Costa Rica	9.4
Lithuania	9.3

Environment

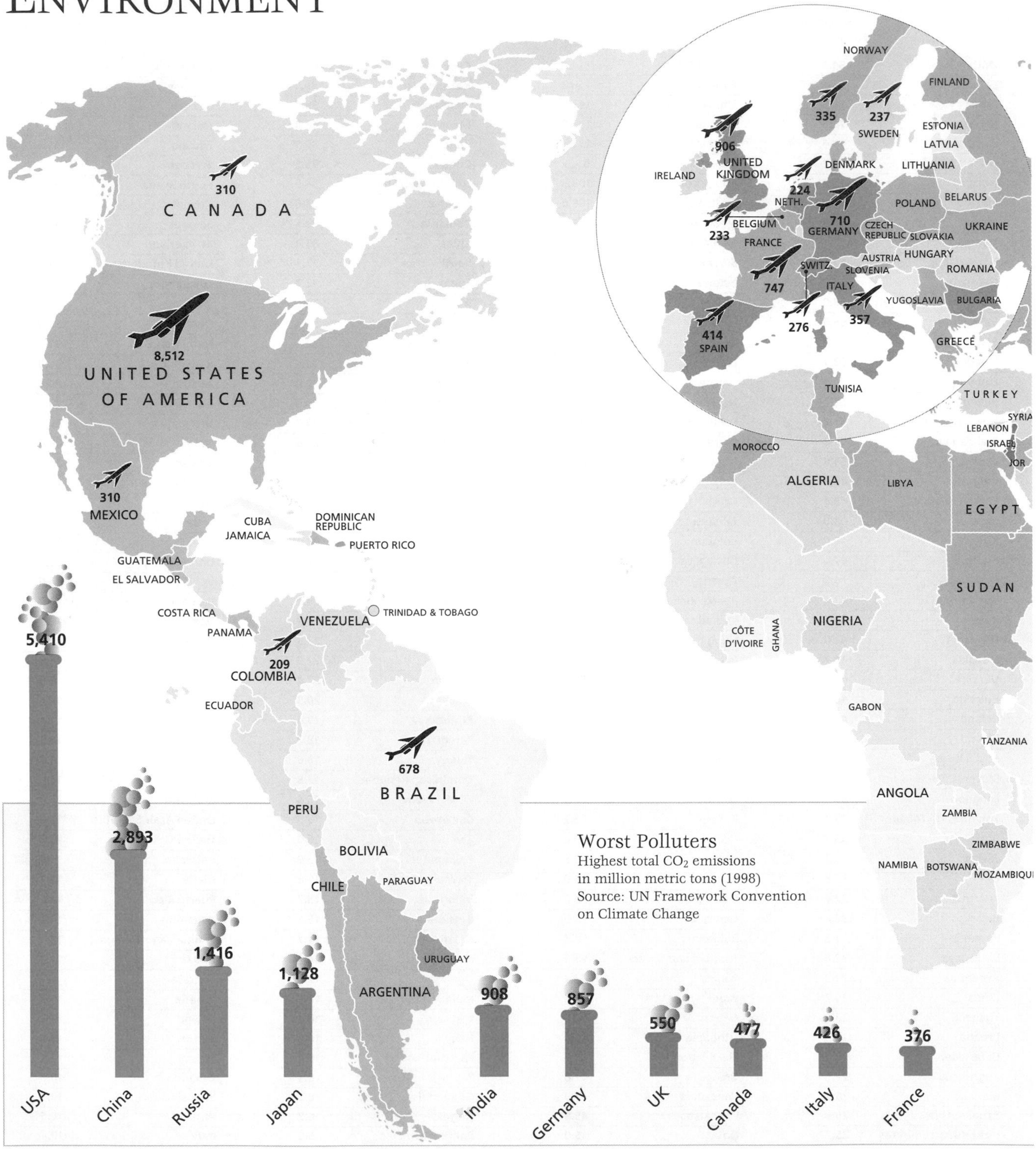

CANADA 310
UNITED STATES OF AMERICA 8,512
MEXICO 310
COLOMBIA 209
BRAZIL 678
NORWAY 335
SWEDEN 237
UNITED KINGDOM 906
DENMARK 224
NETH.
BELGIUM 233
GERMANY 710
FRANCE 747
SWITZ. 276
ITALY 357
SPAIN 414

IRELAND, FINLAND, ESTONIA, LATVIA, LITHUANIA, POLAND, BELARUS, UKRAINE, CZECH REPUBLIC, SLOVAKIA, AUSTRIA, HUNGARY, SLOVENIA, ROMANIA, YUGOSLAVIA, BULGARIA, GREECE, TUNISIA, TURKEY, SYRIA, LEBANON, ISRAEL, JOR, MOROCCO, ALGERIA, LIBYA, EGYPT, SUDAN, NIGERIA, CÔTE D'IVOIRE, GHANA, GABON, TANZANIA, ANGOLA, ZAMBIA, ZIMBABWE, NAMIBIA, BOTSWANA, MOZAMBIQUE, CUBA, JAMAICA, DOMINICAN REPUBLIC, PUERTO RICO, GUATEMALA, EL SALVADOR, COSTA RICA, PANAMA, VENEZUELA, TRINIDAD & TOBAGO, ECUADOR, PERU, BOLIVIA, CHILE, PARAGUAY, URUGUAY, ARGENTINA

Worst Polluters

Highest total CO_2 emissions in million metric tons (1998)
Source: UN Framework Convention on Climate Change

USA	5,410
China	2,893
Russia	1,416
Japan	1,128
India	908
Germany	857
UK	550
Canada	477
Italy	426
France	376

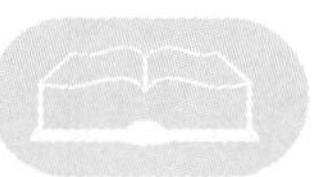

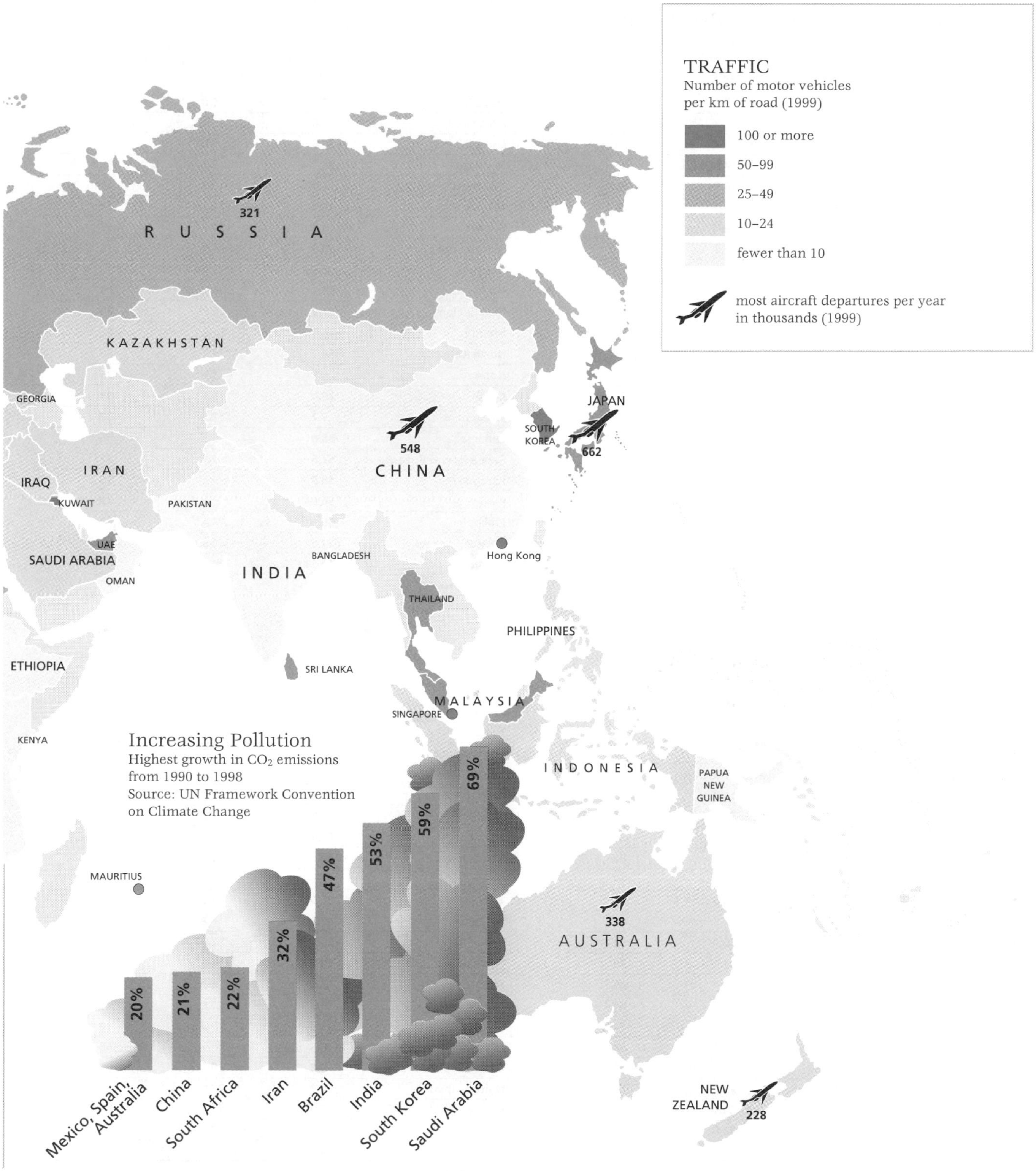

TRAFFIC

Number of motor vehicles per km of road (1999)

- 100 or more
- 50–99
- 25–49
- 10–24
- fewer than 10

most aircraft departures per year in thousands (1999)

RUSSIA 321
KAZAKHSTAN
GEORGIA
IRAN
IRAQ
KUWAIT
PAKISTAN
UAE
SAUDI ARABIA
OMAN
INDIA
BANGLADESH
CHINA 548
SOUTH KOREA
JAPAN 662
Hong Kong
THAILAND
PHILIPPINES
SRI LANKA
MALAYSIA
SINGAPORE
ETHIOPIA
KENYA
INDONESIA
PAPUA NEW GUINEA
MAURITIUS
AUSTRALIA 338
NEW ZEALAND 228

Increasing Pollution

Highest growth in CO_2 emissions from 1990 to 1998
Source: UN Framework Convention on Climate Change

Mexico, Spain, Australia	20%
China	21%
South Africa	22%
Iran	32%
Brazil	47%
India	53%
South Korea	59%
Saudi Arabia	69%

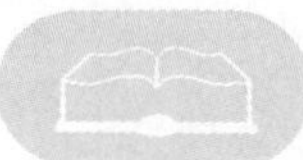

Forest Cover, Arable Land, and Urban Population

	Forest area (% of total land area) 2000	Arable land (% of total land area) 1998	Urban population (%) 1999
Algeria	0.9	3.2	60
Angola	56.0	2.4	34
Argentina	12.7	9.1	90
Australia	20.6	7.0	85
Austria	47.0	16.9	65
Bangladesh	10.2	61.4	24
Belarus	45.3	29.8	71
Belgium	22.2	24.8	97
Bolivia	48.9	1.8	62
Botswana	21.9	0.6	50
Brazil	63.0	6.3	81
Bulgaria	33.4	38.8	69
Cameroon	51.3	12.8	48
Canada	26.5	4.9	77
Chile	20.7	2.6	85
China	17.5	13.3	32
Colombia	47.8	2.0	74
Costa Rica	38.5	4.4	48
Côte d'Ivoire	22.4	9.3	46
Croatia	31.9	26.1	57
Cuba	21.4	33.1	75
Cyprus	13.0	12.0	56
Czech Republic	34.1	40.1	75
Denmark	10.7	55.7	85
Dominican Republic	28.4	22.1	64
Ecuador	38.1	5.7	64
Egypt	0.1	2.8	45
El Salvador	5.8	27.0	46
Estonia	48.7	26.5	69
Ethiopia	4.6	9.9	17
Finland	72.0	7.1	67
France	27.9	33.4	75
Gabon	84.7	1.3	80
Georgia	42.9	11.3	60
Germany	30.7	34.0	87
Ghana	27.8	15.8	38
Greece	27.9	22.1	60
Guatemala	26.3	12.5	40
Hong Kong	20.0	6.0	100
Hungary	19.9	52.2	64
Iceland	1.0	0.0	92
India	21.6	54.3	28
Indonesia	58.0	9.9	40
Iran	4.5	10.4	61
Iraq	1.8	11.9	77
Ireland	9.6	19.7	59
Israel	6.4	17.0	91
Italy	34.0	28.2	67
Jamaica	30.0	16.1	56
Japan	64.0	12.0	79
Jordan	1.0	2.9	74
Kazakhstan	4.5	11.2	56
Kenya	30.0	7.0	32
Kuwait	0.3	0.3	98
Latvia	47.1	29.7	69
Lebanon	3.5	17.6	89
Libya	0.2	1.0	87
Lithuania	30.8	45.4	68
Luxembourg	35.0	24.0	91
Malaysia	58.7	5.5	57
Mauritius	7.9	49.3	41
Mexico	28.9	13.2	74
Morocco	6.8	20.2	55
Mozambique	39.0	4.0	39
Namibia	9.8	1.0	30
Netherlands	11.1	26.7	89
New Zealand	29.7	5.8	86
Nigeria	14.8	31.0	43
North Korea	68.2	14.1	60
Norway	28.9	3.0	75
Oman	0.0	0.1	83
Pakistan	3.2	27.8	37
Panama	38.6	6.7	56
Papua New Guinea	67.6	0.1	17
Paraguay	58.8	5.5	55
Peru	50.9	2.9	72
Philippines	19.4	18.4	58
Poland	30.6	46.0	65
Portugal	40.1	20.5	63
Puerto Rico	25.8	3.7	75
Romania	28.0	40.5	56
Russia	50.4	7.5	77
Saudi Arabia	0.7	1.7	85
Singapore	3.3	1.6	100
Slovakia	42.5	30.6	57
Slovenia	55.0	11.5	50
South Africa	7.3	12.1	50
South Korea	63.3	17.3	81
Spain	28.8	28.6	77
Sri Lanka	30.0	13.4	23
Sudan	25.9	7.0	35
Sweden	65.9	6.8	83
Switzerland	30.3	10.5	68
Syria	2.5	25.6	54
Taiwan	55.0	24.0	–
Tanzania	43.9	4.2	32
Thailand	28.9	32.9	21
Trinidad and Tobago	50.5	14.6	74
Tunisia	3.3	18.7	65
Turkey	13.3	31.8	74
Uganda	21.0	25.3	14
Ukraine	16.5	56.7	68
United Arab Emirates	3.8	0.5	85
United Kingdom	10.7	25.9	89
United States	24.7	19.3	77
Uruguay	7.4	7.2	91
Uzbekistan	4.8	10.8	37
Venezuela	56.1	3.0	87
Vietnam	30.2	17.5	20
Yugoslavia	17.0	40.0	52
Zambia	42.0	7.1	40
Zimbabwe	49.2	8.3	35

Most Forested

	Forest area (% of total land area) 2000
Gabon	84.7
Finland	72.0
North Korea	68.2
Papua New Guinea	67.6
Sweden	65.9
Japan	64.0
South Korea	63.3
Brazil	63.0
Paraguay	58.8
Malaysia	58.7
Indonesia	58.0
Venezuela	56.1
Angola	56.0
Slovenia	55.0
Taiwan	55.0
Cameroon	51.3
Peru	50.9
Trinidad and Tobago	50.5
Russia	50.4
Zimbabwe	49.2
Bolivia	48.9
Estonia	48.7
Colombia	47.8
Latvia	47.1
Austria	47.0
Belarus	45.3
Tanzania	43.9
Georgia	42.9
Slovakia	42.5
Zambia	42.0
Portugal	40.1
Mozambique	39.0
Panama	38.6
Costa Rica	38.5
Ecuador	38.1
Luxembourg	35.0
Czech Republic	34.1
Italy	34.0
Bulgaria	33.4
Croatia	31.9
Lithuania	30.8
Germany	30.7
Poland	30.6
Switzerland	30.3
Vietnam	30.2
Jamaica	30.0

	Forest area (% of total land area) 2000
Kenya	30.0
Sri Lanka	30.0
New Zealand	29.7
Mexico	28.9
Norway	28.9
Thailand	28.9
Spain	28.8
Dominican Republic	28.4
Romania	28.0
France	27.9
Greece	27.9
Ghana	27.8
Canada	26.5
Guatemala	26.3
Sudan	25.9
Puerto Rico	25.8
United States	24.7
Côte d'Ivoire	22.4
Belgium	22.2
Botswana	21.9
India	21.6
Cuba	21.4
Uganda	21.0
Chile	20.7
Australia	20.6
Hong Kong	20.0
Hungary	19.9
Philippines	19.4
China	17.5
Yugoslavia	17.0
Ukraine	16.5
Nigeria	14.8
Turkey	13.3
Cyprus	13.0
Argentina	12.7
Netherlands	11.1
Denmark	10.7
United Kingdom	10.7
Bangladesh	10.2
Namibia	9.8
Ireland	9.6
Mauritius	7.9
Uruguay	7.4
South Africa	7.3
Morocco	6.8
Israel	6.4

Most Arable Land

	Arable land (% of total land area) 1998
Bangladesh	61.4
Ukraine	56.7
Denmark	55.7
India	54.3
Hungary	52.2
Mauritius	49.3
Poland	46.0
Lithuania	45.4
Romania	40.5
Czech Republic	40.1
Yugoslavia	40.0
Bulgaria	38.8
Germany	34.0
France	33.4
Cuba	33.1
Thailand	32.9
Turkey	31.8
Nigeria	31.0
Slovakia	30.6
Belarus	29.8
Latvia	29.7
Spain	28.6
Italy	28.2
Pakistan	27.8
El Salvador	27.0
Netherlands	26.7
Estonia	26.5
Croatia	26.1
United Kingdom	25.9
Syria	25.6
Uganda	25.3
Belgium	24.8
Luxembourg	24.0
Taiwan	24.0
Dominican Republic	22.1
Greece	22.1
Portugal	20.5
Morocco	20.2
Ireland	19.7
United States	19.3
Tunisia	18.7
Philippines	18.4
Lebanon	17.6
Vietnam	17.5
South Korea	17.3
Israel	17.0

	Arable land (% of total land area) 1998
Austria	16.9
Jamaica	16.1
Ghana	15.8
Trinidad and Tobago	14.6
North Korea	14.1
Sri Lanka	13.4
China	13.3
Mexico	13.2
Cameroon	12.8
Guatemala	12.5
South Africa	12.1
Cyprus	12.0
Japan	12.0
Iraq	11.9
Slovenia	11.5
Georgia	11.3
Kazakhstan	11.2
Uzbekistan	10.8
Switzerland	10.5
Iran	10.4
Ethiopia	9.9
Indonesia	9.9
Côte d'Ivoire	9.3
Argentina	9.1
Zimbabwe	8.3
Russia	7.5
Uruguay	7.2
Finland	7.1
Zambia	7.1
Australia	7.0
Kenya	7.0
Sudan	7.0
Sweden	6.8
Panama	6.7
Brazil	6.3
Hong Kong	6.0
New Zealand	5.8
Ecuador	5.7
Malaysia	5.5
Paraguay	5.5
Canada	4.9
Costa Rica	4.4
Tanzania	4.2
Mozambique	4.0
Puerto Rico	3.7
Algeria	3.2

Share of World Mineral Production, 1998

	Bauxite (%)	Coal (%)	Copper (%)	Gold (%)	Iron ore (%)	Lead (%)	Nickel (%)	Palladium (%)	Platinum (%)	Zinc (%)
Australia	36	6	5	12	18	20	13	–	–	14
Brazil	10	–	–	2	21	–	2	–	–	1
Canada	–	1	6	7	4	6	18	6	4	14
China	7	33	4	6	14	19	4	–	–	17
European Union	2	3	2	1	2	7	1	–	–	7
Russia	3	4	4	5	7	–	24	49	16	2
South Africa	–	6	2	18	4	3	3	35	76	1
United States	–	26	15	14	7	16	–	7	2	10

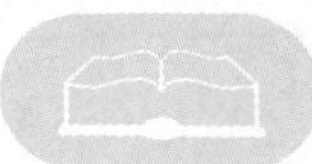

Impact of Motor Vehicles and Aircraft

	Motor vehicles per km of road, 1999	Aircraft departures (000s) 1999
Algeria	14	36
Angola	3	6
Argentina	30	184
Australia	12	338
Austria	22	127
Bangladesh	1	6
Belarus	21	6
Belgium	34	233
Bolivia	7	24
Botswana	11	6
Brazil	6	678
Bulgaria	58	15
Cameroon	–	5
Canada	19	310
Chile	26	93
China	7	548
Colombia	19	209
Costa Rica	14	32
Côte d'Ivoire	9	6
Croatia	–	16
Cuba	6	16
Czech Republic	29	35
Denmark	31	110
Dominican Republic	30	–
Ecuador	13	20
Egypt	28	44
El Salvador	36	32
Estonia	11	11
Ethiopia	3	25
Finland	31	108
France	37	747
Gabon	5	7
Georgia	16	3
Germany	66	710
Ghana	4	5
Greece	28	91
Guatemala	45	7
Hong Kong	276	72
Hungary	15	30
India	3	181
Indonesia	14	135
Iran	15	76
Iraq	23	–
Ireland	12	133
Israel	102	52
Italy	52	357
Jamaica	7	21
Japan	61	662
Jordan	44	16
Kazakhstan	12	18
Kenya	6	25
Kuwait	156	17
Latvia	9	9
Lebanon	205	10
Libya	48	6
Lithuania	16	11
Malaysia	69	165
Mauritius	60	11
Mexico	44	310
Morocco	26	44
Mozambique	0	6
Namibia	2	8
Netherlands	58	224
New Zealand	22	228
Nigeria	14	8
North Korea	–	1
Norway	25	335
Oman	9	22
Pakistan	4	65
Panama	27	21
Papua New Guinea	6	24
Paraguay	4	8
Peru	13	37
Philippines	11	36
Poland	29	44
Portugal	–	104
Puerto Rico	74	–
Romania	17	18
Russia	39	321
Saudi Arabia	20	107
Singapore	170	68
Slovakia	33	6
Slovenia	45	11
South Africa	–	101
South Korea	120	206
Spain	53	414
Sri Lanka	56	10
Sudan	28	7
Sweden	20	237
Switzerland	53	276
Syria	11	11
Tanzania	2	5
Thailand	97	95
Trinidad and Tobago	18	21
Tunisia	25	20
Turkey	14	111
Uganda	–	3
Ukraine	27	28
United Arab Emirates	52	44
United Kingdom	67	906
United States	32	8,512
Uruguay	63	11
Uzbekistan	–	31
Venezuela	21	130
Vietnam	–	29
Yugoslavia	42	–
Zambia	4	1
Zimbabwe	19	13

Highest Motor Vehicle Density

	Motor vehicles per km of road, 1999
Hong Kong	276
Lebanon	205
Singapore	170
Kuwait	156
South Korea	120
Israel	102
Thailand	97
Puerto Rico	74
Malaysia	69
United Kingdom	67
Germany	66
Uruguay	63
Japan	61
Mauritius	60
Bulgaria	58
Netherlands	58
Sri Lanka	56
Spain	53
Switzerland	53
Italy	52
United Arab Emirates	52
Libya	48
Guatemala	45
Slovenia	45
Jordan	44
Mexico	44
Yugoslavia	42
Russia	39
France	37
El Salvador	36
Belgium	34
Slovakia	33
United States	32
Denmark	31
Finland	31
Argentina	30
Dominican Republic	30
Czech Republic	29
Poland	29
Egypt	28
Greece	28
Sudan	28
Panama	27
Ukraine	27
Chile	26
Morocco	26
Norway	25
Tunisia	25
Iraq	23
Austria	22
New Zealand	22
Belarus	21
Venezuela	21
Saudi Arabia	20
Sweden	20
Canada	19
Colombia	19
Zimbabwe	19
Trinidad and Tobago	18
Romania	17
Georgia	16
Lithuania	16
Hungary	15
Iran	15
Algeria	14
Costa Rica	14
Indonesia	14
Nigeria	14
Turkey	14
Ecuador	13
Peru	13
Australia	12
Ireland	12
Kazakhstan	12
Botswana	11
Estonia	11
Philippines	11
Syria	11
Côte d'Ivoire	9
Latvia	9
Oman	9
Bolivia	7
China	7
Jamaica	7
Brazil	6
Cuba	6
Kenya	6
Papua New Guinea	6
Gabon	5
Ghana	4
Pakistan	4
Paraguay	4
Zambia	4
Angola	3
Ethiopia	3
India	3
Namibia	2
Tanzania	2
Bangladesh	1
Mozambique*	0

* less than 0.5 vehicles per km of road

Source: International Road Federation

  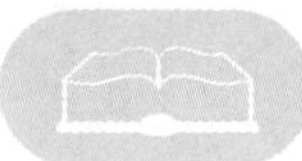    

Most Aircraft Departures

	Aircraft departures (thousands) 1999
United States	8,512
United Kingdom	906
France	747
Germany	710
Brazil	678
Japan	662
China	548
Spain	414
Italy	357
Australia	338
Norway	335
Russia	321
Canada	310
Mexico	310
Switzerland	276
Sweden	237
Belgium	233
New Zealand	228
Netherlands	224
Colombia	209
South Korea	206
Argentina	184
India	181
Malaysia	165
Indonesia	135
Ireland	133
Venezuela	130
Austria	127
Turkey	111
Denmark	110
Finland	108
Saudi Arabia	107
Portugal	104
South Africa	101
Thailand	95
Chile	93
Greece	91
Iran	76
Hong Kong	72
Singapore	68
Pakistan	65
Israel	52
Egypt	44
Morocco	44
Poland	44
United Arab Emirates	44
Peru	37
Algeria	36
Philippines	36
Czech Republic	35
Costa Rica	32
El Salvador	32
Uzbekistan	31
Hungary	30
Vietnam	29
Ukraine	28
Ethiopia	25
Kenya	25
Bolivia	24
Papua New Guinea	24
Oman	22
Jamaica	21
Panama	21
Trinidad and Tobago	21
Ecuador	20
Tunisia	20
Kazakhstan	18
Romania	18
Kuwait	17
Croatia	16
Cuba	16
Jordan	16
Bulgaria	15
Zimbabwe	13
Estonia	11
Lithuania	11
Mauritius	11
Slovenia	11
Syria	11
Uruguay	11
Lebanon	10
Sri Lanka	10
Latvia	9
Namibia	8
Nigeria	8
Paraguay	8
Gabon	7
Guatemala	7
Sudan	7
Angola	6
Bangladesh	6
Belarus	6
Botswana	6
Côte d'Ivoire	6
Libya	6
Mozambique	6
Slovakia	6
Cameroon	5
Ghana	5
Tanzania	5
Georgia	3
Uganda	3
North Korea	1
Zambia	1

Source: International Civil Aviation Organization

Highest Per Capita Carbon Emissions

	CO_2 emissions per capita (tonnes) 1998	Growth in CO_2 emissions (%) 1990–98	Total CO_2 emissions (million tonnes) 1998
United States	20.1	12	5,410
Australia	16.6	20	311
Canada	15.8	13	477
Saudi Arabia	13.1	69	271
Germany	10.4	–11	857
Russia	9.6	–39	1,416
United Kingdom	9.3	–4	550
Japan	8.9	8	1,128
South Africa	8.5	22	354
Poland	8.3	–8	320
South Korea	8.0	59	370
Italy	7.5	6	426
Ukraine	7.1	–47	359
Spain	6.5	20	254
France	6.4	2	376
Iran	4.2	32	260
Mexico	3.7	20	356
China	2.3	21	2,893
Brazil	1.8	47	296
India	0.9	53	908
World	3.9	7	22,726

Fastest Growth in Carbon Emissions 1990–98

	Growth in CO_2 emissions (%) 1990–98	CO_2 emissions per capita (tonnes) 1998	Total CO_2 emissions (million tonnes) 1998
Saudi Arabia	69	13.1	271
South Korea	59	8.0	370
India	53	0.9	908
Brazil	47	1.8	296
Iran	32	4.2	260
South Africa	22	8.5	354
China	21	2.3	2,893
Australia	20	16.6	311
Spain	20	6.5	254
Mexico	20	3.7	356
Canada	13	15.8	477
United States	12	20.1	5,410
Japan	8	8.9	1,128
Italy	6	7.5	426
France	2	6.4	376
United Kingdom	–4	9.3	550
Poland	–8	8.3	320
Germany	–11	10.4	857
Russia	–39	9.6	1,416
Ukraine	–47	7.1	359
World	7	3.9	22,726

Energy

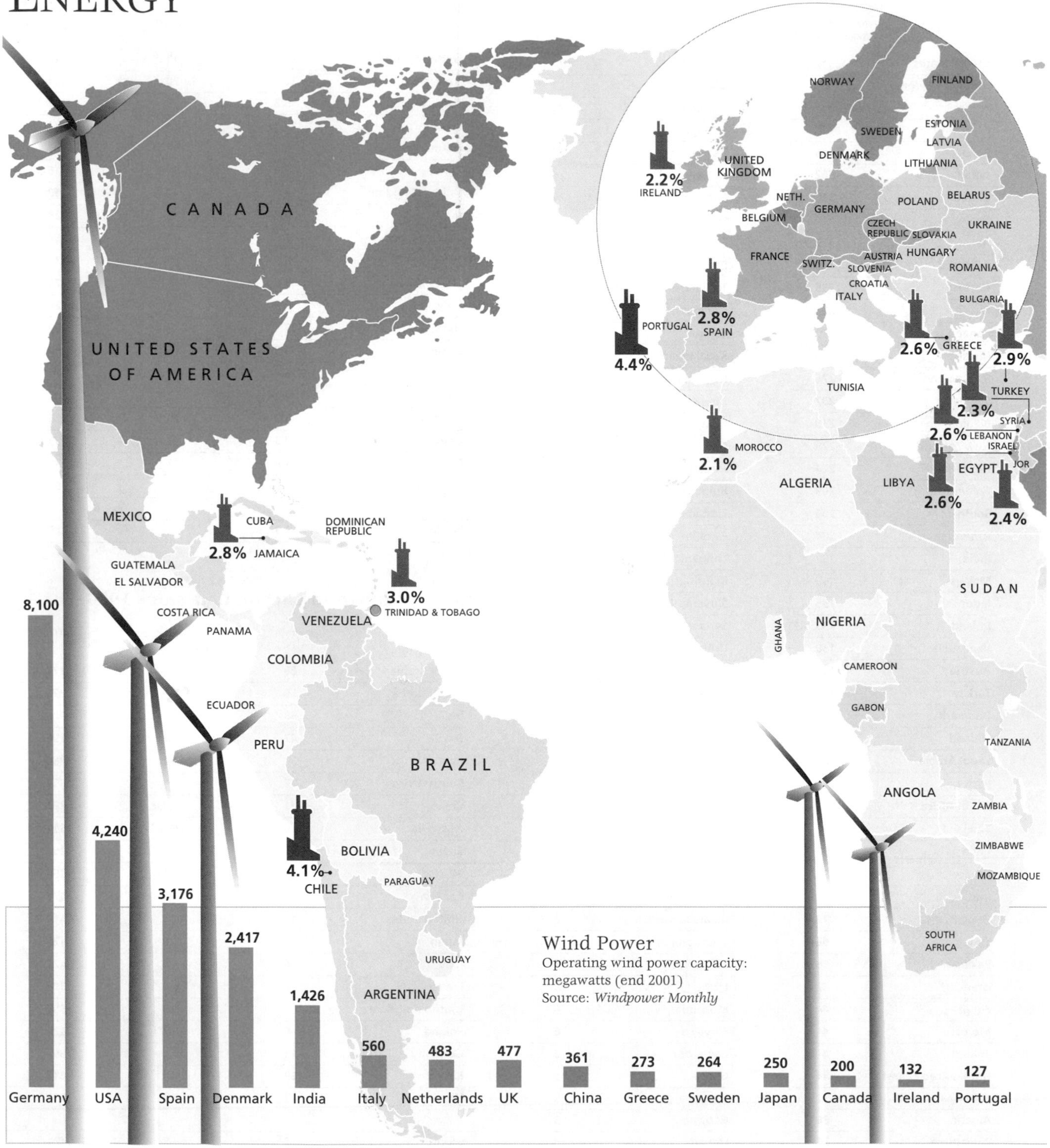

CANADA
UNITED STATES OF AMERICA
MEXICO
CUBA
2.8%
JAMAICA
DOMINICAN REPUBLIC
GUATEMALA
EL SALVADOR
COSTA RICA
PANAMA
3.0%
TRINIDAD & TOBAGO
VENEZUELA
COLOMBIA
ECUADOR
PERU
BRAZIL
4.1%
CHILE
BOLIVIA
PARAGUAY
URUGUAY
ARGENTINA

NORWAY
FINLAND
SWEDEN
ESTONIA
LATVIA
DENMARK
LITHUANIA
2.2%
IRELAND
UNITED KINGDOM
NETH.
GERMANY
POLAND
BELARUS
BELGIUM
CZECH REPUBLIC
SLOVAKIA
UKRAINE
FRANCE
SWITZ.
AUSTRIA
HUNGARY
SLOVENIA
ROMANIA
CROATIA
ITALY
BULGARIA
PORTUGAL
4.4%
2.8%
SPAIN
2.6%
GREECE
2.9%
TURKEY
2.3%
SYRIA
2.6%
LEBANON
ISRAEL
JOR
EGYPT
2.6%
2.4%
TUNISIA
MOROCCO
2.1%
ALGERIA
LIBYA
SUDAN
GHANA
NIGERIA
CAMEROON
GABON
TANZANIA
ANGOLA
ZAMBIA
ZIMBABWE
MOZAMBIQUE
SOUTH AFRICA

Wind Power
Operating wind power capacity: megawatts (end 2001)
Source: *Windpower Monthly*

Germany	8,100
USA	4,240
Spain	3,176
Denmark	2,417
India	1,426
Italy	560
Netherlands	483
UK	477
China	361
Greece	273
Sweden	264
Japan	250
Canada	200
Ireland	132
Portugal	127

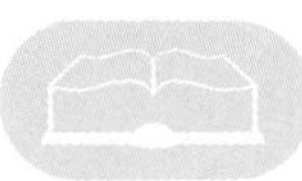

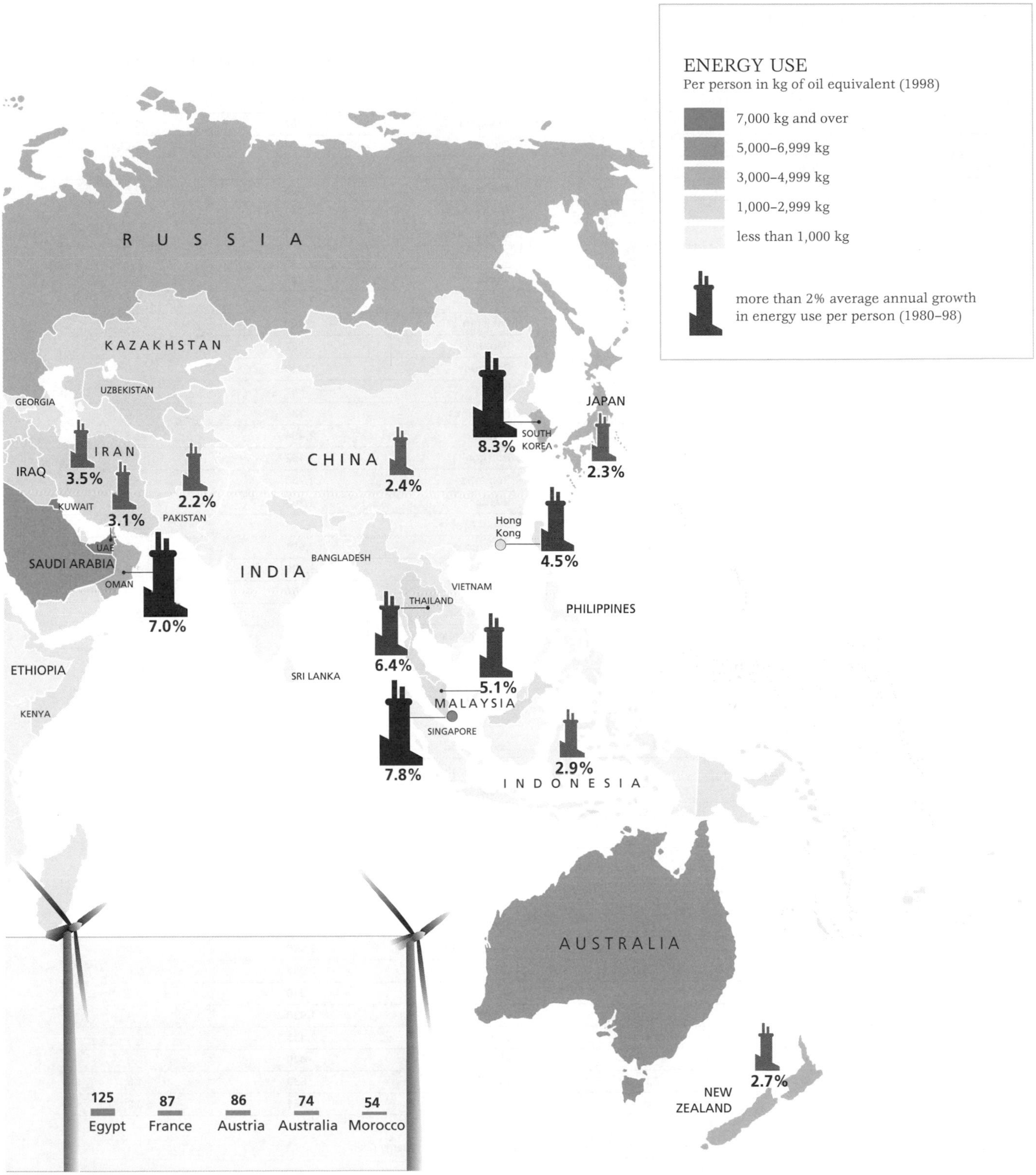

ENERGY USE

Per person in kg of oil equivalent (1998)

- 7,000 kg and over
- 5,000–6,999 kg
- 3,000–4,999 kg
- 1,000–2,999 kg
- less than 1,000 kg

more than 2% average annual growth in energy use per person (1980–98)

RUSSIA
KAZAKHSTAN
UZBEKISTAN
GEORGIA
IRAN 3.5%
IRAQ
KUWAIT 3.1%
2.2%
PAKISTAN
UAE
SAUDI ARABIA
OMAN 7.0%
INDIA
BANGLADESH
CHINA 2.4%
SOUTH KOREA 8.3%
JAPAN 2.3%
Hong Kong 4.5%
VIETNAM
PHILIPPINES
THAILAND 6.4%
SRI LANKA
MALAYSIA 5.1%
SINGAPORE 7.8%
INDONESIA 2.9%
ETHIOPIA
KENYA
AUSTRALIA
NEW ZEALAND 2.7%

125	87	86	74	54
Egypt	France	Austria	Australia	Morocco

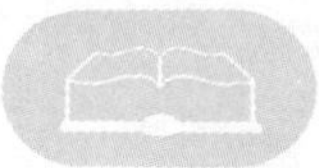

Energy Use and Growth 1980–98

	Energy use per capita (kg of oil equivalent) 1998	Growth in energy use per capita (% p.a.) 1980–98
Algeria	898	1.0
Angola	595	–0.2
Argentina	1,726	0.9
Australia	5,600	1.0
Austria	3,567	1.1
Bangladesh	159	1.4
Belarus	2,614	–
Belgium	5,719	1.5
Bolivia	581	0.7
Brazil	1,055	0.9
Bulgaria	2,418	–2.1
Cameroon	432	–0.3
Canada	7,747	0.4
Chile	1,594	4.1
China	830	2.4
Colombia	753	0.8
Costa Rica	789	1.5
Croatia	1,808	–
Cuba	1,066	–2.8
Czech Republic	3,986	–1.2
Denmark	3,925	0.7
Dominican Republic	676	0.3
Ecuador	737	0.3
Egypt	679	2.4
El Salvador	640	0.5
Estonia	3,335	–
Ethiopia	284	–0.4
Finland	6,493	1.3
France	4,378	1.6
Gabon	1,413	–3.4
Georgia	464	–
Germany	4,199	–0.5
Ghana	396	0.6
Greece	2,565	2.6
Guatemala	579	0.5
Hong Kong	2,497	4.5
Hungary	2,497	–0.7
India	486	1.9
Indonesia	604	2.9
Iran	1,649	3.5
Iraq	1,342	1.7
Ireland	3,570	2.2
Israel	3,165	2.6
Italy	2,916	1.3
Jamaica	1,575	2.8
Japan	4,035	2.3
Jordan	1,063	0.6
Kazakhstan	2,590	–
Kenya	505	–0.9
Kuwait	7,823	–0.7
Latvia	1,746	–
Lebanon	1,256	2.6
Libya	2,343	0.7
Lithuania	2,524	–
Malaysia	1,967	5.1
Mexico	1,552	0.2
Morocco	336	2.1
Mozambique	405	–2.6
Netherlands	4,740	0.9
New Zealand	4,525	2.7
Nigeria	716	–0.3
Norway	5,736	1.3
Oman	3,165	7.0
Pakistan	440	2.2
Panama	862	–0.2
Paraguay	819	1.5
Peru	581	–0.9
Philippines	526	1.4
Poland	2,494	–1.8
Portugal	2,192	4.4
Romania	1,760	–3.0
Russia	3,963	–
Saudi Arabia	5,244	0.9
Singapore	7,681	7.8
Slovakia	3,136	–1.8
Slovenia	3,354	–
South Africa	2,681	–0.1
South Korea	3,519	8.3
Spain	2,865	2.8
Sri Lanka	389	0.9
Sudan	526	0.5
Sweden	5,928	0.8
Switzerland	3,742	0.8
Syria	1,133	2.3
Tanzania	456	–1.1
Thailand	1,153	6.4
Trinidad and Tobago	6,964	3.0
Tunisia	812	1.5
Turkey	1,144	2.9
Ukraine	2,842	–
United Arab Emirates	10,035	3.1
United Kingdom	3,930	0.8
United States	7,937	0.4
Uruguay	910	0.6
Uzbekistan	1,930	–
Venezuela	2,433	0.0
Vietnam	440	0.9
Zambia	630	–1.6
Zimbabwe	861	–0.2

Source: International Energy Agency

Largest Energy Use Per Person

Country	Energy use per capita (kg of oil equivalent) 1998
United Arab Emirates	10,035
United States	7,937
Kuwait	7,823
Canada	7,747
Singapore	7,681
Trinidad and Tobago	6,964
Finland	6,493
Sweden	5,928
Norway	5,736
Belgium	5,719
Australia	5,600
Saudi Arabia	5,244
Netherlands	4,740
New Zealand	4,525
France	4,378
Germany	4,199
Japan	4,035
Czech Republic	3,986
Russia	3,963
United Kingdom	3,930
Denmark	3,925
Switzerland	3,742
Ireland	3,570
Austria	3,567
South Korea	3,519
Slovenia	3,354
Estonia	3,335
Israel	3,165
Oman	3,165
Slovakia	3,136
Italy	2,916
Spain	2,865
Ukraine	2,842
South Africa	2,681
Belarus	2,614
Kazakhstan	2,590
Greece	2,565
Lithuania	2,524
Hong Kong	2,497
Hungary	2,497
Poland	2,494
Venezuela	2,433
Bulgaria	2,418
Libya	2,343
Portugal	2,192
Malaysia	1,967
Uzbekistan	1,930
Croatia	1,808
Romania	1,760
Latvia	1,746
Argentina	1,726
Iran	1,649
Chile	1,594

Country	Energy use per capita (kg of oil equivalent) 1998
Jamaica	1,575
Mexico	1,552
Gabon	1,413
Iraq	1,342
Lebanon	1,256
Thailand	1,153
Turkey	1,144
Syria	1,133
Cuba	1,066
Jordan	1,063
Brazil	1,055
Uruguay	910
Algeria	898
Panama	862
Zimbabwe	861
China	830
Paraguay	819
Tunisia	812
Costa Rica	789
Colombia	753
Ecuador	737
Nigeria	716
Egypt	679
Dominican Republic	676
El Salvador	640
Zambia	630
Indonesia	604
Angola	595
Bolivia	581
Peru	581
Guatemala	579
Philippines	526
Sudan	526
Kenya	505
India	486
Georgia	464
Tanzania	456
Pakistan	440
Vietnam	440
Cameroon	432
Mozambique	405
Ghana	396
Sri Lanka	389
Morocco	336
Ethiopia	284
Bangladesh	159

Fastest Growth in Energy Use Per Person 1980–98

Country	Growth in energy use per capita (% p.a.) 1980–98
South Korea	8.3
Singapore	7.8
Oman	7.0
Thailand	6.4
Malaysia	5.1
Hong Kong	4.5
Portugal	4.4
Chile	4.1
Iran	3.5
United Arab Emirates	3.1
Trinidad and Tobago	3.0
Turkey	2.9
Indonesia	2.9
Spain	2.8
Jamaica	2.8
New Zealand	2.7
Israel	2.6
Greece	2.6
Lebanon	2.6
China	2.4
Egypt	2.4
Japan	2.3
Syria	2.3
Ireland	2.2
Pakistan	2.2
Morocco	2.1
India	1.9
Iraq	1.7
France	1.6
Belgium	1.5
Paraguay	1.5
Tunisia	1.5
Costa Rica	1.5
Philippines	1.4
Bangladesh	1.4
Finland	1.3
Norway	1.3
Italy	1.3
Austria	1.1
Australia	1.0
Algeria	1.0
Saudi Arabia	0.9
Netherlands	0.9
Argentina	0.9
Brazil	0.9
Vietnam	0.9
Sri Lanka	0.9
Sweden	0.8
United Kingdom	0.8
Switzerland	0.8
Colombia	0.8
Denmark	0.7
Libya	0.7

Country	Growth in energy use per capita (% p.a.) 1980–98
Bolivia	0.7
Jordan	0.6
Uruguay	0.6
Ghana	0.6
El Salvador	0.5
Guatemala	0.5
Sudan	0.5
United States	0.4
Canada	0.4
Ecuador	0.3
Dominican Republic	0.3
Mexico	0.2
Venezuela	0.0
South Africa	–0.1
Panama	–0.2
Zimbabwe	–0.2
Angola	–0.2
Nigeria	–0.3
Cameroon	–0.3
Ethiopia	–0.4
Germany	–0.5
Kuwait	–0.7
Hungary	–0.7
Peru	–0.9
Kenya	–0.9
Tanzania	–1.1
Czech Republic	–1.2
Zambia	–1.6
Slovakia	–1.8
Poland	–1.8
Bulgaria	–2.1
Mozambique	–2.6
Cuba	–2.8
Romania	–3.0
Gabon	–3.4

Contribution of Hydropower and Nuclear Power

	Hydropower (%) 1998	Nuclear power (%) 1998
Algeria	3	–
Angola	90	–
Argentina	36	10
Australia	8	–
Austria	67	–
Bangladesh	7	–
Belarus	0	–
Belgium	1	56
Bolivia	41	–
Brazil	91	1
Bulgaria	8	41
Cameroon	99	–
Canada	59	13
Chile	47	–
China	18	1
Colombia	67	–
Costa Rica	82	–
Croatia	50	–
Cuba	1	–
Czech Republic	2	20
Denmark	0	–
Dominican Republic	19	–
Ecuador	66	–
Egypt	19	–
El Salvador	41	–
Estonia	0	–
Ethiopia	97	–
Finland	21	31
France	12	77
Gabon	71	–
Georgia	79	–
Germany	3	29
Ghana	100	–
Greece	8	–
Guatemala	77	–
Hungary	0	38
India	17	2
Indonesia	12	–
Iran	7	–
Iraq	2	–
Ireland	4	–
Israel	0	–
Italy	16	–
Jamaica	1	–
Japan	9	32
Jordan	0	–
Kazakhstan	13	–
Kenya	68	–
Latvia	75	–
Lebanon	9	–
Lithuania	2	79
Malaysia	8	–
Mexico	14	5
Morocco	12	–
Mozambique	99	–
Netherlands	0	4
New Zealand	65	–
Nigeria	36	–
Norway	99	–
Pakistan	36	1
Panama	49	–
Paraguay	100	–
Peru	74	–
Philippines	12	–
Poland	2	–
Portugal	33	–
Romania	35	10
Russia	19	13
Slovakia	17	45
Slovenia	25	37
South Africa	1	7
South Korea	2	38
Spain	18	31
Sri Lanka	69	–
Sudan	53	–
Sweden	47	47
Switzerland	54	42
Syria	41	–
Tanzania	97	–
Thailand	6	–
Tunisia	1	–
Turkey	38	–
Ukraine	9	44
United Kingdom	2	28
United States	8	19
Uruguay	96	–
Uzbekistan	13	–
Venezuela	72	–
Vietnam	51	–
Zambia	100	–
Zimbabwe	29	–

Source: International Energy Agency

Largest Use of Hydropower

	Hydropower (%) 1998
Paraguay	100
Ghana	100
Zambia	100
Mozambique	99
Norway	99
Cameroon	99
Ethiopia	97
Tanzania	97
Uruguay	96
Brazil	91
Angola	90
Costa Rica	82
Georgia	79
Guatemala	77
Latvia	75
Peru	74
Venezuela	72
Gabon	71
Sri Lanka	69
Kenya	68
Colombia	67
Austria	67
Ecuador	66
New Zealand	65
Canada	59
Switzerland	54
Sudan	53
Vietnam	51
Croatia	50
Panama	49
Chile	47
Sweden	47
Bolivia	41
Syria	41
El Salvador	41
Turkey	38
Argentina	36
Nigeria	36
Pakistan	36
Romania	35
Portugal	33
Zimbabwe	29
Slovenia	25
Finland	21
Egypt	19
Russia	19
Dominican Republic	19
China	18
Spain	18
Slovakia	17
India	17
Italy	16
Mexico	14
Kazakhstan	13
Uzbekistan	13
Indonesia	12
Morocco	12
Philippines	12
France	12
Lebanon	9

	Hydropower (%) 1998
Ukraine	9
Japan	9
Australia	8
Greece	8
Malaysia	8
United States	8
Bulgaria	8
Iran	7
Bangladesh	7
Thailand	6
Ireland	4
Algeria	3
Germany	3
Lithuania	2
Czech Republic	2
Iraq	2
South Korea	2
Poland	2
United Kingdom	2
Jamaica	1
Tunisia	1
Cuba	1
South Africa	1
Belgium	1

Greatest Dependence on Nuclear Power

	Nuclear power (%) 1998
Lithuania	79
France	77
Belgium	56
Sweden	47
Slovakia	45
Ukraine	44
Switzerland	42
Bulgaria	41
South Korea	38
Hungary	38
Slovenia	37
Japan	32
Finland	31
Spain	31
Germany	29
United Kingdom	28
Czech Republic	20
United States	19
Canada	13
Russia	13
Argentina	10
Romania	10
South Africa	7
Mexico	5
Netherlands	4
India	2
China	1
Brazil	1
Pakistan	1

Wind and Solar Power

	Total operating wind power capacity (megawatts) end 2001	Operating solar power capacity added in 2001 (megawatts)
Germany	8,100	70
United States	4,240	34
Spain	3,175	1.5
Denmark	2,417	–
India	1,426	18
Italy	560	4
Netherlands	483	–
United Kingdom	477	–
China	361	–
Greece	273	–
Sweden	264	–
Japan	250	120
Canada	200	6
Ireland	132	–
Portugal	127	–
Egypt	125	–
France	87	–
Austria	86	–
Australia	74	15
Morocco	54	–
Costa Rica	51	–
Ukraine	40	–
Finland	39	–
New Zealand	37	–
Brazil	20	2
Turkey	20	–
Belgium	18	–
Norway	16	–
Poland	16	–
Argentina	14	–
Czech Republic	12	–
Iran	11	–
Luxembourg	10	–
Israel	8	–
South Korea	8	–
Mexico	5	2
Russia	5	–
Sri Lanka	3	–
Switzerland	3	–
Taiwan	3	–
Jordan	2	–
Latvia	1	–
Romania	1	–
World	23,270	273

Sources: BTM Consult ApS, PV Energy Systems Inc.

Largest Wind Power Capacity Per Capita

	Operating wind power capacity per capita (watts) end 2001	Total operating wind power capacity (megawatts) end 2001
Denmark	458	2,417
Germany	99	8,100
Spain	80	3,176
Ireland	36	132
Netherlands	31	483
Sweden	30	264
Greece	26	273
Luxembourg	23	10
United States	15	4,240
Portugal	13	127
Costa Rica	13	51
Austria	11	86
Italy	10	560
New Zealand	10	37
United Kingdom	8	477
Finland	8	39
Canada	6	200
Australia	4	74
Norway	4	16
Japan	2	250
Egypt	2	125
Morocco	2	54
Belgium	2	18
India	1	1,426
France	1	87
Ukraine	1	40
Czech Republic	1	12
Israel	1	8
Latvia	0.4	361
Poland	0.4	20
Switzerland	0.4	20
Argentina	0.4	16
Jordan	0.3	14
Turkey	0.3	11
China	0.3	8
South Korea	0.2	5
Iran	0.2	5
Sri Lanka	0.2	3
Taiwan	0.1	3
Brazil	0.1	3
Mexico	0.05	2
Romania	0.04	1
Russia	0.03	1

BUSINESS ENVIRONMENT

CANADA
UNITED STATES OF AMERICA
MEXICO
DOMINICAN REPUBLIC
GUATEMALA
EL SALVADOR
COSTA RICA
PANAMA
VENEZUELA
TRINIDAD & TOBAGO
COLOMBIA
ECUADOR
BRAZIL
PERU
BOLIVIA
CHILE
URUGUAY
ARGENTINA
ICELAND
NORWAY
SWEDEN
FINLAND
ESTONIA
LATVIA
LITHUANIA
DENMARK
UNITED KINGDOM
IRELAND
NETH.
BELGIUM
GERMANY
POLAND
CZECH REPUBLIC
SLOVAKIA
UKRAINE
LUXEMBOURG
AUSTRIA
HUNGARY
SLOVENIA
FRANCE
ROMANIA
CROATIA
ITALY
BULGARIA
PORTUGAL
SPAIN
SWITZERLAND
GREECE
TUNISIA
TURKEY
ISRAEL
JOR.
EGYPT
CÔTE D'IVOIRE
GHANA
NIGERIA
CAMEROON
UGANDA
TANZANIA
ZAMBIA
ZIMBABWE
NAMIBIA
BOTSWANA
SOUTH AFRICA

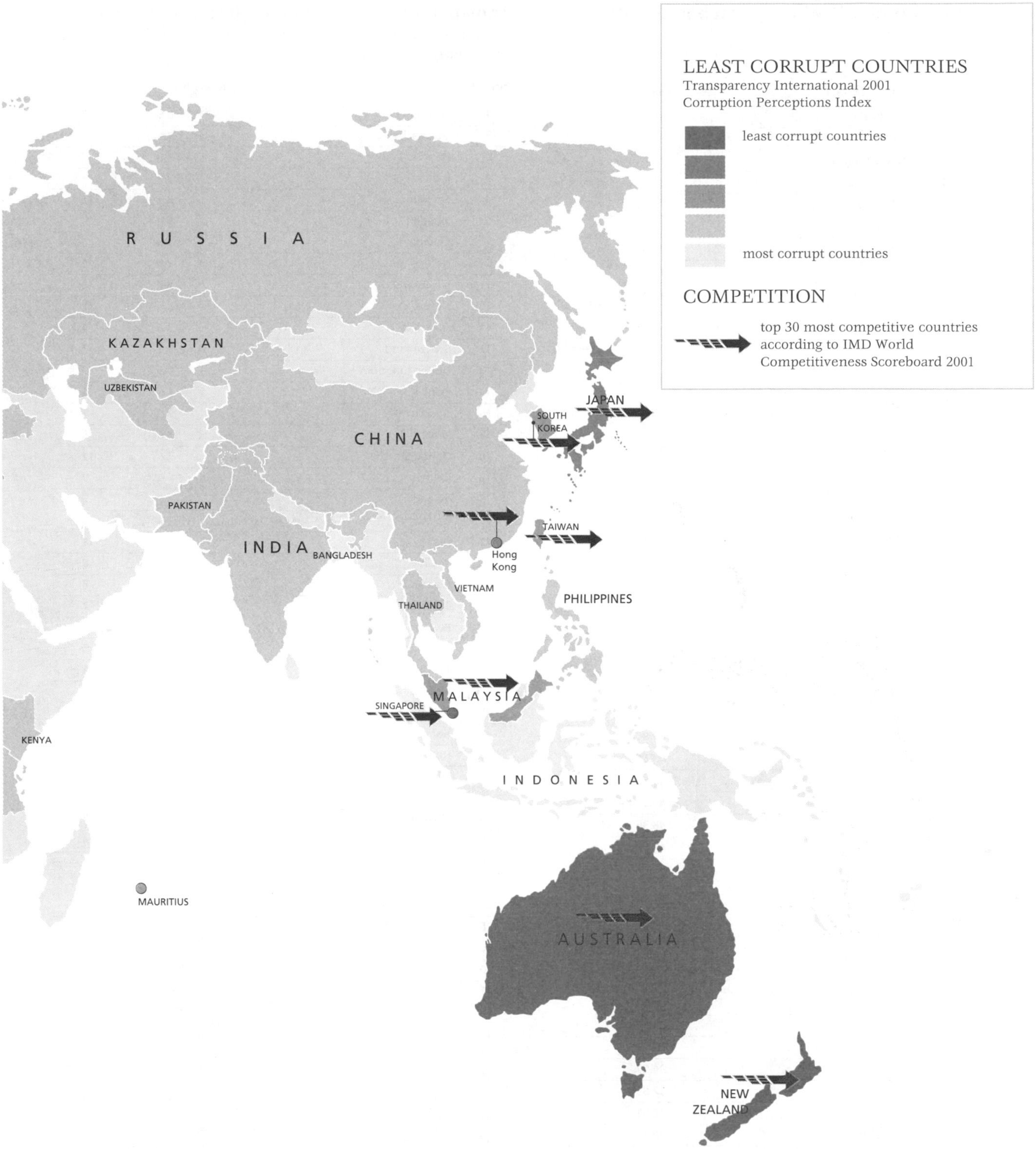
LEAST CORRUPT COUNTRIES
Transparency International 2001
Corruption Perceptions Index
least corrupt countries
most corrupt countries
COMPETITION
top 30 most competitive countries according to IMD World Competitiveness Scoreboard 2001
RUSSIA
KAZAKHSTAN
UZBEKISTAN
CHINA
JAPAN
SOUTH KOREA
PAKISTAN
INDIA
BANGLADESH
Hong Kong
TAIWAN
VIETNAM
THAILAND
PHILIPPINES
MALAYSIA
SINGAPORE
KENYA
INDONESIA
MAURITIUS
AUSTRALIA
NEW ZEALAND

  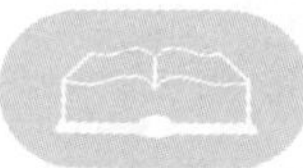    

IMD World Competitiveness Scoreboard 2001

Rank 2001	Rank 2000		Score 2001
1	1	United States	100.00
2	2	Singapore	87.66
3	4	Finland	83.38
4	6	Luxembourg	82.81
5	3	Netherlands	81.46
6	12	Hong Kong	79.55
7	5	Ireland	79.20
8	14	Sweden	77.86
9	8	Canada	76.94
10	7	Switzerland	76.81
11	10	Australia	75.87
12	11	Germany	74.04
13	9	Iceland	73.75
14	15	Austria	72.54
15	13	Denmark	71.79
16	21	Israel	67.92
17	19	Belgium	66.03
18	20	Taiwan	64.84
19	16	United Kingdom	64.78
20	17	Norway	63.10
21	18	New Zealand	61.73
22		Estonia	60.20
23	23	Spain	60.14
24	25	Chile	59.84
25	22	France	59.56
26	24	Japan	57.52
27	26	Hungary	55.64
28	28	South Korea	51.08
29	27	Malaysia	50.03
30	34	Greece	49.96
31	31	Brazil	49.66
32	32	Italy	49.58
33	30	China	49.53
34	29	Portugal	48.36
35	40	Czech Republic	46.68
36	33	Mexico	43.67
37		Slovakia	43.59
38	35	Thailand	42.67
39	36	Slovenia	42.48
40	37	Philippines	40.60
41	39	India	40.41
42	43	South Africa	38.61
43	41	Argentina	37.51
44	42	Turkey	35.44
45	47	Russia	34.57
46	45	Colombia	32.84
47	38	Poland	32.01
48	46	Venezuela	30.66
49	44	Indonesia	28.26

Source: *The World Competitiveness Yearbook 2001*, IMD, Switzerland, www.imd.ch/wcy

Transparency International 2001 Corruption Perceptions Index

Least corrupt countries

Rank 2001		Corruption Perceptions Index 2001	No. of surveys used
1	Finland	9.9	7
2	Denmark	9.5	7
3	New Zealand	9.4	7
4	Iceland	9.2	6
4	Singapore	9.2	12
6	Sweden	9.0	8
7	Canada	8.9	8
8	Netherlands	8.8	7
9	Luxembourg	8.7	6
10	Norway	8.6	7
11	Australia	8.5	9
12	Switzerland	8.4	7
13	United Kingdom	8.3	9
14	Hong Kong	7.9	11
15	Austria	7.8	7
16	Israel	7.6	8
16	United States	7.6	11
18	Chile	7.5	9
18	Ireland	7.5	7
20	Germany	7.4	8
21	Japan	7.1	11
22	Spain	7.0	8
23	France	6.7	8
24	Belgium	6.6	7
25	Portugal	6.3	8
26	Botswana	6.0	3
27	Taiwan	5.9	11
28	Estonia	5.6	5
29	Italy	5.5	9
30	Namibia	5.4	3
31	Hungary	5.3	10
31	Trinidad and Tobago	5.3	3
31	Tunisia	5.3	3
34	Slovenia	5.2	7
35	Uruguay	5.1	4
36	Malaysia	5.0	11
37	Jordan	4.9	4
38	Lithuania	4.8	5
38	South Africa	4.8	10
40	Costa Rica	4.5	5
40	Mauritius	4.5	5
42	Greece	4.2	8
42	South Korea	4.2	11
44	Peru	4.1	6
44	Poland	4.1	10
46	Brazil	4.0	9
47	Bulgaria	3.9	6
47	Croatia	3.9	3
47	Czech Republic	3.9	10
50	Colombia	3.8	9
51	Mexico	3.7	9
51	Panama	3.7	3
51	Slovakia	3.7	7
54	Egypt	3.6	7

  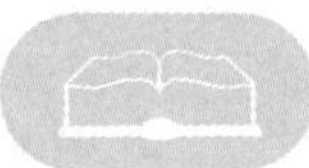    

Rank 2001		Corruption Perceptions Index 2001	No. of surveys used
54	El Salvador	3.6	5
54	Turkey	3.6	9
57	Argentina	3.5	9
57	China	3.5	10
59	Ghana	3.4	3
59	Latvia	3.4	3
61	Thailand	3.2	12
63	Dominican Republic	3.1	3
65	Guatemala	2.9	4
65	Philippines	2.9	11
65	Zimbabwe	2.9	6
69	Romania	2.8	5
69	Venezuela	2.8	9
71	India	2.7	12
71	Kazakhstan	2.7	3
71	Uzbekistan	2.7	3
75	Vietnam	2.6	7
75	Zambia	2.6	3
77	Côte d'Ivoire	2.4	3
79	Ecuador	2.3	6
79	Pakistan	2.3	3
79	Russia	2.3	10
82	Tanzania	2.2	3
83	Ukraine	2.1	6
84	Bolivia	2.0	5
84	Cameroon	2.0	3
84	Kenya	2.0	4
88	Indonesia	1.9	12
88	Uganda	1.9	3
90	Nigeria	1.0	4
91	Bangladesh	0.4	3

Transparency International 2001 Corruption Perceptions Index

Most corrupt countries

Rank 2001		Corruption Perceptions Index 2001	No. of surveys used
91	Bangladesh	0.4	3
90	Nigeria	1.0	4
88	Indonesia	1.9	12
88	Uganda	1.9	3
84	Bolivia	2.0	5
84	Cameroon	2.0	3
84	Kenya	2.0	4
83	Ukraine	2.1	6
82	Tanzania	2.2	3
79	Ecuador	2.3	6
79	Pakistan	2.3	3
79	Russia	2.3	10
77	Côte d'Ivoire	2.4	3
75	Vietnam	2.6	7
75	Zambia	2.6	3
71	India	2.7	12
71	Kazakhstan	2.7	3
71	Uzbekistan	2.7	3
69	Romania	2.8	5
69	Venezuela	2.8	9
65	Guatemala	2.9	4
65	Philippines	2.9	11
65	Zimbabwe	2.9	6
63	Dominican Republic	3.1	3
61	Thailand	3.2	12
59	Ghana	3.4	3
59	Latvia	3.4	3
57	Argentina	3.5	9
57	China	3.5	10
54	Egypt	3.6	7
54	El Salvador	3.6	5
54	Turkey	3.6	9
51	Mexico	3.7	9
51	Panama	3.7	3
51	Slovakia	3.7	7
50	Colombia	3.8	9
47	Bulgaria	3.9	6
47	Croatia	3.9	3
47	Czech Republic	3.9	10
46	Brazil	4.0	9
44	Peru	4.1	6
44	Poland	4.1	10
42	Greece	4.2	8
42	South Korea	4.2	11
40	Costa Rica	4.5	5
40	Mauritius	4.5	5
38	Lithuania	4.8	5
38	South Africa	4.8	10
37	Jordan	4.9	4
36	Malaysia	5.0	11
35	Uruguay	5.1	4
34	Slovenia	5.2	7
31	Hungary	5.3	10
31	Trinidad and Tobago	5.3	3
31	Tunisia	5.3	3
30	Namibia	5.4	3
29	Italy	5.5	9
28	Estonia	5.6	5
27	Taiwan	5.9	11
26	Botswana	6.0	3

WEALTH

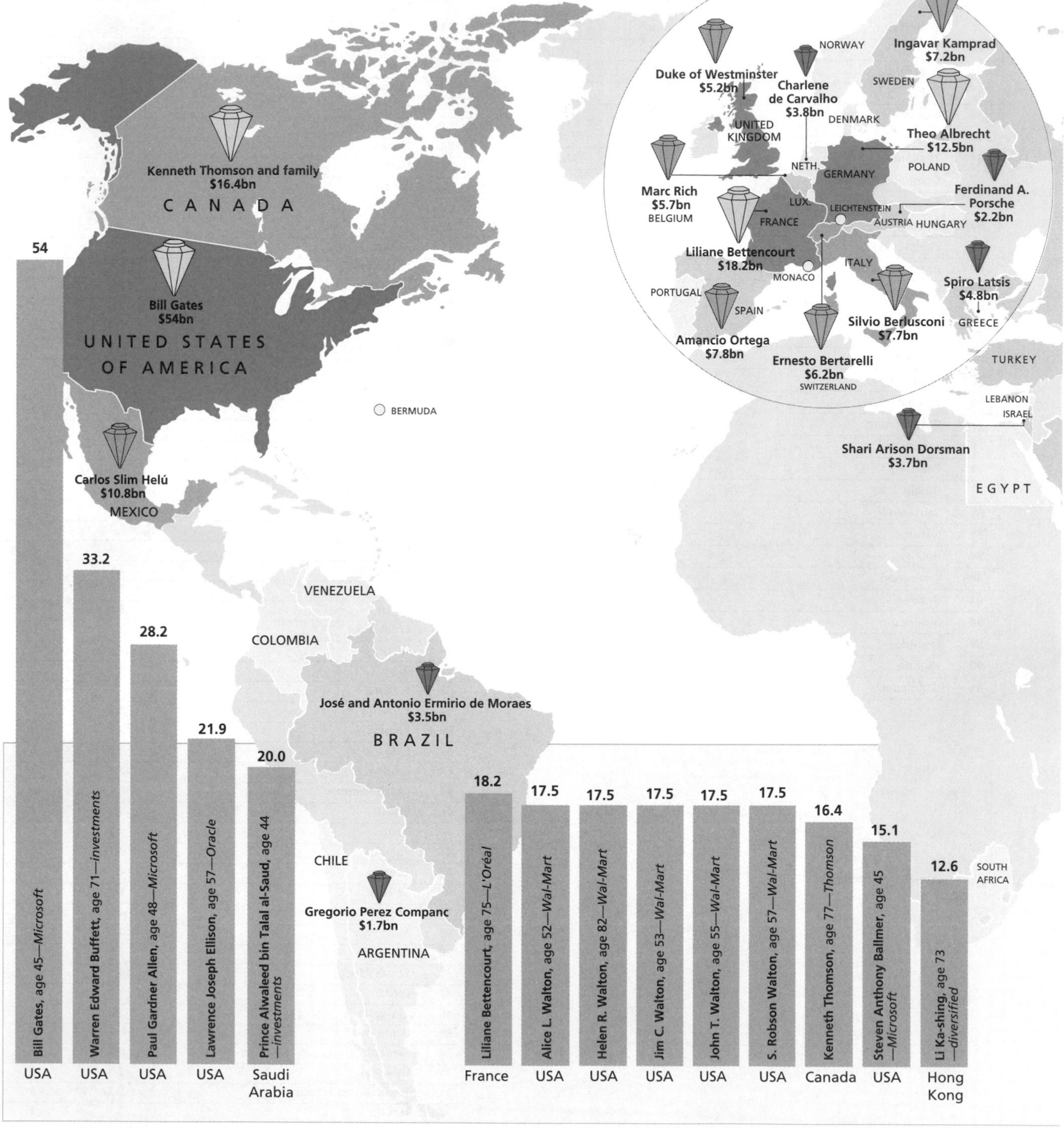

- Kenneth Thomson and family $16.4bn — CANADA
- Bill Gates $54bn — UNITED STATES OF AMERICA
- Carlos Slim Helú $10.8bn — MEXICO
- BERMUDA
- VENEZUELA
- COLOMBIA
- José and Antonio Ermirio de Moraes $3.5bn — BRAZIL
- CHILE
- Gregorio Perez Companc $1.7bn — ARGENTINA
- Duke of Westminster $5.2bn — UNITED KINGDOM
- Charlene de Carvalho $3.8bn — NETH.
- NORWAY
- Ingavar Kamprad $7.2bn — SWEDEN
- DENMARK
- Theo Albrecht $12.5bn — GERMANY
- POLAND
- Marc Rich $5.7bn — BELGIUM
- LUX.
- Liliane Bettencourt $18.2bn — FRANCE
- LEICHTENSTEIN
- AUSTRIA
- Ferdinand A. Porsche $2.2bn — AUSTRIA
- HUNGARY
- MONACO
- ITALY
- PORTUGAL
- Amancio Ortega $7.8bn — SPAIN
- Ernesto Bertarelli $6.2bn — SWITZERLAND
- Silvio Berlusconi $7.7bn — ITALY
- Spiro Latsis $4.8bn — GREECE
- TURKEY
- LEBANON
- Shari Arison Dorsman $3.7bn — ISRAEL
- EGYPT
- SOUTH AFRICA

Name	Value ($bn)	Country
Bill Gates, age 45—*Microsoft*	54	USA
Warren Edward Buffett, age 71—*investments*	33.2	USA
Paul Gardner Allen, age 48—*Microsoft*	28.2	USA
Lawrence Joseph Ellison, age 57—*Oracle*	21.9	USA
Prince Alwaleed bin Talal al-Saud, age 44—*investments*	20.0	Saudi Arabia
Liliane Bettencourt, age 75—*L'Oréal*	18.2	France
Alice L. Walton, age 52—*Wal-Mart*	17.5	USA
Helen R. Walton, age 82—*Wal-Mart*	17.5	USA
Jim C. Walton, age 53—*Wal-Mart*	17.5	USA
John T. Walton, age 55—*Wal-Mart*	17.5	USA
S. Robson Walton, age 57—*Wal-Mart*	17.5	USA
Kenneth Thomson, age 77—*Thomson*	16.4	Canada
Steven Anthony Ballmer, age 45—*Microsoft*	15.1	USA
Li Ka-shing, age 73—*diversified*	12.6	Hong Kong

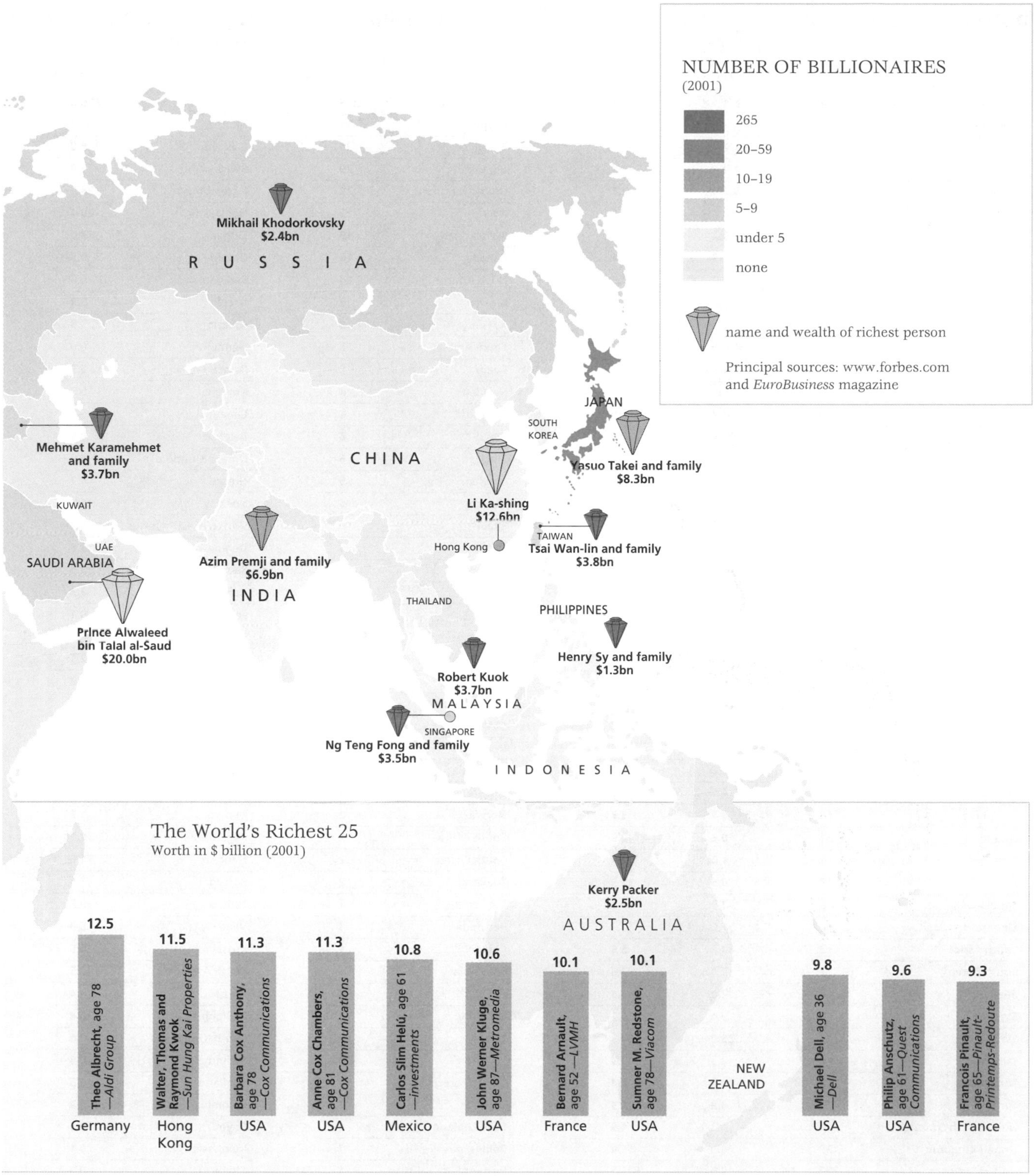

NUMBER OF BILLIONAIRES
(2001)

- 265
- 20–59
- 10–19
- 5–9
- under 5
- none

name and wealth of richest person

Principal sources: www.forbes.com and *EuroBusiness* magazine

RUSSIA
Mikhail Khodorkovsky **$2.4bn**

Mehmet Karamehmet and family **$3.7bn**

KUWAIT

UAE

SAUDI ARABIA
Prince Alwaleed bin Talal al-Saud **$20.0bn**

INDIA
Azim Premji and family **$6.9bn**

CHINA

Hong Kong
Li Ka-shing **$12.6bn**

SOUTH KOREA

JAPAN
Yasuo Takei and family **$8.3bn**

TAIWAN
Tsai Wan-lin and family **$3.8bn**

THAILAND

PHILIPPINES
Henry Sy and family **$1.3bn**

MALAYSIA
Robert Kuok **$3.7bn**

SINGAPORE
Ng Teng Fong and family **$3.5bn**

INDONESIA

AUSTRALIA
Kerry Packer **$2.5bn**

NEW ZEALAND

The World's Richest 25

Worth in $ billion (2001)

12.5	Theo Albrecht, age 78 —*Aldi Group*	Germany
11.5	Walter, Thomas and Raymond Kwok —*Sun Hung Kai Properties*	Hong Kong
11.3	Barbara Cox Anthony, age 78 —*Cox Communications*	USA
11.3	Anne Cox Chambers, age 81 —*Cox Communications*	USA
10.8	Carlos Slim Helú, age 61 —*Investments*	Mexico
10.6	John Werner Kluge, age 87—*Metromedia*	USA
10.1	Bernard Arnault, age 52 —*LVMH*	France
10.1	Sumner M. Redstone, age 78—*Viacom*	USA
9.8	Michael Dell, age 36 —*Dell*	USA
9.6	Philip Anschutz, age 61—*Quest Communications*	USA
9.3	Francois Pinault, age 65—*Pinault-Printemps-Redoute*	France

Distribution of Billionaires

	No. of billionaires in 2001	No. of billionaires per 10 million people in 2001	Total worth of billionaires ($ billion) 2001
Argentina	4	1.1	5.3
Australia	3	1.6	6.0
Austria	6	7.3	9.5
Belgium	5	4.9	13.3
Bermuda	1	160.0	2.1
Brazil	6	0.4	14.1
Canada	16	5.2	46.7
Chile	2	1.3	2.6
China	1	0.0	1.3
Colombia	1	0.2	1.5
Denmark	2	3.8	4.2
Egypt	1	0.1	1.0
France	31	5.3	98.5
Germany	57	6.9	189.9
Greece	5	4.7	13.0
Hong Kong	14	20.4	50.6
Hungary	1	1.0	2.2
India	4	0.0	14.2
Indonesia	2	0.1	3.0
Israel	5	8.2	9.9
Italy	19	3.3	40.7
Japan	29	2.3	89.3
Kuwait	1	5.3	6.0
Lebanon	1	3.1	3.1
Liechtenstein	2	625.0	5.7
Luxembourg	1	23.5	3.4
Malaysia	4	1.8	7.3
Mexico	13	1.3	34.1
Monaco	1	303.0	4.3
Netherlands	4	2.5	11.5
New Zealand	1	2.6	1.0
Norway	2	4.5	2.6
Philippines	3	0.4	3.7
Poland	1	0.3	2.9
Portugal	1	1.0	2.0
Russia	8	0.5	12.3
Saudi Arabia	8	3.8	40.8
Singapore	6	17.0	11.3
South Africa	2	0.5	5.8
South Korea	2	0.4	2.6
Spain	8	2.0	19.3
Sweden	8	9.0	30.2
Switzerland	19	25.9	57.3
Taiwan	5	2.3	11.3
Thailand	2	0.3	2.4
Turkey	5	0.8	13.3
United Arab Emirates	1	4.2	1.9
United Kingdom	29	4.9	59.4
United States	265	9.6	841.5
Venezuela	2	0.8	9.8
World	620	–	1,825.7

Most Billionaires

	No. of billionaires in 2001
United States	265
Germany	57
France	31
Japan	29
United Kingdom	29
Italy	19
Switzerland	19
Canada	16
Hong Kong	14
Mexico	13
Russia	8
Saudi Arabia	8
Spain	8
Sweden	8
Austria	6
Brazil	6
Singapore	6
Belgium	5
Greece	5
Israel	5
Taiwan	5
Turkey	5
Argentina	4
India	4
Malaysia	4
Netherlands	4
Australia	3
Philippines	3
Chile	2
Denmark	2
Indonesia	2
Liechtenstein	2
Norway	2
South Africa	2
South Korea	2
Thailand	2
Venezuela	2
Bermuda	1
China	1
Colombia	1
Egypt	1
Hungary	1
Kuwait	1
Lebanon	1
Luxembourg	1
Monaco	1
New Zealand	1
Poland	1
Portugal	1
United Arab Emirates	1
World	620

Highest Density of Billionaires

	No. of billionaires per 10 million people in 2001
Liechtenstein	625.0
Monaco	303.0
Bermuda	160.0
Switzerland	25.9
Luxembourg	23.5
Hong Kong	20.4
Singapore	17.0
United States	9.6
Sweden	9.0
Israel	8.2
Austria	7.3
Germany	6.9
France	5.3
Kuwait	5.3
Canada	5.2
Belgium	4.9
United Kingdom	4.9
Greece	4.7
Norway	4.5
United Arab Emirates	4.2
Denmark	3.8
Saudi Arabia	3.8
Italy	3.3
Lebanon	3.1
New Zealand	2.6
Netherlands	2.5
Japan	2.3
Taiwan	2.3
Spain	2.0
Malaysia	1.8
Australia	1.6
Chile	1.3
Mexico	1.3
Argentina	1.1
Hungary	1.0
Portugal	1.0
Turkey	0.8
Venezuela	0.8
Russia	0.5
South Africa	0.5
Brazil	0.4
Philippines	0.4
South Korea	0.4
Poland	0.3
Thailand	0.3
Colombia	0.2
Egypt	0.1
Indonesia	0.1
China	0.0
India	0.0

Sources: www.forbes.com, *EuroBusiness* magazine

Total Worth of Billionaires Per Country

	Total worth of billionaires ($ billion) 2001
United States	841.5
Germany	189.9
France	98.5
Japan	89.3
United Kingdom	59.4
Switzerland	57.3
Hong Kong	50.6
Canada	46.7
Saudi Arabia	40.8
Italy	40.7
Mexico	34.1
Sweden	30.2
Spain	19.3
India	14.2
Brazil	14.1
Belgium	13.3
Turkey	13.3
Greece	13.0
Russia	12.3
Netherlands	11.5
Singapore	11.3
Taiwan	11.3
Israel	9.9
Venezuela	9.8
Austria	9.5
Malaysia	7.3
Australia	6.0
Kuwait	6.0
South Africa	5.8
Liechtenstein	5.7
Argentina	5.3
Monaco	4.3
Denmark	4.2
Philippines	3.7
Luxembourg	3.4
Lebanon	3.1
Indonesia	3.0
Poland	2.9
Chile	2.6
Norway	2.6
South Korea	2.6
Thailand	2.4
Hungary	2.2
Bermuda	2.1
Portugal	2.0
United Arab Emirates	1.9
Colombia	1.5
China	1.3
Egypt	1.0
New Zealand	1.0
World	1,825.7

Sources: www.forbes.com, *EuroBusiness* magazine

Richest Person/Family Per Country

	Richest person/family, age in 2001	Worth ($ billion)	Source of wealth
Argentina	Gregorio Perez Companc, 66	1.7	oil and gas
Australia	Kerry Packer, 63	2.5	media
Austria	Ferdinand A. Porsche, 66	2.2	automotive (Porsche)
Belgium	Marc Rich, 67	5.7	finance (Marc Rich & Co Investment)
Bermuda	Ernest E. Stempel, 85	2.1	insurance (AIG)
Brazil	José and Antonio Ermirio de Moraes	3.5	diversified
Canada	Kenneth Thomson and family, 77	16.4	media (Thomson)
Chile	Andronico Luksic and family, 74	1.3	mining
Chile	Eliodoro Matte and family, 55	1.3	paper
China	Rong Yiren and family	1.3	investments
Colombia	Luis Carlos Sarmiento Angulo, 68	1.5	finance
Denmark	Maersk Mc-Kinney Møller, 87	2.3	shipping (A.P. Møller)
Egypt	Onsi Sawiris and family, 71	1.0	diversified
France	Liliane Bettencourt, 75	18.2	cosmetics (L'Oréal)
Germany	Theo Albrecht, 78	12.5	food retailing (Aldi Group)
Greece	Spiro Latsis, 54	4.8	finance (EFG Bank Group)
Hong Kong	Li Ka-shing, 73	12.6	diversified
Hungary	George Soros, 71	2.2	finance (Soros Fund Management)
India	Azim Premji and family, 55	6.9	IT/software
Indonesia	Rachman Halim and family, 53	1.7	tobacco
Israel	Shari Arison Dorsman, 43	3.7	diversified
Italy	Silvio Berlusconi, 64	7.7	media (Fininvest)
Japan	Yasuo Takei and family, 71	8.3	consumer finance
Kuwait	Nasser al-Kharafi and family, 58	6.0	diversified
Lebanon	Rafik al-Hariri and family, 57	3.1	construction
Liechtenstein	Prince Hans-Adam II, 56	4.4	investments (Liechtenstein Royal Family)
Luxembourg	Grand Duke Jean of Luxembourg, 80	3.3	investments (Luxembourg Royal Family)
Malaysia	Robert Kuok, 78	3.7	diversified
Mexico	Carlos Slim Helú, 61	10.8	investments
Monaco	Lily Safra, 66	4.3	finance (Republic Bank)
Netherlands	Charlene de Carvalho, 51	3.8	beverages (Heineken)
New Zealand	John Todd and family, 73	1.0	energy
Norway	Stein-Erik Hagen, 44	1.4	finance (Canica)
Philippines	Henry Sy and family, 76	1.3	shopping malls
Poland	Jan Kulczyk, 52	2.9	diversified (Kulczyk Holdings)
Portugal	Antonio Champalimaud, 82	2.0	finance (Champalimaud Group)
Russia	Mikhail Khodorkovsky, 38	2.4	energy (Yukos)
Saudi Arabia	Prince Alwaleed bin Talal al-Saud, 44	20.0	investments
Singapore	Ng Teng Fong and family, 72	3.5	real estate
South Africa	Nicky Oppenheimer and family, 56	4.5	mining (De Beers)
South Korea	Lee Kun Hee and family, 59	1.6	electronics, diversified
Spain	Amancio Ortega, 65	7.8	fashion (Inditex)
Sweden	Ingavar Kamprad, 75	7.2	retailing (Ikea)
Switzerland	Ernesto Bertarelli, 36	6.2	pharmaceuticals (Serono)
Taiwan	Tsai Wan-lin and family, 76	3.8	insurance
Thailand	David Bromilow, 58	1.2	sports clothing and footware (Adidas)
Thailand	Thaksin Shinawatra, 51	1.2	diversified
Turkey	Mehmet Karamehmet and family, 47	3.7	telecoms
United Arab Emirates	Abdul Aziz al-Ghurair, 47	1.9	finance
United Kingdom	Duke of Westminster, 50	5.2	real estate (Grosvenor Estates)
United States	William Gates, 45	54.0	IT/software (Microsoft)
Venezuela	Gustavo Cisneros and family, 56	5.3	media

 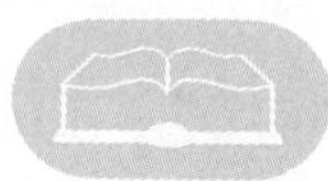    

DEMOCRACY AND SECURITY

GREENLAND
ICELAND
FAEROE ISLANDS
NORWAY
FINLAND
SWEDEN
ESTONIA
LATVIA
LITHUANIA
UNITED KINGDOM
DENMARK
IRELAND
ISLE OF MAN
BELARUS
POLAND
NETH.
GERMANY
BELGIUM
CHANNEL ISLANDS
CZECH REPUBLIC
SLOVAKIA
UKRAINE
LUX.
LIECHTENSTEIN
FRANCE
AUSTRIA
HUNGARY
SWITZ.
SLOVENIA
ROMANIA
CROATIA
YUGOSLAVIA
BULGARIA
ANDORRA
MONACO
ITALY
PORTUGAL
SPAIN
GREECE
GIBRALTAR
TUNISIA
MALTA
TURKEY
CYPRUS
SYRIA
LEBANON
ISRAEL
JOR
MOROCCO
ALGERIA
LIBYA
EGYPT
SUDAN
CANADA
UNITED STATES OF AMERICA
BERMUDA
MEXICO
CUBA
BAHAMAS
TURKS & CAICOS
DOMINICAN REP.
PUERTO RICO
VIRGIN ISLANDS (UK)
CAYMAN ISLANDS
ANTIGUA & BARBUDA
BELIZE
VIRGIN IS. (US)
GUADELOUPE
GUATEMALA
JAMAICA
ST KITTS & NEVIS
DOMINICA
MARTINIQUE
EL SALVADOR
ARUBA
ST LUCIA
NETH. ANTILLES
BARBADOS
COSTA RICA
GRENADA
TRINIDAD & TOBAGO
PANAMA
VENEZUELA
FRENCH GUIANA
COLOMBIA
ECUADOR
BRAZIL
PERU
BOLIVIA
CHILE
PARAGUAY
URUGUAY
ARGENTINA
CÔTE D'IVOIRE
GHANA
NIGERIA
CAMEROON
GABON
UGANDA
TANZANIA
ANGOLA
ZAMBIA
ZIMBABWE
NAMIBIA
BOTSWANA
MOZAMBIQUE
SOUTH AFRICA

  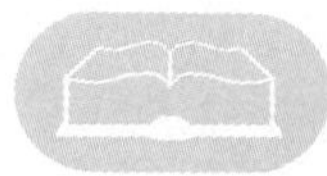  

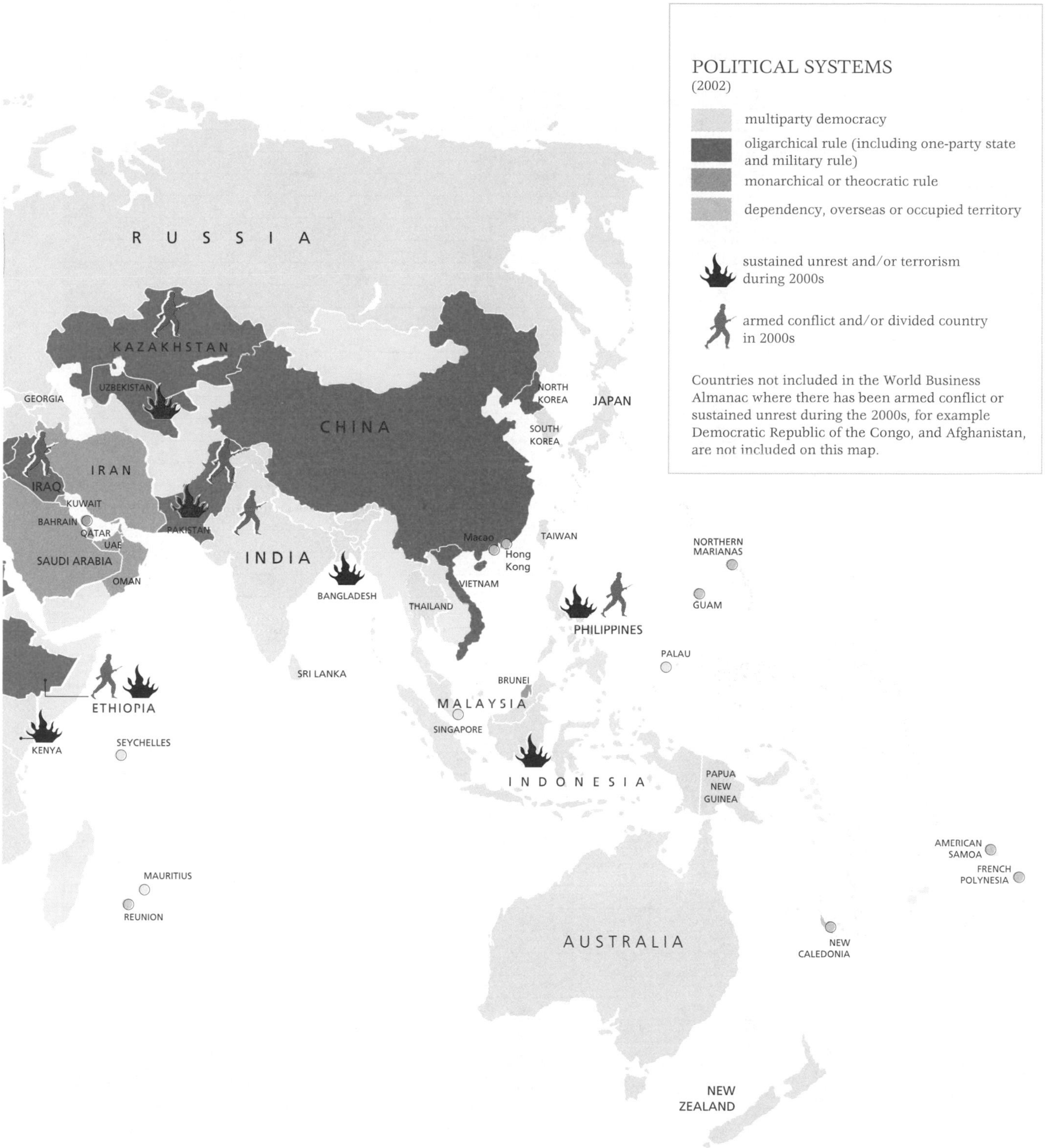

POLITICAL SYSTEMS
(2002)

- multiparty democracy
- oligarchical rule (including one-party state and military rule)
- monarchical or theocratic rule
- dependency, overseas or occupied territory

- sustained unrest and/or terrorism during 2000s
- armed conflict and/or divided country in 2000s

Countries not included in the World Business Almanac where there has been armed conflict or sustained unrest during the 2000s, for example Democratic Republic of the Congo, and Afghanistan, are not included on this map.

RUSSIA
KAZAKHSTAN
UZBEKISTAN
GEORGIA
CHINA
NORTH KOREA
SOUTH KOREA
JAPAN
IRAN
IRAQ
KUWAIT
BAHRAIN
QATAR
UAE
SAUDI ARABIA
OMAN
PAKISTAN
INDIA
BANGLADESH
Macao
Hong Kong
TAIWAN
NORTHERN MARIANAS
GUAM
VIETNAM
THAILAND
PHILIPPINES
PALAU
SRI LANKA
BRUNEI
MALAYSIA
SINGAPORE
ETHIOPIA
KENYA
SEYCHELLES
INDONESIA
PAPUA NEW GUINEA
AMERICAN SAMOA
FRENCH POLYNESIA
MAURITIUS
REUNION
AUSTRALIA
NEW CALEDONIA
NEW ZEALAND

Political Systems

	Total population (thousands) 1999	Population per km² 1999	Multiparty democracy	Oligarchical rule	Monarchical or theocratic rule	Dependency, overseas, or occupied territory	Sustained unrest/ terrorism in 2000s	Armed conflict/divided country in 2000s
Algeria	30,774	13		•			•	•
American Samoa	64	324				•		
Andorra	75	162	•					
Angola	12,479	10		•				•
Antigua and Barbuda	67	151	•					
Argentina	36,577	13	•				•	
Aruba	69	356				•		
Australia	18,705	2	•					
Austria	8,177	99	•					
Bahamas	301	22	•					
Bahrain	606	873			•			
Bangladesh	126,947	975	•				•	
Barbados	269	624	•					
Belarus	10,274	50		•			•	
Belgium	10,152	308	•					
Belize	235	10	•					
Bermuda	63	1,202				•		
Bolivia	8,142	8	•					
Botswana	1,597	3	•					
Brazil	167,988	20	•					
British Virgin Islands	19	125				•		
Brunei	322	61			•			
Bulgaria	8,279	75	•					
Cameroon	14,693	32	•					
Canada	30,857	3	•					
Cayman Islands	39	152				•		
Channel Islands	–	–				•		
Chile	15,019	20	•					
China	1,266,838	136		•				
Colombia	41,564	40	•					•
Costa Rica	3,933	77	•					
Côte d'Ivoire	14,526	46		•			•	
Croatia	4,477	80	•					
Cuba	11,160	102		•				
Cyprus	778	85	•					•
Czech Republic	10,262	133	•					
Denmark	5,282	125	•					
Dominica	71	95	•					
Dominican Republic	8,364	173	•					
Ecuador	12,411	45	•					
Egypt	67,226	68		•				
El Salvador	6,154	297	•					
Estonia	1,412	33	•					
Ethiopia	61,095	54		•			•	•
Faeroe Islands	45	32				•		
Finland	5,165	17	•					
France	58,886	107	•					
French Guiana	168	2				•		
French Polynesia	233	60				•		
Gabon	1,197	5	•					
Georgia	5,006	72	•					
Germany	82,178	235	•					
Ghana	19,678	86	•					

Political Systems (continued)

	Total population (thousands) 1999	Population per km² 1999	Multiparty democracy	Oligarchical rule	Monarchical or theocratic rule	Dependency, overseas, or occupied territory	Sustained unrest/ terrorism in 2000s	Armed conflict/divided country in 2000s
Gibraltar	29	4,462				•		
Greece	10,626	82	•					
Greenland	60	0				•		
Grenada	93	270	•					
Guadeloupe	428	240				•		
Guam	152	278				•		
Guatemala	11,090	102	•					
Hong Kong	6,850	6,273				•		
Hungary	10,076	109	•					
Iceland	279	3	•					
India	998,056	336	•					•
Indonesia	209,255	116	•				•	
Iran	66,796	41			•			
Iraq	22,450	51		•				•
Ireland	3,705	54	•					
Isle of Man	74	130				•		
Israel	6,101	296	•				•	•
Italy	57,343	195	•					
Jamaica	2,560	237	•				•	
Japan	126,505	336	•					
Jordan	6,482	73			•			
Kazakhstan	16,269	6		•				•
Kenya	29,549	52	•				•	
Kuwait	1,897	107			•			
Latvia	2,389	38	•					
Lebanon	3,236	317		•				•
Libya	5,471	3		•				
Liechtenstein	32	200	•					
Lithuania	3,682	57	•					
Luxembourg	426	165	•					
Macao	437	18,530				•		
Malaysia	21,830	66	•					
Malta	386	1,222	•					
Martinique	381	338				•		
Mauritius	1,150	617	•					
Mexico	97,365	51	•					
Monaco	33	16,923	•					
Morocco	27,867	62			•			
Mozambique	19,286	25	•					
Namibia	1,695	2	•					
Netherlands	15,735	464	•					
Netherlands Antilles	248	310				•		
New Caledonia	215	11				•		
New Zealand	3,828	14	•					
Nigeria	108,945	120	•				•	
North Korea	23,702	197		•				
Northern Marianas	75	158				•		
Norway	4,442	14	•					
Oman	2,460	12			•			
Pakistan	152,331	198		•			•	•
Palau	19	41	•					
Panama	2,812	38	•					
Papua New Guinea	4,702	10	•					

Political Systems (continued)

	Total population (thousands) 1999	Population per km² 1999	Multiparty democracy	Oligarchical rule	Monarchical or theocratic rule	Dependency, overseas, or occupied territory	Sustained unrest/ terrorism in 2000s	Armed conflict/divided country in 2000s
Paraguay	5,358	13	•					
Peru	25,230	20	•					
Philippines	74,454	250	•				•	•
Poland	38,740	127	•					
Portugal	9,873	108	•					
Puerto Rico	3,884	427				•		
Qatar	589	54			•			
Reunion	718	282				•		
Romania	22,402	97	•					
Russia	147,196	9	•					
St Kitts and Nevis	39	149	•					
St Lucia	152	247	•					
Saudi Arabia	20,899	10			•			
Seychelles	77	169	•					
Singapore	3,522	5,435	•					
Slovakia	5,382	112	•					
Slovenia	1,989	99	•					
South Africa	39,900	33	•					
South Korea	46,480	471	•					
Spain	39,634	79	•					
Sri Lanka	18,639	289	•					
Sudan	28,883	12		•			•	•
Sweden	8,892	22	•					
Switzerland	7,344	185	•					
Syria	15,725	86		•				
Taiwan	22,113	611	•					
Tanzania	32,793	37	•					
Thailand	60,856	119	•					
Trinidad and Tobago	1,289	253	•					
Tunisia	9,460	61		•				
Turkey	65,546	85	•					
Turks and Caicos Islands	17	34				•		
Uganda	21,143	106	•					•
Ukraine	50,658	87	•					
United Arab Emirates	2,398	29			•			
United Kingdom	58,744	243	•					
United States	276,218	30	•					
Uruguay	3,313	19	•					
US Virgin Islands	120	330				•		
Uzbekistan	23,942	58		•			•	
Venezuela	23,706	27	•					
Vietnam	78,705	242		•				
Yugoslavia	10,637	104	•				•	
Zambia	8,976	12	•					
Zimbabwe	11,529	30	•				•	

Sustained Unrest/Terrorism in 2000s

	Total population (thousands) 1999	Population per km^2 1999	Sustained unrest/ terrorism	Armed conflict/ divided country	Multiparty democracy	Oligarchical rule	Monarchical or theocratic rule	Dependency, overseas, or occupied territory
Algeria	30,774	13	•	•		•		
Argentina	36,577	13	•		•			
Bangladesh	126,947	975	•		•			
Belarus	10,274	50	•			•		
Côte d'Ivoire	14,526	46	•			•		
Ethiopia	61,095	54	•	•		•		
Indonesia	209,255	116	•		•			
Israel	6,101	296	•	•	•			
Jamaica	2,560	237	•		•			
Kenya	29,549	52	•		•			
Nigeria	108,945	120	•		•			
Pakistan	152,331	198	•	•		•		
Philippines	74,454	250	•	•	•			
Sudan	28,883	12	•	•		•		
Uzbekistan	23,942	58	•			•		
Yugoslavia	10,637	104	•		•			
Zimbabwe	11,529	30	•		•			

Armed Conflict/Divided Country in 2000s

	Total population (thousands) 1999	Population per km^2 1999	Armed conflict/ divided country	Sustained unrest/ terrorism	Multiparty democracy	Oligarchical rule	Monarchical or theocratic rule	Dependency, overseas, or occupied territory
Algeria	30,774	13	•	•		•		
Angola	12,479	10	•			•		
Colombia	41,564	40	•		•			
Cyprus	778	85	•		•			
Ethiopia	61,095	54	•	•		•		
India	998,056	336	•		•			
Iraq	22,450	51	•			•		
Israel	6,101	296	•	•	•			
Kazakhstan	16,269	6	•			•		
Lebanon	3,236	317	•			•		
Pakistan	152,331	198	•	•		•		
Philippines	74,454	250	•	•	•			
Sudan	28,883	12	•	•		•		
Uganda	21,143	106	•		•			

Multiparty Democracies and Unrest/Armed Conflict

	Total population (thousands) 1999	Population per km^2 1999	Sustained unrest/ terrorism in 2000s	Armed conflict/ divided country in 2000s
Argentina	36,577	13	•	
Bangladesh	126,947	975	•	
Colombia	41,564	40		•
Cyprus	778	85		•
India	998,056	336		•
Indonesia	209,255	116	•	
Israel	6,101	296	•	•
Jamaica	2,560	237	•	
Kenya	29,549	52	•	
Nigeria	108,945	120	•	
Philippines	74,454	250	•	•
Uganda	21,143	106		•
Yugoslavia	10,637	104	•	
Zimbabwe	11,529	30	•	

Oligarchical Rule and Unrest/Armed Conflict

	Total population (thousands) 1999	Population per km^2 1999	Sustained unrest/ terrorism in 2000s	Armed conflict/ divided country in 2000s
Algeria	30,774	13	•	•
Angola	12,479	10		•
Belarus	10,274	50	•	
Côte d'Ivoire	14,526	46	•	
Ethiopia	61,095	54	•	•
Iraq	22,450	51		•
Kazakhstan	16,269	6		•
Lebanon	3,236	317		•
Pakistan	152,331	198	•	•
Sudan	28,883	12	•	•
Uzbekistan	23,942	58	•	

ALGERIA

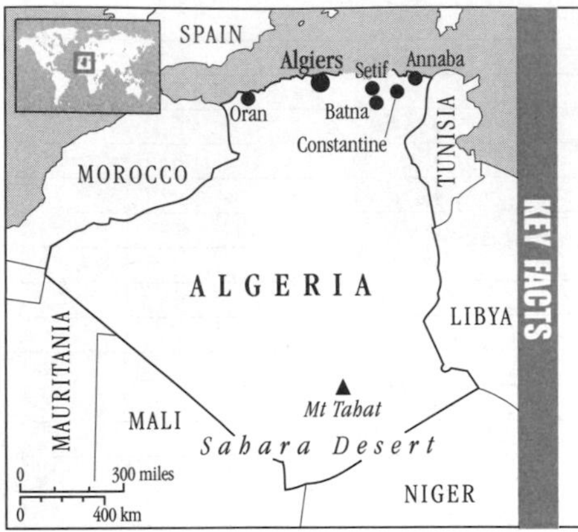

KEY FACTS

GNI: **$46,548 million; world's 52nd**
GNI pc: **$1,550; world's 117th**
Head of government: **president**
Currency: **Algerian dirham (DA)**
Capital: **Algiers**
Population: **30,774,000, growing at 2.3% p.a.**
Land area: **919,574 square miles**
Population density: **33 per square mile**
Life expectancy: **69 years**
Infant mortality: **36 per 1,000 live births**
Language: **Arabic (official), French, Tamazight (Berber)**
Best buy: **textiles, leather goods, jewelry**

ECONOMIC STRUCTURE

France colonized Algeria in 1830. In 1954 the National Liberation Front (FLN) launched a war of independence, which was won in 1962. The FLN took power and established a single-party Arab-Islamic socialist state, in which the military has played a key role. France transferred ownership of the Saharan oilfields to Algeria. Oil and gas resources were developed, agriculture was reformed, and industry established. Increasing social pressures led to riots in the 1980s in favor of democracy and a return to Islamic traditions. The conflict between government and Islamic militants continues, exacerbated by rising unemployment.

Hydrocarbons contributed 40.8% of GDP in 2000, followed by services (29.3%), construction (8.6%), agriculture (8.1%) and non-hydrocarbons manufacturing (7.3%). Refined petroleum products and liquefied natural gas are the main manufacturing industries. Nitrogenous and phosphate fertilizers, steel, cement, construction materials, transport equipment, household appliances, cigarettes, and processed foods are also produced. Natural gas and crude and refined petroleum accounted for 97% of export value in 2000. Dates and wine are among the main food exports. The main markets were Italy (24%), the United States (13%), and France (11%).

The public sector accounts for 80% of industry. State enterprises were restructured into smaller, more specialized units from the early 1980s. State holding companies were established in 1996, and from 1997 the state banks were more closely involved in the restructuring of state companies. A privatization program, involving share offers to workers and partnerships with foreign firms, was launched in 1995. In 1998 89 companies were offered for sale, but by early 2001 less than 15% had found buyers. The lack of success was blamed on the holding companies, which were to be replaced by sector-based conglomerates in late 2001. In early 2001 the government proposed streamlining privatization procedures, and drew up a new list of 181 companies to be sold off. They include the state airline, hotels, agro-industry, mechanical and electrical engineering, and electronics. The government ended the domestic electricity and gas monopoly of Sonelgas in late 2001 and introduced competition in telecommunications. It licensed new private banks and foreign banks, but the main banks remain firmly in state hands.

ECONOMIC POLICY

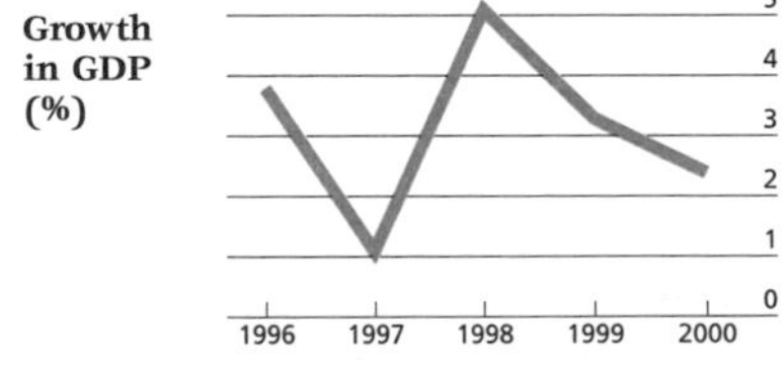

The government has followed an IMF-backed structural adjustment program since 1994 with the aim of reducing the government debt and debt service, budget deficit, and inflation. A key part of the program has been tighter financial management of state companies and a move towards market economics. During this time socio-economic pressures have been increasing with rising unemployment, rapid population growth and escalating political violence.

The program has been successful, with a reduction in the ratio of debt service to export receipts from 80% in 1993 to an estimated 21.6% in 2001. The foreign debt fell from 71.9% of GDP in 1996 to 40.7% in 2001. The foreign trade surplus remains consistently buoyant. The pace of change to market economics has been slow, however. The government intends private business to the main source of job creation and growth in the three-year economic plan launched in 2001. It is strengthening the legislative framework and investing in infrastructure to support this goal.

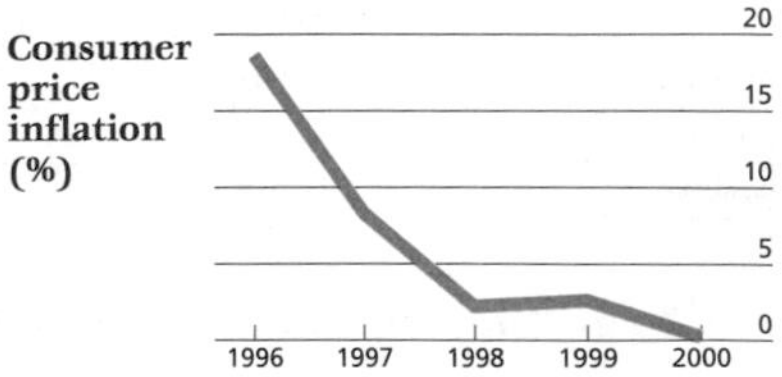

Annual GDP growth averaged 3.4% in 1996–2000. It was expected to be 3.8% in 2001, boosted by government spending. Inflation fell from 29.8% in 1995 to 0.3% in 2000. Unemployment is high, and rose from 28% in 1996 to 30% in early 2000.

GEOGRAPHY/RESOURCES

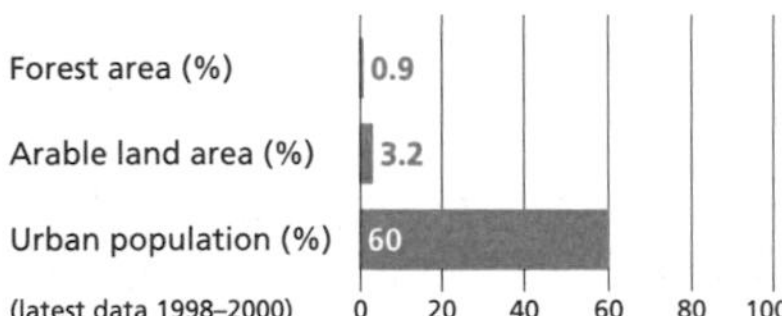

Algeria has four geographic regions running west to east: the fertile Tell northern coastal strip and the foothills of the Atlas mountains; the mostly barren high plateau, which contains the lowest point of 131 feet below sea level; the three ranges of the Saharan Atlas mountains; and the Saharan Desert, which covers 90% of the total land area and contains the highest peak (9,850 feet). Dust storms are common in summer, and the country is subject to severe earthquakes.

The main agricultural crops are wheat, potatoes, and tomatoes, but the varied agriculture also includes a range of cereals, vegetables, and fruits. Even so, Algeria imports 60% of its food requirements. Official proven petroleum reserves are 9.2 billion barrels, but the country remains largely unexplored, and potential is much higher. Proven natural gas reserves are 160 trillion cubic feet, placing Algeria in the top ten world sources of gas. There were 44 million

  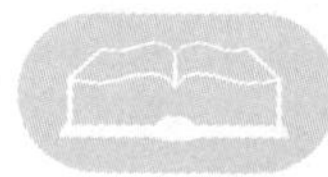    

short tons of recoverable coal reserves in 1998. Non-energy minerals produced include iron ore, lead, zinc, phosphates, silver, and gypsum. There are reserves of gold, diamonds, celestine, and sulfur.

Over half the population are urban and under the age of 20, and 92% live in the Tell region. The majority are Arab (83%), followed by Berber (17%) and Berber-Arab. People of European origin constitute less than 1%.

Communications/Energy

PCs	0.7
Telephone lines	5.7
Mobiles	0.3
Internet users	0.2
(per 100 people, 2000)	0 20 40 60 80 100

The road network comprises 87,000 miles, of which 44,120 miles are paved. The Trans-Sahara Highway, completed in 1985, runs from the Mediterranean coast to the Niger border, providing access to the Sahara oilfields. The rail network is 2,800 miles. Gas pipelines total 4,610 miles and oil pipelines 3,587 miles. There are 13 major sea ports, the largest for general cargo being Algiers. The merchant fleet includes 73 ships over 1,000 grt with a total displacement of 896,911 grt in 2000. There are international airports at Algiers, Constantine, Annaba, Tlemcen, and Oran.

Telecommunications is dominated by the public sector monopoly operator Djazair Telecom. Telephone density is very low, according to government figures only 0.4% of the population in 2000. Domestic and international links are provided by cable, satellite, and microwave radio relay. Mobile telephony was opened to competition in mid-2001 when a license was awarded to the Egyptian company Orascom Telecom. Djazair Telecom and Orascom Telecom will share the market until December 2003, when the next mobile license will be awarded.

In 2000 crude oil production was 66.8 million tons. Refined oil production was 19.6 million tons, with domestic consumption at 6.6 million tons. Natural gas production was 6,000 billion cubic feet, with consumption at 477 billion cubic feet. Coal output was an estimated 20,000 short tons in 1999, while imports were 710,000 tons to meet consumption of 730,000 tons. Four oil refineries produce a range of fuels and feedstocks. In 2000 98% of electricity was produced from fossil fuels, with hydro and other sources accounting for 2%. Solar power is used in remote southern communities.

Education/Employment

Education is compulsory from age 6 to 15. There are 17 universities, 13 university centers, 10 teacher training colleges, and 12 other higher education institutes. There are 400,000 students enrolled in higher education. There are several specialized research centers, with R&D strengths in biotechnology, geophysics, geology, seismology, astrophysics, water engineering, energy (including renewables), and IT.

The labor force has a range of skills. Wages and other employment conditions are determined between the government, employers, and trade unions, with the government taking the leading role.

Fiscal/Financial

The five large commercial banks and four development banks are all state-owned. Insurance is also dominated by the state. The large commercial banks are Banque Al-Baraka d'Algérie, Banque Extérieure d'Algérie, Banque Nationale d'Algérie, Crédit Populaire d'Algérie, and Banque du Maghreb Arabe pour l'Investissement et le Commerce (jointly owned with the Libyan government). Banque d'Algérie is the central bank. With the Finance Ministry it is responsible for regulating the finance sector.

Standard corporation tax is 30%, with a reduced rate of 15% when profits are reinvested. Various other reductions apply to specific sectors and circumstances. The top rate of personal income tax is 40%. VAT applies at various rates.

The government recognizes the need for the banking sector to play a more effective role in economic development, but lending decisions are still politicized, and bad debts are sometimes difficult to recover. The number of foreign banks, especially from other Arab countries, is growing. The Algiers Stock Exchange opened in mid-1999, launched to handle privatization stocks and bonds.

Business Opportunities

Tax and financial incentives are available to investors. There are free trade zones at Skikda, Annaba, Ghazaouet, Mostaganem, Bellara, and Tamanpasset (in the Sahara region). There is a general investment code, and specific codes for minerals and hydrocarbons. The government has selected foreign partners to strengthen the pharmaceuticals and automotive industries and oil exploration. Other sectors due to be opened up in this way include electronics and food processing. Telecommunications and banking have attracted investment from abroad. Government red tape, the newness of market economy laws, a traditional antipathy for market economics and foreign business, and political unrest constitute barriers to inward investment. Opportunities exist in the sectors slated for privatization, in banking, business services, mining, and minerals processing (especially fertilizers). The point of contact for investors is the Agence de Promotion de Soutien et de Suivie des Investissements.

For More Information

Books:

Ruedy, J. *Modern Algeria: The Origins and Development of a Nation.* Bloomington, IN: Indiana University Press, 1992.

Willis, M. *The Islamist Challenge in Algeria: A Political History.* New York: University Press, 1997.

Economist Intelligence Unit. *Country Profile and Quarterly Reports.* London.

Web Sites:

Agence de Promotion de Soutien et de Suivie des Investissements (Algeria Investment Focus): **www.apsi.com.dz**

Banque d'Algérie (central bank): **www.bank-of-algeria.dz**

Government entry point: **www.gouvernement.dz**

  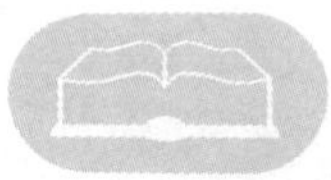    

American Samoa

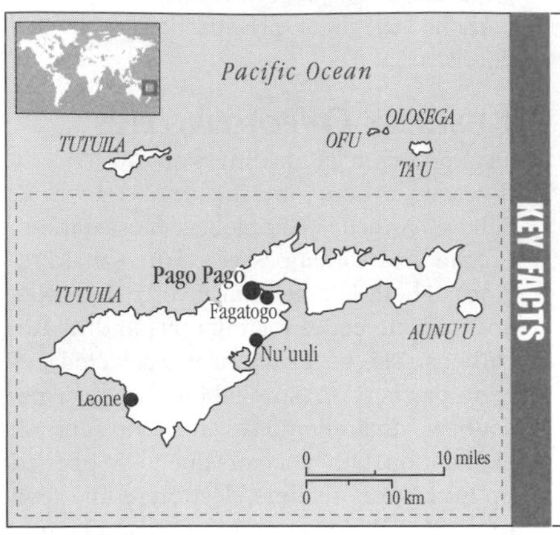

KEY FACTS

Head of government: **governor**
Currency: **U.S. dollar ($)**
Capital: **Pago Pago**
Language: **English, Samoan**
Best buy: **orchids, handcrafts**

Economy

Canned tuna is the main economic activity and export, employing around one-third of the labor force. Sold exclusively to the United States, tuna accounted for 93% of export earnings in 1996. The tuna is landed by U.S., Korean, and Taiwanese boats. Other small-scale manufacturing plants are geared to the needs of the local market. Government services provide employment for about a third of the workforce, while private sector services employ another 7%. Attempts to diversify the economy have proved unsuccessful. Although tourism increased in the early 1990s, it tailed off later in the decade because of cyclones. Much of the population is not in the market economy, but lives from subsistence farming and fishing in traditional communal groups.

The country is dependent on U.S. aid, with annual appropriations of $23.1 million for operational support and $10.1 million for construction in 2000–02. The government received a loan subsidy of $3.1 million in 2001. It is working towards the improvement of financial management and the establishment of long-term infrastructure and operations plans by 2005. In the early 1990s cyclone damage caused increased public expenditure, lower receipts, and rising debt. The 1993 U.S. recovery program was suspended in 1996–97, and resumed in 1998 after the American Samoan government established independent authorities for telecommunications to reduce commercial costs, and for the hospital, to reduce its $10–12 million debt. The hospital debt accounted for 25% of the American Samoan government deficit. Economic growth was estimated at 11% a year in the 1980s. Inflation averaged 14% a year in 1994–96, mainly on account of price increases in imported U.S. goods, which supply basic needs, including food. Unemployment was 13% in 1996.

Geography/Resources

American Samoa is in the Pacific Ocean 2,300 miles southwest of Hawaii and 2,700 miles northeast of Australia. The country consists of five main volcanic islands: Tutuila, Ta'u, Olosega, Ofu, and Aunu'u, and two coral atolls, Swain's and Rose. Tutuila is the largest and most populated island; its highest peak is Lata at 3,168 feet. The volcanic islands have rugged mountains and limited coastal plains. The climate is hot and extremely wet: the average temperature is 80°F, and there are more than 118 inches of rainfall a year. Cyclones and tsunamis are an annual hazard from December to March. The main agricultural crops are coconuts, taro, bananas, yams, pineapples, and breadfruit, and there is an orchid-farming sector. Poultry and pigs are the main sources of meat. Coastal fishing provides subsistence for some communities, and there is also mining for pumice and pumicite. The majority of the population is of Samoan origin.

Communications/Energy

The road network is 217 miles, including 93 miles of paved roads. Drainage of rainfall and strengthening of sea defenses along coastal roads (the majority of the network) are constant costs. The United States allocated $2.2 million for rural road development in 1998–2002. Pago Pago is the main sea port with container, bulk cargo, and passenger facilities. Other main sea ports are at Aunu'u, Auasi, Faleosao, Ofu and Ta'u. The international airport is near Pago Pago, and there are three other airports.

Modern telecommunications links are available via two satellite earth stations. In 1997 there were 13,200 fixed phone lines and 2,550 mobile phones. The American Samoan Power Authority produces and distributes electricity to the five main islands from four power stations, all of which use imported oil. The power stations and oil storage and distribution systems are all constructed to withstand cyclones. Total electricity production was 130 million kWh in 1999.

Fiscal/Financial

Income tax and corporation tax follow the same regime as that of the United States, and monetary policy is set there. Local financial regulation is carried out by the American Samoan government. There are foreign-owned commercial banks, a local development bank, and insurance companies. There is no local stock exchange.

Business Opportunities

The main barrier to foreign investment is the remoteness of the country and the high cost of transporting goods and people. There are investment opportunities in tourism, especially eco-tourism, and in import-substitution industries.

For More Information

Book:

American Samoa Research Group. *A Strategic Assessment of American Samoa* (Strategic Planning Series). San Diego, CA: ICON Group International, 2000.
The State of the Islands Report—1999. Washington, D.C.: U.S. Department of the Interior, Office of Insular Affairs.
Talbot, Dorinda, and Deanna Swaney. *Samoa: Independent and American Samoa.* 3rd ed. Oakland, CA: Lonely Planet, 1998.

Web Sites:

American Samoa Office of Tourism: **www.amsamoa.com/tourism**
American Samoan government: **www.government.as**

ANDORRA

KEY FACTS

GNI pc: **$18,000 (approx.)**
Currency: **Euro (€)**
Capital: **Andorra la Vella**
Population: **75,000, growing at 4.1% p.a.**
Land area: **193 square miles**
Population density: **388 per square mile**
Infant mortality: **6 per 1,000 live births**
Language: **Catalan (official), Spanish, French**
Best buy: **cars, electrical and optical goods, fashion items, leather goods, cigars, cigarettes, alcohol**

ECONOMY

Tourism and the associated retail trade in duty-free and low-duty goods are the main industries, providing 53% of jobs in 1999 and an estimated 80% of GDP. There were 9.5 million visitors in 1999. Imported motor vehicles, electrical, optical and precision goods, fashion items and perfumes, alcohol, and tobacco are among the main exports. Spain and France are the main export markets. Tobacco is the main domestic crop. There are domestic tobacco processing, leather goods, textiles, furniture, alcoholic beverages, coffee roasting and graphic arts industries. Industry and construction accounted for 22% of employment in 1999. Real estate, finance and insurance are important, and the government has introduced new laws to promote these sectors.

The economy is varied with a strong local input: until 1999 foreign ownership of local companies was limited to 33%. The government's promotion of tourism and trade since the 1960s has produced a vibrant economy. The focus of the 1990s has been the development of the finance center, the introduction of regulations along international lines, and the removal of foreign investment restrictions. The 1990 customs union with the EU allows the duty-free export of non-agricultural goods. Andorra has applied to join the World Trade Organization, and currently has observer status. Government receipts are derived from indirect taxes and levies, as there is no income tax. Inflation was 1.6% in 1998 and 2.6% in 1999.

GEOGRAPHY/RESOURCES

Andorra is a small landlocked country in the eastern Pyrenees mountains. The average altitude is 6,547 feet. Over half the land is mountain grassland, with 22% forest and 20% wilderness. Only 4% of the land is farmed. Timber is harvested. Sheep and cattle are the main livestock resources. The majority of food is imported. Stone, alum, iron and lead are mined. The majority of the population is Spanish (43% in 1998), followed by Andorrans (33%), Portuguese (11%) and French (7%).

COMMUNICATIONS/ENERGY

The main means of transport is by the road network of 137 miles, since there are no railways and no airport. There are local helicopter services, and local bus services link to railway stations in Spain and France. The Spanish airport of Seo de Urgel is 12 miles from Andorra la Vella. At end 1999 there were 33,607 fixed phone lines and 20,600 mobile phones. There were 5,000 internet users in 2000. The domestic postal service is free. Most energy products are imported; the domestic hydro-power plant supplied 23% of electricity consumption in 1998, with the rest imported from France and Spain. Varying amounts of electricity have been exported since 1996. Diesel accounted for 46% of energy needs in 1998, followed by electricity (35%), petrol (18%), and propane and butane (1%). Imports of petroleum fuels increased by 4.3% in 1999.

FISCAL/FINANCIAL

There is no income tax. A 1996 law entitles foreign nationals to "passive residential status" if they spend 183 days per year in Andorra and if they place a deposit of 24,1000 Euros with the Andorran National Institute of Finances (INAF), the monetary authority, and pay an annual levy of 6,024 Euros. This facility existed prior to 1996 without the levy. Such residents were estimated to account for 90% of Andorran bank deposits in the mid-1990s.

INAF was set up in 1989 to administer public finances and supervise the finance center. It is autonomous of the government. The 1993 and 1996 Finance Laws set solvency criteria and other rules, including secrecy, for financial institutions and finance professionals. Money laundering was outlawed in 1995. The Agrupacio de Bancs Andorrans (Andorran banking association) became an associate member of the European Union Banking Federation in 1992. In 1999 there were eight commercial banks, all private sector. In 1998 there were 85 finance companies, including the banks, specialized credit institutions, investment companies and insurance companies. Insurance companies are regulated under a 1989 law. There is no stock market.

BUSINESS OPPORTUNITIES

The removal in 1999 of restrictions on foreign ownership of Andorran companies and banks opens new opportunities for investment. There has been significant foreign investment in tourism, import-export trade, finance, and real estate, which may now increase.

For More Information

Book:
Andorra Business and Investment Opportunities Yearbook. 3rd ed. Washington, D.C.: International Business Publications, 2001 (annual).

Web Sites:
Andorran Tourist Office:
www.turisme.ad
Government entry point:
www.andorra.ad
Ministry of Finance Statistics Service:
www.estudis-estadistica.finances.ad

  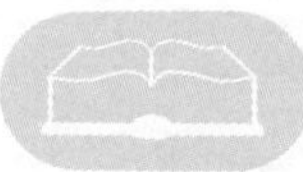    

Angola

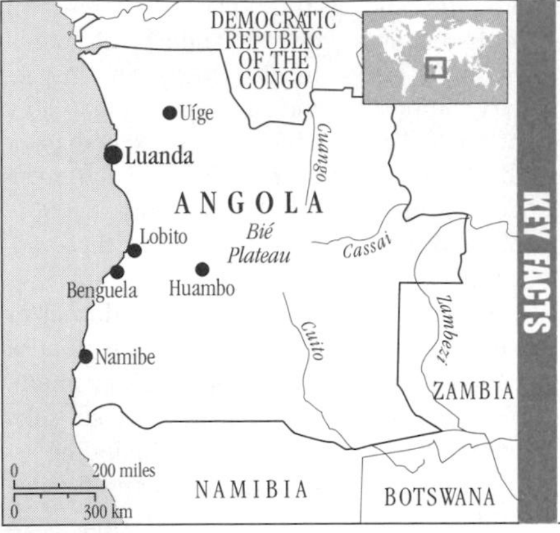

KEY FACTS

GNI: **$3,276 million; world's 130th**
GNI pc: **$270; world's 185th**
Head of government: **president**
Currency: **kwanza (kw)**
Capital: **Luanda**
Population: **12,479,000, growing at 3.4% p.a.**
Land area: **481,351 square miles**
Population density: **26 per square mile**
Life expectancy: **48 years**
Infant mortality: **172 per 1,000 live births**
Language: **Portuguese, U-Mbundu, Ki-Mbundu**
Best buy: **handicrafts**

Economy

Although Angola has huge potential as an oil producer for many years to come, its government is still struggling to overcome the effects of an apparently endless internal war and to implement productive economic policies. Following some recent major discoveries in deep offshore waters, oil is destined to assume even greater importance than it already does—accounting for nearly 90% of official exports. Investment in other areas of the economy is urgently needed but is inhibited by the war.

The long-running conflict between the ruling MPLA party and the UNITA rebel movement has displaced at least a third of the population and has stifled economic prospects in all sectors other than oil—especially agriculture, which once sustained the economy. However, organizations dedicated to building civil society are making renewed efforts to stabilize and rebuild the domestic economy at the grassroots level.

The government, after failing to meet Angola's external debt obligations and after running up unsustainable financial and fiscal deficits, eventually altered its economic policy direction in 2000 and began to enact an adjustment program approved by the IMF, but progress was still not satisfactory by early 2002. In the 1990s, inflation was regularly running at much more than 100% per annum, the fiscal deficit regularly stood at more than 15% of GDP, and the current account deficit in some years exceeded 30% of GDP. Economic growth in 2000 was 2.1%. In 2001, more impressive growth was anticipated, but inflation continued to run out of control.

Geography/Resources

Angola borders the Atlantic Ocean between the mouth of the Congo river and Namibia. Two-thirds of the land area is plateau with an average elevation higher than 3,280 feet above sea level. Before independence in 1975 Angola was a net exporter of food, but since that time much productive land has been lost through war, confiscation, and large-scale movements of population. Although the economy is dominated by the mining of oil and diamonds, Angola also has iron ore, copper, and other minerals; as with agriculture, however, most activities have been brought to a halt by civil war.

Communications/Energy

Only a few major road transport routes are considered safe for public transport, and the railway network has been destroyed by war. In recent years there has been a sharp increase in domestic air transport services. Telephone services are inefficient and undeveloped. Electric power output is below capacity: the construction of new hydroelectric power generation projects has been prevented by the war.

Fiscal/Financial

As the oil production industry is the only dynamic sector of the economy, Angola has tended to become over-dependent on this single commodity as the only significant source of foreign exchange and government revenue. Much still needs to be done to modernize the tax system, widen the tax base, remove the large number of tax exemptions, and improve the tax administration. The financial system is also still undeveloped, although private banks have been permitted to operate since 1995 and four Portuguese banks have established offices in the country. There is no stock market.

Business Opportunities

Angola's largest investment prospects exist in the oil sector, thanks to the recent discovery and ongoing development of some very large offshore fields. Oil companies Chevron and Elf have taken the lead in this investment, which could increase national output from around 800,000 at present to 1.4 million barrels per day by 2005 if it continues at recent levels. In 1999 three major consortia, headed by BP-Amoco, Elf, and Exxon, were awarded new offshore exploration blocks in return for very substantial "signature bonuses" paid to the government.

Privatization of Angola's largest state-owned institutions can be expected to proceed under the influence of the international financial institutions, although progress has been slow. Few foreign investors have yet benefited from the privatization of the smaller enterprises already sold off. There will nevertheless be many new investment opportunities in agricultural, fishing, manufacturing, and mining ventures once the country overcomes its legacy of war and poor governance.

For More Information

Book:

Hodges, Tony, and James Currey. *Angola from Afro-Stalinism to Petro-Diamond Capitalism*. Bloomington, IN: Indiana University Press, 2001.

Web Sites:

African news and information: **www.allafrica.com/business**
Ministry of Industry: **www.mind-angola.com**
National Bank of Angola: **www.ebonet.net/bna/bna.htm**

  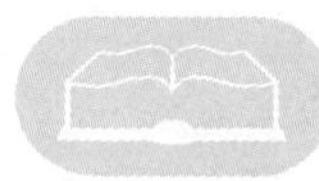    

ANTIGUA AND BARBUDA

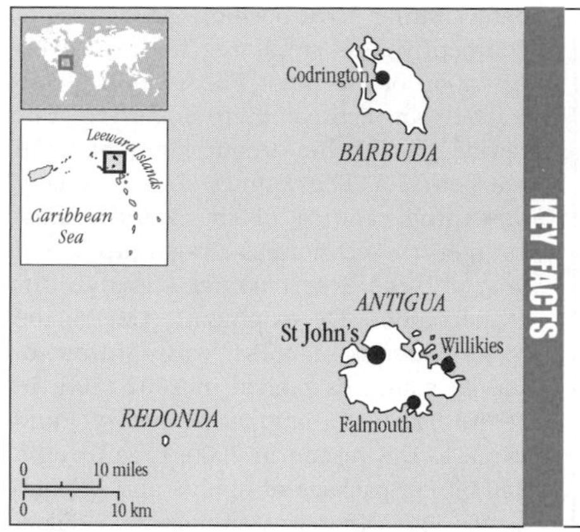

KEY FACTS

GNI: **$606 million**
GNI pc: **$8,990; world's 52nd**
Head of government: **prime minister**
Currency: **Eastern Caribbean dollar (EC$)**
Capital: **St. John's**
Population: **67,000, growing at 0.5% p.a.**
Land area: **170 square miles**
Population density: **394 per square mile**
Infant mortality: **17 per 1,000 live births**
Language: **English**
Best buy: **arts and crafts, clothes**

ECONOMY

The dominant economic sector is tourism, which is a major source both of employment and foreign exchange earnings. Financial services, while less significant as an employer, is a significant foreign exchange earner. The public sector accounted for almost 12,000 jobs in 2000, at a cost of around EC$250 million; it is a major contributor to GDP, followed by hotels and restaurants, which accounted for 12% in 1997. There is a small manufacturing sector, producing construction materials, beer, and other domestic consumer goods, and a similarly small agricultural output of fruit, vegetables, and other foods.

External trade shows a persistent and overwhelming deficit, amounting in 2000 to almost 90% of the import bill; the United States is the principal trading partner.

GDP growth rates fluctuated between 1996 and 2000, with 1996 showing 6.1% growth, attributed to reconstruction after the 1995 hurricane, which had contributed to a 5% GDP decline; from 1997 onwards, there was a falling trend, to 3.5% in 2000. Fluctuations in tourist arrivals were a major factor in the GDP variations. The inflation rate was below 3.5% for most of the 1990s, falling to 1.1% in 1999 and 0.5% in 2000.

GEOGRAPHY/RESOURCES

Antigua and Barbuda are on the outer northeastern curve of the Leeward Islands; their land area is 108 square miles and 62 square miles respectively. Barbuda is 31 miles north of Antigua; the country also includes Redonda, an uninhabited volcanic islet 35 miles southwest of Antigua. Antigua's considerably indented coastline provides several natural harbors; the main port is St. John's, while Nelson's Dockyard in English Harbour, in the south, is preserved as a historic site.

Once dominated by sugar cultivation, the agricultural land now grows some cotton, together with fruit and vegetables, and there is some livestock grazing. St. John's has a population of about 30,000, more than 40% of the national total; out of Barbuda's 1,200 people, about 90% live in the main settlement, Codrington. The population is mainly of African origin; the remainder includes those of European and mixed descent. Adult literacy is estimated at 90–95%.

COMMUNICATIONS/ENERGY

Many international airlines connect Antigua with the main world centers and numerous regional destinations. Ferries provide links to Montserrat and Dominica; transport between Antigua and Barbuda is by air. In Antigua, a network of bus services operates from St. John's.

Overseas telecommunications are provided by Cable & Wireless, and domestic services by the state Antigua Public Utilities Authority; C&W also operates the mobile phone system. APUA is responsible for the electric power supply.

FISCAL/FINANCIAL

The government finances are marked by persistent deficits, which in 2000 reached 12% of GDP, up from 9.25% in 1999. In addition, the government is more than a decade in arrears with its accounts; the audited accounts for 1989, the most recent available, were only tabled in parliament in October 2000. In April 2001 the government started discussions with the IMF over possible changes to the tax system; for 2001/02, an estimated 20% of recurrent expenditure was earmarked for debt servicing, and in April 2001, prime minister Lester Bird froze ministerial travel and telephone allowances after the IMF warned the government to bring the fiscal deficit under control.

The government has also been under sustained international pressure to tighten its supervision of the offshore financial sector; both the United States and the United Kingdom issued advisory notices to investors in 1999, expressing concern about aspects of the country's offshore finance sector, notably its operation of Internet gambling. As a result, the government made a number of changes in its offshore supervisory structures and personnel, and the advisory notices were lifted in 2001.

BUSINESS OPPORTUNITIES

There is no personal income tax, but small domestic businesses pay a 2% gross receipts tax, while incorporated companies pay a 40% profit tax. Foreign investors are offered tax holidays of up to five years for hotels and up to 15 years for new industrial development, together with import duty exemption and free repatriation of profits and capital. Tax rebates are applicable to profits from exports. There is no capital gains or inheritance tax.

With uncertainty surrounding the offshore finance sector—in Antigua and elsewhere in the region—tourism may offer more secure investment prospects, although stayover business has stagnated since 1998. A more promising sector could be telecommunications, with the prospect of competition entering the sector by the end of 2002.

For More Information

Book:

Antigua and Barbuda Business Intelligence Report. 2nd ed. Washington, D.C.: International Business Publications, 2001.

Web Sites:

Antigua and Barbuda government: **www.antigua-barbuda.org**
Caribbean Development Bank: **www.caribank.org**
Eastern Caribbean Central Bank: **www.eccb-centralbank.org**

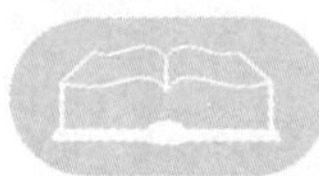

ARGENTINA

KEY FACTS

GNI: **$276,097 million; world's 17th**
GNI pc: **$7,550; world's 58th**
Head of government: **president**
Currency: **peso (Ps)**
Capital: **Buenos Aires**
Population: **36,577,000, growing at 1.3% p.a.**
Land area: **1,056,640 square miles**
Population density: **35 per square mile**
Life expectancy: **73 years**
Infant mortality: **19 per 1,000 live births**
Language: **Spanish**
Best buy: **leather goods**

ECONOMIC STRUCTURE

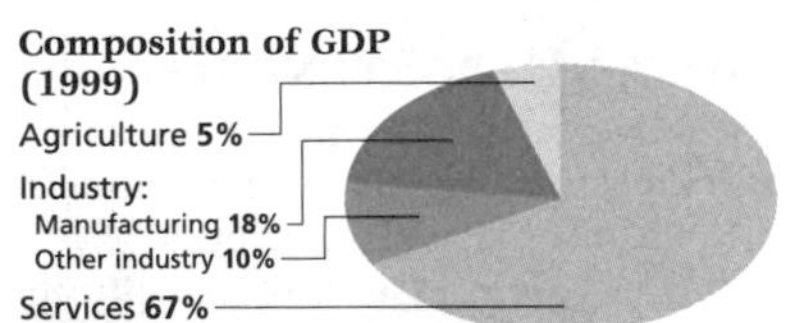

Argentina returned to democracy in 1983 after a long period of military rule. Between 1930, the year of the first military coup, and 1982 the country had 24 presidents. The generals led the country into war with Britain in 1982 after Argentina invaded the Falkland Islands. Hyperinflation was the dominant economic feature of the "lost decade" of the 1980s, with the country staggering from one stabilization program to another. The devaluation was so large in 1985 that the value of the country's currency evaporated, and it was necessary to create a new monetary unit, the austral. Inflation peaked at 4,924% in 1989. The peso replaced the austral in 1992, and was pegged at one-to-one to the U.S. dollar. Inflation in 1993–2001 was below 8%. The burden of a $155 billion total public foreign currency debt led the government of President Fernando de la Rúa, elected for a four-year term in 1999, to impose, in December 2001, tight restrictions on the public's access to dollars and to bank deposits. This sparked riots and looting, which left 28 people dead and forced the president to resign. The crisis claimed three interim presidents in two weeks until a government of "national salvation" was formed, headed by Eduardo Duhalde, the losing Peronist presidential candidate in 1999. It faced a daunting task in rebuilding the shattered economy after the largest sovereign debt default in history.

Services generate 67% of GDP, industry 28%, and agriculture 5%.

The main industries are food, steel, petrochemicals, chemicals, cars, textiles, construction, paper and cellulose, cement, rubber, and plastics. The principal exports are minerals, vegetables, transport material, electrical machinery, live animals and related products, and chemicals. The largest market is neighboring Brazil, with whom Argentina, Uruguay, and Paraguay form the Mercosur free trade area.

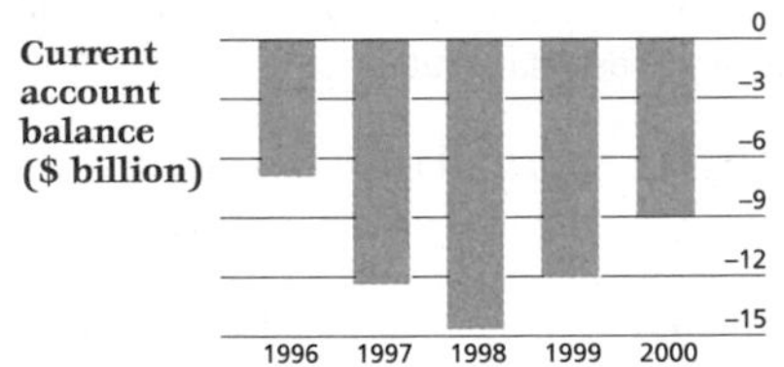

More than 200 companies and service concessions, including YPF, the giant oil monopoly, and Aerolíneas Argentinas, the national airline, were privatized during the 1990s. The $36 billion privatization program was among the most sweeping in Latin America.

ECONOMIC POLICY

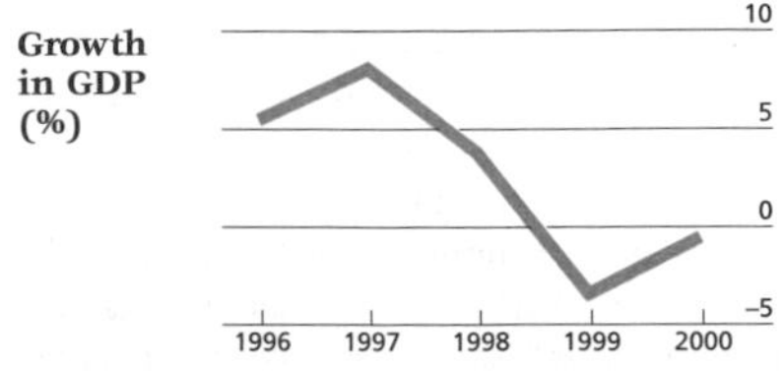

After strong annual average GDP growth of 5.7% from 1991–98 (–0.4% in 1979–89), Argentina was in a deep recession from 1999 to 2002 as a result of a financial crisis, a deteriorating fiscal position, and a loss of competitiveness stemming from an overvaluation of the peso. The economy contracted an estimated 10% during this period, and the unemployment rate reached 20%. The country slipped rapidly down the ranking of the world's most competitive economies drawn up every year by the International Institute for Management Development (IMD), the Swiss business school. It was 43rd out of the 49 countries ranked in 2001 (30th in 1998). The International Monetary Fund came to the rescue in 2000, organizing a $40 billion package of public- and private-sector loans that was supposed to dispel fears that Argentina would be unable to service its public debt.

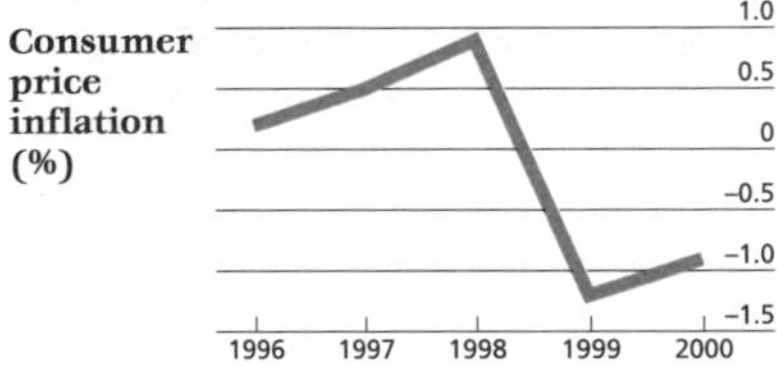

The weakening of the fiscal position stemmed from the privatization of the pension system in 1994, which deprived the state of revenue and was one element which resulted in a ballooning of total public debt (internal and external) from $83.7 billion in 1994 to $155 billion in 2001 (five times annual exports and 55% of GDP). The level of debt was unsustainable at real interest rates of more than 10% and with an economy in recession. Mexico's public debt, in comparison, was less than 100% of exports and one-quarter of GDP. The competitiveness of Argentina's exports was severely eroded by the surge of the dollar—and hence the peso—against the Euro, the yen, and Brazil's real, the currencies of Argentina's main markets. Merchandise exports represented less than 10% of GDP. Another problem was that of weak tax collection (revenue represents less than 15% of GDP).

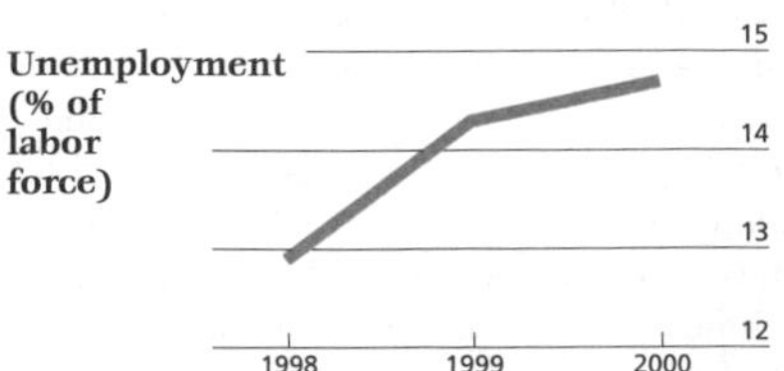

The currency-board system, the keystone of economic policy, was rigidly adhered to

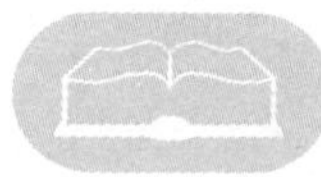

between 1991 and June 2001, when the government tinkered with it: it introduced a floating exchange rate for foreign trade by establishing a system of subsidies for hard-pressed exporters and tariffs for importers. The December 2001 crisis killed convertibility. Argentines, made nervous about the peso by the prolonged recession and government insolvency, rightly believed that a dollar in a domestic bank was not as good as one in New York. There was a risk that populist policies would return Argentina to hyperinflation if money was printed to satisfy the popular desire for spending, and if tight control was not kept on the budget.

Geography/Resources

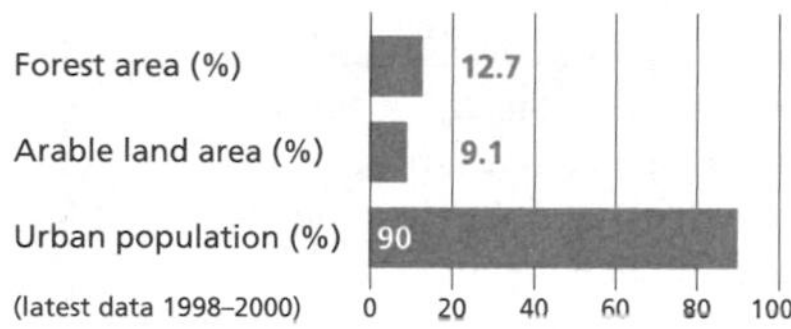

Argentina is the second-largest country in South America after Brazil. It extends from the snow-capped Andes in the west to the Atlantic Ocean in the east and shares borders in the north with Bolivia, in the northeast with Paraguay, to the east with Brazil and Uruguay, and to the west with Chile (3,298 miles long). Two-thirds of the country is either arid or semi-arid, or endures prolonged periods of drought; one-third is humid, of which some 30% are woods and sub-tropical forest; the rest is pampas plains (231,660 square miles). Three river systems flow south and east across the country to the Atlantic. The largest is the Río de la Plata system, formed by the Paraná, Paraguay, and Uruguay rivers. Large ocean-going ships can travel up the Paraná through Rosario to Santa Fe.

Around 70% of the population (36.7 million), 80% of agricultural production, and 85% of industrial activity is in the pampas zone, which covers parts of the provinces of Buenos Aires, Santa Fe, Córdoba, and La Pampa. This temperate region produces wheat, corn, soya (world's third-largest producer), grapes (world's fifth-largest wine producer), and alfalfa, among many other crops, as well as large cattle herds for beef and dairy production. There are many more cattle and sheep than people; beef and lamb are major exports. The northern provinces are hotter and grow rice, sugar cane, cotton, and tropical crops.

Mineral production has been rising, but the sector's contribution to GDP is minute, and it is a small employer. Iron ore is the main mineral extracted, mostly in the Río Negro province, but output does not meet domestic needs. The largest mining project is the Alumbrera copper and gold mine in Catamarca province. Other minerals include lead, zinc, tin, and uranium.

Immigration to Argentina since the 19th century from Italy, Spain, France, Germany, Armenia, Poland, Turkey, and Russia (among other countries) has produced a rich ethnic variety. Italian is widely understood. The indigenous population is small.

Communications/Energy

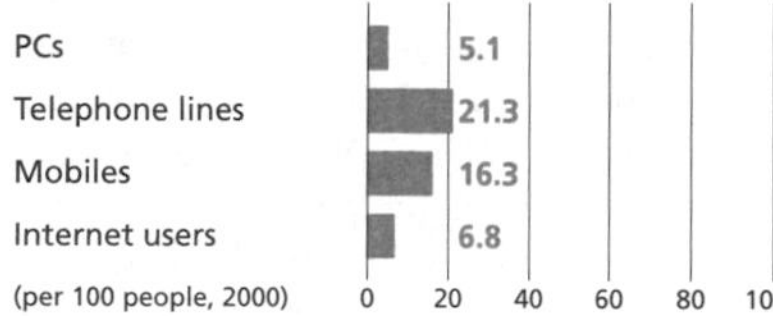

The transport system is well developed but unevenly distributed. Four branches of the Pan-American Highway run from Buenos Aires to the borders of Bolivia, Brazil, Chile, and Paraguay. About a quarter of the 155,350 miles of roads are paved. The upgrading of roads in the 1990s was undertaken through privatization and the tendering-out of concessions to the private sector in the most developed regions. This left many regions behind. A government plan envisaged investments of $20 billion in 2000–05, including new roads and an upgrade of existing infrastructure for road, rail, and air transport. Ensenada (La Plata) and nearby Buenos Aires have large ports. The main port in the south is the naval base of Bahía Blanca. Aerolíneas Argentinas, the bankrupt national carrier, was sold by the Spanish government which had acquired it to the Marsans Group, a Spanish travel company, in 2001.

Argentina is self-sufficient in oil, and crude oil imports ceased in 1983. There are also substantial natural gas deposits, and coal is mined in the Río Turbio area. Installed electricity generating capacity has been largely increasing with the development of dams. The Yacyreta dam on the Parana River on the border between Argentina and Paraguay is one of the largest hydroelectric projects in the world. The number of wind-powered plants is also increasing, and they are forecast to generate around 10% of local demand by 2010. There are agreements with Chile, Argentina, and Brazil for integrating their respective energy grids, creating a common market in electricity between the countries. Nuclear capacity has also been developed: around 10% of domestic electricity generation comes from three nuclear energy plants.

The telephone duopoly, controlled since 1991 by the incumbent companies Telefónica de Argentina (TASA) and Telecom de Argentina (Telecom), ended in 2000, opening up Latin America's third-largest telecommunications market to new players. The government estimated new investment in the sector could top $6.5 billion, $4.1 billion of which was already committed, mostly for corporate data services. SECOM, the regulatory body, withstood pressure from TASA and Telecom and set one of the lowest settlement rates in Latin America. Tariffs were set to decline steeply in 2001–03. In 2000 there were 21 fixed lines and 14 mobile phones per 100 people. As a percentage of the adult population, Internet penetration was the highest in Latin America at 4% in 2000 and a projected 11% for 2003, according to eMarketer.

Education/Employment

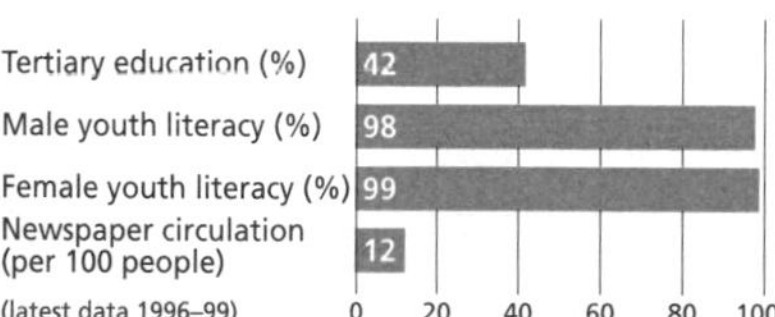

Education is compulsory and free from the age of 6 to 15. Argentina has one of the highest literacy rates in Latin America, with only 3% of those over the age of 15 classed as illiterate in the UN Human Development Index. A high number of students go on to university. Another positive factor is the number of qualified engineers available in the labor market. Spending on R&D, however, which is coordinated by the Secretariat for Technology, Science and Innovation, is low at 0.4% of GDP.

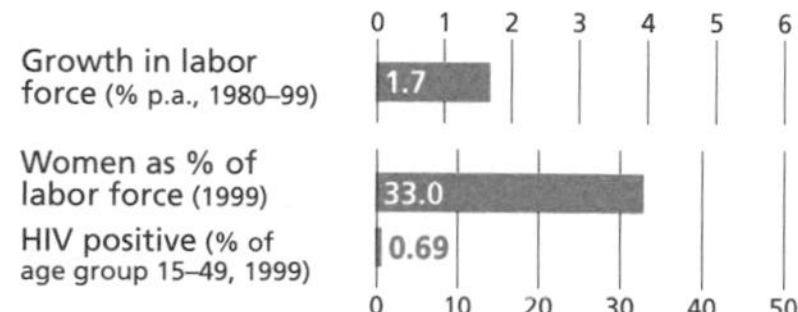

Fiscal/Financial

The banking system was shaken by the 1995 Mexican currency crisis, when around $8 billion of deposits were withdrawn, and confidence was again severely dented by Argentina's crisis in December 2001, when

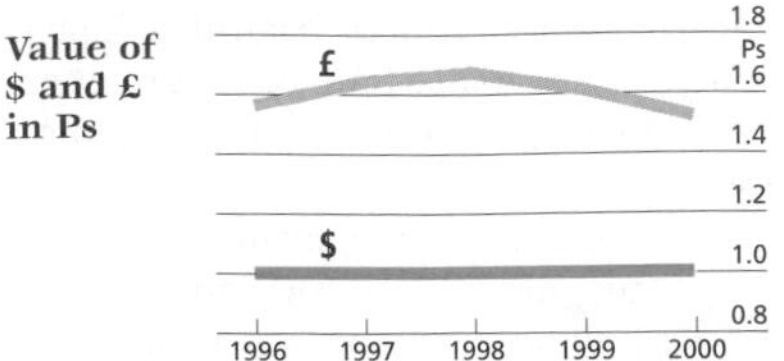

restrictions were imposed on access to deposits to stop people draining their cash. The government responded to the 1995 crisis by allowing weak banks to close and by redoubling regulatory efforts. The meltdown in 2001 was expected to produce a further shakeout among banks. Foreign investment in the banking system was substantial and helped, together with mergers, to reduce the large number of financial institutions. There were more than 110 financial institutions in 2001, almost 90 of them banks. The largest bank in asset terms is the state's Banco de la Nación Argentina. Banco Río de la Plata and BBVA Banco Francés are respectively owned by Spain's Banco Santander Central Hispano and Banco Bilbao Vizcaya Argentaria, and between them control around 20% of the system.

Corporate tax and the top rate of personal income tax are both 35%, and VAT is 21%.

The Buenos Aires Stock Exchange is not very developed: market capitalization is less than 20% of GDP.

Business Opportunities

Growth in output (% p.a., 1990–99)

Services	5.0
Industry	4.6
Manufacturing	3.5
Agriculture	3.8

The liberal foreign investment regime attracted considerable direct investment. FDI averaged $2.2 billion a year in 1985–95, and rose to $12.9 billion in 1997–2000. The amount peaked at $24.1 billion in 1999, when Spain's Repsol acquired the privatized oil company YPF for $14.9 billion. Spanish companies invested more than $30 billion in Argentina between 1990 and 2001, about 10% of the country's GDP. The oil sector has been the main recipient of FDI, followed by manufacturing (chiefly food processing), electricity, gas and water, and banking.

With little privatization left to do, the bulk of new FDI inflows will be channeled into takeovers or greenfield investments once the country's economic mess is sorted out and the economy returns to growth. The deregulation of telecommunications could spur investment in this sector, and the long-term prospects also look promising for electricity generation, oil, natural gas, and mining.

For More Information

Books:

Burns, Jimmy. *The Land That Lost its Heroes*. New York: Bloomsbury, 2002.
Chatwin, Bruce. *In Patagonia*. New York: Vintage Books, 1998.
Financial Times Country Surveys. *Argentina*. London: Financial Times.
France, Miranda. *Bad Times in Buenos Aires*. New York: Phoenix Press, 1999.
Tulchin, Joseph, ed. *Argentina: The Challenges of Modernization*. Wilmington, DE: Scholarly Resources, 1998.
Williamson, Edwin. *Borges*. New York: Viking Books, 2002.

Web Sites:

Buenos Aires Herald (English language newspaper): **www.buenosairesherald.com**
Buenos Aires Stock Exchange: **www.bcba.sba.com.ar**
Central Bank of the Republic of Argentina: **www.bcra.gov.ar**
IMF reports: **www.imf.org/external**
Ministry of Finance: **www.mecon.gov.ar/econom.htm**
National Statistical Institute: **www.indec.mecon.ar**
U.S. State Department Country Commercial Guide: **www.state.gov/e/eb/rls/rpts/ccg**

  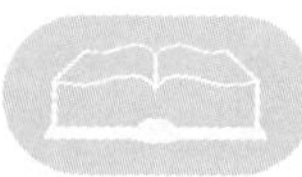    

ARUBA

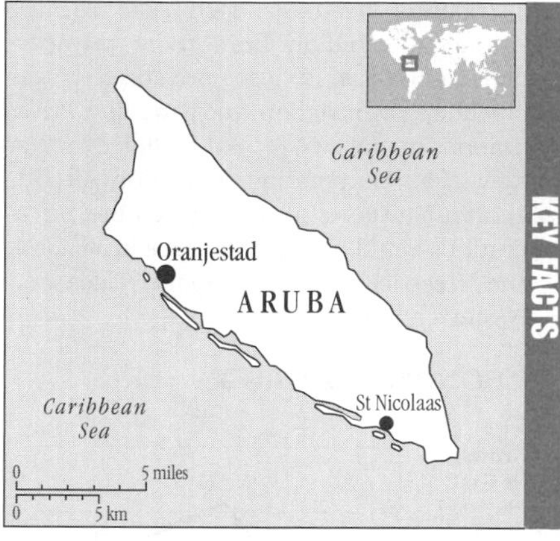

KEY FACTS

GNI pc: **$22,000 (approx.)**
Head of government: **prime minister**
Currency: **Aruba florin**
Capital: **Oranjestad**
Population: **68,700**
Land area: **74.5 square miles**
Population density: **922 per square mile**
Language: **Dutch (official), Papiamento (daily use). English, Spanish, and Portuguese widely spoken**
Best buy: **jewelry, perfumes**

ECONOMY

Along with Netherlands Antilles and the Netherlands itself, Aruba forms one of the three theoretically equal constituents of the Kingdom of the Netherlands. The island government—headed by the prime minister—is responsible for internal affairs, including management of the economy, while the Kingdom—represented by a locally-born governor—is responsible for external affairs and defence. In 1986 Aruba was granted "status aparte" as a separate member of the kingdom, outside the Netherlands Antilles. Relations with the neighboring island of Curaçao, Netherlands Antilles, have not always been easy.

Aruba is one of the most prosperous economies in the Caribbean, with a record of rapid growth since the mid-1980s, reaching double digits in 1987–92, but averaging 4% annually from 1996 to 2000, when the rate declined to 2.5%.

The main foreign exchange earner is tourism, which has grown rapidly since an economic crisis which followed the closure of the oil refinery in 1985, and contributes nearly 38% of GDP and 35% of employment.

The large oil refinery at San Nicolas in the south of the island was originally built in 1929 by Standard Oil (now Exxon) to process Venezuelan oil for the U.S. market; it has now been reopened by Coastal with throughput capacity close to 280,000 barrels a day. Transshipment is also an important activity, and a small petrochemicals sector includes a $100 million liquefied petroleum gas. Oil-related exports totaled $2,385 million in 2000, a year-on-year increase of 107%.

Although the situation has improved since the formation of a coast guard in 1997, illegal activities still play a significant role in the economy.

With unemployment low and growth rates high, economic overheating is a source of concern. Price levels are generally high; however, inflation has been moderate, and has remained in the range 2.0–3.5% since 1995.

GEOGRAPHY/RESOURCES

Aruba is located close to the South American mainland, 15.5 miles off the Venezuelan coast. Curaçao is 42 miles to the east.

Aruba's main resources are its geographical location, its warm, sunny climate, clear offshore waters, and sandy beaches. The population is concentrated around Oranjestad (pop. 21,000), with some other settlements throughout the island. The population is of mixed Amerindian, Dutch, and Hispanic descent, with an Afro-Caribbean minority as well as more recent Hispanic and Filipino migrants, many of whom work in tourism.

COMMUNICATIONS/ENERGY

The Reina Beatrix international airport has direct links to destinations in North America, Venezuela, and Colombia, as well as Amsterdam, Puerto Rico, and Santo Domingo. However, the local carrier, Air Aruba, was declared bankrupt in 2000.

There are ports at San Nicolas (oil), Oranjestad (cruise ships and cargo), and Barcadera (container cargo). There are plans to establish a single free zone spanning both Barcadera and the airport.

There is a well developed internal road network, telecommunications system, and electricity supply system. Fresh water is provided by the world's second-largest desalination plant.

FISCAL/FINANCIAL

The domestic financial sector is supervised by the Centrale Bank van Aruba. The Financial Center, established in 1996, is responsible for the regulation and development of the offshore financial sector. This plays an important role in the local economy, but is not large by some Caribbean standards, and includes registration of trust and management companies. Aruba was listed as a "tax haven" by the Organization for Economic Cooperation and Development in June 2000, but unlike some Caribbean centres was not listed as a "non-cooperative" jurisdiction on money laundering by the Paris-based Financial Action Task Force.

Tax incentives for businesses include accelerated depreciation allowances. The Free Zone allows transshipment and processing of goods without passing through local customs. Certain activities also qualify for a reduced-rate 2% profit tax.

BUSINESS OPPORTUNITIES

Overseas investment is encouraged. The main opportunities are in the tourism sector and related industries. The government is also attempting, so far with very limited success, to promote light industries and high technology enterprises.

State industries earmarked for privatization include the state telecommunications company Setar, the refuse company Serlimar, the water company, and the airport.

For More Information

Web Sites:
Aruba Financial Center:
www.arubafinancialcenter.com
Curaçao daily newspaper, in Dutch, regular coverage on Aruba:
www.amigoe.com
Ministry of Economic Affairs:
www.ministry.arubaeconomicaffairs.com

AUSTRALIA

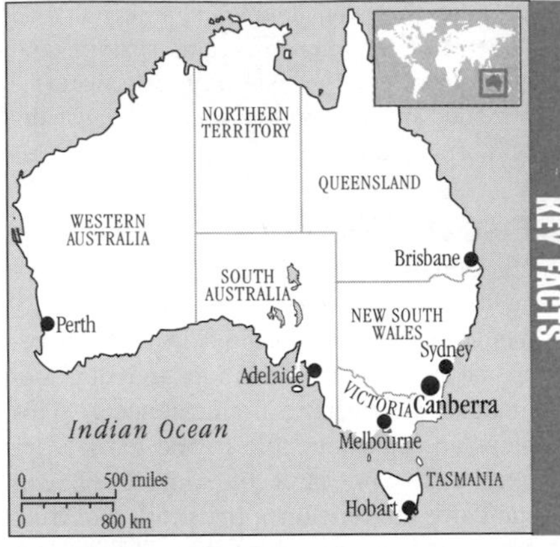

KEY FACTS

GNI: **$397,345 million; world's 15th**
GNI pc: **$20,950; world's 27th**
Head of government: **prime minister**
Currency: **Australian dollar (A$)**
Capital: **Canberra**
Population: **18,705,000, growing at 1.1% p.a.**
Land area: **2,966,136 square miles**
Population density: **6 per square mile**
Life expectancy: **78 years**
Infant mortality: **5 per 1,000 live births**
Language: **English**
Best buy: **vintage wine; gold jewelry, gems, designer clothing, Aboriginal art**

ECONOMIC STRUCTURE

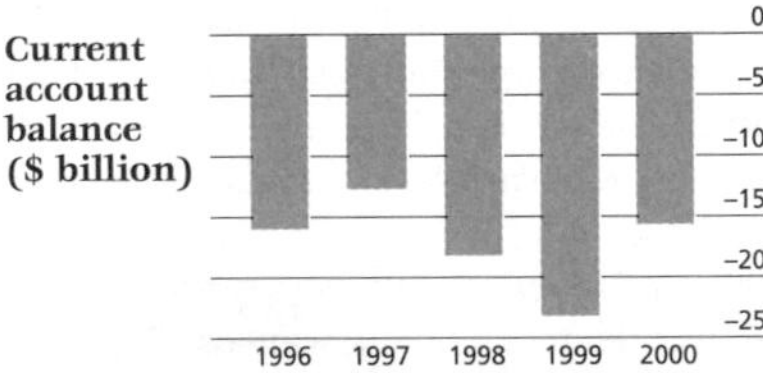

The Aboriginal people of Australia have the longest continuous cultural history in the world, going back to the last ice age. Britain colonized the country in the eighteenth century and established an economy based on agriculture and mining. In 1901, Australia became a federal nation of six states–New South Wales, Victoria, Queensland, South Australia, Western Australia and Tasmania–and two territories, Northern Territory and the Australian Capital Territory, where Canberra is situated. Economic policy implementation is shared between the federal, state and territorial governments. After World War II manufacturing became the dominant sector, and stronger trade links were established with Asia and the United States. Since the 1960s the services sector has led growth.

Services contributed 73.4% of GDP in 1999–2000, followed by manufacturing (12.2%), construction (5.6%), mining (4.2%), and agriculture (3%). The largest services sector was finance, real estate, and business services (18.5% of GDP), followed by trade (10.7%), and transport and communications (8.7%). Communications is fast-growing, and tourism is important. Machinery was the leading manufacturing sector, contributing 22% of manufacturing production in 1999–2000. Manufacturing is diversified, and includes minerals processing, chemicals, food and timber processing, textiles, and leather. Three eastern states account for over three quarters of GDP: New South Wales (34%), Victoria (25%), and Queensland (18%). The leading exports in 1999–2000 were metals and minerals (21%), coal and petroleum (20%), machinery (11%), and gold (5%). Australia is the world's top coal exporter. Other important exports are wool, sheepskins, cereals, meat, and wine. Mining and agriculture, and processed products from these sectors, account for over 70% of exports. In 1999–2000 Japan was the top market (19%), followed by the ASEAN countries (13%), European Union countries (12%), the United States (10%), and South Korea (8%).

From the 1980s federal and state governments pursued privatization programs, selling A$85 billion of public assets by end-1999. Most were in federal assets (A$45 billion), followed by the State of Victoria (A$30 billion). Electricity and gas accounted for 39% of the total, the flotation of half of telecommunications company Telstra for 33%, finance (17%), airports (3%), transport operators and ports (3%), and gambling (2%). Apart from Telstra, other large federal divestitures included Commonwealth Bank (A$9 billion), major airports (A$4 billion), and airline, rail, shipping, and port companies, including Qantas (A$2 billion). Victoria sold its electricity and gas businesses for A$28 billion, and other enterprises in gambling, ports, rail transport, plantations, and equity in an aluminum smelter. In South Australia, electricity privatization raised over A$4 billion. The government also privatized banks, gambling, and ports. New South Wales and Queensland sold banks and insurance companies, and Western Australia sold its gas distribution business, each state earning around A$2 billion from these privatizations. Queensland also privatized a gas pipeline, power station, and gambling. Privatizations in progress in 2001 included the National Rail Corporation, Essendon Airport, and four airports at Sydney. Future privatizations could include hospitals in Victoria, and electricity in New South Wales and Western Australia.

ECONOMIC POLICY

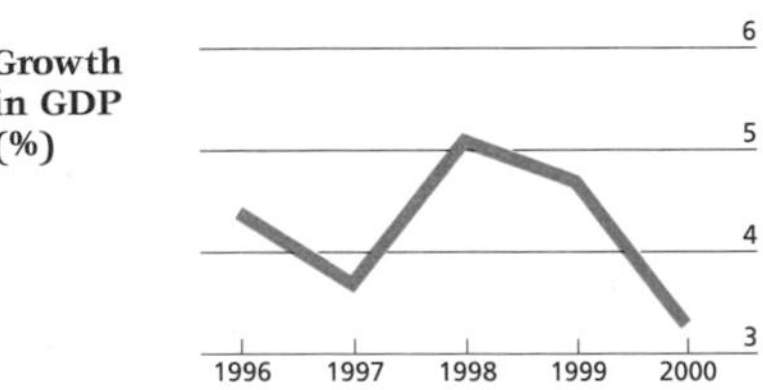

Economic policy shifted in the 1990s from protecting domestic industry to greater international openness and competition. Monetary policy focuses on maintaining a competitive exchange rate for exports without fueling inflation from essential imports, and also on ensuring that interest rates provide a measured stimulus for economic growth. The accumulation of public debt and the need to reduce public expenditure fueled the privatization programs. The states with the highest debt, Victoria and South Australia, pursued privatization more vigorously than others. Federal net debt fell from 19% of GDP in the mid-1990s to 6.4% in 2000–01. From 1996–97 there have been small federal budget surpluses.

Part of future public spending on infrastructure will be conducted in partnership with the private sector. The government introduced a compulsory funded superannuation scheme to cope with the extra pensions cost of an ageing population, but the prospect of much higher public health spending for older people still poses a problem. Labor productivity increased and inflationary pressures from wage demands eased following the introduction of a flexible wage bargaining framework from 1997. Welfare reforms regarding temporary and part-time work are under way to reduce structural unemployment.

Annual GDP growth averaged 4.2% in 1996–2000, a level maintained for nine years to June 2000. Growth slowed to 2% for 2000–01 because of slower growth in main export markets, and the impact on investment and consumption of the new sales tax.

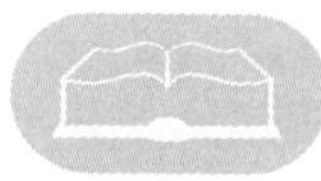

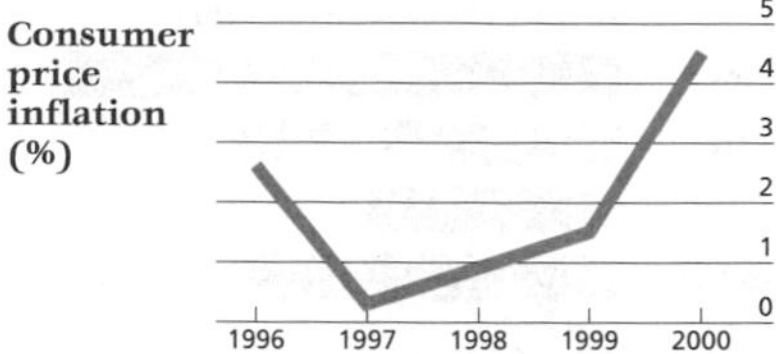

Growth is expected to revive to 3.1% in 2001–02. Inflation averaged 2% in 1996–2000, rising to 6% in the second half of 2000 on account of the sales tax and higher oil prices. Wage moderation should help bring inflation within the government's target of 2–3% in 2001 and 2002. Unemployment fell from 8.6% in 1996–97 to around 6% in mid-2001.

GEOGRAPHY/RESOURCES

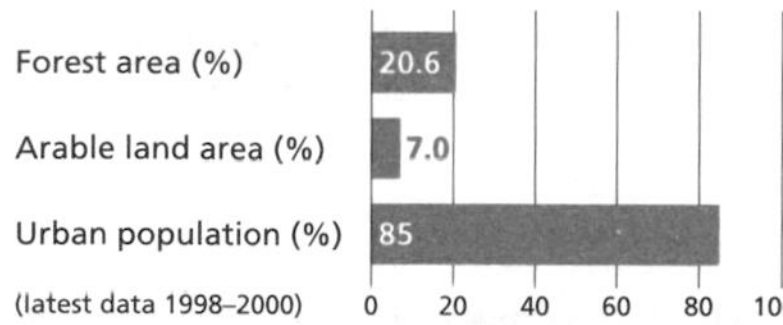

The country comprises the largest island in the world, plus the island state of Tasmania to the southeast of the mainland, and a number of much smaller islands. Much of the center of the mainland is desert, and 80% of the land has rainfall of less than 24 inches, while half has rainfall of less than 12 inches. Temperatures range from 122°F to below 32°F. Most of the land is low plateau, with deserts and fertile plains in the southeast. The low point is Lake Eyre at 49 feet below sea level, while the high point is Mount Kosciuszko at 7,510 feet. Natural hazards include cyclones and droughts.

Australia is self-sufficient in food. The main crops are sugar cane, wheat, barley, other grains, rapeseed, legumes, vegetables, fruit, and cotton. Sheep are the main livestock, followed by chickens, cattle, pigs, horses, and goats. Meat, dairy, honey, leather, and wool are important. Hardwood and softwood timber is harvested for wood and paper processing. Australia has the third largest fisheries zone in the world. The catch is varied, but the volume is small by international standards.

Although mining is an important industry, vast tracts of the country are still unexplored. Exploration continues for most minerals, and proven reserves of petroleum and natural gas, especially, are expected to increase substantially. Proven reserves of petroleum and natural gas were 2.9 billion barrels and 44.6 trillion cubic feet respectively at January 2001. In 1998 Australia had 7% of world recoverable coal resources (100 billion tons), and this is the largest mining sector. Australia had the largest world resources of low-cost uranium (26% of the world total), lead (26%), zinc (18%), silver (15%), and nickel (12%). It is the largest world producer of bauxite, the largest exporter of alumina, and the third largest exporter of aluminum. It is the largest world producer of diamonds, tantalum, rutile, ilmenite, and zircon. It has the third largest reserves of copper, and is the fifth world producer. It is the sixth world producer of manganese ore. Iron ore is a major export, as well as providing a basis for domestic manufacturing. Other minerals produced include tin, antimony, clay, sand, gravel, construction stone, and gemstones.

The population and most of the economic activity is concentrated into the southeastern coastal area. Canberra (population 310,000) is the capital and the center of federal administration. Other chief cities are Sydney (3,990,000 in New South Wales), Melbourne (3,370,000 in Victoria), Brisbane (1,575,000 in Queensland), Perth (1,340,000 in Western Australia), Adelaide (1,090,000 in South Australia), and Hobart (in Tasmania). The majority of people are of European origin (92%), followed by Asian (7%), and Aboriginal (1%).

COMMUNICATIONS/ENERGY

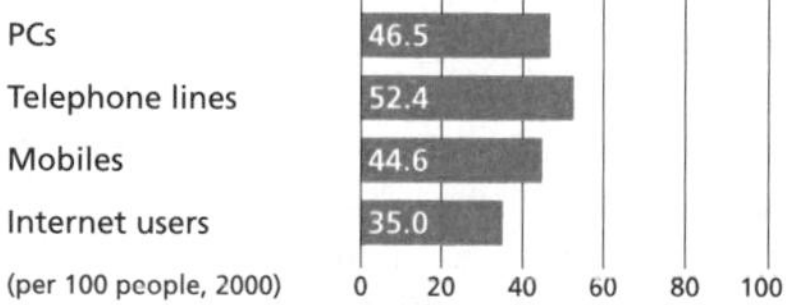

The road network was 500,746 miles in June 2000, of which 201,783 miles was paved. Vehicles traveled a total 110.4 billion miles in 1998/99. Trucks and vans accounted for 37% of this, business travel by car and bus for 20%, and private travel for 43%. The rail network (including metropolitan light rail) was 24,813 miles at June 1999. In 1998–99, 595.2 million passengers and 492 million tons of freight traveled by rail. The pipeline network includes 3,480 miles for natural gas, 1,554 miles for crude oil, and 311 miles for refined petroleum products. The main sea ports are Adelaide, Brisbane, Cairns, Darwin, Devonport (Tasmania), Fremantle, Geelong, and Hobart. In 2000 the merchant fleet over 1,000 grt comprised 54 ships with a total displacement of 1.6 million grt. At March 2000 there were nine international airports and 269 other airports, most of which are commercial.

Telecommunications were opened to competition in 1997 when the Australian Communications Authority (ACA) and Australian Competition and Consumer Commission (ACCC) were appointed guardians of the sector. The number of operators increased from 3 at June 1997 to over 70 in late 2001, but Telstra remains the dominant player. Domestic links are provided by satellite and radiotelephone, while international links are assured by cable and satellite. In late 2001, 96% of households had fixed phones, and 50%—and 56% of businesses—had an internet connection; 40% of the population owned mobile phones.

Australia is a net exporter of energy and is self-sufficient for all its energy needs except oil. Oil and gas meet 54% of domestic demand, with coal accounting for around 39%, and renewables around 7%. Electricity is generated from fossil fuels, mostly coal (89.9%), hydro (8.4%), and other renewable sources (1.7%). Power plants absorb around 29% of indigenous energy output. Oil production was 810,655 barrels per day in 2000, but was expected to settle around 600,000 barrels per day in 2001 and 2002. Oil consumption was 855,000 barrels per day in 2000. Traditionally there is 75% self-sufficiency in oil, but in 2000 Australia became a net oil exporter for the first time. Natural gas production was 1.1 trillion cubic feet in 1999, with consumption at 763 billion cubic feet. Gas is due to take a larger share of energy use in the medium-term, but there are distribution problems following deregulation. Coal output was 320.6 million tons in 1999 with consumption at 142.3 million tons.

EDUCATION/EMPLOYMENT

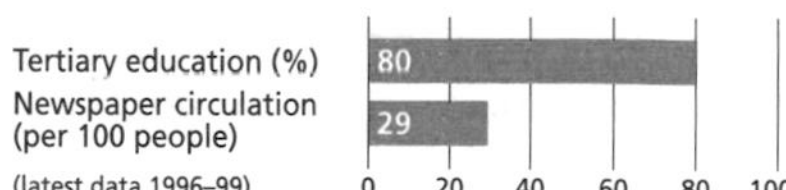

Education is compulsory and free in state schools from age 6 to 15 (16 in Tasmania). Schools and vocational colleges are managed by state governments, and higher education by federal government. There were 36 public universities and 392 other government-funded higher education institutions in 1999, and two private universities. There were 686,300 students in higher education. Student loans are available.

The government launched the comprehensive R&D funding program Backing Australia's Ability in January 2001 to help overcome bottlenecks in innovation. The program includes R&D tax incentives to companies, training schemes, and technology incubator schemes. R&D spending by

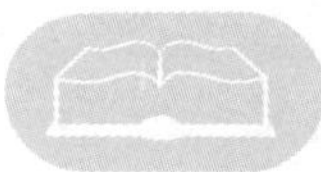

manufacturing industry fell by 7% in 1998–99. R&D strengths include automotive and other transport equipment; electronics and electrical equipment; IT; petroleum, coal and chemical products; metals; biotechnology; and food industries.

Wages and other employment conditions are determined between employers and employees, often on a collective basis, but agreements are decentralized since the Workplace Relations Act came into force in 1997. Previously benchmark wages and conditions were centrally set by government, trade unions, and employers. The new system focuses on Australian Workplace Agreements (AWAs), which are subject to government approval. AWAs are conducted in companies of all sizes and sectors, and their scope varies accordingly. They cover wages, working hours, hiring and dismissal, annual leave, sick leave, pension provision, health and safety, performance targets, and training, but not necessarily all of these. The average working week is 39 hours.

Fiscal/Financial

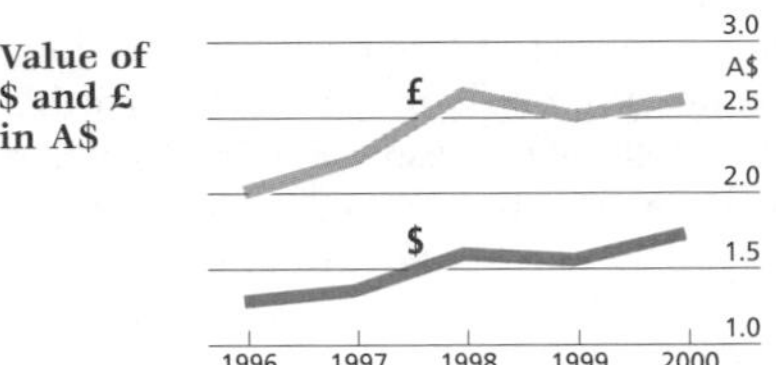

The major banks (all private sector)—Commonwealth Bank, ANZ Bank, National Australia Bank, Westpac—account for over half of banking sector assets. Westpac is also involved in life insurance. Insurance companies include some of the world's largest.

Financial sector reform, implemented from 1997, has focussed on streamlining the regulatory authorities and on opening the sector to greater competition. At the same time the banking and insurance assets of federal and state governments were privatized. Harmonized rules for licensing, disclosure and conduct of finance institutions, disclosure for products, and regulations for clearing and settlement facilities are being introduced over two years from late 2001. These rules stipulate a 15% ownership limitation on financial markets and facilities deemed to be of national significance.

Supervision is conducted by three authorities, which coordinate their activities. The Reserve Bank of Australia, the central bank, is responsible for overseeing the monetary and payments systems and ensuring the stability of the financial system. The Australian Prudential Regulation Authority supervises all deposit-taking institutions. The Australian Securities and Investments Commission regulates conduct and information disclosure in the financial markets, and is responsible for consumer protection.

Corporation tax was reduced to 30% in January 2001, with the loss of government revenue being funded by the elimination of accelerated depreciation of assets in corporate tax returns. Personal income tax was also reduced on salaries below A$60,000 a year, but the OECD warned that the discrepancy between corporation tax and the highest personal tax rate (47%) could lead to a redefinition of the latter. The federal government levies 1.5% on salaries for healthcare. Withholding tax on repatriated income is 10%. The former wholesale sales tax on goods was replaced in July 2000 by a comprehensive 10% goods and services tax. Further tax reforms are expected in 2003.

The finance sector is sophisticated and internationalized. At mid-2000 there were 55 banks, with 5,003 branches and total assets of A$815.6 billion. Non-bank institutions, with total assets of A$189.9 billion, included building societies, credit cooperatives, money market corporations, pastoral finance companies (rural lending), and cash management trusts. There were 50 life insurance companies including 6 re-insurers, and 162 non-life insurance companies, in 1999.

The first stock exchange was set up in Melbourne in 1884. In 1987 the Melbourne, Sydney, Adelaide, Brisbane, Hobart, and Perth exchanges merged to form the Australian Stock Exchange, which was demutualized in 1998. The exchange handles a wide range of instruments. Market capitalization was boosted in the 1990s by the privatization programs, but it remains small compared to that of the global leaders. Trading is electronic, and increasing online. A cross-border trading platform for Asian and other international securities, developed in collaboration with the Singapore Exchange, was due to go into operation from early 2002.

Business Opportunities

Tax and financial incentives are offered to investors. Special encouragement is given to high-tech operations and multinational company regional headquarters. The Darwin Trade Development Zone in Northern Territory, and the Manufacturing-in-Bond scheme elsewhere, allow duty-free imports for processing and re-export. Many former foreign investment restrictions have been eliminated. Restrictions remain on the media, civil aviation, urban real estate, and uranium production. Investments in assets worth over A$50 million are examined by the Foreign Investment Review Board. Sectors attracting the most investment in the late 1990s were mining, manufacturing, communications, and transport. The United States, the United Kingdom, and Japan accounted for some 55% of total FDI. The points of contact are the state and federal governments.

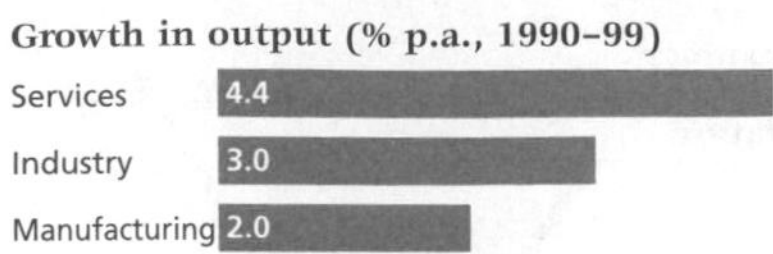

For More Information

Books:

Australia: The Complete Encyclopedia. Toronto, Ontario: Firefly Books, 2001.

Hampshire, David. *Living and Working in Australia.* Oxford: Survival Books.

Irving, H., ed. *The Centenary Companion to the Australian Federation.* New York: Cambridge University Press, 2000.

Knightley, Philip. *Australia: A Biography of a Nation.* New York: Jonathan Cape, 2000.

MacIntyre, Stuart. *A Concise History of Australia.* New York: Cambridge University Press, 2000.

Merrett, David, ed. *Business Institutions and Behaviour in Australia.* New York: Frank Cass, 2000.

Web Sites:

Australian Bureau of Statistics: **www.abs.gov.au**

Australian Financial Review (financial daily newspaper): **www.afr.com.au**

Australian Stock Exchange: **www.asx.com**

Commonwealth Government entry point: **www.australia.gov.au**

National Office for the Information Economy: **www.noie.gov.au**

Reserve Bank of Australia (central bank): **www.rba.gov.au**

AUSTRIA

KEY FACTS

GNI: **$205,743 million; world's 21st**
GNI pc: **$25,430; world's 14th**
Head of government: **chancellor**
Currency: **Euro (€)**
Capital: **Vienna**
Population: **8,177,000, growing at 0.7% p.a.**
Land area: **31,930 square miles**
Population density: **256 per square mile**
Life expectancy: **77 years**
Infant mortality: **4 per 1,000 live births**
Language: **German**
Best buy: **leather goods, glassware, porcelain**

ECONOMIC STRUCTURE

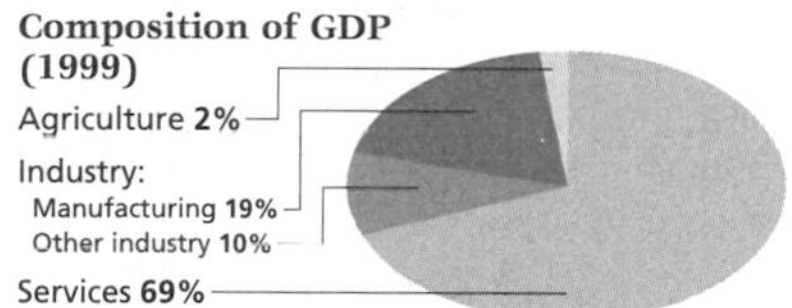

Until defeat in World War I, Austria was a leading world political power for many centuries, and developed a sophisticated economy. After the end of World War II, Austria's primary industries, including metals and minerals, chemicals and hydrocarbons, and telecommunications and transport infrastructure, were rebuilt largely under state ownership. The state participated with private industry in manufacturing. It provided the bulk of R&D funding and facilities, and entered into some areas of high-tech manufacturing, notably semiconductors. Like most small countries, Austria is dependent on external trade. It cultivated strong trading links with other Western European countries, first through the European Free Trade Association (EFTA), and since 1995 through the European Union. It also developed strong banking and trading links with its former Soviet bloc neighbors. The relationship has continued to flourish since the demise of Communism.

Services accounted for 67.4% of GDP in 1999 and for around two-thirds of jobs. Manufacturing accounted for 30.4% of GDP, while agriculture accounted for 2.2%. Austria's mountain scenery, grand history, and culture make it an important tourist destination. Business services, including banking, insurance and trade-related services, are well developed. E-commerce is a growing area. Primary products and manufacturing cover a broad range of sectors. Particular strengths include road transport equipment and industrial machinery. The main export markets in 2000 were Germany, Italy, Switzerland, and Hungary. Main exports were road vehicles, machinery, iron and steel products, chemicals, wood and paper, and processed food.

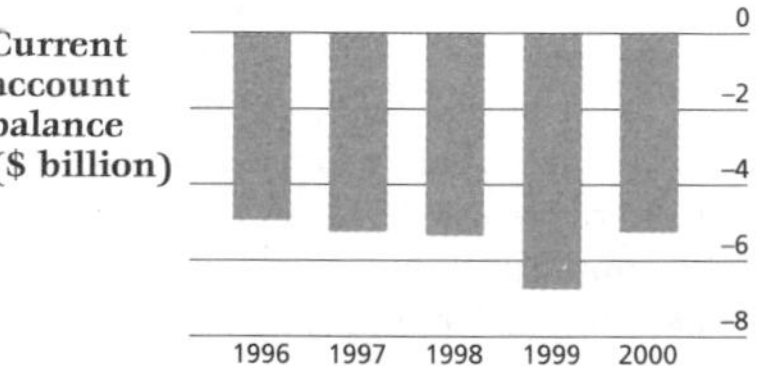

Österreichische Industrieholding Aktiensgesellschaft (ÖIAG), the state holding company, has sold all or part of its interests in a number of key companies to the private sector since 1987. By the end of the 1990s it retained holdings in ÖIAG Bauholding (100%), petroleum and chemicals group ÖMV (35%); steel maker VA Stahl (38.8%); Böhler-Uddeholm (25%), and VA Technologie (24%). In 1988, 49% of electricity-generating company Verbundgesellschaft, which supplies half of Austria's electricity, was privatized. In 1997 salt producer Österreichische Salinen was privatized. In the same year Bank Austria absorbed another leading state-owned bank Creditanstalt Bankverein, prior to privatization. The Post and Telecommunications service has been partly privatized.

ECONOMIC POLICY

The government changed key aspects of its economic policy when Austria joined the European Union in January 1995. It provided compensation for farmers adversely

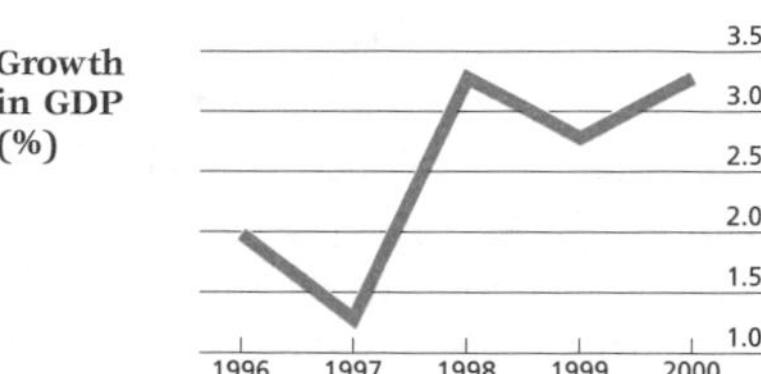

affected by EU membership, and embarked on an austerity program to reduce public expenditure, the national debt, and the government deficit. Having adopted the Euro since January 1999, Austria agreed to reduce the national debt and federal government deficit to 60% and 1.5% of GDP respectively by 2005. The government expected to meet the first target, and to achieve a federal budget deficit of near zero, in 2002.

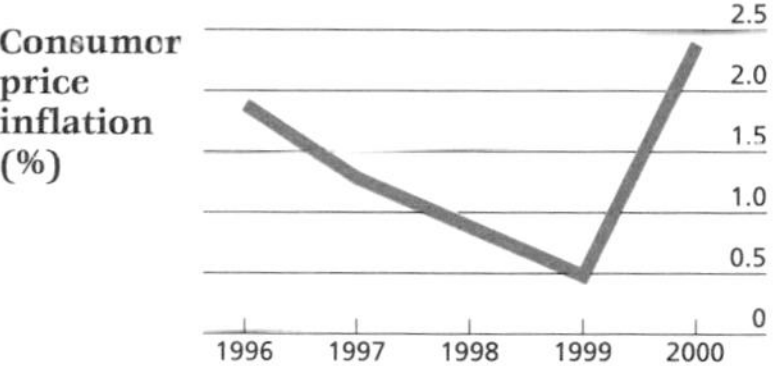

In 1999, prior to the general elections, the government increased family allowances and halted reforms to pensions and healthcare. Austerity was restored to health insurance in the 2000–03 budget with planned reforms requiring all patients, except the poorest, to contribute to health costs. Pension reform (the system is one of the most expensive in the EU) had not resumed by late 2001. The government reduced taxes to bring them more in line with those of other EU nations. The 2000–03 budget policy statement includes the principle that counter-financing must be sought to match new budget expenditures. In 2000 the new center-right coalition government, including the extreme right-wing Freedom Party, incurred the wrath of other EU countries, some of which briefly imposed bilateral sanctions. International relations remain uneasy. Internally the social partnership between government and trade unions disintegrated over health reforms, raising the possibility of industrial action for the first time in decades.

Economic growth was an annual average of 2.5% for 1996–2000. It fell to 1.5% in 2001, but is expected to revive to 1.8% in 2002 and 2.2% in 2003. Growth has been fueled by privatization, an expansion of higher education, income tax cuts, and

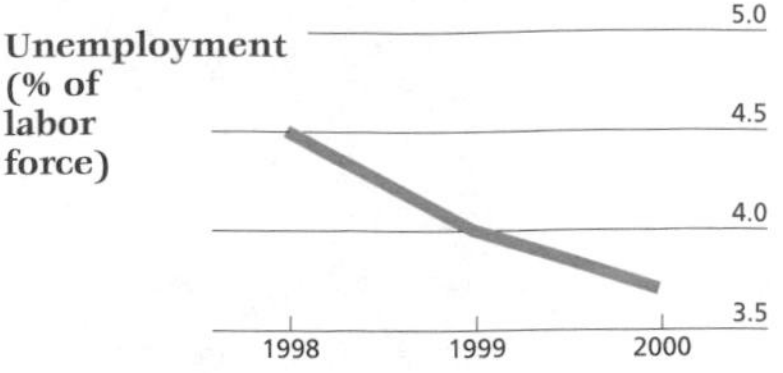

enhanced external trade through EU membership. Inflation fell steadily in the 1990s from 3.3% in 1990 to 0.5% in 1999. It reached 2.4% in 2000–01 on account of higher world oil prices, and was expected to fall to 1.6% in 2002. Job creation was low but positive at 1% in 1999, down from 1.9% in 1990. Unemployment rose from 3.2% in 1990 to 4.5% in 1998, falling to 3.6% in 2000. Labor costs declined slightly through the 1990s to 2000. Under the 2000–03 economic program, the Public Employment Service for the unemployed will be reorganized along the lines of a private company, and will work with private employment agencies to reduce the number of unemployed.

Geography/Resources

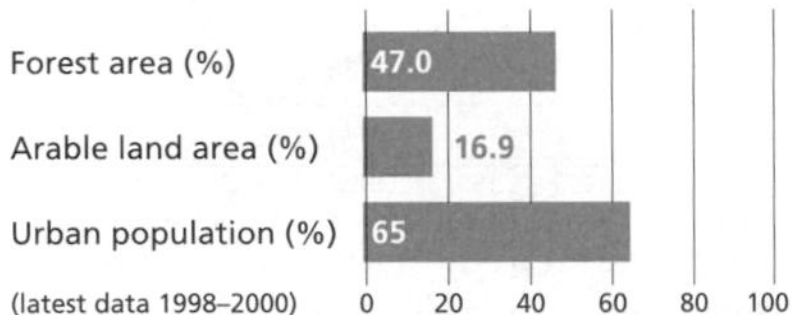

A landlocked country in south central Europe, Austria borders Germany and the Czech Republic to the north, Slovakia and Hungary to the east, Slovenia and Italy to the south, and Switzerland and Liechtenstein to the west. It is mountainous to the west and south—almost two-thirds of the country—and has plains in the north along the Danube river and heathland in the south-east. The highest mountain is the Grossglockner at 12,457 feet. There are three climatic regions: alpine with high precipitation and a continental climate, the eastern heathland with low rainfall and a continental climate, and the rest, which is temperate and wet. Most of the population live in the plains of the north and east, and 98% are of Germanic origin. There are six officially recognized ethnic minorities: Croats and Hungarians, Slovenes, Czechs, Slovaks, Romanies, and Sinti.

The main agricultural region is the northern plain bordering the Danube. Many arable crops are grown, beef and dairy cattle are raised, and there are orchards and vineyards. Forestry covers 46% of the land, and timber is a significant commodity in domestic consumption and export. Natural gas and oil are produced, the oil accounting for almost 10% of domestic demand. Tungsten deposits are some of the largest in the western world. Other minerals produced include iron ore, lignite, coal, magnesite, salt, kaolin, talc, and gypsum.

Communications/Energy

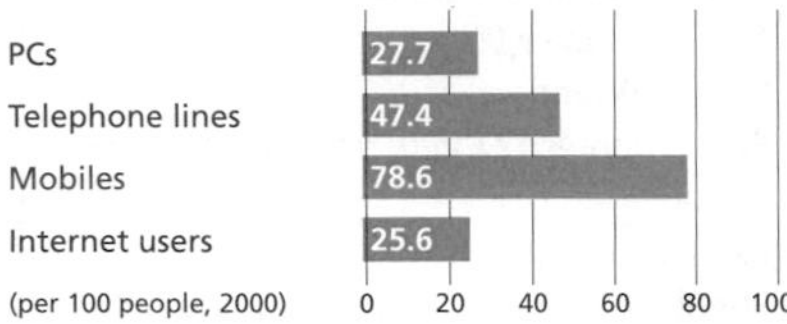

There are 1,240 miles of motorways out of a road network of 124,280 miles. The rail network comprised 3,787 miles in 2001, including 2,264 miles of electrified track. New rail and road routes are being planned from Vienna to the east and south to extend the trans-European transport network to the EU candidate countries in Central and Eastern Europe. Vienna's airport Schwechat has been expanded to cope with increasing traffic, especially from Eastern Europe. The pipeline network comprises 483 miles for crude oil and 522 miles for natural gas. The Danube offers 218 miles of navigable waterway, and barges carry up to 1,800 tons, usually of basic products such as petroleum, coal, iron ore, steel, timber, and grain. The Rhine-Main-Danube canal opened in 1992, providing a navigable waterway across Europe from the North Sea to the Black Sea.

Telecommunications links are provided via fiber-optic cable and satellite with fully digital switching. Mobile telephony has been open to competition since 1997, and fixed line telephony since 1998. From 1998 to 2000 over 120 licenses were approved by the independent regulatory authority Telecom Control GmbH for fixed networks, switching technologies, mobile telephony, and paging systems. There were 4 million fixed phone lines in 1999, and 4 million mobile phones at June 2000. There were 2.6 million Internet users in 2000. In June 2000 interconnection fees from alternative providers to the main provider, Telecom Austria, were reduced by 43%, cuts which followed on previous price reductions to subscribers.

Hydroelectric power accounts for 60% of electricity supply, followed by gas (12%) and coal (9%). There was a policy decision not to build nuclear power stations. Austria is in the top 10 world electricity exporters (14 TWh in 1999) and importers (12 TWh). There is a small indigenous production of oil and natural gas. Oil exploration continues north of the Alps, but deposits are deep and costly to exploit. Austria imports gas by pipeline from Russia, and oil by pipeline from the Italian port of Trieste.

Education/Employment

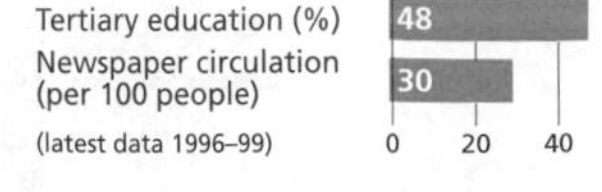

Education is largely funded and provided by the state. It is compulsory from age 6 to 15. Higher education courses are free for Austrians, and there are means-tested state grants for the needy. Central control over the school system is exercised by the Federal Ministry of Education and Cultural Affairs, while that of universities and higher education colleges falls under the aegis of the Federal Ministry of Science and Transport. The 12 universities, six fine arts colleges, and a growing number of professional colleges have had a greater measure of autonomy in decision-making since 1993. In its 2000–03 economic program, the government is committed to reducing staffing costs but not staffing levels in schools, colleges, and universities. It launched a new vocational qualification in the 1990s, the Berufsmatura, to enable people in work to attend university or college to study courses connected with their profession. Further education at specialized colleges is also promoted in order to raise the skills base.

There are close links between public and private sector R&D, with over 400 scientific institutes involved in industrial research. The Austrian Academy of Sciences is an independent corporation, originally set up by the state, which runs 13 specialized research institutes. Specialties include psychology, geriatric research, demography, urban and regional research, energy physics, biophysics, molecular biology, limnology, and information processing. There are various other research institutes attached to different government ministries. Areas of private industry R&D include information technology (including semiconductors and software), telephone equipment, automotive components, biotechnology, chemicals, video and audio equipment, and paper. In the last decade private funding of R&D has risen from 35% to 65% of the total.

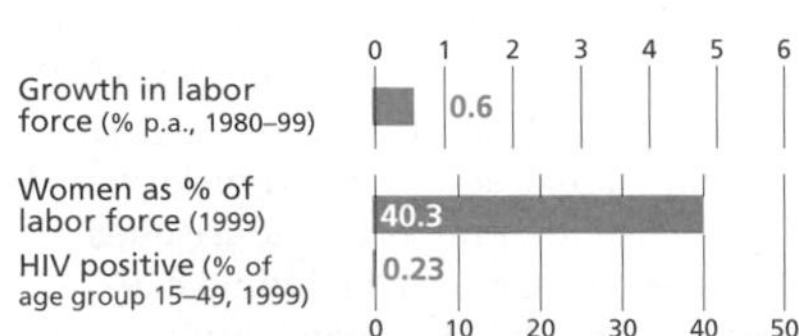

Wages and employment conditions are determined through negotiations between employers and trade unions. Although the government is not officially involved, the leaders of both social partners are often members of parliament, and introduce labor legislation. This system has led to industrial peace. Austria is in the process of adopting EU employment law, which covers safety at work, wages and working hours, industrial relations, employment incentives, and unemployment provision. Under the 2000–03 economic program, the government will adjust the rules for termination of contract payments and pensions pertaining to such contracts to ease the cost on companies. It will also raise the minimum age for early retirement.

Fiscal/Financial

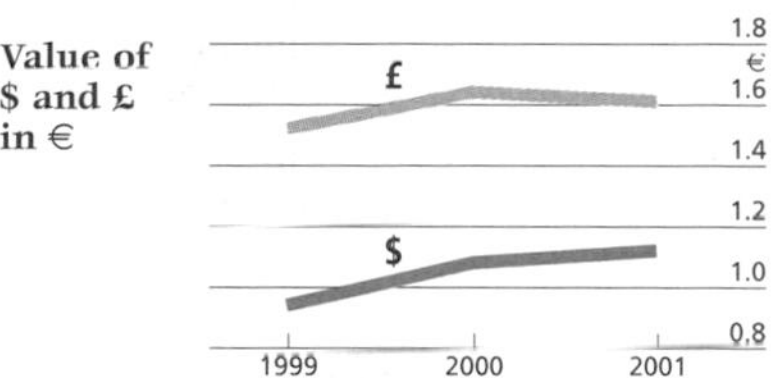

Major banks are Bank Austria (wholly owned by Germany's Hypo-Vereinsbank), Erste Bank, Bank für Arbeit und Wirtschaft (with significant German equity in late 2001), Österreichische Volksbanken (25% German equity in late 2001), and RZB. Leading insurance companies include Wiener Städtische Allgemeine Versicherung, Allianz Elementar, Wüstenrot Versicherungs-AG and Generali Versicherung. Österreichische Nationalbank is the central bank and supervisory authority. It is also part of the European System of Central Banks, which with the European Central Bank sets the policy for the Euro. The Banking Act of 1993 governs Austrian banking operations. Corporation tax is 34%, but will be cut to 31% in 2003. Maximum personal income tax is 50%, and the personal tax on income from dividends is 25%.

Austria has several categories of commercial bank, including joint stock, private banks, specialized credit institutions, savings banks, cooperative banks, provincial mortgage banks, and building societies. Consolidation, privatization, and German investment have provided the platform for expansion and improved profitability. However, the loss of state guarantees by privatized banks led to slippage in their international credit ratings. Business finance is well developed for trade and investment, but the use of risk capital is low. Banking benefits from some of the toughest secrecy laws in the world. Private banking for individuals and corporations is a strong area, but international moves to increase openness in banking and curb the activities of tax havens may force change in the future. The insurance sector covers all classes including reinsurance. The Vienna Stock Exchange was established in 1771. After 1946 it suffered from the level of state ownership of industry, but privatization boosted activity from the late 1980s. The Österreichische Termin- und Optionenbörse is a separate exchange for futures and options within the Vienna Stock Exchange. A joint venture with the Deutsche Börse, Newex AG, was launched in 2000 to develop trading in Central and Eastern European stocks from Vienna.

Business Opportunities

Growth in output (% p.a., 1990–99)

Services	2.0
Industry	1.9
Manufacturing	1.5
Agriculture	0.4

Tax reforms give tax relief on merger operations. Investment tax allowances include a reduction of 20% of tax on acquisitions or production costs of depreciable fixed assets. Actuarial reserves and provisions for insurance costs are tax-deductible. The Tax Reform Group, a government-appointed task force, made proposals at end-2000 for simplifying the tax system and increasing the attractiveness of Austria as a business location for inward investment. A database on state aids is to be set up to improve the efficiency and transparency of granting state aids.

Chemicals, cars, audio-visual equipment, semiconductors, telephone equipment, biotechnology, and paper are some of the main sectors which have attracted inward investment. Investors include German, Scandinavian, Dutch, and American multinational firms. Privatization has encouraged inward investment. The entire railway sector is due to undergo reorganization during the 2000–03 economic program. Privatization of property held by the Federal Real Estate Company will be speeded up during this period. The Austrian Business Agency is actively promoting the creation of distribution centers for Central and Eastern European countries which are applicants for EU membership.

For More Information

Books:

Austria, Belgium, Cyprus, Denmark, Eire, Finland (Major Companies of Europe, vol. 1). 21st ed. London: Graham & Whiteside, 2001.

Brook-Shepherd, G. *The Austrians: A Thousand-Year Odyssey*. New York: Carroll & Graf, 1998.

Honan, Mark. *Austria*. 3rd ed. Oakland, CA: Lonely Planet, 2002.

Pick, Hella. *Guilty Victim: Austria from the Holocaust to Haider*. New York: I. B. Tauris, 2000.

Web Sites:

Austrian Business Agency: **www.aba.gv.at**

Austrian Government entry point: **www.austria.gv.at**

Der Standard (Vienna, daily newspaper): **www.derstandard.at**

Federation of Austrian Industry: **www.industriellenvereinigung.at**

Kurier (Vienna, daily newspaper): **www.kurier.at**

Österreichische Nationalbank: **www.oenb.co.at**

Statistik Austria (Austrian Statistics Office): **www.statistik.at**

Verband Österreichischer Banken und Bankiers (Association of Austrian Banks and Bankers): **www.voebb.at**

Verband der Versicherungsunternehmen Österreichs (Association of Austrian Insurance Companies): **www.vvo.at**

Wiener Börse (Vienna Stock Exchange): **www.wbag.at**

Bahamas

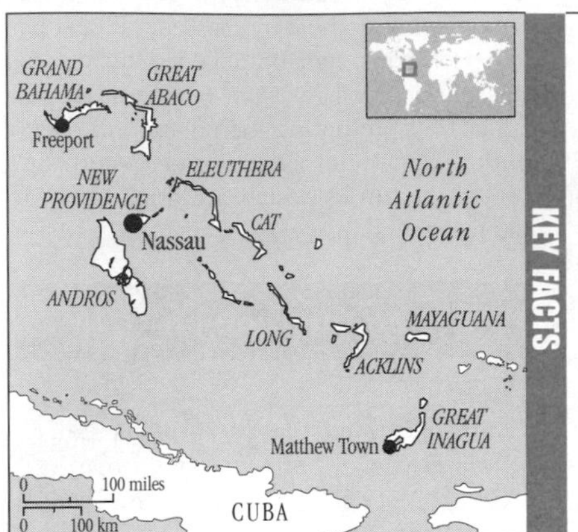

KEY FACTS

GNI pc: **$20,100 (approx.)**
Head of government: **prime minister**
Currency unit: **Bahamas dollar (B$)**
Capital: **Nassau**
Population: **301,000, growing at 1.8% p.a.**
Land area: **3,861 square miles**
Population density: **78 per square mile**
Life expectancy: **74 years**
Infant mortality: **18 per 1,000 live births**
Language: **English**
Best buy: **tableware, jewelry, batik prints**

Economy

The dominant economic sectors are tourism and financial services, which between them account for more than half of GDP, the majority of foreign exchange earnings, and about 40% of employment. Another significant sector is maritime services: the Bahamas is the world's third largest shipping registry, and there is a major freight container transshipment center and shipyard at Freeport, Grand Bahama. Manufacturing and agriculture are both of minor significance.

The country runs a very large annual trade deficit, amounting in 2000 to $1.35 billion, partly offset by revenue from tourism and financial services; investment from overseas was sufficient between 1997 and 1999 to produce an overall payments surplus, followed by a deficit in 2000.

The Free National Movement government, in office since 1992, has sought to reform the extensive state sector, which had become a byword for waste and corruption, contributing to large fiscal deficits. The reform program has included the sale of state-owned hotels and public utilities, together with stricter controls on government expenditure and improvements in revenue collection.

Geography/Resources

The 700 islands and 2,000 cays which comprise the Bahamas cover a large area, about 500 miles long, stretching southeast off the Florida coast, parallel with the north coast of Cuba. Fewer than 20 islands are inhabited; the bulk of the population lives in New Providence and Grand Bahama, which account for approximately 68% and 16% of the total respectively. New Providence is the seat of government and main business center. An estimated 80–85% of the population are of African descent, and the remainder of European or mixed background.

The islands are composed mainly of limestone, with no rivers and few reservoirs of fresh water, except on Andros, which supplies water to Nassau. These natural factors explain the external orientation of the Bahamian economy, aided by the country's proximity to the United States: Grand Bahama is only 62 miles from the Florida coast.

The adult literacy rate is estimated at 98%. Higher education is provided by the College of the Bahamas, and there are specialized colleges offering vocational training in law, tourism, and technical subjects.

Communications/Energy

External air services operate to and from Nassau and Grand Bahama, while some other islands are served by flights to and from Florida and some other destinations. The country has about 11,180 miles of paved roads.

Telecommunications are provided by the Bahamas Telecommunications Corporation, which had 80,000 lines in service in 2000; the corporation was due for privatization during 2002. The Bahamas Electricity Corporation, listed for privatization by 2003, had generating capacity of 488 MW in 1998, using imported oil.

Fiscal/Financial

The Bahamas runs a substantial international banking system, which in 1998 managed assets of B$270 billion: Nassau is the world's third largest Euro-lending center after London and Zurich. In 1999 there were 415 licensed banks and trust companies, and more than 100,000 international business companies. A securities exchange opened in May 2000.

Following the country's listing by international organizations in June 2000 as offering "harmful tax competition" and being "uncooperative" in respect of money laundering, the government introduced legislation to tighten its banking regulations and increase the powers of the regulatory authorities. The country was removed from the Financial Action Task Force list in 2001.

The government's finances show a persistent annual deficit, covered by borrowing, but in the second half of the 1990s there was stricter expenditure control, which led to a reduction in the deficit and in the external debt.

Business Opportunities

Investment incentives include the absence of corporation tax, personal income tax, capital gains tax, or estate duty; there are no restrictions on repatriation of capital, interest or dividends. Companies with less than 60% Bahamian capital pay an annual license fee of $1,000, while banks pay up to $100,000. Offshore banks are exempt from exchange control.

New hotel developers get long-term tax and duty exemptions; similar concessions apply to investors in industry and agriculture. Special incentives apply to investments in the Freeport free zone, including exemption from customs and excise duties and a wide range of taxes until 2054.

For More Information

Books:

Annual Report and Quarterly Statistical Digest. Central Bank of the Bahamas.
Bahamas Handbook 2002. Philadelphia, PA: Taylor & Francis, 2001.
Economist Intelligence Unit. *Country Profile and Quarterly Reports*. London.

Web Sites:

Bahamas Investment Authority: **www.interknowledge.com/bahamas/investment**
Economist Intelligence Unit: **www.eiu.com**

BAHRAIN

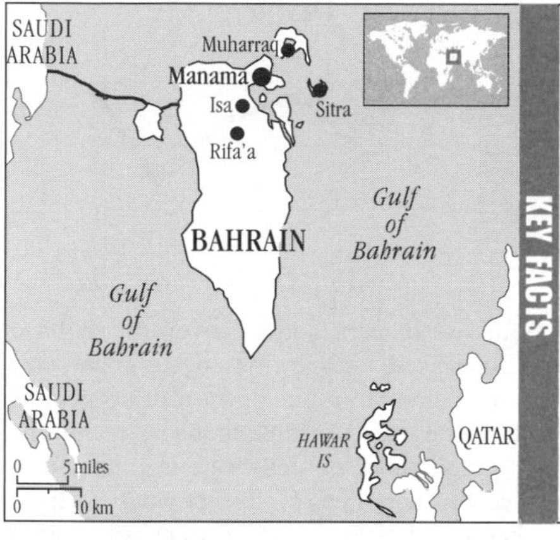

KEY FACTS

GNI pc: **$7,640 (approx.)**
Head of government: **prime minister**
Currency: **Bahraini dinar (BD)**
Capital: **Manama**
Population: **606,000, growing at 2.4% p.a.**
Land area: **270 square miles**
Population density: **2,244 per square mile**
Life expectancy: **73 years**
Infant mortality: **13 per 1,000 live births**
Language: **Arabic (official), English, Farsi, Urdu**
Best buy: **textiles, pottery, electronic goods, pearls**

ECONOMY

Services accounted for 59.8% of GDP in 2000, petroleum and natural gas 27.9%, and manufacturing 11.4%. Finance was the leading services sector (21.4% of GDP). Tourism is fast-growing with 3.3 million visitors in 1999. The main manufacturing industries are oil refining, petrochemicals, aluminum and aluminum products, iron and steel, shipbuilding and repair, and electronics assembly. Petroleum accounted for 70% of total export value in 2000. Metals (especially aluminum) and metal products accounted for 14.5%, and textiles for 5.9%.

The government has invested in infrastructure and industry (the main companies are majority state-owned). Previously it protected domestic industry with high tariffs. Now it is moving toward free trade within the Gulf Cooperation Council region is also a member of the World Trade Organization. The Bahraini dinar has been pegged to the U.S. dollar at a fixed rate since 1980. The government has been successful in attracting foreign investment and has identified tourism and IT, along with finance, as industries that will increase the number of jobs for Bahraini nationals in order to ease political unrest at the increasing numbers of expatriates in the workforce. With dwindling oil and gas reserves, the country is set to become a net gas importer in the medium term. Oil and gas represented 73% of government revenues in 2000. Government financial borrowing is almost exclusively domestic. However, Saudi Arabia provides aid (the income from the Abu Sa'fa oilfield), and Saudi Arabia, United Arab Emirates and Kuwait provide project grants. GDP recovered from a decline of 0.5% in 1998 to growth of 4.3% in 1999 and 5.3% in 2000. Inflation was –0.7% in 2000.

GEOGRAPHY/RESOURCES

An archipelago of 36 islands, Bahrain is in the Arabian Gulf. Bahrain Island, the largest, is linked to the Saudi Arabian mainland, the second-largest island Muharraq, and to the industrial island of Sitra via causeways. A territorial dispute over the Hawar Islands was settled in favor of Bahrain in 2001.

Dates are the main agricultural crop, and fishing is an important traditional industry, with a wide range of fish and crustaceans caught. Pearls are a high-value resource. Proven petroleum reserves were 148 million barrels at January 2001, with natural gas reserves of 3.9 trillion cubic feet. Exploration continues on- and offshore.

COMMUNICATIONS/ENERGY

The road network is 1,966 miles, over three-quarters of which is paved. There are no railways. The pipeline network consists of 35 miles for crude oil, 10 miles for refined oil products, and 20 miles for natural gas. The construction of a new gas pipeline from Qatar to Bahrain is under consideration. The main sea ports are Manama, Mina Salman, and Sitra. Bahrain International Airport is the main airport.

Bahrain Telecommunications Company (Batelco) holds the monopoly for local, long-distance and Internet services. It is 37% owned by the government, 43% by shareholders on the Bahrain Stock Exchange, and 20% by British company Cable & Wireless. Switching is fully digital and integrated. At mid-2000, fixed phone line penetration was 24% of the population, with mobile phones at 25.3% and Internet connections at 5.6%.

In 2000, production of crude oil was 13.8 million barrels and natural gas was 412 billion cubic feet, all consumed locally. Imports of Saudi crude were 80.3 million barrels. Refined oil production by Bahrain Petroleum Company was 93.7 million barrels, mostly for export but also for domestic consumption. Upgrading of the refinery will be completed in 2004. Electricity is generated entirely from fossil fuels. Current expansion is focused on gas-fired stations.

FISCAL/FINANCIAL

Bahrain has been the main financial center of the Middle East for two decades. The consolidated balance sheet of the banking system at end-2000 was U.S.$106.4 billion, with 51 offshore banking units accounting for 87.4% of the total, 19 commercial banks for 9.4%, and 31 investment banks for 3.2%. Islamic banking is fast-growing. The Bahrain Securities Exchange, established in 1989, had a market capitalization of BD 2.5 billion at end-2000. The Bahrain Monetary Agency is the central bank. There is no personal, corporate, or withholding tax.

BUSINESS OPPORTUNITIES

There are many incentives to investment: lack of tax, excellent telecommunications and transport infrastructure, proximity to larger Middle East markets, exemption from import duties for re-exports, sophisticated financial services, a stable and convertible local currency, and sound regulatory environment. There are free trade zones at Mina Salman and Sitra. Although 100% foreign ownership is now allowed for many sectors, government approval procedures can be slow. Areas of inward investment include the aluminum smelter, ship repair, oil exploration, tourism, computer software systems, and telecommunications. Current opportunities exist in finance, insurance, tourism, IT, and infrastructure projects. The point of contact is the Bahrain Promotion and Marketing Board.

For More Information

Books:

Al Khalifa, H. bin I. *First Light: Modern Bahrain and its Heritage*. London: Kegan Paul International, 1995.

Greenway, Paul, and Gordon Robison. *Bahrain, Kuwait and Qatar*. Oakland, CA: Lonely Planet, 2000.

Web Site:

Government entry point:
www.bahrain.gov.bh

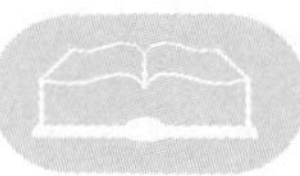

BANGLADESH

KEY FACTS

GNI: **$47,071 million; world's 50th**
GNI pc: **$370; world's 170th**
Head of government: **prime minister**
Currency: **taka (Tk)**
Capital: **Dhaka**
Population: **126,947,000, growing at 1.6% p.a.**
Land area: **50,270 square miles**
Population density: **2,525 per square mile**
Life expectancy: **59 years**
Infant mortality: **58 per 1,000 live births**
Language: **Bengali**
Best buy: **rural handloomed cloth**

ECONOMIC STRUCTURE

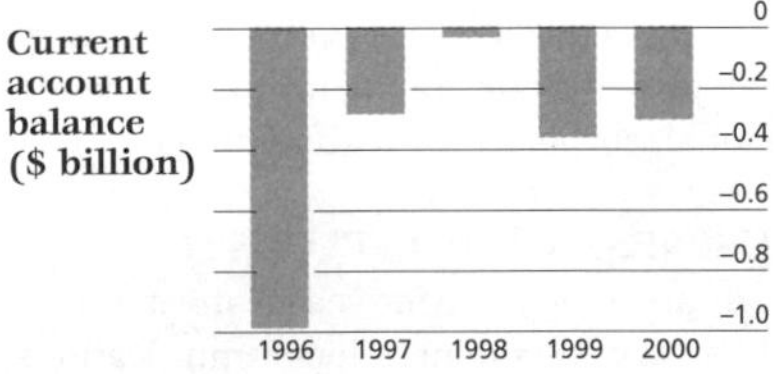

When India was freed from colonial rule and partitioned in 1947, predominantly Muslim east Bengal became East Pakistan but, from the start, had an uneasy relationship with richer West Pakistan. The secessionist Awami League (AL) led by Sheik Mujibur Rahman grew consistently, and in 1970 won national assembly elections. In 1971 the AL seized power and full-scale civil war broke out; this ended with intervention by the Indian army and Rahman's declaration of Bangladeshi statehood. Rahman was assassinated in a military coup in 1975. For the next two decades politics was dominated by army interventions and rivalry between the AL and the Bangladesh National Party (BNP). The 1996 election returned the AL to power. The party is credited with easing relations with India by signing a treaty on sharing the Ganges waters, and making peace with tribal insurgents in Chittagong. Progress was also made in rebuilding the economy after disastrous flooding in 1998. At the October 2001 elections the AL lost power to a four-party alliance headed by the BNP.

Agriculture is the primary occupation of 70% of the Bangladeshi population, and accounted for 35% of GDP in 2000, down from 40% in the 1980s. The main products are rice for domestic consumption, tea for export, and jute for both industrial processing and export (Bangladesh is the world's largest jute exporter). Gas is expected to become a major export after 2002.

Manufacturing industry accounted for 12% of GDP in 2000: traditional activities, including jute and tea processing, food processing and chemicals, have been supplemented since the 1980s by the proliferation of export-oriented garment manufacture, which by 2000 employed 1.4 million workers, 90% of them female.

Poor prices for its principal exports, and dependence on imports for essential goods, mean that Bangladesh suffers from a chronic balance of trade deficit. Export growth is concentrated in ready-made garments and knitwear, which accounted for 76% of total exports in 2000, while traditional exports—jute, jute manufactures, tea, and hides, all highly susceptible to world price fluctuations—have declined. Principal export destinations are the United States (33% in 2000), Germany (11%), the United Kingdom (7%), and France (5%). Leading imports in 2000 were textiles and yarn (mainly for the garment industry), machinery and transport equipment, and cereal and dairy products; the principal sources were India (10% in 2000), Japan (9%), Singapore (8%), and China (7%).

In 1972, the AL government carried out wholesale nationalization. A denationalization drive began in the mid-1980s but was dropped, mainly due to lack of investor interest. The World Bank has estimated that state enterprises comprised 25% of fixed capital formation but only 6% of GDP; these enterprises' chronic losses, and investors' hesitation—rather than political opposition—obstructed privatization in the late 1990s.

ECONOMIC POLICY

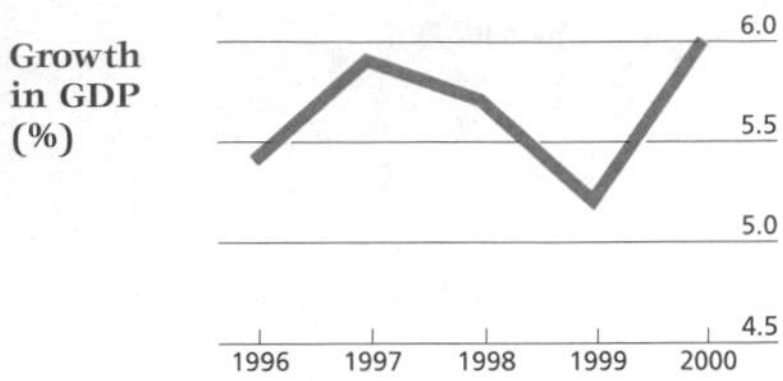

Successive Bangladeshi governments have been faced with trying to stimulate economic growth in one of the world's poorest countries: the World Bank, using a counting method based on daily calorie intake, estimated that 45% of the population lived below subsistence level in 1999. Bangladesh received $36.6 billion in foreign aid (46% in grants and 54% in loans) between 1971 and 1997, but successive governments have tried to reduce dependence on it, and by 2000 it had fallen to 2% of GDP. Through the 1990s there was also political consensus on the need to raise domestic food grain production to ensure self-sufficiency; to cut back the state's role in the economy; and to encourage private-sector development and foreign investment.

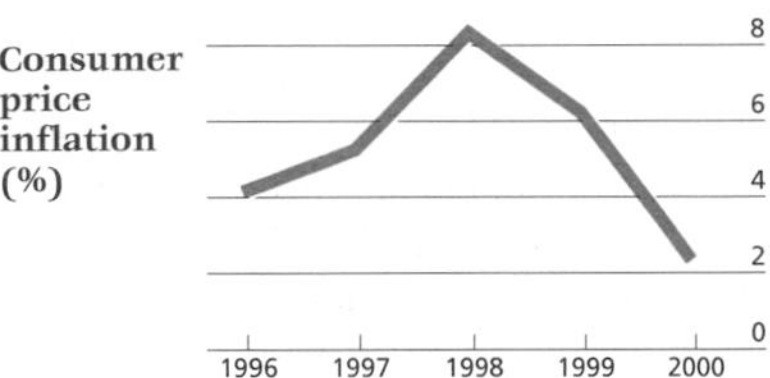

Liberalization in the early 1990s gave an impetus to GDP growth, which averaged 4.8% in 1991–2000 and reached 6% (estimated) in 2001. The 1998 floods had a disastrous impact on agriculture, but it rebounded sharply to lead GDP growth in 1999–2000, aided by good weather conditions and structural changes (use of hybrid seeds, substitution of cash crops for rice cultivation, and improved transport). Manufacturing contributed less to the post-flood recovery, but was restrained by the limited availability of a steady electricity supply and continuous financing. Consumer price inflation has been restrained, and ran at 2.3% in 2000 and 2.8% (estimated) in 2001.

GEOGRAPHY/RESOURCES

Bangladesh has a coast fronting the Bay of Bengal to the south. It borders India to the northeast, north and west, and Burma to the southeast. Its low-lying landscape is domin-

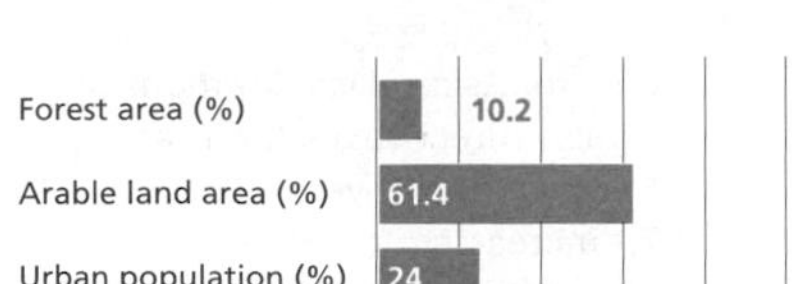

ated by the confluence of three river systems—the Ganges, Brahmaputra (Jamuna), and Meghna—that empty into the Bay of Bengal. Climate has a dramatic effect on the economy, indeed on life and death: the monsoon (June to October) brings heavy rain on which agriculture depends, but also often causes floods that destroy crops, livestock, and human life, and soil erosion that changes the course of the rivers' many tributaries. The coastline—which boasts the 75-mile Cox's Bazar beach, the world's longest—is prone to cyclones and other high-intensity storms, the last serious one of which, in 1970, killed hundreds of thousands of people.

More than two-thirds of Bangladesh's land is arable and one-fifth is irrigated; one-sixth of the land area is covered by forest. Agriculture is dominated by crop farming. State-supported irrigation projects undertaken in the 1990s sought to reduce dependence on the vagaries of the monsoon, while economic planning has encouraged double and triple cropping, intercropping, and increased use of fertilizers to heighten yields. Overall, through the 1990s, food security was enhanced, with food grain supplies growing at a much faster rate (17%) than population (8%), while crop farming grew less rapidly than the small agricultural subsectors (fisheries, livestock, and forestry).

Bangladesh's main energy resource is gas: 20 fields have been discovered, with total reserves of 23 trillion cubic feet. International oil companies, including Unocal, Halliburton, Shell, and Cairn Energy, have begun to develop these fields under production-sharing contracts (PSCs). In late 2001 the producers were expecting to open up a significant new market as the result of a decision to permit gas exports to India; discussions on the construction of a pipeline were under way. Bangladesh's mineral resources are negligible: the bituminous coal deposits discovered in 1995 at Dighipara in Dinajpur, now being developed by the state mining company with Chinese assistance, are the most significant.

It is the most densely-populated country in the world excluding city states such as Singapore. The urban population growth rate is twice that of the countryside, and a quarter of the total now live in towns. However, even rural areas are so thickly settled that it is often difficult to distinguish patterns of individual villages. Ethnically and linguistically, Bangladesh's population is relatively homogenous; more than 98 per cent are ethnically Bengali, and Bengali is their mother tongue. In terms of religion it is mixed: 85% follow Islam (which was made the state religion in 1988), about 10% are Hindus, and among tribal groups in the Chittagong area, most are Buddhists.

COMMUNICATIONS/ENERGY

PCs	0.1
Telephone lines	0.3
Mobiles	0.2
Internet users	0.03
(per 100 people, 2000)	0 20 40 60 80 100

Poor infrastructure is considered a primary obstacle to development in Bangladesh. Advances are being made, however, such as the 1998 opening of the $1 billion multipurpose bridge over the Brahmaputra river, which previously divided the country in two.

Passenger and freight transport is dominated by roads and waterways. The 22,370-mile road network is in good condition; 15% of roads are national highways, 8% regional highways, and half of the rest are unpaved. There is a substantial private trucking industry. There are 5,160 miles of waterways (only 2,360 miles in the dry season); in some outlying areas water is the primary means of transport. The railways, which carried 2.4 billion passenger-miles in 1999–2000, have been in decline throughout the 1990s as a result of failure to control costs or collect fares. External trade is conducted mainly through two major sea ports, at Chittagong and Mongla, and five smaller inland ports. Container handling at Chittagong has risen rapidly, doubling between 1994 and 1999. Bangladesh has two international airports and 12 others (domestic and military). Air transport is dominated by the national airline, Bangladesh Biman, which carried 600,000 passengers and 16,415 tons of cargo in 1997–98, and is suffering from the sector being opened up to competition in 1996.

Bangladesh has one of the lowest telephone densities in the world: five lines per 1,000 inhabitants in 2001. Of these, 35% are analog, and the connection rate is poor. Private investment has been permitted in the sector since 1992, and in mid-2001 a U.S. company was licensed to build, own, and operate a 300,000-line digital network in Dhaka. Around 60% of mobile subscribers can connect only to other mobiles and not to fixed lines. Some Internet service providers were established in Dhaka in 1999–2001.

Bangladesh's inadequate power supply is a major brake on economic growth and a deterrent to foreign investors. Power cuts mean that the Water and Sewage Authority is unable to operate pumps properly, factories are frequently forced to halt production, and domestic users face constant power cuts. The national generator, the Power Development Board, has sizable debts to the oil and gas company Petrobangla, which in turn is indebted to international gas producers operating in Bangladesh. Despite 940 MW of new generating capacity coming on stream in 1997–2000, the power crisis is likely to persist. The World Bank is funding a major power restructuring program in the decade beginning 2000.

EDUCATION/EMPLOYMENT

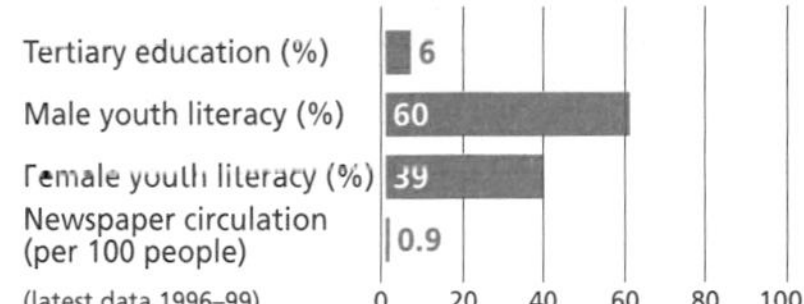

Bangladesh has a total labor force of 60 million, of which 40 million are in agriculture; just 4.8 million workers are in the formal sector, including 1.4 million in state-owned enterprises. According to a U.S. trade department survey in 2001, low registered unemployment (2.5% in 1999) obscures "huge and growing" underemployment, and Bangladesh's comparative advantage in supplying cheap labor for manufacturing was offset by low skills and poor management. The jute, textile, and transportation sectors have strong trade unions which have pushed up wages by militant action. Production can be affected by political general strikes ("hartals") called by opposition parties, which resulted in 22 days lost in 2000.

Between 1980 and 2000 more than 1.5 million Bangladeshis emigrated to work, mainly to the Middle East. Remittances from foreign workers are a key contributor to the Bangladesh economy: they rose rapidly from the mid-1990s, and between 1999 and 2001 rose by about one-fifth to $2 billion officially, plus an estimated $1 billion unofficially, i.e. 30% of export earnings.

Bangladesh is far from attaining universal literacy. Adult literacy rose from 24% in 1991 to 64% in 2000, with urban–rural and male–female disparities remaining. During the 1990s improvements made to education included the introduction of five years of free schooling for boys and eight years for girls, and increased budgetary allocations.

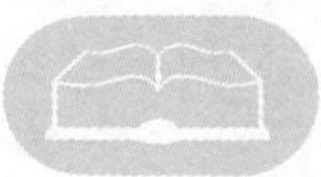

The number of primary school pupils rose from 12 million in 1990 to 17.7 million in 2000, although official statistics throw doubt on the quality of education, recording that only 10% of pupils leave with useful skills. Widespread child labor is an obstruction to educational improvement.

There are more than 600 colleges, mostly affiliated to the universities of Dhaka, Rajshahi, and Chittagong, and several medical educational institutes. Universities received generous government subsidies, but the quality of education is poor when compared with other south Asian countries.

Fiscal/Financial

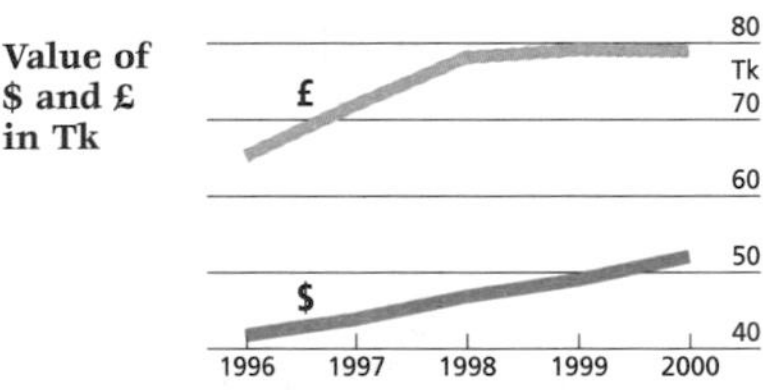

Bangladesh's financial services sector is small and undeveloped, contributing about 2% to GDP in 2000. It is dominated by the four nationalized commercial banks (the Agrani, Janata, Rupali, and Sonali banks), which in 2000 accounted for about 60% of total deposits and 50% of total advances. Despite the Financial Sector Reform Program of 1990–96, chronic lack of credit discipline remains, together with inefficiency and overstaffing, and lending by these banks is often politically directed. The private banking sector has grown slowly since the 1980s, and the private banks, including some joint ventures with foreign banks, increased their proportion of deposits from 20% in 1986 to 28% in 1996, and of advances from 17% to 26% in the same period. In 1997 their rate of defaulted loans was estimated at 48%. By contrast with most other banks, the Grameen Bank founded by Professor Mohammed Yunus has earned a worldwide reputation for its micro-credit program and has kept its default rate down to 2%.

Bangladesh's stock markets, the Dhaka and Chittagong stock exchanges, are among the world's smallest. Their total market capitalization in June 2001 was $1.1 billion and $1 billion respectively. The insurance sector is also embryonic, dominated by two nationalized insurers, the Jiban Bima Corporation (life insurance) and Sadharan Bima Corporation (general insurance).

In the late 1990s import controls were reduced, corporate taxation simplified, and sectors previously reserved for the state opened to private business. A Value Added Tax was introduced in 1992, revenue from which has helped bring domestic contributions to the Annual Development Plan, the state's fund for development projects, to 46% in 1998–99.

Business Opportunities

Growth in output (% p.a., 1990–99)

Services	4.4
Industry	7.4
Manufacturing	7.5
Agriculture	2.5

The Bangladeshi government describes its incentives for foreign investors as the most liberal in Asia. They include 100% ownership in most sectors; tax holidays; reduced import duties on capital machinery and spares; duty-free imports for 100% exporters; and tax exemptions on interest on foreign loans and capital gains by portfolio investors. Trade has been liberalized and duties reduced from an average of 17% to less than 14% in the five years to 2001, although import duties remain high, constituting the largest single source of government revenues. Free repatriation of profits is allowed, and the taka is almost fully convertible on the current account. No prior approval is required for foreign direct investment except registration with the Board of Investment. Deterrents to investment include poor infrastructure, corruption, and labor militancy, but the biggest is Bangladesh's reputation as an undeveloped country subject to frequent and devastating natural disasters. This is partly a misconception, since its annual floods are not just destructive: they also make it one of the world's most fertile countries, which, before the political instability of the 1950s, was one of the wealthiest in Asia.

Export Processing Zones with extra tax, foreign exchange, customs, and labor incentives have been extremely successful: the first two zones, in Chittagong and Dhaka, respectively attracted total investments of $305 million and $165 million in mid-2001, and had workforces of 68,000 and 41,000. South Korea is the largest investor in the zones, where industries range from garments and textiles to electronics, sporting goods, and services. Four further zones were under construction in 2001.

According to Asian Development Bank figures, foreign direct investment averaged a paltry $7–8 million a year between 1990 and 1997, increasing to $249 million in 1998, $198 million in 1999, and $280 million in 2000. In 2001 it was expected to grow rapidly in the energy sector. The United States is the largest foreign investor in Bangladesh, followed by Malaysia, Japan, and the United Kingdom In 2001 the U.S. trade department identified the best prospective sectors for investment as gas exploration and production, power generation and related equipment, telecommunications, computers, aircraft parts and ground support equipment, textile machinery and equipment, and architecture/construction/engineering services. The government remains prepared to consider privatization sales, particularly in the energy sector, when serious prospects of investor interest become evident.

For More Information

Books:

Bornstein, David. *The Price of a Dream: The Story of the Grameen Bank*. Chicago, IL: University of Chicago Press, 1997.
Kabeer, Naila. *Power to Choose: Bangladeshi Women and Labor Market Decisions in London and Dhaka*. New York: Verso, 2000.
Kabir, Muhammad Ghulam. *Changing Face of Nationalism: The Case of Bangladesh*. Denver, CO: International Academic Publishers, 2001.
Sisson, Richard, and Leo E. Rose. *War and Secession: Pakistan, India, and the Creation of Bangladesh*. Berkeley, CA: University of California Press, 1991.

Web Sites:

Bangladesh government site: **www.bangladeshgov.org/pmo**
Bangladesh Net information portal: **www.bangladesh.net**
Bangladeshonline Internet portal: **www.bangladeshonline.com**
Business Bangladesh information site: **www.users.globalnet.co.uk/~imran**
Daily Star (online newspaper in English): **www.dailystarnews.com**
Dhaka-BD portal: **www.dhaka-bd.com**
Dhaka stock exchange: **www.dsebd.org**
Securities and Exchange Commission of Bangladesh: **www.secbd.org**

BARBADOS

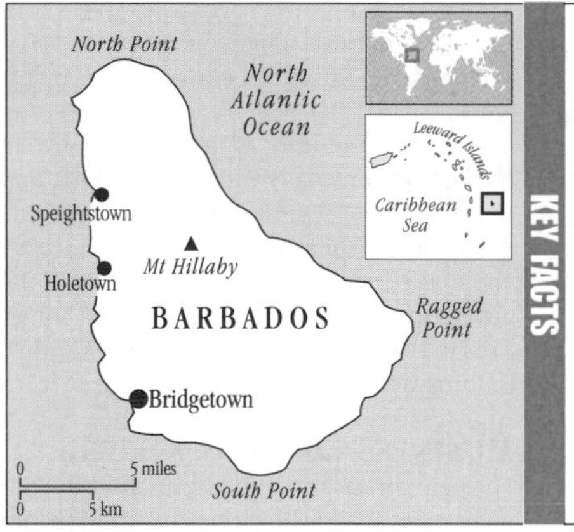

KEY FACTS

GNI: **$2,294 million**
GNI pc: **$8,600; world's 53rd**
Head of government: **prime minister**
Currency unit: **Barbados dollar (Bds$)**
Capital: **Bridgetown**
Population: **269,000, growing at 0.5% p.a.**
Land area: **154 square miles**
Population density: **1,747 per square mile**
Life expectancy: **77 years**
Infant mortality: **14 per 1,000 live births**
Language: **English**
Best buy: **clothes, arts and crafts, rum**

ECONOMY

The leading sectors are the long-established tourist business and two newer sectors, financial services and manufacturing. The formerly important sugar industry produced export earnings of only B$52.2 million in 2000, compared with B$100.6 million from manufacturing, a sector which during the 1990s attracted investment from domestic and overseas companies producing garments, electronic goods, chemicals, furniture, and foodstuffs. The main foreign exchange earner is tourism, which in 1999 reported income of $700 million, or 54% of all earnings from goods and services. Trade and business services accounted for 37.9% of GDP in 2000, against 15.4% for tourism, 9.7% for manufacturing and 6.2% for agriculture.

Government policy is to develop the manufacturing, technology, and communications sectors, while continuing to support tourism; a particular effort is being made to develop technological skills in the working population. Following an economic downturn in the early 1990s, which led to an IMF-backed austerity program, the economy showed average growth of 3.5% between 1994 and 2000, accompanied by an increase of 140% in the external reserves, which reached $475 million at the end of 2000. The inflation rate averaged 1.1% over the same period.

In 2000, the United States supplied 41% of imports and received 15.3% of exports from Barbados; 13.2% of exports went to the United Kingdom, and 43.2% to Caribbean Community countries.

GEOGRAPHY/RESOURCES

Lying to the east of the main Caribbean island chain, Barbados is densely populated along its western and southern coasts. The capital and port city of Bridgetown lies at the southwestern corner of the island. The Atlantic coast is less built up, since it is mainly unsafe for bathing, in contrast to the tourist beaches of the south and west.

The traditional sugar-cane farming areas are increasingly being converted to housing and other use, including golf courses. Barbados is a minor oil producer (see following section).

The population is well educated, with an adult literacy rate of 99%. Education to university level is free, and the government also provides support for independent schools. The University of the West Indies has a campus at Cave Hill, and there are three other tertiary education colleges.

COMMUNICATIONS/ENERGY

Barbados is the airline hub of the Eastern Caribbean, with services from Europe and North America connecting into regional networks. The main road artery connects the airport with Bridgetown and the west coast; inland roads are often narrow and winding. There is a comprehensive bus service based on Bridgetown.

Telecommunications are provided by Cable & Wireless, but the sector is to be progressively opened to competition by July 2003.

The Barbados National Oil Corporation produced 1,800 barrels of oil per day in the year ending on 31 March 2001, about a third of national requirements. In 1999, 1,660 million cubic feet of gas were produced. Barbados Light & Power is the sole electricity utility.

FISCAL/FINANCIAL

The offshore financial sector benefits from concessions, including a maximum tax rate of 2.5% on profits of offshore companies. Foreign sales corporations are exempt from taxes and exchange controls, while international business companies pay 2.5% profits tax, with exemption from capital gains and other taxes. Exempt insurance companies and those engaged in shipping, shipbuilding, and maintenance also enjoy concessions.

The Central Bank is responsible for banking regulation; there is an authority to prevent money laundering. The Securities Exchange, established in 1987, had 23 companies listed at the end of 1999, with capitalization of B$6.1 billion.

BUSINESS OPPORTUNITIES

Tax exemption is offered for new industrial projects, while companies exporting their production outside the Caribbean get profit tax relief. There are special incentives for hotel developers. Investors are allowed full repatriation of profits, dividends, and capital, and can obtain foreign currency without restriction in order to pay invoices and other expenses. Overseas investors may form joint ventures with Barbadian partners or buy shares in domestic companies. The Barbados Industrial Development Corporation offers advice and assistance to prospective investors. In 1999, long-term private capital inflow was a reported B$150 million; at the end of 2000, there were 456 international business companies registered, an increase of 130 during the year.

For More Information

Books:

Barbados Business and Investment Opportunities Yearbook. 3rd ed. Washington, D.C.: International Business Publications, 2001 (annual).

Central Bank of Barbados Annual Report. *Annual Statistical Digest, Economic Review*.

Economist Intelligence Unit. *Country Profiles and Quarterly Reports*. London.

Web Sites:

Barbados Investment and Development Corporation: **www.bidc.com**

Government of Barbados: **www.primeminister.gov.bb**

BELARUS

KEY FACTS

GNI: **$26,299 million; world's 61st**
GNI pc: **$2,620; world's 94th**
Head of government: **president**
Currency: **Belarusian ruble (BRb)**
Capital: **Minsk**
Population: **10,274,000, growing at 0% p.a.**
Land area: **80,116 square miles**
Population density: **128 per square mile**
Life expectancy: **68 years**
Infant mortality: **23 per 1,000 live births**
Language: **Belarusian, Russian**
Best buy: **samovars, amber, lacquer boxes**

ECONOMY

Until World War II, Belarus was a predominantly rural economy; after the war it developed a strong industrial base. After the collapse of Soviet Russia, Belarus was cut off from major export markets, and industrial output fell by 38% between 1991 and 1994. The slump was reversed from the mid-1990s, and since 1996 there have been year-on-year increases both in GDP (growth averaged 6% in 1996–2000) and in industrial output, mainly for export to Russia and other CIS countries. The principal industries are automotive, machine-building, electronics, defense, chemicals, and civil engineering.

Belarus has carried out fewer pro-market reforms than any other European state of the former USSR. Progress in privatization has slowed since the mid-1990s, and the private sector remains marginal. Price controls on a large range of goods remain in place, although their scope was reduced in April 2001. Despite them, inflation spiraled to 250% in 1999, but fell to 107% in 2000 and 40% (estimated) in 2001. In 1999–2000 measures were taken to liberalize access to foreign exchange, and in 2001 a crawling peg to the Russian ruble was introduced. Seeking closer union with Russia is a central plank of economic policy, and in 1999 a new union treaty was signed between the two countries, providing for currency union within five years.

GEOGRAPHY/RESOURCES

Landlocked Belarus has more than 30 different mineral resources, including potassium, peat, and oil; it is Europe's second-largest potassium salt producer. There are also large reserves of granite, coal, iron and nonferrous ores, rock salts, and phosphates.

The Chernobyl reactor disaster of 1985 had a serious impact on southern Belarus, particularly the towns of Homyel and Mogilev.

COMMUNICATIONS/ENERGY

Belarus has 3,180 miles of road. The number of passenger cars rose from 5.7 per 100 inhabitants in 1990 to 13.1 in 1999.

Belarus had 26.1 telephone lines per 100 inhabitants in 1999. Its state-owned telephone network is undergoing modernization, including the installation of automatic exchanges, but facilities such as rapid data transmission are very limited. In 1999 it got its first GSM-based cellular system.

Belarus has few indigenous energy resources. It imports electricity from Russia and Lithuania, and imports all its coal and most of its oil and gas, mostly from Russia. Belarus has substantial energy debts to Russia, despite low prices; its debt for gas was estimated at $250 million in May 2000. In 1999 Belarus postponed for at least ten years plans to build its own nuclear power station.

FISCAL/FINANCIAL

There are 27 banks, 6 of which control 86% of the sector's assets. Four of these largest banks are state-owned. Lending to the private sector, and bond operations, are limited by the slow pace of privatization and of private-sector growth; credit to the private sector at March 2000 amounted to just 9% of GDP.

The only significant tradeable securities are government treasury bills and short-term commercial paper issued by the central bank. The stock exchange trades once a week.

The major sources of tax revenue are internal taxes on goods and services, VAT, and excise duties. Direct taxes on revenue, profit, and capital growth amount to only about 15% of total revenue. In 1998–99 the government introduced a series of measures to simplify the tax system and improve enforcement mechanisms.

BUSINESS OPPORTUNITIES

Foreign direct investment in Belarus has been very low, averaging $215 million per year in 1996–2001. The most popular forms of investment are joint ventures and wholly foreign-owned businesses. These contribute about 2% of GDP; the major sources of FDI are Germany, the Netherlands, the United States, Poland, and Italy.

There are free economic zones designed to attract foreign investment at Brest, Minsk, and Homyel-Raton. A new investment code adopted in June 2001 provided for government support and guarantees for investors. There are no legal obstacles to ownership by foreigners in companies, although 50% of declared capital must be paid in the first year and the entire amount within two years. There are tax breaks on foreign investments comprising more than 30% of the business's capital and in priority industries.

For More Information

Books:

Garnett, Sherman, and Robert Legvold. *Belarus at the Crossroads.* Washington, D.C.: Carnegie Endowment, 2000.

Savchenko, Andrew. *Rationality, Nationalism and Post-Communist Market Transformations: A Comparative Analysis of Belarus, Poland, and the Baltic States.* Burlington, VT: Ashgate Publishing, 2000.

Web Sites:

ICL Guide to Belarus: **www.uni-wuerzburg.de/law/bo_indx.html**

The Virtual Guide to Belarus: **www.belarusguide.com**

BELGIUM

KEY FACTS

GNI: **$252,051 million; world's 19th**
GNI pc: **$24,650; world's 18th**
Head of government: **prime minister**
Currency: **Euro (€)**
Capital: **Brussels**
Population: **10,152,000, growing at 0.2% p.a.**
Land area: **11,783 square miles**
Population density: **862 per square mile**
Life expectancy: **77 years**
Infant mortality: **6 per 1,000 live births**
Language: **Dutch (Flemish), French, German**
Best buy: **diamonds, lace, crystal, chocolates, beer**

ECONOMIC STRUCTURE

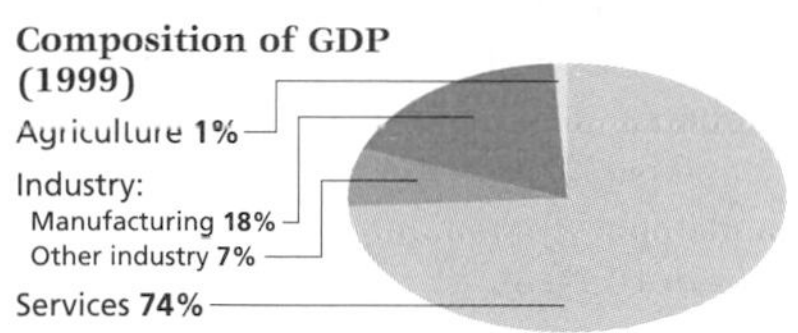

Trade has provided Belgium with its main source of wealth for centuries, firstly in cloth from Bruges in the tenth century, then from Ghent, and in the sixteenth century in a wide variety of European and Asian goods from Antwerp. Independence from foreign domination in 1830 established Brussels as the capital city. The rise of Wallonia's iron and steel industries later in the century allowed for the development of a wide range of industries, including engineering, chemicals, and glass, often based on Belgian patents. Colonial acquisition of the Congo made Antwerp one of the world's leading copper and diamond centers. The establishment of the European Commission and other EU institutions in Brussels in the 1950s brought multinational companies to Belgium and promoted the services sector. Linguistic division and rivalry between Flanders and Wallonia has existed since early history. In 1989 the present devolved political and administrative structure of three regions (Flanders, Wallonia, and Brussels), three linguistic communities (Flemish, Francophone, and German), and national institutions produced relative peace.

Services account for over two-thirds of GDP, followed by industry (about 22%), and agriculture, forestry, and fisheries (around 1%). Financial, real estate and business services are the leading services, followed by commerce, transport and communications, and public services and education. Industry is diversified, encompassing chemicals, pharmaceuticals, motor vehicles, aeronautics, office machinery, power and telecommunications equipment, electronics, armaments, textiles, food, primary metals, and metal products. The petrochemicals and fine chemicals industries have grown since the 1970s, based near the port of Antwerp. Belgium is a major smelter of copper, zinc, and aluminum. It trades 85% of the world's rough diamonds. The main merchandise exports in 2000 were electronic and electrical goods, followed by chemicals and pharmaceuticals, transport equipment, machinery, food and live animals, and metals. The main markets were Germany, France, Netherlands, Italy, the United Kingdom, and the United States Exports of goods and services accounted for 88% of GDP. Integrated industrial production between Belgium, Netherlands, Germany, and France accounted for 45% of Belgian foreign trade in 2000.

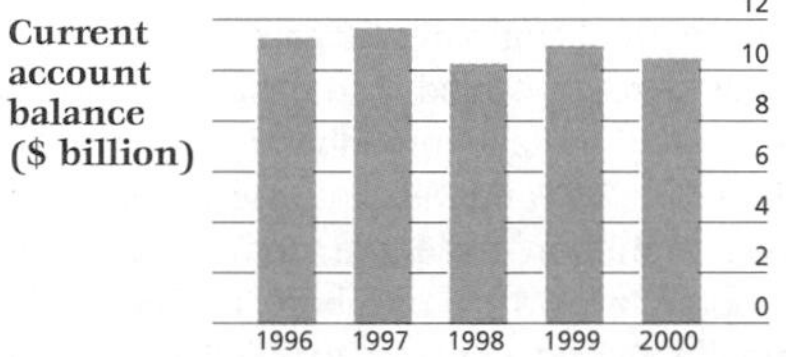

Although the electricity, gas, and telecommunications sectors were opened to competition in the late 1990s, and the state sold off part of its assets in the former monopolies, these companies still occupy a dominant position. The slowness in opening up these markets is partly attributable to the complexities of devolved government decision making. In late 2000 the government announced plans to privatize 150 companies in share deals worth around €17.4 billion. They include a further block of shares in telecoms company Belgacom (50.1% state-owned), electricity company Electrabel, Brussels Airport (65% state-owned), and in hotels, real estate, the lottery, and the post office.

ECONOMIC POLICY

Growth in GDP (%)

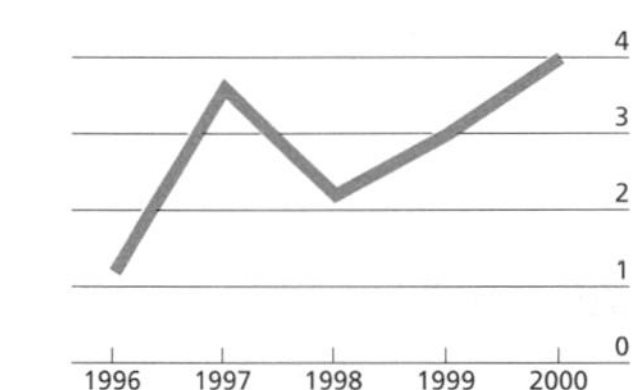

Budget austerity has been a key feature of government economic policy to reduce the public debt, which was 131.2% of GDP in 1995. This was cut to 110% in 2000, but remains one of the highest in the EU. The Stability Program for 2001–05 aims to cut the debt to 90% in 2005. Government surpluses will continue to be used mainly to pay off the debt. In addition, the government plans tax and welfare reform and to create a fund for population aging. The fund will be financed by privatizations and licenses for the UMTS mobile telecommunications network. Health spending will be increased after several years of restraint. The main thrust of tax reform in 2001–04 will be to reduce income tax for low-income groups to encourage greater labor market participation. In addition, the two top tax bands (55% and 52.5%) and the crisis surcharge on income tax will be phased out during this period. Public expenditure has been trimmed, but not sufficiently in the view of the OECD. Public administration costs are amongst the highest in the OECD, and this contributes to the need for relatively heavy taxation. The government has launched a sustainable economic development program in line with EU environmental directives.

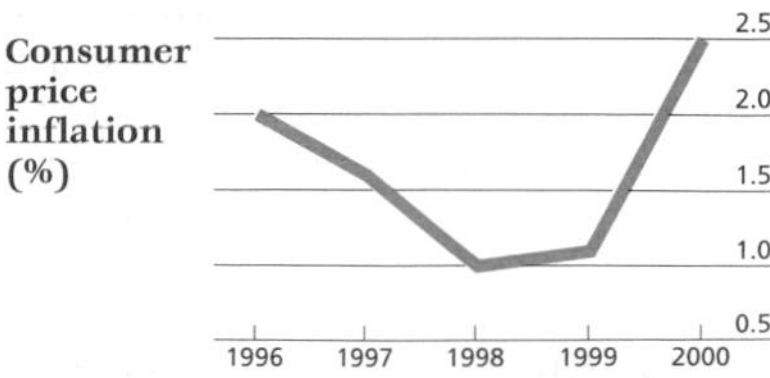

Annual GDP growth recovered from the recession years of the early 1990s to 2.7% in 1996–2000. It was expected to be 1.8% in

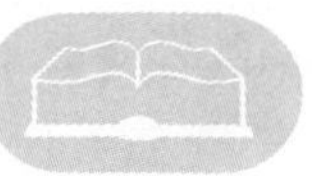

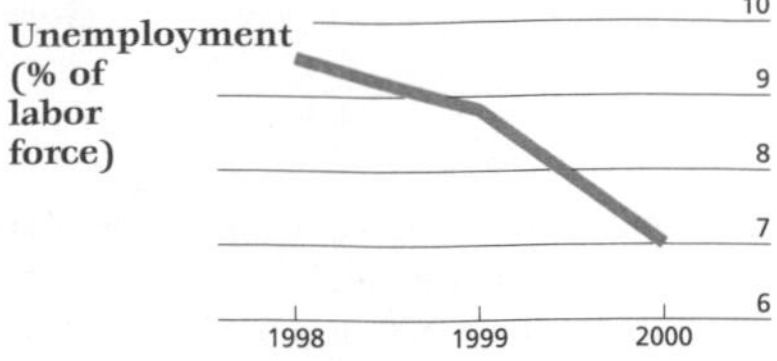

2002. Annual inflation was kept low at 1.6% in 1996–2000 by wage restraint. Inflation rose slightly in 2000 on account of oil price hikes, but was expected to fall in 2001. Unemployment fell from 10% in 1994 to 7.1% in 2000, with an expected decline to 6.1% in 2002. However, structural unemployment persists among older workers and in the disadvantaged areas of the south and east.

Geography/Resources

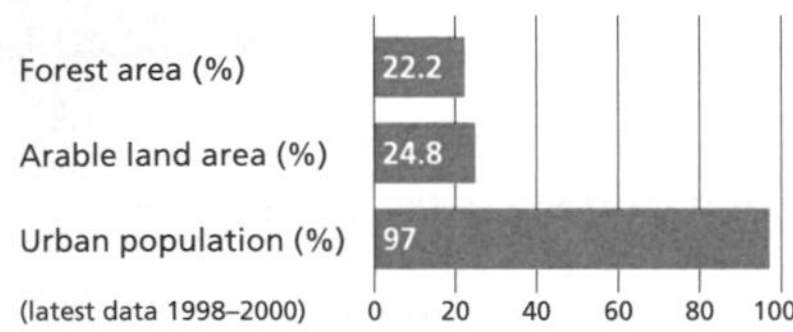

Belgium is a small country in northwest Europe, bordering the Netherlands to the north, Germany and Luxembourg to the east, France to the south and the North Sea to the west. The climate is temperate and wet. Much of the land is flat with low hills. The Scheldt and Maas rivers run north through Belgium, providing important transport links and cooling for nuclear power stations.

About half the land is cultivated. Farming is varied, and Belgium is more than self-sufficient in meat, most dairy products, vegetables, potatoes, and sugar beet. Most farms are family businesses providing work for around 3% of the labor force. There are coal fields in the south and in the northeast, but mining ceased in 1992. Sandstone, limestone, quartzite, marble, and uranium are produced.

Over one-third of the population (3.5 million people) lives in the greater Brussels area, and 28.5% are of foreign origin, although the average of foreigners in the total population is 9%. The second city is Antwerp with 913,000 inhabitants. Liège is the third largest with 476,000. In Flanders the majority of people are of Germanic origin, while in Wallonia the majority are of Gallic origin. The main foreign groups are Italians, Moroccans, French, Turks, Dutch, and Spaniards.

Communications/Energy

Belgium's extensive transport networks are heavily used. The roads carry roughly 450 million tonnes of freight a year, inland

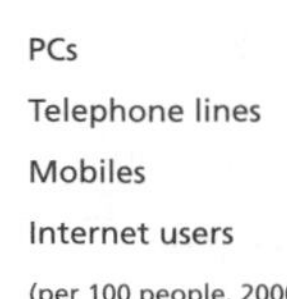

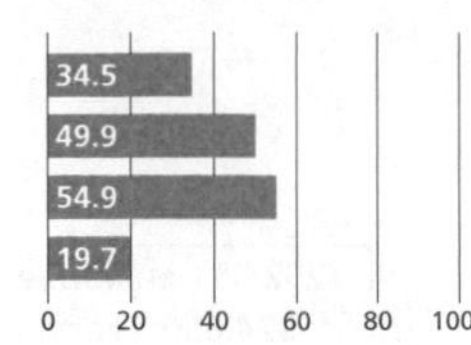

waterways 100 million tons, and railways 60 million tons. The railways carried 153.3 million passengers in 2000, and Brussels Airport had a throughput of 21.8 million passengers. There are nearly 90,725 miles of roads, including 1,045 miles of motorways which link to neighboring countries. At 2,157 miles the rail network is one of the densest in the world, and 1,529 miles is electrified. There is a north–south high-speed rail link to the Netherlands and France, and east–west from Germany to the port of Ostend. Separate track is being built to raise the speed. The 950-mile inland waterway network links the main industrial centers of Antwerp, Brussels, Charleroi, and Liège. Although inland, Ghent is regarded as a sea port because the Ternuezen canal from the Scheldt estuary is wide and deep enough for ocean-going ships. Antwerp is the third largest port in Europe. It handles 100 million tons of freight a year, mostly in bulk goods. At end-2000 it opened a new rail hub with a capacity of one million containers. Zeebrugge specializes in liquefied natural gas and containers, while Ostend is the largest passenger port, and also handles containers in transit to and from the United Kingdom. The merchant fleet comprised 21 ships over 1,000 grt with a total displacement of 32,912 grt in 2000. The pipeline network includes 2,050 miles for natural gas, 725 miles for petroleum products, and 100 miles for crude oil. There are international airports at Brussels, Antwerp, Charleroi, Liège, and Ostend.

Telecommunications is open to competition, but the main operator is the partly state-owned company Belgacom. The country is densely cabled, and cables have been upgraded to take broadband communications for TV and the Internet. There are over 5 million fixed-line phones; Belgium adopted nine-digit numbers in 2000. The mobile phone network was 3.2 million in 1999. There were 2.7 million Internet users in 2000.

Imported oil accounts for 41% of energy needs, imported natural gas for 26%, indigenous nuclear power for 19%, and imported coal for 13%. Around 60% of electricity is generated by seven nuclear power stations, but the government plans to phase out nuclear energy from 2015. Fossil fuels produce just under 40% of electricity, with hydro generating 0.4%.

Education/Employment

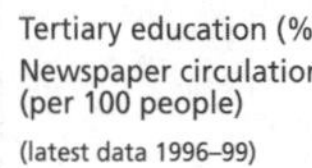

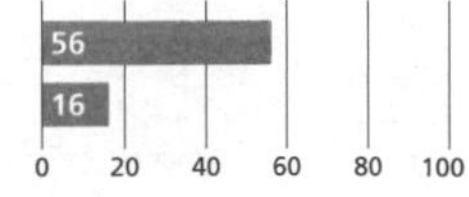

Full-time education is compulsory from age 6 to 16, and part-time education for another two years. Education is the administrative and financial responsibility of the three language communities, Flemish, French, and German (nine municipalities in eastern Belgium). Schools and colleges have autonomy in decision making. Education is free, and grants are available to students in higher education. There are 19 universities and university centers. In addition, technical colleges provide vocational training. There were 299,000 students in higher education in 1998/99, including 133,000 in universities and 166,000 in technical institutes.

Universities are responsible for basic research. Specialties include microelectronics (Louvain, Namur), biotechnology and medicine (Louvain, Antwerp, Brussels), biotechnology and plants (Ghent, Gembloux), materials science and lasers (Antwerp), and space research (Liège). Private sector R&D includes applications in chemicals, electronic and electrical equipment, machinery, metallurgy, transport equipment, rubber, and plastics.

Growth in labor force (% p.a., 1980–99)

Women as % of labor force (1999)

HIV positive (% of age group 15–49, 1999)

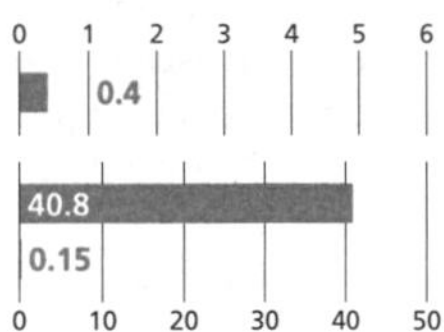

The labor force is well-educated and multilingual. Wages and other employment conditions are determined by tripartite negotiation between the government, employers, and trade unions at the national level, followed by agreements at sectoral and company level. Wages rise automatically in accordance with the consumer price index, but in 1994 key factors, especially energy prices, were taken out of the index. Belgium applies EU employment law, which covers safety at work, wages and working hours, industrial relations, employment incentives, and unemployment provision.

Fiscal/Financial

The largest banks according to total balance sheet at end-1999 were Fortis Banque, fol-

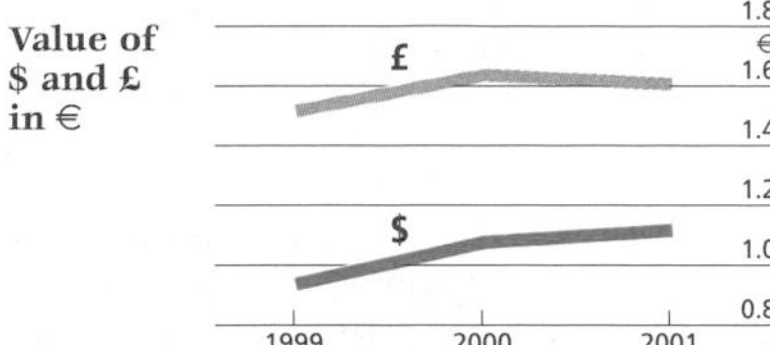

lowed by KBC Bank, Dexia Banque Belgique, and Banque Bruxelles Lambert. Fortis is also a leading player in the insurance sector. The largest insurance company is AXA Royale Belge. The regulatory authority is the Banking and Finance Commission. The National Bank of Belgium is the central bank, which is also part of the European System of Central Banks. This body and the European Central Bank set the policy for the Euro.

At end-2001, corporate tax was 40.17% and maximum personal income tax 56.65% (including the crisis surcharge applied from 1994, which is being phased out). Tax on dividends is 25%, and VAT 21%. Traditionally, income tax is heavily offset by deductions and administrative procedures. Tax incentives further reduce the tax burden on companies, but social security payments are relatively high.

The banking sector was transformed by internal consolidation and international mergers in the second half of the 1990s. The largest retail and wholesale bank Generale de Banque merged with the largest savings bank ASKL CGER in 1999 to form Fortis Banque, which has a significant Dutch shareholding. Banque Bruxelles Lambert was bought by Dutch bank ING in 1997. Dexia was formed through a merger of Belgium's Crédit Communal and France's Crédit Local in 1996. The insurance sector has been similarly affected, with the largest insurer Royale Belge now owned by French firm AXA. At end-1999, 73 of the 134 financial institutions were foreign-owned.

Deregulation and internationalization have created a more dynamic, sophisticated sector. Restrictions on stockbroking firms opting for the status of securities bank were lifted at end-2000, enabling them to engage in leasing and money transmission services. The Brussels Stock Exchanges (BXS) merged with those of Paris and Amsterdam to form Euronext, giving the individual exchanges greater operating scope and reducing trans-frontier trading costs. Euronext Brussels includes the New Market for high-tech firms as well as the main board. It has a cooperation agreement with the Luxembourg Bourse.

Business Opportunities

Growth in output (% p.a., 1990–99)

Services	1.8
Industry	1.5
Manufacturing	1.4
Agriculture	1.2

Grants, training, R&D incentives, and reduced social security and tax are offered to foreign and domestic companies under certain conditions. Companies locating in designated EU Development Zones (in the more disadvantaged regions) receive larger benefits, partly funded by the EU structural funds. Information and assistance is provided by the Flanders Foreign Investment Office (FFIO), Wallonia Office for Foreign Investors, and the Brussels Regional Development Agency. The Federal Government Web site Invest in Belgium gives an overview.

Banking, life sciences, electronics, telecommunications, logistics, and administrative headquarter operations have attracted an influx of foreign investment in recent years. The car industry, chemicals, and pharmaceuticals are more traditional sectors for foreign investment. U.S., Japanese, German, Swedish, Dutch, and U.K. firms are present. Investment opportunities continue in the high-tech and finance sectors. The privatization program and the government's pledge to speed up liberalization of the utilities markets will open new opportunities.

For More Information

Books:

Duprez, K., and L. Vos. *Nationalism in Belgium: Shifting Identities, 1780–1995.* New York: Macmillan, 1998.

Economist Intelligence Unit. *Country Profile and Quarterly Reports.* London.

European Economy: Report and Studies Series. European Union.

IMF Country Report. *Belgium.* Washington, D.C.: IMF.

OECD Economic Surveys. *Belgium.* Paris: OECD.

Web Sites:

Belgian Foreign Trade Office: **www.bdbh.fgov.be**

Brussels Region government entry point: **www.brussels.irisnet.be**

Brussels Regional Development Agency: **www.brda.be**

Federal government entry point: **www.fgov.be**

Flanders Foreign Investment Office: **www.ffio.be**

Flanders Region government entry point: **www.flanders.be**

French-speaking Community: **www.cfwb.be**

National Institute of Statistics: **www.statbel.fgov.be**

Wallonia Office for Foreign Investors: **www.ofisa.be**

Wallonia Region government entry point: **www.wallonie.be**

  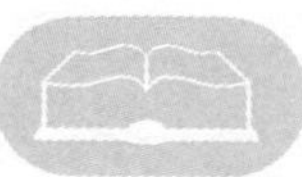    

BELIZE

KEY FACTS

GNI: **$673 million**
GNI pc: **$2,730; world's 91st**
Head of government: **prime minister**
Currency unit: **Belize dollar (Bz$)**
Capital: **Belmopan**
Population: **235,000, growing at 2.5% p.a.**
Land area: **8,803 square miles**
Population density: **27 per square mile**
Life expectancy: **75 years**
Infant mortality: **35 per 1,000 live births**
Language: **English, Spanish**
Best buy: **wood carvings, handicrafts**

ECONOMY

Agriculture and fishing are the leading contributors to employment and exports, but tourism is developing rapidly, with cruise ship calls supplementing the longer-established yachting business in the offshore cays, and eco-tourism inland. A relatively small manufacturing sector produces construction materials and consumer goods, while a free zone adjacent to the Mexican border produces garments and other goods for export. The main export items are sugar, citrus fruit and juice, bananas, and marine products; the United States and European Union account for almost 90% of export revenue, with the United Kingdom the leading EU customer; the United States and European Union supply around 60% of imports, although Mexico is slightly ahead of the EU as a source of imports.

The People's United Party government, elected in 1998, instituted a reform program which returned the national budget from deficit to surplus in two years. Privatization of state utilities has included the sale of the electricity, water, and telecommunications corporations. Belize receives substantial overseas loans and grants for infrastructural and social development programs.

Real GDP growth rates were modest during most of the 1990s, but 1999 showed a rate of 6.4%, and the rate for 2000 was estimated at 10.5%; the inflation rate, which had risen to 6.4% in 1996, fell sharply in the succeeding years, registering a deflation of about 1% in 1998 and 1999, and inflation of 0.6% in 2000.

GEOGRAPHY/RESOURCES

Belize is situated on the Central American coast of the Caribbean sea, bordered by Mexico to the north and Guatemala to the west and south. Guatemala maintains a territorial claim to Belize which periodically leads to border incidents; negotiations are taking place to resolve the issue. Much of the country is mountainous and heavily forested. There is a hydroelectric plant on the Mollejon River in the west.

The largest town and principal port is Belize City; other main towns are Orange Walk and Corozal in the north, San Ignacio and Santa Elena in the west, and Belmopan, established 50 miles inland after Belize City was badly hit by Hurricane Hattie in 1961. At the 1991 census, an estimated 44% of the population were Spanish-speaking, 30% of African background, 11% Maya, and 7% Garifuna, descended from Vincentian Caribs.

The main commercial crops are sugar, citrus fruit, and bananas, while cattle farming and seafood production are also significant activities. Mineral and hydrocarbon resources, as explored to date, are insignificant in commercial terms.

COMMUNICATIONS/ENERGY

Main roads provide connections to Mexico and Guatemala, but large areas are isolated from the main towns. International financial aid has been required for the modernization of the road network. Air services operate to the United States, neighboring countries, and internally, and there is a ferry connection to Guatemala from Punta Gorda in the south.

The telecommunications service is provided by Belize Telecommunications Ltd., majority-owned by Carlisle Holdings; competition in the sector was to be introduced in January 2003. Electric power is supplied by two companies, Belize Electricity Ltd. (BEL) and Belize Electricity Co. (Becol), both of which are majority-owned by a Canadian company, Fortis Inc. BEL receives some electric power from Mexico, and Becol operates the Mollejon hydro plant.

FISCAL/FINANCIAL

There are three foreign-owned commercial banks—Barclays, Nova Scotia and Atlantic—and the Belize Bank, owned by Carlisle Holdings, Lord Ashcroft's Belize-based company. There is no stock market: capital is provided to the public sector by the state Development Finance Corporation, the intermediary for finance from international agencies. There is a growing offshore financial sector, with more than 10,000 registered international business companies.

A value-added tax was introduced in 1996 by the United Democratic Party government, but abolished in 1999 by the present administration; it was replaced by a sales tax.

BUSINESS OPPORTUNITIES

International business companies may receive tax holidays of up to 15 years, and tax exemptions on income including dividends and capital gains. Extra incentives are offered for new industries in less developed areas and for those introducing new technology or oriented towards exporting. Imported machinery and other inputs are eligible for duty exemption, while repatriation of investment and earnings is guaranteed. Priority investment sectors are agriculture, forestry, light manufacturing, and tourism.

For More Information

Books:

Central Statistical Office. Annual Abstract of Statistics.
Economist Intelligence Unit. *Country Profile and Quarterly Reports.* London
Glassman, Paul. *Belize Guide.* 10th ed. New York: Open Road Publishing, 2001.

Web Sites:

Belize Tourism Board: **www.travelbelize.org**
Government entry point: **www.belize.gov.bz**
Trade and Investment Development Service: **www.belizeinvest.org.bz**

BERMUDA

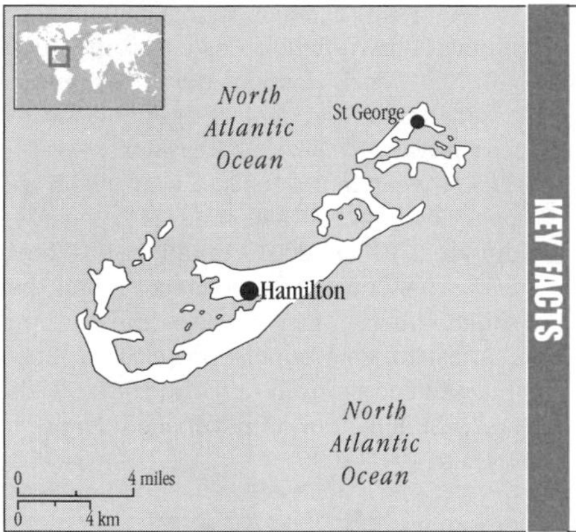

KEY FACTS

GNI pc: **$35,590 (approx.); world's 4th**
Head of government: **premier**
Currency: **Bermuda dollar (Bda$)**
Capital: **Hamilton**
Population: **62,500**
Land area: **20 square miles**
Population density: **3,125 per square mile**
Language: **English**
Best buy: **handicrafts, paintings**

ECONOMY

The dominant economic sectors are the financial sector and tourism, which between them provide the bulk of foreign exchange income and about half the employment for Bermudians; non-Bermudians account for 20% of the workforce. International financial services are strongly focused on the insurance sub-sector, which in 1998 had total capital of Bda$57 billion. At the end of 2000, there were 15,164 international business companies registered, an increase of 32% during the year; foreign exchange earnings by the financial sector amounted to Bda$1,160 million in 1999.

Stayover tourism showed a declining trend in arrivals from almost 477,000 in 1987 to just over 328,000 in 2000, a loss of 31% in 13 years. Conversely, cruise passenger arrivals almost doubled between 1990 and 2000, from 111,000 to 209,000.

Other sectors contributing to employment and GDP are public administration, wholesale and retail trade, transport and communications, and construction. Manufacturing and agriculture are both on a very small scale. Government finances showed an increasing surplus during 1998–2000. During this period, real GDP growth was just over 3% annually, and inflation averaged 2.4%.

GEOGRAPHY/RESOURCES

Located in the Atlantic about 560 miles east of Cape Hatteras, North Carolina, Bermuda comprises 20 inhabited islands, of which seven are linked by bridge or causeway to form the main island group. There are another 130 very small uninhabited islands. The inhabited area is densely populated.

An estimated 395 acres of agricultural land are used for stock rearing and cultivation, 3% of the total land area. Bermuda imports about 90% of its food, and local fishing supplies an estimated 30% of the demand for fish. The country has a subtropical climate, with annual rainfall of about 55 inches.

An estimated two-thirds of the population are of African descent, the remainder of British or Portuguese extraction. More than a quarter of the total population was born outside Bermuda. The offshore financial sector ran short of qualified labor during the 1990s, and the government launched a reform plan, aimed at modernizing and expanding the tertiary education sector.

COMMUNICATIONS/ENERGY

Bermuda's international airport provides services to and from London and several North American destinations. The main sea port is in Hamilton, and two other ports at the east and west ends of the country handle cruise ships and freight traffic. Bermuda has the world's fifth largest shipping register.

Telecommunications service was until recently a monopoly of Cable & Wireless, but the sector was opened to competition in 1997. Electricity is produced by the Bermuda Electric Light Co., using imported oil.

FISCAL/FINANCIAL

There is no personal or corporate income tax, and about 40% of government revenue comes from customs duties. Other revenue sources include a payroll tax, company fees, various license fees, consumer taxes, and a passenger departure tax.

The Bermuda Monetary Authority is responsible for currency issue and exchange control. The Foreign Exchange Control Board is the authority for approval of overseas payments, except those for exempt companies, which are permitted to operate bank accounts in Bermudian currency for local transactions, but are not allowed to deal in Bermuda dollars. There are three domestic commercial banks.

BUSINESS OPPORTUNITIES

Offshore finance, notably insurance, remains the major investment attraction in Bermuda, but other sectors now opening up include telecommunications and light industry, together with tourism and residential property development. In an effort to reverse the decline in stayover tourist arrivals, the government launched a $40m promotional campaign in 1999, aimed at increasing the number to more than 500,000 by 2002; under new legislation passed in mid-2000, the government was authorized to offer tax concessions for new hotel construction.

Legislation has also been introduced to encourage electronic commerce, and an investment licensing and protection act took effect in early 2000. Other new legislation permits insurance companies to transfer risks to the capital market. The government, which strengthened its legislation to counter money laundering in 1998, maintains that any financial crime must be subject to domestic judicial proceedings before any external investigation can take place. Bermuda was *not* included on two lists published by international agencies in mid-2000, naming jurisdictions allegedly uncooperative in connection with money laundering and offering "unfair" tax competition.

For More Information

Books:

Drower, George. *Overseas Territories Handbook.* London: Stationery Office, 1998.
Economist Intelligence Unit. *Country Profile and Quarterly Reports.* London.
Jones, Liz, and James Ziral. *The Insiders' Guide to Bermuda.* 2nd ed. Manteo, NC: Insiders' Publishing, 1999.

Web Sites:

Bermuda Monetary Authority: **www.bma.bm**
Economist Intelligence Unit: **www.eiu.com**

BOLIVIA

KEY FACTS

GNI: **$8,092 million; world's 94th**
GNI pc: **$990; world's 134th**
Head of government: **president**
Currency: **boliviano (Bol)**
Capital: **La Paz (administrative), Sucre (judicial)**
Population: **8,142,000, growing at 2.4% p.a.**
Land area: **418,687 square miles**
Population density: **19 per square mile**
Life expectancy: **62 years**
Infant mortality: **64 per 1,000 live births**
Language: **Spanish, Quechua**
Best buy: **handicrafts**

ECONOMIC STRUCTURE

Bolivia had almost 200 coups between independence from Spain in 1825 and 1981. Since 1982 the country has enjoyed its longest period of stable democracy. General Bánzer, a former military dictator turned democrat, won the 1997 elections and continued the free market policies that began during the 1980s. The 75-year-old Bánzer stepped down in August 2001 because of illness, and was replaced by Jorge Quiroga. Successive World Bank and IMF-backed structural reforms since then have helped to achieve macroeconomic stability (inflation plummeted from 11,700% in 1985 to less than 10% as of 1996), but have failed to lift the rural poor—who comprise more than 40% of the population—out of extreme poverty. The country, with an average per capita income of less than $1,000, qualifies for the Highly Indebted Poor Countries (HIPC) relief program. Public external debt of $4.4 billion in 2000 represented 57% of GDP. A U.S.-backed program to eradicate coca, the shrub from which cocaine is derived, achieved considerable success but led to violent clashes with peasants deprived of their livelihood. In the 1990s Bolivia was the world's second largest coca leaf producer, a $500 million a year business.

Agriculture (excluding coca by-products) generates around 15% of GDP and employs 40% of labor. The rural poor are largely subsistence farmers. The primary food crops are bananas, barley, cocoa beans, coffee, corn, potatoes, rice, soya beans, sugar cane, and wheat. The primary meat products are beef and veal, chicken, duck, lamb, pork, rabbit, and turkey. Industry accounts for about 30% of GDP, mining up to 20%, and services 35%. The country's relatively low level of industrialization makes Bolivia highly dependent on imports. The principal exports are natural gas, tin, zinc, silver, gold, coffee, and soya beans. With its large oil and natural gas potential, Bolivia is becoming an increasingly important player in South America and the energy hub for the Southern Cone. The United Kingdom and the United States are the largest export trading partners. Bolivia enjoys free trade with the Andean Pact nations, and exports products such as clothing and textiles to the United States under the Andean Trade Preference Act.

The state airline, telephone, railroad and electric power companies were privatized in the 1990s. The privatization of Yacimientos Petroliferos Fiscales Bolivianos (YPFB), the state oil company, has been a gradual process since 1994. The privatization program—under which investors acquire a 50% stake and management control in return for a commitment to undertake capital expenditure equivalent to the company's net worth—produced commitments of $1.7 billion in foreign direct investment for 1996–02.

ECONOMIC POLICY

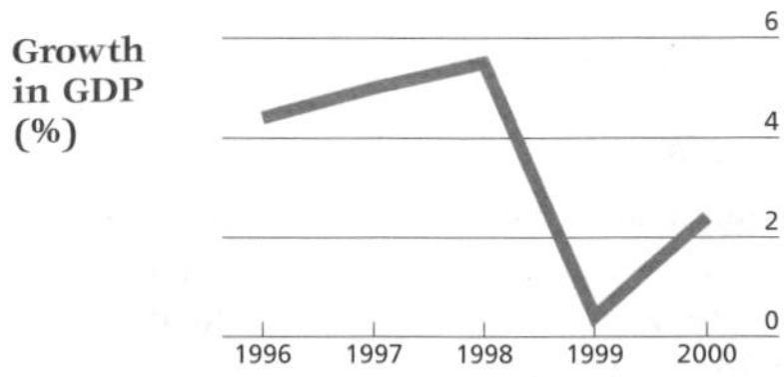

Bolivia began to implement free market reforms after the 1982 Latin American debt crisis, whose impact on the country was intensified by the collapse of international prices of tin, a major source of hard currency. Hyperinflation was overcome, price controls lifted, foreign trade restrictions eased, and a large part of the public sector was privatized. Real GDP growth averaged 3.8% a year in 1991–2000, well up on the paltry 0.2% in 1981–90, but was expected to dip to 0.5% in 2001. Inflation has been below 5% since 1998. Average annual per capita growth, which takes into account the fast-growing population (close to 2% a year) increased from –1.9% in 1981–90 (the steepest fall after impoverished Haiti) to 1.4% in 1991–2000.

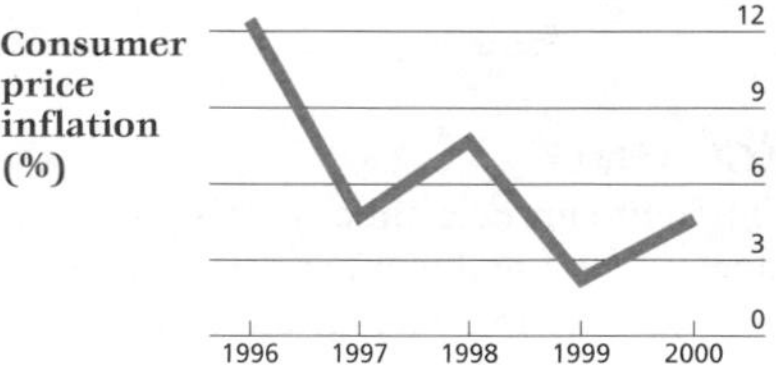

The pay-as-you-go state pension scheme was replaced in 1997 by a system of privately-managed, individually-funded retirement accounts. The reform was a significant step towards lasting fiscal consolidation in Bolivia. Its high transitional cost, however, helped to push up the budget deficit to 4% of GDP in 2000 (close to 6% in 2001), and made it necessary to renegotiate parts of the government's program with the IMF. Most of the deficit is financed by foreign aid. Tax revenue is around 14% of GDP.

GEOGRAPHY/RESOURCES

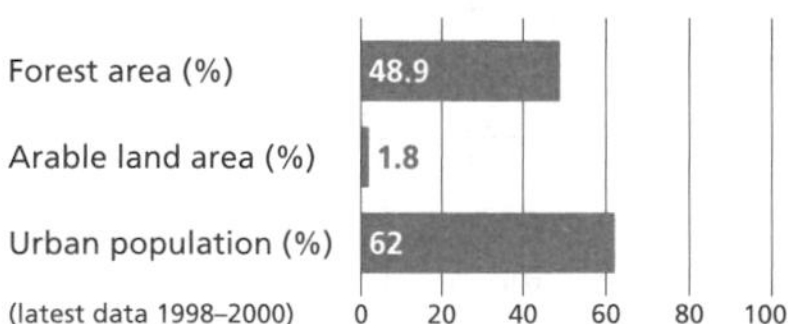

Bolivia is one of only two landlocked South American countries, the other being Paraguay, with whom it has a border to the southeast. To the northeast Bolivia has a frontier with Brazil, while Peru and Chile form the western border, and Argentina lies to the southwest. Three-fifths of the country is lowland, with great plains stretching from the Amazonian lowlands in Brazil, across the frontier, westward towards the Andes mountains. The great bulk of the population—mestizo (30%), Quechua (25%), Aymar (17%), other indigenous groups (16%), and white (12%)—live in the "altiplano," or highland plain, between two

mountain ranges called the Eastern and Western Cordilleras. La Paz is the world's highest capital city (11,810 feet above sea level).

It was gold and silver which lured the Spaniards to Bolivia, and they are still produced today. The mining sector accounts for up to half of total export earnings. The country is the world's largest producer of antimony and a major producer of tungsten. Other minerals extracted include tin, zinc, and copper, while large reserves of iron ore, lithium, and potassium ore are as yet unexploited.

Over half the workforce is employed in the informal economy.

Communications/Energy

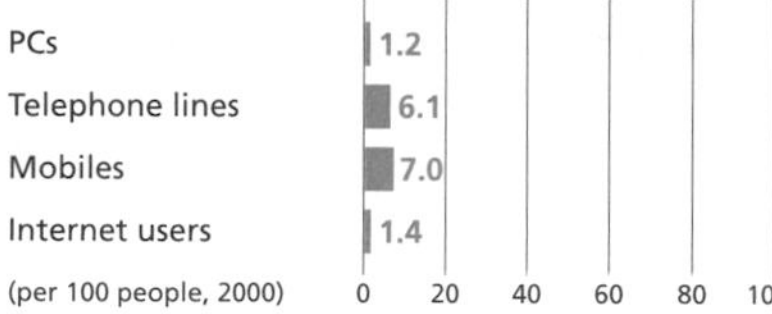

The main population centers of La Paz, Santa Cruz, and Cochabamba are connected by improved highways, but less than 5% of 30,700 miles of roads are paved. Travel during the rainy season (November to March) is particularly hazardous, as most routes are potholed and many roads and bridges are washed out. Road projects were under way in the departments of Santa Cruz, Potosí, La Paz, and Tariji. The railway system, which consists of two independent lines that are separated by the eastern Andes, is in a state of decay. There is an international airport at La Paz. The poor state of transport infrastructure is one of the major obstacles to greater economic development.

Bolivia is self-sufficient in oil and has significant proven natural gas reserves (4.34 trillion cubic feet in 2000, with likely reserves estimated at over 30 trillion cubic feet). The reserves are believed to be the second largest in South America after Venezuela. A pipeline to Brazil came on stream in 1999, and a second one could be built, depending on growth in demand in the vast neighboring market. Bolivia has four gas fields that are estimated to be larger than 5 trillion cubic feet: San Alberto, San Antonio, Itau, and Margarita (with the participation of Brazil's Petrobras and TotalFinaElf, and Spain's Repsol YPF).

Just over 40% of power generation in Bolivia is hydroelectric and the rest fossil fuel. Bolivia's hydroelectric potential is estimated at 38,857 MW, of which 34,208 MW is accounted for in its Amazon region. The country has the potential to export electricity to Brazil, which in 2001 had to impose emergency power rationing measures because of insufficient supply.

Telephone penetration is very low, with two fixed lines per 100 inhabitants, most of them in La Paz. The number of mobile phones has been growing rapidly.

Education/Employment

Education is compulsory from age 7 to 14, but the great majority of people do not complete it, particularly in rural areas where 70% of the total illiterate population live. The disparity between educational attainment in urban and rural areas is enormous, and even in cities and towns less than half of the urban primary school intake progress beyond the fifth grade. The state is the main provider of educational services. Private education accounts for around 12% of total national enrollments. Less than 2% of boys and 1% of girls in rural areas finished secondary education in the mid-1990s, according to UNESCO.

Fiscal/Financial

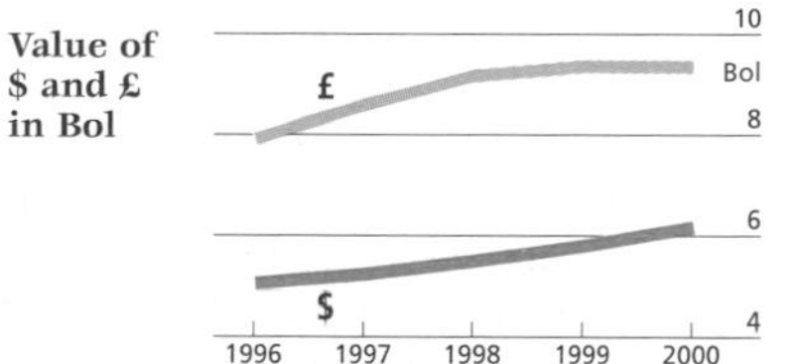

Three banks were recapitalized and restructured under new ownership in the mid 1990s with support from the government's Special Fund for Strengthening the Financial System. Supervision has been tightened, and since 1998 is concentrated in one entity, the Committee of Prudential Financial Regulations (Confip). There are 15 commercial banks, none of which are government-owned. The largest is Banco Bisa. There is a small stock exchange in La Paz.

Bolivia has a flat income tax of 13% and a top corporate tax rate of 25%. VAT is 13%.

Business Opportunities

Bolivia actively encourages foreign direct investment (FDI). There are few restrictions, and those that apply to the oil and mining industries are minimal. The ban on foreigners owning property within 50 kilometers of the country's borders was removed in 1999. Foreign investors receive the same treatment as national ones, and there is no screening process. There is free convertibility of currency. FDI increased from an average of $100 million in 1985–95 to $900 million a year in 1997–2000. Around half of the FDI went into oil and gas, stimulated by the pipeline taking Bolivian gas to São Paulo in Brazil. Corruption is a problem for investors, particularly at lower levels of government and throughout the judiciary. This continues to weaken the rule of law and property rights protection. Bolivia was ranked at 84 out of 91 countries in the 2001 Corruption Perceptions Index drawn up every year by Transparency International, making it the lowest-ranking of all Latin American countries.

For More Information

Books:

Crabtree, John, and Laurence Whitehead, eds. *Towards Democratic Viability: The Bolivian Experience*. New York: St. Martins Press, 2001.

Jemio, Luis Carlos *Debt, Crisis and Reform in Bolivia*. New York: Palgrave Macmillan, 2001

Murphy, Alan. *Bolivia Handbook*. Bath, Somerset: Footprint, 2000.

Web Sites:

Banco Bisa: **www.grupobisa.com**

Central Bank: **www.bcb.gov.bo**

IMF reports: **www.imf.org/external**

National Institute of Statistics: **www.ine.gov.bo**

U.S. State Department Country Commercial Guide: **www.state.gov/e/eb/rls/rpts/ccg**

  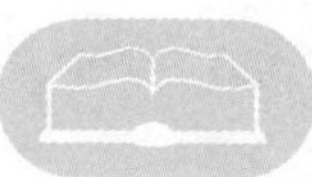    

BOTSWANA

KEY FACTS

GNI: **$5,139 million; world's 109th**
GNI pc: **$3,240; world's 87th**
Head of government: **president**
Currency: **pula (P)**
Capital: **Gaborone**
Population: **1,597,000, growing at 2.5% p.a.**
Land area: **218,803 square miles**
Population density: **7 per square mile**
Life expectancy: **45 years**
Infant mortality: **46 per 1,000 live births**
Language: **Setswana, English**
Best buy: **handicrafts, jewelry**

ECONOMY

A large semi-desert country with a small population and substantial mineral wealth, Botswana has succeeded in maintaining positive economic growth for most of its history as an independent country. This growth has been driven by the discovery and development of substantial diamond resources, which are mined under a joint venture between the government and the South African mining company De Beers. Known as Debswana, this provides about 30% of De Beers' diamonds traded worldwide

The contribution of agriculture to GDP diminished from about 40% at independence in 1966 to only 4% in 1999. By contrast, the mining sector, which was nonexistent at independence, now contributes about 35% of GDP, and there has also been significant growth in trade and financial and government services. A similar shift has occurred in the composition of exports: diamonds have risen from zero to about 75% of the value of exports, and beef sales have fallen from more than 90% to less than 3%. Recurring drought and occasional outbreaks of disease have also affected the beef industry, but it remains an important source of employment.

Government macro-economic policy has been cautious and consistent, and governed by a managed exchange rate that tries to maintain the international competitiveness of non-mining products. The introduction of incentives for foreign investors has stimulated some investment in manufacturing, although this trend is not yet firmly established. Economic development outside the mining sector is more likely to be focused on services, including financial services, and tourism. Government expenditure on the health sector has risen sharply in response to Botswana's HIV/AIDS epidemic. The country's sexually-active population has the highest incidence of the virus in the world, at 38.5%.

The economic outlook remains healthy, with growth sustained at an average of about 5% per annum for several years, rising to 7.8% in 2000–01. Inflation averaged 8.6%.

GEOGRAPHY/RESOURCES

Botswana occupies the Kalahari basin, with an average altitude of 2,950 feet. The Kalahari desert covers most of the south and west of the country. The east and north, with higher rainfall and better soils, are best suited to grazing and arable farming. A shortage of water is one of the main disincentives to further development of Botswana's natural resources. The main diamond production centers are at Jwaneng and Orapa. There is a major copper/nickel mine at Selebi-Phikwe. There are unexploited coal reserves at Mmamabula and Greater Morupule.

COMMUNICATIONS/ENERGY

The main transport corridor links Gaborone in the southeast with Francistown in the east, near the Zimbabwe border. The new Trans-Kalahari Highway serves as a link between South Africa and Namibia. There is growing road and rail traffic, and the country is also served by small airfields. The national airline, Air Botswana, is among possible candidates for privatization, along with the power and telecommunications utilities.

FISCAL/FINANCIAL

The government has implemented a succession of tax reforms so as to widen its revenue base and to improve the tax climate for investors. There is a low corporate tax rate, and there are special tax exemptions for international financial services companies setting up in Botswana. Government revenues have nevertheless been under increasing pressure, forcing cutbacks in expenditure.

There is a small stock market, although most of the listed companies are also traded on the Johannesburg stock exchange.

BUSINESS OPPORTUNITIES

The Botswana Export Development and Investment Authority (BEDIA), established in 1999 as an autonomous organization to promote investment in Botswana, had by the end of 2000 attracted over $10 million in new investment, creating 3,000 new jobs. A total of 11 companies, many of them of Indian or Sri Lankan origin, were helped to start up.

Earlier investments in vehicle assembly were called into question after the collapse of the Hyundai assembly operation in 1999, but new investments can be expected in areas such as textiles, gem-polishing, jewelry, leather products, and pharmaceuticals.

Botswana has applied for a sovereign credit rating that would allow Botswana entities to borrow from international markets.

For More Information

Books:

Botswana Investment & Business Guide. 2nd ed. Washington, D.C.: International Business Publications, 1999.

Dale, R. *Botswana's Search for Autonomy in Southern Africa.* Westport, CT: Greenwood Publishing Group, 1995.

Web Sites:

African news and information: **www.allafrica.com/business**
Botswana Institute for Development Policy Analysis: **www.bidpa.bw**
Botswana Online: **www.botswana-online.com**
Government entry point: **www.gov.bw**

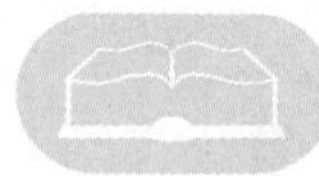

BRAZIL

GNI: **$730,424 million; world's 8th**
GNI pc: **$4,350; world's 73rd**
Head of government: **president**
Currency: **real (R)**
Capital: **Brasília**
Population: **167,988,000, growing at 1.4% p.a.**
Land area: **3,286,488 square miles**
Population density: **51 per square mile**
Life expectancy: **67 years**
Infant mortality: **34 per 1,000 live births**
Language: **Portuguese, Spanish**
Best buy: **high-quality coffee**

ECONOMIC STRUCTURE

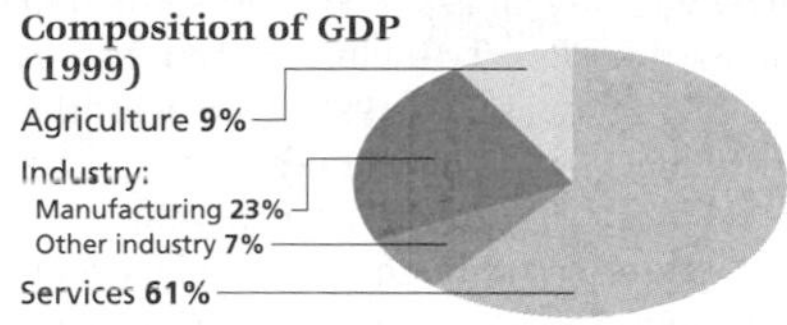

Brazil returned to democracy in 1985 and a new constitution was ratified in 1998, the seventh since independence from Portugal in 1822. This gigantic country, the largest in Latin America, is almost as big as the whole of Europe.

Services generate 60% of GDP, industry 32% (with manufacturing at 23%), and agriculture 8%. The industrial sector, following the promotion during the 1960s and 1970s of import-substituting industrialization (ISI), is the most developed in Latin America. The ISI model, whose protectionist policies made the economy inward-looking and inefficient, began to lose steam in the late 1970s, but it was not until 1990 that rapid trade liberalization began, following a large devaluation of the real. In just four years almost all non-tariff barriers were removed and import tariffs were slashed.

The principal exports are coffee (world's largest exporter), sugar cane (world's largest exporter), soybeans (second largest after the United States), orange juice (Brazil supplies 85% of the world market for orange juice concentrates), tobacco, cocoa, cattle (around 10% of total world trade), iron and steel products, and transportation equipment. Agricultural products account for around one-third of total exports. The share of exports of goods and services in GDP, however, is still small (around 12% in 2000). One reason for this is severe underinvestment, particularly in infrastructure, which has resulted in high costs and inefficiencies in transport and communications. The leading markets are the United States, Argentina, and Germany. Brazil is a member of the Mercosur free trade group with Argentina, Paraguay, and Uruguay.

The economy began to be opened up in the 1990s, when the government moved away from the development policies of previous administrations. These policies covered not only state entities but also wage, price, and credit policies, and subsidy and fiscal incentive programs. The government retains an important economic role, but it has been gradually reducing its presence in the economy and concentrating on public health, safety, and education. Brazil's income distribution is one of the most uneven in the world (the highest 10% of the population have 46.7% of income and the lowest 10% only 1.0%, according to the World Bank).

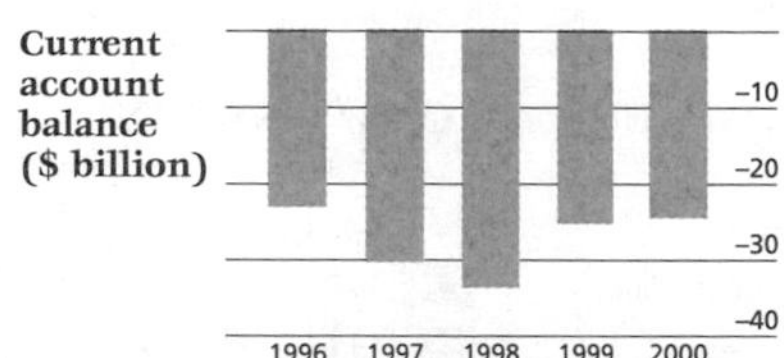

The engine of economic growth is, increasingly, the private sector. In the electricity sector, state entities began to be privatized in 1995. In the oil and gas sector, the government has discussed the privatization of Petrobras, the state-owned oil giant. It lost its monopoly rights in oil exploration, refining, extraction, and distribution in 1998, when the National Petroleum Agency announced that over 90% of Brazil's oil basins were to be sold. Full privatization of Petrobras, however, requires a constitutional amendment. The state's monopoly in telecommunications was ended in 1995; the Telebras telephone monopoly was split up and sold in 1998 in the largest privatization so far. In the transportation sector, the government privatized all seven railway companies in 1997–98, and has either privatized or turned over to the states most of the federal highway network. The pace of privatization since then has been slowed by a spate of legal injunctions and political wrangling.

ECONOMIC POLICY

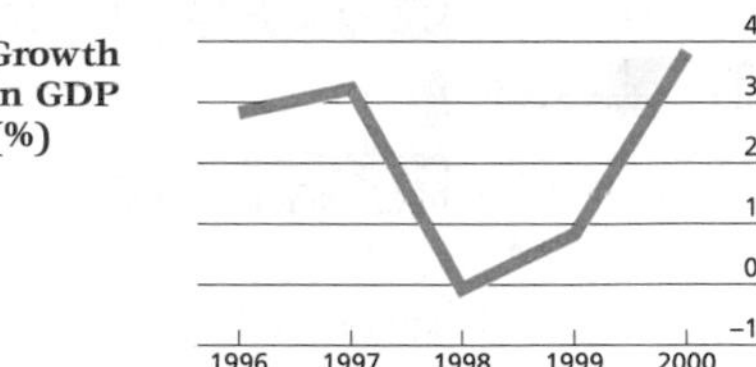

Until the early 1990s and the advent of trade liberalization and the Real Plan, Brazil was one of the West's most closed and inflation-ridden economies. This plan brought inflation down from a peak of 2,500% in 1993 to deflation of 1.8% in 1998 and 4.4% in 2000, when the Central Bank incorporated inflation-targeting into its monetary policy. The economy averaged real annual GDP growth of 2.2% in 1997–2000 (4.5% in 2000) and slowed down in 2001 (an estimated 1.2%). In January 1999 massive capital flight led the Central Bank to switch from a fixed to a floating-rate currency regime, and the real plummeted. The IMF and G7 nations came to the rescue with a 3-year fiscal stabilization plan and $41.5 billion in assistance. The fiscal deficit reached 10% of GDP in 1999 and dropped to 4.5% in 2000 under the impact of reforms and a return to higher growth by the resilient economy which boosted revenue. The deficit grew again in 2001, but the government's commitment to generate a primary surplus (i.e. before debt payments) of 3.5% of GDP in 2001 and 2002 was expected to enable it to continue to service its debt. Tax revenue is around 20% of GDP.

While the economy still remains relatively closed to external trade (import penetration in 2000 was only around 12%), some progress has been made in improving competitiveness. The country moved from 35th in 1998 to 31st in 2001 in the ranking

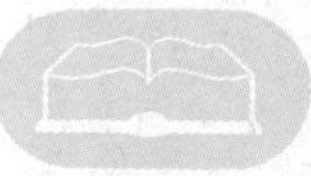

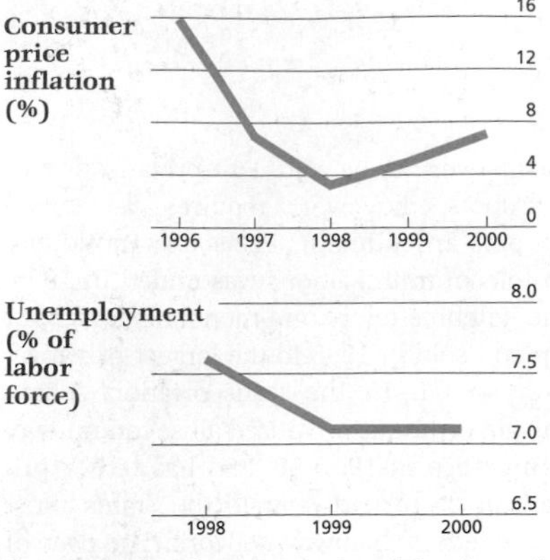

drawn up by the International Institute for Management Development (IMD).

Geography/Resources

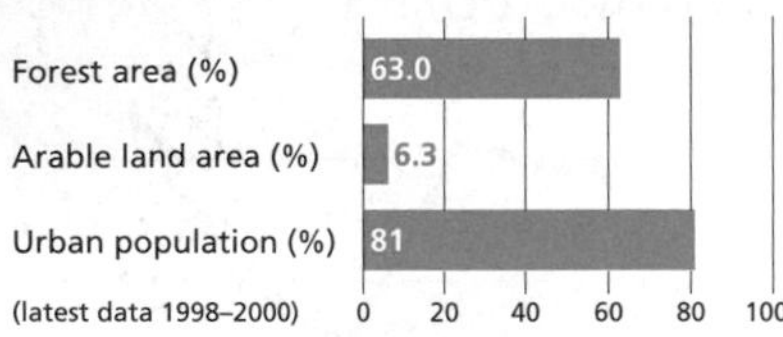

Brazil (3,286,488 square miles) occupies nearly half of South America, and touches all of the other countries except Ecuador and Chile. It is a country of great rivers such as the Amazon and the Paraná (a great tributary of the Río de la Plata). The Iguaçu Falls are one of the country's most famous natural wonders. In such a vast territory the differences in climate and vegetation are considerable. The Amazon basin, which covers some 40% of the territory, has the world's largest tropical rainforest. Over the past 30 years or so, more than 15% of the Brazilian part of Amazonia has been deforested, an environmental disaster (about a third of the Amazon rainforest is in other countries). Trees have been felled to clear pasture for cattle-raising, encouraged by subsidies and tax incentives. A law passed in 1998 introduced stiff penalties for cutting trees without permission from Ibana, Brazil's environmental-protection agency, but it has made little difference to the rate of deforestation, the highest in the world.

The climate in Amazonia is 79°F on average, with no seasonal variation. To the south, on Brazil's great plateau, which covers over half the country, it is hot during the day and cool at night. Towards the Atlantic the plateau ends in mountains which slope down to the fertile coastal plains. More than 70% of the population (170.6 million) live in the southern plateaus and the coastal regions, with over 17 million in São Paulo, the business capital, and 13 million in Rio de Janeiro. In contrast, the Amazon basin has only three inhabitants per square mile.

The country is rich in natural resources. In addition to having an abundance of agricultural products, Brazil's timber reserves are estimated to be the third largest in the world, in particular pine and eucalyptus, which mainly supply local pulp and paper industries, while hardwoods are felled for exports. Minerals include iron ore, bauxite, manganese, coal, zinc, lead, copper, gold, and tin. It is the world leader in the production of tantalite. The country's dominant position in coffee is gradually dwindling as other producers, notably Vietnam, are making incursions into Brazil's world market share (41% in 1955 and 21% in 2000).

Agriculture generates around 8% of GDP and accounts for one-third of exports. Less than 10% of the total land area is cultivated (20% of the arable land). Most large-scale farming is in the south and southeast of the country

Brazil is also self-sufficient in oil (third-largest producer in Latin America after Mexico and Venezuela). Offshore fields account for over 80% of known reserves. Petrobras aims to double production to around 2 million barrels per day by 2005. All price controls and import restrictions on gasoline and diesel were removed in January 2002 in the final step towards full liberalization of the petrol market. This enabled private oil companies, which distributed fuel purchased at government-set wholesale prices, to import and trade at free-market prices.

Around 54% of the population is white, 39% mixed race, 6% black, and 1% Japanese. An estimated 200,000 indigenous Indians live in the Amazon region. Brazil is the largest Catholic country in the world. Almost half of Brazilians are 24 or under, creating a market of tremendous potential but also requiring the creation of millions of jobs.

Communications/Energy

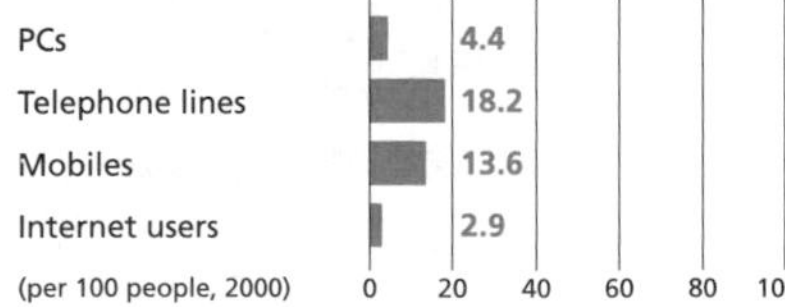

Transport has always been one of Brazil's big problems. Except in the south and the far north, mountains make access from the coast to the interior difficult. As a result, roads were built rather than railways, which are mostly in the coastal districts. For the more remote regions, air travel is vital, particularly in the Amazonian forest. The country's rivers provide 26,720 miles of waterways, along most of which there is a regular goods and passenger service of river craft. Most imports reach Brazil by sea and pass through the inefficiently-run ports, where bureaucracy can be a serious impediment. The main port is Santos, Latin America's largest. The highway network is being increasingly privatized, but only reaches first-world standards in the state of São Paulo, the country's economic powerhouse.

The telecommunications sector is the second largest in the developing world after China. Teledensity, however, is low at less than 15 fixed lines per 100 inhabitants.

The precarious state of the electricity system was exposed in 2001 when the government, faced with an energy shortage, imposed emergency rationing measures to cut consumption by 20% and avoid regular blackouts. An exceptional drought drained the country's hydroelectric dams, which supply virtually all its electricity. Rainfall in southeastern Brazil (including São Paulo) and the northeast in 1998–2001 was the lowest since the 1970s. Another factor was the failure to expand the transmission grid, limiting the capacity to export electricity from dams in the south (not stricken by drought) to the industrial areas of heavy power consumption. Faster privatization of power companies would also have released the government from spending constraints. The government planned to construct 49 thermoelectric plants by 2005, which could supply up to 20% of power, and may revive plans to build a third nuclear power plant in Rio de Janeiro state (originally proposed in 1970).

Education/Employment

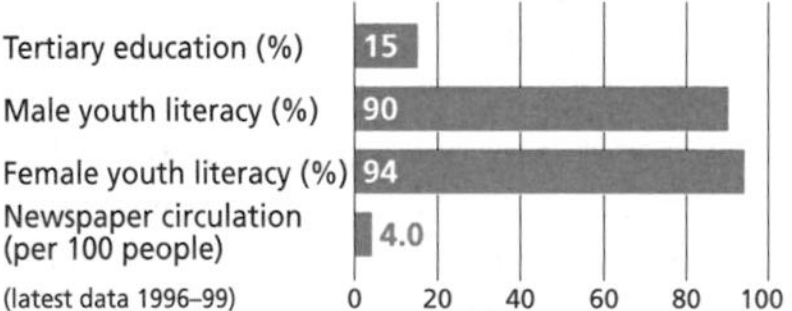

Education is compulsory from age 7 to 14, but most students do not complete the mandatory eight years of basic education. Dropout rates are low at first, but increase sharply as the students get older. Higher education has expanded rapidly, with a five-fold increase in students to 1.5 million between the mid-1960s and 1980, and slower growth since then. However, Brazil has only about 10% of the relevant age group enrolled in higher education, against 20–30% for many countries in Latin America. The private sector provides a significant share of education at all levels. Most places in higher

education are in private institutions of generally low quality. About 30% of places are in public institutions, which are usually better. Spanish is increasingly being taught in schools: Brazil is the only country in Latin America where Spanish is not the official language. Spending on R&D is comparatively high at around 0.7% of GDP.

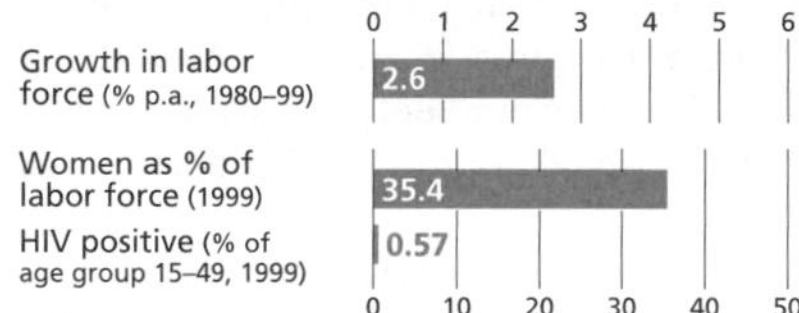

There is a vast pool of labor in Brazil, but not enough of it is skilled. Close to one-quarter of the labor force still works in agriculture, but produces less than 10% of GDP. Unemployment was 7.0% in 2001, but the real level is much higher. Underemployment is widespread.

Fiscal/Financial

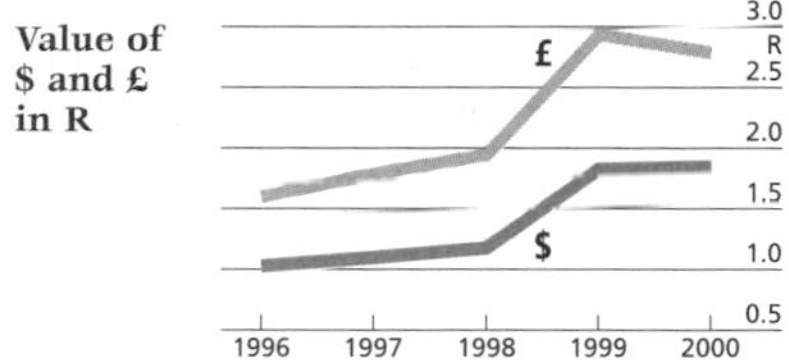

There were a series of bank failures, mergers and acquisitions in 1996 and 1997 following liquidity problems. Foreign banks have invested heavily in the country, owning more than 25% of total banking assets and over two-fifths of private-sector bank assets. By far the largest acquisition was the $4.8 billion purchase by Spain's Banco Santander Central Hispano (BSCH) of Banespa which, together with an earlier purchase of Banco Meridional, made BSCH the third-largest private-sector banking group. The largest bank in terms of assets is the state-owned Banco do Brasil.

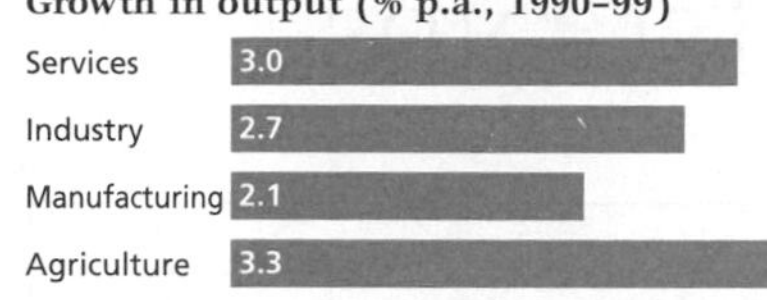

The country, surprisingly, is on the cutting edge in the development of secure e-commerce technology, and has created one of the most advanced home-banking systems in the world, of which Bradesco, the largest private-sector commercial bank, was the pioneer. The use of the Internet in banking is higher than in Asia.

Corporate tax is 15% or 25% depending on the size of the profits, and the top rate of income tax is 27.5%. The São Paulo stock exchange is one of the most active in Latin America. A new law in 2001 strengthened minority investor rights and sharpened the teeth of the securities regulator. Amidst signs that Brazil's risk perception was decoupling from that of crisis-hit neighboring Argentina, corporate heavyweights raised more than $3 billion at the end of 2001.

Business Opportunities

Brazil has attracted considerable foreign direct investment (an annual average of $28 billion in 1997–2000, up from $1.8 billion in 1985–95), a significant share of it through privatizations. Among the most favored sectors are electricity, the car industry, telecommunications, and banking. However, investment began to dry up in 2001 after a record $33.5 billion in 2000.

For More Information

Books:

Box, Ben, and Mick Day. *Brazil Handbook*. 2nd ed. Bath, Somerset: Footprint Handbooks, 2000.

Crocitti, John J., and Robert M. Laine, eds. *The Brazil Reader*. London: Latin America Bureau, 1999.

Fausto, Boris. *A Concise History of Brazil*. New York: Cambridge University Press, 1999.

Financial Times Country Surveys. *Brazil*. London: Financial Times.

OECD Economic Surveys. *Brazil*. Paris: OECD, 2001.

Font, Mauricio A. *Brazil: Development, Industrialization, and Social Transformation*. Lanham, MD: Rowman & Littlefield, 2002.

Noble, John, et al. *Brazil*. 5th ed. Oakland, CA: Lonely Planet, 2002.

Web Sites:

Banco Bradesco: **www.bradesco.com.br**

Central Bank: **www.bcb.gov.br**

Government entry point: **www.brasil.gov.br**

IMF reports: **www.imf.org/external**

Official statistical site: **www.ibge.gov.br**

São Paulo Stock Exchange: **www.bovespa.com.br**

U.S. State Department Country Commercial Guide: **www.state.gov/e/eb/rls/rpts/ccg**

BRITISH VIRGIN ISLANDS

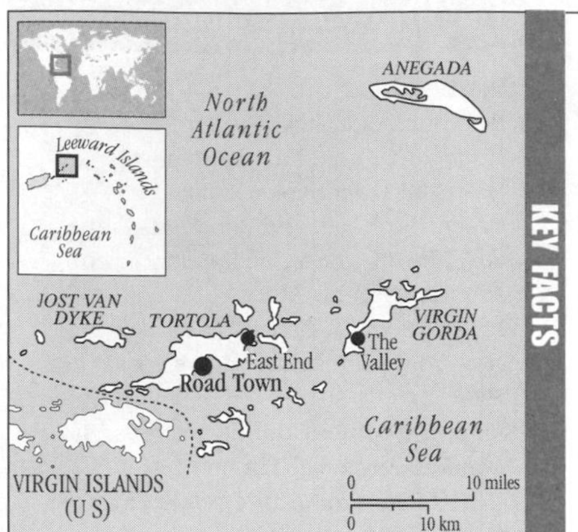

KEY FACTS

Head of government: **chief minister**
Currency unit: **U.S. dollar ($)**
Capital: **Road Town, Tortola**
Population: **19,200**
Land area: **59 square miles**
Population density: **325 per square mile**
Language: **English**
Best buy: **handicrafts, rum**

ECONOMY

Tourism and financial services are the dominant economic sectors, with very limited agriculture, some fishing, and a handful of manufacturing enterprises including a rum distillery. The islands cater for upmarket tourism including yachting, but also for cruise ship visitors; tourist expenditure in 1999 was $279 million, equivalent to 43% of GDP, and more than twice the government's recurrent budget expenditure.

The financial services sector is dominated by the registration of international business companies, which numbered 360,597 at the end of 1999, showing a 32% annual increase since 1994; total bank deposits at the end of 1998 were $863 million, and annual licence fees accounted for around a third of the government's current revenue between 1995 and 1998.

Annual economic growth rates ranged from an estimated 1.8% to 6.4% between 1995 and 1999, averaging 4.1%; the inflation rate also averaged 4.1% between 1996 and 2000. The islands' small export capacity results in an annual trade deficit which in 1999 amounted to $173 million, equal to 87% of the import bill. However, a large surplus on the services account resulted in a positive current account balance, averaging $50 million during 1995–99. The external public debt in 1998 was a modest $34 million.

GEOGRAPHY/RESOURCES

Sited about 50 miles east of Puerto Rico and just east of the U.S. Virgin Islands, the British Virgin Islands comprise about 50 islands and cays, of which 16 are inhabited. The largest island is Tortola, where about 80% of the estimated 20,000 population live; other significant islands are Virgin Gorda, once the main population centre, and Beef Island, which houses the main airport.

More than 80% of the population are of African descent, the remainder being principally from the United States or Europe. The population increased rapidly in the 1980s as a result of the expansion of the tourist infrastructure, but the rate of increase is thought to have slowed in the 1990s. Educational standards are high, and there is very little unemployment.

COMMUNICATIONS/ENERGY

International flights connect the British Virgin Islands with Puerto Rico, the U.S. Virgin Islands, Antigua, St Maarten, and several eastern Caribbean islands. Virgin Gorda and Anegada have airstrips, with some regional as well as domestic services. Ferry services connect several islands with each other and with the U.S. Virgin Islands, and freight services to the United States and Europe. The road system, amounting to about 100 miles in total, includes a bridge between Tortola and Beef Island.

Telecommunications are provided by Cable & Wireless. In 1997 there were about 11,000 lines in operation, plus a mobile phone system operated by CCT Boatphone. The electricity service is provided by the BVI Electricity Corporation, which operates two power stations with a combined capacity of 25.8 MW.

FISCAL/FINANCIAL

For several years, current revenue has exceeded expenditure, providing a surplus which helps support the capital budget, as well as contributing to reserves. The 2001 budget projected a current surplus of $40.3 million; the capital budget amounted to $109.4 million, of which external financing of $71.1 million was expected. Capital projects under way included the Beef Island airport expansion and the reconstruction of the bridge between Beef Island and Tortola; a new hospital, costing $45 million, was planned.

There are four international commercial banks operating in the islands, plus the Virgin Islands Development Bank. Although new legislation governing the offshore financial sector came into effect in 1998, the Organisation for Economic Co-operation and Development listed the British Virgin Islands in June 2000 as a country offering "harmful" tax competition.

BUSINESS OPPORTUNITIES

Investors in the hotel sector, and those investing in "special need" enterprises, are eligible for ten-year tax exemption and duty-free import of capital equipment. The financial services sector offers tax exemption for companies registered in the British Virgin Islands but operating outside the islands.

Areas offering scope for investment in the near and medium term include tourism and infrastructural development; telecommunications, a sector which is to move towards a competitive regime on a timescale not yet established; and fishing, which is increasing as a leisure interest and commercial proposition. The financial services sector will also continue to offer attractions, regardless of the current international pressures on its operation.

For More Information

Books:

Cameron, Sarah. *Caribbean Islands Handbook*. 13th ed. Bath, Somerset: Footprint Handbooks, 2001.

Economist Intelligence Unit. *Country Profile and Quarterly Reports*. London.

Web Sites:

BVI Chamber of Commerce & Hotel Association: **www.bvihotels.org**

Economist Intelligence Unit: **www.eiu.com**

  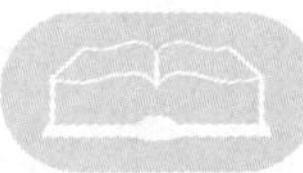    

BRUNEI

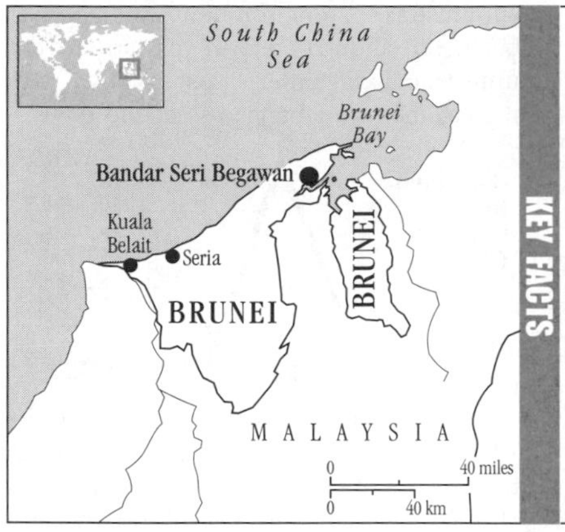

GDP: **$4,852 million**
GDP pc: **$15,070**
GNI pc: **$24,630 (approx.); world's 20th**
Head of government: **the Sultan**
Currency: **Brunei dollar (B$)**
Capital: **Bandar Seri Begawan**
Population: **322,000, growing at 2.5% p.a.**
Land area: **2,046 square miles**
Population density: **157 per square mile**
Life expectancy: **76 years**
Infant mortality: **8 per 1,000 live births**
Language: **Malay (official), English**
Best buy: **ornamental traditional weapons, brass kettles and gongs**

ECONOMY

Petroleum and natural gas dominate the economy, contributing about 50% of GDP, 80–90% of exports, and 75–90% of government receipts. Petroleum refining is the main manufacturing industry. In 1998 agriculture accounted for 2.8% of GDP, trade and tourism for 12.6%, and finance for 8.3%. The top export in 1999 was liquefied natural gas (of which Brunei is the fourth largest world producer), followed by crude petroleum, machinery and transport equipment, and refined petroleum products. The main export market was Japan, followed by the United States, South Korea, and Thailand.

To promote recovery following the Asian financial crises of the late 1990s, the government increased public expenditure in infrastructure and diversification of the economy. Import substitution, tourism, and international financial services are the main focus for development. GDP fell by 1% in 1992 on account of world recession. It revived with growth of 0.5% in 1993, rising to 4.5% in 1998, and was estimated at 3% in 2000. Annual inflation of 3–4% for most of the 1990s fell to 1% in 1999.

GEOGRAPHY/RESOURCES

Situated in the northwest of the island of Borneo, Brunei is two separate enclaves surrounded by the Malaysian state of Sarawak. It has a northern coastline on the South China Sea.

Imports cover 80% of domestic food requirements, and forestry is geared only to the local market. Fisheries, including sea fishing and aquaculture, are growing in importance. Brunei's proven petroleum reserves at January 2000 of 1.4 billion barrels were set to last until 2018 at a production rate of around 160,000 barrels per day. Crude oil output was 191,000 barrels per day in the first eight months of 2000. Natural gas reserves of 13.8 trillion cubic feet are expected to last until 2033. Production was 300 billion cubic feet in 1998. A new marine seismic study indicated further deep sea reserves, for which exploration licenses were issued in 2001.

COMMUNICATIONS/ENERGY

The road network is 1,570 miles. There are no public railways. The main general cargo international sea port is at Muara. Kuala Belait in the extreme west handles general cargo and has a petroleum jetty. There is an LNG jetty at Lumut. The international airport at Berakas near the capital has a capacity of 1.5 million passengers and 50,000 tons of freight a year.

The telecommunications system is modern, and includes digital switching and high speed Internet access. There were 28,000 Internet users in 2001, and in 1999 one-third of the population had access to a phone. Indigenous energy resources supply all local needs. Brunei produces a range of refined petroleum products for the local market as well as for export. Electricity production was 2.4 billion kWh in 1999, entirely from gas-fired power stations.

FISCAL/FINANCIAL

Corporation tax is 30%, but various reductions are available. There is no personal income tax and no tax on personal dividends. There are also no export, sales, payroll, or manufacturing taxes. Withholding tax is 20% on interest paid to non-resident companies. Special tax rules apply to petroleum and gas companies.

Central bank functions and financial service regulation are carried out by Ministry of Finance departments. Legislation includes client privacy, measures against money laundering, and consumer protection in securities trading. The government is eager to promote the financial services sector. The Brunei dollar is at par with the Singapore dollar, and there are no foreign exchange controls. Total bank assets were B$8.5 billion in 1998. Bank interest rates are set by the Association of Banks. There is no local stock market, but securities and other instruments are traded on the Singapore and other international stock exchanges.

BUSINESS OPPORTUNITIES

The government encourages foreign investment in joint venture with local enterprises for industries related to national food security and local resources. Full foreign ownership is allowed for industries selling to the local market and export industries. There are 12 industrial sites. Approved foreign investors are eligible for an eight-year corporation tax holiday. Current opportunities include IT, biotechnology, steel manufacture, oil- and gas-related industries, financial services, transit trade, and tourism. The point of contact is the Industrial Promotion and Tourism Development Division of the Ministry of Industry and Primary Resources.

For More Information

Books:

Cleary, M., and S. Y. Wong. *Oil, Economic Development and Diversification in Brunei*. New York: Palgrave Macmillan, 1994.

Ledesma, Charles, et al. *Rough Guide to Malaysia, Singapore and Brunei*. 3rd ed. New York: Rough Guides, 2001.

Web Sites:

Government entry point: **www.brunei.gov.bn**

Ministry of Finance: **www.finance.gov.bn**

Ministry of Industry and Primary Resources: **www.industry.gov.bn**

BULGARIA

KEY FACTS

GNI: **$11,572 million; world's 81st**
GNI pc: **$1,410; world's 121st**
Head of state: **president**
Head of government: **prime minister**
Currency: **lev (Lv)**
Capital: **Sofia**
Population: **8,279,000, growing at –0.6% p.a.**
Land area: **42,703 square miles**
Population density: **194 per square mile**
Life expectancy: **72 years**
Infant mortality: **14 per 1,000 live births**
Language: **Bulgarian**
Best buy: **wine, cigarettes**

ECONOMIC STRUCTURE

Five centuries of Turkish domination of Bulgaria ended with the Russo-Turkish war of 1876–78, after which Bulgaria was ruled by monarchs of German descent. A pro-Nazi wartime regime was toppled in 1944 by the Communist Party with nationalist allies; from 1947 to 1990 it ruled without them, making Bulgaria a loyal Soviet satellite. Agriculture prospered, and industrialization inclined towards an overemphasis on heavy industry. Post-communist governments of technocrats (1990–91 and 1992–94) and anti-communists (1991–92) were unable to match the reforms prevailing across Eastern Europe, while the government of former communists (1994–97) was unwilling to do so. The resulting policy vacuum hastened an economic crisis. In February 1997 this culminated in financial collapse, bank closures, and massive devaluation of the currency.

In May 1997 the first pro-market-reform government was elected. After Bulgaria took a pro-western stance over Kosovo, it was invited to start EU and NATO accession negotiations. Dramatic progress was made with privatization in 1999: the year started with 42% of privatizable assets sold, and ended with 70% sold, including the oil refinery Neftochim, the fertilizer producer Agropolychim, and Balkan Airlines. By 2000 almost 100% of land had been restored to its pre-communist owners. In 2001 the political map changed: parliamentary elections in June brought into office a populist coalition led by the former king, Simeon Saxe-Coburg, and the presidential poll in November was won by Georgi Purvanov, a former communist. However, reform stayed on course, and the privatization program, suspended before the parliamentary elections, resumed.

Agriculture accounts for 14% of Bulgaria's GDP (2000 figures); industry, which accounts for 28% of GDP, includes important metal mining and processing, food processing (especially tobacco and wine), and oil refining sectors. Electronics and telecommunications are considered to have potential, as is the services sector, notably tourism.

Bulgaria is highly dependent on trade which, in the last decade, has switched away from the former Soviet bloc; it has been a member of the WTO since 1996. Metals, mineral ores, machinery, and consumer goods (especially foodstuffs) are important exports.

ECONOMIC POLICY

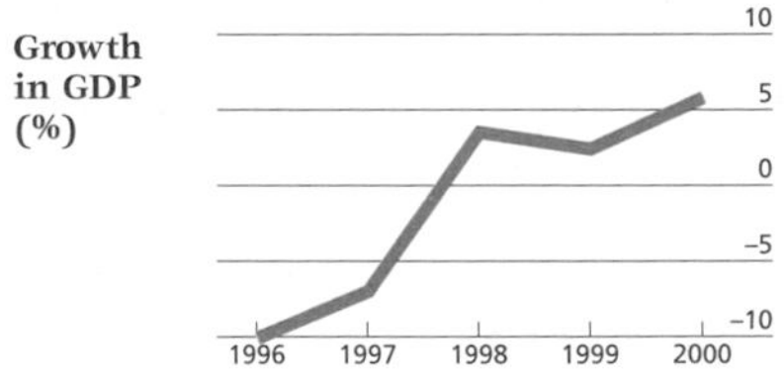

The reformist government soon achieved macro-economic stabilization after the 1997 financial crisis. It introduced a currency board in July 1997, tying the lev to the German mark and later the Euro, and started to tackle a budget deficit built up in 1990–97, mainly comprising high interest payments on government debt. State extra-budgetary funds were closed, soft credits to unprofitable enterprises stopped, most banks privatized, and financial sector regulation introduced. The reforms were strongly supported by the IMF, which started an extended fund facility agreement in 1998. However, in 2001 much still remained to be done to improve the regulatory and administrative environment for private business, and to reform privatized but unrestructured enterprises, many with managements unchanged since the 1980s.

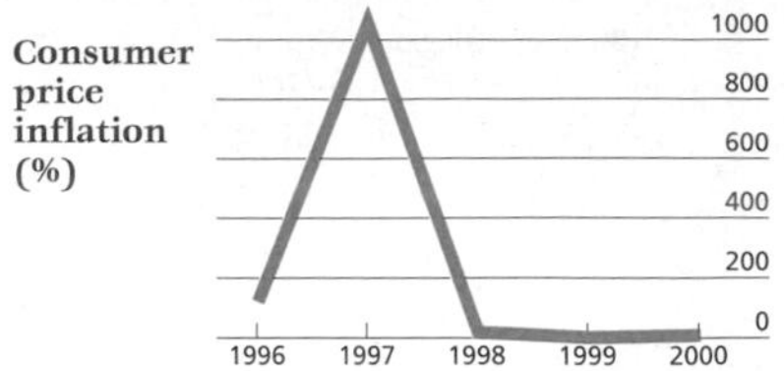

In 1999 Bulgaria's GDP was at 65% of its 1989 level—a decline as serious as that in many parts of the former U.S.S.R.—but had already begun to recover. GDP rose by 2.4% in 1999, 5.8% (estimated) in 2000, and 4% (projected) in 2001, despite adverse external factors including the 1998 Russian crisis and the Kosovo war, which damaged trade and the transport sector. Under the currency board, inflation was cut dramatically, from more than 1000% in 1997 to 22% in 1998; it has remained low and stood at 8% in 2001.

GEOGRAPHY/RESOURCES

Bulgaria's Black Sea coastline, one of Eastern Europe's favorite resorts, comprises its eastern border; the Danube river, separating it from Romania, is the northern border; Yugoslavia and Macedonia lie to the west, and Greece and Turkey to the south.

Two-fifths of Bulgaria's land is arable and a quarter of this is irrigated; one-fifth of the country is pastureland and one-third forested. Bulgaria's main crops are wheat and barley. There are also sunflowers, sugar beet, and tobacco. Its mineral resources include ferrous (iron ore), non-ferrous (lead, zinc, copper), and precious (gold) metals.

The population (total 8.1 million in 2000) is 85.6% Bulgarian; the significant ethnic minorities are Turks (9.4%) and Roma (3.7%). A strong healthcare system under communist rule increased life expectancy, which peaked at 71.3 years in the mid-1970s. In the post-communist decade it fell from 68.2 in 1986 to 67.2 in 1997. The population is aging, and there was net emigration throughout the 1990s.

COMMUNICATIONS/ENERGY

Bulgaria's geographical position makes transit trade, and therefore transport, vital. Its 23,000 miles of roads and 4,020 miles of rail track have suffered from low spending in recent years, but should gain from the EU- and EBRD-supported development of the

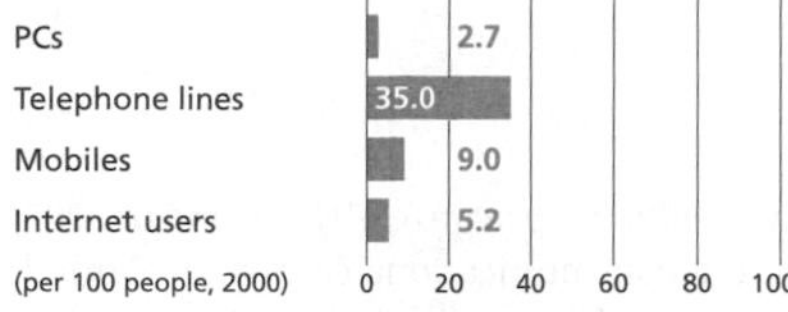

European rail and road transport corridors, four of which are meant to pass through Bulgaria. The Black Sea merchant fleet functions well, and the main shipping company, Navibulgar, has stayed financially healthy. Modernization at the Black Sea ports, Varna and Burgas, is being supported by German, Japanese, Belgian, Dutch, and Italian investment. Air transport is less significant, and the national carrier, Balkan Airlines, remained financially troubled in 2001. There are international airports at Sofia, Varna, and Burgas.

Bulgaria inherited one of the highest telephone line densities of the former Soviet bloc—54 telephones per 100 inhabitants in 1989—but the national monopoly, Bulgarian Telecommunications, failed to develop the system in the 1990s. A planned privatization failed in 2000, and was due to be re-attempted in 2002. The sector was liberalized by a 1998 law, and a long-term digitalization program has begun.

Bulgaria relies heavily for power on the Kozlodui nuclear power station (which it is under EU pressure to downsize), on an inefficient coal sector, and on natural gas imports from Russia, particularly for its synthetic chemical industry. In early 2001 parliament approved an Energy Law providing for market liberalization, and a significant $1.4 billion investment contract for the Maritaz East power station was signed with AES and Entergy of the United States.

Education/Employment

Bulgaria's education system, which attained a high standard under Communism, has declined in the 1990s. There is low pay and low morale among school teaching staff; their numbers fell from just under 120,000 in 1997 to 113,000 in 2000. But the number of students in tertiary education has increased substantially in the post-communist period: from 183,500 in 1989–90 to 258,230 in 2000. Elite foreign-language secondary schools play an important part in providing students for the best universities.

Wage costs in Bulgaria remain low (average $101 per month in late 2000) and unemployment high (18% in mid-2001). However, neither of these figures takes into account a "gray" economic sector that some observers say accounts for 50% of GDP, and the role of self-sufficiency, i.e. food grown by non-farmers for family consumption.

Bulgaria has started to bring labor legislation into line with that of the EU. A new labor code adopted in March 2001 has been criticized by some employers' associations as being too pro-labor: it restricted the use of fixed-term contracts, banned age discrimination, provided legal backing for industry-wide wages negotiations, and preserved compulsory length-of-service pay increases. On the other hand it allowed employers greater flexibility to change working hours.

Fiscal/Financial

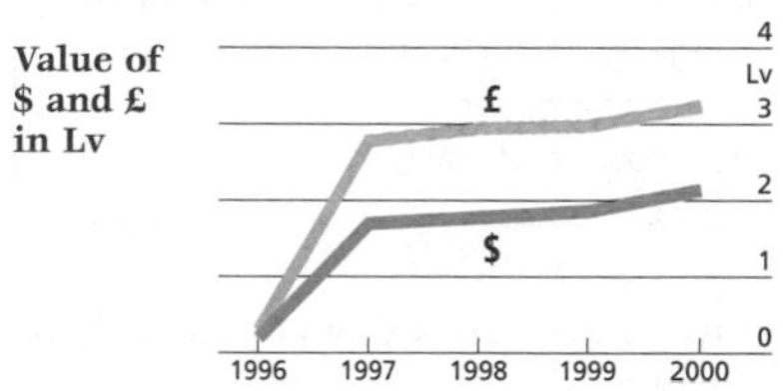

The sale in 1999–2000 of 98% of Expressbank to Société Générale, 98% of HebrosBank to the Regent Pacific Group, and a controlling share of Bulbank (the country's largest) to a consortium including UniCredito and Allianz, meant that only two significant banks remained in state hands, Biochim Bank and the State Savings Bank. However in 2001 substantial reforms in the banking sector remained outstanding. Although central bank refinancing of banks is ruled out under the currency board, and regulation and supervision have been tightened since 1997, the sector is failing to finance industry.

Bulgaria's insurance sector has undergone restructuring and regulatory tightening since 1997. It was opened up for foreign companies in 1998, and both Allianz, which bought a controlling stake in one of the largest companies, and AIG have entered the market.

The tax system is starting to be brought in line with that of the EU, and a 1999 VAT law largely follows EU guidelines. The 2001 Budget Law substantially reduced the tax burden to encourage job creation and the development of the private sector. Corporate income tax was cut from 25% to 20%—there was already a 20% concessionary rate for enterprises with taxable profits of less than Lv50,000 (about $30,000)—and there is also a 10% municipal tax, deductible from the taxable base for corporate income tax. All personal income tax rates were reduced by 2%.

Business Opportunities

Foreign direct investment was negligible (averaging $85 million a year) in 1992–96, averaged $625 million per year in 1997–99, peaked at $1,000 million in 2000, and fell to an estimated $500 million in 2001. Most of this was in green-field projects, while large-scale privatization sales, such as that of Neftochim refinery to Lukoil of Russia for $101 million (the biggest of 1999), played a lesser role. There is significant FDI into trade, the largest single investment of 1999 being the $77 million put into retail by Metro Cash & Carry of Germany.

In 2001 opportunities for investment in privatizations, in green-field manufacturing projects, and in the service sector appeared good. The legal framework is well developed: profits may be freely repatriated upon presentation of a receipt for taxes paid, and although foreign nationals may not own land, 100%-foreign-owned Bulgarian companies may. Investment incentives include the six duty-free zones and corporate income tax breaks for companies investing in regions of high unemployment. On the other hand, obstructions to foreign investment remain: the chief ones identified in 2000 by the Bulgarian International Business Association were the underdevelopment of the capital market, and some remaining unpredictability in the tax system.

For More Information

Books:

Bristow, John A. *The Bulgarian Economy in Transition*. Northampton, MA: Edward Elgar Publications, 1996.

Coenen-Huther, Jacques, ed. *Bulgaria at the Crossroads*. Huntington, NY: Nova Science Publishers, 1996.

Crampton, R. J. *A Concise History of Bulgaria*. New York: Cambridge University Press, 1997.

Melone, Albert P. *Creating Parliamentary Government: The Transition to Democracy in Bulgaria* (Parliaments and Legislatures Series). Columbus, OH: Ohio State University Press, 1998.

Natov, Nikolai. *Foreign Investments in Bulgaria*. Norwell, MA: Kluwer Academic Publishers, 2000.

Web Sites:

Bulgaria International Business Association: **www.biba.mobikom.com**

Bulgarian Foreign Investment Agency: **www.bfia.org**

Bulgarian National Bank: **www.bnb.bg**

Southeast Europe Economic Forum: **www.biforum.org**

CAMEROON

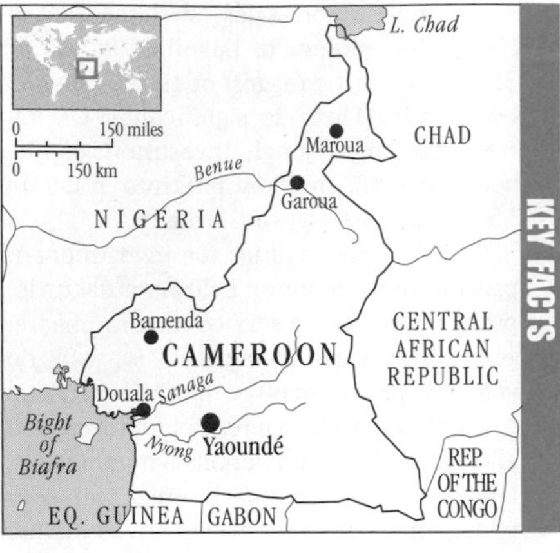

KEY FACTS

GNI: **$8,798 million; world's 88th**
GNI pc: **$600; world's 150th**
Head of government: **president**
Currency: **CFA franc (CFA)**
Capital: **Yaoundé**
Population: **14,693,000, growing at 2.7% p.a.**
Land area: **179,691 square miles**
Population density: **81 per square mile**
Life expectancy: **54 years**
Infant mortality: **95 per 1,000 live births**
Language: **French, English, numerous local languages**
Best buy: **handicrafts**

ECONOMIC STRUCTURE

After a prolonged and severe economic decline in the 1980s and early 1990s—aggravated by mounting external debts, persistent economic mismanagement, political uncertainty, and a long-overvalued exchange rate of the CFA franc—Cameroon has managed to make a recovery in more recent years, helped both by the 1994 devaluation of the CFA franc and by the 1997 appointment of Paul Mafany Musonge as the country's prime minister. Politically, Cameroon has faced difficulties in maintaining an acceptable formula for unity, and there have been outbreaks of political tension, accompanied by reports of official human rights violations. President Biya's government has nevertheless survived in office since 1982 despite a period of civil unrest that accompanied the introduction of multi-party politics in 1991. A number of leading opposition parties boycotted the last elections in 1997. During the 1990s, a new movement to declare independence for the English-speaking Southern Cameroons was firmly repressed. In addition, in recent years Cameroon has been in dispute with Nigeria over ownership of the Bakassi Peninsula, a matter of sovereignty and an issue which provoked a series of armed confrontations between the two countries. However, the prospects are improving for its resolution through the International Court of Justice.

Under the premiership of Mr. Musonge, an English-speaking former manager of the Cameroon Development Corporation, the emphasis of economic policy has been placed on macro-economic adjustment, including privatization of several potentially profitable state enterprises. The government has also attempted to reverse a long decline in the standard of educational and health services.

Cameroon's economy has the inherent strength of being supported by a variety of export products, unlike many African countries where there are often only one or two principal products. In addition to the key natural resources of crude oil and timber, there is also a diverse agricultural sector producing cocoa, coffee, cotton, sugar, grain, and livestock. The agriculture, forestry, and fishing sectors together contribute more than 40% to GDP, compared with the contribution of services at 35%, manufacturing at 12%, and mining (including oil) at 6.5%.

The principal destinations for Cameroon's exports are Italy, Spain, and France, and the country's leading suppliers are France, Belgium, Nigeria, and Italy. Cameroon is expected to receive a boost of inward investment from the anticipated start of work on a pipeline designed to link newly-developed oil fields in Chad to the coast through central Cameroon. The long-term traffic that the Chad oil project will generate for Cameroon will help to compensate for the expected depletion of Cameroon's own oil reserves in the medium term.

The public sector is being gradually reduced in size as commercial enterprises are handed over to the private sector. Privatization has been more extensive in Cameroon than in most other countries in Africa. During 2001 the electricity company, Sonel, became managed and part-owned by a U.S. company. A French/South African consortium has taken over the main railway company and is investing in the rehabilitation of the main line from Douala to Ngaoundere. The national airline, Camair, is expected to be privatized by the end of 2002; the telecommunications company, Camtel, has begun the same process, with its mobile telephone services being already privately operated.

ECONOMIC POLICY

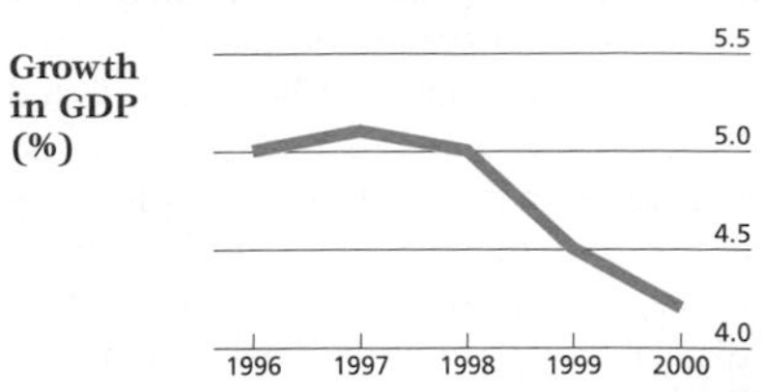

Since 1997 the government has introduced comprehensive macro-economic reforms with the support of international donors and the domestic business community. In 2000 Cameroon was accepted as a candidate for the World Bank's Highly-Indebted Poor Countries (HIPC) initiative which, once implemented, will reduce Cameroon's debt service obligations from 23% to 12% of export earnings. The agreement requires the government to spend its debt service savings on health, primary education, and programs to counteract HIV/AIDS. The government has also been under pressure to prevent and expose corruption, which has long been a feature of economic life in the country. Measures were taken in 2001 to introduce a serious reform of the police service.

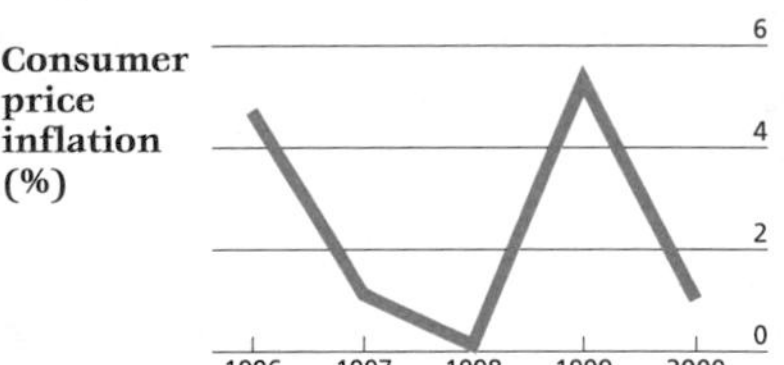

In 2000–01, economic growth reached 5.3%, while inflation was 2.0%. There was a positive trade balance although the current account balance was negative.

GEOGRAPHY/RESOURCES

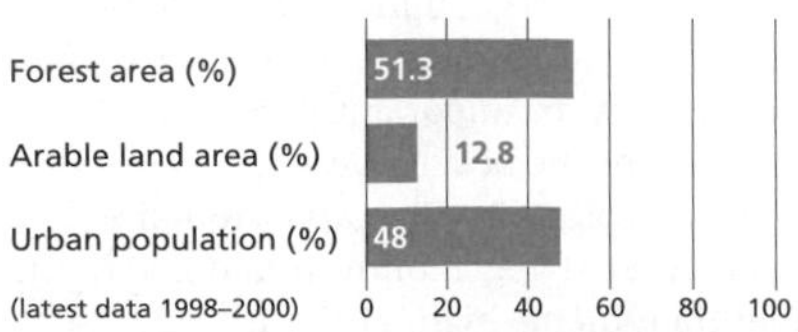

A wedge-shaped country running from its apex in dry savannah lands near Lake Chad into the heart of Africa's western equatorial

forest, Cameroon incorporates several different climatic zones. It sits astride the volcanic belt that separates West Africa from Central Africa, and has mountains of up to 13,120 feet, while the average altitude of the Adamaoua plateau in the north is about 3,280 feet. Fertile volcanic soils in the southwest have encouraged a high population density in this region, while the dense rainforest of the south is much more thinly populated. Annual rainfall varies from 200 inches in the south to little more than 24 inches in the far north of the country. Almost half the country is covered by forest, and Cameroon is the largest producer of logs in Africa. The largest cities are Douala and Yaoundé.

Thanks to the survival of long-lasting farming traditions in Cameroon, peasant farmers still dominate agricultural production, whether for subsistence, local marketing, or export. The country is self-sufficient in millet, sorghum, corn, and rice. The main export crops are cocoa, coffee, bananas, cotton, rubber, and palm oil. The cotton industry has experienced a significant revival in recent years.

Mineral resources include petroleum, which is produced in shallow waters near the Nigerian border, and bauxite, of which there are large deposits that have not yet been developed. Cameroon is also able to exploit its rivers for hydroelectric power, which meets 95% of national electricity demand.

Communications/Energy

PCs	0.3
Telephone lines	0.6
Mobiles	1.0
Internet users	0.1

(per 100 people, 2000) 0 20 40 60 80 100

Cameroon's road network has not been well maintained, and there are only 2,486 miles of paved roads in the country, with the rest being graded laterite or rural tracks. Road maintenance has recently been transferred to the private sector in order to improve effectiveness. Following the privatization of the railway company Camrail, the rail network is also being revitalized, having not received any significant investment since the 1970s. The performance of the country's principal port, Douala, which also handles much trade with landlocked Central African Republic and Chad, has been significantly improved in recent years.

New investment in the telecommunications sector is being made through the development of a mobile network under a joint venture between MTN of South Africa and the national telecommunications company Camtel.

A major innovation in 2001 was the part-privatization of the electricity generation company, Sonel, whose management was taken over by AES of the United States. Expansion of hydroelectric power generation is expected to begin with a new project planned at the Nachtigal falls on the Sanaga river. Cameroon's oil reserves stand at about 250 million barrels, sufficient for about five more years of production. Although special incentives are offered to companies undertaking new exploration and production, Cameroon's oil prospects are not considered as attractive as those of most of its neighboring countries.

Education/Employment

Educational provision has not kept pace with population growth, and primary school enrolment, which approached 99% of school-age children in the early 1980s, had slipped back to only 62% by the late 1990s. Education is provided by the government, missionary societies, and private concerns. There are six universities, producing some 70,000 graduates a year. The quality of the education offered has been adversely affected by reduced funding from central government.

The total labor force was estimated in 1997 as 5.6 million, of which 3.5 million were employed in agriculture. The largest sectors of formal employment are those concerned with community and social services, manufacturing, trade, and tourism.

Fiscal/Financial

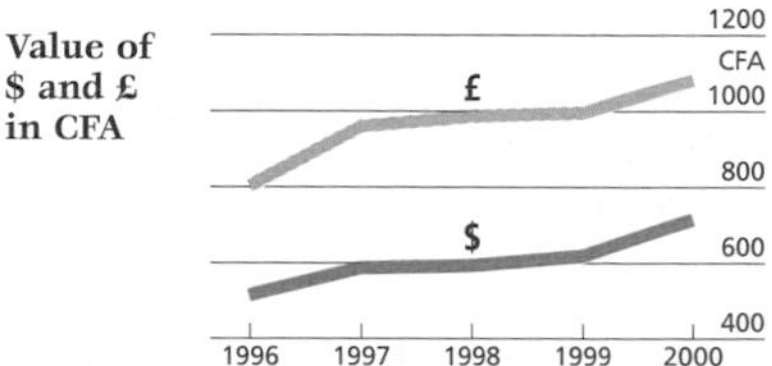

The central bank is the Banque des États de l'Afrique Centrale (BEAC), which is also the bank of issue for Central African Republic, Chad, Congo, Equatorial Guinea, and Gabon. The principal foreign banks represented in Cameroon are Citibank, Crédit Lyonnais, Société Générale, and Standard Chartered. The largest domestic bank, Banque Internationale du Cameroun pour l'Épargne et le Credit (BICEC), has been scheduled for participation by private interests.

There are plans to establish a stock market for the Central African region.

VAT has been in place since 1999. Companies exporting finished or semi-finished products attract special tax incentives.

Business Opportunities

Cameroon is receiving new investment as a result of the steady progress of its privatization program, which encompasses almost all commercial activity formerly owned and managed by the government. The economy is expected to benefit from the development of the Chad oil fields, which require the building of a pipeline through the heart of Cameroon. There are further opportunities in services, tourism, and manufacturing, especially in the production of finished wood products.

For More Information

Books:

Bayart, J.-F. *L'Etat au Cameroun*. Paris: Presses de la Fondation Nationale des Sciences Politiques, 1985.

Gaillard, P. *Le Cameroun*. Paris: Harmattan, 1989.

O'Brien, Donal Cruise, John Dunn, and Richard Rathbone. *Contemporary West African States*. New York: Cambridge University Press, 1990.

Schatzberg, M. G., and I. W. Zartman. *The Political Economy of Cameroon*. Westport, CT: Praeger Publishers, 1986.

Web Sites:

African news and information: **www.allafrica.com/business**

Investir en Zone Franc: **www.izf.net**

Norwegian Council for Africa, Index on Africa: **www.afrika.no**

Political Resources on the Net: **www.politicalresources.net**

Société Générale de Surveillance: **www.sgs.com/sgsgroup.nsf/pages/cameroon.html**

CANADA

KEY FACTS

GNI: **$614,003 million; world's 9th**
GNI pc: **$20,140; world's 30th**
Head of government: **prime minister**
Currency: **Canadian dollar (C$)**
Capital: **Ottawa**
Population: **30,857,000, growing at 1.2% p.a.**
Land area: **3,560,228 square mile**
Population density: **9 per square miles**
Life expectancy: **79 years**
Infant mortality: **6 per 1,000 live births**
Language: **English, French**
Best buy: **native art, pottery, pewter, leather goods, jade jewelry**

ECONOMIC STRUCTURE

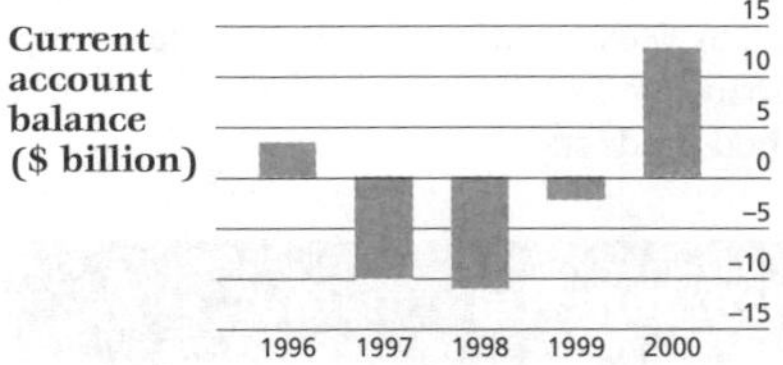

The Aboriginal people who settled Canada thousands of years ago were hunters, farmers and fishermen. These industries and minerals underpin the economy today. The British and French settled in the seventeenth century and established international trade. Eastern Canada became a British colony in 1759, but French law, and cultural and religious freedom were guaranteed in the province of Québec. In 1848 the Canadian government was granted autonomy over national affairs, and the federal system was established in 1867. New provinces and territories joined the federation in the nineteenth and twentieth centuries, the latest (in 1999) being the northern territory of Nanuvut, meaning "our land" in the Inuit language Inuktitut. In 1931 Canada's autonomy from Britain was confirmed by the Statute of Westminster. Canada industrialized during World War II. Government health and welfare programs were established after the war as the economy continued to grow.

Services contributed 67.3% of GDP in 2000, followed by manufacturing (18.2%), construction (5.4%), mining (3.5%), and agriculture (2.3%). Finance and real estate was the top services sector, accounting for 16.1% of GDP, followed by trade (12.9%), business services (6.3%), government services (6%), health (5.9%), education (5.2%), transport (4.6%), and communications (3.8%). The manufacturing base is diversified. The leading industry is transport equipment, followed by electrical and electronic products, food, chemicals, and metal products. The top exports in 2000 were machinery and equipment, followed by automotive products, energy products, forestry products, food, metals and metal products, and chemicals. The predominant market is the United States, which accounted for 85.8% of exports in 1999, followed by the European Union and Japan.

The economy is predominantly private-sector. Public-sector companies, especially in utilities and infrastructure, are owned by federal, provincial, and municipal governments. Most electricity generation and transmission companies are provincial public-sector monopolies. In the 1990s a few provinces liberalized the electricity sector, and some introduced privatization plans, Alberta's being the most advanced. Provincial and local governments are responsible for managing and pricing water supply. Liberalization of telecommunications began in 1979 and the process continues, guided by federal laws. Provincial public-sector companies are involved in general insurance, accounting for 32% of total road vehicle insurance in 1999. Some school boards, hospitals and universities have established self-insurance exchanges. Airports were privatized in 1994 and the air traffic control system in 1996. A program to transfer ownership of sea and inland ports to local not-for-profit organizations began in 1998. There are provincial and federal public-sector railway companies.

ECONOMIC POLICY

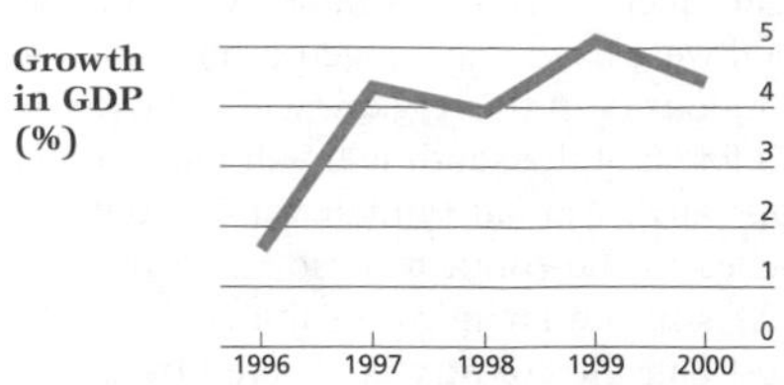

The government pursued fiscal austerity from 1993 to reduce the public debt from 120% of GDP in the mid-1990s to 106% in 2000, with general government budget surpluses from 1997 used to pay off the debt. From 2001 the government decided to allocate half of the budget surplus to new spending initiatives and half to debt reduction. Cuts in government spending in the 1990s were accompanied by tax cuts to boost the economy, a process which continues. Monetary policy targeted core inflation from 1991, the current target being 1–3%. Performance is expected to stay within this range. The main regulatory reforms carried out in the 1990s focused on improving competition and strengthening Canadian industry to compete globally, especially in finance, communications, and utilities, which affect the rest of the economy. Trade and investment restrictions for foreign companies are being rolled back in accordance with the North American Free Trade Agreement and World Trade Organization rules, but foreign investment remains restricted in key sectors, such as media and telecommunications.

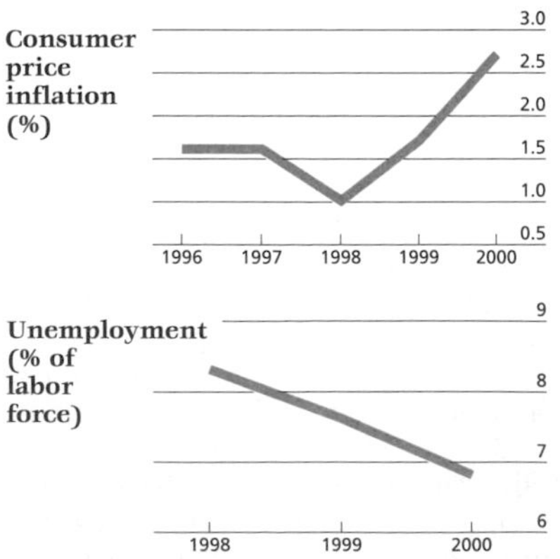

From an annual average 5.6% in the 1960s, GDP growth fell to 4.4% in the 1970s, and 2.9% in the 1980s. The recession of the early 1990s was followed by recovery to growth of 4.5% in 2000. It is expected to be

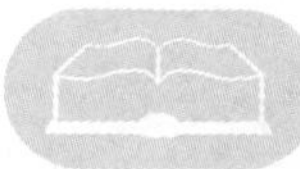

1.3% in 2001 and 1.7% in 2002, reflecting the economic situation in the United States. Inflation was an average 2.2% in 1990–99, rising to 2.7% in 2000 and 3% in early 2001. Unemployment fell from 9.6% in 1996 to 6.8% in 2000, its lowest level since the 1970s, but rose to 7.2% by September 2001.

Geography/Resources

Occupying the northern half of North America, Canada is the second largest country in the world with one of the lowest population densities: 9 people per square mile. It has land borders to the south and northwest with the United States, and borders the Atlantic Ocean in the east, the Arctic Ocean to the north and the Pacific Ocean to the west. In the southeast, Canada shares the Great Lakes with the United States. There are several distinct regions and climates: the temperate wet West Coast; the high mountains (highest point 19,546 feet) with heavy precipitation; the elevated prairies with cold winters, hot summers, and light precipitation; the lower-lying Great Lakes and St. Lawrence River region with cold winters, hot, humid summers, and heavy precipitation; the rugged Atlantic region with cool summers, cold winters, and heavy precipitation; and the north which is frozen for most of the year but has light precipitation. Boreal forest spans the entire country in the sub-Arctic region. There are about 2 million lakes, and it is estimated that Canada has one-seventh of the world's fresh water. The population is mostly urban (77% in 2000), and over half live in the Great Lakes–St. Lawrence region. An estimated two-thirds of Canadians are of European origin (including 17% of British Isles and 9% of French origin), with North American Indians, Métis (of mixed Native and European origin), and Inuit accounting for 3%, and African, Asian, and Arab communities for 6%.

Only 7% of the land is used for agriculture, but Canada is one of the world's leading food producers, especially of grains, oilseed, vegetables, meat, and dairy products. Wheat is the main crop, followed by barley, rapeseed, oats, peas, corn, soya, lentils, flaxseed, rye, canary seed, mustard seed, and sunflower seed. Fruit, vegetables, and legumes are also grown. Meat, dairy products, and eggs are important. Fisheries are significant, with herring the main species, but Atlantic fish stocks are under restriction orders. Forestry is a major industry, and Canada is one of the world's main producers of paper and board.

Canada is richly endowed with minerals. Reserves of main minerals in 1998 included 49 billion cubic feet of petroleum, 64 trillion cubic feet of natural gas, 8,122 million cubic feet of bitumen, 8.6 billion tons of coal, 10.2 million tons of zinc, 8.4 million tons of copper, 5.7 million tons of nickel, 1.8 million tons of lead, 312,000 tons of uranium, 121,000 tons of molybdenum, 15,738 tons of silver and 1,415 tons of gold. Other minerals produced include iron ore, cobalt, cadmium, bismuth, platinum, selenium, sulfur, potash, gypsum, asbestos, salt, nepheline, stone, and gravel.

Communications/Energy

The road network is over 559,260 miles, with 15,535 miles of national highways. The 4,536 miles Trans-Canada Highway links all 10 provinces. There are 18 major road gateways to the United States. Cross-border truck traffic accounts for 70% of U.S.–Canadian goods trade. The rail network is around 31,070 miles. CN Rail and the rail companies spun off from CP Rail account for most freight services. VIA Rail Canada, a federal state-owned company, provides national passenger services. Regional and local services are provided by 77 smaller companies. The pipeline network includes 13,643 miles for petroleum and 46,593 miles for natural gas. The main ports are Vancouver, Montreal, Halifax, Saint John, and Québec, with container terminals at the first three linking directly to rail. In 2000 the merchant fleet numbered 121 ships over 1,000 grt, with a total displacement of 1.8 million grt. The 2,300-mile Great Lakes/St. Lawrence Seaway system is the longest inland waterway in the world open to ocean shipping. There are nine major international airports, including Toronto, Vancouver, Calgary, Winnipeg, Edmonton and Ottawa and 300 smaller airports. About 400 million tons of freight travel by road. The railways handled 284.8 million tons of freight in 1998 and 4.2 million passengers in 2000. Ports handled 344 million tons of freight in 1999, while the major international airports handled around 450,000 tons.

Telecommunications services are fully competitive, with the exception of remote areas. Prices are capped by the federal government, with a levy on southern services to subsidize remote northern services, but this process was under review in 2001. International and domestic links are provided by cable and satellite. The 40 GB/sec CA*Net3, the world's first all-optical network dedicated to Internet traffic, was extended to much of Canada by mid-2000 and was due for completion in 2001. Internet access costs are low. At end-2000 there were 1.3 million subscribers to high-speed Internet services, 917,000 of whom used cable and about 500,000 used digital subscriber lines. A further 3.7 million households were connected to the Internet, and 8 million subscribed to cable TV. There were 18.5 million fixed phone lines and 3 million mobile phones in 1999.

Electricity was 60% generated by hydroelectric power in 1999, 26% by thermal power (oil, gas, and coal), 12% by nuclear, and 1% by geothermal energy. Canada was the largest producer of hydroelectricity in the world in 1999. It exported 44.9 billion kWh and imported 16 billion kWh. It is a significant net energy exporter, exporting 30% of energy production, mostly to the United States. In 1999 natural gas accounted for 36% of primary energy production, petroleum 23%, hydropower 20%, coal 11%, and nuclear 4%. In 2000 oil production was 2.2 million barrels per day and natural gas 6.3 trillion cubic feet. Alberta contributes two thirds of Canada's primary energy, especially gas and oil, and is also a major consumer. As Alberta's oil reserves are becoming depleted, companies are producing "synthetic" crude oil from the Athabasca oil sands deposit in northern Alberta, with output expected to reach 1.8 million barrels per day in 2010. There are several major untapped oil and gas fields on the western and eastern seaboards, and in the Arctic.

Education/Employment

Education is compulsory from age 6 or 7 to 15 or 16. There are 100 universities and 200 technical institutes and community colleges. Enrollment is around 1 million students, 60% of whom attend university. Education is the responsibility of provincial governments, which set standards and curricula, and provide most of the financing for institutions. Municipal authorities and the federal government also fund institutions, and the federal government provides financial assistance to students. Fees contributed a greater share of funding from the 1990s as public budgets were cut.

Universities conduct R&D for companies. The government agency Industry Canada coordinates several R&D programs between the public and private sectors. The National Research Council launched regional technology cluster schemes in 2000 in Nova Scotia and Newfoundland, focusing on IT, genomics, biotechnology, medical diagnostics, and marine sciences. Other R&D strengths include geology, materials science, space sciences, forestry, agriculture, and pharmaceuticals.

The labor force is well educated. Wages and other employment conditions are

determined between employers and employees or trade unions. Trade union membership is 18.2% of the private-sector workforce and 71% of the public-sector workforce. Provincial employment law applies to most industries, and provincial governments also set minimum wages. Federal law, the Canada Labor Code, governs airlines, railways, and banks. It also sets general benchmarks for provincial legislation.

Fiscal/Financial

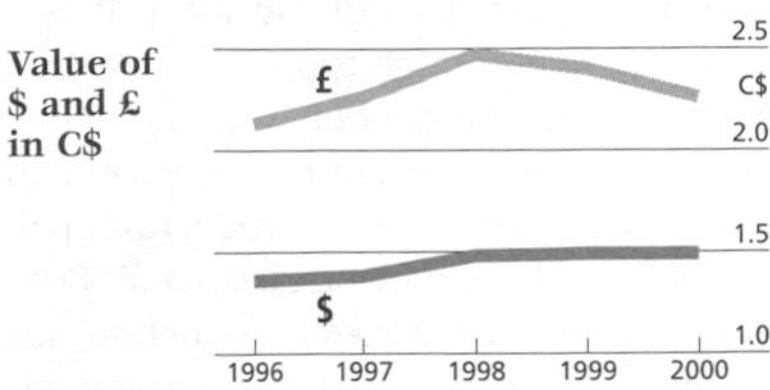

The largest banks at end-1998 were Canadian Imperial Bank of Commerce, followed by Royal Bank of Canada, Bank of Nova Scotia, Bank of Montreal, Toronto-Dominion Bank, and National Bank of Canada. All are private-sector. The largest insurance companies were Great-West & London Life, General Accident, Mutual & Metropolitan Life, Cooperators Group, and Royal & SunAlliance Canada. All are private-sector. General Accident and Royal & SunAlliance are British-owned.

The Bank of Canada is the central bank. Banking supervision is a federal responsibility conducted by the Office of the Superintendent of Financial Institutions. Under the 1999 framework for financial sector change, the 10% shareholding restriction for the largest banks will be raised to 20% to enable them to compete better globally. Banks own insurance and securities-trading subsidiaries. Four large life insurance companies recently announced decisions to demutualize. Other reforms will include a broader range of permitted investments for banks and trust companies; revision of capital taxes; and more flexible structures for life insurance companies, credit unions, securities dealers, mutual funds, and trust companies.

Standard federal corporate profits tax is 27%, with 21% for small businesses as of 2001. Provincial governments levy a minimum corporation tax of 10%, and the federal government allows a 10% tax credit for this. The top federal rate of personal income tax is 29%. Top provincial rates are around 9–11%.

In early 2001 the six main banks accounted for 79% of business loans, 67% of finance institution deposits, 60% of mortgage loans, and 62% of consumer credit. They had over 8,000 nationwide branches and held around 88% of banking industry assets. In addition, 40% of their net revenue derived from foreign operations. The five smaller domestic banks accounted for 2% of bank assets and included the "virtual" Citizens Bank of Canada, which operates via telecommunications technology, and First Nations Bank, which is due to become wholly owned by the aboriginal community in 2006. The 42 foreign bank subsidiaries, offering wholesale financing services, accounted for 10% of bank assets. Since June 1999, foreign banks have been allowed to open lending branches, which may not take deposits, or full-service branches, which can take deposits greater than C$150,000. HongKong Bank of Canada is the largest foreign bank, and has an extensive branch network. In early 2000 the 2,200 credit unions had 10 million members—one-third of the population—and total assets of C$110 billion. The movement is most developed in Québec, Saskatchewan, and British Columbia. The insurance industry is divided into general and life sectors. Foreign companies dominate the former, which comprised 230 firms in early 2001, and domestic companies the latter, which included 132 firms. The life insurance sector has a strong international business.

The Canadian stock market was born in a Montreal coffee house in 1832 where railway shares were traded. The Montreal Stock Exchange opened in 1874. Other exchanges followed in Toronto, Alberta, Winnipeg, and Vancouver. In the late 1990s the Toronto Stock Exchange (TSE) became the sole market for equities, the Montreal Exchange (ME) for derivatives, and the Canadian Venture Exchange (CDNX, a merger of the Vancouver, Alberta and Winnipeg exchanges) for small high-growth firms. The TSE was the world's seventh largest stock market in 1999. There were 188 securities firms at end-1999, including 7 full-service firms owned by banks, 53 serving the institutional market, and 128 the retail market. Internet trading is increasing.

Business Opportunities

There are a wide range of federal and provincial investment incentives, including tax breaks and financial and practical assistance, for targeted sectors which include IT,

Growth in output (% p.a., 1990–99)

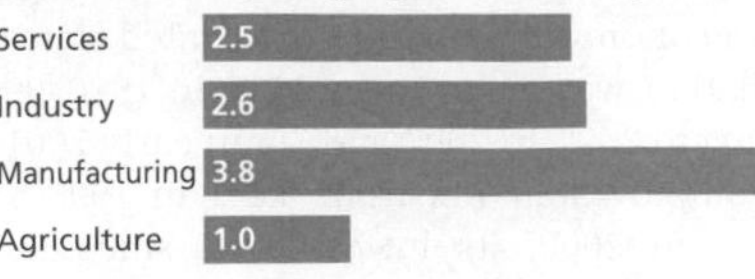

biotechnology, R&D, and regional development. Incentives are available to foreign and Canadian firms, but there are limits on foreign investment in financial services, cultural industries, commercial aviation, mining, telecommunications, fishing, electricity, health care, and real estate. The Investment Canada Act regulates foreign investment. Special arrangements apply to U.S. investment under the North America Free Trade Agreement. There is one free trade zone at Cape Breton, Nova Scotia. The mining (including oil and gas), telecommunications, banking, insurance, and automotive industries, among others, have attracted inward investment from the United States, European Union, Japan, China, and other countries. Opportunities exist in these and other sectors, and to a lesser extent in privatization programs. The point of contact for investors is Investment Canada, part of Industry Canada.

For More Information

Books:

Canada (Eyewitness Travel Guide). Rev. ed. New York: Dorling Kindersley, 2001.

Economist Intelligence Unit. *Country Profile and Quarterly Reports*. London.

IMF Country Report. *Canada*. Washington, D.C.: IMF.

Jackson, R. J. *Politics in Canada: Culture, Institutions, Behaviour and Public Policy*. 4th ed. Upper Saddle River, NJ: Prentice Hall, 1998.

Lightbody, Mark, Thomas Huhti, and Ryan Ver Berkmoes. *Canada*. 7th ed. Oakland, CA: Lonely Planet, 1999.

OECD Economic Surveys. *Canada 2000*. Paris: OECD, 2001.

Web Sites:

Canadian Tourism Commission: **www.canadatourism.com**

Communication Canada: **www.cio-bic.gc.ca**

Government entry point: **www.canada.gc.ca**

Toronto Stock Exchange: **www.tse.com**

Cayman Islands

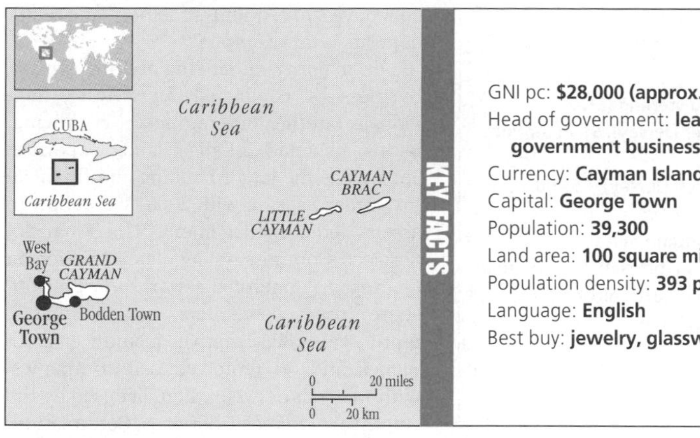

GNI pc: **$28,000 (approx.); world's 11th**
Head of government: **leader of government business**
Currency: **Cayman Islands dollar (CI$)**
Capital: **George Town**
Population: **39,300**
Land area: **100 square miles**
Population density: **393 per square mile**
Language: **English**
Best buy: **jewelry, glassware**

Economy

Offshore financial services and tourism dominate the Cayman economy, accounting between them for the bulk of foreign exchange earnings. Construction is another significant sector, providing considerable employment as the hotel and office building boom continues, along with domestic property development. Manufacturing is of minor importance, with production of construction materials and tourism-related goods heading the sector's output. Agriculture is constrained by poor soil and urbanization, producing fruit, vegetables, and some meat; fishing is likewise a small-scale activity.

The islands run an overwhelming trade deficit, exports in 1999 amounting to only CI$1 million, against imports of CI$457 million. The United States is the principal supplier of imported goods.

Economic policy is based on continued promotion of the externally-oriented sectors, revenue from which offsets the habitual trade deficits. Inflation has stayed at around 3% per annum through most of the 1990s, but public debt increased in the second half of the decade, leading to pressure for a reduction in government employment and expenditure.

Geography/Resources

There are three islands, Grand Cayman, Cayman Brac, and Little Cayman. Almost the entire population lives in Grand Cayman, with about 2,000 in Cayman Brac, and fewer than 100 in Little Cayman. Grand Cayman is about 175 miles south of Cuba and the same distance west of Jamaica; the two smaller islands are about 80 miles northeast of Grand Cayman. The islands contain no rivers, but there is a large mangrove swamp in Grand Cayman, which also has extensive coral reefs.

Approximately half the population live in George Town on Grand Cayman, and there is considerable pressure on available building land in the area of the capital. The continuing development of the tourist and business sectors has created a labor shortage which has been filled by immigration: at the 1999 census, 47% of the population was of non-Caymanian origin. About 25% of the population is of African descent, 20% of European descent, and the remainder of mixed origin. There are strict controls on permanent immigration, and most migrant workers are on short-term permits.

Communications/Energy

International airlines provide links with London, various U.S. cities, the Bahamas, Jamaica, and Honduras. Grand Cayman and Cayman Brac have international airports. The three islands are linked by air, but not by passenger ferry. There are about 200 miles of paved road.

The main telecommunications service is provided by Cable & Wireless, with Mercury also operating a link to Britain. Electric power in Grand Cayman is supplied by the Caribbean Utilities Co., which has 90 MW of installed capacity; the Cayman Brac Power and Light Co. operates on that island, with 3.5 MW capacity.

Fiscal/Financial

There are no direct taxes on personal or corporate income, and the main sources of government revenue are import and stamp duties, business registration and licensing fees, tourist taxes, and airport departure tax. Import duty accounts for about half of total revenue. Administration and supervision of the financial system is the responsibility of the Cayman Islands Monetary Authority, established in 1997. The stock exchange was established at the same time, and at the end of 1999 had 210 companies listed, with market capitalization of $21 million. Out of 580 banks and trust companies registered at the end of 2000, six offered retail banking services.

In addition to banking, the financial sector includes a substantial offshore insurance sub-sector, specializing in health insurance; a mutual funds register containing more than 3,000 entries at the end of 2000; a shipping register; and a general offshore company register accounting for almost 60,000 companies at the end of 2000.

Business Opportunities

The financial sector offers the most advantageous investment prospects in the islands, followed by tourism. There is no corporation tax, capital gains tax, or estate duty, and exempt companies obtain a 20-year guarantee of freedom from direct taxation, renewable for 10 years. There are no restrictions on repatriation of capital or remittance of earnings, and company registration is a swift and straightforward process.

The Cayman Islands was listed by the Financial Action Task Force of the Group of 7 developed countries in mid-2000 as a jurisdiction described as "non-cooperative" in relation to money laundering. The government declared its intention of working closely with the FATF to obtain its removal from the list.

For More Information

Books:

Cameron, Sarah. *Caribbean Islands Handbook*. 13th ed. Bath, Somerset: Footprint Handbooks, 2001.
Quarterly Reports and Annual Profiles. London: Economist Intelligence Unit.
Smith, Roger C., Gene A. Smith, and James C. Bradford. *The Maritime Heritage of the Cayman Islands*. Gainesville, FL: University Press of Florida, 2001.

Web Sites:

Department of Tourism:
www.caymanislands.ky
Economist Intelligence Unit:
www.eiu.com

CHANNEL ISLANDS

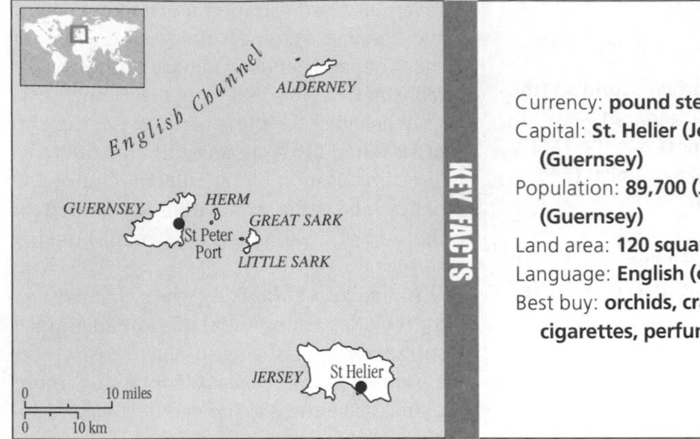

KEY FACTS

Currency: **pound sterling (£)**
Capital: **St. Helier (Jersey), St. Peter Port (Guernsey)**
Population: **89,700 (Jersey); 65,400 (Guernsey)**
Land area: **120 square miles**
Language: **English (official), French (legal)**
Best buy: **orchids, crafts, alcohol, cigarettes, perfume**

ECONOMY

Offshore finance and insurance are the main sectors, followed by tourism. Agriculture provides the main exports. Finance accounts for around 60% of GDP in Jersey and agriculture for 5%. Finance contributed 64% of Guernsey's GDP in 1999, followed by real estate (13%), tourism (12%), industry (8%), and horticulture (3%). Guernsey's industrial and trading sector includes electronics, plastics, pharmaceuticals, boat building, textiles, printing, crafts, LPG gas distribution, and an international optician chain. Light industrial products are Guernsey's main exports, followed by flowers and vegetables, mostly for the U.K. market. Jersey's main exports are agricultural products, especially potatoes and tomatoes, also for the United Kingdom.

Both bailiwicks have tightened up financial regulation, including anti-money-laundering measures, to meet the concerns of the OECD, EU, and IMF. There is an ongoing dialogue with the OECD regarding cooperation with other authorities on tax matters. The two bailiwicks have built up substantial public financial reserves. They have balanced budgets and no public debt. They have invested in a fiber-optic cable to provide the basis for e-commerce, and have also invested in a joint stock exchange. Otherwise Jersey and Guernsey are rivals. Jersey set limits on public spending for 2001–03 to help reduce inflation from 4.4% in 2000 to 2.5%. Guernsey's inflation peaked at 4.5% in September 2000 but fell to 2.6% in September 2001. Tax changes in 2002 in Guernsey were aimed at encouraging property investment and easing personal taxes, while increasing the government's overall tax revenues to pay for investment in tourism, schools, hospitals and transport infrastructure. Tourism is seen as essential for maintaining air and ferry links to the islands, which are vital to the finance centers. Guernsey has plans for hotel refurbishment, a casino, and a new airport as part of a public–private partnership strategy.

GEOGRAPHY/RESOURCES

The Channel Islands are a group of islands close to northwest France. Jersey is the largest and Guernsey the second-largest. There are no significant mineral resources. The majority of people are of Norman origin, but many high net worth individuals, mostly of United Kingdom and other European origin, have settled in the Channel Islands. Business professionals of European origin work in the finance sectors.

COMMUNICATIONS/ENERGY

There are roads on most of the islands but no railways. Jersey and Guernsey both have airports and sea ports. Jersey Telecoms and Guernsey Telecom had monopolies until competition was introduced in 2000 and 2001 respectively to reduce prices and facilitate e-commerce. Guernsey Telecom and London-based Digital Mobility launched a service providing mobile-phone financial, travel, sports and other information at end-2000. Energy needs, principally oil and LPG, are imported. Electricity is produced locally.

FISCAL/FINANCIAL

Income and corporation tax is low, and has often been tailored to individuals and particular companies, a practice criticized by the United Kingdom and international organizations. There is no VAT or sales tax. Non-resident income from financial trusts, collective investment schemes, and bank deposits is tax-exempt.

The majority of banking and investment business is conducted for private individuals, but the corporate sector is growing, taking advantage of the islands' expertise. Jersey has the larger banking and financial investment sector, with £300–350 billion in assets under management. The Financial Services Commission regulates the sector. Guernsey is one of the world's largest offshore insurance centers. At March 2001 there were 323 captive insurance companies and 30 protected cell companies, with 143 cells between them licensed by the Guernsey Financial Services Commission. In addition there were 44 domestic insurers and 52 intermediaries at end-2000. Securitization of insurance assets is a growth area. At end-2000 Guernsey had 77 banks with total deposits of £68.5 billion. The Channel Islands Stock Exchange, based in Guernsey, began operations in October 1998.

BUSINESS OPPORTUNITIES

Banking, insurance, real estate, tourism, and light industry have attracted foreign investment. Investment in real estate is restricted by residency requirements, currently under review. E-commerce is being promoted by the Jersey Information Society Commission and the Guernsey Board of Industry. The latter is also the point of contact for foreign investment in industry and tourism.

For More Information

Books:

Annual Report. Jersey Financial Services Commission.
2001 Economics and Statistics Review. Advisory & Financial Committee, Economics Unit, States of Guernsey.

Web Sites:

Channel Islands Stock Exchange: **www.cisx.com**
Guernsey Financial Services Commission: **www.gfsc.guernseyci.com**
Guernsey government entry point: **www.gov.gg**
Jersey Financial Services Commission: **www.jerseyfsc.org**
Jersey government entry point: **www.gov.je**

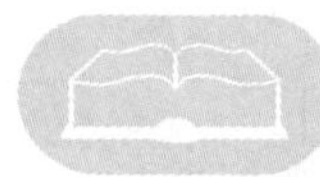

CHILE

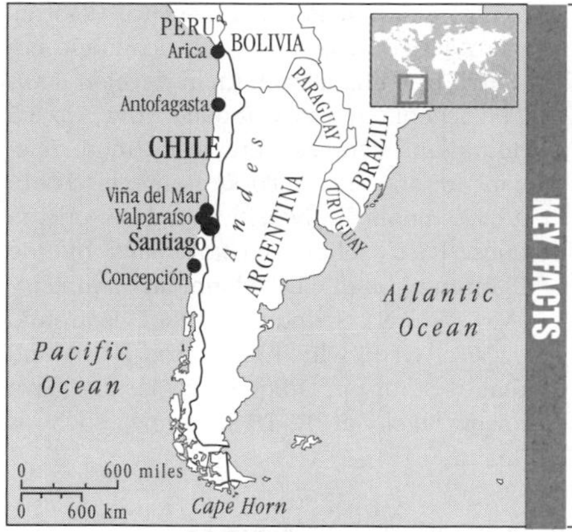

KEY FACTS

GNI: **$69,602 million; world's 43rd**
GNI pc: **$4,630; world's 70th**
Head of government: **president**
Currency: **peso (Ps)**
Capital: **Santiago**
Population: **15,019,000, growing at 1.5% p.a.**
Land area: **289,112 square miles**
Population density: **52 per square mile**
Life expectancy: **75 years**
Infant mortality: **11 per 1,000 live births**
Language: **Spanish**
Best buy: **lapis lazuli jewelry, handicrafts**

ECONOMY

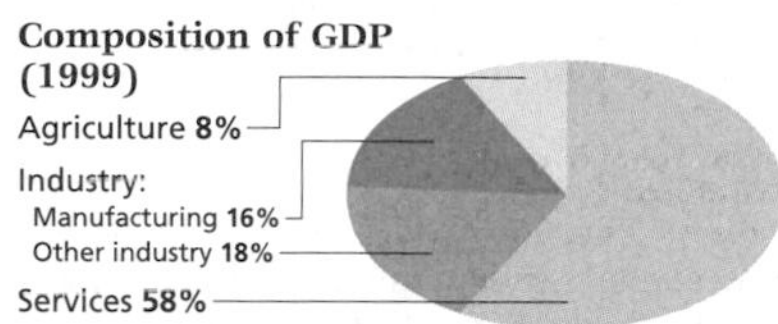

The 1973 coup by General Augusto Pinochet, which overthrew the leftist government of Salvador Allende, brought to an end 150 years of practically uninterrupted civilian and democratically-elected government. Democracy returned in 1989 following a referendum and elections, although in 2001 the military still enjoyed a privileged position. Defense, including military pensions, represents around 16% of total public expenditure, a very high figure. The Pinochet regime replaced the largely state-run economy with a free-market system, pioneering many of the reforms that later galvanized Latin America, notably privatization, export-led growth, debt-equity swaps, and private pension funds. Chile is an associate member of Mercosur, the free-trade block comprising Argentina, Brazil, Paraguay, and Uruguay. In 1994 it became the first South American country invited to join the North American Free Trade Agreement (NAFTA) but by the end of 2001 "fast-track" negotiations had still not started. Chile's single import tariff rate was cut from 9% in 2000 to 8% in 2001, and was scheduled to drop to 7% in 2002 and 6% in 2003.

Chile has been the star economy of Latin America. Services generate 60% of GDP, agriculture 8%, and industry 32%. The International Institute for Management Development (IMD, a Swiss business school) ranked Chile the 24th most competitive economy in the world in 2001 and the first in Latin America. Mining, forestry, and fresh fruit are the biggest export industries. Copper has long been the biggest single export. In the 1980s Chile emerged from almost nowhere to become the southern hemisphere's leading fruit exporter. The main export markets are Japan, the United States, the United Kingdom, and Brazil.

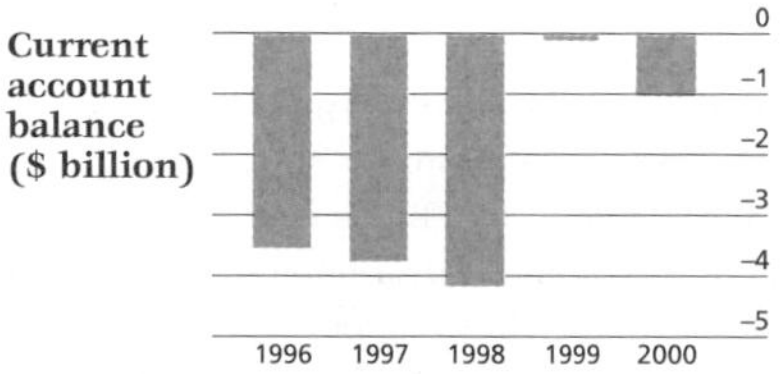

The 1973–90 military-led government reduced the state's share of GDP from 39% to 16%, and this remained virtually unchanged over the next decade. Moves to privatize water utilities and ports began in 2001.

ECONOMIC POLICY

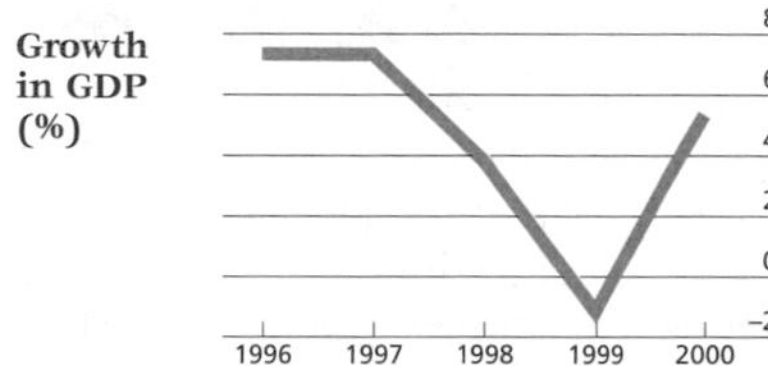

Liberalization has made Chile the best-performing Latin American economy: real GDP growth averaged 3.5% in 1979–89 and accelerated to 7.6% in the ten years to 1998. The economy went into recession in 1999 (–1.1% growth), recovered in 2000 (+5.4%), and then slowed in 2001 (3.0%), partly because of depressed copper prices. Despite diversification, the economy is still dangerously dependent on the metal (two-fifths of exports in 2000). The government, however, has operated a counter-cyclical fiscal policy since 1989. Whenever the copper price is above a certain level, the government puts part of the earnings of the state-owned Codelco into a stabilization fund which it draws on when the price is low. Inflation has been in single figures since 1994. Fiscal surpluses were generated during most of the 1990s (5.6% of GDP in 1996), and a small deficit in 2001. Tax revenue is quite strong at 18% of GDP. Sound finances earned the country an investment-grade credit rating. Income distribution, however, has hardly improved. The top 10% of earners receive 47% of income, and the poorest 10% less than 2%, according to the latest World Bank figures.

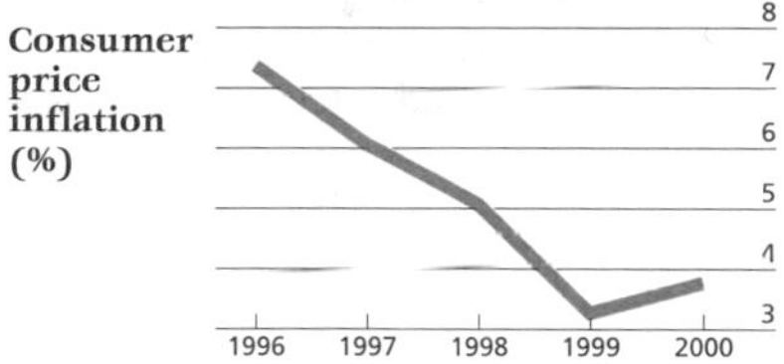

A significant factor behind the relatively healthy public finances has been the creation of private pension fund administrators (AFPs) to supplant the state social security system, and the promotion of private health insurance to supplement public health care (ISAPREs). The AFPs transferred large amounts of funds under the control of the state to the private sector for investment, and provided incentives for workers to save. AFP investment limits were made more flexible in 2001.

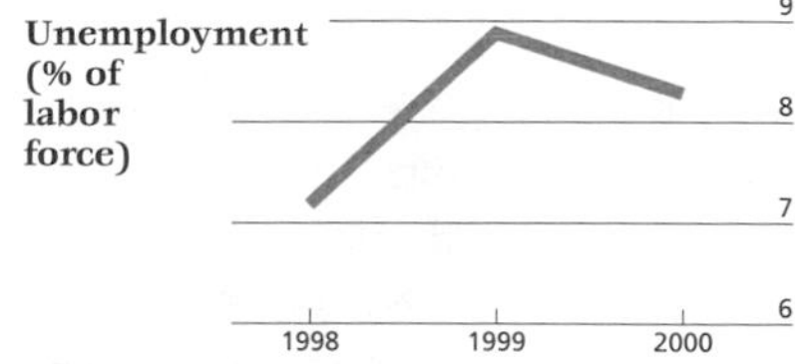

As an export-oriented economy, Chile has a strong external sector. The trade account was in surplus in 1973–2000 apart from in three years when the deficits were largely due to changes in the international prices of Chile's main export commodities (copper, fishing, forestry, fresh produce). The current account deficit was relatively low in 2000 at 1.4% of GDP, and remained at close to this level in 2001. External debt was

estimated at $37.3 billion in 2001 (59% of GDP and 203% of exports).

GEOGRAPHY/RESOURCES

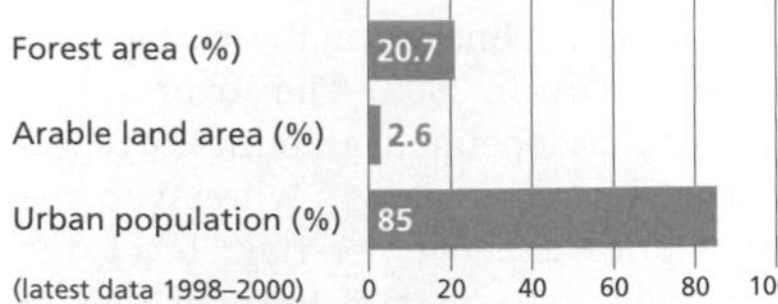

Chile curves snake-like down 2,670 miles of coastline between the Pacific and the Andes. The country is 225 miles wide at its broadest point, and 60 miles at the narrowest. It is so narrow that at some points it is possible to see the snow-capped peaks of the Andes in the east and the Pacific in the west at the same time. Chile is bounded by Peru to the north, Bolivia and Argentina to the east, and the Pacific to the west. The westernmost territory is Easter Island, which was incorporated into Chile in 1888.

Mixed European and indigenous peoples (mestizos) account for about 75% of the population (15 million in 2000); 23% are of European descent and 2% Indians, mainly Mapuches.

Agriculture employs about 12% of the workforce. The main export crops are corn, beans, asparagus, onions, and garlic. Table grapes, wine, citrus fruits, avocados, pears, nectarines, and nuts are also strong exports. The mining sector, led by Codelco, the world's largest copper producer and the mainstay of the economy, generates close to 10% of GDP. Chile has around 20% of world copper reserves. There is also mining of silver, gold (the El Indio mine is one of the highest grade mines in the world), iron ore, lithium, manganese, and mercury.

COMMUNICATIONS/ENERGY

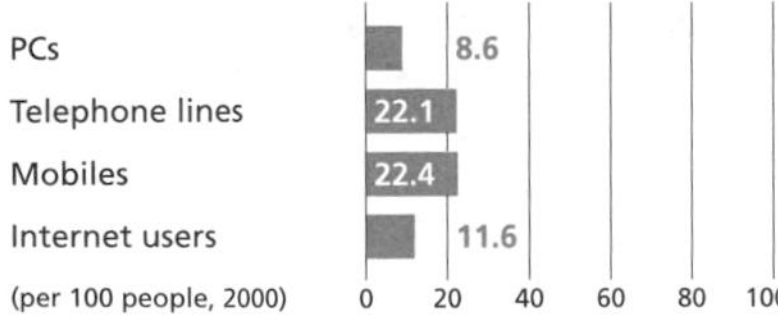

Chile had 14,200 miles of roads in 1999 and 5,557 miles of rail track. Probably out of gratitude to truck drivers, whose strike in 1973 crippled the economy and helped the military to power, the "leftist" railways were starved of money and became rundown. This situation began to change in 2001 under an investment program by the state-run EFE to develop and improve passenger-train suburban services into Santiago from towns on the line south. EFE is responsible for the southern system, the most populous area, and Ferronor runs the network covering the mining areas between Iquique in the northern First Region to La Calera in the Fifth Region. Almost all (95%) of Chile's foreign trade is handled by ports. About 80% goes through the four main ports: Antofagasta in the mining north, Valparaiso and San Antonio in the central part of Chile, and San Vicente in the south. Most cities have an airport for domestic flights. Santiago is the main international airport.

Chile produces around 40% of domestic energy consumption. Hydroelectric power is the main source, with dams supplying more than 60% of power to the main central Chile grid. The largest project under way, and scheduled to be inaugurated in 2004, is the 570 MW Ralco project, owned by Spain's Endesa, Chile's leading generator. Imported natural gas is the single fastest-growing energy source. With completion of pipelines from Argentina and, in the future, Bolivia's highlands, its share of energy is expected eventually to reach 28%. Coal reserves are located in the center and southern central regions and in the far south. Reserves of crude oil are minimal, although there are offshore fields at the Straits of Magellan and onshore at Tierra del Fuego.

The telecommunications industry was transformed during the 1990s by privatization and deregulation. By 2003 the number of fixed telephone lines was expected to reach 32.6 per 100 inhabitants (24.5 in 2000), the highest teledensity in Latin America, and it was predicted that 15 out of every 100 Chileans would have a mobile phone. There were just over 1 million Internet subscribers in 2000.

EDUCATION/EMPLOYMENT

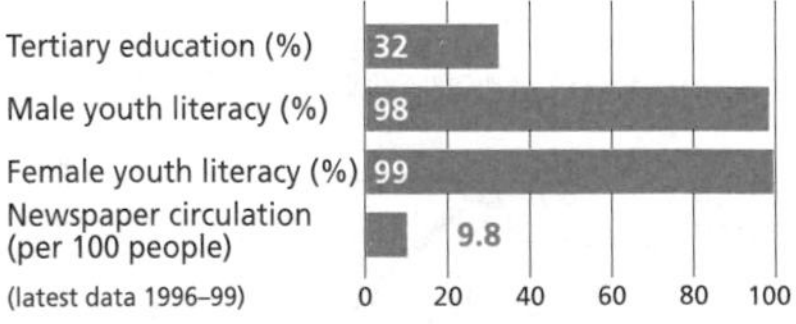

According to the UN Development Program, Chile is in first place in Latin America for fostering "human development" (combining economic achievements with standards of education, health, and equity in income distribution). Spending on education, which is compulsory and free from age 6 to 14, doubled in real terms over the 1990s, and in 2000 stood at a high 7% of GDP, although almost half of that is spent by parents, either on higher education or on private schooling for the 10% of children who do not go to state schools. Over 80% of children complete secondary education, and the government's aim is to increase that to almost 100% by 2006. One-fifth of secondary school children go to university. Reforms were aimed at boosting the economic potential by enhancing human development. The school day was extended from 5 to 8.5 hours, and courses were made more relevant to labor market requirements. There are 25 public universities and 45 private ones. R&D policy is coordinated by the Planning and Development Ministry (MIDEPLAN). Spending on R&D is around 0.7% of GDP, which is not too far behind that of European Union countries that have lower levels of R&D spending, such as Spain.

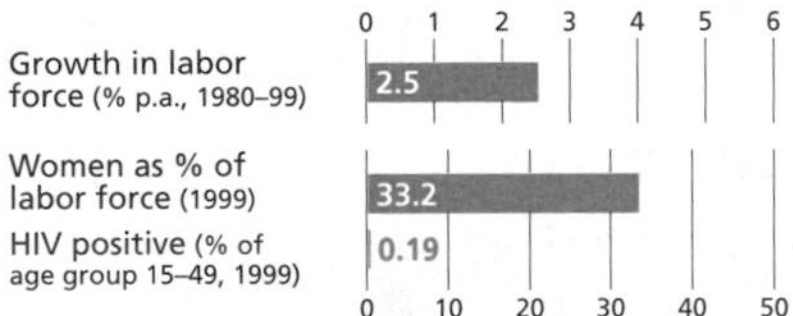

Chilean workers have a reputation for discipline and hard work. Another strength is the availability of qualified information technology employees. Traditionally there is a large degree of state intervention in determining wages and employment conditions. A new labor law in 2001 raised the cost of laying off workers. Unionized labor is strongest in state companies, particularly Codelco, whose Copper Workers Union is an elite within the labor force. In addition, 10% of Codelco's export earnings revert by statute to the armed forces (averaging about $250 million a year during the 1990s). These are two factors that make the privatization of Codelco difficult.

FISCAL/FINANCIAL

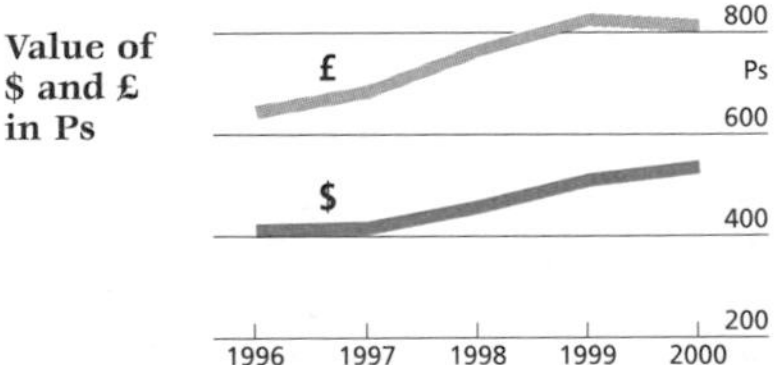

The two largest private-sector commercial banks, Banco Santiago and Banco Santander Chile, are owned by Spain's Banco Santander Central Hispano. Together they have around one-quarter of total deposits. There are five other main banks, including the state's Banco del Estado de Chile. The thriving banking sector is a far cry from 1982, when the financial system almost collapsed because of loose intra-group lending practices and the coun-

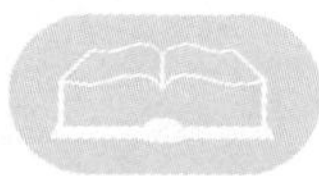

try's economic problems. Solvency ratios are now in line with international requirements, and credit risk indices and non-performing loan rates are low by Latin American standards, a hallmark of post-1982 reforms. The Central Bank enjoys a European-Union-style independence from the government.

The market capitalization of the Santiago Stock Exchange represented a high 88% of GDP in 2000. Despite being an open economy, Chile had capital controls and a confusing exchange rate policy with multiple exchange rates during the 1990s. These were introduced to discourage short-term speculative investment, and were credited with having insulated Chile from the international financial contagion suffered by Latin America on repeated occasions. The last remaining controls on cross-border capital flows were lifted in 2001, as they were anachronistic in a globalized business environment and a disincentive to foreign investment. The reforms also included the elimination of capital gains tax for foreigners for both equity and fixed-income investments. This met the need of foreign investors to be able to move quickly. Legal and administrative procedures were also streamlined, and the "encaje" (reserve requirement) eliminated for banks.

More than 25 companies, representing around two-thirds of stock market capitalization, are quoted abroad in ADR form.

Corporate tax is 15%, the top rate of personal income tax 45%, and VAT 18%.

Business Opportunities

Growth in output (% p.a., 1990–99)

Services	7.6
Industry	6.2
Manufacturing	5.0
Agriculture	1.1

Chile has been one of the most favored Latin American economies for foreign direct investment (FDI). It received an annual average of $5.6 billion in 1997–2000, up from $1.1 billion in 1985–95. Most of the FDI, which peaked in 1999 at $9.4 billion, went into the banking, mining, telecommunications, and electricity sectors. There are no restrictions on foreign investment, although Codelco is off-limits for political reasons. However, private involvement in the copper industry is growing, by putting to tender the exploitation of new infrastructure projects such as transportation. Energy is a key sector that requires foreign investment if Chile is to continue to increase its electricity capacity and avoid power shortages. Spain overtook the United States in the late 1990s as the largest investor.

The bureaucracy involved in setting up companies is stifling; a bill to cut the red tape made slow progress through Congress in 2001.

For More Information

Books:

Bernhardson, Wayne. *Chile and Easter Island.* 5th ed. Oakland, CA: Lonely Planet, 2000.

Caistor, Nick. *Chile in Focus.* Northampton, MA: Interlink Publishing Group, 2002.

Chislett, William. *Chile Stability and Progress.* New York: Euromoney Institutional Investor, 1993.

Economist Intelligence Unit. *Country Profile and Quarterly Reports.* London.

Financial Times Country Surveys. *Chile.* London: Financial Times.

Márquez, Gabriel García. *Clandestine in Chile.* New York: Penguin, 1989.

O'Shaughnessy, Hugh. *Pinochet: The Politics of Torture.* New York: New York University Press, 2000.

Web Sites:

Central Bank of Chile: **www.bcentral.cl**

Foreign Investment Committee: **www.cinver.cl**

IMF reports: **www.imf.org/external**

National Statistics Institute: **www.ine.cl**

Santiago Stock Exchange: **www.bolsadesantiago.com**

Santiago Times (English language newspaper): **www.chipnews.cl**

U.S. State Department Country Commercial Guide: **www.state.gov/e/eb/rls/rpts/ccg**

CHINA

KEY FACTS

GNI: **$979,894 million; world's 7th**
GNI pc: **$780; world's 142nd**
Head of government: **president**
Currency: **yuan (Y: external), renminbi (RMB: internal)**
Capital: **Beijing**
Population: **1,266,838,000, growing at 1.0% p.a.**
Land area: **3,601,309 square miles**
Population density: **352 per square mile**
Life expectancy: **70 years**
Infant mortality: **33 per 1,000 live births**
Language: **Mandarin, Yue (Cantonese), minority languages**
Best buy: **silk, leather goods, jade**

ECONOMIC STRUCTURE

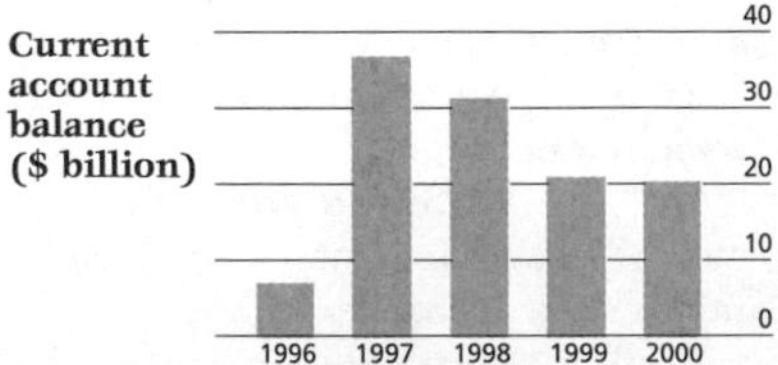

China was one of the earliest civilizations, with developed scientific, engineering, commercial, and artistic skills. The People's Republic of China was formed as a communist state in 1949. Initially centralized along Soviet lines, its main thrust was to develop heavy industry. Neglect of agriculture led to famine, and in the 1960s powers were devolved to local government to invest in agriculture and light industry. The centrally-inspired, but very locally-applied, Cultural Revolution in 1966–76 curbed local power and also held back economic development. In 1976 reforms began towards a more market-oriented economy. From 1979 foreign investment was encouraged in export manufacturing from special economic zones, and by the 1990s foreign companies could manufacture for the domestic market. Restructuring of state-owned enterprises began in the mid-1980s, and private enterprise increased. In the 1990s, labor-intensive industry relocated from Hong Kong, Taiwan, and other countries to mainland China. Control of Hong Kong from 1997 gave China a strong financial and trading base for future development.

Industry, including manufacturing, mining, energy, and water, accounted for 44.3% of GDP in 2000, followed by services (33.2%), agriculture (15.9%) and construction (6.6%). Within the services sector, finance and public administration contributed 19.5% of GDP, trade 8.2%, and transport and communications 5.5%. China is one of the world's largest producers of cotton clothing and textiles. Other textiles include woolens, silks, and acetates. Chemicals, steel, cement, machinery, electronics, bicycles, and other transport equipment are important in a broad-based manufacturing sector. The main exports in 2000 were machinery and transport equipment (42.3%), followed by clothing (14.5%), computer and telecommunications equipment (10.8%), and textiles yarn and fabrics (6.5%).

At mid-2001, state-owned enterprises (SOEs) accounted for an estimated two-thirds of GDP and jobs. The long-term plan is to privatize all corporations except those in sectors considered essential to national security. Such sectors include telecommunications, energy, and transport, although there has been liberalization in each of these. It is estimated that 70–80% of small SOEs at county and municipal level have been privatized or corporatized, and that most such sell-offs have been to insiders. Privatizations of large SOEs in 2000 and 2001 included steel, chemicals, a mobile phone operator, and the second-largest petroleum company. Other sectors likely to be privatized include textiles, furniture, trade, and other services.

ECONOMIC POLICY

The government sets prices for a wide range of products and services. It also sets interest rates and fees in the financial system. Chinese enterprises are required to exchange foreign currency for renminbi, and to apply to the banks for foreign exchange when they need it. Foreign enterprises are allowed to

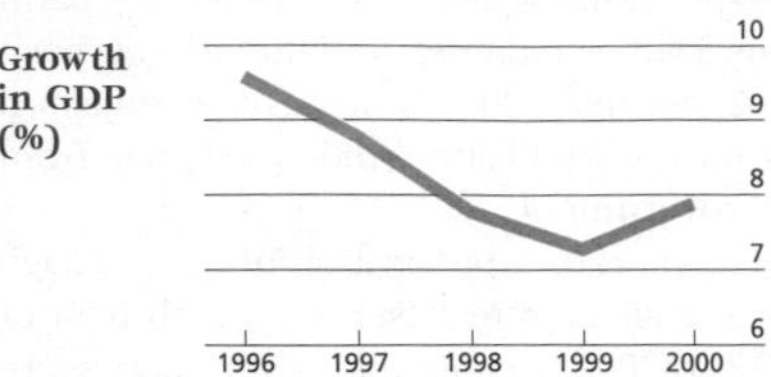

keep foreign exchange accounts. The government has IMF backing to make the renminbi fully convertible once the Chinese economy is better integrated with the global economy.

The transformation of the state sector to market conditions to comply with WTO membership poses a major challenge. Reforms to contract law and corporate governance are being implemented to bring legal structures in line with international standards. The weight of state-sector financing and public debt is not fully reflected in central or local government budgets, since many operations are financed off-budget. The cost of social services, including housing, health, pensions, and other welfare payments—even the police in some cases—was borne by SOEs in the past. Local governments now have to finance these services, but there is a shortfall of funds. Two market consequences—the rapid growth of housing loans and insurance—have not been matched by adequate risk management assessment by the banks or capitalization of the insurers. In 2000 the government established a National Social Security Fund to finance pensions. Individual contributions and allocation to the fund of 10% of the proceeds of privatization is mandatory. A Trust Law for institutional investors was enacted in April 2001, but further framework legislation is needed to underpin the institutional investment market and to define the role and scope of the National Social Security Fund, which will be a major player in this market. The government's emphasis on industrializing the rural areas, where most people live, and on developing the disadvantaged regions, offers better prospects for alleviating poverty.

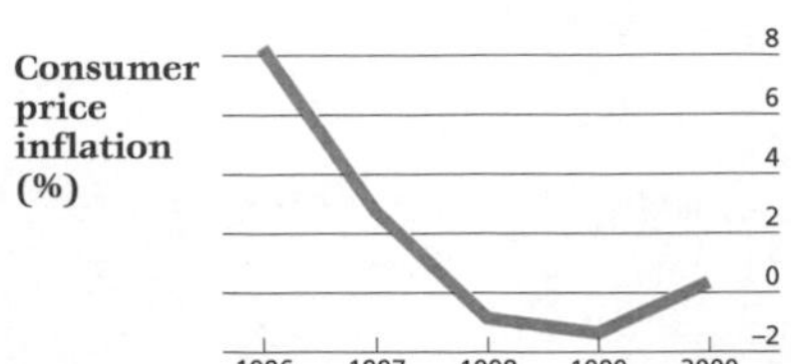

GDP growth was an annual average 8.6% in 1995–2000, driven by domestic consump-

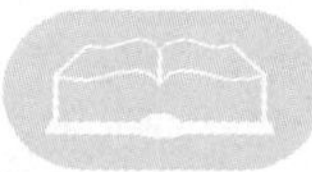

tion and investment. It is expected to average 7.2% a year in 2001–03. Inflation fell from 17.1% in 1995 to 2.8% in 1997. There was deflation of 0.8% and 1.4% in 1998 and 1999 respectively. Inflation resumed at 0.4% in 2000, rising to around 1% in 2001, and is expected to be 2% to 3% in 2002–03. Registered urban unemployment rose from 2.9% in 1995 to 3.2% at mid-2001, or 6.6% including workers dismissed following state enterprise reforms. However, there is significant urban unemployment among the 60–80 million "floating population." In 2000, the World Bank estimated that 230 million (18.5% of the total population) were living in poverty.

Geography/Resources

China is the third-largest country in the world. Two-thirds of the population are rural, mainly in the eastern plains. China is the most populous country in the world. The majority of people (92%) are of Han Chinese origin, the rest comprising more than 20 other indigenous nationalities.

There is a wide range of agricultural crops, although only 10% of the land is arable. Pasture accounts for 43% and woodland for 14%. Forestry is significant, especially for fuel wood and industrial wood. Crustaceans, anchovies, and mackerel are main marine fisheries species. Freshwater fish account for 10% of the fish catch.

The main minerals produced are petroleum, natural gas, coal, iron ore, salt, phosphates, manganese, bauxite, zinc, lead, magnesite, copper, graphite, sulfur, tungsten, potash, tin, antimony, molybdenum, silver, mercury, and gold. There are reserves of uranium, vanadium, and wolfram. At January 2001 proven oil reserves were 24 billion barrels while natural gas reserves were 48.3 trillion cubic feet. Recoverable coal reserves were 126.2 billion tons. Exploration indicates significant new gas reserves and some new prospects for oil.

Communications/Energy

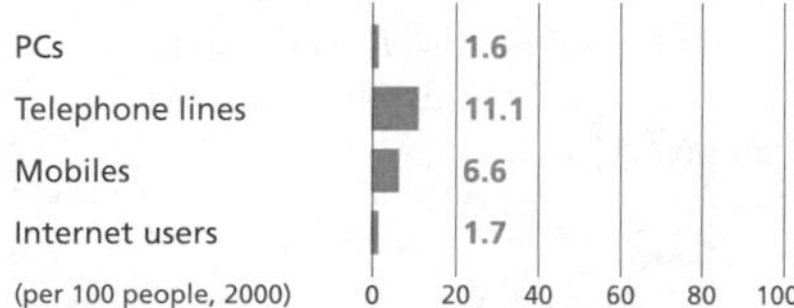

The road network was 838,890 miles in 1999, of which 789,178 miles were paved. There were 5,644 miles of motorways. The rail network was 35,993 miles, of which 7,322 miles were electrified. The inland waterway network was 68,540 miles, with 70 major inland ports and over 5,000 shipping companies. The petroleum and gas pipeline network was a total of 15,473 miles In 1999, 9.9 billion tons of freight went by road, 1.67 billion tons by rail, 1.15 billion by inland waterway, 202.3 million by pipeline, and 1.7 million by air. Road accounted for 39 billion passenger-miles, rail for 41.36 billion, waterways for 10.7 billion, and air for 8.57 billion. There are over 2,000 sea ports, the main ones being Shanghai and Guangzhou. There were 143 civilian airports at end-2000, over 80 of which can handle long-haul aircraft. Thirty new airports are due for completion by 2005.

Domestic and international telecommunications links are provided by fiber-optic cable and satellite, but provincial access is uneven. The sector was partly opened to competition in 1999, but China Telecom remains dominant. The number of fixed phone lines was 160 million, and there were 111 million mobiles at May 2001. There were 8.9 million Internet subscribers and 22.5 million Internet users at end-2000. The cable TV network was 1.5 billion miles in 2000. There were 80 million cable subscribers and 5,300 operators, mostly owned by local governments and communities. The network carries high-speed Internet access and telephony. After WTO accession China will phase out restrictions on foreign operators.

China is the largest world producer and consumer of coal (23% of the 1999 total), and the second-largest energy consumer after the United States. Net oil and coal imports are expected to increase, especially from Russia. Gas consumption is set to triple by 2010, and will include imports as well as new domestic production. Coal consumption will double by 2020. Electricity demand is expected to increase by 5.5% a year until 2020. Electricity is mostly generated from fossil fuels (79.8% in 1999), followed by hydro (19%) and nuclear (1.2%). Coal production was 1 billion tonnes in 2000, with consumption at a little less and net exports at 59 million tons. Petroleum production was 3.2 million barrels per day, with consumption at 4.6 million barrels per day. Natural gas production and consumption were 850 million cubic feet in 1999. In 1999 coal accounted for 68.2% of total energy production, oil for 20.9%, hydro for 7.8%, and natural gas for 3.1%.

Education/Employment

Education is compulsory from age 7 to 16, but it is not free. Government funding provided 82.7% of the total education budget in

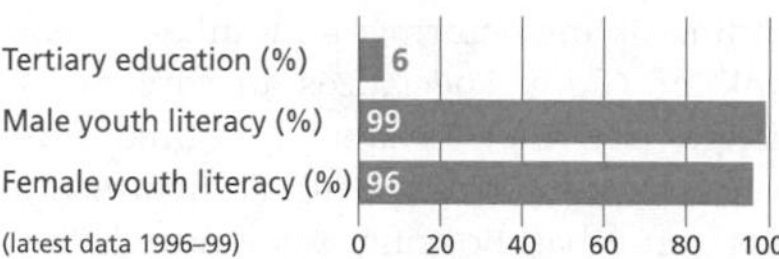

1999, while tuition fees accounted for 6.8%, donations and fund raising for 5.5%, and other funds—including those from social organizations and citizens—for the rest. The Ministry of Education and the governments of the provinces, autonomous regions, and municipalities are responsible for education. There were 1,074 higher-education institutions in 1999, the majority of which were specialized by subject. The largest categories were scientific and engineering (264), teacher training (227), short-term vocational training (161), medicine (118), and economics and finance (74). There were 74 comprehensive universities. Universities are developing distance-learning programs to increase the number of graduates. Scholarships are available for students in higher education.

In 1999 there were 17,498 high-technology enterprises with 2.2 million workers and exports of $11.9 billion. Expenditure by the state-owned enterprises on natural science and technical R&D was Y47.6 billion, 67.5% of which was provided by the government. Y6.35 billion was spent on R&D in higher education. The National Natural Science Foundation of China funds basic and applied research. Biotechnology and microelectronics are priority R&D sectors.

The labor force is well-educated, but there are shortages of skilled labor. Minimum wages are set by local authorities. Under the Labor Law, wages, working conditions, insurance, and welfare are negotiated between employers and the official All-China Federation of Trade Unions, the only permitted trade union. Collective agreements apply in around 90% of foreign companies. Enterprises are often required to provide subsidized housing and health care. Employers' contributions to pension funds can be up to 20% of the total wage bill.

Fiscal/Financial

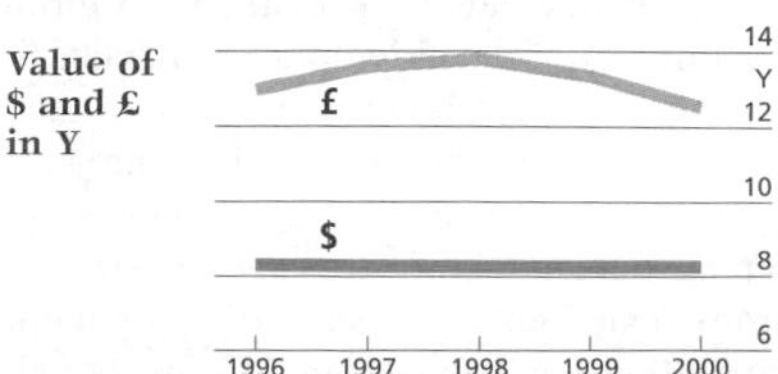

The four main commercial banks are state-owned and specialized. The Industrial & Commerce Bank of China is the largest,

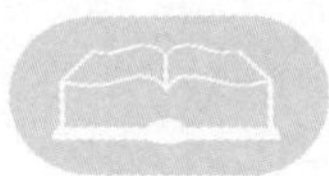

funding manufacturing and urban areas. Bank of China specializes in foreign exchange and trade financing. China Construction Bank finances infrastructure projects and urban housing. Agricultural Bank of China finances farming and other rural operations. The leading insurance companies are all state-controlled. People's Bank of China is the central bank and regulates the financial sector. China Securities Regulatory Commission supervises the stock markets, and China Insurance Regulatory Commission the insurance sector. The creation of a single supervisory agency is under consideration.

Standard profits tax is 33%. In the 14 coastal open cities it is 25%, and in the special economic zones 15%. Other preferential rates apply in the 52 economic and technological zones, and in disadvantaged regions. New foreign enterprises benefit from three years of reduced tax. VAT is applied at 17%. The government will phase out the two-tier tax system for domestic and foreign companies after WTO accession, with the result that many tax breaks will be eliminated. However, lower levels of VAT for high-tech industry and other priority sectors will be introduced. Tax collection was centralized in late 1999.

Resolving nonperforming loans (NPLs), the legacy of planned finance, is a major component in reforming and strengthening the financial sector. According to World Bank estimates, total NPLs accounted for around 41% of GDP in 2000. Although the four asset management corporations (AMCs) established in 1999 for SOE reform absorbed Y1,300 billion in NPLs in 2000, the major banks still had bad loans representing up to 50% of their total lending. Special bonds were issued in 1998 to recapitalize these banks, but government-ordered interest rate reductions eroded the benefit. Interest rates were liberalized for domestic banks in September 2000. Transparency and disclosure rules for banks listed on the stock exchange were tightened in November 2000. Second-tier domestic commercial banks have successfully raised equity through the Shanghai Stock Exchange.

Three policy banks, specializing in infrastructure, rural development, and trade financing, were established in 1994 to take over the government investment projects formerly financed by the four main commercial banks. There are several smaller commercial banks. Trust and investment corporations, which suffered from a high level of NPLs, were barred from raising funds overseas and required to separate their stockbroking and other business in 2000. The separation led to the creation of large securities investment firms. Growth areas of finance include housing loans—although many of these had turned sour by end-2000—mutual funds, pension funds, and Internet banking. Insurance is also expanding rapidly, but the World Bank considers most insurers to be undercapitalized. Access of insurance companies to the stock market has been restricted, but liberalization is planned. Second-tier insurance companies are restricted geographically; these limits will be phased out after WTO accession. At end-2000 there were 13 domestic Chinese insurers, including four SOEs and nine joint stock companies. There were 17 foreign firms, and foreign investment in one domestic insurer. The insurance industry grew at an annual average rate of 26.7% from 1980 to 1999. It is expected to grow by 13% a year in 2001–06.

There are plans for the two stock markets, at Shanghai and Shenzhen, to be merged, with all main board operations handled in Shanghai and a board for high-growth companies to be launched in Shenzhen. Foreign currency listings were opened to domestic investors in early 2001. The restriction on foreign investment in renminbi listings will be phased out. Trading and disclosure rules were tightened in 2001.

Business Opportunities

Growth in output (% p.a., 1990–99)

Services	9.2
Industry	14.4
Manufacturing	13.9
Agriculture	4.3

Tax incentives are offered, but corporation tax rebates must be reinvested in China for at least five years. There are special economic zones at Shenzhen, Shantou, Zhuhai (near to Macau), Xiamen and Hainan, and in 14 coastal cities. In addition there are designated development zones and cities, free ports, and bonded zones, all with separate investment incentives. After WTO accession the number of investment incentives will be reduced, and barriers to foreign investment in many sectors—including banking, insurance, distribution and telecommunications—will be phased out. Red tape constitutes a barrier to investment. Present investment priorities include high-tech industries, the central and western regions, transport, communications, energy, electronics, metallurgy, construction materials, machinery, chemicals, pharmaceuticals, medical equipment, and environmental protection. Manufacturing absorbed most foreign direct investment in 1998–99, followed by real estate, utilities, social services, transport and telecommunications, construction, and trade. The main investor was Hong Kong, followed by the United States, Japan, Singapore, Taiwan, South Korea, and the United Kingdom.

For More Information

Books:

Chang, David Wen-Wei, and Richard Y. Chuang. *The Politics of Hong Kong's Reversion to China*. New York: Palgrave Macmillan, 1999.

China (Macroeconomic Update). Paris.

China (Macroeconomic Update). Washington, D.C.: World Bank.

China Council for the Promotion of International Trade. *China Business Guide*. Beijing: Huaxia Publishing House, 1996.

Cook, Sarah, Shujie Yao, and Juzhong Zhuang, eds. *The Chinese Economy Under Transition*. New York: Palgrave Macmillan, 2000.

MacFarquhar, R., ed. *The Politics of China: The Eras of Mao and Deng*. 2nd ed. New York: Cambridge University Press, 1997.

Seligman, Scott D., and Edward J. Trenn. *Chinese Business Etiquette: A Guide to Protocol, Manners and Culture in the People's Republic of China*. New York: Warner Books, 1999.

Shen, Xiaobai. *The Chinese Road to High Technology*. New York: Palgrave Macmillan, 1999.

Spence, Jonathan D. *The Chan's Great Continent: China in Western Minds*. W. W. Norton, New York, 1998.

Yeung, Henry Wai-Cheung, and Kristopher Olds, eds. *The Globalization of Chinese Business Firms*. New York: Palgrave Macmillan, 1999.

Web Sites:

China Council for the Promotion of International Trade: **www.ccpit.org**

Ministry of Foreign Affairs: **www.fmprc.gov.cn/eng**

COLOMBIA

KEY FACTS

GNI: **$90,007 million; world's 37th**
GNI pc: **$2,170; world's 100th**
Head of government: **president**
Currency: **peso (Ps)**
Capital: **Bogotá**
Population: **41,564,000, growing at 1.9% p.a.**
Land area: **401,042 square miles**
Population density: **104 per square mile**
Life expectancy: **71 years**
Infant mortality: **26 per 1,000 live births**
Language: **Spanish**
Best buy: **emeralds**

ECONOMIC STRUCTURE

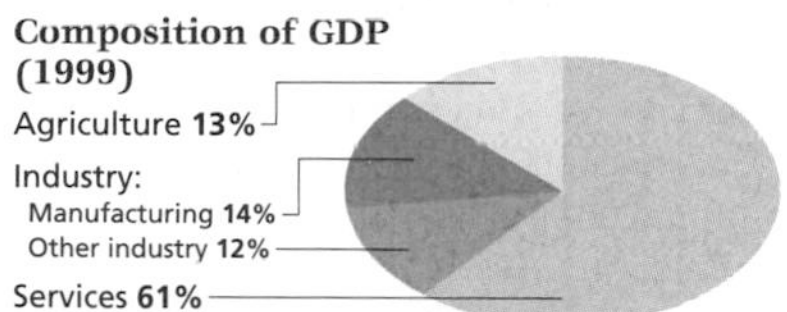

Colombia has been wracked by political violence since the 1950s. During the 1990s an estimated 35,000 people—most of them civilians—were killed or disappeared in the war between, on the one hand, the Revolutionary Armed Forces of Colombia (FARC) and the smaller National Liberation Army (ELN), the world's oldest Marxist guerrilla movements, and, on the other, the security forces aided by bands of right-wing paramilitary vigilantes. Peace talks began in a demilitarized zone in 2001. Under the $7.5 billion U.S.-supported 'Plan Colombia', one element in the intricate peace process, the Colombian armed forces aimed to control the rebel-dominated coca-growing regions which supply the bulk of the cocaine used in the United States. Estimates for the size of the illegal drug trade vary from $1 billion to more than $5 billion per year.

Services account for around 63% of GDP, industry 25%, and agriculture 12%. The largest industries are food processing, beverages, and textiles, followed by chemicals, leather goods, shoes, and clothing. The principal exports are crude oil and derivatives, coffee (Colombia is the world's second-largest producer after Brazil), coal (the world's fourth-largest exporter), and exotic items such as cut flowers (the world's second-largest supplier). As recently as 1986, coffee accounted for more than half of exports, and still accounts for one-third of rural employment. In the early 2000s, coal was set to overtake coffee as the second-largest export. The United States takes more than one-third of exports, many of which enjoy tariff-free entry to the U.S. market under the Andean Trade Preference Act. Colombia forms part of the Andean Pact, a free trade agreement between Peru, Bolivia, Ecuador, and Venezuela.

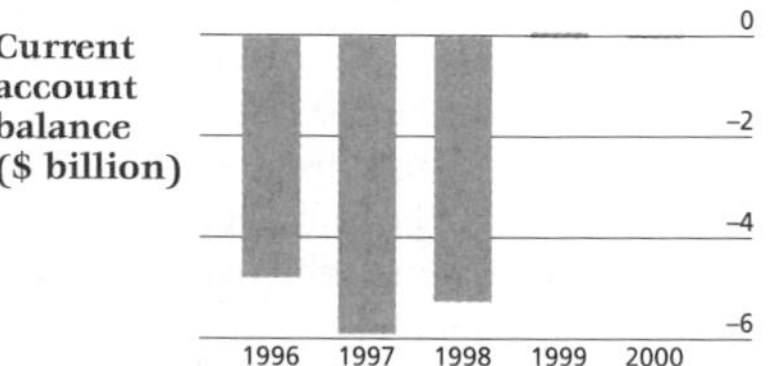

The economy began to be opened up during the 1990s with the privatization of sea ports, highways, electric power generation and distribution firms, telecommunications, and banks. Privatization of ISAGEN, the third-largest power generator with a market share of 14%, and the power grid ISA, was in process in 2001–02.

ECONOMIC POLICY

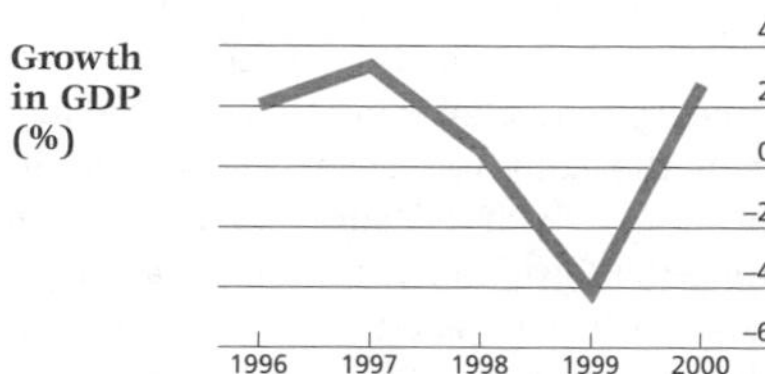

Average annual real GDP growth was 3.4% in 1979–99, one of the most sustained in Latin America during that period. In 1999, the economy went into its first recession (–4.1%) since the 1930s. Unemployment reached a record 20%, and the fiscal deficit reached 7.5% of GDP. The economy recovered modestly in 2000 (2.8%), with inflation close to 9% and a lower budget deficit (5.9% of GDP). GDP growth in 2001 was less than 2%. The International Monetary Fund (IMF) came to the rescue in 1999 with a three-year $2.7 billion agreement which targeted spending cuts, social security reform, and much-needed pensions reform. Labor market reform, further energy and telecommunications privatizations, and restructuring of the financial sector were also planned. The Central Bank adopted an inflation-targeting framework, following its shift to a managed currency float in 1999.

In order to ease the domestic debt burden, a debt swap in 2001 amounting to at least 1.2% of GDP reduced amortizations and improved the schedule for the next four years. The external debt of was estimated at $36 billion at the end of 2001 (45.0% of GDP and 278% of exports, up from 30% and 262% respectively in 1997).

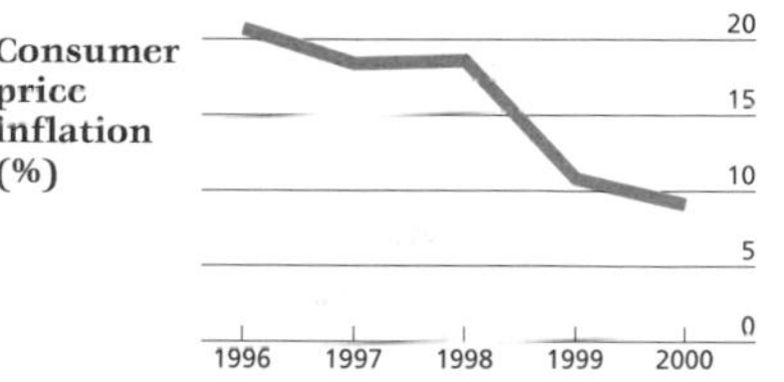

Fiscal solvency depends largely on reducing the transfers from the central government to local governments, and on reforming the state pension system. Tax revenue is around 13% of GDP. The government wanted to raise both pension contributions and the retirement age, and to eliminate special regimes for members of Congress, teachers, oil workers, and the armed forces. Spending on pensions rose from 0.8% of GDP in 1991 to 2.3% in 2000, yet less than one-third of those eligible are covered. High unemployment means that many workers are unable to make contributions.

GEOGRAPHY/RESOURCES

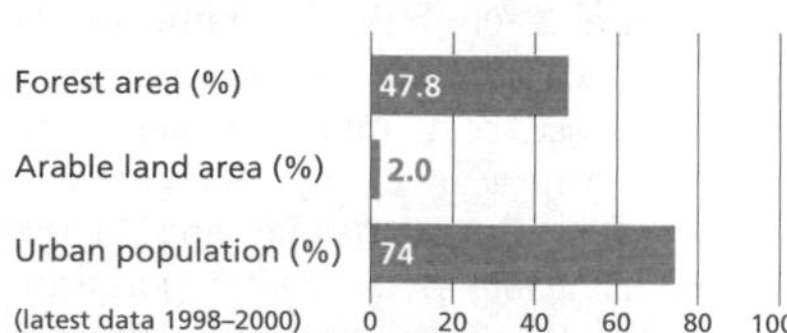

Colombia is bounded to the north by the Caribbean Sea, and by the Pacific Ocean in the west. Panama separates the two waters

and connects the country with Central America. Colombia also borders Venezuela, Brazil, Peru, and Ecuador. Three ranges of the Andean mountain system cut through the western half of the country—the Western, Central and Eastern Cordilleras, which join to form a single range at the border of Ecuador. Tributaries of the Amazon and the Orinoco rivers cross the lower eastern plain. Over half of Colombia is covered in immense forests. The country is prone to earthquakes; the one in 1999 which devastated the coffee-producing region of Eje Cafetero killed 1,185 people and left 150,000 homeless.

Mining, mainly oil and coal, generates 5% of GDP. There is also iron ore, nickel, gold, copper, and over 90% of the world's top-grade emeralds. The Muzo mine in the Eastern Andes is the world's largest emerald mine.

Around 58% of the population (42 million) are mestizo (mixed Amerindian and white), 20% white, 14% mulatto, 1% Amerindian and 8% other races. On the coast live black peoples, who are the descendants of slaves.

Communications/Energy

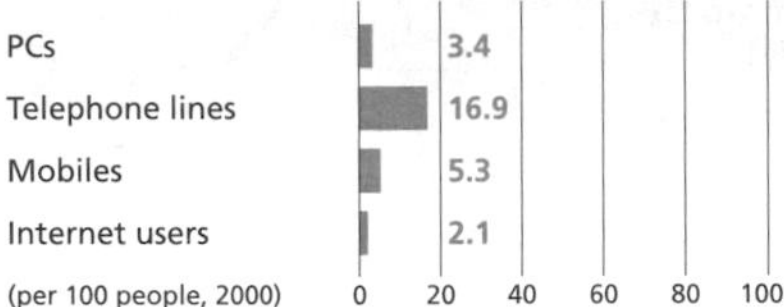

The difficulty of transport is one reason why it has been difficult to develop the country. Bogotá, for example, is 8,530 feet above sea level. Until the Atlantic Railway was built, goods not carried by air had to be loaded and unloaded many times between Bogotá and the Caribbean coast. There are more than 71,460 miles of roads, of which some 8,700 are paved. The road network suffers from lack of maintenance: in 1999 only 37% of the paved roads were considered to be in good condition. The government has opened new highway concession projects calling for the construction, rehabilitation, and maintenance of 4,031 miles of roads.

There are 2,100 miles of railways—93 miles of which connect the Cerrejon high-tech open-cast coal mine managed by Exxon, an American energy company, to the port at Bahia de Portete—and 11,185 miles of navigable rivers. Other ports are Barranquilla, Buenaventura, and Cartagena. There are international airports at Bogotá, Barranquilla, Cartagena, Cali, and Medellín. Air transport has long been important in Colombia, which boasts the world's second-oldest scheduled airline.

Hydroelectricity supplies around 70% of power. In order to meet the growing demand for electricity in 2001–10 that is expected to grow by an average of 5.9% each year, Colombia needs to add 6,200 MW to its installed capacity. Sabotage to the electricity grid cost an estimated $175 million in 2000.

Oil production peaked in 1999 at 815,000 barrels per day (100,000 barrels per day in 1980) following the discovery of new reserves at Cusiana and Cupiagua. The country has about 2.6 billion barrels of proven reserves, and possibly ten times this amount in potential reserves, but progress in exploration has been slow. The state oil giant Colombian Petroleum Corporation (Ecopetrol) warned that the country could become a net oil importer by 2005 if sufficient new deposits were not discovered. Oil pipelines have been frequently attacked by guerrillas. Oil is gradually being replaced by other energy sources, in particular hydroelectric power and coal.

The telecommunications market opened for long-distance and international calling in 1998, with two private consortia competing with the state telecommunications monopoly. Teledensity is the third highest in Latin America after Chile and Argentina. There are almost 20 fixed lines per 100 inhabitants, most of them in the largest cities, and over 2 million mobile phone subscribers. The network is expected to be fully digital by 2005. The government committed itself to a plan to attract $100 billion in investment for the sector over the 1997–2007 period.

Education/Employment

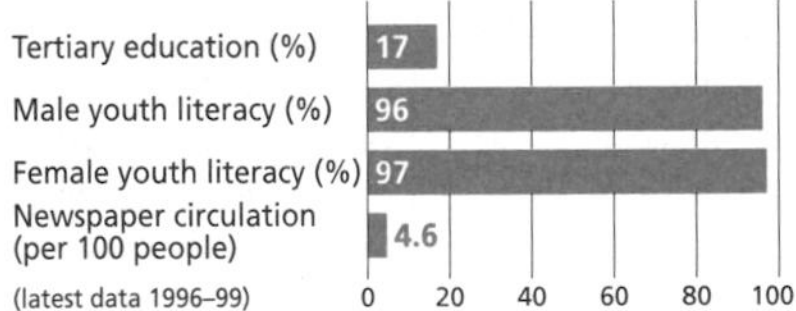

Colombia can boast nearly universal primary education among its urban labor force, but less than half of its children go on to secondary schooling. This is in part the legacy of the country's scant investment in education, which in per capita terms is among the lowest in Latin America. Many state schools operate on two and even three shifts, and around 40% of the secondary schools are privately owned and run. The World Bank helped to fund a short-term incentive program in the late 1990s to provide individual student vouchers which could be used in private schools.

The best known universities are the University of the Andes (private) and the National University (public). Spending on R&D is marginal.

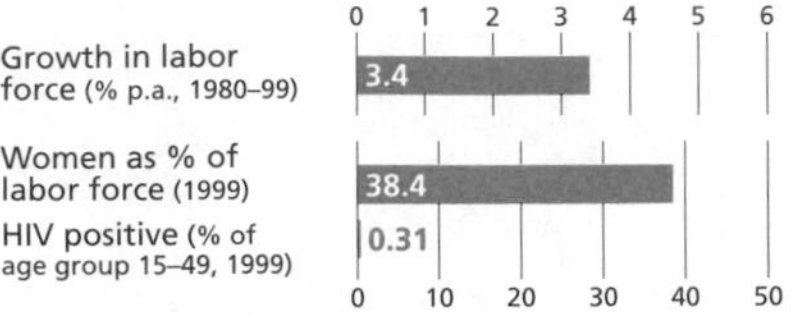

Much of the high unemployment is structural, reflecting the mismatch between the skills of Colombian employees and the education-skill requirements of the labor market. This gap has widened since the economy began to be liberalized in 1991. The country also suffers from a brain drain, largely due to harassment and violence in the workplace, and the inadequate protection of personal security and private property. Colombia's murder rate in proportion to the population is the world's highest. The well-educated tend to emigrate. Legislation does not establish salary levels for specific occupations or professions, but it is mandatory to pay the minimum wage ($124 per month in 2001).

Fiscal/Financial

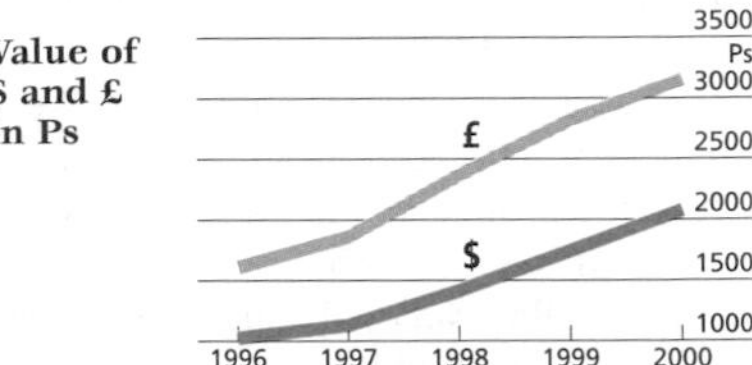

Colombia's banking crisis in the late 1990s, following a credit boom and insufficient supervision, led to the closure, merger, or takeover of 70 financial institutions in 1997–2000 (one-third of total bank/non-bank institutions). Politicians plundered state-owned banks and under restructuring their number was reduced from nine to four. Estimates of the total financial cost of bailing out the banks ranged from 6% of GDP to as much as 15%. The largest privately-owned banks are Bancolombia, Banco de Bogotá, and the Spanish-owned BBVA Banco Ganadero. The largest state bank is Bancafe. Minimum capital requirements for the creation of new financial entities were increased as of 1999, and supervision tightened. Banco de la República, the central bank, is independent of the government.

Both corporate tax and the top rate of personal income tax are 35%, and VAT is 15%. There are stock markets in Bogotá (the largest), Medellín, and Cali. The three were expected to merge.

  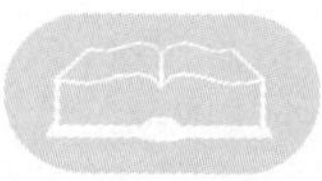    

Business Opportunities

Growth in output (% p.a., 1990–99)

Services	5.2
Industry	1.4
Manufacturing	−2.9
Agriculture	−2.0

Foreign investors are treated in basically the same way as national ones, and 100% foreign ownership is allowed in virtually all sectors. Exceptions include national security and the disposal of hazardous waste products. Investment in public services, mining, and hydrocarbons was still subject in 2002 to concession agreements with the appropriate government entity. The government restricts the movement of personnel in certain professional areas such as architecture, engineering, law, and construction. For firms with 10 employees, no more than 10% of the workforce and 20% of specialists can be foreign nationals. There is a gradual move to liberalize those areas where restrictions still remain. There are 15 duty-free zones where firms have large-scale production operations. Foreign direct investment rose from a yearly average of $400 million in 1985–95 to $2.8 billion in 1997–2000.

The government improved the terms of contracts of association in 1999 between foreign firms and Ecopetrol, the state oil company, in a bid to attract greater foreign investment and meet the goal of producing 1.5 million barrels per day by 2010. On average, the state's take drops by 15–40% compared with the former regime. Under the first such contract, a consortium of U.S. Western Atlas, Canadian-Venezuelan Technopetrol, and Ecopetrol agreed to explore the Cesar province. By July 2001 Ecopetrol had signed 54 such contracts, enhancing Colombia's prospects of self-sufficiency and increasing its chances of exporting more oil.

Another promising area is telecommunications and the introduction of new technologies (personal communications services and digital television, for example). However, the government continues to limit foreign ownership of telecommunications companies.

For More Information

Books:

Galvis, Constanza Ardila. *The Heart of the War in Colombia*. Bloomfield, CT: Kumarian Press, 2002.

Márquez, Gabriel García. *News of a Kidnapping*. New York: Penguin, 1998.

Nicholl, Charles. *The Fruit Palace*. New York: Vintage Books, 1998.

Pollard, Peter. *Colombia Handbook*. 2nd ed. Bath, Somerset: Footprint Handbooks, 2001.

Web Sites:

Bogota Stock Exchange: **www.bolsabogota.com.co**

Central Bank: **www.banrep.gov.co**

IMF reports: **www.imf.org/external**

Investment in Columbia Corporation: **www.coinvertir.org.co**

National Bureau of Statistics: **www.dane.gov.co**

U.S. State Department Country Commercial Guide: **www.state.gov/e/eb/rls/rpts/ccg**

COSTA RICA

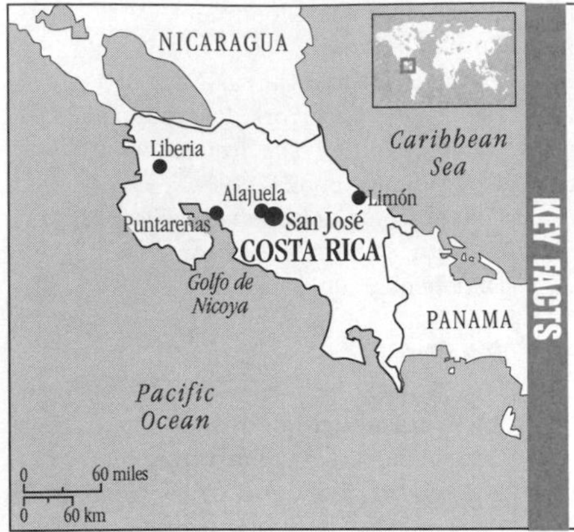

KEY FACTS

GNI: **$12,828 million; world's 79th**
GNI pc: **$3,570; world's 80th**
Head of government: **president**
Currency: **Costa Rican colón (¢)**
Capital: **San José**
Population: **3,933,000, growing at 2.8% p.a.**
Land area: **19,730 square miles**
Population density: **189 per square mile**
Life expectancy: **76 years**
Infant mortality: **13 per 1,000 live births**
Language: **Spanish**
Best buy: **handicrafts, especially pottery and hand-woven textiles**

ECONOMY

Costa Rica became independent of Spain in 1821 when it became part of the newly-created Mexican empire. In 1824 it joined the Central American Federation, and in 1848 became independent. The country is the only one in Central America and Panama with a long tradition of democratic government. It has elected its president and legislature since 1889. Free and compulsory education was established in 1879 and social security in 1942. The army was abolished in 1948.

Costa Rica's industrial base began to outstrip agriculture in the 1990s as the primary contributor to GDP. Real GDP growth averaged 7.4% in 1997–99, and then dropped sharply to 1.7% in 2000 and to less than 1% in 2001, largely because of falling exports, both traditional ones (coffee, bananas, and sugar) and newly-emerging high-tech products. Inflation fell to 10% in 2000 from a yearly average of 15% in 1994–99. The current-account and public-sector deficits, however, have been high.

Some state-owned enterprises have been privatized, notably the San José international airport, currently operated under a 20-year concession by a U.S.-led consortium.

The opening of Intel Corporation's microprocessor assembly plant and testing facility in 1998 was a milestone in the country's transition from being a producer of coffee and bananas to high-technology industry. This was followed by investments by Abbott Laboratories and Procter & Gamble. Other industries include food processing, textiles and clothing, construction materials, fertilizer, and plastic products, as well as a thriving tourism sector. The service sector generates about 64% of GDP, followed by manufacturing (22%) and agriculture (14%). Exports enter the United States duty-free under the Caribbean Basin Initiative (CBI).

GEOGRAPHY/RESOURCES

Costa Rica is the southernmost country in Central America, bordered to the north by Nicaragua and to the south by Panama (which is not formally part of the region). It has both a Caribbean and a Pacific coast. A series of volcanic mountain chains runs from the Nicaraguan border in the northwest to the Panamanian border in the southeast. Between these mountain ranges is a high-altitude plain, with coastal lowlands, separated by rugged mountains, on either side.

Costa Rica's largest trading partner is the United States, which accounts for around half of the country's exports, followed by Europe (22%) and Central America (10%).

COMMUNICATIONS/ENERGY

Costa Rica has opted for phasing in private-sector investment in telecommunications. ICE, the Costa Rican Institute of Electricity, which holds a constitutional monopoly, will not be sold, however. There is a modern telecommunications system. Internet service is becoming widespread. About 80% of Costa Rica's power is hydroelectric, and 10% is generated from imported fossil fuels.

Costa Rica's 590-mile railway system includes 280 miles of main and secondary passenger and cargo rail tracks connecting the Caribbean and Pacific coasts.

There are over 4,350 miles of principal highways and roads, and some 10,000 miles of rural roads. The major airport is near to San José. There are over 100 small airports. The port of Limón-Moin on the Caribbean/Atlantic coast handles approximately 80% of Costa Rica's exports. Puntarenas-Caldera is the main port on the Pacific coast.

FISCAL/FINANCIAL

The largest universal bank is the state-owned Banco Nacional de Costa Rica, which is also the biggest in Central America in asset terms. There is a small stock exchange. The corporate tax rate is 30%, and the top rate of personal income tax is 25%.

BUSINESS OPPORTUNITIES

Costa Rica, with a 95% literacy rate, is attracting hi-tech firms such as electronics companies and healthcare products manufacturers.

Foreign direct investment rose from a yearly average of $171 million in 1985–95 to $507 million in 1997–2000. Incentives are fairly limited, consisting mainly of tax holidays; the free zone system, which is a tax-exemption vehicle; and the temporary admission system whereby processed raw materials are imported into Costa Rica free of duties, in order to have them finished locally and exported as a final product.

For More Information

Book:

Booth, John A. *Costa Rica: Quest for Democracy*. Boulder, CO: Westview Press, 1999.

Web Sites:

General business: **www.businesscostarica.com**
IMF reports: **www.imf.org/external**
U.S. State Department Country Commercial Guide: **www.state.gov/e/eb/rls/rpts/ccg**

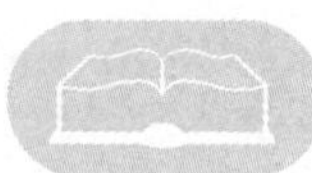

CÔTE D'IVOIRE

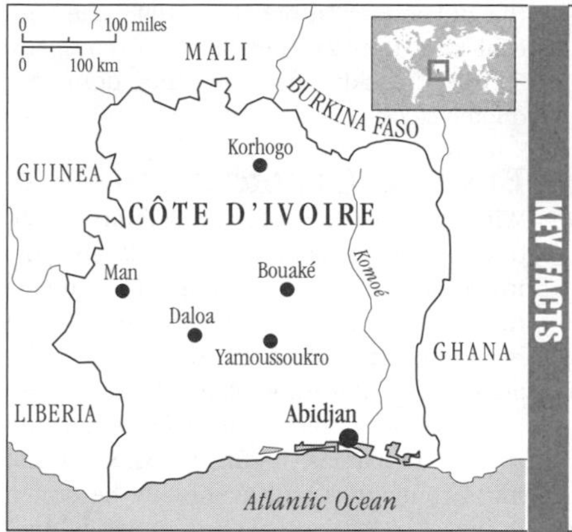

KEY FACTS

GNI: **$10,387 million; world's 84th**
GNI pc: **$670; world's 147th**
Head of government: **president**
Currency: **CFA franc (CFA)**
Capital: **Abidjan**
Population: **14,526,000, growing at 2.5% p.a.**
Land area: **122,780 square miles**
Population density: **118 per square mile**
Life expectancy: **47 years**
Infant mortality: **102 per 1,000 live births**
Language: **French, Akan, Dioula**
Best buy: **traditional textiles and jewelry**

ECONOMIC STRUCTURE

A country that for a long time was considered an "economic miracle" on account of its relatively high level of development compared with all the other countries in West Africa, Côte d'Ivoire has more recently succumbed to some of the African continent's familiar political and economic problems. The monopoly of power long enjoyed by the late president Félix Houphouët-Boigny and his successor Henri Konan Bédié was ended in December 1999 by a period of military rule, which itself collapsed after a blatantly rigged electoral process in October 2000. An uprising in Abidjan allowed the most credible claimant of victory in the election, Laurent Gbagbo, to take power. However, the threat of further military intervention did not disappear, and there was an outbreak of xenophobic feeling with some violence against immigrants, who constitute about one-third of the population. This period of political uncertainty was a sharp setback to international confidence, which had earlier been improving as a result of the country's strong economic recovery in the mid-to-late 1990s. The political crisis triggered a sharp economic slump in 2000 and 2001.

The main contributors to GDP are agriculture, livestock, forestry, and fisheries, which together generate 30%, trade and services which generate a further 30%, and manufacturing which generates 13%. The dominant national product is cocoa, which accounts for about 40% of exports, but Côte d'Ivoire is also Africa's largest producer of robusta coffee. Other significant exports include timber, fish products, crude oil, cotton, bananas, rubber, and palm oil. The diversification of the export base has helped the country survive the long-term downturn in the world cocoa market. The manufacturing sector has grown in importance but has not yet been able to establish important export markets.

Starting in the 1980s, there was substantial privatization of public-sector companies and monopolies, including the sale of majority holdings in the electricity and water industries and the telecommunications company. In 1999, it was announced that the state cocoa and coffee marketing board, Caistab, was to be dissolved and replaced by a producer-dominated regulatory body; domestic cocoa pricing was also to be fully liberalized. These reforms and the ongoing divestiture program were, however, halted by the political crisis in 1999 and 2000, during which time the state-owned energy utilities plunged deeper into deficit.

ECONOMIC POLICY

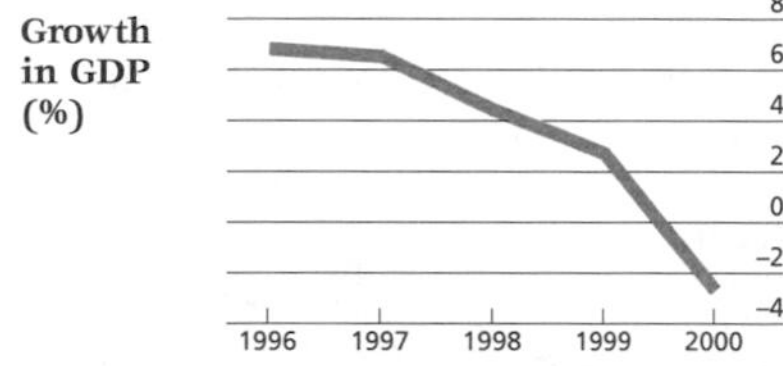

The strong boost to the Ivorian economy provided by the devaluation of the CFA franc in 1994 allowed for impressive economic growth of 6% per annum in the mid-1990s, which slowed to 4% in 1999, partly as a result of poor world cocoa prices. With the political crisis then following at the end of that year, there was a sharp loss of government revenue and of international financial assistance, especially from France and the EU, which suspended financial support throughout 2000. In the light of previous problems and disagreements between the government and the IMF, and a new increase in payments arrears, there was little prospect of immediate financial rescue.

The international financial institutions have sought to persuade the government to strengthen monitoring of its expenditure procedures, to improve revenue collection, and to complete its audit of the dissolved commodity marketing board, Caistab. Although the previous government had been committed to extending privatization to include the state oil refinery and a major bank, the political upheaval brought the process to a halt. The authorities were reluctant to increase energy prices to economic levels, causing public finances to come under enormous strain. Some relief was provided by a resumption of EU financial support during 2001, as the government of President Gbagbo began work on preparing a poverty-reduction strategy paper that might encourage more substantial international support over the medium term.

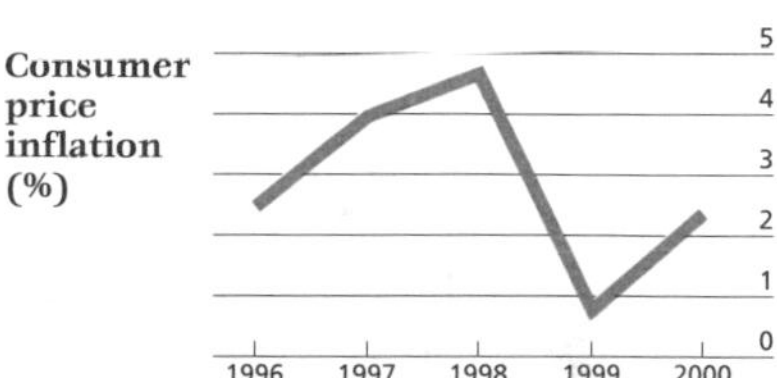

Economic growth turned negative in 2000, with a fall of 2.5% in GDP, and the value of exports fell sharply from $4.5 billion in 1999 to $3.8 billion in 2000. However, under the stabilizing influence of the regional central bank, the BCEAO, inflation remained low at only 2.5%.

GEOGRAPHY/RESOURCES

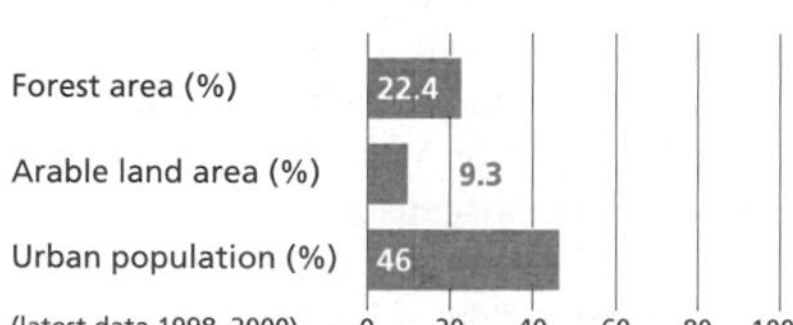

Most of Côte d'Ivoire's land area is relatively low-lying, with the highest hills in the west, bordering Liberia and Guinea. Rainforest, supported by an equatorial climate, formerly covered most of the south of the country, but much of the timber has been felled, except in the southwest. The cleared forest lands have been intensively planted with crops. The coastline consists of a long

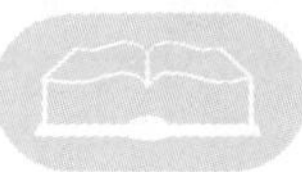

sandbar and lagoons towards the east, and rocky promontories and bays in the west. There is a considerable mineral endowment of iron ore, nickel, and gold, with petroleum and natural gas found offshore.

Much agricultural production, especially of food crops, cocoa, and coffee, is undertaken by smallholder farmers with the help of migrant labor, but there are also large commercial plantations for bananas, pineapples, rubber, and sugar. Livestock is reared in the north, but significant numbers are also imported on the hoof from Burkina Faso.

Offshore petroleum deposits were first discovered in the 1970s, but production from the first two oil fields peaked in 1984 and ceased in 1990. Further discoveries were made in the 1990s, and the new Lion field started production in 1994 with the objective of producing crude oil for export. The Panthère gas field is also being tapped to supply electricity generation plants at Vridi and Azito.

The population is concentrated in the south of the country and in the main city of Abidjan. The second-largest city is Bouaké. More than half of the population is actively employed in agriculture.

Communications/Energy

	(per 100 people, 2000)
PCs	0.6
Telephone lines	1.8
Mobiles	3.0
Internet users	0.3

(per 100 people, 2000) 0 20 40 60 80 100

There is a well-developed road network, and this is being extended with the construction of new toll roads in the vicinity of Abidjan. A railway line connects Abidjan with Ouagadougou in Burkina Faso. There are air services to the major centers of population, but the national airline Air Ivoire has failed to attract investor interest. Management of the international airport at Abidjan has been in the hands of a French company since 1999. The sea port at Abidjan, which handles traffic for a large part of West Africa, is undergoing extension of its capacity.

Since 1997 the national telecommunications company Côte d'Ivoire Télécom has been managed by France Télécom, which competes with private ventures in developing the mobile telephone market. The use of mobile phones has grown rapidly. The main companies providing these services are SIM, Télécel de Loteny, and Sifcom.

More than half of national electricity supply is provided by hydroelectric plants, but there has been increasing investment in natural gas stations, fueled by the Panthère offshore gas field. The national electricity company CIE, which is managed by a French company, has announced plans to start extending supply into rural areas, very few of which are yet connected.

Education/Employment

After significant expansion of educational facilities up to the 1980s, Côte d'Ivoire has seen a decline in standards, with more students failing their school-leaving examinations than ever before, and persistently low levels of literacy. The Bédié government resisted international and local pressure to increase spending on education, and there have on occasions been some violent student protests. In 1995 there were 1.6 million primary students, 464,000 secondary students, and 44,000 students at university level.

Fiscal/Financial

Abidjan, which hosts the headquarters of the African Development Bank and a fledgling francophone West African regional stock exchange, serves as a financial center for all of West Africa. There are 12 commercial banks, some of which are subsidiaries of major French banks, and a similar number of insurance companies. In the past the key economic and financial institution in the country was the Caisse de Stabilisation (Caistab), which has been dissolved to make way for a privately-run marketing board, the Bourse du Café et du Cacao. However, the transition occurred at a time of particularly low world cocoa prices, causing unwelcome losses to cocoa farmers and the government alike.

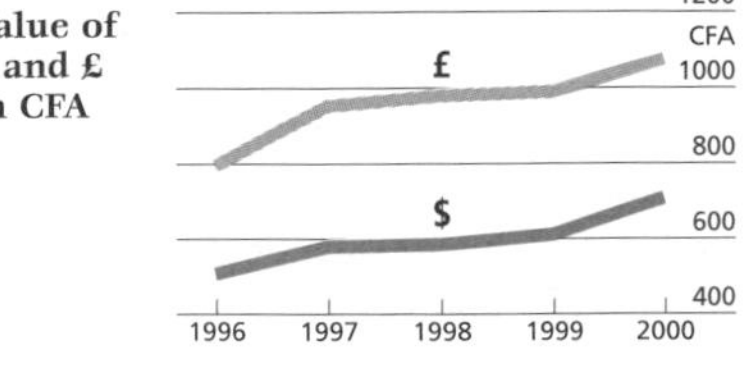

The regional stock market, the Bureau Régionale des Valeurs Mobilières (BRVM), has not yet developed its potential because of the lack of liquidity of most stocks. After the BRVM was launched in 1998, the Senegalese telecommunications company Sonatel quickly became the dominant quoted stock.

Business Opportunities

With continuing political stability, Côte d'Ivoire has considerable potential for new investment in services, tourism, manufacturing, and mining. Industrial production has grown strongly since the 1994 devaluation of the CFA franc. After the successful privatizations of the main sugar, cotton, and rubber companies, it can be expected that more companies will eventually be drawn to invest in local processing of agricultural produce. The U.S. group Cargill is among companies establishing new cocoa processing facilities. In the mining sector, recently installed gold operations have not been proving profitable, but there has been investor interest in diamonds. Other mining projects under consideration include nickel and iron ore.

For More Information

Books:

Ivory Coast Research Group. *Executive Report on Strategies in Ivory Coast* (Strategic Planning Series). San Diego, CA: ICON Group International, 1999.

O'Brien, Donal Cruise, John Dunn, and Richard Rathbone. *Contemporary West African States.* New York: Cambridge University Press, 1990.

Web Sites:

Africa Online: **www.africaonline.com/site/ci**

African news and information: **www.allafrica.com/business**

Investir en Zone Franc: **www.izf.net**

Norwegian Council for Africa, Index on Africa: **www.afrika.no**

Political Resources on the Net: **www.politicalresources.net**

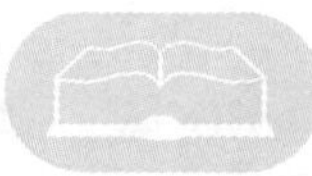

CROATIA

KEY FACTS

GNI: **$20,222 million; world's 64th**
GNI pc: **$4,530; world's 71st**
Head of government: **prime minister**
Currency: **kuna (HRK)**
Capital: **Zagreb**
Population: **4,477,000, growing at –0.1% p.a.**
Land area: **21,582 square miles**
Population density: **207 per square mile**
Life expectancy: **73 years**
Infant mortality: **8 per 1,000 live births**
Language: **Croat**
Best buy: **lace, embroidered textiles, aromatic herb products, wine, olive oil**

ECONOMIC STRUCTURE

Post World War II Croatia became the second richest state in communist Yugoslavia after Slovenia because of its petroleum and natural gas resources, tourism, and pharmaceuticals and shipbuilding industries. In 1991, Croatian nationalists engaged in civil war with Croatian Serbs, who were backed by the Serb-dominated Yugoslav army. A UN-backed peace in 1992 gave Croatia independence from Yugoslavia, but left demilitarized Croatian Serb areas under UN control. Croatian forces were involved in the Bosnian civil war from 1992 to 1995, and regained control of many of the Croatian Serb areas in 1995, thus winning back major tourist venues. A 1995 agreement also restored Eastern Slavonia, the oil region, to government control, but this did not become effective until 1998. The death of nationalist President Franjo Tudjman in December 1999, and the election of a coalition government in January 2000, paved the way for smoother relations with the west, including the IMF. In 2000 Croatia began negotiations for an Association Agreement with the European Union.

Services, including tourism, trade, transport, and public services, accounted for 57.7% of GDP in 2000. Manufacturing contributed 23.2%, mining, power, and construction 9.8%, and agriculture, forestry, and fishing 9.5%. Tourism, traditionally the top foreign exchange earner, revived in 2000. Manufacturing is varied, and includes pharmaceuticals, chemicals, shipbuilding, machinery, household appliances, cement, furniture, food and beverages, textiles, and footwear. Transport equipment was the main export category in 1999, followed by textiles, chemicals, food, petroleum, and gas. The main export markets were Italy (18%), Germany (15.7%), Bosnia and Herzegovina (12.8%), Slovenia (10.6%), and Austria (6.2%).

Before 1991 Croatian industry and financial services were socially owned as state or cooperative enterprises. In the 1990s around 2,000 enterprises were privatized, with shares mostly distributed to employees. The largest companies and over 500 other enterprises remained under state control. Many of these were insolvent or had significant debts; 321 insolvent state companies were made bankrupt in 2000–01, and the government expected to sell 327 other companies by end-2001. Restructuring programs were put in place in 2001 for the shipyards, railways, oil and gas, electricity, and telecommunications companies prior to partial privatization. By mid-2001 51% of HT, the telecommunications company, had been sold to Deutsche Telekom. The production and distribution operations of oil company INA and electricity firm HEP were divided into separate companies prior to privatization by end-2003. The government will decide on a the level of subsidies to be granted to the railways and shipyards before privatization.

ECONOMIC POLICY

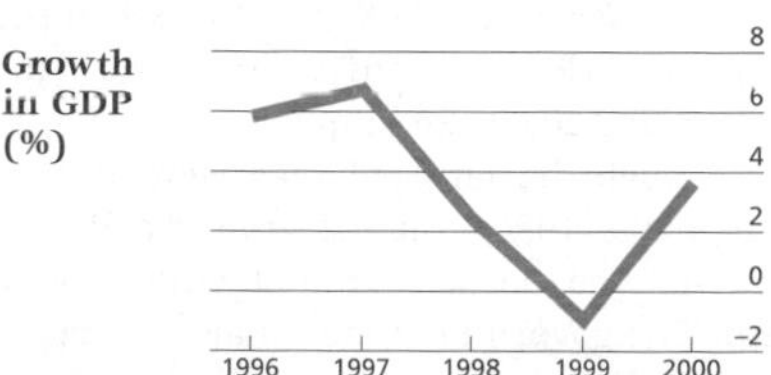

In 1994 the government introduced a new currency, the kuna, and allowed it to float, to overcome the financial crisis caused by the civil war and the continuing military expenditure in Bosnia. The 1993 stabilization program aimed at balanced budgets with massive privatization and financial sector restructuring. The government has run deficits since 1997, peaking at 7.4% of GDP in 1999 and falling to 5.3% in 2001. The targets for 2002 and 2003 are 4.25% and 1.4% respectively. The government's program for 2000–03 focuses on tax reductions and public spending cuts, coupled with privatization receipts to achieve macroeconomic targets agreed with the IMF. The Croatian National Bank has built up foreign currency reserves to contain inflation and strengthen the exchange rate. The public-sector wage bill has been capped. Healthcare, welfare, pensions, and education are due for reform in 2002–03. The external debt rose from 20.8% of GDP in 1995 to 53.2% in 2000, but is expected to fall back to 50.4% in 2001.

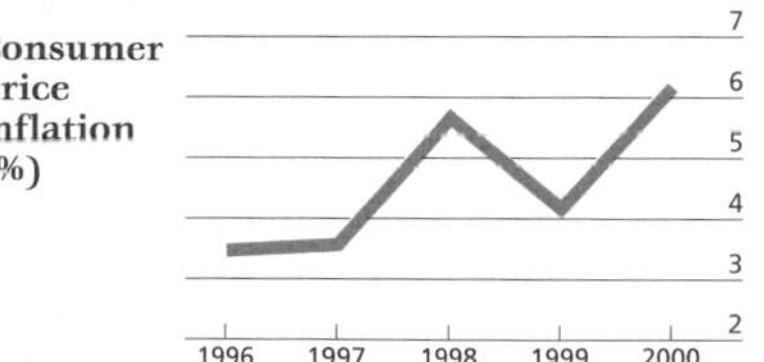

GDP growth averaged 6.5% a year in 1995–97, easing to 2.5% in 1998, then stagnation in 1999. Growth recovered to 3.7% in 2000, continuing at 4% in 2001. It was forecast at 4.2% for 2002 and 4.5% for 2003. Inflation was an annual average of 4.1% in 1995–99, rising to 7.4% in 2000 because of higher oil prices, and falling to 4.5% by end-2001. It is expected to fall to 3.5% by 2003. Unemployment increased from 10% in 1996 to around 14.5% by end-2001.

GEOGRAPHY/RESOURCES

A southeast European state, Croatia borders Slovenia to the northwest, Hungary to the northeast, Serbia (Yugoslavia) to the east, Bosnia and Herzegovina to the south in a long arc, Montenegro (Yugoslavia) to the extreme south, and the Adriatic Sea to the west. The climate is divided by the mountains—Mediterranean at the coast, and continental inland, with cold winters, mild summers, and heavier precipitation.

Agriculture is varied. Wheat, corn, sugar beet, potatoes, and grapes are the main crops, but many other grains, vegetables, and fruit are grown. Meat and dairy are important. Forestry covers 38% of the land,

and timber is produced for industrial wood, pulp, and fuel. Petroleum and natural gas are the main mineral resources. Oil reserves are estimated at 92 million barrels, and gas at 1.2 trillion cubic feet. Exploration continues for both. Small amounts of coal are also mined. There are reserves of bauxite, barite, and salt.

In the 1991 census Croats were 78.1% of the population and Serbs 12.2%, Muslims 0.9%, Hungarians and Slovenes 0.5% each, with smaller communities of Czechs, Albanians, Montenegrins and others.

Communications/Energy

The road network was 17,469 miles in 2001, including 248 miles of motorways. 64.8 million bus passengers and 5.2 million tons of freight went by road in 1999. The rail network was 1,694 miles in 1999 and carried 17.3 million passengers and 11.25 million tons of freight. The 416 miles of oil pipeline carried 5.7 million tons of crude oil, while the 193-mile natural gas pipeline network transported 2 million tons. A new 555-mile gas pipeline is under construction. The 488 miles of navigable waterways accounted for 832,000 tons of freight. A main inland port is Vukovar on the Danube. The most important of the many sea ports is Rijeka. The sea ports handled 6.6 million passengers and 33.1 million tons of freight in 1999. The 10 international airports, 12 domestic airports, and 45 airstrips handled 1.8 million passengers.

Hrvatske Telekomuniacije (HT: Croatian Telecommunications) has a monopoly on fixed line telephony until 2005. A new telecommunications law was enacted in early 2001 to regulate the market and ensure fair prices. Most switching and distribution is digital, and fast Internet access is available. Fiber-optic projects are under way to connect with Germany, Slovenia, Albania, and Greece. The penetration of fixed phone lines was 35% of the population in 2001. There were 100,000 Internet users in 1999, and 187,000 mobile phones at end-1998. Croatia is dependent on oil and gas imports for most of its energy needs. In 1999 oil covered 48% of energy demand, followed by natural gas (24%), hydroelectricity (16%), net electricity imports (9%), and coal (2%). In 2000 domestic oil production was 24,450 barrels per day, and gas production was 612 billion cubic feet. In 1999 59% of electricity was generated by hydro power and 41% by thermal power stations.

Education/Employment

Education is compulsory and free in state schools between the ages of 7 and 15. There

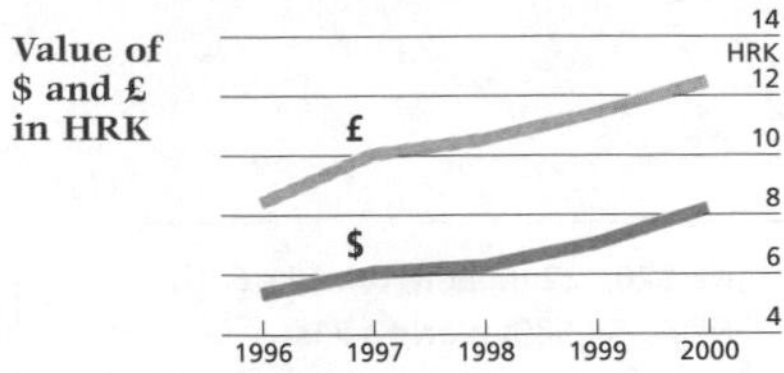

were 93 higher-education institutes with 95,976 students in 1998/99, including 7 polytechnics, 19 schools of higher learning, one private college, and 66 university faculties and institutes. There are four universities: Zagreb, Rijeka, Osijek, and Split. The Ministry of Education is responsible for policy and most funding. Educational institutions are managed autonomously. Spending on R&D has been 0.83% of GNP in recent years, 59% provided by the federal budget, with 36% from the private sector, 4% from foreign investment, and 1% from non-governmental organizations. Technology transfer centers coordinate university and industrial research. Zagreb Technology Park, established in 1994, had 18 small high-tech businesses in early 2001 specializing in electronics, Internet telephony, radar technology, robotics, software, and diagnostic systems for power plants. Industrial R&D also includes pharmaceuticals.

The labor force is well educated. Wages are nominally determined by negotiation between management and workers, but in practice they are set by central government. A tripartite dialog between management, workers, and government has been set up. The 1995 Law on Labor is the basic employment law.

Fiscal/Financial

The top banks are all private sector, and all include strategic foreign partners: Zagrebacka Banka Zagreb, Privredna Banka Zagreb, Splitska Banka, Rijecka Banka, and Slavonska Banka. They control 68.5% of total bank assets. The state-owned Croatian Insurance Company controlled 50% of the insurance market in early 2001 and was due for privatization in 2002. The National Bank of Croatia is the central bank and supervisory authority. Corporation tax is 20%. Tax on dividends is 15%. VAT is 22%. Social security contributions are 20.957% for employers and 20.6% for employees.

Although the largest banks were privatized in the 1990s, only Zagrebacka Banka survived the decade without government help. The government took majority stakes in six leading banks in exchange for taking on their bad loans during the 1998–2000 banking crisis. After instigating tighter control procedures within the banks, the government sold its holdings in four of them to foreign banks in 2000. Another 17 smaller banks were made bankrupt, and a further 9 banks had their licenses revoked from 1998 to spring 2001. There were a total 42 banks in 2001, and further consolidation is expected. The restructuring of the finances of the largest state enterprises and their subsequent privatization should further strengthen the finance sector and operations on the Zagreb Stock Exchange, which had market capitalization of $2.58 billion in 1999. The new National Clearing System for interbank payments began operating in February 2001.

Business Opportunities

The 2000 Investment Incentive Law offers tax and financial incentives, training, and location assistance. High wage levels, a heavy tax burden, and—especially in tourism—land ownership disputes present problems for investors, but the government is working to alleviate these. Foreign investment is seen as a spur to economic growth and job creation. Total foreign investment in 1993–2000 was $4.68 billion. The leading investors were the United States, followed by Germany, Austria, Luxembourg, Netherlands, Italy, Sweden, Switzerland, and the United Kingdom. Banking and telecommunications attracted large investments, while construction, natural resources, and services received smaller sums. The privatization program presents a wealth of opportunities for foreign investors. The point of contact is the Investment Promotion Department at the Ministry of Economy.

For More Information

Books:

Croatia: Administrative Barriers to Foreign Investment. Washington, D.C.: Foreign Investment Advisory Service, World Bank and International Finance Corporation, 2001.

IMF Country Report. *Croatia*. Washington, D.C.: IMF.

Oliver, Jeanne. *Croatia*. Oakland, CA: Lonely Planet, 1999.

Web Sites:

Croatian National Bank (excellent links): **www.hnb.hr**

Government entry point: **www.vlada.hr**

CUBA

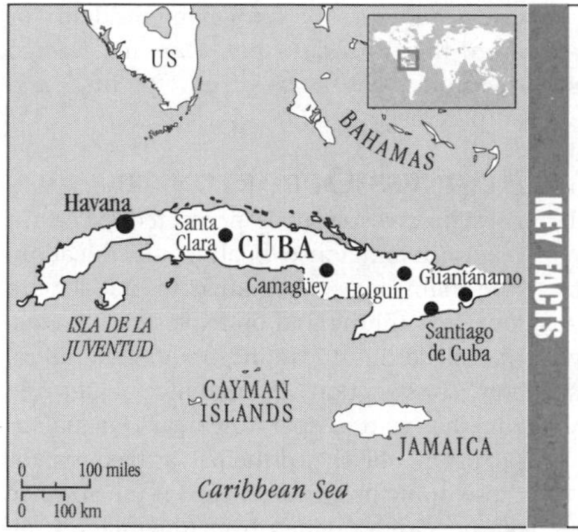

KEY FACTS

GDP: **$22,100 million (approx.)**
GDP pc: **$1,980 (approx.)**
Head of government: **president**
Currency: **peso (Ps)**
Capital: **Havana**
Population: **11,160,000, growing at 0.5% p.a.**
Land area: **42,394 square miles**
Population density: **263 per square mile**
Life expectancy: **76 years**
Infant mortality: **6 per 1,000 live births**
Language: **Spanish**
Best buy: **cigars, Havana Club rum, recorded music**

ECONOMIC STRUCTURE

Before the 1959 revolution, substantial sectors of the Cuban economy were owned by United States companies. The new government nationalized U.S.-owned property in 1960, and the U.S. government imposed a trade embargo on Cuba, breaking off diplomatic relations in 1961 and organizing an invasion attempt in April of that year. The Cuban government turned to the U.S.S.R. for support, and for the next 30 years the bulk of Cuba's trade was with the U.S.S.R. and other Comecon countries. With the collapse of the Soviet system after 1991, the Cuban economy suffered a severe downturn, but succeeded in readjusting and restructuring, internally as well as externally.

The major changes included the development of tourism as a major economic sector, which by 2000 accounted for 43% of hard currency income, with 1,774,000 stay-over visitors and 35,400 hotel rooms in use. In the economy as a whole, 400 companies from 38 countries had investments, led by Spain, Canada, France, Italy, and Mexico. With a majority of the working population employed in the public sector, trade and services (including tourism) accounted for 55% of GDP in 2000, with manufacturing (including sugar production) accounting for 29%, agriculture 8%, and construction 4%.

While in gradual decline, sugar cane cultivation and sugar production continue to provide employment for about 500,000 people, and sugar export earnings in 1999 totaled $458 million, ahead of $394 million for nickel, $237 million for tobacco, and $128 million for seafood. Russia remains the main export customer, taking 23.3% of all exports in 2000, followed by the Netherlands with 14.5% and Canada with 12.9%. Spain was the largest source of imports, at 19.5%, ahead of France (14.0%), Canada, China and Italy (each around 8%).

ECONOMIC POLICY

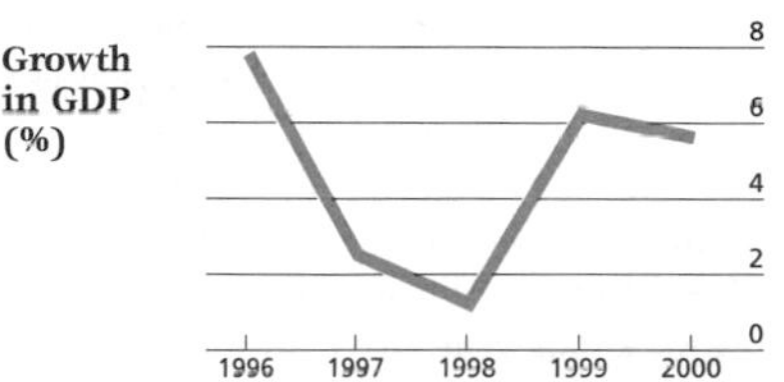

Cuba's economic policy during the 1990s, aimed at overcoming the shock of the Soviet collapse, involved diversifying its trade and investment partners while maintaining the country's independence in the face of a U.S. trade and economic blockade. While public ownership of the core economic sectors has been maintained, limited private enterprise has developed in areas including tourism, catering, and retail trade; joint ventures between state enterprises and private overseas investors have introduced elements of competition and brought a new drive for management efficiency. The introduction of the U.S. dollar as a means of payment and exchange in key economic sectors has been accomplished without depreciation of the Cuban peso, with an inflation rate of 2.8% in 1998, falling to –0.5% in 1999 and –2.6% in 2000.

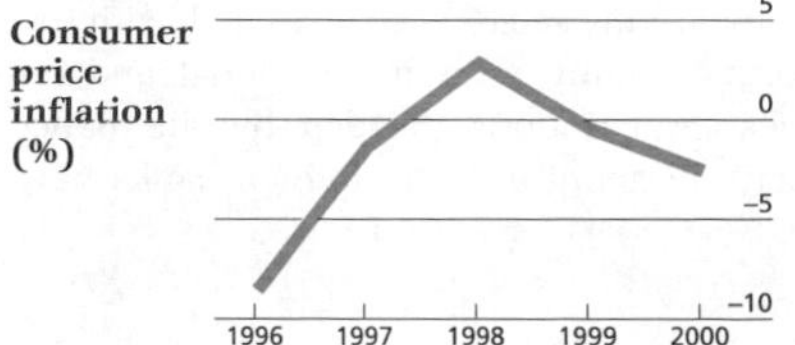

Following reductions in real GDP of 19% in 1992 and 12% in 1993, the recovery accelerated to 7.8% in 1996, falling back to 1–2% in the next two years before returning to 6.2% in 1999 and 5.6% in 2000. In the latter year, agriculture showed a growth rate of 11.6%, and mining 14.4%. The unemployment rate in 2000 was an estimated 5.5%, and in 1998, out of a working population of 3.75 million, 418,000 worked in the private sector or were self-employed. The establishment of producers' cooperatives in former state farms, together with free markets in some agricultural produce, was accompanied by a restructuring of the government apparatus. This involved the abolition of a number of ministries, together with reforms in the management of state enterprises.

GEOGRAPHY/RESOURCES

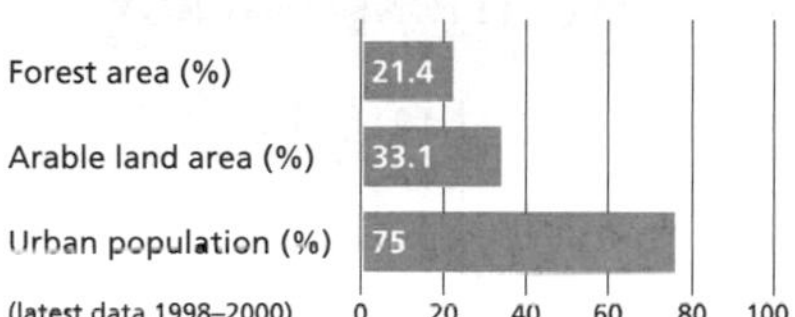

The largest island in the Caribbean, Cuba covers almost 42,394 square miles. It lies at the western end of the Greater Antilles, with Havana only about 93 miles south of the U.S. Florida Keys. The country contains three main mountainous areas: the Sierra Maestra in the east, which includes the Pico de Turquino (6,477 feet), the country's highest peak; the central Escambray Sierra; and the Cordillera de Guaniguanico in the west. The land is about two-thirds limestone, while the Sierra Maestra is volcanic in origin. Rainfall varies from an annual 35 inches in the east to 69 inches in Havana, with the main rainy season from May to October. There are about 200 rivers, few of which are of economic significance; about 75% of the land area is below 1,000 feet in height, and almost 25% is forested.

Mineral resources include substantial deposits of nickel and cobalt in eastern Cuba, mined by a joint venture with Sherritt of Canada: nickel production in 2000 was 71,400 tons, ranking sixth in world terms, with cobalt production equal to about 10% of the world total. Gold, copper, chromium, and industrial minerals are also produced. Agriculture suffered badly in the crisis of the early 1990s, but has been gradually recovering since then, although production of sugar and other crops was affected by

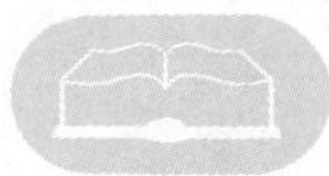

drought in 2000–01, with sugar declining from 4.06 million tons in 2000 to below 3.6 million tons in 2001. Tobacco is a significant export crop, and production of fruit and vegetables for domestic consumption has recovered since 1994, aided by incentives to cooperatives and private farmers. Dairy production, however, remains below the pre-crisis level.

The population, which is about 75% of European or mixed European and African descent, with 25% of African descent, has a relatively low rate of increase; the 1991–94 crisis led to an increase in the population of Havana, which now accounts for an estimated 2.2 million or more people. Other main cities are Santiago de Cuba, with 432,000 inhabitants in 1995, and the provincial capitals of Las Tunas, Camagüey, Holguín, Santa Clara, and Guantánamo, all with more than 200,000. Cuba enjoys high health standards, with universal free provision of health care.

Communications/Energy

PCs	1.0
Telephone lines	4.4
Mobiles	0.1
Internet users	0.5
(per 100 people, 2000)	0 20 40 60 80 100

Cuba has international air links with eight European countries, Canada, and a wide range of Caribbean and Latin American countries; the only air connection with the United States is a weekly charter service between Miami and Havana. International flights serve Havana, Varadero, Holguín, Santiago de Cuba, Cayo Largo, and Ciego de Avila; domestic air services also operate. Havana, Cienfuegos, and Santiago are ports equipped to receive cruise ships.

There are about 37,000 miles of roads, of which more than 2,500 miles are main roads; a road improvement program is under way. Passenger rail services operate between Havana and Santiago in the east and Pinar del Río in the west, together with several branch lines. There is an extensive network of sugar industry railways, some of which are open to passengers as a tourist attraction.

The formerly inadequate telecommunications system is being modernized and extended by the state corporation, Etecsa. An Italian-Canadian company, Fintel, was selected as Etecsa's external traffic operator, and a Spanish company, Soluciones, was chosen to operate mobile phone services.

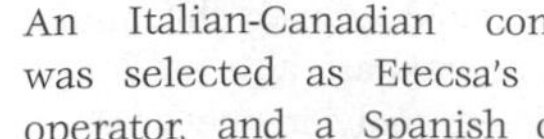

Electric power is predominantly generated from oil and—to a lesser extent—from gas. The traditional use of Soviet oil, supplied in exchange for sugar, was sharply reduced after 1991, and alternative suppliers had to be found at commercial prices; at the same time, domestic oil exploration and production was increased, with foreign companies making investments estimated at more than $300 million in the sector by 1998. In May 2001, more than 70% of Cuba's electricity was generated from domestically-produced oil or gas. The sugar industry uses sugar-cane bagasse to generate its electricity.

Education/Employment

Education is free at all levels, and compulsory between the ages of 6 and 14. There is widespread provision of day nurseries and pre-school education, while at the tertiary level there are four universities, together with numerous other colleges, with an emphasis on technical, medical, and vocational studies. Cuban-trained doctors and other graduates work in many developing countries as part of the country's overseas assistance program. Illiteracy in Cuba is estimated at 3%. The education system is operated and financed by the state.

The opening of the economy in the early 1990s to small-scale private enterprise and cooperatives reduced the proportion of those working in state enterprises and institutions to an estimated 75% by 1998. The disparity in earnings between the dollar and peso sectors led to a situation of over-qualified people working in jobs in areas such as tourism, or entering self-employment in similar occupations. In the state sector, trade union activity is directed towards achievement of production targets and dealing with working conditions and welfare matters.

Fiscal/Financial

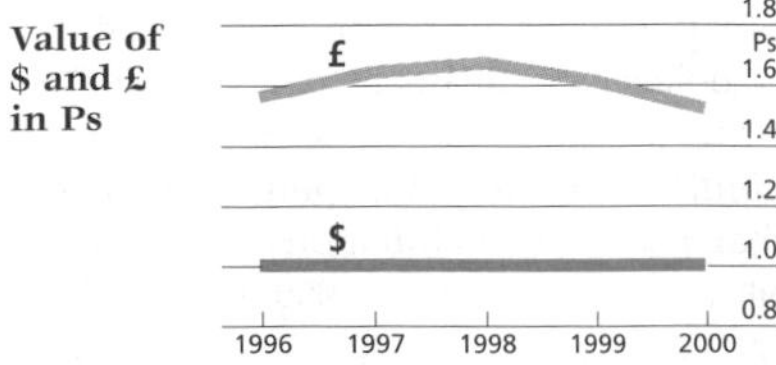

The banking sector is state-owned, with five banks dealing with international and domestic operations, headed by the Banco Central; about a dozen foreign banks have offices in Cuba. A commercial insurance sector started operating under a financial reform initiated in 1994, including some joint ventures with foreign companies. Income tax is payable by foreigners resident for more than 180 days per year, and foreign investors pay taxes on profits and employment.

Business Opportunities

Foreign investment is permitted except in the areas of defense, health, and education. The main investment areas in practice are tourism, mining and oil exploration, industry, telecommunications, power generation, and construction. A manufacturing free zone has started operating near Havana airport. One of the principal attractions for those doing business in Cuba is the absence of the United States from the market, although U.S. pressure on potential investors can act as a deterrent. The process of negotiating joint ventures or other investment proposals can be complex and lengthy.

For More Information

Books:

Cameron, Sarah. *Cuba Handbook.* 2nd ed. Bath, Somerset: Footprint Handbooks, 2001.

Cuba Business (monthly). Cuba Business Solutions Ltd., London.

Department of Trade and Industry. *Hints to Exporters Visiting Cuba and the Dominican Republic.* London: DTI Export Publications, 1999.

Country Profile and Quarterly Reports. Economist Intelligence Unit. London.

Granma International (weekly). Havana.

Hatchwell, Emily, and Simon Caldwell. *Cuba in Focus.* Northampton, MA: Interlink Publishing Group, 1999.

Web Sites:

British Trade International:
www.businesslink.co.uk

Economist Intelligence Unit:
www.eiu.com

Granma (newspaper):
www.granma.cubaweb.cu

Ministry of Foreign Trade:
www.infocex.cu/cepec

Telecom directory:
www.infocom.etecsa.cu

Trade Partners U.K.:
www.tradepartners.gov.uk/cuba

CYPRUS

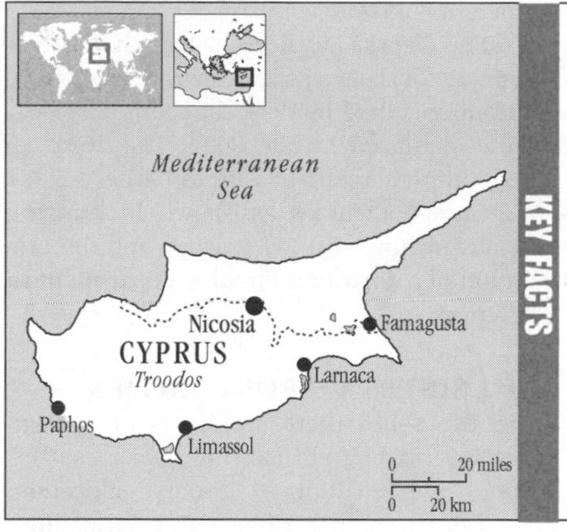

KEY FACTS

GNI: **$9,086 million; world's 87th**
GNI pc: **$11,950; world's 47th**
Head of government: **president**
Currency: **Cyprus pound (C£), Turkish lira (TL)**
Capital: **Nicosia**
Population: **778,000, growing at 1.5% p.a.**
Land area: **3,552 square miles**
Population density: **219 per square mile**
Life expectancy: **78 years**
Infant mortality: **7 per 1,000 live births**
Language: **Greek, Turkish, English**
Best buy: **leather goods, textiles, ceramics, copperware, silverware, lace, wine, liqueurs**

ECONOMIC STRUCTURE

In 1960 Cyprus gained its independence from Britain on condition that it did not unite with either Greece or Turkey. A Greek military-backed coup, which ousted President Makarios in 1974, was followed by a Turkish military invasion, resulting in Turkish control over the northern third of the island. The international community refused to recognize the Turkish Republic of Northern Cyprus (TRNC). International isolation has held back economic development there, while the south has prospered. International efforts since 1974 to achieve a political settlement between the two communities have so far failed. In 1998 the official government began negotiations for full membership of the European Union, which it hopes will take effect in 2004.

In the south, services accounted for 75.5% of GDP in 2000, while industry accounted for 13.1%, construction 6.9%, and agriculture 4.5%, levels which were expected to be maintained in 2001. Tourism and trade were the largest services sector, followed by finance and government services. Food and beverages, clothing and footwear, and metal products are the main manufacturing sectors. Publishing, chemicals, machinery, and electrical goods are growth industries. The main export market in 1999 was the United Kingdom (17.3%), followed by Greece (9.7%), Russia (7%), and Lebanon (5.2%). Clothing was the top export, followed by pharmaceuticals, potatoes, cigarettes, and cement. In the north, services accounted for about 74% of GDP in 1998, including financial and business services (20%), tourism, and government services. In 1996 agriculture contributed 11.4% and industry 12.9%. Finance and higher education have been growth areas. Food and beverages and textiles are the main manufactures and main exports. The main export markets are Turkey and the United Kingdom.

In the south, the government owns the electricity and telecommunications companies, but these sectors will be liberalized to meet EU criteria. It has partly privatized its interests in tourism (including Cyprus Airways) and pipelines. According to the European Union, the TRNC public sector accounts for over half of fixed capital investment, and the government has direct ownership of an airline, electricity, telecommunications, tobacco products, shipping, and fuel supply. It also has a monopoly on agricultural purchasing. Turkish aid has increased the size of the public sector.

ECONOMIC POLICY

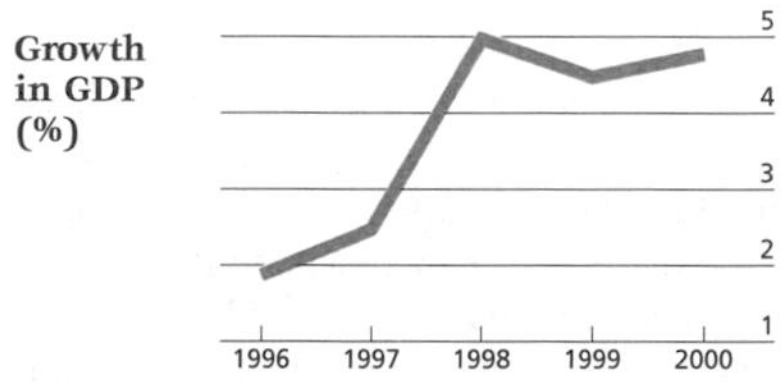

Complete liberalization of short term capital flows in the south is due to be in place by January 2003. The government abolished the ceiling on interest rates in January 2001, and lifted restrictions on medium- and long-term borrowing abroad by residents. The Cyprus pound is pegged to the Euro. The government deficit was reduced to 3.5% in 2000 from a peak of 5.5% in 1998, with a target of 2.5% in 2002 and balance by 2004. The public debt reached 61.6% of GDP in 1999. Price controls remained in place in 2000 on fuel, basic foods, and cement. The government reduced health care costs in 2000 but will increase welfare slightly in 2002 to spread the benefits of tax reform. The northern government is dependent on Turkish aid, and many economic policies are set in Turkey, for example tax increases, welfare spending cuts, and privatization to reduce the fiscal deficit, which reached 20% of GDP in 1999. Banking problems in Turkey in late 1999 created a crisis in the TRNC's five domestic banks, and the TRNC government took control of them. Widespread capital flight will limit the financial sector and prospects for private sector investment in the medium term.

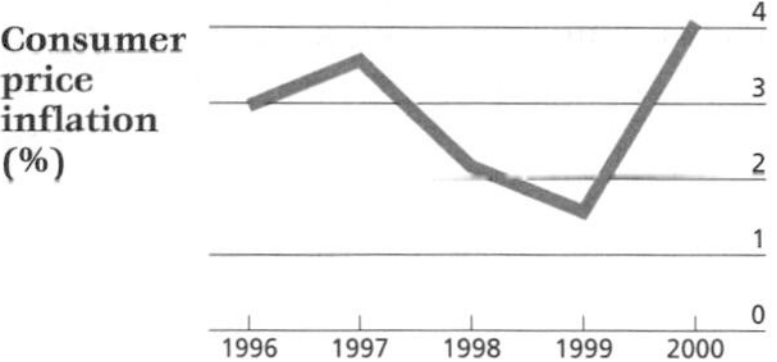

In the south, GDP growth was an annual average of 4.8% in 1998–2000. It is expected to be 4% in 2001. Inflation was an annual average 2.6% in 1995–99, rising to 5.4% in 2000 because of oil prices and the depreciation of the Euro, and falling to an expected 2% in 2001. Unemployment remained at an average 3.3% in 1995–2000, with 3% expected in 2001. The strategic development plan 1999–2003 sets an annual target growth rate of 4%, inflation at 2.5%, and unemployment below 3%. In the north, estimated GDP growth was an annual average 3.3% in 1991–97 and 5% in 1999. Average annual inflation was estimated at 87% in 1990–97 and 60% in 1999, in line with Turkish inflation. Official unemployment was an annual average of 1% in 1990–96.

GEOGRAPHY/RESOURCES

An island in the eastern Mediterranean, Cyprus has mountain ranges in the south (with a high point of 6,408 feet) and the north (highest peak 3,360 feet) divided by the large Messaoria plain. The climate is dry, and the lack of water is an economic constraint. The government in the south has plans for a desalination plant to meet the rapidly rising demand for water.

The Messaoria plain provides most of the agricultural land, and most of the plain is in the TRNC. Meat and dairy products are important. Aquaculture is increasing in importance. Limestone, gypsum, havara, construction stone, clay, sand and gravel, bentonite, umber, ochre, and copper are mined in the south. The copper mine opened in 1996 and exploration for new copper deposits continues.

The majority of the population are of Greek origin (between 66% and 85%, depending on the statistical source). The second-largest group (12% to 33%) are of Turkish origin.

Communications/Energy

The road network in the south was an estimated 6,626 miles in 1998, including 3,883 miles of paved roads, while that of the north was an estimated 1,460 miles in 1996, including 851 miles of paved roads. Limassol, Larnaca, and a new industrial port at Vassiliko are the main sea ports in the south, handling most passenger and cargo traffic to and from the island. Limassol and Larnaca are trans-shipment points for the eastern Mediterranean, Black Sea, and Middle East markets. The Cypriot shipping register, with 1,328 ships over 1,000 grt representing 22.9 million grt in 2000, was the sixth largest in the world. Magosa (Famagusta) and Girne (Kyrenia) are the main sea ports in the north, with most traffic to and from Turkey. Capacity at the south's two international airports, Larnaca and Paphos, is being expanded to 7.5 million and 2 million passengers a year respectively by 2005. Services from the two airports in the north, at Ercan and Gecitkale, link with international routes via Turkey.

Cyprus north and south has fiber-optic and satellite links for international fixed-line and mobile phone connections and Internet access. Domestic and international switching is fully digital in the south, where there were 425,500 fixed phone lines in 1999 and 80,000 Internet subscribers in 2000. The southern sector will be fully liberalized in January 2003 to meet the requirements for EU membership. The north had 83,162 fixed phone lines in 1998 and 70,000 mobile phones in 1999. Imported oil accounts for most energy needs. Electricity is generated entirely from oil in the south. In 1999, electricity production was 2.95 billion kWh in the south. In the north, electricity consumption was 557 million kWh in 1997.

Education/Employment

Education is compulsory and free from age 5½ years to 12 years in the south. There are over 16,000 students in higher education, but most study overseas. Around 7,000 were enrolled in local colleges and the University of Cyprus in 1997–98. The Higher Technical Institute (HTI) specializes in engineering and computer sciences. It conducts applied research projects in computer-aided engineering, and in solar energy in collaboration with companies and international organizations. Agricultural and fisheries research is conducted by specialist institutes. In the north there are five universities, a teacher training college, and an Open University. Policy and funding is set by the government.

The labor force in both north and south is well educated. In the south it is multilingual. Wages and employment conditions are determined by tripartite negotiation between employers, trade unions, and government in the south. The Republic of Cyprus is in the process of enacting EU employment laws.

Fiscal/Financial

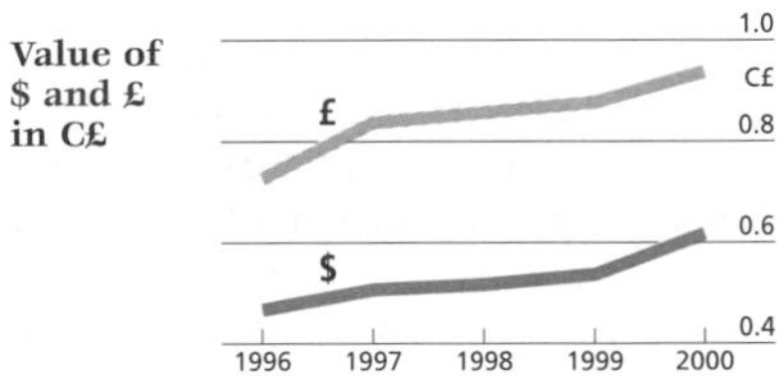

In the south, Bank of Cyprus is the largest domestic commercial bank with assets of C£5 billion in 2000, followed by Cyprus Popular Bank and Hellenic Bank. There is a large offshore banking and insurance sector. Monetary policy, financial regulation, and supervision are the remit of the Ministry of Finance. Central bank operations are conducted by the Central Bank of Cyprus. In the north the Council of Ministers conducts foreign exchange policy and supervisory control over 35 commercial banks and 38 offshore banks. Monetary policy is set by Turkey. Central bank operations are carried out by Central Bank of TRNC.

In the south, corporation tax is 10%, withholding tax 15%, the top rate of personal income tax 28%, and VAT 13% as at 2002. Previous exemptions and lower taxes for the offshore sector have been abolished or are being phased out. VAT will rise to 15% in 2003 to comply with EU membership conditions. The government will clamp down on tax evasion to improve tax receipts. In the north corporation tax is 25%, with an additional tax of 15% for locally-registered companies, but special terms apply to offshore companies.

The financial services industry in the south is sophisticated, and the domestic sector has gained more international scope as a result of the offshore sector. In late 2000 the government launched a five-year program to tighten supervisory provisions in order to comply with EU and OECD requirements regarding tax evasion and money laundering. Anti-money-laundering legislation was enacted in 1996. There are over 40,000 registered offshore companies.

The Cyprus Stock Exchange (Greek Cypriot sector) began official operations in 1996. Trading surged in 1999, dipped in 2000–01, and stabilized in late 2001. The 2000 cooperation agreement with the Athens Stock Exchange includes assistance in bringing rules in line with EU practice and the creation of a derivatives trading department in Cyprus.

Business Opportunities

In the south there are limits on foreign equity holdings in existing banks, real estate, public utilities, tertiary education, broadcasting, publishing, and agricultural concerns. New bank, insurance, financial services and tourism projects are considered case by case. Restrictions are being phased out. Finance, insurance, tourism, shipping, textiles, machinery, and publishing have attracted foreign investment. The government encourages investment in re-export industries in the free trade zones at Limassol and Larnaca, as well as shipping, regional headquarters operations, finance, tourism, IT and e-commerce. The point of contact for foreign investors is the Ministry of Commerce, Industry and Tourism's Investment Center. In the north, offshore banking and companies, together with textiles, have attracted foreign investment. The administration is also promoting foreign investment in tourism and agriculture.

For More Information

Books:

Calotychos, V. *Cyprus and its People: Nation, Identity and Experience in an Unimaginable Community 1955–1997.* Boulder, CO: Westview Press, 1998.
Hellander, Paul. *Cyprus.* Oakland, CA: Lonely Planet, 2000.
IMF Country Report. *Cyprus.* Washington, D.C.: IMF.
Regular Report from the Commission on Cyprus' Progress towards Accession. European Union.

Web Sites:

Government (Greek sector) entry point: **www.pio.gov.cy**
Government (Turkish sector) entry point: **www.pubinfo.gov.nc.tr**

CZECH REPUBLIC

KEY FACTS

GNI: **$51,623 million; world's 48th**
GNI pc: **$5,020; world's 66th**
Head of state: **president**
Head of government: **prime minister**
Currency: **koruna (Kc)**
Capital: **Prague**
Population: **10,262,000, growing at 0% p.a.**
Land area: **30,449 square miles**
Population density: **334 per square mile**
Life expectancy: **74 years**
Infant mortality: **5 per 1,000 live births**
Language: **Czech**
Best buy: **Bohemian glass**

ECONOMIC STRUCTURE

Composition of GDP (1999)

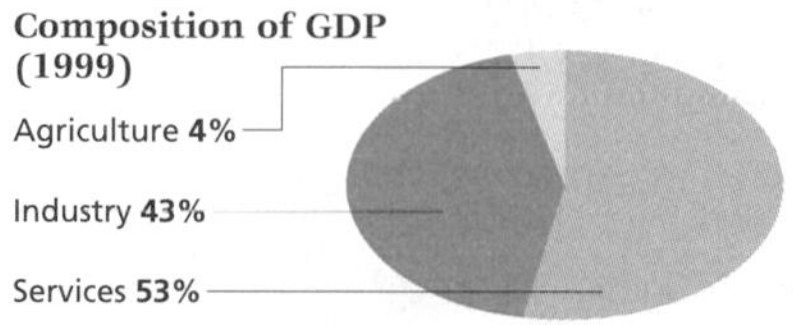

Czechoslovakia, which came into existence in 1918, inherited 70% of the Habsburg empire's industrial capacity. It was occupied by Nazi Germany in 1938 and liberated by the Soviet Red Army in 1945; from 1948 it was a single-party Communist state and became the chief supplier of heavy equipment and other manufactured goods to the Soviet bloc, and one of Eastern Europe's most highly industrialized countries.

The "velvet revolution" of 1989, so called because of its peaceful character, transferred power to pro-Western reformers. In the first post-communist government, extreme market liberals clashed with advocates of more evenly-paced change. The latter moderated, but did not delay, the reformist economic policy adopted: price liberalization, the freeing of exports and imports, drastic cuts in subsidies to enterprises, sharp devaluation and partial convertibility of the koruna, restrictive monetary and fiscal policies, and the freeing of some but not all prices. In 1993 Czechoslovakia was partitioned, at the wish of Slovak and Czech politicians rather than the majority of citizens. This proved to be a highly effective economizing measure for the Czech side, whose economy was relatively diversified (while Slovakia had too many redundant arms factories), and which had a larger share of state assets. The Czech Republic rapidly established itself as a western ally, joined NATO in 1999, and is a candidate for EU membership.

Industry remains the cornerstone of the Czech economy, accounting for 36.6% of GDP, against agriculture's 5.2%. Through the mid- and late 1990s the automotive, car components, and electronics industries powered ahead, while the engineering and metallurgy industries have avoided the catastrophic slump that affected similar sectors elsewhere in Eastern Europe. Industrial output continued to rise in 2001, although telecommunications disappointed expectations. The private sector accounted for 80% of GDP by 2001, but further major selloffs, primarily of utilities, are planned for 2002–03.

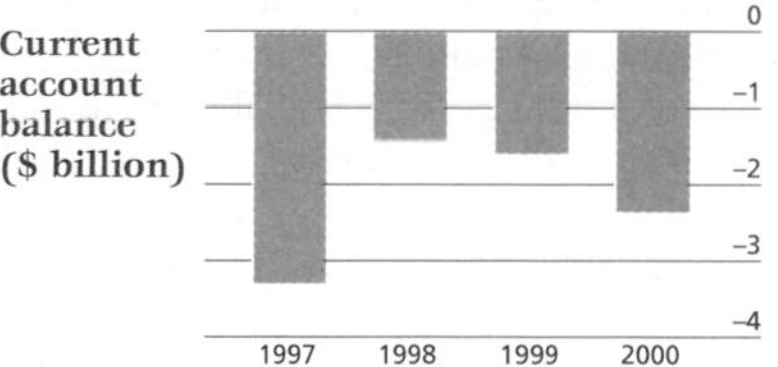

The Czech Republic's principal exports are machinery and transport equipment (44% of the total), chemicals (7%), and intermediate manufactured goods (25%). Its main trading partner is the EU, which accounts for 69% of exports and 62.3% of imports (with Germany taking the largest share at 41% and 32.6% respectively). Most other trade is with fellow members of the Central European Free Trade Area, which account for 17% of exports and 12.9% of imports.

ECONOMIC POLICY

From 1992, Czech politics, and thus economic policy, was dominated by the center

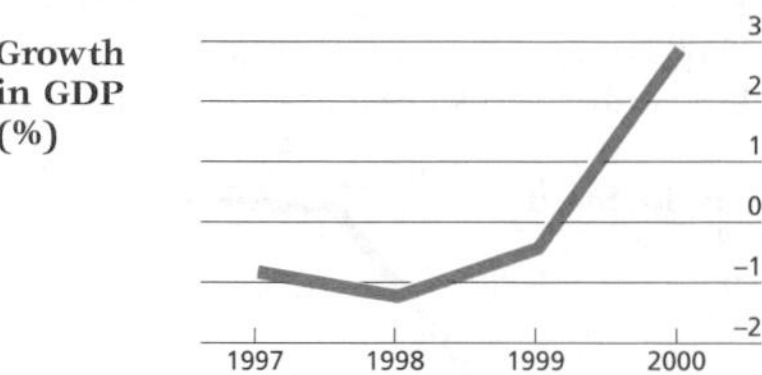

right Civic Democratic Party and its leader Václav Klaus. After the rapid liberalization of 1991–92, the government pressed ahead with two rounds (in 1993 and 1995) of "voucher privatization," a method that supposedly shared ownership among employees but, as in Russia, often resulted in enterprises being taken over by investment funds of uncertain ownership and governance. The resulting accusations of corruption, the failure to reform the banking system, and a growing budget deficit combined to produce a serious financial crisis in May 1997. The Central Bank then floated the koruna, while Mr. Klaus's government introduced two IMF-backed emergency policy packages to try to get reform back on track. In 1998 his party lost power and was succeeded by a minority Social Democratic government (expected to remain in office at least until the 2002 general election), which endorsed the main elements of reformist macro-economic policy, including prudent regulation of capital markets and adoption of a working bankruptcy framework.

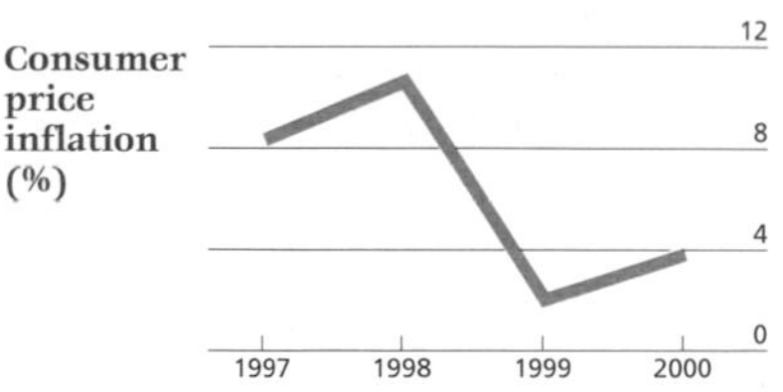

After steady GDP growth in 1993–96, the Czech Republic went into recession, with growth at –1% in 1997, –2.2% in 1998 and –0.2% in 1999. In 2000–01 the country achieved a gradual economic recovery, with GDP growth at 3.1 in 2000 and a projected 3.5% in 2001. Initially net exports, followed by strong capital investment, were the main drivers of growth, and domestic consumption also increased. However, the poor fiscal position (with a projected 9% budget deficit in 2001) concerned international institutions and economists, who regard it as a threat to macro-economic stability.

The problem of large, loss-making enterprises has persisted longer in the Czech republic than in some other transition states.

  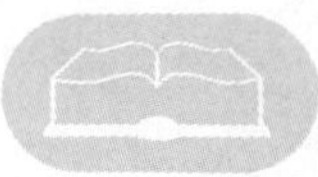    

In 1999–2000 a government restructuring strategy was revitalized, and in May 2000 a stronger bankruptcy law passed; even so, only 14% of bankruptcy cases outstanding in 2000 were dealt with, and many loss-making enterprises are allowed to continue.

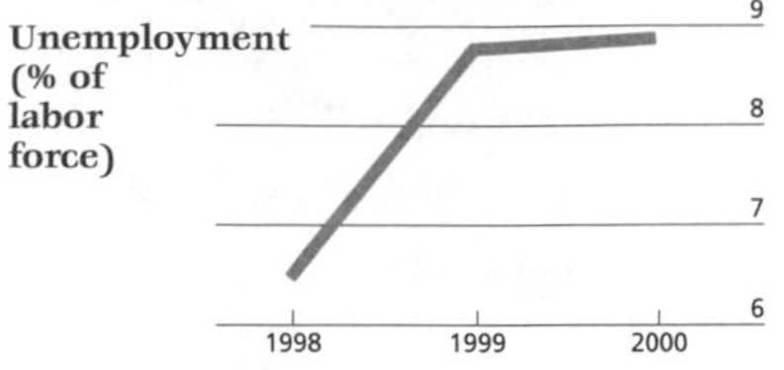

In 2001 inflation was 5.1%, stoked by fuel and food prices, and rising wages. A decision to complete price deregulation by the end of 2002 could also generate inflationary pressure. Unemployment remains high (8.2% in 2001), with wide regional variations.

Geography/Resources

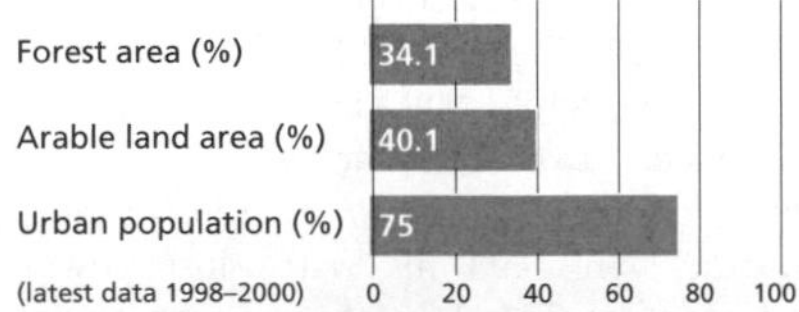

The Czech Republic, which comprises 30,449 square miles, is bordered by Poland to the north, Slovakia to the east, Austria to the south, and Germany to the west and northwest. Its dominant topographical feature is the Bohemian Massif, a large, roughly oval, elevated basin, encircled by mountains that divide into six major groups.

Forests cover one-third of the land area; reforestation efforts of the early 1980s were offset by the effects of acid rain. Agricultural land accounts for 54% of the total, and the country's farms grow wheat, other cereals, sugar beet, and potatoes, and raise cattle, pigs, sheep, and poultry. Although land has almost entirely been returned to private ownership, the cooperative structure widespread under communism has largely been retained.

The Czech Republic has reserves of bituminous, anthracite and brown coal, which are mined in significant quantities. It also has important iron ore deposits, as well as lead and zinc ores, and a significant deposit of gold at Mokrsko, south of Prague. The sand and rock quarries, important to the construction industry, have largely been taken over by foreign companies.

The Czech Republic's population (10.3 million in 2000) has been virtually stable for 20 years, although there was a slight decline between 1994 and 1997. The demographic profile shows a sharply aging population, and the government has begun taking measures to address the resultant labor shortage and extra burden on the state budget. Roughly 95% of the republic's people are Czech, although many Moravians regard themselves as a distinct group. There are Slovak and Polish minorities, and some Germans still live in northwestern Bohemia although most were expelled just after World War II. There is a small minority of Roma, registered at 0.3% of the population in the 1991 census but undoubtedly much larger.

Communications/Energy

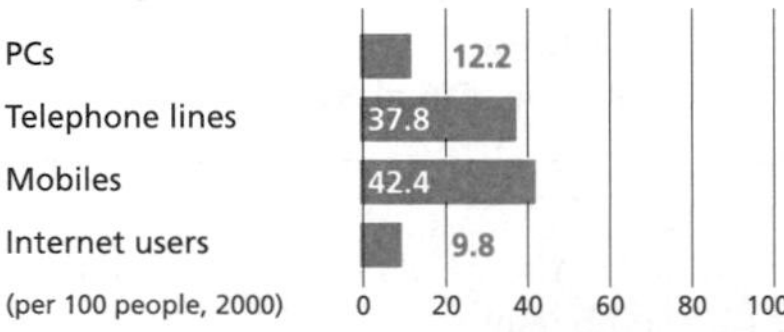

The Czech Republic has a high level of telephone penetration by Eastern European standards—37 fixed lines per 100 inhabitants in 1999, compared to 26 in Poland and 20.4 in Russia—plus the highest proportion of mobile phone users in Eastern Europe (almost 40% of the population by the end of 2000, expected to rise to 60% by late 2001). The government had counted on the sector to help boost economic growth and provide handsome privatization revenues in 2001, but it did neither, mainly due to the weakness of the telecoms sector internationally. The country's second-largest provider, Ceske Radiokomunikace, was sold in September 2001 to the only bidder, a Danish-German consortium, for a mere $177 million, well under half the initial target price. This has clouded the outlook for planned sales of a majority stake in the largest provider, Cesky Telekom, and of UMTS licenses.

The Czech Republic's transport infrastructure is well advanced. It has the densest rail network and longest extent of motorway per capita of any Eastern European country. The first privately-financed motorway construction contract was awarded to an Israeli investor in March 2001, while work on the D5 Prague–Nuremberg motorway and the D8 Prague–Dresden–Berlin motorway, both parts of the pan-European transport network, continued. The harmonization of road transport to EU regulations is well advanced. Change on the railways is slower: a restructuring plan for the state company, whose debts are equivalent to 1.6% of GDP, was delayed in 2000. As for air transport, in April 2001 the national carrier, Czech Airlines, joined the SkyTeam alliance, dominated by Air France and Delta Airlines of the United States, and Air France has indicated an interest in taking a minority stake in it.

In energy, the Czech Republic has made considerable progress in diversifying energy sources away from coal, the primary contributor, towards natural gas and nuclear. It has also diversified energy import routes away from dependence on Russian gas by building a new oil pipeline connection with Germany and signing a long-term gas supply agreement with Norway. An Energy Law adopted in 2000 established the framework for energy reform, including full liberalization by 2007. In December 2001 two major privatization sales were completed—of the monopoly gas importer Transgas and stakes in eight regional distributors to RWE Gas of Germany, and control of petrochemicals producer Unipetrol to local fertilizer maker Agrofert—but a third, of the main power utility, CEZ, was delayed.

Education/Employment

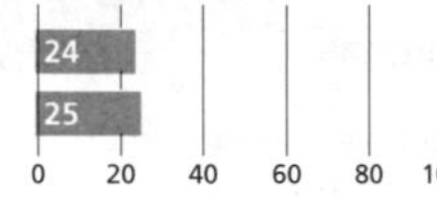

High skill rates, unemployment, and flexibility have made the Czech labor market one of the country's principal attractions to European industrial investors. As the CzechInvest foreign investment agency stated in 2001: "The Czech labor force has established a track record of implementing flexible and innovative working practices including continuous production." It reported a national survey of foreign investors that suggested that more than half of manufacturing firms with foreign participation have a non-unionized workforce, a quarter of them operate seven days a week, and almost a quarter do "significant R&D" in Czech subsidiaries. In wages terms there is an increasing differential between for-profit sectors, where wages increased by 3.8% in 2000, and the public sector and non-profit service organizations, which recorded a 1.1% decline, despite a significant pay increase for teachers and healthcare workers.

The Czech education system consists, as it did before 1989, of nine-year schooling, feeding into middle schools with either a technical or academic bias. About 65% of children (1999 figures) attend nursery schools. In the 1990s there were some notable changes in the middle schools: by the end of the decade 11% of them were private or church-run, and an increasing proportion

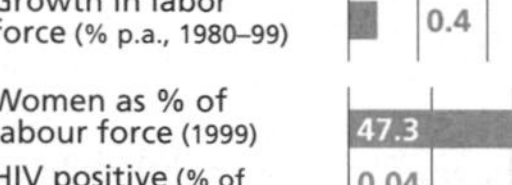

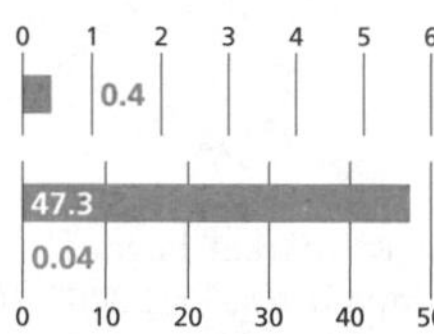

of them integrated academic and technical curricula. Problems of low teacher pay and the increasing average age of teachers remained in 2000–01.

There were 145,097 students in higher education in 1997–98, 16% of the relevant age group and well below the West European level. Although the number of small, specialist higher education institutions is increasing, the EBRD drew attention in 2001 to the need for extra funding.

Fiscal/Financial

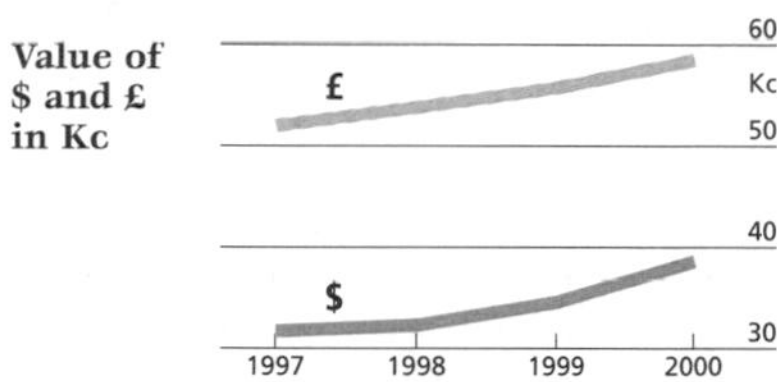

By late 2001 the Czech Republic's banking sector was dominated by a small number of foreign-owned banks accounting for more than 90% of assets, following the successful privatization sales in 2000–01 of the three largest banks: Komercni bank to Société Générale of France for $1 billion, CSOB to KBC of Belgium for more than $1.1 billion, and of a controlling stake in Ceska Sporitelna, the savings bank, to Erste Bank of Austria for $500 million. Regulation has reached a high level of harmonization with EU directives and other standards. A key financial problem remains in the shape of the Consolidation Agency (formerly the Consolidation Bank), a state body for managing non-performing assets transferred from the banking sector. At the end of 2000 it held bad loans equivalent to about 10% of GDP, and was expected to take over those from the failed IPB bank, equivalent to a further 7% of GDP.

The Czech pension industry consists of a pay-as-you-go system and a small but growing voluntary pension fund system. The insurance sector is highly concentrated, with one company, Ceska Pojistovna, accounting for about 40% of the market.

The republic's equity market, the Prague Stock Exchange, was founded in 1993, and is advanced by regional standards. The number of actively traded stocks is still low, however, with telecommunications and bank stocks accounting for nearly two-thirds of turnover, and there has never been an initial public offering on the market. Measures to improve the regulatory framework, including the establishment in 1998 of a semi-independent securities commission, and legislation in 2001 to align regulation with EU standards, have helped.

Czech tax codes are generally in line with EU policies. As of January 2000 the corporate tax rate was lowered from 35% to 31%, and the top rate of personal income tax came down from 40% to 32%. VAT is generally 22%, with some exceptions; employers' and employees' social insurance contributions are 35% and 12.5% respectively.

Business Opportunities

Growth in output (% p.a., 1990–99)

Services	1.0
Industry	–0.1
Agriculture	2.7

The Czech Republic has the highest cumulative levels of foreign direct investment in the Central and Eastern European region, attracting an average of $1.5 billion per year in 1992–98, and a total of about $14 billion in 1999–2001. The principal destinations for investment in the 1990s were financial services, wholesale trade, and manufacturing industry; observers expect the emphasis in the decade to 2010 to be on the telecommunications, financial services, electronics, and automotive sectors.

The FDI boom has been characterized not only by large bank takeovers (see above), but also by major greenfield investments by foreign manufacturers, the largest being Philips' construction of a $624 million flat-screen TV plant in north Moravia, which started in late 2000. Another feature has been the recapitalization of Czech manufacturers, the best example being the $900 million investment in Skoda, the Czech Republic's largest car maker, by Volkswagen, which has held a stake in it since 1991 and owned 100% since 2000.

The impetus for the FDI boom of recent years was twofold: the privatization program was accelerated, and substantial investment incentives were introduced. Under a law of May 2000, inward investors were given a tax holiday of ten years for new companies and five years for expansions of existing companies; job creation grants in high-unemployment regions; training and re-training grants; and other incentives. There are also eight free-trade zones offering other advantages. In January 2001 commercial law was amended to strengthen minority shareholder rights in takeovers, increase disclosure requirements for public companies, and streamline bond issuing procedures.

For More Information

Books:

Clark, Ed, and Anna Soulsby. *Organizational Change in Post-Communist Europe: Management and Transformation in the Czech Republic* (Routledge Studies of Societies in Transition). New York: Routledge, 1999.

Fawn, Rick. *The Czech Republic: A Nation of Velvet*. New York: Routledge, 2000.

Jolly, Adam, ed. *Doing Business in the Czech Republic*. 2nd ed. London: Kogan Page, 1997.

Kundera, Milan. *The Book of Laughter and Forgetting*. New York: Harper Perennial, 1999.

Schutte, Clemens. *Privatization and Corporate Control in the Czech Republic* (Studies in Comparative Economic Systems). Northampton, MA: Edward Elgar, 2000.

Shepherd, Robin H. *Czechoslovakia: The Velvet Revolution and Beyond*. New York: Palgrave Macmillan, 2000.

World Bank Country Study. *Czech Republic: Completing the Transformation of Banks and Enterprises*. Washington, D.C.: World Bank, 2000.

Web Sites:

ABC Business Portal: **www.abc.cz**

American Chamber of Commerce: **www.amcham.cz**

Association for Foreign Investments: **www.afi.cz**

CzechInvest (official investment promotion agency): **www.czechinvest.org**

Doing Business in the Czech Republic: **www.doingbusiness.cz**

Government of the Czech republic: **www.vlada.cz**

Ministry of Industry and Trade: **www.mpo.cz**

Prague.com (daily news): **www.prague.com**

The Prague Post online: **www.praguepost.cz**

Denmark

KEY FACTS

GNI: **$170,685 million; world's 23rd**
GNI pc: **$32,050; world's 6th**
Head of government: **prime minister**
Currency: **Danish krone (DKr)**
Capital: **Copenhagen**
Population: **5,282,000, growing at 0.3% p.a.**
Land area: **16,371 square miles**
Population density: **323 per square mile**
Life expectancy: **76 years**
Infant mortality: **4 per 1,000 live births**
Language: **Danish**
Best buy: **amber jewelry, porcelain, glassware**

Economic Structure

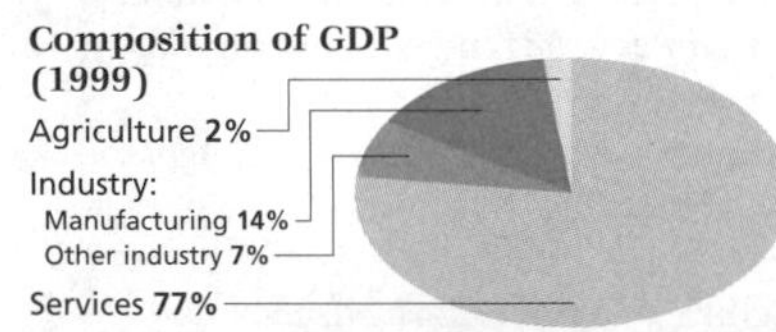

Agriculture and trade have been the mainstays of the Danish economy for many centuries, but the Danes have had to fight hard to keep possession of their land. That they succeeded is expressed through the monarchy, one of the oldest in the world, which goes back in an unbroken line to the tenth century. In the nineteenth century Denmark supplied industrial Britain with grain. Food processing, shipbuilding, cement, and transport industries were established. When the United States and Russia took control of the world grain markets in the 1880s, Denmark turned to processed foods for its export income, especially pigmeat and dairy products. By the 1960s industrial exports exceeded agricultural exports owing to the success of Danish patents and niche market sectors such as applied art, toys, automatic controls, and audio equipment. Denmark joined the European Union in 1973. With the new capitalism of the Balkan nations, Denmark is promoting itself as a hub for the Baltic Region.

Services accounted for 71% of GDP in 2000 and about the same proportion of jobs, whereas industry (including manufacturing, mining, power, construction, and water) contributed around a quarter of each, and agriculture 3.5%. The main services sector is the wholesale and retail trade, followed by real estate (including structural engineering, architecture, and rental services), transport and communications, business services, and public services. Public services account for 30% of total employment, one of the highest levels in the OECD. Communications and IT services are rapidly increasing. Machinery—especially for the processing, storage, and transport of food—and food are the main manufacturing sectors. Other sectors include cars, office machinery, telecommunications and audiovisual equipment, medical equipment, pharmaceuticals, shipbuilding, and refined petroleum products. Denmark is one of the top world producers of insulin. It has around 25% of the world market in hearing aids and is one of the world leaders in industrial acoustics measurement equipment. It is the largest world exporter of pigmeat. Machinery and transport equipment is the largest export category, followed by food and live animals, basic manufactures (paper, textiles, and steel) and chemicals. Germany is by far the largest export market, followed by Sweden, the United Kingdom, Norway, France, and the Netherlands.

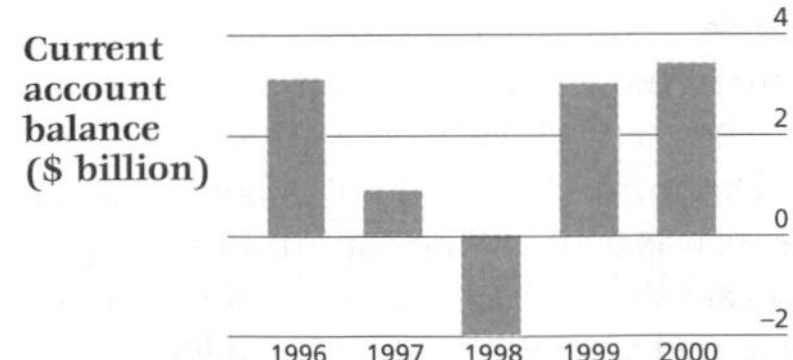
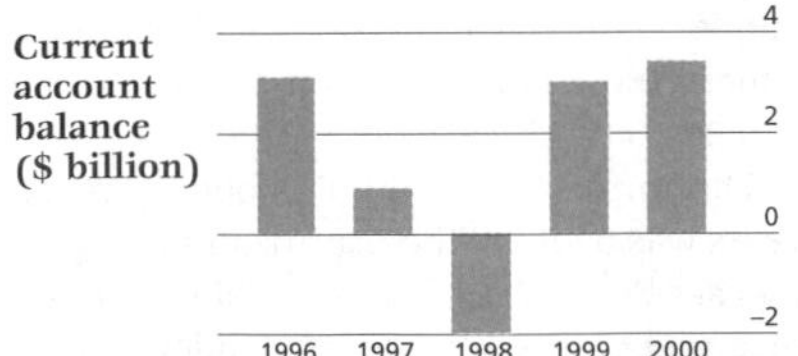

The state ownership of industry was focused on utilities and finance. The state insurance company Danica was privatized and sold to Den Danske Bank in 1990. The telecommunications company Tele Danmark was privatized in 1998 when the sector was liberalized. Liberalization of the electricity market began in 1999, and will be completed at end-2002. The gas sector was liberalized in 2000. Responsibility for railways infrastructure and operations has been separated, and Danish State Railways, the operator, was privatized in 1999. The government strengthened the Competition Act in 2000 to reduce market dominance and high consumer prices in around 51 sectors.

Economic Policy

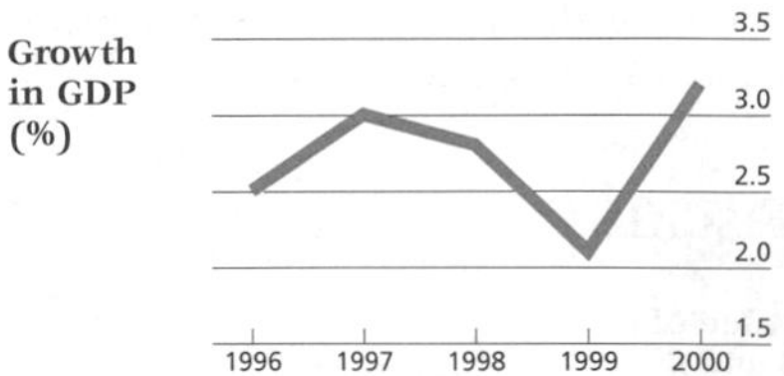

Expansionary monetary conditions in the mid-1990s boom led to an overheating of the economy, which was dampened in 1999 by raising interest rates and by the effective exchange rate with the Euro. Denmark has not joined the Euro because of public opposition, but the fixed exchange rate between the kroner and the Euro—in a narrow band of 2–2.5%—has allowed Denmark to benefit from the Euro's export competitiveness since 1999. Other measures adopted in 1998 aimed at improving public-sector savings and resource allocation in the medium term. The budget surplus of 3% of GDP achieved in 1999 eased to 2.4% in 2000, and is forecast to be remain at this level through 2003. The government will limit public investment growth to 1% a year in 2001–05. The public debt was reduced from a peak of 78% of GDP in 1993 to 47.3% in 2000. The cuts continue with an expected debt level of 42% by 2002.

Consumer price inflation (%)
3.0
2.5
2.0
1.5
1996 1997 1998 1999 2000

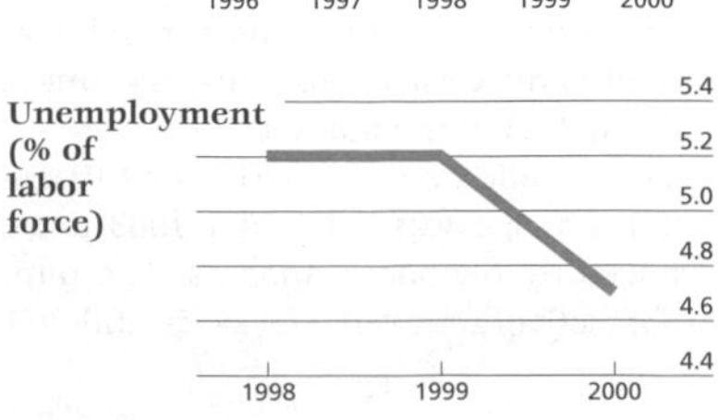

GDP growth averaged 2.3% a year in 1996–2000. It was expected to be 1.3% in 2001, 1.7% in 2002, and 1.8% in 2003. Inflation averaged 2.3% in 1996–2000. It was expected to be 2.2% in 2001 and 1.7% in 2002–03, following wage moderation, a trimming of social benefits, and lower oil prices after the 1999–2000 high. Unemployment fell from 8.2% in 1994 to 5.4% in 2000, and is expected to stay at around this level through 2003.

GEOGRAPHY/RESOURCES

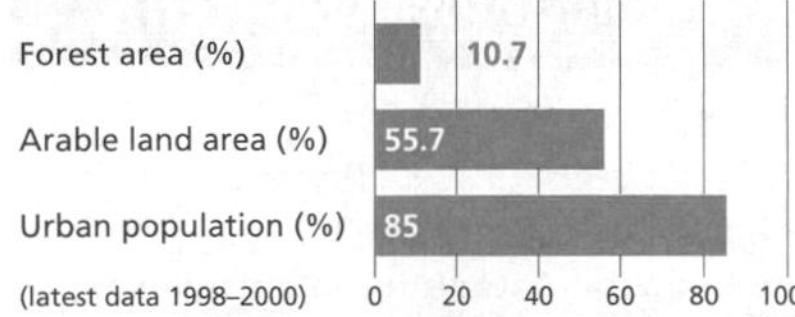

A small country in northwestern Europe, Denmark borders Germany to the south, the North Sea to the west and north, and the Baltic to the east. It is the southernmost of the Scandinavian countries. The land consists of the Jutland peninsula and 406 islands. Most of the country is low-lying and flat. The climate is wet and cold–temperate, with mild summers and cold winters.

Agriculture is varied and highly developed, with a dynamic export sector. Livestock, meat, and dairy are particular strengths. The main arable crops are wheat, barley, potatoes, and sugar beet. Fisheries and forestry are also important. Denmark has offshore oil and natural gas in the North Sea, with reserves at January 2001 of 1.1 billion barrels and 3.4 trillion cubic feet respectively. These reserves are forecast to be depleted by 2020, but exploration continues. Salt, sulfur, and limestone are also produced. There are reserves of titanium, zirconium, and yttrium.

Almost one-third of the population live in or near the capital, Copenhagen. Other large cities include Aarhus (216,564 inhabitants), Odense (144,940), and Aalborg (119,431). The majority of people are of Scandinavian origin. Just over 2% of the population is of foreign origin, mostly from other EU countries.

COMMUNICATIONS/ENERGY

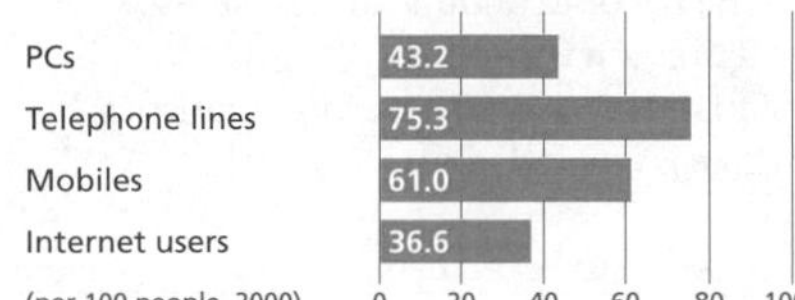

There are 44,492 miles of roads, including 547 miles of highways. The 11-mile Oresund road and rail bridge connecting Denmark and Sweden was opened in July 2000. The rail network operated by Danish State Railways comprises 1,460 miles, 373 miles of which is electrified. A further network of 327 miles is operated by private companies. A high-speed rail link is planned linking Copenhagen, Stockholm, and Berlin. Copenhagen Airport handles around 15 million passengers and 300,000 tons of freight each year. There are 89 commercial ports, the main ones being Fredericia, Copenhagen, Kalundborg, Arhus, and Alberg. Total seaborne freight handled by the ports was 54.7 million tons in 1998. Car ferries are an important means of transport.

There are six telecommunications providers, and costs have fallen since the sector was liberalized in 1996. Consumers in all parts of the country have access to at least two suppliers. The number of fixed phone lines was 4.7 million in 1999, almost 90% of the population. In December 2000 65% of the population had a mobile phone. There are three fiber-optic network operators, and many municipalities have invested in their own fiber-optic networks. In spring 2000 two-thirds of Danish homes had personal computers, over 60% of the population had access to the Internet at home, and 16% of families used e-commerce. The government aims to use e-commerce for one-third of procurement within a few years, and for all procurement in the long term.

Denmark's production of North Sea oil and gas was sufficient to meet domestic energy demand until the latter half of the 1990s, when imports covered around 5% of needs. In 2000 Denmark became a net energy exporter through exports of natural gas to Sweden. Oil production was 361,000 barrels per day and exports 141,000 barrels per day in 2000, while gas production was 276 billion cubic feet with exports of 95 billion cubic feet. Dansk Olie og Naturgas is a consultancy, the operating and distribution companies being foreign-owned. Electricity is generated by imported coal, mostly domestic oil or gas, combined heat and power, and wind turbines. Gas and biomass will account for 20% of electricity production, with a reduction in coal use, by 2003. The electricity sector is being liberalized to meet EU requirements.

EDUCATION/EMPLOYMENT

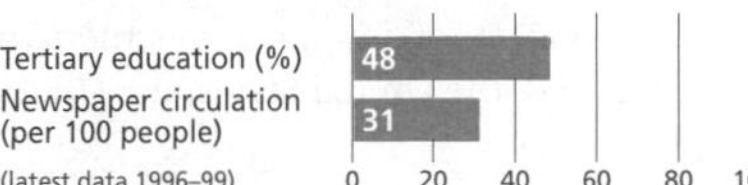

Education is compulsory from age 7 to 16. There are five multi-faculty universities, ten universities specializing in engineering, veterinary science, pharmacy, art, architecture, and business studies, and two academies of music. In addition there are over 100 colleges offering professional courses in teacher training, social work, physiotherapy, nursing, engineering, design, music, and other subjects. The state finances and regulates most higher-education institutes. Grants and loans are available to Danish students. Doctorate level students can conduct their studies in English. Oresund University was established in 1997 to integrate research and education at eight Danish universities and three Swedish universities at each side of the Oresund bridge.

In 1997 the government launched a three-year Technology Incubator program to promote exchange between public R&D institutions, entrepreneurs, established companies, and sources of finance. In 1998–99, 172 high-tech companies were formed, around 100 of these based on patented ideas mainly in the IT and biotechnology sectors. The program was expanded and extended for another three years in 2000. Other R&D strengths include food technology, environmental protection, and energy conservation. There are three e-commerce clusters around Copenhagen, Aarhus, and Aalborg. Smart technology is being developed for a variety of applications including architecture, audiovisual equipment (Bang & Olufsen), and toys (Lego).

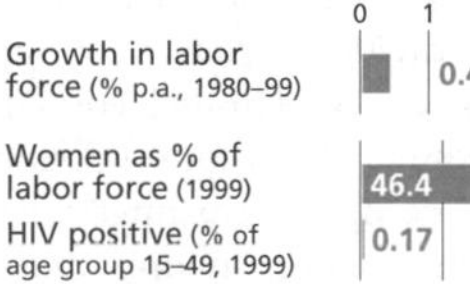
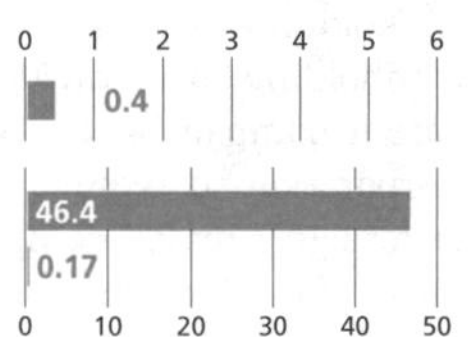

The labor force is skilled and multilingual. Over 75% of the population speak English, and many have mastered two main international languages. Wages and employment conditions are determined in a national framework by employers, trade unions, and government. Negotiations then take place at sectoral and company levels. Employees pay most of their social security contributions through income tax, leaving a small contribution to be made by employers. Denmark applies some of EU employment law, which covers safety at work, wages and working hours, industrial relations, employment incentives, and unemployment provision. A notable exception is the absence of limits on the number of hours in the working week.

FISCAL/FINANCIAL

The largest bank Den Danske Bank absorbed the third-largest, BG Bank, in November

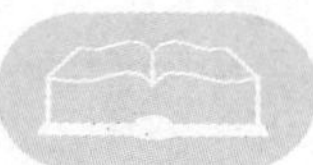

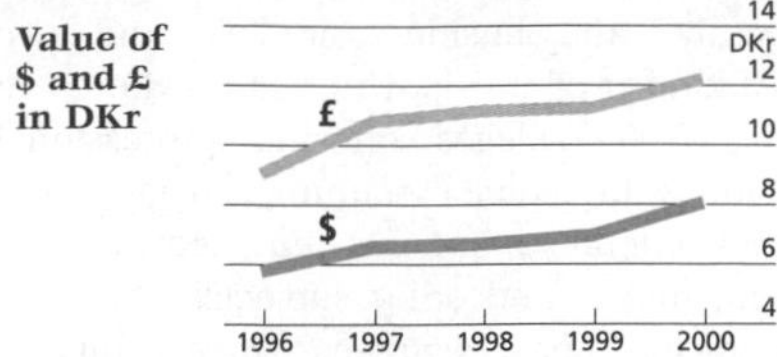

2000. The second-largest bank Unibank merged with the Swedish–Finnish bank Merita-Nordbanken in spring 2000. This financial group, now called Nordea and including Christiana Bank of Norway, is the largest in Scandinavia. The third-largest bank is Jyske Bank. In 1999 Unibank merged with leading Danish non-life insurance company Tryg-Baltica, which is also third in life and pensions insurance. The second and third non-life insurance companies are Topdanmark and Alm Brand. Danica, owned by Den Danske Bank, is second in pensions and life insurance, with PFA Pension leading this sector. Supervision of the finance sector is carried out by the Danish Financial Supervisory Authority. The Danish National Bank is the monetary authority and central bank.

Corporate tax is 26% from 2002, maximum personal income tax is 58.2%, withholding tax is 30%, land tax levied on all properties is a maximum 34% of land value, and building tax is a maximum 10% of the building value. From 1998 a special regime for holding companies exempts them from withholding tax on dividends paid to foreign parent companies. The Controlled Foreign Corporation tax regime allows consolidation of foreign finance company earnings with those of the Danish parent company under certain conditions.

The 1990s was a period of mergers for the banking industry. At end-1999 there were 190 commercial and savings banks, including 20 foreign financial institutions. International transactions are increasingly important. The depth and sophistication of the market has increased. E-banking is growing. The government is making efforts to bring small industry to the stock market, thus ensuring a more varied range of financing options. It launched innovation funds to enable institutional investors to participate in financing technology firms. Venture capital financing of Danish firms and of foreign firms by Danish venture capitalists has grown significantly.

The Danish stock market is not as strong as the bond market on account of the small size of most Danish firms. However, equity trading rose in 2000 while bond trading fell. This reflected direct Internet access for the general public, the lifting of the ban on institutional investors trading directly on the exchange, a modernized share trading system with international scope, and increased use of equity by the government for financing business development. In 1998 the Copenhagen and Stockholm exchanges entered into the Norex agreement to establish a fully Nordic securities market. The Iceland and Oslo exchanges joined in 2000, and the Baltic states have signaled their intention to join. In June 2001 the Copenhagen exchange adopted Standard & Poor's classification of companies. Det nye Marked is the exchange for new high-growth companies. There is also a derivatives exchange.

Business Opportunities

Growth in output (% p.a., 1990–99)

Services	2.6
Industry	1.6
Manufacturing	1.2
Agriculture	3.2

Grants, loans, services, and tax breaks are available to new firms for R&D, design revamps, job training and job rotation, and for regional development. The Ministry of Trade and Industry's Business Development Finance agency offers equity cofinancing and loan guarantees to projects involving innovation or an improvement of competitiveness. The technology incubator scheme involves a private-public financing partnership for firms aiming to be self-supporting. EU aid is available for projects over DKr100,000 involving small and medium-sized manufacturing, tourism and service firms in Northern Jutland. There are ten ports with free zone facilities. Invest in Denmark is the government agency for information and assistance to foreign investors.

E-business and telecommunications, food processing, distribution centers, and customer service centers are key sectors for foreign investment from Sweden (which accounted for 71% of foreign investment in 2000), Finland, the United States, the United Kingdom, Germany, and Switzerland, among others. These sectors offer a growing market. Other investment opportunities include environmental protection and energy conservation. New energy-efficient building regulations are likely come into effect in 2005. The liberalization of the electricity and gas markets provides opportunities for new entrants.

For More Information

Books:

Denmark Business and Investment Opportunities Yearbook. 3rd ed. Washington, D.C.: International Business Publications, 2001 (annual).

Denmark: The Gateway to a Market of 100 Million People. Copenhagen, Denmark: Invest in Denmark, Foreign Trade Council.

Economist Intelligence Unit. *Country Profile and Quarterly Reports*. London.

European Union: European Economy: Report and Studies Series.

IMF Country Report. *Denmark*. Washington, D.C.: IMF.

OECD Economic Surveys. *Denmark*. Paris: OECD.

Taxation, a series of factsheets produced by Copenhagen Capacity.

Turner, Barry, ed. *Scandinavia Profiled*. New York: St. Martin's Press, 2000.

White Paper on E-opportunities in Denmark. Copenhagen, Denmark: Invest in Denmark, Foreign Trade Council, 2001.

Wireless Opportunities in Denmark. Copenhagen, Denmark: Invest in Denmark, Foreign Trade Council.

Web Sites:

Government entry point: **www.denmark.dk**

Invest in Denmark: **www.investindk.com**

Ministry of Economic and Business Affairs: **www.oem.dk**

Statistics Denmark (national statistics office): **www.dst.dk**

DOMINICA

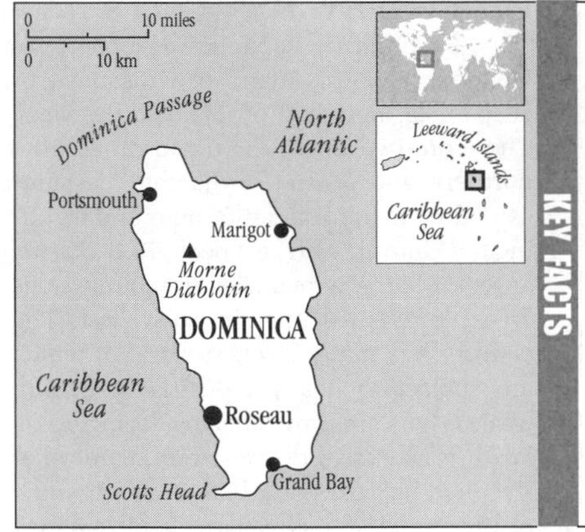

KEY FACTS

GNI: **$238 million**
GNI pc: **$3,260; world's 86th**
Head of government: **prime minister**
Currency: **Eastern Caribbean dollar (EC$)**
Capital: **Roseau**
Population: **71,000, growing at 0% p.a.**
Land area: **309 square miles**
Population density: **230 per square mile**
Infant mortality: **16 per 1,000 live births**
Language: **English, Creole**
Best buy: **handicrafts, paintings**

ECONOMY

The principal economic sector is agriculture, which contributed 19% of GDP in 2000, employing a quarter of the workforce. The manufacturing sector, which accounted for 9% of GDP, is agriculture-based; the main company in the sector produces soaps and other items derived from coconut palm. There is a growing tourism sector, in which cruise visitors outnumber stayover tourists. Half the workforce is engaged in services, including tourism, transport, trade, and commerce. An offshore banking sector was launched in 1997.

The principal export is bananas, accounting in 1998 for 60% of the total; the remainder is mainly composed of other agricultural produce and the coconut-based soaps and cosmetics. Exports routinely total about half the value of the country's imports. Dominica is self-sufficient in fruit and vegetables, and the main import items are machinery and equipment, other foods, and manufactured goods.

Economic policy is aimed at building up the newer economic sectors, principally tourism, in order to reduce dependency on agriculture. The banana industry saw a 32% decline in export tonnage between 1996 and 2000, and a 22% decline in export earnings in 1996–99, while the number of banana farmers fell from 5,799 in 1993 to 2,130 in 2000, a drop of 63%. Real GDP growth averaged 2.2% annually between 1996 and 1999, but fell to -1.0% in 2000, while annual inflation averaged 1.8% in 1996–2000.

GEOGRAPHY/RESOURCES

The northernmost of the Windward Islands, Dominica is predominantly mountainous and heavily forested. About a quarter of the land is suitable for agriculture. Dominica is a world heritage site, and the forest reserves are protected against logging, but tourist trails are being opened in some areas.

The capital, Roseau, is on the southwest coast, with a population of 16,000 at the 1991 census, 22% of the national total. The second largest town is Portsmouth, in the northeast. Education and health services are well developed, with continuing modernization programs; the adult literacy rate is estimated at 90%. The bulk of the population is of African descent, but there are about 2,000 descendants of the pre-Columbian Carib people, who live in a dedicated Carib Territory.

COMMUNICATIONS/ENERGY

Dominica's mountainous nature has hitherto prevented construction of an airport capable of accommodating full-size long-haul aircraft, although plans for one are under consideration. Regional airlines provide services to neighboring islands, plus Puerto Rico and Barbados. There is a ferry service to Guadeloupe and Martinique. There are about 300 miles of paved road, and 150 miles unpaved. Bus services are mainly centered on Roseau, operating principally during school and market hours.

Telecommunications were until recently a monopoly of Cable & Wireless, but new legislation was passed in late 2000, opening the sector up to competition. About 20,000 lines are in operation. Electricity is provided by Dominica Electricity Services, which was privatized in 1996 and is now majority-owned by the Commonwealth Development Corporation. A hydroelectric plant operates at Trafalgar Falls, northeast of Roseau, and there are two diesel-fueled plants.

FISCAL/FINANCIAL

Personal income tax is charged on incomes of EC$15,000 and more, with a basic rate of 20%, rising to 40%. The corporate tax rate is 30%, and there is no capital gains tax or estate duty. Introduction of a value-added tax was being considered in early 2001, to replace existing consumption and sales taxes. The government budget normally runs on a recurrent surplus but an overall deficit, financed by borrowing and overseas aid.

There is a relatively small offshore financial sector, comprising 5,831 international business companies and six offshore banks in 1999. The Dominica Labour Party government elected in 2000 has revoked one bank's license, following fraud allegations; the former government had operated an "economic citizenship" program, criticized by the DLP as a channel for corruption.

BUSINESS OPPORTUNITIES

Investment incentives include exemptions from import duty and some taxes, profit repatriation, property protection, and tax holidays ranging from 10 to 15 years. Overseas investors are permitted to own domestic companies. There are three industrial estates on which facilities are available to foreign investors.

Sectors particularly welcoming foreign investment include tourism, manufacturing (including agricultural processing), infrastructural modernization, processing of agricultural produce, and offshore finance.

For More Information

Books:

Cameron, Sarah. *Caribbean Islands Handbook*. 13th ed. Bath, Somerset: Footprint Handbooks, 2001.

Dominica Business and Investment Opportunities Yearbook. 3rd ed. Washington, D.C.: International Business Publications, 2001 (annual).

Eastern Caribbean Central Bank: *Economic and Financial Review* (quarterly); *Statistical Digest* (annual).

Web Sites:

Dominica Export–Import Agency: **www.dexiaexport.com**

National Development Corporation: **www.dominica.dm**

Dominican Republic

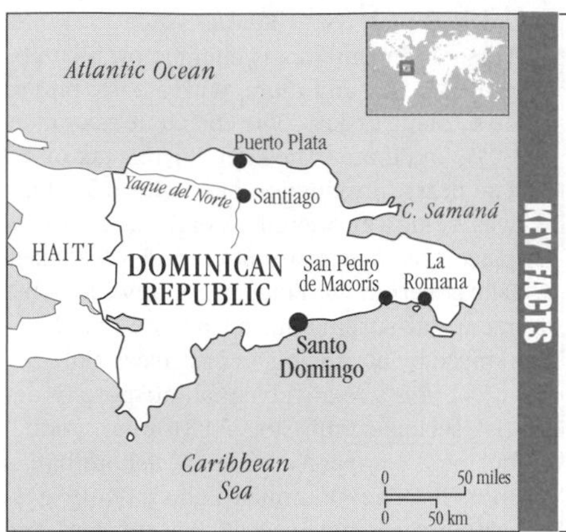

KEY FACTS

GNI: **$16,130 million; world's 74th**
GNI pc: **$1,920; world's 105th**
Head of government: **president**
Currency: **peso (RD$)**
Capital: **Santo Domingo**
Population: **8,364,000, growing at 1.8% p.a.**
Land area: **18,687 square miles**
Population density: **447 per square mile**
Life expectancy: **71 years**
Infant mortality: **43 per 1,000 live births**
Language: **Spanish**
Best buy: **coral, cigars, rocking chairs**

Economic Structure

Traditionally dominated by agriculture, in particular sugar, the Dominican economy started to develop and diversify after the assassination of the dictator Rafael Trujillo in 1961 and the subsequent political conflicts. Gold, silver and nickel mining started in the 1970s, and by 1990 the mining sector had displaced agriculture as the main export earner. Tourism and manufacturing, notably the development of industrial free zones, were the new growth sectors in the 1990s, providing a fillip to other sectors, notably construction. In 2000, manufacturing contributed 17.0% of GDP, construction 13.1%, wholesale and retail trade 13.0%, and agriculture and mining 12.9%.

With sugar in long-term decline, coffee, cocoa, and tobacco have assumed more significance as traditional crops, while new export production includes fruit, vegetables, and flowers. Rice, beans, corn, other vegetables, and fruit are grown for domestic consumption, and cattle, pigs, and chickens are reared in substantial numbers. In the manufacturing sector, cement, clothing, and food processing (including sugar refining) are significant domestic activities, while the export production of the free zones consists of garments, footwear, electronic goods, and other items.

Tourism is the main earner of foreign exchange, amounting to $2.9 billion in 2000, from 3.0 million arrivals (including 0.5 million Dominicans living overseas). In 2000, net free zone earnings were $1.02 billion, while the main traditional export earner was ferro-nickel, at $237 million. The dominant trading partner is the United States, which took 66.1% of the country's exports in 1999 and supplied 25.7% of imports. The Netherlands, Canada, and Russia were second-rank export customers, while Venezuela and Mexico, which supply oil, accounted for 13.2% of imports between them.

Economic Policy

Until the election of the Partido de la Liberación Dominicana (PLD) government in 1996, headed by President Leonel Fernández, the Dominican economy had been dominated by sluggish and inefficient state monopolies in key areas, including sugar production, mining, and utilities, with the deficiencies of the state electricity corporation seriously affecting national life in the mid-1990s. The PLD government instituted a divestment program, under which the electricity corporation was divided up and privatized, with part-privatization of the sugar industry following; foreign investment in the mining sector was being sought in 2001, under the social democratic administration of President Hipólito Mejía, elected in 2000.

A long-standing tradition in the Dominican Republic has been the rewarding of political supporters and the creation of employment opportunities through prestige construction projects, which have contributed to substantial government deficits. Several areas of the economy were closed to foreign investment until 1997, when a new investment law opened the economy to all but a few areas. Tourism, utilities, communications, free zone manufacturing, mining, and agriculture benefited from the liberalization, contributing to an average GDP growth rate of 7.7% between 1996 and 2000. Over the same period, the inflation rate was 6.5%.

Geography/Resources

The Dominican Republic occupies the larger part of the island of Quisqueya or Hispaniola, bordered by Haiti to the west. There are two major mountain ranges, the northern and central cordilleras, the latter extending to the Haitian frontier and featuring the country's highest peak, Pico Duarte, at 10,417 feet. There are lesser mountainous areas in the east and the southwest. The country has many rivers, several of which are subject to heavy industrial pollution, while others are threatened by drying-up related to extensive deforestation. Somewhat less than half the country is forested; much of the remainder is pasture land. Average annual rainfall in Santo Domingo is 55 inches; the main rainy season is from May to November, and June is the wettest month. The main mineral resources are in the center of the country.

Santo Domingo is the country's chief business center and port as well as its capital and political center; its population is an estimated 2.5 million. The second city, Santiago de los Caballeros, houses an estimated 400,000 people; it is the center of the increasingly urbanized northern area which embraces La Vega and San Francisco de Macorís, while the south coast growth area stretches west of Santo Domingo to San Cristóbal and Baní westward, and to San Pedro de Macorís and La Romana eastward. Extensive tourist development is taking place on the north coast, based on Puerto Plata, and in several other coastal areas.

An estimated 75% of the population is of mixed African and European descent, with 15% of European and 10% African descent.

Communications/Energy

The main international airport is Las Americas, east of Santo Domingo. Other airports offering international connections are at Puerto Plata, Santiago, La Romana, Barahona, and Punta Cana. North America, Europe, Latin America, and the Caribbean all maintain direct air links, although travel to and from the Commonwealth Caribbean involves changing in Puerto Rico. There are extensive internal air services.

There is a rapidly expanding road network, including new motorways, although some rural areas retain unpaved roads. There is a high accident rate, caused principally by aggressive overtaking and speeding. A railway is to be built between the port of Haina, close to Santo Domingo, and

  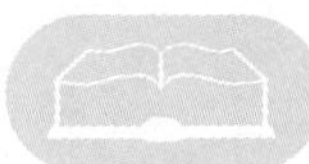    

Santiago, with a target completion date of mid-2004.

The largest telecommunications company is the Compañía Dominicana de Teléfonos (Codetel), owned by a United States corporation, GTE. Other operators are Tricom, part-owned by Motorola, and All-American Cable. The telecommunications sector is undergoing rapid expansion and modernization; in May 2000 there were 900,000 lines operating, plus 705,000 mobile lines.

The state electricity corporation was privatized in 1999, with two Spanish companies, Union Fenosa and AES, taking control of the main generating and distribution operations. Installed capacity is around 2,000 MW, but breakdowns and technical deficiencies remain a problem. Electricity generation is mainly from imported oil, plus some hydroelectric and gas turbine plants.

Education/Employment

Education is free and compulsory between the ages of 7 and 14; secondary education is financed wholly or partly by the state. Primary school enrollment is estimated at more than 90%, falling to a lower level in the secondary phase: an estimated 58,000 children under 14 were working in 1994. The adult literacy rate in 1996 was 77%; the 1993 census found that 1.5 million people had never been to school. There are eight universities, four of which are religious in character. The Autonomous University of Santo Domingo was founded in 1538.

Unemployment was put at 13.9% in 2000, compared with 20.3% in 1992. Tourism and free-zone manufacturing are the main growth areas for employment. In traditional areas such as cane cutting in the sugar harvest, there is a shortage of labor, filled by the seasonal recruitment of Haitians.

Fiscal/Financial

The financial services sector is relatively undeveloped. The banking system contains three foreign-owned banks (Chase Manhattan, Citibank, and Nova Scotia) and a dozen Dominican-owned ones including the state Banco de Reservas. There are several development banks, and the sector is regulated by the Central Bank, which sets the foreign exchange rate and controls foreign exchange transactions. Its monetary board (junta monetaria) controls interest rate policy and money supply. In 2000, the profits of the banking sector increased by 36%, reaching approximately $150 million.

The insurance sub-sector contains almost 40 companies, more than 10 of them foreign-owned. A securities exchange was established in 1992 as a step towards the development of a stock exchange. Registered foreign investment at the end of 1999 amounted to $1.35 billion.

The government finances have shown a positive balance on the current side in recent years, which reached RD$11.2 billion in 2000. Traditionally, large-scale capital expenditure has produced an overall deficit, which in 1999 was RD$1.7 billion, but an increase in capital revenue in 2000, attributed to privatization proceeds, led to an overall positive balance of RD$3.1 billion.

Business Opportunities

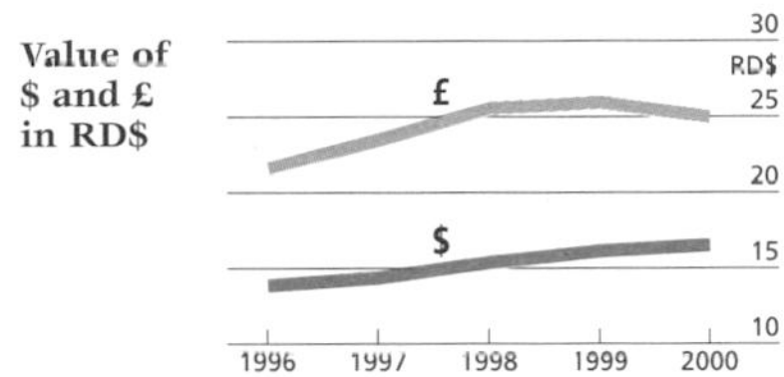

The traditionally protected economy has been progressively opened to foreign investment since the 1980s, led by tourism and the manufacturing free zones. However, cumbersome and lengthy bureaucratic procedures remain in place in some areas, including external trade, although the government is continuing its drive to streamline the processes. A value-added tax, ITBIS, is charged on commercial transactions at 12%, and companies pay a 1.5% tax on gross sales of more than RD$2 million a year. There is a maximum customs tariff of 20%, with three lower rates. Registered investors may repatriate capital and earnings.

In the free-zone sector, companies have a 20-year tax exemption, and their imports of equipment and materials are free of duty. Other concessions relate to the provision of factory buildings and facilities, while the output from the factories has preferential access to the United States.

The government's privatization and deregulation program offers opportunities in the electricity and telecommunications sectors, the sugar industry, mining, and elsewhere. Transport and other infrastructure is another area likely to generate considerable investment for the foreseeable future, but the tourist sector now appears over-extended: with more than 50,000 hotel rooms available in 2000, the occupancy rate was only 70%.

For exporters, agricultural machinery, vehicles and parts, construction equipment, pharmaceuticals, food and drink, clothing and textiles, chemicals, and electrical equipment are promising areas.

For More Information

Books:

Cameron, Sarah. *Dominican Republic Handbook*. Bath: Footprint Handbooks, 2001.

Department of Trade and Industry. *Hints to Exporters Visiting Cuba and the Dominican Republic*. London: DTI Export Publications, 1999.

Economist Intelligence Unit. *Country Profiles and Country Reports*. London.

Howard, David. *Dominican Republic in Focus*. London: Latin America Bureau, 1999.

Howard, David. *Dominican Republic: A Guide to the People, Politics and Culture*. Northampton, MA: Interlink Publishing Group, 1999.

International Financial Statistics. IMF: Washington, D.C.

South America, Central America and the Caribbean. 10th ed. New York: Europa Publications, 2001.

Web Sites:

Central Bank: **www.bancentral.gov.do**
Centre for the Promotion of Exports: **www.cedopex.gov.do**
DR One, news service: **www.drl.com**
Economist Intelligence Unit: **www.eiu.com**
Listín Diario (newspaper): **www.codetel.net.do/listin-diario**
Office for the Promotion of Investment: **www.dr-opin.com**
Tourism Board: **www.domrep-hotels.com.do**

Ecuador

KEY FACTS

GNI: **$16,841 million; world's 72nd**
GNI pc: **$1,360; world's 123rd**
Head of government: **president**
Currency: **U.S. dollar ($)**
Capital: **Quito**
Population: **12,411,000, growing at 2.1% p.a.**
Land area: **106,872 square miles**
Population density: **116 per square mile**
Life expectancy: **70 years**
Infant mortality: **27 per 1,000 live births**
Language: **Spanish, Quechua, Jarvo**
Best buy: **naïf paintings and handicrafts**

Economic Structure

Ecuador returned to democracy in 1979 after two decades when presidents were usually elected and appointed by the armed forces, few of whom saw out their full terms in office. President Jamil Mahoud was ousted in January 2000 by Indians opposing his liberal economic policies, in an unholy alliance with part of the military, which was against Mahoud's resolution of a long-standing territorial dispute with neighboring Peru. Mahoud was replaced by Gustavo Noboa, the vice president, who reached an agreement with the International Monetary Fund (IMF) and continued his predecessor's dollarization plan.

The country is dependent on a small number of primary products for export earnings, leaving it vulnerable to external shocks caused by lower international prices for commodities. The principal exports are oil, discovered in the 1970s and the driving force of the economy, bananas (Ecuador is the world's largest producer), shrimp, coffee, tinned fish, and flowers. Agriculture accounts for around 12% of GDP, industry 32%, and services 56%. The United States is the largest market. After oil, which accounts for roughly 50% of public-sector revenue and of export earnings, the main industries are textiles, wood, and paper, while the contribution of chemicals, machinery, food, and beverages has declined.

Ecuador has been slow to embrace the market-oriented reforms that have taken place elsewhere in Latin America. It joined the World Trade Organization in 1996 but failed to comply with many of its accession commitments. The state sold its stakes in La Cemento Nacional, the biggest cement company, and in Fertisa, a fertilizers company, during the 1990s, but little else of significance. The public sector is notoriously inefficient, and economic progress has also been paralyzed by the country's fragmented, corrupt and polarized political system. According to UNICEF, 70% of the population lived in poverty in 2000, up from 32% in 1995. A law was passed in 2000 which allowed for privatization in the electricity, telecommunications and oil sectors, and the government hoped to move ahead during 2001. The armed forces are major economic players, with interests in aviation, agriculture, banking, transportation, shrimp, and flowers.

Economic Policy

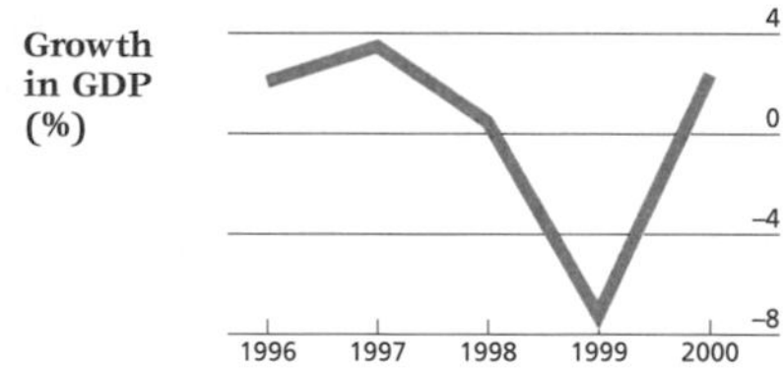

The economy began to decline in 1995 after real GDP growth averaged 3.8% a year in 1991–94. The steep fall in world oil prices, the crises in emerging markets, and the devastation wrought by the El Niño weather phenomenon plunged the economy into recession in 1999 (–7.3% growth), when inflation rose 60.7%. In a desperate measure to stave off hyperinflation, the government replaced the sucre with the U.S. dollar, but without a strong banking system—one of the prerequisites for success—in place. Nevertheless, dollarization has led to a marked deceleration in inflation (96% in 2000 and half that in 2001). Severe belt-tightening measures including the ending of fuel subsidies, combined with tax reform, reduced the non-financial public-sector deficit (excluding the provinces and municipalities) to zero in 2000, when tax revenue reached 14% of GDP.

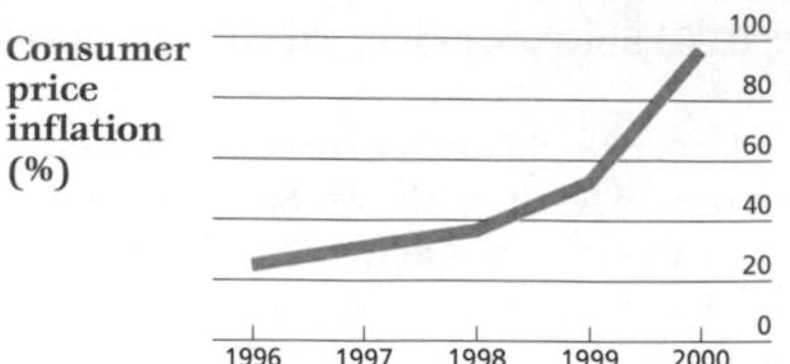

Excessive foreign borrowing during the country's oil boom in the 1970s and the 1990s, the economy's poor performance in the 1980s, and the accumulation of debt arrears between 1987 and 1999 caused the stock of public-sector external debt to reach $13.4 billion in 2000 (80% of GDP).

Geography/Resources

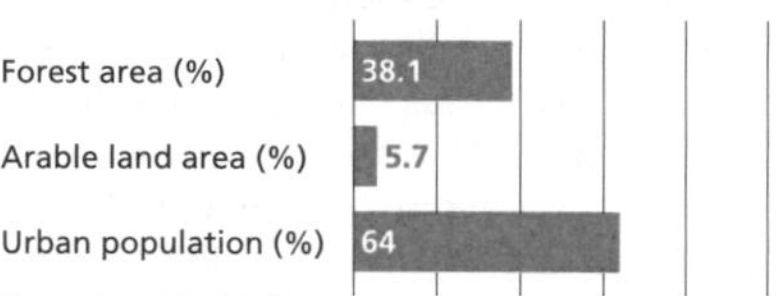

Ecuador is located on the northwest edge of South America and is bordered by Colombia in the north, Peru in the east and south, and in the west by the Pacific Ocean. The country is bisected north to south by the Andes. The mountains reach over 20,000 feet, so high that ice and snow lie on the summits all year round. Cotopaxi, which towers over Quito, is the world's highest active volcano. Across the north of the country passes the equator, after which Ecuador is named. On the equator, about 600 miles off the coast, lie the 18 Galápagos Islands, which belong to Ecuador. The main river is the Guayas, which flows through the Pacific coastal region, with many tributaries along the way. The longest river is the Napo, which is a tributary of the Amazon.

The country has abundant natural resources and is astonishingly varied, with a unique diversity of climatological zones, fauna, and flora. There are four distinct regions: the tropical lowlands of the Pacific coast, the mountains and valleys of the Andean Sierra, the Amazon rain forest of the Oriente, and the Galápagos Islands. Virtually the whole of the country is suitable for some form of agriculture. The main crops are bananas, cocoa, coffee, oil palms, sugar

cane, cotton, rice, and corn. There is extensive, but underdeveloped, mining potential (gold, silver, and copper). A new mining law to encourage development came into force in 2001.

Just over 40% of the population are mixed Indian and white, 29% Indian, 10% white, 5% black, and others 5%. The indigenous Indian population consists of eight main groups, five in the Oriente and three on the coast, each with its own language.

Communications/Energy

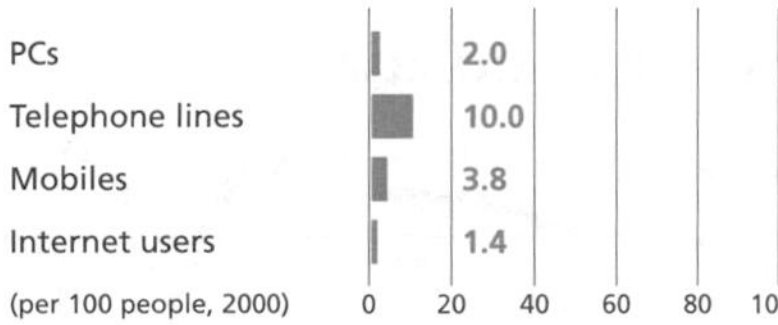

The Pan American Highway runs through Ecuador, but there are few other good roads because of the mountainous terrain. In much of the coastal lowlands and the Oriente, rivers form the main routes of communication. The railways are in a state of decay. There are international airports at Quito, the seat of government, and Guayaquil, the bastion city of the private sector. There were plans to build a new airport for Quito. The containerized port at Guayaquil handles most exports and imports. Manta on the central coast handles a large proportion of the cocoa and coffee exports, as well as almost all tuna exports.

About three-quarters of electricity generation is hydropower and the remainder fossil fuel. Roughly half of the electricity comes from one hydroelectric plant (Paute). Power demand has been growing rapidly, but generation capacity, and transmission and distribution infrastructure, are failing to keep pace. About 25% of the population does not have access to electricity. The failure to open the electricity sector to private investment in the 1990s led to severe power shortages when drought reduced hydroelectric output.

The government approved the building of a second national oil pipeline in July 2001. The $1.1 billion Transandean Heavy Oil Pipeline from the interior to the Pacific Ocean was expected to double production to 800,000 barrels per day by 2003. Capacity constraints on the Trans-Ecuadorian pipeline from the Lago Agrio area in the Oriente to the Balao terminal near the port city of Esmeraldas forced operators to produce at 100,000 barrels a day below capacity.

The privatization of state telephone companies has been slowly progressing since 1993. Empresa Estatal de Telecomunicaciones (EMETEL), the telecommunications monopoly, was divided into two companies, ANINATEL and PACIFICTEL, each with different regional coverage. The telecommunications market began to be opened to free competition for all services during 2001. Teledensity is low, with around 10 fixed lines per 100 inhabitants and 3 mobile subscribers per 100 inhabitants.

Education/Employment

The system of education, compulsory for age six to fifteen, was hard hit by the economic crisis of the 1990s. Public investment in education declined from 5.6% of GDP in 1980 to around 3% in 2000, one of the lowest rates of spending in Latin America. Dropout rates in primary and secondary schools are very high. Universities are generally of a poor quality. Not surprisingly, businessmen complain that the degrees which graduates are attaining are inadequate, and that basic skills still have to be taught after people are taken on by companies. Families who can afford it send their children to universities in the United States.

Fiscal/Financial

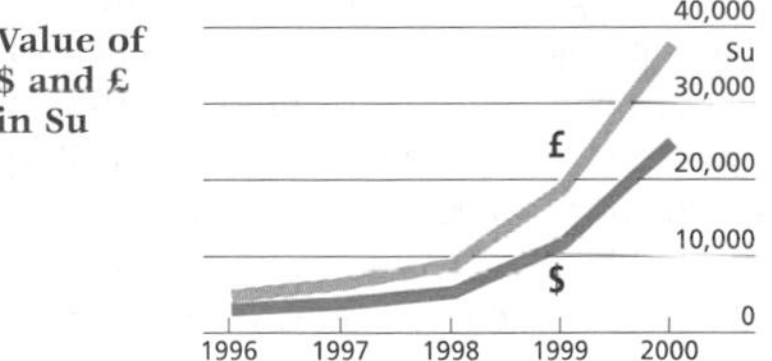

The government closed all banks for a week in 1999 at the height of the economic crisis and a run on the sucre which plunged 26% against the U.S. dollar. More than six banks had to close because of liquidity problems, including Banco Popular, the largest bank; in a similar number of other cases closure was averted by government intervention in an attempt to shore up the financial sector. The Financial Institutions law established fully consolidated financial disclosure rules, and raised the capital stock requirement for new banks to $6 million (existing banks had to meet this requirement by 2002).

There are small stock markets in Quito and Guayaquil. The corporate tax rate is 25%, with an obligatory 15% pre-tax profit to be set aside for workers. The top rate of personal income tax is 25%, and VAT is 12%.

Business Opportunities

Although the government is publicly eager to attract foreign direct investment (FDI), the economy remains one of the most statist and protected in Latin America. FDI, which averaged $200 million in 1985–95 and increased to $700 million in 1997–2000, has been mostly concentrated in the oil sector. The construction of the new pipeline in 2001–03 will produce inward investment of around $3.5 billion. Outside oil, FDI is modest, and is focused on financial services, food processing, chemicals, and vehicle manufacturing.

For More Information

Books:

Chislett, William. *Ecuador: The Economic Modernisation*. London: Euromoney Books, 1995.
Economist Intelligence Unit. *Country Profiles and Country Reports*. London.
Rachowiecki, Rob. *Ecuador*. Oakland, CA: Lonely Planet, 2000.
Roos, Wilma, and Omer Van Renterghem. *In Focus Ecuador: A Guide to the People, Politics and Culture*. Northampton, MA: Interlink Publishing, 2000.

Web Sites:

Banco Pacifico: **www.bp.fin.ec**
Central Bank: **www.bce.fin.ec**
Export and Investment Development Corporation: **www.corpei.org**
IMF reports: **www.imf.org/external**
Official statistical site: **www.inec.gov.ec**
U.S. State Department Country Commercial Guide: **www.state.gov/e/eb/rls/rpts/ccg**

EGYPT

KEY FACTS

- GNI: **$86,544 million; world's 39th**
- GNI pc: **$1,380; world's 122nd**
- Head of government: **president**
- Currency: **Egyptian pound (E£)**
- Capital: **Cairo**
- Population: **67,226,000, growing at 2.0% p.a.**
- Land area: **384,362 square miles**
- Population density: **175 per square mile**
- Life expectancy: **67 years**
- Infant mortality: **41 per 1,000 live births**
- Language: **Arabic, English**
- Best buy: **gold jewelry, spices, carpets**

ECONOMIC STRUCTURE

Composition of GDP (1999)

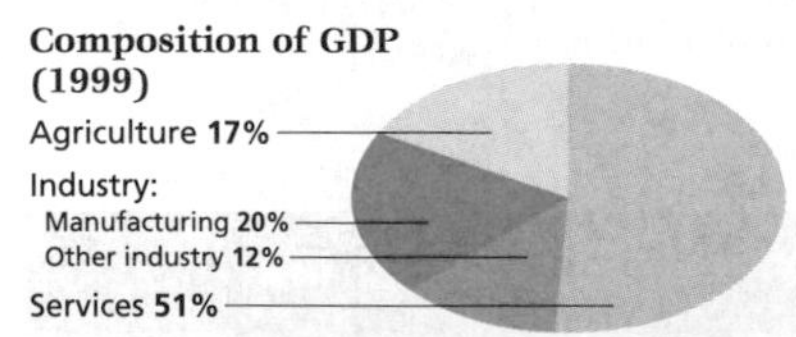

Egypt established one of the earliest world civilizations with impressive engineering, scientific, and cultural achievements. After construction of the Suez Canal was completed in 1869, Britain took increasing financial control of Egypt, and political control in 1882, which it officially relinquished in 1922. However, it continued to exert influence and pressure. After full independence from Britain in 1956 under President Nasser, Egypt developed a socialist command economy led by the military, with an orientation away from the West towards the Soviet Union. Nasser's successor, Anwar Sadat, reversed this in 1974 by launching the "infitah" or open-door policy to Western private sector investment. He concluded the historic peace agreement with Israel in 1979, which led to his assassination in 1981. Other Arab states ostracized Egypt, and financial aid from the Arab oil countries was replaced by U.S. aid. Sadat's successor Hosni Mubarak maintained openness to the West and peace with Israel. He also rebuilt good relations with moderate Arab states. However, the state of emergency introduced after Sadat's assassination is still in force, and defense expenditure is relatively high. Egypt signed a free trade agreement with the European Union in June 2001.

Services, including public services, accounted for around 50% of GDP in 2000–01, followed by industry and mining (20%), agriculture (16%), construction, and energy. The informal sector—encompassing agriculture, waste collection and recycling, construction, manufacturing, trade, and other services—is estimated to account for around 30% of GDP. Tourism and receipts from the Suez Canal are key services sectors which, with workers' remittances and oil and gas revenues, provide the bulk of foreign exchange earnings. Metal products (especially aluminum and steel), textiles, food processing, cement, automotive, household appliances, petroleum products, and fertilizers are the main manufacturing industries. Egypt is a publishing and film production center for the Arab and Islamic world. In 2000–01 petroleum, gas, and petroleum products were the main exports (37.2%), followed by raw cotton, cotton yarn, textiles and clothing (8.7%), aluminum, and iron and steel products (4.5%). The main markets were the United States (40.8%), European Union (28%), Asia (11.4%), and Arab countries (11%).

Current account balance ($ billion)

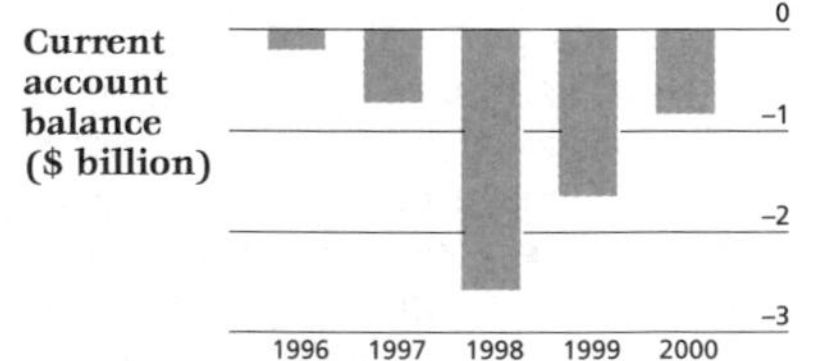

The privatization program started in 1994 but stalled as a result of state companies' debts, fears for the political fallout from worker layoffs, and problems in changing the command economy culture. By late 2001, 126 companies of the 315 put up for privatization had been privatized, bringing the government $3.94 billion, most of which was used to pay for worker dismissal and pension schemes. A large number of loss-making companies were closed. Banking, utilities, energy and transport concerns, and part of the food sector remained in state hands, but these sectors are being opened up to private investment. In 2001 the government prepared to sell its equity in joint venture banks, part of Telecom Egypt, and part of the insurance sector.

ECONOMIC POLICY

Growth in GDP (%)

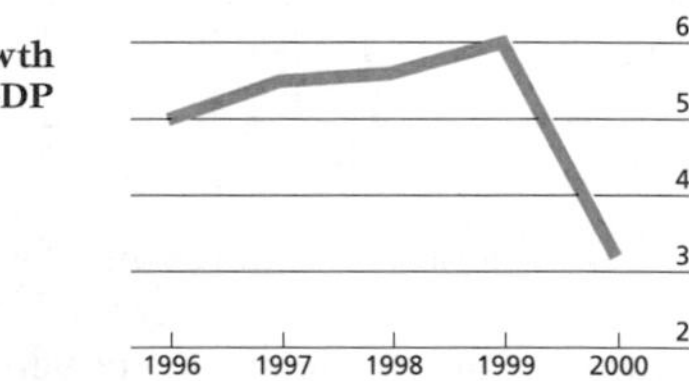

Persistent trade deficits have put pressure on government finances and the financial system. From 1986, IMF-backed reforms were adopted, and in 1990 a $7 billion debt-forgiveness package was directly linked to the structural adjustment program. The pound was pegged to the U.S. dollar. Consumption patterns stabilized in the 1990s as food and other subsidies were phased out. Inflation fell from 55% in 1990 to 8% in 1995, and continued to fall to 2.4% in 2000–01. The budget deficit fell to 13% of GDP in 1995 and 3.7% in 2000. Government spending has been reduced by the privatization program. However, the high level of public debt (26% of GDP to foreign creditors and 38% of GDP to domestic creditors in 2000) and non-performing loans of both public and private sector remain a problem.

Consumer price inflation (%)

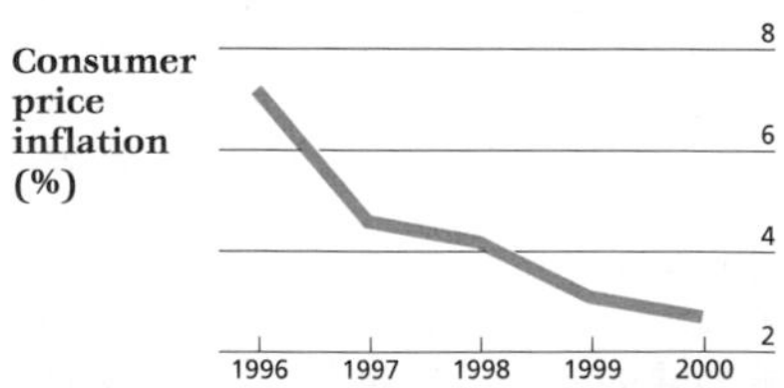

The downturn in oil and tourism earnings in the late 1990s put renewed pressure on the financial system, and the government tightened liquidity. The result was slower growth and rising unemployment. Annual GDP growth declined from an average 6% in the first half of the 1990s to 5.1% in 1996–2000. It is expected to be 3.5% in 2001–03. Unemployment (more accurately under-employment) is unofficially estimated at 20%, although its impact is mitigated by the vibrant informal sector. With the labor force

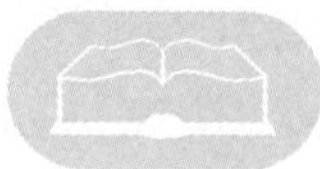

increasing at 2.7% a year, job creation is imperative. The best prospect for that is tourism, which is a government priority for investment. The plan is to double tourism revenues to $8 billion by 2010. Agriculture and small-scale industry are the other priorities, along with IT. Market economy reforms and the privatization program continue.

Geography/Resources

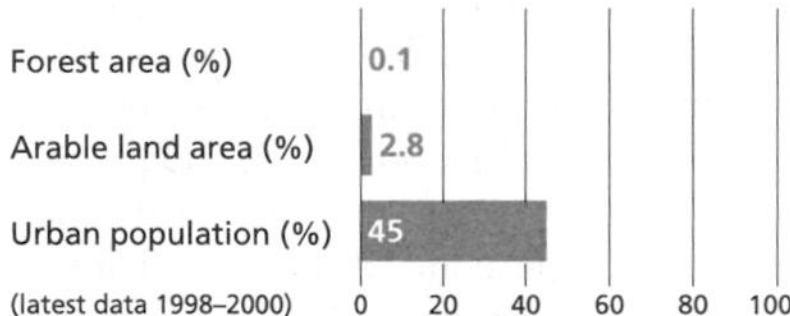

Egypt consists of a 600 mile square on the African continent through which the Nile flows north from Lake Nasser to the Mediterranean, together with the Sinai peninsula. It is bounded by the Gaza Strip and Israel in the northeast, the Red Sea and Gulf of Aqaba in the east, Sudan in the south, Libya in the west, and the Mediterranean Sea in the north. Most of the land is desert with hot dry summers and mild winters. There are winter rains in the coastal plain, but rainfall elsewhere is negligible. The western desert is mostly plateau dotted with oases, while the Sinai is mountainous. The low point is the Qattara Depression at 371 feet below sea level, and the high point Mount Catherine at 8,626 feet.

Less than 4% of the land, mainly the Nile valley and the delta, is cultivated. The main agricultural crop is wheat, followed by sugar cane, rice, cotton, tomatoes, barley, sorghum, sugar beet, citrus fruits, and melons. Many other grains, fruit, and vegetables are grown. Chickens are the main livestock, followed by ducks, sheep, buffaloes, goats, cattle, asses, camels, horses, and pigs. Meat, dairy, honey, leather, and wool are produced. Sea and river fish and fuel wood timber are also important. The most important minerals are petroleum and natural gas. Proven reserves at January 2000 were 2.9 billion barrels and 42.5 trillion cubic feet respectively. Probable gas reserves from new finds were 120 trillion cubic feet. Estimated oil reserves from new finds and improved recovery rates were 8.2 billion barrels. Phosphate rock, iron ore, gypsum, coal, salt, and kaolin are also mined. There are reserves of gold, manganese, and uranium. Exploration continues for various minerals, especially gas and oil.

Around 75% of the population lives in the Nile delta, and most of the rest live in the Nile valley. More than half are urban and under the age of 20. A further 1.9 million work and live abroad, mainly in the Arabian Peninsula. Some 90% of the population is Sunni Muslim, the rest being mainly Christian Copts. Egyptians, Bedouins, and Berbers account for 99% of the population, with Nubians, Greek, Armenian, Italian, and French accounting for 1%.

Communications/Energy

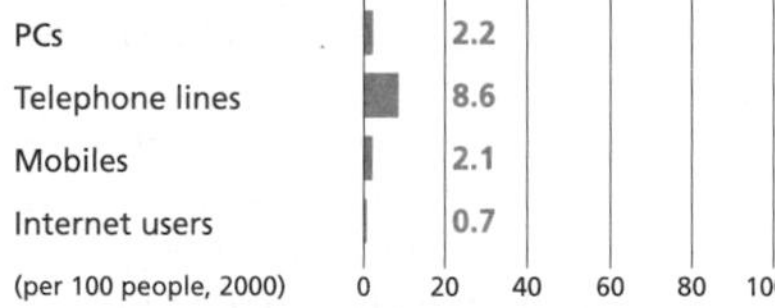

Egypt's 27,300 miles of mixed-quality paved road carries 85% of the country's freight and 60% of its passenger traffic. Road links between the major cities are reasonably good. The Nile valley road has been upgraded, a transcontinental highway is under construction from Alexandria to Tangier to open up the Mediterranean coast, and privately financed BOT (build-operate-transfer) projects are planned. The heavily-subsidized railways system, which boasts 5,800 miles of track, is also to be opened up to private investment. Egypt has 2,100 miles of waterways, of which half are canals. The pipeline network consists of 728 miles for crude oil, 370 miles for petroleum products, and 286 miles for gas. The main sea port is Alexandria, which is operating at less than half its capacity of 50 million tons per year. A major new private-sector container terminal has opened at Port Said, serving a new free trade zone as well as canal traffic. The main international airport is at Cairo, with other international airports at Alexandria and Nuzhah. Foreign carriers are now allowed to fly scheduled fights to any of Egypt's provincial airports, eroding state carrier EgyptAir's dominance. Bids are planned on a BOT basis for several new regional airports.

State-owned Telecom Egypt is the main telecommunications operator, but it is excluded from mobile telephony until November 2002. It is seeking a strategic partner and investor to help develop its mobile network from end-2002. Meanwhile mobile networks are operated by Click and MobiNil. In March 2001 there were 7 million fixed phone lines and 2.5 mobile phones. Telecom Egypt aims to increase local-loop lines by 1 million a year through 2005. At mid-2001 there were 70,000 Internet subscribers and 560,000 Internet users. Fees for Internet access were due to be reduced to encourage greater participation.

Oil production at 794,000 barrels per day in 2000, down from 922,000 barrels per day in 1996, reflects the depletion of reserves. Without new proven reserves Egypt could become a net oil importer by 2010. Domestic oil consumption was 573,000 barrels per day in 2000. Gas production was 2.3 billion cubic feet per day by end-1999, and is expected to double by end-2002 with many new gas fields coming on-stream. Gas exports are planned for Europe with the construction of new LNG processing plants and export terminals due for completion in 2004. The construction of a gas pipeline to Israel and on to Turkey is under consideration. Around 84% of electricity is generated from thermal power plants, most of which have been converted from oil to gas. Hydroelectricity accounts for 16%. New gas-fired power stations, being built with private finance under the BOT scheme, are planned to meet the 7–8% a year increase in electricity demand. The sector is thus being liberalized, although the dominant operator remains state-owned Egyptian Electricity Authority. The Egyptian grid was linked with that of Jordan in 1998 and Libya in 1999. Links with Syria, Turkey, and Iraq were due for completion by 2002. Further links with other Arabian Peninsula countries are planned.

Education/Employment

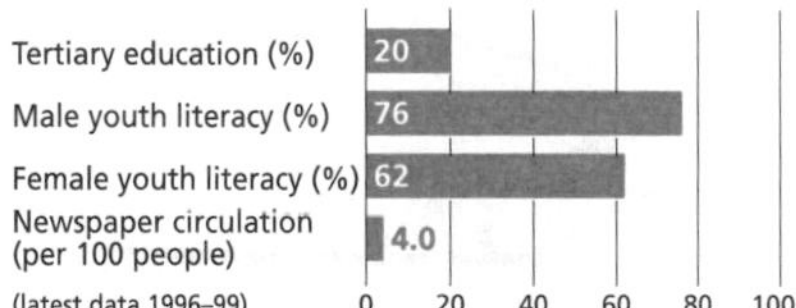

Education is compulsory from age six to fourteen. It is free at all levels, but only 8% achieve university degrees. There were 1.3 million students enrolled at 14 universities and 342 other higher-education institutes in 1998–99. Education policy and funding is the remit of the Ministry of Education. Male adult illiteracy is 34% and female 57%, imposing a major constraint on manpower development. The government is concentrating on improving the range and quality of education, including vocational training, with an emphasis on IT.

The National Technology program was launched in 1982 to develop national R&D capacity with international cooperation. Research takes place at specialized research centers, universities, and companies. Decentralized units have been established to take part in projects and help overcome regional development problems. R&D strengths include agriculture, biotech-

  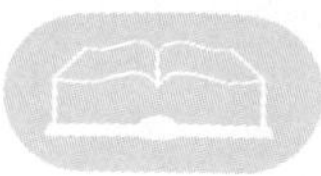    

nology, medical, water, desertification, environment protection, seismology, metallurgy, materials science, energy, transport, civil engineering, and IT. International cooperation includes agreements with the United States, China, Germany, Italy, and the EU.

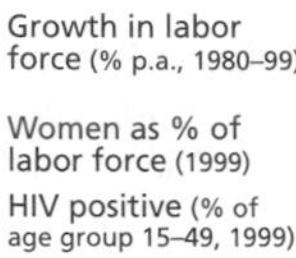

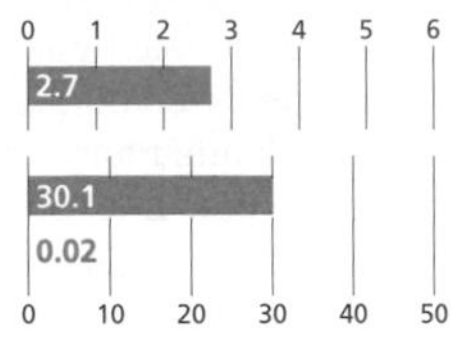

The labor force has a range of skills, but those with high qualifications are in short supply. Wages and other employment conditions are determined by employers and employees. Around 27% of the labor force is unionized, mostly in state industries. Strikes are legally banned, but take place occasionally nonetheless. The government sets health and safety standards, but inspection is infrequent. Labor law makes dismissal difficult. A new labor law giving employees the right to collective bargaining, freedom of association and prenotified strikes, and employers the right to dismiss staff, was given preliminary cabinet approval in May 2001 prior to further debate.

Fiscal/Financial

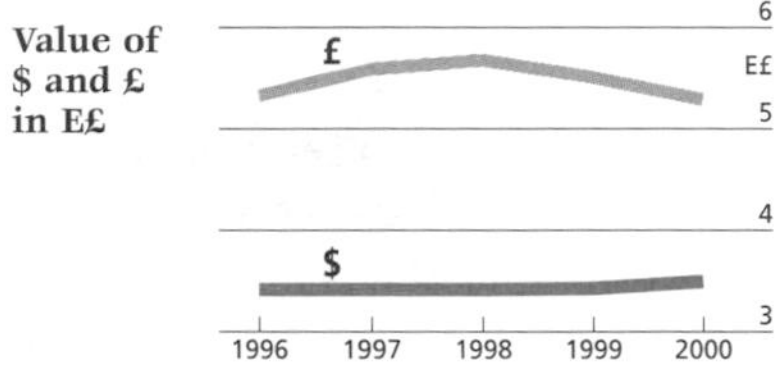

The largest banks are National Bank of Egypt, Banque du Caire, Bank of Alexandria and Banque Misr. All are state-owned, and together they accounted for 65% of total banking sector assets in late 2001. State-owned companies also dominate the insurance sector. The Central Bank of Egypt was given greater independence from government in formulating monetary and credit policies in late 2001. The CBE supervises the banking and insurance sectors, while the Capital Markets Authority regulates the stock market. In June 2001 the OECD added Egypt to the list of countries it considers to have insufficiently strict laws against money laundering.

Corporation tax is 32% for industrial and export operations and 40% for non-industrial operations, but new foreign investment projects can qualify for a tax holiday of 5–20 years. Sales tax was introduced in 1991, and the government is in the process of replacing it with VAT, which will apply to businesses with annual turnover above E£150,000. Tax collection has improved, but tax evasion is still rife.

In late 2001 there were around 80 commercial banks, but retail banking is largely undeveloped, with the majority of the population using a cash economy. The banks have not yet developed sophisticated IT systems. The main banks conduct operations for all sectors of the economy, and have extensive branch networks. Their ratios of non-performing loans are reckoned to be high, but internal reforms have been instigated and loan management has improved. The government intends to sell its remaining equity in joint venture banks to the private sector, but its plans to privatize the big banks are on hold at least until internal reforms are completed. In the meantime, the government has extended the operations of foreign banks, including local acquisitions. Money-market operations are sophisticated. New opportunities are opening up in corporate banking. Foreign insurance companies are now allowed to fully own domestic insurers. Preparations are under way for the privatization of state insurance companies.

The Cairo and Alexandria Stock Exchange, relaunched in 1992, is one of the largest bourses in the region with over 1,000 companies listed in 2001. Automated trading began in May 2001. Companies are required to follow international accounting rules for information disclosure. The stock market has performed badly following a promising start because of the slow pace of privatization and the liquidity squeeze caused by the deteriorating exchange rate, which led to a decline in the number of institutional investors. The lack of institutional investors has in turn slowed privatization.

Business Opportunities

Growth in output (% p.a., 1990–99)

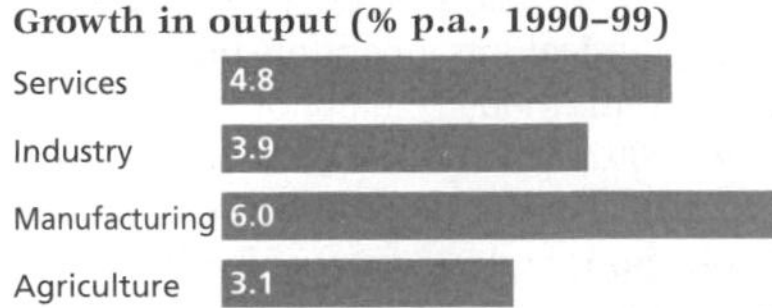

Tax incentives are offered to investors. At mid-2001 there were six free trade zones, and new ones were planned. Although investment application procedures have been streamlined, red tape can still be a problem. The effective elimination of all foreign exchange controls in 1998 removed a major operational hazard. Manufacturing and mining (especially oil and gas) have attracted the most foreign investment, followed by tourism. Other sectors include finance, insurance, power plants, transport infrastructure, and agriculture. Saudi Arabia is the top foreign investor, followed by the United Arab Emirates, United Kingdom, United States, Panama, Netherlands, Switzerland, and Libya. Investment opportunities continue in tourism, infrastructure, power, finance, insurance, oil and gas, IT, car assembly, specialized steel mills, glass-making, textiles, consumer goods, and agribusiness. Liberalization of state-dominated sectors and privatizations offer further opportunities. The point of contact for investors is the General Authority for Investment & Free Zones (GAFI) within the Ministry of Economy and Foreign Trade.

For More Information

Books:

Abdel-Khalek, G. *Stabilization and Adjustment in Egypt*. Northampton, MA: Edward Elgar, 2001.

Capmas Statistical Year Book. Cairo.

Daly, M. W. *The Cambridge History of Egypt*, 2 vols. New York: Cambridge University Press, 2000.

McDermott, Anthony. *Egypt from Nasser to Mubarak: A Flawed Revolution*. London: Croom Helm, 1988.

Raymond, André. *Cairo*. Cambridge, MA: Harvard University Press, 2001.

Rodenbeck, Max. *Cairo: The City Victorious*. New York: Picador, 1998.

Web Sites:

Al-Ahram Weekly (English weekly digest of the largest daily newspaper): **www.ahram.org.eg/weekly**

Cabinet Information and Decision Support Centre (government entry point): **www.idsc.gov.eg**

Cairo and Alexandria Stock Exchanges: **www.egyptse.com**

Central Agency for Public Mobilization and Statistics: **www.capmas.gov.eg**

Central Bank of Egypt: **www.cbe.org.eg**

EGF Hermes Egypt Country Report 2000: **www.egf-hermes.com**

Egyptian State Information Service: **www.sis.gov.org**

Ministry of Economy and Foreign Trade: **www.tpegypt.gov.eg**

  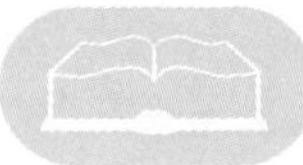    

El Salvador

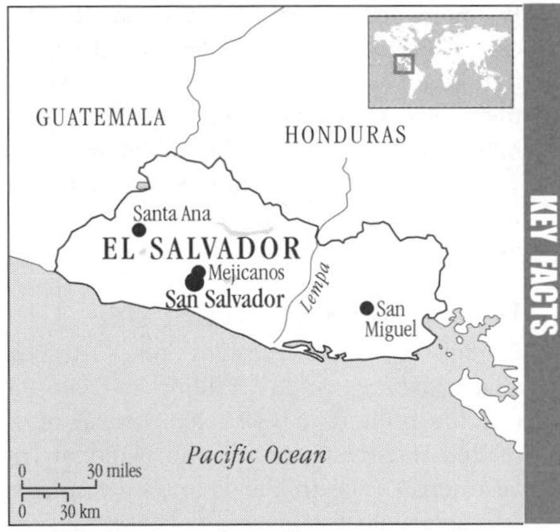

KEY FACTS

GNI: **$11,806 million; world's 80th**
GNI pc: **$1,920; world's 105th**
Head of government: **president**
Currency: **U.S. dollar ($)**
Capital: **San Salvador**
Population: **6,154,000, growing at 2.1% p.a.**
Land area: **7,992 square miles**
Population density: **770 per square mile**
Life expectancy: **70 years**
Infant mortality: **35 per 1,000 live births**
Language: **Spanish**
Best buy: **handicrafts**

Economic Structure

A 12-year civil war which claimed 70,000 lives, most of them civilian, ended in 1992 with UN-brokered peace accords. From 1932 until 1980 every president, with one exception, was an army officer. During this period the land-owning economic elite, known as the 14 families, ruled the country in conjunction with the military and rightist vigilante death squads. The Farabundo Marti National Liberation Front (FMLN), the former guerrilla organization, won the legislative elections in 2000 and became the main opposition to the right-wing Arena party, in power since 1989.

The economy, traditionally based on coffee-growing, has become more diversified, particularly since the introduction of sweeping free market reforms during the 1990s. El Salvador was ranked a very high twelfth out of 124 countries in the 2001 Index of Economic Freedom drawn up by the U.S. Heritage Foundation, and its status was upgraded from "mostly free" to "free." But, in stark contrast, it was ranked ninety-fifth out of 162 countries in the world human development ranking of the United Nations Development Program (UNDP). The neo-liberal policies have done little to improve the skewed income distribution.

Services generate 65% of GDP, industry 22%, and agriculture 13% (the latter employs 25% of the work force). Apart from coffee the principal products are sugar, rice, beans, and cotton. Industrial activities include food and beverage processing, textiles, footwear and clothing, chemical products, and electronics. Historically, El Salvador has been the most industrialized nation in Central America, though this position was weakened during the 1980–92 civil war. The industrial sector has shifted since 1993 from a primarily domestic orientation to include free zone ("maquiladora" assembly plants) manufacturing for export. The maquiladoras, which import most of their inputs and export the finished product—for example shirts or computer components—account for a growing share of exports. The other principal and traditional exports are coffee, sugar, and shrimp. The major market is the United States (up to 60%). Canada began to negotiate a free trade deal with El Salvador in November 2001.

The five banks nationalized in 1980 were sold in 1989 and this was followed by the privatization of several sugar mills, the four electricity distribution companies, and the telecommunications companies INTEL and ANTEL. The "pay as you go" state pension system was also phased out and replaced by one of individual capitalization based on the model in Chile.

Economic Policy

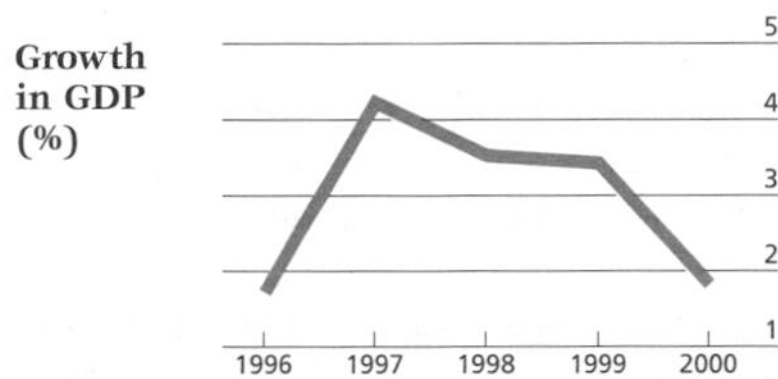

The civil war devastated the economy. It was not until 1994 that real GDP, as measured in 1990 constant colones, returned to its pre-war level. Free-market reforms and prudent fiscal management produced strong growth in the 1990s, albeit from a low base. Real GDP growth averaged 5.0% in 1992–1999, fell to 2% in 2000, and fell again in 2001. Inflation has been below 5% since 1997 (deflation of 1% in 1999), the fiscal deficit was around 3% of GDP in 2001, and external debt is less than 25% of GDP. Tax revenue reached 11% of GDP in 2000 (8% in 1991). The official unemployment rate is around 7% but is much higher in rural areas. Underemployment and child labor are widespread.

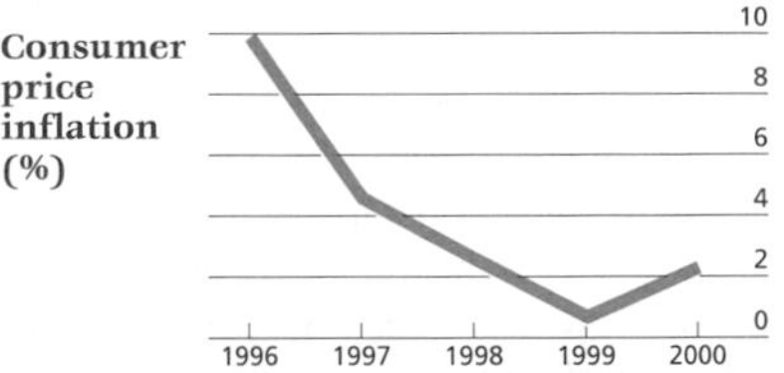

The exchange-rate regime was changed at the beginning of 2001. After seven years of Central Bank intervention to keep the colon at 8.75 per $, the Banco Central de Reserva (BCR) decided to peg the currency to the dollar at this rate and make the dollar full legal tender. By the middle of 2002 the colon had been fully withdrawn from circulation. Dollarization reduced lending risk, but it means the BCR cannot use monetary policy as an instrument to fend off external shocks.

Geography/Resources

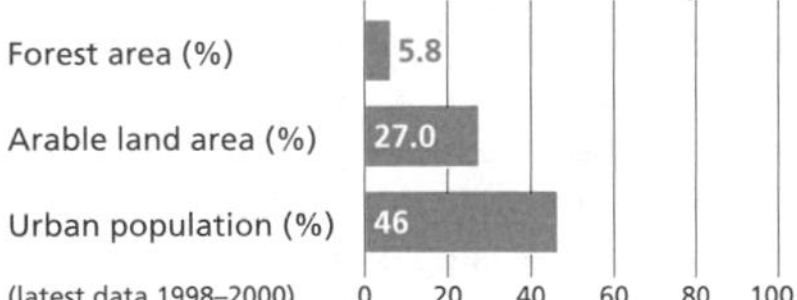

El Salvador is the smallest country in Central America and, with more than 750 inhabitants per square mile, the most densely populated in Latin America. It borders Guatemala to the west and Honduras to the north, both Honduras and Nicaragua to the east, divided in part by the Gulf of Fonseca, and the Pacific Ocean to the south. It is the only Central American country that does not have an Atlantic coast.

The country is divided almost evenly between mountainous and fairly level land. Two mountain ranges cross the country from west to east. The northern range, near the Honduran border, rises at some points to 7,900 feet. The southern range is formed by a chain of more than 20 volcanoes, the highest of which, Santa Ana, rises more than 7,500 feet above sea level. Some of the volcanoes are active. The central plain between the two ranges is an area of plateaux about 2,000 feet above sea level. The country's

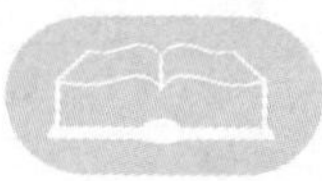

longest river, the Lempa, flows through this region to the Pacific Ocean. The country is subject to earthquakes and hurricanes. The two earthquakes in 2001 killed more than 1,200 people, and destroyed or badly damaged 335,000 homes, one-quarter of the country's stock of housing, much of it makeshift. Hurricane Mitch left 374 people dead or missing in 1998. The damage wrought in 2001 was estimated at $2 billion (15% of GDP).

El Salvador is part of an extraordinarily rich ecological area (Central America formed the bridge on which, long ago, South American monkeys met North American squirrels under the tropical canopy), but it ranks just behind Haiti as the Western hemisphere's most environmentally-degraded country. Less than 2% of the original tropical forest cover is left, and another 7% of the land is only partially protected by coffee trees.

Gold, silver, sea-salt, and limestone are mined or quarried, and there are deposits of copper, iron ore, lead, mercury, sulfur, and zinc. The mining sector's contribution to the economy, however, is tiny (an estimated 0.1% of GDP).

Around 94% of the population (6.2 million) are mestizo (mixed Amerindian and white), 5% Amerindian, and 1% white. Emigration during the civil war reached such a level that an estimated 20% of the population now live abroad, mostly in the United States. The annual inflow of cash remittances is exceptionally high for such a small country (more than $1.6 billion), and they are a key driver of growth and the largest single source of foreign exchange.

Communications/Energy

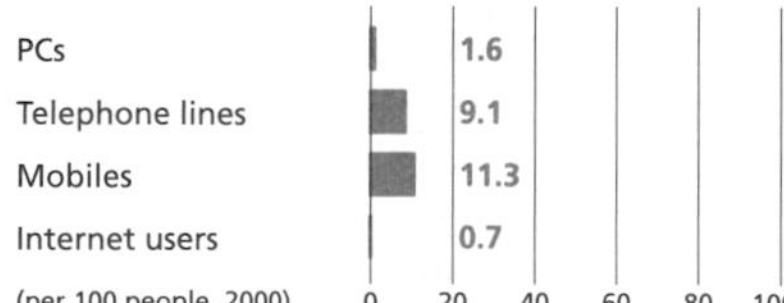

The country's 7,800 miles of roads, 1,200 miles of which are paved, and 374 miles of railways took a battering during the civil war. While the roads have been improved, the railways are in a poor state, with some sections abandoned or unusable. Acajutla on the Pacific coast is the only port in service, but it has tidal conditions that make loading and unloading difficult. Ports in Guatemala and Honduras are used. The international airport at San Salvador is the most modern in Central America and has become an important hub thanks to the success of TACA, El Salvador's privately-owned airline and the third-largest in Latin America (after Varig of Brazil and Aeromexico), which has a regional network of interlinked airlines.

Electricity is produced by four hydroelectric plants and one geothermal plant. Imported oil accounts for around one-third of energy needs. The electricity sector was also hard hit by the civil war, and a major expansion program was under way to increase capacity from 950 MW to 2015 MW by 2010. A Central American electricity interconnection system, stretching from Guatemala to Panama, is being established. Cel, the leading electricity company, expected to become a net exporter to the Central American grid.

San Salvador has more than 20 fixed telephone lines per 100 persons, but the rest of the country has less than 6 lines per 100 persons.

Education/Employment

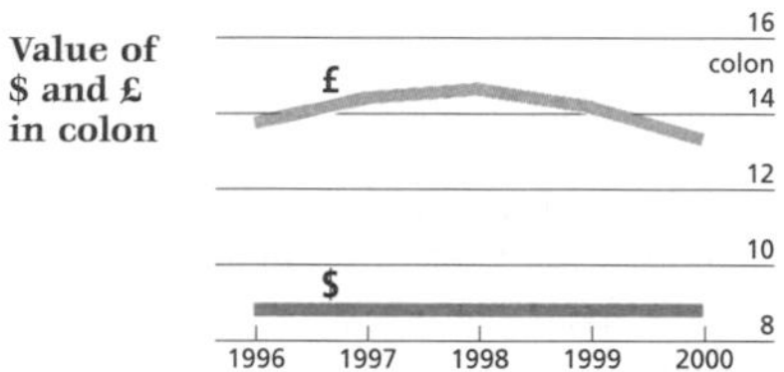

Investment in education remains a high priority. Education is obligatory from age seven to sixteen. The illiteracy rate, according to official figures, was cut from 50% to 16% during the 1990s through programs largely in rural areas. The emphasis has switched from primary to secondary education. Close to 20% of school-age children stop their studies and work to help their families survive. There is one public university and 30 private ones. The best known is the Jesuit-run University of Central America.

The labor force is hard-working and enterprising when given the opportunity. There are many examples of Salvadorans who emigrated to the United States and have become successful entrepreneurs.

Fiscal/Financial

El Salvador's banks are the largest in Central America, and are expanding domestically and within the region. The main banks are Banco Agrícola Comercial and Banco Cuscatlan. Banco Central de Reserva, the Central Bank, is independent of the government. A constitutional reform in 1998 prohibits it from lending to the public sector.

The top income tax rate is 30% and corporate tax is 25%. VAT is 13%. The stock exchange in San Salvador is very small.

Business Opportunities

Foreign direct investment rose from a yearly average of $17 million in 1985–95 to $394 million in 1997–2000, most of it related to privatizations. The National Investment Office in the Economy Ministry is responsible for investments. Key incentives include income tax exemption, duty-free importation of machinery and inputs, no limits on foreign capital, and full currency convertibility. A growing problem for foreign firms in the country is public security: crime rates are very high.

For More Information

Books:

Browning, David. *Landscape and Society*. New York: Oxford University Press, 1971.
Chislett, William. *El Salvador: A New Opportunity*. London: Euromoney Books, 1998.
Dunkerley, James. *Power in the Isthmus*. New York: Verso, 1987.
Luciak, Ilya A. *After the Revolution*. Baltimore, MD: Johns Hopkins University Press, 2001.
Wood, Elizabeth J. *Forging Democracy from Below*. New York: Cambridge University Press, 2000.

Web Sites:

Central Bank: **www.bcr.gob.sv**
Foundation for Economic and Social Development: **www.fusades.com.sv**
IMF reports: **www.imf.org.external**
Investment Promotion Agency: **www.proesa.com.sv**
U.S. State Department Country Commercial Guide: **www.state.gov/e/eb/rls/rpts/ccg**

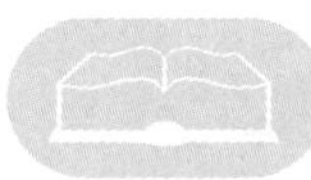

ESTONIA

KEY FACTS

GNI: **$4,906 million; world's 112th**
GNI pc: **$3,400; world's 83rd**
Head of government: **prime minister**
Currency: **kroon (EEK)**
Capital: **Tallinn**
Population: **1,412,000, growing at –1.2% p.a.**
Land area: **17,423 square miles**
Population density: **81 per square mile**
Life expectancy: **69 years**
Infant mortality: **17 per 1,000 live births**
Language: **Estonian, Russian**
Best buy: **antiques, classic Estonian knitwear**

The Estonian stock exchange, established in 1996, soon became more active than those of other former Soviet states. Its total capitalization at the end of 1999 was about $1.9 billion. Legislation has been introduced to encourage participation in private pension schemes, and the insurance market, like banking, experienced consolidation and became majority foreign-owned in 1997–2000.

Estonia's tax system has been comprehensively reformed in line with its EU membership application. Individual income tax and corporate (profit) tax are charged at a 26% flat rate and VAT at 18%; as of 2000, reinvested profit is not taxed.

ECONOMY

Estonia is regarded as the former Soviet state that has moved furthest towards the market system. In the mid 1990s it completed economic liberalization. In the late 1990s most major industries were privatized, external economic imbalances curbed, the increase in external debt halted and inflation reduced to EU levels. In 2001 some remaining capital controls were abolished. EU and Euro membership are expected to bring further macro-economic benefits.

Estonia grew its service sector, especially transport and tourism, through the 1990s, while agriculture declined. Its largest industries are food processing, machine building, forestry, textiles, and chemicals; in general these successfully reoriented away from Russia after the 1998 Russian crisis. By 2000 Finland and Sweden both surpassed Russia as both importers and as an export market. Estonian exports to the EU continued to increase in 2000–01 despite the EU slowdown.

GEOGRAPHY/RESOURCES

Estonia has a land area of 17,423 square miles. Its population fell throughout the 1990s, by 8.1% to 1,439,000 between 1989 and 2000; at the end of the 1990s the death rate still exceeded the birth rate. According to the 1989 census the population was 61.5% Estonian and 30.3% Russian, with smaller groups of Ukrainians, Belarusians, Finns, and other nationalities.

COMMUNICATIONS/ENERGY

Transit trade is crucial to the Estonian economy and comprises an estimated 80% of the cargo handled in its 101 sea ports. This trade overcame the adverse effects of the 1998 Russian crisis; cargo volumes increased by 23.5% between 1998 and 1999, and continued to rise the following year. Sea passenger traffic increased greatly in the 1990s. The railways and roads, by contrast with the ports, remained in urgent need of development at the end of the 1990s.

By 2000 Estonia had 35 telephone lines per 100 inhabitants, high by Eastern European standards, and the highest mobile telephone penetration of any former Soviet state. The telecommunications industry has been partially privatized, with investment by Finnish and Swedish strategic investors. In 2001 the fixed-line market was liberalized.

Oil shale, which supplies most of Estonia's energy needs, has helped it to achieve energy independence from Russia, but is a highly pollutant fuel. In 2001 resulting environmental concerns had still to be resolved prior to Estonia joining the EU, and costs of clean-up measures are high. Gas is likely to increasingly replace oil shale as fuel. Energy sector restructuring and privatization were given an impetus by the 1998 Energy Act, and privatization of the largest power-generating company was mostly completed in 2001.

FISCAL/FINANCIAL

The Estonian banking sector has been one of the fastest-growing sectors in the Baltic states. By the end of 1998 it had become the most concentrated banking sector in the region, with the number of banks shrinking from 11 to 5; it also became 90% Scandinavian-owned, which added to its stability.

BUSINESS OPPORTUNITIES

Estonia is regarded as having one of the most favorable investment climates in Eastern Europe, comparable with Slovenia and Hungary. It attracts one of the highest amounts of foreign direct investment per capita. The main sources of FDI were Finland, Sweden, the United States, Norway, and the Netherlands, and it amounted to 5% of GDP in 1999.

Estonia's legal framework is largely in line with the EU's; there are no exchange controls or restrictions on foreign investment, and foreigners enjoy equal rights with domestic investors, which are legally fully developed. Transparency International has rated Estonia as the least corrupt country in Central and Eastern Europe.

Privatization is already well advanced, but Estonia has many investment opportunities in banking and other financial services, transport and tourism, and all manufacturing sectors.

For More Information

Books:

Lieven, Anatol. *The Baltic Revolution: Estonia, Latvia, Lithuania and the Path to Independence*. New Haven, CT: Yale University Press, 1994.

Raun, Toivo U. *Estonia and the Estonians*. 2nd ed. Stanford, CA: Hoover Institution Press, 2002.

Web Sites:

Bank of Estonia: **www.ee/epbe**
Estonian state Web center: **www.riik.ee**

ETHIOPIA

KEY FACTS

GNI: **$6,524 million; world's 99th**
GNI pc: **$100; world's 207th**
Head of government: **prime minister**
Currency: **birr (B)**
Capital: **Addis Ababa**
Population: **61,095,000, growing at 2.7% p.a.**
Land area: **435,185 square miles**
Population density: **135 per square mile**
Life expectancy: **44 years**
Infant mortality: **118 per 1,000 live births**
Language: **Amharic, Orominya, Tigrinya**
Best buy: **leather, textiles, jewelry, coffee**

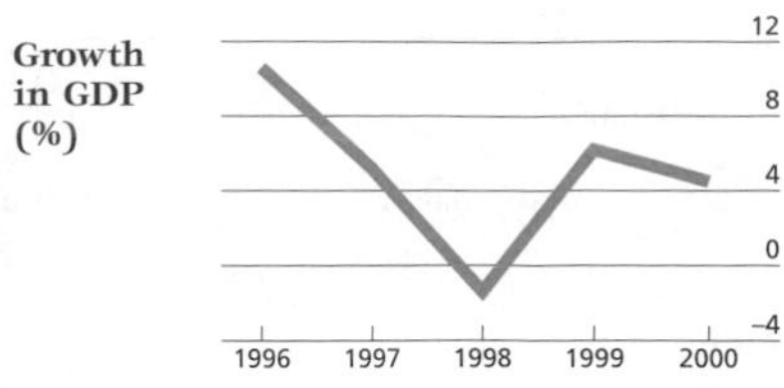

ECONOMIC STRUCTURE

As one of the few regions of Africa not to have been subjected to foreign rule, Ethiopia has a proud but turbulent history. In recent years the country's fortunes have been determined by the rise to power of the Ethiopian Revolutionary People's Democratic Front (EPRDF) in 1991, by the independence granted to Eritrea in 1993, by the subsequent Ethiopian-Eritrean war (1998–2000), and by other ongoing regional political struggles within Ethiopia itself.

Although there are vocal opposition groups representing the rights of the Oromo and Amhara people of central Ethiopia, and armed opposition groups operate in some of the more remote parts of the country, nationwide elections held in 2000 resulted in the EPRDF winning 89% of the seats in the federal legislature. In 2001, however, there was evidence of an ongoing power struggle within the EPRDF, and several formerly close allies of prime minister Meles Zenawi resigned or were removed from office. There were strong disagreements over the government's strategy towards Eritrea. The ceasefire agreed between the two countries in 2000 was holding, but there was continuing mutual suspicion, and very little progress in the demarcation of the common border. Additionally, in late 2001 there was a rise in tension on the long border with Somalia, where the absence of an effective central government posed the potential risk of terrorist activity by Islamic extremists.

Despite the inevitably negative impact of the upheavals of the 1990s on such a poor country, there has been intermittent progress on the economic front. Ethiopia's fortunes are always constrained by its erratic rainfall patterns, mountainous terrain, and poor infrastructure, but the liberalization policies adopted in the past decade have encouraged at least some new investment in a modernization process that can only be very gradual in such an underdeveloped economy.

Agriculture, hunting, forestry, and fishing contribute about 50% of Ethiopia's GDP. The next most important contributors are the public administration (10%), and trade, hotels and restaurants (8%). As an overwhelmingly rural people, 85% of Ethiopians are directly or indirectly dependent upon the land for their living, and their day-to-day living conditions are often extremely harsh. The country's principal export product is coffee, followed by hides, skins, and qat. Coffee normally provides about 60% of the country's foreign exchange earnings. The largest market for Ethiopian exports is Germany, followed by Japan, Saudi Arabia, Italy, and the United States.

The economy has undergone substantial reform since the early 1990s, and the process has largely been dictated by Ethiopians themselves rather than by the international agencies. The most important reforms have included dismantling direct government controls, deregulation of trade, a revised taxation system, financial liberalization, and gradual privatization. The government has not yielded to domestic and foreign demands that it bring an end to the system of state ownership of land.

ECONOMIC POLICY

Economic reforms were first introduced in 1992, with strong support from the World Bank, the IMF, and other donors. However, the initially-expected scale of international financial support has not been sustained, although nearly all government operations are highly dependent on direct financial aid from the international community. Privatization of shops, hotels, restaurants, and some larger-scale enterprises has, however, brought in some new investment, and hundreds of new projects have received investment approval. Many of Ethiopia's bilateral debts, especially those to the former Soviet Union, have been canceled.

The fortunes of the economy remain critically dependent on climatic developments and the size of the national harvests. Economic activity has been interrupted and distorted by the repeated flare-up of Ethiopia's border conflict with Eritrea. Growth averaged above 5% in the late 1990s and reached 7.5% in 2000–01. Inflation has been kept under control, and turned negative in 2000 thanks to good harvests and a high inflow of food aid.

Improved management of the agricultural sector will be essential if any real prosperity is to be brought to Ethiopia's overcrowded rural communities. Agricultural production yields are low and erratic as a result of soil erosion, limited use of fertilizers and pesticides, and lack of irrigation. Although market liberalization has improved production incentives, there is as yet no comprehensive program to improve or update traditional production methods. Lack of rain in 1997 and 1999 resulted in serious crop failures.

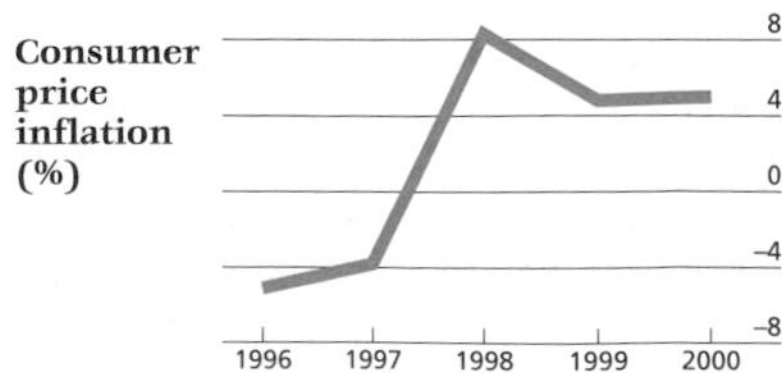

Following the release of $150 million in economic rehabilitation funds by the World Bank in 2001, some reforms were stepped up, including the ending of the central bank's foreign exchange monopoly and the introduction of a liberalized foreign exchange market. Further reforms were anticipated in the wake of nationwide con-

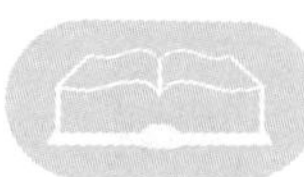

sultations on a poverty reduction strategy, which was due to be presented to donors in the course of 2002.

Geography/Resources

Ethiopia is Africa's most mountainous country, but it is bounded by harsh desert and semi-desert regions. The mountains feed some large rivers, including the Blue Nile. The central and western regions attract the most reliable rainfall, and it is here that most of the country's food is grown. Coffee is a leading crop in central and southern areas. Over-intensive cultivation and a heavy reliance on firewood for fuel have resulted in deforestation and soil erosion. There is now widespread concern to ensure conservation and environmental protection.

There are substantial mineral resources, although relatively little has been done to develop them. Investors have shown particular interest in gold, precious metals, oil, and gas. Current output of gold stands at more than 3 tons per annum, and the government estimates that this could be expanded tenfold with relatively modest new investment. There are reserves of coal, iron ore, tantalum, bicarbonate, and potassium. At present, the leading mining activities are those of limestone, clay, and marble.

More than 60 million people live in Ethiopia. The two largest ethnic groups are the Oromo, who account for about one-third of the population, and the Amhara, who account for about 24%. Although there are numerous smaller groups, and perhaps 250 distinct languages, the federal constitution recognizes only nine different nationalities. There are 14 administrative regions with their own regional assemblies.

Communications/Energy

	(per 100 people, 2000)
PCs	0.1
Telephone lines	0.4
Mobiles	0.03
Internet users	0.02

(per 100 people, 2000) 0 20 40 60 80 100

Ethiopia has an underdeveloped transport network based on road and rail links between various Red Sea ports and Addis Ababa, and on roads radiating outwards from the capital. About 20% of the national capital budget is regularly devoted to road construction and repairs. The recent war with Eritrea has forced Ethiopia to depend on Djibouti as its major maritime outlet—although this route is served by an inadequate and decaying railway line—and to explore the development of closer trading relations with Sudan.

Telecommunications services are only just beginning to be modernized. A mobile telephone service was introduced in 1999 in the vicinity of Addis Ababa by the state-owned Ethiopian Telecommunications Corporation, in a joint venture with Ericsson of Sweden.

There is room for further development of Ethiopia's energy potential. Studies have been carried out on the construction of some major hydroelectric dams on the Blue Nile and Awash rivers.

Education/Employment

After years of underfunding of the educational sector, the government has attempted to increase spending, but there are still very low levels of enrollment, with only 28% of children attending primary school and only 15% attending secondary school. There is a university in Addis Ababa and an agricultural university at Alemaya. About 30,000 students attend these institutions.

Fiscal/Financial

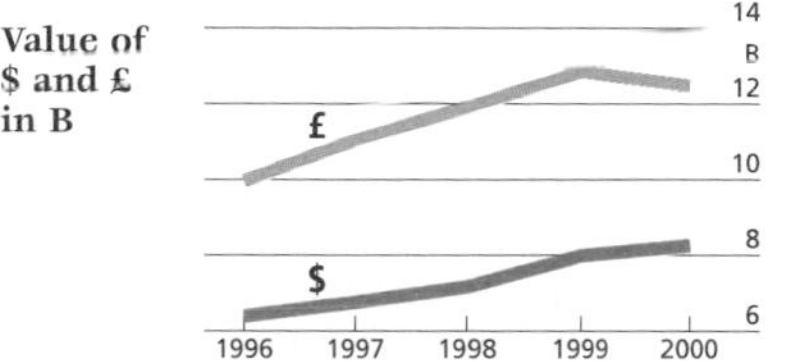

The National Bank of Ethiopia is the central bank. There are nine commercial banks, the largest of which is the state-owned Commercial Bank of Ethiopia. Financial sector liberalization has proceeded slowly, but there was a breakthrough in 2001 with the lifting of foreign exchange controls. The introduction of market-determined interest rates was expected to follow.

Ethiopia is a candidate for debt relief under the World Bank's Highly Indebted Poor Countries (HIPC) initiative, and many bilateral creditors have already announced the cancellation of the country's debts to them.

Taxation is levied by the central government, which raises about 85% of domestic revenue, and by the regional authorities, which are nevertheless financially dependent upon subsidies from the central government. Revenue collection has improved as the process of collecting sales and excise taxes has been simplified.

Business Opportunities

Privatization of state-owned enterprises has been the main avenue for attracting foreign investment in recent years. Having disposed of shops, restaurants, and hotels, mainly in and around Addis Ababa, the government has now embarked on privatizing breweries, state farms, and agro-industries. There is a good prospect of investment by Ethiopians resident abroad. The leading investor in recent years has been the Midroc group, which is controlled by Sheikh Alamoudi of Saudi Arabia, whose mother is Ethiopian.

The mining sector has excited some preliminary interest from foreign investors, both in solid minerals and hydrocarbons. Up to 1998, both the telecommunications and energy sectors were the preserve of the government. Investment in the potentially very lucrative tourism industry was beginning to pick up strongly before the outbreak of the Ethiopian-Eritrean war in 1998. If the UN-brokered peace agreement holds, it is likely that the industry will resume its activities.

For More Information

Books:

Abraham, K. *Ethiopia: From Bullets to the Ballot Box.* Lawrenceville, NJ: Red Sea Press, 1994.
Clapham, C. *Transformation and Continuity in Revolutionary Ethiopia.* New York: Cambridge University Press, 1988.
Connell, D. *Against all Odds: A Chronicle of the Eritrean Revolution.* Lawrenceville, NJ: Red Sea Press, 1993.
Erlich, H. *Ethiopia and the Middle East.* Boulder, CO: Lynne Rienner Publishers, 1994.

Web Sites:

African news and information: **www.allafrica.com/business**
African Studies Internet Resources: **www.columbia.edu/cu/libraries/indiv/area/Africa/Ethecon.html**
COMESA country information: **www.comesa.int/states/ethiopia/qethindx.htm**
Norwegian Council for Africa, Index on Africa: **www.afrika.no/index**
Political Resources on the Net: **www.politicalresources.net**

Faeroe Islands

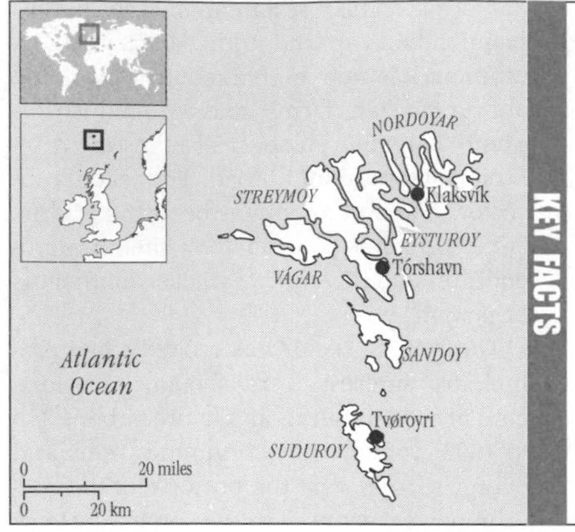

KEY FACTS

GNI pc: **$16,000 (approx.)**
Head of government: **prime minister**
Currency: **Danish kroner (DKr)**
Capital: **Tórshavn**
Population: **45,400**
Land area: **546 square miles**
Population density: **83 per square mile**
Language: **Faeroese, Danish**
Best buy: **knitwear, fish**

Economy

Fisheries are the main industry, with blue whiting, herring, saithe, and cod the main species. Fisheries accounted for 92% of exports in 2000, followed by ships (6.7%). Ship building, servicing and repair are important industries connected with fishing. In 2000 services contributed 60.7% of GDP, followed by fishing and agriculture 27.9% (fishing accounted for about 27%), construction 5.4%, manufacturing (especially fish processing and textiles) 3.5%, energy and water 2.2%, and mining 0.3%. Fish farming, mostly of salmon, is increasingly important. The government is backing research into the farming of cod and haddock to replace production from fragile ocean stocks. Annual GDP decline averaged 10% in 1990–93, but in 1994–2000 there has been growth averaging 7.4% a year. Inflation averaged 3.5% a year in 1991–2000. Unemployment fell from 12% in July 1996 to 4% in February 2001. Government finances are dependent on Danish state aid, but since the recession credit, wage, and welfare restrictions have reduced the net foreign debt from DKrF8.5 billion in 1990 to DKr4.7 billion in 2000. The 1998 debt agreement between Denmark and the Faeroe Islands acknowledged the aim of the latter to attain full sovereignty.

Offshore oil offers hope of diversifying the economy. In 2000 the government awarded seven exploration licenses for an area next to the United Kingdom sea border, close to where oil has been found in U.K. territory. The licenses were awarded only to companies agreeing to establish Faeroese subsidiaries and train Faeroese workers. The Faeroese company Atlantic Oil has a minor stake in one of the licenses. The license agreements and revenues deriving from them are governed by a new Hydrocarbons Law.

Geography/Resources

The Faeroe Islands are an archipelago of 18 islands in the North Atlantic between the Shetland Islands and Iceland.

About 6% of the land is farmed. The country is self-sufficient in milk, and other dairy products meet 75% of domestic demand. Most meat is imported. Potatoes and other vegetables are grown. Fisheries, including ocean fish, shellfish, and aquaculture, are the dominant industry. Whale hunting is an important industry. Coal is mined. The main prospective mineral resource is offshore oil.

Communications/Energy

The road network is 288 miles. Shipping is the main mode of freight transport between islands and for international destinations. There is a weekly passenger service to Denmark, Iceland, Shetland, and Norway in summer, and a year-round freight service to Denmark. The main port is the capital, Tórshavn. In 2000 the fleet comprised 248 ships with a total displacement of 97,500 grt. The airport at Vágar, served by local airline Atlantic Air, Air Iceland, and Danish airline Mærsk Air, handled 143,208 passengers in 2000, an 11% increase on 1999 as a result of oil exploration and tourism. Atlantic Air operates domestic air services with helicopters.

There were 24,851 fixed phone lines and 10,761 mobile phones in 1999, and 3,000 Internet users in 2000. Electricity is generated mostly from imported oil (58.8% in 1999), followed by hydroelectricity (41.2%).

Fiscal/Financial

The Faeroe Islands are part of the monetary union of the Kingdom of Denmark. Thus monetary and exchange rate policy are conducted by the Danish National Bank and Danish government. Banking supervision is the remit of the Danish Financial Supervisory Authority. Since 1997 insurance has been regulated by the Faeroese government. A new company Trygd began business in 1998 offering house and car insurance. The recession led to the bankruptcy of the smallest bank Fossbankin in 1993, and the merger of the two other commercial banks Sjóvinnubankin and Føroya Banki in 1994 under the latter's name. There are also three savings banks. Public finance institutions, including a venture-capital holding company, account for 10% of total Faeroese financial assets. Asset management and investment banking operations are increasing. A local stock exchange was due to launch in 2002. The Home Rule Government issued bonds for the first time in 1994 which are quoted on the Copenhagen Stock Exchange. Corporation tax is 20% for most companies, 27% for oil companies. Maximum personal income tax is 37%, but with municipal taxes and social security, the final burden can reach 60%.

Business Opportunities

Oil exploration and services related to it offer opportunities to foreign investors willing to fulfil training of Faeroese personnel and other local economy requirements. If and when oil production begins, a host of new opportunities will open up.

For More Information

Books:

Cornwallis, G., and D. Swaney. *Iceland, Greenland, and the Faroe Islands*. 4th ed. Oakland, CA: Lonely Planet, 2001.

The Faroe Islands. Copenhagen, Denmark: Royal Danish Ministry of Foreign Affairs.

Statistical Bulletin 2000 of The Faroe Islands. Argir, Faeroe Islands: Statistics Faeroe Islands.

Web Sites:

National Bank: **www.landsbank.fo**
Statistics Faeroe Islands: **www.hagstova.fo**

FINLAND

KEY FACTS

GNI: **$127,764 million; world's 29th**
GNI pc: **$24,730; world's 17th**
Head of government: **prime minister**
Currency: **Euro (€)**
Capital: **Helsinki**
Population: **5,165,000, growing at 0.4% p.a.**
Land area: **117,600 square miles**
Population density: **44 per square mile**
Life expectancy: **77 years**
Infant mortality: **4 per 1,000 live births**
Language: **Finnish, Swedish**
Best buy: **gold and silver jewelry, ceramics, glassware, cloudberry liqueur**

ECONOMIC STRUCTURE

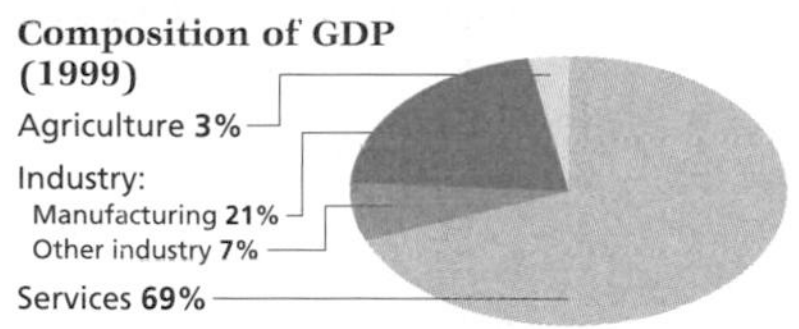

Finland gained its independence in 1917, after a century of being a semi-autonomous region within the Russian Empire and, before that, six centuries of Swedish rule. Its main economic wealth has been forestry, but metalworking was already developed during Swedish rule using imported Swedish metals. In 1910 major copper, zinc, lead, and iron ore deposits were discovered at Outökumpu in southeast Finland, providing the base for industrialization. Foreign trade has been vital to prosperity, and Finland developed close trading relationships with Russia and the Baltic States during the Soviet era. These links remain, and Finland has become a center for multinational companies eager to do business with the Baltic region. Since the runaway success of local company Nokia's mobile phone technology, Finland is also a testing ground for new communications systems.

Services accounted for 61.2% of GDP in 1999. Government services accounted for one-third of services. Industry (including manufacturing, construction, and power) accounted for 34.2% of GDP. Agriculture, forestry and fishing, and mining accounted for 4.6% of GDP. Trade and tourism, followed by communications, transport, and storage, were the main services sectors. Electronics and telecommunications products are the main manufacturing sector, ahead of engineering and metals. Nokia is the leading world manufacturer of mobile telephone products, and the company's growth has increased the share of manufacturing in GDP. Forestry is the main agricultural product. The National Forest Program aims at doubling the value of exports and the use of wood products for domestic energy by 2010. Biotechnology is fast-growing, and Finland ranks sixth in Europe in this sector. In 2000 the main exports were electrical and optical equipment (31%), machinery, transport equipment and metal products (24.7%), pulp and paper (21.7%), and chemicals, rubber, and plastics (7%). The main export markets were Germany, Sweden, United Kingdom, United States, and France.

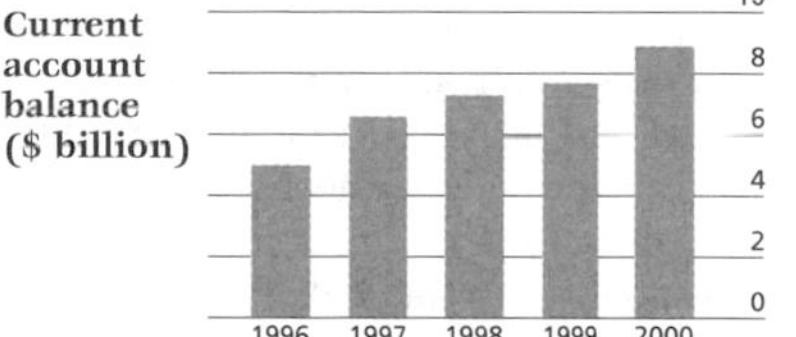

At mid-2001 the government held equity in 46 major companies, including 40% of mining and metals group Outökumpu, 42% of steelmaker Rautaruukki, 53.4% of chemicals company Kemira, 76% of energy group Fortum, most of telecommunications operator Sonera, and national airline Finnair. The electricity market was opened to competition in January 1997. The government sold a small part of Sonera in 2000, and is considering full privatization. It has also sold part of its mining interests and may privatize more in the future. The state-owned Finnish Rail Administration owns the rail network and its equipment, but the rail operator VR Group was transformed into a joint stock company in 1995. In June 2001 the Finnish parliament approved divestiture of part of alcohol company Altia Group and of 49.9% of the peat and wood company Vapo.

ECONOMIC POLICY

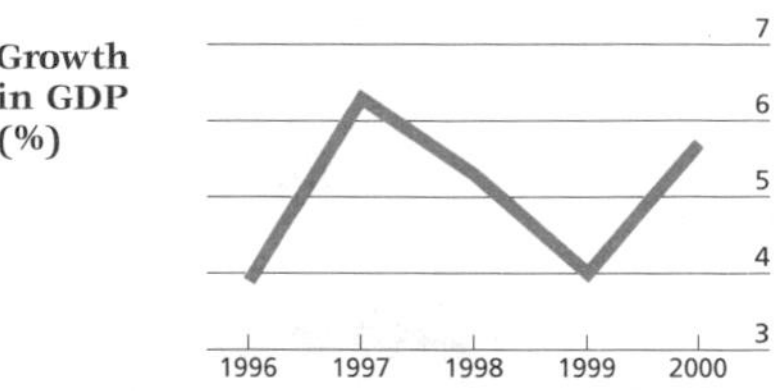

Government spending rose rapidly during the severe recession of the early 1990s as a result of generous social provisions, but net borrowing was restrained. The public sector debt peaked at 58.8% of GDP in 1994 but declined to 39.4% in 2001. This performance is due to better-than-expected growth and tax receipts, and wage moderation to keep inflation low. The resulting government surpluses since 1998 have been used to pay off the debt. Surpluses are expected to increase in the coming years. Modest income tax cuts have been offered in return for wage restraint. However, the OECD and IMF point to the high overall tax burden and the need to reform the social security system, especially to reduce early retirement and structural unemployment problems. Reforms in the public housing sector should lead to increased labor mobility.

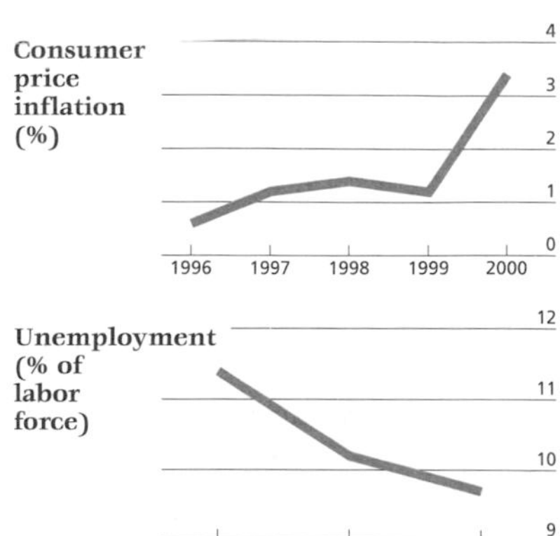

Average annual GDP growth was 5.1% in 1996–2000, but fell dramatically to 0.9% in 2001 because of the economic slowdown in main export markets. The 1990s recovery was led by exports of mobile phones in particular, and demand for these eased. Growth is expected to revive to 2.7% in 2002 and

3.2% in 2003. Inflation fell from an annual average of 2.3% in 1991–95 to 1.3% in 1996–99, rising to 3% in 2000 on account of high oil prices and higher interest rates. Inflation eased to 2% in 2001 with a strengthening of the Euro against the dollar and lower oil prices. It was expected to fall in 2002. Unemployment rose to a peak of 16.6% in 1994; since then it fell steadily to 9.9% in 2000. It is expected to continue falling to 7.5% in 2004.

Geography/Resources

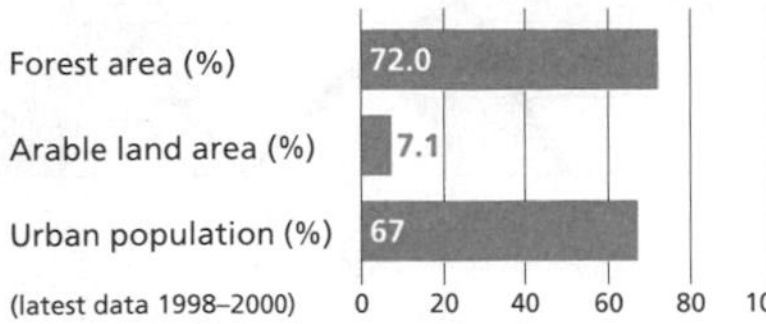

Finland lies in eastern Scandinavia, and shares frontiers with Sweden in the northwest, Norway in the north, and Russia in the east. It has western and southern coasts on the Gulf of Bothnia and the Baltic Sea. Almost a quarter of the land lies within the Arctic Circle. The country is mostly flat and low-lying, with hills in the south, west and north. Lakes occupy one-tenth and forests three-quarters of the land. The climate is very wet, with cold winters and warm summers. Daylight varies from zero hours in winter to 24 hours in summer in the north.

Only 8% of the land is used for agriculture. The main products are meat and dairy, barley, oats, potatoes, and sugar beet. Finland is a significant producer of nickel, copper, zinc, chromium, iron, cobalt, and vanadium. Gold, pyrite, lime, talc, feldspar, and quartz are also produced.

Around 65% of the people live in urban areas, especially the capital Helsinki and neighboring towns of Espoo and Vantaa. Other important towns are Tampere and Turku, and in the north Oulu. The majority of people are of Finnish origin. About 6% are of Swedish origin, and there are communities of a few thousand Lapps in the north. There were 85,000 immigrants (1.6% of the total population) living permanently in Finland in 1999, mostly of Russian, Estonian, and Swedish origin.

Communications/Energy

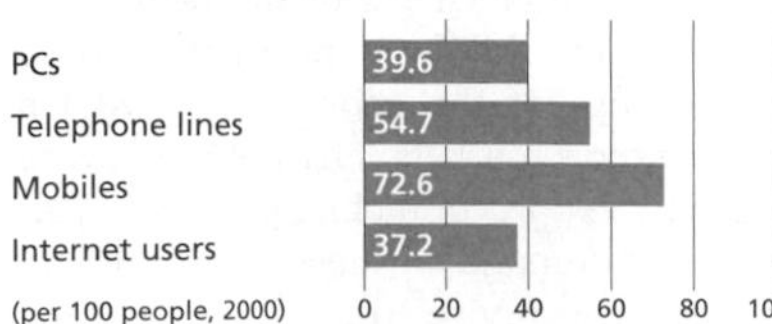

The road network comprised 48,350 miles in 1999, including 294 miles of highways. The rail network was 3,626 miles, 1,388 miles of which was electrified. It connects with the Swedish and Russian railways. While the number of passengers using public transport has remained roughly the same since 1980, the use of cars has increased significantly. The roads accounted for 41.2 billion ton/miles of freight in 1999, against 15.8 billion for the railways. There are 4,100 miles of inland waterways. There are 360 miles of natural gas pipeline. Almost 90% of exports are dispatched by sea from Finland's 29 ports, which are kept free of ice throughout the winter. The main export port is Kotka, while the main import port is Helsinki. The main international airport is at Helsinki. There are 26 other commercial airports.

Finland was the first country in the world to launch a digital network for mobile communications. Mobile phone penetration was 73% of the population in 2000, the highest in the world, and it is still growing fast. Mobile phone subscribers outnumbered fixed-line subscribers in 1999, the latter accounting for just over half of the population. Because the telecommunications sector has been open to competition for a long time, phone costs for fixed and mobile phones are well below the OECD average. Finland was the first country in the world to grant licenses for multimedia mobile communications, and the network was due to start operation at the beginning of 2002. Finland has one of the highest Internet penetrations in the world, with around 60% of the population having access in 2001. Encryption strategies are robust, and information technology has been integrated into manufacturing, public services, and home life. ASDL fast Internet connections are available to 95% of Finns. The country's biggest media company SanomaWSOY transmits the Internet on cable. It has obtained licenses for two new digital TV channels.

There are 370 power stations. The main source of indigenous electricity is combined heat and power (CHP: waste heat recovery and distribution—33%), followed by nuclear (27%), hydroelectric (19%), and coal (9%). The remaining 12% of requirements was imported from the Swedish, Norwegian, and Russian grids. With the economy growing fast, the reliance on imported electricity has risen. The government forecasts the share of CHP will increase to 40% by 2010. It may approve a fifth nuclear power station to keep imports at bay. Deregulation of the electricity market has brought significant cost savings to consumers since 1998. Oil imports accounted for 28% of energy requirements in 1999, indigenous wood fuel for 20%, imported natural gas and coal for 11% each, and indigenous peat for 5%.

Education/Employment

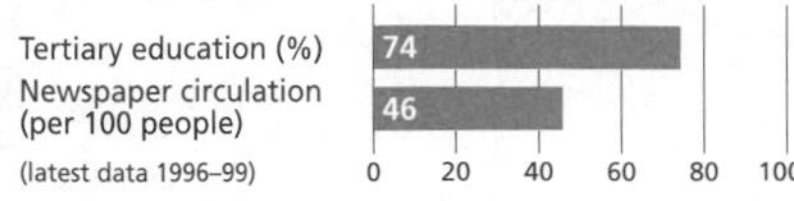

Education is compulsory from age seven to sixteen. There are 20 universities, including 10 which are multidisciplinary, three specializing in technology, three in economics and business administration, and four art academies. The number of university students has increased by 40% in the last decade to 147,000. In the 1990s many higher education colleges were transformed into polytechnics, offering degrees in occupational skills. The polytechnics are planned to quadruple the number of students from the 2000–01 level of 24,000. About one million people follow vocational adult education courses. All universities are owned and funded by the Ministry of Education, but decision-making is autonomous. Universities receive private-sector funding for research. Polytechnics and other colleges are administered by municipalities or private organizations, with funding split between central and local government. Students receive state grants and loans through to doctorate level.

Finland invested 3.1% of GDP in R&D in 1999. Private industry accounted for two-thirds of this, and the public sector for one-third. R&D strengths are telecommunications and mobile phone technology (Nokia), computer software such as the Linux operating system, and neural networks, biotechnology and medical research, forest and paper technology, new materials, and technologies related to cold weather, ranging from agriculture to icebreaking ships. Public-sector research focuses on the universities, which provide centers of excellence for spin-off companies.

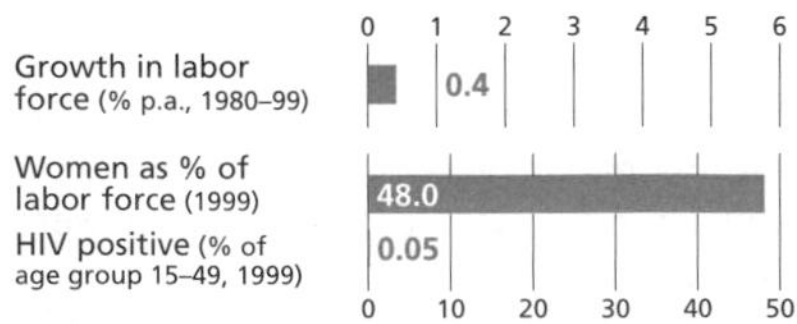

The labor force is highly skilled, and there is ready acceptance of new technology. Over 90% of Finns under the age of 30 speak English. Wages and employment conditions are negotiated nationally by the labor unions, employers, and the government, then at the sectoral and company levels. They include wage increases, income tax cuts, social security contributions, working hours, and training. Finland applies EU employment law, which covers safety at work, wages and working hours, industrial relations, employment incentives, and unemployment provision. In recent years there has been more recourse to short-term contracts to increase flexibility in the labor market.

Fiscal/Financial

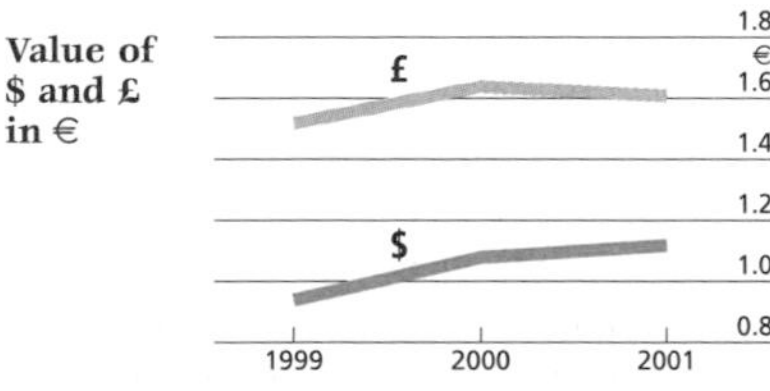

The largest bank, Merita, is part of the Nordea banking and insurance group which also includes Christiana Bank of Norway, Nordbanken of Sweden, and Unidanmark (Unibank) of Denmark. Nordea is the largest bank in Scandinavia. The second-largest bank in Finland is Okobank (the Cooperative Bank group), and the third is Leonia. Leonia merged with the largest Finnish insurance company, Sampo, at end-2000, creating the second-largest finance sector group after Nordea. Ilmarinen is the third-largest insurance company. The Financial Supervision Authority is the regulatory authority for the finance markets. It is independent of the Bank of Finland, but works in cooperation with the central bank. The Bank of Finland is part of the European System of Central Banks. This body and the European Central Bank set the policy for the Euro.

Corporation tax is 29%, while the maximum personal income tax rate is 30%. The government is committed to reducing income tax and labor tax. VAT is 22%. The island of Åland is self-governing, and has third-country status for excise tax and VAT. Reduced tax rates apply to shipping. Tax reforms have been enacted to facilitate lending against underlying assets and to favor equity over debt in order to improve the liquidity of the capital markets.

At end-2000 there were 337 domestic banks, including eight commercial banks, 246 member banks of Oko, 43 local cooperative banks, and 40 savings banks. There were 6 foreign banks and 6 foreign credit institutions. The banking sector has become more sophisticated and internationalized as the economy has grown. The government has encouraged the use of venture capital, and has eased restrictions on pension fund investments. Large industries can use electricity as an underlying asset to hedge risk. E-banking is so well established that it outstrips conventional banking in the retail sector: Finland is the world leader in e-banking. While 95% of companies use e-commerce, they have been much slower to adopt e-banking, despite the lower cost of transactions. Merita was the first bank in the world to offer WAP banking services in 1999. Most Finnish banks now offer WAP service, which includes bank transfers, bills payment, shopping, stock exchange share price information, and trading.

The Helsinki Exchanges group (HEX) has seen activity skyrocket because of trading in the shares of Nokia and Sonera. Turnover rose from €32 billion in 1997 to €150 billion at end-August 2000, making Helsinki the ninth largest stock exchange in Europe. Over half of the new trade has been international. HEX has links with the Eurex derivatives stock exchange. The EL-EX electricity exchange operates in close cooperation with the Norwegian-Swedish Nord Pool to support active markets for trading in electricity.

Business Opportunities

Growth in output (% p.a., 1990–99)

Services	1.8
Industry	4.2
Manufacturing	5.8
Agriculture	1.1

Grants, loans, tax benefits, equity participation and guarantees, and employee training are offered as investment incentives for companies locating in northern and central Finland and in the smaller, lower-income towns of the south. Priority is given to small firms. Foreign and Finnish firms are eligible. Under separate programs run by the public finance institutions Finnish National Fund for Research and Development (Sitra) and the Technology Development Center (Tekes), equity participation, grants of up to 50%, and loans of up to 60% of costs are offered to R&D firms. Invest in Finland Bureau is the point of contact for foreign firms.

Electronics, IT and communications, biotechnology, pharmaceuticals, healthcare equipment, logistics, banking, and insurance have attracted foreign investment from the United States, United Kingdom, Japan, Sweden, Germany, and Italy. Communications technologies—including mobile and Internet connectivity, and encryption and antivirus software—will get a further boost when the mobile multimedia network comes on-stream in 2002. Further opportunities will be offered by the proposed liberalization of the rail network and possible selloff of state shares in major companies.

For More Information

Books:

Turner, Barry, ed. *Scandinavia Profiled.* London: Macmillan, 2000.
Business Finland 2001. Helsinki: Helsinki Media, 2000.
European Union: European Economy: Report and Studies Series.
Finland—The Investor's Opportunity. Helsinki: Invest in Finland Bureau, 1995.
Finland in Figures. Helsinki: Statistics Finland (annual).
Economist Intelligence Unit. *Country Profiles and Country Reports.* London.
IMF Country Report. *Finland.* Washington, D.C.: IMF.
O.E.C.D. Economic Surveys. *Finland.* Paris: OECD.
Singleton, Fred, and A. F. Upton. *A Short History of Finland.* 2nd ed. New York: Cambridge University Press, 1998.
Swallow, Deborah. *Culture Shock! Finland: A Guide to Customs and Etiquette.* Portland, OR: Graphic Arts Center Publishing Co., 2001.

Web Sites:

Bank of Finland: **www.bof.fi**
Contact Finland (business guide): **www.contactfinland.fi**
Economic Information Bureau: **www.tat.fi**
Federation of Finnish Insurance Companies: **www.vakes.fi.svk**
Finland Trade Centre: **www.ftcla.com**
Finnish Bankers' Association: **www.pankkiyhdistys.fi**
Finnish Tourist Board: **www.mek.fi**
Government entry point: **www.finland.fi**
Helsinki Exchanges (stock exchange): **www.hex.fi**
Helsingin Sanomat (main daily newspaper): **www.helsinginsanomat.fi**
Invest in Finland Bureau: **www.investinfinland.fi**
Research Institute of the Finnish Economy: **www.etla.fi**
Statistics Finland: **www.stat.fi**

FRANCE

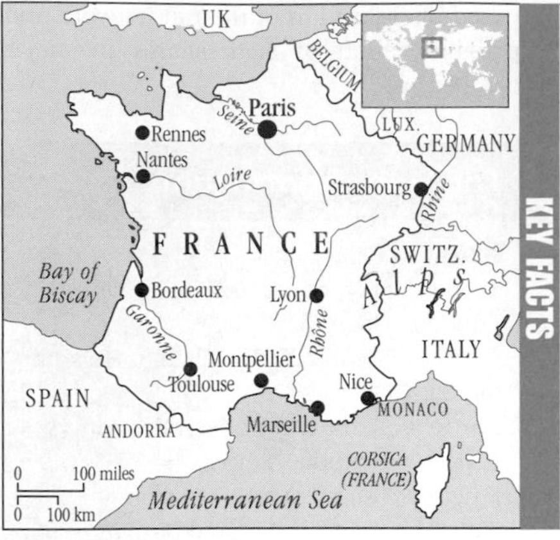

GNI: **$1,453,211 million; world's 4th**
GNI pc: **$24,170; world's 21st**
Head of government: **prime minister**
Currency: **Euro (€)**
Capital: **Paris**
Population: **58,886,000, growing at 0.4% p.a.**
Land area: **212,394 square miles**
Population density: **277 per square mile**
Life expectancy: **78 years**
Infant mortality: **5 per 1,000 live births**
Language: **French**
Best buy: **designer clothes, silk items, perfume, wine, truffles**

ECONOMIC STRUCTURE

France has been rich in agricultural resources from early history, and this provided the base for a diverse economy and trade by both land and sea. For several centuries power has been heavily centralized. Revolution at the end of the 18th century and republicanism in the 19th century increased the control of the center. Industrialization in the 19th century was strengthened by raw materials from the colonies. In World War II France was divided and partly occupied, thus losing its role as a leading world diplomatic power. After liberation the new government took control of the reconstruction effort, with a determination to restore French pride and France's position in the world. Governments since then have succeeded in promoting French interests, particularly through the European Union, of which France remains the leading political power with Germany.

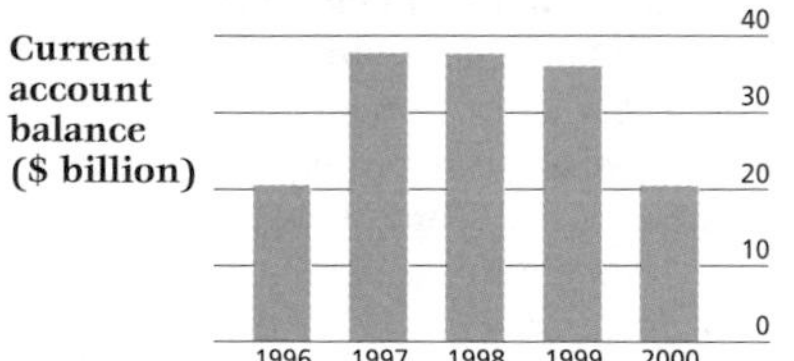

Services account for around 72% of GDP, followed by manufacturing (16%), construction (4%), and agriculture and energy (3% each). Tourism is a key services sector. Government services account for 17% of GDP, and the civil service accounts for 25% of employment. Industry is varied, ranging from the traditional steel, textiles, and shipbuilding to chemicals, machinery, cars, consumer goods, and high-tech goods. France is the second-largest agricultural exporter in the world after the United States, benefiting from EU farm subsidies. Food processing and wine are important industries. There is a strong domestic film industry. Manufactured goods accounted for 85% of merchandise exports in 2000 (intermediary goods 31.9%, machinery 26%, cars and consumer goods 13.4% each), processed foods for 8.6%, agricultural goods for 3.2%, and energy products for 3%. Services accounted for 10.4% of total exports in 1999, the main category being business services, followed by transport. The main export markets in 2000 were Germany, the United Kingdom, Spain, and Italy.

There has been extensive state involvement in finance and business through direct ownership, cross-shareholdings, and subsidies. Most privatizations in the 1990s offered minority shareholdings to the private sector. The notable exceptions were in the banking and insurance sectors, where companies were fully privatized. Many French state-controlled companies rank among the largest in Europe, and many have forged alliances with foreign companies to enable them to operate on a global scale. In early 2001 the state controlled IT firm Bull, STMicroelectronics, Thomson Multimedia (consumer electronics), Thales (telecommunications equipment), France Télécom, carmaker Renault, Eléctricité de France, Société Nationale des Chemins de Fer, Air France, and many other companies. Cross-shareholdings of state companies and banks have mostly been unraveled. The liberalization of the telecommunications, electricity, and gas markets—in compliance with EU directives—has been conducted on a minimum level. The level of state aid to industry continues to be higher than in other EU countries despite pressure from the European Commission to phase out these subsidies.

ECONOMIC POLICY

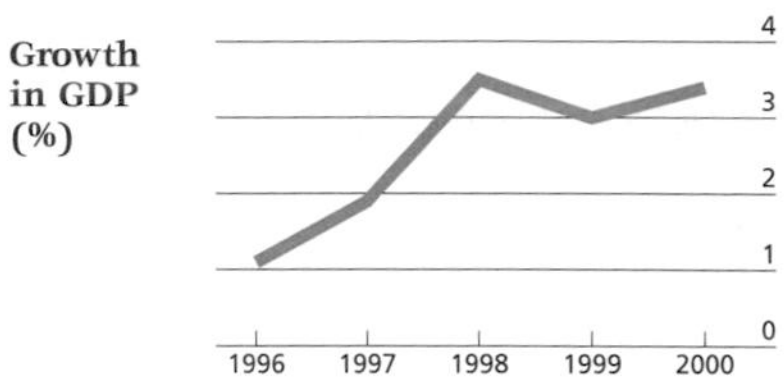

The government has pursued cautious budgetary policies for several years to reduce the general government deficit from 4.1% of GDP in 1996 to 1.5% in 2001, but the deficit is expected to rise in election year 2002. The government aims to achieve budgetary balance in 2004. The public debt fell from 59.3% of GDP in 1997 to 57.9% in 2001. Wage moderation has helped keep inflation low. Job creation to reduce the high unemployment level resulted from the reduction of the working week from 39 to 35 hours in 2000. Reduction of social security contributions from employers and employees accompanied the shorter working hours, lowering the heavy tax burden. There were cuts in direct taxes and VAT in 1999, 2001, and 2002. Further reforms to social security rates and taxes, together with simplified business procedures, are planned in order to make industry more competitive. The government established a pension reserve fund in 1999 and announced reforms to the pensions system in 2000, to reduce the burden of an ageing population which will begin to be felt by 2005. Minor spending cuts have been made to the costly healthcare system.

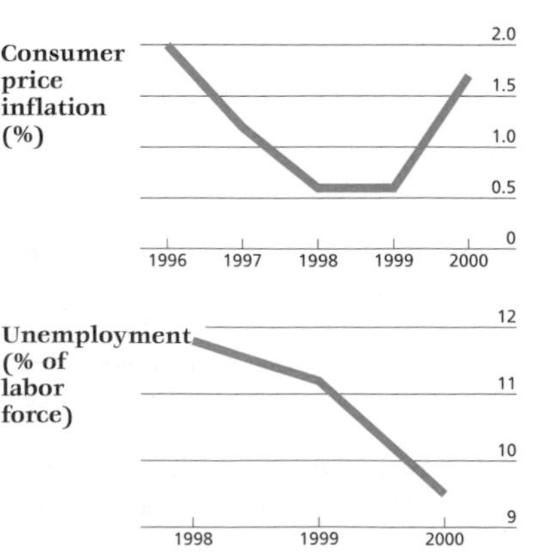

GDP growth picked up from 1997, fueled by domestic demand, after a prolonged period of sluggish performance from 1991. Average annual growth doubled from 1.1% in 1991–96 to 2.8% in 1997–2000. Growth was 2% in 2001 and was expected to be 1.3% in 2002. Inflation fell from an average 3.1% in 1991–95 to 1.2% in 1996–99, rose to 1.8% in 2000–01, and was expected to ease slightly in 2002. Unemployment remained high at around 11.3% throughout the 1990s, falling to 9.8% in 2000 and an expected 8.6% in 2001. New jobs have been created almost exclusively in the services sector.

Geography/Resources

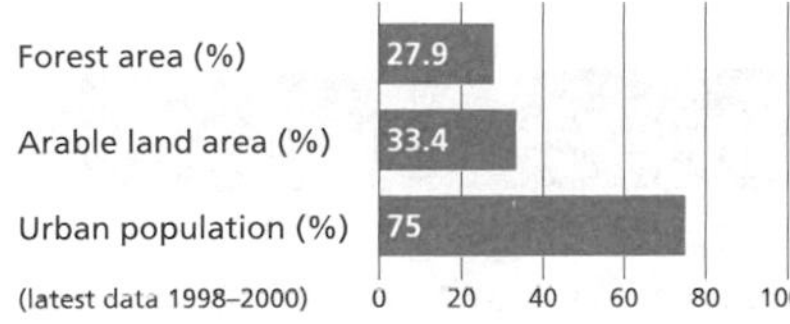

On Europe's western seaboard, France has western coasts on the Atlantic Ocean and English Channel, and southern coasts on the Mediterranean. It has land borders with Belgium, Luxembourg, Germany, Switzerland, Italy, Monaco, Spain, and Andorra. French territory includes the Mediterranean island of Corsica. France also has overseas territories in the Caribbean and in the Pacific and Indian Oceans. Most of mainland France is characterized by plains and low hills, but there are high mountains in the east (Vosges, Jura, and Alps), in the southwest (Pyrenees) and in the Massif Central in south central France. The climate varies from temperate and wet in the west and north to continental in the east (greater extremes of temperature and drier than the west), and dry Mediterranean in the south.

Agriculture is varied. The main crops are wheat, corn, barley, sugar beet, potatoes, grapes, pulses, apples, and sunflower seeds. A large range of other grains, vegetables, and fruit are also grown. Meat and dairy produce is important, as are forestry and fishing. The main minerals are coal, lignite, petroleum, and natural gas, but production is not large. Iron ore, potash, zinc, silver, gold, uranium, bauxite, gypsum, arsenic, mica, talc, limestone, slate, and salt are mined. There are also reserves of copper, lead, wolfram, sulfur, barytes, and fluorite.

The majority of people are of mixed Gallic origin. There are distinct communities and languages in Brittany (Celtic), in Alsace and Lorraine (Germanic), in the southwest (Basque), and south-center (Occitan). There is a relatively large immigrant community from North and sub-Saharan Africa, the Far East, and Eastern Europe.

Communications/Energy

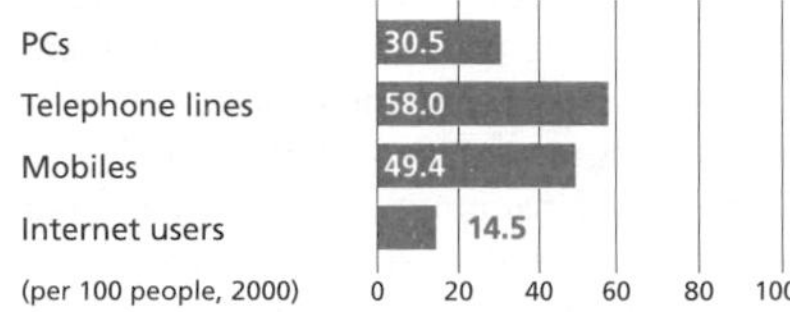

The road network consists of around 6,000 miles of highways and about 560,000 miles of other roads. The rail network was around 16,000 miles in 2000. There are 5,300 miles of navigable inland waterways. The main seaports for freight are Marseille (the second-largest in Europe), Le Havre, and Dunkerque. The main passenger seaport is Calais. There are international airports at Paris, Lyon, Marseille, Strasbourg, Toulouse, Bordeaux, Nice, and Lille. Road transport accounts for most domestic and transit freight (75%), international freight to and from other EU countries (56%), and domestic passengers (89%). The share of rail is 16%, 8%, and 8% respectively. Seaports account for 80% of international freight from non-EU countries. There are high-speed rail links from Paris west to Calais and the Channel Tunnel, southwest to Poitiers, north to Belgium, east to Germany, and south to Marseille. The high-speed network is planned to continue from Marseille to the Spanish border, and from Lyon to Switzerland and from there to Italy, with a 35-mile tunnel under Mont Blanc.

Despite market liberalization from 1998, state-controlled France Télécom remains the dominant player in fixed-line and mobile communications, and Internet service provision. As of December 2000, 30% of long-distance phone calls were open to competition. Competition for local services began in 2000. France Télécom's fixed-line network is fully digitized, and its Minitel system (an electronic phone book, information and online shopping service) has been provided to all subscribers for about 20 years. Internet use has been relatively slower to take off than in other countries, partly because of Minitel. Mobile phone penetration from all providers was 49% in December 2000, while fixed phone lines reached 58% of the population and the Internet 14.4%. UMTS mobile networks will be in operation from 2002.

Crude oil accounted for 59% of energy imports in 2000, refined oil products for 22%, gas for 16%, and coal for 3%. Domestic production of coal and lignite met 17% of national demand, while domestic oil and gas output met 16% and 4% respectively. Output of all these products is in decline. Nuclear power contributed 77% of electricity production, followed by hydroelectricity (14%) and thermal power, mostly coal (9%). France exports electricity to Italy. It also exports refined oil products. The Cogema nuclear fuel reprocessing plant reprocesses spent nuclear fuels for French and foreign power stations.

Education/Employment

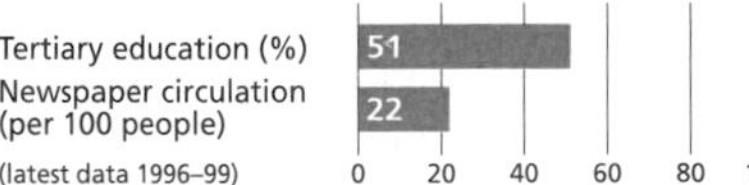

Education is compulsory from age 6 to 16. Pre-school education is available from age 2. There are 78 state universities, 3 polytechnics, over 80 specialized elite professional institutes (known as the Grandes Écoles) from which most of France's administrators have graduated, 6 Catholic universities, and about 100 independent specialized professional colleges. Control and funding of French education has been highly centralized, but there have been moves in recent years to devolve both funding and decision making to the regional level. There were a total 2.1 million students in higher education in 1999–2000, the vast majority in university.

R&D spending is just over 2% of GDP, one of the higher levels in the OECD area. The government foots 47% of the bill and industry (state and private-sector) around 50%. The government has created national innovation technology networks to further R&D synergy between public-sector and private-sector research. The telecommunications network was established in 1998, nano-technology in 1999, and in 2000 networks for software, materials and processes, health, audiovisual and multimedia, water and environment, and earth and space. Each network has a budget and conducts projects. Other government-sponsored programs include transport, biotechnology, and the use of IT and e-commerce by small firms.

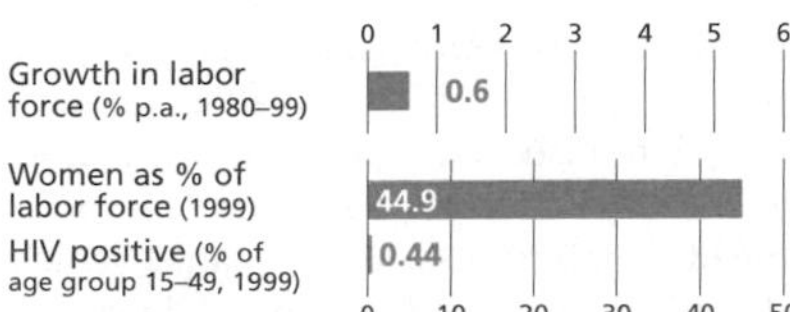

The labor force is well educated. Wages and employment conditions are determined by tripartite agreement between the government, employers, and trade unions. There

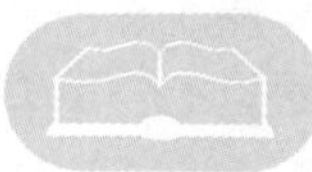

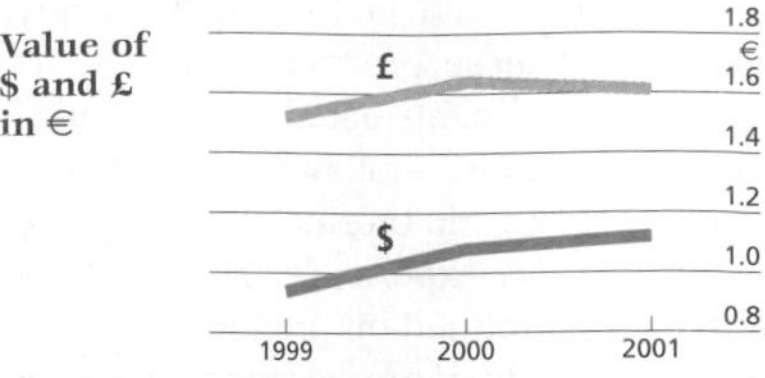

have been recent moves by employers to negotiate more directly with trade unions. The law reducing the working week from 39 hours to 35 hours from February 2000 allowed employers greater freedom in negotiating temporary, part-time and fixed-term contracts and other working conditions. France applies EU employment law, which covers safety at work, wages and working hours, industrial relations, employment incentives, and unemployment provision.

Fiscal/Financial

The largest banks in late 2001 were Crédit Agricole, BNP-Paribas, Société Générale, and Crédit Lyonnais. AXA is the largest insurance company in France and also one of the largest in the world. The central bank is the Banque de France, which is also part of the European System of Central Banks. This body and the European Central Bank set the policy for the Euro. The Banque de France, which was made independent of the state in 1993, holds sway over the various regulatory bodies for the banking, insurance, and stock exchange sectors.

The standard rate of corporation tax is 33.3%, with 15% for small business, and maximum personal income tax at 53.25%. Personal income tax rates are to be cut in 2002 and 2003 apart from the top rate. VAT is applied at 19.6% and 5.5%. Corporation tax can be offset by a wide range of reductions. In addition, lower rates of corporation and personal income tax are available to multinational companies and their employees for headquarters, finance, and logistics operations.

The number of banks fell from 2,000 in 1990 to 1,143 in 1999. Consolidation is likely to intensify with the proposed takeover of Crédit Lyonnais by Crédit Agricole and the possibility of a renewed bid for Société Générale by BNP-Paribas. Mutual status for banks and insurance companies is protected, but insurance companies are now more open to scrutiny and competition for some of their business. Mutual banks, which included Crédit Agricole, accounted for 60% of savings and 50% of loans at mid-2001, but this proportion will change once Crédit Agricole conducts its planned stock market flotation. Crédit Agricole and BNP-Paribas are expected to dominate French banking in the future and to play a larger international role in Europe with their alliances and shareholdings in Italian, German, and British banks and insurance companies. French finance is sophisticated and international, but less developed in personal financial instruments, such as private pensions, than other EU countries. The consequent lack of large private pension funds as institutional investors in the corporate sector has allowed foreign banks to fill the gap. All French debit and credit cards contain embedded chips with identification codes, making transactions, including e-banking and e-commerce, more secure. France is ahead of other countries in this, but it has yet to translate this gain to e-commerce.

The Paris Bourse merged with the stock exchanges of Amsterdam and Brussels in September 2000 to create Euronext, the first pan-European stock exchange, with a single trading system and single payments clearing system established in 2001. The value of equity trades on the Euronext exchanges rose by almost 60% in 2000, and market capitalization reached €2.4 trillion. The exchanges have agreed to integrate their derivatives trading in the Next derivatives system from 2002. They launched the Next-Track tracking system for index funds in January 2001.

Business Opportunities

Growth in output (% p.a., 1990–99)

Services	1.5
Industry	0.9
Agriculture	1.9

Financial and tax incentives are available to investors locating in special investment zones, in regions of high unemployment, and in R&D. The government sees foreign investment as a means of job creation, but it imposes some restrictions on foreign investment in agriculture, aerospace and defense industries, transport, nuclear energy, media, banking, insurance, telecommunications, and tourism. Invest in France is the point of contact for foreign investors within the planning and investment promotion agency DATAR (Délégation à l'Aménagement du Territoire et à l'Action Régionale).

There is foreign investment in a wide range of industries including agribusiness, chemicals, IT and electronics, mechanical engineering, metals, transport equipment, paper and wood, energy, textiles, construction, tourism, trade distribution, media and leisure, insurance, and business services. In 1997–99 the Netherlands was the leading foreign investor, followed by the United States, United Kingdom, Germany, Switzerland, and Belgium. There are new investment opportunities in the liberalization of the electricity and gas sectors, in further privatizations and unbundling of cross-shareholdings, and also in cross-border alliances.

For More Information

Books:

Agulhon, Maurice. *De Gaulle: Histoire, Symbole, Mythe*. Paris: Plon, 2000.

Ardagh, John. *France in the New Century: Portrait of a Changing Society*. New York: Viking, 1999.

European Union: European Economy: Report and Studies Series.

Friend, Julius W. *The Long Presidency: France in the Mitterrand Years, 1981–95*. Boulder, CO: Westview Press, 1999.

Goldea, R. *France Since 1945*. New York: Oxford University Press, 1996.

IMF Country Report. *France*. Washington, D.C.: IMF.

Ministry of the Economy, Finance and Industry. *Energies et Matières Premières*. (Monthly newsletter.)

OECD Economic Surveys. *France*. Paris: OECD.

Web Sites:

Banque de France: **www.banque-france.fr**

Euronext Paris: **www.bourse-de-paris.fr**

Institut National de la Statistique et des Etudes Economiques (National Statistics Office): **www.insee.fr**

Invest in France: **www.investinfrance.com**

Ministry of Economy, Finance and Industry: **www.minefi.gouv.fr**

Ministry of Foreign Trade: **www.dree.org**

French Guiana

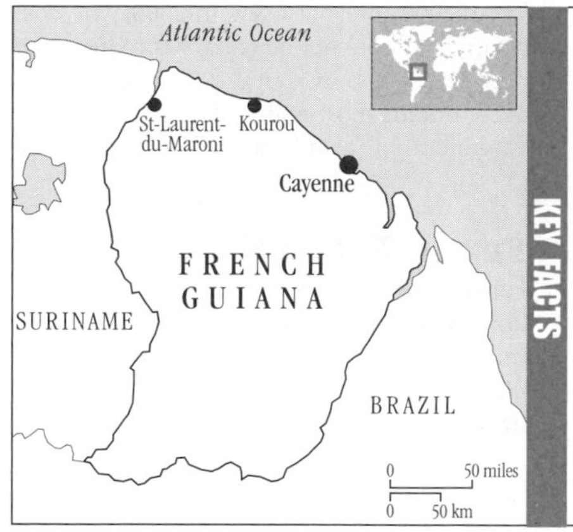

KEY FACTS

GNI pc: **$6,000 (approx.)**
Currency: **Euro (€)**
Capital: **Cayenne**
Population: **168,000**
Land area: **32,252 square miles**
Population density: **5 per square mile**
Language: **French, Creole**
Best buy: **handicrafts**

Economy

As a department of France, French Guiana enjoys substantial subsidies from the French government, and government services accounted for more than 20% of GDP in 1992, the most recent estimate available. Finance, property, transport, communications, and tourism accounted for 37% between them, with construction, mining, manufacturing, and agriculture mustering 27% between them. In terms of employment, services (excluding government services, for which no statistic was available) accounted for 54.2% in 1990, against 12.1% employed in construction and 11.4% in agriculture; the unemployment rate in 1998 was 21.4%. The main boost to the economy since World War II has been the establishment of the satellite-launching space station at Kourou, on the coast northwest of Cayenne. In recent years the department has attracted large-scale migration from Brazil and Suriname, mostly involving freelance gold prospectors.

Gold is the leading export, with sales of €40.4 million in 1999, followed by shellfish (€22.5 million) and space vehicle parts (€7.4 million); total exports of €105.8 million were outweighed by imports of €519.1 million, leaving a deficit of €413.4 million. The main export customer was metropolitan France, accounting for €57.7 million, or 54.6% of the total; France supplied 52.1% of the department's imports (€270.6 million), while another 15.7% (€81.7 million) came from Trinidad & Tobago and four EU countries.

Average real GDP growth between 1990 and 1996 was 4.3%, while inflation between 1996 and 1999 averaged only 0.6%.

Geography/Resources

French Guiana's natural resources include gold, bauxite, and timber, but their exploitation is restricted by the difficulties of the terrain; there are 15 sawmills, while gold production in 1998 reached 2.8 tons. The main food crop produced in 1998 was rice, with 31,000 tons of paddy harvested; livestock rearing is small-scale, and is mainly confined to the coastal area.

Out of a 1999 census population of 157,213, Cayenne housed 50,594 people, and the coastal strip accounted for 92% of the total; other sizeable towns included St Laurent-du-Maroni, near the mouth of the Maroni river (19,211), Kourou (19,107), and Matoury, near Cayenne (18,032). The population is of diverse origin, with differing estimates of its background according to the categories used: those from metropolitan France form about 20% of the total, with a similar proportion from Haiti, slightly fewer from Laos, about 12% from Brazil, and 6% from Suriname. Ethnically, those of African descent form an estimated 35–40% of the population (60–65% including those from Haiti), those of Asian descent 15–20%, and those of European descent 10%, with an estimated 4% of Amerindian descent.

The literacy rate in 1992 was 83% male, 81% female. Education is free and compulsory between 6 and 16 years of age, and there is a university college in Cayenne, plus colleges for technical studies, agriculture, and teacher training.

Communications/Energy

The department has direct air connections with France, Brazil, Suriname, and other Latin American countries, together with internal flights. The main port is Dégrad-des-Cannes, on the River Mahury, about 7 miles from Cayenne. In 1995 there were 268 miles of main roads, principally the one connecting Cayenne with St Laurent, plus 239 miles of secondary roads; very few roads exist in the interior, where travel is by river or air.

Telecommunications are operated by the French national enterprise, France Télécom. The state-owned Electricité de France supplies the department's power from three generating stations in Cayenne, Kourou, and St Laurent.

Fiscal/Financial

French financial and tax structures apply, with the addition of an *octroi de mer*; tax on imported goods, levied at a standard rate of 12%. French national and departmental banks operate, under state regulation. There is no separate stock market.

Business Opportunities

Projects generating employment and development qualify for tax exemptions, while national and regional grants are available for such investments. Gold mining is the most promising investment sector, but construction and engineering also offer possibilities, together with tourist development–both conventional seaside operations and inland "eco-tourism" or adventure holiday schemes.

For More Information

Book:

French Guiana Research Group. *A Strategic Profile of French Guiana* (Strategic Planning Series). San Diego, CA: ICON Group International, 2000.

Web Sites:

Departmental Chamber of Commerce and Industry: **www.guyane.cci.fr**
Ministry of the DOM-TOM: **www.outre-mer.gouv.fr**
Radio Caraibe Internationale: **www.fwinet.com/rci.htm**
Radio France Outre-Mer (RFO): **www.rfo.fr**
Tourist Board: **www.tourisme-guyane.gf**

French Polynesia

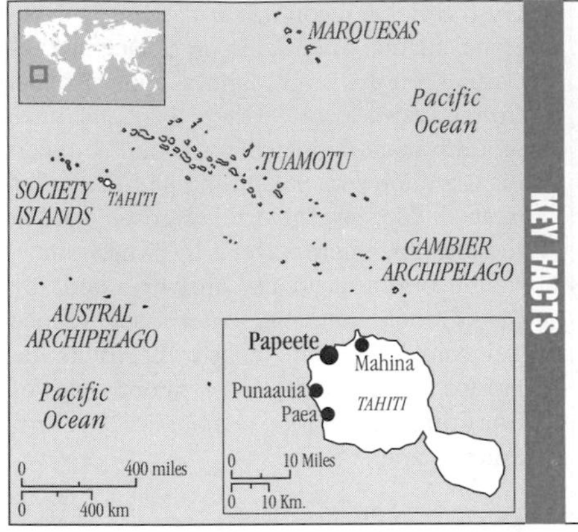

KEY FACTS

GNI: **$3,908 million**
GNI pc: **$16,930; world's 35th**
Head of government: **president of the council of ministers**
Currency: **Pacific franc (PF)**
Capital: **Papeete**
Population: **232,800**
Land area: **1,400 square miles**
Population density: **166 per square mile**
Language: **French (official), Tahitian (official)**
Best buy: **black pearls, craft textiles**

Economy

Services contributed 73.8% of GDP in 1998, followed by manufacturing (13.8%), construction (7.3%), and agriculture, fisheries and pearls (5%). Tourism is the main industry, with 260,000 visitors in 2000, mainly from France, the United States, and Japan. Small-scale local industry includes food processing, copra oil and monoi cosmetics, textiles, clothing, machinery, handicrafts, and art. Agriculture and coastal fishing provide the only source of income for many people. Copra is exported; other agricultural exports include pineapples and flowers. The government licenses Japanese and Korean industrial fishing of tuna. French Polynesia is the second world exporter of black pearls after Australia. They constitute the main goods export, accounting for 28% of export revenue in 1998. The government introduced regulation of the black pearl trade in 1998 to strengthen prices, which had been falling.

The economy is dependent on French aid which, at PF93.6 billion in 1999, covered 54% of total resources, down from 79% in 1992. The aim is for the local economy to generate 50% of total resources by 2005, including PF60 billion from tourism (up from PF47.2 billion in 1999), PF30 billion from black pearls (up from PF20 billion in 2000). Agriculture is planned to generate PF8.7 billion in 2003 (up from PF6.5 billion in 2000). An annual PF18 billion French aid program (1996–2005), to cover loss of income from nuclear weapons activities, provides investment capital, especially for the tourism sector. New luxury hotels have been built in Papeete and on Bora Bora, and smaller hotels on more remote islands. Annual GDP growth averaged 3.8% in 1995–2000. Annual inflation averaged 1.3% in 1991–2000. Unemployment was 13.2% in 1996.

Geography/Resources

French Polynesia consists of 118 volcanic or coral islands. Coconuts are the main agricultural products. Vegetables, fruit, vanilla, and coffee are also grown, and there is livestock rearing for meat and milk. However, local food production only covers 20% of needs. Black pearls are the most important marine resource, but traditional coastal fishing and fish farming, especially of shrimp, provides food for the islanders and the tourist trade. Industrial fisheries are increasing. There are few mineral resources of commercial value. Over 40% of the population are under age 20. The majority are of Polynesian origin. Other distinct groups include people of European and Chinese origin.

Communications/Energy

The paved road network totals 492 miles, 164 miles of which is paved. The main sea port is at the capital Papeete on Tahiti. Total sea freight was 746,737 tons, and 1 million passengers traveled between the islands in 1998. The international airport at Tahiti links with 40 airstrips on other islands. The airlines handled 554,560 international and 462,960 domestic passengers in 1998. In 1997 there were 52,000 fixed phone lines, giving phone access to over 70% of the population, and 5,427 mobile phones. Since then the government has invested in a fiber-optic cable and ASDL links to provide Internet access for all the main islands. There were 5,000 Internet users in 2000. The cost of international phone calls was reduced by between 8–45% in March 2001. Imported oil accounts for most energy needs. Electricity is generated from oil (51%) and hydro (49%).

Fiscal/Financial

Personal income tax and corporation tax are low. Tax receipts have depended on elevated import duties of up to 160%. Reforms to replace these gradually with VAT by 2002, and thus reduce the cost of living, were launched in 1998. From 2002 the main VAT rate has been 16% (sale of goods), with lower rates of 10% (services) and 6%. A local development tax was introduced to protect local industries. Monetary policy is set in France. There are five local banks and seven finance companies. These are regulated by the local branch of the Association française des Banques, which sets local interest rates. The publicly-owned development bank Socredo has agencies on many islands. There is no local stock market.

Business Opportunities

The tourism industry and related trade have attracted foreign investment, and continue to offer opportunities as the government attempts to achieve its ambitious plans for the sector. Industrial fishing offers additional opportunities.

For More Information

Books:

French Polynesia Research Group. *A Strategic Profile of French Polynesia* (Strategic Planning Series). San Diego, CA: ICON Group International, 2000.
Polynesia French Country Study Guide. 3rd ed. Washington, D.C.: International Business Publications, 2001.
Wheeler, Tony, and J.-B. Carillet. *Tahiti and French Polynesia*. 5th ed. Oakland, CA: Lonely Planet, 2000.

Web Sites:

Government entry point: **www.presidence.pf**
Tahiti Tourisme: **www.tahiti-tourisme.pf**

  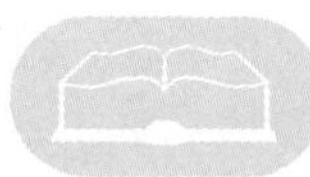    

GABON

KEY FACTS

GNI: **$3,987 million; world's 118th**
GNI pc: **$3,300; world's 85th**
Head of government: **president**
Currency: **CFA franc (CFA)**
Capital: **Libreville**
Population: **1,197,000, growing at 2.7% p.a.**
Land area: **99,500 square miles**
Population density: **12 per square mile**
Life expectancy: **52 years**
Infant mortality: **85 per 1,000 live births**
Language: **French, Fang and other local languages**
Best buy: **wood carvings and other handicrafts**

ECONOMY

Although Gabon has only a small population, the country's substantial national income from more than 30 years of crude oil production has been spread unevenly and has failed to benefit the majority. The rural economy has been undermined by migration to the urban areas and by inadequate incentives for agricultural producers. There has been very little diversification of the economy, and the government has a poor record for economic management. Now that a decline in oil output has begun, a relative rise in the importance of other mining, forestry, and tourism can be expected.

Oil contributes 40% of GDP, while other contributors include government services (9%), commerce (8%), manufacturing (6%), and agriculture (5%). Oil is also the leading export, representing 70% of foreign exchange earnings. Other exports include timber, manganese, and uranium.

Economic growth has been low in recent years, and was estimated to have declined by 1.0% in 2000. Faced with a mounting financial crisis, the government instituted an economic reform program in 1999 and subsequently reached a new agreement with the IMF. Inflation, which has been kept under control since the devaluation of the CFA franc in 1994, stood at 2% in 2000.

GEOGRAPHY/RESOURCES

The climate of Gabon is equatorial, with annual rainfall of up to 120 inches, high humidity, and high temperatures. Very few areas of the country are agriculturally developed, the main cash crops being cocoa, coffee, and palm oil. The principal mining zone around Masuku contains manganese and uranium, and there are also known deposits of iron ore, gold, and diamonds.

More than half the population live in the main cities of Libreville, Port-Gentil, and Masuku. The country's main ethnic groups are Fang (30%) and Eshira (25%).

COMMUNICATIONS/ENERGY

The main transport artery is the Transgabonais railway, which runs for 442 miles between Libreville and Masuku, mainly to facilitate the export of logs and minerals. Plans for the construction of a branch line between Booué and Belinga have been suspended. The road network is poorly developed, with only 391 miles paved and the remaining 4,350 miles unsurfaced and therefore subject to rain damage throughout much of the year. There are five airports and numerous small airstrips. There is only a small fixed-line telephone network, with 32,000 lines, and mobile telephone services have proved popular.

The main energy provider, SEEG, a privately-owned company, generates power from hydroelectric (72%) and gas (28%) sources. Gabon's oil is produced both offshore and onshore. Production has now gone into decline, although there are hopes of new offshore discoveries and production.

FISCAL/FINANCIAL

Under a new team of economic reformers appointed in 1999, the government envisages improved revenue collection by restructuring the tax and customs administration and by broadening the tax base away from the oil sector, which has been the dominant source of government income in the past. The government has also been reducing recurrent expenditure by privatizing state-owned companies and by laying off surplus public-sector employees.

The central bank is the Banque des États de l'Afrique Centrale (BEAC), based in neighboring Cameroon, and there are five commercial banks. There are plans to open a stock exchange for the Central African region.

Gabon has built up substantial arrears on its external debts and has negotiated successive rounds of debt rescheduling with its creditors.

BUSINESS OPPORTUNITIES

Gabon has always been successful in attracting foreign investment into the oil industry, but the appeal of its other sectors is limited because of the small size of the domestic market and the continuous political and economic instability in the surrounding Central African region, particularly in the two Congos and Angola. However, the privatization program has provided new opportunities for foreign companies. The first major sell-off was that of the power and water utility, SEEG, followed by that of the railway company, Octra. The next in line for sale include the post and telecommunications office, the national airline, the ports company, the government's timber-exporting interests, and the national rubber and sugar plantations.

For More Information

Books:

Gabon Business and Investment Opportunities Yearbook. 3rd ed. Washington, D.C.: International Business Publications, 2001 (annual).

Yates, D. *The Rentier State in Africa: Oil Dependency and Neocolonialism in the Republic of Gabon*. Lawrenceville, NJ: Africa World Press, 1996.

Web Sites:

African news and information: **www.allafrica.com/business**

Investir en Zone Franc: **www.izf.net**

GEORGIA

KEY FACTS

GNI: **$3,362 million; world's 128th**
GNI pc: **$620; world's 149th**
Head of government: **president**
Currency: **lari (Lari)**
Capital: **Tbilisi**
Population: **5,006,000, growing at –1.0% p.a.**
Land area: **26,900 square miles**
Population density: **186 per square mile**
Life expectancy: **73 years**
Infant mortality: **19 per 1,000 live births**
Language: **Georgian, Russian**
Best buy: **Georgian wine**

ECONOMY

In Soviet times, Georgia underwent large-scale industrial development and became a center for tourism. When Soviet Russia collapsed in 1991, Georgia lost markets and suffered an economic slump; it also experienced civil wars and unrest.

Georgia's role as an oil and gas transit center between the Caspian and Europe is seen as the key to economic development. Its own natural gas and oil reserves also have promise, as do its mining, agricultural, and tourism sectors. Real GDP grew by 2.7% in 1998–2001.

Georgia has pursued a pro-market reform policy, and in 2000 became the fourth post-Soviet state to join the WTO. Outside the energy sector, however, large-scale privatization and foreign direct investment remain hampered by lack of transparency, and by uncertainty about regulation and taxes. In January 2001 the IMF approved a three-year loan program, which also set budget and tax collection targets. Inflation is low (5.6% in 2001) and the currency stable, but there is extreme poverty.

GEOGRAPHY/RESOURCES

In addition to the Black Sea coastline and its tourist potential, Georgia has one of the richest manganese deposits in the world (estimated reserves of 200 million tons), and reserves of non-ferrous metals, arsenic, agate, and obsidian. Development of Georgia's oil and gas deposits may allow it to become a net exporter of energy. There are significant mineral water sources. Agricultural land covers 43% of the land area; principal products are wine, nuts, and citrus fruits.

Georgia's population was estimated at 5.0 million in 2000, but data is unreliable due to war and related population movements.

COMMUNICATIONS/ENERGY

Georgia's geographical position gives it potential as a trade center between central Asia, Turkey, Iran, and Russia. While its 984 miles of rail track and 12,900 miles of roads are in a state of disrepair, the country is already receiving fees from pipelines crossing its territory, and this is a key potential source of future income. The pipeline from Baku (Azerbaijan) to the Georgian port of Supsa was opened in 1999. A further main export pipeline from Baku to Ceyhan (Turkey) via Tbilisi is planned.

Georgia depends on imports for most of its own energy requirements: oil and gas from Russia, gas from Turkmenistan, and electricity from Russia and Azerbaijan. It has made progress towards independence in energy supplies by developing its own oil resources.

Georgia's fixed-line telecommunications network has only limited coverage outside Tbilisi. Density is 20 lines per 100 inhabitants in urban areas and only 4 lines per 100 in rural areas. There are three mobile networks.

FISCAL/FINANCIAL

In 1999, Georgia's tax revenues were just 14% of GDP. Although some tax reform measures were taken in 2000, arrears remain at about one-third of tax revenue and tax evasion remains endemic. This in turn has aggravated the problem of high public debt (75% of GDP at the end of 1999) and of external debt arrears, mostly for gas from Turkmenistan.

Georgia's banking sector has undergone consolidation in 1998–2000, under pressure of strong regulatory measures by the National Bank of Georgia. International accounting standards became compulsory in January 2001.

The market in treasury bills was suspended in 1998 and restarted in 1999. A small stock market opened in 1999, but in 2001 had yet to take on significance for the economy.

BUSINESS OPPORTUNITIES

Foreign direct investment was well over $200 million per year in 1997–98, but decreased to around $100 million per year in 1999–2001after the Baku-Supsa pipeline was completed. Oil and gas exploration, electrical power distribution and food processing, including wine making, have been key recipients of FDI; these industries, as well as mining and tourism, are considered to have potential.

Although Georgia has no specific incentives for foreign investors or free economic zones, it has a liberal foreign investment policy, allows unlimited repatriation of capital and profits, and has a legal framework, drafted with the help of international advisers, that gives foreign investors equal treatment. However, despite government support for foreign investment, there are considerable difficulties: those listed by the EBRD in 2001 were widespread corruption, including a culture of bribery in enterprises; predatory tax enforcement; lack of confidence in the competence of lower court judges; and the absence of reliable property registers.

For More Information

Books:

Avez, Jonathan. *Georgia: From Chaos to Stability?* London: Royal Institute of International Affairs, 1996.

Rosen, Roger, and Eduard Shevardnadze. *Georgia: A Sovereign Country of the Caucasus.* New York: Odyssey Publications, 1999.

Web Sites:

Georgia on the Net portal: **www.georgia.net.ge**

Industrial Georgia site: **www.industry.ge**

GERMANY

GNI: **$2,103,804 million; world's 3rd**
GNI pc: **$25,620; world's 13th**
Head of government: **chancellor**
Currency: **euro (€)**
Capital: **Berlin**
Population: **82,178,000, growing at 0.4% p.a.**
Land area: **134,900 square miles**
Population density: **609 per square mile**
Life expectancy: **77 years**
Infant mortality: **5 per 1,000 live births**
Language: **German**
Best buy: **optical goods, porcelain, pewter, fine art prints, beer**

ECONOMIC STRUCTURE

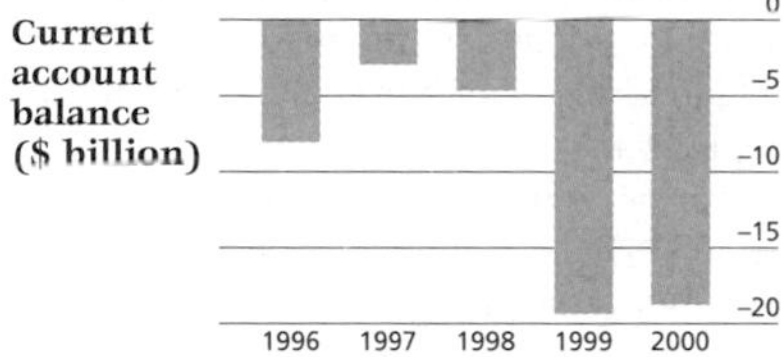

Germany has been a collection of wealthy states for several centuries. From the 17th century they built up industrial, cultural, scientific, and military strengths in rivalry with one another. By the time of federal unification in 1871, Germany was a leading world economic power with strong steel and engineering industries, but its economic power was not matched by political influence. Defeat in two world wars in the 20th century left Germany divided between western capitalism and Soviet communism in 1945. Denied significant military spending by the "winners" of World War II, both Germanies flourished, becoming the leading economic powers of Western and Eastern Europe. West Germany has gained political prominence through the European Union, but reunification with East Germany since 1990 has proven a difficult and costly transformation.

Services accounted for 65.2% of GDP in 1999, manufacturing for 23.9%, construction for 5.3%, and agriculture for 1.3%. The leading services sector was banking and finance, contributing 28.6% of GDP, while tourism and transport accounted for 17.2%. Manufacturing is diverse, including electronics, mechanical and electrical engineering, machine tools and other precision instruments, transport equipment, chemicals, pharmaceuticals, and medical equipment. Germany is the world's second-largest exporter. The main export markets in 2000 were France (8.3%) and Italy (7.5%); the 15 EU countries absorbed 56.6% of exports. Machinery was the main export category (33.5%), followed by automotive (17.6%) and chemicals (13.7%).

There is extensive public ownership of banks and utilities at the state (länder) and municipal levels, but the elimination of state guarantees for public banks in mid-2005 will strengthen competition in the finance sector. Although most industry is private-sector, the banks and major companies have a network of cross-shareholdings which have kept German industries largely in German ownership until recent years. From 2002 the elimination of tax on sales of these holdings will accelerate divestitures. The telecommunications and electricity sectors were opened to competition and some of the former state monopolies were privatized in 1998.

ECONOMIC POLICY

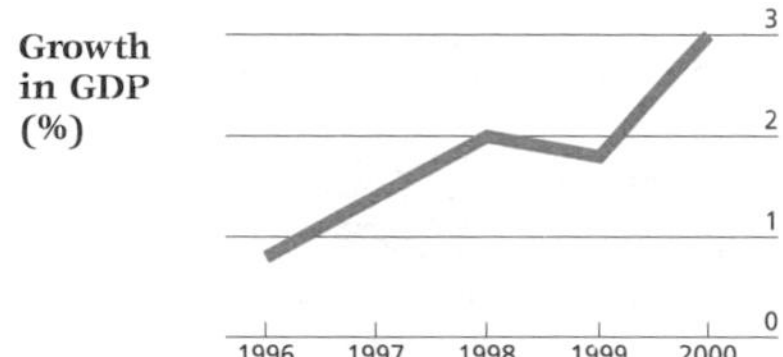

Government spending rose in the early years of reunification as a result of industrial restructuring in the east and increased welfare for those whose jobs disappeared, but spending has been trimmed since 1997. Government debt rose from 43.5% of GDP in 1990 to 61% in 1999, but fell to 59.6% in 2001. The government deficit fell from 3.5% of GDP in 1993 to 1.2% in 2000, but it rose to 2.2% in 2001. The licensing of UTMS mobile phone networks produced a surplus of 1.6% of GDP in 2000. Wage moderation has kept inflation low from the mid-1990s. Unemployment remains a persistent problem.

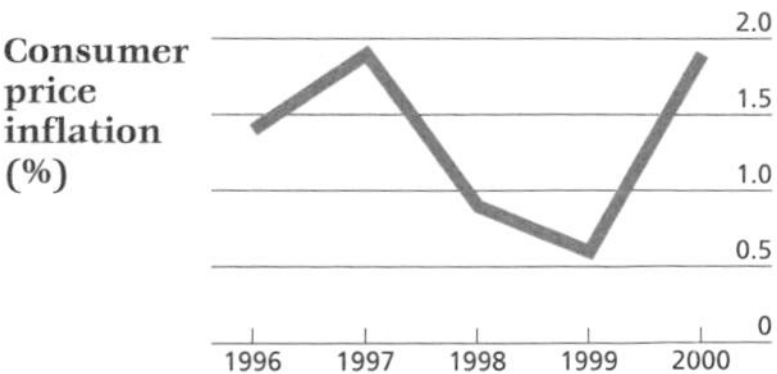

In 1999 the government embarked on a series of reforms to the tax and social security systems. Tax and social security costs have been eased for small businesses, large businesses, and individuals. Direct tax cuts were accompanied by a broadening of the tax base for business through the elimination of various tax reliefs. From 2002 funding of pensions shifted towards an equity base, with employees encouraged to invest 1% of gross wages in private savings instruments, including insurance, stocks, and bonds. This rate is due to increase to 2% in 2004, 3% in 2006, and 4% in 2008.

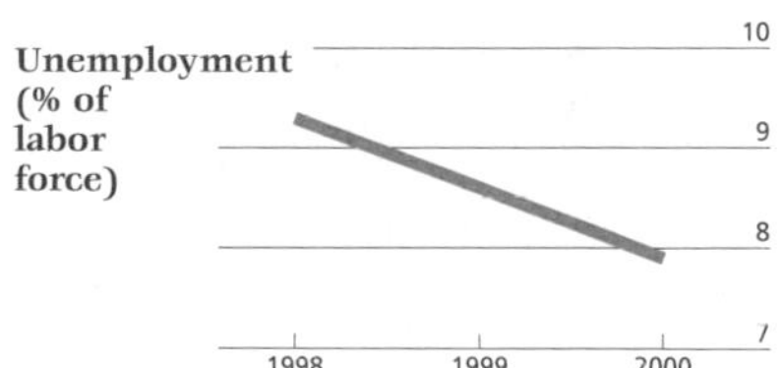

GDP rebounded in 2000 with growth of 3%, led by exports and productive investment, following a decade of sluggish performance with average annual growth of 1.75%. However, growth slowed to 0.8% in 2001 and was expected to be 1.5% in 2002 because of the world economic slowdown. The malaise of the 1990s resulted from slow demand in export markets, and it also reflected the difficulties of reunification. Inflation was brought down from an average 3.5% in 1991–95 to 1% in 1996–99. It rose to 2.3% in 2000–01 because of higher oil prices. Unemployment rose from an average 7.3% in 1991–95 to a peak of 9.9% in 1997. Falling to 7.9% in 2000 and 2001, it remains one of the highest in the EU. Employment gains have been concentrated in the west, while structural problems have persisted in the east.

GEOGRAPHY/RESOURCES

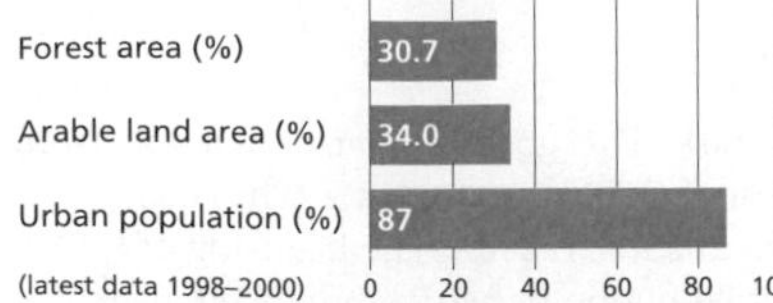

In central Europe, Germany borders Poland and the Czech Republic to the east, Austria and Switzerland to the south, France, Luxembourg, and the Netherlands to the west, and Denmark to the north. It has coasts on the North and Baltic Seas. Several major rivers flow through Germany, including the Rhine, Main, Danube, Elbe, Ems, and Oder. The river valleys form plains and depressions across the country, except for the south which is mountainous. The main plain is in the north. The climate varies from cool temperate in the north to continental mountain climate in the south.

About half of the land is farmed. Agriculture is varied and includes cereals, vegetables and root crops, fruit, meat, and dairy. One-third of the land is forested, and domestic timber meets two-thirds of demand. Lignite and hard coal is mined in the west and east. Proven recoverable reserves of lignite and hard coal are 44 billion tons and 24 billion tons respectively. At January 2001 proven oil reserves were 380 million barrels, and gas reserves were 11.5 trillion cubic feet. Salt is the main other mineral produced. Uranium mining stopped at the end of the 1980s. There are reserves of bauxite, zinc, copper, iron, nickel, lead, barite, fluorite, graphite, potash, and gypsum.

With 609 people per square mile, the country is densely populated and has the highest concentration in the west. One-third of the population live in the 84 cities of over 100,000, but the majority live in small towns and villages. There is a population peak around age 35–45, and a lesser peak around age 60. The people are mostly of mixed Nordic origin, with about 10% of foreign origin. Immigration pressure from the former Soviet bloc countries of eastern Europe and from the Balkan region has caused social tensions in recent years.

COMMUNICATIONS/ENERGY

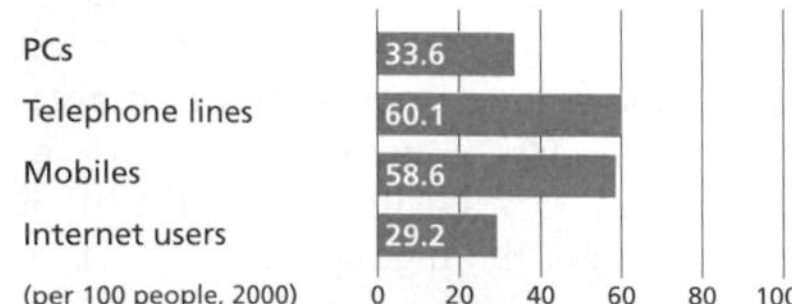

There were 7,200 miles of highways in early 2000, 143,400 miles of other main roads out of a total road network of around 404,000 miles. The 28,548 miles of railways includes high-speed track for train speeds of up to 155 mph. Construction of track to take trains at up to 300 mph between Berlin and Hamburg will be completed in 2005. Some 20% of domestic freight is carried on the 4,640 miles of inland waterways, including the River Rhine and Main-Danube canal. The pipeline network includes 1,550 miles for crude oil. The main sea ports are Hamburg, Bremerhaven, Wilhelmshaven, Rostock, and Lübeck. The largest airport is at Frankfurt, which handled 42 million passengers in 1998. Berlin has three airports, and a fourth will be completed in 2004–07. Other main airports are at Düsseldorf, Hamburg, and Munich. The majority of federal transport infrastructure spending until 2012 is going into waterways and railways to relieve pressure on the roads.

The telecommunications industry has expanded rapidly since liberalization of the sector in 1998: 99.5% of households in the former West Germany and 96.5 % in the former East Germany had a fixed-line phone in 1999. About 59% of the population had mobile phones, and Internet penetration was about 29% at end-2000. UMTS mobile networks are due to go live in 2002. Cable Internet access is also growing; 90% of homes had cable or satellite TV in 2000.

Energy needs are mainly met through imported oil, followed by imported gas, indigenous lignite and coal, domestic nuclear power, and renewable sources, including solar and wind. In 2000 oil production was 134,000 barrels per day, and gas production was 823 billion cubic feet. Net imports were 2.7 million barrels per day and 2.2 trillion cubic feet. Almost two-thirds of electricity is generated by coal and lignite, with nuclear power accounting for 30%, hydroelectricity for 3.6%, and other sources for 2.8%. The government has pledged to phase out nuclear power.

EDUCATION/EMPLOYMENT

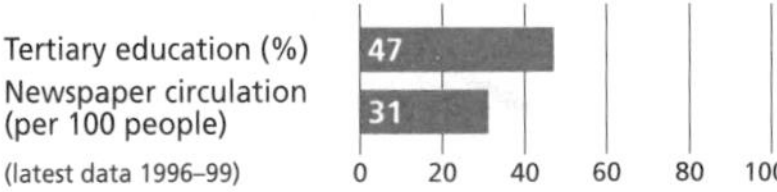

Full-time education is compulsory from age 6 to 15, and part-time education until age 18. The Federal Government-Länder Commission for Educational Planning and Research Promotion is responsible for higher education and research policy. There are over 300 higher-education institutes, mostly run and financed by the länder, but administration is autonomous to the institute. Means-tested financial assistance is available for students. The universities and technical universities are the largest higher-education sector, followed by university-level professional institutes, professional training colleges, and amalgamated universities, providing both university and professional courses. Private universities are a growing sector. New institutes have been established with corporate financing and as joint ventures with American universities.

The universities and technical universities conduct basic research, and the professional colleges applied R&D. Federal, länder and EU finance is available. There are 16 national research centers, which cover a wide range of research disciplines. In 1999 the government's risk capital program provided various forms of finance including equity for R&D firms specializing in computer software and hardware, communications, machinery, biotechnology, consumer goods, trade, medicine, and financial services. Other sectors targeted by the program include renewable energy, energy conservation, and environmental protection. Private industry contributes about 60% of R&D spending.

The labor force is well-educated, with a high level of female participation. Wages are either determined by collective agreement between employers and trade unions or by individual agreements between employer and employee. Collective wage agreements are valid for individual companies or for specific regions. Framework agreements cover such conditions as notice and dismissal, holiday entitlement, sick pay, parental leave, and dispute conciliation procedures. Germany applies EU employment law.

FISCAL/FINANCIAL

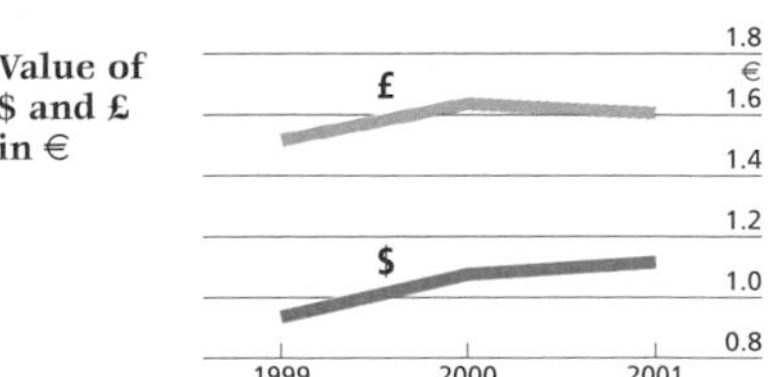

The largest commercial banks are Deutsche Bank, HVB Group, Dresdner Bank, and Commerzbank, all of which are private-sector. At the end of 2001 Westdeutsche Landesbank, the largest public-sector bank, was in the process of splitting its operations into a publicly-owned parent company and a commercially-operated private bank. Insurance and banking are closely linked. The largest insurer Allianz owns Dresdner Bank.

The second-largest insurer Munich Re is linked with HVB. The Federal Agency for Financial Market Supervision, advised by the Deutsche Bundesbank (the central bank), is due to take over financial sector supervision. The Federal Banking Supervisory Office, Federal Insurance Supervisory Office, and Federal Supervisory Office for Securities oversee financial market operators. Deutsche Bundesbank is part of the European System of Central Banks: this body and the European Central Bank set the policy for the Euro.

Federal corporation tax is 25% as of 2001, with maximum personal income tax at 48.5%, and maximum investment income tax at 33.5%. In addition there are wage taxes, a special solidarity levy to pay for the cost of German reunification, and local trade and property taxes. The standard rate of VAT is 16%, with 7% for basic items such as food and books. The top rate of personal income tax will be reduced to 47% and the basic rate from 19.9% to 17% in 2003. Further cuts to 42% and 15% are planned by 2005. The personal tax threshold will also be raised. Capital gains tax on the sale by companies of cross-shareholdings was abolished in January 2002.

Although four of the leading commercial banks are private-sector, two-thirds of domestic deposits are placed with public-sector and cooperative banks. The landesbanks' state guarantees give them top credit ratings, allowing them to lend at lower interest rates than the commercial banks. As a result 7 of the 12 landesbanks rank in the top 15 German banks. The cost to the commercial banks of maintaining a large number of branches to compete in this market has eroded profits. The government has agreed with the European Commission to phase out state guarantees by July 2005. The big four private-sector banks continued to seek alliances abroad for more profitable operations, and with IT producers at home for domestic e-banking. The investment cost for telephone and e-banking has led to consolidation in the public bank and cooperative bank sector. Financial instruments for business are sophisticated and international. Equity finance and mutual funds have attracted a growing portion of household investment as pensions are seen to be insufficient, and as e-banking increases. Public bodies are also eager to make the most of pension funds and other locked-in finance, which has been under-utilized in the past.

The Deutsche Börse is centered on Frankfurt, the main stock market, but there are also stock exchanges in Berlin, Hamburg, Bremen, Düsseldorf, Munich, and Stuttgart. The proposed merger between the Deutsche Börse and the London Stock Exchange, and an alliance with New York's Nasdaq for new technology stocks, failed in 2000. The Deutsche Börse's Eurex derivatives exchange, which it set up with Switzerland in 1998, has become the largest derivatives market in Europe, mainly on account of the secondary market in German treasury bonds. The Neuer Markt is an exchange for small high-tech firms. The Börse's Xetra electronic trading system has featured in a number of cooperation agreements with Dublin and Vienna, among others. Börse activity has been boosted by mergers and consolidations, also by the unraveling of cross-shareholdings and pension reform.

BUSINESS OPPORTUNITIES

Growth in output (% p.a., 1990–99)

Services	1.9
Industry	0.3
Manufacturing	–0.3
Agriculture	2.2

The government adopted the half-income method of taxable income calculation in 2001 to stimulate investment and job creation by companies with trans-border operations. There are over 600 schemes to provide assistance to firms for start-up, investment, environmental protection, regional development, R&D, training, and foreign trade. Foreign and German firms are eligible. Finance comes from the federal and länder governments and the EU. There is a special EU allocation for East Germany. The point of contact for foreign investors is the Commissioner for Foreign Investment in Germany, or—for the former East Germany—the Industrial Development Council.

Services, especially telecommunications, banking and insurance, holding companies, and shareholdings in a wide range of manufacturing and service industries are the main areas of foreign investment. The largest investors are other EU states—especially the United Kingdom and France—and the United States, but the list of countries is long. Many German businesses continue to present investment opportunities as the cross-shareholdings of the major companies and banks unravel. Apart from equity, these organizations are seeking foreign alliances for global operations. East Germany presents a range of infrastructure, business, and environmental protection opportunities. It is also developing as a business center for links between the EU and Eastern Europe, especially the EU candidate countries (Poland, Czech and Slovak Republics, and Hungary). Further privatization may take place in banking and utilities.

For More Information

Books:

European Union: European Economy: Report and Studies Series.

Federal Ministry of Economics and Technology. *Economic Report '99*

Germany Partner of the World: The Federal Republic of Germany 50 Years on. Documentation of Economy and Export Special Edition, 1999.

Germany—Your Business Partner. Cologne, Germany: Federal Office of Foreign Trade Information, 2000.

Heneghan, Tom. *Unchained Eagle: Germany after the Wall.* Upper Saddle River, NJ: Financial Times Prentice Hall, 2000.

IMF Country Report. *Germany.* Washington, D.C.: IMF.

Merkl, Peter H., ed. *The Federal Republic of Germany at Fifty: The End of a Century of Turmoil.* New York: New York University Press, 1999.

OECD Economic Surveys. *Germany.* Paris: OECD.

Web Sites:

Commissioner for Foreign Investment in Germany: **www.business-in-germany.de**

Deutsche Bundesbank: **www.bundesbank.de**

Die Welt (daily newspaper): **www.welt.de**

Economist Intelligence Unit: **www.eiu.com**

Federal Ministry of Economics: **www.bmwi.de**

Federal Office of Statistics: **www.statistik-bund.de**

Federation of German Industries: **www.bdi-online.de**

Financial Times Deutschland (in German): **www.ftd.de**

Frankfurter Allgemeine Zeitung (English language version): **www.faz.com**

Government entry point: **www.government.de**

Handelsblatt (daily business newspaper): **www.handelsblatt.com**

Industrial Investment Council: **www.iic.de**

GHANA

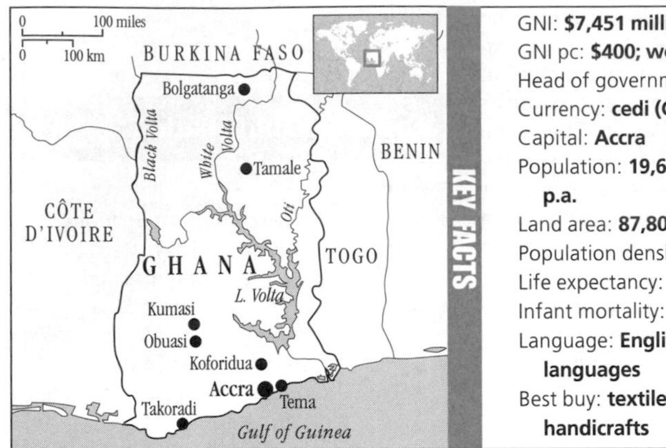

GNI: **$7,451 million; world's 97th**
GNI pc: **$400; world's 166th**
Head of government: **president**
Currency: **cedi (C)**
Capital: **Accra**
Population: **19,678,000, growing at 2.9% p.a.**
Land area: **87,800 square miles**
Population density: **224 per square mile**
Life expectancy: **61 years**
Infant mortality: **63 per 1,000 live births**
Language: **English, Twi, Fanti, other languages**
Best buy: **textiles, gold jewelry, handicrafts**

Economic Structure

Ghana appeared to have returned to solid democratic governance with the outcome of elections in December 2000, when an entirely civilian president, John Kufuor, leader of the New Patriotic Party (NPP), replaced the 20-year rule of President Jerry Rawlings. Since its independence in 1957, Ghana has experienced three periods of military rule, during the last of which the Rawlings government (in power for nearly 20 years) introduced multiparty politics in 1992, at which point the country began its fourth experiment with democracy. The achievement of a peaceful transition between one government and another bodes well that the country may now have come to terms with the demands of democracy.

After an almost complete collapse in the 1970s, Ghana's economy over the past 20 years has begun to make an apparently sustainable if slow recovery, helped by substantial public and private investment and foreign assistance. The persistence of an inflationary environment, resulting principally from poor financial management by government, has tended to undermine the country's attempts to achieve a high level of economic growth, but there is strong potential for improvement. Agriculture is the largest contributor to GDP, representing 37%, followed by trade and public services, which account for 32%. Industry, including manufacturing and mining, contributes 25%. Ghana's leading exports are gold, cocoa, and timber, and there has been growth in other exports, including tropical fruit. The largest importers of Ghanaian produce are Switzerland, the United Kingdom, the Netherlands, and Spain, while the principal suppliers are the United Kingdom, the United States, Germany, Nigeria, and Japan.

Ghana's public sector has been substantially reduced in size since the 1980s, with the sale of government stakes in gold mines, state-owned factories and farms, banks, and telecommunications. However, there is further potential to reduce state ownership and control in key sectors and, especially, to improve the efficiency of the civil service machinery. The new government of President Kufuor declared itself in favor of establishing greater competitiveness in the market.

Economic Policy

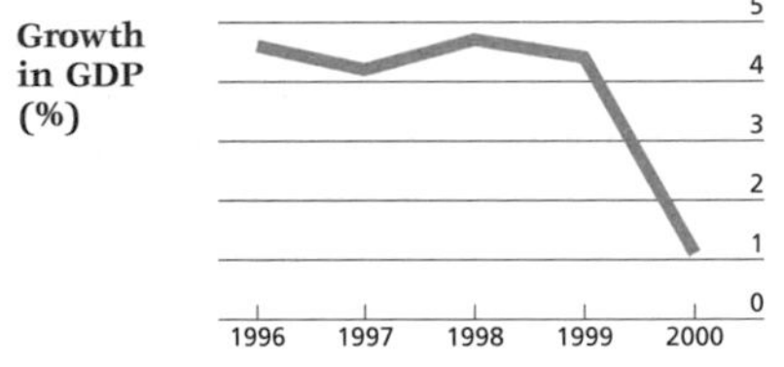

In 1983, the Rawlings government introduced a economic recovery program, with support from the World Bank and the IMF. Investment was successfully attracted into the gold mining industry, which experienced a strong revival. The program allowed for a series of privatizations and for much-needed financial sector adjustment, and a stock exchange was established in 1989. However, a loss of fiscal discipline after 1992 undermined the confidence of international investors and donors until a new enhanced structural adjustment facility was approved by the IMF in 1999. Performance since then, however, has been below target, with economic growth slipping from 4.4% in 1999 to 3.7% in 2000, and with inflation averaging 25% in 2000 and continuing to rise in early 2001. The incoming government of President Kufuor succeeded in slowing the resultant decline of the national currency but was faced with difficult choices in restoring the economy's fortunes. The private sector has been constrained from contributing to higher growth by the high level of government borrowing and inflationary deficit financing.

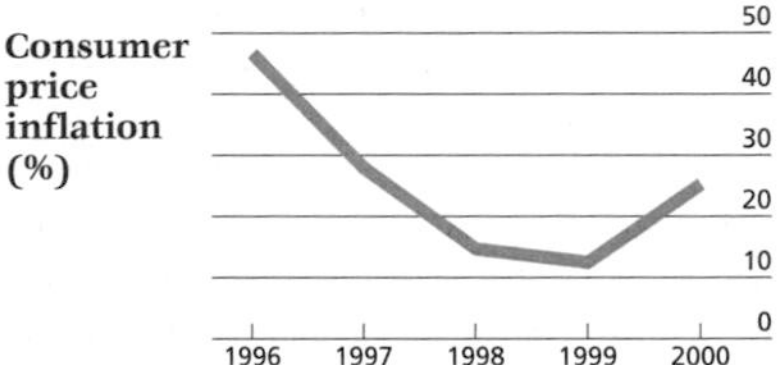

More than half of the economically active population is employed in farming, forestry, and fishing. Poverty is widespread, especially in Ghana's rural areas of the center and north, but also in most urban areas.

Geography/Resources

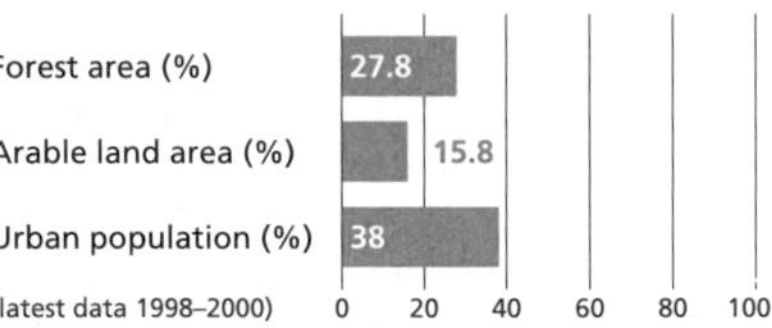

Ghana comprises much of the Volta river basin, surrounded by hill and mountain ranges rising to 1,000–3,000 feet above sea level. Some of the more ancient rocky outcrops and plains contain minerals such as gold, diamonds, manganese, and bauxite. The Volta river has been dammed at Akosombo, forming a large lake covering part of the center and east of the country and providing substantial quantities of electric power to Ghana and neighboring countries. The regions of the south and west are partially forested, although farming and logging have severely reduced forest cover. Rainfall is highest in the south, where there are two wet seasons each year. In the north there is less rainfall, occurring in a single season between April and September. Ghana's principal food crops are cassava, yams, plantains, and corn, while the main cash crops are cocoa, coconuts, groundnuts, and sugar.

The largest ethnic groups are Akan (including Ashanti, Fanti, and others) who make up 52% of the population, Mossi (16%), Ewe (12%), Guan (12%), and Ga (8%). The population grew at just under 3%

per annum through the 1990s. The largest cities are Accra and Kumasi.

Communications/Energy

PCs	0.3
Telephone lines	1.2
Mobiles	0.6
Internet users	0.2
(per 100 people, 2000)	0 20 40 60 80 100

The road network of 24,000 miles carries most of the country's domestic freight and passenger traffic. The main trunk roads are being improved and generally maintained, in contrast to the neglect they suffered in the 1970s. A railway network connects Accra, Kumasi, and Sekondi-Takoradi. The ports at Tema and Takoradi have been expanded and upgraded to handle a growing throughput of foreign trade. Tema handles much of the import trade, while Takoradi is used for the export of timber, manganese, and bauxite. The Ghana Ports and Harbour Authority (GPHA) is planning to privatize most of its shore activities.

The international airport at Accra handles direct flights to Europe, the United States, Southern Africa, and most of West Africa. Telecommunications growth in Ghana has been spearheaded by a number of mobile telephone companies, while the fixed-line network has grown more slowly.

Electricity generated by the Akosombo and Kpong hydroelectric facilities has been proved to be vulnerable to fluctuations in rainfall, and there was a severe electricity shortage in 1998. As a result, there has been significant new public and private investment in power generated by oil and gas. In normal times, Ghana is an exporter of electricity to neighboring countries. Oil and gas discoveries have been made in the offshore Tano basin, near the border with Côte d'Ivoire. Plans to pipe gas from Nigeria through an offshore pipeline have not yet been put into effect.

Education/Employment

Although Ghana was among the first countries in Africa to introduce free education, it has subsequently failed to maintain reasonable standards or to achieve universal provision. During the 1990s, the government shifted the emphasis of educational policy towards free basic education, if possible to all children of primary school age, while encouraging cost recovery in the later stages of education. There are more than 11,000 primary schools and 400 secondary schools. There are 4 universities, 6 polytechnic colleges, 21 technical colleges and 38 teacher training institutions.

Of the economically active population of 9 million, about 57% are employed in farming, forestry, and fishing. The other main sources of employment are trade, restaurants and hotels, manufacturing, community services, transport, and construction. The mining industry, although important to the national economy, employs relatively small numbers of workers, estimated at about 40,000 in total. There is considered to be a high level of unemployment, although it has also been demonstrated that most people without formal employment make a living by petty trading and the "informal economy."

Fiscal/Financial

The Bank of Ghana is the central bank. The four largest banks are Ghana Commercial Bank (GCB), Standard Chartered, Social Security Bank (SSB), and Barclays. The government has sold its controlling stake in GCB and SSB.

The poor record of fiscal control by the previous government presented a difficult challenge to the incoming government of President John Kufuor to restore discipline and to reduce the size of the central government's budgetary deficit. The government aimed to reduce the deficit from 7.2% of GDP in 2000 to 2% in 2003, and its first budget for 2001 sought to rein in government departments' indiscriminate use of credit facilities. There was some success in stabilizing the currency in 2001 after its earlier rapid depreciation. Sustained donor support for further government reform can be expected, especially after Ghana qualifies for Highly-Indebted Poor Country (HIPC) status.

VAT was introduced in 1999 at an initial rate of 10%; the rate was subsequently raised to 12.5% and is likely to be raised again. The budget for 2001 reduced the rate of corporate tax payable by companies listed on the Ghana stock exchange.

The banking sector has been comprehensively reformed. New commercial banks, including Trust Bank, Prudential Bank, International Commercial Bank, and Metropolitan and Allied Bank, have entered the market in the last decade. The government-owned National Investment Bank and the Agricultural Development Bank have been scheduled for privatization. There has been expansion of the insurance industry and the non-bank financial sector.

The Ghana stock exchange, established in 1989, has 22 listed companies. It is dominated by the Ashanti Goldfields Corporation, which accounts for about 65% of market capitalization.

Business Opportunities

Substantial investment can be expected in the telecommunications sector, especially in developing mobile telephone networks. Another sector of ongoing activity is electricity generation, where a government plan of action issued for the sector in 1998 identified the need to build larger thermal power-generation facilities through joint ventures between state-owned power utilities and foreign strategic investors. U.S. companies have taken the lead in building thermal power stations in the west of the country. The market could be further stimulated by the delivery of gas from Nigeria and Côte d'Ivoire under projects being negotiated.

Investments have begun at the Tema export processing zone near Accra. One of the first projects on the site was the installation of modern cocoa-processing facilities.

Investment in new financial services and banking card systems has commenced as the country begins to make the switch to technological solutions. Tourism has experienced steady growth since the late 1980s, and is expected to stimulate more hotel building and new investment in tourist sites and locations.

For More Information

Book:

Herbst, J. *The Politics of Reform in Ghana, 1982–1991*. Berkeley, CA: University of California Press, 1994.

Web Sites:

Africa Online:
www.africaonline.com/site.gh
African news and information:
www.allafrica.com/business
ghanaweb.com: **www.ghanaweb.com**
Government entry point:
www.Ghana.gov.gh
Norwegian Council for Africa, Index on Africa: **www.afrika.no/index**
Political Resources on the Net:
www.politicalresources.net

GIBRALTAR

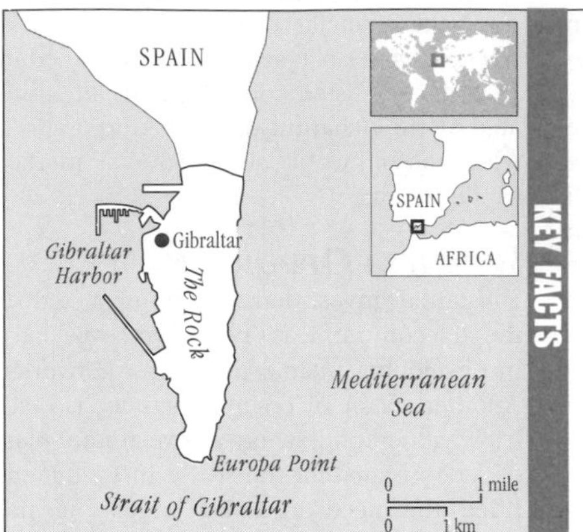

GNI pc: **$5,000 (approx.)**
Head of government: **chief minister**
Currency: **Gibraltar pound (G£)**
Capital: **Gibraltar**
Population: **29,000**
Land area: **2.5 square miles**
Population density: **11,600 per square mile**
Language: **English (official), Spanish**
Best buy: **consumer goods, petrol, alcohol, tobacco**

ECONOMY

The main industries are finance and insurance, tourism and retail trading in duty-free or low duty goods, ship bunkering, and repair. Offshore electronic gambling is a fast-growing sector. There are small local manufacturing industries in beverages and crafts.

An agreement between the United Kingdom and Spain in April 2000 eased some of the restrictions on the Gibraltar economy. The adequacy of anti-money-laundering measures was reviewed and endorsed by an IMF task force in June 2000. The United Kingdom and Spain aimed to conclude a comprehensive agreement regarding Gibraltar in mid-2002. This would lead to the incorporation of Gibraltar into the European Union and the obligation to apply EU laws, procedures and tax structures.

GEOGRAPHY/RESOURCES

Gibraltar is a small peninsula at the tip of southwest Spain, and forms the entrance from the Atlantic Ocean to the Mediterranean Sea. The climate is relatively dry, with mild winters and warm summers. There is no agricultural land and no significant mineral resources. Food is imported.

COMMUNICATIONS/ENERGY

There are 8 miles of main roads and a total network of 28 miles. There is no railway. The airport has a capacity of 1 million passengers per year, but only handled 186,000 in 1999 because Spain restricts air transport to Gibraltar. Gibraltar is Europe's largest bunkering port, handling 6,000 ships in 1999. Gibraltar's merchant fleet over 1,000 grt comprised 49 ships in 2000, with a total displacement of 669,056 grt. The telecommunications network is restricted because Spain has blocked the allocation of new numbers, and Gibraltar is covered by the Spanish national code. There were 27,178 fixed land lines in 1998. Mobile phone users either use the Spanish code or Gibraltar's code, from which they can phone anywhere in the world except Spain. The European Commission has taken action against Spain for breach of competition rules with regard to telecommunications. Electricity is generated entirely by imported fossil fuels. Other energy products are also imported. Petrol and ship fuel are re-exported.

FISCAL/FINANCIAL

Local tax is low, and there are exemptions and reductions for certain categories of business, non-resident individuals, and trusts administered for non-residents. Financial transactions—including betting and real estate, the shipping register, and other shipping activities—benefit from preferential tax rates. The government is considering introducing a harmonized tax rate of between 8 and 12% to satisfy OECD concerns about tax havens. Following an Anglo-Spanish agreement, Gibraltar might have to introduce VAT.

In September 2001 there were 19 banks with total assets of £5.6 billion, 17 insurance companies, 27 insurance intermediaries, 28 investment firms, 83 groups providing company managment and professional trustee services, and 7 insurance managers licensed by the Financial Services Commission. The banks are mostly U.K., other European, and U.S. There was a fall in the number of banks in 2000 because of consolidation elsewhere. The banks provide local real estate mortgages. Third-party funds managed by the banks account for at least as much again as assets, and totaled around £5.5 billion in March 2000. Many of these funds are engaged in stock market transactions around the world. There is direct trading on the German–Swiss Eurex futures exchange. The Financial Services Commission is responsible for supervision, and is regularly reviewed by the U.K. authorities for equivalence of standards.

BUSINESS OPPORTUNITIES

Finance, betting, real estate, trade, and shipping activities continue to attract inward investment. The growth of the betting business demonstrates that Spanish restrictions on infrastructure can be overcome. E-commerce and e-banking are likely to grow anyway, but will grow much faster if Spanish restrictions are removed, as would tourism and air transport if air traffic limits were lifted.

For More Information

Books:

The Gibraltar Research Group. *A Strategic Profile of Gibraltar*. San Diego, CA: ICON Group International, 2000.
Morris, D. S., and R. H. Haigh. *Britain, Spain and Gibraltar: The Eternal Triangle*. New York: Routledge, 1992.

Web Sites:

Gibraltar Statistics Office: **www.1gibraltarplaza.gi/gibraltar/statistics.html**
Government entry point: **www.gibraltar.gi**

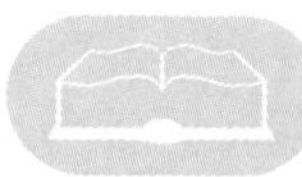

GREECE

KEY FACTS

GNI: **$127,648 million; world's 30th**
GNI pc: **$12,110; world's 46th**
Head of government: **prime minister**
Currency: **Euro (€)**
Capital: **Athens**
Population: **10,626,000, growing at 0.4% p.a.**
Land area: **49,800 square miles**
Population density: **213 per square mile**
Life expectancy: **78 years**
Infant mortality: **6 per 1,000 live births**
Language: **Greek**
Best buy: **onyx, alabaster, silver jewelry, textiles, ouzo**

ECONOMIC STRUCTURE

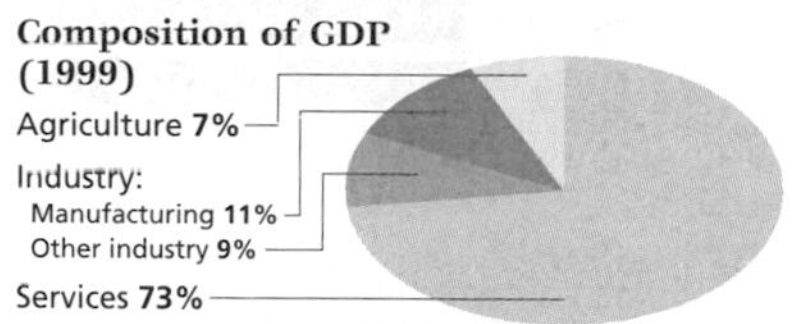

The cradle of western democracy in ancient history, Greece was then and is now a nation characterized by independent minds and business enterprise. The geographical isolation of Greek communities, caused by the mountains and islands, has made shipping and trade of vital importance down the ages. EU membership in 1981 made land transport through the former Yugoslavia to other EU countries the key to development and prosperity. From the early 1990s this was disrupted by civil wars and international military action. From the mid-1990s the government made a virtue out of necessity, organizing a forum of Balkan nations to try and resolve disputes and plan economic recovery for the region. The government has promoted Greece as a regional hub for trade and development.

Services accounted for 72% of GDP in 1999, followed by industry (including manufacturing, construction, and utilities 20%), and agriculture, forestry, and fishing (7%). Manufacturing accounted for 11%. Tourism and shipping are key service industries, but banking and business services are growing fast. Greece has one of the largest merchant fleets in the world with 780 ships over 1,000 grt, representing 25.6 million grt in 2000. Food processing is the main manufacturing sector, followed by metals and metal products, textiles and clothing, oil refining, and chemicals. The majority of Greek companies and farms are small.

Germany is the main export market followed by Italy, the United Kingdom, France, the United States, and Cyprus. Basic manufactures (including textiles, minerals, and metals) are the main exports, followed by food and live animals, petroleum products, olive oil, and chemicals. Textiles exports to other EU countries benefit from special trade preferences which will be phased out by 2005 under World Trade Organization rules. Trade with Turkey is on the increase following moves by the two countries to remove traditional rivalries.

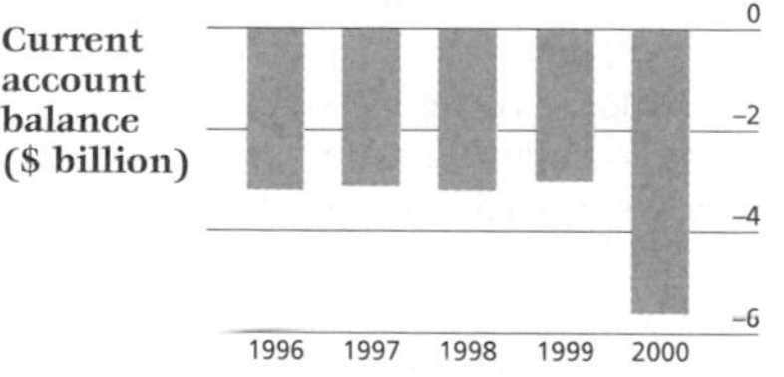

Since the reconstruction of the country after World War II, the state has dominated infrastructure and key resources such as finance, oil, and gas to provide a measure of protectionism to Greek industry. Privatization began in the 1980s and gathered pace in the latter half of the 1990s. By mid-2001, 20 state enterprises and banks had been fully or partly privatized. A further 10 were due for privatization, including air transport, the ports of Piraeus and Thessaloniki, and power, gas and aerospace companies. The state has retained shareholdings in the main telecommunications, banking, energy, and transport companies to give them the scope to expand their operations—in conjunction with private-sector partners—to other countries in the Balkans, thus producing the economies of scale absent in the domestic market. At mid-2001 the telecommunications industry was fully deregulated. Gas distribution may be liberalized by 2004 and electricity by 2005.

ECONOMIC POLICY

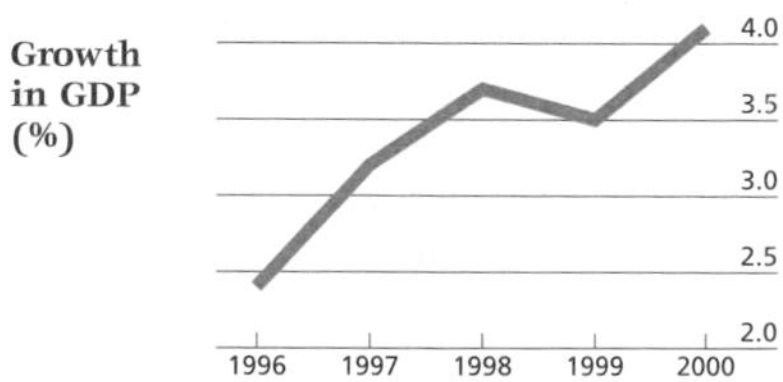

The government has applied wage constraints, increased competition and privatization, and tight monetary policies for several years in order to improve public finances and economic fundamentals sufficiently to qualify for Euro membership, which was achieved in 2001. The budget deficit fell from 13.8% of GDP in 1993 to 1.2% in 2000, with a surplus of 0.5% planned in 2001. The public debt was reduced from 138.8% of GDP in 1993 to around 100% in 2001. It is expected to ease in 2002 if GDP growth and tax receipts strengthen. A single unified health fund will be created to promote more uniform provision of healthcare and better control over costs. Measures to reduce unemployment include the reduction of social security contributions for employers hiring from disadvantaged groups, especially the young and women, and the removal of barriers to part-time work. Negotiations between the government, employers, and trade unions on social security reforms, pension reforms, and privatization were launched in autumn 2001 following adverse reactions from the trade unions.

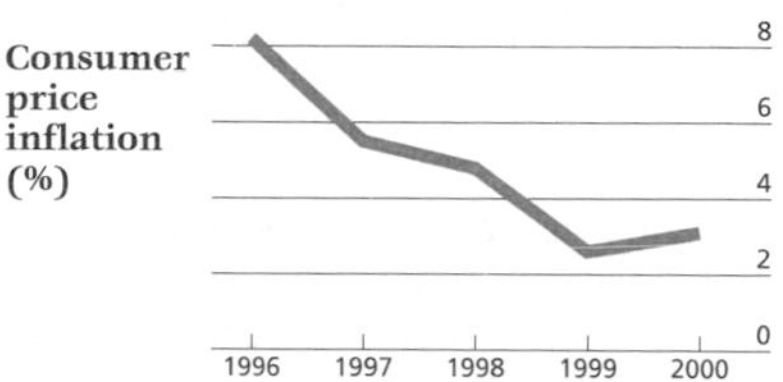

Economic growth gathered momentum in the second half of the 1990s, averaging 3.3% a year for 1996–99 against 1.2% for 1991–95. Growth was 4.1% in 2000 and around 3% in 2001. Growth in 1999 and 2000 was led by private investment and consumption, but exports also played an important part. Improved performance as a result of cheaper credit and more stable

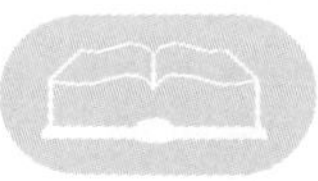

interest rates is anticipated following Greece's adoption of the Euro from January 2001. Domestic demand is expected to far outstrip supply, leading to the risk of increased inflation. Inflation fell from an annual average 13.9% in 1991–95 to an average 5% in 1996–99, reaching a low point of 2% in September 1999. It rose to 3% in 2000 mainly on account of oil prices, easing slightly to 2.7% in 2001. It was expected to fall slightly in 2002. Modest gains in jobs did not keep pace with increases in the labor force. Unemployment rose from 8.3% in 1991–95 to 10% in 1996–2000. It is expected to stay at around this level, or slightly below it, in the medium term.

Geography/Resources

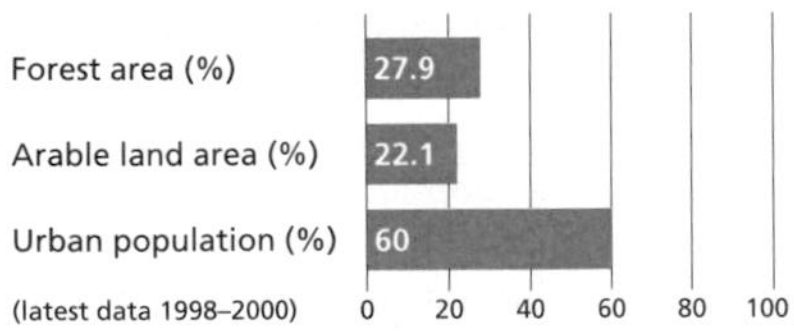

At the extreme southeast of Europe, Greece borders the Ionian Sea in the west, the Mediterranean in the south, and the Aegean in the east. It has northern land borders with Albania, Macedonia, Bulgaria, and Turkey. The climate is dry with hot summers and mild winters. The land is characterized by mountains and islands. 169 islands are inhabited by 17% of the population. 39% of the land is rocky scrub and pasture, 29% is arable, 20% is forest, and 12% urban.

Cotton and tobacco are the main industrial crops. Other important products include wine and grapes, olives and olive oil, melons, peaches, oranges, tomatoes, wheat, corn, rice, alfalfa, sugar beet, timber, and wood pulp. About 40% of cultivated land is irrigated. Farmed sea bass and sea bream are becoming important fisheries products. Greece is a major producer of bauxite with reserves of over 650 million tons. Magnesite, gypsum, iron ore, lignite, kaolin, marble, salt, silver, zinc, lead, petroleum, and natural gas are also produced. Proven oil reserves were 10 million barrels at January 2001, with natural gas reserves of 35 billion cubic feet. Lignite reserves were 3.17 billion tons in 1996.

The main concentrations of people are around the two largest cities, Athens and Thessaloniki. At the 1991 census, 55% of the population were urban. The majority of people are of Greek origin, but there has been a significant increase in immigration as a result of the conflicts in neighboring Balkan states.

Communications/Energy

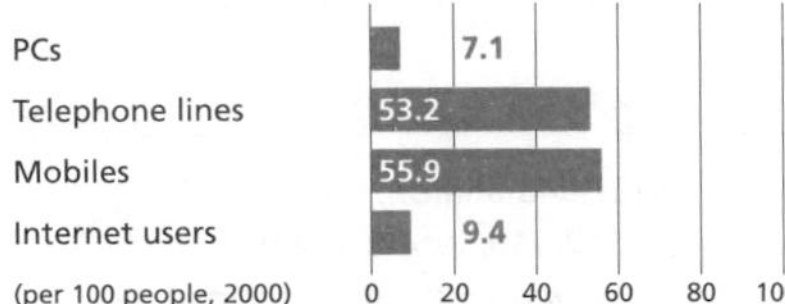

Transport networks are benefiting from major investment in preparation for the Olympic Games to be held in Athens in 2004. The new $2 billion airport for Athens opened in March 2001 with a new highway and rail connection to the capital. State-owned Olympic Airways has bought new Airbus aircraft, and the airline is being reorganized to make it, and the new airport, the key to air travel in the Balkan and east Mediterranean region. Hellenic Railways Organization (OSE) is investing $500 million in electrification, new rolling stock, and station improvements for the 1,591 miles rail network. The Athens metro, with a capacity of 140 million passengers a year, opened in January 2000. The road network consists of 5,751 miles of highways and 18,238 miles of provincial roads. The new Egnatia highway across northern Greece will be completed by 2006. Greece has 123 sea ports handling freight and passengers. The largest are Piraeus, Patras, and Thessaloniki. The two main international airports are at Athens and Thessaloniki. There are 25 domestic airports.

The telecommunications sector was fully opened up to competition by end-2000. The main company OTE, which is majority state-owned, invested €792 million in 2001 to complete digitalization and fast Internet access on the main network. The number of fixed phone lines is increasing so rapidly that ten-digit numbers will be phased in by October 2002. At end-2000 there were 5.7 million fixed phone lines and 1 million Internet users. There were over 6 million mobile phones in early 2001. OSE owns a separate telecommunications network, which it will develop with foreign partners.

Oil imports accounted for 60% of energy requirements in 2000, while natural gas accounted for 5%. Domestic oil production was 8,750 barrels per day in 2000. Gas production was 70 million cubic feet and lignite production was 67.2 million tons in 1999. In 1999, 89.6% of electricity was generated by thermal power stations (mostly lignite with some oil), 9.7% by hydroelectric power, and 0.7% by solar and wind power. Solar and wind power will be increased, especially to serve the islands. The Greek electricity grid links with the grids of Italy, Albania (and—via Albania—Kosovo), Macedonia, and Bulgaria. A link with Turkey is under construction and will be supplied by a new gas-fired power station being built by Greek and Turkish companies in Greece. Most new power stations under construction will use gas, demand for which is planned to double, and oil imports are expected to increase at around 4.4% a year in the next decade. There are plans to build a new gas pipeline from Italy to Greece. State-owned Hellenic Petroleum is exploring for oil and gas both offshore and onshore in western Greece. It has shares in consortia drilling for oil and gas in Iran and Albania. It will undertake studies for the Burgas (Bulgaria) to Alexandroupolis (Greece) pipeline, which is planned to be a main conduit to the west for crude oil from the massive Caspian fields.

Education/Employment

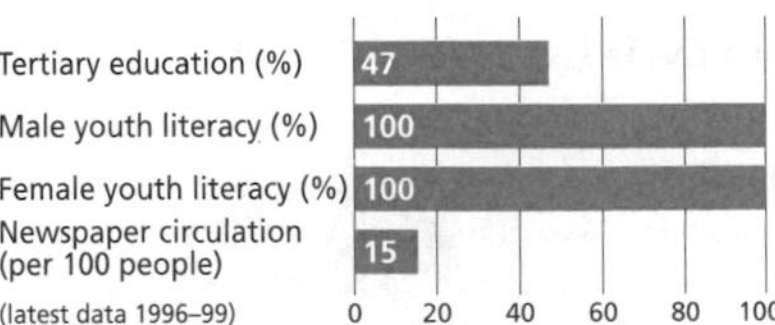

Education is compulsory from age 6 to 15. Courses and books are provided free by the state at all levels. There are 17 universities and 14 technological educational institutes. The range of courses was expanded in 1998–99. Until 2001–02 there were around 160,400 university students and 58,600 technological college students; from autumn 2001 the intake increased, as all students with secondary-school leaving certificates were allowed to enroll in higher education. The Ministry of National Education and the Pedagogical Institute set education policy and goals; private-sector schools and vocational colleges are required to follow national standards.

There are 30 research centers, some connected to the universities. Nine industrial R&D companies have been established in marine technology, renewable energy sources, ceramics and refractories, aquaculture, and industrial property, to offer services and solve production problems for small and medium-sized enterprises. Technology parks have been created in Attica, Thessaloniki, Crete, and Patras, providing high-grade facilities for innovative firms. Expenditure on R&D is only 0.46% of GDP, and the government recognizes the need for higher spending from both the public and private sectors.

Labor costs are the second lowest in the EU, and Greece combines a pool of skilled and unskilled workers. 11% of the population have university degrees. Most

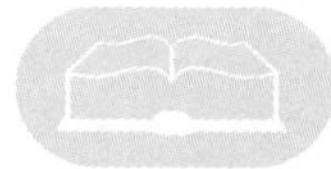

graduates have studied abroad and speak at least one other language, especially English. The labor force increased in the late 1990s, with new young people and immigrants from Balkan countries coming on to the job market. Strikes in the public sector have accompanied the privatizations and other changes introduced in the 1990s.

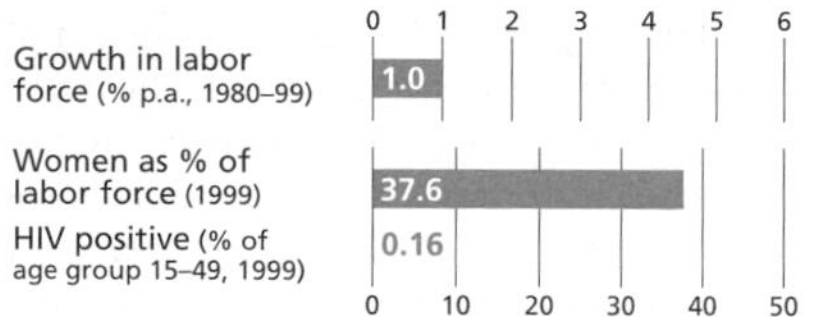

Wages and working conditions are set through negotiations between trade unions and employers at national level and then at sectoral level. The government has encouraged enterprise-level negotiations in areas of high unemployment. Greece applies EU employment law, which covers safety at work, wages and working hours, industrial relations, employment incentives, and unemployment provision. Greek labor laws are particularly strict regarding overtime, part-time work, and dismissals. In 2001 the government introduced legislation to ease employment protection for part-time workers in order to open up more job opportunities.

Fiscal/Financial

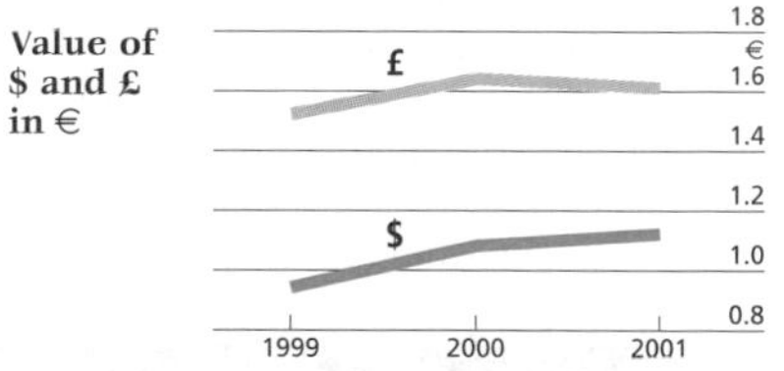

The largest bank with 32% market share, National Bank of Greece was partly privatized in 2000. Private-sector Alpha Credit Bank is the second largest, followed by Agricultural Bank of Greece, another state bank partly privatized in 2000. The regulatory authority for banks is the Bank of Greece, which is also part of the European System of Central Banks. This body and the European Central Bank set the policy for the Euro. The Capital Market Commission supervises the capital market and non-bank capital market firms. The Ministry of Development is responsible for the supervision of insurance companies.

The government measures from the late 1990s to broaden the tax base have gone in tandem with efforts to combat tax evasion, the latter proving reasonably successful. From 2002 the standard rate of corporation

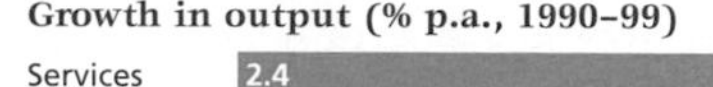

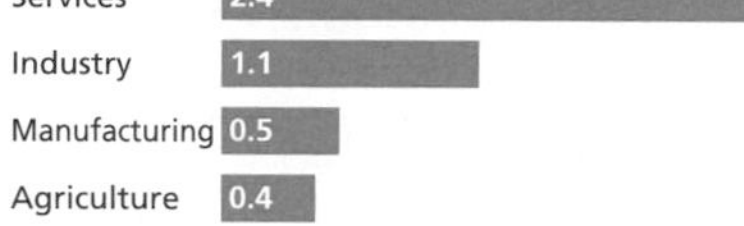

tax was 35%. Maximum personal income tax was reduced to 40%. Further tax cuts were planned. Offshore branches of foreign companies, which are used by shipping companies, are exempt from corporation tax. VAT is applied at 18%.

The government restructured the financial regulatory framework, privatized many state-owned banks, and approved mergers in the sector in preparation for Euro membership in January 2001. Increased competition led to the greater sophistication and internationalization of financial services, a process which will continue, leading eventually to consolidation. At mid-2001 there were 33 commercial banks, four investment banks, one specialized bank (Agricultural Bank), 9 local cooperative banks, and the Postal Savings Bank. State-controlled banks and specialized institutions accounted for 63% of deposits and 58% of loans, while private banks controlled 29% and 31% respectively, and foreign banks (including EU and U.S. banks) 8% and 11%. From July 2000 bank liquidity increased as the Bank of Greece allowed banks to release part of their reserves. Credit to industry thus became cheaper and more readily available. The government has launched a €500 million venture capital fund to assist new companies.

Privatization and increased competition boosted activity on the Athens stock exchange, but share values tumbled in 2000 prior to Euro membership. Trading slumped again in 2001 when emerging market funds left the exchange following its upgrading by the Morgan Stanley Capital International index from emerging-market to developed-market status. The Athens Derivatives Exchange was launched in 1999. A new market for Balkans companies, Eagek, was launched at end-2001 in Thessaloniki.

Business Opportunities

The Hellenic Center for Investment (ELKE) provides information and assistance to foreign investors. The government offers grants, interest-rate subsidies, and tax-free reserves to productive investments. Priority sectors include new technologies and products, modernization of existing industry, and environmental control and energy conservation. Location and job creation are additional criteria for the level of incentives. Maximum grants—cash up to 65% and tax deductions of 60–100% of the investment—are offered for projects in Thrace. EU grants are also available to investors.

In 1999–2000 the main industries attracting foreign investment were chemicals, metallurgy, food processing, textiles, energy, tourism, IT, and banking. Hotels, restaurants, and other visitor services connected with the Olympic Games offer investment opportunities. The privatization programs continue to offer prospects in the sectors of banking, transport, power, telecommunications, and military defense systems.

For More Information

Books:

Douskas, George, and Pericles Smerlas, eds. *About Greece*. Athens: Ministry of Press and Mass Media, 2001.

European Union: European Economy: Report and Studies Series.

IMF Country Report. *Greece*. Washington, D.C.: IMF.

OECD Economic Surveys. *Greece*. Paris: OECD, 2001.

Stathoulopoulos, Stavros, et al., eds. *Greece in the World: A Global View of Foreign and Security Policy*. Athens: Ministry of Press and Mass Media, 1999.

Tsardanidis, Charalambos. *Greece and the South-Eastern European States: Economic Dynamics, Cooperation and Prospects*. Athens: Institute of International Economic Relations, 2000.

Web Sites:

Association of Insurance Companies: **www.eaee.gr**

Athens News (daily English language newspaper): **www.athensnews.dolnet.gr**

Athens Stock Exchange: **www.ase.gr**

Economist Intelligence Unit: **www.eiu.com**

General Secretariat for International Economic Relations: **www.dos.gr**

Government entry point: **www.government.gr**

Hellenic Bank Association: **www.hba.gr**

Hellenic Center for Investment (ELKE): **www.elke.gr**

Ministry of National Economy: **www.ypetho.gr**

National Statistical Service of Greece: **www.statistics.gr**

  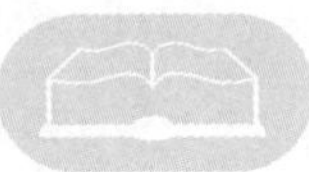    

Greenland

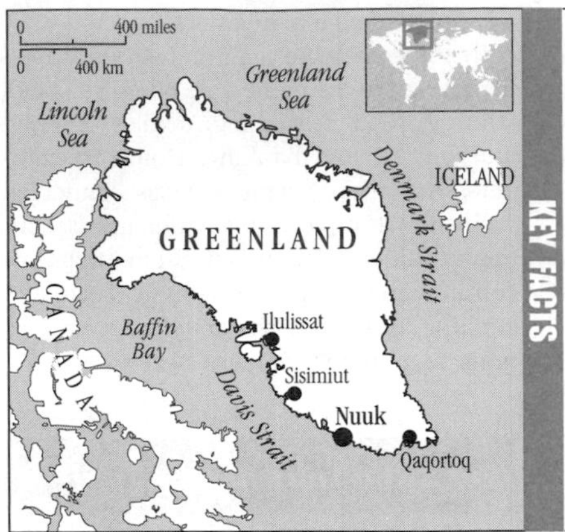

KEY FACTS

GNI pc: **$16,100 (approx.)**
Head of government: **prime minister**
Currency: **Danish Krone (DKr)**
Capital: **Nuuk**
Population: **59,800**
Land area: **840,000 square miles**
Population density: **0.07 per square mile**
Language: **Greenlandic, Danish**
Best buy: **cold-weather clothing, handicrafts**

Economy

Fisheries is the main industry, with shrimp and halibut the main products and exports. Prawns accounted for 63% and halibut for 17% of export earnings in 2000. Revenue is also derived from the licensing of foreign fishing in Greenlandic waters. However, the government has limited fish catches to conserve stocks. Shipyards provide maintenance and repair for a broad range of ships and for onshore industrial installations. Traditional seal and whale hunting provide the main income for about one-fifth of the population. There is a specialized clothing industry in traditional garments and modern cold-weather items. Tourism is a growing industry. It is government strategy to promote tourism and minerals as the sectors with the most potential for diversifying the economy.

Greenland government finances are derived from Danish grant aid, taxes, and excise revenues. In 1987 the government instigated a long-term program of public spending cuts in order to reduce the foreign debt of the government and of the large number of state enterprises, which stood at DKr2.1 billion in 1996. The enterprises were restructured and managed along the lines of private-sector companies, but the government retained full or significant ownership. GDP growth fluctuates with the status of fisheries and investment projects. Annual average GDP growth was 1.4% in 1986–95, with substantial peaks and troughs. Growth was 7.8% in 1998. Average annual inflation in 1986–95 was about 3%. In 1999 it was 1.7%, rising to 3.2% in July 2001. Unemployment rose from 7% in 1999 to 10% in 2000.

Geography/Resources

Greenland is one of the largest islands in the world, 81% of it permanently under ice several miles thick. Most of the island is also surrounded by ice. The summer is too short to grow most crops. Animal husbandry, especially sheep and reindeer, are the main agricultural sectors. Seal hunting and whaling provide meager self-sufficiency for some communities. There has been no mining production since 1990, but there are deposits of gold, zinc, diamonds, nickel, lead, iron ore, petroleum, natural gas and other minerals. In 1997 22 minerals companies and 11 oil companies held exploration licenses.

Most Greenlanders are a mixture of Inuit who migrated from North America 1,000 years ago, and Europeans who migrated from the early 18th century. They live in the capital, 16 small towns, and 60 settlements. The rest of the land is uninhabited.

Communications/Energy

There are no roads or railways between settlements; air is the main mode of transport from six airports, and helicopters are used for most settlements. Coastal ships carry passengers and freight along the west coast and elsewhere when the ice allows. At end-1999 there were 25,617 fixed phone lines, 12,676 mobile phones, and 4,000 Internet users. Fully digitalized links are provided by satellite, cable, and microwave radio relay.

The Buksefjorden hydro power station has supplied the capital Nuuk with electricity since October 1993, replacing around one-third of imported oil used for electricity. District heating provides electricity in 12 towns. However, imported oil remains the main energy source for electricity and transport. Indigenous oil and natural gas are not produced at present.

Fiscal/Financial

Greenland is part of the monetary union of the Kingdom of Denmark, so monetary and exchange rate policy are conducted by the Danish National Bank and Danish government. Banking supervision is the remit of the Danish Financial Supervisory Authority, as Danish and Greenlandic banks operate in Greenland. The two Greenlandic commercial banks, Bank of Greenland and Nuna Bank, merged in 1997, adopting the name of the former. Lending activity by the banks and Danish mortgage credit institutes declined in the 1990s. Project finance is provided by these institutions and by the Nordic Investment Bank. There is no stock market in Greenland. Corporation tax is 35%, but the government is planning to reduce it to 30%, possibly from 2002. Personal income tax consists of Home Rule tax and municipal tax, which combined averages around 40%.

Business Opportunities

The main companies are wholly or partly owned by the government and some, such as shipping company Royal Arctic Line, have been granted monopolies. The government is open to foreign investment in minerals exploration and production. The new Minerals Resource Act strengthens the rights of private-sector companies. The point of contact is the Bureau of Minerals and Petroleum.

For More Information

Books:

Greenland: A "Spy" Guide (World Offshore Investments and Business Library). 3rd ed. Washington, D.C.: International Business Publications, 2001.

Statistical Yearbook 2000–2001. 30th ed. Nuuk, Greenland: Statistics Greenland, 2001.

This Is Greenland 2000–2001. Copenhagen, Denmark: Royal Danish Ministry of Foreign Affairs, 2001.

Web Sites:

Greenland Home Rule government: **www.gh.gl**

Statistics Greenland: **www.statgreen.gl**

GRENADA

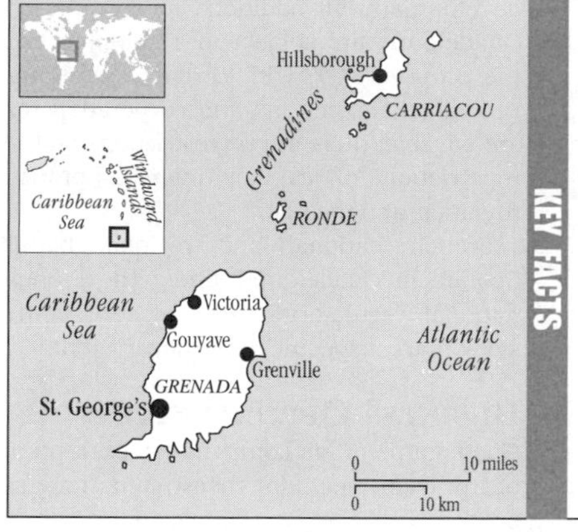

KEY FACTS

GNI: **$334 million**
GNI pc: **$3,440; world's 82nd**
Head of government: **prime minister**
Currency: **Eastern Caribbean dollar (EC$)**
Capital: **St. George's**
Population: **93,000, growing at 0.2% p.a.**
Land area: **116 square miles**
Population density: **801 per square mile**
Infant mortality: **22 per 1,000 live births**
Language: **English**
Best buy: **spices, perfumes**

ECONOMY

Tourism and agriculture are the principal economic sectors, in terms of both employment and foreign exchange earnings. Agriculture accounts for half of Grenada's export income, and a fifth of the population depend on farming for their living. In the mid-1990s there were an estimated 12,000 farmers, with 31,000 acres devoted to prime agriculture, but since then there has been a severe decline in two export crops, nutmeg and bananas, in the face of increased competition in world markets. In 1997, hotels and restaurants accounted for 8.9% of gross domestic product, agriculture 8.1%, and manufacturing 7.3%; the manufacturing sector includes agricultural processing, brewing, garments, and pharmaceuticals. Fishing has been developed in recent years, and in 1997 it employed 1,500 people and accounted for 16% of export revenue.

The main export earner is nutmeg (including nutmeg oil and other derivatives). Grenada's main export customers are Britain, Germany, and the Netherlands, while the United States and Britain supply the bulk of its imports, followed by Caribbean Community countries such as Barbados and Trinidad & Tobago. In the services sector, stayover tourist arrivals increased during the 1990s, reaching almost 129,000 in 2000, while cruise ship traffic fluctuated, reaching 266,000 arrivals in 1998, but falling to 180,000 in 2000; earnings in 1998 were $169 million.

The economy underwent a structural adjustment in the early 1990s, subsequently showing increased growth, which exceeded 7% in both 1998 and 1999 and 6% in 2000, partly through the development of an offshore finance sector. The increased growth rates in the late 1990s were accompanied by a reduction in inflation, which averaged 1.4% per year during 1997–2000.

GEOGRAPHY/RESOURCES

Grenada is the most southerly country in the Windward Islands. As well as the main island, it comprises Carriacou and Petit Martinique, plus several islets, almost all uninhabited. The population was estimated at 100,000 in 2000, of whom about 6,000 lived in the two smaller islands; about 85% are of African descent, the remainder including those of European, Asian, or mixed descent.

Grenada is mountainous, and heavily forested in the interior, the highest point being Mt. St. Catherine, in the northern part of the island, at 2,756 feet. Average annual rainfall is 59 inches in coastal areas, 150 inches inland; the rainy season lasts from June to December. The island is the world's second-largest nutmeg producer, and a profusion of other spices, fruit, and vegetables is to be found.

Traditionally poor, with a high emigration rate, Grenada has undergone rapid changes in the last two decades. Adult literacy is estimated at 85%. There are 18 secondary schools and several higher-education establishments, grouped together as a national college, with a strong emphasis on vocational training.

COMMUNICATIONS/ENERGY

Grenada has frequent air services to and from Britain, the United States, and many Caribbean countries, plus domestic inter-island links. Bus routes are mainly centered on St. George's. There are about 620 miles of roads, of which 435 miles are paved.

Telecommunications service is provided by Cable & Wireless, and electric power by the Grenada Electricity Co., formerly state-owned but privatized in 1994.

FISCAL/FINANCIAL

There is no income tax, and the budget is heavily dependent on revenue from a general consumption tax. There is a company tax of 30%, and a variety of other taxes on motor vehicles, foreign exchange purchases, property, travel, and foreign trade.

An offshore services sector, which was developed in the mid-1990s, housed 1,652 international business companies and 31 offshore banks in 1999. The following year, a scandal concerning an offshore bank led to new legislation to combat money laundering, together with the creation of a financial investigation unit of the police force.

BUSINESS OPPORTUNITIES

Incentives for investment from overseas include exemption from company tax for periods ranging from 10 to 15 years, together with waivers of duties and taxes on imported plant, equipment, materials, and vehicles. Companies may be fully foreign-owned, or joint ventures with Grenadian investors. Repatriation of capital is permitted, and investors also benefit from exemption from consumption and foreign exchange taxes, license fees, and other requirements. Export-oriented manufacturing is the priority sector for investment, but tourist-related projects are also a sector offering good investment prospects, both for operators and construction companies.

For More Information

Books:

The Caribbean Handbook. London: FT Caribbean (BVI) Ltd. (annual).
Grenada Business and Investment Opportunities Yearbook. 3rd ed. Washington, D.C.: International Business Publications, 2001 (annual).

Web Sites:

Chamber of Industry and Commerce: **www.spiceisle.com/homepages/gcic**
Economist Intelligence Unit: **www.eiu.com**

GUADELOUPE

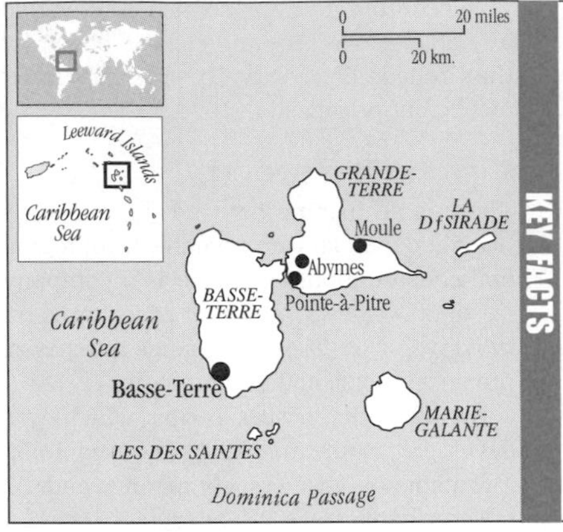

KEY FACTS

GNI pc: **$9,200 (approx.)**
Currency: **Euro (€)**
Capital: **Basse-Terre**
Population: **428,000**
Land area: **687 square miles**
Population density: **622 per square mile**
Language: **French, Creole**
Best buy: **rum, handicrafts**

ECONOMY

Tourism is the major source of revenue and employment in Guadeloupe, one of two French overseas departments in the Caribbean; the economy is strongly oriented towards services and closely linked with mainland France, which provided 83% of tourist arrivals in 1998. While government services accounted for 26.5% of employment in 1992, trade, restaurants and hotels accounted for 16.2%, finance 11.3% and other services 16.3%. Agriculture employed only 6.7%, a figure which declined to 3.8% in 1998; bananas and sugar cane were the main crops. Sugar and rum are the main traditional manufactures, but construction materials, cereals, and boats are also produced. There is an industrial free zone in the port area of Pointe-à-Pitre.

More than 60% of the department's trade is with mainland France; the main exports are bananas, sugar and rum, plus non-traditional items. Between 1990 and 1996, GDP declined by an annual average of 4.1%, and unemployment in 1998 was 28.8%; financial support from the central government is fundamental to the department's well-being. In 1999, the trade deficit was €1.4 billion; imports totaled €1,580 million and exports only €144 million.

GEOGRAPHY/RESOURCES

Lying between the Leeward and Windward Islands in the eastern Caribbean, Guadeloupe is divided into two parts, Basse-Terre and Grande-Terre. The former is mainly mountainous, with the Grande Soufrière volcano (4,813 feet) the highest peak; Grande-Terre is predominantly flat, with a central hilly area reaching a maximum of 443 feet. The bulk of agricultural production is in Grande-Terre. There are no significant mineral resources.

Tourism and fishing are the main activities. On the mainland, the chief urban area is Pointe-à-Pitre and its suburbs (Les Abymes, Baie-Mahault and Le Gosier), which between them numbered 132,751 inhabitants at the 1999 census, 31.4% of the total population. Basse-Terre, although the administrative center, had only 12,410 inhabitants.

The population is mainly of African or mixed African and European descent; others are of European descent, principally from the French mainland. There is free compulsory education from 6 to 16 years of age, and extensive pre-school nursery provision; the literacy rate is more than 90%.

COMMUNICATIONS/ENERGY

International air links are provided by Air France and other French airlines, with destinations including Miami and Caracas as well as a variety of French and Caribbean airports. Canadian, Cuban and United States airlines also operate. A ferry service connects Guadeloupe with Dominica and Martinique. Bus services operate throughout the island; out of 1,524 miles of roads, 202 miles are main roads.

Telecommunications and electricity are provided by French state enterprises; electrical power is generated from imported fuel oil, except for two small hydroelectric plants.

FISCAL/FINANCIAL

Guadeloupe and its dependencies are generally covered by the French national tax structures, which include a value-added tax on most transactions, with exemptions for items such as building materials and inputs for agricultural, industrial and tourist development. In addition, goods entering Guadeloupe are subject to a shipping tax, the *octroi de mer*, with certain exceptions. Individual income tax and corporation tax are payable; there are no restrictions on the repatriation of capital, interest, profits, royalties, and the like.

French national and regional banks operate in Guadeloupe, under the French national regulatory system. There is no stock market specific to the department.

BUSINESS OPPORTUNITIES

Guadeloupe offers company tax exemption of up to ten years for investments in agriculture, fisheries, small-scale industry, energy, and tourism, and five-year tax reductions on individual income for individual investors, while the industrial free zone in Pointe-à-Pitre provides duty-free concessions on inputs for manufacturers. The Guadeloupe administration may impose countervailing duties on imports regarded as unduly low-priced and thus offering unfair competition to local products.

However, exports from European Union countries normally enter Guadeloupe free of duty, as do commercial samples. Opportunities for joint ventures exist, and public-sector procurement, carried out by tender, provides export opportunities. Appointment of an agent is recommended. For exporters, agricultural machinery, construction equipment, and consumer goods are recommended as promising categories of goods, while the hotel and restaurant sector offers opportunities for investors. Import licenses are not required for most products.

For More Information

Books:

Frémy, Dominique, and Michèle Frémy. *Quid 2002*. Paris: Editions Robert Laffont, 2002.

The Guadeloupe Research Group. *A Strategic Profile of Guadeloupe* (Strategic Planning Series). San Diego, CA: ICON Group International, 2000.

Web Sites:

Basse-Terre Chamber of Commerce and Industry: **www.basse-terre.cci.fr**
General Council: **www.cg972.fr**
Ministry of the DOM-TOM: **www.outre-mer.gouv.fr**
Regional Council: **www.cr-guadeloupe.fr**

GUAM

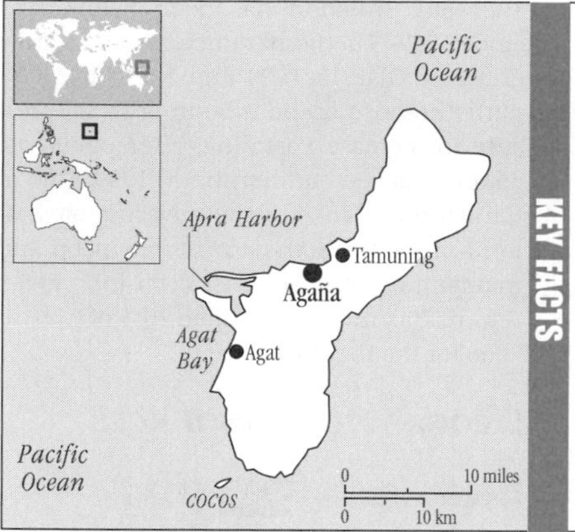

KEY FACTS

GNI pc: **$19,000 (approx.)**
Head of government: **governor**
Currency: **U.S. dollar ($)**
Capital: **Agaña**
Population: **151,700**
Land area: **210 square miles**
Population density: **722 per square mile**
Language: **English (official), Chamorro, Japanese**
Best buy: **duty-free goods, handicrafts**

ECONOMY

Tourism, and the trade in duty-free and other goods associated with it, are the main industries. Tourism was hit by the Asian financial crisis as 80% of visitors are Japanese, but began to recover in late 1999. U.S. military spending, and aid for infrastructure projects and social programs, are major contributors to the economy. Military spending was reduced from $748 million in 1993 to $507 million in 1998. Construction has benefited from the tourist boom and the conversion of the economy from military to private-sector orientation. Around 70% of jobs were private sector in 1999, with 22% of jobs in local government and 8% for the U.S. federal government. Local industries include commercial ship repair and servicing, food processing, textiles, concrete products, printing, publishing, and discounted sales of designer clothes. Fish is processed and exported. A new fish-farming project is also aimed at export. The main export markets are Japan, Micronesia, and Palau.

There were significant local job losses, and a loss of tax receipts, as a result of military downsizing. The government operated deficits from 1994 to 1996, with increased borrowing, including a bond issue. Balanced budgets have been the policy aim since 1997. The United States provided $56 million a year in 2000–02 to improve tax collection. The government continued to strengthen infrastructure. Over $200 million in capital improvement projects were due to be completed or started in 2000. Tourism, duty-free shopping, banking, insurance, and telecommunications are growth areas targeted by government policy. Since 1992 GDP has been stagnant at around $3 billion following 75% growth from 1988 to 1992, but it is likely to revive as the major Asian economies recover. Consumer prices increased by 0.4% in 1999 and fell by 0.62% in the first quarter of 2000, according to Guam government figures.

GEOGRAPHY/RESOURCES

Guam is the southernmost island of the Marianas group in the Pacific Ocean, some 1,200 miles south of Japan. Agricultural crops include cassava, sweet potatoes, coconuts, breadfruit, bananas, watermelons, and sugar cane for local consumption. Sea fisheries are significant, with catches landed by U.S., Japanese, and Taiwanese vessels. There are no significant mineral resources.

COMMUNICATIONS/ENERGY

The road network is estimated at around 930 miles, including 426 miles of military roads not for public use. Of the public network, 420 miles is paved. Apra Harbor has a container and bulk cargo port. A new passenger terminal was completed in 1996 at the international airport to provide better facilities for the 1.4 million visitors a year. Modern telecommunications, including the Internet and mobile and fixed telephony links, are available via undersea fiber-optic cables and satellite. Fiber-optic cable was laid in 2001. In 1998 there were 84,134 fixed phone lines and 55,000 mobile phones. There were 5,000 Internet users in 2000. The Guam Power Authority's electricity generation and distribution facilities were upgraded in the 1990s to meet the fast pace of economic development. Imported petroleum supplies most energy needs, including electricity.

FISCAL/FINANCIAL

U.S. federal income and corporation tax rules apply, with additional local taxes. The main local tax is the 4% levy on gross business receipts. There are various exemptions and reductions for specific industries to encourage investment. Banking, financial trusts, and insurance benefit from 100% profit-tax rebates for 20 years. To ensure transparency, the tax is held and invested for 180 days by the government before being returned. The finance system is regulated by the Guam government, but monetary policy is set in the United States. The banking sector is well developed, with U.S., Japanese, Taiwanese, Philippines, Hong Kong, and local banks. Bank deposits totaled $1.46 billion in 1997, and bank loans increased to $2.58 billion. Captive insurance is a growing sector. The Bank of Guam became the first local bank to list its stocks in 2000. The listing on San Francisco's Pacific Exchange gives the bank access to U.S. capital markets.

BUSINESS OPPORTUNITIES

Tax and financial incentives are offered to investors. Tourism, construction, transshipment operations, fish farming, finance, and insurance have attracted foreign investment and continue to offer opportunities. Guam Economic Development Authority, the point of contact for foreign investors, has four industrial parks where it leases land on easy terms in return for employment guarantees.

For More Information

Book:

The State of the Islands Report—1999. Washington, D.C.: U.S. Department of the Interior, Office of Insular Affairs.

Web Sites:

Government entry point: **www.ns.gov.gu/government.html**
Guam Economic Development Authority: **www.investguam.com**

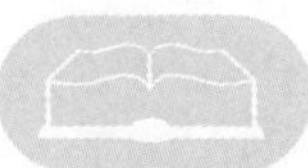

GUATEMALA

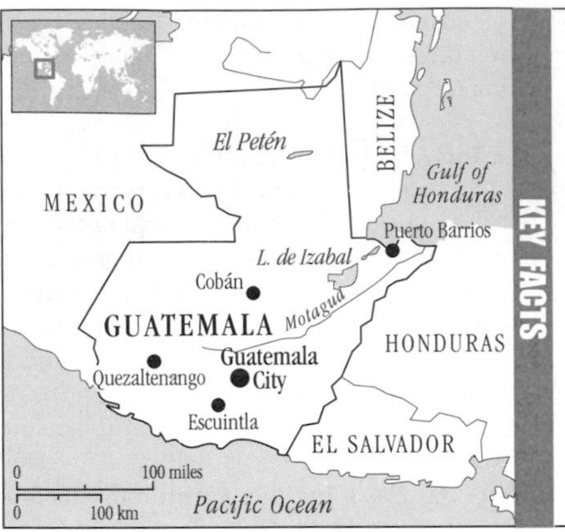

KEY FACTS

GNI: **$18,625 million; world's 68th**
GNI pc: **$1,680; world's 112th**
Head of government: **president**
Currency: **quetzal (Q)**
Capital: **Guatemala City**
Population: **11,090,000, growing at 2.6% p.a.**
Land area: **41,850 square miles**
Population density: **264 per square mile**
Life expectancy: **65 years**
Infant mortality: **45 per 1,000 live births**
Language: **Spanish, Quiché**
Best buy: **textiles, painted wooden masks**

ECONOMIC STRUCTURE

A peace treaty in 1996 ended a 36-year war between right-wing (and U.S.-backed) governments (most of them military) and left-wing rebels, in which an estimated 200,000 people were killed, most of them indigenous Mayans. The conflict followed the CIA-sponsored overthrow of the reformist President Jacobo Arbenz in 1954. The deadline for full implementation of the peace accords—a complex series of measures to transform Guatemala into a civilian democracy—was put back from December 2000 to 2004. The predominantly agricultural economy (one-quarter of GDP, two-thirds of exports, and employing half the labor force) is still largely in the hands of an estimated 20 families. Three-quarters of the population live below the poverty line; the wealthiest 10% have 46% of income and the poorest 10% have 1.6%. The overall illiteracy rate is more than 30%.

Industry (including a 14% manufacturing contribution) generates 20% of GDP, and services account for 55%. Tourism is becoming increasingly important, attracted by the spectacular Mayan pyramids. Coffee is the largest source of export earnings (up to 40% of the total), followed by sugar, bananas, and small cardamom (Guatemala is the world's largest producer of this spice). Manufacturing comprises food and drink processing, textiles, pottery, furniture, and assembly of electronic products by *maquiladora* plants. Guatemala has a free trade agreement with Mexico, El Salvador, and Honduras, and is a member of the Central American Common Market along with El Salvador, Costa Rica, Honduras, and Nicaragua. The main market is the United States (almost half of total exports). Exports enjoy preferential access to the U.S. market through the Caribbean Basin Initiative (CBI) and the Generalized System of Preferences (GSP).

Privatization began in 1996 when the government embarked on a modernization program that included the sale, concession, and privatization of inefficient companies that had hindered the development of key sectors of the economy. The Guatemalan Electricity Company (EEGSA), the main distribution company, the Guatemalan Electrical Institute (INDE), the generation company, and the Guatemalan Telecommunications Company (TELGUA) were all sold, while concessions were granted to build, renovate, and operate two ports and the international airport at Guatemala City.

ECONOMIC POLICY

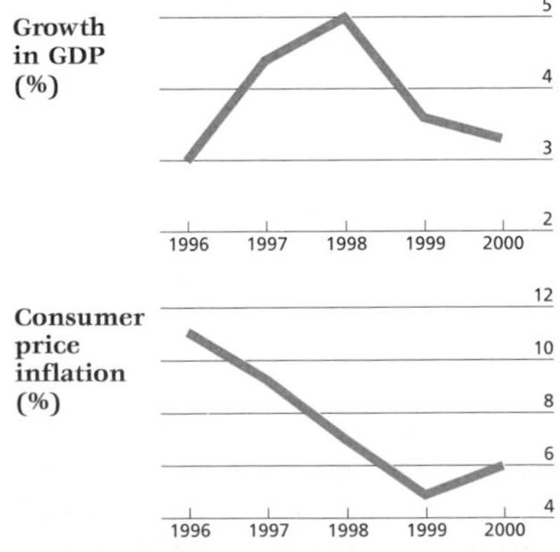

A degree of macroeconomic stability has been achieved since the ending of the civil war in 1996 which has laid the foundations for stronger growth. Real GDP expanded 4.1% a year on average in 1991–2000, albeit from a very low base (a meager 0.9% in 1981–90). Inflation has been below 10% since 1997. The fiscal deficit began to grow (2.8% of GDP in 1999 and 1.9% in 2000), partly because of the mounting social pressure to increase spending, after public accounts reached equilibrium in 1996. One of the central planks of the government's efforts to improve the lot of the poor and maintain a reasonable fiscal position is tax reform. Tax revenue reached 10% of GDP in 2000 for the first time ever.

GEOGRAPHY/RESOURCES

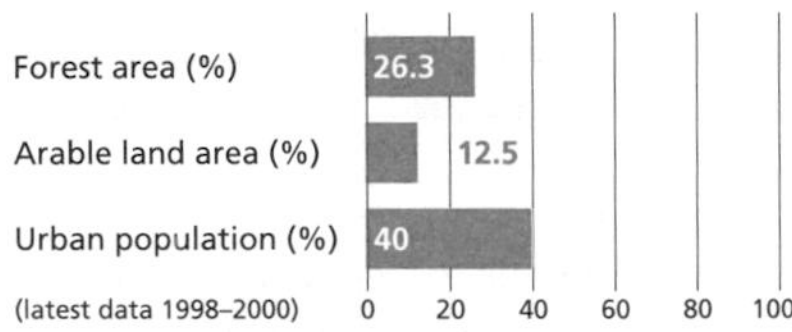

Guatemala is the largest and most northerly of the Central American countries. To the west and north lie Mexico, and to the east of it are Belize, an Atlantic coastline of 70 miles (Gulf of Honduras), and Honduras and El Salvador. In the south Guatemala has a Pacific coastline of 200 miles. A range of volcanic mountains called the Sierra Madre runs from east to west across the southern part of the country. In the center are flat-topped highlands. The remote northern region is a plain covered with grass or forest (El Petén).

Sugar cane, bananas, and pineapples grow in the coastal lowlands, and coffee and tobacco in the central highlands, where sheep and cattle are also raised. Copper, antimony, and tungsten are mined on a small scale. There are also reserves of marble and sulfur. Guatemala is the only oil-producing country in Central America. Several oil deposits have been found in Petén, but development has been slow because of reluctance by foreign companies to invest. Oil production is no more than a couple of thousand barrels a day.

More than 45% of the population belong to 22 Mayan ethno-linguistic groups. Most of them live in small villages, growing corn and beans as their main food. Power lies with the people descended from the Spaniards or of mixed Spanish and Indian ancestry (mestizos).

COMMUNICATIONS/ENERGY

Transport infrastructure was damaged during the 36-year civil war and also by Hurricane Mitch in 1998. The Pan-American

  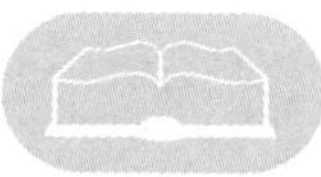    

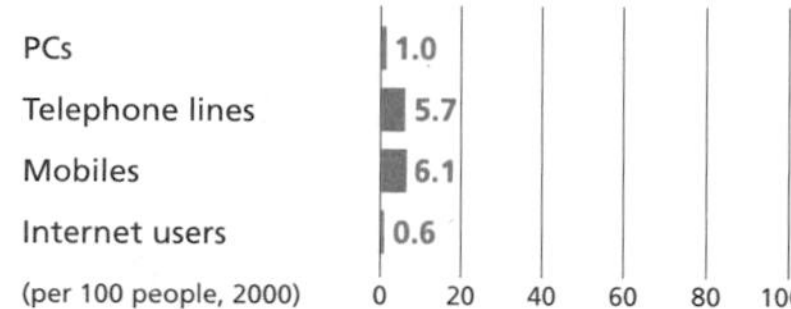

Highway runs through the country, but many roads are unpaved. A Mexican company was awarded a 25-year concession in 1997 to operate the Palín–Escuintla toll highway. The 568 miles track of the moribund Guatemalan Railroad Company (FEGUA) is being revitalized and operated by an affiliate of the Railroad Development Corporation of Pittsburgh, initially for freight traffic. The first part to be rebuilt was the old line between Puerto Barrios, the main port on the Atlantic, and Guatemala City. At its height, the rail network was the most important in Central America, despite operating on a substandard 42-inch gauge (neighboring countries have 56½-inch systems). The chief port on the Pacific is San José. Transport to the El Petén region is chiefly by air.

As well as some oil, Guatemala also has small proven natural gas reserves. A natural gas pipeline is planned from southern Mexico, where there are plentiful natural gas reserves, to Guatemala; it could also extend to other Central American countries which, like Guatemala, are heavily dependent on hydroelectric power. Less than half the population has access to electricity. There is also a planned connection with Mexico's power grid, and Guatemala and five other Central American nations have agreed on a project (SIEPAC) that would interconnect their transmission grids, allowing power to flow between the countries. With Panama already linked to Colombia's grid, SIEPAC could eventually result in the connection of the North and South American power grids. Central America's first coal-fired power plant, the San José plant in Guatemala, came on stream in December 1999.

The telecommunications market was liberalized in 1996. Teledensity is very low.

Education/Employment

Education, which in theory is compulsory between the ages of 7 and 14, in practice covers less than two-thirds of the population. The absence of formal education has long been a factor of exclusion and social marginalization of broad sectors of the population, especially Indians in remote areas. The 1996 peace agreement set educational reform as one of the priorities for the process of democratic consolidation, and seeks to increase coverage, particularly at primary levels, with the emphasis on rural areas and education for girls. The illiteracy rate for women in the late 1990s was put at 43%, and 28% for men. One U.S.-funded scheme was the "New Multigrade School," a community- and democracy-based learning curriculum designed for the single teacher in the one-room schools that predominate in rural Guatemala.

The formal work force is estimated at more than 3.5 million, with at least another 1 million in the informal sector. The availability of a large, unskilled, and inexpensive labor force (the legal daily minimum wage in most sectors is less than $4) has led many employers, particularly in the construction and agriculture sectors, to use labor-intensive production methods.

Fiscal/Financial

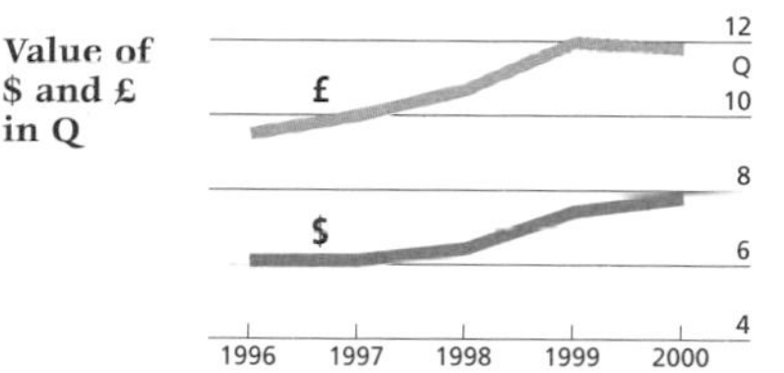

The development of capital markets has been quite rapid, but they remain shallow. There are more than 30 private-sector commercial banks, with the top five controlling around 40% of total assets. The collapse of several "financial houses" in 1998 and 1999 hit several commercial banks holding paper issued by these unregistered intermediaries. The government tightened up supervision and approved a deposit insurance program.

Corporate tax and the top rate of income tax are both 31%, and VAT is 10%.

Business Opportunities

There are no obstacles to the formation of joint ventures or the purchase of local companies by foreign investors, but Guatemala's lack of a stock market in which shares are traded makes acquisitions or takeovers of private-sector companies difficult. The stock exchange in Guatemala City deals almost exclusively in commercial paper and government bonds. Most foreign companies operate as locally incorporated subsidiaries. In the case of the large state companies that have been sold, the sales were directly arranged between the government and the purchaser. Foreign direct investment (FDI) is only restricted in a few areas regarded as strategic, for example in domestic airlines (to 60%) and ground transport companies (to 51%). In the case of the latter, the restriction is being gradually decreased until 2004 when 100% ownership will be allowed. Subsurface minerals and oil belong to the state. Concessions for exploitation are granted through production-sharing contracts which, in the past, were negotiated in a non-transparent manner. FDI averaged $110 million a year in 1985–95, and increased to $285 million in 1997–2000. There is a "one stop investment window" which streamlines investment procedures.

Although there are no legal restraints on the amount of remittances by foreign companies or on any other capital flows, the Central Bank does have the power to impose restrictions, and has used it at times. Corruption is a serious problem, particularly at ports and borders.

For More Information

Books:

Kinzer, Stephen, and Stephen Schlesinger. *Bitter Fruit: The Untold Story of the American Coup in Guatemala.* Cambridge, MA: Havard University Press, 1999.

Lovell, W. George. *A Beauty That Hurts.* Rev. ed. Austin, TX: University of Texas Press, 2001.

Stewart, Iain, and Mark Whatmore. *Rough Guide to Guatemala.* 2nd ed. New York: Rough Guides, 2002.

Web Sites:

Central Bank: **www.banguat.gob.gt**

Guatemala News Watch: **www.quetzalnet.com/newswatch**

Guatemalan Development Foundation: **www.fundesa.guatemala.org**

IMF reports: **www.imf.org/external**

U.S. State Department Country Commercial Guide: **www.state.gov/e/eb/rls/rpts/ccg**

 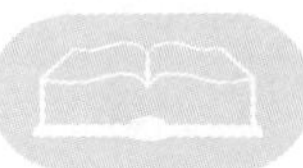    

HONG KONG

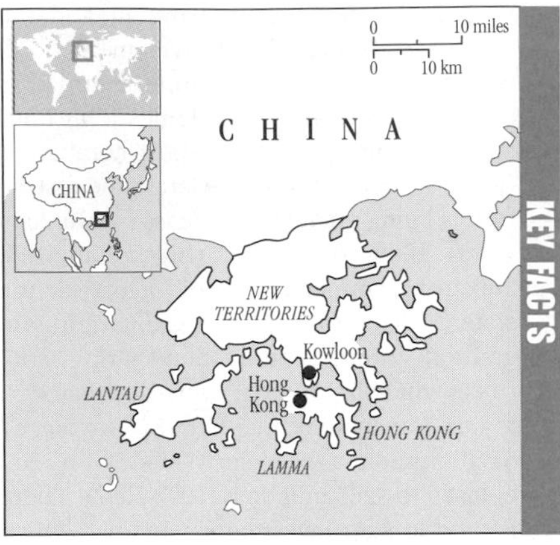

KEY FACTS

GNI: **$165,122 million; world's 24th**
GNI pc: **$24,570; world's 19th**
Head of government: **chief executive**
Currency: **Hong Kong dollar (HK$)**
Population: **6,850,000**
Land area: **422 square miles**
Population density: **16,232 per square mile**
Language: **Yue (Cantonese) (official), English (official), Mandarin**
Best buy: **clothing, cameras, electronic goods, music CDs and tapes, sports equipment, jewelry, porcelain, carvings, scroll paintings, silk fabrics and goods**

ECONOMIC STRUCTURE

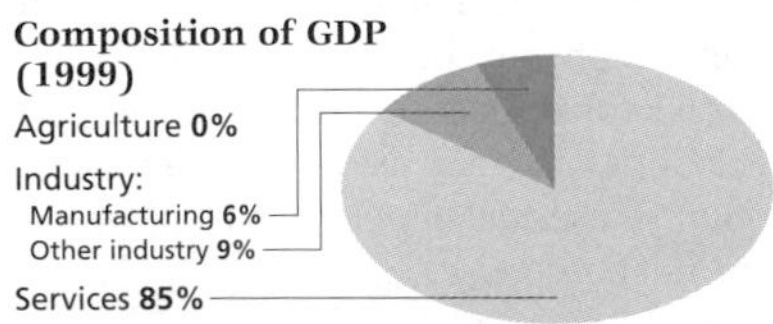

The Chinese ceded Hong Kong Island to the British in 1842. The British acquired Kowloon and the New Territories on a 99-year lease in 1898. When the lease expired in July 1997 the British handed all of Hong Kong territory back to China under an agreement, enshrined in the Basic Law for the region, that Hong Kong's free-market economic system should remain intact for a further 50 years at least. China formed the Hong Kong Special Administrative Region guaranteeing the territory a large degree of autonomy in all matters except defense and foreign affairs. From the 1950s to the 1970s Hong Kong developed labor-intensive manufacturing, especially in textiles and precision industries such as clock making. In the 1980s and 1990s Hong Kong companies relocated their labor-intensive industries to Guandong Province in China, and Hong Kong developed as a major financial, business services and trading center, spurred by the opening up of China to the west.

Services accounted for 85.4% of GDP in 1999, industry for 14.5% and agriculture for 0.1%. Commerce was the largest services sector, contributing 25.2% of GDP, followed by finance and business services at 23.2%, community and personal services at 21.5%, real estate at 14.1%, and transport at 9.6%. In the industrial sector construction accounted for 5.8% of GDP, followed by manufacturing at 5.7%, and electricity, gas and water at 3%. As a major gateway to China, Hong Kong's activities in transport, communications, finance, and multinational business services are rapidly growing. Exports of services were a total $34.9 billion in 1999, easily outweighing Hong Kong's $5.6 billion merchandise trade deficit. The leading sectors were transport, trade-related and travel services (including tourism), followed by finance, insurance, and business services. The main merchandise exports in 2000 were clothing (42.8%), followed by electrical machinery (15.8%), textiles (5.1%), office machinery parts (3.2%), and watches and clocks (1.7%). The main markets were the United States (30.1%), followed by China (29.9%), the United Kingdom (5.9%), Germany (5.1%), and Taiwan (3.4%).

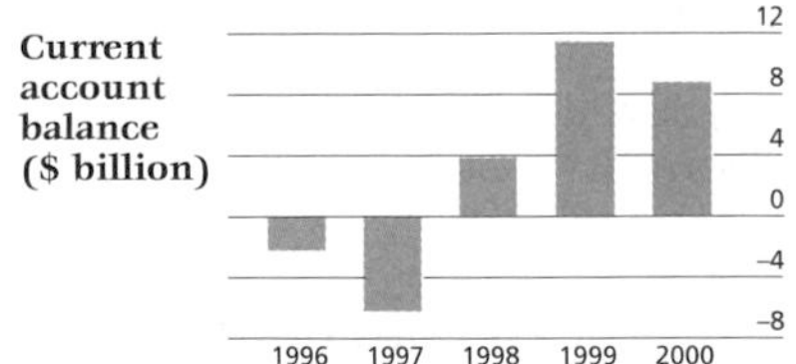

There is traditionally little direct state ownership of the economy, and the Basic Law ensures that free market structures will continue. Most service sectors, including electricity, gas, and transport, are operated by private companies. Water and railways are publicly owned, and one broadcaster is publicly funded.

ECONOMIC POLICY

In 1983, after the initial Chinese-British negotiations over Hong Kong caused a run on the Hong Kong dollar, the government

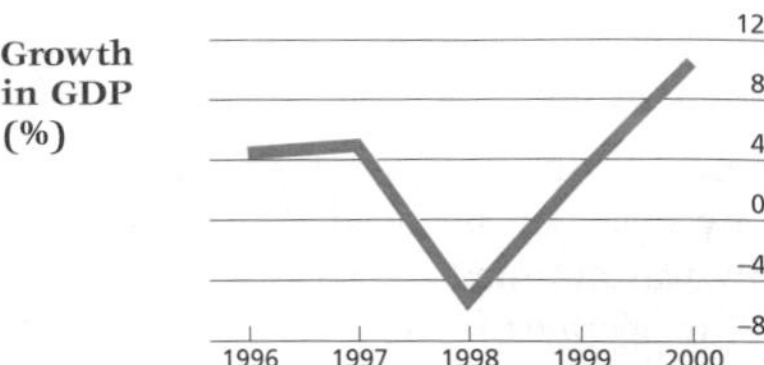

pegged the currency to the U.S. dollar. This imposed constraints on monetary and fiscal policy in return for exchange rate stability. The government maintained a prudent public expenditure policy and accumulated HK$150 billion (around $19 billion) in reserves from a decade of budget surpluses. The 1997–98 Asian financial crisis caused a $15 billion intervention by the authorities in August 1998 to support the currency, after which the peg with the U.S. dollar was restored. The government brought forward major investment projects to strengthen the economy, and ran slight budget deficits in 1998 and 2000. It imposed interest rate restrictions, which were removed progressively by July 2001. In February 2001 the IMF commended progress in government sales of equities it had acquired through the 1998 stock market intervention.

Regulation of the economy is strictly applied. Given Hong Kong's lack of natural resources and large population, the government has taken the lead in modernizing transport and telecommunications infrastructure, and in housing development and healthcare, both of which are subsidized. Other forms of welfare are not highly developed, but a contributory retirement pensions scheme was established in the late 1990s. The Asian recession of the late 1990s highlighted the problems of Hong Kong's dependence on regional services and trade. The government has launched funds to promote the growth of R&D and high-tech industries to broaden the economic base. This policy fits in with the role of Hong Kong investment in furthering mainland Chinese development.

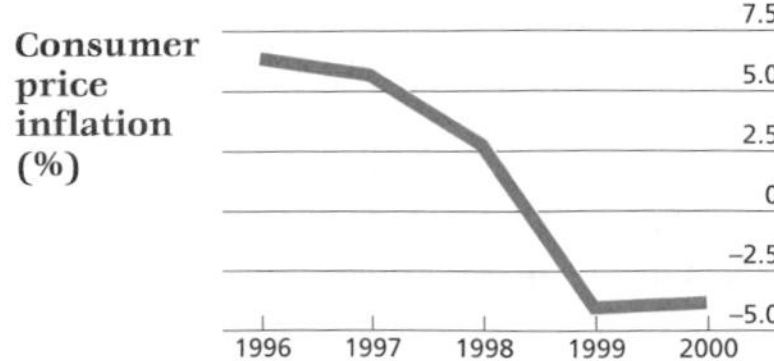

GDP growth was an annual average 4.5% in 1995–97. GDP fell by 5.1% in 1998 as a result of the Asian financial crisis, revived to 3.1% in 1999 and 10.5% in 2000. Growth was

about 0.7% in 2001 as a result of the downturn in export markets, but it was expected to revive to 3.6% in 2002. Inflation was an annual average 6% in 1995–98, followed by deflation of 3.9% in 1999–2000. Further deflation occurred in 2001, but inflation was expected to resume in 2002. Unemployment was an average 4% in 1995–2000, with a peak of 6.3% in 1999.

Geography/Resources

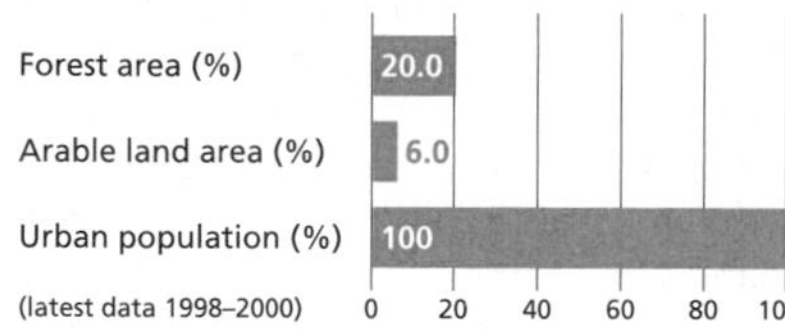

A peninsula and several islands, Hong Kong lies to the south of the Chinese mainland with coasts on the South China Sea. Most of the land consists of steep mountains, with a high point of 3,143 feet. There are plains in the north near the Sum Chun River which marks the border with Guandong Province. The climate is tropical, hot and humid with most rainfall in spring and summer. Average rainfall is 87 inches. Temperatures range from 50°F in winter to 88°F in summer. There are typhoons between May and October. The population is mostly Chinese (95%), with resident foreigners accounting for 5%.

With 72% of the land unusable hillside there is little space for agriculture, and most food is imported. In 1999 local production accounted for 18% of poultry consumption, 22% of pork, and 12% of vegetables. Vegetables and flowers are the main crops. A wide variety of exotic fruits are grown. Chickens are the main livestock, followed by pigeons, pigs, quail and ducks. Aquaculture, and coastal and deep sea fisheries accounted for 57% of local marine fish and 10% of freshwater fish consumption in 1999. There is no significant minerals production, but there are reserves of feldspar.

Communications/Energy

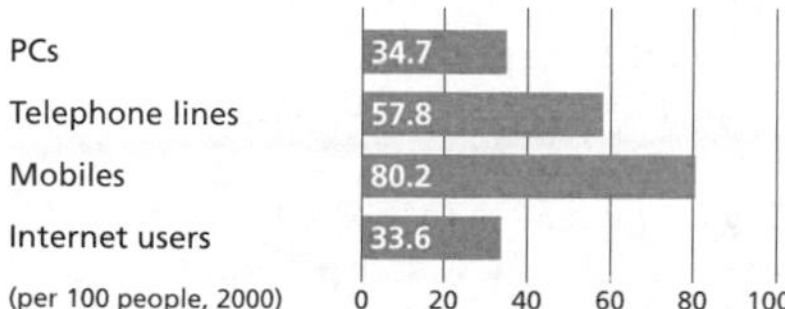

The road network was 1,183 miles at end-2000, 266 miles on Hong Kong Island, 276 miles in Kowloon, and 640 miles in the New Territories. With 516,782 licensed vehicles, Hong Kong had one of the highest vehicle densities in the world. Several new roads were opened in the late 1990s, some to facilitate access to the new international airport at Chek Lap Kok on Lantau Island, which opened in 1998. The airport can handle 45 million passengers and 3 million tons of cargo a year. In 1999 it ranked fifth busiest in the world for passengers and first for cargo. The airport is being expanded to take up to 87 million passengers and 9 million tons of freight. The 89-mile rail network includes the Kowloon-Canton Railway (21 miles of electrified track), Mass Transit Railway (46 miles), Airport Express Line (21½ miles opened in 1998), the Light Rail Transit (20 miles), and Tramway and Peak Tram (10 miles). The government plans to extend the network by 41 miles by 2005, and to a total 155 miles by 2016. Hong Kong has one of the busiest container sea ports in the world, handling 18.1 million teus in 2000. An additional 2.6-million-teu terminal, due to open in 2002, will be expanded to 14 million teus by 2004. Hong Kong is a major center for ship owning and management. At January 2001 the merchant fleet comprised 587 ships representing 11.1 million grt, including ships belonging to owners in Europe, North America, China, and Japan. In 1999 1.97 million tons of freight traveled by air, 128.2 million tons by sea, 40.6 million tons by river, 466,000 tons by rail, and 38.6 million tons by road.

The telecommunications sector is liberalized. At early 2001 Hong Kong had nine submarine cables, including fiber-optic cables, connecting it to elsewhere in Asia, North America, Europe, and the Middle East. There were 41 satellite earth stations. There were 3.9 million fixed phones at end-2000, 5.4 million mobile phones, and 2.3 million Internet accounts. All businesses and over 80% of homes had broadband access by mid-2000, and there were 178 Internet service providers.

The two private-sector electricity companies are expanding power-generating capacity. CLP Power Hong Kong supplies Kowloon, the New Territories, Lantau, Cheung Chau, and most of the outlying islands from four fossil-fuel power stations, the newest using natural gas from Hainan Island. CLP has a grid connection with Guandong Power in mainland China. It exports electricity to Guandong Power and imports from Guandong Daya Bay nuclear power station. Hongkong Electric Company supplies electricity to Hong Kong Island, Ap Lei Chau, and Lamma Island from Lamma Power station. The company has a grid connection with CLP. Town gas is manufactured in Hong Kong from naphtha and distributed via a 1,682-mile pipe network by Hong Kong & China Gas Company. Petroleum and other fuels are imported.

Education/Employment

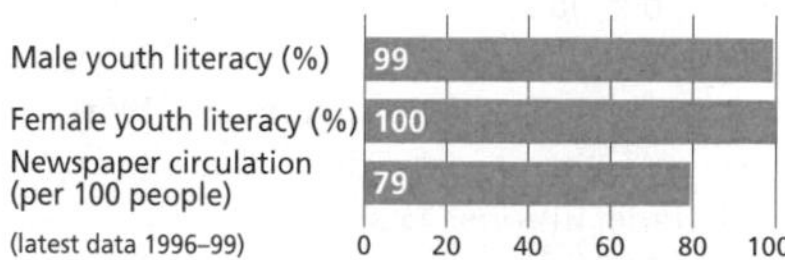

Education is compulsory and free from age 6 to 15. Government financial assistance is available for students continuing their education after age 15. There are 10 university-level institutions, including 8 universities, the Hong Kong Academy for Performing Arts, and the Open University of Hong Kong. In addition the Institute of Vocational Education, comprising 9 former technical colleges and institutes, provides professional and technical courses. There were 105,461 full-time and 60,000 part-time students enrolled in higher education in 1999–2000. Most higher education is funded by the government, but the Open University is self-funding, and there are some private institutions providing specialized courses.

The Innovation and Technology Commission (ITC), established in 2000, provides liaison for R&D between universities, government departments, and industry. It also manages funding schemes and is responsible for developing R&D infrastructure. It promotes R&D in biotechnology, electronics, environmental protection, and IT. In addition it encourages R&D in the traditional textile, clock-making, and plastic products industries. The Innovation and Technology Fund supports the upgrading of local industry through R&D projects. The Applied Research Fund provides venture capital for local technology. The Hong Kong Applied Science and Technology Institute provides R&D for products and processes. In order to offer a streamlined R&D support package, the new Hong Kong Science Park, due to open end-2001, was merged with the Hong Kong Industrial Estates Corporation, which manages four industrial estates, and with the Hong Kong Industrial Technology Center Corporation, which provides business incubation services to new technology-based companies.

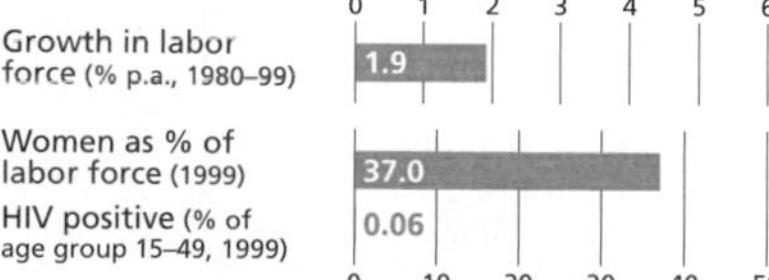

The labor force is well educated, hard working, and adaptable to new technology. Wages are determined between employers and employees. There is no minimum wage. The Employment Ordinance is the main labor law, covering wages, employment contracts and terms, and the operation of employment agencies. Workers have the right to join one of the 626 registered trade unions. Disputes between employers and employees are resolved by the Labor Tribunal. Hong Kong has implemented several International Labor Organization conventions.

FISCAL/FINANCIAL

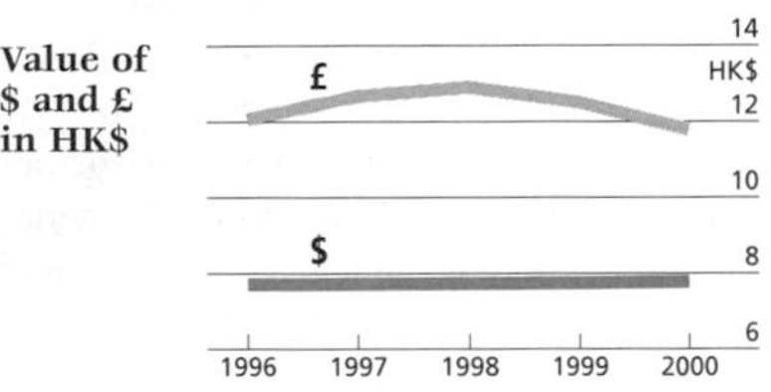

The largest banks by total assets at end-1999 were Hong Kong & Shanghai Banking Corporation, followed by Bank of China Group, Hang Seng Bank, Bank of East Asia, and Dao Heng Bank. Insurance companies include some of the world's largest. All banks and commercial insurance companies are private sector. The financial sector is open to foreign investment and transactions. The Hong Kong Monetary Authority acts as de facto central bank and regulates the banking system. The other regulators are the Office of the Commissioner of Insurance, the Securities and Futures Commission (for the stock exchange), and the Mandatory Provident Fund Schemes Authority. Banking supervision is in accordance with Basle Core Principles since the 1997–98 crisis, including a move to risk-based supervision. Corporate profits tax is 16%, while tax on unincorporated enterprises at 15% is the same as maximum personal income tax. There are no taxes on capital gains, dividends, or interest. The Mandatory Provident Fund raises a minimum contribution of 5% from both employer and employee for pensions.

The banking sector weathered the financial crisis reasonably well, although lending growth remained low in early 2001. Companies used reserves and the equity market to finance investment. Non-performing loans peaked at 10.5% in 1999, but bank capitalization averaged 18%, well above the Basle standard, and profitability improved. At end-2000 there were 154 licensed banks (with full commercial operations), 48 restricted-license banks (merchant banking and capital markets operations), 61 deposit-taking finance companies, and 118 offices of foreign banks (including 80 of the world's largest 100 banks) from over 40 countries. At end-February 2001 there were 205 insurers, including 100 Hong Kong companies and 105 from 25 other countries. The main foreign insurers are U.S. companies, with U.K. companies in second place. Gross premia in 1999 were HK$58 billion. Hong Kong is a regional center for portfolio management. At end-2000 there were 1,860 unit trusts and mutual funds with a total net asset value of HK$2,410 billion. The Mandatory Provident Fund System, introduced to the financial markets in December 2000, provides a long-term investment vehicle for retirement pensions.

The Hong Kong stock market is the 10th largest in the world by market capitalization. At end February 2001 the 739 companies listed on the main board of the Stock Exchange of Hong Kong had capitalization of HK$4.8 trillion. They included 48 Chinese state-owned enterprises. The Growth Enterprise Market, established in November 1999, had 60 firms with capitalization of HK$67 billion. The computerized trading and payments system was upgraded in October 2000 to fully integrate online trading. The Hong Kong Futures Exchange became fully electronic in June 2000. The two exchanges and three clearing houses were merged in March 2000. The resulting company, Hong Kong Exchanges & Clearing, was demutualized and listed on the main board in June 2000. Apart from the two exchanges, there is an active over-the-counter market in trades swaps, forwards, and options related to equities, interest rates, and currencies. The Hong Kong dollar debt market in Exchange Fund bills and notes had average daily turnover of HK$24.6 billion in December 2000, and private-sector issues totaled HK$180.6 billion in 2000. The Chinese Gold and Silver Exchange Society operates one of the largest gold bullion markets in the world.

BUSINESS OPPORTUNITIES

There are no specific investment incentives, but the government is encouraging R&D investment. Hong Kong is a duty-free zone. Foreign investment is restricted in certain sectors: mass transit, electric power generation, medical services, legal services, telecommunications, and broadcasting. The government is negotiating bilateral investment protection and promotion agreements with the governments of major foreign investors. Commerce absorbed most inward investment, followed by banking; investment holdings, real estate and business services; communications; non-bank financial institutions; manufacturing; transport; and insurance. The leading investors at end-1999 were China (40. %), followed by the Netherlands (10.2%), the United Kingdom (9.7%), the United States (8.4%), Singapore (7%), Bermuda (6.2%), Japan (5.5%), Switzerland (1%), and Taiwan (0.9%). Service sectors and R&D industries offer investment opportunities.

For More Information

Books:

Brown, Judith M., ed. *Hong Kong's Transitions, 1842–1997*. New York: Palgrave Macmillan, 1997.

Grzeskowiak, Andrew. *Passport Hong Kong: Your Pocket Guide to Hong Kong Business, Customs and Etiquette*. Novato, CA: World Trade Press.

Harper, Damian, and Steve Fallon. *Hong Kong, Macau, and Guangzho*. 10th ed. Oakland, CA: Lonely Planet, 2002.

IMF Country Report. *Hong Kong*. Washington, D.C.: IMF.

Lo, Shio-Hing. *The Politics of Democratisation in Hong Kong*. New York: Palgrave Macmillan, 1997.

Web Sites:

Economist Intelligence Unit: **www.eiu.com**

Far East Economic Review (business weekly): **www.feer.com**

Government Information Service (entry point): **www.info.gov.hk**

Hong Kong Monetary Authority: **www.info.gov.hk/hkma**

Hong Kong Tourist Association: **www.hkta.org**

Hong Kong Trade Development Council: **www.tdc.org.hk**

South China Morning Post (daily newspaper): **www.scmp.com**

Stock Exchange of Hong Kong: **www.sehk.com.hk**

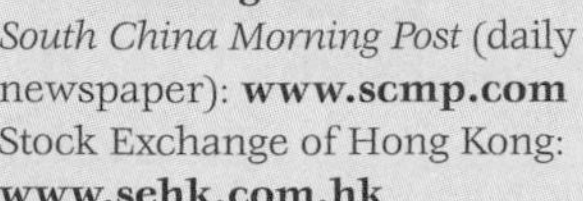

HUNGARY

KEY FACTS

GNI: **$46,751 million; world's 51st**
GNI pc: **$4,640; world's 69th**
Head of government: **prime minister**
Currency: **forint (Ft)**
Capital: **Budapest**
Population: **10,076,000, growing at –0.3% p.a.**
Land area: **35,640 square miles**
Population density: **282 per square mile**
Life expectancy: **71 years**
Infant mortality: **9 per 1,000 live births**
Language: **Hungarian**
Best buy: **fruit brandies**

ECONOMIC STRUCTURE

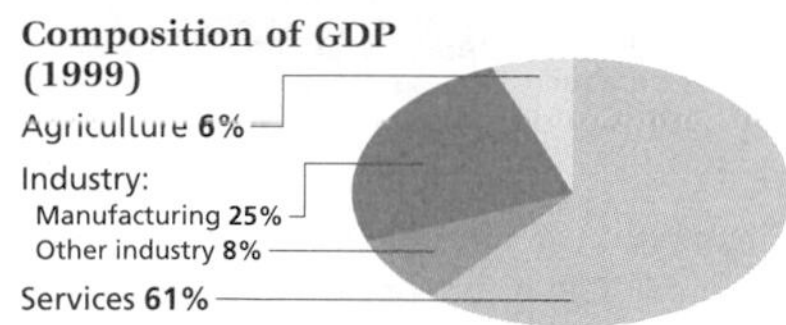

Hungary, which emerged in its present form after World War I, remained a principally agrarian country until after World War II. The communist Hungarian Socialist Workers' Party, which took power in 1948, undertook forced industrialization. Millions of new industrial jobs were created, including many for women: by the time communism fell in 1989, the proportion of the workforce in agriculture had fallen from more than half to about a quarter, and that in industry had grown to nearly one-third. Iron, steel, and engineering were prioritized, while modern infrastructure, services, and communication lagged behind. Hungary introduced mixed economy policies from the 1960s, and by 1989 the private sector already accounted for one-third of GDP.

Post-communist Hungary inherited an enormous external debt, accumulated after 1973 as a result of price increases for oil and modern technology, and also because of noncompetitive export sectors. The sudden opening-up to world markets and abolition of subsidies in 1989 triggered economic collapse. Agricultural production declined by half, much of heavy industry folded, unemployment rose from nearly zero to 14%, the proportion of people living below the poverty line rose from 10% in 1988 to 30% in 1995, and GDP sank by 30%.

The economy recovered rapidly from the mid-1990s as new industries surged past old ones. Electronics and car manufacture are the most dynamic, telecommunications and energy in 2001 had the potential for rapid expansion; food processing and wine are profitable; and tourism—which grew threefold in the 1990s, with annual foreign visitor numbers rising past the 20 million mark—continues to expand. Foreign direct investment has powered growth: in the decade to 2000, Hungary received more FDI per capita than any other country in Central and Eastern Europe, and nearly one-third of total FDI flows into the region. Privatization is more complete than anywhere else in Eastern Europe, and the private sector accounts for 80% of GDP, more than in many EU countries. A significant part is played in the economy by small, mostly family-owned enterprises, which by 2000 numbered 750,000.

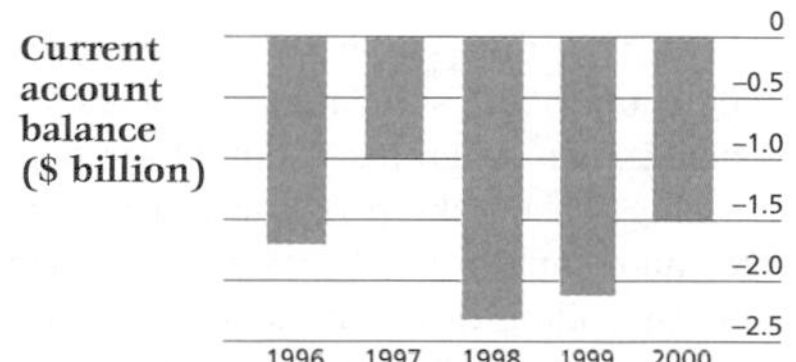

Hungary's principal trading partner is the EU, which in 2000 took a 75.7% share of exports and 58.7% of imports (Germany, with 37.9% and 26% respectively, was the leader among EU countries); the Central European Free Trade Area, of which Hungary is a founding member, took 8.2% and 7.5%, the CIS 2.4% and 8.9%. Hungary belongs to the WTO and NATO, and is a strong candidate among east European countries for EU membership.

ECONOMIC POLICY

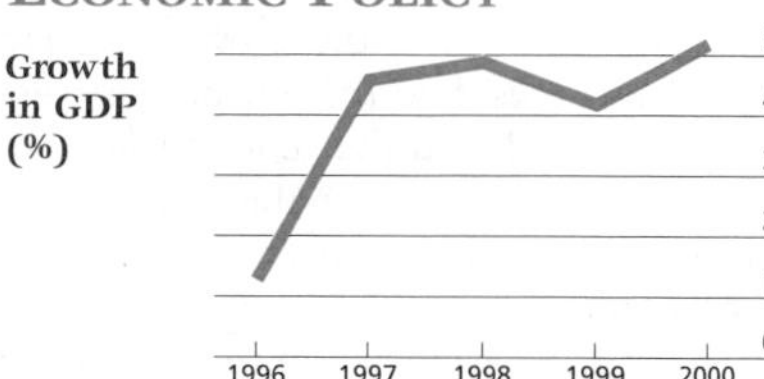

Hungary's first post-communist government, formed in 1990 by the center-right Hungarian Democratic Forum, launched a reform program that liberalized foreign trade, freed prices, reduced subsidies, and strengthened the legal framework for business. In 1995 it was succeeded by the Hungarian Socialist Party, which not only continued pro-market reforms but also imposed a radical austerity program designed to tackle high state spending and Hungary's current account deficit. By 1997 these policies produced results in terms of both the budget balance and GDP growth, which was 4.6% in 1997 and has remained at 4.5–5% annually since then. Unemployment fell from 11.6% in 1997 to 9% in 2000; inflation has fallen steadily from 23.6% in 1996 to 9.1% in 2001 (EBRD projection).

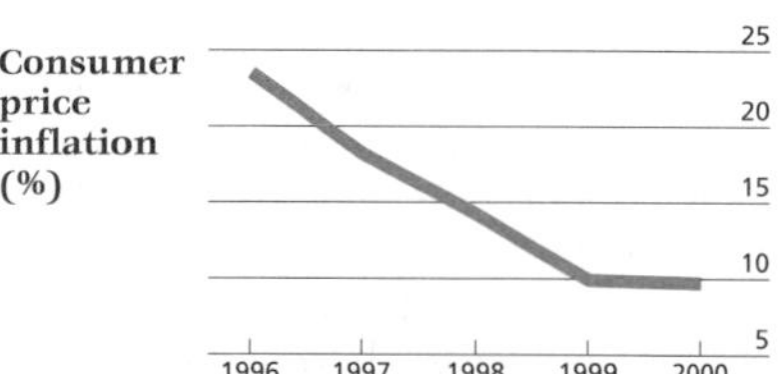

A center-right coalition elected in 1998 presided over further economic stabilization, and emphasized support for small and medium-sized enterprises and the spreading of prosperity to less-developed rural areas. The Szechenyi Plan, a national economic development plan issued by the government in 2000, set out programs to develop enterprise, tourism, housing, information technology, infrastructure, and the regions. Prospects for stabilization were judged to have improved in 2001 when the forint, which had been tied to the Euro within a narrow band, was made fully convertible.

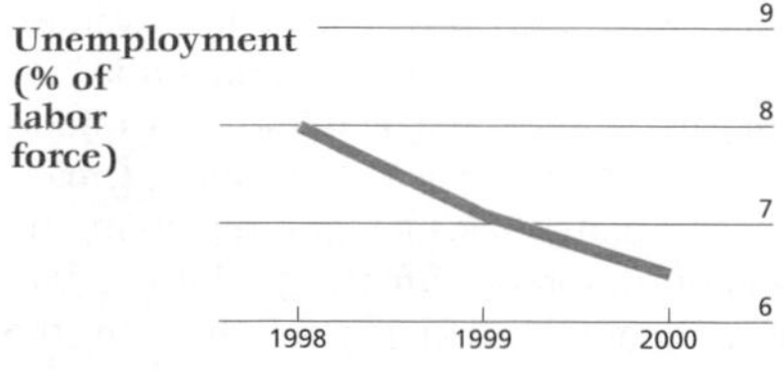

In 2001 the EBRD identified urgent economic policy tasks as: adherence to a tighter fiscal policy; the reform of public finances, especially with regard to healthcare and local government; "fighting the gray economy"; and addressing the growing divide between Budapest and the prosperous west on the one hand, and the economically depressed areas in the east on the other. There was progress in this respect during 2001: construction of the M3 motorway was restarted (and was expected to reach Miskolc by 2002), and foreign companies such as Flextronics of Singapore and Butler of the United States moved east, attracted by labor which is about 25% cheaper than in western Hungary.

Geography/Resources

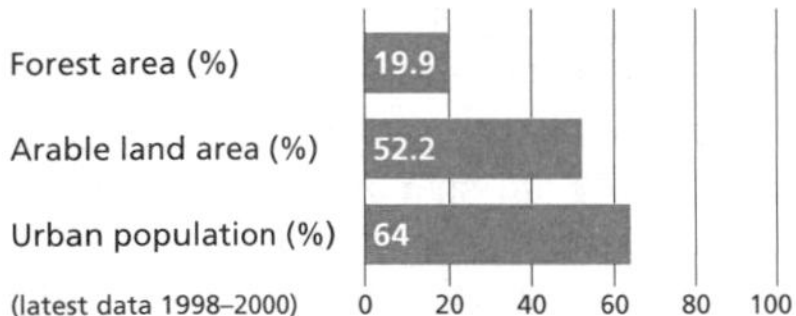

Hungary is one of the smallest European countries, comprising 35,640 square miles and bordered by Slovakia to the north, Ukraine to the northeast, Romania to the east, Yugoslavia, Croatia and Slovenia to the south, and Austria to the west. A low mountain system stretches across Hungary from southwest to northeast, made up of the Transdanubian and Northern Mountains. Between them runs the Visegrád Gorge along which the Danube river flows. Hungary has only limited fossil fuel resources, including anthracite, brown coal, and a little oil and natural gas. It has some limited deposits of bauxite and manganese, and undeveloped reserves of copper and zinc.

Half of Hungary's land is arable, less than one-fifth covered by woods, and two-thirds is under cultivation. Despite the decline of agriculture Hungary is almost self-sufficient in food: wheat and corn are the main crops, followed by sugar beet, sunflower seeds, and potatoes. Cattle, sheep, and pigs are raised, although herds were substantially reduced in the 1990s.

Hungary's population peaked at 10.7 million in 1980. Since then it has declined gradually, to about 10 million in 2000. Death rates exceeded birth rates, the decline of which was analogous to that in advanced European countries. The population is 92% Hungarian, 3% Roma, and 5% other minorities (including Slovaks, Romanians, Croats, and Germans). Because of emigration and Eastern Europe's constantly shifting borders, 3 million Hungarians live in the neighboring states of Romania, Slovakia, Croatia, and Serbia, and about 1.3 million further afield. In the early 1990s the outflow reversed: 100,000 Hungarians arrived in Hungary from Romania and Yugoslavia.

Two-thirds of Hungary's population live in towns, about 2 million of them in Budapest, which is several times larger than the other major cities (Miskolc, Debrecen, Szeged, Pécs and Györ). Apart from these, most towns have populations of less than 40,000 and only began to expand towards the end of the 20th century.

Communications/Energy

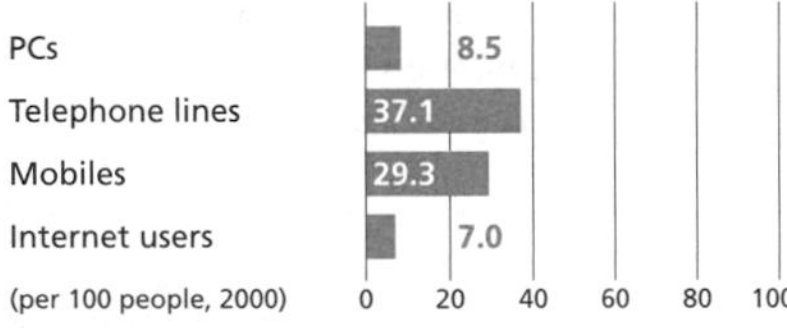

Telecommunications was one of the fastest-growing sectors of the Hungarian economy in the 1990s; the number of lines per 100 inhabitants rose from 10 to 40 through the decade. The primary operator, Matav, was privatized in 1993, and after some subsequent trading in shares Deutsche Telekom took control. This, together with a deregulation program that was expected to culminate in full liberalization in January 2002, made possible modernization of the basic infrastructure. Alternative fixed-line and long-distance operators include PanTel, Vivendi, Novacom, and GTS. The mobile telephone market is well developed, with substantial foreign investment, and market penetration had reached 25% by September 2000. Internet services are also expanding. In 2001 the sector grew less rapidly than had been expected, and forecasts of long-term growth were revised downwards, as they were in many countries.

Hungary's transport networks are being brought up to EU standards by a series of modernization programs. A rail reform plan, involving the break-up of the loss-making state rail company MAV, was agreed in late 1999. Upgrading of the motorway network has been an infrastructure priority since the start of transition; in 2000 a ten-year development plan provided for 87 miles of new highways and 358 miles of other major roads. In air transport, an attempt to privatize the state carrier, Malev, was postponed indefinitely in 2001 after persistently failing to attract interest. The only international airport, Ferihegy near Budapest, completed a major expansion in the late 1990s that raised capacity to 5.5 million passengers per year.

Hungary has modest coal, oil, and natural gas resources, but imports more than 50% of its energy needs, mostly from Russia. The energy sector has been undergoing far-reaching market reforms in the late 1990s and the early years of the present decade. The privatization of the sector, regarded as the most radical in continental Europe, resulted in all six electricity distribution companies being sold to foreign investors, and all but two of the power generation companies being privatized. The largest Hungarian power group, MOL, refocused on upstream hydrocarbons production and downstream fuel retailing. Liberalization of the energy market was expected to start in 2002, and is generating political concern over the resulting inflationary pressure.

Education/Employment

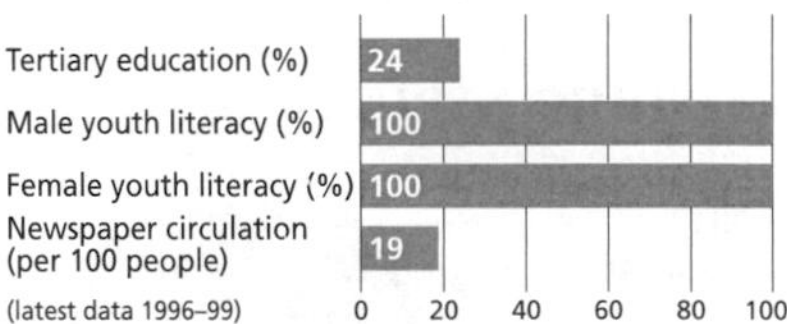

Hungary has a skilled and well-educated workforce. The entry of new graduates into the market is reducing the problem of shortages of such skills as knowledge of Western languages and business techniques. While unemployment remains high in the east, in 2001 the labor market in Budapest and other western areas was tightening considerably. Earnings were driven down by the austerity policies of 1995–98, but began to rise rapidly after that, with substantial increases in the minimum wage.

Hungarian industrial relations are governed by a 1992 Labor Code, which adapts Western European principles to the Hungarian environment. The Code allows unions workplace access and gives them negotiating status, although they cannot discriminate against non-members or force them to join. There are also legally-prescribed workers' councils at all enterprises with more than 50 employees.

There is free education at all levels in Hungary. It is compulsory between the ages of 6 and 16. Secondary education, including vocational training (for about two-thirds of the relevant age group) and preparation for higher education, became virtually universal by the late 1980s.

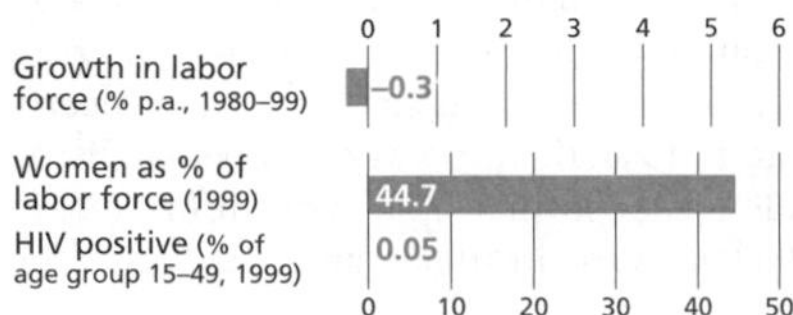

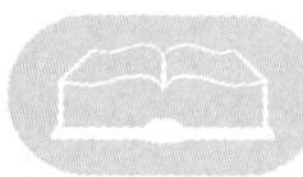

Between 1990–91 and 1999–2000, the proportion of 18–22-year-olds in higher education more than doubled, from 8.5% to 17.5%. Tuition fees were reintroduced under the austerity program of the mid-1990s but were abolished again in 1998. In 1998 the government began implementing a World Bank-backed plan to reform and develop the higher education system, which includes hundreds of specialized schools and colleges as well as universities. Education at lower levels, 96% of which is in state schools, has been badly hit by cuts in funding: state spending on education has declined from 7% of GDP in the early 1990s to 4.2% in 1999. At secondary school level, the number of students in industrial training has fallen, from 42% in 1990 to 23% in 1998, reflecting the diversification of the economy away from industry.

Fiscal/Financial

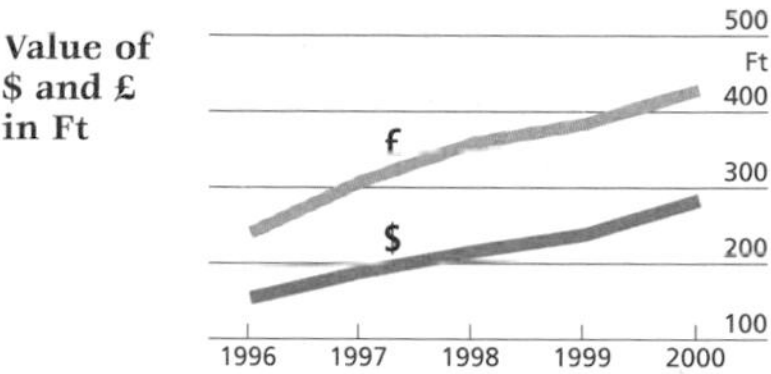

The Hungarian financial sector is one of Eastern Europe's most mature. The banking sector is mainly privately-owned; foreign and joint-venture banks, such as CIB Bank (majority owned by Banca Commerciala Italiana), Bank Austria-Creditanstalt, and Citibank of the United States control around 35% of total assets. In 2001 it was expected that the number of banks would decrease steadily: two mergers announced in 2000—of the Hungarian subsidiaries of KBC of Belgium with ABN Amro of the Netherlands, and of Bank Austria-Creditanstalt with Hypo Vereinsbank of Germany—were seen as indicative. The role of foreign institutions in the insurance market is even more predominant: in 2001 they controlled about 90% of annual premiums.

Since 1998 Hungary has operated a three-pillar pension system based on a pay-as-you-go state system, contributions to private funds, and voluntary mutual pension funds. By the end of 2000, private funds attracted more than 2 million members (50% of the economically active population) and about $4.5 billion in assets.

The Budapest Stock Exchange, although relatively small by international standards, is one of the most liquid in Eastern Europe. Its supervisory structure is largely harmonized with EU standards, and meets the requirements of OECD membership. In 2000 the exchange—the most liquid shares on which are Matav (telecoms), MOL (oil and gas), OTP Bank, and Richter Gedeon (pharmaceuticals)—introduced fully-automated futures and options trading. However, a punitive flat-rate 20% capital gains tax, introduced in January 2001, has dampened market performance.

Hungary has relatively high individual income taxes, with a top rate of 40%, but the corporate tax rate of 18% is one of the lowest in the region. The basic VAT rate (at 2001) was 25%, with a preferential rate of 12% on food, energy, and some other items. The employers' social security contribution rate was 33% in 2000, and was reduced to 31% in early 2001.

Business Opportunities

Growth in output (% p.a., 1990–99)

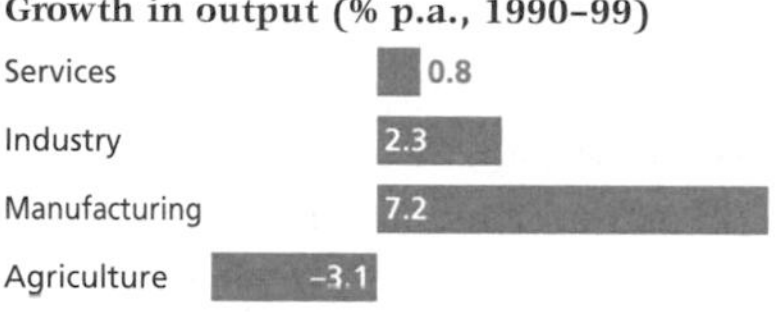

Hungary's FDI boom exploded in 1995, when $4.4 billion arrived; in 1996–2001 it averaged more than $1.6 billion per year. Foreign-owned companies generated 77% of Hungary's exports, 33% of its GDP, and 25% of private-sector employment by end of 2000.

Hungary's key attractions to inward investors have been regarded as special tax incentives (up to 1995), transparent and commercially viable privatization, high economic growth, and well-developed financial and commercial infrastructure. Investment by foreigners is governed by a 1988 law that allowed for the establishment and operation of companies with foreign participation, granted significant rights and benefits to foreign investors, and abolished general requirements for government approval.

At the end of the 1990s the government shifted to a strategy of supplying investors with more direct support, rather than general tax and grant incentives, in an effort to harmonize the investment framework with EU regulations. The lack of protection for investors-specifically in the case of minority shareholders faced with takeovers-was, however, highlighted in 2000 by the battles between MOL and Gazprom of Russia for control of the petrochemicals companies Borsochem and VTK. New regulations were introduced in July 2001 to address these problems, but some portfolio investors have been waiting to see how they are implemented.

The leading destinations for FDI have been manufacturing (38.4% aggregate FDI to 1998), electricity, gas, steam, and water supply (14.8%), trade and repairs (12.3%), financial intermediation (10.9%) and real estate and renting activities (9.8%). As the privatization program has neared its end, investment has increasingly been replaced by greenfield investments. Opportunities to look forward to include the further liberalization of the energy, telecoms, and healthcare sectors, and membership of the EU. The automotive, information technology, tourism, electronics, and research and development sectors were expected to continue attracting investment.

For More Information

Books:

Andor, Laszlo. *Hungary on the Road to the European Union: Transition in Blue.* Westport, CT: Praeger Publishing, 2000.

Antal-Mokos, Zoltan. *Privatization, Politics, and Economic Performance in Hungary.* New York: Cambridge University Press, 1998.

Beracs, Jozsef, and Attila Chikan, eds. *Managing Business in Hungary: An International Perspective (Transition, Competitiveness and Economic Growth, 1).* Budapest: Akademiai Kiado, 1999.

Braun, Aurel, and Zoltan Barany, eds. *Dilemmas of Transition.* Lanham, MD: Rowman & Littlefield Publishing, 1999.

Halpern, Laszlo, and Charles Wyplosz, eds. *Hungary: Towards a Market Economy.* New York: Cambridge University Press, 1998.

Lieber, Joseph S., Christina Shea, and Erzsebet Barat. *Frommer's Budapest & the Best of Hungary.* New York: Hungry Minds, 2000.

Web Sites:

Budapest Business Journal: **www.bbj.hu**

Budapest Sun (English language newspaper): **www.budapestsun.com**

Hungarian Investment and Trade Development Agency: **www.itd.hu**

List of Hungarian gopher servers: **www.fsz.bme.hu/hungary/gopher.htm**

List of information servers: **www.fsz.bme.hu/hu-infoservers.html**

Ministry of Economic Affairs: **www.gm.hu/kulfold**

Prime minister's office: **www.meh.hu**

ICELAND

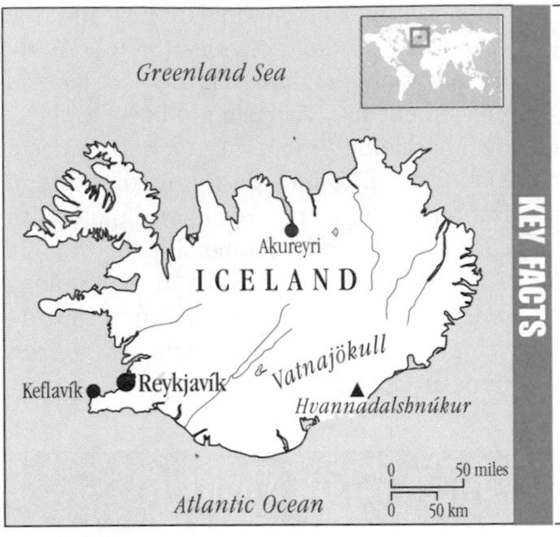

GNI: **$8,197 million; world's 92nd**
GNI pc: **$29,540; world's 10th**
Head of government: **prime minister**
Currency: **Icelandic króna (ISK)**
Capital: **Reykjavík**
Population: **279,000, growing at 1.0% p.a.**
Land area: **38,700 square miles**
Population density: **7 per square mile**
Life expectancy: **79 years**
Infant mortality: **5 per 1,000 live births**
Language: **Icelandic**
Best buy: **sweaters, sheepskin leather goods, ceramics**

ECONOMIC STRUCTURE

As a colony first of Norway and then of Denmark, Iceland was an impoverished land. It gained sovereignty in a union with Denmark in 1918. When Denmark was occupied by German forces in 1940, the British occupied Iceland, followed by the Americans who established bases. The occupation years brought unprecedented prosperity from the demand for fish, paid for in U.S. dollars, and in infrastructure investment. Iceland declared itself a republic in 1944, when Denmark was still under German occupation, and also declared itself neutral, demanding the withdrawal of occupation forces. The government invested its wartime wealth in modernizing the fishing fleet.

Services accounted for 62.6% of GDP in 2000, including private services (43.3%, the main sectors being finance and real estate, followed by trade and hotels) and public services (19.3%). Manufacturing, construction, and utilities contributed 25.6% of GDP, fish and fish processing 9.9%, and agriculture 1.8%. Aluminum and ferro-silicon manufacture from imported inputs is based on Iceland's abundant natural energy. The industrial sector includes food and beverages, construction materials, chemicals, plastics, and machinery. Computer services, telecommunications, and biotechnology are rapid growth areas. Fish and crustaceans, including processed fish products, are the main exports (63.3% in 2000), followed by aluminum (19.4%) and ferrosilicon (2.6%). Tourism accounted for 14% of foreign exchange earnings in 2000. Other important exports include canned products, diatomite, tanned leather, and woolen products. The main markets are the United Kingdom, followed by Germany, the United States, Spain, Norway, Japan, and Switzerland.

The government embarked on a privatization and market liberalization program in the late 1990s. Four state credit institutions were merged into the FBA (Icelandic Investment Bank) in 1998. FBA was fully privatized in 1999, and merged with private-sector Islandsbanki in 2000 as a commercial bank. In 1999 the government partly privatized two state-owned commercial banks, Landsbanki íslands and Búnadarbanki íslands, with the intention of full privatization in the long term. In 1998 the postal services and telecommunications authority was divided into two limited liability companies owned by the state. The telecommunications sector was opened to competition. Electricity generation and distribution remain in the public sector, but split between central and local government ownership.

ECONOMIC POLICY

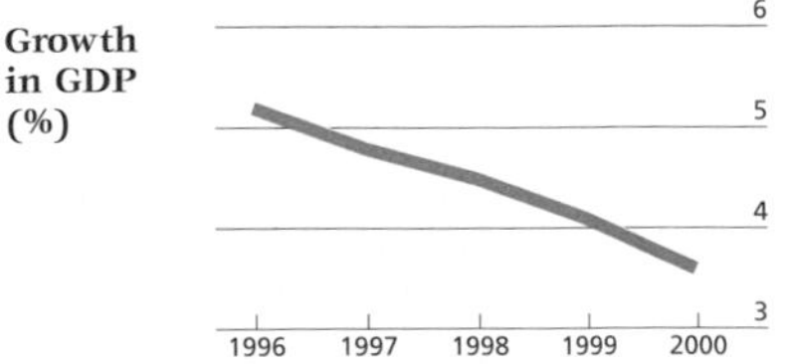

In March 2001 the government allowed the króna to float, and adopted inflation targeting as the focus of monetary policy. The government consolidated public finances in the 1990s following heavy deficit spending in the 1980s. The deficit was eliminated in 1997. Annual surpluses averaged 2% in 1998–2001. Government debt fell from 53.2% of GDP in 1997 to 40.2% in 2001. Inflation has been contained by wage restraint agreed between the social partners. Diversification of the economy away from dependence on fisheries exports is a key point of government policy, the main sectors targeted being finance, telecommunications, and biotechnology.

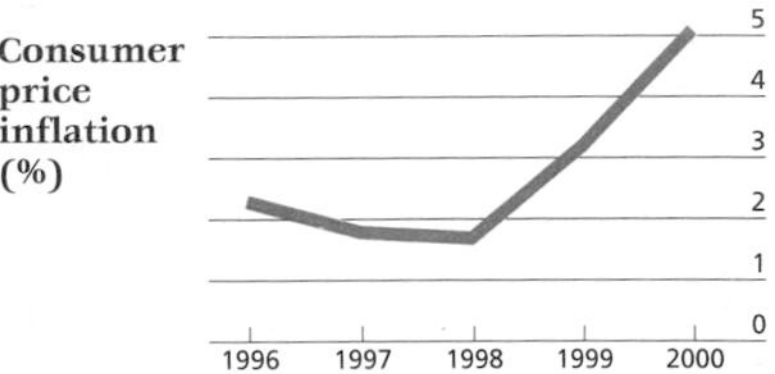

GDP stagnated in 1990–95 because of recession in European markets, reviving to an average 4% in 1998–2000, but easing back to 2.2% in 2001, with an average 2.25% expected for 2001–04. Inflation fell from a peak of 6.8% in 1991 to 3.4% in 1999, reviving to 6.3% in 2000–01. 3.5% was expected in 2002. Unemployment is traditionally low, averaging 2.7% in 1993–2000. It was 2.1% at April 2001.

GEOGRAPHY/RESOURCES

The main island of Iceland is the second-largest in Europe, and lies in the north Atlantic Ocean between Greenland, Norway, and Scotland. It is one of the most volcanically active places on earth, with hot springs, geysers, volcanic eruptions, and earthquakes. A fault line runs through the main island from northeast to southwest, and volcanic activity is concentrated on the eastern side of this, both onshore and under the sea. Ice covers 11% of the land, lava 1.5%, post-glacial lava 10%, lakes 3%, glacial plains 4%, and forest 1%. Three-quarters of the land has no vegetation. Over half of the land is above 1,300 feet, with the mountains reaching a high point of 6,952 feet. The Gulf Stream moderates winter temperatures, producing an average 31°F in Reykjavík in January. The summer average is 52°F. There is heavy precipitation, and rapid storms pose a hazard.

The main agricultural crops are potatoes, turnips, and other root vegetables grown outdoors, and tomatoes and cucumbers grown in greenhouses heated by hot springs. Iceland is self-sufficient in meat and dairy products. The main fish species caught are blue whiting, followed by capelin, herring, cod, Atlantic redfishes, crustaceans, and haddock. The main minerals are diatomite, pumice, and salt. Iceland has

3% of the world market in diatomite, which is used in the filtration of organic liquids ranging from beer to aviation fuel. Geothermal brine output is 10,000 tons a year.

Around 62% of the population live in the capital, Reykjavík. The population is one of the most homogeneous on earth, descended mostly from 9th century Norwegian colonists and a smaller number of Celts. Family records have been kept since the 12th century, the longest continual recording of human genealogy. People of other European, Asian, American, and African origin accounted for 2.6% of the population in 1999.

Communications/Energy

The road network is 7,900 miles, including 2,700 miles of main roads. Sea ports are important for heavy freight transport between coastal towns and regions. The merchant fleet was 1,014 ships totaling 230,354 grt at January 2000, 841 of which were fishing vessels. There are 12 airports, including the international airport at Keflavík near to Reykjavík, and 74 airstrips. Air transport is a vital means of domestic travel.

Telecommunications is deregulated, and costs are among the lowest in the OECD. The phone network is fully digitalized. ISDN links have been available since 1995. The fiber-optic network operates internationally and to all urban communities. There are also satellite links for international communications. There were 197,000 fixed phone lines, 188,200 mobile phones, and 168,000 Internet users at end-2000. At September 2000 79.1% of the population used mobile phones and 52.8% used SMS text messages, while 77.8% had access to a computer with an Internet connection, and 64.7% had the Internet at home. 19% had engaged in e-commerce.

Geothermal energy provides 32% of total energy requirements, hydroelectric power 40%, and fossil fuels 28%. Geothermal energy replaces electricity or fossil fuels for heating in 85% of homes, and in many industrial and agricultural applications. There are four geothermal electricity plants, which produced 15.84% of electricity in 1999. Hydroelectricity accounted for 84.1% and oil for 0.06%.

Education/Employment

Education is compulsory from age 6 to 16. There are seven universities, the largest of which is the University of Iceland with 6,000 students. The University College of Education has 1,200 students, and the Icelandic College of Engineering and Technology has 600. The other universities have 50 to 500 students and include specific institutes for agriculture and the arts. Higher education is the remit of the Ministry of Education, and most funding is provided by the state. There is liaison between independent research institutes and the universities. The Fisheries Research Institute carries out research for the fishing industry. The Nordic Volcanological Institute develops software systems for analysis of large data sets, as well as other R&D applications. Human and fish biotechnology are special strengths. Icelandic researchers are taking part in a multinational analysis of information on genetic human diseases derived from Iceland's unique genealogical records.

The labor force is well educated and well adapted to new technology. Over 85% is unionized. Framework wage and employment conditions are determined by tripartite negotiation between employers, unions, and the government, with specific conditions set at the sectoral or workplace level. The key aspects of employment law are broadly similar to those in other European countries.

Fiscal/Financial

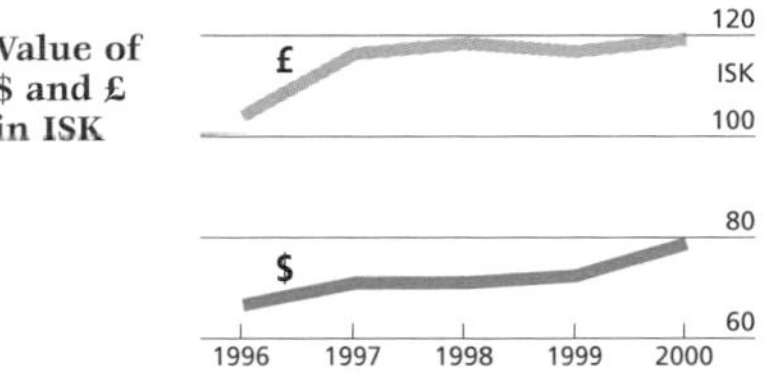

There were four commercial banks in early 2001. Landsbanki íslands and Bunadarbanki íslands were majority-owned by the government, while Islandsbanki-FBA (formed by the merger of four government investment funds and Islandsbanki) was entirely private-sector, and Sparisjodabanki íslands (Icebank) was owned by the 29 savings banks. The savings banks are mostly private-sector, as are most insurance companies. The central bank is Sedlabanki íslands. Regulation of the finance sector is carried out by the Financial Supervisory Authority, which was established in 1999. Stricter supervisory rules were introduced in 1993 in line with EU laws as a result of Iceland's membership of the European Economic Area (EEA).

Corporation tax is 18%. The regular rate of personal income tax is 38.34%. There is a levy of 0.08% of operating income on industrial activities, and there are also property taxes. Payroll tax is 5.14%. The standard VAT rate is 24.5%, but 14% applies to food, newspapers, and some other items.

In addition to commercial and savings banks, cooperatives have their own savings departments, and there is the Post Giro. A new State Housing Fund was created in 1999 to rationalize state housing finance. In 2000 there were 14 locally-incorporated insurance companies and 156 foreign insurance companies with licenses to provide services in Iceland. Pension funds are well established as the most important source of long-term finance. The Iceland Stock Exchange (ISE) became a limited liability company in 1999, and its monopoly on exchange operations was abolished. Electronic securities registration began, and ISE became a member of the Nordic Stock Exchange, NOREX, in 2000. There is a non-regulated market in unlisted shares. ISE market capitalization was ISK1,330 billion at end-1999.

Business Opportunities

Special tax reductions and grants are available to film companies using Iceland as a location. The aluminum smelters are owned Swiss and U.S. companies, while the ferro-silicon plant is an Icelandic-Norwegian-Japanese joint venture. The government is eager to attract more such energy-intensive industries. Insurance is a fully international sector. Future banking privatization, and liberalization of the telecommunications market, will offer opportunities to foreign investors. Direct foreign investment is banned in fishing and fish processing, and indirect investment is limited to 33%. Investment from outside the EEA in energy production and distribution requires parliamentary approval, and is limited to 49% in aviation. The point of contact for investors is Invest in Iceland, part of the Trade Council of Iceland.

For More Information

Books:

Gylfadóttir, Þóra. *Iceland in Figures*. Reykjavík: Statistics Iceland, 2000.

Iceland Business, quarterly magazine. (Sample copies available online at http://icelandreview.com.)

Karlsson, Gunnar. *The History of Iceland*. Minneapolis, MN: University of Minnesota Press, 2000.

OECD Economic Surveys. *Iceland 2000–2001*. Paris: OECD, 2001.

Web Sites:

Central Bank of Iceland: **www.sedlabanki.is**
Government entry point: **www.stjr.is**
Iceland Stock Exchange: **www.vi.is**
Statistics Iceland: **www.statice.is**
Trade Council: **www.icetrade.is**

INDIA

GNI: **$441,834 million; world's 11th**
GNI pc: **$440; world's 163rd**
Head of government: **prime minister**
Currency: **rupee (Rs)**
Capital: **New Delhi**
Population: **998,056,000, growing at 1.8% p.a.**
Land area: **1,147,950 square miles**
Population density: **869 per square mile**
Life expectancy: **63 years**
Infant mortality: **70 per 1,000 live births**
Language: **Hindi, English, other local and regional languages**
Best buy: **embroidered silk scarves**

ECONOMIC STRUCTURE

Composition of GDP (1999)
Agriculture **28%**
Industry:
Manufacturing **16%**
Other industry **10%**
Services **46%**

Having been colonized mainly by the East India Company, India was a directly-ruled British colony from 1858 until 1947. Independent India has been governed mainly by the Congress Party (which held power for 45 of the 53 years after independence), headed by the dynasty of its first prime minister Jawarhlal Nehru and his daughter Indira Gandhi, who was prime minister in 1966–77 and 1980–84. A state-led development strategy was adopted, which brought gigantic improvements in education and health and created a broad, if uneven, industrial sector. In agriculture, this strategy culminated in the so-called Green Revolution (introduction of high-yield seeds and mechanization) of the 1960s, and achieved self-sufficiency in rice and wheat. From 1991 state-led development was broadly replaced by a strategy of liberalization. In the late 1990s, Congress Party domination was broken by a series of coalition governments and, in 1999, by a majority government of the Hindu Bharatiya Janata Party (BJP). The challenge now is whether growth of the economy can keep pace with that of the population, which in 2000 soared past 1 billion. It is the second largest in the world after China's, and is expected to overtake China around 2030.

Agriculture, forestry, and fishing account for about 30% of India's GDP; three-quarters of the population depend on it. India's strongest industrial sectors include steel, and consumer goods manufacturing (cars, scooters, consumer electronics, computer systems, and white goods), which expanded rapidly in the 1990s. The information technology industry is India's sensational success. It grew from nothing in 1991 to sales of $8.3 billion in 2000, when it employed 400,000 people, comprised 15% of exports, and accounted for 80% of the world's software development outsourced offshore.

The export mix has changed dramatically since the 1970s. Tea and jute, India's traditional exports, have declined from 40% to 2%; manufactured goods including gems, leather goods, garments, chemicals, and pharmaceuticals accounted for 75% of exports by 2000. India's leading export destinations in 2000 were the United States (22.7%), the United Kingdom (6.0%), Germany (4.8%), and Japan (4.5%). Import substitution policies have hit imports of consumer goods, while demand for raw materials and intermediate goods (including fertilizers, paper, steel, and non-ferrous metals) has risen. Leading importers in 2000 were the United States (7.7%), the United Kingdom (5.8%), Belgium (7.4%), Japan (5.0%), and Germany (4.0%).

Current account balance ($ billion)

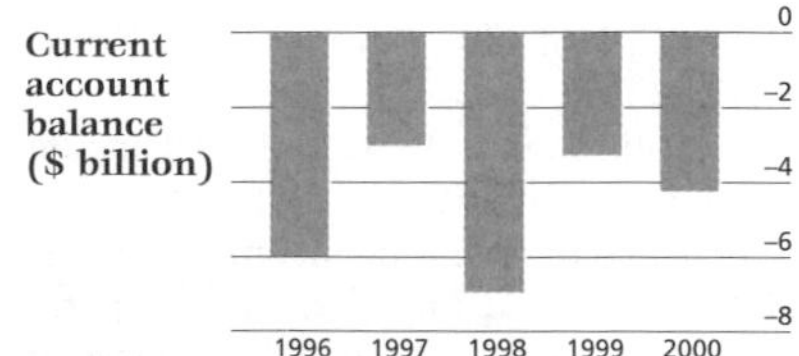

Indian governments have indicated support for privatization (officially, "divestment") throughout the 1990s, but little has taken place. In 2001 the BJP government was expressing what appeared to be more serious intentions to privatize Air India, the international carrier, and the car maker Maruti.

ECONOMIC POLICY

Growth in GDP (%)

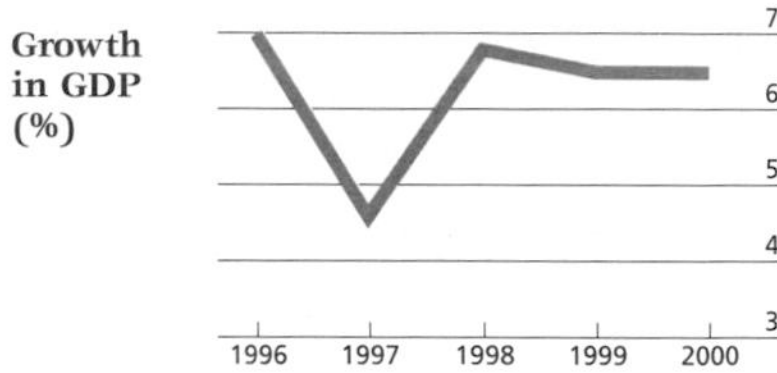

A severe financial crisis in 1991 culminated in India being forced to seek emergency IMF funding. The resulting negotiations provided an impetus for the reform program, which in the following decade opened more sectors to private—including foreign-investment, including power, steel, oil refining and exploration, road construction, air and sea transport, telecommunications, and the financial sector. It encouraged foreign direct investment with majority equity, and liberalized trade policy, converting some import quotas into tariffs and reducing tariffs. It also decontrolled and delicensed most industries.

India's major economic policy problem is its fiscal deficit. After running a borrowing requirement over 5% of GDP in the 1980s, successive governments attempted unsuccessfully to cut it back. In 2000 the deficit exceeded 10% of GDP. Reform of the inefficient state sector is considered to be a large part of the problem: in 2001 it employed 70% of the 28 million workers in organized employment, but accounted for just one-third of economic output.

Consumer price inflation (%)

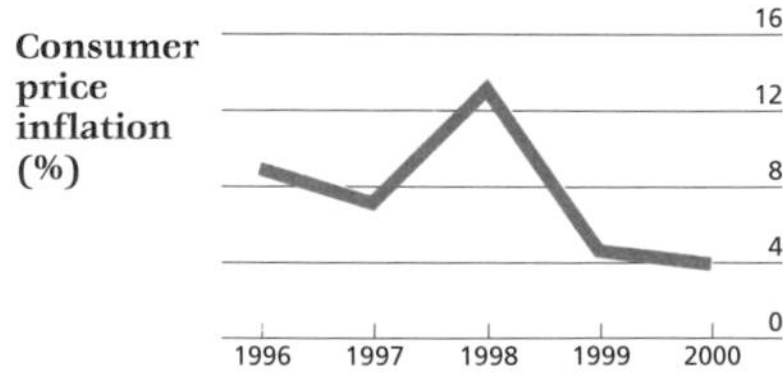

In the early 1990s growth had slowed, but it surpassed 5% in 1994–98, peaked at 6.5% in 1999, and slowed again to 6% in 2000 and 5.6% (projection) in 2001. Observers say that the Asian economic crisis and world slowdown hit export performance, and the government's failure to reform restrictive labor laws and to curtail costly public-sector subsidies has aggravated matters. There were negative impacts on the Indian econ-

omy from the September 11 attacks and their aftermath—which affected software, tourism, and worker remittances from the Middle East—and from renewed fears of war with Pakistan after a stand-off in December 2001. Consumer price inflation (to which India's majority, the poor rural population, is especially sensitive) has fallen from 13.2% in 1998 to 4.3% in 2000.

GEOGRAPHY/RESOURCES

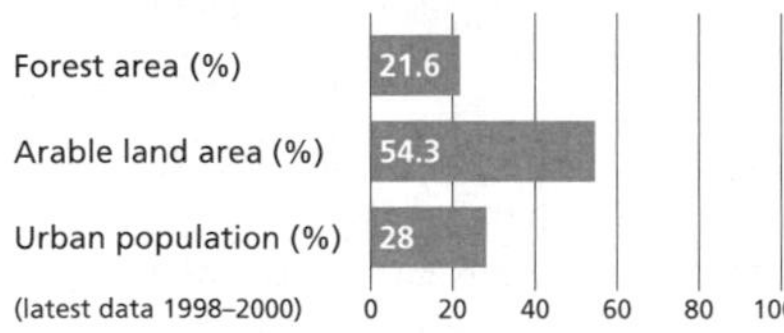

India, the sixth-largest country in the world by land area, forms—together with Bangladesh and Pakistan—the south Asian subcontinent, set off from the rest of Asia by the Himalayas and other mountain ranges. Its northern neighbors, from west to east, are Pakistan, China, Nepal, Bhutan, and Burma; Bangladesh in the east sits between Indian territory and the Indian Ocean. Topographically, India may be divided broadly into the Himalayas, the Indo-Gangetic plain, and the variegated southern region. Politically India comprises 26 states (which have control over important aspects of social and economic policy and limited powers of taxation), and six union territories. During the 1990s economic differences between wealthier states (e.g. Gujarat and Maharashtra) and poorer ones (e.g. Uttar Pradesh and Bihar) have widened.

India's vast population (1,002.8 million in 2000) is extremely diverse: ethnically (with roots in European, Indo-European, Central Asian, Tibetan and Burman, and Australoid ethnic groups); linguistically (Hindi and English are the lingua francas, but Assamese, Bengali, Gujarati, Kashmiri, Konkani, Marathi, Nepali, Oriya, and Punjabi enjoy official status at state level, and Sindhi and Urdu are spoken by many millions); by religion (the Hindu majority of 83% is itself divided, and there are also Muslims (11%), Sikhs, and Christians); and by caste and class. Life expectancy at birth increased from 32 years in 1951 to 62 years for men and 63 years for women in 1996. India is less urbanized than most developing Asian countries: 60% of its people live in villages with a population of less than 5,000.

Agriculture remains India's most important resource; rice and wheat are the main crops. In the 1970s India put starvation behind it and accumulated buffer grain stocks sufficient to weather several disastrously bad monsoons. Production of coarse grains and pulses, however, stayed stable or decreased, and the threat of food scarcity was not eliminated. In 1991–99, agricultural growth was estimated at 3.5% per year, but in 2000–01 immense problems remained: just over a quarter of farmers produce 60% of output, with most of the rest farming for subsistence on private plots too small to make mechanization worthwhile.

India's mineral resources are modest. Iron ore and ferro-alloys, notably manganese and chromite, are widely distributed over peninsular India. There is also copper, bauxite, zinc, lead, gold, and silver. There are abundant reserves of coal and some oil fields in eastern Assam, in Gujarat, and offshore in the Arabian Sea.

COMMUNICATIONS/ENERGY

PCs 0.5
Telephone lines 3.2
Mobiles 0.4
Internet users 0.5
(per 100 people, 2000) 0 20 40 60 80 100

India has the world's most extensive railway system, covering 38,850 miles (31% of it electrified) and employing 1.6 million staff. Freight traffic in 2000–01 was 428 million tons, up 8.4% on the previous year. Private-sector participation has been encouraged by government initiatives to provide containers and an "Own-Your-Wagon" scheme. Safety spending was increased after almost 300 people died in a rail accident in August 1999. However, more investment goes into India's 2 million miles of roads, of which half are unsurfaced and only 35,420 are highways. The National Highways Authority raised $1.4 billion in bonds in 2000–01 for the national Integrated Highway Project to link Delhi, Mumbai, Chennai, and Kolkata. India also has 11 major and 139 minor ports, which handle 90% of its foreign trade. Its domestic air traffic amounts to 11.6 million passengers (1997), of which one-third is handled by private operators.

Indian telecommunications expanded rapidly from the late 1990s; by 2001 it had 36.7 million lines and 30 million working lines, about 50% up on the 1998 level, plus 3.6 million mobile phones. Competition was introduced to the national long-distance service market in August 2000, and the basic service segment in January 2001.

In 2000–01, total power generation was 497 billion kWh, but there were serious shortages (a 6.2% overall shortage and 12.4% peak shortage). Power-sector restructuring was identified by the Asian Development Bank in late 2001 as one of India's most urgent challenges: 35–40% of generated power is lost in transmission and distribution, including theft; the electricity distributors, the State Electricity Boards (SEBs), are largely bankrupt, partly because of large subsidies to domestic and agricultural users; and foreign investors in the sector have found themselves in conflict with distribution companies.

EDUCATION/EMPLOYMENT

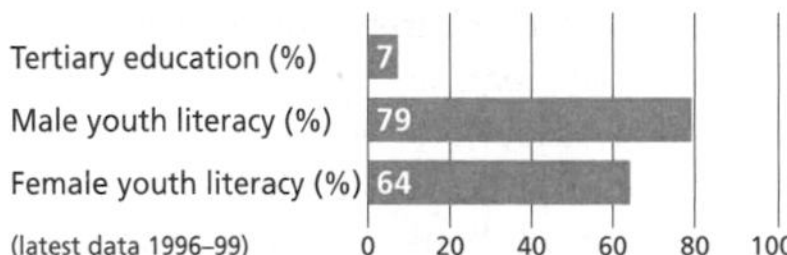

Of India's 1 billion people, only 68.26 million are counted within the organized labor force, and of these 40.09 million are registered as unemployed (Asian Development Bank figures, 1998). This excludes almost the entire rural population and many urban laborers. The pool of unemployed includes many workers with higher education or vocational training, and many English-speakers. The labor force is largely non-union, but where unions exist, principally in the state sector, they have well-established bargaining rights.

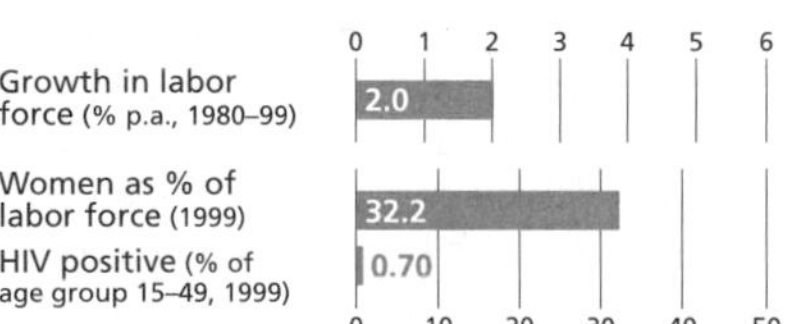

India's literacy rates have risen considerably in the last decade. At the 2001 census there was 65% literacy, with a large gap between males (76%) and females (54%), and wide regional differences (e.g. 91% literacy in Kerala and 48% in Bihar). The rate of enrollment in primary schools had risen by 1991 to 98% of boys and 83% of girls, secondary school enrollment to 44% overall, and university enrollment to 9%, the highest by far for a low-income developing country. The number of students in higher education continued to grow during the 1990s: 6.4 million were enrolled in 1995–96, although access to places depends largely on caste, religion, and wealth rather than ability.

FISCAL/FINANCIAL

India's public-sector banks account for more than 80% of banking activity, and the banking sector is subject to controls: domestic

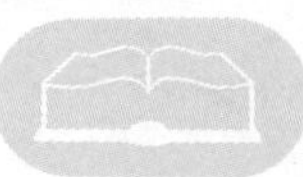

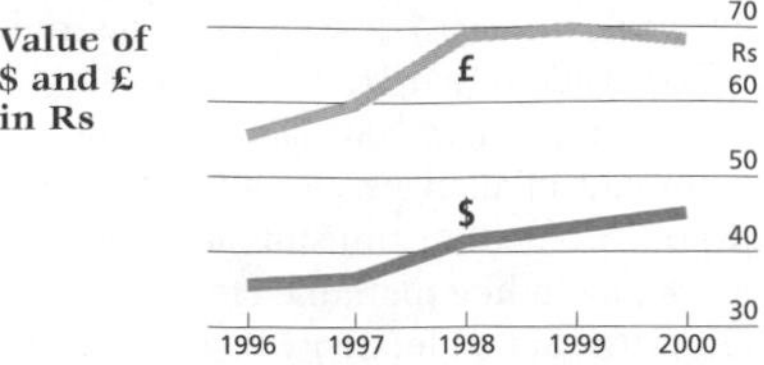

banks are required to extend 40% of loans to "priority" borrowers, foreign-owned banks 32%; the upper limit on external commercial borrowing for companies is $200 million for eight years or $400 million for 16 years. The gross non-performing assets of the 27 public-sector banks were estimated at 14.3% of total loan assets in March 2001. Households account for 90% of national savings, and by 1991–92 40% of these were held in financial form (bank accounts, shares, insurance policies) rather than physical form, up from 10% in 1980–81.

The growth of India's capital markets has been due largely to the presence of foreign institutional investors, which are able to register on the stock exchanges and hold up to 10% of any Indian company. Total foreign portfolio investment is limited to 49% of any company. There are 6,000 companies listed on the largest exchange, the Bombay Stock Exchange, but only 500 are actively traded; total market capitalization was $1.5 billion in 1998. In 2001 the exchanges experienced a series of insider-dealing scandals, including some involving employees of large international banks. As a result of these, regulation has been tightened, with the traditional five-day settlement system being replaced with the international norm of compulsory rolling settlement, and exchanges being instructed to demutualize.

India charges long-term (more than three years) capital gains tax at a flat rate of 20%, with a number of concessions and exemptions. It operates double taxation avoidance agreements with many countries. In 2001 its system of special excises was simplified, the peak customs duty of 35% being retained but a surcharge of 10% on the basic duty removed. The government also declared its intention of further "people-friendly and reform-oriented" improvements to the tax system.

Business Opportunities

Growth in output (% p.a., 1990–99)

Services	7.8
Industry	6.7
Manufacturing	7.5
Agriculture	3.4

Levels of foreign direct investment were under $1 billion per year in the early 1990s, and consistently higher than $2 billion in the late 1990s. The most promising investment opportunities are in oil and gas development, insurance, drugs and pharmaceuticals, and healthcare services. India's membership of the WTO and the Multilateral Insurance Guarantee Agency, its bilateral investment protection agreements with major investing countries, and the changes it has made, in particular, to intellectual property rights legislation, are seen as positive.

Deregulation and liberalization has created a much improved environment for foreign investment. Incentives include: automatic approval for foreign equity participation of up to 51% in some sectors and 100% in others; permission to freely repatriate profits and capital investment, except in specified consumer goods industries; permission to use foreign brand names and trademarks; and special investment and tax incentives in certain sectors including power, electronics, software, and food processing. A Foreign Investment Promotion Board has been formed. It was hoped in late 2001 that restrictions on 100% foreign investment in garments manufacture, and more than 49% foreign investment in telecoms, would be removed. However, remaining controls, as well as problems with corruption, are given as reasons why inward investment remains slow.

The creation of a Divestment Department in 1999, and the sale of the government's stake in Bahrat Aluminium company to Sterlite Industries for $118 million in 2000, showed the government's determination to overcome political opposition to privatization. However, in 2001 the principal obstacle to any further deals of this kind was hesitation by foreign investors.

For More Information

Books:

Ackerley, Joe Randolph, and Eliot Weinberger. *Hindoo Holiday: An Indian Journal* (New York Review of Books Classics). New York: New York Review Books, 2000.

Chadha, Yogesh. *Gandhi: A Life*. New York: John Wiley, 1999.

Cohen, Stephen P. *India: Emerging Power*. Washington, D.C.: Brookings Institution, 2001.

Das, Gurcharan. *India Unbound*. New York: Knopf, 2001.

Dreze, Jean, and Amartya Sen. *India: Economic Development and Social Opportunity*. New York: Oxford University Press, 1999.

Harrison, Selig, Paul Kreisberg, and Dennis Kux. *India and Pakistan: The First Fifty Years*. New York: Cambridge University Press, 1999.

Sachs, Jeffrey D., and Nirupam Bajpai. *The Decade of Development: Goal Setting and Policy Challenges in India*. Cambridge, MA: Harvard University Center for International Development, 2001. (Also available online at www2.cid.harvard.edu/cidwp/062.pdf.)

Schofield, Victoria. *Kashmir in Conflict: India, Pakistan and the Unfinished War*. New York: I. B. Tauris, 2000.

Wolpert, Stanley A. *India*. Berkeley, CA: University of California Press, 1999.

Web Sites:

Directory of government sites: **goidirectory.nic.in**
Economic Times (newspaper): **www.economictimes.com**
India Today (magazine): **www.india-today.com**
Ministry of Commerce Directorate of Foreign Trade: **dgft.delhi.nic.in**
Ministry of Commerce and Industry: **commin.nic.in**
Reserve Bank of India: **www.rbi.org.in**
Web India business portal: **www.webindia.com**

INDONESIA

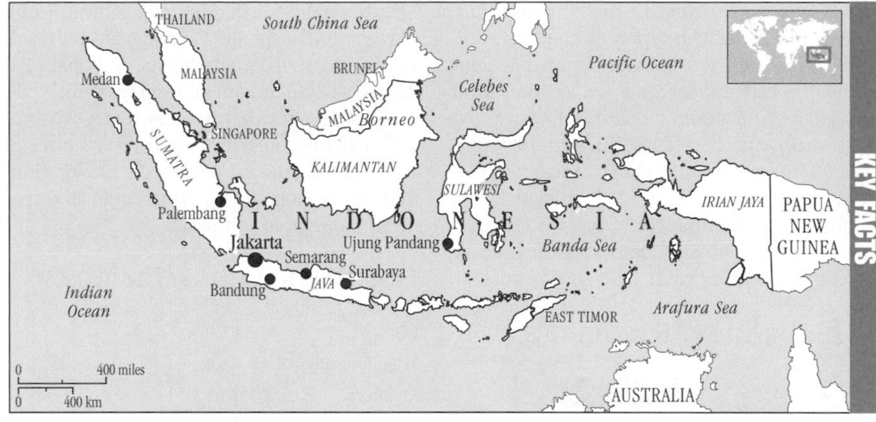

GNI: **$125,043 million; world's 31st**
GNI pc: **$600; world's 150th**
Head of government: **president**
Currency: **rupiah (Rp)**
Capital: **Jakarta**
Population: **209,255,000, growing at 1.5% p.a.**
Land area: **699,460 square miles**
Population density: **299 per square mile**
Life expectancy: **66 years**
Infant mortality: **38 per 1,000 live births**
Language: **Bahasa Indonesia, local languages (500)**
Best buy: **batik, filigree silverware, gems**

ECONOMIC STRUCTURE

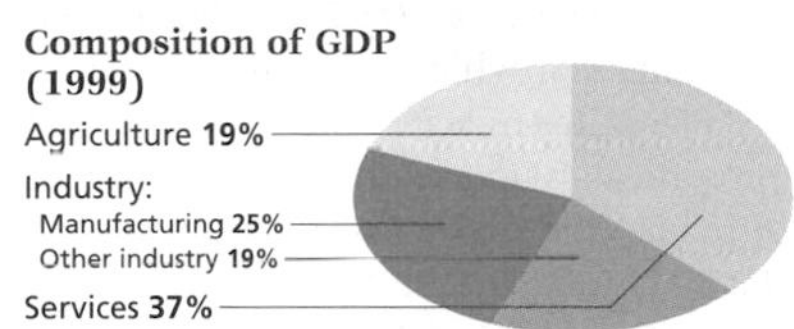

The Indonesian islands had a highly-developed agriculture and maritime trade with the rest of Asia from early history. From the 17th century to World War II they were colonized by the Dutch. Oil was discovered in 1883. Following the departure of Japanese occupation forces in 1945, Indonesia declared its independence, and this was internationally recognized in 1950. Political unrest across the huge country resulted in an army-backed dictatorship, initially under the civilian President Sukarno and—from 1965—under General Suharto. General Suharto's encouragement of foreign investment resulted in rapid economic growth, based first on metals, timber and oil, then on textiles and import-substitution industries backed by protective tariffs. From the late 1980s non-oil exports were the focus of industrialization, and in the 1990s industry with higher added-value grew rapidly. Despite foreign investment, state-owned industries controlled by the political elite dominated the economy from the 1970s. Following the Asian financial crisis in 1997, President Suharto was forced to resign in 1998.

Services accounted for 39.9% of GDP in 2000, followed by manufacturing (26.4%), agriculture (16.7%), mining (9.4%), and construction (6%). Trade was the leading services sector, contributing 16% of GDP, followed by transport (7.4%), finance (6.9%), and public administration (5.7%). Tourism is important but has been adversely affected by separatist violence and, from autumn 2001, by domestic antipathy to the West's war in Afghanistan. Petroleum and gas refining, fertilizers, chemicals, pharmaceuticals, metals refining, processed timber, paper, and textiles are among the leading manufacturing industries. Indonesia is one of the leading world exporters of LNG (liquefied natural gas), rubber, and palm oil. Petroleum was the top export in 2000, followed by natural gas, textiles, electrical appliances, manufactured wood products, machinery, and food. The main market was Japan (23.2%), followed by the United States (13.6%), Singapore (10.6%), South Korea, Netherlands, and China.

The state owns the petroleum and natural gas production company Pertamina, as well as companies involved in domestic gas distribution, electricity production and distribution, and water supply. However, utilities sectors have been liberalized and have attracted foreign investment, especially from the United Kingdom The railway operator was privatized in 1991 but retains the monopoly. Air transport has been liberalized, but the state owns the main airline Garuda.

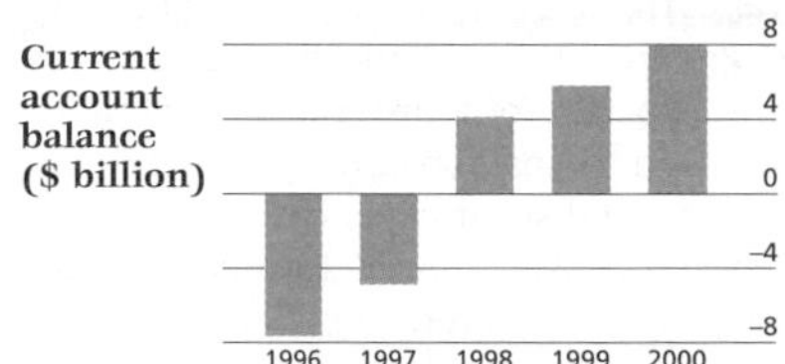

The telecommunications sector was partly privatized in 1994–95. In June 2000 the government relaunched its ambitious program to sell out majority state holdings in 164 enterprises. The initial companies to be sold are in mining, plantations, airport operations, and fertilizers. However, by mid-2001 only two small divestitures in pharmaceuticals companies had taken place. At end-2000 the state held 95% of commercial bank equity as a result of the recapitalization program following the collapse of the sector in 1998. Divestiture is due to be completed by 2004. The government is determined that the banking sector will be more independent than in the past, and that the previous concentration of bank ownership within leading private-sector business groups will not be repeated.

ECONOMIC POLICY

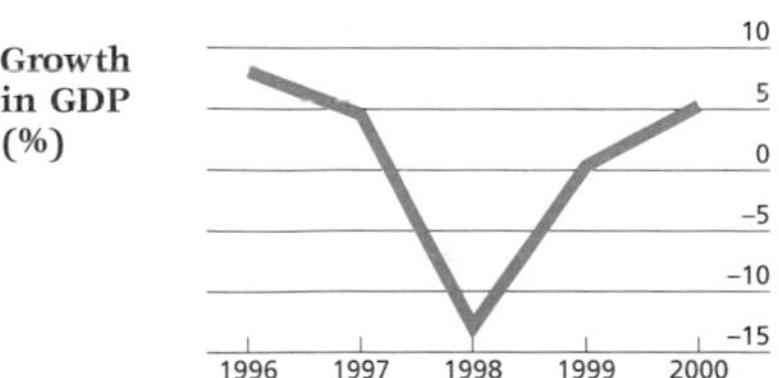

Before the 1997–98 financial crisis, the government conducted a prudent debt policy, borrowing abroad for development projects, mostly from public-sector sources, to avoid inflation at home. Inflation averaged 8.9% in 1994–97. The government's exchange-rate and interest-rate policies were less prudent. The rupiah was allowed to depreciate by an annual average of 3.9% in 1990–96 in order to keep exports competitive. Interest rates on loans and deposits were high, driving Indonesian corporations to seek finance abroad and encouraging foreign investors to place deposits and make loans in Indonesia. The government decided not to intervene

to support the rupiah during the 1997 crisis, which led to a 73% depreciation of the currency and 77.6% inflation in 1998. Inflation fell to 2% in 1999 and 0.9% in 2000 as a result of depressed economic activity, reviving to 5.6% in the first six months of 2001. The 2002 budget was based on inflation of 9% and growth of 4%. Annual GDP growth averaged 3.9% in 2000–01, after stagnation in 1999, a decline of 13.2% in 1998, and annual average growth of 7.6% in 1990–97. Official unemployment was an annual average of 4.4% in 1990–99, but official estimates of underemployment and unemployment were 38% of the labor force in March 2000. Job creation and the reduction of underemployment, especially through foreign investment, are key policy goals.

However, political uncertainty resulting from anti-Western sentiment over the war in Afghanistan, from separatist movements, and from the decentralization of tax and investment approval in 2001 are disincentives to foreign investment. The government's program to review the decentralization framework in 2002 to ensure economic stability has IMF backing, which extends to the rest of the government's economic program. But the rupiah remains volatile because of the government's slow progress in restructuring the corporate sector and in paying off its estimated $65 billion in foreign debt. This has created a vicious circle, raising the cost of debt and restructuring and causing further delays. Government debt servicing, at 27% of government expenditure in 2000, outweighed the development budget at 21%.

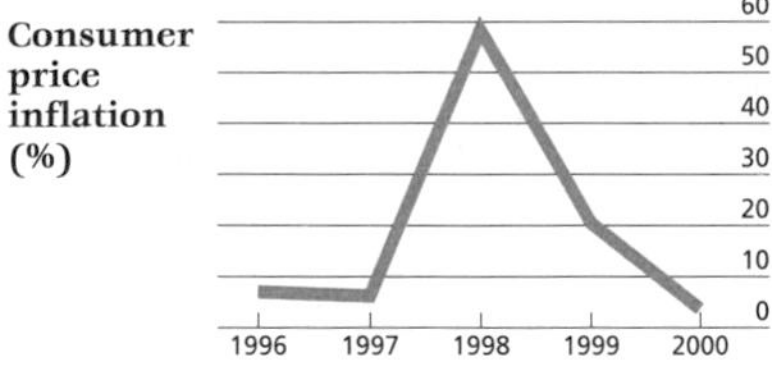

The 1997 crisis left the banking sector and much of the corporate sector paralyzed. The Indonesian Bank Restructuring Agency (IBRA) was established in 1998 to take control of failing banks, restructure and sell them, restructure bad loans taken over from the banks, and sell assets pledged by the banks as collateral for emergency central bank liquidity credits issued in 1997–98. The government recapitalized 37 banks in 1999–2000, raising Rp430.4 trillion through bonds. It also issued stricter capital adequacy requirements and other prudential measures, including better corporate governance. Banks were required to increase their capital again in 2001, and international standards of banking supervision (Basle Core Principles) were to be in place by end-2002. The government's Blanket Guarantee Scheme for bank deposits will operate until the Deposit Insurance Scheme comes into effect in 2004. The legacy of the crisis and the constraints of tighter regulation kept new corporate lending below the level needed for economic revival. However, the government created facilities in 1998 and 1999 in agreement with foreign governments to assure basic trade financing. It also introduced a framework program for bank lending to small businesses in 1999, initially on a compulsory basis, with good results.

Geography/Resources

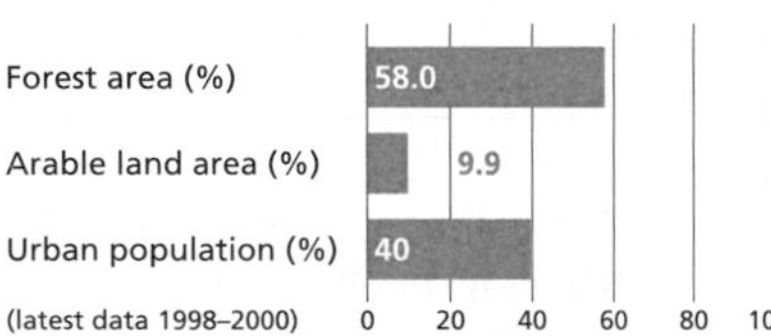

In southeast Asia, Indonesia is an archipelago of 17,508 islands, 6,000 of which are inhabited, lying on the Equator between the Indian Ocean to the west and south, the South China Sea to the north, and the Pacific Ocean to the east. The main islands are Java (the most populated), Sumatra (the largest), Irian Jaya (part of New Guinea, which it shares with Papua New Guinea), Kalimantan (two-thirds of the island of Borneo, with Malaysia and Brunei in the north), and Sulawesi. Most of the country is mountainous (the highest point is 16,503 feet) with coastal plains. There are around 400 volcanoes, a quarter of which are active. Tropical forest covers more than half of the land. The climate is hot, and humidity ranges between 73% and 87%. There is abundant rainfall. The average temperature is 82°F on the plains and 77°F in the mountains. The population is mostly of Javanese origin (45%), followed by Sundanese (14%), Madurese (7.5%), Malays (7.5%), and others belonging to the country's 500 tribes. Indonesia is the largest Muslim country in the world.

Rice is the main agricultural crop. Cassava, corn, and a wide range of other crops are grown for the domestic market. The main export crops are rubber, palm oil, coffee, tea, cocoa, tobacco, spices, bananas, coconuts, and sugar cane. Chickens are the main livestock, followed by ducks, goats, cattle, and pigs. Production of fuel wood, furniture timber, and other industrial timbers is significant. Fishing covers a wide range of species, with most of the catch from deep-sea fishing in the Pacific and Indian Oceans. There are extensive mineral resources, of which petroleum and natural gas are the most valuable. Other main mining products are coal, copper, nickel, bauxite, gold, silver, tin, manganese, iron, granite, and asphalt. Gemstones produced include diamonds, amethysts, and opals. At January 2000, proven oil reserves were 5 billion barrels and natural gas reserves were 72.3 trillion cubic feet. Coal reserves were 5.75 billion tons at end-1996. Exploration and the expansion of production in all three energy minerals continues.

Communications/Energy

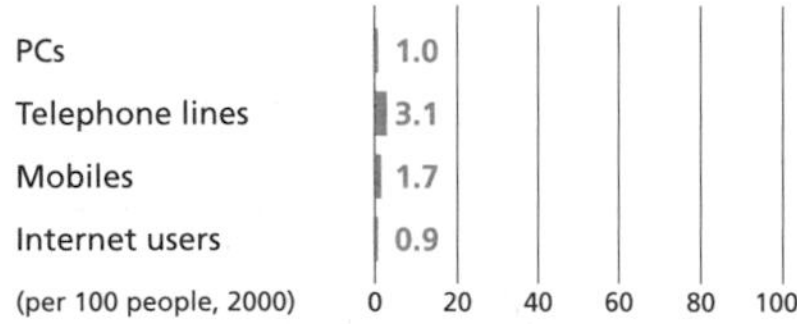

The road network was 215,541 miles in 1998 (93,925 miles of which was paved), including 16,686 miles of state roads, 29,749 miles of provincial roads, and 169,105 miles of local roads. The rail network on the islands of Java, Sumatra, and Madura was 4,013 miles in 1996. New track in Sumatra totaling 496 miles will be completed in 2011. A new high-speed rail link in Java from Jakarta to Surabaya is under construction. The river and lake transport network totals 13,409 miles on the five main islands. There were 672 sea ports in 1998, 25 of which are regarded as strategic. There were 127 airports, including 7 major international airports, and 319 airstrips in 1999. In 1998 airports handled 7.5 million domestic and 3.9 million international passengers, and 140,502 tons of domestic and 171,141 tons of international cargo. Sea ports handled 418.8 million tons of international and inter-island freight and 46.7 million passengers. Inland waterways carried 40.6 million passengers and 11,254 tons of freight, while 169 million passengers and 18.1 million tons of freight traveled by rail.

International telecommunications links are provided via satellite, and domestic links are provided by satellite, microwave, and high-frequency radio. Majority state-owned companies predominate. There were 6.7 million fixed phone lines, 3.7 million mobile phones, and 2 million Internet users at end-2000.

Most electricity is generated by oil, but natural gas, coal, geothermal, and hydroelectric power stations were built in the 1990s to reduce dependence on oil. In 2000 fossil fuels accounted for 82% of power generation, hydroelectricity for 15%, and

geothermal for 3%. Proposals to build a nuclear power station were postponed indefinitely in 1998. Crude oil production was 440.5 million barrels in 1999, while 9.6 million barrels of condensates, 519.5 million barrels (equivalent) of natural gas, and 64.6 million tons of coal were produced. Around 65% of oil, 60% of natural gas, and 76% of coal is exported. Some refined petroleum products and coal are imported.

Education/Employment

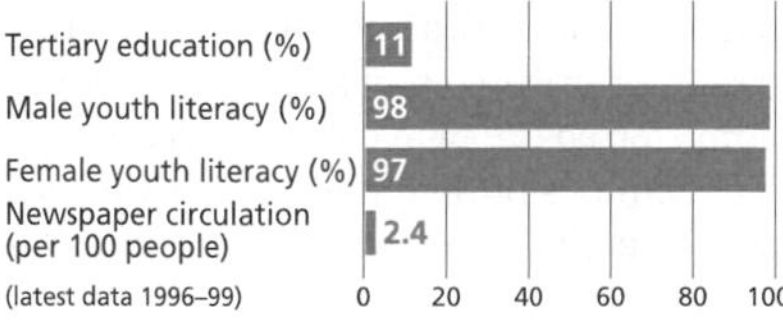

Education is compulsory from age 7 to 16. There were 1,634 higher education institutions, including 321 universities, in 1999 with 3.1 million students enrolled. There were also 36,881 private-sector and 15,567 public-sector vocational senior secondary schools providing business and technical courses to 1.3 million and 657,462 students respectively. The Ministry of National Education is responsible for education policy and for the funding and supervision of public educational institutions. The Indonesian Institute of Sciences is responsible for science and technology policy covering natural sciences, technology, social sciences, testing, and standardization. There are R&D centers for biology, biotechnology, geotechnology, oceanology, limnology, metallurgy, telecommunications, applied physics, and applied chemistry.

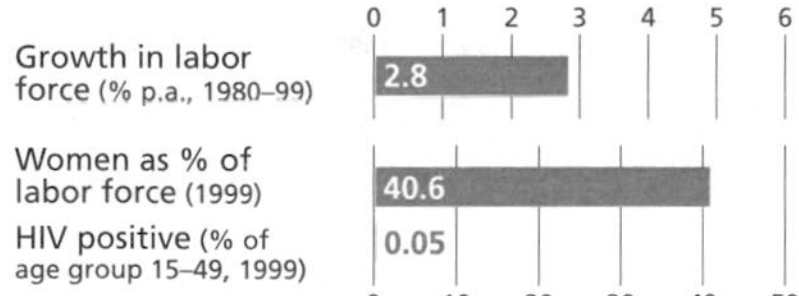

The labor force has skills ranging from top business management and technical know-how to unskilled. The government sets minimum wages by region, but these have often not been applied. Corporate compliance with and legal enforcement of labor law is erratic, and this, combined with massive redundancies since the crisis, has led to strikes. Independent trade unions began to register after the 1998 law granting them recognition. New legislation on the rights of trade unions, and a system for resolving industrial disputes, was drafted in 2000.

Fiscal/Financial

Value of $ and £ in Rp

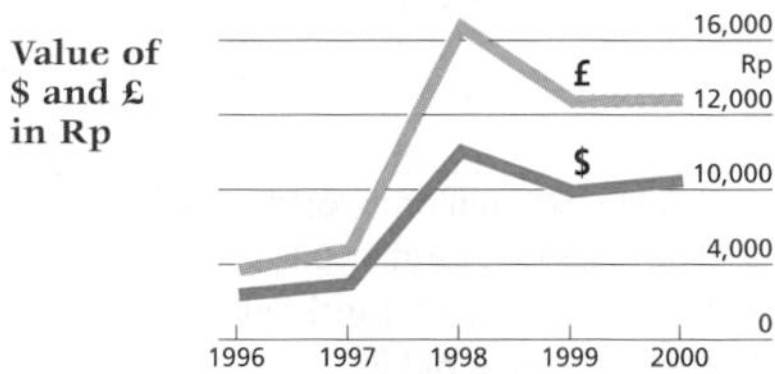

The leading commercial banks, which were recapitalized by the government in 1999–2000, are Bank Mandiri, Bank Negara Indonesia, Bank Central Asia, and Danamon. The fifth-largest bank, Bank Internasional Indonesia, was merged with Bank Mandiri in mid-2001. Some leading banks have insurance company subsidiaries. Bank Indonesia is the central bank and supervisory authority for the finance sector. The Insurance Supervisory Authority of Indonesia and the Capital Markets Supervisory Agency regulate the insurance industry and the stock markets respectively. The 49% equity limitation on foreign bank ownership of domestic banks was lifted in 1999. A similar ruling for stockbrokers was removed in 1998. Maximum income tax is 30%, but from 2001 local administrations have been empowered to raise taxes. The standard rate of VAT is 10%, with a maximum of 35% on luxury goods.

There were 238 banks before the 1997 crisis, but at end-2000 the number was reduced to 151, including five public-sector national banks, 26 public-sector regional development banks, 81 private-sector banks (although most of these are temporarily owned by the government), and 10 foreign banks. The government is encouraging further consolidation. In addition there were 7,764 rural credit banks, but their business with small organizations has been invaded by the commercial banks.

The Jakarta Stock Exchange is the main stock market. There is also a stock exchange at Surabaya and a parallel market. Equities trading grew significantly in the 1990s, but the bond market remains thin. The fixed interest rates of the government's bank recapitalization bonds were not popular while market rates remained high.

Business Opportunities

Tax incentives are available to investors in specific sectors. Foreign investors are expected to train and develop their Indonesian workers. Sectors which are closed to foreign investment include germ plasm cultivation,

Growth in output (% p.a., 1990–99)

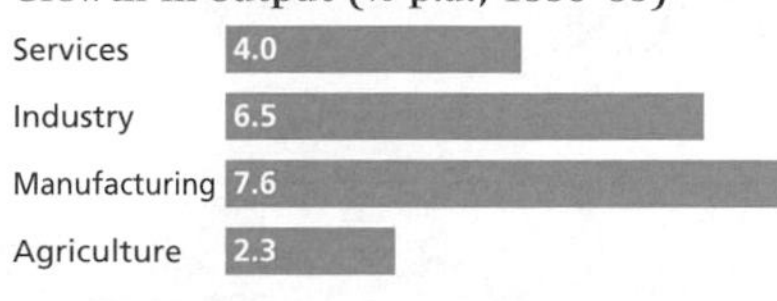

forestry and wood processing, media, bus and taxi transport, small-scale shipping, trading, and services. Special investment conditions apply to hydrocarbons and minerals. Physical security concerns are a disincentive to foreign investment.

Chemicals and pharmaceuticals have attracted the most foreign direct investment, followed by paper, services (including finance and utilities), metal goods, transport, real estate, hotels, and mining (including petroleum and gas). The top investor was Japan, followed by the United Kingdom, Singapore, Taiwan, Hong Kong, and the United States. These sectors, and the privatization program, offer current opportunities for investment. The point of contact for foreign investors is the Board of Investment, but investment approvals are now the remit of local administrations.

For More Information

Books:

Asian Development Bank, Country Economic Review. *Indonesia*. 2000.
IMF Country Report. *Indonesia*. Washington, D.C.: IMF.
Ricklefs, Merle C. *A History of Modern Indonesia since c.1200*. Stanford, CA: Stanford University Press, 2001.
Schwarz, Adam. *A Nation in Waiting*. Boulder, CO: Westview Press, 1999.

Web Sites:

Bank Indonesia (central bank): **www.bi.go.id**
Central Bureau of Statistics: **www.bps.go.id**
Department of Foreign Affairs (government entry point): **www.dfa-deplu.go.id**
Department of Trade and Industry: **www.dprin.go.id**
Economist Intelligence Unit: **www.eiu.com**
Indonesian Tourism Promotion Board: **www.itpb.go.id**

IRAN

KEY FACTS

GNI: **$113,729 million; world's 33rd**
GNI pc: **$1,810; world's 109th**
Head of government: **president**
Currency: **Iranian rial (IR)**
Capital: **Tehran**
Population: **66,796,000, growing at 1.9% p.a.**
Land area: **626,250 square miles**
Population density: **106 per square mile**
Life expectancy: **70 years**
Infant mortality: **37 per 1,000 live births**
Language: **Farsi, Turkic, Kurdish, Luri, Balochi, Arabic, Turkish**
Best buy: **textiles, carpets and rugs, leather goods, woolen goods, jewelry**

ECONOMIC STRUCTURE

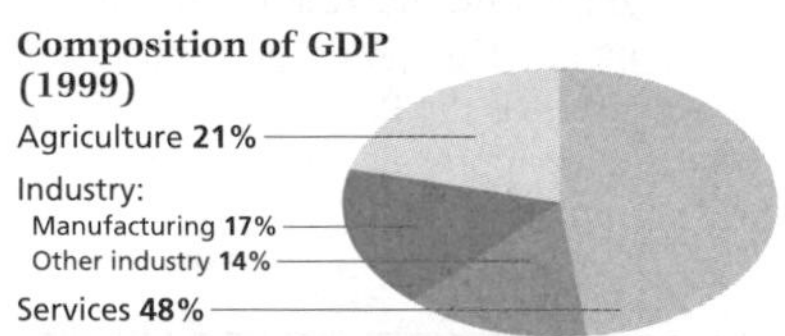

Persia was one of the world's earliest civilizations, with developed scientific, engineering, commercial, banking, and artistic skills. Scientific centers expanded later under Islamic influence. In the 19th century the weak Qajar monarchy allowed Britain and Russia to dominate economic development, which focused on minerals and finance. In 1901 the British gained the concession to exploit Iranian oil, and production by the Anglo-Iranian Oil Company began in 1908. The Abadan refinery, which started operations in 1912, was the first in the Middle East. A British-sponsored coup in 1921 overthrew the Qajar monarchy in favor of the Pahlavi monarchy, which was characterized by the increasing strength of the armed forces (in the 1970s it had the largest arsenal of U.S. arms in the world outside the United States), centralized control, and foreign influence. The oil sector was nationalized in 1951 but an international consortium was formed in 1954 following the collapse of the industry due to international sanctions. Large state companies and banks dominated the economy from the mid-20th century because of trade with the Soviet Union. Until the 1979 Islamic Revolution they coexisted with private-sector banks and companies, including foreign entities. The 1979 constitution stipulates that all minerals entities, other major industries, utilities, communications infrastructure, banks, and insurance companies should be in the public sector and administered by the state. The anti-U.S. stance of the regime was established early, and suspicion between the two countries continues. The 1980s were dominated by the war with Iraq. War damage and international isolation have weighed on the economy, which remains dependent on oil despite efforts to diversify in medium-term development plans from 1949.

Services accounted for 47.9% of GDP in 1999, followed by industry (31.2%) and agriculture (20.9%). Trade and hotels are the main services sector, followed by government services, financial services and real estate, transport, and communications. Petroleum and natural gas contribute around 10–20% of GDP. Refined petroleum products include LPG, naphtha, petrol, aviation gasoline, kerosene, jet fuel, diesel oil, other fuel oils, lubricating oils, asphalt and white spirit. Petrochemicals products include rubber, tires, detergent, acid, fertilizers, glue, synthetic fibers, pesticides, and paint. Nonhydrocarbons industries include metals processing, armaments, transport equipment, machinery, household appliances, communications equipment, cement, textiles, carpets and rugs, cigarettes, and food processing. In 1999–2000 oil and gas represented 82.5% of export value, followed by carpets (3.5%), and fresh and dried fruit (2.6%). Japan was the leading market, absorbing 20.5% of exports, followed by Italy (7%) and U.A.E. (5.9%).

Most economic activity is dominated by the 505 state companies and banks, which were allocated 66% of the 2001–02 national budget. The private sector is mainly limited to small-scale trading and service companies. The first privatization law in 1975 stipulated that 99% of non-basic industries and 49% of private company stocks should be transferred to blue-collar workers and other members of the public, but it was not enacted. In 1989 the legal basis for the separation of the government's regulatory and executive responsibilities was adopted. Decrees in 1991 and 1992 set out guidelines and guide prices for transferring shares to workers. Further legal obstacles were resolved by 1999. In 2000 shares worth IR648 billion in 180 manufacturing units were transferred to 359,270 workers. The industries involved were foods, pharmaceuticals, chemicals, textiles, home appliances, entertainment, automotive, and nonmetallic mining. IR1.8 trillion was allocated to further privatization in 2001–02.

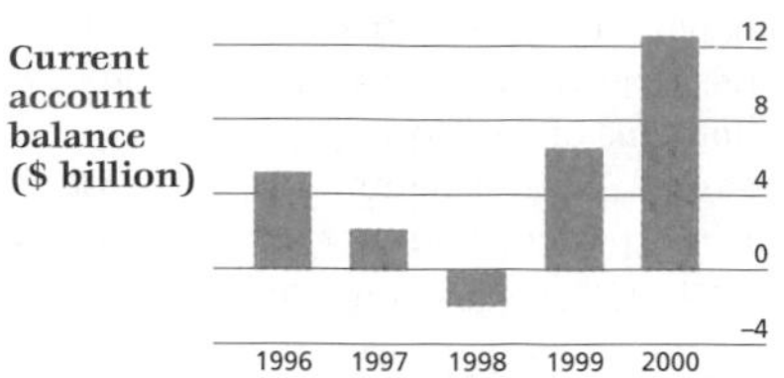

ECONOMIC POLICY

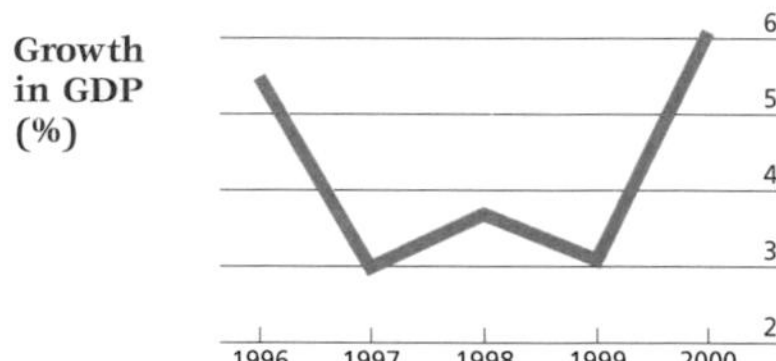

Macro-economic policy has been prudent since 1979, taking account of the large foreign debt inherited from the monarchy, the 1980–88 war with Iraq, and international trade sanctions. International sanctions eased in recent years except those imposed by the United States, which tightened in 1996 to include investments. This resulted in U.S. oil and gas operations being taken over by other foreign companies. Economic policy is essentially socialist, following five-year development plans. Investment is tailored to international oil prices, which led to project delays in the late 1990s but allowed foreign debt reduction. The public debt fell from 36% of GDP in 1998 to 30% in 2000. Recent major oil and gas investments have been conducted with foreign firms on an oil "buy-back" basis to comply with the law preventing foreign companies from holding minerals concessions.

  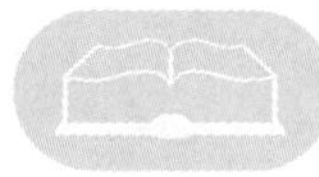      

The key aims of the 1995–2000 plan—privatization and reduction of the size of state organizations, elimination of tax exemptions for state firms, and the establishment of a single rate for foreign exchange—were not achieved, but have been restated in the 2000–05 plan, along with diversification of the economy and the creation of 3.8 million new jobs. Funds allocated to state companies increased in 1995–2000, but the legal basis for privatization was established. The productivity gains are already apparent from the 2000 privatizations. The 2000 law eliminating tax exemptions for state firms has not yet been enacted. The government adopted programs to recapitalize state-owned commercial banks and phase out subsidies. An Oil Stabilization Fund was created in 2000–01 to protect the economy from unforeseen events. The May 2001 foreign investment law provides foreign investment safeguards and dispute settlement procedures. A single foreign exchange rate, to be organized on a managed float basis, was due to be introduced by March 2002.

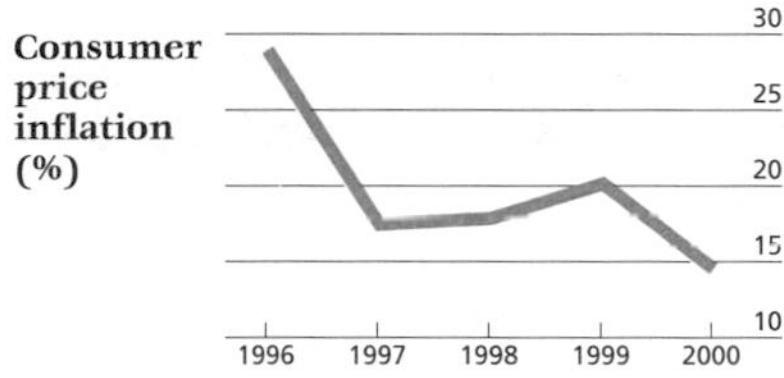

Real GDP growth averaged 3.5% a year in 1996–2000, while inflation averaged 19.5%. Growth was 5.6% for the year ending March 2001. It is expected to weaken in 2001–02 and revive in 2002–03. Strong oil receipts are expected to sustain the trade surplus in 2002. Inflation was 12.6% in March 2001. Unemployment was an average 12.5% in 1997–2001.

Geography/Resources

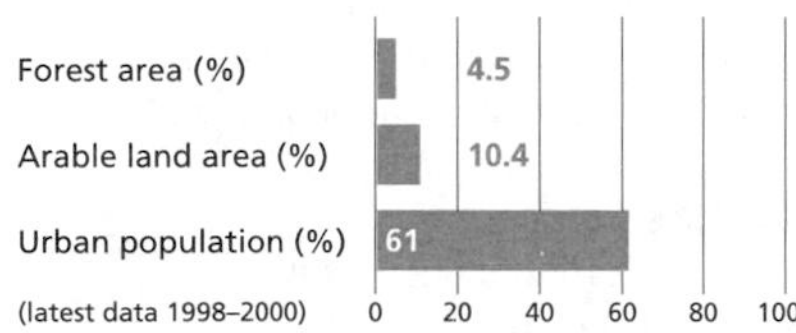

In western Asia, Iran borders Armenia, Azerbaijan, the Caspian Sea, and Turkmenistan in the north, Afghanistan and Pakistan in the east, the Arabian Gulf in the south, and Iraq and Turkey in the west. Most of the land is mountainous, with high mountains and a high point of 18,606 feet, a central plateau, narrow coastal plains, and a low point of –92 feet at the Caspian Sea. The climate is mostly arid with a temperature range of 131°F to 0°F. Natural hazards include droughts, floods, dust storms, and earthquakes on the western border and in the northeast. A major dam on the longest river, the Karkheh, opened in 2001 and will reduce flooding and increase water supply. The majority of the population is of Persian origin (51%), while Azeris constitute 24%, Gilaki and Mazandarani 8%, Kurds 7%, Arabs 3%, and Luri, Balochi, and Turkmens 2% each.

Agriculture is varied, strengthened by major investment in irrigation. The main cash crops are fruit, nuts, and flowers. Wheat, rice, barley, corn, potatoes, legumes, sugar beet, sugar cane, vegetables, tea, tobacco, and cotton are grown. Chickens are the main livestock, followed by sheep, goats, cattle, asses, buffaloes, horses, camels, and mules. Meat, dairy, wool, and leather are produced. Fisheries—including high-value products such as caviar and shellfish—and forestry are important.

Iran is richly endowed with mineral resources. Petroleum, natural gas, coal, chromium, copper, iron, lead, manganese, zinc, magnesite, fluorspar, barytes, salt, and gypsum are produced. There are also reserves of sulfur, gold, chromite, bauxite, strontium, and asbestos. In January 2001 proven oil reserves were at least 90 billion barrels (about 9% of the world total), while proven natural gas reserves at 812 trillion cubic feet were the second largest in the world after those of Russia. New oil finds in the 1990s could add 30 billion barrels to reserves. These new fields are being developed with foreign companies. Recoverable coal reserves were 213 million tons in 1997.

Communications/Energy

PCs	1.0
Telephone lines	3.1
Mobiles	1.7
Internet users	0.9
(per 100 people, 2000)	0 20 40 60 80 100

The road network was 104,400 miles in March 2001, including 1,200 miles of motorways. Paved roads accounted for 58% of the total. The rail network was 5,000 miles in March 2001. State-owned Iranian Islamic Republic Railways carried 10.26 million passengers and 21.6 million tons of freight in 1997. The pipeline network includes 3,700 miles for crude oil, 2,400 miles for petroleum products, and 4,345 miles for natural gas. A further 1,307 miles of gas pipelines will be built under the current development plan. There are 562 miles of inland waterways, including Lake Rezaiyeh in northwest Iran, and the Karun and Shatt al-Arab rivers. The main sea ports for general cargo are Bandar Shahid Rajai, Bandar Khomeini, Bushehr, Bandar Abbas and Chah Bahar. The main oil port is at Kharg Island. The main Caspian Sea ports are Bandar Anzali and Bandar Nowshahr. The merchant fleet over 1,000 grt numbered 152 ships in 2000, representing a total displacement of 4.1 million grt. Iran has OPEC's largest oil tanker fleet. The main international airports are at Tehran and Abadan. There are 47 other commercial airports. In 1998–99 Tehran's Mehrabad Airport handled 8 million passengers and 49,714 tons of freight.

Domestic telecommunications links are provided by microwave radio relay. Major investment in the system extended phone services to 26,615 rural communities and Internet services to 90 cities by 2000, with 80% of the systems design and equipment produced in Iran. International links are provided by fiber-optic cable, microwave radio relay, and satellite. There were 9.3 million fixed phone lines and 875,000 mobile phones in March 2001.

Iran is largely self-sufficient in energy resources, but in 2001 it began importing natural gas from Turkmenistan for consumption in the north, far from its own gas fields. It also conducts oil swaps with international oil companies for Turkmen, Kazakh, and Azeri oil to supply northern refineries. It imports refined oil products, but is expanding domestic refining capacity to meet rapidly increasing domestic demand. Natural gas accounts for 44% of total domestic energy needs, oil for 54%, and coal for 1%. Electricity is mostly generated from fossil fuels (oil and gas 92.3%), with hydroelectric power accounting for the rest. Two 1.3 GW nuclear power stations are under construction at Beshehr, with completion due in March 2004. Crude oil production was 3.9 million barrels per day in 2000–01. In 1999 natural gas output was 1.87 trillion cubic feet and coal production was 1 million tons.

Education/Employment

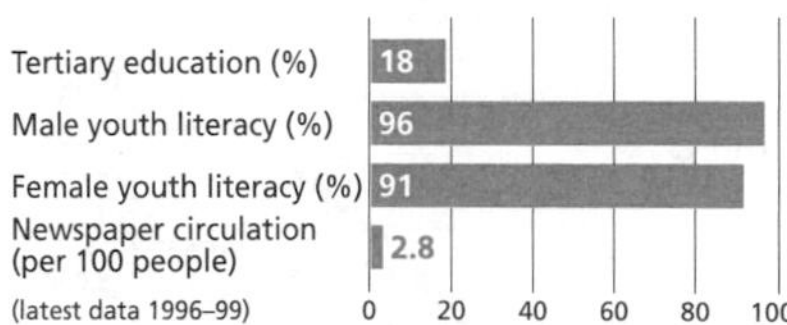

Education is compulsory and free from age 6 to 10. Teacher training and vocational training take place at secondary school level, and enrolment was 21,210 and 347,008 respectively in 1994–95. There are 50 universities affiliated to the Ministry of Culture and Higher Education, and 33

affiliated to the Ministry of Health Treatment and Medical Education. These two ministries are responsible for planning education policy and programs and for supervising higher education establishments, including non-governmental universities and the 53 government universities connected with other ministries. They are also responsible for the 29 research institutes. Higher education enrolment was 600,000 students in the state sector and 650,000 students in the non-state sector in 1996–97. There were also 200,000 students following distance learning courses. From 1991 employers and employees have been allowed to establish guilds which issue vocational licenses.

Iran has developed R&D strengths in earthquake science, oceanography, computing, telecommunications, metallurgy, materials science, chemicals, mechanical engineering, structural engineering, medicine, and agriculture.

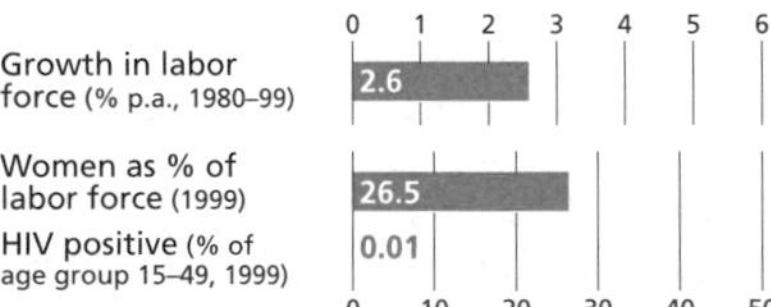

The labor force has a wide range of skills, which include a high level of technical expertise. The Supreme Labor Council sets annual minimum wages for each industrial sector and region. The Labor Code stipulates a six day working week with a maximum of 48 hours, one rest day a week (usually Friday), and a minimum 12 days of paid annual leave with public holidays in addition. Safety committees are established in organizations with over 10 employees. The only authorized workers' organization is the Worker's House, established in 1982. Its representatives liaise with Islamic labor councils, which include worker and management representatives and which are present in organizations with over 35 employees.

Fiscal/Financial

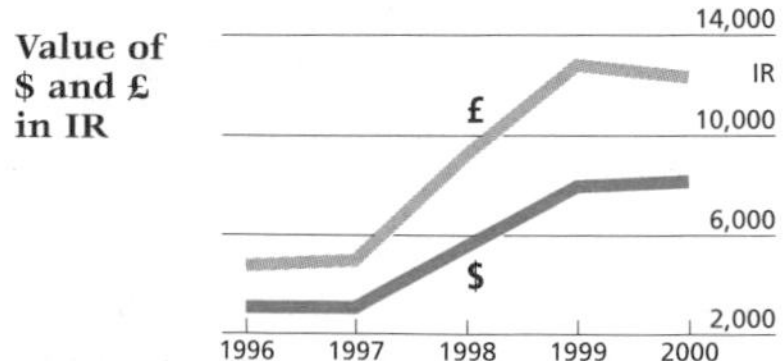

Bank Melli Iran is the largest bank in terms of deposits, followed by Bank Mellat and Bank Tejarat. All banks and insurance companies were nationalized following the 1979 Revolution. The first private bank since the Revolution was licensed in September 2001. Bank Markazi Jomhouri Islami Iran is the central bank. The Council of Money and Credit regulates all Iranian banks, and sets interest rates and other financial conditions. The insurance industry is regulated by reinsurance company Bimeh Markazi Iran, the only authorized reinsurer. Insurance companies are obliged to reinsure half of their life insurance business and 25% of their general insurance. State companies enjoy tax exemption. A 2000 law ends this status in accordance with current policy, but tax exemptions for state firms were written into the 2001–02 budget. Private-sector companies can deduct from tax any profits held back for productive investment.

The banking sector applies Islamic law, which prohibits "usury" or high interest rates. The set interest rates on bank loans and deposits are often below the rate of inflation. Higher rates apply to commercial operations, and the banks have geared their funds to the business sector. However, banks are also obliged to extend credit, sometimes at low rates, to sectors prioritized by the development plan. There is a high ratio of bad debts, and banks incur heavy expenses trying to collect amounts due. Low interest rates are a disincentive to private investors to place money with the banks. There are nine commercial banks, two development banks (for industry and mining, and exports), and a housing bank (formed through the merger of all pre-Revolution credit institutes). In December 1995 the central bank authorized the first of four new private-sector non-bank credit institutes for savings and loans. Other credit institutes not licensed by the central bank are also in operation. There are no foreign bank branches operating in Iran, but around 30 have representative offices. Iran's first credit card was launched in mid-2001. The Tehran Stock Exchange reopened in 1992.

Business Opportunities

Bureaucracy, financial restrictions, and international trade and investment sanctions are disincentives to foreign investment, which totaled only $40 million in 1993–97. Because of past British and U.S. political interference concerning minerals interests in Iran, all minerals concessions must now be held by nationals, but development is conducted with foreign firms on a "buy-back" basis. The 2001 foreign investment law improves the climate for foreign investment. The government also hopes to attract Iranian private capital back to Iran. Free zones have been established which offer facilities, and tax and other incentives. The Kish Island Free Trade Zone has attracted German and French investment. Major oil, gas, and petrochemicals contracts with French, Malaysian, Russian, Italian, Canadian, and Anglo-Dutch operating companies have been signed since 1998. In 2001 Kuwait announced it would invest in fish farming, agriculture, industry, and construction. These and other sectors continue to offer opportunities to investors.

Growth in output (% p.a., 1990–99)

Services	4.7
Industry	2.8
Manufacturing	4.8
Agriculture	4.2

For More Information

Books:

Abdelkhah, Fariba. *Being Modern in Iran.* New York: Columbia University Press, 1999.

Amuzegar, Jahangir. *Iran's Economy under the Islamic Republic.* New York: I. B. Tauris, 1997.

IMF Country Report. *Islamic Republic of Iran.* Washington, D.C.: IMF.

Pahlavi, Reza. *Winds of Change: The Future of Democracy in Iran.* Washington, D.C.: Regnery Pub., 2002.

Sciolino, Elaine. *Persian Mirrors: The Elusive Face of Iran.* New York: Free Press, 2000.

Wright, Robin B. *The Last Great Revolution: Turmoil and Transformation in Iran.* New York: Vintage Books, 2001.

Web Sites:

Economist Intelligence Unit: **www.eiu.com**

Government entry point: **www.gov.ir**

Iran National Tourist Organization: **www.iran-tourism.com**

Islamic Republic News Agency: **www.irna.com**

Netiran (links to print and broadcast media): **www.netiran.com**

Iraq

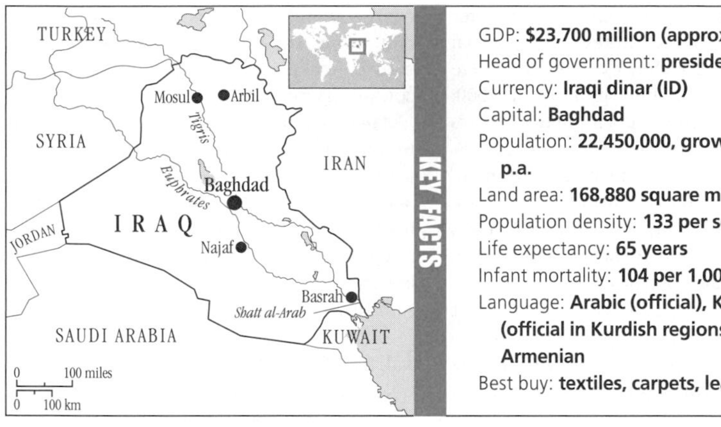

GDP: **$23,700 million (approx.)**
Head of government: **president**
Currency: **Iraqi dinar (ID)**
Capital: **Baghdad**
Population: **22,450,000, growing at 2.4% p.a.**
Land area: **168,880 square miles**
Population density: **133 per square mile**
Life expectancy: **65 years**
Infant mortality: **104 per 1,000 live births**
Language: **Arabic (official), Kurdish (official in Kurdish regions), Assyrian, Armenian**
Best buy: **textiles, carpets, leather goods**

Economic Structure

Modern Iraq covers the territory of ancient Mesopotamia, one of the earliest civilizations. Until the Mongol invasions of the 13th century Baghdad was the capital of the Islamic Empire which extended from Morocco to the Indian subcontinent. Iraq subsequently became part of the Ottoman Empire until 1917, when it came under British control. A monarchy was established at independence in 1932, but this was overthrown in 1958. Land was nationalized and collective farms established. Another coup in 1968 brought the nationalist and socialist Ba'ath Party to power. Foreign-owned companies, which controlled most industry including oil, were nationalized in the mid-1970s. War with Iran from 1980 to 1988 focused resources on the arms industry. The invasion of Kuwait in 1990, and withdrawal in 1991 enforced by an international coalition, was followed by United Nations trade and investment sanctions. These soon began to be broken, and this process continues, but the sanctions remain officially in place.

Petroleum, natural gas, and petrochemicals are the mainstay of the economy, but a large part of the population relies on agriculture. Oil refining, liquid natural gas processing, petrochemicals, and phosphate fertilizers are the main large-scale manufacturing industries. Iron, steel, cement, agricultural and transport equipment, armaments, electronic goods, and paper are also produced. Small-scale manufacturing includes textiles, leather goods, furniture, processed food, and cigarettes.

Crude and refined petroleum accounted for 95% of official exports in 1998 under the UN oil-for-food program. The United States accounted for around 40% of official oil exports in 2000, France for 13%, and Italy for 10%. Syria, Jordan, and Turkey are leading markets for unofficial oil exports, with Syria and Jordan accounting for an estimated $1 billion a year each, and Turkey for $3 billion. There is a UN-approved barter trade between Iraq and Jordan.

The state controls most aspects of the economy. Socialist economic principles are written into the constitution. All large companies are state-owned. The government ended its monopoly on banking in 1991. Private banks were established from 1992, but the sector remains dominated by state entities.

Economic Policy

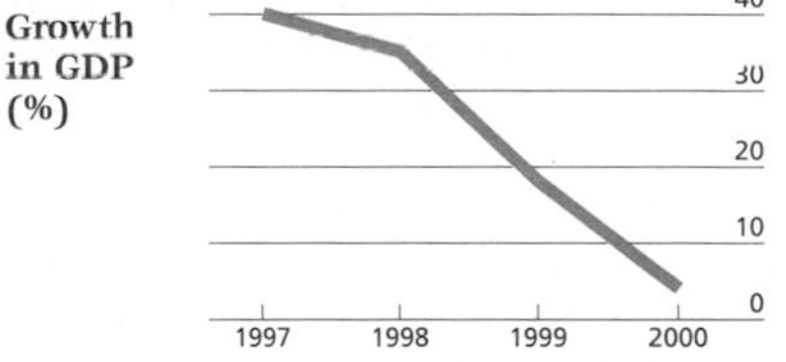

The main thrust of economic policy since 1991 has been to overcome international trade sanctions diplomatically and through the strengthening of trade links with neighboring countries. In mid-2001, following the failure of U.S. and U.K. initiatives at the United Nations to tighten sanctions, trade links with Arab and Islamic countries increased. They included the signing of free trade zone agreements with Syria, Egypt, Tunisia, and Yemen, progress on building a new oil pipeline to Jordan and a new gas pipeline to Turkey, and the opening of air links with Syria and Yemen. Germany and Japan reopened embassies in Baghdad in 2000, and trade delegations from European and Asian countries visited. Links with Russia and China are strong.

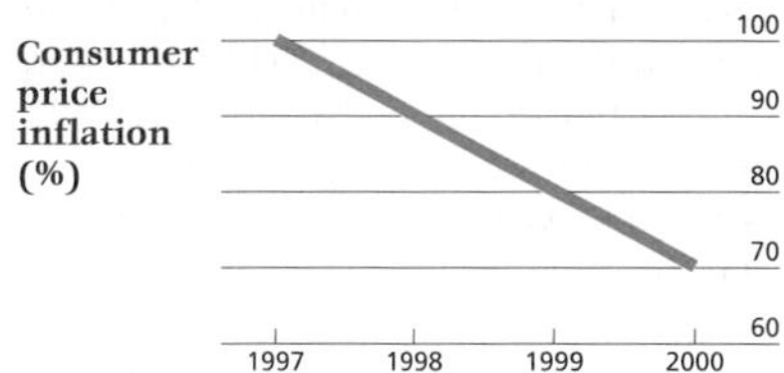

Annual GDP growth was 11% in 1995–99, while annual inflation was 190%. In the early 1990s GDP was estimated to be in severe decline. Growth was estimated at 4% in 2000 and 6% in 2002, with 7% expected in 2002. Inflation was estimated at 70% in 2000. Estimates of unemployment are high.

Geography/Resources

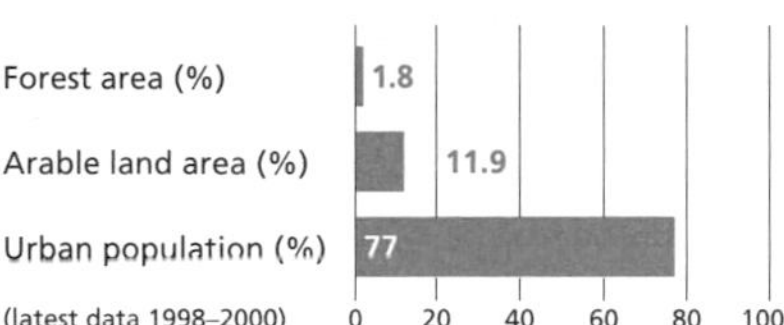

A Middle Eastern state, Iraq has a very small coastline at the north of the Arabian Gulf. It has land borders with Kuwait to the southeast, Saudi Arabia to the south, Jordan to the southwest, Syria to the west, Turkey to the north, and Iran to the east. The mighty Euphrates and Tigris rivers run from central Syria and from the Syrian-Turkish border respectively across the country, converging in the Shatt al-Arab river which reaches the Arabian Gulf at Faw on the Iranian border. The rivers provide broad, fertile alluvial plains. The Zagros mountains in the north have a high point of 12,232 feet. The low-lying swamps of the southeast have been extensively drained in the last decade. Desert to the west of the Euphrates constitutes 35% of the land. The climate is continental and dry, with hot summers, especially in the south, and cold winters, especially in the north. Temperatures in Baghdad range from 122°F to 48°F. The central plains have annual rainfall of less than 6 inches, while the desert has no rainfall. Precipitation is heaviest in the northern mountains.

Irrigation between the Euphrates and Tigris rivers allows for a diversified agriculture, but irrigation infrastructure fell into disrepair in the 1990s. Rain-fed agriculture is stronger in the northern Kurdish region. Wheat, barley, rice, corn, vegetables, fruit,

tobacco, and cotton are grown. Iraq was the world's largest producer and exporter of dates before the imposition of international trade sanctions. The main livestock is poultry, followed by sheep, goats, cattle, asses, buffaloes, horses, mules, and camels. Meat, dairy, wool, and leather are important products. There are small forestry and fishing industries. Before the Gulf War, Iraq imported 70% of its food needs. The UN-controlled oil-for-food program has been in place since 1996, but Iraq has not fully used this facility.

The main minerals produced are petroleum and natural gas, followed by gypsum, salt, phosphates, and sulfur. There are small reserves of iron, gold, lead, copper, silver, platinum, and zinc, and larger reserves of lignite. Proven oil reserves were 112.5 billion barrels at January 2001, the second largest in the world after Saudi Arabia. There are a further 215 billion barrels of probable reserves. Proven gas reserves were 110 trillion cubic feet at January 2001, with a further 150 trillion cubic feet in probable reserves, mostly associated with oil. Part of the Western Desert oil-bearing formations still remains to be explored.

The majority of people (70%) live in urban areas. About 80% are of Arab origin, while 15% are of Kurdish origin, and there are smaller minorities of Jazirah Bedouins, Turkomans, Sabaeans, Jews, and Yazidis.

Communications/Energy

Telephone lines (per 100 people, 2000): 2.9 (scale 0 20 40 60 80 100)

At end-1996 the road network comprised 29,454 miles, of which 25,328 miles was paved. The rail network operated by State Enterprise for Iraqi Railways was 1,261 miles in 1996. The pipeline network comprised 2,703 miles for crude oil, 450 miles for refined oil products, and 845 miles for natural gas. It is being extended. Inland waterways total 631 miles and link to the sea port of Basrah. The main sea port is Umm Qasr, close to the Kuwaiti border. The oil port of Faw on the Iranian border ceased to be used by Iraq during the Iraq-Iran war. In 2000 the merchant fleet comprised 30 ships over 1,000 grt with total displacement of 453,273 grt. Airports and airstrips suffered heavy damage during the Gulf War. The international airports are at Baghdad and Basrah. National carrier Iraqi Airways has been grounded since the Gulf War, as former allies against Iraq imposed no-fly zones in the north and south of the country. New air links with Syria were opened in 2001.

The telecommunications network was severely damaged during the Gulf War, but has been largely rebuilt. Cable and microwave radio relay links provide domestic and international connections, the latter via Jordan, Syria, and Turkey. International links are also provided by satellite. There were 675,000 fixed-line phones in 2000. Internet connection is limited, and is government-controlled.

Electricity is generated mostly from indigenous fossil fuels (98%), with hydroelectricity producing the rest. However, power plants were extensively damaged in the Gulf War, and power cuts are frequent. Oil production was 2.29 million barrels per day in 2000–01, with consumption at 0.4–0.5 million barrels per day. Natural gas production and consumption were 112 billion cubic feet in 1999.

Education/Employment

Primary education from age 6 to 12 is compulsory and free. Secondary education from age 12 to 18 is free, but not compulsory. In the late 1980s higher education establishments had enrollment of around 209,800 students, but the level is estimated to have fallen in the 1990s. There are seven universities, an institute of administration, an institute of applied arts, 22 technical institutes, and several teacher training institutes. The Ministry of Education has overall responsibility for education, and there is a separate Minister for Higher Education and Scientific Research. All education is state-funded. Iraq has developed R&D strengths in weapons technology, including biological, chemical, and nuclear applications.

The labor force has a range of skills. An amendment to the 1987 Labor Law adopted in April 2000 provides for a committee to set and conduct an annual review of minimum wages. The new law also limits working time to 300 hours a year, and requires employers to allow employees to take annual leave. Trade union rights are recognized under the constitution.

Fiscal/Financial

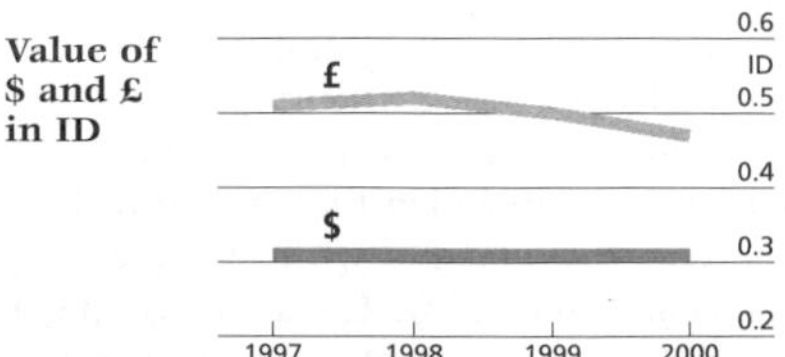

The largest banks are state-owned. They are Rafidain Bank, followed by Rashid bank and Real Estate Bank of Iraq. Two of the three insurance companies are state-owned, Iraq Life Insurance Company and Iraq Reinsurance Company. Central Bank of Iraq is the central bank and has responsibility for regulating the financial sector. It sets commercial bank interest rates and other conditions for different types of accounts.

Apart from the two state-owned commercial banks, there are two private-sector commercial banks, two general investment banks, two agricultural banks, an industrial investment bank, an Islamic bank and the real estate bank. The Baghdad stock market is managed by the Capital Markets Authority.

Business Opportunities

UN sanctions constitute significant barriers to investment and trade, but the international community has a diminishing appetite for applying them. Iraq's rehabilitation with its neighbors and other Arab and Islamic countries is gathering momentum, leading to increased trade. Investment is needed in the oil industry and agriculture, as well as in healthcare and education, and in most industries. But progress will depend on the willingness of foreign countries to break sanctions. Political uncertainty has increased since Iraq was accused of involvement in the September 11, 2001 terrorist attacks in the United States. Investment from Russia, China, and France is involved in the development of oil and gas.

For More Information

Books:

Baram, Amatzia, ed. *Cultural History and Ideology in the Formation of Ba'athist Iraq, 1968–89*. New York: Palgrave Macmillan, 1991.

Mackay, Sandra. *The Reckoning: Iraq and the Legacy of Saddam Hussein*. New York: W. W. Norton, 2002.

Marr, Phebe. *Modern History of Iraq*. Boulder, CO: Westview Press, 2002.

Thesiger, Wilfred. *Arabian Sands*. New York: Viking Books, 1985.

Web Sites:

Iraq News Agency: **www.uruklink.net/iraqnews**

Iraq Resources Information Site: **www.geocities.com/iraqinfo**

Ministry of Foreign Affairs: **www.uruklink.net/mofa**

  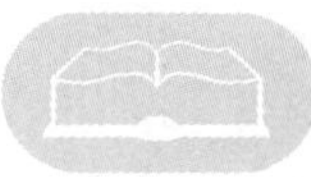  

IRELAND

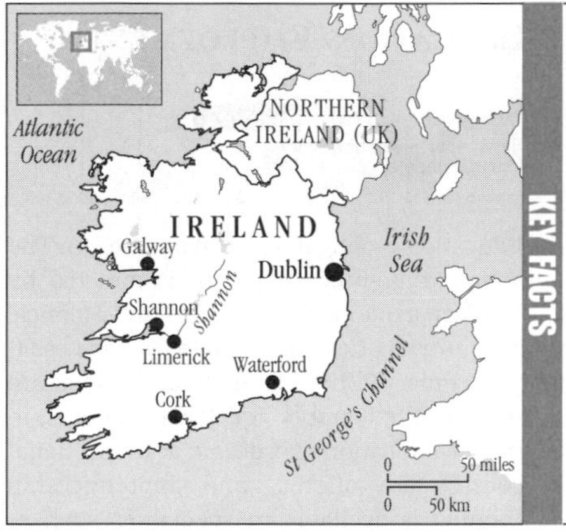

KEY FACTS

GNI: **$80,559 million; world's 40th**
GNI pc: **$21,470; world's 24th**
Head of government: **prime minister**
Currency: **Euro (€)**
Capital: **Dublin**
Population: **3,705,000, growing at 0.6% p.a.**
Land area: **27,136 square miles**
Population density: **139 per square mile**
Life expectancy: **77 years**
Infant mortality: **6 per 1,000 live births**
Language: **Irish, English**
Best buy: **Waterford crystal, Aran sweaters, Irish whiskey**

ECONOMIC STRUCTURE

Composition of GDP (1999)

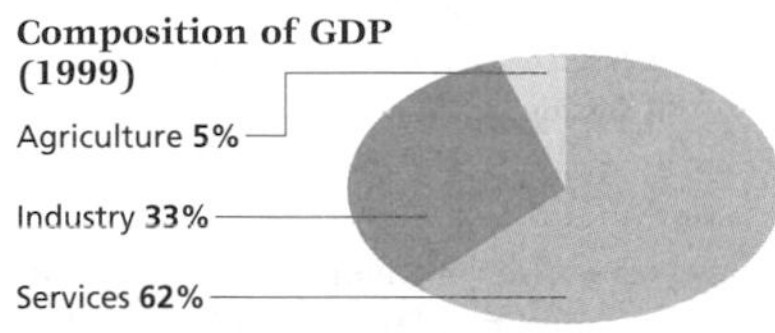

When the Irish State was founded in 1922 the industrial sector was small and based on farming, for example textiles, food, and drink. Production was for the home market. In the 1930s protectionist measures failed to promote industrial expansion as intended. In 1958 the government introduced the first export incentives. The Industrial Development Authority was given the role of helping indigenous industry and encouraging foreign inward investment in export goods such as electronics, engineering, and pharmaceuticals. Exports rose from 37% of GNP in 1973 to 86% in 1998. The importance of agriculture, both in production and employment, has fallen gradually, and although it remains an important sector, services and manufacturing have dominated the economy since the early 1990s.

Services (private and public) accounted for 58% of GDP and 63% of jobs in 1999. The largest sector of services includes banking and insurance, tourism, telephone call centers, and other private-sector services. Manufacturing, mining, construction, and utilities contributed 38% of GDP and 28% of jobs. Manufacturing is the largest component in this group. Agriculture and forestry accounted for 4% of GDP and 8.5% of jobs. The main export markets in 2000 were the United Kingdom (19.8%), followed by the United States (17.1%), Germany (11.3%), France (7.7%), and Netherlands (5.6%). The main exports were pharmaceuticals and chemicals (34%), followed by computer equipment and software (23%), machinery (16%), and livestock and food (7%). Ireland and the United States are the largest exporters of computer software in the world, the Irish software going to other EU countries.

Current account balance ($ billion)

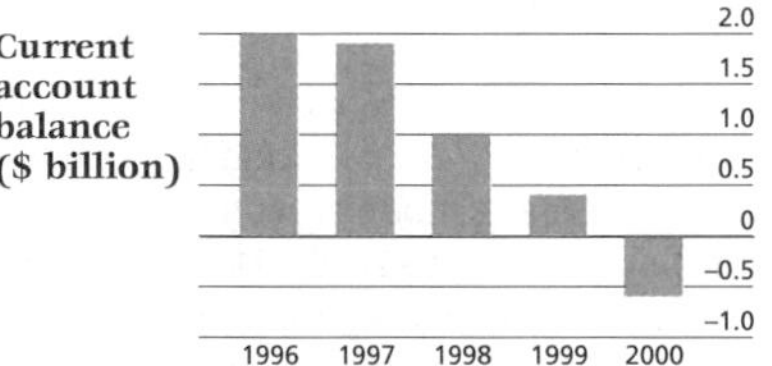

At the end of the 1990s there were 100 state-sponsored organizations, employing over 60,000 people. Telecom Eireann, the telecommunications company, was fully privatized in 1999 under a new name, Eircom, this sector having been fully opened to competition in December 1998. The Electricity Regulation Act came into effect in July 1999, providing an independent regulator for the industry and preparing the introduction of competition to 28% of the sector by February 2000 and 100% by 2006. The Electricity Supply Board and the Bord Gais are to be formed into public limited companies. New operators had access to the gas network from 2000. Inland bus and air transport have been liberalized, but the railways and urban buses remain largely under state control. The privatization of state-owned banks began in 2000. The partial privatization of Aer Lingus, the national airline, had to be postponed in 2001 on account of the worldwide crisis in air transport.

ECONOMIC POLICY

Growth in GDP (%)

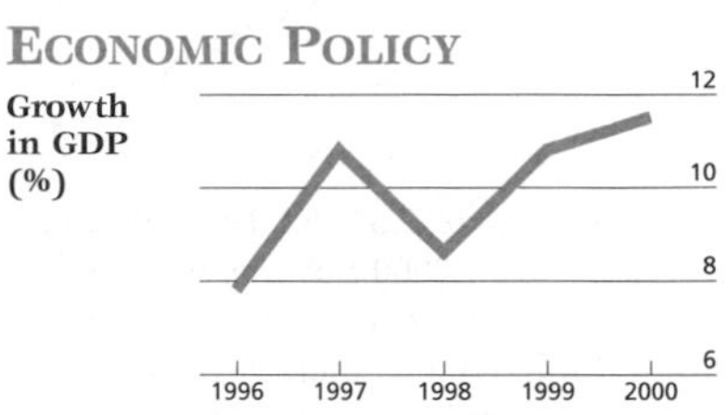

Careful management of the economy, especially through wage restraint, fiscal measures, and the promotion of industry and services, has enabled the government to reduce the high level of public debt from 97% of GDP in 1986–90 to an expected 36% of GDP by 2002. Government deficits were transformed to surpluses from 1997, and have grown since then to an expected 2.7% in 2001. This strong performance of public finances has been achieved through rapid economic growth and buoyant tax receipts. Inflation has been kept low through wage restraint and tax cuts. Under the 2000–06 National Development Plan, the government is planning to remove transport bottlenecks through increased public investment, overcome structural labor force problems through tax reforms, and foster greater competition through further deregulation and privatization. The government has embarked on public–private finance initiatives to improve project management and to spread the risks of infrastructure costs.

Consumer price inflation (%)

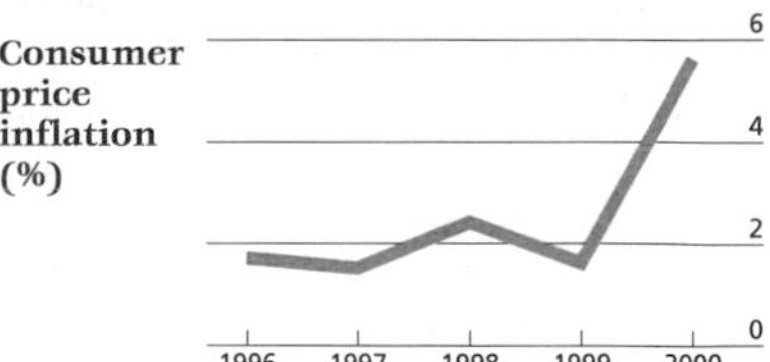

Ireland has the fastest-growing economy of the European Union and of the OECD area. Annual average growth was 9.9% in 1996–2000. Growth levels of 5.7% and 5.1% are expected in 2002 and 2003. Rapid growth was spurred by high-tech export industries, especially chemicals and computers, and more latterly by domestic demand, as real disposable incomes and private consumption have risen following tax cuts. The slower growth expected in the medium term is the result of capacity limitations in the labor market and manufacturing plant, and of the slowdown in export markets.

Inflation has maintained an annual average rate of 2.1% from 1995 to 2000, down

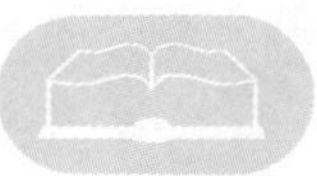

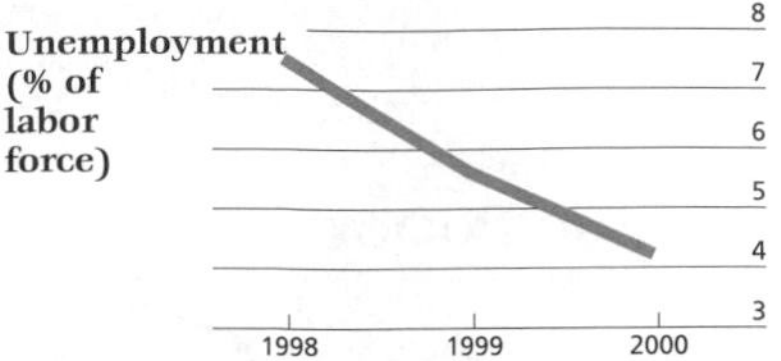

from an average of 2.5% for 1991–95. Inflation was 5.6% in 2000 but was expected to ease in 2001. Property prices increased sharply. Employment increased rapidly in the closing years of the 1990s, with growth of 5.1% in 1999, up from the annual average of 1.9% in 1991–95. Jobs were expected to increase by 3.5% and 2.7% in 2000 and 2001. Unemployment has fallen from traditionally high levels of around 15% from 1986–95 to 5.8% in 1999, and levels of 4.2% in 2000 and approximately 4% in 2001.

Geography/Resources

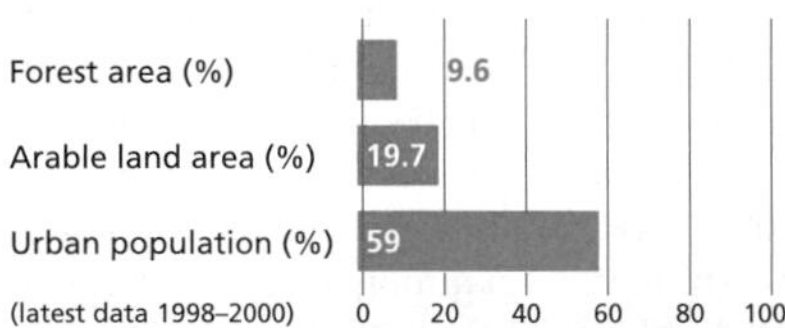

The Republic of Ireland covers most of the island of Ireland to the south and west of Northern Ireland, and has a total area of 27,136 square miles. It has a mild Atlantic climate with relatively high rainfall and few extremes of temperature. The land comprises a central lowland area of limestone with a relief of hills, some containing bog land, and coastal mountains, which consist mainly of red sandstone and granite.

About 71% of the land is farmed or forested. Cattle raising and dairy farming account for 85% of agricultural output. Crops include barley, wheat, sugar beet, potatoes, and mushrooms. High-value farmed shellfish and salmon are a feature of fisheries. Timber production was 88 million cubic feet in 1999. Sand, gravel, and stone are quarried for the construction industry. Ireland is the leading European producer of zinc. New mines coming onstream were expected to double production from the 1998 levels of 181,000 tons of zinc and 36,000 tons of lead. Silver, natural gas, and peat are also produced.

The population was 3.7 million in 1999, with 41% under age 25. Since the late 1990s there has been net immigration. In 1999 55% of immigrants were returning Irish nationals, 17% were British, and 14% were from other EU countries. The main centers of population are the Dublin area (1 million at the 1996 census), Cork (180,000), Limerick (79,000), Galway (57,000), and Waterford (44,000). The majority of people are of Celtic origin.

Communications/Energy

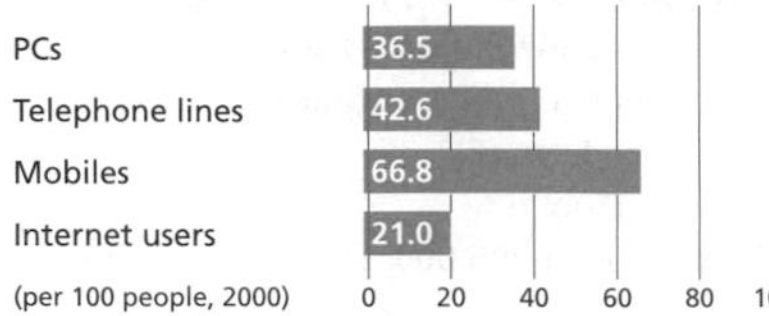

There is heavy dependence on the 57,500 miles of roads because of the traditionally rural, low-density nature of the population. There are bus services throughout the country, and Bus Eireann carries 84 million passengers a year. The 1,240-mile rail network carried 32 million passengers in 1998. A rapid transit light rail system is being built in Dublin. Coras Iompair Eireann (CIE) is the state-owned company responsible for public rail and bus transport, and for the 435 miles of inland waterways. There are international airports at Shannon, Cork, and Dublin. The state-owned airline Aer Lingus carried 6 million passengers and 42,000 tons of freight in 1999. The main private airlines are Ryanair and CityJet.

The Office for the Director of Telecommunications licenses and oversees telecoms service providers, cable TV, and radio networks. There are seven fixed-line phone operators. There were 1.59 million fixed phone lines, 2.5 million mobiles, and 784,000 Internet users at end-2000. Domestic and international links are assured by cable, satellite, and microwave radio relay. Switching is digital. Regulations were introduced in 1999 to facilitate broadband communications and integrated services. In 2000 the government underwrote a $80 million high-speed Internet link with the United States to ensure that multinational companies had a sufficiently powerful e-commerce infrastructure. The government's strategy is to make high-speed Internet access more available generally at much reduced cost.

The Electricity Supply Board (ESB) operates 24 power stations and the supply grid. Demand is growing by 5% a year, and the ESB has launched a major power station construction program. The interconnector with Northern Ireland was recommissioned in 1995. Natural gas accounted for 41% of power generation in 1999, coal for 20%, oil for 19%, hydro for 11.5%, and peat for 7%. Offshore natural gas reserves supplied 20% of domestic demand. Reserves were due to be depleted by 2004, but the prospects for new discoveries looked good in 2000. Oil and coal are imported. There are extensive peat reserves, and annual production amounts to 900,000 tons of oil equivalent.

Education/Employment

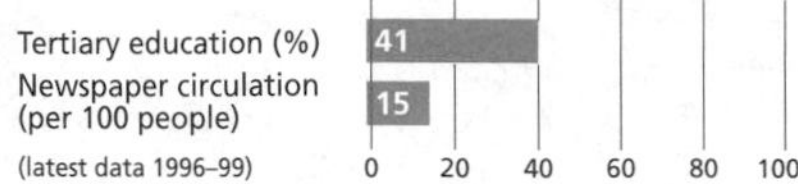

Education is obligatory from age 6 to 15. The largely state-funded system is directed by the Department of Education and Science, but universities and colleges are self-governing. Tuition is free, and there are means-tested grants for Irish students in higher education. Academic and vocational courses are offered, and apprenticeship training is available in specialties such as engineering, construction, printing, and furniture-making. The government is promoting adult education. In 1997 it established a fund to develop technology education at all levels and a separate project to link every school in the country to the Internet.

There are four universities: the University of Dublin (Trinity College), the National University of Ireland (with colleges in Dublin, Cork, Galway, and Maynooth), the University of Limerick, and Dublin City University. There are 12 institutes of technology offering courses in business, engineering, technology, science, and paramedicine. In recent years several private colleges have opened, offering business courses. Half of young people go into higher education, and half of these take degrees.

Pharmaceuticals and information technology are private-sector R&D strengths. Private R&D spending rose to the EU average by 1999. The government has allocated €2.48 billion for R&D in the 2000–06 National Development Plan to raise its hitherto low participation. Specialties in the public sector include agriculture and food, peat, health, and physics.

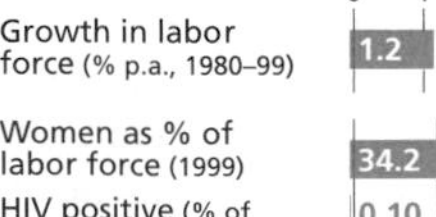

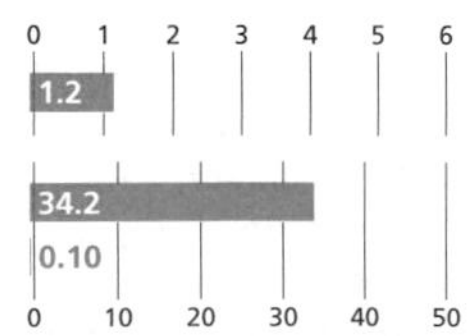

Ireland has one of the youngest labor forces in Western Europe: the baby-boom generation of the 1970s has come on to the job market in the last decade. Real unit labor costs have fallen, and productivity has risen constantly since 1961. Costs fell by 2.6% a year and productivity rose by an annual

4.1% in 1996–99. Negotiations between the government, trade unions, and employers are enshrined in partnership agreements which include tax cuts as well as pay increases and labor conditions. The current agreement is the Program for Prosperity and Fairness 2000–02, which has the competitiveness of the Irish economy and social inclusion at its core. In addition 1% of GNP per annum has been set aside by the government to prefund pensions when the population ages. Ireland applies EU employment law, which covers safety at work, wages and working hours, industrial relations, employment incentives, and unemployment provision.

Fiscal/Financial

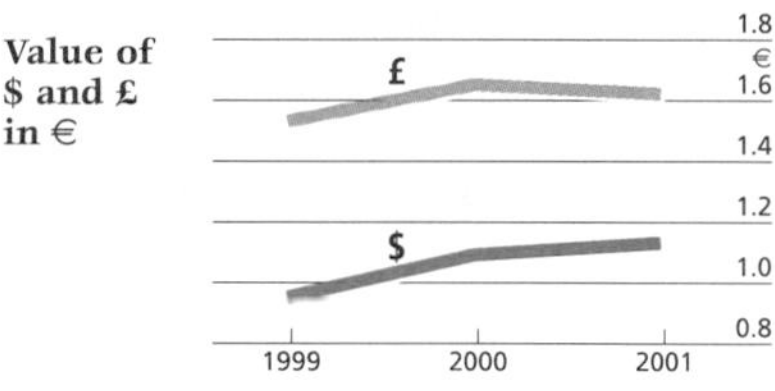

The main banks include private-sector retail clearing banks AIB Group, Bank of Ireland Group, National Irish Bank, TSB Bank, and Ulster Banks. The leading life insurance companies at end-1999 were Irish Life, Friends First Life, and Ark Life. The leading non-life insurance firms were AXA PMPA, Allianz, and Hibernian Insurance.

Standard corporation tax was 20% in 2001 and 16% in 2002, and will be reduced to 12.5% by January 2003. Until end-2002 most domestic and foreign companies are operating with an effective rate of 10%. Three regimes currently qualify for the 10% rate: manufacturing, the Shannon Airport Zone, and the International Financial Services Center (IFSC) in Dublin. Manufacturing and some service companies complying with these conditions will retain the 10% rate until 2010. Financial services companies and Shannon industrial zone companies will retain the 10% rate until 2005. However, projects established after July 22, 1998 will be subject to the new standard rate in January 2003. The tax regime has been altered following EU pressure, but Irish corporation tax will probably remain the lowest in the EU. Capital gains tax is 20%.

The regulatory authority is the Bank Ceannais na Eireann, which is also part of the European System of Central Banks. This body and the European Central Bank set the policy for the Euro. The government is pledged to reform the domestic regulatory structure, and may establish a single authority for all branches of finance. In early 2001 there were over 370 Irish and foreign banks and credit institutions at the IFSC, which was established in 1987. The advent of foreign banks has developed the sophistication and internationalism of the sector to provide all corporate banking needs. Insurance services are also well developed, with several major international players present. Venture capital funding of domestic industry experienced significant growth in the 1990s. Credit unions, of which there were 438 in 1998, are set to play a larger role, as they will be licensed to offer a wider range of services. E-banking and e-commerce are fast-growing areas.

The Irish Stock Exchange is part of the Euro block of European stock exchanges. It uses the Xetra electronic trading platform of the Deutsche Börse in a strategic alliance with the German exchange. It has a main market, a developing companies market, and an exploration securities market. FINEX Europe, part of the New York Cotton Exchange group, began trading currency futures in Dublin in 1994. A branch of the New York Futures Exchange was established in 1998.

Business Opportunities

Apart from the advantage of the lowest tax rate in the EU, investors can benefit from Irish government and EU finance for various projects. As per capita income is still below the EU average, Ireland qualifies for EU Cohesion Fund aid and for EU structural and regional grants, most of which require matching funds. The government offers support to R&D projects and for the professional training of employees. The current privatization programs in the banking, energy, and transport sectors offer investment opportunities. The Irish Development Agency is the point of contact for potential foreign investors.

Over 1,140 foreign firms have established manufacturing bases in Ireland. Since 1980 Ireland has attracted 40% of U.S. direct foreign investment in electronics in Europe. There is also U.S. investment in pharmaceuticals, biotechnology, banking, and graphic design for the film industry. Other main investors include the United Kingdom, Germany, other EU countries, and Switzerland. The main sectors for foreign investment are computer hardware and software, pharmaceuticals, medical products, fine chemicals, cosmetics, banking, insurance, and call centers.

For More Information

Books:

Ardagh, John. *Ireland and the Irish: Portrait of a Changing Society*. New York: Penguin U.S.A., 1997.

Butler, Joe, ed. *Business Ireland*. Dublin: Irish Development Agency. (Quarterly newsletter; also available online from the Irish Development Agency Web site.)

IMF Country Report. *Ireland*. Washington, D.C.: IMF.

Irish Development Agency: *Business Ireland*. (Quarterly newsletter in print and online.)

Keogh, Dermot. *Twentieth-century Ireland: Nation and State*. Dublin: Gill & Macmillan, 1993.

Lee, Joseph. *Ireland 1912–85: Politics and Society*. New York: Cambridge University Press, 1989.

Ministry of Foreign Affairs. *Ireland in Brief*.

National Treasury Management Agency. *Ireland Information Memorandum*. Dublin: March, 2001.

OECD Economic Surveys. *Ireland*. Paris: OECD, 2001.

Web Sites:

Central Bank of Ireland: **www.centralbank.ie**

Central Statistics Office: **www.cso.ie**

Irish Banks' Information Service: **www.ibis.ie**

Irish Development Agency: **www.ida.ie**

Irish government entry point: **www.irlgov.ie**

Irish Independent (newspaper): **www.independent.ie**

Irish Insurance Federation: **www.iif.ie**

The Irish Times (newspaper): **www.ireland.ie**

Ministry of Foreign Affairs: **www.irlgov.ie/iveagh**

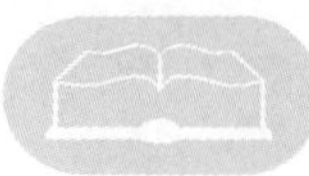

Isle of Man

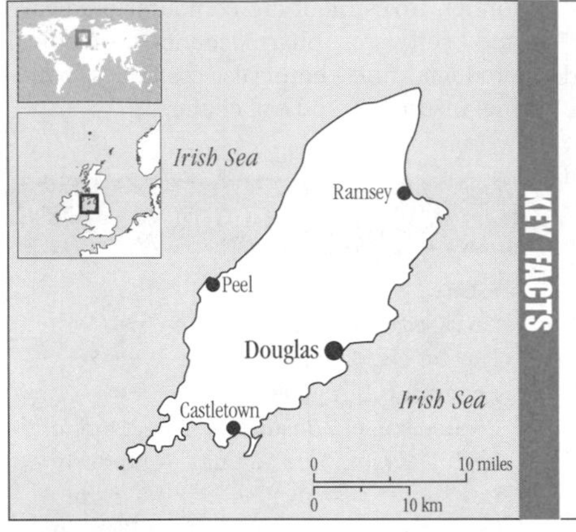

Head of government: **chief minister**
Currency: **pound sterling (£)**
Capital: **Douglas**
Population: **74,100**
Land area: **221 square miles**
Population density: **335 per square mile**
Language: **English, Manx**
Best buy: **handcrafts**

Economy

Services accounted for 86% of GDP in 2000, followed by manufacturing (7%), construction (6%) and agriculture (1%). Finance contributed 41%, with private banking and investment for overseas individuals the main activity. Tourism contributed 6%. International ship management and e-commerce are fast-growing sectors. The shipping register had 240 merchant ships, totaling 5.5 million tons in 2000.

The government has tightened financial regulation, transparency of operations, and the tax regime to meet international pressure from the OECD and EU. Tax information will be shared with other authorities if there is suspicion of fraud. A new pensions law is to be promulgated to increase the scope for pension fund business. The government has invested in fiber-optic cabling to ensure the growth of e-commerce, and in the development of a conference center and hotel accommodation to boost the tourism industry. Annual GDP growth averaged about 9% from 1983 to 1998, rising to 13.5% in 1999. It was expected to be 8.5% in 2000, 6% in 2001, and 3% in 2002. Inflation was 0.2% and unemployment 0.5% in November 2001.

Geography/Resources

A small island in the Irish Sea, the Isle of Man has plains in the north and south and hills in the center, with the highest point Snaefell at 2,037 feet. Two-thirds of the land is cultivated. Grains and potatoes are the main crops, while sheep are the main livestock. Scallop fishing is important. There are no significant mineral resources. The population is largely of Celtic and English origin.

Communications/Energy

The road network totals over 310 miles. The rail network comprises 22 miles of electrified track and a 15-mile steam railway. The three sea ports at Douglas, Peel, and Ramsey handle freight. Douglas is the main port for passengers. The airport handles 700,000 passengers and about 400 tons of freight and mail a year. Manx Airlines is the local carrier. In 2000 there were 25,000 mobile phones, and 13,000 households had a personal computer. There were 46,000 fixed phone lines in 1996. Manx Telecom was vying with Japan's DoCoMo to be the first to launch commercial services over the third generation of mobile phones in spring 2002. Most energy demand is met by imported oil and LPG. Electricity is generated locally by the Manx Electricity Authority, whose smallest power plant is a hydroelectric unit. A cable from the United Kingdom was commissioned in 2000, and there are plans to import natural gas for power generation.

Fiscal/Financial

Corporation tax and maximum personal income tax are 18%, with a lower profits and income bracket of 12%. Certain types of company are eligible for tax exemption but must pay an annual fee of at least £480. Income from trusts whose beneficiaries are Manx residents are taxed at 18%, but if the beneficiaries are non-resident there is no tax.

Assets under management in the financial services industry total around £100 billion. The insurance sector accounts for another £22 billion in assets, including life, general, and captive insurance (where an offshore subsidiary handles all or part of the insurance operations of an overseas corporation). Finance sector deposits were £26.54 billion in June 2001. At September 2001 there were 60 banks, 2 building societies, 50 investment companies and 100 collective investment schemes licensed by the Financial Supervision Commission. Non-financial companies are also regulated by the FSC. The insurance industry and pension schemes are regulated by the Insurance and Pensions Authority. Investments are traded globally. There is no local stock exchange.

Business Opportunities

Investment grants are available, but special tax rules are the main incentive, and these apply to banking, insurance, trusts, pension schemes, and certain corporate financial activities; also to shipping and to the film and construction industries. There is foreign investment in these sectors, and in hotels and real estate, from the United Kingdom and other EU countries, the United States, Japan, and Hong Kong and other Asian countries. New opportunities exist in e-commerce and e-finance.

For More Information

Books:

Belchem, John, ed. *A New History of the Isle of Man, vol. 5: The Modern Period 1830–1999*. Liverpool: Liverpool University Press, 2001.

Harrison, S., ed. *100 Years of Heritage*. Douglas, Isle of Man: Manx Museum, 1996.

Kneale, Trevor, and Derek Croucher. *Isle of Man* (travel guide). Cincinnati, OH: David & Charles, 2001.

Web Sites:

Financial Services Commission: **www.fsc.gov.im**

Government entry point: **www.gov.im**

Insurance and Pensions Authority: **www.gov.im/ipa**

Manx Tourist Board: **www.gov.im/tourism**

ISRAEL

KEY FACTS

GNI: **$99,574 million; world's 35th**
GNI pc: **$16,310; world's 36th**
Head of government: **prime minister**
Currency: **new shekel (NIS)**
Capital: **Jerusalem**
Population: **6,101,000, growing at 3.0% p.a.**
Land area: **7,954 square miles**
Population density: **767 per square mile**
Life expectancy: **78 years**
Infant mortality: **6 per 1,000 live births**
Language: **Hebrew (official), Arabic, English**
Best buy: **jewelry, diamonds, silver and copper goods, olive wood items**

ECONOMIC STRUCTURE

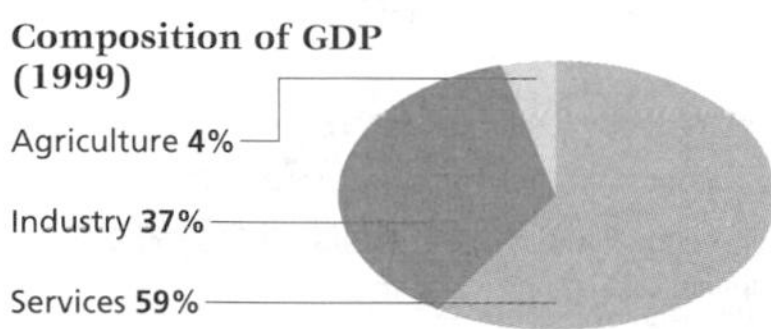

Since the creation of Israel as the Jewish homeland in 1948, the economy has been affected positively by immigration and negatively by conflict with neighboring Arab states and with the Palestinians for whom the land is also home. Israel industrialized in the 1950s and also developed a robust agricultural export sector. Neighboring Arab states invaded in 1967 and were defeated, losing part of their territory. Israel's gain boosted the economy with additional water resources, agricultural land, and Palestinian labor. The 1973 Yom Kippur war confirmed Israeli military superiority, but OPEC retaliated with two world oil shocks. State intervention in the economy increased in order to combat soaring inflation. Israel made peace with Egypt in 1980, giving back the Sinai Peninsula. Its invasion of Lebanon in 1982 failed to crush Palestinian paramilitary operations. The focus on security led to a strong arms industry and sophisticated telecommunications and computing sectors. Mass Jewish immigration from the former Soviet Union from 1990 produced economic growth, but also put more pressure on the land. The 1995 peace agreement between Israel and the Palestinians, after which the Palestinian National Authority (PNA) was established to administer the West Bank and Gaza Strip, was not fully implemented. Lack of agreement on the most sensitive issues led to renewed violence between the communities and the destruction of infrastructure in the West Bank and Gaza, undermining the economies of Israel and the Palestinian territories, and eroding international investor confidence.

Services accounted for 47% of GDP in 2000, followed by the public sector (34%), manufacturing (21%), construction (6%), and agriculture (1.8%). Finance and business services are the main services sectors. Israel exports 75% of GDP. Arms manufacture is an important industry and a key export. Cut diamonds were the largest single export in 2000, but the largest category was electrical, electronic, and transport equipment, followed by chemicals, metal goods, and machinery. The main markets were the United States, Germany, the United Kingdom, Netherlands, Italy, and France. The main exports from the West Bank and from Gaza—citrus and flowers—go primarily to Israel, and secondly to Egypt. The Palestinian economy is dependent on Israel for these earnings and essential services (telecommunications, electricity, etc), and these are disrupted when the internal borders are closed as they were from September 2000 into 2002. Remittances from Palestinians in other countries, and tourism receipts, are also important. Internally, services are the most important sector, followed by construction, agriculture, and manufacturing.

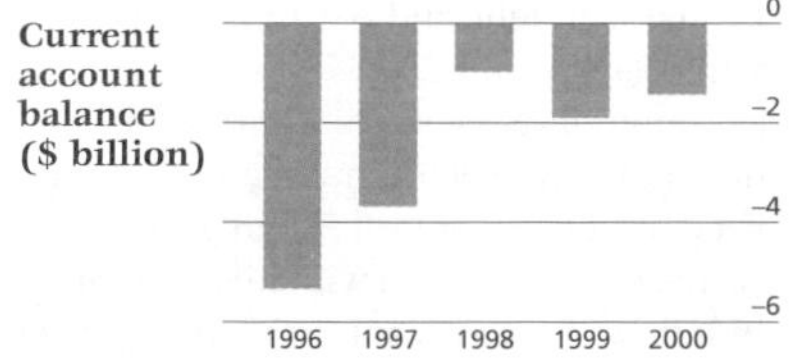

The Israeli state has had a significant role in the economy through military expenditure, project investment, and state-owned companies and banks. A privatization program was launched in 1986, and by mid-2001 77 state companies and banks had been sold off, bringing in $7.7 billion. In 2000 the government sold some shares in Israel Chemicals, Wertex, Bezeq, Bank Leumi, and Bank Mizrahi, and its remaining public shareholding in Bank Hapoalim, the main bank. Bezeq, the main telecommunications operator, was due to be fully privatized in 2001. The sale of the state's controlling interest in Bank Leumi was approved mid-2001. The public sector is dominant in broadcasting, electricity, air, sea and rail transport, the aeronautical industry, and refineries.

ECONOMIC POLICY

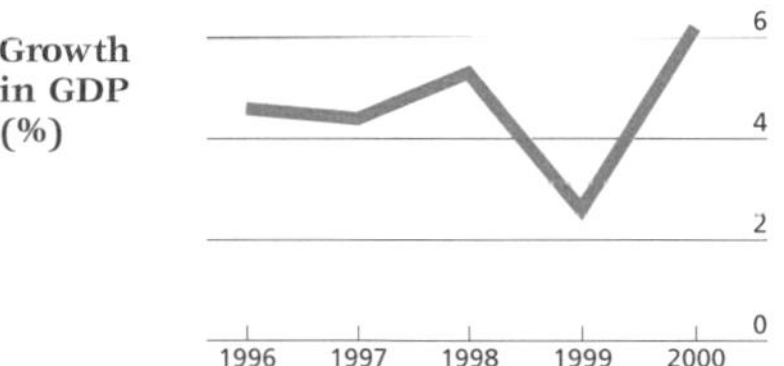

The government has exercised monetary and fiscal austerity to reduce inflation, the budget deficit, and foreign debt. From 1985 all new government finance, apart from receipts, has been raised through bonds. Inflation was reduced from 445% in 1984 to zero in 2000, but rose to 2.5% in 2001. The 2002 level is expected to be close to the government's target ceiling of 3%. After rapid GDP growth in the early 1990s, the pace slowed to an annual average 2.4% in 1997–99 before reviving to 6% in 2000, led by high-technology exports. Growth in 2001 was 2.6% following the slowdown in high-tech markets (especially the United States) and the deteriorating internal security situation and its resultant loss of tourism earnings. Export markets remained depressed and security in disarray into 2002. Israel is unlikely to reach its strong growth, investment, and export potential until the security problem is resolved. Other aspects of the economy will suffer the longer the crisis continues, but the government has prepared a tight management program to deal with shocks as well as possible. The government deficit was 2.9% of GDP in 2001—up from zero in 2000—following lower tax receipts and the postponement of new

mobile telephone licensing and of privatizations. The public debt was 92.8% of GDP in 2000. The persistent balance of trade deficit is largely offset by U.S. government aid. Reduction of personal income tax and simplification of capital taxes, including the elimination of some exemptions, are planned by 2003, but progress was delayed in 2001. Unemployment in Israel (which excludes Palestinians working in Israel and foreign workers) rose from 6.8% in 1995 to 8.8% in 2000. It was 8.6% at mid-2001. Around 80% of Palestinians working in Israel were prevented from going to work on account of the security situation in 2001, leaving some Israeli sectors short-staffed and producing 51% unemployment among Palestinians.

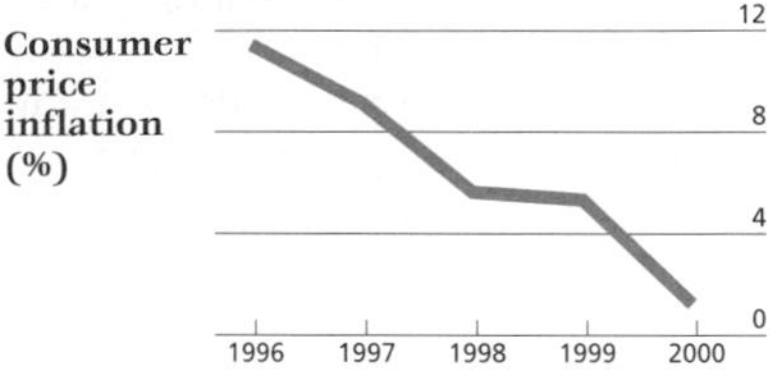

The PNA has focused on creating the administrative capability to channel international financial aid from the EU, the United States, Japan, Saudi Arabia, Norway, and the World Bank into infrastructure investment. It is also updating commercial law and strengthening the regulatory environment to boost private-sector investment in productive industries and services. GDP growth was estimated at 2.1% in 1998, with inflation at 5.6% (down from 7.9% in 1996) and unemployment at 14.4%. The economy was under siege from September 2000 through to 2002 with loss of production and infrastructure. The PNA focused its efforts on relief of mass poverty, and on reconstruction when possible.

GEOGRAPHY/RESOURCES

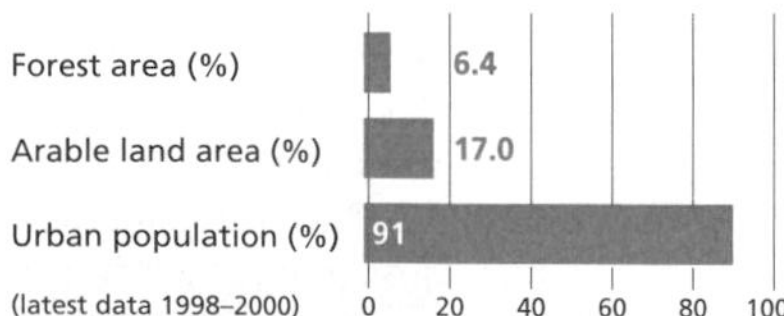

Israel has coastlines on the east Mediterranean and the Red Sea, and land borders with Lebanon and Syria to the north, Jordan to the east, and Egypt to the southwest. The country includes four territories occupied by Israel since 1967: the Golan Heights (formerly part of Syria), East Jerusalem and the West Bank of the Jordan River (formerly part of Jordan), and the Gaza Strip on the Mediterranean coast (formerly part of Egypt). Much of the land is rugged and dry. The Negev Desert dominates the south. The Mediterranean coastal plain and the Jordan valley north of the Dead Sea provide the best farmland. The central mountains have a high point of 13,963 feet. The Dead Sea is 1,339 feet below sea level. Summers are hot and dry, winters mild and wet, with a temperature range of 41°F to 122°F.

Through irrigation Israel is more than self-sufficient in food, although only one-third of the land is usable for agriculture. Vegetables are the main domestic crop, while citrus fruit are the main crop for export. Potatoes, wheat, bananas, avocados, melons, cotton, and olives are among the many other crops grown. Poultry are the main livestock, followed by cattle, sheep, pigs, and goats. Phosphates, potash, magnesium, and bromides are mined. Israel is the world's main exporter of bromine. There are reserves of copper and gold, and small amounts of petroleum and natural gas.

In 1998 about 42% of the population was under age 20. Jews were the largest community (79%), followed by Muslims (15%), Christians (2%), and Druze (1.6%). Of the Jewish community, around 32% were of European or American origin, 14.6% of African origin, 12.6% of Asian origin, and 21% were Israeli-born. The non-Jewish communities are mostly of Arab origin.

COMMUNICATIONS/ENERGY

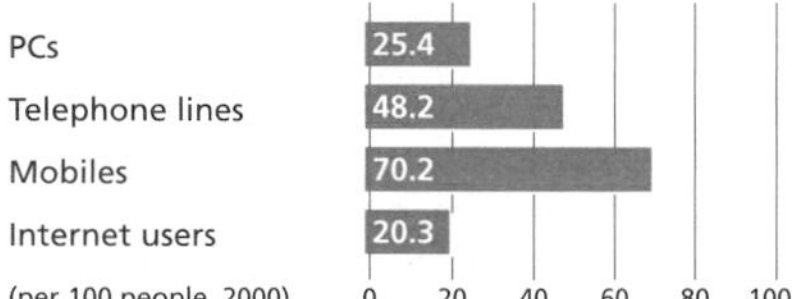

The paved road network in Israel was 9,921 miles in 1998, including 35 miles of motorways. There were a further 1,680 miles of roads in the West Bank and 104 miles in Gaza. The rail network is 380 miles. The pipeline network comprises 490 miles for crude oil, 180 miles for oil products, and 55 miles for natural gas. The main sea ports are Haifa, Ashdod, and Eilat. The merchant fleet comprised 17 ships over 1,000 grt, totaling 631,582 grt in 2000. The main international airport is at Tel Aviv, and there is one each in Gaza and the West Bank. There were 28 other airports and 25 airstrips in Israel in 2000. The railways carried 9.2 million tons of freight and 6.4 million passengers in 1998, while 280,447 tons of freight and 7.9 million passengers went by air.

International telecommunications are liberalized, and competition is being extended to domestic links. All switching is digital, provided by coaxial cable and microwave for domestic calls, and by submarine cable and satellite for international calls. There were 3 million fixed phone lines, 4.4 million mobile phones, and 1.3 million Internet users in Israel at end-2000. In the West Bank and Gaza there were 95,729 fixed phone lines in 1997 and 23,520 Internet users in 1999.

Israel is dependent on imported primary energy sources, especially petroleum and natural gas, although indigenous solar power has been developed. The state-owned Israel Electric is the predominant power company. Independent producers are allowed to generate 10% of total electricity, and imports of a further 10% are permitted. Electricity is almost entirely generated by fossil fuels (99.9%), with hydroelectricity supplying 0.1%. Gaza and the West Bank are dependent on Israeli electricity, although the West Bank towns of Nablus and Janin have small local generators.

EDUCATION/EMPLOYMENT

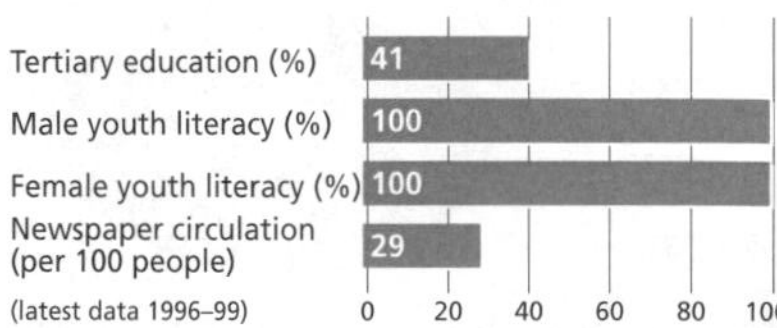

Education is compulsory and free from age 5 to 15 in Israel. There are 6 universities, an institute of technology, an institute of science, 44 teacher training colleges, and over 200 other tertiary education institutions. In 1998 there were 108,900 Jewish students in university and 153,400 in other forms of higher education. The Ministry of Education is responsible for higher education in Israel. In the West Bank and Gaza, there are eight universities and 20 community colleges. The PNA Ministry of Higher Education is responsible for tertiary education. The United Nations Relief and Works Agency operates four vocational training centers and provides university scholarships. There were 39,921 Arab students in higher education in 1996.

The Israeli Ministry of Science coordinates government R&D programs. The government-funded supercomputer center at Tel Aviv University provides services to universities, research centers, and industry. R&D strengths include electro-optics, IT, microelectronics, materials science, remote sensing and control, aerospace, ballistics, and biotechnology. Spending on civilian R&D was 3.5% of GDP in 1999. U.S. computer firms Microsoft, Cisco, and Motorola have R&D centers in Israel. Israel is eligible for participation in European Union-funded R&D projects.

Growth in labor force (% p.a., 1980–99)

Women as % of labor force (1999)

HIV positive (% of age group 15–49, 1999)

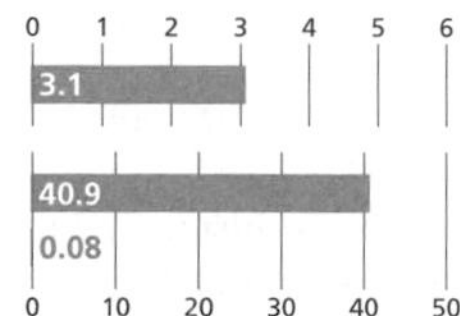

The labor force is well educated with a range of skills. Wages and other employment conditions are determined by employers and trade unions, most of which belong to the General Federation of Labor (Histadrut). The majority of the labor force is covered by collective bargaining agreements. The minimum wage is set by law at 47.5% of the national average wage, and updated according to changes in the latter and in inflation. The normal working week is 47 hours, after which overtime must be paid. Weekly rest must be 36 consecutive hours, including the Sabbath.

Fiscal/Financial

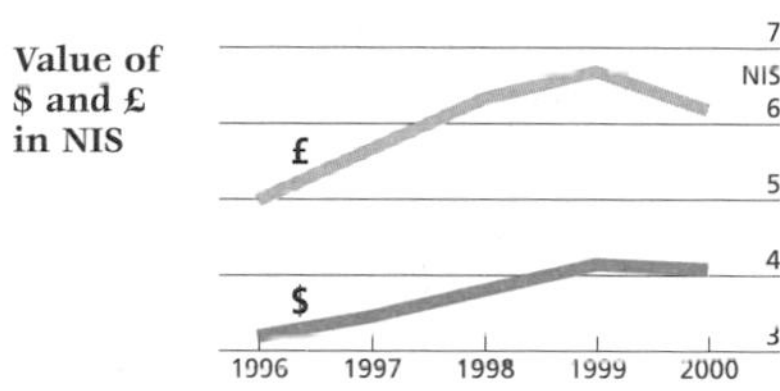

The largest bank by total assets at end-March 2001 was Bank Hapoalim, followed by Bank Leumi, Israel Discount Bank, United Mizrahi Bank, and First International Bank of Israel. Formerly state-owned, Bank Hapoalim was privatized in 2000. The state has equity in Bank Leumi and United Mizrahi Bank. Bank Leumi owns Migdal Insurance Company, one of over 30 Israeli insurance companies. The Bank of Israel, the central bank, is responsible for implementing monetary policy and for financial sector regulation in Israel. The Israel Securities Authority supervises the stock market. The Palestinian Monetary Authority (PMA) is responsible for monetary policy and financial sector regulation in the West Bank and Gaza.

The standard rate of corporation tax is 36%. Withholding tax on dividends, interest, and royalties is 25%. The top rate of personal income tax and social security is 50%. Sales taxes of 25% to 95% are levied on many goods, although the government eliminated such taxes on 600 goods in 2000. Further tax reform is due in 2002–03.

In early 2001 Bank Hapoalim controlled 30.6% of the banking system, followed by the 8 mortgage banks with 28.7%. There were 23 locally-incorporated commercial banks, 3 foreign branches, 2 merchant banks, 1 investment finance company, and 6 finance companies. Restrictions on the range of investments used by provident and pension funds and insurance companies were lifted in 2001. Limits on foreign exchange transactions were removed in 2000. There were 23 local and foreign commercial banks in the territory of the PMA. The Palestine Mortgage and Housing Corporation, established with assistance from the World Bank, provides medium- and long-term financing for the Palestinian banking system and its role in reconstruction and in social and economic development.

The Tel Aviv Stock Exchange (TASE) has a main board and a derivatives market. Trading is fully automated, and there is Internet access. There were 681 companies listed on the TASE in 2000. In October 2000 a regulation allowed Israeli securities traded on the U.S. exchanges (NYSE, Amex, and Nasdaq-MN) to trade on TASE without additional listing requirements. The Palestinian Securities Exchange at Nablus has been in operation since 1997, and listed 28 companies at mid-2001. Trading is automated and Internet access is being arranged.

Business Opportunities

The breakdown of the peace process in Israel, the West Bank, and Gaza, the hardening of political attitudes, and the consequent lack of security are a major disincentive to investment.

The Israeli government encourages foreign joint venture investment in export and high-technology industries and in tourism. Tax incentives and grants are offered under the Capital Investment Encouragement Law and for foreign investment in and spending on R&D. The city of Eilat is a free trade zone, and there are free ports at Eilat, Haifa, and Ashdod, where companies are exempt from indirect tax and can qualify for other tax breaks. There are restrictions on foreign investment in banking, insurance, and defense industries. Electric and electronic equipment, finance, insurance, real estate, business services, trade, tourism, and food manufacturing have attracted foreign investment from the United States, the United Kingdom, Switzerland, and many other countries. These sectors and certain privatizations continue to offer opportunities. The point of contact is the Investment Promotion Center.

In 1996 Israel and the PNA agreed to establish three industrial estates at Carni in Gaza and Jenin and Tulkarem on the West Bank, a project welcomed by international donors. The Palestinian territories have attracted foreign investment in banking and water services management from Jordan, Egypt, Kuwait, the United Kingdom, and France among other countries. Manufacturing, service industries—especially tourism to religious sites—and infrastructure offer investment opportunities. The point of contact is the Palestinian Economic Council for Development and Reconstruction.

For More Information

Books:

IMF Country Report. *Israel*. Washington, D.C.: IMF.

Investment Promotion Center. *Seven Reasons to Invest in Israel*. (Available online from the Investment Promotion Center Web site.)

Israel Business and Investment Opportunities Yearbook. 3rd ed. Washington, D.C.: International Business Publications, 2001 (annual).

Ministry of Industry and Trade. *The Israeli Economy at a Glance*. (Available online from the Ministry of Industry and Trade Web site.)

Netanyahu, Benjamin. *A Durable Peace: Israel and its Place Among the Nations*. New York: Warner Books, 2000.

World Bank. *West Bank and Gaza at a Glance*. Washington, D.C. (See also the World Bank Web site.)

Web Sites:

Bank of Israel: **www.bankisrael.gov.il**

Central Bureau of Statistics: **www.cbs.gov.il**

Government gateway: **www.israel.gov.il**

Investment Promotion Center: **www.moit.gov.il/ipc.htm**

Jerusalem Post (daily newspaper): **www.jpost.com**

Ministry of Industry and Trade: **www.moit.gov.il**

Palestinian Central Bureau of Statistics: **www.pcbs.org**

Palestinian Economic Council for Development and Reconstruction: **www.pecdar.org**

Palestinian Monetary Authority: **www.pma-palestine.org**

World Bank: **www.worldbank.org**

ITALY

GNI: **$1,162,910 million; world's 6th**
GNI pc: **$20,170; world's 29th**
Head of government: **prime minister**
Currency: **Euro (€)**
Capital: **Rome**
Population: **57,343,000, growing at 0.1% p.a.**
Land area: **113,552 square miles**
Population density: **505 per square mile**
Life expectancy: **78 years**
Infant mortality: **6 per 1,000 live births**
Language: **Italian**
Best buy: **clothes, leather goods, Venetian glass, art, wine**

ECONOMIC STRUCTURE

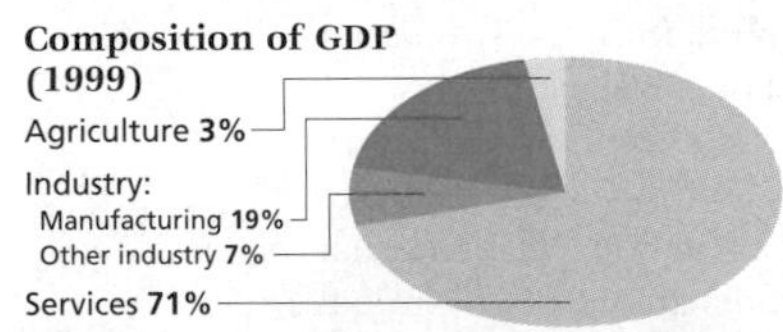

Italy became a national entity in the late 19th century to rid itself of foreign domination. The unification between the wealthy north and center and the poor south was uneasy, and the divide remains to this day. Between the fall of the Roman Empire in the 5th century and 19th century unification, Italy was characterized by separate principalities and city states, often at war with one another. Variety, independence, and dissent are still predominant today. Wealth in medieval times came primarily from trade and banking, but textiles, metals, and ceramics were established industries. The Italian states led the western world in science, invention, and art during the Renaissance of the 14th and 15th centuries. During the 19th century, engineering industries owned by wealthy families developed in the north. The state intervened in industry during the Fascist era in the first half of the 20th century. At the end of World War II it took over the reconstruction of the country and established control of key sectors. The rest of the economy has been based mainly on family business, large and small.

Services accounted for 66.5% of GDP and 61.8% of jobs in 1999, industry for 26.2% of GDP and 25% of jobs, building construction for 4.8% of GDP and 7.6% of jobs, and agriculture for 2.6% of GDP and 5.5% of jobs. Tourism is a major source of foreign exchange and jobs. Italy receives around 57 million visitors a year. Finance and business services are increasingly important. Industry is diversified, ranging from steel, chemicals, and food to heavy and light engineering, electronics, textiles, clothing, decorative glass, and other fine objects. Cars, office equipment, and oil, gas and petrochemicals plant are particular strengths. Government incentives for electronics and information technology firms to expand business in the south have begun to narrow the wealth gap between north and south for the first time. However, the unofficial economy is thought to be around 25% of GDP, one of the largest in the EU. In 2000 the leading exports were engineering products (29.6%), textiles, clothing and leather goods (15.4%), transport equipment (11.6%), and chemicals (9.3%). The main markets were Germany (15.1%), France (12.6%), the United States (10.4%), and the United Kingdom (6.9%).

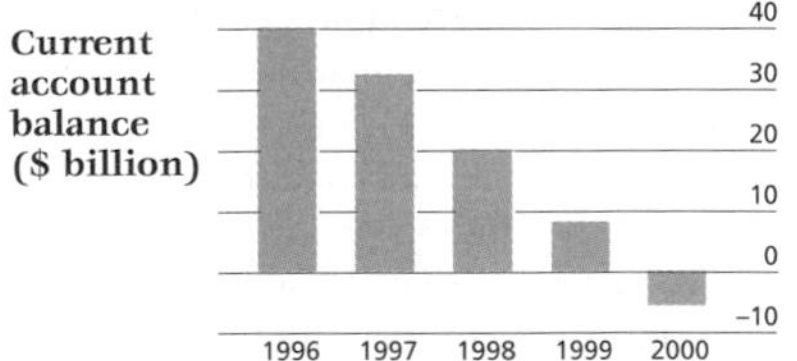

Italian manufacturing, utilities, and banking have been characterized by a high level of state ownership, alongside a few large private-sector companies in manufacturing and banking and a host of small ones. Cross-shareholdings are a feature of major public- and private-sector companies. Some of these have unraveled due to privatization, but many still remain. Most state firms were owned by the massive state holding company IRI, which was dissolved by the Treasury Ministry in June 2000. Part privatizations included oil and gas holding company ENI, electricity firm ENEL, highways company Autostrade, defense industry holding company Finmeccanica, former local government enterprises, most of the main telecommunications operator Telecom Italia (97% sold), and most of two large banks, Banca Nazionale del Lavoro and Banca di Roma. At end-2000 the government maintained control of or substantial stakes in the electricity sector, energy and chemicals production and imports, airports, railways, highways, shipyards, airline Alitalia, aeronautics and defense equipment manufacturing, the post office, broadcaster RAI, and—to a lesser extent—banks. Several banks, utilities, and airports were owned or controlled by local governments. Tobacco manufacturer Ente Tabacchi was due to be sold off in late 2001. Alitalia, and more of the energy sector companies, were being prepared for privatization.

ECONOMIC POLICY

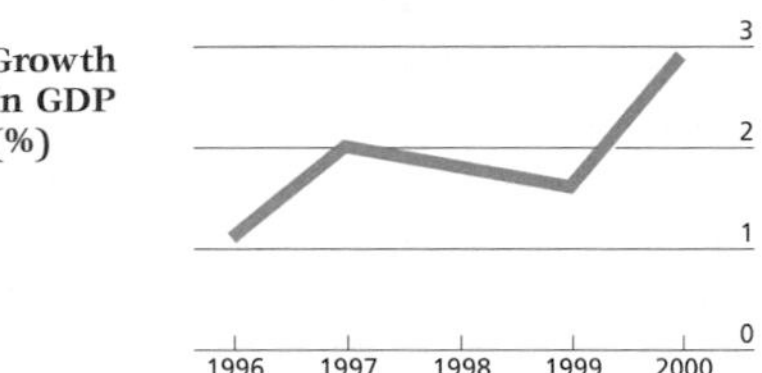

Austerity measures reduced the government structural deficit from 9.8% of GDP in 1992 to 2.8% in 1997. Consolidation has continued, and the government is aiming to achieve budget balance by 2003. At this point the public debt will be around 100% of GDP, one of the highest in the Euro area, down from a peak of 124.9% in 1994. The OECD considers this target to be a minimum if Italy is to maintain international competitiveness. However, spending cuts and reforms, including privatization and the reduction of red tape for businesses, have proved difficult to implement at the local level. Pensions absorb two-thirds of welfare spending, but reforms have been tardy, complex, and unpopular, exempting around 40% of workers. Social security charges are some of the highest in the OECD area. Tax reforms have reduced the cost of capital to industry, but the tax burden remains heavy. There have been modest personal income tax cuts to sweeten wage moderation. Political leaders have promised to speed up implementation of the privatization program,

which is vital to improve competitiveness and to pay off the public debt.

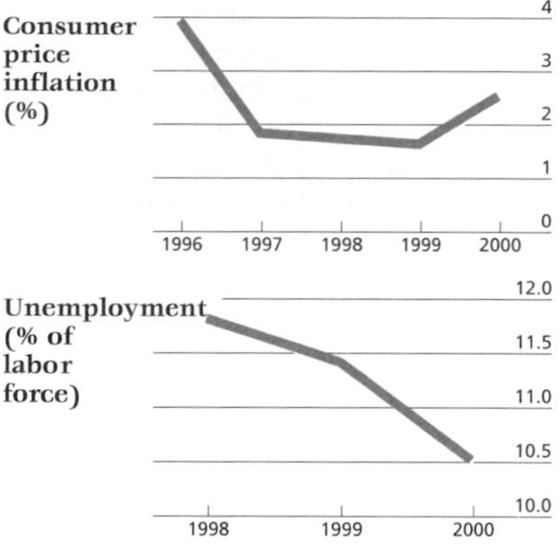

GDP growth has picked up from an annual average of 1.5% in 1991–95 to 2.6% in 1996–2000, led by exports and investment. Growth was 1.8% in 2001, and was expected to be 1.4% in 2002. Inflation fell from an annual average rate of 5% in 1991–95 to an average 2.3% in 1996–2000, with 2.6% in 2001. Unemployment increased in the second half of the 1990s from an average 10.1% in 1991–95 to 11.5% in 1996–2000, falling back to 9.5% in 2001, but still one of the highest in the Euro area. Regional disparities persist, with unemployment in the south above 20%, but national unemployment has fallen gradually since 1999, and this trend is expected to continue as a result of new investment and more flexible labor contracts.

Geography/Resources

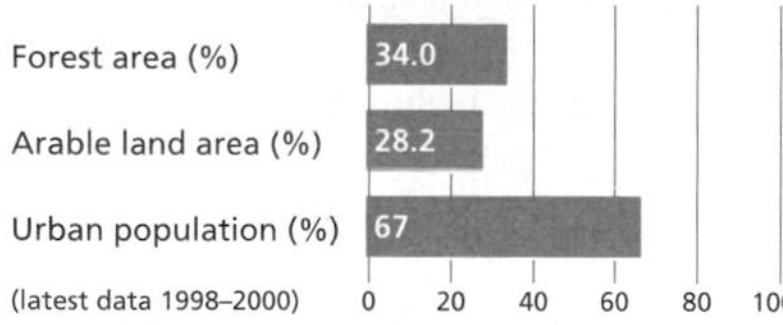

A southern European country with a mild winters (except in the northern mountains) and hot summers, Italy consists mainly of a large peninsula, a continental hinterland bordering France, Switzerland, Austria, and Slovenia, and several islands, the largest of which are Sicily and Sardinia. The land is divided by mountains, which ring the land borders and run through the center of the peninsula from northwest to southwest. The highest point is 15,772 feet. The central Apennine range lies in southern Europe's earthquake zone. The main plain is in the northern Po river valley. About 23% of the land is forested.

There is a varied agriculture on predominantly small, family-run farms. Almost 55% of farms are in the south, 28% in the north, and 17% in central Italy. The main crops are wheat, corn, tomatoes, vegetables, sugar beet, olives, grapes, and citrus fruits. Italy is a significant producer of wine. It is also one of the top world producers of silk. Meat and dairy produce are important. Natural gas in the Po valley is the main mineral resource, followed by petroleum in the north and center and in Sicily. Gas reserves at January 2000 were 8.1 trillion cubic feet, and proven oil reserves were 622 million barrels. New oil production at the Val d'Agri field began in 2000. Marble is a significant high-value mineral product. Rock salt, feldspar, talc, lignite, barites, lead, and zinc are also produced.

The majority of the population is urban. The largest cities are the capital Rome (2.6 million in 1998), Milan (1.3 million), Naples (1 million), and Turin (909,717). The majority of people are of Latin origin, but there are Germanic communities in the northern Dolomite region, and Slavs in the northeast. In the 1990s immigration has increased, especially in the south, as a result of refugees from the Balkan wars.

Communications/Energy

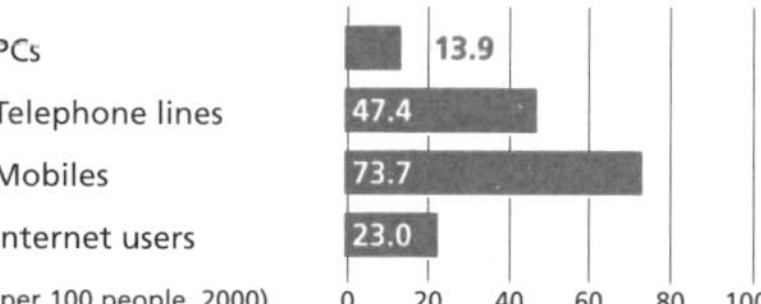

The 190,075 miles road network includes 5,900 miles of highways, most of which are toll roads. The highways criss-cross the country, providing access to most areas. The rail network extends to 12,096 miles, over half of which is electrified. High speed rail links are being built between Naples and Rome and Rome and Milan. The high-speed network is planned to include Turin, Genoa, and Venice. The pipeline network consists of 1,058 miles for crude oil, 1,335 miles for refined oil products, and 12,055 miles for natural gas. The main sea ports are Genoa, Livorno, Naples, Palermo, Trieste, and Venice. The merchant fleet over 1,000 grt numbered 445 ships, with a total displacement of 8 million grt in 2000. There are 19 international airports and 17 main domestic airports. Milan and Rome handle the largest volumes of international and domestic traffic.

The telecommunications sector was liberalized in 1997. Since then telephony has blossomed, with several operators in the market, leading to reduced prices. Telecom Italia, the former state company, was taken over by private-sector company Olivetti at the turn of the millennium. Olivetti's fixed-line phone business was later shed to Germany's Mannesmann. At end-2000 there were 27.2 million fixed phone lines, 42.2 million mobiles, and 13.2 million Internet users. E-commerce is growing quickly.

Around 80% of energy requirements are met by imports, including oil, natural gas, and electricity. Imported electricity from France and Switzerland accounted for 16% of consumption in 1999. Domestic power is generated mostly by oil and natural gas, 79% in 1999, with hydroelectricity contributing 20%. Natural gas accounted for 31% of energy demand in 1999, but this is expected to rise to 37% in 2010, mainly for power generation. Domestic gas production contributed 27% of demand, and imports from Algeria, Russia, and the Netherlands accounted for 73%. Power generation is expected to double by 2010 with substantial investment in combined-cycle plants. Although the electricity and gas sectors were opened to competition in 1999 and 2000 respectively, ENEL remains the dominant operator in electricity and ENI in gas and oil. Manufacturing industries produce their own electricity, 681 firms accounting for 23.8% of total electricity production in 1999.

Education/Employment

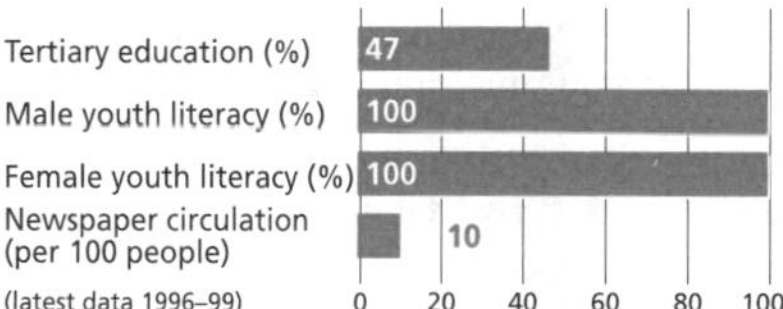

Education is compulsory from age 6 to 16. Schools and universities are mostly state-owned, and education is free. Universities come under the aegis of the Ministry of Universities and Scientific Research, and must fulfil the tasks of teaching and research, but decision making is autonomous. There are 42 state universities, 6 private universities, 3 technical universities, and 12 university institutes. Four new universities were created recently. Italy has the world's oldest university, Bologna, established in 1088. Of the 251,012 students enrolled at university for degree courses (4–6 years) in 1999–2000, law was the main subject, followed by economics and engineering. The most popular subjects for diploma courses (2–3 years) were medicine, economics, and engineering.

The universities conduct research, often in collaboration with companies. Science parks provide a framework for public/private R&D partnerships. Strengths include biotechnology, telecommunications,

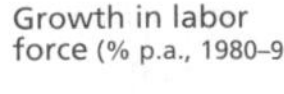
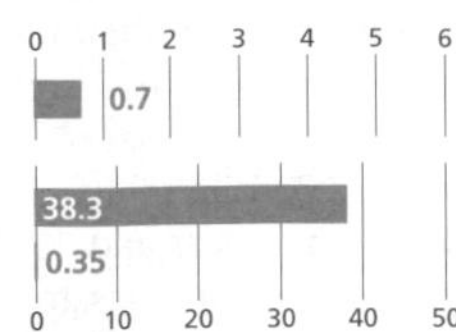

electronics, and multimedia. Large private-sector companies in the electronics, office equipment, automotive, chemicals, pharmaceuticals, steel, and textiles sectors invest in R&D, but the majority of private-sector firms have a low R&D participation. In 2001 the government launched a new fund to support IT and biotechnology research, financed partly from the proceeds of the UMTS mobile phone licensing round.

The labor force is two-thirds male, reflecting a low level of female participation. Wages and employment conditions are determined through negotiation between employers and trade unions. Job protection for permanent employment is tightly regulated. To reduce unemployment the government relaxed the rules for temporary contracts. This has led to a growing number of such contracts, and a sharp division of the labor force between those who have substantial rights and those who do not. Italy applies EU employment law, which covers safety at work, wages and working hours, industrial relations, employment incentives, and unemployment provision.

Fiscal/Financial

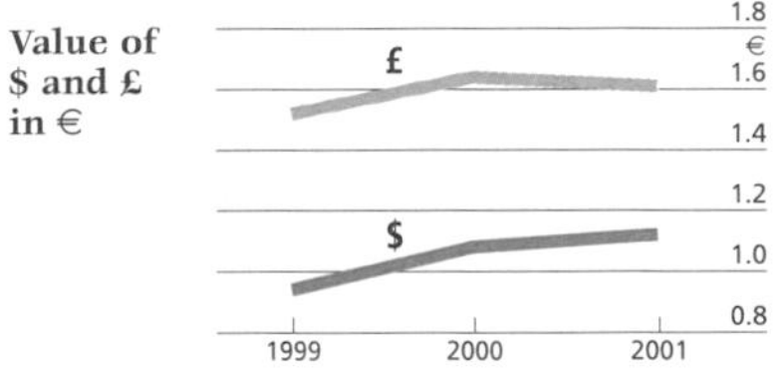

The main commercial banks are Banca Commerciale Italiana, Banca di Roma, Banca Nazionale del Lavoro, Banca Monte dei Paschi di Siena, and CARIPLO (a savings bank). The Banca d'Italia is the supervisory authority and central bank. It is also part of the European System of Central Banks. This body, and the European Central Bank, set the policy for the Euro. The Commissione Nazionale per le Società e la Borsa (CONSOB) regulates the stock exchange.

Corporation tax was reduced to 36% in early 2001 and will be cut to 35% in 2003. Regional tax rates for small firms were reduced. Personal income tax has been cut at the lower levels, and more comprehensive cuts are pledged for 2002 and 2003. The dual corporate income tax system offers lower tax rates on equity increases, especially equity obtained through the stock market. Eligibility for the system will be broadened in future years.

The bank privatization program, which began in 1990, led to a spate of mergers and to a greater internationalization of the sector. This in turn led to greater efficiency. Mergers and privatizations in other sectors have boosted banking and stock market activity. Bank loans are still preferred to equity, and there has been a substantial increase in the level of lending—also in venture capital, particularly for high-tech industry. The greater transparency in reporting procedures and accounting, and the relative stability afforded by the Euro have increased investor confidence. More households now invest in mutual funds, equity, and bond holdings. In September 2000 the Italian Banking Association launched an e-banking initiative to create specific standards and secure payment systems for e-commerce.

Since its privatization the Borsa Italiana in Milan, the most important of Italy's ten stock exchanges, has seen a spectacular increase in trading. Although large corporations still dominate the market, more small companies now seek finance through the Borsa. Capitalization rose from €96 billion at end-1992 to €852 billion at end-2000. The exchange launched a new market for small companies, STAR, in spring 2001. Its Nuovo Mercato for high-growth, high-technology companies, like other such exchanges, suffered when the dot.com bubble burst. A new electricity exchange is planned.

Business Opportunities

Growth in output (% p.a., 1990–99)

Services	1.5
Industry	1.1
Manufacturing	1.5
Agriculture	1.7

Grants, loans, and tax incentives are offered to companies locating in regions of high unemployment, such as the south, or in specific sectors such as R&D. Tax credits are offered to firms engaging in e-commerce. Finance is partly provided by the EU structural funds. Tax incentives include accelerated depreciation of assets, and tax credits and reductions. Electronics, information technology and telecommunications, biotechnology, motor vehicles, engineering, energy equipment, chemicals, banking, and insurance have attracted foreign investment from the United States, Germany, France, Netherlands, the United Kingdom, Luxembourg, Switzerland, and other countries. The Italian Trade Commission is the point of contact for investors.

The privatization program is due to gather momentum, and it will engender further internationalization and consolidation in a number of sectors. Further shares in the electricity company, ENEL, are due to be sold. ENEL and ENI are seeking international alliances to meet new competition on the Italian market from foreign and Italian firms. Rome Airport and the highways company are being prepared for sale. Local governments are likely to divest more shares in utilities and banks.

For More Information

Books:

Economic Bulletin (quarterly). Bank of Italy. (Economic performance update, available in English.)
European Union, European Economy: Report and Studies Series.
Fodor's Italy. New York: Fodors Travel Publications, 2001.
Frei, Matt. *Getting the Boot: Italy's Unfinished Revolution*. New York: Times Books, 1995.
Ginsborg, Paul. *A History of Contemporary Italy: Society and Politics, 1943–1988*. New York: Penguin, 1990.
IMF Country Report. *Italy*. Washington, D.C.: IMF.
Italy Business and Investment Opportunities Yearbook. 3rd ed. Washington, D.C.: International Business Publications, 2001 (annual).
Italy Country Study Guide. 3rd ed. Washington, D.C.: International Business Publications, 2001.
OECD Economic Surveys. *Italy*. Paris: OECD, 2001.

Web Sites:

Bank of Italy: **www.bancaditalia.it**
Commissione Nazionale per le Società e la Borsa (CONSOB): **www.consob.it**
Il Sole 24 ore (leading business newspaper): **www.englishedition/ilsole24ore.com**
Italian Trade Commission: **www.ice.it**
La Repubblica (main daily newspaper): **www.repubblica.it**
Ministry of Finance: **www.finanze.it**
Ministry of Treasury, Budget and Economic Planning: **www.tesoro.it**
National Institute of Statistics: **www.istat.it**

JAMAICA

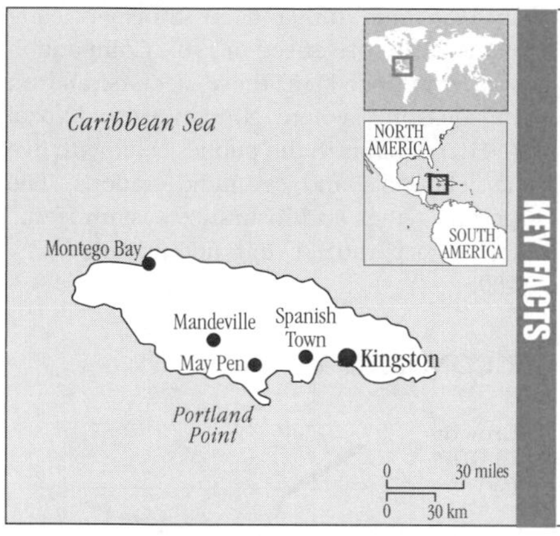

KEY FACTS

GNI: **$6,311 million; world's 101st**
GNI pc: **$2,430; world's 95th**
Head of government: **prime minister**
Currency: **Jamaican dollar (J$)**
Capital: **Kingston**
Population: **2,560,000, growing at 0.9% p.a.**
Land area: **4,170 square miles**
Population density: **614 per square mile**
Life expectancy: **75 years**
Infant mortality: **10 per 1,000 live births**
Language: **English**
Best buy: **Blue Mountain coffee, rum**

ECONOMY

Jamaica has a diversified economy in which tourism, manufacturing, mining, finance, and agriculture are all significant sectors. Distribution, which includes the tourism sector, accounted for 22.5% of GDP in 1999, manufacturing 16.9%, and finance 14.5%. Stopover tourist arrivals numbered 1.32 million in 2000, with almost 908,000 cruise ship passengers, producing $1.38 billion in foreign exchange earnings, compared with $1.33 billion from exports.

The mining industry produces bauxite, most of which is refined into alumina before export, and the manufacturing sector produces a wide range of goods including chemicals, fertilizers, construction materials, foodstuffs, garments, and electronic equipment. Three industrial free zones produce goods for export, and further development of this sub-sector is planned.

The major export earner is the mining sector, with alumina and bauxite sales totaling $795 million in 2000; the second-largest earner was sugar, accounting for $109 million.

During the 1990s the economy was marked by very low or negative growth, inflationary pressures, and high unemployment, together with a major crisis in the financial sector. A structural adjustment program, which received substantial international financing, stabilized the exchange rate by the end of the decade, and a return to positive growth of about 1% was recorded in 2000. In the same year, the inflation rate was 8.2%; it had been in single figures in four of the years since 1995 when it was at 35%; foreign investment, which had weakened in the early 1990s, recovered to $350 million in 1998.

GEOGRAPHY/RESOURCES

Lying south of Cuba and west of Haiti, Jamaica has two main mountainous areas, and much of the island is limestone. Almost 30% of the population live in Kingston.

The bauxite deposits are in the central limestone areas. About 25% of the land area is cultivated, and 15–20% forested, although deforestation is a cause of anxiety. As well as sugar, agricultural production includes bananas and other fruit, and coffee.

Adult literacy is estimated at around 70%; in 1996, primary schools had 93% enrollment, but secondary enrollment was only 65%. In 2000 the unemployment rate was about 15%.

COMMUNICATIONS/ENERGY

Several international airlines—including the national carrier, Air Jamaica—serve the United States, Canada, Europe, and many Caribbean countries. There are domestic flights between Kingston and Montego Bay. The road system is extensive, but many roads are in poor condition, although improvements are scheduled.

Telecommunications services are provided by Cable & Wireless, while an Irish company, Mossel, launched a mobile phone service in April 2001. A fully competitive regime is to be introduced by the end of 2002.

Jamaica depends on imported oil for its energy requirements. Electricity production is in the hands of the Jamaica Public Service Company, formerly a public corporation. It was agreed in February 2001 to sell 80% of its shares to a U.S. corporation, Mirant (formerly Southern Electric), which has undertaken to increase generating capacity from 660 to 1,035 MW.

FISCAL/FINANCIAL

A crisis in the financial sector in 1996–97 obliged the government to take several banks and other institutions under the control of a Financial Sector Adjustment Company, with the support of international financial institutions. Several of the banks and other finance houses concerned were wound up or amalgamated in a government scheme to rationalize the sector; in March 2001, legislation was passed to allow a Financial Services Commission to be established, responsible for supervising the sector.

The Stock Exchange, founded in 1968, has 42 companies listed, with market capitalization of J$147 billion.

BUSINESS OPPORTUNITIES

Extensive liberalization of the foreign exchange, taxation, and business licensing systems took place in the 1990s. There is a fully-floating exchange rate, with no restriction on foreign exchange accounts. Import licensing is confined to a small number of items. Investment incentives include tax holidays of up to 15 years, import duty exemption, tax reductions on profits from exports, and special agricultural investment incentives. There is a free zone in Kingston for export production. Special incentives are offered for investment in tourism, and there is no capital gains tax.

For More Information

Books:

Bank of Jamaica. *Economic Statistics* (monthly). Bank of Jamaica. (Available online from the Bank of Jamaica Web site.)
Jamaica Business and Investment Opportunities Yearbook. 3rd ed. Washington, DC: International Business Publications, 2001 (annual).
Mason, Peter. *In Focus Jamaica: A Guide to the People, Politics and Culture*. Northampton, MA: Interlink Publishing Group, 2000.

Web Sites:

Bank of Jamaica: **www.boj.org.jm**
Government of Jamaica: **www.jis.gov.jm**

JAPAN

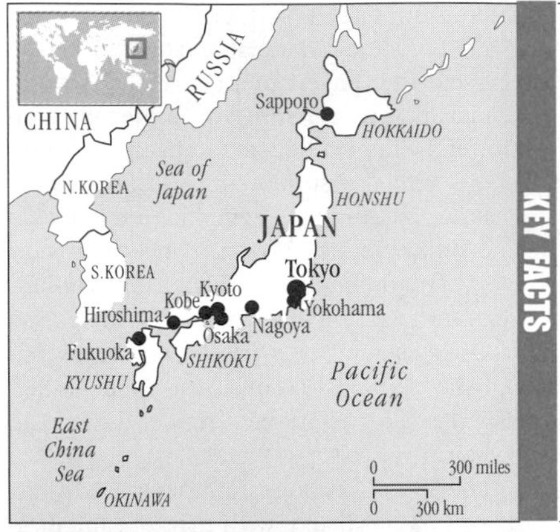

KEY FACTS

GNI: **$4,054,545 million; world's 2nd**
GNI pc: **$32,030; world's 7th**
Head of government: **prime minister**
Currency: **yen (¥)**
Capital: **Tokyo**
Population: **126,505,000, growing at 0.3% p.a.**
Land area: **145,367 square miles**
Population density: **870 per square mile**
Life expectancy: **80 years**
Infant mortality: **4 per 1,000 live births**
Language: **Japanese**
Best buy: **cameras, electronic goods, computers, watches, pearls, silk goods, woodblock prints, lacquerware**

ECONOMIC STRUCTURE

Composition of GDP (1999)

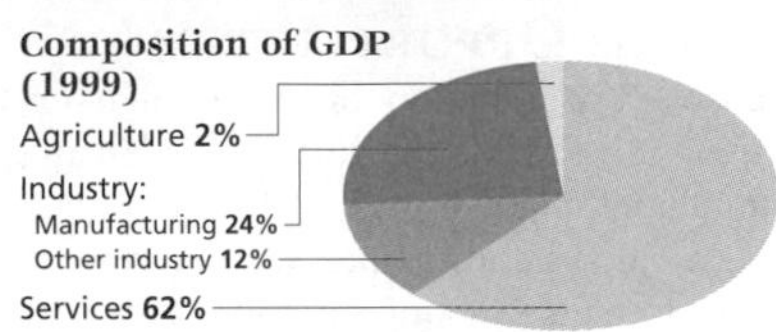

Japan's industrial revolution, which began after the Meiji Restoration in 1868, was spearheaded by the government to ensure that Japan caught up with the West. Western technology and methods were imported. The government focused on transport, communications and financial infrastructure to underpin capitalism, and on light industry and armaments. Heavy industry, iron and steel, and shipbuilding gained momentum from the end of the 19th century. Industrial combines ("zaibatsu") with broad-ranging industrial and financial interests, owned by merchant families, flourished under the Meiji government program. The largest were Mitsui, Mitsubishi, and Sumitomo, which increased their control over finance and over smaller companies during the financial crises of the 1920s and 1930s. They introduced lifetime employment and wage increases according to seniority in order to keep their trained workers. Smaller companies became subcontractors to the zaibatsu. The zaibatsu were dissolved after World War II, but to ward off corporate takeovers they bought each other's shares. In the 1970s the keiretsu—groups of companies working under the umbrella of one major manufacturer—provided the stability for the pursuit of sales expansion and new technology rather than profits. Booming stock prices in the late 1980s were based on an extension of this practice, creating a bubble that burst in the early 1990s. By then, however, this special brand of capitalism had made Japan the second world economic power.

Services account for 63% of GDP, followed by manufacturing (23%), construction (9%), and agriculture (1.7%). Real estate is the main services sector (13% of GDP), followed by commerce (12%), public administration (8%), transport (6%), and finance (5%). Electronics and cars are the main manufacturing industries. Japan is the world's third-largest machine tool maker, and second-largest steel producer after South Korea. Other important industries are machinery, chemicals, petroleum products, textiles, and shipbuilding. The leading exports in 2000 were electrical machinery (25.5%), followed by general machinery (20.7%), transport equipment (20.2%), chemicals (7.1%), and metals and metal products (5.3%). The top export market was the U.S. (29.7%), followed by Taiwan (7.5%), China (6.4%), South Korea (6.3%), and Hong Kong (5.7%).

Current account balance ($ billion)

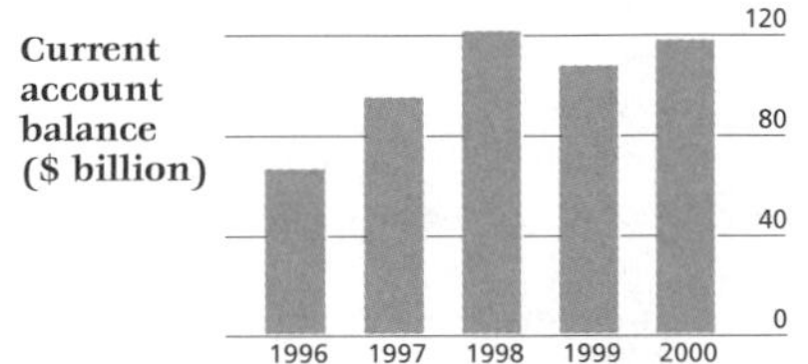

Although the government has little direct ownership of the economy, it has extensive influence through policy and rules. Deregulation has increased through the 1990s. Ministries were streamlined in 2001, and the civil service will be reduced. The telecommunications monopoly NTT was privatized in 1985, and rail and air transport companies were privatized in 1987. Competition was introduced in these sectors and in broadcasting, where Nippon Hoso Kyokai (NHK) remains in the public sector with five TV channels and six radio stations. The postal savings and insurance system is due to be corporatized, but not privatized, by 2003.

ECONOMIC POLICY

Growth in GDP (%)

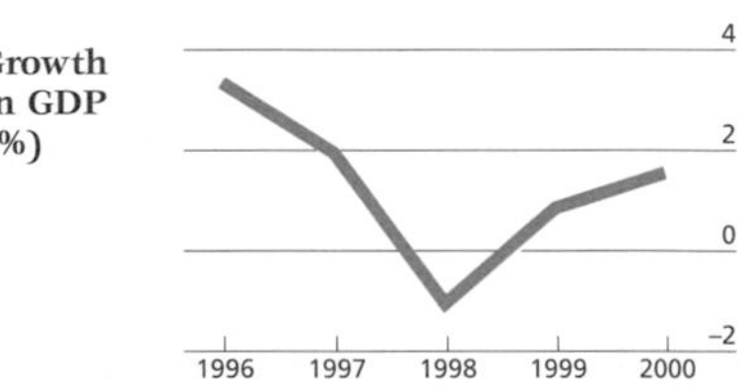

Low central bank discount rates have been a cornerstone of monetary policy for many years to provide Japanese industry with low-cost credit. The high rate of domestic savings facilitated low interest rates. In August 2000 the Bank of Japan raised the discount rate for the first time in ten years—from 0.25% to 0.5%—to provide the incentive for industry to change to a more profit-based culture. The government needs to reduce the level of gross public debt, which was the highest in the OECD at 130% of GDP in late 2001. The level of public debt increased in the late 1990s as a result of the government's recapitalization of the banking sector in order to shore up some banks against non-performing loans. Several banks remained under state control in 2000 because of bad loans.

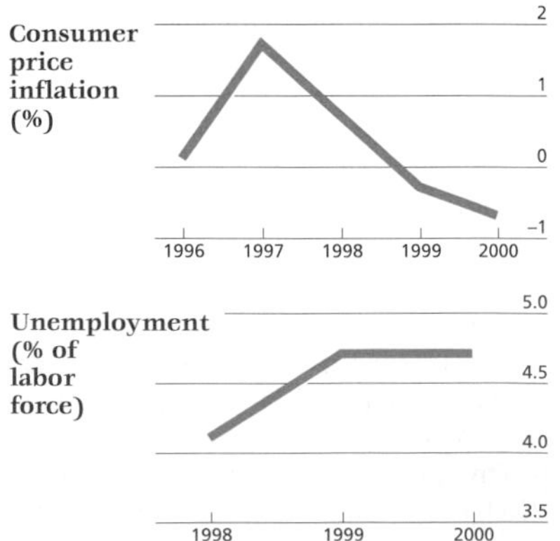

GDP growth has been sluggish in recent years, averaging 1.1% in 1994–2000, in contrast to the 4% average of the 1980s. GDP fell by 0.6% in 2001 and is expected to rise

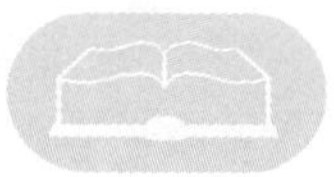

by 0.8% in 2002. Inflation was low at an annual average of 0.3% in 1994–2000, including two deflationary years. Deflation returned in 2001 at 0.4%, and is expected to continue at 0.3% in 2002. Unemployment is low, but rose on account of the recession from 2.9% in 1994 to 4.8% in 2000 and 2001. It is expected to stay at this level in 2002.

Geography/Resources

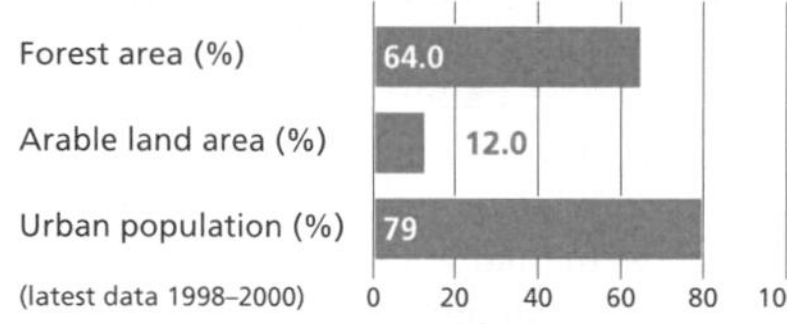

Japan is a chain of four major islands, Hokkaido, Honshu, Shikoku, and Kyushu, and 6,848 smaller islands. The Sea of Japan separates the main islands from Russia and the Korean peninsula to the west. The East China Sea separates the southern smaller islands from China. The Pacific Ocean lies to the east. The large islands are mainly mountainous, with Mount Fuji the high point at 12,389 feet. The lowest point is 13 feet below sea level. There are some active volcanoes, and the country is prone to major earthquakes, tsunamis, and typhoons. The climate is largely temperate. About 40% of the population live in 86 large cities. There are two population peaks, from age 45–60 and age 20–34. The vast majority of people (over 99%) are of Japanese origin. There is a small Korean community.

The main agricultural crop is rice, followed by spinach, potatoes, sugar beet, cabbages, small citrus fruits, sugar cane, onions, and sweet potatoes. Poultry are the main livestock, followed by pigs and cattle. Meat and dairy products are important. Japan is one of the top world fishing nations, with a wide variety of species caught, mostly from deep sea fishing in the Pacific. Aquaculture is increasingly important. General food self-sufficiency was 40% in 1998. Forest covers two-thirds of the land, and timber production includes industrial lumber, pulpwood, and fuel wood. Limestone and silica are the main mineral products. Small amounts of natural gas, petroleum, and coal are produced. Proven oil reserves were 59 million barrels and gas reserves were 1.4 trillion cubic feet at January 2001. Other mineral production includes lead, copper, zinc, gold, and iron ore. There are reserves of wolfram and talc.

Communications/Energy

There were 4,584 miles of motorways in March 1999 out of an estimated total road

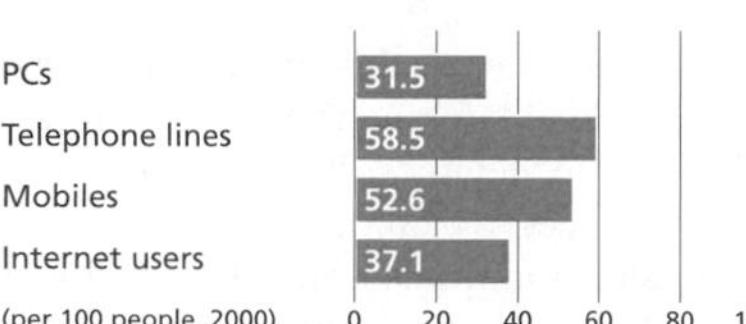

network of around 0.75 million miles. The rail network was 14,708 miles in 1994, 8,308 miles of which was electrified. The world's first operating superconductive, magnetically-levitated train recorded a test speed of 343 mph in April 1999. There are about 1,100 miles of navigable waterways. The pipeline network includes 1,118 miles for natural gas, 200 miles for petroleum products, and 52 miles for crude petroleum. The main sea ports are Tokyo, Yokohama, Nagoya, Osaka, and Kobe. The merchant fleet comprised 630 ships over 1,000 grt, representing a total of 11.7 million grt in 2000. There were 142 airports, 31 airstrips, and 16 heliports in 2000. There are international airports at Tokyo (Narita) and Osaka (Kansai). Air fares were completely deregulated in 2000. In 1998, 54.5% of domestic freight (300.7 billion tons/mile) and 67% of passengers (1,536.5 billion passenger/mile) traveled by road, 41.2% (227 billion tons/mile) and 0.3% (7.4 billion passenger/mile) by coastal ship, and 4.2% (22.9 billion tons/mile) and 27.3% (625.8 billion passenger/mile) by rail. Domestic air travel accounted for 5.3% (122 billion passenger/mile) of passengers.

Telecommunications services are deregulated, but the former state monopoly NTT remains dominant. At end-2000 there were 74.3 million fixed phone lines, 66.8 million mobile phones, and 47.1 million Internet users. In 2000 medium- and high-speed links accounted for 85% of international data connections. Cable TV networks are expanding, and provide Internet access. The government's National Information Infrastructure plan aims to link all homes, offices, schools, and government offices to fiberoptic cable by 2005.

Japan is dependent on imports for around 80% of its energy needs. Domestic oil production was 76,620 barrels per day in the first quarter 2001. In 1999 gas production was 80 billion cubic feet and coal output was 4.1 million tons. Oil consumption in 2001 was 5.6 million barrels per day. In 1999 gas consumption was 2.6 trillion cubic feet and coal consumption was 149.5 million tons. In 1999 electricity was generated mainly from imported oil, gas, and coal (59%), with nuclear providing 30% from 52 power plants, hydroelectricity 8%, and other sources (including waste incineration and solar and wind energy) 3%. Nine new nuclear power plants will add 11.3 GW to capacity by 2008 despite public concern over safety incidents in recent years. The electricity market was opened to competition from 1995. Large industrial companies have supplied surplus electricity to the grid from 1999. This source, incineration, and the use of solar panels by households are set to increase their share of the energy supply.

Education/Employment

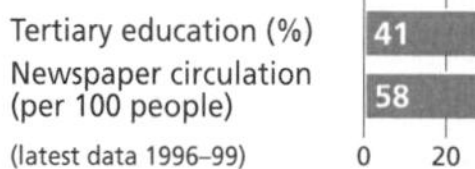

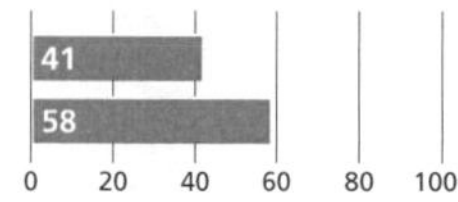

Education is compulsory from age 6 to 15. In 1999 there were 62 technical colleges with 56,436 students, 585 junior colleges with 377,852 students, 622 universities with 2.7 million students, 3,565 special training schools with 753,740 students, and 2,361 vocational schools with 230,502 students. In addition, 73,000 people were enrolled on distance courses provided by the University of the Air. Law and economics were the most popular higher education subjects, followed by science and technology, and liberal arts. Most higher education is funded by the government, and policy is the remit of the Ministry of Education.

R&D relies traditionally on private-sector investment. In 1992–95 this fell because of the recession. The 1995 Science and Technology Basic Law requires national and local governments to promote R&D. Total R&D spending revived in 1996 and rose to ¥16 trillion in 1999, 3.12% of GDP. The private sector accounted for ¥12.4 trillion, 77.8% of the total. Companies accounted for ¥10.6 trillion, universities and colleges ¥3.2 trillion, and research institutions ¥2.17 trillion. Basic research comprised 14.1% of activity, applied research 23.6%, and development 62.3%. Electrical machinery, chemicals, and transportation equipment accounted for 63% of company R&D. Other key areas include biotechnology, IT, and new materials.

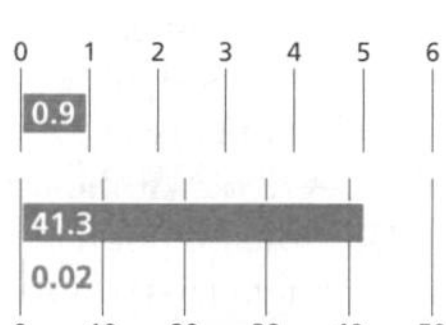

The labor force is well educated. Wages and other employment conditions are determined between employers and trade unions in the larger companies, and by employers and workers in non-unionized situations. In 2000 only 23% of workers were

unionized. Employment practices in the large companies are still built around lifetime employment and seniority-based wage increases, but in 1998 a quarter of large companies had a performance-based pay structure. Recently there has been greater recourse to fixed-term and part-time contracts. The Labor Standards Law is the key employment law.

Fiscal/Financial

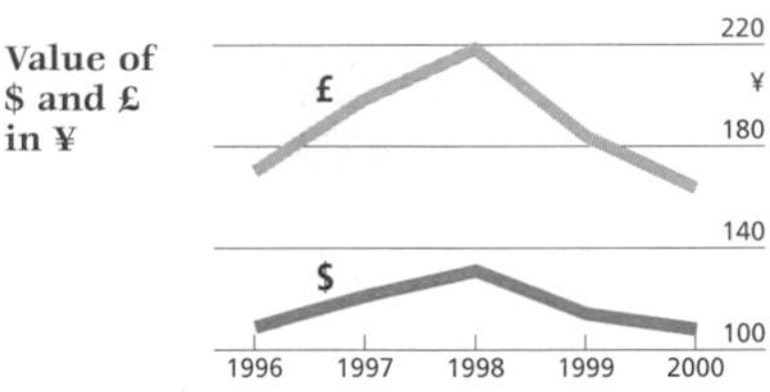

There are four huge banking groups and one huge insurance group, all in the private sector. The largest bank is Mizuho Financial Group, formed from a merger in late 2000 between Dai-Ichi Kangyo Bank, Fuji Bank, and the Industrial Bank of Japan. Mizuho was the second-largest bank in the world at mid-2000. The second-largest Japanese bank (third largest in the world at mid-2000) is the result of a merger in April 2001 between Sanwa, Tokai, and Asahi Banks. The third-largest Japanese group consists of Sumitomo and Sakura Banks, due to merge in spring 2002. The fourth is Tokyo Mitsubishi Bank. The largest insurance group is Millea Insurance Group, the result of a merger in early 2001 between the largest non-life insurer, Tokio Marine & Fire Insurance, seventh-largest non-life insurer Nichido Fire & Marine Insurance, and fifth-largest life insurer Asahi Mutual Life Insurance.

Regulation of the financial services sector is conducted by a single entity, the Financial Services Agency (FSA) created in 1998, which has tightened up inspection of all financial organizations to bring practice in line with U.S. and European standards. The Bank of Japan is the central bank, responsible—with the Ministry of Finance—for monetary policy. Corporation tax is 30%. The effective rate, including local and national taxes, is 40.87%. The top rate of personal income tax is 37% and local residential tax is 13%. Withholding tax on dividends is 20%. Consumption tax is 5%.

The financial services industry is undergoing radical change. The "city" banks—the leading commercial banks before the 1990s recession—have merged to confront international competition. Foreign banks have gained increasing access, and the sector is adapting to Western accounting and stock market practices. The cross-shareholdings between banks and industry are unraveling. Japanese retail banking is changing from a cash basis to debit cards as of 1999, and more advanced e-banking. Checks are still rare. Cash withdrawals from ATM machines are done online, with a lower security risk than offline operations. New bank operators, such as Japan Net Bank and Sony Corp., are focused on Internet banking.

Banking and stockbroking activities are separated under present laws, but the unitary regulatory FSA allows for better assessment of risk management and consequently better integration of banking and investment operations, including stock market activity. In 1999 a new registration system for securities intermediaries led to an increase in off-exchange trading in securities via banks, non-banks, general trading companies, and electrical manufacturers. At the same time Internet trading increased stock market operations, and deregulation of stockbroking commissions lowered costs, again with a diversity of new service providers. These developments offer the prospect of a greater opening up to risky instruments such as derivatives trading, which has been underused. Foreign bank consultancy on mergers and acquisitions has promoted this aspect of stock market activity. New laws prevent a bank from holding more than 5% of the equity in a corporation: as banks merge, so the number of shares they need to sell off increases. The Tokyo Stock Exchange introduced less stringent listing criteria for emerging companies in 1999. The Osaka Stock Exchange opened a joint venture with New York's NASDAQ exchange in 2000: NASDAQ Japan for smaller dynamic companies. In 2000 revisions were made to the way in which the Nikkei stock market index is calculated, giving priority to IT and other high market liquidity firms over the traditional heavy industry sectors.

Business Opportunities

Growth in output (% p.a., 1990–99)

Services	2.2
Industry	0.8
Manufacturing	1.2
Agriculture	−1.6

The government offers tax incentives, soft loans, credit guarantees, subsidized training for employees, and assistance in location and other practical details for new companies, including foreign firms. Technology-intensive investment is encouraged through the Technopolis scheme. There are many barriers to foreign inward investment, including restricted industrial sectors, legal constraints (which are diminishing), standards verification and other official procedures, and consumer preference for Japanese suppliers. Finance and insurance, machinery manufacturing, commercial services, trade, telecommunications, and chemicals manufacture were the main destinations of foreign inward investment from 1950 to 2000. The United States was the leading foreign investor, followed by the Netherlands, France, Germany, Switzerland, Canada, the United Kingdom, and Singapore. Distribution and logistics, information and communications, medical equipment, and biotechnology are among the many high-growth areas. The point of contact for foreign investors is the Japan External Trade Organization (JETRO).

For More Information

Books:

Facts and Figures of Japan. Tokyo: Foreign Press Center (biannual).
IMF Country Report. *Japan*. Washington, D.C.: IMF.
Japan Business and Investment Opportunities Yearbook. 3rd ed. Washington, D.C.: International Business Publications, 2001 (annual).
Japan Foreign Policy and Government Guide. 3rd ed. Washington, D.C.: International Business Publications, 2001.
The Japanese Economy: Recent Trends and Outlook 2000. Economic Planning Agency, Japanese government.
Nariai, Osamu. *History of the Modern Japanese Economy* (About Japan Series, 2). Tokyo: Foreign Press Center, 1999.
OECD Economic Surveys. *Japan*. Paris: OECD, 2001.
Rowthorn, Chris, et al. *Japan*. 7th ed. Oakland, CA: Lonely Planet, 2000.
World Trade Organization. *Trade Policy Review: Japan*. Lanham, MD: Bernan Press, 2002.

Web Sites:

Bank of Japan: **www.boj.or.jp**
Japan National Tourist Organization: **www.jnto.go.jp**
Japanese Chamber of Commerce and Industry: **www.jcci.or.jp**
Ministry of Foreign Trade (government entry point): **www.mofa.go.jp**
Ministry of International Trade and Industry: **www.miti.go.jp**
Statistics Bureau: **www.stat.go.jp**
Yomiuri Shimbun (daily newspaper): **www.yomiuri.co.jp/daily**

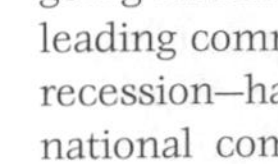

  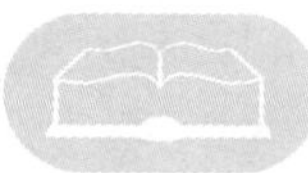    

JORDAN

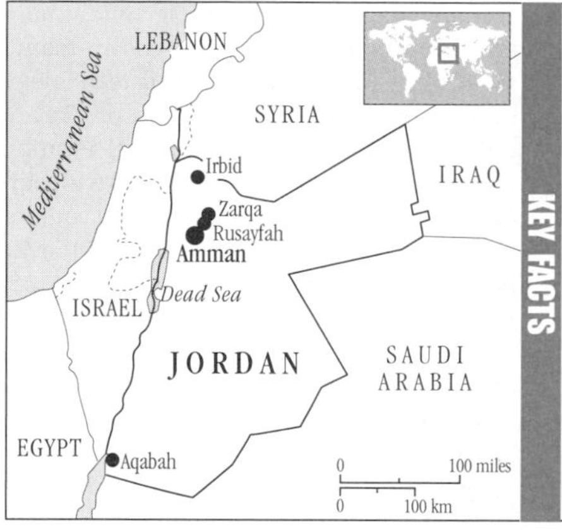

KEY FACTS

GNI: **$7,717 million; world's 96th**
GNI pc: **$1,630; world's 115th**
Head of state: **monarch**
Head of government: **prime minister**
Currency: **Jordanian dinar (JD)**
Capital: **Amman**
Population: **6,482,000, growing at 3.8% p.a.**
Land area: **34,324 square miles**
Population density: **188 per square mile**
Life expectancy: **71 years**
Infant mortality: **29 per 1,000 live births**
Language: **Arabic, English widely spoken**
Best buy: **olive wood objects, textiles, carpets, dates**

ECONOMIC STRUCTURE

Modern Jordan, established by Emir Abdullah in 1921 as a self-governing territory under British mandate, became the independent Hashemite Kingdom of Jordan in 1946. Formal union with the West Bank (of the Jordan River) was declared in 1950, but the West Bank was lost to Israel in 1967. King Hussein ibn Talal (1953–99) maintained a difficult peace with neighboring countries and with Jordan's increasingly large population of Palestinian refugees. King Hussein supported Iraq in the 1990–91 Gulf War to please the Palestinians. Jordan has participated in unofficial and official trade with Iraq since then, with trade at such a high level that the UN has approved barter arrangements between Jordan and Iraq. The 1994 peace treaty with Israel led to increased trade from 1996. Jordan's wealth is based on potash and phosphates. Key industries have been state-owned as a means of developing the economy and providing social welfare. King Abdullah, who succeeded King Hussein, has maintained Jordan's quest for peace through diplomacy, and has accelerated economic and political reform.

In 2000 services accounted for 73% of GDP, followed by industry (including manufacturing, mining, construction and utilities 24.8%), and agriculture 2.2%. Finance, insurance, and real estate are the leading services sectors, followed by transport and communications, and government services. Tourism is important but has suffered from the violence in neighboring Israel. Manufacturing contributed 15.6% of GDP and covers a wide range of activities. Chemicals, especially fertilizers and pharmaceuticals, are established as the leading industries, but textiles and clothing are growing quickly. Jordan is the world's third-largest exporter of raw phosphates. In 2000 potash was the leading export (12.8%), followed by pharmaceuticals (10.3%), raw phosphates (8.4%), clothes (7%), phosphoric acid (6.8%), machinery and transport equipment (6.4%), fertilizers, and vegetables (5.5% each). India was the leading market (15.9%), followed by Iraq (9.3%), Saudi Arabia (8.5%), Israel (5.1%), and the U.A.E. (4.4%).

Public-sector ownership was extensive before the privatization program of the 1990s. From 1995 the government divested all or most of its equity in holding companies of banks, tourism, hotels, ceramics, textiles, tanning, paper, tobacco manufacturing, and agriculture, as well as 48% of Jordan Telecom and one-third of Jordan Cement Factories. Private management has been introduced for Amman water and the Aqabah Railway. Privatization is planned for the power sector, national airline, and Aqabah port in 2002. It is also envisaged for the phosphate and potash mines and for the postal system.

ECONOMIC POLICY

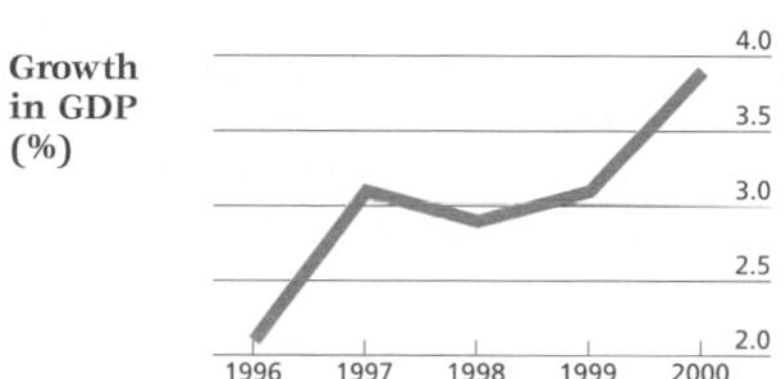

Since 1991 the government has applied a structural adjustment program sanctioned by the IMF to reduce debt levels from 203.4% of GDP in 1990 to 100.7% in 2000. The reduction of subsidies on bread and oil, coupled with privatization, led to increased hardship for many people. Unemployment was as high as 30% in 2000, although the official rate was half that. The government is the largest employer, and the continued streamlining of public administration is likely to lead to more unemployment. In addition the government is committed to reforming the pensions system in the medium term to reduce costs. However, the government increased expenditure for the poor through the National Aid Fund and Social Productivity Program (community projects) in 2001.

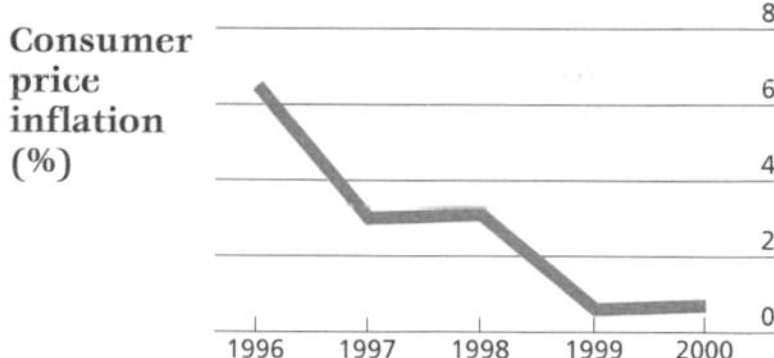

Monetary policy is focused on a stable exchange rate to keep inflation low. The dinar has been pegged to the U.S. dollar at JD1.41 = $1 since 1995. Inflation averaged 0.9% in 1999–2001. Annual GDP growth averaged 3.4% in 1998–2001, and is forecast at 4.6% for 2000–04. The external balance is usually in surplus because of grants from Arab oil states and workers' remittances. Privatization has added to government income in recent years, totaling 7% of GDP in 2000. In 2000 VAT replaced the general sales tax, and the tax administration was strengthened. The government aims to eliminate the budget deficit by 2005 and to reduce total debt to 65% of GDP.

GEOGRAPHY/RESOURCES

In the Middle East, Jordan borders Iraq, Saudi Arabia, the Gulf of Aqabah, Israel, the West Bank, and Syria. The land is mostly desert plateau with highlands in the west, with a high point of 5,689 feet and a low point at the Dead Sea of 1,339 feet below sea level (the lowest point on land in the world). The climate is dry, with average rainfall of 2½ inches in the northwest and ½ inch in the east. Chronic lack of water is a problem for the increasing population and for industry and agriculture. Temperatures range from freezing on high ground in winter to 120°F in the Jordan Valley in summer.

The main agricultural area is the Jordan

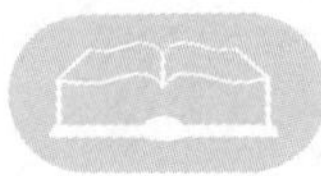

Valley, where a wide range of vegetables and fruit are grown. The main crops are tomatoes, cucumbers, potatoes, citrus, olives, watermelons, almonds, figs, grapes, and apricots. Small quantities of wheat and barley are grown. Poultry is the main livestock, followed by sheep, goats, cattle, camels, asses, horses, and mules. Meat and dairy are important.

Phosphates, potash, salt, construction stone, petroleum, and natural gas are produced. Phosphate reserves total 7 billion tons. At January 2001 there were proven oil reserves of 890,000 barrels and gas reserves of 230 billion cubic feet. Production from oil shale reserves of 40 billion tons is under consideration. Oil and gas exploration continues.

Most of the population live in the Amman area and in the Jordan valley: 70% are under age 30, 60% are Palestinians, and 98% are of Arab origin, with 1% Circassian and 1% Armenian. About 1 million foreign workers live in Jordan.

Communications/Energy

The paved road network was around 4,500 miles in 1999. The 500-mile rail network is being upgraded and expanded. Phosphates are transported on the 71 miles of Aqabah Railway. The original Hedjaz–Jordan Railway connected Damascus in Syria with Medina in Saudi Arabia, and there have been many plans to reopen the entire line. An express rail service was inaugurated between Amman and Damascus in 1999. The only sea port, Aqabah, is equipped with modern cargo facilities. It handled 12.6 million tons of freight in 1998. There are two international commercial airports at Aqabah and Amman.

Majority state-owned Jordan Telecommunications Company is the main operator, but private mobile phone operators have been authorized since 1995. Full competition is planned for the sector in 2004. Links are provided by cable, satellite, and microwave radio relay. Digital switching has increased. At end-2000 there were 620,000 fixed phone lines, 388,900 mobiles, and 127,300 Internet users.

Jordan is dependent on imported oil, mostly from Iraq. In 1999 oil accounted for 93.2% of energy consumption, and natural gas for 4.8%. Hydroelectricity contributed 0.2% of electricity production, the rest generated by oil. Electricity demand has grown at 5% a year since 1995. There are links with the Egyptian and Syrian grids. A new power station, to be operated by Belgian company Tractebel, will be completed in 2004.

Education/Employment

Education is compulsory and free from age 6 to 15. There were 21 universities with 89,000 students enrolled in 1997–98, and 34,000 students attended other higher education institutes. The Ministry of Education is responsible for education. Higher education produces 2,400 graduates a year in IT-related subjects. The Higher Council for Science and Technology is responsible for research policy, project coordination, and funding. Public-sector finance accounts for 60% and private-sector finance 40% of R&D funding. R&D strengths include minerals, engineering, environment protection, agriculture, and medicine.

The labor force is well educated and has a range of skills. Wages are determined between employers and employees or trade unions. About 30% of the work force is unionized, including the civil service and professional associations. Strikes must have government approval. Labor law covers contractual obligations, dismissal, working time, paid leave, and safety at work in compliance with international law.

Fiscal/Financial

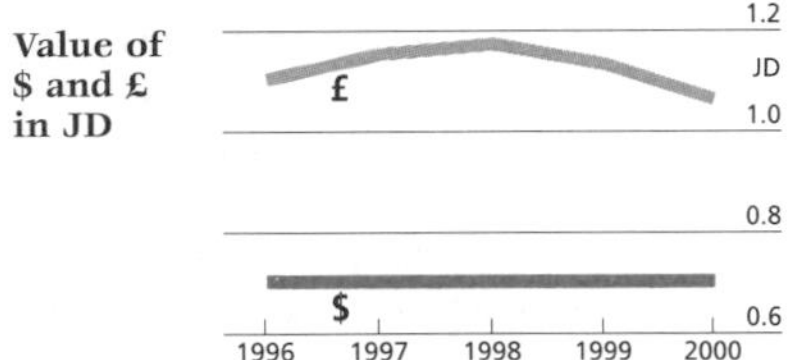

The largest banks by assets at end-2000 were Arab Bank (JD18.5 billion) and Housing Bank (JD1.6 billion). The Middle East Insurance Company and Jordan Insurance Company are the largest by capital. The Central Bank of Jordan regulates the financial sector. The Jordan Securities Commission oversees the stock exchange. The 2000 banking law protects depositors, guards against concentration of lending, and contains sections on e-commerce, e-banking, and money-laundering.

At mid-2001 there were 14 commercial banks (including 5 branches of foreign banks), 5 investment banks, 2 Islamic banks, one industrial development bank, several specialized credit institutions (including the Housing Bank), and 76 money lenders. Arab Bank, which has worldwide operations, accounts for 60% of the total assets and dominates the sector. Some banks offer telebanking and e-banking. The Central Bank is encouraging consolidation. The Amman Stock Exchange became privately managed in 1999, and established electronic trading in 2000 and an independent automated settlement system in 2001. Listing requirements are being updated.

Business Opportunities

Jordan is eager to attract foreign investment in IT, tourism, and services, and in manufacturing which uses advanced technology or local materials. A range of tax breaks are offered according to geographical location and industrial sector. Export goods with Jordanian, Israeli, West Bank, and Gaza content from Qualifying Industrial Zones (QIZs) benefit from duty-free access to the U.S. market. Aqabah port has a special economic zone, and there are free zones at Zarqa, Sahab Industrial Estate, and Queen Alia International Airport. Foreign ownership is banned in road transport, security services, construction stone quarrying, and sports clubs. It is limited to 50% in the case of construction and contracting companies, wastewater treatment, sea, air and rail transport, travel agencies, wholesale and retail trade, import-export, advertising, food services, and various other business services.

QIZs have attracted Asian textile and manufacturing companies facing quota restrictions in the United States. Their success prompted Hong Kong-based Bocan International to build a cybercity in Hassan Estate QIZ for 200 light-industry and media companies. Privatization led to investment from French, U.S., Belgian, Spanish, and other firms in rail transport, water treatment, retail and power. Further privatization offers more opportunities for foreign investment.

For More Information

Books:

El-Said, Hamed, and Kip Becker. *Management and International Business Issues in Jordan*. New York: International Business Press, 2002.

Jordan Business and Investment Opportunities Yearbook. 3rd ed. Washington, D.C.: International Business Publications, 2001 (annual).

Piro, Timothy J. *The Political Economy of Market Reform in Jordan*. Lanham, MD: Rowman & Littlefield, 1998.

Web Sites:

Government entry point: **www.nic.gov.jo**

Jordan Export Development and Commercial Centers Corp: **www.jedco.gov.jo**

Kazakhstan

KEY FACTS

GNI: **$18,732 million; world's 67th**
GNI pc: **$1,250; world's 126th**
Head of state: **president**
Head of government: **prime minister**
Currency: **tenge (Tenge)**
Capital: **Astana**
Population: **16,269,000, growing at –0.3% p.a.**
Land area: **1,031,157 square miles**
Population density: **15 per square mile**
Life expectancy: **68 years**
Infant mortality: **35 per 1,000 live births**
Language: **Kazakh, Russian**
Best buy: **Kazakh cognac**

Economic Structure

In Soviet times Kazakhstan specialized in agriculture, metallurgy, and mineral extraction. After the dissolution of the USSR in 1991 its economy collapsed into slump; the slow recovery has been driven mainly by oil, gas, and metals exports. More than $10 billion was invested in hydrocarbons in the 1990s: production rose to 706,650 barrels per day of oil and gas condensate in 2000, and is expected to continue rising to 1 million barrels per day. Most oil is produced by joint ventures with foreign participation. In 2001 Kazakh refineries were working at one-third of capacity, and most oil is exported. Exports were further boosted by cost cuts when the Caspian pipeline came into operation in late 2001.

After hydrocarbons, mining and processing of metals—including steel, aluminum and alumina, copper, chrome, and gold—is the second-largest exporter and recipient of foreign direct investment.

Relatively few people are employed in the oil sector (mainly near the Caspian coast) and in metals (mostly in large enterprises that dominate nearby towns). Manufacturing industries include aviation, cement, chemical fertilizers, textiles, and food products. Agriculture remains the third-largest export sector and largest employer, employing a quarter of the workforce, although it has suffered from poor harvests (in 1991, 1995, and 1998) and badly-implemented reforms. Kazakhstan is self-reliant in major foodstuffs, although it imports fruit and vegetables from Kyrgyzstan and Uzbekistan.

Kazakh exports consist predominantly of natural resources: hydrocarbons account for 40% and metals for 25%. Russia remains Kazakhstan's prime trade partner, accounting for 19.5% of exports and 48.7% of imports in 2000, but the proportion of trade with non-CIS countries has grown, from 46.2% of exports and 30.5% of imports in 1996 to 73.8% and 45.4% respectively in 2000.

Economic Policy

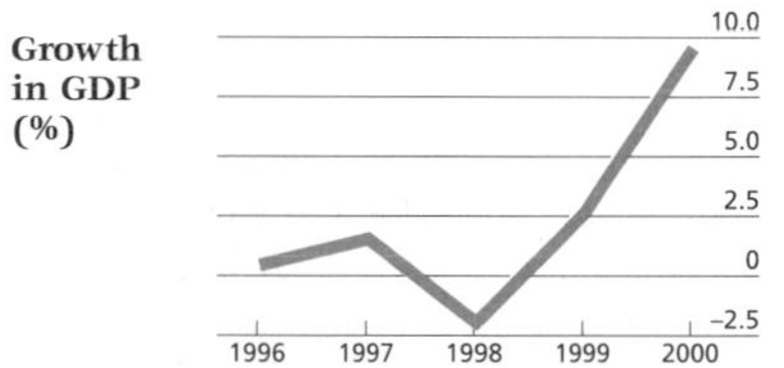

The post-Soviet economic collapse resulted in GDP falling by 44% between 1990 and 1994. Industry and agriculture continued to decline after that: industry's share of GDP fell from 31% (1992) to 22.5% (1998), and agriculture's from 34.9% (1990) to 8.8% (1998). Stabilization from the mid-1990s was interrupted by the Asian crisis of 1997 and the oil price dip and Russian crisis of 1998, but by 2000 the economy was growing rapidly. GDP growth averaged 9.8% in 2000–01.

Economic policy has favored market reforms. In April 1999, following a period of heavy intervention to sustain the exchange rate after the Russian crisis, the tenge was allowed to depreciate and lost 75% of its value against the dollar. In 2000 fiscal revenue surpassed 20% of GDP for the first time, indicating that long-standing tax collection problems were being addressed. Matters were improved by tight fiscal policy, some quick sales of state assets, resumption of an IMF lending program, a return to international debt markets, and strong oil prices. A national fund, in which windfall oil profits are accumulated for strategic investment, was established in 2000, and by May 2001 totaled $1.2 billion. A one-month amnesty for flight capital in June 2001 brought $485 million back into Kazakhstan.

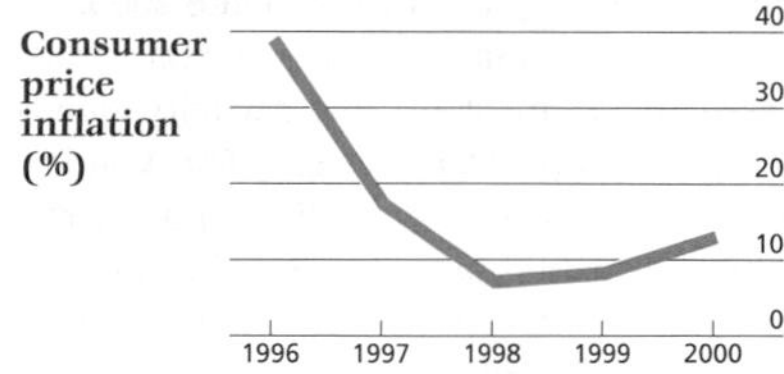

Privatization, mainly by direct sale, expanded the private sector in the late 1990s but slowed in 2000–01. The private sector accounted for 25% of GDP in 1995 and 60% in 2001. Slow progress on other aspects of market reform, including infrastructure and tax administration reform and land ownership rights, has been criticized by international institutions.

Geography/Resources

Kazakhstan is a vast tableland bordering the Caspian Sea to its southwest, rising to high mountains in the southeast along the border with Kyrgyzstan and China. It is bordered in the northwest by the southern Urals region of Russia, and to the north by western Siberia. Lowlands account for more than one-third of the total area and hilly plains for nearly half; the rest is mountainous.

Much of southern and western Kazakhstan needs extra water supplies, and overuse of the Syr Darya and other feeder rivers has caused the Aral Sea between Kazakhstan and Uzbekistan to shrink. Another serious environmental problem is radioactive contamination of the area around Semipalatinsk in the northwest, used for nuclear testing in Soviet times.

Kazakhstan's oil and gas reserves are its most valuable resource. Although some earlier estimates were exaggerated, proven reserves by the end of the 1990s were 15.5 billion barrels of oil and 250 million cubic feet of gas, with further reserves in the north Caspian. There are also rich reserves of copper, lead, zinc, gold, and iron.

Because of a low birth rate, Kazakhstan's natural rate of population increase is 6.5 per 1,000 (against a world average of 15.7), leading to a fall in overall numbers in post-Soviet times to 14.9 million in 2000.

Communications/Energy

Kazakhstan's oil industry is dominated by foreign-controlled joint ventures such as the Tengizchevroil production company and the

Offshore Kazakhstan International Operating Company which is carrying out exploration work in the North Caspian. Most of its production is exported. The state's shift in focus in the oil industry from production—where it has not competed well with the foreign companies—to transport was marked by the formation of the pipeline monopoly Kaztransneftegaz in late 2000.

Despite being a net oil exporter, Kazakhstan meets most of its electricity needs through imports from Russia. The volume and cost of these is falling, but inter-enterprise debts have resulted in debts to Russian suppliers, and in power cuts. Similar debts have built up for Uzbek gas imports (which have been continued because they are cheaper than gas transported across Kazakhstan). About 80% of power generation is based in the industrial northwest. Power transmission and distribution networks are badly in need of investment.

Communications are poor. There are 15 fixed telephone lines per 100 inhabitants; the use of mobile telephones is growing rapidly from a small base. The largest provider, Kazakhtelecom, was partly privatized in 1997.

Transportation relies heavily on the railways, which need modernizing: a restructuring program began in 2001. Road investment is also needed as only 25% of the motorways are usable.

Education/Employment

The sharp contraction in output in the early 1990s had a negative impact on the workforce. Real wages have fallen by more than 50%, and unemployment has risen to around 14%. New labor force entrants and unskilled workers suffered worst from unemployment, while emigration has eroded the skilled workforce. A quota system on foreign workers has been introduced, aimed in the first instance at Turkish and Indian construction contractors with their own supply of labor which is even cheaper than that available locally. A labor law that came into force in 2000 provides for the regulation of locally-agreed contracts. Equal pay for equal work is required between Kazakh and foreign employees. The law also gives employers the right to dismiss workers for organizing illegal strikes, and removes Soviet-era special status for trade unions.

Kazakhstan has almost universal literacy (97.5%), and more than two-thirds of the population has completed secondary or tertiary education. However, a substantial reduction in education spending—from 7% of GDP in 1990 to 3.3% in 2000—bodes ill for the future. Kazakhstan has 61 tertiary education institutions, but a fall in enrollment in tertiary institutions (from 1.7% of the population to 1.6%) and in vocational and specialized secondary education in the early and mid-1990s has not been reversed. The private educational sector has grown, from 137 institutions in 1996 to 382 in 2000, but even then it only accounted for 5% of students.

Fiscal/Financial

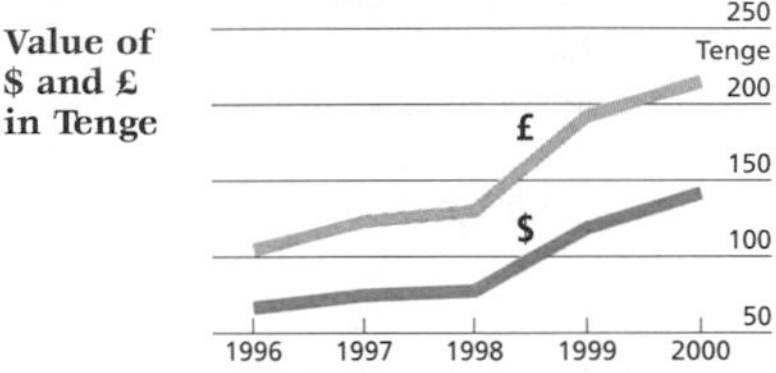

Kazakhstan's banking sector weathered the 1999 credit squeeze better than expected. Confidence in it has grown, due to reformist initiatives by the National Bank chairman Grigorii Marchenko. From 2000, partial conversion of deposits to other currencies and limited deposit insurance were introduced. In the first half of 2001, banking sector assets grew by 80%. By mid-2001 total bank loans had grown to $2.7 billion, and banking sector equity to $678 million. Three domestic banks—Kazkommertsbank, Turan-Alem Bank, and Halyk Savings Bank—dominate the sector and account for more than 50% of its assets. The foreign bank sector, led by ABN Amro and Citibank, has grown: from 2000, foreign ownership of banks was permitted to rise to 50%.

Kazakhstan's stock exchange opened in 1997. In early 2001 the total capitalization of the stock market was under $1.4 billion, and there were 58 licensed brokers. In 1998 the government began to encourage the formation of private pension funds, and by July 2001 the newly-established funds had accumulated $1 billion of assets, but most of these were invested in government bonds. The insurance sector is in its infancy.

Tax reform is continuing. From July 2001 employers' social contributions were reduced from 26% to 21%, VAT was lowered from 20% to 16%, and the destination principle applied to all VAT payments, so that oil exports to CIS countries, for example, will be VAT-free. Income from foreign companies permanently in Kazakhstan is taxed locally; foreigners do not pay income tax if their salaries are paid by a non-resident entity.

Business Opportunities

Foreign investment averaged $1.4 billion p.a. in 1996–2001. The United States is the largest foreign investor, mainly into the upstream oil and gas sector. Kazakhstan has given preferential status, with substantial tax breaks for investors, to industries including industrial infrastructure, residential construction, tourism, and agriculture. A State Agency for Investments, and a Foreign Investors Council chaired by the president, have been established.

Foreign exchange surrender has been abolished and full currency account convertibility introduced. International institutions are working with Kazakhstan to overcome potential obstacles to inward investment.

Equipment and services procurement for the oil and gas sectors offers the biggest opportunities. Apart from the major hydrocarbons joint ventures, there has been successful inward investment via the sale of stakes in major metals producers, including in the Ispat-Karmet steelworks sold to Ispat International of the United Kingdom, in Kazakhmys copper works to Samsung of Korea, and in the Ust-Kamenogorsk titanium works to Belgian interests. Privatization purchases and partnerships are also available in infrastructure businesses (power and other utilities, telecoms, the national airline, etc). Joint stock companies and limited liability partnerships are preferred forms for inward investment.

For More Information

Books:

George, Alexandra. *Journey into Kazakhstan: The True Face of the Nazarbayev Regime*. Lanham, MD: University Press of America, 2001.

Kazakhstan Business and Investment Opportunities Yearbook. 3rd ed. Washington, D.C.: International Business Publications, 2001 (annual).

Olcott, Martha Brill, ed. *Kazakhstan: Unfulfilled Promise*. Washington, D.C.: Carnegie Endowment for International Peace, 2002.

Rigi, Jakob. *Post-Soviet Chaos and the New Capitalism: Kazakhstan, a Case Study*. London: Pluto Press, 1999.

Svanberg, Ingvar, ed. *Contemporary Kazaks*. New York: Palgrave, 1999.

Web Sites:

Kazakh stock exchange: **www.kase.kz/eng**

Kazakhstan business information site: **www.kazecon.kz**

Khabar news agency: **www.khabar.kz**

National Bank of Kazakhstan: **www.nationalbank.kz/eng**

Official presidential site: **www.president.kz**

World Bank in Kazakhstan: **www.worldbank.kz**

KENYA

KEY FACTS

GNI: **$10,696 million; world's 83rd**
GNI pc: **$360; world's 172nd**
Head of government: **president**
Currency: **Kenya shilling (KSh)**
Capital: **Nairobi**
Population: **29,549,000, growing at 2.5% p.a.**
Land area: **219,729 square miles**
Population density: **134 per square mile**
Life expectancy: **51 years**
Infant mortality: **76 per 1,000 live births**
Language: **Swahili, English, Kikuyu, Luo, other languages**
Best buy: **carvings, beadwork, textiles, coffee, flowers**

ECONOMIC STRUCTURE

Kenya has been ruled since independence in 1963 by the Kenya African National Union (KANU), at first under President Jomo Kenyatta and, since 1978, under President Daniel arap Moi. The country has a reputation for stability despite periods of political and ethnic unrest, but the government has been repeatedly criticized both for its tolerance of corruption and for its inefficient economic policies, factors which have tended to deter new investment. Elections for a new parliament and president are scheduled for 2002.

The country remains a focal point for tourism in East Africa, but after political disturbances during the mid-1990s the number of visitors went into decline, and has not fully recovered since then. Tourism is the country's principal source of foreign exchange, but agriculture—which accounts for about 30% of GDP—is still the backbone of the economy. There is also an active industrial sector, contributing about 14% of GDP. Tea and coffee constitute Kenya's most valuable exports, while horticulture has developed strongly. However, both agriculture and industry have proved to be vulnerable to periods of drought. During 2000 there was severe electric power rationing when hydroelectric plants were affected by low water levels.

The largest customers for Kenya's exports are Uganda, Tanzania, the United Kingdom, Germany, and the Netherlands. However, exports have been in decline since 1997 because of the depressed state of the economy and low world prices for tea and coffee.

The public sector has been reduced in size, with the sale of many small and medium-sized businesses, although the government has been reluctant to relinquish control of some of the more important monopolies. Some of the most prominent companies still scheduled for privatization are the Kenya Ports Authority, Kenya Railways, and Telkom Kenya.

ECONOMIC POLICY

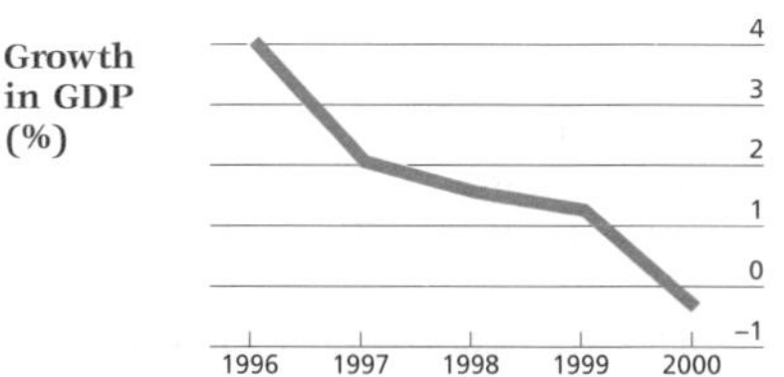

Macro-economic policy has been subject to considerable variability and ongoing negotiation with the international financial institutions. In 1993, the government enacted a program of economic liberalization, including the removal of import licensing, price controls, and foreign exchange controls. Although this at first led to an improvement of economic performance, the government's subsequent failure to maintain the pace of reform or to weed out corruption led to a collapse of international confidence. Economic growth slowed to 1.5% in 1999 and again to –0.3% in 2000. A new economic management team was put in place during 1999 with a brief to revitalize reform, tackle corruption, and reduce the size of the civil service, but this was again dismantled in 2001.

Despite some buoyancy in tourism, foreign exchange earnings from other sources have been depressed, and Kenya has suffered a mounting external current account deficit. The Paris Club of official creditors agreed in November 2000 to reschedule

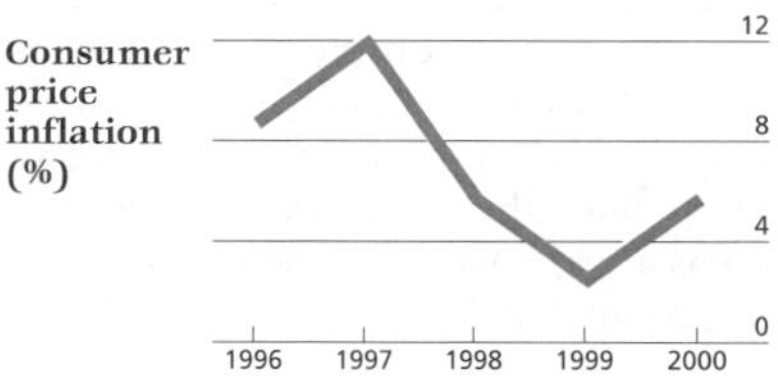

Kenya's foreign debts, cutting due repayments by one-third. Inflation has been kept under control since the mid-1990s but began to move upwards during 2000 to an estimated 5.9% under the influence of an increase in the VAT rate and of rising fuel prices.

GEOGRAPHY/RESOURCES

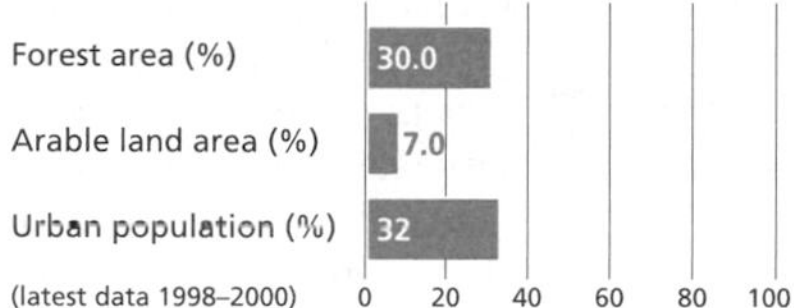

Kenya is a large country with considerable geographical and climatic variations within its borders, from semi-desert conditions in the north to significant highlands in the center and west. The Great Rift Valley runs north to south, with a width of 40 miles in places, and is bounded by high escarpments. In the southwest lies Lake Victoria. Rainfall is highest in the west and at the coast. The highlands of the west receive rain in a single long season, while in the east there is a pattern of two rainy seasons. Large tracts of land are given over to game parks, where there is an abundance of wild animals. Nevertheless, under pressure from increased human cultivation of available land there has been a sharp deterioration in biodiversity, and both deforestation and soil erosion are becoming serious problems. Water resources are also under pressure from over-use.

The principal food crops are corn, sorghum, cassava, and bananas, while the main export crops are tea, coffee, pyrethrum, and sisal. The livestock industry is substantial. Minerals include limestone, soda ash, salt barites, fluorspar, gold, and precious stones, but mining is not a significant contributor to the economy.

Kenya had an extremely high population growth rate until the early 1990s but this has tended to be reduced by family planning campaigns and by the impact of HIV/AIDS. There has, however, been a refugee influx from countries to the north, and the population currently stands at around 30 million.

  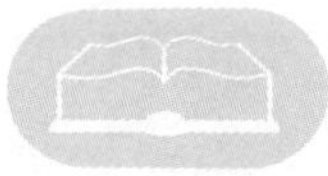  

The main centers of population are located in the central and western regions of the country and around Mombasa.

The indigenous population is a mix of Bantu, Nilotic, and Cushitic ethnic groups, with the Kikuyu and Luo being the largest single groups. There has long been Arab influence along the Indian Ocean coast, and there is a small but economically important Asian population.

Communications/Energy

	(per 100 people, 2000)
PCs	0.5
Telephone lines	1.1
Mobiles	0.4
Internet users	0.7

(per 100 people, 2000) 0 20 40 60 80 100

There are 39,600 miles of roads, of which 5,510 miles are surfaced, although poor maintenance has caused the most heavily-used roads to deteriorate rapidly. A narrow-gauge railway line links the port at Mombasa with the capital, Nairobi, and beyond to Kenya's landlocked neighbor, Uganda. Mombasa port is a vital hub of the economy but has developed a reputation for inefficiency and delay; increasing quantities of goods for the East African region are being shipped through Dar es Salaam.

There are two major international airports, at Nairobi and Mombasa, while a third has been built at Eldoret. The Dutch airline KLM manages, and has shares in, the national airline, Kenya Airways.

The national telecommunications provider is Telkom Kenya, which has been investing in new equipment and laying off surplus staff ahead of eventual privatization.

The Kenya Power and Lighting Company (KPLC) is dependent on hydroelectric generation for most of its power, but is undertaking an ambitious expansion program to build diesel and geothermal power stations across the country. There are also plans to increase imports of electricity from Uganda and from the Southern African power pool. Kenya has no oil reserves. Fuel is supplied by the Mombasa oil refinery or imported.

Education/Employment

Government provision of educational facilities has come under budgetary pressure, and parents have been required to cover an increasing part of the costs of education. In the late 1990s there was a decline in enrollment in both primary and secondary education. There is also a high drop-out rate, with less than half of those who initially enroll going on to complete their primary education. Primary enrollment amounted to 5.9 million children in 15,900 schools in 1999. Secondary enrollment was 638,500 pupils in 2,900 schools. There are about 40 technical colleges, 30 teacher training colleges, 5 public universities, and 12 private universities.

Of a potential total labor force of 14.5 million people, an estimated 77% are employed in agriculture, hunting, forestry, and fishing. About 15% work in services and 7% work in industry.

Fiscal/Financial

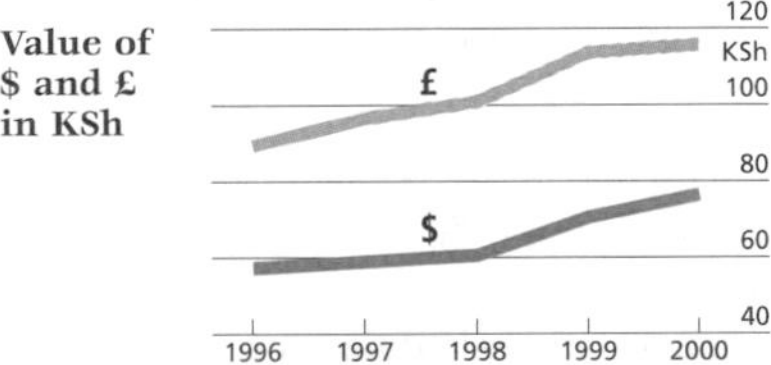

The tax regime is intended to favor new investors, especially in industry and tourism. In order to improve the efficiency and propriety of revenue collection, the Kenya Revenue Authority has been reorganized.

The central bank is the Central Bank of Kenya. The four largest commercial banks are Barclays Bank of Kenya, Kenya Commercial Bank, National Bank of Kenya, and Standard Chartered Bank Kenya. Until the late 1990s, the market was highly competitive, but once it began to shrink there was an urgent need to restructure and merge institutions. In 1998, the central bank placed five banks under statutory management after they failed to meet their financial obligations. In 2000 there were 56 commercial banks, 44 foreign exchange bureaux, 8 representative offices of foreign banks, and 13 non-bank financial institutions. The viability of the smaller banks has been adversely affected by government attempts to regulate interest rates.

The Nairobi Stock Exchange has recorded declining levels of profitability among its leading stocks, accompanied by a substantial outflow of investor funds.

Business Opportunities

There are generous investment allowances for investors in the manufacturing and tourism sectors. Enterprises operating in export processing zones enjoy tax holidays and exemptions, and reduced tax rates. Growth areas in manufacturing include textiles and engineering, and there is potential to increase areas of industry such as vehicle assembly, electronics, plastics, chemicals, and construction goods. The fastest-growing agricultural sector is the growing of fruit, vegetables, and flowers for export. However, the introduction of further diversification and sophistication of the agricultural sector is also possible, especially to bring improvements in packaging, storage, and transportation.

Tourism has received very little new investment in recent years, especially after visitor numbers went into steady decline in the mid-1990s in reaction to negative publicity about the country.

For More Information

Books:

Kenya Business and Investment Opportunities Yearbook. 3rd ed. Washington, D.C.: International Business Publications, 2001 (annual).

Le Carré, J. *The Constant Gardener* (novel). New York: Pocket Books, 2001.

Miller, N., and R. Yeager. *Kenya: The Quest for Prosperity*. Boulder, CO: Westview Press, 1993.

Ochieng, W. R., and R. M. Maxon. *An Economic History of Kenya*. Nairobi: East African Educational Publishers, 1992.

Ogot, B. A., and W. R. Ochieng, eds. *Decolonisation and Independence in Kenya, 1940-93*. Athens, OH: Ohio University Press, 1995.

Trillo, Richard. *The Rough Guide to Kenya*. 7th ed. New York: Rough Guides, 2002.

Web Sites:

Africa Online: **www.africaonline.com/site/ke**

African news and information: **www.allafrica.com/business**

Investment Promotion Center: **www.ipckenya.org**

Kenyaweb.com: **www.kenyaweb.com**

Norwegian Council for Africa. Index on Africa: **www.afrika.no/index**

Political Resources on the Net: **www.politicalresources.net**

  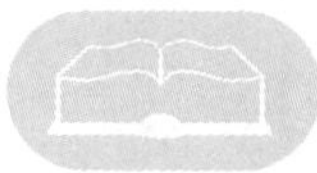    

KUWAIT

KEY FACTS

GDP: **$29,572 million**
GDP pc: **$15,590**
Head of state: **emir**
Head of government: **prime minister**
Currency: **Kuwaiti dinar (KD)**
Capital: **Kuwait**
Population: **1,897,000, growing at –1.4% p.a.**
Land area: **6,872 square miles**
Population density: **273 per square mile**
Life expectancy: **76 years**
Infant mortality: **11 per 1,000 live births**
Language: **Arabic (official), English widely spoken**
Best buy: **luxury goods, dates**

ECONOMIC STRUCTURE

The al-Sabah dynasty was established in the mid-18th century, when Kuwait was a province of the Ottoman Empire. During the 19th century Kuwait was a thriving port, with general trade, fishing, pearls, and shipbuilding its main strengths. A protectorate treaty with Britain was signed in 1899. Oil was discovered in 1938, and production expanded after independence in June 1961. Since then Kuwait's oil wealth has financed an ultra-modern physical infrastructure and state-run social infrastructure. The state manages around three-quarters of the economy. The Kuwait Investment Authority, established in 1982, has built up a massive portfolio of foreign holdings estimated at over $60 billion. This proved invaluable in keeping Kuwaiti assets out of Iraqi hands during the 1990–91 Iraqi invasion, and in providing resources for reconstruction after the Gulf War liberation.

In 1999 services accounted for 52.2% of GDP, followed by oil and gas (37.1%), and manufacturing (12.2%). Social, community, and personal services were the largest services sector (25.2% of GDP), followed by finance, insurance and business services (14.2%), trade and hotels (7.2%), and transport and communications (5.6%). The main manufacturing industries are oil refining and petrochemicals. Oil and oil products accounted for 90% of exports in 1999, followed by chemicals (5.7%). The main markets were Saudi Arabia (11.5%), followed by the U.A.E. (9.3%), India (8.6%), Switzerland (7.5%), and the United States (4.6%).

Privatization has been mooted for some years to introduce greater efficiency and allow access to the latest foreign technology. However, privatization is unpopular because 93% of Kuwaitis work for the public sector, and public services, housing, and utilities are heavily subsidized. In June 2001 the government divested over half of its holdings in the Mobile Telecommunication Company. The government has sold its equity in most of the nation's banks and insurance companies. These holdings were acquired following the stock market crashes of 1979 and 1982 and during the 1992 Bank Stabilization Program to wipe out bad debts, restructure the banks, overhaul management practices, and provide development capital. The five-year privatization plan announced in July 2001 includes the national airline, petrol stations, telecommunications, ports, public transport, power, water, and the Petrochemical Industries Company (PIC), but each privatization must be approved by the National Assembly. Several build-operate-transfer projects involving the private sector are under way in healthcare, water treatment, and real estate development. Foreign participation in upgrading the northern oilfields was due to be agreed by 2002. The state-owned PIC is expanding in joint ventures with the Kuwaiti private sector and U.S. company Union Carbide.

ECONOMIC POLICY

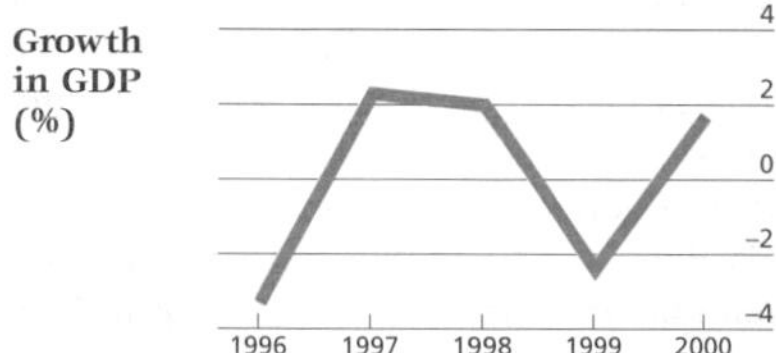

Kuwait has huge financial reserves and is well managed, but its very wealth militates against structural change that would inject more dynamism into the domestic economy. Investment income from overseas has waned since spring 2000, reflecting the downturn in the international economy. The domestic economy remains heavily dependent on oil, and reforms to strengthen downstream manufacturing and diversification have been slow to take shape. The 2001 law lifting restrictions on foreign direct and portfolio investment should give more momentum to change.

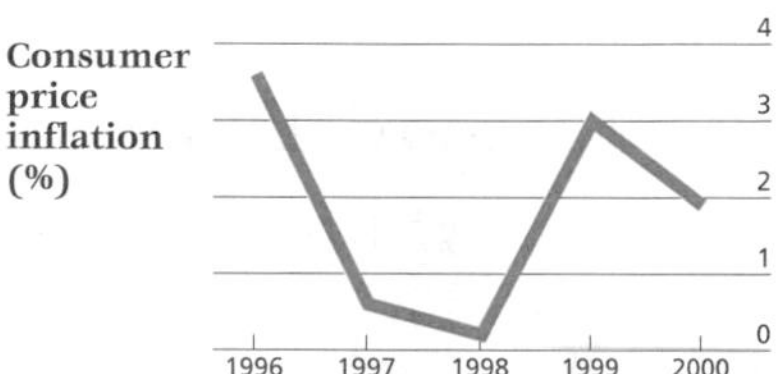

Following streamlining of the public sector, there are fewer public-sector jobs available to the growing number of young Kuwaitis entering the job market, but they are not eager to join the private sector. In April 2000 the government extended social benefits previously reserved for the public sector to private-sector Kuwaiti employees to help improve private-sector recruitment. It also established unemployment benefit for Kuwaitis looking for work in either the public or private sector. The benefits will be funded from a levy on firms. Annual GDP growth, heavily dependent on oil prices, averaged 2% in 1997–2001. It is expected to decline by 1.3% in 2002. Inflation averaged 1.6% in 1997–2001 and is expected to rise to 3.3% in 2002.

GEOGRAPHY/RESOURCES

At the head of the Persian Gulf, Kuwait is bordered by Iraq to the north and Saudi Arabia to the south. The land is low-lying desert, with a high point of 984 feet. Summers are intensely hot and winters cool. With only 1–7 inches of annual rainfall, most water comes from desalination plants. Most of the population (56.8%) are expatriates, but the high birth rate will double the Kuwaiti population to around 1.4 million by 2015. 60% of Kuwaitis are under age 25. Other Arab nationalities account for 35% of the population, South Asian for 9%, Iranian for 4%, and other nationalities 7%. Most food is imported, but the small agricultural sector produces vegetables, cereals, dates, meat, dairy, and leather. There is a small fishing industry, with a wide variety of species caught.

At January 2001, proven oil reserves in Kuwait and its half-share of the neutral zone (shared with Saudi Arabia) were 96.5 billion barrels (9% of the world total) with natural gas reserves of 52.7 trillion cubic feet. Saudi Arabia and Kuwait agreed in 2000 to share equally the offshore Dorra gas field, but this is also claimed by Iran, and negotiations with Iran continue. Exploration for oil and gas continue. In 2000 Iraq renewed its accusation, denied by Kuwait, that Kuwait was stealing its oil through horizontal drilling at the Ratqa oil field on the border close to Iraq's huge Rumaila field. Iraq's claim was one of its reasons for invading Kuwait in 1990.

Communications/Energy

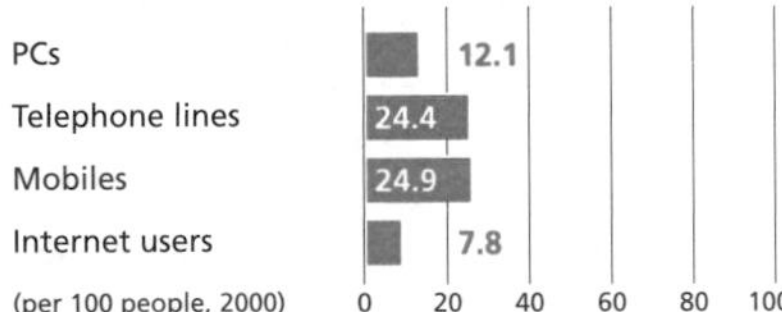

The road network was a total 2,765 miles, 2,230 miles of which was paved, in 1999. The pipeline network comprises 545 miles for crude oil, 25 miles for petroleum products, and 102 miles for natural gas. There are three general cargo sea ports—Shuwaikh, Shuaiba and Doha—and an oil port at Mina al-Ahmadi. The merchant fleet comprised 45 ships over 1,000 grt, representing a total 2.5 million grt in 2000. Kuwait International Airport handled 3.7 million passengers in 2000.

Modern telecommunications links are provided by cable, satellite, and microwave radio relay. At end-2000 there were 467,100 fixed phone lines, 476,000 mobile phones, and 150,000 Internet users.

Oil production was 2.2 million barrels per day in 2000, including Kuwait's share of the neutral zone, while consumption was 192,000 barrels per day. Production capacity is targeted to rise to around 3 million barrels per day by 2005, although Kuwait's OPEC quota was cut to 1.9 million barrels per day in 2001. Refinery capacity is due for expansion to take up the difference and give added value to exports. Gas production and consumption was 290 billion cubic feet in 1999. Consumption is targeted to increase, especially for power generation, in order to free up more oil for export. Gas import deals signed with Qatar and Iran in 2001 are due to take effect by 2005. Electricity demand is growing at 7–9% a year. Electricity prices are some of the lowest in the world, and the government is considering reducing subsidies to encourage energy savings. There are five power plants, mostly using oil. Two gas-fired plants are under construction, with five more planned.

Education/Employment

Education is compulsory from age 6 to 14. Under the Ministry of Education, there is one university, a technical college, and a teacher training college. There were 16,000 university students in 1996–97, and 4,500 others studying abroad. The government is also giving priority to vocational training. The government promotes and funds scientific research, and is eager to work with foreign firms.

The labor force, both Kuwaiti and expatriate, has a range of skills from top management to unskilled. Palestinians, who constituted a large part of middle management before the Gulf War, have been replaced by other nationalities on account of their support for Iraq. There are separate labor laws for the public and private sectors, and for the oil industry. Minimum wages apply in the public sector, with Kuwaitis awarded substantially more than non-Kuwaitis. There is no minimum wage in the private sector, where remuneration and other conditions are determined between employers and employees. Private-sector workers have the right to collective bargaining and strikes (limited by compulsory negotiation and dispute settlement). The working week is 48 hours, annual paid leave is 14 days, and there are provisions for safety at work.

Fiscal/Financial

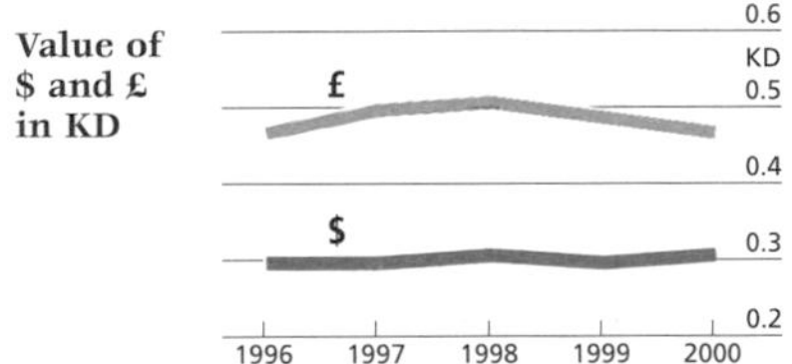

The largest bank by total assets at end-2000 was National Bank of Kuwait, followed by Gulf Bank, Commercial Bank of Kuwait, al-Ahli Bank, Burgan Bank, and Bank of Kuwait and the Middle East. There are around 20 local and foreign insurance firms operating in Kuwait. The Central Bank of Kuwait (CBK) closely regulates the financial sector. There is no corporation tax for local companies, but since 2000 there are levies for social benefits. The government proposed legislation in 2001 to reduce maximum corporate tax rates for foreign firms from 55% to 25%.

The seven commercial banks include Kuwait Finance House (KFH), an Islamic bank with 49% government and 51% private-sector capital. There are three specialized state banks providing loans for industry, agriculture, housing, and real estate. The range of services provided by the commercial banks is sophisticated and international. E-banking and e-commerce have been slow to take off, however. The Kuwait Stock Exchange, which listed 77 Kuwaiti companies and 9 from other Gulf States, had market capitalization of $20 billion at mid-2001. Foreign participation has been allowed since 2000.

Business Opportunities

The 2001 Foreign Investment Law allows full foreign ownership in certain sectors, and 49% ownership of banks. It removes the previous obligation to have a Kuwaiti agent, and grants a ten-year tax holiday and other incentives. There is a free trade zone at Shuwaikh port. Foreign investment is prohibited in the minerals sector. There is foreign investment in oil, petrochemicals, and insurance by the United States, Japan, and other countries. Healthcare, real estate development, water treatment, petrochemicals, telecommunications, IT, and food processing offer investment opportunities.

For More Information

Books:

Cordesman, Anthony H. *Kuwait: Recovery and Security after the Gulf War*. Boulder, CO: Westview Press, 1997.

Kennedy, Paul D. *Doing Business with Kuwait*. London: Kogan Page, 1997.

Kuwait Business and Investment Opportunities Yearbook. 3rd ed. Washington, D.C.: International Business Publications, 2001 (annual).

Zahlan, Rosemarie Said, and Roger Owen. *The Making of the Modern Gulf States: Kuwait, Bahrain, Qatar, the United Arab Emirates, and Oman*. Reading, Berkshire: Ithaca Press, 1999.

Web Sites:

Kuwait Information Office, Washington (government entry point with excellent links for English speakers): **www.kuwait-info.org**

Kuwait Stock Exchange: **www.kse.com.kw**

Ministry of Finance: **www.mof.gov.kw**

Ministry of Information: **www.moinfo.gov.kw**

Ministry of Planning: **www.mop.gov.kw**

Latvia

KEY FACTS

GNI: **$5,913 million; world's 106th**
GNI pc: **$2,430; world's 95th**
Head of state: **president**
Head of government: **prime minister**
Currency: **lat (LVL)**
Capital: **Riga**
Population: **2,389,000, growing at –1.3% p.a.**
Land area: **23,977 square miles**
Population density: **99 per square mile**
Life expectancy: **69 years**
Infant mortality: **17 per 1,000 live births**
Language: **Latvian, Russian**
Best buy: **Latvian chocolates**

Economy

Since independence was regained in 1991, Latvia's economy has been characterized by a booming services sector, which grew from 48% of GDP in 1992 to 69% in 1999. Its transport network has expanded, advancing its role as a transit hub for east-west trade. Annual GDP growth was around 6% in 2000–01.

Latvian industry—which used to provide the Soviet Union with telephones, radios, chemicals, and other products—declined in the 1990s; although by the end of the decade a revival had begun in engineering, chemicals, and pharmaceuticals. Forestry and wood processing are key contributors to GDP and account for 40% of exports.

Economic policy since the mid-1990s has been linked to Latvia's EU membership application (accession is expected around 2005). A collapse of the Latvian banking system in 1994–95 was followed by a strong recovery, encouraged by rising world pulp and paper prices. The boom was halted by the 1998 Russian financial crisis. After that, exports to CIS countries fell, while those to the EU increased. Tight fiscal policies were encouraged by IMF standby programs from 1999; these helped to stabilize the economy and bring inflation down to EU levels (3.3% in 2001). Privatization of small enterprises was complete by the late 1990s, but some key large-scale privatizations have been repeatedly postponed.

Geography/Resources

Latvia's most important natural resource is the forests that cover around 47% of its land area. Agriculture declined in the post-Soviet decade, but provides employment and important additional income for many families.

Latvia's population declined throughout the 1990s (to 2.42 million in 2000, 8% lower than 1992).

Communications/Energy

Transit trade, centering on Latvia's ports—Ventspils free port, Ventspils oil terminal, Riga, and Liepaja accounts for around 15% of GDP. Port modernization projects are being undertaken, including construction of a new multi-purpose terminal that began at Ventspils in 2000.

Road construction has also increased, including on the Via Baltica project linking the Baltic states to Germany via Poland. In the 1990s, road use increased and the number of registered car owners doubled. Latvia's only international airport is at Riga.

In 2000 Latvia had a telephone density of 30 lines per 100 inhabitants. Almost one-third of the network was digitalized.

Latvia imports more than three-quarters of its energy, mostly from Russia. The energy sector suffers from high rates of nonpayment, and restructuring has been slow; a plan to restructure the main energy company, Latvenergo, is due for implementation in 2002 after several failed privatization attempts.

Fiscal/Financial

The bank crisis of 1995 and the collapse of Bank Baltija, then Latvia's largest bank, was followed by a strengthening of the supervision regime. The 1998 Russian crisis further weakened Latvian banks. That was followed by a period of consolidation; by April 2000 the number of banks had fallen to 23, the largest of which in 1999–2000 came under Swedish, Finnish, and German control.

The Riga Stock Exchange, which began trading in July 1995, is small (total capitalization was about $300 million in 1999) and in 2000 shares in Unibanka, the largest private bank, often accounted for half of its trading turnover.

The tax structure has largely been brought into line with that of the EU. There is a 25% corporate income tax applicable to all enterprises equally.

Business Opportunities

Foreign direct investment averaged just above $300 million per year in 1997–2000; the largest amounts came from the Nordic countries, the United States, and Germany. The largest investment to date has been Finnish-Danish investment in the telecoms sector, and purchases of stakes in financial institutions.

The Latvian government actively encourages inward investment, and has led efforts to reduce administrative barriers to investment and reduce the costs of creating new business. As well as equal treatment of foreign investors and liberal ownership requirements, the 1991 law on foreign investment granted a variety of other incentives, including VAT and customs duties exemptions, on fixed assets imported as part of a long-term investment.

For More Information

Books:

Dreifelds, Juris. *Latvia in Transition*. New York: Cambridge University Press, 1996.

Latvia Business and Investment Opportunities Yearbook. 3rd ed. Washington, D.C.: International Business Publications, 2001 (annual).

Lieven, Anatol. *The Baltic Revolution: Estonia, Latvia, Lithuania, and the Path to Independence*. 4th ed. New Haven, CT: Yale University Press, 1994.

Williams, Nicola, S. Kokker, and Kate Galbraith. *Estonia, Latvia and Lithuania*. 2nd ed. Oakland, CA: Lonely Planet, 2000.

Web Sites:

Bank of Latvia: **www.bank.lv**
Latnet business portal: **www.latnet.lv**
Latvian Development Agency: **www.lda.gov.lv**
Riga Stock Exchange: **www.rfb.lv**

LEBANON

KEY FACTS

GNI: **$15,796 million; world's 75th**
GNI pc: **$3,700; world's 78th**
Head of state: **president**
Head of government: **prime minister**
Currency: **Lebanese pound (L£)**
Capital: **Beirut**
Population: **3,236,000, growing at 2.6% p.a.**
Land area: **3,938 square miles**
Population density: **821 per square mile**
Life expectancy: **70 years**
Infant mortality: **28 per 1,000 live births**
Language: **Arabic; English and French widely spoken**
Best buy: **jewelry, wine, nuts**

ECONOMIC STRUCTURE

Lebanon was home to the seafaring Phoenicians in ancient history, and the trading culture remains deeply ingrained. The country has been divided between Christians and Muslims since the 11th century, different sects isolated by the mountains. After a bloody civil war in the mid-19th century, Britain and France helped establish a Christian-dominated administration which remained in place during the French protectorate from 1918 to 1943. After independence, Christian control was challenged sporadically by the local Muslim population. The influx of Palestinian refugees from Israel after 1967 led to outright civil war from 1975. The Israeli invasion in 1982 caused massive destruction, failed in its attempt to crush Palestinian strikes on Israel, and exacerbated Lebanon's inter-religious strife. Israel occupied part of South Lebanon from the 1970s until 2000, and has conducted air attacks since then against southern towns and villages. Syria invaded to protect Lebanon in 1982 and helped the government army regain power. An Arab-brokered peace established power-sharing between Christians and Muslims in 1988. Before the civil war, Lebanon was a major banking, business, and tourism center for the Middle East. Many businessmen and bankers transferred their businesses to Europe and elsewhere, but the government hopes to win them back in time.

Services accounted for 66.1% of GDP in 2000, followed by industry (22%), and agriculture (11.9%). Trade and finance are the leading services sectors. Lebanon is a transshipment hub for Syria. Tourism began to revive strongly from 1997, producing a bonus for the construction industry in new hotels and facilities. Manufacturing, which contributed 10.3% of GDP in 2000, includes construction materials, food and beverages, textiles and clothing, furniture, paper and board, chemicals, and metal products. In addition there is a thriving small-scale artisan sector, including jewelry. The main exports in 2000 were food, jewelry, chemicals, electrical goods, metal products, and textiles. The main markets were Saudi Arabia, followed by the U.A.E., the United States, France, Syria, and Kuwait. External receipts include large remittances from Lebanese living abroad.

The public sector encompasses utilities, transport, airports, and ports, but the government has always encouraged private business. There are plans to privatize telecommunications, electricity, water, public transport including Middle East Airlines, Beirut International Airport, and Beirut Port. Strategic partners were sought for Liban Télécom and Électricité du Liban to provide new technology. There is private-sector involvement in the upgrading and expansion of both sectors.

ECONOMIC POLICY

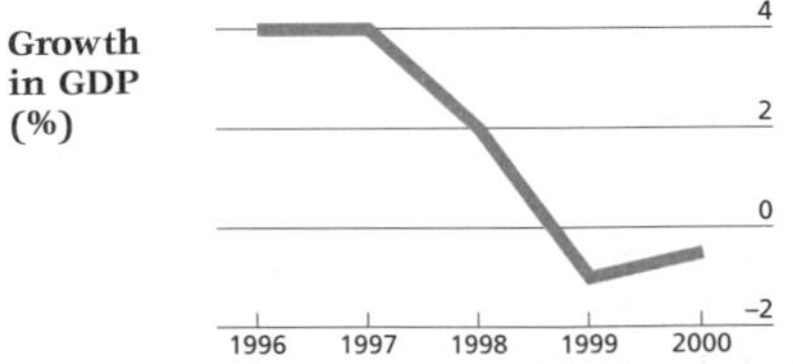

In 1992 the government launched a reconstruction program financed initially by bond issues and other domestic revenues. Program management is conducted by Solidère, a government-backed private company formed in 1994. From 1996 the program was underpinned by international aid from the World Bank, Arab Funds, European Union, and the United States. However, the government continued to issue bonds, and gross public debt rose to 160% of GDP in mid-2001, with debt servicing representing more than 90% of government revenues. Most of this is in local currency, but foreign exchange reserves have been depleted to finance government operations, which include relatively high military expenditure. The government aims to reduce its deficit from 21.7% of GDP in 2000 to 15% by 2003 through spending cuts and the introduction of VAT in 2002. Increased private and foreign investment resulting from the privatization program are aimed at reviving growth.

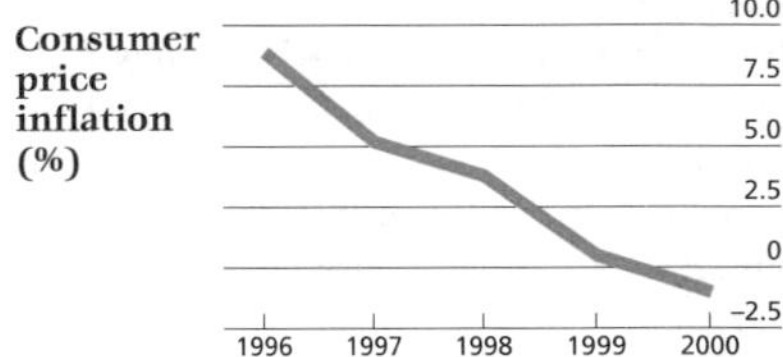

Tight monetary policy reduced inflation from 120% in 1991 to zero in 2000; it rose to 2% in 2001. Construction led economic growth in the early 1990s, which averaged 6.5%, but average annual growth fell to 2.3% in 1996–2001. Unemployment was officially estimated at 15–20% in 2001, down from 20–25% in 1999 and 2000.

GEOGRAPHY/RESOURCES

Lebanon borders the Mediterranean Sea to the west, Syria to the north and east, and Israel to the south. There are four geographical regions: the coastal plain, the Lebanese mountains, with the highest point at 10,138 feet, the Bekaa valley, and the Anti-Lebanon mountains. Summers are hot and dry, winters cool with snow on the higher mountains. The Anti-Lebanon range is arid.

Agriculture is varied, and is concentrated on the coastal plain and in the Bekaa valley. The main crops are vegetables, citrus and other fruits, potatoes, pulses, and sugar beet. Wine is made and exported. Wheat, barley, tobacco, and illegal hashish are also grown. Meat, dairy, leather, and honey are important. There are small but significant timber and fisheries industries.

One-third of the population lives in or around Beirut, half are under age 21, and

95% are of Arab origin, with 4% of Armenian origin. Christian communities are now outnumbered by Muslims following the influx of around 300,000 Palestinian refugees. More than 1.2 million Lebanese live abroad, several hundred thousand of whom emigrated during the civil war.

Communications/Energy

The road network comprised 4,500 miles, 3,946 miles of which was paved, in 1999. Reconstruction following war damage is a major ongoing task. A reconstruction program has been drawn up for the 256-mile rail network, which is in limited use. The main sea port for general cargo is at Beirut. Tripoli is the second port. Both are undergoing reconstruction, as are the lesser ports of Tyre and Sidon. Beirut International Airport has been rebuilt; 35 international carriers have returned, and the new terminal can handle 6 million passengers a year.

The telecommunications network has been upgraded during reconstruction following civil war damage. Links are provided by cable, satellite and microwave radio relay. Projects still to be completed include fast Internet access, integrated multimedia, and extension to rural areas. At end-2000 there were 681,000 fixed phone lines, 743,000 mobile phones, and 300,000 Internet users.

Most energy needs are met by imported petroleum, but gas will have a larger role in electricity generation once construction of a pipeline from Syria is completed. In 1999, 91% of power was generated by oil and 9% by hydroelectric power. Electricity demand is projected to grow by 4–6% a year. Domestic electricity production is set to expand. In addition a grid link with Syria was established in 2001, and there are plans to take part in a regional network including Turkey, Iraq, Jordan, and Egypt.

Education/Employment

Education is not compulsory, but it is free in state schools, and literacy is over 90%. The main higher education institutes are private-sector. There were 88,000 students enrolled at university in 1996–97, including Beirut's five universities. There are also technical and vocational training institutes. The Ministry of Education is responsible for education policy. The Lebanese National Council for Scientific Research is a public body which initiates, coordinates, and funds scientific research. It has divisions and centers for environmental science, engineering and basic technology, agriculture, medicine, marine science, geophysics, remote sensing, and nuclear energy.

The labor force is well educated, and unskilled workers are in short supply, these jobs being filled mostly by immigrants. Wages and other employment conditions are determined between employers and employees in accordance with the 1964 Labor Law. Collective bargaining is allowed, but it is regulated by the Ministry of Labor. Only Lebanese citizens can join trade unions. The Labor Law covers contracts, paid leave (15 days annual holiday and 45 days maternity leave), a maximum 48-hour working week, and dismissal terms.

Fiscal/Financial

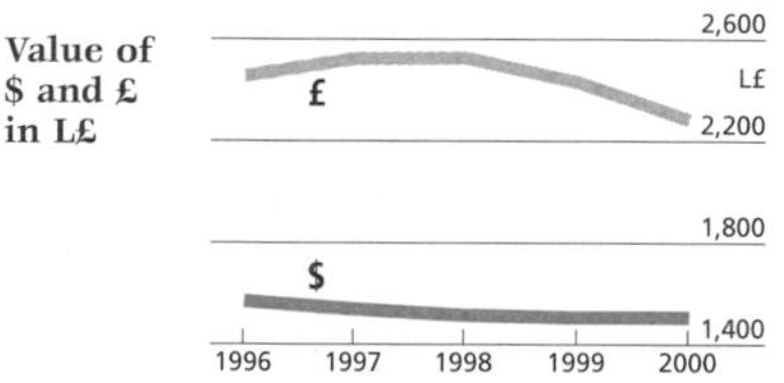

The largest banks by deposits in 1999–2000 were Banque de la Méditerranée, followed by Banque Audi, Byblos Bank, Fransabank, Société Générale Libano Européenne de Banque, and Crédit Libanais. The Bank of Lebanon is the central bank and oversees the regulation of financial services. The Banking Control Commission regulates banking, applying internationally accepted Basle Core principles. Lebanese banks also apply international accounting procedures for transaction disclosure. Despite this, and anti-money-laundering legislation adopted in 2001, Lebanon remained on the money-laundering blacklist of the industrial nations' Financial Action Task Force at early 2002. The Bank of Lebanon continues to effect changes in order to achieve removal from the blacklist. Corporation tax is 15%, with payroll tax at 21.5%; maximum personal income tax is 21%. Dividend and interest withholding tax is 10%, while dividend distribution is subject to 5% tax. VAT is 10%.

There are 67 commercial banks, with a total balance sheet at September 2001 of L£71 trillion, and 38 investment houses and broking firms with a total balance sheet of L£444.5 billion. Consolidation is in progress. There are around 70 insurance companies, and these are also likely to undergo consolidation. Financial services are sophisticated, international, and increasingly online. Foreign banks are well represented, as they were before the civil war, and their focus is on local and Syrian operations. Government treasury bonds have proved lucrative to banks, yielding 35% interest. The Beirut Stock Exchange reopened in 1995. It consists of a main board, a Junior Market for small companies, and an over-the-counter market. It installed electronic trading in 2000. Reconstruction company Solidère accounts for 98% of main board trades. There are links with the Cairo and Kuwait Stock Exchanges.

Business Opportunities

Tax and other incentives are available to investors. At mid-2001 there were two free zones at Beirut and Tripoli. Two more were planned for the north. Red tape has been a disincentive to industrial investment, as is the war-torn nature of the country. Foreign investment is restricted in broadcast media. Construction and real estate, hotels, clothing, fast food, finance, and insurance have attracted foreign direct investment, which is estimated to have totaled some $1.1 billion in 1996–2000. Of the 44 new foreign companies registered in 2000, most were European, followed by Arab, U.S., and Bermudan, and one each from Japan and China. Services—including finance, insurance, advertising, and tourism—offer investment opportunities, as do prospective privatizations. The point of contact for investors is the Industrial Development Authority of Lebanon.

For More Information

Books:

Hollis, Rosemary, and Nadim Shehadi, eds. *Lebanon on Hold: Implications of a Middle East Peace*. London: Royal Institute of International Affairs, 1996.

Lebanon Business and Investment Opportunities Yearbook. 3rd ed. Washington, D.C.: International Business Publications, 2001 (annual).

Mannheim, Ivan. *Syria and Lebanon Handbook*. 2nd ed. Bath, Somerset: Footprint Handbooks, 2001.

Saeedi, Nasser, and Samir Nasr. *The Development of Lebanon's Capital Markets*. Beirut: Center for Economic Policy and Analysis, 1995.

Web Sites:

Beirut Stock Exchange: **www.bse.com.lb**

Central Bank of Lebanon, also has good links: **www.bdl.gov.lb**

The Daily Star (English language newspaper): **www.dailystar.com.lb**

Industrial Development Authority of Lebanon: **www.idal.com.lb**

Office of the Minister of Planning for Administrative Reform, government entry point with excellent links: **www.omsar.gov.lb**

LIBYA

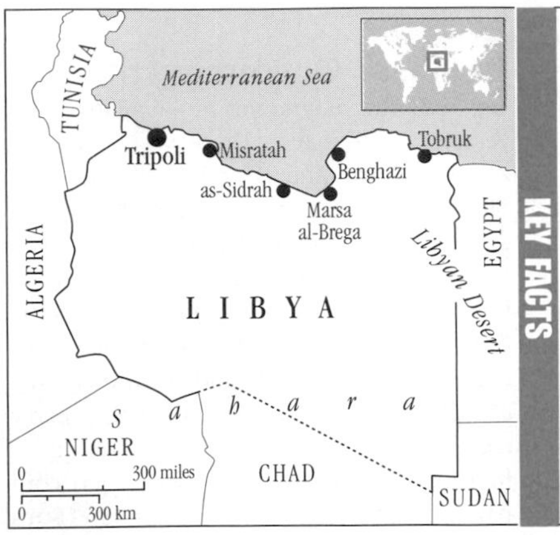

KEY FACTS

GNI pc: **$6,700 (approx.)**
Head of government: **revolutionary leader**
Currency: **Libyan dinar (LD)**
Capital: **Tripoli**
Population: **5,471,000, growing at 2.4% p.a.**
Land area: **679,343 square miles**
Population density: **8 per square mile**
Life expectancy: **70 years**
Infant mortality: **19 per 1,000 live births**
Language: **Arabic (official), Berber, English, Italian**
Best buy: **leather goods, pottery, copperware, fabrics, carpets**

ECONOMY

Services contribute 42% of GDP, followed by petroleum (33%), non-oil manufacturing and construction (20%), and agriculture (5%). Crude oil, refined oil products, and lubricants account for around 95% of export earnings and 70–90% of state revenues. Petrochemicals are important. Other manufacturing includes iron, steel, aluminum, cement, machinery, consumer appliances, textiles, leather goods, and food and tobacco processing.

Libya has an Islamic socialist economy, with all main productive industries owned by the state. The government wants to reduce dependence on oil, with diversification into natural gas, manufacturing, tourism, and agriculture, and increased private-sector participation in manufacturing. UN sanctions imposed from 1992, and temporarily lifted in 1999 (Libyan agents were accused of bombing a U.S. airliner in 1988), caused economic decline in the 1990s. Long-term oil export contracts remained in force, but foreign investment in key natural gas, iron mining, and water distribution projects were delayed. U.S. sanctions were renewed for five years from mid-2001.

GEOGRAPHY/RESOURCES

In North Africa, Libya borders the Mediterranean Sea, Egypt, Sudan, Chad, Niger, Algeria, and Tunisia. Most of the land is desert, part of the Sahara. Tripoli has temperatures of 46°F to 80°F, and average annual rainfall of 15 inches. The south has virtually no rain, and has daytime temperatures of 59°F to over 122°F.

Imports meet 75% of food requirements. Irrigated arable farming is centered on three oases in the south. The main crops are tomatoes, citrus fruits, barley, wheat, potatoes, olives, figs, apricots, and dates. Sheep, goats, cattle, camels, and poultry are raised. Proven petroleum reserves were 29.5 billion barrels, with gas reserves of 46.4 trillion cubic feet, in January 2001. There are large untapped oil reserves both off- and onshore, and exploration continues. Gypsum and salt are produced.

COMMUNICATIONS/ENERGY

The road network is about 12,000 miles, 56% of which is paved. There are no railways. The pipeline network includes 2,724 miles for crude petroleum, 275 miles for refined petroleum products, and 1,210 miles for natural gas. The main sea ports are Marsa al-Brega and as-Sidrah for oil, Tripoli, Benghazi, and Misurata. The main international airport is at Tripoli, with smaller airports at Benghazi, Sebha, and Misurata. International air travel was curtailed by UN sanctions in 1992–99.

The state-owned General Posts & Telecommunications Company provides digitized international and domestic links via cable, satellite, and microwave relay. At end-2000 there were 605,000 fixed phone lines, 40,000 mobile phones, and 10,000 Internet users.

Libya uses about 10% of its oil for domestic needs. Most electricity is generated from oil, but gas has taken an increasing share in order to free more oil for export. A link to the Tunisian grid was under construction in mid-2001, and there are plans to connect with the Egyptian grid. Oil production was 1.5 million barrels per day in the first five months of 2001. Oil refineries had a capacity of 343,400 barrels per day. Half of refinery output is used for domestic consumption and half is exported. Gas production was 220 billion cubic feet, and consumption was 180 billion cubic feet in 1999. New gas fields are due to come onstream in 2003.

FISCAL/FINANCIAL

The Central Bank of Libya is the bank of issue, and operates exchange controls. It has full ownership of, or controlling interests in, the commercial banks. Jamahiriya Bank, National Commercial Bank, Umma Bank, Wahda Bank, Sahara Bank, and Savings & Real Estate Investment Bank conduct domestic operations. Libyan Arab Foreign Bank conducts foreign exchange and international operations. The state-owned Libyan Insurance Company handles all classes of insurance. There is no stock exchange.

BUSINESS OPPORTUNITIES

Trade and investment sanctions constitute barriers to inward investment. The 1997 foreign investment law offers tax breaks and other benefits to joint venture projects in industry, tourism, services, health, and agriculture. Technology transfer is a requirement. Petroleum and gas projects are covered by a separate law, and have attracted investment from Italy, Germany, France, Austria, Tunisia, and South Korea. Joint venture opportunities exist in construction materials, chemicals, plastic products, transport equipment, packaging, wood, paper, and food. The point of contact is the General Industrialization Corporation.

For More Information

Books:

Azema, James. *Libya Handbook*. Bath, Somerset: Footprint Handbooks, 2001.
Libya Business and Investment Opportunities Yearbook. 3rd ed. Washington, D.C.: International Business Publications, 2001 (annual).
Terterov, Marat, ed. *Doing Business with Libya*. London: Kogan Page, 2002.
Vandewalle, Dirk. *Libya since Independence*. Ithaca, NY: Cornell University Press, 1998.

Web Sites:

General Industrialization Corporation: **www.giclibya.com**
Government gateway: **www.libyanet.net**
Independent business information site: **www.libyaninvestment.com**

  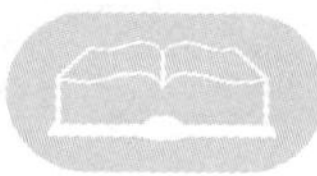    

LIECHTENSTEIN

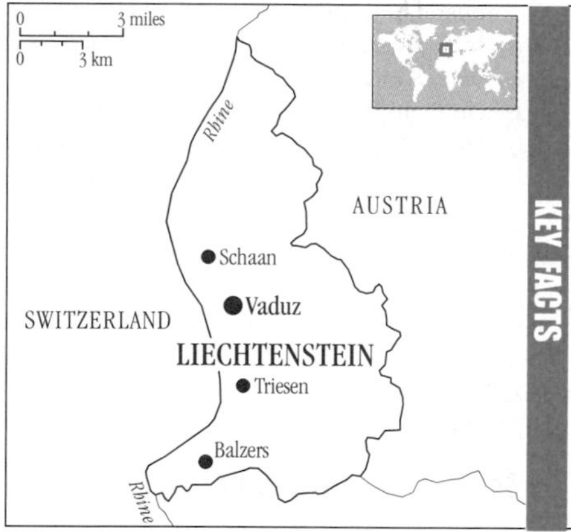

KEY FACTS

GNI pc: **$40,000 (approx.); world's 2nd**
Head of government: **prime minister**
Currency: **Swiss franc (SFr)**
Capital: **Vaduz**
Population: **32,000, growing at 1.1% p.a.**
Land area: **62 square miles**
Population density: **516 per square mile**
Infant mortality: **10 per 1,000 live births**
Language: **German (official), Alemannic**
Best buy: **postage stamps, ceramics, chocolates, wine**

Economic Structure

An independent principality, Liechtenstein has been ruled by the same dynasty since 1699. The present constitution, including the democratic enfranchisement of the population, was enacted in 1921, and an agreement on customs and monetary union was signed with Switzerland in 1923. Since the end of World War II Liechtenstein has transformed itself from an agrarian- to an industrial- and then to a service-based economy. It joined the European Economic Area in 1995, following a popular vote in favor in 1992, while the Swiss voted against. Prince Hans Adam II, the current monarch, campaigned for the "yes" vote, and takes an active role in running the country. The government has a program to enact laws in keeping with those of the rest of Europe.

Services are the main source of GDP and the main source of employment (53.5% at end-1999). Industry, mining, energy and water supply, and construction provided 45.2% of jobs at end-1999, and agriculture 1.3%. Finance and tourism are the main service industries and main sources of foreign exchange. Most visitors are German, followed by Swiss, Americans, Austrians, Italians, and French. Tourists come for winter sports and for hiking in the summer. The leading manufacturing industries are metallurgy and mechanical and precision engineering. Pharmaceuticals, textiles, ceramics, and food processing are important. Liechtenstein is one of the world's top producers and exporters of false teeth. Electronics is a fast-growing sector. Most manufacturing is export-oriented. The principal exports are specialist machinery, dentistry materials—including artificial teeth—and frozen foods. Germany, the United States, and Switzerland are the main markets, followed by France, Italy, and Japan. The EU accounts for almost half of exports.

There is little direct state ownership of the economy. The state owns a bank, an insurance company (for pensions), a bus company, and the postal services company. Water services are owned by the communes (local authorities). The state subsidizes agriculture.

Economic Policy

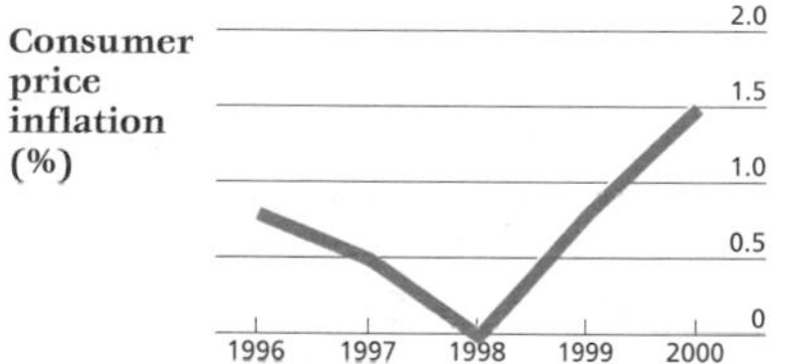

Macro-economic policy is geared to the prudent management of a small private-enterprise economy with open borders and low taxes. In 1999, 78.2% of government receipts were derived from taxation and customs duties credited by Switzerland. In 1996–99 there were substantial surpluses on the central government budget. Local authority budgets were in surplus in 1995–97 (latest available data). The level of public investment has fallen over the years, but the ratio remained higher at local level (45.5%) than at national level (15.4%) in 1997. Key areas of national expenditure in 1999 were finance and taxation (35.8%), social welfare (17%), and education (15.1%). Social security is well developed through insurance for pensions, incapacity, accident and sickness, and unemployment, and well supported with almost full employment.

Income from gainful employment grew by 6.8% from 1990 to 1999, reaching SFr1.83 billion according to government figures. United Nations statistics show annual average nominal GDP growth of 5.6% in 1992–96. GDP was $1.26 billion in 1996. Inflation fell from 4% in 1980 to 0.8% in 1999, with a peak of 6.5% in 1981 and a trough of zero in 1998. Unemployment rose from zero in 1980 to 2% in 1998, before falling to 1.2% in 1999. As only 40% of the workforce are of Liechtenstein origin (foreign residents and commuters from Austria and Switzerland are the majority), the government responded to local pressure to set limits on foreign labor. However, it recognizes the continuing need for foreign workers.

Geography/Resources

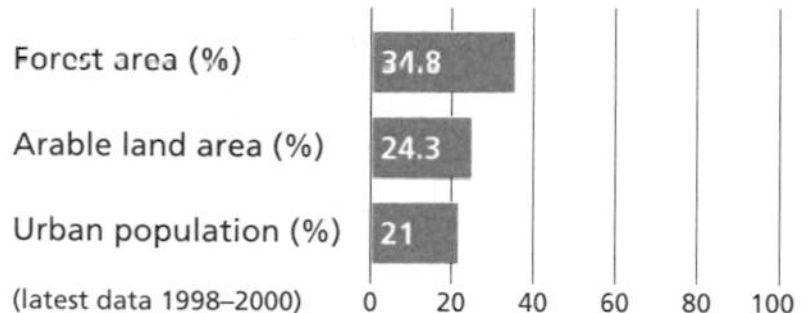

A small land-locked Central European country, Liechtenstein has borders with Switzerland to the west and south, and Austria to the east and north. The River Rhine forms the western border. Most of the land consists of the high Rhatikon Mountains, part of the Alps, with a high point of 8,527 feet. The northern region has lower mountains and plains, the lowest point being 1,411 feet. The climate is relatively mild, with an average annual temperature of 50°F, but the mountains have ample snow for winter sports. Average annual precipitation is 51 inches.

Farmed land accounts for 24.3% of the total area, mountain pasture for 15.7%, and forestry for 34.8%. Dairy production accounts for two-thirds of total farm income, and Liechtenstein is more than self-sufficient in dairy produce. The main agricultural crops are fodder maize, wheat, barley, and potatoes. Grapes and wine production are important. Forestry, which covers 19% of the land, supplies industrial timber and fuel wood. There are no significant commercial mineral resources.

Towns, although small—the largest is Schaan with 5,262 inhabitants—form autonomous communities. There is a population age peak at 30–50 years. The majority of people are of Liechtenstein origin (62%), with communities of Swiss (16%), Austrians (7%), Germans (4%), Italians, and Turks.

Communications/Energy

The road network comprises 155 miles and links all the towns and villages of the country. Five main roads cross the Rhine to Switzerland. The roads to Austria are concentrated in the north. Austrian Federal Railways operates services on the 11½-mile rail network which crosses the northern plain and passes within a few miles of Vaduz. The network is fully electrified. Liechtenstein is on the main line from Vienna to Paris. There are three stations in Liechtenstein at Schaan (the closest station to Vaduz), Nendeln, and Schaanwald. There is no airport.

Telecommunications services are provided via Swiss companies to LTN Liechtenstein TeleNet AG. Since 1999 Liechtenstein has had its own country code. There were 19,763 fixed phone lines in 1999 linked to the Swiss network via cable. There is a microwave relay station for mobile phones. Liechtenstein benefited from the 115 Internet service providers operating in Switzerland and Liechtenstein in 1999. In 1999, 93% of energy needs were imported. Natural gas accounted for 24.2% of energy consumption, electricity (295,031 MWh) for 23.6%, fuel oil 23.5%, petrol 19.2%, diesel oil 8.2%, firewood 1.2%, and coal and liquid gas 0.1%. Firewood and some electricity are produced domestically, equivalent to 88,051 MWh in 1999.

Education/Employment

Education is compulsory from age 7 to 16. Higher education institutes include a technical college, philosophy college, a music school, art school, and a continuing education center, which enroll several thousand students each year. Professional courses include financial services, IT, and architecture. There is no university: Liechtensteiners usually attend university in Switzerland or Austria. The government is responsible for education, but local authorities and individual institutes have a broad measure of autonomy. Continuing adult education, including a wide range of distance-learning courses, is encouraged and supported by state aid. Liechtenstein is eligible to take part in EU R&D programs. R&D is mostly private-sector. There were 692 R&D personnel in foreign-owned industrial firms (3.5% of employees in these firms) at end-1999. R&D strengths include dentistry products, electronic equipment, precision tools, and materials science. The labor force is well educated and adaptable. Wage and other employment conditions are determined by employers and employees, and the relationship is harmonious.

Fiscal/Financial

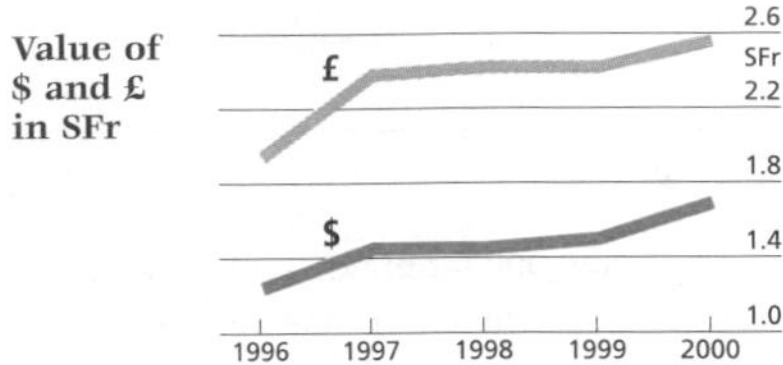

The three largest banks by deposits at end-1998 were LGT Bank in Liechtenstein (SFr10 billion), Liechtensteiner Landesbank (SFr9.5 billion), and Verwaltungs- und Privat-Bank (SFr6.3 billion). Liechtensteiner Landesbank is state-owned and the others are private-sector. Insurance companies include some of the world's largest. Monetary policy is set in Switzerland. The government regulates the finance sector. Although anti-money-laundering laws, and laws relating to the professional conduct of banks and bankers, were tightened in 1996, Liechtenstein has been accused by three international agencies—supported by the world's largest economies—of insufficient supervision and lack of cooperation with the authorities of other countries. The government has resisted this pressure to change: banking and tax secrecy are strictly guarded. As there are no double-taxation treaties with other countries, there is no reporting requirement between tax authorities.

Maximum personal income tax is 17%, with a local property tax of 8.5%. Standard VAT is 7.5% with reduced rates of 3.5% and 2.3%. The maximum income tax for domestic companies is 20%, with a 2% capital tax. Foreign insurance companies pay no capital or earnings taxes, but pay 1% of premium receipts from life and old-age insurance, and 2% of premium receipts from other classes of insurance. Coupon tax on capital interest is 4%. There is no profit or income tax for the estimated 75,000 "offshore" corporations, holding companies, and foundations. Instead they pay a 1% tax on capital and reserves. This category of company is guaranteed absolute fiscal secrecy: there is no need for official authorization in order to set up in business (although they must register), and the capital provider and recipients remain anonymous. The activities they can undertake include management of international capital and economic interests, control of direct investments, real estate management, all types of services, exploitation of licenses, private investment and investment management, and distribution of investment income to family welfare bodies and charities.

The financial sector provides the services required by these companies, as well as private banking for high net worth individuals, together with the full range of domestic and international investment and trade financing operations. The insurance industry covers life, pensions, non-life, marine, and reinsurance. There were 13 banks with total assets under management of SFr110.3 billion in 1999. Net client deposits and trust funds under management of the 11 largest banks were SFr70.7 billion and SFr11.8 billion respectively. The balance sheet and net profit of all banks was SFr34.9 billion and SFr451.1 million respectively in 1999. There is no local stock market.

Business Opportunities

Low tax, good infrastructure, access to European markets, and special conditions for foreign holding companies and foundations are investment incentives. Manufacturing industry, finance, insurance, and business services have attracted inward investment from many countries including Switzerland, the United States, and Austria. Opportunities continue to exist in all these sectors.

For More Information

Books:

Liechtenstein Business and Investment Opportunities Yearbook. 3rd ed. Washington, D.C.: International Business Publications, 2001 (annual).

Liechtenstein in Figures. Vaduz: Office of National Economy, 2000.

Liechtenstein: Principality at the Heart of Europe (brochure). Vaduz: Press and Information Office.

The Liechtenstein Research Group. *A Strategic Assessment of Liechtenstein* (Strategic Planning Series). San Diego, CA: ICON Group International, 2000.

Seger, Otto. *A Survey of Liechtenstein History*. Vaduz: Press and Information Office, n.d.

Where to Go in Liechtenstein. Vaduz: Liechtenstein Tourism.

World Trade Organization. *Trade Policy Review: Switzerland and Liechtenstein*. Lanham, MD: Bernan Press, 2001.

Web Sites:

Chamber of Commerce: **www.lihk.li**

Government information point: **www.firstlink.li**

  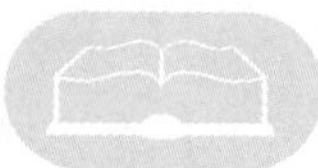    

LITHUANIA

KEY FACTS

GNI: **$9,751 million; world's 85th**
GNI pc: **$2,640; world's 92nd**
Head of state: **president**
Head of government: **prime minister**
Currency: **litas (LTL)**
Capital: **Vilnius**
Population: **3,682,000, growing at –0.2% p.a.**
Land area: **25,019 square miles**
Population density: **147 per square mile**
Life expectancy: **71 years**
Infant mortality: **18 per 1,000 live births**
Language: **Lithuanian, Russian, Polish**
Best buy: **amber jewelry**

ECONOMY

Lithuania adopted a comprehensive market reform program immediately after regaining independence in 1991. It tightened fiscal policies, and adopted a new currency, the litas, which since 1994 has been pegged to the U.S. dollar. Economic liberalization and privatization followed.

In 1991–94, Lithuania suffered a typical post-Soviet slump; industrial output fell by about one-third and much manufacturing industry closed. Agriculture was badly hit by an ill-considered reform program. In the late 1990s agriculture remained stagnant, but industry recovered and services expanded rapidly, accounting for 56% of GDP by 2001. The improvement was interrupted by the 1998 Russian financial crisis. Lithuania struggled with a budget deficit in the mid- and late 1990s, and the IMF started a lending program in 2000. GDP fell in 1998–99 and began to recover in early 2000. Lithuania joined the WTO in 2000 and is an applicant for EU and NATO membership.

GEOGRAPHY/RESOURCES

Lithuania is the largest of the three Baltic states. Lithuania's forests take up 27% of the land area and provide its most important natural resource, timber. The timber industry increased output by 54% in the decade from 1991. Lithuania has small offshore oil reserves (estimated at 360 million barrels) and some peat reserves.

Lithuania's population is the largest of the Baltic States. Unlike Latvia and Estonia, Lithuania does not have a large Russian minority: about 8% of the population are Russian and 7% Polish.

COMMUNICATIONS/ENERGY

Post-Soviet Lithuania has made road construction a priority in a bid to re-establish itself as a regional transport hub: the road network grew by 46.5% to 44,352 miles in the decade to 2000. Lithuania's port, Klaìpeda, handled a large proportion of Baltic trade in Soviet times but has recently faced tough competition.

Telephone access is close to the regional average, with 30 lines per 100 inhabitants in 2000. The 1998 sale of a 60% share in Lithuania Telekom to a Swedish–Finnish consortium was one of Lithuania's most successful privatizations.

Lithuania's main suppliers of power are two nuclear reactors, which provide 80% of its energy needs and exports to Belarus and Latvia. The stations reduce Latvia's energy reliance on Russia, its chief supplier of oil and gas. Oil refining at the Mazeikiu refinery plays a key role in the economy, accounting for about 10% of GDP. The 1999 privatization of Mazeikiu Nafta—which owns the refinery, a pipeline system, and an oil terminal—caused a political crisis and occasioned a battle between Williams International of the United States, which bought a 33% stake, and Russian oil companies. In 2001 Williams reached a deal with Yukos of Russia, which took a 27% stake, concluded crude oil supply contracts, and is participating in an investment program.

FISCAL/FINANCIAL

Lithuania's banking sector underwent consolidation in 1998–99, after which the three largest banks owned 86% of the assets. The largest, Vilniaus Banka, which has assets of $1.2 billion, was by 2000 42%-owned by SEB of Sweden. The financial services sector remains underdeveloped. In 2000 a regulatory structure for the pensions industry was put in place.

The National Stock Exchange of Lithuania (NSEL) had a market capitalization of $3.5 billion at the end of 1999. It lists 1,200 stocks, but in 1999 only 170 were traded.

Corporate profit tax was cut from 29% to 24% in January 2000. A flat income tax rate of 33% is applied, standard VAT is 18%, and employers pay 31% of the payroll in national insurance contributions.

BUSINESS OPPORTUNITIES

Lithuania's preparations to join the European Union have resulted in far-reaching changes to its legal framework and to official encouragement of foreign investment. Legally, foreign investors enjoy equal rights. There are no specific tax holidays for foreign investors, but in 2000 legislation was drafted for tax breaks for those investing more than $50 million.

Foreign direct investment has averaged $510 million per year in 1997–2001; Scandinavian countries account for about one-third of this.

As well as banking, telecoms, and other infrastructure sectors which have attracted most FDI in recent years, manufacturing sectors such as food processing, electronics, and textiles, and also construction and tourism, offer opportunities.

For More Information

Books:

Lieven, Anatol. *The Baltic Revolution: Estonia, Latvia, Lithuania and the Path to Independence*. New Haven, CT: Yale University Press, 1993.

Lithuania Business and Industrial Directory. 2nd ed. Washington, D.C.: International Business Publications, 2001.

Lithuania Business and Investment Opportunities Yearbook. 3rd ed. Washington, D.C.: International Business Publications, 2001 (annual).

Web Sites:

Bank of Lithuania: **www.lbank.lt**
Government of Lithuania: **www.lrvk.lt**
State Property Fund: **www.vtf.lt**

LUXEMBOURG

KEY FACTS

GNI: **$18,545 million; world's 69th**
GNI pc: **$42,930; world's 1st**
Head of government: **prime minister**
Currency: **Euro (€)**
Capital: **Luxembourg**
Population: **426,000, growing at 1.2% p.a.**
Land area: **998 square miles**
Population density: **426 per square mile**
Life expectancy: **77 years**
Infant mortality: **5 per 1,000 live births**
Language: **Luxembourgish, French, German**
Best buy: **chocolates, petrol, consumer goods (low tax)**

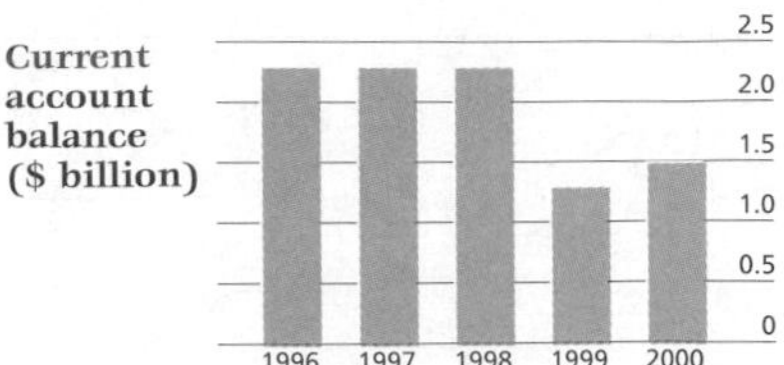

ECONOMIC STRUCTURE

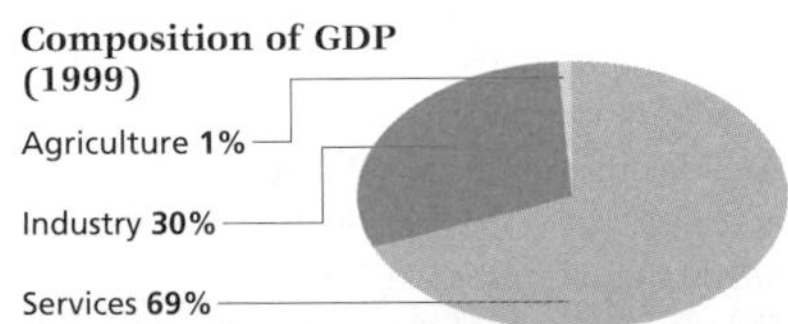

Since steel put Luxembourg on the world map in the 1870s, the economy has generated wealth far beyond the country's small size. Luxembourg has the highest GDP per capita in the world, according to World Bank figures. The steel industry was based on huge iron ore deposits which are now depleted. The steel company Acieries Réunies de Burbach, Esch et Dudelange (ARBED) was the largest in Europe and the third-largest in the world before it merged with France's Usinor and Spain's Aceralia in 2001 to become the largest in the world. The headquarters remained in Luxembourg with some diplomatic help from the government. Luxembourg also became the world's largest satellite communications operator in 2001. Its broadcasting entity RTL is the largest in Europe following the 2000 merger with Germany's Bertelsmann and U.K. group Pearson. The conference and hotel industry was strengthened from the 1950s by Luxembourg's role as a capital city for institutions of the European Communities. From the 1970s the finance center grew rapidly to become the leading economic sector, the main employer, and an important center in world terms. With the introduction of the Euro, Luxembourg became the business, financial, and logistical hub for a major industrial region comprising France's Lorraine, Germany's Saarland, and the Grand Duchy.

Private services are the main contributor to GDP, accounting for 63.4% of gross added value (output at basic prices plus intermediate consumption) in 1999. Within this sector finance contributed 23.4%; hotels, catering, transport and communications 22.8%; and services to companies 17.2%. Public services accounted for 17% of gross added value, while manufacturing industry contributed 11.6% (including 3.1% from steel).

The finance center specializes in private banking business, investment funds, Eurobond issues, and services to the administrative headquarters of multinational companies. Insurance has developed strongly in recent years, and pension funds are set to become a key activity in the future. The many European Union institutions present in Luxembourg contribute to the healthy services industry in travel, communications, and the hotel business. Broadcasting is a significant activity, with over 20 TV and radio stations transmitting programs in nine languages. Raw steel and rolled-steel products account for most of ARBED's output. The Goodyear Tire and Rubber Company produces rubber and plastic goods.

The finance center's business is mainly international, and the surplus on invisibles far outweighs the trade deficit. Other members of the European Union account for well over 80% of Luxembourg's foreign trade. The main export markets for manufactured goods are Germany, France, Belgium, the United Kingdom, and Italy. Main manufactured goods exports are metals, machinery, rubber and plastics, and textiles.

In 1995 the separation of ownership and management of the railways led to a significant reduction in state subsidies. Since then, state aids to the steel industry and to the regions are being dismantled, and price regulation has been abolished. From 1998 the government opened the telecommunications and electricity industries to private competition. By January 2001 the entire telecommunications network and 40% of the electricity market were liberalized. More of the electricity market will be opened to competition under the 2000–05 economic plan. Although the government has reduced its direct participation in industry, it has played a key role in maintaining jobs. Its investment with the private sector in satellite company SES Astra in 1985 put Luxembourg into the satellite communications sector. In the early 1990s it persuaded Goodyear not to close its tire plant and research center, which employed 3,740 people in 2000. Jobs underpinned its argument for keeping the headquarters of the new steel conglomerate in Luxembourg. ARBED had 7,880 workers in 2000, making it the largest single employer after the government.

ECONOMIC POLICY

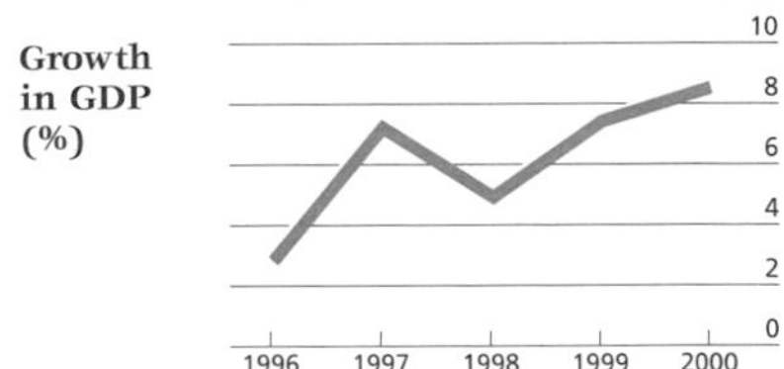

For 30 years the government has registered a surplus on the current account. The debt-to-GDP ratio is the lowest in the EU and the OECD, falling from a peak of 6.4% in 1998 to 5.1% in 2001, with a further decline to 4.9% expected in 2002. Government net financial assets of 30% of GDP at end-1999 were expected to rise to over 40% by 2003. The government has ordered a report into the long-term outlook for financing pensions, which could place a heavy burden on the state from 2010 if greater recourse to private pension funds is not used. The net financial assets will provide a cushion, but will not be enough if structural problems in local employment and social benefits are not resolved.

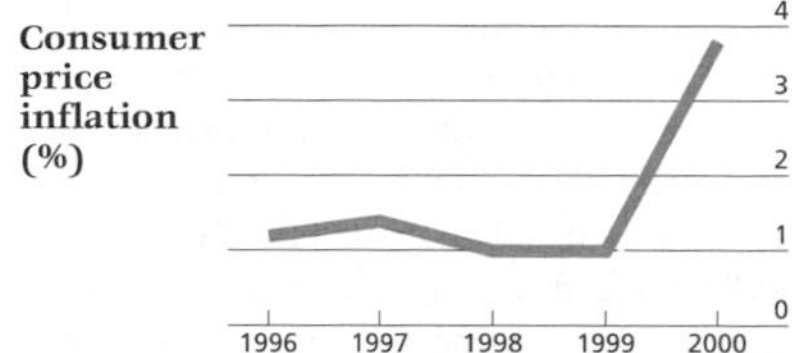

Annual GDP growth averaged 1.5% in 1991–95 and 6.1% in 1996–2001. It was expected to be 5.5% in 2002. Investment and labor productivity are strong. Wages rose by an annual average of 3.2% in 1991–99 and by 5% in 2000 because of the tight job market. Inflation was an annual average of 2% in 1991–99. It rose to 3.8% in 2000 as a result of high oil prices, but eased to 2.5% in 2001.

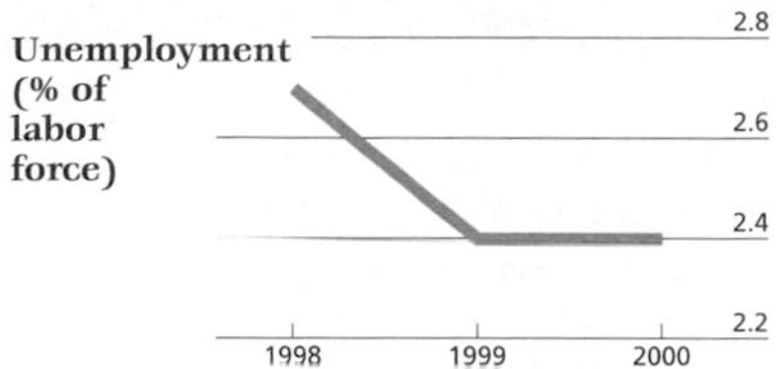

Unemployment averaged 2.3% a year in 1991–2001, and is expected to fall to 1.8% in 2002. The number of jobs rose by 3.2% a year in the 1990s, with stronger growth in 2000 and 2001. Trans-frontier workers from France, Germany, and Belgium constitute 30% of the workforce, and mask structural weaknesses in the local labor force. The 1999 National Action Plan for Employment introduced measures to increase the participation of older workers, women, and the long-term unemployed in the job market.

Geography/Resources

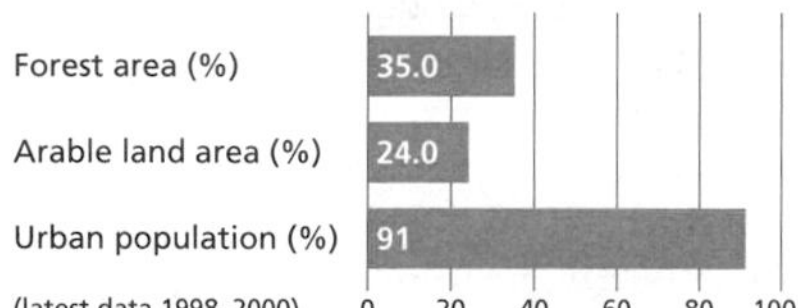

Luxembourg is the smallest member of the European Union. It is landlocked, and borders Belgium, Germany, and France. The land divides naturally into the northern Oesling region, part of the Plateau de l'Ardennes, and the southern Gutland region, part of the Parisian plain. The climate is continental but temperate, given that the English Channel coast is about 190 miles to the west.

The north is forested, and most of the timber produced is exported. A larger amount of timber is imported. There is a varied and efficient agricultural sector, with dairy and meat the main subsectors. Farm size grew by one-third to an average 128 acres from 1990 to 1999, while the number of farms and families engaged in agriculture fell by about one-third. The Moselle river valley forms a natural border with Germany in the southeast. It offers ideal slopes for vine-growing. Most of the wine is consumed within the home market. The river also provides hydroelectric power which is exported to Germany, and an inland waterway linking to the Rhine. The iron ore deposits near the southern border with France formed part of the massive Lorraine iron ore field.

In 2000 nearly 37% of the population were of foreign origin. By far the largest group of foreigners are Portuguese, followed by Italians, French, Belgians, Germans, other EU, and non-EU. The main towns are in the south, Luxembourg city (80,700) and seven towns in the steel-making region (105,800).

Communications/Energy

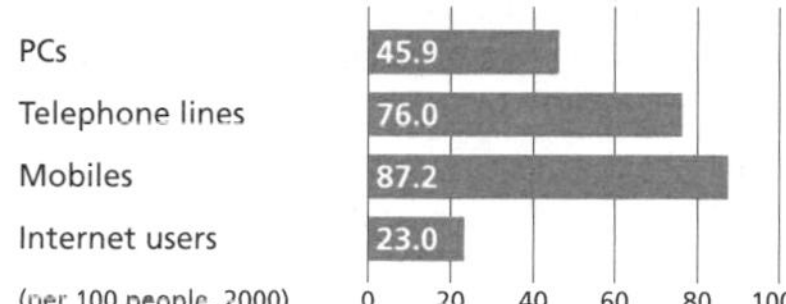

Good transport links are vital to enable the workforce living in neighboring countries to cross into Luxembourg to work, and to enable over 80% of goods to be exported. The 71-mile highway network runs from the western border with Belgium, around Luxembourg city, and on to the eastern border with Germany, and south through the steel region to France. Smaller roads criss-cross the country, bringing the total road network to 3,210 miles. The Société Nationale des Chemins de Fer Luxembourgeois (CFL) operates local services and international links on its 170-mile electrified network. Luxembourg city is on the main lines connecting Scandinavia to Italy and France and Belgium to Moscow. CFL carried 498 million passenger-miles and 1,062 million freight ton-miles in 1999. Luxembourg International Airport offers connecting flights to all parts of the world. In 1999 it handled 1.6 million passengers and 448,000 tons of freight. Cargolux is one of the world's top cargo airlines. The River Moselle provides 28 miles of inland waterway, linking the port of Mertert with the River Rhine and the North Sea. The merchant fleet comprised 50 ships over 1,000 grt, representing a total 988,450 grt in 2000.

The telecommunications network has digital switching and extensive fiberoptic and ISDN provision. There were 331,000 fixed phone lines, 380,000 mobile phones, and 100,000 Internet users at end-2000. Most energy needs are imported, with oil products accounting for over 61% of the total, followed by natural gas (20%) and electricity (14%). Local electricity production, however, increased by 10% in 1999–2000. In 1999 hydroelectricity accounted for 53% of output, followed by fossil fuels (37%), and renewables (10%). Luxembourg exports small amounts of electricity to Germany.

Education/Employment

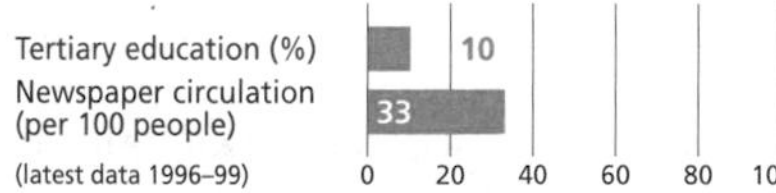

Education is compulsory from age 6 to 15, and is delivered in German and French, making Luxembourgers at least trilingual. Luxembourgish is a dialect of German. Luxembourg does not have a full university. The Centre Universitaire offers training course for teachers and lawyers, and one-year courses in a range of subjects. There is also the College for Management and the Superior Institute of Technology, both of which have an enrollment of around 250 students. Over 4,000 Luxembourgers attended university abroad on government grants in 1998–99. This is welcomed by industry as well as being government policy, since it provides a means of keeping up with international innovation and developments. The two largest manufacturing companies, ARBED and Goodyear, have research and development centers for their products. Broadcasting firm CLT and satellite company SES Astra develop the expertise of their employees in broadcasting and satellite communications.

The labor force is multilingual, multinational, and highly skilled. Wages are negotiated through tripartite agreements between the government, employers, and trade unions. In addition to negotiated pay increases, wages are linked to the inflation index, and rise automatically when prices exceed a given level. The IMF and OECD have advised the government to take oil prices out of the index, or to scrap it altogether. Luxembourg applies EU employment law, which covers safety at work, wages and working hours, industrial relations, employment incentives, and unemployment provision. National laws, though—especially regarding dismissal and the use of fixed-term contracts—are less favorable to business than those of many other EU countries.

  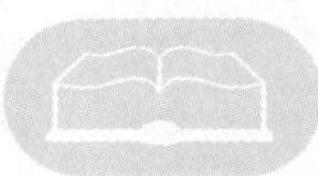    

Fiscal/Financial

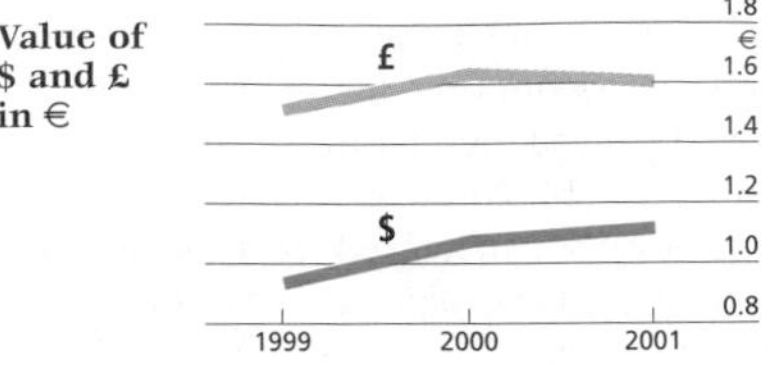

The leading banks (ranked by net profit by the Association des Banques et Banquiers Luxembourg) are Drexia Banque Internationale à Luxembourg, Kredietbank SA Luxembourgoise, Banque Générale du Luxembourg, Dresdner Bank Luxembourg, and Deutsche Bank Luxembourg. Insurance companies include main international players such as AON and AXA. All are private-sector. The government owns the industrial development bank Société Nationale de Crédit à l'Industrie (SNCI) and savings bank Banque et Caisse d'Épargne de l'État. In 1998 the government replaced the Institut Monétaire Luxembourg with the Banque Centrale du Luxembourg. This has full central bank powers for clearing transactions, a task formerly conducted for Luxembourg by the Belgian central bank. The new central bank is part of the European System of Central Banks. This body, and the European Central Bank, set the policy for the Euro. The regulatory authority for Luxembourg banking is another new body, the Commission de surveillance du secteur financier (CSSF).

Corporate tax is 30% as of January 2002, with maximum personal income tax at 38%. There are substantial corporate tax incentives, especially in the assessment of taxable income. International financial holding companies can allocate taxable profits to foreign or local subsidiaries. Investment funds pay a "registration" tax rather than corporate tax. Re-insurance companies can set aside tax-free reserves subject to certain limitations. Manufacturing or service companies can qualify for a 14% tax credit for investment in machinery. The credit can be carried forward for ten years, and this does not reduce the depreciation allowance. The EU wants to tax interest income, a move opposed by Luxembourg and the United Kingdom. In 2000 the government agreed to work towards improving access to bank information for tax purposes. It also enacted one of the toughest laws against money-laundering anywhere in the world in order to quash international criticism of its banking secrecy laws.

At March 2001 there were 197 banks with a total balance sheet of €672 billion. The financial sector is adapting to take advantage of greater openness in financial operations across Europe. Fund management and securities clearing operations have grown in importance relative to private banking, with 1,816 funds and €863 billion under management at end-2000, making Luxembourg the leading European center for fund management. The government set a minimum reserve requirement for finance companies for the first time in 1999, but the sector continued to grow. New laws on real estate banking and pension funds are designed to attract this business to the center. The government program for e-commerce, including infrastructure investment and training, will facilitate e-banking. The number of insurance companies is increasing rapidly. They include re-insurance firms and "captive" insurance firms of global corporations.

The Luxembourg Stock Exchange lists over 19,000 international securities, mostly Eurobonds, issued by several thousand companies from over 90 countries. Trading volume was €2.8 billion in 2000. It has links with Euronext, the merged exchanges of Paris, Amsterdam, and Brussels. Clearstream International, the clearing system adopted by the Deutsche Börse and Cedel group in 1999, is headquartered in Luxembourg and provides a standardized platform for operations and credit ratings. The aim is to create a pan-European clearing house.

Business Opportunities

The government provides land on favorable terms at the 14 national industrial parks, or in the many municipal and regional industrial parks. SNCI offers grants, loans, and venture capital to companies locating in development areas, small and medium-sized companies, R&D firms focusing on new products or services, and firms involved in environment protection. It channels government and EU project finance, and sometimes takes equity for a brief period of time. There is foreign investment in many sectors, including automotive, chemicals, textiles, machinery, media, banking, insurance, and business services. The United States is the main investor in manufacturing, followed by France, Belgium, Japan, and Germany. Finance sector investments have come from Germany, Italy, Switzerland, France, Scandinavia, Japan, the Middle East, the United Kingdom, and the United States among others. Regional manufacturing, IT, media, finance, and business services continue to offer investment opportunities. The opening of competition and expansion of electricity generation and distribution present additional opportunities.

For More Information

Books:

Grand Duchy of Luxembourg: Sights and Attractions. Luxembourg: Luxembourg National Tourist Office.

IMF Country Report. *Luxembourg*. Washington, D.C.: IMF.

Luxembourg Business and Investment Opportunities Yearbook. 3rd ed. Washington, D.C.: International Business Publications, 2001 (annual).

Luxembourg in Figures. Central Service for Statistics and Economic Research (STATEC).

Michelin the Green Guide: Belgium [and] Grand Duchy of Luxembourg. 3rd ed. Greenville, SC: Michelin Travel Publications, 2001.

OECD Economic Surveys. *Luxembourg*. Paris: OECD, 2001.

Web Sites:

Association des Banques et Banquiers Luxembourg: **www.abbl.lu**

Central Service for Statistics and Economic Research: **www.statec.lu**

Chamber of Commerce: **www.cc.lu**

Government of Luxembourg entry point: **www.etat.lu**

Luxembourg National Tourist Office: **www.ont.lu**

Luxemburger Wort/La Voix du Luxembourg (main daily newspaper): **www.wort.online.lu**

Ministry of the Economy: **www.etat.lu/ECO**

Société Nationale de Credit à l'Industrie: **www.snci.lu**

  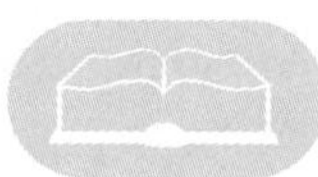    

Macao

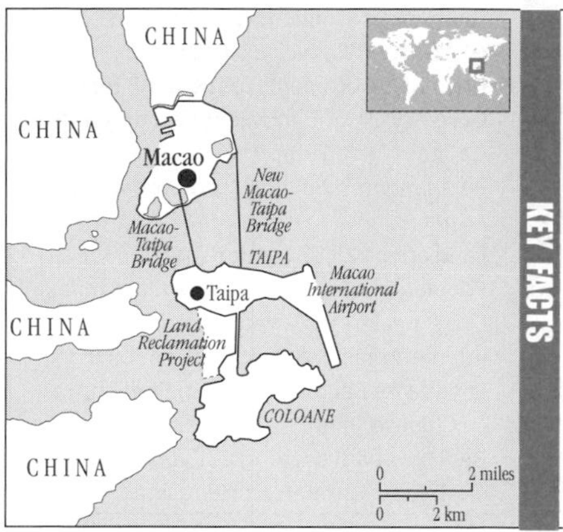

KEY FACTS

GNI: **$6,161 million; world's 103rd**
GNI pc: **$14,200; world's 41st**
Head of government: **chief executive**
Currency: **pataca (MPtc)**
Capital: **Macao City**
Population: **437,300**
Land area: **9 square miles**
Population density: **48,055 per square mile**
Language: **Cantonese, Mandarin, Portuguese, English**
Best buy: **cameras, watches, jewelry, tobacco and cigars, clothing**

Economy

Services account for over three-quarters of GDP, and manufacturing for most of the rest. Tourism and gambling are the main activities: decline in these sectors caused recession in 1996–99. GDP growth revived by 4.6% in 2000. There were 9.16 million visitors in 2000, mostly from Hong Kong, followed by China, Taiwan, Japan, the United States, and the United Kingdom. Visitors increased by 13.1% in the first eight months of 2001. Trade, transport and storage, finance, and insurance are other important services sectors. The main manufacturing industries and merchandise exports in 2000 were garments, followed by textiles, footwear, electronics, and toys.

Formerly an overseas province of Portugal, Macau became a Special Administrative Region of China in 1999, but its free market economy is guaranteed for at least 50 years. The government is committed to diversifying the economy towards high-tech industry and multinational company hub operations. The government's prudent fiscal policy, and its defense of the exchange rate between the pataca and the Hong Kong dollar (the main trading currency), produced stability through the Asian financial crisis. Traditional government budget surpluses fell slightly, but balance of trade surpluses strengthened. Annual inflation of 2.7% in 1995–98 turned to deflation of 2.4% in 1999–2000. Unemployment rose from 4% in the late 1990s to 6.3% in April 2001.

Geography/Resources

The Macao peninsula is divided from China by the Pearl River. The land is largely flat with a high point of 570 feet. Average temperatures range from 59°F in January to 84°F in July. Only 2% of the land is used for agriculture. There are no minerals of commercial significance.

Communications/Energy

The road network is around 95 miles. New roads are planned linking Macao with the mainland and Hong Kong. Macao's first railway, a 115-mile high-speed electrified link from Guangzhou on the mainland, will have a branch line to the container terminal at Ka Ho port and a link to Macao International Airport. Sea ports handled 2 million tons of freight in 1999, while 409,596 tons were transported by land and 44,261 by air. Container traffic at Ka Ho and Inner Harbour ports was 21,942 containers in 2000.

Companhia de Telecommunicaçoes (CTM) is the main telecommunications operator, but competition was introduced in late 2000. Local calls are free from private phones. Switching is fully digital. International links are provided by Hong Kong and Chinese companies via satellite and cable. Broadband transmission extended to 90% of the region by end-2000. There were 300,100 fixed phones at end-1999, 60,000 Internet users at end-2000, and 155,086 mobile phones at May 2001. The Macau Electric Company produced 1.4 billion kWh of electricity entirely from fossil fuels in 2000. A small amount of electricity was imported from the mainland, and 3% of demand was met from waste incineration. Oil and gas are imported.

Fiscal/Financial

The Monetary and Foreign Exchange Authority of Macau is the de facto central bank, and regulates the financial sector. The banks were sufficiently well capitalized to handle the rise in non-performing loans following the Asian financial crisis. Bank of China, one of the two banks of issue for the pataca, introduced local e-banking in 2000. At mid-2001 there were 24 banks, including 12 local, 11 foreign bank branches, and one offshore banking unit. The largest local bank at end-2000 was Banco Tai Fung, followed by Banco Seng Heng and Luso International Banking. There were 24 insurance companies, including 9 life insurers and 15 non-life insurers. General insurers include some of the world's largest. There is no local stock market, but securities trading is active on the Hong Kong Exchange and other international exchanges. Companies pay a fixed annual levy of MPtc300 on each activity conducted, and an average 15% on profits. Personal income tax is a maximum 15%. Offshore companies and banks benefit from complete tax exemption.

Business Opportunities

Tax and financial investment incentives are available, especially for high tech and IT industries, environmental protection, and export companies. Macao is a duty-free zone. Finance, insurance, and trade have attracted foreign investment from China, Hong Kong, Taiwan, Portugal, France, Germany, the United States, Japan, and Bermuda, among other countries. These sectors continue to offer opportunities. The point of contact for investors is the Macao Trade and Investment Promotion Institute.

For More Information

Books:

Brown, Jules. *The Rough Guide to Hong Kong and Macau.* 5th ed. New York: Rough Guides, 2002.
Macao Business and Investment Opportunities Yearbook. 3rd ed. Washington, D.C.: International Business Publications, 2001 (annual).
Macau Economic Bulletin. Macao: Statistics and Census Service (quarterly).

Web Sites:

Macao Government Information Services (entry point): **www.macau.gov.mo**
Macao Trade and Investment Promotion Institute: **www.ipim.gov.mo**

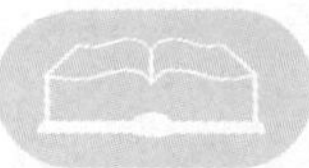

MALAYSIA

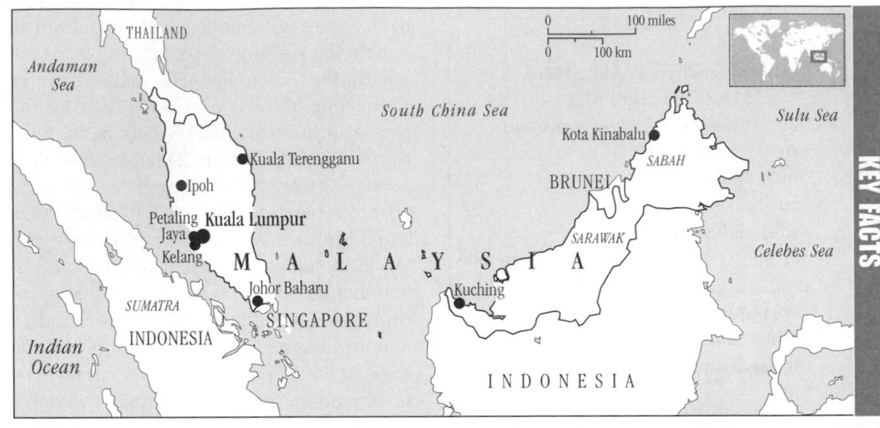

KEY FACTS

GNI: **$76,944 million; world's 42nd**
GNI pc: **$3,390; world's 84th**
Head of government: **prime minister**
Currency: **ringgit or Malaysian dollar (M$)**
Capital: **Kuala Lumpur**
Population: **21,830,000, growing at 2.2% p.a.**
Land area: **126,872 square miles**
Population density: **172 per square mile**
Life expectancy: **72 years**
Infant mortality: **8 per 1,000 live births**
Language: **Bahasa Malaysia, English, Chinese, Tamil**
Best buy: **batik, sarongs, silverware, shadow puppets, carvings**

ECONOMIC STRUCTURE

Malaysia became an international trading nation two thousand years ago, selling tin to India. This was still the most valuable product when the British established a colony there in the early 19th century. In 1957 the federated states of the Malaysian peninsula gained independence. They were joined by Sarawak, Sabah, and Singapore in 1963, but Singapore left in 1965. Economic development focused first on natural resources, which Malaysia has in abundance, and light manufacturing. Heavy manufacturing of petroleum, petrochemicals, and natural gas products followed in the 1980s after the oil and gas fields came into production. The high technology content of manufacturing and service industries grew rapidly in the 1990s. The Asian currency crisis of 1997–98 highlighted weaknesses in the finance sector and prompted radical restructuring.

Services accounted for around 47% of GDP in 2001, followed by manufacturing (31%), mining (9%), agriculture (8%), and construction (4%). Trade was the leading services sector, followed by finance, transport and communications, and public administration. Electronic goods are the leading manufacturing industry and top export. Car production benefits from a strong domestic market, and Malaysian cars dominate in the ASEAN region. Furniture is another key industry with strong exports to ASEAN. Despite the abundance and variety of Malaysian hardwoods, U.S. timber is imported. Malaysia is the top world exporter of palm oil. In 2000, electronics and electrical machinery accounted for 58.8% of exports, followed by gas and petroleum (6.8%), chemicals (4%), palm oil (3.9%), timber and wood products (2.7%), textiles, and clothing and footwear (2.3%). The United States was the main export market, followed by Singapore, the European Union, Japan, Hong Kong, and Taiwan.

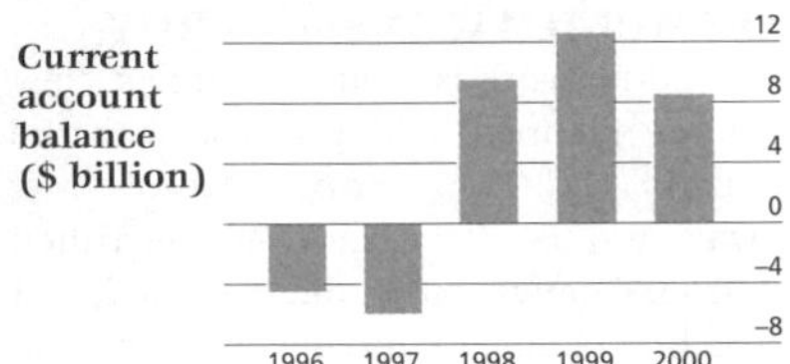

The government has control over a wide range of industries, including hydrocarbons firm Petronas, steel, cement, electronics, plantations and forestry, and infrastructure and holding companies. However, many corporations have been privatized under a program launched in 1986. The financial crisis of 1997–98 caused the government to recapitalize failing banks, in which it took temporary shareholdings. It provided additional assistance for key sectors, notably telecommunications, urban infrastructure, transport, and steel. The power and telecommunications sectors have been opened to competition, but former monopolies remain dominant. Some sea ports and roads have been privatized.

ECONOMIC POLICY

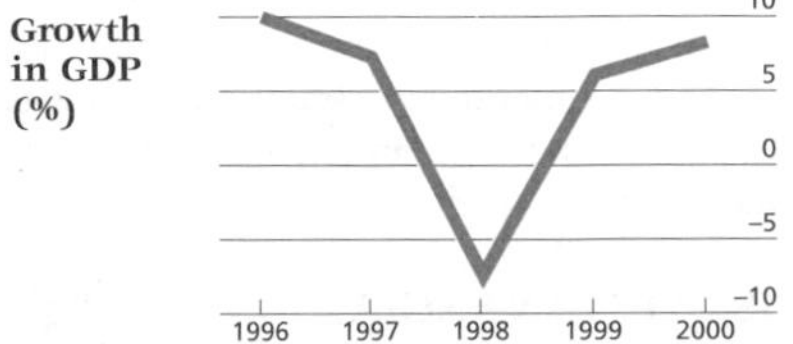

The government directs the economy with five-year plans, which include an increasing role for the private sector. The Eighth Plan covers 2001–2005. The government's strict monetary measures, its restructuring of the financial sector, and the reduction of public spending facilitated a relatively rapid recovery from the 1997–98 financial crisis. A consistently positive trade balance helped restore official reserves and underpin the value of the currency. However, capital controls—imposed in 1998 to prevent further speculation—had the effect of reducing foreign direct aid. The IMF also warned in mid-2000 that the ringgit was undervalued. Government measures to revive the economy in 1998 included reductions in the base lending rate, the amount of reserves banks were required to deposit with the central bank, and interest rates on consumer credit cards, mortgages and car loans; it also created new funds to help small business.

Danaharta (National Asset Management Company) was established in 1998 to acquire and dispose of non-performing loans (NPLs), with the Corporate Debt Restructuring Committee (CDRC) to adjudicate. Danamodal injected M$7.1 billion into ten banks, but this was reduced to M$4.9 billion by May 2000 as banks repaid the debt. At November 2001, M$40.7 billion of Danaharta's portfolio of M$47.8 billion NPLs had been resolved with an expected recovery rate of 57%.

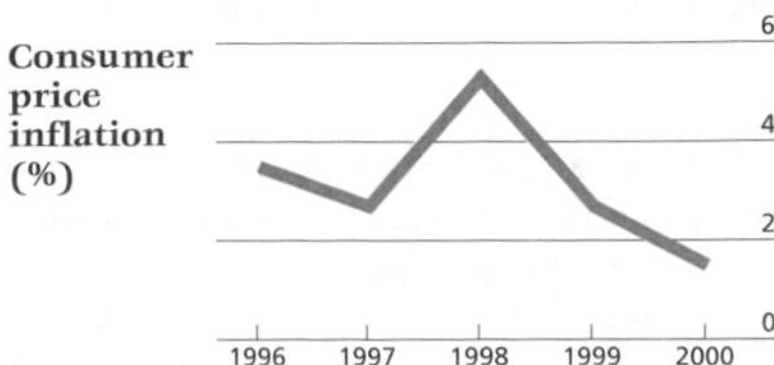

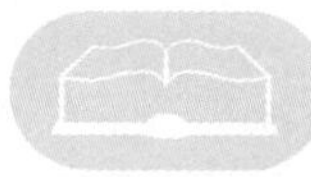

Annual average GDP growth was 7.2% in 1990–99 despite a 7.5% fall in 1998 because of the financial crisis. Growth was 8.3% in 2000 and 0.4% in 2001, and was expected to be 2.5% in 2002. Inflation averaged 3.6% a year in 1990–99 with a peak of 5.8% in 1998. It fell to 1.5% in 2000–01. Unemployment was an annual average of 3.4% in 1990–2001.

Geography/Resources

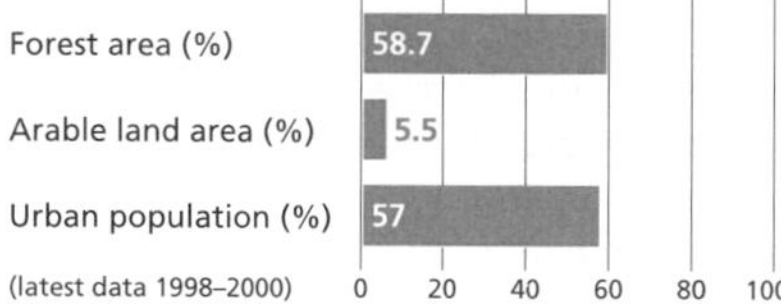

Malaysia is in southeast Asia and consists of the southern Malay peninsula and, across the South China Sea, Sarawak and Sabah in northwest Borneo. The peninsula borders Thailand to the north, Singapore to the south, and the Straits of Malacca to the west. Sarawak and Sabah border the Indonesian territory of Kalimantan to the south. Sarawak surrounds the land borders of Brunei on the northern coast. The peninsula has a central mountain range and alluvial plains. Sabah and Sarawak are mountainous, with the highest mountains over 13,000 feet. Malaysia is heavily forested, with average annual rainfall of 95 inches. There is a monsoon season from November to March, and a dry season from June to October. Temperatures range between 71°F and 91°F. The main population group is Malay (47%), followed by Chinese (24%), non-Malay indigenous groups who are especially predominant in Sabah and Sarawak (11%), Indian (7%), foreign residents (7%), and citizens of mixed descent (4%).

The main agricultural products are export crops, palm oil and kernels, rubber, copra and coconut oil, and timber. Rice is the top domestic crop. Other important crops are cassava, sugar cane, bananas, pineapples, other fruits, vegetables, corn, sweet potatoes, cocoa, coffee, tea, and tobacco. Chickens are the main livestock, followed by ducks, pigs, cattle, goats, sheep, and buffaloes. Forestry is a major industry, mostly in hardwood for furniture and fuel wood, although hardwood production has been restricted since 1993 to ensure forest sustainability. Other timber categories include heavy industrial timber and pulpwood. There is a small deep-sea fishing sector.

The main mineral resources are natural gas and petroleum, with reserves of 81.7 trillion cubic feet and 3.9 billion barrels respectively at January 2001. Malaysia is a leading world producer of tin, but the main non-hydrocarbon minerals by volume produced are bauxite and iron ore. Other important minerals are ilmenite, kaolin, copper, barytes, zirconium, coal, gold, and silver. Coal reserves were 1,050 million tons in 2000. A new offshore gas field jointly owned with Thailand came onstream in 2002. Minerals exploration continues.

Communications/Energy

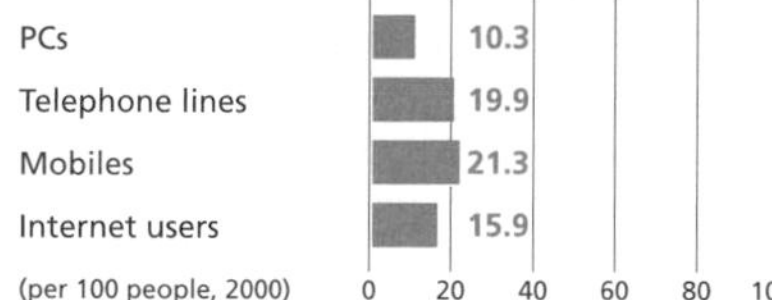

The road network was 40,888 miles in 2000, including over 370 miles of motorways and 30,200 miles of paved rural roads. Private funding has been used to build motorways, and a further 60 miles of privatized motorways are planned by 2005. The rail network was 1,119 miles in 2000, including 112 miles of electrified track. KTMB (Malayan Railways), which has been managed by a private consortium since 1997, handled 0.9 billion passenger-miles on inter-city routes and a total of 4.98 million tons of freight on all routes in 2000. The pipeline network includes 812 miles for crude oil and 235 miles for natural gas. There are 1,988 miles of navigable waterways on the Malaysian peninsula, 976 miles in Sabah, and 1,565 miles in Sarawak. The main sea ports are Kelang in Selangor state (near to Kuala Lumpur), which handled 65.3 million tons of freight in 2000, Johor (near to Singapore: 29 million tons), Bintulu (Sarawak: 24.9 million tons), and Penang (20.5 million tons). There are many smaller ports. All main port capacity is due for expansion under the 2001–05 development plan. The merchant fleet numbered 3,200 ships in 2000, representing 6.5 million grt. There are 36 airports and numerous airstrips. The main international airport is the new Kuala Lumpur International Airport, which began operations in 1998. Other international airports include Penang and Langkawi on the peninsula, Labuan (Sabah), and Kuching (Sarawak). Airport expansion and upgrading continues in order to meet increased passenger and freight traffic. In 2000 32.9 million passengers and 773,861 tons of freight traveled by air, and this volume is expected to rise by 5.2% and 7.3% a year respectively in 2001–05.

International and domestic telecommunications are provided via satellite, cable, and microwave radio relay. Switches and routers are digitalized. Fiberoptic links were to be upgraded for high-speed data transmission by 2005. E-commerce is growing for retailing, entertainment, travel, and finance. The 1997 Digital Signature Act, and the licensing in 2000 of two verifying companies for such signatures, provided security and immediacy for online transactions. There were 4.65 million fixed phone line subscribers, 5 million mobile phones, and 3.7 million Internet users at end-2000.

Petroleum accounted for 53.1% of primary energy supply in 2000, natural gas for 37.1%, coal and coke 5.4%, and hydroelectricity 4.4%. By 2005 the shares are expected to be 50.8%, 39.9%, 5.9%, and 3.4% respectively. Malaysia is expected to cease to be a net petroleum exporter in 2010. Petroleum for domestic consumption is largely imported, whereas 81% of gas used is domestically produced. Gas production was 4.95 billion cubic feet per day and oil production 606,000 barrels per day in 2000. Coal output was 400,000 tons in 1999. Coal mined in Sarawak is used at the local Sejingkat power station. Gas accounted for 78.7% of electricity generation in 2000, hydro power 8%, coal 7.9%, oil 5.3%, and other means for 0.1%. By 2005 the shares are expected to be 61%, 5.4%, 30.3%, 3%, and 0.3% respectively. Three new coal and one new hydroelectric station are due to come onstream in that time. There is a grid link with Thailand. Further links with Indonesia, Brunei, and Philippines are planned.

Education/Employment

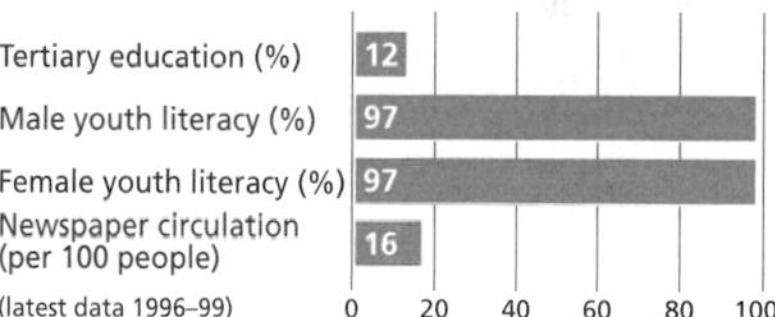

Education is compulsory from age 6 to 16. There were 56 higher education institutions in 2000. The public sector included 10 universities, 6 polytechnics, and 31 teacher training colleges with total enrollment of 321,729 students. There are also private universities and colleges. Eleven universities oversee a distance learning program for 20,000 students. The Ministry of Education is responsible for educational policy and for most public-sector higher education institutions. The government has encouraged private sector participation in the funding and management of public universities. The government provides financial assistance for students in both public- and private-sector higher education. The government is promoting vocational training to provide the technical skills for the information age.

There are 194 vocational training institutes, with 292 new ones planned by 2005, which fall under the remit of several ministries.

The National Council for Scientific Research and Development and the Malaysian Technology Development Corporation (which provides venture capital) promote R&D linkages between universities and research institutes and industry. There are technology parks located close to universities. Precision manufacturing, biotechnology, electronics, IT, and energy are key strengths. In 1998 public R&D spending was M$1.1 billion, or 0.4% of GDP, while private-sector R&D spending was M$746 million. Government R&D spending in 2001–05 will be M$4.7 billion.

The labor force is well educated. Guidelines for wages and employment conditions are set by the National Labor Advisory Council, composed of representatives of government, employers, and trade unions. Present wage increases are linked to productivity. National trade unions are banned, but there are national confederations of trade unions. Although strikes are not banned, they are severely discouraged by the government. The Employment Act of 1955 is the basic labor law. The standard working week is 48 hours, with no more than 8 hours in the working day, after which time and a half must be paid on normal days, double time on rest days and treble time on public holidays. Annual leave is 8 to 16 days, with 14–16 days of paid sick leave per year, 10 paid public holidays, and 60 days maternity leave. Compulsory contributions to the Employee Provident Fund are 12% for employers and 11% for employees. The Fund provides retirement pensions for private-sector workers.

Fiscal/Financial

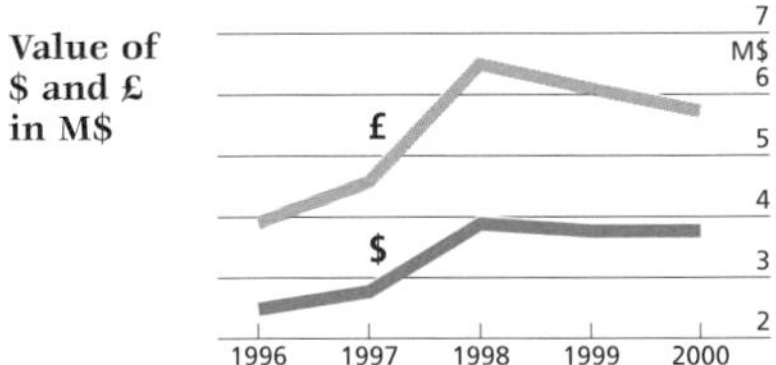

Malayan Banking (Mayban) is the largest banking group, followed by Bumiputra-Commerce Bank, RHB Bank, and Public Bank. There were six other "anchor" banks following the end-2000 consolidation. Insurance companies were also consolidated at end-2000. Malayan Banking group and other anchor banks have insurance subsidiaries. Bank Negara Malaysia, the central bank, is responsible for regulation of the onshore finance and insurance sector. The Securities Commission regulates the stock exchange. The Labuan Offshore Financial Services Authority (LOFSA) regulates the offshore banking and insurance center at Labuan in Sabah. Corporation tax for most companies is 28%, but 38% applies to the petroleum sector. The top rate of personal income tax is 29%. Withholding tax for fees is 10% and 15% for interest. General sales tax is 10%.

The finance sector is in better shape since the 1997–98 crisis, with a stronger capital base and economies of scale following the consolidation. Greater transparency of accounting, and tighter regulation in line with international standards, has been introduced. An anti-money-laundering law was passed in early 2001. E-banking and e-trading on the stock markets are growth activities. The government required the 54 financial institutions to consolidate in ten anchor banks by January 2001. At end-March 2001 there were 26 domestic and foreign commercial banks, and two Islamic banks, with 12 finance companies and 10 merchant banks affiliated to the 10 domestic commercial banks. At December 2000 five mergers involving 10 insurers were completed and nine others involving 17 companies were in the pipeline. The Labuan International Offshore Finance Center had 60 banks, 19 leasing companies, 39 insurance companies, 8 fund management companies, 20 trust companies, over 2,000 trading companies, 20 audit firms, and 15 liquidator firms at end-2000. The center is growing, and the government is encouraging Islamic banking and funds to do business there.

The present Kuala Lumpur Stock Exchange was established in 1973, and had close links with the Singapore Stock Exchange, which overshadowed its development. In 1990 the two exchanges ceased listing firms incorporated in each other's territory, and trading on the KLSE took off. It operates a main board and second board, the Kuala Lumpur Options and Financial Futures Exchange (KLOFFE) for derivatives, a central clearing house, and fully electronic settlement system. The KLSE's Listing Information Network is available on the Internet, and e-trading is available through ATMs. There are two other exchanges: the Commodity and Monetary Exchange of Malaysia, which trades in commodities and derivatives, and the Malaysian Exchange for Securities Dealing and Automated Quotation (MESDAQ), which deals with small high-growth firms. The Securities Commission is encouraging consolidation of the 69 stockbroking companies into a core of well-capitalized universal brokers. Foreign participation in portfolio investment is due to be fully liberalized by 2003.

Business Opportunities

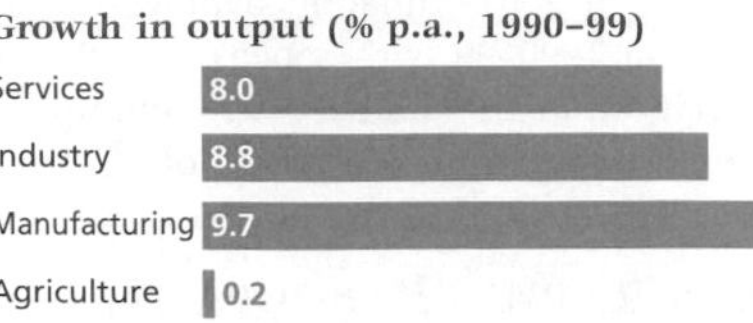

The government offers tax and training incentives for investment. There are over 200 industrial sites, 14 free industrial zones for export processing and re-export activities, and technology parks for R&D investment. The Multimedia Super Corridor (MSC) is a program to attract investment in IT. Electronics have attracted the most foreign direct investment in recent years, followed by petroleum, paper and printing, and a wide variety of other industries, including chemicals, basic and fabricated metals, transport, finance, and insurance. Opportunities continue to exist in these industries. The top investor in 1996–2000 was the United States ($7 billion), followed by Japan ($4.13 billion), Singapore ($3.52 billion), Taiwan ($1.34 billion), Germany ($1.22 billion) and Switzerland ($1.05 billion). The point of contact for foreign investors is the Malaysian Industrial Development Agency.

For More Information

Books:

The Eighth Economic Development Plan 2001–2005. Government of Malaysia.
IMF Country Report. *Malaysia*. Washington, D.C.: IMF.
Malaysia. Asian Development Bank, Country Economic Review.

Web Sites:

Bank Negara Malaysia (central bank): **www.bnm.gov.my**
Department of Statistics: **www.statistics.gov.my**
Kuala Lumpur Stock Exchange: **www.klse.com.my**
Labuan Offshore Financial Services Authority: **www.lofsa.gov.my**
Malaysian Industrial Development Authority: **www.mida.gov.my**
Malaysian Science and Technology Information Center: **www.mastic.gov.my**
Ministry of International Trade and Industry (government entry point): **www.miti.gov.my**

MALTA

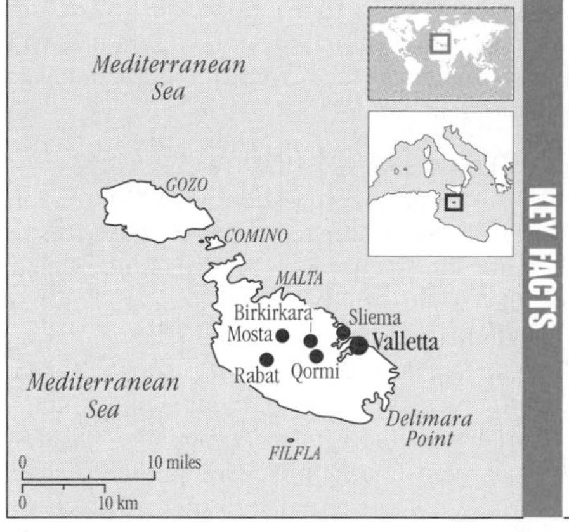

KEY FACTS

GNI: **$3,492 million; world's 128th**
GNI pc: **$9,210; world's 51st**
Head of government: **prime minister**
Currency: **Maltese lira (Lm)**
Capital: **Valletta**
Population: **386,000, growing at 1.0% p.a.**
Land area: **122 square miles**
Population density: **3,163 per square mile**
Life expectancy: **78 years**
Infant mortality: **6 per 1,000 live births**
Language: **Malti (first official language), English (second official language), Italian**
Best buy: **lace, gold and silver filigree objects, pottery, embroidered fabrics**

ECONOMIC STRUCTURE

As a British colony from 1814 to 1964, the Maltese economy was focused on provisioning and repairing British Navy ships. Since the British naval base closed in 1979, successive governments have sought to diversify the economy with the development of tourism, manufacturing for export to the European market, and the establishment of an international financial center. Shipbuilding and repair remain important, especially in terms of employment, absorbing large amounts of state aid, which must be phased out before Malta can join the European Union. Malta's 1970 Association Agreement with the EU gave its exports preferential access. In February 2000 Malta began negotiations for full membership, but opinions are divided on whether to join. The Labour Party is opposed. The Nationalist Party, presently in government, has promised to hold a referendum over the issue in 2002.

Services, including tourism, trade, finance, and public services, accounted for 70.4% of GDP in 1999. Industry contributed 24.8%, agriculture 2.5%, and construction 2.3%. Tourism is the largest single sector. Manufacturing is diverse, with around 500 foreign and Maltese firms producing for export. Smaller firms produce a range of goods for the domestic market. Electronics, telecommunications equipment, and finance are fast-growing sectors. Machinery and communications equipment are the main exports, followed by manufactured goods and semi-manufactures. The main market is the United States, followed by Germany, France, the United Kingdom, and Italy.

The state is heavily involved in the traditional sectors of the economy, such as the shipyards and utilities. The domestic economy has been protected from the outside by import duties and other restrictions, and there has been a tendency to create new monopolies for private-sector firms in new areas such as cable TV and mobile phones. All of this is now changing. The government sold shareholdings in two banks before setting up a unit in 2000 to oversee the rest of its ambitious privatization program, which is due to be completed in 2005. On the list are Malta Freeport Terminals, telecommunications company Maltacom (in which the state holds 60%), Malta International Airport, Air Malta, Mediterranean Offshore Bunkering Company, the Public Lotto Department, 25% of the Bank of Valletta, water and electricity companies, a film studio, printing plant, broadcasting company, a dairy products factory, a casino, and a tourism complex.

ECONOMIC POLICY

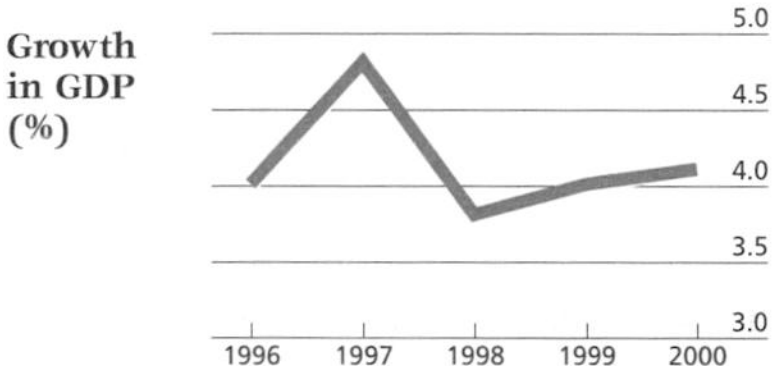

Public-sector wages, social services, state aids to industry, and investment in infrastructure have kept government spending high. Policy targets to reduce the number of public-sector employees to 25–30% of the labor force were not met in 2000, largely because the privatization program did not go ahead as quickly as planned. Even so, the public sector accounted for 34% of the labor force, down from 39%, at end-2000. The labor force is increasing, and the government believes that privatization will create the jobs needed. In the meantime the government deficit rose from 3.5% of GDP in 1995 to 8.5% in 1999, and is expected to continue to grow in the medium term despite public spending cuts, improved direct tax collection, and the introduction of VAT in 1999. Government debt was 60% of GDP in June 2000, while the gross foreign debt of the whole economy was estimated at over 200% of GDP. Privatization receipts should improve public finances, but protective import duties are due to be phased out in 2003. Monetary policy aims at the stability of the lira, low inflation, and the maintenance of export competitiveness. The lira is weighted against a basket of currencies including the Euro, dollar, and sterling.

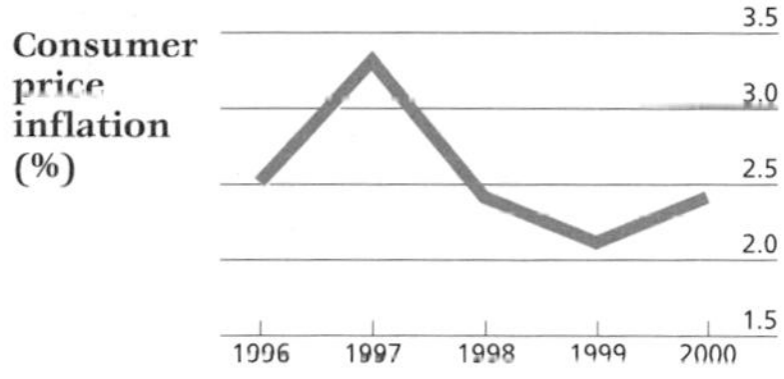

GDP growth slowed from 6.2% in 1995 to an annual average of around 4% in 1996–2000. It was estimated at 3.5% in 2001, and could be less in 2002 because of the adverse international environment. Inflation fell from 4% in 1995 to an annual average of 2.5% in 1996–2001. Unemployment is traditionally low: it rose from 3.7% in 1995 to 5.3% in 1999, but fell to 4.5% by September 2001.

GEOGRAPHY/RESOURCES

An archipelago in the Mediterranean Sea just south of Sicily, Malta has three inhabited islands—Malta, Gozo, and Comino—and two uninhabited islands, Cominotto and Filfla. The terrain is rugged but low-lying. The climate is warm and dry, with average temperatures of 73°F in summer and 57°F in winter, and average annual rainfall of 23 inches. The population is ethnically mixed, mostly of Italian and Arab origin, with small British, Greek, Syrian, and Indian communities.

About 80% of food is imported. Most agricultural crops are grown in the rainy winter season. Potatoes are grown for export. Other crops include tomatoes and other vegetables, wheat, barley, and fruit. Meat and dairy are important. A small inshore fishing industry catches dorado and swordfish. Limestone and sand are quarried, and sea

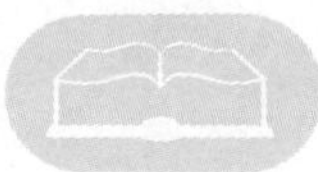

salt is extracted. There are offshore petroleum and natural gas reserves, which are being explored.

Communications/Energy

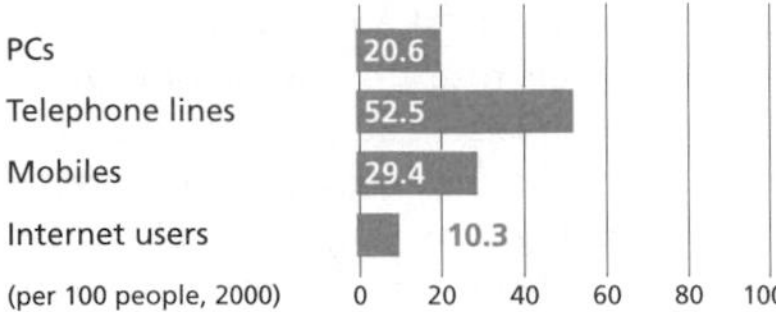

The road network totaled 1,219 miles in 1998, including trunk roads between the main towns and links to ferries between the three main islands. The main sea ports are at Valletta and Marsaxlokk. Malta Freeport transshipment zone at Valletta handles 1 million teus of containers a year. Valletta also has bunkering and ship repair facilities. Some 300 cruise ships visited Valletta in 2000. The Maltese shipping register is one of the largest in the world, with 3,189 ships totaling 28.6 million grt at end-1999. Rules for flag of convenience ships from 49 countries were tightened in 2000. The international airport is near to Valletta, and there is a regular helicopter shuttle service from there to Gozo island.

There were 205,200 fixed phone lines in September 2000, and 114,400 mobile phones and 40,000 Internet users at end-2000. State-owned Maltacom is the main operator. The sector will be fully liberalized by January 2003. Maltacom's mobile phone subsidiary Go Mobile was launched end-2000 to challenge Vodaphone's mobile monopoly. Cable TV company Melita Cable is likely to offer fixed-line telephony when its cable broadcasting monopoly expires in 2003. An independent regulatory authority was established in July 2000 with separate directorates for telecommunications, data protection, and e-commerce. Energy needs are met mainly by petroleum imported from Libya and by coal, which is used exclusively for electricity generation.

Education/Employment

Education is compulsory from age 5 to 16. Higher education is delivered at the University of Malta; three technical institutes specializing in mechanical engineering, naval and technical engineering, and surveying and technical drawing; and several professional institutes offering apprenticeship programs. The university has faculties of engineering, computer science, and medicine, among others. Education is the responsibility of the Ministry of Education, and funding is provided by the state. Student grants are available. The government promotes R&D links between the university and industry. Many of the foreign companies that have established manufacturing plants in Malta conduct R&D there. Commercial R&D includes computer-based industrial and automotive control systems, pharmaceuticals, and medical equipment. From 2001 Maltese companies are eligible for EU-funded R&D projects.

The labor force is well educated, multilingual, and adaptable. Wages and employment conditions are determined by negotiation between employers, workers, and the government. Malta is gradually enacting EU employment law in preparation for EU membership.

Fiscal/Financial

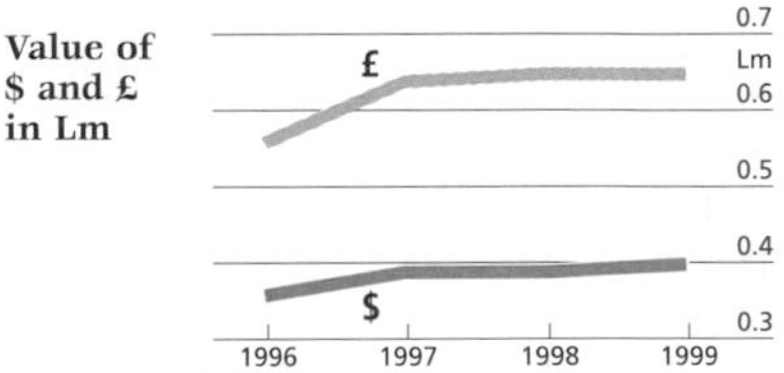

In early 2001 there were three deposit banks, Bank of Valletta (partly state-owned and due for further privatization), APS Bank, and Mid-Med Bank (privatized). There were 15 insurance companies. The Central Bank of Malta conducts monetary policy which is set by the government. The Malta Financial Services Center is the single regulator for the financial sector as of January 2002. Foreign exchange restrictions were lifted in 2002 to meet EU rules. In 2001 the government established a Financial Intelligence Unit to combat money-laundering in line with OECD requirements.

Standard corporation tax is 35%, but concessionary rates of 5%, 10%, and 15% apply under the Business Promotion Act 2001. Withholding tax on capital-generated income is 15%, but exemptions apply for collective investment schemes and for securities traded on the Malta Stock Exchange. VAT is 15%. Under-reporting of taxable income, especially by individuals and small businesses, is a major problem. The government established a Tax Compliance Unit in 2001 to follow up its success in improving tax collection in 2000.

Apart from the three deposit banks, there were three other domestic commercial financial institutions and 14 foreign banks in early 2001. The government set out to attract foreign finance and insurance companies in the early 1990s. It stopped issuing offshore company licenses in 1996, but the number of blue-chip companies and banks continues to rise. The few remaining offshore units are due to end their operations in 2004. The finance sector is sophisticated and internationalized. Activity on the Malta Stock Exchange has increased with the development of the financial center, especially in products deriving from the investment fund and insurance sectors. Operations will strengthen as the privatization program gets into gear.

Business Opportunities

Foreign direct investment was $780 million in 1999. Companies from the United Kingdom, Germany, France, Netherlands, the United States, Austria, and other countries have established manufacturing plants for electronics products, steel products, automotive components, industrial machinery and components, plastics, pharmaceuticals, medical equipment, toys, and service centers for software development and aero engine repairs. Greenfield investment is encouraged, and privatization will add to opportunities.

The Business Promotion Act 2001 offers reduced corporation tax, investment tax credits and capital allowances, soft loans, loan guarantees, exemption from import duties, employment incentives, and training assistance to eligible companies making electronic and telecommunications equipment, computer software, machinery and engineering products, certain metal manufactures, rubber and plastic items, pharmaceuticals, medical equipment, optical instruments, audiovisual productions, and jewelry, or involved in the maintenance of aircraft, ships and cranes, biotechnology, aquaculture, waste treatment, and R&D. The point of contact for foreign investors is the Malta Development Corporation (MDC). The MDC administers 12 industrial estates with facilities for a wide range of enterprises. Two new estates specifically for marine industries and aviation services are planned.

For More Information

Book:

Malta: Regular Report from the Commission on Malta's Progress towards Accession. Brussels: European Union.

Web Sites:

Central Bank of Malta:
www.centralbankmalta.com
Government entry point:
www.magnet.mt
The Malta Business Weekly:
www.business-line.com
Malta Development Corporation:
www.investinmalta.com

MARTINIQUE

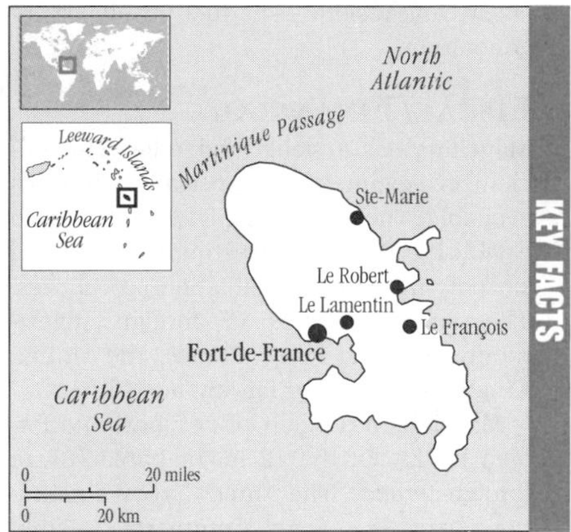

KEY FACTS

GNI pc: **$10,700 (approx.)**
Head of government: **president of the general council**
Currency: **Euro (€)**
Capital: **Fort-de-France**
Population: **381,300**
Land area: **417 square miles**
Population density: **876 per square mile**
Life expectancy: **78 years**
Infant mortality: **8 per 1,000 live births**
Language: **French, Creole**
Best buy: **rum, handicrafts**

ECONOMY

The principal economic sector is tourism, a major source of foreign exchange and employment, although government services are the leading contributor to GDP, with 24.8% of the total, according to 1992 statistics. Stopover tourist arrivals numbered 531,515 in 2000, and cruise ship passengers 290,097; in 1997, tourism revenue was an estimated $400 million. About 80% of hotel guests come from metropolitan France, with the U.S. the second-largest market. Trade, restaurants and hotels had an 18.4% share of GDP in 1992, closely followed by other services, while manufacturing held 7.1% and agriculture only 5.1%.

Industrial production is mainly based on food processing, including the production of sugar and rum; there is an oil refinery, a cement factory, and a polyethylene plant, and others producing construction materials and packaging materials. The agricultural sector remains largely dominated by sugar cane cultivation, which saw production of 189,000 tons in 1998; the sugar output is principally used for rum production. Banana production is substantial, at 321,000 tons in 1998, while newer crops include pineapples, citrus fruits, melon, avocados, egg plant, and cut flowers.

Much of this production is for export; in 1997, banana exports totaled 70.5 million, or 36.6% of total exports; refined petroleum products accounted for 16%, and rum 10%. Other exports included soft drinks and pleasure boats, while the main imports were transport equipment and machinery, manufactured goods, chemicals, and fuels. In 1999 the trade deficit amounted to 1.4 billion (84% of the import figure). Metropolitan France supplied 64% of imports and took 47% of the department's exports, while Guadeloupe accounted for 22% of exports.

French government expenditure supports the trade and fiscal deficit, the subsidy comprising about 70% of GNP and cushioning the steady GDP decline, which averaged 4.7% annually between 1990 and 1996.

The inflation rate averaged 1.05% between 1996 and 1999, and the unemployment rate was 28.8% at the end of 1997, out of a labor force of 165,000.

GEOGRAPHY/RESOURCES

Situated in the southern part of the lesser Antilles, Martinique is a volcanic island, the north dominated by Mt. Pelée (4,583 feet), which devastated the town of St. Pierre in an eruption in 1902. There is a lesser mountainous area to the south, with lower ground in the center.

The land area is 417 square miles. The administrative and economic center, Fort-de-France, accounted for 94,049 people at the 1999 census, almost 25% of the total population. The second-largest populated area was Le Lamentin, near the airport, with 35,460 inhabitants; six other areas had populations between 15,000 and 21,000.

Education is free and compulsory between 6 and 16 years of age; there is a high literacy rate. A campus of the University of the French Antilles offers degrees in law, economics, medicine, and the humanities, and there are several vocational colleges. Students from Martinique can pursue higher education in metropolitan France.

COMMUNICATIONS/ENERGY

Direct flight connections with Paris and other French cities operate, together with services to the United States and a number of Caribbean and Latin American destinations. There is a hydrofoil service linking Martinique with St. Lucia, Dominica, and Guadeloupe. The road network includes 166 miles of motorways and main roads, plus 382 miles of secondary roads and 500 miles of local roads.

Telecommunications are provided by the French state enterprise, and electricity by a Martinique company, which operates two generating stations powered by imported oil.

FISCAL/FINANCIAL

The tax system generally corresponds to the national French pattern, with some exceptions, including a reduced rate of value-added tax in Martinique. Corporate taxation is based on the number of employees and other company indices. Imports pay a tax known as the *octroi de mer*, charged at varying rates according to the category of goods. French national and regional banks operate in the department, under French regulation.

BUSINESS OPPORTUNITIES

There are no restrictions on transfers of profits, interest, and royalties, and imports from European Union member countries enter free of duty. Licensing arrangements and opportunities for joint ventures exist. There is a tendering system for government contracts.

Export opportunities to Martinique include agricultural and construction machinery and equipment, together with consumer goods. Possible areas of investment include the hotel and restaurant sector, agricultural processing and other industrial development, and construction.

For More Information

Book:

British Trade International. *Hints to Exporters Visiting the Eastern Caribbean.*
Quid. Paris: Editions Robert Laffont, n.d.

Web Sites:

British Trade International:
www.brittrade.com
Departmental Chamber of Commerce and Industry: **www.martinique.cci.fr**
General information:
www.martinique.org
Ministry of the DOM-TOM: **www.outre-mer.gouv.fr**

MAURITIUS

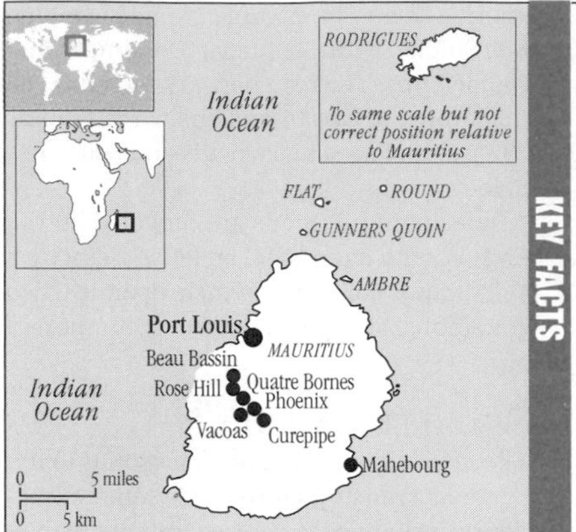

KEY FACTS

GNI: **$4,157 million; world's 117th**
GNI pc: **$3,540; world's 81st**
Head of government: **prime minister**
Currency: **Mauritius rupee (MRs)**
Capital: **Port Louis**
Population: **1,150,000, growing at 0.9% p.a.**
Land area: **713 square miles**
Population density: **1,613 per square mile**
Life expectancy: **72 years**
Infant mortality: **19 per 1,000 live births**
Language: **Creole, French, English**
Best buy: **clothing, textiles, jewelry, spices**

ECONOMY

The economy of this small island state is based on sugar, tourism, garment manufacture, and financial services. The main contributors to GDP are services (61%), industry (29%), and agriculture (10%). The main goods exported are clothing and sugar, and the leading export market is the United Kingdom, followed by France, the United Sates, Germany, and Italy. The country has a strong democratic tradition and there have been regular changes of government over the years. A coalition led by veteran politicians Sir Anerood Jugnauth and Paul Berenger took power in September 2000.

Mauritius has long followed pragmatic economic policies designed to exploit the country's special attributes. The growth of the export processing zone (EPZ), in which companies manufacturing for export do not pay import duties for their essential inputs, has been a major success. There has also been progress in establishing financial services. The coalition government is working towards improving the economy's international competitiveness and attracting new foreign investment, especially in information and communications technology. It aims to curb the budget deficit while reducing corporate tax rates and import duties for non-EPZ businesses.

Economic growth averaged about 5% a year in the mid-1990s, but fell back to only 2.6% in 1999 and 3.6% in 2000 after drought badly affected the sugar crop. Growth is expected to recover more strongly in the coming years. Inflation averaged little more than 4% in 2001.

GEOGRAPHY/RESOURCES

A small Indian Ocean island with extinct volcanoes and rolling plains surrounded by coral reefs, Mauritius was intensively settled and developed in the 19th century both as a maritime staging post and as a center of sugar production, bringing most of its labor force from South Asia. Sugar is grown over nearly all the available arable land, leaving little space for food and other crops. There is also concern to conserve the environment so that tourism can continue to thrive. The seas within the exclusive economic zone are exceptionally rich in fish.

The population of 1.3 million is drawn predominantly from Hindu South Asian origins, but also from the Far East, Africa, and Europe. The Creole population makes up about 27%. The population is concentrated in Port Louis and towns on the central plateau. There is very low unemployment.

COMMUNICATIONS/ENERGY

The road network of 1,168 miles is of good quality and is well maintained. Port Louis is the commercial port, and has been substantially developed. The international airport is served by 15 international airlines including Air Mauritius, which is still government-owned although scheduled for privatization. Mauritius Telecom has invested successfully in developing telecommunications on the island, and was part-privatized in 2000, with France Telecom taking a 40% stake. Mauritius imports nearly all its energy requirements, but there is a hydroelectric power station, and there has been investment in using bagasse—crushed sugar cane residue—as a fuel for electricity generation.

FISCAL/FINANCIAL

Mauritius has a stable and relatively efficient tax regime, with especially low rates available to new investors. There are plans to establish a Board of Investment that would simplify investment facilitation procedures. The largest sources of foreign investment are Hong Kong, France, the United Kingdom, Germany, Taiwan, and China.

Mauritius has a network of local and foreign banks. Of the 12 major banks, 8 are foreign-owned. The three largest institutions are the State Commercial Bank, Barclays, and Mauritius Commercial Bank. Offshore banking was launched in 1989, and the main offshore operators are major banks from Japan, France, the United Kingdom, and India. The offshore center handles a considerable amount of investment into India. A stock exchange commenced operations in 1989.

BUSINESS OPPORTUNITIES

The principal investment opportunities lie in the existing strengths of the economy, especially the EPZ industries, tourism, and sugar. EPZ activity is dominated by the textiles and clothing industry, with Hong Kong as the leading source of investment. There has been steady expansion of tourism, and there are now 92 hotels offering 8,255 rooms. The construction industry also has strong potential because of the need to improve and develop the island's infrastructure, especially in and around Port Louis.

For More Information

Book:
Singh, Sarina, and Joe Bindloss. *Mauritius, Reunion & Seychelles.* 4th ed. Oakland, CA: Lonely Planet, 2001.

Web Sites:
African news and information:
www.allafrica.com/business
Indian Ocean Rim Network:
www.iornet.org/newiornet/mauritius.htm

MEXICO

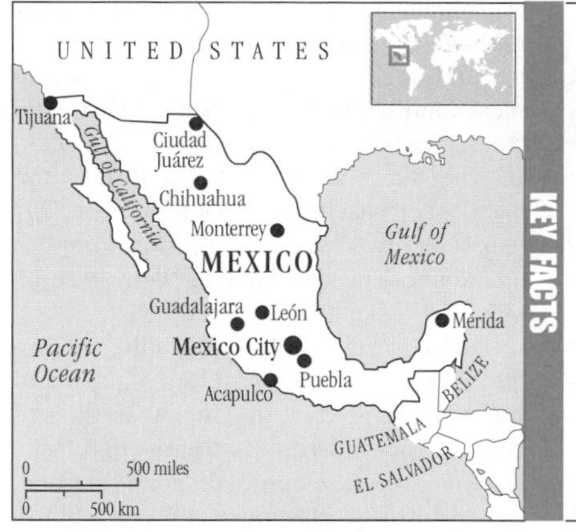

KEY FACTS

GNI: **$428,877 million; world's 12th**
GNI pc: **$4,440; world's 72nd**
Head of government: **president**
Currency: **Mexican peso (Ps)**
Capital: **Mexico City**
Population: **97,365,000, growing at 1.7% p.a.**
Land area: **736,949 square miles**
Population density: **132 per square mile**
Life expectancy: **73 years**
Infant mortality: **27 per 1,000 live births**
Language: **Spanish and indigenous languages (Náhuatl, Maya, Zapoteco)**
Best buy: **gold and silver jewelry, onyx, ceramics, handicrafts**

ECONOMIC STRUCTURE

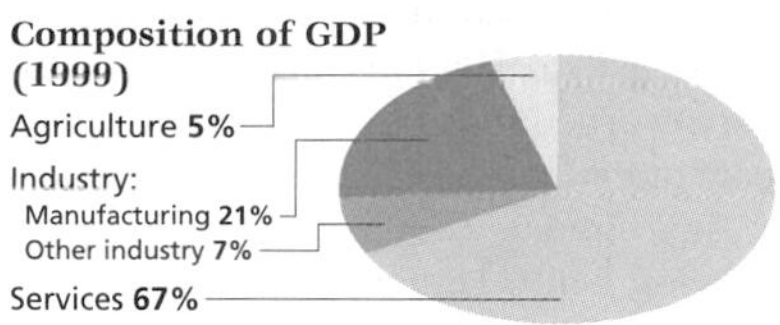

The 1910 revolution overthrew the dictatorship of General Porfirio Díaz, who had seized power in 1876. It was followed by a long period of strife and disorder until the creation in 1929 of the Institutional Revolutionary Party (PRI) which united the warring factions and removed the military from politics. The PRI, the world's longest-ruling political party, kept control through regular and generally rigged elections, by not allowing presidents to stand for more than one six-year term and by buying the loyalty of different social groups. It became known as the "perfect dictatorship" until it was defeated by the center-right National Action Party (PAN) of Vicente Fox in the historic July 2000 presidential election. The PRI, however, remains the largest party in Congress.

In 1994 Mexico, the largest Latin American economy and the ninth in the world, became the first developing country to join the Organisation for Economic Co-operation and Development (OECD), and that year it also formed part of the North American Free Trade Agreement (NAFTA) with the United States and Canada. The very same day that NAFTA came into force, the pipe-smoking, Balaclava-wearing self-styled Insurgent Subcommander Marcos led an uprising by Indian Zapatista rebels in the impoverished, indigenous southern state of Chiapas. Nothing better epitomized the modern and ancient worlds that Mexico straddles. More than 40 million Mexicans are poverty-stricken.

NAFTA has increasingly tied the Mexican and U.S. economies together. The United States takes more than 85% of Mexico's exports and an estimated 300,000 illegal Mexican immigrants a year. NAFTA has helped Mexico to diversify its economy away from its previous excessive dependence on oil (the country is the largest non-OPEC producer, and has the world's tenth-largest proven reserves) to a more manufacturing-based economy. Services generate two-thirds of GDP, industry close to 30%, and agriculture the rest. Manufacturing comprises base metals, construction materials, paper and paper products, textiles and apparel, food processing, cars, electro-domestic appliances, and machinery. The principal exports are oil and oil products, cars, and a range of agricultural and manufactured goods. One of the drivers of the manufacturing-based economy are *maquiladoras*, the assembly plants concentrated on the border with the United States that make goods from imported materials for re-export. There is a free-trade deal similar in coverage to NAFTA with the European Union.

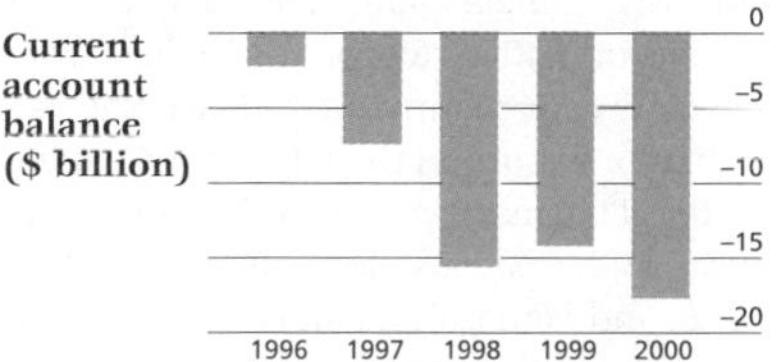

The state, traditionally heavily involved in the economy, has gradually loosened its control since the re-privatization of the banks and the privatization of Telmex, the telephone company, in the 1990s. Pemex, the hugely overstaffed state oil company, and the Federal Electricity Commission (CFE), remain off limits for political reasons.

ECONOMIC POLICY

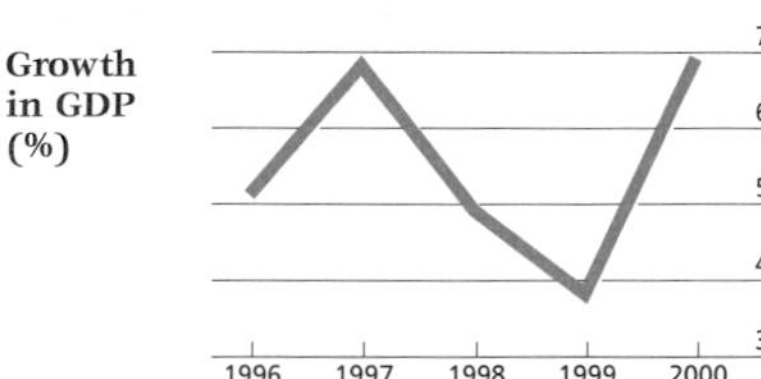

Mexico triggered the external debt crisis in developing countries when it defaulted on its own massive debt in 1982, shaking the world financial system and plunging the country into its worst ever economic crisis. Two decades later, orthodox economic policies and stabilization programs had achieved a degree of macro-economic stability not seen since the 1960s, as well as more manageable external debt ratios. The external public-sector debt in 2001 was estimated at $156 billion (25.6% of GDP and 93% of exports, down from 37.2% and 135% respectively in 1997).

Real GDP growth averaged 4.8% in 1989–99, and in 2000 it was 6.9%. The economy entered recession in 2001 when it felt the pinch from the U.S. recession, just as it had previously benefited from America's 10-year boom. Inflation was around 6.0% in 2001 and the fiscal deficit 0.9% of GDP.

The central pillar of President Fox's 2000–06 economic agenda, and the key issue for enhancing Mexico's capacity to meet its growing social needs, is a sweeping tax reform, but the government's proposals were watered down under pressure from opposition parties who control the Congress. At 11% in 2000, Mexico's tax revenue as a proportion of GDP is behind even India's. Tax evasion is widespread. Higher tax revenues would reduce the state's heavy dependence on oil earnings.

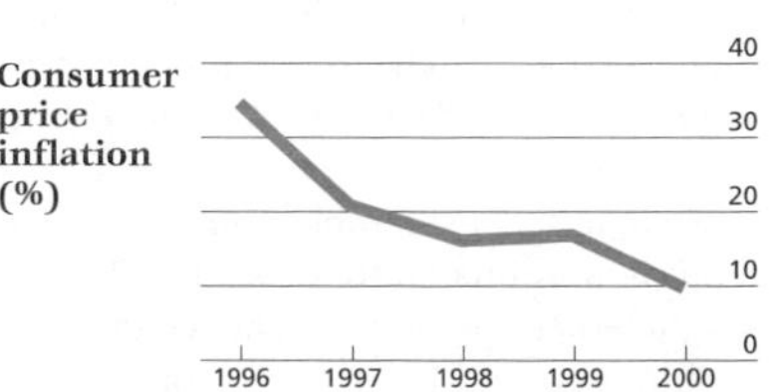

The official unemployment rate is less than 3.5%, but this masks the millions of people who are underemployed or who work in the underground economy.

Geography/Resources

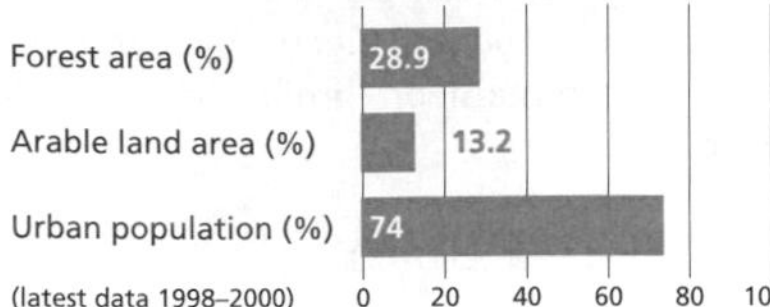

Mexico borders the U.S. states of California, Arizona, New Mexico, and Texas to the north, and Guatemala and Belize to the south. The Rio Grande river forms a large part of the northern border. On the west is the Pacific Ocean, and on the east the Gulf of Mexico and the Caribbean. Most of Mexico consists of a broad central plateau, which is highest in the south and rises to 2,990–8,010 feet above sea level. The highest mountain, Citlaltepetl, near the east coast, is a snow-capped cone 18,700 feet high. It, and most of the other great peaks such as Popocatepetl and Ixtacihuatl, were once volcanoes. Volcanic activity still occurs. As in most volcanic countries, earthquakes are quite common in Mexico, especially near the Pacific coast. The last big one was in 1985 which left thousands dead, injured, and homeless in Mexico City. Between 1993 and 2000 the annual forest loss to logging, fires, and the expansion of farms was 6.75 million acres, the second-highest rate of deforestation in the world after Brazil, according to Mexico's Environment Ministry.

The tropical southern region and coastlands are hot and wet, while the highlands of the central plateau are temperate. Temperature in Mexico City ranges from 41–77°F, with occasional sharp frosts in winter (December–February).

Agriculture contributes around 5% of GDP but it employs close to one-quarter of the workforce. Farming is small-scale. About half of total cultivatable land (47 million acres) is held by *ejidos*, rural communities farming on small individual/collective lots. The only large commercial farms are in the export-oriented regions of the northwest and some coffee estates in the south. Main crops are corn, sorghum, wheat, rice, barley, potatoes, soybeans, and dry beans. The principal export crops are coffee, cotton, fresh fruit, tobacco, and tomatoes.

Mexico has considerable mining potential, but it is estimated that less than 15% of areas have been explored. The sector only contributes around 1% of GDP. The country is the world's largest producer of silver, and there are big deposits of uranium and gold. Other minerals include celestine and sodium sulfate, mercury, antimony, cadmium, zinc, lead, copper, manganese, graphite, feldspar, and barite.

Over half (55%) of the population of around 100 million are mestizo, 29% native American, and 16% white. More than four million Mexicans work legally or illegally in the United States, and their cash remittances are the second-largest source of foreign exchange after oil sales. Remittances topped $9 billion in 2001, up from $6.3 billion in 2000. One-fifth of the population live in Mexico City, including the megalopolis. Other large cities are Guadalajara (2.9 million) and Monterrey (2.5 million). The population growth rate is more than 1%, down from an annual average of 1.7% in 1993–99, but still adding more than 1 million people to the country every year. Mexico needs to create 1.2 million jobs a year just to keep up with the growth in the population. Migration to the United States is a crucial safety valve for labor market pressures.

Communications/Energy

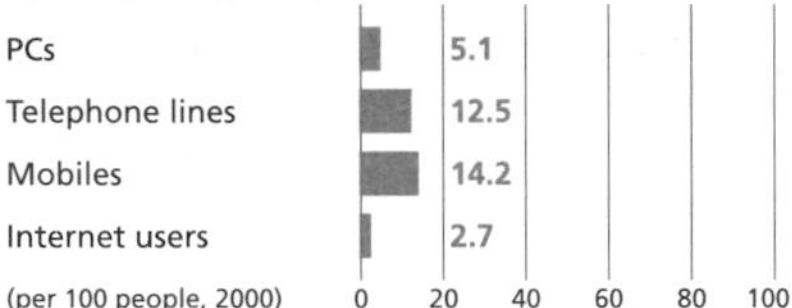

The road network was 204,771 miles in 1999, including 67,164 miles of paved roads. There were 29,948 miles of motorways, 3,995 miles of which were toll roads. The rail network remained unchanged between 1996 and 1999 at 16,543 miles. It is in need of a massive overhaul and modernization. The government's efforts have gone into the building of roads, particularly encouraging the private sector to build toll roads. The country is well served by airports. There are 61 of them, 47 of which are international. Each of the 31 states and the Federal District (Mexico City) has at least one airport. The main international airports are Mexico City, Monterrey, Guadalajara, and Acapulco. A new airport at Texcoco, 19 miles from Mexico City, is planned to replace the Benito Juarez airport on the edge of the capital in 2005. The main ports are Veracruz, Altamira, and Coatzacoalcos in the Gulf of Mexico, and Manazanillo and Salina Cruz on the Pacific.

The telecommunications sector, following the privatization of Telmex and the loss of its monopoly, grew four times faster than the economy between 1990 and 1999. Many new service concessions have been granted for local and long-distance wired and wireless services. The number of mobile lines (13 million) overtook fixed phone lines (12.3 million) in 2000. Teledensity is still very low, although the number of fixed lines almost doubled between 1990 and 2000 to 12.5 per 100 inhabitants. There were 1.5 million Internet subscribers in 2000, and the number was forecast to reach 6.4 million in 2004 (8.6% of the population), according to eMarketer. The backbone network was almost 100% digitalized in 2000.

Mexico is the world's fifth leading oil producer. Oil and gas account for some 90% of primary energy requirements, with the rest coming from hydroelectricity and geothermal power. Energy demand, particularly electricity growing at 6% per annum, was rising faster than total GDP in 2000, making necessary large investments in the future. Daily consumption of gas was forecast to double to 9 billion cubic feet by 2010. Experts warned that Mexico would have to import more than half its gas by 2007 if foreign investment could not be attracted to develop fields. Pemex does not have the funds. Under a preliminary agreement signed in December 2001, up to 800 million cubic feet of liquefied natural gas per day will be shipped from Bolivia to Baja California by 2005.

Education/Employment

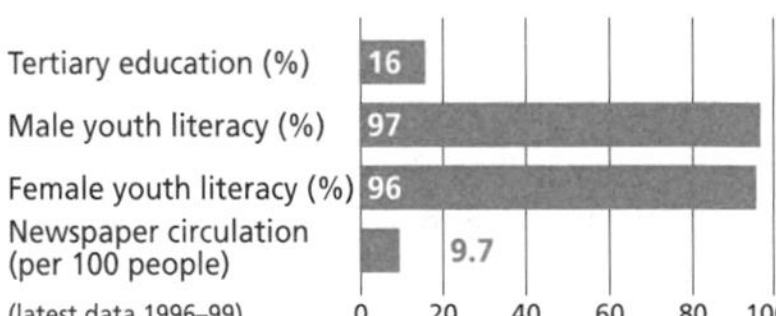

Education is in compulsory and free from age 6 to 14. There are more than 100 universities and technological institutes, with student enrollment in higher education of over 1.8 million. The main universities are in Mexico City, Guadalajara, and Monterrey. The poorly-funded state universities are in crisis: the National Autonomous University of Mexico (UNAM), the biggest in the Americas (270,000 students), was shut for most of 1999 because it was occupied by students protesting at an increase in the annual tuition fee of 20 centavos (two U.S. cents).

The National Council of Science and Technology (CONACYT) coordinates basic and applied R&D. Spending on R&D is low at around 0.3% of GDP. The International Institute for Management Development, a Swiss business school, listed—in its 2001 *World Competitiveness Yearbook*—the weakest

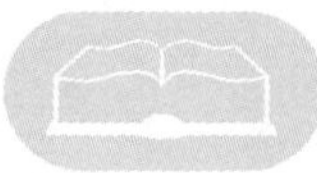

Growth in labor force (% p.a., 1980–99)

Women as % of labor force (1999)

HIV positive (% of age group 15–49, 1999)

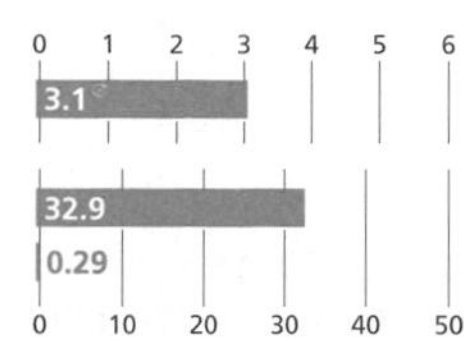

criteria in Mexico's infrastructure as being lack of development, poor application of technology, and insufficient technological cooperation between companies.

There is a plentiful supply of unskilled and highly educated labor, with the top jobs increasingly filled by Mexicans who have graduated from U.S. universities. The legal minimum daily wage is very low (around $4). The wage and employment conditions set by the government for the public sector are the benchmark for the private sector. Unionized labor is strong in certain state sectors, particularly the oil and electricity industries and education. The government estimates there are more than 9 million people working in the informal economy (close to one-quarter of the active population).

Fiscal/Financial

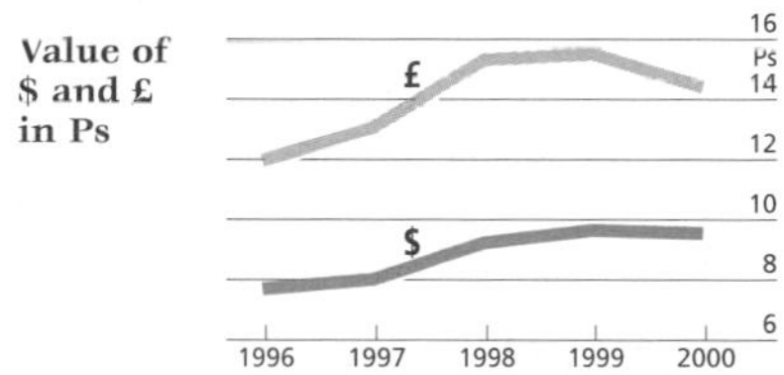

The banking system was re-privatized in 1990 after being nationalized in 1982. The three largest private-sector commercial banks—Banamex, Bancomer and Serfin—are U.S.- or Spanish-owned. Citigroup paid $12.5 billion for Banamex, the largest bank, in 2001. Close to 80% of the total assets of the banking system are estimated to be under foreign ownership. The banking crisis of 1995, caused by the turmoil of peso devaluation and lax lending regulations, led to a government bail-out that cost more than $70 billion. Banking laws and supervision have been since tightened. Moody's, the rating agency, raised Mexico to investment grade status in 2000 for the first time in its history. The state owns specialized banks for agriculture, exports, and public works.

Corporate tax and the top rate of personal income tax are both 35%. VAT is 15%. The Mexico City stock exchange, the best performer in Latin America in 2001, lists 200 of the country's largest companies. A municipal and state bond market was launched at the end of 2001.

Business Opportunities

Growth in output (% p.a., 1990–99)

Services	2.5
Industry	3.5
Manufacturing	4.0
Agriculture	1.6

Mexico received an annual average of $12.6 billion of foreign direct investment (FDI) in 1997–2000, up from $5.3 billion in 1985–95. In 2001 it was expected to top $18 billion. FDI is particularly strong in the automotive, banking, pharmaceuticals, electronics, and tourism industries. One of the main attractions for foreign companies is to take advantage of Mexico's NAFTA membership and use the country as a springboard for exporting to the United States. The government is eager to lure foreign investment to develop new capacity in the electricity sector and develop natural gas reserves. Government proposals to give energy companies total control over gas-drilling projects for up to 20 years, the most extensive access since the country expelled foreign oil companies in 1938, threatened to unleash a constitutional battle between the government and opposition parties.

For More Information

Books:

Castaneda, Jorge G. *The Mexican Shock*. New York: New Press, 1996.

Krauze, Enrique. *Biography of Power*. New York: HarperCollins, 1997.

Oppenheimer, Andres. *Bordering on Chaos*. New York: Little, Brown, 1996.

Riding, Alan. *Distant Neighbours*. New York: Vintage Books, 2000.

OECD Economic Surveys. *Mexico*. Paris: OECD.

Financial Times Country Surveys. *Mexico*. London: Financial Times.

Web Sites:

Bank of Mexico (central bank): **www.banxico.org.mx**

IMF reports: **www.imf.org/external**

Inegi (national statistics institute): **www.inegi.gob.mx**

Mexico City Stock Exchange: **www.bmv.com.mx**

Ministry of Finance: **www.shcp.gob.mx**

The News (English language newspaper): **www.thenewsmexico.com**

U.S. State Department Country Commercial Guide: **www. state.gov/e/eb/rls/rpts/ccg**

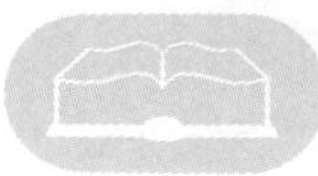

MONACO

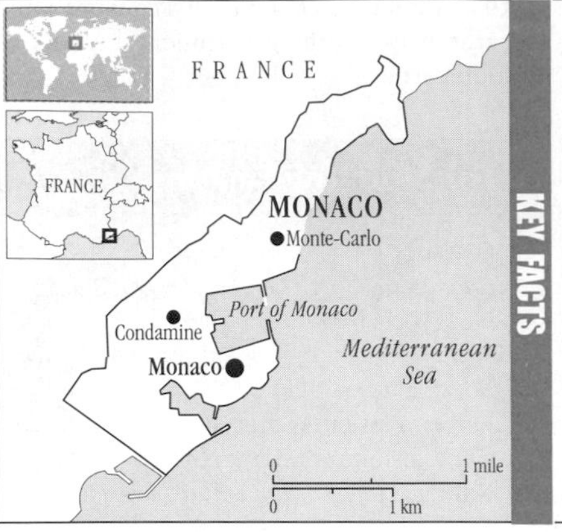

GNI pc: **$25,000 (approx.); world's 15th**
Head of government: **minister of state**
Currency: **Euro (€)**
Capital: **Monaco**
Population: **33,000, growing at 1.1% p.a.**
Land area: **¾ square mile**
Population density: **44,000 per square mile**
Infant mortality: **5 per 1,000 live births**
Language: **French**
Best buy: **crystal, silverware, perfumes, porcelain, Formula 1 Grand Prix memorabilia**

ECONOMY

Tourism and trade accounted for 40% of national turnover (national finances are established on the basis of total business turnover rather than GDP) in 2000, while banking and finance contributed 18%, manufacturing 10%, and shipping 4%. Chemicals, pharmaceuticals, and cosmetics form the largest manufacturing sector, accounting for 49% of industrial turnover in 2000, followed by plastic components for motor vehicles (22%), electrical and electronic goods (10%), printing (6%), mechanical and precision goods (5%), and textiles and clothing (3%). France and Italy are the main export markets in these goods and for the import-export trade in consumer goods. E-commerce, multimedia services and telephone call centers are new activities since the acquisition of a 51% stake in Monaco Telecom by French group Vivendi in June 2000. Vivendi, which also owns the Monagasque broadcasting company Somera, will use Monaco as a test ground for new Internet and multimedia services destined for the French and other European markets.

Monaco is the only non-EU country to have the Euro as its currency. This results from its monetary union with France. VAT rates, an important part of government receipts, mirror those of France, and are being reduced to converge with other Euro countries. There is no formal Monagasque public debt, and the state had estimated reserves of €1.5 billion in 2000. The VAT shortfall may be replaced by receipts from new business as the government pursues ambitious public works programs to extend the territory and provide new business facilities. The latest projects include the Grimaldi Forum conference center and the Condamine port floating jetty extension, both of which will enhance tourism and trade. The government also promotes the finance center, which now benefits from fast Internet links. Economic growth dwindled in the mid-1990s in tandem with that of France, but is estimated to have revived more strongly than that of its neighbor since 1997.

GEOGRAPHY/RESOURCES

Monaco is surrounded by southeastern France. The country is a thin 2½-mile strip along the Mediterranean Sea coast. The land rises steeply from the coast. There is no agricultural land and no mineral resources, but there is a fish farm for sea bream.

COMMUNICATIONS/ENERGY

There are 31 miles of roads and 1 mile of railway. The main railway line from France to Italy runs through Monaco and is operated by French railways, SNCF. Scheduled helicopter services operate from the Principality's heliport at Fontvieille to Nice International Airport. There were 33,000 fixed phone lines in 2000 and 12,000 mobile phones. Energy sources are imported.

FISCAL/FINANCIAL

There is no personal income tax. Corporation tax is 33.33% if at least 25% of a company's turnover is derived from foreign operations. There is exemption from this tax for the first two years of operation in Monaco, and reduced rates for the next three years. Standard VAT is 19.6%, with a reduced rate at 5.5%. Monaco is under pressure from the EU and OECD to introduce tax on investment income and to provide more information on residents' and non-residents' bank accounts to the tax authorities of other countries.

Banking activity, with around 85% of customers from outside Monaco, has increased at around 18% a year since the creation of a special anti-money-laundering unit in 1994 following a money-laundering scandal. The money-launderer received a 12-year jail sentence. Other regulation of banks is conducted by the French Banking Commission, and central bank functions by the Bank of France. Total assets under management by 45 banks were €56.2 billion at end-2000, while equity and bonds totaled €37.6 billion and deposits €18.6 billion. Private banking is the main sector benefiting from the 1997 portfolio management law. Other activities include real estate, corporate banking, and shipping. A new law on investment funds will promote fund management. There is no local stock market.

BUSINESS OPPORTUNITIES

Sectors which have attracted foreign investment include broadcasting, telecommunications, finance, insurance, and fish farming, and manufacturing of perfumes, porcelain, chemicals, food, textiles and precision instruments. Low effective corporation tax and modern facilities are incentives. The point of contact for investors is the Direction de l'Expansion Économique. New opportunities arise in e-commerce, multimedia, tourism, and finance.

For More Information

Book:

Campbell, Siri. *Inside Monaco*. New York: Post Oak Press, 2000.

Web Site:

Government entry point:
www.monaco.gouv.mc

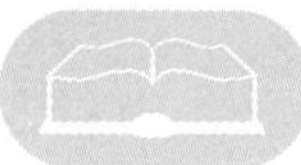

Morocco

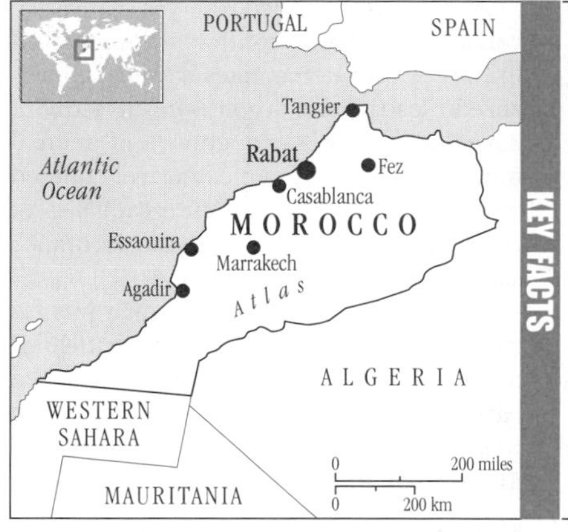

KEY FACTS

GNI: **$33,715 million; world's 55th**
GNI pc: **$1,190; world's 129th**
Head of government: **monarch**
Currency: **Moroccan dirham (Dh)**
Capital: **Rabat**
Population: **27,867,000, growing at 1.7% p.a.**
Land area: **172,316 square miles**
Population density: **161 per square mile**
Life expectancy: **67 years**
Infant mortality: **45 per 1,000 live births**
Language: **Arabic (official), Berber, French, Spanish**
Best buy: **pottery, textiles, leather goods, jewelry**

Economic Structure

The Berbers of Morocco have been ruled by Arab kings for several centuries. In 1912 France established a protectorate over most of the country, and the Spanish established a protectorate in Western Sahara. Morocco regained its independence in 1956, but factions in Western Sahara fought against Moroccan rule. The United Nations' attempts to register voters for a referendum to settle the dispute are proving torturous. The 1996 Free Trade Agreement with the European Union and membership of the World Trade Organization have accelerated legal and economic reforms. King Mohammed VI has also instigated judicial and social reforms since succeeding to the throne in 1999.

Services contributed 54.3% of GDP in 2000, followed by manufacturing (17.6%), agriculture (13.5%), energy and water (7.5%), construction (5.1%), and mining (2%). Tourism is the main services sector. The main manufacturing industries are phosphate fertilizers, petroleum refining, food processing, and textiles. Morocco is the leading world producer of phosphate rock and the third-largest exporter. It is the leading world exporter of phosphoric acid. The top export in 2000 was textiles, followed by shellfish, phosphoric acid, phosphate rock, fertilizers and canned fish. The main market was France, followed by Spain, the United Kingdom, Italy, Germany, India, and Japan. Workers' remittances were $2.1 billion in 2000.

Key sectors, especially phosphate mining, telecommunications, air and rail transport, and utilities are under state control. In 1997 public enterprises accounted for 13% of GDP and 22% of total investment. By early 2001 about half of the companies intended for privatization in the 1993 program had come to the market. Sectors included finance, oil refining, cement, steel, mining (cobalt, fluorine, copper, and silver), chemicals, textiles, hotels, road haulage, and telecommunications. Agreements were signed for the private-sector operation of electricity power plants. State holdings in transport, hotels, sugar refineries, banks, a fertilizer company, and telecommunications are due to be divested.

Economic Policy

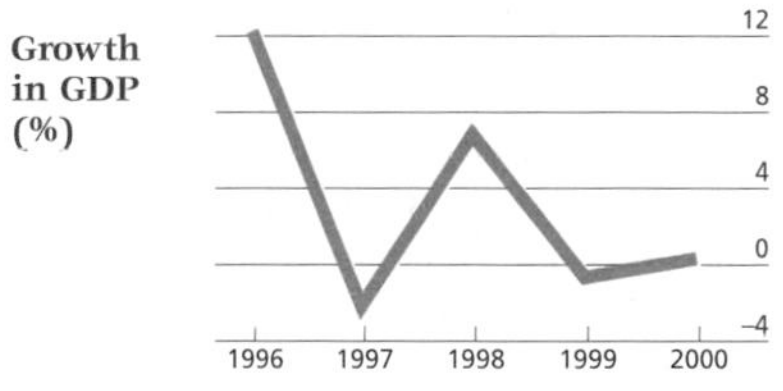

In the last decade prudent monetary policy has focused on foreign debt reduction, replacing this with domestic debt. The foreign debt fell from 75% of GDP in 1991 to 50% by 2000, while the overall central government debt rose from 75.6% of GDP in 1996 to 77.8% in 2000. The budget deficit has been maintained at less than 3% of GDP. Civil service salaries absorb nearly half the state budget, and the government has limited recruitment to the public sector. Foreign investment laws are being strengthened to provide the basis for future productive investment to help overcome high unemployment and dependence on agriculture. The liberalization of the finance system has proved slow, and the small business sector (an important vehicle for job creation) is still bereft of funding. A low level of public spending on education is being addressed. Poverty reduction programs for the rural communities are backed by the World Bank and other international agencies.

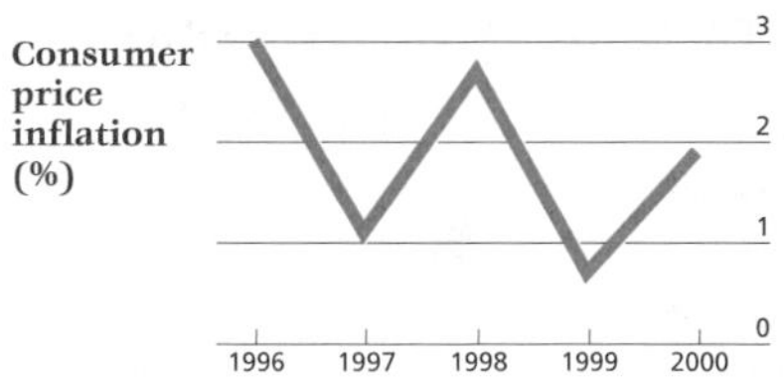

Annual GDP growth averaged 3.3% in 1999–2000. Better rainfall in 2001 led to increased farm output and 6.5% GDP growth. Inflation rose to 2.5% from an average 1.9% in 1996–2000. Urban unemployment rose to 23% from an annual average of 19.1% in 1996–2000.

Geography/Resources

In north west Africa, Morocco borders the Mediterranean Sea, the Strait of Gibraltar, and the Spanish enclaves of Ceuta and Melilla in the north, the Atlantic Ocean to the west, the disputed area of Western Sahara (formerly Spanish Sahara, annexed by Morocco in 1979) and then Mauritania to the south, and Algeria to the east. There are four geographic regions: the Rif Mountains in the north, the Atlas Mountains (with highest point of 13,665 feet), the coastal plains, and the Sahara desert in the southeast.

Agriculture employs about 40% of the workforce, and Morocco is a net exporter of fruit and vegetables. Most crops are rain-fed, but have suffered from drought in recent years. Wheat, barley, sugar beet, potatoes, tomatoes, and citrus fruits are the main crops, but a wide range of cereals, legumes, vegetables, and fruit are grown. Poultry are the main livestock, followed by sheep, goats, and cattle. Forestry (especially cork wood) and fishing (especially pilchards and sardines) are important. The sale of fishing licenses to foreign fleets earns foreign exchange.

Morocco has about 75% of known world reserves of phosphates. In addition barytes, manganese, lead, fluorine, silver, iron ore, copper, zinc, gold, cobalt, marble, salt, and clay are mined. There are reserves of antimony, tin, titanium, and wolfram. At end-2000 there were proven petroleum reserves of 1.2 million barrels and proven gas reserves of 100 trillion cubic feet. An oil discovery in 2000 indicated additional reserves of 10 million barrels. Gas reserves in the Essaouira

Basin could be extensive. Exploration continues.

Over 70% of the population is under the age of 30. The majority is Berber (40%) or of Berber origin (35%), followed by Arabs, and smaller communities of black African and European descent.

Communications/Energy

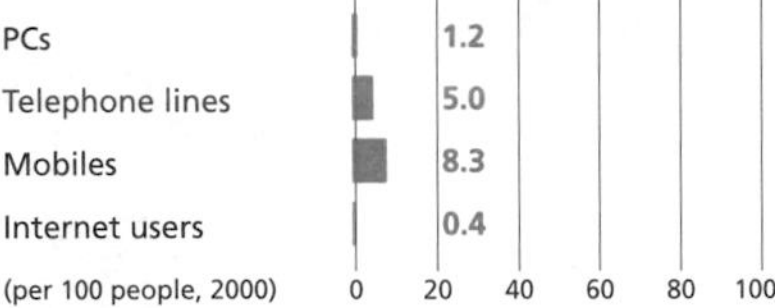

The road network comprises 3,678 miles of paved roads. The 1,185-mile rail network carried 13.1 million passengers and 27.1 million tons of freight in 2000. There are 225 miles of crude oil pipelines and 150 miles for natural gas (the Maghreb-Europe Gas pipeline from Algeria to Spain). The 24 sea ports, the largest of which is Casablanca, handled 52.9 million tons of cargo in 1999, but only 23.4 million tons in 2000. The merchant fleet comprised 496 ships in 1998, with a total displacement of 444,000 grt. There are 11 international and 16 domestic commercial airports. In 2000 the main airports handled 7 million passengers and 53,447 tons of freight.

Telecommunications links are provided via cable, microwave radio relay, and satellite. Switching is fully digital. Maroc Telecom, the main operator, was 35% privatized in early 2001. The sector is due to be fully liberalized by 2003. There were 1.4 million fixed phone lines, 2.3 million mobile phones, and 100,000 Internet users at end-2000.

Electricity is produced from fossil fuels (77% in 2000), hydroelectric (5%), and wind (0.5%). There is a small indigenous production of crude petroleum (13 million tons in 2000), natural gas (1,766 million cubic feet) and coal (28,700 tons). Only natural gas output is sufficient to meet demand. Oil production will increase when the Talsinnt field comes onstream in 2003. Most oil is imported from Saudi Arabia, Iran, Iraq, and Nigeria. Two oil refineries produce fuels for the domestic market and are being expanded. Most coal for power generation is imported from South Africa. Electricity demand is growing at 7% a year. The government has an ambitious program for rural electrification, and is considering a link with the Spanish grid.

Education/Employment

Education is compulsory from age 7 to 13, but half of the population is illiterate. Current reforms aim at the universalization of primary education by 2003. There are 13 universities, with an enrollment of 250,000 students, and 27 other higher education institutes. The Vocational Training Agency administers 166 institutions, including 59 institutes of applied technology, 86 centers of professional qualification, and 24 training centers. Student enrollment in vocational training was 132,000 in 2000–01, including 56,000 in the private sector. Most education is provided and funded by the government and is the responsibility of the Ministry of Higher Education, Professional Training and Scientific Research. R&D strengths include chemicals, agriculture, water engineering, mechanical and electrical engineering, and IT.

The labor force has a range of skills. The Social Dialog between government, employers, and trade unions agrees guidelines for employment conditions and sets the national minimum wage. Individual agreements are negotiated between employers and employees, or in larger companies between trade unions and employers. In unionized sectors workers are usually paid between 13 and 16 months' salary a year.

Fiscal/Financial

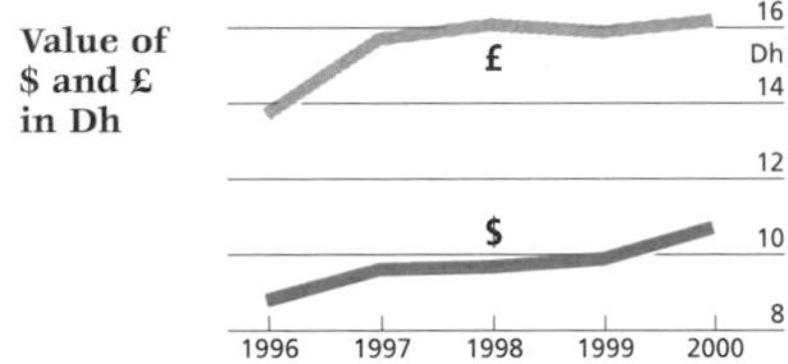

The largest banks by assets are Crédit Populaire du Maroc (51% state-owned), followed by Banque Marocaine du Commerce Extérieure, Banque Commerciale du Maroc, and Wafabank (all private-sector). Two of the largest insurance companies are Royale Marocaine d'Assurances and Al-Amane. The central bank is Bank Al-Maghrib, which regulates the finance sector. Its current policy is to issue no new banking licenses. An independent commission oversees the stock market. The basic rate of corporation tax is 35%, and the top rate of personal income tax is 44%. VAT applies at 20%, 14%, and 7%. The government intends to reduce the tax burden on corporations and individuals, and to simplify company tax incentives to reduce tax avoidance.

There are 15 commercial banks, including three specialized development funds with commercial bank status. The three largest commercial banks accounted for almost two-thirds of banking assets and deposits, and 55% of lending in 2000. The large banks offer electronic banking to large corporate clients. A 1992 law established offshore banking in Tangier. The 1993 banking law reduced domestic bank reserve requirements from 25% to 10% but obliged them to invest the freed reserves in treasury bonds. Direct credit controls were removed in 1991. Most interest rates have been liberalized. Restrictions on outward investment have led to the rapid growth of mutual funds, but these are not extensively offered on the stock market. Venture capital is of increasing importance, and the insurance sector offers room for growth.

The Casablanca Stock Exchange was established in 1929 and privatized in 1996. It has had a cooperation agreement with the Paris Bourse since 1996. Electronic trading was introduced in 1997. Capitalization was $13.5 billion in 1999.

Business Opportunities

The 1995 Investment Code applies to national and foreign investors, but foreign exchange provisions are more favorable to foreign investors. Foreign investment is not allowed in agricultural land, phosphate mining, and tobacco production. The government is considering adding insurance to the list. There is an export free zone at Tangier Free Zone, and financial and tax incentives are available for projects elsewhere in Morocco. France is the leading investor ($981 million in 1996–2000), followed by Portugal, Netherlands, the United States, and Spain. Telecommunications attracted foreign direct and portfolio investment of $1.8 billion in 1996–2000, followed by manufacturing and banking. Telecommunications, water resources management, manufacturing and environmental protection industries, and privatizations offer investment opportunities. The Department for Foreign Investments is the point of contact.

For More Information

Book:

Bourqia, Rahma, and Susan Miller Tilson, eds. *In the Shadow of the Sultan: Culture, Power and Politics in Morocco.* Cambridge, MA: Harvard University Press, 1999.

Web Sites:

Direction de Statistique:
www.statistic.gov.ma
Government entry point:
www.mincom.gov.ma
Ministry of Economy, Finance, Privatization and Tourism:
www.mfie.gov.ma

Mozambique

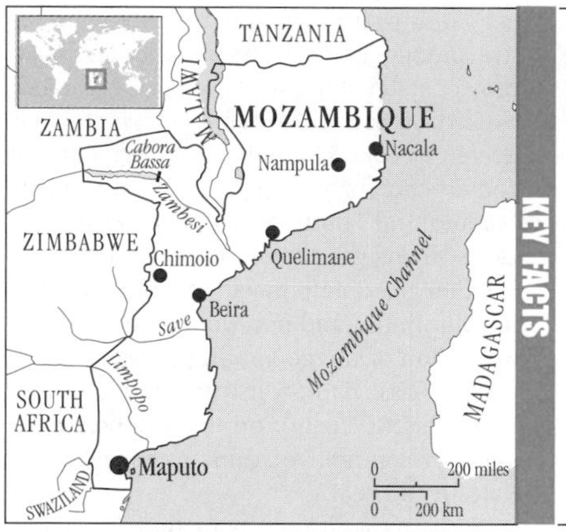

KEY FACTS

GNI: **$3,804 million; world's 122nd**
GNI pc: **$220; world's 195th**
Head of government: **president**
Currency: **metical (MT)**
Capital: **Maputo**
Population: **19,286,000, growing at 3.4% p.a.**
Land area: **302,741 square miles**
Population density: **64 per square mile**
Life expectancy: **42 years**
Infant mortality: **127 per 1,000 live births**
Language: **Portuguese, numerous local languages**
Best buy: **Makonde carvings, semi-precious stones, basketwork**

Economic Structure

One of the world's poorest countries, and one whose transition to independence was blighted by regional tensions and a brutal civil war, Mozambique has made significant economic advances since the return of peace and the holding of its first democratic elections in 1994. Mozambique is an important point of transport access for much of Southern Africa, and it has good economic potential as a major producer of agricultural, mineral and industrial goods.

The principal economic activities are agriculture and livestock (contributing 28% of GDP), trade (22%), transport and communications (11%), manufacturing (8.5%) and construction (7.5%). The agricultural sector is a long way from realizing its full potential, having been disrupted by recurring drought and floods as well as by the upheavals of the long civil war. Much of the land in the more developed southern half of the country is of poor quality, while the most fertile areas in the northern half are isolated because of poor transport infrastructure. Many of the population are engaged in subsistence farming of cassava, corn, and bananas. The major cash crops are cotton, cashew nuts, sugar, and copra. The larger plantations for such crops have been privatized and rehabilitated since the early 1990s. Mozambique's leading exports are shrimps and prawns, cotton, cashew nuts, and sugar. Its main customers are Spain, South Africa, India, the United States, and Portugal. The country's principal source of imports is South Africa.

Mozambique has undertaken substantial privatization of its state-owned enterprises since the 1980s, with more than 1,000 such companies now in private ownership. The privatization process has included firms in the industrial and agricultural sectors, the national airline, and the major banks.

Economic Policy

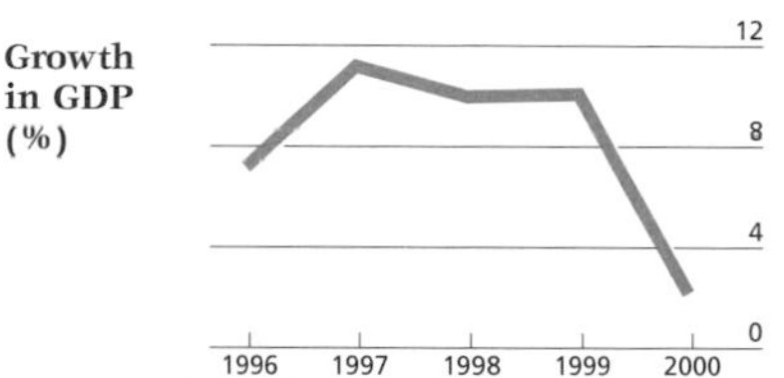

The Mozambican government won praise for its achievement of macro-economic adjustment and stabilization in the 1990s. This helped to achieve average annual growth of 8.5% between 1995 and 1999 as an inflow of foreign investment in manufacturing and transport stimulated a construction and property boom. The emphasis of policy has been to restrain inflation, reform the customs and tax systems, reform the judiciary, strengthen budget administration, and pursue poverty reduction. With the support of international donors, there is increasing spending on health and education. Increased government spending will be facilitated by Mozambique's qualification for debt relief under the Heavily Indebted Poor Countries (HIPC) initiative, which has reduced debt servicing to manageable levels. The government's overall targets are to maintain real GDP growth of 7–10% a year, and to limit inflation to 5–7% a year.

As part of its public enterprise restructuring, the government has encouraged the private sector to engage in the provision of goods and services, including transport, electricity, telecommunications, and agricultural marketing. Meanwhile, foreign investment is continuing to flow into major aluminum, iron, and steel projects, a gas pipeline, electricity, sugar, mining, and tourism.

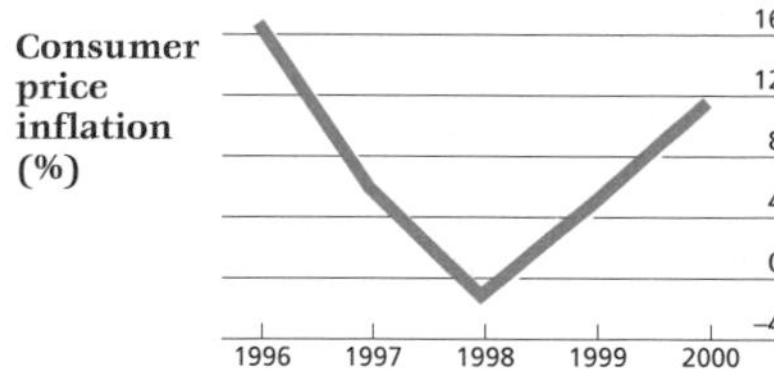

About 80% of the economically active population are employed in agriculture, fishing, and forestry. There is also a buoyant informal trading sector. Large numbers of Mozambicans live and work in South Africa. Nevertheless, there is widespread poverty in Mozambique.

Geography/Resources

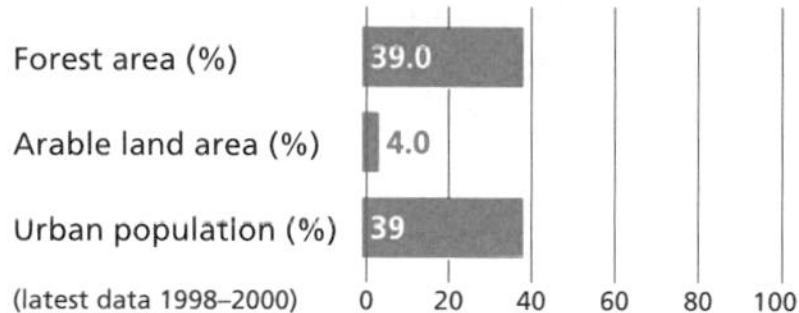

Mozambique is a large country bordering the Indian Ocean and bounded to the south by South Africa and Swaziland, to the west by Zimbabwe, Zambia, and Malawi, and to the north by Tanzania. Its transport infrastructure is of great importance to most of these neighbors. The low-lying coastal region is more extensive in the south than the north of the country, and nearly half of the land lies below 3,300 feet, although there are numerous inland hill and mountain ranges in both north and south. Several major rivers, including the Zambezi and Limpopo, flow through Mozambique to the sea.

The climate is mainly tropical, with a wet season during the southern summer months. There was severe drought in the 1980s and early 1990s, but in 2000 and 2001 the country was afflicted by severe flooding. The most reliable rainfall occurs in the central and northern regions, which support a high population density and produce a surplus of food and cash crops. Although the land is well served by rivers, there has been little use of irrigation, water control measures, or hydroelectric development. There is substantial potential for more dam building. Mineral resources include coal, gas, iron ore, ilmenite, and gold.

The most densely populated provinces

are Zambezia and Nampula, in the northern half of the country, while the largest cities are Maputo and Beira. The largest ethnic groups in the north of the country are the Makua and the Lomwe, and those in the south are the Tonga and the Shona.

Communications/Energy

PCs	0.3
Telephone lines	0.4
Mobiles	0.1
Internet users	0.2
(per 100 people, 2000)	0 20 40 60 80 100

The ports of Maputo, Beira, and Nacala are the focal points of Mozambique's transport system. They are linked with neighboring countries by railway lines, which managed to survive the many years of civil war. The road network serving the domestic economy is more poorly developed, however, and in addition many trunk roads were badly damaged by the floods of 2000. An alternative means of transport is provided by coastal shipping services, which were opened to private participation in 1996. Port management is also being opened up to private companies.

The first stage of the Maputo Corridor linking the Mozambican capital with South Africa's Gauteng province consists of the operation of a toll road by a consortium of private companies. Subsequently, private investors are to be assisted to locate new businesses along the corridor. Similar transport and development corridors are being planned in other locations.

The government planned in 2001 to sell a minority stake in the state telecommunications company TDM, which has had limited success in expanding its network and services to meet demand. Mobile telephone services have been developing strongly.

The largest source of electric power is the Cabora Bassa dam on the Zambezi. It supplies Zimbabwe and the northern towns of Nampula and Quelimane. Following reconstruction of pylons destroyed during the civil war, agreement was reached in 2000 on the resumption of power supplies to South Africa.

In 2000 the state energy company ENH reached agreement with South Africa's Sasol to build a gas pipeline of 227 miles from Pande and Temane gas fields at a cost of $600 million. The pipeline will feed the proposed Maputo iron and steel project, and will also provide gas for the South African market.

Education/Employment

The government's efforts at developing the educational system after independence from Portugal in 1975 were set back by the civil war, in which many schools were destroyed. In the 1990s there was a renewal of investment in education and an increase in primary school enrollment, but facilities at the secondary and tertiary levels have remained very poorly developed. While there are more than 6,000 primary schools with 1.9 million pupils, there are only 75 secondary schools with just over 50,000 students. There are three university-level institutions with 7,200 students.

Fiscal/Financial

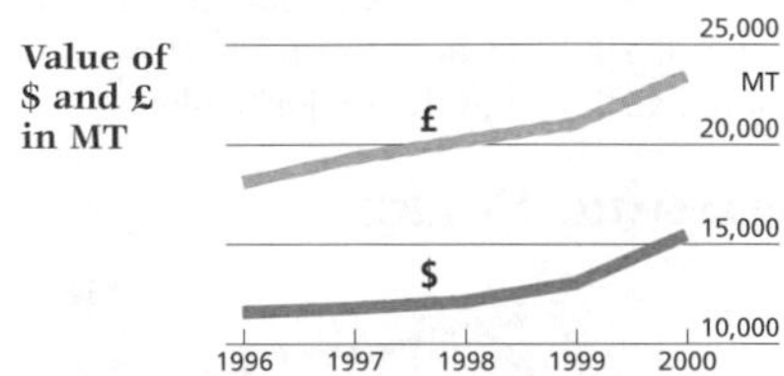

The state-dominated banking system of the 1980s and early 1990s has been radically reformed. Majority shares in the largest state-owned banks, BCM and BPD, were sold to foreign banks and private investors in 1996 and 1997. New private banks have also been licensed to operate, including BSTM, BFE, BIM, and BCI. This opening-up of the financial sector has stimulated the opening of new branch networks. There is also a venture capital fund, backed by the Commonwealth Development Corporation.

The central bank has been committed to moving from direct to indirect monetary controls. Interest rates have remained high as a result of remaining central bank controls and the limited availability of loan collateral.

A stock market, the Bolsa de Valores de Mocambique, opened in 1999. The market is expected to remain small in for the time being, but it could become an effective means of mobilizing savings.

Business Opportunities

Investment projects worth billions of dollars have been proposed, and some of these are at an advanced stage of development. The Mozal aluminum smelter in Maputo, in which $1.3 billion was invested in a first phase, is now being doubled in size to produce more than 500,000 tons of aluminum per annum; it is already a highly competitive producer of the metal. Another major project is the Maputo Iron and Steel Project, backed by South Africa's IDC, which is expected to cost $2.2 billion. Agreements for construction of a gas pipeline from Pande to Maputo and South Africa have been finalized. Oil and gas exploration are ongoing.

Other possible projects include establishing aluminum and iron production at Beira, expansion of the generating capacity of the Cabora Bassa dam, construction of a further hydroelectric facility on the Zambezi river, and development of mining, especially ilmenite and coal.

In the agricultural sector there has been investment in four separate sugar refineries. There has also been ongoing investment in tourism, with the opening of luxury hotels in Maputo and the development of coastal lodges in the southern half of the country. Private investors have opened hunting and nature reserves in remote central and northern locations.

For More Information

Books:

Finnegan, W. A. *A Complicated War: The Harrowing of Mozambique*. Berkeley, CA: University of California Press, 1992.

Minter, W. *Apartheid's Contras: An Inquiry into the Roots of War in Angola and Mozambique*. London: Zed Books, 1994.

Newitt, M. D. D. *A History of Mozambique*. Bloomington, IN: University of Indiana Press, 1995.

Synge, R. *Mozambique: United Nations Peacekeeping in Action*. Washington, D.C.: United States Institute of Peace, 1997.

Vines, A. *Renamo: From Terrorism to Democracy in Mozambique*. 2nd ed. Oxford: James Currey, 1996.

Web Sites:

African news and information: **www.allafrica.com/business**

Norwegian Council for Africa, Index on Africa: **www.afrika.no/index**

Political Resources on the Net: **www.politicalresources.net**

  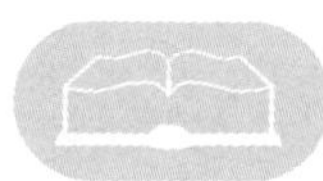    

NAMIBIA

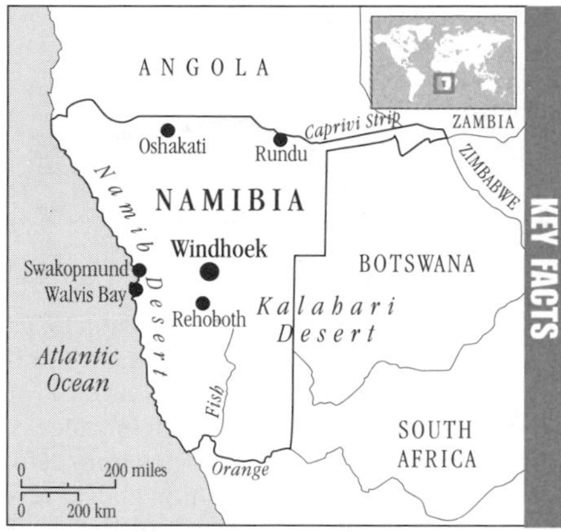

GNI: **$3,211 million; world's 132nd**
GNI pc: **$1,890; world's 107th**
Head of government: **president**
Currency: **Namibia dollar (N$)**
Capital: **Windhoek**
Population: **1,695,000, growing at 2.5% p.a.**
Land area: **317,876 square miles**
Population density: **5 per square mile**
Life expectancy: **48 years**
Infant mortality: **56 per 1,000 live births**
Language: **English, Afrikaans, German, Oshivambo**
Best buy: **fabric, handicrafts, fish and meat products, beer**

ECONOMY

Since achieving its long-delayed transition to independence from South African political control in 1990, Namibia has made progress in economic, social and political development. The government has expanded its investment in education and health facilities, while seeking to attract private capital to develop the economy. The main contributors to GDP are government services (20%), financial services (12.7%), mining and quarrying (11.4%), and agriculture and fisheries (11.4%). Namibia's principal exports are diamonds and fish. The main markets for Namibian goods are the United Kingdom and South Africa, while South Africa alone provides 84% of all Namibia's imports.

The government's economic policy has sought to achieve an increase in income per head for the poorest people, including landless workers. It has also sought to provide employment by diversifying the productive sector. There has been very little privatization, although the government plans to dilute the ownership of state-owned enterprises.

Economic growth averaged just below 5% per annum in the first half of the 1990s, slowing to an average of only 2.5% per annum thereafter. New investment continues at a modest level in the minerals sector and in manufacturing. Inflation has been influenced by developments in South Africa, and averaged 8.6% in 1999 and 9.3% in 2000.

GEOGRAPHY/RESOURCES

Much of Namibia's large land area is covered by two deserts. Between these deserts lies the central plateau, with an average altitude of 3,608 feet. There are few permanent watercourses other than the Orange river, which forms the southern border with South Africa, and the Kunene, forming the northern border with Angola. The availability of water is a major determinant of demographic patterns. Most of the population live on the central plateau, with the greatest concentration in the best-watered northern region. The central highlands around Windhoek have attracted large-scale farming settlers, who depend on boreholes and seasonal water courses. There is concern about the adequacy of these sources to meet the needs of the rapidly growing population of the capital city.

The country's mineral wealth is varied and scattered. In addition to alluvial diamonds, which are found both along the coast and offshore, there are deposits of uranium, tin, copper, salt, lead, and zinc.

With Windhoek as the only major town, Namibia is extremely thinly populated. The largest ethnic group is the Ovambo, who comprise about half the population and whose ancestral lands are in the north of the country. Europeans comprise only about 6% of the population but play a leading role in the economy.

COMMUNICATIONS/ENERGY

The transport network is relatively well developed. There are 3,100 miles of tarred roads and 16,800 miles of gravel roads. The largest developments in recent years have been the construction of the Trans-Kalahari and Trans-Caprivi highways. There are efficient rail, port, and air services. The principal port is Walvis Bay, where the authorities have undertaken substantial modernization. A good telecommunications network has stimulated rapid growth in Internet and mobile telephone usage. Electricity generation is undertaken by the Namibia Power Corporation, which takes power from the Ruacana hydroelectric facility on the Kunene river and from smaller thermal stations. It also imports power from South Africa.

FISCAL/FINANCIAL

Namibia operates favorable tax regimes for foreign investors, especially those engaged in mining and petroleum activities and manufacturing. Investors in export processing zones pay no corporate tax for an indefinite period and have exemption from indirect taxes and import duties on goods and inputs for exports outside the Southern African Customs Union. VAT was introduced on domestic trade in 2000.

The Bank of Namibia is the central bank. There are six commercial banks. There is a small stock exchange.

BUSINESS OPPORTUNITIES

The principal areas of opportunity exist in diamond mining, fish processing, manufacturing, and tourism. The constraints on new investment include a shortage of skilled labor, the small size of the domestic market, and the high costs of transportation.

For More Information

Books:

Leys, C., and J. S. Saul. *Namibia's Liberation Struggle: The Two-Edged Sword.* Oxford: James Currey, 1995.

Sparks, D., and D. Green. *Namibia: The Nation after Independence.* Boulder, CO: Westview Press, 1992.

Web Sites:

African news and information: **www.allafrica.com/business**

Norwegian Council for Africa, Index on Africa: **www.africa.no/index**

Political Resources on the Net: **www.politicalresources.net**

NETHERLANDS

KEY FACTS

GNI: **$397,384 million; world's 14th**
GNI pc: **$25,140; world's 16th**
Head of government: **prime minister**
Currency: **Euro (€)**
Capital: **Amsterdam**
Population: **15,735,000, growing at 0.6% p.a.**
Land area: **13,089 square miles**
Population density: **1,202 per square mile**
Life expectancy: **78 years**
Infant mortality: **5 per 1,000 live births**
Language: **Dutch**
Best buy: **Delft porcelain, diamonds, cheese**

ECONOMIC STRUCTURE

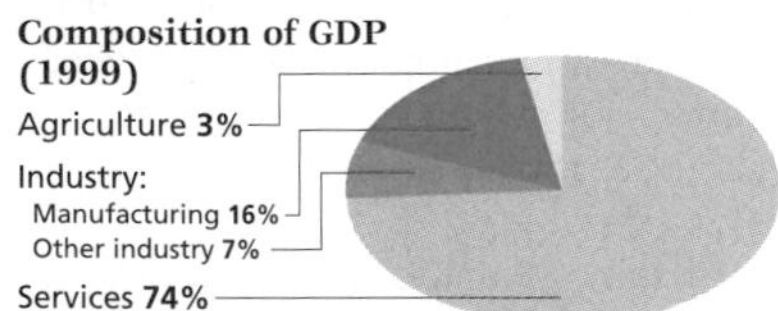

The Netherlands and its merchant rulers owed their independence from foreign domination in the 16th century to their seafarers and to the Rivers Scheldt, Maas, and Rhine, which formed natural barriers against invading armies. Strength at sea led to the development of colonies in Asia, the Caribbean, and Latin America. The country's economic strength continues to be derived from trading with the outside world, especially through the port of Rotterdam on the Eastern Scheldt estuary. The exploitation of vast offshore gas reserves from the 1970s helped underpin the economy, but high technology now dominates.

Services accounted for 70% of GDP in 2000, followed by industry (26%) and agriculture (3%). Manufacturing contributed 16% of GDP. Trade and distribution were the main services sector, followed by tourism and finance. Rotterdam is the largest port in the world, handling 30% of EU sea freight, with major logistics infrastructure for forwarding freight to other countries. Oil is a key import commodity, and there are pipeline links to Germany and Belgium for oil, gas, and chemical products. Marine services are important. The Netherlands is the world leader in maritime salvage operations and dredging. Food processing leads the manufacturing sector, followed by chemicals and machinery (especially office equipment). The Dutch are leaders in environmental control systems because of the country's vulnerable low-lying environment. The Netherlands is the European Union's main gas exporter. North Sea gas and the importation of oil for major consumers has led to a thriving industry in designing turnkey plant for gas and oil production, refining, and distribution. Horticulture is the largest agricultural sector. The main exports in 2000 were machinery and transport equipment (33.4%), chemicals (15.8%), processed food, beverages and tobacco (14.6%), fuels (8.7%), and agricultural products (5.4%). The main markets were Germany (25.8%), followed by Belgium (11.8%), the United Kingdom (10.8%), and France (10.5%). The European Union accounted for 77.3% of exports.

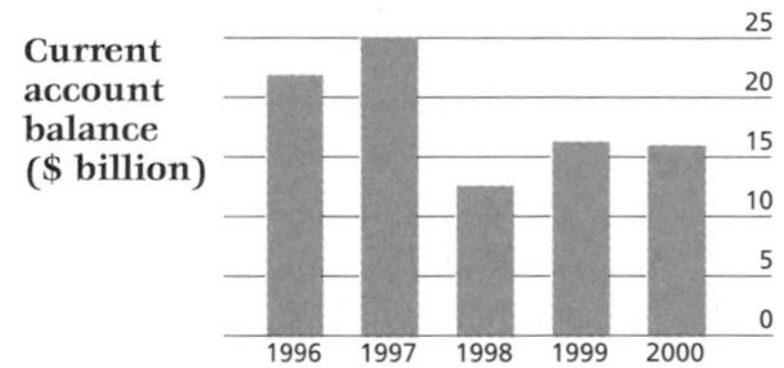

The Dutch State retains a shareholding in Nederlandse Gasunie, the company which exploits and markets North Sea gas. The Posts and Telecommunications Authority was privatized in 1989. Privatization of urban and regional transport is under way, and one-third of the network is due to be contracted out to private companies by 2003. The main airport, Schipol, is to be privatized. The main airline, KLM, is 14% state-owned. Liberalization of the domestic gas and electricity distribution sector is in progress. The employment service for those on welfare was privatized in the 1990s social security reforms.

ECONOMIC POLICY

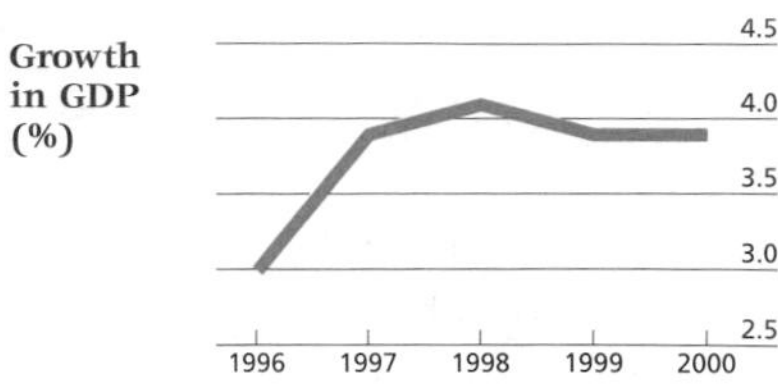

Strong economic growth in the late 1990s and in 2000 allowed the government to reduce the public debt from 70% of GDP in 1997 to 52.1% in 2001, and to cut income tax and social security contributions from 2001 with a net loss of €2.3 billion in budget revenues. The general government deficit of 4.2% of GDP in 1995 was transformed into small surpluses of 1.2% each year in 1999–2001. The government is planning to maintain surpluses at an average annual 1% to eliminate the public debt in 25 years' time. It has tightened eligibility criteria for welfare benefits, but the ratio of benefit recipients to the workforce remains relatively high. It introduced measures to reduce early retirement. The Netherlands meets all the underlying fundamentals required by the EU in preparation for the Euro, and stands to benefit substantially from the single currency.

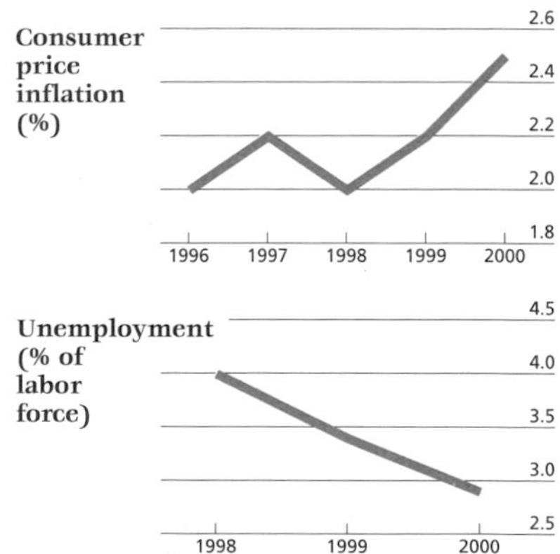

Economic growth picked up from the first half of the 1990s, when it was 2.1% a year, to 3.7% in 1996–2000. The increase was led by domestic demand. When this and export markets deteriorated in 2001, growth fell to 0.8% and is expected to stay low at 0.6% in 2002, before reviving to 2.6% in 2003. Inflation rose from an annual average of 2.2% in 1996–2000 to 4.2% in 2001. The low-valued Euro has raised the cost of imports and production. Job creation strengthened to 2.6% a year in 1996–99

from just 1.1% in 1991–95. It is expected to maintain this momentum in 2000 and 2001. Unemployment fell from 6.2% in 1997 to 3.7% in 2001.

Geography/Resources

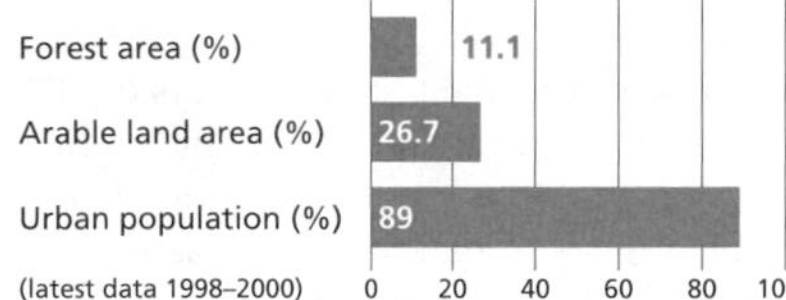

The Netherlands borders the North Sea to the west and north, Germany to the east, and Belgium to the south. The climate is temperate maritime. The country is mostly flat, except in the southeast where it is hilly with heath and woodland terrain. Three major rivers, the Rhine, Scheldt, and Maas have their estuaries in the Netherlands. The land is also criss-crossed by canals, which serve to control water levels and to provide transport and leisure activities. As 25% of the land is below sea level and another 25% is low-lying, there is severe risk of flooding from the rivers at times of high rainfall or snow melt from the Swiss Alps, and also from the sea as global warming causes sea levels to rise. The Major Rivers Project strengthened flood defenses on these rivers. The Delta Project involves the construction of flood barriers across the estuaries.

Horticulture is the leading agricultural activity, mostly under glass in heated conditions. Intensive agriculture has been practiced for several decades, but there have been moves to reduce this in recent years to lower pollution from agricultural chemicals. Leading agricultural produce includes flowers, vegetables, potatoes, cereals, sugar beet, dairy, and meat. There are small but significant fishing and forestry industries. The main minerals resources are natural gas and oil, which were discovered in the 1950s. Proven reserves of gas and oil were 62.5 trillion cubic feet and 107 million barrels respectively at January 2001. Coal mining in the southeastern province of South Limburg ceased in 1975. Limestone, clay, sand, and gravel are produced. Salt is processed from brine.

The country is one of the most densely populated in the world. Most of the people are of Germanic and mixed origin, as the country has attracted immigrants for centuries. Modern immigrants from Italy, Turkey, Morocco, and the former Dutch colonies of Indonesia, Suriname, and the Netherlands Antilles account for 5.1% of the population.

Communications/Energy

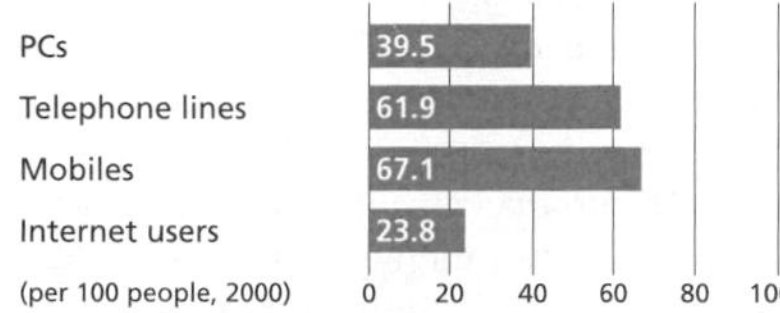

The 1,400 miles of highways, out of the total 75,000-mile road network, are suffering from congestion as most domestic and external freight is transported by road. Car use has increased rapidly since the 1970s, accounting for three-quarters of passenger journeys in the mid-1990s, despite the existence of frequent trains on the 1,750-mile rail network, and of buses, trams, and metros in Amsterdam and Rotterdam. To alleviate the pressure on the roads, the Betuwe freight rail link from Rotterdam to the German border is under construction and will be completed in 2005. The government is encouraging passengers to make more use of public transport. Over 3,000 miles of inland waterways provide the second most important means of freight transport after roads, carrying 219.7 million tons in 1998. Rotterdam is the largest port, handling around 3 billion tons of freight in 1998, but there are many others on the coast and inland. The merchant fleet numbered 596 ships over 1,000 grt, with a total displacement of 4.3 million grt in 2000. The pipeline network includes 6,400 miles for natural gas, 600 miles for petroleum products, and 260 miles for crude oil. The main international airport is Schipol, which serves Amsterdam and handled 36.4 million passengers in 1999. There are plans to build a fifth runway at Schipol. There are other international airports at Rotterdam (607,000 passengers in 1999), Maastricht (293,000), Eindhoven (289,000), and Groningen 99,000). There are major integrated transport plans, including all modes, for Amsterdam and Rotterdam.

Telecommunications networks are highly developed, digital, and increasingly integrated. The sector is privatized, but the privatized former state monopoly KPN Telecom was still the main operator in 2001. Measures to liberalize the sector are progressing. The government was one of the first in the world to develop an e-commerce Code of Conduct, which was approved by the International Chamber of Commerce. E-commerce totaled $2.45 billion in 2000 and is set to increase rapidly. Several large and small internationally-oriented e-commerce service companies operate from the Netherlands. Internet connectivity was the highest in Europe at mid-2001. At end-2000 there were 9.9 million fixed phone lines, 10.7 million mobile phones, and 3.9 million Internet users. Over 90% of households were connected to cable television, which allows for telephony, data transmission, and interactive television.

The Netherlands is the largest European producer of natural gas after Russia. Gas production was 2.6 trillion cubic feet in 1999, but output is being scaled down to lengthen the life of reserves. About two-thirds of gas production was used for domestic needs in 1999, including electricity, direct residential use, and industrial feedstock. Oil production was 112,000 barrels per day in 2000, but most oil is imported. Most electricity is generated from gas (around 90%), with nuclear accounting for 4%, and various renewable energy sources for 5.5%. The share of renewable energy is set to increase in the future.

Education/Employment

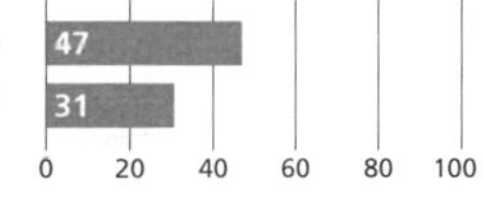

Full-time education is compulsory from age 5 to 16. Part-time education is compulsory for a further two years. Education is largely state-funded and overseen by the Ministry of Education. The Ministry of Agriculture funds the Agricultural University at Wageningen and agricultural technical colleges. The 13 universities and 58 university-level vocational colleges are self-governing. Most universities and technical colleges have links with business to ensure that training meets commercial needs. More than one-third of women and men between the ages of 20 and 24 are in higher education, with 34% in economics and business programs and 32% in sciences and math. Foreign-language training is part of all curricula.

Universities and teaching hospitals are obliged by law to conduct research, part of which is funded by the government. The Netherlands Organization for Scientific Research (NWO) and the Royal Netherlands Academy of Arts and Sciences (KNAW) fund specific projects. The universities also conduct contract research for companies. The private sector's share of this category is 15%, but the government wants to involve industry more and to increase the commercialization of public research. The leading research institutes include TNO (Netherlands Organization for Applied Scientific Research) with a wide range of programs from nutrition to industrial technology, Delft International Institute of Hydraulic Engineering, RIVM (National Institute of

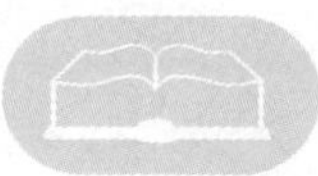

Public Health and Environmental Protection), ECN (Netherlands Energy Research Center), and the National Aerospace Laboratory. About 45% of private-sector R&D is conducted by five Dutch multinational companies: Philips, Unilever, Shell, DSM, and AKZO. However, smaller companies are beginning to increase their share.

The government is promoting e-commerce through public/private-financed projects, Twinning Venture Capital Network (including guidance and funds), and the creation of Internet clusters in Amsterdam, Rotterdam, Enschede, The Hague, and Eindhoven. The government has speeded up patent procedures and created centers of excellence in biotechnology based on the universities and research institutes in Groningen, Leiden, Utrecht, Wageningen, and Amsterdam. The $50 million Life Sciences Action Plan will provide up to $5 million of government money per company, to be matched by private funds.

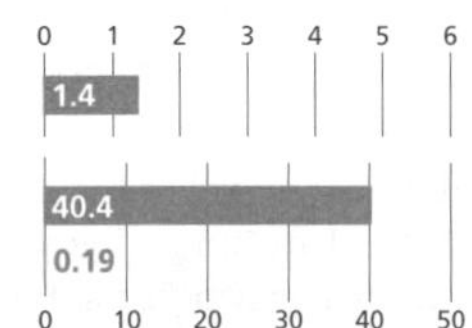

The labor force is well-educated and multilingual. Almost two-thirds of the population are of working age (20 to 65), but there is a preponderance in the upper age group. Wages and other employment conditions are determined by tripartite negotiation between the government, employers, and trade unions. The Netherlands applies EU employment law, which covers safety at work, wages and working hours, industrial relations, employment incentives, and unemployment provision.

Fiscal/Financial

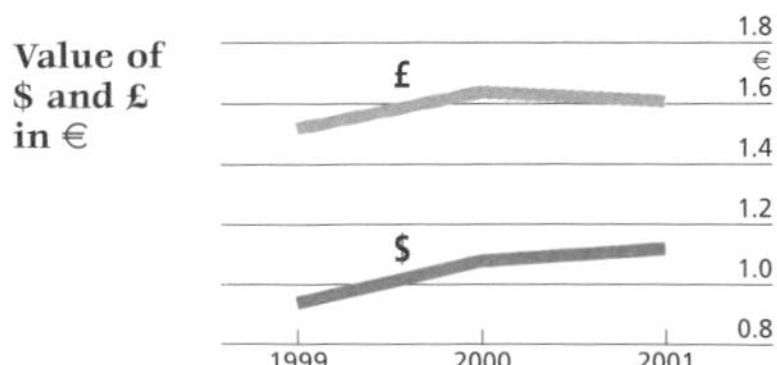

The largest banks are ABN Amro, ING, and Rabobank (all private-sector). Major insurance companies include AEGON Insurance Group and ING Vezekering. The regulatory authority and central bank is De Nederlandsche Bank, which is also part of the European System of Central Banks. This body and the European Central Bank set the policy for the Euro.

Corporation tax is 34.5%, assessed on a consolidated basis. There are provisions for tax-free reserves and free depreciation of assets for certain categories of investment relating to environmental protection, R&D, group finance, and shipping. Losses can be carried forward indefinitely or back for three years. The government offers special tax concessions to holding and financing companies. The standard rate of VAT is 19%, with a reduced rate of 6%.

Financial services are sophisticated and internationally-oriented. The three largest Dutch banks are among the world's largest, and account for 75% of domestic lending. The government's move to attract foreign financial holding companies to establish headquarters, and measures for greater use of venture capital, have strengthened local financial services. The Amsterdam exchanges merged with those of Paris and Brussels to form Euronext, giving the individual exchanges transnational operating scope. Rotterdam is an important trading center for petroleum spot prices. Euronext has links with Luxembourg and other exchanges. Euronext Amsterdam has a main board, and exchanges for futures, options, and derivatives.

Business Opportunities

Growth in output (% p.a., 1990–99)

Services	3.1
Industry	1.7
Manufacturing	2.2
Agriculture	2.1

According to the EIU business environment rankings, the Netherlands is expected to be the best place in the world to conduct business over the next five years (2002–06). The increasingly tax-friendly environment for corporations, with tax cuts and reduction of social security contributions under the present reform program, and the excellent infrastructure and international orientation of banks and companies are incentives to invest, offsetting relatively high labor costs. Foreign investors are excluded from air and rail transport and public broadcast media, but have equal rights with domestic firms to invest in any other sector. Tax and financial incentives are offered to investors. New rules for holding and financing companies include: no formal debt-to-equity requirement; tax exemption for dividends received and capital gains derived from qualifying share holdings; the allocation by group finance companies of up to 80% of income from financing activities to a reserve (thus reducing taxable income); and the absence of Controlled Foreign Company rules which prohibit the use of low-tax centers for group activities.

The Netherlands has attracted about 25% of total foreign direct investment to the EU, and is one of the eight top recipients of FDI in the world. The main sectors are IT, biotechnology, medical technology, food processing, high-tech manufacturing assembly, chemicals, distribution, call centers, services centers, and European headquarters operations. These sectors continue to offer investment opportunities. Around 60% of Japanese and U.S. European Distribution Centers are located in the Netherlands. Over half of investments come from EU countries, with more from other European and non-European countries. The point of contact is the Netherlands Foreign Investment Agency.

For More Information

Books:

Andeweg, Rudy, and Galen Irwing. *Dutch Government and Politics*. New York: Macmillan, 1993.
Dutch Ministry of Transport, Public Works and Water Management. *Water Management in the Netherlands*. 1999.
IMF Country Report. *Netherlands*. Washington, D.C.: IMF.
Netherlands Ministry of Foreign Affairs. *The Netherlands in Brief*.
OECD Economic Surveys. *Netherlands*. Paris: OECD.
Wolters, M., and P. Coffey, eds. *The Netherlands and EC Membership Evaluated*. London: Pinter, 1990.

Web Sites:

Central Bureau of Statistics: **www.cbs.nl**
De Nederlandsche Bank: **www.dnb.nl**
De Telegraaf (national daily newspaper): **www.telegraaf.nl**
De Volkskrant (national daily newspaper): **www.volkskrant.nl**
Euronext Amsterdam (stock exchanges): **www.aex.nl**
Ministry of Economic Affairs: **www.minez.nl**
Ministry of Foreign Affairs, government entry point: **www.minbuza.nl**
Netherlands Foreign Investment Agency: **www.nfia.nl**

NETHERLANDS ANTILLES

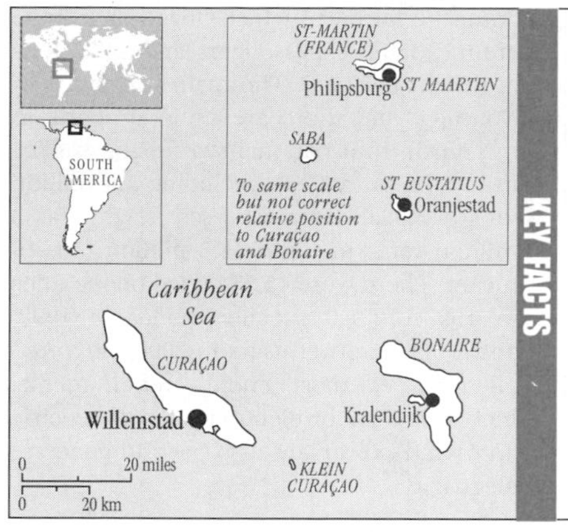

KEY FACTS

GNI pc: **$11,500 (approx.)**
Head of government: **premier**
Currency: **Netherlands Antilles guilder (NAG)**
Capital: **Willemstad**
Population: **247,800**
Land area: **309 square miles**
Population density: **801 per square mile**
Language: **Dutch (official language), Papiamento (daily use, Curaçao and Bonaire), English (daily use, St. Maarten, St. Eustatius and Saba)**
Best buy: **jewelry, perfumes, Curaçao liqueur**

ECONOMY

The five-island federation of the Netherlands Antilles forms a self-governing component of the Kingdom of the Netherlands, along with the Netherlands itself and neighboring Aruba.

The Netherlands Antilles has a fairly high standard of living by Caribbean standards. However, the economy of the largest island, Curaçao, has been in severe difficulties since 1996 following a clampdown on cocaine transshipment. GDP fell by a cumulative 10% in 1996–2000. Underlying weaknesses include a fiscal deficit rising at times to more than 5% of GDP, a stagnant tourism sector, and high labor, interest, transport and communications costs. Partly because of long-awaited tax increases, inflation was an estimated 5.8% in 2000 after two years of virtual price stability.

In 2000 the IMF agreed NAG110 million ($61 million) of support for an economic adjustment and reform program, which is also assisted by the Netherlands. Attempts have been made to cut the public-sector deficit, and there are hopes of renewed economic growth from 2002–03.

The main foreign exchange earner is tourism; of total stopover arrivals in 2000, 28% went to the most populous island, Curaçao, 62% to St. Maarten, 7% to Bonaire, and 3% to St. Eustatius and Saba. St. Maarten also receives close to 900,000 cruise passengers a year, with a further 230,000 going to Curaçao.

In Curaçao the other main industry is oil refining. The former Shell refinery, originally built in 1915 to process Venezuelan crude for the U.S. market, is now operated by the state-owned Venezuelan oil company, Petroleos de Venezuela (PdVSA) as the Refineria Isla (Curazao) under a 20-year lease expiring in 2015, and processes Venezuelan heavy crude oil. Expansion and upgrading are now in progress. Storage and transshipment of crude oil is also an important activity on Bonaire and St. Eustatius.

There is a small and heavily-protected manufacturing sector on Curaçao, including a brewery, as well as a large free zone, for warehousing, wholesaling, and re-export of imported manufactured goods. On Bonaire, sea salt, the traditional economic mainstay, is still produced by evaporation.

GEOGRAPHY/RESOURCES

Curaçao and Bonaire are 31 miles apart, 37 miles off the coast of Venezuela. St. Maarten, 550 miles from Curaçao, shares a 34 square-mile island with French St. Martin; Saba and St. Eustatius are respectively 28 and 37 miles from St. Maarten.

The main resources of the Netherlands Antilles are the geographical location of the islands, their warm, sunny climate, clear offshore waters, and sandy beaches. Commercial agriculture is not well developed, although aloe (aloe barbadiensis) is grown for use by the pharmaceuticals industry. The islands have some hills, and are covered with scrub vegetation.

Curaçao and Bonaire lie outside the hurricane belt, but St. Maarten and its neighbors have suffered several direct hits in recent years.

The majority of the population is of Afro-Caribbean origin.

The education system is well developed, with high levels of literacy. Many of the population are fluent in several languages.

COMMUNICATIONS/ENERGY

The main international airports are on Curaçao and St. Maarten, and have direct connections to Europe, the Caribbean, and North and South America. Bonaire, Saba, and St. Eustatius have short-haul flights. Telecommunications and electricity supply are adequate, and much of the fresh water supply is producted by desalination.

FISCAL/FINANCIAL

Curaçao's offshore financial sector now specializes in trade brokerage, countertrade finance, trusts, and private companies, but has not grown as strongly as some of its Caribbean rivals. Controls on money-laundering were tightened from 1995.

The Netherlands Antilles was listed as a tax haven by the Organisation for Economic Co-operation and Development in June 2000. As a result, the government was forced to reassess a corporate tax package, the Nieuw Fiscaal Ramwerk or New Fiscal Regime.

BUSINESS OPPORTUNITIES

The major business opportunities are in tourism and related service industries. Curaçao also has an industrial park, but high costs are a deterrent to manufacturing industries. State enterprises marked for privatization include the high-cost dry dock on Curaçao, and the loss-making and heavily indebted state airline, ALM.

For More Information

Books:

Cijntje, D. E., ed. *Netherlands Antilles Business Law: Legal, Accounting and Tax Aspects of Doing Business in the Netherlands Antilles*. The Hague: Kluwer Law International, 1999.

Curaçao Chamber of Commerce and Industry. *Curaçao Business Information Guide*.

Netherlands Antilles Offshore Investment and Business Guide (World Offshore Investment and Business Library). Washington, D.C.: International Business Publications, 2001.

The Netherlands Antilles Research Group. *A Strategic Profile of Netherlands Antilles* (Strategic Planning Series). San Diego, CA: ICON Group International, 2000.

Web Sites:

Curaçao Chamber of Commerce and Industry: **www.Curacao-chamber.an**
General site for Curaçao: **www.Curacao.com**

NEW CALEDONIA

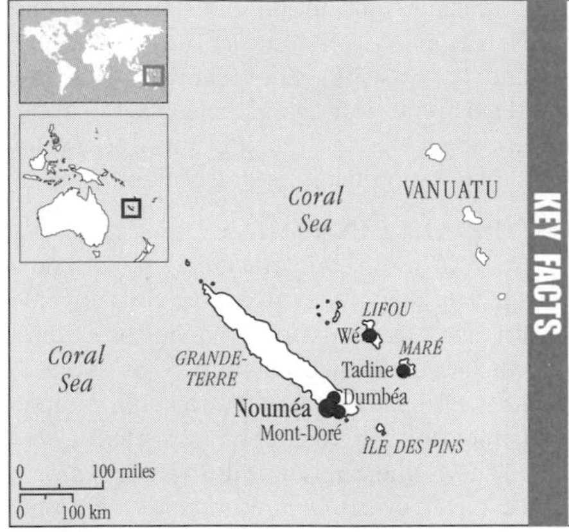

KEY FACTS

GNI: **$3,169 million**
GNI pc: **$15,160; world's 38th**
Head of government: **president**
Currency: **Pacific franc (PF)**
Capital: **Nouméa on Grande-Terre**
Population: **215,200**
Land area: **7,234 square miles**
Population density: **30 per square mile**
Language: **French (official), Melanesian languages**
Best buy: **wood and soapstone carvings, sand and bark paintings, nickel artifacts, shells**

ECONOMY

Nickel mining (at 12 centers on the main island, Grande-Terre) and smelting is the dominant industry, accounting for about 10% of GDP and 90% of exports. Output of nickel ore was 7.5 million tons in 1998, 60% of which was exported unprocessed to Japan, Australia, the United States, and France. Nickel prices rose sharply in 1999–2000. Production increased and continued to increase in 2001, although nickel prices fell again. The SLN smelter at Doniambo produced 56,502 tons of refined nickel in 1998. Tourism is the second industry, contributing another 10% of GDP. A variety of small industries, including copra, construction materials, mechanical engineering, food processing, beverages, and soap, contribute 14% of GDP. Most serve the local market. Copra is exported. Craft industries provide 18% of jobs, while construction provides 40% and metallurgy, mechanical engineering, and electricity 20%. Coffee plantations employ 28% of the workforce, but all agriculture accounts for less than 2% of GDP. Most agriculture is subsistence farming, but locally-produced food only accounts for 47% of requirements. Farmed shrimp are the second export after nickel. Tuna is also exported to Japan.

Government receipts rely on grant aid from France. Aid has increased since the 1988 Matignon Accord ended direct control by France over the territory's budget and fiscal policy, local economic development, land reform, and cultural matters. French government equity in nickel is being transferred to local interests. There is a significant trade deficit, with only 41.3% export cover of imports in 1998. Local banking sources put average GDP growth for 1990–99 at 1.5%. It probably strengthened in 2000 but eased in 2001 in tandem with world nickel prices. Inflation was 2.7% in September 2001.

GEOGRAPHY/RESOURCES

New Caledonia, in the Pacific Ocean 930 miles east of Australia, comprises one large island, Grande-Terre, the Belep archipelago, the Loyauté islands, and the île des Pins. Grande-Terre is divided by a central mountain range, with the highest point Mount Panié at 5,250 feet. To the east of the mountains the climate is wet with abundant vegetation. The western side is drier, and is characterized by pasture and plains. About 60% of the population live in or near the capital, Nouméa.

Coconuts, corn, yams, sweet potatoes, pumpkins, and coffee are the main agricultural crops. The main livestock products are beef, pork, and chicken. Fish farming (especially of shrimp), traditional coastal fishing, industrial fisheries (especially tuna), and leisure fishing for the tourist industry are important. There are rich mineral resources, including nickel, chrome, cobalt, iron, manganese, copper, lead, zinc, jasper, and gold. New Caledonia accounts for 20% of world nickel reserves and 12.3% of world production. It is a major cobalt producer. Chrome is also mined. In 1999 a huge natural gas deposit was found.

COMMUNICATIONS/ENERGY

The road network on Grande-Terre is around 3,500 miles, with a further 300 miles of roads on the smaller islands. Nouméa has an international airport and a separate domestic airport, which together handle around 350,000 passengers and 5,000 tons of freight per year. The main sea port is at Nouméa, and there are minerals ports in the north. International sea freight was 6.8 million tons in 1997, including 5.4 million tons of nickel. Domestic sea freight was 3 million tons, including 2.8 million tons of nickel. There were 45,574 fixed phone lines in 1997, 13,040 mobile phones in 1998, and 5,000 Internet users in 2000. Imported oil provides most energy requirements, including 79% of electricity. Hydroelectric and wind power are also used to generate electricity.

FISCAL/FINANCIAL

Personal income tax and corporation tax are low. Personal tax averaged just over 7% in the mid-1990s. Monetary policy is set by France. The local branch of the Association Française des Banques oversees banking and financial regulation. There are seven banks and 10 finance companies. There is no stock market.

BUSINESS OPPORTUNITIES

There is foreign investment in the nickel mining sector, tourism, and trade. International companies are considering establishing a new nickel smelter and related infrastructure, including an airport, sea port, and roads. The government is eager to encourage investment in tourism, especially new hotels, and in fish processing. The point of contact for foreign investors is the New Caledonia Economic Development Agency.

For More Information

Books:

Logan, Leanne, and Geert Cole. *New Caledonia*. 9th ed. Oakland, CA: Lonely Planet, 2001.

New Caledonia Country Study. Washington, D.C.: International Business Publications, 2000.

Web Sites:

Chamber of Commerce and Industry: **www.cci.nc**

Government entry point: **www.gouv.nc**

New Caledonia Economic Development Agency: **www.adecal.nc**

NEW ZEALAND

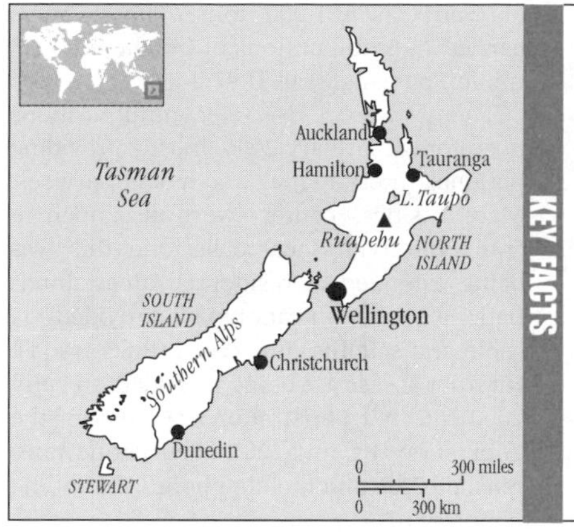

KEY FACTS

GNI: **$53,299 million; world's 47th**
GNI pc: **$13,990; world's 43rd**
Head of government: **prime minister**
Currency: **New Zealand dollar (NZ$)**
Capital: **Wellington**
Population: **3,828,000, growing at 1.4% p.a.**
Land area: **103,475 square miles**
Population density: **37 per square mile**
Life expectancy: **77 years**
Infant mortality: **6 per 1,000 live births**
Language: **English, Maori**
Best buy: **woolen goods, leather goods, Maori handcrafts, wine**

ECONOMIC STRUCTURE

Composition of GDP (1999)

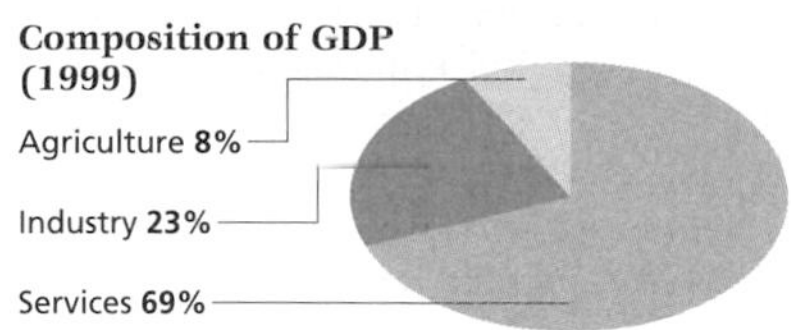

New Zealand was colonized by British missionaries and traders in the early 19th century. By 1858 Europeans outnumbered the indigenous Maori population, and sheep farming was the key economic sector. Gold, petroleum, and gas were discovered in the 1860s. Free compulsory education was introduced in 1877, and government pensions for the poor in 1898. New Zealand was the first country in the world to give women the vote in 1893. The introduction of freezer ships from the 1880s allowed for the export of meat and dairy products to the United Kingdom, a trade which dominated the economy until the United Kingdom joined the European Community in 1973. New Zealand gained independence in 1947. The loss of the British market in the 1970s led to intense government investment in industry and subsidies to farming and industry. Soaring inflation was followed by a wage and price freeze. From 1984 interventionism was cast aside. The exchange rate was floated, foreign exchange controls were lifted, and the financial markets were deregulated. Import duties were cut, the top rate of income tax was halved, subsidies to industry and farming eliminated, and a radical program of privatization was launched. The economy remained focused on exports of agricultural, forestry, and mining products, although high technology increased rapidly in the 1990s.

Services accounted for 69% of GDP in 1998–99, followed by industry (23%), and agriculture (8%). Trade and tourism is the leading services sector. Tourism is also a leading source of foreign exchange. Finance, insurance, and business services are the second services sector, followed by transport and government services. Food, wine and beer, textiles, footwear, wood products, pulp and paper, cars, machinery, aluminum, and carpets are important manufacturing industries. Boat building has been given a boost by New Zealand's hosting of the prestigious America's Cup yacht race. IT and telecommunications are rapidly growing industries, with New Zealand used as a test market for new applications. In 2000 dairy products were the top exports (15.7%), followed by meat (12.6%), timber and wood products (11.2%), fish, machinery, and aluminum. Australia was the leading market, absorbing 20.4% of exports, followed by the United States (14.5%), Japan (13.5%), the United Kingdom, South Korea, China, Hong Kong, and Germany.

Current account balance ($ billion)

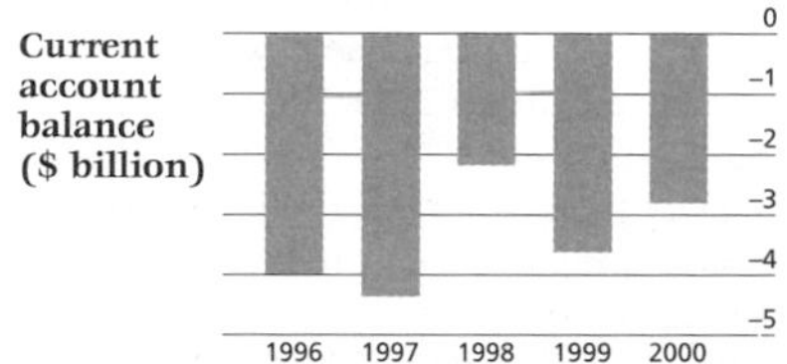

At mid-2001 there were 39 state-owned enterprises in energy, insurance, broadcasting, transport, and other sectors. The privatization program of the previous 16 years included Air New Zealand (1989), Telecom Corporation of New Zealand (1990), New Zealand Rail (1993), part of the broadcasting network (1996), and Auckland airport (2000). The telecommunications sector was liberalized in 1989 and broadcasting in 1995 with the division of the state broadcaster into private and public broadcasting companies. In 1996 the Electricity Corporation of New Zealand was split into two state-owned enterprises to introduce competition into wholesale electricity distribution. Entry of a private company into this sector failed in 2001. Workplace accident insurance was renationalized in 2000. There were plans in mid-2001 to privatize Wellington airport. Other sectors due for privatization include water and sewage systems, forests, sea ports and bus and truck companies owned by regional governments.

ECONOMIC POLICY

Growth in GDP (%)

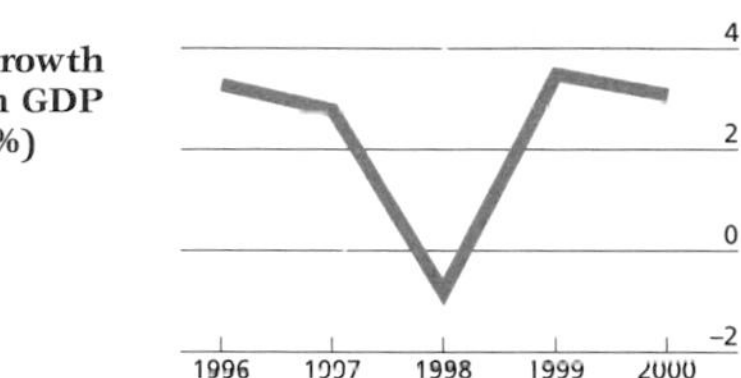

From the mid-1980s government policy moved from one of tight regulation to greater deregulation in order to reduce inflation and improve GDP growth. These targets have been largely achieved, with GDP growth roughly double its pre-reform level and inflation relatively low. The Reserve Bank of New Zealand has targeted inflation as the key to its monetary policy, which it handles independently of the government. Government budget surpluses were used to reduce the public debt to 20% of GDP in 2000. However, net foreign liabilities are 90% of GDP because of the low level of domestic savings and investment. The government is committed to maintaining the public debt at 20% of GDP or less and government spending at 35% of GDP. Although there are no subsidies to agriculture and industry, government marketing boards set prices for agricultural produce and have the monopoly on overseas sales. New Zealand's dependence on foreign trade, and the greater degree of protectionism in its main export markets than at home, are constant problems. They underscore New Zealand's interest in providing the World Trade Organization with its first Director General, Mike Moore.

Although the state sector was reduced through the privatization program, and welfare eligibility was tightened in the 1990s,

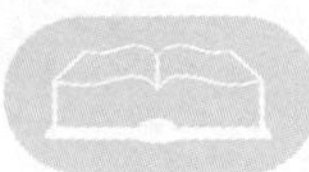

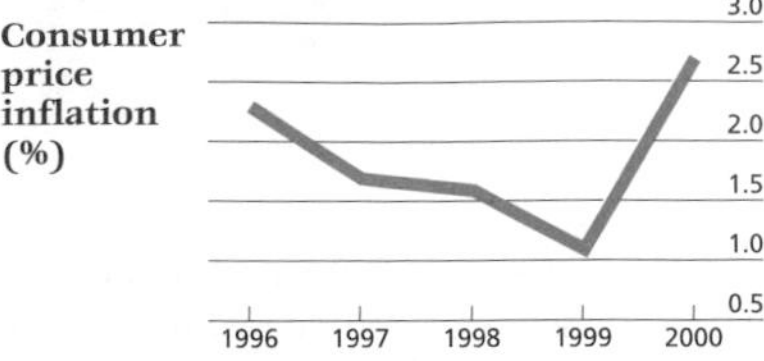

government spending accounts for 40% of GDP, higher than the OECD average. The increased gap between rich and poor as a result of the reform program resulted in measures aimed at improving social cohesion in 2000, such as the new Employment Relations Act and the creation of Industry New Zealand to spearhead the government's drive for increased industrialization. Education reforms are aimed at increasing professional and technical skills. Health sector reforms are aimed at cutting bureaucracy. Pre-funding of pensions is planned to prepare for population aging. However, the OECD considers that this issue would be better addressed through tax incentives to private savings.

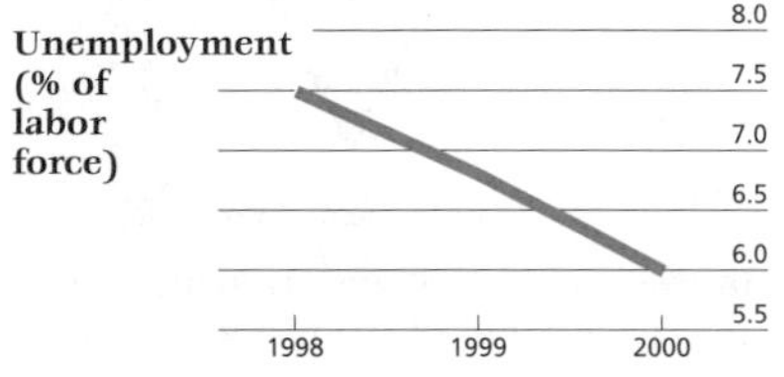

GDP growth was an average 3% in 1992–2000, with a slight decline in 1998 as a result of the Asian financial crisis. It was 2% in 2001 and is not expected to revive much before 2003. Inflation increased from an annual average 1.7% in 1996–99 to just over 3% in 2000, falling slightly in 2001. It is to be within the government's target of less than 3% in 2002. Unemployment was an average 6.6% in 1996–2000.

GEOGRAPHY/RESOURCES

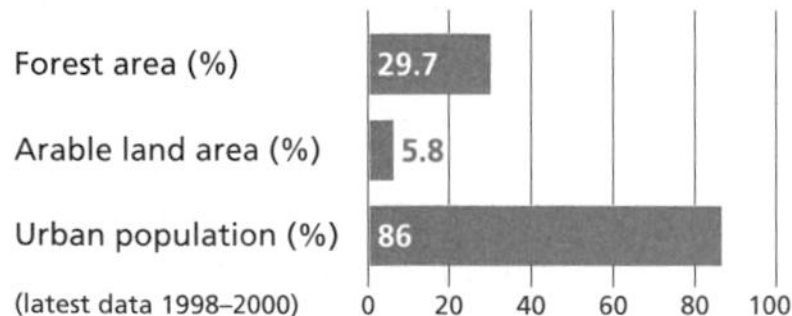

In the southern Pacific Ocean, New Zealand consists of two large and several smaller islands. Volcanic mountain ranges and hills dominate North and South Island. There is volcanic activity on North Island where geysers, hot springs, and mudpools are a feature. South Island has fjords and glaciers. There are coastal plains on both islands. The climate is temperate with average temperatures of 46°F in winter and 63°F in summer, but temperatures can reach 86°F in summer. Mean average rainfall varies from 4 inches to 472 inches. The majority of people are urban and live on North Island. Most people are of European origin (79.6%), while the indigenous Maori population is 14.5% of the total, followed by Pacific Islanders (5.6%), and Chinese (2.2%) and Indian (1.2%) communities.

The main agricultural crops are apples (an important export), potatoes, barley, wheat, and corn. Other grains, fruit, and vegetables are grown. Dairy and meat are particularly important, as are wool and leather. Sheep and cattle are the most important livestock. Poultry, pigs, goats, deer, ostriches, and llamas are also raised. Production of pine and exotic hardwoods is significant. Fisheries are important; hoki is the main species caught.

New Zealand is richly endowed with minerals, but the local market is small and export is restricted to high-value minerals on account of the country's distance from its main markets. Minerals produced include petroleum, natural gas, coal, gold, aggregates, titanomagnetite ironsand, limestone, marble, silica, zeolite, pumice, diatomite, and specialty clays. Perlite, sulfur, and serpentinite are mined intermittently. Petroleum, coal, titanomagnetite, halloysite clays, ilmenite, limestone, and lime are exported. Coal reserves are about 15 billion tons, of which 8.6 billion are economically recoverable. Petroleum and natural gas reserves at mid-2000 were 100 million barrels and 2.2 trillion cubic feet respectively.

COMMUNICATIONS/ENERGY

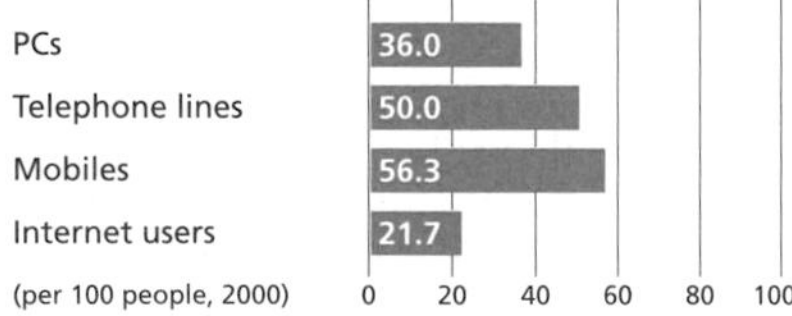

The 57,000-mile road network accounts for most domestic traffic. There were 2.7 million road vehicles in 1999. The rail network was 2,431 miles in 1999, of which 322 miles was electrified. Tranz Rail, the privatized operator, provides multimodal transport, including road services, warehousing and logistics, and links with shipping. There are 13 main sea ports, the largest ports being Auckland, Tauranga, Wellington, Lyttleton (for Christchurch), and Port Chalmers (for Dunedin). At end-1998 the merchant fleet numbered 173 ships, representing 336,278 grt. The pipeline network includes 620 miles for natural gas, 93 miles for LPG, and 100 miles for petroleum products. There are three international airports at Auckland, Christchurch, and Wellington, 41 other airports, and 67 airstrips. In 1999 sea ports handled 32.1 million tons of overseas freight and airports 181,000 tons. The railways carried 11.5 million tons of freight and 11.6 million passengers in 1997.

There were 15 telecommunications operators at January 2000, mostly providing national, international, and mobile services. Main business centers were also open to competition for local calls, and this was being extended to residential areas. International communications are provided via cable and satellite. Broadband links for fast Internet access are being extended. In early 2000 Internet penetration was 51% of the population. By mid-2001 fixed phone lines reached 72% and mobile phones 95% of the population.

New Zealand is self-sufficient in all energy forms apart from petroleum. Gas accounted for 28.9% of primary energy in 2000, followed by imported oil (27.5%), geothermal (17.6%), hydro (10.6%), other renewables (6.3%), coal (5.8%), and indigenous oil (3.3%). In 2000, 36% of electricity was generated from geothermal, followed by fossil fuels, mostly gas (32%), hydro (25%), and other renewable sources including wood, biogas, steam, and wind (7%). By 2020 hydro is expected to account for 52% of electricity, natural gas for 15%, and coal for 14%. Coal production was 85.5 PJ (petajoules) in 2000. Natural gas output was 235.2 PJ, 42% of which was used for petrochemical feedstock. Current gas reserves are expected to be depleted by 2014. Crude petroleum and condensate production was 95.5 PJ in 2000.

EDUCATION/EMPLOYMENT

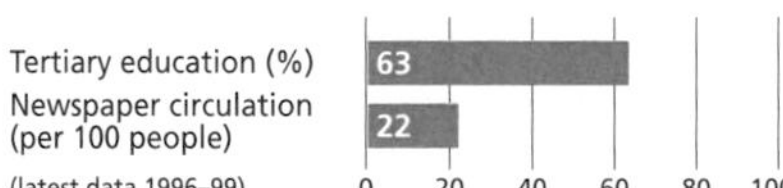

Education is compulsory from age 6 to 16. There are 8 universities, 23 polytechnics, 4 teacher training colleges, 2 Wānanga (Maori higher education institutions), 800 private training establishments, and a number of not-for-profit tertiary education centers. Continuing education is provided through the universities, polytechnics, schools, and voluntary organizations. There were 248,123 students in higher education in 1998. In 2001, 13.1% of higher education students had opted for math, science, and engineering. The Ministry of Education is responsible for education policy and for overseeing educational institutions, includ-

ing those in the private sector. State-sector education is government-funded. Financial assistance is available to students on a means-tested basis.

Universities and polytechnics conduct research. In addition there are nine government research institutes which specialize in various aspects of biotechnology, environment protection, manufacturing, energy, geology, and nuclear science. There are several government R&D funds. Technology New Zealand is targeted at helping businesses to develop and adopt new technology. Private-sector R&D includes IT and telecommunications.

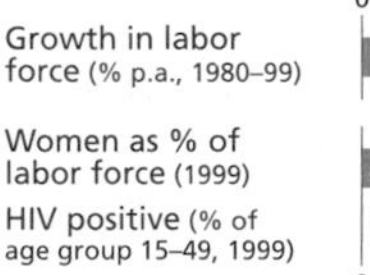

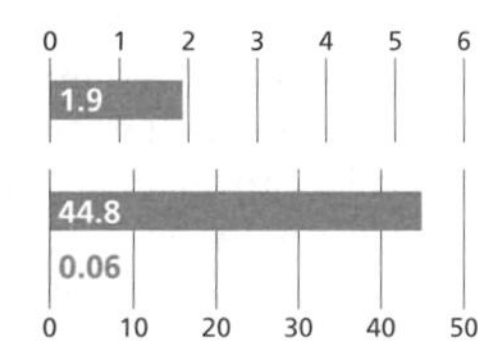

The labor force is well educated. Wages and other employment conditions are negotiated between employers and workers. Compulsory unionism was ended in the Employment Contracts Act of 1991. Coercive and sympathy strikes by workers not involved in a particular dispute are banned, but the 2000 Employment Relations Act strengthens the role of collective bargaining, particularly in respect of multi-company employment contracts. It also tightens notice and dismissal procedures. The government sets minimum wage levels and health and safety rules.

Fiscal/Financial

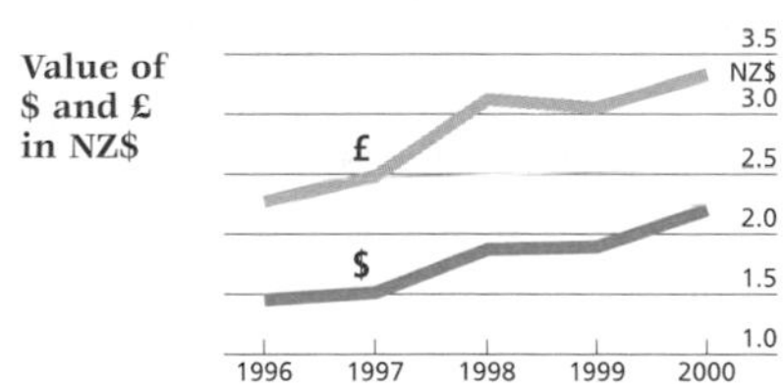

The largest bank by total assets at September 2000 was Bank of New Zealand, followed by National Bank of New Zealand, ANZ Banking Group (New Zealand), Commonwealth Bank of Australia (New Zealand), and ASB Bank. All are private-sector. The 29 insurance companies include some of the world's largest. The Reserve Bank of New Zealand sets and implements monetary policy and supervises the banking sector. Capital adequacy is above the minimum required by Basle principles, but customers' deposits are not insured. Banks are required to obtain and publish a credit rating. Finance companies, building societies, insurance companies, and the stock exchange are regulated by the Securities Commission, but insurance companies are largely self-regulated by the Insurance Council of New Zealand. Corporation tax is 33% for resident companies or 38% for non-resident companies. The maximum rate of personal income tax is 39%. Sales tax is 12.5%.

There were 17 banks at mid-2001, including seven locally-incorporated banks and 10 overseas-incorporated banks. However, most local banks are foreign-owned. Foreign banks regarded as systemically important or whose retail deposits exceed NZ$200 million are obliged to incorporate locally. Financial services are sophisticated and internationalized. As individuals use finance houses, insurance companies, and the stock market more, foreign and inter-bank business has featured more strongly in bank operations. E-banking is a growth area for business and individuals. All main classes of insurance are available, including re-insurance. In 2000 the government renationalized work place accident insurance cover, which is now provided by the state-owned Accident Compensation Corporation.

The New Zealand Stock Exchange was formed at Wellington in 1981. At early 2002 it was preparing to demutualize. Total capitalization at January 2002 was NZ$43.6 billion. There is a main board and the New Capital Market which lists small high-growth companies. Foreign exchange and derivatives have attracted increasing interest. Trading is electronic, and there is Internet and WAP access. The Exchange encourages individuals to invest, by providing information on how to choose stocks and an online trading game with prizes, called "Stock Market Challenge." This simulates real trading to give investors and schools a taste of how events unfold.

Business Opportunities

There are financial incentives and practical assistance available to foreign investors through Investment New Zealand, part of Trade New Zealand. Various investment programs for New Zealand businesses, including the technology incubator, small business and regional development programs, are coordinated by Industry New Zealand. Finance, insurance, telecommunications, IT, minerals, automotive, and food processing have attracted investment from Australia, the United States, the United Kingdom, Japan, Canada, and Hong Kong, among other countries. Opportunities continue to exist in these sectors and in biotechnology, wood processing, food processing, and tourism.

Growth in output (% p.a., 1990–99)

Services	3.7
Industry	2.4
Agriculture	2.7

For More Information

Books:

Birks, S. and S. Chatterjee, eds. *The New Zealand Economy, Issues and Policies.* 3rd ed. Palmerston North: Dunmore Press, 1997.

Brash, D. *New Zealand's Remarkable Reforms.* London: Institute of Economic Affairs, 1996.

IMF Country Report. *New Zealand.* Washington, D.C.: IMF.

OECD Economic Surveys. *New Zealand.* Paris: OECD.

Web Sites:

Government entry point: **www.govt.nz**

Insurance Council of New Zealand: **www.icnz.org.nz**

Ministry of Economic Development: **www.med.govt.nz**

Ministry of Foreign Affairs and Trade: **www.mft.govt.nz**

New Zealand Herald (largest daily newspaper): **www.nzherald.co.nz**

New Zealand Stock Exchange: **www.nzse.co.nz**

Reserve Bank of New Zealand: **www.rbnz.govt.nz**

Statistics New Zealand: **www.stats.govt.nz**

Tourism New Zealand: **www.tourisminfo.govt.nz**

Trade New Zealand: **www.tradenz.govt.nz**

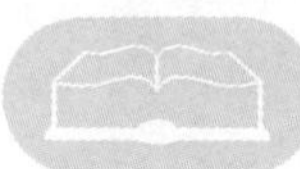

NIGERIA

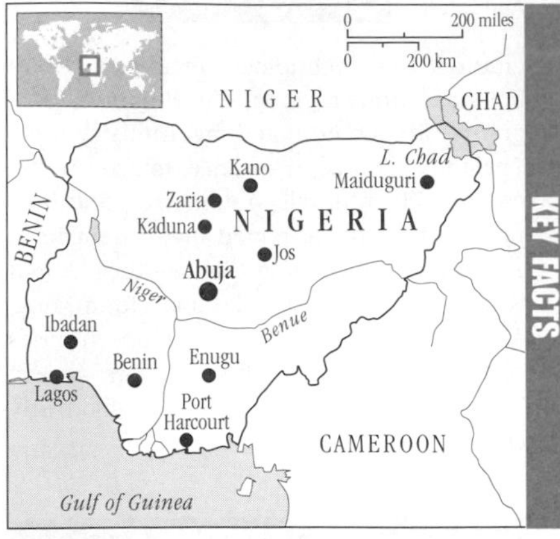

KEY FACTS

GNI: **$31,600 million; world's 57th**
GNI pc: **$260; world's 187th**
Head of government: **president**
Currency: **naira (N)**
Capital: **Abuja**
Population: **108,945,000, growing at 2.5% p.a.**
Land area: **351,660 square miles**
Population density: **310 per square mile**
Life expectancy: **50 years**
Infant mortality: **112 per 1,000 live births**
Language: **English, Hausa, Yoruba, Ibo, and other languages**
Best buy: **textiles, jewelry, carvings**

ECONOMIC STRUCTURE

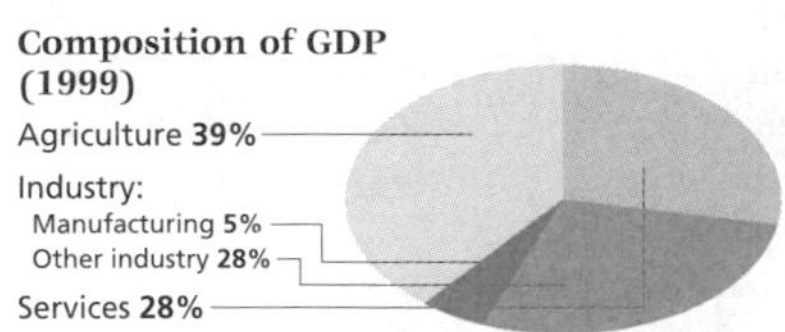

Africa's most populous country, Nigeria has undergone a series of political and economic upheavals since its independence in 1960. Having survived a civil war, in which the Ibos of the southeast sought to break away but were eventually forced to surrender in 1970, the country subsequently fell increasingly under the control of military rulers. Successive experiments with democracy tended to founder because of the interaction of complex regional, ethnic, and religious differences across the country. After the latest period of military dictatorship—under Generals Ibrahim Babangida (in power 1985–93) and Sani Abacha (in power 1993–98)—the country's reputation for economic mismanagement and corruption worsened considerably but, after the sudden death of Abacha in 1998, a new experiment with democracy was begun in 1999. A former military ruler, Olusegun Obasanjo, was voted in as president with declared objectives to root out corruption and to restore good economic management. The federal government is the dominant political force in the country, although there are also 36 state governments and about 800 local government areas.

Formerly reliant on its agricultural productivity and diversity, since the early 1970s the Nigerian economy has been dependent almost entirely on crude oil exports, and as a result has suffered a series of economic "booms and busts." Between 1972 and 1974 the federal government's earnings from oil jumped by a factor of five, and oil has ever since accounted for at least 65% of government revenues and 90% of national exports. While the domestic economy continued to be dominated by agriculture for many years, even this pattern has begun to change, with the oil industry now contributing 40% of GDP and agriculture only 28%. In addition, the manufacturing sector has not kept pace despite very heavy investment in industry in the 1970s and early 1980s. The contribution of manufacturing to GDP currently stands at only 4%.

The heavy financial influence of the government has tended to discourage the growth of a genuine private sector in Nigeria, and it has also undermined the efficiency and delivery of basic services. The government's accumulation of heavy foreign and domestic debts in the financing of projects, most of which failed to deliver financial returns, has also became a severe deterrent to new initiatives. A succession of financial and political crises in the 1980s and 1990s severely undermined investor confidence and, although there was a gradual liberalization of legislation governing foreign investment, the business climate failed to improve. Since the early 1980s, the only attraction for significant foreign investment has been in the oil and gas industry, and this pattern seems set to continue, especially as several major new finds of oil and gas have been made in offshore waters.

In the 1980s and 1990s there was only very limited privatization across the economy. The most significant withdrawal of government ownership occurred in the

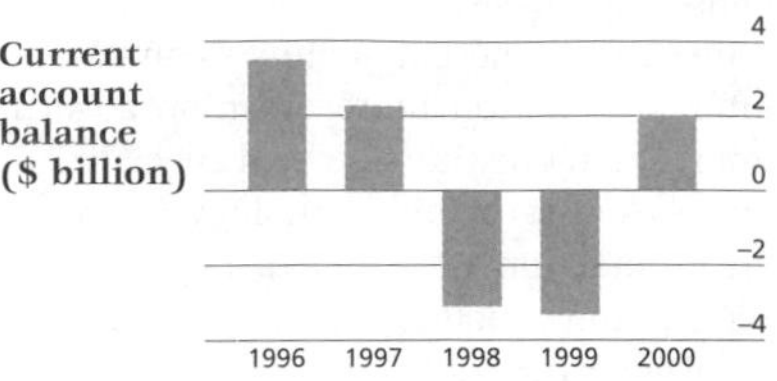

banking sector. The largest state-owned companies, and particularly the Nigerian National Petroleum Corporation (NNPC), the National Electric Power Authority (NEPA), and Nigeria Telecommunications (Nitel), persistently failed to perform the tasks for which they were established as monopoly providers. Although their continued existence was a matter of national pride for successive governments, their functioning tended to become distorted by political influences, which not only left the financial accounts of these state-owned companies in disarray, but also undermined any efforts to privatize them. In view of their controversial history, any sale of shares in these largest enterprises could be expected to prove equally contentious. Arrangements to privatize NEPA and Nitel were, however, beginning to move forward in early 2002.

ECONOMIC POLICY

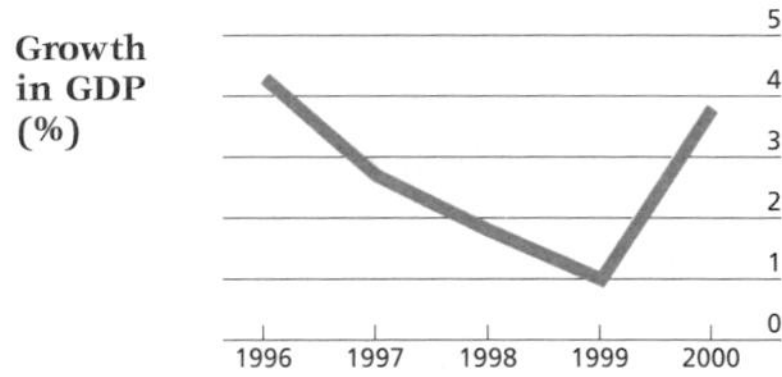

In the 1970s, Nigeria adopted methods of central planning for government-owned projects in nearly all the economic sectors. Most of these projects were designed on a large scale—with the hope of preparing Nigeria for intensive industrial and agricultural development—but they were subject to delays, inefficiency, and corruption in both their preparation and their realization. As a result the largest projects, including a multi-billion-dollar iron and steel complex and some petrochemicals plants, were incapable of starting production, although the fiction that they were "nearing completion" was maintained for many years. Many of the largest government investments collapsed and fell into disuse, including the steel rolling mills, vehicle assembly plants, and giant irrigation schemes in Nigeria's arid northern states. Debts

were payable on these projects even though they were failing to earn any revenue. Even the key facilities to generate electricity and to refine Nigeria's oil for the domestic fuel market were allowed to fall into disrepair.

Negotiations with the IMF and World Bank led to the first of Nigeria's structural adjustment programs, which was launched with a substantial devaluation of the naira in 1986. Import licensing and the allocation of foreign exchange were liberalized, and the agricultural marketing boards were abolished. Although these reforms helped to free up the business environment, they had very little impact on the real economy and failed to stimulate the intended development of non-oil exports. Manufacturing companies achieved some success in developing their local sources of raw materials, but the depressed domestic economy could not provide the essential growth in the market that would justify continuous reinvestment.

Economic management lapsed in the early 1990s, partly under the influence of the boost to oil prices provided by the Gulf War crisis, and partly in response to domestic political developments. Aborted elections in 1993 produced a new political crisis, followed by a change of government and a return to economic nationalism, with the imposition of fixed exchange and interest rates and a prolonged failure either to honor or to renegotiate the government's debt-service obligations. From 1996 there was a renewed statement of commitment to economic adjustment, although the key decisions on the most pressing structural matters were repeatedly deferred. The civilian government of President Obasanjo, which took office in May 1999, indicated its commitment to liberal market reforms but faced strong political opposition to any rapid implementation of its fuel price liberalization strategy and of its privatization program. Its declared policies in favor of making Nigeria a "fast-growth economy"—in which basic services would be improved and poverty would be eliminated—were not implemented.

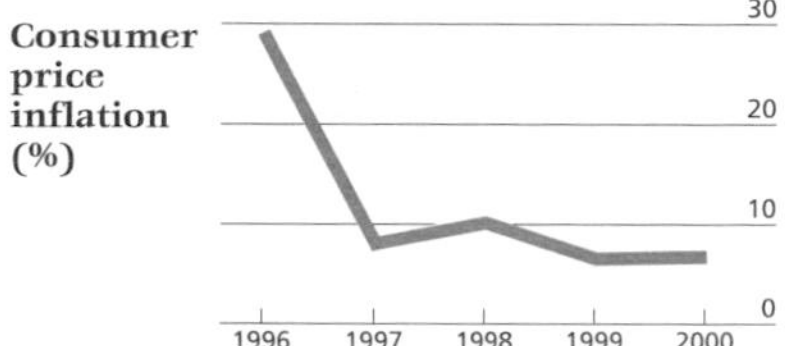

Economic growth was insignificant in the 1980s and averaged an annual rate of 2.7% in the 1990s. GNP per capita remained almost unchanged at little more than $300. GDP growth was recorded at 2.8% in both 1999 and 2000. Although oil exports flowed at maximum capacity, the economy continued to be depressed by deficient infrastructure, low non-oil investment, poor industrial capacity utilization, rising unemployment, and increasing poverty. Inflation, which was 30% in 1999, fell to 15% in 2000. The prevailing high interest rates began to fall somewhat in 2000. The value of the naira continued to slide in early 2001.

Geography/Resources

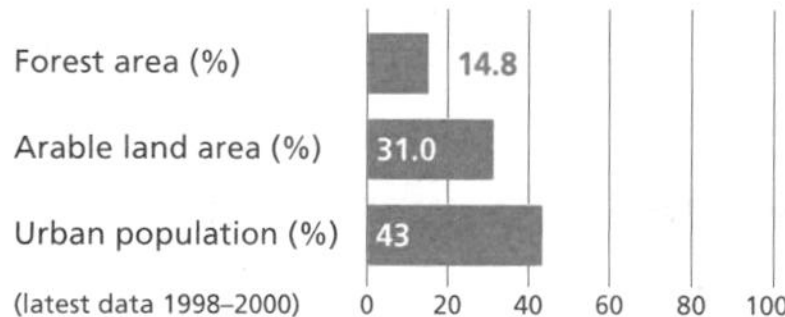

Nigeria encompasses the lower Niger-Benue basin and the Niger delta, with highlands rising along its eastern border with Cameroon and on the Jos plateau, which is surrounded by plains with large rocky outcrops. Toward the coastline, much of the land is low-lying at less than 1,000 feet. The climate is both equatorial and tropical, with high rainfall in the south, where there are two wet seasons, and a single rainy season followed by a long dry season in the north. There are many areas of high soil fertility throughout Nigeria. The vegetation ranges from mangrove and rain forests in the south to savannah and grassland in the north. Agricultural activity is widespread, predominantly conducted by traditional methods. There is also substantial livestock rearing, especially of cattle in the north.

The principal mineral resource is of hydrocarbons, both onshore and offshore from the Niger Delta. High-grade crude oil and natural gas are gathered from small wells, although much of the gas is simply burned off into the atmosphere. Solid minerals include tin, columbite, iron ore, coal, gold, and gemstones.

The population consists of about 250 ethnic groups, although ten of these constitute about 80% of the total—these are the Yoruba, Hausa, Fulani, Ibo, Ijaw, Kanuri, Tiv, Edo, Nupe, and Ibibio. Much of the population is concentrated in the southern part of the country, especially around the largest cities, which include Lagos, Ibadan, Benin, Port Harcourt and Enugu. There is also considerable density of population around Kano, the largest city of the north. The newly-built capital city of Abuja, located in the so-called Middle Belt, has grown rapidly since the early 1990s.

Communications/Energy

Nigeria has a fairly extensive road network, with about 22,500 miles having been paved. However, poor vehicle maintenance and low safety standards mean that the country has a very high accident rate. The antiquated railway network of 2,200 miles has undergone some piecemeal rehabilitation but provides very inefficient services. There are extensive daytime domestic air services between 11 airports in major cities, and there are three international airports at Lagos, Abuja, and Kano.

A privatization process for the telecommunications company Nitel commenced in 2001, and two mobile telephone companies were awarded licenses to start operations.

Electricity provision is in the hands of NEPA, which has been subject to persistent inefficiency and breakdown. Crucial generating facilities at the giant Kainji hydroelectric plant and the largest thermal power station at Egbin, Lagos, have been more often out of action than in service. Plans to restructure and privatize NEPA were being put together in 2001.

The oil industry is focused almost entirely on maintaining Nigeria's high level of exports. The NNPC has a joint venture stake of 60% in most of the production operations, which are run principally by Shell, Chevron, ExxonMobil, Texaco, TotalFinaElf, and Agip. Total national production has been close to 2 million barrels per day for several years. The government has awarded numerous new licenses to companies to develop both large offshore and small onshore fields. Natural gas exports have also begun to expand since the start of operations of the Shell-managed company Nigeria LNG.

Education/Employment

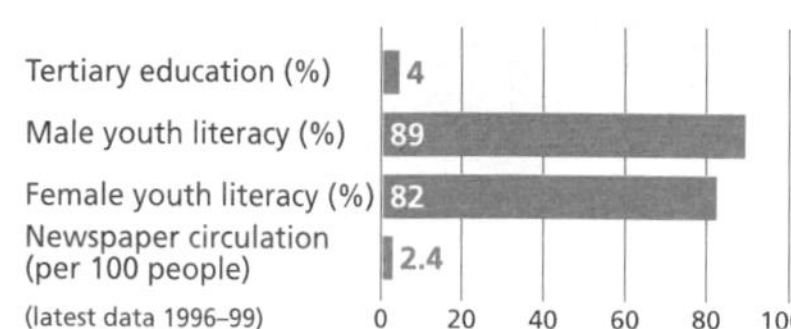

The federal and state systems of education suffered a sharp decline in recurrent and capital resources from 1982 onwards. Pri-

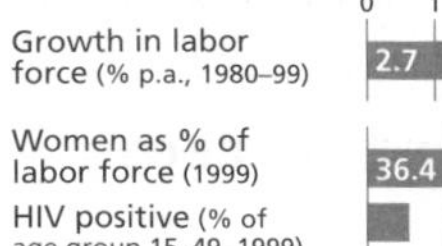

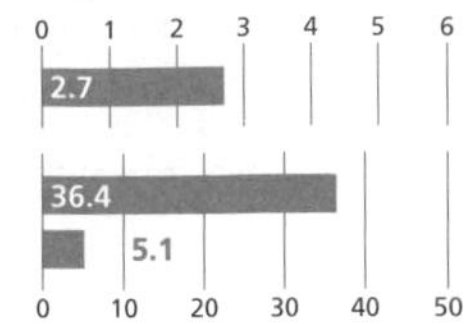

mary schooling has been maintained at a basic level, but the standards of secondary and tertiary education have tended to decline. Many of the country's best teachers have emigrated in search of higher salaries and better career prospects. Pupils in primary school numbered 16 million in 1994, while there were 4.4 million secondary students and 380,000 students in higher education.

The largest employment sectors are agriculture (about 40% of the economically active population), trade (about 25%), and government and other services (about 17%).

Fiscal/Financial

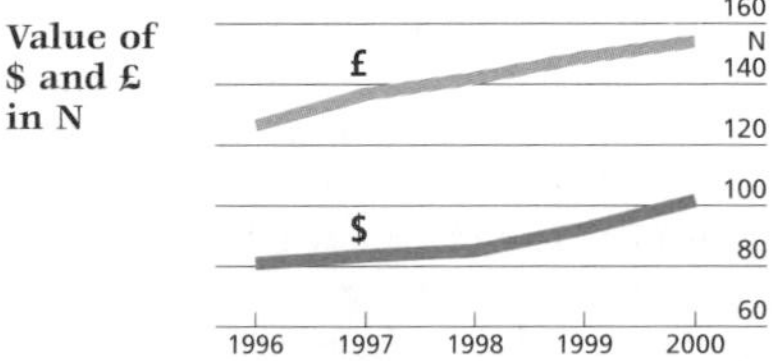

The Central Bank of Nigeria operates with a degree of independence from the federal government. The largest banks are United Bank of Nigeria, United Bank for Africa, and First Bank of Nigeria, all of which are predominantly Nigerian-owned. Several foreign-owned banks have operations in Nigeria. A universal banking system came into force in 2001 whereby banks can engage in unrestricted financial services without requiring specific commercial or merchant banking status.

After many years in the doldrums, the stock market began to recover strongly in the course of 2000, with a recovery in company profits and an increase in market capitalization. However, foreign portfolio investment in Nigeria remained extremely limited, and was considered unlikely to pick up until greater progress was made in the privatization program.

Attempts to rationalize the taxation system have tended to be undermined by the efforts of state governments to raise their own revenues and by popular resistance to the introduction of VAT. Levels of corporate taxation have been progressively reduced, but companies still have to pay for non-delivered services, such as electricity, and also have to spend heavily on providing these services for themselves. Such considerations have negated the effectiveness of official incentives offered to foreign investors.

Business Opportunities

Growth in output (% p.a., 1990–99)

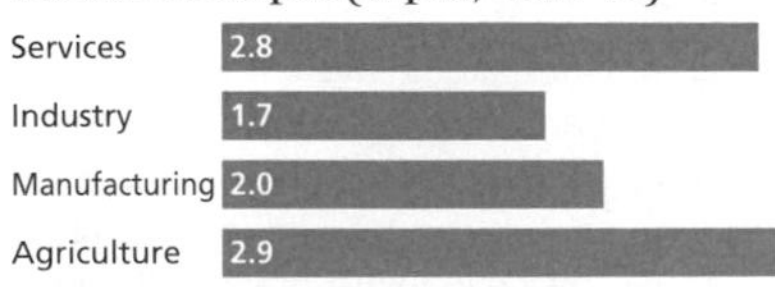

There would be good prospects for new investment on all fronts were a political and economic framework established within which Nigerians could agree to live. In the absence of this framework, the principal foreign investors have been, and will continue to be, the major oil companies, which are interested primarily in offshore oil and gas developments. Telecommunications companies have also shown some interest, and companies were awarded licenses to operate mobile services in 2001. Potential investors in other sectors hope for substantive improvements in the running of Nigeria's fuel and power infrastructure.

The long-term investment prospects are considerable across the whole spectrum of the Nigerian economy, whether in agriculture, manufacturing, distribution and retail, financial services, transportation, or tourism. Meanwhile, different areas of Nigeria are moving at different speeds, according to their location and relative economic power. Although the capitals of the states in the Niger delta that host onshore or offshore oil operations have assumed a strategic importance, the economic center of gravity continues to rest in Lagos, which remains Nigeria's dominant financial and industrial center.

For More Information

Books:

Beckett, P., and C. Young, eds. *Dilemmas of Democracy in Nigeria*. Rochester, NY: University of Rochester Press, 1997.

Enahoro, P. *The Complete Nigerian*. Lagos: Malthouse Press, 1992.

Falola, T., and J. Ihonvbere. *The Rise and Fall of Nigeria's Second Republic 1979–84*. London: Zed Books, 1985.

Forrest, T. *Politics and Economic Development in Nigeria*. Boulder, CO: Westview Press, 1993.

Maier, Karl. *This House Has Fallen: Nigeria in Crisis*. London: Allen Lane Penguin, 2001.

Omotoso, K. *Just before Dawn*. Ibadan: Spectrum Books, 1997.

Saro-Wiwa, K. *A Month and a Day: A Detention Diary*. New York: Penguin, 1996.

Web Sites:

African news and information: **www.allafrica.com/business**

Ernst and Young investment profiles: **www.mbendi.co.za/ernsty/cyaf.htm**

News: **www.gamji.com**

Nigeria Connections: **www.nigeriaconnections.net**

Norwegian Council for Africa, Index on Africa: **www.afrika.no/index**

Political Resources on the Net: **www.politicalresources.net**

NORTH KOREA

KEY FACTS

GNI pc: **$1,000 (approx.)**
Head of government: **president**
Currency: **won (Won)**
Capital: **Pyongyang**
Population: **23,702,000, growing at 1.6% p.a.**
Land area: **46,500 square miles**
Population density: **510 per square mile**
Life expectancy: **73 years**
Infant mortality: **23 per 1,000 live births**
Language: **Korean**
Best buy: **ginseng, cosmetics, textiles**

ECONOMIC STRUCTURE

Resource-rich North Korea was industrialized under Japanese colonial rule from 1910 to 1945. The division of the Korean peninsula between communism in the North and capitalism in the South from 1945 was unresolved by the 1950–53 Korean War, which devastated both countries. Aid from the Soviet Union and China helped rebuild the Northern economy with the focus on heavy industry, machinery, and weapons to provide self-reliance, or "juche." In the 1970s the government embarked on industrial modernization importing western technology, but defaulted on the debt. Nuclear weapons development, and terrorist incidents for which North Korea was blamed, added to the country's international isolation. North and South Korea have maintained an intermittent dialog since 1971. They signed a reconciliation agreement in 1992. In 1994 the government agreed with the United States to freeze its nuclear weapons development program in return for the construction of two nuclear power stations by 2003 and for the delivery of 500,000 tonnes of petroleum a year until then. The project, which also involves South Korea and the European Union, has been dogged by mistrust and delays but appeared to make some progress from 1999. Other inter-Korean projects made headway from 2000. Various countries restored diplomatic relations with North Korea in 2001, and the government signed international agreements against terrorism.

Industry was estimated to contribute 42% of GDP in 1999, followed by agriculture (30%), and services (28%). Military spending is an estimated 25–33% of GDP. Mining, metallurgy, and machinery (including armaments) are the leading industries. Chemicals, pharmaceuticals, cement, textiles, and food and timber processing are important. In 1999 the main exports were minerals, metal products, machinery, armaments, textiles, and food. The top market in 1995 was Japan, followed by South Korea, China, Germany, and Russia. Processing and assembly of goods for South Korean firms, microelectronics, and IT are growth sectors.

State-owned enterprises and collective farms account for an estimated 90% of GDP, and control is mostly centralized. Free enterprise farmers' markets have been permitted for several decades to increase food supplies. Reforms began in 1997 with the decentralization of some decision-making, decollectivization of some farms, and the creation of a private-sector trading zone at Wonjong. The Rajin-Sonbong free economic and trade zone, established in 1991, is now a model for change. It is included in the UNIDO-backed regional economic program for the Tumen River area (linking Russia, China, Mongolia, and North Korea). From 1997 state enterprises in the zone were granted more autonomy to form joint ventures with foreign private investors. A foreign investment law for the zone was enacted in 1999. By 1998 the zone had attracted $88 million in foreign investment, and there were 50 local light manufacturing firms established there. In 2000 agreements were signed with South Korea to set up free economic zones at Kaesong and Nampo, and joint ventures with South Korean private-sector companies elsewhere.

ECONOMIC POLICY

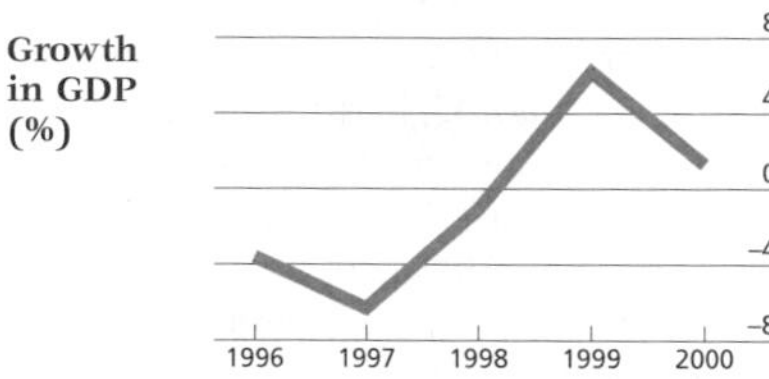

The economy is centrally planned, with five-year plans setting production and development targets and resource allocation. Prices, wages, and other monetary factors are fixed by the government in accordance with planning goals. Welfare is provided by state enterprises, collectives, government bodies, and state funds. Employment is regarded as essential to welfare. The won is non-convertible. Economic growth was an estimated 6.2% in 1999 and 1.3% in 2000, following year-on-year decline from 1990 as a result of the collapse of communism in the former states of the Soviet bloc, which were the main trading partners.

GEOGRAPHY/RESOURCES

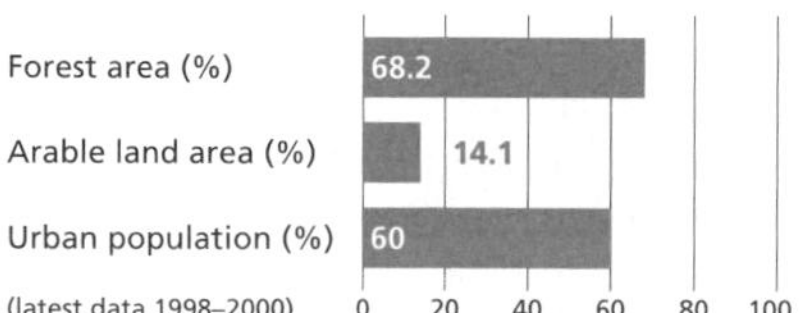

The Democratic Peoples' Republic of Korea occupies the northern half of the Korean peninsula, bordering South Korea to the south, Russia to the extreme northeast, China to the north, the Sea of Japan to the east, and the Korea Bay and Yellow Sea to the west. About 80% of the land is rugged mountains with a high point of 9,003 feet. In the east there is a narrow intermittent coastal plain, and in the west there are hills interspersed with deep valleys and plains. Winters are long, cold, and dry, and summers short, wet, and humid.

Rice is the main agricultural crop. Natural calamities, and a lack of fertilizers and machinery parts have left a shortfall of around 1 million tons a year, which has been met by food aid. Other crops include potatoes, corn, wheat, barley, soya, cotton, tobacco, and hemp. Poultry is the main livestock, followed by pigs, goats, cattle, and sheep. Arable land accounts for 14% of the total surface area, permanent crops for 2%, forests for 61%, and other land for 23%. Forestry and fishing are important.

North Korea is estimated to have nearly half of world magnesite reserves, 661 million tons of coal (1996), 400 million tons of iron ore (1993), and over 1,000 tons of gold. Other minerals produced include zinc, lead, tungsten, mercury, copper, bentonite, graphite, uranium, manganese, phosphates, sulfur, silver, fluorite, barite, limestone, talc, and apatite. Joint development of a tantalum mine was agreed by North and South Korea in mid-2001. Other joint mining projects include feldspar and potassium. Offshore exploration in the Korea Bay has indicated the presence of oil.

Communications/Energy

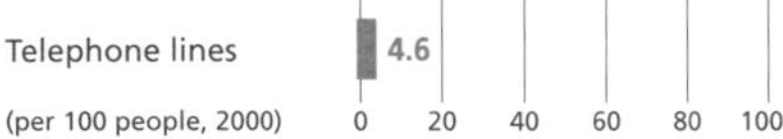

The railway network was 3,240 miles in 1997, 78% of which was electrified. It is the main means of transport for freight, carrying 74% in 1997. It links with the Chinese and Russian railways. Work began in 2001 to restore the rail and road links with South Korea. The 19,000-mile road network is only 8% paved. It included 424 miles of motorways in 1997. There are 14,000 miles of navigable inland waterways. The main sea ports are at Nampo, Songnim, Haeju, Wonsan, Chongjin, and Hungnam (for Hamhung). There is an international airport at Sunnan for Pyongyang. Another is under construction for the Rajin-Sonbong economic zone. There are plans to upgrade the domestic airport at Hamhung for international traffic.

State-owned Korea Posts and Telecommunications Corporation is the main operator. Northeast Asia Telephone and Telecommunications, a joint-venture with Thai private-sector company Loxley Pacific, is developing the telecommunications for the Rajin-Sonbong economic zone, including a fiberoptic cable link to China, mobile and fixed telephony, a pager system, and Internet connections. Elsewhere international links are via satellite only with relatively high charges. In 1995 there were 1.1 million fixed-line phones.

Severe electricity shortages curtailed manufacturing and distribution in the 1990s in a vicious circle, since coal for power stations is delivered by electrified railways. Generating capacity is divided equally between coal and hydroelectricity, but hydro plants have been affected by drought. Coal accounted for 77% of primary energy in 1999, followed by hydro (13%) and imported oil (10%). Net coal imports are 3% of consumption. Electricity consumption in 1999 was 55% of the 1991 level. Hydro contributed 65% of production, followed by thermal (35%). An oil-fired power station serves the Rajin-Sonbong economic zone, and similar projects are planned for new economic zones and for the capital Pyongyang. Electricity supply from South Korea will not be practicable until the North Korean grid is upgraded. The first of the four nuclear power stations is scheduled for completion in 2008, unless there are further delays. The construction of a natural gas pipeline from Russia's Kovykta field through China and North Korea to South Korea is under discussion.

Education/Employment

Education is compulsory and free for 11 years from age 5 to 16. There are over 500 higher education institutes, including universities and specialized colleges for IT, science, engineering, medicine, and other disciplines. Adult education, including IT, is strongly encouraged and supported at factory and farmers' colleges, at special schools, and in distance learning, with the result that most people are in education, and the literacy rate is 99%. The Ministry of Education is responsible for education policy, management and funding. North and South Korea agreed in 2001 to establish the Pyongyang College of Information, Science, and Technology. Universities, specialized colleges, and enterprises have research facilities and staff. Military research is well funded. Other R&D areas include metallurgy, chemicals, pharmaceuticals and traditional medicine, textiles, and machinery. New areas of R&D conducted in cooperation with South Korea include IT, microelectronics, and agriculture.

The labor force is well educated and accustomed to updating its skills. Technical training is required from foreign investors. The government sets minimum wages and other conditions of employment. Detailed wage levels and other employment matters are negotiated between employers and trade unions.

Fiscal/Financial

There were six state banks in 1998. Until the 1970s the Central Bank, Farmers' Bank and Foreign Trade Bank conducted all financial transactions. The seven banks formed with overseas Korean residents and foreign finance houses following the 1984 Joint-Venture Act handle foreign exchange, external trade, and inward foreign investment.

Two foreign banks were set up following the 1993 Foreign Investment Banking Act. The State Insurance Bureau and Korea Foreign Insurance Company are the main insurance companies, both state-owned. The government regulates the financial system. There is no stock market.

Standard corporation tax is 25%, but this is reduced to 10–14% for foreign companies in the Rajin-Sonbong economic zone. Foreign managers and technicians in the zone pay a top rate of 20% personal income tax. There is a 20% withholding tax on royalties, interest, and dividends. Sales taxes apply except for exported goods.

Business Opportunities

Tax incentives and infrastructure facilities are offered to foreign investors. Red tape and the backwardness of most infrastructure areas constitute barriers to foreign investment. Chemicals, mining, automotive, IT, pharmaceuticals, beverages, fish processing, tourism, finance, and telecommunications have attracted inward investment from South Korea, the United Kingdom, Sweden, Australia, and Thailand, among other countries. Further opportunities exist in these sectors, plus utilities, building materials, timber processing, textiles, leather goods, paper, and electric and electronic goods. The point of contact for investors is the National Economic Cooperation Federation.

For More Information

Book:

Smith, H., et al., eds. *North Korea in the New World Order*. New York: Palgrave Macmillan, 1996.

Web Sites:

Korea Central News Agency: **www.cna.co.jp**

Korea Web Weekly (North and South Korea): **www.kimsoft.com/korea.htm**

Ministry of Unification (South Korea): **www.unikorea.go.kr**

  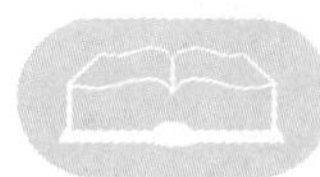    

NORTHERN MARIANAS

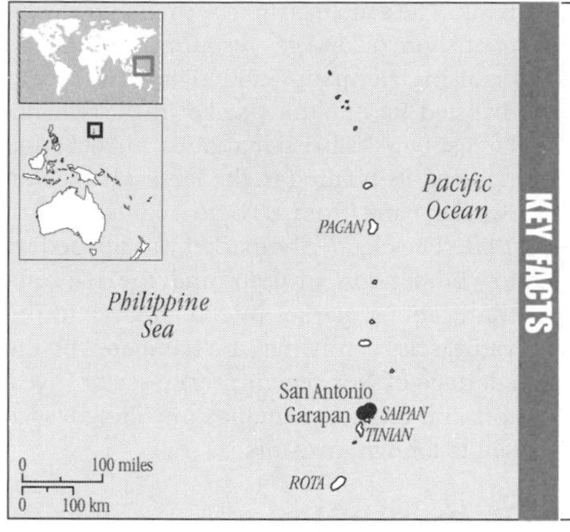

GNI pc: **$11,500 (approx.)**
Head of government: **governor**
Currency: **U.S. dollar ($)**
Capital: **Saipan**
Population: **75,300**
Land area: **184 square miles**
Population density: **409 per square mile**
Language: **English (official), Chamorro, Carolinian**
Best buy: **duty-free goods, Tinian hot chili pepper sauce**

ECONOMY

From the mid-1990s garment manufacturing took over from tourism as the main economic activity. In the early 1990s tourism and related trade, especially in duty free goods, contributed 50% of GDP and provided 45% of paid jobs. Over 70% of garment industry workers are foreign (mostly Chinese), which contributed to a jump in local unemployment from 6.6% in 1990 to 16.1% in 1999. The low wages in the garment industry and alleged labor malpractices by the employers are currently the subject of a major U.S. lawsuit filed by human rights groups, casting doubt over the sector's future. Garments exports to the United States, worth over $1 billion a year in 1998 and 1999, account for almost all export earnings. Some vegetables and meat are exported. Tinian is a major fish transshipment center, with processing facilities at the harbor. Tourism declined in 1997–98 because of the Japanese recession. Construction employs around 18% of the workforce.

The economy receives U.S. aid for infrastructure projects, but the government must find matching funds. Economic decline in the late 1990s left the government unable to produce matching funds until it launched a bond in 2001. Many projects were delayed. The government drew up a multi-annual capital investment program in 1999, including school and library improvements, and port, power, and road projects. In 1998 it launched a task force to broaden the economy and its own receipts, as lost revenues from the tourism industry were not offset by the export fees levied on the garment industry. Sectors targeted for expansion include banking and insurance, the import-export trade, and new areas of tourism, such as Tinian's casino which opened in 1995, and eco-tourism and golf on Rota.

GEOGRAPHY/RESOURCES

The Northern Marianas consist of 14 islands, six of which are inhabited. They are volcanic or limestone. The highest land point, 3,166 feet on Agrihan, is 32,800 feet if measured from the ocean floor. The northern islands have active volcanoes. Other hazards are earthquakes and cyclones (August to December). The climate is tropical, with an average temperature of 80°F and average rainfall of around 60 inches. Coconuts, breadfruit, tomatoes, melons, beef, and pork constitute the main agricultural products. There is a small commercial fishing industry. Volcanic ash from the island of Pagan has been mined as an additive to cement. The population more than tripled from 1980 to 1995.

COMMUNICATIONS/ENERGY

In the early 1990s the islands' road network was 200 miles. Road construction and upgrading are ongoing, including four-lane highways to major tourist areas on Saipan. There are commercial sea ports on Saipan, Rota, and Tinian. There is also a U.S. navy base at Tinian. The international airport is at Saipan, with domestic airports at Tinian and Rota. Undersea fiberoptic cables and satellite links provide the full range of modern digital telecommunications, including the Internet, integrated voice and data systems, mobile and fixed-line phones, fax, and paging systems. There are seven telecommunications companies. There were 21,000 fixed phone lines in 1996 and 1,200 mobile phones in 1995. Electricity is generated by diesel. There are two power plants on the island of Saipan, one on Tinian, and one on Rota. Petroleum products for electricity and other energy needs are imported.

FISCAL/FINANCIAL

Basic U.S. tax rules apply as well as local taxes. However, tax exemptions or reductions apply to specific industries. Notably, the garment industry pays no corporation tax. There are ten commercial local and foreign banks. There are several finance companies, security brokers, trust companies, remittance companies, and foreign exchange dealers. The sector is internationalized and there is no restriction on repatriation of funds. In 1998 there were 49 licensed insurers conducting on- and offshore business. The local government regulates the finance and insurance sectors in accordance with U.S. rules. Monetary policy is set in the United States. There is no local stock market.

BUSINESS OPPORTUNITIES

Textiles, banking, insurance, telecommunications, import-export trade, and tourism have attracted foreign investment and—with the possible exception of textiles—still offer opportunities. The point of contact for foreign investors is the Commonwealth Development Authority.

For More Information

Books:

The State of the Islands Report. Washington, D.C.: U.S. Department of the Interior, Office of Insular Affairs.

Willens, Howard P., and Deanne C. Siemer. *An Honorable Accord.* Honolulu, HI: University of Hawaii Press, 2001.

Web Sites:

CNMI Guide: **www.cnmi-guide.com**

Commonwealth Development Authority: **www.cda.gov.mp**

Government entry point: **www.saipan.com/gov**

NORWAY

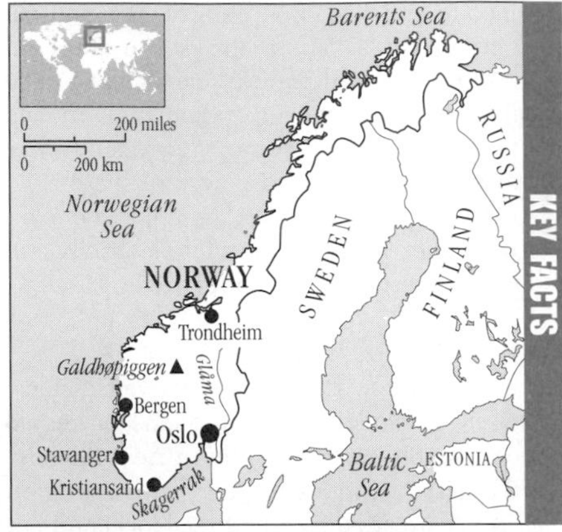

KEY FACTS

GNI: **$149,280 million; world's 26th**
GNI pc: **$33,470; world's 5th**
Head of government: **prime minister**
Currency: **Norwegian krone (NKr)**
Capital: **Oslo**
Population: **4,442,000, growing at 0.5% p.a.**
Land area: **118,485 square miles**
Population density: **37 per square mile**
Life expectancy: **78 years**
Infant mortality: **4 per 1,000 live births**
Language: **Norwegian**
Best buy: **knitwear, pewter, silver and enamel jewelry**

ECONOMIC STRUCTURE

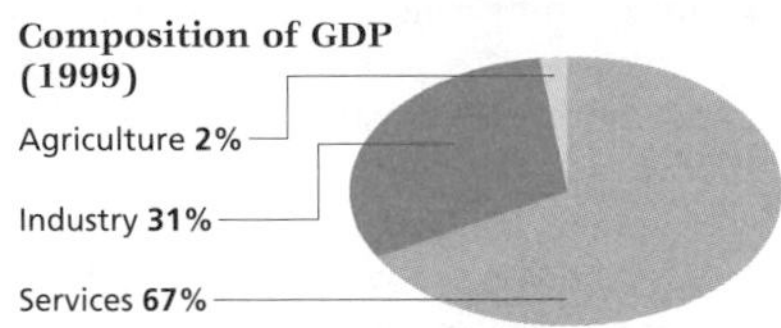

Norway has been a seafaring nation of explorers and traders since early history. In the mid-nineteenth century Norwegians owned the third-largest merchant fleet in the world, a position they still hold today. Economic wealth came also from indigenous raw materials, especially metals and timber, and the products made from them. The dependence on trade and raw materials made the country vulnerable to swings in the world economy. After World War II the government took control of the reconstruction effort and established the welfare state. Since the early 1970s oil and natural gas have made Norway one of the richest nations in the world through the government's careful management of the sector. Norway is a member of the European Economic Area, which also includes the European Union, Iceland, and Liechtenstein.

Services accounted for 51.2% of GDP in 2000, followed by oil and gas (23.4%), manufacturing (9.1%), and agriculture, fisheries and forestry (1%). Private-sector services contributed 36.7% and government services 14.5%. Trade is the leading services sector, followed by finance and real estate, transport, and business services. The manufacturing sector includes refined oil products, petrochemicals, metal industries and engineering, fish and food processing, timber, and paper products. Engineering specialties include oil rigs and other oil and gas equipment. The state-owned oil and gas company Statoil is active in hydrocarbons exploration, production, and transport in various parts of the world as well as in Norwegian territory. Norway has a large share of the world's gas, oil, and chemicals tankers, and of cruise ships. The main exports in 2000 were crude oil, gas, and refined oil products (63.9%), manufactured goods (11.2%), machinery and transport equipment (including motor vehicles and components and specialized ships: 9.4%), food, especially fish (6.3%), and chemicals (4.9%). The main export market was the U.K. (20.7%), followed by Netherlands (11.4%), Germany (10.3%), France (10%), and Sweden (8.4%). The EU absorbed 76.8% of exports.

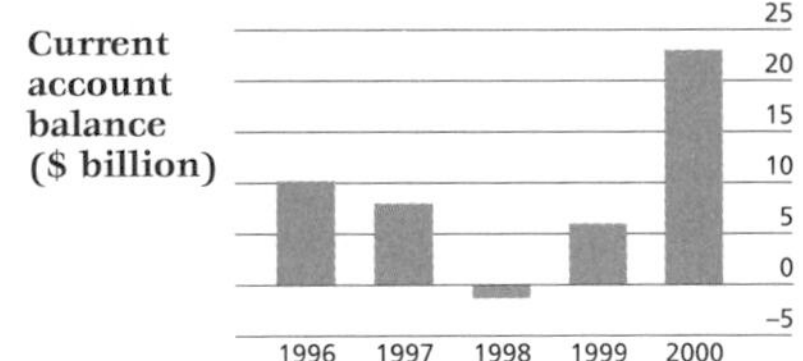

There is extensive government involvement in industry and banking, including direct control of the five largest entities in the Norwegian economy, and investment in other companies through state bank financing. In early 2001 the main direct state shareholdings were in the hydrocarbons production and sales company Statoil (partly privatized in 2001); Norsk Hydro (a diversified conglomerate with interests in fertilizers, chemicals, oil, gas, metals, biomedicine and aquaculture); telecommunications company Telenor (partly privatized in 2000); electricity producer Statkraft; and the country's largest bank Den Norske Bank. The state has direct ownership of 40% of offshore oil and gas resources through the licensing company SDFI. The government divested its one-third stake in the second-largest bank, Christiana Bank, in 2000, and reduced its holding in the largest bank Den Norske Bank from 60% to 46.6% in April 2001. The electricity market was opened up to competition in 1997 and the telecommunications market in 2001. Moves to privatize state companies are hampered by the shortage of Norwegian private-sector investors and the government's unwillingness to sell to foreign investors.

ECONOMIC POLICY

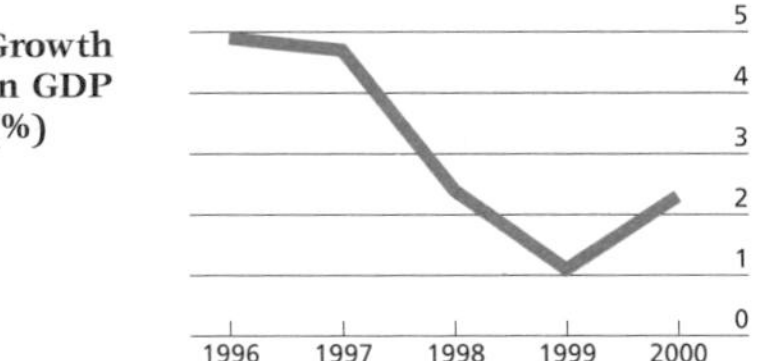

Economic policy is geared towards maintaining a stable exchange rate (especially between the krone and the Euro) via an inflation target of 2.5%, and towards a judicious rise in public spending and wages along with an easing of the tax burden to meet voter aspirations without overheating the economy. The crushing defeat of the Labor government in the October 2001 elections delivered a strong message from voters that public spending, especially on education, health and the elderly, was insufficient and that taxes were too high.

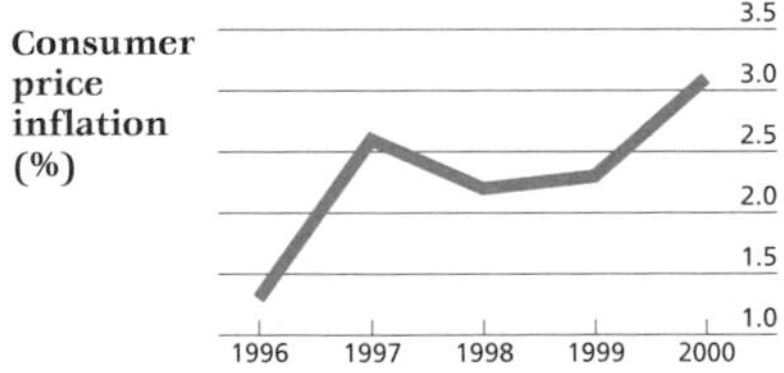

Annual budget surpluses from oil revenues, which were a comfortable 5.3% of GDP in 1997–99, shot up to 15.75% in 2000–01 because of high oil prices. Part of the surpluses has been invested in the Petroleum Fund to finance future pensions. The Fund, which had assets of $60 billion in 2001, is mostly invested in foreign markets. Public spending on healthcare and education rose rapidly in the 1990s, and taxes were increased to cover part of the cost. These, coupled with above-inflation wage rises since the mid-1990s, pushed up labor costs.

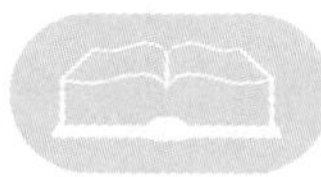

Taxes may be trimmed but wages are ikely to remain relatively high as a result of public pressure and labor shortages in some skills.

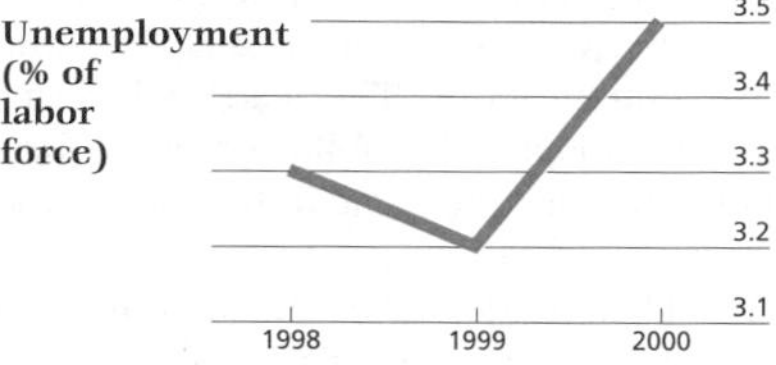

The long-term goal to reduce dependence on the oil and gas sector seems unlikely to be achieved in the medium term, and the economy will continue to fluctuate according to world oil prices. There was severe recession from 1986 to 1993, followed by a boom until 1998 with GDP growth averaging over 4% a year. Growth fell to 0.8% in 1999, due to tight labor market conditions and other capacity constraints, but revived to 2.3% in 2000–01 because of strong oil prices, and is expected to reach 3% in 2002. Annual average inflation rose from 2.3% in 1998–99 to 3.1% in 2000–01. Most new jobs in recent years were created in public-sector services, especially in health and education. Unemployment fell from 6.1% in 1993 to 3.4% in 2000–01.

Geography/Resources

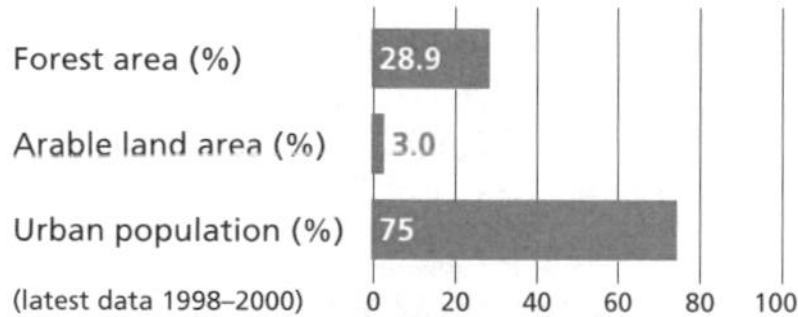

In the extreme northwest of Europe, Norway occupies the western third of the Scandinavian peninsula, with the North Sea and Skagerrak strait to the south, the Atlantic Ocean to the west, and the Arctic Ocean and Barents Sea to the north. Norway shares land borders with Russia, Finland, and Sweden. Its territory also includes the Svalbard (Spitzbergen) archipelago and Jan Mayen Island in the Arctic Ocean. Mainland Norway is mountainous, with an immensely long coastline because of the fjords and thousands of islands. About one-third of the land is in the Arctic Circle. Forest covers 23% of the land, and only 3.5% is farmed. The climate is milder than that of most such northern countries because of the Atlantic Gulf Stream. It is also very wet.

Livestock and dairy produce are the main focus of agriculture, but cereals, potatoes, and other crops are grown. Fisheries are important, especially fish farming of trout and salmon as sea fishing has declined. The main mineral resources are offshore petroleum and natural gas. Proven reserves of oil and gas at January 2001 were 9.4 billion barrels and 44 trillion cubic feet respectively, providing several decades of output without any new finds. Cumulative oil extraction from the Norwegian Continental Shelf by end-1999 was estimated to be one-third of reserves, and gas production only 9%. Exploration continues, especially in the Barents Sea. There are considerable reserves of copper and zinc, and lesser amounts of iron ore, lead, and coal, all of which are mined. There are also reserves of molybdenum, nickel, titanium, talc, olivine, dolomite, quartzite, and limestone.

The majority of the population is homogeneously Scandinavian; there are distinct communities of Lapps and Finns in the north. Less than half the population live in major towns, and the average population density is only 37 people per square mile. Many communities are isolated by the mountains, and rely on ferry and jetfoil transport.

Communications/Energy

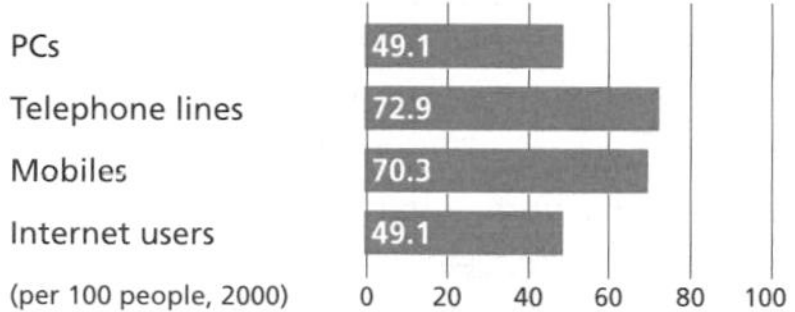

There are 56,386 miles of roads, including 66 miles of highways and 16,536 miles of national main roads. The rail network is 2,499 miles, 1,526 miles of which is electrified, but only 81 miles is double track. There are 54 airports which take scheduled flights. The main international airports are at Oslo, Bergen, and Stavanger. In 1999 there were 4,430 Norwegian-registered ships, totaling 22.8 million grt. The Norwegian-owned fleet for foreign operations numbered 1,687 ships, totaling 49.8 million grt in September 2000. Shipping carried 22.7% of domestic freight (excluding offshore oil and gas and supplies) in 1998, while roads accounted for 28.1% and rail 4.3%. However, 86.7% of passengers traveled by road, against 6.9% by air, 5% by rail, and 1.4% by ship.

At end-2000 there were 3.3 million fixed phone lines, 3.2 million mobile phones, and 2.2 million Internet users, several hundred thousand of whom had ISDN links. The telecommunications sector was opened to competition in 1997, but the state-owned company Telenor remains the main operator. In 2001 Telenor became the world's largest mobile phone satellite provider following its acquisition of COMSAT from U.S. firm Lockheed Martin Global Telecommunications. IT and Internet penetration is one of the highest in the world according to analysis bureau IDC. Retail and construction companies are actively pursuing e-commerce. In early 2001 there were 800,000 cable TV subscribers, with a high proportion of users belonging to networks owned by housing cooperatives and other non-trading groups.

Norway is one of the largest net oil and gas exporters in the world. Oil output was 3.3 million barrels per day, with net exports of 3.1 million barrels per day in 2000. Gas production was 1.8 trillion cubic feet in 1999, 1.6 trillion cubic feet of which was exported. Gas exports to Europe are expected to triple from 1999 levels by 2005. Hydroelectric power accounts for 99% of domestic electricity, but most new power plants will be gas-fired since Norway needs to import electricity in low-rainfall years. Norway exports and imports electricity through the grid link with Sweden. Coal production on Spitzbergen was 400,000 tons in 1999, most of which was used to supply the power plant there. There are plans to increase coal output and electricity to raise Spitzbergen's level of energy self-sufficiency.

Education/Employment

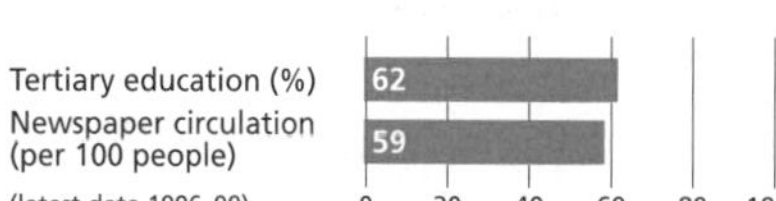

Education is compulsory from age 6 to 15. From 1994–95 all students aged 16–19 have the right to upper secondary education, which includes apprenticeship and other vocational studies. The Ministry of Education is responsible for universities and university colleges, while the National Education Office and local authorities are responsible for adult education and schools. There is academic and administrative autonomy at the college level. The state finances most tertiary education, with the exception of some private university colleges. There are 11 universities and specialized university institutions, 26 state university colleges (offering mainly shorter vocational courses), and 45 higher education colleges. In 1998–99 there were 81,128 students enrolled at university level and 102,935 students in other colleges. The government is promoting adult education to provide the new skills needed in industry.

The universities, university institutions and state university colleges conduct R&D. The Research Council of Norway coordinates R&D strategy for basic and applied re-

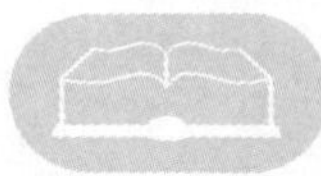

search. Norway takes part in EU R&D programs. In 1997 industry accounted for 47% of R&D spending, while universities and colleges contributed 27% and other organizations 26%, but total R&D spending was under 2% of GDP. Norway has particular R&D strengths in shipping, deep-sea minerals exploration and production, marine biology, energy, environmental technology, and IT connected with all of these.

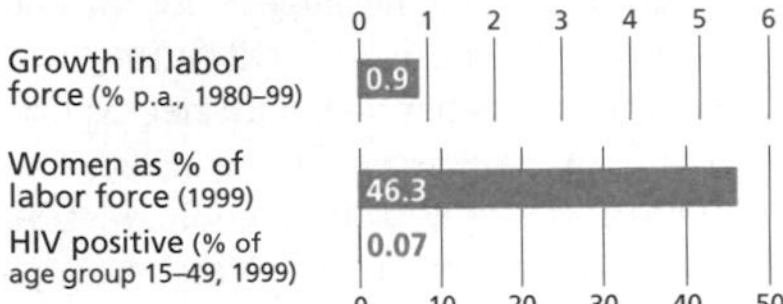

The labor force is well educated and adaptable, with a high participation of women and older people. Framework agreements for wages and employment conditions are determined at the national level by government, employers, and trade unions, and specific agreements are negotiated at industry level. Labor laws have been protective of workers' rights, but greater flexibility has been introduced in recent years, with greater recourse to temporary contracts. Retirement age is 67, higher than in most OECD countries.

Fiscal/Financial

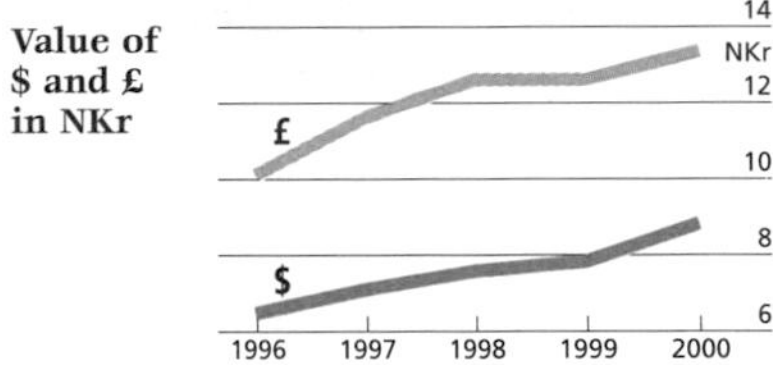

The largest bank is Den Norske Bank (46.6% state-owned). The second largest, Christiana Bank, merged with the Swedish-Finnish-Danish banking group Nordea after the government sold its minority stake. Nordea is the largest financial group in Scandinavia. The third bank, Union Bank of Norway, the largest savings bank, is due to be demutualized. Storebrand, the largest insurance company, is partly state-owned, as is finance and insurance group Orkla. The state also owns investment funds. The central bank Norges Bank executes monetary policy. Supervision of the banking, insurance, and stock exchange sectors is conducted by the Banking, Insurance, and Securities Commission.

Combined state and municipal corporation tax is 28%. Depreciation of fixed assets varies from zero to 25% depending on the type of asset. Withholding tax of 25% is applied to dividends paid by Norwegian companies to non-resident companies and individuals. The top marginal income tax rate is 55.3%. In 2001 a 14% dividend tax was introduced and the standard VAT rate was raised by 1% to 24%. Reduced VAT of 12% applies to food and other essential items.

The finance sector underwent consolidation in the 1990s, but Norwegian banks and insurance companies remain small by international standards. Further consolidation among the top banking and insurance groups is likely, but an agreed bid by Finland's Sampo for Storebrand was blocked by the government in 2001. The investment finance market has been sophisticated and international for many years because of government investments from the proceeds of oil, and because of the oil and shipping industries which attract international investors. The use of equity finance and venture capital is increasing in non-oil sectors. Banks have formed joint ventures with supermarkets for e-banking and e-commerce.

The Oslo Stock Exchange (OSE) was privatized in summer 2001. The Oslo exchange joined the Norex alliance with the Stockholm and Copenhagen bourses in 1999. It introduced electronic trading that year, and securities trading increased by 38.3%. Total derivatives turnover rose by 107%. Market surveillance rules were tightened. Statoil became the largest company on the OSE following the share floatation in June 2001, pushing state telecoms company Telenor, which was listed in December 2000, into second place. Total share values were $57 billion at October 2001.

Business Opportunities

Growth in output (% p.a., 1990–99)

Services	3.6
Industry	4.2
Agriculture	2.6

The Norwegian Industrial and Regional Development Fund (SND) provides equity capital, low-risk loans, venture capital, grants, and guarantees to Norwegian-based companies. It has two internationally-oriented funds for companies investing in northwest Russia and Central and Eastern Europe. The government has demonstrated a negative attitude to foreign investment in strategic entities such as financial institutions. The main foreign investment sectors in 1995–99 were hydrocarbons and mining, followed by finance, manufacturing, trade, hotels and restaurants, construction, transport, and telecommunications. The leading investor was the United States, followed by Netherlands, Sweden, the United Kingdom, and France.

The liberalization of the telecommunications, electricity, and financial markets offers investment opportunities. Expansion of gas and oil production and distribution will create new business in several different sectors. Other opportunities include intensified deep-sea hydrocarbons exploration, the negotiation of cooperation agreements with Russia for the exploitation the Barents Sea reserves, and privatization of state organizations. The Norwegian Trade Council is the point of contact for foreign investors.

For More Information

Books:

Derry, T. K. *A History of Scandinavia: Norway, Sweden, Denmark, Finland and Iceland*. Minneapolis, MN: University of Minnesota Press, 1979.
Elder, N., A. H. Thomas, and D. Arter. *The Consensual Democracies? The Government and Politics of Scandinavian States*. Malden, MA: Blackwell, 1988.
Miles, L., ed. *The European Union and the Nordic Countries*. New York: Routledge, 1996.

Web Sites:

Aftenposten (daily newspaper, includes online English version): **www.aftenposten.no**
Dagbladet (daily newspaper, includes financial news): **www.dagbladet.no**
Norges Bank (central bank): **www.norges-bank.no**
Norwegian Financial Services Association: **www.fnh.no**
Norwegian government entry point: **www.odin.dep.no**
Norwegian Trade Council (government agency): **www.ntc.no**
Oslo Stock Exchange: **www.ose.no**
Statistics Norway: **www.ssb.no**
Statoil (oil company Web site in English): **www.statoil.com**

OMAN

KEY FACTS

GDP: **$15,000 million (approx.)**
GDP pc: **$6,100 (approx.)**
Head of government: **the Sultan**
Currency: **Omani rial (OR)**
Capital: **Muscat**
Population: **2,460,000, growing at 3.6% p.a.**
Land area: **82,046 square miles**
Population density: **30 per square mile**
Life expectancy: **71 years**
Infant mortality: **14 per 1,000 live births**
Language: **Arabic, English**
Best buy: **consumer goods, dates, spices**

ECONOMY

Under Sultan Qaboos's leadership Oman has moved from feudal sultanate to modern state. The country's oil wealth is being used to modernize infrastructure and to diversify from oil into manufacturing for export (including gas-based LNG, chemicals and fertilizers, and a range of finished goods), logistics for the Middle East region, and tourism. In 2000 oil accounted for 49% of GDP, 77% of government revenues, and 90% of exports. Other exports included LNG, fish, metals and textiles. The main manufacturing industries were oil and copper refining, cement, and LNG. Government services and agriculture were the main sources of employment for Omanis. When current oil reserves run dry in 2020, the government intends oil to contribute 9% of GDP, gas 10%, and non-oil industry 29%.

Privatization and foreign investment are key to this plan, as is "Omanization" to ensure that the growing Omani workforce has sufficient jobs. The government is strengthening commercial law to comply with World Trade Organization rules. Oman joined the WTO in 2000. Public and private foreign ownership has worked successfully in the oil and gas sectors, port management, and power stations. The privatization program includes the rest of the electricity network, airports, and telecommunications operator Omantel.

GEOGRAPHY/RESOURCES

Oman borders Yemen, Saudi Arabia, U.A.E., the Gulf of Oman, and the Arabian Sea. Most of the land is low-lying desert. Spectacular scenery and beaches offer considerable tourism potential.

Oman produces around half of its food needs. Dates are the main agricultural crop, followed by vegetables, other fruit, cereals, and tobacco. Meat, dairy, and fish are important. Proven oil reserves were 5.5 billion barrels, and gas reserves were 29.3 trillion cubic feet at January 2001. New oil and gas discoveries in 2001 could significantly increase reserves. Gold, limestone, copper, marble, gypsum, chromite, silver, and salt are produced. There are large coal reserves.

COMMUNICATIONS/ENERGY

The 20,400-mile road network includes 340 miles of expressways. The pipeline network—800 miles for crude oil and 640 miles for natural gas—is being extended. Port Salalah, one of the world's largest container ports, handled 1 million teus in 2000, mostly in transshipment trade between Asia and Europe. Mina al-Fahal is the second port. Both handle oil exports and general cargo. A new port at Sohar is under construction for gas. The two international airports at Muscat and Salalah are being expanded. Telecommunications links are provided by cable, satellite, microwave radio relay, and radiotelephone. At end-2000 there were 225,000 fixed phone lines, 164,000 mobile phones, and 90,000 Internet users.

Oil production was 946,000 barrels per day in 2000, with 893,000 barrels per day in net exports and 53,000 barrels per day in domestic consumption. Production is due to rise to 1million barrels per day by 2003. Oil is refined for domestic use and export. Gas output and consumption were 197 billion cubic feet and 181 billion cubic feet respectively in 1999. LNG was exported for the first time in 2000. New private-sector gas-fired power plants are coming onstream by end-2003 to meet the 5% a year growth in electricity demand.

FISCAL/FINANCIAL

The largest local commercial bank at end-2000 was Bank Muscat (total assets $3.4 billion), followed by Oman International Bank, National Bank of Oman, Oman Arab Bank, Bank Dhofar Al Omani Al Fransi, and Majan Bank. There are nine foreign-owned commercial banks, four local specialized banks, and several investment companies. The November 2000 banking law established stricter supervision by the Central Bank of Oman. The Muscat Securities Market opened in 1989. Standard corporation tax is 12% for Omani companies and 30% for foreign companies, but such discrimination is due to end in 2003.

BUSINESS OPPORTUNITIES

Tax and financial incentives are offered to investors. There are plans to create free zones at Salalah and Sohar. Restrictions on investment by majority foreign-owned firms are being eased. Priority is given to tourism and to projects engaging local materials and Omani workers. Oil, gas, accountancy, banking, hotels, port management, industrial machinery, and power have attracted investors from the United States, the United Kingdom, Japan, India, Hong Kong, Iran, Denmark, and other countries. These sectors, non-hydrocarbon minerals and privatization offer further opportunities. The point of contact is the Oman Center for Investment Promotion & Export Development.

For More Information

Books:

Allen, Calvin H., and W. Lynn Rigsbee II. *Oman Under Qaboos*. Portland, OR: Frank Cass, 2000.

Riphenburg, Carol J. *Oman: Political Development in a Changing World.* Westport, CT: Praeger Publishers, 1998.

Web Sites:

Ministry of Information (government entry point): **www.omanet.com**

Oman Center for Investment Promotion and Export Development: **www.ociped.com**

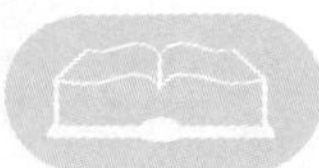

Pakistan

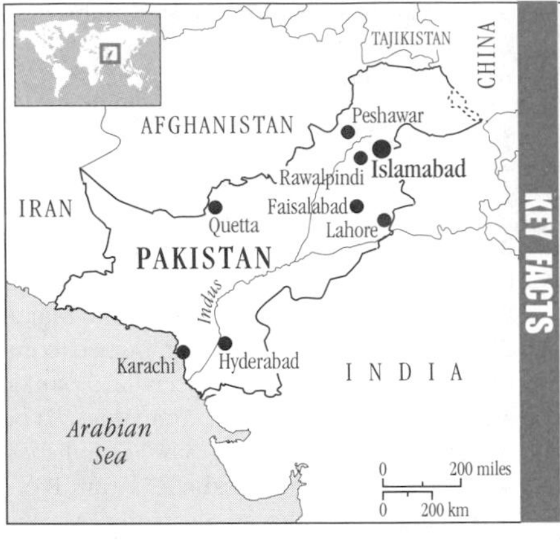

KEY FACTS

GNI: **$62,915 million; world's 44th**
GNI pc: **$470; world's 160th**
Head of government: **president**
Currency: **Pakistan rupee (PRs)**
Capital: **Islamabad**
Population: **152,331,000, growing at 2.7% p.a.**
Land area: **297,644 square miles**
Population density: **511 per square mile**
Life expectancy: **65 years**
Infant mortality: **84 per 1,000 live births**
Language: **English (official), Urdu (national)**
Best buy: **snakeskin purses, silk scarves**

Economic Structure

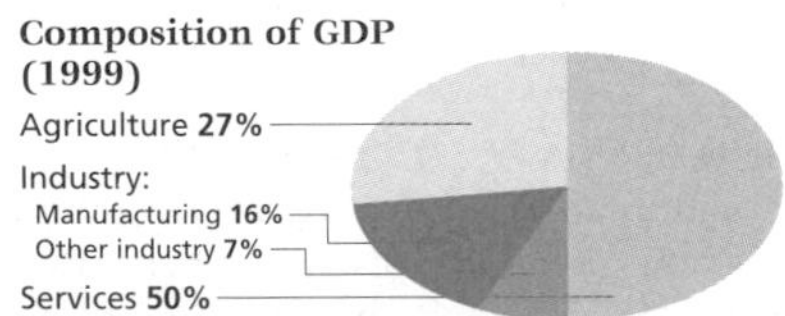

Pakistan was formed out of the bloody partition of British India in 1947 as a homeland for Indian Muslims. It comprised two wings separated by 995 miles of Indian territory: West Pakistan (now the Islamic Republic of Pakistan) and East Pakistan (now Bangladesh). Pakistan's first general election in 1970 resulted in victory for the Pakistan People's Party led by Zulfikar Ali Bhutto in the west, and for the Awami League in the east. Bhutto's unwillingness to accept a Bengali-led government, a civil disobedience campaign by the Awami League, and a military crackdown in response, led to Indian army intervention in the east and secession by Bangladesh. Since then Pakistan has alternated between military and civilian rule: four civilian governments, including the first, led by Bhutto, and two led by his daughter Benazir, were prematurely dissolved by army intervention.

The most recent military takeover, prompted by a flare-up of Pakistan's perennial conflict with India over Kashmir, brought down Nawaz Sharif's Pakistan Muslim League government in October 1999. General Pervez Musharraf, who led the coup, ruled first as chief executive and then as president. In 2001 elections were announced for October 2002 in preparation for a return to civilian rule. The allied military action in Afghanistan following the September 11 attacks in the United States provoked unrest in Pakistan; the resulting political instability, and recession in Pakistan's export markets, had a negative impact on the economy in late 2001.

Agriculture accounts for 26% of Pakistan's GDP, and provides employment for at least half of the labor force and a livelihood for three-quarters of the population. The economy remains highly dependent on cotton, Pakistan's principal cash crop.

Before 1947 Pakistan had no manufacturing industry to speak of. Since then, successive governments have supported industrialization drives. The principal industries are textiles, leather and leather goods, sugar, paper, and tobacco; by 2001 manufacturing accounted for 16% of GDP. A privatization drive from 1991 resulted in the sale of some state-owned manufacturing companies, but foreign investors' enthusiasm remained limited.

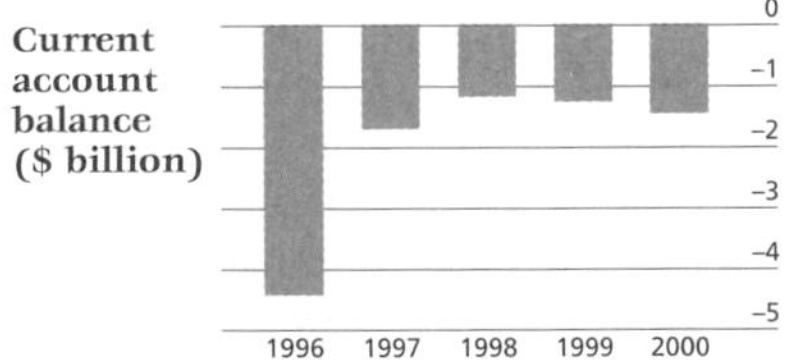

Pakistan has recorded a trade deficit every year since 1972. It has a narrow export base, relying heavily on rice (of which it is the world's third-largest exporter after the United States and Thailand), raw cotton, cotton yarn, cotton cloth, and garments and hosiery. The leading export destinations in 2000–01 were the United States (with 24.2% of the total), the United Arab Emirates (6.4%), the United Kingdom (6.1%), and Germany (5.4%). Main imports are capital goods and raw materials; leading importers were the United Arab Emirates (11.9%), Saudi Arabia (11.8%), Kuwait (9.3%), and the United States (5.5% each).

Economic Policy

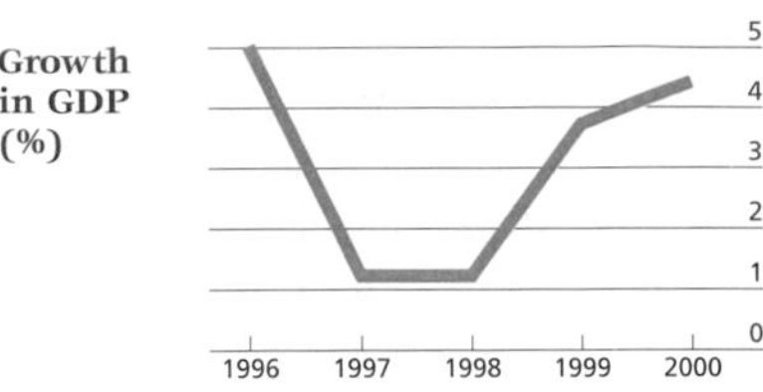

Between 1947 and 1990, Pakistan's economy grew by four times and its population by three-and-a-half times, while per capita income doubled. Pakistan achieved self-sufficiency in wheat in the 1970s, and although GNP per capita is low, the proportion of people living in absolute poverty in Pakistan is small compared with other South Asian countries. Nevertheless, growth is impeded by macro-economic imbalances and by dependence on cotton and cotton-based manufacturing, which renders the country vulnerable to external factors such as adverse weather. GDP growth slowed from an average of 6% per year in the 1980s to 3% per year in the late 1990s—3.9% in 2000, when a drought hit farm output—and 2.6% in 2001. Investment growth has slowed seriously, from an annual average of 17.1% in 1984–94 to 7.9% in 1994–2000. Inflation, although exacerbated by excessive public-sector domestic borrowing, has fallen from double digits in the mid-1990s to 4.7% in 2001.

Pakistan's economy reels under the burden of repayments on $64 billion of foreign and domestic debt. A restructuring agreement was reached with sovereign and private international creditors in January 2001. Additional financial help to Pakistan was promised by the United States and other Western governments contingent upon its pro-Western stance on the war in Afghanistan: in September–November 2001 alone it received $800 million in politically-driven grants.

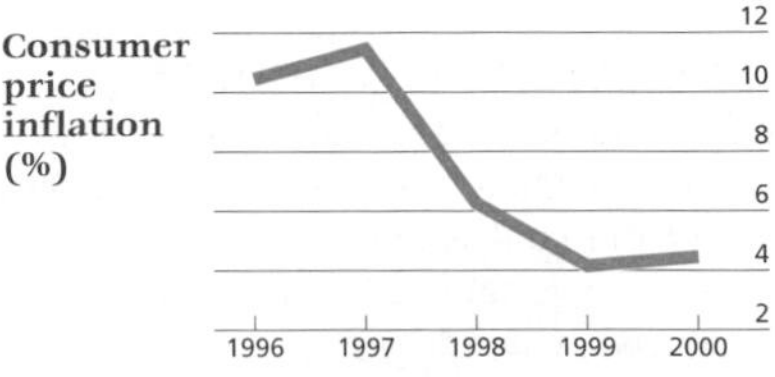

  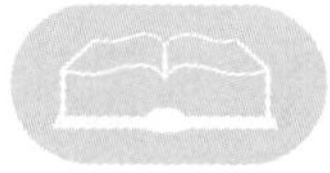     

At the same time Pakistan's relations improved with the IMF and World Bank which, during the 1990s, worked with successive governments on the details of economic liberalization programs. During that decade several Pakistani governments started IMF lending programs but failed to comply with their conditions, ending them again before the second stage. General Musharraf's government has made more progress: by settling the dispute over tariffs paid by the state power transmission company to the electricity generation company Hubco (recipient of Pakistan's largest-ever foreign investment package), by imposing a general sales tax, and by cutting subsidies to the energy sector.

Geography/Resources

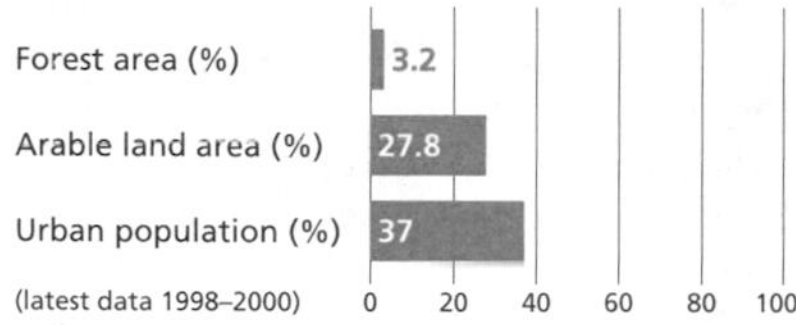

Pakistan is bounded by Iran to the west, Afghanistan to the north, China to the northeast, India to the east and southeast, and the Arabian Sea to the south. Topographically, Pakistan comprises the western end of the Indo-Gangetic plain, bounded to the north by the mountain wall of the Great Himalayan mountain ranges and their offshoots; administratively, it is made up of four linguistically and culturally distinct provinces: Sindh, Punjab, the North-West Frontier Province, and Balochistan. The territory of Jammu and Kashmir, along the western Himalayas, remains in dispute between Pakistan and India. Both countries hold sectors, and have fought three wars over it in 1948–49, 1965, and 1971.

Pakistan's crude oil reserves, estimated in the late 1990s at 225 million barrels, in 2000 supported production of 56,140 barrels per day but were expected to decline in the succeeding decade. Gas reserves are much more substantial but have not been fully developed. In Balochistan, negotiations on drilling charges between international companies and local tribespeople have broken down. There are some coal deposits and mining; there is also an extensive range of non-fuel minerals including limestone (which supports a significant cement industry), chromite, celestite, antimony, aragonite, gypsum, rock salt, and marble.

Pakistan's agricultural resources are concentrated in three well-irrigated areas—around Lahore, the Canal Colony areas, and Sindh—which produce more than half its wheat and virtually all its cotton and rice. Elsewhere, where there is little or no irrigation, agricultural holdings are smaller and fragmented, and overpopulation and poverty have stimulated migration into the towns or armed forces, or abroad.

Ethnically, the population is broadly Punjabi (the majority, more than 55%), Sindhi (20%), Pathan (10% each), and Baloch (5%). Linguistically it is heterogeneous, the main languages being Urdu, Punjabi, Sindhi, Pashto, Balochi, and Brahui. It is more than 98% Muslim. The population has been molded by waves of immigration (of 8 million Indian Muslims in 1947, of refugees from Bangladesh after separation and from Afghanistan after the Soviet invasion of 1979), and of emigration, the largest wave having been the 3 million laborers, mostly men, who went to the Middle East during the 1970s oil boom. Extremely rapid population growth rates, averaging 3.1% in 1972–81, have slowed slightly to 2.7% over 1990–99 and 2.2% in 1999. Infant mortality, too, was falling. A male–female disparity of 108–100 is due, demographers believe, to continuing female infanticide.

Communications/Energy

PCs	0.4
Telephone lines	2.3
Mobiles	0.3
Internet users	0.1
(per 100 people, 2000)	0 20 40 60 80 100

Roads carry 63% of Pakistan's total freight and passenger traffic, even though highways comprise only 4,500 miles of the 155,500-mile road network. The roads' importance has been increased by chronic under-investment in Pakistan Railways' outdated, outworn network. The government has been criticized for eschewing a comprehensive road development plan in favor of heavy spending on motorways between Lahore and Islamabad, and Peshawar and Islamabad. Pakistan International Airways is the sole carrier of domestic air traffic and also runs international flights; the principal airports are at Karachi, Lahore, Rawalpindi, Quetta, and Peshawar.

Energy production is 66.7% thermal (mostly oil and gas) and 32.7% hydro, with an extremely small input of nuclear power. Electricity generation is dominated by two state power generation and distribution companies, the Water and Power Development Authority (WAPDA) and the Karachi Electricity Supply Corporation (KESC). In 1999–2000 they supplied 11,701 MW, and private producers contributed another 4,674 MW. A dispute over pricing between the government and the independent power producers, including foreign investors, flared in 1997. It centered on Hubco, which is jointly owned by National Power of the United Kingdom and WAPDA. The Musharraf government has resolved this dispute and announced plans to break up WAPSA—which generates, transmits, and distributes most of Pakistan's electricity, but is mired in debt—into three generation companies, eight distributors, and a transmission company.

Despite the low level of telephone coverage, the telecoms sector is highly profitable, and in late 2001 the government persisted in its hope of partially privatizing Pakistan Telecommunications Company Ltd. (PTCL), the national telecoms company.

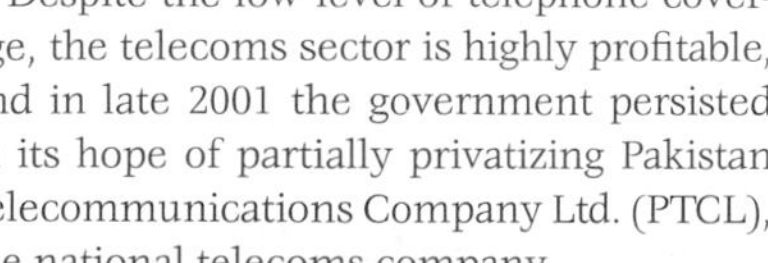

Education/Employment

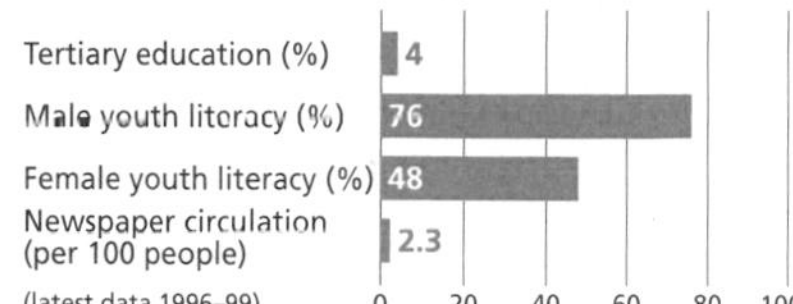

Pakistan's labor force comprises a relatively small proportion of the population; a study by the International Labour Organization concluded that in 1997, of a population of 135 million, there was a labor force of 37 million, including 4 million underemployed (working less than 35 hours a week) and 2 million unemployed. Workforce numbers were depressed by emigration by workers, the small number of women working, and the even smaller number reported to statisticians. The study also found that 44% of the employed workforce was self-employed, most of these very poor rural farmers.

While literacy rates among workers have been improving (from 35.3% in 1987 to 43.2% in 1995), levels of literacy and education overall remain among the lowest in the world. According to UNICEF, Pakistan scored 37% literacy in 1997, 160th of 174 countries measured; the literacy rate among women is far lower than among men. In 1996–97 less than 40% of Pakistani children completed five years of schooling: enrollment rates among boys were just above 60%, and among girls just above 40%. Education is not compulsory.

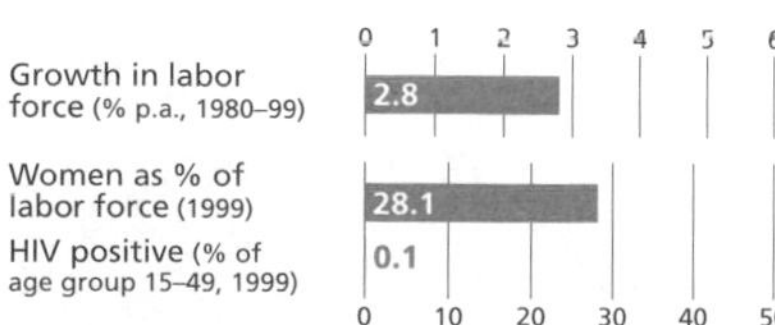

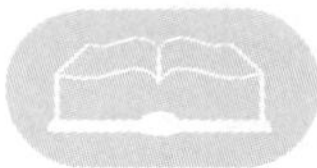

Higher education is available at universities, technical schools, and vocational schools. It was severely disrupted by being nationalized in the 1970s and then privatized again in the 1980s. From the 1980s the government concentrated on encouraging the Islamization of the curriculum, and the use of Urdu as opposed to English. A gulf has grown between state-run Islamic schools and universities, and privately-run Western-leaning institutions that usually teach in English and often prepare students for entry examinations for U.K. and U.S. universities.

Fiscal/Financial

The core of Pakistan's financial system remains the commercial banks, which hold about 90% of deposits and provide more than two-thirds of total financing. There are three large state-owned commercial banks (the National Bank of Pakistan, Habib Bank, and United Bank), 21 other domestic commercial banks, and 21 branches of foreign banks. Financial services liberalization measures in the early 1990s were supplemented by a bank reform program announced in 1997, but problems such as high levels of non-performing loans persist. Capital mobilization through the bond and stock markets had reached 43% and 22% of GDP respectively by the end of 1997, but these figures are deceptively high: treasury bonds accounted for 99% of the bond market, and stock trading at Pakistan's three exchanges (Karachi, Lahore, and Islamabad) is dominated by a tiny number of corporates, with Hubco and PTCL accounting for more than half of market turnover.

Fiscal policy is constrained above all by low rates of tax collection. General Musharraf's government has improved matters by introducing a general sales tax on retail trade, despite widespread protests, and clamping down on tax evaders, achieving a year-on-year increase in tax revenues of nearly 50 billion rupees ($785 million) between 1999–2000 and 2000–01.

The financial system's difficulties have been aggravated by a Supreme Court decision in December 1999 outlawing all forms of interest, and ordering the government to establish Islamic financial institutions by June 2001. Successive governments avoided confrontation with the court over the religiously-charged issue until March 2001, when United Bank, supported by the government, appealed against the decision. The finance minister and other officials have routinely assured investors that the Supreme Court's position will be overturned, but the threat of its implementation—and a consequent run on deposits—has not yet been fully removed.

Business Opportunities

Growth in output (% p.a., 1990–99)

Services	4.4
Industry	4.0
Manufacturing	3.7
Agriculture	4.4

While Pakistan has a full range of policies designed to encourage inward investment, more general political and economic conditions act as a powerful deterrent. The openness to investors has been fully enshrined in legislation, including a Foreign Private Investment Act (1976) that outlaws inferior treatment of foreign investors, and a series of measures taken in the 1990s including relaxation of foreign exchange controls; blanket permission for foreign-owned entities to undertake export and import trade; full safeguards protecting foreign investment; withdrawal of work permit restrictions for foreign staff; and abolition of approvals procedures in all but a small group of security-related industries. The Board of Investment acts as a one-stop shop for foreign investors. The deterrent factors include the instability resulting from the war in Afghanistan; political and religious violence and general lawlessness; and the predominance of corruption.

Foreign direct investment rose from an average of $325 million in 1990–95 to $1106 million in 1996, and went down again to an average of $566 million in 1997–99. The leading contributors were the United Kingdom and the United States, who in the late 1990s each accounted for about one-third of the total. In 1997 agriculture, services, and infrastructure joined manufacturing as sectors open to foreign investment on a repatriable basis, and although this has not yet resulted in large-scale inflows of capital, it was hoped in 2001 that it would be made possible in future with an improvement of Pakistan's political and economic climate. In late 2001 the government was planning to offer nine oil and gas fields, followed by two state oil companies, for privatization, as well as PTCL.

For More Information

Books:

Harrison, Selig, Paul Kreisberg, and Dennis Kux. *India and Pakistan: The First Fifty Years* (Woodrow Wilson Center Series). New York: Cambridge University Press, 1998.

Husain, Ishrat. *Pakistan: The Economy of an Elitist State*. New York: Oxford University Press, 1999.

Khan, Bashir Ahmad, and Syed Mubashir Ali, eds. *Corporate Finance in Pakistan: Case Studies from the Emerging Market*. New York: Oxford University Press, 2000.

Looney, Robert. *The Pakistani Economy*. Westport, CT: Praeger Publishers, 1997.

Schofield, Victoria. *Kashmir in Conflict: India, Pakistan and the Unfinished War*. New York: I. B. Tauris, 2000.

Zaidi, S. Akbar. *Issues in Pakistan's Economy*. New York: Oxford University Press, 1999.

Web Sites:

Asian Development Bank Pakistan page: **www.adb.org/Pakistan/default.asp**

Board of Investment of Pakistan: **www.pakboi.gov.pk**

Business Recorder (newspaper): **www.brecorder.com**

E-Pakistan internet portal: **www.epakistan.com/epakhome.nsf**

Karachi Stock Exchange: **www.ksc.com.pk**

Pakistan ministry of finance: **www.finance.gov.pk**

PALAU

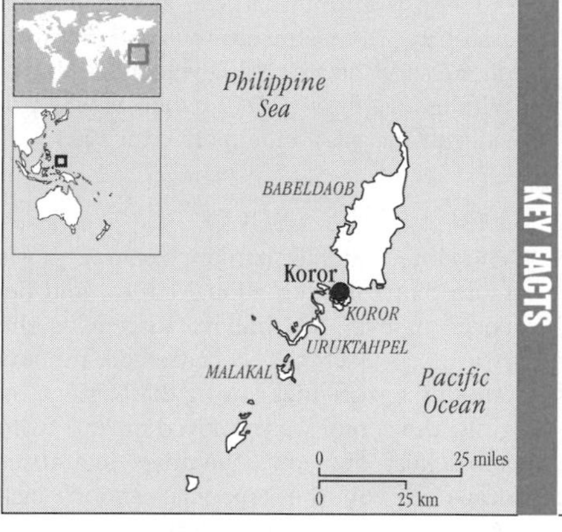

GNI pc: **$5,000 (approx.)**
Head of government: **president**
Currency: **U.S. dollar ($)**
Capital: **Koror**
Population: **19,000, growing at 2.6% p.a.**
Land area: **177 square miles**
Population density: **107 per square mile**
Life expectancy: **69 years**
Infant mortality: **17 per 1,000 live births**
Language: **English (official), Palauan (official)**
Best buy: **storyboards (carvings of legends), hats, baskets, purses**

ECONOMY

Tourism is the main industry, accounting for about half of GDP, with the majority of visitors coming from Taiwan, Japan, and the United States. The service sector, including tourism and public-sector services, contributes over 80% of GDP. The government employs around 30% of the workforce, many of whom are engaged in administering U.S. aid programs. Construction is the main industrial activity, accounting for 9% of GDP. Agriculture and fisheries contribute about 5% of GDP. Manufacturing of textiles and handcrafts contributes 0.8%. The main exports are fish, garments, and handcrafts, and the main export markets are the United States, Japan, and Taiwan.

Palau was a Pacific Trust Territory of the United States until 1994 when it became an independent republic. At that time it entered the Compact of Free Association with the United States, under which it will receive grant aid totaling over $500 million until 2009. Aid is targeted at infrastructure projects that will underpin the long-term health of the economy. The government has created a trust fund to be drawn upon after U.S. aid ends. In addition the government limited the budget deficit to 4% of GDP in 2000, and planned to eliminate it in the medium term through public-sector cuts. Tax reforms were drafted in 1999 with IMF assistance to broaden the tax base and improve tax collection. The government made plans to simplify foreign investment laws in 2000. With the dollar as its currency, Palau has been at a competitive disadvantage for Asian tourism, especially since the Asian financial crisis of the late 1990s. GDP growth was spectacular in 1994–96 on account of U.S. aid and a boost in tourism. It slid into stagnation by 1999 but revived in 2000. Inflation was estimated to be in single figures, similar to those of the United States and Japan in recent years.

GEOGRAPHY/RESOURCES

Palau consists of eight main islands and 250 smaller ones in the Pacific Ocean.

Main agricultural crops are coconuts, bananas, cassava, sweet potatoes, and other root crops. Other sectors include eggs and meat (largely chickens and pigs). Tuna fishing licenses are sold to fleets from Taiwan, the United States, Japan, and the Philippines. There is a small mining and quarrying industry.

Around 70% of the population lives in the capital Koror on Koror Island. The constitution requires a new capital to be built on the much larger adjacent island, Babeldaob. Most Palauans are of Micronesian origin.

COMMUNICATIONS/ENERGY

There is a new 53-mile road on Babeldaob. Previously the majority of Palau's 22 miles of paved roads were on Koror. There are a further 15 miles of coral and gravel-surfaced roads. There is a 700-foot bridge between Babeldaob and Koror, providing an essential link between the two islands. The international airport is in southern Babeldaob near to Koror. There are airstrips on Angaur and Peleliu. Malakal Island, across a causeway from Koror, has a deep-water port with container and bulk handling facilities. The government-owned ferries operate between Koror and the other populated islands. There are modern telecommunications links, including local, inter-island and international connections. There is Internet access. Electricity production totaled 208 million kWh in 1995 from two diesel-run power plants. A third power plant was under construction in 1999. Oil and gas are imported.

FISCAL/FINANCIAL

Taxation is low, and there are preferential rules for offshore banks since 1998. The National Banking Review Commission was established in 1999 to regulate the financial services industry, following IMF advice for financial regulation along international lines. In 2001 there were eight banks, including two U.S. banks, the Bank of Guam, and Palau's National Development Bank. Credit unions are an established source of local finance. There is no local stock market.

BUSINESS OPPORTUNITIES

Apart from banking, the government is actively promoting tourism. There is already foreign investment in both these sectors. The government is also working to resolve unsettled claims regarding land ownership and lease rights, which have held back investment. Construction will continue as infrastructure is improved. There are plans to expand cargo handling facilities at Malakal Harbor. Trade and development agreements were signed in the 1990s with Taiwan and the Philippines.

For More Information

Books:

Galbraith, Kate, et al. *Micronesia*. 4th ed. Oakland, CA: Lonely Planet, 2000.

Leibowitz, Arnold H. *Embattled Island: Palau's Struggle for Independence*. Westport, CT: Praeger Publishers, 1996.

Palau Business and Investment Opportunities Yearbook. 3rd ed. Washington, D.C.: International Business Publications, 2001 (annual).

Web Sites:

Palau National Communications Corporation (information and government entry point): **www.palaunet.com**

Palau Visitors' Authority: **www.visit-palau.com**

  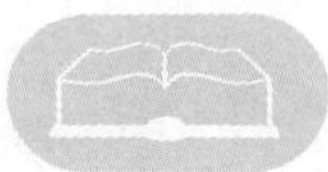    

Panama

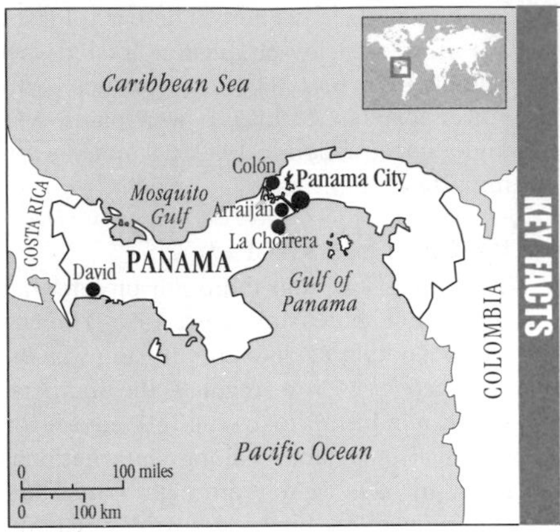

KEY FACTS

GNI: **$8,657 million; world's 89th**
GNI pc: **$3,080; world's 89th**
Head of government: **president**
Currency: **balboa (B)**
Capital: **Panama City**
Population: **2,812,000, growing at 1.8% p.a.**
Land area: **28,726 square miles**
Population density: **98 per square mile**
Life expectancy: **74 years**
Infant mortality: **21 per 1,000 live births**
Language: **Spanish**
Best buy: **molas (colorful native textiles), ceramics**

Economy

Panama seceded from Colombia in 1903 with U.S. backing. The building of the Panama Canal in 1914 and the accompanying controversial treaty gave the United States control over the canal and important segments of Panama's territory and economy until 1999, when the canal was turned over to the government of Panama. The United States invaded the country in 1989 to overthrow the six-year dictatorship of General Manuel Antonio Noriega, and the armed forces were abolished.

Panama's service-based economy (75% of GDP) revolves around the canal, flagship registry, offshore banking, the Colón Free Zone—the world's second-largest free trade zone after Hong Kong—and tourism. The U.S. dollar (known locally as the balboa) is the legal tender, resulting in low inflation and no foreign exchange risk. Real GDP growth averaged 3.3% in 1995–99 and dipped to 2.7% in 2000 and lower in 2001, partly because of the economic impact of the U.S. pullout and the slowdown in world trade, while inflation has rarely been above 2.0 %. The main exports are bananas, coffee, sugar, and shrimp.

The canal's toll revenues grew by only 0.9% in the 2000–01 financial year because of slowing world commerce. Tolls for the year to September 30, 2001 amounted to $579.5 million. Cargo volume at the canal—which carried 4% of global trade—was almost unchanged from the year before, at 193.6 million tons. The trend towards larger ships led the canal to invest $1 billion to increase capacity by 20%. The widening of the canal's narrowest point was due to be completed in 2002.

The Colón Free Zone (which represents a market much larger than Panama's entire internal market) has stagnated. Imports dropped 1.2% in the first nine months of 2001 to $3.4 billion over the same 2000 period, and re-exports increased 0.3% to $3.8 billion. The Zone plans to become the largest Multimodal Logistics Center in the Americas.

Geography/Resources

The tiny S-shaped country links South and Central America. It borders on the Atlantic in the north, the Pacific in the south, Colombia in the east, and Costa Rica in the west. At its narrowest point the country is less than 50 miles wide. Most of the country lies below 2,300 feet.

There is some copper mining, but the sector as a whole accounts for an insignificant part of GDP.

About one-third of the country's population (close to 3 million) lives in Panama City; 70% is mestizo.

Communications/Energy

There are over 7,000 miles of highways in Panama, but only about 2,500 miles are paved. The passenger rail sector is underdeveloped, with about 200 miles of tracks. The hemisphere's oldest transcontinental railroad, between Balboa near Panama City on the Pacific coast and Cristobal near Colón on the Atlantic, was re-launched in 2001 for both passengers and cargo. Colón on the Atlantic coast is Latin America's largest container port. The railroad, first built in 1855, was sold in 1998 to a joint venture partnership of Kansas City Southern Industries and Mi-Jack.

There is an international airport at Panama City. Domestic and international telephone services are well developed. Cable & Wireless acquired INTEL when it was privatized, and has a monopoly until 2003.

Fiscal/Financial

The international banking center hosts more than 70 international banks, and deposits of over $38 billion. Known as the "washing machine" because of money-laundering activities during the Noriega regime, the center was removed in 2001 from a blacklist of "noncooperative" countries drawn up by the Financial Action Task Force on Money Laundering, an intergovernmental body. Banco Nacional de Panama acts as the central bank, though it cannot issue U.S. dollars. Primer Banco del Istmo is the largest Panamanian bank. Both corporate tax and the top personal income tax rate are 30%.

Business Opportunities

Foreign direct investment averaged $850 million in 1997–2000, up from $19 million in 1985–95. The bulk of investment has gone into telecommunications and tourism, particularly hotels.

For More Information

Books:

Jones, Kenneth J. *Panama Now*. Panama City: Focus Publications (Int.), 2000.

McCullough, David G. *The Path Between the Seas: The Creation of the Panama Canal, 1870–1914*. New York: Simon & Schuster, 1999.

Web Sites:

Colón Free Zone: **www.colonfreezone.com**

Council for Investment and Development: **www.businesspanama.com**

Legal information: **www.legalinfo-panama.com**

Panama Banking Association: **www.asociacionbancaria.com/english**

Panama Canal: **www.pancanal.com/eng**

Papua New Guinea

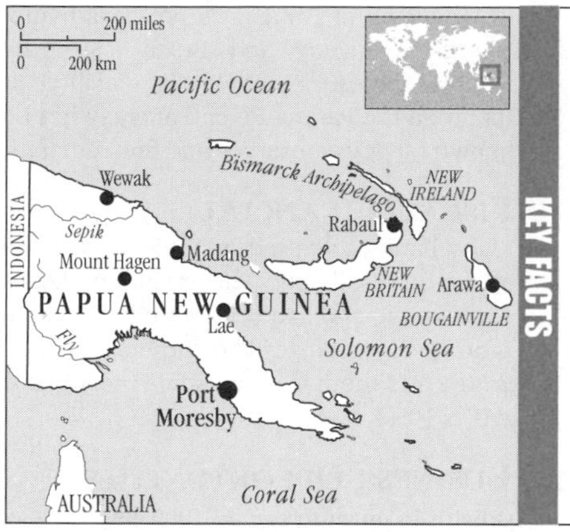

KEY FACTS

GNI: **$3,834 million; world's 121st**
GNI pc: **$810; world's 140th**
Head of government: **prime minister**
Currency: **kina (Kina)**
Capital: **Port Moresby**
Population: **4,702,000, growing at 2.3% p.a.**
Land area: **174,865 square miles**
Population density: **27 per square mile**
Life expectancy: **59 years**
Infant mortality: **79 per 1,000 live births**
Language: **English, Tok Pisin, Hiri Motu**
Best buy: **carvings, story and spirit boards, pottery, bilums (string bags)**

Economy

Mining and processing of gold, copper, and petroleum are the leading activities, contributing 26% of GDP in 1999. Agriculture, forestry, and fisheries—especially subsistence farming and fisheries—provide income for over 80% of the population and contribute 25% of GDP. Cash crops are coffee, palm and copra oil, copra, tea, rubber, cane sugar, timber, and cocoa. Non-minerals-related manufacturing, which accounts for 9% of GDP, is focused on the local market. Services, including tourism, trade, transport and communications, finance, and public services, contribute around 30% of GDP. The main exports are gold (71% in 2001), copper, petroleum, timber, palm oil, and coffee. The main export markets are Australia, Japan, Germany, the United Kingdom, Korea and China.

Despite its rich endowment of natural resources, Papua New Guinea is dependent on foreign aid because of geographical and social obstacles to development, and volatile international commodity prices. GDP fluctuated from double-digit growth in 1991–93 to decline of 4% a year in 1997–98 because of the Asian crisis and drought. The new government launched reforms to improve public administration and finances in 1999. Total public debt was reduced to 60.8% of GDP in 2000 from 65.8% in 1998. Annual GDP growth averaged 3.3% in 1999–2001. Annual average inflation was 8.3% in 1990–2001. Only one in eight of the potential labor force of 2 million is employed in the formal sector. The IMF-backed government program for 2000–03 includes privatization of finance, telecommunications, electricity and airline companies, and tax reform. The National Provident Fund (pension fund) and Papua New Guinea Banking Corporation (PNGBC) were privatized in 2001. The World Bank is financing programs to strengthen government departments' capacity to take development projects forward.

Geography/Resources

Papua New Guinea consists of the eastern part of the island of New Guinea (which it shares with the Indonesian territory of Irian Jaya), the islands of New Britain, New Ireland, and Bougainville, and many smaller islands. The climate is hot with heavy rainfall, but it has also suffered from drought in recent years.

Apart from agricultural cash crops, sorghum, corn, bananas, and cassava are produced for local consumption. Pigs are the main livestock. Foreign fleets are licensed to fish for tuna. Local fishing includes shrimp, which is exported. Exploitable forest covers about 40% of the land. There are rich mineral resources on many islands and offshore, including 22.5 trillion cubic feet of gas and several oil fields. Exploitation depends on agreement between the government and local landowners. There are plans to construct a 2,000-mile gas pipeline to Australia once agreement for gas development is reached. Other projects include oil, nickel, and new copper and gold mines. There are reserves of chromite, cobalt, silver, and quartz.

Communications/Energy

In 1996 the road network was estimated at 12,000 miles, only 426 miles of which was paved. There are 16 major sea ports and 492 airports, including the three international airports near Port Moresby, Lae, and Mount Hagen. There are projects to upgrade 9 other airports. There were 47,000 fixed phone lines in 1997. Radiotelephone is the main domestic telecommunications link. International links are provided via cable, satellite, and international radio communications. There were 2,000 Internet users in 2000. Most electricity is generated from oil (70% in 1998) with the rest from hydro. A new oil power station was being built in 1999. Oil is imported.

Fiscal/Financial

Tax incentives for foreign investment have been simplified in recent years to render the system more transparent and to produce more tax revenues. VAT has been introduced. The Bank of Papua New Guinea is the central bank and regulator of the financial sector. Supervisory laws have been strengthened recently. There are local and foreign-owned banks and insurance companies with branches on different islands. The Papua New Guinea Stock Exchange, which has links with the Australian Stock Exchange, began operations in 1999.

Business Opportunities

There has been foreign investment in all the export industries, finance, and insurance. New opportunities exist in construction, minerals, agriculture, fishing, and tourism. The privatization program also offers opportunities. The point of contact for foreign investors is the Investment Promotion Authority.

For More Information

Books:

Kelly, Robert C., et al., eds. *Papua New Guinea Country Review 2000*. Houston, TX: CountryWatch.com, 1999.

Lipscomb, Adrian, et al. *Papua New Guinea*. 6th ed. Oakland, CA: Lonely Planet, 1998.

Web Sites:

Department of Treasury and Planning: **www.treasury.gov.pg**

Government entry point: **www.pngonline.gov.pg**

Paraguay

KEY FACTS

GNI: **$8,374 million; world's 91st**
GNI pc: **$1,560; world's 116th**
Head of government: **president**
Currency: **guarani (G)**
Capital: **Asunción**
Population: **5,358,000, growing at 2.7% p.a.**
Land area: **153,400 square miles**
Population density: **35 per square mile**
Life expectancy: **70 years**
Infant mortality: **27 per 1,000 live births**
Language: **Spanish, Guarani**
Best buy: **handicrafts, especially delicate cobweb lace (nanduti)**

Economy

Paraguay gained its independence from Spain in 1811 and was then ruled for about 80 years by dictators, one of whom waged a war against Argentina, Uruguay, and Brazil (War of the Triple Alliance, 1865–70) in which Paraguay lost half its population. In the 1930s and 1940s, a period of extreme political instability, Paraguayan politics were defined by the Chaco War against Bolivia, a civil war, and more dictatorships. General Alfredo Stroessner took power in May 1954 and ruled until 1989. In May 1993, Paraguay elected its first civilian president in almost 40 years in a free election. President Luis Gonzalez Macchi became president in March 1999.

Paraguay's economy is about one-half service-based, with the balance split fairly evenly between agriculture and industry. Isolation due to three decades of authoritarian rule under General Stroessner left Paraguay relatively underdeveloped while other countries in the region experienced much faster economic growth. Corruption is another factor that has held back the country. Real GDP grew by a yearly average of only 0.7% between 1996 and 2000 (–0.4% in 2000), partly because of falling exports. With a population growth rate of 2.6%, national income per head declined 1.8% a year during this period. Inflation averaged 8.6%. The government signed a pact with the IMF in 2001 promising higher taxes, lower spending, and privatization.

Agriculture sustains over 50% of the population in rural areas, many farming at a subsistence level. The main exports are soybeans, cotton, meat, and edible oil, and some manufactured products such as toys, sports equipment, and furniture. There is a large informal economy involved in the re-export of imported consumer goods to neighboring countries as well as street vendors. The country is a member of the Mercosur free trade bloc with the other "southern cone" Latin American countries.

Geography/Resources

Paraguay is landlocked: no part of its territory is closer than 590 miles to the ocean. It is surrounded by Argentina, Brazil and Bolivia. The country is divided into two by the Paraguay River. Over a quarter of Paraguay's population live in the Asunción area. Most other Paraguayans live in the numerous small towns to the east.

About 95% of the population is mestizo.

Communications/Energy

There are approximately 12,000 miles of highways in Paraguay, about half of which are paved. However, many paved highways, even in cities, develop potholes which generally go unrepaired for months. The country has only about 620 miles of railroads. There are international airports at Asunción and Ciudad del Este, but neither has a fully-functioning radar system. The main ports are at Asunción and Villeta (to the south of Asunción) on the Paraguay river, and at Encarnación on the Paraná river.

The telecommunications sector is very underdeveloped, giving it the greatest expansion potential in Mercosur. There are only 5 phone lines per 100 inhabitants. Private mobile operators have been quick to take advantage of the inefficiency of Antelco, the state-run telephone company. Paraguay is the only country in Latin America with twice as many mobile phones as functioning fixed phone lines.

Almost all of Paraguay's power is hydroelectric. Paraguay and Brazil share the world's largest hydroelectric facility at Itaipú on the Parana River. Paraguay has no known oil or gas reserves and few minerals.

Fiscal/Financial

Many banks collapsed in 1995–98, and the effects are still felt. The credit market is weak and loan default rates are high. There is no stock exchange. The corporate tax rate is 30% and there is no personal income tax. VAT is 10%.

Business Opportunities

Growth in output (% p.a., 1990–99)

Services	4.4
Industry	4.0
Manufacturing	3.7
Agriculture	4.4

Paraguay has attracted little foreign direct investment. Inflows averaged $175 million a year in 1997–2000, up from $100 million in 1985–95. The sectors which the government identifies as ripe for investment are those areas which have proved successful for both local and export markets. These include dairy products, cattle raising, soybean, and cotton. The government offers investment incentives (tax breaks, duty-free import of capital goods, and unlimited repatriation of capital) and the lowest factor costs (particularly energy) in the region. The first important *maquila* (assembly) operation began in 2000 with the export of leather car seats to France.

For More Information

Books:

Bao, Sandra, ed. *Argentina, Uruguay and Paraguay.* 4th ed. Oakland, CA: Lonely Planet, 2002.

Paraguay Business and Investment Opportunities Yearbook. 3rd ed. Washington, D.C.: International Business Publications, 2001 (annual).

Web Sites:

Central Bank: **www.bcp.gov.py**
General information: **www.worldskip.com/paraguay** and **www.paraguay.com**
ProParaguay (investment and export promotion): **www.proparaguay.gov.py**

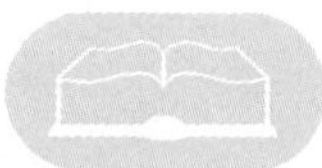

PERU

KEY FACTS

GNI: **$53,705 million; world's 46th**
GNI pc: **$2,130; world's 101st**
Head of government: **president**
Currency: **new sol (Ns)**
Capital: **Lima**
Population: **25,230,000, growing at 1.7% p.a.**
Land area: **494,200 square miles**
Population density: **51 per square mile**
Life expectancy: **69 years**
Infant mortality: **42 per 1,000 live births**
Language: **Spanish, Quechua, Aymara**
Best buy: **silver, gold, articles of clothing made of alpaca**

ECONOMIC STRUCTURE

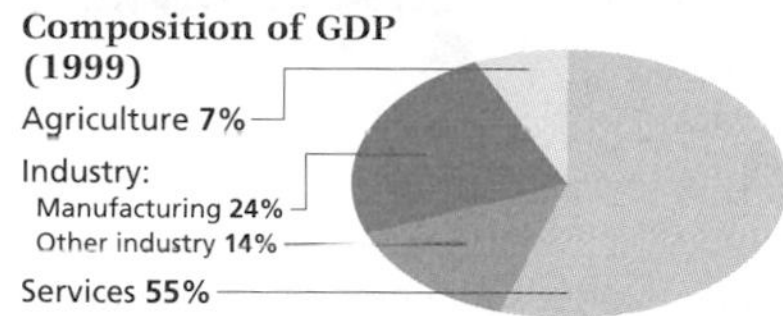

During 1968–80, under left-wing military government, there was extensive nationalization. With the return of civilian rule in 1980, the government became engaged in a protracted conflict with Shining Path, one of the world's most ruthless terrorist movements, which continued until 1992. During this period an estimated 25,000 people died, and 10,000 disappeared.

The 1990 victory of Alberto Fujimori ushered in free-market reforms and led to almost a decade of growth. The authoritarian Fujimori was re-elected in 1995, and in 2000 beat Alejandro Toledo for an unprecedented third term, though the result was very controversial. Fujimori went into exile in his native Japan from where he resigned by fax, while Vladimiro Montesinos, his disgraced spy chief, fled abroad. He was captured after eight months on the run, and returned to Peru to face charges of massive corruption, drug-trafficking, and money-laundering.

Toledo, a centrist Harvard-educated Native American, narrowly won the June 2001 presidential election. His *Perú Posible* party, which does not have a majority in parliament, faced a daunting task in rebuilding institutions, almost all of them corrupted, and alleviating some of Latin America's most extreme poverty. More than half the population is below the poverty line: according to the World Bank, the wealthiest 20% of the population has 51% of the national income.

Services generate 56% of GDP, industry 37%, and agriculture 7%. Manufacturing is mainly centered in Lima and Callao, and includes food processing, fishmeal (used for animal feed and fertilizer), chemicals, petrochemicals, rubber, plastics, basic metallurgy, cement, textiles, and paper products. The principal exports are mining (almost 50% of the total in 2000), fisheries, and agricultural products such as mangos and limes. The main markets are the United States and Japan. Peru is one of the world's largest producers of the coca leaf, most of which is shipped to neighboring Colombia, Brazil, and Bolivia for processing into cocaine.

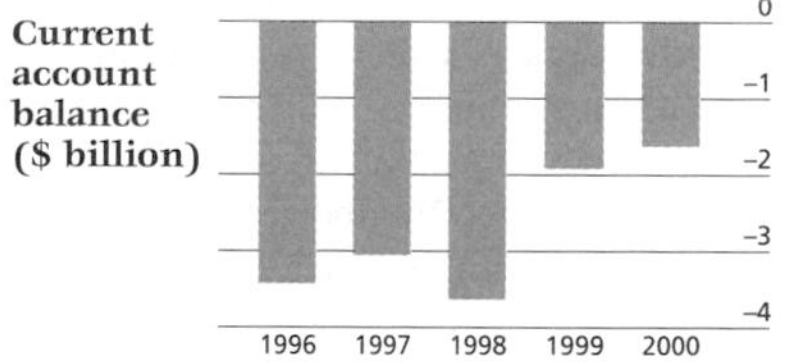

Privatization began in 1994 with the Compañía Peruana de Teléfonos (CPT), which was acquired by Spain's Telefónica. The state also sold stakes in mining and electricity companies and in two banks, but the process came to a virtual halt after 1997. The Toledo government restored privatization, but faced opposition on the water and sanitation infrastructure because of the tariff rises needed to fund improvements and extensions to the network, and to construct water treatment plants to reduce pollution. Privatization of the urban electricity industry was also planned so that the government could concentrate on rural electrification.

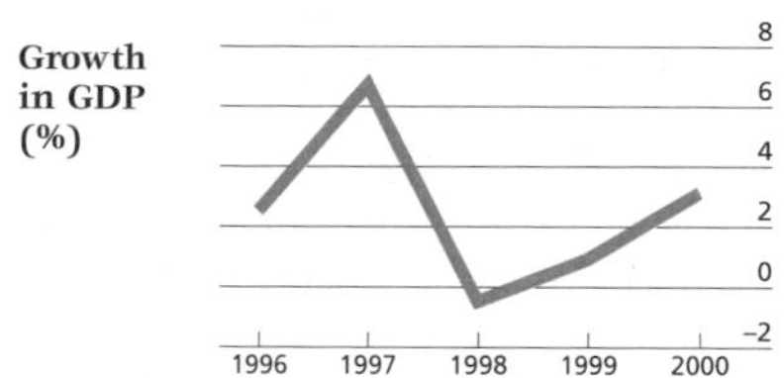

ECONOMIC POLICY

Liberalization during the 1990s unleashed a period of high growth and low inflation. However, real per capita GDP of $2,350 was no higher in 2000 than in 1970. Growth averaged 0.5% a year in 1979–88 and then accelerated to 4.3% in 1989–99. The economy dipped into recession in 1998 (–0.5%), picked up in 1999 (+0.9%) and 2000 (+3.1%), and in 2001 was at a standstill. Inflation was down to 1.0% in 2001. The fiscal balance has been in deficit since 1998 (0.8% of GDP) and was around 2.5% of GDP in 2001. Tax revenue represents 14% of GDP. The external debt remains a heavy burden (at an estimated $28.4 billion in 2001 it represented 51% of GDP and 306% of exports). The International Monetary Fund signed a two year standby agreement with Peru in January 2002.

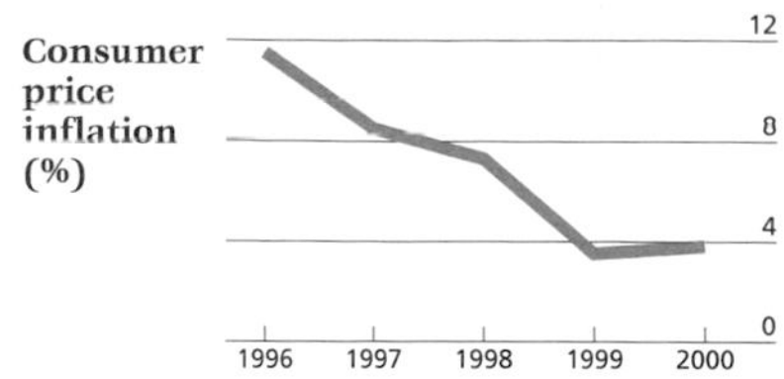

The government adopted a more socially-oriented economic policy while remaining committed to macro-economic stability and honoring the foreign debt. This included the creation of 2.5 million jobs in 2000–05 through an emergency employment program and by promoting intensive farming, food processing, tourism, foreign investment, and construction. The authorities are aiming at 2.5 million tourist arrivals a year by 2005, up from 1million in 2000. The official rate of unemployment is 8%, but only around 50% of the labor force of 8 million could be considered to be fully employed.

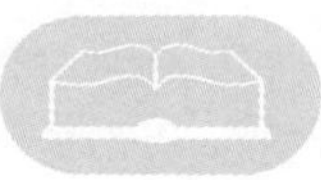

GEOGRAPHY/RESOURCES

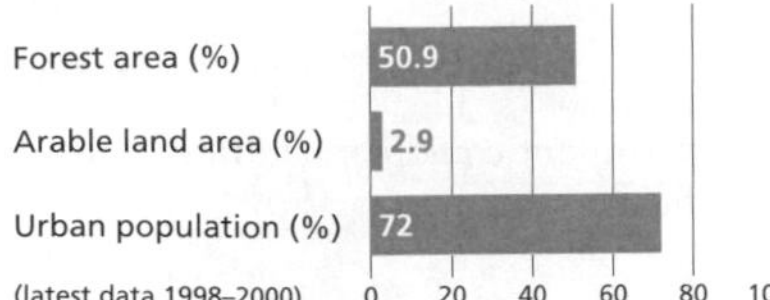

Peru is bounded by Ecuador and Colombia to the north, by Brazil and Bolivia to the east, and by Chile to the south. To the west is the Pacific Ocean. Two chains of the Andes Mountains, running parallel to the Pacific coast, divide the country into three very different regions. These are the coastal zone; mountainous areas consisting of very high chains called *cordilleras* (Huscaran is 22,265 feet high), high plateaus, and deep valleys; and heavily forested slopes east of the mountains, leading to the low-lying Amazonian plain. The Atacama Desert, to the south, is one of the driest places in the world. In contrast, on the borders of Peru and Bolivia is Lake Titicaca, the world's highest navigable lake (12,497 feet above sea level). The country is subject to earthquakes: a huge one measuring 8.1 on the Richter scale killed more than 100 people in 2001 and left an estimated 74,000 homeless. Peru also suffers from the effects of *El Niño,* a disruption of the ocean atmosphere system in the tropical Pacific with major consequences for weather and climate, which produced extensive floods in 1997–98.

The cold Peru Current flowing north along the coast is rich in fish. Peru is one of the world's leading fishing nations. Indians living high in the sierra grow corn, potatoes, beans, and wheat to feed themselves. In the river valleys of the coastal belt, cotton and sugar are the chief crops. Coffee and quinine are grown in the eastern lowlands. The agricultural sector employs around 30% of the population, but its contribution to GDP is small.

When it was part of the Spanish Empire (1535–1821), Peru was famous for its gold and silver, and they are still mined in large quantities: the country is the world's second-largest silver producer. The Yanacocha mine in Cajamarca, a joint venture between Newmont Gold of the United States and Peru's Buenaventura, is Latin America's largest gold mine, and one of the world's lowest-cost gold producers. The country is virtually self-sufficient in oil; copper (fifth-largest producer), lead, zinc, vanadium (used for hardening steel), and bismuth are also mined. The main mining regions are Sierra and on the southern coast. International companies are particularly active in the copper sector. Cambior of Canada was developing the La Granja copper deposit in Cajamarca and Grupo Mexico, the Mexican mining giant, owned more than half of the Southern Peru Copper Corporation, one of the world's largest private-sector copper mining companies. In 2001 Southern Peru launched a $600 million project to modernize and expand its smelter in Ilo. Protests by local inhabitants over pollution in mining areas are becoming a growing problem for some firms.

About 45% of the population are Native American, 37% mestizo, 15% white, and 3% black, Asian, or other. Life is harsh for highland farmers (infant mortality rates approach 100 per 1,000 live births).

COMMUNICATIONS/ENERGY

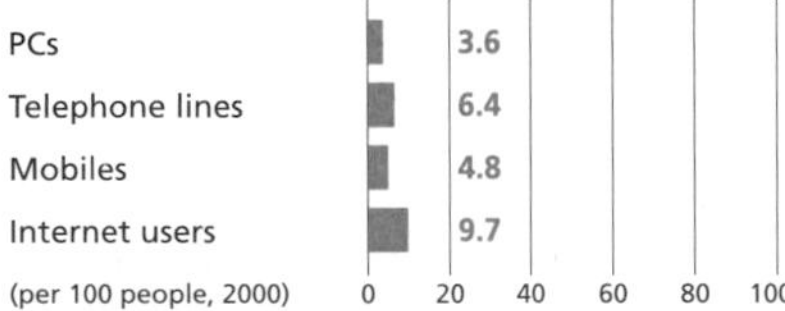

The country's topography makes transport difficult, and successive governments, with limited funds available, have been restricted in their capacity to improve infrastructure. There are 45,300 miles of roads, only 5,400 miles of which were paved in 1999. A coastal road forms part of the Pan-American Highway, and the Trans-Andean Highway runs from Lima across the mountains to the Amazonian port of Pucallpa. The Amazon has 5,350 miles of navigable tributaries. Highways between the coast and mountain regions are often blocked by landslides in the rainy season. There are several railways, some of them built to join inland towns with the nearest port. The railway running inland from Lima reaches a height of almost 15,100 feet at La Cima, making it the highest full-sized railway in the world. The main ports are at Callao, Chimbote, Ilo, Salaverry, and Pisco. The international airport is at Lima.

A build-operate-transfer (BOT) concessions system was introduced to encourage private-sector investment in transport, energy, water, and sanitation. The maintenance and development of the railways and the main highways were expected to be auctioned to private operators through BOT concessions.

Around 80% of electricity-generating capacity is hydroelectric, the remainder being fossil fuel. With more investment in its oil industry, Peru could stop importing crude. The country's offshore basins are largely unexplored. A consortium formed by Argentina's Pluspetrol, U.S. Hunt Oil, and SK of South Korea won the 40-year concession in 2000 to develop the Camisea natural gas fields. The same group, plus Techint of Argentina, Algeria's state-owned Sonatrach, and Peru's Grana y Montrero won the downstream phase. Gas is expected to be flowing to Lima by 2004.

The telecommunications market was opened to full competition in 1998. Teledensity is very low, even in Lima, the capital. In 2000 there were more than 1 million cellular telephones, over half as many as the number of fixed-line telephones. There were less than one million Internet users. Close to 100% of the telephone network is digitalized.

EDUCATION/EMPLOYMENT

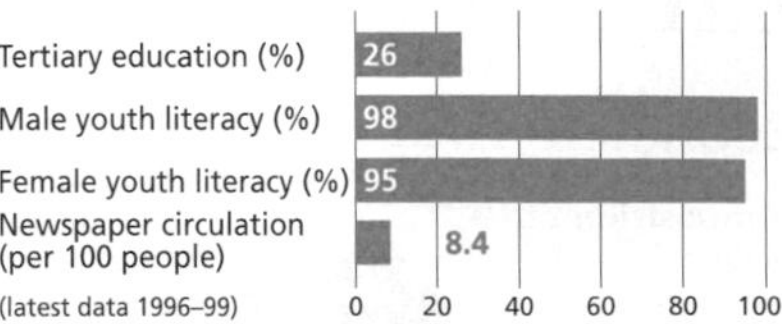

Education is compulsory and free from age 6 to 15, but a relatively large proportion of the population is illiterate, especially in the interior of the country. There are 75 universities, 45 of which are privately owned. There has been considerable growth in private universities, some of which, like the Universidad Pacífico, offer high-quality courses in business administration. The National University of San Marcos in Lima is the oldest university in Latin America. Spending on R&D is insignificant.

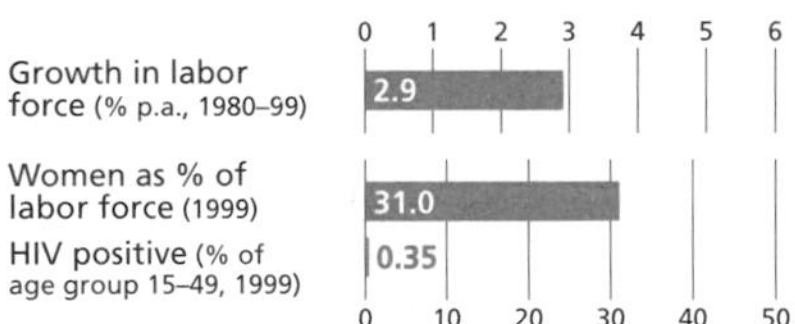

There is an abundant supply of labor, but qualified workers are in short supply. Child labor is widespread.

FISCAL/FINANCIAL

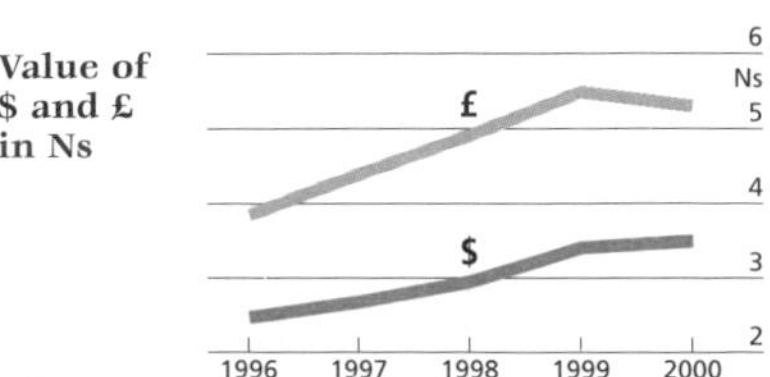

Two banks were privatized in the 1990s (Interbank and Continental), leaving the system entirely in the hands of the private sector apart from Banco de la Nación and

COFIDE, a second-tier bank. Close to half the total capital of banks is owned by foreign entities. Spain's Banco Bilbao Vizcaya Argentaria (BBVA) and Banco Santander Central Hispano (BSCH) own the third- and fourth-largest banks (BBVA Continental and BSCH Perú). Banco Central de Reserva, the Central Bank, is autonomous from the government, and is held up as an example of the level of political independence which other public sector institutions should strive to achieve.

Corporate tax and the top rate of income tax are both 30%, and VAT is 18%. The Lima Stock Exchange is small.

Business Opportunities

Growth in output (% p.a., 1990–99)

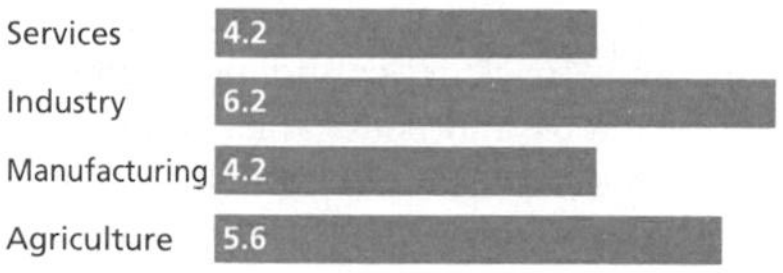

Services	4.2
Industry	6.2
Manufacturing	4.2
Agriculture	5.6

Despite all its problems, Peru is investor-friendly and has a liberal foreign investment regime. Foreign direct investment (FDI) rose from a yearly average of $600 million in 1985–95 to $1.5 billion in 1997–2000. Repatriation procedures are simple, and there is unrestricted access to foreign currency and a flexible exchange rate. A problematic area for investors, however, is the poor reputation and corruption of the judicial system. The principle of equal treatment for local and foreign companies is enshrined in the Peruvian constitution, and the government has tried to reinforce this, and to make up for the defects of the legal system, through investment promotion and protection accords such as one signed with Chile in 2000. These bilateral agreements offer alternatives for settlement of disputes, including the possibility of insuring investments against non-commercial risks with the World Bank's Multilateral Investment Guarantee Agency, or with agencies such as the Overseas Private Investment Corporation of the United States.

The government has planned specific incentives for sectors it wants to develop, such as tourism. The incentives would be temporary, and similar to the exemption of reinvested earnings from corporate taxes that helped to attract large-scale investments to develop the mining sector. The largest single foreign investment, a $2.3 billion copper-and-zinc concern called Antamina, began producing in 2001. Peru hoped to receive a further $11 billion in mining investments in 2001–10.

For More Information

Books:

Box, Ben, and Alan Murphy. *Peru Handbook*. 3rd ed. Bath, Somerset: Footprint Handbooks, 2001.
de Soto, Hernando. *The Other Path: The Invisible Revolution in the Third World.* New York: Basic Books, 2002.
Peru Business and Investment Opportunities Yearbook. 3rd ed. Washington, D.C.: International Business Publications, 2001 (annual).

Web Sites:

Central Bank: **www.bcrp.gob.pe**
CONITE (Foreign Investment Agency): **www.mef.gob.pe/peruinv/ingles/peruinv1.htm**
IMF reports: **www.imf.org/external**
Lima Stock Exchange: **www.bvl.com.pe**
National Institute of Statistics: **www.inei.gob.pe**
Peru Times (English language newspaper): **www.perutimes.com**
U.S. State Department Country Commercial Guide: **www. state.gov/e/eb/rls/rpts/ccg**

  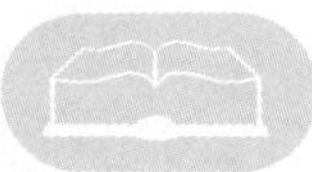    

PHILIPPINES

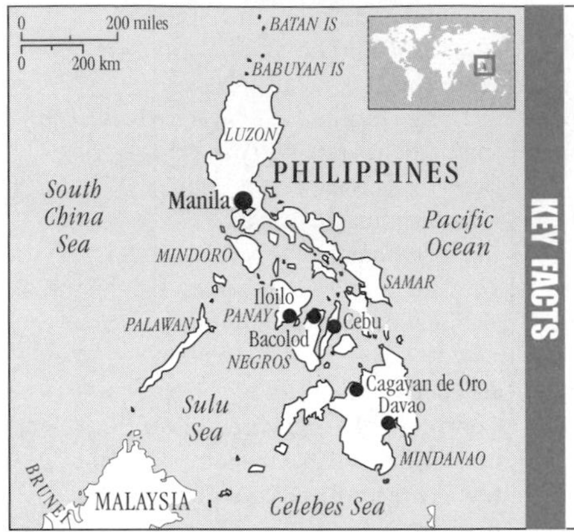

KEY FACTS

GNI: **$77,967 million; world's 41st**
GNI pc: **$1,050; world's 133rd**
Head of government: **president**
Currency: **peso (P)**
Capital: **Manila**
Population: **74,454,000, growing at 2.3% p.a.**
Land area: **115,135 square miles**
Population density: **646 per square mile**
Life expectancy: **69 years**
Infant mortality: **31 per 1,000 live births**
Language: **English, Pilipino**
Best buy: **textiles, brassware, wooden artifacts, coral jewelry**

ECONOMIC STRUCTURE

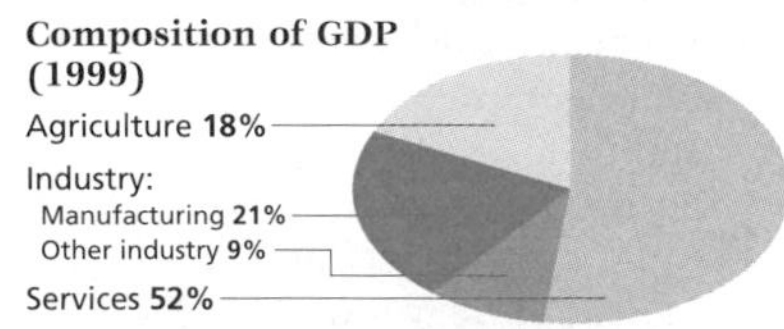

A Spanish colony from 1565 to 1898, the Philippines was ruled by the United States from 1898 to 1946 when the country gained independence. The few families which had dominated land ownership and wealth during colonial times became the new ruling elite. The majority of the population gained little from independence, and violent insurrection has been a constant threat. The armed forces backed President Marcos's rewriting of the constitution in 1973 to keep himself in power, since this provided stability. Economic development gathered pace in the 1970s when industrialization targeted export industries, abandoning the import substitution policy of the 1950s and 1960s. Capital-intensive heavy industry was developed, thus neglecting the poor once again and raising debt levels. The Marcos family and their associates controlled the economy through monopolies and cartels. The ousting of Marcos in 1986 was followed by IMF-backed reforms which emphasized labor-intensive industry and agriculture. In the 1990s, state intervention in the economy was reduced. The Asian financial crisis of 1997–98 caused delays in the privatization program, but led to improvements in the banking sector.

Services contributed 45.7% of GDP in 2000, followed by industry (34.4%), and agriculture (19.9%). Trade accounted for 16%, finance and housing 10%, and transport and communications 7.1%. Tourism is important. IT services are rapidly growing, with many U.S. and other multinational companies locating hub operations in design, data processing, and telephone call centers to Manila. Remittances of Filipinos working overseas were $6 billion in 2000. Manufacturing contributed 28.9% to GDP, construction 5%, and mining 1.1%. Electronics and electrical equipment are the key manufacturing industries, accounting for 58.2% of total exports in 2000. Machinery and transport equipment accounted for 15.5% of exports, clothing 6.7%, minerals 1.7%, and coconut products 1.6%. The top market was the United States (31.2%), followed by Japan (15.1%), Singapore (7.5%), the Netherlands (6.3%), and Hong Kong (4.8%).

Reform of state enterprises, corporate governance, and state finances began in the late 1980s following the removal of President Marcos. The first wave of privatization included the shares in the state airline, steel and petrol companies, and the Philippine National Bank (PNB). Liberalized sectors include sea ports, and the telecommunications and electricity industries, but the former state monopolies still predominate. State-owned National Power Corporation (NPC) owns 52% of electricity generating capacity, and it is scheduled for privatization. Although the privatization program was delayed by the Asian financial crisis, in the late 1990s the government turned to private-sector finance for and subsequent operation of infrastructure projects, including power generation, water supply in Manila, roads, and a new international airport terminal.

ECONOMIC POLICY

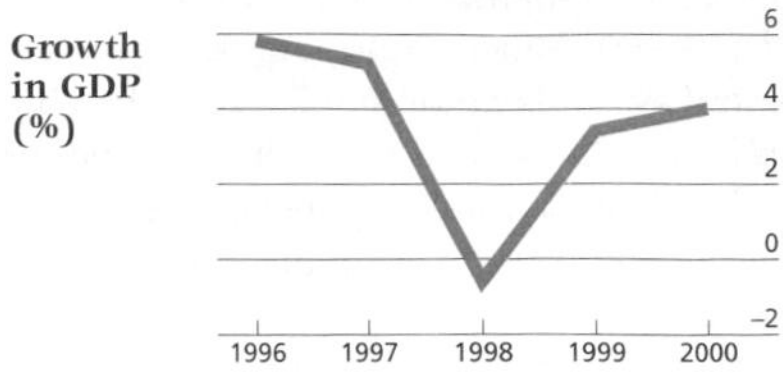

Under-investment in infrastructure, widespread poverty (36.7% of the population in 1997), and insufficient tax collection are persistent problems. Governments since 1986 have tried to resolve these problems with varying degrees of success, recognizing the restrictions they place on economic development, investor confidence, government revenues, and political harmony. The government has also tried to reduce subsidies on petrol, electricity, water, transport, and rice but has made little progress on account of public anger.

The government has sought and found private investment for infrastructure. Recent agrarian programs to reduce poverty have succeeded in raising the standard of living but not in reducing the gap between rich and poor. Current plans to extend electricity and roads in rural areas should help. Improvements in corporate governance and a major program to improve tax administration led to increased tax receipts in the mid-1990s, enabling the government to turn its chronic deficit to surpluses in 1994–96, but the end of the decade saw the return of tax shortfalls and deficits. The tax reform program intensified. Monetary policy has focused on reducing inflation to encourage long-term saving and investment, and on a freely floating exchange rate for the peso. The ratio of non-performing loans as a result of the 1997–98 financial crisis reached 16.3% of total loans at March 2001. The government required banks to recapitalize and make better provision for bad loans. Compliance was achieved without the injection of public funds into the banking system.

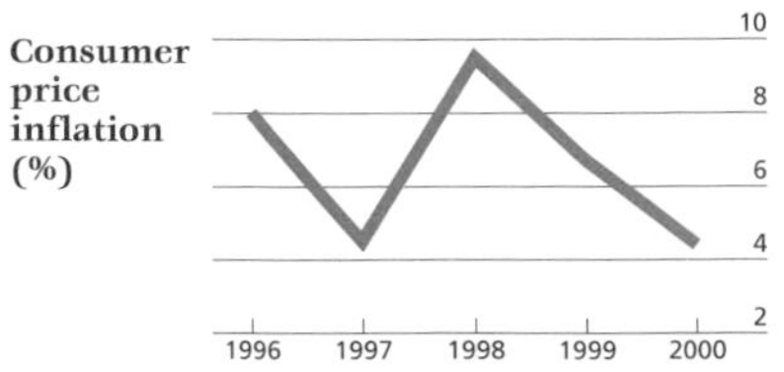

GDP growth was 3.3% in 1990–2001, with two falls of 0.6% in 1991 and 1998. Growth is expected to be 3% in 2002. Inflation was an

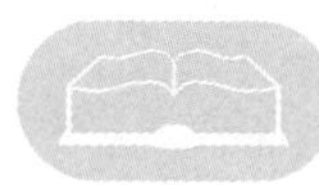

annual average 8.7% in 1990–99, with peaks in 1991 and 1998. It fell to 4.4% in 2000, rose again to 7% in 2001, and is expected to be 6% in 2002. Unemployment was an average 8.6% in 1990–99, rising to an average 11.2% in 2000–01.

Geography/Resources

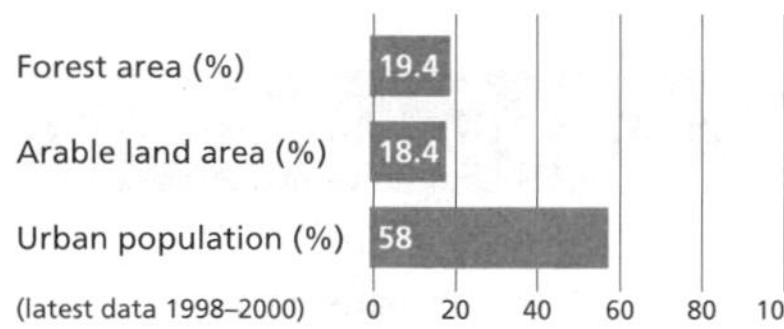

The Philippines is an archipelago of over 7,000 islands in the west Pacific Ocean. The main islands are Luzon in the north and Mindanao in the south, both of which are mountainous and volcanic with a high point of 9,692 feet. The climate is tropical: hot and humid at the lower levels, with abundant rainfall. There are two monsoon seasons, November–April and May–October. Natural hazards include 5–6 typhoons a year, volcanic eruptions, earthquakes, tsunamis, and landslides. Forests cover 46% of the land, arable land accounts for 31%, and pasture for 4%. The region around the capital, Manila, accounted for 14% of the population in 1997, but one-third of GDP. There were 32% of the population living below the poverty line. The majority of the population is of Malay origin, and most are Christian (91.5%), while 4% are Muslim and 1.5% are of Chinese origin.

Sugar cane is the top agricultural product, followed by coconuts, rice, corn, bananas, rubber, coffee, and abaca. Chickens are the most important livestock, followed by ducks, pigs, goats, buffaloes, and cattle. Forestry is significant, especially for fuel wood. A wide variety of fish are caught, especially in deep-sea operations. Coal, chromite, copper, nickel, iron, gold, silver, petroleum, limestone, salt, petroleum and—from 2001—gas are the main minerals extracted. There are reserves of gypsum and manganese. Coal reserves were 300 million tons at end-1996. At January 2001, proven gas and oil reserves were 2.8 trillion cubic feet and 289 million barrels respectively. Most gas is at the Malampaya offshore field, which also holds some oil. Exploration continues at this site, but has been limited elsewhere.

Communications/Energy

The road network is around 99,500 miles, of which 17,400 miles are strategic national roads. These roads are being upgraded under the 1999–2004 Development Plan.

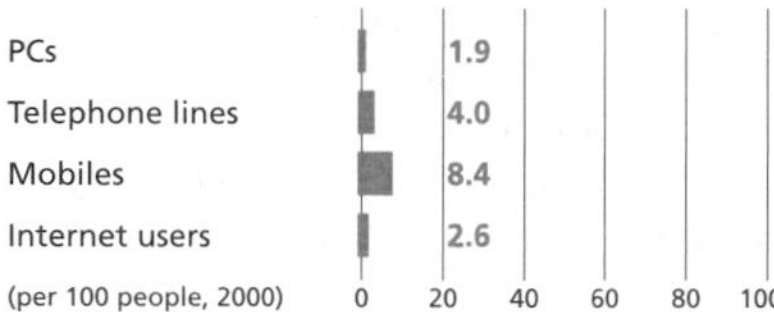

About 300 miles of new privately-operated toll motorways are being built. The rail network on the main island of Luzon is around 120 miles. A further 250 miles of track were non-operational. Investment is focused on doubling the Manila light rail system to 17 miles by 2004, and on restructuring the state-owned Philippine National Railways. Almost 98% of freight is handled by sea ports, of which there were 624 under public ownership and 300 under private ownership in 1999. Long-term projects are focused on linking land, air, and sea transport at 42 ports. By 2004, 11 international ports, 4 ro-ro terminals, 6 transfer ports, and 36 feeder ports will be developed. The merchant fleet numbered 1,726 ships, with total displacement of 8.5 million grt in 1998. Container traffic was a total 3.1 million teus in 2000. There were 92 public and 103 private airports in 1999, including 9 international airports. The Medium-Term Plan provides for the development of 37 international airports by 2004.

The domination of the telecommunications sector by the Philippine Long Distance Telephone Company was extended when it acquired cable and Internet companies to add to its mobile and fixed phone subsidiaries. The company will install cable for fast Internet access. Other operators of fixed, mobile, and multimedia telephony merged to give sufficient scale for future investments. International links via satellite and cable are good, but the domestic network requires upgrading and extension. There were 6.8 million fixed-line phones in 1999. At end-2000 there were 6.5 million mobile phones and 2 million Internet users. The 2000 E-Commerce Act gives priority to this fast-growing sector.

At end-1999 most electricity power plants used oil (30%), followed by coal (26%), hydro (19%), geothermal (17%), and other renewables including biomass, solar, wind, wood, and waste (1%). Power-plant expansion—including gas, coal, hydro, geothermal, solar, and wind—is under way to meet an anticipated 41% increase in demand from 1999 to 2004. Three new gas fired power stations are using gas from the new Malampaya field from 2002. Plans to build a nuclear power station have been shelved. Electricity distribution is being extended to reach 88% of households in 2004, up from 76% in 1999. Indigenous oil and coal contribute to energy supply, but most oil and coal is imported. Oil production was 4,000 barrels per day and consumption was 377,000 barrels per day in 2000. Coal production was 1 million tons, with consumption at 5.7 million tons, in 1999.

Education/Employment

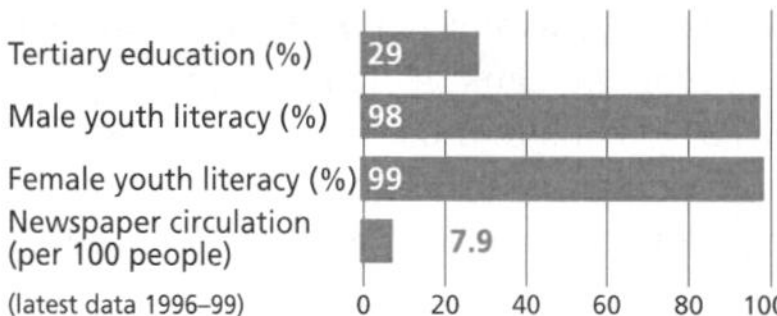

Education is compulsory from age 7 to 13. There are 28 public- and private-sector universities and colleges with a total enrollment of around 2 million students. The Department of Education is responsible for public higher-education institutes. The 1999–2004 Medium-Term Development Plan outlines reforms to give institutes a greater degree of autonomy in pursuing instruction and research which will equip graduates with the technical skills needed for the information age.

Universities and research institutes conduct basic and applied research. Strengths include food, agriculture, forestry, biotechnology, metals, industrial processes, and IT. There are government-supported programs for private-sector R&D in IT, food and nutrition, forest industries, metals industries, textiles, and industrial technology. The government is encouraging the formation of science parks to link university research with industrial applications.

The labor force is well educated, adaptable, and multilingual. English and Spanish are the most widely spoken second languages. Wages and other employment conditions are determined by employers and trade unions or employees. Just over half a million workers are covered by collective agreements. Most trade unions are willing to consider productivity as part of the wage bargaining process, and the number of strikes has fallen steadily since the 1980s. Minimum wages are set annually by the 16 regional government Wage and Productivity Boards.

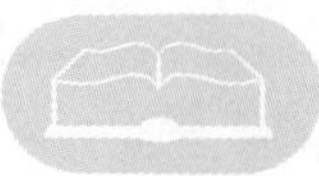

FISCAL/FINANCIAL

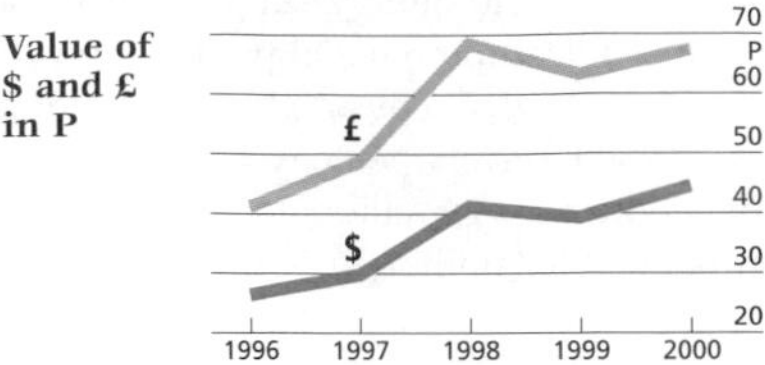

At end-March 2001 the largest bank in terms of total assets, deposits, and loans was Metropolitan Bank & Trust Company, followed by Bank of the Philippines. The third bank in total deposits was the state-owned Land Bank of the Philippines, followed by Equitable PCI Bank. Three of the top four banks are private-sector. Bank of the Philippines and Equitable PCI Bank are the result of mergers in 1999. Metropolitan and Equitable have insurance company subsidiaries. U.S.-owned Citibank was the fifth largest, and the partly state-owned Philippine National Bank the sixth, in terms of deposits. Bangko Sentral ng Pilipinas (BSP), the central bank, is responsible for implementing monetary policy and financial sector regulation. The Insurance Commission supervises the insurance sector, while the Securities and Exchange Commission regulates the stock market. Corporate income tax is 32%, and the top rate of personal income tax is 35%. VAT is 10%.

As a result of the 1997–98 financial crisis, BSP required banks to recapitalize and set aside larger loan-loss provisions. Restrictions on foreign bank equity were lifted to allow greater access to private capital. The 2000 General Banking Law sets international standards of risk management, bank reporting and transparency, and bank supervision. Anti-money-laundering laws were tightened in 2000 and 2001, but banking secrecy remains protected. The level of non-performing loans (NPL) acted as a brake on lending operations. BSP is encouraging bank consolidation. At March 2001 there were 45 commercial banks, including 19 foreign banks, which account for 90% of total banking resources; 111 thrift banks (including savings banks, private debt banks, and stock savings and loans associations); over 787 rural banks; and 13 offshore banking units.

The corporate sector has traditionally relied on short- to medium-term loans to raise finance. The government is promoting longer-term instruments, especially bonds, and greater recourse to the stock market. Use of securities is increasing, but the equities market is thin. Stock market capitalization and turnover plummeted as a result of the financial crisis, declining further through 2000–01 as a result of domestic political problems and high-profile kidnappings of foreign tourists by anti-government dissidents in the south. In 1993 the Manila Stock Exchange and Makati Stock Exchange merged to form the Philippines Stock Exchange. The consolidation was completed with the introduction of electronic trading and links between the two exchanges in 1994. A real-time computerized settlement system for equities, fixed-income securities, money and foreign exchange operations was being installed by banks in 2001.

BUSINESS OPPORTUNITIES

Growth in output (% p.a., 1990–99)

Services	4.0
Industry	3.2
Manufacturing	2.9
Agriculture	1.4

The Philippine Economic Zone Authority (PEZA) administers four public-sector and 40 private-sector special economic zones where companies are eligible for tax and other incentives, especially for export industries. Two other private-sector economic zones on Mindanao island and in Cagayan province are administered separately. PEZA encourages the establishment of IT parks, as IT is the top investment priority. Foreign investment is excluded or restricted in several sectors. The main destinations of foreign direct investment are finance, food production, hydrocarbons production and processing, chemicals, and communications infrastructure and operation. The United States was the top investor in 1998–2000, followed by Japan, Netherlands, Switzerland, the United Kingdom, and Hong Kong. Current opportunities exist in IT, telecommunications, electricity, roads, finance, and manufacturing. Privatizations offer further opportunities. The point of contact for foreign investors is the Board of Investment.

For More Information

Books:

Asian Development Bank, Country Economic Review. *Philippines.*
Economist Intelligence Unit. *Country Profile and Quarterly Reports.* London.
IMF Country Report. *Philippines.* Washington, D.C.
Jealous, Virginia, et al. *Philippines.* 7th ed. Oakland, CA: Lonely Planet, 2000.
Philippines Country Study Guide. 2nd ed. Washington, D.C.: International Business Publications, 2000.
Philippines Foreign Policy and Government Guide. 3rd ed. Washington, D.C.: International Business Publications, 2001.

Web Sites:

Bangko Sentral ng Pilipinas (central bank): **www.bsp.gov.ph**
Board of Investment: **www.boi.gov.ph**
Department of Foreign Affairs: **www.dfa.gov.ph**
Department of Science and Technology: **www.dost.gov.ph**
Department of Tourism: **www.tourism.gov.ph**
Manila Bulletin (English language daily newspaper): **www.mb.com.ph**
National Economic and Development Authority (government entry point): **www.neda.gov.ph**
National Statistics Office: **www.census.gov.ph**
Philippine Stock Exchange: **www.pse.org.ph**

POLAND

KEY FACTS

GNI: **$157,429 million; world's 25th**
GNI pc: **$4,070; world's 74th**
Head of state: **president**
Head of government: **prime minister**
Currency: **zloty (Zl)**
Capital: **Warsaw**
Population: **38,740,000, growing at 0.2% p.a.**
Land area: **117,350 square miles**
Population density: **329 per square mile**
Life expectancy: **73 years**
Infant mortality: **9 per 1,000 live births**
Language: **Polish**
Best buy: **glass, tableware**

ECONOMIC STRUCTURE

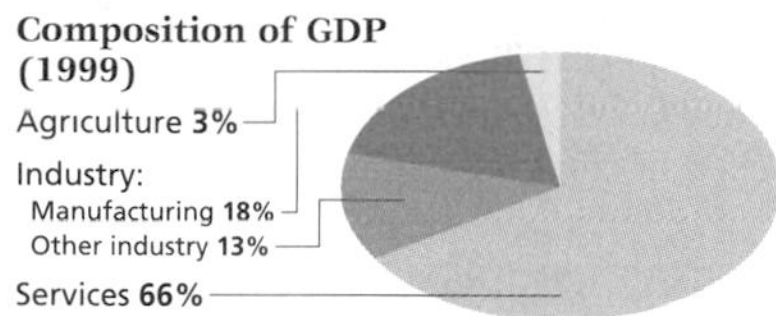

Poland's shape and size has changed constantly over its 1000-year existence; in the mid-1500s, for example, it was Europe's largest state. In 1939 Germany and the Soviet Union agreed to partition Poland, and Germany's invasion is usually regarded as the opening of World War II. The state that emerged from the war in 1945 was ruled by the (communist) Polish United Workers Party from 1948 to 1989, when a decade of campaigning by the Solidarity trade union movement resulted in free elections, and the communists lost power. The Polish market reforms of the 1990s were regarded, along with the Czech and Hungarian, as the most successful in the transition states. Despite several changes of government—the latest, resulting from the September 2001 general election, bringing to power a left-of-center coalition headed by the reformist former communists (SLD)—Poland's pro-Western orientation stayed constant. It has joined the WTO (in 1995), the OECD (1996), and NATO (1999). In 2001 it remained among the most promising East European candidates for EU membership, with agricultural reform presenting the main stumbling block.

In the 1990s, industry's share of GDP has declined (from 41.7% in 1988 to 23.6% in 1999) and that of services increased. However, manufacturing retains a central role: the food processing, beverages and tobacco, and chemicals and pharmaceuticals sectors have grown, and have attracted substantial foreign investment. The automotive and car components industry also expanded rapidly in the late 1990s but fell back sharply in 2000–01. Warsaw's development as Eastern Europe's leading business center has boosted construction, although that, too, slowed in 2000–01. Poland's shipbuilding industry is the world's fourth largest; it had a $4 billion order book in 2001. The coal and steel industries, based mainly in southeast Poland, are being restructured but remain crucial. A successful privatization program, which boosted foreign direct investment (FDI) levels in the late 1990s and took private-sector share of GDP to 65% (in 2000–01), is expected to near completion in 2002–03.

A key economic problem is agriculture, which employs more than 20% of the workforce but accounts for only 5% of GDP. Farms are small (19.3 acres on average in 1997). EU entry negotiations reached stalemate in 2000 due to Brussels refusing to accept Warsaw's proposals that Polish farmers, in return for accepting the Common Agricultural Policy, must receive EU-level subsidies from the moment of accession.

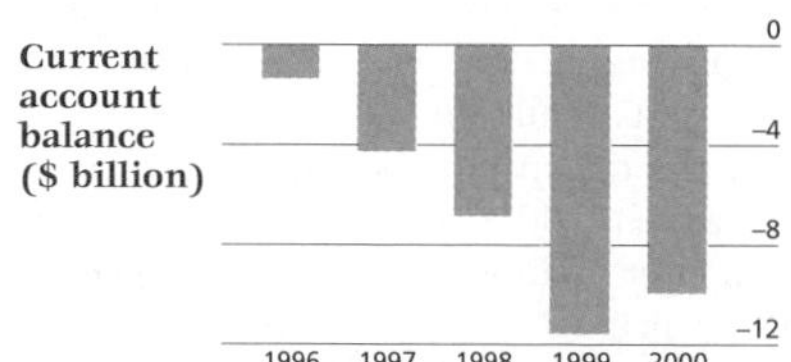

Poland's most important exports are cars and car parts, wood and timber products, and machinery and equipment; the food industry's share dropped in the late 1990s. Poland's main trading partner is the EU, with 70% of exports and 61.2% of imports. The leading export destinations (2000 figures) are Germany (34.9%), Italy (6.3%), France (5.2%), and the Netherlands (5.1%), and main sources of imports Germany (23.9%), Russia (9.4%), Italy (8.3%), and France (6.4%). Poland's partners in the six-nation Central European Free Trade Agreement account for very little of its trade.

ECONOMIC POLICY

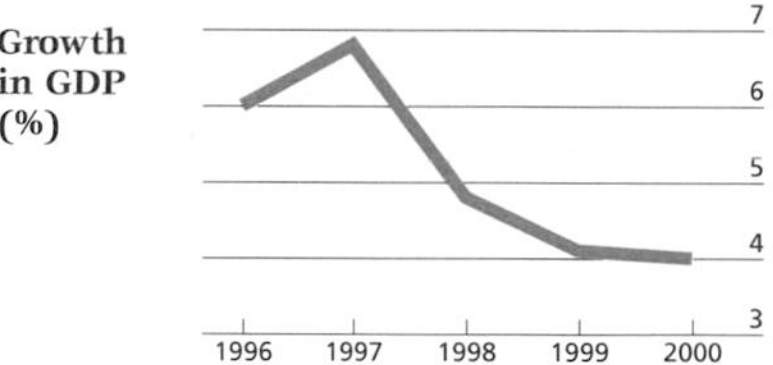

Poland has boasted uninterrupted growth since 1992. Although it recently slowed, from 5–6% in the mid-1990s to 4% in 2000 and 2% in 2001, this was mainly due to tight monetary policy designed to control inflation, which ran at 7.3% in 1999 and 10.1% in 2000, but fell to 5.6% (EBRD projection) in 2001. Poland's principal economic policy concern was seen in late 2001 by the EBRD as the need to implement fiscal consolidation, in the face of falling EU demand and the expected loss of an important source of capital inflows as the privatization program nears completion.

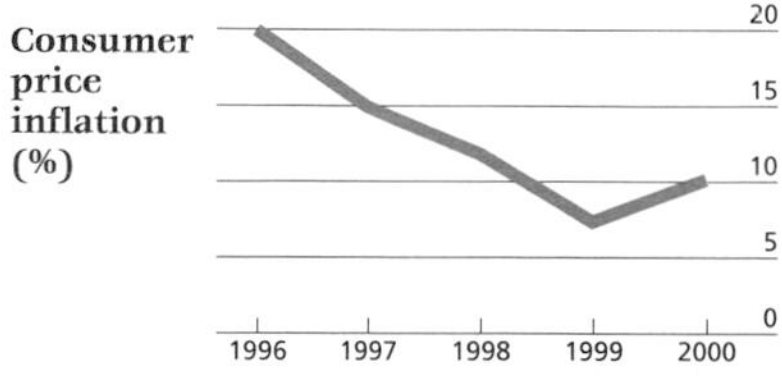

The way to Poland's long spell of steady growth was paved by the "shock therapy" imposed in 1990 by the first post-communist finance minister, Leszek Balcerowicz, which tipped the economy into a deep recession in 1991–92. Since then Poland has been seen as a standard-bearer for market reform: in 1991 it restructured its communist era international debt (postponing much of the repayment burden to the decade from 2000); after applying for EU membership in 1994 it has based fiscal policy on the Maastricht criteria and introduced EU-compatible legislation; it carried

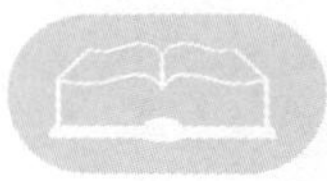

through currency, tax, and banking reforms, and in 1997 made the Central Bank constitutionally independent of government.

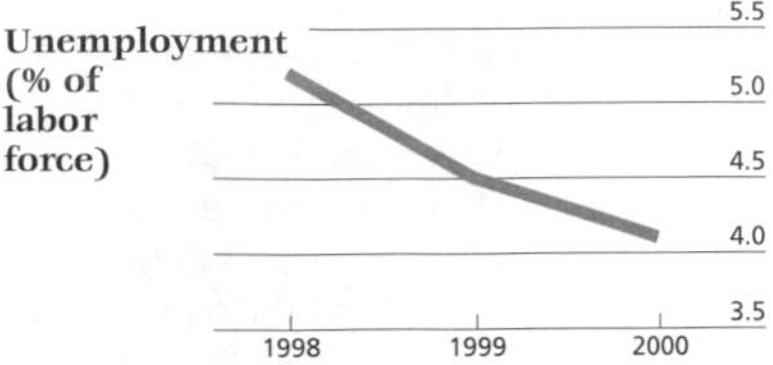

Poland retains a large "gray" economy, which accounts for 10–20% of GDP, and unemployment has risen sharply from 8.6% in 1997 to 16% in 2001 (first half). There are also sharp regional differences: a prosperous zone stretching from Gdansk to Warsaw and thence to Krakow in the south contrasts sharply with the poor agricultural areas of the east. In general, cities contrast with the countryside, attracting labor from it and struggling with a resultant housing shortage; among industrial conurbations, Katowice (where wage levels are 25% above average) contrasts with the rest.

Geography/Resources

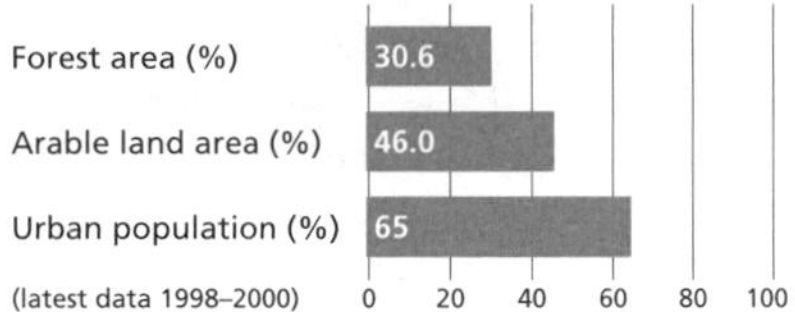

Poland is bordered to the north by the Baltic Sea, to the northeast by Russia, and Lithuania and to the east by Belarus and Ukraine. The southern border follows the line of the Beskid, Carpathian, and Sudeten mountains, separating Poland from the Czech and Slovak republics, and the western border with Germany runs partly along the Neisse and Oder rivers. Except for the southern mountains, the country consists almost entirely of lowlands.

Poland has rich natural resources. Its principal mineral asset is bituminous coal, but it has smaller quantities of brown coal, oil, and natural gas, and minerals including sulfur, barite, salt, and kaolin. Its copper resources are sufficient to make it a major world producer; silver is a by-product. Despite agriculture's decline in the 1990s, Poland remains one of the world's leading producers of rye and potatoes. Its other principal crops are wheat and sugar beet. Farming is mixed: Poland has large herds of beef cattle, dairy cows, and pigs.

Poland's population was spared the damaging demographic impact of the post-communist slump experienced by most of Eastern Europe. It is expected to grow gradually, reaching 40 million by 2010, and also to become older, with a continuing increase in the working-age population in 2001–05, and a steady increase in the proportion of pensioners after that. Poland has been urbanizing for half a century and continues to do so: in 1946 the rural population outnumbered townspeople by two to one; by 1996 the position was reversed.

Poland's population is one of the world's most ethnically homogeneous: ethnic Poles comprise more than 98%. Prewar Poland was notable for its rich and varied multiethnicity, but during the war it lost about 11 million people: almost all Jews were killed, and other ethnic groupsBelarusians, Ukrainians, Germans, Lithuanians, and the Poles themselves—were reduced both by war and by forced and voluntary emigration.

Communications/Energy

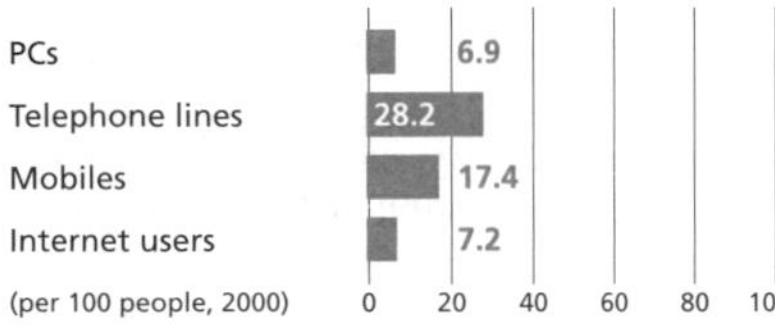

Of Poland's 220,000 miles of roads, only 21% are in good condition. Major investment is required, and hundreds of millions of dollars are being lent, or donated, for this under various EU programs. The first EU-supported, 54-Zlbillion, 15-year scheme, starting in 2001, envisages the modernization of 2,988 miles of roads. On the railways, financial restructuring is judged the priority; in 2000 the state rail company's debts were equivalent to 1% of GDP, and parliament approved plans to break it up, privatize most parts, and reduce its workforce by a quarter, although observers doubt whether the new SLD-led coalition will carry out this program. Poland's Baltic ports are key trade assets: cargo handling was 55 million tons in 2000, and there are plans to double this by 2010. As for air traffic, Poland has agreed with the EU to liberalize the market by 2004. In preparation, the national airline LOT has been reducing fares, improving services, and increasing the number of destinations, and Warsaw's Okecie airport has been undergoing modernization, to increase capacity to 6.5 million passengers per year. After the collapse in October 2001 of Swissair, which held 37.6% of LOT, the government was seeking a new strategic partner for the airline.

Poland's telecommunications sector has grown steadily. The number of fixed lines per 100 inhabitants has risen from 9.3 in 1992 to 22.8 in 1999 and 26 in 2000. Mobile telephone penetration had reached 17.8% by the end of 2000. The sector is being deregulated to meet EU accession criteria: the local and domestic long-distance markets are due to be fully liberalized in 2002, the international market by 2003. TPSA, the state telecoms company, was joined in 2000 by strong competitors in the local markets.

Most of Poland's energy provision is from coal: it accounts for 90% of primary energy production and 70% of total consumption. Imported oil and natural gas, mostly from Russia, also play a role. In 2001 the government signed contracts to lay a Baltic gas pipeline with a view to diversifying supply away from Russia towards Denmark, Norway, and others. The energy sector—comprising 17 power plants, 19 combined heat and power plants, 33 distribution companies and the national grid—is being restructured. By February 2001 three power plants and six CHPs had been privatized; the government hoped to sell the rest by the end of 2002. Liberalization of the energy market is being held up by long-term contracts that cover 70% of it.

Education/Employment

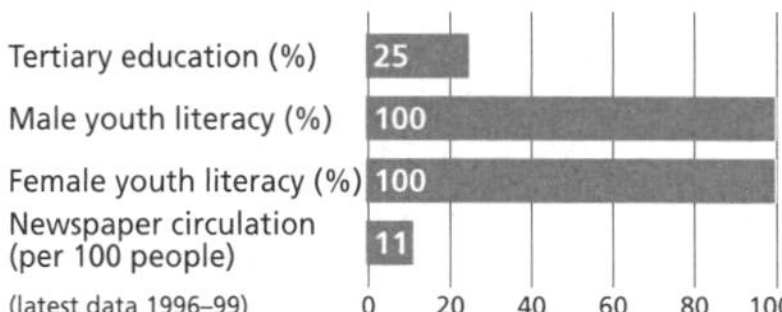

Poland's workforce of nearly 15 million people is relatively highly skilled. Productivity is low by Western standards but rising; the average gross monthly wage in 1999 was $524. The state sector still provides 30% of employment, but private-sector employment continues to rise. High unemployment, combined with a high minimum wage, had combined by late 2001 to produce what the EBRD described as "structural imbalances" in the labor market that needed to be addressed. Poland's industrial relations are governed by a Labor Code, revised in 1996; the unions remain powerful, continue to have a say in decisions on restructuring, and will usually require an agreement with new owners of any privatized enterprise.

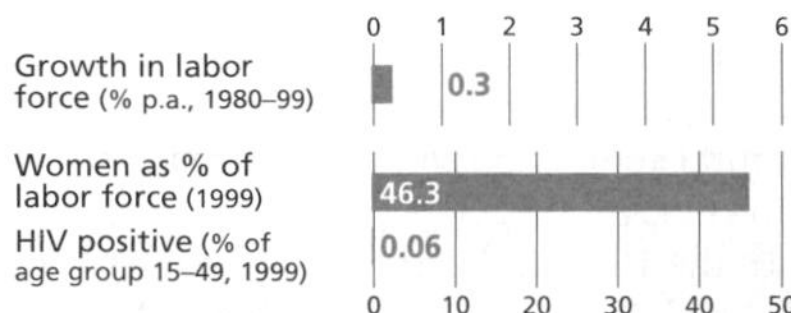

Poland's state-funded, freely-available education system is organized on the German model: basic schooling (ages 7–14),

vocation or further schooling (15–18), and higher education (19–24). High standards of education and literacy prevailed in the communist period, and have suffered less from subsequent upheavals than they did elsewhere in Eastern Europe. Participation in higher education has increased, from 10–12% of the relevant age group in the 1980s to 28% in 1999–2000. Although the constitution guarantees higher education free of charge, and a system of cheap loans for students was introduced in 1998, many state universities charge some fees. They also face a challenge from strong private higher education institutions, many of them business schools, which in 2000–01 provided 37% of the 460,000 new student places. With state academic salaries falling sharply behind those in this private sector, it has become common for state-employed teachers to take second jobs in private colleges.

Fiscal/Financial

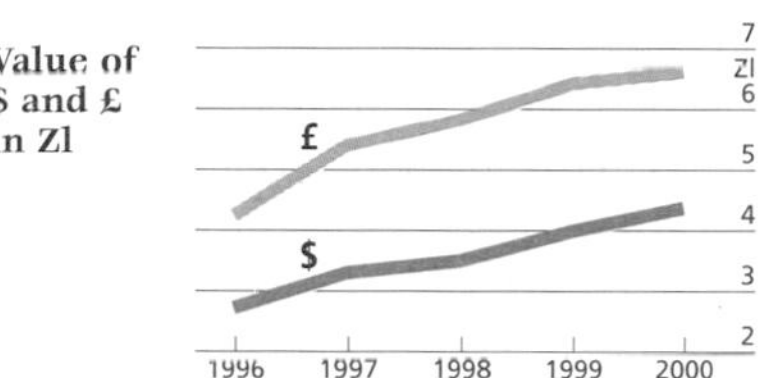

Poland's banking sector is one of Eastern Europe's most advanced: the problem of bad loans, present in the early 1990s, was largely overcome through the establishment of regulatory institutions and some recapitalization. Privatization of the sector is well advanced, and foreign owners control the majority of banking assets. A significant round of sell-offs in 1997–2000 left only two large banks to be privatized: PKO BP, the largest savings bank, and BGZ, the agricultural bank. There was also considerable consolidation in the late 1990s: by 2000 Pekao SA and PKO BP held 32% of banking assets, with other large banks, including the third, Bank Handlowy, holding 4–5% each.

Poland's equity market is well developed. The Warsaw Stock Exchange, which opened in 1991, is now Central and Eastern Europe's largest, with a capitalization of about $30 billion (about 20% of GDP), which is comparable to the smaller EU exchanges.

The pension reform that began in 1999 initiated a system based on the Latin American model, whereby individuals put payroll deductions into individual retirement accounts in privately managed funds. More than 80% of the population were participating by early 2001. The pension system, which invests heavily in local shares and has contributed to stock market development, is dominated by three funds created by Polish-foreign partnerships: Commercial Union (United Kingdom), Nationale Nederlanden (Netherlands), and PZU Zlota Jesien. The insurance market, of which life insurance is the most important component, also has a strong foreign ownership element: in 2000, 41 of the 69 insurance companies were majority foreign-held, but the former state monopoly, PZU, still has a 58% market share.

After a major tax reform in January 2000, corporate income tax was lowered from 34% to 30%, and is due to go down to 22% by 2004. Tax incentives and a complex system of investment allowances were eliminated, and some rules regarding depreciation of assets and revaluation of fixed assets simplified. The VAT tax base was broadened, and in July 2000 VAT at a reduced rate was introduced for agricultural products.

Business Opportunities

Growth in output (% p.a., 1990–99)

Services	4.1
Industry	3.8
Agriculture	–0.1

Poland has become a leader among Central and Eastern European countries in terms of FDI inflow. By the end of 2000 it had reached a record $9.3 billion for the year and an aggregate total of $35.5 billion since 1991. The leading inward investors are, by volume, Germany, the United States, the Netherlands, and France, who between them accounted for 70% of FDI up to 2001. Since 1997, flows have been enhanced by large-scale privatization sales, which are expected to fall again by 2002–03; the largest such deal was the $4.3 billion sale in 2000 of 35% of TPSA, the telecoms company, to a French-Polish consortium. Another large sale, of a stake in PZU, the insurance company, to pan-European insurer Eureko, was finally completed in late 2001 after becoming mired in a legal dispute. The privatization program for Huta Katowice, the largest steel mill, failed and was abandoned in 2001.

Up to 1998 the largest amount of FDI went into the manufacturing sector, led by food processing and the automotive industry, followed by wood processing, printing and publishing, and manufacture of non-metal goods. But since 1997 manufacturing's share has fallen, and that of the financial services sector in particular has risen, particularly with the opening of the insurance and pension sectors to foreign investors. The financial, telecoms, light manufacturing, and tourism sectors were in 2001 expected to provide further FDI opportunities; so were (in 2001) the expected sale of a controlling stake of Rafineria Gdanska, Poland's second-largest oil refinery and (in 2002–03) partial privatization of the PGNiG gas distribution company and the rail company PKP.

Most legislation governing investment is in line with EU requirements. Foreign-owned companies enjoy equal treatment to Polish entities. Some legal barriers to takeovers and other investment activity were removed by laws enacted in January 2001, including the Law on Commercial Activity and the Code of Commercial Partnerships. Poland also has an Agency for Foreign Investment to liaise with foreign business, and 17 Special Economic Zones with advantageous conditions for inward investors.

For More Information

Books:

Armstrong, Diane. *Mosaic: A Chronicle of Five Generations.* New York: St. Martin's Press, 2001.

Davies, Norman. *Heart of Europe: The Past in Poland's Present.* New York: Oxford University Press, 2001.

Gupta, Kanhaya, and Robert Lensink. *Financial Reforms in Eastern Europe: A Policy Model for Poland.* New York: Routledge, 1998.

Hunter, Richard, and Leo Ryan. *From Autarchy to Market.* Westport, CT: Praeger Publishers, 1998.

Johnson, Simon, and Gary Loveman. *Starting Over in Eastern Europe: Entrepreneurship and Economic Renewal.* Cambridge, MA: Harvard Business School Press, 1995.

Jolly, Adam, Nadine Kettaneh, and Nick Sljivic, eds. *Doing Business with Poland.* 3rd ed. Sterling, VA: Kogan Page, 2000.

Szerlip, Barbara, ed. *Passport Poland: Your Pocket Guide to Polish Business, Customs & Etiquette.* Novato, CA: World Trade Press, 1999.

Web Sites:

Industrial Development Agency: **www.arp.com.pl**

Ministry of Economy: **www.mg.gov.pl**

Polish Agency for Foreign Investment: **www.paiz.gov.pl/indexm.html**

Polish Stock Exchange: **www.gpw.com.pl**

Warsaw Business Journal: **www.wbj.pl**

Warsaw Voice magazine: **www.warsawvoice.pl**

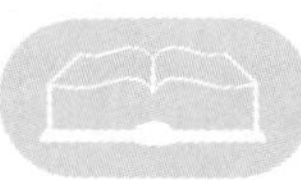

Portugal

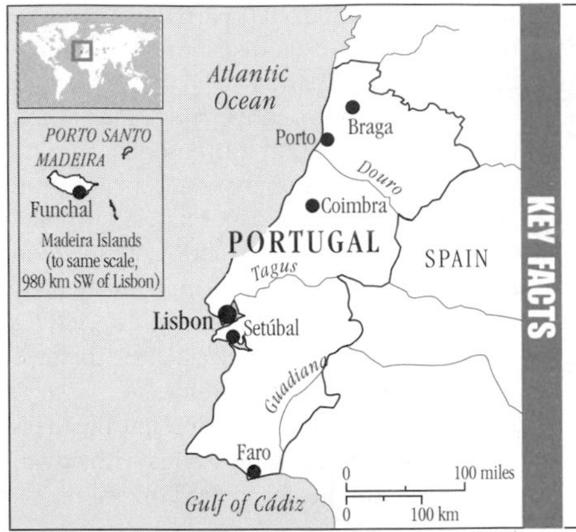

KEY FACTS

GNI: **$110,175 million; world's 34th**
GNI pc: **$11,030; world's 49th**
Head of government: **prime minister**
Currency: **Euro (€)**
Capital: **Lisbon**
Population: **9,873,000, growing at 0.0% p.a.**
Land area: **35,330 square miles**
Population density: **280 per square mile**
Life expectancy: **76 years**
Infant mortality: **5 per 1,000 live births**
Language: **Portuguese**
Best buy: **leather goods, ceramics, wine, port**

Economic Structure

Composition of GDP (1999)

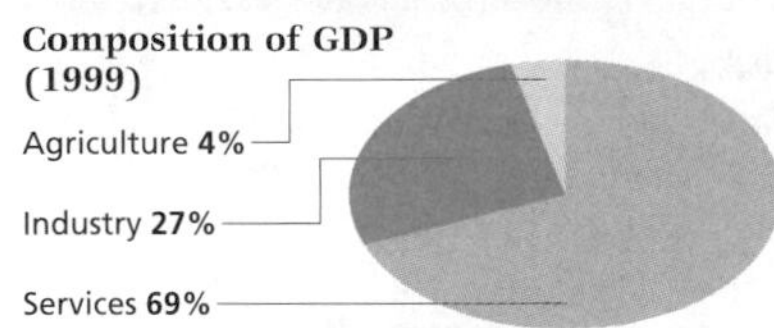

Portugal was one of the earliest European colonial powers. Following maritime exploration in the 14th century, the Portuguese established trading colonies in Africa, Brazil, and the Far East in the 15th and 16th centuries. However, the monarchy and the elite merchants kept the wealth for themselves, and Portugal itself remained undeveloped. Political unrest prevailed in the 19th and early 20th centuries, culminating in the military dictatorship of 1926. Control was centralized, and relied on the army and secret police; the Portuguese people remained poor. At the end of this era in 1976, a new constitution enshrined socialist principles of nationalization and redistribution of wealth. This did not produce prosperity. Accession to the European Union in 1986 created the conditions for releasing state control and increasing wealth.

Services contributed around 60% of GDP in 1999, while manufacturing, power, construction, and mining accounted for 36%, and agriculture, forestry, and fisheries 4%. Tourism is the main services sector, followed by finance, insurance and real estate, and business services, including call centers. In 2000, 28 million visitors spent $5.7 billion. Textiles, clothing, and leather goods have been the main manufacturing sectors, but automotive and electronics industries are growing fast while the traditional industries are in relative decline. Wine and food processing remain strong. Portuguese banks and telecommunications, electricity, retail, and cement companies have invested in Brazil to create global links; they are expected to earn more from Brazilian than Portuguese operations in a few years' time. The main export market in 2000 was Spain (19.3%), followed by Germany (18%), France (12.7%), the United Kingdom (10.9%), Belgium and Luxembourg (6%), and the United States (5.8%). The main exports were machinery (19.7%), clothing and footwear (17.3%), road vehicles and parts (15%), wood, cork and paper (10.4%), chemicals (7.8%), leather (7.4%), food including sardines (7.2%), and metals (6.3%).

Current account balance ($ billion)

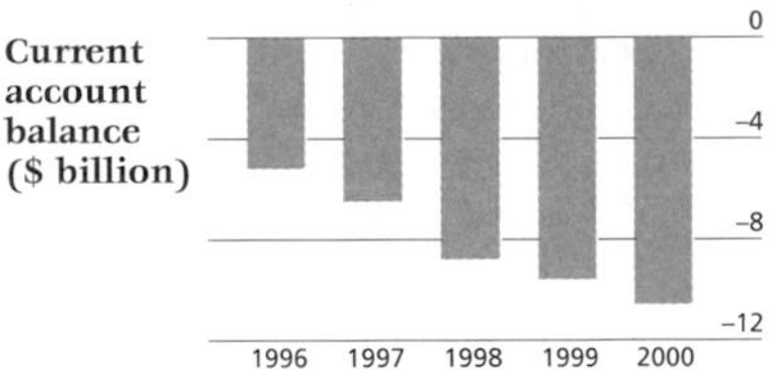

The government began a massive privatization program in 1989. By 2001 it had sold off part or all of more than 100 organizations in finance, insurance, energy utilities, telecommunications, cement, wood pulp, chemicals, and highways. Entities due for privatization, some of which are debt-laden, include air transport, agribusiness, paper, shipyards, ports, and the railways. The government plans to keep its strategic minority shareholdings in Portugal Telecom, Electricidade de Portugal, and cement company Cimpor, and majority control of the largest savings bank Caixa Geral de Depositos. CGD provides finance to industry and agriculture, and owns insurance companies, but these might be partly privatized.

Economic Policy

Growth in GDP (%)

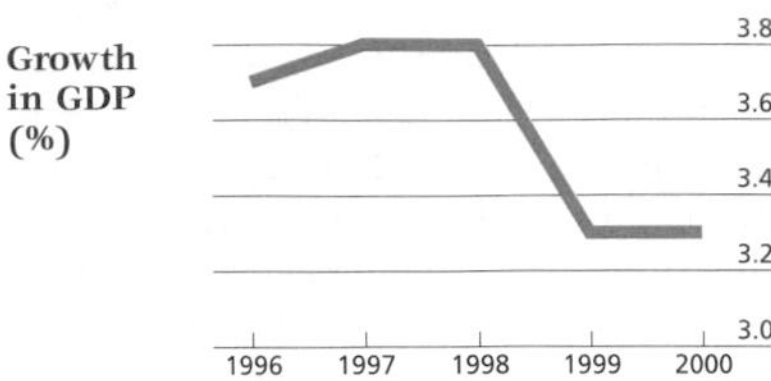

The privatization proceeds of almost $20 billion to 1999 were used to pay off the public debt, reducing it from 64.5% of GDP in 1995 to 55.1% in 2000. The government aims to reduce it to 48.1% of GDP in 2004. The general government deficit fell from 2.5% of GDP in 1997 to 1.5% in 2000, but rose to 2% in 2001 because of lower tax revenues. The government is committed to achieving a balanced budget by 2004. Public spending was reduced in 1993–99 to ensure compliance with EU eligibility criteria for the Euro, but it increased after 1999 until lower economic growth in 2001 forced the government to introduce new cuts, including limits on public-sector recruitment and a tougher stance on public-sector wage increases. The government has had success in combating tax evasion, and reforms in 2000 included measures to combat under-reporting of income by small firms and individuals. Corporation tax for small companies was simplified, and banking secrecy can now be lifted under certain circumstances. There have been significant gains in opening the economy to competition and in creating employment to offset the huge job losses resulting from privatization. The job-creation program was achieved through a 1996 pact between government, employers, and trade unions to improve education and training and to introduce flexible work contracts and practices. The 2001–04 stability program targets improvements in education, health, public administration, and new technologies. In particular IT is being used to simplify public administration procedures, and Internet links are being extended to schools and small shops.

Unemployment (% of labor force)

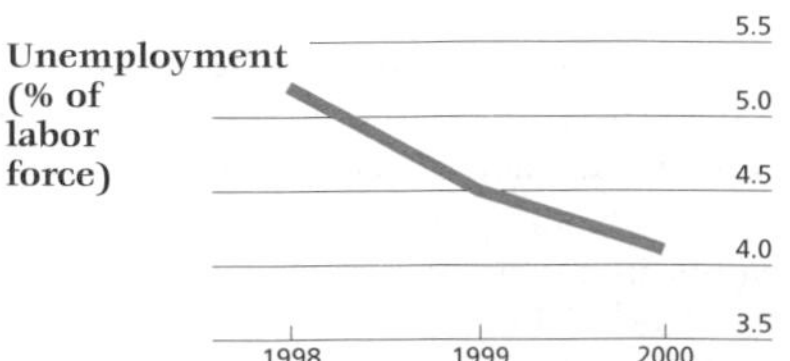

GDP growth picked up from the mid-1990s, rising from an annual average of

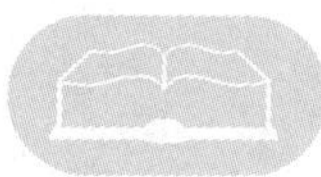

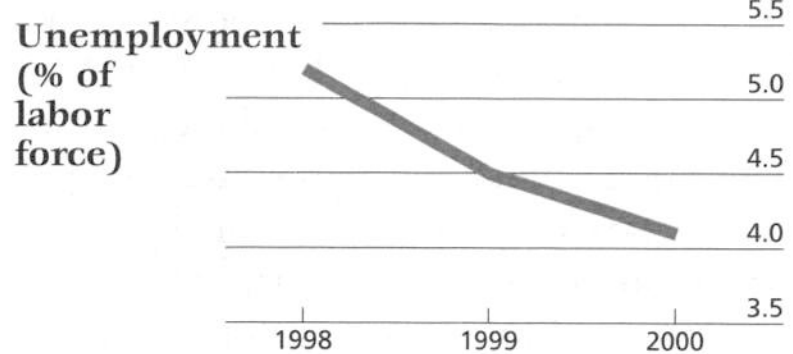

1.8% in 1991–95 to 3.6% in 1996–2000, led initially by exports, then by private consumption and investment, then by exports again. With weaker exports growth fell to 1.8% in 2001, and 1.5% is expected in 2002. Inflation fell from an average 7.1% in 1991–95 to 2.6% in 1996–2000. It rose to 4.3% in 2001 but is expected to fall to 2.6% in 2002. Unemployment fell from a peak of 7.3% in 1996 to 4.1% in 2000, and is expected to stay at around 4% in the medium term.

Geography/Resources

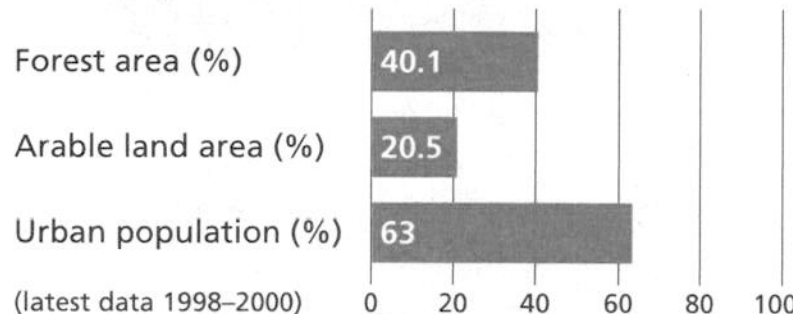

Portugal is in the extreme southwest of Europe with the Atlantic Ocean to the west, the Mediterranean to the south, and land borders with Spain to the east and north. Portuguese territory also includes the islands of Madeira and the Azores in the Atlantic. The climate is mild in winter, hot in summer, and dry inland. There are mountains in the northern half of the country, while most of the south is low-lying, with hills in the south in the coastal region around Lisbon and near the central border with Spain. About one-third of the land is forested.

Agriculture is varied. Main crops include sweet potatoes, onions, corn, grapes, olives, oranges and other fruit, and sugar beet. Meat and dairy are also important, with a preponderance of sheep in the livestock sector. Forestry products include sawlogs, pulpwood, and fuel wood. Fishing is important, covering a wide range of sea fish and crustaceans. Sardines are a key product. Copper, limestone, and granite are the main minerals; uranium, marble, and gold are also significant. Tin, tungsten, silver, clay, salt, and gypsum are also mined. There are reserves of manganese, lead, wolfram, barite, feldspar, talc, and coal.

The majority of people live in the Lisbon and Porto areas. Most are of Mediterranean origin, with a small number of immigrants from Portugal's former African colonies. As a result of the tight labor market there has been a wave of immigration recently from North Africa and Eastern Europe, which has caused social tensions.

Communications/Energy

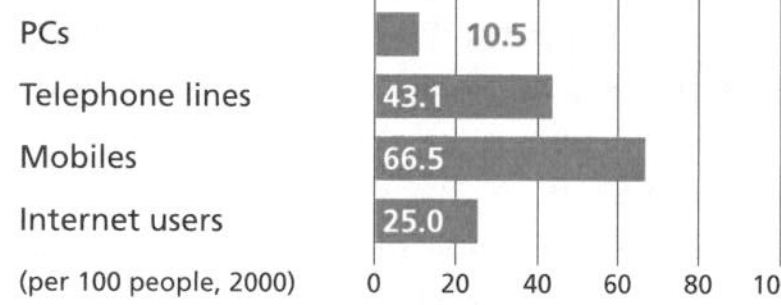

There are 6,077 miles of roads, including 495 miles of motorways. The railway network comprises 1,888 miles. A high-speed link was opened between Lisbon and Porto in 1999, but upgrading the track for full speed will not be completed until 2006. The pipeline network includes over 450 miles for gas, 36 miles for oil products, and 14 miles for crude oil. There are six international airports at Lisbon, Porto, Faro, Funchal (Madeira), Santa Maria, and São Miguel (both in the Azores). A second airport is being built at Lisbon. The main maritime ports are Lisbon, Leixoes (Porto), Setubal, and Funchal. Mainland sea ports handle 30 million tons of cargo a year. The merchant fleet comprised 158 ships over 1,000 grt, totaling 1 million grt in 2000.

In September 2000 there were 3.6 million analog fixed phone lines, and 181,000 ISDN lines. Phone costs have fallen since liberalization of the sector, which was completed in 2000. There were 6.7 million mobile phones at end-2000, accounting for 67% of the population, and 2.5 million Internet users, representing a massive growth in this area since 1998. About 10% of the population had cable TV. Free Internet access has been offered by some companies from 1999, and Internet access through cable TV has been available since 2000. UMTS mobile phone networks are expected to greatly increase Internet use from 2002.

Portugal is heavily dependent on energy imports. Imported oil accounted for 68.4% of energy consumption in 1999, followed by imported coal (15.4%), and gas via pipeline from Algeria (8.4%). Gas is due to take on a larger role. In 1999 electricity was mostly generated thermal power, especially oil and coal (80%), followed by hydro (17%), and other renewables, including biomass, geothermal, solar, and wind (2.8%). In higher rainfall years, the share of hydroelectricity is higher. Electricity prices fell slightly following liberalization of the sector from 1996. There is a link with the Spanish grid, and Portugal was a net exporter of electricity in 1999.

Education/Employment

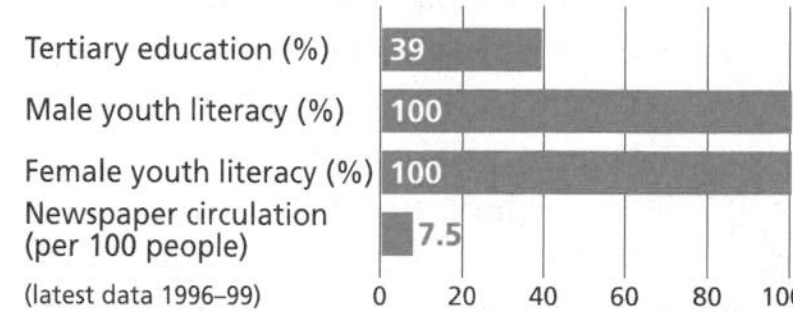

Education is compulsory from age 6 to 15. Pre-school education from age 3 to 6 is available. There are 15 public and 13 private universities, 45 polytechnics, 8 military schools, and 106 vocational colleges. The polytechnics offer courses in medicine, tourism, technology, business management, teacher training, and fine arts. There are eight technical universities. State education is the remit of the Ministry of Education. Education is free at all levels in state schools and public higher education institutes. Student grants and loans are available for state higher education courses. There were 1.6 million students enrolled at university in 1999–2000, including 6% in the private sector. Law was by far the most popular subject, followed by technology and science. The government increased the provision for adult education in 2001 in its ongoing effort to reduce illiteracy and also to help the labor market adjust to structural changes. In 2001 only 35% of the population aged 25 to 29 had completed secondary education, and only 10% had pursued higher education, a factor holding back modernization.

R&D investment is low, only 0.4% of GDP, and the government has taken steps to redress this. There are five science business parks linked to technical universities: three in the Lisbon area and two in the Porto area. The system will be extended to other centers. In 1997 the government introduced tax breaks for R&D firms in industrial, agricultural, and service activities.

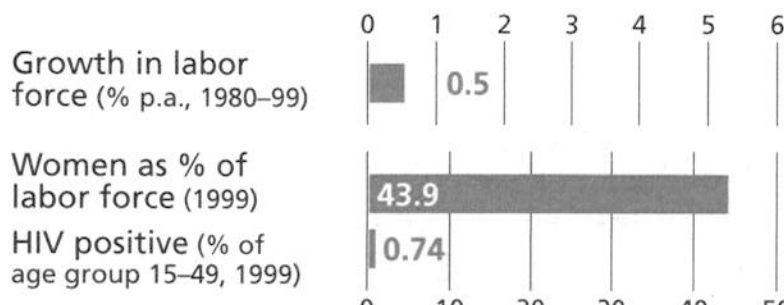

The labor force is hard-working and adaptable to change. There has been a gradual increase in skills. Traditionally the majority of workers were low-skilled and low-paid, but many such jobs have been cut, and those that remain are taken increasingly by immigrants. The frameworks for wages and employment conditions are determined annually at the national level by tripartite negotiation between government, employers, and trade unions. Industry-level

negotiations set actual wages and conditions. There is little absenteeism, and strikes are rare because problems are usually resolved in the annual tripartite round. Portugal applies EU employment law, which covers safety at work, wages and working hours, industrial relations, employment incentives, and unemployment provision.

Fiscal/Financial

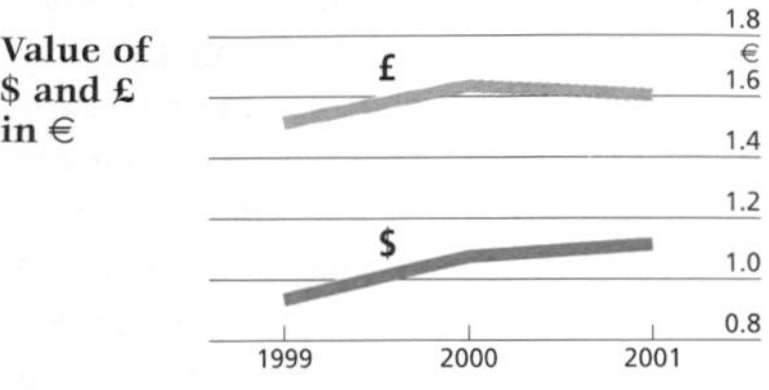

The largest bank is Caixa Geral de Depositos (CGD) which is state-controlled, followed by Banco Comercial Portugues (BCP), Banco Espirito Santo (BES), Banco Santander Central Hispano, and Banco Portugues de Investimento (BPI). Most of the banking sector is under private ownership. Many of the leading international insurance companies are present in Portugal. Some of the leading banks have insurance subsidiaries. The regulatory authority for banks is the Bank of Portugal, which is also the central bank and part of the European System of Central Banks. This body and the European Central Bank set the policy for the Euro. The insurance sector is regulated by the Insurance Institute of Portugal and the stock exchange by the Stock Exchange Commission.

Corporate tax is 32% but this rises to 35.2% after local tax, with maximum personal income tax at 40%. There are plans to cut corporate tax to 30% or 28% by 2003. The International Business Center of Madeira has a special tax regime whereby financial institutions, holding companies, trusts, and international service and shipping companies established there are exempt from corporate income tax until December 31, 2011.

The financial services industry underwent consolidation in the latter half of the 1990s, but the five large banks which account for 90% of the domestic market remain small in European terms. A bid for BPI by BES failed in 2000, but further consolidation is likely. After Spanish Banco Santander's Portuguese acquisitions placed it among the top five banking groups, the government blocked another proposed Spanish takeover. However, cooperation between Portuguese and Spanish banks is increasing, especially for e-banking. The largest banks have teamed up with the main Portuguese electricity and telecommunications companies to launch e-banking subsidiaries with Spanish banks. BCP and CGD are investing in Poland. There is increasing integration between banking and insurance. Since privatization of the sector, there are more foreign banks operating in Lisbon, and the range of business finance has achieved international sophistication. Portuguese banks are better placed for e-commerce than banks in many other countries, since they share the same electronic payments system. Portugal's ATM network is one of the most sophisticated in the world, allowing account holders to pay bills, book train tickets, and make bank transfers. The next generation of ATMs will include computer keyboards and Internet access.

The privatization program has transformed stock market activity. Stock market capitalization rose from $39 billion in 1997 to $67 billion in 1999, with privatized companies accounting for half of capitalization and most of trading. Equity capitalization exceeded bond capitalization for the first time in 1997. Foreign share listings began in 2000. The Portuguese market index was added to the Dow Jones Global Indices in 1997. In 1999 electronic trading was introduced and links established with the São Paulo exchange in Brazil. The Lisbon Stock Exchange and Porto Derivatives Exchange were combined and privatized in 2000. The Portuguese exchange will join the Paris, Brussels, and Amsterdam exchanges in Euronext, the first Euro-zone cross-border trading platform, once legislative procedures have been completed. In the meantime the Portuguese exchange has added three new indices: for new telecommunications, media and technology; for financial intermediaries; and for industry.

Business Opportunities

Growth in output (% p.a., 1990–99)

Sector	% p.a.
Services	2.4
Industry	2.7
Agriculture	0.4

Tax and financial incentives are available to investors. Investment projects worth $4.5 million or more qualify for tax credits of 5–20% of investment cost in corporation tax, exemption from or reduction in property taxes and local tax, interest-free loans for industrial activities, training subsidies, and exemption from social security payments for the long-term unemployed and first-time employees. Broad tax reductions are offered to R&D firms. A special tax regime exists for the International Business Center in Madeira. There are two free trade zones at Medeira and the Azores. In mainland Portugal there are 24 industrial parks, including six science parks. The first point of contact for foreign investors is the government agency Investment, Commerce and Tourism Portugal (ICEP).

Foreign investment rose from €8.9 billion in 1997 to €20 billion in 2000. The automotive sector, electronic and telecommunications equipment, textiles, footwear, and agribusiness have attracted investment from the United States, Japan, Germany, the Netherlands, France, Italy, the United Kingdom, and South Korea, among others. New opportunities exist in e-business, and in sectors that are being liberalized or privatized, specifically gas and energy, transport, agribusiness, shipbuilding, and paper.

For More Information

Books:

Chislett, William. *Portugal Investment and Growth*. London: Euromoney Books, 1997.

Economist Intelligence Unit. *Country Profile and Quarterly Reports*. London.

European Union. *European Economy*. Report and Studies Series.

IMF Country Report. *Portugal*. Washington, D.C.

OECD Economic Surveys. *Portugal*. Paris: OECD.

Portugal Export, Import, and Business Directory. 3rd ed. Washington, D.C.: International Business Publications, 2001.

Portuguese Ministry of Finance. *Portugal--Economic Indicators*.

Web Sites:

Bank of Portugal: **www.bportugal.pt**

Council of Ministries, government entry point: **www.pcm.gov.pt**

Diario de Noticias (daily newspaper): **www.dn.pt**

Diario Economico (business newspaper): **www.de.iol.pt**

Investment, Commerce and Tourism Portugal (ICEP): **www.portugal.org**

Lisbon Stock Exchange: **www.bvl.pt**

Ministry of Finance and Economy: **www.dgep.pt**

Ministry of Science and Technology: **www.mct.pt**

National Statistics Institute: **www.ine.pt**

Portuguese Industrial Association: **www.aip.pt**

Puerto Rico

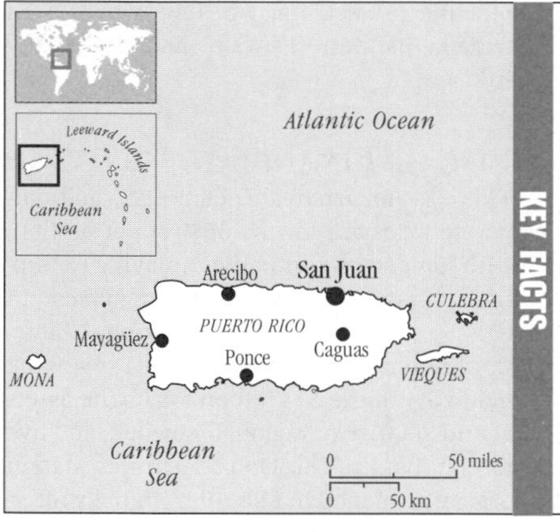

KEY FACTS

GNI pc: **$8,200 (approx.)**
Head of government: **governor**
Currency: **U.S. dollar ($)**
Capital: **San Juan**
Population: **3,884,000**
Land area: **3,515 square miles**
Population density: **1,104 per square mile**
Life expectancy: **76 years**
Infant mortality: **11 per 1,000 live births**
Language: **Spanish, English**
Best buy: **musical instruments, lace**

Economy

Manufacturing is the dominant economic sector, comprising 44% of GDP in 2000; production includes pharmaceuticals, electronic goods, scientific instruments, textiles, and clothing. The second-largest sector is financial and other services, accounting for 33% of GDP; this sector includes tourism, which in 1999–2000 saw 3.3 million stopover arrivals, plus 1.2 million arrivals by cruise ship passengers and U.S. military personnel, with total expenditure of $2.4 million. In 1999–2000 public services employed 249,000 people, 21.5% of the total in employment; commerce employed 239,000, and manufacturing 159,000.

Manufactured goods account for 97% of both exports and imports; the United States is the dominant export customer, accounting for 90% of Puerto Rico's exports and supplying 60% of its imports in 1998–99. There was a trade surplus of $6.7 billion in 1999–2000, outweighed by a deficit of $22 billion on the services account, partially offset by U.S. federal transfers and a capital account surplus. However, the government's external debt in 2000 totaled $23.8 billion.

In the second half of the 1990s, economic growth averaged just over 3% annually, with little variation between years, while the inflation rate averaged just over 5%. Government economic policy focused in the late 1990s on the privatization of state enterprises, but made slow progress, with only the Banco Popular and the telecommunications enterprise being sold.

Geography/ Resources

Puerto Rico lies east of the Dominican Republic, about 1,000 miles southeast of Miami. It is a "Commonwealth" of the United States, which maintains military bases in Puerto Rico and Vieques, the latter being used for naval bombing target practice. There are 54 major rivers, but few with hydroelectric potential. The island is strongly urbanized in the greater San Juan area; other main towns are Ponce on the south coast, Mayagüez on the west coast, and Caguas, south of San Juan.

There are no known oil or gas reserves, and agriculture accounts for only 1% of GDP, employing about 30,000 people. Traditional crops, now of limited significance, include coffee and sugar; a newer sector focuses on meat, dairy products, eggs, fruit, and vegetables.

The majority of the population is of Spanish descent. The literacy rate is about 90%, but the unemployment rate remains relatively high—11% in 2000—despite a reduction from 13.6% in 1998. Education is free to secondary level, while scholarships and grants are available to assist students to enter tertiary education colleges.

Communications/Energy

San Juan is the main airline interchange point in the Caribbean, with extensive services to the United States and to regional destinations, as well as links with Canada, the United Kingdom, Spain, and other European countries. There are also direct flights to Mexico and several other Latin American countries. Ferry services operate to the Dominican Republic and the U.S. Virgin Islands. Internal flights connect San Juan with Vieques, Ponce, and Mayagüez, and there are urban and long-distance bus services; a rapid rail transit system is under construction in San Juan, with opening scheduled for 2002. There are 8,450 miles of paved roads.

The former state-owned Puerto Rico Telephone Co. was privatized in 1998, with the GTE Corporation of the United States taking a majority holding; it operates more than 1.4 million lines. Under an equal access requirement introduced in 1999, companies including AT&T, MCI, Sprint, and Telefónica Larga Distancia of Spain have entered the market.

Almost all the island's electricity is generated and distributed by the state-owned power authority, which has installed capacity of 4,500 MW. Its four main power plants are oil-fired.

Fiscal/Financial

The Puerto Rican government is heavily dependent on U.S. financial transfers; domestic revenue accounted for only 69% of government current revenue in 1998–99. Since the government is also a major employer, attempts to reduce current expenditure have met considerable resistance.

There is no central bank. At the end of 1998 there were 17 commercial banks, mainly Puerto Rican or U.S.-owned, but including two Canadian and two Spanish banks.

Business Opportunities

Industrial incentives include a corporation tax rate for manufacturing enterprises of only 7%, together with substantial tax credits for research and development and worker training; special grants are available for enterprises established in high unemployment areas. New investment opportunities are in transport, utilities, technological research, healthcare, environmental protection, and financial services.

For More Information

Book:
Investing into Caribbean Countries Markets Handbook. Washington, D.C.: International Business Publications, 2002.

Web Sites:
Government:
www.fortaleza.govpr.org
Government Development Bank:
www.gdb-pur.com

QATAR

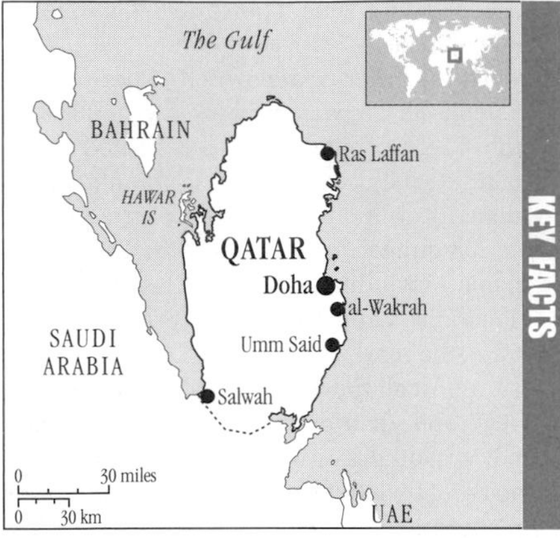

KEY FACTS

GNI pc: **$17,100 (approx.)**
Head of state: **the Amir**
Head of government: **prime minister**
Currency: **Qatari riyal (QR)**
Capital: **Doha**
Population: **589,000, growing at 2.2% p.a.**
Land area: **4,250 square miles**
Population density: **138 per square mile**
Life expectancy: **72 years**
Infant mortality: **12 per 1,000 live births**
Language: **Arabic, English**
Best buy: **luxury goods from duty-free shops**

ECONOMY

Qatar is a major world gas producer, but in 2001 its large oil exports still earned more than gas. Oil income allowed the government to develop gas reserves (the third largest in the world after those of Russia and Iran); downstream industries in oil refining, gas liquefaction, and petrochemicals using gas feedstock; basic industries such as steel and food processing; innovative agriculture; and ultra-modern infrastructure. That infrastructure includes the controversial state-owned al-Jazeera television station, which shot to world prominence with its coverage of Afghanistan and Osama bin Laden, balanced with Western views, in late 2001. Diplomatically Qatar provided a bridge of communication between protagonists in this and other disputes, maintaining good relations with Iran, Iraq and Israel, other Gulf neighbors, and the industrialized nations.

Hydrocarbons, including downstream manufacturing, dominate the economy, accounting for over 40% of GDP. Services account for most of the rest. The state sector has also dominated the economy, but privatization, launched in 1997, has led to private/public partnerships in oil, gas, power, telecommunications, petrochemicals and other sectors. High oil and gas prices boosted economic growth to 35% in 2000 from 19% in 1999 and a decline of 9% in 1998. Growth is expected to be far slower in 2001–02. Long-term gas contracts should help level out such fluctuations in future.

GEOGRAPHY/RESOURCES

Qatar is a low-lying, largely desert peninsula, which borders the Arabian Gulf to the east, United Arab Emirates and Saudi Arabia to the south, and the Gulf of Bahrain to the west. Temperatures range from 122°F in summer to 50°F in winter. Average rainfall is 3 inches. Qatar is nearly self-sufficient in vegetables, the main agricultural crop. Dates and cereals are grown. There are small livestock and fisheries industries. At January 2001 proven oil reserves were 13.2 billion barrels, and gas reserves 396 trillion cubic feet, including the world's largest gas field not associated with an oil field (containing very high-grade gas). Exploration continues.

COMMUNICATIONS/ENERGY

The road network was 764 miles in 1999, connecting to Saudi Arabia and the U.A.E. A causeway to Bahrain is planned. Qatar is served by Doha International Airport and three smaller airports. The main sea ports are Doha for general cargo, Umm Said (general cargo and hydrocarbons), and Ras Laffan (hydrocarbons). At end-2000 there were 160,200 fixed phone lines, 119,500 mobile phones, and 45,000 Internet users. Qatar Telecom was partly privatized in 1999. Gas accounted for 84.4% of energy consumption in 1999, followed by oil (15.6%). Most electricity is generated from gas. In 2000 oil production was 863,000 barrels per day, with consumption at 67,000 barrels per day and net exports of 806,000 barrels per day. Production is planned to be 1 million barrels per day in 2002. In 1999 gas production was 848 billion cubic feet, with consumption at 562 billion cubic feet and net exports of 286 billion cubic feet. Qatar is the key player in an integrated gas pipeline project that will link with U.A.E., Oman, Bahrain, Kuwait, and eventually Pakistan.

FISCAL/FINANCIAL

There is no personal income tax, and corporate taxes are low (5–35% of net profits), with joint stock companies enjoying exemptions. Qatar Central Bank regulates 15 banks: seven local (Qatar National Bank, Commercial Bank of Qatar and Doha Bank held 70% of the $14 billion total bank assets at end-2000), two regionally-owned, and five foreign banks. The Doha Securities Market officially opened in May 1997, initially offering trading to Qatari nationals only. This was extended to Gulf Cooperation Council nationals in March 2000.

BUSINESS OPPORTUNITIES

Most foreign investment is in gas, a total of $10 billion at mid-2001. Other sectors that have attracted foreign investment include oil, and privatized telecommunications, power, steel, fertilizer and petrochemicals firms. Investors include the United States, the United Kingdom, Canada, France, Denmark, Norway, Taiwan, Japan, and Italy. The 2000 foreign investment law allows for full foreign ownership in certain projects (limited to 49% previously). The government is eager to attract investment to tourism, agriculture, health, education, energy, and mining.

For More Information

Books:

Cordesman, Anthony H. *Bahrain, Oman, Qatar, and the U.A.E.—Challenges of Security*. Boulder, CO: Westview Press, 1997.

Zahlan, Rosemarie Said. *Making of the Modern Gulf States: Kuwait, Bahrain, Qatar, the United Arab Emirates and Oman*. Rev. ed. Reading, Berkshire: Garnet Publishing, 1998.

Web Sites:

Ministry of Foreign Affairs: **http://english.mofa.gov.qa**

Qatar Central Bank: **www.qcb.gov.qa**

Réunion

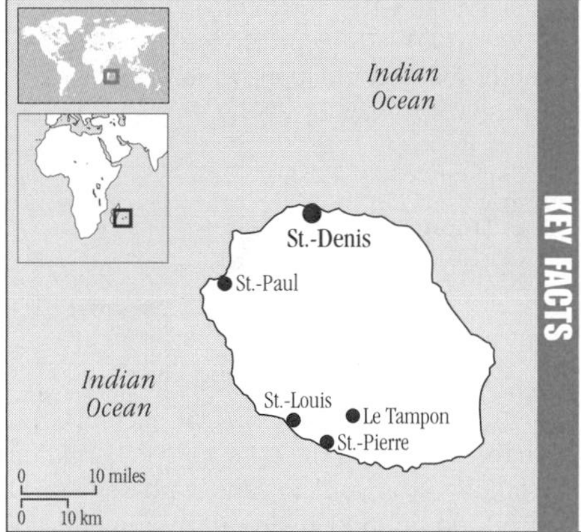

KEY FACTS

GNI pc: **$4,800 (approx.)**
Head of government: **president of the general council**
Currency: **Euro (€)**
Capital: **St.-Denis**
Population: **717,700**
Land area: **983 square miles**
Population density: **675 per square mile**
Life expectancy: **73 years**
Infant mortality: **8 per 1,000 live births**
Language: **French (official), Creole (most used)**
Best buy: **rum, hats, stone carvings, handcrafts**

Economy

The main product and export is cane sugar: 1.7 million tons of refined sugar was produced and 195,025 tons exported in 1998. Rum production was 1.5 million gallons much of which was exported. Other main exports include fish and lobsters, fruit, vanilla, flowers, and essential oils. Tourism is a growing sector. The number of visitors increased from 217,000 in 1992 to 390,643 in 1998. The majority, around 82%, are from France. Most industry is small-scale. The largest companies are in food processing and beverages. There are also wood products, construction materials, mechanical engineering, IT, textiles and leather industries. Public administration and commercial services form the largest component of GDP. There is a rapidly growing IT sector, which includes hardware, software, and services. The commercial services sector is dominated by trading and tourism. Imports far outweigh exports.

The government is dependent on French aid, which constituted 54% of the budget in 2001. Investment projects are aimed at strengthening agriculture and diversifying the economy towards industry and tourism, especially to provide jobs for a rapidly growing labor force. Attempts to establish the country as a location for outsourcing manufactures from Europe and Africa have met with mixed success because the cost of living is high. Unemployment has remained stubbornly high at around 40%. The main infrastructure project in hand is the provision of a water conduit from the west to the east side of the island, tunneling through the mountains, to assure irrigation and drinking water throughout dry seasons. GDP growth fluctuates with the sugar cane harvest. It was an estimated annual average 3% for the first half of the 1990s. Inflation was 1.5% in 1997 and 0.9% in 1998, according to official sources.

Geography/Resources

A tropical island in the Indian Ocean 500 miles to the east of Madagascar, Réunion has two ranges of volcanoes. Average temperatures are 68°F at the coast and 57°F inland. There are night-time frosts above 6,600 feet. The cyclone season lasts from December to April.

About 25% of land is farmed, half of it under sugar-cane plantations. Other important agricultural products include vanilla, essential oils (geranium, vetiver, and ylang-ylang), pineapples, bananas, tobacco, ginger, pimentos, meat, and dairy. There is a small forestry industry. Fisheries are important, and include traditional coastal fishing and industrial fishing for tuna and other fish along with lobsters. There are no commercially significant mineral resources. A French colony from 1638 until it was made an overseas department of France in 1946, Réunion has a diverse population from European, African, Asian, and Madagascan origins. Over two-thirds are urban and 56% are under age 30. There were 16,663 immigrant arrivals from 1990 to 1999.

Communications/Energy

The road network totaled 1,711 miles in 1994, including 230 miles of main roads linking the main towns. There are two international airports, one serving the capital St.-Denis and the other the third-largest town St.-Pierre. They handled 1.5 million passengers and 22,200 tons of freight in 1998. The main sea port is the Port de la Pointe des Galets, which handled 3.1 million tons of freight in 1998. There are two leisure ports at St.-Gilles-les-Bains and St.-Pierre. There were 250,000 fixed phone lines in 1997, reaching around 90% of the population. There were 85,000 mobile phones in 1999 and 10,000 Internet users in 2000. A project to install fast Internet access was launched in 2001. Electricity is generated by thermal (54.5%) and hydro power (45.5%). Oil is imported.

Fiscal/Financial

Personal income tax and corporation tax are low. The Institut d'Emission des Départements d'Outre-mer acts as the local central bank and regulator of the finance sector, but monetary policy is set in France. There are four commercial banks, one development bank, and 20 insurance companies. There is no local stock market.

Business Opportunities

There is substantial grant aid (up to 50% of investment cost) for industrial projects, with additional subsidies for employment and relocation expenses, including leases. Tax holidays of up to ten years are accorded. Aquaculture and textiles projects are being promoted. The government is also eager to attract investment to the tourist industry, sea fishing, flowers, textiles, leather goods, and IT. The point of contact is the Comité de Pilotage de l'Industrie.

For More Information

Book:

Bindloss, Joseph, et al. *Mauritius, Réunion and Seychelles*. 4th ed. Oakland, CA: Lonely Planet, 2001.

Web Sites:

Chamber of Commerce and Industry: **www.reunion.cci.fr**
Comité de Pilotage de l'Industrie: **www.cpi.asso.fr**
Government entry point: **www.cg974.fr**
Government entry point (foreign investment oriented): **www.region-reunion.com**

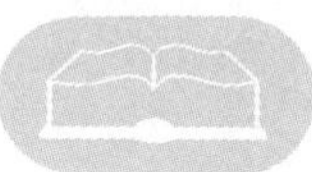

ROMANIA

KEY FACTS

GNI: **$33,034 million; world's 56th**
GNI pc: **$1,470; world's 120th**
Head of state: **president**
Head of government: **prime minister**
Currency: **leu (Lei)**
Capital: **Bucharest**
Population: **22,402,000, growing at –0.4% p.a.**
Land area: **88,920 square miles**
Population density: **252 per square mile**
Life expectancy: **70 years**
Infant mortality: **21 per 1,000 live births**
Language: **Romanian**
Best buy: **frosted and gilded glassware**

ECONOMIC STRUCTURE

Romania gained independence from the Ottoman empire in 1878 and became a kingdom in 1881. The Versailles treaty that ended World War I sanctioned Romania's acquisition of Transylvania, Bessarabia, and other Romanian-inhabited lands, but it lost them all again, except Transylvania, in the settlement that followed World War II. In 1947 the Communist Party took power, and from 1965 the dictator Nicolae Ceaucescu imposed severe privations in order to repay foreign debts. In 1989, the fall of other East European Communist Party regimes triggered Ceaucescu's overthrow and execution, and from then until 1996 Romania was ruled by coalitions of former communists and social democrats who opposed a rapid opening up to the market. A center-right coalition, elected in 1996, made economic reforms recommended by the international institutions, but a recession set in and living standards declined, provoking industrial unrest and violence. In the 2000 parliamentary elections, that government was replaced by a minority administration headed by the former communist Party of Social Democracy, and former communist Ion Iliescu was elected president. This government soon won praise from Western powers for a foreign policy based on EU and NATO accession. Prime minister Ante Nastase described Romania as a "de facto NATO member" in its support for the U.S. anti-terrorism campaign in late 2001. Business has been encouraged by the continuation of market reform.

Romania's services sector comprised only 45.5% of GDP in 2000, lagging behind other East European states. The economy remains dominated by agriculture (11.4% of GDP in 2000) and industry (including important metallurgy, automotive, telecommunications, and oil and gas sectors), whose share of GDP fell from 40% in 1989 to 27.6% in 2000.

Low value-added labor-intensive products from the clothing, footwear, and furniture industries are important exports; so are metallurgical products and machinery. The EU (especially Germany and Italy) is Romania's most important trading partner by far, accounting for 63.8% of exports and 56.6% of imports in 2000. Other countries in the East European trading block CEFTA, to which Romania belongs, account for 8.2% of exports and 9% of imports.

ECONOMIC POLICY

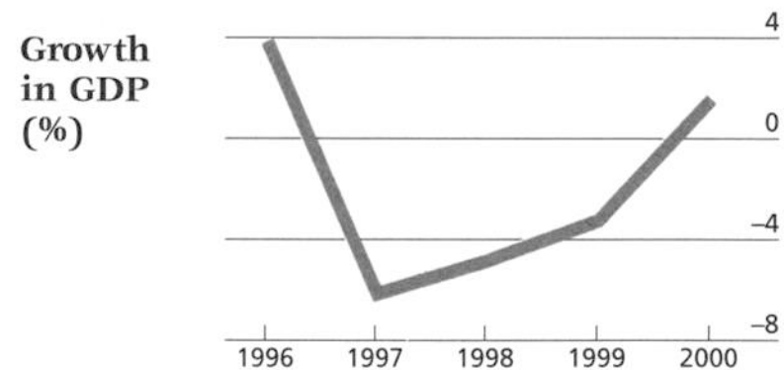

The center-right government of 1996–2000 removed price controls, liberalized the foreign exchange market, unified the exchange rate, and introduced virtually full currency convertibility. It closed loss-making coal mines and restructured some heavy engineering enterprises. Living standards fell, prices for public services were raised, and utilities were restructured as corporations. The changes were criticized as inadequate by the European Commission and the IMF, who argued that increases in industrial subsidies and state-sector wages were steps in the wrong direction. Nevertheless, as Romania emerged from the 1997–99 recession, it achieved GDP growth of 1.6% in 2000 and 4% in 2001 (EBRD projection), and consistently reduced inflation, which ran at 155% in 1997, to 34.2% by 2001.

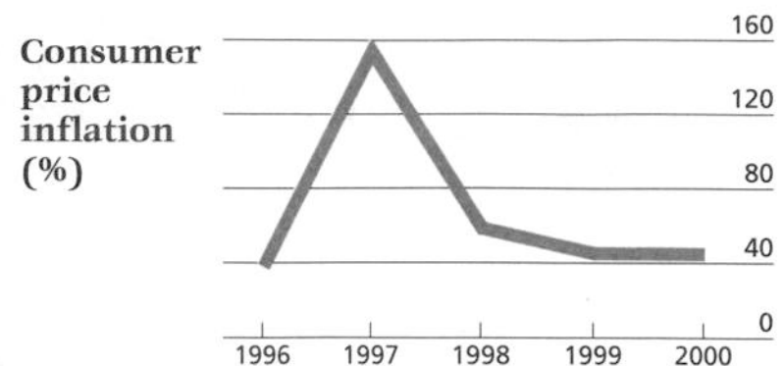

In September 2001, in connection with agreements with the IMF on a $400 million standby arrangement, and with the World Bank on up to $1 billion in funding for development in 2002–04, the Romanian government announced its economic policy priorities as tightening fiscal control, improving the performance of state-owned enterprises, and proceeding with privatization. In the latter respect progress was made with the sale of the largest steel producer, Sidex, to the U.K.-Indian group Ispat. The problems of unemployment (which was 10.5% in 2000) and declining living standards (with an estimated 44% of people living below the poverty line) remained serious in 2001.

GEOGRAPHY/RESOURCES

Romania is bordered by the Black Sea on the east, and in the south by the Danube river, which divides it from Bulgaria. Yugoslavia is to the southwest, Hungary to the west, Ukraine to the north, and Moldova to the northeast. Romania's topography is dominated by the Carpathian Mountains.

More than two-fifths of the land is arable, and 63% of that is cultivated. Natural conditions favor a range of crops including cereals, industrial crops, vegetables, and—particularly in the Subcarpathian region—vines. Romania has significant, but largely undeveloped, oil and gas reserves, and some mineral resources.

Romania's population is second only to that of Poland among Eastern European EU candidate countries. Between 1991 and 2000 the population fell by 760,000; the birth rate, one of Europe's lowest, fell from 13.6 per 1000 inhabitants in 1990 to 10.5 per 1000 in 1998, as a result of economic hardship and newly-available contraception. According to the 1992 census, Romanians comprise 89.4% of the population, Hungarians 7.2%, and Roma (gypsies) 1.8%, but the statistics are believed to exclude much of the Roma population. International bodies have criticized

  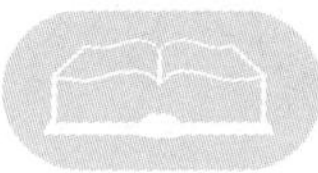    

Romania for continuing discrimination against minorities, particularly the Roma.

Communications/Energy

Romania produces annually about 6 million tons of oil, a figure that will increase when a newly-discovered Black Sea deposit comes on stream, and 494 billion cubic feet of gas. The industry is dominated by two state-owned national entities, Romgaz gas company and Petrom oil company. International oil majors including TotalFinaElf, Shell, and BP Amoco are doing exploration work in Romania.

Romania's oil refining industry is Eastern Europe's largest, and produces a wide range of oil products and chemicals. In the late 1990s it attracted foreign investors including Lukoil of Russia and Dutch interests. The retail petrol market has also attracted foreign companies, which now hold about one-fifth of it.

Despite the hydrocarbon sector's potential, Romania's lopsided heavy industrialization made it a net importer of energy, and in 2001 it still was. A major energy restructuring program, including break-up of the national power company, began in 1999, but privatizations planned for 2001 did not get under way.

The Ceaucescu regime left Romania with badly underdeveloped road and rail transport: 45,524 miles of roads, only 70 miles of which are motorways; and 7,352 miles of railways, only 35% of which is electrified. EU- and World Bank-supported modernization programs have yet to reap rewards. Air transport also requires major investment: the three international and 16 domestic airports are underused. The Romanian port of Constanta is the Black Sea's biggest, and a key Europe–Asia trade link.

Telecommunications are underdeveloped: line density is 17.5%, just a little over half of Bulgaria's. However the fixed-line monopoly, RomTelecom, was privatized in 1998, with 35% going to OTE, the main Greek telecommunications company, and a major investment program started. The mobile telephone industry has also attracted foreign investment.

Education/Employment

Romania's labor market is notable for strong union organizations with collective agreements covering much of manufacturing industry; in other workplaces, individual written contracts are required by law. Although money wages are low by European standards (around $106 a month in mid-2001), legislation prescribes hours of work, minimum wages, statutory holidays, paid holidays, and paid maternity leave, and sets out periods of minimum notice. Employers pay social security contributions at around 26% of salary. In 2000 the government cancelled a planned 80% national wage increase, and in February 2001, as part of its economic development plan, it concluded a one-year no-strike agreement with unions.

The education system is undergoing development. In 2000 public expenditure on education rose to 4% of GDP, still low by European standards. Education is compulsory between the ages of 6 and 16, illiteracy among school-age children is under 1%, and 64% of children aged 4–6 attend kindergartens. In the 1990s the student body in higher education expanded dramatically: in 1991–92, 12.5% of 19–23 year olds were in full-time education, whereas in 1996–97 it was 24%, a total of 355,488 students.

Fiscal/Financial

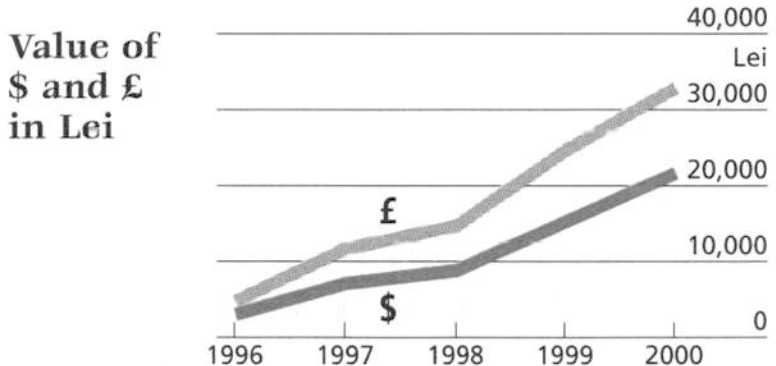

Serious efforts to reform Romania's banking sector began in 1998 with the establishment of a government agency to manage state banks' bad loan portfolios. In 1999 Bancorex, which held two-thirds of the banking system's losses, was closed, and in 2000 the National Bank of Romania's supervisory capabilities were strengthened in law. By the end of 2001 more than two-thirds of banking assets were privatized and about 55% were in foreign hands: of the largest banks, a controlling stake in the Romanian Development Bank was sold in 1998 to Société Générale of France, and Banca Agricola was sold in 2001 to a consortium headed by Raiffeisen bank of Austria. The privatization of the remaining large state-owned bank, Banca Comerciala Romana, was not expected until late 2002.

Confidence in mutual financial intermediaries, already low following pyramid scheme scandals in the early 1990s, was dashed again in May 2000 when the largest investment fund, FNK, collapsed. Banca Populara Romana, the largest credit cooperative, closed a month later after being unable to meet demands for urgent withdrawals.

The Bucharest Stock Exchange, reopened in 1995, and an electronic over-the-counter share market, Rasdaq, has opened, but the BSE's market capitalization, at 5% of GDP, remains low by Eastern European standards.

Tax reforms in 1999–2000 were geared towards lowering tax rates, broadening the tax base, and reducing distortions. In early 2000 tax breaks for foreign investors were suspended in agreement with the international financial institutions. As compensation a general tax reform was implemented, including a new corporate income tax of 25%, reduced from 38%; profit tax of 5% on exports; a global personal income tax system; and a uniform VAT rate of 19% that replaces a two-rate system.

Business Opportunities

Net foreign direct investment averaged $267 million per year in 1992–96, and increased rapidly thereafter, averaging $1.34 billion per year in 1997–2000; it fell slightly to $900 million in 2001. Preferred areas for foreign investment include oil exploration, the automobile and automotive components industry, banking and finance, telecommunications, hotels, consumer products, and the retail sector.

Romania's main advantages for foreign investors are a potentially large domestic market, a good geographical position, a diversified industrial structure, skilled labor, and low wages. Foreign investors now have free access to domestic markets and may have any level of participation in Romanian companies, or establish wholly foreign-owned enterprises. There are six free-trade zones offering tax incentives. However, the Foreign Investor Council stated in its white book in 2001 that it considered taxes, regulations and policy instability to be the most serious obstacles to foreign investment.

For More Information

Books:

Daianu, Daniel. *Transformation of Economy as a Real Process: An Insider's Perspective*. Burlington, VT: Ashgate Publishing, 1999.

Jolly, Adam, and Nadine Kettaneh, eds. *Doing Business in Romania*. Sterling, VA: Kogan Page, 1999.

Roper, Steven D. *Romania: The Unfinished Revolution* (Postcommunist States and Nations). Newark, NJ: Harwood Academic Pub., 2000.

Web Sites:

Bucharest Stock Exchange: **www.bse.ro**

Chamber of Commerce and Industry of Romania and Bucharest: **www.ccir.ro**

Government of Romania: **www.gov.ro**

iRomania links and news site: **iromania.com**

Teleactivities Web portal: **www.teleactivities.net**

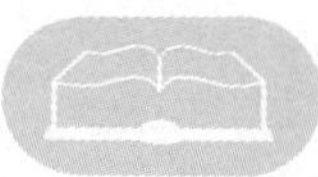

RUSSIA

GNI: **$328,995 million; world's 16th**
GNI pc: **$2,250, world's 99th**
Head of state: **president**
Head of government: **prime minister**
Currency: **ruble (Rb)**
Capital: **Moscow**
Population: **147,196,000, growing at –0.1% p.a.**
Land area: **6,520,650 square miles**
Population density: **23 per square mile**
Life expectancy: **67 years**
Infant mortality: **18 per 1,000 live births**
Language: **Russian**
Best buy: **caviar, fur hats**

ECONOMIC STRUCTURE

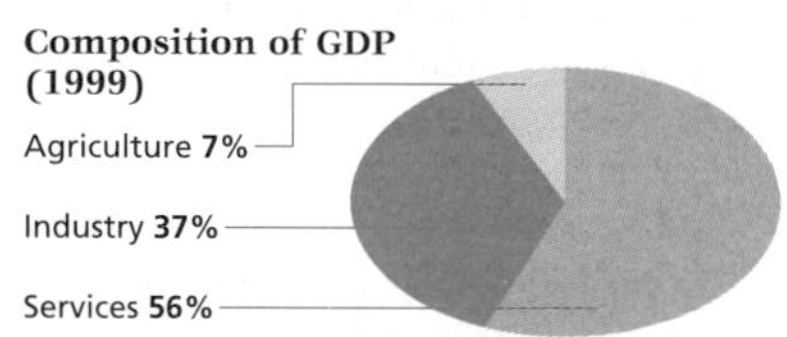

As it emerged from the collapse of the U.S.S.R. in 1991, Russia had, on the one hand, the problems of a great power that suddenly lost its empire; having been deprived of old export markets, it struggled to compete for new ones. On the other hand, it had problems of transition from communism that dwarfed those encountered in Eastern Europe. In 1991–93 Russia experienced an unprecedented economic slump. Industrial collapse, and the hyperinflation that followed from economic "shock therapy," combined to cause social instability. The rule of president Boris Yeltsin (1991–99) was also marked by political instability, as his pro-market administration and the reform-wary parliament were constantly at loggerheads (and, briefly in October 1993, on the verge of armed conflict), and by economic instability, which culminated in the financial crash of August 1998. Parliamentary elections in December 1999, at which the Communist Party and allies lost their majority, and presidential elections in March 2000, in which Vladimir Putin succeeded Yeltsin, opened a new era of stability, helped by an unexpectedly rapid post-1998 economic recovery on the back of strong commodity prices. At home Putin established authority based on collaboration between president and parliament; abroad he achieved a more stable relationship with the Western powers. His politically adept declarations of support for the United States following the attacks of September 11, 2001 led to promises that Russia's WTO accession would be speeded up, and it is now expected in 2003–04.

Retail trade and services have increased their share of GDP from 36% in 1991 to 55% in 2000; in the same period agriculture's share fell from 17% to 6.4%, and industry's from just under 50% to 38.4%. Fuels and energy account for 27% of industrial output, metallurgy for 18.4%, and wood and paper for 4.8%. Of the processing industries, machine-building and metalworking are the largest, comprising 19.2% of industrial output, followed by food processing (14.7%).

Russia's exports are dominated by commodities: oil and gas account for 45%, and metals for 20%, by volume. The former Soviet republics, which in 1990 accounted for 70% of Russian exports and 47% of imports, by 2000 had only 14.9% of exports and 27.7% of imports. The EU has replaced them as Russia's main trading partner, with 38.9% of exports and 36.5% of imports, while the United States accounted for 3.2% of exports and 8.5% of imports.

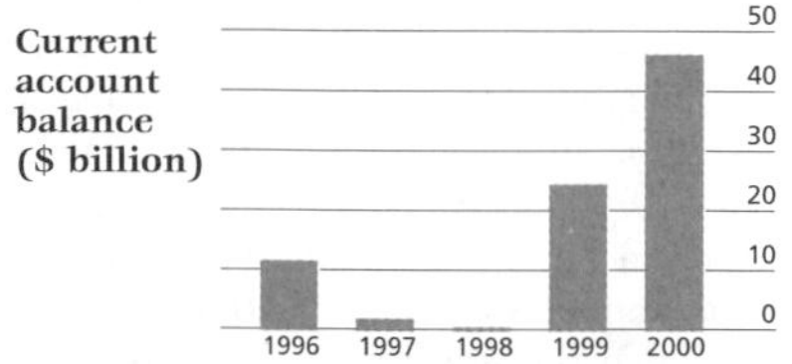

Russia's crash privatization program left most key industrial assets and some of the banking sector—but not the energy or transport infrastructure—in private hands. Since 1997 the private sector has accounted for about 70% of GDP.

ECONOMIC POLICY

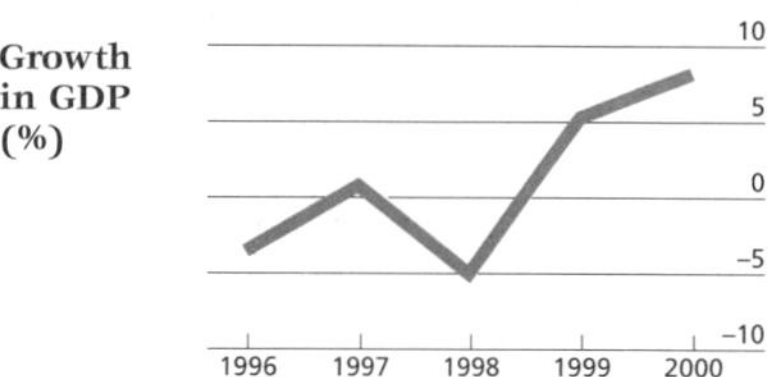

After the initial "shock therapy" in 1992, economic policy was pragmatic at best. Hurried privatization left oil and other key industries in the hands of a powerful class of "oligarchs" (politically influential businessmen). Weak regulation fed the world's greatest-ever wave of capital flight (about $200 billion in the 1990s). Politically-driven lending to Russia, and the growth of a gigantic pyramid in the domestic bond market, culminated in the 1998 crash, when the government defaulted on some classes of debt and devalued the ruble four times.

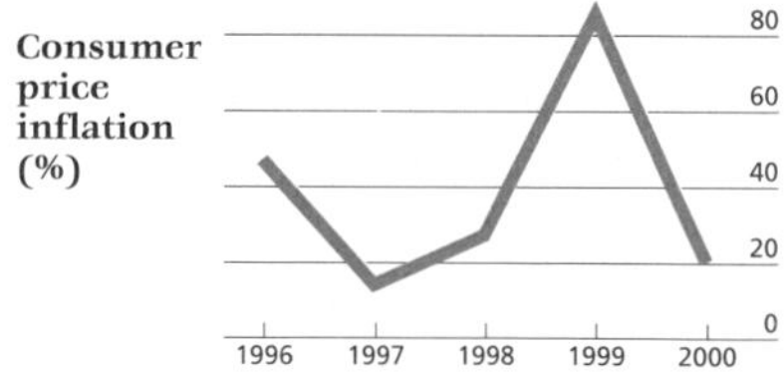

The devaluation made possible an unexpectedly rapid, albeit one-sided, recovery, led by the natural resources exporters whose costs were slashed. Post-crisis Russia remains over-reliant on these exporters, and has not reversed the decline of its manufacturing capacity. The oil-led recovery, however, provided a breathing space in three other crucial respects: first, increased revenues provided for the first non-deficit budget in post-Soviet times; second, foreign

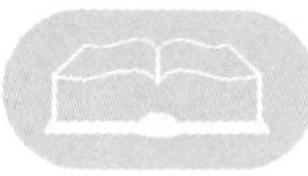

currency reserves grew rapidly to a record $30 billion by mid-2001, enabling Russia comfortably to cover its commitments to the IMF and "Paris club" of sovereign debtors and to stop borrowing from the IMF; third, it enabled the Putin administration to press ahead with structural reforms.

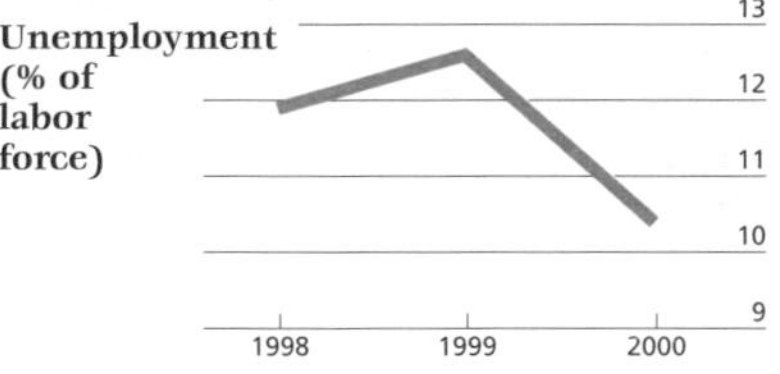

GDP growth was negative until 1998, 5.4% in 1999, 8.3% in 2000 (the best economic performance for 30 years), and a projected 5.5% in 2001. Inflation was dampened but not eradicated after the 1998 crash, to 36% in 1999, 20% in 2000, and 21% in 2001. The recovery of real incomes continued to lag: at the end of 2000 they had not recovered their 1997 level. Poverty is declining slowly: in early 2001 the state statistics agency reported that 30% of the population live below the official poverty line ($42 per month). There is severe inequality of incomes: officially, the top 10% of the population account for one-third of the income and the bottom 10% for less than one-thirtieth. Official unemployment was 9.7% in 2000, actual unemployment higher.

Geography/Resources

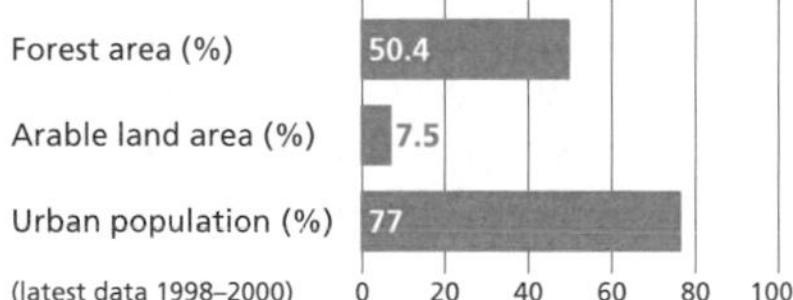

Russia is the world's largest country, covering almost twice the territory of China or the United States, and stretching 5,600 miles across 11 time zones from Kaliningrad, the detached province on Germany's Baltic coast, in the west, to the Pacific coast in the east. There are arctic deserts in the extreme north, tundra to the south of that, and then forest zones that cover about half of the country. South of the forests lie wooded steppe and steppe, and beyond that small sections of semi-desert along the Caspian Sea's northern shore. Politically there are 89 regional administrative units united in the Russian Federation.

Russia has incomparably rich natural resources, including an estimated one-third of the world's natural gas reserves and up to one-tenth of world oil reserves, mostly in west Siberia and the Arctic. It has substantial proportions of world reserves of nonferrous metals such as nickel and cobalt, and of precious metals including gold, platinum, and palladium, and large coal and iron ore reserves. It has the world's largest forestry reserves, and produces more than one-fifth of the world's softwood. Russia's harsh climate means that only about one-sixth of its land is used for farming; three-fifths of this farmland is used to grow crops (half of which is for grain) and the remainder is pasture and meadow.

The post-Soviet recession has been accompanied by a decrease in population unprecedented in peacetime. There was a rapid dip in the birth rate in the early 1990s, and a precipitous fall in life expectancy, especially for men (who were seriously affected by alcoholism and heart disease): in 2000 it was 58.3 years (male) and 71.7 years (female). The population fell from 148.7 million at the end of 1991 to 144.6 million in mid-2001. Russia has 128 recognized nations and ethnic groups, the largest being the Russians (86.6% of the population), Tatars (3.2%), Ukrainians (1.3%), Chuvash (0.9%), Bashkirs (0.6%), Mordovans (0.5%), and Chechens (0.6%).

Communications/Energy

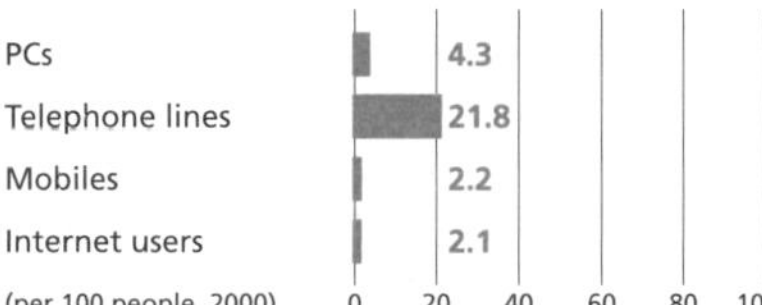

President Putin's administration has identified energy sector restructuring as a key aim. Russia's vast hydrocarbons resources make it self-sufficient in fuel, but its power network—more than 200 gigawatts of generation capacity, interconnected by 1.5 million miles of high-voltage transmission lines—is on average 30 years old and, like much of its infrastructure, suffered from almost no investment in the 1990s. Widespread power cuts in the winters of 2000 and 2001 underlined the urgency of restructuring. Major tariff reform is needed to attract strategic investors: tariffs are now about 1.38 cents per kWh for industrial users (against roughly 6 cents per kWh in the EU) and 0.78 cents per kWh for residential users (against roughly 12 cents).

Similar reforms to the rail network are overdue: 53,400 miles of railways, of which 46.5% are electrified, carries the vast bulk of freight, but railway freight traffic slumped by 59.6% between 1990 and 1998. Air transport plays a comparatively large role, but also suffers from underinvestment: the air fleet is aging, and is on average more than 15 years old. Air passenger transport slumped from 256.7 billion passenger-miles in 1990 to 85 billion in 1999 as a result of fare price increases. Russia has 43 sea ports and major merchant fleets on the Pacific and Arctic Oceans, the Baltic, and the Black Sea.

The number of private telephone lines increased dramatically during the 1990s (53.1% up between 1990 and 1998), although in 2000 there were still only 22 lines per 100 inhabitants. By 2001 there were 3.7 million mobile phone users. Svyazinvest, the state monopoly that controls the long-distance telephone monopoly Rostelekom and most regional phone companies, was partly privatized in 1996–97, but further privatization became mired in political controversy. Two companies that dominate the mobile phone market, Vimpelcom and MTS, are among the small number of Russian companies with New York stock exchange listings.

Education/Employment

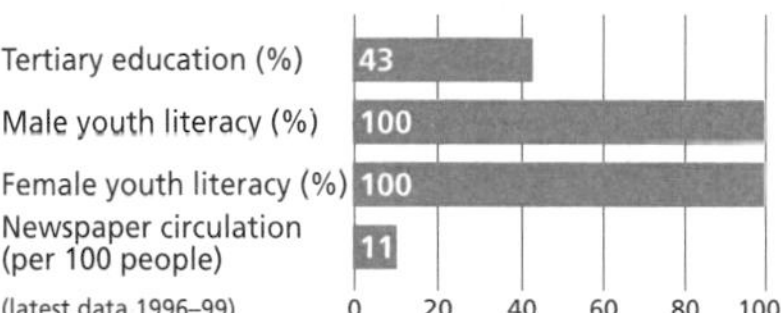

Throughout the 1990s, a free market in labor came into being in many parts of the private sector, and the Soviet labor code fell into disuse. In late 2001, parliament adopted a new labor code which accounts for post-Soviet changes. It shifts the balance in favor of employers, allowing wider use of fixed-term and renewable contracts and more extensive overtime working, strips unions of veto power over dismissals, and circumscribes unions' right to sue employers. Apart from unemployment and declining real wages, the workforce has been adversely affected by an epidemic of late wage payment, estimated at the end of 2000 at an aggregate total of 38.3 billion rubles ($1.4 billion).

Russia has a highly educated workforce: 1994 estimates showed that 15.1% of the population have higher or postgraduate education, a further 77.8% have secondary and some post-secondary education, 20.2% have some secondary education, and 10% only primary education. Despite the extent of the 1990s depression there was no contraction of the education system. In 1998–99 there were 3.6 million students in Russia, studying at 914 institutions. Demand for commercially-oriented qualifications has boomed, and the new private education

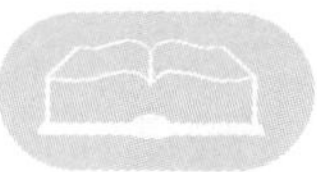

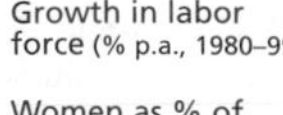
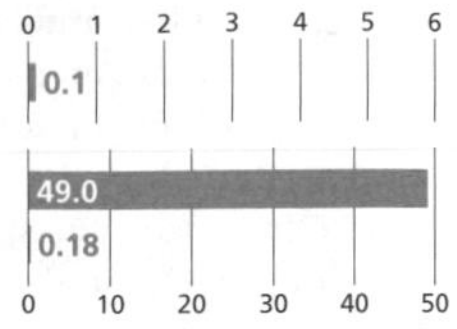

sector has provided most of these. By 1999 it accounted for 20% of the total number of students in higher education. Budget cutbacks have, however, undermined primary and secondary education, and in 1998–2000 there were constant teachers' strikes over underfunding and wages arrears.

Fiscal/Financial

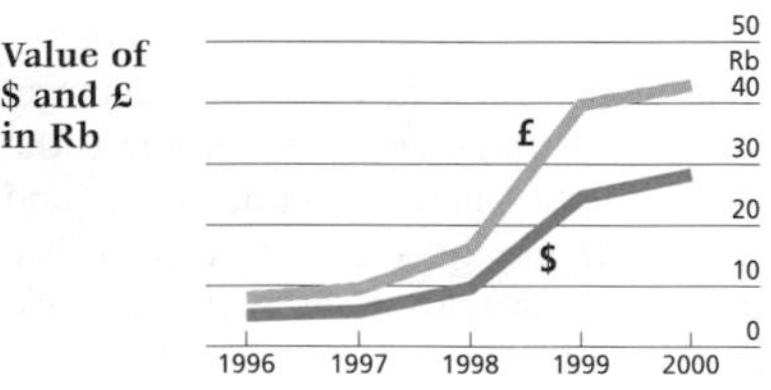

After the 1998 crisis, four types of banks remained active: the state-controlled banks (including the savings bank Sberbank, which in early 2001 held 85% of ruble deposits and 50% of hard currency deposits, and the foreign trade banks Vneshekonombank and Vneshtorgbank which are due for restructuring in 2002); private banks that held sufficiently few treasury bonds at the 1998 default to survive (including Alfa Bank and MDM); the "pocket" banks of large corporates, including some "bridge" banks used to preserve beyond creditors' reach the assets of banks that crashed in 1998; and 19 subsidiaries of foreign banks. In 2001 the sector remained small, and was notable for its failure to provide credit for industrial investment. A package of measures adopted by parliament in May 2001 provided for better regulation and greater transparency.

While many of Russia's largest companies are privately owned or have shares that are largely illiquid, some shares are in free float on the stock market; in some sectors, such as telecoms, there are growing opportunities for portfolio investment. Nevertheless the stock market's total capitalization stood at only 20% of GDP at the end of 2000; about two-thirds of that comprised oil and gas stocks.

Changes to tax laws introduced under Putin represent an improvement for investors. The new tax code adopted in 2000 introduced a flat 13% personal income tax, unified and reduced various social security contributions, reduced turnover tax, and eliminated a number of smaller taxes. In 2001 corporate profit tax was cut from 35% to 24% and most exemptions abolished; accelerated depreciation is to be allowed from 2002, and the scope of deductible business expenses widened.

Business Opportunities

Growth in output (% p.a., 1990–99)

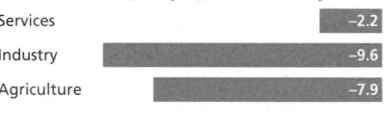

Foreign direct investment into Russia is substantially lower than into other transition states. Cumulative FDI per head, up to 2000, was $160 compared to $2,130 in Hungary and $1,060 in Poland. Gross FDI peaked at $4,864 million in 1997 and averaged $2,925 million in 1998–2000, but considerable investment outflows reduce the net figure, and in 2000 exceeded inflows by $350 million. All the figures must be considered against the background of continuing large-scale capital flight, which was estimated for 2000 at $24–29 billion. Moreover, a small proportion of this returned as inward investment.

There are indications that the protection afforded to inward investors by production sharing agreement (PSA) legislation may be reaping benefits. In November 2001 ExxonMobil announced a $10.5 billion six-year investment program for the Sakhalin Island oil project. The Indian national oil company ONGC took a share in the Sakhalin project for $1 billion in early 2001, also completed under PSA provisions. Such investments contrast sharply with the largest single pre-1998 piece of FDI, the purchase of a 10% stake in Sidanko oil company by BP for $500 million, which was followed by the bankruptcy of Sidanko's parent company, Oneksimbank, and a lengthy legal battle for assets. BP eventually found a commercial, rather than legal, solution.

In 2000 the largest privatization deals were sale of a 9% stake in Lukoil, the largest oil company, to a Cyprus-based trader, and the $1 billion sale of a controlling stake in Onako oil company to Tyumen Oil Company, considered Russia's most transparent tender yet. The large-scale privatization program was suspended temporarily in late 2000, and is due to resume in 2002 with the sale of Rosgossstrakh, the largest insurance company, and Norsi Oil, a medium-sized oil company.

Russia's tremendous supply of natural resources continues to make it highly attractive to inward investors, subject to continuing improvement in the legal and regulatory environment. Its potentially gigantic consumer market also offers opportunities, although investments in this sector have, since the 1998 crisis, concentrated on buying into domestic producers rather than on importing products at an unfavorable exchange rate.

For More Information

Books:

Aslund, Anders, ed. *Russia's Economic Transformation in the 1990s*. New York: Pinter, 1998.

Freeland, Chrystia. *Sale of the Century: Russia's Wild Ride from Communism to Capitalism*. New York: Times Books, 2000.

Klebnikov, Paul. *Godfather of the Kremlin: Boris Berezovsky and the Looting of Russia*. New York: Harcourt, 2000.

Lieven, Anatole. *Chechnya: Tombstone of Russian Power*. New Haven, CT: Yale University Press, 1999.

Putin, Vladimir, with A. Kolesnikov and N. Timakova. *First Person*. New York: Public Affairs Books, 2000.

Rutland, Peter, ed. *Business and the State in Contemporary Russia*. Boulder, CO: Westview Press, 2000.

Service, Robert. *A History of Twentieth Century Russia*. New York: Penguin, 1999.

Yeltsin, Boris N. *Midnight Diaries*. New York: Public Affairs Books, 2000.

Web Sites:

Federal Commission for the Securities Market: **www.fedcom.ru**

Moscow Times (English daily newspaper): **www.themoscowtimes.com**

Russia on the Net portal: **www.ru**

Russian government: **www.government.gov.ru**

Russian Central bank: **www.cbr.ru**

RTS stock exchange: **www.rts.ru**

Troika Dialog investment bank: **www.trodial.ru**

United Financial Group: **www.ufg.com**

SAUDI ARABIA

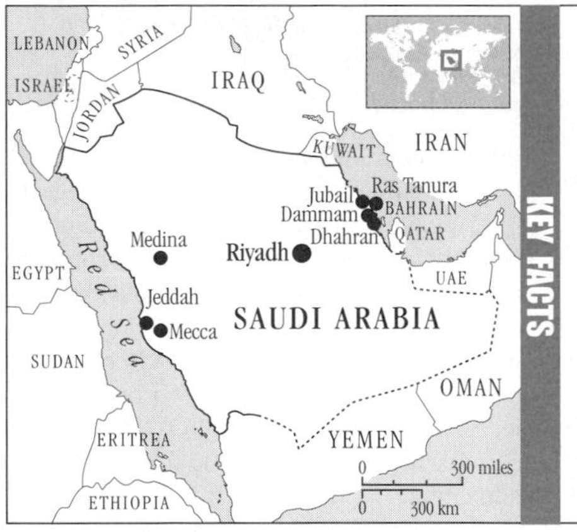

KEY FACTS

GNI: **$139,365 million; world's 27th**
GNI pc: **$6,900; world's 60th**
Head of government: **the King**
Currency: **Saudi riyal (SR)**
Capital: **Riyadh**
Population: **20,899,000, growing at 2.9% p.a.**
Land area: **830,000 square miles**
Population density: **25 per square mile**
Life expectancy: **72 years**
Infant mortality: **20 per 1,000 live births**
Language: **Arabic**
Best buy: **textiles, leather goods, silver jewelry**

ECONOMIC STRUCTURE

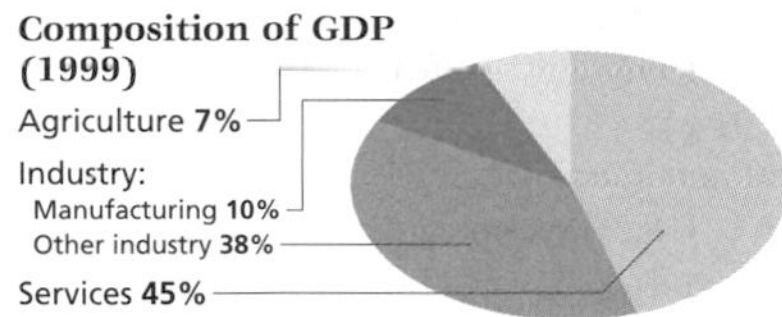

In early history the Arabian Peninsula supported agricultural and hunting communities, between which trade routes developed. The cities of Mecca and Medina, the birthplace of Islam, are the religion's main pilgrimage centers. The modern Kingdom of Saudi Arabia was founded in 1932, following a 30-year campaign by Abdul Aziz bin Abdul Rahman al-Saud to repel the Turks and unify the Arabian tribes against foreign intervention. Oil was used in small quantities for many centuries. Significant oil deposits were found by a U.S. company in 1935, and production began in 1938. In 1973 the Saudi government took a 25% stake in the oil company Aramco, and in 1980 it took full control of the company in agreement with the former U.S. owners. Saudi Aramco, the world's largest oil-producing company, owns pipelines, refineries, and ships, and has taken a key role in providing schools, electric power, and other infrastructure.

Industry (including mining, manufacturing, construction, and power) contributed 48% of GDP in 1998, followed by services (45%) and agriculture (7%). The oil and gas sector contributes around 35–40% of GDP, depending on world prices. Petroleum refining accounted for 31% of manufacturing in 1999. Government consumption accounted for 29% of GDP in 1999. Trade and transport are the other main services sectors, followed by finance and real estate. Non-oil manufacturing includes iron and steel, metal goods, chemicals, construction materials, and food processing. Crude petroleum is the main export, accounting for 68.1% of total export value in 1999, followed by refined petroleum products (15.9%). Japan was the leading market, absorbing 16.8%, followed by the United States (16.1%), France (10.9%), and Italy (6.2%).

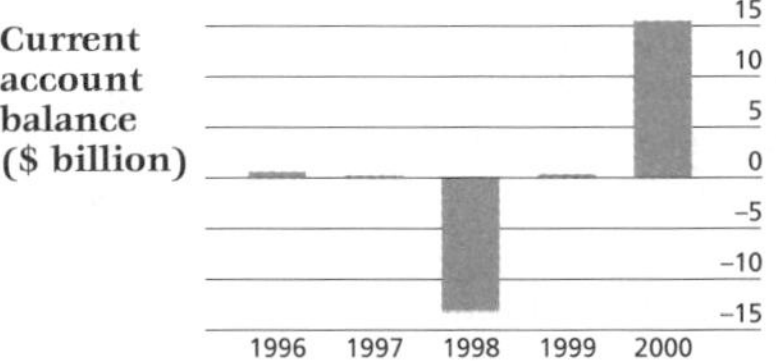

The public sector drives the economy. Saudi Aramco is the second-largest employer after the government. The government has taken the leading role in promoting diversification from oil. It established Saudi Arabian Basic Industries Corporation in the 1970s and Saudi Consulting House (now transferred to the General Investment Commission) to carry out industrialization with the private sector. The government set up the Saudi Arabian Mining Company in 1997 to spearhead non-hydrocarbon minerals development. The state provides development finance through specialized funds, but commercial banks are private-sector. The largest public/private partnership is the development of gas resources. Other sectors in which the government has involved the private sector include new power and telecommunications projects. Privatization of the electricity sector was officially approved in 2000. Saudi Telecommunications Company and the airline Saudia were being prepared for privatization in 2001. The Ministerial Committee for Privatization is considering other divestitures.

ECONOMIC POLICY

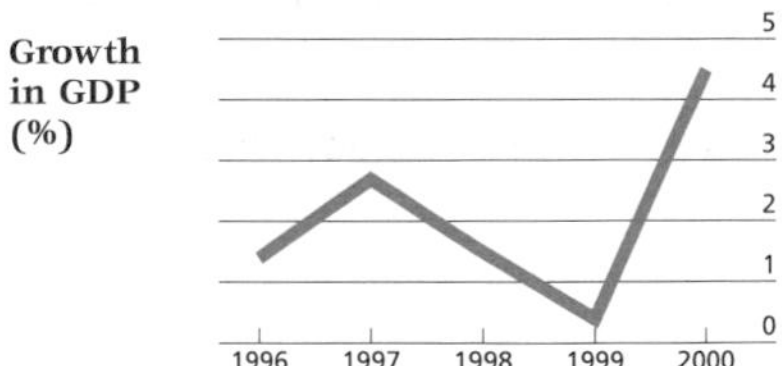

The maintenance of a stable exchange rate is the key to monetary policy. The government takes a prudent approach to oil production to maintain international prices but also to ease inflationary effects in consumer countries when the price rises sharply. Public spending has been trimmed in recent years in line with reduced oil revenues. Government consumption fell from 32.5% of GDP in 1998 to 26% in 2000, and the public debt was reduced from 127% of GDP to 106.4%. Borrowing is mostly domestic. High oil prices in 2000 produced the first budget surplus since 1982, but in 2001 there was a small deficit. The government aims to further reduce debt, achieve a balanced budget, and increase GDP growth to nearer the population growth rate of 3.5%. Average annual GDP growth was 1.3% in 1995–99, rising to 4.1% in 2000, falling to 1% in 2001, with weaker growth expected in 2002. There was deflation of –0.3% in 1996–2000, with zero inflation in 2001. Unemployment among Saudis was estimated at 15% in 2001.

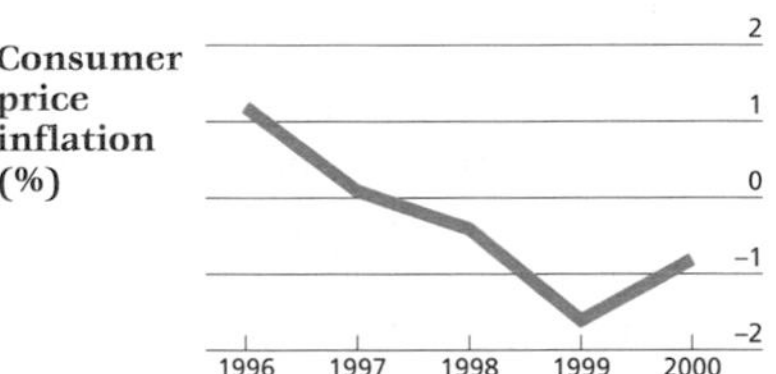

Five-year development plans in operation since 1970 have focused on diversification from oil and the establishment of a wide range of manufacturing industries. In the 1980s agriculture was developed as a means of import substitution, but has been so successful that wheat is now exported. The present focus for diversification is on non-hydrocarbon minerals exploitation and the development of high-technology industries. The state sector is likely to continue to lead economic development, but government policy is to strengthen the role of the private

  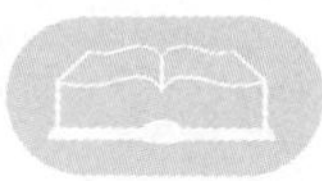    

sector under Saudi ownership. The need for more foreign investment is recognized in the 2000 Foreign Investment Law. Foreign investment and private-sector Saudi investment will drive the major expansion of natural gas production and distribution, and of downstream petrochemicals industries. The government is committed to a generous public welfare system, but expatriates are obliged to take out private health insurance under a 2001 law.

Geography/Resources

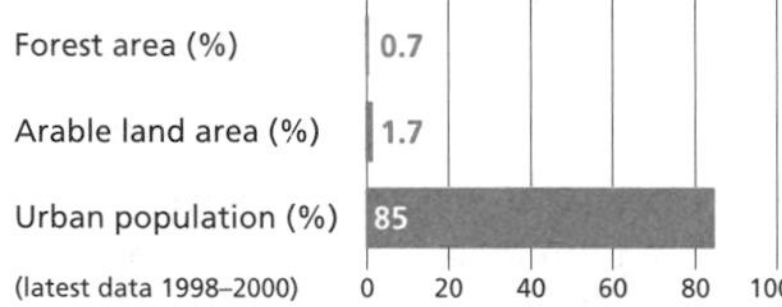

In western Asia, Saudi Arabia borders Jordan to the north, Iraq and Kuwait to the northeast, the Arabian Gulf, Bahrain, Qatar, and the United Arab Emirates to the east, Oman and Yemen to the south, and the Red Sea to the west. Most of the land is arid sandy desert and uninhabited. Some regions have no rain for periods of several years. There are no major rivers. Average rainfall is 4–8 inches in the north and less in the south. Summer temperatures vary from 100°F at the coast to 129°F inland. Winters are mild. There is a broad plain in the north and east, and a narrow coastal plain along the Red Sea. Most of the center and west is mountainous with a high point of 10,279 feet. Most of the population (90%) is of Arab origin, with about 10% of African and Asian origin, and small communities of Europeans and North Americans.

Investment from the 1980s in irrigation increased agricultural production, and Saudi Arabia has exported surplus wheat, the main crop, for over a decade. It is self-sufficient in many dairy products and in chickens, the main livestock. Other important crops are barley, sorghum, potatoes, vegetables, and fruit (especially dates). Sheep, goats, camels, cattle, and asses are raised. There is a small fishing industry. The country has the world's largest proven oil reserves at 259 billion barrels in 2001, one-quarter of world reserves. Estimated recoverable oil reserves are 1 trillion barrels. Proven gas reserves (excluding the neutral zone with Kuwait) were 204.5 trillion cubic feet in 2001, the fourth largest in the world after those of Russia, Iran, and Qatar. Gypsum is also mined. Projects to mine phosphates, bauxite, silica, and kaolin were under way in 2001. There are reserves of iron, gold, and copper.

Communications/Energy

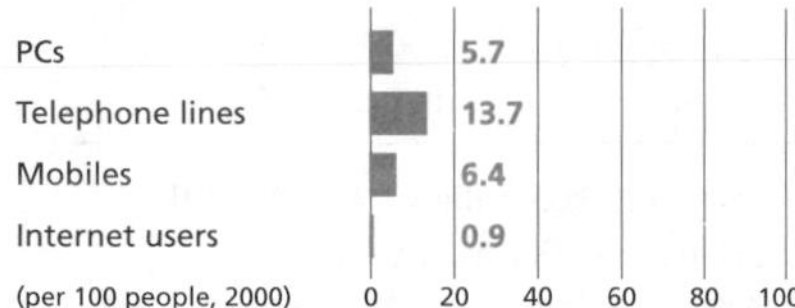

The road network totaled 91,050 miles, including 30,238 miles of paved roads, in 1998. The rail network was 760 miles. The pipeline network includes 3,977 miles for crude oil, 1,367 miles for natural gas, and 93 miles for petroleum products. New roads, railways, and pipelines are being built under the 2000–05 development plan. Jeddah is the main general cargo sea port, followed by Dammam. Jubail and Yanbu handle petroleum, natural gas, and petrochemicals as well as general cargo. Other main sea ports are Gizan and Dhiba. The main oil port, the world's largest, is Ras Tanura. Total non-oil cargo handled by Saudi ports was 95.3 million tons in 2000. The merchant fleet comprised 71 ships over 1,000 grt, with a total displacement of 1.2 million grt. There are three international airports for Mecca, Riyadh, and Dharan, and 22 other commercial airports.

Domestic and international telecommunication links are provided by cable, satellite, and microwave radio relay. There were 3 million fixed phone lines at end-2000, and 1.87 million mobile phones and 250,000 Internet subscribers at mid-2001. By 2005 it is planned there should be 7.5 million fixed and mobile phone lines. Private-sector telecommunications services include Internet and multimedia services, but the Internet server is state-owned. Internet services for the public were launched in 1999. Fast Internet access is available.

Crude oil production was 8.4 million barrels per day in 2000, while consumption was 1.3 million barrels per day. Natural gas production and consumption was an estimated 1.63 trillion cubic feet in 1999. The government is making major investments in gas production expansion to free more oil for export. Electricity is generated entirely from oil and gas, with a total installed capacity of 25 GW in 2001. This will be doubled to 50 GW by 2020 to meet annual growth in demand of 4.5%. Most of the new capacity will be in gas-fired or combined-cycle stations, and includes private-sector projects. Electricity is subsidized by the state, with 85% of supply provided by 10 regional state-owned companies. Plans to increase prices prior to privatization and liberalization of the sector were rescinded in late 2000.

Education/Employment

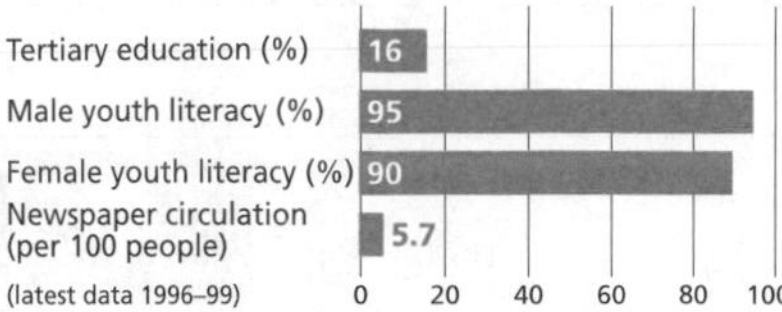

Education is free, but not compulsory at all levels. Primary education begins at age 6, intermediate education at age 12, secondary education at age 15, and higher education at age 18. In 1997–98 there were 296,524 students enrolled in higher education, which included 72 universities, 18 teacher training colleges, and technical and vocational colleges. The Ministry of Higher Education is responsible for directing and funding higher education.

The King Abdulaziz City for Science and Technology is the government organization responsible for science and technology policy and for coordinating applied R&D with universities, other government agencies, and the private sector, including foreign companies and institutions. It oversees research institutes specializing in astronomy and geophysics, natural resources and environmental sciences, petroleum and petrochemicals, energy (including nuclear), and computers and electronics. Other research centers specialize in medicine, agriculture, and water. Most foreign investment agreements include technology transfer and training.

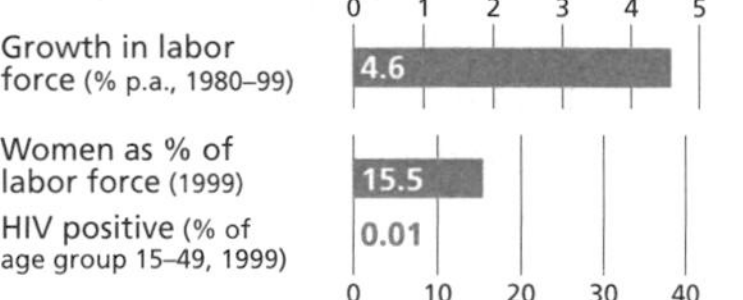

The labor force has a range of skills and includes African, Asian, European, and North American workers. Women are not allowed to work. The minimum employment age is 14. Trade unions, collective bargaining, and strikes are banned. Wages are determined between employers and employees. The Labor and Workmen Law is the main legislation regarding employment conditions. Implementation of the law is handled by the Labor Affairs Agency at the Ministry of Labor and Social Affairs. The working week is a maximum 48 hours (except during Ramadan when it is 36 hours), after which overtime (at time and a half) must be paid. Paid annual leave after one year of service is 15 days, rising to 21 days after 10 years of continuous service.

  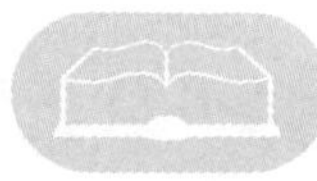    

Fiscal/Financial

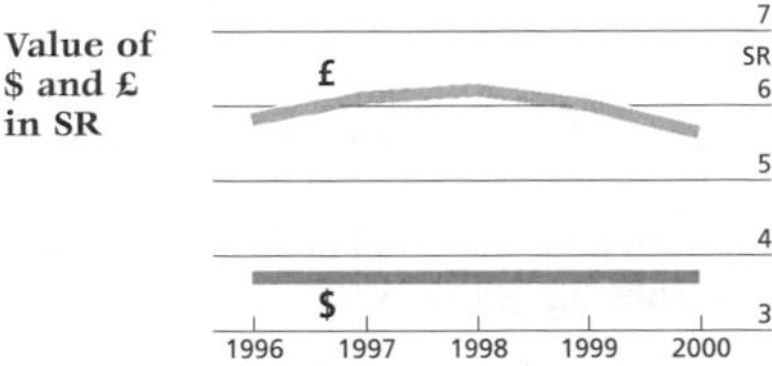

The largest banks by total assets in 2000 were National Commercial Bank, Saudi American Bank, Riyad Bank, Al-Rajhi Banking & Investment Corporation, Saudi British Bank, Arab National Bank, Saudi French Bank, Saudi Hollandi Bank, Saudi Investment Bank, and Bank al-Jazira. All were under majority private-sector ownership except for National Commercial Bank which sold 50% of its shares to the state-owned Public Investment Fund in 1999. One of the largest insurance companies is the state-owned National Company for Cooperative Insurance. The Saudi Arabian Monetary Agency is the central bank. It regulates the finance sector in conjunction with the Ministries of Finance and Commerce.

Saudi citizens and companies pay an Islamic tax, or zakat, of 2.5% of net worth, but no income tax. The top rate of income tax for foreign citizens and enterprises is 30%. Joint-venture companies pay income tax on the foreign portion of the business. Separate tax rules apply to the petroleum and gas sectors. Accounts must be submitted in Arabic to the Ministry of Finance, which establishes a company's tax base from these documents. There is a ten-year tax holiday for foreign joint venture companies which reinvest to expand their industrial operations.

One recent bank merger (Saudi American Bank with United Saudi Bank in 1999) is expected to be followed by further consolidation to face tougher international competition once World Trade Organization rules are applied to Middle East banking. National Commercial Bank could absorb one of the smaller banks before being reprivatized. The country's only Islamic bank, Al-Rajhi Banking & Investment Corporation, is the most profitable. One of the smaller banks, Arab National Bank, was the first to launch Internet banking in February 2000. An extensive network of automatic teller machines provides local banking services. U.S., Egyptian, Iranian, French, Dutch, and British banks have joint venture equity in four of the leading commercial banks. The government's specialized funds finance industrial, infrastructure, agricultural, and real estate projects. There are around 70 insurance firms, but consolidation is expected as new mandatory health insurance and car insurance take effect from 2002.

The Saudi Arabian Stock Market is the largest in the Arab world with a capitalization of $68 billion at end-2000. But capitalization is dominated by banks and SABIC, and—equivalent to 40% of GDP—is small in international terms. From 1997 international investors have been allowed to participate in the market through mutual funds. SAMA operates the stock market through the Electronic Securities Information System, set up in 1990. In October 2001 the trading system was updated to provide Internet access and instant share and company information. Foreign nationals of the Gulf Cooperation Council countries (Kuwait, Qatar, Bahrain, Oman, and U.A.E.) were allowed to participate directly in the market provided they opened an account prior to trading. In 2001 the government proposed to establish an official stock exchange "floor," with an independent regulatory authority to ensure no insider trading, as a means of expanding operations.

Business Opportunities

Growth in output (% p.a., 1990–99)

Sector	% p.a.
Services	2.2
Industry	1.5
Manufacturing	2.7
Agriculture	0.7

Foreign investment in the form of joint ventures is encouraged to create industrial diversification. Tax and financial incentives are available. The 2000 Foreign Investment Law allows foreign companies to have full ownership of Saudi projects for the first time and to be eligible for the same incentives as joint ventures and Saudi-owned projects. The point of contact is the General Investment Commission. Petrochemicals have attracted the most foreign investment to date from European, Asian, and North American companies. This sector, minerals, gas distribution, and high-tech industries offer investment opportunities. Government priorities include process industries using oil and gas feedstock, indigenous agricultural produce, and the manufacture of spare parts and machinery.

Foreign joint venture partners in service and contracting companies set up as limited liability partnerships are required to pay all their contribution to authorized capital in cash or kind. For industrial projects, 25% of the contribution must be paid in and 10% of profits must be set aside each year until this reserve reaches 50% of authorized capital. The workforce must be 75% Saudi unless an exemption has been obtained from the Ministry of Labor. There are several types of commercial operation from which foreign companies are barred. They include petroleum exploration and production, and manufacture of military equipment and civilian explosives. Services from which foreign companies are barred include insurance, telecommunications and audiovisual, education, wholesale and retail trade, transport, and electricity distribution. Saudization is a key component of joint venture projects, the aim being to strengthen Saudi technical and managerial skills and the Saudi private sector for an increasing role in the economy.

For More Information

Books:

Economist Intelligence Unit. *Country Profile and Quarterly Reports*. London.

Humphreys, Andrew, et al. *Middle East*. 3rd ed. Oakland, CA: Lonely Planet, 2000.

Kostiner, J. *The Making of Saudi Arabia: From Chieftaincy to Monarchical State*. New York: Oxford University Press, 1994.

Peters, James. *The Arab World Handbook*. London: Stacey International, 2000.

Web Sites:

Business information site (commercial with links to government): **www.saudia-online.com**

Ministry of Information (government entry point): **www.saudinf.com**

Saudi Arabian Monetary Agency: **www.sama-ksa.org**

  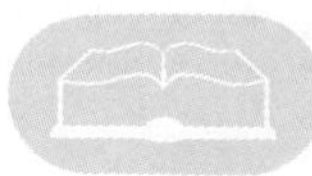    

SEYCHELLES

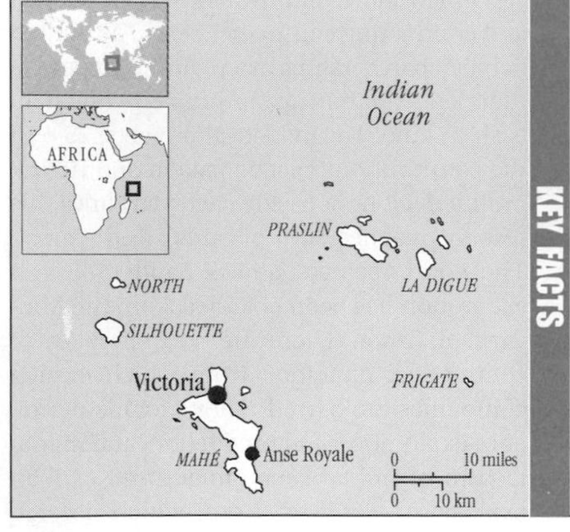

KEY FACTS

GNI: **$520 million**
GNI pc: **$6,500; world's 62nd**
Head of government: **president**
Currency: **Seychelles rupee (SRs)**
Capital: **Victoria**
Population: **77,000, growing at 1.1% p.a.**
Land area: **176 square miles**
Population density: **437 per square mile**
Life expectancy: **71 years**
Infant mortality: **13 per 1,000 live births**
Language: **Creole, French, English**
Best buy: **sea shells, stone carvings, cinnamon**

ECONOMY

An archipelago of Indian Ocean islands scattered over more than a million square kilometers of the ocean's surface, the Seychelles depend primarily on tourism and fishing for their economic survival. Tourism provides a wide range of jobs, brings in foreign currency, stimulates the development of infrastructure, and boosts property values. Conversely, however, any downturn in the industry quickly translates into a setback for the whole economy. After a decline in the late 1990s, visitor numbers recovered marginally to 128,000 in 2000. Because of a shortage of arable land, agriculture cannot provide sufficient foodstuffs for the population and, apart from fish, much of the food consumed in the islands is imported.

Seychelles territorial waters are rich with tuna. Some of these fish are caught by licensed foreign fleets, to be refrigerated and transported to Europe and Asia, but an increasing proportion is also being brought ashore to be canned on Mahé island at a plant owned by the U.S. food company H. J. Heinz. The main markets for Seychelles' exports are the United States, Yemen, and the United Kingdom. The main sources of imports are the United States, the United Kingdom, South Africa, and Singapore.

Despite its problems in balancing the budget, the government of President France Albert René has resisted reforming the state sector of the economy, which suffered an ever-widening deficit during the 1990s. The economy has long suffered balance of payments deficits and foreign exchange shortages-problems affecting foreign and local businesses operating in the islands. State-owned companies account for two-thirds of employment and more than half the country's GDP; the largest, the Seychelles Marketing Board, has a monopoly on many imports.

Economic growth averaged 2.8% per annum in the second half of the 1990s. Inflation was low at the beginning of the period but increased to about 6.5% in 2000. The value of the Seychelles rupee also slipped.

GEOGRAPHY/RESOURCES

The main inhabited islands of Mahé, Silhouette, Praslin, and La Digue are formed from granite rock rising from the ocean floor. About 88% of the islands' small population live on Mahé, where the capital, Victoria, forms a natural harbor. Only limited agricultural activity is possible on the rocky islands; small amounts of copra, cinnamon, and tea are grown as cash crops. Fish from the sea constitute the single most important food resource. The only mining activity is for granite and salt.

The people of the Seychelles are descended from a mixture of French settlers and slaves of African and Indian descent. There has been considerable investment in health and education and there is low unemployment.

COMMUNICATIONS/ENERGY

The roads on Mahé are adequate for the island's low traffic density, and there is a good bus fleet. The main islands are linked by public and private ferries and by domestic air services. Air Seychelles operates inter-island services and international services to Europe and Asia. There are efficient telecommunications services. Domestic power requirements are provided from imported petroleum products. Fuel and electricity are sold at subsidized prices.

FISCAL/FINANCIAL

Nearly half of government revenue comes from taxes on imported goods. The government has sought to bolster its tax administration by reducing tax exemptions and monitoring the concessions it makes under the Investment Promotion Act.

The Central Bank of Seychelles operates under government direction. There are three domestic banks, and four international banks have representative offices. There is an offshore business registry. The government has sought the cooperation of the IMF and the UN in making the country a center of finance for the Indian Ocean region, and says it is committed to combating money-laundering and other financial crime. There is no stock market.

BUSINESS OPPORTUNITIES

The principal attraction for foreign investors will remain the tourism industry, where government policy is geared towards maintaining the special exclusivity of the islands. Two new five-star hotels were opened in 1999 and other luxury resorts are planned. The government also has plans to modernize the international airport on Mahé island.

For More Information

Books:

Benedict, B., and M. Benedict. *Men, Women and Money in Seychelles.* Berkeley, CA: University of California Press, 1982.

Mancham, J. *Paradise Raped: Life, Love and Power in the Seychelles.* New York: Methuen, 1983.

Web Sites:

African news and information: **www.allafrica.com/business**
Indian Ocean Rim Network: **www.iornet.org/newiornet/seychelles.htm**
News and information: **www.worldskip.com/seychelles**

SINGAPORE

KEY FACTS

GNI: **$95,429 million; world's 36th**
GNI pc: **$24,150; world's 22nd**
Head of government: **prime minister**
Currency: **Singapore dollar (S$)**
Capital: **Singapore**
Population: **3,522,000, growing at 1.7% p.a.**
Land area: **250 square miles**
Population density: **14,088 per square mile**
Life expectancy: **78 years**
Infant mortality: **4 per 1,000 live births**
Language: **Malay, Chinese (Mandarin), Tamil, English**
Best buy: **cameras, watches, computers, electrical goods, textiles, antiques**

ECONOMIC STRUCTURE

Composition of GDP (1999)

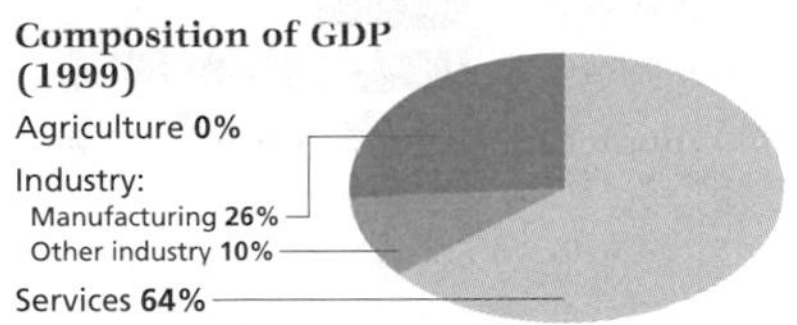

Singapore became a trading center for Asia and Europe under an agreement between the Sultan of Johor, the Malay ruler of the island, and the British East India Company in 1819. It developed rapidly in its new role with an influx of migrant labor, especially Chinese, who came to outnumber the original Malay population. In 1963 Malaya and Singapore gained independence from Britain. Singapore joined the Federation of Malaysia but left in 1965. In the first years of independence Singapore attracted foreign investment into labor-intensive industry to overcome unemployment. Since the early 1970s the government has directed the economy towards capital and skill-intensive industries and services. Its focus on foreign investment has provided a model for other countries of the Association of South-East Asian Nations, of which it is a founder member.

Services accounted for 67% of GDP in 2000 and manufacturing for 26%. The contribution of agriculture was around 0.1% and that of mining was 0.01% in 1998. In 1998 finance and business services accounted for 29% of GDP, trade for 17%, transport and communications for 10%. The electronics industry is by far the most important manufacturing sector. Chemicals and petroleum refining are also key industrial sectors. Finance, insurance, and business services, including global company headquarters operations, are the leading services. The import-export trade generates retail and wholesale trading, logistics and transport activities, and finance and insurance. The main exports in 2000 were office machinery (22.9%), followed by telecommunications equipment (5.5%), petroleum (5.2%), and scientific and optical equipment (2.2%). The main markets were Malaysia (18.2%), followed by the United States (17.3%), Hong Kong (7.9%), Japan (7.6%), Thailand, the United Kingdom, and China.

Current account balance ($ billion)

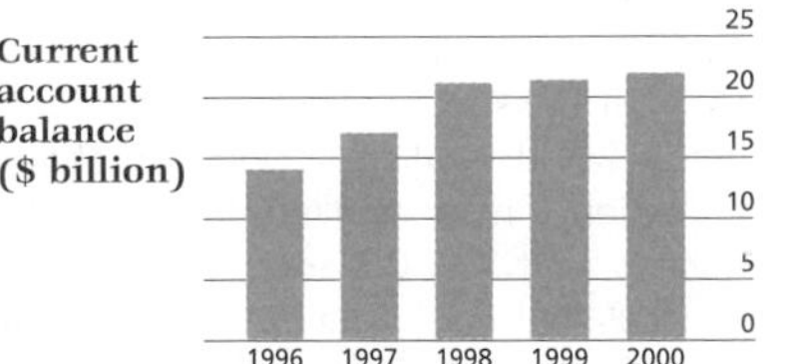

The government has extensive control over the economy, more apparent through regulation than through its strategic shareholdings in a wide range of government-linked companies, including manufacturing and utilities. It has reduced some of these shareholdings. It controls power, water, and telecommunications companies which either have monopolies or are dominant. In the mid-1990s it corporatized these companies, forming separate regulatory authorities for the sectors and a state holding company, Temasek Holdings, at the same time. Temasek Holdings has 100% of electricity and gas company Singapore Power, and 80% of Singapore Telecommunications. The telecoms sector was liberalized in 2000 with the licensing of 150 new service providers. Retail electricity distribution has been partly liberalized. There are plans to privatize two Singapore Power subsidiaries. The 40% equity ceiling on foreign ownership of domestic banks was removed in May 1999. In October 1999 and June 2001 restrictions on foreign bank operations were eased. The 49% limit on foreign ownership in other sectors and some restrictions on foreign operations have also been lifted.

ECONOMIC POLICY

Growth in GDP (%)

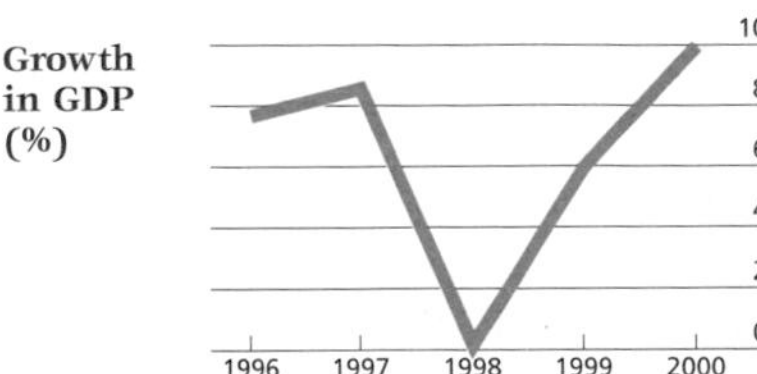

Macro-economic policy is geared to long-term objectives, primarily long-term economic growth and long-term investment. The government has preferred to promote job creation rather than welfare benefits, but its public housing, education and health programs underpin welfare. From the 1970s about one-third of government expenditure has gone into infrastructure projects. Strong economic growth and strict tax collection allowed for budget surpluses averaging 5% of GDP throughout the 1990s. Prudent fiscal policy encouraged a high rate of savings, which rose from 11% of GDP in 1965 to 50% in 1995. This allowed for a high level of investment without incurring foreign debt. It also facilitated ample foreign reserves to underpin the government's policy of stability for the Singapore dollar and prices. The exchange rate is the chosen focus of monetary policy since 1981, and has delivered price stability. It floats freely, and the government intervenes in the market to maintain the value within an undisclosed range set against a basket of currencies of Singapore's main trading partners. The adoption of a basket of currencies, rather than the U.S. dollar, contributed to rapid recovery from the Asian financial crisis in the late 1990s. With a loss of share of regional foreign investment as a result of the opening of China to Western investment, the government has stepped up liberalization measures and invested in ultra-modern communications technology to revamp Singapore's trading capacity.

Although the economy stagnated in 1998 as a result of the Asian financial crisis, annual GDP growth averaged 8.6% in 1965–99. GDP grew by 5.4% in 1999 and 9.9% in 2000 before declining by 3.5% in 2001. A further

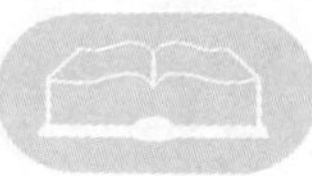

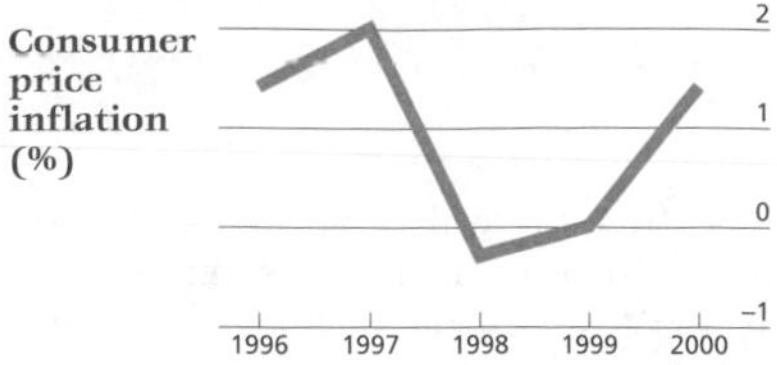

fall of 0.4% was expected in 2002. Inflation averaged 3.2% a year in 1965–99, but was near zero in 1998–99. It was 1.3% in 2000, and 1–2% is expected for 2001 and 2002. Unemployment is characteristically low, but rose from 2% in 1996 to a peak of 4.5% in late 1998 before falling to 3% by 2001. Singapore has more often suffered from insufficient labor supply, and has recruited from overseas to fill the gap.

Geography/Resources

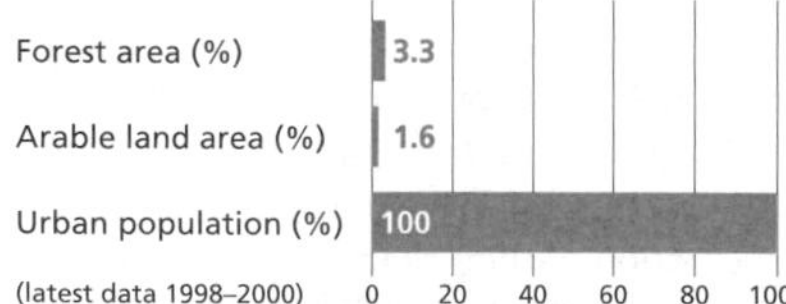

Situated at the southern tip of the Malaysian peninsula, Singapore consists of a main island and 63 smaller islands. A causeway and bridge between Singapore island and Johor in Malaysia carries a road and rail bridge and a water pipe. Another causeway links the main island with Sentosa. Eleven islands are being reclaimed and merged to form Jurong Island. The main island consists of low hills in the center and west (with a high point of 541 feet), and a flat eastern region. Nearly half of the land (49%) is urban. Forest covers 4%, marsh 2%, farmland 1.5%, and other features such as inland water, public gardens and unused land 43%. The climate is equatorial, hot with abundant rainfall averaging 92 inches a year. There are two monsoon seasons: December–March and June–September. Mean daily temperature is 81 °F. The majority of the population are of Chinese origin (77% in 1999), followed by Malay (14%), Indian (8%), and others including European (1%). The median age was 33.4 years in 1999. Population density was 9,500 per square mile.

The main agricultural crops are orchids and other ornamental plants, vegetables, and fruit. Most vegetables are grown under plastic to protect the plants from heavy rain and pests. Poultry meat and eggs are important. Aquaculture includes marine and freshwater food fish and freshwater ornamental fish, of which Singapore is a leading world exporter. There is an import-export business in ornamental fish. The government has established agrotechnology parks on 3,620 acres of land. By end-1999, 2,419 acres had been allocated to 353 farms involving livestock, fish, fruit, vegetables, and plants. There is a small mining industry focused on granite quarrying.

Communications/Energy

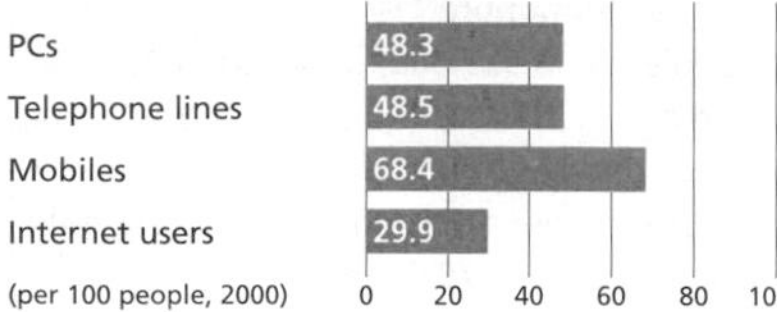

There were 1,940 miles of roads in 1999, 1,888 miles of which were paved. The network included 93 miles of expressways. Singapore operates an electronic road pricing system to reduce congestion on the roads. The Mass Rapid Transit System has 52 miles of electrified track and carries around 1 million passengers a day. In 2000 it had two lines with 48 stations. Two additional lines totaling 16 miles, with 17 stations, are due for completion in 2002 and 2004. One of the new lines will connect with Changi International Airport. The 16-mile railway which links to Malaysia is owned and operated by Malaysian Railways. Singapore has the world's busiest port in terms of tonnage handled. There are container and bulk handling facilities. The port handled 17.04 million teus of containers in 2000. It is a major transshipment hub for 400 shipping lines, with links to 700 ports worldwide. It is a top world bunkering port, supplying 18.9 million tons of bunkers in 1999. The merchant fleet was the seventh largest in the world, with 3,360 ships representing 23.7 million grt in 1999. The Singapore Cruise Center handled over 6 million passengers in 1999 at its international and regional terminals, including 1 million cruise ship passengers. Changi International Airport handled 26 million passengers and 1.5 million tons of freight in 1999. The planned third passenger terminal will expand capacity to 64 million passengers a year. An eighth airfreight terminal was added in 2001.

The telecommunications sector is partly liberalized, but Singapore Telecommunications is the dominant player. Three fiber-optic cables link Singapore to Japan, the Middle East, Africa, and Europe. The country's first satellite, jointly owned by SingTel and Taiwan's Chunghwa Telecom, was launched in 1998 to carry broadcasting and telecommunications signals across Asia. Singapore has the world's first nationwide broadband network, Singapore ONE. At April 2001 99% of homes, companies, and institutions were connected to the high-speed multimedia link. At end-2000 there were 274,000 users out of 2 million Internet subscribers. The government intends Singapore ONE to make the country into a global "infocomms" hub. At end-2000 there were 1.9 million fixed phone lines and 2.7 million mobile phones. Electricity is generated from imported oil and natural gas at five power stations. Electricity demand is forecast to increase by around 5% a year in the next decade. Natural gas is piped to homes. Oil accounted for 95.9% of energy needs in 1999, followed by gas (4.1%). Singapore is a regional center for oil refining, with a 2001 capacity of 1.3 million barrels per day, over half of which is exported.

Education/Employment

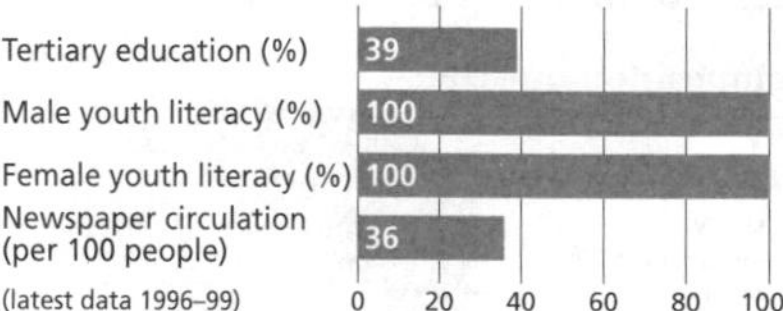

Education is provided for at least ten years from age 6 in at least two languages, English (Singapore's language of administration and commerce) and Chinese, Malay, or Tamil. The 14 vocational institutes and two universities are the responsibility of the Ministry of Education, and funding is provided by the state. There are also 79 commercial schools and 72 language schools, which are either private-sector or not-for-profit. Nanyang Technological University has schools of applied science, communication, civil engineering, electrical and electronic engineering, mechanical engineering, and business. The polytechnics have strong links with industry, especially in electronics, engineering, IT, and biotechnology. They provide continuing education and skills upgrades for people in work, as well as R&D facilities.

The National University of Singapore has 13 affiliated and 40 faculty-based research institutes. Computing, engineering, sciences, architecture, and medicine are among its specialties. Nanyang Polytechnic has established electronic games and e-commerce research centers in collaboration with the private sector. Singapore Polytechnic has R&D strengths in robotics and automotive applications, such as its solar-powered car. Temasek Polytechnic has a Mechatronics Design Center, Hydroponic greenhouse, and food pilot plant.

The labor force is well educated, adapt-

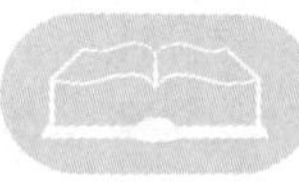

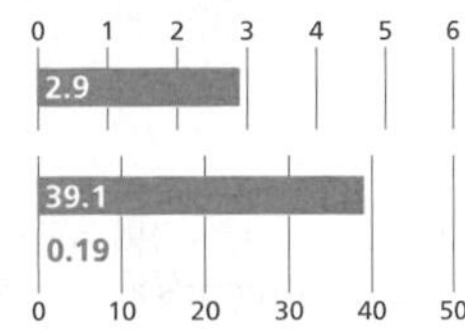

able to new technologies, and well versed in IT. Wages and employment conditions are determined by tripartite negotiation between employers, trade unions, and government. The National Wages Council, which comprises representatives of the social partners, advises the government on the basis for negotiations between employers and unions. Retirement age was raised to 62 years in January 1999, and social security contributions were reduced for workers over 60. The normal working week is 44 hours with one rest day. Workers are entitled to 11 public holidays and 7–14 days of annual leave.

Fiscal/Financial

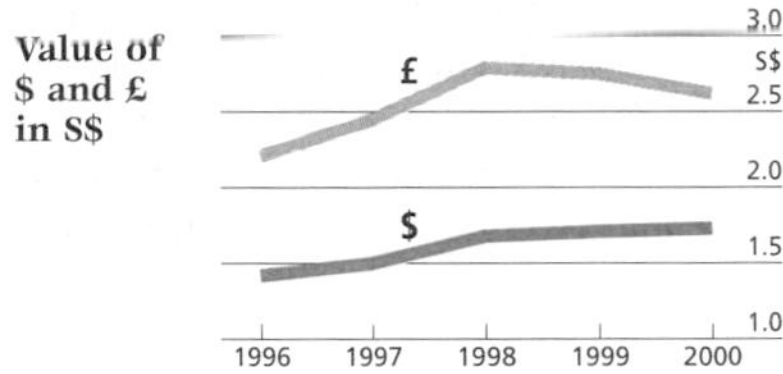

The largest commercial bank is DBS (Development Bank of Singapore), which is 37% government-owned (but the government pledged in 2001 to reduce its stake), followed by OCBC (Oversea-Chinese Banking Corporation), which is private-sector. The two other large domestic commercial banks are OUB (Overseas Union Bank) and UOB (United Overseas Bank), both private-sector. There were 156 insurance companies in 1999, including most of the world's largest. The Monetary Authority of Singapore (MAS) fulfils central bank and supervisory functions. It restricts the use of the Singapore dollar to prevent internationalization of the currency. The Asian Currency Unit replaces the Singapore dollar in the foreign currency role.

Corporation tax is 24.5% as of January 2001. The top rate of personal income tax of 28% will be reduced to 26% from fiscal year 2002–03. There is no capital gains tax except on residential properties sold within three years of purchase. There is a value added Goods and Services Tax of 3%. Tax concessions and exemptions are offered to offshore banking and insurance units, and multinational company headquarters operations.

Singapore is a leading world center for foreign exchange trading, derivatives, and offshore lending. In 1999 MAS launched a 5-year program to liberalize the sector, and strengthen local competition and thus the leading local banks. The aim is for Singapore to play a larger role in Asian regional finance and insurance. DBS's acquisition of Hong Kong's Dao Heng Bank in 2001 will help achieve this goal. MAS removed the 40% limit on foreign equity in domestic banks and the 49% limit for insurance companies. In June 2001 it simplified its bank licensing categories to allow foreign banks to engage in a wider range of operations. There were 31 fully licensed banks in mid-2001, including 8 locally-incorporated banks and 21 branches of foreign banks, 19 wholesale banks (including former restricted banks) and 80 offshore banks (all foreign-owned), 56 merchant banks, and 11 finance companies. At end-1999 there were 57 direct insurers, 47 professional reinsurers, and 52 captive insurers. The domestic market is small. Citibank, ABN Amro, Standard Chartered, and BNP-Paribas were accorded licenses in May 1999 to conduct limited domestic banking operations in order to increase local competition. In 1998 the government merged savings bank POSBank into DBS, but MAS believes there is more room for consolidation. DBS has acquired banks in Thailand and Hong Kong to increase its international scope, while OCBC has bought a Malaysian bank. At end-March 2000, total assets of commercial and merchant banks were S$421.9 billion and total insurance company assets were S$43.4 billion.

Singapore Exchange (SGX) is a demutualized and integrated securities and derivatives exchange which was launched at end-1999 following the merger of the Stock Exchange of Singapore and the Singapore International Monetary Exchange. SGX signed a cross-listing agreement with the Australian Stock Exchange in June 2000. In May 2001 it launched a joint venture with American Stock Exchange to list five Amex exchange traded funds.

Business Opportunities

The government offers grants and tax breaks to investors. It is eager to attract high-tech industries and an R&D component to investments, offering grants for this, and to ensure that IT is widely used. It offers assistance in matching international and local partners and in helping them to devise global strategies. It has promoted clusters in manufacturing: electronics, engineering, chemicals, and others; and in services: ICT and media, logistics, education and healthcare, and headquarters operations. Jurong Town Corporation manages 35 industrial parks with modern facilities for companies. Electronics, computer hardware and software and other IT products, biotechnology and pharmaceuticals, petroleum refining, chemicals, finance, insurance, and shipping are among the many sectors to attract foreign investment. The leading investor at end-1999 was the United States, followed by Japan, Netherlands, the United Kingdom, and Germany. The point of contact for foreign investors is the Economic Development Board.

Growth in output (% p.a., 1990–99)

Sector	% p.a.
Services	8.0
Industry	7.9
Manufacturing	6.7
Agriculture	0.4

For More Information

Books:

Chong, Amelyn, ed. *Business Guide to Singapore.* Woburn, MA: Butterworth-Heinemann, 1997.
Economist Intelligence Unit. *Country Profile and Quarterly Reports.* London.
Genzberger, Christine, ed. *Singapore Business: The Portable Encyclopedia for Doing Business with Singapore.* Novato, CA: World Trade Press, 1994.
IMF Country Report. *Singapore.* Washington, D.C.
Ministry of Information and the Arts. *Singapore Facts and Pictures.*
Singapore Business and Investment Opportunities Yearbook. 3rd ed. Washington, D.C.: International Business Publications, 2001 (annual).

Web Sites:

Department of Statistics: **www.singstat.gov.sg**
Economic Development Board: **www.sedb.com**
Government entry point: **www.sg**
Monetary Authority of Singapore: **www.mas.gov.sg**
Singapore Exchange: **www.sgx.com**
Singapore Tourism Board: **www.stb.com.sg**

  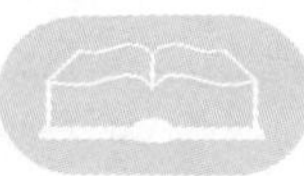    

SLOVAKIA

KEY FACTS

GNI: **$20,318 million; world's 63rd**
GNI pc: **$3,770; world's 77th**
Head of government: **prime minister**
Currency: **Euro (€)**
Capital: **Bratislava**
Population: **5,382,000, growing at 0.3% p.a.**
Land area: **18,930 square miles**
Population density: **290 per square mile**
Life expectancy: **73 years**
Infant mortality: **9 per 1,000 live births**
Language: **Slovak, Hungarian**
Best buy: **slivovica (plum brandy)**

ECONOMIC STRUCTURE

Present-day Slovakia formed, from the 11th century, part of Hungary and then of the Austro-Hungarian empire, upon the collapse of which, in 1918, it united with the Czech lands to form Czechoslovakia. Dismembered by Nazism, Czechoslovakia was reconstituted in 1945 and ruled by the Communist Party from 1948. Slovakia's underdeveloped, agrarian economy benefited from state subsidies and industrialization. It became the center of the Czechoslovak armaments industry. After the "velvet revolution" of 1989 ended communism, the political elite (although not most of the population) favored separation, and in 1993 Slovakia became independent. Prime Minister Vladimir Meciar of the Movement for a Democratic Slovakia (HZDS) ruled from 1994. His unorthodox attitude to reform and authoritarian tendencies alienated international institutions, and in 1997 the EU and NATO excluded Slovakia from the first group of transition countries invited to join. In late 1998 an opposition coalition won parliamentary elections. Relations with the West quickly warmed: in 2000 Slovakia began EU accession negotiations and joined the Organisation for Economic Co-operation and Development. It has expressed determination to join NATO, an aim strongly supported by the United States. It is already a World Trade Organization member.

In the 1990s Slovakia's heavy industry contracted, but manufacturing remains vital to its economy. Metallurgy accounts for 9% of employment and 16% of exports; the automotive industry, and especially automotive components, is growing rapidly; and telecommunications, wood processing, and food processing were thriving in 2001. Agriculture accounts for 4.5% of GDP and 7.4% of total employment (2000 figures). The services sector mushroomed in the 1990s, reaching a 61.4% share of GDP in 2000. The private-sector share of GDP rose to more than 75% by 2000.

Slovakia's trade is heavily oriented to the EU (which accounted for 59.3% of exports and 49.3% of imports in 2000). Its other important trading partner is the Czech republic (with 17.4% of exports and 14.7% of imports in 2000).

ECONOMIC POLICY

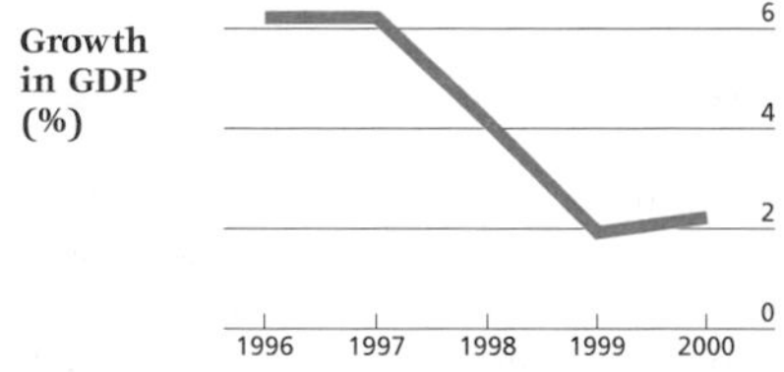

The government elected in 1998, headed by Mikulas Dzurinda, made economic policy changes aimed at tackling a substantial budget deficit. Regulated prices were increased: in the 18-month period to the end of 2000, household electricity prices rose by 135%, heating prices by 112%, and rents by 70%. Efforts were made to reduce the volume of state guarantees, which stood at 16% of GDP in 2000. The issue of new guarantees was strictly limited. An expensive highway construction program was cut back, and the privatization program revised, reducing the number of enterprises classified as "strategic" and therefore unsaleable. The previous policy of "revitalizing" unprofitable enterprises was abandoned, and replaced with stronger bankruptcy procedures as the basis of restructuring.

The koruna has floated since 1998, and the new government's austerity policies affected inflation in two ways: liberalization of fixed prices pushed it up, and wage restraint pushed it down. Overall, inflation rose from 6.7% in 1998 to 10.6% in 1999 and 12% in 2000; it fell to 7.4% in 2001 (EBRD projection).

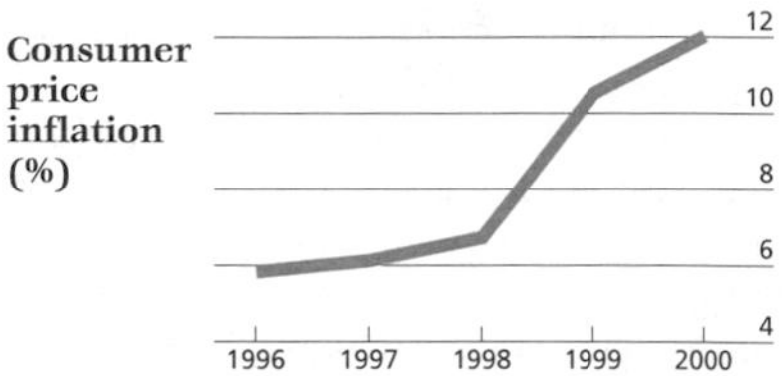

GDP growth, driven by strong industrial production and external demand in 1994–95, and by a surge in public and private consumption in 1996–98, averaged 5.6% during the latter period. It slowed to 1.9% in 1999 and 2% in 2000; in 2001 a recovery in domestic demand helped growth to reach 3% (EBRD projection). However, high unemployment persisted throughout the 1990s and in the early 2000s, and at the end of 2000 it stood at 17.9% nationally, and at 25% or higher in some regions.

GEOGRAPHY/RESOURCES

Slovakia is a small country, just 18,930 square miles, bordered by the Czech republic to the west, Poland to the north, Ukraine to the east, and Hungary and Austria to the south. Forests cover 40% of Slovakia, and support its important timber and wood processing industry. Farmland covers about 50%: wheat, corn, sugar beet, potatoes, sunflowers, and grapes are the main crops. Slovakia has limited resources of lignite and brown coal.

Under communism Slovakia experienced a slowdown of population growth typical of modernizing countries; population rose by just 6.3% in the 1980s. In the 1990s Slovakia avoided the depopulation experienced by many post-communist states, and the population remained at around 5.4 million from 1995 to 2000. The proportion in the productive age group (15–59 years) is expected to grow until around 2010 and then decline.

COMMUNICATIONS/ENERGY

Slovakia relies on imports—primarily of oil, gas, and nuclear fuel supplies from Russia—for more than 80% of its energy. Its own power resources mainly consist of the small brown-coal industry and nuclear generators. During the 1990s little was done to diversify supply: in 1993 below-market prices were negotiated with Russia, and in 1997 an exclusive gas delivery contract was signed between the Slovak gas company Slovesnsky plynarensky priemysl (SPP) and the Russian gas company Gazprom. Major power sector restructuring, including market liberalization and privatization, started in 2000. The Hungarian oil company MOL took a strategic stake in the Slovnaft oil refinery. In December 2001 the Russian oil company Yukos bought 49% of the main oil pipeline operator, Transpetrol. The government was preparing the partial privatization of SPP. Some nuclear capacity is being closed: at the Mochovce plant, partly owned by a French-German-Czech consortium, two reactors are operating but further expansion plans have been canceled. Slovakia's importance to gas transit has increased with Russia's intentions of reducing transit via Ukraine, and in 2001 project finance was secured for pipeline upgrades.

Slovakia's mountainous terrain is a challenge for rail and road transport, especially north-south routes; as of 2001 major investment is still required. The 2,277 miles of railways, less than half of it electrified, operate at a loss. The road network requires upgrading, and the government has started a project to build 410 miles of new motorways. Slovakia has five airports with international capacity—at Bratislava, Košice, Piestany, Sliac, and Poprad—and three ports on the Danube that give access to the pan-European waterway system.

Telecommunications advanced rapidly in the 1990s, when the number of lines per 100 inhabitants rose from 20.8 in 1995 to 30.7, plus 12.3 mobiles, in 1999. The sale to Deutsche Telekom of a controlling stake in Slovak Telecom, the former state monopoly, was Slovakia's largest privatization up to 2001. Two mobile telephone companies, one with French and one with German and U.S. ownership, expanded rapidly in 1999–2001.

Education/Employment

High unemployment is the greatest persistent problem in Slovakia's labor market. There is also a high proportion of long-term jobless, with 50% of the unemployed in 2000 having been without work for more than a year. An underdeveloped housing market means low labor mobility, and there are wide disparities between both employment levels and wage levels in prosperous areas such as Bratislava and poor parts of the country, particularly in the east. A strong social welfare system and low wages combine to deprive low-paid unskilled workers of incentives to find work. Collective bargaining covers much of industry, but unemployment has weakened unions.

The educational attainment of the workforce compares well to that of advanced OECD countries. Tertiary education is well developed, and the number of university students rose from 66,900 in 1994 to 89,608 in 1999. A feature of Slovakia's education system is secondary schools specializing in technical subjects, economics, management, and other vocational subjects, but enrollment in these fell steeply in the late 1990s.

Fiscal/Financial

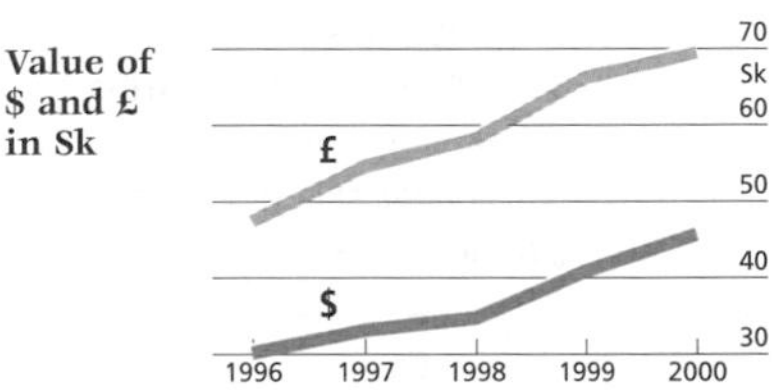

A major privatization program had, by the end of 2001, brought the two largest state banks into private hands: the largest, Slovenska sporitelna, was sold to Erste Bank of Austria for $425 million, and the second-largest, Vseobecna uverova banka, to the Italian group IntesaBCI for €550 million. Sales of the third largest bank, other state banks, and the dominant insurance company were in progress at the end of 2001. The sales ended a period of soft lending and mismanagement in the mid-1990s, which by 1998 had brought the banking sector to a state where it had insufficient capital to deal with non-performing loans. Bad assets equal to more than 10% of GDP were placed in state consolidation agencies, and a significant portion of them sold in June 2001 to an international consortium. A new Banking Act, enacted in 2001, aligned regulation and supervision with EU standards.

The Bratislavia Stock Exchange is underdeveloped and illiquid, even by Eastern European standards; local stock exchange capitalization, at 2.5% of GDP, is low. The insurance market started undergoing liberalization and developed rapidly in the 1990s, with U.S., German, Dutch, and Austrian companies moving into it.

The tax environment for investors was improved by the 1999 tax reform, which reduced corporate income tax from 40% to 29%, and improved tax deductibility of expenses, losses carried forward, and depreciation rules. Income tax rates range from 12% to 42%. The indirect tax category comprises excise taxes and VAT.

Business Opportunities

Foreign direct investment leaped from an average of $185 million per year in 1992–98 to $701 million in 1999, $2,028 million in 2000, and an estimated $2,000 million in 2001. Around half of this went into the manufacturing industry. Important investors included Volkswagen, the largest foreign investor and Slovakia's only car producer, which has announced major expansion plans; Siemens in the automotive sector; U.S. Steel, which bought the production activities of the Katowice steel mill, Slovakia's largest enterprise; German and Norwegian interests that bought control of the Slovalco aluminum smelter; IKEA of Sweden, which has bought the most successful furniture manufacturer; U.K., French, German, and Austrian companies that have invested in sugar; and Dutch and South African investors in beer production.

In January 2001 a series of investment incentives came into force, including five-year corporate tax breaks to majority foreign-owned companies that invest at least €4.5 million, and less than that in high-unemployment areas and in certain sectors; 50% corporate tax relief for a further five years under certain conditions; zero tariffs for manufacturing equipment imports; and state subsidies of between €680 and €3,600 for every job created. Capital movement and payments regimes are being liberalized gradually, as are capital markets operations.

For More Information

Books:

Goldman, Minton. *Slovakia since Independence: A Struggle for Democracy*. Westport, CT: Praeger Publishers, 1999.
Shepherd, Robin. *Czechoslovakia: The Velvet Revolution and Beyond*. New York: Palgrave Macmillan, 2000.
Smith, Adrian. *Reconstructing the Regional Economy: Industrial Transformation and Regional Development in Slovakia* (Studies of Communism in Transition). Northampton, MA: Edward Elgar, 1998.
Toma, Peter, and Dusan Kovac. *Slovakia: From Samo to Dzurinda*. Stanford, CA: Hoover Institution, 2001.
Trade Policy Review: Slovak Republic. Geneva: World Trade Organization, 2002.

Web Sites:

Bratislava stock exchange: **www.bsse.sk/bsseApp/index.asp**
National Bank of Slovakia: **www.nbs.sk**
Slovak government site: **www.government.gov.sk**
Slovak Investment and Trade Development Agency: **www.sario.sk**

Slovenia

KEY FACTS

GNI: **$19,862 million; world's 65th**
GNI pc: **$10,000; world's 50th**
Head of government: **prime minister**
Currency: **tolar (SIT)**
Capital: **Ljubljana**
Population: **1,989,000, growing at 0.4% p.a.**
Land area: **7,760 square miles**
Population density: **256 per square mile**
Life expectancy: **75 years**
Infant mortality: **5 per 1,000 live births**
Language: **Slovenian**
Best buy: **lace, crystal, ski equipment and clothing, honey, wine**

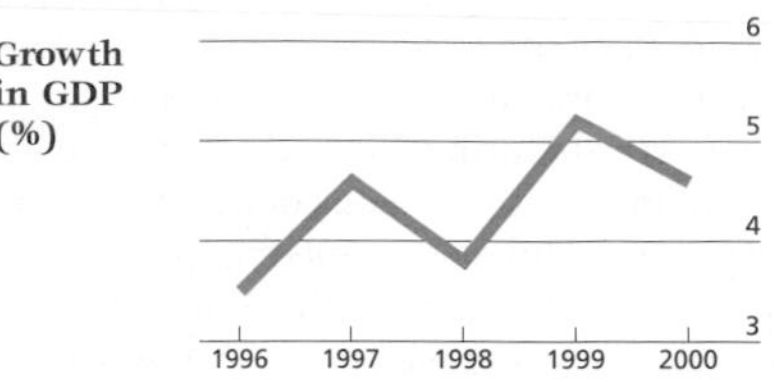

Economic Structure

During the 20th century Slovenia industrialized, and by 1980 was the richest of the Yugoslav socialist republics, sending essential goods to the rest of the Federation and to East European countries. In 1989 the Slovene Assembly voted for greater autonomy of Slovenia within the Yugoslav Federation, which was rejected by the Yugoslav government. In 1991 the Yugoslav army invaded, but accepted an EU-brokered truce. Slovenia gained its independence by the end of that year, and international recognition in early 1992. It began the task of reorienting its economy towards the West and market principles. From 1998 the government has been engaged in negotiations for membership of the EU, to take effect by 2005.

The economy is broad-based. Services, including tourism, trade, transport, finance, and public services, contributed 59.3% of GDP in 2000, followed by manufacturing (27.2%), construction (6%), utilities and agriculture (3.2% each), and mining (1%). The basic manufacturing sector includes paper and wood, hydrochloric and sulfuric acid, petroleum products, steel, aluminum, cement, construction materials, and textiles. Finished goods industries include machinery, optical goods, cars, household appliances, clothing, footwear, pharmaceuticals, food, beverages, and ski equipment and clothing. The ski equipment company Elan supplies 8–10% of world demand. The main exports in 2000 were cars and other road vehicles (12.2%), followed by electrical machinery (11.2%), furniture (6.7%), paper, pharmaceuticals, metal products, and clothing. The top market was Germany (27.2%), followed by Italy (13.6%), Croatia (7.9%), Austria (7.5%), and France (7.1%).

Until 1990 the economy was a decentralized form of communism with state- and cooperatively-owned enterprises. Privatization has been complicated by the 1992 Denationalization Act, whereby assets nationalized under communism are to be returned to their previous owners. By February 2001, 62% of claims had been processed and 58% (representing just over half the value of claims) had been resolved. Many claims were found to be inflated or dubious. The government created a fund, financed by state company shares, to pay for denationalization. By 1997 over 1,000 state-owned companies had been transformed into joint stock companies with priority share distribution given to employees. Foreign investors were prohibited from taking part directly in these privatizations, but restrictions on foreign investment were eased in 1999 and again in 2001. The electricity and telecommunications markets were opened to competition in 2001. The gas sector is due to be liberalized in 2003. The privatization process for Telekom Slovenje began in 2002. Divestitures of banks (including the largest and second-largest) to strategic foreign investors, with the government retaining significant holdings, were due in 2002. Other planned privatizations include Maribor Airport and a steelworks.

Economic Policy

Macro-economic policy is focused on stability and structural adjustment to meet EU criteria. Government expenditure has been prudent, with broadly balanced budgets and low public debt at around 25% of GDP. There have been small budget deficits of about 1% of GDP since 1997. In monetary policy the government has adopted a flexible exchange rate policy and strict limits on money supply. Wages and pensions are indexed to inflation: this has helped keep inflation above 9% since 1994. The government has instituted pension reforms, raising pensionable age from 56.6 years to 61 years for women and 63 for men, and has introduced voluntary contributions to pension and healthcare funding, but it is unlikely to make the unpopular move of cutting the index link. Moderate increases in spending on health and education bring spending levels close to the EU norm. Increased provision for vocational training is aimed at maintaining international competitiveness.

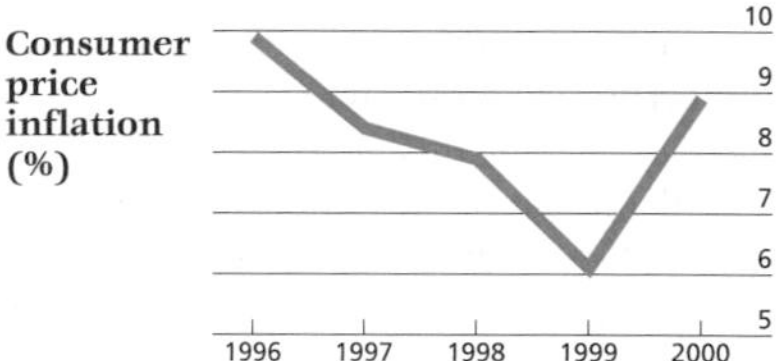

The loss of Yugoslav markets caused hardship in the early 1990s, but GDP remained positive with growth of 2.8% in 1994. Annual average growth, derived both from exports and domestic demand, has been sustained at over 4% in 1994–2001, with 3.3% expected in 2002. Registered unemployment fell from an average 14% in 1994–99 to 12% in 2000, with 11% expected in 2002. The International Labour Organization definition of unemployment gives a much lower figure, which fell from 7.7% in 1998 to 6.7% in 2001.

Geography/Resources

A small Central European republic, Slovenia has a short coastline on the Adriatic Sea, and land borders with Italy to the west, Austria to the north, Hungary to the east, and Croatia to the south. It is mountainous in the west, north, and center, with the highest peaks in the Julian Alps (Mount Triglav reaches 9,393 feet). The climate is temperate except in the high mountains, which have an alpine climate. Annual average precipitation ranges from 32 inches in the east

to 138 inches in the northern mountains. Over 90% of the population is Slovene, and there are small Hungarian, Italian, Roma, Croat, Serb, and Muslim communities.

Main agricultural crops include corn, wheat, potatoes, sugar beet, grapes, and apples, but a wide range of other grains, vegetables, and fruit are grown. Meat and dairy is important. Forestry produces industrial timber for the furniture and construction industries, pulpwood, and fuel wood. Lignite and natural gas are the main mineral resources produced. Brown coal, petroleum, lead, zinc, and salt are also extracted. However, three coal mines are due to close by July 2002 with more to follow. There are reserves of uranium and mercury.

Communications/Energy

The road network was 12,507 miles, including around 10,000 miles of paved roads, in 1999. Motorway construction will create a 322-mile network by 2006. In 2000 the 746-mile rail network included 310 miles of electrified track. A new 25 mile rail link to Hungary opened in 2001. There are 180 miles of oil pipelines and 343 miles of natural gas pipelines. The main sea port is Koper. Izola and Piran are also important. The main airport is Ljubljana's Brnik Airport. There are international airports at Maribor and Portoro, and three domestic airports. In 2000 roads carried 78 million passengers and 4.5 million tons of freight, while rail accounted for 15 million passengers and 15.1 million tons of freight, sea ports for 26.2 million tons of freight and 866,000 passengers, and air travel for 866,000 passengers and 4,556 tons of cargo.

At end-2000 there were 751,800 fixed phone lines, 1.1 million mobile phones (accounting for 55% of the population), and 300,000 Internet users. In 1999 37% of electricity was produced by the nuclear power station at Krško, 34% by thermal power stations and 30% by hydro power. Slovenia is a net exporter of electricity. The electricity sector was liberalized in 2001. Five new hydropower plants are to be built. Slovenia is self-sufficient in coal, but most oil and natural gas are imported. Oil accounted for 44% of energy consumption in 1999, followed by coal (19%), nuclear (16%), hydro (14%), natural gas (13%), and electricity exports (–6%).

Education/Employment

Education is free and compulsory from age 6 to 15. There are 2 universities at Ljubljana and Maribor, and 35 technical and vocational colleges. The Ministry of Education is responsible for education. Most higher education is state-funded, but there are private specialized higher education institutions. In 2000–01 there were 68,427 students enrolled in 44 higher education institutions. In 2000 total R&D funding was 1.5% of GDP. The government funds university research, part of the cost of companies' R&D, and the operating costs of technology parks. Research sectors include electrical engineering and computer science, civil engineering, chemicals and chemical engineering, biomedicine, and agriculture. Slovenia is included in EU R&D programs.

The labor force is well educated. Wages are determined nominally by negotiation between management and workers, but in practice they are set by central government. Employment law is changing to meet EU criteria, but progress has been slow. The EU law on health and safety at work was adopted in 1999.

Fiscal/Financial

The largest bank in mid-2001 was Nova Ljubljanska Banka (NLB), which had 43% of the market, followed by Nova Kreditna Banka Maribor (NKBM: 12%), SKB Banka (10%) and Banka Koper. The main insurance company was state-owned Zavarovalnica Triglav. The Bank of Slovenia is the central bank and the regulatory authority for the financial services industry. The stock exchange is regulated by the Securities and Exchange Commission (SEC). Foreign exchange restrictions were eased in 1999 and 2000, with full liberation due in 2002. Reform was launched in December 1999 of the system of interbank payments to replace the central payment agency with a competition-based system. General corporation tax is 25%, but 10% applies to companies operating in designated economic zones. Tax on capital gains from securities trading was introduced in 1997. VAT was introduced in 1999.

In 1998 there were 31 commercial banks, 113 savings banks, 45 investment companies, and 12 insurance companies. Consolidation reduced the number of commercial banks to 24 by early 2000. NLB acquired six small banks by 2001. In 2001 the private-sector SKB Banka was sold to French bank Société Générale, and the state-owned Banka Koper to Italy's San Paolo IMI. In early 2002 the government was expected to sell 34% of NLB to Belgian bank KBC and a further 14% to portfolio investors. NKBM and smaller banks were also being prepared for privatization. Bank Austria is the longest established foreign bank. The Ljubljana Stock Exchange began operations in March 1990. A precious metals market was added in 1992 and electronic trading in 1993. The first pension fund was listed in 1999. In 2000 six sector indices were launched for pharmaceuticals, food and beverages, chemicals, oil and gas, transport, and trade, and a parallel market was established. A cooperation agreement was signed with the London Stock Exchange.

Business Opportunities

The finance, trade, pulp and paper, chemicals, automotive, petroleum products, rubber and plastics, food processing, and cosmetics industries have attracted investment from Austria, France, Germany, Italy, Czech Republic, the United Kingdom, the United States, and the Netherlands. These sectors continue to offer opportunities. Privatization and liberalization of telecommunications, energy, and finance will offer further opportunities. Tax incentives, grants, and concessional access to facilities and utilities in industrial zones are offered to investors. The point of contact is the Trade and Investment Promotion Office (TIPO).

For More Information

Books:

Emerging Markets Investment Center. *Slovenia Investment and Business Guide*. 2nd ed. Washington, D.C.: International Business Publications, 1999.

IMF Country Report. *Slovenia*. Washington, D.C.: IMF.

Slovenia: Regular Report from the Commission on Slovenia's Progress towards Accession. Brussels: European Union.

Web Sites:

Bank of Slovenia: **www.bsi.si**
Government entry point: **www.sigov.si**
Ljubljana Stock Exchange: **www.ljse.si**
Ministry of Finance: **www.gov.si/mf**
Trade and Investment Promotion Office (TIPO): **www.investslovenia.org**

  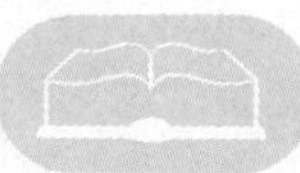    

South Africa

GNI: **$133,569 million; world's 28th**
GNI pc: **$3,170; world's 88th**
Head of government: **president**
Currency: **rand (R)**
Capital: **Pretoria**
Population: **39,900,000, growing at 1.8% p.a.**
Land area: **471,400 square miles**
Population density: **85 per square mile**
Life expectancy: **52 years**
Infant mortality: **54 per 1,000 live births**
Language: **English, Afrikaans, Zulu, Xhosa, Sepedi, Setswana**
Best buy: **wine, fruit, jewelry, handicrafts**

Economic Structure

Composition of GDP (1999)

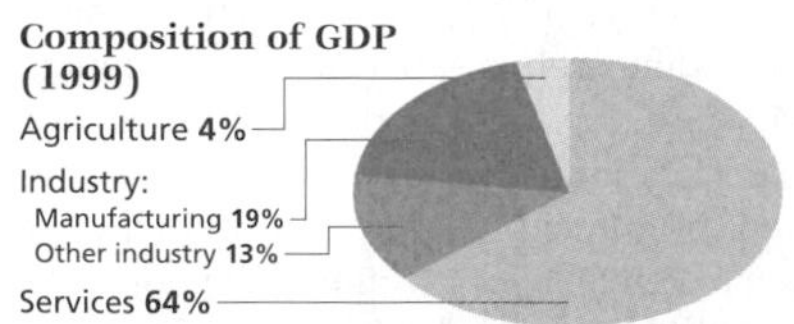

In South Africa's second democratic general election in 1999, Thabo Mbeki was voted in as president to succeed Nelson Mandela. His government has concentrated on maintaining political stability and promoting economic reform and recovery, as well as on developing a leadership role for South Africa across the African continent. It has succeeded in maintaining dialog and cooperation between the country's diverse racial and ethnic groups, although there remain enormous challenges in correcting past injustices and social divisions, and in delivering basic social services to all. South Africa is unlikely to play an effective influential role in the rest of Africa until it has established its domestic stability and has built and diversified its own economic strength.

Although the majority of South Africans live in deprivation and poverty, the country is substantially industrialized and has an impressively diverse economy. The main contributors to GDP are financial and business services (18%), manufacturing (17%), government services (15%), trade (12%), transport (9%), and mining (6%). Agriculture contributes only 3% of GDP, but this sector plays an important role in ensuring the country's self-sufficiency, in supplying foods and fibers to industry, and in generating export earnings.

The country's principal exports are non-metallic mineral manufactures (above 15% of the total), machinery and transport equipment (below 15%), diamonds, coal, chemicals, food and drink, iron and steel, gold, and a variety of manufactures. The main markets for South African goods are the United Kingdom, the United States, Germany, and Japan. The leading sources of imports are Germany, the United States, the United Kingdom, Japan, France, and Italy. In local currency terms, there was a 25% rise in the value of exports in 2000.

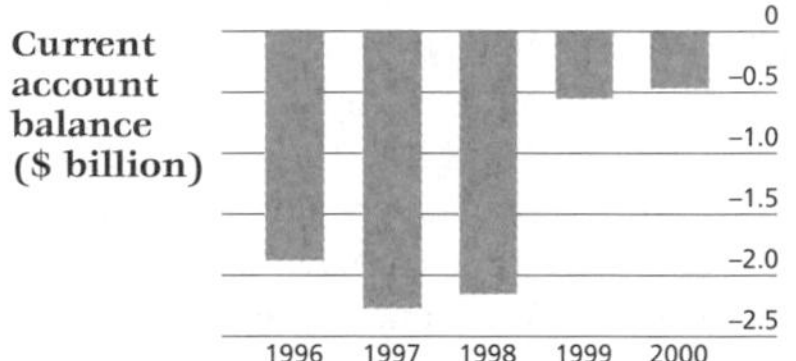

The country's large public sector tended to expand rather than contract after the transition to majority rule in 1994, and the government adopted a very cautious approach to privatization of state-owned enterprises. The main sales of shares to private partners have taken place in South African Airways (SAA) and the telecommunications company Telkom. Privatization has not been popular with the trade unions, and implementation has been slow. Strategic equity partners are still expected to be sought for a wider range of activities, including infrastructure projects, the power and defense industries, and the ports. Since the mid-1990s, foreign investment into South Africa has been at lower levels than predicted, reflecting widespread caution about the rise of corruption, the high incidence of crime, the AIDS problem, and the effectiveness of South Africa's policies in Africa (especially in Zimbabwe).

Economic Policy

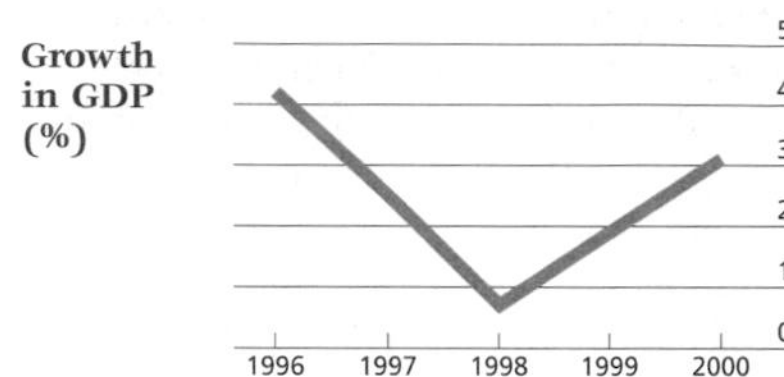

A policy of Growth, Employment and Redistribution (GEAR) was adopted after 1996, with subsequent modifications designed to boost investment and growth. The main objectives of GEAR have been to reduce the fiscal deficit, to introduce labor-market flexibility, to reduce tariffs, to attract investment into growth sectors through tax incentives, and to liberalize exchange controls. The main sectors targeted for growth have been agro-processing, the motor industry, mining technology, clothing and textiles, tourism, agriculture, information and communications technology, and cultural industries. The formulation of monetary policy has been more transparent since a shake-up of the management of the central bank, the South African Reserve Bank. A monetary policy committee meets every month. After a period of sluggish growth and sharp currency depreciation in the late 1990s, growth in the economy began to accelerate in 2000, although high oil prices again stimulated inflation. The government indicated in 2001 that it would increase spending on infrastructure.

Economic growth averaged 2.3% per annum between 1995 and 1999, rising to 3% in 2000 but slipping back to an estimated 2% in 2001. Exports, which had been hurt by the weak gold price, recovered sharply in 2000 to a value of $30 billion and were expected to continue their growth in the following years. There was also a rise in domestic consumer spending. The exchange rate of the rand was, however, under considerable pressure.

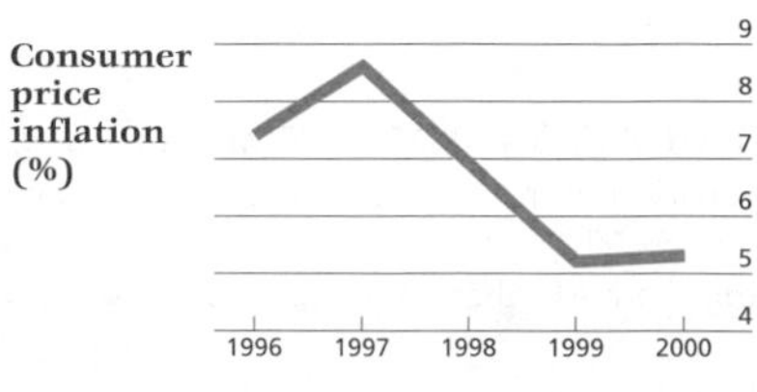

Consumer prices rose by 7.1% during 2000, largely as a result of high world oil prices, but inflation appeared to be under control and likely to diminish in coming years. There is high unemployment, estimated at about 25% of the labor force.

Geography/Resources

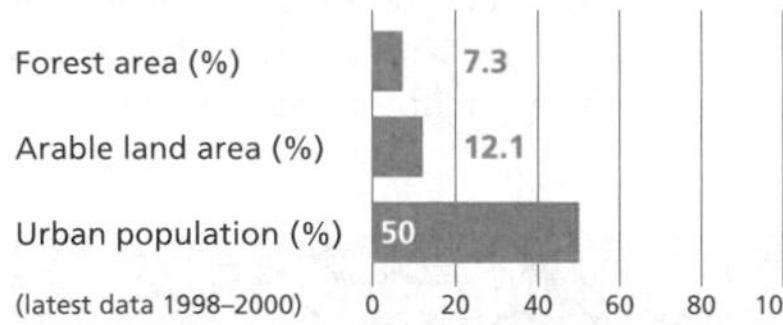

South Africa covers a highly varied geographical area, including semi-desert in the northwest, high plateau lands in the north and center, and extensive mountain ranges in the east and south. The edges of the main plateau region reach altitudes of around 10,000 feet along the Drakensberg mountain range. The stepped ridges of the southwest are known as the Little and Great Karoo. In the east there is a coastal plain in northern Kwazulu/Natal, and the regions adjoining Mozambique are low-lying. The Orange river basin forms South Africa's largest hydrological system; the river rises in the Drakensberg and flows westward into the Atlantic Ocean. The Limpopo river drains most of the Northern Province into the Indian Ocean.

The climate is largely subtropical, while being heavily influenced by ocean currents and by the country's physical features. The east coast is warmed by the Mozambique current, while the west coast is cooled by the Benguela current. The areas of highest rainfall are those with the highest mountains, including the Cape ranges and the Drakensberg. In general, the eastern half the country receives substantially more rain than the west. The prevailing vegetation pattern is grassland, while the most forested region is along the southeastern coastline of the Eastern Cape and Kwazulu/Natal.

Agriculture has been developed by the adoption of intensive production methods, especially for the growing of both tropical and temperate fruit and vegetables. Corn farming dominates the high veld region. Sugar is grown on large plantations, mainly in Kwazulu/Natal. People living in the former tribal homelands grow their own food for subsistence. About 13% of all land is tilled, while 67% is used for grazing. A mineral zone of extraordinary wealth stretches through Northern and North West Provinces, Gauteng, and the Free State into the Northern Cape. The most valuable minerals include gold, silver, diamonds, chrome, nickel, platinum, and vanadium. There are also deposits of manganese, iron ore, uranium, and asbestos.

The African population, which comprises five major ethnic groups, accounts for 77% of South Africa's total population of 40 million. Africans are in the overwhelming majority in seven out of the nine provinces. People of European origin account for 11%, "Cape Coloureds" for 9%, and Asians for 3%. Gauteng, the province that includes the major cities of Johannesburg and Pretoria, is the most intensively populated part of the country. The largest city is Cape Town. Other main centers of population are Durban, Roodepoort, Port Elizabeth, Vereeniging, Springs, and Bloemfontein.

Communications/Energy

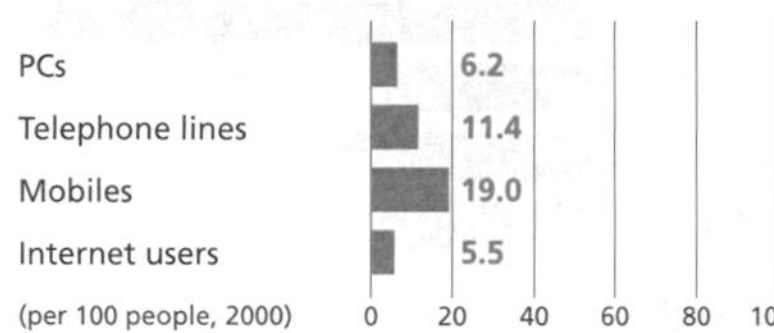

There are extensive and generally well-maintained networks of roads and railways, especially in the vicinity of the major cities, but many rural areas still remain isolated. There are regular domestic air services covering most of the country, while international air links into Johannesburg, Cape Town, and Durban expanded rapidly in the late 1990s. The development of new infrastructure is expressed in the form of Spatial Development Initiatives (SDIs) and industrial development zones, which are intended to create opportunities for Black Economic Empowerment (BEE). Eight SDIs have been identified, including the Maputo Corridor (which links Gauteng to the Mozambican capital), Lubombo, the West Coast, and the Trans-Kalahari/Platinum Corridor. At the same time, transport services throughout the country have been identified for possible privatization.

The telecommunications monopoly of Telkom was first modified in 1994 with the licensing of two mobile telephone operators, which have subsequently built up a very substantial area of new business. Subsequently, Telkom was part-privatized with the sale of shares to Telekom Malaysia and SBC Communications of the U.S. The communications authority deals with new licensing issues.

South Africa produces a very small amount of oil from its own natural sources and rather more from synthetic sources, but it still depends heavily on oil imports from Iran, Kuwait, and Saudi Arabia for most of its industrial and transport needs. Coal is, nevertheless, the country's most important single source of energy, especially for generation by the national electricity provider, Eskom, which is planning for the future by seeking to develop hydroelectric power sources beyond South Africa's borders. The availability of natural gas in neighboring Mozambique has stimulated substantial South Africa investment in developing pipelines and major gas utilization projects in both countries.

Education/Employment

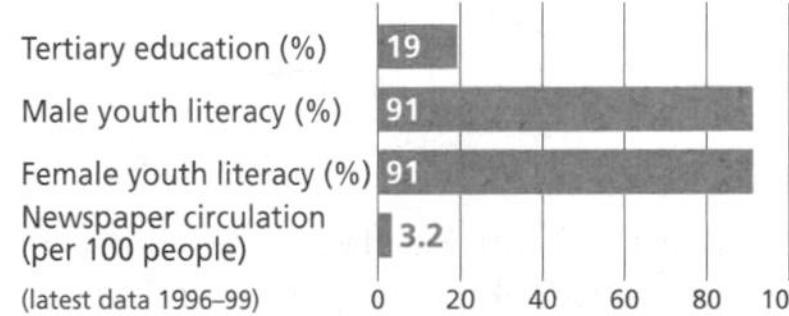

Investment in new education facilities has been stepped up to help the African population catch up with the educational standards that were previously restricted to the white population. A national education policy adopted in 1995 established a unitary education system responsible to a central authority rather than being organized, as before, on a provincial basis. This reorganization of the system has proved complicated and expensive, and has only just begun to address the backlog of educational deprivation. It has been especially difficult to increase the intake at the higher levels of education while standards at the lower level remain poor. There are 36 universities and colleges of technology, a number that the government wants to reduce through mergers.

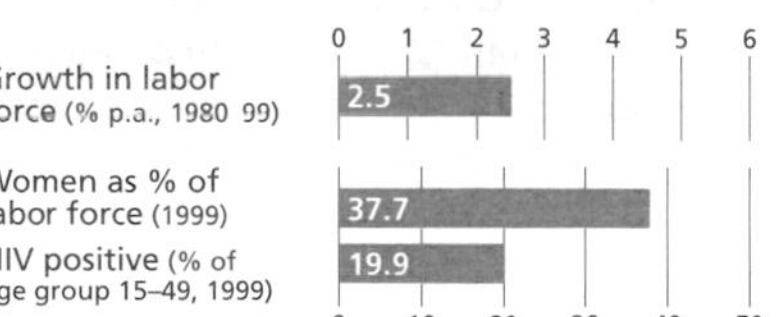

Unemployment is high, at around 25% of the potential workforce, and there is intensive labor migration, including illegal immigration from neighboring countries, which is thought to account for 4 million people, or about 10% of the population. The main sources of employment are trade (15% of the workforce), community and social services (14.5%), manufacturing (11%), agriculture (8%), and domestic work (7%). The mining industry, although still very important to the economy, is no longer a major employer. Since 1994, the government has sought to find ways to generate new employment, particularly through legislation designed to promote affirmative action, but

  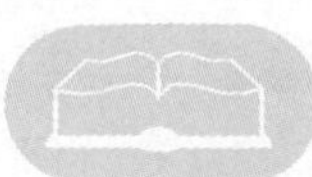  

this strategy did not prevent companies from laying off large numbers of workers in the formal sector throughout the 1990s. The high incidence of HIV/AIDS, affecting more than 10% of the population, has also made it difficult for many people to work. Infection rates among skilled workers are higher than among the unskilled.

Fiscal/Financial

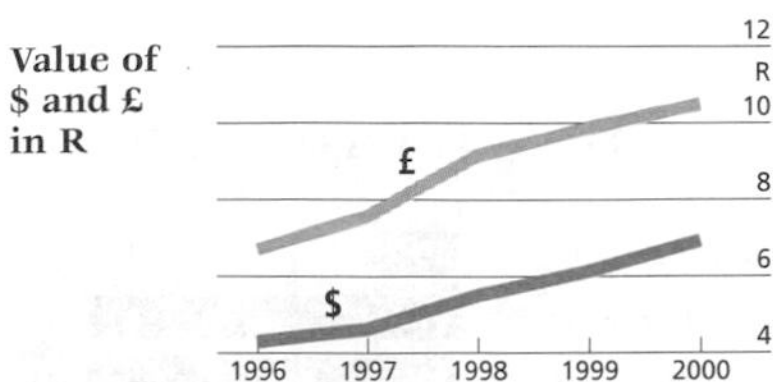

The South African Reserve Bank—the central bank—has a high degree of independence; it determines interest rates by the setting the "repurchase rate" in the money market. The four main banking groups are ABSA, Standard Bank (Stanbic), Nedcor, and FirstRand. They are closely linked with the leading insurance companies in the country. Other leading banks are Investec and NBS/Boland. International banking groups have also moved into the market. South Africa has a sophisticated financial sector, although its impact is not yet felt across the economy, with most of the population beyond the reach of banks or other financial institutions. Savings are limited, representing about 15% of GDP. Consumption tends to be higher than incomes.

The tax regime has been undergoing constant reform since the end of apartheid in 1994. In 2000, tax relief was extended and exemptions from tax on interest income were announced. A capital gains tax was also imposed on profits from the sale of capital assets and investments. The top income tax bracket is 42%. A wide range of incentives is available to new investors, especially those in manufacturing and strategic industrial projects.

The Johannesburg Stock Exchange (JSE) is Africa's largest stock market, but several of the largest business houses have moved their primary listings to London, which has not only required them to change their traditional patterns of cross-ownership but has also tended to reduce the level of share trading done on the JSE. The market remains dependent on a limited number of stocks.

Business Opportunities

Growth in output (% p.a., 1990–99)

Services	2.4
Industry	0.9
Manufacturing	1.1
Agriculture	1.0

The political transition in South Africa has created new opportunities both in the domestic market and for South African companies seeking business in the rest of Africa. The government has sought to boost investment by promising to use state money to develop ports and build new infrastructure, by proposing to restructure the energy sector, and by promoting wider telecommunications and information technology development. New foreign investment is expected to accelerate as the pace of the privatization program is stepped up. Although foreign investors have sometimes been deterred by the high level of crime and by the potential difficulties in labor management, there has been a continuous positive inward flow. There has been considerable activity in vehicle assembly and components manufacture: new plants have been opened in several locations. There has been a surge in the manufacture of catalytic converters for export. The tourism industry has also received continuous investment and the numbers of visitors has grown, with larger numbers coming from Europe and North America. The South African tourist board estimates that one permanent job is created for every eight tourists who visit.

For More Information

Books:

Hain, P. *Sing the Beloved Country: The Struggle for the New South Africa*. London: Pluto Press, 1996.

Johnson, R. W., and L. Schlemmer, eds. *Launching Democracy in South Africa: The First Open Election, April 1994*. New Haven, CT: Yale University Press, 1996.

Marais, H. *South Africa: Limits to Change—The Political Economy of Transformation*. New York: Palgrave Macmillan, 1998.

Web Sites:

African news and information: **www.allafrica.com/business**

Daily Mail & Guardian (English language newspaper): **www.mg.co.za/mg**

Ernst and Young investment profiles: **www.mbendi.co.za/ernsty/cyaf.htm**

Norwegian Council for Africa, Index on Africa: **www.afrika.no**

Political Resources on the Net: **www.politicalresources.net**

South Africa Online: **www.southafrica.co.za**

South Korea

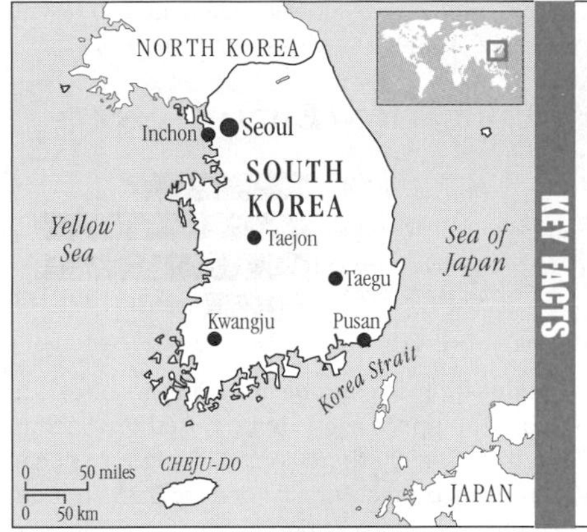

KEY FACTS

GNI: **$397,910 million; world's 13th**
GNI pc: **$8,490; world's 54th**
Head of government: **president**
Currency: **won (W)**
Capital: **Seoul**
Population: **46,480,000, growing at 0.9% p.a.**
Land area: **38,110 square miles**
Population density: **1,220 per square mile**
Life expectancy: **73 years**
Infant mortality: **5 per 1,000 live births**
Language: **Korean**
Best buy: **sports equipment, ginseng, brass, lacquerwork, ceramics**

Economic Structure

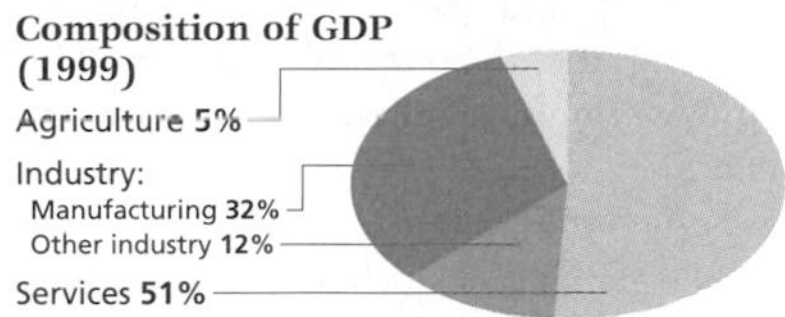

Korea was an established trading nation in the 10th century, but it went into self-imposed isolation in the 19th century when confronted by Western demands for trade relations. In 1910 Japan annexed Korea, a domination which ended with Soviet occupation of the north and U.S. occupation of the south at the close of World War II. The United Nations only recognized the southern republic, and dispatched a multinational force to the Korean War, which devastated both Koreas from 1950 to 1953, leaving the peninsula divided. In the south a military coup brought Major General Park Chung-hee to power in 1961. He embarked on a program of rapid industrialization. The economy became heavily indebted, and the government implemented an IMF austerity plan in 1979 after General Park's death. Industrial expansion continued, however, and by the 1990s South Korea was one of the top ten world industrial nations, with an industrial structure similar to that of Japan. In 1997 the high level of corporate debt made Korea a heavy casualty of the Asian financial crisis, the repercussions of which continue.

Services contributed 52% of GDP in 2000 (financial services accounted for 20% and government services for 7%), followed by manufacturing (32%), construction (8%), and agriculture (5%). The main manufacturing industries are automotive, semiconductors, steel, petrochemicals, shipbuilding, and textiles. Korea is a top world producer in all of these industries. Telecommunications and office equipment are growing sectors. Paper and cement are key sectors subject to downsizing since 1997. In 2000 electronics were the main export (35.9%), followed by chemicals (7%), machinery (6.9%), and metal products (6.6%). The top export market was the United States (21.8%), followed by Japan (11.9%), China (10.7%), and Hong Kong (6.2%).

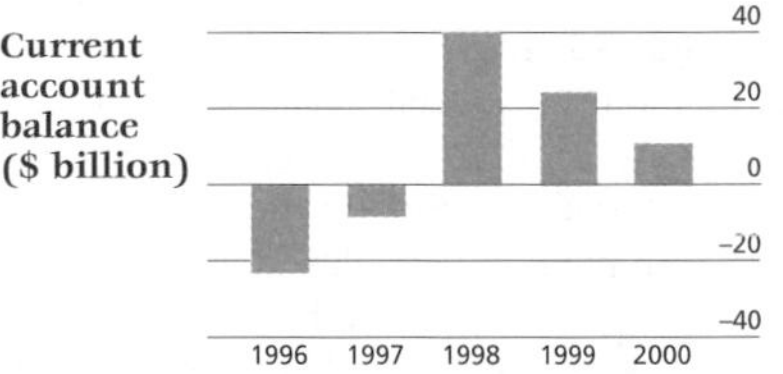

The government's industrialization program from 1962 was achieved through the nationalization of banks to channel capital into export-oriented industries, and through a major construction program to modernize power and transport infrastructure, which was also owned by the state. From the 1970s selected family-owned conglomerates, the chaebol, received government loans to finance industrial development. The government set market share limits for the chaebol, and restricted foreign access to the domestic market and to company ownership. In the early 1990s it began to dismantle limits on foreign participation and to introduce market liberalization measures in order to qualify for membership of the OECD. Banks were privatized, and parts of the gas and telecommunications markets were liberalized. In 1997 a series of large corporate insolvencies combined with the Asian currency crisis to undermine investor confidence and cause capital flight. The government has implemented an IMF-backed restructuring program since then, which involved temporary renationalization of failing banks, resolving non-performing loans, and finding buyers for these and for bankrupt industries. At mid-2001, however, most banks remained under government control. The government has fully or partly privatized companies involved in energy, telecommunications, and heavy and light industry. At mid-2001 it still controlled 101 companies, representing around 7% of GNP, which it planned to divest.

Economic Policy

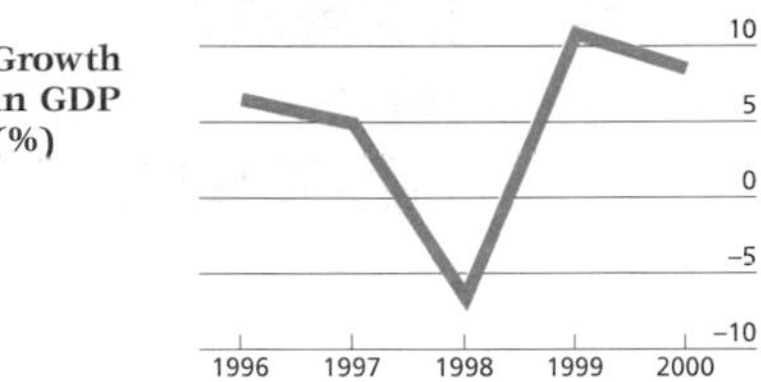

The government maintained a balanced budget policy for many years until 1997. In 1998–99 it pursued an expansionary macroeconomic policy to generate recovery. Interest rates were kept low until the market revived in mid-1999. Government spending increased as a result of its involvement in restructuring of the banking and industrial sectors, and additional welfare provision for the unemployed. The active government role helped rapid recovery of economic growth, which, combined with the strength of overseas investments, helped stabilize the exchange rate. The IMF-backed restructuring program involved lifting restrictions on foreign investment, greater transparency in accounting procedures, and improved productivity and profitability of banks and enterprises. Strategic foreign investors were found to bail out key industries, and Korean businesses scaled back overseas operations, creating a surplus on the capital account. Net foreign debt of $20.2 billion at end-1998 was thereby converted to net foreign credit of $8.8 billion by end-1999, rising to $33.3 billion at April 2001. The pace of restructuring and privatization slackened as a result. The government is investing heavily in transport, telecommunications, and education in partnership with the private sector to secure the country's future competitiveness.

Average annual GDP growth was 7.3% in

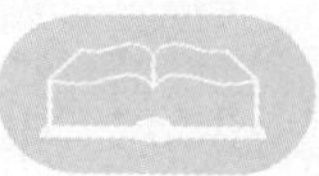

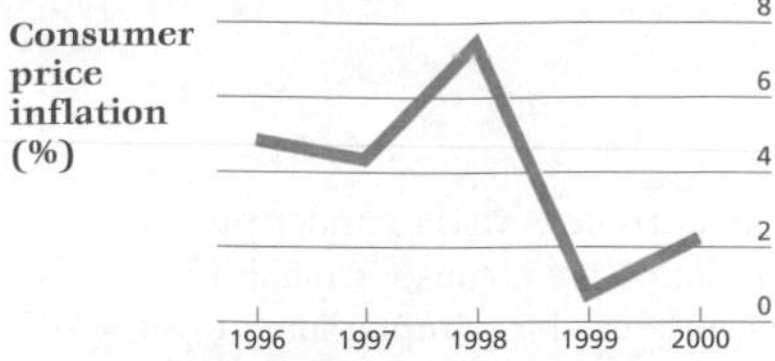

1990–97. In 1998 GDP fell by 6.7% as a result of the crisis. It rebounded with 10.9% growth in 1999 and 8.8% in 2000, followed by 1.8% in 2001. Growth is expected to be 1.3% in 2002. Average annual inflation was 6.1% in 1990–97, rising to 7.5% in 1998. Inflation averaged 2.5% in 1999–2001. Annual average unemployment rose from 2.6% in 1997 to 6.8% in 1998, holding at 6.3% in 1999 and falling to 4.1% in 2000.

Geography/Resources

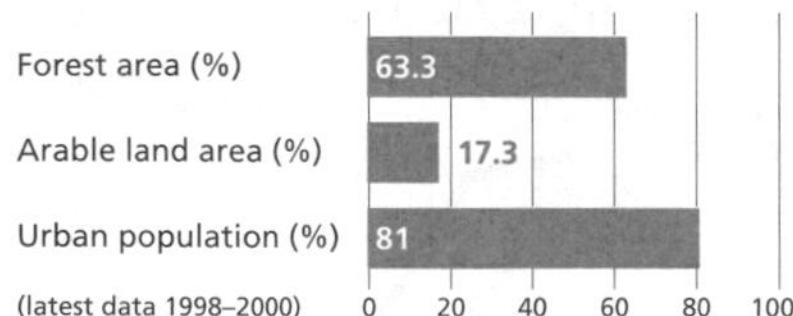

The Republic of Korea, situated on the southern half of the Korean peninsula to the far east of China close to Russia, has a land border with North Korea and coastlines on the Sea of Japan to the east, Korea Strait to the south, and Yellow Sea to the west. Two-thirds of the land is mountainous, with plains in the center and west around Seoul. The Taebaek Sanmaek Mountains run the full length of the east coast, with a high point at 5,604 feet. The south coast has numerous small peninsulas and islands. Cheju-do, a larger island in the Korea Strait, is part of the territory and has the highest mountain at 6,398 feet. The climate is continental with four distinct seasons. Winters are cold (average temperature 31°F) and summers hot and humid (average temperature 77°C).

Arable land comprises about one-fifth of the total area, but Korea achieved its goal of self-sufficiency in rice in 1997. A wide variety of vegetables are grown under vinyl. Fruits are important. Livestock is a major sector, with a particular emphasis on poultry, pigs, cattle, and bees. Meat, dairy, honey, and leather are produced. Forest covers 65% of the land. The government has implemented conservation and reforestation programs, limiting the harvest to 28 million cubic feet a year to prevent soil erosion. The lumber industry provides industrial timber, pulp wood, and fuel wood. Fisheries are important both for domestic consumption and export. Korea is one of the leading deep-sea fishing nations. The main minerals extracted are zinc, lead, anthracite, iron, gold, and silver. A small offshore natural gas field, with 200 billion cubic feet of reserves, will come into production in 2003.

The majority of the population is urban, one-fifth of whom live in or near the capital, Seoul. Other cities with over 1 million inhabitants at the 1995 census were Pusan, Taegu, Inchon, Taejon, and Kwangju. The people are homogeneously Korean in origin, with a very small Chinese community.

Communications/Energy

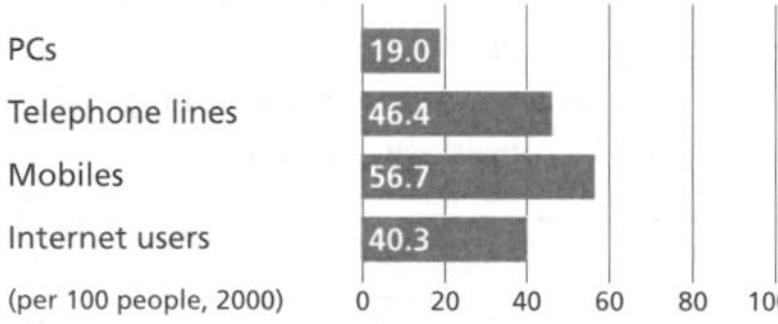

The road network, comprising 54,055 miles and including 1,240 miles of motorways, is being expanded. The railway network is 3,877 miles, including 326 miles of electrified track. There are 1,000 miles of navigable waterways, especially the two main rivers, the Hangang which runs through Seoul, and the Nakdonggang. There is a 283-mile petroleum products pipeline network. The main sea ports are at Pusan, Inchon, Ulsan, Poehang, Chinhae, Masan, Yosu, Mokpeo, and Gunsan. The merchant fleet included 496 ships over 1,000 grt, totaling 5.4 million grt in 2000. The new Inchon International Airport has replaced Seoul's Gimpo Airport as the country's main airport. Gimpo now handles only domestic traffic. There are three other international airports at Pusan, Cheongju, and Cheju. Domestic flights link 16 major cities and carried 40 million passengers in 2000.

The government has encouraged low telecommunications costs, including low-cost subscriptions to fast Internet links via broadband, to place Korea at the forefront of the e-commerce revolution. International telecommunications links are provided by three satellite systems, a microwave system, and submarine cables to Japan, Russia, and China. At end-2000 there were 21.9 million fixed phone lines, 26.8 million mobile phones, and 19 million Internet users, including over 2 million broadband subscribers.

In 1999, 59% of electricity was generated from imported fossil fuels, 39% from nuclear, and 1.6% from hydro. Nuclear power generating capacity is being expanded to help meet the 4.3% a year increase in electricity demand and to reduce dependence on imported oil, natural gas, and coal, which accounted for 97% of primary energy consumption in 1999. Oil accounted for 57.5% of energy consumption, followed by coal (19.5%), and gas (9.1%). Small indigenous gas production, due to begin in 2003, will meet around 2% of gas requirements.

Education/Employment

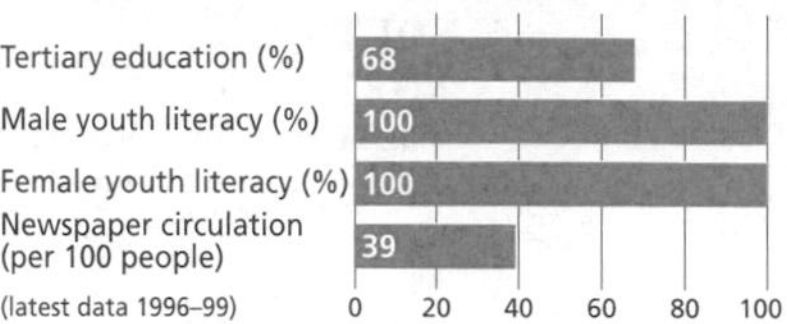

Education is compulsory from age 6 to 12, but the upper age is to be raised to 15 from 2002. In 2000 there were 355 higher education institutes with a total of 3.36 million students. Universities and colleges deliver four-year degree courses, while vocational colleges provide two-year diploma courses. The Ministry of Education is responsible for policy and the majority of funding. The government provides financial assistance to students.

The National Science and Technology Council (NSTC), established in April 1999, coordinates government science and technology policy and sets priorities for R&D programs. The aim is that Korea should become one of the top seven world technology nations by 2025. In 1999 total R&D investment was $10 billion, 2.46% of GDP. The main focus of R&D is on IT, biotechnology, nanotechnology, new materials, environmental technology, and nuclear energy. Government policy is to coordinate private- and public-sector research and to promote labor-force skills.

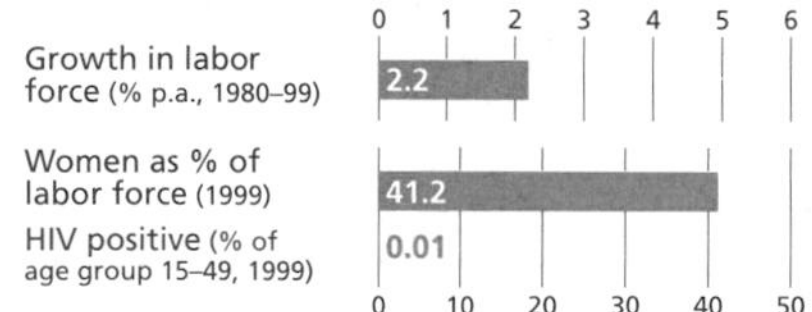

The labor force ranges from highly skilled to unskilled, and is increasingly flexible following the financial crisis and the loss of protected-status jobs. The government extended vocational training, adapted unemployment insurance to cover part-time and temporary workers, and increased job retention and creation measures. It authorized employment agencies for both domestic and overseas jobs. In 1998 it established the Tripartite Commission of employers, unions, and government to agree steps to overcome the crisis, and an equitable sharing of the economic and non-economic costs. The Labor Standards Act was revised

to allow more management flexibility on labor issues, especially regarding the maximum working week of 44 hours and the obligation to pay overtime for extra hours. The Equal Employment Act bans discrimination against women in hiring and promotion opportunities. Wages are determined between employers and workers' representatives, but a minimum wage applies to companies employing more than 10 staff.

Fiscal/Financial

Value of $ and £ in W

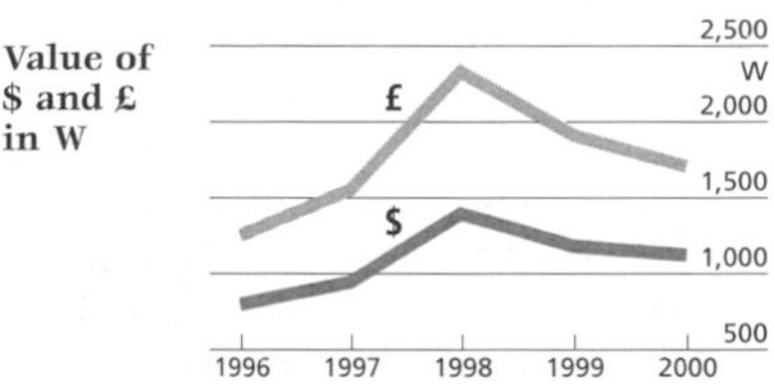

The largest commercial bank at mid-2001 was Kookmin (which merged with another large bank, Housing & Commercial Bank), Shinhan, Hana, and KorAm, all of which were majority state-owned. The central bank, Bank of Korea, recapitalized ailing commercial and merchant banks, and finance and insurance companies, following the 1997 crisis; it established the Korea Deposit Insurance Corporation (KDIC) to hold assets until the situation had been resolved. The government enacted four major pieces of legislation by end-2000 to tighten financial accountability and supervision. The Financial Supervision Commission is the regulatory authority. Corporation tax is 28% for private companies, 25% for public companies, and 10% for agricultural, fisheries, and livestock unit associations. The top rate of personal income tax is 40%. VAT is levied at 10%.

Loans were the preferred form of financing during the industrialization programs. Risk and profitability evaluation by the banks was lax. Government policy focused on world market share, and the focus of the chaebol was to retain family control over their expanding empires. Recourse to the stock market was therefore minimal. In June 2001 financial institutions still had W50 trillion in non-performing loans, a ratio of 8.1%, despite the government's writing off of W98 trillion from 1998. The five main commercial banks held W7.4 trillion in bad loans, amounting to 4% of their loan total. The government drafted legislation in 2001 to increase the use of asset-backed securities to absorb the 44.8% of bad loans, which were collateralized with real estate. The government has undertaken a massive restructuring of the finance sector since 1997. In 1998–2000, 368 companies and banks were closed, 143 were merged, and 39 were created. At end-2000 there were 22 commercial banks (down from 33 at end-1997), 10 merchant banks (down from 30), 43 securities companies (up from 36), 21 investment trust companies (down from 31), 147 mutual savings and finance companies (down from 231), 1,317 credit unions (down from 1,666), and 21 life insurance and 13 non-life insurance companies (down from 31 and 14 respectively). Korea First was the only bank in which the government has sold a majority shareholding to a foreign investor, U.S. equity fund Newbridge Capital.

Although the Korea Stock Exchange has the attributes of a sophisticated market (main board, small business exchange, high-tech companies exchange, markets in bonds, futures and options, automated trading, and links with other major stock exchanges), its market capitalization is small. Limits on foreign participation were lifted in 1998. Samsung Electronics, the world's largest chip maker, accounted for 40% of foreign investment on the stock market in 2000.

Business Opportunities

Growth in output (% p.a., 1990–99)

Services	5.8
Industry	6.2
Manufacturing	7.1
Agriculture	2.1

There are tax and financial incentives for investors, including special provisions for high-tech industries. In spring 2001 there were foreign investment restrictions on 21 industrial sectors, and seven of these were closed to external participation. Key sectors for foreign investment following the removal of barriers from 1998 include automotive manufacturing, chemicals, banking, insurance, and real estate. Total foreign direct investment was $64.7 billion in 2000, up from $803 million in 1990. The main investor is the United States, followed by Japan, Netherlands, Germany, France, the United Kingdom, and Hong Kong. Current opportunities exist in the automotive, chemicals, electronics, machinery, metals, finance, and many other industries. The Korea Trade and Investment Promotion Agency is the point of contact for foreign investors.

For More Information

Books:

Kenna, Peggy, and Sondra Lacy. *Business Korea: A Practical Guide to Understanding South Korean Business Culture*. New York: McGraw-Hill, 1994.

Wilen, Tracey, and Patricia Wilen. *Asia for Women on Business: Hong Kong, Taiwan, Singapore, and South Korea*. Berkeley, CA: Stone Bridge Press, 1995.

Web Sites:

Bank of Korea: **www.bok.or.kr**

Government entry point: **www.korea.net**

Korea National Tourism Organization: **www.knto.or.kr**

Korea Times (business news): **www.koreatimes.co.kr**

Korea Trade & Investment (e-zine): **www.kt-i.com**

Korea Trade and Investment Promotion Agency: **www.kotra.or.kr**

Ministry of Foreign Affairs and Trade (good links): **www.mofat.go.kr**

SPAIN

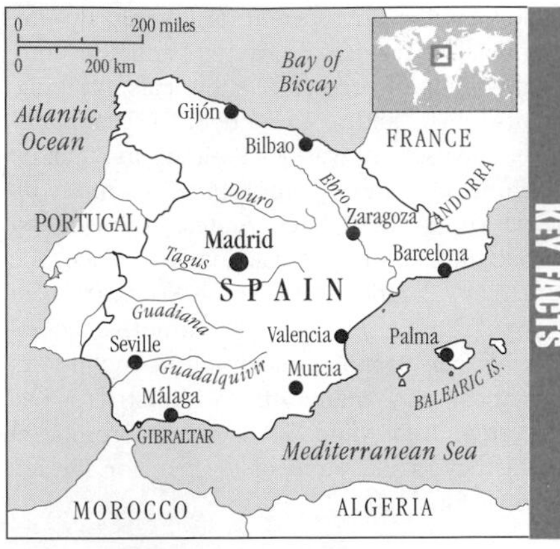

KEY FACTS

GNI: **$583,082 million; world's 10th**
GNI pc: **$14,800; world's 39th**
Head of government: **prime minister**
Currency: **Euro (€)**
Capital: **Madrid**
Population: **39,634,000, growing at 0.1% p.a.**
Land area: **192,820 square miles**
Population density: **205 per square mile**
Life expectancy: **78 years**
Infant mortality: **6 per 1,000 live births**
Language: **Spanish, Catalan, Basque, Galician, Valencian**
Best buy: **shoes, designer fashion clothes, wine, specialty foods**

ECONOMIC STRUCTURE

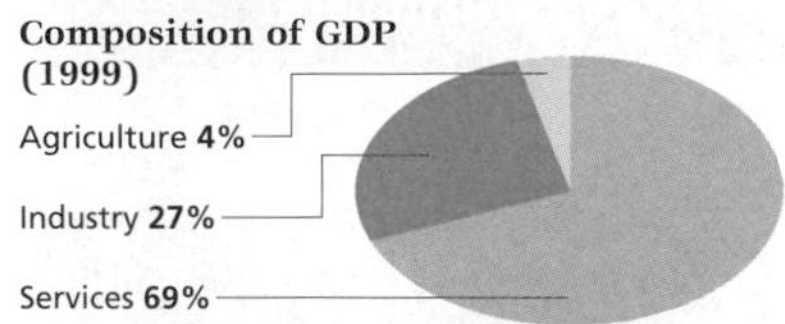

Spain's wealth from its American colonies from the 15th century to the end of the 18th century remained mostly with the aristocracy and the monarchy, and did not create a merchant class with any political power. Thus, when Spain emerged from almost a century and a half of internal strife and civil wars with General Franco's victory over the Republican government in 1939, it was a largely agricultural country. The Francoist government adopted a policy of industrial development by state intervention in key industries such as steel and shipbuilding. The economy was closed to the outside world until the 1960s, when tourism was established. However, economic activity was still protected and heavily regulated by the state. Protection was stripped back in preparation for EU membership in 1986, after which there was a surge of growth in private industry and agriculture, and also in foreign investment.

Services contributed 65.9% of GDP in 2000, followed by industry (including manufacturing, utilities, and mining: 21.7%), construction (8.8%), and agriculture, forestry, and fisheries 3.6%. Tourism is the largest service sector (10% of GDP) with $31 billion income from 74.4 million visitors in 2000. The main manufacturing industries are cars, chemicals and pharmaceuticals, machinery and machine tools, processed foods, and wine. Spain is a major exporter of fresh agricultural and fisheries produce. The main export market in 2000 was France (19.4%), followed by Germany (12.4%), Italy (9.4%), and Portugal (8.8%). The main exports were motor vehicles, nuclear reactors and machinery, electrical equipment, fruit and nuts, plastics, vegetables, mineral fuels, and oils.

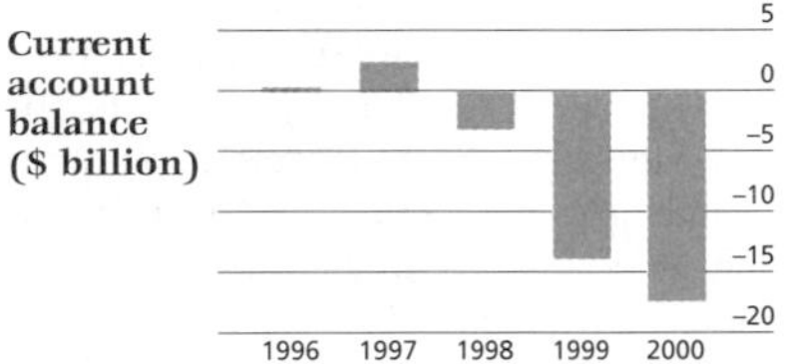

State involvement in key sectors of the economy has been substantially reduced. The petroleum and natural gas production, electricity generating, steel, and banking industries have been fully privatized, while the state retains shareholdings and effective control through regulation over other sectors which have been opened to competition. These include electricity, gas and fuels distribution, air transport, and telecommunications. Rail transport and broadcasting are under state ownership. The government has restricted the voting rights of foreign companies that have bought significant shareholdings in privatized companies, especially where the foreign companies are state-owned or not open to Spanish investment, or where there are other competitive distortions. This has affected French and German investment in Spanish electricity companies.

ECONOMIC POLICY

Consolidation of public finances, combined with structural reforms introducing greater

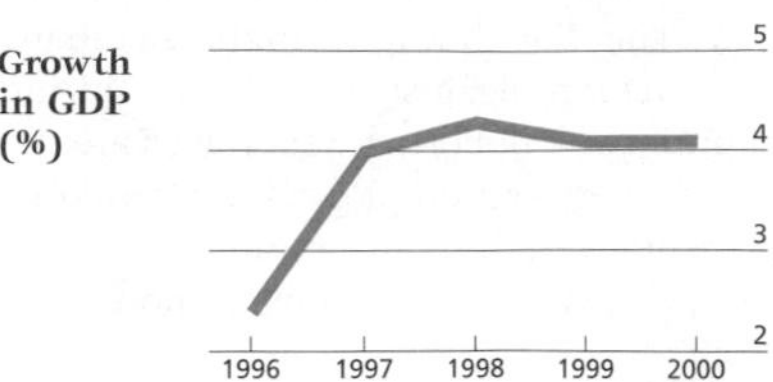

competition, more flexible labor conditions, and more sophisticated financial markets, led to sufficient improvement in economic fundamentals for Spain to adopt the Euro in 1999. The deficit of central and regional governments was reduced from 4.9% of GDP in 1996 to 0.4% in 2000, and the public debt declined from 68.1% to 61.1% of GDP. Budgets were due to be in balance, and the debt reduced to 58.1%, in 2001, but the result was somewhat less good than projected because of the decline in world markets. The proposed central government law on budgetary stability—making balanced budgets a requirement in the future for all levels of government, including social security and public corporations—is opposed by the Basque government which has autonomy in tax raising. The law also requires multi-annual planning, transparency, and the efficient use of public funds. The regional and local governments have played a significant role in deficit reduction, but the central government appeared unwilling to follow OECD and IMF advice to broaden regional and local tax-raising powers to fit in better with new spending responsibilities. Regional governments would like a share of social security budget surpluses, but central government used these in 2000 to create a reserve fund for future pensions as the population ages.

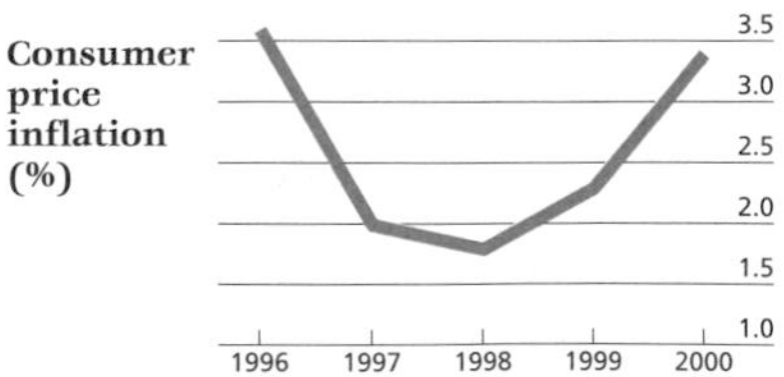

Measures to reduce unemployment include cuts in income tax in 1999 and social security contributions in 2000. Red tape has been reduced for business registration and for tax and social security returns, especially for the small firms which constitute the majority of Spanish businesses and farms. The powers of the competition authority are being strengthened. Greater competition in the retail sector will be

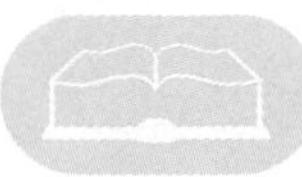

phased in by 2004 through the elimination of restrictions on shops. New rules on pharmaceutical pricing and distribution were introduced in December 2000 to increase competition and lower health-care costs. Planning laws were simplified in 2000 to increase the supply of land for development.

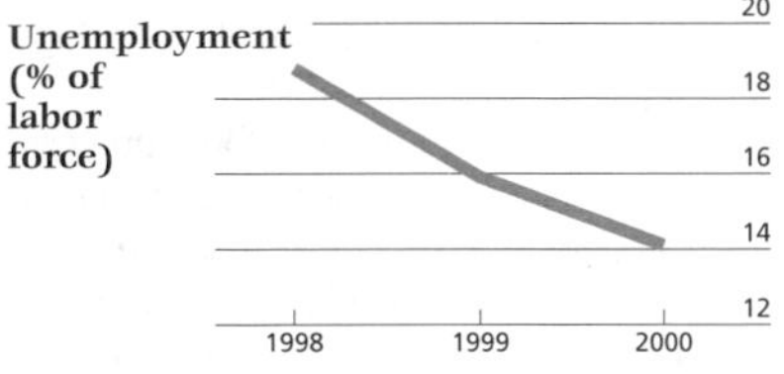

Annual average GDP growth strengthened from 1.3% in 1991–95 to 3.2% in 1996–2001, with 2.4% expected in 2002. Domestic demand, an easing of monetary conditions, and strong exports underpinned the performance. Inflation fell from an average 5.3% in 1991–95 to 3.2% in 1996–2001 owing to wage moderation, lower interest rates, and reduced government spending. Unemployment fell from 24% in 1994 to 13.6% in 2000, but it remains the highest in the OECD area. It is expected to continue falling in the medium term.

Geography/Resources

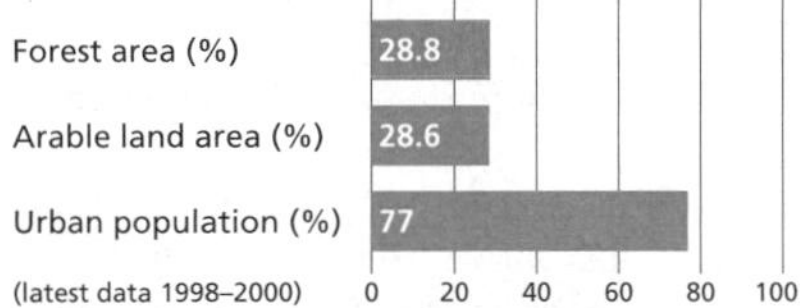

Spain includes most of the Iberian peninsula in southwest Europe, the Balearic Islands in the Mediterranean, the enclaves of Ceuta and Melilla in Morocco, and the Canary Islands in the Atlantic. Mainland Spain is mainly mountainous. There is a central plateau, and high ranges along the border with France, across the north, in the center, and in the south. Spain borders Portugal in the west. It has coasts on the Bay of Biscay in the north, Atlantic Ocean in the west and Mediterranean Sea in the south. The climate is temperate and wet in the Atlantic regions of the north, dry with mild winters and hot summers in the south, while a mountain climate prevails above 4,000 feet. The Canary Islands are sub-tropical. One third of the land is forested.

Agriculture is varied, on predominantly small holdings. In 1998 arable crops were grown on 37% of the land, while 14% was down to pasture. Fruit and vegetables are the main products, but olives, cereals (especially barley), sugar beet, grapes, potatoes, pigmeat, and dairy are also important. Forestry products include industrial timber, pulpwood, and fuel wood. Spain has one of the largest fishing fleets in the world, mostly fishing the Atlantic Ocean, but also in the Mediterranean, Black Sea, and Indian Ocean. Fish farming, particularly of mussels, accounts for 22% of the annual volume of fish. Coal and lignite are the main minerals produced. Small amounts of natural gas and petroleum are extracted from the Bay of Biscay. Gypsum, salt, potash, iron ore and pyrites, fluorspar, zinc, copper, and lead are also produced. There are reserves of gold, silver, and mercury.

Three-quarters of the population are urban. The main cities are the capital Madrid, Barcelona, Valencia, Seville, Zaragoza, Málaga, and Bilbao. There is a peak of population from age 15 to 40. The majority of people are of mixed Mediterranean origin, but large distinct cultural and language groups exist in the Basque region of the northeast, Catalonia in the southeast, and Galicia in the northwest. About 2% of the total population are of foreign origin, with the largest groups from the United Kingdom, Germany, Portugal, and France.

Communications/Energy

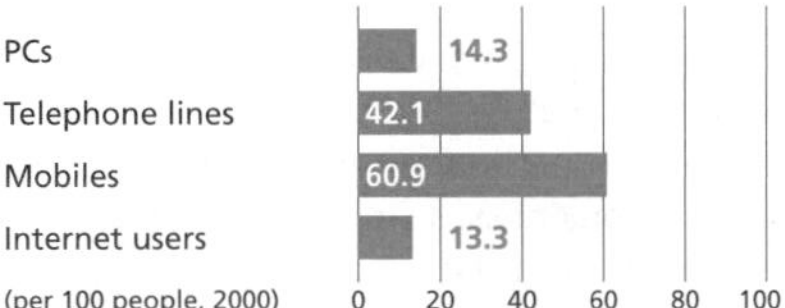

Transport infrastructure is being expanded and modernized under the 1993–2007 Master Infrastructure Plan. In 1999 there were 419,524 miles of roads, including 6,404 miles of motorways. In 1998 the railway network was 8,877 miles, 54% of which was electrified. A high-speed link runs from Madrid to Seville. A high-speed line from Madrid to the French border will be completed in 2004. The pipeline network includes 1,035 miles for natural gas, 1,317 miles for petroleum products, and 173 miles for crude oil. There are 45 maritime and inland ports, the main ones being Barcelona, Bilbao, Gijón and Seville on the mainland, and Santa Cruz and Las Palmas in the Canary Islands. The merchant fleet comprised 135 ships over 1,000 grt, totaling 1.2 million grt in 2000. There are 39 civilian airports, 30 of which cater for international flights. In 1998, 82% of domestic freight was transported by road, 12% by sea, and 4% by rail.

The telecommunications industry was fully liberalized in 1998. The former state monopoly Telefónica was privatized in 1997. Lower prices, down by 7% in 1998–99, led to a 16% rise in fixed-line subscribers and an 11% increase in the average traffic per user. However, fixed-line rental costs are linked to inflation. Mobile phone costs fell by almost 18% in 1999. At end-2000 there were 17.1 million fixed phone lines, 24.7 million mobile phones, and 5.4 million Internet users. Information technology costs can be deducted from personal income for tax purposes as from 2000. E-commerce and e-banking are fast-growing.

Oil accounted for 57% of energy consumption in 1999, followed by coal (14.3%), and natural gas (11.3%). Net oil imports were 1.46 million barrels per day and indigenous production was 20,000 barrels per day in 2000. In 1999 coal production and consumption were 24.5 million tons and 44.5 million tons respectively, and gas production and consumption were 4.1 billion cubic feet and 513.8 billion cubic feet. Electricity was mostly generated from fossil fuels in 1999 (57.7%), followed by nuclear (28.3%), hydro (12.1%), and other renewables including solar (1.9%). Around 3% of electricity is imported from France, but France has blocked a larger grid connection which would fully integrate Spain with European electricity. Natural gas, imported from Algeria and Norway by pipeline and from a host of other suppliers as LNG, is planned to take on a larger role for electricity demand, growing at 6–10% a year, and for chemicals feedstock. Prices have fallen for electricity and gas since market liberalization in 1997 and 2000 respectively.

Education/Employment

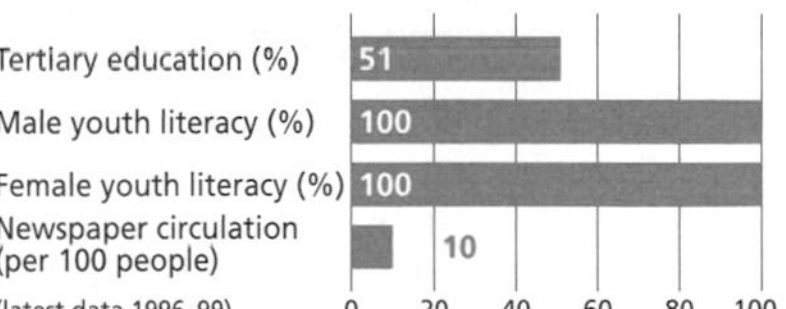

Education is compulsory and free in state schools from age 6 to 16. Most children aged 4–5 attend pre-school. There are 64 universities, including private Catholic universities, and many more colleges and technical schools. Education comes under the Ministry of Education, Culture and Sports, and financing is allocated at regional and local levels. Grants are available to students. In 1997–98 more than 40% of the age group 18–23 attended university. Law, economics, and business studies were by far the most popular subjects in 1999–2000.

The National Plan for R&D 2000–03 targets biomedicine and biotechnology, natural resources, food technology, industrial

design and production, materials, chemical processes and products, IT, and communications technology. There are 17 technology parks. The private sector accounted for 52% of R&D spending in 1998, higher education for 30.5%, state organizations for 16%, and non-profit organizations for 1%. The main sectors for private R&D were electronic and electrical machinery, pharmaceuticals, and aerospace.

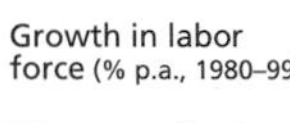

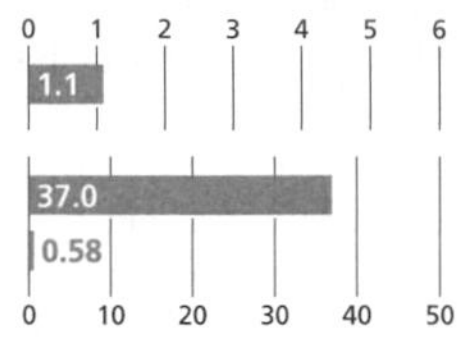

Over half the labor force is in the 20–40 age group. Wages and employment conditions are determined by tripartite negotiation between employers, trade unions, and the government at industry and regional levels. Employers and unions negotiate at company level. There are two basic employment laws, both enacted in 1995: the Workers' Statute, and the Prevention of Labor Risks Law. Spain applies EU employment law, which covers safety at work, wages and working hours, industrial relations, employment incentives, and unemployment provision.

Fiscal/Financial

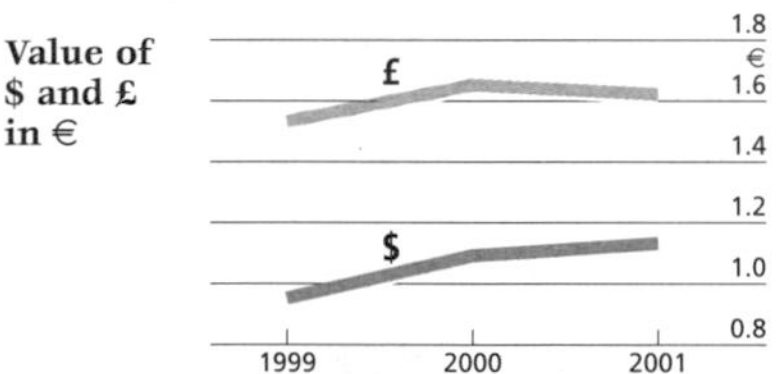

The largest bank is Banco Bilbao Vizcaya Argentaria, followed by Banco Santander Central Hispano. Both are private-sector and have an international presence in Europe and Latin America. Other large banks with branches in Spain and abroad include Banco Español de Credito, Banco Popular Español, and Banco de Sabadell. Insurance companies include some of the world's largest. The regulatory authority for banks is the Bank of Spain, which is also part of the European System of Central Banks. This body and the European Central Bank set the policy for the Euro. The regulatory body for insurance is the Dirección General de Seguros, while the stock exchanges are regulated by the Comisión Nacional del Mercado de Valores. Solvency rules for credit institutions, securities dealers, and brokers were lowered in 2000 to bring them into line with those applied elsewhere in Europe. Transparency rules were tightened.

Standard corporation tax is 35%, with a lower rate of 30% for small businesses. Maximum personal income tax is 39.6% plus 8.4% local tax. Maximum net worth tax is 2.5%. Capital gains tax for corporations and individuals is 18%. Standard VAT is 16%. Oil and gas exploration operations are taxed at 40%. Separate tax rates apply in the Basque and Navarre regions. Non-resident companies or individuals whose worldwide income is derived 75% or more from Spain may opt to be taxed as residents. Non-residents are required to appoint a Spanish resident as their tax representative. There are separate tax regimes for non-resident corporations and individuals, depending on whether or not they have a permanent establishment in Spain.

Private-sector banks and savings banks have the largest volume of business, and are present in all sectors of the economy. Services are sophisticated and internationalized. E-banking and insurance are fast growing. At end-2000 there were 93 Spanish and 53 foreign commercial banks. The 50 savings banks are primarily involved in savings and home mortgage operations, but they also finance major public works and private projects. The government has promulgated new laws and initiatives to improve finance for small businesses, including more flexible rules for mutual funds and venture capital, and a new credit guarantee facility. Rules for new collective investment instruments were due in 2001.

The Spanish Stock Exchange, ranked ninth in the world by trading volume, consists of four main exchanges at Madrid, Bilbao, Barcelona, and Valencia. The Spanish futures and options market MEFF is part of the GLOBEX agreement for derivatives between major international exchanges. The New Market for small high-tech firms was established in December 1999. The Spanish exchange has links with nine European exchanges (Amsterdam, Germany, Helsinki, Lisbon, London, Milan, Paris, Stockholm, and Zurich) and three Latin American exchanges (Argentina, Brazil, and Chile).

Business Opportunities

Financial, tax and other incentives are available for specific industries and regions, and for small and medium businesses, for the purposes of innovation, internationalization, training, and employment. Incentives are available from national, regional, and municipal governments and from EU funds. Specific industry incentives are allocated for improvements to farms, food processing and fisheries operations, energy conservation, minerals exploration, and mine safety. Development regions currently include about 80% of Spanish territory. The point of contact for foreign investors is the Spanish Institute for Foreign Trade.

Motor vehicles, chemicals, food processing, cement, metals, telecommunications, real estate, and financial services are the main sectors for foreign investment. The main investors in 1997–2000 were the Netherlands, France, the United States, the United Kingdom, Germany, and Portugal. Sectors offering investment opportunities include high-tech industries, finance, real estate, retailing, and electricity and gas distribution.

For More Information

Books:

Carr, Raymond. *Modern Spain 1875–1980.* New York: Oxford University Press, 2001.

Hooper, John. *The New Spaniards.* New York: Penguin, 1995.

IMF Country Report. *Spain.* Washington, D.C.

OECD Economic Surveys. *Spain.* Paris.

Spain: A Spy Guide. 3rd ed. Washington, D.C.: International Business Publications, 2001.

Spain Business and Investment Opportunities Yearbook. 3rd ed. Washington, D.C.: International Business Publications, 2001 (annual).

Spain Export, Import, and Business Directory. 3rd ed. Washington, D.C.: International Business Publications, 2001.

Web Sites:

Bank of Spain: **www.bde.es**

El Pais (main daily newspaper): **www.elpais.es**

Ministry of the Economy, government entry point: **www.mineco.es**

National Statistics Institute: **www.ine.es**

Spanish Institute for Foreign Trade: **www.icex.es**

Spanish Stock Exchange: **www.infobolsa.es**

Sri Lanka

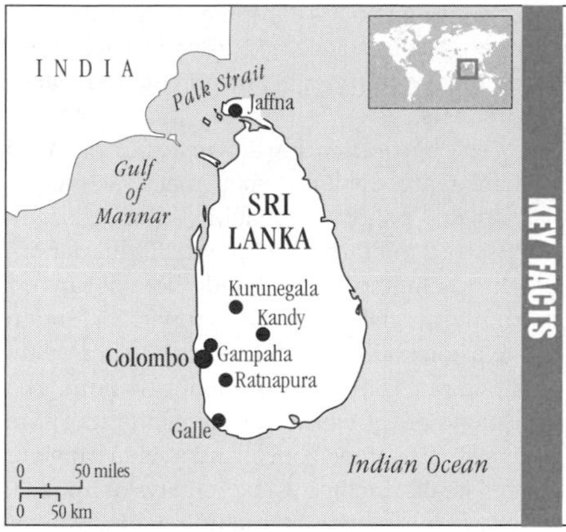

KEY FACTS

GNI: **$15,578 million; world's 76th**
GNI pc: **$820; world's 139th**
Head of state: **president**
Head of government: **prime minister**
Currency: **rupee (SLRs)**
Capital: **Colombo**
Population: **18,639,000, growing at 1.0% p.a.**
Land area: **24,940 square miles**
Population density: **747 per square mile**
Life expectancy: **74 years**
Infant mortality: **17 per 1,000 live births**
Language: **Sinhala, Tamil, English**
Best buy: **gemstones (sapphires, topaz, rubies)**

Economic Structure

Having been colonized by Portugal and Holland in the 16th and 17th centuries respectively, and by Britain in the 19th, Sri Lanka (then called Ceylon) became independent within the Commonwealth in 1948. Clashes between the different nationalistic directions of the Sinhalese majority and Tamil minority, and between state socialism and free market liberalism, have dominated much of its subsequent history. From 1960 socialistic governments nationalized most industry and instituted land reform. In 1977 the United National Party (UNP) government switched economic policy to liberalization—and in the 1978 constitution renamed the country the Democratic Socialist Republic of Sri Lanka—but failed to halt the growing Sinhala-Tamil conflict. Following intercommunal riots in 1983, the conflict escalated into a civil war that has continued since. After winning the violence-marred December 2001 elections, the UNP signed a ceasefire with Tamil groups that raised hopes of longer-term peace.

Agriculture remains the backbone of the economy, accounting for 21% of GDP (in 1999) and one-third of employment. It comprises a plantation sector growing, principally, tea, coconuts, and rubber for export, and a non-plantation sector dominated by subsistence farmers growing paddy rice. Manufacturing, which accounted for 17% of GDP in 1999, is dominated by garment manufacture. There are also significant food processing, chemicals, and rubber-based goods industries.

Sri Lanka's main exports are garments and tea, which together generated 63% of export earnings in 1999. During the 1990s the share of rubber and coconut exports declined, while industrial exports, including rubber products, diamonds, ceramics, and electrical goods, increased. Main destinations for exports are the United States (38.9% in 1999), the United Kingdom (13.1%), the Middle East (7.9%), and Germany (4.7%). Sri Lanka is heavily dependent on imported capital goods and industrial imports, the main sources of which are Japan (9.5% in 1999), India (8.7%), Hong Kong (7.8%), and Singapore (7.6%).

Since 1977, successive governments have sought to reverse the 1960s nationalization of most industry and plantations. During the 1990s, 36 major industrial enterprises, the tea plantations, one-third of the national telecoms monopoly, and 40% of the national airline were put into private hands.

Economic Policy

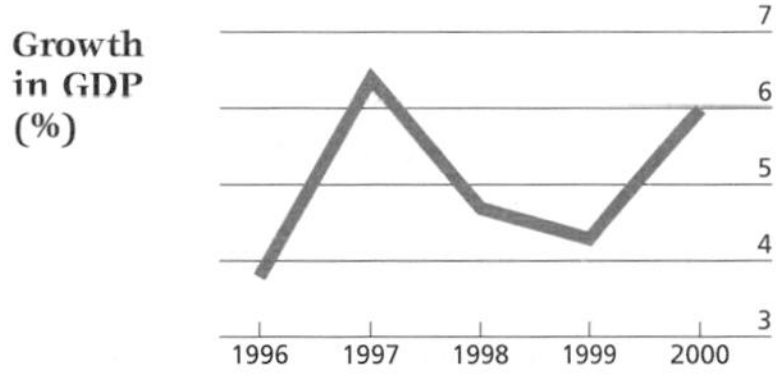

Commitment to economic liberalization has been consistent, but implementation uneven. Since 1996, services and infrastructure have been opened up to private—including foreign—investment, but in 2001 the government had yet to rationalize the antiquated civil service or reform stringent labor laws. Persistently high fiscal deficits, partly caused by high military spending, remain a major obstacle to growth. The deficit was cut to 7.5% of GDP in 1999, rose to 9.9% in 2000—during which year the government spent nearly $1 billion on

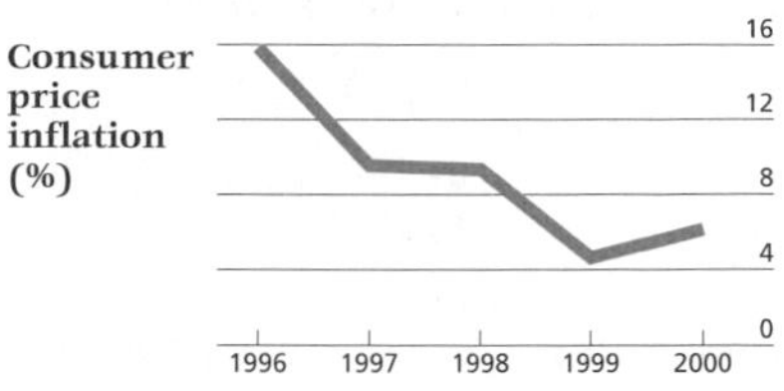

defense—and was projected at 8.5% for 2001.

The civil war has stifled investment, and this has adversely affected overall economic growth. An average annual growth rate of 5.5% in 1990–94 fell to below 5% in 1995–99, rose to 6% in 2000, but was projected to fall to 4.5% in 2001. Price inflation ran at 4.7% in 1999 and 6.2% in 2000. Unemployment was relatively high throughout the 1990s, and stood officially at 8% in 2000.

Geography/Resources

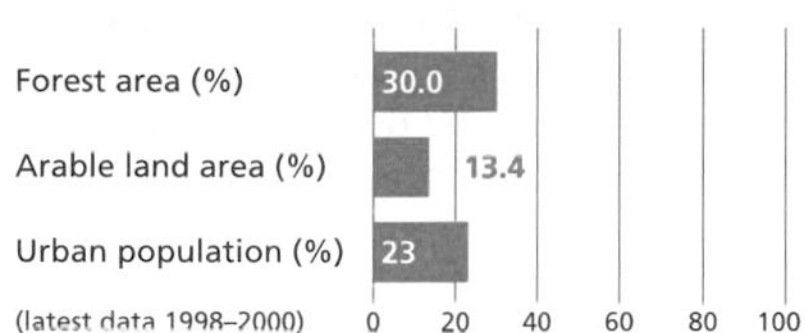

Sri Lanka comprises a compact island—with a maximum north-south length of 268 miles and maximum east-west width of 139 miles—and several small adjacent islands, just off the southern tip of the Indian subcontinent. A diverse physical environment makes Sri Lanka one of the world's most scenic countries, giving it a tourist business that has thrived despite the civil war.

Sri Lanka has a tropical climate, and about one-third of the land area is covered by natural vegetation. Forests have been severely depleted by extensive clearing and indiscriminate tree-felling, but reforestation projects are arresting the decline. Rivers flow down from the elevated central highlands, and freshwater resources are abundant. Sri Lanka has rich mineral resources, including gemstones, graphite, ilmenite, iron ore, quartz, and salt, and small amounts of nonferrous metals including titanium and zircon.

Sri Lanka's population rose from about 6.5 million at independence to 17 million in the early 1990s; between the 1970s and the 1990s population growth slowed from 2.6% per year to about 1.7%. Two-thirds of Sri Lankans live in rural areas. Ethnic, religious, and linguistic distinctions coincide: the Sinhalese, who speak Sinhala and are mostly Buddhists, comprise about 76% of the population; the Tamils, who speak Tamil

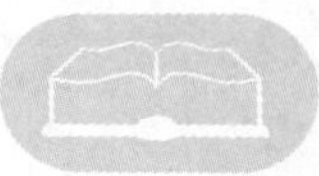

and are mainly Hindu, about 13%; and Muslims of partly Arab ethnic origin about 7.5%.

Communications/Energy

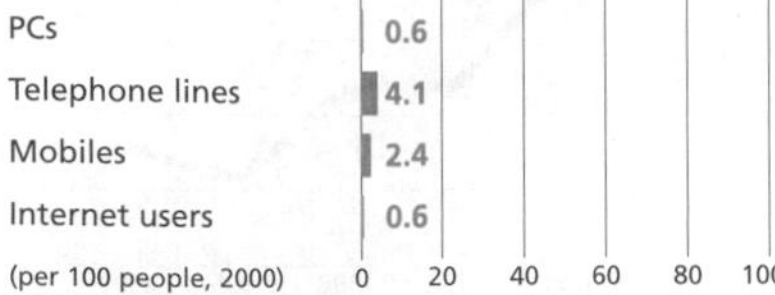

Sea trade through Colombo and two smaller ports has historically been pivotal. In 2001 Colombo port was operating at full capacity (1.7 million teus), and expansion work was under way, the first phase of which was expected to raise capacity by 750,000 teus. Other plans under discussion in 2001 were Japanese-financed development of the north pier at Colombo, or the construction of a new port at Hambantota. Air transport suffered a devastating blow in July 2001 when a Tamil guerrilla attack destroyed much of Colombo airport, the only international one; damage was estimated at $400 million, including the destruction of 13 aircraft. Inland transport is 90% by road. Coverage is above average for developing countries, but investment is badly needed, and a dramatic incrase in vehicle stock in the late 1990s aggravated congestion problems.

Sri Lanka depends on hydroelectric power for 67% of its electricity supply. Since a power crisis in 1996 efforts have been made to expand thermal capacity, which doubled with the addition of 273 MW on a build-operate-transfer basis by private investors. Power sector restructuring was under way in 2001, with generation, transmission, and distribution being unbundled and privatized. Petroleum, all imported, is the second-largest source of power supply after hydroelectricity.

The telecommunications network has grown dramatically since deregulation in 1996 and privatization of Sri Lanka Telecom in 1997. In 1997–99 the number of fixed lines doubled to 671,916, fixed-line phone density rose from 1.69 per hundred people to 3.05 per hundred people, and mobile usage grew by 123% to 256,665 subscribers.

Education/Employment

Sri Lanka's workforce is largely literate and relatively highly skilled; workers have an average of eight years of education. Labor costs are low, but higher than in other south Asian countries. Child labor is virtually nonexistent in the organized sector. Most permanent workers are protected by robust legislation on hours of work, minimum wages, safety and health standards, the right of association, and limitations on employers' right to hire and fire. Sri Lanka has a large expatriate workforce, including many women working in the Middle East as housemaids, from which there is a strong inflow of inward remittances, estimated in 2001 at $1 billion or 6.7% of GDP. But emigration of skilled workers aggravates shortages of some types of skilled labor at home.

With free, compulsory school education, high enrollment rates, and 92% literacy, Sri Lanka is far ahead of other south Asian countries. However in 1999 the government, alarmed at poor examination pass rates, launched a secondary education reform program. University education is severely restricted, with only 15% of eligible students gaining places at the country's 13 universities, and there is inadequate vocational and technical emphasis in courses.

Fiscal/Financial

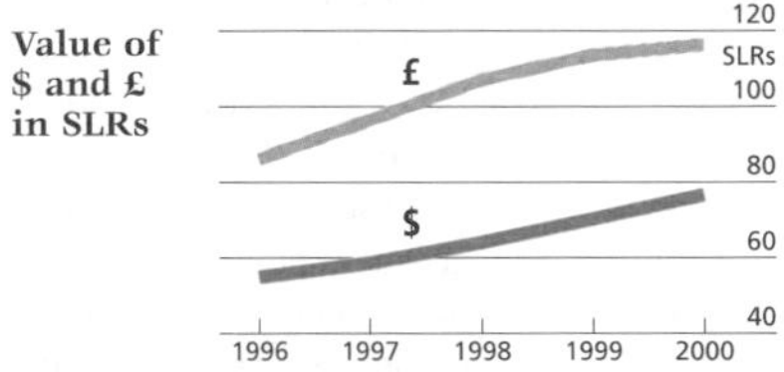

Financial reforms facilitated rapid growth in financial services in the 1990s. In 2000 the sector was further liberalized, with limits on the foreign ownership of banks being raised from 49% to 60%, and foreign ownership of up to 90% of insurance companies being permitted. The commercial banking sector is dominated by two state banks, the Bank of Ceylon and the People's Bank. There are seven private local banks and 17 foreign banks, most of whose business comprises short-term trade finance. Two development banks, the National Development Bank and the Development Finance Corporation of Ceylon, boosted their capital base by raising funds on the international markets in 1998. Sri Lanka also has ten merchant banks, six venture capital companies, five leasing companies, and 25 finance companies. The insurance sector grew rapidly throughout the late 1990s and was deregulated in 2000.

The Colombo Stock Exchange, which has suffered a downward trend since mid-1998—when investors withdrew from the region following the Asian financial crisis—is fully automated, and considered the most efficient in the region.

Business Opportunities

Foreign direct investment averaged just $150 million per year in 1990–98, and was $177 million in 1999. In 2001, increased FDI was expected for a power project and for the telecommunications sector. The U.S. Trade Department considered the most promising sectors for inward investment to be telecommunications equipment, power and energy, electrical and other machinery, medical equipment, and paper and paper products.

The barriers to inward investment in Sri Lanka are evident: poor macro-economic climate, political instability, and the unresolved military conflict with Tamil nationalists. On the other hand there is an extremely high level of state support for foreign investors, administered by the Board of Investment (BoI) and a subdepartment, the Bureau of Infrastructure Investment. There are six free trade zones, and a wide range of tax breaks, including tax holidays of up to 20 years in industries including electronics, light engineering, large-scale export-oriented projects, infrastructure projects, gems or precious stones enterprises, and hospitals; no restriction on repatriation of dividends or profits; and free transferability of shares.

For More Information

Books:

Bullis, Douglas, ed. *The Mahavamsa: The Great Chronicle of Sri Lanka.* Fremont, CA: Asian Humanities Press, 1999.

Lakshman, W. D., and C. A. Tisdell. *Sri Lanka's Development since Independence: Socio-Economic Perspectives and Analyses.* Huntington, NY: Nova Science, 2000.

Rotberg, Robert I. *Creating Peace in Sri Lanka: Civil War and Reconciliation.* Washington, D.C.: Brookings Institution, 1999.

Sri Lanka Business and Investment Opportunities Yearbook. 3rd ed. Washington, D.C.: International Business Publications, 2001 (annual).

Web Sites:

Board of Investment of Sri Lanka: **www.boisrilanka.org**

Central Bank of Sri Lanka: **www.lanka.net/centralbank**

Colombo Stock Exchange: **www.cse.lk**

Daily News: **www.dailynews.lk**

Heladiva news service: **www.heladiva.fsnet.co.uk**

The Island (news): **www.island.lk**

Journey to Sri Lanka (travel information): **www.srilanka-travel.com**

Trade Net SL (trade information): **www.tradenetsl.lk**

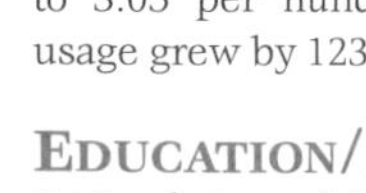

  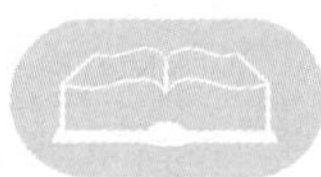    

St. Kitts and Nevis

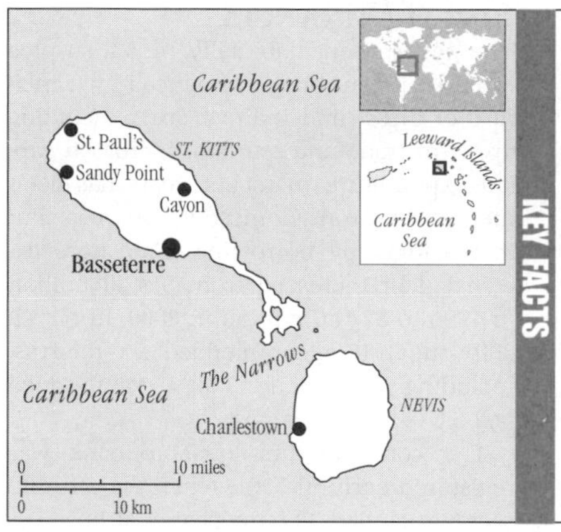

KEY FACTS

GNI: **$259 million**
GNI pc: **$6,330; world's 63rd**
Head of government: **prime minister**
Currency: **Eastern Caribbean dollar (EC$)**
Capital: **Basseterre**
Population: **39,000, growing at –0.8 % p.a.**
Land area: **101 square miles**
Population density: **386 per square mile**
Life expectancy: **71 years**
Infant mortality: **24 per 1,000 live births**
Language: **English**
Best buy: **cotton clothing, handicrafts**

Economy

Traditionally dominated by sugar cultivation and processing, St. Kitts is rapidly developing its tourist sector to replace the declining sugar industry. In Nevis, tourism is the main activity, with offshore finance a recent arrival. Manufacturing, which includes sugar milling, contributed 9.2% to GDP in 1998, just ahead of tourism at 8.7%, while government services and commerce between them accounted for the bulk of GDP and employment. New hotel projects and infrastructural work, including major air and sea port development, have given considerable impetus to the construction sector. Consultations were launched in mid-2000 on the future of the sugar sector, with scaling down or complete closure among the options.

In 1998, however, sugar accounted for 32% of export earnings, followed by garments at 20%; other main export items were electronic goods and other manufactures. Food, fuel, machinery, and manufactured goods were the main imports. In terms of overall foreign exchange earnings, tourism has overtaken sugar as the leading sector, bringing in $75 million in 1998.

Real GDP growth averaged 5% or more annually between 1993 and 1997, but fell to an estimated 1.0% in 1998 under the impact of Hurricane Georges, which caused damage estimated at $400 million. Growth recovered to an estimated 3.7% in 1999 and 7.5% in 2000. The inflation rate was generally below 4% throughout the 1990s, except in 1997 when it rose to 8.3%.

Geography/Resources

St. Kitts and Nevis consists of the islands of St. Christopher (St. Kitts) and Nevis, the latter lying to the southeast of the main island. Respectively 68 and 36 square miles in size, both islands are mountainous. Annual rainfall is about 55 inches.

Basseterre houses around 17,000 inhabitants, almost half the St. Kitts population, while the population of Nevis is more evenly dispersed. Nevis has internal self-government, with its own elected assembly and a premier, while also electing members of the federal parliament. The population is primarily of African descent. Adult literacy is estimated at 80%.

Communications/Energy

Scheduled flights operate between St. Kitts and Antigua, Barbados, Puerto Rico, and St. Maarten, while charter flights operate from London, Toronto, and various U.S. cities. Nevis has flight connections with St. Kitts and regional airports. There are 199 miles of roads on the two islands, of which 84 miles are paved; both islands have bus services, and there is an inter-island ferry. Basseterre houses a deep water port accommodating international shipping.

International and domestic telecommunications are provided by Cable & Wireless. Electric power is generated from imported diesel fuel.

Fiscal/Financial

There is no personal income tax. Corporation tax is 40%, and there is a 10% tax on profit, fees and other payments remitted externally. Capital gains tax of 20% is charged on assets sold within 12 months of their acquisition. There are double taxation treaties with the United Kingdom, the United States, and some other countries. Domestic taxes include a land tax and residential property tax.

Three foreign-owned banks operate in the country: Barclays, Nova Scotia, and Royal Bank of Canada. There are three domestic banks, two of which operate only in Nevis; other banking institutions are the national Development Bank and the regional Eastern Caribbean Central Bank, the headquarters of which are in Basseterre. This bank, which issues the Eastern Caribbean dollar, regulates the banking sector in the Leeward and Windward islands.

There is an offshore finance sector in Nevis, comprising 12,674 international business companies in 1998, plus 1,549 offshore trusts and 180 exempt insurance companies. Legislation aimed at strengthening regulation of the offshore sector was passed in September 2000.

Business Opportunities

Export-oriented companies are eligible for tax holidays varying from 10 to 15 years, according to value added, plus a tax rebate based on the percentage of profits derived from exporting. Companies granted tax holidays are exempted from duty on imported equipment and raw materials; all profits, dividends, and imported capital may be repatriated. Special tax relief and duty concessions apply to companies constructing or extending hotels, including profits tax exemptions for up to ten years.

For More Information

Books:

Cameron, Sarah. *Caribbean Islands Handbook*. 13th ed. Bath, Somerset: Footprint Handbooks, 2001.
Caribbean Development Bank: Annual report.
Eastern Caribbean Central Bank: Statistical Digest and annual report.

Web Sites:

Eastern Caribbean Central Bank: **www.eccb-centralbank.org**
Government information: **www.stkittsnevis.net**
Ministry of Finance: **www.fsd.gov.kn**

  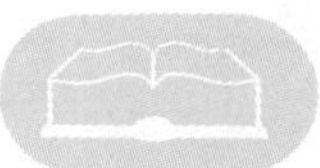  

St. Lucia

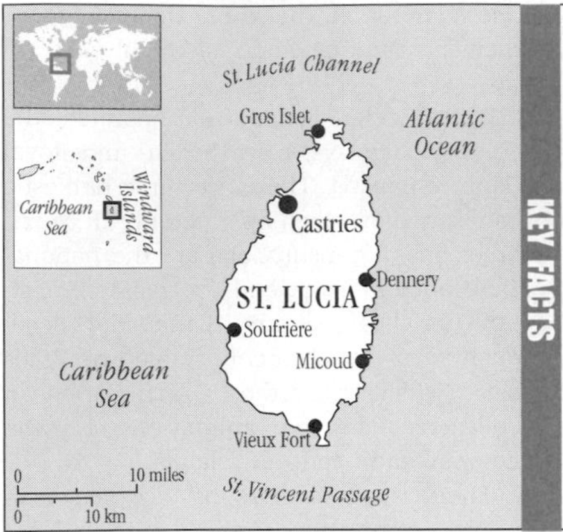

KEY FACTS

GNI: **$590 million**
GNI pc: **$3,820; world's 76th**
Head of government: **prime minister**
Currency: **Eastern Caribbean dollar (EC$)**
Capital: **Castries**
Population: **152,000, growing at 1.4% p.a.**
Land area: **238 square miles**
Population density: **525 per square mile**
Life expectancy: **73 years**
Infant mortality: **17 per 1,000 live births**
Language: **English, Creole**
Best buy: **batik and cotton clothing, tropical flowers**

Economy

Tourism and agriculture are the leading economic sectors, despite difficulties facing banana producers, while construction and manufacturing are also significant contributors to GDP and employment. Data processing, clothing, and agricultural processing are the main manufacturing activities, employing 14% of the work force (estimated at about 90,000 people). St. Lucia's tourism is dominated by large all-inclusive hotels; directly and indirectly, tourism is estimated to account for about half of total employment, while the number of banana farmers was just over 6,000 in 1998. The unemployment rate in 1999 was 18%.

Bananas remain the leading export item, accounting for 62% of total export earnings in 1999, the remainder consisting principally of other agricultural produce and manufactured goods. However, tourism earnings, which totaled $250 million in 1998, are more than three times export revenue. About 75% of exports go to the European Union, with Britain the major customer for bananas.

Government economic policy is to develop tourism and industry in order to compensate for the decline of the banana sector. After three years of low or negative growth in 1994–96, average GDP growth in 1996–2000 was 2%, with a similar average inflation rate, notwithstanding an isolated surge to 6.1% in 1999. St. Lucia has moved cautiously in the area of offshore finance, but is encouraging the development of data processing as a growth sector for employment and foreign exchange earnings.

Geography/Resources

St. Lucia, an island of 238 square miles, lies between Martinique and St. Vincent in the Windward Islands. Rainfall ranges from 63 inches in coastal area to 142 inches in the mountains. The main rainy season is from June to November, but there is no dry season as such. There are numerous rivers, none navigable, and there are no known mineral resources.

Castries has a population of about 60,000; the two other main towns are Vieux Fort in the south and Soufriere in the southwest. Vieux Fort, which houses the main airport, is also the site of an industrial development zone. Several coastal areas are the focus of tourist development, including residential accommodation as well as hotels.

The population is mainly of African descent. Education is compulsory to the age of 15; the literacy rate is an estimated 70%. International agencies are contributing to a program to develop and improve the education system.

Communications/Energy

International air services operate to and from London, Frankfurt, Paris, Miami, New York, and Toronto; there is an extensive network of regional services. A weekly passenger and freight ferry connects St. Lucia with Barbados, St. Vincent, Trinidad, and Venezuela. Domestic public transport is by minibus and taxi. There are an estimated 750 miles of roads, about 620 miles of which are paved.

Telecommunications services are provided by Cable & Wireless; competition is to be introduced into the sector by October 2002. Electric power is generated and distributed by St. Lucia Electricity Services Ltd., whose Castries power plant has a generating capacity of 4.6 MW.

Fiscal/Financial

The government habitually runs a surplus in its recurrent budget, financed by a mixture of direct and indirect taxes, including taxes on trade and tourism. Increased capital expenditure in recent years has been met partly from domestic resources, but increasingly by borrowing. The gross external debt increased from $142.0 million in 1996 to $214.0 million in 2000; in March 2001 the IMF recommended tax reforms, including introduction of a value-added tax.

The country's first offshore bank was registered early in 2001, when the offshore sector included 117 international business companies, three insurance companies, three international trusts, and one mutual fund. Three Canadian and one British commercial bank offer retail banking, together with two St. Lucian banks and one other Caribbean bank.

Business Opportunities

Tax exemption for ten years is offered to investors in industry. Six acts of parliament, covering the full range of financial services, offer tax exemptions and other incentives to investors in offshore banking, mutual funds and other entities. A U.S. company has been engaged to promote the offshore finance sector. Other investment incentives include duty exemption on imports, and free repatriation of profits.

For More Information

Books:

Cameron, Sarah. *Caribbean Islands Handbook*. 13th ed. Bath, Somerset: Footprint Handbooks, 2001.
The Caribbean Handbook 2000. London: FT Caribbean (BVI) Ltd., 2000.
South America, Central America and the Caribbean 2002. 10th ed. New York: Europa Publications, 2001.

Web Sites:

Chamber of Commerce, Industry and Agriculture: **www.sluchamber.com.lc**
National Commercial Bank: **www.ncbstlucia.com**
National Development Corporation: **www.stluciandc.com**

SUDAN

GNI: **$9,435 million; world's 86th**
GNI pc: **$330; world's 175th**
Head of government: **president**
Currency: **Sudanese dinar (SD)**
Capital: **Khartoum**
Population: **28,883,000, growing at 2.0% p.a.**
Land area: **917,400 square miles**
Population density: **31 per square mile**
Life expectancy: **56 years**
Infant mortality: **67 per 1,000 live births**
Language: **Arabic, many African languages**
Best buy: **textiles, perfumes, spices**

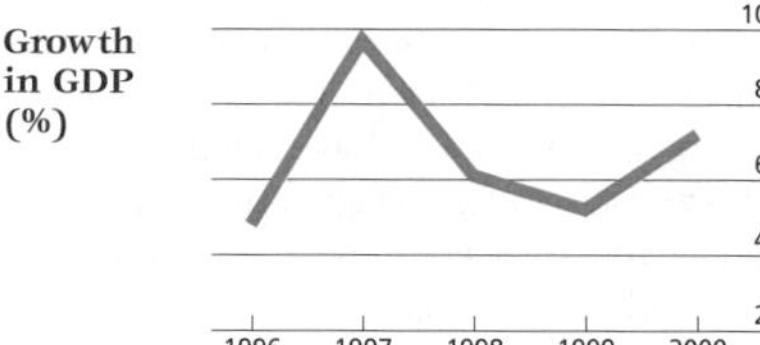

ECONOMIC STRUCTURE

Sudan has sustained a long-running civil war between north and south for most of its independent history since 1956. In part this reflects the fact the country straddles an ethnic, cultural, and religious fault-line between the Middle East and Central Africa, but the war has also been sustained by the persistence of chronic political instability within the dominant northern region where the capital, Khartoum, is located. Sharp and bitter divisions among democratic, nationalist, and religious political groups have encouraged the army both to dominate the power structure and to pursue the war against the southern rebels of the Sudan People's Liberation Army (SPLA). During the 1990s, the military ruler, President Omar al-Bashir, also lent his support to the efforts of Hassan al-Turabi's National Islamic Front (NIF) to impose strict sharia law throughout Sudan, but by 2000 Bashir had begun to distance himself from Turabi, and had opened negotiations with other political parties. In the south, meanwhile, the normal conditions of war still prevailed in 2001 and 2002—once again under the threat of the kind of recurring famine that had already killed hundreds of thousands of southern Sudanese in the past. Despite mediation efforts by a newly-appointed U.S. envoy, the prospects for any kind of peace settlement had not greatly improved by early 2002.

The economy is largely rural, with agriculture providing most employment and contributing heavily to exports. The economy of southern Sudan is entirely undeveloped, having been subject to a debilitating combination of war, drought, and famine. Excluding the south, however, agriculture still accounts for about 45% of the country's GDP, followed by trade and other services (about 30%). The manufacturing base is very small. Crude oil exports began in 1999, and oil can be expected to become a significant factor in the economy in future. Other exports are cotton, sesame seeds, livestock, groundnuts, gold, hides and skins, gum arabic, and sugar. The waters of the Nile have been exploited for irrigation, which has greatly boosted the production of cotton, sorghum, sugar, wheat, and groundnuts, although some irrigation projects have suffered from low investment and poor maintenance, resulting in silting and reduced production.

Sudan's largest export market is Saudi Arabia, followed by the United Kingdom, China, Italy, Egypt, and Thailand. The country's largest suppliers are Saudi Arabia, the United Kingdom, Japan, and France. The United States in 1997 imposed sanctions on most trade between U.S. companies and Sudan, but trade in food was exempted from the sanctions in 1999.

During the 1990s there was only very limited privatization of the state sector of the economy, with the principal exception being the telecommunications company Sudatel. Official plans for further privatization have, however, included the National Electricity Corporation, Sudan Airways, the Gezira irrigation scheme, and four sugar factories.

ECONOMIC POLICY

After a break in relations with the IMF in the early 1990s, the government opened new negotiations on its economic policies in 1997 and began to implement a series of reforms. These included reducing government deficits and trying to boost tax revenues. The government's revenue projections have been helped by the start of oil production and exports, which could lead to an expansion of expenditure in the future. In response to a surge in economic growth in 2000, the Bank of Sudan implemented measures to encourage increased lending by the commercial banks.

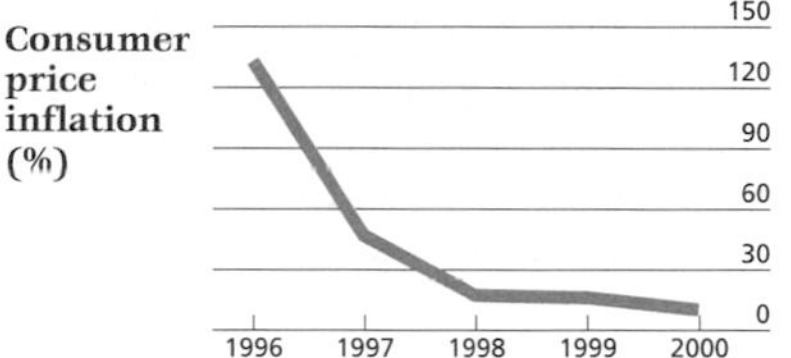

Economic growth averaged about 4% in the second half of the 1990s, rising to 6% in 1999 and 7% in 2000. Investment in the oil industry was an important stimulant to growth. Inflation was brought under control from levels of above 100% in the mid-1990s to 12% in 2000. Most employment is in the agricultural sector, and the oil industry has not had a significant effect on levels of formal employment. Many Sudanese travel abroad, especially to the Gulf states, in search of employment. Consequently, there has been a substantial growth in trade and investment flows between Sudan and Saudi Arabia.

GEOGRAPHY/RESOURCES

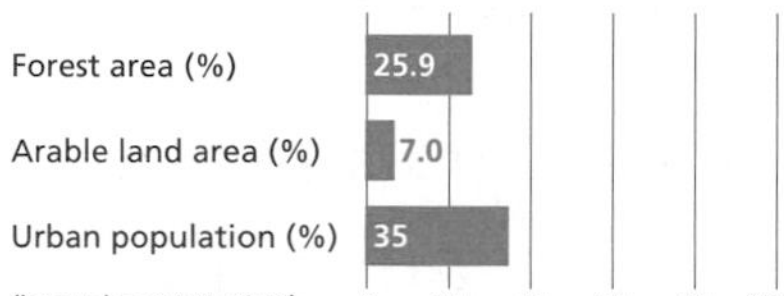

Sudan is Africa's largest single country. From its southern tropical forest and savannah regions it stretches into open desert in the north. The waters of the Nile, which flow into Sudan from Uganda and Ethiopia, and finally northwards into Egypt, are an important element in patterns of human settlement, agriculture, and trade. The steadiest flow of water is that of the White Nile, which flows from Lake Victoria in

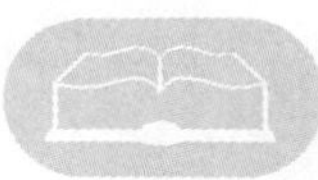

Uganda through the swamps of the Sudd and Machar in southern Sudan, but more than half the Nile's flow derives from the seasonal floods carried by the Blue Nile from Ethiopia, floods which are at their highest between July and October. In the past, Egypt and Sudan have tried jointly to optimize their water usage, but a project to build a canal that would reduce evaporation in the Sudd swamp has not been completed because of the civil war.

Rainfall averages about 39 inches a year in the south, where it occurs between April and October. Further north the annual rainfall is considerably reduced, being only 8 inches at Khartoum, where the wet season occurs in July and August only. The soils of the center and east of the country have relatively good agricultural potential when assisted by irrigation. The natural vegetation in the south includes some tropical rainforest as well as grassland. Apart from the better-watered Nile valley, towards the center and north the vegetation becomes thinner, with short grasses and occasional acacia trees giving way to empty barren desert in the northernmost quarter of the country. Sudan's exploited mineral resources include crude oil in southern and central regions, gold in the Red Sea Hills, and chromite near the Ethiopian border. There are untapped reserves of silver, iron ore, copper, lead, mica, asbestos, talc, tungsten, zinc, diamonds, and uranium.

The people of Sudan are ethnically mixed in the north, where Arabic culture and language predominate, and more distinctly defined by separate ethnic groups and cultures in the south, where the Nuer, Dinka, and Shilluk are the largest such groups. The highest population density occurs along the Nile valley between the Ethiopian and Egyptian borders. The largest cities and towns are Khartoum, Omdurman, Port Sudan, Kassala, al-Obeid, and Wad Medani. The southern region accounts for about 25% of the population.

Communications/Energy

	(per 100 people, 2000)
PCs	0.3
Telephone lines	1.2
Mobiles	0.1
Internet users	0.1

For such a large country, Sudan has a meager land transport network, consisting of 1,964 miles of main roads and only 459 miles of secondary roads, and a collapsing rail network of 2,936 miles. The only major all-weather highway links Port Sudan to Khartoum, a distance of 745 miles. A new highway, paid for by Iran, has opened between Rabak and Malakal to serve the developing oil sector and the government's military operations in the south. Air services are limited. The four main airports are at Khartoum, Port Sudan, al-Obeid and El Fasher. There are plans to build a new international airport for Khartoum. Sudan Airways has been targeted for privatization. The telecommunications network is very limited in coverage. The national provider, Sudatel, has been part-privatized, and there has been some investment in mobile telephone services.

Electric power is drawn largely from hydroelectric sources, especially the Roseires dam on the Blue Nile, while there are also thermal power stations located near Khartoum. Further investment in hydroelectric capacity has often been discussed but has not been implemented. The emphasis of energy policy is being transformed by the development of Sudan's oil reserves since 1997, when the Greater Nile Petroleum Operating Company (GNPOC) was established by Canadian, Chinese, and Malaysian companies in partnership with the Sudanese government to exploit oilfields near Bentiu in the south, and to build a 1,000-mile pipeline to take the oil to Port Sudan on the Red Sea. Oil production reached 200,000 barrels per day in 2000, of which 50,000 barrels per day was required for the domestic market. A new $600 million oil refinery was opened in Khartoum in 2000.

Education/Employment

Educational provision has not been a priority for Sudan's successive governments, except to bolster the Islamic policies adopted in the 1990s. There is very high illiteracy, especially among women. Primary schools cater for barely half the number of school-age children. Secondary and higher education, which are available to limited numbers of students, have been disrupted by the war because many male students have been required to serve in the armed forces. More than 60% of the economically active population work in agriculture. The other principal sources of employment are trade and other services.

Fiscal/Financial

The central bank is the Bank of Sudan. In addition to the two government-owned banks, there are numerous smaller banks and six foreign institutions (from Saudi Arabia, U.A.E., Pakistan and South Korea). Islamic banking regulations have meant that the banks are restricted in the range of

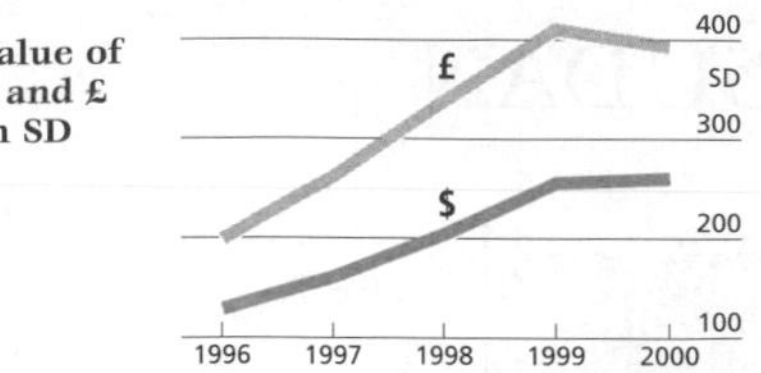

instruments they can use. The tax base is narrow, but allows tax breaks for foreign investors. The government is heavily indebted, and by the end of 2001 had still not reached agreement with creditors on a comprehensive rescheduling. This naturally made it extremely difficult for Sudanese companies to raise finance, other than through direct investment, on international markets. However, starting in 2000, the government's financial position was much improved by the flow of revenues from oil, and new negotiations on debt rescheduling are expected in 2002.

Business Opportunities

Investment in the oil industry is likely to become a dominant factor in the evolution of the economy. It has already led to the construction of a major pipeline and the installation of a modern oil refinery in Khartoum. Although Western investors have been wary of engaging further in Sudan's oil boom in view of the continuation of the war and growing international sympathy with the southern rebels' cause, other major investors from the Middle East, Asia, and the former Soviet Union have begun to step up their activities.

For More Information

Books:

Burr, J. M., and R. O. Collins. *Requiem for the Sudan: War, Drought and Disaster Relief.* Boulder, CO: Westview Press, 1995.

Deng, F. M. *War of Visions: Conflict of Identities in the Sudan.* Washington, D.C.: Brookings Institution, 1995.

Woodward, P. *Sudan 1898–1989: The Unstable State.* Boulder, CO: Lynne Rienner, 1990.

Web Sites:

African news and information: **www.allafrica.com/business**

National web site: **www.sudan.net**

Norwegian Council for Africa, Index on Africa: **www.afrika.no**

UN humanitarian relief news: **www.reliefweb.int**

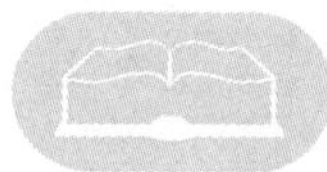

SWEDEN

KEY FACTS

GNI: **$236,940 million; world's 20th**
GNI pc: **$26,750; world's 12th**
Head of government: **prime minister**
Currency: **Swedish krona (SKr)**
Capital: **Stockholm**
Population: **8,892,000, growing at 0.4% p.a.**
Land area: **158,920 square miles**
Population density: **56 per square mile**
Life expectancy: **79 years**
Infant mortality: **3 per 1,000 live births**
Language: **Swedish**
Best buy: **crystal, amber and silver jewelry, birchwood souvenirs, cloudberry jam**

ECONOMIC STRUCTURE

Composition of GDP (1999)

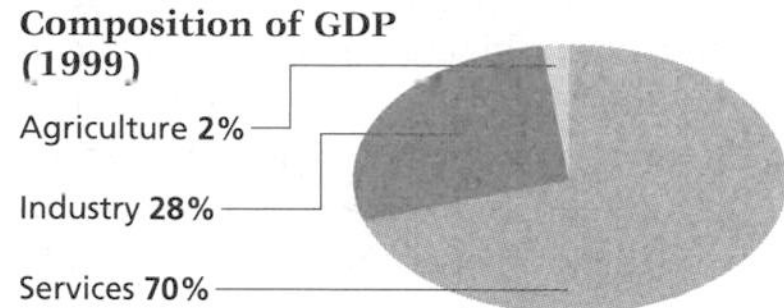

Sweden's economic wealth was built from iron ore and other metals mined 1,000 years ago. These were traded with other European countries. Sweden also became a significant arms manufacturer. The combination of metals, minerals, chemicals, engineering, and foreign trade has maintained Sweden's wealth down the centuries. The concept of the multinational company was born in the mid-19th century when explosives manufacturer Alfred Nobel established foreign subsidiaries as Swedish law banned the export of dynamite. A handful of large privately-owned Swedish companies, based on Swedish technology, have dominated Swedish industry from then to the present day. In recent years, large Swedish firms have been involved in several international mergers. The resulting companies have retained their Swedish manufacturing bases, R&D centers, and often headquarters, although increasingly headquarters are moving out because of high costs. Despite the strength of the private sector, politics since World War II was dominated by the Social Democrat Party, with the result that social services and benefits are highly developed, and labor costs and taxation relatively high. Membership of the European Union from 1995 has oriented the management of the economy more towards market principles. Opportunities offered by the new capitalism of the former Soviet bloc have led Sweden to return to its traditional role as a hub for trading in the Baltic Sea region.

Services accounted for 63% of GDP in 1998, while manufacturing, construction, power, and mining contributed about 28%, and agriculture, forestry, and fishing 2.2%. Private services predominate, including the full range of business and finance services for foreign and domestic trade. Local public-sector services are extensive, employing 25% of the labor force, and include health, education, and welfare. The main manufactured goods are paper, motor vehicles, communications equipment, machinery, chemicals and pharmaceuticals, steel products, and military aircraft. Swedish firm Ericsson, the second-largest producer of mobile phones in the world after Finland's Nokia, is a world leader in developing mobile Internet systems. Sweden is also a world leader in biotechnology products, including medical equipment and treatments. Forest products are important for export and for the domestic market. Agriculture and fisheries are important for the domestic market.

In 2000 Germany was the main export market (10.6%), followed by the United States (9.5%), the United Kingdom (9.1%), Norway (7.5%), and Denmark (5.3%). Exports are expected to increase to the Baltic states and Russia. The top export category was non-electrical machinery (35.2%), followed by electrical and telecommunications equipment (22.7%), wood and paper products (12.3%), and chemicals (9.2%). Other important exports include pharmaceuticals, steel, iron ore, and petroleum products.

Public services, administered at local government level, are extensive; a greater allocation of taxes is directed towards them than in many other EU countries. The state

Current account balance ($ billion)

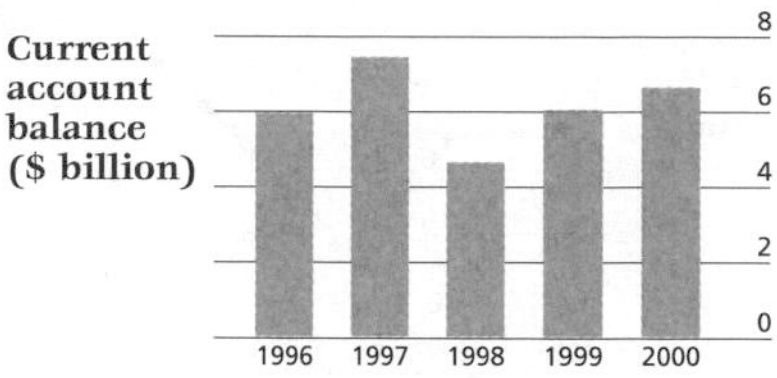

owns companies in the power, water, transport, telecommunications, postal services, broadcasting, gambling, alcohol retailing, real estate, finance, and forestry sectors, among others, where it perceives there to be a public interest: alcohol retailing, for example, became a government monopoly in order to reduce alcoholism. Telecommunications was opened to competition in 1993, electricity in 1996, and the railways in 2000, but state companies or local monopolies still predominate. The Swedish Mint was privatized in January 2002, and the paper factory that supplied the Mint was sold to a separate foreign buyer.

ECONOMIC POLICY

Growth in GDP (%)

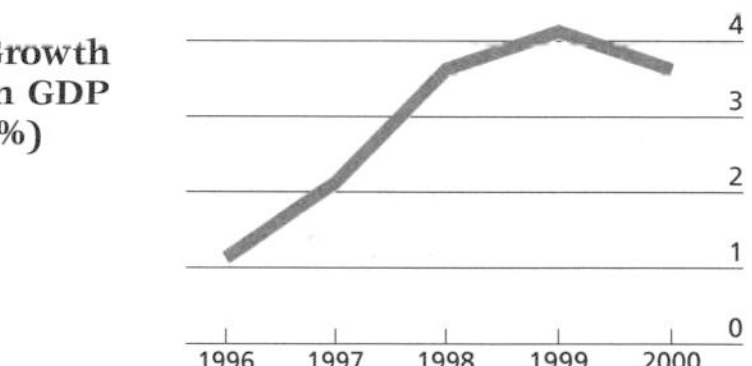

Tight monetary policy and budget austerity have characterized government policy since the recession of the early 1990s. In November 1992 the link between the krona and the European currency unit was removed, allowing the krona to drift down, thus improving export competitiveness. Government spending has been capped since 1997, although discretionary spending has risen slightly above the ceiling to maintain local living standards. Government surpluses, targeted at 2% of GDP a year and achieving 2.9% in 1998–2001, enabled the general government debt to be reduced from 74.5% of GDP in 1997 to 52.4% in 2001. It is expected to fall to 49.4% in 2002. Income tax reforms have involved phased reductions of direct tax from 2000 to offset the 7% pension fee. Wage agreements for 2001–03 incorporate moderate increases to achieve the government's inflation target of less than 3%. However, greater consumer spending power from the buoyant economy, and more costly imports from the weakening of the krona against the Euro, pushed inflation to 2.3% in 2001 up from an annual average

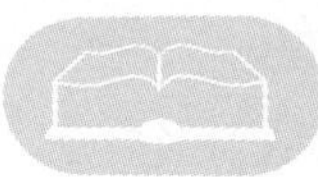

of 0.5% in 1996–2000. Inflation is expected to be 2.2% in 2002. The average for 1991–95 was 4.2%.

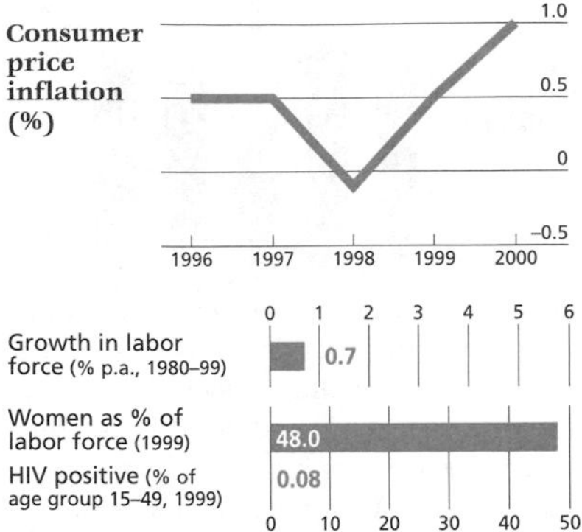

Reducing the weight of regulation to allow greater competition has been a key element of government policy. The Competition Act of 1993 is based on EU competition rules, but block exemptions have protected firms in dominant positions, for example in food retailing. Average annual GDP growth was 2.9% in 1996–2000, with 1.2% in 2001 and 2.5% expected in 2002. The telecommunications boom was the main driver of growth in the late 1990s and in 2000, but in 2001 momentum waned. Telecommunications is still strong, and the role of biotechnology is expected to increase. Unemployment fell from a peak of 9.9% in 1997 to 4.1% in 2001, with 4% expected in 2002.

Geography/Resources

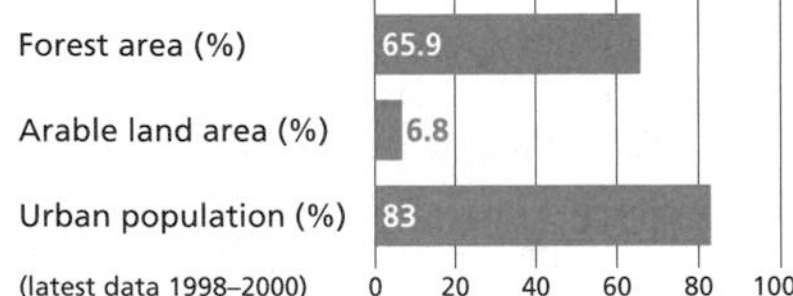

Sweden is one of the largest countries in Western Europe, and one of the least densely populated (56 inhabitants per square mile). The country occupies the eastern two-thirds of the Scandinavian peninsula. It borders Norway to the west and north, Finland to the north, the Gulf of Bothnia and Baltic Sea to the east, and the Øresund strait to the south. About 15% of the land lies within the Arctic Circle. The climate is cold in winter, mild in summer, and relatively dry. Daylight varies from a few hours in the south and none in the north in winter to 22–24 hours in summer. Most of the land is relatively flat with low hills and thousands of lakes. The Kjolen Mountains border Norway in the northwest.

Half of the land area is forested and less than 10% is cultivated, but Sweden is largely self-sufficient in agricultural products. Over two-thirds of farms combine forestry and farming. Many farmers belong to food processing and marketing cooperatives. Meat and dairy products, barley, wheat, oats, and potatoes are important. Sweden produces the largest volume of iron ore, lead, silver, and gold in the EU, and is the second-largest producer of copper and zinc. Minerals exploration is on the increase, with interest focusing on copper, zinc, gold, and diamonds. Most mineral deposits are in the northern half of Sweden.

Most of the population live in the southern third of Sweden. Half of the population is urban, living mostly in Stockholm, Gothenburg, and Malmö. The majority of people are of Scandinavian origin, with small indigenous communities of Lapps in the north. Immigrants account for 5% of the population, the majority of whom are Finns, followed by Bosnians, Norwegians, Iraqis, Yugoslavs, Danes, Iranians, and Turks.

Communications/Energy

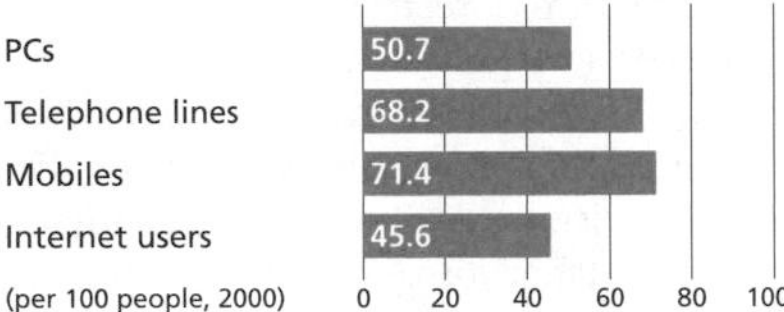

Road transport is dominant for both passengers and freight. The road network comprises 60,900 miles, including 9,070 miles of main roads of which 870 miles are motorways. The road and rail bridge across the 10-mile Øresund strait to Denmark was opened in July 2000. The share of road transport for goods is expected to rise from 40% in 1997 to 47% in 2010, whereas the share of railways is expected to fall slightly from 22% to 21%, and that of shipping from 33% to 31%. The rail network was 7,967 miles in 1998, including 2,233 miles of private railways. One-third of rail passenger traffic was opened to competition in 2000. Gothenburg is the main sea port. The main international airport is Arlanda (Stockholm). There are international airports at Gothenburg and Malmö, and many domestic commercial airports elsewhere.

Sweden invests 7.7% of GDP in IT and communications. At end-2000 there were 6.1 million fixed phone lines serving 68.2% of the population, 6.3 million mobile phones (71.4% of the population), and 4 million Internet users (45.6%), including 2 million people who used the Internet for banking. Almost 70% of Swedish households have a personal computer.

In 1999 one-third of electricity was generated by nuclear power, while oil accounted for another third. Biofuels, peat, wind, hydro, coal, and combined heat and power accounted for the rest. The electricity market between Norway, Sweden, and Finland was restructured and opened to competition in 1996, leading to cheaper electricity and to the closure of high-cost plants. An undersea cable to Poland was commissioned in 2000. Sweden imports oil mainly from Norway: half of total imports are processed and exported. Gas from Denmark's offshore fields is imported by pipeline.

Education/Employment

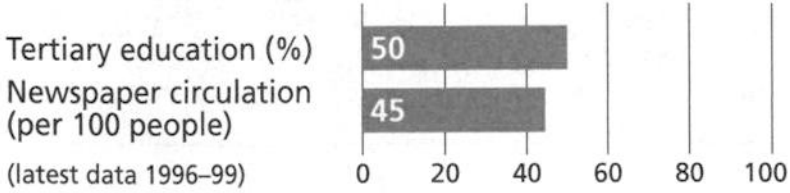

Education is compulsory from age 6 to 14 or 7 to 15. In 1993 a new Higher Education Act came into effect, giving universities and colleges greater autonomy and a wider choice for students. Performance targets are set for institutions, and grants are allocated according to results and student demand. Enrollment in higher education increased by 50% from 1991 to 1997. Over 30% of young people go into higher education within five years of completing secondary school. Study grants and loans are offered to students up to age 45. Most of the 64 universities, university colleges, and specialized higher education institutions come under the Ministry of Education and Science. The University of Agricultural Sciences in Uppsala is the responsibility of the Ministry of Agriculture, Food and Fisheries. The Stockholm School of Economics, Chalmers University of Technology, and the University College of Jonjoping are run by private foundations with government support.

According to an OECD report in 2000, Sweden invests 4% of GDP in R&D, more than any other country. Research is an important part of the higher education system, but about 75% of R&D funding comes from the private sector, especially from Swedish and foreign multinational companies. Particular strengths are IT, telecommunications, electronics and robotics, automotive applications, machinery, chemicals, pharmaceuticals, biotechnology, energy conservation, environmental control, construction materials, and aerospace.

The workforce is highly skilled, and Sweden has the second-largest number of R&D personnel per capita in the world after Switzerland, according to the Invest in Sweden

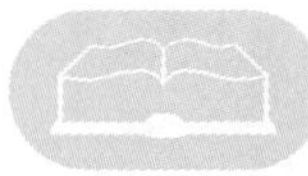

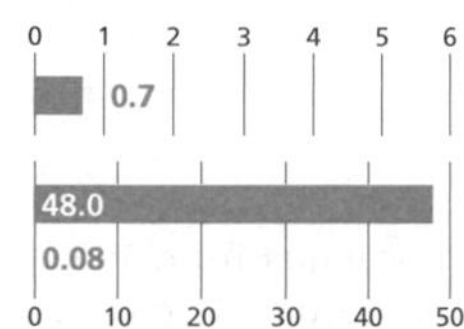

Agency. Over 1 million people, a quarter of the labor force, are employed in local government services, including health, education, and social services. Wages are determined through negotiations between employers and trade unions. Sweden applies EU employment law, which covers safety at work, wages and working hours, industrial relations, employment incentives, and unemployment provision. However, the main legal framework for employment conditions in the workplace is set out in the Work Environment Act of 1978. Amendments in the 1990s have increased the employer's responsibility for providing a safe working environment.

Fiscal/Financial

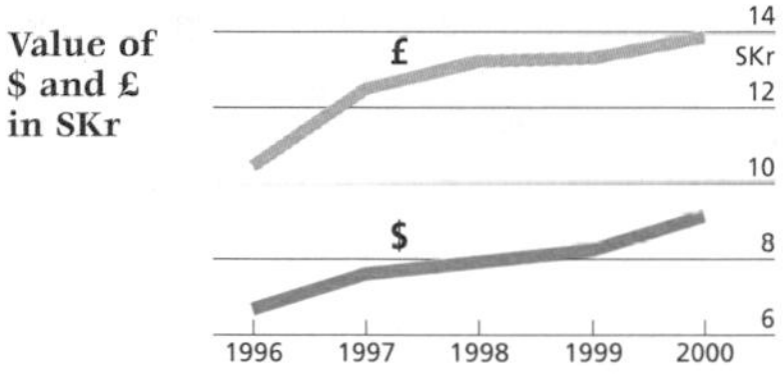

The largest bank according to balance sheet total at end-2000 was Svenska Handelsbanken, followed by SEB, Föreningens-Sparbanken and Nordbanken. Nordbanken is part of the largest Scandinavian banking and insurance group Nordea, which also includes Christiana Bank of Norway, Unidanmark of Denmark, and Merita of Finland. A merger between SEB and FöreningensSparbanken, which would have created the largest Swedish bank, was blocked by the EU Commission in late 2001. The largest Swedish insurance company according to total assets at end-2000 was SPP, followed by Skandia, SEB, and AMF Pension. Sveriges Riksbank (Swedish Central Bank) implements monetary policy. The Finansinspektionen (Financial Supervisory Authority) is the regulatory authority for banks, finance and insurance companies, and the stock exchange.

Corporation tax is 28% one of the lowest in the EU, but at 59% maximum, personal income tax is one of the highest. Social security premiums are high. There is a range of indirect taxes to encourage environmental protection, but these are weighted less heavily on industry to maintain international competitiveness. VAT applies at a standard rate of 25% and a reduced rate of 12%.

The financial services industry grew rapidly in size, sophistication, and international orientation in the 1990s following liberalization and the removal of capital controls in the 1980s. All major banks offer Internet banking. Foreign banks are now well established on the business finance market. At end-2000 there were 41 banks, including commercial and savings banks and foreign banks with a total balance sheet of SKr2.8 billion. Following consolidation several of these banks, although still operating independently, form part of larger finance groups, notably Nordea, Svenska Handelsbanken, and FöreningensSparbanken. Activity on the Stockholm Stock Exchange rose from 1,000 trades a day in 1989 to 100,000 trades a day in 2000. This dramatic expansion followed the government's removal of turnover tax and restrictions on short trading and proprietary trading, and the upgrading of the computerized trading system. In 1998 the Stockholm Stock Exchange merged with the derivatives exchange operated by OM Group. OM has a risk capital exchange in London, which specializes in the Nordic market, and a virtual stock exchange, Jiway, which is a joint venture with U.S. finance house Morgan Stanley Dean Witter.

Business Opportunities

Growth in output (% p.a., 1990–99)

Services 1.2
Industry 3.0
Agriculture 0.0

Sweden offers a special tax regime to non-life insurance companies. Invest in Sweden Agency (ISA) provides assistance to foreign investors. U.S., Japanese, U.K., German, French, Canadian, Dutch, Italian, and Swiss companies have established regional headquarters for the Baltic area (Scandinavia, northern Germany, Poland, Latvia, Lithuania, Estonia, and western Russia). Others have established call centers and distribution centers. The net inflow of foreign direct investment to Sweden in 1991–2000 was SKr142 billion, contrasting with a net outflow of SKr251 billion in 1982–90. The United States has the largest number of companies, followed by Norway, Netherlands, and Denmark. The top investor in 2000 was Finland, followed by the United States, Norway, the United Kingdom, and Switzerland. The leading investment sector in 2000 was energy, followed by real estate, finance, chemicals, telecommunications, and transport. Other sectors include IT, automotive, machinery, pharmaceuticals, and minerals. All these industries, and the further liberalization of the telecommunications, electricity and transport sectors, continue to offer investment opportunities.

For More Information

Books:

Economist Intelligence Unit. *Country Profile and Quarterly Reports*. London.
European Union: European Economy: Report and Studies Series.
IMF Country Report. *Sweden*. Washington, D.C.
Johnsson, Hans-Ingvar. *Spotlight on Sweden*. Stockholm: Swedish Institute, 1999.
Lagerqvist, Lars O. *A History of Sweden*. Stockholm: Swedish Institute, 2001.
OECD Economic Surveys. *Sweden*. Paris: OECD.
Swahn, Jan-Öjvind. *Maypoles, Crayfish and Lucia: Swedish Holidays and Traditions*. Stockholm: Swedish Institute, 1999.

Web Sites:

Central Statistics Office: **www.scb.se**
Dagens Nyheter (main daily newspaper): **www.dn.se**
Government entry point: **www.sweden.gov.se**
Government information point (with links): **www.virtualsweden.net**
Invest in Sweden Agency: **www.isa.se**
Stockholm Stock Exchange: **www.stockholmsborsen.se**
Sveriges Riksbank (central bank): **www.riksbank.com**
Swedish Bankers' Association: **www.bankforeningen.se**
The Swedish Institute (government background information on Sweden): **www.si.se**
Swedish Insurance Federation: **www.forsakringsforbundet.com**

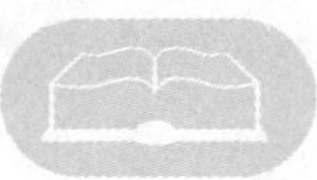

Switzerland

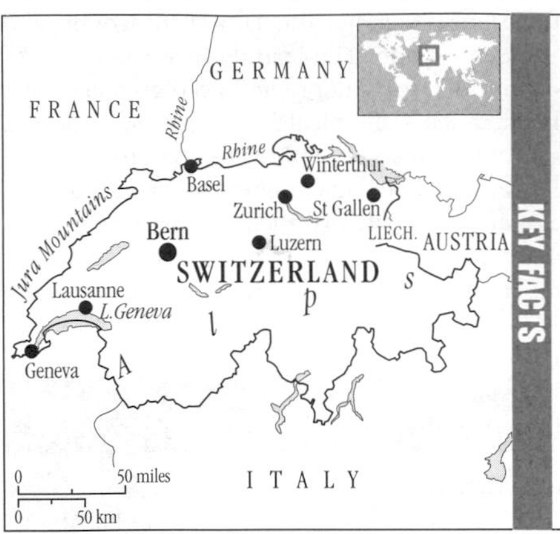

KEY FACTS

GNI: **$273,856 million; world's 18th**
GNI pc: **$38,380; world's 3rd**
Head of government: **president**
Currency: **Swiss franc (SFr)**
Capital: **Bern**
Population: **7,344,000, growing at 0.8% p.a.**
Land area: **15,290 square miles**
Population density: **479 per square mile**
Life expectancy: **79 years**
Infant mortality: **3 per 1,000 live births**
Language: **German, French, Italian, Rhaeto-Romansch**
Best buy: **Swiss Army knife, watches and clocks, jewelry, chocolates**

Economic Structure

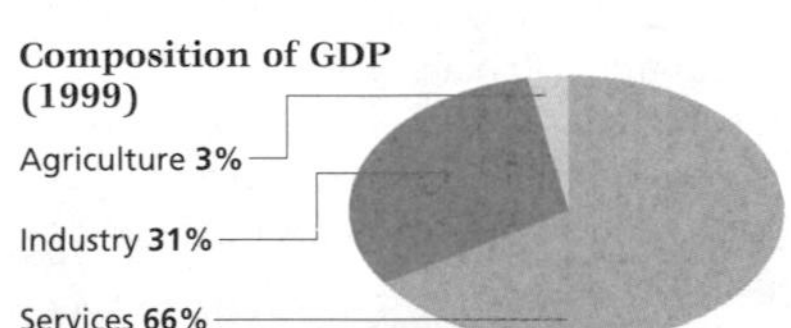

Switzerland has gained from isolation and internationalism down the ages. The mountainous terrain gave communities and cities a natural independence in medieval times. Defense of the territory against outsiders resulted in an element of democracy in the 14th century. Agriculture and trade were the basis of Swiss domestic wealth, while Swiss mercenaries fought for various foreign armies and came back to Switzerland with precision engineering skills. Political neutrality has been guaranteed and respected by other European countries since 1815. Thus Switzerland not only kept its industry intact through the two World Wars of the 20th century, but also gained from trading. The banks seized assets placed with them for safekeeping by Jewish families persecuted by the Nazis in the 1930s and 1940s. These included large amounts of gold, some of which was taken by other European governments after the war. The Swiss government and banks apologized to Jewish families and created a fund for reparation in the late 1990s. Despite this blot on its reputation, Swiss finance continues to flourish and maintain a strong presence in the international arena. Switzerland belatedly joined the IMF and World Bank in 1992, but signed up immediately to the World Trade Organization when it was established in 1995. In the early 1990s a popular referendum rejected government proposals to join either the EU or the European Economic Area, a vote repeated in 2001.

Services account for two-thirds of GDP, industry for 32%, and agriculture for 2%. Banking and insurance are particularly prominent service sectors. Tourism, conferences and health services are also important. The main manufacturing industries are chemicals and pharmaceuticals, machinery, vehicles, electrical, electronic and optical products, metal goods, food, printing, and textiles. Many Swiss companies and banks are global in operations and income: Nestlé, for example, is the largest food manufacturer in the world. In 2000 machinery was the top export category (29.3%), followed by chemicals (28.4%), precision instruments (14.4%), metals and metal goods (8.6%), textiles, clothing, and shoes (3%). The main export market was Germany (22.3%), followed by the United States (11.6%), France (9%), Italy (7.6%), and the United Kingdom (5.4%).

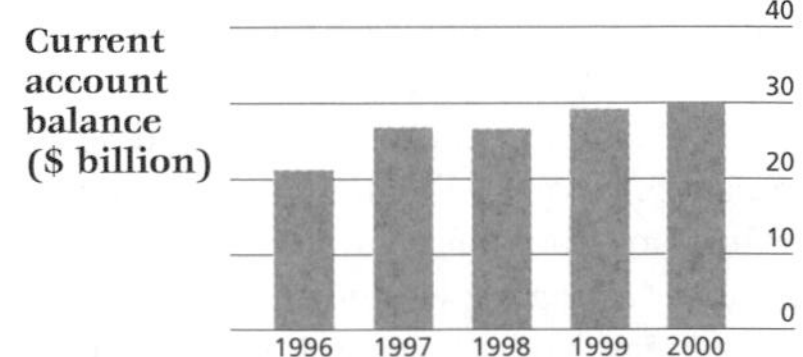

State-owned companies predominate in rail transport, electricity and telecommunications. There are 24 banks owned by the cantons. Agriculture is heavily subsidized, with about 80% of farm income coming from the state, but there is international pressure to reduce this subsidy protection. Dairy products and cereals are protected by import tariffs. Liberalization of telecommunications from 1998 led to price reductions. Partial liberalization of the electricity market began in 2001.

Economic Policy

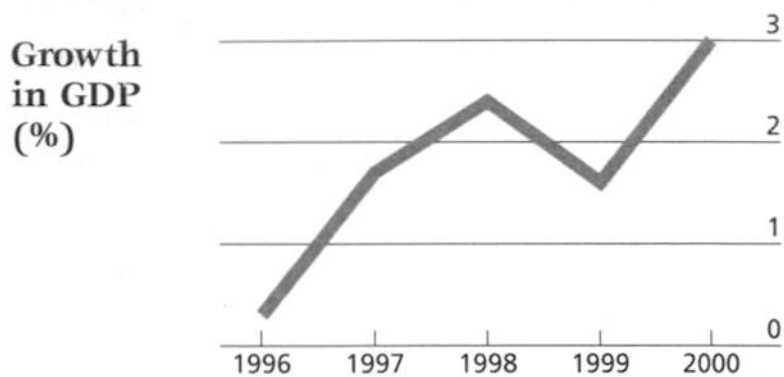

The prolonged economic stagnation of the late 1980s and early 1990s, and the tenfold increase in unemployment from 1990 to 1997 led to reforms in the unemployment benefits system and the upgrading of vocational and technical training. From 2001—following several years of deficits—it was a constitutional requirement for the government to balance its budget. From 2002 federal government expenditure will be capped, while revenues will fluctuate with the business cycle. The public debt rose from 46.9% of GDP in 1995 to 54.4% in 1998 but fell since then to 49.3% in 2001. The Swiss National Bank abandoned monetary targeting in 2000 in favor of an inflation rate ceiling of 2% a year. To avoid currency speculation in the Swiss franc arising as a result of the introduction of the Euro, the National Bank adopted a program for gradually selling off gold reserves and a policy to keep the franc roughly in line with the Euro. Tax reform is under way to produce a unified framework—although not unified tax rates—for the federal, cantonal, and municipal authorities. The subsidies system is also being simplified.

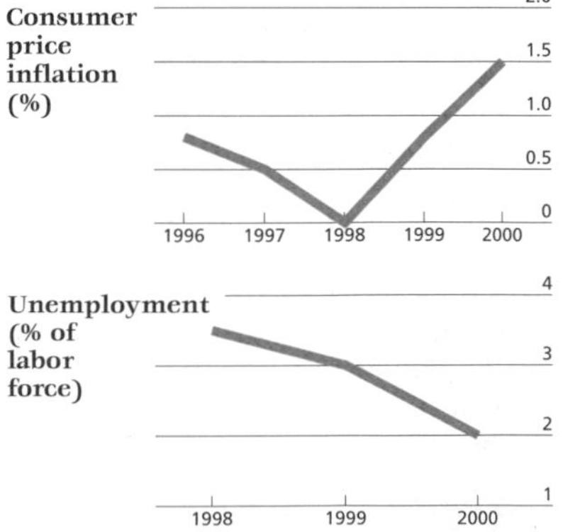

After almost a decade of stagnation, GDP growth rose from 1.7% in 1997 to 3.5% in

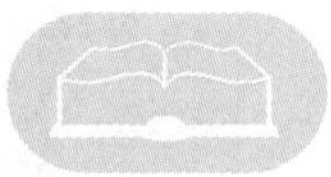

2000. The recovery was led by exports and strong domestic consumption. With the downturn in world markets growth fell to 1.3% in 2001, and is expected to be 0.9% in 2002. Inflation fell from the recession peak of 5.9% in 1991 to zero in 1998 before picking up in 1999 to reach 1.5% in 2000 because of oil price rises and the weakness of the Swiss franc in relation to the dollar. It was 1.4% in 2001 and is expected to stay at this level in 2002. Unemployment fell from a high of 5.4% in spring 1997 to 2% in 2000, rising to 2.2% in 2001. It is expected to be 2.4% in 2002.

Geography/Resources

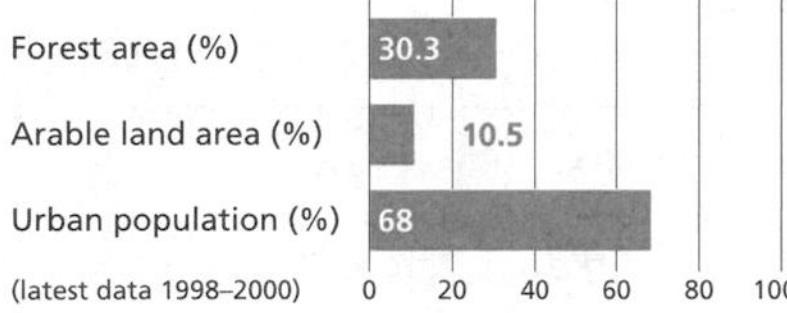

A small country in Central Europe, Switzerland borders France in the west, Germany in the north, Austria and Liechtenstein in the east, and Italy in the south. Two-thirds of the land is mountainous, with the Jura range in the west and north and the Alps across the center and south. There are many lakes, and the River Rhine has its source in Switzerland. The main cities and industry are in the northern plain between the mountain ranges. The climate is wet with cold winters and mild summers. Many peaks are snow-capped all year round and there are 140 glaciers.

Agriculture is varied. Dairy products have international renown. Meat, sugar beet, cereals, potatoes, vegetables, fruit, and wine are also important. Forestry provides construction and fine timbers, pulpwood, and fuel wood. There are few mineral resources, rock salt being the main one, with small amounts of natural gas.

The country is densely populated with 479 people per square mile. Most are urban, and the main cities are Zurich (1.2 million inhabitants), Geneva and Basel (800,000 each), Bern and Lausanne (600,000 each), and St Gallen and Luzern (500,000 each). There are four language and cultural groups. German is spoken in 74% of the territory (in the north, center and east), French in 20% (in the west), Italian in 5%, and Romansch in 1% (in the south). Nearly 20% of the population are of non-Swiss origin.

Communications/Energy

There are 45,000 miles of roads, including 1,000 miles of motorways. Motorway construction of a further 124 miles will be

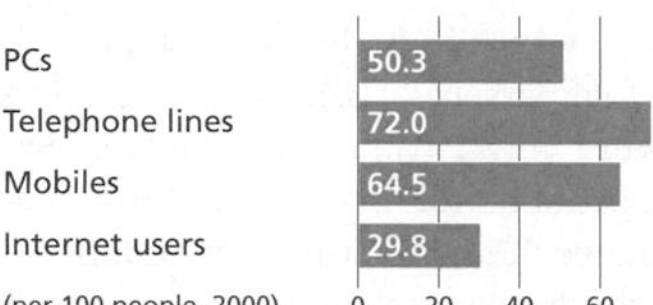

completed in 2010. The 10.5-mile St Gotthard road and rail tunnel provide main European transport links to and from Italy, but transit trucks are subject to weight, quota, and tax restrictions for environmental and safety reasons. The state railways network comprises 1,808 miles, almost all of which is electrified. An additional 1,243 miles of short-distance mountain railways are operated by 56 private companies. The pipeline network includes 195 miles for crude oil and 936 miles for natural gas. There are three international airports at Zurich, Geneva and Basel. Barge traffic on the Rhine and canals carries freight, while lake steamers carry passengers. Basel is a busy freight-handling port with bonded warehouses and integrated facilities for shipment by road, rail, and waterway. The majority of freight is transported by road (56%), followed by rail (34%), and oil and gas pipelines (9%). Nearly 80% of passengers travel by car, with 14% traveling by rail and 2% by air.

Long-distance and international phone costs have fallen since competition was introduced in the late 1990s. However, local calls remain the preserve of Swisscom, and costs are relatively high. Cablecom is the largest provider of cable TV services. At end-2000 there were 5.2 million fixed phone lines and 4.6 million mobile phones, and 95% of the population had access to cable TV. There were 3.5 million Internet users at mid 2001. E-commerce is increasing rapidly.

Switzerland relies on imports for over 80% of energy requirements, oil accounting for more than 60% of energy demand. Switzerland is a net exporter of electricity, mainly to Italy. Net exports doubled in 1999. Hydro generated 61% of electricity output in 1999, nuclear 35%, and conventional thermal power stations 4%. The government has launched a program for energy savings and environmental protection, which includes research projects and "green" taxes.

Education/Employment

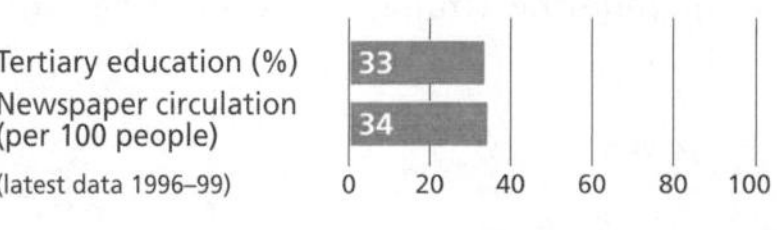

Education is compulsory from age 7 to 16. Responsibility and funding for public higher education is shared between the cantons and the federal government. Closer cooperation has been promulgated in recent years. There are two federal institutes of technology at Zurich and Lausanne, 10 cantonal universities, and numerous colleges specializing in technology, business, social sciences, art, and music. Vocational and technical training has been strengthened since the late 1990s. There were 154,838 students in higher education in 1999–2000. Grants and loans are provided by the cantons for Swiss students and established resident foreign students. Private companies provide a high level of on-the-job training.

Of the $6 billion invested annually in R&D, 70% comes from private industry and 25% from the federal and cantonal authorities. Switzerland participates in the EU framework R&D program. Other funding for R&D comes from non-profit organizations. Most universities and colleges have a technology transfer unit for links with industry. The two federal technical institutes conduct research. Company-based R&D is highly internationalized, with 40% of researchers coming from abroad. Particular strengths are chemicals, pharmaceuticals, biotechnology, medical equipment, precision instruments, electronics, electrical engineering, machine tools, and motor vehicles.

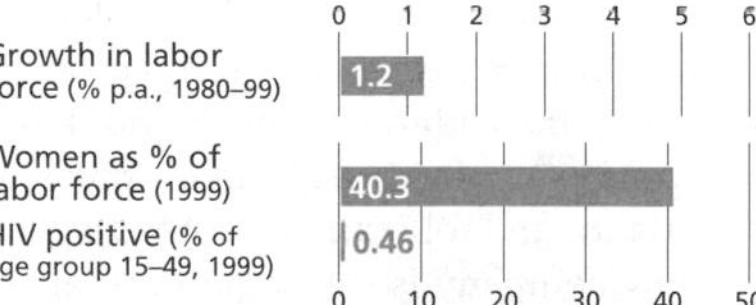

The labor force is well educated and motivated, and multilingual. Absenteeism is low and strikes almost unknown. A large number of managers have international business experience. Foreigners account for one-quarter of the total labor force. Wages are negotiated individually between employer and employee, or by collective agreement with trade unions. About half of private-sector employees are covered by collective agreements. The main laws and rules governing employment are the Labor Law, Law on Sickness and Accident Insurance, Law on Labor Contracts, the Code of Obligations, and collective agreements negotiated between unions and employers. Conditions are broadly similar to those in other European countries.

Fiscal/Financial

The two main banks are world players. UBS was the result of a merger of two of the

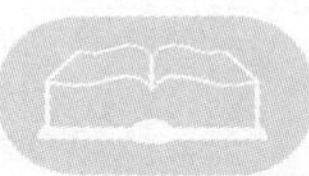

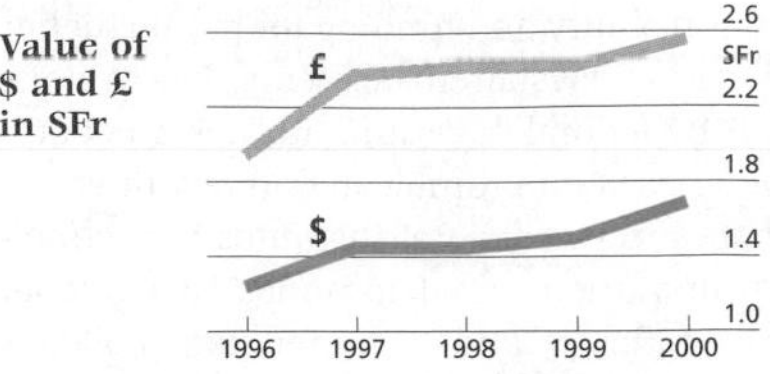

largest three in 1998, Union Bank of Switzerland and Swiss Bank Corporation. Crédit Suisse First Boston (CSFB) also absorbed other Swiss banks in the 1990s. Both UBS and CSFB have bought other international banks. The Raiffeisen (agricultural cooperative) banks have the largest number of branches, 582 in 1999. The main insurance companies are among the largest in the world. They include Swiss Re, Zurich group, and Winterthur Schweizerische Versicherungs-Gesellschaft (part of Crédit Suisse). The Swiss National Bank is the monetary authority and central bank. Supervision of the finance sector is provided by the Federal Banking Commission.

Maximum overall corporate tax is less than 26%, maximum personal income tax is 21.1%, wealth tax is less than 1%, withholding tax on income from financial assets is 35%, and the standard rate of VAT is 7.6% (2.3% on goods for personal consumption). Taxes are levied at the federal, cantonal, and municipal levels. There are three types of corporation in the tax regime: operating company (with activities in Switzerland); holding company (either engaged solely in the management of other companies, or combining this with operations); and domiciliary company (with registered offices in Switzerland and operations abroad). The operating company is subject to normal tax at all three levels. The holding company is eligible for tax relief or exemption at all three levels. The domiciliary company is subject to normal federal tax and exemption or relief at cantonal and municipal levels.

In the 1990s the banking sector underwent significant consolidation, with the number of banks shrinking by 247 to 375 by end-2000. Over 100 financial institutions are foreign-owned. Apart from the two large global banks, there are 24 public-sector cantonal banks specializing in savings and mortgages, private-sector regional banks also specializing in savings and mortgages, the Raiffeisen and Vaudoise rural cooperative banks, private banks specializing in portfolio management, finance companies, foreign banks, and specialized financial institutions, which include the postal check system. Total assets of the Swiss banking system were SFr2.1 trillion at end-2000. Securities portfolios for private banking customers totaled SFr3.7 billion, 55% for foreign and 45% for domestic accounts. Swiss-based banks offer a sophisticated range of business finance instruments. Lending rates are relatively low because of the high level of savings in Switzerland. All types of international trade and investment financing are provided. Private banking is available to corporations and individuals. Secrecy laws can be suspended if there is suspicion of money-laundering or tax fraud. By contrast, tax evasion is not a crime under Swiss law although there is pressure from the European Union for this to change. Information disclosure rules have been tightened following the September 11, 2001 terrorist attacks on the United States and the subsequent search for subversive networks and finance.

The Swiss Stock Exchange is among the top ten world securities exchanges. In 1988 the exchange established the Swiss Options and Financial Futures Exchange, which it transformed ten years later into the largest European derivatives exchange, Eurex, which it owns 50:50 with the Deutsche Börse. In the late 1990s the Swiss Exchange set new rules for small high-growth companies to reduce the cost of listing. In mid-2001 it joined a consortium including UBS, Crédit Suisse and London's Tradepoint to launch Virt-x, a pan-European stock exchange based in London. Some Swiss blue-chip securities are traded through Virt-x.

Business Opportunities

About a quarter of the country, especially western Switzerland, has been designated an economic renewal area, where new businesses qualify for tax reductions or exemptions for up to ten years, financial guarantees of up to one-third of the total project cost for eight years, and interest subsidies on loans of up to one-third of total project cost for up to five years. In addition, grants are available for job creation and training of existing or new staff, and for R&D projects. Location: Switzerland is the contact point for investment assistance and advice (see below).

The top foreign investor in 1997–99 was the United States, followed by the Netherlands, Germany, and France. Other investors include the United Kingdom, Belgium, Japan, Israel, and many other countries. The main investment category in 1997–99 was finance and holding companies, followed by banks, trade, electronics, energy, precision instruments, chemicals, insurance, metals, and machinery. Other sectors attracting foreign investment include hotels, private education, and health services. All these sectors, and the liberalization of electricity and communications, offer further investment opportunities.

For More Information

Books:

Benini, Aldo Albert. *Modern Switzerland* (Comparative Societies Series). New York: McGraw-Hill, 1998.
Butler, Michael, Malcolm Pender, and Joy Charnley, eds. *The Making of Modern Switzerland 1848–1998*. New York: Palgrave Macmillan, 2000.
Economist Intelligence Unit. *Country Profile and Quarterly Reports.* London.
IMF Country Report. *Switzerland.* Washington, D.C.
OECD Economic Surveys. *Switzerland.* Paris: OECD.
State Secretariat for Economic Affairs. *The Advantages of the Swiss Tax System* (annual). Berne.
State Secretariat for Economic Affairs. *Handbook for Investors: Doing Business in Switzerland* (annual). Berne.
State Secretariat for Economic Affairs. *Your Pocket Business Guide to Switzerland.* Berne.
Steinberg, Jonathan. *Why Switzerland?.* 2nd ed. New York: Cambridge University Press, 1996.

Web Sites:

Government entry point: **www.admin.ch**
Location: Switzerland: **www.locationswitzerland.ch**
State Secretariat for Economic Affairs: **www.seco-admin.ch**
Swiss Federal Statistical Office: **www.statistik.admin.ch**
Swiss National Bank: **www.snb.ch**
Swiss Radio International (information site): **www.swissinfo.org**
Swiss Stock Exchange: **www.swx.com**

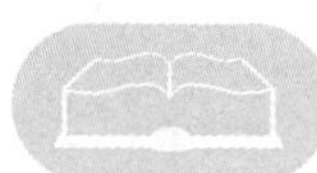

Syria

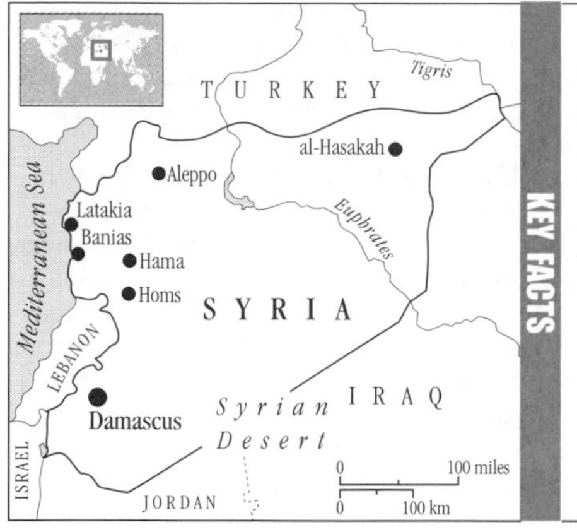

KEY FACTS

GNI: **$15,172 million; world's 77th**
GNI pc: **$970; world's 135th**
Head of government: **prime minister**
Currency: **Syrian pound (S£)**
Capital: **Damascus**
Population: **15,725,000**
Land area: **70,965 square miles**
Population density: **222 per square mile**
Life expectancy: **69 years**
Infant mortality: **25 per 1,000 live births**
Language: **Arabic, Kurdish in the north**
Best buy: **carpets, fine textiles, copper, silver, gold, glassware**

Economic Structure

Syria had one of the earliest civilizations, with achievements in science, engineering, and the arts. It was one of the key centers of early Islamic society. It came under Turkish rule during the Ottoman Empire. From 1922 until independence in 1946 it was ruled by France. After a series of military coups, the Ba'ath Arab Socialist Party came to power with military backing in 1963 and has remained in power since then. The main industries, agricultural sectors and services—including oil, cotton, wheat, banking and insurance—were nationalized in the 1960s and remain under state control. From the 1970s the development of oil resources, and financial aid from wealthier Arab oil states (and until 1991 from the Soviet Union), for Syria's strategic role against Israeli expansion allowed for industrial expansion. Israel's occupation of the Golan Heights since 1967, the invasion of Lebanon by Israel in 1982, and continuing violence in the Israeli border area has kept Syria on a war footing. Syria opposed Iraq during the 1990–91 Gulf War, but has re-established good relations since then. In 1997 the UN approved Syria as a transshipment point for authorized trade with Iraq. Syria and Lebanon have an effective customs union from 2002. Free trade with other Arab countries is progressing, as is a free trade agreement with the European Union. Syria is subject to U.S. sanctions, accused by the U.S. of sponsoring terrorism despite its cooperation with Western governments since the September 11, 2001 terrorist attacks on the United States.

Services contributed 41.1% of GDP in 2000, followed by industry (including manufacturing, mining, utilities, and construction 32.8%) and agriculture (26.1%). Trade is the main services sector, followed by transport and communications, government services, and finance, insurance, real estate and business services. Manufacturing accounted for 29.2% of GDP. Chemicals and oil refining are the main manufacturing industries, followed by food, beverages, and tobacco; textiles, clothing, and leather goods; metal goods, machinery, and transport equipment; and non-metallic minerals processing. Crude oil and refined oil products were the top export in 2000 (66%), followed by agricultural produce, especially vegetables, raw cotton, and wheat (16.4%), and manufactured goods, especially textiles (4%). Other exports included raw phosphates. The main export market in 1999 was Italy, followed by France, Turkey, Saudi Arabia, Spain, and Lebanon. The EU absorbs around half of exports.

The government has no privatization program. Laws in 1985 and 1986 encouraged private-sector investment in tourism and joint-venture agricultural initiatives. The 1991 Investment Law promoted private joint-venture investment in all sectors, offering the same incentives to local and foreign investors; it also limited competition with state industries. In 2000 amendments to this law offered improved terms, and private-sector banks were authorized.

Economic Policy

The economy is centrally planned, and is isolated from external pressures by strict limits on foreign currency and controlled domestic prices, including subsidies on essential items. Although the total foreign debt was 127.6% of GDP in 2000, 66% of the debt was in bilateral transfers, mostly from other Arab states. The trade balance is con-

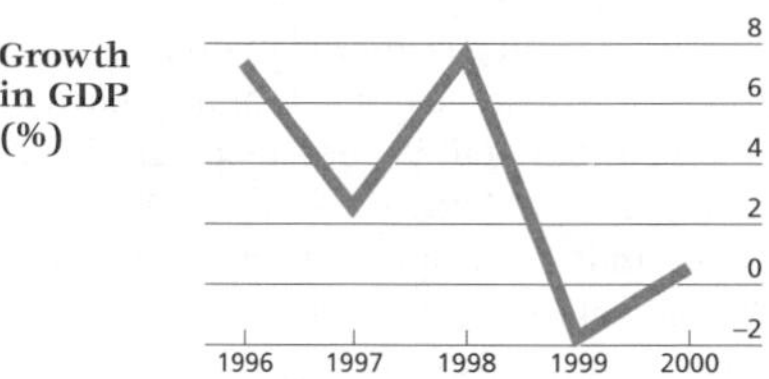

sistently in surplus because of oil exports, but reserves are dwindling. Banking and investment laws in 2000 and the 2001–05 development plan give more momentum to change, especially in the financial sector. Private-sector investment will provide the key to job creation for the young, fast-growing population.

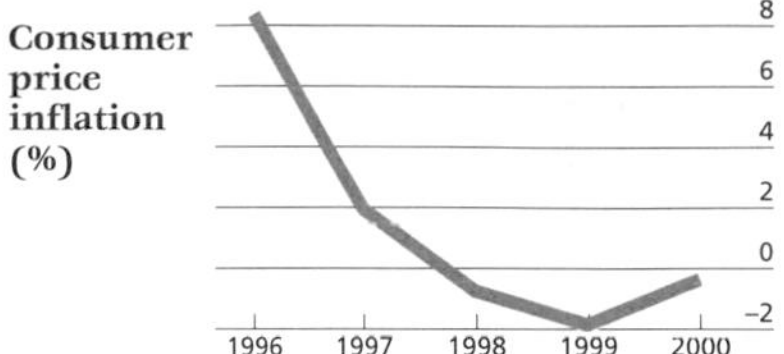

Annual average GDP growth was 5.8% in 1990–2000, with a lower rate in 2001. GDP growth is dependent on oil and agricultural prices, both of which are subject to large fluctuations. Inflation fell from 19.4% in 1990 to 1.1% in 2000, following 2.1% deflation in 1999. Unemployment was officially estimated at 9.5% in 2000, but private-sector economists gave an estimate of 15–20%.

Geography/Resources

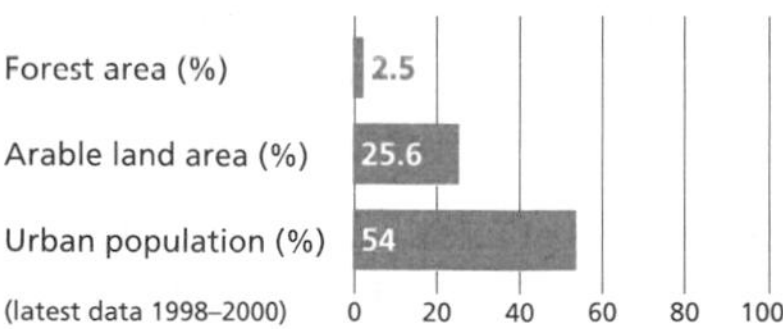

Syria borders the Mediterranean Sea, Turkey, Iraq, Jordan, Israel, and Lebanon. Mountains with a high point of 9,233 feet dominate the west, separating the narrow coastal plain from the interior, much of which is desert plateau. Drought is a problem. The River Euphrates in the north is the main source of water for irrigated agriculture. Around 90% of the population are of Arab origin, with Kurdish and Armenian minorities. Nearly 40% of the population is under age 15.

The main agricultural crops are wheat, cotton, vegetables, sugar beet, fruit, and legumes. Cereals, cotton and sugar beet are produced on the Euphrates plain, while fruit

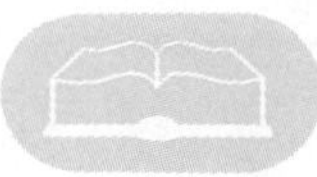

and vegetables are grown at the coast. Chickens are the main livestock, followed by sheep, goats, and cattle. Meat, dairy, wool, and leather are produced.

Petroleum and gas are the main minerals, with proven reserves of 2.5 billion barrels and 8.5 trillion cubic feet respectively at January 2001. There have been no major new oil finds for around a decade, although 60% of potential structures remain unexplored. Syria also produces a significant volume of phosphates, and lesser amounts of rock salt and natural asphalt. There are reserves of iron ore, coal, marble, gypsum, chrome, and manganese.

Communications/Energy

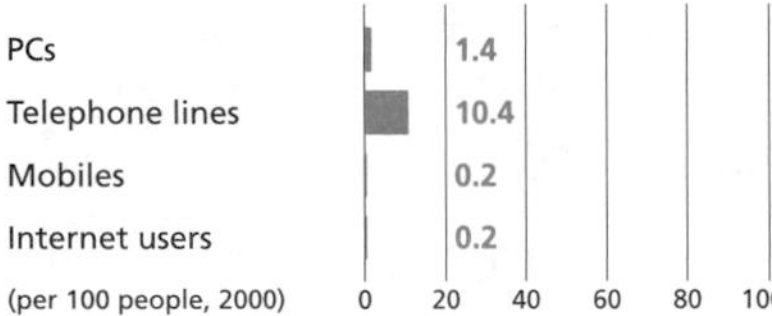

The road network of 25,969 miles in 1998, most of which was asphalted, is being expanded and upgraded. The rail network is 1,709 miles. An express rail service was inaugurated between Amman and Damascus in 1999. Rail links with Iraq were restored in 2000. The pipeline network—which includes 810 miles for crude oil and 320 miles for refined oil products—is being expanded, with a gas pipeline between Palmyra and Aleppo, and a new crude oil pipeline from Iraq. The main sea port is Latakia, followed by Tartous. The main oil port is Banias. There are international airports at Damascus, Aleppo, and Latakia.

The telecommunications network is undergoing extensive modernization including digital switching, fiberoptic cables, voice and data integration, and greater extension to rural areas to be completed by 2004. Liberalization of mobile telephony began in 2000. At end-2000 there were 1.7 million fixed phone lines and 30,000 Internet users. At mid-2001 there were 90,000 mobile phone subscribers.

Oil accounted for 65% of energy consumption in 1999 and gas for 25%. Oil production was 530,000 barrels per day in 2000, with consumption at 255,000 barrels per day and net exports at 276,000 barrels per day. Syria imports oil from Iraq to the value of an estimated $1 billion a year. Gas production and consumption was 213 billion cubic feet in 1999. In 1999 fossil fuels accounted for 57.6% of electricity output, with hydro contributing the rest. The River Euphrates, the main source of hydro power, is also harnessed by Turkey where the river originates. Grid links with Jordan and Egypt were established in 2001, and links with Turkey and Lebanon were due for completion in 2002, with Iraq to follow in 2003.

Education/Employment

Education is compulsory from age 6 to 12. There are four universities at Damascus, Aleppo, Latakia, and Homs, which concentrate on engineering and medicine. Agricultural and technical schools deliver vocational training. In 1996–97 there were 167,186 university students, 48,548 students in other higher education institutes, and 92,622 students in vocational training. Several thousand students pursue higher education abroad. The Ministry of Higher Education is responsible for higher education. Most higher education is public-sector, but private institutes were authorized in 2001.

The labor force is well-educated. Wages and other employment conditions in the public sector are set mainly by the government, but trade unions participate in setting minimum wages for different industry sectors. Private-sector wages are influenced by the public sector. Workers' and trade unions monitor compliance with health and safety and other employment conditions.

Fiscal/Financial

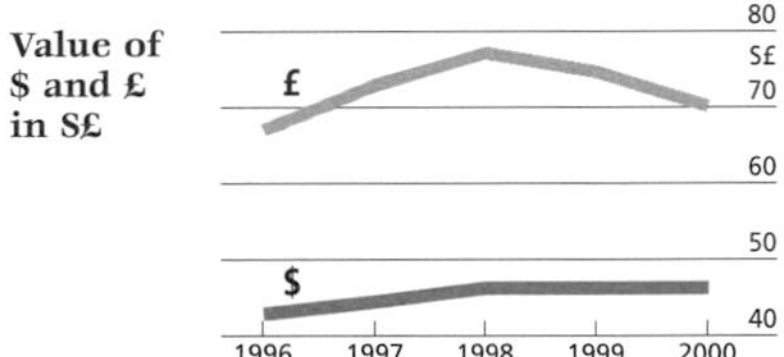

The Commercial Bank of Syria provides most trade financing. In early 2002 it was the only authorized source of foreign exchange along with the Central Bank of Syria, which oversees the financial sector. People's Credit Bank provides banking to the services sector and individuals. Agricultural Cooperative Bank, Industrial Bank, and Real Estate Bank provide investment and other finance for these sectors. Syrian General Organization for Insurance is the only insurance company. All are state-owned. At mid-2001 two private-sector Lebanese banks offered banking services, and five others had representative offices in the Damascus free zone. The tax system is complex, and collection haphazard.

A 2001 law allows private-sector banks and public-private joint ventures to operate in the general market on condition that they have 51% Syrian ownership. These banks will be subject to 25% profits tax. The law allows banking secrecy. Another 2001 law provides for the creation of a stock exchange in cooperation with the Syrian Federation of Chambers of Commerce. Other reforms in the 2001–05 plan include the creation of a new investment bank and a currency exchange company, and the modernization of existing banks and the insurance company.

Business Opportunities

Foreign exchange restrictions and the rigidity of the banking sector have been major disincentives to investors. The easing of currency restrictions for oil and gas exploration companies in the late 1990s and for general investors (including guaranteed repatriation of profits and capital for foreign investors and greater access to foreign exchange for Syrians) under the 2000 investment law amendments, the creation of seven free zones, and the authorization of private-sector banks establish a much improved investment climate.

Tax incentives are available to investors. The Higher Council for Investment vets investment projects. From 1991 to 2001 1,783 investment projects worth S£341 billion were approved, but less than half of these (in value) had been established. Oil, gas, chemicals, food processing, engineering, light manufacturing, transport, trade, hotels, and banking have attracted investment from the United States, Netherlands, the United Kingdom, Germany, France, Japan, Switzerland, Lebanon, and Saudi Arabia among other countries, and from expatriate Syrians. Further opportunities exist in these sectors and in the liberalization of telecommunications, electricity, and higher education.

For More Information

Books:

Kienle, Eberhard. *Contemporary Syria: Liberalization between Cold War and Peace*. New York: St. Martin's Press, 1996.

Mannheim, Ivan. *Syria and Lebanon Handbook*. 2nd ed. Bath, Somerset: Footprint Handbooks, 2001.

Syria Business and Investment Opportunities Yearbook. 3rd ed. Washington, D.C.: International Business Publications, 2001 (annual).

Web Sites:

Government entry point:
www.syriagate.com

Ministry of Economy and Foreign Trade:
www.syrecon.org

TAIWAN

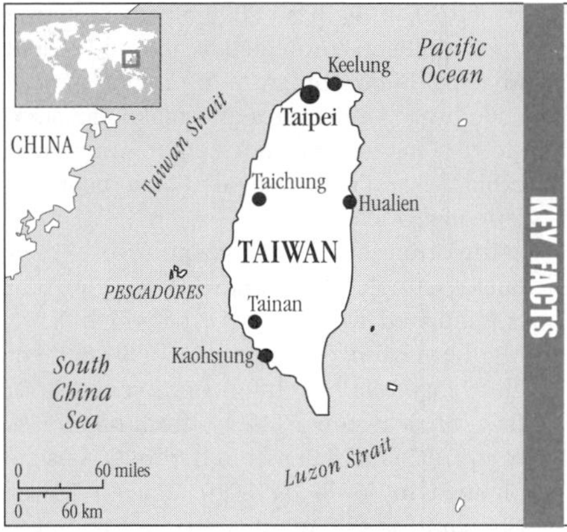

KEY FACTS

GNI: **$290,500 million; world's 17th**
GNI pc: **$13,235; world's 44th**
Head of state: **president**
Head of government: **premier**
Currency: **new Taiwan dollar (NT$)**
Capital: **Taipei**
Population: **22,113,300**
Land area: **13,967 square miles**
Population density: **1,583 per square mile**
Life expectancy: **75 years**
Infant mortality: **6 per 1,000 live births**
Language: **Mandarin Chinese**
Best buy: **jade, ceramics , electronic goods, textiles**

ECONOMIC STRUCTURE

Composition of GDP (1999)

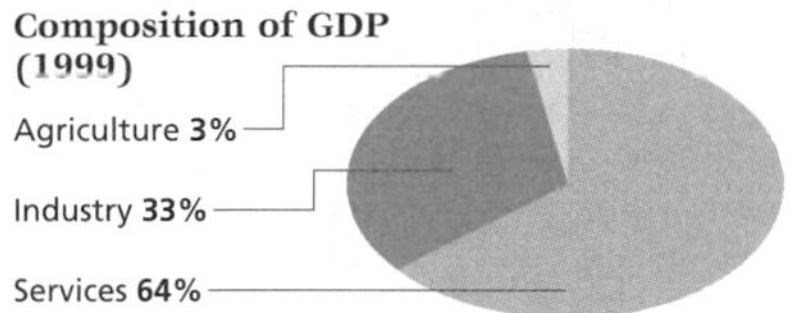

Taiwan became a world trading nation in the 17th century as a result of Spanish and Dutch traders. The Chinese ousted the Dutch colonists in 1662 but ceded the island to Japan in 1895. In 1945 Taiwan became part of China again, until the nationalist Chinese government was ousted by the Communists and formed a separate republic in Taiwan in 1949. U.S. aid underpinned the agrarian reform and industrialization of the 1950s and 1960s aimed at self-sufficiency in basic goods. Labor-intensive export industries followed. In the 1980s and 1990s high-technology industries and services were developed. Taiwan diversified its export markets in the 1990s away from dependence on the United States. Although not officially recognized by most of the international community because of mainland China's refusal to acknowledge its independent sovereignty, Taiwan has become one of the world's leading industrial trading nations. Taiwan joined the World Trade Organization (WTO) in January 2002, following China's membership in late 2001. This provides an opening for better relations between the two countries, and eventual integration of Taiwan in the international community.

Services accounted for 64% of GDP in 1999, industry for 33%, and agriculture for 2.6%. Finance, insurance and real estate are the main services sectors, followed by commerce. Taiwan has a significant feature film industry. The main manufacturing and export industry is computer hardware, with Taiwan ranking third in the world after the United States and Japan. Other electronics, machinery, chemicals, cars, and textiles are important industries. Taiwan supplies around half of world demand for notebook computers, monitors, motherboards, and scanners; machinery and electrical equipment accounted for 53.5% of exports in 2000, followed by textiles (10.3%), base metal products (9.1%), and plastic and rubber goods (5.2%). Other exports include transport equipment, furniture, and fish, especially tuna and eels. The top export market in 2000 was the United States (23.5%), followed by Hong Kong (for China, as direct trade is prohibited, 21.1%), Japan (11.2%), and Germany and Netherlands (3.3% each). Small and medium-sized companies account for 50% of exports, almost 80% of jobs, and 98% of registered firms.

Current account balance ($ billion)

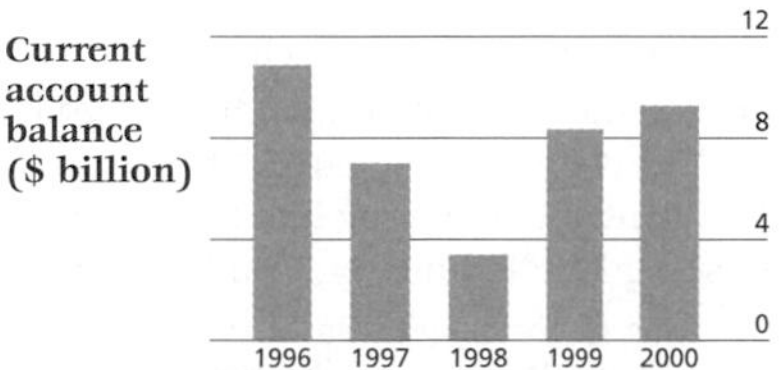

The government exerts a strong influence on the economy through its multi-annual development plans. The main utilities, telecommunications, transport operators, and infrastructure firms are state-owned, but there is liberalization in power generation and telecommunications. Railways and air transport are shared by state and private companies. In late 1999, following two earthquakes, public/private finance was proposed for rebuilding transport infrastructure. By mid-2001 the government reduced its equity to below 50% in 23 entities, including nine banks, three insurance companies, a steel mill, and a fertilizer firm. Further privatizations are planned in the energy, tobacco, wine, rail transport, insurance, and telecommunications sectors.

ECONOMIC POLICY

Growth in GDP (%)

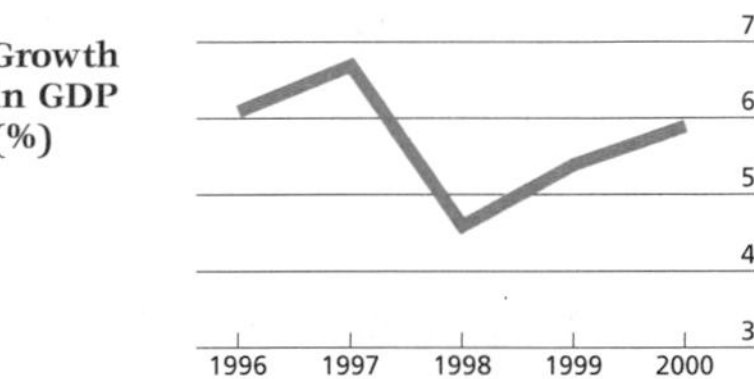

For over 30 years the government has focused policy on maximizing export revenues and foreign exchange reserves. Taiwan built up large trade and financial surpluses with the United States during the 1960s. From the 1970s these reserves enabled the government to issue bonds to pay for economic development, and financial aid from the United States ceased. Prudent financial management and strict control over the domestic economy through monetary and fiscal measures since then have led to sustained economic growth, low inflation, low unemployment, rapid modernization, and rising prosperity. Government bonds made Taiwan Asia's second-largest money market. The Taiwanese government is now an aid donor within the Asian Development Bank, one of the few international organizations it has been able to join. Taiwanese entrepreneurs are significant outward investors, especially in mainland China to which Taiwanese companies switched their labor-intensive light manufacturing operations in the 1990s. The main challenge for economic policy is to adapt to a free international market. Interest rates were fully liberalized in 1989. Limits on foreign capital flows were eased in 1999. As WTO rules are phased in, Taiwan's plethora of small firms and banks will begin to face the full force of international competition, not least from mainland China.

Consumer price inflation (%)

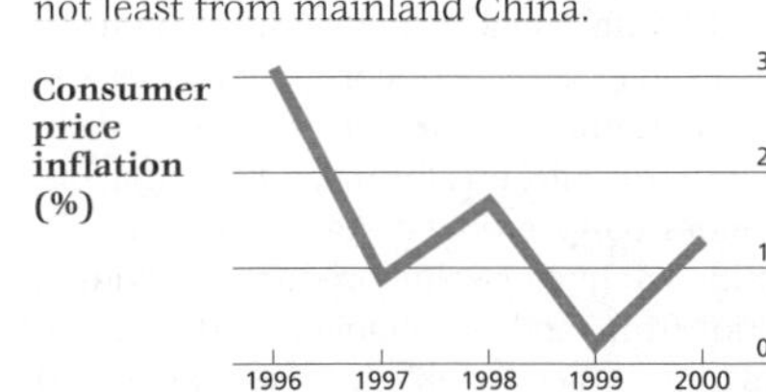

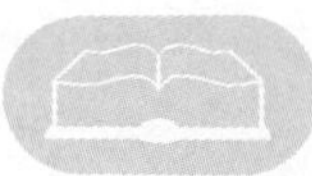

Average annual GDP growth was 5.9% in 1990–2001, despite the disruption of the Asian financial crisis in 1998 and earthquakes in 1999. Reconstruction following the earthquakes diverted government money from other infrastructure projects, but private-sector finance was sought to fill the gap. The public debt remained low at 26% of GDP in 2000 but almost double the 1990 level of 13.6%. With weaker export and domestic demand, GDP growth was below 4% in 2001. Growth is expected to be sluggish in 2002 because of the downturn in export markets. Average annual inflation was 2.2% in 1990–2001. Inflation is expected to be 1.2% in 2002. Unemployment is traditionally low, averaging 2.8% in 1997–2000, rising to 3.8% in 2001.

Geography/Resources

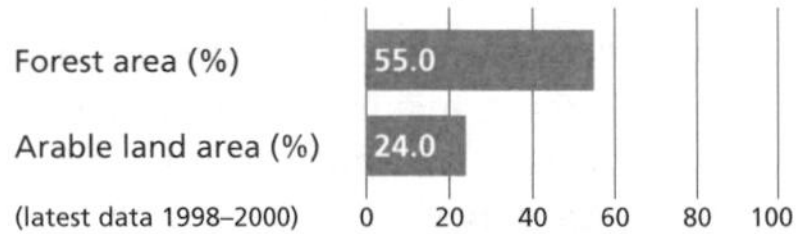

Taiwan consists of one main island and 63 smaller islands in the South China Sea, 137 miles east of China, with Japan to the north and the Philippines to the south. Steep mountains over 3,300 feet in five north-south ranges constitute almost half of the land. There is a coastal plain in the west, which provides valuable agricultural land. The highest peak is Mount Jade at 12,966 feet. Some of the mountains are volcanic, especially the Tatun group overlooking the capital, Taipei. The climate is generally oceanic and subtropical monsoon, with long, hot, humid summers (mean temperature 75–86°F, 80% humidity), and short, mild winters (mean temperature 61°F). The mountain climate is colder. The northeast monsoon brings rain to the north for six months in winter. The southwest monsoon brings rain to the south for five months in summer. Taiwan is hit by three to four typhoons a year from July to September. It is also in an earthquake zone. Two major earthquakes struck in 1999. Almost all of the population are of Han origin (98%), and the remaining 2% are from nine aboriginal tribes and 60 other minority groups.

Rice is the top agricultural crop, followed by betel nuts, sugar cane, peanuts, bamboo shoots, tea, mangoes, corn, watermelons, and sorghum. Pigs are the main livestock, followed by chickens for meat and eggs, and cattle for dairy produce. Agriculture has diversified to higher-value products, including exotic fruit and vegetables and organic foods, to brace itself for tougher world competition as government subsidies are reduced prior to WTO membership. Taiwan is a major fishing nation, with a catch worth $2.8 billion in 1999: 63% from deep-sea fishing, 19% from aquaculture, 15% from offshore fishing, and 3% from coastal fishing. Skipjack tuna and eels were the main species. Mining is a small industry, but significant amounts of marble are produced. Indigenous natural gas, oil, and coal contribute 3% of energy supply. Gas reserves were 2.7 trillion cubic feet and oil reserves 4 million barrels at January 2001. Coal reserves were 1.0 million tons at end-1996. Other minerals extracted include sulfur, dolomite, and salt.

Communications/Energy

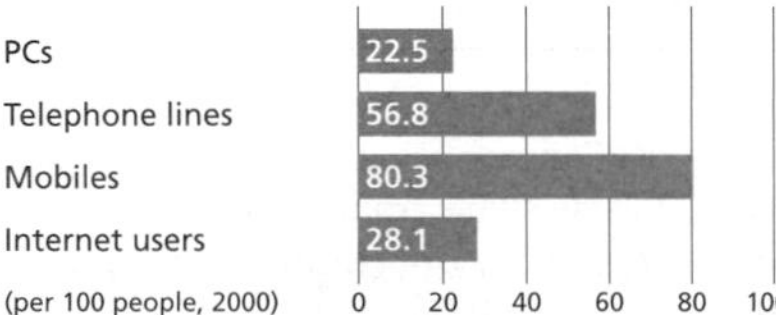

The road network was 12,500 miles in 1998, including around 400 miles of motorways. A further 241 miles of motorway is due for completion in 2003, and another 273 miles is planned. In 1999 1.05 billion people and 350 million tons of freight traveled by road. At end-1999 the rail network was 1,468 miles roughly half operated by Taiwan Railway Administration, and the rest by Taiwan Sugar Corporation and Taiwan Forestry Bureau. Although the last two focus on freight, they also carry passengers. A 211-mile high-speed link between Taipei and Kaohsiung is due for completion in 2003. In 1999 180 million passengers and 16.7 million tons of freight traveled by rail. There are six international sea ports—at Keelung, Suao, Taichung, Hualien, Anping and Kaohsiung—which handled 175.5 million tons of freight in 1999. 112 shipping lines account for most of the merchant fleet, 167 ships over 1,000 grt totaling 4.8 million grt in 2000. Evergreen Marine Corp is the second-largest container shipping line in the world. Kaohsiung handled nearly 7 million teus of containers in 1999, making it the third busiest world container port by volume after Hong Kong and Singapore. There are two international airports, Chiang Kai-shek for Taipei in the north and Kaohsiung in the south, which handled 50.3 million passengers and 1.45 million tons of freight in 1999. There are 15 domestic airports. The government expects domestic air travel to grow by 10% a year to 2005. Domestic and international airports are being expanded.

State-owned Chunghwa Telecom is the dominant company in a partly liberalized telecommunications sector. There were 12.6 million fixed phone lines, 17.9 million mobile phones, and 6.4 million Internet users at end-2000. By June 2000 all trunk phone lines had been connected to fiberoptic cable in a $5.4 billion program to provide nationwide broadband access and make Taiwan a global Chinese Internet center. Integrated cable TV and data networks have been operational since 1997.

Imported fossil fuels account for 97% of energy supply. Total hydropower potential is estimated at 5,047 MW, of which 1,973 MW have been developed. In 1999 38.6% of electricity was generated from coal, 26.6% from nuclear power, 18.4% from oil, 10.2% from LNG, and 6.2% from hydro. Gas use is planned to triple by 2010. Taiwan Power Company is the main electricity operator, but in 1999 six private-sector power stations began operations, and more will come onstream in 2002. Controversy over nuclear power has led to the postponement of privatization of Taiwan Power Company until 2005. In 2000 indigenous oil production was 3,300 barrels per day, while consumption was 782,000 barrels per day and net imports 778,700 barrels per day. In 1999 gas production was 31 billion cubic feet in 1999, with consumption of 220 billion cubic feet and net imports of 203 billion cubic feet, while coal output was 90,720 tons, consumption 40.7 million tons, and net imports 40.6 million tons.

Education/Employment

Education is compulsory from age 6 to 15. Higher education is provided at 36 junior colleges (32 of which are private-sector), 61 independent colleges, and 44 universities. In 1999–2000 994,283 undergraduate and 67,233 graduate students were enrolled. The colleges provide vocational courses. The government provides at least 75% of university funding, with an increasing share of private funds being raised by the universities. Education is under the authority of the Ministry of Education.

The National Science Council promotes scientific and technological development, mostly in academic institutions and its own research centers. Its 2001 budget was $669.4 million: 34% for engineering and applied sciences, 29% for life sciences, 19% for natural sciences and mathematics, and 18% for social sciences. It also funds two high-technology industrial parks at Hsinchu and Tainan, and programs run by private nonprofit research institutes. The Ministry of Economic Affairs funds public/private sector R&D cooperation. Leading companies

have their own R&D centers. R&D strengths include electronics and IT, materials technology, mechanical engineering, chemicals, textiles, energy, aerospace, shipping, and biotechnology.

The labor force is well educated and adaptable. The government has encouraged organizations to negotiate collective agreements covering wages, work hours, layoffs, pensions, compensation for occupational injuries, and procedures for labor complaints and disputes. The employers' federation and trade unions set the minimum wage every August. The key laws are the Labor Union Law, Collective Agreements Law, Settlement of Labor Disputes Law, Labor Insurance Act, Labor Safety and Health Law, and Employment Services Act (against discrimination). The Collective Agreements Law is being amended to make trade unions the sole representatives of workers in collective agreements, with the aim of reducing the number of disputes.

Fiscal/Financial

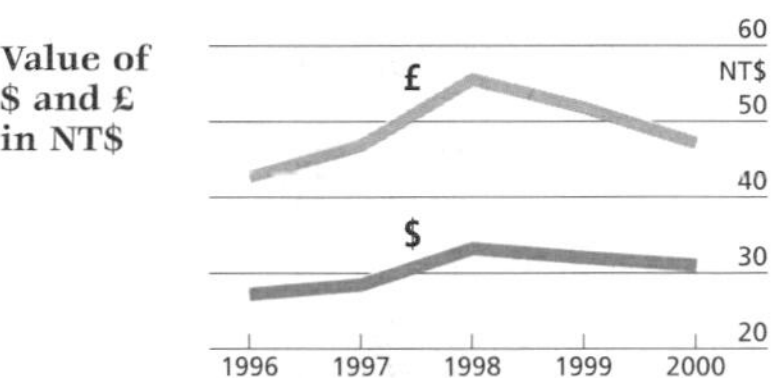

The largest banks by deposits are the state-owned Bank of Taiwan (which was due to merge the third-largest bank Land Bank of Taiwan and state-owned insurance company Central Trust of China in 2001), followed by Taiwan Cooperative Bank, First Commercial Bank, and Chang Hwa Commercial Bank. The Central Bank of China is responsible for monetary policy and issues the currency. The Ministry of Finance supervises the finance sector. The Securities and Futures Commission supervises the stock market. A unified supervisory agency is proposed. Export credit guarantees are provided by the United States, as Taiwan lacks international diplomatic recognition. The top rate of corporation tax is 25% but most companies pay 22%. A 10% surtax is imposed on retained profits. The maximum rate of personal income tax is 40%. Withholding tax on dividends, interest, fees, and royalties is 20%. VAT is applied at 5%.

The finance sector has undergone extensive change since 1987 with the full liberalization of interest rates, the removal of many restrictions on foreign capital and operations, and the reduction of the state banking sector from 61% of total assets (before privatization of nine banks in 1998–99) to 26% held by five banks at end-2000. Financial regulation and supervision have been tightened in line with international standards. The domestic sector will be susceptible to consolidation once the remaining limits on free market operation are lifted, probably after Taiwan joins the World Trade Organization. At end-2000 there were 48 domestic banks, 5 medium business banks, 39 branches of foreign banks, 48 credit cooperatives, 314 credit departments of farmers' and fishermen's associations, the state-owned Postal Savings System, 3 investment and trust companies, 31 life insurance companies, 26 non-life insurance companies, and one central reinsurance corporation. At end-April 2001 there were 69 offshore banking units with total assets of $49.9 billion.

The Taiwan Stock Exchange was established in 1962 to formalize over-the-counter trading in bonds and shares allocated to landlords by the government as part of the 1952 land reform. Computerized trading was introduced in 1988. Futures trading has taken place since 1997. The Taiwan Innovative Growing Entrepreneurs market (TIGER) was launched in April 2000 for small high-tech firms. The TSE had market capitalization of NT$11.8 trillion at end-1999.

It is the second-largest money market in Asia with annual turnover of $1.6 trillion. Limits on foreign portfolio investment were lifted in 2001 except for telecommunications, broadcasting and electricity stocks.

Business Opportunities

Tax and financial incentives are available, with more favorable conditions offered to firms locating in disadvantaged regions and establishing high-tech operations. Foreign ownership of domestic companies is limited in certain sectors, particularly those undergoing privatization, and banned in a few sectors. These restrictions are likely to be lifted after World Trade Organization rules come into effect. In 1952–2000 electronics and electrical appliances manufacturing was the top investment sector ($10.5 billion), followed by finance and insurance ($6.8 billion), trade ($5 billion), chemicals ($3.9 billion) and metals and metal products ($2.3 billion). The top investor was the United States ($10.8 billion), followed by Japan ($9.2 billion), Central America ($6.1 million), Europe ($5.4 billion) and Hong Kong ($3.6 billion). Opportunities continue to exist in these sectors. Liberalization and privatization offer additional opportunities to foreign investors. The point of contact is the Industrial Development and Investment Center.

For More Information

Books:

Asian Development Bank. *Asian Development Outlook 2001.* New York: Oxford University Press, 2001 (annual).
Economist Intelligence Unit. *Country Profile and Quarterly Reports.* London.
Genzberger, Christine, and Edward G. Hinkelman, eds. *Taiwan Business: The Portable Encyclopedia for Doing Business with Taiwan.* Novato, CA: World Trade Press, 1994.
Hughes, C. W. *Taiwan and Chinese Nationalism: National Identity and Status in International Society.* New York: Routledge, 1997.
Kenna, Peggy, and Sondra Lacy. *Business Taiwan: A Practical Guide to Understanding Taiwan's Business Culture.* New York: McGraw-Hill, 1994.
Taiwan Business and Investment Opportunities Yearbook. 3rd ed. Washington, D.C.: International Business Publications, 2001 (annual).

Web Sites:

Central Bank of China (Chinese only): **www.cbc.gov.tw**
Council for Economic Planning and Development: **www.cepd.gov.tw**
Government Information Office: **www.gio.gov.tw**
Industrial Development and Investment Center: **www.idic.gov.tw**
Ministry of Finance: **www.mof.gov.tw**

TANZANIA

KEY FACTS

GNI: **$8,515 million; world's 90th**
GNI pc: **$260; world's 187th**
Head of government: **president**
Currency: **Tanzanian shilling (TSh)**
Capital: **Dar es Salaam**
Population: **32,793,000, growing at 2.8% p.a.**
Land area: **341,160 square miles**
Population density: **96 per square mile**
Life expectancy: **48 years**
Infant mortality: **90 per 1,000 live births**
Language: **Swahili, many African languages**
Best buy: **printed textiles, carvings, jewelry**

ECONOMIC STRUCTURE

For an African country, Tanzania has had unusual political stability, with the same ruling party—known as Chama Cha Mapinduzi (CCM)—remaining in power since independence in mainland Tanganyika in 1961 (in Zanzibar in 1964). For many years the CCM was the only political party in both parts of the country. The first President, Julius Nyerere, was recognized as one of Africa's leading statesmen, and he handed over power to a successor in 1985. After multiparty politics was introduced in 1995 the CCM represented stability and continuity, and won successive elections although its results in the islands of Zanzibar have been strongly contested by the Civic United Front (CUF), leading to recurring political violence on the islands. Despite the moves to broaden democracy, the established authorities in Tanzania have been reluctant to accept change or to take action against corruption.

Agriculture accounts for 46% of GDP and employs most of the work force. Although the country has a wide diversity of crops and growing conditions, severe disruption has occasionally been caused by both drought and floods. There has been very limited diversification of the economy. Tourism is making an increasingly important contribution. The mining and manufacturing industries have not yet realized their potential.

Structural adjustment policies have been applied repeatedly since 1986, although progress in achieving results has been slow. Further radical reforms helped Tanzania to benefit from the Heavily Indebted Poor Countries (HIPC) debt reduction initiative, which came into effect at the end of 2001. Priorities have included reforming the financial system and the agricultural marketing system, and increasing spending on social services. However, government revenues remain limited, and there is a high dependence on donor-financed projects.

The wholesale nationalization of foreign and privately-owned businesses in the 1970s contributed to the country's economic failure in the years that followed. A process of privatization was launched in the 1990s, with the sale of factories, farms, tourist facilities, the telecommunications company, and the major commercial bank to the private sector. Further privatization is anticipated.

ECONOMIC POLICY

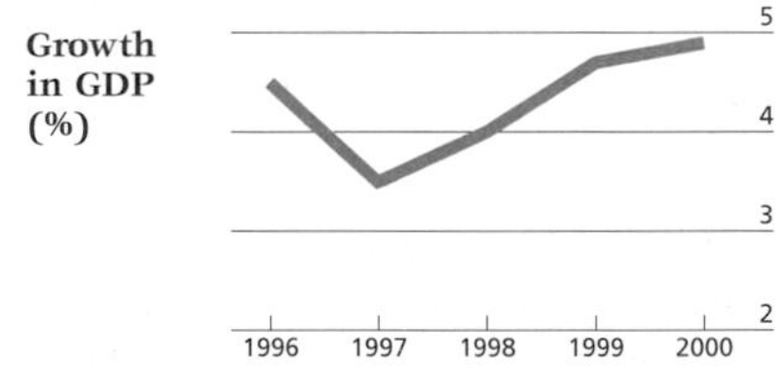

Tanzania is heavily dependent on international aid for its recurrent and capital spending, but has been slow to agree to the conditions accompanying this aid. Under long-term donor pressure, the government eventually reined in its own spending but seemed to have few sources of independent revenue other than foreign aid itself. Under more recent donor pressure in the framework of the government's HIPC negotiations in 2001, the authorities appear to have agreed to allocate the debt service savings towards preventing the further collapse of Tanzania's standards of educational and healthcare provision.

The average GDP growth rate in the late 1990s was about 4% per year. This rose to 4.9% in 2000, when there were reports of an increase in official gold exports and of the beginnings of an improvement in government revenues. The main areas of new investment have been related to the mining industry and a construction boom in Dar es Salaam, but investment in the crucial agricultural sector has been minimal.

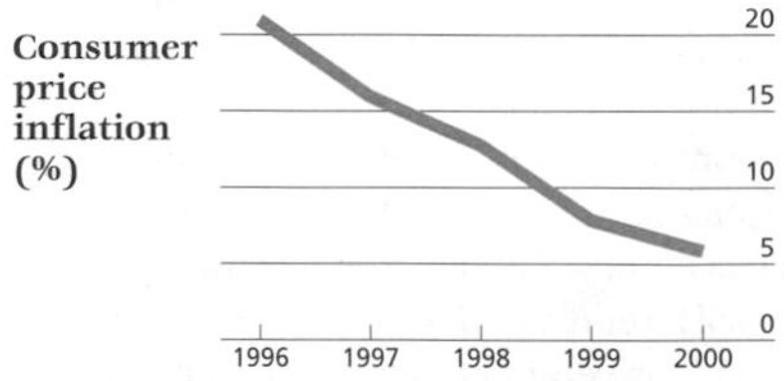

Inflation was brought down from high levels in the mid-1990s to 6% in 2000, and fell to 5.2% in mid-2001.

GEOGRAPHY/RESOURCES

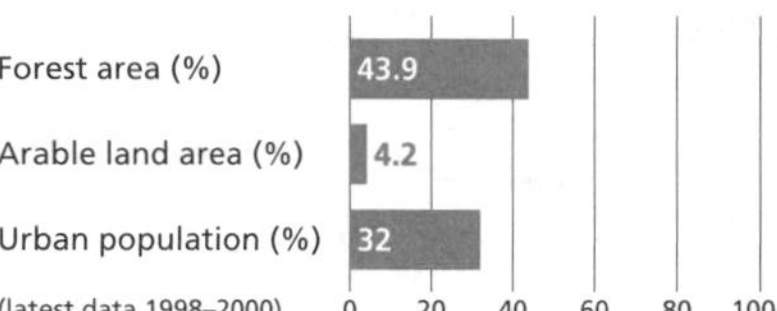

Tanzania stretches from Lake Tanganyika in the west to the Indian Ocean shore in the east and covers a large tropical zone of mountains, valleys, and plains. The mountains include Kilimanjaro, Africa's highest. The largest rivers are the Rufiji, Ruvuma, Ruvu, Wami, and Pangani. Smaller rivers flow into Lakes Tanganyika, Victoria, and Malawi. There are areas of woodland in the south and west of the country, but intense cultivation has changed the natural vegetation in many of the more fertile plateau regions. Game parks and nature reserves cover one-third of the country, and some of these are designated as world heritage sites. Agriculture consists of farming for food and cash crops such as cotton, coffee, cashew nuts, tobacco, tea, and sisal. The most valuable mineral resources include gold, nickel, gemstones, iron ore, coal, and natural gas. Not all of these are exploited, and there is evidence of much greater mineral wealth yet to be developed. The islands of Zanzibar have an area of 950 square miles. Their main resources are fish, and crops such as cloves, copra, seaweed, and food crops. The population of the islands is about 900,000, most of whom adhere to Islam.

Mainland Tanzania has more than 120 different ethnic groups, of which the Sukuma and Nyamwezi are the largest, although no single group constitutes more than 10% of the population. Swahili, a language which originated on the coast, is the national language, spoken by all. In Dar es Salaam and other large towns there is a substantial Asian population. Dar es Salaam is the largest city, with an official population of 1.5 million, although the surrounding semi-urban area is thought to be home to about 10 million people. The other significant towns on the mainland are Mwanza, Tabora, Mbeya, and Tanga.

Communications/Energy

	(per 100 people, 2000)
PCs	0.3
Telephone lines	0.5
Mobiles	0.5
Internet users	0.3

(per 100 people, 2000) 0 20 40 60 80 100

The road transport system is undeveloped, and is confined to a few arterial routes, most them around the periphery of the country, especially in the vicinity of Dar es Salaam and Arusha. A railway system connects Dar es Salaam with the central and northern regions. The Tanzania–Zambia Railway (Tazara) connects Dar es Salaam with Kapiri Mposhi in Zambia, but traffic has declined sharply on this route. There are international airports at Dar es Salaam, Kilimanjaro and Zanzibar, and there are many smaller airfields. Air Tanzania has suffered financial difficulties. The main port at Dar es Salaam serves a number of Tanzania's landlocked neighbors. In 2000, the telecommunications company TTCL was part-privatized, with the sale of 35% of its shares.

The electricity supply company Tanesco may eventually be privatized, but has become controversial because of its management's questionable investment decisions made in the past and because of its persistent failure to ensure reliable power supply to the main towns. Tanesco has not produced a coherent set of investment plans for domestic power provision, although there are numerous potential power sources, including hydroelectric sites, plentiful natural gas, and enormous reserves of coal. The company has preferred to commission plants using aviation fuel and diesel, which have all proved uneconomic and inadequate.

Tanzania imports all its oil needs. Discoveries of offshore natural gas near Pemba and at Songo-Songo have remained undeveloped, although there were reports of a formalization of the investment at the end of 2001. Exploration for oil and gas in coastal offshore areas is continuing.

Education/Employment

The government's efforts to provide free education for all have proved unsustainable. Enrollment in primary schools fell from 68% of the school-age population in 1980 to 48% in 1997. According to government figures, the number attending primary school stood at 5.4 million in 1998, with 300,000 attending secondary schools. Secondary education is provided both by the government and the private sector. About 6,000 students receive higher education at the University of Dar es Salaam.

The agricultural sector is Tanzania's largest source of employment, accounting for the livelihoods of 13 million workers out of a total labor force of 16 million. The industrial sector, located almost entirely in Dar es Salaam, employs about 145,000 workers.

Fiscal/Financial

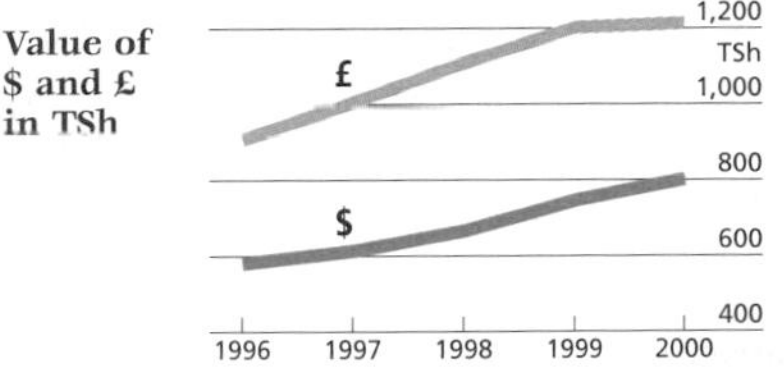

The central bank is the Bank of Tanzania. The largest commercial bank is the National Bank of Commerce, in which a majority stake was sold in 2000 to the South African banking group Absa. Other important institutions are the Cooperative and Rural Development Bank and the National Microfinance Bank. Foreign banks include Standard Chartered, Stanbic, Barclays, and Citibank.

Improvements in the tax environment for foreign business have gradually been introduced, most notably for companies in the mining sector. However, anomalies persist, especially in the administration of taxation between the mainland and Zanzibar, from where many imports are smuggled to the mainland. There has also been a long tradition of corruption in the issue of import duty exemptions.

A stock exchange was launched in Dar es Salaam in 1998 with the listing of four companies. Foreigners are not permitted to invest on the exchange.

Business Opportunities

Investment levels have exceeded $150 million a year in recent years. Investment was stimulated firstly by privatization of the industrial and tourism sectors, and secondly by the discovery of substantial gold reserves in the northwest of the country, where development of new projects has been undertaken largely by Canadian companies. The privatization process is continuing, with 65 companies scheduled for sale by 2003, including Tanzania Railways Corporation, Tanzania Harbors Authority, and the Dar es Salaam Water and Sewerage Authority. The greater involvement of the private sector in all areas of the economy is expected to lead to a construction boom. Tourism is another area of potential investment. The industry experienced a major revival in the 1990s, with the official number of visitors rising from 200,000 in 1992 to more than 600,000 in 1999. Government-owned hotels and lodges were put up for sale in 2000.

For More Information

Books:

Campbell, H., and H. Stein. *Tanzania and the IMF: The Dynamics of Liberalization*. Boulder, CO: Westview Press, 1992.

Forster, P., and S. Maghimbi. *The Tanzanian Peasantry: Further Strides*. Brookfield, VT: Avebury Publishing, 1995.

Hodd, Michael. *East Africa Handbook*. 6th ed. Bath, Somerset: Footprint Handbooks, 1999.

Legum, C., and G. Mmari, eds. *Mwalimu: The Influence of Nyerere*. Lawrenceville, NJ: Africa World Press, 1995.

Tanzania Business and Investment Opportunities Yearbook. 3rd ed. Washington, D.C.: International Business Publications, 2001.

Web Sites:

African news and information: **www.allafrica.com/business**

Ernst and Young investment profiles: **www.mbendi.co.za/ernsty/cyaf.htm**

Norwegian Council for Africa, Index on Africa: **www.afrika.no**

Political Resources on the Net: **www.politicalresources.net**

Tanzania High Commission in London: **www.tanzania-online.gov.uk**

Tanzania Tourist Board: **www.tanzania-web.com**

THAILAND

KEY FACTS

GNI: **$121,051 million; world's 32nd**
GNI pc: **$2,010; world's 103rd**
Head of government: **prime minister**
Currency: **baht (Bt)**
Capital: **Bangkok**
Population: **60,856,000, growing at 1.0% p.a.**
Land area: **197,260 square miles**
Population density: **308 per square mile**
Life expectancy: **69 years**
Infant mortality: **26 per 1,000 live births**
Language: **Thai, Chinese**
Best buy: **silk fabric and goods, textile wallets, coral, jade, jewelry, brass rubbings, orchids**

ECONOMIC STRUCTURE

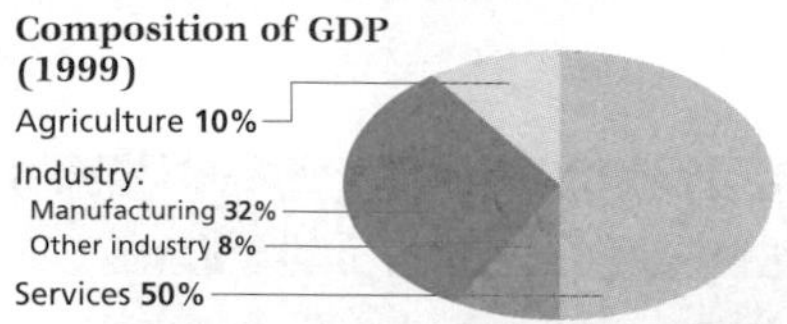

The Kingdom of Thailand was established in the mid-14th century, and has maintained its independence of foreign domination since that time. Industrialization began in the 1960s with the emphasis on import substitution, private-sector ownership, and foreign investment. U.S. involvement in the Vietnam War brought infrastructure investment to Thailand and a boost in tourist-oriented services. Export-oriented labor-intensive industries were the focus of development in the 1980s, leading to an influx of foreign investment and double-digit economic growth. Robust growth continued in the 1990s as industrialization switched to higher technology. However, the trade balance remained chronically negative in both decades, leaving Thailand vulnerable to external shock, which came in the currency crisis of 1997–98. The crisis has been well handled, but essential structural reforms in the financial system, corporate governance, communications infrastructure, and education still have some way to go.

In 2000 services accounted for 49.4% of GDP, followed by industry (including manufacturing, mining, construction and utilities 40.1%) and agriculture (10.5%). The main service industries were trade, followed by transport and communications, finance, and public administration. Tourism is a major industry and foreign exchange earner. There were 9.6 million tourists in 2000, generating $7.1 billion in earnings. In manufacturing, the electronics and automotive industries take the lead. In 1999, 46% of the work force was employed in agriculture. Thailand is the world's top exporter of rice. In 2000 the principal exports were computers (12.2%), followed by textiles (6.8%), integrated circuits (6.5%), and rice (2.4%). The main markets were the United States (21.3%), followed by Japan (14.8%), Singapore (8.7%), and Hong Kong (5%).

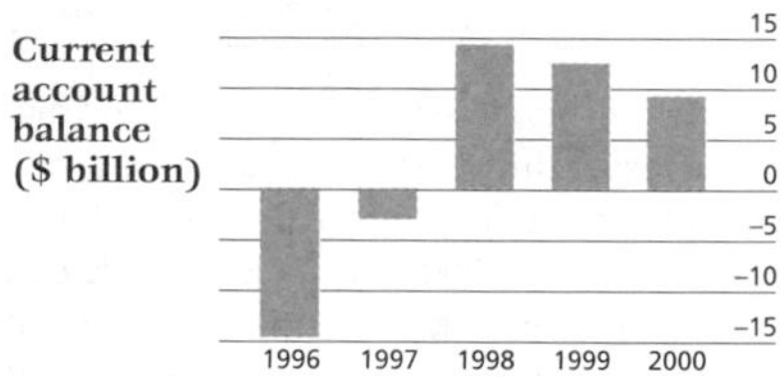

Most direct state ownership of industry is in infrastructure companies, energy, water, telecommunications, and transport. Privatization began in the 1980s but was slow to take effect. As a result of the 1997–98 financial crisis, the government nationalized six banks, but three-quarters of banks remained in private ownership. An agreement with the IMF to privatize 59 state enterprises in 1998–2000 was set back by the crisis and by strong opposition from the workers and from political interests alarmed by the extent of foreign ownership in major Thai companies. Liberalization of the energy and telecommunications sectors is in progress. State companies are being corporatized and restructured to facilitate privatization, and the government has created a holding company for its equity. The government is pursuing a program to sell minority shareholdings in 18 companies in communications, energy, water, transport, tobacco, and finance through the stock exchange in 2001–03.

ECONOMIC POLICY

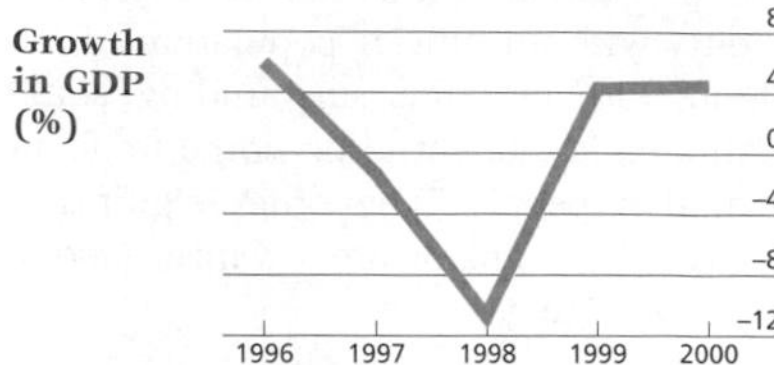

Macro-economic policy is traditionally prudent, geared to fostering economic growth under private-sector ownership. The large trade deficits through the 1980s and the 1990s weakened the baht, and external indebtedness and debt-servicing costs rose. Thus, although strong economic growth and government policy encouraged investment, the financial basis was weak. Pegged to the U.S. dollar, the baht suffered as the dollar strengthened in the mid-1990s, and the government was forced to let it float freely from July 1997. The resulting fall in value led to a large number of non-performing loans, capital flight, and a domino effect on investor confidence elsewhere in Asia, including Thailand's main regional markets. In 1997 the government agreed a financial recovery program underpinned by the IMF, which was successfully concluded in 2000. Reserves were restored to mid-1990s levels by 1999. The balance of payments was in surplus in 1998–2001 for the first time in two decades, and it is expected to remain in surplus in the medium term. Total debt was reduced from $109.3 billion (72.3% of GDP) in 1997 to $70.1 billion (60.2% of GDP) in 2001. The debt service ratio rose from 15.3% of exports to 16.8%.

To restore health to the financial system, the government nationalized ailing banks, closed failing finance companies, and introduced a comprehensive deposit guarantee, requiring banks to recapitalize. It lowered interest rates but reduced the money supply. Bank lending fell, but bank deposits began to recover from 2000. Support for the finance sector increased the public-sector deficit from 2.7% of GDP in 1997 to 5.4% in 2001. The government aims to achieve fiscal balance by 2007, but needs 5% annual GDP growth, 2.7% inflation, and budget spending growth capped at 5% in order to do so.

After average annual GDP growth of 8.5% in 1990–96, GDP went into decline by 1.4%

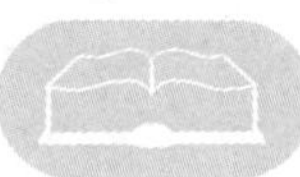

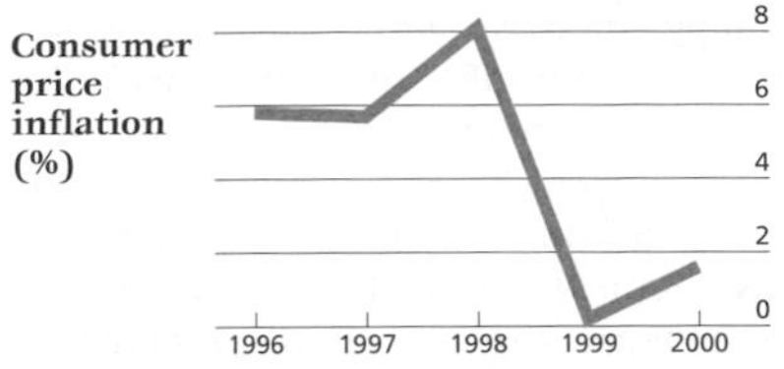

in 1997 and 10.8% in 1998 before recovering with average growth of 4.3% in 1999–2000 and 2% in 2001. It is expected to stay low in 2002 as a result of weak export demand. Inflation was an annual average of 4.9% in 1990–97, rose to 8.1% in 1998 and stagnated at 0.3% in 1999, before rising to 1.5% in 2000 and 2.5% in 2001. Unemployment is traditionally low, and averaged 1.5% in 1990–97. It rose to 4.4% in 1998, falling to 3.6% in 2000.

Geography/Resources

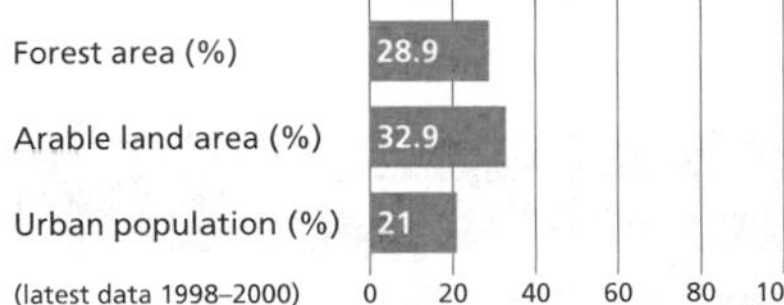

In southeast Asia, Thailand consists of a continental land mass, the Kra isthmus and part of the Malay Peninsula, and several islands. It has land borders with Myanmar to the west and north, Laos to the north and east, Cambodia to the southeast and Malaysia to the south. The eastern coast lies on the Gulf of Thailand and the west on the Andaman Sea. There is a large central plain around the many rivers flowing from the continental land to the Gulf of Thailand. The rest of the country is mountainous, with a high point of 8,452 feet. The climate is tropical, hot and humid with abundant rainfall. The average annual temperature is 84°F. The majority of people are of Thai origin (75%), with a Chinese community of 14% and indigenous communities (11%).

The most important agricultural crop for domestic consumption and export is rice. Sugar cane, cassava, corn, rubber, coconuts, mung beans, pineapples, and bananas are other main crops. Chickens are the main livestock, followed by ducks, cattle, pigs, buffaloes, and goats. Forestry is important, especially fuel wood. Fisheries are significant, with a total catch of 2.9 million tons in 1997. Natural gas, coal, and gypsum are the main minerals. Other minerals produced include petroleum, zinc, lead, iron, fluorite, tin, manganese, antimony, salt, potash, barytes, wolfram, gold, and gemstones. At January 2001 proven reserves of gas and oil were 11.8 trillion cubic feet and 351.6 million barrels respectively. Coal reserves were 2.0 billion tons at end-1996.

Communications/Energy

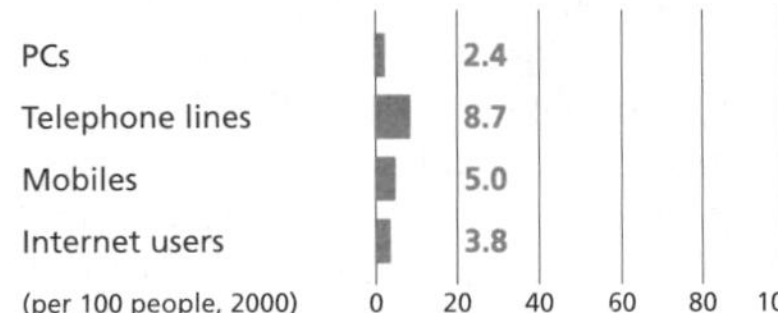

The road network was 31,915 miles in 1999, including 174 miles of inter-city roads, 4,412 miles of primary roads, 6,700 miles of secondary roads, and 20,600 miles of provincial roads. The rail network was 2,512 miles in 1998, including 56 miles of double track. The government has embarked on projects to increase double track by 1,705 miles, and on other upgrading schemes for existing routes. There are plans to build 376 miles of new railways, including a link to China through Laos and Myanmar. The pipeline network included 258 miles for natural gas and 42 miles for petroleum products in 1999. There are 2,500 miles of main navigable waterways. Bangkok and Laem Chabang are the main sea ports, handling 13.2 million and 18 million tons of freight respectively in 2000. The merchant fleet comprised 294 ships over 1,000 grt, with a total displacement of 1.8 million grt in 2000. The main international airports at Bangkok, Chiang Mai, Chiang Rai, Hat Yai, and Phuket handled 33.5 million passengers and 823,476 tons of freight in 1999, 85% of the total. There are two other international airports and 21 domestic commercial airports, and 50 airstrips.

There are submarine cable, satellite, and microwave links for international communications. Investment programs for fiberoptic cable extensions and other communications upgrades were delayed by the recession. At end-2000 there were 5.6 million fixed phone lines, 3.1 million mobile phones, and 2.3 million Internet users.

Natural gas power stations accounted for 36.2% of public-sector electricity generation in 1999, followed by oil (18.4%), coal (17.2%), and hydro (3.8%). Private power companies supplied 22.2% of electricity, and 2.09% was purchased from Laos. Domestic oil output was 171,000 barrels per day, with consumption at 759,000 barrels per day in 2000. Coal production was 17.8 million tons in 2000, and consumption was 20.1 million tons in 1999. Gas production and consumption was 625 billion cubic feet was in 1999. Two major new gas fields will come into production in 2002. Gas is due to play a larger role in power generation.

Education/Employment

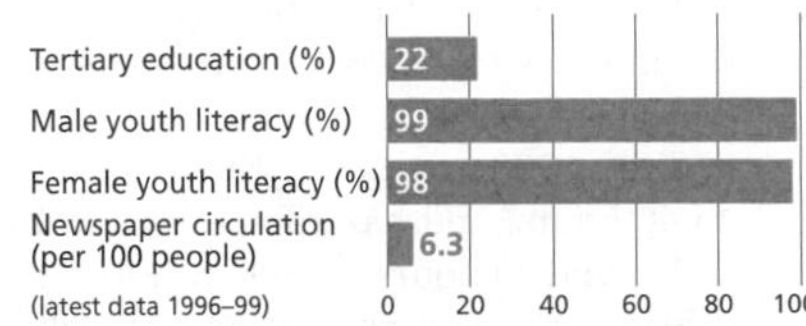

Education is compulsory from age 6 to 15, and Thai children have the right to receive free education to age 18. The literacy rate is high at 94% of the population. The government is making efforts to overcome previous skilled labor shortages resulting from an education system based mainly on rural needs. In 1998 higher education institutes within the responsibility of the Ministry of Education consisted of 409 vocational education centers with 559,658 students, 50 institutes connected with the Rajamangala Institute of Technology with 90,339 students, 11 institutes connected with Mahachulalongkorarajavidyalaya University (7,685 students) and 8 with the Mahamakut Buddhist University (2,264 students). The Ministry of University Affairs is responsible for 24 public-sector universities and 48 private universities. Public universities had 1998 enrollment of 627,237 full-time students and 209,680 students on open university courses. There were 199,464 students enrolled at private universities in 1998. The government is actively encouraging private-sector participation in education. It provides funding and management of public education institutes.

The National Science and Technology Development Agency coordinates the application of R&D policy. It provides grants, soft loans and services—notably testing and quality control—for private-sector and university R&D. A science park at Rangsit has been in operation since 1998, offering facilities for R&D incubator projects and close links between the private sector and university research. R&D strengths include biotechnology, IT, computerized control systems, electric vehicles, and renewable energy.

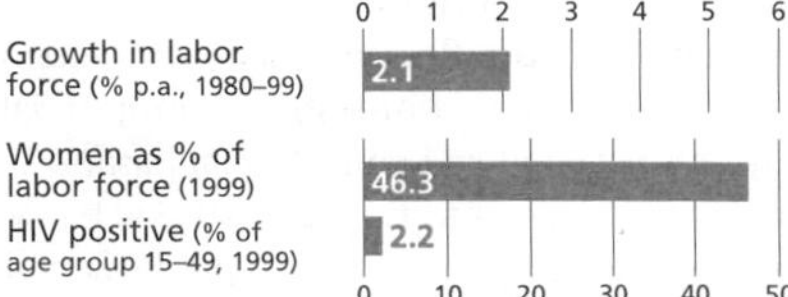

The labor force is hard-working and adaptable, with a variety of skills. However, technical and managerial skills are in short supply. Wages and other employment conditions are determined between employers and employees. Minimum wages are set by

the government and reviewed annually. Only 10% of the industrial labor force is organized, and less than 2% are members of trade unions. The basic labor law was amended in 1998, reducing the working week to 48 hours, and hazardous work to 7 hours a day and 40 hours a week. Minimum annual leave is 6 days plus 13 public holidays. Child labor under age 15 is banned, and there are restrictions on employment of young people aged 15–18. Employers with 10 or more employees must pay 0.2–1.0% of wages into the Workmen's Compensation Fund for workplace injuries. In addition, employers, employees and the government pay into the Social Security Fund.

Fiscal/Financial

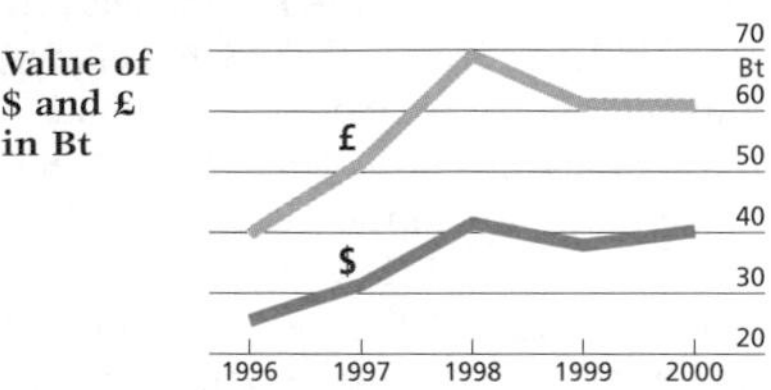

The leading domestic commercial banks are Bangkok Bank, followed by Krung Thai Bank, Siam Commercial Bank, Thai Farmers Bank, Bank of Ayudhaya and Thai Military Bank. All except Krung Thai Bank are private-sector. Some of the leading banks also own insurance companies. The Bank of Thailand is the central bank, and is responsible for regulating the financial sector. The Securities and Exchange Commission supervises stock market operations. The central bank was given greater autonomy for setting monetary measures in the 2001 Bank of Thailand Act. Stricter regulation of the financial sector is assured by three other 2001 laws, the Financial Institutions Act, the Deposit Insurance Act, and the Foreign Currency Act. Standard corporation tax is 30%, but newly listed companies pay 25% and other listed companies pay 25% on profits up to Bt600 million. The top rate of personal income tax is 37%. VAT is 7%, but is planned to increase to 10% from 2003.

At end-2000 the financial sector included 7 private-sector domestic commercial banks, 6 nationalized commercial banks, 21 foreign banks (including international banking facilities), 5 specialized public-sector banks (for small savings, agricultural cooperatives, housing mortgages, industrial development, and export-import trade), 21 finance companies, 10 mortgage lenders, financial cooperatives, and life and non-life insurance. As a result of the financial crisis, the government nationalized 6 failing banks and closed 56 finance companies in 1997. One of the nationalized banks was due to be closed, two to be merged with other financial institutions, and three to be privatized, following recapitalization, but in early 2002 this had not yet happened. To aid recapitalization the law limiting foreign investment in domestic banks to 49% of equity was relaxed for ten years. By end-2000 private banks had raised almost $11 billion in new capital. Non-performing loans reached 52.5% of total lending in April 2001, but fell to 10.4% in December 2001. Most of these loans were in the process of liquidation by the Thai Asset Management Corporation, which began operations in July 2001. The financial sector offers a sophisticated range of services, but the government is eager to reduce the traditional dependence of corporations on bank loans and short-term financing, encouraging them to use the stock market share listings and long-term bonds instead.

The Stock Exchange of Thailand (SET) established Vision 2003 in 1999 to strengthen the market and revive investor confidence after the financial crisis. Stricter information disclosure and accountability rules were introduced. In 1999 SET was a founder member of the Thai Institute of Directors Association to encourage best practice and good corporate governance among listed companies. Measures for investigating alleged misconduct were strengthened. The Market for Alternative Investment for small companies, derivatives trading, and Internet trading were launched in 2000. An information exchange agreement was signed with the Australian Stock Exchange in 1999.

Business Opportunities

Growth in output (% p.a., 1990–99)

Services	4.4
Industry	5.7
Manufacturing	6.7
Agriculture	2.5

The Board of Investment is the point of contact for foreign investors. There are five priority sectors for investment: agribusiness, environmental protection, technology and training, transport infrastructure and services, and specific industries (including electronics, automotive, and tourism). These are eligible for investment incentives, which include tax breaks and guarantees. The BOI has divided the country into investment zones with varying incentives in order to achieve decentralization. There are 11 export processing zones and 37 industrial zones. Commerce attracted the most foreign investment in 1998–2000, followed by machinery and transport equipment, finance, and electrical appliances. Major car manufacturers General Motors and Volkswagen have established manufacturing plants in Thailand. The top investor in 1998–2000 was the United States, followed by Japan, Singapore, Netherlands, Hong Kong, and France. Electronics, IT, trade, finance and transport, and the privatization program offer current opportunities.

For More Information

Books:

A Business Guide to Thailand. Board of Investment: Bangkok.
Costs of Doing Business in Thailand. Board of Investment: Bangkok.
Country Economic Review: *Thailand*. Asian Development Bank.
Cummings, Joe, and Steven Martin. *Thailand* . 9th ed. Oakland, CA: Lonely Planet, 2001.
Economist Intelligence Unit. *Country Profile and Quarterly Reports*. London.
IMF Country Report. *Thailand*. Washington, D.C.: IMF.
Seline, Christopher, ed. *The Business Guide to Thailand*. Woburn, MA: Butterworth-Heinemann, 1999.

Web Sites:

Bangkok Post (English language daily newspaper): **www.bangkokpost.net**
Bank of Thailand: **www.bot.or.th**
Board of Investment (government entry point): **www.boi.go.th**
Ministry of Finance: **www.mof.go.th**
Stock Exchange of Thailand: **www.set.or.th**
Thai Chamber of Commerce: **www.tcc.or.th**
Tourism Authority of Thailand: **www.tourismthailand.org**

Trinidad and Tobago

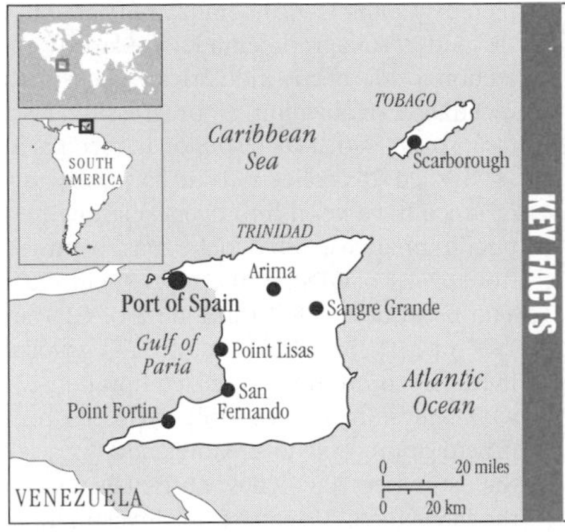

GNI: **$6,142 million; world's 104th**
GNI pc: **$4,750; world's 68th**
Head of government: **prime minister**
Currency: **Trinidad & Tobago dollar (TT$)**
Capital: **Port of Spain**
Population: **1,289,000, growing at 0.7% p.a.**
Land area: **1,969 square miles**
Population density: **654 per square mile**
Life expectancy: **74 years**
Infant mortality: **17 per 1,000 live births**
Language: **English**
Best buy: **rum, pottery, batik**

Economy

Trinidad & Tobago's economy is the largest and most developed in the Commonwealth Caribbean. Its main sector, oil and gas, accounted for 24% of GDP in 2000; in 1999, distribution (16.9%) and finance (13.9%) were also significant sectors. In 1999, the petroleum sector contributed TT$2 billion to government revenue, 20.7% of the total. Industrial development fuelled by natural gas is a further source of employment and foreign exchange, as is tourism.

Mineral fuels and chemicals are the major export earner, accounting for 73% of export revenue in 1999. The United States took 46% of total exports, and the Caribbean Community 26%; the United States supplied 37% of imports and Latin America 22%, of which 8% were from Venezuela.

The economy underwent a serious recession between 1983 and 1993, set off by the international price slump, but it emerged from an IMF restructuring program with positive growth, which reached 5.2% in 1999 and 4.0% in 2000. The inflation rate occasionally reached double figures between 1989 and 1993, but was generally below 4% between 1996 and 2000.

Geography/Resources

Situated 7 miles from the Venezuelan coast, Trinidad is 1,864 square miles in area; Tobago, 19 miles northeast of Trinidad, covers 116 square miles. Average rainfall in the two islands is 63 inches.

Sugar cane, cocoa, coffee and rice are cultivated in Trinidad, together with commercial forestry. The main urban areas are in and around Port of Spain, and in the west and southwest.

The literacy rate is estimated at 90%, although secondary education was only made compulsory in 2000. The unemployment rate in 1999 was 13%, and in 1996 an estimated 35% of the population lived below the poverty line.

Communications/Energy

The privately-owned national airline, BWIA, serves London, Miami, New York, Toronto, and regional destinations, together with U.S., Canadian, and other Caribbean operators. There are several ports used by ocean-going ships, of which Port of Spain and Scarborough (Tobago) accommodate cruise liners; Point Lisas on the west coast is the main cargo port, serving the oil-based industrial zone. There are 2,237 miles of paved road and 2,672 miles unpaved. Domestic and international telecommunications are provided by Telecommunications Services of Trinidad & Tobago, 51% owned by the government and 49% by Cable & Wireless; the mobile phone market is open to private companies. The state electricity corporation distributes power purchased from the Power Generation Co., in which the state has a majority holding; it has a generating capacity of 1,189 MW. A further 225 MW is supplied by a U.S. company, Inncogen.

Trinidad's oil deposits are in the southern part of the country, while there are more extensive oil and gas reserves offshore.

Fiscal/Financial

The fiscal structure combines direct and indirect taxation. Personal income tax is charged on incomes above TT$25,000 per year, while companies pay corporate tax of 35%. Value-added tax is payable on retail sales, and financial transactions are taxable at 15%. The petroleum sector contributed TT$2 billion to total government revenue of TT$9.7 billion in 1999; the budget has shown a current surplus since 1997.

The financial sector is well developed, with six commercial banks and a variety of other financial institutions, regulated by the Central Bank. The government operates several financial institutions which provide development loans for business. The Stock Exchange, founded in 1981, had 28 listed companies in 1999, with market capitalization equal to 67% of GDP.

Business Opportunities

Investment incentives include: tax exemption for up to ten years; duty-free import of equipment and raw materials, where not available domestically; reduced leasing rates for factory premises; repatriation of capital and profits; protection from import competition; training subsidies; export-financing arrangements, including tax-deductible promotion costs; and tax concessions for companies earning foreign exchange. Full foreign ownership is permitted under certain conditions, but joint ventures with domestic companies are favored, and more than 20 categories of business are reserved for Trinidadian investors.

The petroleum-based sector and downstream industrial development offer the most opportunities, together with advanced technology sectors, hotel construction, and transport ventures, such as a new rapid transport system planned for the corridor linking Port of Spain with Piarco airport.

For More Information

Books:

Trinidad and Tobago: A Spy Guide. 3rd ed. Washington, D.C.: International Business Publications, 2001.

Trinidad and Tobago Business and Investment Opportunities Yearbook. 3rd ed. Washington, D.C.: International Business Publications, 2001 (annual).

World Trade Organization. *Trade Policy Review: Trinidad and Tobago.* Lanham, MD: Bernan Press, 1999.

Web Sites:

Central Bank: **www.central-bank.org.tt**

Prime Minister's office: **www.opm.gov.tt**

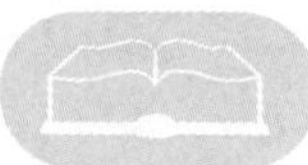

Tunisia

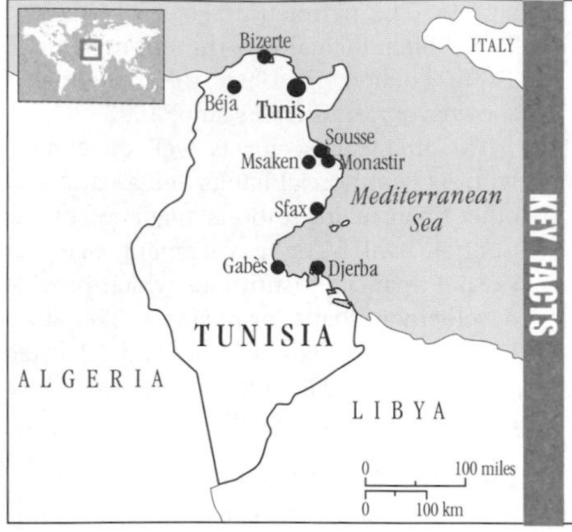

KEY FACTS

GNI: **$19,757 million; world's 66th**
GNI pc: **$2,090; world's 102nd**
Head of state: **president**
Head of government: **prime minister**
Currency: **Tunisian dinar (TD)**
Capital: **Tunis**
Population: **9,460,000, growing at 1.6% p.a.**
Land area: **60,000 square miles**
Population density: **158 per square mile**
Life expectancy: **70 years**
Infant mortality: **24 per 1,000 live births**
Language: **Arabic (official), French (business)**
Best buy: **Berber carpets, pottery, textiles**

Economic Structure

Tunisia was ruled as a colony of France from 1881 until independence in 1956. Relations with France then soured over Tunisia's support for Algerian independence. The UN ordered France to close its military base at Bizerte, and France cut off financial aid to Tunisia. From 1964 Tunisia's ruling party adopted socialism. The economy was based on agriculture and hydrocarbons, but manufacturing and services sectors were developed in the 1980s. Following the 1995 agreement with the European Union to create a free trade area by 2008, and membership of the World Trade Organization, the government began to dismantle protective economic structures.

In 2000 services accounted for 58.9% of GDP, followed by industry (28.8%) and agriculture (12.3%). Trade and business services are the main services, followed by government services, transport and communications, and tourism. Manufacturing contributed 18.2% of GDP in 2000. Textiles, cement, phosphates processing, food processing, and oil refining are the main manufacturing industries. Tourism is the top foreign exchange earner. In 2000 the leading merchandise exports were clothing, followed by hydrocarbons, shoes, and olive oil. The main markets were France (26.8%), followed by Italy (23%), Germany (12.5%), Spain (5.4%), and Belgium (5.1%).

The state sector is extensive. Privatization began in 1987. By end-2000 140 mostly small companies had been partly or fully sold. Some shares were bought by employees and state-owned banks, notably in airline Tunis Air. From 1998 larger companies, including cement works and energy and transport companies, were targeted. Several mixed private- and public-sector companies were fully privatized. Over two-thirds of privatization receipts were from foreign companies. The 2001–02 privatization program includes 41 companies.

Economic Policy

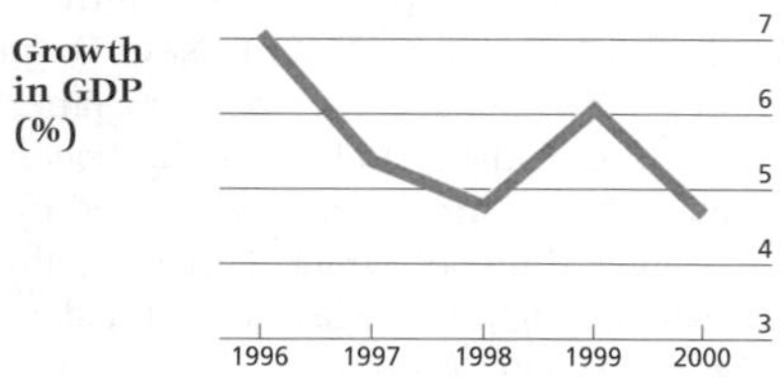

With exports traditionally dependent on oil and food, GDP and the balance of payments were subject to large fluctuations. Tight monetary and fiscal policies coupled with liberalization of the economy were adopted in 1986 in line with the IMF-backed structural adjustment program to reduce debt.

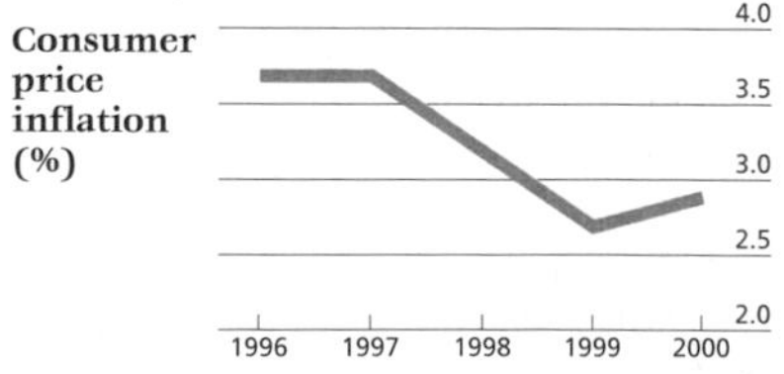

Large state-company payment arrears to the banks were cleared, and debt collection agencies were formed to handle private-enterprise arrears. Privatization moved slowly, with only TD316 million in receipts in 1987–96. However, foreign investment helped establish textiles and tourism as important sources of foreign exchange. The phasing out of favorable quotas and tariffs in client countries for Tunisian textiles under the Multifiber Arrangement will be completed by 2005. Trade liberalization under the EU and WTO agreements has reduced protection for domestic industries and customs receipts. Privatization is progressing at a faster pace, with TD1.09 billion in receipts in 1998–2000. Tax collection and corporate governance have been improved to strengthen public finances. Total debt was trimmed from 62.4% of GDP in 1990 to 48.9% in 2001. The fiscal deficit fell from 4.6% of GDP in 1990 to 2.9% in 2001. However, the government is committed to its comprehensive welfare system, to mitigating job losses from privatization, and to creating new jobs for the estimated 70,000 new entrants a year to the labor force. Private-sector investment is seen as the main source of new jobs. Annual average GDP growth was 3.9% in 1992–96, rising to 5.3% in 1997–2000, while inflation averaged 4.9% and 3.1% respectively. Growth was 5.5% and inflation 3% in 2001. Unemployment is high at an official 15.5%.

Geography/Resources

In North Africa, Tunisia borders the Mediterranean Sea, Libya, and Algeria. Most of the country is low-lying, with the lowest point in the central depression at Shatt al Gharsah 55 feet below sea level. At the northern coast winters are mild and wet, summers hot and dry. The interior is arid, humid because of its proximity to the sea, and hot, with typical temperatures over 100°F. Drought is a natural hazard. Most of the population lives along the coast, which provides the focus for tourism and agriculture. Most are of Arab origin (98%), with a small European community (1%).

Agriculture is varied. Olive oil is the main agricultural export. Olives, citrus, and dates are grown for export, while wheat is the main domestic crop, followed by tomatoes, chilies, other vegetables, and fruit. Tunisia is the world's leading date producer. Poultry are the main livestock, followed by sheep and goats. Meat, dairy, and leather are important. Forestry and fishing are small industries. The main minerals are petroleum, gas, phosphates, zinc, lead, and barytes. Iron ore, salt, and gypsum are also produced. Proven oil reserves were 308 million barrels and gas reserves were 2.75 trillion cubic feet at January 2001. Exploration continues.

Communications/Energy

The road network is 14,350 miles, 11,326 miles of which is paved, including an 87-mile motorway between Tunis and Sousse.

There are plans for another 528 miles of motorways, 280 miles to be operational before 2010. The 1,347-mile rail network transported 12.5 million tons of freight and 34.4 million passengers in 1999. The pipeline network comprises 495 miles for crude oil, 461 miles for gas, and 53 miles for refined oil products. There are seven major sea ports: Tunis, Bizerte, Sfax, Gabès, La Goulette, Sousse, and Zarzis. Total seaborne freight handled in 1999 was 19.9 million tons. There are seven international airports at Tunis, Sfax, Djerba, Monastir, Tabarka, Gafsa, and Tozeur. A new airport at Enfidha will be completed in 2004.

The national telephone network is fully digitized. At end-1999 there were 850,000 fixed phone lines and 55,300 mobile phones; at end-2000 there were 100,000 Internet users.

Energy demand for commercial and industrial purposes is growing by an estimated 7% per year. In 1999 oil accounted for 57.9% of energy consumption, and gas for 41.3%. Electricity is generated almost entirely by fossil fuels (99.2% in 1999), with hydro supplying 0.8%. Oil production was 79,000 barrels per day in 2000, with consumption at 86,000 barrels per day and net imports of 7,000 barrels per day. Gas production was 67 billion cubic feet in 1999, with consumption at 106 billion cubic feet and net imports at 39 billion cubic feet. Tunisia imports gas from Libya. Algeria's Transmed pipeline to Italy runs through Tunisia, for which Tunisia receives transit fees. There are plans to link the Tunisian and Libyan electricity grids.

Education/Employment

Education is compulsory from age 6 to 16. There were 101 higher education institutes in 1999–2000, including three universities, with 180,044 students enrolled. Around 15,000 Tunisian students attend foreign universities and colleges. The Ministry of Higher Education is responsible for higher education policy and funding. There are plans to allow private universities and colleges.

The Ministry of Scientific Research and Technology has 305 research centers and 71 laboratories specializing in IT, health, biotechnology, chemicals and materials science, water, power, environmental protection, agriculture, and marine science. R&D spending was TD121.7 billion (0.45% of GDP) in 2000, 91% from the state and 3.5% from foreign finance. The government aims to increase spending to 1% of GDP by 2004. The Tunis Technology and Communications Park was established in 1997 to link commercial and state R&D in IT.

The labor force has a range of skills. Wages and other employment conditions are set through three-year collective agreements between the national employers' association (UTICA) and the national trade union confederation (UGTT). The agreements set standards which are followed by the public and private sectors. A minimum monthly wage applies to full-time industrial workers.

Fiscal/Financial

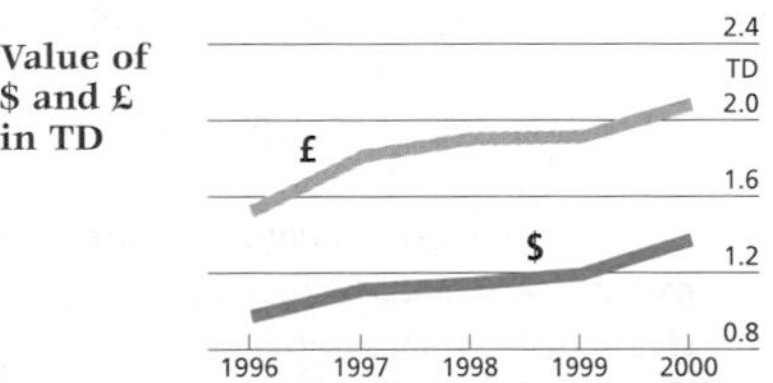

The largest banks by total assets are Société Tunisienne de Banque (STB), Banque Nationale Agricole, Banque Internationale Arabe de Tunisie (BIAT), and Banque de l'Habitat. BIAT is private-sector, the others state-controlled. The Banque Centrale de Tunisie, the central bank, is responsible for regulating the financial sector. Prudential rules have been strengthened in recent years to bring them closer to international accounting standards. The government-run Capital Market Council regulates and manages the stock market. Corporation tax is 35%.

There were 14 commercial banks in early 2002. Ten of these were state-controlled and accounted for two-thirds of lending and half of deposits. The Central Bank has encouraged consolidation. STB absorbed two development banks—Banque de Dévéloppement Économique de Tunisie and Banque Nationale de Dévéloppement Touristique—in 2000. Six development banks remain, mostly joint ventures of the state with Arab partners. Foreign banks include two onshore and six offshore. There are two local investment banks. Non-performing loans accounted for less than 25% of total bank lending in 2000, down from 37% in 1993. Bank loans are the main form of business finance, but the Central Bank is encouraging greater use of the stock exchange through reduced corporate tax of 20% for firms with 30% or more of their shares traded on market.

Operations on the Tunis Stock Exchange—the Bourse des Valeurs mobilières de Tunis (BVMT)—have been strengthened by privatizations. The BVMT has itself been partly privatized. At mid-2001 the market listed a total of 48 companies (including 12 banks), several local investment funds, and bonds. Trading through licensed brokerages is fully electronic.

Business Opportunities

The government favors foreign direct investment in industries that export 80% or more of output. It discourages foreign investment that competes with Tunisian firms on the domestic market. With the exception of tourism, government authorization is needed for foreign participation in domestic companies over 49%. Job creation is a key requirement for new investments, and expatriate labor is restricted. Foreign ownership of agricultural land is proscribed. Tax and financial incentives are available to investors, with higher benefits for investment in health, education, transport, environmental protection, waste treatment, and R&D operations, and for investment in depressed regions. There are free trade zones at Bizerte and Zarzis.

By early 2000 there was TD15 billion in cumulative foreign direct investment. At mid-2001 France was the top foreign investor; other investors included the United Kingdom, the United States, Portugal, Spain, Sweden, Switzerland, Germany, Netherlands, Italy, Japan, and Arab countries. The largest foreign investment sector by value is hydrocarbons, whereas the largest by number of companies and jobs created is textiles. Other key sectors include footwear, food processing, telecommunications, electronics, automotive, aerospace, machinery, cement, power generation, transport, finance, and tourism. New opportunities exist in these sectors and privatizations. The point of contact is the Foreign Investment Promotion Agency.

For More Information

Books:

Murphy, Emma C. *Economic and Political Change in Tunisia: From Bourguiba to Ben Ali.* New York: Palgrave Macmillan, 1999.
Tunisia Business and Investment Opportunities Yearbook. 3rd ed. Washington, D.C.: International Business Publications, 2001 (annual).
White, Gregory. *A Comparative Political Economy of Tunisia and Morocco: On the Outside of Europe Looking in.* Albany, NY: State University of New York Press, 2001.

Web Sites:

Foreign Investment Promotion Agency: **www.investintunisia.tn**
Government entry point: **www.ministeres.tn**
Tunisian National Tourism Office: **www.tourismtunisia.com**

Turkey

KEY FACTS

GNI: **$186,490 million; world's 22nd**
GNI pc: **$2,900; world's 90th**
Head of government: **prime minister**
Currency: **Turkish lira (TL)**
Capital: **Ankara**
Population: **65,546,000, growing at 1.7% p.a.**
Land area: **297,140 square miles**
Population density: **220 per square mile**
Life expectancy: **70 years**
Infant mortality: **40 per 1,000 live births**
Language: **Turkish**
Best buy: **leather goods, onyx, alabaster, carpets, gold and silver jewelry, ceramics, loukum, samovars**

Economic Structure

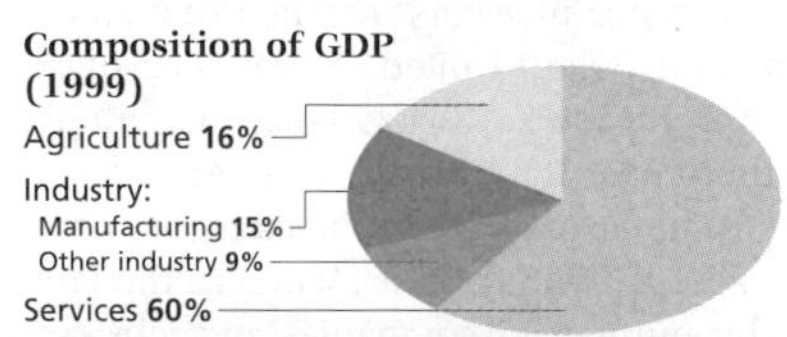

The visionary military leader Mustafa Kemal Attatürk gained international recognition for Republic of Turkey and himself as its first president in 1923. He then launched a radical modernization program of the country's social and legal structures. In 1950 Turkey became a strategic NATO country against Soviet influence. In 1960 the military took direct political power briefly, enacting a new constitution. Planned economic development began in the 1960s and continues today, giving Turkey more the style of a socialist economy than the capitalist state it nominally is. The military took direct power again in 1980 and directed economic change towards liberalization, a process which gathered momentum from the end of the 1990s with the prospect of EU membership. The military is in favor of EU membership, but the EU is ill at ease with the extent of military influence over domestic affairs. It suspended negotiations for 18 months in 1999–2000 because of military measures against the Kurdish minority in the east. The apparent resolution of the Kurdish question in 2000 and the devastating Turkish earthquakes of 1999 led the EU to join other international donors in the reconstruction effort and to resume membership negotiations.

Services accounted for 53% of GDP in 2000, including trade (22%), transport (13%), finance, business services and real estate (9%), and government services (9%). Tourism is important. Industry contributed 28% of GDP, agriculture 14%, and construction 5%. Manufacturing comprises textiles, metal industries, automotive, pharmaceuticals, glass, ceramics, cement, paper, petrochemicals, fertilizers, food, and beverages. The principal exports in 2000 were clothing and textiles (31%), followed by electrical machinery (6.2%), iron and steel (5.8%), fruit and vegetables (5.7%), and transport equipment (5.5%). The top export market was Germany (19.6%), followed by the United States (11.1%) and the United Kingdom (7.5%). The EU absorbed 53.4% of exports.

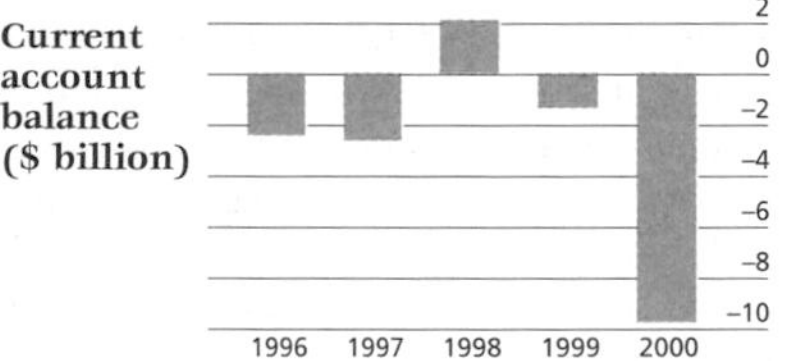

The state has a high degree of control over the official economy, but there are extensive parallel market operations in manufacturing and services. As companies and banks have been privatized, they have usually been absorbed into large industrial conglomerates. An ambitious privatization program was launched in 1985, but by end-2000 only $7.3 billion in sales had been made, $2.7 billion in 2000 alone. The cost to the state of privatization in capital increases, loans, social security, and early retirement payments, was almost equal to revenues. Out of the 219 companies and banks originally included in the privatization portfolio, 162 were privatized; the state retained no holdings in 143 of these. Certain banks that were privatized were taken back into state ownership when they failed in 2000, and other private-sector banks were nationalized to save them from collapse in 2001–02. These and state banks are being restructured prior to divestiture. The 2001 privatization program included Turkish Airlines, two petroleum companies, the Atakoy Group (tourism), petrochemicals, steel, tobacco, and sugar processing companies, but divestments were delayed by weakened stock market conditions. Türk Telekom was being prepared for privatization. The state has significant holdings in utilities, telecommunications, railways, petroleum refining, petrochemicals, steel, tourism, textiles, meat processing, and forestry despite privatization and liberalization. Privatization plans have been complicated by overmanning and outdated capital equipment in many state companies, by restrictions on foreign investment, in certain cases by cancellation following accusations of corruption, and by the financial crisis.

Economic Policy

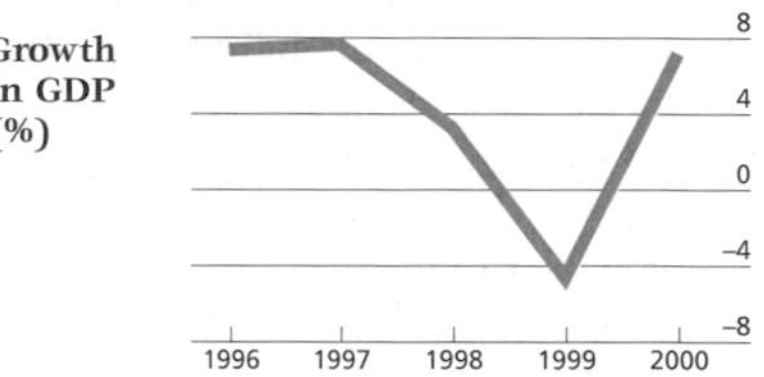

The privatization policy was launched to reduce state expenditure, but slow progress left the financial burden and outmoded structures in place. During the 1990s the government introduced stabilization programs to combat rampant inflation, to support the lira and rebuild foreign exchange holdings, and to consolidate public finances. These had only limited success on account of domestic political pressures, external events and, in 1999, two massive earthquakes affecting regions contributing almost half of industrial added value, half of bank deposits and credits, and 58% of government tax revenues. International multilateral donor support for rebuilding the economy since the earthquakes has given greater momentum to reform. However, exchange rate problems and private capital flight caused a banking crisis in 2000–01. The IMF endorsed a new stabilization program and a floating exchange rate for the lira in May 2001. The government intends to introduce inflation targeting for monetary

policy in 2002. To improve public finances it has cut spending and restricted public sector wages and recruitment, and is phasing out subsidies on electricity and other state enterprise products.

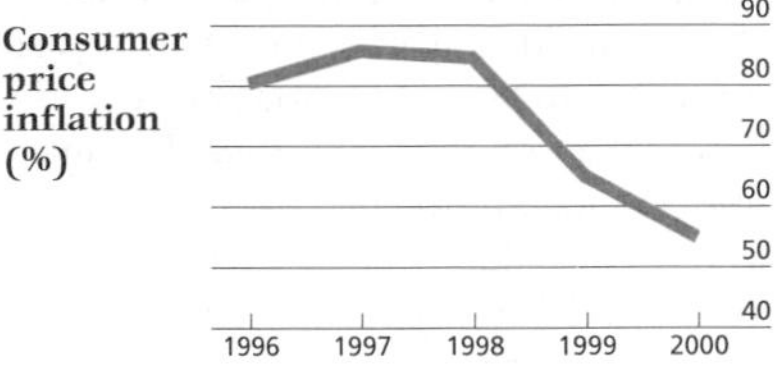

Real GDP growth fell from an annual average 7.2% in 1995–97 to 3.1% in 1998. In 1999 it declined by 6.1% because of the earthquakes, the government's 1998 consolidation program, and the quartering of export revenue from Russia as a result of the 1998 Russian economic crisis. Russia was the second export market in 1997. Growth was 7.1% in 2000, but GDP declined by 8.5% in 2001. Growth is expected to be 4% in 2002. Annual average inflation was 73.7% in 1996–2000. It was 65% in 2001. The inflation target for 2002 is 35%. Unemployment rose from 6.9% in 1997 to 8.3% in 2000. However, participation in the labor force is very low at around 47%, indicating underemployment and parallel market activity.

Geography/Resources

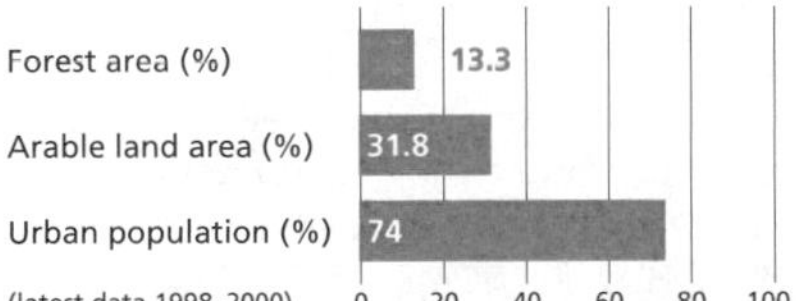

West of the Bosphorus strait from the Mediterranean to the Black Sea, Turkey is European; east of the strait it is Asian. Turkey has land borders with Armenia, Azerbaijan, Georgia, Iran, Iraq, and Syria in the east, and with Bulgaria and Greece in the west. It has coastlines on the Black, Aegean and Mediterranean Seas. The land is mostly mountainous, with a central plateau, a high point of 16,950 feet (Mount Ararat), and coastal plains. The Tigris and Euphrates rivers have their source in Turkey. There is an earthquake fault line across the north of the country from west to east. The climate is dry with hot summers and mild winters, except on the high mountains, which have an alpine climate. The majority of people are of Turkish origin, but there is a Kurdish minority of 20%, most of whom live in the disadvantaged eastern part of the country. Many Turks work abroad; their remittances are an important source of foreign exchange.

The Southeastern Anatolia Project (GAP), which includes 22 dams on the Tigris and Euphrates and their tributaries, aims to provide 4.2 million ares of irrigated land for agriculture in 2005 and to improve earnings for the largely agricultural-based Kurdish population. In 2000 crops accounted for 55% of agricultural output, livestock for 34%, and forestry and aquaculture for 11%. Main crops were wheat, barley, sugar beet, potatoes, grapes, oranges, apples, onions, cotton, olives, sunflower seeds, and tea. Nuts are also important. Sheep are the main livestock, followed by cattle. Dairy, honey, leather, and wool are important.

A wide range of minerals is produced. They include chromite (Turkey is a leading world producer), copper (production of ore is 3.4 million tons per year, concentrate 50,000 tons per year), lead and zinc, boron (Turkey has two-thirds of world reserves, and annual production is around 1 million tons), magnesite, barytes, pumice, feldspar, celestite, emery (Turkish output meets 80% of world demand), clay, and many kinds of dimension stone including marble, onyx, quartzite, slate, limestone, granite, dolomite, basalt, sandstone, travertine, serpentine, diabase, and tuffs. There are unexploited reserves of soda ash, in which foreign investors have shown an interest. Proven oil reserves were 296 million barrels, and gas reserves were 310 billion cubic feet at January 2001. Coal reserves were 1.1 billion tons in 1998.

Communications/Energy

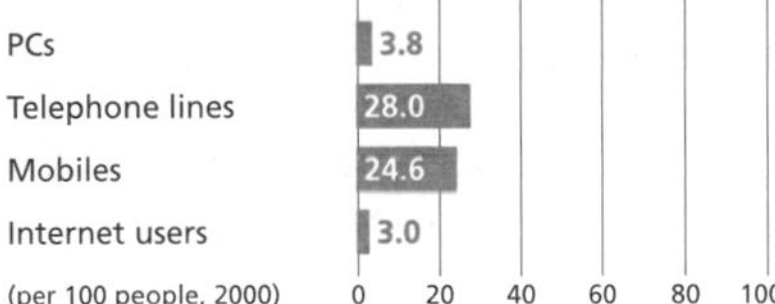

The road network was an estimated 237,621 miles in 1999, including 59,405 miles of paved roads and 1,087 miles of motorways. The rail network was 5,395 miles in 1999, including 1,325 miles of electrified track. There are 746 miles of navigable waterways. The pipeline network included 1,080 miles for crude oil, 1,442 miles for petroleum products, and 440 miles for natural gas in 1999. Several major new pipelines are planned. Seven large sea ports are operated by Turkish State Railways and have direct rail links. Five smaller ports are run by the Turkish Maritime Organization. The merchant fleet comprised 548 ships of over 1,000 grt, totaling 5.6 million grt in 2000. Total freight handled by the sea ports in 1998 was 102.9 million tons. There were 118 airports in 1999, including three international airports at Istanbul, Ankara, and Izmir.

Telecommunications were liberalized in 2000 with the creation of the Telecommunications Authority. However, the main operator Türk Telekom remains dominant. Private-sector companies operate in mobile telephony and Internet access. Türk Telekom also provides these services, and retains the monopoly on fixed telephony until end-2003. There were 18.5 million fixed phone lines, 16.1 million mobile phones, and 2 million Internet users at end-2000.

Imports of petroleum and natural gas accounted for 40% and 17% of energy supply in 2000. Domestic production of lignite contributed 16%, wood 6.4%, petroleum 3.6%, hydroelectricity 3.4%, and gas 0.8%. Thermal (oil, gas, coal) power plants produce 70% of electricity and hydro 30%. The GAP project will increase the share of hydro to 42% from 2005. Gas use is also due to increase. Electricity demand is growing rapidly, and Turkey imports from Bulgaria and Russia (via Georgia and Iran). The electricity sector has been liberalized, with several private-sector power plants coming onstream from 2001. However, prices are subsidized, with state companies producing at a loss. State oil and gas company Botas's monopoly on gas imports was abolished in 2001. New gas import agreements with Iran and Russia were due to come into effect in 2001–02, but both have been subject to delays. An agreement was signed end-1999 between Turkey, Azerbaijan, Georgia, Kazakhstan, and Turkmenistan for the construction of a $1.8–4.0 billion oil pipeline from Baku in Azerbaijan to Ceyhan in Turkey. The pipeline, which could come into operation in 2004 if not subject to delays, offers a major alternative to Russian pipelines from the Caspian oilfields, and foreign exchange earnings for Turkey in transit fees.

Education/Employment

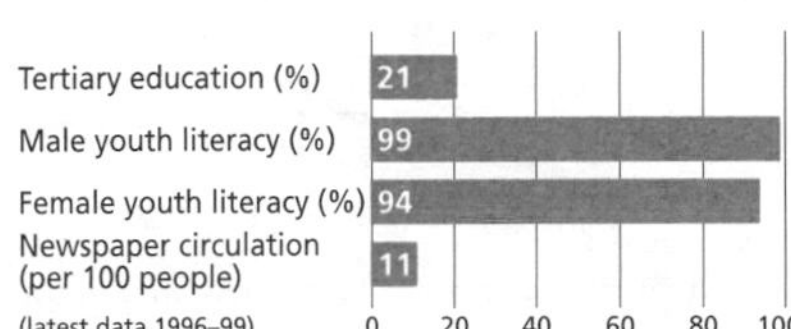

Education is compulsory and free from age 6 to 14. There are around 820 higher education institutes including universities, with total student enrollment of over 1 million. The 15 main universities are in Istanbul, Ankara, and Izmir. Tertiary education is the responsibility of the Higher Education Council, and funding is provided by the state. From 1998 the universities were given greater autonomy, and were encouraged to raise funds from partnerships with industry.

The Scientific and Technical Research Council of Turkey coordinates basic and applied R&D. There are 64 research institutes and organizations. R&D strengths include agriculture, forestry, health, biotechnology, nuclear technologies, minerals, materials, IT, and defense. R&D spending was 0.49% of GDP in 1997. Higher education accounted for 57% of R&D, the commercial sector for 32%, and the public sector 10.5%. The Turkish Science and Technology Policy 1993–2003 aims to increase R&D spending to 1% of GDP by 2003. Turkey takes part in EU R&D programs.

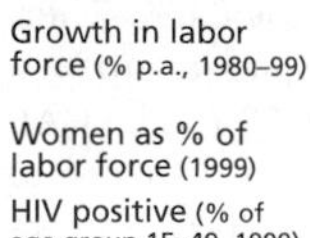

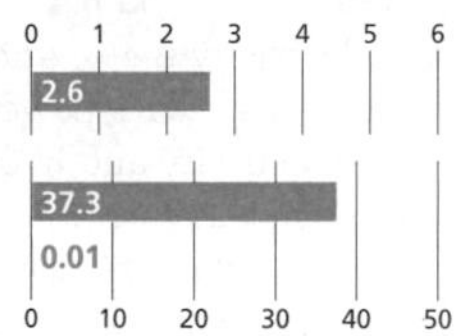

The labor force is flexible, with a wide spectrum of skills from the unskilled to highly educated. Traditionally there is a large degree of state intervention in determining wages and employment conditions. Until recently, unionized labor in state enterprises enjoyed the best conditions. In 2000 public-sector workers' access to unionization and union activity was restricted, bringing it in line with the private sector. The minimum wage is low. Onerous legal safeguards for employees are frequently ignored. The labor black market is estimated at 3 million people, including children. Turkey is obliged to apply EU employment and social laws to qualify for membership, but progress has been slow.

Fiscal/Financial

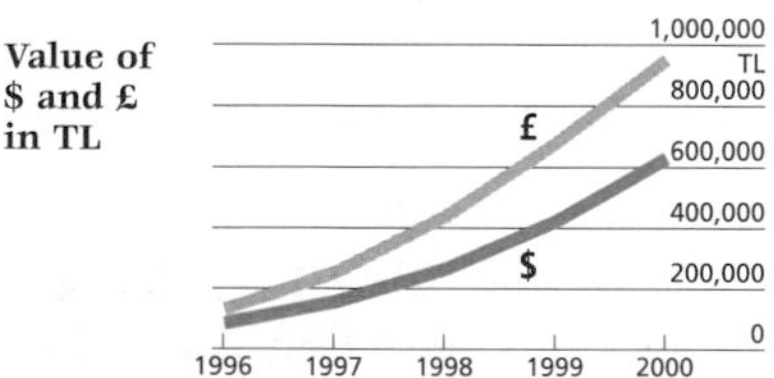

In 2000 there were four large private-sector retail banks: Isbank, Akbank, Yapi Kredi Bank, and Garanti Bank. All are part of wider industrial conglomerates. The state owns large specialized banks for agriculture, real estate, export, and economic development, which in late 2000 accounted for 34.6% of total assets, 26.2% of credit, and 40% of loans. Three state banks and two state funds suffered heavy losses because of the earthquakes. The majority of insurance companies are private-sector. A new state organization—Turkish Catastrophic Insurance Pool—was established with World Bank help in 2000 to handle the new compulsory earthquake cover for properties. Monetary policy and central bank functions are conducted by Central Bank of the Republic of Turkey. The Banking Regulation and Supervision Agency (BRSA), Insurance Supervisory Board, and Capital Markets Board are the supervisory authorities. Basic corporation tax is 25%, and the standard top rate of personal income tax is 40%. Following the 1999 earthquakes an additional 5% was added to profits tax and income tax. VAT rates were raised to 17% and 25%.

There were 81 commercial banks in 2000. As a result of the 2000–01 banking crisis several banks became insolvent and were taken over by the State Deposit Insurance Fund. The government recapitalized most of them, and one of the largest, Demirbank, was sold to Hong Kong & Shanghai Banking Corporation. Others were also reprivatized. Several more insolvent private-sector banks were nationalized and recapitalized in early 2002. Banks were obliged to raise capital adequacy ratios to 8% by end-2001, which resulted in mergers. In the private sector, Körfez Bank and Osmanli Bank merged with Garanti Bank. State banks also underwent restructuring prior to privatization. Banking services are sophisticated and internationalized. The Istanbul Stock Exchange, which has been in operation since 1985, added a Second National Market for small companies and a New Economy Market for high-technology firms in 2000. It is introducing a wide-area electronic network to allow decentralized trading in Istanbul, Ankara, and Izmir. There are no restrictions on foreign portfolio investment. The Istanbul Stock Exchange has minor shareholdings in the Baku and Krgyz Stock Exchanges.

Business Opportunities

Growth in output (% p.a., 1990–99)

Services	3.9
Industry	4.3
Manufacturing	5.1
Agriculture	1.4

Tax and financial incentives are offered to investors. Increased benefits are available for investment in the southeast and east, and in high-tech industries. At mid-2001 there were 17 free zones. Foreign investment in banking, insurance, and petroleum requires special permission, while equity holdings are limited to 49% in air and sea transport and telecommunications, and 20% in broadcast media. From 1980 to March 2001 manufacturing was the main investment sector (54.9%), followed by services, (42.6%), agriculture (1.5%), and mining (0.9%). France was the top investor (18.6%), followed by the Netherlands (13.6%), Germany (12.6%), and the United States (11.5%). In 2000 banking was the top sector (13.9%) followed by trade (8.1%), food, beverage and tobacco processing (6.5%), chemicals (6%), and electronics and electrical machinery (3.5%). There is also foreign investment in the automotive, pharmaceuticals, energy, telecommunications, metals, and tourism industries. All these sectors and privatizations continue to offer investment opportunities. The approval agency for foreign investments is the Undersecretariat for Treasury, General Directorate of Foreign Investment.

For More Information

Books:

Chislett, W. *Turkey: A European Perspective*. London: Euromoney Books, 2000.

European Union. Turkey: Regular Report from the Commission on Turkey's Progress towards Accession.

Pope, H., and N. Pope. *Turkey Unveiled: A History of Modern Turkey*. New York: Overlook Press, 1999.

Turkey 2001 Almanac: Executive's Handbook. 10th ed. Istanbul: InterMedia, 2001 (annual).

Web Sites:

Central Bank of the Republic of Turkey: **www.tcmb.gov.tr**

Dünya Gazetesi (business news with English language version): **www.dunyagazetesi.com.tr**

Istanbul Stock Exchange: **www.ise.org**

Ministry of Foreign Affairs (government entry point): **www.mfa.gov.tr**

Privatization Administration: **www.oib.gov.tr**

State Institute of Statistics: **www.die.gov.tr**

Turkish Daily News (newspaper): **www.turkishdailynews.com**

TURKS AND CAICOS ISLANDS

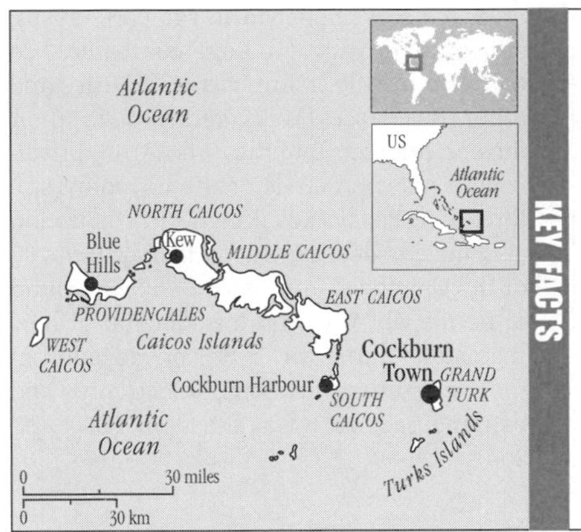

KEY FACTS

GNI pc: **$5,000 (approx.)**
Head of government: **chief minister**
Currency: **U.S. dollar ($)**
Capital: **Cockburn Town on Grand Turk**
Population: **17,000**
Land area: **192 square miles**
Population density: **88 per square mile**
Life expectancy: **74 years**
Infant mortality: **18 per 1,000 live births**
Language: **English**
Best buy: **shell jewelry, paintings**

ECONOMY

Tourism and financial services are the dominant economic sectors, while government services account for about a third of employment. Agriculture and fishing provide jobs for another 20% of those employed, principally fishing: lobster, conch, and other sea creatures are the islands' main export. The growth of tourism has helped develop the construction and quarrying sector. There is a very small manufacturing sector, confined principally to the production of handicrafts for sale to tourists. The main trading partner is the United States, which in 1998 also provided 68% of tourist arrivals.

The islands have maintained high growth rates in recent years, ranging from 7.6% in 1996 to an estimated 11.6% in 1998, before easing to an estimated 6.7% for 1999. Expansion of the offshore financial and tourism sectors was the motor of the economic surge, with associated sectors such as construction also contributing. The GDP growth was achieved without inflationary consequences, the consumer price index averaging 2.7% between 1993 and 1997. However, unemployment increased from an estimated 10% in 1997 to 12.6% in 1999, with almost a third of the potential workforce in North and Middle Caicos unemployed. Providenciales, the main tourist center, however, enjoyed full employment.

GEOGRAPHY/RESOURCES

While Grand Turk is the seat of government, the most populated island is Providenciales, at the west end of the chain. Grand Turk and various cays lie to the southeast, with most of the Caicos islands between Providenciales and Grand Turk. Out of an estimated 1999 population of 24,000, a substantial proportion are of Haitian, Dominican, and U.S. origin. The literacy rate is about 90%.

High salinity in the soil and low rainfall severely restrict the potential for agriculture, and the only other natural resources, the beaches and coral reefs, provide the basis for the tourist trade.

COMMUNICATIONS/ENERGY

The main airport in Providenciales provides connections to London, Miami, New York, the Bahamas, Jamaica, Haiti, and the Dominican Republic. There are four ports of entry for passenger and cargo boats, but no cruise passenger port. The road network includes metalled roads on all the inhabited islands.

Domestic and international telecommunications are provided by Cable & Wireless. Electricity is generated by private companies, with capacity of more than 6 MW on the three main islands.

FISCAL/FINANCIAL

The government's finances have shown a surplus on current operations in recent years, with wages and salaries accounting for half of total spending. As a British dependency, the islands receive British government assistance towards the capital budget. There is no personal or corporate income tax, and no tax on inheritance or capital gains. Customs receipts are the main source of government revenue, together with tourism taxes, company registration fees, and various non-tax sources.

Four commercial banks operate on the island, including two international banks, Nova Scotia and Barclays. The offshore financial sector housed 14,600 companies in 1998. Insurance, trust companies, and accounting and legal firms are other elements in the sector, which is supervised by a unit financed by the British government. Five banks conduct exclusively offshore business. The Turks & Caicos Islands was among the jurisdictions listed in 2000 by the Organisation for Economic Co-operation and Development as offering "harmful tax competition" to OECD members.

BUSINESS OPPORTUNITIES

Investment incentives for "non-Belongers" (those not of island origin) include: duty exemption on imported construction materials and equipment; grant of permanent residence certificates to investors, plus work permits for key staff; availability of long-term government leases at concessionary rents, with freehold purchase available in exceptional circumstances; and remission of freight duties and other taxes. Land purchases of less than $25,000 are duty-free; others carry duty at a maximum of 3%. Crown land is available for lease where the project is for development of hotels, housing, light manufacturing, wholesaling, and other commercial enterprises. Developers are required to give preference in employment to Belongers; work permits for non-Belongers are renewable after five years. Certain activities, mainly in the retail and service sectors, are reserved for Belongers.

For More Information

Books:

Doing Business in the Turks and Caicos Islands. TCInvest, P.O. Box 105, Grand Turk.

A Strategic Profile of Turks and Caicos Islands, 2000 Edition. San Diego, CA: Icon Group International, 2000.

Turks and Caicos Islands Country Study Guide. 2nd ed. Washington, D.C.: International Business Publications, 2000.

Web Sites:

Caribbean Development Bank: **www.caribank.org**

Turks and Caicos Islands Investment Agency (TCInvest): **www.tcinvest.tc**

Turks and Caicos Tourist Board: **www.turksandcaicostourism.com**

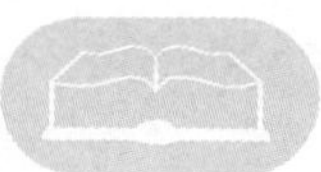

UGANDA

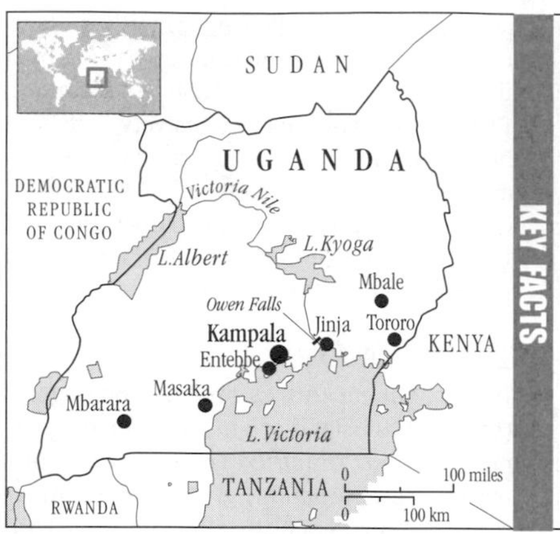

KEY FACTS

GNI: **$6,794 million, world's 98th**
GNI pc: **$320; world's 178th**
Head of government: **president**
Currency: **new Uganda shilling (NUSh)**
Capital: **Kampala**
Population: **21,143,000, growing at 2.8% p.a.**
Land area: **77,100 square miles**
Population density: **274 per square mile**
Life expectancy: **42 years**
Infant mortality: **83 per 1,000 live births**
Language: **English, Swahili, Luganda, Lusoga, other languages**
Best buy: **fabrics, basketwork, carvings, flowers, spices, fruit**

ECONOMIC STRUCTURE

For 15 years, between 1971 and 1986, Uganda underwent a collapse of order and responsible government, triggered by General Idi Amin's seizure of power. Brutal military repression stirred ethnic conflict and caused hundreds of thousands of deaths as well as the forced departure of the economically-important Asian community. The fighting continued even after Amin's overthrow in 1979, and peace was eventually restored by the National Resistance Army, led by Yoweri Museveni, who introduced a "no-party" or "movement" system of government whereby communities elected their representatives without party affiliation. In the early 1990s, a new constitution was drawn up, which established a national parliament but deferred the establishment of multiparty democracy to a later date. Presidential and parliamentary elections in 1996 and 2001 confirmed the continuing popularity of Museveni and the movement system. The former principal parties, the Uganda People's Congress and the Democratic Party, were not permitted to organize through meetings or rallies, but several of their candidates won seats in parliament.

Also during the 1990s, there were armed insurrections in the north and the southwest, led respectively by the Lord's Resistance Army and the Allied Democratic Front. In 1997 both Uganda and Rwanda supported the armed movement which took power in Congo Democratic Republic, but in 1998 that country itself became divided between its different armed factions, and Uganda sent in its own forces to support two of the factions in the north and northeast. In line with UN peacekeeping efforts, Uganda began a partial withdrawal of its troops from the Congo in 2000. In 2001, however, there was a rise in tension between Uganda and Rwanda, although the threat of war was deferred by international mediation.

Uganda has a predominantly agricultural economy in which food is grown for subsistence and for local trade, with some growing of cash crops, especially coffee, tea, and cotton. Agriculture accounts for 43% of GDP, while the other main contributors to GDP are trade, services, construction, and manufacturing. Economic activity is concentrated in the south and southwest of the country where the weather patterns are generally reliable. Helped by the restoration of political stability and the economic reforms introduced since the late 1980s, the economy has recovered well from its collapse of the 1970s. The key sectors of agriculture, manufacturing, trade, transport, and construction have all witnessed a strong recovery.

The most important exports are coffee (which accounts for more than half the value of export earnings), fish, tea, tobacco, corn, cotton, and cut flowers. There are also exports of gold and other minerals brought in from neighboring countries, especially Congo Democratic Republic and Sudan. The main markets for Uganda's exports are the United Kingdom, Belgium, Spain, the United States, and France. Its principal sources of imports are Kenya, the United Kingdom, Japan, India, the U.A.E., and Germany. South Africa is also becoming a major supplier.

Liberalization policies adopted by the government have sharply reduced the state's formerly dominant role in the economy. Its monopoly over prices and exports of coffee was abolished in the early 1990s, allowing private trading companies to compete openly. Many farms, factories and other businesses were returned to their former owners, but the process of privatization in some areas of the economy suffered long delays resulting from corruption and insider dealing. In particular, the sale of the Uganda Commercial Bank was found to be illegal. After the introduction of new regulatory frameworks, full privatization of the telecommunications, electricity and banking sectors went ahead in 2000 and 2001.

ECONOMIC POLICY

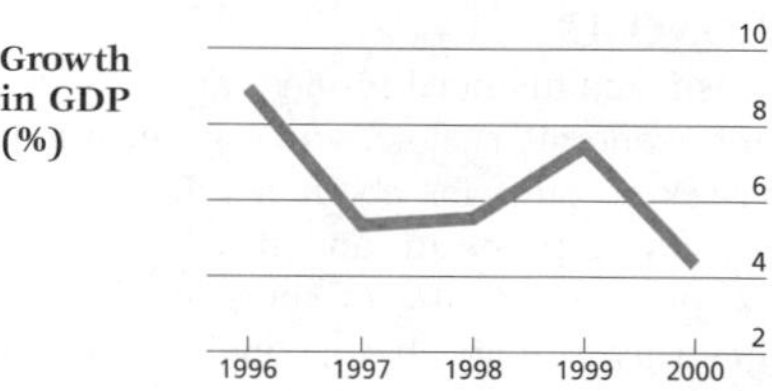

Uganda has adopted far-reaching economic adjustment and reform policies, and has tended to outperform the expectations of international donors and the IMF. The government's budget deficit has been brought under control despite the low level of domestic tax revenue, while a tight monetary policy has been adopted in order to reduce inflation. Investment has been attracted by the abolition of all capital controls. In 2000, Uganda became the first country to comply with the conditions necessary to benefit from the Highly Indebted Poor Countries (HIPC) debt relief initiative. The government has been proactive in redirecting expenditure towards the elimination of poverty by increasing spending on education and health. International donors have supported these programs.

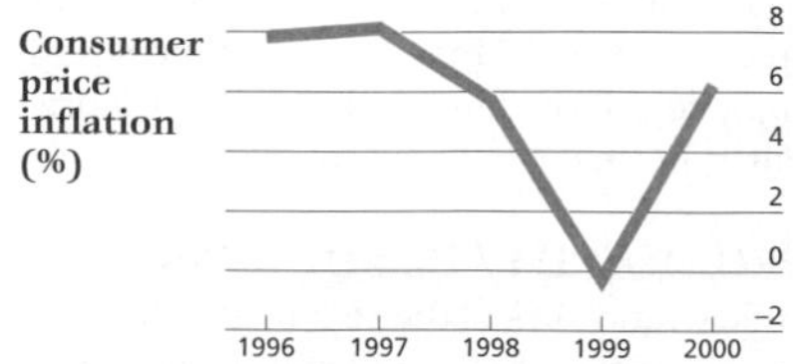

Economic growth, which reached 9% in 1996 and averaged 5% in subsequent years, has remained strong enough to maintain a level of confidence in the country's recovery. Inflation has remained low.

Employment levels have improved in areas of active investment.

Geography/Resources

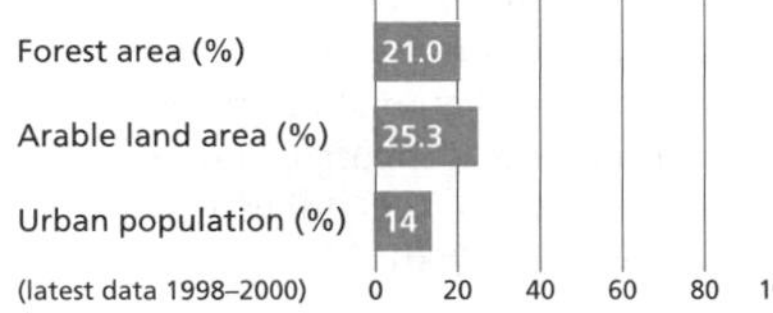

Much of Uganda is located on a high plateau which slopes eastwards from the high peaks of the snow-covered Ruwenzori mountains of the southwest. In the west of the country, the rough terrain and the climate favor the survival of wild flora and fauna, and there are several game parks and reserves. Uganda's borders traverse three large lakes—Victoria, Edward and Albert—and it has its own large lake, Kyoga, formed by the waters of the Nile after it leaves Lake Victoria on its way towards Sudan. High rainfall around Lake Victoria ensures plentiful vegetation and good agricultural conditions in the area. Most of Uganda is more than 3,300 feet above sea level.

Bananas are grown as the staple food throughout much of southern Uganda, while the main crops in the drier more northerly regions are millet and sorghum. There is fairly intensive rearing of livestock throughout the country. Uganda's mineral resources have attracted some mining activity but have not yet proved substantial enough for major investments. Cobalt is being extracted from worked-out copper mines at Kilembe. Exploration for other minerals, including oil, is continuing, and the government has reduced the charges for exploration licenses to encourage further activity.

The population is divided among about 30 ethnic groups, of which the most numerous are Baganda, Basoga, Teso, Banyankole, Langi, and Acholi. Almost 90% of the population live in rural areas. The only city of any size is Kampala, which is home to about 1 million people. Other towns, such as Jinja, Mbarara, Tororo, and Mbale, are of modest size.

Communications/Energy

After the economic destruction of the 1970s and 1980s, substantial investment was made in restoring the network of major and secondary roads, especially those around Kampala and the main trunk road between the Rwanda and Kenya borders. The railway link between Kenya and Kampala is an important lifeline for the economy, but has not

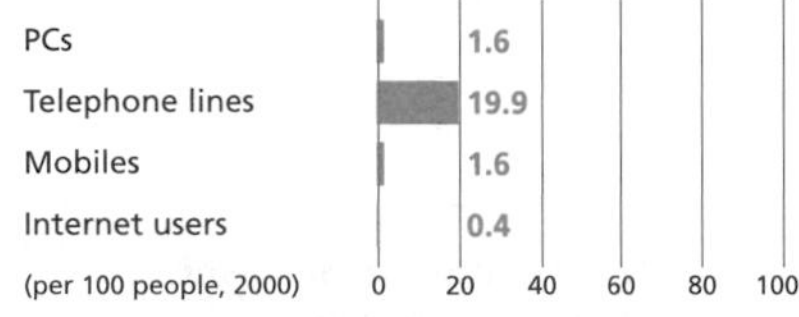

been able to attract the investment needed for modernization. The conditions of the other internal railway lines have deteriorated badly. Transport services on Lake Victoria form an important economic link with neighboring Kenya and Tanzania, and have received some new investment.

The telecommunications sector has been opened to private competition with the licensing of mobile and fixed-line operators. Majority shares in the main provider, Uganda Telecommunications Ltd., were sold in 2000 to a consortium led by Deutsche Telekom.

The electric power network reaches only a small proportion of the population. The main source of power is the Owen Falls dam on the Nile. A new privately-owned power project to be built at Bujagali, a few kilometers downstream from Owen Falls, will double national output. Other private power projects have been under negotiation. Privatization of the Uganda Electricity Board began in 2001. Uganda's fuel requirements are brought in by road and rail from Kenya.

Education/Employment

A program of major investment in primary education was launched in 1998. Although most children now enter primary school there is a high dropout rate, and only 50% of boys and 30% of girls complete their primary schooling. The secondary schooling system has been expanded by private efforts but still caters for only a very small proportion—less than 10%—of school-age children. The higher education sector has expanded significantly with the opening of new private universities. The national university is at Makerere, in Kampala. There are about 20,000 students in higher education.

About 85% of the working population are active in agriculture, forestry, and fishing.

Fiscal/Financial

The Bank of Uganda is the central bank. The only commercial bank with branches throughout the country is the Uganda Commercial Bank, which was sold to South Africa's Stanbic in 2001. Foreign banks, including Standard Chartered, Stanbic, Barclays, and Bank of Baroda, have local operations.

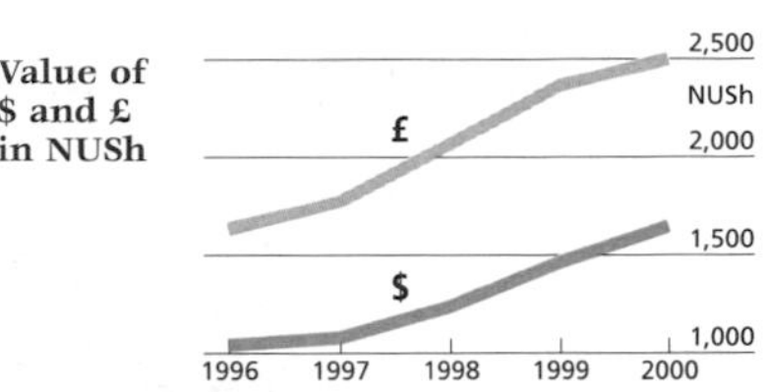

There is a small stock market which started dealing in company stocks in 2000. The tax regime is investor-friendly, and there are no barriers on capital movements.

Business Opportunities

Investment has been attracted from a wide range of companies interested in Uganda's prospects for growth and development. Investment in infrastructure has begun with the telecommunications sector and with the development of a private hydroelectric power facility at Bujagali. There has been investment in agriculture, manufacturing, tourism, and mining from a wide range of international sources, including other African countries such as Kenya, Egypt, and South Africa. In recent years, flower-farming has proved to be one of the most attractive areas for small-scale investors, in view of the perfect climatic conditions and the improvement of reliable transport links to international markets.

For More Information

Books:

Hansen, H. B., and M. Twaddle, eds. *Changing Uganda*. Athens, OH: Ohio University Press, 1991.

Hansen, H. B., and M. Twaddle, eds. *Developing Uganda*. Athens, OH: Ohio University Press, 1998.

Museveni, Y. *Sowing the Mustard Seed: The Struggle for Freedom and Democracy in Uganda*. New York: Macmillan, 1997.

Nzita, R., and Mbanga-Niwampa. *Peoples and Cultures of Uganda* Kampala: Fountain Publishers, 1995.

Web Sites:

African news and information: **www.allafrica.com/business**

Ernst and Young investment profiles: **www.mbendi.co.za/ernsty/cyaf.htm**

The New Vision (daily newspaper): **www.aegis.com/news/nv**

Norwegian Council for Africa, Index on Africa: **www.afrika.no**

Political Resources on the Net: **www.politicalresources.net**

Ukraine

KEY FACTS

GNI: **$41,991 million; world's 53rd**
GNI pc: **$840; world's 138th**
Head of state: **president**
Head of government: **prime minister**
Currency: **hryvnya (HRN)**
Capital: **Kiev**
Population: **50,658,000**
Land area: **223,710 square miles**
Population density: **226 per square mile**
Life expectancy: **69 years**
Infant mortality: **17 per 1,000 live births**
Language: **Ukrainian, Russian**
Best buy: **Ukrainian pepper vodka (pirtsovka)**

Economic Structure

In Soviet times, Ukraine put more in to the Union in terms of industrial and, especially, agricultural output than it took out in the form of investment funds, measured proportionally. Its declaration of independence in 1991, the first by any Soviet state and a key trigger for the U.S.S.R.'s collapse, brought hopes for economic prosperity, but these were dashed in a disastrous slump. Recorded real GDP fell by 70% in the decade to early 2000, the worst decline of any post-Soviet economy not affected by war.

The Soviet breakup left Ukraine with an economy based on heavy industry—chiefly steel, chemicals, machine tools, and armaments—reliant on technology outdated by world standards. High fuel consumption by these industries has made Ukraine over-reliant on imports of energy, particularly gas from Russia. The coal industry, which cannot compete with imports, has not helped, and a far-reaching closure program is under way. Heavy industry has suffered a loss of export markets, and restructuring difficulties. So has agriculture: since independence, harvests have more than halved in Ukraine, which was known as the Soviet Union's "bread basket." Agriculture's share of GDP fell from 25% in 1991 and 12% in 2000.

Russia remains Ukraine's principal trading partner, accounting for nearly two-thirds of imports and one-third of exports, followed by China and Turkey (EBRD estimates).

The private sector now accounts for 55% of GDP. Privatization programs have struggled because of poor economic conditions and lack of transparency. The most successful sale, and the one which attracted by far the largest amount of foreign investment, was that of six regional energy distributors in April 2001.

Economic Policy

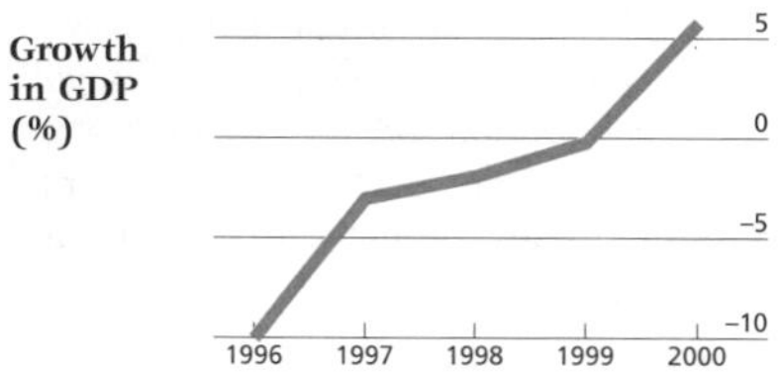

Ukraine's pro-market reforms moved slowly until the election of Leonid Kuchma as president in 1994, under whom foreign exchange and price liberalization were completed by 1997 and many trade restrictions removed. Public finances suffered from a precipitous fall in budget revenue in the early 1990s, and Ukraine became dependent on debt finance. An IMF loan program, started in 1994, was followed by the mushrooming of the government bond market in 1997–78, which collapsed in the wake of the 1998 Russian crisis.

In 1999 the IMF program was suspended. Ukraine had to restructure its external debt of $12 billion and its domestic treasury-bill debt (much of it to the national bank). President, government, and parliament agreed on an austerity budget, which reduced tax exemptions and subsidies to loss-making enterprises, and the IMF program was restored. Ukraine then began negotiations to join the WTO. Reform was invigorated by the government of Viktor Yushchenko, prime minister from 2000 to 2001, who incurred opposition from powerful business groups by addressing the energy sector's intractable problems, including corruption. Yushchenko was removed in early 2001, and reform lost momentum; however, the international financial institutions continued to support Ukraine, and a new IMF standby arrangement was put in place in November 2001.

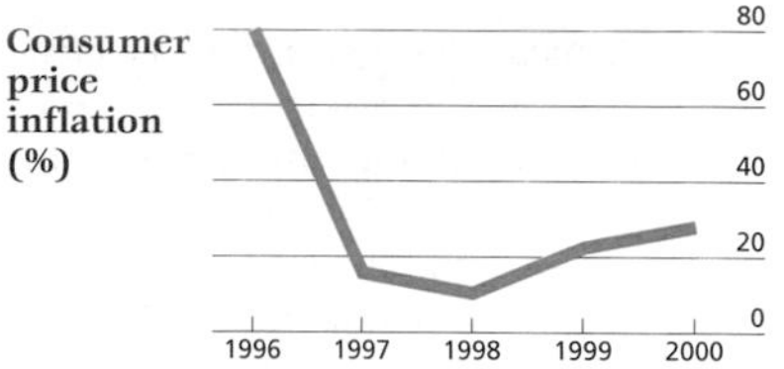

Ukraine's GDP growth became positive for the first time in 2000, when it was 3%; it was estimated at nearly 10% in 2001. Since hyperinflation subsided in 1995, inflation has averaged at 22% annually. Living standards continued to fall until 2000, when real wages had sunk to 40% of the 1992 level and an estimated 41% of the population were below the poverty line. Most observers detected the beginning of an improvement in 2001.

Geography/Resources

Ukraine, the second-largest country in Europe after Russia, is bordered by Romania, Moldova, Slovakia, and Poland in the southeast and east, Belarus and Russia to the north and east, and the Black and Azov Seas to the south.

Eastern Ukraine's industry grew on the foundation of rich mineral resources: iron ore reserves in the southeast; coal in the Donets basin; brown coal (lignite) in the Dnieper river basin; and large deposits of titanium ore, bauxite, mercury ores, and other minerals. There are oil and natural gas deposits in the Subcarpathian and Dnieper-Donets regions, and on the Crimean peninsula. Ukraine's huge swathe of fertile black soil and favorable climate is the basis for its potential to produce crops including wheat, barley, corn, potatoes, sugar beet, fruit, and sunflower seeds.

Ukraine's population, like Russia's, was ravaged by economic collapse and social instability throughout the 1990s. Between 1990 and 2000 the population was reduced by more than 2 million, from 51.6 million to 49.4 million. Falling standards of healthcare and nutrition have cut life expectancy from 65 to 62 for males, and from 77 to 73 for females. In the early 1990s the population decline was offset by immigration, particularly of Crimean Tatars exiled to central Asia

  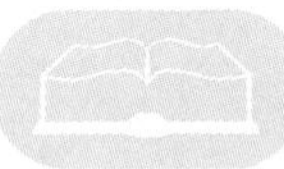  

during World War II. In the late 1990s it was exacerbated by net emigration, particularly of skilled workers.

Communications/Energy

Energy sector restructuring is a key to economic progress. Inefficient industries rely on gas supplies for which they do not pay. Ukraine is so overdependent on Russian gas imports that it has built up a debt to Russia estimated at $1.5–2.0 billion. In the mid-1990s chronic problems of business corruption centered on the gas trading market; these began to be addressed in 2000–01 by the Yushchenko government under which rates of cash settlement rose. The sale of six regional electricity distributors in 2001 was a success offset by an asset-stripping scandal that deprived Ukraine's largest generating company, Donbassenergo, of key assets.

The Chernobyl nuclear power station, site of the 1988 accident, was finally closed in 2000, and financial support is being sought from international institutions, and from Russia, for construction of replacement capacity. Redevelopment of Ukraine's own oil and natural gas producing potential is a key reform objective, as is development of its considerable oil refining sector, which has a capacity of 1.24 million barrels per day.

Ukraine's transport sector is important, given the country's size and location as an east–west gateway. In the 1990s, international financial institutions supported air transport development measures, including refurbishment of Kiev's main airport, Borispol, and thereafter of Odessa, Lviv, and Kharkiv airports, and of the air traffic control authority. Ukraine's railways (14,062 miles, all 60 inch broad-gauge, of which 5,350 miles are electrified) and roads (153,670 miles, of which about two-thirds are highways) urgently need modernization. Marine transport on Ukraine's rivers and the Black Sea is well developed.

Ukraine's telecoms infrastructure is as undeveloped as in other former Soviet republics, with just under 20 lines per 100 people, compared with 25 in Poland and an EU average of around 50. Privatization of the national telecoms monopoly Ukrtelekom has been postponed repeatedly. Private operators are enthused by the growth of the mobile telecoms sector, although at the end of 2000 it had achieved only about 3% market penetration (1.4 million subscribers).

Education/Employment

Ukraine's labor market has retained many Soviet-era inefficiencies, while the workforce has been hard hit by the post-Soviet economic crisis. An ILO study in 2000 concluded that—apart from official unemployment (4%), which is substantially lower than actual unemployment—there is widespread underemployment. The survey found that 38% of firms believed they could maintain output with fewer workers and could cut an average of one in four jobs; that at any time one in three workers is laid off via unpaid "administrative leave," short time working, or extended maternity leave for women workers.

The education system, brought to a high standard in the late Soviet period, has suffered chronic underfunding and the erosion of free education in localities where schools have instituted ad hoc payment systems. The switch to compulsory education in Ukrainian has been hampered by financial problems. Nevertheless a 1999 education ministry survey showed that the vast majority of children complete basic schooling (9 years up to age 15), with regional variations in rates of attendance at secondary schools (ages 15–17) between 33% and 49%. Ukraine's higher education system comprises 81 universities, 48 academies, and a wide range of technical and vocational schools.

Fiscal/Financial

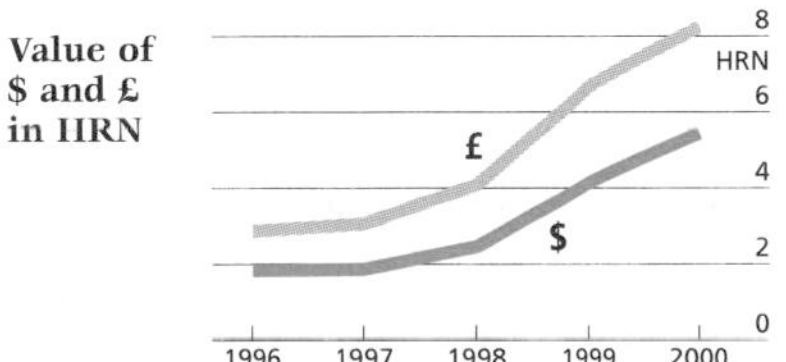

Ukraine has seven major banks, including two still in state hands that account for more than half the sector's assets; 20 medium-sized banks; and a large number of small, undercapitalized banks. From 1999 consolidation was hastened by tighter controls by the National Bank of Ukraine, and by proposed legislation that will strengthen the regulatory framework. Foreign banks play an important part in Ukraine, accounting for one-third of banking capital.

The stock market has undergone a major contraction since 1997–98: in early 2001 the KP-Dragon index, which tracks the ten most-traded large companies, was 60% up year on year, but 85% down on its high of September 1997. Only a handful of the 200 stocks quoted on the market are liquid, and there is a more widespread trade in corporate and government debt, and promissory notes ("veksels").

Since independence, Ukraine has struggled to reform its opaque and over-complex tax system. A new tax code was presented to parliament in June 2000 and passed, in a watered-down form, in 2001.

Business Opportunities

Net foreign direct investment into Ukraine in the five years from 1994 to 1999 averaged $460 million per year; in 2000 it was $595 million. In 2000 some of the large Russian companies, cash-rich from high commodity prices, bought Ukrainian metals and oil refining assets. Other sources of investment are the United States, the Netherlands, the United Kingdom, and Germany. In mid-2001 the government approved a more radical privatization program which may provide opportunities in the energy, telecoms, manufacturing, agricultural, and food processing sectors.

Over-regulation, tax issues, and weaknesses in the judicial and arbitration process are among the reasons for lack of investment. However, a series of Special Economic Zones (SEZs) have been created in which incentives include exemption from customs duty, lower corporate profit tax, a one-third reduction of tax on non-resident profits, abolition or reduction of payments into social security and other state funds, and exemption from compulsory conversion of foreign currency revenue. In October 1999 production-sharing agreement legislation was introduced, which could open the way for foreign investment in oil and gas exploration and development.

For More Information

Books:

Åslund, Anders, and Georges de Ménil, eds. *Economic Reform in Ukraine: The Unfinished Agenda*. Armonk, NY: M.E. Sharpe, 2000.

Szporluk, Roman. *Russia, Ukraine, and the Breakup of the Soviet Union*. Stanford, CA: Hoover Institution Press, 2000.

Zabytko, Irene. *The Sky Unwashed* (novel). Chapel Hill, NC: Algonquin Books, 2000.

Web Sites:

Business in Ukraine: **www.ukrbiz.net**

Infobank news agency and UkraiNet directory: **www.ukrainet.lviv.ua**

National Bank of Ukraine: **www.bank.gov.ua**

Ukraine-Today (business portal): **www.ukraine-today.com**

Ukrainian–European Policy and Legal Advice Centre: **www.ueplac.kiev.ua**

United Arab Emirates

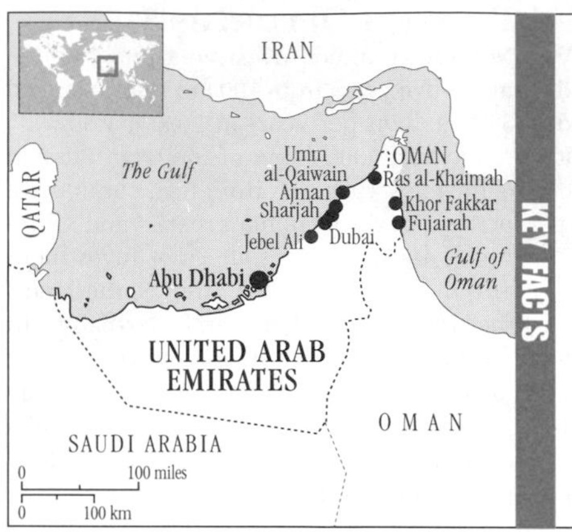

KEY FACTS

GDP: **$52,700 million**
GDP pc: **$21,980**
Head of government: **president**
Currency: **U.A.E. dirham (Dh)**
Capital: **Abu Dhabi**
Population: **2,398,000, growing at 2.5% p.a.**
Land area: **32,280 square miles**
Population density: **74 per square mile**
Life expectancy: **75 years**
Infant mortality: **8 per 1,000 live births**
Language: **Arabic (official), English, Hindi, Farsi**
Best buy: **textiles, leather goods, electronic goods**

Economic Structure

In the early 19th century Britain signed treaties with the leaders of the states of the current United Arab Emirates to protect its shipping routes to India from pirates. Britain handled foreign relations for these "Trucial States." Oil, which transformed the economy of the larger emirates in the 1960s, fuelled the drive for full independence, which was achieved in 1971 with the formation of the federation. Sheikh Zayed bin Sultan Al Nahyan of Abu Dhabi was elected president, a post to which he has been re-elected at five-year intervals since then. The U.A.E.'s membership of the World Trade Organization, which becomes fully effective in 2003, will oblige it to open up more to foreign banks and companies.

Services contributed 48.5% of GDP in 1999, followed by industry (including manufacturing, mining, construction, and utilities 48.1%) and agriculture (3.4%). The oil sector accounted for 25.4%, and non-oil manufacturing 10.3%. The main services sectors were wholesale and retail trading, followed by government services, real estate and business services, transport and communications, and finance. The mining sector is dominated by oil and gas, and the manufacturing sector by downstream processing of these products. Dubai is also a leading world producer of aluminum from imported bauxite, and re-exports accounted for 35% of exports in 1998. Crude oil accounted for 45% of total exports in 1999. Natural gas, dried fish, and dates are also important exports, and tourism a significant foreign exchange earner. In 1999 Japan was the main export market (30%), followed by South Korea (10%), India (6%), Singapore (4.5%), and Oman (3%).

The main companies and banks are majority owned by the governments of the individual emirates, but private enterprise is encouraged. The main oil company, Abu Dhabi National Oil Company, has 40% foreign ownership. In 1995 40% of the Emirates General Petroleum Company was sold to the private sector. This, and the sale of minority stakes in banks, were restricted to U.A.E. nationals. In 1998 the Abu Dhabi government approved the first private-sector power and desalination project. Further projects of this kind are planned.

Economic Policy

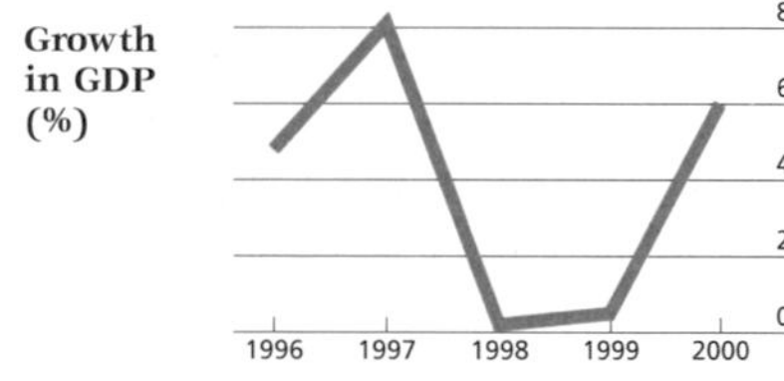

The federal budget accounts for about half of public spending, with the smaller emirates dependent on federal resources. The individual emirates manage their own resources and investment. Monetary policy is centralized, with the dirham pegged to the dollar since 1981. Welfare is generous for Emiri nationals. Power and water consumption is subsidized. Despite high federal budget deficits of 10–12% of GDP, debt is

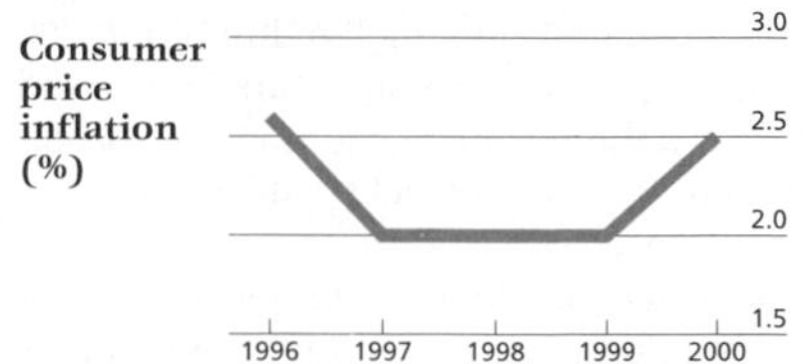

estimated to be well-contained, largely because Abu Dhabi contributes most of the budget, and its surplus wealth is well invested. The current account surplus was 3% of GDP in 1998 when oil prices were low, and will have been higher since then. Much public spending is directed at economic diversification, especially at developing education, IT, and the re-export and services sectors. Dubai, whose oil reserves are fast dwindling, has established itself as the country's non-oil commercial center through its free zones at Jebel Ali port and Dubai International Airport and Dubai Internet City. The U.A.E. has ten free zones which are being expanded for non-oil economic development. Annual GDP growth averaged 4.3% in 1997–2001. Annual average inflation was an estimated 4% in 1999–2001. Unemployment of Emiri nationals is an estimated 2.6%.

Geography/Resources

The United Arab Emirates is a federation of seven emirates: Abu Dhabi (accounting for 86.7% of the total land area), Dubai (5%), Sharjah (3.3%), Ras al-Khaimah (2.2%), Fujairah (1.5%), Umm al-Qaiwain (1%), and Ajman (0.3%). It borders the Arabian Gulf, Oman and the Gulf of Oman, Qatar, and Saudi Arabia. Most of the land is flat, low-lying desert interspersed with oases. The Hajar mountains in the northeast have a high point of 5,010 feet. Daytime temperatures range from 120°F in summer to 78°F in winter. Average rainfall is only 2.5 inches. Substantial investment has been made in seawater desalination plants to provide water for agricultural and urban consumption. Only 19% of the population are Emiri nationals, 60% of whom are under the age of 23. The largest population group are of south Asian origin (50%), followed by non-Emiri Arabs and Iranians (23%), and Westerners and east Asians (8%).

The main agricultural crops are dates, tomatoes, egg plant, melons, cucumbers, chilies, and peppers. Cereals and tobacco are also grown. Dates are a traditional oasis crop. Meat and dairy products are important. Fishing is a traditional industry, and has greatly increased in importance in the last 20 years. The government has banned the export of U.A.E.-caught fish and promoted fish breeding programs using artificial coral reefs to maintain stocks.

Proven petroleum reserves were 97.8 billion barrels (almost 10% of the world total)

and gas reserves were 212 trillion cubic feet (the fifth largest in the world) at January 2001. Abu Dhabi has the largest reserves (92.2 billion barrels and 196.1 trillion cubic feet), followed by Dubai (4 billion barrels and 4.1 trillion cubic feet), Sharjah (1.5 billion barrels and 10.7 trillion cubic feet) and Ras al-Khaimah (100 million barrels and 1.1 trillion cubic feet). Abu Dhabi's reserves have doubled in the last decade through new finds and improved rates of recovery. Non-hydrocarbon mineral resources include sulfur and gypsum.

Communications/Energy

The road network has 2,800 miles of paved roads. The pipeline network includes 516 miles for oil and 540 miles for natural gas. The main sea ports are Port Zayed, Abu Dhabi (which handled 4.7 million tons of freight in 1999), Jebel Ali and Port Rashid (Dubai—39 million tons), Port Khalid and Khor Fakkar (Sharjah—90,972 teus and 989,028 teus respectively), and the Port of Fujairah (565,723 teus). In 1999 the merchant fleet comprised 68 ships of over 1,000 grt, representing a total 1.1 million grt. There are six international airports at Abu Dhabi, Al Ain, Dubai, Sharjah, Ras al-Khaimah, and Fujairah. Dubai, Abu Dhabi, Al Ain, and Sharjah are undergoing expansion. Dubai handled 11.2 million passengers and 498,000 tons of cargo in 1999, while Sharjah handled 580,550 tons of freight and 1 million passengers.

State-controlled Emirates Telecommunications Corporation, which has a monopoly on telecommunications services, applies the lowest mobile phone and Internet fees in the Middle East to promote the U.A.E. as an e-commerce hub through the Dubai Internet City launched in 2000. At end-2000 there were 1 million fixed phone lines, 1.4 million mobile phones, and 735,000 Internet subscribers.

Total crude oil production was 2.15 million barrels per day in the third quarter 2001. Oil consumption was an estimated 331,000 barrels per day, and exports 1.8 million barrels per day in 2001. Natural gas production was 1.34 trillion cubic feet, with consumption 1.11 trillion cubic feet and exports 230 billion cubic feet in 1999. Abu Dhabi National Oil Company operates the U.A.E.'s two refineries. Electricity is entirely generated by fossil fuels. Major investment in the gas sector is aimed at meeting rapidly expanding demand for electricity and for gas feedstock for the petrochemicals industry. The Dolphin Project is aimed at linking the gas grids of U.A.E., Qatar, Oman, and—eventually—Pakistan. Electricity grid connections are planned with neighboring countries.

Education/Employment

Education is compulsory from age 6 to 12. There are three universities at Abu Dhabi, Dubai, and Sharjah. Eleven Higher Colleges of Technology offer technical training in business administration, accounting, IT, engineering, aviation technology, and health sciences. The Center for Excellence for Applied Research and Training offers continuing education. Most higher education is publicly funded, but the private sector is increasing. The Ministry for Higher Education oversees the sector. Student enrollment is around 30,000 (mostly women), with several thousand more studying abroad on government scholarships. The government has instigated IT degrees to provide skilled workers and the basis for IT research.

About 90% of the labor force is expatriate, and the national objective is to increase the participation of Emiris. Laws to achieve this are in effect for the banking and teaching sectors. Wages are determined by employers and employees. Collective bargaining is not allowed. The Ministry of Labor reviews work contracts in accordance with an unofficial minimum wage to ensure an employee's basic needs. Health and safety standards are set by the government. The standard working day is 8 hours and working week 6 days.

Fiscal/Financial

Value of $ and £ in Dh

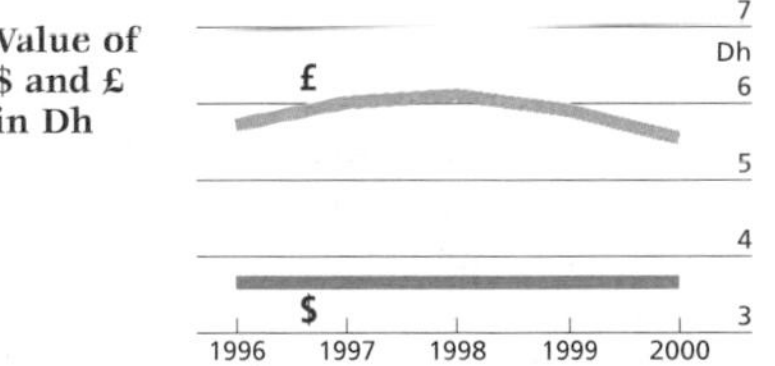

The largest banks by assets are National Bank of Abu Dhabi, National Bank of Dubai, Emirates Bank International, Mashreqbank, and Abu Dhabi Commercial Bank, most of which are majority public-sector with minority private-sector equity. The Central Bank of the United Arab Emirates regulates the finance sector. There is no income tax. Profits tax of 20% is applied to foreign banks. Foreign oil companies holding equity in U.A.E. operations pay taxes and royalties.

At mid-2000 the banking sector comprised 20 locally-owned banks with 207 branches in the U.A.E. and 43 overseas branches, 27 foreign banks with 119 branches, 1 restricted license bank, 2 investment banks, and ten representative offices of foreign banks. Consolidation is likely once World Trade Organization rules apply to banking, and the government will have to lift its freeze on foreign bank licenses. U.A.E. banks finance non-oil investment, since the hydrocarbons sector is funded by government, and find insufficient projects. Internet banking is actively promoted by the government. Abu Dhabi's new financial center, the Saadiyat Financial Market, was launched in summer 2000 and includes banking, financial, commodities and derivatives trading, and insurance. There are two stock exchanges regulated by the Emirates Financial and Commodity Market Authority: the Dubai Financial Market, which launched in March 2000, and the Abu Dhabi Securities Market, which opened in November 2000.

Business Opportunities

The legal framework favors local enterprise. Foreign investors have been excluded from most privatizations, but there are now opportunities for foreign companies to build, own, and operate new power and desalination plants. Free zones offer full enterprise ownership to foreign investors in manufacturing and services. Elsewhere foreign equity is limited to 49%. Most free zones also allow full exemption from import and export duties and commercial levies, as well as full repatriation of profits and capital. The free zone authorities offer premises, utilities, and assistance in recruitment. The largest free zone at Jebel Ali has attracted 1300 companies from 80 countries. The main foreign investors are the United Kingdom, the United States, France, India, Japan, and Germany.

For More Information

Books:

Humphreys, Andrew, et al. *Middle East*. 3rd ed. Oakland, CA: Lonely Planet, 2000.

Peters, James. *The Arab World Handbook*. London: Stacey International, 2000.

Taryam, A. O. *The Establishment of the United Arab Emirates, 1950–1985*. New York: Routledge, 1987.

Web Sites:

Emirates News Agency: **www.wam.org.ae**

Government entry point: **www.uae.gov.ae**

UNITED KINGDOM

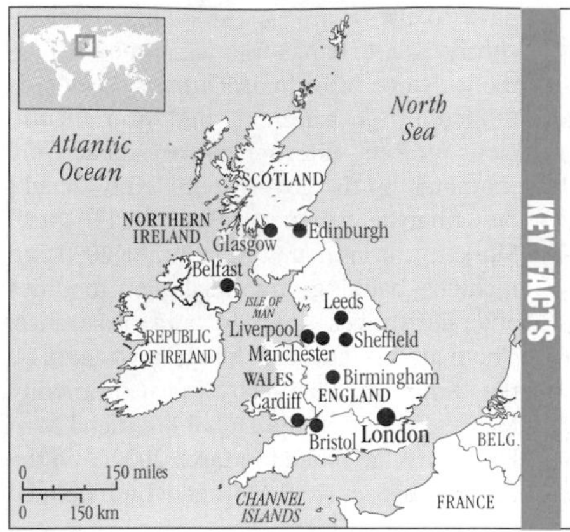

KEY FACTS

GNI: **$1,403,843 million; world's 5th**
GNI pc: **$23,590; world's 23rd**
Head of government: **prime minister**
Currency: **pound sterling (£)**
Capital: **London**
Population: **58,744,000, growing at 0.2% p.a.**
Land area: **93,280 square miles**
Population density: **630 per square mile**
Life expectancy: **78 years**
Infant mortality: **6 per 1,000 live births**
Language: **English, Welsh (official in Wales), Gaelic, Irish**
Best buy: **cashmere sweaters, ceramics, antiques, whisky**

ECONOMIC STRUCTURE

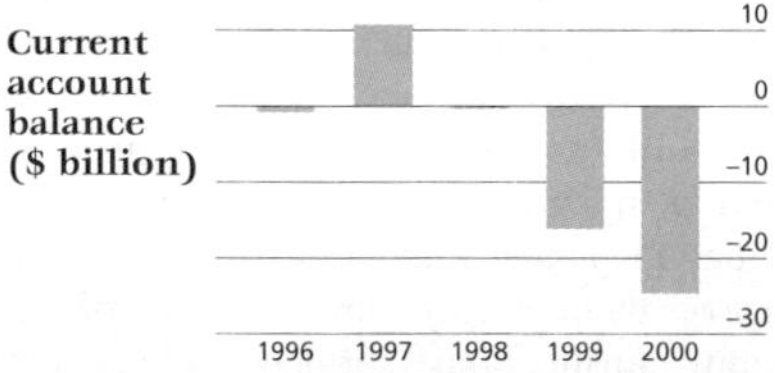

The United Kingdom has thrived on trade and seafaring since early history. Metals and cloth provided the basis for industry. Mercantilism and finance grew in the 16th century with world exploration and trade. The 18th century brought the Industrial Revolution. The rest of the Western world caught up a century later, and the United States and Germany surpassed the United Kingdom in economic strength at that time. However, this was masked by Britain's expansion of overseas empire. The United Kingdom suffered greatly from two world wars in the 20th century, both of which it nominally won. Its failure to join the European Economic Community at the outset in the late 1950s cost it prosperity. Its failure to join the Euro in 1999 may do the same. However, British attempts to make the EU more democratic at the turn of the century could strengthen the Union.

Services accounted for 70.3% of gross value added in 1999, manufacturing for 18.8%, mining (including petroleum and gas) 2.3%, and agriculture 1.2%. Business services and real estate were the main private services sector, contributing 22.4%, followed by commerce 11.8%, transport, storage and communications 8.8%, and finance 5.8%. Tourism is important, and was severely reduced in 2001 by the outbreak of foot-and-mouth disease and consequent closing of the countryside. Public services—including education, health and defense—accounted for 16.9%. The arms industry is significant. Processed food and beverages, electrical and optical equipment, paper and publishing, transport equipment, chemicals, and metal products are the main industries. IT and biotechnology are growing rapidly. The main exports in 1999 were machinery and transport equipment (especially office machinery and telecommunications equipment, cars, and mechanical engineering products), chemicals, processed food and agricultural produce, and minerals. The main markets were the United States, Germany, France, the Netherlands, Ireland, and Belgium.

Privatization of public-sector companies (which included utilities, oil and gas primary production, coal, steel, and transport) began in 1984 with the sale of British Telecom. Gas distribution, electricity, water, bus, and air transport companies followed, along with blocks of shares in oil and gas producer BP. Many other public companies and administrative services have been privatized since then. Most public-sector entities, such as hospitals and local governments, are obliged by law to contract out services to the private sector. The Post Office's traditional operating areas are being opened to competition. Air traffic control was privatized in 2001, but airports remained in the public sector. The rail infrastructure company Railtrack was effectively renationalized in 2001 to prevent bankruptcy and to achieve greater accountability for the public finance role in the privatized rail industry. The government plans to restructure the rail industry.

ECONOMIC POLICY

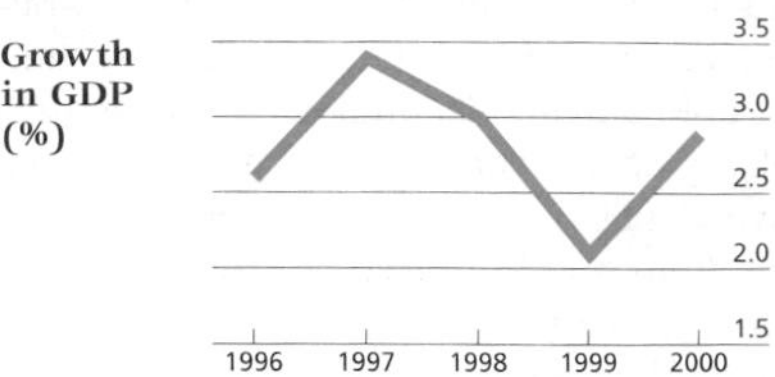

Caution has been the watchword of British macro-economic policy for many years, so much so that the long-term lack of infrastructure investment has caused productivity bottlenecks. In 2001 the government announced major new investment in transport (all modes, but with the highest spending for rail), education, and health, with financing to be provided by both the public and private sectors. In 2002 it announced changes in countryside policy to give greater support to environmental protection and tourism. Government debt increased in the first half of the 1990s, reaching 52.7% in 1996, since when it has declined to around 40% in 2001. The government intends to reduce it to 31% in the medium term. The government's inflation target for monetary stability and sufficient economic growth is 2.5%.

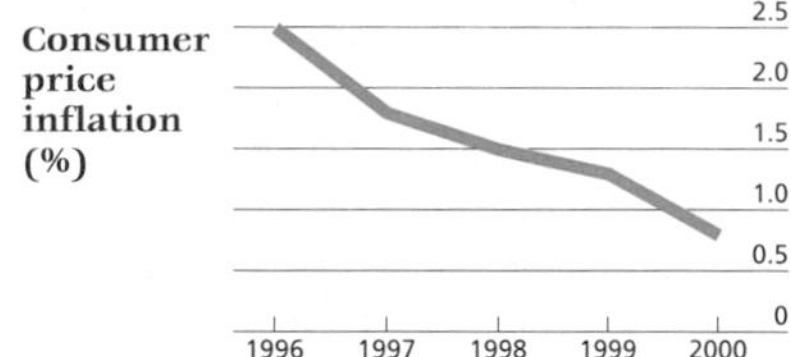

Recovery from the early 1990s recession began in 1994 with GDP growth of 4.4%. Average annual growth for 1991–95 of 1.6% improved to 2.7% for 1996–2000. It was 2.3% in 2001, and is expected to be about 2% in 2002. Inflation fell from an average 3.4% in 1991–95 to 2.6% in 1996–2000. It was around 2% in 2001 and is expected to stay low in 2002. Unemployment fell from a peak of 10.5% in 1993 to 5.3% in 2001, but labor productivity was in decline from 1995 to 1999, reflecting skills shortages, and inadequate investment in industrial equipment and in education. Productivity improved in 2000–01.

GEOGRAPHY/RESOURCES

The United Kingdom is a collection of islands to the west of continental Europe. The mainland and its close islands comprise England, Scotland, and Wales. Northern

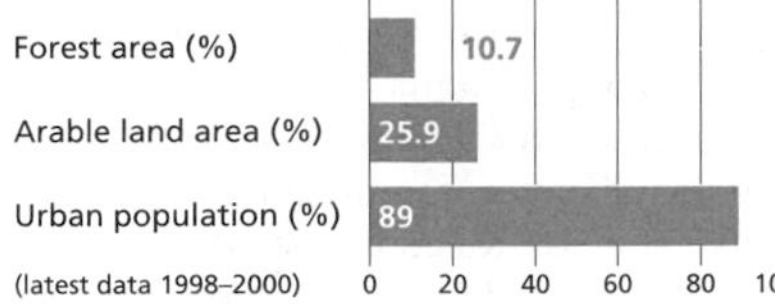

Ireland consists of six counties in the extreme northeast of Ireland. U.K. Crown Dependencies include the Channel Islands, close to France, and the Isle of Man in the Irish Sea. There are other dependent territories in the Atlantic and Pacific Oceans, and the Caribbean and Mediterranean Seas. Most of England and Northern Ireland consists of plains, valleys, and hills. Low mountains cover about half of Scotland and more than half of Wales. The climate is temperate and wet, with colder and wetter weather in the north.

Agriculture is varied. Main crops are wheat and barley, potatoes, sugar beet, oilseed rape, vegetables, and fruit. Meat and dairy produce have been important, but production and exports suffered from the ten-year BSE crisis in beef, followed by a massive foot-and-mouth outbreak in 2001. The main mineral resources are petroleum and natural gas from the North Sea, along with coal, production of which has virtually ceased as a result of cost and environmental considerations. Proven oil reserves were 5 billion barrels and gas reserves were 26.8 trillion cubic feet at January 2001. Coal reserves were 1.5 billion tons at end-1996. Iron ore, clay, slate, limestone, dolomite, chalk, sandstone, gravel, gypsum, fluorspar, barytes, talc, sulfur, potash, tin, and salt are mined. There are reserves of zinc and copper.

There are four main nationalities: English, Welsh, Scottish, and Northern Irish, the latter three sharing Celtic languages, versions of which are also spoken in Cornwall and the Isle of Man. The majority of the population is urban. About 6% are of foreign origin, mainly from the Indian subcontinent, the Caribbean, Africa, and the Far East.

Communications/Energy

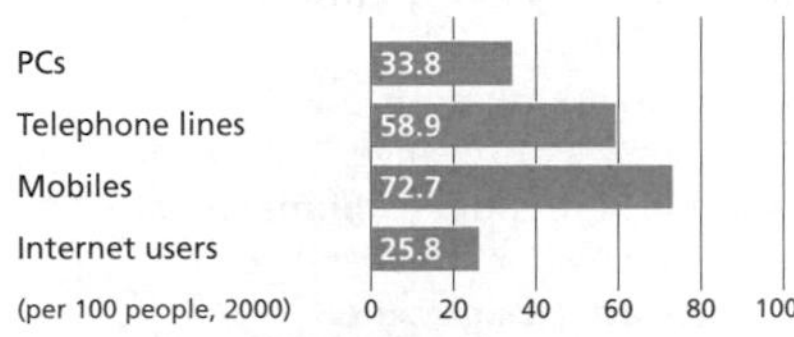

Road transport is dominant for both passengers and freight. In 1999, 93% of domestic passengers traveled by road (1,086 billion passenger-miles), against 6% by rail (74 billion passenger-miles), and 1% by air (11.7 billion passenger-miles); 65% of domestic freight moved on the roads (252.2 billion ton–mile), against 22% by water (85.3 billion ton–mile), 8% by rail (29.6 billion ton–mile), and 5% by pipeline (18.7 billion ton–mile). The road network is 231,107 miles, with 2,087 miles of motorways. The rail network is 10,346 miles, of which 3,173 miles is electrified. Inadequate track and safety maintenance from the early 1990s prior to and after rail privatization caused a series of fatal accidents in recent years and reduced rail operations. The Channel Tunnel, providing rail access to continental Europe, was opened in 1994. There are over 400 sea ports which handled 291.5 million tons of imports and 252.8 million tons of exports in 1999. Most of the 2,000 miles of inland waterways are used for leisure, but 2.8 billion ton–mile of freight traveled by this mode in 1999. The ocean-going merchant fleet numbered 200 ships over 1,000 grt, totaling 3.9 million grt in 2000. The two main airports serving London—Heathrow and Gatwick—are among the busiest in the world. Other main airports are at Manchester, Birmingham, and Glasgow. Over 20 airports offer domestic and international routes. They handled 82 million international passengers in 1999.

Telecommunications has been open to competition for over a decade, lowering prices. British Telecom remains the dominant player in fixed-line telephony and Vodaphone in mobile phone communications. There were 35.2 million fixed phone lines, 43.5 million mobile phones, and 15.4 million Internet users at end-2000. At September 2000 96% of businesses and 45% of households had PCs. The value of e-commerce was estimated at £2 billion in 1999, 40% of which was business-to-business. However, the uptake of fast Internet access has been slower than expected, and total Internet subscriptions fell in 2001.

Oil accounted for 46% of final energy consumption in 1999, gas for 34%, electricity for 15%, and coal and coal products for 3%. Conventional thermal power stations generated 39% of electricity, combined-cycle gas turbine stations 34%, nuclear 25%, and hydro 2%. Oil production was 2.75 million barrels per day, with consumption at 1.7 million barrels per day and net exports at 1.05 million barrels per day in 2000. Gas production was 3.49 trillion cubic feet, with consumption at 3.26 trillion cubic feet and net exports of 20 billion cubic feet in 1999. Coal production was 37.1 million tons and consumption 58.8 million tons in 1999. There is an electricity grid link between Britain and France, and a link between Northern Ireland and the Irish Republic, but there is no link between Britain and Northern Ireland.

Education/Employment

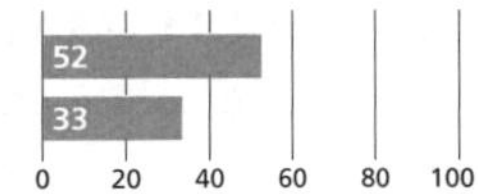

Education is compulsory from age 5 to 16. The government has encouraged parents to make use of preschool classes, available from age 3. There are 89 universities providing degree courses, and over 500 colleges providing specialized professional and vocational courses. The Open University provides distance degree and diploma courses. Many private and local government funded training providers offer National Vocational Qualifications in professional subjects to those in or out of work. Universities are autonomous, but most funding is provided by the Higher Education Funding Councils for England, Scotland, Wales, and Northern Ireland. Other funding comes from fees, research conducted for industry, and from spin-off R&D companies. Responsibility for higher education in Scotland and Northern Ireland is devolved to the respective assemblies, while higher education in England and Wales is the remit of the central government. Loans are available to students.

R&D spending was 1.87% of GDP in 1997, 31% provided by government and 50% by industry. Defense R&D accounted for 40% of total spending. Government R&D spending in 2001–04 gives top priority to aerospace, followed by competiveness and the commercial exploitation of industrial research. There are 54 science and research parks which link business and university R&D. Specialties include IT, medical and biotechnology, pharmaceuticals, optics, and engineering. Foreign private-sector firms have established R&D centers for IT and pharmaceuticals.

The labor force is well educated. Wages are determined at company level between employers and trade unions or employers and employees. Government gives guidelines on wage increases, typically that they should not be above inflation. A minimum wage was introduced in 1999 and raised in 2001. Several foreign firms have negotiated zero industrial action agreements with trade unions in return for guaranteeing jobs over a period of time. Industrial action has been restricted by law since the late 1980s. The use of temporary, part-time, and fixed-term contracts increased markedly following the

  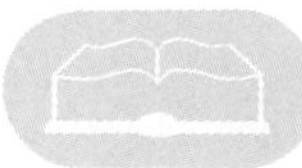    

early 1990s recession. The United Kingdom applies EU employment law, which covers safety at work, wages and working hours, industrial relations, employment incentives, and unemployment provision.

Fiscal/Financial

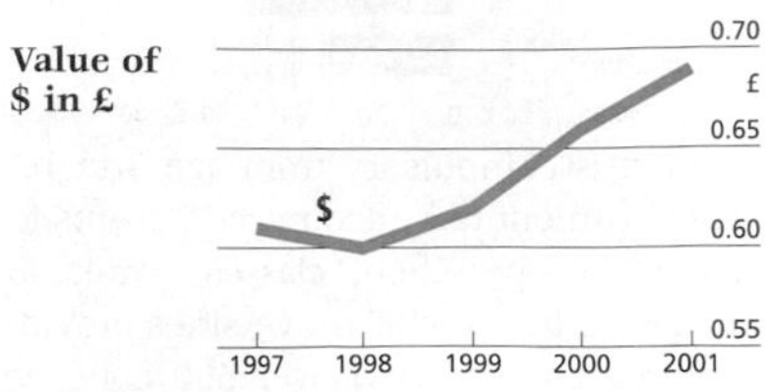

The largest bank by assets and market capitalization in 2000 was HSBC Bank, followed by Barclays Bank and Lloyds TSB. All are private-sector. The largest insurance company is Legal & General. The Bank of England, the central bank, determines monetary policy. The Financial Services Authority regulates the financial and insurance markets and the stock exchange. The main rate of corporation tax is 30% (applicable on annual income above £1.5 million), with maximum personal income tax at 40%, and personal income tax on dividends at 40%. Recent tax reforms introduced 10% and 20% tax bands for smaller businesses, and 10% initial personal income tax. Tax thresholds were raised.

London is one of the world's largest financial markets, accounting for 20% of world cross-border lending and 33% of world foreign exchange dealings. One-quarter of EU banking assets are held in the United Kingdom. There has been consolidation in domestic retail banking, especially as building societies have demutualized to become banks. E-banking is increasing, with several dedicated e-banks established. At end-2000 there were 409 banks with a total balance sheet of £3.14 trillion, including 188 U.K. banks, 97 European institutions, and 124 bank branches from other countries. Personal equity and fund investment gained impetus from privatizations, demutualizations, and the development of private pensions. Tax-free personal investment instruments launched in the 1990s increased the involvement of the public in the stock markets. Online trading from home was established and growing by 2000. Pension and investment fund management in industry is well developed. All aspects of business finance are available. The government encouraged banks to improve their services to small business. It launched venture capital funds for small companies in 2000 and 2001.

The abolition of traditional fixed-fee financial dealings in the City of London in 1987 led to the complete restructuring of investment banking into larger units. By the late 1990s almost all investment banking was controlled by foreign banks. London is the third-largest world insurance market after the United States and Japan. The total value of net premiums for worldwide life and non-life business was £141.3 billion in 1999. Standard & Poor's ranked Lloyd's of London the second-largest business insurer in the world in 1999.

The seven stock markets are the London Stock Exchange (LSE—the largest general stock market), Virt-x (a pan-European stock exchange launched in 2001 by former London-based exchange Tradepoint with the Swiss Stock Exchange and Swiss Banks), LIFFE (financial futures), OM London (specializing in Scandinavia), Jiway (a virtual exchange established by OM and U.S. finance house Morgan Stanley Dean Witter to give access to European and U.S. exchanges), the London Metal Exchange (LME—the world's largest metal exchange), and the International Petroleum Exchange. The LSE's plans to merge with the Deutsche Börse, and to link up with New York's Nasdaq exchange for smaller companies, fell through in mid-2000. The LSE fought off a hostile bid from Sweden's OM later in the year. International capital managed in London in 2000 totaled $2.5 trillion, one of the largest in the world. Turnover was £3.4 trillion, 40% up on 1999. Domestic equity capitalization was $2 trillion, equivalent to 200% of GDP, one of the highest ratios in the world.

Business Opportunities

Growth in output (% p.a., 1990–99)

Services	3.1
Industry	1.3
Agriculture	–0.2

There are financial incentives for investment (especially in regions of high unemployment, and for high-tech firms) from central and devolved governments, from the 12 regional development agencies, and from EU funds. Tax incentives include capital cost allowances in enterprise zones and elsewhere for small businesses. Opportunities exist in the IT, electronics, biotechnology, automotive, finance, and trade sectors among others. Invest U.K. is the point of contact for foreign investors.

The United Kingdom is the world's second-largest destination for inward foreign investment after the United States. It is also the second-largest outward investor. British government agencies claim to have attracted 40% of U.S. and Japanese investment for the EU market in recent years. IT, computer software, electronics, and automotive were the top investment sectors in 2000. Other key investment sectors include finance, insurance, and aerospace. EU and U.S. firms have acquired privatized utilities companies. The leading investors were the United States, Germany, Japan, and France. Other investors include companies from South Korea, Switzerland, Canada, Ireland, Sweden, Netherlands, and India.

For More Information

Books:

Hutton, Will. *The State We're In*. Rev. ed. London: Vintage Books, 1996.

Marquand, David and Anthony Seldon, eds. *The Ideas that Shaped Post-war Britain*. London: Fontana, 1996.

Office for National Statistics. *Britain: The Official Yearbook of the United Kingdom*. Norwich: Stationery Office (annual).

Turner, Barry, ed. *U.K. Today: Essential Facts in an Ever Changing World*. New York: Palgrave Macmillan, 2000.

United Kingdom Business and Investment Opportunities Yearbook. 3rd ed. Washington, D.C.: International Business Publications, 2001 (annual).

Web Sites:

Bank of England: **www.bankofengland.co.uk**

Department of Trade and Industry: **www.dti.gov.uk**

Financial Times (daily business newspaper): **www.ft.com**

Investment Agency: **www.invest.uk.com**

London Stock Exchange: **www.londonstockexchange.com**

Office for National Statistics: **www.statistics.gov.uk**

UNITED STATES

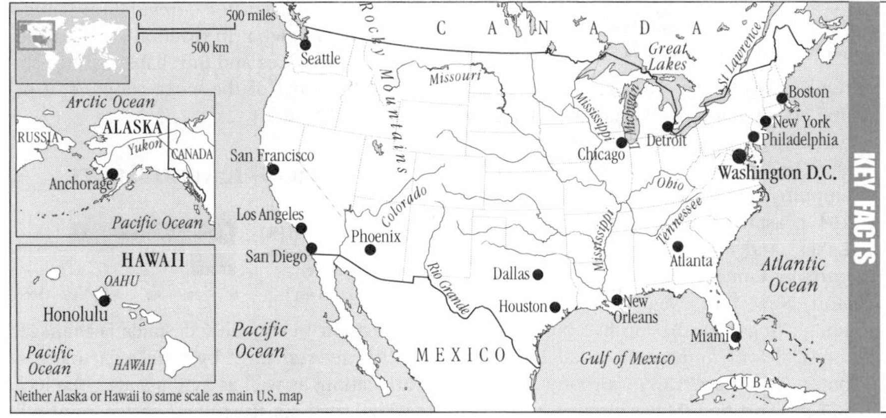

GNI: **$8,879,500 million; world's 1st**
GNI pc: **$31,910; world's 8th**
Head of government: **president**
Currency: **dollar ($)**
Capital: **Washington, D.C.**
Population: **276,218,000, growing at 0.9% p.a.**
Land area: **3,536,330 square miles**
Population density: **78 per square mile**
Life expectancy: **77 years**
Infant mortality: **7 per 1,000 live births**
Language: **English**
Best buy: **electronic equipment, gold and silver jewelry, leather goods, designer clothing, antiques, pottery, bourbon**

ECONOMIC STRUCTURE

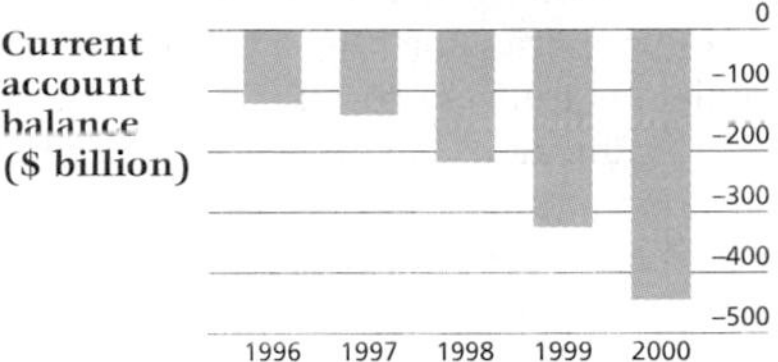

The industrial revolution in the United States, which first mechanized the previously agricultural economy, made the country a significant economic power with the growth of the iron and steel industries in the late 19th century. The expansion of the transportation network during this time allowed the country's significant natural resources to be distributed nationwide, and created pockets of industry in various geographic areas, including iron and steel in the east, meatpacking and other agricultural processing in the midwest, and textiles in the south. As companies were able to compete in national rather than regional markets, regulation of industry passed from the state to the federal level. The country's industrial growth prompted the formation of large corporations, followed in turn by antitrust laws intended to ensure competitive markets by preventing monopolies. The country's rampant industrial growth during and after World War II made it an economic superpower, and it has remained so through the transition to a service economy during the last quarter of the 20th century, despite some stumblings in the 1970s and 1980s.

Services accounted for 76.9% of GDP in 1999, followed by manufacturing (16.1%), construction (4.5%), agriculture, forestry, and fishing (1.3%), and mining (1.2%). Finance, insurance, and real estate was the largest services sector (19.3%), followed by government (11.8%), retail trade (9.2%), transportation and utilities (8.4%), wholesale trade (6.9%), and health services (5.5%). Electronic equipment is the largest manufacturing industry, followed by chemicals, industrial machinery, food products, motor vehicles, and fabricated metals. The top export markets were Canada, Mexico, Japan, the United Kingdom, and Germany. Petroleum was the primary export in 2000, followed by automotive vehicles and parts, semiconductors, computer accessories, telecoms equipment, electric apparatus, industrial machinery, and civilian aircraft.

The government has less direct involvement in the economy than in most countries: the telecommunications, transportation, banking, and electricity industries are all completely, or almost completely, privately owned. Airlines were deregulated in 1978, telecommunications in 1996, and the electric utilities were opened to competition on a state-by-state basis from 2001.

ECONOMIC POLICY

U.S. fiscal and monetary policy is established by the Federal Reserve System, which determines the amount that depository institutions must keep in reserve in Federal Reserve banks, supervises banking operations, and sets the discount rate for borrowing funds from Federal Reserve banks. The Fed steadily decreased the discount rate during the recession of the early 1990s, from 6.5% in 1990 to 3% in mid-1994, then gradually returned it to 6% as the economy improved in the late 1990s. A downturn in the economy prompted a reduction to 1.25% by the end of 2001. Public debt dropped from $3.8 trillion to $3.4 trillion from 1998–2000,

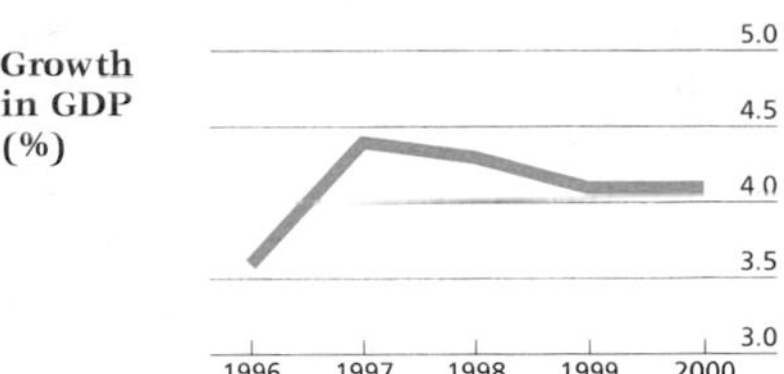

during which time the government had budget surpluses for the first time since 1957. Under the current plan, debt is due to be reduced by $2 trillion by 2010. In 2000, debt was 35% of GDP, a reduction from 1990 but still a higher percentage than in 1970 and 1980.

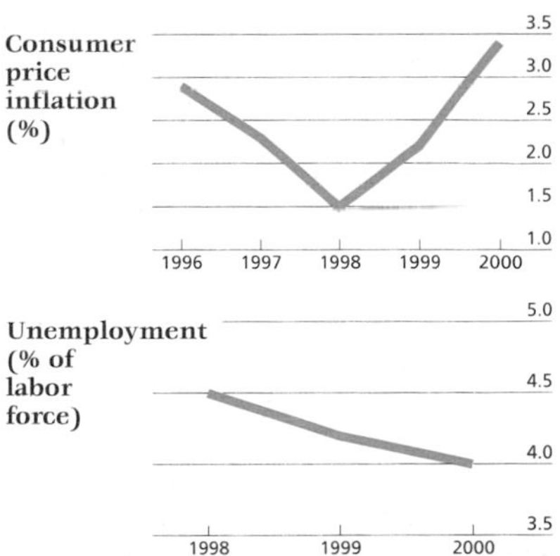

GDP has shown high levels of growth in recent years, averaging 4.1% from 1996–2000, but predictions that this level of growth cannot be sustained seem to be proving true, and growth was 1.2% in 2001. Inflation, after decreasing in 1997 and 1998, rose to 3.4% in 2000 and fell again to 1.6% in 2001. Unemployment, after averaging 6.9% from 1991–94, decreased steadily through the rest of the 1990s to a low of 4.0% in 2000, though it began increasing again in 2001.

GEOGRAPHY/RESOURCES

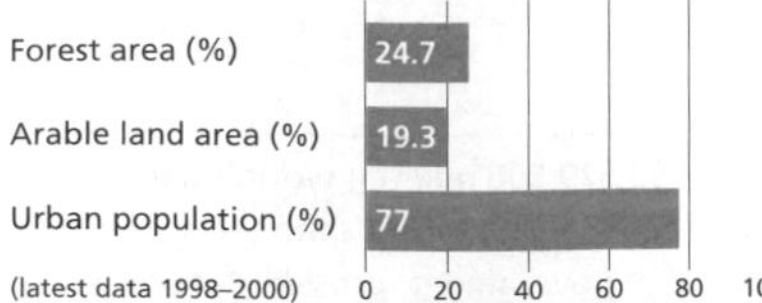

Located across the middle of the North American continent, the United States borders Canada to the north, Mexico to the south, the Atlantic Ocean to the east, the Gulf of Mexico to the southeast, and the Pacific Ocean to the west. The continental United States consists of mountains in the east and west, forests along the eastern and southeastern coasts, fertile plains in the central area, and rangeland in the west. Much of the United States has a temperate climate, but Hawaii and Florida are tropical, Alaska is arctic, the great plains west of the Mississippi River are semiarid, and the Great Basin of the southwest is arid. Major rivers include the Mississippi, the Ohio, the Missouri, the St. Lawrence Seaway, the Tennessee, the Colorado, and the Rio Grande. The Great Lakes, along the northern border in the Interior Plains, are an important shipping resource.

The varied landscape of the United States provides a wide range of natural resources. Cattle are the most significant farm product, followed by poultry and poultry products, dairy products, corn, soybeans, and hogs and pigs. The United States also produces large amounts of hay, tobacco, oranges, potatoes, tomatoes, apples, peanuts, and sorghum. Crude oil, natural gas, and coal are the most significant mineral resources; others, in order of value, are crushed stone, Portland cement, sand and gravel, gold, copper, iron ore, phosphate rock, lime, and salt.

The country's low population density is deceptive, since approximately 75% of the population lives in urban areas, while great tracts of land remain uninhabited. The population is one of the most diverse in the world, representing nearly every country on earth. Immigrants make up 11% of the population, nearly half of whom came to the United States in the 1990s; recent immigrants are primarily from Latin America and Asia. 77.1% of the population is white (from Europe, the Middle East, or North Africa); 12.5% is Hispanic, of any race; 12.3% is black or African-American; and 3.6% is Asian.

COMMUNICATIONS/ENERGY

The United States has a total road network of 3,934,000 miles, of which 60% are major

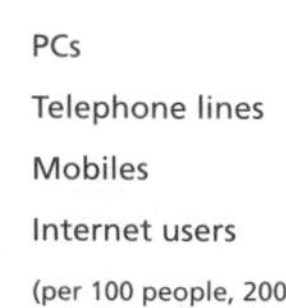

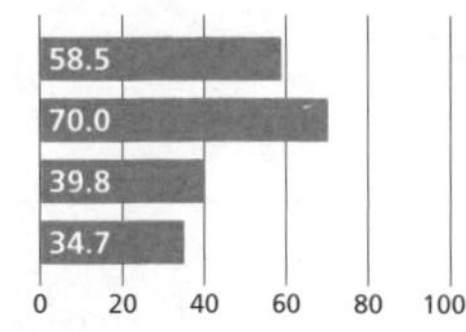

roads. There are 181,311 miles of rail, and 30,500 miles of commercially navigable waterways, including inland waterways and the Great Lakes but not including coastal shipping routes. The country has 321 ports: 194 coastal ports, 82 ports on the Great Lakes, and 45 inland ports. The top five ports by tonnage are South Louisiana, Houston, New York, New Orleans, and Baton Rouge. Together, the top five ports account for 27.8% of tonnage from all U.S. water ports. There are 13,175 airports, of which 577 are certified. Major airports are in Chicago, Dallas/Fort Worth, Los Angeles, Atlanta, and Detroit. There are 1,469,602 miles of pipeline for transporting oil and gas. Road transport accounts for 44.3% of domestic freight; pipeline (crude oil and natural gas), 22.0%; and rail, 20.0%. Water transport accounts for 13.5% of total domestic freight: 24.5% is coastal shipping, 10.5% is on the Great Lakes, and 65.0% is on inland waterways. Air freight only represents 0.2% of domestic freight.

The telecommunications industry is privatized, and regulated by the Federal Communications Commission (FCC). AT&T, a monopoly until it was broken up in 1984, remains a dominant player; WorldCom and Sprint are other significant long-distance providers. The local service providers ("Baby Bells") that resulted from the AT&T breakup still dominate most local markets. Deregulation in 1996 and increasing demand for high-speed transmission services are forcing reorganization within the sector. In 2000, 94.5% of households had a fixed-line phone, 34.5% of the population had wireless telephone service, and 41.5% of households had Internet access.

The United States is one of the world's largest energy producers, consumers, and importers. Oil accounts for approximately 38% of total energy demand, 57% of which is imported; natural gas and coal account for 24% and 23% of total demand, respectively. While coal production has decreased since 1995 and is expected to continue to do so, oil production is expected to increase as the industry recovers from the price collapse of the late 1990s, and natural gas production is expected to increase sharply due to higher demand and higher prices. The electricity market is being opened to competition on a state-by-state basis: as of 2000, 24 states and the District of Columbia had mandated electric industry restructuring, two states had legislation pending, and virtually all other states were considering restructuring. The initial enthusiasm for deregulation has decreased somewhat in reaction to the higher consumer prices and unreliable service suffered by some of the early adopters, especially California.

EDUCATION/EMPLOYMENT

Tertiary education (%)
Newspaper circulation (per 100 people)
(latest data 1996–99)

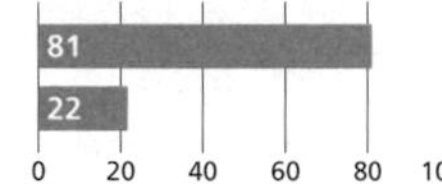

Education in the United States is managed at the federal level by the Department of Education, as well as by the states, the local school systems, the private sector, nonprofit educational research institutions, and community-based organizations. Compulsory education ages vary by state, with age of enrollment ranging from 5 to 8 and age of completion from 16 to 18. Enrollment in higher education has increased steadily since the mid-1970s, to 14,966,061 people in 1999. There were 9,485 higher education institutes in 1999; 65% of these were eligible for federal financial aid, and nearly half of all undergraduates receive some type of financial aid from federal, state, institutional, or other sources, including need-based grants, scholarships, and loans. Of these institutions, 4,500 were degree-granting institutions, from two-year to doctorate level degrees; the other 4,985 non-degree-granting institutions include both trade/vocational schools and professional certificates. In 1997–98, a third of 2-year and 4-year postsecondary education institutions offered distance education courses, and another 20% planned to start offering them within 3 years.

Most R&D investment (75.5%) comes from the private sector, 13.6% comes from colleges and universities, 7.2% from the federal government, and 3.7% from other nonprofit institutions. The bulk of R&D activity is limited to a few states, and tends to be concentrated by type; for example, California is a major center for technology and aerospace R&D, Delaware for pharmaceutical research, Maryland for medical and technological research, Massachusetts for software and biotechnology, Michigan for engineering, New Jersey for technical and pharmaceutical, New York for medical and energy research, and Texas for defense and aerospace. Since 1981 companies are entitled to a 20% tax credit for incremental R&D expenditures.

Growth in labor force (% p.a., 1980–99)
Women as % of labour force (1999)
HIV positive (% of age group 15–49, 1999)

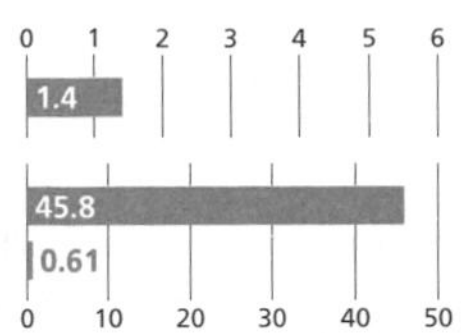

The labor force is largely well educated, although this varies by state. Wages are determined by individual agreements between employer and employee, except in the case of unionized employees; 13.5% of wage and salary workers are union members, a number which has been decreasing throughout the 1990s. Federal labor laws are the Social Security Act and Federal Unemployment Act, the Fair Labor Standards Act, the National Labor Relations Act, the Occupational Health and Safety Act, and the Worker Adjustment and Retraining Notification Act. There is also extensive state regulation is this area.

Fiscal/Financial

The five largest banks in the United States—Citigroup, J. P. Morgan Chase & Co., Bank of America, Wells Fargo, and Bank One—are all private, and represent 43.8% of total U.S. commercial banking assets. Deregulation in the banking industry created a wave of approximately 8,000 mergers from 1980 to 1998, and assisted in the creation of megabanks. The banking industry is supervised by the Federal Reserve, the Comptroller of the Currency, the U.S. Treasury, and the Federal Deposit Insurance Corporation (FDIC). The 1999 Gramm-Leach-Bliley Act, which abolishes barriers between banking and other financial services, increases demands on regulatory structure but is also expected to increase efficiency in both the banking and insurance industries. The largest insurers are State Farm, American International Group Inc., TIAA-CREF, Allstate, and Prudential of America. Although there have been slowdowns in the insurance industry in 1999 and 2000, there should be turnaround based on mergers, better pricing, and efficiency from Internet operations. European insurers are expected to seek stronger positions in the United States.

Federal corporation income tax ranges from 15–39% on a sliding scale, in addition to state and local income tax. Federal unemployment tax is 6.2%, in addition to state unemployment tax. If, however, a corporation pays all state contributions on time, the federal tax is reduced to 0.008%. Employment taxes are 15.3%. Other corporate taxes vary by state. A tax relief plan initiated in 2001 reduces personal income tax to 10–33% in four brackets.

Financial markets and the securities industry are both regulated by the Securities and Exchange Commission (SEC). The major national stock exchanges are the New York Stock Exchange (NYSE) and the American Stock Exchange (ASE or AMEX); there are regional five regional stock exchanges in the Midwest, Pacific, Philadelphia, Boston, and Cincinnati. NASDAQ, a decentralized market for securities not listed on a stock exchange, gained importance in the late 1990s due to the number of technology stocks traded. The market share of traditional exchanges is being eroded by Internet brokerage orders: NYSE and NASDAQ are both looking to expand internationally, and are considering converting to for-profit, stockholder-owned companies. The NYSE is also considering trading NASDAQ stocks for the first time.

Business Opportunities

Throughout the 1990s, most of the states established economic development programs to attract business, including some programs that specifically target foreign investors. State and local incentives include tax credits, tax exemptions, financing assistance, relocation assistance, environmental assistance, training programs, and enterprise zones. Most federal incentives to foreign investors focus on promoting exports of U.S.-manufactured goods.

Barriers to foreign investment in the United States are minimal. Non-U.S. citizens generally do not need approval from government authorities to establish a business. Exceptions to this policy include the television and radio broadcasting industries, domestic air and marine transportation, and fishing, all of which restrict the percentage of foreign ownership, and the banking, insurance, electric and gas, and communications industries, in which foreign investors may be subject to a higher level of scrutiny than U.S. investors.

Growth in foreign investment has been increasing throughout the 1990s. The United Kingdom is the largest foreign investor, accounting for 33.6% of investment outlays in 2000, followed by the Netherlands (14.9%), Canada (8.6%), France (8.3%), and Japan (7.9%). Industries that have attracted the most foreign investment are telecommunications, information services, computer equipment manufacturing, petroleum manufacturing, food manufacturing, mining, utilities, and investment banking, consulting, insurance, financial management, and advertising services.

For More Information

Books:

The Budget and Economic Outlook: Fiscal Years 2002–2011. Washington, D.C.: Congressional Budget Office, U.S. Congress, 2001.
International Economic Review (bimonthly publication). Washington, D.C.: United States International Trade Commission.
Johnson, P. *A History of the American People*. New York: HarperCollins, 1999.
Krugman, P. *The Age of Diminished Expectations: U.S. Economic Policy in the 1990s*. 3rd ed. Cambridge, MA: MIT Press, 1997.
Monetary Policy Report to the Congress. Washington, D.C.: Federal Reserve Board.
OECD Economic Surveys. *United States*. Paris: OECD.
Schick, A. *The Federal Budget. Politics, Policy and Process*. 2nd ed. Washington, D.C.: Brookings Institution, 2000.
Spulber, N. *The American Economy: The Struggle for Supremacy in the 21st Century*. New York: Cambridge University Press, 1997.
Statistical Abstract of the United States. Washington, D.C.: U.S. Census Bureau.
United States Business and Investment Opportunities Yearbook. 3rd ed. Washington, D.C.: International Business Publications, 2001 (annual).
United States Business Law Handbook. 3rd ed. Washington, D.C.: International Business Publications, 2001.
United States Export, Import, and Business Directory. 3rd ed. Washington, D.C.: International Business Publications, 2001.

Web Sites:

Bureau of Economic Analysis: **www.bea.doc.gov**
Department of Commerce: **www.doc.gov**
Department of Labor: **www.dol.gov**
Federal Reserve System: **www.federalreserve.gov**
Federal Trade Commission: **www.ftc.gov**
Government entry point: **www.firstgov.gov**
New York Times (newspaper): **www.nytimes.com**
Wall Street Journal (business newspaper): **www.wsj.com**

Uruguay

KEY FACTS

GNI: **$20,604 million; world's 62nd**
GNI pc: **$6,220; world's 64th**
Head of government: **president**
Currency: **new peso (Ps)**
Capital: **Montevideo**
Population: **3,313,000, growing at 0.7% p.a.**
Land area: **67,490 square miles**
Population density: **49 per square mile**
Life expectancy: **74 years**
Infant mortality: **15 per 1,000 live births**
Language: **Spanish**
Best buy: **leather goods**

Economic Structure

Uruguay has a long tradition of democracy, with the notable exception of military rule in 1972–85 during which period the Tupamaro National Liberation Front, a socialist revolutionary group, was defeated by the army. The country is distinguished by its high literacy rate, large urban middle class, and relatively even income distribution. The country has one of the most comprehensive systems of social security in Latin America, including free education, state medical care, pensions, and unemployment benefits.

The economy is based on agriculture. Although the sector generates 5–8% of GPD, agricultural products account for as much as 80% of export earnings. The principal exports are wool, beef, rice, leather, vegetables, chemicals, shoes, ceramics, glassware, and machinery. Industry generates close to 30% of GDP, and services around 65%. Industry is largely based on agricultural processing. There has been a gradual move from the traditional sectors such as meat processing, wool, and fisheries to other sectors such as dairy products and textiles. The third-largest source of revenue after textiles and meat products is tourism; the industry thrives on visitors from Argentina and Brazil. The country is a member of the Mercosur free trade bloc with the other "southern cone" Latin American countries. The largest export markets are Mercosur (around 45%) and the European Union (20%).

Economic and trade liberalization similar to that in other Latin American countries began during the 1990s. Activities and assets transferred to the private sector included the sale of the national airline PLUNA, gas distribution, road construction, port services, mobile telephony, and the social security system. The sale of the state telephone company, ANTEL, was rejected in a 1992 referendum by 72% of voters. Progress in privatization has been slow compared to most other Latin American countries, partly because many of Uruguay's state-owned companies are more efficiently run than their counterparts in the region.

Economic Policy

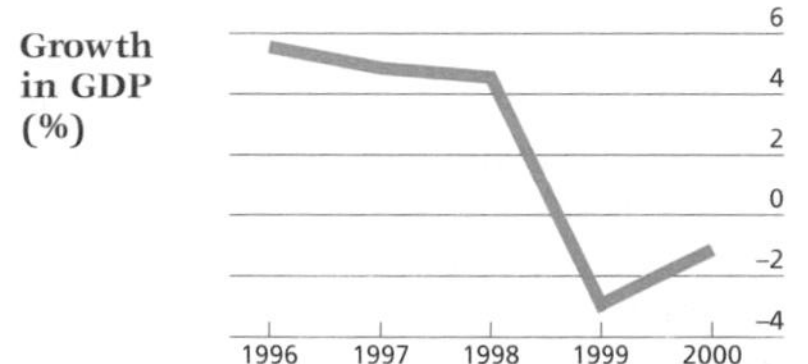

The economy performed well during the 1990s when tariffs were lowered, the budget deficit was reduced, and inflation fell from 129% in 1990 to 5.8% in 2000. Real GDP growth averaged 4.5% a year in 1992–98, and the economy went into recession in 1999 (–3.2%) and 2000 (–1.3%). Growth was zero or slightly negative in 2001. In order to ease the growing burden of social security payments on public finances, reforms were implemented in 1996 to convert the deficit-ridden system into one of public and private providers. Prior to the reform, the government financed an annual social security deficit equivalent to more than 6% of GDP. The reform is expected to reduce the deficit to 1% of GDP. More than 550,000 people out of a working population of 1.5 million have joined private pension schemes. The recession was triggered by the Brazilian devaluation, reduced growth in both Argentina and Brazil (major export markets for Uruguay), and low commodity prices. The budget deficit reached 3.9% of GDP in 2000. Inflation and debt service, however, remained under control. Inflation dropped from 130% in 1990 to around 5% in 2001. Standard & Poor's confirmed Uruguay's investment grade status in May 2001 when it was the only Mercosur country with this rating. Tax revenue represents around 25% of GDP, the highest figure in Latin America. An IMF standby credit of $200 million was in effect until March 2001.

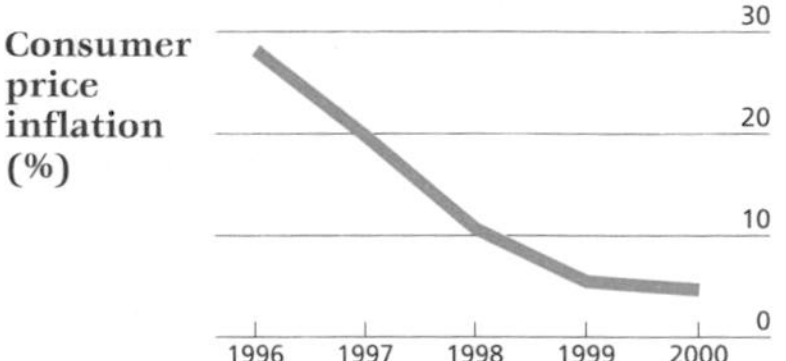

The economy is highly dollarized: around 90% of deposits in private-sector banks are dollar-denominated. The government has a policy of fixed but declining devaluation of the peso against the dollar.

Geography/Resources

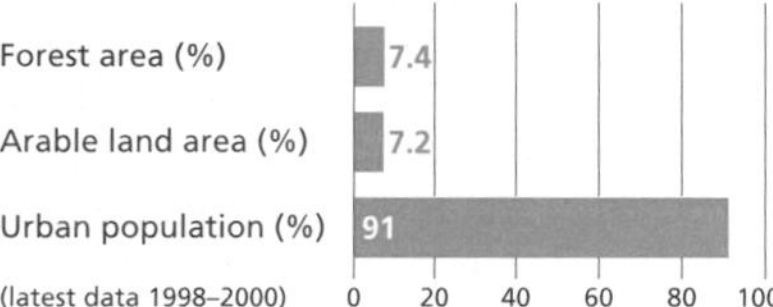

Uruguay is sandwiched between Argentina to the west and Brazil to the north. It is only 310 miles from north to south, and 292 miles from east to west. Most of the country forms part of the pampas region of South America, and consists of low, rolling plain ideally suited for cattle and sheep. The highest point is the Cerro Catedral at 1,686 feet. The River Negro, the main tributary of the River Uruguay, cuts across the center of the country, separating the two main ranges of hills, the Cuchilla de Haedo and the Cuchilla Grande. The climate is temperate, and it rains on average for about 100 days a year. Two short sections of the border with Brazil were still in dispute in 2002—the Arroyo de la Invernada area of the River Cuareim, and the islands at the confluence of the Cuareim.

More than one-third of the population lives in the southeastern part of Uruguay, in and around Montevideo, the only large city

  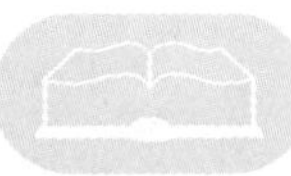    

(1.4 million). The rest of the urban population lives in about 20 towns. A low birth rate by Latin American standards and high emigration, principally to Argentina and Brazil, have created a relatively elderly population.

The country is virtually self-sufficient in food. The main crops are wheat, corn, oats, rice, sugar cane, vegetables, and citrus fruits (mainly oranges and tangerines). There are some deposits of iron ore, gold, diamonds, manganese, copper, zinc, and lead, but the mining sector is undeveloped, generating less than 0.5% of GDP.

More than 90% of the population are of European descent, mainly from Spain and Italy, 5% of African descent, and 1% mestizo.

Communications/Energy

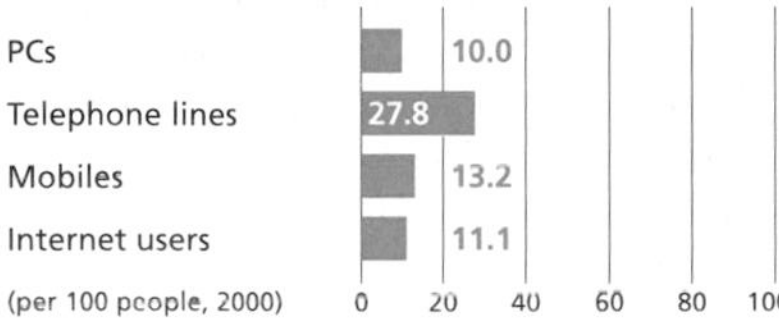

Railways began to be built in the 1860s, and by 1911 Uruguay had more miles of track in proportion to the size of the country than any other South American nation. The railways, like the most important roads, fan out from Montevideo. Parts of the railway may be upgraded in order to transport timber from the interior to ports. The country has 1,288 miles of railways and 5,582 miles of roads, almost all of them paved, and is the natural gateway to the 2,500-mile Parana-Paraguay waterway. The waterway goes north to Paraguay and Bolivia and deep into Argentina and Brazil. Joint use of this waterway for transporting goods from the five countries to the Atlantic Ocean is the largest regional integration project under way. Montevideo is a major port, and smaller ports are located in the Nueva Palmira and Colonia free trade zones.

Uruguay produces about half of its energy needs. All oil is imported. Intermittent oil exploration has been conducted but the results have been disappointing. There are deposits of low-grade coal. Electricity is entirely hydroelectric. Private generation of electricity was approved in 1997. Transmission and distribution rights remain a state monopoly. There is sufficient electricity to meet demand and provide a surplus for export to neighboring countries.

Telecoms infrastructure is among the most advanced in Latin America. The country has around 30 phone lines for every 100 inhabitants, and mobile phone penetration is more than 13%. ANTEL, the state telephone company, has a monopoly on fixed-line services. Cellular service is provided by ANTEL and a private company (Movicom) regulated by ANTEL. Data transmission and some value-added services are in the hands of private companies.

Education/Employment

The adult literacy rate is the highest in Latin America at an estimated 97%, the same as in the United States. All education, including university tuition, is provided free of charge. Education is compulsory for ages 6 to 15. Enrollment in primary and secondary education is typically 90% of the relevant age group, with around 30% in higher education.

The labor force is well educated and able to adapt to modern industrial techniques. The government has technical training programs to meet industry's skilled labor requirements. The social security overhead is high, increasing basic wage costs by almost 50% for an employer. Unionization is high in the public sector (over 80%), and low in the private sector (below 5%). The influence of trade unions has been declining.

Fiscal/Financial

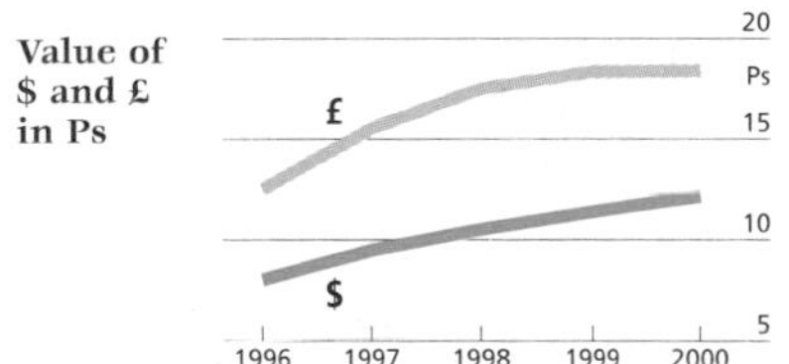

Uruguay has traditionally been a safe haven for capital flight from other Latin American countries during times of financial turmoil. The country's banking system is sound, with a low bad debts ratio and prudent supervision. The largest bank in asset terms is the state-owned Banco de la República Oriental del Uruguay. The Central Bank is not independent of the government. There is a small stock market in Montevideo with predominantly public-sector rather than private-sector securities.

Corporate tax is 30% and VAT is 23%. There is no income tax, but there is a capital tax assessed at the rate of 1.5% on assets in Uruguay less certain debts for companies and farms, 2.8% for banks, and 2% for other entities.

Business Opportunities

Uruguay welcomes foreign direct investment (FDI), but the level has been low. FDI averaged $100 million a year in 1985–95 and $175 million in 1997–2000. A 1998 law established some tax exemptions and incentives for sectors. They include accelerated depreciation, lower social security contributions for employers, exemption from corporate income tax and net worth tax payments for a specified period, and exoneration of import tariffs on equipment which does not compete with equipment produced locally. The growing forestry sector has attracted the attention of several multinationals. The government has ambitions to make the information technology (IT) industry a driver of economic growth, mirroring Ireland and Israel-like Uruguay, small countries with well-qualified labor forces.

For More Information

Books:

Box, Ben. *South American Handbook.* 78th ed. Bath, Somerset: Footprint Handbooks, 2001.

Campomar, Andreas. *Uruguay: Open for Growth.* London: Euromoney Publications, 1999.

Uruguay Business Law Handbook. 3rd ed. Washington, D.C.: International Business Publications, 2001.

Uruguay Investment and Business Guide. 3rd ed. Washington, D.C.: International Business Publications, 2001.

Web Sites:

Central Bank: **www.bcu.gub.uy**
Economist Intelligence Unit: **www.eiu.com**
Government entry point: **www.presidencia.gub.uy**
IMF reports: **www.imf.org/external**
Investment and Export Promotion Agency: **www.uruguayxxi.gub.uy**
U.S. State Department Country Commercial Guide: **www. state.gov/e/eb/rls/rpts/ccg**

  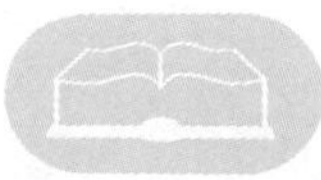    

U.S. Virgin Islands

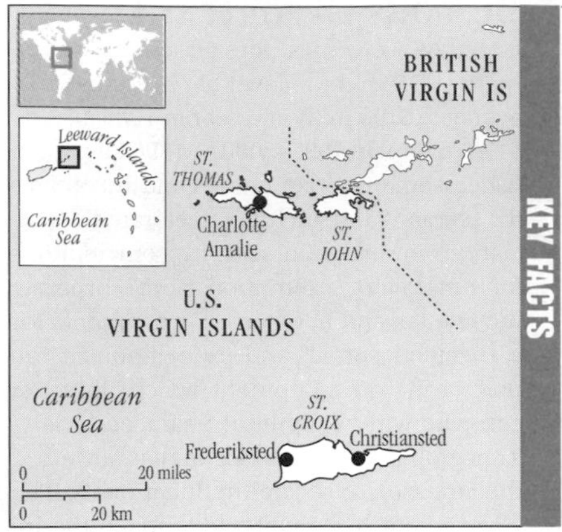

KEY FACTS

GNI pc: **$12,500 (approx.)**
Head of government: **governor**
Currency: **U.S. dollar ($)**
Capital: **Charlotte Amalie on St. Thomas**
Population: **119,800**
Land area: **140 square miles**
Population density: **85 per square mile**
Life expectancy: **78 years**
Infant mortality: **9 per 1,000 live births**
Language: **English**
Best buy: **rum, arts and crafts, jewelry**

Economy

The major employer and source of revenue in the U.S. Virgin Islands is tourism, which registered 628,000 stayover arrivals in 2000, and 1.77 million cruise ship passenger arrivals. The islands have more than 5,000 hotel rooms, and tourism is one of the two main sources of employment, the other being government services, which accounts for a third of the workforce. Unemployment was estimated at 8.5% in 2000. Agriculture is of limited significance, producing fruit and vegetables for domestic consumption, plus some cattle-raising. The major industrial activity is oil refining, conducted at the Hovensa plant in St. Croix, using imported crude. A U.S.-owned alumina refinery sited in St. Croix suspended operations indefinitely early in 2001. Other manufacturing includes the production of textiles, pharmaceuticals, and electronic goods.

The bulk of the islands' trade is with the United States and Puerto Rico, accounting for 90% of both imports and exports. Crude oil is the principal import, and refined petroleum products are the main export.

Geography/Resources

There are more than 50 islands in the group, nearly all uninhabited. They are sited east and southeast of Puerto Rico, with St. Thomas the closest to Puerto Rico. St. Croix, 40 miles south of St. Thomas, has a land area of 83 square miles, compared with 31 square miles for St. Thomas; the two islands between them contain about 96% of the total population, with slightly more people living in St. Croix. The third largest island, St. John, 3 miles east of St. Thomas, covers 20 square miles.

Rainfall averages 39 inches per annum, with wide regional variations. Fresh water supplies are limited; there is a desalination plant in St. Croix. The largely mountainous terrain and the soil salinity in flatter areas inhibit agricultural development.

The capital, Charlotte Amalie, houses more than a quarter of the population of St. Thomas, while St. Croix has two towns, Christiansted in the north and Frederiksted in the west, both sited on the coast. The population is about 40% urban. About two-thirds are of African descent, the remainder European or mixed, plus about 1,000 people of Palestinian origin. Educational standards are high, with free compulsory education to the age of 16, and higher education colleges in St. Croix and St. Thomas.

Communications/Energy

St. Croix and St. Thomas both have international airports, providing connections with the U.S., Puerto Rico, British Virgin Islands, and other regional destinations. Ports in St. Croix and St. Thomas accommodate ocean-going cargo and passenger ships. St. John has a frequent ferry service from St. Thomas. There are 531 miles of roads, varying from modern major roads to rough tracks on mountain areas. St. Croix and St. Thomas have regular bus services.

Telecommunications service is the monopoly of the Virgin Islands Telephone Corporation, owned by Atlantic Tele-Network (ATN), the proprietor of which, Jeffrey Prosser, also owns two cable television companies and the *Virgin Islands Daily News*.

Electric power is generated and distributed by the Virgin Islands Water and Power Authority, which also operates the water desalination plants.

Fiscal/Financial

Corporate and personal income tax are payable, under U.S. tax law, together with a gross receipts tax. However, companies established in the USVI for the purpose of exporting goods or services from the United States to other countries, known under U.S. tax law as foreign sales corporations, are exempt from these taxes, and from customs and excise duty, though they do have to pay nominal annual franchise tax and a license fee. The territory houses more than 3,000 such corporations, estimated at 80% of the world total.

The government's finances have shown mounting deficits in recent years, with the deficit in 1999 reaching $98 million. Government debt was estimated at $1.1 billion in 2000. Regulation of government and private-sector financial operations is the responsibility of territorial and federal inspectorates.

Business Opportunities

As well as the tax exemptions for foreign sales corporations, companies operating in the U.S. Virgin Islands benefit from duty-free entry to the United States for a wide range of products, and some items also qualify for entry to other countries under agreements between these countries and the United States. A variety of tax and duty exemptions is also available to investors in the islands, including those applying to machinery, equipment, building materials, raw materials, and components. There are partial exemptions from corporate income tax and withholding tax on dividends, and full exemption from property tax and gross receipts tax. The main opportunities are in industrial development and tourism, while communications also offer possibilities.

For More Information

Books:

Cameron, Sarah. *Caribbean Islands Handbook*. 13th ed. Bath, Somerset: Footprint Handbooks, 2001.

The Caribbean Handbook 2000. London: FT Caribbean (BVI) Ltd., 2000.

Groene, Janet. *Puerto Rico and U.S. Virgin Islands Guide*. 2nd ed. New York: Open Road Publishing, 2000.

Web Sites:

Tourist Guide: **www.usvi.net**
USVI Government: **www.usvi.org**

Uzbekistan

GNI: **$17,613 million; world's 70th**
GNI pc: **$720; world's 146th**
Head of government: **president**
Currency: **som (Som)**
Capital: **Tashkent**
Population: **23,942,000, growing at 1.7% p.a.**
Land area: **159,920 square miles**
Population density: **150 per square mile**
Life expectancy: **68 years**
Infant mortality: **45 per 1,000 live births**
Language: **Uzbek, Russian**
Best buy: **silk goods**

Economic Structure

The feudal khanates of Bukhara, Khiva, and Kokand, which comprised most of present-day Uzbekistan, were integrated into the Russian empire in the mid-19th century. Uzbekistan was first constituted in 1924, as a Soviet republic. In Soviet times cotton production was prioritized and irrigation, mechanization, and chemical fertilizers introduced. In the postwar period, limited industrialization began. After an earthquake that razed Tashkent in 1966, resources were diverted to reconstruction work. Uzbekistan was the first central Asian republic to declare independence in 1991. In the decade that followed it was comparatively unscathed by the industrial slump that hit other post-Soviet republics, partly because it is one of the least industrialized.

Uzbekistan's economy now relies primarily on cotton and gold. These easily marketable commodities account for 55% of exports and about three-quarters of hard currency export earnings, and figure significantly in the main sources of GDP: agriculture (28% in 1999) and industry (13.9% in 1999). Uzbekistan is also self-sufficient in oil, a net exporter of gas, and a producer of cars. It is attempting to reduce its reliance on trade with the CIS, which in 2000 accounted for 30% of exports and 26% of imports; its principal non-CIS trading partners are South Korea, Germany, the United States, and the United Kingdom.

Uzbekistan has adopted a conservative attitude to market reform in general and privatization in particular; the state remains a majority shareholder in most large enterprises and the EBRD estimated in 2001 that the private sector accounts for only 45% of GDP.

Economic Policy

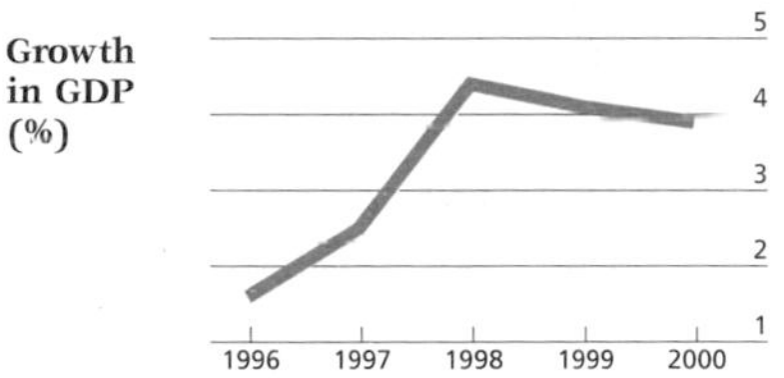

In contrast to other post-Soviet states, Uzbekistan has pursued a statist development policy, characterized by the IMF as "a cautious approach to structural reforms and reliance on administrative measures and government control and intervention." Under the import-substituting industrialization (ISI) policy, credit and hard-currency reserves are allocated administratively to priority industrial sectors. The policy has helped to achieve energy self-sufficiency, but substantial net transfers to support industrialization from agriculture (principally cotton revenues, 80% of which are retained by the government to fund ISI) have been criticized as economically costly. As of 2001, the government's goal of increasing grain production and ending grain imports had not been achieved.

The ISI policy is supported by foreign exchange restrictions in the form of a multiple exchange rate, which is regarded as a key obstruction to foreigners doing business in Uzbekistan. Unification of the official rate and the interbank rate in 2000, and decrees on access to foreign currency issued in 2001 that brought import prices close to the underlying market rate, were significant moves towards convertibility.

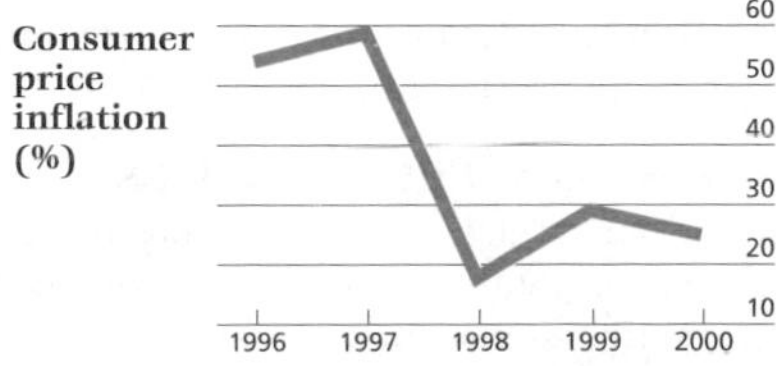

Protectionist economic policy and the dominance of agriculture helped Uzbekistan escape the worst consequences of the post-Soviet recession of the early 1990s: in 1992–97, GDP fell by 14.2%, compared with, for example, 30.3% in Kazakhstan. In 1998–2001 GDP increased by more than 4% a year, although some economists consider these figures to be exaggerated. The official unemployment rate of under 1% is also widely questioned; the UN Development Program estimated in 1998 that hidden unemployment could be as high as 26.5%. Consumer price inflation figures, which have been at 23–28% per year since 1997, are considered to be understated.

Geography/Resources

Uzbekistan lies in the heart of central Asia, bounded to its north and west by Kazakhstan, to the south by Turkmenistan and Afghanistan, and to the east by Kyrgyzstan and Tajikistan (from which Uzbek Islamists mounted armed incursions into Uzbekistan in 1999–2001). Four-fifths of Uzbekistan consists of flat, sun-baked lowlands, rising to high mountain ranges in the south and east. Apart from gold it has sizeable reserves of hydrocarbons, copper, zinc, lead, and uranium (the world's fourth-largest producer). Its agriculture, besides cotton, includes silkworm cultivation and sheep farming.

Two great rivers, the Amu-Darya and Syr-Darya (the ancient Oxus and Jaxartes), flow from the mountains of Tajikistan and Kyrgyzstan through Uzbekistan down to the Aral Sea, and provide 90% of central Asia's water. Rapid Soviet-era population growth increased the burden on water supplies, and in the 1990s inter-state tension has grown over their allocation. Tajikistan and Kyrgyzstan need water to run major hydroelectric power projects upstream, and Uzbekistan and Kazakhstan need it for irrigation. Inefficient irrigation, and excessive use of fertilizers and pesticides, has combined since the 1960s to contaminate the water table and shrink the Aral Sea, the disappearance of which—now a serious possibility—would have catastrophic environmental consequences. Water contamination and reduction of ground water reserves around Tashkent are also causing concern.

Uzbekistan is the most populous central Asian country, with 23.9 million inhabitants. Unlike other post-Soviet states, Uzbekistan experienced population growth in the 1990s (average 1.8% per annum, compared to 2.5% per annum in the 1980s). The population is increasingly young, and increasingly rural.

Communications/Energy

The import substitution strategy has made Uzbekistan self-sufficient in energy. A 189% increase in oil production between 1991 and 1998, to 162,000 barrels per day, eliminated oil imports, although by 2001 production had fallen back to 146,000 barrels per day. Gas production rose by 1,480 billion cubic feet to 2,119 billion cubic feet (estimated) between 1991 and 2001, although most is exported to CIS countries that pay late, if at all. Hydrocarbons production has now reached a plateau: substantial investment will be needed, firstly in the gas pipeline network, to realize the potential of the export business. In December 2001 the government said it intended to offer 49% of the oil and gas monopoly Uzbekneftegaz in a privatization sale.

Telecommunications also require major investment. In 1999 there were only 6.7 telephones per 100 inhabitants. After failing to attract Western investment into the sector, the government was planning in late 2001 to offer 51% of the main telecoms company, Uzbektelecom, for sale.

Uzbekistan is landlocked, and some goods cross three other countries to reach a port. Tashkent international airport, and regional airports at Samarkand, Bukhara, and Urgench (near Nukus), have been upgraded and should be able to handle the traffic increases expected in the next decade. However, little attention has been paid to development of the 2,151 miles rail network, although investment capital may come from the oil industry, which relies on it. There are 50,706 miles of main roads, of which 87% are paved.

Education/Employment

Uzbekistan has a relatively highly-skilled workforce, although the departure of many ethnic Russians—which resulted in net emigration of 845,000 between 1990 and 1999—has left gaps. Since Uzbekistan is a political autocracy, wages and pensions are essentially set by presidential decree. Uzbek employees have high expectations of non-wage benefits, since much of the welfare system has been maintained in the Soviet tradition, continuing to provide family allowances and indirect benefits such as subsidized central heating, urban transport and housing. The mahalla (neighborhood committees), which date from the pre-Soviet era, have in recent years been strengthened and used to administer social welfare.

Uzbekistan's population is well educated, with a literacy rate of more than 99%. Government spending on education has fallen from the very high level of 11.6% of GDP in 1992 to 7.4% in 1998. Uzbekistan's education system deteriorated through the 1990s. Although education remains compulsory between the ages of 6 and 14, the proportion of children receiving pre-school education fell from close to 100% in the 1980s to 30% in 1992 and 16% in 1998. The number of students in tertiary education has fallen: the proportion of 19-year-olds in full-time education fell from 30% in 1992 to 17% in 1998. Since the mid-1980s, resources have been put into switching Uzbek-language education from the Cyrillic alphabet to the Latin alphabet. The centuries-old madrasahs (Islamic theological schools) continue to function.

Fiscal/Financial

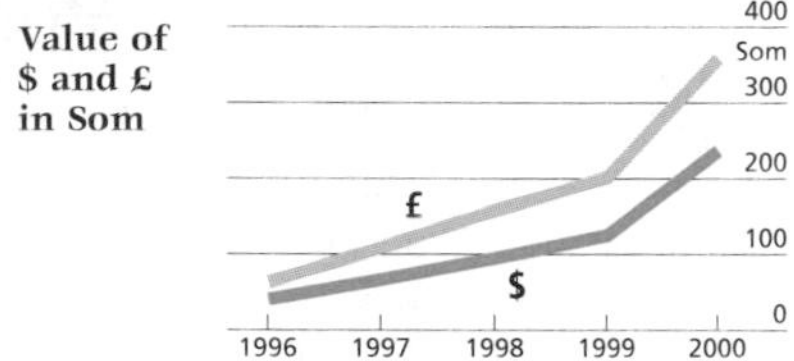

Big state-controlled institutions completely dominate the banking sector. The largest bank, the National Bank of Uzbekistan (NBU), controls 90% of foreign currency transactions and parts of the state foreign currency and gold reserves; the state savings bank, Narodny Bank, holds 80% of all household deposits. Lending policy is state-directed under the National Investment Plan, and about two-thirds of all outstanding loans were extended under state direction, and carry a sovereign guarantee and negative real interest rates. A 1998 decree requiring a reduction of state ownership in the sector has not been implemented; only four small banks out of the 31 operating are privately owned. The one foreign bank active in Uzbekistan, ABN Amro of the Netherlands, operates a joint venture with NBU. There is a small stock exchange, established in 1995, with more than 4,000 shares listed and a relatively low volume of trading. There is no private insurance sector.

Business Opportunities

Uzbekistan welcomes foreign businesses, but many potential investors have been deterred by statist financial and industrial policy, and in particular by the absence of currency convertibility. Foreign direct investment fell from an average of $130 million per year in 1996–99 to $73 million in 2000 and $71 million in 2001.

The most notable foreign investments so far have been into construction projects in the natural resources sector. A $1 billion gas processing plant in the Shurtan field, built by an international consortium led by ABB and Mitsui, is close to completion. Two other projects—to build a compressor station at Shurtan and upgrade the Fergana refinery—are under way. Newmont Mining of the U.S. is involved in a major joint venture with the State Geology Committee and a state-owned gold company to recover gold from 220 million tons of tailings that have accumulated at the Muruntau open-cast mine, one of the world's largest. Daewoo of South Korea has invested heavily in UzDaewooAuto, a joint-venture motor manufacturer.

By early 2001, the privatization program was in the doldrums following the cancellation of the sale of a stake in the Almalyk gold refinery in 1999 and a lack of interest in an oil refinery stake. Sectors designated as strategic (precious metals mining, oil and gas production, aerospace, communications, etc.) are not subject to privatization.

For More Information

Books:

Karimov, President I. A. *Uzbekistan on the Threshold of the Twenty-First Century: Challenges to Stability and Progress*. New York: Palgrave Macmillan, 1998.

MacLeod, C., and M. Bradley. *Uzbekistan: Tashkent, Bukhara, Khiva and the Golden Road to Samarkand*. 4th ed. Corona, CA: Odyssey Publications, 2002.

Rubin, B. R., N. Lubin, and K. Martin. *Calming the Ferghana Valley: Development and Dialogue in the Heart of Central Asia*. New York: Twentieth Century Fund/ Century Foundation, 2000.

Uzbekistan Export, Import, and Business Directory. 3rd ed. Washington, D.C.: International Business Publications, 2001.

Web Sites:

Cyber Uzbekistan: **www.cu-online.com/~k_a/uzbekistan**

Official Uzbek government site: **www.gov.uz**

Times of Central Asia: **www.times.kg**

Uzbekistan Links: **www.cpss.org/sites/uzbek.htm**

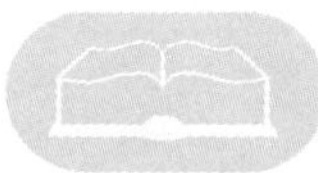

VENEZUELA

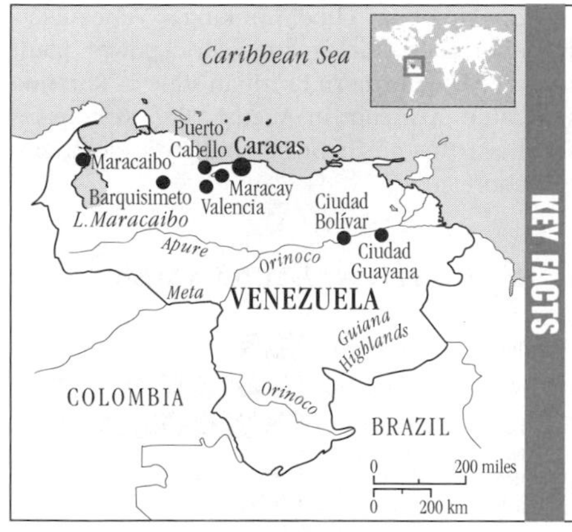

KEY FACTS

GNI: **$87,313 million; world's 38th**
GNI pc: **$3,680; world's 79th**
Head of government: **president**
Currency: **bolívar (Bs)**
Capital: **Caracas**
Population: **23,706,000, growing at 2.2% p.a.**
Land area: **340,580 square miles**
Population density: **70 per square mile**
Life expectancy: **73 years**
Infant mortality: **20 per 1,000 live births**
Language: **Spanish**
Best buy: **hammocks, gold, Margarita Island pearls**

ECONOMIC STRUCTURE

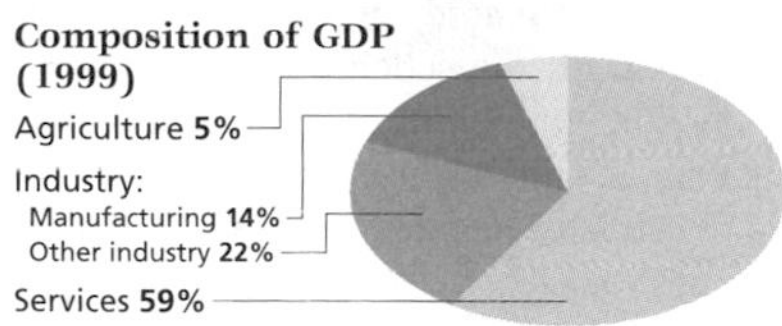

Hugo Chávez, a leftist army officer imprisoned for the failed 1992 coup he led, broke the mould of Venezuelan politics when he became president in 1999. His Movement for the Fifth Republic was swept to power with support from the impoverished and politically inarticulate section of society, fed up with the corrupt ancien régime of the two traditional parties that had ruled the country after the military dictatorship ended in 1958. A new constitution was written and the legislature and judiciary reorganized. Chávez was in the tradition of left-wing nationalist officers in Latin America (for example, Omar Torríjos in Panama). Emigration to the United States by the disaffected middle classes, and capital flight, intensified after Chávez came to power. Some of his policies irritated the Bush administration and antagonized the Venezuelan business and land-owning class. A one-day general strike in December 2001 paralyzed the country.

It remained to be seen whether Chávez would be able to hold office for the full term (until 2006) or whether his "Bolivarian revolution"—named in homage to the (Venezuelan-born) South American independence leader of the early 19th century, Simón Bolívar—would produce more political upheaval.

Services generate around 60% of GDP, industry 34%, and agriculture 5%. The main home market industries are textiles, beverages, food processing, and paper/pulp. Heavy industries that use local commodities are refining of aluminum, petrochemicals (ammonia, sulfuric acid, fertilizers, and plastics), cement, and steel.

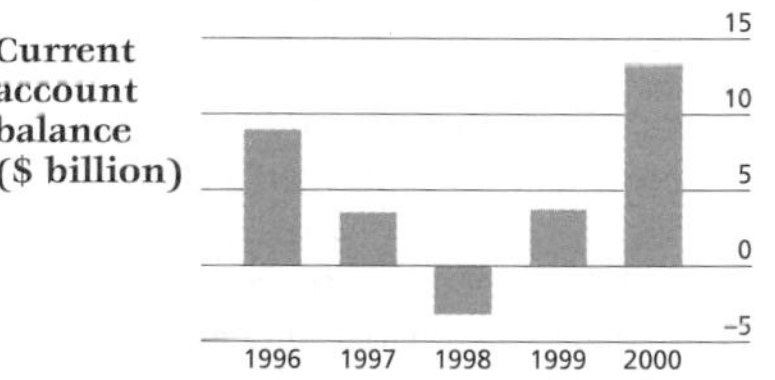

The state's presence in the economy is largely represented by the giant oil monopoly Petróleos de Venezuela (PDVSA), Venalum and Alcasa (aluminum), and Pequiven (petrochemicals). The telecoms company Compañía Anónima Nacional Teléfonos de Venezuela (CANTV) and the steel industry have been privatized to varying degrees. The privatization of other state-run concerns was progressing more slowly. The 1999 constitution enshrined state ownership of PDVSA and of mineral rights over the country's subsoil as being of strategic economic importance to the country, limiting the possibilities for private-sector involvement in the oil sector. This situation was reinforced by a new hydrocarbons decree law passed in 2001 which included a controversial provision requiring all activities relating to exploration, extraction, collection, and transport to be performed by the state directly, through companies majority-owned or exclusively owned by the government. The rate at which royalties are charged was also increased.

ECONOMIC POLICY

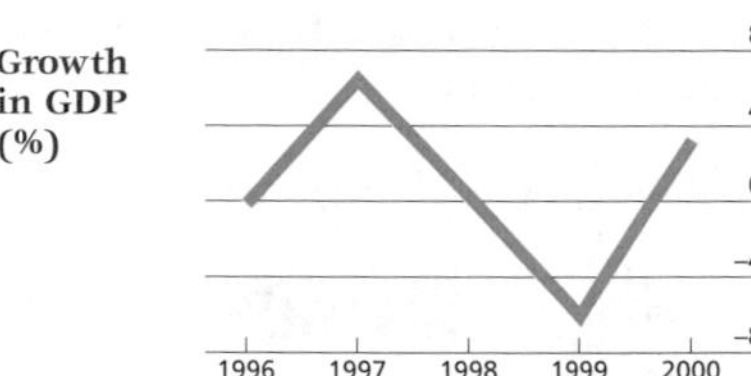

Economic policy has veered between the neo-liberal and the populist, but neither approach has done much to improve competitiveness. The International Institute for Management Development (IMD), a Swiss business school, ranked Venezuela 48th in its 2001 ranking of the world's 49 most competitive countries (44th in 1997). Despite fabulous mineral wealth, growth has rarely been strong, and is often sluggish, especially in the inefficient non-oil economy. Oil revenue, depending on the price, has accounted for up to 80% of export income, over a fifth of GDP, and half of the government's income. Average real GDP expanded 0.5% in 1979–89 and 2.3% in 1989–99. The economy went into recession in 1999 (–6.1%) and picked up in 2000 (+3.2%), thanks to the rise in oil prices which were three times the budgeted level of $9 per barrel. Growth in 2001 was around 3%. Inflation was below 15% in 2000 and 2001. The budget deficit ballooned to more than 5% of GDP in 2001 from 1.8% in 2000.

When oil prices are high the external sector is buoyant. The current account surplus was a massive 11% of GDP in 2000, and dropped to about 4% of GDP in 2001 because of lower oil prices. The external debt has been kept at a manageable level. In 2001 it was estimated at $34.5 billion (26.5% of GDP and 116% of exports, compared with 40.3% and 150.6% respectively in 1997).

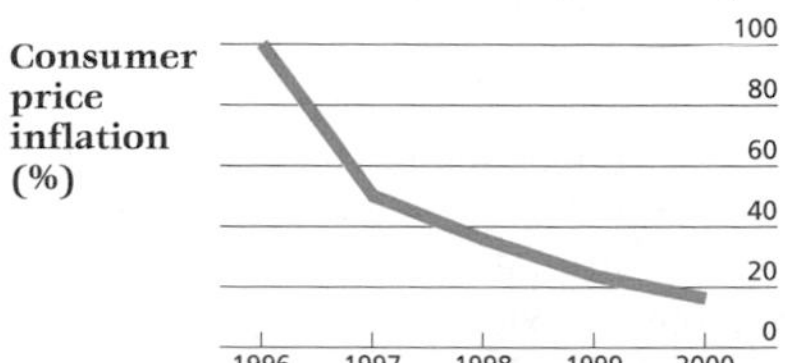

With the external and fiscal accounts vulnerable to volatility in world oil prices, the creation of a Macro-economic Stabilization Fund, which sets aside a percentage of oil revenue when the price is above a certain level, acts as a cushion against lower oil prices. Venezuela needs to diversify its sources of revenue away from oil. The country, moreover, has a low tax collection

record compared with some of its regional peers (revenue represents less than 13% of GDP). Tax evasion is very high at an estimated 60–70%. The government introduced measures to improve collection and enforcement, and to modernize Seniat, the tax and customs agency.

Geography/Resources

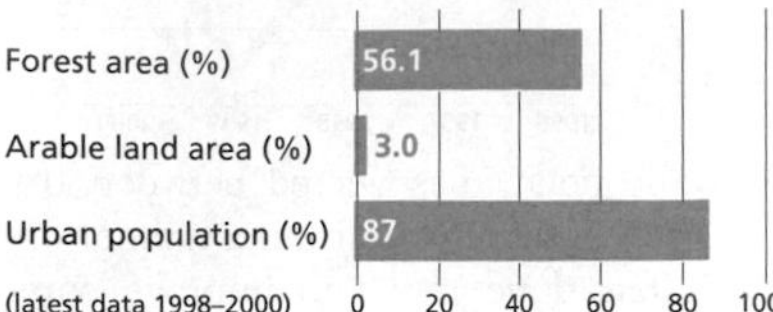

Venezuela is bounded on the north by the Caribbean and has a coastline of 1,900 miles, with many islands. To the west is Colombia, to the east Guyana, and to the south Brazil. It has high mountains, tropical rainforests, and hundreds of rivers. The great Orinoco River rises in the south and makes a wide curve to flow through the center of the country. It is joined by many tributaries and flows out to the Atlantic Ocean through several swampy mouths. North of the Apure River, and part of the Orinoco, are grassy plains called *llanos*, where cattle are raised. In the southeast are the Guiana Highlands, which are covered with forests and little explored, and high on the River Carrao are the Angel Falls, the highest falls in the world (3,212 feet). The country is subject to tropical storms; the one in December 1999 killed up to 30,000 people.

The country has vast mineral wealth which is largely undeveloped except for oil. Venezuela has the largest reserves of oil in the Western hemisphere and the sixth-largest in the world (estimated at close to 80 billion barrels at the end of 2000), and has been a prime mover behind restoring discipline in the organization of Petroleum Exporting Countries (OPEC). PDVSA's average output was 2.9 million barrels a day in 2000. Exploration is focused on the Orinoco heavy oil belt, the Monagas region, and the area southwest of Lake Maracaibo. There are also huge reserves of natural gas and other minerals (iron ore, bauxite, gold, diamonds, coal, lead, nickel, and phosphates). The mining sector (excluding oil) contributes around 1% of GDP.

The chief agricultural products are coffee, cocoa, sugar, tobacco, cotton, and corn. The arrival of oil in the 1920s triggered a gradual decline of the rural economy in favor of industrial development of towns. Venezuela stopped being self-sufficient in food production in the 1980s. One of Chávez's priorities was to try to redress the balance. The National Agrarian Institute estimated that half of the country's 500,000 or so farms occupied less than 2% of arable land, while at the other end of the scale 1% of the farms held 46% of the land—and this in a large country where only 12% of the population live in the interior and there is plenty of space. The former two-party system did nothing to improve the lot of landless peasants. A controversial decree law came into effect in December 2001 which charges a tax on idle or underutilized land and defines the types of land subject to expropriation.

The population increased nearly fivefold between 1958 and 2001, from 5 million to 24.1 million. Mestizos make up 66% of the population; 21% are white, 10% black and 2% Native American. One-third of the population is under the age of 14.

Communications/Energy

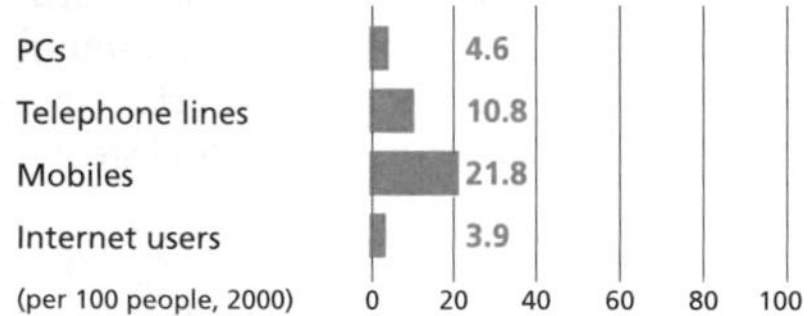

Venezuela has an estimated 59,483 miles of roads, 20,195 miles of which are paved. There are few railways, with the notable exception of the 99 miles track from Puerto Cabello to Barquisimeto and Acarigua, and a system to transport iron ore from mines to Puerto Ordaz. No railways join Venezuela with neighboring countries. There has long been talk of developing a railway system, but by 2001 nothing had happened. Most of the railways and roads are near the towns along the coast. Travel by boat on the Orinoco and its tributaries is still the only means of transport for many people. The river port of Ciudad Bolívar is the commercial center for a large part of the interior of Venezuela. The other main ports are La Guaira (near Caracas), Puerto Cabello, and Maracaibo.

Venezuela was one of the first countries in Latin America in which mobile phones outnumbered those that depend on a fixed-line connection. There were an estimated 19 mobile phones per 100 inhabitants in 2001 compared with 13 fixed-line phones per 100 inhabitants. The monopoly over basic telephony long held by CANTV came to an end in 2000, when licenses to operate in the fixed-line market were granted. The number of Internet subscribers was around half a million in 2000, and is projected to reach 1.3 million in 2003.

Venezuela is self-sufficient in energy. The emphasis is on developing hydroelectric power to replace thermal electricity as the main source of energy. A 423-mile transmission line linking Venezuela's enormous Guri hydroelectric power plant with the northern Brazilian state of Roraima came onstream in August 2001 to help relieve the neighboring country's electricity shortage.

Education/Employment

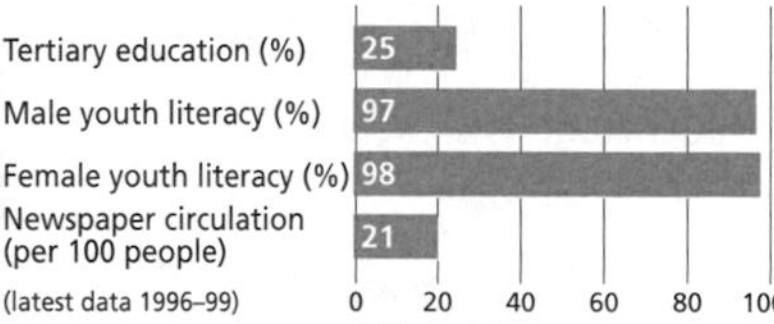

Education is free and compulsory from age 6 to 17. The country used to score well on education compared with its regional neighbors until the schooling system went into decline. One child in ten fails to complete primary school, and almost one in five does not finish secondary education. Those who can afford it send their children abroad for university education. Moreover, the well-educated young have increasingly emigrated. The government began controversial education reforms in 2000, which opponents labeled as "indoctrination": textbooks reflected the government's new version of history. Cuba provides teacher-trainers and materials in exchange for Venezuelan oil sold at below the market price. "Bolivarian schools" were established to provide basic education and three meals a day for poor children.

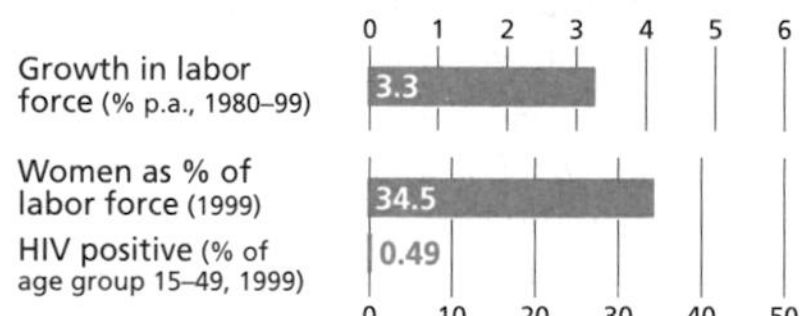

R&D spending is around 0.5% of GDP. The quality of basic research is insufficient to enhance the country's long-term economic and technological development.

Fiscal/Financial

Despite consolidation in the aftermath of the severe 1994–95 banking crisis, which saw nearly half the sector fall into state hands, and despite a flurry of mergers in 2000 triggered by the 1999 recession, the banking sector remained overcrowded. There were 69 financial institutions in 2001, among them 36 banks. The two largest

Value of $ and £ in Bs

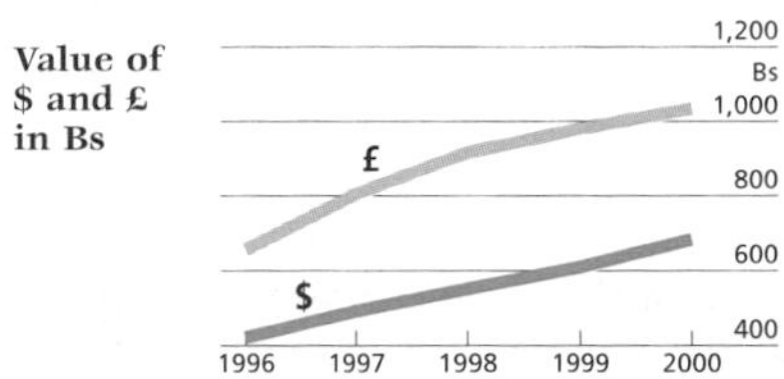

private-sector banks—Banco Provincial and Banco de Venezuela-Grupo Santander—are Spanish-owned, and between them have around 30% of deposits.

The largest state bank is Banco Industrial de Venezuela. Many banks faced pressing problems, including high operating costs and a need to diversify their sources of income in order to secure their positions in a volatile economy. The smaller banks had to find a lucrative niche or risk continued marginalization and even collapse.

Chávez threatened in December 2001 to nationalize banks that did not offer credits in line with his new land law intended to help small farmers. Under the law, banks have to raise the proportion of their loan portfolio for farmers from 8% to 15%, and to accept only a producer's harvest as collateral, rather than land.

Corporate tax and the top rate of personal income tax are 34%, and VAT is 14.5%. The Caracas Stock Exchange is small.

Business Opportunities

Growth in output (% p.a., 1990–99)

Services	0.2
Industry	3.3
Manufacturing	1.3
Agriculture	1.5

Foreign direct investment (FDI) has been on the rise despite the country's poor infrastructure and political uncertainty. The annual average of FDI accelerated from $500 million in 1985–95 to $4.3 billion in 1997–2000. Most of the FDI went into the telecommunications, banking, and energy sectors. The ending of CANTV's monopoly of fixed-line services in November 2000 triggered a flurry of foreign investment in the sector.

The new opportunities are mainly in petrochemicals and gas. Venezuela faced a gas supply deficit by 2004 if it failed to produce more from its own fields. PDVSA developed a strategy to lift output from its own oil fields, encourage contractors to produce more gas from their marginal oilfields, and promote the search for new gas fields. Investment in petrochemicals, under PDVSA's 2000–09 plan, could total $8.7 billion. It focuses on natural gas derivatives, derivatives of refinery flows, and the manufacture of products derived from other raw materials.

For More Information

Books:

Coronil, F. *The Magical State: Nature, Money, and Modernity in Venezuela.* Chicago, IL: University of Chicago Press, 1997.

Financial Times country surveys: *Venezuela.*

Gott, Richard. *In the Shadow of the Liberator: The Impact of Hugo Chávez on Venezuela and Latin America.* New York: Verso, 2000.

Márquez, Gabriel García. *The General in His Labyrinth*, trans. Edith Grossman. New York: Penguin, 1995.

Web Sites:

Caracas Stock Exchange: **www.caracasstock.com**

Central Bank of Venezuela: **www.bcv.org.ve**

CONAPRI (Investment Agency): **www.conapri.org**

Finance Ministry: **www.mf.gov.ve**

IMF reports: **www.imf.org/external**

National Statistics Office: **www.ocei.gov.ve**

U.S. State Department Country Commercial Guide: **www.state.gov/e/eb/rls/rpts/ccg**

VIETNAM

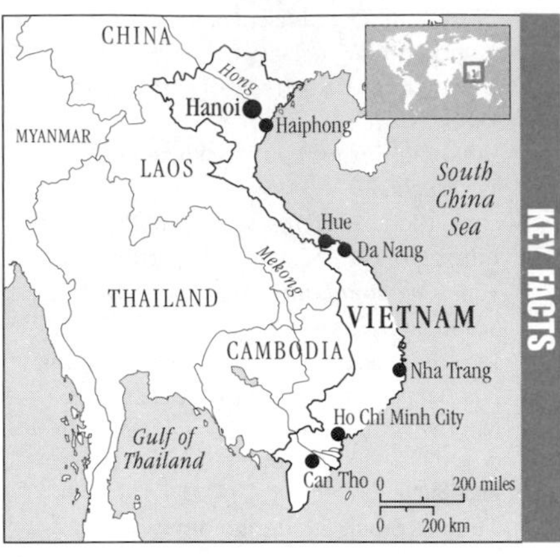

KEY FACTS

GNI: **$28,733 million; world's 60th**
GNI pc: **$370; world's 170th**
Head of government: **prime minister**
Currency: **dong (D)**
Capital: **Hanoi**
Population: **78,705,000, growing at 1.8% p.a.**
Land area: **125,700 square miles**
Population density: **626 per square mile**
Life expectancy: **68 years**
Infant mortality: **31 per 1,000 live births**
Language: **Vietnamese, Chinese, Mon Khmer**
Best buy: **lacquerware, ceramics, mother-of-pearl, paintings, leather goods**

ECONOMIC STRUCTURE

A French colony in the 19th century, and occupied by Japan in World War II, Vietnam gained independence in 1945 as a communist state. France attempted to regain control and was defeated in 1954. The division of the country into the communist north, backed by China and the Soviet Union, and capitalist south, backed by the United States, was internationally recognized. War between north and south resumed in the 1960s, with increasing involvement by the United States. The United States withdrew in 1973. In 1975 the communists defeated the southern capitalists, reunified the country, and extended communism to the south. Vietnam's invasion of Cambodia in 1979 led to international isolation and dependence on Soviet aid. In 1986 the government adopted the Chinese model of economic reform, allowing private enterprise alongside state-owned industries. In 1990 it opened the economy to foreign investment. However, Communist Party policy is that the state sector should predominate, especially in finance, telecommunications, and hydrocarbons.

Services contributed 39.1% of GDP in 2000, followed by industry (36.6%), and agriculture (24.3%). Wholesale and retail trade is the main services sector. Textiles, clothing, and leather footwear are key manufacturing industries. Other main manufactures include farm machinery, motorbikes, machine tools, bricks, cement, chemical fertilizers, cigarettes, and beer. Motorbike assembly is fast growing. In 2000 the main exports were crude petroleum (24.2%), textiles (13.1%), and footwear (10.1%). Vietnam is the world's second-largest exporter of rice. Fish and crustaceans, coffee, and rubber are important exports. The main export markets were Japan (18.1%), followed by China (10.6%), Singapore (8.8%), and Australia (6.1%).

From 1989 to 2000 the number of state-owned enterprises (SOEs) was cut from 12,000 to 5,300. The SOEs' share in industrial output fell from 62% in 1990 to 42% in 2000, and in employment from 2.5 million to 1.6 million jobs. Total official SOE debt at end-1999 was D126 trillion—32% of GDP—much of which consisted of non-performing loans, placing a strain on the state-owned banks. At May 2001, 502 SOEs were equitized, with minority shareholdings sold to the private sector. A further 1,775 SOEs will be equitized in 2001–04. Around 2,000 SOEs have been grouped into 17 general corporations and 77 special corporations in key industries.

ECONOMIC POLICY

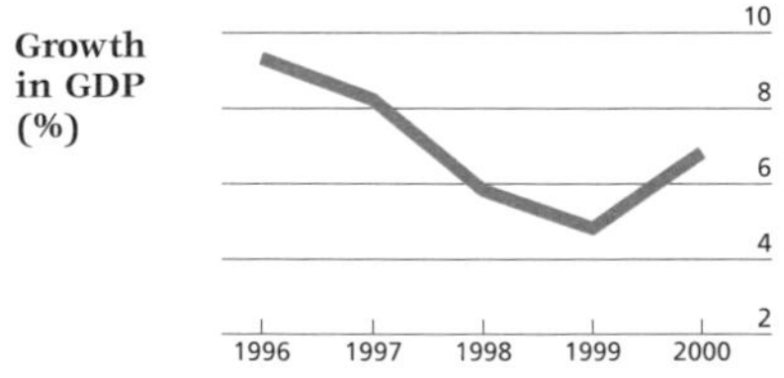

Macro-economic policy is geared to long-term growth and poverty reduction. The present strategy covers 2001–20. In 2001–03 the government aims to contain the budget deficit at 3% of GDP, an increase from 1.8% in 2000, reflecting the cost of restructuring SOEs and other investments. As trade and foreign currency restrictions are eased in the next three to six years, industries and the finance sector need strengthening to withstand increased international competition. The government has international assistance to improve tax collection and the transparency of public-sector accounts. The long-term growth target of 7% a year requires investment at 30% of GDP a year, mostly from private and foreign sources, given the constraints on government spending. Investment was 25.6% of GDP in 2000 and 26.1% in 2001.

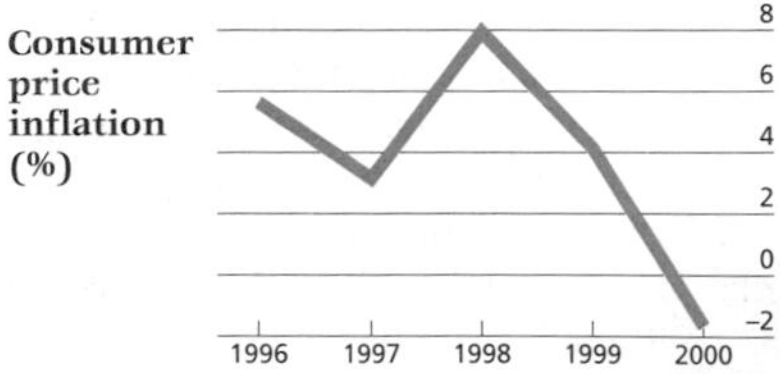

Annual average GDP growth was 9% in 1995–97, slowing to 5.7% in 1998–2000, mainly because of the Asian financial crisis. It was 6.8% in 2001 and is expected to be 5.8% in 2002. Inflation averaged 3.8% in 1996–2000, with 0.8% in 2001. It is expected to be low in 2002. Unemployment estimates range from around 2% to 20%. Agriculture and forestry, much of which is not in the official economy, was estimated to account for 70% of jobs in 1999, but this pattern is changing.

GEOGRAPHY/RESOURCES

In southeast Asia, Vietnam borders China, Laos, Cambodia, and the South China Sea. The climate is humid all year round, 91°F in summer, 55°F in winter, with monsoons from May to September. The Hong River in the north and the Mekong River in the south have major deltas, where most of the population live. Much of the rest of the land is mountainous, with a high point of 10,312 feet. Most people are of Vietnamese origin (85–90%), with 3% Chinese, and the rest of Muong, Thai, Meo, Khmer, Man, and Cham origin.

Rice is the main agricultural crop. Other cash crops include sugar cane, rubber, coffee, and groundnuts, while vegetables, fruit, corn, cassava, sweet potatoes, and coconuts are mostly for domestic consumption. Pigs are the main livestock, followed by cattle and buffaloes. Fuel wood and industrial timber are harvested. Fishing is important. Proven petroleum reserves were 600 million barrels and gas reserves were 6.8 trillion cubic feet at January 2001. New oil finds in 2000 indicated 400 million barrels of additional reserves. Exploration continues for oil and gas. Coal reserves were 149.7 million

tons at end-1996. Salt, chromite, and phosphates are also mined. There are reserves of manganese, bauxite, iron ore, zinc, tin, wolfram, and gold.

Communications/Energy

The road network was an estimated 57,980 miles in 1996, a quarter of which was paved. The rail network was 1,648 miles in 1998. There are 93 miles of pipelines for petroleum products. Navigable waterways total 11,000 miles. The main sea ports are at Haiphong, Da Nang, and Ho Chi Minh City. The main international airports serve Hanoi and Ho Chi Minh City. There are nine domestic airports.

As of 2000 national telecommunications networks were provided by the state-owned Viet Nam Posts & Telecommunications Corp and the Army Electronics & Communications Corp (owned by the military). Saigon Post & Telecom (part state, part private) had a license to provide services in the south. Most switching is digital, and fiberoptic and microwave communications link the main cities and provinces. At end-2000 there were 2.5 million fixed phone lines, 788,600 mobile phones, and 200,000 Internet users.

Oil accounted for 52.2% of energy consumption in 1999, followed by coal (19.9%) and gas (6.3%). Hydro power was the main source of electricity (52%), with the rest generated by fossil fuels. Oil production was 357,000 barrels per day in the first eight months of 2001, with consumption at 153,000 barrels per day and net exports at 204,000 barrels per day. Refined oil products are imported. In 1999 gas production and consumption were 35.3 billion cubic feet, while coal production was 10.8 million tons, with consumption at 5.4 million and net exports of 6.5 million.

Education/Employment

Education is compulsory from age 6 to 11. There were 139 institutes of higher education, including 75 colleges and 64 universities, with 800,000 students enrolled in 1999–2000. Over 50 colleges, 138 training schools, two international training institutions, and over 1,000 training centers provide vocational courses. The Ministry of Education and Training has responsibility for higher education and provides most of the funding. International aid and private-sector finance also support vocational training and a new private-sector university at Ho Chi Minh City, which will provide courses in IT, engineering, business administration, teacher training, and English. The main R&D strengths have been in agriculture, notably exotic fruits and rice. Ho Chi Minh City will be endowed with an IT and Telecom High-Tech Zone, which will include an R&D center.

The labor force is adaptable and well educated, but managerial and technological skills are in short supply. The law requires employers to establish labor unions within six months of incorporating the company. Wages and employment conditions are negotiated between management and unions, and overseen by the government, which sets policy. Vietnam is committed to enact all International Labour Organization conventions, and had completed eight at mid-2001.

Fiscal/Financial

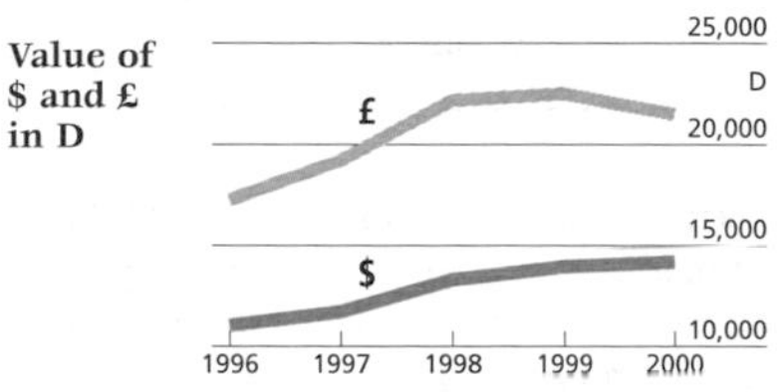

Four state-owned commercial banks (SOCB) dominate the financial sector, accounting for 70% of lending in mid-2001: Bank of Foreign Trade, Vietnam Industrial and Commercial Bank, Vietnam Bank for Agriculture and Rural Development, and Vietnam Bank for Investment and Development. These banks are being restructured in 2002 and will be recapitalized. The largest insurance company is the state-owned Baoviet, which handles all classes of insurance. The State Financial and Monetary Council is responsible for monetary policy. The State Bank of Vietnam, the central bank, supervises the financial sector. Restrictions on foreign capital, foreign bank operations, and currency are being phased out. Corporation tax is 32% for foreign companies, but tax incentives can significantly reduce this. The maximum rate of personal income tax is 50% for expatriates and 60% for local employees of foreign enterprises. VAT is applied at 5%, 10%, and 15%.

Reforms in 1988–91 separated commercial banks from the central bank, and provided for the establishment of joint stock banks (JSBs), joint venture banks, and foreign bank branches. Although 1999 reforms introduced governance rules more in line with international standards, about 30% of loans are non-performing. Half of local business finance transactions are conducted outside the banking sector. There is a substantial parallel market in U.S. dollars and gold. Households and shops act as lenders as well as borrowers. At end-1999 the banking sector included the four SOCBs, the Bank for the Poor, the Housing Development Bank of the Mekong River Delta, 48 JSBs, 26 foreign bank branches, five financial companies, and eight leasing companies. Life insurance is growing quickly, and foreign companies have been established. The Vietnam Stock Exchange opened in Ho Chi Minh City in July 2000. At January 2002 individuals, not enterprises, accounted for most trading. There were 12 listed companies. Foreign ownership of equitized companies listed on the exchange was limited to 20%, and foreign companies were not allowed to list.

Business Opportunities

Bureaucracy and the required use of the U.S. dollar or the non-convertible dong for different types of financing add to the cost and difficulty of investing in Vietnam. Sectors deemed key to national security, such as telecommunications and electricity, are closed to foreign direct investment. Tax and other incentives are offered to direct investors in other sectors, such as banking, insurance, higher education, and manufacturing. At end-2000 total cumulative FDI reached $36.6 billion. The top investor was Singapore ($5.76 billion), followed by Taiwan, Japan, Hong Kong, and South Korea. General manufacturing attracted $12.1 billion for 1,514 projects, followed by tourism, construction, transport, and communications, and petroleum and gas. These sectors and privatization offer new investment opportunities.

For More Information

Books:

Asian Development Bank. *Asian Development Outlook: Vietnam.*

Economist Intelligence Unit. *Country Profile and Quarterly Reports.* London.

Florence, M., and R. Storey. *Vietnam.* 6th ed. Oakland, CA: Lonely Planet, 2001.

Morley, J. W., and M. Nishihara, eds. *Vietnam Joins the World.* Armonk, NY: M. E. Sharpe, 1997.

Web Sites:

Ministry of Foreign Affairs (entry point): **www.mofa.gov.vn**

Vietnam Investment Review: **www.vir.com.vn/virweb site/Output/home.htm**

Vietnam News Agency (government information agency): **www.vnagency.com.vn**

Vietnamonline (portal): **www.vietnamonline.net**

YUGOSLAVIA

KEY FACTS

GNI pc: **$2,300 (approx)**
Head of government: **president**
Currency: **Yugoslav dinar (YuD), Euro in Montenegro**
Capital: **Belgrade**
Population: **10,637,000, growing at 0.5% p.a.**
Land area: **39,420 square miles**
Population density: **270 per square mile**
Life expectancy: **73 years**
Infant mortality: **20 per 1,000 live births**
Language: **Serbian**
Best buy: **slivovice, wine, crystalware, knitwear, mimosas**

ECONOMIC STRUCTURE

The Balkan region has had a turbulent history. Several centuries ago invaders left a legacy of three major competing religions—Orthodox Christianity, Roman Catholicism, and Islam—whose bitter rivalries dominated events in the 1990s and continue to this day. Serbia and Montenegro formed modern Yugoslavia in 1992 after the secession of Slovenia, Croatia, Bosnia-Herzegovina, and Macedonia. Yugoslavia was subject to international economic sanctions and isolation for most of the decade because of its role in the various Balkan wars. There was intensive bombing of Yugoslavia by NATO in the first half of 1999 following events in the province of Kosovo. Peace was signed in June 1999, but UN economic sanctions remained until President Slobodan Miloševic was voted out in late 2000. The April 2001 agreement with the IMF and World Bank ended international isolation.

In 1999 services contributed 37.7% of GDP, followed by industry (including manufacturing, utilities, construction and mining: 35.8%) and agriculture (26.5%). Agricultural output has been reduced by fertilizer shortages and drought. Manufacturing includes metals, chemicals, pharmaceuticals, motor vehicles, textiles, garments, footwear, and food processing. Basic manufactures are the main export category, followed by chemicals, food and live animals, machinery, and transport equipment. In 1998 the main export markets were Bosnia-Herzegovina, Italy, Macedonia, and Germany. Tourism in Montenegro revived in 2000.

From 1945 until the 1990s Yugoslavia had a decentralized socialist economy. Companies and banks were either state-owned or cooperatives. By 1995 the Montenegrin government had transferred majority shareholdings in 350 state-owned companies to state-owned funds prior to privatization, with 300 more companies targeted in 1998. Serbia's 1997 privatization law allowed enterprises to opt for joint stock status, but free shares had to be distributed to management and employees as a priority. Strategic commercial partners were sought only for Telekom Srbija, 49% of which was sold to Greek company OTE and Telecom Italia in 1997. In 2001 most Serbian companies and banks were under state, cooperative, or employee ownership. With multilateral aid agency support, bank restructuring and privatization made progress under the 2001–03 program. Sectors to be privatized include cement, chemicals, aluminum, oil, automotive, agribusiness, tourism, and air transport.

ECONOMIC POLICY

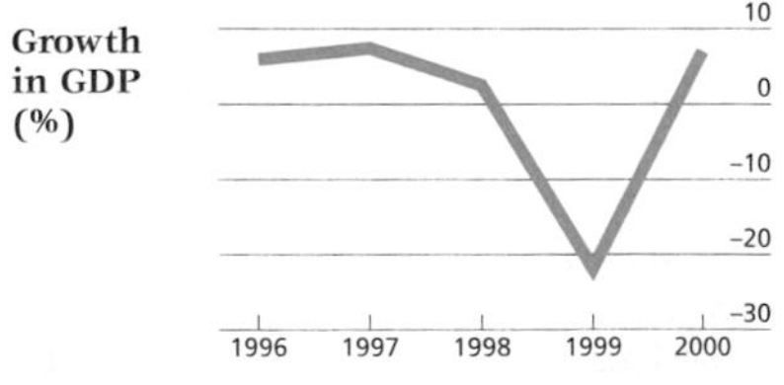

The loss of economic structures with the breakup of the former Yugoslavia in 1992, and the cost of regional war, led to hyperinflation in 1993. Large private foreign-exchange bank deposits were frozen by the authorities, and private banks collapsed. In 1994 a five-year stabilization program was introduced, and the government tried to maintain tight macro-economic policies with partial success. The Telekom Srbija sale brought in revenues of $1 billion by mid-1997. Public-sector cash deficits were contained by spending cuts and an accumulation of arrears. Wage and pension arrears totaling $140 million built up in 2000. In 2000 Montenegro stopped contributing to the federal budget, and the federal budget stopped contributing to Montenegrin pension funds, rendering Montenegrin public finances independent. U.S. and EU grants financed the 2000–01 Montenegrin government deficits. Taxes have been reformed, tax collection improved, and subsidies reduced in both Serbia and Montenegro. Public-sector wages were increased in 2001 and 2002 in line with IMF recommendations. The 2001 IMF agreement includes the repayment of pension and wage arrears, frozen foreign-currency deposits, and external debt. Total debt was 136% of GDP in 2000.

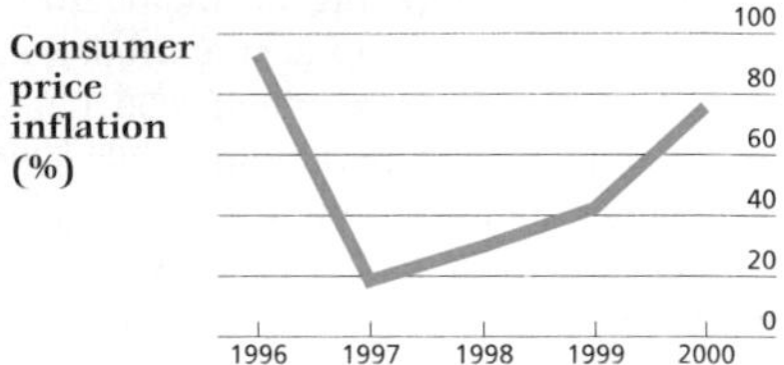

At end-2000 GDP in Serbia was at 40%, and in Montenegro at 53%, of its 1989 level, according to the IMF. The GDP of Serbia and Montenegro grew by an annual average of 5.8% in 1994–98, fell by 15.7% in 1999, and rose by an annual average 5.8% in 2000–01. Growth is expected to be 4% in 2002. Annual average inflation for the federation was 44% in 1994–99. Serb inflation was 113% in 2000 and 40% in 2001, with a target of 20% in 2002. Montenegrin inflation was 26% in 2001, with a target of 8% for 2002. Unemployment averaged 24.6% a year in 1993–98, rising to 40.5% in 2000.

GEOGRAPHY/RESOURCES

In the central Balkan peninsula, land-locked Serbia borders Hungary, Romania, Bulgaria, Macedonia, Albania, Montenegro, Bosnia-Herzegovina, and Croatia. Sandwiched between Bosnia-Herzegovina and Albania, Montenegro provides the federation's outlet to the Adriatic Sea. Northern Serbia is mainly flat, with mountains in the center and south. Major rivers run through Serbia: the Danube, Sava, Tisa, and Morava. Most of Montenegro is mountainous. A narrow coastal plain extends inland around the largest lake, Skadarsko Jezero. Serbia has a large and varied agricultural sector. Main crops are corn, sugar beet, oilseeds, wheat, and potatoes. Meat and dairy are important. Montenegrin agriculture is limited by the amount of suitable land. Forestry supplies construction wood, pulpwood, and fuel. Serbia has an important mining sector producing coal, petroleum, natural gas, copper, bauxite, iron, lead, and zinc. Proven oil reserves were 77.5 million barrels and gas reserves were 1.7 trillion cubic feet at January 2001. Coal reserves were 16.5 billion tons at end-1996.

The majority of people are of Slav origin, but there are significant differences in religious affiliation and ethnic identity. Orthodox Christianity is the main religion, but there are important Muslim and Roman Catholic communities. There are up to 800,000 refugees in Yugoslavia from the various Balkan wars of the 1990s.

Communications/Energy

Investment in the transport infrastructure was minimal from the mid-1980s, and NATO bombing in 1999 severely damaged road, rail and river networks. In 1999 the road network was 27,882 miles, 17,364 miles of which was paved, including the trans-European motorway providing access from western Europe to Macedonia, Greece, Turkey, Bulgaria, and Romania. In 1999 the rail network was 2,522 miles—2,367 miles in Serbia and 155 miles in Montenegro. One-third was electrified. The River Danube, another major link from west to southeast Europe, was closed in 1999 but reopened in 2000. The Sava and Tisa rivers are also navigable. The pipeline network was 957 miles in 1999, including 231 miles for oil. The main sea port is Bar in Montenegro, which has a capacity for 5 million tons of freight a year and a direct rail link with Serbia. There are international airports at Belgrade, Podgorica, and Tivat, and several domestic airports elsewhere.

At end-2000 there were 2.4 million fixed phone lines, 1.3 million mobile phones, and 400,000 Internet users. Telecommunications infrastructure is being rebuilt after war damage. Partly privatized Telekom Srbija dominates in fixed and mobile telephony in Serbia. The Montenegro telecommunications company is due to be privatized by end-2002.

In early 2001 Yugoslavia imported 23% of its electricity requirements, mostly funded by the EU, as a result of bomb damage to power stations and other infrastructure. Before 1999 the country produced one-quarter of its oil and gas needs from the north Serbian Vojvodina fields, and imported the rest from a variety of sources including Russia and the EU. Sanctions and bombing disrupted supplies, and payment arrears to foreign companies constitute an ongoing problem. The Yugoslav state-owned hydrocarbons company Nafta Industrija Srbije stopped exploration because of lack of funds. In 2000 oil production was 16,170 barrels per day, and gas output was 25.7 billion cubic feet. In 1999 coal production was 32.7 million tons. In 1999 coal accounted for 48% of energy consumption, followed by oil (22%), hydro (18%), and gas (11%).

Education/Employment

Education is compulsory and free from age 7 to 15. There were 172,313 students in higher education in 1996–97. There are six universities—five in Serbia and one in Montenegro. The universities are financed by the two governments, which also set education policy. Research institutes are attached to the universities. The University of Belgrade has eight research institutes, specializing in nuclear energy, nuclear sciences, biology, physics, chemistry, metallurgy, computer science, and social sciences. Commercially based R&D has included metallurgy, hydrocarbons, agrochemicals, and pharmaceuticals.

The labor force is well educated. Although wages and employment conditions would normally be settled by collective agreement between management and employees, in practice they have been set by the government in response to financial stringency. Public-sector wages set a benchmark for the private sector, but the link between Montenegro's minimum wage and public-sector wages is due to be severed in 2002.

Fiscal/Financial

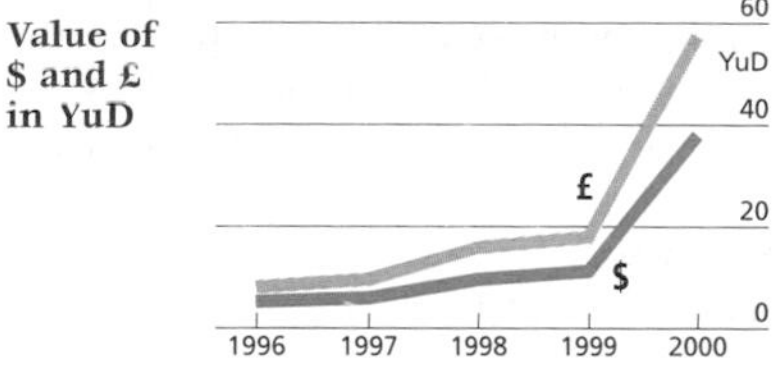

About 80% of Serbian banks were public-sector in early 2001, and most were insolvent. Thirty banks accounted for 70% of assets. Beogradska Banka was the largest with 37% of total bank capital. Two state-owned companies dominated the insurance sector. The National Bank of Yugoslavia is the Serbian central bank, with responsibility for monetary policy and financial regulation. Its supervisory powers were strengthened in 2002. The Bank Rehabilitation Agency is responsible for restructuring Serbian banks and resolving the non-performing loans and tax arrears of state companies. The Central Bank of Montenegro, whose supervisory powers were also strengthened, is restructuring Montenegro's 11 banks, and took control of the largest, Montenegro Banka, in 2001. The Finance Ministry stopped issuing offshore banking licenses in 2000. Bilateral and multilateral aid agencies are supporting bank restructuring in Yugoslavia and, with Dutch and German commercial banks, established the Micro-Finance Bank of the Federal Republic of Yugoslavia to provide finance to small enterprises from April 2001. The basic rate of corporation tax and tax on dividends is 20%. Montenegro's offshore banking rules set profits tax at 2.5%. Privatization has strengthened operations on the Belgrade Stock Exchange. Trading was YuD50.2 billion in 2001. A cooperation agreement was signed with the Athens Stock Exchange in November 2000.

Business Opportunities

There is Italian, Greek, and German investment in telecommunications, Swiss investment in cement, and German, Dutch, French, and Austrian investment in banking. Privatization offers investment opportunities. Other investment sectors include wood industries, mechanical engineering, leather goods, and boat building.

For More Information

Books:

Allcock, J. B. *Explaining Yugoslavia*. New York: Columbia University Press, 2000.
Secretariat of Information of the Republic of Montenegro. *Profile of Montenegro*.
Yugoslavia Business and Investment Opportunities Yearbook. 3rd ed. Washington, D.C.: International Business Publications, 2001 (annual).
Yugoslavia Investment and Business Guide. 3rd ed. Washington, D.C.: International Business Publications, 2001.
The Yugoslav Survey. Yugoslav Survey, Belgrade.

Web Sites:

Belgrade Stock Exchange: **www.belex.co.yu**
Federal government entry point: **www.gov.yu**
Federal Ministry of Foreign Affairs (good links): **www.smip.sv.gov.yu**
Federal Statistical Office: **www.szs.sv.gov.yu**
Montenegro government entry point: **www.montenegro.yu**
Serbian government entry point: **www.serbia.sr.gov.yu**

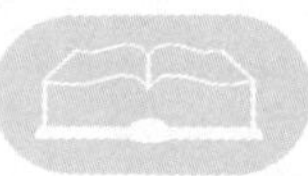

ZAMBIA

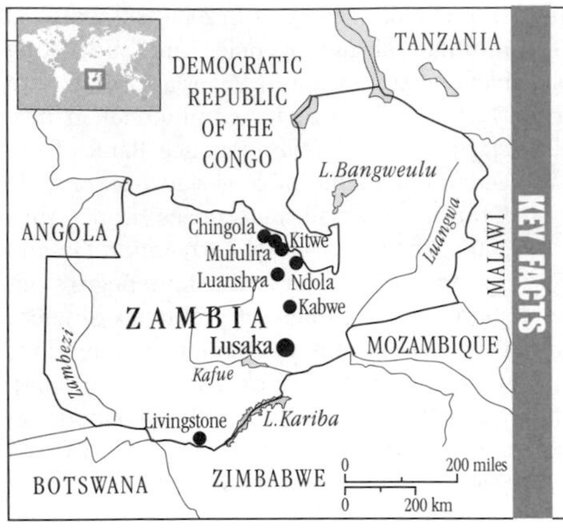

KEY FACTS

GNI: **$3,222 million; world's 131st**
GNI pc: **$330; world's 175th**
Head of government: **president**
Currency: **kwacha (ZK)**
Capital: **Lusaka**
Population: **8,976,000, growing at 2.4% p.a.**
Land area: **287,030 square miles**
Population density: **31 per square mile**
Life expectancy: **41 years**
Infant mortality: **112 per 1,000 live births**
Language: **English, Nyanja, Bemba, Tonga, other languages**
Best buy: **handicrafts, carvings, textiles, coffee**

ECONOMIC STRUCTURE

A landlocked country that has been repeatedly afflicted by the troubles of three of its largest neighbors—Congo, Angola, and Zimbabwe—Zambia has also experienced its own domestic problems, with both political and economic dimensions. The long rule of its first President, Kenneth Kaunda, was brought to an end in 1991 by the unpopularity of his single-party system of government and by the disastrous failure of his economic policies of state control. Although the Movement for Multiparty Democracy (MMD), which swept Kaunda from power in an election in 1991, at first represented the possibility of change and choice, within ten years it too had begun to display monopolistic tendencies, and its economic management record was widely criticized. In general elections at the end of 2001 the MMD held on to power at all levels, and President Frederick Chiluba's chosen successor, Levy Mwanawasa, was voted in by a narrow margin.

Zambia's economic development throughout the 20th century was strongly influenced by the discovery of large reserves of copper in the region known as the Copperbelt, bordering what is now the Democratic Republic of the Congo. Mining has long provided the bulk of Zambia's export earnings, but the industry went into decline through the 1990s, when the government accepted the need to attract private investment by privatizing the mines. However, the government's protracted negotiations with potential buyers contributed to the near-collapse of many operations. Mining contributes about 6% of GDP, agriculture about 15%, and manufacturing about 20%.

Copper accounted for about 50% of exports in 1999. Other exports included cobalt (contributing 14%), electricity, vegetables, flowers, sugar, and cotton. In 1999 Zambia's largest markets were Saudi Arabia, Japan, Thailand, and India. The country's dominant source of imports was South Africa, accounting for 55% of the total, followed by Zimbabwe, the United Kingdom, and the United States

The public sector's extensive interests in the economy were sold off progressively throughout the 1990s, starting with the agricultural and manufacturing companies and continuing with banks, insurance companies and hotels. The mining-sector operations of Zambia Consolidated Copper Mines (ZCCM) proved more contentious politically. After four years of negotiations, a subsidiary of Anglo American Corporation acquired the most valuable properties, the Konkola and Nchanga copper mines, in March 2000. Other major investors in the sector include Phelps Dodge of the United States, Canada's First Quantum Minerals, Switzerland's Glencore International, and South Africa's AngloVaal.

ECONOMIC POLICY

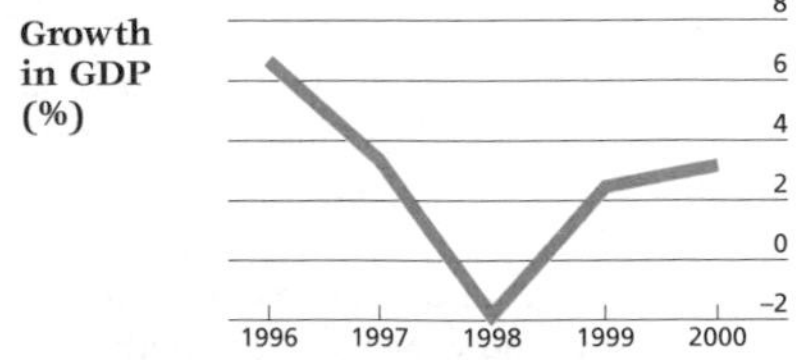

The MMD government pursued a policy of structural adjustment throughout the 1990s, with emphasis on privatization, liberalization of foreign exchange regulations, control of the money supply, reducing public expenditure, and boosting public revenues by more efficient tax collection. Most economic programs are heavily dependent on donor planning and funding, and corruption has not been eradicated. In the agricultural sector, the government has only gradually withdrawn from providing inputs and the buying and distribution of corn.

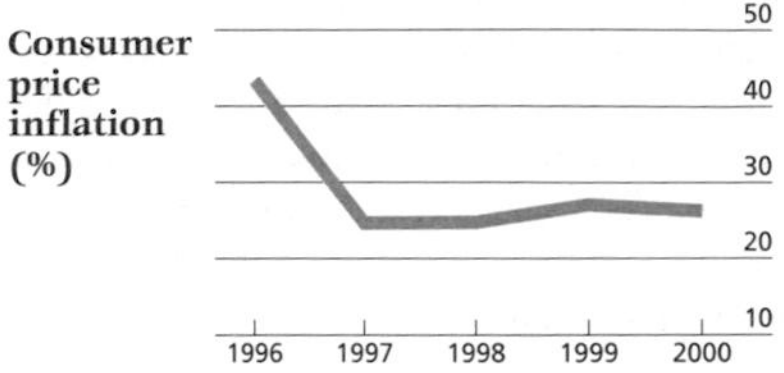

Economic growth was strongly positive in the mid-1990s but was insignificant or negative by the end of the decade, although for 2001 the government was estimating growth of 5%. The long-awaited privatization of the major copper mines in 2000 appeared to have provided a boost to growth. Inflation stood at about 25% in 2000. Small-scale and informal farming activities provide the largest source of employment. Formal employment has fallen in the mining and manufacturing sectors but has grown in services.

GEOGRAPHY/RESOURCES

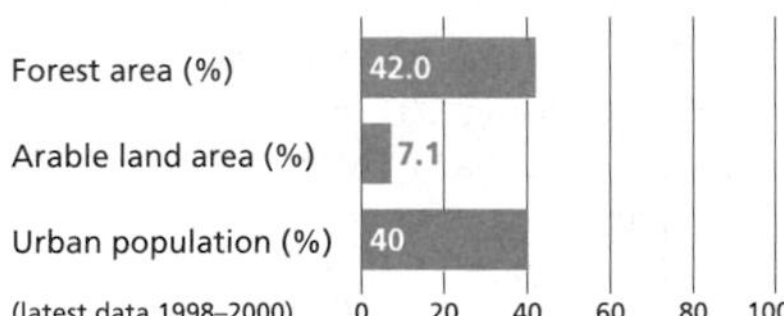

Zambia occupies a large section of the Central African plateau, higher in the east and lower in the west, and interspersed with lakes and swampy river basins. There are tributaries of the Congo and Zambezi rivers, and the latter forms the southern border with Zimbabwe, taking in the dramatic Victoria Falls and the man-made Lake Kariba. Much of Zambia's land is forested. The climate is tropical, with a wet season between November and March, followed a relatively cool dry period from April to August and a hot dry season in September and October.

The Southern and Central Provinces have the most productive land. The main food crops are cassava and corn, and there is also substantial production of groundnuts and sorghum. The spread of agriculture is made difficult by poor soils in the east, by

seasonal flooding in the larger river basins, and by recurring drought in the west. Cattle-rearing is common in the south and center, although in the Kafue and Luangwa basins there is infestation by tsetse fly. Commercial farming activity is concentrated along the transport route between the Copperbelt and Lusaka. There is fishing on the largest lakes and rivers. Zambia has large reserves of copper and cobalt, which are actively mined. Other minerals include lead, zinc, coal, manganese, silver, and gold-all of which have been exploited in the past.

There are about 70 distinct ethnic groups, of which the most numerous are the Bemba, Nyanja, Tonga, and Lozi. About 60% of Zambians live in rural areas, although the urban population is growing rapidly. The towns of the Copperbelt–including Ndola, Kabwe, Kitwe and Chingola–are home to about 20% of the population, while 15% live in Lusaka. There are small numbers of Europeans and Asians. More than 10% of the population are estimated to be HIV-positive, and infection rates are highest in the urban areas.

Communications/Energy

PCs	0.7
Telephone lines	0.9
Mobiles	0.5
Internet users	0.2
(per 100 people, 2000)	0 20 40 60 80 100

There are 39,000 miles of roads, of which about 4,500 miles are surfaced, although many are in a poor condition. Rehabilitation projects have received funding from international donors, and there are plans to upgrade and improve road connections with neighboring Botswana and Namibia. There are 1,345 miles of railway track, with the main line running from the Zimbabwe border to the Copperbelt, and a link at Kapiri Mposhi forming the Tanzania–Zambia railway to Dar es Salaam. A connection with Angola was put out of action in the 1970s. As a landlocked country Zambia has been concerned to secure its rail links with sea ports in both East and Southern Africa. Dar es Salaam was for many years the single most important port of access, but since the return of normal economic dealings in Southern Africa in 1994, Zambia has increased its traffic through Beira (Mozambique) and Durban (South Africa).

The former national airline, Zambia Airways, was liquidated in 1994. In 1999, it was replaced by a private company, Zambian Airways, which operates the main routes to Europe. Private companies compete in the domestic market.

The national telecommunications company Zamtel has been scheduled for partial privatization. Zamtel runs a small mobile telephone network in competition with two private operators.

The state-owned electricity company Zesco, which has been scheduled for privatization, relies on hydroelectric power sources, including the dams at Kafue Gorge, Kariba North Bank, and Victoria Falls. The main consumption is in the mining industry and in the urban areas of the Copperbelt and Lusaka. The surplus is sold to neighboring countries. Zambia's oil imports are normally conveyed by pipeline from Tanzania to a refinery at Indeni, although this was out of action in 2000 following a fire, and the country began to import refined fuel. Zambia has no oil or gas reserves of its own.

Education/Employment

The introduction of school fees in the 1990s has had a negative impact on primary school enrollment, which was formerly amongst the highest in Africa at 96% but is now about 70% per cent. For many, particularly in rural districts, the facilities are poor. Secondary school enrollment covers about 30% of the eligible age group. There are two universities, each with about 4,500 students, and there are several polytechnic colleges and technical schools.

The decline of mining and manufacturing activities has created high unemployment in the formal economy, and has severely reduced the bargaining power of the trade unions. Labor laws have been relaxed as part of the program to attract foreign investment.

Fiscal/Financial

The central bank is the Bank of Zambia. There are about 15 banks, including six foreign institutions. The banks operate under difficult conditions of high interest rates, which make it difficult for them to lend to domestic business. In an attempt to slow the depreciation of the kwacha, new foreign exchange controls were introduced in December 2000, including the restriction of foreign currency purchasing and export, and a requirement on investors to open foreign exchange accounts to hold 75% of their earnings in Zambia. There are tax incentives for foreign investors, and the general level of

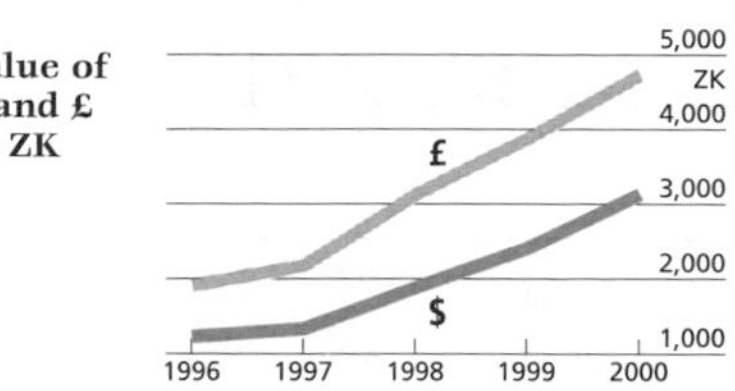

taxation in tourism and mining has been reduced.

The Lusaka stock exchange, established in 1994, has been affected by the unexciting performance of the economy and by the constant depreciation of the kwacha.

Business Opportunities

The investment climate in Zambia is strongly influenced by the fate of the mining industry, where a spate of new investment starting in 2000 began to have a beneficial effect on other economic activities. Zambia has significant potential to develop its tourism industry, which at present accommodates about 600,000 visitors a year. The country attracts high-paying visitors rather than those on limited budgets, and the emphasis of new investment has been on luxury developments and on the refurbishment of game lodges.

For More Information

Books:

Clark, J., and C. Allison. *Zambia: Debt and Poverty*. Oxford, Oxfordshire: Oxfam, 1989.

Ihonvbere, J. O. *Economic Crisis, Civil Society, and Democratization: The Case of Zambia*. Lawrenceville, NJ: Africa World Press, 1996.

Zambia Business and Investment Opportunities Yearbook. 3rd ed. Washington, D.C.: International Business Publications, 2001 (annual).

Zambia Investment and Business Guide. 3rd ed. Washington, D.C.: International Business Publications, 2001.

Web Sites:

African news and information: **www.allafrica.com/business**

Ernst and Young investment profiles: **www.mbendi.co.za/ernsty/cyaf.htm**

Norwegian Council for Africa, Index on Africa: **www.afrika.no**

Presidential web site: **www.statehouse.gov.zm**

Zambia Online: **www.zambia.co.zm**

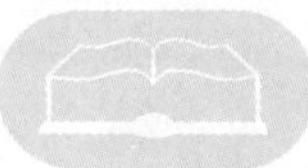

ZIMBABWE

KEY FACTS

GNI: **$6,302 million; world's 102nd**
GNI pc: **$530; world's 154th**
Head of government: **president**
Currency: **Zimbabwe dollar (Z$)**
Capital: **Harare**
Population: **11,529,000, growing at 1.7% p.a.**
Land area: **149,380 square miles**
Population density: **77 per square mile**
Life expectancy: **43 years**
Infant mortality: **60 per 1,000 live births**
Language: **English, Shona, Ndebele**
Best buy: **carvings, textiles**

ECONOMIC STRUCTURE

Zimbabwe achieved political independence in 1980, when the guerrilla forces led by Robert Mugabe ended their war against the white settler government of Ian Smith and were voted into power. Although the Mugabe government espoused Marxism, there was for some years an uneasy truce with the established corporate and settler interests that dominated the economy. In the early years, Mugabe's Zimbabwe African National Union-Patriotic Front (ZANU-PF), mainly representing the Shona majority, was engaged in sharp political rivalry with Joshua Nkomo's Zimbabwe African People's Union (ZAPU), which drew its strongest support in Matabeleland. During the 1980s the government used brutal military force to wipe out dissidents in Matabeleland, and persuaded Nkomo to join in the establishment of a single ZANU-PF party.

The Mugabe government's intolerance of opposition once again came into the spotlight at the end of the 1990s in response to the formation by the Zimbabwe Congress of Trade Unions (ZCTU) of a new political party—the Movement of Democratic Change (MDC), led by Morgan Tsvangirai—to protest at the government's policies. A serious political crisis then arose in the course of 2000, as the government used, and openly encouraged, violence both against the opposition and against the (mainly white) owners of large farms. Mugabe praised and supported the occupation of these farms by gangs of landless peasants and self-proclaimed "war veterans." In September 2001, after negotiations with Commonwealth governments, there was the appearance of an agreement to de-escalate the crisis, although this did not happen. Mugabe won the presidential election, though international observers did not accept it to be free or fair, in March 2002.

The harassment of the large-scale farmers had immediate consequences for the whole economy. There was a mounting shortage of essential foodstuffs and a sharpening collapse of foreign exchange earnings. Inflation soared out of control. During 2001 Mugabe declared that the state would take over any businesses that failed, and effectively restated the Marxist policies that he had always espoused. Prior to this latest crisis, Zimbabwe's economy had been relatively well diversified, with agriculture generating about 20% of GDP, manufacturing about 18%, and mining about 2%. Commercial farming and mining had played an important part in sustaining both exports and employment. The agricultural sector had produced a combination of food, cash crops, and livestock. The staple food, corn, had been supplemented by wheat, millet, sorghum, and barley. Agricultural crops produced for export had included tobacco, cotton, sugar, vegetables, fruit, and flowers. The main mineral in production was gold, but there was also mining for nickel, platinum, coal, copper, chromite, and many others. Manufacturing activities had included steel-making, textiles, clothing, food, and beverages. The tourist industry had also been an important source of foreign exchange for the economy until visitor numbers fell sharply in 2000.

The principal exports in the past consisted of tobacco (about 30% of the total), gold, ferro-alloys, and cotton. The most important markets for Zimbabwean goods were South Africa, the United Kingdom, Malawi, Botswana, and Japan. South Africa was the dominant source of imports, accounting for nearly half of the total, followed by the United Kingdom, China, Germany, and the United States.

Zimbabwe has reformed its public sector only marginally, principally by ending the former monopoly of the agricultural marketing boards, although the Grain Marketing Board was still used as a strategic asset for the government in imposing price controls on staple foods. Under Mugabe's government there was no likelihood that other state-owned corporations, such as those responsible for the railways and for electric power, would be privatized.

ECONOMIC POLICY

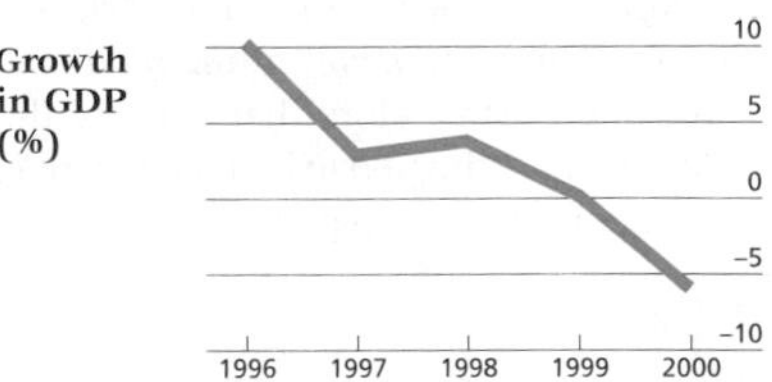

The Mugabe government was selective in its implementation of economic reforms urged by the IMF and the international community. In the 1980s it imposed strict controls on foreign exchange allocations. This was followed in the early 1990s by a gradual liberalization of foreign trade and foreign exchange dealings, although this in turn led to a rapid depreciation of the Zimbabwe dollar, and to ineffective government attempts to maintain an official exchange rate at an unsustainably high value. In the late 1990s, partly as a result of the government's military intervention in the Democratic Republic of the Congo, the authorities lost control of the budget deficit, causing the international community to suspend most forms of financial support. Under conditions of mounting economic crisis, the government resorted to short-term management strategies, including official price controls, to try to slow inflation.

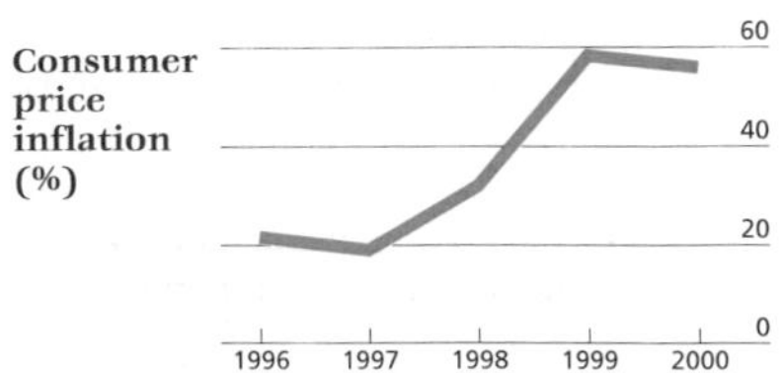

Zimbabwe's economic growth record has been erratic, with years of substantial growth in the 1980s and 1990s interspersed

with sharp falls in output in other years. There was negative growth of -1.4% in 1999 and -5.5% in 2000. Inflation was at high levels in the 1990s, averaging 29% a year in 1994–99, 60% in 2000, and 100% in 2001. A phase of employment creation in the 1980s came to an end in the 1990s.

Geography/Resources

Zimbabwe occupies a series of plateaus between the Zambezi and Limpopo rivers. The highest ground, averaging 4,000 feet above sea level, crosses the country from the southwest to the northeast, following the line of the Great Dyke. The lower ground, below 3,000 feet in altitude, lies in the basins of the main rivers. There are hill ranges along the Great Dyke and in the eastern highlands, where the highest peak is 8,511 feet. Much of the land is sandy and infertile, but there are several zones of high fertility and reliable rainfall. The main rainy season occurs between November and March, and rainfall is highest in the eastern highlands, where the average is 55 inches a year, varying to 31 inches in the northeast and less than 16 inches in the Limpopo valley. About 30% of the most productive land was formerly owned by about 4,000 commercial farmers. Although the extent of communal land holdings has increased as the number of commercial farms has fallen, many of these holdings have suffered from overpopulation and overstocking. The Great Dyke is the source of most of Zimbabwe's minerals, including gold, nickel, chrome, platinum, asbestos, and copper. Coal, iron ore, and phosphate rock are mined for local consumption.

The majority of Zimbabweans belong to sub-groups of the Shona. About one-fifth of the population are Ndebele, who live mainly in the south and west. The white population fell sharply from 275,000 in the 1970s to only 70,000 in 2000. There has been substantial migration from rural to urban areas, to the point that at least one-third of the population now live in the towns and cities, of which the largest are Harare and Bulawayo. It is estimated that about 15% of the population are HIV-positive, and that more than 500,000 people have died of AIDS since the disease arrived in the 1980s.

Communications/Energy

The road network is extensive and well-developed, and includes 9,500 miles of tarred roads. There is also a well-developed rail network, which provides links to Botswana, South Africa, Mozambique, and Zambia. The most important link is through Mozambique to the port of Beira. The national airline, Air Zimbabwe, has been operating at a loss for many years, and the privately-owned Zimbabwe Express Airlines provides competition on domestic and regional routes.

The fixed-line telecommunications network is owned by the Posts and Telecommunications Corporation, but competition is provided by mobile telephone services.

Electric power is provided by the Zimbabwe Electricity Supply Authority, which generates power at Kariba dam and Hwange coal-fired power station, while also importing supplies from Mozambique and South Africa. All the country's oil requirements are imported, principally by pipeline from Beira. The government-owned National Oil Corporation of Zimbabwe, which has a monopoly on oil imports and sells at subsidized prices, has been making substantial losses in recent years. The collapse of all oil imports in 2001 was prevented only by the agreement of Libya to provide oil in exchange for government promises of Zimbabwean products, land, and big-game hunting rights.

Education/Employment

Primary education is available free to all children, and there are places for about 2.5 million pupils at primary level. About 700,000 students are enrolled in secondary education, while about 40,000 students attend higher education.

Growth in employment has lagged far behind population growth, and only 10% of the population have formal jobs. The commercial farms have become major employers of labor, but in 2001 were threatening to lay off more than half their workers in response to Mugabe's land-seizure program. Agriculture also provides informal employment for much of the population. The value of wages has fallen steadily in the 1990s, and there has been recurring industrial unrest.

Fiscal/Financial

The Reserve Bank of Zimbabwe is the central bank. The main commercial banks are Standard Chartered, Barclays, Stanbic, Commercial Bank of Zimbabwe, and Zimbank. The Ministry of Finance has licensed

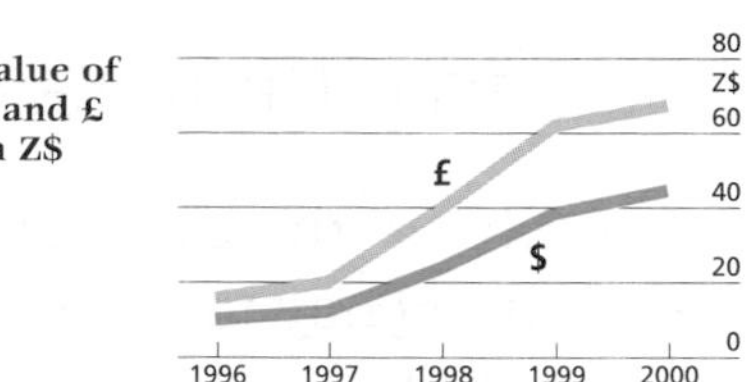

the establishment of many new banks, most of which are poorly supervised. The economic crisis of 2000 and 2001 created the conditions for a thriving black market in foreign exchange, with the Zimbabwe dollar trading at about half its official value.

The Zimbabwe Stock Exchange is one of the oldest and largest in Africa. The market remains an active center of business despite the economic crisis that has enveloped the economy.

Business Opportunities

The disturbed political climate and the restrictions imposed on foreign exchange dealings acted as a strong disincentive to any new investment in Zimbabwe from the late 1990s onwards. Investors who avoided Zimbabwe during the Mugabe era would nevertheless take a close interest following any change of government. The sharp shrinkage of the Zimbabwe economy since 1999 may have served to reduce the value of many assets to such an extent that the country could become a source of bargains for foreign investors. International mining companies have continued to show an interest in acquiring properties even though many mining operations have actually come to a halt.

For More Information

Books:

Moyo, S. *The Land Question in Zimbabwe.* Harare: Southern African Printing and Publishing, 1995.

Weiss, R., and N. Gordimer. *Zimbabwe and the New Elite.* London: British Academic Press, 1994.

Web Sites:

Ernst and Young investment profiles: **www.mbendi.co.za/ernsty/cyaf.htm**

Norwegian Council for Africa, Index on Africa: **www.afrika.no**

Zimbabwe links: **www.zimbabwe.8m.com**

  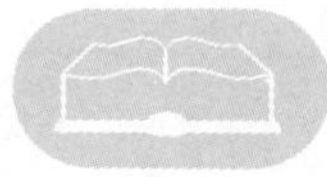    

U.S. State Profiles

The profiles of the U.S. states aim to give you an introduction to each state from a business perspective. They focus in particular on the following aspects:

- economy
- geography/resources
- communications/energy
- fiscal/financial opportunities
- business opportunities

Figures for the ethnic composition of some states add up to more than 100% because a variety of bases for population groups—including language, geographical origin, and ethnicity—is used in the U.S. censuses.

Contents

Key
CT Connecticut
DE Delaware
MA Massachusetts
MD Maryland
NH New Hampshire
NJ New Jersey
RI Rhode Island
VT Vermont
Arctic Ocean
Beaufort Sea
RUSSIA
ALASKA
CANADA
Bering Strait
Yukon
Mt McKinley
Fairbanks
Anchorage
Juneau
Bering Sea
Gulf of Alaska
ALEUTIAN ISLANDS
Pacific Ocean
C A N A D A
Rocky Mountains
Seattle
Olympia
Mt Rainier
WASHINGTON
Salem
OREGON
Boise
IDAHO
Helena
MONTANA
Missouri
WYOMING
Cheyenne
Platte
NORTH DAKOTA
Bismarck
SOUTH DAKOTA
Pierre
NEBRASKA
Lincoln
MINNESOTA
St. Paul
Mississippi
WISCONSIN
Madison
MICHIGAN
Lansing
Detroit
L. Superior
L. Huron
L. Michigan
IOWA
Des Moines
Chicago
Springfield
ILLINOIS
INDIANA
Indianapolis
OHIO
Columbus
Ohio
WEST VIRGINIA
Charleston
MAINE
Augusta
VT
Montpelier
NH
Concord
Albany
MA
Boston
RI
Providence
CT
Hartford
NEW YORK
NJ
New York
Trenton
PENNSYLVANIA
Harrisburg
MD
DE
Dover
Annapolis
Washington DC
Richmond
VIRGINIA
Sacramento
Carson City
San Francisco
NEVADA
Salt Lake City
UTAH
Mt Whitney
CALIFORNIA
Los Angeles
San Diego
Denver
COLORADO
Colorado
KANSAS
Topeka
Arkansas
MISSOURI
Jefferson City
KENTUCKY
Frankfort
NORTH CAROLINA
Raleigh
Nashville
TENNESSEE
Tennessee
ARIZONA
Phoenix
Santa Fe
NEW MEXICO
OKLAHOMA
Oklahoma City
Red
ARKANSAS
Little Rock
Columbia
SOUTH CAROLINA
Atlanta
GEORGIA
ALABAMA
Montgomery
Jackson
LOUISIANA
MISSISSIPPI
Pacific Ocean
Atlantic Ocean
TEXAS
Dallas
Austin
Houston
San Antonio
Rio Grande
Baton Rouge
New Orleans
Jacksonville
Tallahassee
FLORIDA
Miami
Gulf of Mexico
MEXICO
CUBA
0
500 miles
0
500 km
HAWAII
KAUAI
Lihue
NIIHAU
OAHU
Honolulu
MOLOKAI
MAUI
LANAI
KAHOOLAWE
Hilo
Mauna Loa
HAWAII
Pacific Ocean

  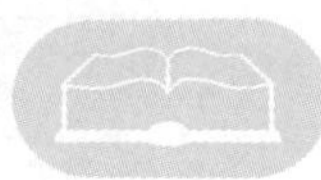    

ALABAMA

KEY FACTS

State capital: **Montgomery**
Population: **4,447,100; 23rd in U.S.; grew 10.1% 1990–2000**
Land area: **50,744 square miles; 28th in U.S.**
Population density: **87.6 per square mile**
GSP: **$115,071 million**
GSP pc: **$25,875.51**
Household income: **$33,105; 45th in U.S.**
Poverty rate: **14.6%**
Unemployment: **4.6%**

ECONOMY

Alabama's cotton-based agricultural economy began to decline early in the 20th century, paving the way for the manufacturing industry to become dominant; it is still a major sector of Alabama's economy, led by paper products, electronic equipment, primary metals, lumber and wood, chemicals, textiles, fabricated metals, industrial machinery, and food products.

The service industry is growing, led by health and business services. The state has identified a number of industries to target for growth and development, including: electronics fabrication and assembly; plastics and resins; aerospace; automotive equipment; wood products; textiles and apparel; food and agribusiness; distribution, warehouse, and back-office facilities; and finance, insurance, and real estate.

Challenges facing Alabama are its historically low educational attainment rate, a high level of poverty, and problems in the healthcare and social arenas.

GEOGRAPHY/RESOURCES

Located in the southeastern United States, Alabama consists mainly of coastal plain in the southern two-thirds of the state, with the fertile Black Belt in the middle of that area; the northern third contains hills and plateaus and is crossed by the Appalachian Ridge.

Poultry and poultry products are the primary agricultural output; other produce includes cattle and calves, nursery and greenhouse crops, cotton, soybeans, corn, hay, and vegetables. Mineral resources are natural gas, crude oil, coal, crushed stone, cement, lime, sand and gravel, bentonite, clay, kaolin, iron oxide pigments, salt, and gemstones. Shrimp is the primary marine resource; others include crab, mullet, oysters, flatfish, menhaden, mackerel, snapper, catfish, and bluefish. Forestry resources include pine, oak, hickory, gum, and mixed upland hardwoods.

There is little in-migration in Alabama; the white population of the state consists mainly of the descendants of 19th-century Irish, English, and German settlers, who came from northern and eastern states; the black population is descended from the slaves of the state's cotton days. The 2000 census shows that 71.1% of the population is white; 26% African American; and 1.7% Hispanic, of any race.

Birmingham is the largest city, with a population of 921,106. Other significant cities include: Mobile (540,258); Huntsville (342,376); Montgomery (333,055); Tuscaloosa (164,875); Decatur (145,867); Florence (142,950); Dothan (137,916); the Auburn/Opelika metro area (115,092); Anniston (112,249); and Gadsden (103,459).

Environmental imperatives for Alabama include reducing air pollution from industrial facilities and reducing water pollution.

COMMUNICATIONS/ENERGY

Alabama has 96 public-use airports, of which two—Birmingham International Airport and Huntsville International Airport/Carl T. Jones Field—are international. There are 14 public ports, the largest of which is the port of Mobile on the Gulf of Mexico. Alabama has 21 railroads operating 6,003 miles of track, and 163,666 miles of roads.

Private industry has provided Alabama with a fairly substantial digital infrastructure, including 63,334 high-speed lines as of 2000. In 2000, 91.3% of Alabama households had telephone service; 35.5% of households had Internet access; and 31.2% of the population had wireless telephones.

Coal is the most-used energy resource in Alabama, followed by petroleum. Electric utilities rely primarily on coal, followed by nuclear energy.

FISCAL/FINANCIAL

Alabama has one of the lowest per-capita state tax burdens in the United States. Of state tax collected in 2000, 32.2% came from individual income tax; 26.4% from general sales tax; 23.7% from selective sales tax; 8.4% from license tax; and 3.8% from corporate income tax. The corporate income tax rate is 6.5%.

Birmingham is one of the financial centers of the South; major financial institutions include ABC Bancorp, Alabama National BanCorporation, The Banc Corporation, BancorpSouth, The Colonial BancGroup, South Alabama Bancorporation, SouthTrust Corp., SunTrust Banks, United Security Bancshares, and Whitney Holding Corp.

BUSINESS OPPORTUNITIES

Alabama began offering incentives for business in the late 1990s, including: tax credits for capital investment and employee education; tax exemptions on business inventory, pollution control equipment, and construction materials; incentives for new and expanding businesses in enterprise zones; and tax credits for increased production of coal.

Alabama is a research center for the aerospace and defense industries; over half of the state's federal R&D funding comes from the Department of Defense. Research centers include: Alabama A&M University; the Army Aeromedical Research Laboratory; the Army Aviation Research, Development, and Engineering Center; the Army Aviation Technical Test Center; the Army Missile Research, Development, and Engineering Center; Boeing; Dyntetics Inc.; the George C. Marshall Space Flight Center; the Missile Guidance Directorate; Nichols Research Corp.; the Southern Research Institute; the Space and Missile Defense Technical Center; Teledyne Industries; Tuskegee University; the University of Alabama; and the University of Southern Alabama.

There are seven *Fortune* 500 companies with their headquarters in Alabama: SCI Systems, Saks, Caremark Rx, HealthSouth, SouthTrust Corp., Regions Financial, and AmSouth Bancorp.

For More Information

Book:

Rogers, William Warren, et. al., eds. *Alabama: The History of a Deep South State*. Tuscaloosa, AL: University of Alabama Press, 1994.

Web Sites:

Alabama Development Office:
www.ado.state.al.us
Alabama State Homepage:
www.state.al.us

ALASKA

KEY FACTS

State capital: **Juneau**
Population: **626,932; 48th in U.S.; grew 14.0% 1990–2000**
Land area: **571,948 square miles; 1st in U.S.**
Population density: **1.09 per square mile**
GSP: **$26,353 million**
GSP pc: **$42,034.86**
Household income: **$50,746; 4th in U.S.**
Poverty rate: **8.3%**
Unemployment: **6.6%**

ECONOMY

Alaska's real economic development began with the discovery of gold in 1880, which was the primary driver of the economy until the discovery of oil in 1968. Oil and gas continue to make up the state's economic base, though government activity is also significant. Timber and fishing likewise continue to contribute, although the state's manufacturing base is declining due to decreases in timber and seafood processing. Transportation and aerospace are growing industries; the state's service sector is also becoming significant, led by healthcare, business services, and tourism.

The main challenge facing the state is its inaccessibility, despite the fact that it is nearly equidistant from Japan, Europe, and the east coast of the United States. Though transportation has steadily improved since the late 1960s and the state has a strong export base, its geographic isolation has led to high outward migration of workers and very little venture capital and R&D investment.

GEOGRAPHY/RESOURCES

Located at the extreme northwest of the North American continent, Alaska consists of mountains in the southeast, the south coastal archipelago and Gulf of Alaska islands, the Aleutian region in the extreme southwest, the tundra-covered Alaska range in the southern third of the mainland, plains north and west of the Alaska range, the Rocky Mountain System of Alaska running west to east north of the central plains, and the Arctic Coastal Plain in the northernmost region.

Salmon is the most important marine resource; others include crabs, pollock, halibut, cod, sablefish, herring, mackerel, rockfish, shrimp, sole, flatfish, and sea urchins. Mineral resources are crude oil, natural gas, coal, zinc, silver, and gold. Forestry resources include spruce, hemlock, cedar, and alder. There is little agriculture in Alaska, but the state produces some oats, barley, potatoes, hay, and vegetables.

The earliest explorers in Alaska were Russian; the United States purchased it as a territory in 1867 and it became a state in 1959. The 2000 census shows that 69.3% of the population is white; 15.6% is Native American and Alaska Native; 4.1% is Hispanic, of any race; 4.0% is Asian; and 3.5% is African American. Anchorage is the largest city, with a population of 260,283.

As the site of one of the most disastrous oil spills in history, one of Alaska's primary environmental imperatives is preventing and responding to spills. Others include forest conservation and wildlife protection.

COMMUNICATIONS/ENERGY

With air travel as a major method of transportation, Alaska has 1,112 airports, seaplane bases, and aircraft landing areas; international airports are Anchorage International Airport, Fairbanks International Airport, Juneau International Airport, and Ketchikan International Airport. Ferry services are an important method of shipping and of transportation for residents. There are 30 ports; Anchorage is the main general cargo port, and Valdez is the main oil transhipment port. Overland travel is more difficult; Alaska has 12,200 miles of public roads, approximately half of which are paved. Highways only provide access to one-third of the state. There is one railroad with 525 miles of track.

Alaska's digital government services consistently rank among the best in the nation, allowing the state to provide services to geographically isolated residents; however, the state had only 934 high-speed lines as of 2000. In 2000 95.5% of households had telephone service and 55.6% of households had Internet access.

Alaska is the second-largest producer of crude oil in the United States, but the state depends most heavily on natural gas to meet its own energy requirements; Alaska's electric utilities rely mostly on natural gas and hydroelectricity.

FISCAL/FINANCIAL

Most of the state's revenue comes from the oil industry; Alaska has no state taxes on income, general sales, or inventory. Of state taxes collected in 2000, 49.8% came from severance tax; 30.8% from corporate net income tax; 9.7% from selective sales tax; 6.4% from license tax; and 3.1% from property tax. The corporate income tax rate is divided into 10 brackets, from 1.0 to 9.4%.

Major financial institutions in Alaska include Alaska Pacific Bancshares, First National Bank of Anchorage, KeyCorp, Northrim Bank, and Wells Fargo & Co.

BUSINESS OPPORTUNITIES

Alaska is attempting to diversify its economy and improve its unemployment rate by offering a number of business incentives: tax credits for hiring welfare recipients and other disadvantaged groups, exploration incentives for mining companies, funding for development in low-income communities, loans for the development or upgrade of electric power facilities, and reimbursement of startup costs for new companies.

The lack of major research facilities is a disadvantage, although there are a few: the Alaska Biological Science Center, the Alaska Synthetic Aperture Radar Facility, the Auke Bay Laboratory, and the University of Alaska.

There are no *Fortune* 500 companies with their headquarters in Alaska.

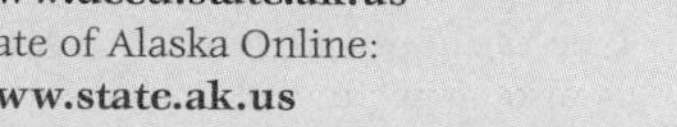

For More Information

Books:

Naske, Claus-M., and Herman E. Slotnick. *Alaska: A History of the 49th State.* Norman, OK: University of Oklahoma Press, 1994.

Strohmeyer, John. *Extreme Conditions: Big Oil and the Transformation of Alaska.* Anchorage, AK: Cascade Press, 1997.

Web Sites:

Department of Community and Economic Development: **www.dced.state.ak.us**

State of Alaska Online: **www.state.ak.us**

Travel Alaska: **www.travelalaska.com**

ARIZONA

KEY FACTS

State capital: **Phoenix**
Population: **5,130,632; 20th in U.S.; grew 40.0% 1990–2000**
Land area: **113,634 square miles; 6th in U.S.**
Population density: **45.1 per square mile**
GSP: **$143,683 million**
GSP pc: **$28,004.93**
Household income: **$41,456; 28th in U.S.**
Poverty rate: **13.6%**
Unemployment: **3.9%**

ECONOMY

Arizona's economy has been defined by the "5 Cs": cattle, copper, citrus, cotton, and climate. The agricultural and mining industries represented by cattle, copper, citrus, and cotton have declined in the latter half of the 20th century, but they still contribute to the economy.

Services are now the dominant industry, driven by business services and tourism, the latter being based on Arizona's warm, dry climate and natural attractions such as the Grand Canyon. Manufacturing, another significant sector (14.4%), has experienced most of its growth through the electronics, communications, aeronautical, and aluminum industries.

A major challenge facing Arizona is to improve the state educational system, and a recent increase in the sales tax has been earmarked as revenue for that purpose. The state also needs to increase R&D expenditures and improve access to venture capital.

GEOGRAPHY/RESOURCES

Located in the southwestern United States, Arizona consists of the Colorado Plateau in the northeast, the Mogollon Rim along the southern border, the Basin and Range region in the southwest, and the rugged Transition Zone in between the latter two.

Copper is the primary mineral resource; others include coal, crude oil, gold, silver, lime, sand and gravel, Portland cement, crushed stone, molybdenum, gemstones, iron oxide pigments, bentonite, and gypsum. Pine is the major forestry resource; there is also some fir and spruce. Marine resources include trout, bass, catfish, sunfish, crappie, bullhead, perch, walleye, and tilapia. Cattle and calves and dairy products are the primary agricultural output; other produce includes cotton, vegetables, citrus fruits, hay, and nursery and greenhouse crops.

There was little European settlement in Arizona until the second half of the 19th century; a swell of Hispanic immigration occurred throughout the 20th century. The 2000 census shows that 75.5% of the population is white; 25.3% Hispanic, of any race; 5.0% Native American; 3.1% African American; and 1.8% Asian.

Nearly two-thirds of the state's population—3,251,876 people—live in the Phoenix/Mesa metro area. Other cities include: Tucson (843,7460); Yuma (160,026); Mohave County, which adjoins Nevada's Las Vegas (155,032); and Flagstaff (116,320).

Water conservation and management is a major environmental concern in Arizona; other environmental imperatives include the waste management and remediation of contaminated and saline soils.

COMMUNICATIONS/ENERGY

Arizona has 83 public-use airports, of which six—Bisbee Douglas International Airport, Laughlin/Bullhead International Airport, Nogales International Airport, Phoenix Sky Harbor International Airport, Tucson International Airport, and Yuma International Airport—are international. There are 53,994 miles of roads. A new passenger rail system is under development, though there are several existing freight lines.

Arizona had 153,500 high-speed telephone lines as of 2000, and is exploring options for further developing its digital infrastructure, especially in smaller communities. In 2000, 94.4% of households had telephone service; 42.5% of households had Internet access; and 35.7% of the population had wireless telephones.

Petroleum is the most-used energy resource in Arizona, followed by coal and nuclear energy. Electric utilities rely primarily on coal and nuclear energy, with some use of hydroelectricity; petroleum is consumed primarily by transportation and industrial use.

FISCAL/FINANCIAL

Arizona has undergone several tax reductions: personal income taxes have been cut by 31% since 1995, and corporate income tax has been decreased twice since 1998. Of state tax collected in 2000, 44.8% came from general sales tax; 28.3% from individual income tax; 12.5% from selective sales tax; 6.5% from corporate income tax; and 3.7% from property tax. The corporate income tax rate is 6.968%.

Major financial institutions in Arizona include the Bank of America, Bank One Corp., Citigroup, Comerica, Compass Bancshares, Fifth Third Bancorp, Golden West Financial Corp., Harris Bankcorp, Marshall & Ilsley Corp., Silicon Valley Bancshares, Sun Community Bancorp, U.S. Bancorp, Washington Federal, Washington Mutual, Wells Fargo & Co., and Zions Bancorporation.

BUSINESS OPPORTUNITIES

Arizona offers several incentives for business, including job training grants, enterprise zones, bonds for the construction of industrial and manufacturing facilities and the purchase of equipment, and tax credits for R&D, pollution control, and IT training.

The majority of federal research spending in Arizona goes to defense. Research facilities include AlliedSignal, Arizona State University, the Army Yuma Proving Ground, Interop Joint Venture, Lockheed Martin, Motorola, Orbital Sciences Corp., the Phoenix Epidemiology and Clinical Research Branch, Raytheon Co., St. Joseph's Hospital and Medical Center, the University of Arizona, and the Western Cotton Research Laboratory.

There are five *Fortune* 500 companies with their headquarters in Arizona: AVNet, Allied Waste Industries, Phelps Dodge, Pinnacle West Capital, and MicroAge

For More Information

Book:

Sheridan, Thomas E. *Arizona: A History*. Tucson, AZ: University of Arizona Press, 1995.

Web Sites:

Arizona Department of Commerce:
www.azcommerce.com
Arizona Guide:
www.arizonaguide.com
Arizona State Homepage:
www.state.az.us

ARKANSAS

KEY FACTS

State capital: **Little Rock**
Population: **2,673,400; 33rd in U.S.; grew 13.7% 1990–2000**
Land area: **52,067.7 square miles; 27th in U.S.**
Population density: **51.3 per square mile**
GSP: **$64,773 million**
GSP pc: **$24,228.70**
Household income: **$30,293; 49th in U.S.**
Poverty rate: **15.8%**
Unemployment: **4.4%**

ECONOMY

Arkansas's agricultural economy became industrialized in the mid-20th century, and the manufacturing sector, which is still growing, is an important sector of the economy. Significant products include food products, electronic equipment, paper products, fabricated and primary metals, industrial machinery, and motor vehicles.

The service sector is growing, led by health and business services; tourism is also important. Industries that Arkansas has targeted for growth and development include distribution, information technology, telecommunications, biotechnology, and tourism. Realizing the importance of knowledge-based industries to a state's economy, Arkansas voted in 1999 to expand business incentives to these industries.

Despite growth in recent years, due in large part to aggressive economic-development policies, Arkansas still faces a number of challenges that will need to be addressed if the state is to attract high-wage jobs. They include a high poverty rate, low educational attainment, a scarcity of venture capital, and a shortage of skilled labor.

GEOGRAPHY/RESOURCES

Located in the central southern United States, Arkansas consists of four geographic regions: the Ouachita Province highlands in the west, the Ozark Plateau in the north, the Mississippi alluvial plain in the east, and the Gulf Coastal Plain in the south.

Poultry and poultry products are the most significant agricultural output; other produce includes soybeans, rice, cotton, cattle and calves, pigs, wheat, dairy products, and corn. Mineral resources include natural gas, crude oil, coal, bromine, silica stone, tripoli, kaolin, gemstones including diamonds, gypsum, sand and gravel, and crushed stone. Pine is the primary forestry resource; others include oak and other mixed upland hardwoods. Marine resources include trout, bass, bullhead, sunfish, catfish, gar, and crappie.

The state's population in the 19th century consisted largely of Scottish, Scotch-Irish, and English settlers from other eastern states, and black slaves; there has been little in-migration in the 20th century, while the black population has decreased. The 2000 census shows that 80% of the population is white; 15.7% African American; and 3.2% Hispanic, of any race.

The Little Rock metro area is the largest in Arkansas, with a population of 583,845; other cities include the Fayetteville/Springdale/Rogers metro area (311,121), Fort Smith (168,318), Pine Bluff (84,278), and Jonesboro (82,148).

Environmental imperatives for Arkansas include restoring land and water damaged by mining activities and regulating waste from the state's manufacturing sector.

COMMUNICATIONS/ENERGY

Arkansas has 101 public-use airports, one of which—Arkansas International Airport —is international. There are five commercial waterways—the McClellan-Kerr Arkansas River Navigation System and the Mississippi, Ouachita, White and Red Rivers—with nine public ports and numerous private ports. The state has 3,170.4 miles of rail served by 25 railroads, and 77,781.3 miles of roads. An initiative begun in 1999 will reconstruct every mile of Arkansas's interstate highway system.

Arkansas had 28,968 high-speed telephones lines as of 2000, 14 fiber parks for businesses, and a developing telecommunications industry. Despite the available infrastructure, however, Arkansas ranks near the bottom of the United States in measures such as number of high-tech jobs and use of technology in state government. In 2000, 90.1% of households had telephone service; 26.5% of households had Internet access (the second-lowest number in the United States); and 27.8% of the population had wireless telephones.

Petroleum is the most-used energy resource in Arkansas, followed by coal and natural gas in nearly equal measures. Electric utilities make primary use of coal, with some nuclear energy; the industrial sector uses primarily wood and waste and natural gas. Transportation uses petroleum almost exclusively.

FISCAL/FINANCIAL

Arkansas reduced its state tax burden in the 1990s, but its per-capita state tax burden is still higher than that of surrounding states. Of state tax collected in 2000, 35.0% came from general sales tax; 30.2% from individual income tax; 13.5% from selective sales tax; 9.9% from property tax; 5.3% from license tax; and 4.9% from corporate income tax. The corporate income tax rate ranges from 1.0 to 6.5% in six brackets.

Major financial institutions include BancorpSouth, Bank of America, Bank of the Ozarks, BOK Financial Corp., First Federal Bancshares of Arkansas, First Tennessee National Corp., Morgan Keegan, Pocahontas Bancorp, Regions Financial Corp., Superior Financial Corp., Union Planters Corp., and U.S. Bancorp.

BUSINESS OPPORTUNITIES

Arkansas has recently begun offering a number of incentives to business, including tax credits for the purchase of recycling equipment, for manufacturers of high-growth energy technologies, for job creation in enterprise zones, for capital investment, for businesses providing daycare, and for businesses in the tourism and biotechnology industries. The state also offers a training incentives program.

Research facilities in Arkansas include Arkansas Blue Cross & Blue Shield, Arkansas Children's Hospital, BEI Sensors & Systems Co., the National Center for Toxicological Research, and the University of Arkansas.

There are five *Fortune* 500 companies with their headquarters in Arkansas: Wal-Mart Stores, Dillard's, Tyson Foods, AllTel, and Murphy Oil.

For More Information

Book:

Johnson, Ben F., III. *Arkansas in Modern America 1930–1999*. Fayetteville, AR: University of Arkansas Press, 2000.

Web Sites:

Arkansas Department of Economic Development:
www.1800arkansas.com
Arkansas State Homepage:
www.state.ar.us

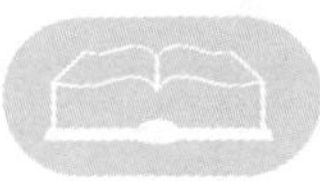

CALIFORNIA

KEY FACTS

State capital: **Sacramento**
Population: **33,871,648; 1st in U.S.; grew 13.6% 1990–2000**
Land area: **155,958.2 square miles; 3rd in U.S.**
Population density: **217.1 per square mile**
GSP: **$1,229,098 million**
GSP pc: **$36,286.93**
Household income: **$46,802; 13th in U.S.**
Poverty rate: **14.0%**
Unemployment: **4.9%**

ECONOMY

California has always had something that draws people from all over the world: gold in the 19th century, the entertainment business in the 20th, and high-tech industries in the 21st. However, these images have never been representative of the state as a whole as there is a wide variety of economic activity in California.

The state's abundant natural resources have led to an economy that ranks among the top ten in the world and is more varied than any other state; California ranks first in the nation in both agricultural and manufacturing output.

The manufacturing sector is led by electronic equipment and instruments, much of it contributing to the state's aerospace industry. Other important industries include industrial machinery, food products, chemicals, printing and publishing, transportation equipment, and petroleum products. The service sector is the largest in the economy, led by business and health services; the state's significant tourism and motion picture industries also fall into this sector. Finance, insurance, and real estate (FIRE) are another important contributor.

The major industry clusters in California are telecommunications, healthcare technologies, multimedia, environmental technologies, entertainment, apparel and fashion design, information technologies of all types, wood products, and diversified manufacturing.

Challenges for California include: improving education and workforce training to meet the needs of the state's industries, especially high-tech businesses; developing a more efficient transportation infrastructure and maintaining existing transportation networks; and building affordable housing in urban areas.

GEOGRAPHY/RESOURCES

Located on the west coast of the United States, California has eight physiographic regions: the Klamath Mountains in the northwest, the Coast Ranges along most of the coast, the Central Valley west of the Coast Ranges in the central part of the state, the Sierra Nevada west of the Central Valley, the Cascade Mountains north of the Sierra Nevada, the Basin and Range Region in the north and west, the Los Angeles Ranges, and the San Diego Ranges.

Crude oil is the primary mineral resource; others include natural gas, sand and gravel, Portland cement, boron minerals, crushed stone, diatomite, feldspar, salt, soda ash, gold, silver, magnesium compounds, titanium, clay, fuller's earth, crude gypsum, kaolin, talc, bentonite, perlite, and gemstones. Marine resources include squid, crab, tuna, sea urchins, salmon, sardines, sablefish, sole, shrimp, lobster, halibut, thornyhead, mackerel, rockfish, cabezon, bass, croaker, and flounder. Citrus and other fruits are the primary agricultural output; other produce includes vegetables, dairy products, nursery and greenhouse products, poultry and poultry products, cattle and calves, cotton, hay, soybeans, and wheat. Forestry resources include pine, redwood, fir, spruce, juniper, oak, and other western hardwoods.

California's population boomed with the discovery of gold in 1848, bringing northern Europeans, mainly from the midwest, to join the state's Spanish and Mexican population. Chinese, Irish, French, Russians, and Japanese also came in the 19th century; 20th-century immigration was mainly from Mexico and various Asian countries. The 2000 census shows that 59.5% of the population is white; 32.4% Hispanic, of any race; 10.9% Asian; 6.7% African American; and 1.0% native American.

The Los Angeles/Riverside/Orange County metro area is the largest in the state, with 16,373,645 people. Other major cities include: San Diego (2,813,833); Oakland (2,393,557); San Francisco (1,731,183); the Sacramento/Yolo metro area (1,796,857); San Jose (1,682,585); Fresno (922,516); Ventura (753,197); Bakersfield (661,645); the Stockton/Lodi metro area (563,598); the Vallejo/Fairfield/Napa metro area (518,821); Santa Rosa (458,614); Modesto (446,997); Salinas (401,762); the Santa Barbara metro area (399,347); the Visalia/Tulare/Porterville metro area (368,021); the Santa Cruz/Watsonville metro area (255,602); the San Luis Obispo metro area (246,681); Merced (210,554); and the Chico/Paradise metro area (203,171).

Environmental imperatives for California include improving air quality in urban areas, reducing solid waste, encouraging infill development, restoring industrial areas, and protecting agricultural land.

COMMUNICATIONS/ENERGY

California has 266 public-use airports, of which 11—Calexico International Airport, Fresno Yosemite International Airport, Los Angeles International Airport, Metropolitan Oakland International Airport, Ontario International Airport, Palm Springs International Airport, Sacramento International Airport, San Bernardino International Airport, San Diego International Airport-Lindbergh Field, San Francisco International Airport, and San Jose International Airport—are international. Major ports include Los Angeles, Long Beach, and San Diego on the Pacific Ocean and San Francisco, Oakland, Redwood City, and Richmond on the San Francisco Bay. The state has 34 freight railroads as well as passenger trains throughout the state, a commuter rail service around Los Angeles, metro systems in Los Angeles and San Francisco, and light rail lines in Sacramento, San Diego, and San Jose. The state has 166,024.3 miles of roads.

California's high-tech industry has encouraged a sophisticated digital infrastructure, especially in areas with high concentrations of technology businesses, which includes 1,386,625 high-speed lines as of 2000—the most by far in the United States. However, as would be expected in the state that was ranked last in the United States in rural/urban disparity, rural communities are still mainly underserved. The state is currently examining its funding options to extend digital infrastructure throughout the state. In 2000, 95.6% of households had telephone service, 46.7% of households had Internet access, and 37.3% of the population had wireless phones.

Petroleum is the most-used energy resource in California, followed by natural gas. The electric utilities rely primarily on hydroelectricity, followed by nuclear energy; the industrial sector relies on natural gas, while transportation depends almost solely on petroleum. Severe energy shortages in California early in the first decade of

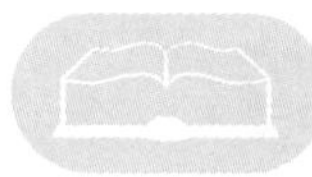

the 21st century caused rolling blackouts throughout the state.

Fiscal/Financial

California has one of the highest per-capita state tax burdens in the United States. Of state tax collected in 2000, 47.2% came from individual income tax; 28.0% from general sales tax; 7.9% from corporate income tax; 7.4% from selective sales tax; 4.4% from license tax; and 4.0% from property tax. The corporate income tax rate is 8.84% (10.84% for financial institutions).

Major financial institutions include BancWest Corp., Bank of America, Bank Plus Corp., Bay View Capital Corp., California First National Bancorp, Citigroup, City National Corp., Comerica, Downey Financial Corp., East West Bancorp, FirstFed Financial Corp., Greater Bay Bancorp, Golden West Financial Corp., Golden State Bancorp, Humboldt Bancorp, ITLA Capital Corp., Mid-State Bancshares, National Mercantile Bancorp, Pacific Capital Bancorp, Silicon Valley Bancshares, Union-BanCal Corp., United California Bank, U.S. Bancorp, Washington Mutual, Wells Fargo & Co., Westamerica Bancorporation, and Zions Bancorporation.

Business Opportunities

California offers a wide variety of incentives to business, including: tax credits for R&D and childcare; a net operating loss carryover for new businesses and businesses in enterprise zones; tax credits, hiring credits, and expensing for companies locating in enterprise zones; various incentives in areas affected by military base downsizing; numerous forms of financing assistance; and investment credits and some tax exemptions for manufacturers.

California is a major research center, ranking first in the United States in federal R&D spending, the majority of it from the Department of Defense, and very high in private investment in R&D. Research centers include the Aeroflightdynamics Directorate, the Aerospace FFRDC, the Air Force Flight Test Center, the Ames Research Center, the Burnham Institute, Boeing, the California Institute of Technology, California State University, the Center for Communications Research, the Charles R. Drew University of Medicine and Science, City of Hope National Medical Center, the Dryden Flight Research Center, the Energy Technology Engineering Center, the Geologic Western Regional Office, the Jet Propulsion Laboratory, the Lawrence Berkeley National Laboratory, the Lawrence Livermore National Laboratory, Lockheed Martin, Loma Linda University, McDonnell Douglas Corp., the Naval Air Warfare Center Weapons Division, Project AIR FORCE, SAIC, the Salk Institute for Biological Studies, Science Applications International Corp., the Scripps Research Institute, the Space and Naval Warfare Systems Center, the Stanford Linear Accelerator Center, Stanford University, TRW, the University of California, the University of Southern California, the Western Ecological Research Center, and the Western Regional Research Center.

The top 20 *Fortune* 500 companies with their headquarters in California are Hewlett-Packard, Chevron, McKesson HBOC, Intel, Safeway, Ingram Micro, Wells Fargo & Co., Walt Disney, PG&E Corp., Bergen Brunswig, Cisco Systems, Sun Microsystems, Occidental Petroleum, Solectron, GAP, Edison International, Pacificare Health Systems, Tenet Healthcare, Fluor, and Oracle.

For More Information

Books:

Lee, Chong-Moon, et al., eds. *The Silicon Valley Edge: A Habitat for Innovation and Entrepreneurship*. Stanford, CA: Stanford University Press, 2000.

O'Leary Morgan, Kathleen, ed. *California in Perspective 2001: A Statistical View of the Golden State*. Lawrence, KS: Morgan Quitno Corp., 2001.

Rawls, James J., and Richard J. Orsi, eds. *A Golden State: Mining and Economic Development in Gold Rush California*. Berkeley, CA: University of California Press, 1999.

Sollen, Robert. *An Ocean of Oil: A Century of Political Struggle over Petroleum Off the California Coast*. Juneau, AK: Denali Press, 1998.

Web Sites:

California State Homepage: **www.state.ca.us**

California Technology, Trade, and Commerce Agency: **www.commerce.ca.go**

California Travel and Tourism: **www.gocalif.ca.gov**

  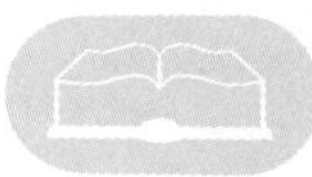    

Colorado

KEY FACTS

State capital: **Denver**
Population: **4,301,261; 24th in U.S.; grew 30.6% 1990–2000**
Land area: **103,718 square miles; 8th in U.S.**
Population density: **41.4 per square mile**
GSP: **$153,728 million**
GSP pc: **$35,740.22**
Household income: **$48,506; 9th in U.S.**
Poverty rate: **8.5%**
Unemployment: **2.7%**

Economy

Colorado's economy, once dependent on agriculture and mining, developed a manufacturing base in the second half of the 20th century that still represents a significant portion of the whole; it is based on electronic equipment and instruments, industrial machinery, printing and publishing, food processing, transportation equipment, and pharmaceuticals. Now, however, the economy is largely service-based, driven by business and other professional services.

The state experienced consistent growth throughout the 1990s; construction, financial and business services, and telecommunications accounted for a significant portion of that growth. The telecommunications industry is expected to continue to be a major contributor to the economy. A significant factor in this industry's growth is Colorado's highly educated workforce.

Challenges for Colorado include conserving its natural resources and maintaining the quality of the educational system in light of rapid population growth.

Geography/Resources

Located in the central western United States, Colorado consists of four physical regions: the Colorado Plateau in the west, the Intermontane Basin in the northwest, the Rocky Mountains in the central part of the state, and the Great Plains in the east.

Mineral resources are natural gas, crude oil, coal, sand and gravel, Portland cement, crushed stone, molybdenum, gold, silver, and gemstones. Cattle and calves are the primary agricultural output; other produce includes corn, wheat, soybeans, nursery and greenhouse crops, hay, dairy products, pigs, poultry and poultry products, sheep and lambs, and vegetables. Marine resources are trout, salmon, walleye, bass, crappie, catfish, bullhead, perch, bluegill, sunfish, crayfish, and whitefish. Forestry resources are pine, aspen, fir, and spruce.

Colorado's population began booming with the discovery of gold in the mid-19th century; it experienced another growth spurt during World War II with the location of military facilities in the state, and another in the 1990s as a high-tech center. The 2000 census shows that 82.8% of the population is white; 17.1% Hispanic, of any race; 3.8% African American; 2.2% Asian; and 1.0% Native American.

Denver is the largest city, with nearly half of the population, or 2,109,282 people. Other significant cities include: Colorado Springs (516,929); Boulder (291,288); the Fort Collins/Loveland metro area (251,494); Greeley (180,936); and Pueblo (141,472).

Environmental imperatives for Colorado include conserving the state's limited water supply, maintaining the state's high air quality as the population increases, and containing waste from livestock operations.

Communications/Energy

Colorado has 79 public airports, one of which—Denver International Airport—is international. There are 8 railroads operating 3,219 miles of track, and 84,485 miles of roads.

Colorado has recently begun initiatives to coordinate the growth of the state's telecommunications infrastructure, to avoid duplication in certain areas while others, particularly rural areas, do not have the facilities they need. Overall, however, Colorado is fairly well connected, with 104,534 high-speed lines in 2000. In 2000, 95.2% of households had telephone service; 51.8% of households had Internet access; and 43.2% of the population had wireless telephones.

Petroleum is the most-used energy resource in Colorado, followed by coal and natural gas. The electric utilities are powered almost exclusively by coal; the industrial sector makes use of natural gas and petroleum, while transportation primarily uses petroleum.

Fiscal/Financial

Colorado has a fairly low state tax burden. There are no state property taxes, though local areas may impose them. Of state tax collected in 2000, 51.4% came from individual income tax; 26.1% from general sales tax; 12.2% from selective sales tax; 4.7% from corporate income tax; and 4.2% from license tax. The corporate income tax rate is 4.63%.

Major financial institutions in Colorado include Bank One Corp., CoBiz, Comerica, Commercial Federal Bank, Compass Bancshares, Golden West Financial Corp., Keycorp, TCF Financial, Union Bankshares, U.S. Bancorp, Wells Fargo & Co., and Zions Bancorporation.

Business Opportunities

Colorado offers some incentives for business, including tax credits for investment in enterprise zones and sales tax exemptions on some manufacturing equipment or machine tools, component parts, fuels and electricity, packaging materials, aircraft parts used in general maintenance, interstate long-distance telephone charges, ink and newsprint, and farm equipment and machinery. The state has fairly low unemployment insurance premiums.

There is a well-developed R&D infrastructure in Colorado, particularly in the defense and aerospace industries. Research centers include the AMC Cancer Research Center and Hospital, Antarctic Support Associates, Ball Aerospace and Technologies, the Colorado School of Mines, Colorado State University, the Geologic Central Regional Office, ITT Systems and Sciences Corp., Lockheed Martin, the National Center for Atmospheric Research, the Natural Resources Research Center, the University of Colorado, and the University of Denver.

There are four *Fortune* 500 companies with their headquarters in Colorado: Qwest Communications, Transmontaigne, Ball, and Western Gas Resources.

For More Information

Book:

Ubbelohde, Carl, Maxine Benson, and Duane A. Smith. *A Colorado History*. Boulder, CO: Pruett Publishing Co., 1995.

Web Sites:

Colorado Office of Economic Development and International Trade: **www.state.co.us/gov_dir/oed.html**

Colorado State Homepage: **www.state.co.us**

CONNECTICUT

KEY FACTS

State capital: **Hartford**
Population: **3,405,565; 29th in U.S.; grew 3.6% 1990–2000**
Land area: **4,845 square miles; 48th in U.S.**
Population density: **702 per square mile**
GSP: **$151,779 million**
GSP pc: **$44,567.94**
Household income: **$50,360; 5th in U.S.**
Poverty rate: **7.6%**
Unemployment: **2.3%**

ECONOMY

Connecticut has been a strong industrial state since the late 19th century, emphasizing manufacturing and trade. Like much of New England, it had economic troubles in the mid-20th century when much of the manufacturing sector moved south; it was also hard hit by the recession in the early 1990s, when its defense industry suffered from the end of the cold war.

Today, finance, insurance, and real estate (FIRE) is the largest sector in the economy, and contributes a higher percentage of GSP than in most states. The service sector is also significant, particularly business, health, and legal services. Connecticut has identified five clusters it would like to attract and develop: biosciences, aerospace, software/information technology, metal manufacturing, and maritime.

Challenges that the state must address include continuing to improve the transportation infrastructure, particularly the highways; increasing the state's pool of skilled labor through education and recruitment; and diversifying the economy to decrease reliance on the financial markets.

GEOGRAPHY/RESOURCES

Located in the northeastern United States, Connecticut consists of three regions: the hilly Western and Eastern Uplands and the valley formed by the Central Lowland. Agriculture has not been an important part of the economy since the late 19th century, but the state does export some tobacco and also produces dairy products, poultry and poultry products, livestock, mushrooms, pears, apples, berries, vegetables, greenhouse and nursery crops, and maple syrup. Oysters and lobster are the primary marine resources; others include clams, scallops, hake, goosefish, squid, and flounder. Mineral products include sand, gravel, stone, feldspar, clay, and mica. Forestry resources are birch, beech, hemlock, hickory, maple, oak, and pine.

The state's original English settlers were joined by Irish immigrants in the mid-19th century, French Canadians and southern and eastern Europeans in the late 19th century, African Americans in the mid-20th century, and Latin Americans in the late 20th century. The 2000 census shows that 81.6% of the population is white; 9.4% Hispanic, of any race; 9.1% African American; and 2.4% Asian.

Though much of the state is urban, the population is not concentrated into a few large cities. Hartford is the largest city, with 1,183,110 people; the New London metro area, which includes Norwich, RI, has 293,566 people.

Connecticut's primary environmental imperatives are restoring the land and groundwater damaged by the state's industrial history, and cleaning up the coastal waters to redevelop the state's oyster industry.

COMMUNICATIONS/ENERGY

Connecticut's aging transportation infrastructure was improved by extensive investment in the 1990s, but highway congestion is still a major problem. The state has 24 public-use airports, one of which—Bradley International Airport—is international. Its three major ports are Bridgeport, New Haven, and New London. Connecticut lies directly in the New York-to-Boston rail corridor, and has 570 miles of railroad track. There are 20,609 miles of highways.

Connecticut is still building a telecommunications infrastructure that can handle the demands of its high-tech industry; as of 2000, the state had 111,792 high-speed lines. The state's schools, in particular, are among the least wired in the United States, and a few businesses have made complaints about the high cost of Internet access.

In 2000, 95.4% of households had telephone service; 51.2% of households had Internet access; and 37.5% of the population had wireless telephones.

Petroleum is the major energy source consumed in Connecticut, primarily in the form of motor gasoline, distillate fuel, and residual fuel. Nuclear energy and petroleum power most of the electric utilities.

FISCAL/FINANCIAL

Despite some tax cuts in the late 1990s, Connecticut still had the highest per-capita state tax burden in the United States in 2000. Of state tax collected in 2000, 39.1% came from individual income tax; 33.7% from general sales tax; 16.1% from selective sales tax; 4.2% from corporate income tax; and 3.6% from license tax. The corporate income tax rate is 7.5%.

Major financial institutions in Connecticut include the American Bank of Connecticut, American Financial Holdings, Banknorth Group, Comerica, First Federal Savings & Loan, First International Bancorp, First Union Corp., FleetBoston, The Hartford Financial Services Group, Hudson United Bancorp, NewMil Bancorp, and Webster Financial Corp.

BUSINESS OPPORTUNITIES

Connecticut offers a number of incentives for businesses, including tax credits for businesses locating in designated areas, for hiring individuals receiving government assistance, for financial institutions constructing new facilities or adding new employees, and for R&D expenditures.

R&D is growing in the state, led by Yale University. Other research facilities include Analysis & Technology Inc., Electric Boat Corp., Hughes Danbury Optical Systems Inc., United Technologies Corp., the University of Connecticut, and the U.S. Coast Guard Research and Development Center.

There are 13 *Fortune* 500 companies with their headquarters in Connecticut: General Electric, Aetna, United Technologies, Tosco, Xerox, Hartford Financial Services, Union Carbide, Northeast Utilities, Praxair, Pitney Bowes, Oxford Health Plans, Ames Department Stores, and Emcor Group.

For More Information

Book:

Fraser, Bruce. *Land of Steady Habits: A Brief History of Connecticut*. Hartford, CT: Connecticut Historical Commission, 1988.

Web Sites:

Connecticut Business & Industry Association: **www.cbia.com**
State of Connecticut Web site: **www.state.ct.us**

DELAWARE

KEY FACTS

State capital: **Dover**
Population: **783,600; 45th in U.S.; grew 17.6% 1990–2000**
Land area: **1,954 square miles; 49th in U.S.**
Population density: **401 per square mile**
GSP: **$34,669 million**
GSP pc: **$44,243.24**
Household income: **$50,154; 6th in U.S.**
Poverty rate: **9.8%**
Unemployment: **4.0%**

ECONOMY

Delaware's agricultural history gave way to manufacturing early in the 20th century, and chemical manufacturing in particular by the mid-20th century. Wilmington is a center for chemical research and production; other manufacturing industries include motor vehicles, food products, paper products, rubber and plastics, electronic equipment, and petroleum products.

The finance, insurance, and real estate (FIRE) sector is the largest in the economy, due to a tax and legislative environment favorable to financial institutions. The service sector is the second largest, led by health and business services. With more scientists and engineers per capita than any other state, Delaware is well positioned to continue developing its knowledge-based industries.

Challenges for Delaware include: maintaining affordable housing and healthcare in the face of high population growth; encouraging industrial diversity; increasing venture capital; and maintaining the state's transportation infrastructure.

GEOGRAPHY/RESOURCES

Located in the northeastern United States, Delaware consists of two main land regions: the Atlantic Coastal Plain, which covers most of the state, and the hilly Piedmont at the northern tip.

Crabs are the primary marine resource; others include weakfish, snails, bass, clams, finfish, eel, and shad. Forestry resources are mixed upland hardwoods, primarily pine and oak; mineral resources are sand and gravel, magnesium compounds, and gemstones. Poultry products are the primary agricultural output; other produce includes soybeans, corn, vegetables, dairy products, and nursery and greenhouse crops.

Delaware has been characterized by diverse immigration since colonial times; Swedes, Finns, Dutch, and African slaves were the earliest settlers, joined by immigrants from all over Europe in the 18th and 19th centuries and Puerto Ricans in the 20th. The 2000 census shows that 74.6% of the population is white; 19.2% African American; 4.8% Hispanic, of any race; and 2.1% Asian.

The Wilmington/Newark metro area is the largest in the state, with 500,265 people; Dover is another significant city, with 126,697 people.

Environmental imperatives for Delaware include preventing urban sprawl from interfering with the agricultural and tourism industries, redeveloping abandoned industrial sites, and conserving wetlands.

COMMUNICATIONS/ENERGY

Located near most of the major cities on the eastern seaboard, Delaware has 11 public-use airports, none of which are international. The state's major port, the Port of Wilmington, lies on the Delaware River. There are six railroads operating 271 miles of rail, and 5,050 miles of roads.

With 7,492 high-speed lines as of 2000, Delaware has a solid telecommunications infrastructure with high-speed access in most of the state, especially in the northern, industrialized area. In 2000, 97.4% of households had telephone service; 50.7% of households had Internet access; and 47.3% of the population had wireless telephones.

Petroleum is the primary energy source used in Delaware, followed by natural gas. Electric utilities rely mainly on coal and natural gas; the industrial sector uses primarily petroleum and natural gas.

FISCAL/FINANCIAL

Because of its fair tax system and liberal incorporation laws, an unusually high number of companies are incorporated in Delaware. Of state tax collected in 2000, 36.4% came from license tax; 34.4% from individual income tax; 13.6% from selective sales tax; and 11.2% from corporate income tax. Delaware has no general sales tax. The corporate income tax rate is 8.7%; for banks and trust companies, the income tax rate is 1.7–8.7% in five brackets. Certain investment and holding companies are exempt from corporate income tax.

Major financial institutions in Delaware include Allfirst Financial, Commerce Bancorp, First Union Corp., First USA Bank, Fulton Financial Corp., MBNA, Mellon Financial Corp., Mercantile Bankshares Corp., Sovereign Bancorp, and Wilmington Trust Corp.

BUSINESS OPPORTUNITIES

Delaware offers a number of incentives to business, including no tax on inventories and process machinery or equipment. It offers tax credits on bank franchises, corporate income tax credits and reduction of gross receipts taxes for new and expanded businesses, property tax relief for new construction and improvements of existing property, and tax credits for R&D, waste reduction, and recycling initiatives. Corporate income tax credits and gross receipts tax reductions are available to: manufacturers, wholesalers, laboratories and R&D facilities, computer processors, engineering firms, consumer credit reporting services, telecommunications services, and aviation services.

Delaware is a major research hub, ranking second in the United States in private R&D investment, although it ranks 47th in federal R&D spending. Research centers include the Advanced Technology Center for Medical Devices, Alloy Surfaces Co., AstraZeneca, Astropower, the Center for Nanomachined Surfaces, ICI Americas Inc., ILC Dover, the Delaware Biotechnology Institute, Delaware State University, Du Pont, Hercules Inc., Montell Polyolefins, the University of Delaware, and W. L. Gore and Associates.

There are three *Fortune* 500 companies with their headquarters in Delaware: E.I. Du Pont De Nemours, MBNA, and Conectiv.

For More Information

Book:

Munroe, John A. *History of Delaware*. Newark, DE: University of Delaware Press, 2000.

Web Sites:

Delaware Economic Development Office: **www.state.de.us/dedo**
Delaware State Homepage: **www.state.de.us**

District of Columbia

KEY FACTS

Population: **572,059; 50th in U.S.; grew –5.7% 1990–2000**
Land area: **56 square miles; 51st in U.S.**
Population density: **10,215 per square mile**
GSP: **$55,832 million**
GSP pc: **$97,598.32**
Household income: **$38,752; 33rd in U.S.**
Poverty rate: **17.3%**
Unemployment: **5.8%**

Economy

The business of Washington, DC is the business of government. Government activity, primarily federal civilian government, is the largest sector of the economy and contributes more to the District's economy than it does to any of the states'. The service sector is the second largest, led by legal, business, health, and educational services. Tourism is also important, contributing a great deal to retail sales.

Private-sector activity has increased since the end of the 1990s, and the District has targeted a number of industries it would like to attract and develop, including: business/professional/financial/association services; hospitality/entertainment/tourism/specialty retail; biomedical research/health services; media/publications; and information technology/telecommunications.

Challenges facing the District include the need for affordable housing, high crime rates, disparities in income distribution, and an extremely high poverty rate. One explanation for all of these problems is that the majority of the people who work in the city of Washington live and pay taxes in the surrounding suburbs of Maryland and Virginia, leaving the city to face the troubles familiar in most major metropolitan areas without the state resources available to other cities.

Geography/Resources

Located in the central area of the eastern seaboard, the District of Columbia was created in 1791 from land donated by Maryland and Virginia and has both urban and suburban areas within its boundaries.

The District's African-American population, which originated after the Civil War and experienced another wave of growth in the 1960s, is larger than any state's and most American cities'. The white population represents a fairly accurate cross-section of the rest of the country. The 2000 census shows that 60% of the population is African American; 30.8% white; 7.9% Hispanic, of any race; and 2.7% Asian.

Environmental imperatives for the District include proper waste disposal, eliminating illegal dumping, improving the sewer system to maintain water quality, and improving air quality.

Communications/Energy

The District of Columbia has two public-use airports, one of which—Washington Dulles International Airport—is international. It has an 81-mile metro, two commuter rail networks, and 1,102 miles of roads.

The District's telecommunication infrastructure is developing rapidly, with 27,757 high-speed lines as of 2000. However, the economic divides evident between neighborhoods also apply to digital infrastructure, with high-speed access more prevalent in business districts and affluent areas. In 2000, 91.0% of households had telephone service; 39.6% of households had Internet access; and 58.4% of the population had wireless telephones.

Petroleum and natural gas are the most-used energy resources in the District, in nearly equal measures. Electric utilities rely solely on petroleum; it is also the main resource for the industrial sector. The residential sector primarily uses natural gas.

Fiscal/Financial

Of District tax collected in 2000, 35.3% came from individual income tax; 22.3% from property tax; 19.9% from general sales tax; 7.1% from corporate income tax; and 4.5% from public utility tax. The corporate income tax rate is 9.975%.

The District of Columbia's financial sector is an unusual mix of local banks and international behemoths. Major financial institutions include Abigail Adams National Bancorp, Allfirst Financial, Bank of America, BB&T Corp., Chevy Chase Bank, Citigroup, the Federal Reserve System, First Union Corp., Greater Atlantic Financial Corp., Independence Federal Savings Bank, the International Monetary Fund, MBNA, Provident Bankshares Corp., Riggs National Corp., SunTrust Banks, United Bankshares, Virginia Commerce Bancorp, and the World Bank.

Business Opportunities

The District of Columbia offers a number of incentives to business, including: tax credits, exemption from capital gains taxes, increased expensing allowance, and access to tax-exempt financing for businesses locating in enterprise zones; employee training funds for District residents; tax credits for hiring employees previously on government assistance; financing for housing development; and tax-increment financing for public infrastructure redevelopment.

The District of Columbia is a major R&D center, housing the headquarters for a number of institutions with branches throughout the country. Research centers include Advanced Power Technologies, the Agricultural Research Service Headquarters, the American Institutes for Research, the American Registry of Pathology, the American University, the Armed Forces Institute of Pathology, the Catholic University of America, the Center for Food Safety and Applied Nutrition, the Cooperative State Research, Extension, and Education Service, Georgetown University, George Washington University, Howard University, the Joint Oceanographic Institutions, Lockheed Martin, the National Academy of Sciences, the National Aeronautics and Space Administration Headquarters, the National Center for Environmental Research and Quality Assurance, the National Institute of Justice, the Naval Research Laboratory, the Science and Technology Policy Institute, the Smithsonian Institution Libraries, the University of the District of Columbia, the U.S. National Arboretum, and the Walter Reed Army Institute of Research.

There are two *Fortune* 500 companies with their headquarters in the District of Columbia: Fannie Mae and Danaher.

For More Information

Book:
Greenfield, Meg. *Washington*. New York: Public Affairs, 2001.

Web Sites:
District of Columbia Homepage: **www.washingtondc.gov**
Official Tourism Web site of Washington DC: **www.washington.org**
Planning and Economic Development: **www.dcbiz.dc.gov**

FLORIDA

KEY FACTS

State capital: **Tallahassee**
Population: **15,982,378; 4th in U.S.; grew 23.5% 1990–2000**
Land area: **53,927 square miles; 26th in U.S.**
Population density: **296 per square mile**
GSP: **$442,895 million**
GSP pc: **$27,711.46**
Household income: **$37,998; 36th in U.S.**
Poverty rate: **12.1%**
Unemployment: **3.6%**

ECONOMY

Florida's agricultural economy in the 19th century was transformed by the discovery of phosphate in 1881; this brought railroads to the state, followed in turn by manufacturing and tourism. Today, tourism is the leading industry, based on the state's tropical weather, natural attractions, and Walt Disney World, which is the largest single tourist attraction in the country. The services sector as a whole benefits from tourism; wholesale and retail trade also profit. Manufacturing contributes much less than these; the electronics industry is the leading manufacturing activity, followed by printing and publishing. The aerospace industry is also important.

Improving the educational system, particularly in regard to technology, is a major challenge for the future; Florida's workforce is currently less educated on average than that of the nation. Another challenge for startup industries in Florida is a lack of available early-stage venture capital.

GEOGRAPHY/RESOURCES

The southernmost state on the eastern coast of the United States, Florida consists mainly of coastal lowlands, with the exception of the western highlands, the Marianna lowlands, the Tallahassee hills, and the central highlands; these four areas go from west to east across the northern part of the state.

Florida is the number one citrus-producing state in the United States; agricultural output includes fruit and vegetables, livestock, dairy products, poultry and poultry products, and thoroughbred horses. Forestry resources include pine, oak, cypress, tupelo, hickory, and mixed hardwoods. Marine resources include shrimp, crabs, lobster, mackerel, swordfish, snapper, oysters, scallops, dolphin, sharks, tuna, and tilefish. Phosphate rock is the most significant mineral resource; others include crude oil, natural gas, crushed stone, sand and gravel, peat, zircon, and ilmenite.

The earliest European settlers were Spanish; others included Greeks, Italians, and Eastern Europeans. In the late 20th century, most immigrants were Latin Americans and retirees from other states. The 2000 census shows that 78.0% of the population is white; 16.8% Hispanic, of any race; 14.6% African American; and 1.7% Asian.

Miami/Ft. Lauderdale is the largest metro area, with 3,876,380 people; others include: Tampa/St. Petersburg/Clearwater (2,395,997); Orlando (1,644,561); West Palm Beach/Boca Raton (1,131,184); Jacksonville (1,100,491); Sarasota/Bradenton (589,959); and Daytona Beach (493,175).

Environmental imperatives include protecting endangered species, preventing further erosion of the wetlands, and managing the state's supply of fresh water.

COMMUNICATIONS/ENERGY

Florida has 131 public airports, 13 of which are international: Daytona Beach, Ft. Lauderdale-Hollywood, Jacksonville, Key West, Melbourne, Miami, Orlando, Palm Beach, Panama City/Bay County, St. Petersburg-Clearwater, Sarasota Bradenton, Southwest Florida, and Tampa. Of the 14 deepwater ports, the most significant are Canaveral, Everglades, Jacksonville, Miami, and Tampa. There are 114,000 miles of roads, and almost 3,000 miles of track serving 13 railroads.

The state also has a sophisticated telecommunications network, including 460,795 high-speed lines as of 2000, since the country's land networks of fiber optic lines and undersea telecommunications links converge in Florida. In 2000, 92.4% of households had telephone service; 43.2% of households had Internet access; and 39.9% of the population had wireless telephones.

The state produces crude oil and natural gas for its own energy needs; Florida's electric utilities are powered primarily by coal, with some use of nuclear power. There is also limited use of hydroelectricity.

FISCAL/FINANCIAL

Florida has a favorable tax environment, with no personal income tax, no property tax on business inventories, and no corporate income tax for certain corporations. Of state taxes collected in 2000, 60.5% came from general sales tax; 16.6% from selective sales tax; 6.1% from license tax; 5.8% from documentary and stock transfer tax; 4.8% from corporate income tax; and 3.1% from property tax. The corporate income tax rate is 5.5%.

Major financial institutions include AmSouth, Bank of America, Bank One Corp., Comerica, Compass Bancshares, Fifth Third Bancorp, First Union Corp., FNB Corp., Golden West Financial Corp., Harris Bankcorp, Huntington Bancshares, Regions Financial Corp., SouthTrust, SunTrust Banks, and Union Planters Corp.

BUSINESS OPPORTUNITIES

Florida offers special business incentives for targeted industries, such as communications, R&D, and electronic equipment, as well as tax incentives for development in rural and inner-city communities and a capital investment tax credit. A major area of concern in Florida's business environment is the state's workers' compensation rates, which are among the highest in the nation.

A great deal of the research conducted in Florida benefits the aerospace and defense industries. Major research centers include the Air Force Development Test Center, the Atlantic Oceanographic and Meteorological Laboratory, the John F. Kennedy Space Center, Lockheed Martin, United Technologies Corporation, the University of Florida, the University of Miami, and the University of South Florida.

There are 12 *Fortune* 500 companies with their headquarters in Florida: AutoNation, Tech Data, Publix Super Markets, Winn-Dixie Stores, Office Depot, FPL Group, Ryder System, Lennar, Spherion, Darden Restaurants, Jabil Circuit, and Hughes Supply.

For More Information

Book:

Gannon, Michael, ed. *The New History of Florida*. Gainesville, FL: University Press of Florida, 1996.

Web Sites:

Enterprise Florida: **www.eflorida.com**
Florida State Web site: **www.state.fl.us**

GEORGIA

KEY FACTS

State capital: **Atlanta**
Population: **8,186,453; 10th in U.S.; grew 26.4% 1990–2000**
Land area: **57,905 square miles; 21st in U.S.**
Population density: **141 per square mile**
GSP: **$275,719 million**
GSP pc: **$33,679.91**
Household income: **$42,887; 23rd in U.S.**
Poverty rate: **12.5%**
Unemployment: **3.7%**

ECONOMY

Georgia's agricultural history, based around rice and cotton, is still evident in the state's agribusiness sector; likewise, the manufacturing boom that occurred in the mid-20th century still impacts the state's economy. The manufacturing sector today is led by textiles, food processing, chemicals, electronic equipment, industrial equipment, motor vehicles, paper products, and tobacco products.

The service industry dominates the economy, led by business and health services; finance, insurance, and real estate (FIRE) is a significant contributor, as Atlanta is one of the financial centers of the southeast. A variety of initiatives are focused on developing the state's broadband communications, biotechnology, and environmental technology industries.

The major challenge facing Georgia is the slow economic development of its rural areas, which the state is addressing with economic development programs funded by a settlement to the state from the tobacco industry.

GEOGRAPHY/RESOURCES

Located on the southeast coast of the United States, Georgia consists of the Appalachian Plateau, the Appalachian Ridge and Valley Region, and the Blue Ridge in the north; the East Gulf Coastal Plain in the southwest; the Atlantic Coastal Plain along the coast; and the hilly Piedmont throughout the rest of the state.

Poultry and poultry products are the major agricultural output; other produce includes cotton, vegetables, cattle and calves, nursery and greenhouse crops, dairy products, tobacco, pigs, and corn. Mineral resources are kaolin and other clays, crushed stone, sand and gravel, Portland cement, barite, fuller's earth, mica, iron oxide pigments, and feldspar; marine resources include shrimp, crabs, snails, finfishes, and snapper. Forestry resources include pine, oak, cedar, maple, sweetbay, sweetgum, poplar, and mixed upland hardwoods.

Georgia's original English, Scottish, Austrian, and black inhabitants made up the majority of the population through the early 20th century; outward migration increased throughout the 20th century until the growth of Atlanta in the 1960s. The 2000 census shows that 65.1% of the population is white; 28.7% African American; 5.3% Hispanic, of any race; and 2.1% Asian.

Atlanta is the largest city and an urban center for the whole southeastern United States, with 4,112,198 people. Other significant cities include Macon (322,549), Augusta (310,294), Savannah (293,000), Columbus (224,868), Athens (153,444), and Albany (120,822).

Environmental imperatives for Georgia include water conservation, reducing ozone levels in the Atlanta metropolitan area, and cleaning up hazardous waste deposits.

COMMUNICATIONS/ENERGY

Georgia has 110 public-use airports, two of which—Hartsfield Atlanta International Airport and Savannah International Airport—are international. There are two deepwater ports, at Savannah and Brunswick. The state has 19 railroads operating on 4,734 miles of rail, in addition to commuter rail, and 111,797 miles of roads.

The state has 203,855 high-speed telephone lines as of 2000, but rural communities are currently underserved. Both the schools and the state government lag behind much of the nation in their use of technology resources. In 2000, 91.9% of households had telephone service; 38.3% of households had Internet access; and 33.5% of the population had wireless telephones.

Petroleum is Georgia's most-used energy resource, followed by coal. The electric utilities rely mainly on coal, followed by nuclear energy; the industrial sector makes use of wood and waste, followed by natural gas and petroleum.

FISCAL/FINANCIAL

Georgia's state tax burden is lower than in many states, but higher than in most of the surrounding states. Of state tax collected in 2000, 47.1% came from individual income tax; 34.3% from general sales tax; 8.3% from selective sales tax; 5.3% from corporate income tax; and 3.5% from license tax. The corporate income tax rate is 6.0%.

Major financial institutions include ABC Bancorp, AmSouth Bancorporation, Bank of America, BB&T Corp., Colony Bankcorp, Comerica, Fidelity National Corp., First Union Corp., PAB Bankshares, Regions Financial Corp., SouthTrust Corp., SunTrust Banks, and Synovus Financial Corp.

BUSINESS OPPORTUNITIES

Georgia offers a number of incentives for business, including: tax credits for investment in the manufacturing and telecommunications industries; for employee retraining in new technologies; for providing childcare; for R&D; for increasing shipment through Georgia's ports; for establishing or relocating headquarters to the state; and for job creation, especially in the manufacturing, warehousing and distribution, processing, telecommunications, tourism and R&D industries.

Georgia ranks fourth in the United States in terms of federal investment in R&D, mainly from the Department of Defense. Research centers include Boeing, Clark Atlanta University, Emory University, the Georgia Institute of Technology, Georgia State University, Lockheed Martin Aeronautical Systems, the Richard B. Russell Agricultural Research Center, Scientific Research Corp., and the University of Georgia.

There are 15 *Fortune* 500 companies with their headquarters in Georgia: Home Depot, United Parcel Service, BellSouth, Southern, Georgia-Pacific, Coca-Cola, Delta Airlines, Coca-Cola Enterprises, AFLAC, SunTrust Banks, Genuine Parts, First Data, Flowers Industries, Cox Communications, and Mohawk Industries.

For More Information

Book:

Terterov, Marat, ed. *Doing Business with Georgia*. New York: Kogan Page, 2001.

Web Sites:

Georgia Department of Community Affairs: **www.dca.state.ga.us**
Georgia State Homepage: **www.state.ga.us**

  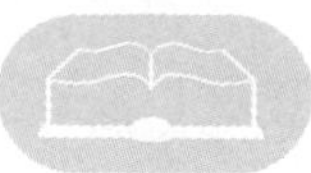    

HAWAII

KEY FACTS

State capital: **Honolulu**
Population: **1,211,537; 42nd in U.S.; grew 9.3% 1990–2000**
Land area: **6,423 square miles; 47th in U.S.**
Population density: **187 per square mile**
Household income: **$48,026; 10th in U.S.**
Poverty rate: **10.5%**
GSP: **$40,914 million**
GSP pc: **$33,770.33**
Unemployment: **4.3%**

ECONOMY

Hawaii's economy took a severe downturn in the 1990s, owing to international competition in the pineapple industry and to the disruption of the Asian economies, which reduced tourism. It has since recovered slightly, and tourism remains a significant industry.

Hawaii is building up its technological infrastructure and expanding its research facilities in an attempt to draw industries including information technology, telecommunications, biotechnology, astronomy and space science, ocean research and development, and engineering research and development. Other targeted industries include film and television production, sports, and floral and specialty food products.

Major challenges for Hawaii are the shortages and high prices caused by its isolation, leading to a high cost of living. This is particularly an issue in housing, since land is in short supply and building materials are expensive.

GEOGRAPHY/RESOURCES

Located approximately 3,840 km from the west coast of the United States, Hawaii is a string of 137 islands. The eight major islands among them are Niihau, Kauai, Oahu (home to the capital, Honolulu), Molokai, Lanai, Kahoolawe, Maui, and Hawaii. The islands are the tops of volcanic mountains, domelike in some areas, and marked by cliffs, caves, valleys, and plains in others.

Hawaii is one of the largest producers of sugarcane in the United States; pineapple was an important cash crop until international competition forced it out of the market, although it still contributes. Other agricultural output includes flowers and nursery products, macadamia nuts, coffee, dairy and poultry products, and cattle. The state's only mineral resources are cement, sand and gravel, and crushed stone. The primary commercial fish is tuna; others include swordfish, mahi-mahi, marlin, ono, opa, akule, snapper, and lobster.

The state's indigenous population was radically decreased by diseases brought by colonists, and most of the population now consists of the descendants of settlers. 41.6% of the population is Asian; 24.3% is white; 21.4% is of two or more races; 9.4% is Native Hawaiian and other Pacific Islander; 7.2% is Hispanic or Latino of any race; 1.8% is black or African American; and 1.3% is of some other race. Honolulu, the only legally incorporated city in the state, has 876,156 people.

Environmental imperatives include improving sustainability practices for the state's fishing industry, preventing beach erosion, and waste disposal.

COMMUNICATIONS/ENERGY

Hawaii has 14 public-use airports and heliports, three of which—Honolulu International Airport, Hilo International Airport, and Kona International Airport at Keahole—are international. Honolulu is the major port; others include Kalaeloa Barbers Point Harbors, Kewalo Basin, Port Allen, Nawiliwili Harbors, Kahului Harbor, Hilo, Kawaihae, Kaunakakai, and Kaumalapau. There are 3,943 miles of paved roads, concentrated on the eight main islands.

Hawaii has 30 telecommunications satellites and 46,400 km of fiber optic cable, more per capita than any other state. In 2000, 93.6% of households had telephone service; 43.0% of households had Internet access; and 43.3% of the population had wireless telephones.

Hawaii has the lowest energy use per person and in its residential and commercial sectors in the United States, perhaps because it has the highest price for motor gasoline and the second-highest for electricity. Its primary source is petroleum, though its electric utilities use small amounts of hydroelectric power. Because Hawaii is nearly completely dependent on imports, its top priorities are conservation and developing alternate fuel sources.

FISCAL/FINANCIAL

Hawaii ranked second in the nation in per-capita state tax collections in 2000, though it does not have a personal property tax. Of state taxes collected in 2000, 46.1% came from general sales tax; 31.9% from individual income tax; 15.5% from selective sales tax; 3.3% from license tax; and 2.3% from corporate income tax. The corporate income tax rate is 4.4–6.4% (7.92% for financial institutions).

Major financial institutions include BancWest Corp., CB Bancshares, CPB Inc., Hawaiian Electric Industries, and Pacific Century Financial Corp.

BUSINESS OPPORTUNITIES

Hawaii has initiated a number of reforms in an attempt to correct the decline of the 1990s, including reducing the regulatory burden on businesses, initiating a tourism policy with larger and dedicated funding, and reforming the civil service. It also offers tax incentives, including no state tax on goods manufactured for export and a credit against taxes paid on the purchase of capital goods, machinery, and equipment. At this point, however, there are no *Fortune* 500 companies with their headquarters in Hawaii.

The state's extensive research centers should prove a draw to several tech-related industries. They include the High Technology Development Corporation, the Maui Research & Technology Center, the Natural Energy Laboratory Of Hawaii Authority, the Pacific Center for High Technology Research, the Hawaii Natural Energy Institute, the Subaru Telescope Facility, and the University of Hawaii.

For More Information

Book:

Hitch, Thomas Kemper, and Robert M. Kamins, eds. *Islands in Transition: The Past, Present, and Future of Hawaii's Economy*. Honolulu, HI: University of Hawaii Press, 1994.

Web Sites:

Hawaii Department of Business, Economic Development, and Tourism: **www.state.hi.us/dbedt**
Hawaii Tourism Authority: **www.hawaii.gov/tourism**
State of Hawaii Web site: **www.state.hi.us**

IDAHO

KEY FACTS

State capital: **Boise**
Population: **1,293,953; 39th in U.S.; grew 28.5% 1990–2000**
Land area: **82,746 square miles; 11th in U.S.**
Population density: **16 per square mile**
Household income: **$37,462; 38th in U.S.**
Poverty rate: **13.3%**
GSP: **$34,025 million**
GSP pc: **$26,295.39**
Unemployment: **4.9%**

ECONOMY

Considering that Idaho is a state known best for its potatoes, it is perhaps rather surprising that it is also home to a rapidly expanding high-tech industry. In the last decade Idaho has had the fastest growth rate in the United States for high-tech manufacturing, and the third-highest for overall manufacturing. Other sectors include food processing, lumber and wood, and chemical manufacturing.

Although the state's traditional industries—agriculture, logging, and mining—have declined from their historic peaks, they still contribute to the state's bottom line. Tourism is another major economic driver, thanks to Idaho's winter sports and other outdoor attractions.

Although the state's economy as a whole is on an upswing, not all of Idaho's residents have reaped the benefits: growth has been primarily an urban phenomenon, and there are disparities in employment, income, and the availability of social services between the urban and rural areas. The state is focusing its efforts to level the playing field on telecommunications and education.

GEOGRAPHY/RESOURCES

Located in the northwestern United States, Idaho is divided into four regions: the Northern Rocky Mountains in the northern half of the state, the Middle Rocky Mountains along the southeastern border, the Basin and Range Province in the rest of the southeast, and the Columbia Basin in the southwest.

Potatoes are Idaho's largest cash crop; the state also produces hay, sugarbeets, barley, wheat, legumes, cattle and calves, dairy products, and sheep and lambs. The primary commercial trees are Douglas fir, ponderosa pine, and western white pine. Gold, the original impetus for Idaho's mining industry, no longer exists in significant quantities, but the state is still an important producer of silver, lead, antimony, molybdenum, and phosphates.

Many of today's Idaho residents are descendants of 19th-century gold-rush settlers, Confederate refugees, and Mormons. 91.0% of the population is white; 7.9% is Hispanic or Latino of any race; 4.2% is of some other race; 2.0% is of one or more races; and 1.4% is Native American and Alaska Native.

The largest cities are Boise City, with 432,345 people, and Pocatello, with 75,565 people. Idaho ranks first in the United States in air quality, although there has been some water pollution from mining and logging activities. There is some concern about deforestation as well.

COMMUNICATIONS/ENERGY

Transportation through Idaho has traditionally been difficult, due to the mountains and the wilderness. The state has 120 public-use airports, two of which—Boise International Airport and Eckhart International Airport—are international. There is one port, in Lewiston, from which ships can reach the Pacific via the Snake and Columbia rivers. There are four transcontinental railroads operating on 1,910 miles of rail, and 59,924 miles of roads.

Idaho's have/have-not divide is evident in access to telecommunications infrastructure, which is more developed in urban areas; the state had only 15,908 high-speed lines as of 2000. In 2000, 93.7% of households had telephone service; 42.3% of households had Internet access; and 26.6% of the population had wireless telephones.

Idaho's numerous rivers make it the fifth-largest generator of hydroelectric power in the United States, and its electricity comes solely from that source. The industrial sector uses petroleum, natural gas, and wood and waste; transportation uses primarily petroleum, with some natural gas.

FISCAL/FINANCIAL

Idaho has a stable tax structure, with per-capita state tax collections consistent with those in surrounding states. Of the taxes collected by the state in 2000, 40.6% came from individual income tax; 31.4% from general sales tax; 12.9% from selective sales tax; 9.1% from license tax; and 5.3% from corporate income tax. The corporate income tax rate is 8.0%.

Major banks and institutions in Idaho include AmericanWest Bancorporation, Banner Corp., Glacier Bancorp, KeyCorp, Sterling Financial Corp., U.S. Bancorp, Washington Federal, Washington Mutual, Wells Fargo & Co., and Zions Bancorporation.

BUSINESS OPPORTUNITIES

Idaho offers some business incentives, including: tax credits for new investments made in the state; property tax exemptions for inventories, livestock, property in transit, pollution control facilities, and the first $50,000 of the value of a primary residence; and tax increment financing for businesses locating within designated urban-renewal districts. Idaho has also implemented several measures of reform to bring in business: both unemployment insurance taxes and workers' compensation rates decreased steadily throughout the 1990s.

A draw for high-tech businesses in Idaho is the Idaho National Engineering and Environmental Laboratory, where 2,600 scientists conduct research in the basic sciences and technology, applied engineering and science, and environmental management. Other research centers include the Small Grains and Potato Germplasm Research Laboratory, the Northwest Watershed Research Center, the U.S. Sheep Experiment Station, the Northwest Irrigation and Soils Research Laboratory, the University of Idaho, Boise State University, and Idaho State University.

There are three *Fortune* 500 companies with their headquarters in Idaho: Albertson's, Boise Cascade, and Micron Technology.

For More Information

Book:

Morgan, Kathleen O. *Idaho in Perspective 2001: A Statistical View of the Gem State.* Lawrence, KS: Morgan Quitno Corp., 2001.

Idaho Investment and Business Guide. Washington, DC: International Business Publications USA, 2001.

Web Sites:

Access Idaho: **www.state.id.us**
Idaho Department of Commerce: **www.idoc.state.id.us**
Idaho Travel and Tourism Guide: **www.visitid.org**

  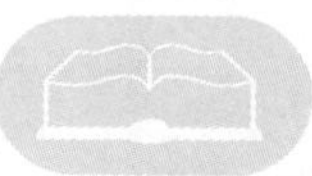    

ILLINOIS

KEY FACTS

State capital: **Springfield**
Population: **12,419,293; 5th in U.S.; grew 8.6% 1990–2000**
Land area: **55,583 square miles; 24th in U.S.**
Population density: **223 per square mile**
GSP: **$445,666 million**
GSP pc: **$35,884.97**
Household income: **$46,435; 14th in U.S.**
Poverty rate: **10.5%**
Unemployment: **4.4%**

ECONOMY

Illinois's economy was dominated by agriculture in the early 20th century. By the middle of that century heavy industry and manufacturing had taken over, and processing the state's agricultural output is still the primary manufacturing activity. Other manufacturing leaders include industrial machinery, plastics products, electric lighting and wiring, motor vehicles and equipment, and metal fabrication.

Service industries are now the largest segment of the economy, led by business services, tourism and travel, entertainment, and health care. Due to Illinois's central location, transportation and warehousing are also important. The state hopes to grow its sciences industry.

The major challenge facing the state is improving its infrastructure, especially road and rail. This will be necessary if Illinois is to continue as a transportation hub. In the late 1990s the state began a five-year, $12 billion investment in infrastructure improvements and environmental cleanup.

GEOGRAPHY/RESOURCES

Located in the midwestern United States, Illinois consists of three geographical areas: the Central Plains covering the majority of the state, the Shawnee Hills in the south, and the Gulf Coastal Plain at the southern tip. Most of the state has rich, fertile soil, contributing to the agricultural output of corn, soybeans, sorghum, hay, wheat, oats, apples, peaches, asparagus, potatoes, pigs, cattle, dairy products, sheep, wool, and poultry and poultry products. Forestry resources include oak, hickory, ash, elm, maple, beech, and birch. Mineral resources are coal, crude oil, crushed stone, Portland cement, sand and gravel, limestone, and tripoli. Marine resources include chub, bass, trout, salmon, pike, mussels, perch, smelt, and whitefish.

Illinois has been influenced by various waves of immigration, including Western Europeans in the mid-19th century, Eastern Europeans in the late 19th and early 20th centuries, African Americans from the south after World War I, and Asians and Latin Americans in recent years. The 2000 census shows that 73.5% of the population is white; 15.1% African American; 12.3% Hispanic, of any race; and 3.4% Asian.

The Chicago metro area, which includes parts of Gary, IN, and Kenosha, WI, is the largest in the state, with 9,157,540 people. Other significant cities include Rockford (371,236); the Peoria/Pekin metro area (347,387); Springfield (201,437); and the Champaign/Urbana metro area (179,669).

Environmental imperatives for the state include improving the quality of the groundwater, which has been contaminated in many industrialized areas; reducing air pollutants; and cleaning up abandoned landfills and other solid-waste hazards.

COMMUNICATIONS/ENERGY

Illinois has 122 public-use airports, four of which—Chicago O'Hare International Airport, Clow International Airport, Lawrenceville-Vincennes International Airport, and Quad City International Airport—are international. Chicago is the major port, linking the Great Lakes to the Mississippi River via several smaller rivers. The state has 16,100 miles of rail serving approximately 45 railroads, and 137,639 miles of roads.

Illinois's technological network, with 242,239 high-speed lines as of 2000, is uneven, with high-tech industry flourishing in the metropolitan areas while schools and government remain among the least-wired in the United States. In 2000, 93.0% of households had telephone service; 40.1% of households had Internet access; and 41.4% of the population had wireless telephones.

Illinois produces important quantities of crude oil, coal, and nuclear power. Coal-fired generation and nuclear power dominate the electric utilities.

FISCAL/FINANCIAL

Illinois's tax system is friendly to retirees, with no state tax on social security payments, government retirement plans, and qualified retirement plans. Of state taxes collected in 2000, 33.5% came from individual income tax; 28.1% from general sales tax; 19.6% from selective sales tax; 9.9% from corporate net income tax; and 6.9% from license tax. The corporate income tax rate is 7.3%.

Major financial institutions in Illinois include Associated Banc-Corp, Bank of America, Bank One Corp., Charter One Financial, Citizens Banking Corp., Comerica, Commerce Bancshares, Fifth Third Bancorp, First Midwest Bancorp, Golden West Financial Corp., Harris Bankcorp, National City Corp., Northern Trust Corp., TCF Financial, Union Planters Corp., U.S. Bancorp, Wells Fargo & Co., and Wintrust Financial Corp.

BUSINESS OPPORTUNITIES

Illinois counts on the commercial infrastructure developed by earlier industries to attract new business; it also offers tax increment financing and a tax credit for new business.

Research facilities will also be a draw for knowledge industries. Major centers in Illinois include Argonne National Laboratory-East, Loyola University, Northrop Grumman, Northwestern University, the University of Chicago, and the University of Illinois.

The top 20 *Fortune* 500 companies with their headquarters in Illinois are: State Farm Insurance Cos., Sears Roebuck, Motorola, AllState, Bank One Corp., Walgreen, Sara Lee, Caterpillar, UAL, McDonald's, Abbott Laboratories, Deere, Archer Daniels Midland, Household International, Illinois Tool Works, Smurfit-Stone Container, NaviStar International, Exelon, AON, and Baxter International.

For More Information

Book:
Illinois Investment and Business Guide. International Business Publications USA, 2001.

Web Sites:
Enjoy Illinois: **www.enjoyillinois.com**
Illinois Department of Commerce and Community Affairs:
www.commerce.state.il.us

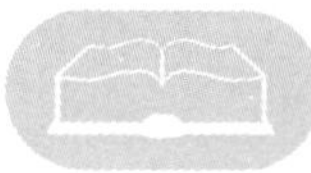

INDIANA

KEY FACTS

State capital: **Indianapolis**
Population: **6,080,485; 14th in U.S.; grew 9.7% 1990–2000**
Land area: **35,866.8 square miles; 38th in U.S.**
Population density: **169.5 per square mile**
GSP: **$182,202 million**
GSP pc: **$29,965.04**
Household income: **$39,717; 30th in U.S.**
Poverty rate: **8.2%**
Unemployment: **3.2%**

ECONOMY

Indiana has been a heavy industrial and manufacturing state since the mid-19th century, and manufacturing is still a major sector of the economy, led by transportation equipment, electronic equipment, machinery, primary and fabricated metals (particularly steel), rubber and miscellaneous plastics, household appliances, pharmaceuticals, surgical supplies, and musical instruments.

There has been growth in the service sector since the late 1980s, health services accounting for a large part of the increase.

Though Indiana's economy grew faster than the national average in the 1990s, that may change unless the state takes measures to allow it to participate in the new economy. Because there are relatively few management and professional jobs, many graduates of the state's universities migrate to other states, leaving Indiana with fewer residents with a college degree than most other states. Other challenges include a lack of startup capital for small and non-manufacturing businesses, and a need to bring infrastructure—water, wastewater, transportation, and telecommunications—to the same level in rural areas as they are in urban areas.

GEOGRAPHY/RESOURCES

Located in the midwestern United States, Indiana consists of three regions: the northern lake and moraine region, the fertile Till Plains in the central part of the state, and the southern hills and lowlands.

Agricultural output includes corn, soybeans, wheat, oats, rye, hay, tobacco, potatoes, tomatoes, cucumbers, snap beans, cantaloupe, pigs, cattle, sheep, poultry, and dairy products. Forestry resources include oak, maple, beech, birch, ash, elm, cherry, cedar, pine, and mixed hardwoods. Marine resources are bass, pike, perch, catfish, bluegill, crappie, tilapia, trout, and sunfish. Coal is the most important mineral resource; others are crude oil, Portland cement, sand and gravel, and crushed stone.

The population consists mainly of the descendants of English, Scottish, Irish, and German settlers; ethnic minorities are primarily concentrated in urban regions. The 2000 census shows that 87.5% of the population is white; 8.4% African American; 3.5% Hispanic, of any race; and 1.0% Asian.

Indianapolis is the largest city, with 1,607,486 people; others include: Fort Wayne (502,141); the Evansville metro area, which includes Henderson, KY (296,195); South Bend (265,559); Lafayette (182,821); the Elkhart/Goshen metro area (182,7910; and Terre Haute (149,192). The population of Gary, another major city, is included in the population of Chicago, IL's metro area.

Environmental imperatives for Indiana include reducing air and water pollution caused by steel mills in the northwestern part of the state, and protecting and developing the coastal area's natural resources.

COMMUNICATIONS/ENERGY

Indiana has 117 public-use airports, three of which—Fort Wayne International Airport, Indianapolis International Airport, and Terre Haute International Airport—are international. There are three ports: Indiana's International Port on Lake Michigan and Southwind Maritime Center and Clark Maritime Center on the Ohio River. Indiana is a major overland transportation center, with 20,078.3 miles of highways; it also has 4,252.2 miles of railroad track served by approximately 40 freight railroads.

Indiana is still developing its telecommunications infrastructure, which included 60,494 high-speed lines in 2000, with assistance from private industry in the state. In 2000, 95.7% of households had telephone service; 39.4% of the households in the state had Internet access; and 28.2% of the population had wireless telephones.

The state ranks ninth nationally in coal production, and its electric utilities depend almost completely on coal. Natural gas and petroleum are the other most prevalent energy sources.

FISCAL/FINANCIAL

Indiana has a stable tax environment. Of state taxes collected in 2000, 37.1% came from individual income tax; 35.4% from general sales tax; 14.4% from selective sales tax; 9.2% from corporate income tax; and 2.4% from license tax. Corporate income tax is 7.9% (8.5% for financial institutions).

Major financial institutions in Indiana include 1st Source Corp., Bank One Corp., Comerica, Community Bank Shares of Indiana, Fifth Third Bancorp, First Financial Corp., First Indiana Corp., First Merchants Corp., Flagstar Bancorp, Indiana United Bancorp, KeyCorp, National City Corp., Old National Bancorp, TCF Financial, Union Planters Corp., U.S. Bancorp, and Wells Fargo & Co.

BUSINESS OPPORTUNITIES

Indiana offers a number of business incentives, many of them developed in the late 1990s. They include: an employee training program providing financial assistance to new and expanding companies; industrial development grant funds to meet the infrastructure needs of new and expanding businesses; tax incentives in enterprise zones; and tax credits for college and university contributions, R&D, and industrial recovery.

Research in the state receives little federal funding; most R&D is funded by the state and private industries. Research facilities include the ARS Research Center at Purdue University, Indiana University, ITT Industries Inc., Light Helicopter Turbine Engine Co., M.A. Laboratory Animals, the Naval Surface Warfare Center Crane Division, Notre Dame University, Purdue University, Raytheon Co., and Rolls-Royce Allison.

There are five *Fortune* 500 companies with their headquarters in Indiana: Eli Lilly, Anthem Insurance, Conseco, Cummins Engine, and NiSource.

For More Information

Book:

Madison, James H. *The Indiana Way: A State History*. Bloomington, IN: Indiana University Press, 1990.

Web Sites:

Access Indiana: **www.state.in.us**
Indiana Department of Commerce: **www.in.gov**
Enjoy Indiana: **www.enjoyindiana.com**

  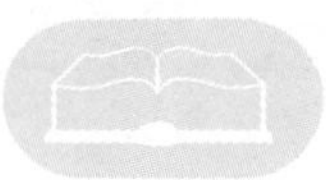    

IOWA

KEY FACTS

State capital: **Des Moines**
Population: **2,926,324; 30th in U.S.; grew 5.4% 1990–2000**
Land area: **55,868.7 square miles; 23rd in U.S.**
Population density: **52.3 per square mile**
GSP: **$85,243 million**
GSP pc: **$29,129.72**
Household income: **$42,993; 21st in U.S.**
Poverty rate: **7.9%**
Unemployment: **2.6%**

ECONOMY

National perception of Iowa is largely of an agricultural state. But, while agriculture does contribute more to Iowa's economy than it does to the economies of many states, the manufacturing and service sectors are much more significant. They are led by agricultural processing, electronic equipment and instruments, industrial machinery, chemicals, fabricated metals, and motor vehicles, and by health and business services, respectively.

The state has identified three industry clusters it would like to target for growth: life sciences, including value-added agricultural products and drugs and pharmaceuticals; advanced manufacturing, including plastics, metals, printing paper or packaging products, measuring devices and medical instruments, and recycling and waste management; and information solutions, including insurance and financial services, software development, and telecommunications.

Challenges facing Iowa include a tight labor market and a low percentage of entrepreneurial endeavors.

GEOGRAPHY/RESOURCES

Located in the midwestern United States, Iowa consists of three physical regions: the Dissected Till Plains in the south, the fertile Young Drift Plains in the northern and central parts of the state, and the rough, hilly Driftless Area in the northeast.

Agricultural output includes corn, pigs, soybeans, cattle and calves, poultry and poultry products, dairy products, hay, and nursery and greenhouse crops. Forestry resources include oak, hickory, ash, elm, and maple. Mineral resources are crushed stone, Portland cement, sand and gravel, lime, gypsum, and clay. Marine resources are bass, crappie, bluegill, sunfish, catfish, trout, pike, and perch.

Much of the population is descended from the 19th-century immigrants who came to Iowa from states to the south and east, largely of German, British, Irish, and Scandinavian heritage; there has been an influx of African Americans to the urban areas in the 20th century. The 2000 census shows that 93.9% of the population is white; 2.8% Hispanic, of any race; 2.1% African American; and 1.3% Asian.

Des Moines is the largest city, with 456,022 people. Other significant cities include Cedar Rapids (191,701); the Davenport metro area (158,668); the Waterloo/Cedar Falls metro area (128,012); Sioux City (124,130); and Iowa City (111,006).

Environmental imperatives for Iowa include: cleaning up and preventing future leaks from underground petroleum storage tanks; maintaining standards for wastewater treatment; and protecting groundwater from chemicals used in agricultural cultivation.

COMMUNICATIONS/ENERGY

Iowa has 114 airports, one of which—Des Moines International Airport—is international. Major ports include Burlington, Clinton, Davenport, Dubuque, Fort Madison, Keokuk, McGregor, and Muscatine on the Mississippi River, and Council Bluffs and Sioux City on the Missouri River. There are 4,276.9 miles of rail operated by 17 railroads, and 113,145.3 miles of roads.

Iowa has 5,152 km of fiber optic cable installed by the state, to which private telecommunications companies can connect; it links the state's schools, hospitals, libraries, and government agencies, with the result that Iowa's schools are among the most wired in the nation. As of 2000, there were 58,199 high-speed lines. However, there is some debate about how to find the funding to make necessary upgrades. In 2000, 96.5% of households had telephone service; 39.0% of households had Internet access; and 28.4% of the population had wireless telephones.

Iowa consumes petroleum and coal in nearly equal measures, followed by natural gas. Electric utilities are powered almost entirely by coal, with some use of nuclear energy; the industrial sector uses petroleum, natural gas, and coal.

FISCAL/FINANCIAL

Iowa's state tax burden is consistent with surrounding states; it has no property tax. Of state tax collected in 2000, 36.5% came from individual income tax; 33.2% from general sales tax; 14.6% from selective sales tax; 9.5% from license tax; and 4.1% from corporate income tax. The corporate income tax rate is in four brackets, from 6.0 to 12.0%; the rate is 5% for financial institutions.

Major financial institutions in Iowa include the Bank of America, Citizens Banking Corp., First Midwest Financial, Mahaska Investment Co., North Central Bancshares, Principal Financial, Union Planters Corp., and U.S. Bancorp.

BUSINESS OPPORTUNITIES

Iowa offers a number of incentives for business, including: tax credits, tax exemptions, and financial assistance for companies that create new jobs or invest capital; enterprise zones; state investment in agribusiness; financial assistance to early-stage technology companies; funding for necessary infrastructure development; and tax increment financing.

R&D in the state is limited, concentrated mainly on health and human services and agriculture. Research centers include Ames Laboratory, the ARS Research Facility, the Krell Institute, Midwest Power Systems, Rockwell International Corp., the University of Iowa, and Iowa State University.

There are two *Fortune* 500 companies with their headquarters in Iowa: Principal Financial and Maytag.

For More Information

Book:

Davis, Judy McCoy, ed. *Greater Des Moines: Iowa's Commercial Center*. Memphis, TN: Towery Publications, 1999.

Web Sites:

Iowa Department of Economic Development: **www.state.ia.us/ided**
Iowa Division of Tourism: **www.traveliowa.com**

KANSAS

KEY FACTS

State capital: **Topeka**
Population: **2,688,418; 32nd in U.S.; grew 8.5% 1990–2000**
Land area: **81,814.6 square miles; 13th in U.S.**
Population density: **32.8 per square mile**
GSP: **$80,843 million**
GSP pc: **$30,070.84**
Household income: **$37,705; 37th in U.S.**
Poverty rate: **10.4%**
Unemployment: **3.7%**

ECONOMY

Kansas has a fairly diversified economy, with aircraft, communications, and services all making contributions. The manufacturing sector did not outstrip agriculture until the 1950s; in the 1990s, certain manufacturing segments—aircraft, food and kindred products, and printing and publishing—have grown faster in Kansas than in the rest of the United States. Business and health services are the primary contributors to the service sector, which has recently become the largest in the state.

Kansas has identified a number of industries that it would like to attract or maintain: aviation, plastics, value-added agriculture, call centers, administrative service centers, and wholesale, packaging, and distribution.

The state has a number of challenges to face in attracting new, and especially startup, businesses. First among them is Kansas's lack of financial capital: Venture capital in the state is one-third the national average. Others include placing a greater emphasis on technology in the educational system, retaining the science and engineering students graduating from Kansas universities, improving telecommunications access throughout the state, and increasing access to global trade.

GEOGRAPHY/RESOURCES

Located in the Great Plains of the United States, Kansas consists of high plains in the far west, the Gypsum Hills in the south-central part of the state, the Flint Hills in the east-central part, and hilly, timbered land in the northeast.

Wheat is the primary agricultural output; others include alfalfa, corn, grain, sorghum, hay, soybeans, sugar beets, sunflowers, apples, peaches, beans, oats, cattle, dairy products, hogs, poultry, and poultry products. Forestry resources include walnut, maple, beech, birch, cherry, ash, elm, oak, and hickory; while there is no commercial fishing, Kansas's lakes have bass, crappie, catfish, bluegill, trout, and walleye. Mineral resources are coal, crude oil, natural gas, Portland cement, salt, crushed stone, sand and gravel, and helium.

The earliest European settlers in Kansas were Anglo-Saxons by way of New England; after the Civil War, the new railroads brought Central European immigrants. The 2000 census shows that 86.1% of the population is white; 7.0% Hispanic, of any race; 5.7% African American; and 1.7% Asian.

Wichita is the largest city, with 545, 220 people; others include Topeka (169,871) and Lawrence (99,962). Kansas City, which is in Missouri with a metropolitan area that overflows into Kansas, has 1,776,062 people.

Environmental imperatives in Kansas include: limiting pesticide and fertilizer damage to the state's soil and groundwater; understanding the effects of planting genetically engineered crops; making provisions for drought; and the disposal of waste products from livestock industry.

COMMUNICATIONS/ENERGY

Kansas has 144 public airports, of which Wichita Mid-Continent Airport is the largest; there are no international airports. There are three major ports on the Missouri River: Atchison, Leavenworth, and Kansas City. Kansas is a major trucking hub, with 11,005 miles of highways; there are 6,111.7 miles of railroad track used by 3 major and 17 secondary rail carriers.

Kansas is set for future telecommunications infrastructure development, with a central location that puts it in the middle of several of the nation's fiber optic networks; there were 68,743 high-speed lines as of 2000. In 2000, 94.1% of households had telephone service; 43.9% of households had Internet access; and 29.8% of the population had wireless telephones.

Kansas is the sixth-largest producer of natural gas and the eighth-largest producer of crude oil in the United States. The state primarily uses petroleum, natural gas, and coal for its own energy needs; most electric utilities are powered by coal and nuclear power.

FISCAL/FINANCIAL

Kansas has had a stable tax environment for the latter half of the 20th century. Of state taxes collected in 2000, 38.3% came from individual income tax; 35.8% from general sales tax; 11.9% from selective sales tax; 5.6% from corporate income tax; and 4.9% from license tax. The corporate income tax rate is 4.0% plus a 3.35% surtax over $50,000; for banks, it is 2.25% plus a 2.125% surtax over $25,000.

Major financial institutions include the Bank of America, Capitol Federal Financial, Commerce Bancshares, First Independence Corporation, First Kansas Financial, Gold Banc Corp., Golden West Financial Corp., Team Financial Inc., UMB Financial, and U.S. Bancorp.

BUSINESS OPPORTUNITIES

Kansas offers a number of incentives to businesses in the state, including: tax credits for job expansion and capital investment; tax incentives for businesses locating in non-metropolitan enterprise zones; various incentives for employers who invest significantly in employee training and pay higher than average wages; property tax exemptions; sales tax exemptions on manufacturing equipment; R&D tax credits; and tax credits for businesses that pay for or provide childcare to their employees.

One drawback to Kansas is the lack of research facilities compared to other states. Research centers include Boeing, the Centers of Excellence, the Center for Research, Eagle Picher Industries, the Grain Marketing and Production Research Center, Kansas State University, and the University of Kansas.

Sprint and Yellow are the only *Fortune* 500 companies with their headquarters in Kansas.

For More Information

Book:

Richmond, Robert W. *Kansas: A Land of Contrasts*. Wheeling, IL: Harlan Davidson, 1999.

Web Sites:

Kansas Department of Commerce & Housing: **www.kansascommerce.com**
State of Kansas Homepage: **www.accesskansas.com**
Traveling in Kansas: **www.kansas-travel.com**

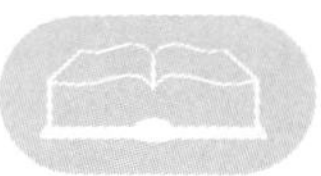

KENTUCKY

KEY FACTS

State capital: **Frankfort**
Population: **4,041,769; 25th in U.S.; grew 9.6% 1990–2000**
Land area: **39,727.8 square miles; 36th in U.S.**
Population density: **101.7 per square mile**
GSP: **$113,539 million**
GSP pc: **$28,091.41**
Household income: **$37,186; 39th in U.S.**
Poverty rate: **12.5%**
Unemployment: **4.1%**

ECONOMY

Kentucky's fastest-growing industry is manufacturing, with a 5% growth in the number of manufacturing establishments from 1990 to 1998. Automotive manufacturing has led that growth; the state also has a strong industrial base in steel, aluminum, chemicals, and machinery production.

Warehousing and distribution is another fast growing industry, prompted by Kentucky's central location in the United States. It is the only state with two overnight air cargo and package hubs. Its high-tech industry, while not yet a significant contributor to the state's economy, has registered growth in the last several years, particularly in data processing and preparation, computer programming, and commercial nonphysical research.

Kentucky has addressed many of the technological weaknesses that plague other states in the region, but its most important challenge remains its physical environment. Although it has made improvements in the last decade, the quality of the state's air and water continue to be a concern.

GEOGRAPHY/RESOURCES

Located in the geographical center of the eastern United States, Kentucky has three geographical regions: the Appalachian highlands in the east, containing the state's coalfields; the interior lowlands in the center; and the coastal plain along the Mississippi River in the west.

Tobacco is a major cash crop, and the state is internationally known for its thoroughbred horses. Other agricultural output includes cattle and calves, dairy products, soybeans, corn, and pigs. The state's mineral resources are coal, crude oil, natural gas, asphalt, and lime. Forestry resources are oak, pine, hickory, cedar, and mixed upland hardwoods.

The state's Native American inhabitants virtually disappeared with the coming of white settlers from the north, south, and east. 90.1% of the population is white; 7.3% is black or African American; and 1.5% is Hispanic, of any race. Louisville is the largest city, with 1,025,598 people; other cities include Lexington (479,198) and Owensboro (91,545).

A major concern is the presence of toxic pollutants in the state's air and water. The major sources of pollution in the water are agricultural, coal, and sewage byproducts. Major air pollutants are carbon monoxide, nitrogen oxide, and sulfur dioxide emissions.

COMMUNICATIONS/ENERGY

Kentucky has 63 public-use airports, three of which–Cincinnati/Northern Kentucky International Airport, Louisville International Airport at Standiford Field, and Bluegrass Airport–are international. Six public inland ports–Henderson, Louisville, Owensboro, Paducah, Hickman, and Lyon County–operate on the Mississippi, Ohio, and Tennessee Rivers. There are three major railroads operating on 2,893.2 miles of rail, and 73,033.1 miles of roads.

Kentucky has recently developed a sophisticated telecommunications infrastructure, with fiber optic cable; wireless-radio, digital-microwave, and satellite technologies; and 32,731 high-speed lines as of 2000. In 2000, 93.9% of households had telephone service; 36.6% of households had Internet access; and 23.3% of the population had wireless telephones.

Kentucky is the third-highest coal producer in the United States, and the majority of the state's electricity is coal-powered. It also produces some natural gas, crude oil, and electricity from hydroelectric power.

FISCAL/FINANCIAL

A large part of Kentucky's efforts to bring business to the state has focused on tax reform. The state offers tax credits for new and expanded manufacturing projects, as well as occupational and skills upgrade training costs. Kentucky's tax rate on real property has decreased steadily since 1979, and recent reform has included property tax relief for leased manufacturing machinery, reduced inventory for distribution centers, and lower tax rates for private aircraft.

Of state taxes collected in 2000, 35.1% came from individual income tax; 28.2% from general sales tax; 17.4% from selective sales tax; 7.0% from license tax; 5.1% from property tax; and 4.0% from corporate income tax. The corporate income tax is 4.0–8.25%, with five tax brackets.

Major financial institutions in Kentucky include AREA Bancshares, Bank One Corp., BB&T Corp., Community Trust Bancorp, Farmers Capital Bank Corp., Fifth Third Bancorp, National City Corp., Old National Bancorp, Republic Bancorp, Union Planters Corp., and U.S. Bancorp.

BUSINESS OPPORTUNITIES

In addition to tax reform, Kentucky's push to be business-friendly has included workers' compensation reform and the Kentucky Networking Initiative, which encourages collaboration among companies as well as between business and government. These measures, in addition to the state's location in the middle of "Auto Alley", have contributed to Kentucky's manufacturing growth.

While the state has always had some tourism thanks to the Kentucky Derby, it has recently introduced incentives to businesses in that industry, offering new and expanded privately-owned tourist attractions a tax credit of up to 25% on their investment.

Research centers in the state include the University of Kentucky, the University of Louisville, Kentucky State University, the Mounted Maneuver Battlespace Battle Laboratory, and the Armored Forces Research Unit.

Four *Fortune* 500 companies have their headquarters in Kentucky: Humana, Ashland, Tricon Global Restaurants, and Lexmark International.

For More Information

Book:

Cauthen, Steve. *Northern Kentucky: Looking to the New Millennium* (Urban Tapestry Series). Memphis, TN: Towery Publishing, 1999.

Web Sites:

Commonwealth of Kentucky Home Page: **www.kydirect.net**
Kentucky Cabinet for Economic Development: **www.edc.state.ky.us**

  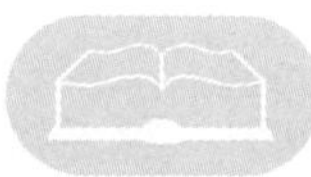    

LOUISIANA

KEY FACTS

State capital: **Baton Rouge**
Population: **4,468,976; 22nd in U.S.; grew 5.9% 1990–2000**
Land area: **43,561.7 square miles; 33rd in U.S.**
Population density: **102.6 per square mile**
Household income: **$30,219; 50th in U.S.**
Poverty rate: **18.6%**
GSP: **$128,959 million**
GSP pc: **$28,856.50**
Unemployment: **5.5%**

ECONOMY

Louisiana's economy has traditionally relied on the oil and gas industries, with significant income from the petrochemical industry as well. Manufacturing is also a significant sector; it includes shipbuilding, light truck assembly, aerospace and aviation facilities, automobile equipment manufacturing, food processing, and apparel manufacturing.

The service sector, the largest in the state, is led by health and business services. Tourism is also important, with jazz music, Cajun and Creole cuisine, hunting and fishing, boating, water skiing, sailing, and historical sites as the main features.

Louisiana has a lot of work to do before it can achieve its vision of being a viable participant in the information economy. Challenges include the state's low levels of educational attainment, a shortage of technologically skilled employees, a poor digital infrastructure, and high poverty rates.

GEOGRAPHY/RESOURCES

Located in the southern United States on the Gulf of Mexico at the mouth of the Mississippi River, Louisiana is a gateway into the industrialized Mississippi River Valley and a point of export for the Midwest. It is divided into two regions: the Mississippi flood plain in the north, and the Gulf coastal plain in the south. There is a wide band of swampland along the coast.

Louisiana is the largest producer of salt in America, a major producer of crude oil, natural gas, coal, sulfur, lime, and silica sands, and it has 13.8 million acres of hardwood and softwood forests. It is among the ten largest producers in the United States of cotton, sugar cane, yams, rice, and pecans, and its fishing industry—including shrimp, menhaden, crabs, oysters, crayfish, tuna, snapper, and swordfish—accounts for 26% of all seafood landed in the country.

The state is more racially diverse than most of the South, due in part to immigration through its ports. 63.9% of the population is white; 32.5% is black or African American; 2.4% is Hispanic, of any race; and 1.2% is Asian.

New Orleans is the largest city in the state, with 1,337,726 people. Other significant cities include: Baton Rouge (602,894); the Shreveport/Bossier City metro area (392,302); Lafayette (385,647); Houma (194,477); Lake Charles (183,577); Monroe (147,250); and Alexandria, (126,337).

The primary environmental issues facing Louisiana are the erosion of the wetlands—increasing the risk of flood to residential and commercial districts, damage to transportation infrastructure, and intrusion of salt water into water supplies—and toxic emissions in the air and water.

COMMUNICATIONS/ENERGY

Louisiana has 82 public-use airports, three of which—Alexandria International Airport, Chennault International Airport, and New Orleans International Airport—are international. The state's five largest deep-water ports—Greater Baton Rouge, Lake Charles, New Orleans, Plaquemines, and South Louisiana—handle more than 450 million tonnes of U.S. waterborne commerce a year. There are six railroads operating on 2,787.9 miles of rail, and 60,048.3 miles of roads.

The telecommunications infrastructure, however, is not of the same caliber; its 74,950 high-speed lines, as of 2000, are mainly concentrated in urban areas. In 2000, 90.9% of households had telephone service; 30.2% of households had Internet access; and 29.2% of the population had wireless telephones.

Louisiana is an energy exporter, with 11% of U.S. oil reserves and 19% of the country's natural gas reserves. The state is also the second-largest refiner of petroleum in the United States. Electric utilities rely on natural gas and coal; the industrial sector uses primarily natural gas and petroleum.

FISCAL/FINANCIAL

Two factors negatively impact Louisiana's ability to compete: high taxes on corporations relative to other Southern states, and low bond ratings that make it difficult for the state to raise capital. Of state taxes collected in 2000, 31.6% came from general sales tax; 25.5% from selective sales tax; 24.3% from individual income tax; 7.5% from license tax; 5.8% from severance tax; and 3.4% from corporate income tax. The corporate income tax rate is 4.0–8.0%, in five brackets.

Major financial institutions in the state include AmSouth Bancorporation, BancorpSouth, Bank One Corp., Comerica, Hancock Holding Co., Hibernia Corp., IBERIABANK Corp., Regions Financial Corp., Union Planters Corp., and Whitney Holding Corp.

BUSINESS OPPORTUNITIES

Louisiana offers several incentives to business in the state: low energy costs for industrial users; pre-employment and on-the-job update training through public sources; nonadversarial environmental procedures include preplanning meetings with new industries; industrial property tax exemptions; and tax credits for new jobs created in underdeveloped areas.

Entergy is the only *Fortune* 500 company in Louisiana.

Research centers in the state include Louisiana State University, Grambling State University, Louisiana Tech, Tulane University, the University of Louisiana, Southern University, and the National Wetlands Resource Center.

For More Information

Book:

Morgan, Kathleen O. *Louisiana in Perspective 2001: A Statistical View of the Pelican State*. Lawrence, KS: Morgan Quitno Corp., 2001.

Web Sites:

Louisiana's Official State Government Information and Services: **www.state.la.us**
Louisiana Department of Economic Development: **www.lded.state.la.us**
Louisiana Travel Promotion Association: **www.ltpa.org**

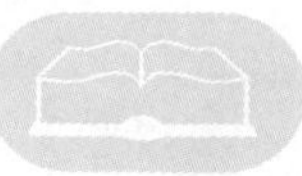

MAINE

KEY FACTS

State capital: **Augusta**
Population: **1,274,923; 40th in U.S.; grew 3.8% 1990–2000**
Land area: **30,861.8 square miles; 39th in U.S.**
Population density: **41.3 per square mile**
Household income: **$41,597; 27th in U.S.**
Poverty rate: **9.8%**
GSP: **$34,064 million**
GSP pc: **$26,718.48**
Unemployment: **3.5%**

ECONOMY

Situated outside the flow of the northeast's commercial traffic, Maine's economy has long depended primarily on its natural resources. The textile and shoe industries, which were major sources of income in the early 20th century, moved south and overseas in the 1980s; manufacturing, which is now the third-largest sector in the state, is dependent on processing lumber and paper from Maine's extensive forests. The service sector is the largest in the state, thanks in part to the tourism industry that is based on winter sports and natural attractions. Farm and fishery products also contribute to the overall economy.

Maine is attempting to revitalize its economy by drawing in growth industries such as information technology. The state hopes that recent investments in R&D will increase the small number of technology firms in the state and make knowledge-based industry a more significant contributor to the economy.

A major challenge for Maine is corporate perception of the state: that it is primarily a vacation spot unsuitable for business, that its extreme weather conditions will impact industry, that it has a subpar transportation infrastructure, and that the population is too low for a solid employee base. In addition to inviting investors from all over the country to showcases intended to combat these stereotypes, Maine is investing in its infrastructure, importing labor, and exploring methods of keeping the current labor force in the state.

GEOGRAPHY/RESOURCES

Located in the northeastern corner of the United States, Maine consists of three regions: an extension of the Appalachian Mountain chain in the southwest, a rugged upland region in the north, and the Atlantic Seaboard in the east.

Agricultural output includes potatoes, apples, blueberries, cranberries, poultry, and dairy products. Forestry products include spruce, fir, hardwoods, aspen, birch, pine, oak, hickory, elm, ash, and red maple. Lobster is the primary marine resource; others include sea urchins, clams, herring, goosefish, scallops, plaice, shrimp, pollock, bloodworms, flounder, hake, cod, and tuna. Mineral resources are sand and gravel, peat, crushed stone, Portland cement, lead, clay, copper, silver, and zinc.

The original settlers were English and Scotch-Irish Protestants, and their descendants still make up the majority of the population. The 2000 census shows that 96.9% of the population is white.

Portland is the largest city, with 243,537 people; other significant cities include Bangor (90,864) and the Lewiston/Auburn metro area (90,830). Maine's most important environmental imperative is to conserve the natural resources that contribute to its economy, particularly the forests and fisheries, which are popular with tourists.

COMMUNICATIONS/ENERGY

Maine has 46 commercial airports, two of which—Bangor and Portland—are international. It has 32,014.5 miles of roads and seven short-line railroads operating 1,400.6 miles of track, in addition to two rail-truck intermodal facilities. Of its seven seaports, the three largest cargo-shipping ports are Eastport, Searsport, and Portland.

The state's telecommunications system has 100% digital switching and 26,266 high-speed lines as of 2000, though high-speed broadband access is only available in some areas. In 2000, 98.5% of households had telephone service; 42.6% of households had Internet access; and 28.2% of the population had wireless telephones.

Maine produces some hydroelectric power, but petroleum is the most important source of energy, particularly for residences and commercial enterprises. Industry makes important use of wood and waste as sources of power.

FISCAL/FINANCIAL

Though Maine has instituted an aggressive business development initiative and offers a number of incentives to industry, it still has high individual income tax rates. Of state taxes collected in 2000, 40.5% came from individual income tax; 31.8% from general sales tax; 12.9% from selective sales tax; 5.6% from corporate income tax; and 5.0% from license tax. There are four brackets for corporate income tax rates, ranging from 3.5 to 8.93%; the rate is 1% for financial institutions.

Major financial institutions in the state include Banknorth Group, Camden National Corporation, Chittenden Corp., FleetBoston, KeyCorp, MBNA New England, Norway Savings Bank, and Union Trust.

BUSINESS OPPORTUNITIES

Maine's incentives to draw business include a business-property tax reimbursement for new businesses, a tax credit for R&D, and exemptions on sales and use taxes for equipment used in production or R&D. Additionally, the state has had a 35% decrease in workers' compensation costs, saving approximately $60 million.

There are no *Fortune* 500 companies with their headquarters in Maine.

Maine ranks among the last of the states in terms of federal funding for R&D. Research centers in the state include the Bigelow Laboratory for Ocean Sciences, the Jackson Laboratory, the Maine Medical Center, and the University of Maine.

For More Information

Books:

Morgan, Kathleen O. *Maine in Perspective.* Lawrence, KS: Morgan Quitno Corp., 2001.

Rolde, Neil. *Maine: A Narrative History.* Gardiner, ME: Tilbury House Publishers, 1990.

Web Sites:

Maine Economic and Community Development: **www.econdevmaine.com**

Maine Office of Tourism: **www.visitmaine.com**

State of Maine Homepage: **www.state.me.us**

MARYLAND

KEY FACTS

State capital: **Annapolis**
Population: **5,296,486; 19th in U.S.; grew 10.8% 1990–2000**
Land area: **9,773.9 square miles; 42nd in U.S.**
Population density: **541.9 per square mile**
GSP: **$174,710 million**
GSP pc: **$32,986.02**
Household income: **$51,695; 1st in U.S.**
Poverty rate: **7.3%**
Unemployment: **3.9%**

ECONOMY

Maryland's position on the seaboard made it a center of trade and transportation in its earliest days; manufacturing grew rapidly during the Industrial Revolution. Today, the services industry accounts for the majority of employment in the state, thanks mainly to government employment in nearby Washington DC and a large transportation-services industry; employment in the health, legal, and education fields rounds out this sector.

Manufacturing remains an important part of the state's economic base, however, with strengths in aerospace, food processing, chemicals, computers and electronics, transportation equipment, primary metals, machinery, metal products, and printing and publishing. Biotechnology is growing rapidly, thanks to research centers in the region; information technology is another growth industry, focused on software services, data processing, and information services.

Challenges going forward include improving Maryland's status as an exporter, especially in international markets; another area for improvement is the state's regulatory and permit requirements, which remain complicated despite reform in the mid-1990s.

GEOGRAPHY/RESOURCES

Located in the Middle Atlantic region of the eastern seaboard, Maryland is divided into eastern and western halves by Chesapeake Bay, an arm of the Atlantic Ocean. The Coastal Plain in the eastern half of the state is sandy in the south, fertile in the north; the Piedmont Plateau in the western half of the state is arable land except for belts of clay.

Poultry is the primary agricultural output; other produce includes greenhouse and nursery products, dairy products, vegetables, livestock, feed crops, soybeans, and tobacco. Maryland has the largest crab haul in the United States; other marine resources include oysters, clams, bass, shad, and catfish. Forestry resources include beech, birch, cherry, hemlock, hickory, maple, pine, poplar, oak, and ash. Mineral resources are crushed stone, coal, Portland cement, sand and gravel, clay, and natural gas.

Maryland has been marked by its ethnic diversity since the mid-19th century; first because of immigration from all over Europe, then because it was more friendly to the free African-American population after the Civil War than the states immediately to the south. The 2000 census shows that 64.0% of the population is white; 27.9% African American; 4.3% Hispanic, of any race; and 4.0% Asian.

Baltimore is the largest city, with 2,491,254 people; other significant cities include Hagerstown (127,791) and Cumberland (98,231). One major metro area, Newark, overlaps with Wilmington, DE; the combined population is 571,420 people.

Environmental imperatives include protecting the eroding shoreline and conserving the forests, which are currently being harvested at a faster rate than regrowth.

COMMUNICATIONS/ENERGY

Centrally located in the eastern corridor, Maryland has one international airport—Baltimore/Washington International Airport—and six regional airports. There is one major port, the Port of Baltimore; there are two Class I and four short-line railroads, and 47,116.7 miles of roads.

The state had 124,465 high-speed lines as of 2000. A recent initiative is bringing the quality of telecoms infrastructure in the technology corridor to rural areas. In 2000, 96.4% of households had telephone service; 43.8% of households had Internet access; and 35.8% of the population had wireless telephones.

Maryland produces coal, electricity from nuclear power, and hydroelectric power; the generation of electricity by utilities comes mostly from coal and nuclear power. Petroleum is the most-used source of energy, mostly in the form of motor gasoline and distillate fuel.

FISCAL/FINANCIAL

The early 1990s were a difficult time for Maryland, with federal funding cuts, private-sector job losses, and a sluggish economy. To combat the situation, the state reduced or eliminated 14 taxes, reformed its government, and instigated some regulatory reform to draw business. Of state taxes collected in 2000, 44.6% came from individual income tax; 24.1% from general sales tax; 18.0% from selective sales tax; 4.2% from corporate income tax; 3.7% from license tax; and 2.5% from property tax. The corporate income tax rate is 7.0%.

Major financial institutions in Maryland include Allfirst Financial, Bank of America, BB&T Corp., Chevy Chase Bank, F&M National Corp., First Mariner Bancorp, First Union Corp., Mercantile Bankshares Corp., Provident Bankshares, and SunTrust Banks.

BUSINESS OPPORTUNITIES

Maryland has introduced a number of tax credits to improve the business climate, including credits for job creation, building in underdeveloped areas, and R&D. The state's major draw for business, however, is its research facilities; Maryland has the second-highest level of R&D funding in the United States. The state is especially strong in medical and technological research; centers include the Adelphi Laboratory Center, the Army Medical Research Institute of Infectious Disease, the Edgewood Chemical Biological Center, the Food and Drug Administration, the Goddard Space Flight Center, Johns Hopkins University, Morgan State University, the National Institutes of Health, Standards and Technology, and the University of Maryland.

The *Fortune* 500 companies with their headquarters in Maryland are Lockheed Martin, Marriott International, Crestline Capital, Sodexho Marriott Services, Black & Decker, Allegheny Energy, and Constellation Energy.

For More Information

Book:
Maryland Investment and Business Guide. International Business Publications USA, 2001.

Web Sites:
Choose Maryland:
www.choosemaryland.org
Maryland State Homepage:
www.state.md.us

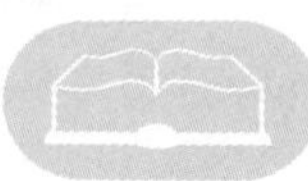

MASSACHUSETTS

KEY FACTS

State capital: **Boston**
Population: **6,349,097; 13th in U.S.; grew 5.5% 1990–2000**
Land area: **7,839.9 square miles; 45th in U.S.**
Population density: **809.8 per square mile**
GSP: **$262,564 million**
GSP pc: **$41,354.54**
Household income: **$46,947; 12th in U.S.**
Poverty rate: **10.2%**
Unemployment: **2.6%**

ECONOMY

Because of its rocky soil, which makes agriculture difficult, Massachusetts has been primarily an industrial state since the 17th century. Fishing in the surrounding Atlantic waters has always been important, but the once prosperous whaling industry declined early in the 20th century; the textile industry has largely relocated to southern states.

Service industries now predominate and growth areas are high-tech manufacturing, financial services, and healthcare, drawing on the resources of the educational institutions around Boston.

The most significant challenge facing industry is a shortage of skilled labor, combined with low population growth and a tight housing market; state government has increased investment in education, pursued education reform and funded new housing.

GEOGRAPHY/RESOURCES

Located in the northeastern United States, Massachusetts's rocky coast gives way to a hard land surface inland, becoming stony upland near the central part of the state. Farther west are the Connecticut River valley, the Berkshire Hills, and the Taconic and Hoosac ranges. Forestry resources include sugar maple, northern red oak, white ash, white pine, and hemlock. The principal crops are cranberries and greenhouse products. Main minerals are sand, gravel, crushed stone and lime. Scallops and lobster are the primary marine resources; others include goosefish, cod, flounder, tuna, clams, haddock, plaice, pollock, hake, swordfish, crabs, squid, skate, herring, and bass.

Although Massachusetts was one of the first states in the union and has strong Puritan roots, the influx of Irish and Italian immigrants in the late 19th and early 20th centuries is still evident in the population. The 2000 census shows that 84.5% of the population is white; 6.8% Hispanic, of any race; 5.4% African American; and 3.8% Asian.

The Boston metro area is the largest in the state, with 3,406,829 people. Other significant cities include: Springfield (591,932); Worcester (502,511); Lowell (290,772); Lawrence (264,873); Brockton (255,459); New Bedford (175,198); the Barnstable/Yarmouth metro area (162,582); and the Fitchburg/Leominster metro area (142,284).

COMMUNICATIONS/ENERGY

Massachusetts has 45 public-use airports; Logan International Airport is the only international airport, and is the largest passenger and air cargo terminal in New England. Boston, Fall River, Gloucester, New Bedford, and Salem are the major ports. There are approximately 1,305 miles of rail, in addition to metro, light rail, and commuter networks around Boston, and 34,740.6 miles of roads.

As the state that now bills itself the "dot-Commonwealth" and boasts a $3 billion telecommunications industry, Massachusetts had 289,447 high-speed lines as of 2000, and more than 3,000 IT companies are located there. In 2000, 94.0% of households had telephone service; 45.5% of households had Internet access; and 41.7% of the population had wireless telephones.

Petroleum is the most-used energy resource, followed by natural gas. Electric utilities rely primarily on nuclear energy, followed by hydroelectricity and coal. With the recent deregulation of the electricity industry, the Commonwealth is concerned about increased pollution from its several power plants. Accordingly, it has implemented a generation performance standard, limiting each plant's emissions based on how much power it is generating.

FISCAL/FINANCIAL

Badly hit by the recession at the start of the 1990s, Massachusetts made substantial business and personal tax cuts throughout the decade, yet in 2000 it still ranked fifth in the nation for state tax collections per capita. Of state taxes collected in 2000, 56.0% came from individual income tax; 22.1% from general sales tax; 9.3% from selective sales tax; 8.1% from corporate income tax; and 2.8% from license tax. Corporate income tax rates are 9.5% (10.5% for financial institutions), among the highest in the United States.

Investment companies manage more than $730 billion worth of mutual fund services and the state exports $662 billion worth. Major financial institutions in Massachusetts include Allmerica Financial, Banknorth Group, CCBT Financial Companies, Charter One Financial, Citigroup, Eastern Bank Corp., FirstFed America Bancorp, FleetBoston Financial, John Hancock Financial Services, and State Street Corp.

BUSINESS OPPORTUNITIES

To encourage investment and stimulate economic growth, unemployment insurance, workers' compensation premiums, and capital gains tax have all been reduced and investment tax credit tripled. In addition, the state offers a 3% tax credit on depreciable capital assets and a tax credit for corporations engaged in R&D.

The presence of world-renowned research centers, such as Harvard University, the Massachusetts Institute of Technology, and Boston University, has encouraged clusters of knowledge-based industry, notably in software and biotechnology. Other important research centers in the state include the Air Force Research Laboratory Space Vehicles Directorate, the John A. Volpe National Transportation Systems Center, and the Astrophysical Observatory.

Massachusetts is home to thirteen *Fortune* 500 companies: FleetBoston Financial, Raytheon, Liberty Mutual Insurance Group, Massachusetts Mutual Life Insurance, Staples, Gillette, TJX, EMC, John Hancock Financial Services, State Street Corp., BJ's Wholesale Club, Thermo Electron, and Allmerica Financial.

For More Information

Book:

Brown, Richard D., and Jack Tager. *Massachusetts: A Concise History.* Amherst, MA: University of Massachusetts Press, 2000.

Web Sites:

Business Assistance Resource Center: **http://corp.sec.state.ma.us**
Commonwealth of Massachusetts: **www.state.ma.us**

  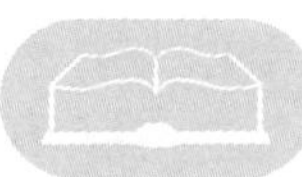  

Michigan

KEY FACTS

State capital: **Lansing**
Population: **9,938,444; 8th in U.S.; grew 6.9% 1990–2000**
Land area: **56,803.7 square miles; 22nd in U.S.**
Population density: **174.9 per square mile**
Household income: **$46,181; 15th in U.S.**
Poverty rate: **10.2%**
GSP: **$308,310 million**
GSP pc: **$31,021.96**
Unemployment: **3.6%**

Economy

Dominated by mining in the north and agriculture in the south during the 19th century, Michigan became the home of the automotive industry fairly early in the 20th century. Manufacturing still contributes a quarter of GSP, led by the automotive industry, but with significant contributions from office furniture, chemicals, pharmaceuticals, machine tools, and plastics.

Michigan has been building on its strengths in traditional manufacturing, particularly its capacities for engineering and research, to attract industries such as life sciences, information technologies, and advanced manufacturing. The existing IT sector in the state includes telecommunications, software products and services, and software consulting. The service sector is the second largest in the state, led by health and business services and by tourism, which relies primarily on Michigan's outdoor sports and attractions.

The necessity of these expansion efforts was made clear in the 1980s, when international competition in the automobile industry caused Michigan's state economy to bottom out. Diversifying its economy and reducing its dependence on the automotive industry remains an ongoing challenge for the state.

Geography/Resources

Located in the middle west of the United States, Michigan is divided into the rugged, mineral-rich Upper Peninsula and the Lower Peninsula. Agricultural output includes apples, beans, corn, cherries, blueberries, cucumbers, nursery plants, and Christmas trees; primary forestry products include birch, aspen, pine, and oak. The state produces nearly one-third of the nation's iron ore; other mineral resources are natural gas, crude oil, gypsum, and salt. Marine resources include whitefish, trout, chub, perch, and catfish.

Originally a French colony, Michigan had a number of German and Irish immigrants in the 19th century, and high growth in the black population during the 20th. 80.2% of the population is white; 14.2% is African American; 3.3% is Hispanic, of any race; and 1.8% is Asian. Detroit/Ann Arbor/Flint is the largest metro area, with 5,456,428 people; other large cities include: the Grand Rapids metro area (1,088,514); the Kalamazoo metro area (452,851); Lansing (447,728); and the Saginaw metro area (403,070).

Environmental imperatives include developing guidelines for sustainable land use, such as protecting farmlands, decreasing the amount of synthetic fertilizers, pesticides, and fungicides used, and preventing the loss of topsoil, as well as preventing deforestation.

Communications/Energy

Michigan has 1,232.8 miles of interstate highway, and four Class I and 25 regional railroads. There are 99 airports, 15 of which offer commercial air passenger and freight service; the major airports are Detroit Metro Airport and Kent County International Airport. Michigan also has 38 deepwater ports, connected to the Great Lakes shipping system, the Gulf of Mexico and Mississippi River barge system, and the Atlantic Ocean via the St. Lawrence Seaway.

Michigan, which had 198,230 high-speed lines in 2000, is in the midst of an initiative to coordinate and expand its digital infrastructure. In 2000, 95.8% of households had telephone service; 42.1% of households had Internet access; and 35.1% of the population had wireless telephones.

Michigan is the tenth-largest producer of natural gas in the country, and its natural gas use ranks sixth; it also produces crude oil. Electric utilities rely mainly on coal and nuclear power, but hydroelectric power is a secondary source for the production of electricity.

Fiscal/Financial

Michigan's business tax burden is higher than the national average, although tax cuts have reduced it by 20% over the last decade. Of state taxes collected in 2000, 33.7% came from general sales tax; 31.6% from individual income tax; 10.5% from corporate income tax; 9.3% from selective sales tax; 7.5% from property tax; and 5.3% from license tax. The state has a single business tax of 2.0%.

Major financial institutions include 1st Source Corp., Bank One Corp., Charter One Financial, Chemical Financial Corp., Citizens Banking Corp., Comerica, Fifth Third Bancorp, Flagstar Bancorp, KeyCorp, National City Corp., Sky Financial Group, TCF Financial, and Wells Fargo & Co.

Business Opportunities

The need to reform Michigan's economy prompted the state to offer several non-tax incentives for businesses, including job training and business-property search services. Costs for unemployment insurance and workers' compensation have also been reduced in the last decade. Tax incentives include tax free renaissance zones, state and local property-tax abatements, tax credits for job creation, and tax-increment financing.

Research centers, particularly those focusing on engineering, are also a draw; major centers include the Great Lakes Environmental Research Laboratory, the Great Lakes Science Center, the Van Andel Institute, the University of Michigan, Wayne State University, Michigan State University, Michigan Technological University, Oakland University, and Western Michigan University.

There are 19 *Fortune* 500 companies with their headquarters in Michigan: General Motors, Ford Motor, KMart, Delphi Automotive, Dow Chemical, Lear, Whirlpool, CMS Energy, Masco, Kellogg, Federal-Mogul, DTE Energy, ArvinMeritor, United Auto Group, Kelly Services, Pulte, Comerica, Steelcase, and the Borders Group.

For More Information

Book:

Folsom, Burton W. Jr. *Empire Builders: How Michigan Entrepreneurs Helped Make America Great*. Traverse City, MI: Rhodes & Easton, 1998.

Web Sites:

Michigan Economic Development Corporation: **http://medc.michigan.org**

State of Michigan: **www.state.mi.us**

Minnesota

KEY FACTS

State capital: **St. Paul**
Population: **4,919,479; 21st in U.S.; grew 12.4% 1990–2000**
Land area: **79,609.6 square miles; 14th in U.S.**
Population density: **61.8 per square mile**
GSP: **$172,982 million**
GSP pc: **$35,162.67**
Household income: **$50,865; 3rd in U.S.**
Poverty rate: **7.8%**
Unemployment: **3.3%**

Economy

Minnesota's traditional industries—agriculture and mining—declined during the second half of the 20th century. Services now make up the largest segment of the economy, driven by health, business, and agricultural services. Manufacturing is a close second, led by industrial machinery, scientific instruments, and electronic equipment.

Minnesota has targeted several industries it would like to attract or further develop, including: healthcare, biosciences, and information technology.

Challenges for the state include a worker shortage, caused by low levels of in-migration, and geographic distance from markets. To compensate for these issues, the state is creating a partnership between higher education and industry to provide workers in needed industries. Other measures will include simplifying tax and regulatory systems and making the treatment of capital gains more favorable to business.

Geography/Resources

Located in the northern central United States, Minnesota consists of four major regions: the rocky Superior Upland in the north, the fertile Young Drift Plains in the northwest, the Dissected Till Plains in the southwest, and the Driftless Area in the southeast.

Agricultural output includes corn, soybeans, wheat, hay, nursery and greenhouse crops, sugar beets, potatoes, pigs, dairy products, poultry and poultry products, cattle and calves. Forestry resources are aspen, maple, beech, birch, spruce, elm, ash, oak, hickory, fir, tamarack, cedar, and pine. Marine resources are herring, walleye, pike, trout, bass, catfish, crappie, bluegill, and salmon. Iron ore is the most significant mineral resource; others include sand and gravel, limestone, and peat.

Minnesota's first settlers were English, Irish, and Scots from New England; Germans, Swedes, and Norwegians came in the later 19th century. The early 20th century brought immigrants from all over Europe, as well as blacks and Hispanics, and recent immigrants include Vietnamese and Laotians. The 2000 census shows that 89.4% of the population is white; 3.5% African American; 2.9% Hispanic, of any race; 2.9% Asian; and 1.1% Native American.

The Minneapolis/St. Paul metro area is the largest in Minnesota, with 2,868,847 people; other cities include Duluth (200,528), St. Cloud (167,392), and Rochester (124,277).

While Minnesota's air quality has improved since the 1970s, the state is still looking for ways to further reduce toxic emissions. Other environmental imperatives include reducing soil erosion and conserving wetlands.

Communications/Energy

Minnesota has 142 public-use airports, six of which—Baudette International Airport, Duluth International Airport, Falls International Airport, Minneapolis/St. Paul International Airport, Rochester International Airport, and Warroad International Airport—are international. There are five ports, of which St. Paul and Savage are the largest. The state has 23 railroads operating on 4,608.1 miles of track, and 130,672.2 miles of roads.

Minnesota has a fully digital telecommunications network and 117,894 high-speed lines as of 2000, which the state plans to develop further in the first decade of the century, particularly in rural areas. In 2000, 97.8% of households had telephone service; 43.0% of households had Internet access; and 35.4% of the population had wireless telephones.

Petroleum is the most-used energy resource in Minnesota, followed by natural gas and coal in nearly equal measure. Electric utilities are powered primarily by coal, with some use of nuclear energy.

Fiscal/Financial

Minnesota is improving its tax structure to make itself more welcoming to business, with measures including reductions in property tax, workers' compensation tax, and unemployment insurance tax; as of 2000, however, Minnesota had the fourth-highest per-capita state tax burden in the United States. Of state tax collected in 2000, 41.6% came from individual income tax; 27.9% from general sales tax; 15.4% from selective sales tax; 7.3% from license tax; and 6.0% from corporate net income tax. The corporate income tax rate is 9.8%, one of the highest in the United States.

Major financial institutions include Associated Banc-Corp, Citizen's Banking Corp., HMN Financial, Northern Star Financial, TCF Financial Corporation, U.S. Bancorp, Wells Fargo & Co., and Wells Financial Corp.

Business Opportunities

Minnesota offers diverse incentives to businesses locating or expanding in the state, including a tax credit for R&D, tax exemptions for inventory, machinery, and equipment, enterprise zones, job-skills training programs, and low-interest loans to tourism businesses.

Much of Minnesota's federal research funding comes from the Department of Defense. Research facilities in Minnesota include Alliant TechSystems Inc, the ARS Research Facility, General Dynamics Corp., Honeywell, Lockheed Martin, the Mayo Foundation, United Defense LP, and the University of Minnesota.

There are 16 *Fortune* 500 companies with their headquarters in Minnesota: Target, United Health Group, Supervalu, Minnesota Mining & Mfg., Best Buy, Xcel Energy, Northwest Airlines, U.S. Bancorp, St. Paul Cos., Cenex Harvest States, General Mills, Medtronic, Nash Finch, Hormel Foods, ADC Telecommunications, and Lutheran Brotherhood.

For More Information

Book:

Bockelman, Wilfred, ed. *Culture of Corporate Citizenship: Minnesota's Business Legacy for the Global Future.* Lakeville, MN: Galde Press, 1999.

Web Sites:

Minnesota Department of Trade and Economic Development:
www.dted.state.mn.us
State of Minnesota Homepage:
www.state.mn.us

Mississippi

KEY FACTS

State capital: **Jackson**
Population: **2,844,658; 31st in U.S.; grew 10.5% 1990–2000**
Land area: **46,906.7 square miles; 31st in U.S.**
Population density: **60.6 per square mile**
GSP: **$64,286 million**
GSP pc: **$22,598.85**
Household income: **$31,528; 48th in U.S.**
Poverty rate: **15.5%**
Unemployment: **5.7%**

Economy

Mississippi's agricultural history isn't as historically distant as in most states; it was only in the mid-20th century that revenues from industrial activity surpassed those of agriculture. The state's agricultural sector is still important to the economy, as are its other traditional industries: mining—especially of crude oil and natural gas—and forestry.

The manufacturing sector is significant, led by electronic equipment, lumber and wood, food products, furniture and fixtures, chemicals, industrial machinery, petroleum products, paper products, transportation equipment, and rubber and plastics. The service industry is growing, led by health and business services and tourism. The state hopes to create a cluster of communications and information technology companies.

Mississippi faces numerous challenges in its economic growth, not the least of which is low educational attainment and a relatively unskilled workforce. Other issues that the state must face are its low job quality, low earnings, high poverty rate, low capital investment, and the little investment in R&D by its industry.

Geography/Resources

Located in the southeastern U.S., Mississippi lies entirely in the Gulf Coastal Plain, with the exception of the North Central Hills in the northeast corner of the state.

Natural gas and crude oil are the most significant mineral resources; others include coal, sand and gravel, Portland cement, fuller's earth, clay, bentonite, and crushed stone. Shrimp is the primary marine resource; others include menhaden, finfishes, crab, mullet, flatfish, snapper, trout, catfish, and drum. Forestry resources include pine, oak, gum, hickory, elm, ash, and tupelo. Poultry and poultry products are the primary agricultural output; other produce includes cotton, soybeans, cattle and calves, corn, dairy products, hogs and pigs, and nursery and greenhouse crops.

There is little in-migration in Mississippi; the black population has decreased significantly in the 20th century, and the white population consists mainly of the descendants of the state's British, Irish, and other northern European 18th- and 19th-century settlers. The 2000 census shows that 61.4% of the population is white; 36.3% African American; and 1.4% Hispanic, of any race.

Jackson is the largest city, with 440,801 people. Other cities include the Biloxi/Gulfport/Pascagoula metro area (363,988) and Hattiesburg (111,674).

Environmental imperatives for Mississippi include decreasing industrial waste in the state's waters, conserving wetlands, and sustaining marine wildlife.

Communications/Energy

Mississippi has 83 public-use airports, three of which—Stennis International Airport, Jackson International Airport, and Trent Lott International Airport—are international. There are 13 river ports on the Mississippi River and the Tennessee-Tombigbee Waterway, and two deepwater ports on the Gulf of Mexico at Pascagoula and Gulfport. There are 20 railroads operating 2,842.2 miles of track, and 47,736.5 miles of roads.

Hoping to attract a telecommunications industry cluster, Mississippi has begun establishing a digital infrastructure. However, rural areas are still underserved, and the state had only 12,305 high-speed lines as of 2000. In 2000 Mississippi had the lowest percentage of households in the U.S. with telephone service, at 88.9%, and the lowest percentage of households with Internet access, at 26.3%. 27.7% of the population had wireless telephones in 2000.

Petroleum is the most-used energy resource in Mississippi, followed by natural gas. Electric utilities mainly use coal, natural gas, and nuclear energy; the industrial sector uses natural gas, coal, and wood and waste. Transportation is powered primarily by petroleum with some use of natural gas.

Fiscal/Financial

Mississippi had a fairly low state tax burden in 2000. Of state tax collected in 2000, 49.5% came from general sales tax; 21.4% from individual income tax; 17.3% from selective sales tax; 5.9% from license tax; and 4.8% from corporate income tax. The corporate income tax rate is 3.0–5.0%, in three brackets.

Major financial institutions include AmSouth Bancorporation, BancorpSouth, Citizens Holding Company, First Tennessee National Corp., Hancock Holding Company, Hibernia Corp., The Peoples Holding Company, SouthTrust Corp., Trustmark Corp., Union Planters Corp., United Security Bancshares, and Whitney Holding Corp.

Business Opportunities

Mississippi has only recently begun offering some incentives to business, including: incentive payments for businesses creating high-paying jobs; tax credits for job creation, R&D, and workforce training; tax exemptions for companies locating in underdeveloped counties; tax exemptions on pollution-control equipment; and tax credits and incentives for agribusiness.

Research centers in Mississippi include Alcorn State University, the Institute for Technology Development, Jackson State University, the Jamie Whitten Delta States Research Center, the John C. Stennis Space Center, the Mississippi/Alabama Sea Grant Consortium, the Mississippi State Research Center, Mississippi State University, the University of Mississippi, the University of Southern Mississippi, and the Waterways Experiment Station.

Worldcom is the only *Fortune* 500 companies with its headquarters in Mississippi.

For More Information

Book:
Ownby, Ted. *American Dreams in Mississippi: Consumers, Poverty, & Culture, 1830–1998*. Chapel Hill, NC: University of North Carolina Press, 1999.

Web Sites:
Mississippi Development Authority: **www.decd.state.ms.us**
Mississippi Division of Tourism: **www.visitmississippi.org**
Mississippi State Homepage: **www.state.ms.us**

Missouri

KEY FACTS

State capital: **Jefferson City**
Population: **5,595,211; 17th in U.S.; grew 9.3% 1990–2000**
Land area: **68,885.6 square miles; 18th in U.S.**
Population density: **81.2 per square mile**
GSP: **$170,470 million**
GSP pc: **$30,467.13**
Household income: **$47,462; 11th in U.S.**
Poverty rate: **9.7%**
Unemployment: **3.65%**

Economy

Missouri's historical dependence on agriculture and mining gave way to manufacturing, which was the dominant sector for most of the 20th century. The industry is led by aerospace and transportation manufacturing, followed by metals and chemicals. The processing of agricultural products is also important, and high-tech manufacturing is on the rise. Services comprise the largest sector of the economy, led by business services. Tourism and recreation have become increasingly important to this industry.

Industries that Missouri has targeted for retention, growth, and development include business and financial services, manufacturing, health products and services, information and media services, food processing, wood and paper products production, and tourism.

The state faces challenges to development including an undereducated workforce, the emigration of young skilled workers, inefficient use of renewable resources, and low capital investment, especially in manufacturing.

Geography/Resources

Located in the southern midwestern United States, the state of Missouri is divided by the Missouri River, which runs west to east across it. North of the river the land is characterized by plains and prairie; the southern half of the state, which contains the Ozark Mountains, is mainly rough and hilly, except for alluvial plains in the southeast.

Missouri is the top lead-producer in the United States; other mineral resources include coal, crude oil, crushed stone, Portland cement, lime, sand and gravel, silver, clay, copper, zinc, and iron ore. Agricultural output includes corn, soybeans, winter wheat, grain sorghum, oats, rice, tobacco, potatoes, cotton, hay, fruit, poultry and poultry products, cattle and calves, and hogs and pigs. Marine resources include bass, trout, catfish, sunfish, bluegill, crappie, walleye, and carp. Oak is the primary forestry resource; others include hickory, maple, beech, birch, elm, ash, cottonwood, cedar, and pine.

The state's original French settlers gave way to immigrants from the east coast in the 18th century; the 19th and early 20th centuries brought in immigrants from all parts of Europe and blacks from the rural south. The 2000 census shows that 84.9% of the population is white; 11.2% African American; 2.1% Hispanic, of any race; and 1.1% Asian.

St. Louis is the largest city, with 2,603,607 people; other major cities include Kansas City (1,776,062); Springfield (325,721); Joplin (157,322); Columbia (135,454); and St. Joseph (102,490).

Environmental imperatives for Missouri include controlling the release of hazardous chemicals from manufacturing plants into the soil, water, and air.

Communications/Energy

Missouri has 140 public airports, two of which—Lambert St. Louis International and Kansas City International—are international. Of the 14 ports, the most significant are Kansas City and St. Louis. There are 122,671.7 miles of roads and 17 railroads operating on 6,648 miles of track.

Missouri's telecommunications infrastructure is still in the process of being developed. Most of the cities have adequate telecom access; the state had 100,403 high-speed lines as of 2000. However, rural areas are still underserved. In 2000, 95.5% of households had telephone service; 42.5% of the households had Internet access; and 31.6% of the population had wireless telephones.

Petroleum is the most-used resource in Missouri, followed closely by coal and then by natural gas. Missouri produces some coal; coal is the primary resource for electricity, with some use of nuclear energy.

Fiscal/Financial

Missouri has a competitive tax structure for business and one of the lowest per-capita state tax burdens in the United States. Of state tax collected in 2000, 41.4% came from individual income tax; 32.5% from general sales tax; 14.5% from selective sales tax; 6.7% from license tax; and 3.1% from corporate income tax. The corporate tax rate is 6.25% (7% for financial institutions); businesses can deduct 50% of federal taxes before computing income taxable by the state.

Major financial institutions in Missouri include the Bank of America, Commerce Bancshares, Gold Banc Corp., Great Southern Bancorp, UMB Financial Corp., Union Planters Corp., and U.S. Bancorp.

Business Opportunities

Missouri offers a number of tax credits to attract industry: for infrastructure, transportation, or industrial development; for the rehabilitation of historic structures; for new enterprises; for R&D; for new or expanding businesses in enterprise zones; and for hiring long-time welfare recipients. The state also, in its attempt to target life-sciences companies, offers tax exemptions for purchases made by those companies.

Defense research accounts for most federal R&D funding in Missouri. Research centers include Barnes-Jewish Hospital, the Columbia Environmental Research Center, Engineered Air Systems Inc., McDonnell Douglas Corporation (now part of the Boeing Company), the Mid-Continent Mapping Center, the Midwest Research Institute, St. Louis University, the University of Missouri, and Washington University.

There are 13 *Fortune* 500 companies with their headquarters in Missouri: Utilicorp United, Emerson Electric, May Department Stores, Anheuser-Busch, Farmland Industries, Premcor, Express Scripts, Graybar Electric, Leggett & Platt, Ameren, Trans World Airlines, Interstate Bakeries, and Charter Communications.

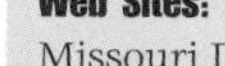

For More Information

Book:
Meyer, Duane G. *Heritage of Missouri.* Springfield, MO: Emden Press, 1998.

Web Sites:
Missouri Department of Economic Development:
www.ecodev.state.mo.us
Missouri State Homepage:
www.state.mo.us

Montana

KEY FACTS

State capital: **Helena**
Population: **902,195; 44th in U.S.; grew 12.9% 1990–2000**
Land area: **145,551.3 square miles; 4th in U.S.**
Population density: **6.2 per square mile**
GSP: **$20,636 million**
GSP pc: **$22,873.10**
Household income: **$32,045; 47th in U.S.**
Poverty rate: **16.0%**
Unemployment: **4.9%**

Economy

Historically, Montana's economy has relied on mining, starting with metals in the 19th century and moving on to coal, petroleum, and natural gas in the 20th. Mining is still an important sector of the economy, as are agriculture and forestry, its historical counterparts. Manufacturing is a relatively small sector as compared to other states, and is mainly confined to Montana's traditional industries: leading industries include lumber and wood, petroleum products, printing and publishing, and food products.

The services sector is now the largest, led by health services; tourism is also a significant contributor. There has been little development as yet in knowledge-based industries in the state.

Challenges facing Montana include the fact that it has the worst annual pay in the United States, low teacher salaries, a high unemployment rate, and limited development of new businesses. Lower shipping costs worldwide now force industries in the state to compete with global competitors, eliminating the market-cornering advantage of the state's relative isolation.

Geography/Resources

Montana is located in the northwestern United States. A section of the Rocky Mountains takes up the western two-fifths of the state, and the Great Plains account for the remainder.

Mineral resources include coal, natural gas, crude oil, palladium, copper, gold, Portland cement, molybdenum, talc, platinum, silver, crushed stone, lime, zinc, lead, bentonite, industrial garnets, and gemstones. Cattle and calves are the primary agricultural output; others include wheat, barley, hay, and dairy products. Forestry resources include fir, pine, spruce, hemlock, and cedar. Marine resources are trout, walleye, crappie, bass, stonecat, minnow, and chub.

The population is primarily Western European in origin, including people of British, Irish, German, French, Dutch, Scandinavian, and Polish descent; the state also has one of the largest Native American populations in the country. The 2000 census shows that 90.6% of the population is white; 6.2% Native American; and 2.0% Hispanic, of any race.

Billings is the largest city, with 129,352 people; other cities include Missoula, with 95,802 people, and Great Falls, with 80,357.

Environmental imperatives for Montana include: continuing to repair damage to the land, air, and groundwater from mining operations; restoring abandoned mine sites; and complying with EPA standards for the disposal of animal waste.

Communications/Energy

Montana has 125 public-use airports, seven of which—Billings Logan International Airport, Wokal Field/Glasgow International Airport, Great Falls International Airport, Glacier Park International Airport, Missoula International Airport, Whetstone International Airport, and Ross International Airport—are international. The state has 69,568.6 miles of roads and 3,301.5 miles of rail.

Digital infrastructure is primarily limited to metropolitan areas; the state had 7,378 high-speed lines as of 2000. In 2000, 95.1% of households had telephone service and 40.6% of households had Internet access.

Montana uses coal and petroleum in nearly equal measures, followed by hydroelectricity. Electric utilities depend on coal and hydroelectricity; the industrial sector relies primarily on petroleum. Most energy resources are produced within the state.

Fiscal/Financial

Montana has a fairly low per-capita state tax burden, and no general sales tax. Of state tax collected in 2000, 36.6% came from individual income tax; 24.4% from selective sales tax; 15.5% from property tax; 8.7% from license tax; 7.1% from corporate income tax; and 6.0% from severance tax. The corporate income tax rate is 6.75%.

Major financial institutions include Eagle Bancorp, Empire Federal Bancorp, Glacier Bancorp, Sterling Financial Corp., United Financial Corp., U.S. Bancorp, and Wells Fargo & Co.

Business Opportunities

Recent initiatives by the state to attract business have included lowering business equipment taxes, easing regulatory compliance, and improving access to long-term fixed-rate loans. The state offers tax credits for recycling, new and expanding industries, R&D, energy conservation, and mineral exploration; it offers reduced tax rates for oil, natural gas, and coal production.

Montana ranks near the bottom of the list in terms of federal spending on R&D; research centers include the McLaughlin Research Institute, Montana State University, Montec Associates, MSE Technologies, the Rocky Mountain Laboratories, and the University of Montana.

There are no *Fortune 500* companies with their headquarters in Montana.

For More Information

Books:

Morgan, Kathleen O. *Montana in Perspective 2001: A Statistical View of the Treasure State*. Lawrence, KS: Morgan Quitno Corp., 2001.
Toole, K. Ross. *20th Century Montana: A State of Extremes*. Norman, OK: University of Oklahoma Press, 1983.

Web Sites:

Montana Department of Commerce: **www.commerce.state.mt.us**
Montana State Homepage: **www.state.mt.us**
Montana Tourism: **www.visitmt.com**

NEBRASKA

KEY FACTS

State capital: **Lincoln**
Population: **1,711,263; 38th in U.S.; grew 8.4% 1990–2000**
Land area: **76,871.6 square miles; 15th in U.S.**
Population density: **22 per square mile**
GSP: **$53,744 million**
GSP pc: **$31,406.04**
Household income: **$38,574; 34th in U.S.**
Poverty rate: **10.6%**
Unemployment: **3.0%**

ECONOMY

Nebraska's traditional dependence on agriculture has given way to a service-based economy, though agriculture remains more important to the economy than in most states. The service sector is led by health services, followed by business services; business services include telemarketing, which is a growth industry in the state. The most significant segments of the manufacturing sector are food processing, electronic equipment, chemicals, and industrial machinery.

The state has targeted six industries it would like to attract or develop, based on its existing strengths: agribusiness, financial services, metal products, biotechnology, electronics manufacturing, and software development.

The most significant challenges facing Nebraska are the loss of youth throughout the state due to limited opportunities; another important consideration is Nebraska's lack of an entrepreneurial mindset. The state can offer new businesses little venture capital, few new investors, and only a vaguely articulated economic development plan. The state also needs to further develop its telecommunications infrastructure in rural areas.

GEOGRAPHY/RESOURCES

Located in the midwestern United States, Nebraska consists mainly of prairies, with two physical regions: the Central Lowlands and the Great Plains.

Agricultural output includes cattle and calves, corn, soybeans, hogs and pigs, wheat, hay, poultry and poultry products, dairy products, sorghum, and potatoes. Mineral resources are crude oil, Portland cement, sand and gravel, crushed stone, and uranium. Forestry resources are maple, beech, birch, pine, cottonwood, cherry, cedar, and mixed upland hardwoods. Marine resources are bass, perch, catfish, trout, sunfish, and chub.

Nebraska saw a wave of immigration from Germany, Scandinavia, Bohemia, and Great Britain in the mid-19th century, and these influences are still evident in the population. The 2000 census shows that 89.6% of the population is white; 5.5% Hispanic, of any race; 4.0% African American; and 1.3% Asian.

Omaha is the largest city, with 629,294 people; Lincoln has 250,291 people.

Environmental imperatives for Nebraska include improving the quality of surface water and groundwater, and compliance with new EPA regulations for disposal of waste from the livestock industry.

COMMUNICATIONS/ENERGY

Nebraska has 93 public airports, one of which—Omaha International Airport—is international. There are 19 barge terminal facilities operating on the Missouri River. There are 11 railroads operating 3,654.6 miles of rail, and 89,840.7 miles of roads.

Having deregulated its telecommunications industry in 1987, earlier than most states, Nebraska has a sophisticated network for a state with a relatively small high-tech industry; however, access varies by county to the 54,085 high-speed lines the state had as of 2000. In 2000, 98.1% of households had telephone service; 37.0% of households had Internet access; and 38.5% of the population had wireless telephones.

Petroleum is the most-used energy resource in Nebraska, followed by coal. Electric utilities are powered primarily by coal, with some use of nuclear energy; industrial energy use consists of natural gas and petroleum in nearly equal parts. Transportation depends almost solely on petroleum.

FISCAL/FINANCIAL

Nebraska's state tax burden is in line with other states in the region. Of state tax collected in 2000, 39.4% came from individual income tax; 34.5% from general sales tax; 14.0% from selective sales tax; 6.4% from license tax; and 4.7% from corporate income tax. The corporate income tax rate is in two brackets, from 5.58 to 7.81%.

Major financial institutions in Nebraska include Citigroup, Commercial Federal Corp., Community First Bankshares, Compass Bancshares, First National of Nebraska, J. P. Morgan Chase & Co., KeyCorp, Team Financial, UMB Financial Corp., U.S. Bancorp, and Wells Fargo & Co.

BUSINESS OPPORTUNITIES

Nebraska offers a few incentives to business, including tax credits and exemptions for new and expanding businesses, for R&D, and for companies engaged in data processing, telecommunications, insurance, or financial services. The state also offers low-interest financing for economic development.

Nebraska has little industry investment in R&D. Research centers include Creighton University, Duncan Aviation, the Roman L. Hruska U.S. Meat Animal Research Center, Sterling Software, and the University of Nebraska.

There are five *Fortune* 500 companies with their headquarters in Nebraska: Berkshire Hathaway, ConAgra, Union Pacific, Peter Kiewit Sons', and Mutual of Omaha Insurance.

For More Information

Book:

Olson, James C., and Ronald C. Naugle. *History of Nebraska*. Lincoln, NE: University of Nebraska Press, 1997.

Web Sites:

Nebraska Department of Economic Development: **www.neded.org**
Nebraska State Homepage: **www.state.ne.us**
Visit Nebraska: **www.visitnebraska.org**

Nevada

KEY FACTS

State capital: **Carson City**
Population: **1,998,257; 35th in U.S.; grew 66.3% 1990–2000**
Land area: **109,825.5 square miles; 7th in U.S.**
Population density: **18.2 per square mile**
GSP: **$69,864 million**
GSP pc: **$34,962.47**
Household income: **$44,755; 18th in U.S.**
Poverty rate: **10.0%**
Unemployment: **4.1%**

Economy

Nevada's mining boom in the mid-19th century, when silver and gold were discovered, gave way to a tourism boom in the 1930s, based on entertainment and legalized gambling, factors that still define the state's economy. Mining remains an important industry, and Nevada produces more gold than any other state. Agriculture, which is dependent on irrigation in this arid state, has never been a major contributor. The manufacturing sector, which expanded at the end of the 20th century but remains a minor part of the economy, is led by printed materials, food products, machinery, electronic equipment, and rubber and plastics.

The major challenge facing Nevada's economy is its dependence on outside factors, such as the national economy, which impacts levels of tourism, and the price of gold, which affects Nevada's mining industry. Nevada is attempting to remedy this problem by touting its favorable tax system and plentiful real estate to diversify the economy, especially by attracting high-tech companies from nearby Silicon Valley.

Geography/Resources

Located in the western United States, most of Nevada lies in the Great Basin region of the Basin and Range Province; there is also the Mojave Desert in the south, the Columbia Plateau in the northeast, and the Sierra Nevada mountain range in the southwest.

Gold is the primary mineral resource; others include silver, copper, sand and gravel, lime, crushed stone, Portland cement, diatomite, lithium minerals, magnesite, brucite, mercury, and crude oil. Forestry resources include pine, fir, and aspen. Marine resources are trout, bass, crappie, perch, sunfish, walleye, and wiper. Most of Nevada's agricultural output consists of livestock, primarily cattle and calves, pigs, and dairy products; the state also produces some hay, wheat, corn, potatoes, rye, oats, alfalfa, barley, and vegetables.

The initial population boom in Nevada occurred in the mid-19th century and was based around the mining industry. The 2000 census shows that 75.2% of the population is white; 19.7% Hispanic, of any race; 6.8% African American; 4.5% Asian; and 1.3% native American.

Las Vegas is the largest city, with 1,408,250 people, or 70% of the state's population. Reno has 339,486 people.

Environmental imperatives for Nevada include the reclamation of lands damaged by mining, limiting pollution in the face of the state's rapidly growing population, and preventing contamination of the state's groundwater from underground septic tanks.

Communications/Energy

Due to its size, Nevada is largely dependent on air travel; it has 98 airports, two of which—McCarran International Airport and Reno/Tahoe International Airport—are international. There are 1,272.5 miles of rail operated by 3 railroads, and 49,724.5 miles of roads.

Nevada was an early adopter of fiber optic technology and digital switching, and the state has an extensive network—albeit concentrated in urban areas—that included 59,879 high-speed lines as of 2000. It is being further developed by the high-tech companies that have come to Nevada from California in search of cheap real estate. In 2000, 95.4% of households had telephone service; 41.0% of households had Internet access; and 34.3% of the population had wireless telephones.

Petroleum is the most-used energy resource in Nevada, followed by coal and natural gas. Electric utilities are powered primarily by coal, with some use of natural gas; petroleum is used mainly for transportation.

Fiscal/Financial

Nevada has a favorable tax environment, with no corporate income tax, no personal income tax, no franchise tax on income, no inheritance or gift tax, and no admissions tax; there is a business tax of $25 per FTE per quarter. Of state tax collected in 2000, 52.2% came from general sales tax; 32.6% from selective sales tax; 9.8% from license tax; 2.5% from property tax; and 2.0% from death and gift tax.

Major financial institutions in Nevada include the Bank of America, Citigroup, Comerica, Golden West Financial Corp., Marshall & Ilsley Corp., Sun Community Bancorp, U.S. Bancorp, Washington Federal, Washington Mutual, Wells Fargo & Co., and Zions Bancorporation.

Business Opportunities

Nevada has begun offering a number of business incentives in an effort to diversity its economy, including a sales and use tax abatement on machinery and equipment, a sales tax deferral on some capital equipment, a business tax abatement for new and expanding industries, a property tax abatement for recycling businesses, job training, and industrial development bonds.

The majority of research funding in Nevada goes to energy-related projects. Research facilities include Bechtel, the Environmental Sciences Division, GPS Solutions, Hodges Transportation, Sierra Nevada Corp., and the University and Community College System of Nevada.

There are three *Fortune* 500 companies with their headquarters in Nevada: Park Place Entertainment, Harrah's Entertainment, and MGM Mirage.

For More Information

Book:

Burbank, Jeff. *License to Steal: Nevada's Gaming Control System in the Megaresort Age.* Revo, NV: University of Nevada Press, 2000.

Web Sites:

Nevada Commission on Economic Development:
www.expand2nevada.com
Nevada Commission on Tourism:
www.travelnevada.com
Nevada State Homepage:
www.state.nv.us

NEW HAMPSHIRE

KEY FACTS

State capital: **Concord**
Population: **1,235,786; 41st in U.S.; grew 11.4% 1990–2000**
Land area: **8,967.9 square miles; 44th in U.S.**
Population density: **137.8 per square mile**
GSP: **$44,229 million**
GSP pc: **$35,790.18**
Household income: **$48,928; 8th in U.S.**
Poverty rate: **7.4%**
Unemployment: **2.8%**

ECONOMY

Though New Hampshire's economy, formerly based on agriculture and manufacturing, became more diversified by the mid-20th century, manufacturing is still a larger sector of the economy than in many states. In the 1990s, the sector shifted from low-value-added nondurable goods, such as lumber and paper, to high-value-added durable goods, such as electronic and industrial equipment.

The finance, insurance, and real estate (FIRE) sector, however, is the largest, followed by the service sector, which is led by business and health services. Industries targeted for growth include electronic components, commercial physical research, printed circuit boards, computer programming and related services, employment agencies, and analytical instruments.

The major challenge facing New Hampshire is the shortage of labor, both skilled and unskilled; the state is addressing the problem with out-of-state recruitment and collaboration between businesses and the state's educational system to provide employers with needed workers.

GEOGRAPHY/RESOURCES

Located in the northeastern United States, New Hampshire consists of three physical regions: the Coastal Lowlands in the southeast, where the state borders the Atlantic; the Eastern New England Upland in the south; and the White Mountains Region in the north.

Forestry resources are maple, beech, birch, pine, hemlock, spruce, oak, ash, fir, aspen, and mixed upland hardwoods. Dairy products and nursery and greenhouse products are the primary agricultural output; there are some poultry and poultry products, fruits, vegetables, hay, and cattle and calves. Mineral resources are limited to sand and gravel, crushed stone, and granite. Marine resources are lobster, tuna, hake, cod, crabs, shrimp, trout, bass, mackerel, salmon, flounder, perch, pike, haddock, and crappie.

The original settlers in New Hampshire were English, followed by Scotch-Irish in the 18th century, French Canadians in the mid-19th century, and Central and Eastern Europeans throughout the 19th and 20th centuries. The 2000 census shows that 96.0% of the population is white; 1.7% Hispanic, of any race; and 1.3% Asian.

The Portsmouth/Rochester metro area is the largest in the state, with 199,323 people; other cities are Manchester (198,378) and Nashua (190,949).

Environmental imperatives for New Hampshire include preventing urban sprawl and loss of forest lands as the state's economy grows; upgrading wastewater treatment and sewage facilities; and reducing air pollutants blown in from states to the west and south as well as the state's own emissions of ozone.

COMMUNICATIONS/ENERGY

New Hampshire has 26 airports, one of which—Pease International Tradeport—is international. The Port of New Hampshire is the only port. The rail system, which has grown smaller throughout the second half of the 20th century, now consists of 14 railroads operating 459.2 miles of rail. There are 16,894.3 miles of roads.

New Hampshire has a fairly extensive telecommunications network; there were 42,364 high-speed lines as of 2000, though service is more easily available in urban areas than rural. In 2000, 98.0% of households had telephone service; 56.0% of households had Internet access (the highest in the United States); and 31.3% of the population had wireless telephones.

Petroleum is the primary source of energy in New Hampshire, followed by nuclear energy. The electric utilities are powered primarily by nuclear energy, followed by coal; the industrial sector uses wood and waste, petroleum, and hydroelectricity. Transportation is powered exclusively by petroleum.

FISCAL/FINANCIAL

New Hampshire has no general sales tax, use tax, capital gains tax, inventory tax, or property tax on machinery or equipment, and consequently has one of the lowest per-capita state tax burdens in the United States. Of state tax collected in 2000, 32.8% came from selective sales tax; 27.9% from property tax; 18.4% from corporate income tax; 8.4% from license tax; 5.0% from documentary and stock transfer tax; and 3.9% from individual income tax. The corporate income tax rate is 8.0%; there is a 0.5% business enterprise tax.

Major financial institutions in New Hampshire include Banknorth Group, Chittenden Corp., First Essex Bancorp, FleetBoston Financial Corp., Granite State Bankshares, KeyCorp, New Hampshire Thrift Bancshares, Northway Financial, Royal Bank of Scotland, Sovereign Bancorp, and Webster Financial Corp.

BUSINESS OPPORTUNITIES

In addition to low unemployment and workers' compensation tax rates, New Hampshire offers business incentives including credits against the business enterprise tax, loans to high-risk small businesses, tax credits for capital investment and job creation, tax-free industrial development bonds, and asset guarantee programs for financial institutions.

There are no *Fortune* 500 companies with their headquarters in New Hampshire.

New Hampshire has a solid base of R&D facilities, with a large portion of federal R&D spending going to defense research. Research centers include the Cold Regions Research and Engineering Laboratory, Creare Inc., Dartmouth College, Lockheed Sanders, Sonetech Corp., Telzen K.K., and the University of New Hampshire.

For More Information

Book:

Heffernan, Nancy Coffey, and Ann Page Stecker. *New Hampshire*. Hanover, NH: University Press of New England, 1996.

Web Sites:

New Hampshire Department of Resources and Economic Development:
www.dred.state.nh.us
New Hampshire Division of Travel & Tourism Development:
www.visitnh.gov
State of New Hampshire Homepage:
www.state.nh.us

  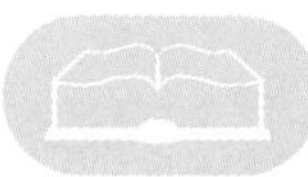    

New Jersey

KEY FACTS

State capital: **Trenton**
Population: **8,414,350; 9th in U.S.; grew 8.6% 1990–2000**
Land area: **7,413.9 square miles; 46th in U.S.**
Population density: **1,134.9 per square mile**
GSP: **$331,544 million**
GSP pc: **$39,402.21**
Household income: **$51,032; 2nd in U.S.**
Poverty rate: **8.1%**
Unemployment: **3.8%**

Economy

New Jersey has been primarily an industrial state throughout the 20th century, and was hit harder than many states by the recession in the early 1990s. Since then, it has completed the transition to a primarily service-oriented economy, driven by business services, health services, and tourism to the state's beaches; the finance, insurance, and real estate (FIRE) sector has grown in part owing to the state's proximity to New York City.

Manufacturing is still important to New Jersey's economy: The state ranks first in the United States in the manufacturing of pharmaceutical products; electronic equipment and food processing are also significant. Growing industries are telecommunications and biotechnology.

Challenges for the state include continuing to improve its business climate and tax structure, which impose a heavy burden on businesses locating there.

Geography/Resources

Located on the northeastern coast of the United States, New Jersey consists of four regions: the Ridge and Valley section in the northwest, the New England section which begins in the northeast and runs southwest, the central Piedmont, and the Atlantic Coastal Plain.

Nursery and greenhouse crops are the most profitable agricultural output; other produce includes tomatoes, blueberries, peaches, peppers, cranberries, soybeans, corn, wheat, barley, oats, poultry and poultry products, dairy products, cattle and calves, and hogs and pigs. Forestry resources are pine, oak, cedar, ash, elm, maple, and mixed upland hardwoods. Mineral resources are crushed stone, sand and gravel, peat, and greensand marl. Clams are the primary marine resource; others include scallops, squid, goosefish, crabs, flounder, lobster, mackerel, menhaden, tuna, swordfish, and oysters.

The 19th and early 20th centuries brought immigrants from all over Europe; blacks from the south came to the state during and after World War II, and many Puerto Ricans and Cubans immigrated during the second half of the 20th century. The 2000 census shows that 72.6% of the population is white; 13.6% African American; 13.3% Hispanic, of any race; and 5.7% Asian.

Newark is the largest city, with 2,032,989 people; others include the Bergen/Passaic metro area (1,373,167); the Middlesex/Somerset/Hunterdon metro area (1,169,641); the Monmouth/Ocean City metro area (1,126,217); and Jersey City (608,975).

While the quality of New Jersey's air and water improved during the 1980s and 1990s, pollution control is an ongoing concern due to the state's high population density, level of industrial activity, and proximity to major cities.

Communications/Energy

New Jersey has 49 public-use airports, two of which—Newark International Airport and Atlantic City International Airport—are international. There are 76 ports and terminals, the largest of which are Newark-Elizabeth and Camden. 1,600.7 miles of track serve New Jersey's passenger rail service, freight railroads, a metro link to New York City, and commuter railways around Newark, and there are 35,015.9 miles of roads.

New Jersey has a sophisticated telecommunications network, with 285,311 high-speed lines as of 2000. In 2000, 94.5% of households had telephone service; 47.8% of households had Internet access; and 42.5% of the population had wireless telephones.

Petroleum is the most-used resource in New Jersey, followed by natural gas and nuclear energy. Electric utilities are powered primarily by nuclear energy.

Fiscal/Financial

Despite some tax reform in the 1990s, New Jersey still has a fairly high per-capita state tax burden. Of state tax collected in 2000, 39.7% came from individual income tax; 30.4% from general sales tax; 14.8% from selective sales tax; 7.4% from corporate income tax; and 4.4% from license tax. The corporate income tax rate is 9.0% (7.5% for corporations with net income less than $100,000).

Major financial institutions include Chase Manhattan Bank, Community Bancorp of New Jersey, First Sentinel Bancorp, First Union Corp., FleetBoston Financial, Golden West Financial Corp., Liberty Bancorp, OceanFirst Financial Corporation, the PNC Financial Services Group, Sovereign Bancorp, and the Trust Company of New Jersey.

Business Opportunities

New Jersey offers a number of business incentives, including tax credits for new-job creation, investing in enterprise zones, R&D, high-tech business investment, redevelopment of underused areas, ride-sharing, and childcare.

The state has a solid network of technological and pharmaceutical research facilities, including the Center for Communications Research, Computer Sciences Corporation, the Garden State Cancer Center, the Institute for Advanced Study, Lockheed Martin Corporation, the Princeton Plasma Physics Laboratory, Princeton University, Rutgers University, Sarnoff Corporation, and the William J. Hughes Technical Center.

The top 20 *Fortune* 500 companies with their headquarters in New Jersey are Lucent Technologies, Merck, Johnson & Johnson, Honeywell International, Prudential Insurance Company of America, Pharmacia, American Home Products, Toys 'R' Us, Schering-Plough, Ingersoll-Rand, American Standard, Chubb, Public Service Enterprise Group, Automatic Data Processing, Campbell Soup, Engelhard, GPU, Foster Wheeler, Pathmark Stores, and Becton Dickinson.

For More Information

Book:

Lurie, Maxine N., ed. *A New Jersey Anthology*. Newark, NJ: New Jersey Historical Society, 1994.

Web Sites:

New Jersey Commerce and Economic Growth Commission:
www.newjerseycommerce.org
State of New Jersey Homepage:
www.state.nj.us

New Mexico

KEY FACTS

State capital: **Santa Fe**
Population: **1,819,046; 36th in U.S.; grew 20.1% 1990–2000**
Land area: **121,355.4 square miles; 5th in U.S.**
Population density: **14.9 per square mile**
Household income: **$35,254; 43rd in U.S.**
Poverty rate: **19.3%**
GSP: **$51,026 million**
GSP pc: **$28,050.97**
Unemployment: **4.9%**

Economy

New Mexico's mining sector is on the decline owing to rising costs and reduced profits, though it still contributes more to GSP than in most states. Manufacturing declined from 1997 to 1999, but electric and electronic manufacturing companies should bring this sector new growth. The service sector, which is the largest in the state, is led by health and business services.

The state has also become an important research center, beginning with federal nuclear R&D and expanding into commercial research. Technology clusters have emerged in microelectronics, information technology, optoelectronics, biomedicine and biotechnology, and advanced materials.

A major challenge facing New Mexico is the dichotomy between the relatively high percentage of science and engineering professionals and the percentage of the population that lives in poverty. The state plans to increase education budgets and to bring Internet access to every community.

Geography/Resources

New Mexico, located in the southwestern United States with part of its southern border adjoining Mexico, has the Great Plains in the eastern third of the state, the Rocky Mountains in the central third, and mountainous plateaus in the western third.

Agricultural exports from New Mexico include cattle and calves, dairy products, other livestock and livestock products, hay, vegetables, and fruits. While crude oil and gas are the most important mineral resources, the state also produces coal, potash, uranium, silver, and copper.

New Mexico was home to several Native American tribes before the arrival of Spanish colonists, and both facets of this history are still evident in the state's demographics. 66.8% of the population is white; 42.1% is Hispanic, of any race; 9.5% is Native American; 1.9% is African American; and 1.1% is Asian. Albuquerque is home to nearly 40% of the population, or 712,738 people; other major cities include Las Cruces (174,6820) and Santa Fe (147,635).

The primary environmental issues in New Mexico, such as contaminated groundwater, are the result of former mining, milling, oil and gas production, and manufacturing sites. The Environmental Protection Agency has offered New Mexico federal assistance in cleaning up and redeveloping these sites.

Communications/Energy

New Mexico has two international airports, in Albuquerque and Las Cruces, in addition to three cross-border points of entry to Mexico at Santa Teresa, Antelope Wells, and Columbus. There are two mainline and three short-line railroads operating 1,868.5 miles of rail, and 61,316.6 miles of roads, including three interstate highways.

There are more than 900 high-tech companies in New Mexico, which have contributed to its infrastructure; however, the state had only 28,497 high-speed lines as of 2000. In 2000, 91.3% of households had telephone service; 35.7% of households had Internet access; and 24.4% of the population had wireless telephones.

New Mexico ranks third in the country in natural gas production, seventh in oil production, and twelfth in coal production. Its electric utilities depend on coal, natural gas, and a small amount of hydroelectricity. Twenty of New Mexico's 33 counties have geothermal energy sources, and the state is also developing its solar, wind, biomass, and hydropower energy potential.

Fiscal/Financial

New Mexico's tax incentives include no tax on 800/WATS and other private communications services, and a corporate tax credit of 30% of the cost of daycare provided by corporations. Of state taxes collected in 2000, 40.1% came from general sales tax; 23.5% from individual income tax; 13.5% from selective sales tax; 11.7% from severance tax; 5.5% from license tax; and 4.3% from corporate income tax. The state corporate income tax rate is 4.8–7.6%, in three brackets.

Major financial institutions in the state include the Bank of America, BOK Financial Corp., Community First National Bank, Compass Bancshares, Los Alamos National Bank, Sun Community Bancorp, Wells Fargo & Co., and Zions Bancorporation.

Business Opportunities

In an attempt to alleviate the state's high unemployment rate, New Mexico has created the Industrial Development Training Program, which provides funding to new or expanding businesses that are willing to hire and train residents of the state as employees.

The primary draw for business in New Mexico is the state's extensive research facilities. Major research centers include the Air Force Research Laboratory Directed Energy Directorate, Sandia National Laboratories, White Sands Test Facility, the Jornada Experimental Range, Los Alamos National Laboratory, White Sands Missile Range, the University of New Mexico, New Mexico State University, New Mexico Highlands University, and the New Mexico Institute of Mining and Technology.

There are no *Fortune* 500 companies with their headquarters in New Mexico.

For More Information

Books:

New Mexico Investment and Business Guide. International Business Publications USA, 2001.

Morgan, Kathleen O. *New Mexico in Perspective 2001: A Statistical View of the Land of Enchantment State*. Lawrence, KS: Morgan Quitno Corp, 2001.

Web Sites:

New Mexico Department of Tourism: **www.newmexico.org**

New Mexico Economic Development Department: **www.edd.state.nm.us**

New Mexico State Homepage: **www.state.nm.us**

  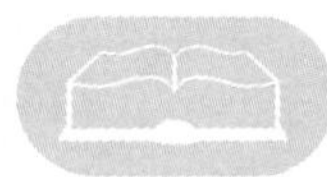    

New York

KEY FACTS

State capital: **Albany**
Population: **18,976,457; 3rd in U.S.; grew 5.5% 1990–2000**
Land area: **47,196.4 square miles; 30th in U.S.**
Population density: **402 per square mile**
GSP: **$754,590 million**
GSP pc: **$39,764.54**
Household income: **$41,605; 26th in U.S.**
Poverty rate: **14.7%**
Unemployment: **4.6%**

Economy

New York's central location on the eastern seaboard has made the state a center of commerce since its founding. Agriculture, which contributed historically to the economy, has been greatly reduced. The state's economy is now highly diversified, with the upstate region dependent on manufacturing, including scientific instruments, electrical equipment, machinery, clothing, fabricated metal products, food products, paper products, and transportation equipment.

New York City, in the south, is service-oriented. Finance, insurance, and real estate (FIRE), which constitute the largest segment of the state's economy, are mainly focused in New York City. Other major service industries include travel and tourism, business services, and health services. Printing and publishing and communications also contribute to the city's economy.

Challenges for New York include compensating for the job losses upstate in the 1980s and 1990s, primarily in manufacturing, and further reducing the tax burden on businesses and individuals.

Geography/Resources

Located in the eastern United States, New York consists of nine geographic regions: the Adirondack Upland in the northeast, the St. Lawrence Lowlands along the northern border, the Hudson-Mohawk Lowland on the west bank of the Hudson River, the New England Upland on the east bank of the Hudson, the Atlantic Coastal Plain on Long Island and Staten Island, the Piedmont on the southernmost west bank of the Hudson, the Appalachian Highlands that extend west from the Hudson-Mohawk Lowland to cover half of the state, the Erie-Ontario Lowlands north of the Appalachian Highlands, and the Tug Hill Upland in the northwest.

Dairy products are New York's primary agricultural output; other produce includes nursery and greenhouse crops, fruits and vegetables, wheat, cattle and calves, and poultry and poultry products. Forestry resources are maple, beech, birch, pine, cedar, oak, hemlock, spruce, and mixed upland hardwoods. Marine resources are lobster, clams, squid, hake, flounder, tilefish, tuna, bass, and goosefish. Mineral resources include crude oil, natural gas, crushed stone, salt, Portland cement, sand and gravel, zinc, wollastonite, industrial garnet, talc, and limestone.

New York has always been a gateway for immigrants of all nations. The 2000 census shows that 67.9% of the population is white; 15.9% African American; 15.1% Hispanic, of any race; and 5.5% Asian.

With nearly two-thirds of the state's population, the New York City metro area is the largest in New York with 12,348,298 people. Other major cities include the Buffalo/Niagara Falls metro area (1,170,111); Rochester (1,098,201); the Albany/Schenectady/Troy metro area (875,583); Syracuse (732,117); Newburgh (341,367); the Utica/Rome metro area (299,896); and Binghamton (252,320).

Environmental imperatives for New York include upgrading outdated sewage treatment plants, increasing solid waste recycling, closing environmentally unsound landfills, and improving air quality.

Communications/Energy

New York has 147 public-use airports, of which nine—Albany International Airport, Buffalo Niagara International Airport, Greater Rochester International Airport, John F. Kennedy International Airport, Massena International Airport, Ogdensburg International Airport, Stewart International Airport, Syracuse Hancock International Airport, and Watertown International Airport—are international. There are 33 ports; the major ones are the Port of New York and New Jersey, Albany, Buffalo, Hempstead Harbor, and Port Jefferson. There are 112,766.6 miles of roads and 4,616 miles of rail, in addition to metro rail systems.

New York's telecommunications infrastructure reflects the economic divisions between the cities and rural areas. While the state had 603,487 high-speed lines in 2000, they were largely concentrated in urban areas. In 2000, 96.1% of households had telephone service; 39.8% of households had Internet access; and 30.2% of the population had wireless telephones.

Petroleum is the most-used energy source in New York, followed by natural gas. Electric utilities are powered primarily by nuclear energy, followed by hydroelectricity and natural gas; petroleum is used primarily for transportation purposes.

Fiscal/Financial

Despite tax cuts in the late 1990s, New York still has a fairly high per-capita state tax burden. Of state tax collected in 2000, 55.6% came from individual income tax; 20.5% from general sales tax; 11.4% from selective sales tax; 6.6% from corporate income tax; 2.5% from death and gift tax; and 2.3% from license tax. The corporate income tax rate is 8.0% (7.5% for corporations whose income is less than $200,000).

New York is a global financial capital, with representatives from most of the world's major financial institutions. They include the Bank of America, Bank of New York, Brown Brothers Harriman & Co., Canadian Imperial Bank of Commerce, Citigroup, Comerica, The Dai-Ichi Kangyo Bank, Deutsche Bank AG, First Union Corp., Goldman Sachs Group, HSBC Bank USA, J. P. Morgan Chase, Lehman Brothers Holdings, M&T Bank Corp., Merrill Lynch, Morgan Stanley Dean Witter, North Fork Bancorporation, and UBS AG.

Business Opportunities

New York reduced workers' compensation and unemployment insurance costs in the 1990s and streamlined regulatory processes. The state offers diverse incentives to business, including: tax credits for investment, R&D, and development in enterprise zones; sales tax exemptions; property tax abatement; no personal property tax; and special incentives for businesses in industries including technology, banking, insurance, and telecommunications.

The top 20 *Fortune* 500 companies with their headquarters in New York are Citigroup, International Business Machines (IBM), AT&T, Verizon Communications, Philip Morris, J. P. Morgan Chase, Texaco, American International Group, Morgan Stanley Dean Witter, Merrill Lynch, TIAA-CREF, Goldman Sachs Group, MetLife, Pfizer, International Paper, Lehman Brothers Holdings, American Express, New

York Life Insurance, Bristol-Myers Squibb, and Loews.

The majority of federal research spending in New York is split between health and human services, defense, and energy. Research facilities include the Albert Einstein College of Medicine, the Benet Laboratories, the Brookhaven National Laboratory, Cold Spring Harbor Laboratory, Columbia University, Cornell University, General Electric, the Goddard Institute for Space Studies, Health Research Inc., ITT Industries, Lockheed Martin, the Memorial Sloan-Kettering Cancer Center, Mount Sinai School of Medicine, New York University, Northrop Grumman, the Research Foundation for Mental Hygiene, Rockefeller University, the State University of New York, and the University of Rochester.

For More Information

Books:

Klein, Milton M., ed. *The Empire State: A History of New York*. Ithaca, NY: Cornell University Press, 2001.

Morgan, Kathleen O. *New York in Perspective 2001: A Statistical View of the Empire State*. Lawrence, KS: Morgan Quitno Corp., 2001.

Web Sites:

Empire State Development: **www.empire.state.ny.us**

New York State Homepage: **www.state.ny.us**

New York Tourism: **www.iloveny.state.ny.us**

  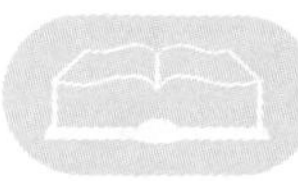    

North Carolina

KEY FACTS

State capital: **Raleigh**
Population: **8,049,313; 11th in U.S.; grew 21.4% 1990–2000**
Land area: **48,710.7 square miles; 29th in U.S.**
Population density: **165.2 per square mile**
GSP: **$258,592 million**
GSP pc: **$32,125.97**
Household income: **$38,829; 32nd in U.S.**
Poverty rate: **13.2%**
Unemployment: **3.6%**

Economy

North Carolina's agricultural economy, developed around cotton, tobacco, rice, and indigo in colonial times, prevailed until the early 20th century, when manufacturing, especially textiles, became the dominant economic sector. It still plays a significant role, driven by electronic equipment, chemicals, tobacco products, apparel and textiles, motor vehicles, and rubber and plastics. Health, business, and educational services are expected to be the major growth drivers in the service sector in the early part of the second millennium; other clusters targeted for growth are metalworking, vehicle manufacturing, electronics and computers, printing and publishing, and packaged foods.

The challenges facing North Carolina's economy are: a low level of education among the workforce as a result of North Carolina's history as a low-wage, low-skill economy; an inadequate telecommunications infrastructure in rural areas; and low rates of capital investment.

Geography/Resources

Located on the southeastern coast of the United States, North Carolina consists of three physical regions: the Atlantic Coastal Plain, the hilly Piedmont in the central part of the state, and the Mountain Region in the west.

Agricultural output includes pigs, poultry products, tobacco, nursery and greenhouse crops, cotton, soybeans, corn, dairy products, cattle, wheat, vegetables, sweet potatoes, and peanuts. Mineral resources are crushed stone, phosphate rock, sand and gravel, feldspar, mica, pyrophyllite, clay, olivine, gemstones, and dimension stone. Forestry resources are pine, mixed upland hardwoods, oak, hickory, sweetgum, poplar, sweetbay, and maple. Crabs are the primary marine resource; others are flounder, clams, croaker, menhaden, tuna, mackerel, mullet, snapper, spot, bluefish, trout, swordfish, oysters, bass, and anglerfish.

North Carolina has been populated by the descendants of Europeans—especially Germans, English, Irish, and Scotch-Irish—and by African Americans since the 17th century. The 2000 census shows that 72.1% of the population is white; 21.6% African American; 4.7% Hispanic, of any race; 1.4% Asian; and 1.2% Native American.

The Charlotte metro area is the largest in the state, with 1,334,679 people. Other major cities include the Greensboro/Winston-Salem metro area (1,251,509); the Raleigh-Durham/Chapel Hill metro area (1,187,941); the Hickory/Morganton/Lenoir metro area (341,851); Fayetteville (302,963); Wilmington (233,450); and Asheville (225,965).

Environmental imperatives for North Carolina include reducing agricultural and urban pollution in the state's water and protecting coastal ecosystems.

Communications/Energy

North Carolina has 82 public airports, three of which—Raleigh-Durham International Airport, Piedmont Triad International Airport, and Charlotte International Airport—are international. There are 2 deepwater ports, at Wilmington and Morehead City. There are 26 railroads operating 3,285.4 miles of rail, and 96,852.9 miles of roads.

Though the Research Triangle area of North Carolina is a home to high technology and is one of the most wired regions in the United States, telecommunications infrastructure is inadequate in most rural areas of the state, though there were 136,981 high-speed lines in 2000. In 2000, 93.5% of households had telephone service; 35.3% of households had Internet access; and 38.6% had wireless telephones.

Petroleum is the most-used energy source in North Carolina, followed by coal. The electric utilities are powered primarily by coal, with some use of nuclear energy; the industrial sector makes use of petroleum and natural gas.

Fiscal/Financial

North Carolina has a higher per-capita state tax burden than most of the surrounding states. Of state tax collected in 2000, 46.6% came from individual income tax; 22.1% from general sales tax; 17.5% from selective sales tax; 6.5% from corporate income tax; and 6.0% from license tax. The corporate income tax is 6.9%.

North Carolina is a banking center for the southeast. Major financial institutions include Bank of America, Bank of Granite Corp., BB&T Corp., Comerica, First Citizens BancShares, First Union Corp., Peoples Bancorp of North Carolina, and SouthTrust Corp.

Business Opportunities

North Carolina provides several incentives to business, including: tax credits for job creation, investment, worker training, and R&D; industrial revenue bonds for some manufacturing companies; business energy loans for facilities or projects that demonstrate energy efficiency; a fund to build roads that provide access to new facilities; and grant funding to finance railroad access tracks required by a new or expanded industry.

North Carolina has an established research community, dedicated to high technology in some areas and health and human services in others. Research centers include Digital Optics Corp., Duke University, Family Health International, the National Exposure Research Laboratory, the National Health and Environmental Effects Research Laboratory, the National Institute of Environmental Health Sciences, North Carolina State University, NSI Technology Services Corp., the Research Triangle Institute, and the University of North Carolina.

There are 13 *Fortune* 500 companies with their headquarters in North Carolina: the Bank of America Corp., Duke Energy, First Union Corp., Lowe's, R.J. Reynolds Tobacco, Wachovia Corp., Sonic Automotive, VF, B. F. Goodrich, BB&T Corp., Nucor, Progress Energy, and Jefferson-Pilot.

For More Information

Book:

Gaddy, Charlie. *Celebrating a Triangle Millennium*. Memphis, TN: Towery Publications, 1999.

Web Sites:

North Carolina Department of Commerce: **www.nccommerce.com**
State of North Carolina Homepage: **www.ncgov.com**

NORTH DAKOTA

KEY FACTS

State capital: **Bismarck**
Population: **642,200; 47th in U.S.; grew 0.5% 1990–2000**
Land area: **68,975.6 square miles; 17th in U.S.**
Population density: **9.3 per square mile**
GSP: **$16,991 million**
GSP pc: **$26,457.49**
Household income: **$35,349; 42nd in U.S.**
Poverty rate: **12.7%**
Unemployment: **3.0%**

ECONOMY

North Dakota's agricultural history is still in evidence, although mechanized farming and large holdings have largely replaced the traditional family farm. Mining remains an important industry, as it has been since the discovery of oil in the state in the mid-20th century. Manufacturing accounts for a relatively small percentage of the economy, led by industrial machinery, food products, motor vehicles, and printing and publishing. The service sector, led by health services, is the largest; the government sector is also important, owing in part to the presence of military bases.

North Dakota's attempts to diversify its economy have included targeting certain industries for growth and development, including: food processing; industrial and agricultural equipment manufacturing; electronics manufacturing; and information technology, including computer programming services, software manufacturing, electronic commerce, and shared service centers.

Despite economic development efforts in the latter half of the 1990s, the challenges facing North Dakota include a low rate of job creation, low-paying existing jobs, a need to diversify the economy, and a lack of venture capital.

GEOGRAPHY/RESOURCES

Located in the northwestern United States, North Dakota is divided into two physiographical regions: the Central Lowlands in the eastern half of the state and the Great Plains in the western half.

Crude oil is the primary mineral resource; others include coal, natural gas, sand and gravel, clay, crushed stone, scoria, leonardite, and uranium. Marine resources include salmon, catfish, perch, paddlefish, bass, bluegill, crappie, muskellunge, sauger, and trout. Wheat is the primary agricultural output; others include cattle and calves, soybeans, barley, corn, dairy products, hay, rye, and oats. Forestry resources are maple, aspen, and mixed hardwoods.

North Dakota's population still shows evidence of the French, Scottish, English, and Canadian immigrants who settled the state in the 18th century and the Norwegians and Germans who came in the 19th century. The 2000 census shows that 92.4% of the population is white; 4.9% Native American; and 1.2% Hispanic, of any race.

The Fargo metro area is the largest in the state, with 123,138 people. Other significant cities include Bismarck (94,719) and Grand Forks (66,109).

Environmental imperatives for North Dakota include proper disposal of hazardous waste, maintenance of underground storage tanks, and water conservation.

COMMUNICATIONS/ENERGY

North Dakota has 92 public-use airports, of which four—Grand Forks International Airport, Hector International Airport, Minot International Airport, and Sloulin Field International Airport—are international. There are five railroads operating 3,859.7 miles of rail, and 86,847.4 miles of roads.

North Dakota has begun to develop a solid digital infrastructure, with 61,180 km of fiber optic cable. High-speed access, however, is mainly limited to the urban areas, with only 6,380 high-speed lines as of 2000. In 2000, 94.8% of households had telephone service and 37.7% of households had Internet access, as did more than 90% of the state's schools.

Coal is the primary energy resource used in North Dakota. Electric utilities rely primarily on coal, with some use of hydroelectricity; the industrial sector uses coal and petroleum.

FISCAL/FINANCIAL

The corporate income tax rates in North Dakota have been the same since 1983, and unemployment taxes were reduced in the 1990s. Of state tax collected in 2000, 28.2% came from general sales tax; 27.7% from selective sales tax; 16.9% from individual income tax; 12.3% from severance tax; 7.4% from license tax; and 6.7% from corporate income tax. The corporate income tax rate is from 3.0 to 10.5%, in six brackets; for financial institutions, the rate is 7%.

Major financial institutions include Bank of North Dakota, BNCCORP, Community First Bankshares, First International Bank and Trust, First Southwest Bank Holding Co., First State Bank, Security First Bank of North Dakota, Security State Bank of ND, United Community Bank of North Dakota, U.S. Bancorp, Wells Fargo & Co., and Western State Bank.

BUSINESS OPPORTUNITIES

Recognizing the need to diversify the state's economy, North Dakota has offered a number of incentives to business, including: job training assistance; property tax exemptions for new and expanding businesses; sales and use tax exemptions for building materials used to construct agricultural commodity processing facilities; no sales and use tax on processing and manufacturing machinery or equipment; corporate income tax exemption for some primary-sector businesses; and assistance with financing, including the North Dakota Development Fund.

There is little R&D activity in North Dakota, and much of research that does take place is related to agriculture. Research centers include Blue Cross/Blue Shield of North Dakota, the Grand Forks Human Nutrition Research Center, North Dakota State University, the Red River Valley Agricultural Research Center, the University of North Dakota, and Wheeler Contracting.

There are no *Fortune* 500 companies with their headquarters in North Dakota.

For More Information

Book:
Robinson, Elwyn B. *History of North Dakota*. North Dakota Institute for Regional Studies, 1995.

Web Sites:
North Dakota State Homepage: **www.state.nd.us**
North Dakota Economic Development and Finance: **www.growingnd.com**
North Dakota Travel and Tourism: **www.ndtourism.com**

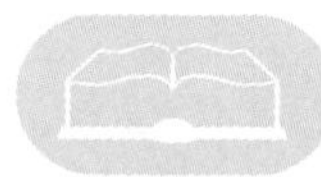

OHIO

KEY FACTS

State capital: **Columbus**
Population: **11,353,140; 7th in U.S.; grew 4.7% 1990–2000**
Land area: **40,947.8 square miles; 35th in U.S.**
Population density: **277.2 per square mile**
GSP: **$361,981 million**
GSP pc: **$31,883.78**
Household income: **$43,894; 19th in U.S.**
Poverty rate: **11.1%**
Unemployment: **4.1%**

ECONOMY

By the early 19th century Ohio's economy was no longer solely agricultural, but already included mining; in the early 20th century it was dominated by manufacturing. The globalization pressure and increased competition facing the primary manufacturing industries have caused Ohio's growth rate to lag behind the nation's. The service sector is driven by health and business services.

Ohio is targeting a number of industries to retain and develop in order to boost the state's economic growth. They include: metal- and material-working; advanced manufacturing equipment; transportation equipment; information and knowledge-based industries; advanced medicine and services; agriculture, natural resources, and environmental industries; finance and real estate; the infrastructure, engineering and architecture industries; and travel, tourism, entertainment, and leisure.

The challenges facing Ohio include an unequal distribution of incentive dollars, which are mainly received by manufacturing industry, and a limited supply of skilled and technical labor, which the state is attempting to remedy through education initiatives.

GEOGRAPHY/RESOURCES

Located in the midwestern United States, Ohio is divided into two parts. The Appalachian Plateau covers the eastern half of the state, and the western half consists of the Central Lowlands, which are also divided in two parts: the Lake Plains in the east and the Central Plains in the west.

Agricultural output consists of soybeans, corn, hay, wheat, barley, oats, tobacco, vegetables, poultry products, dairy products, pigs, and cattle. Coal is the primary mineral output: others include oil, gas, crushed stone, sand and gravel, limestone, Portland cement, and salt. Forestry resources are maple, beech, birch, oak, hickory, poplar, ash, elm, cherry, sycamore, and mixed upland hardwoods. Marine resources are perch, bass, whitefish, carp, walleye, trout, and catfish.

The earliest settlers in Ohio were primarily Scotch-Irish immigrants from the eastern seaboard; immigrants from all over Europe as well as Asia and Latin America began appearing after 1880. The black population also grew significantly in the late 19th and early 20th centuries. The 2000 census shows that 85% of the population is white; 11.5% African American; 1.9% Hispanic, of any race; and 1.2% Asian.

The Cleveland/Akron metro area is the largest in Ohio, with 2,945,831 people. Other significant cities include: the Cincinnati metro area (1,979,202); Columbus (1,540,157); the Dayton/Springfield metro area (950,558); Toledo (618,203); the Youngstown/Warren metro area (594,746); and the Canton/Massillon metro area (406,934).

Environmental imperatives include improving the state's air, water, and soil, which have been damaged by decades of heavy industry in Ohio.

COMMUNICATIONS/ENERGY

Ohio has 165 public airports, four of which—Rickenbacker, Dayton, Cleveland-Hopkins, and Columbus—are international. There are 9 commercial ports on Lake Erie. There are 116,271.5 miles of roads, and 32 railroads operate on 5,802.6 miles of track.

Ohio's cities are mainly wired for high-speed access, with 223,845 high-speed telephone lines as of 2000, but rural areas lag severely behind. In 2000, 94.8% of households had telephone service; 40.7% of households had Internet access; and 35.1% of the population had wireless telephones.

Ohio consumes coal and petroleum in nearly equal measures, followed by natural gas; most oil and gas are imported. Electric utilities are powered mainly by coal, with some use of nuclear energy. There is some industrial use of wood and waste.

FISCAL/FINANCIAL

Ohio is a higher-cost state in which to conduct business than many of those with which it regularly competes. It has relied on an economic development strategy based on incentives to counteract the high costs of its business taxes. Of state tax collected in 2000, 41.9% came from individual income tax; 31.8% from general sales tax; 14.2% from selective sales tax; 7.9% from license tax; and 3.2% from corporate income tax. The corporate tax rate is 5.1–8.5%.

Major financial institutions in Ohio include Bank One Corp., Citigroup, Comerica, Fifth Third Bancorp, Huntington Bancshares, KeyCorp, MBNA Corporation, Merrill Lynch, National City Corp., Old National Bancorp, Sky Financial Group, U.S. Bancorp, and Wells Fargo & Co.

BUSINESS OPPORTUNITIES

Incentives to business in Ohio include enterprise zones, tax credits for job creation and machinery and equipment, business development grants and loans, roadwork development grants, industrial jobs training, community reinvestment areas, and tax increment financing districts.

A great deal of research in Ohio focuses on defense and aerospace. Research centers include Battelle Memorial Institute, Case Western Reserve University, Camp Inc., the Cleveland Clinic Foundation, General Electric, the Glenn Research Center, Lockheed Martin, the Medical College of Ohio, the National Risk Management Research Laboratory, Ohio State University, Systems Research Laboratory, the University of Cincinnati, the University of Dayton, and Wright State University.

The top *Fortune* 500 companies with their headquarters in Ohio include Kroger, Procter & Gamble, Cardinal Health, Federated Department Stores, TRW, Goodyear Tire & Rubber, American Electric Power, Eaton, KeyCorp, Cinergy, FirstEnergy, Progressive, NCR, Owens-Illinois, Parker Hannifin, and Sherwin-Williams.

For More Information

Book:
Ohio Investment and Business Guide. International Business Publications USA, 2001.

Web Sites:
Ohio Department of Development: **www.odod.state.oh.us**
Ohio State Homepage: **www.state.oh.us**

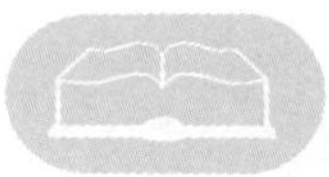

Oklahoma

KEY FACTS

State capital: **Oklahoma City**
Population: **3,450,654; 27th in U.S.; grew 9.7% 1990–2000**
Land area: **68,666.6 square miles; 19th in U.S.**
Population density: **50.2 per square mile**
GSP: **$86,382 million**
GSP pc: **$25,033.52**
Household income: **$32,445; 46th in U.S.**
Poverty rate: **14.1%**
Unemployment: **3.0%**

Economy

While Oklahoma reduced its traditional dependence on agriculture and mining in the 1990s, those sectors still contribute more to Oklahoma's economy than they do to the economies of most states. The manufacturing sector has grown, led by machinery, including oilfield machinery, construction machinery, and refrigeration and heating equipment, and with electrical equipment, transportation equipment, fabricated metal products, food products, and rubber and plastic products also featuring strongly. The services sector is slightly larger than the manufacturing sector, led by health and business services.

Initiatives for economic development include further expansion of the manufacturing sector, as well as increased tourism. The challenges facing Oklahoma in pursuing these goals include the need to increase capital investment, especially in manufacturing, and a digital infrastructure that lags behind that of most states.

Geography/Resources

Located in the southern central United States, Oklahoma is a motley collection of physiographic types, with ten subregions contained in the three major regions: the Interior Highlands in the east, the Coastal Plain in the south, and the Interior Plains covering the rest of the state.

Cattle and calves are the primary agricultural resource; others include wheat, poultry and poultry products, pigs, dairy products, corn, sorghum, hay, pecans, peanuts, peaches, and nursery and greenhouse crops. Mineral resources are natural gas, crude oil, coal, crushed stone, Portland cement, sand and gravel, gypsum, clay, helium, iodine, salt, tripoli, and feldspar. Marine resources are crappie, catfish, bluegill, trout, bass, sunfish, saugeye, and walleye. The primary forestry resources are oak, hickory, and pine.

Oklahoma's homesteading origins have contributed to a diverse population, with immigrants from Asia and Latin America as well as Europe settling in the late 19th and early 20th centuries. The 2000 census shows that 76.2% of the population is white; 7.9% Native American; 7.6% African American; 5.2% Hispanic, of any race; and 1.4% Asian.

Oklahoma City is the largest metropolitan area, with 1,083,346 people. Other major cities include Tulsa (803,235), Lawton (114,996), and Enid (57,813).

Environmental imperatives for Oklahoma include water conservation, the reclamation of land damaged by mining, the reduction of chemicals in the environment from pesticides and fertilizers, and the reduction of runoff from urban developments into the water supply.

Communications/Energy

One of Oklahoma's advantages is its location: equidistant from New York City and Los Angeles, Mexico and Canada. The state has 159 public airports, of which two—Will Rogers World Airport and Tulsa International Airport—are international. There are two ports, Catoosa and Muskogee, on the McClellan-Kerr Waterway. Oklahoma has 14 railroads operating on 3,868.7 miles of track, and 112,085.9 miles of roads.

Oklahoma began an initiative in 1992 to develop its telecommunications infrastructure and bring high-speed communications to public schools, colleges and universities, public libraries, government, court systems, rural health care delivery systems, and research programs. As of 2000, however, Oklahoma had only 95,138 high-speed lines. In 2000, 90.3% of households had telephone service; 34.3% of households had Internet access; and 65.8% of the population had wireless telephones.

Natural gas is the most-used energy resource in Oklahoma, followed closely by petroleum and then coal. Electric utilities are powered primarily by coal and natural gas; the industrial sector makes use of natural gas and petroleum.

Fiscal/Financial

Since 1995 Oklahoma has initiated measures to reduce its tax burden, including the first state personal income tax cut in 50 years and tax relief for the oil industry. Of state tax collected in 2000, 36.5% came from individual income tax; 24.6% from general sales tax; 14.4% from license tax; 12.6% from selective sales tax; 6.7% from severance tax; and 3.3% from corporate income tax. The corporate income tax rate is 6%.

Major financial institutions in Oklahoma include BancFirst Corp., Bank of America, Bank One Corp., BOK Financial Corp., Gold Banc Corp., Local Financial Corp., Southwest Bancorp, Superior Financial Corp., and UMB Financial Corp.

Business Opportunities

After the oil industry bust in the early 1980s, Oklahoma took steps to diversify its economy and promote development. The state now offers incentives including enterprise zones, tax credits for new jobs, specialized sales tax refunds for manufacturers and aircraft facilities, income tax credits/exemptions for certain environmental initiatives, tax exemptions for manufacturing and R&D, and special federal tax treatment.

One disincentive to business may be Oklahoma's level of R&D activity, which ranks near the bottom of the 50 states. Research centers include Aeromet, DCT, the Civil Aeromedical Institute, the Oklahoma Medical Research Foundation, Oklahoma State University, and the University of Oklahoma.

There are five *Fortune* 500 companies with their headquarters in Oklahoma: Phillips Petroleum, Williams, Oneok, Kerr-McGee, and OGE Energy.

For More Information

Book:

Gibson, Arrell Morgan. *Oklahoma: A History of Five Centuries*. Norman, OK: University of Oklahoma Press, 1981.

Web Sites:

Oklahoma Department of Commerce: **www.odoc.state.ok.us**
Oklahoma State Homepage: **www.state.ok.us**
Oklahoma Tourism and Recreation Department: **www.travelok.com**

  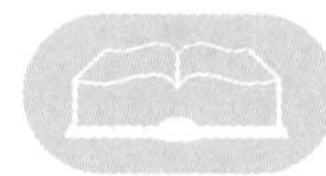    

OREGON

KEY FACTS

State capital: **Salem**
Population: **3,421,399; 28th in U.S.; grew 20.4% 1990–2000**
Land area: **95,996.5 square miles; 10th in U.S.**
Population density: **35.6 per square mile**
GSP: **$109,694 million**
GSP pc: **$32,061.15**
Household income: **$42,440; 24th in U.S.**
Poverty rate: **12.8%**
Unemployment: **4.9%**

ECONOMY

Oregon's timber industry has been a mainstay of the its economy since the 19th century; the region boomed during World War II when the war effort made use of Oregon's timber and shipyards, and continued to do so during the nationwide construction spike in the 1960s and 1970s. In the early 1990s, Oregon began making an effort to diversify its economy, targeting 14 industries: aerospace, agriculture and processing, bioscience, environmental technology, film and video, fisheries, forest and secondary wood products, graphic communications, high technology, primary and fabricated metals, plastics, professional services, software, and tourism.

Manufacturing is a major sector of the economy, driven by electronic equipment, lumber products, food processing, industrial machinery, paper products, and printing and publishing. The services sector is led by business services and health services.

Oregon's major challenge is the rapid growth of income disparity caused by declines in the resource-based economy of the rural areas compared to the industrial growth of the urban areas. Another challenge is the perception of Oregon as a resource-intensive economy unsuited for knowledge-based industry.

GEOGRAPHY/RESOURCES

Located in the northwestern U.S., Oregon consists of nine physical regions: the Coast Range on the northern coast; the Klamath Mountains on the southern coast; the Willamette Valley in the northwest; the Cascade Range covering a north-south strip east of the coast; the Deschutes-Umatilla Plateau in the northern central part of the state; the Blue-Wallowa Mountains in the northeast; the High Lava Plains in the central part of the state; the Great Basin in the south; and the Malheur-Owyhee Upland in the southeast.

Forestry resources include fir, pine, alder, hemlock, spruce, madrone, cedar, and other western hardwoods. Significant marine resources are crabs, rockfish, shrimp, sablefish, hake, sole, salmon, oysters, and tuna. Mineral resources are crushed stone, sand and gravel, pumice, lime, Portland cement, gemstones, emery, diatomite, zeolites, and perlite. Agricultural output consists of nursery and greenhouse products, cattle, hay, dairy products, and soybeans.

Many of Oregon's inhabitants are descendants of the German, English, Irish, French, Swedish, and Norwegian immigrants of the 1840s and 1850s. The 2000 census shows that 86.6% of the population is white; 8.0% Hispanic, of any race; 3.0% Asian; 1.6% African American; and 1.3% Native American.

Portland is the largest city, with 1,572,771 people. Other significant cities include Salem (347,214), the Eugene/Springfield metro area (322,959), and the Medford/Ashland metro area (181,269).

Environmental imperatives for Oregon include developing sustainability practices for Oregon's forests, which have been depleted by the extensive timber industry; another priority is to improve the state of watersheds to protect marine resources.

COMMUNICATIONS/ENERGY

Oregon has 99 airports, two of which—Portland International Airport and Klamath Falls International Airport—are international. There are 23 ports on the coast and the Columbia River; major ports include Coos Bay, Newport, Astoria, St. Helens, Portland, Morrow, and Umatilla. Oregon has 21 railroads operating on 2,573.1 miles of track, and 83,982.1 miles of roads.

Oregon is still developing its telecommunications infrastructure, having decided in 1999 to begin investigating gaps in rural access to telecommunications services. A major priority is to coordinate the use of public and private resources for greater network efficiency. In 2000 there were 76,839 high-speed lines; 94.2% of households had telephone service; 50.8% of households had Internet access; and 35.1% of the population had wireless telephones.

Hydroelectricity is the most-used energy resource in Oregon, followed by petroleum and then natural gas. Electric utilities are powered almost entirely by hydroelectricity; the industrial sector makes the most use of natural gas, while transportation primarily uses petroleum.

FISCAL/FINANCIAL

Oregon has a favorable tax climate, including no general sales tax. Of state tax collected in 2000, 68.9% came from individual income tax; 12.2% from selective sales tax; 10.2% from license tax; and 6.8% from corporate income tax. The corporate income tax rate is 6.6%.

Major financial institutions in Oregon include the Bank of America, Cascade Bancorp, First Washington Bancorp, Keycorp, Klamath First Bancorp, Oregon Trail Financial Corp., Umpqua Holdings Corp., U.S. Bancorp, Washington Mutual, and Wells Fargo & Co.

BUSINESS OPPORTUNITIES

Oregon offers a number of business incentives, including property tax incentives for capital investment, for construction, and in enterprise zones; tax credits for pollution control, energy-efficient equipment, recycling, R&D, and dependent care; financing assistance; workforce development assistance; and infrastructure expansion assistance.

Research facilities include the Corvallis Forestry Sciences Laboratory, the Oregon Graduate Institute of Science and Technology, Oregon Health Sciences University, the Oregon Research Institute, the Oregon Social Learning Center, Oregon State University, Providence Health System, Templex Technology Corp., and the University of Oregon.

There are two *Fortune* 500 companies with their headquarters in Oregon: Nike and Willamette Industries.

For More Information

Book:

Arrieta-Walden, Michael, ed. *The Oregon Story: 1850–2000*. Portland, OR: Graphic Arts Center Publishing Co., 2000.

Web Sites:

Oregon Economic and Community Development Department:
www.econ.state.or.us
Oregon State Homepage:
www.state.or.us

  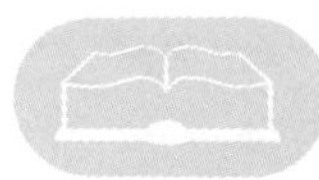    

PENNSYLVANIA

KEY FACTS

State capital: **Harrisburg**
Population: **12,281,054; 6th in U.S.; grew 3.4% 1990–2000**
Land area: **44,816.7 square miles; 32nd in U.S.**
Population density: **274 per square mile**
Household income: **$43,742; 20th in U.S.**
Poverty rate: **9.9%**
GSP: **$382,980 million**
GSP pc: **$31,184.62**
Unemployment: **4.2%**

ECONOMY

Pennsylvania's early dependence on agriculture declined when the state became a leading producer of iron in the 19th century and a center for steel production in the 20th. The state is currently in the midst of a transition to a modern economy focused on the service and technology industries.

Manufacturing is still a strong sector, but the historical focus on iron and steel has expanded to food products, chemicals, machinery, and electronic equipment; the services sector is led by health services. Biotechnology and biopharmaceuticals are growing fields thanks to state research facilities. Telecommunications and software are fueling the state's high-tech growth.

The challenge facing Pennsylvania is the poverty that still exists in communities that were resource-dependent. The Pennsylvania Industrial Development Authority and the Pennsylvania Economic Development Partnership are responsible for bringing the prosperity of the urban areas to the rest of the state.

GEOGRAPHY/RESOURCES

Located in the mideastern United States, Pennsylvania is bisected diagonally from northeast to southwest by the Allegheny Front and Allegheny Mountains. There is a plateau region in the north and west, bordering Lake Erie, while the southeast is occupied by the Coastal Plains.

Major agricultural output consists of dairy and poultry products, cattle, mushrooms, corn, hay, apples, grapes, potatoes, winter wheat, oats, vegetables, and tobacco. Marine resources include carp, perch, trout, salmon, and bass. Pennsylvania is one of the nation's largest coal producers; other mineral resources include cement, stone, natural gas, crude oil, iron ore, limestone, silver, gold, copper, cobalt, zinc, and salt.

The original settlers of Pennsylvania were from northern Europe, and there is still a large German presence in the state. 85.4% of the population is white; 10.0% is black or African American; 3.2% is Hispanic or Latino of any race; and 1.8% is Asian.

The Philadelphia metro area is the largest city, with 6,188,463 people. Other large cities include Pittsburgh (2,358,695), the Allentown metro area (637,958), the Harrisburg metro area (629,401), and the Scranton metro area (624,776).

The state's environmental challenges include: preserving farmland; cleaning up abandoned mines; restoring water tables; and upgrading water and sewer systems.

COMMUNICATIONS/ENERGY

Pennsylvania has 141 public airports, six of which—Lehigh Valley International Airport, Erie International Airport, Harrisburg International Airport, Philadelphia International Airport, Pittsburgh International Airport, and Wilkes-Barre/Scranton International Airport—are international. There are four ports—Philadelphia, Camden, Erie, and Pittsburgh—on the Ohio and Delaware Rivers. There are 70 railroads operating 5,381.3 miles of rail, in addition to commuter networks around Philadelphia and Pittsburgh, as well as 119,333 miles of roads.

Pennsylvania had 176,670 high-speed telephone lines as of 2000, which are fairly well distributed. In 2000, 97.3% of households had telephone service; 40.1% of households had Internet access; and 32.7% of the population had wireless telephones.

Pennsylvania ranks first nationally in the production of nuclear energy, and its electric utilities primarily use nuclear power and coal. Secondary sources of energy include crude oil, natural gas, and hydroelectric power. Its electric utilities were deregulated in 1998.

FISCAL/FINANCIAL

The per-capita state tax burden is lower in Pennsylvania than in most of the surrounding states. Of state taxes collected in 2000, 31.4% came from general sales; 30.1% from individual income; 15.1% from selective sales tax; 10.1% from license tax; 7.6% from corporate income tax; and 3.6% from death and gift tax. The corporate income tax rate is 9.99%, one of the highest in the country.

Major banks and financial institutions include Allfirst Financial, Commonwealth Bancorp, First Commonwealth Financial Corp., First Union Corp., Harleysville National Corp., M&T Bank Corp., Mellon Financial Corp., Mercantile Bankshares Corp., National City Corp., the PNC Financial Services Group, Sky Financial Group, Sovereign Bancorp, Sterling Financial Corp., and Waypoint Financial.

BUSINESS OPPORTUNITIES

In the late 1990s, Pennsylvania improved its business climate through tax cuts and workers' compensation reform, and reduced red tape for businesses expanding or relocating in the state. Tax incentives for business offered in Pennsylvania include a $1,000 tax credit for each new job created, up to $250,000 of tax credits in enterprise zones, and a 10% tax credit for new R&D investments.

R&D facilities, focusing on medical research in Philadelphia and scientific and technical research in Pittsburgh, are a draw for business. Major research centers include the Philadelphia District Laboratory, the Software Engineering Institute, the Pittsburgh Research Laboratory, the National Energy Technology Laboratory Pittsburgh, the University of Pennsylvania, Pennsylvania State University, the University of Pittsburgh, Thomas Jefferson University, MCP Hahnemann University, Temple University, and Carnegie Mellon University.

The top *Fortune* 500 companies with their headquarters in Pennsylvania include USX, Alcoa, Cigna, Rite Aid, Sunoco, Amerisource Health, H.J. Heinz, PPG Industries, Comcast, PNC Financial Services Group, Crown Cork & Seal, Aramark, Unisys, Rohm & Haas, Mellon Financial Corp., PPL, Ikon Office Solutions, and Hershey Foods.

For More Information

Book:
Pennsylvania Investment and Business Guide. International Business Publications USA, 2001.

Web Sites:
Pennsylvania Department of Community and Economic Development: **www.dced.state.pa.us**
Pennsylvania's Home Page: **www.state.pa.us**

  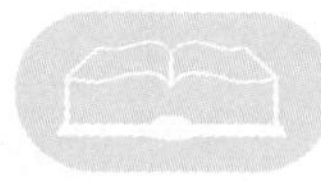    

Rhode Island

KEY FACTS

State capital: **Providence**
Population: **1,048,319; 43rd in U.S.; grew 4.5% 1990–2000**
Land area: **1,044.9 square miles; 50th in U.S.**
Population density: **1,003.2 per square mile**
GSP: **$32,546 million**
GSP pc: **$31,045.89**
Household income: **$42,973; 22nd in U.S.**
Poverty rate: **10.0%**
Unemployment: **4.1%**

Economy

Rhode Island's economic history is based around commerce and industry, as a result of its coastal location and poor soil that inhibits agriculture. The manufacturing sector, which led the economy throughout the 19th and early 20th centuries, has been on the decline since the mid-20th century, though the state still produces electronic equipment, fabricated metals, textiles, and industrial machinery.

The finance, insurance, and real estate (FIRE) sector is the largest in the economy, followed by services, which is led by health and business services; tourism is also significant. The state encourages the following industry clusters: arts and entertainment, financial services, jewelry, high-tech manufacturing, ocean industries, support services, and technology.

Challenges facing Rhode Island include the replacement of high-paying manufacturing jobs with minimum-wage service jobs, high business costs, a small labor force, and minimal venture capital.

Geography/Resources

Located in the northeastern United States, Rhode Island consists of the hilly New England Upland in the western two-thirds of the state and the Narragansett Lowland along the coast.

Lobster is the most profitable marine resource; others include squid, goosefish, clams, flounder, assorted shellfish, hake, herring, porgies, butterfish, mackerel, cod, and crab. Mineral resources are crushed stone and sand and gravel. Forestry resources include oak, pine, ash, maple, and mixed upland hardwoods. Nursery and greenhouse crops are the primary agricultural output; other produce includes dairy products and poultry and poultry products.

Rhode Island has had several waves of immigration: the English in the colonial era; Irish in the early 19th century; French Canadians, Scandinavians, Germans, and Portuguese in the mid-19th century; Eastern Europeans, Greeks, Armenians, and Italians early in the 20th century; and blacks, Hispanics, and Southeast Asians in the late 20th century. The 2000 census shows that 85% of the population is white; 8.7% Hispanic, of any race; 4.5% African American; and 2.3% Asian. The Providence metro area is home to 955,549 people, over 90% of the state's population.

Environmental imperatives for Rhode Island include preventing damage to the land and water from underground storage tanks, conserving wetlands, and continuing to reduce air pollution in Rhode Island and surrounding states.

Communications/Energy

Rhode Island has six general-aviation airports, one of which—T. F. Green International Airport—is international. The state's two major ports are Providence Port and Quonset/Davisville Port and Commerce Park. There are 515.2 miles of rail, operated by one regional railroad, and 5,895.6 miles of roads.

Rhode Island has nearly complete fiber optic coverage, with the exception of some rural areas; it had 30,919 high-speed lines as of 2000. In 2000, 94.6% of households had telephone service; 38.8% of households had Internet access; and 33.9% of the population had wireless telephones.

Petroleum is the most-used energy resource in Rhode Island, followed by natural gas. The electric utilities use hydroelectricity almost exclusively; the industrial sector relies on natural gas, while the residential sector and transportation make use of petroleum.

Fiscal/Financial

In 1985, the state reduced the tax burden and unemployment and workers' compensation costs, which had limited economic development within the state; it now has the lowest per-capita state tax burden in the region. Of state tax collected in 2000, 40.7% came from individual income tax; 30.5% from general sales tax; 18.8% from selective sales tax; 4.5% from license tax; and 3.7% from corporate income tax. The corporate income tax rate is among the highest in the U.S., at 9.0%.

Major financial institutions include Bancorp Rhode Island, FirstFed America Bancorp, First Financial Corp., FleetBoston Financial Corp., Merrill Lynch, Sovereign Bancorp, State Street Corp., and Washington Trust Bancorp.

Business Opportunities

Rhode Island has developed a generous tax credit program as an incentive to business, including tax credits for manufacturers for new facilities, machinery, and equipment; for software developers and service industries for purchased or leased equipment; for companies operating in enterprise zones; for R&D; for job training; and for daycare. The state also offers tax reductions for the creation of new jobs.

Most of Rhode Island's federal R&D investment comes from the Department of Defense and is spent in the private sector. Research centers include the Atlantic Ecology Division, Brown University, Rhode Island Hospital, Memorial Hospital, Miriam Hospital, the Raytheon Company, the Slater Center for Biomedical Technology, Textron, and the University of Rhode Island.

There are three *Fortune* 500 companies with their headquarters in Rhode Island: CVS, Textron, and Hasbro.

For More Information

Book:

McLoughlin, William G. *Rhode Island: A History*. New York: W.W. Norton & Co., 1986.

Web Sites:

Rhode Island Economic Development Corporation: **www.riedc.com**
Rhode Island State Homepage: **www.state.ri.us**
Rhode Island Tourism: **www.visitrhodeisland.com**

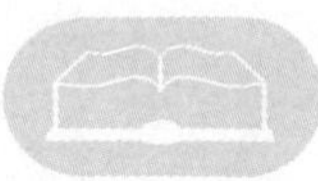

SOUTH CAROLINA

KEY FACTS

State capital: **Columbia**
Population: **4,012,012; 26th in U.S.; grew 15.1% 1990–2000**
Land area: **30,109.8 square miles; 40th in U.S.**
Population density: **133.2 per square mile**
Household income: **$37,119; 40th in U.S.**
Poverty rate: **11.9%**
GSP: **$106,917 million**
GSP pc: **$26,649.22**
Unemployment: **3.9%**

ECONOMY

Manufacturing is a major economic presence in South Carolina; textile manufacturing has been an important part of the state's economy since slavery in the early 19th century made it possible to produce large amounts of cotton, but chemical, clothing, and paper manufacturing are also present.

Tourism, generated by the state's beaches, golf courses, and historical sites, is an important industry and contributes to the services sector and to retail sales. Agriculture is a historical contributor and has led to growth in agricultural services.

The state suffers from a shortage of knowledge workers and technological infrastructure, which it is addressing with the South Carolina Information Technology Institute and other initiatives.

GEOGRAPHY/RESOURCES

Located in the southeastern United States, South Carolina consists of two regions: the broad Coastal Plain along the Atlantic Ocean, with islands separated from the mainland by marshes, and the rolling Piedmont farmland in the west.

Agricultural resources include tobacco, cotton, soybeans, peanuts, hay, oats, wheat, poultry, cattle and calves, and other livestock products. Mining products include cement, clays, stone, and sand and gravel. Shrimp is the primary marine resource; others include crabs, clams, swordfish, oysters, snapper, and scamp. Forestry resources are pine, oak, hickory, sweetgum, and mixed hardwoods.

Although more than half of the state's population after the Civil War was African American, that number has dropped due to the political disenfranchisement of the black population prior to the Civil Rights movement. 67.2% of the population is white; 29.5% is African American; and 2.4% is Hispanic, of any race.

The Greenville/Spartanburg/Anderson metro area is the largest in the state, with 962,441 people. Other significant cities include the Charleston metro area (549,033), Columbia (536,691), Myrtle Beach (196,2690), Florence (125,761), and Sumter (104,646).

Environmental imperatives in the state include the erosion of the wetlands along the coast and toxic emissions in the air and water from manufacturing plants.

COMMUNICATIONS/ENERGY

South Carolina has 68 public-use airports, three of which—Charleston International Airport, Greenville-Spartanburg International Airport, and Myrtle Beach International Airport—are international. The state's 41,537 miles of highway and two Class I railroads facilitate transportation from its three deep-water ports—Charleston, Georgetown, and Port Royal—which moved 1.56 million tonnes of cargo in 2000.

The state has only recently begun any technology initiatives, although it had 63,914 high-speed lines by 2000. In 2000, 94.3% of households had telephone service; 32.0% of households had Internet access; and 34.7% of the population had wireless telephones.

Utilities in the state depend primarily on nuclear power and coal for electricity generation, ranking third in the nation in terms of the generation of electricity from nuclear power. The industrial sector uses natural gas, wood and waste, and petroleum.

FISCAL/FINANCIAL

South Carolina has a fairly low per-capita state tax burden. Of state tax collected in 2000, 38.5% came from general sales tax; 38.3% from individual income tax; 12.3% from selective sales tax; 5.9% from license tax; and 3.6% from corporate income tax. Its 5% corporate income tax rate (4.5% for banks, 6.0% for savings and loans) is the lowest in the southeast.

Major banks and institutions in South Carolina include the Bank of America, BB&T Corp., First Citizens Bancorporation of South Carolina, First Financial Holdings, First National Corp., First Union Corp., RBC Centura Banks, Regions Financial Corp., The South Financial Group, and SouthTrust Corp.

BUSINESS OPPORTUNITIES

South Carolina is currently in the process of creating an alliance between the state's colleges and universities and its industries, in an attempt to bring more high-tech business into the state and to increase its number of technology workers. However, manufacturing and the spinoff jobs it creates remain the dominant industries and will continue to offer the greatest opportunity for growth until South Carolina's technology initiative is more advanced. The state has relatively low rates for workers' compensation benefits and unemployment insurance; it offers tax incentives to companies that locate their headquarters in the state and that provide childcare for employees, a five-year abatement from county property taxes for new industries, and exemptions from property tax for pollution control equipment and inventories.

Major research centers in the state include the Savannah River Technology Center, the Space and Naval Warfare Systems Center Charleston, the U.S. Vegetable Laboratory, the Cotton Quality Research Station, the University of South Carolina, the Medical University of South Carolina, Clemson University, and South Carolina State University.

Scana is the only *Fortune* 500 company with its headquarters in South Carolina.

For More Information

Book:
Edgar, Walter B. *South Carolina: A History*. Columbia, SC: University of South Carolina Press, 1998.

Web Sites:
South Carolina State Web site: **www.myscgov.com**
South Carolina Economic Developers Association: **www.sceda.org**
Travel Guide to South Carolina: **www.travelsc.com**

SOUTH DAKOTA

KEY FACTS

State capital: **Pierre**
Population: **754,844; 46th in U.S.; grew 8.5% 1990–2000**
Land area: **75,884.6 square miles; 16th in U.S.**
Population density: **9.9 per square mile**
Household income: **$36,172; 41st in U.S.**
Poverty rate: **9.3%**
GSP: **$21,631 million**
GSP pc: **$28,656.25**
Unemployment: **2.3%**

ECONOMY

Agriculture, a traditional staple of South Dakota's economy, is still an important source of income for the state. Mining, which had been a major source of economic activity since the gold rush in 1875, declined toward the end of the 20th century as a result of low gold prices and the increased cost of environmental compliance.

Tourism brings in nearly $1.3 billion per year and is a major driver of the state's retail sales and services income. Manufacturing, much of it resulting from the state's traditional dependence on agriculture, has emerged since the 1980s as an important industry. The largest manufacturing segments are machinery and equipment and food products.

The major challenge facing South Dakota is an exodus of young people owing to a lack of economic opportunity, which it hopes to remedy with a lenient tax structure.

GEOGRAPHY/RESOURCES

South Dakota has three physical sections: the Prairie Plains in the east; the Great Plains in the west; and the Black Hills, also in the western part of the state. The Missouri River runs from north to south through the center of the state.

The state is a leading producer of oats, rye, flaxseed, sunflower seeds, and hay. It also exports corn, wheat, barley, sorghum, and soybeans. Livestock production is the largest source of agricultural income, from cattle and calves, hogs and pigs, and sheep and lambs. South Dakota's mineral resources include gold, crude oil, dimension stone, limestone, quartzite, shale, iron ore, gypsum, bentonite, and sand and gravel.

South Dakota is mainly populated by descendants of the 19th-century Northern European settlers, as well as of its original Native American inhabitants. 88.7% of the population is white; 8.3% is Native American; and 1.4% is Hispanic, of any race. The largest cities in the state are Sioux Falls, with 172,412 people, and Rapid City, with 88,565 people.

One environmental concern for South Dakota is a recent proposal that would change how animal feeding operations are regulated, possibly at some cost to the state's livestock producers. Another recent initiative is the government's promise to remove hazardous waste containers from private property in an effort to increase the quality of the state's groundwater.

COMMUNICATIONS/ENERGY

Although passenger rail service has declined significantly, freight train transportation on the state's 1,856.1 miles of rail has increased since the 1980s. South Dakota has 83,451.5 miles of highways. There is regular airline service to Sioux Falls and other major cities, though none of the 68 public-use airports is international.

The state has only recently begun preparing for the information economy. The majority of the state is now wired with fiber optic cable, though there were only 11,799 high-speed lines as of 2000. In 2000, 95.3% of households had telephone service and 37.9% of households had Internet access.

South Dakota's energy comes primarily from hydropower, produced by the four dammed areas of the Missouri River, and petroleum, with natural gas and coal as secondary fuels. Three-quarters of the state's electric utility output is hydroelectric.

FISCAL/FINANCIAL

South Dakota is the only state in the nation that does not have corporate income tax, personal income tax, personal property tax, business inventory tax, or inheritance tax. Banks and financial corporations are the only exceptions: they pay corporate income taxes at a graduated rate from 6% to 1%. Of state taxes collected in 2000, 52.6% came from general sales tax; 26.4% from selective sales tax; 12.8% from license tax; 4.9% from corporate income tax; and 3.1% from death and gift tax.

Major banks and institutions include Citigroup, Community First Bankshares, First Midwest Financial, First National of Nebraska, HF Financial Corp., U.S. Bancorp, and Wells Fargo & Co.

BUSINESS OPPORTUNITIES

South Dakota offers special incentives to telecommunications companies: The state has no sales/use tax on out-of-state services or interstate phone calls; no restrictions on interest rate charges, late fees, or the hours that telemarketers are allowed to call; and one-party consent recording.

New-economy companies looking to locate in South Dakota may be discouraged by the state's lack of technological research facilities. South Dakota ranked last in the country in terms of federal research grants, though there are research centers at South Dakota State University, the University of South Dakota, the South Dakota School of Mines and Technology, the Northern Grain Insects Research Laboratory, and the Forestry Sciences Laboratory.

There are two *Fortune* 500 companies with their headquarters in South Dakota: IBP and Northwestern.

For More Information

Books:

South Dakota Investment and Business Guide, International Business Publications USA, 2001.

Morgan, Kathleen O. *South Dakota in Perspective 2001: A Statistical View of the Mount Rushmore State*. Lawrence, KS: Morgan Quitno, 2001.

Web Sites:

South Dakota Governor's Office of Economic Development: **www.sdgreatprofits.com**

South Dakota Home Page: **www.state.sd.us**

South Dakota Travel Information: **www.travelsd.com**

TENNESSEE

KEY FACTS

State capital: **Nashville**
Population: **5,689,283; 16th in U.S.; grew 16.7% 1990–2000**
Land area: **41,216.8 square miles; 34th in U.S.**
Population density: **138 per square mile**
GSP: **$170,085 million**
GSP pc: **$29,895.68**
Household income: **$33,885; 44th in U.S.**
Poverty rate: **13.3%**
Unemployment: **3.9%**

ECONOMY

Like many southern states, Tennessee's early dependence on cotton and tobacco gave way to manufacturing. The manufacturing sector—consisting primarily of printing, publishing, chemicals, fabricated metals, food products, industrial and commercial machinery, electronics, rubber and plastics, furniture, and transportation equipment—is still significant; the service sector is driven by tourism, entertainment, health services, and business services. Warehousing and distribution, based on Tennessee's central location, is also an important industry.

Tennessee has identified eight industry clusters that it would like to develop: transportation equipment; industrial and commercial machinery; rubber and plastics; printing and publishing; business, transportation, and health services; entertainment; tourism; and agriculture and forestry.

The major challenge facing Tennessee is the education level of its workforce, which ranks among the lowest of the states. Highway congestion and necessary rail repairs are other important issues.

GEOGRAPHY/RESOURCES

Located in the central southeastern United States, Tennessee consists of six regions running from east to west: the Unaka Mountains, the Great Valley, the Cumberland Plateau, the Interior Low Plateau, the eastern Gulf Coastal Plain, and the Mississippi alluvial plain.

Agricultural output includes cattle, poultry and poultry products, soybeans, nursery and greenhouse crops, dairy products, cotton, tobacco, corn, and pigs. Forestry resources are oak, hickory, cedar, pine, poplar, and mixed upland hardwoods. Marine resources are trout, bass, crappie, sunfish, catfish, sauger, and walleye. Coal is the most important mineral resource; others include crude oil, crushed stone, sand and gravel, Portland cement, salt, zinc, barite, copper, lead, silver, lime, and petroleum.

The earliest European settlers were mainly Scotch-Irish and English; blacks have also been present since the early 19th century. The 2000 census shows that 80.2% of the population is white; 16.4% African American; 2.2% Hispanic, of any race; and 1.0% Asian.

Nashville is the largest city, with 1,231,311 people; other major cities include Memphis (977,549), Knoxville (687,249), the Johnson City/Kingsport metro area (388,218), Chattanooga (335,672), and Clarksville (134,7680).

Environmental imperatives for Tennessee include reducing ground-level ozone, decreasing the level of chemicals in groundwater aquifers, and reducing damage caused by hazardous waste.

COMMUNICATIONS/ENERGY

Tennessee has 81 airports, two of which—Memphis International and Nashville International—are international. River traffic is an important part of the transportation infrastructure, and there are 30 ports on the Tennessee, Mississippi, and Cumberland Rivers. There are 3,152.4 miles of rail, operated by three Class I and 14 shortline railroads, and 85,637.8 miles of roads.

Tennessee is in the process of identifying its existing telecommunications infrastructure. An important initiative is to connect the systems used by the government, the educational system, and private industry to make the best use of existing networks, including the 122,481 high-speed lines in place in 2000. In 2000, 96.3% of households had telephone service; 36.3% of households had Internet access; and 34.5% of the population had wireless telephones.

Petroleum is the most-used energy resource in Tennessee, followed closely by coal. Electric utilities are powered primarily by coal, followed by nuclear energy; transportation runs almost completely on petroleum, while the industrial sector uses natural gas, petroleum, and coal.

FISCAL/FINANCIAL

Tennessee does not collect income tax on wages or salaries—only on stocks, bonds, and notes receivable—which is a source of the state's competitive advantage; it has one of the lowest per-capita state tax burdens in the United States. Of state tax collected in 2000, 57.4% came from general sales tax; 17.6% from selective sales tax; 11.6% from license tax; 7.9% from corporate income tax; and 2.3% from individual income tax. The corporate income tax rate is 6.0%.

Major financial institutions in Tennessee include AmSouth Bancorporation, BancorpSouth, Comerica, First Tennessee National Corp., National Commerce Financial Corporation, Old National Bancorp, Regions Financial Corp., SFB Bancorp, SouthTrust Corp., SunTrust Banks, Union Planters Corp., and U.S. Bancorp.

BUSINESS OPPORTUNITIES

Tennessee offers business incentives including tax credits for the purchase of industrial machinery, the purchase of equipment associated with a distribution or warehouse facility, job creation, and corporate provisions for daycare; tax exemptions for pollution equipment; and varied tax incentives for manufacturers and operations.

Half of the federal research funds received by Tennessee come from the Department of Energy. Research facilities include Accurate Automation Corp., the Arnold Engineering Development Center, Boeing, Meharry Medical College, Micro Craft, the Oak Ridge National Laboratory, St. Jude Children's Research Hospital, the University of Memphis, the University of Tennessee, and Vanderbilt University Hospital.

There are six *Fortune* 500 companies with their headquarters in Tennessee: FedEx, HCA, UnumProvident, Eastman Chemical, Dollar General, and AutoZone.

For More Information

Book:

Corlew, Robert Ewing. *Tennessee: A Short History*. Knoxville, TN: University of Tennessee Press, 1990.

Web Sites:

State of Tennessee Homepage:
www.state.tn.us
Tennessee Department of Economic and Community Development:
www.state.tn.us/ecd

TEXAS

KEY FACTS

State capital: **Austin**
Population: **20,851,820; 2nd in U.S.; grew 22.8% 1990–2000**
Land area: **261,795.7 square miles; 2nd in U.S.**
Population density: **79.6 per square mile**
GSP: **$687,272 million**
GSP pc: **$32,959.81**
Household income: **$39,842; 29th in U.S.**
Poverty rate: **14.9%**
Unemployment: **4.2%**

ECONOMY

While the agricultural industry that supported Texas's economy in the 19th century and the mining boom that began at the turn of the 20th century are still important to the economy—mining, especially, contributes more in Texas than in most U.S. states—they are less important than the manufacturing industry, which is growing in Texas as it declines in other states. Important products include electronic equipment, chemicals, industrial machinery, food products, primary and fabricated metals, petroleum products, transportation equipment, rubber and plastics, printing and publishing, textiles, and lumber and wood.

The service sector is now the largest in the economy, led by business and health services; other significant services include architectural engineering, software, film production, and tourism-related industries. Communications and knowledge-based industries are growing rapidly, led by clusters in metropolitan areas.

The challenges facing Texas are its high poverty rate, poor income distribution, disparity between rural and urban areas in categories including economic development and infrastructure, and low educational attainment rates.

GEOGRAPHY/RESOURCES

Located in the southwestern United States, Texas consists of five geographical regions: the Gulf Coastal Plains in the east and along the southern border; the Prairie Plains, Rolling Plains, and Great Plains running from east to west in the central part of the state; and the Basin and Range Region in the west.

Mineral resources include crude oil, natural gas, coal, Portland cement, crushed stone, sand and gravel, lime, salt, magnesium metal, Frasch sulfur, helium, talc, clay, zeolites, greensand marl, gypsum, raw steel, primary aluminum, and copper. Cattle and calves are the primary agricultural output; other produce includes cotton, poultry and poultry products, dairy products, corn, nursery and greenhouse crops, sorghum, wheat, vegetables, and hay. Shrimp is the primary marine resource; others include oysters, crab, drum, snapper, tuna, flatfish, croaker, grouper, and mackerel. Forestry resources include pine, oak, hickory, and other hardwoods.

Texas has a diverse population, reflecting the migratory patterns of the 19th century when Europeans came from the north and east and Spanish and Mexican settlers came from the west and south. The black population began to grow after the Civil War. The 2000 census shows that 71% of the population is white; 32% Hispanic, of any race; 11.5% African American; and 2.7% Asian.

The Dallas/Fort Worth metro area is the largest in the state, with 5,221,801 people. Other significant cities include: the Houston/Galveston metro area (4,669,571); San Antonio (1,592,383); the Austin/San Marcos metro area (1,249,763); El Paso (679,622); the McAllen/Edinburg/Mission metro area (569,462); the Beaumont/Port Arthur metro area (385,090); Corpus Christi (380,783); the Brownsville/Harlingen/San Benito metro area (335,227); the Killeen/Temple metro area (312,952); Lubbock (242,628); the Odessa/Midland metro area (237,132); and Amarillo (217,858).

Environmental imperatives for Texas include reducing air pollution, especially ozone, from the industrial sector, the disposal of hazardous waste, and cleaning up abandoned industrial sites.

COMMUNICATIONS/ENERGY

Texas has 383 public-use airports, of which Dallas-Fort Worth International and George Bush Intercontinental are the largest. There are 29 ports; the most significant is the Port of Houston. There are 44 railroads operating on 12,005.4 miles of track, and 296,320.5 miles of highways in addition to the largest network of local roads in the United States.

Despite a strong high-tech industry and impressive digital infrastructure in technology corridors around major cities such as Austin and Dallas, Texas ranks near the bottom of the United States in statewide digital infrastructure. This is due in part to the sheer size of the state, but also to a high economic discrepancy between urban and rural areas. In 2000, Texas had 522,538 high-speed lines; 93.5% of households had telephone service; 38.3% of households had Internet access; and 35.9% of the population had wireless telephones.

Texas is a major oil-producing state, and petroleum is its most-used energy resource, followed by natural gas. Electric utilities rely primarily on coal and natural gas, with some use of nuclear energy; the industrial sector consumes petroleum and natural gas.

FISCAL/FINANCIAL

Texas has no individual income tax, corporate income tax, or state-level property tax; consequently, it has one of the lowest per-capita state tax burdens in the United States. Of state tax collected in 2000, 51.1% came from general sales tax; 29.9% from selective sales tax; 13.9% from license tax; and 4.1% from severance tax. There is a franchise tax of 4.5% of earned income.

Major financial institutions include BancorpSouth, Bank of America, Bank One Corp., BOK Financial Corp., Coastal Bancorp, Comerica, Compass Bancshares, Cullen/Frost Bankers, First Financial Bankshares, First USA Bank, Golden West Financial Corp., International Bancshares Corp., J. P. Morgan Chase & Co., MetroCorp Bancshares, Prosperity Bancshares, Sterling Bancshares, SouthTrust Corp., Southwest Bancorporation of Texas, Temple-Inland Inc., Texas Regional Bancshares, Union Planters Corp., Washington Mutual, and Wells Fargo & Co.

BUSINESS OPPORTUNITIES

Texas offers a number of incentives for business, including industrial revenue bonds, tax incentives for businesses in enterprise zones and in communities that have been adversely impacted by the downturn in the defense industry, training grants, and several financing programs.

The state ranks fifth in federal R&D spending, mainly from the Department of Defense and the National Aeronautics and Space Administration. Research centers include Baylor College of Medicine, Bell Helicopter Textron, Boeing, the Cancer

 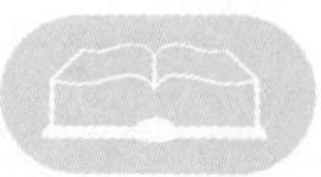    

Therapy and Research Center, the Center for Nuclear Waste Regulatory Analyses, the Human Effectiveness Directorate at Brooks Air Force Base, the Lyndon B. Johnson Space Center, Lockheed Martin, Raytheon, Rice University, Southern Methodist University, the Southern Plains Agricultural Research Center, the Southwest Foundation for Biomedical Research, Texas A&M University, Texas Engineering Experiment Center, Texas Instruments, Texas Tech University, the University of Houston, the University of North Texas, and the University of Texas.

The top 20 *Fortune* 500 companies with their headquarters in Texas are Exxon Mobil, SBC Communications, Compaq Computer, J. C. Penney, Conoco, Dell Computer, Dynegy, Reliant Energy, TXU, El Paso, AMR, Sysco, Electronic Data Systems, Valero Energy, Fleming, Ultramar Diamond Shamrock, Kimberly-Clark, Halliburton, Waste Management, and Texas Instruments.

For More Information

Book:

Richardson, Rupert N., ed. *Texas*. Upper Saddle River, NJ: Prentice Hall College Division, 2000.

Web Site:

Texas Department of Economic Development: **www.tded.state.tx.us**

  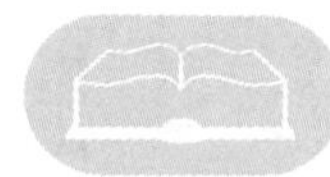    

UTAH

KEY FACTS

State capital: **Salt Lake City**
Population: **2,233,169; 34th in U.S.; grew 29.6% 1990–2000**
Land area: **82,143.6 square miles; 12th in U.S.**
Population density: **27.1 per square mile**
GSP: **$62,641 million**
GSP pc: **$28,050.27**
Household income: **$45,230; 17th in U.S.**
Poverty rate: **8.1%**
Unemployment: **3.2%**

ECONOMY

Utah's early dependence on agriculture and light industry was supplanted by mining in the late 19th century; the defense and aerospace industries became significant during and after World War II. Today, services are the largest and fastest-growing sector, driven by business services.

The state is taking advantage of its proximity to Silicon Valley and other high-tech centers to grow that sector of the economy. High-tech growth areas include biotechnology; computer applications; networking, hardware, and software companies; Internet call centers; and chip production and testing. Merchandise exports, agriculture, energy, and minerals showed stable growth in the late 1990s, and construction and tourism, which were staples of the economy in the 1990s, were down at the beginning of the 21st century.

A major challenge facing Utah is the expected boom in school-age children in the first decade of the 21st century, which will be larger in Utah than most other states. The state must find a way to provide an educational system appropriate for a high-tech workforce and for a larger number of children, without compromising its tax climate. Another concern is the need for renovations to Utah's transportation infrastructure, especially its roads.

GEOGRAPHY/RESOURCES

Utah is located in the western United States. Nearly half of the state is covered by the Colorado Plateau. The desertlike Great Basin is in the western third; the Great Salt Lake is in the northeast, with the Great Salt Lake Desert to its southwest; and the Middle Rockies are also in the northeast.

Copper is Utah's most significant mineral resource; others are crude oil, natural gas, coal, gold, silver, magnesium, potash, molybdenum, phosphate, helium, beryllium, silver, bentonite, perlite, salt, gemstones, crushed stone, and sand and gravel. Forestry resources are aspen, fir, spruce, pine, and hemlock. Marine resources are trout, bass, salmon, perch, catfish, sunfish, bluegill, whitefish, carp, and crappie. Cattle and calves and dairy products account for approximately two-thirds of Utah's agricultural output; other produce includes poultry and poultry products, hogs and pigs, grains, hay, vegetables, and nursery and greenhouse crops.

Utah was settled in the mid-19th century by Mormons, and they still exert a cultural influence on the state. The 2000 census shows that 89.2% of the population is white; 9.0% Hispanic, of any race; 1.7% Asian; and 1.3% Native American.

The Salt Lake City/Ogden metro area is the largest in Utah, with 1,333,914 people, or nearly 60% of the population; the Provo/Orem metro area has 368,536 people.

Environmental imperatives for Utah include high levels of ozone pollution in the air, the reclamation of abandoned mines, and the reduction of hazardous waste from mining and refining operations.

COMMUNICATIONS/ENERGY

Utah has 49 airports, one of which—Salt Lake City International Airport—is international. There are 43,174.6 miles of roads, and two railroads operate 1,700.7 miles of rail.

Utah has a telecommunications infrastructure adequate to support its burgeoning high-tech industry. Cities are mainly wired with fiber optic cable, although rural areas are not; the 35,970 high-speed lines in place as of 2000 are mainly confined to urban areas, as the small numbers of people in rural areas prevent cost-effective installation of high-speed transmissions. In 2000, 95.8% of households had telephone service; 48.4% of households had Internet access; and 33.6% of the population had wireless telephones.

Coal is the most-used energy source in Utah, followed by petroleum and then natural gas. Electric utilities are powered almost entirely by coal; petroleum is used mainly for motor gasoline and distillate fuel.

FISCAL/FINANCIAL

Utah has a stable tax climate and a per-capita state tax burden consistent with surrounding states. Of state tax collected in 2000, 41.5% came from individual income tax; 35.8% from general sales tax; 12.6% from selective sales tax; 4.4% from corporate income tax; and 3.5% from license tax. The corporate income tax rate is 5.0%.

Major financial institutions in Utah include Bank One Corp., Citigroup, Countrywide Credit, Glacier Bancorp, KeyCorp, Merrill Lynch, U.S. Bancorp, Washington Federal, Washington Mutual, Wells Fargo & Co., and Zions Bancorporation.

BUSINESS OPPORTUNITIES

Utah offers a few incentives to business, including sales and use tax exemption for manufacturers, enterprise zones, tax credits for recycling, an industrial assistance fund for relocation costs, and training funds for new or expanding companies.

The majority of R&D spending in Utah is focused on the defense industry. Research facilities include Alliant Techsystems Inc., the Dugway Proving Ground, L-3 Communications, Lockheed Martin, Thiokol Corp., and the University of Utah.

Autoliv is the only *Fortune* 500 company with its headquarters in Utah.

For More Information

Book:

Hinton, Wayne K. *Utah: Unusual Beginning to Unique Present*. Sun Valley, CA: American Historical Press, 2001.

Web Sites:

The Official Travel Site of the State of Utah: **www.utah.com**
Utah Department of Community and Economic Development: **www.dced.state.ut.us**
Utah State Homepage: **www.state.ut.us**

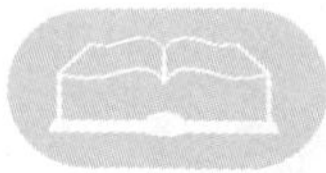

VERMONT

KEY FACTS

State capital: **Montpelier**
Population: **608,827; 49th in U.S.; grew 8.2% 1990–2000**
Land area: **9,249.9 square miles; 43rd in U.S.**
Population density: **65.8 per square mile**
GSP: **$17,164 million**
GSP pc: **$28,191.92**
Household income: **$38,150; 35th in U.S.**
Poverty rate: **10.1%**
Unemployment: **2.9%**

ECONOMY

The agricultural activity that characterized Vermont's history declined during the 20th century, as family farms have become expensive to maintain; however, the image of Vermont as a rural state remains. The service sector is now the largest in Vermont, driven by health and business services; the tourism that results from Vermont's natural attractions and winter sports also falls into this category.

Manufacturing is another important sector. Traditionally, the industry has depended on processing agricultural and forestry products; while these are still important, machinery, metal products, transportation equipment, and plastics and rubber now contribute as well. As in most of New England, a great deal of Vermont's textile and apparel manufacturing has moved to the southern United States and overseas.

The state's complicated permitting process represents an obstacle to businesses looking to locate in Vermont, and the state is looking into reform. The small population has led to a shortage of skilled workers, which the state is trying to remedy through education initiatives.

GEOGRAPHY/RESOURCES

Located in the northeastern United States, Vermont is mostly covered by the Green Mountains, the northeastern extension of the Appalachian range. The state's small amount of level, fertile land lies in the Champlain Valley, in the northwestern part of the state.

Dairy products are the primary agricultural resource; others include maple syrup, cattle, sheep, hogs and pigs, poultry, hay, apples and some other fruits, vegetables, and berries. Forestry resources are maple, beech, birch, spruce, pine, hemlock, and fir. Marine resources are trout, bass, pike, perch, pickerel, catfish, and panfish. Vermont is known for its granite, marble, and slate; other mineral resources are asbestos, talc, and sand and gravel.

Much of the population is descended from the early Anglo-Saxon settlers; there were influxes of Irish immigrants in the mid-19th century and French Canadians in the early 20th century. The 2000 census shows that 96.8% of the population is white.

Most residents live in large towns or in rural areas. Burlington is the largest city, with 169,391 people.

Environmental imperatives include redeveloping land that has been used and abandoned by industry, in order to reduce the urban sprawl that is occurring rural areas.

COMMUNICATIONS/ENERGY

Vermont has 17 public-use airports, one of which—Burlington International Airport—is international. There are 14,006.3 miles of road, and 11 railroads operate on 793.3 miles of rail.

Vermont has a backbone of approximately 13,000 miles of fiber optic cable, but it does not currently extend to most rural areas in the state. The state is exploring options in wireless coverage to remedy the lack of telecommunications infrastructure in certain areas. In 2000, there were 7,773 high-speed lines; 95.6% of households had telephone service; and 46.7% of households had Internet access.

Petroleum is the most-used energy resource in Vermont, mainly in the form of motor gasoline and distillate oil; electric utilities use nuclear and hydroelectric power almost exclusively. Vermont's energy consumption is the lowest in the United States.

FISCAL/FINANCIAL

Vermont's per-capita state tax burden is one of the highest in the United States, though lower than several other states in the region. Of state tax collected in 2000, 29.4% came from individual income tax; 27.5% from property tax; 17.4% from selective sales tax; 14.6% from general sales tax; 4.6% from license tax; and 3.0% from corporate income tax. The corporate income tax rate is 7.0–9.75%, in four brackets.

Major financial institutions in Vermont include the Advest Group Inc., Banknorth Group, Charter One Financial, Chittenden Corp., FleetBoston, and KeyCorp.

BUSINESS OPPORTUNITIES

Vermont offers a number of tax credits: for financial services companies, R&D, workforce training, and exports; it also offers additional credits and incentives for small businesses. There are tax exemptions on sales of building materials, on sales of certain fuels, on machinery and equipment, on industrial fuels and raw materials, and on pollution-control equipment, and property tax exemptions on alternative energy sources used to generate electricity.

Research facilities include Concepts ETI Inc., the George A. Aiken Forestry Sciences Laboratory, Kaiser Aerospace & Electronics, North Dancer Labs Inc., and the University of Vermont.

There are no *Fortune* 500 companies with their headquarters in Vermont.

For More Information

Book:

Sherman, Joe. *Fast Lane on a Dirt Road: A Contemporary History of Vermont*. White River Junction, VT: Chelsea Green Publishing, 2000.

Web Sites:

Vermont Department of Economic Development:
www.thinkvermont.com
Vermont State Homepage:
www.state.vt.us
Vermont Tourism:
www.1-800-vermont.com

VIRGINIA

KEY FACTS

State capital: **Richmond**
Population: **7,078,515; 12th in U.S.; grew 14.4% 1990–2000**
Land area: **39,593.8 square miles; 37th in U.S.**
Population density: **178.7 per square mile**
GSP: **$242,221 million**
GSP pc: **$34,219.18**
Household income: **$50,069; 7th in U.S.**
Poverty rate: **8.1%**
Unemployment: **2.2%**

ECONOMY

Traditionally an agricultural economy with an emphasis on tobacco, and with large-scale mining and commercial fishing, Virginia has grown into a service-oriented state, business services and tourism account for a large portion of the service sector.

Proximity to the nation's capital has resulted in a high number of government jobs. Manufacturing, which has grown in Virginia as it has declined in most of the nation, comprises electronic equipment, lumber, industrial equipment, apparel, transportation equipment, textiles, food processing, rubber and plastics, and furniture. Transportation is another significant industry.

Virginia's economy was under threat in the early 1990s because of it relied heavily on the defense industry, which suffered from cutbacks at the end of the Cold War; that has been remedied by the state's burgeoning high-tech industry. Virginia's complicated regulatory system was also simplified in the 1990s.

GEOGRAPHY/RESOURCES

Located in the middle of the east coast of the United States, Virginia consists of three mountainous provinces (from west to east, the Appalachian Plateau, the Ridge and Valley province, and the Blue Ridge), the Coastal Plain along the Atlantic coast, and the Eastern Shore, which is separated from the rest of the state by Chesapeake Bay.

Tobacco is the most significant agricultural output; others include soybeans, corn, peanuts, wheat, potatoes, small grains, tomatoes, snap beans, cucumbers, peppers, peaches, apples, cotton, poultry products, beef, dairy products, pork, and horses. Menhaden, scallops, and crabs are the primary marine resources; others include croaker, flounder, clams, bass, snails, spot, weakfish, oysters, and goosefish. Pine is the major forestry resource, followed by ash, birch, cedar, hickory, maple, mixed hardwoods, oak, and sycamore. Coal is the most important mineral resource; others are natural gas, crude oil, crushed stone, sand and gravel, limestone, granite, and titanium.

The earliest European settlers in Virginia were English, French, Welsh, Scotch-Irish, and German, and their descendants still compose a sizable amount of the population. The 2000 census shows that 72.3% of the population is white; 19.6% African American; 4.7% Hispanic, of any race; and 3.7% Asian.

The Norfolk/Virginia Beach/Newport News metro area is the largest in the state, with 1,569,541 people. Other significant cities are the Richmond/Petersburg metro area (996,512), Roanoke (235,932), and Lynchburg (214,911).

Environmental imperatives include cleaning up hazardous chemicals in the state's water supply and preventing further contamination from industrial properties.

COMMUNICATIONS/ENERGY

Strategically located in the northeastern corridor, Virginia has 70 airports, of which two—Norfolk International Airport and Richmond International Airport—are international. Major ports are Newport News, Norfolk, Portsmouth, and Chesapeake. There are 55,625.2 miles of roads, and 13 rail companies operating 3,189.6 miles of track.

Home to the largest computer-software industry on the east coast and the "birthplace of the Internet," Virginia has a sophisticated telecommunications infrastructure, with 139,915 high-speed lines as of 2000. In 2000, 94.9% of households had telephone service; 44.3% of households had Internet access; and 34.6% of the population had wireless telephones.

Virginia uses diverse energy sources, including petroleum, natural gas, coal, electricity, and wood and waste. Electricity is generated primarily by nuclear power and coal, both of which are produced by the state.

FISCAL/FINANCIAL

Virginia has a stable tax structure, showing little change in the last half of the 20th century. Of state taxes collected in 2000, 54.0% came from individual income tax; 19.5% from general sales tax; 14.9% from selective sales tax; 4.5% from corporate income tax; and 4.1% from license tax. The corporate income tax rate, which has not increased since 1972, is 6.0%.

Major financial institutions include Allfirst Financial, Bank of America, BB&T Corp., F&M National Corp., First Citizens BancShares, First Virginia Banks, First Union Corp., Mercantile Bankshares Corp., RBC Centura Banks, and SunTrust Banks.

BUSINESS OPPORTUNITIES

Virginia offers a number of advantages to businesses, including access to venture capital, enterprise zone incentives, numerous exemptions to property and sales and use taxes, low workers' compensation insurance costs, infrastructure development grants, and tax credits for job creation.

Virginia receives the third-highest amount of federal R&D funding in the United States, most of which goes to defense research. Major research centers include the Army's Operational Test and Evaluation Command, the Aviation Applied Technology Directorate, Bell-Boeing, the Center for Advanced Aviation System Development, the Computer Sciences Corporation, the Defense Technical Information Center, the Institute for Defense Analyses Studies, the Logistics Management Institute, the Office of Naval Research, the Thomas Jefferson National Accelerator Facility, the University of Virginia, Virginia Commonwealth University, and the Wallops Flight Facility.

There are 16 *Fortune* 500 companies with their headquarters in Virginia: Freddie Mac, Circuit City Stores, General Dynamics, U.S. Airways Group, Dominion Resources, CSX, AES, Gannett, Norfolk Southern, Nextel Communications, Capital One Financial, Smithfield Foods, Pittston, USA Education, Owens & Minor, and Universal.

For More Information

Book:
Virginia Investment and Business Guide. International Business Publications USA, 2001.

Web Sites:
Commonwealth of Virginia Homepage: **www.state.va.us**
Virginia Economic Development Partnership: **www.yesvirginia.org**

  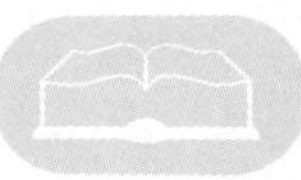    

WASHINGTON

KEY FACTS

State capital: **Olympia**
Population: **5,894,121; 15th in U.S.; grew 21.1% 1990–2000**
Land area: **66,543.6 square miles; 20th in U.S.**
Population density: **88.5 per square mile**
Household income: **$42,024; 25th in U.S.**
Poverty rate: **9.4%**
GSP: **$209,258 million**
GSP pc: **$35,502.83**
Unemployment: **5.2%**

ECONOMY

The agriculture, forestry, and fishing industries that comprised Washington's economy in the 19th and early 20th centuries have declined, giving way to manufacturing and services after World War II. Manufacturing is still significant; aerospace manufacturing is the largest industry in the sector, but shipbuilding, cars and trucks, electronics, scientific and medical instruments, and food processing also contribute.

The state experienced an economic slowdown during the 1980s and 1990s, particularly in communities dependent on lumber and agriculture. Washington's economic recovery during the early 1990s was based on the high-tech and telecommunications industries and on its service industries, which include software development, publishing, and medical services; these now constitute the largest part of the economy.

The greatest challenge for the state is to diversify the industries and employers within the state, an issue made clear in the late 1990s when a downturn in the aerospace sector affected the whole state's economy. Expanded effort in international trade and increased investment in telecommunications infrastructure to draw that industry will begin to remedy the problem.

GEOGRAPHY/RESOURCES

Washington, located in the northwestern corner of the United States and bordering Canada, consists of the Olympic Mountains in the northwest; the Puget Sound Lowland east of the Olympic Mountains; the Cascade Range in the northern-central part of the state; the Columbia Basin in most of the central region; the Okanogan Highlands in the northeast; and the Blue Mountains in the southeast.

Agricultural output includes wheat, fruit, hay, hops, potatoes, sugar beet, peas, dry beans, and flower bulbs; the primary commercial forest products are Douglas fir and western hemlock. While mineral and marine resources contribute little to the overall economy, these resources include coal, Portland cement, sand and gravel, stone, lead, zinc, magnesium, and gold on the one hand; and crabs, clams, oysters, halibut, salmon, sablefish, shrimp, mussels, and tuna on the other.

The majority of Washington's immigration has occurred within the last century, many migrants arriving from Canada and Scandinavia, although the state does have a larger Asian population than most. 81.8% of the population is white; 3.2% is black or African American; 1.6% is Native American and Alaskan Native; 5.5% is Asian; 0.4% is Native Hawaiian and Pacific Islander; 3.9% is of some other race; 3.6% is of two or more races. The Seattle/Tacoma/Bremerton metro area, with 3,554,760 people, is the most populous in the state; Spokane has 417,939 people.

Environmental imperatives include protecting the state's forests and their wildlife, regulating safety standards for natural-gas pipelines in the state, protecting coastal regions from pollution and erosion, and decreasing oil-tanker traffic in Puget Sound.

COMMUNICATIONS/ENERGY

Washington has 756.8 miles of highways and 3,470.5 miles of Class I railroad track. It has 138 public airports, seven of which—Bellingham International Airport, Grant County International Airport, William R. Fairchild International Airport, Jefferson County International Airport, Seattle-Tacoma International Airport, Boeing Field/King County International Airport, and Spokane International Airport—are international. Its four major ports are Seattle, Tacoma, Kalama, and Longview.

Washington has only recently undertaken a survey of the extent of telecommunications infrastructure in the state. There were 195,628 high-speed lines in place in 2000. Likewise in 2000, 93.7% of households had telephone service; 49.7% of households had Internet access; and 38.8% of the population had wireless telephones.

Washington is first in the United States in hydroelectric net generation, which accounts for 88% of electric output; some electricity is exported to other states. Secondary sources are petroleum, natural gas, wood and waste, coal, and nuclear power. Recent energy shortages, due to water shortages and other factors, have caused higher prices and downturns in dependent industries.

FISCAL/FINANCIAL

Washington has no individual income tax and no corporate income tax, although it does charge companies gross-receipts tax ranging from 0.011 to 5.029%. Unemployment insurance tax is 0.50–5.42%, which is slightly higher than most states. Of state taxes collected in 2000, 61.6% came from general sales tax; 15.5% from selective sales tax; 13.5% from property tax; 4.8% from license tax; and 3.5% from documentary and stock transfer tax.

Major financial institutions include Bank of America, Washington Mutual Bank, U.S. Bank of Washington, Keycorp, U.S. Bancorp, Washington Trust Bank, and Zions Bancorporation.

BUSINESS OPPORTUNITIES

Equidistant between Europe and Asia, Washington offers opportunities for companies engaging in international trade. An educated workforce is a draw for high-tech companies, and many non-tax incentives such as business incubator projects are offered on a county-by-county basis.

Major research centers include the Seafood Product Research Center, the Naval Undersea Warfare Center Keyport Division, the Marrowstone Marine Field Laboratory, the Pacific Northwest National Laboratory, the University of Washington, and Washington State University.

Washington is home to the following *Fortune* 500 companies: Boeing, Costco Wholesale, Microsoft, Weyerhaeuser, Washington Mutual, Paccar, Avista, Safeco, Nordstrom, Puget Energy, and Airborne Freight.

For More Information

Book:

Sell, T. M. *Wings of Power: Boeing and the Politics of Growth in the Northwest*. Seattle, WA: University of Washington Press, 2001.

Web Sites:

Access Washington Home Page: **www.state.wa.us**

State of Washington Office of Financial Management: **www.ofm.wa.gov**

  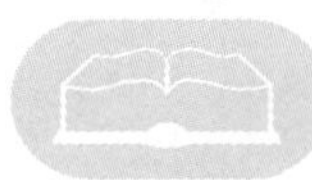  

West Virginia

KEY FACTS

State capital: **Charleston**
Population: **1,808,344; 37th in U.S.; grew 0.8% 1990–2000**
Land area: **24,077.9 square miles; 41st in U.S.**
Population density: **75.1 per square mile**
GSP: **$40,685 million**
GSP pc: **$22,498.48**
Household income: **$29,052; 51st in U.S.**
Poverty rate: **15.8%**
Unemployment: **5.5%**

Economy

After its industrial boom in the late 19th century led by its natural resources—coal, oil, natural gas, and timber—West Virginia has suffered virtually continual decline in the mid- to late 20th century, owing to the mechanization of industry, which resulted in job losses, and a national decline in coal use. Mining still contributes to the state's economy, and manufacturing is a significant sector, led by the chemical industry; other manufacturing industries include primary and fabricated metals; lumber; stone, clay, and glass; industrial machinery; petroleum products; and rubber and plastics.

The services sector is the largest in the state, led by health services. Industries the state is hoping to attract and develop include plastic materials and resins, fabricated plastics, teleservices, wood furniture, warehousing and distribution, automotive parts, medical laboratories, packaging machinery, and industrial organic chemicals.

Challenges facing the state include improving infrastructure, including telecommunications access, air and waterway transportation facilities, and municipal water service; diversifying the industrial base; and raising the state's educational attainment levels. The state has recently undertaken a number of initiatives between education and industry designed to provide workers with the necessary skills.

Geography/Resources

Located in the central eastern United States, West Virginia is a mountainous state with two physiographic regions: the Appalachian Ridge and Valley Region in the east and the Appalachian Plateau over the rest of the state.

Coal is the primary mineral resource; others include natural gas, crude oil, crushed stone, Portland cement, sand and gravel, lime, and salt. Forestry resources include oak, poplar, maple, beech, birch, cherry, and mixed upland hardwoods. Agricultural output includes poultry and poultry products, cattle and calves, nursery and greenhouse crops, apples, peaches, and hay. Marine resources include catfish, bass, crappie, minnows, saugeye, walleye, bluegill, and trout.

Most of West Virginia's population consists of descendants of the German, Irish, Scotch-Irish, and English settlers who came in the 18th and 19th centuries, and the Italian, Hungarian, Polish, and African-American immigrants of the late 19th and early 20th centuries. The 2000 census shows that 95% of the population is white and 3.2% is African American.

Charleston is the largest city, with 251,662 people. Others include Wheeling (153,172); Huntington (139,687); Parkersburg (63,251); and Weirton (58,114).

Environmental imperatives for West Virginia include reclamation of abandoned mines and reducing toxic releases in groundwater.

Communications/Energy

West Virginia has 38 public-use airports, none of which are international. Jackson County Maritime and Industrial Center is the major port, in addition to private shipping facilities; the state is attempting to attract developers for new ports. There are 14 railroads operating 2,645.1 miles of track in addition to commuter rail around Martinsburg, and 37,424.9 miles of roads, with more highway mileage under construction.

Though West Virginia currently ranks close to last in the nation in digital infrastructure, government and private industries are working together to develop it further and have currently laid approximately 161,000 km of fiber optic cable. However, high-speed access is mainly limited to urban areas; there were 6,498 high-speed lines in 2000. In 2000, 93.3% of households had telephone service; 34.3% of households had Internet access; and 19.7% of the population had wireless telephones.

Coal, which West Virginia produces in abundance, is the most-used energy resource in the state. The electric utilities use coal almost exclusively; the industrial sector relies primarily on coal, followed by petroleum and natural gas.

Fiscal/Financial

West Virginia has a per-capita state tax burden in line with those of surrounding states. Of state tax collected in 2000, 28.9% came from individual income tax; 27.4% from general sales tax; 26.4% from selective sales tax; 6.5% from corporate income tax; 5.2% from license tax; and 4.6% from severance tax. The corporate income tax rate is 9.0%, among the highest in the United States.

Major financial institutions include American Bancorporation, Bank One Corp., BB&T Corp., Belmont Bancorp, Camco Financial Corp., City Holding Company, Classic Bancshares, Community Trust Bancorp, First Citizens BancShares, First United Corp., First West Virginia Bancorp, F&M National Corp., Huntington Bancshares, Peoples Bancorp, Premier Financial Bancorp, Sky Financial Group, United Bankshares, and WesBanco.

Business Opportunities

West Virginia offers a few incentives to business, including tax credits for job creation, headquarters location, capital investment, expansion of manufacturing businesses, and R&D, and financing assistance.

Energy-related research is the major R&D sector in West Virginia. Research centers include Bombardier Services Corp.; the Canaan Valley Institute; the Health and Human Services' Division of Safety Research, Division of Respiratory Disease Studies, and Health Effects Laboratory; Marshall University; the National Energy Technology Laboratory; the National Radio Astronomy Observatory; and West Virginia University.

There are no *Fortune* 500 companies with their headquarters in West Virginia.

For More Information

Book:

Rice, Otis K., and Stephen W. Brown. *West Virginia: A History*. Lexington, KY: University Press of Kentucky, 1993.

Web Sites:

West Virginia Development Office:
www.wvdo.org
West Virginia State Homepage:
www.state.wv.us
West Virginia Tourism:
www.callwva.com

WISCONSIN

KEY FACTS

State capital: **Madison**
Population: **5,363,675; 18th in U.S.; grew 9.6% 1990–2000**
Land area: **54,309.7 square miles; 25th in U.S.**
Population density: **98.7 per square mile**
Household income: **$45,349; 16th in U.S.**
Poverty rate: **8.8%**
GSP: **$166,481 million**
GSP pc: **$31,038.61**
Unemployment: **3.5%**

ECONOMY

The development of Wisconsin's economy in the 19th century was divided between iron mining and agriculture. Manufacturing, which is a significant sector of the economy, began with the production of goods from the state's raw materials, and continued to grow even after the mining industry declined. The majority of manufacturing is durable goods, balanced by the production of agricultural and forest products, especially paper. The services industry is boosted by tourism, concentrated in the forests in the northern part of the state and the public parks in the south. There is also a growing biotechnology industry, focusing mainly on agricultural, medical, environmental, and industrial biotechnology.

While Wisconsin has a strong base of traditional industries, it is addressing a number of challenges to fulfill its goal of bringing more high-tech business to the state. Primary concerns include attracting venture capital and improving air travel.

GEOGRAPHY/RESOURCES

Located in the northern Midwest, Wisconsin consists of five physical regions: the broad upland of the Northern Highland; the narrow plain of the Lake Superior Lowland; the Central Plain; the Western Upland in the southwest; and the Southeastern Ridge.

Dairy products are the primary agricultural output, but the state also produces corn, hay, soybeans, oats, and wheat. Forestry resources include aspen, red oak, hard maple, elm, and pine. Wisconsin's primary mineral resources are crushed stone, sand and gravel, silica stone, and lime; metallic minerals, including iron, copper, gold, and silver, are no longer produced. Marine resources, for commercial and sport fishing, include whitefish, chub, perch, smelt, panfish, trout, herring, bass, walleye, northern pike, muskellunge, salmon, and sturgeon.

Despite the state's early French origins, the influx of German immigrants in the mid-19th century provided the most lasting influence on the state's population, followed by Poles, Scandinavians, and British. The 2000 census shows that 88.9% of the population is white; 5.7% is African American; and 1.7% is Asian.

The largest city in Wisconsin is the Milwaukee/Racine metro area, with 1,689,572 people; other major metro areas include the populations of cities in other states, such as the Kenosha metro area, with 9,157,540 people, and the St. Paul metro area, with 2,968,806 people.

The state's forests were decimated by commercial timbering in the late 19th and early 20th centuries. Although reforestation and the tourist industry have both contributed to the forests' recovery since the mid-20th century, regrowth continues to be an environmental priority.

COMMUNICATIONS/ENERGY

Wisconsin has 134 public airports, two of which—Austin Straubel International Airport and Milwaukee's Mitchell International Airport—are international. It has over 111,550.6 miles of roads and 4,201.9 miles of railroad with six major railroad lines; of its 17 commercial ports on the Great Lakes, the four most significant are Duluth-Superior, Milwaukee, La Crosse, and Green Bay.

Wireless providers and cable television companies are investing in technological infrastructure and expanding networks, including the 76,257 high-speed lines in place in 2000. In 2000, 94.0% of households had telephone service; 40.6% of households had Internet access; and 29.8% of the population had wireless telephones.

Petroleum, coal, and natural gas are key sources of energy for the state as a whole; Wisconsin's industries also employ some wood and waste. Utilities mostly use coal and nuclear power for electricity generation.

FISCAL/FINANCIAL

Wisconsin's business climate has improved consistently since the 1970s, although the personal income tax rate remains among the highest in the United States and the state tax burden per capita is one of the highest in the nation. Of state taxes collected in 2000, 47.1% came from individual income tax; 27.7% from general sales tax; 13.0% from selective sales tax; 5.4% from license tax; and 4.6% from corporate net income tax. The corporate income tax rate is 7.9%.

Major institutions in Wisconsin include AMCORE Financial, Anchor BanCorp Wisconsin, Associated Banc-Corp, Bank One Corp., Citizens Banking Corp., First Federal Capital Corp., Marshall & Ilsley, TCF Financial, U.S. Bancorp, and Wells Fargo & Co.

BUSINESS OPPORTUNITIES

Wisconsin has made a number of efforts to draw business to the state since the early 1990s. Workers' compensation premium rates have declined by 33% since 1994, saving over $1 billion. The state also offers property tax exemptions for computers, manufacturing machinery and equipment, inventories, and pollution-control equipment; tax credits for energy used in manufacturing and for R&D; and a 60% capital gains exclusion.

Research centers in the state primarily support the state's agricultural and forestry industries; they include the Madison Forest Products Laboratory, Marquette University, the Medical College of Wisconsin, the National Wildlife Health Center, the Plant Disease Resistance Research Laboratory, the University of Wisconsin, and the Upper Midwest Environmental Sciences Center.

Fortune 500 companies with their headquarters in Wisconsin are Johnson Controls, Northwestern Mutual, Manpower, Rockwell International, Firstar Corp., Kohl's, American Family Insurance Group, Shopko Stores, Aid Association for Lutherans, and Wisconsin Energy.

For More Information

Book:

Morgan, Kathleen O. *Wisconsin in Perspective 2001: A Statistical View of the Badger State.* Lawrence, KS: Morgan Quitno Corp., 2001.

Web Sites:

Forward Wisconsin:
www.forwardwi.com
Travel Wisconsin:
www.travelwisconsin.com

  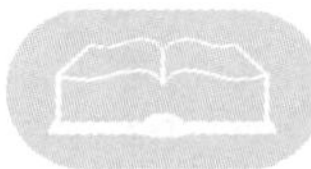    

WYOMING

KEY FACTS

State capital: **Cheyenne**
Population: **493,782; 51st in U.S.; grew 8.9% 1990–2000**
Land area: **97,099.5 square miles; 9th in U.S.**
Population density: **5.1 per square mile**
GSP: **$17,448 million**
GSP pc: **$35,335.43**
Household income: **$39,026; 31st in U.S.**
Poverty rate: **11.0%**
Unemployment: **3.9%**

ECONOMY

Wyoming's history as a cattle-ranching state, which dates back to the mid-19th century, still has an impact on the state's economy; mining—primarily of coal, natural gas, oil, and uranium—is the largest sector of the economy, and contributes more than in any other state. Tourism, driven by winter sports and natural attractions such as Yellowstone National Park, is an important industry that boosts the service sector and retail trade. Manufacturing is a small sector, dependent on processing the state's natural resources.

Of all the states, Wyoming's economy is the most different from the national economy. As a result of its reliance on mining and agriculture, the state benefits from high prices on these commodities while the national economy suffers. This means that Wyoming's economy was boosted during the national economic slowdown in the early 1990s; growth slowed in the mid- to late 1990s, and began increasing again in 1999–2000.

As Wyoming attempts to diversify its economy, services, wholesale trade, and retail trade are expected to be the fastest-growing sectors; growth in the service sector in the 1990s was due mainly to business services, social services, and engineering and management services.

Wyoming faces significant challenges in attracting new business, particularly in new-economy industries. There is a shortage of labor, especially skilled labor, because of the small population base, slow population growth, and difficulty in attracting out-of-state employees. The telecommunications infrastructure, particularly in rural parts of the state, is not sufficient for high-volume data transmission, and access by air is limited. There are initiatives in place to remedy these disadvantages, but they will take time to complete.

GEOGRAPHY/RESOURCES

Located in the western United States, Wyoming consists of the Black Hills in the northeast, the Great Plains in the east, the Southern, Middle, and Northern Rocky Mountains, and the Wyoming Basin between the Southern and Middle Rocky Mountains.

Mineral resources include coal, crude oil, natural gas, uranium, soda ash, bentonite, helium, Portland cement, sand and gravel, crushed stone, and lime. Pine is the primary forestry resource; others are aspen, spruce, and fir. Marine resources include trout, bass, walleye, crappie, perch, sauger, ling, channel catfish, and bluegill. Meat animals, primarily cattle, are the primary agricultural output; others are feed crops, hay, sugar beet, barley, vegetables, wheat, oats, corn, beans, potatoes, vegetables, and dairy products.

Wyoming's population, which fluctuates with the strength of the mining industry, consists primarily of the descendants of early European settlers, though the Mexican population is growing. The 2000 census shows that 92.1% of the population is white; 6.4% Hispanic, of any race; and 2.3% Native American. Cheyenne is the largest city, with 81,607 people; Casper has 66,533 people.

Environmental imperatives include repairing damage to the soil and groundwater caused by mining activity and livestock processing.

COMMUNICATIONS/ENERGY

Highways and railroads are the dominant modes of transport in Wyoming; the state has 34,130.4 miles of highways and 47,395.4 miles of railroad. Wyoming has 30 public-use airports, none of which are international. Major airports include Cheyenne, Larami, Jackson Hole, and Yellowstone.

Wyoming is still developing its telecommunications infrastructure, and insufficient coverage has resulted in problems with high-speed data transmission. A number of initiatives are under way to remedy these problems. In 2000, 94.8% of households had telephone service and 44.1% of households had Internet access.

Coal is the dominant energy resource, and electricity is generated almost completely by coal. Natural gas and petroleum are the other most-consumed resources.

FISCAL/FINANCIAL

Wyoming is a low-tax state, with no individual or corporate income tax and no inventory tax. Of state taxes collected in 2000, 38.3% came from general sales tax; 25.5% from severance tax; 11.2% from selective sales tax; 10.5% from property tax; 9.3% from license tax; and 5.3% from death and gift tax.

Major financial institutions in Wyoming include Wyoming Community First Bankshares Inc., U.S. Bancorp, and Wells Fargo & Co.

BUSINESS OPPORTUNITIES

Wyoming offers several incentives for business, including a revolving loan fund for new and expanding businesses, gap financing for business relocation, workforce training grants, grants for tradeshow marketing, rural enterprise business grants, and grants for infrastructure development.

However, the lack of research facilities acts as a disincentive to new businesses, especially those outside the state's traditional industries; Wyoming ranks last among the states in terms of federal research funding, and most research is focused on mining and agriculture. Research centers include the Arthropod-Borne Animal Diseases Research Laboratory, the High Plains Grasslands Research Station, the University of Wyoming, and the Western Research Institute.

There are no *Fortune* 500 companies with their headquarters in Wyoming.

For More Information

Book:
Larson, T. A. *History of Wyoming*. Lincoln, NE: University of Nebraska Press, 1993.

Web Sites:
State of Wyoming Homepage:
www.state.wy.us
Wyoming Business Council:
www.wyomingbusiness.org
Wyoming Tourism Events and Activities:
www.wyomingcompanion.com

Industry Profiles

AUTOMOTIVES

1769	First true automobile, a steam truck designed by Nicole-Joseph Cugnot, for the French army.
1801	World's first passenger-carrying vehicle, built by Richard Trevithick in the United Kingdom.
1884–1885	Karl Benz of Mannheim builds two-seater tricycle powered by four-stroke gasoline engine.
1885	André Michelin of France produces first pneumatic car tire.
1902	Ford Motor Company formed.
1908	Ford pioneers first moving assembly line with Model T Ford.
1925	Mercedes and Benz companies merge.
1938	Volkswagen Beetle enters production.
1958	Mini small car launched in Britain.
1961	Jaguar Cars of Coventry produces first 150mph production car, the E-Type.
1972	Sales of VW Beetle reach 15 million.
1986	Toyota of Japan overtakes VW to claim best-selling vehicle, the Corolla.
1994	BMW of Germany acquires Rover Group, Britain's largest car maker.
1998	Daimler-Benz acquires Chrysler Corp in world's largest industrial merger.
2000	BMW breaks up Rover Group; GM acquires 20% of Fiat Auto; Ford buys Land Rover.
2001	Profit warnings at Ford, Renault, Volvo Trucks, DaimlerChrysler, Fiat, Delphi, Visteon.
2002	Major restructuring launched by Big Three U.S. car makers.

The global motor industry has entered the 21st century with a business model not far removed from that of the early 20th century.

The world's single largest manufacturing industry—in terms of revenue and employment—is still defined by high fixed costs, low profit margins, heavily unionized labor, intense price competition, volatile demand, and state-subsidized companies in several countries.

While the business model may not have changed much, the product has. It is true that today's automobile still has the same basic characteristics as the horseless carriage pioneered in the 1880s by Karl Benz and Gottlieb Daimler—four wheels, mostly gasoline-powered engines, low weight, and relative speed—but the changes that have been made are dramatic.

Over the past 120 years or so, but more especially in the past 70, the motor car has transformed society and personal mobility. In 1890, the average Briton—then a citizen of the world's most industrialized society—traveled about 13 miles a year. According to figures compiled by U.K. industry consultants Autopolis, that figure had reached about 13 miles a day by the 1990s.

Autopolis calculate that there were 800 cars on the road at the end of the 19th century. By 1910, that number had increased to almost 460,000, with more than 300 car makers setting up business. Ten years later, there were 8 million vehicles on the road. Even then, the industry was heavily weighted in production and usage toward the United States.

As production grew, so prices fell. By the outbreak of World War II, the entire industry had embraced the concept of mass production, dominated by Henry Ford's ubiquitous Model T in the 1920s. Only after the war, however, did the industry truly begin to gain global proportions; it was partly forced to do so by the need to move large volumes of material and people by road over longer distances.

Best selling automobiles of all time: totals to 2001 (million)

Toyota Corolla, 1966–	23.0
VW Beetle, 1937–	21.5
VW Golf, 1974–	20.0
Lada Riva, 1972–97	19.0
Ford Model T, 1908–27	16.5
Honda Civic, 1972–	14.0
Nissan Sunny/Pulsar, 1966–94	13.6
Honda Accord, 1976–	11.5
VW Passat, 1973–	10.4

Growing personal wealth and international trade created new export markets in North America, Japan, and Western Europe. That drive, at least after the oil crisis of 1973, has been dominated by the production techniques, quality manufacturing, and sales of Japanese manufacturers. Their global scale, along with those of their American rivals General Motors (GM), Ford, and Chrysler, underpinned an industry which, by 2000, was producing 59.7 million vehicles annually.

In the 1990s and the early years of the new millennium, the industry has been characterized by growing consolidation among car and truck manufacturers and by the emergence of the environment as a key issue in vehicle engineering and production. The costs involved in meeting new environmental legislation—mainly focusing on a reduction in emissions—have fueled a sharp rise in product development spending, which only the richest companies can fully afford. That, in turn, has proved one of the main factors behind mergers and acquisitions in the industry. Those without the financial muscle to fund new products or expansion into new markets are either swallowed up or disappear completely.

Those that remain, however, are committed to developing vehicles running on much cleaner engines. A century revolutionized by the combustion engine could, therefore, make way for a new era defined by zero-emission vehicles using a completely different technology.

The similarly fragmented commercial vehicle industry also contracted during the 1990s into a handful of global manufacturers. In heavy trucks, the sector is dominated by DaimlerChrysler, followed by Volvo of Sweden. However, a sharp downturn in U.S. orders, a shortage of drivers, and falling residual values have combined in the 2000s to undermine profits in the sector, and have led to a wave of restructuring and cutbacks among manufacturers.

The light commercial vehicle sector, however, has been less affected. Demand for vans and small trucks has been fueled by the growth of mail order and home delivery services. Ford, Renault, and Iveco—part of Fiat—have emerged as the market leaders in Europe.

COMPANIES

A sector that began as a fragmented cottage industry, relying initially on traditional coachbuilding skills, is now dominated by a handful of global players. Of almost 60 million cars and trucks produced in 2000, less than a dozen companies account for more than 47 million, or about 80% of all output.

The industry is led by General Motors and Ford, which together assemble and

Top companies by sales, 2000 ($ million)

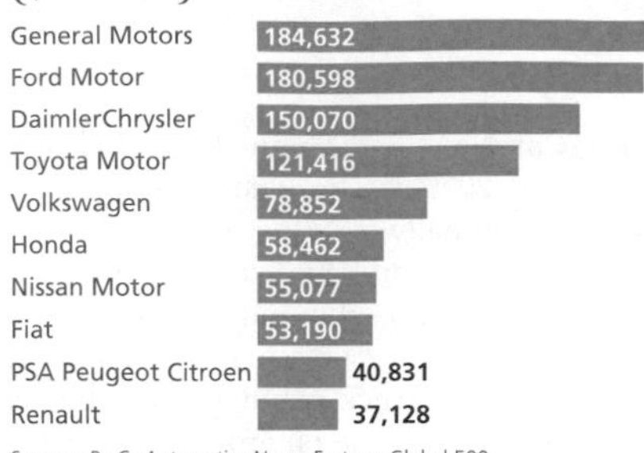

Sources: PwC, *Automotive News*, Fortune Global 500

Top companies by profits, 2000 ($ million)

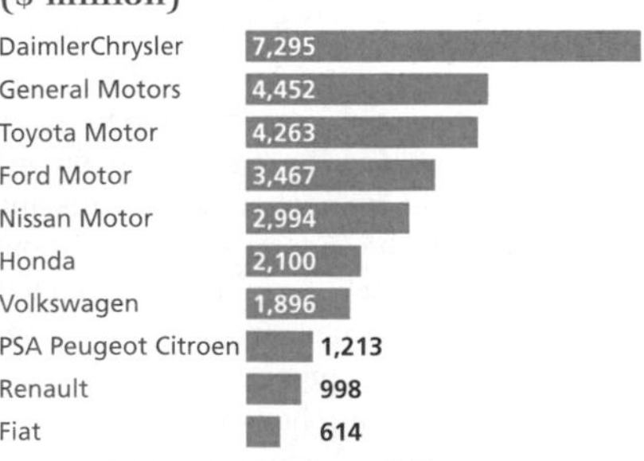

Sources: PwC, *Automotive News*, Fortune Global 500

sell about 16 million vehicles a year. However, although the two U.S. giants boast the greatest scale—serving the largest market—no other car maker among the top 20 has its headquarters in North America. This is largely because many of the smaller U.S. brands, such as Buick, Dodge, Cadillac, Lincoln and Mercury, have been swallowed up by GM and Ford themselves, but it also reflects the tremendous growth of Japanese and European car makers—not least in winning market share in the United States.

Although Toyota of Japan is the world's third-largest manufacturer, it is number one in terms of market capitalization and financial strength. Toyota is also unique in having stood aside from the wave of mergers and acquisitions that has swept the industry in recent years. When it wanted to move into the luxury car market, it developed a new brand, Lexus. When it wanted to expand in small cars, it used its wholly-owned Daihatsu subsidiary. Most other car makers have taken part in the trend towards consolidation. In 1998, Daimler-Benz of Germany began the latest series of deals by agreeing a "merger of equals" with Chrysler of the United States. That was followed by Ford's acquisition of Volvo Cars for about $6 billion. Renault of France subsequently acquired 36.8% of Nissan Motor, the Japanese car maker that was almost crushed by a mountain of debt. DaimlerChrysler, the newly merged German-U.S. group, then snapped up a controlling stake in Mitsubishi Motors of Japan.

In Europe, BMW of Germany jettisoned its loss-making Rover subsidiary during 2000. It sold the off-road Land Rover part of the business to Ford for almost $2 billion, and the troubled car business to a local consortium of U.K. businessmen. Elsewhere, General Motors agreed to acquire 20% of Italy's Fiat Auto, and also increased its stakes in Suzuki and Isuzu of Japan. GM took full control of Saab Automobile, and launched an offer for Daewoo, the bankrupt South Korean car manufacturer.

This activity was mirrored in the commercial vehicle sector, where Volvo—the industrial business that was not part of the Ford deal—acquired Renault's heavy truck arm. DaimlerChrysler acquired Western Star of Canada. Fiat's Iveco unit took control of Renault's bus-building division.

Such deals were funded largely by cash generated following a sharp upturn in the industry during the 1990s, but growth and profitability have started to slow in the 2000s. The three main markets of North America, Western Europe, and Japan are showing signs of flat or falling vehicle demand.

The mass-market car sector has been hit particularly hard, with manufacturers resorting to costly discounting or incentive schemes in their attempts to retain market share. The luxury or premium sector, led by car makers such as BMW and Mercedes, has proved far more resilient. Margins at BMW are about 9%, the highest for any large-volume manufacturer. Porsche, the specialist sports car group, boasts even better margins, but it is relatively small-scale.

The industry giants of Ford and GM, however, have much lower margins: only 4–5% at peak times. They are much more vulnerable to volatile demand. In an effort to compensate at least to some extent, they have moved into the premium sector with brands such as Cadillac and Jaguar, striving to achieve the sort of profitability enjoyed by BMW. So far they have only been modestly successful in that effort.

MARKETS

The United States is by far the largest car and truck market in the world. At its peak in 2000, it was sustaining sales of 17.4 million units a year. Although it is not expected to regain those levels for some time, the annualized selling rate is expected to settle at about 14.5–15.0 million units a year.

Western European sales were 17.03 million in 2000, and fell only modestly in 2001. Of the European markets, the five largest are Germany, the United Kingdom, France, Spain, and Italy. The German market alone, at about 3–3.3 million cars a year, is larger than the entire market of Eastern Europe—about 2.7 million a year—and Latin America, where about 2.5 million cars a year are sold.

After North America and Western Europe, Asia Pacific accounts for 12–13 million units a year, dominated by Japan with 4–4.3 million units a year. The Japanese market, in terms of size, is almost double the combined markets of the entire Middle East and Africa, with annual sales of 1.7 million and 900,000 units respectively.

Emerging markets, nevertheless, are expected to account for the largest growth in demand during the 2000s. Countries such as China, India, and Russia are likely to generate some of the fastest sales increases. However, low average disposable income will mean that most of the demand will be for entry-level small cars, a sector where most car makers find it very difficult to make significant profits.

TECHNOLOGY

In recent years, vehicle technology has been dominated by the drive to develop cleaner, lower-emission engines. Ultimately, car makers hope to develop fuel-cell technology for volume cars. Although fuel cells themselves are not new—they were used in the Apollo moon rockets—car

Largest markets for automobiles, 2000

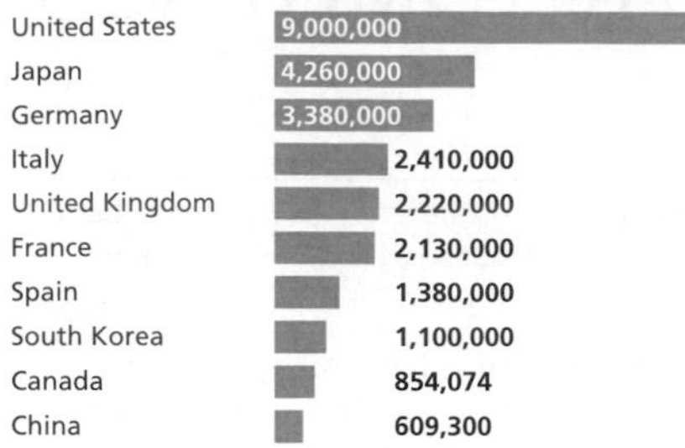

Largest markets for commercial vehicles, 2000

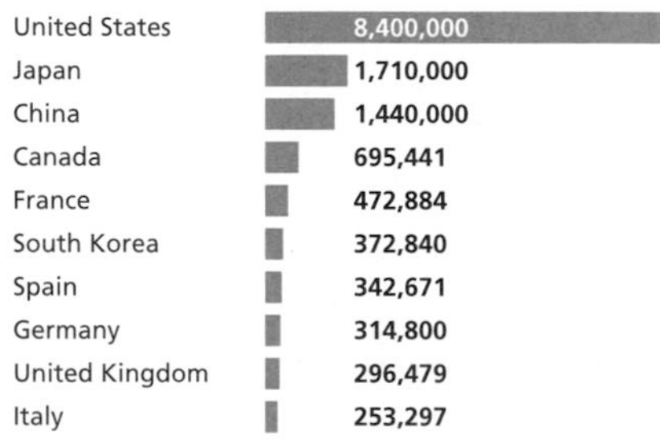

makers are only just beginning to use the technology for road transport.

Fuel cells combine hydrogen and oxygen to produce an electrical current. That current is used to drive an electrical engine, emitting steam as its only by-product. So far, car makers and fuel providers have failed to agree an industry standard for fuel cells, particularly on which fuel to use to provide the hydrogen necessary. There are safety reservations about using hydrogen directly at fuel pumps, with most manufacturers preferring instead to use methanol or gasoline and then to extract the hydrogen using a reformer on the vehicle.

Until an industry standard is reached, car makers are likely to develop alternative fuel vehicles using liquefied petroleum gas or compressed natural gas. Others are developing hybrid vehicles, which combine ordinary gasoline engines with electric motors.

Apart from new cleaner engines, the industry has started to harness the Internet and satellite technology to develop navigation and other services for drivers.

New Products

As the industry leader, the North American market has defined the market for new vehicles. In the United States, more than half of all vehicles sold are now "light trucks"—sports utility vehicles, pick-up trucks, and minivans.

The best-selling light truck is the Ford Explorer, which has annual sales of about 400,000–500,000 units.

The success and relatively high margins of that sector have stimulated the development of a range of similar new models, such as BMW's X5 and X3 sports utility vehicles (SUVs), the new Range Rover (developed at a cost of $1.4 billion), and the Dodge Ram.

Outside North America the market is more oriented to ordinary passenger cars. Arguably the most successful European car is BMW's 3-series model, which has become the benchmark for the mid-size sector. The 3-series sells about 330,000 units a year in Europe and almost 100,000 in North America, but it is facing a new challenge from vehicles such as Jaguar's X-Type small car and the Mercedes C-Class. Audi, Lexus, and VW are also moving into this sector.

The Japanese car makers continue to dominate the small-car segment, with Toyota's Yaris proving a best-seller. The frequency of new launches by specialist groups—the new Mini (BMW), a new mid-size Bentley, and a revived Maserati—has sharply increased.

Employment

The motor industry as a whole is one of the world's largest employers, generating hundreds of thousands of jobs among manufacturers, as well as many more for suppliers, dealers, advertisers, and so on. In the United Kingdom alone, estimates suggest that the industry accounts for about 800,000 jobs. The U.S. auto industry sustains at least 2 million direct jobs, including manufacturers, component suppliers, and dealers. Many more jobs are described as "induced labor," in that their existence depends on demand generated by the auto sector.

Largest employers, 2000

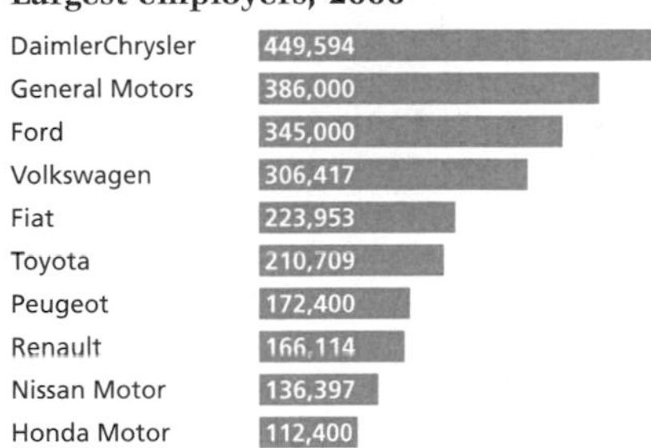

Sources: FT 500, 2000 annual reports

The largest employers, by company, are General Motors and Ford, both of which have global workforces of about 350,000.

No wholly accurate figures exist for the complete workforce of the industry, ranging from suppliers to used car salesmen, but conservative estimates suggest it could be around 15 million people.

In recent years, however, the emphasis has been on cutting rather than creating jobs. Chrysler alone announced 26,000 job losses in 2001, mainly through early retirement and voluntary separation packages.

Nevertheless, the industry remains highly unionized, which makes savage job cuts difficult. This is particularly the case in Europe, where many car makers have to observe co-determination rules: union representatives sit on their supervisory boards and have to be consulted on strategic cutbacks.

Impact of the Internet

Vehicle manufacturers embraced the Internet and e-commerce boom along with every other industry at the end of the 1990s. However, the sharp downturn in the technology sector has made car makers reassess their "e-ambitions."

Internet dealerships, for example, have proved less popular than regular showrooms. Most motorists still want to "kick the tires" of a car and test it before buying. Where Internet showrooms exist, they are used mostly as a search tool to compare prices.

The Internet has made inroads into "telematics"—the provision of e-services in the car, such as navigation systems, emergency call services, and e-mail. Route guidance and real-time traffic information is proving one of the most popular features in new cars.

The other area where e-business is having an effect is parts purchasing. Several leading manufacturers, led by GM, Ford, and DaimlerChrysler, have formed Covisint, an online trade exchange where suppliers bid over the Internet for large purchase orders. Although some component companies have expressed reservations, other car makers have set up their own trade exchanges. VW, for example, says it is already conducting about 25% of all its purchasing over the Internet.

For More Information

Books and Directories:

DRI.Wefa. *World Car Industry Forecasts.* London: DRI.

Maxton, Graeme, and John Wormald. *Driving Over a Cliff? Business Lessons from the World's Car Industry.* Boston, MA: Addison Wesley Publishing Company, 1995.

Vlasic, W., and B.A. Stertz. *Taken for a Ride: How Daimler-Benz Drove Off with Chrysler.* New York: HarperCollins, 2001.

Womack, James P. et al. *The Machine That Changed the World.* New York: Macmillan, 1990.

Magazines and Journals:

Automotive News: **www.automotivenewseurope.com**

AutoExpress: **autoexpress.co.uk**

Web Sites:

American Alliance of Automobile Manufacturers: **autoalliance.org**

Automotive Sector Insights: **www.pwcglobal.com/insights/auto**

European Association of Automobile Manufacturers: **www.acea.be**

German Vehicle Manufacturers Association (VDA): **www.VDA.de**

Japanese Automobile Manufacturers' Association: **Jama.or.jp**

Society of Motor Manufacturers and Traders: **smmt.co.uk**

AVIATION

1903	First powered flight.
1922	First transcontinental crossing of the United States.
1927	Charles Lindbergh made the first solo flight across the Atlantic; Pan-American Airways set up its first service flying between Key West and Florida.
1944	Chicago Conference set the pattern of restrictive international aviation regulation, which still persists today.
1946	Pan-American made the first scheduled transatlantic flight.
1952	The De Havilland Comet, the world's first jetliner, entered service with BOAC in the United Kingdom.
1958	The first Boeing jetliner, the 707, entered revenue service with Pan American.
1969	First flight of the Boeing 747, capable of carrying more than 400 passengers.
1970	Establishment of Airbus, the first step towards integration of Europe's civil aviation industry.
1971	Southwest Airlines, the pioneer low-cost airline, founded in the United States.
1976	Entry into service of Concorde, the only supersonic civilian airliner.
1978	Sweeping deregulation of U.S. airline industry.
1987	Privatization of British Airways.
1993	Single aviation market in the European Union largely in place, process completed in 1997.
1997	Boeing takeover of McDonnell Douglas.
2000	Industrial launch of 555-seat Airbus A380 superjumbo, due to enter service in 2006.
2000	Crash of Air France Concorde near Paris. All Concordes grounded for 15 months. Flights resumed in late 2001.
2001	September 11 terrorist attacks in U.S. trigger world aviation crisis.
2001	Financial collapse of Swissair and Sabena.

In the century since Wilbur and Orville Wright took to the skies in December 1903, aviation has become one of the most powerful single influences on world development. Relatively low-cost, safe, and efficient jet travel has cut journeys that took days and sometimes weeks to just hours, in the process vastly accelerating the expansion of trade and economic integration worldwide.

The growth in air travel has been startling, with the number of passengers traveling on scheduled services climbing from 78 million in 1956 to 1.65 billion in 2000.

A dark shadow passed across air travel on September 11, 2001 with the terrorist attacks in the United States. Never before had civil airliners been hijacked by suicide squads and turned into flying bombs.

The impact on the airline industry and its suppliers, led by the commercial aircraft makers, has been profound. The events of September 11 and the heavy blow they dealt to confidence in air travel led to the first year-on-year fall in international scheduled traffic in 2001 since 1991, the year of the Gulf war.

The airline industry has always been highly cyclical. In four years in the early 1990s, airlines in the International Air Transport Association (IATA) lost $15.6 billion on their international scheduled services, more than wiping out the total profits they made in the 44 preceding years. In the second half of the 1990s the airline sector again recorded strong profits, although margins remained modest by comparison with many business sectors; by 2000 its fortunes were already in decline. In particular in the United States, which alone accounts for 40% of the world aviation market, 2001 became the worst year in the industry's history.

Even before September 11 airlines were already suffering from the downturn in the U.S. economy and in particular from a steep fall in lucrative business travel. The terrorist attacks caused a further sudden—and exceptionally severe—fall in demand for air travel, however, leading to unprecedented losses of around $15 billion for the world airline industry in 2001, according to IATA estimates.

On the basis of its experience after the Gulf War, the aviation industry is looking to a gradual recovery in its fortunes during 2002, but the recession is expected to last much longer in the commercial aerospace industry, where the dearth of new orders is expected to result in falling production of large civil aircraft well into 2003–04.

AIRCRAFT MAKERS

The civil aircraft industry has become highly concentrated, with a duopoly created in the supply of large aircraft of 100 seats and above between the respective champions of the United States and Europe, Boeing and Airbus. Boeing account for around 80% of all the aircraft over 100 seats operating in the world. Airbus, which is 80% owned by the European Aeronautic Defense and Space company (EADS) and 20% by BAE Systems of the United Kingdom, won 375 new orders in 2001 for aircraft above 100 seats, compared with the 335 won by Boeing. These included its first 85 firm orders for the A380 superjumbo.

Aerospace groups by aero sales, 2000 ($ million)

Source: *Flight International*

The overall aircraft market has contracted sharply as airlines have restricted new orders, first in response to the global economic slowdown and second in the aftermath of the September 11 attacks. Total deliveries by both Boeing and Airbus are expected to be about 650 in 2002, a 24% fall on 2001. In the wake of September 11, Boeing cut up to 30,000 jobs—almost a third of its commercial airplanes workforce.

Civil aircraft sales, 2000 ($ million)

Boeing, U.S.	31,171
EADS (Airbus), France/Germany	13,692
Bombardier, Canada	7,112
BAE Systems, U.K.	4,340
Raytheon, U.S.	3,220
General Dynamics (Gulfstream), U.S.	3,029
Embraer, Brazil	2,925
Textron (Cessna), U.S.	2,750
Dassault Aviation (Falcon), France	2,280
Fairchild Dornier, U.S./Germany	629

Source: *Flight International*

Boeing estimates that the world aircraft fleet will double to almost 33,000 jets by 2020, comprising almost 18,400 new aircraft for market growth, 5,100 replacement aircraft, and more than 9,500 aircraft that are currently flying. This forecast was based on an expected average annual growth in world air travel of 4.7% a year, plus 6.4% annual growth in air cargo: air freight accounts for over a third of the value of world merchandise trade, and during the past two decades the number of all-cargo aircraft has more than tripled.

According to the Boeing, forecast regional growth rates in air travel will vary around the world between 3.1 and 7.7%, with Latin America expected to be the fastest-growing market. Boeing projected that airlines will invest $1.7 trillion in new commercial aircraft, which equates to 23,500 aircraft deliveries during the next 20 years. It believes that the events of September 11 have only postponed this expansion, that economic growth will return, and that traffic growth will return to its long-term trend.

Airlines

Despite the global nature of air travel, the airline industry remains far more fragmented than most business sectors, largely as a result of the barriers to consolidation set by international aviation regulation and competition policy. The result of current restrictions is that even the world's largest carrier, American Airlines, has a global market share of little more than 7%.

Airlines still operate under a set of ground rules established at a conference in Chicago in 1944. International route rights are governed by a web of bilateral treaties, and still based on an airline's national identity. (Foreign ownership is often limited by law: to 25% in the case of U.S. airlines, and to 49% in the European Union.) The treaties allocate route rights, and can decide frequencies and even influence fare levels

Airlines by revenues, 2000 ($ million)

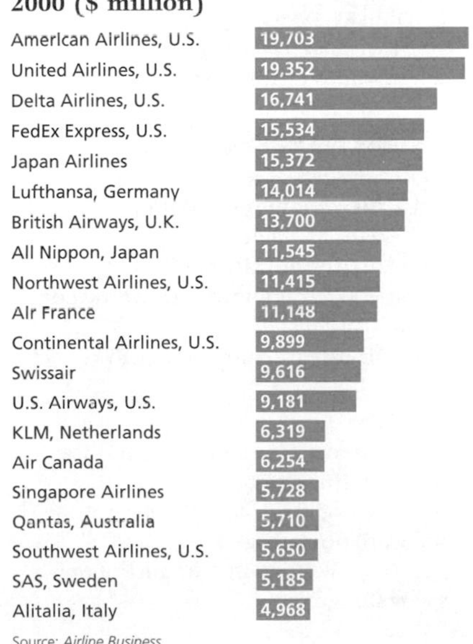

Source: *Airline Business*

Bermuda II, the present U.S./U.K. bilateral air services treaty, which dates back to 1977, is one of the most restrictive in international aviation. Under this agreement, only two British airlines—British Airways and Virgin Atlantic—and two American carriers—United Airlines and American Airlines—are allowed to fly direct transatlantic routes out of London's Heathrow airport. The United States has made reform of the Bermuda II treaty its top priority for opening access to foreign markets. The European Commission has set the long term aim of negotiating a transatlantic common aviation area with the United States, which would bring together the two biggest aviation markets in the world and could finally remove the ownership and traffic rights regulations which hitherto have hampered the consolidation of the international airline industry.

Airlines by operating margin, 2000 (%)

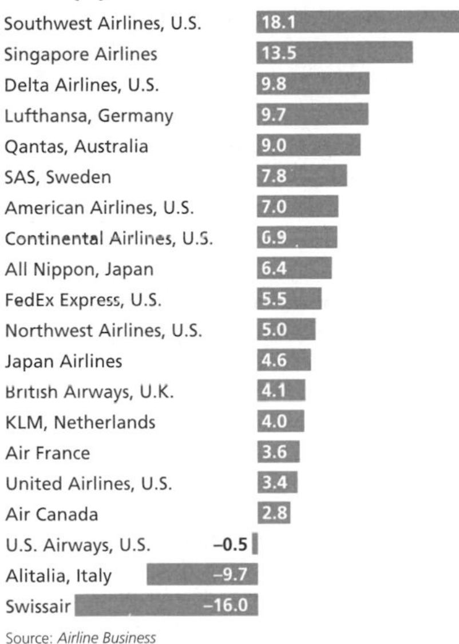

Source: *Airline Business*

International aviation rules on traffic rights played a big part in thwarting British Airways' planned takeover of KLM, the Dutch national carrier, in the second half of 2000: this would have produced the world's largest carrier measured by turnover, and would have kick-started the consolidation process in Europe. For the moment, consolidation is happening more as a result of corporate collapse and operations shrinkage rather than through mergers and acquisitions.

For the first time in 2001 two European flag carriers, Swissair and Sabena, suffered financial collapse, but in both cases entrenched local interests succeeded in salvaging successor national airlines out of the wreckage.

In the United States it is the competition regime that has halted a further concentration of the U.S. industry, and in 2001 led to United Airlines having to drop its planned acquisition of U.S. Airways. The one step that has been accomplished is American Airlines' takeover in 2001 of TransWorld Airlines, which allowed American to leapfrog United Airlines to become the world's largest carrier. The deal only became possible, however, after TWA collapsed.

The belief among carriers in the need for consolidation is unchanged, as the big network airlines try to deal with growing pressures from low-cost startup carriers, overcapacity, volatile fuel prices, rising labor costs, and regional deregulation. However, the obstacles to big mergers and acquisitions also remain unchanged.

Alliances

Denied the mechanism of large-scale mergers and acquisitions to consolidate and rationalize, airlines have instead been forced to invent the device of the "alliance" in order to offer customers the experience of seamless air travel around the globe and between different networks. Three main alliance groupings have emerged: oneworld under the leadership of American Airlines and British Airways, Star led by Lufthansa and United Airlines, and SkyTeam led by Air France and Delta Air Lines. Here too, however, competition concerns and international regulation threaten the scope of the alliances' activities.

American Airlines and British Airways were forced to withdraw their application to the U.S. Department of Transportation for antitrust immunity for a joint venture across the North Atlantic in early 2002. The carriers have joined forces in a campaign to persuade the U.S. government and the European Commission to begin negotiations on establishing a "truly open" aviation market between the United States and Europe. They are seeking to persuade governments to move quickly to establish the transatlantic common aviation market, with all issues open for negotiation from operating freedoms to ownership and control.

Low-cost Carriers

While the network carriers seek to develop alliances to improve their global competitiveness, they are facing tough and increasing competition within their home regions from the growing band of low-cost airlines. The crisis that hit large parts of the global airline community during 2001 and 2002 presented the low-cost, no-frills carriers with an unprecedented window of opportunity, particularly in Europe.

Ryanair, the fast-growing, leading low-cost airline in Europe, believes that over the next five years the European airline industry will consolidate with the emergence of "three large mega-connecting carriers"—British Airways, Lufthansa, and Air France—together with one or maybe two very large, low-fare, point-to-point carriers (taking customers direct to their destination, rather than via time-consuming transfers through busy hub airports). Ryanair expects that most other airlines will become either subsidiaries or feeders of the three big alliances, or will disappear altogether.

While the traditional flag carriers were forced to cut back, the low-cost airlines have continued to expand, successfully stimulating traffic through low-fare promotions. They are holding to their highly ambitious growth plans. In the case of Ryanair this includes a firm order placed with Boeing in January 2002 for 100 new aircraft to support planned growth of 25% a year, which could make it the biggest short-haul airline in Europe by 2010 with 40 million passengers a year.

Investors also appear to believe in the future of the low-cost model in Europe, where Ryanair has become the second-largest airline by market capitalization, valued at the end of 2001 well ahead of British Airways and not far behind Germany's Lufthansa. EasyJet, which floated on the London stock market in November 2000, saw its value rise by almost 50% in a year.

In the United States, a market capitalization of around $14.9 billion at the end of 2001 made Southwest worth more than the six biggest U.S. airlines combined, which together managed a total market valuation of only $11.7 billion. Southwest's financial performance in 2001 marked the group's 29th consecutive year of profitability, a record of consistency unmatched in an industry better known for its cyclical nature. Southwest was the only big U.S. carrier to make both net and operating profits during the last crisis in the airline industry in the early 1990s, a record it could repeat in the crisis of 2001–02.

Technology

Airbus and Boeing are following strikingly different strategic routes in the development of new aircraft.

Boeing's concept for the next generation airliner is the sonic cruiser, that could fly at speeds up to 98% of the speed of sound and cover distances greater than any plane flying today. The faster speeds could reduce flight times by 15–20%, shortening air journeys by about one hour for every 4,800 km flown. Boeing is aiming, however, for a fuel consumption per passenger comparable to today's best-performing widebody, twin-engined airliners. The sonic cruiser would fly at an altitude of more than 12,500 m, significantly higher than current aircraft, and some versions could have a range of 16,500 km or more. The target date for entry into service of the aircraft is around 2008.

Aerospace groups by R&D spend, 2000 ($ million)

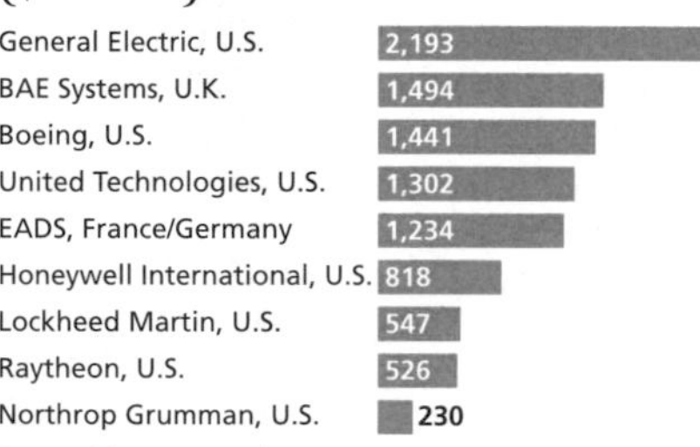

Source: *Flight International*

Airbus is also researching the market for a new 200–250 seat plane that could replace its own outdated twin-aisle A300 as well as the ageing Boeing 767. It believes that the airlines have set their priorities on the economics of operation and on environmental performance, rather than on speed.

After years of hesitation, Airbus committed itself at the end of 2000 to the $10.7 billion development of the 555-seat A380 superjumbo, the most ambitious project ever undertaken by the European civil aerospace industry. The A380, which is due to enter service in 2006 with Singapore Airlines, will be the biggest civil aircraft ever built, and is designed to fly on the world's busiest air routes between congested hub airports, where takeoff and landing slots are already at a premium. Airbus believes that airlines will need larger-capacity aircraft to fly the densest trunk routes around the world connecting the main hub airports of Asia, North America, and Europe.

The A380 poses a great challenge to Boeing, as it is set to break the U.S. group's more than 30-year monopoly of the very large aircraft market with its 747 jumbo jet, which entered service in 1970. The Airbus aircraft's planned capacity for 555 seats compares with the 416 of the present Boeing 747–400, the largest passenger aircraft flying today. Airbus says that the A380 will provide 15–20% lower operating costs than the 747–400, and will have 10–15% more range, as well as lower fuel burn, less noise, and lower emissions. The double-decker design will offer 49% more available floor space than the 747–400 but only 35% more seating, which implies that seating space and aisles will be more spacious.

The future for supersonic travel looks a little less bleak than it did in the summer of 2000, when the crash of an Air France Concorde shortly after takeoff near Paris threatened to bring a quarter of a century of technological achievement to an abrupt end.

The consensus in the industry is that any supersonic airliner of the future will be a business jet. A viable project would need a market of at least 300 aircraft, and even then it still faces the problem of persuading an engine maker to share the risk. In addition it would either need a change in regulations that would lift the ban on commercial aircraft creating sonic booms over land—a large part of any future demand is in the U.S. transcontinental market—or advances in engine technology that would eliminate the problem completely.

For More Information

Books and Directories:

Doganis, Rigas. *The Airline Business in the 21st Century*. New York: Routledge, 2000.

Sabbagh, Karl. *21st Century Jet*. New York: Macmillan, 1996.

World Aviation Directory: **www.wadaviation.com**

Magazines and Journals:

Airline Business: **www.airlinebusiness.com**

The Airline Monitor: **www.airlinemonitor.com**

Aviation Week: **www.aviationnow.com**

Flight International: **www.flightinternational.com**

Web Sites:

Air Transport Association of America: **www.airlines.org**

Airports Council International: **www.airports.org**

U.S. Federal Aviation Administration: **www.faa.gov**

BANKING

1821	Gold standard established in the United Kingdom.
1929	Wall Street crash.
1933	Glass-Steagall Act.
1944	Bretton Woods agreement foresees the IMF and World Bank.
1963	U.S. interest equalization tax gives impetus to the offshore dollar market.
1971	U.S. dollar comes off the gold standard.
1972	Currency futures launched in Chicago.
1973	Oil crisis: OPEC quadruples oil price.
1979	Lifting of U.K. exchange controls.
1981	Eurodollar future launched in Chicago.
1982	Third world debt crisis; Mexico and Brazil default.
1986	London's Big Bang.
1994	Dollar interest-rate shock.
1998	Russia defaults, collapse of Long-Term Capital Management.
1999	Repeal of Glass-Steagall Act in United States.
1999	Creation of a single EU currency: the Euro.
2000	Merger of JP Morgan and Chase; merger of Citicorp and Salomon Smith Barney.

The concept of a bank has not changed much since medieval times. A bank takes deposits from customers, pays a low interest for use of the money, and lends it as credit at a higher rate of interest. It also deals with other banks, transferring payments, and with a central bank, which regulates the supply of money. In contrast, the corporate structure of banks has undergone enormous change. The biggest banks employ thousands of people around the globe; they deal with all kinds of customers, from the smallest depositor to multinational companies and government ministries. They are part of an international structure as well as a national payment system. Apart from cash, they deal in securities and derivatives (which are promises to pay cash according to the performance of an index, for example on interest rates, foreign exchange, securities, or commodities). Almost all of what they do is—or can be—done electronically.

COMPANIES

In the last 15 years there has been widespread consolidation in the banking industry. The United States still has 8,300 banks, but in 1991 it had around 12,000. Whereas there used to be at least 15 major money-center banks in the United States, there are now three dominant banks—Citigroup, JP Morgan Chase, and Bank of America—each with core capital of more than $40 billion.

Largest banks by tier one capital, July 2001 ($ billion)

Source: *The Banker*

In Europe there has been a similar concentration at the top, and most European countries are now dominated by no more than two banks. Cross-border mergers are less common, however, except in Scandinavia, where language and cultural barriers are low. This has not, however, prevented the enormous spread of banks' international banking operations in other countries. Citigroup, for example, is present in 46 countries.

International banking and financial markets began a phase of rapid development in the 1960s. Foreign exchange was traded across borders by telephone and telex. A market for offshore dollar deposits grew. To avoid a domestic tax (imposed in 1963), offshore subsidiaries of U.S. companies borrowed dollars abroad by issuing so-called Eurobonds.

International bond issues outstanding at September 2001 ($ billion)

Financial institutions	4,255
Government	1,404
Companies	1,036
All bonds	7,085

International banks also dealt in offshore deposits, placing and taking deposits, generally of three-month to six-month maturity. These deposits were used to fund medium-term loans to international companies and sovereign states. Banks would club together in syndicates to lend tens of millions of dollars to these international borrowers. In the mid-1970s, after the oil crisis quadrupled the price of oil, newly rich oil-producing countries deposited their wealth with Western banks, which in turn lent the money to developing countries hungry for capital. Inflation soared in Western countries, which responded in 1981 by raising interest rates as high as 20%. Dozens of the developing countries could no longer service their loans at these rates and had to reschedule them. It took a decade (1982–92) to develop a method of rescheduling these debts, in some cases by converting them into bonds (Brady bonds, named after Nicholas Brady, the U.S. treasury secretary in the late 1980s).

RISK MANAGEMENT

With such extreme interest rates and such strong movements in exchange rates, banks and company treasurers had to learn to live with more volatile financial markets. Financial engineers created new products, which were sold to protect buyers from volatile rates. There were swaps, which allowed borrowers to exchange debt repayment flows—for example from fixed-rate to floating short-term rate—or even to change the currency of their debt. There were interest-rate and currency options and futures, traded with banks and on American

and British exchanges. Stock index futures were also traded. In 1988 the first electronic options exchange started up in Switzerland, followed by Germany. Other more traditional exchanges believed that trading by open outcry in pits was more efficient; it took nearly ten years for them to be proved wrong.

Increasingly powerful computers and faster communications meant that borrowers, lenders, investors, and seekers of capital were offered products tailored more accurately than ever before to their financial needs—in theory, at least. In practice, these products had almost no track record and were poorly understood. Markets became increasingly linked, so that feelings in one would quickly transmit themselves to the others. Buyers and traders of derivatives were caught out many times, sometimes expensively, by the highly geared nature of gains and losses that they produced. At times of panic, such as a severe correction in the U.S. stock market in October 1987, the shock spread quickly to other markets around the world. A similar, but more severe, global panic was seen in August 1998, when Russia defaulted on its domestic bonds. Even some of the most heavily traded government bonds became illiquid for a while as traders sought cover. That in turn led to the collapse of a huge but unregulated hedge fund, Long-Term Capital Management (LTCM), which for a time seemed in danger of dislocating major sections of the financial system. Fourteen banks were persuaded to intervene and to recapitalize LTCM before winding it down. It was a lesson to financial regulators worldwide that the financial markets at the turn of the century had become so integrated and so immediately responsive to information flows that they would function smoothly only if they had their own inbuilt checks and balances. Intervention by governments or central banks would never be powerful enough on its own.

While regulators worried about systemic effects, creative bankers continued to develop and trade financial products ostensibly designed to transfer risk to those most equipped to handle it. With asset-backed securities, banks were able to sell receivables from credit cards, car loans, mortgages, and even music royalties, in the form of a security, transferring the risk of non-payment back to the investing public. The banking sector has tended, over three decades, to become a vehicle for these risks rather than the bearer of them. The risk has been passed to insurance companies, pension funds, mutual funds, and private investors.

In many ways this is a healthy development, and has resulted in a stronger banking sector. It has also resulted in the blurring of dividing lines between banks, investment banks, insurance companies, corporate treasury departments, and even asset managers. All are concerned with the trade-off between financial risk and return on the one hand, and acquiring the financial exposures they are most comfortable with on the other. Regulators have had difficulty in ironing out anomalies in regulation that give one type of financial institution a competitive advantage over other types. The distinction between banks and investment banks became so blurred that the United States in 1999 abolished the 1933 Glass-Steagall Act, which had prevented banks from dealing in securities, and investment banks from taking deposits. In 2001 the U.K. super-regulator, the Financial Services Authority, began to develop common prudential rules for banks and insurance companies.

Investment banks by share of equity issues market, 2001 (%)

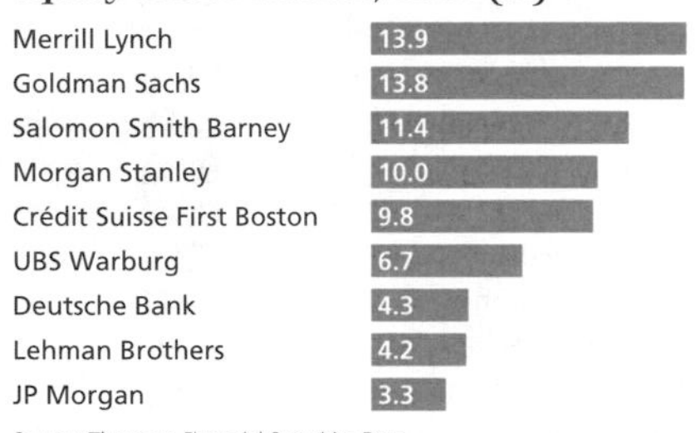

Source: Thomson Financial Securities Data

Investment banks by share of low-risk bond issues market, 2001 (%)

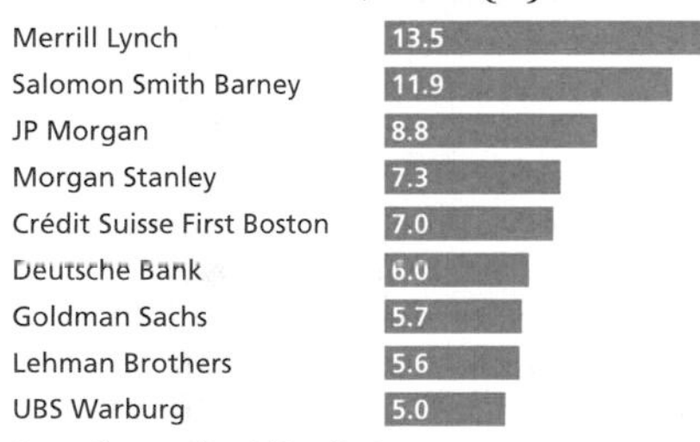

Source: Thomson Financial Securities Data

Paradoxically, while this integration of financial markets and their institutions continues, the European financial markets remain relatively fragmented despite the introduction of the Euro in 1999. Circulation of Euro notes and coins from January 2002 may have given integration new momentum, but the 12 different jurisdictions of the Euro zone, and vested interests in each capital market, have so far prevented optimum flows of capital through the region

Investment banks by share of high-risk bond issues market, 2001 (%)

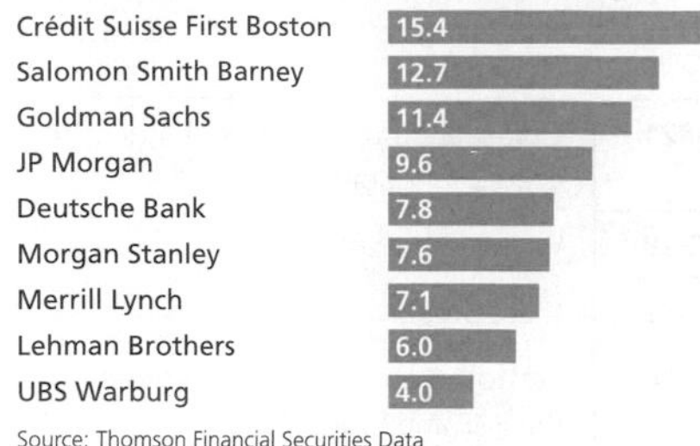

Source: Thomson Financial Securities Data

Investment banks by share of mergers and acquisitions market, 2001 (%)

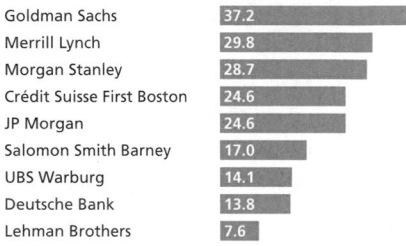

Source: Thomson Financial Securities Data

to the points of highest demand. This may help explain why the Euro seemed to underperform as a reserve currency during its first three years.

MARKETS

Competition between financial centers once depended on the volume of local economic activity. New York, London, and Tokyo were the premier financial centers of the 1980s, and have retained that position despite the decline in the Japanese economy and the consolidation of European currencies in the Euro.

Global foreign exchange market turnover: daily averages in April 2001 ($ billion)

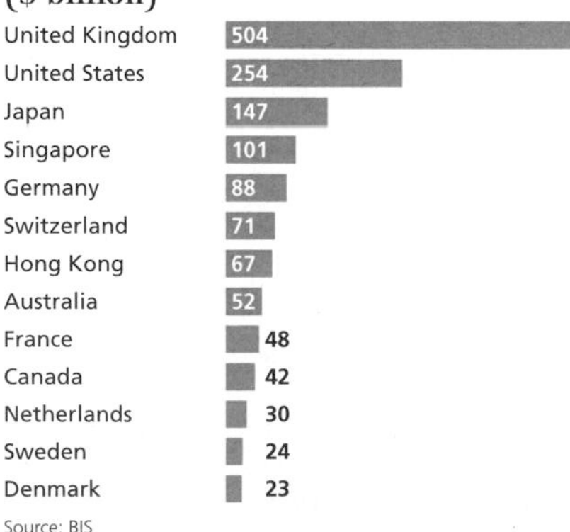

Source: BIS

Now these centers thrive on the sophistication and size of investment institutions, such as banks, insurance companies, and mutual funds; the liquidity and transparency of financial markets; and the

Global foreign exchange and derivatives market turnover: daily averages by instrument ($ billion)

1995 | 1998 | 2001

Total foreign exchange market turnover

1,190
1,490
1,210

of which:	1995	1998	2001
Spot transactions	494	568	387
Outright FX forwards	97	128	131
Foreign exchange swaps	546	734	656

Total over-the-counter derivatives turnover

200
375
575

of which:	1995	1998	2001
Foreign exchange instruments	45	97	67
Interest-rate instruments	151	265	489

Source: BIS

user-friendliness of regulation. They also depend on the pool of skills available, from derivatives dealers to lawyers, printers, and computer wizards. On this basis Frankfurt, Paris, Hong Kong, Singapore, and Tokyo are a long way behind London and New York. The main market for currency and derivatives dealing is in London. Trading of securities and short-term deposits in Euros is also predominantly in London, even though the most actively traded futures contracts in the world—on German government bonds—are traded electronically on Eurex, the Frankfurt-based futures exchange.

Exchanges and Payment Systems

In theory all the stock exchanges and other financial exchanges in the world could be wired and integrated, so that a trader could trade from a single screen, and this is in fact happening to some extent. Exchanges are merging, or linking themselves electronically. However, national barriers such as tax and bankruptcy laws and market practices, get in the way. Although trading across borders can be done easily, clearing and settling those trades is a more difficult challenge. Competition between exchanges, and the egos of those who run them, are further obstacles to integration. The German and London stock exchanges failed to complete a proposed merger in 2000; however, Euronext, the successful merger of the Belgian, Dutch, and French exchanges, was followed by a merger with the London futures exchange Liffe. In the meantime the German exchange, Deutsche Börse, has integrated vertically with Clearstream, an international securities depository based in Luxembourg.

At some stage in 2002, a new system of clearing and settling foreign exchange transactions is expected to come into operation: the much-delayed CLS Bank is designed to settle foreign exchange trades continuously throughout the day, reducing the huge outstanding payments flows which for decades have settled towards the end of each day. CLS Bank is expected to affect the way banks manage their daily cash flows in seven major currencies.

Technology

In some ways the story of modern finance is the story of ever-increasing computer power. More sophisticated information technology in finance has increased the sophistication of financial products and the ability to process historical data, and to calculate from it the probabilities of certain market outcomes. However, the cost and complexity of handling these products has increased, and these costs are passed on to the customer: companies, investment funds, and private individuals. For customers it has become increasingly difficult to avoid these costs in one form or another, although over all the developments have resulted in a greater, and almost overwhelming, choice of financial products.

All companies above a certain size can have access to sophisticated cash management. All investment funds can outsource custody of their investments, including day-to-day response to tax calls, share splits, exercise of options, and other actions that require constant vigilance.

Despite this sophistication there is still tremendous resistance among banks to giving customers the full benefit of what technology can do, particularly for transferring funds from one account to another. In December 2001, the European Commission fined five German banks for overcharging customers for cross-border payments in Euros. European banks in general have been slow to reduce such charges and the time taken in transit. Technically the cost is negligible and the transfer instantaneous, but banks have clung on to practices which still move at medieval speed.

Internet payment systems such as PayPal have recruited many customers, but these customers are not able to use it as an alternative banking system. To turn Internet payments back into cash still requires a bank account and a cumbersome bank transfer.

Looking Ahead

Regulators and the banks themselves may feel that giants such as JP Morgan Chase and Citigroup, with assets of $713 billion and $902 billion respectively, have grown as big as they should. Already their size means that they will probably have maximum exposure to any large corporate failure, as was the case with Enron in November 2001. But the convergence of what banks, investment banks, and insurance companies do will continue. Supermarkets, garages, consultancies, and data providers will join the fray to provide banking services.

On the other hand, the community of regulated banks is likely to be ever more vigilant about the source of funds coming into the system, which may put large areas of the banking and informal payment system out of bounds. Whether that will restrict the funding of global terrorism, or simply send it deeper underground, is not certain. The spread of credit cards and prepaid or loadable payment cards will mean a reduction in the use of cash. The Octopus card, which can be used at shops and ticket barriers on Hong Kong's mass-transit system, was an early pioneer. The logic of making payments by mobile phone may eventually prevail, but physical cash—including this year's new Euro notes and coins—will be around for some time to come.

For More Information

Magazines and Journals:

American Banker, New York.
Bank of England: *Financial Stability Review*, London:
www.bankofengland.co.uk
The Banker, London (monthly).
Euromoney, London (monthly):
www.euromoney.com
Global Finance, New York.
Institutional Investor, New York.

Web Sites:

Bank for International Settlements:
www.bis.org
Bank of England:
www.bankofengland.co.uk
Deutsche Bundesbank:
www.bundesbank.de
European Banking Federation, Brussels:
www.fbe.be
European Central Bank: **www.ecb.de**
Federal Reserve Bank of New York:
www.newyorkfed.org
Federal Reserve Board, Washington:
www.federalreserve.gov
Institute of International Finance, Washington: **www.iif.com**

Chemicals

1749	Lead chamber method to produce sulfuric acid, United Kingdom.
1802	DuPont founded to manufacture gunpowder in Delaware, United States.
1850	First petroleum refinery built in Pittsburgh, United States.
1866	Dynamite patented by Alfred Nobel.
1860s	Celluloid becomes first synthetic plastic.
1895	Air liquefaction technique developed by Linde.
1901	*Handbook of Chemical Engineering* by George Davis.
1908	Greenhouse effect from burning coal and oil first postulated. Bakelite discovered.
1915	Pyrex glass produced by Corning.
1925	Fischer-Tropsch process synthesizes petroleum fuels from coal.
1931	Neoprene synthetic rubber.
1935	Nylon (originally called hexamethylenediamine).
1942	Polyester resins.
1944	Teflon (polytetrafluoroethene) is mass-produced.
1965	Kevlar.
1987	BASF produces a polyacetylene with twice the electrical conductivity of copper.
2001	Synthetic zeolite catalyst reportedly improves process yield from 1% to 98%.

The development of the chemical industry was intimately intertwined with the start of the industrial revolution in the mid-18th century. The demands of the new manufacturing industries, in particular the textile industry, for larger quantities and consistent qualities of chemical products such as sulfuric acid and synthetic dyes gave rise to a scientifically based chemical manufacturing industry. A measure of the scientific advance which has driven the development of the industry can be seen in the increase in known organic chemicals. In 1800, approximately 500 of these were recognized, many of them being simple acid salts. By 1900, the number had grown to 150,000, and by 2000 to about 10 million.

Sulfuric acid is generally regarded as the first bulk chemical product, and remains an important commodity chemical today. With an annual production of over 150 million tons (late 1990s), it is the largest volume product of the chemical industry and is used in a diverse range of processes, including the manufacture of fertilizers, detergents, paints, and explosives.

The development of the industry accelerated in the 19th century, as the science of chemistry became better understood and new proprietary processes for the manufacture of specific chemicals were developed. An example is the 1863 development of the Solvay process for producing alkali, exploiting chemistry discovered 60 years earlier but for the first time scaling up successfully to achieve commercial volume production. Scaling up from laboratory to industrial production is still a key skill of the chemical engineer.

Companies

By the early 20th century, the chemical companies themselves had undergone a scaling-up process with the emergence of the industrial giants, notably I G Farben in Germany, DuPont in the United States, and Imperial Chemical Industries (ICI) in the United Kingdom. I G Farben, created in 1925 from the merger of six already large chemical concerns, was closely associated with the Nazi regime in Germany, and after World War II it was broken up and its assets transferred to Bayer, Hoechst, Agfa, and BASF.

The industry today encompasses an extremely diverse range of activities including pharmaceuticals, fibers, and foodstuffs, as well as the manufacture of chemicals and plastics. Its global sales are worth about $1,700 billion, making it one of the largest and most dynamic of the manufacturing industries. Chemical manufacturing accounts for almost 2% of U.S. GDP, and about 2.4% of EU GDP.

Globally there are well over 100,000 companies active in the field, with the 30 largest accounting for about 30% of world chemical sales. A handful of American and European

Top chemical companies by sales, 2000 ($ billion)

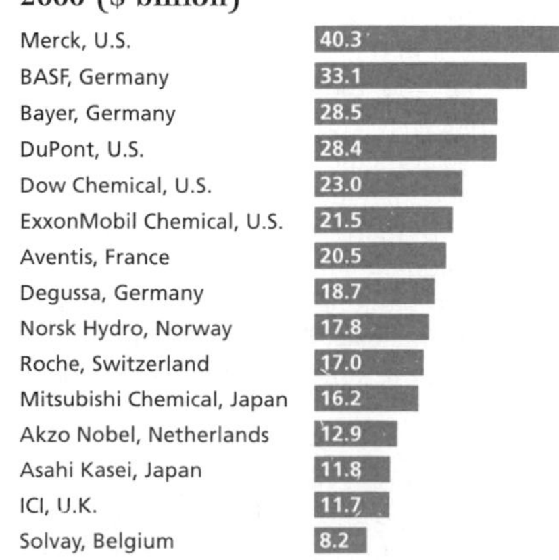

Top chemical companies by profit, 2000 ($ billion)

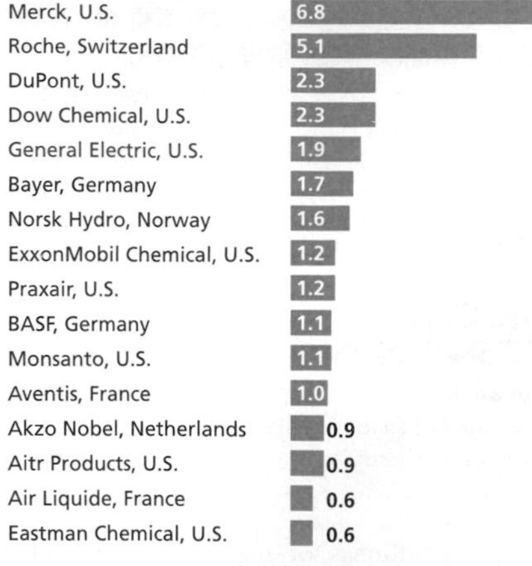

Top chemical industry employers, 2000

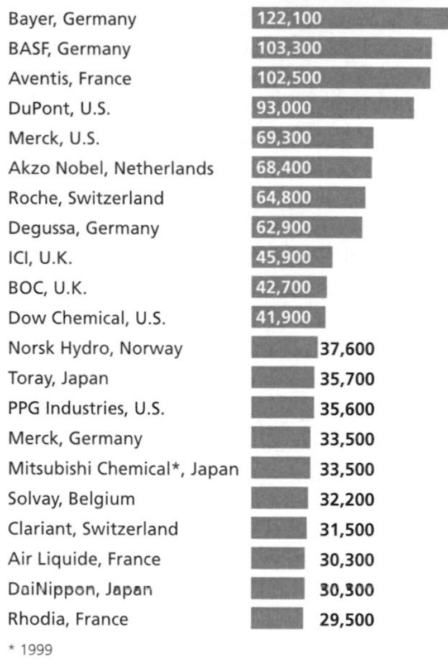

* 1999

companies claim some dominance, although each of the biggest four (Merck, BASF, Bayer, and DuPont) achieves only a 2–3% share of the global market. A fifth company, Dow Chemical, has staked a claim to a position in this superleague after acquiring Union Carbide in 2000. Each one of these companies is about twice as big, in terms of sales, as the largest non-Western chemical company, Japan's Mitsubishi Chemical.

The late 20th century saw a rash of mergers and acquisitions in the sector, most notably typified by a move away from broadly based conglomerate structures in favor of a focus on a particular segment of the sector. Thus, for example, ICI—once the most powerful industrial concern in the United Kingdom—divested its successful pharmaceutical operations (Zeneca, later merging to form AstraZeneca) and its commodity chemicals businesses, while acquiring the specialty chemicals operations of Unilever. The company has effectively reinvented itself as a manufacturer of food ingredients, personal care products, and paints—the "lighter" end of the industry, which is attractive because it is believed to be less cyclical and more profitable than bulk chemical manufacture.

Other major restructurings, mainly during the second half of the 1990s, were driven by a similar belief that only globalized and tightly focused organizations could be competitive. In the oil sector, U.S. giants Exxon and Mobil merged, while BP acquired both Amoco and Arco. Mitsui and Sumitomo merged to mount a challenge to Mitsubishi for the top position in the Japanese chemical sector. Hoechst and Rhône-Poulenc merged their life sciences businesses to form a new Franco-German giant, Aventis. Another life sciences company, Novartis, was formed from Ciba and Santos; Novartis then merged its agricultural chemicals business with that of AstraZeneca to create Syngenta. In the specialty chemicals sector, Clariant was formed as a spinoff from Sandoz, Henkel similarly spun off Cognis, and Rhône-Poulenc made its specialty chemicals business independent as Rhodia. The acquisition of SKW Trostberg saw Degussa become the world's largest specialty chemicals company.

A similar strategy has been followed, to a greater or lesser degree, by most of the major companies in the industry. The most notable exceptions are the German giants BASF and Bayer, which have resisted pressure to abandon the diversified approach. Bayer remains the only company to maintain market-leading positions in both chemicals and pharmaceuticals, while BASF's "Verbund" (integrated) industrial structure allows it to use the product of one process as the raw material for the next. It thus keeps its supply chains largely internal, which enables it to add value at several stages.

The general trend in developed countries, nevertheless, has been the expansion of high-margin, low-volume fine and specialty chemicals businesses and the demise of the "old-fashioned" bulk or commodity chemicals industries. A number of factors have influenced this trend, not least the growing effect on world markets of low-cost producers in developing countries, particularly in Asia, the Middle East, and Mexico. Manufacturers in these countries have capitalized on three significant advantages they have over their European and American competitors: lower wage costs, local availability of feedstocks (crude oil and other raw materials), and less stringent environmental restrictions.

Markets

The world chemical market is dominated by Western Europe and the United States, each responsible for about 30% of global production, and each employing over a million people in chemicals manufacturing. Within Europe, Germany remains the biggest producer, responsible for about one quarter of the continent's output. The other major industrial powers within Europe-France, the United Kingdom, and Italy—are also major chemical producers, while Belgium, Spain, and the Netherlands complete the so-called "big seven" European chemical-producing nations. That group may soon have to be expanded to include Ireland, which has seen a rapid expansion of its chemical industry in recent years. Fueled by European Union assistance and national investment incentives, the country saw its chemical production more than quadruple during the 1990s. It now claims perhaps 5% of the total European market.

World chemical production by region, 2000 (%)

Western Europe (EU + Switzerland)	31
United States	30
Japan	14
Asia	13
Central and Eastern Europe	4
Latin America	3
Rest of world	5

A relatively new player in the global bulk chemicals business is Sabic (Saudi Arabian Basic Industries), created in 1976 as part of a drive by the Saudi government to diversify its economy. Sabic was established to process—and add value to—the country's abundant natural hydrocarbon supplies, and in so doing it has become a leading international petrochemicals manufacturer and the top-ranked Middle Eastern company by market capitalization.

Chemical production by country, 2000 ($ billion)

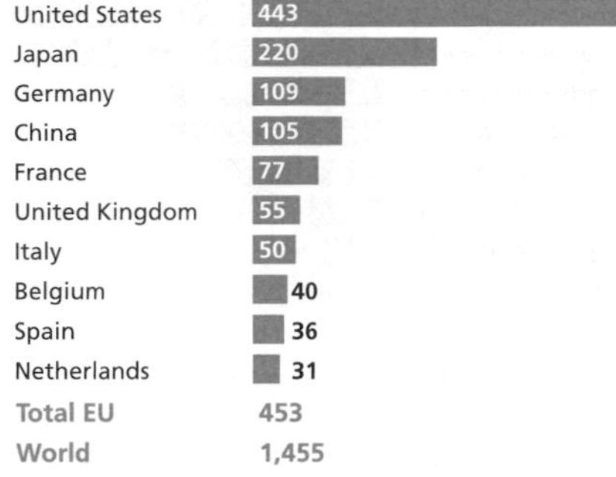

The growing Mexican chemical industry has been boosted by significant investment from the United States, in terms of both capital and technology. Like other oil-producing developing nations (including Saudi Arabia and Malaysia), it is capitalizing on two natural resources: hydrocarbon feedstocks and cheap labor. It has been calculated that labor costs in Mexico are about one third of those in the United States or Western Europe, although this advantage is somewhat offset by lower productivity.

Technology

Chemical manufacturing is traditionally based on what are known as unit operations —individual processes which effect some change on the material being processed. These can be quite basic (like filtration or evaporation), or more complex (fractional distillation, catalytic reaction). A series of unit operations transforms the raw material from a low-value input to a higher-value output, and this output is quite likely to become an input material for some other industrial process. As an example, a chemical plant may transform caprolactam, a gasoline-like hydrocarbon, into nylon. The output material becomes the raw material for a later manufacturing process, to make fibers to be woven into garments. The caprolactam itself may have been the output from some other chemical manufacturer.

Early chemical processes were invariably batch processes, in which fixed quantities of materials were subjected to various unit op-

Chemical industry sectors in Europe, 2000 (%)

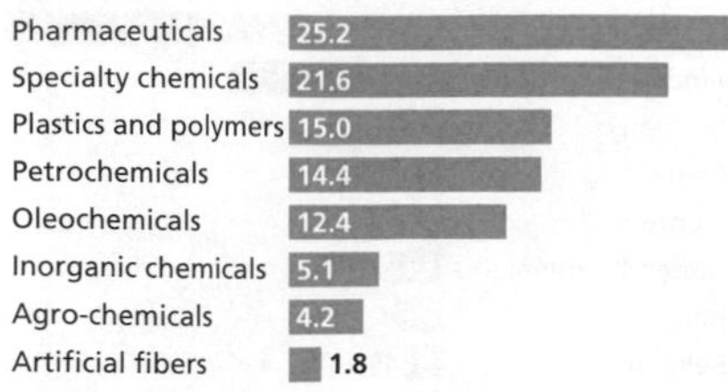

erations and reacted together to create a batch of product. With improved technology and engineering skill, the concept of the continuous process became important. Here, the raw materials are fed steadily into the chemical plant, where they are transported through the various vessels and pipes which house the unit operations. The result is a steady stream of output product. Both approaches are still used today, although most commodity chemical production is performed on a continuous basis.

Recent advances in technology are allowing the traditional unit operations to be combined, typically in smaller and cheaper manufacturing equipment. Known as "process intensification," this method has yet to see widespread adoption but does appear to offer faster and more economical chemical manufacturing. Other new technologies on the horizon take the concept of process intensification further, greatly reducing the scale of the pipes and vessels of a chemical plant to sub-millimeter sizes. These "microfluidic" devices can be considered analogous to electronic circuits, rather than the vacuum tubes and capacitors of a conventional chemical plant. Chemical manufacturing has a reputation as a notoriously capital-intensive business, a perception which may need to be modified if the promise of these approaches is realized.

A technology of growing importance, regardless of the processing method employed, is catalysis. The ability of certain materials (often metals) to stimulate and modify a chemical reaction has long been recognized and exploited in the industry. In recent years it has become possible to tune specific catalysts for desired properties, providing a significant boost to the economics of a chemical process.

Products

The industry's products fall into a number of major groupings. The largest single group today is pharmaceuticals, accounting for about one quarter of sales. The second-largest is another large and growing area: specialty chemicals, including pigments, high-purity materials for electronics manufacture, and other chemicals used in small volumes. Plastics and polymers include materials such as polyethylene (polythene), polypropylene, and synthetic rubber. Petrochemicals are the intermediate products made from hydrocarbons (including ethylene and propylene), often used in turn in the manufacture of polymers. Oleochemicals may be made from natural (vegetable) or synthetic (oil) raw materials, and include surfactants (used in the manufacture of soaps and detergents) and cosmetic products. Finally, agrochemicals consist of fertilizers and crop protection chemicals.

Impact of the Internet

The chemical industry tends to be regarded as an archetypal "old-economy" sector, so it may be surprising to learn that it has been at the forefront of the e-business revolution. Part of the reason for this is the sheer size of the industry, and its traditionally low margins, meaning that even small savings in transaction costs have a worthwhile effect on profitability. Internet-based trading systems have been launched and supported by consortia of all of the major manufacturers, primarily for their own use in integrating with each others' buying and selling activities. The early years of the 21st century are expected to see online transactions account for around 15% of the industry's sales, leading to an annual volume of e-business of as much as $250 billion.

For More Information

Magazines and Journals:
Chemical Week: **www.chemweek.com**
Chemical News & Intelligence: **www.cnionline.com**
The Chemical Engineer: **www.tce-online.com**

Web Sites:
American Chemical Society: **www.chemistry.org**
Chemical Industries Association: **www.cia.org.uk**
ChemIndustry (search engine for the chemical industry): **www.chemindustry.com**
Dechema (Germany): **www.dechema.de**
European Chemical Industry Council (CEFIC): **www.cefic.be**

Construction

8000B.C.	Stonehenge, Wiltshire, England.
2700B.C.	Construction of the Great Pyramid of Giza, Egypt.
A.D.120	Pantheon, Rome (lightweight concrete dome).
1779	Ironbridge, United Kingdom (first iron bridge).
1869	Suez Canal, Egypt.
1883	Brooklyn Bridge, New York.
1885	Home Insurance Building, Chicago (first modern skyscraper).
1889	Eiffel Tower, Paris.
1890	London Underground starts.
1914	Panama Canal.
1931	Empire State Building, New York.
1937	Golden Gate Bridge, San Francisco.
1973	World Trade Center, New York.
1981	Humber Bridge, United Kingdom.
1994	Channel Tunnel, United Kingdom–France.
1997	Petronas Towers, Kuala Lumpur (tallest building, 1,482 feet).
1998	Akashi Kaikyo Bridge, Japan (longest span, 6,527 feet).

The construction industry is, almost by definition, as old as civilization itself. Remains of very ancient structures have been found which date back at least 200,000 years. The most impressive surviving examples of structures from ancient times belong to the Roman era. While earlier civilizations had demonstrated superb craftsmanship in stone (such as the Parthenon in Athens, the great pyramids of Egypt, and Stonehenge in England), the Romans were the first to exploit the versatile properties of concrete, and the first to develop a sophisticated infrastructure of roads, drainage, water supply, and so on. Much of the expertise developed by Roman engineers was lost when its empire fell, and it was not until the industrial revolution started in Europe in the mid-18th century that this knowledge was relearned.

What we can now recognize as the beginning of the modern construction industry can be traced to the growth of the guild system in Europe, perhaps as early as the 8th century and certainly by the 11th. Under the guilds, many of the traditional construction crafts—such as masonry and carpentry—developed into the modern trades which still play a role in the sector. Somewhat later, around the 18th century, the demarcation between the "professions" (architect, engineer) and the "trades" (skilled craftsmen) became more formalized.

The development of new construction centers was encouraged largely by the growth of commerce, which demanded transportation infrastructure, including railways, canals, bridges, and tunnels, manufacturing facilities such as factories and warehouses, and housing for the newly urbanized communities. These forces are still, to a great extent, the drivers of today's construction industry.

Companies

The industry remains largely divided between the professions and the trades. The professional groups include the design community (architects, responsible for conceptual and aesthetic design), civil and structural consulting engineers (responsible for technical design and supervision of construction), and quantity surveyors. The trades—the people who actually perform the construction work—are the contractors.

In practice, however, these distinctions are becoming less clearly defined. The late 20th century saw the introduction of new hybrid organizations which merged some of the traditional groups under a single umbrella, or at least blurred the distinctions between them. Several new descriptions were used for these organizations and the new types of contract they undertook, although these descriptions are not always used consistently.

Largest international contractors by sales, 2000 ($ million)

Bouygues, France	16,280
Kajima, Japan	16,050
Taisei, Japan	15,861
Vinci, France	15,500
Bechtel, U.S.	14,300
Shimizu, Japan	12,449
Obayashi, Japan	10,567
Skanska, Sweden	10,337
Fluor, U.S.	10,000
Takenaka, Japan	8,752
Hochtief, Germany	8,113
Halliburton KBR, U.S.	6,380
ABB, Switzerland	5,900
Philipp Holzmann, Germany	5,823
Bovis Lend Lease, U.K.	5,700
Toda, Japan	5,130
Fujita, Japan	5,094
Hollandsche Beton, Neth.	5,075
Hyundai E&C, South Korea	5,069
China State C&E	4,704

Largest international consulting firms by sales, 2001 ($ million)

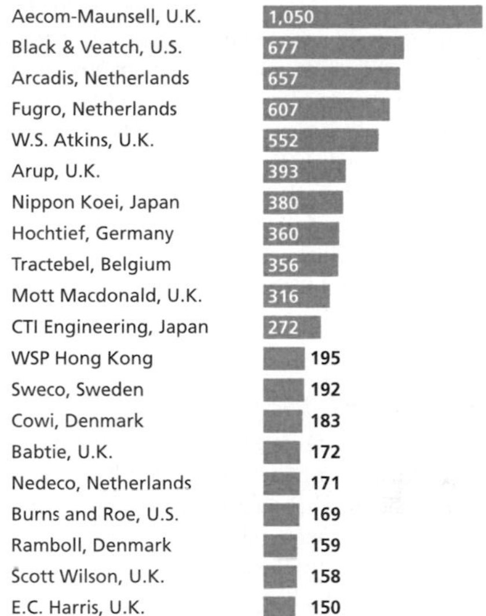

In a design and build contract, as the name implies, the contractor is given responsibility for the both design and construction. This type of contract is most often associated with projects such as warehouses, factories, and other large but fairly basic building types with little architectural ambition. Under a project management contract, the project manager (usually a contractor) actually performs little work directly, but sub-contracts effectively all the construction work to others while retaining a supervisory role. A project manager (sometimes called a construction manager, especially in North America) will usually also be responsible for employing the professional designers and surveyors—a reversal of the traditional construction contract arrangements, where the contractor would report to the engineer. A management contractor is broadly similar, but typically does not employ the design professionals.

Employment

The range of company sizes in the sector is extremely wide, from one-man operations

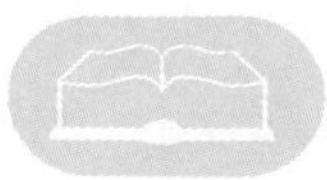

to multinational corporations employing several thousand individuals, and this diversity encompasses both the trades and the professions. In the United Kingdom, for example, there are almost 200,000 contracting companies, half of which are single-person organizations. Only 5% of these 200,000 employ more than seven people. Nevertheless, over 40% of the value of construction work in the country is performed by large companies (those employing 80 or more people). Total U.K. construction industry employment is about 1.4 million, while in the much larger U.S. market between six and seven million are employed. In Europe and the United States the industry accounts for roughly 10% of all employment and 10% of GDP.

Markets

The major markets for the construction industry can be divided into three broad sectors: residential (housing); commercial and industrial (offices, shops, factories); and major works (highways, bridges, tunnels, airports, and the like).

The main geographic markets are the principal industrialized countries (America, Japan, and in Europe), and developing nations like China and South Korea. Countries in southeast Asia in particular have been investing heavily in infrastructure since towards the end of the 20th century, with many large-scale projects to build highway systems, airports, ever-higher office buildings, and ever-longer bridges. The worldwide economic difficulties of the late 1990s, however, had a significant cooling effect on this market.

Largest construction markets by total spend, 2001 ($ billion)

United States	876
Japan	628
Germany	247
China	190
Brazil	141
United Kingdom	113
France	109
Italy	97
Spain	88
South Korea	74
Canada	72
India	65
Australia	47
Mexico	46
Russia	42
Netherlands	42
Taiwan	35
Argentina	33
Austria	31
Belgium	30

Largest construction markets by spend per capita, 2001 ($)

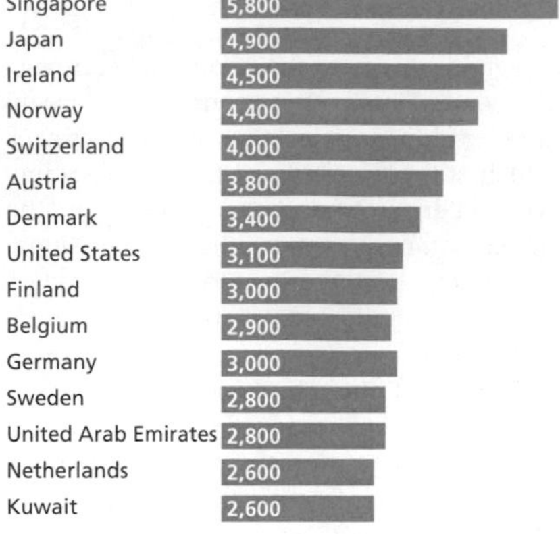

As with other industrial sectors, construction has seen accelerated merger activity in the 1990s. One significant factor here has been the increasing integration of construction companies in Europe, and the growth of cross-border working as a result of the escalating effect of the European single market. Nevertheless, the industry remains much more fragmented than many others, with companies for the most part concentrating on their home markets, and increasingly on specific niches within these markets. While there remain a great many general contractors who will undertake a broad range of work, there is a noticeable trend towards the specialist contractor who might concentrate on, for example, earthmoving, brickwork, window installation, or electrical fitting.

Technology

Although construction is often considered a low-technology activity, it does employ some very sophisticated techniques and, increasingly, advanced materials. Perhaps the most important technology in the sector is that of concrete, a substance much derided in the popular imagination but which is undoubtedly the most versatile building material ever devised. Plain concrete is made from a mixture of cement (a product of limestone), water, fine aggregate (sand), and coarse aggregate (gravel or stone chippings). It sets to form a hard, rock-like material which, when properly made, is strong, durable, and—above all—cheap.

Concrete has good strength in compression (squeezing forces), but little or no strength in tension (stretching). Steel, on the other hand, has good strength in tension. If the two materials are combined, with a lattice of steel bars enveloped in a concrete matrix, the resulting reinforced concrete becomes an extremely useful structural material. A further development of reinforced concrete is prestressed concrete, where the steel reinforcement is placed in tension while the concrete is poured around it. A further variation is post-tensioning, where the steel is placed inside ducts in the concrete and is not tensioned until the concrete has set; the overall effect is much the same.

Concrete's great rival for large structural projects is large steel sections, most familiar as H- or I-sections popularly (but inaccurately) referred to as "girders." The major advantages over concrete are that a steel section will be much lighter than a concrete component carrying the same load, and it can be more readily connected to other components. Early steel structures relied on metal rivets to make connections but, in the second half of the 20th century, this gave way to bolts and welding.

More recently, plastic materials have begun to make an impression on the industry. Advanced fiber-reinforced composites are used in nonstructural applications such as external cladding, and increasingly as direct replacements for steel components including structural sections, cables (such as in suspension bridges), and as reinforcement for concrete. They remain expensive, but offer far higher corrosion resistance and far lower weight than steel, and are expected to become more widely used in the early 21st century. Some of the enormous structures proposed for this period, such as bridges with extremely long spans (more than 3 miles), would be impossible to build without the use of these materials.

The technology of construction equipment is equally important as that of construction materials. During the 20th century, construction machinery developed from tractor derivatives and basic block-and-tackle lifting equipment to ever larger and more powerful—and more specialized—equipment. Today's contractor can call on an armory of dedicated machines to perform activities such as earth moving, excavation, lifting, tunneling, road laying, and so on. Concrete pumps can deliver material across large distances and to heights of more than 1,640 feet. Slipforming techniques—in which the molds (formwork) into which concrete is cast are steadily moved upwards while the concrete sets, and new material is continuously added at the top—enable tower structures to be raised with startling speed. Slipforming is employed on projects as diverse as tall buildings, bridge towers, concrete dams, and offshore oil production platforms.

The moving of earth is an important early stage of almost every above-ground construction project, and is fundamental in the case of below-ground projects. Traditionally, the profile of the ground required was marked with wooden pegs and boards to show the machine operator where to cut and where to fill. Recently, global positioning system (GPS) technology has been employed with sophisticated computer modeling to align the machine's blades automatically. This system is now capable of accuracy within one centimeter. Surveying technology has also advanced through the use of electronic distance measurement (EDM) and automated instruments that can record and position sensors to within a millimeter over a kilometer or more.

Products and Projects

Construction is probably unique among the world's major industries in that, with the exception of housing, its products are for the most part bespoke, one-off projects. Even where a number of superficially similar structures are built, for example a series of bridges across a new motorway, each may be subtly different from the others because of variations in the underlying ground.

Progress in construction can be measured by easily understood records, such as the height of the tallest buildings or the clear span of the longest bridges. The location of these edifices also gives an indication of the economic success—or at least ambition—of the countries which build them. Thus the record for the world's tallest buildings passed from Europe to the United States for most of the 20th century, but has now gone to Asia with the completion of the Petronas towers in Kuala Lumpur, Malaysia, in 1998. Similarly, the longest-span suspension bridge record, variously held in Europe and the United States during the 20th century, now rests in Japan for its Akashi Kaikyo bridge. Currently seven of the top ten buildings and four of the ten longest spans, including the outright record holder in each, are in Asia.

Impact of the Internet

The nature of the industry means that it does not lend itself readily to electronic commerce. Individual projects are typically bid for by a process of tendering—a type of blind auction—and the materials and equipment required to complete the job are purchased from the best local source. While materials and components are sometimes shipped large distances, simple economics usually mean that these high-weight, low-value items are purchased as close as possible to the construction site.

New technology is, however, employed in many facets of the industry, such as using new communications systems to allow designers to work remotely from the actual construction site. This can be particularly important for fast-track construction projects, where the design work proceeds only just ahead of the actual construction. In some cases, teams of engineers and other designers are located in two or three different places, each progressing the design during their working day before passing the work to another office in a different time zone. The result is that three full shifts of professional expertise can be applied to a project in a 24-hour day. These designers make full use of advanced computer-aided design (CAD) technologies.

For More Information

Reflecting the fragmented nature of the industry, construction trade associations and other industry bodies are formed around either specific (usually national) territories, or specific subdivisions and specializations within the industry. European and American construction companies are served by a bewildering number of associations, promoting the professions (such as civil engineers and architects), trades, and machinery and materials. International associations are aligned to specific construction activities such as roadbuilding (International Road Federation).

Magazines and Journals:

Engineering News Record (United States): **www.enr.com**

New Civil Engineer (United Kingdom): **www.nceplus.com**

Web Sites:

American Road and Transportation Builders Association: **www.artba.org**

American Society of Civil Engineers: **www.asce.org**

Construction Industry Manufacturer's Association (CIMA): **www.cimanet.com**

International Association for Bridge and Structural Engineering (IABSE): **www.iabse.ethz.ch**

International Federation of Consulting Engineers (Fidic): **www.fidic.org**

International Road Federation: **www.irfnet.org**

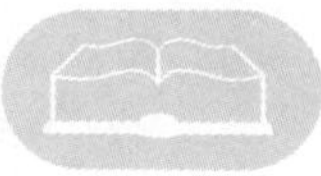

DEFENSE

1903	Wright Brothers make first flight at Kitty Hawk, North Carolina.
1915	Glenn L. Martin Company delivers trainer planes to U.S. Army Signal Corps.
1918	Boeing Airplane Company sells 50 seaplane trainers to U.S. Navy.
1918	Loughead (later renamed Lockheed) sells flying boats to U.S. Navy.
1922	U.S. Navy orders torpedo bombers from Douglas Company.
1940	45 U.S. aircraft companies build tens of thousands of aircraft for World War II, then suffer huge job losses after war.
1958	McDonnell makes first flight of F-4 Phantom.
1961	Glenn L. Martin Company merged with American-Marietta Corp to form Martin Marietta.
1967	McDonnell and Douglas companies merge.
1974	General Dynamics F-16 fighter makes first flight.
1977	British Aerospace formed as nationalized corporation by merger of British Aircraft Corporation, Hawker Siddeley Aviation, Hawker Siddeley Dynamics, and Scottish Aviation.
1981	British Aerospace privatized.
1988	United States discloses existence of F-117, first stealth fighter, developed by Lockheed.
1993	Lockheed acquires aircraft division of General Dynamics.
1994	Northrop acquires Grumman to form Northrop Grumman.
1995	Lockheed and Martin Marietta merge to form Lockheed Martin.
1996	Boeing acquires defense and space divisions of Rockwell International.
1997	Boeing acquires McDonnell Douglas.
1999	British Aerospace buys defense interests of General Electric Company to form BAE SYSTEMS.
2001	Lockheed Martin wins contract to build F-35 Joint Strike Fighter.

War is good for weapons manufacturers. When peace is declared, their fate becomes uncertain, and rationalization takes place. Industry shake-ups occurred after all the big wars of the 20th century, including the Cold War.

However, this never happens along purely market-driven lines, because the governments that are the customers of weapons makers have vital interests and concerns. First, security: they seek to prevent the technology developed by the industry from falling into the hands of enemies who might use it against their citizens. Second, strategic interests: they cannot allow companies to go bankrupt without being certain that they and their allies can still buy essential armaments. Third, domestic politics: they are put in office by voters who expect government orders to provide jobs at home. The effect of all this is that the defense industry will never be quite like any other sector of an economy.

These issues have also restricted the extent to which defense companies can make acquisitions and enter into joint ventures or mergers across national borders. The United States, by far the largest defense market, placed huge barriers around its technological advances in order to prevent them from falling into communist hands. So too did the Soviet Union. Meanwhile European countries, which had spent hundreds of years fighting each other, were preserving national, mostly state-owned, armaments industries which became increasingly uneconomic, especially as many countries opted to buy U.S. products.

However, the decade after the end of the Cold War saw huge changes. Economic forces became so powerful that governments had to adjust or even put aside their traditional concerns. On the one hand, the technology needed to produce modern weapons became so advanced that development costs soared. On the other, demand for new armaments collapsed because there appeared to be no threat of large-scale conflict. Governments reaped the "peace dividend," slashing defense spending. The effect was felt most acutely in Europe, but it was the United States, with its more flexible economy and more hard-nosed approach to obtaining value for money, that acted first. During the 1990s an extraordinary wave of mergers transformed the U.S. defense industry. Belatedly, Europe followed; its restructuring is still in progress. In the early part of the 21st century, the focus is on building transatlantic links.

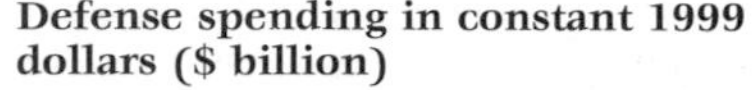
Defense spending in constant 1999 dollars ($ billion)

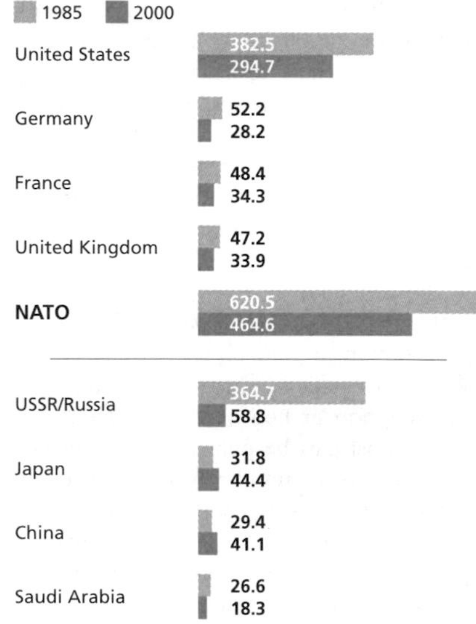

Source: International Institute of Strategic Studies, U.K.

COMPANIES

Although the defense business can be viewed separately from other activities because of the particular nature of large, long-term government contracts, it is not so easy to view the companies that engage in it as a distinct sector. This is because companies with defense interests often have other activities as well. Boeing, the world's second biggest defense contractor in 2000, earned only one third of its turnover from defense because of its large civil aircraft production. Lockheed Martin, BAE Systems, and Raytheon mostly concentrate on defense, but the defense interests of United Technologies and TRW are small in relation to their civil activities. Each company has adopted its own strategy.

In Europe the ownership structure is more complex. For example, DaimlerChrysler, the German car maker, and Lagardère, the French media group, do not appear on the list below, but both are significant shareholders in the European Aeronautic Defense and Space Company and therefore have a keen interest in defense. BAE Systems and EADS are separate companies and rivals, but their businesses are closely intertwined because of common interests in missiles and space systems

Defense spending as a share of GDP (%)

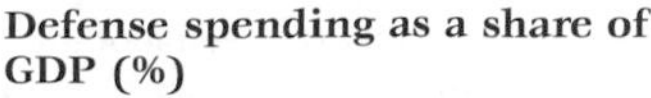

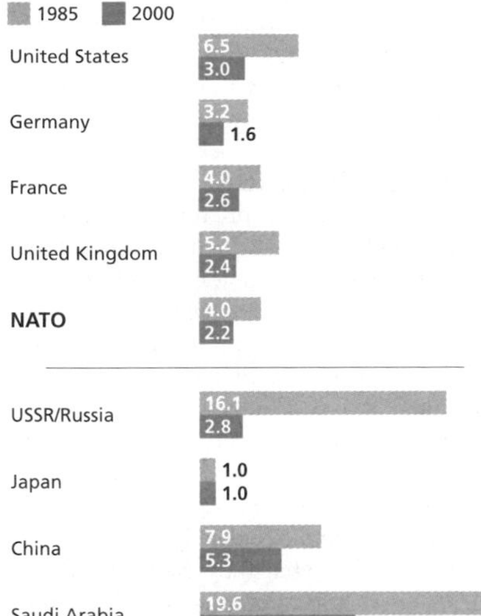

Source: International Institute of Strategic Studies, U.K.

Top defense manufacturers by defense sales, 2000 ($ billion)

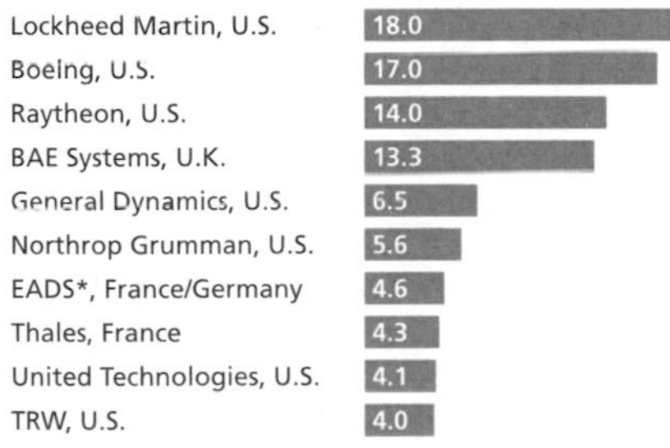

* European Aeronautic Defence and Space Company; year-end 30 June
Source: *Defense News*

ventures, as well as their joint production of the Eurofighter combat aircraft—not to mention Airbus, the civil aircraft builder (just starting up in military aircraft), of which EADS owns 80% and BAE 20%. Though the European aerospace industry has been restructured, the land and naval sectors have not, so there are still national companies—some still state-owned—struggling to survive.

A handful of U.S. companies dominates the world's defense industry. Each is the result of multiple mergers and acquisitions spanning almost a century. However, the rationalization was accelerated to an unprecedented degree by a "last supper" held at the U.S. Department of Defense in 1993, at which top executives of all the larger defense companies were told that the Pentagon wished to see fewer of them in future. It wanted to be supplied by larger companies with the financial clout to undertake very large programs, able to achieve economies of scale. The companies, and their merchant bankers, obliged by entering into an extensive series of deals.

Top U.S. DoD contractors by value of new prime contracts awarded, fiscal 2000 ($ billion)

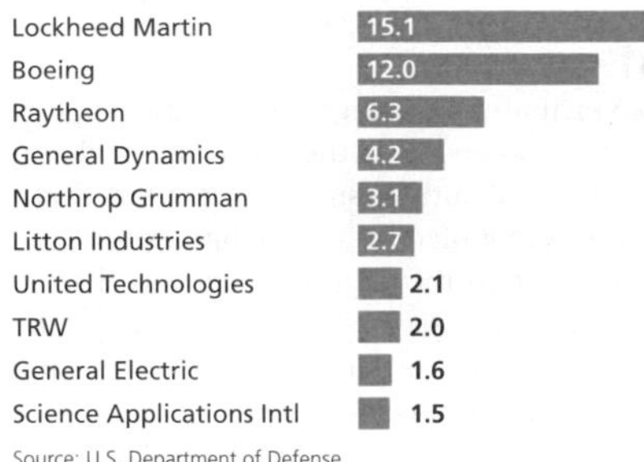

Source: U.S. Department of Defense

General Dynamics, which built the F-16 fighter at its Fort Worth, Texas, plant, sold the aircraft business to Lockheed. Lockheed also acquired Loral, and merged with Martin Marietta, which built the C-130 Hercules transport aircraft at its Marietta, Georgia factory. Lockheed Martin now includes no less than 17 "heritage" businesses.

Boeing is similar. It acquired Rockwell International's aerospace and defense businesses, and later bought McDonnell Douglas. Raytheon meanwhile acquired several businesses—including the defense activities of Texas Instruments and Hughes Aircraft—thereby becoming a very large producer of missile systems. Northrop Grumman is the product of Northrop's purchase of Grumman, followed by Westinghouse's electronic systems business Logicon, Litton Industries, and Newport News Shipbuilding.

The consolidation process among larger defense companies came to an abrupt halt in 1998, when the Pentagon and the Justice Department blocked Lockheed Martin's proposed acquisition of Northrop Grumman on competition grounds. The Pentagon made clear that in most sectors it wanted at least two competitors. However, consolidation continues apace among smaller-sized defense manufacturers: the reshaping of the U.S. defense industry is not yet over.

The industry consolidation has proved extremely difficult to manage for all the U.S. companies, especially as it occurred during a time when new large acquisition programs for the U.S. armed forces were scarce. Many thousands of jobs were lost. Lockheed Martin and Raytheon have suffered the most from integration problems, each suffering share price slumps in the late 1990s. Both had built up large debts as a result of their acquisitions, and both began a recovery with the start of the new decade.

In contrast to the United States, the rationalization of Europe's defense industries did not turn out quite as governments had expected. By the end of 1997, the governments of the United Kingdom, France, and Germany realized that urgent action was necessary if they were to preserve a military aircraft industry. They called for rationalization; their clear idea was that a single company should be created around Airbus, already Boeing's close rival in civil aircraft. This required one key precondition: the privatization of Aérospatiale, which would form the French component. Without this step, British Aerospace (BAe) and DaimlerChrysler Aerospace (Dasa)—respectively the prospective U.K. and German components—would not take part, because they felt that a significant French government stake would spell inefficiency and political interference in management.

BAe and Dasa meanwhile pursued a two-way merger as the first step towards a tripartite grouping. Negotiations took place through 1998, but foundered on how control would be balanced between the two sides, although these difficulties could probably have been overcome in time. The unexpected event was the decision by General Electric Company (GEC), the United Kingdom's other large defense manufacturer, to put its defense business, Marconi Electronic Systems (MES), up for sale. BAe was concerned that an American company might step in and buy MES, thus giving it a big rival on its own doorstep while it pursued mergers abroad. So it stepped in to buy MES for £6 billion, infuriating Dasa's chiefs. The effect was that the United Kingdom had a defense company, renamed BAE Systems, that dwarfed its European rivals, which all remained without merger partners. It did not take long for other European governments and companies to put together EADS, including Dasa of Germany, Aérospatiale and Matra of France, and Construcciones Aeronáuticas of Spain. The result was that the United Kingdom had taken a different path from the rest of Europe—one which took it closer to the United States.

As noted above, BAE and EADS are rivals, though they have many common interests in Europe. Each has a different focus, however: BAE, thanks to large U.S. acquisitions, has become a significant supplier to the Pentagon, and could become a still more important player in the U.S. defense market. EADS's primary business is civil—Airbus—but it aims to build a bigger defense base and is also looking for U.S. links. Over time, the strict 50/50 balance between France and Germany in EADS seems likely to shift in favor of France.

Technology

The long-term future of every company in the defense business depends on its ability to develop new technologies at prices that governments can afford. The responsibility on industry has increased over the past 10 years as many governments have reduced their own research budgets and asked companies to shoulder more of the burden of integrating complex technologies into weapons systems as "prime contractors"—albeit funded by government money.

Much of the technology at the center of the latest developments comes from the civil world, particularly computers, electronics, and communications. The emphasis in the United States armed forces is on a seamless and very fast-moving network of "sensors" and "shooters." Sensors are the means of finding out what an enemy is doing, and where and when he is doing it: intelligence, surveillance, and target acquisition (known as ISTAR). They may be human eyes and ears; images captured from satellites or spy planes; data gathered by listening devices; or any other means of keeping tabs on the opposition. The "shooters" are precision weapons, mostly fired from a distance with extreme accuracy to reduce the risk of casualties among all but opposing military forces. Digital and satellite technologies make all these things possible. The additional pieces in the puzzle are the elaborate information, communication, and computer systems which channel the mass of data to commanders, synthesize it into information upon which they can act, and then enable them to do so with extreme speed. After the 1991 Gulf war, when Iraqi Scud missiles were fired at U.S. forces in Saudi Arabia and there was a strong desire to eliminate launchers as soon as they were pulled out of hiding, the Pentagon set a "sensor-to-shooter" target of 10 minutes—the time between information being gathered and a weapon being fired. The signs are that in the 2001 Afghanistan conflict, the target was close to being achieved.

All surviving defense companies are involved in these technologies, whether for use on aircraft or ships, or as land-based systems. These are increasingly becoming no more than the platforms on which sensors or weapons can be placed with as much flexibility as possible. Increasingly, the platforms will be unmanned, like the Predator and Global Hawk pilotless spy planes used over Afghanistan.

Markets

Governmental willingness to spend money on new weapons is the main factor determining the future size of the market for defense manufacturers. Though exports are important in the defense business, hardly any program gets under way without the domestic government of a defense company funding development.

There are signs that, after the "procurement holiday" of the 1990s, budgets are beginning to turn upwards. President George W. Bush has stepped up U.S. defense spending. The largest new program, developed during the 1990s but pushed forward by Mr. Bush, is the F-35 Joint Strike Fighter to be built by Lockheed Martin in partnership with Northrop Grumman and BAE Systems. The program, which could be worth $200 billion or more, is innovative in several respects: the aircraft was designed around a price, instead of being designed first and costed later; it is "joint"—in other words, intended to equip the U.S. airforce, navy, and marine corps, each of which previously ordered aircraft separately; it is the first large transatlantic collaboration, with the U.K. government having a large say in a U.S.-led program. All these factors are likely to be copied on other projects, further shaping the industry and putting pressure on companies to establish transatlantic partnerships.

Mr. Bush has also signaled a faster U.S. naval shipbuilding program, and changes to the army to make it more mobile and flexible in conflict. He wants to develop new defenses against ballistic missiles. These changes will bring new business to U.S. companies.

In Europe, aircraft companies have reached the production stage for Eurofighter, Europe's next combat aircraft, which will enter service in the United Kingdom, Germany, Italy, and Spain in the next few years. However, the pressure for rationalization is on governments as well: France still has its own new fighter, the Rafale, while Sweden's Gripen has so far been the most successful of the three in winning export sales. European governments have, however, set up a joint procurement agency, and are showing signs of collaborating more effectively on weapons acquisition and technology-sharing after some dismal failures. Meanwhile, times are hard for naval shipbuilders and the armored vehicle industry in most of Europe.

War on Terror

The terrorist attacks on the United States on September 11, 2001 have altered the perspective for the defense industry. Its customers have been awakened to new threats. However, countering terrorism does not necessarily mean a need for new weapons.

Governments are studying what is involved in improved homeland defense. The biggest impact for the armed forces of Nato countries, though, is likely to be a reinforcement of what they were already attempting. After Afghanistan, they now know that they may have to fight anywhere in the world, at very short notice. The emphasis will therefore be on having highly deployable, capable, and flexible troops armed with precision weapons, and on the means to get them wherever they need to be quickly, and then to sustain them when they are in place.

Transport, logistics, intelligence, command and control systems, and the most effective weapons: the military has needed all these for thousands of years. The challenge for the defense industry is to continue to provide them all with the latest technology, at a price governments can afford—and still make money.

For More Information

Web Sites:

Aerospace Industries Association (United States): **www.aia-aerospace.org**

BAE Systems: **www.baesystems.com**

Boeing: **www.boeing.com**

European Aeronautic Defence and Space Company: **www.eads.net**

French defense ministry: **www.defense.gouv.fr**

Lockheed Martin: **www.lockheedmartin.com**

U.S. defense ministry: **www.defenselink.mil**

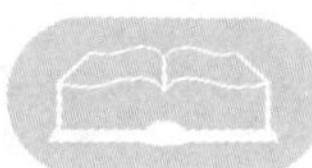

E-COMMERCE

1969	First experiments with ARPAnet.
1978	CompuServe founded as a time-sharing service; grows into information service; invention of public-key cryptography.
1983	Invention of the domain name system, for example ibm.com.
1985	Internet set up to link five regional super-computing centers; precursor of AOL (Qlink) founded.
1989	World Wide Web invented at CERN.
1992	First dial-up ISPs begin offering Internet access to consumers.
1993	Internet opened for commercial traffic.
1994	Yahoo! begins indexing the Web; graphical Web browsers begin to appear.
1995	Amazon.com and eBay founded; Netscape browser released; Microsoft "gets Net."
1999	Stock market and dot-com boom peak.
2000	70 million people download Napster to trade music files.
2001	Gnutella network created; leading music companies announce online services.

E-commerce as we know it began in 1994. The Internet was restricted to academic and research use until 1993. The first e-commerce sites went up in 1994, typically set up by people who had been around the Internet since its earliest days. Existing businesses began to take note when these newer companies started to attract substantial amounts of business (and even more substantial initial public offerings—IPOs). By August 2001, best estimates were that 513.4 million users worldwide were on the Internet, and that e-commerce globally had become a trillion-dollar economy.

The Internet itself belongs to no one. It is traditionally a cooperative structure that works because it is to everyone's benefit to adopt the same open standards. The World Wide Web, invented in 1989 by Briton Tim Berners-Lee at CERN as a way of making it easier to share information with colleagues, is the most easily adapted Internet application for e-commerce. This is partly due to the domain name system that makes it easy to assign memorable, marketable names to sites, and partly because, by its nature, it is suited for one-to-many communication—unlike many other parts of the Internet. The Web's further development is led by Berners-Lee via the non-profit World Wide Web Consortium, based at the at the Massachusetts Institute of Technology.

Even so, large corporate interests do own significant chunks of the Internet. MCI Worldcom, through purchases of companies such as UUNet and Pipex, owns most of the world's Internet backbone. AOL Time-Warner is the single largest content provider and Internet service provider (ISP), passing the 32-million-user mark in November 2001. Cable and telephone companies are rolling out permanent broadband connections that will eventually dominate domestic and small-business access to the Internet. Cisco makes 90% of the special-purpose computers that route data traffic around the Net. Finally Microsoft dominates the desktop computers connected to the Internet, and is gaining ground in the Web server market, where the most significant competition is free software known as Apache.

COMPANIES

The early days of e-commerce were marked by a rush to achieve the biggest market share in the shortest possible time, regardless of how much money a company lost in the process. Accordingly, Amazon.com branched out into CDs, DVDs, and videos, and bought up U.K. and German competitors even before achieving profitability in its original category: online book sales. To some extent, hindsight validates this first-mover-advantage mentality: the biggest online brand names—Amazon.com, eBay, and Yahoo!—are all companies that started early and built big customer bases. But the death of some 500-plus companies (or their e-commerce operations) in 2000 and 2001 showed what a high-risk strategy it was. Yahoo!'s early lead translated into profits ($80 million per quarter in late 2000), primarily via advertising revenues. Badly hit by the advertising downturn, Yahoo!, back into the red in 2001, scrambled to refocus on business and premium services (about 20% of its revenues by the end of 2001), and on e-commerce via commissions on transactions enabled by its shopping search engine, auctions, and Web sites.

Yahoo! wasn't alone. After the downturn,

E-commerce companies by profit/loss in 12 months to mid-2001 ($ million)

eBay (auctioneer)	88
Expedia (travel agent)	–52
Travelocity (travel agent)	–79
Yahoo! (portal)	–182
E*Trade (stockbroker)	–262
Amazon.com (retailer)	–1,100
Cisco (hardware—routers)	–2,100
AOL Time-Warner (ISP/content owner)	–2,291
Commerce One (B2B supplier)	–2,600
Ariba (B2B supplier)	–2,800
i2 Technologies (e-business software)	–7,890
Verisign (digital trust services)	–14,267

Source: Yahoo Marketguide/Multex Network

E-commerce companies by market capitalization in November 2001 ($ billion)

Cisco (hardware—routers)	158.0
AOL Time-Warner (ISP/content owner)	157.1
eBay (auctioneer)	17.9
Yahoo! (portal)	9.2
Verisign (digital trust services)	8.0
Amazon.com (retailer)	4.3
E*Trade (stockbroker)	3.0
i2 Technologies (e-business software)	2.8
Expedia (travel agent)	1.8
Ariba (B2B supplier)	1.4
Travelocity (travel agent)	1.0
Commerce One (B2B supplier)	1.0

Source: Yahoo Marketguide/Multex Network

online advertising sales—$243.7 billion in the United States in 2000—were down 8.4% in 2001, while TV advertising in the United States fell by 24.9%. However, U.K. online ad sales—only 1% of the industry in 2001 (more than cinema advertising)—were up 42% from 2000, to £90.2 million.

That these risks seemed worth taking is understandable. Beginning at zero in August 1995, for example, e-commerce in 2001 accounted for 7.5% of overall U.S. book sales (as compared to 22% via book clubs). Expedia, the Microsoft-founded travel site, was one of the world's top 40 travel agencies after only 18 months. The airlines themselves have 58% of online ticket sales, amounting to 9% of airline sales in 2000. By March 2000, e-commerce was taking $53 billion in the United States alone, or roughly 1.7% of the country's $3.1 trillion retail sector.

The same aspects of the Internet that benefit e-commerce companies—increased global reach, lower costs, and greater access to information—benefit their customers

even more. Special-purpose search engines let customers compare prices on different sites in a few seconds, while content providers compete with free sites. The result is the driving-down of prices, while at the same time increasing customer demands for excellent service.

For e-commerce companies, acquiring customers and revenues at high speed has come at a high cost. Few of these companies make money, though many are fueled by the cash from IPOs at the height of the stock market boom. The profitable exception is eBay, a broker providing the infrastructure for millions of individuals to bid for items at auction. Unlike Amazon.com, which lost more than $2 billion in its first six years, eBay was profitable from the start, has no offline counterpart, and is difficult to compete against because the most important key to its success is not its pricing but the size of its customer base.

For physical-world companies extending into cyberspace, the emphasis is different. Even if their e-commerce operations don't pay off directly in online sales, the sites help drive customers into stores by providing advance product information, pricing, and availability. This is especially true in the automobile sector: by 2001, 13% of total new car sales were initiated on the Internet (though they were all completed offline), and 4% of used-car buyers were matched to sellers by e-commerce sites.

The received wisdom in the early days was that pure e-commerce operations would have significant cost advantages over physical world retailers. By 2001 the advantage was on the side of existing physical-world chains, which already had revenues, customers, distribution infrastructures, and brand names into which they could integrate e-commerce. The U.K. grocery store chain Tesco began online services in 1996, fulfilling orders from a single store and recovering delivery costs by charging customers a flat fee of about $7.50. By 2001, Tesco had extended the service to 290 stores nationwide at a cost of $58 million over four years, and was booking $30 billion worth of online grocery sales annually—1.5% of its overall revenues. By contrast, the U.S. start-up Webvan spent $1 billion between 1999 and 2001 before filing for bankruptcy.

Among online successes, Dell Computer's direct sales business translated so effectively to the Web that, as early as 1998, its sales were worth $1 million a day. In 2001 it booked fully half its sales online. EasyJet, the U.K.-based, cut-price direct sales airline, sells more than 90% of its seats online.

In the business-to-business marketplace, few apart from the largest computer companies—IBM, Dell, Cisco (until early 2001), and Oracle—made money from the principle that the successes during the gold rush were those who sold picks and shovels to miners. Companies providing infrastructure for online procurement, business exchanges, and supply chain management, such as i2 Technologies, Ariba, and Commerce One, all lost substantial amounts, as hundreds of b2b marketplaces crashed.

Consolidation is a way of life in such a young industry, both for companies struggling to survive financially and for those seeking entry into new markets. AOL's acquisition of media giant Time-Warner was a rare exception of a new media company capitalizing on its high-flying stock price to pick up an older, more mature company with solid revenues.

In the second category are companies like Cisco, which acquired 73 companies between 1993 and 2001, mostly start-ups working on new technologies that Cisco could use to aid its own development. Peak years for the company's acquisitions were 1999 (18) and 2000 (23), when its stock price was at its height. Amazon.com and eBay both acquired non-U.S. competitors to expand into markets such as the United Kingdom, Germany, and France.

Markets

The United States indubitably leads the world in e-commerce, with a spend of $3.6 billion in October 2001 alone (Forrester Research). The next biggest markets are the United Kingdom, Germany, and France, followed by the Netherlands and Sweden. However, the United States' share of global e-commerce dropped throughout the late 1990s as more and more countries came online; in 2001 it dropped below the 50% mark for the first time.

The size of a given country's e-commerce market tends to vary directly with the speed at which PCs were adopted by consumers, but other factors affecting the geographical breakdown are language and tax issues, plus consumer confidence. A French online radio station's audience will come not only from France but from Canada and large parts of Africa. An English-language site based in the United Kingdom can reasonably serve Scandinavia and the Netherlands, as both those countries have high percentages of English speakers, but an e-commerce company targeting Germany or France must provide a site in those languages.

Business use of Internet, 2000 (% of all companies)

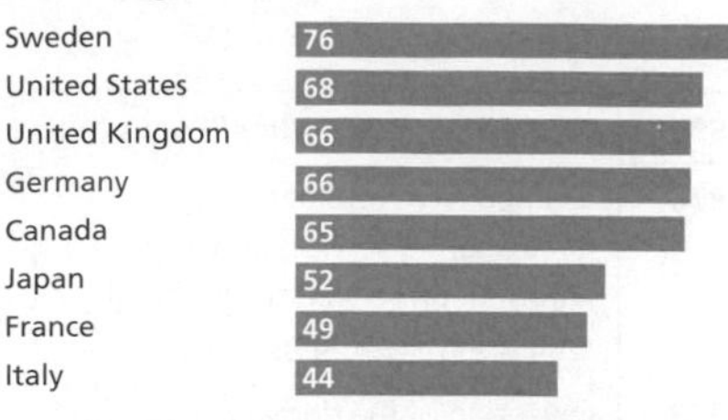

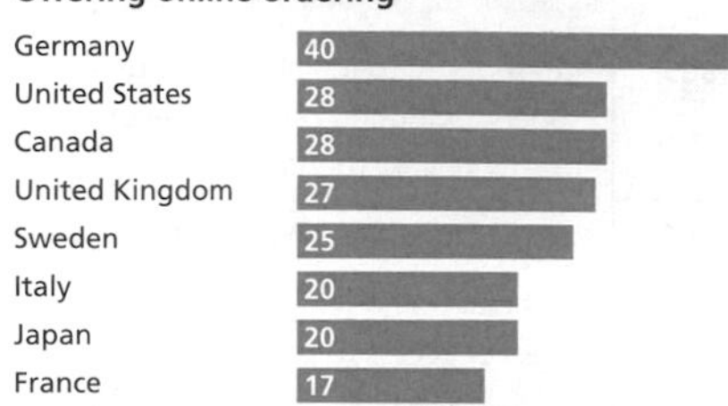

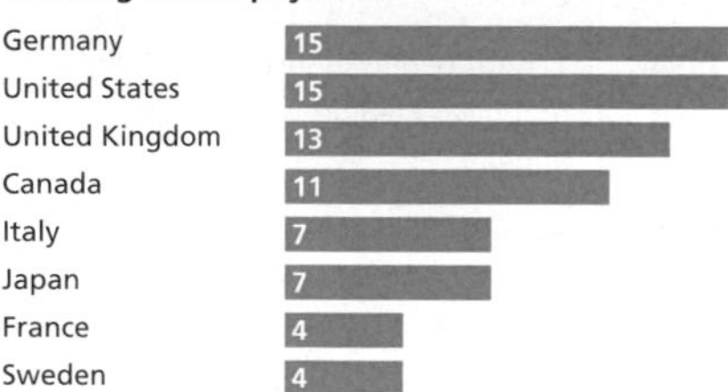

Source: Department of Trade and Industry, U.K.

Technology

Every couple of years, the Internet reinvents itself. As peer-to-peer networking makes direct connections a fact of online life, and the Web becomes machine-readable, new Web-based services will emerge to collate data from multiple sources, repackage it in new ways, and resell it. In addition, these technologies are designed to allow industry sectors to create common vocabularies for the exchange of data so that—for example—a pharmacist, GP, and hospital can all exchange patient data, even though they run disparate applications.

Several initiatives are battling it out to become the dominant e-commerce platform: Microsoft's .NET (which the company hopes to use to turn software into a rental service), IBM's WebSphere (based on the free operating system Linux), and Sun ONE. Microsoft's Hailstorm, which offers centralized authentication, is XML-based and is designed to allow .NET services to offer device-independent authentication, competing with the similar functions AOL offers its users.

In countries with low PC penetration rates (such as Italy and Greece), mobile

Forecast e-commerce sales by region for 2004 ($ billion), with 2001 sales in parens

North America (25.3)	3,500
Asia-Pacific (3.86)	1,600
Western Europe (8.85)	1,500
Latin America	82
Rest of World	69

Sources: Gartner, Forrester Research

E-commerce sales in the U.S. by retail product during October 2001 ($ million)

Airline tickets	485.8
Computer hardware	386.0
Apparel	284.0
Hotel reservations	282.5
Consumer electronics	225.9
Books	149.8
Music	126.6
Toys/video games	124.1
Car rentals	123.5
Office supplies	102.2

Source: Forrester Research

phones are an important way of using Internet services and of making small payments, although designing applications that work well on such small screens is a significant challenge.

In the digital content areas, designing cryptographic systems to prohibit copying of intellectual property is both a legal and a technical challenge.

New Products

Surprisingly, given that e-commerce claimed it was going to reinvent the world, genuinely new products have been slow to emerge and slower to catch on. E-commerce is ideally suited to selling downloaded digital copies of books, music, software, and even films, yet by the end of 2001 e-books had only captured 0.1% (under $500,000) of book sales. Bertelsmann, active in e-commerce via BOL (books online) and its acquisition CDNow, among others, closed its e-publishing unit, AtRandom, for lack of demand, and AOL Time-Warner closed its e-book division, iPublish.

The biggest challenge is getting consumers to pay for content, when the Internet is filled with free material and consumers have the means to make their own digital copies. Sales of physical CDs and downloads took off rapidly, reaching 18% of U.S. music sales in 2001. As the record labels launched commercial music services, they continued to fight legal and technical battles against free services allowing users to swap files. This pattern is repeated in the video and film industry, as flat-rate high-speed connections are developed, and disk storage space continues to drop in price.

Major media companies have had some of e-commerce's biggest failures. Time-Warner lost millions on portals (Pathfinder) and news services (The Netly News) before being acquired by AOL, under whose aegis it then failed with iPublish. Disney failed just as notably with portals (Go.com), search engines (Infoseek), and news (Mr Showbiz).

Employment

It is extremely difficult to know exactly how many people are employed in e-commerce at any one time. Older companies do not generally separate those employees from their overall numbers; very small online businesses are difficult to count, and purely electronic companies are usually either growing, or laying people off, very quickly. What is known is that by July 2001, 135,925 people (*The Industry Standard*) had been laid off in the U.S. high-tech sector as part of the dot-com collapse, and many more companies went under or were acquired after that. In January 2001, the 1,300 employees laid off by Amazon.com were estimated to form about 15% of its workforce, which would give the company total staff numbers of about 8,500. In the Internet economy as a whole at that point, start-ups employed only 15.6% of the estimated 3 million workers with jobs related to the Internet. However, many of those jobs were nontechnical positions such as sales and marketing, administration, and manufacturing.

Challenges

The big difficulty remains that of persuading people to pay for content. Solving the micropayments problem—providing a cost-effective means for customers to make one-off very small payments—is one key. However, users will only be persuaded to pay for online content if it is unique (and so not available elsewhere for free), precisely targeted (exactly what they need), timely (so that copying is not an issue), and high-quality. Profitable early e-commerce businesses capitalized on the Internet's unique ability to serve niche markets and directly connect users to each other. These are the key characteristics of the Internet as a medium.

E-commerce as a simple translation of mail order catalogues will plateau, following the slowing growth of PC penetration and the advent of new shopping channels based on more familiar-seeming technologies such as interactive TV.

Many issues remain to be resolved, including the application of existing national tax structures to e-commerce, the safeguarding of consumers' privacy, and how (and whether) it will be possible to police the movement of material that contravenes local censorship laws. The U.S. moratorium on Internet taxes extends to 2003, but within the European Union the lack of harmonized VAT structures places a great burden on e-commerce companies attempting to compete internationally. Unless this is resolved, U.S. companies have a clear advantage in Europe.

For More Information

Books and Directories:

Grossman, Wendy M. *From Anarchy to Power: The Net Comes of Age.* New York: New York University Press, 2001.

Hagel, John, and Arthur G. Armstrong. *Net Gain: Expanding Markets through Virtual Communities.* Boston, MA: Harvard Business School Press, 1997.

Lewis, Michael. *Next: The Future Just Happened.* New York: W.W. Norton, 2001.

Plant, Robert T. *eCommerce: Formulation of Strategy.* Upper Saddle River, NJ: Financial Times Prentice Hall, 2000.

Magazines and Journals:

Business Week (United States), McGraw-Hill: **www.businessweek.com**

The Economist (United Kingdom): **www.economist.com**

Financial Times (United Kingdom) **www.ft.com**

Web Sites:

Amazon.com: **www.amazon.com**

CyberAtlas: **cyberatlas.internet.com**

eCentre: **www.ecentre.org.uk**

Elab: **www.elabweb.com**

Electronic Commerce Association: **www.theeca.org**

Interactive Advertising Bureau: **www.iab.net**

The International E-commerce Association: **www.inteca.org**

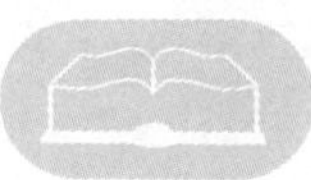

ELECTRONICS

1746	The Leyden jar—the prototype for the capacitor—is simultaneously invented by Pieter van Musschenbroek of the University of Leyden in the Netherlands and Dean E. J. von Kleist of Cammin, Pomerania.
1876	Alexander Graham Bell receives a U.S. patent for the telephone.
1904	John Ambrose Fleming files for a patent for the vacuum tube.
1924	Zenith Electronics produces the first portable radio.
1927	Farm boy Philo Farnsworth applies for a patent on his electronic television. Bell Telephone Labs demonstrates wireless TV.
1945	Arthur C. Clarke proposes a geosynchronous communications satellite system, which became reality 20 years later.
1946	AT&T introduces the first mobile telephones.
1947	William Shockley, John Bardeen, and Walter Brattain invent the transistor at Bell Telephone Labs.
1958	Jack Kilby of Texas Instruments and Robert Noyce of Fairchild Semiconductors separately invent the integrated circuit.
1958	Arthur Schawlow and Charles Townes develop the laser at Bell Labs.
1966	Professor Charles Kao and his team at STL in Harlow, United Kingdom, publish a paper which led to the development of fiberoptic communications.
1971	Ted Hoff designs Intel's first microprocessor, the 4004, which is used in the Busicom calculator.
1992	Tim Berners-Lee at CERN develops hypertext mark-up language (HTML) and effectively invents the World Wide Web.

The global electronics market is immense, totaling some $1.0 trillion a year in value (2000). This market includes worldwide sales of semiconductors, components, subsystems, finished systems, and related software and services.

While Dr. William Gilbert first coined the word "electricity" in 1600, it was not until the 20th century that electronic technology was commercially exploited in consumer goods.

The center of the electronics world is Silicon Valley, established on a large patch of farmland south of San Francisco.

William Shockley, born in London, gained a Ph.D. from Massachusetts Institute of Technology, before going on to work on developing the transistor at Bell Labs in New Jersey in 1936. It was first demonstrated in 1947, and by 1954 nearly a million were being delivered for use in a variety of products, from hearing aids to a battery-powered radio. Shockley's disillusion at not receiving any royalties for the discovery, and a desire to return to California, led him to set up Shockley Semiconductor Laboratory in 1956. He based himself near the Stanford Industrial Park that already boasted the fast-growing instrument producer Hewlett-Packard, and close to an IBM research lab that was to design the first disk memory for computers. It is said that all semiconductor design in Silicon Valley can be traced back to Shockley's company.

This "start-up" philosophy has continued to this day, and has been exported around the world. Many countries have tried to replicate the success of the Silicon Valley phenomenon, including Silicon Glen in Scotland, with varying degrees of success.

COMPANIES

Electronics is a truly diversified market. There are thousands of types of products, with most Western companies concentrating on producing a few well, rather than having a wide portfolio. Since the 1990s, in particular, there has been a concentration on core competencies. Asian companies, however, are more integrated, manufacturing as many parts of their products in-house as possible and producing a wider range of products.

Companies that manufacture and market products are referred to as OEMs (original equipment manufacturers), although this is becoming a misnomer, as these companies increasingly subcontract the manufacture of their products to the CEMs (contract electronics manufacturers) while retaining their marketing and sales channels. Some traditional manufacturers—such as Ericsson and Motorola—have sold manufacturing facilities to large contract manufacturing organizations like Flextronics and Solectron.

Top electronics OEMs by sales, 2000 ($ million)

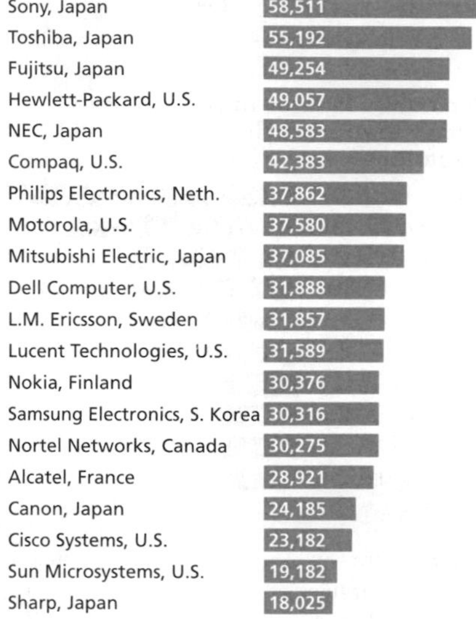

Around 20% of global electronics assembly is done by contract manufacturers, so there is room for this trend to continue for some time. CEMs work on low margins of between 4 and 8%, and are trying to increase this by offering additional, higher-value services such as design.

Mergers and acquisitions in the contract electronics manufacturers sector

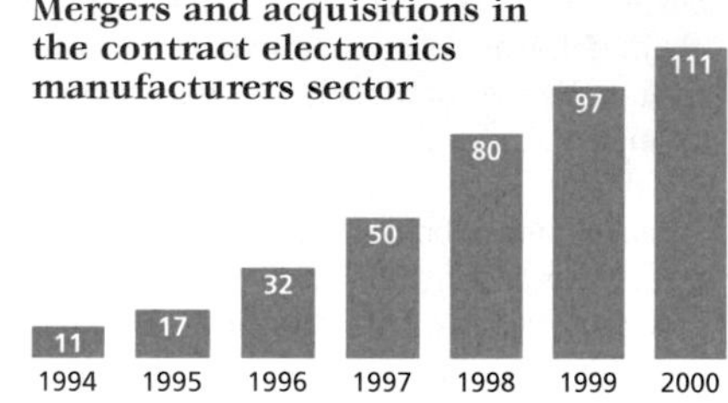

Electronic products are made up of three main types of device: passive components, including resistors and capacitors; electromechanical components, including switches and connectors; and semiconductors that account for up to 90% of the cost.

Very many components are used in the manufacture of consumer electronic equipment, but the most important group is semiconductors. The worldwide semiconductor market was around $140 billion in 2001. The leading manufacturers are also spread throughout the world, often with manufacturing plants outside their home continent. In 2001, the collapse of the dot-com boom sector and difficulties in the

Semiconductor sales, 2000 ($ billion)

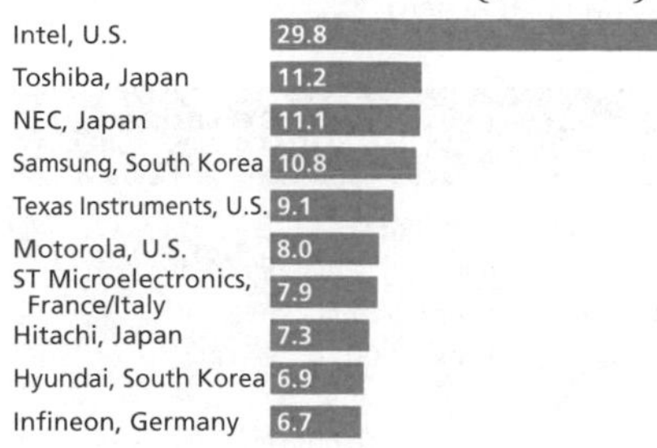

Connector sales, 2000 ($ million)

Tyco Electronics, U.S.	5,841
Molex, U.S.	2,438
FCI (Europe)	2,251
Delphi Connector Systems, U.S.	1,145
Amphenol, U.S.	1,034
Foxconn, U.S.	930
Hirose, Japan	835
Yazaki, Japan	770
3M, U.S.	740
JAE, Japan	713

communications market led to a 30% drop in semiconductor sales.

Connectors are used between modules and as the interface with the outside world. The connector manufacturing industry comprises many small suppliers, though in recent years there have been some mergers and acquisitions among the larger companies. Tyco has led this, making 22 acquisitions between 1998 and March 2001. There are around 1,245 manufacturers of connectors worldwide, with sales of some $32 billion a year. The top 10 companies accounted for 53% of this total, while the top 100 supplied 84%.

PCB sales, 2000 ($ million)

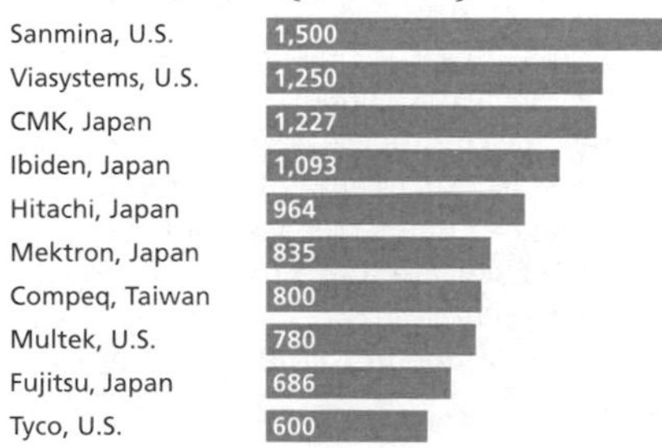

Components are assembled onto printed circuit boards. In the 1990s, the PCB market was worth 20% of the semiconductor market, down from around 30% in the 1980s. In 2000 this market was worth $42 billion, but there was no European company in the top 25 PCB manufacturers.

Markets

The worldwide semiconductor market most accurately indicates the changing fortunes of the electronics sector. Most semiconductors are made on silicon wafers in expensive fabrication facilities (fabs), which now cost up to $3 billion to set up. According to the SIA (Semiconductor Industry Association), global wafer capacity utilization declined to 64.2% in the third quarter of 2001 compared to 92.8% in the fourth quarter of 2000, hitting its lowest level since the early 1990s. In 2000, twice as much capacity came online as did in 1999. Semiconductor manufacturers have been closing down old fabs and delaying the commissioning of new ones, but are caught in a trap: to produce better and faster components they need to use the latest equipment and manufacturing techniques.

World electronic equipment production by product sector, 2000 ($ billion)

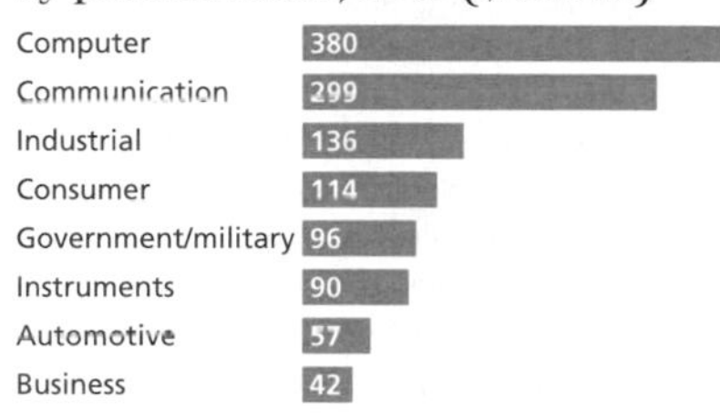

World electronic equipment production by region, 2000 ($ million)

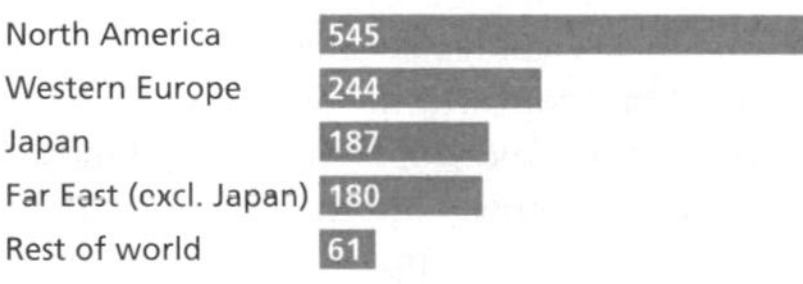

Forecast semiconductor sales in 2002 by region ($ billion)

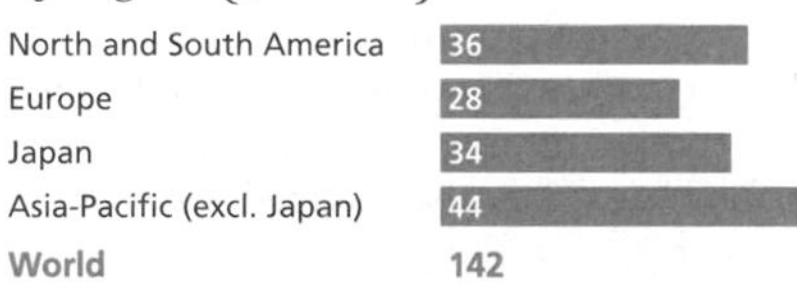

The driving force behind many economies in the last couple of years has been mobile communications and computer equipment. Both these markets came under severe pressure early in 2001, which has had a knock-on effect for the suppliers of components. The world market for semiconductors was forecast to decline by over 30% in 2001, with a very small improvement in 2002. It will be a long time before the market recovers: it is predicted that semiconductor revenues in 2004 will fail to match those in 2000, and this slow comeback will be replicated through most product types.

Technology

Traditionally, electronics companies invest 10–15% of turnover on research and development. Around five years ago, companies started to exploit their knowledge by licensing this intellectual property (IP) to other companies. This has now become an industry of its own, with worldwide revenue for independent IP providers jumping 40% to $617 million in 2000, from $439 million in 1999. By the end of 2005, revenue in this market is forecast to exceed $1.6 billion. This use of IP has spurred the growth of companies producing basic designs to which others can add modules to differentiate their products and reduce costs.

Displays are one area where companies are improving their products. By 2007, flat panel units should replace cathode ray tubes in computer monitors, but the technology is being taken up much faster in other products such as camcorders, digital cameras, and TVs.

One type, based on organic light-emitting diode (OLED) materials, is expected to provide a market worth $714 million in 2005. This was developed by Kodak but has been licensed to a number of other companies.

In the production of semiconductors, both companies making their own devices and foundries (companies making integrated circuits for others) are starting to use 300mm (11 inch) silicon wafers. Larger wafers allow more devices to be manufactured with one piece of equipment, and thus reduce costs.

New Products

The electronics sector relies on new products for market growth. In 2001–02 it was third-generation mobile communications products. However, growth was held back by delays in providing the corresponding video and audio services to consumers.

Computers have also had a difficult time: worldwide market growth peaked in early 1999 at just over 25%, and has dropped to below 10%. The release of the XP operating system from Microsoft late in 2001 stimulated the market as it requires more memory and faster processors, but this will probably be just a temporary phenomenon.

In the automotive sector, component suppliers are increasingly cooperating on designs that will expand the market. In-

  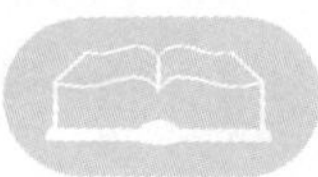    

dependent organizations like the FlexRay Consortium, set up to develop a standard for high-speed bus systems for distributed control applications in automobiles, received support from many of the major producers.

In 2001, while the worldwide semiconductor market was expected to decline 30%, the automotive semiconductor market was set to grow by 7%. This is driven by the adoption of more extensive safety measures, including plans for external airbags and increasing demand for in-car entertainment consoles.

The communications sector looks likely to revive, with wireless interconnection of equipment being a key driver. The Bluetooth initiative attracted 2,500 member companies but seemed to be slow to capitalize on its early impact.

Many electronic equipment makers are relying on a dramatic growth in the increasing proliferation of electronics in the home. The integration of entertainment appliances (TV, DVD, satellite decoders, and so on) with home computers and increasingly intelligent white goods provides exciting opportunities for companies to expand outside their traditional sectors.

To make products more attractive to purchasers, increased attention has been paid to the human-machine interface, with increased use of flat panel displays.

Employment

At the end of 2001, subcontractors who had benefited from the shift to outsourced manufacturing started to rationalize their acquisitions, resulting in job losses. They are able to move production to the most cost-effective manufacturing sites, whether in Eastern Europe, the Far East, or Latin America.

In 2001–02, tens of thousands of jobs were cut in the electronics industry worldwide. Britain's Engineering Employers' Federation estimated that the total number of engineering job cuts in the United Kingdom in 2001 would be around 50,000, with an additional 60,000 jobs to go in 2002–27,000 of them in the electronics sector. In the United States, component manufacturers cut 65,000 jobs in the first five months of

Leading electronics OEMs by employment, 2000/01

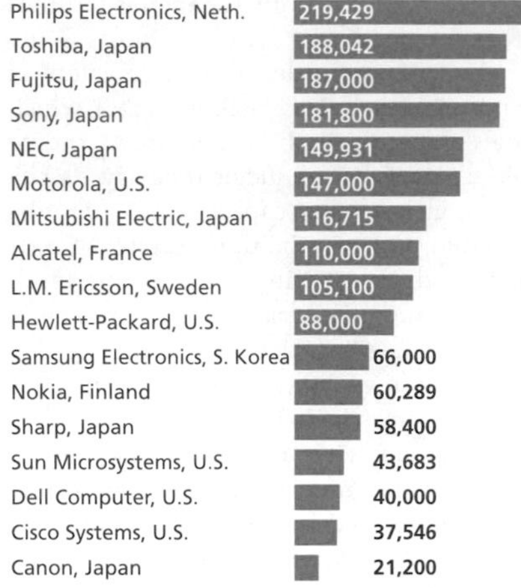

2001. In mid-2001 Hitachi announced that it was cutting 14,700 jobs in Asia alone.

Impact of the Internet

The electronics sector has been quick to adopt new technologies, especially if they produce cost savings. In the 1990s there was a growth in electronic data interchange, whereby suppliers and customers could exchange stock information, orders, and progress reports, initially via dedicated computer systems, and then via the Internet. In the late 1990s, some 300 major companies established RosettaNet, an independent consortium dedicated to the development and deployment of standard electronic business interfaces to align the process between supply chain partners on a global basis. Basically this means that product descriptions and orders are done in a common language in order to cut costs of procurement. Much of the early work was done in the United States, but major European and Asian companies have now also adopted RosettaNet's standards.

The major area in which the Web has come into its own, besides making it easier for design engineers to source technical information, has been in tracking components and products during times of shortage, a situation that ceased to exist during the second half of 2001.

For More Information

Books and Directories:

Kaplan, David A. *The Silicon Boys and Their Valley of Dreams*. New York: HarperCollins, 2000.

Langdon, Christopher, and David Manners. *Digerati, Glitterati: High-tech Heroes*. New York: John Wiley, 2001.

Lubar, Steven. *Info Culture: The Smithsonian Book of Information Age Inventions*. Boston, MA: Houghton Mifflin Company, 1993.

Reid, T.R. *The Chip: How Two Americans Invented the Microchip and Launched a Revolution*. New York: Simon & Schuster, 1984.

Global Semiconductors Report 1998–2002, Miller Freeman: **www.cmp-europe.com**

Magazines and Journals:

Electronic Buyers' News, CMP: **www.ebnonline.com**

Electronic Engineering Times, CMP: **www.eet.com**

Electronics Business, Cahners: **www.e-insite.net/eb-mag**

Web Sites:

American Electronics Association: **www.aeanet.org**

Electronics Industry Knowledge Network: **www.e-insite.net**

The Federation of the Electronics Industry (United Kingdom): **www.fei.org.uk**

Institute of Electrical and Electronics Engineers (IEEE) (United States): **www.ieee.org**

The Institution of Electrical Engineers (IEE) (United Kingdom): **www.iee.org.uk**

Japan Electronics and Information Technology Industries Association (JEITA): **www.jeita.or.jp**

SiliconValley.com: **www.siliconvalley.com**

ENGINEERING

2500B.C.	Horse and cart, Mesopotamia.
664	Windmill, Persia.
c.1300	Clock, Europe.
1440	Printing press, Germany.
1705	Steam pump, United Kingdom.
c.1730	Centigrade thermometer, Sweden.
1857	Elevator, United States.
1860	Automatic machine tool, United States.
1867	Typewriter, United States.
1885	Car, Germany.
1923	Factory transfer line, United Kingdom.
1944	Space rocket, Germany.
c.1945	Gas turbine, United Kingdom.
1946	Electronic computer, United States.
1947	Transistor, United States.
1960	Computer-controlled machine tool, United States.
1973	Computer tomography scanner, United Kingdom.
1991	GSM cellular telephone, Europe.

Engineering is one of the oldest and most pervasive of global industrial sectors. It is divided into a huge variety of product types, and as a result of its breadth is difficult to define statistically. Many other large industrial sectors—including automotive, aircraft, and information and communications technologies (ICT) products (including computers and mobile telephones)—can, by some definitions, be considered part of engineering.

However, the most useful definition of engineering products is that they include all types of machinery (apart from ICT and office equipment), fabricated metal and plastic components, and transport systems and components, excluding road vehicles and aircraft. Out of world manufacturing output of some $6,000 billion a year (measured according to net output), engineering using this definition accounts for output of $1,400 billion, according to estimates adapted from OECD data. To put this into perspective, total world GDP—defined as net world economic output—adds up to some $30,000 billion a year.

The main types of engineering products are listed below. The data in this table are based on gross output, rather than the net figures used earlier. Gross output is the sum of the turnovers of all the companies involved in specific kinds of engineering production: for many engineering companies, their net figure is between 30% and 70% of gross output.

Sales of leading engineering products, 2000 ($ billion)

Product	$ billion
Car parts and systems	500
Electronic parts/systems	500
Medical equipment	150
Ships/aircraft	100
Industrial control equipment (including electric motors)	100
Construction machines	70
Electricity generators	65
Semiconductor manufacturing equipment	50
Batteries	40
Taps/valves	40
Agricultural equipment	35
Machine tools	35
Industrial bearings	22
Locks	20
Pumps	20
Printing machines	10
Textile machines	10
Lighting	10
Compressors	5

Note: sales include spare parts and some service activities, eg maintenance of existing equipment

Engineering has its roots in activities going back to the dawn of civilization. Many of the important mechanical principles used by machines today can be traced back to basic inventions—including the wheel, gears, and anti-friction bearings—that have been around for centuries. The advent of electricity to provide power and control, from the end of the 19th century onwards, plus the invention of the electronic computer after World War II, stimulated important advances in worldwide engineering development. In a continuation of this process, during the past 30 years many older-established mechanical engineering products have fused with more recent areas of electrical engineering, leading to the development of "mechatronic" products (containing mechanical and electronic parts) which are among the most important engineering artifacts in use today. Examples include industrial control systems, many types of car parts (such as sensor-activated airbags and bearing systems), and elevators and escalators.

Most engineering products are used by other industries, not consumers. Because such products are generally hidden from view—and are often rather complicated—engineering does not have a very glamorous public image. However, many engineering products and parts are essential to everyday life. It is estimated that in mechanical engineering alone—not including electrical engineering—there are roughly 20,000 separate product types, ranging from pumps to rocket components.

COMPANIES

As might be expected from an industry with such a varied range of products, there is a huge number of engineering companies. Europe alone has about 20,000 mechanical engineering companies, of which only 800 have a workforce above 500; 15,000 of them have fewer than 100 employees. In contrast to the trend towards agglomeration seen in big companies in many other sectors, many engineering companies wish to become smaller and more specialized rather than larger and more diverse.

Top engineering companies by sales, 2000 ($ billion)

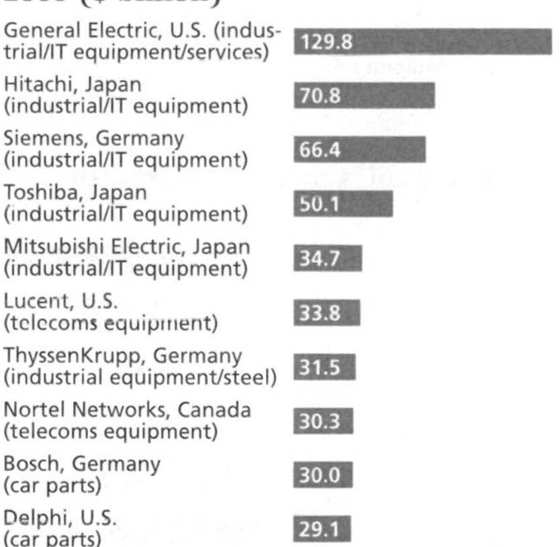

Note: companies may encompass activities other than engineering
Source: *Business Week*

Because of the diversity of the product range, there is a trend in engineering towards the domination of particular product niches, often on a worldwide basis, by specific companies. As a result, a feature of the industry is the "sliver" companies, which maintain a leading position in a narrow product sector that could be worth only a few hundred million dollars on a worldwide basis. Examples of such sliver companies include Munters, a Swedish business which is the world leader in making specialist

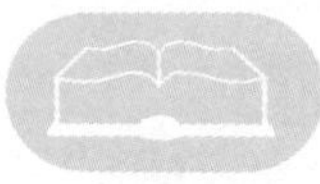

Top companies by after-tax return on sales, 2000 (%)

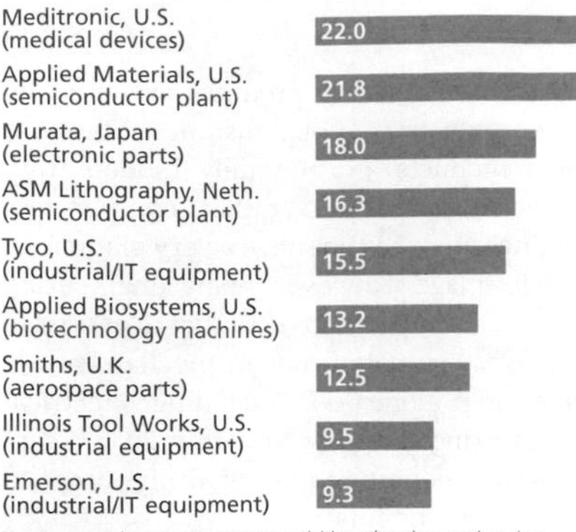

Note: companies may encompass activities other than engineering
Source: *Business Week*

Top engineering companies by market capitalization in July 2001 ($ billion)

Company	$ billion
General Electric, U.S. (industrial/IT equipment/services)	486.7
Tyco, U.S. (industrial/IT equipment)	101.7
Siemens, Germany (industrial/IT equipment)	63.7
Meditronic, U.S. (medical devices)	51.9
3M, U.S. (industrial products)	47.1
Applied Materials, U.S. (semiconductor plant)	40.5
United Technologies, U.S. (elevators/aircraft engines)	39.2
Honeywell, U.S. (industrial equipment)	38.6
Hitachi, Japan (industrial/IT equipment)	34.3
Alcatel, France (telecoms equipment)	30.7

Note: companies may encompass activities other than engineering
Source: *Business Week*

Top companies by after-tax return on equity, 2000 (%)

Invensys, U.K. (industrial/IT equipment)	54.0
Smiths, U.K. (aerospace parts)	38.2
ASM Lithography, Neth. (semiconductor plant)	35.4
Vestas, Denmark (wind turbines)	35.6
Applied Materials, U.S. (semiconductor plant)	34.6
Waters, U.S. (instruments)	34.1
General Electric, U.S. (industrial/IT equipment/services)	29.5
Tyco, U.S. (industrial/IT equipment)	29.2
ABB, Switzerland (industrial/IT equipment)	28.4
3M, U.S. (industrial products)	28.0

Note: companies may encompass activities other than engineering
Source: *Business Week*

dehumidifying equipment used in applications from supermarkets to gyms, and has sales of only about $300 million a year.

Another feature of engineering companies is that many, particularly in continental Europe, remain privately owned, despite the trend in many other areas of industry. Managers of many engineering companies—particularly in product niches—like to remain private because this form of ownership enables then to concentrate on their own areas of expertise on a long-term basis, free from interference from outside shareholders. Germany has more medium-sized, private engineering companies with strong global positions than anywhere else: about 20, all of them with sales of more than $1 billion a year. The biggest is Bosch, the world's second-largest maker of vehicle components, with annual sales of more than $30 billion. Other examples include Liebherr, a major manufacturer of construction equipment, and ZF, the world's largest producer of automatic gearboxes, excluding those groups controlled by car makers.

Most of the largest engineering companies span several sectors, in contrast to the concentration on niches seen in the industry as a whole. The biggest, by market capitalization and sales, is General Electric of the United States, which makes a range of engineering products including aircraft engines, medical systems, home appliances, and lighting. GE is also a large services company: more than half its sales are accounted for by financial services products and TV operations. Other major players are other conglomerates such as Siemens of Germany and Hitachi of Japan. Sales of such companies include significant volumes of ICT products which, strictly speaking, do not belong to the definition of engineering as set out above. However such companies are, at heart, mechanical/electrical engineering businesses.

The breadth of product types in engineering can be appreciated from other companies in the top 10 tables below. These include Medtronic, the biggest company in the world in medical devices (which has total sales of $150 billion a year), and Applied Materials, the biggest manufacturer of machines for semiconductor production. Most of the major engineering companies—and also many of the smaller ones—are highly global. It is common to find organizations in this sector which have more than half—and often up to 75%—of their sales in countries outside their home territory.

Markets

Roughly speaking, the world can be divided into four as regards sales of engineering products: North America, Western Europe, Japan, and the rest of the world. The United States is the most important market, not just because it accounts for about one quarter of sales of engineering products but because it is generally in the lead in terms of technical innovation. Because of this, most leading European engineering companies aim to have 25–30% of their sales in the United States. Roughly 75–90% of all sales of engineering products are made directly to other engineering or industrial companies, with a very small proportion going to consumers (exceptions to this include domestic appliances, where consumer involvement is high). Most engineering companies, therefore, rely for their sales on specialist teams of engineers/sales staff who liaise with customers on a technical level. For these reasons, few engineering companies advertise at consumer level.

Technology

A key to product development at leading engineering companies is the increasing cross-linkage between different areas of technology. For instance, it is common to find that many such companies have chemists, materials scientists, manufacturing experts, and software specialists working together in efforts to devise new products in fields such as engines, pumps, compressors, and other systems that form part of modern machine technology.

In many mechanical engineering companies it is not unusual for one quarter of the people working on new product development to be specialists not in mechanical areas of engineering, but in electronics—such is the importance of ICT-related disciplines in many areas of engineering. Examples of this are the sectors of agricultural machines (including tractors) and kitchen appliances (white goods). In the former, companies are increasingly equipping their products with satellite receiving systems so that the machinery can download details of its location. In white goods, the equipment often incorporates computer programs that control parameters such as operating cycles and times; in some cases these can be transmitted to the product via the Internet or using a mobile telephone.

In the most high-tech areas of engineering, such as production of specialized semiconductor manufacturing machinery, a quarter of company staff are likely to have engineering or other high-level qualifications.

New Products

Because the base on which the engineering industry rests is so broad and historically so deep, many of today's new products have their roots in ideas that first emerged 100 years ago. This underlines the fact that engineering ideas move ahead in an evo-

lutionary, step-by-step way, rather than by sudden leaps.

Often, too, ideas need a very long gestation time before they develop into products that are commercially significant. For instance, the fuel cell—a device that produces electricity by combining oxygen from the air with hydrogen—was devised in outline about 150 years ago, but appeared as a viable product only in the 1960s; even now, fuel cells are not used in mass markets because of their high costs.

Employment

Accurate figures for engineering employment do not exist, but total world employment in engineering in 2000 was estimated at about 40 million. Half of these people were in the developed countries of the OECD. The biggest engineering companies in the world have employees measured in hundreds of thousands: General Electric has 313,000 workers; Toshiba has 188,000; and Mitsubishi Electric has 116,000. These employees are likely to be spread across the globe. Of Siemens' 450,000 employees, for example, only 170,000 are in its home country of Germany; a further 85,000 are based in the United States, and there are 25,000 in China.

The activities of engineering companies are becoming increasingly technological, so more and more engineering workers are likely to be technically qualified. It is common for only about 40% of the workforce to be involved in relatively low-skilled factory-floor manufacturing jobs; of the rest, a large proportion will have good technical or scientific qualifications, and will be involved in areas such as product development, marketing, or customer support.

Another trend is that many more engineering employees than 20 years ago are in service activities, such as equipment maintenance and the operation of call centers providing advice to customers. Of the 220,000 employees of Tyco, one of the world's biggest engineering companies, 42% work in service-related fields. In the next 10 years, most commentators expect the number of engineering jobs in the rich OECD countries to stay fairly stable, or go down slightly. Basic production jobs will move, as many have done already, to lower-cost countries in parts of east Asia or Eastern Europe; the jobs that remain in the richer nations will be mainly in high-level development or in production that makes use of automatic machinery and has a higher skill level than old-style manual manufacturing methods.

Impact of the Internet

The growth of the Internet has helped boost worldwide engineering activity by making it possible for companies to manufacture their products more effectively. One way in which this can happen is through the use of new telecommunications links with suppliers and customers. Such links can enable an engineering company to receive orders about specific products from distributors, make changes in the design of the product in question, and transmit specifications for particular types of parts to suppliers. In this way, reaction times can be greatly reduced, enabling the company to reduce stocks of goods and offer a better service to customers. Use of the Internet and other means of telecommunications (often involving greater use of computer-aided design) is expected to increase over the next few years.

For More Information

Web Site:

Orgalime (Brussels-based umbrella organization for engineering companies to which most national engineering trade associations are affiliated): **www.orgalime.org**

  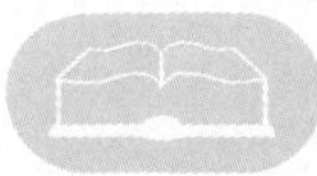    

FOOD AND AGRI-BUSINESS

1780	First U.S. chocolate mill opens.
1867	Swiss Henri Nestlé begins developing infant formula milk.
1876	Budweiser brand launched by Anheuser-Busch.
1886	Coca-Cola invented by Dr. John S. Pemberton in Atlanta, United States.
1896	Henry J. Heinz begins promoting his "57 varieties" of canned sauces and pickles.
1899	First large-scale bottling of Coca-Cola in United States.
1905	First patents for use of ionizing radiation to kill food bacteria.
1906	W.K. Kellogg founds the Bottle Creek Toasted Corn Flake Co.
1930	Clarence Birdseye patents flash freezing of prepared foods.
1937	Nestlé launches Nescafé powdered coffee.
1950	Kraft unveils first commercially-packed sliced processed cheese.
1960s	Pillsbury develops HACCP quality assurance system for NASA, now the safety benchmark for all food producers.
1965	Launch of Gatorade sports drink.
1970s	NASA uses irradiation to sterilize foods for astronauts.
1985	Coca-Cola becomes first soft drink in space.
1988	Kraft bought by Philip Morris Inc. to create world's largest consumer products group.
1996	BSE devastates U.K. meat industry.
1997	Guinness and Grand Metropolitan merge to create Diageo, the world's biggest spirits group.
1999	P&G's Sunny Delight becomes United Kingdom's most successful soft drink launch.
1999	In Europe, green activists oppose genetically-modified crops and foods.

Globalization of food is nothing new: the great explorers and merchant-venturers of the 16th and 17th centuries helped open the intercontinental trade routes for food, building on millennia of lively but relatively small-scale and localized trading.

However, food and drink products present an obstacle that most other major commodities do not, and that is perishability. Only in the last couple of centuries have we moved beyond salting, drying, and brining as the chief means of preserving foodstuffs, and only in the last 100 years have techniques been perfected such as freezing, bottling, canning and, latterly, aseptic and modified-atmosphere packaging.

There has been another obstacle to the true globalization of our food supply: price. Most foodstuffs do not command sufficient market value to justify the costs of shipping them over long distances. As a result, those multinationals that have emerged in the past 30–40 years have largely followed one of two models: buying raw materials from lowest-cost producers, usually in the developing world, and shipping them to developed nations for added-value processing; or building/acquiring overseas factories and distribution systems, often in joint ventures or licensing deals with local businesses, to serve local markets.

Historically, brands have been important. Companies such as Kellogg, Cadbury, Heinz, and Coca-Cola have built reputations that outstripped the true value of their products. Food companies, particularly in the latter part of the 20th century, set the benchmark in brand marketing. Coca-Cola is perhaps the ultimate example: a simple mix of water and syrup that, through inspired marketing and regional bottling partnerships, has conquered the world.

Big brands are only part of the story. In the United States, Canada, and the United Kingdom, and increasingly in other parts of Europe, the mounting strength of retail multiples has seen the emergence of the private label or retailer own brand: goods manufactured on the retailers' behalf (sometimes by major brand owners) and carrying no indication of the maker. With no need for heavy advertising they have successfully undercut traditional manufacturers' brands in many key segments.

The growth of the private label has recast the relationship between manufacturer and client. Brand leaders have been forced to reassess their strategy. For many, price has become an unavoidable weapon against own-label brands, leaving less money for advertising and brand-building promotions. As a result, manufacturers have been forced to cut back on their product ranges and concentrate on "power brands" strong enough to repel the threats of own labels and low prices.

In such circumstances, staying small is not an option. Manufacturers have been forced to consolidate, and the industry is polarizing between a few dozen true multinationals, of which Switzerland's Nestlé is probably the largest, and a very large number of small to medium-sized businesses with only a local or regional customer base. Many of the latter will almost certainly become acquisition targets in due course.

COMPANIES

There was a wave of mergers and acquisitions within the food and beverages industry in the 2000s. Beginning with the $24-billion buyout of U.S.-headquartered Bestfoods by the Anglo-Dutch conglomerate Unilever, 2000 alone saw PepsiCo gobble up Quaker Oats for $13.4 million, Cadbury Schweppes spend $900 million on Snapple Beverage Group, and General Mills pay $5.1 billion for Pillsbury. According to some commentators: "Food companies with only $10 billion in revenues are now looking small, with $20-plus billion quickly becoming the minimum size threshold to be considered a global industry player." (Arthur Andersen, 2001)

Large food and beverage mergers by business enterprise value* of target ($ billion), with target in parens

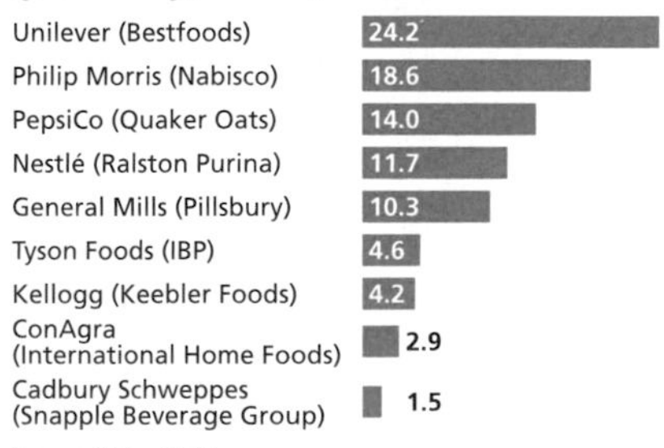

* sum paid plus liabilities
Note: all acquisitions announced between Feb 2000 and Jan 2001
Source: Arthur Andersen Industry Insights

This high level of mergers followed a decade of relative calm, and saw the U.S. Standard & Poor index of global food and agribusiness companies outstripping the all-industry S&P 500 by 37%. Over the previous two years, by contrast, food had underperformed the rest of the 500 by 70% be-

Top companies by food and beverage sales, 1999/2000 ($ billion)

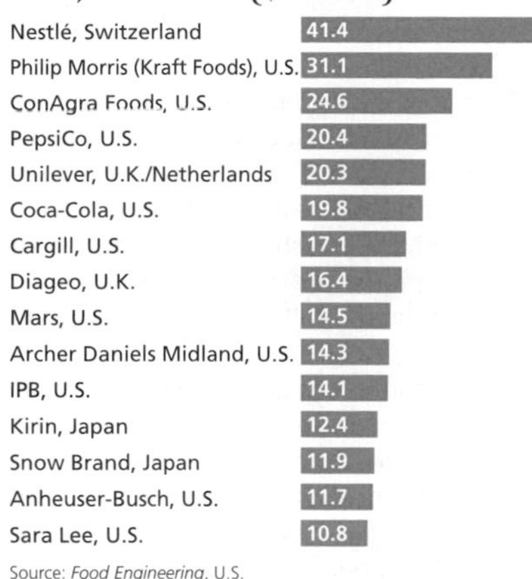

Source: *Food Engineering*, U.S.

Top food and beverage companies by market capitalization, May 2001 ($ million)

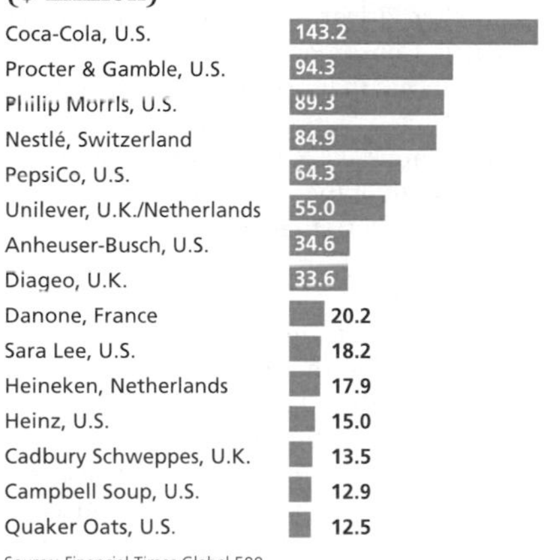

Source: Financial Times Global 500

cause the markets were more interested in technology stocks than tea bags.

The confidence displayed by brands in the 1970s and early 1980s was already beginning to look misplaced by the mid-1990s: manufacturers were starting to need retailers more than retailers needed them. By the early 2000s, only a relatively small number of producers remained in a position of market power which was equal to or greater than that of their biggest customers. Wal-Mart, the world's biggest retailer, ranks sixth in the Financial Times Global 500, higher than any food company. Retailers 7–11 of Japan and Carrefour of France, and fast food group McDonalds, ranked higher than all but six food companies in the same listing. Only eight food manufacturers ranked higher than retailers Tesco (U.K.), Safeway (U.S.), or Ahold (Netherlands).

The shift towards retailers' own-brand products in the more developed European and North American markets has emphasized the diminishing power of all but the biggest manufacturers to control their own destiny. When a supermarket retailer's sales exceed $10 billion annually, few suppliers can claim equivalent market power.

Markets

In 2000, research company Euromonitor estimated the world market for packaged foods—the type of products that most global companies are handling—to be worth $1,322 billion. The market had grown just 3.4% in real terms since 1995. The most spectacular growth came from savory snacks (just under 109%). Meal replacement drinks grew by more than 50% in the same period, and snack bars, spreads, and confectionery all grew by over 30%.

Total retail sales of packaged food, 2001 ($ billion)

North America	270
Western Europe	322
Asia-Pacific	271
World	1,137

Source: Euromonitor International

Total retail sales of soft drinks, 2001 ($ billion)

North America	69
Western Europe	43
Asia-Pacific	59
World	232

Source: Euromonitor International

Taken together, the countries of Western Europe were the world's largest market, accounting for 27.5% of sales in 2000, followed by North America (24.3%), and Asia-Pacific (23.2%).

Technology

The relentless price pressure faced by manufacturers supplying the retail multiples such as Wal-Mart, Germany's Aldi, or the United Kingdom's Tesco has forced attention back on to the factories and renewed the search for savings. Manufacturers are seeking improvements in efficiency by reducing labor costs and by using better machinery and practices to make savings on equipment downtime, product changeover time, maintenance, and wastage.

There have been major advances in production and packaging machinery in recent years. One labeling system launched in 2001 was able to label beverages bottles at speeds of up to 900 a minute. Another could add caps to bottles at up to 500 per minute. These speeds were unheard of just a few years ago, and—provided the equipment is priced competitively—mean companies can turn out far more product in far less time.

Another key word is flexibility. With a typical retail superstore carrying over 15,000 distinct food and drink products, the ability of manufacturers to offer variety without compromising on price has become essential. Most manufacturers—even those operating on a global basis—are still batch producers to some extent. They are looking for equipment solutions to minimize the cost of switching between products and pack formats.

If the cost pressure points firmly downward, regulatory pressure is rising, and this again is reflected in the demands made on equipment suppliers. The industry has already come to terms with the broad demands of food hygiene, but the increasing call for the monitoring and recording of all aspects of the processing operation are an added challenge.

In the meat sector, for example, the consequences of BSE and foot-and-mouth disease in Europe include moves to provide full traceability of meat from the live animal, through carcasses and primal cuts, right up to packaged meat on the supermarket shelf. This will increasingly mean incorporating barcode readers and, in due course, radio frequency tag readers into production lines, not just in bulk and carton handling systems.

Although most major operators now use sophisticated enterprise resource planning software, plus materials and manufacturing resource planning packages, there are still relatively few fully networked factories. Software is available to help with recipe formulation and the monitoring of equipment performance in the factory, but many companies are still struggling to fully integrate this data with their existing systems. Multilevel IT systems, allowing board directors access to the most important factory floor data such as line efficiencies, are more of an aspiration than a reality at the present time.

New Products

Tens of thousands of new food and beverage products are launched each year. In the United States, the Food Marketing Institute (FMI) recorded 16,390 new flavors, colors, or varieties of products introduced in 2000. Several research organizations, including Mintel International, now sell access to global databases of new products to help the industry track launches worldwide.

Billion-dollar global food, drinks, and tobacco brands by 12 months' sales to Q1 2001 in 30 countries ($ billion)

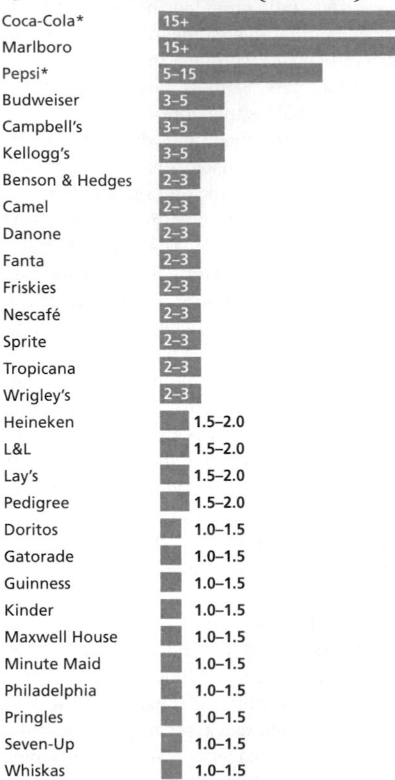

* regular Coca-Cola, Diet Coke, regular Pepsi and Diet Pepsi are all billion-dollar brands in their own right
Source: A.C. Nielsen

The numbers look huge, but so is the range of products now available in supermarkets. According to the FMI, the average number of products carried by a typical U.S. supermarket more than tripled between 1980 and 1999, from 14,145 to 49,225.

The degree of true innovation, however, is less impressive: most new launches are variations on existing products, and new products capable of global success—for example, Procter & Gamble's Sunny Delight juice drink—are rare.

A list of "billion dollar brands," produced by researcher A. C. Nielsen in October 2001, showed food and drink to be the dominant forces in global megabrands. Out of 43 labels that topped $1 billion in sales, 24 were food and beverage brands. However, the list included few names that would have been unfamiliar in the 1980s.

Perhaps the most exciting area of genuine new product development is "better for you" foods. As the developed world has moved away from its traditional carbohydrate-rich diet to more fatty snacks and convenience foods, increased awareness of the associated health risks led first to a parallel boom in sales of low-calorie, low-fat, low-sodium, and vitamin- and mineral-enriched foods.

Now, the industry is developing sophisticated products that not only do less potential harm but can offer positive benefits. They include products which aim to reduce the risk of coronary heart disease, strip out blood cholesterol, or help counter common problems such as osteoporosis. These are usually described as functional foods and beverages, but have also been bundled together with dietary supplements and foods for special dietary use under the new heading of "neutraceuticals." According to research company Frost & Sullivan, this market—still in its infancy—was already worth $50 billion in the United States alone by 2000: one tenth of the entire U.S. food market.

Biotechnology may yet offer even greater opportunities if the characteristics of plants or animals can be manipulated to add human health benefits or to remove harmful elements. However, the massive consumer backlash, particularly in Europe, against genetic modification has given biotechnology a bad image. It may take a long-term consumer education campaign to undo the damage caused by the over-hasty introduction of GM crops.

EMPLOYMENT

Estimates from the World Labor Organization have put global employment in food and agribusiness at around 20 million. In developed countries, employment has fallen despite increased output, as a result of restructuring, rationalization, and some gains from new technology. However, food production (more than drink production) remains relatively labor-intensive. One problem is the prevalence of batch production: machines cannot be set up and left to run unsupervised, and therefore require constant human intervention. Another is the requirement from consumers for increasingly complex products, often with a handmade appearance.

Although many basic food processes can now be carried out automatically, the availability of cheap labor and the relatively low margins in food distribution have been a bar to the replacement of people by expensive machines. A typical large food plant may employ 500–1,200 people, 60–70% of them in relatively low-skilled operations.

Nestlé employs 224,500 people across 80 countries. ConAgra, which is the biggest domestic supplier in the United States, employs 80,000 worldwide in 34 countries. Heinz has 45,000 people in over 200 locations.

IMPACT OF THE INTERNET

Multinationals have been the only segment of the food and beverage industry to benefit significantly from e-commerce. This is partly because smaller companies have been unwilling to shoulder the financial risk, and partly because of a lack of IT awareness and skills inside most food companies.

Up to a point, however, global companies have been driven into e-commerce by the enthusiasm of their customers. Retailers that had been dealing with several thousand suppliers using a mix of traditional paper-based and EDI (electronic data interchange) systems were keen to move to Web-based systems. It is only a short step from Web-based ordering and inventory tracking to Internet auctions and B2B exchanges.

Another driver of e-markets has been Efficient Consumer Response, a management process that originated with Wal-Mart in the United States and is now spreading across Europe. ECR aims to strip unnecessary cost out of the consumer goods supply chain. Moving transactions online and providing inventory tracking data in real time has been shown to offer cost reductions at numerous points in the chain. The only question, from the manufacturer's viewpoint, is whether those benefits are shared or are gobbled up by the retailer.

By 2001, four Internet exchanges had been flagged as most likely to succeed among the initial flurry of exchange launches. These were CPGmarket.com, Globalnetxchange, WorldWide Retail Exchange and Transora. Three were set up by consortia of manufacturers, but the WorldWide Retail Exchange was established as a buying tool by a group of retailers.

For More Information

Magazines and Journals:
Food Processing:
www.foodprocessing.com
Progressive Grocer:
www.progressivegrocer.com

Web Sites:
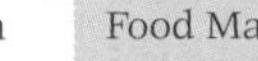
Food Marketing Institute: **www.fmi.org**
Food Navigator:
www.foodnavigator.com
Institute of Food Technology:
www.ift.org

INFORMATION TECHNOLOGY

1896	Herman Hollerith founds the Tabulating Machine Company, now known as IBM.
1943	Colossus, first electronic computer, at Bletchley Park, United Kingdom.
1946	ENIAC: first general-purpose computer, University of Pennsylvania, United States.
1968	Douglas Engelbart demonstrates system of keyboard, mouse, and windows, San Francisco, United States.
1974	First widely sold microcomputer, the Altair, launched.
1976	First Apple computer, the Apple 1.
1977	Commodore PET, Radio Shack TRS-80.
1979	First spreadsheet, VisiCalc, drives adoption of personal computers.
1981	IBM PC launched, setting industry standard; BBC Acorn.
1984	Apple launches the Macintosh; UNIX developed at AT&T.
1985	Microsoft launches Windows.
1991	First release of Linux.
1994	Internet opened to commercial traffic; graphical browser opens the Web to mainstream users.
1997–1999	Remediation of year 2000 problem.
2001	Microsoft narrowly misses being broken up over antitrust violations.

Modern computing is generally held to be about 50 years old. The IT industry itself is arguably older, since the company now known as IBM was originally founded in 1896 by Herman Hollerith, who developed punch card tabulation in order to handle the volume of data produced by the 1880 U.S. Census. The growth of IT has been driven ever since by the increasing volumes of data that companies have to deal with, and senior IT personnel are now key figures in every large company.

In 1975, an IBM mainframe computer that cost $10 million could process 10 million instructions per second. By 1995, a video games console that cost $500 could process 500 million instructions per second.

COMPANIES

The IT industry breaks down into several sub-sectors: hardware, software, and services. However, these are becoming increasingly interdependent as computing, broadcasting, and telecoms converge. IBM is bigger—four times the revenues, 40% higher profits—but Microsoft is the current leader of the industry. Microsoft's operating systems and office applications software dominate 90% of the desktop computer market; it has manipulated its market share to control office software and Web browsers, and is now bidding for digital rights management and content delivery. The company (like IBM before it) spent much of the 1990s defending itself against accusations of monopolistic behavior. The number two software company, Oracle, is a specialist in large databases; the third, SAP, specializes in business management software. Other notable software companies include Intuit (personal finance), Novell (network operating systems), and Symantec (utilities and antivirus).

Leading IT companies by sales, 2000/01 ($ billion)

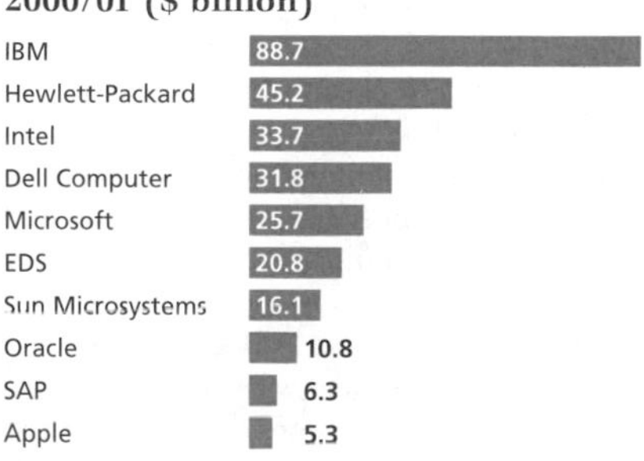

In 2001 Microsoft moved into hardware by producing the Xbox games platform (competing with Sony and Nintendo). Its .NET platform for Web services is intended both to support Windows' continued dominance on the desktop, and to use Windows as leverage to gain control of the burgeoning market for Internet servers and development tools. Sun, which sells high-end workstations running Solaris (its version of the UNIX operating system), competes with Microsoft via its Java technology, which poses a threat to Windows' dominance by creating software that can run on any operating system without being rewritten. The personal digital assistant (PDA) market is currently lead by Palm, Psion, and machines running a cut-down version of Windows (Compaq, Sony).

Global market share, workstations, Q3 2001 (%)

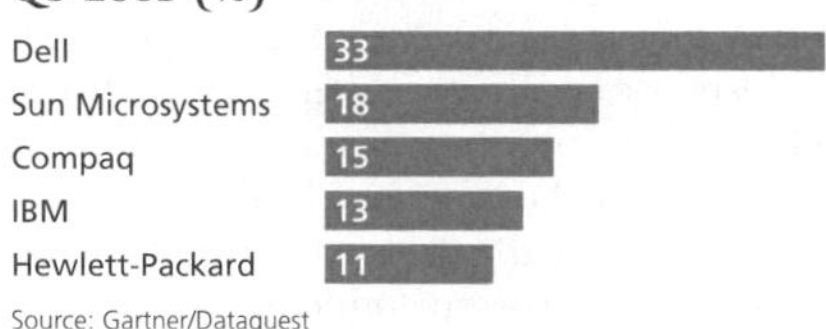

Source: Gartner/Dataquest

Top PC makers, 2001 (%)

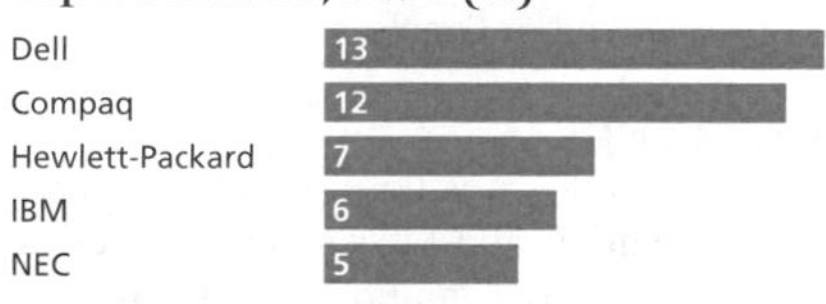

Source: Gartner/Dataquest

The difficulty in the IT industry is not primarily in identifying winning players but in knowing which technologies will cease to matter. Giants of the 1980s such as Digital Equipment Corporation (bought by Compaq in 1999) and Data General (storage vendor EMC) failed to adapt to changing conditions and new approaches. IBM's failure to adapt to a world dominated by PCs resulted in the company's difficulties in 1993. It made a major business mistake in 1980 when it allowed Microsoft to retain the right to license its new PC operating system to other manufacturers, opening the way for a huge new third-party software vendor market.

A significant problem for technology companies is developing a second product after their first has been successful. Mergers and acquisitions help them overcome this by allowing them to extend their existing success into new markets. Microsoft bought its way into databases (FoxBase) and operating systems (DOS, acquired as QDOS from the Seattle Computer Company).

The most important merger of 2001 was Hewlett-Packard's bid, opposed by the heirs of the company's founders, to buy Compaq Computer, the first IBM clone manufacturer. Compaq is an example of why such acquisitions are regarded with skepticism by industry analysts: its 1998 acquisition of DEC is largely blamed for its subsequent crash.

As IT systems become more complex, while hardware prices and margins keep falling, the services market—worth $517 billion in 2000 and approximately $554 billion in 2001—is an increasingly important part of the business of both hardware and software companies. By 2001, IBM, derived nearly 43% of its revenues from services.

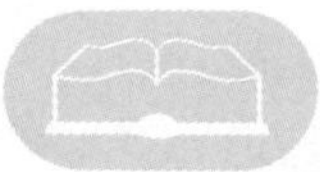

It is, however, almost impossible to gauge the overall size of the IT industry, although best estimates put it in at least the trillion-dollar range. One reason is that IT is becoming more and more difficult to separate from overall company functions; another is that many computer operations are very small indeed. We know, however, that IBM—the biggest IT company—was number 19 on Fortune's list of the top 500 global companies; that nine out of the top ten richest self-made men under 40 were founders of IT or e-commerce companies; and that three of the world's four richest men derive their wealth from Microsoft or Oracle.

Markets

The United States is both the IT industry's biggest market and biggest supplier, using 28.32% (or 164.1 million) of the world's computers in 2000 compared to 8.62% for the second-largest market, Japan. Most of the leading companies driving development—IBM, Microsoft, Oracle, Intel, Apple—are American, or have made deliberate attempts to appear so (by, for example, moving their headquarters) because the United States is notoriously resistant to buying technology from other countries.

Share of world's computers in use, 2000 (%)

United States	28.3
Japan	8.6
Germany	5.3
United Kingdom	4.5
France	3.8
Italy	3.0
Canada	2.8
China	2.8
Brazil	1.5
India	1.1

Source: U.S. Department of Commerce

There are exceptions. Japan's success in consumer electronics carries over into portable computers (Toshiba, NEC, Sony), monitors (Mitsubishi, Sharp), peripherals (Hitachi), and smaller devices (Sony). The country is the second-largest IT market, and boasts more leading IT companies than any other outside the United States.

Much of the manufacturing of electronic components, and of larger parts such as disk drives and monitors, takes place in low-cost manufacturing centers such as Taiwan and South Korea (which is also home to Samsung, maker of one-fifth of the world's computer monitors). Manufacturing is also increasingly being carried out in China, with its low-cost labor force and potentially huge domestic market. Computer companies themselves typically assemble standard parts they source elsewhere; one reason Dell's progress has been so successful is its dedication to efficient production, installing systems that allow it to operate on a "last-minute" basis.

Largest IT software markets, 1999/2000 ($ billion)

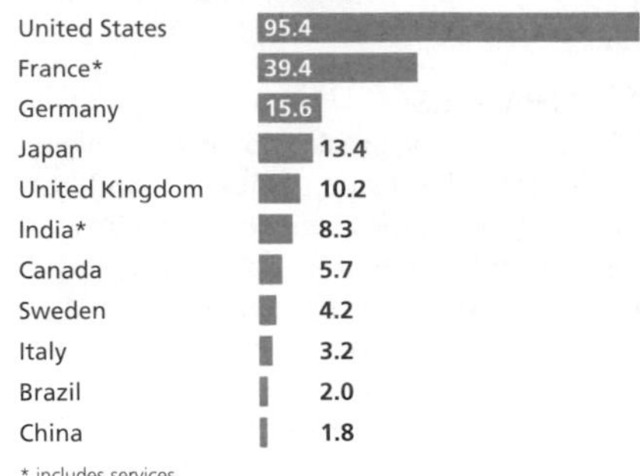

* includes services
Sources: U.S. Department of Commerce; SIIA, U.S.

India's thriving software industry carried out much of the work implementing the switch from two-digit to four-digit years (the Year 2000 problem); its Tata Consultancy Services earns $689 million in revenues annually. Within Europe, Scotland and the Republic of Ireland have built substantial high-tech economies by using tax breaks and other incentives to lure U.S. manufacturers like Compaq, Hewlett-Packard, IBM, Dell, and Microsoft into setting up factories and telephone support operations. Germany is home to several large companies, notably Siemens (which teams with Fujitsu to produce PCs and laptops) and business management software supplier SAP.

However, the world leader in software is still the United States, with the two largest software-only companies, Microsoft and database specialist Oracle. (The third-largest is Germany's SAP.) The size of the software market is a measure of how much the IT world has changed: until personal computers, software was bundled with hardware or written by end users. IBM, which competes with Oracle in databases, with Microsoft in desktop and server software, and with leading consultancies such as EDS in services, is second only to Microsoft in software revenues.

The United States lead in IT was largely created by military's commitment, after Soviet success in space, to fund basic research through its Advanced Research Projects Agency (ARPA). The climate so created helped establish three world-class research organizations-AT&T Bell Labs (UNIX, networking), Xerox PARC, and IBM's Thomas J. Watson Research Lab (hard drives, chips). Research alone, however, is not enough. Xerox—whose PARC pioneered laser printing, ethernet networking (3Com), PostScript (Adobe), and graphical interfaces (Apple and later Microsoft)—failed to capitalize on any of them, and its core photocopier business is becoming a niche market.

Britain retains a world-famous research and development community centered in Cambridge, which in the 1990s fostered such companies as ARM (which designs chips for manufacture by other companies under license), Autonomy (knowledge management software), and Openwave (Internet access software for mobile phones). The United Kingdom's indigenous hardware companies have almost all either disappeared (Sinclair); spun off assets (Acorn, which parented ARM), or been absorbed by foreign buyers (Fujitsu's ICL). The exception is Psion, which pioneered the PDA in 1980, and has formed Symbian as a joint venture with Nokia, Ericsson, Matsushita, and Motorola, to develop and license its operating system software to mobile phone and PDA manufacturers.

The fastest-growing markets for computer and Internet technology for the next few years seem likely to be China, which recently became the world's largest user of mobile phones, and developing countries in Latin America and Africa. The U.S. market, while always responsive to new technology, is likely to recover slowly from the triple impact of the Enron scandal, the September 11 terrorist attacks, and the already existing economic downturn. Europe's Internet growth is expected to slow soon, and high prices for broadband have delayed its adoption. Much of the focus has shifted to wireless technologies and smaller devices.

Technology

The computer industry is dominated by Moore's Law (named for Intel co-founder Gordon Moore), which holds that the amount of information storable on a given amount of silicon doubles roughly every 12 months. Although this is not completely accurate, the industry's products are continually becoming massively more powerful and much cheaper at the same time.

The result is that no company can ever feel secure, no matter how apparently dominant it is. Throughout the 1980s and 1990s both hardware and software were sufficiently underpowered to ensure that there was always a market for new products. This is no longer true. Another factor is that constant change imposes severe time pressure to launch new products before they become obsolete. This reality is thought to favor smaller companies, on the grounds that they can change direction more quickly and get products to market faster than their older, larger, and less flexible counterparts.

EMPLOYMENT

It is impossible to tell at any one time how many people are employed in IT. IBM's employee figure of 316,303, Fujitsu's 187,000, and Apple's of 9,000 are clear enough, but more varied companies like Toshiba or Hitachi do not specify their IT employees; similarly, IT is so completely woven into many companies' structures that it is impossible to isolate the numbers of staff involved.

Leading IT companies by employment, 2001

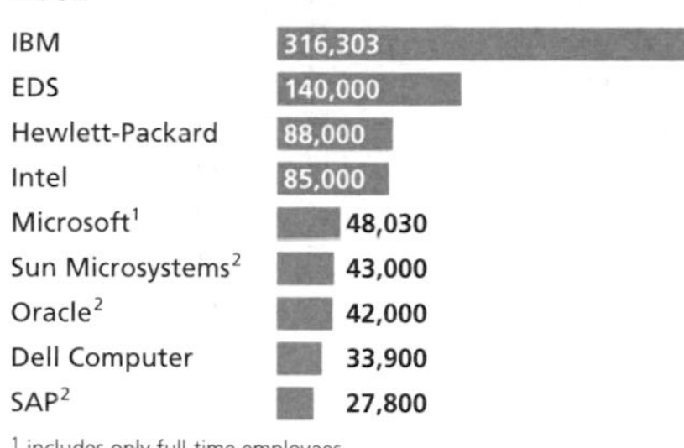

[1] includes only full-time employees
[2] conservative figure

There are countless two-person companies supplying machines, software, and expertise all over the world. Another reason for the lack of clarity is the widespread industry practice of hiring "permatemps": employees who are officially temporary but work full-time on a long-term basis, usually without benefits, and often next to full-timers doing the same job. Microsoft's figure of 48,030 employees is therefore deceptively low, and the company has faced legal actions over its employment policies.

NEW PRODUCTS

One of the paradoxes of the IT industry is that its constant dedication to the newest, fastest technology sometimes involves rediscovering old ideas. The new operating system of 1999, Linux, was a clone of the new operating system of 1984, UNIX. Moreover, it was free, inspiring thousands of developers around the world to work on improving it. By 2001, IBM had adopted Linux for a number of its products. Issuing free copies of source code is anathema to most software companies, especially Microsoft, but proponents of this development model point out a number of public benefits to having software code open, readable, and—most importantly—fixable. In less wealthy countries, Linux is of increasing importance for cost reasons.

Even more surprising, the artificial intelligence field has failed to produce the intelligent robots dreamed of by generations of science fiction writers. Techniques such as neural networking, fuzzy logic, parallel processing, and increasingly powerful silicon chips all produced huge advances in computing, and great strides were made in the late 1990s toward natural language processing, speech recognition, machine translation, and software agents. However, a split remains within the human-computer interface community, who focus on issues of usability: should software be stupid, acting predictably to known commands, or smart, trying to guess what its users want on the basis of what they had wanted in the past.

Internet users by region in August 2001 (million)

North America	181
Europe	155
Asia-Pacific	144
Latin America	25
Middle East	5
Africa	4
World	**513**

Source: www.nua.ie

The increasing push is to make computing ubiquitous and invisible. It is becoming possible to design wearable computers based on the use of metallic thread. Major areas of interest are home networking—smart appliances that can communicate both with each other and with their owners remotely—and personal networking.

Internet users by country in August 2001 (million)

United States	166
Japan	47
United Kingdom	33
Germany	29
China	27
South Korea	22
Italy	19
Canada	14
Brazil	12
France	12

Source: www.nua.ie

The September 11 attacks are driving increased interest in security; the IT industry's contribution is an important one, particularly in biometric recognition systems, networked CCTV and facial recognition, and database technology for such proposals as national ID cards (Britain) and police systems.

IMPACT OF THE INTERNET

The biggest driver of the runaway high-tech boom of the late 1990s was the development of the Internet and the demand it created for computing power (Dell, Sun), data storage (EMC), networking (Cisco), e-commerce infrastructure (Verisign, Microsoft), and consultancy services (IBM).

Because the IT industry was the source of the goods and services that enabled the building of the Internet, these companies were the first beneficiaries of the Internet's ability to extend an organization's reach and cut costs. In addition, these companies grew rapidly due to the hugely increased market for both existing and new products and services such as Web hosting, infrastructure integration, and supply chain management software to enable other companies to engage in e-commerce.

For More Information

Books and Directories:

Hagel, John, and Arthur G. Armstrong. *Net Gain: Expanding Markets through Virtual Communities*. Boston, MA: Harvard Business School Press, 1997.

Lewis, Michael. *Next: The Future Just Happened*. New York: W.W. Norton, 2001.

Plant, Robert T. *eCommerce: Formulation of Strategy*. Upper Saddle River, NJ: Financial Times Prentice Hall, 2000.

Magazines and Journals:

Technology Review: **www.techreview.com**

Web Sites:

Association for Computing Machinery: **www.acm.org**

C'Net: **www.cnet.com**

The Register: **www.theregister.com**

ZDNet: **www.zdnet.com**

INSURANCE

1666	The Great Fire of London prompts the formation of fire insurers.
1688	The beginnings of Lloyd's, the insurance market, in a coffeehouse in London.
1752	Benjamin Franklin sets up the "Philadelphia Contributorship," the first insurance company in the United States.
1871	The society of Lloyd's is incorporated by the Lloyd's Act.
1871	Otto von Bismarck's liability law paves the way for collective accident insurance for workers; a few years later he introduces state accident insurance and mandatory health insurance.
1906	San Francisco earthquake.
1912	The sinking of the Titanic.
1992	Hurricane Andrew produces the biggest natural-catastrophe losses ever.
2001	Terrorist attacks on September 11 result in the biggest insured losses in history.

Risk is the business of insurance and reinsurance companies. Not all risk is insurable: an insurable risk must be measurable in financial terms and exist in large homogeneous groups. Moreover, the probability of loss must be calculable, the loss must be accidental and beyond the control of the insured, and the transfer of a risk must be achievable at a reasonable rate for the individual. War risk, for instance, is a risk that cannot be insured by private companies: either the rates for war insurance would be too high for policyholders, or the financial risk would be too great for the insurance company.

Insurance has three broad categories: life insurance, property and casualty insurance, and reinsurance, which is insurance for insurers. Many insurers operate in two or even all three areas, though there are strong believers in "pure play." Swiss Re, for instance, only writes reinsurance policies. U.S. International Group writes all three types of insurance.

The first "modern" insurance contracts were struck in the most perilous trades in the Middle Ages: the sea trade, mining, and carpentry. An early form of marine insurance was launched in Pisa in 1318. Marine insurance became highly developed in the 15th century. It was known in Spain, Portugal, the Hanseatic cities, the Baltic countries, Holland, and England. In the 16th century the stock exchanges in Bruges, Antwerp, and Amsterdam even speculated with marine insurance.

London established itself early as the center of the world insurance market. Marine insurance companies set up shop in London at the end of the 17th century, and the great fire of London in 1666 prompted the formation of fire insurance companies.

Lloyd's of London, the insurance market, had its beginning in a coffeehouse owned by Edward Lloyd, where underwriters, speculators, merchants, and ship owners congregated in the 1680s. The term "underwriter" dates back to these days, as each risk-taker of the Lloyd's group wrote his name on a piece of paper under the proportion of risk that he was prepared to guarantee. With the growth of Britain's sea power, Lloyd's became the world's leading insurer for marine risk during the 18th and 19th centuries.

In the past century domination of global insurance shifted to the United States, though it lost some of its pre-eminent position from the 1970s. In 1970 the United States still accounted for some 70% of total global insurance premiums; today U.S. insurers control about 35% of total premiums.

London continues to be an important hub for insurers, and Lloyd's exists to this day, although in a much reduced form after near-bankruptcy in the 1990s. Lloyd's was just about to recover in 2001 after some fundamental reforms when the terrorist attacks in September 2001 dealt the market another huge blow.

COMPANIES

Like most industries, the insurance industry has been consolidating in the past few years. Large global players such as Allianz, Axa, Swiss Re, and Munich Re already dominate Europe. The U.S. market remains more fragmented.

European companies are making extensive cross-border acquisitions, mainly in the United States. Aegon, a Dutch insurer, has pursued a particularly expansive strategy in the United States with the acquisition of Transamerica in 1999. Today about 70% of its revenue and 60% of its profits are created by its U.S. operations. ING, Fortis, and

Largest insurance companies by market capitalization in February 2002 ($ billion)

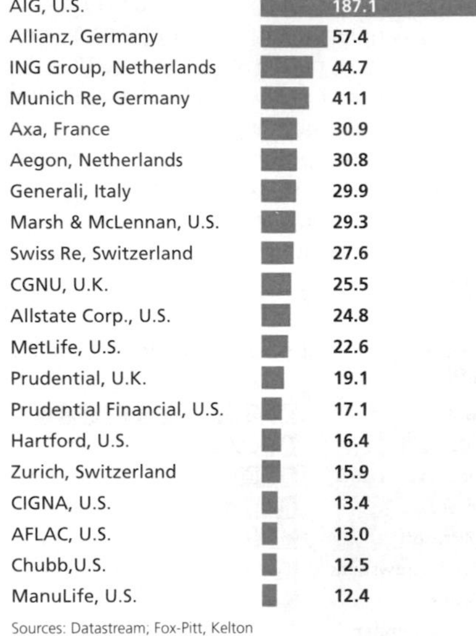

Sources: Datastream; Fox-Pitt, Kelton

Largest life insurance companies by revenues, 2000 ($ billion)

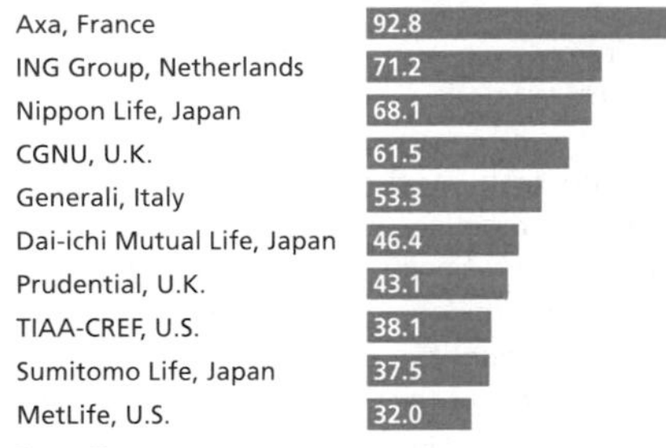

Source: *Fortune*

Largest property/casualty insurance companies by revenues, 2000 ($ billion)

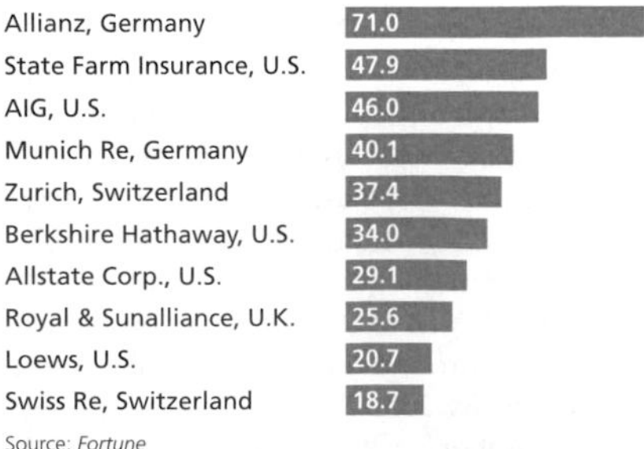

Source: *Fortune*

Zurich Financial Services are other European insurers with a considerable part of their business in the United States: ING bought United Life & Annuity in 1999 and

Largest insurance brokers by revenues, 2000 ($ million)

Marsh & McLennan, U.S.	6,915
Aon Corp., U.S.	5,137
Willis Group, U.K.	1,305
Arthur J. Gallagher & Co., U.S.	716
Wells Fargo Insurance Brokerage, U.S.	610
Jardine Lloyd Thompson Group, U.K.	462
HLF Insurance Holdings	406
Alexander Forbes, South Africa	385
USI Insurance Services Corp., U.S.	360
Hilb, Rogal & Hamilton Co., U.S.	260

Source: *Business Insurance*

Reliastar and Aetna in 2000; Fortis took over the U.S. Bankers Insurance Group in 1999 and U.S. Memorial Life in 2000; and Zurich Financial Services took over Farmers in 1999.

U.S. companies, on the other hand, remain relatively under-represented abroad: only 10% of 6,000 or so insurance companies in the United States have foreign operations. One exception is U.S. International Group, the largest commercial and industrial insurer in the United States, which has a relatively strong global network; its focus overseas is the Asian and the Latin U.S. insurance markets.

U.S. parochialism is partly due to the sheer size of the domestic market. Moreover, insurance in the United States is regulated on a state level, which can be an obstacle to the formation of the very large insurance companies that are interested in international expansion. In addition, many U.S. insurers are still mutually owned, though there has been a strong trend to demutualize in the past few years.

Despite their size, Japanese insurers have tended to concentrate on the domestic market. Japan's depressed economy, industry deregulation, and declining investment returns made for dire business conditions for insurers.

The United Kingdom has been in the front line of mergers and takeovers. Two of its five largest composite insurers are in the hands of the French and the Swiss: Axa bought Guardian Royal Exchange in 1999, and Zurich Financial Services was formed in 1999 after Zurich took over BAT Industries' financial services arm. In 2000 the United Kingdom's biggest composite insurer was born: CGU and Norwich Union merged to CGNU.

The industry is set to grow in European life insurance, and in life and non-life insurance in emerging markets, which are still underdeveloped. Pension reform and the need to privatize the provision of pensions is the main driver of the industry's expansion in Europe. In the United States the bulk of pensions are already provided by the private sector.

Most large insurers are also building up their own asset-management arm. Allianz bought Pimco in 1999 and Nicholas Applegate in the following year. Both are U.S. fund-management companies. Alliance Capital, which is owned by Axa, took over Sanford Bernstein, and Old Mutual, United Asset Management in 2000.

MARKETS

North and South America together generate about 37% of total premium income worldwide, with the overwhelming majority of income generated in North America. Europe is the world's second-largest insurance market with about 33% of global total premium income. Japan accounts for 21% of total premiums, and the rest of Asia 6%.

Largest insurance markets by premium income, 2000 ($ million)

United States	865,327
Japan	504,005
United Kingdom	236,960
Germany	123,722
France	121,910
Italy	63,062
South Korea	58,348
Canada	46,587
Spain	37,617
Netherlands	36,450
Australia	35,739
Switzerland	29,950
Taiwan	22,790
South Africa	21,167
Belgium	20,518
China	19,278
Sweden	17,874
Ireland	16,551
Brazil	12,554
Finland	11,345

Source: Fox-Pitt, Kelton

Asia (excluding Japan) is set to be one of the fastest-growing insurance markets in the world in both life and non-life insurance. This is mainly due to globalization and deregulation gathering steam in the region, and to the gradual opening up of the Chinese and Indian insurance markets.

There is also high growth potential in other emerging markets such as Latin America, South Africa, and Eastern Europe. Foreign direct insurers have more than doubled their share in these markets during the 1990s. Life insurance in particular has enormous growth potential; it is still in its infancy in most emerging markets.

Largest insurance markets by premium income as a percentage of GDP, 2000 (%)

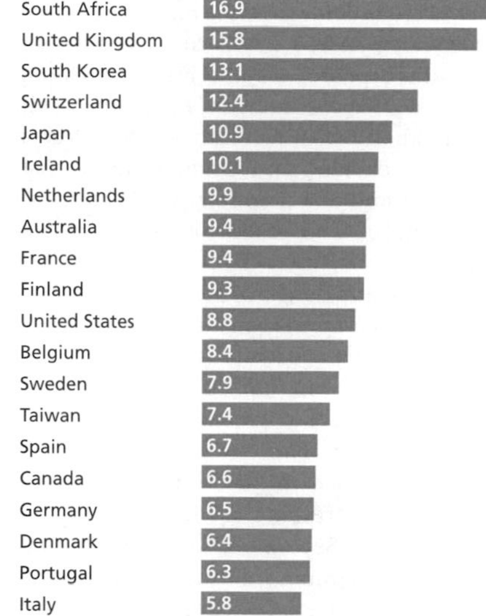

Source: Fox-Pitt, Kelton

Largest insurance markets by premium income per capita, 2000 ($)

Switzerland	4,154
Japan	3,973
United Kingdom	3,759
United States	3,152
Ireland	2,552
Netherlands	2,290
Finland	2,192
France	2,051
Sweden	2,014
Denmark	1,936
Australia	1,859
Belgium	1,855
Norway	1,559
Canada	1,517
Germany	1,491
Luxembourg	1,476
Austria	1,313
South Korea	1,234
Hong Kong	1,162
Italy	1,084

Source: Fox-Pitt, Kelton

Until the 1990s insurance markets were tightly regulated. This kept competition low and profit margins high. Most insurance companies concentrated on volume; insurers were mainly assessed through market share. This has changed thanks to deregulation and globalization during the 1990s. Competition has intensified, and profit margins are much lower.

Profitability is volatile because the insurance and reinsurance industry is extremely cyclical—few businesses see greater swings in supply and demand than insurance companies. The forces that create demand, such as catastrophes and the movement in values of assets in the capital market, are the same forces that destroy supply, and vice versa.

When demand increases rates are hardening (which means prices for insurance go up), and capital flows into insurance. More players enter the industry, competing with each other by undercutting prices. As a result rates fall until some insurers that cannot afford to write unprofitable business go bankrupt, and prices for insurance rise again.

The ups and downs of the insurance cycle are catalyzed by man-made or natural catastrophes. Prices for catastrophe insurance, for instance, went up 60% in 1993 after Hurricane Andrew wreaked havoc in California in 1992. They increased by almost 100% in France in 2000 after the storms Lothar and Martin in the winter of 1999.

Before the September 2001 terrorist attacks, the insurance industry was at the end of a soft cycle. Rates had dropped so low that the industry was effectively writing losses in economic terms. Some of the weaker companies—notably in Australia—collapsed. Rates were starting to harden when the industry was confronted with a double blow: the terrorist attacks in the United States, and huge losses in assets thanks to falling equity markets. As a result prices went up considerably for property and casualty insurance and reinsurance, in particular in certain segments such as insurance for aviation and commercial property. Even so, it is likely to take several years before the industry's equilibrium is restored.

The insurance sector is difficult to value, as traditional measurements such as sales or gross margins are not very helpful. Moreover, the actual profits in some segments of the industry, such as life insurance, may not be known for years: the actual profit that is made from—for example—a 20-year endowment that pays out a sum to the policyholder at maturity or upon death is not known precisely until the contract is fulfilled.

The evaluation of insurance companies uses such concepts as embedded and appraisal values and combined ratios. Embedded value calculates the value of existing business as the discounted future statutory profits that are expected to emerge in the business. Combined ratio is the sum of an insurer's claims or loss ratio and the expense ratio. If the figure is below 100%, an underwriting profit has been achieved.

New Products

Insurers use securities and derivative contracts to hedge risk in their investment portfolio. The first "cat," or catastrophe, bonds came to the market in 1994. A typical cat bond is, for example, a ten-year bond that yields more than double the typical return of bonds—but it is also not as low-risk an investment as an ordinary bond contract. If a catastrophe occurs, the investor forfeits all or part of his principal.

Insurance derivatives are still very much a niche market, but this could change. Derivatives are futures, options, and other financial instruments whose value is partly based on some underlying asset. Exchange-traded derivatives are attractive to insurers for a number of reasons: their prices are public while the price of some insurance contracts is not. Derivatives can be bought and sold at all times to alter the amount of protection against a risk; insurance is less flexible. And there is no legal risk with derivatives; insurance claims are often disputed in court.

The other big attraction of derivatives is that, as they are easily traded, they attract large amounts of money from institutional investors. The nominal value of outstanding derivative contracts for all types of risk is now several trillion dollars. Compared with that, the several billions of capital behind the global insurance industry are relatively insignificant. Derivatives could help tackle the problem of uninsurable risk; after the terrorist attacks in the United States, the extent to which capital markets can absorb terrorist risk has been hotly debated.

Even so, widespread use of derivatives in insurance is unlikely. Most insurers are conservative by inclination, and many of them do not fully understand derivatives. They have also been frightened by large losses related to derivatives in the past.

Except for a few countries such as France and Spain, bancassurance—the selling of insurance by banks—is still only marginal. The concept is trickier than it sounds, as Citibank discovered when it took over Travelers Group in 1998, hoping to sell Travelers' insurance products to its bank clients. The integration of Citigroup and Travelers' banking and insurance operations worked only in parts. In December 2001 Citibank decided to spin off Travelers Property Casualty unit, a large provider of commercial, home, and car insurance.

One of the reasons for the mixed record of bancassurance is that many insurance products are more complex than straightforward banking services, so it is difficult to sell them through a bank clerk with no specialist training. Moreover, banking and insurance products are very different, and even well-trained staff have had little success in selling them together. Finally, bank and insurance chiefs do not agree on whether it is necessary to own a bank or an insurance company to cross-sell products, or whether alliances will do. Axa has distribution agreements with various banks in France; Citigroup thought it was necessary to own an insurance company.

Impact of the Internet

The Internet's impact on the global insurance industry has been minimal to date. It is mainly used to inform clients about the company and its products, and to communicate within the company. The main reason for the Internet playing only a marginal role is that many insurance products are too complex to be sold via the Internet. Moreover, most people still prefer to talk to a human being when they buy such products. Finally, there are "channel conflicts" between an insurance company's standalone Internet operation and its existing network of agents and brokers.

Even so, some non-life insurance products, such as car or travel insurance, are well suited to the Internet because they are fairly standardized and they can be cheaply and efficiently distributed electronically. Internet insurance brokers could become a serious threat to established companies, because there are considerable cost savings to be achieved by replacing a network of insurance brokers and agents with an easily accessible Web site.

For More Information

Reports:

Fox-Pitt, Kelton. United Kingdom: **www.fpk.com**

SIGMA reports. Swiss Re: **www.swissre.com**

Web Sites:

"Best's Review" (insurance issues and analysis): **www.bestreview.com**

"Business Insurance": **www.businessinsurance.com**

Insurance News Network: **www.insurancenewsnet.com**

The Insurance Services Office (United States): **www.iso.com**

The U.S. Council of Life Insurers: **www.acli.com**

The Association of British Insurers: **www.abi.org.uk**

The British Insurance Brokers' Association: **www.biba.org.uk**

Lloyd's, the London insurance market: **www.lloydsoflondon.com**

  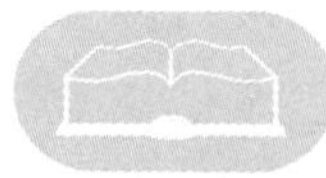    

MEDIA

Key dates: newspapers and books

868	Earliest printed book produced in China.
1040	Pi Sheng invents movable type in China.
1420	Korea's King Sejong sets up printing with metal type.
1438	Johann Gutenberg independently invents movable type in Germany.
1814	*The Times* in London installs the first steam-powered press.
1886	New York *Tribune* automates typesetting with Ottmar Mergenthaler's Linotype machine.
1939	Photocomposition speeds typesetting; followed by first computer typesetting from 1965.
1987	QuarkXPress software allows typesetting and layout on personal computers.

Key dates: sound and picture recording

1877	Thomas Alva Edison records on waxed paper.
1880s	Étienne Jules Marey in France, George Eastman in United States, and William Friese-Greene in United Kingdom all work on moving pictures.
1888	Emile Berliner, United States, demonstrates sound recording with flat disks; mass-produced from 1892.
1895	Louis and Auguste Lumière open first public movie theater, Paris.
1905	First purpose-built movie theaters opened in United States.
1917	Technicolor introduces primitive color process.
1927	Hollywood's first sound movie, "The Jazz Singer."
1948	Introduction of 33 rpm long-playing record and 45 rpm single record; both replace earlier 78 rpm standard.
1963	Philips, Netherlands, introduces compact audio cassette.
1975	Sony introduces Betamax home video taping system, later eclipsed by JVC's VHS standard.
1979	Sony introduces the Walkman portable audio tape player.
1979	Philips and Sony demonstrate CD and digital compact audio disk.
1995	Philips, Sony, Matsushita, and Toshiba announce DVD.

Key dates: radio and television

1894	Italian inventor Guglielmo Marconi sends first radio signals.
1920	Westinghouse sets up first radio station.
1925	Charles Francis Jenkins demonstrates television in Washington D.C., followed in 1926 by John Logie Baird, London.
1930	Motorola makes first car radio.
1935	German company Fernseh begins first regular electronic TV programs, followed by BBC in London 1936 and RCA in New York 1939.
1949	David Sarnoff's RCA develops electronic color TV system; transmissions start 1953.
1954	Introduction of transistor radio.
1962	First intercontinental satellite relays of TV programs.
1972	Magnavox, United States, launches first video game.
1976	First specialist cable-only TV channels launched in United States.
1982	New company Satellite Television starts pan-European broadcasts; renamed Sky in 1984.
1989	Sky Television begins U.K. multi-channel television transmitted direct-to-home from satellites.

As the three tables of key dates show, the media industry is really a number of different industries, which range from printing developed in the late Middle Ages to the launch of the DVD at the end of the 20th century.

It accounts for an enormous expenditure of time and money. According to the newsletter *Screen Digest*, the average U.K. citizen in 2001 spent 53 hours a week "consuming" media—by far the biggest use of people's leisure time, including 25 hours watching TV and 21 hours listening to the radio.

For much of their history, the separate industries which are together regarded as "the media" remained independent, and many could trace their origins back for a century or more. In some cases the big players in the industries owed their origins to the inventors or developers of the technology: companies such as General Electric (founded by Edison), RCA, and Westinghouse.

In the last two decades of the 20th century, however, there was a significant trend towards the consolidation of companies across the mass media, as the industry is termed. This has also extended across national boundaries, so that, for example, Sony—founded in Tokyo after World War II to make electronic equipment—now owns record companies and movie company Columbia TriStar, produces PlayStation electronic games, makes CDs and DVDs, owns 40% of a U.S. theater chain, and manufactures wireless phones. Rupert Murdoch's Australia-based News International group owns *The Times*, founded in 1785, plus the U.S. movie studio Twentieth-Century Fox, and British Sky Broadcasting. A series of mergers brought the publishers of *Time* and other magazines into a group with movie studio Warner Bros, the Turner group (which owned the CNN news channel), and Internet service AOL.

COMPANIES

The media industry has always had a complex relationship with governments and their appointed regulators, even in the United States, where the freedom of the press has been enshrined in the constitution since the earliest days.

Largest U.S. media companies by television revenues, 2000 ($ million)

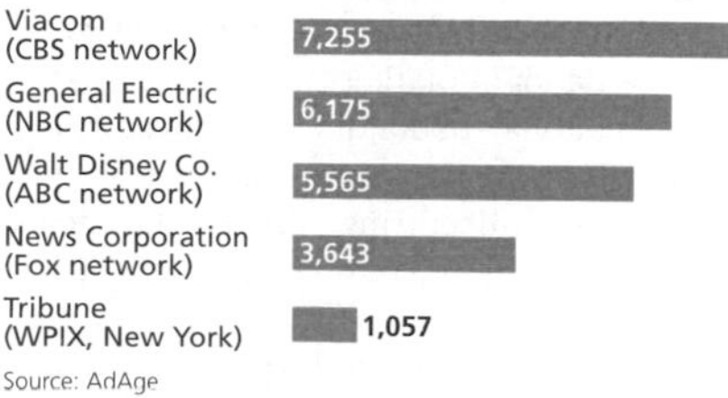

Source: AdAge

In the United States, for example, TV and radio broadcast licenses are regulated by the Federal Communications Commission. Under its rules, no single TV service may

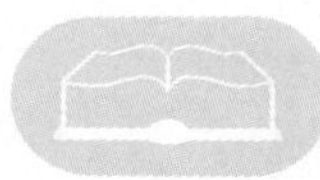

Largest U.S. media companies by cable television revenues, 2000 ($ million)

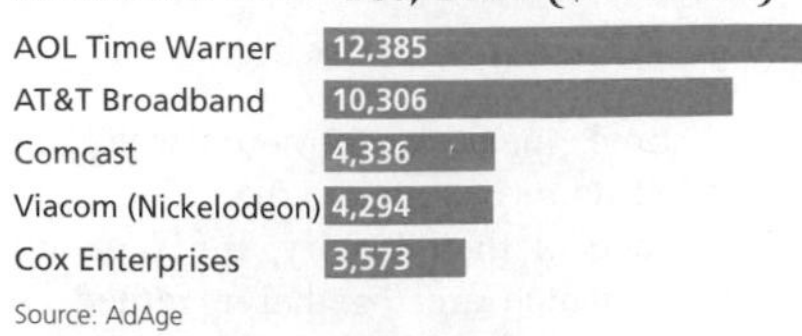

Source: AdAge

Largest U.S. media companies by newspaper revenues, 2000 ($ million)

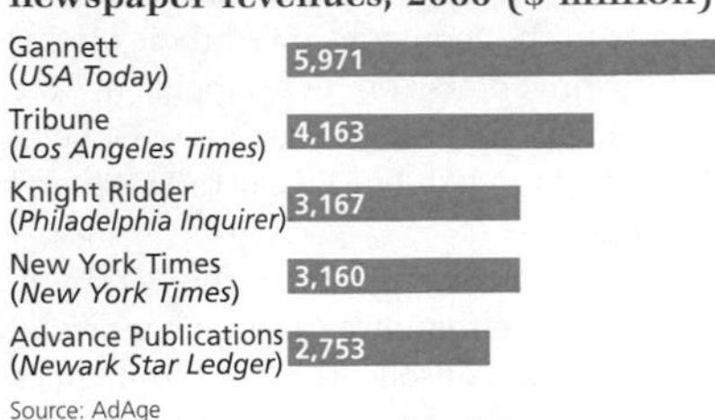

Source: AdAge

have a share of the national audience exceeding 35%, no cable TV network may serve more than 30% of the national audience, and no daily newspaper owner may own a radio or TV broadcaster in the same geographical area.

Other countries have their own variations on these rules. In France a cross-media owner may have no more than two of the following: a TV audience of more than 4 million, a radio audience of 30 million, a cable audience of 6 million, and a 20% national daily newspaper circulation.

Foreign ownership of broadcasters is banned in the United States and many other countries, though not in Denmark, Germany, Ireland, Italy, Netherlands, the United Kingdom, and Portugal. In Sweden even periodical publishers must only be from the European Economic Area.

Outside the United States, there is a tradition for many of the major broadcasters to be publicly owned, albeit often at arm's length: in the United Kingdom, for example, three of the five nationally broadcast networks, BBC1, BBC2, and Channel Four, are publicly owned, as are the BBC's five national radio networks.

This situation, combined with differences in culture and language, has tended to reinforce national markets in the media, with more national operators and fewer transnational companies than in, for example, oil, car manufacturing, drugs, chemicals, computers, or electronic and electrical equipment.

As a result the three biggest U.S. television networks, ABC, CBS, and NBC, have little international presence; Germany's state and commercial channels can be received across Europe by satellite but do not seek audiences except in German-speaking Austria and Switzerland; Silvio Berlusconi, who owns the biggest Italian commercial channels—and as prime minister of the country also controls the three state channels—has little media presence outside Italy.

Magazine publishing is more internationalized. European companies Bertelsmann (Germany), Hachette (France), United Business Media (United Kingdom), VNU (Netherlands), Reed Elsevier (United Kingdom/Netherlands), and Emap (United Kingdom) appear in the list of top 20 U.S. magazine publishers, and U.S. publishers such as AOL Time Warner, Hearst, IDG, Reader's Digest and Ziff Davis all have widespread international interests.

Markets

The last third of the 20th century marked an astonishing increase in the markets for radio and television, particularly in the developing world.

Radio sets, 1970 and 1997 (million)

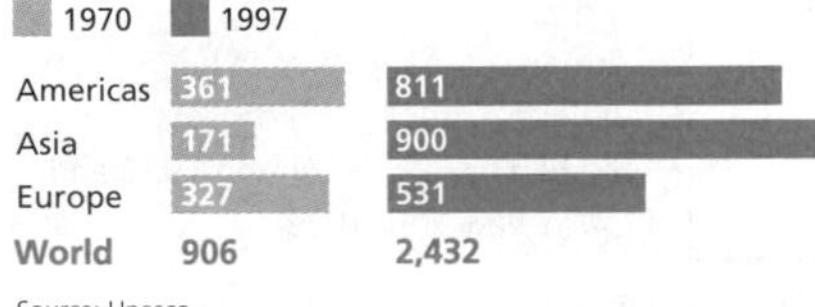

Source: Unesco

Television sets, 1970 and 1997 (million)

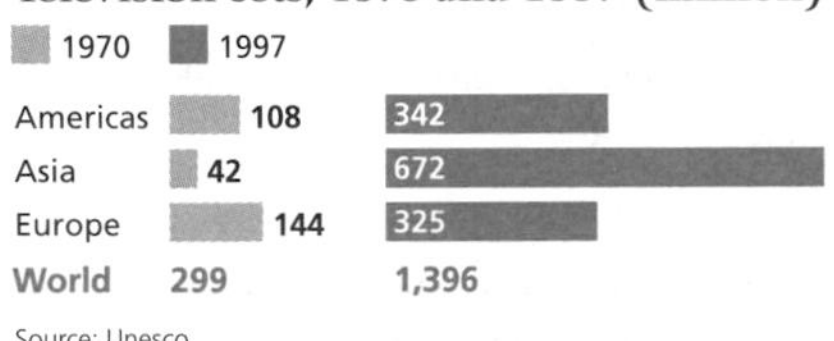

Source: Unesco

Movie theaters, 1995

United States	26,586
France	4,295
Germany	3,861
Italy	3,617
Russia	2,066
United Kingdom	1,969
Spain	1,888

Source: Unesco

Movie theater attendance per capita, 1995

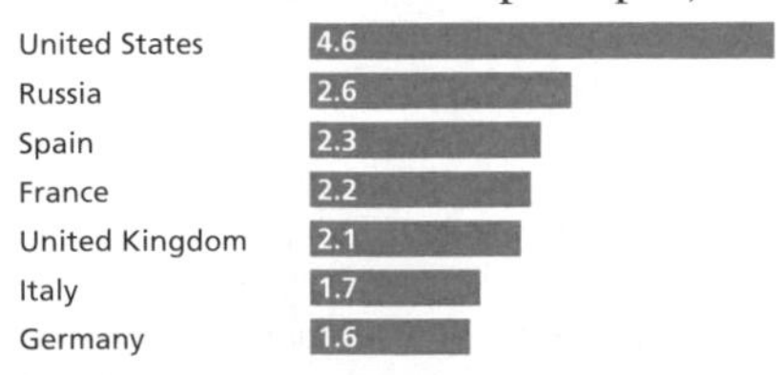

Source: Unesco

In developing countries, according to Unesco figures, there were 240 million radios and 26 million TV sets in 1970, but 1,124 million and 720 million respectively by 1997. These latter figures mean that for every 1,000 inhabitants there were 245 radios and 157 TV sets.

Markets in the developed world were largely mature, but still showed a substantial growth as two- or three-set households became the norm: in Europe there were 729 radios and 446 TV sets per 1,000 people by 1997. In the Americas there were more radio sets than people by 1997—811 million radios, equivalent to 1,017 per 1,000 people.

The United States is by far the largest market in the Western world for movies: the average American attends a movie 4.6 times a year, more than double the rate of most other developed countries.

Attendance in movie theaters in most countries was in a long-term decline, but appears to have undergone a recovery from the mid-1990s onwards. Again, the United States is the exception, where the number of cinemas in operation doubled from 1970 to 1994, and—after a brief decline in attendance to a low of 3.7 visits per person in 1992—ticket sales have risen to 1970s and 1980s levels.

In Europe though, the trend has been down. The French visited the movies an average of 3.7 times each a year in 1970s, but only 2.2 times in 1995. British ticket sales fell from 3.5 a year for each person in 1970 to only 2.0 in 1995. The fall in Spain was steeper: from 9.8 per person in 1970 to 2.4 in 1995.

Around 548 million newspapers are printed and sold each day around the world, a figure that has stayed roughly level since the mid-1980s. The rapid increase in the

Daily newspaper titles, 1996

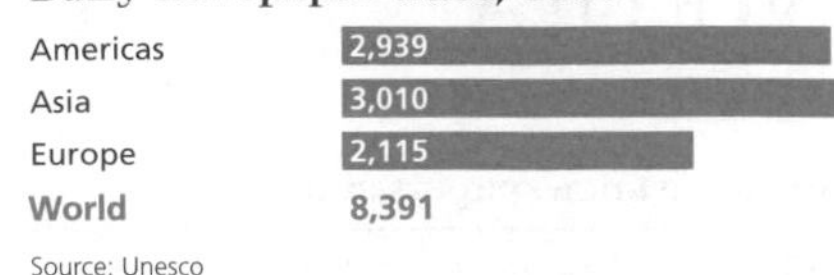

Source: Unesco

Daily newspaper circulation, 1996

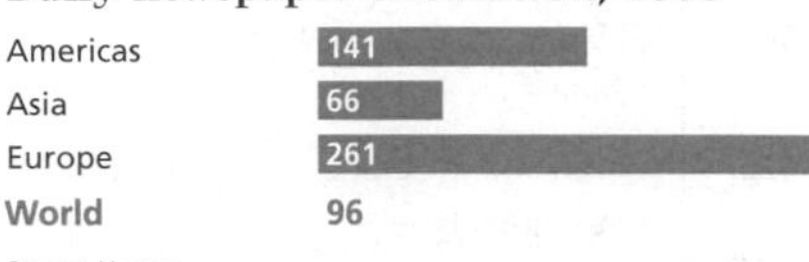

Source: Unesco

Top five U.S. daily newspapers by circulation, September 2000

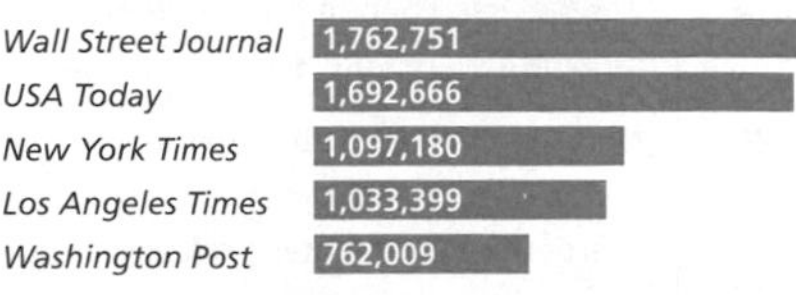

Source: Audit Bureau of Circulations

world's population over the same period, however, means that only 96 copies were sold per 1,000 people in 1996, compared with 107 in 1970.

Daily newspaper circulation reflects wealth around the world. In Europe there are 261 daily newspaper sales per 1,000 people—a figure that has fallen from a peak of 340 in 1990, though that followed a steep rise from 281 in 1970. Sales in the Americas have been steadier, at around 140–150 per 1,000 since the mid-1980s. Developing country sales are much lower, according to Unesco: an average of 60 copies per 1,000 in developing countries worldwide, and only 16 in Africa.

The pattern of daily newspaper circulation varies widely in different parts of the world. The U.S. market, for example, is dominated by many small, city-based newspapers, with only two genuinely national titles—the specialist *Wall Street Journal* and *USA Today*—and only four having daily sales above one million copies.

The United Kingdom, by contrast, is dominated by largely London-based dailies which circulate nationwide: the biggest is the *Sun*, which sells 3.3 million a day, with the *Daily Mirror* and the *Daily Mail* both printing more than 2.4 million a day, the *Daily Telegraph* and the *Daily Express* around 1 million, and *The Times*, the *Financial Times*, the *Guardian*, the *Daily Star*, the *Daily Record*, and the *Independent* ranging from 200,000 to 700,000.

There are few figures for all forms of media across all markets. One of the few surveys which brings together all media spending was conducted for the United Kingdom by the newsletter *Screen Digest* and the bank ABN Amro in late 2001. It showed that the total U.K. market for all forms of media in 1985 was £7 billion, and forecast a rise to £56 billion by 2010, or to £84 billion if new media opportunities could be exploited.

Print's share of the spending will fall in the 25-year period, suggested the survey: from 48% in 1985 to 15% in 2010. Subscriptions to media—mainly TV licenses in 1985, but including pay-TV and Internet costs by 2010—would rise from 11% of the total at the beginning of the period to 50% at the end.

Technology

The media industry has always been technology-driven, beginning in the middle of the 15th century when a Mainz goldsmith, Johann Gensfleisch zum Gutenberg, borrowed 1,600 guilders to develop a printing system and start a book-publishing business. Nearly four centuries later, in 1814, *The Times* of London funded the inventors of steam-powered printing, and introduced the technology behind the backs of the existing print workers—an interesting parallel to the same newspaper's action in 1986, when it brought in computerized production in a similar way.

Computers allowed huge efficiencies in what was an enormously labor-intensive process. Now newspapers are written and laid out using computers; instead of presses being located in the basement of the building—very often in expensive city-center premises—the actual production has now been removed to cheaper industrial sites, and many titles are printed simultaneously in many locations worldwide.

As the technologies have continued to develop, the industries have had to adjust rapidly to the changing market. For example, international printing means that the *Wall Street Journal* and the *Financial Times*, whose sales were once limited to overnight truck or train distribution from New York or London, are now sold on newsstands side by side in their home cities and in Tokyo, Frankfurt, Los Angeles, and elsewhere throughout the world.

In electronic media, TV markets are no longer restricted by the amount of bandwidth available for over-the-air transmission. Cable networks and direct-to-home satellite services have brought new competitors for the original networks. Digital transmission, introduced in the late 1990s, has increased the potential number of competitors from dozens to hundreds.

Despite predictions that this new market would be dominated by transnational channels, only a few of these have developed—mainly news channels—though there are local versions of channels such as MTV for the United Kingdom, France, and elsewhere.

New Products

As the tables of key dates show, a succession of new products has been introduced into the media industry: tape cassettes in 1963, video cassettes in 1975, CDs in 1979, satellite TV in the mid-1980s, and digital television in the mid 1990s.

The process continues, most recently by the introduction of the DVD in the late 1990s. At the beginning of the 21st century, the DVD is being hailed as the most successful consumer electronics launch ever. According to *Screen Digest*, Western European sales of DVD movie titles will go from €420 million in 1999 to €5.3 billion in 2003, forcing a drop in sales of titles on VHS tapes, now a 25-year-old technology, from €5.7 billion in 1999 to €2.8 billion in 2003.

Employment

Because of its diversified nature, coherent statistics on the worldwide media business are difficult to obtain. In the United States, cable TV, broadcast TV, and radio broadcasting employed 430,500 people in 1998, a figure that was increasing by over 3% each year. The TV and radio communications equipment industry employed a further 121,900 people, though this figure was declining by about 0.75% a year.

Impact of the Internet

The successful development of broadband telecommunications networks will—if it happens—have an undoubted effect on the mass media. There was a huge investment in intercity and international broadband optical fiber networks in the developed world in the late 1990s, and this is now being followed by the construction of local networks: broadband cable, optical fiber to the home in some cases, and technologies such as digital subscriber line (DSL) which allow conventional copper domestic phone wiring to carry video signals.

Development of DSL started in the early 1990s with the aim of allowing phone companies to offer video on demand—a sort of electronic video rental service, with the TV set coupled to the phone network. By 2001 DSL was being installed in many countries, but largely for high-speed Internet access: a video-on-demand market has still not developed. However, the market research company Frost & Sullivan predicted in 2001 that there will be 8.5 million subscribers in Europe by 2006, with annual sales worth €2.7 billion. Even if this is accurate, however, it will still be relatively small compared with the size of the overall media industry.

For More Information

Web Sites:

AdAge: **www.adage.com**
European Commission Information Society Project: **www.europa.eu.int/eeurope**
Frost & Sullivan: **www.frost.com**
Idate Foundation: **www.idate.fr**
Jupiter MMXI: **www.jupitermmxi.com**
Newspaper Association of America: **www.naa.org**
Screen Digest: **www.screendigest.com**
Unesco: **www.unesco.org**
U.S. Federal Communications Commission: **www.fcc.gov**

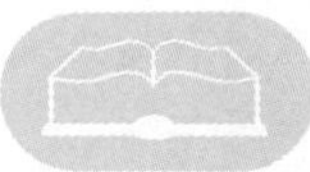

MINING

15th century	Larger furnaces introduced for smelting iron ore; new ways found to separate gold and silver.
17th century	Explosives introduced to the West.
18th century	Coke (from coal) starts to replace charcoal (from wood) in smelting iron (1709); steam pumps introduced to remove water from mines.
19th century	Mechanical rock drills introduced; Hall-Heroult electrolytic process for smelting aluminum discovered (1886).
20th century	Flotation process to separate ore minerals from waste invented in Broken Hill in Australia; large-scale factory-sized production units pioneered at Bingham Canyon in the United States (1903); hydro-metallurgical extraction methods come into use.

Top 20 mined commodities* by production, 1999 ($ billion)

Commodity	$ billion
Coal	60–70
Aluminum	32.2
Gold	23.1
Copper	22.5
Iron ore	15.3
Zinc	9.0
Nickel	6.3
Phosphate	5.5
Platinum group	4.5
Silicon	4.5
Potash	3.8
Lead	3.1
Silver	2.9
Kaolin	2.5
Sulfur	1.9
Magnesium	1.6
Manganese	1.6
Tin	1.3
Cobalt	1.1
Uranium	1.1

* excluding gem diamonds
Source: *Minerals Handbook*

Mining has been around almost as long as civilization.

The mining of industrial commodities developed more slowly, often in response to technological breakthroughs. When Abraham Darby, a Quaker iron founder in Shropshire, United Kingdom, used coke rather than charcoal to smelt iron in 1709, he invented what is today one of coal's two major markets.

The idea that large-scale factory-style production could make it worth exploiting lower-grade ores was pioneered at Bingham Canyon in the United States early in the last century; earlier miners had concentrated on high-grade ores. Nowadays almost all new mines start as large open pits, employing enormous trucks and shovels: sometimes they literally move mountains.

Today the global mining industry is a mixture of some reasonably large businesses and a large number of small entrepreneurial operators.

There are big differences even among the conventional Western-style corporations. One division is between the major companies and the smaller operations. Since all mining exploits, and ultimately destroys, its own assets, new deposits are always needed. Small, equity-backed exploration and development companies have traditionally done much of the initial work of looking for promising deposits. There are hundreds of these companies, traded on stock exchanges such as Vancouver, but very few make worthwhile finds.

Another division is between companies that mine gold and those that mine other metals and commodities. Most gold-mining companies are specialists, and they attract a different type of investor from normal mining companies.

A further difference is between large companies that focus on a single metal, and those with a portfolio of different metals. Broadly, North American investors have tended to prefer single-metal companies, such as Alcoa in aluminum, Inco in nickel, and Phelps Dodge in copper. The United Kingdom, which plays a surprisingly important part in mining finance given the paucity of its own resources, has tended to prefer diversified companies such as Rio Tinto.

The mining industry has a reputation for being excessively fragmented, but in practice the degree of fragmentation varies considerably from one commodity to another. In diamonds, for example, De Beers remained the dominant seller of rough stones throughout the last century. Recent consolidation has meant that most international trade in both iron ore and coal is now in the hands of a small number of large companies: CVRD (Brazil), Rio Tinto, and BHP Billiton for iron ore; and BHP Billiton, Rio Tinto, Glencore (a Swiss metals trader), and Anglo American in coal. At the end of 2000, however, the top ten gold miners accounted for only 41% of total production.

Mining is an industry which almost inevitably produces international acrimony, since many resources are mined in the less developed countries for the use and benefit of people in the developed world. Mines can be damaging both to the environment and to the host communities. The larger mining companies are now paying considerable attention to the fashionable concept of sustainable development, and have sponsored several bodies to improve the industry's practices and image.

COMPANIES

The industry has a reputation as a destroyer of corporate value. For years chief executives measured success by the number of tons of rock they shifted and the quantities of metals and minerals produced. Mining company annual reports are still remarkable for the fact that many of them start with pages of production statistics before they get on to the financial figures. This approach to business was particularly unfortunate in an industry where the long-term trend in most product prices was downwards. Over the past 20 years a production index covering 50 commodities shows a rise in volume of over 40%; over the same period real prices dropped by 60%.

However, a handful of companies, such as Alcoa in the United States and Rio Tinto in the United Kingdom, have long concentrated on achieving good results for shareholders. Both have a reputation for employing a hard-nosed commercial approach to business both inside the company and outside, with cost-cutting a way of life. This investor-friendly approach, with the emphasis on "shareholder value," is now being imitated by most of the other substantial publicly-owned companies.

One of the reasons for the recent consolidation in the industry is that C.E.O.s want to increase their market share without increasing the industry's output and thereby undermining the prices of their products. Justifying mergers on the grounds of synergy is more difficult in mining than in many industries, since it is not possible to move mines. In commodities such as iron ore and coal, where expensive infrastructure is necessary to transport high-volume, low-value commodities, proximity

Top non-ferrous metals producers by market capitalization, November 2001 ($ billion)

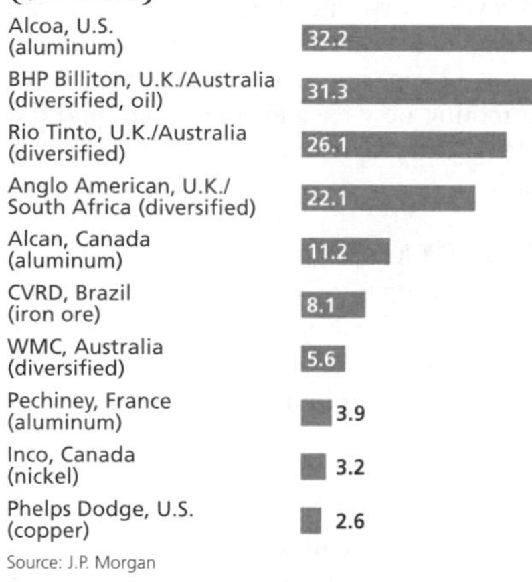

Top precious metals producers by market capitalization, November 2001 ($ billion)

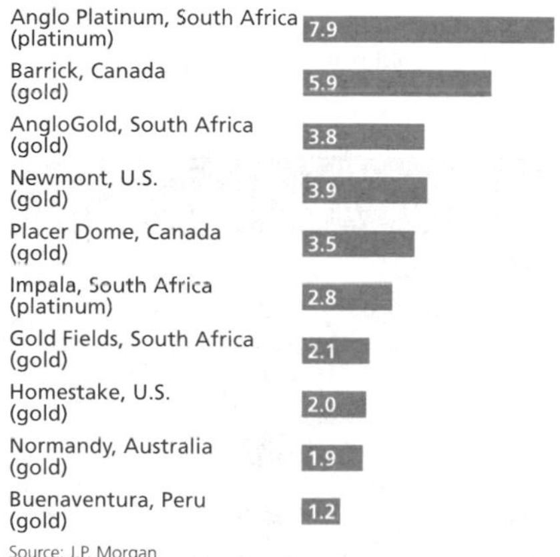

savings can be substantial. Companies such as BHP Billiton, however, also argue that having a small number of large producers should result in a more disciplined market.

As Opec has found, producer restraint can be hard to implement successfully in markets where some substantial producers are not interested in cooperation. Russian and Chinese producers have sometimes been accused of flooding various markets, such as zinc and several of the minor metals, by exporting regardless of demand, and so driving down prices.

But in many markets concentration of ownership does appear to be linked to higher returns. Iron ore, alumina (the feedstock for aluminum) and diamonds are three unusually concentrated markets, and the returns have also been unusually high.

Unsurprisingly, concentration of ownership has also attracted the attention of the competition authorities in Europe and the United States. The aluminum industry, where both Alcoa and Alcan proposed major mergers in 1999, was hit particularly hard by the European Commission. It effectively blocked Pechiney's participation in the Alcan/Alusuisse merger, and made Alcoa agree to substantial disposals before its acquisition of Reynolds was allowed to proceed.

Gold-mining companies have been participating in the merger wave, and some of them have hopes of importing discipline to their part of the industry too, but they have some particular problems to contend with. Although gold is technically still part of many countries' official reserves, it no longer has a real role in the financial system, and its industrial uses are insignificant. In theory it is a metal in deficit, since newly-mined supply is well short of demand, but the enormous quantities of gold already above ground—held by banks and savers—sometimes come on to the market. Gold mining has generally been one of the less rewarding parts of the industry.

Markets

Mining operates in a series of discrete markets, most of which have little in common. The geographical diversity of both the commodity sources and the customer bases underpins the industry's claims to be genuinely global.

Some commodities are linked, however, either because they occur together or because they are sold to the same customers. Cobalt, for instance, is mainly produced as a byproduct of copper or nickel, which means that its output tends to be relatively independent of its own supply/demand balance. But what the industry calls "by-product credits" can be important to the viability of the mainstream projects. Thus, assumptions about the probable price that could be obtained for cobalt were highly relevant in the calculations for a new nickel project in Australia.

Iron ore and coking coal have a natural affinity because both are sold to steel mills. BHP Billiton has recognized this by grouping the two together under "carbon steel materials," while steam coal (for power stations) is in a separate division. Similarly, it puts nickel and ferrochrome into "stainless steel materials" because they, too, have a common customer base.

Another popular way to group commodities is by whether they are or are not traded on a major exchange, such as the London Metal Exchange or Comex in New York. Prices of exchange-traded metals, such as aluminum, copper, zinc, nickel, lead, and even tin, tend to fluctuate markedly: they exaggerate both the top and the bottom of cycles. They respond rapidly to changes in demand and stock levels, and to world financial and political events.

Main aluminum markets by market share, 1999 (%)

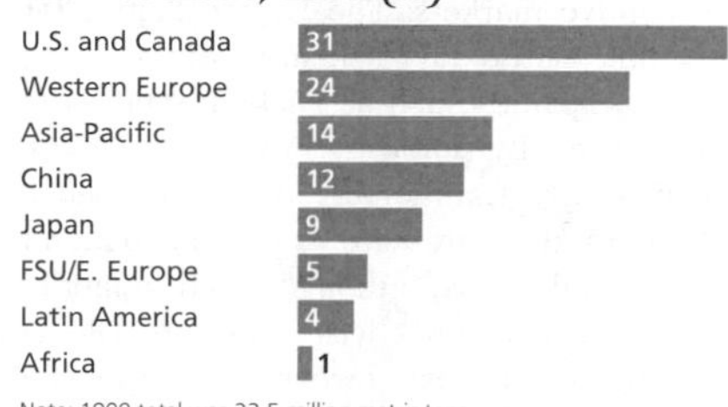

Main gold fabricating areas by market share, 2000 (%)

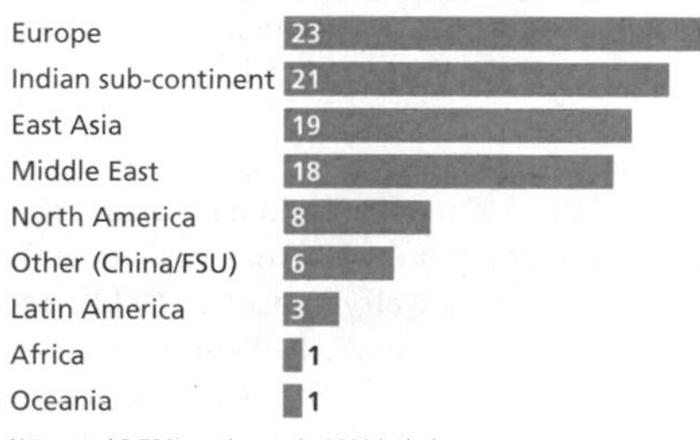

Main markets for copper by market share, 1999 (%)

Most of the actual metal is sold through annual supply contracts, but the pricing of those contracts is based on LME or Comex prices. As a result, profits of mines which concentrate on exchange-traded commodities are often considerably more volatile than those priced in consumer/producer negotiations.

One partial exception to this generalization is aluminum, where the atypical, vertically-integrated nature of large specialist companies such as Alcan and Alcoa means that they are often their own most important customers. This might appear to be beneficial, but some industry experts argue that vertical integration has actually made it harder for the companies to monitor the efficiency of the different units.

The most important mined commodities not traded on exchanges are coal and iron ore. In both cases there are large domestic or captive markets. The United States, for example, is broadly self-sufficient in coal, and companies such as Peabody and Arch are essentially domestic. Many steel companies have traditionally owned or had a share in their iron-ore suppliers, both at home and abroad, though such relationships are becoming less common. Global mining companies, however, are primarily interested in internationally traded commodities. In both cases, most trades come under long term contracts, with prices negotiated annually. Benchmark prices tend to emerge from Australia early in the new year.

Another traditional split is between precious and base metals. Gold, silver, and the platinum group metals are rivals in both industrial and jewelry markets. Gold's industrial uses are small. Palladium (mainly produced in Russia) is only used for industrial purposes, notably for auto catalysts, where it has stolen market share from platinum. However, the erratic marketing tactics of the Russians at the turn of the century, resulting in supply shortages and rocketing prices, were regarded as commercially suicidal.

Platinum (mainly produced in South Africa), with a stake in both industrial and jewelry markets, is one of the very few metals which can be deemed a marketing success. Taking some tips from De Beers, the mining companies (essentially Anglo Platinum) have run a successful campaign to support its use in jewelry. Gold miners have long sponsored a marketing body, the World Gold Council, but financial support for it has always been patchy and relatively meager, and it often appears unsure of its target market.

Technology

Mining techniques are being constantly refined, but major changes only come about occasionally. The last significant advance, in the second half of the 20th century, was the introduction of SX-EW (solvent extraction-electro-winning) processing methods. These are an alternative to the traditional costly smelting process, and are widely used to extract metals, particularly copper, from low-grade surface ore or waste dumps, which could not be processed economically by smelting.

BHP Billiton and Codelco have a new experimental bioleaching project, which uses micro-organisms to treat ores which were hitherto only amenable to smelting to make them suitable for the SX-EW process.

Another interesting development is the introduction of airborne magnetic surveying techniques, which should make it easier to find mineral deposits in large areas of inhospitable country.

New Products

New minerals are rare. One of the few discovered last century was a dark- and light-blue marbled stone called "Dianite" after the late Princess Diana. It was found in Yakutia in eastern Siberia in the 1970s, but it was not until 1998 that all the geological tests to prove its uniqueness were completed. It is unlikely, however, that the discovery of Dianite has any commercial importance.

Mining companies are far more interested in finding new deposits of popular minerals. To be of any interest to a major company, the deposit needs to be large, low-cost, and available in sufficient quantities to make it a long-term prospect. Good geology is not enough, though. When dealing with high-value/low-volume gold or diamonds, infrastructure does not matter as the miners can fly in and out. But with a low-value/high-volume commodity such as bauxite or iron ore, logistics are important. A deposit in the center of a continent is far less attractive than one near a port or existing railway or road system. The companies are also mindful of their prospective tenure and tax position.

New uses for metals can have a considerable influence on mining companies' turnover and profits. Aluminum usage has grown much faster than that of its rival metals, although it is not clear whether its superior growth is directly connected with the fact that the large aluminum companies are vertically integrated, and active in finding new uses for their metal.

Anglo Platinum's marketing agent, Johnson Matthey, is active in research into fuel cells, which could provide a major new market for platinum. Most mining groups, however, have little involvement at the downstream end of their business, although Chilean copper producers are talking about promoting new uses for the metal, and the gold industry is looking at industrial uses for gold.

Employment

Mining companies are large employers of mainly unskilled labor. Anglo American, for instance, had 249,000 employees at the end of 2000 (excluding those working for joint ventures and associates), Rio Tinto had 34,000 (including its share of those in joint ventures and associates) at the same date, and BHP Billiton had 59,000 in mid-2001. The majority of Anglo's employees were in Africa, where traditional deep gold and platinum mines have always been labor-intensive and have a high accident rate: around 180 people are killed underground in gold mines each year.

For More Information

Book:

Crowson, Phillip, ed. *Minerals Handbook* (annual). New York: Macmillan, 1996.

Magazines and Journals:

American Metal Market.
Metal Bulletin.
Metals Week.
Mining Journal (weekly), Mining Journal Ltd.: **www.mining-journal.com**
Mining Review.
The Northern Miner (weekly: North American mining): **www.northernminer.com**
World Gold (monthly), Mining Journal Ltd.

Web Sites:

Infomine Inc.: **www.infomine.com**
London community of mining and exploration: **www.minesite.com**
Precious metals information and trading: **www.thebulliondesk.com**

OIL AND GAS

1859	First oil well drilled at Titusville, Pennsylvania.
1870	John D. Rockefeller forms Standard Oil Company.
1871	First oil wells drilled at Baku on the Caspian Sea.
1907	Shell and Royal Dutch form combined company.
1908	Tricone drill bit invented.
1911	U.S. Supreme Court orders break-up of the New Jersey-based Standard Oil Trust.
1938	Oil discovered in Kuwait and Saudi Arabia.
1948	Biggest ever oil field discovered at Ghawar in Saudi Arabia.
1956	Start of seismic surveying for oil.
1959	First ever shipment of liquefied natural gas landed in the United Kingdom.
1960	Organization of Petroleum Exporting Countries formed.
1968	Oil discovered on Alaska's North Slope.
1973	OPEC oil embargo and ensuing crisis.
1975	First oil from United Kingdom sector of North Sea.
1983	Oil futures trading starts in New York.

Oil, in the form of bitumen seeping to the surface, has been known for thousands of years in the Middle East, where it was used for caulking boats. Its commercial exploitation, however, really started in the United States in the mid-19th century, when it was drilled in Pennsylvania and sold as kerosene for lighting. Other centers developed: in central Asia, where the Rothschilds and Nobels built up the oil industry at Baku, and in Asia where Royal Dutch discovered oil in Sumatra in the 1880s.

For the first two thirds of the 20th century the industry was dominated by the international oil companies. U.S. companies had not only the advantage of their enormous home market, but also reaped the benefit of the dominant geopolitical position of the United States after World War II. European oil companies developed within the framework of their colonial empires.

This changed with the rise in nationalism in the 1970s, particularly in the Middle East where most of the world's proven oil reserves have been found to lie. Oil-rich countries were no longer content to have the international oil companies tell them what the price of oil should be, or what share of the revenue they should have. These countries formed OPEC in 1960, and within 15 years they had effectively nationalized the local assets of the international companies.

As a result, the international companies—though they are some of the biggest publicly-quoted businesses in the world—now account for less than half the world's oil and gas production and reserves. Most of the world industry is in the hands of state-owned national oil companies. However, the pendulum is now swinging back a little in favor of the international companies, as some OPEC countries—Iran, Saudi Arabia, and Kuwait—invite the international oil and gas companies back in to explore for oil and gas.

The industry faces two main challenges. One is over the future of oil and gas reserves. There are some who believe that oil is a renewable resource, because it has been—and still is being—created deep inside the earth; almost everyone else agrees that it will run out at some point. But when? The world has already consumed 850 billion barrels of oil; its proven reserves currently stand at just over 1,000 billion barrels. The optimists say that the industry will go on finding new reserves, just as it always has done; the pessimists believe that world production will peak during the 2000s, just as production in the United States—once the world's largest producer—did in the early 1970s. New techniques have been developed that permit the discovery and exploitation of smaller finds, but the more pessimistic view is that increasing the rate of recovery from oil fields merely accelerates their decline. At current production levels, world oil reserves of 1,046 billion barrels would last about 40 years. Gas would last a little longer: world reserves of 5,300 trillion cubic feet would last 61 years at present levels of output.

The other challenge is environmental. The industry has made great strides in recent years in controlling oil spills and in developing cleaner fuels, with less sulfur and nitrous oxides, to prevent the build-up of fumes and smog in cities. The problem posed by climate change is of even greater magnitude. Carbon is an intrinsic part of hydrocarbons like oil, but it is also the major component of greenhouse gases which are damaging the planet's cooling system. The aim of the Kyoto protocol, which all industrialized countries, except the United States, have said they will ratify, is to reduce the level of carbon emissions. The response of most oil companies has been to increase their efforts to find natural gas, which is less polluting than oil, and to look at other, renewable forms of energy such as solar power.

Largest oil reserves, 2000 (billion barrels)

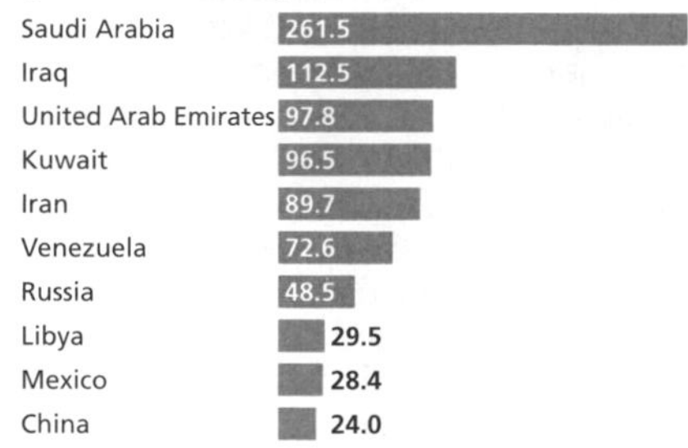

COMPANIES

The oil industry was once dominated by the "seven sisters," most of them American and created at the time of the break-up of Standard Oil. In fact, today's largest company is the result of Standard Oil of New Jersey (Exxon) eventually merging with Standard Oil of New York (Mobil). It is one of three super-majors—the other two being Shell and BP—which are present, to some degree, everywhere in the world where outside oil investment is permitted.

The top end of the industry has recently seen a wave of consolidation. Companies have sought to increase their scale to cope with new technical challenges such as prospecting for oil in deep water off West Africa and Brazil, and with the economic challenges of dealing with fluctuations in the price of oil: this rose, for example, from $10 a barrel in spring 1999 to a peak of $35 in autumn 2000, and fell back to about $20 in late 2001. Since 1998 Exxon has merged with Mobil; BP has bought Amoco, Arco, and Burmah Castrol; and the two French companies of Total and Elf have merged and swallowed up Petrofina of Belgium. In the United States, Chevron and Texaco have merged, and Conoco and Phillips agreed in November 2001 to do the same.

Largest oil and gas producers, 2000 (million barrels of oil equivalent a day)

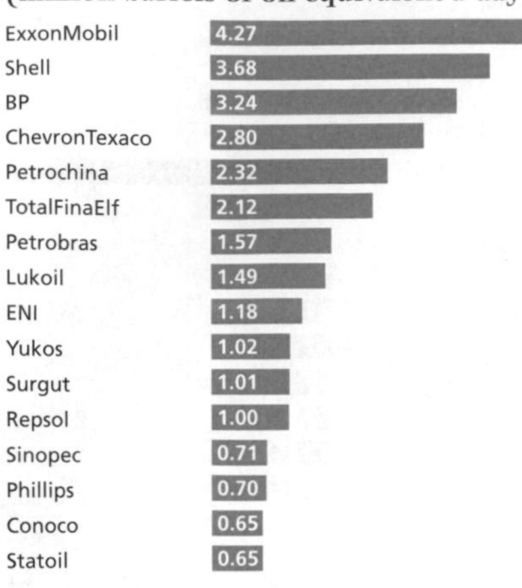

Top Western companies by market capitalization in mid-2001 ($ billion)

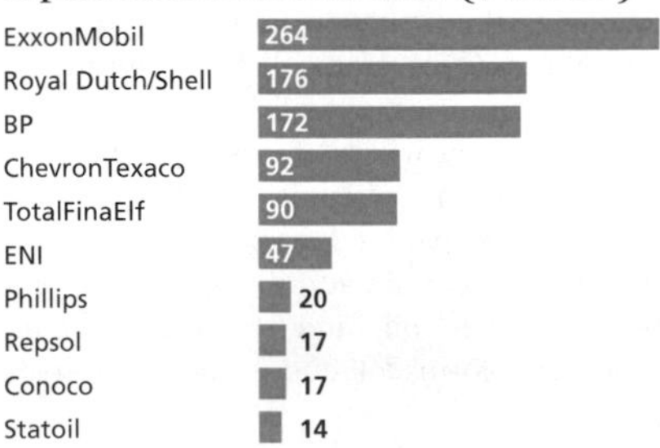

Top Western companies by pretax profits, 2000 ($ billion)

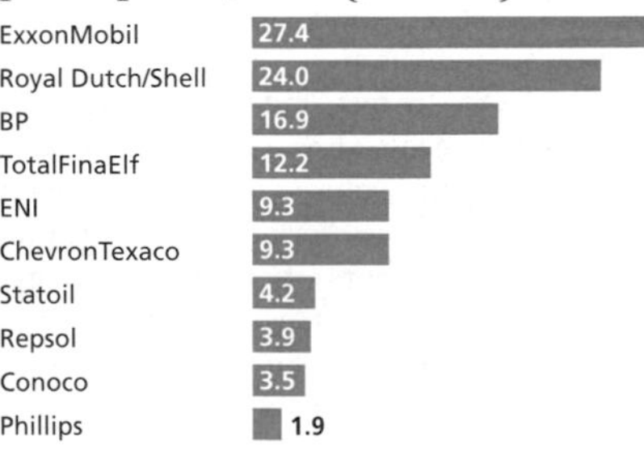

Top Western companies by employment at end-2000

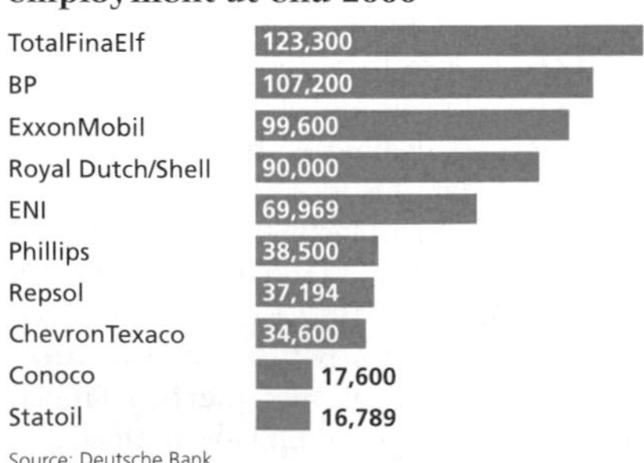

Source: Deutsche Bank

All these companies are "integrated" oil companies that combine the upstream exploration and production of oil with downstream refining and marketing of fuels in their own chains of gas stations. Refining involves distilling or separating crude oil into products like gasoline, diesel, kerosene, naphtha, liquefied petroleum gas, and lubricants. A further stage involves using gas or naphtha to make petrochemicals, from which plastics, synthetic rubber and fibers, and a wide range of other products are made. The oil industry has been involved in refining from the outset, and in petrochemicals since the 1920s. These activities provide a useful commercial counterbalance to upstream oil and gas production; however, since the profit margins in refining and petrochemicals are often thin and volatile, integrated majors now generally tend to limit their exposure in these sectors. Recent years have seen the birth of companies entirely devoted to exploration and production, the biggest of which are Anadarko in the United States and Enterprise Oil in the United Kingdom. They are known as "independents," in the sense that their upstream production is independent of any downstream activity.

Increasingly, the oil companies tend to hire oil service contractors like Halliburton of the United States and Schlumberger, a Franco-American company, to perform many of the tasks they used to carry out in-house. The essential risk in finding oil is still borne by the oil companies, but even here the oil companies increasingly share the risks. Indeed, one of the unusual features of the oil and gas industry is the degree to which companies—which are bitter commercial rivals, and are closely watched by anti-trust authorities for any sign of price-fixing—collaborate to minimize upstream exploration risk. A striking example is the formation of a consortium by nine leading oil and gas companies to exploit the Kashagan field in the north Caspian Sea.

Some non-Western companies are also beginning to make an impact beyond their national boundaries. They include some state oil companies from OPEC countries, notably Saudi Aramco, Petroleos de Venezuela, and Kuwait Petroleum, which are mainly interested in establishing foreign refining and marketing operations for their crude oil. Russia, not a member of OPEC, has several large oil companies, in particular Lukoil and Yukos which have foreign ambitions upstream as well as downstream, and one giant gas company, Gazprom. On the same pattern as Russia, China has created several listed oil companies: Petrochina, Sinopec, and the China National Offshore Oil Corporation.

Markets

Despite recent improvements in energy efficiency, world demand for oil has grown enormously in recent years to a current level of around 77 million barrels per day, and is forecast to reach 115 million barrels per day by 2020. Gas demand is rising even faster, largely for environmental reasons, and as a result many oil companies have sought to increase their production of gas, either by organic growth or by acquisition: BP, for example, has become North America's biggest gas producer by buying Amoco.

The oil market has become increasingly international. Forty years ago, when OPEC was first formed, only five countries produced more than 1 million barrels per day, oil was consumed mainly in industrialized countries, and the physical trade in oil was around 10 million barrels per day. Now some 17 countries pump more than 1 million barrels per day, the growth in demand is mainly in Asia and the developing world, and some 40 million barrels per day is traded. By contrast, gas has developed far more slowly into a world market because it can only be transported by pipeline or in the form of liquefied natural gas (LNG), and both are expensive.

In terms of supply, the bulk of the increase in oil and gas supply is coming from Russia, the Gulf of Mexico, Canada, and deep-water Angola, as well as from OPEC countries. However, after 2010 the increase in non-OPEC supplies will tail off, and the market will turn in favor of OPEC countries, particularly those in the Middle East, which have over half the world's oil reserves. In terms of demand, nearly half the increase over the next 20 years will come from China, India, and the rest of Asia. The really important flow, therefore, will be of OPEC oil going east to Asia.

The volatility of the oil price is a problem for the oil market. Upward spikes in the oil price are bad for the world economy, and were a contributing factor to the recessions of 1974–75, 1980–82 and 1990–91. Downward plunges are bad for the industry. The often erratic cycles of the oil price make it difficult for companies to plan long-term investment, despite the stabilization efforts made by OPEC.

Inescapably, the oil industry's fate depends to a considerable extent on OPEC. The cartel seeks to stabilize the oil revenues of its 11 members by regulating production, expanding it when demand increases and reducing it when demand falls. To fulfill this adjustment role, all OPEC members must be prepared to maintain spare capacity, though

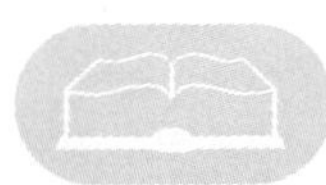

Top oil-consuming countries, 2000 (million barrels a day)

Country	Million barrels a day
United States	19.80
Japan	5.48
China	4.79
Germany	2.76
Russia	2.44
Canada	2.14
Brazil	2.12
South Korea	2.11
Mexico	2.04
India	1.98

Top gas-consuming countries, 1999 (billion cubic metres)

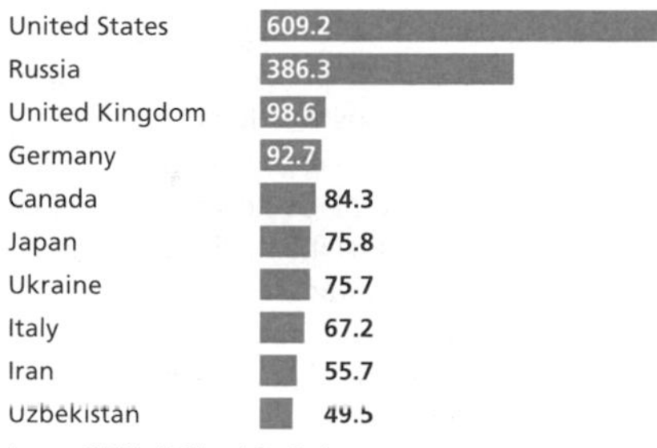

Source: *ENI World Oil and Gas Review*

Largest oil producers, 2000 (million barrels a day)

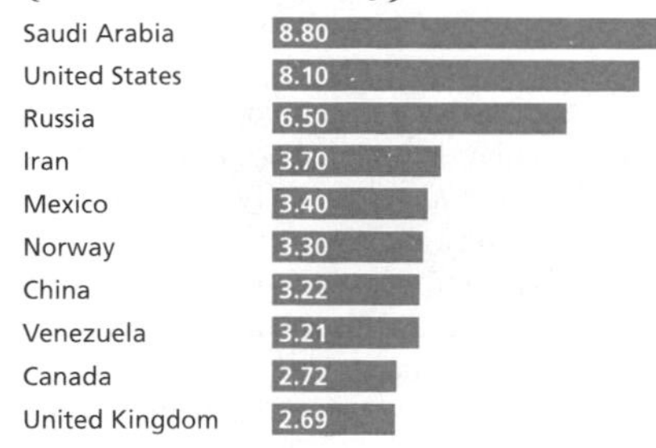

Largest gas producers, 2000 (billion cubic metres)

Country	Billion cubic metres
Russia	584.0
United States	535.8
Canada	181.9
United Kingdom	117.8
Algeria	90.3
Indonesia	69.4
Netherlands	66.4
Uzbekistan	57.9
Norway	54.1
Iran	50.9

in practice it is only Saudi Arabia, the cartel's leading producer, which does so.

However, OPEC's track record is mixed. Its efforts are often undermined by its own members, who cheat on their individual quotas by over-producing, and by rising production from non-OPEC producers. In 1997 OPEC made a bad problem worse by increasing output when demand was in fact falling. Its efforts from spring 1999 to mid-2000 were more fruitful, because for most of that period demand was growing faster than non-OPEC production was rising. However, the dramatic collapse of oil demand in the wake of the September 11 terrorist attacks on the United States saw OPEC being forced to appeal to non-OPEC producers to join it in taking oil off the market in order to stabilize the price.

Technology

New technology in the oil and gas industry is focused on processing, rather than on the product itself. The first technology landmark came in the early 1900s with the development of the tricone drilling bit. Until then drillers had relied on percussive drilling bits, which were dropped into wells and frequently snapped before the rock did. The tricone bit chewed the rock into small bits.

The second major advance came with the introduction of seismic surveys in the mid-1950s, which allowed geologists to find oil and gas before actually drilling. This became particularly important as the search for oil and gas went offshore. Three-dimensional seismic surveys, and even 4-D surveys which factor in the element of time to see how reservoirs flow, allow companies to produce holographs mapping out entire oilfields. As a result, oil and gas can be found using seismic techniques, and need the drill only for confirmation.

At the same time, the industry has devised better ways of reaching the hydrocarbon pockets which seismic techniques can spot, in particular the ability to drill horizontally and at many different angles. This ability enables an operator to reach several small reservoirs from one well, and also to reduce the size of his environmental footprint on the surface of the land or sea.

For the gas industry, the major advance has been the freezing of natural gas into a liquid (LNG) which occupies 1/600th of the volume of the fuel in its gaseous form. This frozen liquid is carried around the world in special insulated LNG carriers. Today LNG is traded worldwide, accounting for about 5% of the global gas market.

A broader technology challenge faced by the oil companies is the result of rising concern over global warming and the contribution made to that problem by the burning of hydrocarbons. Most oil companies are now becoming involved in renewable energy: two of the super-majors—Shell and BP—are vaunting their "greenness" as part of their corporate image. Both are involved in solar cell manufacture. ExxonMobil, a company with a more conservative image, says it still does not believe renewable energy is a commercial proposition, but it has joined other oil majors in funding ways to use gasoline as a source for hydrogen cells in cars. The age of oil is far from over, but to protect themselves for the future many oil companies now call themselves energy—not just "oil"—companies.

Impact of the Internet

Online procurement has been of considerable assistance to a worldwide industry such as the oil and gas sector, particularly because much of its equipment is standardized. The main impact, though, has been on energy trading. Oil future trading on London's International Petroleum Exchange and on the New York Mercantile Exchange has traditionally been by open outcry, but is increasingly moving to electronic screens. The liberalization of gas and electricity markets has also led to a sharp increase in the trading of these commodities. Indeed, energy trading has become necessary in order to balance the inputs and outputs of electricity grids and gas pipelines once the latter are separated from the old monopolies.

For More Information

Book:

Yergin, Daniel. *The Prize: The Epic Quest for Oil, Money and Power*. Carmichael, CA: Touchstone Books, 1993.

Web Sites:

American Petroleum Institute: **www.api.org**

International Energy Agency: **www.iea.org**

Organization of Petroleum Exporting Countries: **www.opec.org**

PHARMACEUTICALS

1899	Bayer's aspirin becomes first mass-marketed drug.
1941	Penicillin.
1946	General anesthesia.
1949	Cortisone.
1953	Francis Crick and James Watson discover structure of DNA.
1957	Factor VIII for hemophilia.
1960	Oral contraceptive pill.
1976	SmithKline launches Tagamet for ulcers after James Black's pioneering work on H2 receptors.
1978	Genentech, a U.S. biotechnology company, clones human insulin.
1988	Astra launches Losec for ulcers.
1993	SmithKline Beecham sign pioneering genomics collaboration with Human Genome Sciences.
1996	Triple therapy for HIV/AIDS.
1998	Pfizer launches Viagra for impotence: first "lifestyle" drug to make headlines.
1998	Genentech launches Herceptin, arguably first post-genomics drug.
2000	Cox-2 inhibitors for pain and inflammation become huge sellers for Merck and Pharmacia.
2001	Drug companies receive big legal setbacks over patent protection in both the developed and the developing world.
2001	Advances in stem cell biology provoke both scientific excitement and ethical disquiet.

The pharmaceutical industry in its modern form emerged at the turn of the 19th century, when mainly German and Swiss chemical manufacturers began to gain an understanding of the medicinal properties of synthesized chemicals.

A good example is the case of aspirin, "discovered" by Bayer of Germany in 1899. At the time, Bayer was principally a dye maker, but it had set up a pharmacological institute to examine the potential of using chemicals as medicines. It had started with diacetylmorphine which, because it made recipients feel heroic, had been given the name heroin. Once the addictive qualities of that particular drug became manifest, Bayer turned its attentions to acetylsalicylic acid, better known as aspirin.

Acetylsalicylic acid is found naturally in myrtle leaves and willow bark, and its qualities had been recognized by the ancient Egyptians who used it for back pain. Bayer's unique contribution to the modern drugs industry was to isolate the active ingredient and synthesize it. Aspirin also became the first mass-marketed drug and one of the first to be compressed into convenient doses—tablets.

In the first half of the 20th century, the industry was dominated by Europeans, with companies such as Schering of Germany and Hoffmann La Roche of Switzerland among the leaders. The shift to the United States, the industry's current center of gravity, began partly as a result of World Wars I and II: aspirin was expropriated by the United States in the treaty of Versailles. Merck, then a tiny U.S. subsidiary of a distinguished German pharmaceuticals manufacturer, was also ceded. Today, Merck of Germany is a bit player, while Merck of the United States, though no longer the biggest company in the sector, is a $200 billion giant, still considered by many to be at the forefront of the industry.

The shift to the United States and, to a lesser extent, the United Kingdom, has been accompanied by big technological developments as pure chemistry has given ground to biology. Largely as a result of the pioneering work in Cambridge, England, of Francis Crick and James Watson in discovering the helical structure of DNA, knowledge of biology exploded.

The biotechnology industry, now an integral part of pharmaceutical research, was founded in California in the late 1960s. By 2001 it accounted for around a quarter of the pharmaceutical industry's spending on basic research. In late 2001, Amgen, one of the oldest biotechnology companies, was planning to take over Immunex to create a group bigger than many traditional pharmaceutical companies. In corporate terms, this was seen by many as biotechnology's coming of age.

The prescription drugs industry in 2001 is worth some $250 billion, and even more if hospital and generic drugs (those that have lost their patent) are counted. In spite of pressure to control government spending on healthcare, especially pharmaceuticals,

Sales by main therapeutic category, year to September 2001 ($ billion)

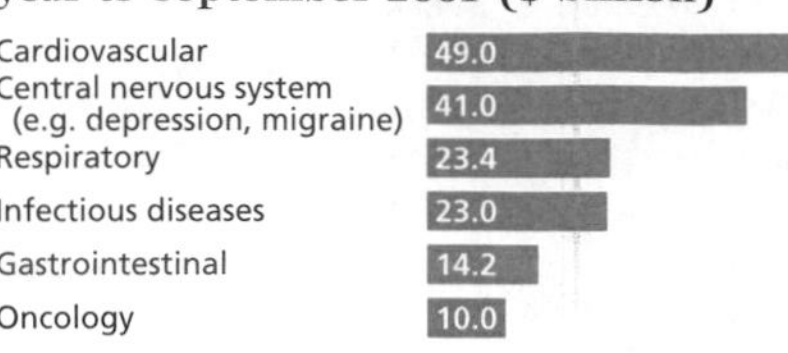

the industry has been one of the most profitable and best performing during several decades. The top 20 pharmaceutical companies, which mostly have operating margins above 30%, aspire to annual sales and profit growth of at least 10%. Most achieve that comfortably. Pharmaceutical companies were among the least affected by the 2001 stock market fallout precipitated by the bursting of the Internet bubble and compounded by the September 11 terrorist attacks on the United States.

During the 20th century, the industry became the most regulated in the world, with the U.S. Food and Drug Administration (FDA) the principal arbiter in the delicate balancing of risk and reward. Regulators insist on increasingly comprehensive trials to prove a drug's safety and efficacy, a process that normally lasts at least five years. Nine out of ten drugs entering clinical trials fail. It costs around $500 million to bring each new drug to market, including the costs of those that fell by the wayside. By 2001, the low number of new drug approvals led to frustrated calls by the industry that the burden of regulation had become too heavy.

COMPANIES

By the standards of other industries, the pharmaceutical sector remained highly fragmented in late 2001, with no single company having anywhere near 10% of market share. That situation prevailed in spite of years of steady consolidation. The creation of GlaxoSmithKline in 2000, for example, brought about the amalgamation of what, until 1990, had been four separate companies: Glaxo, Wellcome, SmithKline Beckman, and Beecham. Franco-German group Aventis marked the coming together of still more companies including Hoechst of Germany and Marion Merrel Dow of the United States as well as Rhône-Poulenc Rorer, Roussel Uclaf, and Pasteur Merieux of France.

Yet Aventis has less than 5% of global market share and Pfizer, the number one by

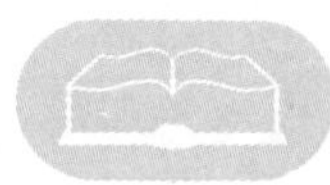

Top companies by market share, year to November 2000 (%)

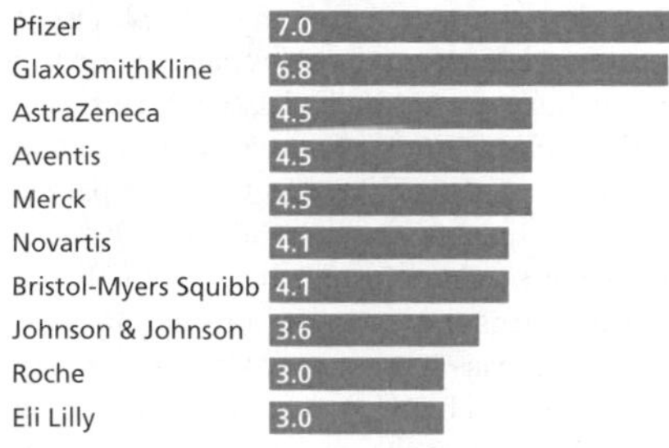

Top companies by market capitalization in December 2001 ($ billion)

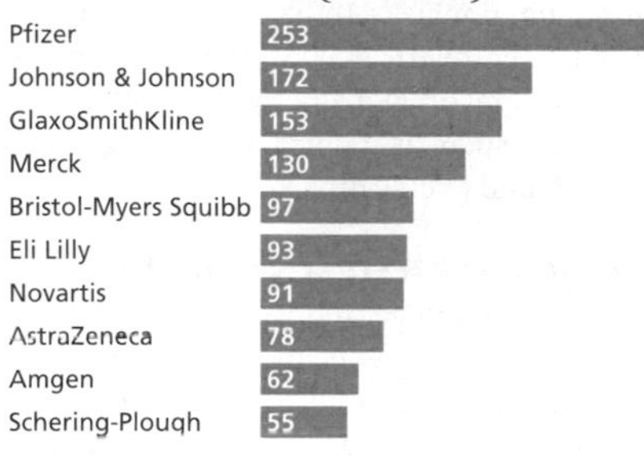

Top companies by operating margin, 1999 (%)

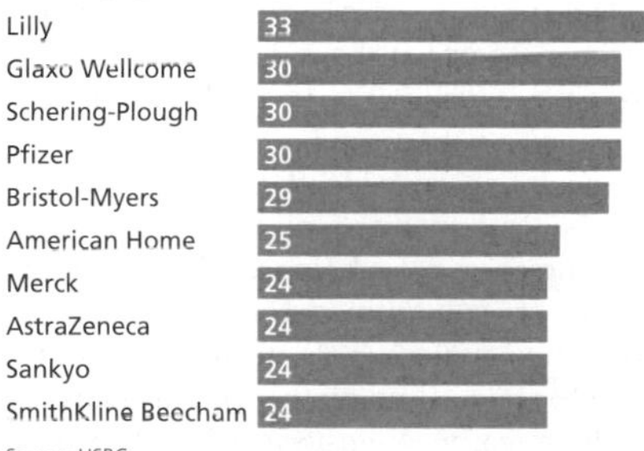

Source: HSBC

sales, about 7%. This is because the drugs industry more naturally breaks down into therapeutic categories, such as cardiovascular, which alone is worth nearly $50 billion in annual drug sales.

Apart from the proposed Amgen-Immunex tie-up, the most significant deal of 2001 may prove to be Roche's takeover of Japan's Chugai to form that country's fifth-largest drugs group. The deal added to growing evidence that the world's second-largest pharmaceuticals market is becoming more open to Western companies.

The general belief is that the industry will continue to consolidate until there are perhaps half a dozen companies with a global market share exceeding 10% and a wide geographical and therapeutic reach. These companies would be involved in all activities from basic research through clinical trials to the increasingly important activity of branding and marketing. Other smaller companies would have niche roles, either in specific sections of the value chain (for example basic research, clinical trials) or in particular therapeutic areas (diabetes, contraception). There is a contrary view that industry consolidation will eventually break down, leading to the creation of a series of smaller, more focused companies. They might be complemented by a few "virtual companies," possessing a strong brand and wide marketing reach, but with little in-house research and development capability.

Markets

The global market for pharmaceuticals divides naturally into four blocks: the United States, Japan, Europe, and the rest of the world.

Top markets for pharmaceuticals, 2001 ($ billion)

Market	$ billion
United States	127
Japan	48
Germany	15
France	14
Italy	9
United Kingdom	9
Canada	6
Spain	6
Mexico	5
Brazil	5
Argentina	3
Australia/NZ	3

Source: IMS Health

The United States dominates every global company's calculations: it accounts for approximately 40% of sales and 60% of profits. The United States is the only "free market" for prescription pharmaceuticals. When a drug is approved by the FDA, it goes on sale immediately at whatever price companies can extract from competing private insurers, managed care organizations, and employee health schemes. The quid pro quo for high initial prices is that the United States has a fiercely competitive generics market. When a drug goes off patent and generic manufacturers enter the fray, prices drop by as much as 90% overnight.

By contrast Japan is far more protected. Until recently, Japanese regulators have insisted that companies conduct extensive clinical trials in Japan on the grounds that Japanese people metabolize drugs differently from Westerners. The effect has been that Western companies have found it hard to break into Japan, which accounts for about 13% of global sales. The environment has been made more difficult by regular government-imposed price cuts, adopted to counter the potentially devastating impact of an aging population on the national drugs bill. However, Japan's growing commitment to accept foreign trial data, coupled with a greater willingness by individual corporations to consider international mergers (see above) are signs of significant change.

Europe is different again. Supposedly a single market, it is in fact a patchwork of different pricing and regulatory environments, although the latter are being harmonized by the EMEA, Europe's equivalent of the FDA, founded in 1995. Most European governments have some mechanism for setting drug prices, a process that can be extremely bureaucratic and one that may delay the launch of a drug by several months or even years. European governments, most of which implement a form of socialized healthcare, are reluctant to adopt the U.S. system of free pricing for fear their drug bills will become unmanageable.

From a commercial perspective, the least important markets are in the rest of the world, although Brazil, Mexico, Argentina, and South Korea are sizeable. India and China could become extremely important, particularly if they adhere to World Trade Organization rules clamping down on patent infringement.

However, even commercially insignificant markets, for example in sub-Saharan Africa, cannot be ignored by drug companies as the AIDS epidemic illustrates. Pressure has grown on drug manufacturers to make potentially life-saving medicines available at marginal cost in poor countries. In 2001, drug companies withdrew controversial legal challenges to the governments of South Africa and Brazil, which were both threatening to override patent protection in the interests of public health. Drug companies are nervous about giving ground on the question of intellectual property, but are, equally, acutely aware of the bad publicity that ensues when they are criticized for denying life-saving drugs to those who need them. Many slashed prices of AIDS drugs in the developing world, at least in part as a way of trying to improve their public image.

Technology

For most of the last century, discovering a new drug was a haphazard affair dominated by luck or one scientist's intuition. Companies screened huge chemical libraries against known biological targets that were suspected of playing a role in disease. All drugs invented to date either block or stimulate one of about 500 targets.

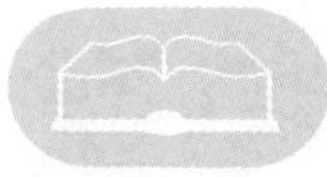

The leap in biological knowledge, epitomized by the deciphering of the human genome in 2000, promises to revolutionize the way drugs are discovered and the type of new medicines that become available. The discovery of new genes should lead to the unearthing of hundreds, if not thousands, of new "druggable" targets. Greater understanding of biology should also help scientists get to the root cause of disease, rather than merely treating its symptoms, and to classify diseases currently lumped together (diabetes, breast cancer, and so on,) into subtypes according to their molecular mechanism. Eventually, treatment may be tailored to a patient's individual genetic make-up. The use of embryonic stem cells, which is still highly controversial, promises the possibility of growing replacement tissue to help treat age- or accident-related health problems.

The new biology has led to the explosion of drug-discovery techniques, many of them linked to the equally impressive flourishing of computer technology. Instead of one scientist synthesizing one chemical, for example, combinatorial chemistry can produce tens of thousands of molecules that can be tested by robots against several targets at once in a technique known as high-throughput screening. Promising molecules can be tested in animals genetically altered to simulate human disease, or even in computers with software designed to simulate a disease process.

The genomics revolution might have led to more confusion than clarity initially, but it is expected that it will vastly improve the hunt for new medicines in the future. A good example is Herceptin, a drug discovered by Genentech of California, which targets a particularly virulent subtype of breast cancer in which a protein called Her2 is over-expressed. Use of the drug, administered only when a test confirms over-expression of Her2, greatly improves the chance of survival. Herceptin is an antibody, a new type of drug derived from the antibodies that every human being possesses to fight off disease.

New Products

The other great technological revolution in the pharmaceuticals industry has been to make drugs from proteins, as opposed to traditional small molecules. In the 1980s, companies such as Genentech and Amgen learnt how to isolate and clone recombinant proteins, such as insulin, growth hormone, and erythropoetin. Many scientists hope that genes, which make proteins, will one day be made into drugs, though many technical obstacles remain.

Proteins notwithstanding, the drugs industry is still heavily biased towards small molecules, which are very cheap to make and available in tablet, rather than injectable, form.

Best-selling products, 1999 ($ billion)

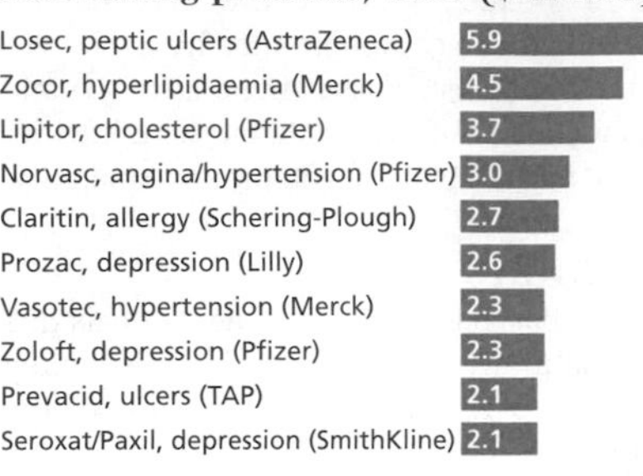

Cardiovascular disease has been the industry's biggest money spinner. In hypertension, Ace inhibitors and beta-blockers are still a mainstay. In the 1990s, statins, a class of drug to lower cholesterol, became a phenomenon. Several companies had billion-dollar products, but all were eclipsed when Warner-Lambert and Pfizer launched Lipitor in the late 1990s. Based on evidence that it lowered cholesterol faster and more effectively than competitors, it became one of the most successful drugs of all time. A change in 2001 by U.S. medical authorities as to what constitutes high cholesterol could further bolster cardiovascular drug sales.

Ulcer medicines have also been a big driver of the industry, first with SmithKline's Tagamet, then with Glaxo's Zantac (on which the company's global status was built), and latterly with Losec, Astra's protein-pump inhibitor with annual sales of $6 billion. In 2001, AstraZeneca launched Nexium, a supposedly even more effective drug than Losec. Diseases of aging are another big area. Pfizer's Viagra, for erectile dysfunction, captured the headlines when it was launched in 1998, beginning a trend for "lifestyle" drugs. Arthritis has become another huge area, particularly with the Cox-2 inhibitors, drugs that target inflammation without suppressing Cox-1, an enzyme that controls acid secretion. Thus patients can take Cox-2s, such as Pharmacia's Celebrex and Merck's Vioxx, with less risk of internal bleeding.

Employment

The big pharmaceutical companies employ 60,000 to 100,000 people each, about 15% of whom are typically scientists. The rest are sales, marketing, and administrative staff, and those in legal, manufacturing, and other technical functions. The drugs industry is global, albeit heavily skewed towards the United States. Most companies employ staff in 50 or 60 countries. A typical company might have five principal laboratories, two in the United States, two in Europe, and one in Japan. Most of the big U.S. companies are based in New Jersey, where many of the Europeans also have their U.S. headquarters. It is increasingly common to have a research base in Boston or California to tap into the biotechnology revolution unfolding in both regions. Drug companies recruit internationally. Many big pharmaceutical and biotechnology companies, for example, employ nationals of India, which has strong IT and chemistry skills. Manufacturing is also undertaken globally, with big plants in locations such as Puerto Rico, Singapore, Ireland, and even China.

Impact of the Internet

The biotechnology industry is one manifestation of the new economy that is transforming the drugs industry. Technology is moving so fast that drug companies do not try to keep up; instead they outsource a significant portion of basic research by forming multiple alliances.

The Internet also promises to change various aspects of the industry. Companies are already using it to forge closer relationships with patients, who have traditionally been kept at arm's length by regulation and by the intermediary physician-prescriber. The Internet is also being used, albeit tentatively, to communicate with doctors, to speed up clinical trials, to help refine research, and to simplify the United States' incredibly complex insurance-based healthcare system. However, healthcare Internet companies have not been spared from the new technology shake-out.

For More Information

Books:

Le Fanu, James. *The Rise and Fall of Modern Medicine.* New York: Little, Brown and Company, 1999.

Ridley, Matt. *Genome.* London: Fourth Estate, 1999.

Web Sites:

Electronic Medicines Compendium: **emc.vhn.net**

Latest regulatory news: **www.fda.gov**

U.S. National Institutes of Health: **www.nih.gov**

  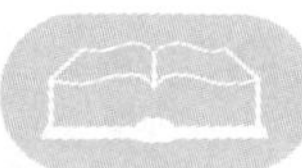    

POWER

1882	The Pearl Street system in the United States inaugurates the modern power industry.
1930s	Global trend to centralization and state ownership of power accelerates.
1978	Purpa legislation in the United States introduces the independent power producer (IPP) model.
1988	Chile pioneers the implementation of power privatization.
1997	Asian economic crisis challenges the IPP model.
1999	The right to choose their energy supplier is extended to all U.K. customers.
2000	California energy crisis results in global reassessment of deregulation.
2001	China becomes the world's second-largest power user after the United States.

The power industry became a commercial reality with the inauguration of Edison's Pearl Street system in New York in 1882. By the turn of the century, power companies had been established in major urban centers throughout the Americas, Europe, and Asia Pacific. In most cases the companies were privately or municipally owned.

In the course of the 20th century, power supply was progressively extended from the cities to outlying areas, with electrification programs being implemented in successively less developed economies. In the process local companies were merged into regional or national companies which, in most cases, received exclusive rights to generate, transmit, distribute, and supply power in specific areas.

The creation of large, integrated monopolies was driven by the belief that this was the best way to ensure the secure power supplies regarded as essential for national and economic well-being. The security concerns also resulted in increased state control of the system, either through nationalization or by stringent regulation of investor-owned utilities.

By the middle of the 20th century, the global power industry consisted almost entirely of regulated monopolies. However, dissatisfaction with their performance increased from the 1970s. The absence of competition was seen as having an adverse affect on prices, while the companies appeared unable to respond quickly to changing circumstances.

This led to a reassessment of policy in several countries. The Purpa legislation passed in the United States in 1978 represented one of the first attempts to reform the industry. The act established the concept of the independent power producer (IPP), a self-standing generator which sells its power to a utility under a long-term agreement. IPPs awarded as a result of competitive bidding were expected to have lower capital and operating costs than new capacity built by the utilities themselves.

IPPs became widespread throughout the global market in the 1980s and 1990s, with their use being backed by agencies such as the World Bank. However, critics argued that IPPs merely complemented the host utility's own capacity, and did not compete with it. They also argued that IPPs were of little value without parallel investment in transmission and distribution, and without reform of tariff and revenue collection structures to create economically sustainable power systems.

These arguments were borne out during the Asian economic crisis of 1997, when several countries defaulted on their IPP obligations. As a result, the multilateral agencies switched their focus from IPPs to the reform of distribution and tariff structures in the late 1990s.

IPPs nevertheless remain an integral part of the power programs of many countries, and have provided an entry into over a hundred markets previously closed to private investors.

IPPs also helped dispel the belief that security of supply could only be guaranteed by monopoly utilities. From the 1980s, increasingly ambitious liberalization policies were pursued in countries including Chile, New Zealand, Britain, and the United States. While accepting that transmission and distribution is a natural monopoly, and should thus be regulated, the proponents of reform argued that the generation and supply businesses should be open to competition. In the case of state-owned systems, moves towards liberalization usually went hand in hand with the privatization of the system.

Competition between generators was first implemented in Chile in 1988. By the beginning of 2002, wholesale competition in various forms had been instituted in a large number of countries. Competition to supply final users had also been implemented in a substantial number of countries by 2002, although in many cases only large energy users are contestable, rather than all customers.

Some national power markets were also opened to cross-border competition from the 1990s, notably in Europe. However, the level of international competition remains limited by transmission and, in some cases, by political and economic constraints.

Although power liberalization has made considerable strides since the 1980s, the belief that electricity is no different from any other commodity remains far from universal. This was demonstrated by the responses to the power shortages in California in 2000. The view that the sector is of strategic importance, and should be owned or closely regulated by the state, retains substantial support both in the United States and beyond.

COMPANIES

The global power market has changed from a business consisting almost entirely of monopolies to a patchwork of structures ranging from state monoliths to fully competitive markets. This was accompanied by a change in the composition of the players as large areas of the market opened up to foreign and private investment.

New companies entering the market included independent power developers and equipment manufacturers, energy producers and engineering and construction companies, looking for an outlet for their wares. However, the business remains dominated by companies from a power utility background, albeit companies who have become international players and who have changed from their domestic focus as their home markets are liberalized.

The utilities have maintained their dominance through a wave of acquisitions,

Power companies by total capacity, 2001 (GW)

UES, Russia	155
EdF, France	136
SPC, China	74
Tokyo EPC, Japan	58
Enel, Italy	53
AEP, U.S.	38
Kansai, Japan	38
Duke Energy, U.S.	37
Endesa, Spain	37
Hydro Quebec, Canada	37

 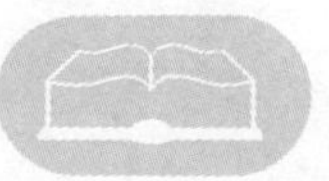    

Power companies by sales, 2001 (TWh)

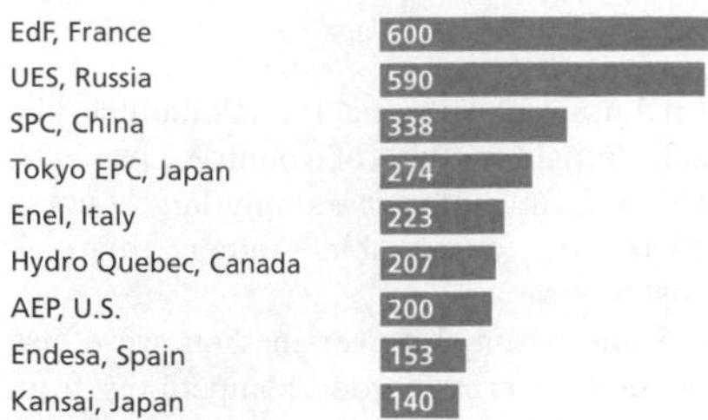

in particular in Europe and North America. The larger companies bought gas suppliers, smaller electricity utilities, and independent power developers from 1997 onwards to entrench their positions ahead of market liberalization.

As a result, the concentration of ownership has increased markedly at regional level, especially in Europe. However, concentration of ownership at global level remains low. UES and EdF, although by far the largest power generators, each account for under 4.5% of global production. Concentration in the global transmission, distribution, and retail businesses is even lower.

Markets

Until recently, most power was used in the heavy industrial sector. This was especially the case in the former Soviet Union, where large energy users accounted for up to 70% of total consumption.

The share of power consumed by industrials has declined—over many years and in almost all regions—in relation to that used by commercial and residential customers. This has resulted in increased peaks and troughs in daily demand. There have also been changes in seasonal demand, notably because of the spread of air conditioning. These changes had significant implications for power suppliers, especially in the need for a greater amount of peaking capacity.

There has also been a shift in the regional breakdown of global consumption in recent decades. The growth of demand in less developed economies easily outstripped growth in the developed economies.

The trend is projected to continue in the coming decades, with a large proportion of the opportunities for new business coming from Asia-Pacific, Latin America, Africa, and the Middle East. However, the low growth projected for advanced economies should not disguise the fact that they start from a high base and that they still offer substantial business opportunities for new and replacement capacity.

World power consumption, 1999 (TWh)

Africa	367
Asia-Pacific	3,480
FSU/Eastern Europe	1,387
Latin America	700
Middle East	389
North America	3,905
Western Europe	2,606
World	**12,833**

Source: Energy Information Administration, U.S.

Growth of world power consumption 1990–99 (% p.a.)

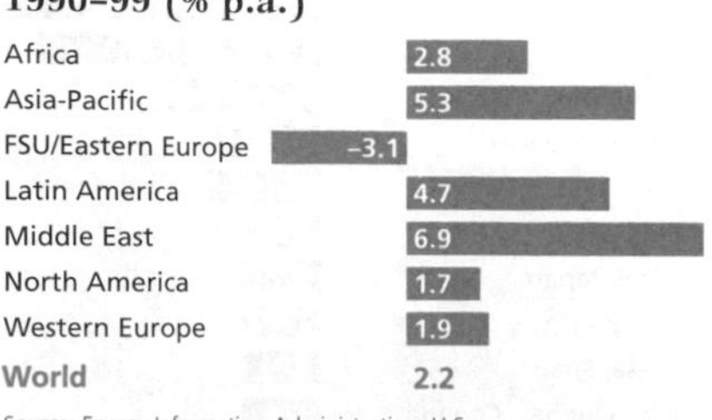

Source: Energy Information Administration, U.S.

New and replacement capacity needed by region, 1997–2020 (GW)

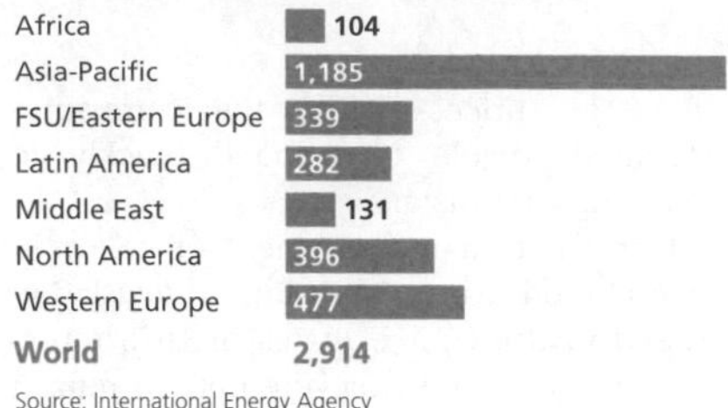

Source: International Energy Agency

Investment in new and replacement capacity needed by region, 1997–2020 ($ billion)

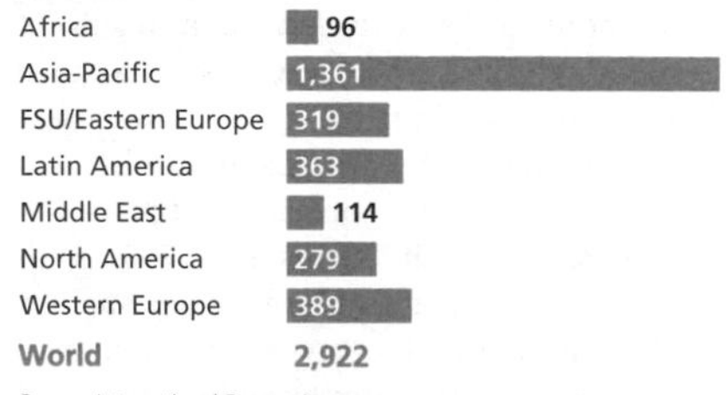

Source: International Energy Agency

Technology

Coal has been the main power station feedstock from the early days of the industry, and remains the largest single source of global generation. Hydroelectric power was also tapped from an early stage, while oil use increased from the middle of the 20th century until the oil price shocks of the 1970s halted its growth.

Nuclear power took up much of the slack during the 1980s. However, natural gas became increasingly important from the late 1980s, and is now the fuel of choice throughout the global power business.

This resulted from a combination of factors. The fuel is well suited for use in combined cycle gas turbine (CCGT) plants, in which power is generated from gas turbines and the waste exhaust heat is used to drive steam turbines. This increases the efficiency of fuel use to between 50% and 58%, compared to the 34%-43% available from steam or gas turbines operating alone.

CCGTs are cheaper and quicker to build than coal, hydroelectric, or nuclear plants. They also produce lower emissions and tend to arouse less environmental opposition than these other sources.

The proportion of gas-fired capacity is expected to increase over the next two decades. Nuclear capacity will decline over the same period as new builds fail to keep

Share of global power production and generation capacity by fuel source, 1997 (%)

Power production

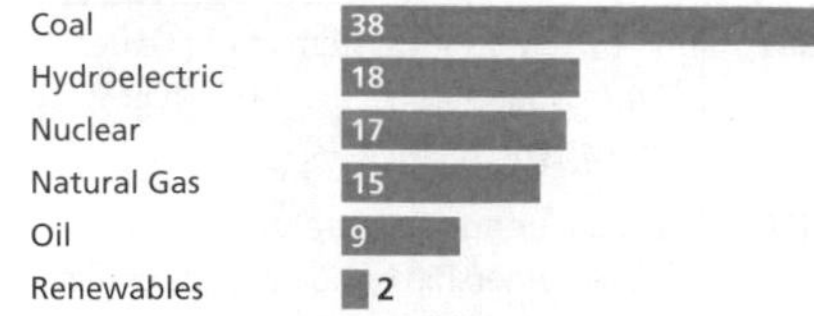

Power generation capacity

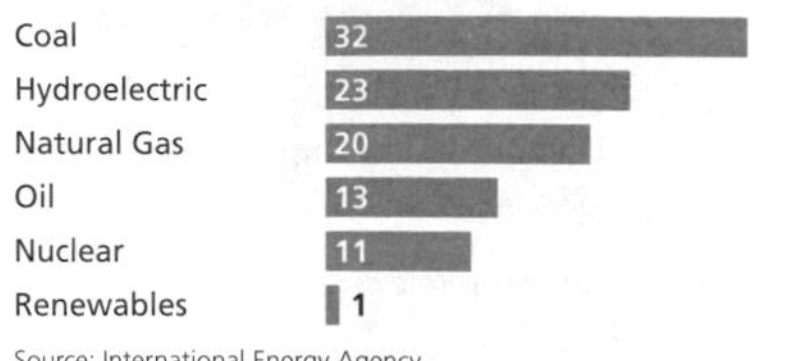

Source: International Energy Agency

Forecast share of global power production and generation capacity by fuel source, 2020 (%)

Power production

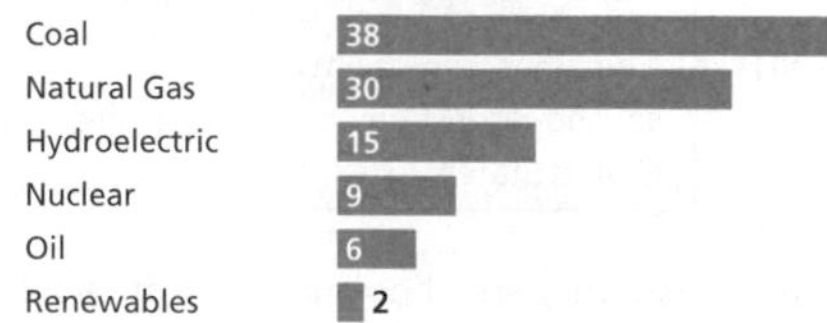

Power generation capacity

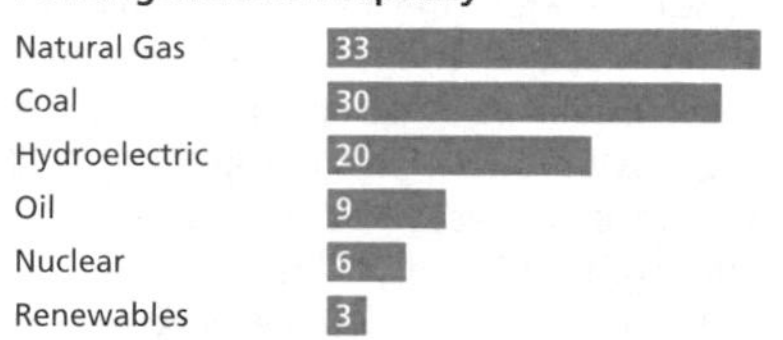

Source: International Energy Agency

Capital cost, lead times, and efficiency of new U.S. plant in 2001			
Technology	$ per kW	Years	%
Combined cycle gas turbine	580	3	54
Open cycle gas turbine	465	3	43
Pulverized coal	1,100	4	38
Circulating fluidized bed, coal	1,200	4	34
Nuclear	2,400	7	n/a

Source: Deutsche Bank, Alex. Brown (Global Utilities, August 2001)

pace with decommissioning, while hydroelectric output is expected to retain its position because of its importance in markets such as Brazil.

Coal-fired plant is expected to grow significantly in actual, if not proportional, terms because of its importance in markets such as China, India, and Indonesia. Renewable sources are projected to increase strongly, but will remain marginal in global terms in the near to medium term.

The trend to consolidation noted for power companies is equally true of equipment suppliers. The second half of the 1990s saw a small number of manufacturing companies emerge from a series of mergers. However, while the industry is dominated by companies such as GE, Alstom, Siemens, and Mitsubishi, a significant number of companies occupy specialist niches, for instance in the diesel and wind turbine sectors.

EMPLOYMENT

The diverse nature of the industry means that employment trends are difficult to project. State-owned monopolies in some regions are notorious for over-employment. The general trend has been for employment levels to fall, often steeply, as industries are privatized and liberalized, with no indication that this pattern is likely to change.

FUTURE PROSPECTS

The power business has been transformed since the 1980s. Liberalization and internationalization are expected to continue, although the pace will be uneven over time and between regions. The process is expected to result in further consolidation among the industry players.

In the longer term an even more radical transformation is predicted by many industry observers. The move to ever larger companies may be reversed, with small businesses and households moving into the production of power, both for their own use and for sale. The change from central to distributed generation is projected to occur as systems which for the most part already exist—such as micro-turbines and fuel cells—fall in price and become competitive. The process would also be driven by the increased cost and difficulty of securing environmental approval for new generation and transmission infrastructure in advanced economies.

For More Information

Magazines and Journals:
Global Power Report, Power in Asia: **www.platts.com**

Web Sites:
Central Research Institute of Electric Power Industry: **http://criepi.denken.or.jp**
Edison Electric Institute: **www.eei.org**
Energy Information Administration. **eia.doe.gov**
Eurelectric: **www.eurelectric.org**
International Energy Agency: **www.iea.org**
Tat Energy Research Institute, India: **www.teriin.org**

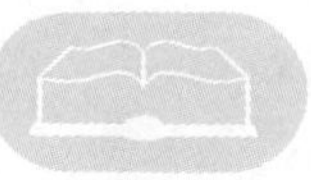

Real Estate

1945–1960	Post-war reconstruction creates European real estate industry.
1960s	Pension funds/insurance companies move into real estate.
1970s	Bretton Woods agreement ends; international investment expands.
1980s	Japanese investment into Europe/United States/Southeast Asia; Dutch funds expand across Europe/the United States; Scandinavian investors expand across Europe; REITS take off in United States.
1990s	Japanese withdraw to home markets; Southeast Asian international investment expands, then eases; fall of Berlin wall opens up Central/Eastern Europe; U.S./U.K. vulture funds move into Europe/Southeast Asia; REITs suffer downturn, then recover.
2000s	Global economic slowdown; REIT consolidation; vulture funds continue European expansion; occupiers/governments begin asset sale to private sector.

The old joke in real estate is that the three most important factors are "location, location, location." Appearances are important, naturally, but for investors the critical factor is how much buyers or occupiers will pay, and this in turn depends on a complex pattern of demand and supply.

The balance varies not just from country to country, nor even from city to city, but right down to neighborhoods and streets. Architects can create almost identical buildings in different cities, but the value of those buildings will vary enormously. Local knowledge of the forces which determine rents and investment value is critical, which is why real estate has always been the most local of industries.

Gradually, however, national boundaries are dissolving. International diversification took off in the 1970s following the demise of the Bretton Woods system (which had controlled capital flows) and other deregulation measures. This was reinforced by developments in financial economics which showed how risk could be reduced by diversifying across borders.

Real estate has played a significant role in the upsurge of international capital flows both through direct development and investment in equities. Short-term investors have often been forced out of home markets when the weight of capital exceeded local opportunities. Middle-Eastern oil states and Japanese conglomerates made heavy inroads into the United States and United Kingdom in the 1970s and 1980s, followed by the Dutch, Scandinavians, Germans, and Southeast Asians. Insurance companies and pension funds have become heavily involved as they seek to spread risk, improve long-term performance, and use tax advantages.

Commercial real estate, 2001 ($ billion)

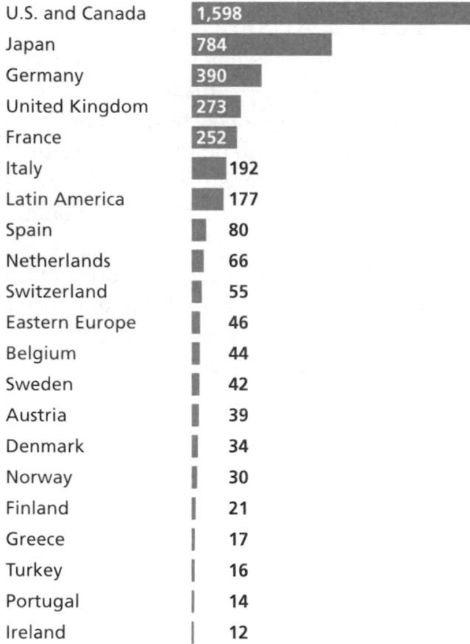

Sources: Economist Intelligence Unit, Prudential Real Estate Investors

Capital began to flow in the opposite direction as the 20th century closed. The fall of the Berlin wall attracted U.S. interest to former Soviet bloc countries, but the main influence came from vulture funds swooping into the United Kingdom and France to take advantage of cheap assets left by the widespread economic slump. By the turn of the century, foreign investors owned close to 20% of French real estate after being involved in around half the transactions in the late 1990s.

This fell away as the world economy slowed, but was still running at $4.5 billion by the third quarter of 2001, with U.S. investors accounting for 45% of all cross-border investment in Europe. The United Kingdom attracted 38% of investment, followed by France at 27%.

A further influence is that major occupiers like IBM, Mitsubishi, Coca-Cola, and Microsoft have come to treat the world as a single market and demand similar provision of real estate everywhere. International mergers have reinforced this trend, and the real estate industry has raced to match the demands. Advisors went through their own mergers, forming global networks like Jones Lang LaSalle, Insignia, and CB Richard Ellis.

They worked closely with financial groups such as Morgan Stanley, CSFB, and Goldman Sachs in guiding U.S. capital to new opportunities. Even after the sharp economic downturn, some $25 billion was earmarked to flow into Europe and Southeast Asia in 2001, although some of this could also be diverted into emerging markets like Latin America. Meanwhile—despite the slowing world economy—German open-ended investment funds need an outlet for more than $1 billion pouring in from private investors every month. With around $50 billion already invested in property ranging from British offices to Spanish shopping centers, the funds have looked again at opportunities in U.S. real estate. Other buyers include Dutch pension fund managers, Israeli private investors, and Australian investment funds.

Structure

The change in approach to real estate investment still has a long way to go to erode the traditional structure of the industry, however. The money flowing out of the United States is not significant in a total market worth around $3 trillion. The biggest players are real estate investment trusts (REITs)—tax shelters which won the favor of private investors and institutions alike, and soared in value from $8 billion to around $150 billion in 10 years. They suffered setbacks in the late 1990s, but came back into favor as technology stocks collapsed.

Most of them focus on home markets, but high net-worth players and institutional funds spread their interest further afield in the 1990s. Expertise gained in handling billions of dollars worth of property debts after the collapse in the late 1980s and early 1990s of the U.S. savings and loan movement led the big financial groups to set up pooled funds which took advantage of similar opportunities in Europe, Japan, and Southeast Asia.

International real estate investment

	Investment trusts	Real estate companies
Australia	dominant	small
Canada	dominant	small
Germany	dominant	small
France		dominant
Hong Kong		dominant
Japan		dominant
Malaysia		dominant
Netherlands	dominant	small
Singapore		dominant
Spain		small
Sweden		small
Switzerland	dominant	small
United Kingdom		dominant
United States	dominant	small

Source: Jones Lang Wootton, 1999

At first they concentrated on distressed debt in countries like France, but companies such as Security Capital, PRICOA, and GE Capital became bolder, setting up teams to look for potential investments in Europe. They tend to buy portfolios or developers with the intention of selling out within five to seven years.

Within Europe, the Netherlands pioneered international investment by taking advantage of regulations that allowed companies tax transparency, provided they distributed all their income: prime examples of these companies are Rodamco and Wereldhave. Open- and closed-end funds also provide opportunities for international investment, and REIT-style vehicles have developed in the Netherlands, Belgium (SICAFI), and Spain.

Despite having one of the most sophisticated and substantial real estate markets, the United Kingdom has struggled to develop the kind of vehicle which offers liquidity, security, and management skills to investors. Unit trusts have been around for some time, but are of minor importance compared to their position in Australia. Nor are there the open-ended investment funds such as in Germany, which also provide access for ordinary investors into commercial real estate.

Financial groups in the United Kingdom have dabbled with securitized single-asset vehicles and property derivatives, but the most significant progress has been in limited partnerships and offshore investment trusts, which had drawn in more than £10 billion ($14 billion) by the beginning of 2002. This is partly because traditional real estate companies are losing their attraction. Share prices have always traded at discounts to asset values, but this gap grew to 30% or more in the 1990s as investors tired of poor performance and liquidity. Many companies have been privatized, including MEPC, one of the United Kingdom's top five names.

Markets

United States

Real estate, like the economy, saw its longest ever bull market through the 1990s. City-center and suburban offices were among the major benefactors as rental values soared, with particular hotspots in technology centers such as New York and San Francisco. Ironically, the dot-com phenomenon brought this to an end. First, real estate investment trust (REIT) prices dived as technology stocks stole the limelight. The NASDAQ crash swung back the balance, but also tipped the economy into recession, driving down demand by occupiers.

Largest U.S. REITs by market capitalization in November 2001 ($ billion)

Equity Office Properties Trust	12.3
Equity Residential Properties Trust	7.8
Plum Creek Timber Company	5.4
Simon Property Group	5.0
Archstone Communities Trust	4.5
Public Storage	3.9
ProLogis Trust	3.8
Vornado Realty Trust	3.8
Boston Properties	3.4
AvalonBay Communities	3.3
Apartment Investment and Management Company	3.3
Kimco Realty Corp.	3.3
Duke Realty Corp.	3.1
Host Marriott Corp	2.2
AMB Property Corp.	2.1
Liberty Property Trust	2.1
General Growth Properties	2.1
Health Care Property Investors	2.1
The Rouse Company	2.0
Crescent Real Estate Equities Co.	1.9

Source: National Association of Real Estate Investment Trusts, U.S.

Rents began dropping and vacancy rates rising in 2001, dragging the REIT Index from double-digit increases into decline. Lower rents and growing vacancies were expected to result in growth of the Index in 2002, but uncertainties following the terrorist attacks and the Afghan war in 2001 pushed recovery back.

Few expect the kind of problems seen in previous recessions, however, because developers did not overbuild, nor lenders overspend, as they have in the past. Pain will be most intense in sectors such as retailing, which was already over-supplied before the threat of online shopping arose. High-tech centers and new media markets will also struggle.

Europe

European markets recovered more slowly than the United States after the early 1990s recession, and have declined again more gently. This is one of the reasons why so many dollars have crossed the Atlantic. However, the global slowdown was still expected to cut activity across the continent by half in 2002. The U.K. cycle lies somewhere between those of the United States and continental Europe, so investors have juggled resources between the three markets. Office rents in London, for instance, peaked in 2001, well before those in Paris, Berlin, and Rome.

European real estate companies by market value in November 2001 ($ billion)

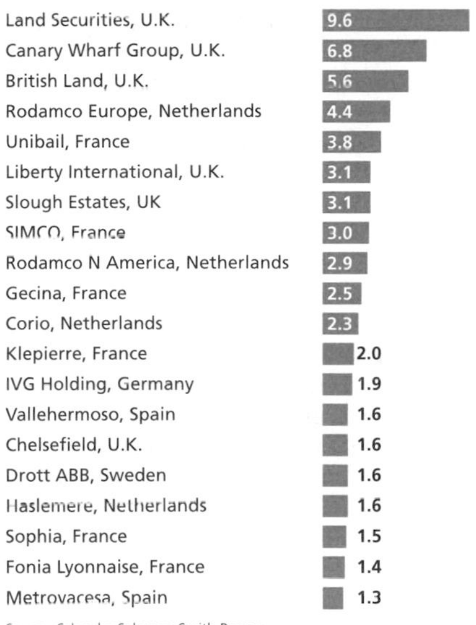

Source: Schroder Salomon Smith Barney

Like the United States, the recession will be less severe than in the past because development was more restrained during the 1990s boom than in previous cycles. Rental growth is expected to continue to exceed inflation even if demand falls.

A European "superleague" of cities was identified by Ernst & Young, based on international companies' investment intentions. The top five were London, Paris, Barcelona, Amsterdam, and Dublin, which accounted for 18% of investment in 2000. One problem is that this came from sectors such as software, telecommunications, and business and financial services, so recovery will hinge on how well these sectors can overcome their own problems.

The severity of the downturn is being

eased by filling gaps in the real estate market. Cross-border development was growing even before the introduction of a single currency across most of Europe, so investors were transferring attention from—for example—London offices to Spanish shopping centers much more readily. Retailing remains an uncertain sector, however, with polarization between high-demand prime sites and weaker secondary property.

Central and Eastern Europe will offer further new opportunities as countries like Hungary, Poland, and the Czech Republic improve their economies and join the European Community, but they are vulnerable to downturns in dominant markets such as Germany.

The central attraction for opportunistic investors is likely to be the growing trend among governments and major companies to outsource property. Financial re-engineering of real estate is likely to be the dominant factor of the early 21st century. Some 70% of property is owned by occupiers—twice the level of the United States—and this will be exchanged for cheap capital to invest in core operations.

Asia

After the excesses of over-borrowing and over-development in the late 20th century, the region was looking at slow recovery until caught in the backlash of the September 11 attacks on the United States. The potential of 1.6 billion people, rapidly diversifying economies, and relatively high GDP is an undoubted attraction to investors, but the future will depend on whether governments will be strong enough to clear up the problems of the 1997 financial crisis.

Asia will emerge as the world's growth engine if it can sort out a huge backlog of non-performing loans, according to a study carried out in early 2002; unfortunately these debts grew from $1.5 trillion to $2.0 trillion in 2001. Restructuring will open up enormous opportunities for global real estate investors, however, as assets are packaged for sale into investment trusts, much as they were when European countries went through a similar—if less severe—crisis. Japanese banks alone were estimated to have $1.3 trillion of assets on their books.

Impact of the Internet

New technology has had a major impact on real estate. A computer on every desk made existing offices obsolete as companies required extra space for cabling and heat extraction. High-tech companies almost single-handedly drove development out of towns and cities into greenfield business parks, first in the United States and then across the world. Then came the Internet, adding a new layer of telecommunications occupiers, and promising to transform building services by linking every company via high-speed networks.

However, the revolution has been postponed. The dot-com crash left acres of empty buildings and failed projects. Internet-based brokerage gained a foothold in places like the United States, where vast distances can separate buyers and sellers, but struggled elsewhere. Landlords ran out of resources to thread high-speed cable links to every building, and creation of a new kind of real estate to hold clusters of computer servers ground to almost a complete halt as telecom companies ran into trouble.

Changes will continue, however. As economies recover, cabling and wireless connections will accelerate, further changing the nature of buildings. Call centers and Web hosting "hotels" will mature into a new real estate sector. One downside could be the impact on retailing, as customers become more accustomed to ordering from computers. U.S. shopping centers are already under threat because of oversupply. Europe has much less space per head and can feel more secure. High streets around the world will also survive by concentrating on "touch and feel" products like fashion and food.

For More Information

Web Sites:

British Property Federation:
www.bpf.propertymall.com
European Property Federation:
www.epf-fepi.com
International Real Estate Federation:
www.fiabci.net
National Real Estate Investor (U.S.):
www.nreionline.com

RENEWABLE ENERGY

1880	First hydroelectric power station at Niagara Falls.
1887	Charles F. Brush erects first wind turbine for electricity generation.
1897	Poul la Cour pioneers wind generation in Denmark.
1905	Einstein explains photoelectric effect.
1922	First geothermal power station in the United States at The Geysers.
1960s	U.S. space program provides impetus to develop photovoltaics.
1973–1979	Oil crises result in increased R&D spending on alternatives.
1980–1985	First California wind boom.
1992	UN Framework Convention on Climate Change signed at Rio Earth Summit.
1995	Japanese Sunshine solar program launched.
1996	German *Einspeisungsgesetz* (power supply) renewables law.
2001	New German renewable energy law, E.U. renewables directive, details of Kyoto Protocol all agreed.

While the use of energy forms such as wood fuel, wind, and water flows stretches back to prehistory, most of the modern renewable energy industry can be traced back to the oil crises of the 1970s. In the wake of supply disruptions, research and development money was poured into alternatives to fossil fuels, forming the basis of a new energy sector. The money dried up when the oil price collapsed in the mid-1980s, but the nascent industry was given a boost in the 1990s as environmental concerns rose up the political agenda. The sector is now poised to be one of the major energy suppliers of the 21st century.

It is slightly misleading to refer to a single renewable energy industry: it is in fact a collection of disparate industries based on different technologies. Hydroelectricity is an established technology. Low-impact small hydro has potential, and is generally counted as a "new" renewable, along with wind, solar power, geothermal energy, wave, and tidal. The use of biomass on open fires is as old as humanity, but a number of new and modern technologies are emerging, for both power generation and transport fuels.

These technologies are in different stages of development. The most advanced sectors are wind, solar, and biomass, which are all growing at annual rates of up to 25–30% from small bases. Geothermal power is a semi-mature technology, but its potential is limited unless "hot dry rock" techniques can be perfected that do not depend on existing underground aquifers. Wave and tidal power are in earlier stages of development, and will not make significant contributions before the 2010s.

The rise of new renewable energy also belongs in the context of other technological and institutional developments. Combined heat and power, and more efficient end-use technologies, have the potential to curb or even reverse the growth in energy demand, while the liberalization of electricity industries gives opportunities to exploit distributed renewable energy supplies. In the longer term, the development of fuel cells for automotive or stationary use throws up the possibility of the "hydrogen economy," which would result in completely emission-free energy supply.

The new renewable energy technologies have, to varying degrees, higher costs than conventional supplies. This means that their introduction is dependent on public support in the medium term: wind may compete directly in 2–3 years, while other technologies could need funding until at least the 2010s. The reasons justifying this expenditure are many: the pressing need to reduce humanity's impact on the environment, particularly carbon emissions; the finite nature of fossil fuel resources; avoiding fuel price volatility (renewable supplies have very stable prices); reduction of energy import costs; and, particularly important after the terrorist attacks of September 2001, security of supply.

MARKETS

Due to the need for public funding, the markets for renewable energy are where this support is strongest. The European Union has the most advanced markets, though the level of support varies across the member states. Since the EU has taken the lead in the UN climate change negotiations, it has a political need to deliver carbon reductions, and renewable energy is a key part of the equation. Germany is in the lead, with a generous system of support that has made it a large market for wind, solar, and biomass. Spain and Denmark have advanced wind sectors, and most other EU states are establishing wind industries. Solar power is also attracting attention for its huge long-term potential, even though it is still relatively expensive now. Biomass has an important place in official European targets, and it is widely used in Austria, Finland, and Sweden: biomass provides one sixth of Sweden's total primary energy supply.

Contribution of renewable energy sources in the EU, 1995 (MW)

Large-scale hydro	82,500
Small-scale hydro	9,500
Wind	2,500
Geothermal electric	500
Photovoltaic	30

Source: European Union

Forecast contribution of renewable energy sources in the EU, 2010 (MW)

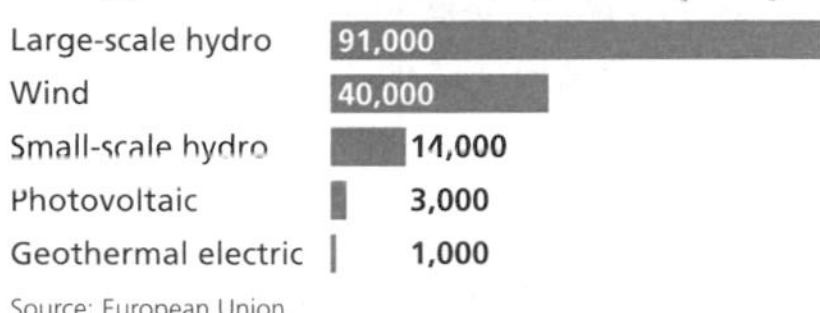

Source: European Union

Share of energy from renewable sources in the EU, 1997 (%)

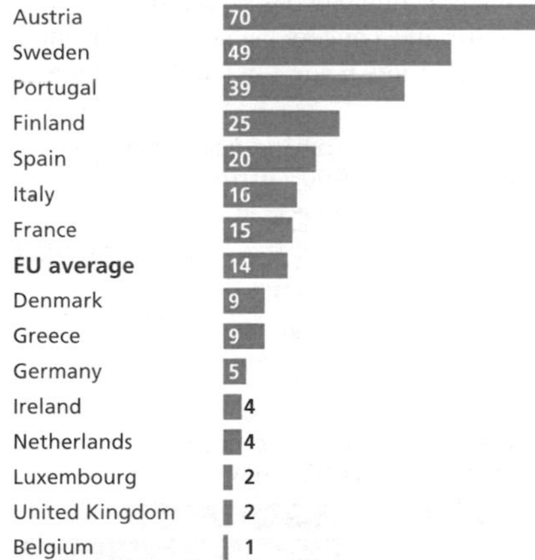

Japan has made solar power a priority, and is the largest market in the world for this technology. It also has a small wind sector, but otherwise Japan is not in the forefront of renewable development. The United States had an early lead in wind and solar, but has let this slip during the 1990s. Renewed concerns over security may change this, but since environmental

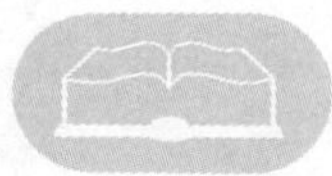

concerns carry less weight in Washington than in Brussels it will probably be left to individual states to support renewables, leading to widespread variations in policy. In the Western United States, the need for new generating capacity is leading to new development, but in general America is likely to lag behind.

There are many opportunities for renewables in Eastern Europe and the CIS as these countries renew their infrastructure, and the Kyoto Joint Implementation mechanism will allow the value of carbon reductions to be captured. Much work remains to be done, however, before these become major markets. Developing countries also have pressing need for energy supplies to fuel their development, and the second Kyoto project mechanism, the Clean Development Mechanism, will again allow emission reductions there to be valued. Renewables, particularly solar power, also have much promise in bringing modern energy services to the two billion people that at present have no electricity supply.

Technology

The leading sectors of wind, solar, and biomass are in varying technological stages, though all will see reductions in cost as techniques are refined and economies of scale production are realized. The feedback loop from experience in deployment to improvements in design and cost reduction is particularly rapid for most renewables.

Wind technology has settled on the "Danish" turbine concept, which is horizontal-axis with three blades, upwind of the tower.

Sales of wind turbine generators by turbine size, 2000 (units)

1MW and above	1,293
500–999 kW	4,087
Less than 500 kW	311
Total	**5,691**

Source: BTM Consult ApS

Sales of wind turbine generators by turbine size, 2000 (MW)

1MW and above	1,779
500–999 kW	2,685
Less than 500 kW	84
Total	**4,548**

Source: BTM Consult ApS

Other models may come to the fore as commercial research bears fruit, but three-bladed machines will dominate for the foreseeable future. Wind turbines have increased in size rapidly, with the average size installed now approaching 1MW. There

Leading wind generators, end-2001 (MW)

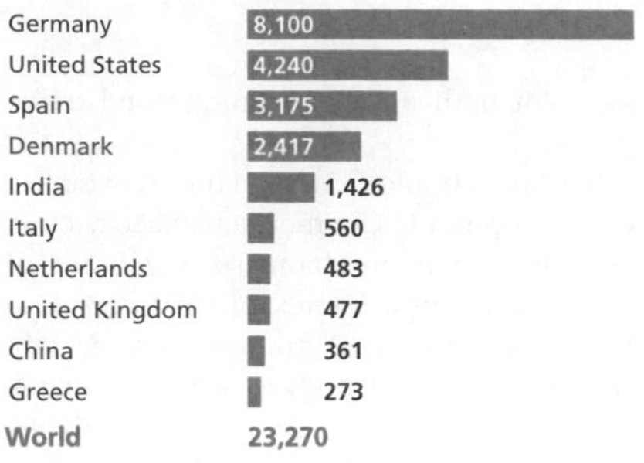

are several models commercially available of 1MW and over; the largest in serial production is 2.5MW. Machines of up to 5MW are planned, which should be available in 2003–04. These giant models will be able to exploit the more consistent winds offshore, offsetting the extra costs of building at sea and without the constraints on size that apply onshore.

For the best sites, and where competing energy supplies are high-cost, wind is now the cheapest power source available. In northern Europe and some other regions, the seasonal peak wind generation period coincides with peak power demand in the winter, and advances in weather forecasting should improve the predictability of wind on a daily or weekly basis. This will limit the need for reserve generation to smooth out the intermittency of wind. Advances in monitoring and control technology are also making the integration of wind into existing grids easier, and if commercial power storage technologies become widespread there will be no technical barrier to significant penetration of wind into the electricity mix. Assuming consistent policy support to underpin the growth of the industry, wind could take as much as 15% of the total world market for new power generation capacity during the 2000s.

Solar electric power—photovoltaic (PV) technology—is a branch of solid-state electronics. Most technologies use silicon, with monocrystalline and polycrystalline forms the most widespread. Most supplies of solar-grade silicon come from unsuitable or surplus production for the wider semiconductor industry. With the recent slowdown in the information technology market, supplies have been plentiful for the growth of PV, but there could be a supply shortfall in 2003–04 if the computer industry recovers, as it is expected to do. Other, "thin-film" solar technologies are being commercialized, which use less silicon, or compounds such as cadmium telluride or gallium arsenide. Such technologies offer

Photovoltaic production by technology (kW)

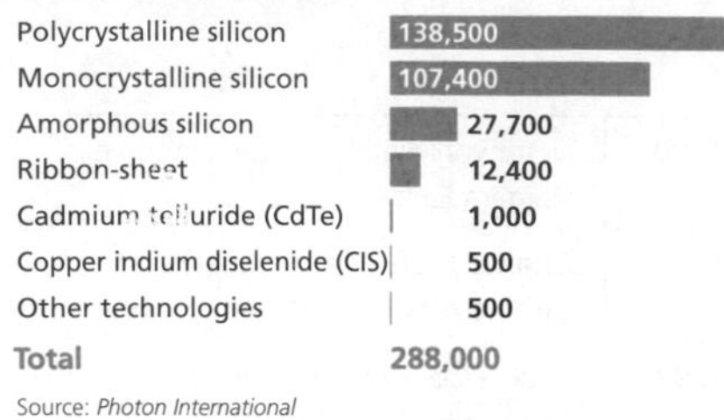

Source: *Photon International*

much lower production costs than crystalline silicon, which offset their lower efficiencies. They also hold out the prospect of integration with construction materials, leading to buildings of similar cost to conventional designs which produce power as a free byproduct. Thin-film has only a small market share at the moment, however.

The cost of power from solar cells is still high—up to $0.25/kWh—but is falling rapidly, and there is plenty of scope for further economies. It is important to note that, in general, solar power is competing with the delivered cost of conventional electricity rather than the wholesale price. This is because it is naturally a distributed resource, with most solar electricity used where it is generated. In sunny regions, where PV is most economic, the peak power demand for air conditioning coincides with the peak output from solar capacity, adding to its value

In contrast to wind and solar, development of the biomass industry is less dependent on high technology. Feasibility depends primarily on securing sufficient fuel supplies at reasonable prices. New technologies are being developed and commercialized using sophisticated techniques, however, which do offer increased efficiency and better economy. Fluidized bed combustion is being transferred from the fossil fuel sector, where it has been proved, as is gasification, which is earlier in the commercialization process. Gasifying biomass fuels allows the use of combined-cycle power production technology, which dominates the market for gas-fired generation with its high efficiency. Pyrolysis techniques, also in the early stages of commercialization, convert biomass feedstocks into high-quality oil which can be used for power production or transport uses, using conventional technologies. Use of biomass for small heating loads like domestic residences is made easier by using wood pellets: sawdust that has been compressed into a consistent fuel. The improved handling qualities of pellets over sawdust or logs allow automatic operation of boilers.

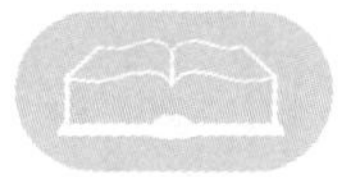

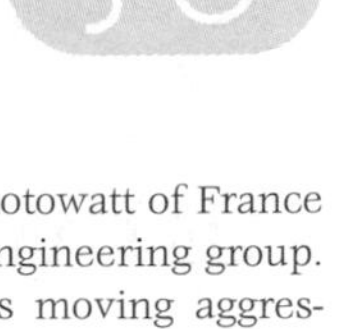
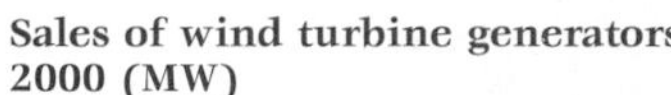

Anaerobic digestion of human and animal wastes produces methane gas, which can be used for power production on site, or perhaps fed into the natural gas grid or used to fuel vehicles. This also helps deal with the problem of disposing of these wastes, which pose an environmental challenge—in fact, the solid residue resulting from the digestion process can be used as a high-nutrient fertilizer. Opportunities to use these and other organic waste streams depend on the integration of energy and waste policies, which is complex. However, landfill sites are becoming more and more difficult to find, increasing the urgency of finding alternatives.

Biomass also poses a challenge for agricultural policy. The early development of modern biomass technologies is based on the use of existing fuel supplies—paper and timber industry wastes, plus forestry and crop residues. There is considerable scope to increase the use of these, but there will also be a need to grow dedicated energy crops. Fast-growing species like willow (in short-rotation coppice), miscanthus, and switchgrass can be planted to fuel power generation, while rape or other oil crops can be used as feedstock to make biodiesel. Corn and sugar are already widely used to make ethanol, particularly in Brazil and the United States. These crops will provide a new income stream for farmers, but they need to be supported through the establishment of the new crop, and must have an assured market for their products. Integration into the European Common Agricultural Policy and U.S. federal farm programs is essential if energy crops are to take off.

Companies

As in the various technologies, there are differences in the corporate structures of the renewable energy industries. For all of them, however, the situation is in flux, with much merger and acquisition activity likely in the coming years, as well as entry by new players.

The wind industry now has annual turnover in excess of $5 billion, and its biggest players are substantial companies by any measure. World leader Vestas of Denmark, with about 20% of the market, had market capitalization at the end of 2001 of over $3 billion, and posted a pre-tax profit of over $100 million in 2000. It is now going head-to-head with its former partner Gamesa. The two dissolved a seven-year technology transfer alliance at the end of 2001, and the Spanish company is now branching out from its home market to consolidate its position. NEG Micon, the result of a merger between Danish companies Nordtank and Micon in 1998, is still a major player despite a serious financial crisis in 1999. German Enercon is by far the leader in its home market, and its compatriot Nordex is gaining market share with its range of MW-class turbines. Outside of Europe and the United States, Suzlon of India is the only manufacturer of note, though all the major players are looking to set up businesses in markets around the world.

Sales of wind turbine generators, 2000 (MW)

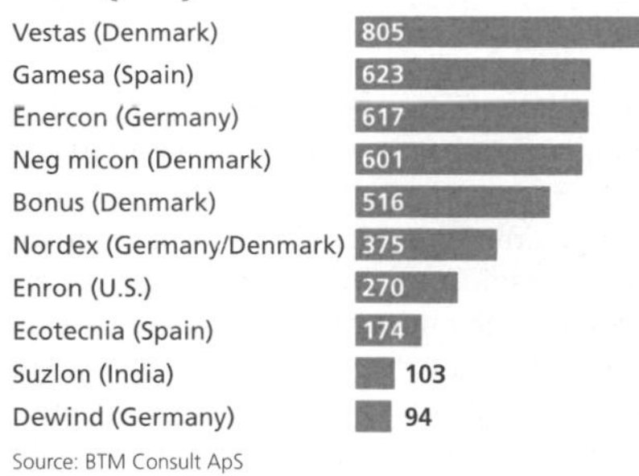

Source: BTM Consult ApS

On the project development side, a number of dedicated renewable companies are emerging, such as EHN in Spain (due to be integrated with the renewable activities of utility Iberdrola), SeaWest in the United States, and Umweltkontor, Plambeck, Energiekontor and P&T Technology in Germany. Subsidiaries of large energy companies are setting up in the wind sector, with Erga (the green power unit of Enel of Italy), Nuon (in the Netherlands), and Shell as notable examples.

The situation in the solar industry is quite different from wind, where independent manufacturers dominate. Most PV production capacity is owned by large conglomerates, with Sharp and Kyocera of Japan in first and second positions in the market due to the strength of their home market. Of the top nine solar companies, only AstroPower is wholly independent: Photowatt of France is owned by a Canadian engineering group. SolarWorld of Germany is moving aggressively, however, in its strategy to become the first integrated solar company, from raw silicon to complete systems, and is sure to figure strongly in the years ahead.

Production of solar generators, 2000 (MW)

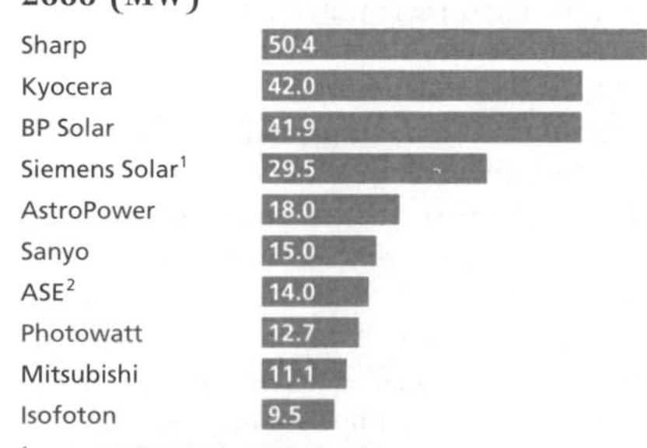

[1] merged with Shell Solar in February 2001
[2] renamed RWE Solar in September 2001
Source: *Photon International*

Most biomass equipment manufacturers are established power engineering companies who are transferring their skills from the fossil fuel market or from advanced biomass markets like Finland and Sweden, for example Alstom and Foster Wheeler. The new technologies described above are generally being developed by start-up companies such as DynaMotive of Canada and Ensyn of the United States in pyrolysis, and Farmatic of Germany in biogas. In ethanol there are some big names involved, such as agricultural giant Archer Daniels Midland in the United States and engineering company Abengoa in Spain.

Impact of the Internet

While renewable resources are among the earliest that were used for energy supply, the means now used to exploit them are high-tech. Remote monitoring and control through the Internet allows easier integration of distributed, small, intermittent renewables into power grids.

Despite this, renewable energy industries are old-fashioned in that they are about making things from mostly standard materials. However, they are manufacturing with Internet-like levels of growth. This should attract the venture-capital money that has been looking for a new home after the bursting of the dot-com bubble. What is required to sustain this level of growth is a consistent policy foundation that signals that entrepreneurs can make money in the sector.

For More Information

Directories:

World Directory of Renewable Energy Suppliers and Services. James & James: **www.jxj.com/yearbook/index.html**

World Market Update 2000, BTM Consult: **www.btm.dk/wmu2000/wmu.htm**

Web Sites:

American Wind Energy Association: **www.awea.org**

U.S. Department of Energy, Energy Efficiency, and Renewable Energy Network: **www.eren.doe.gov**

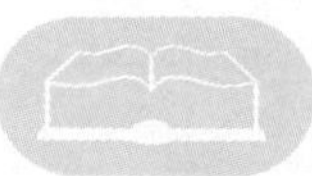

Retailing

1900–1929	Rapid growth of chain specialty stores.
1930s	Rapid growth of supermarket chains.
	Emergence of gasoline stations.
	First modern shopping center opens.
1940s	Post-war retail surge.
1950s	Growth of self-service drug stores.
	First credit cards issued.
	World's first enclosed shopping mall.
1960s	First hypermarket opens.
	First retail barcode scanner.
1970s	DIY home improvement centers.
1980s	Retail merger & acquisition era begins.
	Private label/vertical integration.
	TV home shopping.
1990s	Globalization of retailing.
	E-retailing era begins.
	Amazon sells its first book (1995).
2000s	Euro introduced in Europe, creating single market.

The era of modern department store retailing (single store with multiple departments) and chain store retailing (single concept with multiple units) had its beginnings in the latter half of the 19th century. The rapid growth and initial success of these concepts was fueled by the Industrial Revolution and the development of the railroad, which made possible the mass production of goods and the wide distribution of merchandise. Advertising and promotions, charge accounts, and formal return policies were introduced.

Retailing has traditionally been local in nature because it has always required a knowledge of the needs and habits of specific groups of consumers. This is difficult on a regional or global scale, as evidenced by the failure of many who have tried it. Since the early 1990s, however, a significant increase in world trade, the introduction of market economics to previously planned economies, rising standards of living around the world, the globalization of popular culture, and new developments in technology have made retailing on a global scale far more feasible.

Another factor driving industry consolidation and globalization is that some leading retailers are approaching saturation in their home markets. In many mature markets, such as the United States and Western Europe, there is already too much retail space, leaving no room for marginal performers. The elimination of weaker players has resulted in the concentration of retail sales among fewer, but larger, more efficient, and better managed companies. To continue growing, many of these companies have begun to aggressively pursue global expansion opportunities. Retail consolidation has begun to shift from home country consolidation to regional and even global consolidation.

Retailers are not only getting bigger, they are acting bigger, centralizing their operations and buying organizations to achieve economies of scale and transfer of knowledge across the globe. This has raised the level of competition still further, and will force out all but the strongest companies. Many retailers now have sufficient volume to commission manufacturing, which has shifted the power in the distribution channel from the manufacturer to the retailer. As product sourcing has become more centrally coordinated rather than being left to individual national subsidiaries, retailers have become more aware of international differences in prices, terms, and conditions.

Companies

Wal-Mart topped the list of the world's largest retailers in 2000 (as measured in U.S. dollars) in impressive fashion. Wal-Mart generated nearly three times the sales volume of France's Carrefour, the second-largest retailer in the world.

Since the late 1980s, retailers with global operations have steadily accounted for a larger share of sales throughout the world. Among the top 100 retailers worldwide, those with operations outside their geographic region accounted for 52% of top 100 sales in 2000, up significantly from 45% in 1996 and just 29% in 1986.

Wal-Mart's growth aspirations have been slowly shifting from U.S. to foreign markets during the past several years. To date, the world's largest retailer has experienced success in Canada, Mexico, and the United Kingdom, though it failed to generate acceptable financial results in Germany. Regardless, Wal-Mart's acquisitions in Europe—most notably Asda in the U.K. in late 1999—signaled a momentous occasion

Largest retailers by sales, 2000 ($ billion)

Wal-Mart Stores, U.S.	180.8
Carrefour, France	61.0
The Kroger Company, U.S.	49.0
The Home Depot, U.S.	45.7
Royal Ahold, Netherlands	45.7
Metro, Germany	44.2
Kmart Corporation, U.S.	37.0
Sears, Roebuck & Co., U.S.	36.8
Albertson's, U.S.	36.8
Target Corporation, U.S.	36.4

Fastest compound annual growth, 1996–2000 (%)

Royal Ahold	31
Carrefour	29
Albertson's	28
The Home Depot	24
The Kroger Company	18
Wal-Mart Stores	16
Metro	10
Target Corporation	9
Kmart Corporation	4
Sears, Roebuck & Co.	2

Most stores, 2000

Carrefour (hypermarkets)	8,130
Royal Ahold (supermarkets)	8,112
Wal-Mart Stores (discount stores)	4,189
The Kroger Company (supermarkets)	3,541
Sears, Roebuck & Co. (department stores)	3,021
Albertson's (supermarkets)	2,512
Metro (diversified)	2,169
Kmart Corporation (discount stores)	2,105
Target Corporation (discount stores)	1,307
The Home Depot (hardlines specialty stores)	1,134

Market capitalization at end 2001 ($ billion)

Wal-Mart Stores	257
The Home Depot	119
Carrefour Group*	46
Target Corporation	37
Royal Ahold	24
The Kroger Company	17
Sears, Roebuck & Co.	15
Albertson's	13
Metro	11
Kmart Corporation	3

* market capitalization is as of year-end 2000

for the global retail marketplace. Because of its expanding presence, retailers around the world have focused on improving the efficiency of their operations. In addition, a recent increase in worldwide merger and acquisition activity has been partially in response to Wal-Mart's ambitious global expansion plans.

In spite of the overall trend toward globalization, some single-country retailers may never expand beyond their geographic borders. In particular, due to the vastness of the U.S. economy, U.S. retailers with operations solely in their home country will be much less likely than their international counterparts to leave home. In addition, there are numerous challenges related to entering a new country. These include cultural and language differences, adverse government regulations, reporting practices (e.g. customs), and supply chain complexities.

By line of retail trade, supermarket retailers account for the largest share of companies and sales among the top 100 retailers worldwide, but their share of sales has declined in recent years, largely because of competition from mass-channel retailers. Diversified retailers (so classified because they do not derive a majority of sales from any single line of trade) and department stores also account for a smaller share of top 100 sales today. Many historically diversified retailers have sold off non-core and often struggling retail businesses in order to concentrate their resources on core areas of expertise and to realize greater operational synergies. In 1996, 16 of the world's largest retailers were classified as diversified companies, compared to only ten in 2000.

In contrast, the biggest gainers are the mass retailers, including hypermarkets, supercenters, discount department stores, and warehouse clubs (largely due to Wal-Mart), hardlines specialty stores, and drug stores. The ascent of hardlines specialty stores corresponds with the rollout of the "category killer" concept within several product categories, including books, consumer electronics, home furnishings, home improvement, office supplies, and toys. Category killers are retailers that offer a deep selection within a broad product category housed in big-box locations. Demographic trends are partly responsible for the rising drug store wave: the global population is aging, naturally increasing the demand for the products and services offered by drug stores.

MARKETS

Retailing is big business. Worldwide retail sales in 2000 are estimated at $7.2 trillion. In the developed countries, the industry is largely mature and growth is slowing. For example, in the United States, the largest retail market, sales grew at an average annual rate of 5.1% in the 1990s, down from 6.7% in the 1980s and 9.9% in the 1970s. Growth is projected to slow to just 2.6% per year during 2001–05. Above average rates of growth in any retail sector or by any retail company will, of necessity, come at the expense of another competitor or competitive format.

Total retail sales, 2000 ($ billion),
with % of GDP in parens

Country	$ billion
United States (23)	2,251.0
Japan (23)	1,089.0
Germany (24)	446.6
China (36)	392.0
United Kingdom (22)	313.1
France (22)	286.2
Italy (24)	257.6
India (47)	221.8
Canada (18)	131.0
Mexico (17)	95.2

Sources: U.S. Census Bureau, IMF, Euromonitor, Retail Forward

On the other hand, in the emerging economies, the middle class is expanding rapidly, creating new and growing retail demand. Despite ephemeral business cycle fluctuations, the long-term outlook is for relatively strong economic and consumer spending growth in these countries. However, there are restrictions on expansion by foreign retailers into some of these countries. Thus the process of retail globalization will be a gradual one, and may never reach the level already achieved by consumer product manufacturers.

Around the globe, economic and political developments are forcing retailers to deal with a wide range of challenging situations. The economic slowdown in the United States has spread throughout much of the rest of the world.

Meanwhile, there is the constant risk of financial deterioration and the subsequent social unrest in emerging countries, particularly in Southeast Asia and Latin America. Many countries, such as Poland, Thailand, and Argentina, have enacted or considered legislation that restricts the development of large stores and the type of foreign investment, hindering expansion plans for some retailers. These limitations are often implemented to protect small, local business owners, regardless of the potential benefits local consumers may experience when foreign operators become active, such as lower prices and greater selection.

EMPLOYMENT

In the United States, the retail sector was the second-largest employer in 2000 among the broad employment sectors, accounting for nearly 18% of total employment. That compares with a 31% share for the overall services sector. The government and manufacturing sectors were next on the list, registering shares of 16% and 14%, respectively.

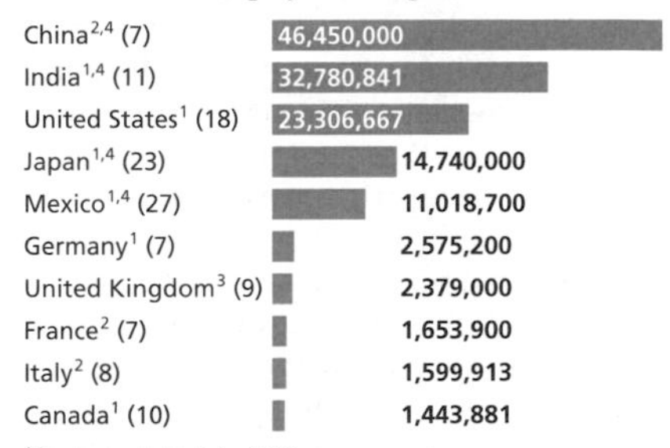

[1] Employment data is for 2000
[2] Employment data is for 1998
[3] Employment data is for mid 1990s
[4] Employment data includes employment in wholesale trade
Sources: U.S. Bureau of Labor Statistics, Retail Intelligence, Euromonitor, Japan Statistics Bureau, Haver Analytics, China National Bureau of Statistics, Retail Forward

Largest employers (thousands),
with sales per employee in parens ($ thousand)

Wal-Mart Stores, U.S. (145)	1,244
Royal Ahold, Netherlands (121)	377
Carrefour, France (185)	330
Sears, Roebuck & Co., U.S. (114)	323
The Kroger Company, U.S. (157)	312
Target Corporation, U.S. (143)	254
Kmart Corporation, U.S. (147)	252
Albertson's, U.S. (156)	235
The Home Depot, U.S. (201)	227
Metro, Germany (196)	225

Within the United States retail sector, eating and drinking places garnered the largest employment share, representing 35% of all retail employees. Food stores, such as grocery stores and supermarkets, had the next highest share—15%. The general merchandise channel, which includes department stores, supercenters, warehouse clubs, and dollar stores, was next with a 12% share. Among the other key retail channels, the smallest share belonged to building materials and garden supply stores (4%).

Compared with other large retail markets, such as Germany, the United Kingdom, and Canada, the United States has typically had a significantly higher share of employment in the retail sector. Some major retail markets, such as Japan and Mexico, combine their wholesale and retail employment estimates and are therefore not strictly comparable with countries that estimate retail employment separately.

New Concepts and Strategies

The types of formats and strategies that retailers operate have been changing rapidly in many parts of the world. These changes are driven by technology, changes in consumer shopping patterns, and the success of various innovations. Technology is making larger, more complex organizations possible. The growth of a professional female labor force is reducing the amount of time spent shopping and the frequency of shopping. This necessitates larger destination-oriented stores that can satisfy more needs in one shopping trip. Consequently, large hypermarkets that offer one-stop convenience for multiple goods have become a dominant global format. Moreover, value consciousness on the part of consumers has led to the rise of low-price formats at the expense of traditional high-cost formats such as department stores.

As the retailing industry in mature markets has become saturated, and excess capacity has emerged, retailers have attempted to differentiate themselves from one another through such strategies as a greater focus on "own-brand" products and developing the retail store itself as a brand. They are adopting a stronger value orientation as consumers everywhere become more concerned with getting more for their money. Multi-channel retailing through stores, catalogs, and the Internet is emerging as the dominant business model, providing consumers with greater access to stores, brands, products, and information.

Competition, once confined to other retailers offering similar goods in a similar format and operating under a similar economic model, is now being replaced with convergence on the part of different retail formats. Convergence is occurring as retailers pursue a strategy of broadening their offer of goods and services to meet more of the diverse needs of individual shoppers (e.g. financial services at supermarkets and petrol at hypermarkets), or to create solutions to a shopper's specific problem (e.g. installation, home maintenance services, tool rental, home improvement loans as part of home improvement center offering). This one-stop shopping phenomenon will continue as the retail industry becomes more consolidated and competitive giants collide in their efforts to sustain growth.

Technology

The retail industry has become increasingly reliant on information technology for business management. The focus of technology has changed from automation in the 1960s to integration to facilitate e-business today. Much of the IT investment of the past five years went toward internal systems integration. The next phase is expected to involve the integration of supply chain systems—linking retailers and their trading partners, largely via business-to-business and e-market initiatives—and multi-channel integration—connecting store, catalog, and online systems.

Store systems continue to evolve as retailers embrace more open hardware and software, new operating systems, Web access, and wireless capabilities. Advanced point-of-sale functionality is taking on more importance as retailers begin to look for new ways to drive customer traffic and enhance the shopping experience.

In the supply chain arena, the Internet is replacing costly proprietary systems with a more accessible platform that enables greater collaboration between a wide range of trading partners. Emerging e-markets and private e-hubs will play a much more prominent role in the future.

For the most part, retailers are eschewing ERP (enterprise resource planning) systems, which were chosen by many manufacturers, in favor of packaged software for enterprise applications. Data warehouse and data dissemination are the top IT investment priorities, being driven largely by the non-integrated nature of the systems most retailers currently have in place. Other critical initiatives include CRM (customer relationship management) and multi-channel integration. All of these investments are ultimately designed to enhance the ability of retailers to differentiate themselves from competitors, engender greater loyalty on the part of their customers, and reduce the cost of operations by aligning inventory management with customer needs.

Retailers spent about 1.7% of revenue on information technology in 2001. Although this pales in comparison to the average IT budget of most other industries (e.g. 6.6% for financial services, 5.7% for telecommunications, 4.3% for healthcare), retailers' understanding of the strategic value of IT to business performance appears to be growing steadily.

Impact of the Internet

The next economy will be populated by businesses that are neither "old economy" nor "new economy," but a synthesis of both. These businesses will take the technology of the new economy—the scope and functionality afforded by a networked environment—and apply it to some proven opportunities of the old, including a renewed focus on customers, supply chain, people, and competitors, to generate sales and profits. The next economy will be driven by innovation. The focus of this innovation will be not so much in the creation of new technologies as in the discovery of new applications for existing technologies. Upgrading retail technology will be an essential step.

For More Information

Directories:

European Retail Handbook:
www.mintel.com
Retail Trade International:
www.euromonitor.com

Magazines and Journals:

Chain Store Age:
www.chainstoreage.com
European Retail Analyst:
www.conciseb2b.com
Internet Retailer:
www.internetretailer.com

Web Sites:

Direct Marketing Association:
www.the-dma.org
Direct Selling Association:
www.dsa.org
Electronic Retailing Association:
www.electronicretailing.org
Food Distributors International:
www.fdi.org
Home Improvement Research Institute:
www.hiri.org
International Association of Department Stores: **www.iads.org**
International Council of Shopping Centers: **www.icsc.org**
National Grocers Association:
www.nationalgrocers.org
Private Label Manufacturers Association: **www.plma.com**

STEEL

1500B.C.	The Hittites smelted iron ore with charcoal to make iron.
A.D.1709	Abraham Darby, a U.K. iron maker, substituted coke for charcoal and added limestone to make iron on a large scale in blast furnaces.
1855	Henry Bessemer (United Kingdom) and William Kelly (United States) independently develop processes to make steel by blowing air through molten iron.
1867	Open-hearth furnace invented, in which flames from burning coke burn away excess carbon.
1999	U.S. Steel formed in Pittsburgh by Andrew Carnegie.
1960s	Mini-mills introduced.
1988	British Steel privatized.
1992	Wangyang steel plant, biggest steel production site in the world, opened in South Korea.

Steel is one of the world's most widely used materials, vital to many industries including cars, domestic appliances, construction, packaging, and general engineering. World consumption in 2001 was about 858 million tons, compared to about 1 billion tons for concrete, 125 million tons for plastics, 22,000 tons for aluminum, and a roughly similar amount for all other metals.

Steel is made in a process that has changed little in its underlying principles for 100 years; as a result, many companies around the world have entered the steel business. Prices have been pushed down to extremely low levels: many types of steel are sold at prices that have barely changed in the past 20 years. In 2001 basic steel (called hot-rolled band) sold in many markets for $200-$250 a ton, compared to about $300 a ton in 1981. Not surprisingly, profitability in the industry is poor.

There are hundreds of types of steel. Many, such as special coated or treated steels, sell for considerably more than the price of basic hot-rolled band. As a result, average revenues per ton for the biggest steel makers came to $515 in 2000. However, many steel makers have found it hard to push up prices, even for the relatively high-value types of steel. In 1990 the average price per ton of steel shipped worldwide by the most important steel makers was $616, significantly above the 2000 figure.

Gross output for the whole of the steel industry worldwide in 2000 is estimated at $300 billion. Net output (steel industry value added) for the same year is estimated at $100 billion. This means the steel industry accounts for roughly 0.3% of world GDP.

The ease of access to steel-making technology explains why the developing world has gradually become a much more important producer of steel. Today, steel is made in 80 countries.

In 1970 Asia produced just 20% of the world's steel, but today the figure is around 40%. China is the single most important country for steel production, accounting for about 15% of total output. Even so, the EU as a whole is the most important region in the world for steel production, making some 160 million tons a year.

Asia and other developing regions are today easily the fastest-growing areas in terms of steel consumption, as befitting steel's use in vital infrastructure (such as bridges and steel framed buildings) and machinery-based products. Total steel output today is about four times the figure in 1950, underlining the importance of the industry to the world economy over the past half century.

The United Kingdom was responsible for several crucial early innovations in steel making. The most important was the Bessemer converter, developed in 1855, which made the mass production of steel possible. The converter takes liquid pig iron produced in a blast furnace (from iron ore and a reducing agent such as coke) and adds hot air, so aiding the conversion to steel. (Ordinary steel is iron plus roughly 2% carbon.) Other key techniques included the Siemens-Martin open-hearth process (devised in the United Kingdom in 1867) which increased productivity, and the Gilchrist-Thomas process which made it possible to use new ores in steel manufacturing.

The United Kingdom was initially well ahead of other countries, in 1850 producing about 50,000 tons of steel out of world production of 70,000 tons. Other nations, however, quickly caught up, and then overtook, the United Kingdom. In 1880, the United Kingdom made 3.9 million tons of steel and Germany 1.9 million tons. The United States had by then inched ahead with 4 million tons. By 1910, Germany also had overtaken the United Kingdom's total: in that year Germany produced 18 million tons, to the United Kingdom's 9 million tons and the United States' 34 million tons.

After the Bessemer process, the single biggest breakthrough in steel production was the advent of the mini-mill from the 1960s onwards. Mini-mills use an electric arc furnace (EAF) to melt scrap steel and re-use the metal. The process means that steel makers no longer have to start production using virgin iron ore. Because their energy costs are lower and raw materials are relatively cheap, mini-mills have the potential to cut the costs of steel production substantially. Some 35% of world steel production is derived from mini-mills, and most pundits believe the figure will grow over the next few years.

Perhaps because of the importance of steel making to basic industry, governments around the world commonly viewed the sector as strategically important. As recently as 1985, about two-thirds of the world steel industry was controlled by government corporations—an astonishingly high figure. In Europe the figure was 55%. Since then there has been widespread privatization of state-owned steel industries. One of the first big privatizations was that of British Steel, which became a stock-market-quoted company in 1988, and the process was continued throughout the 1990s. By 1999, 72% of the world steel industry was controlled by private companies; the figure for Europe was 92%.

However, the fact that many large steel producers today have their origins in government-owned entities continues to have an impact on the industry; many steel plants owe their existence to generous capital payments by governments in the days of state ownership, and probably would not have been financed had the operators been in the private sector from the outset.

COMPANIES

Steel is a highly fragmented industry, with hundreds of producers scattered around the world. The biggest producer, Arcelor, which is due to start operation in early 2002, will account for just 6% of world production with an output of some 45 million tons a year. Arcelor's formation was announced in early 2001, and results from the merger of three of Europe's biggest steel producers: Usinor (France), Arbed (Luxembourg), and Aceralia (Spain).

Top steelmakers by production, 2000 (million tons)

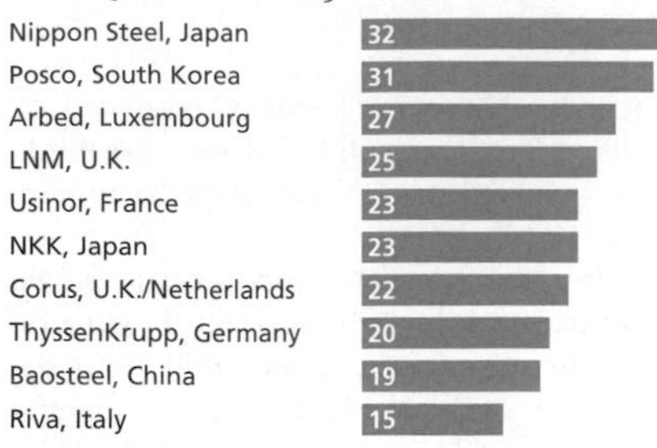

Sources: World Steel Dynamics, U.S.; *Metal Bulletin*, U.K.; *Financial Time*

Top steelmakers by revenues per ton, 2000 ($)

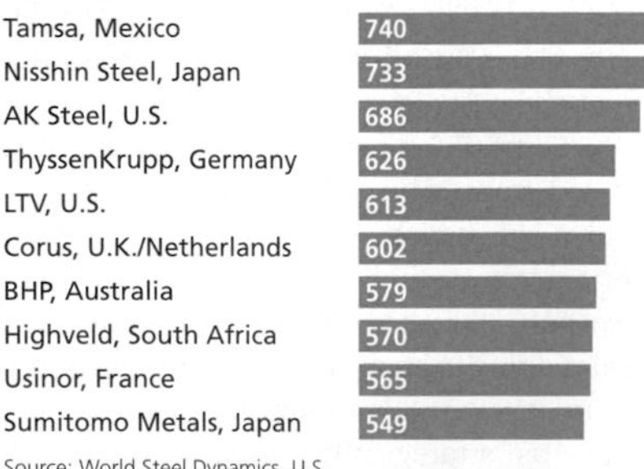

Source: World Steel Dynamics, U.S.

Top steelmakers by operating profit per ton shipped, 2000 ($)

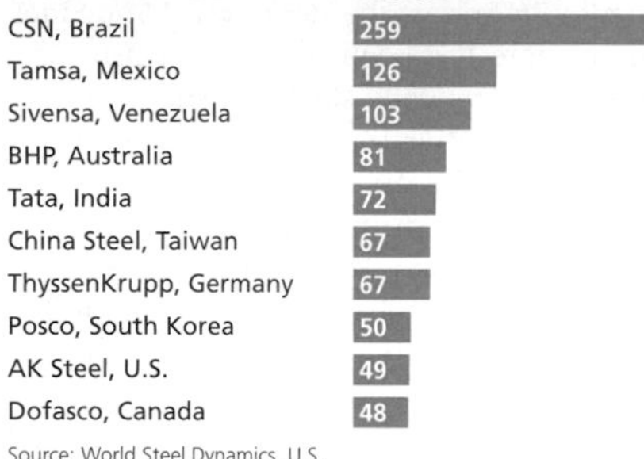

Source: World Steel Dynamics, U.S.

The lack of consolidation among steel companies generally is particularly evident in the United States, which is, after China, the second most important country for steel consumption. The United States is also the third-biggest steel producing nation, after China and Japan. Despite these factors there is no U.S. steel maker among the world's top 10 steel companies. The biggest U.S. steel groups—U.S. Steel and Nucor—both have annual production of about 10 million tons, roughly half as much as ThyssenKrupp and Corus, two large European steel makers.

Europe, in contrast to the United States, has seen relatively swift moves to consolidation in the steel sector. Both ThyssenKrupp and Corus were formed from mergers announced over the past five years. In Europe the five largest steel makers controlled just 32% of production in 1985; by 1999, however, this figure had increased to 53% as a result of consolidation in the industry linked to mergers. It will increase considerably in the future, partly due to the formation of Arcelor.

Prior to the formation of Arcelor, the two biggest steel makers in the world by tonnage are Nippon Steel and Posco (Pohang Iron and Steel). Arcelor is expected to have annual sales of some 30 billion, with more than 100,000 employees. Assuming its annual production is about 45 million tons, the average selling price per ton produced for this company will be about $600, towards the higher end of the spectrum for prices. As stated in the overview section, the price per ton of basic steel has remained very low, at between $200 and $300—about the same as jam or bottled water.

Profits in the industry generally follow prices. It follows that companies wanting to maximize profits will need to aim their marketing and production strategies at grades of steel which command higher prices (for example, special coatings for the automotive and white goods industries). The higher a company's average price per ton, the greater the company's success in applying this strategy. In 2000, Tamsa (Mexico) and Nisshin Steel (Japan) gained the highest revenues per ton in the steel industry—more than $800. In 2000 the best company in terms of operating profit per ton shipped was CSN (Brazil).

Profitability in the worldwide steel industry in 2000 is estimated, pre-tax, at about $22.6 per ton shipped (before extraordinary items). This is a very low figure, given the average price of steel, and works out at about 4% of sales. The best recent year for steel industry profits was 1995, when the comparable figure was $47.3 per ton shipped; in 1990 the figure was $33, while in 1980 and 1985 the industry recorded losses on an average worldwide basis. Since the steel industry is highly cyclical, with prices following the flow of world economic fortunes, profits tend to fluctuate according to the state of the global economy.

From a profits point of view, return on capital employed looks even worse when judged by the standards of many other industries. In 2000, the only large steel makers making a return on capital employed of more than 10% were CSN of Brazil, China Steel (Taiwan), Iscor, Nucor (United States), and Posco of South Korea.

Markets

Steel is a highly traded commodity: about 40% of steel is consumed in industries outside the country where it is made. In 2000, the biggest trade surplus on steel of any single region was that of the former Soviet Union, which had an excess of exports over imports of more than 50 million tons. Japan had a surplus of 22 million tons, Brazil of nearly 10 million tons, the European Union of 3 million tons, and South Korea of 1 million tons. The biggest trade deficits for steel are in the United States (28 million tons) and China (21 million tons).

Recent steel industry mergers/acquisitions	
1997	Krupp Hoesch and Thyssen Stahl merged to form ThyssenKrupp
1998	Usinor (France) bought Cockerill Sambre (Belgium)
1999	British Steel and Hoogovens (Netherlands) merged to form Corus
2000	AvestaPolarit formed as a result of a merger between Avesta Sheffield (United Kingdom/ Sweden) and stainless steel division of Outokumpu (Finaldn). The company becomes the second biggest in the world in stainless steel
2001	Usinor (France), Arbed (Luxembourg) and Aceralia (Spain) agree merger to form Arcelor (headquartered in Luxembourg, and due to become operational in 2002)
2001	NKK and Kawasaki Steel, two of Japan's biggest steel makers, agree a merger, to be effective by 2002–03

Crude steel production, 2000 (million tons)

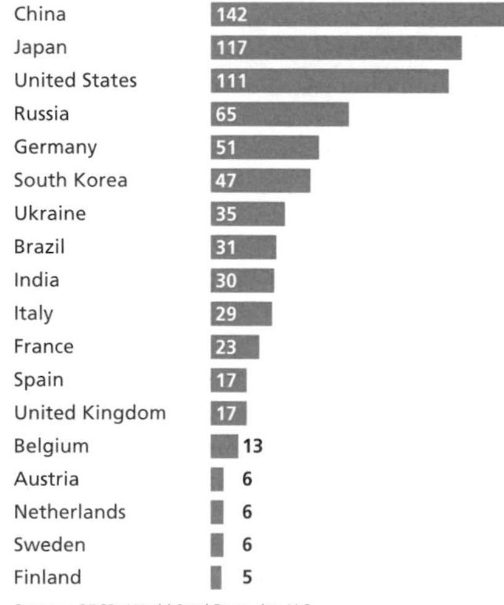

Sources: OECD; World Steel Dynamics, U.S.

Countries with big steel exports such as the Ukraine and Russia are often helped by lower cost structures compared with their counterparts in the United States and Europe. This has given rise to efforts by steel manufacturers, particularly in the

United States, to stop exports of steel into their countries from certain regions as a way of protecting jobs in domestic steel production sites.

About half of world steel production is flat products (such as panels for car bodies or washing machines) and the rest long products (such as bars used in the building industry, or wire rods used in anything from coat hangers to paper clips).

Technology

Steel is an "old technology" industry, in that the essential process for steel—the blast furnace—dates back to the 19th century. However, the advent of the mini-mill (electric arc furnace) in the 1960s has changed the economics of much of the industry. It is estimated that, using EAF methods, a ton of steel can be produced at 80–90% of the cost compared to the blast furnace method.

Other relatively new processes in the industry include:

- Thin-slab casting. Steel sheet is normally made by a two-stage process: first the steel is rolled when hot into slabs, and after cooling it is rolled again to form thinner sections. New processes make it possible to roll thin steel sections (of less than 1 mm) in a single process. In the past 20 years companies such as ThyssenKrupp (Germany), Nucor (United States), BHP (Australia), and Finarvedi (Italy) have used this process to reduce the costs of making thin sections of steel. The technique promises to become more important over the next 20 years.
- Direct-reduced iron. This process uses natural gas rather than coke as a reducing agent in the blast furnace. Costs can be brought down, but the technology is more complicated.
- Laser welding. Laser welding of steel pieces to make thicker sections from two thinner sheets promises to be important in industries such as cars.

Employment

Steel industry productivity has increased enormously in the past 30 years. In the United Kingdom alone, the steel industry employed 300,000 in 1970, but by 2001, this number had fallen below 50,000. The vast workforce of 1970 produced 26 million tons of steel, but the 2000 output of 15 million tons was higher in proportion to the size of the workforce. In 2000, according to industry estimates, average output of steel per person in the U.K. steel industry was 587 tons, more than twice the 213 tons in 1974. For plants in the leading industrialized nations, the increase in output per person was even greater; over the same period, the figure for the EU went up to 454 tons from 172 tons, and for the United States it rose to 630 tons from 208 tons.

Most productive companies, 2000 (tons per employee)

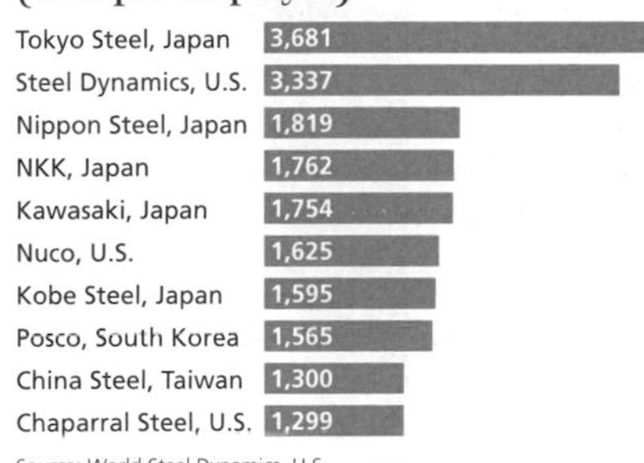

Source: World Steel Dynamics, U.S.

Most productive companies, 2000 ($ thousand added per employee)

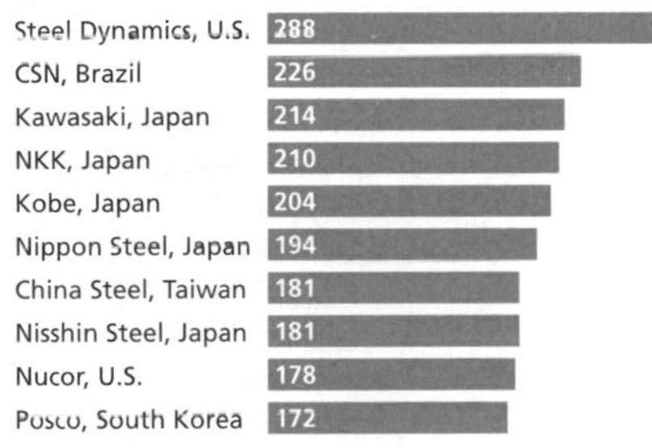

Source: World Steel Dynamics, U.S.

In 2000 the most productive workers were at Tokyo Steel, a leading Japanese mini-mill producer. Here output per person employed in 2000 was 3,340 tons. Another measure of productivity is value added per person: on this basis the most productive company is CSN of Brazil.

Accurate figures for world steel industry employment are not available. It appears that there were about 1.5 million people working in the steel industry worldwide in 2000, considerably fewer than 40 years earlier. Arcelor, the biggest steel company in the world, has some 100,000 employees, while other large employers include Corus, which employs about 50,000, and ThyssenKrupp, which employs a similar number in the steel part of its business.

New Products

Stainless steel is one relatively new product that has become more important in the past 20 years. Stainless steel contains trace amounts of nickel and other materials. It is used in a variety of consumer and industrial areas, such as cutlery, medical instruments, and furniture. Demand is increasing at about 5% a year, with particularly strong growth prospects in Southeast Asia and Latin America.

While the stainless steel industry produces only about 20 million tons a year—2.5% of total steel industry output—selling prices of stainless steel are 5–10 times higher than those of conventional carbon steel.

New flat steel products for the auto industry are also increasingly important. They provide extra strength and durability, and are based on adding small quantities of other metals to steel.

New types of steel plate and beams are also becoming important, increasingly in the United States, for steel-framed housing. Another development is steel roof tiles, which are becoming gradually more widespread in the United States.

Impact of the Internet

E-commerce involving steel companies promises to reduce the costs of trading steel from producer to customer. A number of steel-trading Web sites are in operation, but in early 2002 it appears that this area of development still has some way to go before making an impact on the industry.

For More Information

Web Sites:

American Iron and Steel Institute: **www.steel.org**

Eurofer, Brussels: **www.eurofer.org**

International Iron and Steel Institute, Brussels: **www.worldsteel.org**

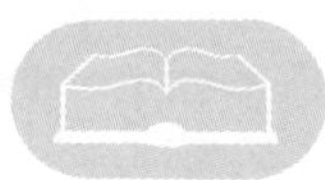

TELECOMMUNICATIONS

1845	Morse establishes Magnetic Telegraph Company in United States; William Cooke sets up Electrical Telegraph Company in United Kingdom.
1861	Western Union Telegraph Company opens first U.S. coast-to-coast service.
1866	First transatlantic telegraph cable.
1876	Alexander Graham Bell patents telephone.
1896	Guglielmo Marconi demonstrates radio.
1901	Marconi transmits first radio signals across the Atlantic.
1927	Transatlantic radio telephone service began.
1956	Transatlantic telephone cable carries up to 36 simultaneous calls.
1962	Telecommunications satellite carries first international phone calls.
1969	Precursor of the Internet set up by U.S. Department of Defense.
1972	First e-mail system (using @ sign).
1973–1976	Robert Metcalfe invents the Ethernet local area network.
1977	Motorola starts experimental cellular mobile phone system in United States.
1984	British Telecom privatized.
1989	Tim Berners-Lee proposes use of Internet hyperlinks; invents name "World Wide Web" the following year.
1990	First GSM (digital) cellular phone networks set up in Europe.
1993	First GSM text message sent.
1994	Netscape formed to develop commercial web browser.
2001	Number of cellular phone subscribers worldwide reaches 800 million, and the rapid convergence of telecoms and computing technologies triggers an explosion of innovation and opportunity.

Top telecoms operators by market capitalization in January 2001 ($ billion)

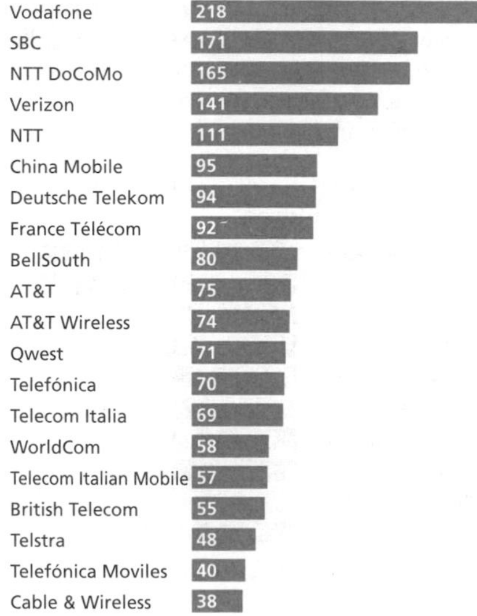

Source: UBS Warburg, London

Top telecoms equipment makers by telecoms sales, 2000 ($ billion)

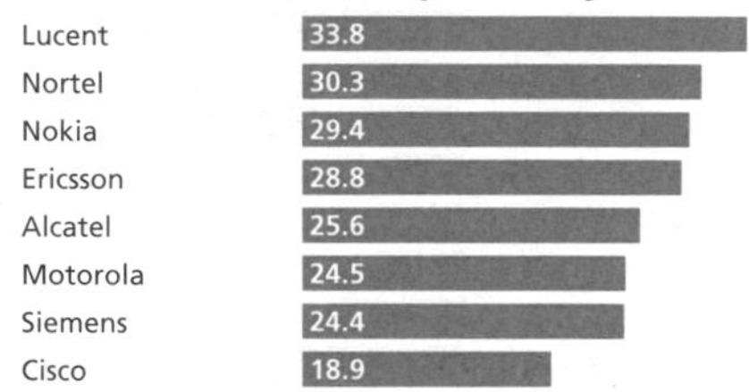

Source: Idate, Montpellier, France

COMPANIES

Commercial development of telecommunications began almost as soon as the systems were invented in the United Kingdom and the United States. The timing was fortuitous: it was only a few years since the first steam railways had speeded up land transport.

Commercial companies were set up to offer telegraph services to the public and to the business community. In the United States, Western Union quickly built a near-monopoly, while in Europe and elsewhere companies were largely taken under the control of government-owned post offices—a situation that persisted in the telecommunications industry until the 1980s.

The telephone business followed a similar pattern. The inventor, Alexander Graham Bell, commercialized the invention, and his company became AT&T, with a near-monopoly in the United States until 1984. Operators were largely government-controlled in the rest of the world until the United Kingdom began the privatization trend when, also in 1984, it sold shares in the previously state-owned British Telecom.

The domination of the operations side of the telephone industry by a few groups—whether commercial or state-owned—led to a close relationship with a limited number of suppliers. In the United States, AT&T relied on its own manufacturing division, Western Electric, now called Lucent. In Canada, Bell Canada—an unrelated company—controlled its supplier, Northern Telecom, now Nortel. In Europe government-owned phone companies gave contracts to domestic companies, such as Siemens in Germany, Plessey and GEC (both now merged under the name Marconi) in the United Kingdom, and France's CGE, now Alcatel. Unlike companies dominating many long-established industries, telecommunications suppliers have so far remained surprisingly resistant to mergers and other reorganizations.

These companies still dominate the supply of fixed telecommunications equipment in the early 21st century, though they now have two significant rivals: Cisco, founded in 1984 by a group of computer scientists from Stanford University, which makes the routers that switch Internet traffic; and Nokia, a paper manufacturer from Finland which in the late 1980s began to transform itself into the world's biggest maker of mobile phones.

MARKETS

Fixed telephone lines per 100 people, end 2000

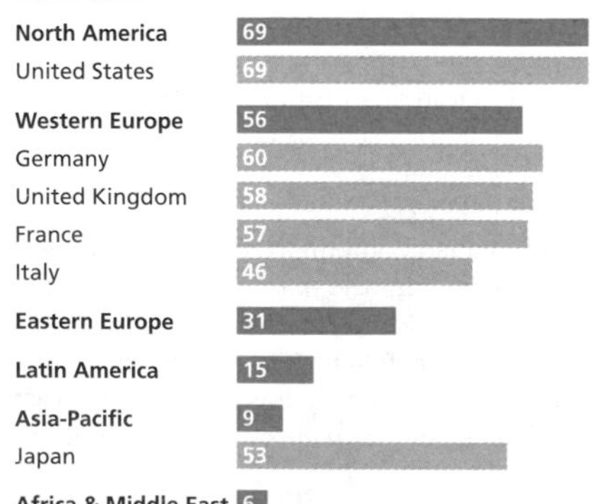

Source: Idate, Montpellier, France

Telecommunications represented about 2.3% of the gross domestic product of the world's developed economies in 1995, according to the Organisation for Economic

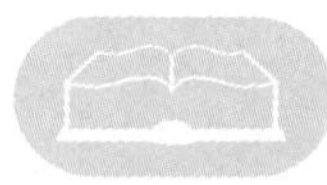

International voice telephone traffic, 1995 (billion minutes of outgoing calls)

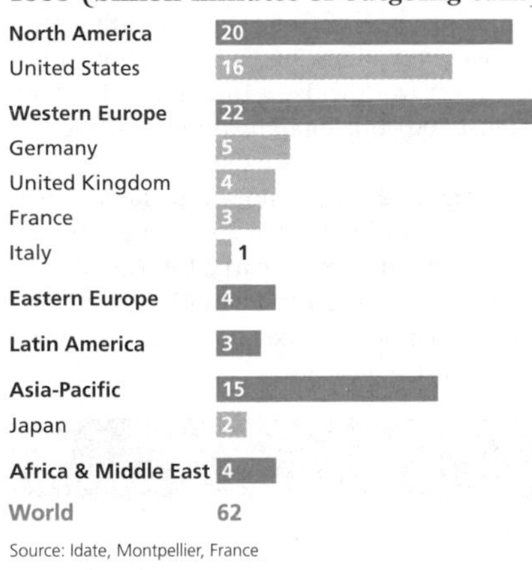

International voice telephone traffic, 2001 (billion minutes of outgoing calls)

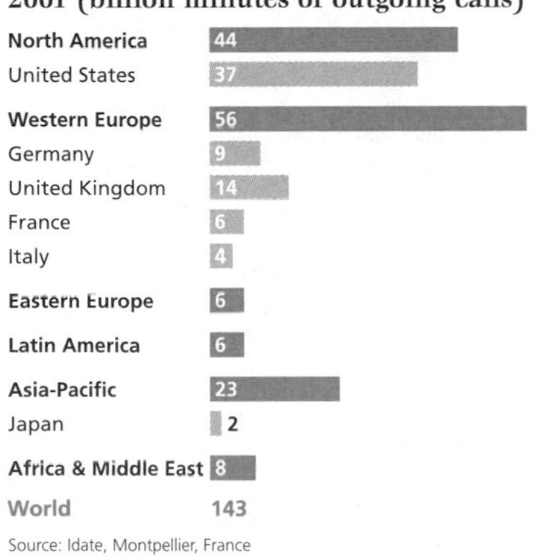

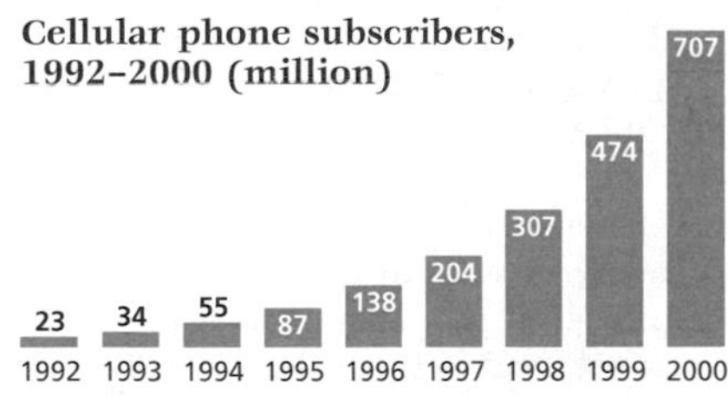

Forecast cellular phone subscribers, 2005 (million)

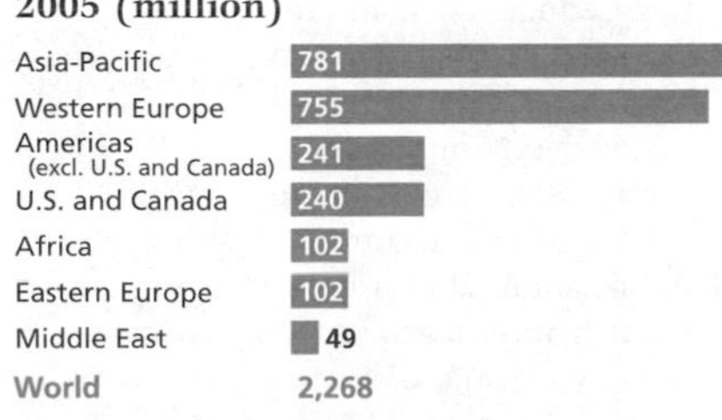

Co-operation and Development—a figure which had risen from 1.9% in 1980 and 2.0% in 1990. In individual countries the actual 1995 figure varied from a surprising 3.1% in Portugal and 2.9% in Ireland—the two highest—through 2.7% in Switzerland, 2.6% in Sweden, the United Kingdom and the United States, to 1.7% in France and 1.6% in Belgium. These percentages should, however, be regarded with caution: as in Ireland and Portugal, they could also represent higher than average telecommunications prices.

Technology

Telecommunications gives the impression of being driven by technological development, but this is really only a recent phenomenon. Until the arrival of the Internet and mobile phones, the domination of supply by a few companies led to an inevitable technological conservatism, traces of which can still be seen in the older-established companies. An example of resistance to technological change is AT&T, which did not adopt dial phones until 1919, a full 30 years after their invention.

Lack of competition meant that cost of calling fell only slowly until the late 1990s. The first transatlantic calls in 1928 cost more than a week's wages for an average person for a three-minute call. Some industry analysts now believe that technology and competition will halve call costs almost every year over at least the first few years of the 21st century. This appears to be following a similar pattern to the steadily declining cost of computer components—halving every 18 months—in the latter 20th century.

The use of optical fibers, which is bringing about this fall in costs, has enabled a complete digitization of telecommunications. Computer techniques were borrowed from the mid-1970s to switch calls more effectively than equipment that was often almost unchanged from the first automatic exchanges designed in the 19th century. Calls could now be transmitted digitally virtually throughout the network, with no loss of quality; in a few cases only the "last mile" (as the industry calls it) from exchange to user is analog, often on traditional copper cables which are little different from those Bell would have used.

New Products

Optical fiber technology made extraordinary strides in the 1990s. The Flag Atlantic 1 cable, one of several which went into operation across the Atlantic in 2001, can alone carry the equivalent of up to 30 million simultaneous phone calls. On land, dozens of rival companies built intercity networks in North America and Europe through the 1990s until the 2001 recession, driving down the cost of connections beyond the level at which many could earn a return on their investment.

Demand for telecommunications has fueled this growth in capacity. In the developed economies of the world the number of fixed telephone lines shows no signs of approaching saturation. The United Kingdom, for example, had 45 lines per 100 inhabitants in 1990, but more than 58 a decade later. Areas with a lower teledensity in 1990 showed even faster growth: Latin America almost tripled the number of phone lines relative to population, but still had only 14.7 per 100 in 2000.

International traffic has soared even faster: the United Kingdom's phone users made 12 billion minutes of outgoing international calls in 2000, equivalent to an extraordinary 200 minutes per inhabitant.

However, it was the astonishing success of mobile cellular services that was the big driver of telecommunications in the last decade of the 20th century, and the growth shows no signs of abating into the first decade of the 2000s.

Until the 1980s, car telephones were limited in range to the centers of large cities, and they were expensive to buy and use. Motorola, famous from the 1920s onwards for its car radios, proposed a network of mobile phone base stations, each covering a cell—which could be a few buildings in a busy city or several square miles in a flat, rural area. The idea was successful beyond Motorola's dreams, especially once digital techniques—such as the widely used but not universal GSM standard—increased capacity and capability from the late 1980s. By the end of 2001 the industry calculated that there were 800 million cellular phones in service—about one for every five of the world's population.

At the rates of growth being achieved in 2000–01, there will be more cellular phones than conventional fixed-line phones in use in the world by about 2003. Already in some countries this milestone has been achieved, including some developing countries which have traditionally had poor fixed telecommunications infrastructure. South Africa, notably, had just under five million fixed phones in service at the end of 2001 but more than 10 million cellular phones.

The next generation of cellular phones—the third (3G), beginning with the analog networks of the mid-1980s—promises far greater call capacity for the networks,

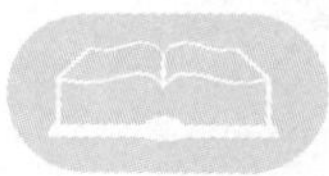

something that will be welcomed by many operating companies that are reaching the limits of their second-generation systems. However, operators are also hoping that 3G networks will achieve great commercial success by carrying business data services and moving video, either in the form of video phone calls or even television clips or programs. This is why operators in some countries paid large sums for licenses, and will need to spend even more on building networks. They see 3G mobile services as creating a "wireless internet."

Employment

The U.S. telecommunications industry (operators, rather than equipment suppliers) employs about 1.2 million people, a figure that has grown about 20% in 20 years. However, as the chart shows, technology and the effects of competition brought down employment figures in the conventional industry from 1.0 million in 1981 to a low of almost 800,000 in 1995. Since then employment has expanded dramatically, and at the same time the cellular telephone industry has grown from around 20,000 in the 1980s to over 250,000 in 2001.

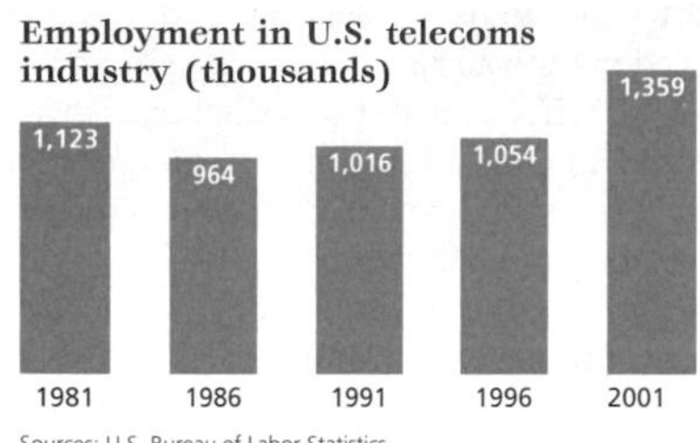

Sources: U.S. Bureau of Labor Statistics, National Cable Television Association

In addition, the U.S. cable industry—which can be regarded as part of either the media industry or the telecommunications industry—has increased its employee numbers from 45,000 in 1981 to 131,000 in 2001.

Changes in employment figures for the rest of the world are not readily available, but in 1999 the largest 25 operators in the world by revenue, including eight U.S. operators, employed around 2.1 million people. As the United States has 20% of the world's fixed telephone lines, it could be estimated that the worldwide industry employs about 20 million people—perhaps rather more, as competition has tended to make U.S. companies more efficient in terms of employment.

Manufacturing employment is harder to calculate. U.S.-based makers of telecommunications equipment and optical fiber cables employed about 805,000 people in 1998, a figure growing at over 3% a year. This excludes non-U.S. employees of North American suppliers such as Nortel and Lucent. Many employees of computer hardware and software companies such as Cisco, Compaq, Hewlett-Packard, Microsoft, and Sun in fact supply telecommunications operators.

Impact of the Internet

The Internet is an almost unrivalled example of an astonishingly successful product which developed almost by accident. It is now revolutionizing not only the telecommunications industry that carries it, but many other sectors of society—from media to retail, from education to government.

Internet users by region in August 2001 (million)

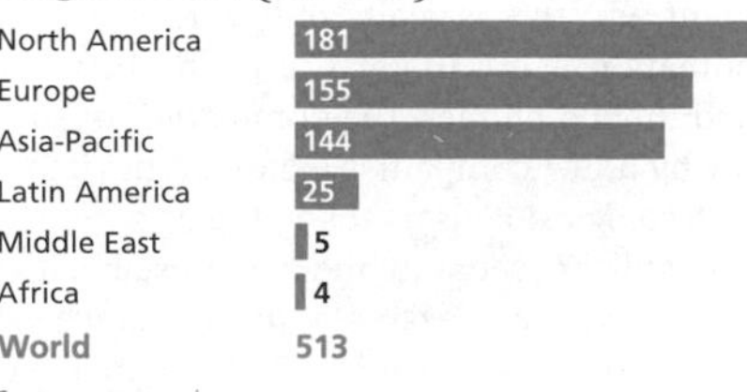

Source: www.nua.ie

Internet users by country in August 2001 (million)

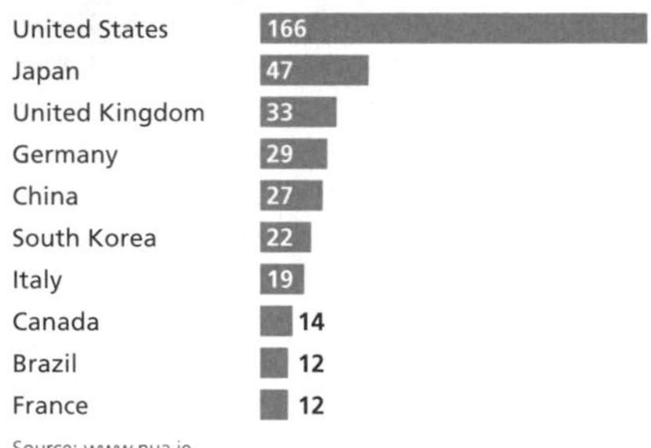

Source: www.nua.ie

It owes its origins to the Cold War, when the U.S. Department of Defense built an interconnected network of computers that would be secure against nuclear attack. The Internet was extended to the whole academic scientific community from the mid-1980s, but began to create an information revolution from the 1990s when Tim Berners-Lee, a consultant at the CERN nuclear research laboratory in Geneva, invented the idea of using the network to make available in graphical form documents that were interconnected using hyperlinks.

Commercial use of the Internet began seriously from around 1995, with the growing important of electronic mail in business and private life. Most commercial organizations set up Web sites, mainly for information purposes, although some are used for the electronic buying and selling of goods and services.

Statistics show clearly that, at the turn of millennium, the Internet was established as the fastest growing telecommunications service ever: there were 222 million Internet users worldwide at the end of 1999; by August 2001 this figure had increased to 513 million.

Meanwhile telecommunications operators, committed to higher and higher capital expenditure to carry Internet traffic, were looking at the possibilities of moving their existing services to their Internet-protocol (IP) networks.

For More Information

Books and Directories:

Cairncross, Frances. *The Death of Distance 2.0*. Boston, MA: Harvard Business School Press, 2001.

Standage, Tom. *The Victorian Internet*. New York: Berkley Publishing Group, 1999.

Magazines and Journals:

Communications International: **www.totaltele.com**

Global Telecoms Business: **www.globaltelecomsbusiness.com**

Wired: **www.wired.com**

Web Sites:

Analysys, Cambridge, United Kingdom: **www.analysys.com**

EMC, United Kingdom: **www.emc-database.com**

European Commission Directorate General for Information Society: **www.europa.eu.int/eeurope**

GSM Association, Dublin, Ireland: **www.gsmworld.com**

Idate, Montpellier, France: **www.idate.fr**

International Telecommunication Union: **www.itu.int**

Internet Society: **www.isoc.org**

Ovum, London, United Kingdom: **www.ovum.com**

Total Telecom: **www.totaltele.com**

U.K. Office of Telecommunications: **www.oftel.gov.uk**

U.S. Cellular Telecommunications Industry Association: **www.wow-com.com**

U.S. Federal Communications Commission: **www.fcc.gov**

U.S. National Telecommunications and Information Administration: **www.ntia.doc.gov**

World Wide Web Consortium: **www.w3.org**

TOURISM AND HOTELS

1834	Lord Henry Brougham "discovers" Cannes in the south of France.
1841	Thomas Cook organizes his first tour.
1889	The opening of the Savoy Hotel in London.
1890s	Henry Lunn credited with developing the ski industry in Switzerland.
1919	Conrad Hilton buys his first hotel in Cisco, Texas.
1927	J. Willard Marriott opened his first catering business.
1952	The first Holiday Inn hotel was opened in Memphis.
1975	Establishment of the United-Nations-affiliated World Tourism Organization in Madrid.
1997	The Monopolies and Mergers Commission concludes the package holiday industry is "broadly competitive."
1999	The European Commission blocks the Airtours bid for First Choice.
2001	A sharp downturn in international travel and tourism follows the September 11 terrorist attacks in the United States, and the industry recovers only slowly during 2002.
2002	The world's two largest cruise lines, Carnival Corporation and Royal Caribbean, battle for the U.K.'s P&O Princess Cruises.

Tourism is one of the world's largest and fastest-growing industries, with revenues in 2000 of $476 billion. The industry has grown rapidly since World War II, fueled by the growth of cheap air travel in the 1960s and 1970s.

Revenues from international travel have increased every year over the past 50 years. Even conflicts such as the 1991 Gulf War, economic crises, and ecological disasters such as the explosion of the Chernobyl nuclear reactor failed to halt the trend. However, a combination of the attacks on the United States on September 11 2001 and a global economic slowdown threatens to break that growth record in 2002.

Although travel for pleasure can be traced back to the ancient world, the roots of modern tourism lie in the Grand Tours undertaken by Europeans to explore Greece and Italy, the birthplace of European civilization. While these tours were confined to the wealthy and aristocratic, mass-market tourism began in the 19th century. Thomas Cook, the founder of the package vacation group that still bears his name, was an early pioneer, originally organizing excursions in Britain to rally support for the temperance movement to which he belonged.

The development of tourism follows a similar pattern in every country. People travel for pleasure domestically, then visit neighboring countries, before embarking on longer-distance travel. This pattern explains the large proportion of travel undertaken within a given region. Just over 80% of travel is intra-regional, with long-haul accounting for only 20%, though long-haul is the fastest-growing segment. Continued increases in disposable income and lifespans are the basis for expectations that tourism will continue to grow.

The hotel industry has grown on the back of the rise in tourism. About 40% of hotel nights sold are for business travel; all the rest are leisure.

The development of the hotel industry in North America was linked to the growth of motor and air travel, hence the tradition of roadside motels, while airlines such as Pan Am and TWA opened hotels along their international routes. In Europe, the industry has historically been based on the family vacation market and middle-management business travelers. Many hotels are still family-owned and, unlike the United States where more than 75% of hotels are part of a large chain, less than 20% in Europe are "branded."

Asia has had a tradition of small inns, but the largest hotel groups are still small by international standards. These include Prince Hotels, Tokyu Hotel group and Nikko International in Japan, and Hong Kong-based groups Shangri-La and Mandarin Oriental.

COMPANIES

The largest tour operating market is in Europe. Until six years ago the largest companies were to be found in the United Kingdom, Germany, and Scandinavia, but the industry has consolidated and is now dominated by German companies. Preussag, the former industrial company, and C&N Touristic—which in 2000 changed its name to that of its most recent acquisition—Thomas Cook, are the two largest groups.

Top European tour operators by sales, 2000 ($ billion)

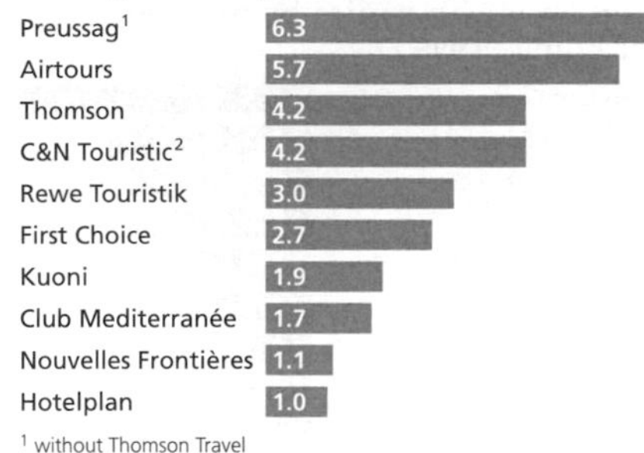

[1] without Thomson Travel
[2] without Thomas Cook
Source: FVW International

The structure of the industry in Germany and the United Kingdom is based on vertical integration—the in-house ownership of the main elements in the supply chain. The principal elements are tour operators, travel agents, airlines, and hotels in resort destinations.

This structure has provoked complaints from the smaller tour operators and travel agents of unfair practices by the industry's giants. In the United Kingdom, the matter was referred in 1997 to the Monopolies and Mergers Commission, which found the industry to be "broadly competitive" and suggested minor changes to the industry's structure, such as prohibiting the practice of making discounts on vacation prices dependent on the compulsory purchase of in-house travel insurance.

Two years later, in 1999, the European Commission blocked the proposed acquisition by Airtours, then the United Kingdom's second-largest package holiday group, of First Choice, its smaller rival. The top four companies—Thomson Travel, Airtours, Thomas Cook, and First Choice—controlled about 60% of the market, and the Commission argued that reducing the number of large players from four to three could lead to uncompetitive practices.

Profit margins are slim—traditionally around 3%. The industry is highly dependent financially on the summer, when about 75% of profits are made. Unlike many other industries, the financial health of tour operators cannot be gauged by the level of sales: the key to profitability lies in getting the supply/demand balance correct for package vacations each year.

In years when the supply of vacations exceeds demand, the industry is forced to give

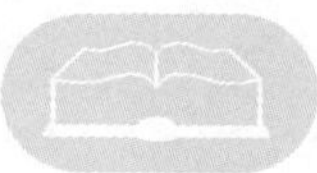

discounts in order to get rid of last-minute vacancies, and this can lead to losses. By reducing the number available for sale, it can charge higher prices for packages, and thus support profits.

Top hotel companies by number of hotels, 1999

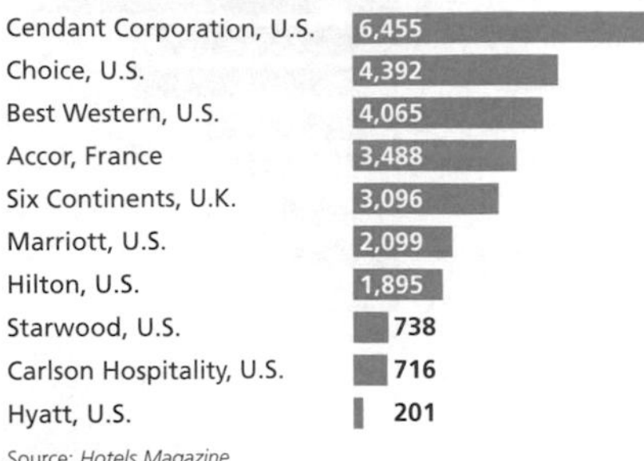

Source: *Hotels Magazine*

Top hotel companies by number of rooms, 1999

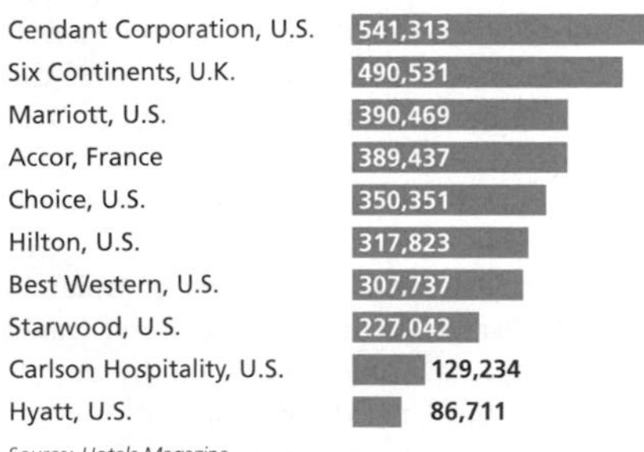

Source: *Hotels Magazine*

The hotel industry is one in which the United States has come to dominate. Out of the top 10 hotel groups, eight are U.S.-based.

Hotel operators can own their properties, manage them on behalf of an owner for a fee, or franchise them. Many have a combination of all three, such as Six Continents, the group formerly known as Bass. Cendant and Choice are franchisers, with brands which include Howard Johnson, Days Inn and Clarion (Cendant), and Quality and Comfort (Choice).

There has been growing consolidation within domestic markets. Cross-border consolidation is expected to increase, spurred primarily by the needs of the global business traveler who wants to stay at a familiar hotel when in unfamiliar territory, and requires access to facilities such as fax machines and the Internet. Some of the largest cross-border deals in recent years include Bass's purchase of Inter-Continental from Japan's Saison group for £1.8 billion ($2.5 billion) in 1998; Accor's £700 million ($1 billion) acquisition of U.S.-based Red Roof Inns, and Hilton Group's acquisition of Scandic, the Swedish group, in 2001 for £612 million ($870 million).

The hotel industry has high operational gearing. Its fixed costs are relatively great, but profits made above the breakeven threshold go straight to the bottom line. However, when demand is weak, costs can only be reduced by a relatively small amount, making it difficult to prevent losses.

Markets

The four largest tourist-generating countries are the United States, Germany, Japan, and the United Kingdom, which account for 40% of international travel. Within Europe, Germany is the largest market, followed by the United Kingdom and Scandinavia.

Top tourism spenders, 2000 ($ billion)

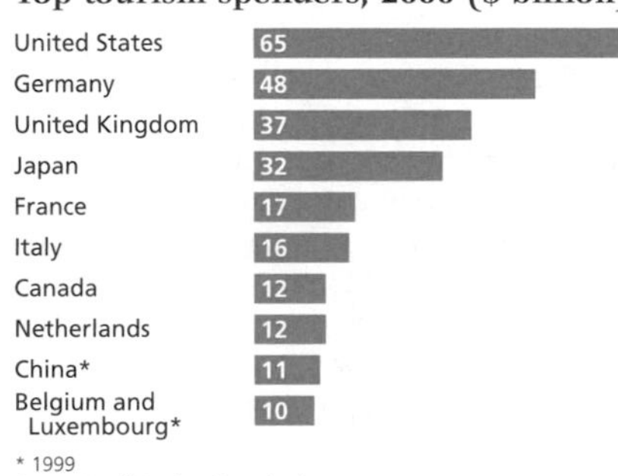

* 1999
Source: World Tourism Organization

International tourism arrivals, 2000 (million)

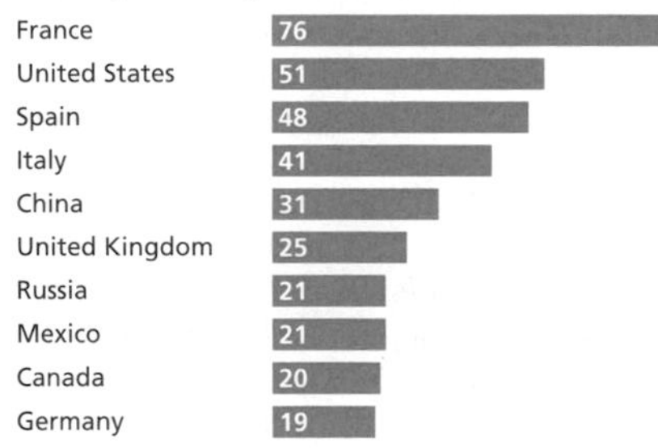

Source: World Tourism Organization

Share of international tourism arrivals, 2000 (%)

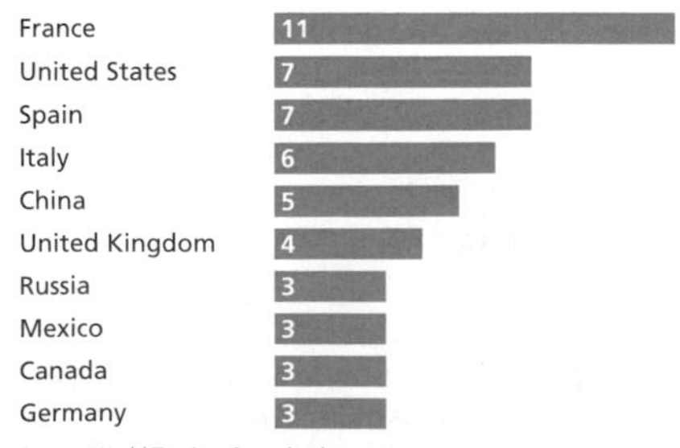

Source: World Tourism Organization

Package vacation companies operate domestically, with companies tailoring their holidays to the market in question. The

Top tourism earners, 2000 ($ billion)

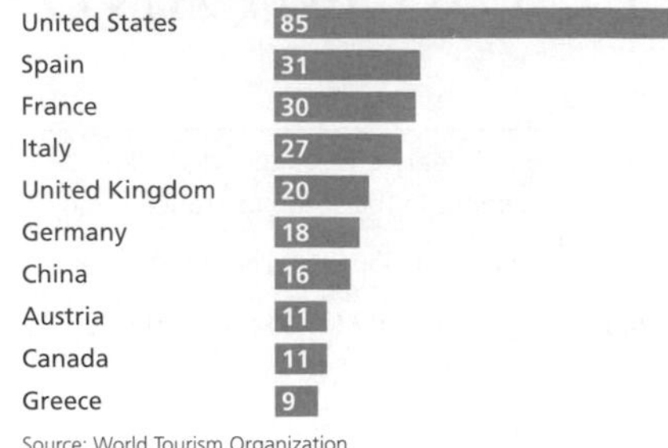

Source: World Tourism Organization

Top tourism earners, 2000 (% of world spend)

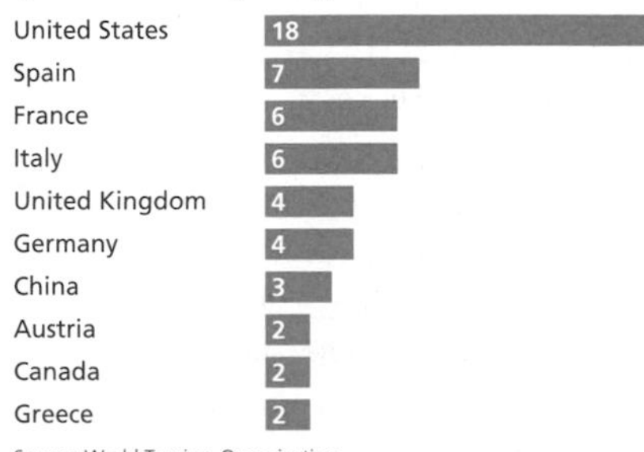

Source: World Tourism Organization

main destination for package tourists in northern Europe is Spain. The United States is the second most popular destination for travelers from the United Kingdom, with Florida as the most popular area visited. The popularity of destinations further east or south, such as Turkey, Egypt, Tunisia, and Morocco, tends to be more volatile and dependent on political events. In recent years, long-haul travel has been one of the fastest growing segments, with the Caribbean figuring prominently.

European tour operators have tried to enter new markets, principally through acquisition, to reduce dependence on the home market and help smooth out their earnings over the year. Thus Airtours and First Choice both operate in Canada, where people tend to take their vacation in winter. Thomas Cook also aims to look outside Europe for expansion, beginning with Cuba and India.

Airtours established a startup business in the United States, but has so far failed to reap the potential benefits. The nature of vacations in the United States is fundamentally different from the United Kingdom, where the industry is airline-led. Vacation allowances of two weeks are far shorter than the five or six weeks enjoyed in Europe, giving less opportunity for selling two or three vacations a year to the same customer.

In the hotel industry, most demand is domestic, sometimes accounting for 85% of room nights sold. However, in 5-star hotels in large international cities, such as New York, London and Paris, overseas visitors can account for up to 70% of room nights sold.

Europe has more hotel rooms than any other region, with more than 40% of the world total, while North America has about 30% and Asia-Pacific 16%. This means that Asia-Pacific's hotel sector is only half the size of North America's, but it is growing more rapidly.

The group with the widest international coverage is Six Continents, the world's second-largest hotels group, which has hotels in 98 countries. Cendant and Choice are almost entirely U.S.-domestic, and even Marriott International, the third largest, has only 15% of its rooms outside North America. For most of the branded chains, the goal is to increase their representation globally to cater to the needs of business travelers, sometimes through partnerships but more usually through takeovers and mergers.

Technology

The technology employed to sell holidays and room nights is surprisingly unsophisticated, something which the industry recognizes and is trying to change. In recent years investment has been directed at e-commerce and the establishment of online booking sites, but the technology needed for customer relationship management is relatively poor.

Although bookings are automated, they do not capture enough information about the customer. Few of the big package travel companies are able to identify their customers, or have available data showing how many holidays were taken by a given individual or how much was spent in the past with the company. This is an area in which the industry intends to increase investment.

The hotel industry is more advanced in this area than the package travel companies, but even here it is not necessarily the case that all hotels within a chain are linked to one system. The best-equipped groups are able to call up customers' preferences when taking a booking. Hotel loyalty schemes are an established and important source of data collection.

Over the past five years the hotel industry has focused on installing technology enabling it to apply the "yield management" techniques employed by the airline industry to room nights. This means that a room can vary considerably in price depending on demand at the time of enquiry. The groups with the most active yield management claim to have improved profit margins considerably as a result of employing the technique.

New Products

Tour operators have broadened their portfolio of vacations to increase their appeal to people who would not usually think of buying a package vacation. Although beach vacations are the mainstay of the European mass-market operators, they also offer an increasingly greater choice of more exclusive holidays, including skiing, city breaks, cruises, and adventure vacations.

Independent travel has increased at the expense of the package vacation in recent years, prompting operators to increase flexibility so that, for an additional fee, it is possible to book airline seats in advance, stay in an upgraded hotel room, and have a choice of flight times. The trend towards providing greater choice can be expected to continue, especially given the increasing interest in eco-tourism and agri-tourism.

The focus for the hotel industry has been on devising rooms which are both functional for the business traveler–such as equipping rooms with modems at desk height-while also trying to make them "homely."

In recent years, boutique or "designer" hotels have emerged to challenge the more mundane chains. Designer hotels found a ready market with the dot-com generation, and have also been popular with those in the music and film industries. Their success is such that Starwood, owner of the Sheraton and Westin chains, has launched its own rival, named W, and serves as a reminder that the large groups cannot afford to be complacent.

Employment

These industries are large employers, providing jobs for 207 million people, equivalent to 8% of global employment. The World Travel and Tourism Council, a private-sector industry group, estimates that by 2011, travel and tourism will support 260 million jobs and account for 9% of total employment.

As employers, the industry is valuable in drawing from all cultures and educational levels. However, it is characterized by high staff turnover, which it recognizes should be countered by providing more structured career paths, better pay, and increased training for employees.

Impact of the Internet

Tourism and the Internet work well as partners. The Internet allows consumers to research destinations more thoroughly than is possible with a brochure, and enables travel companies to provide information and to process bookings at lower cost.

Internet sales account for 15% of total tourism bookings, and are forecast to grow to 25% within five years by the World Tourism Organization. Although North America has the highest proportion of online bookings, it could be surpassed by Asia-Pacific by 2003.

Online bookings for air travel are higher than for hotels or package vacations. Some airlines only sell online or over the telephone, cutting out the travel agent completely. Since the Internet puts consumers in touch directly with hotel companies or the tour operators, travel agents are potentially threatened. Nevertheless, a new breed of online travel agents has emerged, and the large travel agency groups have gone online themselves. In general, though, travel agents will have to offer value-added services or niche marketing to survive.

Growth in online travel has been so rapid that it could represent nearly half of all e-commerce within the next three years. The main challenge for smaller and medium-sized companies is in keeping up with the investment and with the Internet's rapid technological advances.

For More Information

Directories:

The European Hotel Industry. London: Travel Research International.
The International Hotel Industry. London: Travel & Tourism Intelligence.

Magazines and Journal:

Hotels magazine, Cahners Business Information: **www.hotelsmag.com**

Web sites:

Euromonitor International: **www.euromonitor.com**
World Tourism Organization: **www.world-tourism.org**
World Travel and Tourism Council: **www.wttc.org**

Water

1619	New River Company incorporated to serve London.
1853	Foundation of the French Compagnie Générale des Eaux (CGE)—now the core of Vivendi Universal's Vivendi Environnement company.
1880	CGE wins Venice supply concession.
1880	Foundation of Société Lyonnaise des Eaux, now the core of France's Suez Ondeo.
1881	Lyonnaise wins Barcelona contract.
1946	Lyonnaise des Eaux nationalized.
1972	Lyonnaise buys Degremont engineering company.
1989	Water companies of England and Wales privatized.
1996	Lyonnaise buys U.K.'s Northumbrian Water.
1997	Merger of Lyonnaise des Eaux with Compagnie Suez, original developers of the Suez Canal.
1998	Compagnie Générale des Eaux renamed Vivendi.
1998	U.S.'s now defunct Enron launches Azurix; Azurix purchases U.K.'s Wessex Water.
1999	Vivendi buys U.S. Filter and Berlin Water.
1999	Suez Ondeo buys U.S.'s industrial service companies Nalco & Calgon.
2000	Partial flotation of Vivendi Environnement from Vivendi Universal.
2000/1	Azurix folded back into Enron.
2001	Thames is bought by German multi-utility, RWE; RWE buys American Water Works.

Water serves three primary functions: personal use, agriculture, and industry. Although agriculture accounts for more than 70% of global water use, the water industry developed as a result of the requirements of domestic and industrial water use. However, attitudes to domestic and industrial use are still considerably affected by the current or past reliance of much of the population on agriculture: the concept that water is free is still ingrained amongst many water consumers, notably in cities in developing countries, expanding rapidly as a result of migration from the countryside.

In Europe and North America, a relatively long history of urban water supply has made it easier to convey the concept that the provision of water should carry a price, although in some quarters there is still considerable resistance to the concept that it is a commodity like any other, to be bought and sold by private corporations for profit. In developing countries, most notably in the large conurbations of Africa and South Asia, urban water systems—developed in colonial times for what were then much smaller communities—have come under great strain as populations have soared. The issues of water provision in these markets are often very different from those of Europe and North America; however, both regions face a common problem in the inability or unwillingness of governments to pay for renovating or extending the infrastructure required for the delivery of clean water to households (and perhaps ultra-clean water to industry), and for proper sewerage and treatment services for waste water and sewage.

Most of the major cities of the West began to lay down water and sewerage networks following public health scares in the late 19th century. By the mid-20th century these networks were crumbling. In municipal hands, services had been overmanned and inefficiently run, with leakage rates often running at around 40%. In 1973 in England and Wales, responsibility for water supply was placed in the hands of ten Regional Water Authorities who took over the work previously carried out by 157 water undertakings, 29 River Authorities, and 1,393 sanitary authorities, whose jurisdiction was based on river catchment areas.

By the mid-1970s, the European Community was beginning to draw up a series of water quality directives, together with the setting of target dates for compliance. However, the lack of a sound regulatory regime meant that progress in attaining environmental objectives was difficult to monitor.

Underinvestment and the expensive system upgrades required by various environmental directives from the European Union led the government to privatize the water and sewerage services in England and Wales in 1989—the only full privatization in the world, in which the assets of the water companies moved completely from the public to the private sector. The industry's debt of £5.2 billion was written off, and it received a "green dowry" of £1.5 billion from the government. Tax allowances of £7.7 billion were granted to the companies, which were then floated on the stock exchange; these companies joined major European players in competing for contract business worldwide. The European giants have had plenty of experience: France's Compagnie Générale des Eaux was founded in 1853, and Suez Lyonnaise des Eaux in 1880.

Structure

Around the world, most water activities are still controlled by state or municipally owned companies. It is the drying up of funds for these companies that has prompted, and continues to prompt, increasing activity by private corporations. The world water industry consists, generally speaking, of a handful of major companies or groups, and of the various specialist technical and equipment companies that serve them.

Top companies by market capitalization in December 2001 ($ billion)

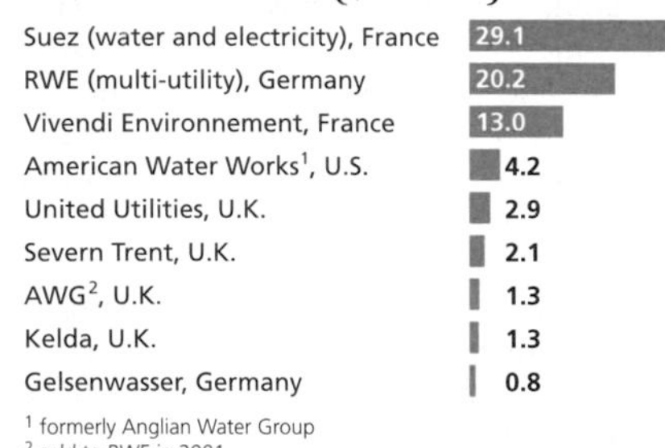

[1] formerly Anglian Water Group
[2] sold to RWE in 2001
Source: Platts *Global Water Report*

Top water and wastewater companies by domestic population served, 2001 (million)

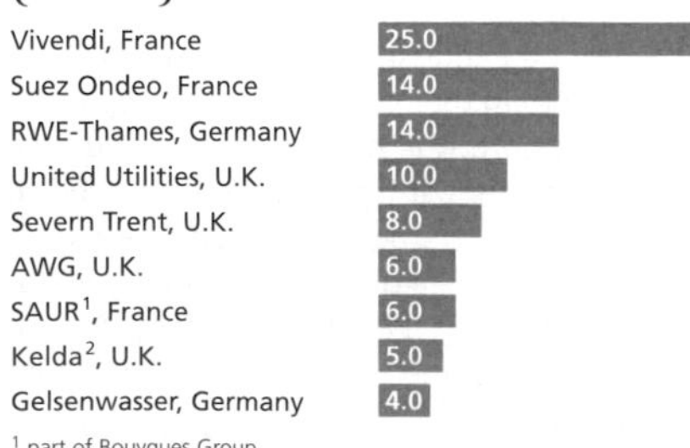

[1] part of Bouygues Group
[2] formerly Yorkshire Water Group
Source: Platts *Global Water Report*

The industry is dominated by a few companies which grew big from their possession of large domestic markets. The two biggest companies, Suez/Ondeo and Vivendi

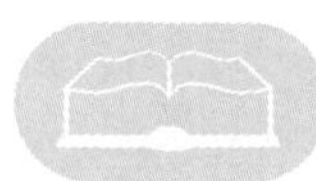

Top water and wastewater companies by international population served, 2001 (million)

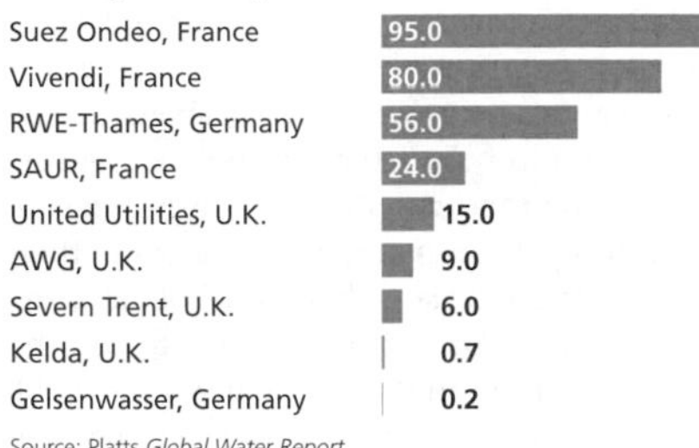

Source: Platts *Global Water Report*

Environnement, are both French. The next biggest company is Germany's RWE, which in 2001 absorbed Thames, the largest U.K. water company (in terms of international business). A handful of U.K. companies and a few firms from Germany almost complete the picture as far as cross-border activities are concerned. Spanish companies are active in Latin America, but generally in partnership with, or as subsidiaries of, the French giants. The most prominent U.S. company, in terms of its overseas activities, was Azurix, a company developed by Enron, spun off from Enron and then re-absorbed prior to the collapse of the disgraced U.S. gas-trading giant in 2001.

It is to this small group of companies that national governments, municipal authorities, and such financial institutions as the World Bank, the Asian Development Bank, and the Latin American Development Bank look when seeking to solicit bids for the operation and/or expansion of urban water infrastructure in the developing world.

In pursuit of this aim they are in part seeking to emulate the start of a major era of water infrastructure regeneration begun in Europe in the 1980s. This has involved the overhaul of water operations and structures in such countries as the United Kingdom, France, and Germany, subsequently extended to Spain, Portugal, and Italy. Water reform has also been carried out in Belgium and the Netherlands, and is a significant item on the political and financial agendas of EU applicant countries in Central and Eastern Europe. It has yet to affect much of the former Soviet Union (the Baltic states are an exception), and in much of the developing world progress towards reform has been patchy.

The two big French companies dominate the international water scene, although some major contracts have also been won by the other four members of the select group of six who currently serve more customers overseas than in their own home countries.

There are currently around 10 companies which are routinely active in the international arena: Vivendi Environnement and Suez/Ondeo; the German-British RWE-Thames (now including American Water Works); the United Kingdom's United Utilities, AWG, Kelda, and Severn Trent; France's Saur; and Germany's Gelsenwasser.

One significant additional player is International Water, the international water arm of the U.S. engineering giant, Bechtel. International Water was founded in 1994 as a joint venture with the United Kingdom's United Utilities, but UU sold back its stake in 1999. It is currently running two globally significant operations: the contract for the eastern half of the Philippines capital of Manila, and the contract for the Bulgarian capital of Sofia. It also has concessions in Poland, Estonia, Australia, and Malaysia, and Private Finance Initiative (PFI) projects in Scotland.

The other major U.S. player of the late 1990s, Azurix, was folded back into its parent company, the controversial Enron, in 2001. As of January 2002, Enron/Azurix still owned the United Kingdom's Wessex Water. However, thanks to OFWAT (Office of Water Services, the U.K. regulatory body), Wessex Water's finances are ring-fenced and the company is currently looking for a buyer.

Markets

Global Need

Former U.S. President Bill Clinton noted that "a billion people go to bed hungry every night and a billion and a half people—one quarter of the people on earth—never get a clean glass of water." That is the scope of the global water market. Two billion do not have adequate sanitation. In 1980 The United Nations launched its Water Supply and Sanitation Decade, and during that time $100 billion was spent on infrastructure projects worldwide. At the end of the decade, though, these projects were little more than a drop in the ocean. In 2000, 38% of African households had no access to water or sewerage; in Asia the figure was 19%. In Europe, however, 96% of urban households have domestic water supplies and 92% have sewerage.

Developing World

According to the World Bank, between 1990 and 1999 more than 121 developing countries introduced private participation in at least one infrastructure sector. Those countries awarded over 1,900 projects that involved investment commitments of $580 billion. Yet, in spite of the investment of vast sums, the situation for the poorest does not improve. The number of people living in

Municipal water, wastewater, and related services market ($ billion)

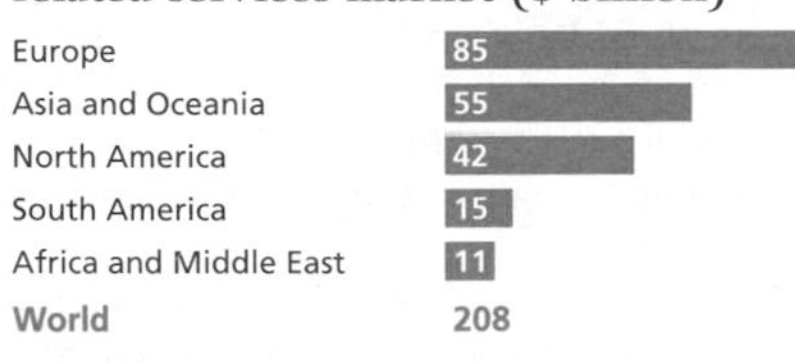

Source: *Masons Water Yearbook*

water-stressed countries is projected to climb from 470 million to nearly 3 billion by 2025. Intensification of agriculture and rapid urban expansion are putting tremendous pressure on water resources. City population in developing economies is forecast to grow by 160% between 1990 and 2030. Many agricultural ministries are unwilling to charge true cost, or even any cost, for irrigation water, deeming it wiser to placate farmers rather than risk political upheaval and perhaps be voted out of office.

Total private-sector water and sewerage projects in developing countries by region, 1990–97

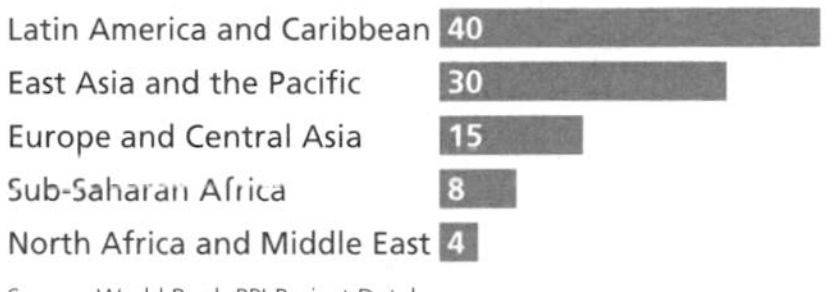

Source: World Bank PPI Project Database

Private-sector investment in water and sewerage projects in developing countries, 1990–97 ($ billion)

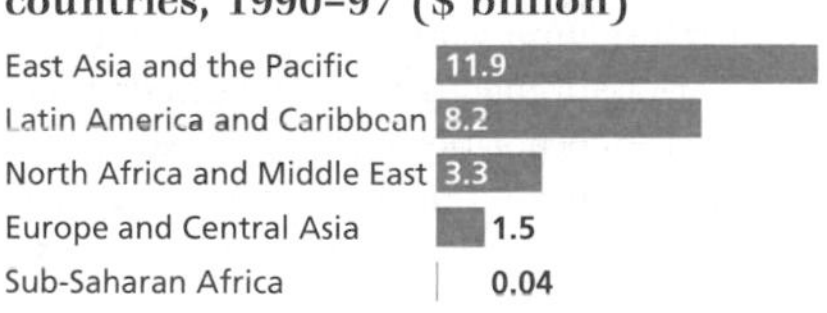

Source: World Bank PPI Project Database

Moreover, in urban areas there is increasing concern in many countries about the ability of customers to pay for their water during an economic downturn. When companies cut off water for non-payment of bills, the people are forced on to the black market, where they may have to pay as much as ten times the true cost. However, companies argue that it is not a question of people being unable to pay, but rather of the politics of the rate increase. Politicians do not want to be seen to increase prices during an economic downturn.

The World Bank believes that some $700 billion is required in order to meet the demand for services in water supply and sanitation, irrigation, and power over the next ten years. Around $300 billion of in-

vestment will be required from the private sector, the rest to be found from bodies such as the World Bank. In 1997, total investment in water-related infrastructure in developing countries was around $65 billion, with $25 billion being spent on water supply and sanitation.

The need for capital in both the developed and developing worlds is so great that local and national governments have had little choice but to look to the private sector for infrastructure funding and development. However, whilst there is a great need, it takes great skill to draw up a contract which anticipates all the major risks over the 30-year life of a concession. For example, the valuation of existing assets in a country is difficult because most of these assets—the pipework—are hidden underground. Governments change and city councils hope to be re-elected. Tariff increases are often unpopular, even if, historically, the poor have often paid massively for black-market water, or privately supplied water-tanker supplies. Water requires vast capital sums to be invested in massive infrastructure upfront, with a long waiting period before profits can be retrieved.

Faced with a combination of burgeoning populations, lack of indigenous capital for infrastructure, inefficient or corrupt local administrations, and pressure from international funding institutions for significant institutional reforms, a number of major international cities have turned to the private sector to maintain, develop, and extend their water supply and sewerage systems.

A variety of mechanisms have been used. Some city authorities have awarded simple management contracts, in which they pay the contractor a fee for running the city's water supply while themselves remaining in charge of tariff collection. Others have opted for Build, Own, Operate, Transfer (BOOT) contracts, under which the private company transfers the assets back to the municipality at the end of the contract period. A further group has awarded outright concession contracts, which allow companies the right to operate utility services for a certain period of time, after which the assets are transferred to the municipality.

European Union

Under EU regulations, the current 15 members of the European Union will have to spend hundreds of billions of dollars to comply with various directives from the European Commission, notably the Urban Wastewater Directive and the Bathing Water Directive. The United Kingdom alone will need to invest more than $60 billion in order to comply with European Union regulations.

Some southern European countries are seeking to postpone compliance with the demands of the Urban Wastewater Directives. The EU has the power to fine member states over $100,000 a day for non-compliance.

Eastern Europe

The Eastern European countries seeking membership of the EU (Bulgaria, Czech Republic, Estonia, Hungary, Latvia, Lithuania, Poland, Romania, Slovakia, and Slovenia) are driven towards Private Sector Participation (PSP) by the need to improve environmental standards prior to accession, remedying years of environmental neglect during the communist era. They will also have to improve basic water supply, treatment, and sewerage for many of their cities. There is a substantial amount of EU financing being put toward developing the infrastructure in these countries, but more financing will be required—hence the wish to involve the private sector.

United States

This is an extremely fragmented market, with a few large regional water companies and many small municipal suppliers. About 80% of water is municipally owned. Of the 60,000 municipal systems, 95% serve fewer than 10,000 people. The 1974 Safe Drinking Water Act required all supplied water to be treated, but most municipalities have not yet built the necessary treatment plants. Many pipes are over a hundred years old. Faced with aging infrastructure, city bosses are turning to the private sector in order to bring in outside funding, although some municipalities have faced resistance from unions concerned about layoffs. In 1998, 48 million people—12% of the population—received services from the private sector.

Foreign companies want to take advantage of opportunities to buy small systems in order to consolidate them, thus creating economies of scale. Aquarion was bought by the United Kingdom's Kelda Group. E'Town was bought be RWE-Thames Water, as was American Water Works. United Water Resources was bought by Suez Ondeo.

According to the American Water Works Association, water supply is estimated as worth around $27 billion a year, with sewerage and waste water worth around $25 billion. According to the U.S. company, CH2M Hill, the addressable market (water and waste water contracts at $35 per service per person per year) is worth $13.4 billion a year.

There are new concerns regarding projections by the Environmental Protection Agency (EPA) that around $300 billion needs to be invested in U.S. water and waste water infrastructure over the next 20 years. Companies are also anxious about a new EPA requirement that water companies must send reports on water quality and contaminants to consumers along with their bills, but some see this as a business opportunity as municipalities are forced, by the regulation, to deal with any water quality problems. Security concerns, in the light of the terrorist attacks of September 11, will also lead to higher costs.

Latin America

In Latin America there is a struggle between a government's desire to offload expensive water and sewerage provision and the strength of the labor unions. There is corruption, which must be set against the great need for water. The economic crisis taking place in Argentina will impact on consumers' ability to pay their water and sewerage bills. Brazil has proved frustrating with its political stop-go attitude to privatization; it is estimated that $40 billion must be spent in Brazil on upgrading sewerage by 2005. In Rio there have been charges of corruption, together with union opposition, and international companies are awaiting the establishment of a sound regulatory regime. Chile's good regulatory regime has meant that several international companies have entered the market successfully.

For More Information

Books and Directories:

Who's Who in the Water Industry. London: Water Services Association.

Masons Water Yearbook. London: **www.masons.co.uk**

Magazines and Journals:

Platts Global Water Report. London: Platts (a division of McGraw-Hill): **www.platts.com**

Web Sites:

American Water Works Association: **www.awwa.org**

News and information about environmental and engineering issues: **www.waterinfocenter.com**

Online information for the water treatment professional: **www.waterandwastewater.com**

The International Private Water Association: **www.ipwa.org**

Business Information Sources

BUSINESS INFORMATION SOURCES

Providing the Quickest and Easiest Route to the Best Business Information Available

Business Information Sources is a highly selective source of sources: it's designed to give you the quickest and easiest route to the information you need, in a variety of media.

This section identifies over 3,000 sources of the best business information from around the world, organized into over 100 subject areas. These include the best management Web sites, the most informative books, magazines, and journals, and the most authoritative organizations.

ACCOUNTING

BOOKS

Accounts Demystified: How to Understand and Use Company Accounts
ANTHONY RICE
Upper Saddle River, New Jersey: Financial Times Prentice Hall, 1999
239pp (Smarter Solutions Series)
ISBN: 0273601547
This book provides a practical guide to the basics of accounting, covering balance sheets, profit and loss accounts, and cash-flow statements. Separate sections deal with the interpretation of accounts and annual reports and the financial analysis of company accounts. A glossary of accounting terms is also included.

After the Merger: Seven Strategies for Successful Post-merger Integration
MAX M. HABECK, FRITZ KRÖGER, MICHAEL R. TRÄM
Upper Saddle River, New Jersey: Financial Times Prentice Hall, 2000
146pp ISBN: 0273643541
Drawing on their experience as management consultants, the authors offer seven rules for merger success: vision, leadership, growth, early wins, cultural differences, communication, and risk management, with a focus on the integration process. An assessment of future trends in mergers and acquisitions is also made.

Cost and Effect
ROBERT S. KAPLAN, ROBIN COOPER
Boston, Massachusetts: Harvard Business School Press, 1997
357pp ISBN: 0875847889
This book demonstrates how the principles of activity-based costing and other advanced cost management techniques can drive business performance. It includes examples from a variety of leading companies worldwide.

Finance and Accounting for Nonfinancial Managers 4th ed.
WILLIAM G. DROMS
Cambridge, Massachusetts: Perseus, 1998
265pp ISBN: 0201311399
This helpful book demystifies the complex world of finance and accounting and makes it accessible to managers of all levels.

The Finance Manual for Non-financial Managers: The Power to Make Confident Financial Decisions
PAUL MCKOEN, LEO GOUGH
Philadelphia, Pennsylvania: Trans-Atlantic Publications, 1999
319pp (Smarter Solutions Series)
ISBN: 0273625594
The book aims to give the non-financial manager a practical introduction to financial management and control. It explains the basics of accounting and financial reports, with separate chapters covering costing, pricing, project analysis, corporate taxation, financing, and risk management. The accounting implications of acquisitions are also discussed.

How to Read a Financial Report 5th ed.
JOHN A. TRACEY
New York: John Wiley, 1999
176pp ISBN: 0471329355
Tracey provides guidance on interpreting company accounts (with relation to U.S. practice), with particular reference to the three essential parts of every financial report—the balance sheet, the income statement, and the cash-flow statement. His explanations are illustrated with many examples.

Intermediate Accounting
DONALD E. KEISO, JERRY J. WYGANDT, TERRY D. WARFIELD
New York: John Wiley, 2001
1438pp ISBN: 0471363049
The book is used in over 70% of the intermediate accounting courses taught in post-secondary institutions in the United States. It covers the conceptual framework underlying financial accounting, financial reporting standards and statements, and more complex topics and transactions that are encountered in today's business environment. Specific guidance is provided for numerous topics including accounting for cash and receivables, inventory, intangible assets, current and long-term liabilities, income taxes, leases, shareholders' equity, and revenue recognition.

Managerial Accounting 2nd ed.
JAMES JIAMBALVO
New York: John Wiley, 2000
448pp ISBN: 0471238236
The book presents the fundamental concepts of managerial accounting including job-order and process costing, cost-volume-profit analysis, cost allocation and activity-based costing, capital budgeting decisions, and standard cost and variance analysis. Unlike many cost and managerial accounting texts that focus on accounting skills, the book approaches the subject matter from a manager's perspective.

Relevance Lost: The Rise and Fall of Management Accounting
H. THOMAS JOHNSON, ROBERT S. KAPLAN
Boston, Massachusetts: Harvard Business School Press, 1991
269pp ISBN: 0875842542
This book, first published in 1987, has won two major awards from the accounting profession, and has become a manifesto for managers in accounting and control. It explores the evolution of management accounting in U.S. business and how this relates to modern corporations.

2002 FASB (Financial Accounting Standards Board) Current Text
FINANCIAL ACCOUNTING STANDARDS BOARD
New York: John Wiley, 2002
ISBN: 0471218561 (vol 1) 0471218545 (vol 2)
This book is a collection of generally accepted accounting principles (GAAP) organized by topic. Material in the book is drawn from the Financial Accounting Standards Board's Statements on Financial Accounting Standards and Interpretations, the AICPA's Accounting Research Bulletins, and APB Opinions. Volume 1 is a collection of GAAP that has general applicability to all businesses. Volume 2 contains standards that apply to specific industries and nonprofit organizations. The book is updated annually to reflect new standards promulgated during the year.

Unlocking Company Reports and Accounts
WENDY MCKENZIE
Upper Saddle River, New Jersey: Financial Times Pitman, 1998
496pp ISBN: 0273632507
McKenzie provides a key to understanding company reports and accounts from first principles, explaining every point through the use of worked examples. She takes extracts from published accounts, including those of overseas companies, to illustrate accounting presentation, and enables the reader to understand and analyze a company's accounts and so build a comprehensive picture of its financial state.

MAGAZINES

Accountancy
ISSN: 0001–4664
Institute of Chartered Accountants in England and Wales

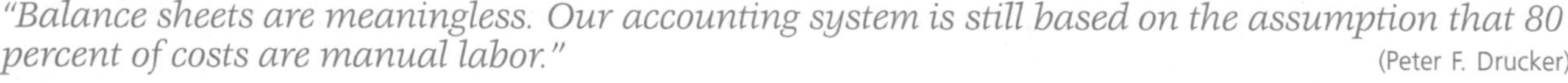

"Balance sheets are meaningless. Our accounting system is still based on the assumption that 80 percent of costs are manual labor."
(Peter F. Drucker)

Chartered Accountants' Hall, P.O. Box 433, London, EC2P 2BJ, U.K.
T: +44 (0) 20 7833 3291
F: +44 (0) 20 7833 2085
www.accountancymagazine.com
Published by the ICAEW, the magazine contains a wide range of news and articles relating to the practice of accountancy and fields such as auditing, taxation, finance, business, and management, as well as news about the ICAEW itself as a professional body.

Accountancy Age
ISSN: 0001-4672
VNU Business Publications Ltd.
VNU House, 32–34 Broadwick Street, London, W1A 2HG, U.K.
T: +44 (0) 20 7316 9000
F: +44 (0) 20 7316 9440
www.accountancyage.co.uk
Accountancy Age contains news on all aspects of accountancy practice, including financial reporting, taxation, law, business recovery, software programs, and auditing.

Accounting and Business
ISSN: 1460-406X
Association of Chartered Certified Accountants
29 Lincoln's Inn Fields, London, WC2A 3EE, U.K.
T: +44 (0) 20 7396 7000
F: +44 (0) 20 7396 7070
www.accaglobal.com/publications/accountingandbusiness
This magazine publishes articles on all aspects of, and developments in, professional accounting, and is aimed at executive agencies and professional partnerships as well as at accounting and financial professionals.

Accounting Horizons
ISSN: 0888-7993
American Accounting Association
5717 Bessie Drive, Sarasota, Florida, 34233
T: +1 941 921 7747
F: +1 941 923 4093
www.rutgers.edu/Accounting/raw/aaa/pubs.htm
Published quarterly, this reviewed magazine thoroughly covers all aspects of banking and finance, business, and accounting. The theory and application of business finance is paramount in this journal.

Accounting Review
ISSN: 0001-4826
American Accounting Association
5717 Bessie Drive, Sarasota, Florida, 34233-2399
T: +1 941 921 7747
F: +1 941 923 4093
http://accounting.rutgers.edu/raw/aaa/pubs/acctrev.htm
The *Review* contains news and articles on all aspects of teaching and research in the field of accounting.

Accounting Technician
ISSN: 1358-6297
Centurion Publishing
1 Benjamin Street, London, EC1M 5QG, U.K.
T: +44 (0) 20 7296 4236
F: +44 (0) 20 7296 4218
www.accountingtechnician.co.uk
Aimed at members and students of the Association of Accounting Technicians, the magazine covers all aspects of business and accounting of interest to accounting professionals.

Accounting Today
ISSN: 1044-5714
Accountants Media Group/Thomson
P.O. Box 966, Fort Worth, Texas, 76101
T: +1 800 260 2793
F: +1 817 252 4400
www.electronicaccountant.com
Published bimonthly, this magazine is an essential resource for accounting professionals. Covering the latest trends in finance, it is a timely source for finding current information.

American Economist
ISSN: 0569-4345
American Economist
P.O. Box 1486, Hattiesburg, Mississippi, 39403
www.bus.lsu.edu/students/organizations/ode/theamericaneconomist.htm
Published twice annually, this is the journal of the International Honor Society in Economics. The journal will appeal to anyone working in the field of economics as it highlights the latest developments in pure and applied economics.

Financial Management
ISSN: 0025-1682
Chartered Institute of Management Accountants
63 Portland Place, London, W1B 1AB, U.K.
T: +44 (0) 20 7637 2311
F: +44 (0) 20 7631 5309
www.cimaglobal.com
The magazine of the Chartered Institute of Management Accountants, *Financial Management* features news from the field of management accounting and articles on all aspects of the subject.

Journal of Accountancy
ISSN: 0021-8448
CPA2Biz, Inc.
1211 Avenue of the Americas, New York, 10036
T: +1 212 596 6200
F: +1 212 596 6213
www.aicpa.org/pubs/jofa/index.htm
Published monthly, this journal provides articles, interviews and legislative updates on all aspects of accounting. The magazine is the publication of the American Institute of Certified Public Accountants.

INTERNET

Accountants World

www.accountantsworld.com
This is an extensive portal based in the United States with links to a wide range of Web sites of interest to accountants. It relates mainly to U.S. accounting practice.

Accounting Web
www.accountingweb.co.uk
This site is an extensive online resource based in the United Kingdom. It contains material from a number of providers intended for accountancy and finance professionals. It has received an award as the New Media Business Web Site of the Year.

American Institute of Certified Public Accountants
www.aicpa.org
With 330,000 members, this organization and its Web site provide information, continuing education, accreditation, advocacy, and leadership to certified public accountants in the United States. The AICPA publishes Accounting Trends and Techniques, Statements of Position, Practice Bulletins, Accounting Interpretations, and other guidance for financial accounting and reporting.

Financial Accounting Standards Board
www.fasb.org
This is the Web site for the Financial Accounting Standards Board, the independent private-sector entity that establishes generally accepted accounting principles (GAAP). The Board issues formal accounting guidance on the treatment and reporting of financial transactions and performance.

The Dyer Partnership
http://netaccountants.com
The site provides a wide range of information on U.K. tax and accounting matters and other issues of interest to owners and managers of U.K. businesses.

ORGANIZATIONS

USA
American Institute of Certified Public

"Economics is as much a study in fantasy and aspiration as in hard numbers—maybe more so."
(Theodore Roszak)

Accountants
1211 Avenue of the Americas, New York, 10036
T: +1 212 596 6200
F: +1 212 596 6213
www.aicpa.org
With more than 330,000 members, the AICPA is the premier national professional association for certified public accountants in the United States.

National Society of Accountants
1010 North Fairfax Street, Alexandria, Virginia, 22314
T: +1 703 549 6400
F: +1 703 549 2984
www.nsacct.org
The National Society of Accountants is a nonprofit organization of some 17,000 professionals who provide accounting, tax preparation, financial and estate planning, and management advisory services to an estimated 19 million individuals and business clients. Most of the Society's members are independent practitioners or partners in small to midsize accounting and tax firms.

Europe

Association of Accounting Technicians
154 Clerkenwell Road, London, EC1R 5AD, U.K.
T: +44 (0) 20 7837 8600
F: +44 (0) 20 7410 0906
E: aatuk@dial.pipex.com
www.aat.co.uk
The AAT awards certificates in accounting at NVQ levels 2, 3, and 4. An accounting technician is qualified to a slightly lower level than a fully qualified accountant.

Association of Chartered Certified Accountants
29 Lincoln's Inn Fields, London, WC2A 3EE, U.K.
T: +44 (0) 20 7396 7000
F: +44 (0) 20 7396 7070
E: info@accaglobal.com
www.acca.co.uk
The Association is a professional and examining body in accountancy, recognized under the Companies Act 1989 by the U.K. Department of Trade and Industry.

Chartered Institute of Management Accountants
26 Chapter Street, London, SW1P 4NP, U.K.
T: +44 (0) 20 7663 5441
F: +44 (0) 20 7663 5442
www.cimaglobal.com
CIMA is the leading U.K. professional organization for management accountants.

CIPFA (Chartered Institute of Public Finance and Accountancy)
3 Robert Street, London, WC2N 6RL, U.K.
T: +44 (0) 20 7543 5600
F: +44 (0) 20 7543 5700
E: cipfa@westminster.com
www.cipfa.org
CIPFA is a U.K. professional accountancy body whose main aim is to train managers to understand public finance and manage public money. Its members are drawn from both the public and private sectors. In addition to providing membership services, running courses, and awarding certification, it organizes conferences and produces publications.

Institute of Chartered Accountants in England and Wales
Chartered Accountants' Hall, P.O. Box 433, Moorgate Place, London, EC2P 2BJ, U.K.
T: +44 (0) 20 7920 8100
F: +44 (0) 20 7920 8547
E: dsbds@icaew.co.uk
www.icaew.co.uk
This, the largest professional accountancy organization in Europe with over 120,000 members, is responsible for educating and training chartered accountants and maintaining standards of professional conduct among its members.

Institute of Chartered Accountants in Scotland
CA House, 21 Haymarket Yards, Edinburgh, Scotland, EH12 5BH, U.K.
T: +44 (0) 131 347 0100
F: +44 (0) 131 347 0105
E: enquiries@icas.org.uk
www.icas.org.uk
The ICAS is the leading professional accounting body in Scotland, and the oldest professional body of accountants in the world.

For More Information

☆ **Managing 21st Century Finances (pp. 127–28)**
Auditing and Management Audit (pp. 1908–09)
Budgeting (pp. 1913–15)
Taxation (pp. 2119–21)

Acquisitions, Takeovers, and Mergers

BOOKS

The Art of M and A Integration: A Guide to Merging Resources Processes and Responsibilities
Alexandra Reed Lajoux
New York: McGraw-Hill, 1998
439pp ISBN: 0786311274
A comprehensive treatment of postmerger integration is provided, covering the following areas: planning and communications; integration of resources; processes and management systems; technology and innovation; and commitments to customers, suppliers, shareholders, and employees.

Break Up: When Large Companies Are Worth More Dead Than Alive
David Sadtler, Andrew Campbell, Richard Koch
New York: Free Press, 1997
230pp ISBN: 1900961008
The authors consider the reasons behind a growing trend toward demerger and break-up in Western business and give advice on when a company should break up and how to profit from a break-up.

Capitalize on Merger Chaos: Six Ways to Profit from Your Competitors' Consolidation and Your Own
Thomas M. Grubb, Robert B. Lamb
New York: Simon & Schuster, 2000
212pp ISBN: 068486777X
The authors suggest that, although merger mania is at an all-time high, up to 80% of mergers fail because of culture clashes, mismanagement, and the chaos that ensues. They examine the growth and profit opportunities that can arise from competitors' merger chaos, and identify strategies which managers can adopt to exploit them. They further illustrate their argument by considering the winning strategies devised by companies such as AOL, General Electric, Dell, and Vodafone, and the failures at Coca-Cola, Boeing, and Compaq.

Complete Guide to Mergers and Acquisitions: Process Tools to Support M and A Integration at Every Level
Timothy J. Galpin, Mark Herndon
San Francisco, California: Jossey-Bass, 2000
249pp (Jossey-Bass Business and

"I learned then what a bunch of gangsters the banks are. They really are gangsters." (Alan Sugar)

Management Series)
ISBN: 0787947865
The authors provide a guide to the process of managing a merger, focusing on due diligence, change management, integration task forces, communication, retaining key people, structure and staffing decisions, cultural factors, and human resources.

Corporate Financial Reporting: Text and Cases 4th ed.
E. Richard Brownlee, Kenneth R. Ferris, Mark E. Haskins
New York: McGraw-Hill, 2000
816pp ISBN: 0072316365
The book is written for those who require a substantial appreciation and understanding of the issues, problems, and practices of financial accounting. The topics covered are: the institutional setting and fundamental concepts of accounting; the measurement and reporting of income, financial position, and cash flows; the measurement and reporting of assets, liabilities, and stockholders' equity; selected reporting and disclosure issues; and assessing the quality of reported earnings and financial position.

HR Know-how in Mergers and Acquisitions
Sue Cartwright, Cary L. Cooper
New York: Beekman, 2000
116pp (Developing Practice Series)
ISBN: 0846451751
The authors offer guidance on the human factors involved in mergers and acquisitions. The topics they cover include: influencing the decision to merge; establishing effective communication; handling job insecurity; pay and benefits; downsizing, early retirement, and relocation; support systems and counseling; creating a new corporate culture; and establishing new roles and training. Case studies of the Halifax and Leeds Permanent Building Societies, AstraZeneca, and Marconi Communications are included.

Mergers and Acquisitions: Managing the Transaction
Joseph C. Krallinger
New York: McGraw-Hill, 1997
300pp ISBN: 0786311665
This guide takes you through the entire merger and acquisition process whether you are a buyer or a seller. It explains such matters as: how to avoid the fatal flaw; the standard pitfalls; venturing, cross-licensing, and partnering; the accurate valuation of a business or a product line; and the human factor.

The Morning After: Making Corporate Mergers Work After the Deal is Sealed
Stephen J. Wall, Shannon Rye Wall
Cambridge, Massachusetts: Perseus, 2000
256pp ISBN: 0738203718
This book deals with merger management. It offers insights for recognizing when a merger is in danger, and advice on issues such as communicating effectively with stakeholders. It includes several case studies.

Successful Acquisition of Unquoted Companies: A Practical Guide 4th ed.
Barrie Pearson
Brookfield, Vermont: Gower, 1999
156pp ISBN: 0566080990
A practical guide designed to help those undertaking the acquisition of unquoted companies and subsidiaries of quoted companies, this book explains the process of investigating a potential acquisition and provides a checklist. Management buyouts and buyins and the process of selling a business to maximize shareholder value are also covered.

Successfully Integrating Two Businesses
Hans J. C. Bakker, Jeroen W. A. Helmink
Brookfield, Vermont: Gower, 2000
208pp ISBN: 056608368X
Drawing on the experiences of directors from a range of companies, the authors put forward a best practice approach to merger and acquisition integration. They also consider the role of strategic decision making and give advice on avoiding common pitfalls.

MAGAZINES

Acquisitions Monthly
ISSN: 0592–3618
Thomson Financial
Aldgate House, 33 Aldgate High Street, London, EC3N 1DL, U.K.
T: +44 (0) 20 7369 7000
F: +44 (0) 20 7369 7373
www.acquisitions-monthly.com
This monthly journal for financial executives, directors, bankers, and accountants provides information on international mergers, acquisitions, and management buyouts.

Mergers and Acquisitions Report
ISSN: 1099–3428
Securities Data Publishing
195 Broadway, 10th Floor, New York, 10007
T: +1 646 822 3295
www.mareport.com
The *M&A Report* is a weekly publication covering mergers, acquisitions, restructurings, and bankruptcies. Details of pending and ongoing deals, industry trends and strategies, news stories, and analysis are included.

Mergers and Acquisitions: The Dealmaker's Journal
ISSN: 0026–1101
Securities Data Publishing
195 Broadway, 10th Floor, New York, 10007
T: +1 212 765 5311
F: +1 212 956 0112
www.sdponline.com
This monthly journal offers complete listings of all M&A deals, including pricing, deal structure, and the sales and profit levels of merger partners. In-depth feature articles cover trends in the industry and provide practical advice.

INTERNET

Acquisitions Monthly
www.acquisitions-monthly.com
The site provides M&A news and data worldwide and information on trends, industries, and sectors. Some services are subscription-based.

Antitrust Division Department of Justice
www.usdoj.gov/atr
This U.S. government site provides information on antitrust enforcement, case filings, and links to competition authorities worldwide.

Antitrust Policy 
www.antitrust.org
This site is sponsored by the Owen Graduate School of Management and aims to bring together economic and legal perspectives on antitrust policy, law, and practice in the United States. Its comprehensive collection of information includes cases, news, research, speeches, bibliographies, and discussion groups.

BizBuySell
www.bizbuysell.com
As well as databases of businesses for sale and e-mail notification of listings, this U.S.-based site includes articles on how to go about buying or selling a business. A subscription-based Workbook that includes forms, checklists, and tips is also offered.

@BRINT
www.brint.com
This extensive portal and community network for e-business, information, technology, and knowledge management contains news, articles, book reviews, and links to relevant Web sites in the featured areas.

Company Mergers and Acquisitions
www.ventureeconomics.com
This database contains details of over 1,900 deals in the United States from 1970 onwards,

"As a publisher, we've not done acquisitions." (Duncan Edwards)

drawn from quarterly and annual fund reports, news sources, and telegrams. It is produced by Venture Economics, a Thomson Financial Company

Competition Policy
www.dti.gov.uk/cp/monopolyguide.htm
This site provides information and guidance on U.K. and E.U. legislation and procedures from the U.K. Department of Trade and Industry.

European Commission Competition
http://europa.eu.int/comm/competition
This site provides information on European competition policy and legislation.

MergerNetwork
www.mergernetwork.com
This site, a subsidiary of Dealstream Inc. founded in 1995, acts as a marketplace for buyers and sellers of companies, predominantly in North America but increasingly also in Europe, Asia, and South America. Users may search the databases of buyer profiles and businesses for sale free of charge but pay for contact information.

Worldwide Merger and Acquisitions
www.tfsd.com
This comprehensive and authoritative database of over 273,000 transactions, dating back to 1979 for the United States and 1985 for other countries, provides profiles of target and acquirer companies, and covers such matters as deal terms, value, and status. The database is subscription-based and available via the Internet or through online database hosts. It is produced by Thomsons Financial Securities Data

ORGANIZATIONS

USA

Alliance of Merger and Acquisition Advisors (AMAA)
T: +1 800 869 0491 ext.302
E: *miken@advisor-alliance.com*
www.advisor-alliance.com
This association was formed to bring together all professionals who work with mergers and acquisitions. AMAA provides national certification for members as well as various opportunities for networking with other organization members.

M&A Source
401 North Michigan Avenue, Suite 2200, Chicago, Illinois, 60611
T: +1 888 686 4222
F: +1 312 673 6599
E: *admin@ibba.org*
www.masource.org
Founded in 1991, M&A Source proclaims itself to be the world's largest organization of middle market intermediaries. With a focus on the enhancement of member skills and abilities, this body provides members with the guidance needed to assist clients. M&A Source keeps its members current on the latest issues and trends in mergers and acquisitions, and strives to enhance their professional development.

International

International Association of Merger & Acquisition Professionals (IMAP)
525 SW Fifth Street, Des Moines, Iowa, 50309
T: +1 512 282 8192
F: +1 512 282 9117
E: *imap@imap.com*
www.imap.com
Founded in 1971, this organization was formerly the International Association of Merger and Acquisition Consultants. A global networking organization with over 50 members, this organization is dedicated to helping middle-market companies obtain confidential business information on available merger and acquisition prospects. IMAP assists individuals in a variety of financial transactions: the sale of private or public companies, the purchase of product lines, leveraged buyouts, financing and investment banking services, and mezzanine financing.

For More Information

☆ **Organic Growth versus Acquisition (pp. 79–80)**
Corporate Strategy (pp. 1944–46)
Interfirm Cooperation, Strategic Alliances, Joint Ventures (pp. 2005–07)
Organization and Organization Structure (pp. 2059–61)
Venture Capital (pp. 2131–33)

ADVERTISING

BOOKS

Advertising Management 5th ed.
DAVID A. AAKER, RAJEEV BATRA, JOHN G. MYERS
Englewood Cliffs, New Jersey: Prentice Hall International, 1996
754pp ISBN: 0133057151
This is a comprehensive and detailed book on advertising management for both advertising students and those working in the field. Case studies are included.

Advertising: What It Is and How to Do It 2nd ed.
RODERICK WHITE
New York: McGraw-Hill, 1999
320pp ISBN: 0077070771
This informative and detailed introduction to all aspects of advertising is aimed at organizations new to advertising, as well as people training in the area. It discusses the necessity and cost of advertising, the use of agents, the definitions and theories of advertising, planning advertisements, the media, and international and multinational advertising. Further sources of information are also listed.

Copywriting 2nd ed.
JONATHAN J. GABAY
New York: McGraw Hill, 2001
335pp (Teach Yourself Series)
ISBN: 0658012010
The author offers a step-by-step guide to writing powerful copy. All aspects of creative advertising and promotion are covered, including direct mail, the Internet, radio and TV, business-to-business, the press, PR, charities, and posters. The book is written for both the beginner and the more experienced copywriter.

Disruption: Overturning Conventions and Shaking Up the Marketplace
JEAN-MARIE DRU
New York: John Wiley, 1996
256pp ISBN: 0471165654
This book aims to enable advertising and marketing professionals to break the usual conventions in their field and produce a new vision of a product, brand, or service. It examines advertising across the globe and highlights examples of especially effective and ineffective advertising campaigns.

The Elements of Copywriting: The Essential Guide to Creating Copy That Gets the Results You Want
GARY BLAKE, ROBERT W. BLY

"A good ad should be like a good sermon: It must not only comfort the afflicted—it must afflict the comfortable!"
(Bernice Fitz-Gibbon)

  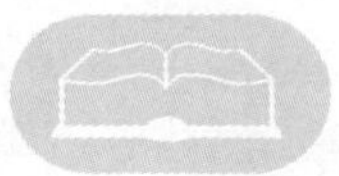    

New York: Longman, 1997
192pp ISBN: 0028626303
A tightly written overview of copywriting, this book concentrates on the use of words that have exceptional impact on consumers. It is an especially useful text because it addresses several direct-marketing forms that are still comparatively new—press releases, electronic messages, and Web advertising. It also deals with traditional marketing forms such as brochures, catalogs, and print ads.

My Life in Advertising and Scientific Advertising: Two Works
Claude C. Hopkins
New York: McGraw-Hill, 1986
336pp (Classic Reprint Edition)
ISBN: 0844231010
This book is a classic in the advertising genre. Originally published some 80 years ago, its succinct advice on reaching customers effectively has never been bettered—which accounts for its dominance in the field. *Scientific Advertising* is the more important of the two reprints here: it details methods for copywriting and test marketing, and introduces many more ideas that have come to be accepted as the building blocks of successful advertising campaigns. Hopkins coined the phrase, "Advertising is salesmanship"; these texts are the touchstone for all advertising texts that followed.

Ogilvy on Advertising
David Ogilvy
New York: Vintage, 1987
224pp ISBN: 039472903X
David Ogilvy's firm, Ogilvy and Mather, changed the way advertising firms work. His advertising ideas became cultural icons. The text is written in a conversational way, making it an easy read—yet it contains profound truths about advertising as a business, as an art form, and as a creative outlet.

Tested Advertising Methods 5th ed.
John Caples, Fred E. Hahn
Upper Saddle River, New Jersey: Prentice Hall, 1998
320pp ISBN: 0130957011
This classic text has been reissued because its influence has been so far-reaching. Caples has had some 60 years of experience in advertising and gives clear, easy-to-understand examples of advertising that works and advertising that fails. Fred Hahn, the listed coauthor, has updated the book to reflect some more current trends in advertising, but the basic principles are still the same and still very sound.

MAGAZINES

Advertising Age
ISSN: 0001–8899
Crain Communications, Inc. (MI)
1400 Woodbridge Street, Detroit, Michigan, 48207–3187
T: +1 313 446 6000
www.adage.com
This is the flagship magazine of the Ad Age Group. Widely regarded as the authoritative source for articles on national and international marketing, *Advertising Age* is the premier U.S. journal for in-depth information and current trends regarding marketing news. This weekly magazine is a must read for individuals working in advertising and marketing.

AdWeek
ISSN: 0199–2864
VNU Business Publications
770 Broadway, New York, 10003–9595
T: +1 646 654 4500
F: +1 646 654 4480
www.adweek.com
Published in six regional editions, this magazine provides specialized information for industry professionals. The same publishing company is responsible for *AdWeek*, *BrandWeek*, and *MediaWeek*, all of which cover aspects of advertising and are aimed at advertising executives. As a result, the information is often a little arcane for the layperson, but invaluable for those familiar enough with methods, layout, and advertising jargon to decipher the text. The magazine includes feature articles, trend analysis, and news about industry events.

American Demographics
ISSN: 0163–4089
Brill's Media Ventures, L.P.
521 Fifth Avenue, 11th Floor, New York, 10175
T: +1 800 529 7502
www.demographics.com/Publications/AD
Formerly called *Marketing Tools*, this monthly magazine is a key title for marketing executives wanting credible and timely information regarding the latest consumer trends. The journal is dedicated to demographical studies in the United States. Each issue offers in-depth analysis of the latest current events and how this influences the public consumer. This magazine is filled with the latest techniques for advertising and marketing research.

Journal of Advertising Research
ISSN: 0021–8499
Advertising Research Foundation
641 Lexington Avenue, New York, 10022
T: +1 212 751 5656
F: +1 212 319 5265
www.arfsite.org/webpages/JAR_pages/JARhome.htm
This is the bimonthly journal of the Advertising Research Foundation, featuring reports of field or laboratory research and case studies.

Marketing Management
ISSN: 1061–3846
American Marketing Association
311 S. Wacker Drive, Suite 5800, Chicago, Illinois, 60606
T: +1 800 262 1150
www.marketingpower.com
This journal, published every other month by the American Marketing Association, was developed with the purpose of providing middle- to senior-level marketing executives with thought provoking discussions on emerging issues in the marketing profession. It provides indepth coverage of many aspects of the profession, including national and international strategies.

INTERNET

AdForum
www.adforum.com
This gateway Web site offers links to advertising agencies, press releases, videos of ads in production, advocacy agencies, consultants, the trade press, and more.

Admark
www.admark.org.uk
The site gives details of an opt-in scheme for member advertisers and publishers who want online advertising.

Advertising Educational Foundation 
www.aef.com
This is an advertising resource that includes information on careers, academic courses, industry news and events, plus a library and an online journal.

Advertising World
http://advertising.utexas.edu/world
Extensive resources for advertising and marketing professors, students, and teachers are to be found on this site.

B to B: The Magazine for Marketing and E-commerce Strategists
www.Btobonline.com
This is the electronic counterpart to the print magazine. It provides a good overview of online marketing strategies and news on developing issues in this area. The site features polls, surveys, and lists of top advertisers and top advertising venues. It is recommended for those trying to target advertising and for those interested in ad analysis.

"It is not necessary to advertise food to hungry people, fuel to cold people, or houses to the homeless."
(J. K. Galbraith)

  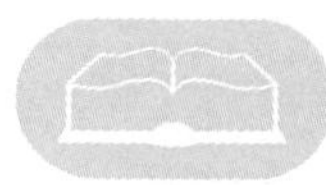    

The British Codes of Advertising and Sales Promotion
www.cap.org.uk/codes
The latest edition of The British Codes of Advertising and Sales Promotion.

The Journal of Advertising Research
www.arfsite.org/webpages/JAR_pages/JARhome.htm
Sponsored by the Advertising Research Foundation, this Web site combines the academic and the commercial. The site is interesting for those looking to spot advertising trends and for statistical analysis of advertising methods.

ORGANIZATIONS

USA

Advertising Council, Inc.
261 Madison Avenue, 11th Floor, New York, 10016
T: +1 212 922 1500
F: +1 212 922 1676
E: Info@adcouncil.org
www.adcouncil.org
This is the foremost creator of public service announcements in the United States. The Advertising Council is a nonprofit organization that was created in 1942 out of the remnants of the War Advertising Council. Its work focuses on primarily quality-of-life issues, preventive health, and community issues. Some of the most influential ad campaigns in the United States originated from this organization.

Advertising Research Foundation
641 Lexington Avenue, New York, 10022
T: +1 212 751 5656
F: +1 212 319 5265
E: info@arfsite.org
www.arfsite.org
A nonprofit corporate membership association which arranges conferences, workshops, and other events, and promotes research and development in the field of advertising.

American Advertising Federation
1101 Vermont Avenue, NW, Suite 500, Washington, D.C., 20005–6303
T: +1 202 898 0089
F: +1 202 898 0159
E: aaf@aaf.org
www.aaf.org
The Federation has a network of local chapters and clubs. It administers a prestigious award, the Advertising Hall of Fame, as well as other awards, conferences, and exhibitions.

American Association of Advertising Agencies
405 Lexington Avenue, 18th Floor, New York, 10174
T: +1 212 682 2500
F: +1 212 682 8391
E: donahue@aaaa.org
www.aaaa.org
This is an industry organization for advertising agencies. Lobbyists under AAAA auspices work for the industry on Capitol Hill. The Web site features upcoming events, news, tutorials, and the programs and publications of the group.

American Marketing Association
311 S. Wacker Drive, Suite 5800, Chicago, Illinois, 60606
T: +1 800 262 1150
E: feedback@MarketingPower.com
www.marketingpower.com
This association is an advocacy group providing resources to marketing professionals. Their site gives access to a job directory, provides courses for skill upgrades, and permits the tracking of trends in the industry. It also includes articles and tutorials for registrants.

The Direct Marketing Association
1120 Avenue of the Americas, New York, 10036–6700
T: +1 212 768 7277
F: +1 212 302 6714
E: lmastria@the-dma.org
www.the-dma.org
This group is the largest trade organization for companies involved in direct marketing, database marketing, and interactive global marketing. It is involved in lobbying efforts, promoting direct marketing, and disseminating trade information on Capitol Hill, with governmental agencies, and within all U.S. states. It is also expanding to work on international trade issues. It is well known for its work on telemarketing and is spearheading the national campaign to remove disgruntled customers from telemarketer call lists.

Europe

Advertising Association (AA)
Abford House, 15 Wilton Road, London, SW1V 1NJ, U.K.
T: +44 (0) 20 7828 2771
F: +44 (0) 20 7931 0376
E: ic@adassoc.org.uk
www.adassoc.org.uk
The AA is a federation of 26 trade associations and professional bodies representing advertisers, agencies, the media, and support services. Its remit is to promote and protect the rights, responsibilities, and role of advertising in the United Kingdom.

European Advertising Standards Alliance
10a rue de la Pépinière, 1000 Brussels, Belgium
T: +32 2 513 7806
F: +32 2 513 2861
www.easa-alliance.org
The Alliance is a coordinating body for 28 self-regulatory organizations within Europe. Its main task is to administer a cross-border complaints procedure.

Institute of Practitioners in Advertising (IPA)
44 Belgrave Square, London, SW1X 8QS, U.K.
T: +44 (0) 20 7235 7020
F: +44 (0) 20 7245 9904
E: info@ipa.co.uk
www.ipa.co.uk
The mission of the IPA is to serve, promote, and anticipate the collective interests of advertising agencies, and, at the same time, to define, develop, and help maintain the highest possible standards of professional practice within the advertising business.

International Advertising Association (U.K. Chapter) Ltd. (IAA)
166 Finchley Road, London, NW3 6BP, U.K.
T: +44 (0) 20 7431 7701
F: +44 (0) 20 7431 7098
www.iaaukchp.co.uk
The Association promotes the critical role and benefits of advertising as the vital force behind all healthy economies and the foundation of diverse, independent, and affordable media in an open society.

Outdoor Advertising Association of Great Britain Ltd. (OAA)
Summit House, 27 Sale Place, London, W2 1YR, U.K.
T: +44 (0) 20 7973 0315
F: +44 (0) 20 7973 0318
E: enquiries@oaa.org.uk
www.oaa.org.uk
The OAA is the central reference point for the outdoor advertising industry. It seeks to advance and protect the interests of members, enhance an image which is professional and proactive, and encourage the growth of business.

International

Interactive Advertising Bureau
420 Lexington Avenue, Suite 2656, New York, 10170
T: +1 212 949 9030
F: +1 212 949 9035
www.iab.net
This interactive advertising association

"It is pretty obvious that the debasement of the human mind caused by a constant flow of fraudulent advertising is not a trivial thing."
(Raymond Chandler)

undertakes a variety of activities. These include: evaluating and recommending guidelines and best practice; funding research to document the effectiveness of interactive media; and educating the advertising industry about the use of interactive advertising and marketing.

For More Information

- **Customer Relations/Customer Service (pp. 1948–50)**
- **Direct Marketing (pp. 1953–54)**
- **Market Research and Competitor Intelligence (pp. 2042–44)**
- **Marketing Management (pp. 2045–48)**
- **Product and Brand Management (pp. 2081–83)**

Analytical Techniques and Statistics

BOOKS

Applied Statistical Decision Theory
Howard Raiffa, Robert Schlaifer
New York: John Wiley, 2000
356pp (Wiley Classics Library)
ISBN: 047138349X
This book is aimed at people who are interested in using statistics as a tool in practical decision making under conditions of uncertainty, and who also have the necessary training in mathematics and statistics to employ the relevant analytical techniques. It focuses on experimentation and decision, general theory, extensive-form analysis, and distribution theory.

Basic Business Statistics: Concepts and Applications 7th ed.
Mark L. Berenson, David M. Levine
Upper Saddle River, New Jersey: Prentice Hall, 1998
1114pp ISBN: 0137956185
This textbook deals with the techniques of analyzing and presenting business data. The authors explain probability, normal distribution, estimation, hypothesis testing, analysis of variance, and linear and multiple regression models. It includes a CD-ROM.

Dictionary of Economics
Jae K. Shim, Joel G. Siegel
New York: John Wiley, 1995
373pp ISBN: 0471013145
This is an economic forecasting and analysis textbook that is geared for the lay reader. It is remarkably jargon-free and features paraphrased basic English descriptions of complex economic terms. It is also notable for its unusual feature of including slang terms. Likewise of note are the extremely clear graphics: there are many charts and diagrams that are very useful in understanding complicated concepts. While not exactly a guide to performing statistical analysis, this book is essential for those intending actually to understand the reports they have commissioned on the subject.

Doing Research in Business and Management: An Introduction to Process and Method
Dan Remenyi, et al.
Thousand Oaks, California: Sage, 1998
336pp ISBN: 0761959505
Highlighting first the different contexts and purposes, strategies and tactics, and programs and processes of management research, the authors then move on to a more detailed review of the relevant research approaches and methods. They discuss the interrelationship of theoretical and empirical research, and examine how these different approaches are used in practice. The implications of using quantitative and qualitative methods are examined, and the book also contains practical advice on available analysis techniques and software packages.

Effective Use of Statistics: A Practical Guide for Managers 2nd ed.
Tim Hannagan
Milford, Connecticut: Kogan Page, 1999
160pp (Business Skills Series)
ISBN: 0749429690
Hannagan provides a statistical foundation for managers, focusing on integrating statistical information into everyday work and presenting it effectively. An appendix offers basic math for managers, and the book comes with an accompanying computer disk with a data file in Microsoft Word for Windows.

Essential Quantitative Methods for Business Management and Finance 2nd ed.
Les Oakshott
New York: Palgrave, 2001
432pp ISBN: 0333963350
This is a student guide to the major topics likely to be taught on a quantitative methods course. The areas covered include index numbers, investment appraisal, sampling methods, presentation of data, profitability, normal distribution, hypothesis testing, correlation and regression, time series analysis, linear programming, critical path analysis, and simulation.

Implementing Global Performance Measurement Systems: A Cookbook Approach to Evaluation
Ferdinand Tesoro, Jack Tootson
San Francisco, California: Jossey-Bass/Pfeiffer, 1999
256pp ISBN: 078794744X
This practical guide presents a step-by-step approach to evaluating and measuring ongoing business performance. Following an overview of performance measurement, the areas covered include establishing the business case, identifying the right performance metrics, implementing the performance measurement system, and leveraging results to improve performance. Guidance is offered on constructing a line graph, a cause–effect diagram, and a scatter diagram. A CD-ROM is included.

101 Great Mission Statements: How the World's Leading Companies Run Their Businesses
Timothy R. V. Foster, ed.
Milford, Connecticut: Kogan Page, 1993
144pp ISBN: 0749409525
The compiler provides an introduction to the main elements of an effective mission statement, together with a collection of 101 particularly successful examples.

Practical Business Statistics 4th ed.
Andrew Siegel
New York: McGraw-Hill, 1999
730pp ISBN: 0072337559
Though this is a college textbook, it is not simply filled with formulas and equations. Offering a less theoretical approach to statistics, this text focuses on examples using real data, applications, and the underlying reasons for using statistical analysis in business. It is especially useful because the text acknowledges that much of what is done in business statistics and analysis is now done by computer programs, rather than by unhappy, squinting workers in visors with scientific calculators.

Quantitative Approaches in Business Studies 5th ed.
Claire Morris
Upper Saddle River, New Jersey: Financial

"There should be some professional exam for these analysts. Most of the time they talk through their backsides."
(Alan Sugar)

  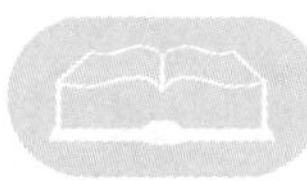    

Times Prentice Hall, 1999
500pp ISBN: 0273638289
Using a problem-driven approach, this textbook for students on business courses aims to demonstrate the effectiveness of quantitative methods. The four parts cover: handling numbers; numbers as a means of communication; numbers as a basis for deduction; and numbers as a tool of planning. This edition includes a chapter on multiple regression and the use of statistical methods for a substantial student project or dissertation.

Quantitative Methods: A Business Perspective
DIANA BEDWARD
Woburn, Massachusetts: Butterworth-Heinemann, 1999
384pp ISBN: 0750640936
Writing for students, researchers, and managers, the author presents a whole toolkit of techniques. She introduces and explains financial mathematics, collecting business information, effective business presentations, business analysis, uncertainty in decision making, linear relationships in business, and the fundamentals of business forecasting. The book comes with a disk containing exercises in Excel.

Root Cause Failure Analysis
R. KEITH MOBLEY
Woburn, Massachusetts: Newnes, 1999
360pp (Plant Engineering Maintenance Series)
ISBN: 0750671580
The author outlines the concepts needed to carry out industrial troubleshooting investigations effectively and explains the principles of Root Cause Failure Analysis (RCFA). He also provides extensive information on equipment design and equipment troubleshooting.

Statistics Data Analysis and Decision Modelling
JAMES R. EVANS, DAVID L. OLSEN
Upper Saddle River, New Jersey: Prentice Hall, 2000
329pp ISBN: 0130205451
This book covers the basic concepts of business statistics, data analysis, and management science in a contemporary spreadsheet environment. It particularly emphasizes the practical applications of its approaches to business decision making. A software package on CD is included.

Time Series Models for Business and Economic Forecasting
PHILIP HANS FRANSES
New York: Cambridge University Press, 1998
280pp ISBN: 0521586410
Generally regarded as one of the best introductory texts on economic forecasting, this book nonetheless requires a bit more background in business and economics than the average lay-person usually possesses. Focus is placed on economic time series analysis, which is a fancy way of saying that it explains statistical analyses of trends, seasonality, and other nonlinear series. The book uses real market examples, rather than simulated data and simple equations. There is also emphasis on model identification and diagnostics, which baffle many business forecasters. This book is definitely skewed to the academic, yet is far easier for most readers to use than standard econometrics texts.

MAGAZINES

Journal of the American Statistical Association
ISSN: 0162-1459
American Statistical Association
1429 Duke Street, Alexandria, Virginia, 22314-3461
T: +1 703 684 1221
F: +1 703 684 8069
www.amstat.org/publications/jasa
JASA was established in 1888 and is published in March, June, September, and December. Subjects covered include statistical applications and statistical education.

Journal of the Royal Statistical Society
Blackwell Publishers
108 Cowley Road, Oxford, Oxfordshire, OX4 1JF, U.K.
T: +44 (0) 1865 791100
F: +44 (0) 1865 791347
www.blackwellpublishers.co.uk
The *Journal* was established in 1838. It is divided into Series A: Statistics in Society (ISSN: 09641998); Series B: Statistical Methodology (ISSN: 13697412); Series C: Applied Statistics (ISSN: 00359254); and Series D: The Statistician (ISSN: 00390526). Each is available as a separate journal. Series A is produced three times a year; Series B, C, and D are quarterly.

INTERNET

Milner Library, Illinois State University
www.mlb.ilstu.edu/learn/stat
This is an online tutorial called "Finding Statistics." Via a series of Internet pages, it covers (a) finding statistics, (b) understanding them, and (c) evaluating their usefulness. A self-assessment tool, or quiz, is included in each section. On this site, the reader can answer a number of basic questions, such as what the general definitions and terminology are in statistical research, how to locate statistics easily, how to determine whether statistics are reliably relevant, and what statistical databases are available. This is an excellent primer on the subject.

ORGANIZATIONS

USA

American Statistical Association
1429 Duke Street, Alexandria, Virginia, 22314-3461
T: +1 703 684 1221
F: +1 703 684 8069
E: asainfo@amstat.org
www.amstat.org
Founded in 1839, this is an educational society for professional statisticians which boasts Florence Nightingale, Alexander Graham Bell, and Andrew Carnegie as former members. It now has some 16,000 members in the United States, Canada, and throughout the world. The ASA publishes or copublishes a number of journals, including the Journal of the American Statistical Association. The Association's Web site has a searchable database of relevant events.

Europe

Royal Statistical Society
12 Errol Street, London, EC1Y 8LX, U.K.
T: +44 (0) 20 7638 8998
F: +44 (0) 20 7614 3905
E: rss@rss.org.uk
www.rss.org.uk
The RSS has over 7,200 members divided into local groups and organizes over 150 meetings a year, including an annual international conference. It offers several professional qualifications to members. The society also publishes the Journal of the Royal Statistical Society (in four series), and a monthly news magazine, RSS News.

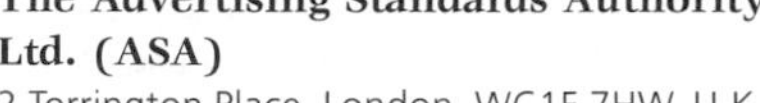

The Advertising Standards Authority Ltd. (ASA)
2 Torrington Place, London, WC1E 7HW, U.K.
T: +44 (0) 20 7580 5555
F: +44 (0) 20 7631 3051
E: inquiries@asa.org.uk
www.asa.org.uk
The ASA exists to protect the public by ensuring that the rules in the British Codes of Advertising and Sales Promotion are followed by everyone who prepares and publishes advertisements. Its declared aim is to promote the highest standards in advertising.

"There are two kinds of statistics, the kind you look up and the kind you make up." (Rex Stout)

For More Information

☆ Benchmarking (pp. 295–96)
☆ Lean Manufacturing (pp. 183–84)

Benchmarking (pp. 1911–13)
Business Process Reengineering (pp. 1921–23)
Market Research and Competitor Intelligence (pp. 2042–44)

Process Control and Statistical Process Control (pp. 2079–80)

Auditing and Management Audit

BOOKS

The Auditor's SAS Field Guide 2002
Dan M. Guy, Douglas R. Carmichael
New York: John Wiley, 2002
272pp ISBN: 0471137030
The book outlines the core Statement on Auditing Standards and provides guidelines for ensuring that fieldwork complies with requirements. It supplements generally-accepted auditing standards and is provided as a reference tool for auditors.

Information System Auditing and Assurance
James A. Hall
Cincinnati, Ohio: South-Western College Publishing, 1999
425pp ISBN: 0324003188
The book and its accompanying software provide a comprehensive understanding of how to audit accounting information systems. It takes a risk analysis approach to auditing and suggests audit tests that mitigate the threats to data integrity related to operating systems, database management, and application and system development.

The Internal Auditing Handbook
K. H. Spencer Pickett
New York: John Wiley, 1997
656pp ISBN: 0471969117B
The book is a comprehensive guide to audit standards, internal controls, planning and risk analysis, statistical sampling, client interviews and flowcharting. It provides many examples of the application of audit theory by means of case studies and assignments with suggested solutions. The handbook also deals with special engagements and topics including computer audits, fraud investigations, establishing an audit function, and training audit staff. It is organized in four major parts that cover theory, techniques, internal audit management, and specialist auditing.

The Management Audit: How to Create an Effective Management Team
Michael Craig-Cooper, Philippe De Backer
Upper Saddle River, New Jersey: Prentice Hall, 1993
224pp ISBN: 0273600044
This book describes how the management audit can be used to manage change effectively and contribute to the efficiency of boards and executive teams. The issues and questions it covers include: managing change; deciding when management audits are appropriate; the management audit as a vital management tool; and the benefits of an audit. It also includes contributions from leading entrepreneurs, and case studies.

Montgomery's Auditing 12th ed.
Vincent M. O'Reilly, et al.
New York: John Wiley, 2001
336pp ISBN: 0471327425
The book outlines all the information needed to understand and apply generally accepted auditing standards. It assists auditors in developing an enterprise plan, testing specific accounting cycles and accounts, and producing the final audit report. The book is organized in five parts that cover the audit environment, theory and concepts, auditing specific accounts, completing the audit and reporting results, and auditing specialized industries.

Quantitative Analysis for Management 7th ed.
Barry Render, Ralph M. Stair
Upper Saddle River, New Jersey: Prentice Hall, 1999
766pp ISBN: 0130215384
This textbook for students combines coverage of traditional management science techniques with modern technology solutions.

MAGAZINES

ABI Journal
American Bankruptcy Institute
44 Canal Center Plaza, Suite 404, Alexandria, Virginia, 22314
T: +1 703 739 0800
F: +1 703 739 1060
www.abiworld.org
The *ABI Journal* is published ten times a year. It is written by experts from the insolvency community and addresses issues such as consumer bankruptcy, the intersection of state laws and the Bankruptcy Code, valuation, turnaround management concerns, and recent legislative developments.

Internal Auditing and Business Risk
Institute of Internal Auditors—United Kingdom & Ireland
13 Abbeville Mews, 88 Clapham Park Road, London, SW4 7BX, U.K.
T: +44 (0) 20 7819 1925
F: +44 (0) 20 7978 2492
www.iia.org.uk
This magazine, the journal of the IIA—U.K., covers all aspects of internal auditing and of risk assessment and risk management.

Internal Auditor
ISSN: 0020-5745
Institute of Internal Auditors, Inc.
247 Maitland Avenue, Altamonte Springs, Florida, 32701-4201
T: +1 407 830 7600
F: +1 407 831 5171
www.theiia.org
This magazine, the journal of the IIA in the United States, covers auditing techniques and applications, internal control systems, corporate governance, and contains practical case studies.

Managerial Auditing Journal
ISSN: 0268-6902
MCB University Press Ltd.
60/62 Toller Lane, Bradford, West Yorkshire, BD8 9BY, U.K.
T: +44 (0) 1274 777700
F: +44 (0) 1274 785200
www.emeraldinsight.com/maj.htm
The *Managerial Auditing Journal* addresses the changing function of the auditor and examines both the professional and the managerial aspects of the role. Its articles are mainly concerned with developments in auditing theory and practice, research, and case studies.

INTERNET

Information Systems Audit and Control Association
www.isaca.org/isacafx.htm
This is the Web site of the Information Systems Audit and Control Association, a recognized leader in information technology assurance, control, and governance. With 23,000 members

"The most important thing American industry needs to do is reduce the number of management layers."
(Kenneth Iverson)

  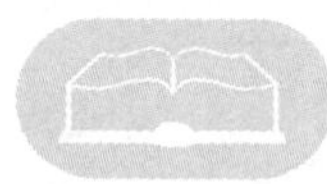    

in more than 100 countries, the organization provides CISA (Certified Information Systems Auditor) certification and develops worldwide standards for information systems auditing and control.

The Institute of Internal Auditors
www.theiia.org
This is the Web site of a nonprofit organization with 70,000 members representing over 100 countries. Its purpose is to serve as the profession's international watchdog and primary resource for certification, continuing education, research, and technological issues related to internal audits.

Internal Auditing World Wide Web
www.bitwise.net/iawww
The main value of this site is the long list it offers of other associations with an interest in internal auditing. The URLs to these are not hyperlinks and have to be manually keyed.

The American Institute of Certified Public Accountants
www.aicpa.org
This is the Web site of an organization with 330,000 members which provides information, continuing education, accreditation, advocacy, and leadership to certified public accountants in the United States. The AICPA's Audit and Attest Standards team directs and develops standards for audit, attestation, and review services performed by CPAs.

ORGANIZATIONS

USA

AACSB International Association for Management Development
600 Emerson Road, Suite 300, St. Louis, Missouri, 63141–6762
T: +1 314 872 8481
F: +1 314 872 8494
www.aacsb.edu
Founded in 1916, the AACSB was formerly known as the American Assembly of Collegiate Schools of Business. It acts as an accrediting agency for bachelor's, master's, and doctoral degree programs in business administration and accounting. It currently has over 850 members, including 650 educational institutions in the United States and 160 abroad.

American Accounting Association
5717 Bessie Drive, Sarasota, Florida, 34233–2399
T: +1 941 921 7747
F: +1 941 923 4093
E: *office@aaahq.packet.net*
www.aaa-edu.org
The AAA is a professional body with a particular interest in developments in the teaching of accountancy.

The Institute of Internal Auditors
247 Maitland Avenue, Altamonte Springs, Florida, 32701–4201
T: +1 407 830 7600
F: +1 407 831 5171
E: *custserv@theiia.org*
www.theiia.org
The IIA is the leading professional body for internal auditors in the United States and has some 70,000 members worldwide.

Europe

Institute of Internal Auditors—United Kingdom
13 Abbeville Mews, 88 Clapham Park Road, London, SW4 7BX, U.K.
T: +44 (0) 20 7498 0101
F: +44 (0) 20 7978 2492
E: *info@iia.org.uk*
www.iia.org.uk
The IIA is the U.K. professional body for internal auditors. It offers its members information and advice on all aspects of internal auditing, and presents their views to the government and other national and international bodies.

For More Information

- ✓ **Internal Audit (pp. 564–65)**
- **Accounting (pp. 1899–1901)**
- **Bankruptcy and Business Failure (pp. 1909–11)**
- **Business Ethics and Codes of Practice (pp. 1918–20)**
- **Social Responsibility of Management (pp. 2115–17)**
- **Taxation (pp. 2119–21)**

BANKRUPTCY AND BUSINESS FAILURE

BOOKS

Buying a Company in Trouble: A Practical Guide 2nd ed.
IAN E. WALKER
Brookfield, Vermont: Gower, 1992
144pp ISBN: 0566072890
This book provides practical guidance for those planning to buy a company that is formally insolvent or close to insolvency. It considers the reasons for buying such a company and discusses how to recognize a company in trouble, decide when to buy, and negotiate the offer, as well as the other matters that should be taken into account.

Corporate Failure by Design: Why Organizations Are Built to Fail
JONATHAN I. KLEIN
Westport, Connecticut: Quorum Books, 2000
328pp ISBN: 1567202977
Despite all that has been written on the subject of making organizations succeed, the reality is that an overwhelming majority of businesses fail within five years and almost all fail within ten years. The author suggests that this tendency is inherent in the organization and explains his theory of organizational self-destruction. Besides analyzing the causes and processes of failure, however, he also points out the lessons that can be learned from it.

Corporate Financial Distress and Bankruptcy: A Complete Guide to Predicting and Avoiding Distress and Profiting from Bankruptcy 2nd ed.
EDWARD I. ALTMAN
New York: John Wiley, 1993
356pp (Wiley Finance Edition)
ISBN: 0471552534
A leading expert on bankruptcy examines the trends in this field, reflecting the atmosphere in corporate America. He also presents models that can be used to analyze companies and their financial options and includes a number of relevant case studies.

Corporate Turnaround: How Managers Turn Losers into Winners
DONALD B. BIBEAULT
Frederick, Maryland: Beard Group, 1998
482pp ISBN: 1893122026
This is a reprint of a classic book that remains a source of effective advice on financial crisis management. It distills the experiences of close to 100 managers who successfully restored companies to profitability and adds up to a guide to practical management strategies to prevent bankruptcy.

Creating Value through Corporate Restructuring: Case Studies in Bankruptcies, Buyouts, and Breakups
STUART C. GILSON

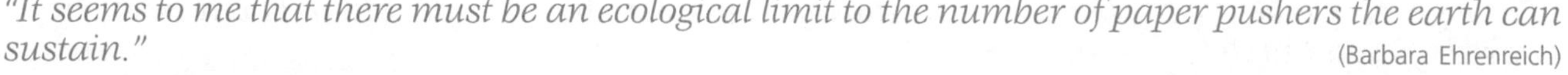

  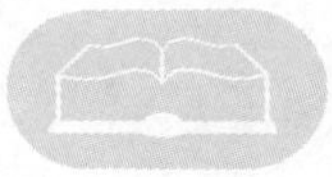    

New York: John Wiley, 2001
528pp ISBN: 0471405590
Management buyouts are a common form of business restructuring. This collection of recent case studies from the United States and several other countries illustrates the real-world techniques and strategies that are common to all types of restructuring. It demystifies complex financial issues surrounding business valuation and gives the reader a better understanding of the possibilities when dealing with corporate restructuring.

Elements of Bankruptcy 3rd ed.
Douglas G. Baird
New York: Foundation Press, 2000
236pp ISBN: 1566628687
Baird's book gives an overview of current law and practice in the United States. Recent changes in the law and topical issues are discussed and placed in context.

The Executive Guide to Corporate Bankruptcy
Thomas J. Salerno, Jordan A. Kroop, Craig D. Hansen
Frederick, Maryland: Beard Group, 2001
735pp ISBN: 1587980266
This book was written to provide a comprehensive resource for managers of financially troubled companies facing Chapter 11 bankruptcy proceedings. The authors outline the history of American bankruptcy law and bankruptcy terminology for the lay person, then provide a step-by-step guide to the bankruptcy and reorganization process, including sample documents.

The Turnaround Manager's Handbook
Richard S. Sloma
Frederick, Maryland: Beard Group, 2000
244pp ISBN: 1893122409
Designed for the corporate manager, this book provides specific details on actions undertaken to achieve a turnaround in a failing business. The author addresses operational issues and provides recommendations and tools to restore a business to profitability.

MAGAZINES

Insolvency Intelligence
ISSN: 0950–2645
Sweet and Maxwell
100 Avenue Road, Swiss Cottage, London, NW3 3PF, U.K.
T: +44 (0) 20 7393 7000
F: +44 (0) 20 7393 7010
www.smlawpub.co.uk
This magazine, published ten times a year, contains news and views on insolvency law for lawyers and accountants.

Insolvency Law and Practice
ISSN: 0267–0771
Butterworths Tolley
Halsbury House, 35 Chancery Lane, London, WC2A 1EL, U.K.
T: +44 (0) 20 7400 2500
F: +44 (0) 20 7400 2842
www.butterworths.co.uk
Aimed at legal practitioners, students, and accountants, this magazine covers all aspects of insolvency law and accountancy. It appears six times a year.

International Insolvency Review
ISSN: 1180–0518
John Wiley
Wiley InterScience Coordinator, Subscriptions Department, 605 Third Avenue, New York, 10158–0012
T: +1 800 825 7550
F: +1 212 850 6021
www.interscience.wiley.com
The *IIR* is published three times a year, in association with INSOL, and provides an international perspective on developments in insolvency law and practice, in addition to covering issues relating to cross-border insolvency.

INTERNET

ABIWorld
www.abiworld.org
ABIWorld is sponsored by the American Bankruptcy Institute and is a major source of U.S. bankruptcy information. The site includes news and statistics, information and opinions on bankruptcy cases, information on international bankruptcy legislation, an interactive newsletter, and information on how to find a bankruptcy professional. Some sections are restricted to ABI members.

American Bankruptcy Institute
www.abiworld.org
The American Bankruptcy Institute is a nonprofit, nonpartisan organization promoting education, research, and the analysis of bankruptcy issues. Its Web site provides access to current news and legislation pertaining to bankruptcy and business failures, an interactive newsletter, and research and analysis.

Business Bankruptcy Info
www.creditworthy.com/topics/bankruptcy.html
This Web site, hosted by Creditworthy Co., provides links to business bankruptcy information covering the United States, Canada, and United Kingdom. It includes information on, and links to, U.S. bankruptcy courts, an overview of the U.S. Bankruptcy Code, and statistics and research on bankruptcy filings.

InsolvencyAsia
www.insolvencyasia.com
This site, based in Hong Kong, provides insolvency-related news together with information on bankruptcy legislation and listings of consultants, associations, and regulatory authorities in Asian countries.

Insolvency.co.uk
www.insolvency.co.uk
This Web site is the major Internet source of information on bankruptcy and insolvency in the United Kingdom. It provides access to databases of companies in liquidation, receivership, and administration, and of specialist legal firms. It contains links to legislation and other relevant sites, as well as offering a range of services including news, FAQs, mailing lists, and training courses.

Insolvency Services
www.insolvency.gov.uk
This government-sponsored site provides practical information and advice on personal and corporate insolvency in the United Kingdom, including statistics and a database of insolvency practitioners.

InterNet Bankruptcy Library
www.bankrupt.com
This site, sponsored by the Bankruptcy Creditors' Service and the Beard Group, is aimed particularly at creditors. It includes a news archive, a database of bankruptcy professionals, information on legal rules in American states, and details of publications, as well as providing access to discussion groups.

World Internet Insolvency and Bankruptcy Resources
www.insolvency.com
This site includes a listing of U.S. and U.K. mailing lists and newsgroups connected with insolvency.

ORGANIZATIONS

USA

American Bankruptcy Institute
44 Canal Center Plaza, Suite 404, Alexandria, Virginia, 22314
T: +1 703 739 0800
F: +1 703 739 1060
E: *info@abiworld.org*
www.abiworld.org
The ABI was founded in 1982 to provide the U.S. Congress and public with unbiased information on bankruptcy issues. Its activities include

"Through the fat years, the bankers were always right there by our side. But in bad times they backed off in a hurry."
(Lee Iacocca)

research, conferences, training programs, and publications; opportunities for the exchange of information and ideas are also provided. The membership of 7,500 includes attorneys, auctioneers, bankers, judges, accountants, and other professionals.

Europe

Bankruptcy Association of England and Wales
4 Johnson Close, Abraham Heights, Lancaster, Lancashire, LA1 5EU, U.K.
T: +44 (0) 1524 64305
F: +44 (0) 1524 389717
E: bankruptcyassociation@gbandi.freeserve.co.uk
www.theba.org.uk
The Association was founded by John McQueen in 1983 to provide information and advice to debtors and bankrupts in the United Kingdom and to campaign for reform of insolvency legislation.

Insolvency Practitioners Association
Bow Bells House, 11 Bread Street, London, EC4M 9BE, U.K.
T: +44 (0) 20 7329 0777
F: +44 (0) 20 7329 2204
E: secretariat@ipa.uk.com
www.ipa.uk.com
The IPA, founded in 1961, is a professional organization for insolvency practitioners. Its main objectives are to promote training and education in insolvency administration and to maintain the standards of performance and conduct of those working in the field.

R3, The Association of Business Recovery Professionals
4th Floor, Halton House, 20–23 Holborn, London, EC1N 2JD, U.K.
T: +44 (0) 20 7831 6563
F: +44 (0) 20 7405 7047
E: association@r3.org.uk
www.r3.org.uk
R3 (Rescue, Recovery, Renewal), founded in 1990 and formerly known as the Society of Practitioners of Insolvency, is a professional organization for insolvency practitioners and turnaround managers which places a growing emphasis on reconstruction, turnaround management, and corporate recovery. Its activities include courses, conferences, and producing publications—including the quarterly journal *Recovery*.

International

INSOL International—International Federation of Insolvency Professionals
2–3 Philpot Lane, London, EC3M 8AQ, U.K.
T: +44 (0) 20 7929 6679
F: +44 (0) 20 7929 6678
E: tina@insol.ision.co.uk
www.insol.org
INSOL is a grouping of member associations that aims to facilitate the exchange of information and ideas and to encourage international cooperation within the insolvency profession. It participates in governmental advisory groups, supports research, and promotes the development of international guidelines and codes of practice. Its activities include the organization of seminars and conferences and the publication of newsletters, reports, and a journal.

For More Information

- **Accounting (pp. 1899–1901)**
- **Auditing and Management Audit (pp. 1908–09)**

BENCHMARKING

BOOKS

Benchmarking
Sylvia Codling
Brookfield, Vermont: Gower, 1998
168pp ISBN: 0566079267
The book is designed for readers who want to know what benchmarking is and what the real benefits are to them and to their organizations. It falls into three sections, which focus upon planning and analysis, implementation, and a case study of the U.K. Employment Service's use of benchmarking. It includes checklists, tables, questionnaires, and answers.

Benchmarking: A Practitioner's Guide for Becoming and Staying Best of the Best
Gerald Balm
Schaumberg, Illinois: QPMA Press, 1992
178pp ISBN: 0963216708
This book is a practical guide for understanding benchmarking strategies, and applying them in an efficient, effective way to various types of organizations, such as industry, healthcare and government. It explains the benchmarking process used at award-winning IBM-Rochester, and includes bibliographical references and an index.

Benchmarking for Best Practices: Winning through Innovative Adaptation
Christopher Bogan, Michael English
New York: McGraw-Hill, 1994
312pp ISBN: 0070063753
This book presents a nine-step benchmarking model for management. It aims to tailor benchmarking to a firm's unique identity. It features timesaving tips, evaluation charts, graphs, ethics, and antitrust guidelines and includes bibliographical references and indexes.

The Benchmarking Sourcebook: How to Find the Right Benchmarking Partners
Michael Cross
London: Batsford, 1998
432pp ISBN: 0713484403
Besides acting as an introduction to the concept of benchmarking, this book identifies sources of information on the technique. These include handbooks and texts, articles, clubs and associations, courses and conferences, and reports and studies. Sources of information on potential benchmarking partners are similarly reviewed.

Benchmarking Strategies: A Tool for Profit Improvement
Rob Reider, Harry Reider
New York: John Wiley, 2000
276pp ISBN: 0471344648
This book provides a practical manual to benchmarking principles, techniques, and implementation. It examines how corporations perform various tasks in identifying and implementing internal and external best practices in a program of continuous improvement. It includes an index.

Best Practices: Building Up Your Business with Customer-focused Solutions
R. Hiebeler, T. B. Kelly, C. Ketteman
New York: Simon & Schuster, 1998
240pp ISBN: 0684834537
From case studies of over 40 best practice companies, this book draws lessons on how to focus on customers, create growth, reduce costs, and increase profits. The topics it discusses are: new insights beyond benchmarking; best practices auditing; how to understand markets and customers; involving customers in the design of products and services; selling products and services; how best

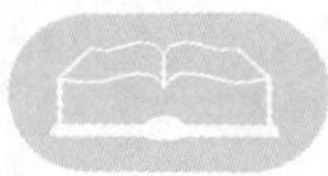

to serve customers; managing customer information; and putting best practices to work.

Effective Management of Benchmarking Projects: Practical Guidelines and Examples of Best Practice
MOHAMED ZAIRI
Woburn, Massachusetts: Butterworth-Heinemann, 1998
348pp ISBN: 0750639873
This book begins with a profile of Rank Xerox—where the benchmarking story started. It examines the strategic application of benchmarking for best practice, as well as such topics as partner selection, the ethics of benchmarking, and the value of industrial visits and benchmarking awards. It also describes the process of benchmarking in practice.

High Performance Benchmarking: 20 Steps to Success
H. JAMES HARRINGTON, JAMES S. HARRINGTON
New York: McGraw-Hill, 1995
173pp ISBN: 007026774X
The aim of this book is to provide a complete understanding of how the total benchmarking process in any organization ought to be managed. It explains the process of benchmarking, data collection and analysis, organizing for benchmarking, and the five phases of benchmarking, presenting helpful hints and tips along the way. Case studies and checklists illustrate the key issues.

The Manager's Guide to Benchmarking: Essential Skills for the New Competitive Cooperative Economy
JEROME P. FINNIGAN
San Francisco, California: Jossey-Bass, 1996 (Jossey-Bass Business and Management Series)
ISBN: 0787902799
Jerome P. Finnigan, a leading authority on quality and benchmarking at the Xerox Corporation, here presents his readers with a valuable toolkit for planning and conducting a benchmarking project in the form of a proven four-phase approach that managers can use to to improve productivity, redesign work processes, and contribute to a culture of learning and change. Using examples from Xerox, Motorola, AT&T, General Electric, and other successful companies, Finnigan effectively balances the "hard" analytical process of gathering information with the "soft" intuitive side of managing the process.

Managing by Measuring: How to Improve Your Organization's Performance Through Effective Benchmarking
MARK T. CZARNECKI
New York: AMACOM, 1999
240pp ISBN: 0814403905
Targeted to the IT professional, this practical how-to guide provides industry-specific tools and programs for creating the kind of organization you desire by measuring the key values. It includes real-world examples and sample forms, and a step-by-step process for conducting benchmarking studies, including the research and data analysis needed to isolate best practices.

Winning Business: How to Use Financial Analysis and Benchmarks to Outscore Your Competition
RICH GILDERSLEEVE
Woburn, Massachusetts: Gulf Professional Publishing Company, 1999
334pp ISBN: 0884158985
Financial analysis, with all its detailed measurements and calculations, is often overlooked as a benchmarking tool. Gildersleeve provides clear explanations of the fundamental terms used to analyze and understand financial statements and demonstrates their value in benchmarking companies. The benchmarking indicators in this book can be used to track key measurements or as a metric by which to measure your company against others.

MAGAZINES

Benchmarking: An International Journal
ISSN: 1463–5771
MCB University Press
60/62 Toller Lane, Bradford, West Yorkshire, BD8 9BY, U.K.
T: +44 (0) 1274 777700
F: +44 (0) 1274 785200
www.emeraldinsight.com/bij.htm
The journal focuses on the theory and practice of benchmarking, with articles on recent academic research as well as real-life case studies of benchmarking activities by companies. Contributors are from a wide range of countries.

INTERNET

APQC's Benchmarking and Best Practice
www.apqc.org/best
This site summarizes the benefits of benchmarking, outlines a methodology, and lists the keys to success in the area. The "free resources" section includes articles, case studies, and white papers to guide you through the benchmarking process.

Avoid These Ten Benchmarking Mistakes
www.benchmarkingplus.com.au/mistakes.htm
Many sites tell you how to benchmark. This site lists the ten most common mistakes in benchmarking so that you can avoid making them yourself.

Benchmarking Exchange
www.benchnet.com
This is an extremely comprehensive site with a lot of information on benchmarking practices for both members and nonmembers. Members can conduct benchmark surveys online and have the information collected and returned through the Exchange as replies are received.

Benchmarking Network
www.benchmarkingnetwork.com
This is another comprehensive site. Members share information about best practice in a wide range of operations across all industry sectors.

Best-Practice.com
www.Best-Practice.com
Providing a range of information on benchmarking, this site has links to more detailed research and tools that can be purchased direct from the various partners in the network. Membership is free.

Global Benchmarking Council
www.globalbenchmarking.com
Members have access to a benchmarking database, regular meetings, and research reports, plus a range of other services and detailed information.

ORGANIZATIONS

USA

American Productivity and Quality Center
123 North Post Oak Lane, 3rd Floor, Houston, Texas, 77024
T: +1 800 776 9676
F: +1 731 681 1182
E: apqcinfo@apqc.org
www.apqc.org
This nonprofit organization works with people and other organizations around the world to improve productivity and quality. Nearly 500 companies, government organizations, and educational institutions support it. It provides the tools, information, expertise, and support needed to discover and implement best practices in a variety of areas, including

"Copying other organizations' activities sounds like industrial espionage to some people, but the truth is that benchmarking is perfectly legal and ethical."
(Warren Bennis)

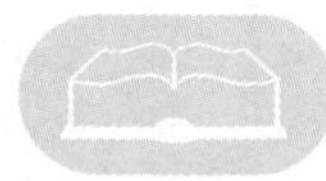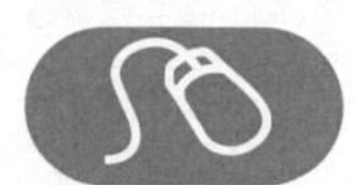

knowledge management, benchmarking, and performance measurement.

Europe
Best Practice Club
Wolseley Business Park, Kempston, Bedfordshire, MK42 7PW, U.K.
T: +44 (0) 1234 853605
F: +44 (0) 1234 854499
E: michelle@bpclub.com
www.bpclub.com
This organization, which has an international membership, promotes organizational excellence through members networking and comparing their practice. Member companies come from both the manufacturing and the service sectors and pool their experience.

Centre for Interfirm Comparison
CIFC Ltd., 32 Thomas Street, Winchester, Hampshire, SO23 9HJ, U.K.
T: +44 (0) 1962 844144
F: +44 (0) 1962 843180
E: projects@cifc.co.uk
www.cifc.co.uk
The Centre helps businesses of all types and in all sectors to assess their performance through confidential, detailed comparison of their financial ratios and other data with those of similar businesses, and to target improvements in specific areas of their operations. The Centre provides a wide range of benchmarking and related consulting services.

For More Information

☆ **The Balanced Scorecard (pp. 303–04)**
Business Appraisal and Performance Measurement (pp. 1915–17)
Quality and Total Quality Management (pp. 2096–98)

BUDGETING

BOOKS

Budgeting for Non-financial Managers: How to Master and Maintain Effective Budgets
IAIN MAITLAND
Philadelphia, Pennsylvania: Trans Atlantic Publications, 2000
206pp (Smarter Solutions Series)
ISBN: 0273644947
This book takes you through each stage of the budgeting process, explaining all you need to know about it. From understanding the procedures for making budgets and forecasts to developing realistic contingency plans, it shows how to turn your budgeting strategy into a valuable management tool. It also contains a wide range of model forecasts, forms, and budgets, and comes complete with checklists and case studies.

Capital Budgeting: Theory and Practice
PAMELA P. PETERSON, FRANK J. FABOZZI
New York: John Wiley, 2002
243pp ISBN: 0471218332
The book covers the underlying principles of capital budgeting including discounted net cash flows, risk assessment, and leases. It explains the importance of making wise decisions when investing in long-lived assets and provides quantitative decision-making tools that assist managers in choosing between options.

Cashflow Reengineering: How to Optimize the Cashflow Timeline and Improve Financial Efficiency
JAMES SAGNER
New York: AMACOM, 1997
256pp ISBN: 0814403611
Sagner shows how to diagnose a company's cashflow situation accurately and prescribe the correct treatment. He presents ten management principles and procedures which, he suggests, have saved many companies large amounts of money.

Credit Risk Management: A Guide to Sound Business Decisions
H. A. SCHAEFFER, JR.
New York: John Wiley, 2000
288pp ISBN: 0471350206
This book examines the steps leading to a sound business credit decision. It is divided into four main sections: analysis for creative credit management; building up essential business credit information; considering all factors that affect the business credit decision; and making a decision or recommendation. Twelve detailed case studies are provided, illustrating common problems along with their solutions.

Driving Value Using Activity-based Budgeting
JAMES A. BRIMSON, JOHN ANTOS, R. STEVEN PLAYER, JAY COLLINS
New York: John Wiley, 1998
288pp ISBN: 0471086312
The book introduces activity-based budgeting (ABB) and feature costing as methods to create value and establish linkage between daily operations and strategic objectives. It covers the essentials of ABB including fundamental concepts, methods of forecasting revenue based on activities, gap analysis, and capacity management. Using examples, case studies, and target-setting techniques, the book illustrates the shortcomings of the traditional budget approach and provides guidance on implementing ABB effectively.

Handbook of Budgeting 4th ed.
ROBERT RACHLIN
New York: John Wiley, 1998
976pp ISBN: 0471183504
Targeted to controllers and budget directors, this book demonstrates how to create a broad range of budgets, from the traditional budget to the activity-based budget. The handbook is divided into five major categories that cover the budgeting process, tools and techniques, preparation of specific budgets, budgeting applications, and industry budgets.

Improving Cash Flow and Profits: A Guide to Effective Credit Management
BARRY EDWARDS
Cambridge, Massachusetts: Director Books, 1993
246pp ISBN: 1870555732
The book outlines the principles of credit risk and its management in the context of both domestic and international trade. In addition, it covers formulating a credit policy, consumer credit, using credit collection agencies, and cash-flow management.

Managing Budgets
STEPHEN BROOKSON
New York: DK Publishing, 2000
72pp (Essential Managers Series)
ISBN: 0789459698
This introductory guide to managing budgets explains the technique of budgeting and examines the processes of preparing, writing, and monitoring a budget.

Managing by the Numbers
CHUCK KREMER, RON RIZZUTO, JOHN CASE
Cambridge, Massachusetts: Perseus, 2000
224pp ISBN: 0738202568
This is a handy and practical guide to reading

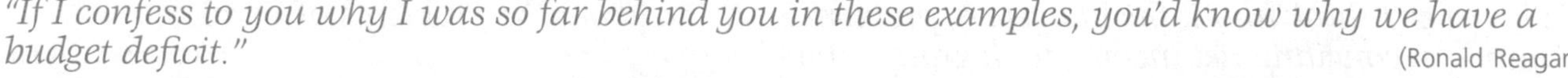

"If I confess to you why I was so far behind you in these examples, you'd know why we have a budget deficit."
(Ronald Reagan)

  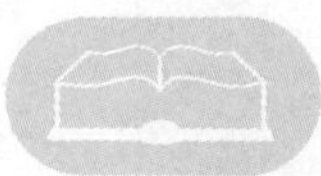    

and using balance sheets, income statements, and cash flow statements to drive business growth and profitability.

Mastering Spreadsheet Budgets and Forecasts: How to Save Time and Gain Control of Your Business
MALCOLM SECRETT
Upper Saddle River, New Jersey: Financial Times Prentice Hall, 1999
260pp (Smarter Solutions Series)
ISBN: 0273644912
This step-by-step, jargon-free guide demonstrates the advantages and potential of using spreadsheets to prepare and present budgets and forecasts. It includes examples of budgets and forecasts, followed through completely from beginning to end.

Total Business Budgeting: A Step-by-step Guide with Forms 2nd ed.
ROBERT RACHLIN
New York: John Wiley, 1999
321pp ISBN: 0471351032
Rachlin provides an introduction to a wide range of budgetary techniques and applications and shows how to analyze outside influences, develop performance targets and budgeting segments, and administer the right budgeting processes. He includes detailed instructions, forms, examples, schedules, and formats.

INTERNET

Accountants World
www.accountantsworld.com
This is an extensive portal based in the United States with links to a wide range of Web sites of interest to accountants. It relates mainly to U.S. accounting practice.

Accounting Web
www.accountingweb.co.uk
This site is an extensive online resource based in the United Kingdom. It contains material from a number of providers intended for accountancy and finance professionals. It has received an award as the New Media Business Website of the Year.

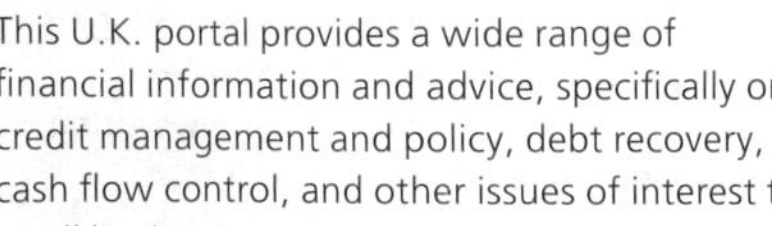

Credit to Cash
www.credit-to-cash.com
This U.K. portal provides a wide range of financial information and advice, specifically on credit management and policy, debt recovery, cash flow control, and other issues of interest to small businesses.

Dyer Partnership
www.netaccountants.com
The site provides a wide range of information on U.K. tax and accounting matters and other business issues of interest to owners and managers of U.K. businesses.

Institute of Management Accountants
www.imanet.org
This is the Web site of the Institute of Management Accountants (IMA), a professional organization that promotes management accounting and financial management. The IMA is responsible for the education and certification of professionals involved in management accounting, including operational and capital budgeting responsibilities. Members of the IMA receive information and educational materials on financial budgeting and control, capital budgeting, and management accounting topics.

LTU I-University
www.iuniversityonline.com
The Web site for LTU's online university provides online courses in effective planning, budgeting and control, corporate finance, and management accounting.

ORGANIZATIONS

USA

American Accounting Association
5717 Bessie Drive, Sarasota, Florida, 34233–2399
T: +1 941 921 7747
F: +1 941 923 4093
E: office@aaahq.org
www.aaa-edu.org
The AAA is a professional body with particular interest in developments in the teaching of accountancy.

American Institute of Certified Public Accountants
1211 Avenue of the Americas, New York, 10036
T: +1 212 596 6200
F: +1 212 596 6213
www.aicpa.org
With more than 330,000 members, the AICPA is the premier national professional association for certified public accountants in the United States.

National Society of Accountants
1010 North Fairfax Street, Alexandria, Virginia, 22314
T: +1 703 549 6400
F: +1 703 549 2984
E: jhemphill@nsacct.org
www.nsacct.org
The National Society of Accountants is a nonprofit organization of some 17,000 professionals which provides accounting, tax preparation, financial and estate planning, and management advisory services to an estimated 19 million individuals and business clients. Most of the Society's members are independent practitioners or partners in small to midsize accounting and tax firms.

Europe

Association of Chartered Certified Accountants
29 Lincoln's Inn Fields, London, WC2A 3EE, U.K.
T: +44 (0) 20 7396 7000
F: +44 (0) 20 7396 7070
E: info@accaglobal.com
www.acca.co.uk
The Association is a professional and examining body in accountancy, recognized under the Companies Act 1989 by the U.K. Department of Trade and Industry.

Chartered Institute of Management Accountants
26 Chapter Street, London, SW1P 4NP, U.K.
T: +44 (0) 20 7663 5441
F: +44 (0) 20 7663 5442
www.cimaglobal.com
CIMA is the leading U.K. professional organization for management accountants.

Institute of Chartered Accountants in England and Wales
Chartered Accountants' Hall, P.O. Box 433, Moorgate Place, London, EC2P 2BJ, U.K.
T: +44 (0) 20 7920 8100
F: +44 (0) 20 7920 8547
E: dsbds@icaew.co.uk
www.icaew.co.uk
This, the largest professional accountancy organization in Europe with over 120,000 members, is responsible for educating and training Chartered Accountants and maintaining standards of professional conduct among its members.

Institute of Chartered Accountants in Scotland
CA House, 21 Haymarket Yards, Edinburgh, Scotland, EH12 5BH, U.K.
T: +44 (0) 131 347 0100
F: +44 (0) 131 347 0105
E: enquiries@icas.org.uk
www.icas.org.uk
The ICAS is the leading professional accounting body in Scotland, and the oldest professional body of accountants in the world.

Institute of Credit Management
The Water Mill, Station Road, South Luffenham, Oakham, Leicestershire, LE15 8NB, U.K.
T: +44 (0) 1780 722900
F: +44 (0) 1780 721333
E: info@icm.org.uk
www.icm.org.uk
The Institute of Credit Management (ICM) is the

"Whenever I think about the budgetary problems, I think about the problems of Errol Flynn. . .reconciling net income with gross habits." (Malcolm Rifkind)

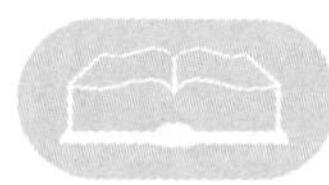

largest organization of credit professionals in Europe, and the focal point in the United Kingdom for all matters relating to credit management and its ancillary functions. The ICM sets professional standards and tests and assesses those who wish to gain its professional qualification. It also provides advice to government and other national bodies.

Institute of Financial Accountants
Burford House, 44 London Road, Sevenoaks, Kent, TN13 1AS, U.K.
T: +44 (0) 1732 458080
F: +44 (0) 1732 455848
E: *mail@ifa.org.uk*
www.ifa.org.uk
The Institute of Financial Accountants, established in 1916, is the largest professional body of its type in the world. It represents members and students in more than 80 countries around the world and provides a qualification and continuing professional development for those who want to become financial accountants. It also sets both technical and ethical standards within the profession.

For More Information

☆ **Allocating Corporate Capital Fairly (pp. 123–24)**
☆ **Budgeting (pp. 117–18)**
✔ **Controlling a Budget (pp. 546–47)**
✔ **Controlling Costs (pp. 548–49)**
✔ **Controlling Credit (pp. 550–51)**
Accounting (pp. 1899–1901)
Forecasting and Scenario Planning (pp. 1986–87)

Business Appraisal and Performance Measurement

BOOKS

The Balanced Scorecard
ROBERT S. KAPLAN, DAVID P. NORTON
Boston, Massachusetts: Harvard Business School Press, 1996
322pp ISBN: 0875846513
This book demonstrates to managers how to utilize their people to fulfill the company's mission. It shows how to channel the energies, abilities, and specific knowledge belonging to each individual into the achievement of long-term strategic goals for the company. It is a measurement tool, and is also a management tool for investing in the long term in customers, employees, new product development, and systems.

Business Health Check: Identify Symptoms of Business Ill-health and Build a Lasting Structure for Growth
CAROL A. O'CONNOR
Chicago, Illinois: Independent Publishers Group, 2001
131pp ISBN: 1854181580
This practical book describes the tools and techniques needed to conduct a companywide analysis. It puts minor issues into perspective and ensures that bigger problems are properly addressed. O'Connor introduces the tools needed to evaluate the overall health of your business—including an 80-item questionnaire to identify key areas for attention—and suggests strategies for in-depth improvement.

Corporate Valuation: Tools for Effective Appraisal and Decision Making
BRADFORD CORNELL
New York: McGraw-Hill, 1993
303pp (Business One)
ISBN: 1556237308
This book illustrates the best practices for measuring and predicting value by combining the science of business appraisal with the art of perceived value. As such, it provides a tool for comparing various valuation techniques. It shows how to rethink the investment process today and into the 21st century. It includes an index.

Evaluation in Organizations: A Systematic Approach to Enhancing Learning, Performance, and Change
DARLENE RUSS-EFT, HALLIE PRESKILL
Cambridge, Massachusetts: Perseus, 2001
416pp ISBN: 0738202681
A guide to the context and implementation of evaluation, in a three-phase system. The book includes an audit mechanism and comprehensive resources.

Harvard Business Review on Measuring Corporate Performance
Boston, Massachusetts: Harvard Business School Press, 1998
224pp (Harvard Business Review Paperback Series)
ISBN: 0875848826
A collection of articles from leading management thinkers, this book shows how to evaluate performance measures and discusses the importance of aligning corporate strategy with performance measures. It includes discussion of the balanced scorecard, customer relationships, internal business processes, and employee learning.

Implementing Global Performance Measurement Systems: A Cookbook Approach to Evaluation
FERDINAND TESORO, JACK TOOTSON
San Francisco, California: Jossey-Bass/Pfeiffer, 1999
256pp ISBN: 078794744X
This practical guide presents a step-by-step approach to evaluating and measuring ongoing business performance. Following an overview of performance measurement, the areas covered include establishing the business case, identifying the right performance metrics, implementing the performance measurement system, and leveraging results to improve performance. Guidance is offered on constructing a line graph, a cause–effect diagram, and a scatter diagram. A CD-ROM is included.

Measuring Business Performance
ANDY NEELY
London: Profile Economist Books, 1998
208pp ISBN: 1861970552
The author looks at why businesses should measure their performance, what should be measured, and how measurements should be made.

Natural Capitalism: Creating the Next Industrial Revolution
PAUL HAWKEN, AMORY LOVINS, L. HUNTER LOVINS
New York: Little Brown & Company, 1999
396pp ISBN: 0316353167
In this title, the coauthors discuss how top companies are carrying out a modern form of industrialism which runs more smoothly, increases profits, lessens damage to the environment and creates more jobs. They call this system "natural capitalism" and give several

"The pursuit of alibis for poor industry performance is one of the great Australian art forms."
(John Button)

examples of organizations which have benefited the environment.

Oliver Wight ABCD Checklist for Operational Excellence 5th ed.
Oliver Wight International
New York: John Wiley, 2000
167pp ISBN: 047138819X
The Oliver Wight ABCD Checklists are a widely recognized tool used by organizations as part of an appraisal of their performance. The aim of this checklist is to become an industry standard for operational performance measurement. Beginning with an explanation of the use of the performance measures, the assessment tool then focuses on the following areas: strategic planning; people and teams; total quality and continuous improvement; new product development; and planning and control.

Operational Performance Measurement: Increasing Total Productivity
Will Kaydos
Delray Beach, Florida: St. Lucie Press, 1998
272pp ISBN: 1574440993
A practical approach to performance measurement, this book makes the case for implementing measurement in all business activities. It describes measurement methods, standards, and techniques, enumerates requirements for successful measurement, outlines how to implement, analyze, and interpret measures, and gives examples from leading companies. It is targeted at managers at all levels.

The Organizational Measurement Manual
David Wealleans
Brookfield, Vermont: Gower, 2001
178pp ISBN: 0566083493
Divided into three parts—the concept of measurement, establishing a process measurement program, and looking beyond the basics—this book gives a guide to performance measurements at the working level. It identifies procedures for using measurements and shows how to relate them to organizational objectives and initiatives. Wealleans demonstrates a best practice approach, and illustrates his text with figures and tables throughout.

Performance Scorecards
Richard Y. Chang, Mark W. Morgan
San Francisco, California: Jossey-Bass, 2000
224pp ISBN: 0787952729
The authors contend that many corporations have too many performance measurements, which causes them to lose sight of the ones which are important, and advocate customizing performance scorecards to suit an organization's strategy. The book uses a fictional storyline to illustrate the six steps that go into performance scorecards: collect, create, cultivate, cascade, connect, and confirm.

Valuing a Business: The Analysis and Appraisal of Closely Held Companies 4th ed.
Shannon P. Pratt, Robert F. Reilly, Robert P. Schweihs
New York: McGraw-Hill, 2000
1291pp ISBN: 0071356150
This latest edition, originally published in 1981, includes significant revisions and ten new chapters. Its coverage now extends to topics such as credentials and standards, analyzing financial statements, control and acquisition premiums, valuing debt securities and litigation support. The book is a standard reference for defining the methodology of business valuation—for businesses of all sizes—and then arriving at an accurate and supportable estimation of value.

Vital Signs: Using Quality, Time, and Cost Performance Measurements to Chart Your Company's Future
Steven M. Hronec
New York: AMACOM, 1993
247pp ISBN: 0814450733
The author claims that many traditional performance measurements focus too heavily on effects to the exclusion of causes, thereby promoting a short-term view of a company's effectiveness. He advocates measurements that emphasize the larger picture and can be more closely tied to strategy. Measures discussed include benchmarking, competitor and market analysis, surveys, and focus groups.

MAGAZINES

Balanced Scorecard Report
ISSN: 1526-145X
Harvard Business School Publishing and Balanced Scorecard Collaborative
60 Harvard Way, Boston, Massachusetts, 02163
T: +1 800 988 0886
F: +1 617 783 7555
www.hbsp.harvard.edu/products/bsr
This bimonthly report is produced by Robert Kaplan and David Norton, creators of the Balanced Scorecard, in order to keep BSC implementers up to date with the latest developments.

Business Valuation Review
ISSN: 0882-2875
American Society of Appraisers
P.O. Box 19237, Denver, Colorado, 80219
T: +1 303 975 8895
F: +1 303 975 8897
www.bvappraisers.org/bv_review
This quarterly journal features articles on the practice and theory of appraisal. The articles present various opinions on the latest trends in business. The journal will be beneficial for any business valuation professional.

Financial Management
ISSN: 1471-9185
Chartered Institute of Management Accountants
26 Chapter Street, London, SW1P 4NP, U.K.
T: +44 (0) 20 7663 2311
F: +44 (0) 20 7663 5442
www.cimaglobal.com/main/about/financial
This magazine provides practical articles on a wide range of issues of interest to management accountants, including business performance and appraisal.

The Valuation Examiner
National Association of Valuation Analysts
111 Brickyard Road, Suite 200, Salt Lake City, Utah, 84106
T: +1 801 486 0600
F: +1 801 486 7500
www.nacva.com
This bimonthly magazine focuses on the latest developments regarding industry issues. It covers a variety of industry related topics, such as trends, forecasts and the latest technology resources, and provides the resources needed for business appraisal professionals.

INTERNET

Balancedscorecard.Com
www.balancedscorecard.com
The site provides members with access to a version of the Balanced Scorecard, a method of assessing business performance by means of a range of performance indicators. The site also includes a bookstore, which recommends books on this and related topics.

Center for Business Innovation
www.cbi.cgey.com
Sponsored by Ernst & Young, the site offers various resources on performance measurement, including a journal, and

"It is not only by the questions we have answered that progress will be measured, but also by those we are still asking."
(Freda Adler)

information on upcoming events and networking opportunities.

College of Performance Management
www.cpm-pmi.org
Sponsored by a nonprofit professional organization, the site offers speeches, articles, abstracts, news, information about events and conferences, and links.

Interthink Consulting, Inc.
www.interthink.ca
Sponsored by a Canadian consulting firm, the site includes research on topics including assessment, processes, training, and implementation, and a newsletter of industry events.

U.S. Business Exchange
www.usbx.com
The site provides access to a comprehensive business evaluation service that includes assessing how well a company is performing in relation to its industry average. Advice on improving performance is also available.

ORGANIZATIONS
USA
American Society of Appraisers (ASA)
555 Herndon Parkway, Suite 125, Herndon, Virginia, 20170
T: +1 703 478 2228 or 1 800 272 8258
F: +1 703 742 8471
E: asainfo@appraisers.org
www.appraisers.org
Founded in 1952, this organization has more than 6,500 members. ASA is a professional appraisal educator and represents all the disciplines of appraisal specialists. The society requires a mandatory certification program for all of its members, including the ASA Ethics Exam and the Uniform Standards of Professional Appraisal Practice Examination.

Institute of Business Appraisers (IBA)
P.O. Box 17410, Plantation, Florida, 33318
T: +1 954 584 1144
F: +1 954 584 1184
E: ibahq@go-iba-org
www.instbusapp.org
Established in 1978, the Institute of Business Appraisers is the oldest professional society devoted to the appraisal of closely-held businesses. This nationally recognized organization has a membership of over 3,000. The IBA seeks to educate the public in all aspects of business valuation and appraisal and is involved in monitoring and supporting national legislation that affects the business valuation community.

Measure.net
2008 Vinewood Boulevard, Ann Arbor, Michigan, 48104
T: +1 734 997 7072
F: +1 435 304 8452
E: info@measure.net
www.measure.net
This organization is concerned with extending and improving corporate performance measurement strategies. It provides information for measuring performance within a company, and for managing a business. Measure.net is involved in research, education and consulting services, and also conducts various seminars and courses.

Europe
Best Practice Club
Wolseley Business Park, Kempston, Bedfordshire, MK42 7PW, U.K.
T: +44 (0) 1234 853605
F: +44 (0) 1234 854499
E: michelle@bpclub.com
www.bpclub.com
This organization, which has an international membership, promotes organizational excellence through members networking and comparing their practice. Member companies come from both the manufacturing and the service sectors and pool their experience.

British Chambers of Commerce
Manning House, 22 Carlisle Place, London, SW1P 1JA, U.K.
T: +44 (0) 20 7565 2000
F: +44 (0) 20 7565 2049
E: info@britishchambers.org.uk
www.britishchambers.org.uk
This is an umbrella body for a network of about 150 locally based chambers of commerce, serving local businesses which provide advice on business appraisal and appraisal services to their member companies. Its Web site provides links to the local chambers.

British Quality Foundation
32–34 Great Peter Street, London, SW1P 2QX, U.K.
T: +44 (0) 20 7654 5000
F: +44 (0) 20 7654 5001
E: mail@quality-foundation.co.uk
www.quality-foundation.co.uk
The BQF assists member organizations to assess their performance and target continuous improvements in specific areas through the use of the U.K. Excellence Model (which is based on the European Excellence Model—see below). The model is used to assess company performance in nine key areas, such as quality of leadership, customer care, or employee development, over and above the usual financial parameters.

Centre for Interfirm Comparison
CIFC Ltd., 32 Thomas Street, Winchester, Hampshire, SO23 9HJ, U.K.
T: +44 (0) 1962 844144
F: +44 (0) 1962 843180
E: projects@cifc.co.uk
www.cifc.co.uk
The Centre helps businesses of all types and in all sectors to assess their performance through confidential, detailed comparison of their financial ratios and other data with those of similar businesses, and to target improvements in specific areas of their operations. The Centre provides a wide range of benchmarking and related consulting services.

European Foundation for Quality Management (EQFM)
Avenue des Pléiades 15, B-1200 Brussels, Belgium
T: +33 2 775 35 11
F: +33 2 775 35 35
E: info@efqm.org
www.efqm.org
The EFQM originally introduced the European Excellence Model in the early 1990s to help businesses assess and improve their performance.

The Small Business Service
Kingsgate House, 66–74 Victoria Street, London, SW1E 6SW, U.K.
T: +44 (0) 114 259 7788
F: +44 (0) 114 259 7330
E: gatewayenquiries@sbs.gsi.gov.uk
www.sbs.gov.uk
The SBS (formerly Business Link) provides advice and consulting services to small businesses. It is a network of about 150 locally based organizations sponsored by the British Department of Trade and Industry. Further details can be obtained from the Web site.

For More Information

- ☆ The Balanced Scorecard (pp. 303–04)
- ✔ Establishing a Performance Measurement System (pp. 496–97)
- ✔ Implementing the Balanced Scorecard (pp. 510–11)
- Benchmarking (pp. 1911–13)

  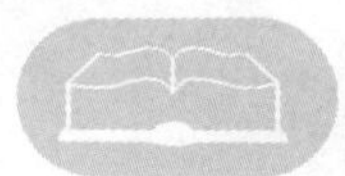    

Business Ethics and Codes of Practice

BOOKS

Business Ethics 5th ed.
Richard T. de George
Upper Saddle River, New Jersey: Prentice Hall, 1999
626pp ISBN: 0130797723
This book, now in its fifth edition, explores approaches to ethical theory and the relationship between business and morality. Each chapter begins with a case study, such as Love Canal or Malden Mills, that illustrates the topic being studied. The topics range from special obligations, safety and public risk, liability, shareholder obligations, and environmental harm, to the legal ramifications of actions.

Business Ethics: The State of the Art
R. Edward Freeman, ed.
New York: Oxford University Press, 1993
225pp ISBN: 0195081986
This long-respected volume contains a series of essays by such leading thinkers as Kenneth Goodpaster, Norman Bowie, and Joanne Ciulla, which explore the myriad facets of the role of ethics in business. The essays cover such areas as ethical imperatives, corporate leadership, corporate rights and responsibilities, and the complexity of ethics in multinational and multicultural settings. They also deal with broader subjects such as the role of businesses when it comes to literacy.

Cases in Ethics and the Conduct of Business
John R. Boatright, ed.
Upper Saddle River, New Jersey: Prentice Hall, 1994
330pp ISBN: 013120601X
The author provides an introduction to ethical theory and considers a range of ethical questions relating to the employee and the firm, employee relations, consumers, and the role of the corporation in society. These include topical issues such as whistle-blowing, privacy, discrimination and affirmative action, marketing and advertising, consumer protection, health and safety, and international business.

Defining Moments: When Managers Must Choose between Right and Right
Joseph L. Badaracco, Jr.
Boston, Massachusetts: Harvard Business School Press, 1997
176pp ISBN: 0875848036
This book explores the difficult questions managers confront, questions which can produce multiple answers depending on which responsibility they are trying to live up to—personal or corporate. Through case studies and examples, the author tries to help managers understand the issues involved, describing steps that can be taken to resolve the dilemma and offering a flexible framework that can be used to determine the right decision.

The Ethical Imperative: Why Moral Leadership Is Good Business
John Dalla Costa
Cambridge, Massachusetts: Perseus, 1999
354pp ISBN: 0738201308
This book explores the importance of incorporating ethics into company strategy, and looks at the ways in which companies can benefit from such an investment. It includes evidence and examples drawn from a wide range of subjects and case studies.

Ethics for Managers
Philip Holden
Brookfield, Vermont: Gower, 2000
206pp ISBN: 0566081156
Holden looks at the relationship between ethics and business and examines how companies reconcile concerns for profitability with morality. Specific areas he discusses include personal standards, leadership, marketing, and environmental issues.

Leading with Soul 2nd ed.
Lee G. Bolman, Terrence E. Deal
New York: John Wiley, 2001
224pp ISBN: 0787955477
This is a contemporary parable about an executive's quest for passion and purpose in work and in life. The authors draw upon many spiritual traditions, poetry, philosophy, and social science teachings on leadership and organizations. The book demonstrates how to lead with soul, and to ignite the soul of an organization. This edition has a new introduction, new material, and includes letters written by readers of the first edition.

Managing Values and Beliefs in Organisations
Tom McEwan
Upper Saddle River, New Jersey: Financial Times Prentice Hall, 2001
560pp ISBN: 0273643401
In this textbook, for the use of students up to MBA level, the areas of corporate social responsibility, business ethics, and corporate governance are examined. Its major sections look at how ethics affect, and are affected by, the internal organizational environment, the external environment, and global issues. Each chapter can be treated as a separate module that includes its own learning objectives, case studies, and discussion questions.

Strategy Safari: A Guided Tour through the Wilds of Strategic Management
Henry Mintzberg, Bruce Ahlstrand, Joseph Lampel
New York: Simon & Schuster, 1998
304pp ISBN: 0684847434
This book provides a thorough critique of the contributions and limitations of ten different approaches to strategic planning. These include such schools of thought as entrepreneurial, cognitive, cultural, and environmental. The book then goes on to show how these alternative schools can be merged and shaped to produce one coherent approach to strategy formation.

Working Ethics: Strategies for Decision Making and Organizational Responsibility
Marvin T. Brown
San Francisco, California: Jossey-Bass, 1990
219pp ISBN: 1555422802
This book explores the role of ethics as a tool in decision making, showing how ethical behavior can improve organizational effectiveness by fostering open communications, resolving disputes, and enhancing employee–management relations. It highlights the fact that arguments centering around an open expression of disagreements can lead to better relations, and provides examples and practical exercises for building an organization that makes morally and socially responsible decisions.

MAGAZINES

Business & Professional Ethics Journal
ISSN: 0277–2027
Robert J. Baum
P.O. Box 15017, Gainsville, Florida, 32604
T: +1 325 392 2084
F: +1 325 392 5577
Published four times per year, this journal contains articles written with a focus on the ethical issues encountered by business professionals working in large organizations.

Business Ethics: A European Review
ISSN: 0962–8770
Blackwell Publishers
350 Main Street, Malden, Massachusetts, 02148
T: +1 781 388 8200
F: +1 781 388 8232

"A well-run business must have high and consistent standards of ethics." (Richard Branson)

www.blackwellpublishers.com/asp/listofj.asp
Although largely an academic research journal, *Business Ethics* contains some items that may be directly applicable to those in business. It does not have an exclusively European focus, and covers ethical issues affecting both global and national organizations.

Business Ethics Quarterly: The Journal of the Society for Business Ethics
ISSN: 1052–150X
Philosophy Documentation Center
Society for Business Ethics, Philosophy Documentation Center, P.O. Box 7147, Charlottesville, Virginia, 22906–7147
T: +1 804 220 3300
F: +1 804 220 3301
www.pdcnet.org/beq.html
This learned journal explores the application of ethics to international business. The nature of the journal means that it is of more relevance to academics than to practicing managers.

Journal of Business Ethics
ISSN: 0167–4544
Kluwer Academic Publishing
101 Philip Drive, Assinippi Park, Norwell, Massachusetts, 02061
T: +1 781 871 6600
www.kluweronline.com
This is the premier U.S. journal on business ethics. Articles cover a vast array of ethical issues and their business context. A monthly journal, it provides timely information ranging from marketing and advertising to organizational behavior. All articles are analyzed and written to highlight the moral viewpoint. This journal will appeal to scholars of business ethics as well as executives and consumer watch groups.

Public Relations Tactics
ISSN: 1080–6792
Public Relations Society of America
33 Irving Place, New York, 10003–2376
T: +1 212 995 2230
www.prsa.org/Tactics/tactinfo.html
This monthly publication covers the latest trends in public relations. Designed to meet the current needs of public relations professionals, the timely information found in this newspaper will help any professional improve their PR skills, and remain competitive in the field of public relations.

INTERNET

Business Impact
www.business-impact.org
This site contains information from Business in the Community's Business Impact task force, including case studies and general information on corporate social responsibility.

Center for the Study of Ethics in the Professions
www.iit.edu/departments/csep/PublicWWW/codes
This site makes available 850 codes of ethics from professional societies, corporations, government, and academic institutions, as well as a literature review and a user guide.

DePaul University Institute for Business and Professional Ethics
www.depaul.edu/ethics
A collection of resources including a newsletter, articles, and a list of relevant institutes is available from this site, together with access to *Business Ethics* magazine at www.business-ethics.com.

Ethics Connection
www.scu.edu/SCU/Centers/Ethics
This site offers case briefings, articles, and dialogue in all fields of applied ethics, including business and technology ethics. It also contains readings and related links.

Ethics Resource Center
www.ethics.org
A range of resources from this Washington-based ethics education organization can be accessed here. These include articles from *Ethics Today* magazine, a mailing list, book reviews, and details of training resources and events. Summaries of the National Business Ethics surveys are also available.

Global Business Society Resource Center
www.bsr.org/resourcecenter
Business for Social Responsibility offers an introduction to issues of social responsibility and business ethics on this site. The site also includes a news archive, information about company practices and policies, award and recognition programs, and publications. A special feature is the facility it provides for creating reports on selected topics.

ORGANIZATIONS

USA

Business for Social Responsibility
2nd Floor, 609 Mission Street, San Francisco, California, 94105–3506
T: +1 415 537 0888
F: +1 415 537 0889
www.bsr.org
Founded in 1992, this membership organization provides resources—including information, news, publications, training, and consulting—designed to help companies succeed in business while respecting ethical values. Based in the United States, BSR has developed regional networks and global alliances with similar organizations worldwide.

Society for Business Ethics
Management Department, School of Business Administration, Loyola University Chicago, 820 N. Michigan Avenue, Chicago, Illinois, 60611
T: +1 312 915 6994
F: +1 312 915 6988
www.luc.edu/depts/business/sbe
The SBE is an international association of over 1,000 scholars and professionals that aims to promote the study of business ethics, to improve the way they are taught, and to provide a forum for the exchange of ideas in the field. It publishes the journal *Business Ethics Quarterly*.

Europe

Business in the Community
137 Shepherdess Walk, London, N1 7RQ, U.K.
T: +44 (0) 870 600 2482
F: +44 (0) 20 7486 1700
E: information@bitc.org.uk
www.bitc.org.uk
Business in the Community is a voluntary organization, formed in 1982, with a strong focus on corporate social responsibility. Its membership of 650 U.K. companies is committed to measuring and improving the impact of their business on the environment and the community, and to making a contribution to social and economic regeneration. Its activities include the organization of the Awards for Excellence and a Business Impact task force.

European Business Ethics Network
EBEN Secretariat, c/o Tone Mikkelsen, NMH-BI, P.O. Box 4636, Sofienberg, Oslo, N-0506, Norway
T: +47 22 98 50 56
F: +47 22 98 50 02
E: eben@bi.no
www.eben.org
The Network is a nonprofit association founded in Brussels in 1987 to promote ethical awareness in business decision making through research, training, education, networking, and the dissemination of information. The membership, which is predominantly European, includes individuals, companies, and academic institutions. National networks have been established in a number of European countries.

Institute of Business Ethics
24 Greencoat Place, London, SW1P 1BE, U.K.
T: +44 (0) 20 7798 6040
F: +44 (0) 20 7798 6044
E: info@ibe.org.uk
www.ibe.org.uk
Launched in 1986 by the then Lord Mayor of London, Alderman Sir Allan Davis, the Institute aims to emphasize the essentially ethical nature

"It's possible to live in this country and create wealth legally and ethically." (Narayana Murthy)

of wealth creation, to encourage the highest standards of behavior by companies, and to publicize the best ethical practices. Its activities include research, conferences, seminars, and the development of codes of practice and resource material.

International

The Institute for Global Ethics
P.O. Box 563, 11 Main Street, Camden, Maine, 04843
T: +1 207 236 6658
F: +1 207 236 4014
E: *webethics@globalethics.org*
www.globalethics.org
A nonsectarian membership organization funded by private foundations, sponsors, and members, the Institute fosters public discussion of and practical action on ethical issues and promotes the teaching of ''Ethical Fitness.'' It has an international board of directors, an international advisory council, and branch offices in the United Kingdom and Canada. Its activities are centered on three areas: corporate services, educational programs, and public policy.

For More Information

- ☆ **Business Ethics (pp. 231–32)**
- ✔ **Codes of Ethics (pp. 456–57)**
- **Social Responsibility of Management (pp. 2115–17)**

Business Plans and Planning

BOOKS

By the Numbers: Using Facts and Figures to Get Your Projects, Plans, and Ideas Approved
Joseph McLeary, et al.
New York: AMACOM, 2000
286pp ISBN: 0814404995
The authors demonstrate how to present a winning business case based on figures. They explain how to research a company strategy, determine whether an idea is in keeping with industry trends, build alliances and support before a formal presentation, and prepare answers to critical questions.

The Complete Book of Business Plans: Simple Steps to Writing a Powerful Business Plan
Joseph A. Covello, Brian J. Hazelgren
Naperville, Illinois: Sourcebooks, 1994
320pp ISBN: 0942061411
This classic presents the key questions to bear in mind when writing a plan for a new business, and encourages the reader to look for the answers to the kinds of questions that investors ask, to develop marketing strategies and financial presentations, and to find ways to stay ahead of the competition.

The Definitive Business Plan: The Fast Track to Intelligent Business Planning for Executives and Entrepreneurs 2nd ed.
Richard Stutely
Upper Saddle River, New Jersey: Financial Times Prentice Hall, 1999
288pp ISBN: 0273639307
This text is written for both the newcomer and the experienced planner. It provides a concise guide to the business planning process, and focuses attention on strategic planning and strategic and operational controls. The practical aspects of constructing various types of business plan are explained in some detail.

Dynamic Planning: The Art of Managing Beyond Tomorrow
Beverly Goldberg, John G. Sifonis
New York: Oxford University Press, 1994
288pp ISBN: 0195083083
This volume takes the reader through the entire planning process—from doing an analysis of the competitive environment, through selecting a direction from the various options the company has for growth, to formulating a vision and designing a mission statement. It goes on to explore the problems of incorporating the right technologies, managing change when new directions are selected, and watching for changes in the outside world that will require new roads to success.

The Fast Forward MBA in Business Planning for Growth
Philip Walcoff
New York: John Wiley, 1999
212pp (Fast Forward MBA Series)
ISBN: 0471345482
Walcoff's step-by-step guide to the process of creating a business plan that ensures growth and profitability identifies and resolves key issues that block a company's growth and develops strategies and tactics that foster it.

How to Really Create a Successful Business Plan 3rd ed.
David E. Gumpert
Boston, Massachusetts: Inc. Publishing, 1996
212pp ISBN: 1880394235
This book provides a step-by-step method for completing a high-quality business plan. It also provides models of business plans from a number of highly successful U.S. companies.

How to Write a .com Business Plan: The Internet Entrepreneur's Guide to Everything You Need to Know about Business Plans and Financing Options
Joanne Eglash
New York: McGraw-Hill, 2001
191pp ISBN: 007135753X
Written for entrepreneurs, business owners, and Web site owners, this text provides a practical guide to developing a business plan for an Internet-based business. Eglash focuses on the factors which distinguish online businesses from conventional enterprises, and covers the areas of mission statements and company descriptions, competition, markets and customers, products and services, marketing and sales, operations, financial projections, and financial management. A sample business plan and an extensive directory of helpful Web sites are included.

Morrisey on Planning: A Guide to Long-range Planning: Creating Your Strategic Journey
George L. Morrisey
San Francisco, California: Jossey-Bass, 1995
109pp ISBN: 0787901695
This, the second in a three-volume series, follows Morrisey's exploration of strategic thinking and precedes his work on tactical planning. It is aimed at organizations that are willing to embark on a three-to-five-year planning process, and focuses on long-term objectives and how to place them in the context of the organization's vision and mission.

Plan to Win: A Definitive Guide to Business Processes
John Garside
West Lafayette, Indiana: Purdue University Press, 1999
304pp ISBN: 1557531633
The author provides a clear and practical approach to creating and implementing cost-

"A lot of companies. . .find planning more interesting than getting out a salable product."
(Ed Wrapp)

effective business processes. Focusing on the key elements of a robust business plan, he defines and describes the core business processes needed in a successful process-driven organization, supporting his descriptions with diagrams and checklists of essential criteria for process design. Garside brings to this work an extensive experience of business planning with various major companies, including Dunlop, GKN Technology, and Lucas Aerospace.

The Successful Business Plan: Secrets and Strategies 3rd ed.
RHONDA M. ABRAMS
Palo Alto, California: Running R Media, 2000
409pp ISBN: 0966963520
This book is designed to help readers create a business plan that will attract the funding they need to get started. It presents insights from some 200 business owners, venture capitalists, and C.E.O.s, but, in addition, contains worksheets and sample business plans, provides tools to help in number-crunching, and offers guidance on the length of an ideal plan and the way it should be worded and formatted.

INTERNET

Business Planet
www.bizplanet.com
BizPlanet provides a range of resources including a newsletter, a virtual business plan, and reviews of business planning software and books.

Business Plan Guide
www.business-plans.co.uk
This site, sponsored by Miller Consultancy, provides information on business planning resources. It includes books, links to Web sites, articles, and an e-mail newsletter.

Business Plans
www.bplans.com
This site, created by Palo Alto Software, offers planning advice for small businesses and a substantial range of sample plans, which subscribers to bplans' software can download and edit. It also includes a resource center with links to other Web sites, as well as an ''ask the experts'' section.

More Business
www.morebusiness.com
This site has a lengthy business and marketing plans section and provides some useful sample business plans.

Small Business Association
www.sba.gov
This Web site, run by the U.S. government organization dedicated to helping small business owners, provides sources for technical, managerial, and financial advice and assistance.

Strategic Planning—University of Nebraska at Omaha
www.unomaha.edu/UNO/stratplan
This site provides some interesting material for use in strategic planning, as well as giving a good overview of the process. It includes a section that defines the terms used in strategic planning.

U.S. Small Business Administration
www.sba.gov/starting/indexbusplans.html
The SBA's site provides a model business plan, addresses relevant FAQs, and offers general information on startups.

Venture Capital Resource Library
www.vfinance.com
This site provides a business plan template, general articles, and texts of SEC and UCC rules and regulations, as well as leads to sources of venture capital.

ORGANIZATIONS

USA

American Management Association (AMA)
1601 Broadway, New York, 10019
T: +1 212 586 8100
F: +1 212 903 8168
E: egreenberg@amanet.org
www.amanet.org
Founded in 1923, this association has over 80,000 members. The AMA provides business forums and seminars worldwide. With a focus on practical training, members can enhance their business skills and develop successful planning strategies by studying the best practices of various world-class organizations. Seminars are geared for every professional level, from C.E.O. to administrative assistant. The AMA also publishes valuable print resources that cover a wide range of topics including business plans, career building, and technology.

Chief Executive Officers' Club
457 Washington Street, New York, 10013
T: +1 212 925 7911
F: +1 212 925 7463
E: info@ceoclubs.org
http://main.ceoclubs.org
Established in 1978, this association serves as a management resource for entrepreneurs and their professional advisers. Membership is by invitation only. Members must be C.E.O.s of businesses that have over $2,000,000 in annual sales. The organization selects publications on developing business plans and conducts seminars on the entrepreneurial process.

For More Information

✓ **Writing a Business Plan (pp. 486–87)**
Budgeting (pp. 1913–15)
Corporate Strategy (pp. 1944–46)
Forecasting and Scenario Planning (pp. 1986–87)
Small and Growing Businesses (pp. 2112–15)

BUSINESS PROCESS REENGINEERING

BOOKS

The Aftermath of Reengineering: Downsizing and Corporate Performance
TONY CARTER
Binghamton, New York: The Haworth Press, 1999
165pp ISBN: 0789007207
Carter takes a much needed, thorough look at the effectiveness of reengineering and both its positive and negative human, strategic, and societal consequences. Every chapter concludes with a case study that illustrates the topic, and the final chapter of the book provides an evaluation of reengineering best practices from a variety of companies and industries.

Beyond Reengineering: How the Process-centered Organization Is Changing
MICHAEL HAMMER
New York: HarperCollins, 1997
304pp ISBN: 0887308805
This book explores the strategy and structure of the process-centered organization, and the consequences of reengineering.

Business Process Redesign: A View from the Inside
ASHLEY BRAGANZA, ANDREW MYERS, EDS.
London: International Thomson Business Press, 1997

"An important technology first creates a problem and then solves it." (Alan Kay)

  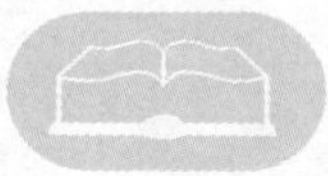    

210pp ISBN: 1861521871
The authors draw on the experience of a number of case-study companies in America and Europe, and provide guidance on building a successful reengineering program.

The Process Edge: Creating Value Where It Counts
PETER G. W. KEEN
Boston, Massachusetts: Harvard Business School Press, 1997
185pp ISBN: 0875845886
The author takes a multidisciplinary approach to reengineering and stresses the need to focus on those processes that add value. He also includes a description of a salience/worth matrix model designed to help companies determine their most critical processes, as well as a number of company case studies.

Process Mapping: How to Reengineer Your Business Process
V. DANIEL HUNT
New York: John Wiley, 1996
274pp ISBN: 0471132810
This book provides a detailed guide to the techniques of process mapping and its role in reengineering. The contents include: assessing the need for process improvement; deciding if is right for you; creating a process mapping team; selecting the best software tools for the job; using the data to build process maps; and using the maps to improve business performance.

The Reengineering Alternative: A Plan for Making Your Current Culture Work
WILLIAM E. SCHNEIDER
New York: McGraw-Hill, 1999
173pp ISBN: 0071359818
Reengineering has virtually become business dogma, yet there are viable, and perhaps even preferable, alternatives. Mechanistic approaches to reengineering often fail to take into account one of a company's most vital and enduring resources—its culture. This book describes an approach to change management that focuses on a company's unique existing strengths and corporate objectives, and shows how to work effectively to foster improvement according to four basic corporate culture types.

Re-engineering at Work 2nd ed.
MICHAEL LOH
Brookfield, Vermont: Gower, 1997
225pp ISBN: 0566079410
The author suggests that the reason why many reengineering programs fall short of expectations is that insufficient attention is paid to the human element. A four-stage framework for introducing a reengineering program is presented to overcome this problem and the process is illustrated with examples from a wide range of organizations in different cultures.

Reengineering Business for Success in the Internet Age: Business-to-business E-commerce Strategies
DEBRA CAMERON
Charleston, South Carolina: Computer Technology Research Corporation, 2000
197pp ISBN: 1566070848
The publisher is now out of business—another casualty of the e-commerce nosedive—but this report may still be purchased through online booksellers. It applies reengineering strategies to the dynamic e-business environment. Topics range from integrating legacy systems to implementing B2B security strategies, with special emphasis on the unique role of XML in reengineering for e-business.

Reengineering Management: The Mandate for New Leadership
JAMES A. CHAMPY
New York: HarperCollins, 1996
288pp ISBN: 0887307965
James Champy, coauthor of *Reengineering the Corporation*, focuses on the challenges of reengineering for managers, especially the loss of control implicit in the necessity of delegation.

Reengineering the Corporation: A Manifesto for Business Revolution
MICHAEL HAMMER, JAMES A. CHAMPY
New York: HarperCollins, 2001
257pp ISBN: 0066621127
Hammer and Champy have updated their classic—and controversial—text on reengineering to deal with the challenges of the new millennium. The reengineering process requires a reinvention of the post-industrial organization through visionary leadership, optimization by means of information technologies, working in close consultation with suppliers to reduce inventories, and integrating decision-making into the nature of the work for all employees.

MAGAZINES

Business Process Management Journal
ISSN: 1463–7154
MCB University Press
60/62 Toller Lane, Bradford, West Yorkshire, BD8 9BY, U.K.
T: +44 (0) 1274 777700
F: +44 (0) 1274 785200
www.emeraldinsight.com/bpmj.htm
This journal is published in association with the European Centre for Total Quality Management. Contributions from both academics and practitioners are included, and the focus is on the management of business processes for efficiency and competitive success.

Knowledge and Process Management
ISSN: 1092–4604
John Wiley
Wiley InterScience Coordinator, Subscriptions Department, 605 Third Avenue, New York, 10158–0012
T: +1 800 825 7550
F: +1 212 850 6021
www.interscience.wiley.com
This quarterly journal, formerly called *Business Change and Reengineering: Journal of Corporate Transformation*, aims to meet the needs of executives responsible for organizational performance improvement. Articles focus on the areas of knowledge management, organizational learning, core competences, and process management. The emphasis is placed on practical lessons learned from the experience of organizations.

INTERNET

BPR (Business Process Reengineering) Online Learning Center
www.prosci.com
This online learning center features seven series of multiple online tutorials on various aspects of business process reengineering, together with best practice benchmarking studies, a change management resource library, a project trouble shooter, and much more.

bprc
http://bprc.warwick.ac.uk
This site, provided by the Business Process Resource Centre at the University of Warwick, gives details of research programs, courses, articles, mailing lists, discussion groups, and other Internet resources.

Brint.com Business Process Reengineering
www.brint.com/BPR.htm
A comprehensive collection of links to BPR resources.

Business Guide to Reengineering Books
www.reengineering.net
This site offers a set of links to books, handbooks, and reports on reengineering and change management as a reference resource for those engaged in reengineering projects.

Business Process
www.c3i.osd.mil/org/bpr.html

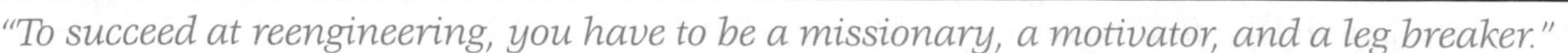

"To succeed at reengineering, you have to be a missionary, a motivator, and a leg breaker."
(Michael Hammer)

This is a library of BPR resources provided by the Office of the Assistant Secretary of Defense and the Defense Technical Information Center in the United States. It includes the Electronic College of Process Innovation and the BPR Internet Resources Kiosk.

National Center for Public Productivity
http://newark.rutgers.edu/~ncpp
Affiliated with Rutgers University, the Web site for this center is a gateway to federal, state, and international resources on productivity in the public sector, and for "citizen-driven government performance."

Reengineering Resource Center
www.reengineering.com
This site offers a library of articles and a marketplace for information on BPR software and tools, together with a diary of events. It is provided by Coe-Truman Technologies.

ORGANIZATIONS

USA

Business Process Management Initiative
1155 South Havana Street, #11–311, Aurora, Colorado, 80012
T: +1 303 364 8595
E: *info@bpmi.org*
www.bpmi.org
The BPMI is a business interest group involved in promoting and developing the use of business process management. It was founded in August 2000 by a small group of companies and is currently working on the development of Business Process Modeling Language (PRML) and Business Process Query Language (BPQL).

International

Business Process Management Group
Oak House, 82 Charterhouse Drive, Solihull, West Midlands, B91 3FH, U.K.
T: +44 121 711 7099
F: +44 121 711 7219
E: *enquiry@bpmg.org*
www.bpmg.org
The BPMG is a business interest group, established in the United Kingdom in 1992, which now has over 1,400 members worldwide. Its aims are to advance the understanding and application of business process management, to raise business awareness of BPM, and to provide a forum for the exchange of information relevant to BPM.

Workflow and Reengineering International Association
2436 North Federal Highway 374, Lighthouse Point, Florida, 33064
T: +1 954 782 3376
F: +1 954 782 6365
E: *waria@waria.com*
www.waria.com
WARIA is a nonprofit organization concerned with issues at the intersection between BPR, knowledge management, electronic commerce, and workflow management. It encourages the sharing of information on issues common to these fields by providing networking opportunities.

For More Information

- **Business Appraisal and Performance Measurement (pp. 1915–17)**
- **Corporate Strategy (pp. 1944–46)**

CHANGE MANAGEMENT

BOOKS

All Hat and No Cattle
CHRIS TURNER
Cambridge, Massachusetts: Perseus, 2000
272pp ISBN: 0738203661
This book takes a humorous look at current corporate wisdom. It is a critique of total quality management that offers anecdotes of managerial incompetence and challenges the status quo.

The Dance of Change: The Challenges to Sustaining Momentum in Learning Organizations
PETER M. SENGE, ET AL.
New York: Doubleday, 1999
224pp ISBN: 0385493223
Written for managers at all levels, this book addresses ways in which the challenges brought by profound change can be met. In a clear and practical format, methods are described for building personal and organizational capabilities to accomplish long-term change initiatives. Exercises, practical advice, and case studies are included.

Leader's Change Handbook: An Essential Guide to Setting Direction and Taking Action
JAY A. CONGER, GRETCHEN M. SPREITZER, EDWARD E. LAWLER, EDS.
San Francisco, California: Jossey-Bass, 1998
320pp ISBN: 0787943517
This handbook contains chapters by various leading contributors to the field, introducing new thinking on ways in which leaders, managers, consultants, and human resource specialists can implement change within their organizations. It outlines the main elements of effective change management, expands traditional ideas of leadership, and discusses the future of organizational change.

Leading Change
JOHN KOTTER
Cambridge, Massachusetts: Harvard Business School Press, 1996
187pp ISBN: 0875847471
This book identifies the most common mistakes in effecting organizational change, and offers an eight-step process to overcoming such obstacles.

The Manager As Change Agent
JERRY W. GILLEY, ET AL.
Cambridge, Massachusetts: Perseus, 2001
208pp ISBN: 0738204625
This book offers a practical approach to developing the skills necessary for leading change in an organization, including motivating people who are resistant to change, resolving conflict, and building consensus.

Managing Change: A Strategic Approach to Organisational Dynamics 3rd ed.
BERNARD BURNES
Upper Saddle River, New Jersey: Financial Times Prentice Hall, 2000
565pp ISBN: 0273641662
This is a comprehensive and readable text on the theory and practice of organizational change. It provides a broad and in-depth exploration of the context, complexity, and processes involved in managing change, using case study examples.

Managing Change in the Workplace: A 12-step Program for Success
RALPH L. KLIEM, IRWIN S. LUDIN
New York: HNB Publishing, 1998
139pp ISBN: 0966428617
One chapter of this book is devoted to each of the 12 steps involved in accomplishing change.

"Most of us are about as eager to be changed as we were to be born, and go through our changes in a similar state of shock."
(James Baldwin)

  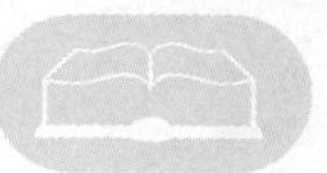    

The book provides a practical approach for managers who are planning or implementing organizational change.

Smart Things to Know about Change
DAVID FIRTH
Oxford: Capstone, 2000
238pp (Smart Series)
ISBN: 1841120359
This book aims to improve managers' understanding and performance of change initiatives by distilling collective wisdom on change management. The concept of change is explained, and seven steps for aligning the organization are examined.

Ten Keys to Successful Change Management
JOHN PENDLEBURY, BENOIT GROUARD, FRANCIS MESTON
New York: John Wiley, 1998
318pp ISBN: 0471979309
This book describes ten keys that can be used to unlock the tools and techniques needed to manage change. The approach is a practical one, aimed at managers accomplishing organizational change. The dynamics of change are described, with consideration given to its causes, its pitfalls, and the criteria for success. Case studies are used to illustrate the main points.

MAGAZINES

Change Manager
Lance A. Berger and Associates Ltd., LBA Consulting Group
17 Courtney Circle, Bryn Mawr, Pennsylvania, 19010
T: +1 610 525 5332
F: +1 610 525 9785
www.users.voicenet.com/~lberger
The *Change Manager* is a newsletter containing articles relating the experiences of executives and experts on the change management process. It is published quarterly and the most recent articles are on the Web site.

Focus on Change Management
ISSN: 1352–9501
Informa Publishing Group
19 Portland Place, London, W1B 1PX, U.K.
T: +44 (0) 20 7553 1000
F: +44 (0) 20 7553 1100
www.informa.com
This journal considers change management and related issues, with an emphasis on case studies and practical advice. It is published ten times a year and aimed at practicing managers.

Industrial and Corporate Change
ISSN: 0960–6491
Oxford University Press
Journals Customer Services, 2001 Evans Road, Cary, North Carolina, 27513
T: +1 919 677 0977
F: +1 919 677 1714
www.oup.com
This journal presents and interprets evidence on corporate and industrial change, drawing from interdisciplinary approaches. It is an academic quarterly journal.

Journal of Organizational Change Management
ISSN: 0953–4814
Emerald (North America)
4th Floor, 44 Brattle Street, Cambridge, Massachusetts, 02138
T: +1 888 622 0075
www.emeraldinsight.com/jocm.htm
The articles in this journal set out for managers the agenda for organizational change and development. They analyze new approaches and present new research theories.

Strategic Change
ISSN: 1086–1718
John Wiley
Wiley InterScience Coordinator, Subscriptions Department, 605 Third Avenue, New York, 10158–0012
T: +1 800 825 7550
F: +1 212 850 6021
www.interscience.wiley.com
The journal has international scope. It aims to publish authoritative and topical papers on sources of change, options for responding to change, and the implementation and management of change processes.

Strategic Management Journal
ISSN: 0143–2095
John Wiley
Wiley Interscience Coordinator, Subscriptions Department, 605 Third Avenue, New York, 10158
T: +1 800 825 7550
F: +1 212 850 6021
www.interscience.wiley.com
Published 13 times per year, this journal covers all aspects of business and management. Articles focus on advances in strategic management and communications. Major topics of interest include entrepreneurship, business environments, organization structure, and strategic business processes.

Training and Development
ISSN: 1055–9760
American Society for Training and Development
1640 King Street, Box 1443, Alexandria, Virginia, 22313
T: +1 703 683 8100
F: +1 703 683 1523
www.astd.org
Published 12 times per year, this magazine is the publication for the American Society of Training and Development. Articles are written with an emphasis on business professionals involved in the training, development skills, and management guidance of their employees.

WorkingUSA
ISSN: 1089–7011
M. E. Sharpe, Inc.
80 Business Park Drive, Armonk, New York, 10504
T: +1 800 541 6563
F: +1 914 273 2106
www.mesharpe.com/usa_main.htm
Published quarterly, this journal serves as a forum for labor management professionals.

INTERNET

Change Management 101: A Primer
http://home.att.net/~nickols/change.htm
Fred Nickols, a consultant based in New Jersey, provides a broad overview of the concept of change management. Coverage is given to definitions of change, the problem of change, skill requirements, four change strategies, and ways of managing change.

Change Management Resource Library
www.change-management.org
Sponsored by ProSci, this site includes a collection of articles posted by consultants, book lists, best practice in managing change, benchmarking tools, and links.

Management First
www.managementfirst.com
This site from Emerald includes a section devoted to full text articles on change management.

ORGANIZATIONS

USA

Center for Management Effectiveness (CME)
P.O. Box 1202, Pacific Palisades, California, 90272
T: +1 310 459 6052 or 888 819 0200
F: +1 310 459 9307
E: *info@cmeinc.org*
www.cmeinc.org
Specializing in training programs, this education and research center is dedicated to helping organizations of all sizes improve output and performance. With a unique focus on change and the management of change, the programs offered are geared toward current topics such as strategic decision

"Thinking about change is a redundancy. All thinking is about change." (Edgar Bronfman, Jr.)

making, stress management and managing change. Programs utilize books, videos and active participation. The Center provides training for commercial business, nonprofit and government agencies.

For More Information

☆ **Managing Dynamic Change (pp. 277-78)**

☆ **Switching Strategies (pp. 93-94)**

☆ **Turnaround Strategies (pp. 251-52)**

COACHING, COUNSELING, AND MENTORING

BOOKS

Action Coaching: How to Leverage Individual Performance for Company Success

DAVID L. DOTLICH, PETER C. CAIRO
San Francisco, California: Jossey-Bass, 1999
287pp (Jossey-Bass Business and Management Series)
ISBN: 0787944777
The authors aim to teach people at the executive, managerial, and group levels to become extraordinary coaches. Action coaching strategically links the progress of individuals to specific organizational issues and thereby becomes a powerful tool for organizational change.

Coaching and Mentoring

NIGEL MACLENNAN
Brookfield, Vermont: Gower, 1995
316pp ISBN: 0566075628
This comprehensive textbook explores the subject from basic skills to designing and implementing a tailor-made coaching and mentoring system. It explains the factors that determine achievement and presents a seven-stage model designed to enable managers and supervisors to encourage people to improve. The problems commonly encountered are also identified, and the process of overcoming them or, in some cases, turning them to positive account is considered.

Coaching for Growth: How to Bring Out the Best in Your Team and Yourself

PETER BOLT
Dublin, Republic of Ireland: Oak Tree Press, 2000
160pp ISBN: 1860761690
Bolt investigates every aspect of coaching from the manager's point of view. He includes: the coaching process itself and the coaching session; the key skills involved; the different approaches the coach can take; the various types of individual the coach might encounter; and coaching downward, sideways, and upward within the organization. The book also deals with coaching individuals during times of turbulent change, whether this is personal or organizational. A particular emphasis is placed on coaching leaders and potential leaders, although the importance of coaching the whole person is continually stressed.

Coaching for Leadership: How the World's Greatest Coaches Help Leaders Learn

MARSHALL GOLDSMITH, LAURENCE LYONS, ALYSSA FREAS, EDS.
San Francisco, California: Jossey-Bass/Pfeiffer, 2000
392pp ISBN: 0787955175
This book brings together the thinking of a number of experienced coaches with the aim of giving both an insight into the importance of coaching as a route to leadership, and an understanding of what can be achieved through coaching. It is intended for those who provide or receive coaching and those who sponsor or design coaching programs. It explains the foundations of coaching, the roles adopted by those who participate in it, and coaching situations that arise from moments of transition, besides examining the practice and techniques involved. A number of case studies are included.

Coaching Illustrated: A Proven Approach to Real-world Management

MARK DAVID
San Mateo, California: The Mark David Corporation, 1999
88pp ISBN: 1893778002
Coaching Illustrated is a practical guide for managers on how to become better coaches for their business teams. It is built upon 30 principles of effective leadership. The book is written in a concise and user-friendly style that defines each principle and gives an example of how it is applied in a business setting.

Coaching: Winning Strategies for Individuals and Teams

DENNIS C. KINLAW
Brookfield, Vermont: Gower, 1997
190pp ISBN: 0566078880
This guide looks at the variety of ways in which coaching is currently understood and applied. It develops a model to help in the development of coaching skills, identifies the generic skills that successful coaches use, and explains and illustrates how to apply these skills in working with both individuals and teams.

Counselling in the Workplace

JENNY SUMMERFIELD, LYN VAN OUDTSHOORN
New York: Beekman, 2000
240pp (Developing Practice Series)
ISBN: 0846450208
This book examines the role of counseling within an organization. It argues that counseling skills should be developed by managers not only to deal with specific problems, but also to aid the enhancement of employee performance levels and the realization of departmental goals. It is divided into three sections. The first examines the advantages of counseling at work and shows how to decide on appropriate counseling strategies; the second examines the range of personal problems that often occur with employees; while the third provides guidelines for appropriate training in counseling skills.

Developing High-performance People

OSCAR G. MINK, KEITH OWEN, BARBARA MINK
Cambridge, Massachusetts: Perseus, 1993
271pp ISBN: 0201563134
This book addresses the changing role of managers in the today's business world. It deals with emerging management challenges, including self-managed work teams, empowerment of employees, and organizational learning.

Executive Coaching with Backbone and Heart: A Systems Approach to Engaging Leaders with Their Challenges

MARY BETH O'NEILL
San Francisco, California: Jossey-Bass, 2000
224pp (Jossey-Bass Business and Management Series)
ISBN: 0787950165
Drawing on her own experience of coaching high-powered executives, the author outlines a systems approach to coaching which takes account of "force fields"—the political and emotional climate within organizations that affects decision making. The book provides both a way of thinking about coaching and a methodology for it.

Handbook of Coaching: A Comprehensive Resource Guide for

Managers, Executives, Consultants, and Human Resource Professionals
FREDERIC M. HUDSON
San Francisco, California: Jossey-Bass, 1999
264pp ISBN: 0787947954
Coaching is viewed as a fundamental element of any successful organization. This handbook offers coaches a complete guide to the emerging field of professional adult coaching. The author introduces the concept of coaching, reviews its theoretical roots, develops a conceptual model for it, and explains how it can be applied throughout the adult years. A ''basic library for coaches'' is provided at the end of each chapter.

Handbook of Counselling in Organizations
MICHAEL CARROLL, MICHAEL WALTON, EDS.
Thousand Oaks, California: Sage, 1997
363pp ISBN: 0761950877
This handbook presents a collection of articles covering all aspects of counseling within an organizational context. It provides a thorough examination of the key issues and concerns within the field, includes models of counseling in organizations, and deals with understanding counseling provision and introducing counseling into an organization.

The Heart of Coaching: Using Transformational Coaching to Create a High-performance Culture
THOMAS G. CRANE
San Diego, California: FTA Press, 2001
220pp ISBN: 0966087402
The Heart of Coaching is a comprehensive overview of the practice of executive coaching derived from Tom Crane's 15 years of experience as an executive coach. His message is to move from a hierarchical organization of bosses and subordinates to a collaborative organization of coaches and learners.

Improving On-the-job Training and Coaching
KAREN LAWSON
Alexandria, Virginia: American Society for Training and Development, 1997
94pp ISBN: 1562860623
This is a comprehensive and usable manual on how to provide on-the-job training. Practical advice and guidance is offered on training adults, selecting the trainer, developing a training plan, conducting and evaluating training, and on-the-job coaching.

The IPD Guide on Counselling at Work
INSTITUTE OF PERSONNEL AND DEVELOPMENT
New York: Beekman, 2000
20pp ISBN: 084645681X
After defining the concept of counseling, this work focuses on counseling skills, the limitations to their use, and referral and workplace counseling. It then introduces models of workplace counseling and explains the process of setting up a workplace counseling scheme. Its overall aim is to promote the best possible standards in the use of workplace counseling.

Masterful Coaching: Extraordinary Results by Impacting People and the Way They Think and Work Together
ROBERT HARGROVE
San Francisco, California: Jossey-Bass/ Pfeiffer, 1995
320pp ISBN: 0893842818
This book shows how to reach breakthrough goals and implement transformational change in the workplace. It emphasizes the core coaching skills of sponsoring, counseling, acknowledging, teaching, and confronting. It provides ideas, methods, and tools for implementing the model, and examples from leading companies.

Masterful Coaching Fieldbook
ROBERT HARGROVE
San Francisco, California: Jossey-Bass, 1999
372pp ISBN: 0787947555
This fieldbook delivers how-to guidelines for becoming a successful coach and mentor. It can be used alone, or alongside Hargrove's *Masterful Coaching* as a practical, hands-on guide for coaching individuals and groups through multiple media.

Mentoring Executives and Directors
DAVID CLUTTERBUCK, DAVID MEGGINSON
Woburn, Massachusetts: Butterworth-Heinemann, 1999
167pp ISBN: 0750636955
This is one of the few books to focus specifically on the role of mentoring in the development of senior managers and directors. The authors explore the issue of mentoring for executives and present 22 case study examples. The lessons to be learned from the case studies are discussed.

Mentoring Manager: Strategies for Fostering Talent and Spreading Knowledge
GARETH LEWIS
Philadelphia, Pennsylvania: Trans-Atlantic Publications, 2000
192pp (Smarter Solutions Series)
ISBN: 027364484X
The author reviews the history and purposes of mentoring and describes the attributes and skills needed by mentors in order to help others to learn. He also provides a practical guide to getting started in mentoring and developing mentoring relationships and programs.

Mentoring Manual
MIKE WHITTAKER, ANN CARTWRIGHT
Brookfield, Vermont: Gower, 2000
202pp ISBN: 0566081474
This book includes eight related OHP slides, questionnaires, forms, and a mentoring workshop outline, and offers the theories and materials needed for providing a mentoring scheme or for improving an existing one.

Stop Managing, Start Coaching!
JERRY W. GILLEY, NATHANIEL W. BOUGHTON
New York: McGraw-Hill, 1995
250pp ISBN: 0786304561
This book highlights the critical skill of performance coaching. It demonstrates how managers can improve productivity in the workplace by balancing the roles of trainer, mentor, career coach, and confronter. It is a guide to ensuring performance improvement by mastering the art of employee ''self-esteeming,'' the next step beyond employee empowerment.

Transformational Mentoring: Creating Development Alliances for Changing Organizational Cultures
JULIE HAY
Watford: Sherwood Publishing, 1999
183pp ISBN: 0952196476
The author introduces what she considers to be a totally new approach to developing employees. She argues that traditional mentoring techniques are no longer valid as traditional organizations are replaced with flatter ones. Transformational mentoring offers a much more flexible alternative where peers, unrelated work colleagues, or even external business people can create alliances to enhance personal development. She outlines the concept of the developmental alliance and explains its implementation. Its benefits and drawbacks are also evaluated. Checklists and an example of a 12-step mentoring program complete the package.

Workplace Counselling: A Systematic Approach to Employee Care
MICHAEL CARROLL
Thousand Oaks, California: Sage, 1996
247pp ISBN: 0761950214
Carroll provides a practical introduction to the whole area of providing counseling in the workplace. The topics he covers include: understanding workplace counseling; models of workplace counseling; setting up workplace counseling; and supervising workplace counselors.

"The information age is one in which workers give way to professionals and managers are replaced by coaches."
(Michael Hammer)

MAGAZINES

Counselling

ISSN: 0264–9977
British Association for Counselling and Psychotherapy
1 Regent Place, Rugby, Warwickshire, CV21 2PJ, U.K.
T: +44 (0) 870 443 5252
F: +44 (0) 870 443 5160
www.bac.co.uk

The monthly professional journal for U.K. counselors is sent to members free of charge ten times a year. It contains articles on the theory and practice of counseling, plus features on setting up in practice, getting the most out of study, professional matters (accreditation, supervision, training), the growing importance of IT in counseling, and, finally, the widening research base for the profession.

INTERNET

Coach Universe

www.coachuniverse.com

Coach Universe is a comprehensive guide to resources for corporate coaches. It offers links to training services, profiling services, discussion groups, articles on coaching, and coaching-related businesses.

European Mentoring Centre

www.mentoringcentre.org

Members have access to the EMC library, while nonmembers can download copies of recent research reports as pdf files. Details of the annual European Mentoring Conference can also be viewed.

Mentoring Group

www.mentoringgroup.com

The Group is a division of the nonprofit corporation, the Coalition of Counseling Centers, and was founded in 1980. Besides promoting various products and services, the site also provides freely available information on starting a program, best practice, ethics in mentoring, and the reasons for being a mentor.

MentorsForum.co.uk

www.mentorsforum.co.uk

The Mentors Forum is an interactive site hosted by Business Link Hertfordshire. It not only looks at individual mentoring schemes, but also studies mentoring as a ''generic'' subject. A section called Discovering Mentoring provides access to case studies of mentoring programs and links to research documents. The Tools section provides lists of relevant software, publications, and factsheets, which can be downloaded. An interactive world map provides links to mentoring activities and organizations worldwide.

The Knowledge Base of Coachville.com

www.topten.org

This site offers an interesting and large collection of knowledge ''nuggets'' on coaching and business life in general. The ''nuggets'' are short articles and can be easily located through topic lists.

ORGANIZATIONS

USA

American Counseling Association

5999 Stevenson Avenue, Alexandria, Virginia, 22304–3300
T: +1 703 823 9800
F: +1 703 823 0252
E: *membership@counseling.org*
www.counseling.org

The American Counseling Association is a nonprofit professional and educational organization that is dedicated to the growth and enhancement of the counseling profession. Founded in 1952, the ACA is the world's largest association exclusively representing professional counselors in various practice settings. By providing leadership training, publications, continuing education opportunities, and advocacy services to nearly 55,000 members, the ACA helps counseling professionals develop their skills and expand their knowledge base.

Europe

Association for Counselling at Work

Eastlands Court, St. Peter's Road, Rugby, Warwickshire, CV21 3QP, U.K.
T: +44 (0) 131 667 9171
F: +44 (0) 131 667 0110
E: *acwdesk@talk21.com*

The ACW promotes and supports the professional practice of counseling and counseling skills in the workplace. It provides a forum and mutual support network, as well as a journal and professional development opportunities.

British Association for Counselling and Psychotherapy

1 Regent Place, Rugby, Warwickshire, CV21 2PJ, U.K.
T: +44 (0) 870 443 5252
F: +44 (0) 870 443 5160
E: *bac@bac.co.uk*
www.bac.co.uk

The BACP has been the United Kingdom's leading representative organization for counseling professionals since 1977. It provides a range of member services, including training and development, and accredited professional recognition. The BACP also maintains the United Kingdom Register of Counsellors.

Employee Assistance Professionals Association

Premier House, 85 High Street, Witney, Oxfordshire, OX8 6LY, U.K.
T: +44 (0) 800 783 7616 (U.K. only)
F: +44 (0) 1993 200401
E: *info@eapa.org.uk*
www.eapa.org.uk

The EAPA is the professional body for Employee Assistance Programs (EAPs). It represents the interests of professionals concerned with employee assistance, and with the psychological health and the well-being of employees in the United Kingdom. It exists to provide leadership in promoting and developing EAPs in the United Kingdom, to set national standards of practice and professional guidelines for EAPs, and to provide support and stimulation for the professional development of its members. It has close links with Employee Assistance Programs International.

The European Mentoring Centre

Burnham House, High Street, Burnham, Buckinghamshire, SL1 7JZ, U.K.
T: +44 (0) 1628 661919
E: *emc@item.co.uk*
www.mentoringcentre.org

The European Mentoring Centre aims to promote mentoring in business, education, and the community at large. It brings together practitioners, researchers, and institutions internationally to explore and foster best practice. The EMC also undertakes a research program, maintains a library, and runs the annual European Mentoring Conference. David Clutterbuck is one of its directors.

The Industrial Society

Peter Runge House, 3 Carlton House Terrace, London, SW1Y 5DG, U.K.
T: +44 (0) 20 7479 1000
F: +44 (0) 20 7479 1111
E: *customercentre@indsoc.co.uk*
www.indsoc.co.uk

The Industrial Society is an independent body with over 80 years' experience in management development and training. The Society operates under the belief that business success goes hand in hand with fair management practices. The services offered to members include an information service and employment law helpline, a publishing program of books, research reports, and videos, plus a training and consulting service which includes the School of Coaching.

International

Canadian Counselling Association

116 Albert Street, Suite 702, Ottawa, Ontario, K1P 5G3, Canada
T: +1 613 237 1099

F: +1 613 237 9786
E: info@ccacc.ca
www.ccacc.ca
The Canadian Counselling Association is a national association of professionally trained counselors engaged in the helping professions. Its members work in many diverse fields—education, employment and career development, social work, business, industry, mental health, public service agencies, government, and private practice. The CCA was founded in 1965.

For More Information

☆ Coaching (pp. 328–29)
☆ Mentoring (pp. 326–27)
✔ Coaching for Better Performance (pp. 344–45)
✔ Mentoring in Practice (pp. 368–69)
Motivation (pp. 2050–52)
Performance Appraisal (pp. 2064–66)
Personnel Management and HR Management (pp. 2067–71)

COMPETENCES

BOOKS

Achieving Corporate Success through People: Making Competencies Impact on the Bottom Line
Derek A. Burn
Philadelphia, Pennsylvania: Trans-Atlantic Publications, 1997
132pp (Management Briefings)
ISBN: 0273633066
With its practical, nonacademic approach, this briefing outlines a realistic and effective way of applying competences and competency frameworks within an organization. The focus is on showing how they can impact on corporate success by providing linkage from mission through the corporate plan to the identification of departmental targets and employee objectives. The pivotal role of the HR department in the implementation and monitoring of a competency system is also discussed. Case studies include the Bank of Scotland, and Desoutter.

Art and Science of Competency Models: Pinpointing Critical Success Factors in Organizations
Antoinette D. Lucia, Richard Lepsinger
San Francisco, California: Jossey-Bass, 1999
197pp ISBN: 0787946028
Lucia and Lepsinger examine the what, why, and how of competency models. They look at how competency models can enhance HRM systems, and discuss developing a competency model from scratch, finalizing and validating it, integrating it into an HRM system, and gaining support for it within the organization.

Building Robust Competencies: Linking Human Resource Systems to Organizational Strategies
Paul C. Green
San Francisco, California: Jossey-Bass, 1999
213pp ISBN: 0787946494
Building Robust Competencies offers a practical guide to tying organizational competencies to human resource development and hiring practices. The book outlines a method for determining the strategic core competencies of an organization and then focuses on hiring to enhance organizational competencies.

Competence and Organizational Change: A Handbook
Shirley Fletcher
Sterling, Virginia: Stylus Publishing, 1997
224pp ISBN: 074942141X
Fletcher examines how organizations can develop, implement, and evaluate integrated performance management and measurement systems. She deals with the role of competence in performance management and organizational change programs, using case studies of companies including ICL, Mazda Cars, and TGI Friday's to illustrate the various approaches to change management. A toolkit designed to make competence-based change more effective is also provided.

Competency-based Recruitment and Selection
Robert Wood, Tim Payne
New York: John Wiley, 1998
214pp (Wiley Series in Strategic Human Resource Management)
ISBN: 0471974730
This guide is one of the few works to examine the place of competency in recruitment, and it offers a comprehensive approach to its subject. It considers application forms, competency-based interviewing, psychometric tests, and the use of assessment centers.

Designing Competence-based Training 2nd ed.
Shirley Fletcher
Sterling, Virginia: Stylus Publishing, 1997
128pp (Practical Trainer Series)
ISBN: 0749421967
Aimed at those responsible for identifying training needs or designing, delivering, and evaluating training, this book uses case studies to demonstrate how training programs can be tailored to the needs of organizations. By providing details of competency models and NVQ standards, it also offers a methodology for mapping training programs to competence.

Developing Managerial Competence
Jonathan Winterton, Ruth Winterton
New York: Routledge, 1999
324pp ISBN: 0415183464
The Wintertons take a comprehensive and analytical look at the field of modern management development, discussing, among other questions, how to measure development and how it can benefit corporate strategy. Their aim is to demonstrate the value of the occupational standards for managers developed by the Management Charter Initiative and also the value of Investors in People. The book offers a conceptual framework for evaluating the business advantages of management development and gives 16 detailed case studies of organizations, across different sectors, to show how this works in practice. The overview approach makes it suitable for both practicing managers and students.

Sustaining Corporate Growth: Harnessing Your Strategic Strengths
A. T. Kearney
Boca Raton, Florida: CRC Press, 2000
120pp ISBN: 1574442899
Sustaining Corporate Growth highlights eight global corporations with case studies that clearly demonstrate a common theme of sustained growth and success. Corporate strategists can use this book to learn how to identify the core competencies their company possesses and those that they need to develop for the future.

MAGAZINES

Competency and Emotional

"Leadership competence. . .is a matter fundamentally of competence in the specific role that carries the leadership accountability."
(Elliot Jaques)

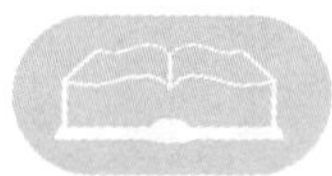

Intelligence
ISSN: 1351–5802
Industrial Relations Services
Eclipse Group, 18–20 Highbury Place, London, N5 1QP, U.K.
T: +44 (0) 20 7354 6746
F: +44 (0) 20 7354 8106
www.irsonline.co.uk/pub_subjects/index_pub_human.htm
Competency and Emotional Intelligence comprises five publications: 1. *Competency and Emotional Intelligence Quarterly*, a practical journal including case studies, features, and research articles (ISSN: paper format 1469–333X; electronic format 1469–3321); 2. *Competency and Emotional Intelligence Benchmarking* surveying current practice, key issues, and emerging trends, and presenting extracts from named employers' competency frameworks, with an overview article (ISSN: paper format 1469–3348; electronic format 1469–3356); 3. *Competency and Emotional Intelligence Monthly* offering news, comment, and analysis (ISSN: electronic format 1469–3313); 4. *Competency and Emotional Intelligence Literature*, a directory of books, articles, and reports, published on the Internet; 5. *Competency—the Cumulative Index*, an index to subjects, authors, and employers for the early issues of *Competency* which were not published electronically.

INTERNET

Bain & Company
www.bain.com/bainweb/about/insights/mtt/core_competencies.asp
This site contains a short article on core competencies which defines the concept, explains the strategic value of core competencies, and provides some helpful information for taking action.

UC Berkeley—Management Core Competencies
www.campus.chance.berkeley.edu/partnership/managecorecomp
This URL accesses a detailed report prepared for UC Berkeley on their effort to develop the core competencies of their management team. It may be of use to anyone considering a similar project.

For More Information

Personnel Management and HR Management (pp. 2067–71)

Competition

BOOKS

The Agenda: What Every Business Must Do to Dominate the Decade
Michael Hammer
New York: Crown Business, 2001
288pp ISBN: 0609609661
This book is more of an outline of what companies need to do to remain competitive than a complete specification. Nevertheless, it is a valuable tool for keeping track of the important things and the reasons why they are important. The book focuses on customer service, but it also covers the more recent strategies of virtual organizations and collaboration with other companies.

Competitive Advantage through People: Unleashing the Power of the Work Force
Jeffrey Pfeffer
Boston, Massachusetts: Harvard Business School Press, 1994
304pp ISBN: 0875844138
This book explores the extent to which a genuine commitment to the workforce can provide companies with competitive advantage. It considers the implications of this shift in competitive focus, discusses potential barriers to its success, and examines strategies for overcoming these barriers and implementing change.

Differentiate or Die: Survival in Our Era of Killer Competition
Jack Trout, Steve Rivkin
New York: John Wiley, 2000
230pp ISBN: 0471357642
Differentiate or Die focuses on the specific attributes of a company and its products or services that set it apart from the competition. It is a book, aimed at all business readers, about becoming known for being different and better in the eyes of customers. It starts off with several chapters describing strategies that do not lead to differentiation and then moves on to discuss the many ways to differentiate, including globally.

Gaining and Sustaining Competitive Advantage
Jay B. Barney
Des Moines, Iowa: Prentice Hall, 2001
600pp ISBN: 0130307947
Barney's book is focused on the strategic aspects of competition. It covers both the external and internal strategies that are needed to remain competitive. It does this from both a "what to do" and a "what to avoid" perspective, offering good coverage of the topic for both advanced business students and current managers.

Getting Everything You Can Out of All You've Got: 21 Ways You Can Out-think, Out-perform, and Out-earn the Competition
Jay Abraham
New York: St. Martin's Press, 2000
376pp ISBN: 0312204655
This book by marketing guru, Jay Abraham, presents sound competitive strategies for creating and capturing market share. It focuses on how to implement these strategies, illustrating each point with plenty of real-life stories. Any small to medium-size business that wants to be truly competitive can learn from this book. Larger companies that want to revitalize their competitiveness may find useful information here as well.

Mission Critical: Realizing the Promise of Enterprise Systems
Thomas H. Davenport
Boston, Massachusetts: Harvard Business School Press, 2000
352pp ISBN: 0875849067
This book presents an authoritative and no-nonsense view of the ES opportunities and challenges, and provides a set of guidelines to help managers evaluate the benefits and risks for their organizations. The author describes in detail the changes that should be formulated in advance of ES adoption and monitored throughout its implementation—changes in an organization's information systems, business processes, and business strategy—and gives extensive real-world examples.

On Competition
Michael E. Porter
Boston, Massachusetts: Harvard Business School Press, 1998
320pp (Harvard Business Review Book Series)
ISBN: 0875847951
This book brings together 11 of Michael Porter's landmark articles on competition and

"We became uncompetitive by not being tolerant of mistakes."

(Roberto Goizueto)

complements them with two entirely new ones. The articles are grouped under three headings: competition and strategy—the core concepts; the competitiveness of locations; and competitive solutions to societal problems.

Wharton on Dynamic Competitive Strategy
GEORGE S. DAY, DAVID J. REIBSTEIN, EDS.
New York: John Wiley, 1997
400pp ISBN: 0471172073
A comprehensive guide to handling competitive situations, this book covers a range of strategies that can be used to assess and challenge the competitors who challenge your organization. The book provides guidelines formed from a history of research into competitive strategy.

MAGAZINES

Advances in Competitiveness Research
ISSN: 1077–0097
American Society for Competitiveness
P.O. Box 1658, Indiana, Pennsylvania, 15705
T: +1 724 357 5928
F: +1 724 357 7768
http://ecobweb.ecob.iup.edu/asc/acr.htm
The annual research journal of the American Society for Competitiveness, this publication considers conceptual, theoretical, and empirical advances in competitiveness and their effects on global economic and management issues.

Butterworths Competition Law
Butterworths Tolley
Halsbury House, 35 Chancery Lane, London, WC2A 1EL, U.K.
T: +44 (0) 20 7400 2500
F: +44 (0) 20 7400 2842
www.butterworths.co.uk
This publication consists of a five-volume loose-leaf base, with quarterly updates. Written by an expert legal team, it focuses on facets of competition law and legislation in the European Community and the United Kingdom, viewed both from a national and an industry sector perspective.

Competition and Change: The Journal of Global Business and Political Economy
ISSN: 1024–5294
Routledge
11 New Fetter Lane, London, EC4P 4EE, U.K.
T: +44 (0) 20 7583 9855
F: +44 (0) 20 7842 2298
www.tandf.co.uk/journals/titles/10245294.html
This quarterly journal examines the changing nature of global business and competition processes and their relationship to economic, political, and social forces.

Competitiveness Review
ISSN: 1059–5422
American Society for Competitiveness
P.O. Box 1658, Indiana, Pennsylvania, 15705
T: +1 724 357 5928
F: +1 724 357 7768
http://ecobweb.ecob.iup.edu/asc/acr.htm
This journal is published biannually and is devoted to exploring, developing, and understanding global competitiveness and related issues, from national competitiveness and strategic management to innovation and business intelligence.

OECD Journal of Competition Law and Policy
ISSN: 1560–7771
Organisation for Economic Cooperation and Development
2 rue André Pascal, 75775 Paris 16, France
T: +33 1 45 24 82 00
www.oecd.org
This is a quarterly journal written for competition experts in business, the law, economics, consulting, and academia. It provides insight into the thinking of competition-law enforcers while also focusing on the practical application of competition law and policy.

World Competition
ISSN: 1011–4548
Kluwer Law International
101 Philip Drive, Assinippi Park, Norwell, Massachusetts, 02061
T: +1 781 871 6600
F: +1 781 871 6528
www.kluwerlaw.com
This quarterly journal publishes articles on the latest developments in international competition legislation. Drawing on both legal and economic disciplines, it presents a rounded view of the implications of competition issues on a global scale.

INTERNET

Competition Commission
www.competition-commission.org.uk
This Web site belongs to the regulatory body that protects the interests of U.K. consumers and businesses. It includes details of current and past inquiries, publications and resource listings, and links to other competition sites.

European Union—Competition Directorate General
www.europa.eu.int/comm/dgs/competition
This is the official Web site of the European Union Competition Directorate, whose role is to establish a coherent competition policy across E.U. member countries. The site includes links to relevant competition bodies throughout the world.

MarketingProfs.com
www.marketingprofs.com
This Web site is aimed at marketing professionals and professors. It is a membership site, but membership is free and without hassle. There are a variety of articles on competition that can be accessed through its search engine.

Your Success Store
www.yoursuccessstore.com
This is a commercial site with some good free content. It offers a number of articles related to competition and business success in its resource section. The articles are organized by author and the author list includes some well-known business experts.

ORGANIZATIONS

USA

American Society for Competitiveness
P.O. Box 1658, Indiana, Pennsylvania, 15705
T: +1 724 357 5928
F: +1 724 357 7768
E: ASC@grove.iup.edu
www.eberly.iup.edu/asc
The Society's main aim is to encourage education in and knowledge of the theory and practice of competitiveness. It seeks to achieve this aim through the exchange of information and ideas by assisting in research activities and by providing teaching and practice materials.

U.S. Department of Justice—Antitrust Division
950 Pennsylvania Avenue NW, Washington, D.C., 20530–0001
T: +1 202 307 6665
F: +1 202 514 8862
E: ANTITRUST@usdoj.gov
www.usdoj.gov/atr
The role of the Antitrust Division of the U.S. Department of Justice is to promote and protect the U.S. economy and its competitive processes through the enforcement of antitrust laws. It is committed to preserving the rights of both company and consumer, and provides information and guidance on competition issues.

Europe

Competition Commission
New Court, 48 Carey Street, London, WC2A 2JT, U.K.
T: +44 (0) 20 7271 0100
F: +44 (0) 20 7271 0367
E: info@competition-commission.org.uk
www.competition-commission.org.uk
An independent public body established in 1999

"We need to re-establish the blue water between ourselves and the competition." (Roger Holmes)

to replace the Monopolies and Mergers Commission, the Commission has two main functions: to follow up any inquiries from outside bodies relating to monopolies, mergers, and the economic regulation of utility companies; and to hear appeals against decisions by other tribunals respecting infringements of the law on anti-competitive agreements and activities.

Competition Directorate General—European Union
Commission of the European Communities, DG Competition, 70 Rue Joseph II, Brussels, B-1049, Belgium
E: infocomp@cec.eu.int
www.europa.eu.int/comm/dgs/competition
The mission of the Competition Directorate General is to establish and implement a coherent competition policy across the countries of the European Union. Its main focus is on antitrust activity, merger control, liberalization and state intervention, and state aid.

Office of Fair Trading
Fleetbank House, 2–6 Salisbury Square, London, EC4Y 8JX, U.K.
T: +44 (0) 20 7211 8000
F: +44 (0) 20 7211 8800
E: enquiries@oft.gov.uk
www.oft.gov.uk
The Office of Fair Trading is a U.K. government body whose various divisions are responsible for monitoring and investigating competition policy and consumer affairs, and for regulating and enforcing legislation in these areas.

Organisation for Economic Co-operation and Development
2 rue André Pascal, 75775 Paris 16, France
T: +33 1 45 24 82 00
E: DAFCLP.contact@oecd.org
www.oecd.org
Made up of 30 member countries, all of which are committed to the market economy and pluralistic democracy, the OECD provides governments with a forum in which to discuss and develop economic and social policy, and with the information, data, and analysis needed to support these discussions. It includes a division and committee assigned to competition law and policy.

World Trade Organization
154 rue de Lausanne, CH-1211 Geneva 21, Switzerland
T: +41 22 739 5111
F: +41 22 731 4206
E: enquiries@wto.org
www.wto.org
The WTO is an international member-based organization whose role is to deal with the rules of trade between member nations. It aims to help producers of goods and services, and exporters and importers, to conduct their business effectively. It includes the Working Group on the Interaction between Trade and Competition Policy.

For More Information

- **Corporate Strategy (pp. 1944–46)**
- **Marketing Management (pp. 2045–48)**

Computers, Information Technology, and E-commerce

BOOKS

Doing IT Right: Technology, Business, and Risk of Computing
Harold Lorin
Greenwich, Connecticut: Manning Publications, 1996
402pp ISBN: 1884777090
This volume explores such strategic and managerial technology issues as creating systems architecture, networking, choosing the right software and software development, and the intricacies of systems management. It then goes on to show the reader ways to deal with the problems of due diligence and risk assessment in the ever-changing information technology environment.

Information Rules: A Strategic Guide to the Network Economy
Carl Shapiro, Hal R. Varian
Boston, Massachusetts: Harvard Business School Press, 1998
352pp ISBN: 087584863X
The advent of technological advances is not a new phenomenon—it has happened before, say the authors, who also note that when such advances occur, economic rules and cycles do not disappear, thus making it critical for managers to avoid focusing on technology to the exclusion of all else. What managers need to do, they suggest, is to find ways to deal with such issues as the distribution and marketing of goods in a networked economy and to resolve problems such as compatibility and standards to ease an organization's road to the information age.

IT Investment: Making a Business Case
Dan Remenyi
Oxford: Digital Equipment Corp., 1999
210pp (Computer Weekly Professional Series)
ISBN: 0750645040
The author presents clear arguments for preparing an IT business case and includes model questionnaires and forms that managers can use in preparing a case of their own. He stresses in particular the importance of demonstrating the improvements an IT project can make to business processes, practice, and efficiency, and introduces a five-factor model which ties the project into an organization's corporate strategy.

Learning to Succeed in Business with Information Technology
Tim Lane, David Snow, Peter Labrow
Manchester: NCC Education, 2000
192pp ISBN: 1902343328
Aimed at managers within industry, this book addresses the reasons why it is important to invest in the IT skills of the workforce. Changes within the workforce, business attitudes to IT education, IT certification and accreditation, and methods of learning are examined in detail. The authors also make recommendations regarding best practice in IT skills training in organizations and for the IT training industry.

Leveraging the New Infrastructure: How Market Leaders Capitalize on Information Technology
Peter Weill, Marianne Broadbent
Boston, Massachusetts: Harvard Business School Press, 1998
294pp ISBN: 0875848303
This book, which is based on research at more than 100 major multinational corporations, shows how various information technology strategies have brought these organizations huge rewards. Promoting the idea

"We couldn't afford to miss the computer revolution." (Stan Shih)

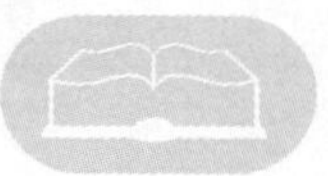

that information technology must be treated as another asset for success, it offers guidelines to follow, questions to resolve, and ways to measure results when dealing with your information investment.

Mission Critical: Realizing the Promise of Enterprise Systems
THOMAS H. DAVENPORT
Boston, Massachusetts: Harvard Business School Press, 2000
352pp ISBN: 0875849067
This book presents an authoritative and no-nonsense view of the Enterprise Systems opportunities and challenges, and provides a set of guidelines to help managers evaluate the benefits and risks for their organizations. The author describes in detail the changes that should be formulated in advance of ES adoption and monitored throughout its implementation—changes in an organization's information systems, business processes, and business strategy—and gives extensive real-world examples.

Overcoming High-tech Anxiety: Thriving in a Wired World
BEVERLY GOLDBERG
San Francisco, California: Jossey-Bass, 1999
187pp ISBN: 0787910228
This book starts from the idea that putting in place all the computers and information technology in the world will not make a difference if you cannot find employees with the skills to use them. It then offers help in turning those with computer anxiety into comfortable, productive workers who can make the difference between success and failure. Aimed at individuals as well as human resource managers and trainers who have to break through resistance to technology, it offers tips for bringing about the changes in mindset critical to learning new technologies.

Software Encyclopedia
New Providence, New Jersey: Bowker, 2001
3500pp ISBN: 0835243966
Over 32,000 software packages are listed in this two-volume reference work. Products are indexed by title, application, and operating system.

Using the PC to Boost Executive Performance
MONICA SEELEY
Brookfield, Vermont: Gower, 2000
240pp ISBN: 0566081105
This book is primarily aimed at managers who wish to improve their confidence and competence in using computers effectively. An examination of how and why managers use PCs is undertaken, with brief questionnaires to prompt readers to think about their use of a PC. The book concludes by presenting a strategy for attaining PC fitness.

The Valuation of Information Technology: A Guide for Strategy Development, Valuation, and Financial Planning
CHRISTOPHER GARDNER
New York: John Wiley, 2000
297pp (Wiley Financial Management Series)
ISBN: 0471378313
Written for practicing managers, but from a stakeholder's perspective, this book presents a way of analyzing and quantifying whether an IT system will add value to an organization. It stresses the importance of seeking the opinion of the end-customer and includes real-world examples of the process in action.

MAGAZINES

Computerworld
ISSN: 0010–4841
Computerworld, Inc.
500 Old Connecticut Path, Framingham, Massachusetts, 01701–9171
T: +1 508 879 0700
F: +1 508 626 2705
www.computerworld.com
This magazine is published 50 times per year. Written for professionals working with computers, business executives, and managers of information systems, it focuses on the very latest developments in the advanced technologies of desktop and workgroup computing. Features include reviews of the latest in developments in computer products and services.

Information Resources Management Journal
ISSN: 1040–1628
Idea Group Publishing
1331 East Chocolate Avenue, Hershey, Philadelphia, 17033–1117
T: +1 717 533 8879
F: +1 717 533 8661
www.idea-group.com/journals
Intended for both researchers and practitioners in the field of information technology management, the *Information Resources Management Journal* includes applied research findings, case studies, and interviews, and covers subjects such as the success and failure of IT projects and the strategy, policy, and application of IT within organizations.

Information Systems Management
Auerbach Publications, Inc.
345 Park Avenue South, Floor 10, New York, 10010
T: +1 800 737 8034, ext. 6407
www.auerbach-publications.com
Published four times per year, this magazine focuses on problem-solving strategies and techniques for managers of corporate information systems. This magazine is a must have for all information technology professionals.

Journal of Information Technology Management
ISSN: 1042–1319
Maximilian Press Publishers
P.O. Box 64841, Virginia Beach, Virginia, 23467–4841
T: +1 804 479 5363
F: +1 804 479 0656
Aimed at a nontechnical audience, the *Journal of Information Technology Management* is concerned with the application of information technology to areas such as information systems planning, network management, database design and administration, and with the human resources aspects of IT. Case study material is included, as well as surveys, research, and reviews.

Wall Street & Technology
ISSN: 1060–989X
CMP Media LLC
3 Park Avenue, New York, 10016
T: +1 212 600 3000
F: +1 212 600 3045
www.wallstreetandtech.com
This journal is published 13 times per year and is written for those working in the financial technology marketplace. IT professional, traders, investment advisers, and analysts can quickly and easily track the latest developments and trends in information technology. The magazine also offers detailed product information.

INTERNET

@Brint.com
www.brint.com
This extensive portal and community network for e-business, information, technology, and knowledge management contains news, articles, book reviews, and links to relevant Web sites in the featured areas.

CMC Information Sources
www.december.com/cmc/info
This site, which focuses on computer-mediated

"The one thing computers have done is let us make bigger mistakes. We have to be careful not to depend on our machines."
(Michael Bloomberg)

communications, offers a set of links to essential Web sites concerned with computer training, applications, technology, and culture.

ORGANIZATIONS

USA

Association of Information Technology Professionals
315 South Northwest Highway, Suite 200, Park Ridge, Illinois, 60068
T: +1 847 825 8124 or 800 224 9371
F: +1 847 825 1693
E: aitp_hq@aitp.org
www.aitp.org
This association is the founder of the Certificate in Data Processing examination. The management of information resources is a vital aspect of today's business world, and the AITP provides various resource materials, such as self-study and videotape management development courses, to aid managers and support staff in developing an information resource department.

Association of the Institute for Certification of Computing Professionals
2350 East Devon Avenue, Suite 115, Des Plaines, Illinois, 60018
T: +1 847 299 4227 or 800 843 8227
F: +1 847 299 4280
E: office@iccp.org
www.iccp.org
Founded in 1973, this association has over 50,000 members. The prestigious Certified Computing Professional (CCP) designation from the Institute for Certification of Computing Professionals (ICCP) is the only internationally recognized certification program in the profession. Employers value CCP certification as the highest standard of computer knowledge and professional competence. ICCP certifications exhibit comprehension and knowledge of stringent industry fundamentals.

Information Technology Association of America
1401 Wilson Boulevard, Suite 1100, Arlington, Virginia, 22209
T: +1 703 522 5055
F: +1 703 522 2279
E: hwarfield@itaa.org
www.itaa.org
This organization, founded in 1982, has over 300 members. The ITAA is America's leading trade association for the information technology industry. With a special focus on computers and communications, the ITAA has developed numerous resources for anyone in the information technology field, and its information is timely and relevant in this fast-paced and ever-changing area.

Europe

British Computer Society
1 Sanford Street, Swindon, Wiltshire, SN1 1HJ, U.K.
T: +44 (0) 1793 417424
F: +44 (0) 1793 480270
E: bcshq@hq.bcs.org.uk
www.bcs.org.uk
Founded in 1957, the British Computer Society is a professional and learned society with members from both the United Kingdom and overseas. It aims to provide a voice for the IT industry in discussions with the U.K. government. In addition, it offers both its own certifications and others accredited by the Engineering Council that can lead to Chartered Engineer status.

National Computing Centre Limited
Oxford House, Oxford Road, Manchester, M1 7ED, U.K.
T: +44 (0) 161 242 2121
F: +44 (0) 161 242 2499
E: info@ncc.co.uk
www.ncc.co.uk
Founded in 1966, the National Computing Centre is an international, membership-based organization that aims to promote the effective use of IT and computers. Its areas of particular interest include systems design, computer security, communications, and training.

International

Information Resources Management Association
1331 East Chocolate Avenue, Hershey, Philadelphia, 17033–1117
T: +1 717 533 8879
F: +1 717 533 8661
E: member@irma-international.org
www.irma-international.org
IRMA is a nonprofit, independent, professional body that aims to develop the practices of information technology management within organizations. It also publishes a number of journals, organizes seminars, conventions, and training programs on subjects relating to IT and information resources, and hosts an annual international conference.

For More Information

☆ **Enterprise Information Systems (pp. 139–40)**
☆ **Marketspaces (pp. 154–56)**
Information Management (pp. 1998–2000)
Knowledge Management (pp. 2018–20)

Conditions of Employment

BOOKS

Drawing Up Employment Contracts 3rd ed.
Olga Aikin
New York: Beekman, 2001
336pp (Developing Practice Series)
ISBN: 0846452324
This comprehensive book deals with creating contracts of employment that will promote professional relationships, meet business needs, and retain enough flexibility to cope with change. In all it covers 18 different types of contract, including contracts for self-employed workers. It also addresses issues such as confidentiality, working hours, and intellectual property, and discusses how to change contracts and deal with breaches.

Employer Perceptions of the Psychological Contract
David E. Guest, Neil Conway
New York: Beekman, 2001
56pp ISBN: 0846451670
This booklet examines the use and interpretation of the psychological contract from the employer's perspective. The issues it deals with include: how employers believe they fulfill their employees' expectations; how they communicate the psychological contract; what happens when it is broken; and how important it is to the employment relationship.

Get Paid What You're Worth: The Expert Negotiator's Guide to Salary and Compensation
Robin L. Pinkley, Gregory B. Northcraft
New York: St. Martin's Press, 2000
240pp ISBN: 0312242549
This book offers advice on how and why to

"The best balance of morale for employee productivity can be described this way: happy, but with low self-esteem."
(Scott Adams)

  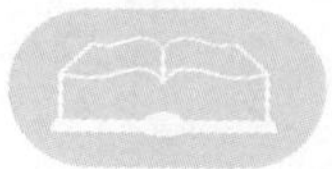    

negotiate salary and job issues. It explains which kind of job issues can be negotiated, and advises how to prepare for and conduct a negotiation and how to close the deal. It also advises ways to respond to various offers and how to avoid "deal killers."

101 Salary Secrets: How to Negotiate Like a Pro
DANIEL POROT, FRANCES BOLLES HAYNES
Berkeley, California: Ten Speed Press, 2001
240pp ISBN: 1580082300
This is a pocket-sized guide to getting a better salary. It shows how to tackle all types of salary-related negotiations, including starting salaries and benefits packages, future advancement, and raises and changes in benefits for the already employed. It provides sample language for saying the things that are hardest to say in salary negotiation.

The 100 Best Companies to Work for in America
ROBERT LEVERING, MILTON MOSKOWITZ
New York: Plume, 1994
ISBN: 0452271231
This is the revised edition of the 1984 bestseller. It summarizes the results of thousands of employee interviews, resulting in a list of 100 U.S. companies where employees are happy and fulfilled. The companies are profiled and rated with regard to several categories, including salary and benefits, promotion opportunities, fairness and openness, and pride in the workplace. The result is a 100-strong list of the best companies to work for in the United States, of which ten are then picked out as the best of the best.

Perks and Parachutes
JOHN J. TARRANT
New York: Crown Business, 1997
338pp ISBN: 0812926773
This book is a guide for people looking to further their career through promotion, or secure employment deals to their best advantage. The author offers advice on how to negotiate such factors as stock-, and profit-sharing opportunities, as well as potential benefits and job-security issues. Aimed at a range of individuals, from new job-seekers to established executives, this book gives practical information on how to access the "perks" of your employment situation.

The Workplace Law Advisor
ANNE COVEY
Cambridge, Massachusetts: Perseus, 2000
257pp ISBN: 0738203742
This is a useful, comprehensive resource for managers and executives. It offers sound advice on the legal rights and responsibilities of both employers and employees in the workplace. It shows the various reasons why employers often get sued, and advises on how to avoid such situations. It discusses relevant Acts such as The Americans with Disabilities Act and The Family and Medical Leave Act.

MAGAZINES

Employee Rights and Employment Policy Journal
Chicago-Kent College of Law
Illinois Institute of Technology, 565 West Adams Street, Chicago, Illinois, 60661–3691
T: +1 312 906 5000
F: +1 312 906 5280
www.kentlaw.edu/ilw/erepj
Published jointly by Chicago-Kent College and the National Employee Rights Institute since 1997, this journal includes articles on legal and law-related issues that affect the wellbeing of employees in the workplace. It has a multidisciplinary approach, and its articles are peer-reviewed.

Employee Rights Quarterly
ISSN: 1532–1304
Aspen Publishers
7201 McKinney Circle, Frederick, Maryland, 21704
T: +1 800 234 1660
F: +1 800 901 9075
www.aspenpub.com
This journal is sponsored by the National Employee Rights Institute. It provides news and analysis of developments in employee rights law. It is written from an employee's perspective and aims to address controversial subject matter and political views.

INTERNET

elaws

www.dol.gov/elaws
Employment law assistance for workers and small businesses is given by the U.S. Department of Labor in question and answer format on this site. The information provided by virtual advisers can be searched in a variety of ways, including by keyword and topic.

TIGER (Tailored Interactive Guide on Employment Rights)
www.tiger.gov.uk
This is a U.K. government site providing information on employment issues.

TUC Online
www.tuc.org.uk
The official Web site of the U.K. Trades Union Congress has a section of advice and information entitled "Know Your Rights."

Your Rights@Work
www.aflcio.org/rightsatwork
This section of the AFL—CIO (American Federation of Labor—Congress of Industrial Organizations) Web site provides information on workers' rights to safe, healthy, and fair conditions at work.

ORGANIZATIONS

USA

Work in America Institute
700 White Plains Road, Scarsdale, New York, 10583
T: +1 914 472 9600
F: +1 914 472 9606
E: *info@workinamerica.org*
www.workinamerica.org
The Institute is a nonprofit research organization, with support from business, labor, and government, which aims to advance productivity and the quality of working life. Through a program of site visits, round tables, research, education and training, and policy studies, it promotes best practice in human resource management.

Workplace Fairness
600 Harrison Street, Suite 535, San Francisco, California, 94107
T: +1 800 469 6374
www.nerinet.org
Workplace Fairness, founded in 1994 as the National Employee Rights Institute, is a nonprofit organization that promotes employee rights and provides information to workers and their advocates. The name was changed in 2001 to reflect wider concerns and efforts to link the work of legal and nonlegal organizations in this field. The NERI continues as the publishing arm of Workplace Fairness, producing books and journals on employee rights.

Europe

European Foundation for the Improvement of Living and Working Conditions
Wyattville Road, Loughlinstown, Dublin, 18, Republic of Ireland
T: +353 1 2043100
F: +353 1 2826456
E: *postmaster@eurofound.ie*
www.eurofound.eu.int

"Had the employers of past generations all of them dealt fairly with their employees there would have been no unions."
(Stanley Baldwin)

  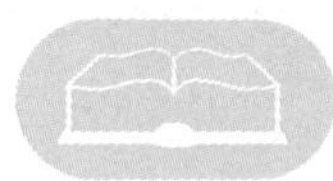    

The Foundation was set up in 1975 to provide information to European institutions and social partners that would support the improvement of living and working conditions. It promotes and coordinates research projects, including the European Surveys of Working Conditions.

Labour Research Department
78 Blackfriars Road, London, SE1 8HF, U.K.
T: +44 (0) 20 7928 3649
F: +44 (0) 20 7928 0621
E: info@lrd.org.uk
www.lrd.org.uk
The LRD is an independent, trade-union-based research organization, founded over 80 years ago. Its function is to provide information to support negotiations and campaigns, and around 2,000 labor union organizations are affiliated to it. Its publications include journals, advice booklets, and an online pay database.

International

International Labour Organization
4, route des Morillons, CH 1211, Geneva 22, Switzerland
T: +41 22 799 6111
F: +41 22 798 8685
E: ilo@ilo.org
www.ilo.org
The ILO is a UN specialized agency, founded in 1919 to promote social justice and human and labor rights. It formulates international labor standards, sets minimum standards for basic workers' rights, provides technical assistance in related areas, and supports the development of employers' and workers' organizations.

For More Information

- ☆ **Fringe Benefits (pp. 21–22)**
- ✔ **Drawing Up a Contract of Employment (pp. 530–31)**
- **Employee Benefits/ Compensation (pp. 1959–61)**
- **Employee Relations (pp. 1964–66)**
- **Employment Law (pp. 1967–69)**
- **Finding Out What You're Worth: Remuneration/Salaries (pp. 1982–84)**
- **Personnel Management and HR Management (pp. 2067–71)**
- **Remuneration (pp. 2103–05)**

Conferences and Exhibitions

BOOKS

Event Management in Leisure and Tourism
David C. Watt
Upper Saddle River, New Jersey: Longman, 1998
211pp ISBN: 0582357063
This book, written by an experienced industry practitioner, is designed for students studying event management. It considers a wide variety of events, including exhibitions. The text covers planning and administration, fundraising and budgeting, marketing and advertising, and features case studies of good practice. Sources of further information and assistance are also listed.

Event Planning: The Ultimate Guide to Successful Meetings, Corporate Events, Fundraising Galas, Conferences, Conventions, Incentives and Other Special Events
Judy Allen
New York: John Wiley, 2000
288pp ISBN: 0471644129
A guide to planning conferences, exhibitions, and meetings, this is written as a how-to book, with many tables and lists to track the myriad details that often determine whether an event is a success or failure. The author runs a full-service event company, and the book includes information on choosing the venue, preparing and managing the budget, scheduling and staffing, coordinating food and beverages, decor and entertainment, and working with professionals such as public relations firms and creative directors.

The Exhibitor Companion
Phil Long
New York: Robert Jansen, 2000
132pp ISBN: 0970426208
A how-to book on preparing for exhibitions, this guide is filled with tips concerning what to do, what to bring, and what not to bring to a trade show. A good overview for a novice exhibitor, the book's humorous tone places it in the category of friendly advice. Illustrations are included in several chapters, clearly showing how to go about performing basic tasks such as setting up a display and registering participants.

Guerrilla Trade Show Selling
Jay Conrad Levinson, Mark S. A. Smith, Orvel Ray Wilson
New York: John Wiley, 1997
320pp ISBN: 0471165689
This book applies guerrilla sales and marketing tactics to the high-pressure environment of the trade show floor. It contains lots of insider secrets, tips, and techniques on how to use trade shows as an effective marketing weapon.

Open Space Technology: A User's Guide 2nd ed.
Harrison Owen
San Francisco, California: Berrett-Koehler, 1997
173pp ISBN: 1576750248
This is a guide for organizing meetings for between five and 1,000 participants. Owen is the originator of a technique called Open Space Technology, which many managers find useful for organizing large groups of people, especially when these groups are being called upon to think about complex issues. The text includes descriptions of how to set up large rooms, break up participants into smaller groups, and how to organize space physically during conferences.

INTERNET

British Exhibition Contractors Association
www.beca.org.uk
This site belongs to a membership organization for exhibition designers, contractors, and materials/service suppliers. It has a searchable database of members.

Business 2.0
www.business2.com
A subsection of this Web site (under "Guide Topics," "Business," and "Conferences") will direct you to an online resource for conferences and events. This is a comprehensive gateway site leading to listings of conferences and events. It is also a full-service business journal site.

Exhibition Bulletin: Exhibitions and Event Services Directory
www.eventservicenet.co.uk

"Never dump a good idea on a conference table. It will belong to the conference." (Jane Trahey)

Published by Tarsus Martex, this is a directory of over 1,300 exhibitions and event services in the United Kingdom, searchable either by company name, or by service or product.

Expo24-7.Com
www.expo24-7.com
This site provides comprehensive online business information and Internet solutions for people who visit, organize, and exhibit at trade shows worldwide.

Expo Guide
www.expoguide.com
Alphabetical, chronological, and geographic listings for exhibitions and conferences are listed at this site, which is an online source for trade show listings and information.

Trade Fairs and Exhibitions U.K.
www.exhibitions.co.uk
Sponsored by Trade Partners U.K., a government organization, this site gives a comprehensive listing of all trade exhibitions in the United Kingdom. It is available in several languages.

Trade Show News Network (TSNN)
www2.tsnn.com
A business-to-business portal that has listings of trade shows and conferences, this site is searchable by city, topic, date, and many other variables. The site also has clickable links for planning, features, management, travel, and suppliers. There is also a section on exhibit management. Expo Files, a monthly e-mail newsletter, is available through the Web site.

Venuefinder.com
www.venuefinder.com
Run by CMP International, this Web site contains a comprehensive listing of venues for all types of event in the United Kingdom.

ORGANIZATIONS

USA

Exhibit Designers and Producers Association (EDPA)
5775 G Peachtree-Dunwoody Road, Suite 500, Atlanta, Georgia, 30342
T: +1 404 303 7310
F: +1 404 252 0774
E: edpa@kellencompany.com
www.edpa.com
Formed in 1955, this organization has over 250 members. The EDPA is an internationally recognized trade association designed to provide networking opportunities for workers involved in the design, manufacture and installation of displays and exhibits.

Exposition Operations Society (EOS)
P.O. Box 949, Framingham, Massachusetts, 01701
T: +1 508 544 1367 or 877 232 3976
F: +1 508 435 0290
E: info@ExpoOps.com
www.expoops.com
This recently formed society has over 75 members. EOS is a professional network where members can share ideas, experiences, and challenges commonly found in the exhibition industry. Networking opportunities allow members to share experiences and solutions.

International Association for Exhibition Management
P.O. Box 802425, Dallas, Texas, 75380–2425
T: +1 972 458 8002
F: +1 972 458 8119
E: iaem@iaem.org
www.iaem.org
The Association is open to all individuals with business interests in the exhibition industry. It offers a range of products and services.

National Association of Consumer Shows (NACS)
147 SE 102nd St., Portland, Oregon, 97216
T: +1 503 253 0832 or 800 728 6227
F: +1 503 253 9172
E: shows@teleport.com
www.publicshows.com
The National Association of Consumer Shows (NACS) was founded in 1987 for the advancement of the consumer (public) show industry and to further the growth and professionalism of those involved in the production of consumer shows. The association has more than 250 members.

Europe

Association for Conferences and Events
Riverside House, High Street, Huntingdon, Cambridgeshire, PE18 6SG, U.K.
T: +44 (0) 1480 457595
F: +44 (0) 1480 412863
E: ace@martex.co.uk
www.martex.co.uk/ace
The benefits of membership of ACE include seminars, inspection visits, social and networking events, the monthly newsletter, a job vacancy list, a calendar of industry events, and free entry to the ACE Internet site. The Association's other services are a confidential helpline, representation on industry bodies, and the Aceplan Insurance Scheme.

Association of British Professional Conference Organisers
6th Floor, Charles House, 148–149 Great Charles Street, Birmingham, B3 3HT, U.K.
T: +44 (0) 121 212 1400
F: +44 (0) 121 212 3131
E: information@abpco.org.uk
www.abpco.org.uk
The aims of the Association are: to provide a forum where leading British professional conference organizers can share knowledge and information; to train personnel; to monitor regulations; and generally to ensure that conference organizing is organized to the highest ethical and professional standards.

Association of Exhibition Organisers Ltd.
113 High Street, Berkhamsted, Hertfordshire, HP4 2DJ, U.K.
T: +44 (0) 1442 873331
F: +44 (0) 1442 875551
E: info@aeo.org.uk
www.aeo.org.uk
The Association is the trade body for those who conceive, create, develop, manage, market, sponsor, supply, or service trade and consumer exhibitions. Membership benefits include events, surveys, latest issues, access to research and training, legal advice, and sponsorship and advertising opportunities.

The Meetings Industry Association
34 High Street, Broadway, Worcestershire, WR12 7DT, U.K.
T: +44 (0) 1386 858572
F: +44 (0) 1386 858986
E: mia@meetings.org
www.meetings.org
The Association seeks to strengthen the position of members' businesses in an increasingly competitive environment and to raise the profile of the United Kingdom as an international conference destination. It pursues the best interests of members and meeting buyers alike by encouraging excellence and ethical standards. It also publishes a quarterly magazine.

For More Information

- **Direct Marketing (pp. 1953–54)**
- **Marketing Management (pp. 2045–48)**

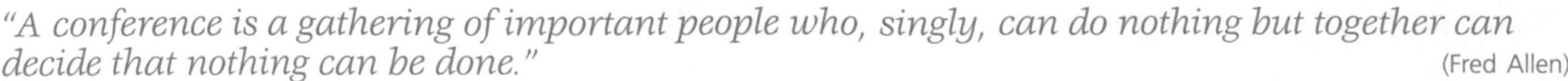
"A conference is a gathering of important people who, singly, can do nothing but together can decide that nothing can be done."
(Fred Allen)

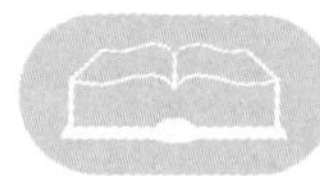

CONSULTING SERVICES/MANAGEMENT CONSULTANTS

BOOKS

Clients for Life
JAGDISH N. SHETH, ANDREW SOBEL
Columbus, Ohio: Fireside, 1997
272pp ISBN: 0684870304
This title uses the results of over 100 case studies and numerous interviews with chief executives to reveal what clients really want and how those who serve them can gain the skills needed to be successful in a challenging, modern society.

Concise Guide to Becoming an Independent Consultant
HERMAN HOLTZ
New York: John Wiley, 1999
320pp ISBN: 0471315737
This abridged version of *How to Succeed as an Independent Consultant* is packed with expert advice, helpful tips, and industry secrets that can lead to successful self-marketing. It provides the crucial tools and techniques needed to survive and thrive in this highly competitive field. It also includes material on founding the business, writing proposals, negotiating fees, and vital consulting skills

The Consultant's Scorecard: Tracking Results and Bottom-line Impact of Consulting Projects
JACK PHILLIPS
New York: McGraw-Hill, 1999
400pp ISBN: 0071348166
You want to know that the money you pay a management consultant will bring measurable success to your company. You want the same return on this investment as on any other. Good consultants are just as interested in demonstrating that ROI to you. This book is a general overview of the metrics both sides can use to evaluate the business impact—and return on investment—of any consulting project.

Consulting Demons: Inside the Unscrupulous World of Global Corporate Consulting
LEWIS PINAULT, STEPHEN M. POLLAN
New York: HarperCollins, 2000
284pp ISBN: 0066619971
This tale of Pinault's 12-year career as a management consultant is a stunning exposé of some of the most prestigious and respected names in the business. An intriguing story, it is both an alarming reflection on the major consulting firms and contains a wealth of information on how best to deal with them. This rare insider's view of global management consulting is useful information that the reader needs to evaluate critically.

Consulting on the Inside: An Internal Consultant's Guide to Living and Working Inside Organizations
BEVERLY SCOTT
Alexandria, Virginia: American Society for Training and Development, 2000
264pp ISBN: 156286131X
Many people routinely operate as internal consultants to their employer, often without recognition as such. This book is a practical guide for them. Whether you are just starting as an internal consultant or have years of experience, this book's eight-step consulting process guide and real-life stories from current and former internal consultants will be a valuable toolkit and reference.

Developing Knowledge-based Client Relationships: The Future of Professional Services
ROSS DAWSON
Woburn, Massachusetts: Butterworth-Heinemann, 2000
296pp ISBN: 0750671858
This book provides consulting and other professional services firms with a new model for doing business. In essence, it encourages such firms to focus on adding value to the client through the transfer of knowledge. This is not a particularly radical shift, since knowledge is the trade of professional services firms—but they need to be aware of the consequences of not fully sharing that knowledge.

Directory of Management Consultants 2002, Inc. 10th ed.
KENNEDY INFORMATION
Fitzwilliam, New Hampshire, 2001
984pp ISBN: 1885922698
This directory profiles over 2,000 North American consulting firms, indexed by service, industry, geographical location, and key contact name. The details given include numbers of staff employed and charging structures.

Flawless Consulting: A Guide to Getting Your Expertise Used 2nd ed.
PETER BLOCK
San Francisco, California: Jossey-Bass, 1999
400pp ISBN: 0787948039
Flawless Consulting is essentially a how-to book on the subject of consulting from the perspective of a successful management consultant. It covers every aspect of the consultancy process, from defining what it is to be a consultant through disengaging from the client. It offers sound, theoretically grounded advice in a simple and friendly manner. This book is extremely useful for consultants both internal and external to the clients they serve.

High Income Consulting: How to Build and Market Your Professional Practice 2nd ed.
TOM LAMBERT
Naperville, Illinois: Nicholas Brealey, 1997
324pp ISBN: 1857881699
This practical workbook is designed to help consultants build and sustain a high-quality, profitable professional practice. It contains guides for action, summaries of key information, an extensive resource glossary of business ideas and terms, and an equally extensive bibliography of books about consulting.

How to Succeed As an Independent Consultant 3rd ed.
HERMAN HOLTZ
New York: John Wiley, 1993
416pp ISBN: 047157581X
This book is considered by many to be a classic on the subject of consulting. In it Holtz essentially presents his ideas on what an independent consultant should do, how the various tasks should be approached, and, in particular, how the work of consulting should be marketed to different business sectors.

McKinsey Mind: Understanding and Implementing the Problem-solving Tools and Management Techniques of the World's Top Strategic Consulting Firm
ETHAN M. RASIEL, PAUL FRIGA
New York: McGraw-Hill, 2001
272pp ISBN: 0071374299
McKinsey & Company is one of the most respected consulting firms in the world. This book is an implementation manual for putting McKinsey concepts and skills into action. It describes the step-by-step techniques and strategies used to solve core business problems. Real-world examples and exercises are designed to help the reader begin to think in McKinsey's rigorous, structured manner.

The McKinsey Way: Using the Techniques of the World's Top Strategic

"The consultants are the thinkers and the strategists. And the managers have the most bizarre job."
(Eileen C. Shapiro)

  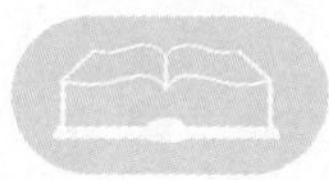    

Consultants to Help You and Your Business
ETHAN M. RASIEL
New York: McGraw-Hill, 1999
187pp ISBN: 0070534489
McKinsey & Company is one of the best-known management consultancies in the world, with a reputation for recruiting and developing some of the world's greatest management thinkers and business leaders. The author, a former McKinsey analyst, introduces some of the tools and techniques used by the company to approach and solve many business problems, as well as providing an insight into the working life of a McKinsey consultant.

Management Consultancy in the 21st Century
FIONA CZERNIAWSKA
West Lafayette, Indiana: Purdue University Press, 2000
256pp ISBN: 1557531781
The author assesses how management consultancy is likely to develop, covering such issues as clients becoming more demanding, managing intellectual capital to survive, networking and alliances, the effects of globalization, and threats, challenges, and critical success factors.

The Trusted Advisor
DAVID H. MAISTER, CHARLES H. GREEN, ROBERT M. GALFORD
Carmichael, California: Touchstone Books, 2001
240pp ISBN: 0743212347
The Trusted Advisor is a guide for consulting professionals on how to establish effective relationships with clients through building trust. That trust comes from delivering skilled, quality services in line with the client's needs and wants. The book is filled with practical advice for the consultant, but is an equally valuable tool for those who contract consulting services.

Vault Guide to the Top 50 Consulting Firms
DANIEL MCHUGH, MAGGIE GEIGER
New York: Vault Reports, 2001
552pp ISBN: 1581311281
This is an annually updated guidebook that includes a wealth of information for those seeking to join or contract with a large consulting firm. It offers insights on everything from what firms do well and not so well, to what it is like to work for the firms listed. This is not a resource for gaining theoretical or operational knowledge, but it has very great practical value.

MAGAZINES

Management Consultancy
ISSN: 1351–0924
VNU Business Publications Ltd.
VNU House, 32–34 Broadwick Street, London, W1A 2HG, U.K.
T: +44 (0) 20 7316 9000
F: +44 (0) 20 7316 9440
www.managementconsultancy.co.uk
News, surveys, and reports from the field of management consulting are the mainstay of this magazine, which also carries main feature articles on issues connected with management and consulting.

Management Consultant International
Kennedy Information
1 Kennedy Place, Fitzwilliam, New Hampshire, 03447
T: +1 603 585 6544
F: +1 603 585 9555
www.kennedyinfo.com/mci/mci.html
This monthly newsletter provides current information on management consulting in an international context for senior consultants. Its coverage includes trends in charging, new business areas, and contracts, mergers, and acquisitions.

INTERNET

Association of Internal Management Consultants
www.aimc.org
The AIMC promotes internal consulting as a profession and gives formal recognition to the internal consultant's role. The site provides a place for members to support each other through the exchange of ideas and information.

Association of Management Consulting Firms
www.amcf.org
The AMCF was established in 1929 to foster an understanding of the management consulting profession's scope and purposes. It provides a forum for the exchange of ideas and to confront common challenges. It also serves as a voice of the industry on major issues and represents the profession before government and regulatory bodies.

Institute of Management Consultants USA
www.imcusa.org
The IMC is the national professional association representing management consultants. It certifies and awards the designation of Certified Management Consultant (CMC). The site features a consultant search page that lets you search by type of consulting practice, specialty, or type of industry.

Skidmore College, Saratoga Springs, NY
www.skidmore.edu/administration/career/consulting.htm
This URL will take you to a resource guide on consulting services. It is geared to those interested in pursuing a career with a consulting firm, but also offers links of a more general nature.

ORGANIZATIONS

USA

Institute of Management Consultants of the United States of America
2025 M Street NW, Suite 800, Washington, D.C., 20036–3309
T: +1 202 367 1134
F: +1 202 367 2134
E: *office@imcusa.org*
www.imcusa.org
The IMC was founded in 1968 as a nonprofit, national, professional association to set standards of professionalism and ethics for management consulting. It sponsors workshops, seminars, and conferences at national and regional level and is a member of the International Council of Management Consulting Institutes.

Europe

Institute of Management Consultancy
3rd Floor, 17–18 Hayward's Place, London, EC1R 0EQ, U.K.
T: +44 (0) 20 7566 5220
F: +44 (0) 20 7566 5230
E: *consult@imc.co.uk*
www.imc.co.uk
Founded in 1962 as a professional institute for management consultants in the United Kingdom, the IMC became a member of the International Council of Management Consulting Institutes in 1993 and is involved in developing the Certified Management Consultant qualification. It organizes social and learning networks and special interest groups as part of its service to members.

Management Consultancies Association
49 Whitehall, London, SW1A 2BX, U.K.
T: +44 (0) 20 7321 3990
F: +44 (0) 20 7321 3991
E: *mca@mca.org.uk*
www.mca.org.uk
The MCA was formed in 1956 and acts as a kind of trade body for leading management consulting firms in the United Kingdom. The criteria for membership are high, and there is a rigid code of practice to which members have to adhere. The MCA uses these routes to enhance the standing of the profession and to increase public awareness of the value of bringing in outside advisers.

International

The International Council of

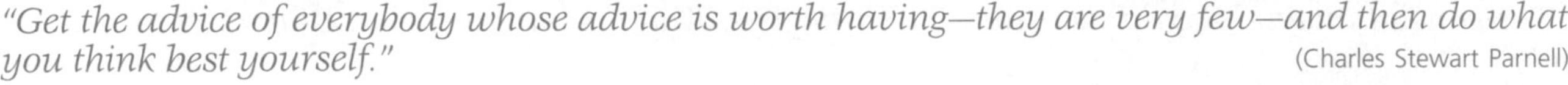

"Get the advice of everybody whose advice is worth having—they are very few—and then do what you think best yourself."
(Charles Stewart Parnell)

Management Consulting Institutes
858 Longview Road, Burlingame, California, 94010–6974
T: +1 650 342 2250
F: +1 650 344 5005
E: icmc@icmci.org
www.icmci.com
The ICMCI is a global association of over 30 national management consulting institutes that administer the Certified Management Consultant qualifications for individual consultants. It upholds an international professional code of conduct, maintains a library of knowledge on consultancy, and promotes the highest standards of ethics and consulting performance.

For More Information

☆ **Using Management Consultants Effectively (pp. 287–88)**
✔ **Using Management Consulting Services Effectively (pp. 526–27)**

CONTINGENCY, CRISIS, DISASTER MANAGEMENT

BOOKS

Business Continuity Planning: A Step-by-step Guide with Planning Forms on CD-ROM

KENNETH L. FULMER
Brookfield, Connecticut: Rothstein Associates, 2000
134pp ISBN: 0964164817

This detailed workbook will help you build a corporate disaster plan. It covers factors such as choosing an alternate location and selecting vendors to enable your organization to resume business as soon as possible. It reviews how to choose a planning coordinator and recovery team and how to write a planning document and stresses the need for testing the plan to be sure it works.

Business Continuity Planning: Protecting Your Organization's Life

KEN DOUGHTY, ED.
Boca Raton, Florida: CRC Press, 2000
408pp (Best Practices Series)
ISBN: 0849309077

Contributions from a range of experts provide a comprehensive overview of business continuity planning. They indicate the importance of analyzing the risks to which an organization is exposed and developing a plan for the resumption of business after a crisis. They also give detailed guidance on building, testing, maintaining, and updating a business continuity plan.

The Definitive Handbook of Business Continuity Management

ANDREW HILES, PETER BARNES, EDS.
New York: John Wiley, 2001
410pp ISBN: 0471485594

This book tackles business continuity from two perspectives: the first part discusses the key concepts and provides an overview of the type of events which can interrupt business; the second takes the form of a practical how-to guide.Further resources, including case studies and standards for business continuity practitioners, are listed in appendices.

Disaster Planning and Recovery: A Guide for Facility Professionals

ALAN M. LEVITT
New York: John Wiley, 1997
432pp ISBN: 0471142050

This book is aims to help facility managers tailor an organization-specific plan involving five steps: identifying possible disasters; determining the level of risk for each possibility; establishing parameters to reduce risk; determining the impact a disaster might have on personnel, plant, and business processes; and developing systems to reduce those impacts.

Disaster Recovery Planning: Strategies for Protecting Critical Information Assets

JON WILLIAM TOIGO
Upper Saddle River, New Jersey: Prentice Hall, 1999
325pp ISBN: 013084506X

This volume provides the information needed to develop a plan to protect your company's data in case of an emergency. Filled with interviews with vendors and practitioners, it walks the reader through the steps that those responsible for an organization's information technology must take to ensure that organizational data will be available in the aftermath of a disaster.

The Essential Guide to Managing Corporate Crises

IAN I. MITROFF, CHRISTINE M. PEARSON, L. KATHARINE HARRINGTON
New York: Oxford University Press, 1997
224pp ISBN: 0195097440

This book provides guidance for all key managers and legal personnel in any size of private or public organization on how to deal with all sorts of crises. It covers how to assess a company's vulnerabilities before a crisis happens, how to handle a crisis once it hits, and how to learn from a crisis to prevent future problems. Based on the authors' experience of studying crises, teaching courses and conducting seminars in CM, and advising firms during the heat of actual crises.

Living with Hazards, Dealing with Disasters: An Introduction to Emergency Management

WILLIAM L. WAUGH
Armonk, New York: M. E. Sharpe, 2000
240pp ISBN: 0765601966

This book provides a concise introduction to emergency management, covering both natural disasters, such as floods and earthquakes, and man-made hazards ranging from structural failures or accidents with hazardous materials to workplace violence, terrorism, and civil disorder. It also gives an overview of the history of emergency management in the United States and considers current policy issues in the field. Each chapter is accompanied by discussion questions and case studies. A bibliography and a listing of additional sources of information, mainly in the United States, are also included.

Manager's Guide to Contingency Planning for Disasters: Protecting Vital Facilities and Critical Operations 2nd ed.

KENNETH N. MYERS
New York: John Wiley, 1999
252pp ISBN: 047135838X

This guide shows how to establish a corporate contingency-plan strategy, following a proven methodology, to ensure minimal disruption to operations in the event of a disaster. The author devotes particular attention to ways of minimizing development time and costs by avoiding extensive information gathering, and to the importance of conducting briefings to communicate aims and objectives before commencing the development process.

Managing Crises Before They Happen

IAN I. MITROFF, GUS ANAGNOS
New York: AMACOM, 2000
172pp ISBN: 0814405630

This book explains the specific features of corporate culture that enable crises to happen.

"I believe that crisis really tends to help develop the character of an organization." (John Sculley)

  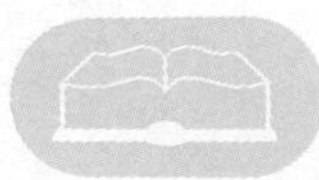    

It presents a framework for preventing such crises happening, and for controlling the damage they cause.

MAGAZINES

Continuity
ISSN: 1460–1451
Business Continuity Institute
P.O. Box 4474, Worcester, Worcestershire, WR6 5YA, U.K.
T: +44 (0) 1886 833555
F: +44 (0) 1886 833845
www.thebci.org
Continuity is the official journal of the Business Continuity Institute. It appears quarterly and includes articles, news, and reports of research projects.

Disaster Prevention and Management
ISSN: 0965–3562
Emerald (North America)
4th Floor, 44 Brattle Street, Cambridge, Massachusetts, 02138
T: +1 888 622 0075
www.emeraldinsight.com/dpm.htm
This journal appears five times a year and focuses on the latest research and practice into the prevention and mitigation of natural and man-made disasters. Each issue includes articles by international experts in the field, news, product reviews, case studies, and details of events, conferences, and resources.

Disaster Recovery Journal
ISSN: 1079–736X
Richard L. Arnold
P.O. Box 510110, St. Louis, Missouri, 63151
T: +1 314 894 0276
F: +1 314 894 7474
www.drj.com
The *DRJ* was founded in 1987 and is published quarterly. It covers the field of business continuity and disaster recovery.

International Journal of Business Continuity Management
Survive International
First Floor, Waterman House, 101–107 Chertsey Road, Woking, Surrey, GU21 5BW, U.K.
T: +44 (0) 1483 710600
F: +44 (0) 1483 710601
www.survive.com
This quarterly journal deals with continuing challenges and topical issues in the field of business continuity and risk management. Articles, including contributions from leading international authorities, cover best practice and new developments.

Journal of Contingencies and Crisis Management
ISSN: 0966–0879
Blackwell Publishers
350 Main Street, Malden, Massachusetts, 02148
T: +1 781 388 8200
F: +1 781 388 8232
www.blackwellpublishers.com/asp/listofj.asp
This is a quarterly journal for managers with responsibilities in the area of risk and crisis management.

INTERNET

ContinuityPlanner.com
www.continuityplanner.com
This is a charged service offering news, e-zines, a discussion list, plans and templates for business continuity, and a job bank. A free trial is available.

Crisis Management and Disaster Recovery Group
www.crisis-management-and-disaster-recovery.com
This site provides information on how to create and maintain a disaster recovery or crisis management plan and provides access to leading support resources.

Disaster Recovery Journal
www.drj.com
This journal's Web site provides access to a great deal of free material and resources including articles, a vendor directory, and chat groups.

Federal Emergency Management Agency
www.fema.gov
This U.S. federal government site from the Federal Emergency Management Agency features GEMS (Global Emergency Management System), a searchable database of reviewed Web sites in fields related to emergency management, and a virtual library including practical guides and checklists.

globalcontinuity.com 
www.globalcontinuity.com
This is a portal site for business recovery and continuity planning information, featuring a database of suppliers and including news, articles, and links.

Survive—The Business Continuity Group
www.survive.com
The Business Continuity Group is a worldwide membership organization of business continuity management professionals. Their site provides links to the events they sponsor, details of forthcoming major educational events, and a directory of disaster recovery and contingency services and products.

ORGANIZATIONS

USA

Contingency Planning Exchange, Inc.
551 Fifth Avenue, Suite 3025, New York, 10176–3099
T: +1 212 983 8644
F: +1 212 687 4016
E: *headquarters@cpeworld.org*
www.cpeworld.org
The CPE is a professional organization for disaster recovery specialists which provides a forum for members to exchange information and represents the views of members to government agencies and the wider business community.

Federal Emergency Management Agency
500 C Street S.W., Room 824, Washington, D.C., 20472
T: +1 202 646 4600
E: *opa@fema.gov*
www.fema.gov
FEMA is an independent agency of the federal government of the United States. It was founded in 1979, but can trace its origins back to the Congressional Act of 1803. The mission of the Agency is to reduce loss of life and property and protect national infrastructure from all types of hazard through an emergency management program that includes preparation, mitigation, response, and recovery.

Europe

Emergency Planning Society
Northumberland House, 11 The Pavement, Popes Lane, London, W5 4NG, U.K.
T: +44 (0) 20 8579 7971
F: +44 (0) 20 8579 7972
E: *headquarters@emergplansoc.org.uk*
www.emergplansoc.org.uk
The Society was formed in 1993 through the merger of the Emergency Planning Association and the County Emergency Planning Officers Society. Its aims are to promote effective emergency planning and management in the United Kingdom and to promote the professional interests of its members, who include representatives of the emergency services, local and central government, the health services, industry, consultants, and voluntary organizations. The Society is active in the areas of training, professional development, networking, representation, and publications.

International

Association of Contingency Planners
Technical Enterprises, Inc., 7044 S. 13th Street, Oak Creek, Wisconsin, 53154
T: +1 414 768 8000
E: *mbrship@techenterprises.net*
www.acp-international.com

"It is on disaster that good fortune perches; it is beneath good fortune that disaster crouches."
(Laozi)

The ACP is a nonprofit trade association for contingency planners, business continuity professionals, and emergency managers. The organization, which began informally in 1983 and was incorporated in 1985, provides an international forum for networking and information exchange. Activities include a branch network, a quarterly newsletter, and an annual international symposium.

Business Continuity Institute
P.O. Box 4474, Worcester, Worcestershire, WR6 5YA, U.K.
T: +44 (0) 1886 833555
F: +44 (0) 1886 833845
E: thebci@btinternet.com
www.thebci.org
The BCI is a professional organization founded in 1994 to promote high standards of professional competence and ethics in the provision of business continuity planning and services. It has developed standards of competence, a code of ethics, and an accreditation scheme for continuity practitioners. Additional activities include seminars, conferences, and the Business Continuity Awards. The organization has over 1,100 members in 32 countries.

Disaster Preparedness and Emergency Response Association
P.O. Box 280795, Denver, Colorado, 80228
T: +1 303 809 4412
E: dera@disasters.org
www.disasters.org
DERA is a nonprofit professional association, established in 1962, whose members include emergency management specialists, government officials, consultants, business managers, volunteers, researchers, and educators. It sponsors research projects in the field and publishes a newsletter, *DisasterCom*.

DRI International
111 Park Place, Falls Church, Virginia, 22046–4513
T: +1 703 538 1792
F: +1 703 241 5603
E: driinfo@drii.org
www.drii.org
Formerly the Disaster Recovery Institute, the DRI was formed in 1988 by a group of professionals in St. Louis, Missouri, who saw a need for education in business continuity. The organization is a nonprofit one; it sets standards of competence for business continuity and has developed a certification program.

Emergency Preparedness for Industry and Commerce Council
1110–1040 West Georgia Street, Vancouver, British Columbia, V6E 4H1, Canada
T: +1 604 687 5522
F: +1 604 681 7530
E: epicc@sfu.ca
www.epicc.org
The EPICC's aim is to help businesses and communities prepare to survive disasters through education and representation. It organizes workshops and forums, and publishes a newsletter.

International Association of Emergency Managers
111 Park Place, Falls Church, Virginia, 22046–4513
T: +1 703 538 1795
F: +1 703 241 5603
E: info@iaem.com
www.iaem.com
The IAEM is a nonprofit educational organization; it created the Certified Emergency Manager program to maintain professional standards in emergency management. Members receive a monthly newsletter and can participate in Internet discussion groups.

Survive International
First Floor, Waterman House, 101–107 Chertsey Road, Woking, Surrey, GU21 5BW, U.K.
T: +44 (0) 1483 710600
F: +44 (0) 1483 710601
E: survive@survive.com
www.survive.com
Survive is a membership group for business continuity management. Founded in 1989, it aims to raise awareness of the need for and value of effective business continuity management, to encourage excellence in the disaster recovery, contingency planning, and business continuity industry, and to support networking and information sharing within this constituency. Survive publishes a quarterly journal and organizes conferences and training events.

For More Information

☆ **Turnaround Strategies (pp. 251–52)**
✔ **Disaster Planning (pp. 492–93)**
Risk Management (pp. 2107–09)

Contracts and Contracting

BOOKS

Business Contracts Kit for Dummies Book/CD-ROM ed.
Richard D. Harroch
New York: Hungry Minds, 2000
330pp ISBN: 0764552368
This kit comprises a book and a CD-ROM providing a reference guide to business contracts, with almost 200 sample documents and contracts.

Concise Business Guide to Contract Law
Charles Boundy
Brookfield, Vermont: Gower, 1998
295pp ISBN: 0566079216
Aimed at all managers, this book introduces the principles of U.K. contract law and the way in which they apply to key elements of business. The book also covers the planning of contracts, the use of standard forms, the international dimension, and what to do when things go wrong. A glossary of legal terms is included.

Contract Law 3rd ed.
Catherine Elliott, Frances Quinn
Harlow: Longman, 1996
327pp ISBN: 0582298784
This is a popular student textbook on U.K. contract law. The authors present a clear explanation of the law of contract, and make reference to contemporary cases and topical issues in the media. They also present guidelines on answering typical examination questions, together with more general advice.

Contract Negotiation Handbook 3rd ed.
P. D. V. Marsh
Brookfield, Vermont: Gower, 2001
320pp ISBN: 0566080214
This textbook sets out a structured approach to all stages of negotiation. It covers the entire process: preparing to negotiate, the opening and development of negotiations, and the closing and recording of the bargain.

Essentials of Contract Law
Martin A. Frey, Phyllis Hurley Frey, Terry H. Bitting
Albany, New York: Delmar Publishing, 2000
303pp ISBN: 0766821455
This textbook provides a functional approach to the study of contract law. It uses a "road map"

"A contract is a mutual promise." (William Paley)

  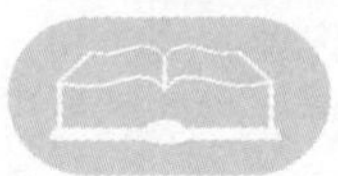    

format to present the law of contracts, discussing each rule of law first conceptually, followed by an example and a concrete problem.

Outsourcing in Brief
MIKE JOHNSON
Woburn, Massachusetts: Butterworth-Heinemann, 1997
200pp (In Brief Series)
ISBN: 0750628766
This practical guide presents an overview of outsourcing, and reviews the pros and cons of the technique. It explains how outsourcing is done, and illustrates specific issues and options by means of checklists and case studies.

MAGAZINES

Contract Management
National Contract Management Association
1921 Woodford Road, Vienna, Virginia, 22182
T: +1 703 448 9231
F: +1 703 448 0939
www.ncmahq.org/pubs/cm/cm.html
This is a monthly publication for government and industry contract managers which is also aimed at other readers, such as executives, lawyers, and owners of small businesses. It covers many aspects of government and business contract management, and contains news and features.

National Contract Management Journal
ISSN: 1045-1668
National Contract Management Association
1921 Woodford Road, Vienna, Virginia, 22182
T: +1 703 448 9231
F: +1 703 448 0939
www.ncmahq.org/pubs/journal/journal.html
This is a biannual, refereed journal, that presents research articles in the area of procurement. Aimed at a diverse readership, it covers policy, legal, and management issues.

INTERNET

Contracting and Organizations Research Initiative
http://cori.missouri.edu
CORI is a research initiative at the University of Missouri. Its mission is to improve understanding of how the economic system works by facilitating empirical research on contracting and organizational structure. It has created a collection of contracts that researchers can use.

ORGANIZATIONS

USA

National Contract Management Association
1921 Woodford Road, Vienna, Virginia, 22182
T: +1 703 448 9231
F: +1 703 448 0939
E: info@ncmahq.org
www.ncmahq.org
Formed in 1959, the NCMA aims to foster the professional growth and educational advancement of contract managers in order to promote business excellence. It is a professional society with individual members. It contains the Contract Management Institute, a nonprofit foundation set up in 1991 to extend NCMA's education and research activities.

Europe

European Institute of Advanced Project and Contract Management
Epci, Prof. Olav Hanssensvei 10, 4021 Stavanger, Norway
T: +47 51 87 66 72
F: +47 51 87 17 11
E: epci@epci.org
www.epci.no
EPCI was founded in 1994 and has an international membership of companies and academic institutions. Member organizations form a network aimed at developing competence in project and contract management.

For More Information

✔ **Deciding Whether to Outsource (pp. 490–91)**
Conditions of Employment (pp. 1933–35)
Employment Law (pp. 1967–69)
Outsourcing (pp. 2061–62)

CORPORATE CULTURE

BOOKS

Built to Last: Successful Habits of Visionary Companies
JAMES C. COLLINS, JERRY I. PORRAS
New York: HarperCollins, 1994
336pp ISBN: 0887306713
This book draws upon a six-year research project at the Stanford University Graduate School of Business, in which 18 truly exceptional and long-lasting companies were examined in depth to see what makes them so successful. It focuses on factors such as their flexibility, ideology, and strong purpose. The book gives practical guidance to those who would like to build landmark companies that stand the test of time.

Corporate Culture and Performance
JOHN P. KOTTER, JAMES L. HESKETT
New York: Free Press, 1992
214pp ISBN: 0029184673
The authors describe their research into the effects of corporate culture on economic performance in international companies. They challenge the belief that strong corporate cultures create excellent business performance, arguing that effective leadership is fundamental to the process of changing organizational culture. Case studies of world-class companies are included.

The Corporate Culture Survival Guide
EDGAR H. SCHEIN
San Francisco, California: Jossey-Bass, 1999
199pp ISBN: 0787946990
This book offers current thinking from a pioneer in the field of corporate culture. The author aims to provide practical advice for frontline managers and change agents and has structured the book around the questions most frequently asked by them. Guidelines are also given on how to evaluate an organization's current culture and effect change.

Cultures and Organizations: Software of the Mind
GEERT HOFSTEDE
New York: McGraw-Hill, 1996
279pp ISBN: 0070293074
The author of this book is known for his pioneering research on national and organizational cultures. The book, first published in 1991, aims to give practicing managers and students an understanding of cultural differences which will assist them in intercultural communication and cooperation in business and society. It examines the nature of culture and cultural differences and considers their implications.

"Contract: an agreement that is binding on the weaker party." (Frederick Sawyer)

  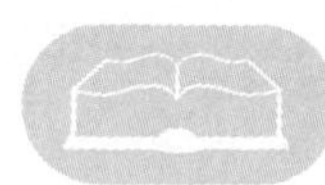    

Diagnosing and Changing Organizational Culture: Based on the Competing Values Framework
Kim S. Cameron, Robert E. Quinn
Reading, Massachusetts: Addison-Wesley, 1998
221pp (Addison-Wesley Series on Organization Development)
ISBN: 0201338718
Written with the aim of helping managers, change agents, and scholars to understand and facilitate cultural and behavioral change within organizations, this book provides a theoretical framework for organizational culture, validated instruments for diagnosing it, and a systematic methodology for changing it.

Evolve!
Rosabeth Moss Kanter
Boston, Massachusetts: Harvard Business School Press, 2001
304pp ISBN: 1578514398
This book explores "e-culture"—a new way of living and working that will transform every aspect of today's organizations. It is for anyone who wants to realize the potential and avoid the pitfalls of the Internet age. It draws on over 300 interviews and a global-scale company survey to provide a framework for adopting the core principles of e-culture.

The New Corporate Cultures: Revitalizing the Workplace after Downsizing, Mergers, and Reengineering
Terrence E. Deal, Allan A. Kennedy
Cambridge, Massachusetts: Perseus, 2000
312pp ISBN: 0738203807
This book examines how changes brought about by economic forces and management trends, such as downsizing, outsourcing, new technology, and globalization, have affected company cultures. The authors consider how companies can approach the task of rebuilding cohesive organizational cultures for greater effectiveness following the fragmentation which has become common.

Organizational Culture and Leadership 2nd ed.
Edgar H. Schein
San Francisco, California: Jossey-Bass, 1997
448pp ISBN: 0787903620
This second edition of a classic work on the dynamics of organizational culture draws on contemporary research to show how leaders can apply the principles of culture change in order to achieve organizational goals.

Riding the Waves of Culture: Understanding Cultural Diversity in Business 2nd ed.
Fons Trompenaars, Charles Hampden-Turner
New York: McGraw-Hill, 1997
416pp ISBN: 0786311258
This book is written by leading authorities on cultural diversity, based on research and experience gained in cross-cultural training programs in 18 countries. The authors contest the view that there is one best way of managing and attempt to give readers a better understanding of their own business culture. The cultural dilemmas facing international organizations are also examined.

MAGAZINES

Cross Cultural Management
ISSN: 1352-7606
Barmarick Publications
Enholmes Hall, Patrington, East Yorkshire, HU12 0PR, U.K.
T: +44 (0) 1964 630033
F: +44 (0) 1964 631716
www.emeraldinsight.com/ccm.htm
Cross Cultural Management is a quarterly academic journal focusing on the cultural aspects of international management.

International Journal of Cross Cultural Management
ISSN: 1470-5958
Sage Publications, Inc.
2455 Teller Road, Thousand Oaks, California, 91320
T: +1 805 499 0721
F: +1 805 499 0871
www.sagepub.com
This academic journal aims to encourage and disseminate research on the cross-cultural aspects of management, work, and organization. It has a particular focus on the impact of cultural factors on theory and practice.

Organization Studies
ISSN: 0170-8406
Walter de Gruyter, Inc.
200 Saw Mill River Road, Hawthorne, New York, 10532
T: +1 914 747 0110
F: +1 914 747 1326
www.degruyter.de/journals/os
This is a scholarly journal covering aspects of organizational theory and practice.

INTERNET

Business.com
www.business.com 
The section on Organization Development under Management includes links to sites covering leading writers and researchers in the field of organizational development theory.

Culture in the Workplace Questionnaire
www.itapintl.com
This questionnaire is based on the work of Geert Hofstede and provided by ITAP International, a consulting company offering crosscultural services for business.

Intermundo
www.intermundo.net
This is the site for an online journal of intercultural communication.

Official Ed Schein Website
http://web.mit.edu/scheine/www/home.html
The site gives information about publications and presentations by Edgar Schein provided by Learning Mastery.

Onepine
www.onepine.demon.co.uk/content.htm
Theories and works of major thinkers are examined under "People & Theories."

ORGANIZATIONS

Europe

Institute for Research on Intercultural Cooperation
P.O. Box 90153, 5000 LE Tilburg, The Netherlands
T: +31 13 466 2816
F: +31 13 466 8018
E: *iric@kub.nl*
www.cwis.kub.nl/~fsw_2/iric/index2.htm
IRIC, an independent research institute affiliated to Tilburg University, was cofounded by Geert Hofstede in 1980. The Institute's main activity is crosscultural research on intercultural cooperation in and between organizations and countries. It organizes a wide range of supporting activities including conferences. It is also the official holder of the Value Survey Module (VSM), a questionnaire for measuring cultural values.

For More Information

☆ **Making Cultures Behave (pp. 51–52)**

"We need a can-do, vibrant, innovation-driven culture. Not wearing a tie is just a snippet of that."
(Paul Walsh)

CORPORATE STRATEGY

BOOKS

The Alchemy of Growth: Practical Insights for Building the Enduring Enterprise
MUHRDAD BAGHAI, STEPHEN COLEY
Cambridge, Massachusetts: Perseus, 1999
250pp ISBN: 0738201006
Using a range of real examples of companies that have turned themselves around, this title is a comprehensive guide on how to maintain a business by means of sustainable growth. The book cites three points that must be addressed if a business is to keep on growing: entrepreneurial ventures, the very basics of a particular business, and the ideas that are most likely to bring profits.

The Art of the Long View: Planning for the Future in an Uncertain World
PETER SCHWARTZ
New York: Doubleday, 1996
258pp ISBN: 0385267320
The author gives practical guidance on the use of scenarios in business, drawn from his experience in a range of contexts from a small-business startup to multinational companies and government institutions. The history of scenario planning, in particular the pioneering work of Pierre Wack at Royal Dutch/Shell, is reviewed, and its continuing relevance explained.

Competing for the Future
GARY HAMEL, C. K. PRAHALAD
Boston, Massachusetts: Harvard Business School Press, 1994
327pp ISBN: 0875844162
In this book the authors put forward a radically new approach to strategy. They introduce the concept of organizational core competencies, suggesting that organizations should examine what it is they do better than others. They particularly highlight the danger of losing competitive advantage by sticking with past achievements, and the importance of unleashing the corporate imagination and developing a dynamic view of the future.

Competitive Strategy: Techniques for Analyzing Industries and Competitors
MICHAEL E. PORTER
New York: Free Press, 1998
432pp ISBN: 0684841487
This work, researched by Porter during the 1970s, is regarded as a management classic and has shaped and influenced mainstream thinking on competition and strategy. The author argues that in order to retain competitive capability companies need to choose from three generic strategies (cost leadership, differentiation, and focus), which are driven by five competitive forces (customers, suppliers, the threat of similar products, existing competition, and the threat of new market entrants).

Contemporary Strategy Analysis: Concepts, Techniques, Applications 3rd ed.
ROBERT M. GRANT
Cambridge, Massachusetts: Blackwell Publishers, 1998
500pp ISBN: 0631207805
This book introduces the concepts of strategy and analyzing markets and competitors, and underlines the importance of competitive analysis. The later editions include additional material on strategy implementation and corporate goals.

The Discipline of Market Leaders: Choose Your Customers, Narrow Your Focus, Dominate Your Market
MICHAEL TREACY, FRED WIERSEMA
Cambridge, Massachusetts: Perseus, 1997
210pp ISBN: 0201407191
This book reveals how altering and increasing the value expectations of your customers can cause severe problems for those who are trying to compete with you. Several examples of companies who are pursuing such a policy are given, including Intel, Wal-Mart, Charles Schwab, and Southwest Airlines.

Every Business Is a Growth Business
NOEL M. TICHY, R.CHARAN
New York: John Wiley, 1999
352pp ISBN: 0471987638
In this title, the authors outline how to turn an ordinary company into one that grows. The book gives two main pointers for successful growth; firstly, to redefine your market and increase demand by seeing things from your customers' point of view, and secondly, to reinvigorate the corporate culture to enable growth. The authors give many real-life examples to support these central points.

Exploring Corporate Strategy 5th ed.
GERRY JOHNSON, KEVAN SCHOLES
Upper Saddle River, New Jersey: Prentice Hall, 1999
972pp ISBN: 0130807400
This classic textbook provides an overview of the principles and practice of corporate strategy in a variety of contexts. The areas of strategic analysis, resource allocation, strategic choice, strategy implementation, and managing strategic change are covered. Recent developments in the field of strategy, including core competence knowledge and learning, have been incorporated into the fifth edition, which also includes a list of recommended key reading and work assignments for students.

Financial Times Guide to Strategy 2nd ed.
RICHARD KOCH
Upper Saddle River, New Jersey: Financial Times Prentice Hall, 2000
314pp ISBN: 027365022X
This title offers executives the help needed to build a strategic structure for a business, to organize a marketplace, and to create a business model. The book also reveals how strategy can help to raise profits and analyzes the views on strategic thinking that have emerged over the last forty years.

Good to Great: Why Some Companies Make the Leap. . .and Others Don't
JIM COLLINS
New York: HarperCollins, 2001
320pp ISBN: 0066620996
Jim Collins asks the question, "Can a good company become great, and if so, how?" His conclusion is that yes, it is possible, but there are no instant answers. Featuring case studies of 11 companies, the book illustrates how it is a strong, disciplined corporate culture that lies at the heart of a successful organization.

Grow to Be Great: Breaking the Downsizing Cycle
DWIGHT L.GERTZ, JOAO BAPTISTA
New York: Free Press, 1995
211pp ISBN: 0028740475
In this book, the two authors, (both of whom work for a major consulting firm, Mercer Management Consulting), challenge accepted ideas about how companies should be run by analyzing information concerning over 1,000 organizations.

The Mind of the Strategist
KENICHI OHMAE
New York: McGraw-Hill, 1991
304pp ISBN: 0070479046
This work, published in Japan in 1975, was

"To start a business and to run it successfully, you have to like people. You have to care about them."
(Bud Hadfield)

  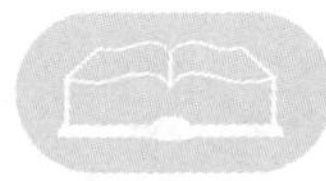    

instrumental in introducing the Japanese approach to strategic thinking to the West during the early 1980s and laid the foundation for more radical approaches to management thinking, including Gary Hamel's work on strategy innovation. The author analyzes strategy in terms of the strategic triangle—corporation, customer, and competition—and sees vision and dynamic leadership as key features of successful business strategy.

The Portable MBA in Strategy 2nd ed.
LIAM FAHEY, ROBERT M. RANDALL
New York: John Wiley, 2000
414pp ISBN: 0471197084
This comprehensive guide features contributions from internationally recognized leaders in strategic thought and practice. Topics covered include: strategic management practices; analysis of customers, markets, and competitors; identification and assessment of strategic alternatives; and threats and opportunities facing business.

The Rise and Fall of Strategic Planning
HENRY MINTZBERG
New York: Free Press, 1993
458pp ISBN: 0029216052
Mintzberg traces the history of strategic planning since the 1960s and gives his own perspective on past failures. The various planning models are reviewed and analyzed, the pitfalls identified, and a new approach is put forward.

The Strategy-focused Organization: How Balanced Scorecard Companies Thrive in the New Business Environment
ROBERT S. KAPLAN, DAVID P. NORTON
Boston, Massachusetts: Harvard Business School Press, 2000
416pp ISBN: 1578512506
The originators of the balanced scorecard examine how 20 companies have implemented and adapted the model and draw out five principles for strategy-focused organizations.

Strategy Process: Concepts, Contexts and Cases 3rd ed.
HENRY MINTZBERG, JAMES BRIAN QUINN
Upper Saddle River, New Jersey: Prentice Hall, 2000
990pp ISBN: 0134558588
This book is designed to support the teaching and practice of strategy formation. A collection of readings covers the concepts and contexts of strategy and is supplemented by U.S. and international case studies. Discussion questions for students are included.

The Strategy Workout: A Journey to the Heart of Your Business
CYRIL LEVICKI
Upper Saddle River, New Jersey: Financial Times Prentice Hall, 1997
288pp ISBN: 0273624423
This title is a step-by-step guide to creating a successful strategy, both for business purposes and for everyday life.

MAGAZINES

Business Strategy Review
ISSN: 0955–6419
Blackwell Publishers
350 Main Street, Malden, Massachusetts, 02148
T: +1 781 388 8200
F: +1 781 388 8232
www.blackwellpublishers.com/asp/listofj.asp
Business Strategy Review is a monthly journal published for the London Business School in association with the Strategic Planning Society of the United Kingdom. The journal includes articles on strategic issues relevant to modern business, taking a multidisciplinary approach, and aiming for accessibility to a wide audience including students and academics.

Harvard Business Review
ISSN: 0017–8012
Harvard Business School Publishing
Customer Service Center, 60 Harvard Way, Boston, Massachusetts, 02163
T: +1 800 545 7685
F: +1 617 783 7666
www.hbsp.harvard.edu/hbr/index.html
The *HBR* is a leading magazine for business leaders and senior executives which emphasizes current best practice and the application of leading-edge research to business problems. Coverage is wide-ranging with a strong focus on strategy. Each issue includes feature articles written by experts and an interview with a business leader.

Journal of Business Strategy
ISSN: 0275–6668
EC Media Group, Thomson Financial
Corporate Communications, 195 Broadway, New York, 10007
T: +1 642 822 2000
www.ecmediagroup.com
This is a bimonthly magazine featuring practical articles on current business topics written by senior executives and strategists.

Long Range Planning
ISSN: 0024–6301
Elsevier Science
Regional Sales Office, Customer Support Department, P.O. Box 945, New York, 10159–0945
T: +1 212 633 3730
F: +1 212 633 3680
www.elsevier.com
LRP is published in association with the Strategic Planning Society and the European Strategic Planning Federation. This is a leading international journal in the field of strategic management, which is aimed at senior managers, administrators, and academics. Articles from academics and practitioners are published.

Sloan Management Review
ISSN: 1532–9194
Sloan Management Review Association, MIT Sloan School of Management
77 Massachusetts Avenue, Room E60–100, Cambridge, Massachusetts, 01239–4307
T: +1 617 253 7170
F: +1 617 258 9739
http://mitsloan.mit.edu/smr
The *SMR* is a quarterly journal founded in 1959 which aims to provide senior managers with the best of current management theory and practice. It has a strong focus on corporate strategy and leadership.

Strategic Change
ISSN: 1086–1718
John Wiley
Wiley InterScience Coordinator, Subscriptions Department, 605 Third Avenue, New York, 10158–0012
T: +1 800 825 7550
F: +1 212 850 6021
www.interscience.wiley.com
Eight issues of *Strategic Change* are published annually. The journal aims to provide authoritative and topical research papers addressing the strategic management of change and its implementation in an increasingly globalized business environment.

Strategic Management Journal
ISSN: 0143–2095
John Wiley
Wiley InterScience Coordinator, Subscriptions Department, 605 Third Avenue, New York, 10158–0012
T: +1 800 825 7550
F: +1 212 850 6021
www.interscience.wiley.com
SMJ is a monthly journal devoted to the theory and practice of strategic management. It is aimed at academics and practicing managers and has a strong emphasis on research.

Strategy and Leadership
ISSN: 1087–8572

"Strategic planning can neither provide creativity nor deal with it when it emerges by other means."
(Henry Mintzberg)

MCB University Press
60/62 Toller Lane, Bradford, West Yorkshire, BD8 9BY, U.K.
T: +44 (0) 1274 777700
F: +44 (0) 1274 785200
www.emeraldinsight.com/sl.htm
This bimonthly journal for business leaders publishes articles describing effective practice in strategy and leadership and new theories that have the potential to advance the art of strategy development and its implementation.

INTERNET

Business.com Strategic Planning
www.business.com
The Strategic Planning section under Management includes a comprehensive collection of links to Web sites, associations, and publications.

Knowledge@Wharton
http://knowledge.wharton.upenn.edu
The section on Strategic Management on this site, sponsored by the Wharton School at the University of Pennsylvania, includes articles, reviews, and links.

Sookoo.com
www.sookoo.com
Sookoo.com is a search engine specializing in business strategy.

Strategic Management Club Online
www.strategyclub.com
This Web site, developed by Dr. Fred David for graduate and undergraduate students, provides links, templates, a discussion forum, and a chat facility.

ORGANIZATIONS

USA

Association for Strategic Planning
12021 Wilshire Boulevard, Suite 286, Los Angeles, California, 90025–1200
T: +1 866 816 2080
E: membership@strategyplus.org
www.strategyplus.org
This professional association aims to promote effective strategic thinking, planning, and action in public and private organizations.

Europe

Strategic Planning Society
17 Portland Place, London, W1B 1PU, U.K.
T: +44 (0) 20 7636 7737
F: +44 (0) 20 7323 1692
E: enquiries@sps.org.uk
www.sps.org.uk
The SPS is a professional organization, founded in 1967, which aims to promote knowledge and understanding of strategic management through publications, training events, conferences, and special interest groups.

International

Global Business Network
5900-X Hollis Street, Emeryville, California, 94608
T: +1 510 547 6822
F: +1 510 547 8510
E: worldview@gbn.com
www.gbn.org
The GBN was founded in 1987 by Peter Schwartz, Jay Ogilvy, Napier Collyns, and Stewart Brand, with the collaboration of European colleagues Kees van der Heijden, Arie de Geus, and Bo Ekman. The founders' aim was to develop a worldwide community of individual members and subscribing organizations interested in increasing their understanding of change in the business environment and developing ideas and tools for planning and innovation. The organization has a strong focus on the use of scenarios.

Strategic Management Society
Executive Office, Purdue University, 1310 Krannert Center, West Lafayette, Indiana, 47907–1310
T: +1 765 494 6984
F: +1 765 494 1533
E: sms@mgmt.purdue.edu
www.smsweb.org
The Strategic Management Society is an international organization founded in 1981 with members in more than 50 countries. It focuses on the development and dissemination of insights into strategic management, combining the contributions of practitioners and academics. An international conference and smaller special interest conferences are held annually, and publications such as the *Strategic Management Journal* and a book series are supported.

Strategos Institute
2460 Sand Hill Road, Suite 202, Menlo Park, California, 94025
T: +1 650 851 2095
F: +1 650 233 1112
E: greim@strategos.com
http://institute.strategosnet.com
The Strategos Institute is a consortium of world-class companies working on the development of tools, processes, and metrics for strategy innovation. Business practitioners, consultants, and business school professors are involved, and the writer and thinker Gary Hamel is the executive director.

For More Information

- ✓ Strategic Planning (pp. 484–85)
- Business Plans and Planning (pp. 1920–21)
- Competition (pp. 1929–31)
- Organization and Organization Structure (pp. 2059–61)

Creating a Résumé

BOOKS

Cyberspace Resume Kit 2001: How to Build and Launch an Online Resume
Mary B. Nemnich, Fred E. Jandt
Indianapolis, Indiana: Jist Works, 2001
362pp ISBN: 1563708086
This guide provides comprehensive information on creating and posting a résumé for persons with little to no experience with Internet-based résumés. Topics include assistance in locating Web-based résumé templates and forms, instructions on creating a résumé to be scanned into a résumé-database, how and where to post your résumé, and evaluations of current résumé sites.

Electronic Résumés: A Complete Guide to Putting Your Résumé Online
James C. Gonyea, Wayne M. Gonyea
New York: McGraw-Hill, 1996
255pp ISBN: 0079121667
This book/disk package helps you post your résumé online so that you can compete successfully in today's job market. The process is explained in simple, step-by-step, nontechnical terms.

The Global Resume and CV Guide
Mary Anne Thompson
New York: John Wiley, 2000
288pp ISBN: 0471380768
This book excels by providing information about

"When I find an employee who turns out to be wrong for a job, I feel it is my fault because I made the decision to hire him."
(Akio Morita)

gaining employment in 40 countries. It addresses the unique requirements of résumés in diverse cultures. For example, in Sweden, a résumé must be signed by someone who attests that all that you've said in the résumé is true. By including country-by-country profiles, résumé specifics, presentation guidelines, work permits/ visas, and advice on how to handle job interviews, *The Global Resume and CV Guide* is a valuable resource for the job seeker with international aspirations.

Job Hunting for the Utterly Confused
JASON R. RICH
New York: McGraw-Hill, 1998
304pp ISBN: 0070526656
This book explains every step of the job-search process, including: defining your personal skills; preparing a résumé; writing a cover letter; marketing yourself; succeeding at interviews; and negotiating a salary. Coverage is also given to using the Internet for job hunting.

The Perfect Cover Letter 2nd ed.
RICHARD H. BEATTY
New York: John Wiley, 1996
192pp ISBN: 0471124001
The Perfect Cover Letter provides an introduction to the purpose of cover letters and describes how employers read and use them. Guidance is given on how to write an effective cover letter for a number of different situations. Example letters are included.

The Resume Handbook 3rd ed.
ARTHUR D. ROSENBERG, DAVID HIZER
Avon, Massachusetts: Adams Media Corporation, 1996
176pp ISBN: 1558506160
This is a concise guide to the principles of writing an effective résumé. It includes examples of cover letters and both well-written and poorly written résumés. Such examples are used to highlight important changes in today's job market.

Résumé Kit 4th ed.
RICHARD H. BEATTY
New York: John Wiley, 2000
368pp ISBN: 0471379492
The author adopts a step-by-step workbook approach that identifies 12 myths of résumé writing. The "electronic résumé" is covered, complete with instructions on the recommended format for online databases. There are over 80 sample résumés and cover letters to cater for a wide range of jobs and a section on job-hunting techniques for the information age, which includes listings and descriptions of the "top 20" career sites on the Web.

Resumes That Knock 'Em Dead
MARTIN YATE
Holbrook, Massachusetts: Adams Media Corporation, 2001
304pp ISBN: 1580624227
A comprehensive guide to creating résumés designed to make a job applicant stand out from all the other applicants. The contents include types of résumés and how to choose the right format for one's field, the ingredients for a basic résumé, creating a scannable résumé for electronic databases, and examples of successful résumés for a variety of careers.

Top Secret Executive Resumes: What It Takes to Create the Perfect Resume for the Best Top-level Positions
STEVEN PROVENZANO
Franklin Lakes, New Jersey: Career Press, 2000
256pp ISBN: 1564144313
Designed for business professionals, this guide provides information on creating résumés for upper management positions. The author, a corporate recruiter, addresses the fundamentals of an executive résumé and provides worksheets to assist in identifying one's skills. The book also prints examples of successful résumés.

INTERNET

Career World
www.career-world.co.uk
Career World provides career development programs to individuals as well as a full range of outplacement services to corporate clients throughout the United Kingdom. New visitors have to register before entering the site, which contains many example résumés, speculative letters, cover letters, and post-interview follow-up letters.

CV and Resume Tips
www.cvandresumetips.com
Straightforward and direct, CV and Resume Tips is the place to visit if you are looking to polish your résumé. It also includes information about the importance of a good cover letter.

GetMYonlineCV.com
www.getmyonlinecv.com
This site focuses on giving you a place and a means to create your online CV. It offers numerous tips and links to other sites for more information and services (paid and/or free). Members of this site have their own personal URL to showcase their résumé.

JobHuntersBible.Com: Job Hunting Online
www.jobhuntersbible.com
This Web site is designed as a companion to the book *What Color Is Your Parachute?* It includes comprehensive links to information on such topics as building a résumé, polishing the quality of a résumé, and posting a résumé online.

Monster Resume Center
www.resume.monster.com
Monster.Com provides online job-searching services, including job postings and company information. Its Resume Center offers a variety of services for job seekers, including résumé writing information such as the elements of a good résumé, how to address potential problem areas such as lack of experience, and career-specific résumés.

Perfect Resume
www.homestead.com/perfectresume
This Web site provides tips and techniques for creating résumés. Its content includes the fundamentals for creating a résumé, tips on selling oneself, mistakes to avoid, selecting the correct résumé type for your career field, creating an electronic résumé, and sites for posting a résumé.

Résumé.com
www.resume.com/content/cv_intl.html
This site offers samples of résumés and services for preparing your résumé (with a link to products and prices). Contact can be made via e-mail or phone.

Rebecca Smith's eRésumés & Resources
www.eresumes.com
Subtitled the "Ultimate Online eRésumé Guide for Winners," Rebecca Smith's site provides step-by-step advice on how to convert paper-based résumés for the Web. There is a gallery of online résumés and a book list, as well as links to job search and résumé sites.

The Chronicle: Career Network
http://chronicle.com/jobs
This site contains features such as the "CV doctor," with critiques and commentaries on a number of résumés, and articles such as "From CV to Resume."

The CV—Index Directory
www.cvindex.com
The CV—Index Directory is a searchable

directory of CVs and résumés which covers every major profession and provides listings in several countries.

Workthing.com
www.workthing.com
This site offers articles and advice on résumés, interviews, and job hunting, tailored to different industry sectors. It also provides access to a database of on- and offline courses. Under the section on Careers Advice, visitors can find a feature which assesses their résumés by means of an interactive quiz.

For More Information

- **Job Hunting (pp. 2017–18)**
- **Planning Your Career (pp. 2075–77)**

Customer Relations/Customer Service

BOOKS

Anytime, Anywhere
Robert Spector
Cambridge, Massachusetts: Perseus, 2002
288pp ISBN: 0738205109
This book is a useful resource for any business whose success depends on excellent customer service. It showcases the pioneering efforts of over a dozen companies that are renowned for their customer focus. It includes guidelines on how to meet and exceed customer expectations via any medium. Hardback.

Customer Relationship Management: A Strategic Imperative in the World of E-business
Stanley A. Brown, ed.
Toronto, Canada: John Wiley, 2000
345pp ISBN: 0471644099
This book asserts that CRM is the key to competitive advantage. It describes the leading trends and best practices in CRM, the successes and failures of organizations around the globe that have implemented it, the 20 key steps in its implementation, and how to define strategies for customers, channels, and products. Case studies are included.

Customer Relationship Management: How to Turn a Good Business into a Great One!
Graham Roberts-Phelps
Chicago, Illinois: John Wiley, 2001
230pp ISBN: 185418119X
This book sets out the essential features of CRM. It examines why customers defect and the economics of customer care, and shows how to define and achieve customer service excellence, manage for customer satisfaction, develop customer-focused selling and marketing skills, and connect with customers in the digital age. It sums everything up in ten keys to outstanding customer service.

Customer Service: A Practical Approach 2nd ed.
Elaine K. Harris
Upper Saddle River, New Jersey: Prentice Hall, 1999
148pp ISBN: 0130826650
Harris takes a practical approach to explaining the dynamics of customer service, covering areas such as barriers to customer service, problem solving, strategy, empowerment, and communications. She also has chapters on coping with challenging customers, motivation, leadership, and customer retention, and includes self-development exercises.

Discovering the Soul of Service
Leonard L. Berry
New York: Free Press, 1999
269pp ISBN: 0684845113
This book is based on a study of 14 mature, highly successful service companies. It presents the concept that the single most important factor in building a lasting service business is not a matter of business practice know-how, but of humane values.

Experiential Marketing: How to get Customers to Sense, Feel, Think, Act, and Relate to Your Company and Brands
Bernd H. Schmidt
New York: Free Press, 1999
288pp ISBN: 0684854236
Experiential marketing, according to Schmidt, is a revolutionary approach to marketing for the branding and information age. The aim of his book is to explain to managers how to create holistic experiences for customers through brands that provide sensory, affective, and creative associations. He also deals with lifestyle marketing and social identity campaigns. He backs up his claims with case studies of cutting-edge companies successfully using these techniques.

Harvard Business Review on Customer Relationship Management
Various
Boston, Massachusetts: Harvard Business School Press, 2001
224pp ISBN: 1578516994
An anthology of eight articles which focus on building a strong, positive customer relationship. Partnering and personalizing the marketing relationship, branding, and providing outstanding customer service and support are outlined as the means to establishing a relationship that fosters customer loyalty.

How to Measure Customer Satisfaction
Nigel Hill, John Brierley, Rob MacDougall
Brookfield, Vermont: Gower, 1999
144pp ISBN: 0566081938
The authors take you through the whole process of measuring customer satisfaction. Starting with setting objectives and project planning, they go on to deal with everything involved in successful exploratory research—questionnaire design, introducing the survey, maximizing response rates, analyzing the results, and benchmarking your performance—that will assist you in ensuring the continued satisfaction, delight, and loyalty of your customers.

The Lifebelt: The Definitive Guide to Managing Customer Retention
John A. Murphy
New York: John Wiley, 2001
304pp ISBN: 0471498181
Research provides evidence that the most sustainable levels of customer loyalty and retention are achieved through consistent excellence in service delivery. This book introduces the Customer Service Integration Framework—the lifebelt—based on four years of research. The author suggests that while many organizations have some good practices in place, most appear to lack synchronization. He gives a detailed case study of N. G. Bailey and Co. to illustrate his argument.

Loyalty.com: Customer Relationship Management in the New Era of Internet Marketing
Frederick Newell
New York: McGraw-Hill, 2000
325pp ISBN: 0071357750
This book outlines what the new technology means for marketers in every field and provides

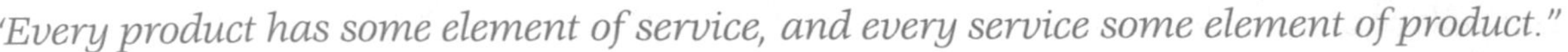

"Every product has some element of service, and every service some element of product."
(Aubrey Wilson)

techniques for creating and implementing CRM strategies. It shows how to give customers what they want to buy as opposed to what you want to sell them, and how to win customer share as opposed to market share.

The Loyalty Effect
Frederick F. Reichheld
Boston, Massachusetts: Harvard Business School Press, 2001
352pp ISBN: 1578516870
This book reveals the secrets of successful companies which base their business strategies on loyal relationships, both internally and externally, with employees, investors, and customers. It demonstrates the measurable results that strong loyalties have on corporate profits.

Loyalty Rules!
Frederick F. Reichheld
Boston, Massachusetts: Harvard Business School Press, 2001
304pp ISBN: 1578512050
Based on extensive research into companies from online start-ups to established institutions, this book looks at the issue of loyalty in industry. It is a practical guidebook, showing how employee and customer loyalty is necessary for lasting success.

Monitoring, Measuring, & Managing Customer Service
Gary S. Goodman
San Francisco, California: Jossey-Bass/ Pfeiffer, 2000
240pp (Jossey-Bass Business and Management Series)
ISBN: 0787951390
Goodman explains how to produce great customer service consistently and identifies the 18 communication factors that promote it. He deals with monitoring customer service, measuring the performance of representatives, team leaders, supervisors, and managers, recruiting, motivating and retaining quality customer service staff, and making a corporate commitment to first-class customer care.

The One to One Manager: Real World Lessons in Customer Relationship Management
Don Peppers, Martha Rogers
New York: Doubleday, 1999
288pp ISBN: 0385494084
Peppers and Rogers document more than two dozen case histories of one-to-one marketing, also known as customer relationship marketing (CRM). They examine the management issues involved in setting up and running one-to-one initiatives, and introduce readers to the groundbreakers, pathfinders, and explorers of customer-focused business strategies.

On Great Service
Leonard L. Berry
New York: Free Press, 1995
292pp ISBN: 0029185556
This book offers a dynamic framework for improving service quality, based on the author's on-site observations in a two-year study of dozens of companies of all sizes renowned for their service excellence. It contains a number of compelling examples of the strategies and practices that these companies implement in delivering great service.

The Service Profit Chain
James L. Heskett, W. Earl Sasser, Jr., Leonard A. Schlesinger
New York: Free Press, 1997
320pp ISBN: 0684832569
This book provides service industry business leaders with practical guidelines on how to manage, market, hire, deliver services, and assess results. It uses detailed case studies to demonstrate how successful companies already use these principles.

Seven Power Strategies for Building Customer Loyalty
Paul R. Timm
New York: AMACOM, 2001
224pp ISBN: 081440569X
Seven strategies are outlined for an organizational approach to customer service that results in valuable customer loyalty. Each strategy is presented in a step-by-step approach which stresses human relationships in what the author terms the "A-Plus" standard. The book addresses important topics such as identifying customer turnoffs, recovering dissatisfied customers, showing corporate personality, and actualizing your strategy. Worksheets, checklists, and case studies are included.

Total Relationship Marketing
Evert Gummesson
Woburn, Massachusetts: Butterworth-Heinemann, 2000
275pp (Marketing Series)
ISBN: 075064463X
As an alternative to the 4Ps of traditional marketing management (product, price, promotion, and place), the author offers 30 relationships, the 30Rs, that are fundamental to the marketing activities of every business. He covers the key relationships in which businesses are involved, from those with customers and competitors to those with government and the media.

MAGAZINES

Customer Interface
ISSN: 0886-9642
Advanstar Communications, Inc.
7500 Old Oak Boulevard, Cleveland, Ohio, 44130
T: +1 440 243 8100
F: +1 440 891 2727
www.c-interface.com/customerinterface
Published 12 times per year, this magazine is a prime source for customer service information. It is aimed at management level executives who are responsible for any aspect of customer service or relations. It highlights the latest changes and trends in this vital business service area.

International Journal of Customer Relationship Management
ISSN: 1461-4561
Winthrop Publications
Brunel House, 55–57 North Wharf Road, London, W2 1LA, U.K.
T: +44 (0) 20 7915 9634
F: +44 (0) 20 7915 9636
www.winthrop-publications.co.uk/crmfrontpage.htm
The *IJCRM* is aimed at marketing and sales managers and directors who are seeking to develop full lifetime value from interactions with customers and suppliers. Its articles are intended to help them improve their relationship management in order to increase the volume and value of their business, ensure an integrated company-wide relationship management strategy, and, through case studies, understand how competitors are successful.

Managing Service Quality
ISSN: 0960-4529
MCB University Press
60/62 Toller Lane, Bradford, West Yorkshire, BD8 9BY, U.K.
T: +44 (0) 1274 777700
F: +44 (0) 1274 785200
www.emeraldinsight.com/msq.htm
This magazine aims to bring ideas, case studies, reviews, and techniques primarily to working managers but also to the scholars and researchers who assist them in helping organizations to improve the quality of their service.

INTERNET

CRM guru
www.crmguru.com
This site carries information on customer relationship management and the CRM industry, and provides a discussion forum and e-mail newsletter. Registration is required.

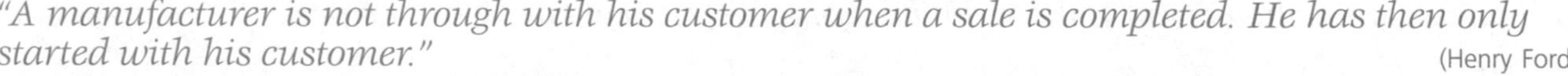
"A manufacturer is not through with his customer when a sale is completed. He has then only started with his customer."
(Henry Ford)

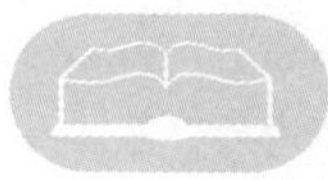

crmindustry
www.crmindustry.com
This free service provides a weekly e-newsletter, industry research, expert online sessions, vendor directory, resource center, and links to other sites.

eCustomerServiceWorld
www.ecustomerserviceworld.com
Sponsored by an international membership organization, the site offers free news, articles, surveys and results, conference information, a speakers' bureau, job information, research articles, and products and services sites.

International Customer Service Association
www.icsa.com
Sponsored by a membership organization, the site offers recent publications, résumé referral, case histories, conference information, merchandise, reports on industry activities, and links to other resources.

The Customer Service Network
www.customernet.co.uk
This virtual community site offers details of events, a discussion forum, and a free complaint benchmarking tool.

ORGANIZATIONS

USA

The Customer Care Institute
17 Dean Overlook, NW, Atlanta, Georgia, 30318
T: +1 404 352 9291
F: +1 404 355 5059
E: *info@customercare.com*
www.customercare.com
The CCI provides customer care professionals with information, research, advisory services, benchmarking, training, and networking opportunities. In addition, it conducts studies, publishes booklets, organizes forums, workshops, and conferences, and offers other programs and services that will enhance the delivery of customer care.

Europe

Institute of Customer Service
2 Castle Court, St. Peter's Street, Colchester, Essex, CO1 1EW, U.K.
T: +44 (0) 1206 571716
F: +44 (0) 1206 546688
E: *enquiries@instcustserv.com*
www.ics-nto.com
The Institute of Customer Service was formed in 1997 primarily to help people and organizations raise customer service standards. It is recognized by the U.K. government as the National Training Organisation for customer service.

For More Information

- ☆ **Managing 1:1 Marketing (pp. 55–56)**
- ☆ **Managing the Customer (pp. 65–66)**
- ✔ **Getting Close to the Customer (pp. 462–63)**
- ✔ **Handling Complaints (pp. 464–65)**
- **Marketing Management (pp. 2045–48)**

Decision Making and Problem Solving

BOOKS

Applied Statistical Decision Theory
Howard Raiffa, Robert Schlaifer
New York: John Wiley, 2000
356pp (Wiley Classics Library)
ISBN: 047138349X
This book is aimed at people who are interested in using statistics as a tool in practical decision making under conditions of uncertainty, and who also have the necessary training in mathematics and statistics to employ the relevant analytical techniques. It focuses on experimentation and decision, general theory, extensive-form analysis, and distribution theory.

Computer-supported Decision Making: Meeting the Decision Demands of Modern Organizations
Charles L. Smith
Norwood, New Jersey: Ablex Publishing, 1998
172pp (Contemporary Studies in Information Management Policy and Services)
ISBN: 1567503578
The author, an expert in the use of computer technology for technical problem solving, presents an overview of the process of decision making and examines the strengths and weaknesses of human and computer-based processes. Guidance on identifying the need for a decision support system and designing, building, and using such a system is provided.

Creative Problem Solving for Managers
Tony Proctor
New York: Routledge, 1999
392pp ISBN: 0415196795
This book focuses on the role of creativity and creative thinking in problem solving. A range of methods and techniques including morphological analysis, brainstorming and its variants, and lateral thinking are described. The text is illustrated with case studies and case histories.

Decision Making: An Integrated Approach 2nd ed.
David Jennings, Stuart Wattam
Upper Saddle River, New Jersey: Financial Times Pitman, 1998
364pp ISBN: 0273628593
This textbook is suitable for business studies students. It provides a comprehensive overview of various approaches to decision making, including systems thinking, simulation, model building, and management science techniques. There is also a strong focus on the factors influencing decision making within groups and organizations. Summaries, case study exercises, glossaries of terms, and suggestions for further reading are included.

Essential Managers: Making Decisions
Robert Heller
New York: DK Publishing, 1999
72pp ISBN: 078942889X
This compact resource offers a quick overview of the essentials of effective managerial decision making. Topics include defining decisions, identifying decision making styles, knowing your corporate culture, analyzing your responsibility, being decisive, identifying issues, and deciding whom to involve in a decision. The book covers both the formal and informal aspects of decision making, and includes practical techniques, checklists, flowcharts, and other illustrations to aid the decision maker.

Leadership and Decision Making
Victor H. Vroom, Philip W. Yetton
Pittsburgh, Pennsylvania: Pittsburgh University Press, 1973
233pp ISBN: 0822932660
The authors describe the model developed by them to demonstrate how leadership styles can be used in solving various types of problem. They also consider the issue of participation in decision making by subordinates and outline different methods for decision making in

"If businessmen always made the right decisions, business wouldn't be business." (J. Paul Getty)

  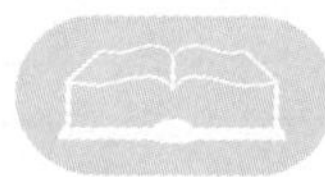    

groups, as well as discussing individual problems.

Making Better Business Decisions
STEVE WILLIAMS
Thousand Oaks, California: Sage, 2001
176pp ISBN: 0761924221
Williams offers insights from behavioral science on the way the mind processes information, and the biological, physiological, and psychological factors that influence thinking. The core of the book focuses on the application of critical thinking skills and creative problem solving to help optimize the quality of solutions to increasingly difficult, complex, and important problems.

Problem Solving 2nd ed.
GRAHAM WILSON
Milford, Connecticut: Kogan Page, 2000
245pp (Fast Track MBA Series)
ISBN: 074943032X
This book, published in association with PriceWaterhouseCoopers, is aimed at executives, managers, and students. It is written in an accessible and participative style and gives practical guidance on dealing with the problems that arise on a day-to-day basis in the context of an organization. It covers a wide range of topics, including: communication as an organizational problem; problem solving in small groups; conflicts and misunderstandings; the role of problem-solving models; and pinpointing the problem.

The Problem Solving Journey: Your Guide for Making Decisions and Getting Results
CHRISTOPHER W. HOENIG
Cambridge, Massachusetts: Perseus, 2000
283pp ISBN: 0738202800
This book is a thorough guide to the art of problem solving that uses examples as varied as NASA and VISA to illustrate how best this can be achieved. Having helped the reader to create a problem solving profile, the author then divides problem solving into a journey made up of six stages, each of which needs to be successfully negotiated. The journey culminates in "Delivering the results."

The 75 Greatest Management Decisions Ever Made and 21 of the Worst
STUART CRAINER
New York: AMACOM, 1999
256pp ISBN: 081440491X
A selection of the greatest management decisions ever made, as nominated by a panel of experts, is presented by a well-known management writer, who also discusses the characteristics that made those decisions great. The cases are drawn from business history through the ages and from all over the world. A collection of 21 disastrous decisions is also included.

Smart Choices: A Practical Guide to Making Better Decisions
JOHN S. HAMMOND, RALPH L. KEENEY, HOWARD RAIFFA
Boston, Massachusetts: Harvard Business School Press, 1998
272pp ISBN: 0875848575
Three world-renowned experts on complex decision making join forces to craft a practical approach to making better decisions in our business, professional, and personal lives. They offer a simple, flexible technique based on a solid triumvirate of research, practical experience, and common sense that supports the decision maker in clearly and effectively assessing options, specifying objectives, identifying creative alternatives, making reasoned tradeoffs, clarifying uncertainties, and evaluating associated risks. Their approach integrates the intuitive and rational analytic approaches.

The Thinking Manager's Toolbox: Effective Processes for Problem Solving and Decision Making
WILLIAM J. ALTIER
New York: Oxford University Press, 1999
219pp ISBN: 0195131967
In this title, the author argues that an understanding of the processes that are being employed in a certain business, and the experience of going through those processes repeatedly over a long period of time, will determine who is a successful leader. He also reveals ways of preventing problems before they occur, and teaches the reader how to create "thinking tools" to help make choices.

Winning Decisions: Getting It Right the First Time
J. EDWARD RUSSO, PAUL J. SCHOEMAKER
New York: Doubleday, 2001
352pp ISBN: 0385502257
Russo and Schoemaker provide a practical four-step method for making winning decisions. The steps in question are: framing decisions effectively; gathering data that does not simply support existing biases; reaching conclusions on effective action based on the data gathered; and learning from experience. *Winning Decisions* is laced with specific tools, questionnaires, how-to's, worksheets, case studies, and anecdotes to help readers apply the method immediately to enhance the quality of their own business decisions.

MAGAZINES

Decision Sciences Journal
ISSN: 0011-7315
Decision Sciences Institute
J. Mack Robinson College of Business, Georgia State University, Atlanta, Georgia, 30303
T: +1 404 651 4073
F: +1 404 651 2804
www.decisionsciences.org/dsj
The *DSJ* is a quarterly journal that focuses on the use of behavioral, economic, and quantitative methods of analysis in decision making in public and private organizations.

Decision Support Systems
ISSN: 0167-9236
Elsevier Science
Regional Sales Office, Customer Support Department, P.O. Box 945, New York, 10159-0945
T: +1 212 633 3730
F: +1 212 633 3680
www.elsevier.com
DSS is an academic journal which appears eight times a year and covers the concept, implementation, and evaluation of decision support systems, together with related studies.

Journal of Behavioral Decision Making
ISSN: 0894-3257
John Wiley
Wiley InterScience Coordinator, Subscriptions Department, 605 Third Avenue, New York, 10158-0012
T: +1 800 825 7550
F: +1 212 850 6021
www.interscience.wiley.com
This is a multidisciplinary journal, broad-based in content and style, that publishes reports, critical review papers, theoretical analyses, and methodological contributions. It presents behavioral research on decision making and provides a forum for the evaluation of complementary, contrasting, and conflicting perspectives.

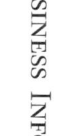

Journal of Multi-criteria Decision Analysis
ISSN: 1057-9214
John Wiley
Wiley InterScience Coordinator, Subscriptions Department, 605 Third Avenue, New York, 10158-0012
T: +1 800 825 7550
F: +1 212 850 6021
www.interscience.wiley.com
The *JMCDA* is published in association with the International Society on Multiple-Criteria Decision Making. The journal appears six times a year and provides an international forum for the presentation and discussion of all aspects of research into, and the application and evaluation of, multi-criteria decision analysis, covering its mathematical, theoretical, and behavioral aspects.

Theory and Decision
ISSN: 0040–5833
Kluwer Academic Publishers
Customer Service Department, P.O. Box 358, 101 Philip Drive, Assinippi Park, Norwell, Massachusetts, 02018–0358
T: +1 781 871 6600
F: +1 781 871 6528
www.kluweronline.com/issn/0040–5833
This academic, cross-discipline journal on the mechanics of decision making focuses on preference and uncertainty modeling, multi-criteria decision making, social choice, negotiation and group decisions, game theory, and gaming and conflict analysis.

INTERNET

Brainstorming.co.uk
www.brainstorming.co.uk
This site offers an introduction to brainstorming, plus information on brainstorming software, a list of recommended books, and a mailing list provided by Infinite Innovation.

Data Warehousing Information Center
www.dwinfocenter.org
This targeted-knowledge portal provides information and education for the layperson on data warehousing and decision support. Primarily an informational site, it does not market any particular product or service. It offers a series of essays, plus links to vendors, helpfully grouped into several categories, and to additional resources and organizations.

DAWeb
http://faculty.fuqua.duke.edu/daweb
The Web site of the Decision Analysis Society provides a range of information in the field of decision analysis including a lexicon of decision making, bibliographies, information on courses and syllabuses, Web-based decision aids, a newsletter, and a mailing list.

Decision Conferencing—Global Decision Conferencing and Decision Analysis Resource Centre
www.decision-conferencing.com
This site provides general information on decision conferencing, including case studies, a reading list, demos of decision-analysis software, and a discussion forum provided by Enterprise LSE at the London School of Economics.

Decision Support Systems Resources
www.dssresources.com
With everything you ever wanted to know about computerized decision-support systems, this knowledge portal, established and maintained by Professor Daniel J. Power, provides tutorials, case studies, decision aids, a glossary of terms, extensive links, and a ''Web-tour'' for newcomers.

MindTools
www.mindtools.com
This site includes introductions to a number of problem-solving techniques, such as brainstorming and decision trees.

Society for Judgment and Decision Making
www.sjdm.org
At this interdisciplinary academic society Web site, non members can access a searchable database of references to books and book chapters on judgment and decision making. The site also provides links to journals, academic programs, and other organizations related to the field, as well as syllabuses for an extensive series of courses ranging from managerial decision making to decision making in government and administration.

ORGANIZATIONS

USA

Decision Analysis Society
c/o INFORMS, 901 Elkridge Landing Road, Suite 400, Linthicum, Maryland, 21090–2909
T: +1 410 850 0300
F: +1 410 684 2963
E: informs@informs.org
http://faculty.fuqua.duke.edu/daweb
The DAS started life in 1980 as a special interest group of ORSA (Operations Research Society of America) and became a section of INFORMS (Institute for Operations Research and the Management Sciences) following a merger with the Institute for Management Sciences in 1995. The Society promotes the development and use of logical methods for the improvement of decision making in public and private enterprise. Members include practitioners, educators, and researchers.

Society for Judgment and Decision Making
c/o Dr. Sandra Schneider, Department of Psychology BEH 339, University of South Florida, 4202 E. Fowler Avenue, Tampa, Florida, 33620–8200
T: +1 813 974 0495
F: +1 813 974 4617
E: sjdm@web.usf.edu
www.sjdm.org
SJDM is an interdisciplinary academic organization dedicated to the study of theories of decision. Its members include psychologists, economists, decision analysts, and decision researchers. The Society was formally established in 1986 and holds an annual meeting for the presentation of research papers.

Europe

European Association for Decision Making
Pieter Koele, Department of Psychology, University of Amsterdam, Roetersstraat 15, 1018 WB Amsterdam, The Netherlands
T: +31 20 525 68 81
F: +31 20 639 00 26
www.psy.uva.nl/ResEdu/EADM
EADM was founded in 1969 as SPUDM (Subjective Probability and Utility Decision Making) and changed to its current name in 1993. The organization is based in Leiden in the Netherlands. Membership currently stands at 240 and is open to academics and students in the field of human judgment and decision making. The current president is Karl Halvor Teigen of the University of Tromsoe in Norway. EADM promotes the advancement and dissemination of knowledge in this area through meetings, workshops, and conferences, publication of a bulletin, and sponsorship of the Bruno de Finetti prize for promising researchers.

International

Decision Sciences Institute
J. Mack Robinson College of Business, Georgia State University, 35 Broad Street, Atlanta, Georgia, 30303
T: +1 404 651 4073
F: +1 404 651 2804
E: dsi@gsu.edu
www.decisionsciences.org
The Institute's aims are to develop and apply methodologies for solving multiple criteria decision making problems and to encourage interaction, cooperation, and research in the field. In pursuit of these aims it organizes workshops, conferences, and student exchanges, and publishes a newsletter. It has a membership of over 3,500. The current president is Professor Thomas W. Jones of the University of Arkansas.

International Society on Multiple Criteria Decision Making
Department of Banking and Finance, Terry College of Georgia, Athens, Georgia, 30602–6253
T: +1 706 542 3782
F: +1 706 542 9434
E: miettine@mit.jyu.fi

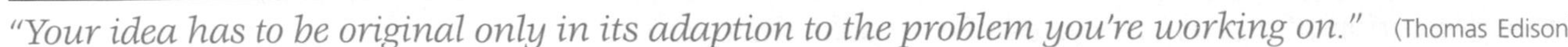
"Your idea has to be original only in its adaption to the problem you're working on." (Thomas Edison)

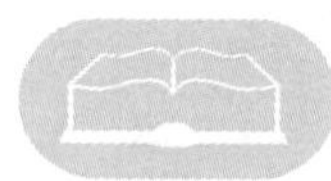

www.terry.uga.edu/mcdm
The Society is an interdisciplinary organization concerned with the methods and procedures by which a concern for multiple conflicting criteria can be formally incorporated into managerial decision making. The organization was founded in 1969 and has a membership of over 1,300 in over 85 countries. The current president is Valerie Belton of Strathclyde University in Scotland. Publications, conferences, and other services are organized with the needs of academics and students in mind.

For More Information

☆ **Developing Exceptional Problem-solving Skills (pp. 338–39)**

✔ **Making Rational Decisions (pp. 566–67)**
✔ **Open Systems Thinking (pp. 568–69)**
✔ **Solving Problems (pp. 408–09)**
Analytical Techniques and Statistics (pp. 1906–08)

Direct Marketing

BOOKS

Commonsense Direct Marketing 4th ed.
Drayton Bird
Milford, Connecticut: Kogan Page, 2000
352pp ISBN: 0749431210
This is a practical textbook, introducing direct marketing, that is packed with international case studies and demonstrations of successful strategies. It covers the following topics: the role of the marketing department; how to acquire and keep customers; how to achieve objectives and evaluate results; what you should sell; how to position products effectively; how to choose an agency and how to do without one; and the Internet, the direct marketer's new tool.

Direct Marketing: Strategy, Planning, Execution 4th ed.
Edward L. Nash
New York: McGraw-Hill, 2000
600pp ISBN: 0071352872
This updated edition is a classic in the direct marketing industry. The author, a direct marketing company executive, presents a thorough overview of all aspects of direct marketing, including strategic planning, media-specific marketing techniques, the economics of direct marketing, and direct marketing considerations for Internet and global marketing.

Enterprise One to One: Tools for Competing in the Interactive Age
Don Peppers, Martha Rogers
New York: Currency/Doubleday, 1997
ISBN: 0385482051
Written by the champions of customer relationship marketing, this is a bestselling guide to using new technology in your quest to get ahead, and stay ahead, of the field.

Exploring Direct Marketing
Lisa O'Malley, Maurice Patterson, Martin Evans
Boston, Massachusetts: International Thomson Business Press, 1998
416pp ISBN: 1861524021
Written for students, this textbook examines the theory of direct marketing and deals in particular with the following subject areas: segmentation and direct marketing, the marketing database, market research, customers, relationship marketing, media including the Internet, creativity, legislation, and social responsibility. Case studies are included.

Making It Personal: How to Profit from Personalization without Invading Privacy
Bruce Kasanoff, Don Peppers, Martha Rogers
Cambridge, Massachusetts: Perseus, 2001
240pp ISBN: 0738205362
This book is a study of how the forthcoming growth in the use of personal information will affect the corporate world. Using research carried out in real life, the author investigates the contradiction that exists in some areas between increasing profits through personal interaction and not invading privacy.

The New Direct Marketing: How to Implement a Profit-driven Database Marketing Strategy
David Shepard Associates
New York: McGraw-Hill, 1999
736pp ISBN: 0070580561
This updated edition serves as a comprehensive reference book on direct marketing for readers of all knowledge and experience levels. The authors thoroughly cover the details and processes of direct marketing, incorporating traditional methods with new technologies such as data mining and use of the Internet.

The New Integrated Direct Marketing
Mike Berry
Brookfield, Vermont: Gower, 1998
256pp ISBN: 0566079607
The central theme of this book is that direct marketing—centered on the creation and profitable exploitation of customer relationships—is the marketing of the future. It evaluates the strengths and weaknesses of the key disciplines of direct marketing, sales promotion, and advertising. In addition, it explains the need for structured and integrated marketing programs using various media and offers advice on the structure of an integrated communications agency. Case studies are also presented.

The One to One Fieldbook: The Complete Toolkit for Implementing a 1 to 1 Marketing Program 288th ed.
Don Peppers, Martha Rogers, Bob Dorf
New York: Bantam Books, 1999
288pp ISBN: 038549369X
A practical resource designed for use with *Enterprise One to One*, full of information on how to identify and develop a loyal customer base for your business.

The One to One Future: Building Relationships One Customer at a Time
Don Peppers, Martha Rogers
New York: Currency/Doubleday, 1997
ISBN: 0385425287
Mass marketing has had its day. This is the era of relationship marketing, where firms expend there energy trying to develop customer loyalty in order to sell more products to fewer people. This milestone work looks to strategies for the future in one to one marketing.

Relationship Marketing: Successful Strategies for the Age of the Customer
Regis McKenna
Cambridge, Massachusetts: Perseus, 1993
256pp ISBN: 0201622408
This title offers advice to organizations on how to dominate and control the market through the construction of highly important relationships with customers.

"We don't so much have a marketing department, as anthropologists working for us." (Anita Roddick)

Successful Direct Marketing Methods 7th ed.
Bob Stone, Ron Jacobs
New York: McGraw-Hill, 2001
608pp ISBN: 0658001450
This newly updated edition provides a classic guide to direct marketing, combining new media with traditional marketing strategies to provide effective direct marketing to consumers. The content includes identifying and meeting consumers' needs, business to business marketing, and e-commerce techniques, such as branding strategies for Internet sites.

2,239 Tested Secrets for Direct Marketing Success
Denny Hatch, Don Jackson
New York: McGraw-Hill, 1999
368pp ISBN: 0844203491
Divided in topic sections for easy reference, this book is an excellent source of direct marketing advice drawn from the experience of experts.

MAGAZINES

Direct Marketing International
ISSN: 0969–6881
Detailextra Ltd.
Media House, Hallidays Yard, Radcliffe Road, Stamford, Lincolnshire, PE9 1ED, U.K.
T: +44 (0) 1780 765960
F: +44 (0) 1780 765904
This is a professional journal focusing on direct marketing worldwide.

Interactive Marketing
ISSN: 1463–5178
Institute of Direct Marketing in conjunction with Henry Stewart Publications
25 Museum Street, London, WC1A 2TJ, U.K.
T: +44 (0) 20 7323 2916
F: +44 (0) 20 7323 2918
www.henrystewart.com/journals/hspindex.htm
This international journal provides a forum for up-and-coming stars of marketing to share experience, ideas, research, and case studies. A legal and regulatory update is also included.

Marketing Direct
Haymarket Business Publications Ltd.
174 Hammersmith Road, London, W6 7JP, U.K.
T: +44 (0) 20 8267 5000
F: +44 (0) 20 8267 4157
www.mxdirect.co.uk
This magazine is targeted at direct marketers and contains news, case studies, a think tank, features, personality profiles, and letters.

INTERNET

Direct
www.directmag.com
This is the site of an American-based online magazine for senior direct marketers that covers all aspects of direct marketing.

Direct Marketing Linked Resources
www.dmlr.org/guide.htm
Many links to useful sites connected with marketing on the Internet are to be found at this address.

DM News
www.dmnews.com
DM News is an online newspaper covering the direct marketing industry. Its Web site provides the latest information on legislative, business, and postal news affecting the industry. This site includes registration for free e-mail newsletters, an online directory of direct marketing businesses, and privacy information.

International Chamber of Commerce
www.iccwbo.org/home/statements_rules/rules/1998/marketcod.asp
The International Chamber of Commerce sets out its code for direct marketing on this site. The code is intended to promote high standards of ethics within marketing.

Response
www.royalmail.com/response
This is an information site that deals with the planning and strategy issues involved in successful direct-marketing campaigns, as well as providing industry news.

Target Marketing
www.targetonline.com
This site houses an America-based online magazine with articles and information on direct marketing.

The Direct Marketing Association
www.the-dma.org
The Direct Marketing Association is a trade association serving the needs of direct marketing users and suppliers. Its Web site provides comprehensive information on direct marketing. This includes: conferences and seminars; professional development; industry guidelines, such as ethics guidelines and online tutorials; directories of direct marketers listed by name and type of service; privacy information; research; and legislative issues.

ORGANIZATIONS

USA

The Direct Marketing Association
1120 Avenue of the Americas, New York, 10036–6700
T: +1 212 768 7277
F: +1 212 302 6714
E: *membership@the-dma.org*
www.the-dma.org
The DMA is a trade association for users and suppliers in the fields of direct, database, and interactive marketing. Founded in 1917, it now has 4,700 member organizations in the United States and 53 other countries. Membership services include events, professional development, representation to government and in public affairs, and a library. The DMA recently acquired two e-commerce trade associations, the Association for Interactive Media and the Internet Alliance.

Europe

Direct Marketing Association
DMA House, 70 Margaret Street, London, W1W 8SS, U.K.
T: +44 (0) 20 7291 3300
F: +44 (0) 20 7323 4165
E: *dma@dma.org.uk*
www.dma.org.uk
The aims of the DMA are to raise the stature of the direct marketing industry and to give the consumer trust and confidence in direct marketing.

Federation of European Direct Marketing
Tervurenlaan, Avenue de Tervuren 439, B-1150 Brussels, Belgium
T: +32 2779 42 68
F: +32 2779 42 69
E: *info@fedma.org*
www.fedma.org
A membership organization for national direct marketing associations, FEDMA aims to promote, protect, and provide information about the European direct-marketing industry.

Institute of Direct Marketing
1 Park Road, Teddington, Middlesex, TW11 0AR, U.K.
T: +44 (0) 20 8977 5705
F: +44 (0) 20 8943 2535
www.theidm.co.uk
The IDM is a professional body for individual direct marketing practitioners. The services it offers to its membership include events, meetings, and networking opportunities, information and research resources, and a national certification program.

For More Information

☆ **Managing 1:1 Marketing (pp. 55–56)**
Marketing Management (pp. 2045–48)

"Your company does not belong in any market where it cannot be the best." (Philip Kotler)

  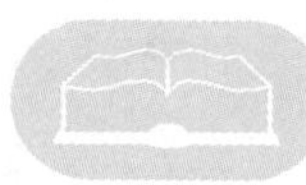    

DIVERSITY

BOOKS

Beyond Race and Gender: Unleashing the Power of Your Total Work Force by Managing Diversity
R. ROOSEVELT THOMAS, JR.
New York: AMACOM, 1992
189pp ISBN: 0814478077
Looking ahead to a time when the U.S. work force will be truly diverse, the author of this classic and groundbreaking book explores the problems facing managers trying to offer equal opportunities to all in order to take advantage of needed talents and skills. He presents an action plan for changing corporate cultures as well as case studies that highlight the problems that emerge once an organization recruits a diverse workforce, especially the failure of those recruited to move up the corporate ladder.

Cultural Diversity in Organizations
TAYLOR COX
San Francisco, California: Berrett-Koehler, 1994
ISBN: 1881052435
This comprehensive text covers all aspects of cultural diversity and its relation to business, including organizational performance, individual and group factors, and guidelines for leadership in managing diversity.

The Diversity Directive: Why Some Initiatives Fail and What to Do About It
ROBERT HAYLES, ARMIDA MENDEZ RUSSELL
New York: American Society for Training and Development, in association with McGraw-Hill, 1997
150pp ISBN: 0786308192
This practical text offers a step-by-step process to help managers to initiate corporate diversity efforts, or to revitalize their existing diversity initiatives. Models, recommended actions, and real-world examples are presented to help organizations to diagnose problems and develop tactical action plans for the diversity change process. Appendices give a sample process outline and schedule for a Diversity Audit.

The Equal Opportunities Guide: How to Deal with Everyday Issues of Unfairness 2nd ed.
PHIL CLEMENTS, TONY SPINKS
Sterling, Virginia: Stylus Publishing, 1997
192pp ISBN: 0749421037
This is a plainly written resource for students, managers, trainers, human resource management staff, teachers, and all those with an interest in equality of opportunity. The text sets out straightforward procedures to guide fair, courteous, and sensitive behavior to others, and includes a summary of recent U.K. legislation and agencies, self-assessment sections, and ways of identifying and preventing institutional discrimination.

Implementing Diversity
MARILYN LODEN
New York: McGraw-Hill, 1995
208pp ISBN: 078630460X
This text is aimed both at those needing to revitalize existing diversity implementation efforts and at those just beginning to initiate diversity management within an organization. It focuses strongly on the mistakes and limited successes of various (unnamed) organizations, seeking to challenge popular assumptions about diversity implementation, and to help managers to anticipate, recognize, and thereby avoid mistakes made within other organizations. Assessment questionnaires for organizations are included.

The IPD Guide on Managing Diversity: Evidence from Case Studies
New York: Beekman, 2001
54pp ISBN: 0846450860
This brief guide for all involved in human resource or strategic management is based on six U.K. company case studies: Bolton Metro, Greenwich Healthcare, the Inland Revenue, Levi Strauss (U.K.), the Littlewoods Organisation, and Sainsbury's supermarkets. A summary of action points is given at the beginning of the guide, and some policy samples and outlines are included.

A Peacock in the Land of Penguins: A Fable About Creativity and Courage
B. J. HATELEY, WARREN H. SCHMIDT
San Francisco, California: Berrett-Koehler, 2001
158pp ISBN: 1576751732
Using the metaphor of a peacock living in the midst of penguins, this book offers a different perspective on valuing and building a diverse workplace. The authors include tips on creating organizational change and training materials to assist in implementing diversity.

Redefining Diversity
R. ROOSEVELT THOMAS, JR.
New York: AMACOM, 1996
275pp ISBN: 0814402283
Disappointed by the limited actions taken within organizations following his earlier classic on diversity, the author offers managers a "paradigm" of eight action options for dealing with diversity issues. The concept of diversity management is widened to include "items" and processes as well as people. Case studies illustrating the uses of the paradigm are central to the book.

When Generations Collide
DAVID STILLMAN, LYNNE C. LANCASTER
New York: HarperCollins, 2002
240pp ISBN: 0066621062
Addressing issues of generational differences as part of workplace diversity, the authors describe the potential problems involved in managing the four generational groups they have identified as members of the work force. The contents include recommendations for bringing each group together as a unified team.

MAGAZINES

Cross Cultural Management
ISSN: 1352–7606
Emerald (North America)
4th Floor, 44 Brattle Street, Cambridge, Massachusetts, 02138
T: +1 888 622 0075
www.emeraldinsight.com/ccm.htm
This is a quarterly journal that gives its editorial objective as the provision of guidance and information for managers about working within national or organizational cultures different from their own, and about the management of people from different cultures.

Diversity Digest
Association of American Colleges and Universities
1818 R Street NW, Washington, D.C., 20009
T: +1 202 387 3760
F: +1 202 265 9532
www.diversityweb.org/digest
This is a quarterly newsletter, available in both online and print versions, targeted at campus practitioners within colleges and universities. It aims to support the facilitation of diversity. It is supported as part of the Diversity Works initiative, financed by grants from the Ford Foundation to AAC&U and the University of Maryland at College Park.

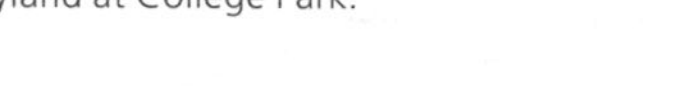

Equal Opportunities International
ISSN: 0261–0159
Barmarick Publications
Enholmes Hall, Patrington, East Yorkshire, HU12 0PR, U.K.
T: +44 (0) 1964 630033

"Diversity raises the intelligence of groups." (Nancy Kline)

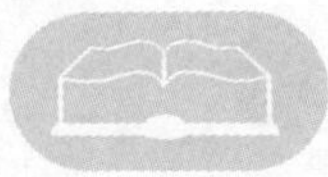

F: +44 (0) 1964 631716
www.emeraldinsight.com/eoi.htm
This is a high-priced subscription journal carrying articles by academics who are involved in equal opportunities teaching or research. The number of issues per year is variable, but eight were published in 2001.

Equal Opportunities Review
ISSN: 0268–7143
Eclipse Group Ltd.
18–20 Highbury Place, London, N5 1QP, U.K.
T: +44 (0) 20 7354 6742
F: +44 (0) 20 7226 8618
www.irseclipse.co.uk
This publication is issued six times a year, and focuses on U.K. equal opportunities legislation and employment practice.

Mosaics
Diversity Initiative
SHRM, 1800 Duke Street, Alexandria, Virginia, 22314
T: +1 703 548 3440
F: +1 703 535 6490
www.shrm.org/diversity
This is a bimonthly journal on diversity management for members of the Society for Human Resource Management (SHRM) Diversity Initiative.

INTERNET

American Institute for Managing Diversity
www.aimd.org
The American Institute for Managing Diversity is a nonprofit organization dedicated to promoting research and education regarding the value of implementing workplace diversity. Its site provides a wealth of resources, including research and resources on managing diversity.

Cultural Diversity at Work Online
www.diversitycentral.com
This is a subscription service bimonthly online journal, described as a virtual toolroom for fostering individual and organizational change. Subscribers also obtain free access to a database of archived articles based on the hard-copy issues of the journal (published from 1988 to April 2000).

Disability on the Agenda
www.disability.gov.uk
This site provides information on disability legislation, including official guidance, press releases, and links. The links include the Web Accessibility Initiative, which aims to make Web technology more accessible to those with disabilities, and also ACDET (Advisory Committee for Disabled People in Training and Employment), an organization that advises ministers and officials on how to secure equality of participation in employment and training opportunities for people who are disabled.

Diversity Central
www.diversityhotwire.com/al
This site provides an array of resources for managers and consultants addressing the issue of workplace diversity. The resources include articles and research on current topics, reports on employment law, online learning activities and tutorials, a directory of consultants, and a fee-based online journal.

Equality North West
www.equality.org.uk
The menu option on this site for the One Stop Shop for Equal Opportunities pilot offers resources to support small and medium-sized enterprises in developing equal opportunities practices in employment and service delivery. Designed for easy usage, its content includes recruitment and selection, policies and procedures, and legislation. It is commissioned by the U.K. Department for Education and Employment.

European Institute for Managing Diversity (EIMD)
www.eimd.org
This is an international network of local consulting organizations in various countries, specializing in diversity management and offering services to address the diversity needs of European organizations.

Race for Opportunity
www.raceforopportunity.org.uk
This is a Business in the Community network initiative to raise business awareness of the case for diversity. It gives information on the employment policies of some member companies; regional and London pages give information about relevant activities and issues.

Society for Human Resource Management (SHRM) Diversity Initiative
www.shrm.org/diversity
This site gives access to articles about diversity, and information on tools and resources. Parts of the site, including the online text of the Mosaics journal on diversity, are accessible to SHRM members only.

University of Maryland Diversity Database
www.inform.umd.edu/Diversity
This site provides an index of multicultural and diversity resources, and of academic material, all from campus, local, national, and international sources.

Workplace Diversity for African, Hispanic (Latino), and Asian Americans
www.ethnicmajority.com/workplace.htm
This Web site addresses workplace diversity issues targeting African Americans, Hispanic Americans, and Asian Americans. Its resources include information about and links to current employment laws, understanding affirmative action, and indicators measuring corporate diversity.

ORGANIZATIONS

USA

American Institute for Managing Diversity
50 Hurt Plaza, Suite 1150, Atlanta, Georgia, 30303
T: +1 404 302 9226
F: +1 404 302 9252
www.aimd.org
This is a national, nonprofit, research-based organization founded in 1984 for the study of diversity issues, offering various services related to diversity management. In November 2000, it was sponsored to establish the Diversity Leadership Academy of Atlanta (DLAA), offering a program for leaders using a tool called the ''Giraffe and Elephant Diversity Process.''

Equal Employment Opportunity Commission
1801 L Street NW, Washington, D.C., 20507
T: +1 202 663 4900
www.eeoc.gov
This body was established by Title VII of the Civil Rights Act of 1964 to enforce federal statutes prohibiting employment discrimination. It began operating on July 2, 1965.

Europe

Commission for Racial Equality
Head Office, Elliot House, 10–12 Allington Street, London, SW1E 5EH, U.K.
T: +44 (0) 20 7828 7022
F: +44 (0) 20 7630 7605
E: *info@cre.gov.uk*
www.cre.gov.uk
This is a publicly funded but nongovernmental body set up under the Race Relations Act 1976 to deal with racial discord and to promote racial equality. It provides information and advice, seeks to raise awareness of relevant issues, and promotes policies and practices to ensure equality of treatment for all.

"Make your employers understand that you are in their service as workers, not as women."
(Susan B. Anthony)

Disability Rights Commission
DRC Helpline, Freepost MID 02164, Stratford-upon-Avon, Warwickshire, CV37 9BR, U.K.
T: +44 (0) 8457 622 633
F: +44 (0) 8457 778 878
E: ddahelp@stra.sitel.co.uk
www.drc-gb.org
Established by an Act of Parliament, the Commission came into operation in April 2000 to ensure that the Disability Discrimination Act 1995 takes effect, to keep disability legislation under review, and to publicize and promote good practice.

Equal Opportunities Commission
Arndale House, Arndale Centre, Manchester, M4 3EQ, U.K.
T: +44 (0) 845 601 5901
F: +44 (0) 161 838 1733
E: info@eoc.org.uk
www.eoc.org.uk
The EOC is a statutory body that works to eliminate unlawful sex discrimination in the United Kingdom, to promote equal opportunities for men and women, and to uphold and review the Sex Discrimination (1975) and Equal Pay (1970) Acts.

Opportunity Now
Business in the Community, 137 Shepherdess Walk, London, N1 7RQ, U.K.
T: +44 (0) 20 7556 8714
F: +44 (0) 20 7253 1877
E: opportunitynow@bitc.org.uk
www.opportunitynow.org.uk
This is a campaign initiative under the umbrella of Business in the Community that works with employers to improve women's opportunities at work.

For More Information

☆ **Boosting Business Success through Diversity (pp. 29–30)**
☆ **Generation Veneration (pp. 39–40)**
Conditions of Employment (pp. 1933–35)
Employee Participation in Management (pp. 1962–64)
Employee Relations (pp. 1964–66)
Employment Law (pp. 1967–69)
Equal Opportunities (pp. 1975–77)
Social Responsibility of Management (pp. 2115–17)

Education Management

BOOKS

Human Resource Management in Schools and Colleges
David Middlewood, Jacky Lumby
London: Paul Chapman, 1999
104pp ISBN: 1853964018
This textbook is designed for those taking courses in education management. It explains the importance of human resource management in education, addresses key issues in the application of HRM principles in the context of educational institutions, and provides practical activities and details of background reading.

Making Managers in Universities and Colleges
Craig Prichard
Buckingham: Open University Press/ Society for Research into Higher Education, 2000
224pp ISBN: 0335204856
The book draws on interviews with over 70 senior managers to illustrate contemporary issues and problems in educational management. It pays particular attention to the role of managers in universities and colleges in the light of moves to operate post-compulsory education in the United Kingdom on a more commercial basis.

Management in Further Education: Theory and Practice
Harriet Harper
London: David Fulton, 1997
1000pp ISBN: 1853464732
This book provides lecturers who are moving into management roles in further education with an understanding of current management theory as it applies to further education colleges. The areas covered include managing people, managing operations, managing resources, and managing information.

Managing Schools
Patrick Whitaker
Woburn, Massachusetts: Butterworth-Heinemann, 1997
221pp (IM Diploma in Management series)
ISBN: 075062194X
This book is one of a series designed for managers wishing to develop their capabilities and is suitable for those undertaking courses leading to the Certificate and Diploma in Management. This volume, written by an educational consultant, provides a strategic approach to educational management and focuses on the application of best practice to the management of schools in the context of rapid change. It defines the role of management in education and gives guidance on developing vision and making and reviewing progress toward objectives.

Reflecting on School Management
Anne Gold, Jennifer Evans
New York: Routledge/Falmer, 1998
160pp (Master Classes in Education)
ISBN: 0750708050
This book is written for teachers, at all levels of responsibility in schools, who wish to reflect on and develop the management aspects of their job. Its style is practical and interactive, and it includes thought-provoking readings and activities. The topics covered include philosophy and values in education management, management and leadership styles, working with people, managing finance and resources, and managing the curriculum.

Standards and Quality in Higher Education
John Brennan, Peter de Vries, Ruth Williams, eds.
Philadelphia, Pennsylvania: Jessica Kingsley, 1997
240pp (Higher Education Policy Series No. 37)
ISBN: 1853024236
This book addresses current debates on academic standards and quality assurance from the perspectives of institutional leaders, national quality bodies, and higher education researchers. A range of contributors review national developments in quality assessment around the world, international initiatives on quality in higher education, and the institutional experience of external quality assessment. The U.K. debate about standards is also featured.

The Use of Performance Indicators in Higher Education: The Challenge of the

"In the early days, it was easy to lead by example. Now it has to be done by structured education and training."
(Tom Farmer)

Quality Movement 3rd ed.
MARTIN CAVE, ET AL.
Philadelphia, Pennsylvania: Jessica Kingsley, 1996
172pp (Higher Education Policy Series No. 3)
ISBN: 1853023450
This book considers the development of performance indicators in British higher education and takes account of recent developments in their use, drawing on evidence from an international research project. A survey of the literature from the United States, the United Kingdom, and OECD countries is included, together with a bibliography.

MAGAZINES

Educational Management and Administration
ISSN: 0263–211X
Sage Publications, Inc.
2455 Teller Road, Thousand Oaks, California, 91320
T: +1 805 499 0721
F: +1 805 499 0871
www.sagepub.com
Educational Management and Administration is the quarterly journal of the British Educational Management and Administration Society. It provides a forum for analysis of all aspects of management, administration, and policy in education, and publishes original research on educational management, administration, and policy in all its forms, including the management of schools and the administration of institutions of further and higher education.

Higher Education Management
ISSN: 1013–851X
OECD Programme on Institutional Management in Higher Education
2 rue André-Pascal, 75775 Paris 16, France
T: +33 1 45 24 92 24
F: +33 1 42 24 02 11
www.oecd.org/els/education/higher
This journal is aimed at policymakers in national and regional authorities, managers of higher education institutions, and researchers.

Higher Education Quarterly
ISSN: 0951–5224
Blackwell Publishers
350 Main Street, Malden, Massachusetts, 02148
T: +1 781 388 8200
F: +1 781 388 8232
www.blackwellpublishers.com/asp/listofj.asp
This journal is primarily concerned with issues of policy and education management. It publishes articles and research with relevance for senior managers and policymakers.

International Journal of Educational Management
ISSN: 0951–354X
Emerald (North America)
44 Brattle Street, 4th Floor, Cambridge, Massachusetts, 02138
T: +1 888 622 0075
www.emeraldinsight.com/iejm.htm
This journal addresses the role of managers in the field of education against a background of changes in structures and philosophy, and diminishing resources. Seven issues appear each year covering topics such as resource allocation, the management and development of professional staff, and the government of educational institutions.

Journal of Educational Administration
ISSN: 0957–8234
Emerald (North America)
44 Brattle Street, 4th Floor, Cambridge, Massachusetts, 02138
T: +1 888 622 0075
F: +44 (0) 1274 785200
www.emeraldinsight.com/jea.htm
This academic journal is published five times a year. It focuses on the challenges facing educational administrators and reports on relevant research in this field. Coverage includes leadership styles, policy formulation, quality and evaluation, performance measurement, and organizational processes in schools.

School Administrator
ISSN: 0036–6439
American Association of School Administrators
1801 North Moore Street, Arlington, Virginia, 22209–1813
T: +1 703 528 0700
F: +1 703 841 1543
www.aasa.org/publications/sa
The official magazine of the AASA is published 11 times a year and aims to provide practical information for district level school administrators in the United States. Each issue focuses on a theme from the area of school system practices, policies, and programs, and includes feature articles, news items, personal profiles, book reviews, and information on resources for school management.

School Leadership and Management
ISSN: 1363–2434
Carfax
Suite 800, 325 Chestnut Street, Philadelphia, Pennsylvania, 19106
T: +1 215 625 8900
F: +1 215 625 8914
www.tandf.co.uk/journals/carfax/13632434.html
This is a quarterly journal that addresses issues relating to school management. Its content consists of articles, research news, and book reviews.

INTERNET

Education 2000
www.education2000.co.uk
Designed for managers and administrators in schools, colleges, and universities, this site provides a directory of Web links, a database of suppliers of goods and services for education, and news.

ERIC Clearinghouse on Educational Management 
http://eric.uoregon.edu
This site offers a comprehensive collection of resources and links for practitioners and policymakers covering issues and trends in educational management. It also contains a directory of organizations and listings of journals and publishers in the field.

Schoolmanager.net
www.schoolmanager.net
This is a free service provided by the U.K. Stationery Office, featuring guidance on management issues relevant to schools, as well as news, links, and an online marketplace for suppliers.

ORGANIZATIONS

USA

American Association of School Administrators
1801 North Moore Street, Arlington, Virginia, 22209–1813
T: +1 703 528 0700
F: +1 703 841 1543
E: info@aasa.org
www.aasa.org
The AASA, founded in 1865, is a professional association for leaders in elementary and secondary education with over 14,000 members. It aims to enhance the professional development of school leaders and support excellence in school administration. It also seeks to raise awareness of educational issues within governmental bodies and the general public. Besides producing publications, it arranges conferences and seminars, and award, recognition, and scholarship programs, and has special interest groups.

American Association of University Administrators
2602 Rutford Avenue, Richardson, Texas, 75080–1470
T: +1 972 248 3957
F: +1 972 713 8209

"Perhaps one of the greatest advantages I have is that I am not educated in the academic sense."
(Jack Petchey)

www.aaua.org
The AAUA is a professional organization, founded in 1970, whose aims are to promote the professional development of those responsible for the administration of higher education, to encourage cooperation, and to represent the interests of its members. The AAUA has developed ethical and professional standards for administrators in higher education. It also publishes a quarterly newsletter and annually sponsors a national assembly.

Europe

Association of University Administrators
AUA National Office, University of Manchester, Oxford Road, Manchester, M13 9PL, U.K.
T: +44 (0) 161 275 2063
F: +44 (0) 161 275 2036
E: aua@man.ac.uk
www.aua.ac.uk
The AUA is a professional body for higher education administrators and managers which promotes excellence in higher education management in the United Kingdom and the Republic of Ireland. It was formed in 1993 through the merger of the Meeting of University Academic Administrative Staff (MUAAS) and the Association of Polytechnic Administrators (APA). Currently the AUA has 4,000 members, offers a range of networking and professional development activities including conferences, and operates a branch network.

British Educational Leadership, Management and Administration Society
BELMAS Office, Sheffield Hallam University, 36 Collegiate Crescent, Sheffield, South Yorkshire, S10 2BP, U.K.
T: +44 (0) 114 225 2328
F: +44 (0) 114 225 2324
E: bemas@shu.ac.uk
www.shu.ac.uk/bemas
The Society seeks to promote the practice, teaching, and study of educational management in the United Kingdom and internationally. Founded in 1971, it brings together practitioners, researchers, and providers of training and consulting in the field. Its activities include publications, conferences, and special interest groups.

Quality Assurance Agency for Higher Education
Southgate House, Southgate Street, Gloucester, Gloucestershire, GL1 1UB, U.K.
T: +44 (0) 1452 577000
F: +44 (0) 1452 557070
E: comms@qaa.ac.uk
www.qaa.ac.uk
The QAA is an independent body established in 1997 to promote public confidence in the quality and standard of educational provision. It conducts reviews and publishes reports on the performance of higher education institutions in the United Kingdom. A code of practice for quality and standards in education has been developed and the QAA is working with the higher education sector to introduce an integrated system of review.

The Staff and Educational Development Association
Selly Wick House, 59/61 Selly Wick Road, Selly Park, Birmingham, B29 7JE, U.K.
T: +44 (0) 121 415 6801
F: +44 (0) 121 415 6802
E: office@seda.ac.co.uk
www.seda.demon.co.uk
SEDA is a professional association for staff and educational developers in the United Kingdom, promoting innovation and good practice in higher education. It was formed in 1993 by the merger of the Standing Conference on Educational Development (SCED) and the Staff Development Group of the Society for Research into Higher Education (SRHE). The Association for Education and Training Technology merged with SEDA in 1996. Activities include the accreditation of professional development, conferences and similar events, and the award of SEDA Research and Development grants. The results of former rounds have been published in various journals and papers.

International

OECD Programme on Institutional Management in Higher Education
2 rue André-Pascal, 75775 Paris 16, France
T: +33 1 45 24 92 24
F: +33 1 42 24 02 11
E: imhe@oecd.org
www.oecd.org/els/education/higher
Founded in 1969, IMHE forms part of the OECD's Directorate for Education, Employment, Labour, and Social Affairs. It provides an international forum for administrators, researchers, and policymakers in higher education. Membership is open to institutions of higher education in OECD member countries. Activities include publications, seminars, study visits, training courses, and a biennial general conference.

Society for Research into Higher Education
3 Devonshire Street, London, W1N 2BA, U.K.
T: +44 (0) 20 7637 2766
F: +44 (0) 20 7637 2781
E: srheoffice@srhe.ac.uk
www.srhe.ac.uk
Established in 1965, the SRHE is an independent society that aims to improve the quality of higher education by stimulating and coordinating research in addition to encouraging debate on issues of policy, the organization and management of educational institutions, the curriculum, and teaching and learning methods. The individual members are researchers, teachers, and managers, while corporate members include higher educational institutions, research institutes, and professional and governmental bodies. Activities include an annual conference, publications, and special interest networks.

For More Information

- **Nonprofit Organizations (pp. 2056–58)**
- **Public Sector Management (pp. 2092–94)**

EMPLOYEE BENEFITS/COMPENSATION

BOOKS

The Compensation Handbook
LANCE A. BERGER, DOROTHY R. BERGER, EDS.
New York: McGraw-Hill, 1999
646pp ISBN: 0071343091
This updated and expanded edition is one of the classic books covering the field of employee compensation. The authors provide authoritative information written by experts in employee benefits and compensation. Topics covered include: base, variable, and executive compensation; measuring performance and compensation; and compensation trends and surveys.

The Executive Handbook on Compensation: Linking Strategic Rewards to Business Performance
CHARLES H. FAY, ET AL.
New York: Free Press, 2001
896pp ISBN: 0684842335
This book is written for managers at all levels of

"If the employees aren't satisfied, they won't promote the product we need." (Herb Kelleher)

  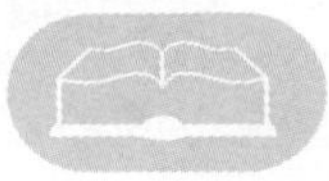    

experience and provides detailed information regarding employee compensation. The authors commissioned international compensation professionals to create this guide on linking employee compensation to performance. Topics include merging compensation and business goals, and designing effective and competitive compensation packages.

Flexible Benefits: A Practical Guide
Russ Watling
Philadelphia, Pennsylvania: Trans-Atlantic Publications, Inc., 1997
76pp (Financial Times Management Briefings)
ISBN: 0273631780
This publication examines the strategy that should underlie a benefits program and identifies the key issues to be considered in any feasibility study of the subject. These include the design of flexible benefits, the ways in which benefits can become flexible, and the employment benefits strategy. A case study of Mercury Communications is provided.

The Handbook of Employee Benefits
Jerry S. Rosenbloom, ed.
New York: McGraw-Hill, 2001
1322pp ISBN: 0071371834
This book is a comprehensive reference tool for creating and implementing employee benefits plans. The author compiled information written by employee benefits experts into a thorough guide for compensation professionals. Topics include current information on benefits legislation, a survey of current benefits issues, and details on creating and maintaining medical, death, flexible, and related benefits plans.

Pensions for Today
Confederation of British Industry
London: Caspian Publishing Ltd. in association with the CBI, 2001
80pp (Business Guide)
ISBN: 1901844218
This Confederation of British Industry guide explains the key issues within the changing pensions marketplace, including the introduction of stakeholder pensions, pan-European pension provision, the changing world of work, communicating the benefits, and pension provision in the future.

MAGAZINES

Benefits and Compensation International
ISSN: 0268–764X
Pension Publications Ltd.
East Wing, 4th Floor, Hope House, 45 Great Peter Street, London, SW1P 3LT, U.K.
T: +44 (0) 20 7222 0288
F: +44 (0) 20 7799 2163
www.benecompintl.com
This monthly magazine provides up-to-date information and analysis concerning employee benefits and remuneration trends aimed at multinational companies. A detailed country report is published twice a year.

Benefits Quarterly
ISSN: 8756–1263
International Society of Certified Employee Benefit Specialists
P.O. Box 209, Brookfield, Wisconsin, 53008–0209
T: +1 262 786 8771
F: +1 262 786 8650
www.iscebs.org
This journal provides an overview of the major issues facing benefits professionals. It covers areas such as employee communication, healthcare cost management, flexible benefits, work and family issues, and post-retirement benefits. Each issue includes a legal update and book reviews.

Compensation and Benefits Review
ISSN: 0886–3687
Sage Publications, Inc.
2455 Teller Road, Thousand Oaks, California, 91320
T: +1 805 499 0721
F: +1 805 499 0871
www.sagepub.com
This bimonthly journal focuses on compensation and benefits and how they affect, and are affected by, the changing nature of the workplace and the way companies do business. Thematic issues are published twice a year.

Employee Benefit News
ISSN: 1044–6265
Thomson Financial & IMG Media
11 Penn Plaza, 17th Floor, New York, 10001
T: +1 888 280 4820
F: +1 301 545 4836
www.benefitnews.com
Published 15 times per year, this magazine is the preeminent source of information on employee benefits. It provides coverage invaluable to employee benefits executives through comprehensive and useful articles that highlight the trends in all aspectss of this area of work.

Employee Benefits
ISSN: 1366–8722
Centaur Communications Ltd.
St. Giles House, 50 Poland Street, London, W1F 7AX, U.K.
T: +44 (0) 20 7970 4000
F: +44 (0) 20 7970 4392
www.centaur.co.uk/public/pub/gb/overview.asp
This monthly magazine aims to provide information to help companies align benefits with corporate objectives. The full spectrum of benefits is covered with news of new ideas and research.

Employee Benefits Journal
ISSN: 0361–4050
International Foundation of Employee Benefit Plans
18700 West Bluemound Road, P.O. Box 69, Brookfield, Wisconsin, 53008–0069
T: +1 262 786 6700
F: +1 262 786 8780
www.ifebp.org
This is a quarterly journal covering employee benefits and trends, mainly containing practical articles written by benefits experts.

Employer's Handbook: Complying with IRS Employee Benefits Rules
Thompson Publishing Group
P.O. Box 26185, Tampa, Florida, 33623–6185
T: +1 800 964 5815
F: +1 800 999 5661
www.thompson.com
This is a comprehensive and authoritative guide to help administrators ensure that benefits comply with federal regulations. Sample forms and documents are provided. The subscription includes a loose-leaf manual and monthly updates and newsletters.

Flex Plan Handbook
Thompson Publishing Group
P.O. Box 26185, Tampa, Florida, 33623–6185
T: +1 800 964 5815
F: +1 800 999 5661
www.thompson.com
This guide shows how to introduce and administer flexible benefits programs. Model plan documents and forms are included. The subscription includes a loose-leaf manual and quarterly updates and newsletters.

Pay and Benefits Bulletin
ISSN: 0143–8328
Industrial Relations Services
Eclipse Group Ltd., 18–20 Highbury Place, London, N5 1QP, U.K.
T: +44 (0) 20 7354 5858
F: +44 (0) 20 7359 4000
www.irseclipse.co.uk
This bulletin provides twice-monthly news on pay and benefits topics, pay reports, and statistical data.

INTERNET

BenefitsAlert.Com
www.benefitsalert.com

"The most un-American phrase in our modern vocabulary is 'take-home pay.'" (Vivian Kellems)

Sponsored by the Alexander Hamilton Institute, this site provides an array of information pertaining to employee compensation and benefits issues. The site includes free reports useful to employers, covering topics such as employee benefits, benefits forms, research, information on benefits laws written for the lay person, discussion areas, e-mail newsletters, and alerts.

BenefitsLink.com 
www.benefitslink.com
This large U.S. site is aimed at employers and provides news, compliance information, a question and answer service, links to articles, and a database of speakers.

Employee Benefit News
www.benefitnews.com
This site provides news and analysis of benefits issues and an e-mail newsletter. Registration is required.

Employee Benefits Interactive
www.employeebenefits.co.uk
The site includes a knowledge bank of articles from *Employee Benefits* magazine and a directory of service providers.

Employee Benefits Survey
www.bls.gov/ncs/ebs
This site provides access to data from the U.S. Bureau of Labor Statistics Employee Benefits Survey in PDF format.

National Employee Benefits Web Site
www.benefitslink.com
This site provides comprehensive information and links related to employee benefits plans and compliance issues for businesses of any size, as well as for employee benefits specialists. The resources include articles with current information, discussion areas involving compensation experts, links to government publications and regulations, conferences, directories of service providers, and a search engine dedicated to employee compensation issues.

Smart Benefits
www.smartbenefits.com
Information and links for benefits administrators are available on this site, including advice on choosing a plan.

ORGANIZATIONS

USA

American Benefits Council
1212 New York Avenue NW, Suite 1250, Washington, D.C., 20005
T: +1 202 289 6700
F: +1 202 289 4582
E: info@abcstaff.org
www.americanbenefitscouncil.org
The American Benefits Council serves as the business community's lobbying arm on employee benefits policy. Professionals in the benefits field can remain current through the organization's weekly e-mail updates on the latest legislative and regulatory developments.

Council on Employee Benefits
4910 Moorland Lane, Bethesda, Maryland, 20814
T: +1 301 664 5940
F: +1 301 664 5944
E: vschieber@ceb.org
www.ceb.org
CEB, founded in 1946, is an association of companies with an interest in the management of employee benefits programs. It provides opportunities for the exchange of ideas, information, and statistics, sponsors research, and runs an annual conference.

Employee Benefit Research Institute
Suite 600, 2121 K Street NW, Washington, D.C., 20037–1896
T: +1 202 659 0670
F: +1 202 775 6312
E: info@ebri.org
www.ebri.org
The EBRI was founded in 1978 with the aim of encouraging and contributing to the development of employee benefits programs through education and research on a nonprofit and nonpartisan basis. It conducts research, collects and disseminates information, and sponsors lectures, debates, discussions, and study groups on employee benefit plans. Publications include the *EBRI Databook on Employee Benefits*, *Fundamentals of Employee Benefit Programs*, and monthly *Notes* and *Issue Brief* studies.

Employers' Council on Flexible Compensation
927 15th Street NW, Suite 1000, Washington, D.C., 20005
T: +1 202 659 4300
F: +1 202 371 1467
E: info@ecfc.org
www.ecfc.org
The ECFC was founded in 1981 by a group of Fortune 500 companies to promote a favorable regulatory climate and public opinion for flexible compensation. The organization engages in lobbying activities and provides up-to-date information for members.

International

International Employee Benefits Association
c/o William M. Mercer, Telford House, 14 Tothill Street, London, SW1H 9NB, U.K.
T: +44 (0) 20 7802 3783
F: +44 (0) 20 7802 3786
www.ieba.org.uk
The IEBA was founded in 1994 to promote professionalism among those involved in the management of international employee benefits. It facilitates the exchange of information as well as providing information on employee benefits issues to governments and other organizations. It holds four meetings a year, including an AGM, and each focuses on a specific issue in the field.

International Foundation of Employee Benefit Plans
18700 West Bluemound Road, P.O. Box 69, Brookfield, Wisconsin, 53008–0069
T: +1 262 786 6700
F: +1 262 786 8780
E: membership@ifebp.org
www.ifebp.org
The IFEBP is a nonprofit educational association that provides training and information for the employee benefits and compensation industry in the United States and Canada. Its membership comprises 35,000 individuals from multiemployer trust funds, corporations, public employee groups, and advisory firms.

International Society of Certified Employee Benefit Specialists
P.O. Box 209, Brookfield, Wisconsin, 53008–0209
T: +1 262 786 8771
F: +1 262 786 8650
E: iscebs@iscebs.org
www.iscebs.org
Employee benefits specialists who have successfully completed the CEBS program of the International Foundation of Employee Benefit Plans are eligible for membership of the ISCEBS. The organization, founded in 1981, provides professional development, networking opportunities, and information resources for its 4,000 members, including the journal *Benefits Quarterly*, an annual symposium, and local chapters.

For More Information

- **Conditions of Employment (pp. 1933–35)**
- **Employee Participation in Management (pp. 1962–64)**
- **Employee Relations (pp. 1964–66)**
- **Employment Law (pp. 1967–69)**
- **Personnel Management and HR Management (pp. 2067–71)**
- **Remuneration (pp. 2103–05)**

"Wages are the price of labor." (John Richard Hicks)

EMPLOYEE PARTICIPATION IN MANAGEMENT

BOOKS

The American Workplace: Skills, Compensation, and Employee Involvement
CASEY ICHNIOWSKI, DAVID I. LEVINE, CRAIG OLSON, GEORGE STRAUSS
Cambridge: Cambridge University Press, 2000
304pp ISBN: 0521650283
This book is a summary of studies aimed at identifying the best practices to date for effective work environments. The authors look at specific industries (for example, the automotive, machine tools, apparel industries) as well as cross-industry studies of financial performance. The research and discussion focuses around three particular areas: the ''modular'' production approach as against the traditional assembly line, employee involvement practices, and TQM programs and their impact on financial performance.

Effective Employee Participation
LYNN TYLCZAK
Milford, Connecticut: Kogan Page, 1990
69pp (Better Management Skills Series)
ISBN: 0749402865
This book focuses on a discussion of the role which employees can play in improving, implementing, and refining processes, productivity, and morale through suggestion schemes and direct involvement. It explores the links between suggestion schemes and key value management tasks using case studies for illustration.

Employee Suggestion Systems: Boosting Productivity and Profits
CHARLES L. MARTIN, ROBERT BASSFORD
Menlo Park, California: Crisp Publications, 1997
103pp (Fifty-Minute Series)
ISBN: 15605 23956
This book offers an exploration of the variety of employee suggestion schemes available to companies.

Flight of the Buffalo: Soaring to Excellence, Learning to Let Employees Lead
JAMES A. BELASCO, RALPH C. STAYER
New York: Warner Books, 1994
355pp ISBN: 0446670081
This popular book uses the analogies of buffalos and geese to explain different ways of viewing leadership and followership. In so doing, the authors explore some of the shifts that are necessary to move from a traditional, hierarchical mode of running your business to one that is primarily employee-driven. Topics covered include leadership as a personal choice, what a ''transfer of ownership'' looks like, and how employees need to redefine their role with their bosses.

Ideas Unlimited: How to Run Suggestion Schemes Successfully
JAMES MCCONVILLE, ANDREW WOOD
London: Industrial Society, 1990
121pp ISBN: 0852904762
The authors introduce the concept of the suggestion plan and outline the practical steps involved in setting up and running a successful plan. Thirteen case studies of some of the most successful plans in the U.K. provide illustrations.

Innovation and Employee Participation through Works Councils: International Case Studies
RAYMOND MARKEY, JACQUES MONAT, EDS.
Burlington, Vermont: Avebury, 1997
474pp ISBN: 1859724345
This is a lengthy, research-based volume of case studies and national monographs on employee participation intended for managers, academics, and others interested in work organization. It focuses on works councils and similar bodies, and aims to contribute to informed discussion and debate in this field. The contributions come from academics and researchers all over the world.

Leading Self-directed Work Teams
KIMBALL FISHER
New York: McGraw-Hill, 1999
339pp ISBN: 0071349243
In this book Fisher describes the change in roles between management and employees that must occur for self-directed work teams (SDWTs) to succeed. Fisher discusses how SDWTs can be perceived as a threat to current management and how supervisors need to rethink their role. He offers results from situations where SDWTs are being used and also explains how technology is helping the movement toward SDWTs.

Managing Employee Involvement and Participation
JEFF HYMAN, BOB MASON
Thousand Oaks, California: Sage Publications, 1995
222pp ISBN: 0803987277
This textbook for students and others interested in management, HRM, and industrial relations offers an introduction to the complex topic of employee involvement and participation. The different ways in which employee influence can be articulated at work are examined, and two main strands of evolution are identified.

The Open-book Experience: Lessons from Over 100 Companies Who Successfully Transformed Themselves
JOHN CASE
Cambridge, Massachusetts: Perseus, 1999
256pp ISBN: 0738200409
This extremely practical, how-to book for business owners and managers reviews the principles of open-book management and explains it as a system, focusing on the implementation process in some detail. The experiences of companies that have implemented open-book management provide much of the basic material on implementation tools.

Open Space Technology: A User's Guide
HARRISON OWEN
San Francisco, California: Berrett-Koehler, 1997
173pp ISBN: 1576750248
This manual describes the author's ''Open Space Technology'' process and the concepts behind it. It is actually a lot simpler than it sounds and is based on the premise that when you bring together large groups of employees to problem-solve, it is better to give them an overall theme, then let them generate the topics of importance within that theme. Finally, instead of forcing them toward a particular topic, you should let them choose which ones they wish to pursue. By these means, the author would argue, you enable employee commitment to come forth naturally.

The Ownership Solution: Toward a Shared Capitalism for the Twenty-first Century
JEFFREY R. GATES
Cambridge, Massachusetts: Perseus, 1998
416pp ISBN: 0201328089
A visionary book dealing with the disparities between the rich and the disempowered in the world today.

Partnerships with People: Improving Business Performance through Your People
INSTITUTE OF DIRECTORS
Milford, Connecticut: Kogan Page, 1999
96pp ISBN: 0749428309

"When participation is suggested in terms of control over overall goals, it is usually a sham."
(Frederick Herzberg)

  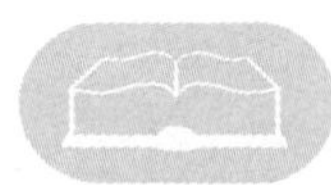    

Written from the executive perspective and aimed at directors and managers, this guidebook offers practical advice on developing a partnership approach that will involve people more in their work and gain their commitment to organizational goals. It contains contributions from various authors who focus upon different areas, relevant to partnership issues, such as corporate image, training, and quality.

MAGAZINES

Ideas Express
Ideas Management
4216 77th Avenue Court NW, Gig Harbour, Washington, D.C., 98335–6542
T: +1 253 265 2137
F: +1 253 265 2138
www.ideasmanagement.com/public.htm
This bimonthly magazine for suggestion plan and recognition professionals reviews the latest practices and trends and offers expert advice and ideas for implementing successful suggestion plans.

IPA Bulletin
Involvement and Participation Association
42 Colebrooke Row, London, N1 8AF, U.K.
T: +44 (0) 20 7354 8040
F: +44 (0) 20 7354 8041
www.ipa-involve.com
This is a monthly bulletin for IPA member companies on developments in partnership and employee involvement.

New Horizons
Employee Involvement Association
525 S.W. 5th Street, Suite A, Des Moines, Iowa, 50309–4501
T: +1 515 282 8192
F: +1 515 282 9117
www.eia.com
This quarterly journal features articles on aspects of the administration, maintenance, and promotion of employee involvement programs. It also provides information about the activities of the Employee Involvement Association and its branches.

INTERNET

Australian Employee Ownership Association
www.aeoa.org.au
This site is run by the Australian Employee Ownership Association. Some of it is open to nonmember visitors interested in employee ownership issues.

Employee Ownership Options
www.employee-ownership.org.uk
The site belongs to a regional consortium network called Employee Ownership Options, is managed by the National Federation of Worker Cooperatives, and was set up with assistance from the EU ADAPT program to provide information on employee ownership options for all those involved with organizations facing closure due to financial or succession problems.

Employee Participation
www.socrates.berkeley.edu/~iir/cohre/darshan/participation
This site, sponsored by the University of California at Berkeley, offers case studies of companies who have had success with employee involvement initiatives. The site also provides background on the theory and history of employee involvement as well as some suggested reading. Lastly, the site provides links to other sites that focus on employee involvement efforts and research.

Ideas Management
www.ideasmanagement.com
This site belongs to an organization providing specialist consulting, training, and software advice on all aspects of company suggestion plans.

Involvement and Participation Association
www.ipa-involve.com/internet/publications/students.htm
The site gives brief information on IPA student services and an opportunity to download free copies of *Towards Industrial Partnership* and IPA case studies.

Ping
www.ping.be/fas
This Internet portal was set up by the European Federation of Employee Shareownership (EFES), based in Brussels, to organize the international exchange of information on employee ownership and participation and to offer links to other relevant databases and sites.

The Association for Quality and Participation
www.aqp.org
This professional association consists of those who are trying to find ways to involve employees more fully in the running of their respective organizations. The site has information about educational programs and seminars, as well as directions for joining the national or a local chapter. It also offers information on publications and a monthly e-newsletter.

ORGANIZATIONS

USA

Employee Involvement Association
525 SW 5th Street, Suite A, Des Moines, Iowa, 50309–4501
T: +1 515 282 8192
F: +1 515 282 9117
E: eia@eianet.org
www.eia.com
Founded in 1948 as the National Association of Suggestion Schemes, this nonprofit professional body became the Employee Involvement Association in 1992. It aims to promote the use of employee suggestion plans and other processes that encourage networking and the exchange of ideas.

National Center for Employee Ownership
8th Floor, 1736 Franklin Street, Oakland, California, 94612
T: +1 510 208 1300
F: +1 510 272 9510
E: nceo@nceo.org
www.nceo.org
A nonprofit, private membership and research organization that seeks to act as a source of unbiased information on employee stock-ownership plans (ESOPs), employee stock options, and employee participation. It offers a library, newsletters, and links from its Web site to related sites.

Europe

Employee Share Ownership (Esop) Centre Ltd.
2 Ridgmount Street, London, WC1E 7AA, U.K.
T: +44 (0) 20 7436 9936
F: +44 (0) 20 7580 0016
E: esop@mhcc.co.uk
www.mhcc.co.uk/esop
The Centre is a nonprofit, membership organization that supports employee share ownership development in the United Kingdom and Europe. It produces publications, organizes events and research, and offers support in starting and operating all forms of broad-based employee share schemes, including SAYE-Sharesave or profit-share schemes, and all-employee share-option or ownership plans (AESOPs).

ICOM (Industrial Common Ownership Movement Ltd.)
74 Kirkgate, Leeds, Yorkshire, LS2 7DJ, U.K.
T: +44 (0) 113 2461737
F: +44 (0) 113 2440002
E: icom@org.uk
www.icof.co.uk/icom
A national, voluntary membership organization for cooperatives and other businesses democratically controlled by employees, ICOM provides legal and registration services, training programs, publications, and information. Its aim

"Many companies say they want to change, but they need to empower people below." (Marvin Bower)

is to promote the democratic control and ownership of enterprises by those who work within them.

ideasUK
Broadway House, 28 Bexley Road, Bangor, Gwynedd, BT19 7TS, U.K.
T: +44 (0) 870 902 1658
F: +44 (0) 870 902 1658
E: enquiries@ideasUK.com
www.ideasuk.com
This nonprofit membership organization is dedicated to supporting and developing the growth of suggestion and employee involvement programs through networking and the exchange of knowledge and best practice. Founded in 1986 as the United Kingdom Association of Suggestion Schemes, it adopted ideasUK as its trading name in 1998.

Involvement and Participation Association
42 Colebrooke Row, London, N1 8AF, U.K.
T: +44 (0) 20 7354 8040
F: +44 (0) 20 7354 8041
E: involve@ipa-involve.com
www.ipa-involve.com
The Association is a nonprofit organization with charitable status that aims to help organizations to develop working practices and strategies for employee involvement and partnership. It acts as a focal point for best practice, and offers advice and support to members, as well as a monthly bulletin on new developments in the field.

Mondragon Cooperative Corporation (Mondragón Corporación Cooperativa)
Pa José Maria, Arizmendiarrieta, No. 5, 20500 Mondragón, Guipúzcoa, Spain
T: +34 943 779 300
F: +34 943 796 632
E: wm@mcc.es
www.mondragon.mcc.es
MCC is a large-scale, cooperatively based business corporation in the Basque country of Spain that also provides education and social welfare for its members.

The Centre for Tomorrow's Company
19 Buckingham Street, London, WC2N 6EF, U.K.
T: +44 (0) 20 7930 5150
F: +44 (0) 20 7930 5155
E: info@tomorrowscompany.com
www.tomorrowscompany.com
The Centre is a research and policy-focused organization, founded in 1996. It aims to enable businesses to achieve success through a more inclusive approach to management.

The European Study Group
Building 2, Brunel Science Park, Kingston Lane, Uxbridge, Middlesex, UB8 3PQ, U.K.
T: +44 (0) 1895 812993
F: +44 (0) 1895 812991
E: info@european-study-group.com
www.european-study-group.com
This nonprofit association of multinational employers was formed originally as the European Works Council Study Group by eight senior HR executives. Now with a wider membership group, it has become a broader forum for considering aspects of employee information and consultation linked to European social policy and legislation.

International Employee Ownership and Incentives Association
3683 West 4th Avenue, Vancouver, British Columbia, V6R 1P2, Canada
T: +1 604 687 3767
F: +1 604 687 3770
E: eoi@esopcanada.org
www.esopcanada.org
The EOIA is a national, nonprofit research and education association in Canada whose objective is to foster broad-based employee ownership, stock options, employee involvement, and nonequity employee incentives. It offers courses, publications, a library, and consulting support for members.

International Co-operative Alliance
15, route des Morillons, 1218 Grand-Saconnex, Geneva, Switzerland
T: +41 (0) 22 929 88 88
F: +41 (0) 22 798 41 22
E: ica@coop.org
www.coop.org/ica
The ICA is an international, nongovernmental organization which unites, represents, and serves cooperatives worldwide. Details of members from Europe and elsewhere are available from the ICA Web site, together with information on the cooperative movement, the development of cooperatives, and related issues.

For More Information

- Conditions of Employment (pp. 1933–35)
- Employee Benefits/ Compensation (pp. 1959–61)
- Motivation (pp. 2050–52)
- Personnel Management and HR Management (pp. 2067–71)

Employee Relations

BOOKS

The Changing Nature of Work
Frank Ackerman, Neva R. Goodwin, Laurie Dougherty, Kevin Gallagher, eds.
Washington, D.C.: Island Press, 1998
417pp ISBN: 1559636653
This volume presents summaries of 86 articles on almost every aspect of work. The book has sections devoted to emerging industrial relations issues such as alternative forms of work organization and work councils. It also covers globalization and labor, new technologies and work organization, diversity in the workplace, and flexibility versus security.

Employee Relations in Context 2nd ed.
David Farnham
New York: Beekman, 2000
432pp ISBN: 0846450410
Employee Relations in Context aims to provide a definitive, single-volume survey of ER in the United Kingdom, taking a managerial perspective on the subject, and including an account of recent legal, political, and social changes. Although it is a lengthy textbook aimed at students and practitioners, the writing is clear and concise, and the handling of the subject is thoughtful.

The Employment Relationship: A Psychological Perspective
Peter Herriot
New York: Psychology Press (Routledge), 2001
256pp ISBN: 1841692395
This book, aimed particularly at managers and occupational psychologists, gives an unusual, psychologist's perspective on employment relations. It discusses some complex ideas, using metaphors to help the understanding of organizational employment relations and to highlight features of the employment relationship and its psychology.

"You cannot love an employee into creativity, although you can. . .avoid his dissatisfactions with the way you treat him."
(Frederick Herzberg)

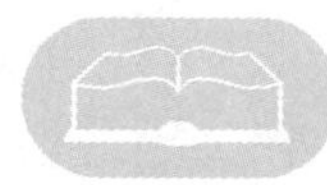

Exploring Employee Relations
Mike Leat
Woburn, Massachusetts: Butterworth-Heinemann, 2001
320pp ISBN: 075064396X
This is a student textbook, aimed at those on undergraduate, postgraduate, and professional courses, which provides a grounding in the theory and practice of employee relations. It focuses on the employment relationship, the nature of work, globalization and employee relations, and the political and legal aspects. Each chapter includes student activities, with answers and feedback, and summaries of key points.

Love 'Em or Lose 'Em: Getting Good People to Stay
Beverly L. Kaye, Sharon Jordan-Evans
San Francisco, California: Berrett-Koehler, 1999
233pp ISBN: 1576750736
This book explores a major problem facing employers: the fact that the best employees, the ones you simply cannot afford to lose, are the ones who find it easiest to move on. The book presents strategies for retaining the best and brightest, including creating connections, providing recognition, telling the truth, sharing information, reconsidering rules, enhancing rewards, yielding responsibility, and listening.

The New Deal at Work: Managing the Market-driven Workforce
Peter Cappelli
Boston, Massachusetts: Harvard Business School Press, 1999
320pp ISBN: 0875846688
A new employment relationship has emerged from the 1990s context of downsizing and restructuring, according to this book for managers, employment relations specialists, and observers of corporate life. In addition to describing the new relationship, the author also discusses the ways in which it is changing the practice of employee management and introducing the force of the market into internal management practices.

Securing Prosperity: The American Labor Market: How It Has Changed and What to Do About It
Paul Osterman
Princeton, New Jersey: Princeton University Press, 1999
240pp ISBN: 0691010110
This book examines the forces that have impacted the American workplace over the past decade, especially globalization and the new market economy, that have shifted the balance of power between workers and managers. It looks at the effects of restructuring organizations to increase productivity, the advent of new technologies, and the effects of these changes on the employment contract. The author recommends new policies for a workforce that is becoming increasingly mobile.

What's Next for Organized Labor? The Report of The Century Foundation Task Force on the Future of Unions
Nelson Lichtenstein
New York: Century Foundation Press, 1998
120pp ISBN: 0870784188
This book contains a report by a task force of business, labor, and political leaders who examined the need for and the future of unions. The task force found that unions are the only mechanism that has proved effective in helping workers gain influence in the workplace over the long term, and made recommendations for rebuilding them, including changes to make them more popular and combat their falling membership. The book includes a background paper that analyzes the history of the labor movement, highlighting its successes and failures.

MAGAZINES

Employee Relations
ISSN: 0142–5455
MCB University Press Ltd.
60/62 Toller Lane, Bradford, Yorkshire, BD8 9BY, U.K.
T: +44 (0) 1274 777700
F: +44 (0) 1274 785200
www.emeraldinsight.com/er.htm
This bimonthly journal is aimed at academics and key HR practitioners, and its main focus is on good employee relations as a commercial necessity for efficiency and productivity. Its coverage draws on the latest ideas and research in employment relations, as well as best practice in the field.

European Industrial Relations Review
ISSN: 0309–7234
Eclipse Group Ltd., Industrial Relations Services
18–20 Highbury Place, London, N5 1QP, U.K.
T: +44 (0) 20 7354 5858
F: +44 (0) 20 7359 4000
www.irseclipse.co.uk
This monthly journal for managers, employers, and employees provides coverage of employment practice and relations across Europe. Its contents usually include analytical articles, case studies, recent news from 18 countries, comparisons, surveys, and legal reviews.

Industrial Relations Journal
ISSN: 0019–8692
Blackwell Publishers
350 Main Street, Malden, Massachusetts, 02148
T: +1 781 388 8200
F: +1 781 388 8232
www.blackwellpublishers.com/journals/irj
Intended for academics, practitioners, and policymakers, the *Journal* is published five times a year and also brings out an annual review and a twice-yearly companion publication called *New Technology, Work and Employment*. It reports on new developments and academic research in the field of industrial relations, seeking to be a bridge between the interests of academics and practitioners.

International Labour Review
ISSN: 0020–7780
International Labour Organization
IIRA Secretariat, c/o RELPROF, International Labour Office, 4, route des Morillons, CH-1211 Geneva 22, Switzerland
T: +41 22 799 7903
F: +41 22 799 6117
www.ilo.org/public/english/support/publ/revue
This quarterly journal, aimed at policymakers and academic and other researchers, contains academic papers on the international labor market and labor issues.

IRS Employment Review
ISSN: 0046–9246
Eclipse Group Ltd., Industrial Relations Services
18–20 Highbury Place, London, N5 1QP, U.K.
T: +44 (0) 20 7354 5858
F: +44 (0) 20 7359 4000
www.irseclipse.co.uk
The *Review* is a twice-monthly publication providing impartial information on industrial relations, personnel and human resource issues, employment law, health-and-safety and environmental questions, occupational health, pay, and pensions, for both employers or managers and employees. It encompasses five journals or bulletins: *IRS Employment Trends*, *Pay and Benefits Bulletin*, *Industrial Relations Law Bulletin*, *Employee Development Bulletin*, and *Employee Health Bulletin*.

INTERNET

Bureau of Labor Statistics
www.bls.gov

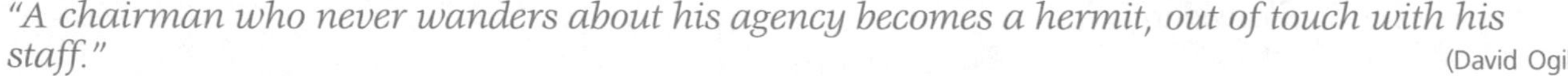
"A chairman who never wanders about his agency becomes a hermit, out of touch with his staff."
(David Ogilvy)

This U.S. government site is a rich source of statistics and data about labor and employment as well as publications and press releases. It provides information about such topics as wages and employment, productivity, health and safety, the state of the economy, and demographics.

ILR Catherwood Library
www.ilr.cornell.edu/library/reference/guides
This site links to a number of informative sites concerned with labor unions, labor law and labor history, industrial action, and online newsletters and magazines related to these issues.

Swarb.co.uk
www.swarb.co.uk
Free legal information is available from this site. It can be searched using the keyword "employment" to find information on employment law and relevant case records.

The Department of Trade and Industry's Employment Relations
www.dti.gov.uk/employment
This, the U.K. Department of Trade and Industry's employment relations site, holds a variety of information on employment issues, including booklets on legislation, gives guidance, and offers links to other Web sites.

ORGANIZATIONS

USA

American Benefits Council
1212 New York Avenue NW, Suite 1250, Washington, D.C., 20005
T: +1 202 289 6700
F: +1 202 289 4582
E: info@abcstaff.org
www.americanbenefitscouncil.org
The American Benefits Council serves as the business community's lobbying arm on employee benefits policy. Professionals in the benefits field can remain current through the organization's weekly e-mail updates on the latest legislative and regulatory developments.

Association of Labor Relations Agencies
110 Second Street, SE, Congressional Office of Compliance, Washington, D.C., 20540
T: +1 202 724 9250
F: +1 202 426 1913
E: tworley@serb.state.oh.us
www.alra.org
This association comprises impartial nonprofit and government agencies that monitor labor-management relations, laws and regulations. The association has a special interest in promoting the public interest in labor relations. The ALRA promotes the peaceful resolution of labor-management disputes.

International Society of Certified Employee Benefit Specialists
P.O. Box 209, Brookfield, Wisconsin, 53008
T: +1 262 786 8771
F: +1 262 786 8650
E: iscebs@iscebs.org
www.iscebs.org
This society of over 3,500 members encourages the professional development of employee benefit practitioners. The society prides itself on providing career-specific materials that cover all areas of employee benefits. This exclusive organization requires members to be graduates of one or more specialized programs.

Europe

Advisory Conciliation and Arbitration Services
Brandon House, 180 Borough High Street, London, SE1 1LW, U.K.
T: +44 (0) 20 7210 3911
F: +44 (0) 20 7210 3708
E: library@acas.org.uk
www.acas.org.uk
ACAS is a U.K. statutory body providing an impartial conciliation and arbitration service for the resolution of employment disputes. It also provides information and advice and seeks to promote good practice in employment and workplace relations.

Central Arbitration Committee
Third Floor, Discovery House, 28–42 Banner Street, London, EC1Y 8QE, U.K.
T: +44 (0) 20 7251 9747
F: +44 (0) 20 7251 3114
E: enquiries@cac.gov.uk
www.cac.gov.uk
The Committee arbitrates disputes over trade union recognition arising from the U.K. Employment Relations Act 1999 and complaints from trade unions regarding employers' failures to disclose information for collective bargaining.

Institute of Employment Rights
177 Abbeville Road, London, SW4 9RL, U.K.
T: +44 (0) 20 7498 6919
F: +44 (0) 20 7498 9080
E: ier@gn.apc.org
www.ier.org.uk
The Institute is an independent think-tank aiming to provide a center for disseminating ideas related to the labor movement and labor law. It is involved in research, conferences, meetings, and seminars, and produces pamphlets on various aspects of labor and employment.

Trades Union Congress
Congress House, Great Russell Street, London, WC1B 3LS, U.K.
T: +44 (0) 20 7636 4030
F: +44 (0) 20 7636 0632
E: info@tuc.org.uk
www.tuc.org.uk
The TUC is the representative organization for the U.K. trade union movement.

International

International Industrial Relations Association
Administration Department, International Labour Office, 4, route des Morillons, CH-1211 Geneva 22, Switzerland
T: +41 22 799 6841
F: +41 22 799 8541
E: perret_n@ilo.org
www.ilo.org/public/english/dialogue/govlab/iira
The Association was established in 1966 to support the exchange of knowledge and information about employment relations at an international level and to create a forum for academic and practitioner discussion and research.

International Labour Organization
IIRA Secretariat, c/o RELPROF, International Labour Office, 4, route des Morillons, CH-1211 Geneva 22, Switzerland
T: +41 22 799 6111
F: +41 22 798 8685
E: ilo@ilo.org
www.ilo.org
The central role of the ILO is to generate and disseminate knowledge about the world of work, and it has offices in many countries in addition to its headquarters in Switzerland.

For More Information

- ☆ **Making Loyalty Work (pp. 289–90)**
- **Conditions of Employment (pp. 1933–35)**
- **Employee Benefits/ Compensation (pp. 1959–61)**
- **Employee Participation in Management (pp. 1962–64)**
- **Employment Law (pp. 1967–69)**
- **Recruitment and Selection (pp. 2099–2101)**

"I'm the boss. I'm allowed to yell." (Ivan Boesky)

EMPLOYMENT LAW

BOOKS

ADA Compliance Guide 2nd ed.
CHARLES D. GOLDMAN, ED.
Washington, D.C.: Thompson Publishing Group
The *Americans With Disabilities Act Compliance Guide* (updated monthly) is a handy reference source for understanding the complexities of the employment provisions of the ADA. Written in plain English, the Guide explains the meaning of ''disability,'' ''reasonable accommodation,'' and ''undue hardship.'' It also contains information on the nonemployment provision accessibility standards.

Covenants Not to Compete: A State-by-state Survey 2nd ed.
BRIAN M. MALSBERGER
Washington, D.C.: BNA Books, 1996 (Supp. 2001)
1275pp ISBN: 157018030X
Written for attorneys, this supplemented volume covers a growing practice area in U.S. law—the protection of an employer's trade secrets and other confidential information. Organized by the state, it covers state statutes governing restrictive covenants and the extent to which a covenant may be forced against an employee.

Employment, Disability, and the Americans with Disabilities Act: Issues in Law, Public Policy, and Research
PETER BLANCK, ED.
Evanston, Illinois: Northwestern University Press, 2000
488pp (Psychological Issues)
ISBN: 081011688X
This is a collection of scholarly essays on employment law, especially as it relates to the Americans with Disabilities Act (ADA). It includes bibliographical references and indexes.

Employment Discrimination 2nd ed.
LEX K. LARSON
New York: Matthew Bender (Lexis), 1994 (Supp. 1999)
ISBN: 0820516260
Larson on *Employment Discrimination* is a law library standard. This is a multivolume treatise (updated with loose-leaf supplements) providing comprehensive coverage relating to employment discrimination based on race, sex, religion, national origin, age, disability and union membership.

Employment Discrimination Law 3rd ed.
BARBARA LINEMANN, PAUL GROSSMANN
Washington, D.C.: BNA Books, 1996 (Supp. 2000)
2356pp ISBN: 0871797917
Employment Discrimination Law has been the long accepted standard treatise in the field. It comprises two hardcover volumes, plus the supplement, and offers a balanced, indepth presentation of issues from legal specialists representing every practice perspective.

Employment Law: New Challenges in the Business Environment 2nd ed.
JOHN JUDE MORAN
Upper Saddle River, New Jersey: Prentice Hall, 2001
594pp ISBN: 0130896071
Aimed at Human Resource Managers and those in the legal profession, this book deals with the subject by taking a simple approach to employment law with a foundation of legal principles explained in language that is easy to understand. The text discusses the overall employment relationship and discrimination topics such as sex, race, age, gender, religion, and AIDS. It looks at the regulatory aspects of employment and presents several sample cases and hypothetical situations in every chapter to illustrate the employment law problems that small businesses confront.

The Fair Labor Standards Act
ELLEN K. KEARNS
Washington, D.C.: BNA Books, 1999 (Supp. 2000)
1750pp ISBN: 1570181058
This is a treatise covering one of the oldest U.S. employment laws, the FLSA, which covers virtually every employee and employer in the United States. This volume provides point-by-point evaluations of each FLSA exemption to determine worker status under the law, as well as possible strategies for dealing with enforcement, remedies, and litigation.

The Family and Medical Leave Act, the Americans with Disabilities Act, and Title VII of the Civil Rights Act of 1964
U.S. EQUAL EMPLOYMENT OPPORTUNITY COMMISSION'S OFFICE OF LEGAL COUNSEL
Washington, D.C.: U.S. Equal Employment Opportunity Commission, 1995
24pp
This fact sheet provides technical assistance and discusses the interrelationship of these three federal statutes. It includes bibliographical references, and is available on order from the Equal Employment Opportunity Commission's Web site (www.eeoc.gov/publications.html).

Foundations of Employment Discrimination Law
JOHN DONOHUE III
New York: Foundation Press, 1997
445pp (Interdisciplinary Readers in Law)
ISBN: 1566629918
This book presents a broad collection of edited readings covering the general development of the law from a variety of perspectives including history, philosophy, economics, law, sociology, politics, and psychology. Its two sections, one on race discrimination and the other on sex discrimination, consider the theoretical and empirical foundations of the law, its operation, and its impact.

Fundamentals of Employment Law
KAREN FORD, KERRY NOTESTINE, RICHARD HILL, EDS.
Chicago, Illinois: American Bar Association Tort and Insurance Practice, 2000
774pp ISBN: 1570738068
This guide serves as an introduction to a rapidly expanding area of litigation. The book is a reference tool written by attorneys at a major employment law firm, offering a clear, concise look at key topics in the employment law field. As well as offering practical advice, it summarizes the federal equal employment opportunity laws that apply to most employment situations, and provides an overview of relevant legislation and court decisions on a variety of topics.

Unjust Dismissal
LEX K. LARSON
New York: Matthew Bender (Lexis), 1984
ISBN: 0820517798
This 3-volume binder set focuses mainly on employment law topics outside of discrimination issues, including employee handbooks and personnel manuals, free speech and privacy in the workplace, whistleblowing, and drug and alcohol screening.

MAGAZINES

HR Magazine
ISSN: 1047-3149
Society for Human Resource Management
1800 Duke Street, Alexandria, Virginia, 22314
T: +1 703 548 3440
F: +1 703 535 6490

"You might as well try to employ a boa constrictor as a tape-measure as to go to a lawyer for legal advice."
(Oliver St. John Gregory)

www.shrm.org
HR Magazine is published by SHRM, the world's largest human resource management association. The magazine is a monthly subscription publication that provides indepth coverage and feature articles on all aspects of the HR profession.

Human Resource Executive
LRP Publications
Human Resource Executive, 747 Dreshner Rd, Ste. 500, Horsham, Pennsylvania, 19044–0980
T: +1 215 784 0941
F: +1 215 784 9639
www.hrexecutive.com
Human Resource Executive is a subscription based monthly magazine focusing on strategic issues in human resources. Its stories cover all elements of human resource management including personnel, benefits, training and development, HR information systems, relocation, retirement planning, workplace security, and healthcare.

Workforce
ISSN: 1092-8332
ACC Communications, Inc.
245 Fischer Avenue, B-2, Costa Mesa, California, 92626
T: 714 751 1883
F: 714 751 4406
www.workforce.com
This is a subscription based monthly magazine that deals with emerging issues in human resources and employment law. Articles range from handling individual employee issues to developing strategic workplace initiatives.

INTERNET

BenefitsLink
www.benefitslink.com
BenefitsLink is one of the oldest law sites on the Web. It offers compliance information and tools about employee benefit plans sponsored by private or governmental employers in the United States. The site contains recent articles on employee benefits, links to key government documents, and an ''ask the experts'' Q&A forum.

Context
www.justis.com
Context provides a vast range of legal material on CD-ROM and on the Internet. From an employment law angle, it provides the internet version of the official employment law case reports, known as ICR, produced by the Incorporated Council of Law Reporting.

Employment Law Information Network
www.elinfonet.com
The Employment Law Information Network is an employment law portal site containing thousands of links to employment law content on the Web. This site contains links to U.S. employment law statutes and regulations, employment law articles, and example human resource policies, forms, and contracts. The site also contains a discussion forum where visitors can post their employment law questions.

Findlaw
www.findlaw.com
Findlaw, the legal media site (now owned by West Group) contains information and links to information on virtually every aspect of U.S. law, including employment law. The employment law section includes links to databases, government agencies, sample legal documents, employment law articles, and related Web sites.

Incomes Data Services
www.incomesdata.co.uk/brief/law.htm
The site offers news, reports, and guidance on a wide range of British employment law issues. There is some free information; otherwise you are directed to the extensive range of IDS published products.

U.S. Department of Labor
www.dol.gov
The U.S. Department of Labor is responsible for the administration and enforcement of over 180 federal statutes, covering areas from wages and hours to family and medical leave. The DOL's Web site was redesigned in August 2001 and contains a vast array of legal compliance information, including ''elaw Advisors''—interactive tools that provide information about federal employment laws.

U.S. Equal Employment Opportunity Commission (EEOC)
www.eeoc.gov
The EEOC is the primary federal agency that enforces the U.S. employment discrimination statutes (protecting employees from discrimination on the basis of protected traits like race, sex, age, and disability status). The Commission's site includes a wide variety of primary source documents on U.S. employment laws, including statutory and regulation text, enforcement guidance, and the Commission's compliance manual. Information is available for both employees and employers, much of which is written in non-technical terms for the layman.

WorkIndex
www.workindex.com
WorkIndex.com provides a comprehensive index of workplace related Web sites (over 3,000) as well as human resource tools and information. The site is produced and maintained by the publishers of *Human Resource Executive* magazine, in cooperation with Cornell University's School of Industrial Labor Relations. It offers business book abstracts, book reviews, a salary calculator, HR news and a place to test HR software. Users can consult a legal clinic, post and search jobs, and read best practice reports.

ORGANIZATIONS

USA

American Management Association (AMA)
1601 Broadway, New York, 10019
T: +1 212 586 8100
F: +1 212 903 8168
E: customerservice@amanet.org
www.amanet.org
One of the world's leading nonprofit membership-based educational organizations, the AMA offers a range of business education and management development programs for individuals and enterprises in the Americas, Europe, and Asia. It identifies best management practices worldwide to provide assessment, design, development, self-development, and instruction services through a variety of print and electronic media and learning methodologies, including conferences and seminars, all designed to enhance the growth of individuals and organizations.

Society for Human Resource Management (SHRM)
1800 Duke Street, Alexandria, Virginia, 22314
T: +1 703 548 3440
F: +1 703 535 6490
www.shrm.org
SHRM is the world's largest human resource management association. It provides education and information services, conferences and seminars, government and media representation, online services, and publications to more than 165,000 professional and student members around the world.

Europe

Advisory, Conciliation and Arbitration Service (ACAS)
Rita Donaghy OBE
Brandon House, 180 Borough High Street, London, SE1 1LW, U.K.
T: +44 (0) 20 7396 5100
www.acas.org.uk
ACAS is a nationwide organization (with its head office in London) of employment relations experts. It has been working with employers, employees, trade unions, and other representatives for more than 25 years. The

organization has a network of telephone helplines giving free help and information, and the Advisory Service works with hundreds of companies every year to develop a joint approach to problem solving. Most cases going to an employment tribunal are first of all referred to ACAS to see if there is a less damaging and expensive way of sorting the problem out. The organization also runs workshops and seminars around the country, targeting small businesses without specialist personnel sections.

Chartered Institute of Personnel and Development
Geoffrey Armstrong, Director General
CIPD House, Camp Road, London, SW19 4UX, U.K.
T: +44 (0) 20 8971 9000
F: +44 (0) 20 8263 3333
E: cipd@cipd.co.uk
www.cipd.co.uk
Formed in 1995 from the amalgamation of the Institute of Personnel Management and the Institute of Training and Development, the CIPD is a professional body for personnel and training professionals which aims to promote good practice in the management and development of people.

International

International Labour Organization (ILO)
Juan Somavia
International Labour Office, 4, route des Morillons, CH-1211 Geneva 22, Switzerland
T: +41 22 799 6111
F: +41 22 798 8685
E: ilo@ilo.org
www.ilo.org
The ILO is the United Nations specialized agency with international responsibilities for work and employment issues. Governments, employers and trade unions all participate in its work and decision making processes. The primary goal of the ILO today is to promote opportunities for men and women to obtain decent work and income, in conditions of freedom, equity, security, and human dignity.

For More Information

- **Conditions of Employment (pp. 1933–35)**
- **Contracts and Contracting (pp. 1941–42)**
- **Employee Benefits/ Compensation (pp. 1959–61)**
- **Employee Relations (pp. 1964–66)**
- **Equal Opportunities (pp. 1975–77)**
- **Personnel Management and HR Management (pp. 2067–71)**

Entrepreneurs

Books

The Adventure Capitalists: The Success Secrets of Twelve High-achieving Entrepreneurs
Jeff Grout, Lynne Curry
Milford, Connecticut: Kogan Page, 1999
224pp ISBN: 0749426381
This book explores the dynamics of entrepreneurial success through the stories of some of Britain's best-known contemporary entrepreneurs. These include: Sir Terence Conran, designer, founder of Habitat and various eating houses; Ron Dennis, head of McLaren International; Peter de Savary; Greg Dyke, former head of the television and media group Pearson; Barry Hearn, sports promoter; Prue Leith, journalist and catering entrepreneur; David Lloyd, famous for his tennis and fitness centers; Rick Parry, sports entrepreneur; Anita Roddick, founder of The Body Shop; Jack Rowell, rugby union coach; Lord Sheppard, former chairman and chief executive of Grand Metropolitan; and Chris Wright, chairman of Chrysalis Group plc.

The Entrepreneurial Mindset: Strategies for Continuously Creating Opportunity in an Age of Uncertainty
Rita Gunther McGrath, Ian MacMillan
Boston, Massachusetts: Harvard Business School Press, 2000
400pp ISBN: 0875848346
This book addresses the question of how large organizations and entrepreneurs can succeed in starting new businesses in an age of increasing uncertainty. It draws on examples from leading entrepreneurs and entrepreneurial companies, and on the results of research projects. It also provides practical guidance on developing an entrepreneurial mindset, identifying business opportunities, and redesigning products.

Entrepreneurship in the Global Firm
Julian Birkinshaw
Thousand Oaks, California: Sage Publications, 2000
256pp (Sage Strategy Series)
ISBN: 0761958096
Birkinshaw examines the dynamics affecting the growth and position of international firms, and shows that many changes result from the initiatives of subsidiary managers.

European Casebook on Entrepreneurship and New Ventures
David Molian, Benoit Leleux
Upper Saddle River, New Jersey: Prentice Hall, 1996
256pp (European Casebook Series on Management)
ISBN: 0133106810
This collection of case studies explores the development of the entrepreneur, the acquisition of resources, taking the business to market, managing the post-startup phase, and valuing and selling the business. The companies featured include Motivation Ltd., Robinson Instruments, Prestel and Minitel, Isis Scientific Software, MTL Instruments Group, Dockspeed Ltd., Advanced Business Computers Ltd., Pizza Pomodoro, and Naf-Naf.

The Guru Guide to Entrepreneurship: A Concise Guide to the Best Ideas from the World's Top Entrepreneurs
Joseph H. Boyett, Jimmie T. Boyett
New York: John Wiley, 2000
400pp ISBN: 0471390844
Drawing on the wisdom and experience of 70 of the world's leading entrepreneurs, this book examines the personal qualities of the successful entrepreneur, and considers what it takes to succeed in business.

The HP Way
David Packard
New York: HarperCollins, 1996
224pp ISBN: 0887308171
In this book, Packard charts the emergence of his technology business: Hewlett Packard. He attributes the company's success to the unique outlook of the firm, "The HP Way," which promotes a combination of openness, honesty, and flexibility. The book should interest both entrepreneurs and technologists alike, in demonstrating the growth of a major contemporary technology company.

Inside Intel: Andy Grove and the Rise of the World's Most Powerful Chip Company
Tim Jackson

"I want Britain to be a nation of entrepreneurs, a nation where talent and ability flourish."
(Tony Blair)

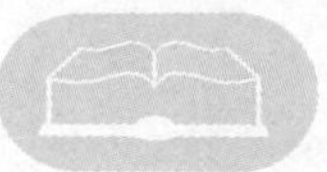

New York: Plume, 1998
432pp ISBN: 0452276438
Most of today's computers operate using Intel chips, and this book provides an account of how the company under CEO Andrew Grove rose to such global dominance. In using both public and private documents and a number of selected interviews, *Financial Times* columnist Tim Jackson charts the story of Intel from its conception to the present day.

Management and Entrepreneurism
John C. Chicken
Stanford, Connecticut: International Thomson Business Press, 2000
192pp (Smart Strategies Series)
ISBN: 1861526393
This book examines the nature of constraints and the role of management in securing maximum benefit from entrepreneurism in both the private and public sectors. It considers the nature of activities requiring management, the forms of entrepreneurism, and the reality of management in the public and private sectors, and suggests how management efficiency can be improved. The book is suitable for students on MBA courses.

Mastering Enterprise
Sue Birley, Daniel F. Muzyka
Upper Saddle River, New Jersey: Financial Times Prentice Hall, 1997
396pp (FT Mastering Series)
ISBN: 0273630318
This book suggests that entrepreneurial spirit is not restricted to people who start their own businesses and encourages managers to strike out as entrepreneurs and realize the business opportunities they see. It gives practical guidance on getting started, managing growth, buying a company, and harvesting.

Matsushita Leadership: Lessons From the 20th Century's Most Remarkable Entrepreneur
John P. Kotter
New York: Free Press, 1997
320pp ISBN: 068483460X
This book chronicles the life of Japanese entrepreneur Konosuke Matsushita, founder of the Matsushita Electric Corporation and Panasonic. It pays particular attention to his visionary management and leadership style, and highlights his views on the social responsibility of business.

The New Alchemists
Charles Handy
London: Trafalgar Square, 2001
238pp ISBN: 0091802156
This is a collection of success stories from a diverse group of people who have achieved something from nothing. The stories cover a wide range of business and community projects, and consider the reasons for the success of these ventures.

The New Global Leaders: Richard Branson, Percy Barnevik, David Simon, and the Remaking of International Business
Manfred F. R. Kets De Vries, Elizabeth Florent-Treacy
San Francisco, California: Jossey-Bass, 1999
188pp ISBN: 0787946575
These pioneering leaders share accounts of how they have created and sustained innovation in their organizations while commanding the respect and loyalty of their employees across continents and cultures. They describe their dreams and visions, their approaches to leadership, and their strategies for building and maintaining competitive global organizations staffed with dedicated enthusiastic people. Despite their distinctly different personal styles and philosophies, these three men exemplify the charismatic and architectural roles of leaders.

The Origin and Evolution of New Businesses
Amar V. Bhide
New York: Oxford University Press, 1999
432pp ISBN: 0195131444
This book develops a comprehensive framework for understanding entrepreneurship by drawing upon anecdote and folklore, intensive research, and modern theories of business and economics. It examines the concept of entrepreneurship, beginning with the improvised business startup, through the radical shifts required to compete in niche markets, to the pursuit of entrepreneurship in large organizations.

Small Firms: Entrepreneurship in the Nineties
David Deakins, Peter Jennings, Colin Mason, eds.
Thousand Oaks, California: Paul Chapman, 1997
192pp ISBN: 1853963615
This collection of 12 papers on entrepreneurship, published on behalf of the Institute for Small Business Affairs, is presented under the following headings: new start, growth, and development; funding; microbusinesses; families in business; women in business; ethnic minorities; and developing policy.

MAGAZINES

Entrepreneur
ISSN: 0163-3341
Entrepreneur Media, Inc.
2392 Morse Avenue, Irvine, California, 92614
T: +1 415 433 0441
www.EntrepreneurMag.com
This magazine, established in 1978, contains articles, interviews, business profiles, financing, marketing, advertising, and legislative news written for the small business owner or those planning to start a new business.

Entrepreneurship and Regional Development
ISSN: 0898-5626
Routledge
Suite 800, 325 Chestnut Street, Philadelphia, Pennsylvania, 19106
T: +1 800 354 1420
F: +1 215 625 8914
www.tandf.co.uk/journals/routledge/08985626.html
This quarterly journal provides a multidisciplinary forum for researchers and practitioners in the field of entrepreneurship and small-business development. It focuses on local and national factors which encourage entrepreneurial vitality.

Inc.
Gruner + Jahr U.S.A. Publishing
38 Commercial Wharf, Boston, Massachusetts, 02110-3883
T: +1 617 248 8000
F: +1 617 248 8090
www.inc.com
Published 18 times per year, this magazine is a premier journal on entrepreneurship. Each issue includes articles on financial and personnel management, marketing, administration, sales, and operations from the unique perspective of small businesses. It is a valuable publication for any executive or manager.

International Journal of Entrepreneurship and Innovation Management
ISSN: 1368-275X
Inderscience Enterprises Ltd.
World Trade Center Building, 29 route de Pre-Bois, Case Postale 896, CH-1215, Geneva 15, Switzerland
T: +44 (0) 1234 240515
F: +44 (0) 22 7910885
www.inderscience.com
This journal publishes original, empirical, and review papers; case studies; and conference reports. It covers the areas of corporate

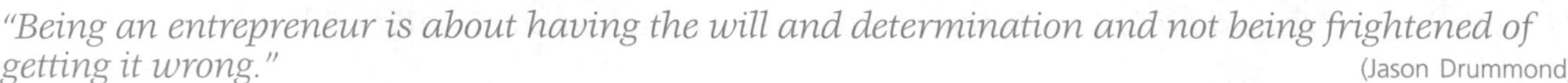
"Being an entrepreneur is about having the will and determination and not being frightened of getting it wrong."
(Jason Drummond)

venturing and intrapreneurship, the international aspects of entrepreneurship, the role of entrepreneurship in economic development, and government policies toward entrepreneurship. It is published quarterly.

International Journal of Management and Enterprise Development
ISSN: 1468–4330
Inderscience Enterprises Ltd.
World Trade Center Building, 29 route de Pre-Bois, Case Postale 896, CH-1215, Geneva 15, Switzerland
T: +44 (0) 1234 240515
F: +44 (0) 22 7910885
www.inderscience.com
This quarterly journal, aimed at professionals, academics, and managers, covers the area of SME startup, and development and related issues.

Journal of Business Venturing
ISSN: 0883–9026
Elsevier Science
Regional Sales Office, Customer Support Department, P.O. Box 945, New York, 10159–0945
T: +1 212 633 3730
F: +1 212 633 3680
www.elsevier.com
This quarterly research journal publishes articles by leading scholars and practitioners, reporting theoretical findings in the areas of entrepreneurship, new business development, industry evolution, and technology management.

INTERNET

CELCEE (Center for Entrepreneurial Leadership Clearinghouse on Entrepreneurship Education)
www.celcee.com
This site provides free access to an extensive database of information relating to entrepreneurship education. The information is drawn from a wide range of sources including articles, books, Web sites, and conferences. Items are indexed and abstracted, and include details of availability.

ENTERWeb
www.enterweb.org
This is an annotated collection of star-rated Web sites on entrepreneurship and related areas, provided by Jean-Claude Lorin. It includes access to the ENTER-L discussion group.

Entrepreneur.com
www.entrepreneur.com
This is a magazine site sponsored by Entrepreneur Media, Inc., offering a comprehensive range of practical information for owners of small businesses. The information includes a search engine, business tools, databases, newsletters, and message boards.

Entrepreneurial Edge
www.lowe.org
The Michigan-based Edward Lowe Foundation provides information and resources for entrepreneurs: news, articles, and an e-mail newsletter.

EntreWorld

www.entreworld.org
This is a collection of resources for entrepreneurs provided by the Kauffman Center for Entrepreneurial Leadership in Kansas City. Three sections focus on starting, growing, and finding support for a business. The site includes articles, a glossary, practical advice, an e-mail newsletter, an events calendar, and a bookstore.

eWeb
http://eweb.slu.edu/eweb.htm
This Web site is provided by St. Louis University, and provides information on entrepreneurial education programs, organizations, research centers, and assistance for entrepreneurs, including advice on business planning.

Global Entrepreneurship Institute
www.gcase.org
The site sponsored by this nonprofit, nongovernmental organization provides open source material for entrepreneurs and managers of small businesses, and includes articles and book lists.

ORGANIZATIONS

USA

Kauffman Center for Entrepreneurial Leadership
Ewing Marion Kauffman Foundation, 4801 Rockhill Road, Kansas City, Missouri, 64110–2046
T: +1 816 932 1000
E: *info@emkf.org*
www.emkf.org
The Kauffman Center promotes entrepreneurship in the United States through education, training, research, and a program of grants. The Center is involved in a wide range of initiatives to develop the concepts and skills of entrepreneurship in young people, and to promote the contribution entrepreneurship can make to community and economic development.

National Business Incubation Association
20 E Circle Drive, Suite 90, Athens, Ohio, 45701–3571
T: +1 740 593 4331
F: +1 740 593 1996
E: *info@nbia.org*
www.nbia.org
The NBIA provides information, education, advocacy, and networking opportunities for those involved or interested in business incubation programs. The organization conducts research, produces statistics and publications on this subject, and runs a referral service. Members include directors of incubator firms, business advisers, consultants, and investors.

National Commission on Entrepreneurship
Suite 399, 444 North Capital Street, Washington, D.C., 20001
T: +1 202 434 8060
F: +1 202 434 8065
E: *ncoe@sso.org*
www.ncoe.org
The NCOE was founded in 1999 to help leaders at local, state, and national level to formulate and implement policies designed to develop and expand an entrepreneurial economy and culture. The organization has a strong focus on the role of entrepreneurship in the national economy, and conducts research in this area.

Europe

National Federation of Enterprise Agencies
Trinity Gardens, 9–11 Bromham Road, Bedford, Bedfordshire, MK40 2UQ, U.K.
T: +44 (0) 1234 354055
E: *alan.bretherton@nfea.com*
www.nfea.com
The NFEA is a network of independent, nonprofit local enterprise agencies for the support of small and growing businesses, especially startups and microbusinesses. The organization aims to identify the needs of such businesses, encourage the government and others to provide the conditions for them to flourish, and provide a forum for members to share best practice. The British Volunteer Mentors Association is an initiative of the NFEA.

Small Firms Enterprise Development Initiative
P.O. Box 1753, The Portergate, Ecclesall Road, Sheffield, South Yorkshire, S11 8WT, U.K.
T: +44 (0) 114 209 6269
F: +44 (0) 114 209 6163
E: *info@sfedi.co.uk*
www.sfedi.co.uk

"Innovation is the specific instrument of entrepreneurship." (Peter Drucker)

The SFEDI has been appointed by the U.K. government to identify standards of best practice for small businesses and to work with providers of small business training, education, and advice to raise standards of support.

U.K. Business Incubation
Aston Science Park, Love Lane, Birmingham, West Midlands, B7 4BJ, U.K.
T: +44 (0) 121 250 3538
F: +44 (0) 121 250 3542
E: info@ukbi.co.uk
www.ukbi.co.uk
UKBI is a public/private sector initiative set up by the Department of Trade and Industry and HM Treasury to provide information and support for the incubator industry in the United Kingdom. The organization runs the incubation network in the United Kingdom, lobbies on behalf of the industry, produces publications, and provides consulting and networking opportunities.

Young Enterprise U.K.
Peterley House, Peterley Road, Oxford, Oxfordshire, OX4 2TZ, U.K.
T: +44 (0) 1865 776845
F: +44 (0) 1865 775671
www.young-enterprise.org.uk
Young Enterprise is a national educational charity founded in 1963 to develop links between schools and industry, and to encourage young people to learn and succeed through involvement in enterprise. Programs organized by Young Enterprise involve thousands of young people and volunteer advisors from local and national businesses. The programs include the Company Programme, Team Enterprise, and the Entrepreneurship Masterclass.

International

National Foundation for Teaching Entrepreneurship
29th Floor, 120 Wall Street, New York, 10005
T: +1 212 232 3333
F: +1 212 232 2244
E: nfte@nfte.com
www.nfte.com
NFTE was founded in 1987 as a program for students, to prevent dropouts and improve academic performance. Now an international nonprofit organization, it aims to help low-income young people by strengthening academic skills and teaching the basics of how to start and run a small business. This is achieved through the development of curricula, training teachers, and the provision of services to alumni.

Young Entrepreneurs' Organization
Suite 200, 1199 Fairfax Street, Alexandria, Virginia, 22314
T: +1 703 519 6700
F: +1 703 519 1864
E: lsurles@yeo.org
www.yeo.org
The YEO is a volunteer group of business professionals under 40 years of age who are the owners and founders of companies with annual sales of over $1,000,000. Founded in 1987, it now has 4,200 members in 94 chapters around the world. The organization's objective is to support, educate, and encourage young entrepreneurs.

For More Information

- ☆ **Intrapreneurial Warriors Versus Traditional Managers (pp. 125–26)**
- **Small and Growing Businesses (pp. 2112–15)**
- **Venture Capital (pp. 2131–33)**

Environmental Management

BOOKS

Corporate Environmental Management 3: Towards Sustainable Development
Richard Welford, ed.
Sterling, Virginia: Stylus Publishing, 2000
184pp (Corporate Environmental Management 3)
ISBN: 1853836419
The author reviews the environmental responsibilities that businesses and organizations must carry in order to ensure a sustainable future. He considers strategies for achieving operations consistent with this goal, focusing on societal, ethical, and social issues.

Corporate Environmental Policies
John Graham, et al.
Lanham, Maryland: Scarecrow Press, 1999
433pp ISBN: 0810835746
This book is a compilation of the complete texts of the environmental policies from 225 corporations from 20 countries throughout the world. Each entry includes brief contact and line-of-business information, as well as information about the corporation's participation with legislation and industry environmental standards. It includes bibliographical references and indexes.

Costing the Earth: The Challenge for Governments, the Opportunities for Business
Frances Cairncross
Boston, Massachusetts: Harvard Business School Press, 1992
ISBN: 0875843158
In this title, the author reveals that the way in which goods are produced is changing in industries across the world and discusses the vital role that government can play in aiding industry and reducing damage to the environment.

The Ecology of Commerce: A Declaration of Sustainability
Paul Hawken
New York: HarperCollins, 1994
ISBN: 0887307043
In this title, the author asserts that powerful, modern companies need to lessen the amount of energy and resources they use. He also suggests that the aims of business should be altered so that the natural world is able to benefit and to ensure that the needs of the planet are catered for.

Environmentalism and the New Logic of Business: How Firms Can Be Profitable and Leave Our Children a Clean Environment
R. Edward Freeman, et al.
New York: Oxford University Press, 2000
160pp ISBN: 0195080939
This book looks at the need for companies to commit to a ''green,'' or environmentally sound, set of business policies, stressing the issues of values and ethics, and at the same time showing that such policies can be profitable. After exploring barriers to taking environmentally sound action, it presents a program for change that can bring financial rewards while protecting the environment, using examples from companies such as The Body Shop, Inc., and DuPont Corp.

Environmental Management and Business Strategy: Leadership Skills for the 21st Century

---

"It is not until a creature begins to manage its environment that nature is thrown into disorder."
(Clifford Simak)

Bruce W. Piasecki, Kevin A. Fletcher, Frank J. Mendelson
New York: John Wiley, 1998
368pp ISBN: 0471169722
The authors explore the factors influencing the development of corporate environmental strategies. The topics covered include: regulatory requirements; environmental policy; environmental accounting; new product development; the use of environmental management systems; and stakeholder expectations. Case studies and further sources of information are appended.

Environmental Risk Management
Paul Pritchard
London: Earthscan, 2000
240pp (Business and Environmental Practitioner Series)
ISBN: 1853835986
Recent developments in environmental risk management are discussed in this book, which focuses on the nature of environmental risks and their relation to property, financial risk transfer, decision making with uncertainty, risk-management integration, and risk-management frameworks.

Environmental Strategies Handbook
Rao Kolluru, ed.
New York: McGraw-Hill, 1994
1030pp ISBN: 0070358583
This handbook contains contributions by over thirty experts from the fields of environmental science, business, and law. They offer insights into issues such as developing environmentally sound products and strategies, projecting a "green" corporate image, and exploiting new environmental investment opportunities.

ISO 14001 and Beyond: Environmental Management Systems in the Real World
Christopher Sheldon, ed.
Sheffield: Greenleaf Publishing, 1997
410pp ISBN: 1874719012
This book examines the creation, use, and limitations of environmental management systems and stresses their importance to the future of industry. It also deals with the background to the ISO14001 standard and important current trends, and includes case studies of tactical responses from the real world.

Lean and Green: Profit for Your Workplace and the Environment
Pamela Gordon
San Francisco, California: Berrett-Koehler, 2001
250pp ISBN: 1576751708
This book shows, through over a hundred examples, how companies can save money by following environmentally sound policies. The author provides a detailed plan of action and discusses issues such as questioning wasteful practices, setting goals to make facilities more energy and cost efficient, gaining management's endorsement for environmentally sound policies by introducing them in business terms, and tracking progress.

Managing Green Issues
Tom Curtin, Jacqueline Jones
New York: St. Martin's Press, 2001
205pp ISBN: 0312237162
The authors explore the potential and the pitfalls of environmental management and analyze green issues to give an insight into why many companies fail to manage them successfully. The book includes strategies, advice, and case studies.

Measuring Corporate and Environmental Performance: Best Practices for Costing and Managing an Effective Environment
Marc Epstein
New York: McGraw-Hill, 1996
319pp ISBN: 0786302305
This book provides information and suggestions on how to develop and implement a corporate environmental strategy. It describes the best and the most up-to-date practices of corporate environmental performance, and includes the results of the largest field study to be conducted in this area.

The Natural Step for Business: Wealth, Ecology, and the Evolutionary Corporation
Brian Nattrass, Mary Altomare
Gabriola Island, British Columbia: New Society Publishers, 1999
222pp ISBN: 0865713847
The book explains the Natural Step Process, a framework for creating environmentally aware companies that are successful enterprises. It is filled with case studies of such companies as IKEA, Scandic Hotels, Electrolux, and Mitsubishi, highlighting how companies can change to a new model of operations.

Principles of Environmental Management: The Greening of Business 2nd ed.
Rogene A. Bucholz
Upper Saddle River, New Jersey: Prentice-Hall, 1998
448pp ISBN: 0136848958
This updated edition focuses on the management of the environment as a business concern. The book provides examples of corporate efforts to respond to specific environmental issues and offers strategic approaches to issues such as ozone depletion, acid rain, air and water pollution, and disposal of hazardous wastes. It examines the regulations corporations must deal with and the public pressure they face as well as highlighting the responsibilities of business for helping create a sustainable society.

Small and Medium-sized Enterprises and the Environment: Business Imperatives
Ruth Hillary, ed.
Sheffield: Greenleaf Publishing, 2000
391pp ISBN: 1874719225
In considering potential ways to improve the environmental performance of small and medium-sized businesses, the author identifies and discusses four main areas. These are: the ways small firms perceive environmental issues and their attitudes toward them; environmental management in the smaller firm; strategies for reaching SMEs; and case studies from around the world.

Sustainability Strategies for the Industry: The Future of Corporate Practice
Nigel Roome, ed.
Washington, D.C.: Island Press, 1998
322pp (Greening of Industry Network)
ISBN: 1559635983
This book contains essays by members of the Greening of Industry Network. These essays examine the emerging picture of sustainability and its implications for industry, as well as for the relationship between industry and consumers, employees, and the community at large.

MAGAZINES

Business and the Environment
ISSN: 1052–7206
Cutter Information Corporation
37 Broadway, Suite 1, Arlington, Massachusetts, 02474
T: +1 800 964 5118 or +1 781 648 8700
F: +1 800 888 1816 or +1 781 648 1950
www.cutter.com
This monthly publication enables worldwide environmental professionals to learn about and debate environmental management issues. It contains case studies, news coverage, and helpful contact information. Each issue also includes the supplemental service BATE's ISO 14000 Update, including news on the status of the ISO 14000 standards and case studies of companies that have implemented the environmental management systems (EMS) standards.

Business Strategy and the Environment
ISSN: 0964–4733

"Accuse not Nature, she hath done her part;/Do thou but thine." (John Milton)

ERP Environment and John Wiley
Wiley InterScience Coordinator, Subscriptions Department, 605 Third Avenue, New York, 10158–0012
T: +1 800 825 7550
F: +1 212 850 6021
www.wiley.com
This bimonthly journal addresses key environmental issues facing managers and industry. It is aimed at environmental managers and strategic planners.

Environmental Engineering
ISSN: 0954–5824
Professional Engineering Publishing Ltd.
Northgate Avenue, Bury St. Edmunds, Suffolk, IP32 6BW, U.K.
T: +44 (0) 1284 718688
F: +44 (0) 1284 768219
This official journal of the Society of Environmental Engineers is aimed at engineers involved in manufacturing, testing, and measurement.

Environmental Quality Management
ISSN: 1088–1913
John Wiley
Wiley InterScience Coordinator, Subscriptions Department, 605 Third Avenue, New York, 10158–0012
T: +1 800 825 7550
F: +1 212 850 6021
www.interscience.wiley.com
Published four times per year, this magazine covers the growing application of total quality management to environmental programs. The magazine highlights such issues as how to improve environmental performance and how to apply TQM to environmental practice. It also features case studies of successful environmental quality programs and includes implementation guidelines.

Environment Business Magazine
ISSN: 1352–8882
Gee Publishing Ltd.
100 Avenue Road, Swiss Cottage, London, NW3 3PG, U.K.
T: +44 (0) 20 7393 7400
F: +44 (0) 20 7393 7915
www.ifi.co.uk
A magazine for senior managers that focuses on environmental management and technology across business and industry.

Environment Information Bulletin
ISSN: 0964–5322
Industrial Relations Services
Eclipse Group Ltd., 18–20 Highbury Road, London, N5 1QP, U.K.
T: +44 (0) 20 7354 5858
F: +44 (0) 20 7359 4000
www.irseclipse.co.uk
This newsletter covers key environmental business issues, particularly legislation and company policy and practice. It is produced for lawyers, and for environmental and health and safety professionals.

International Journal of Environmental Studies
ISSN: 0020–7233
Taylor & Francis
11 New Fetter Lane, London, EC4P 4EE, U.K.
T: +44 (0) 20 7583 9855
F: +44 (0) 20 7842 2298
www.tandf.co.uk/journals/titles/00207233.html
This bimonthly journal for academics, researchers, and environmentalists publishes original papers, review articles, and research on environmental problems and their solutions.

The ENDS Report
ISSN: 0966–4076
Environmental Data Services Ltd.
Finsbury Business Centre, 40 Bowling Green Lane, London, EC1R 0NE, U.K.
T: +44 (0) 20 7814 5300
F: +44 (0) 20 7415 0106
www.ends.co.uk
This is a monthly digest of U.K. and European environmental developments, news, and legislation, aimed at environmental professionals.

INTERNET

Department for Environment, Food and Rural Affairs (DEFRA)
www.defra.gov.uk
This U.K. government Web site combines information on current environmental issues with news of current and forthcoming legislation, government initiatives, regulatory measures, and publications.

SustainableBusiness.com
www.sustainablebusiness.com
This site features news about environmental issues and industry, along with a newsletter, and gives access to information about resources and events, as well as posting press releases from organizations involved in this subject.

Sustainable Enterprise Program—World Resources Institute
www.wri.org/wri/meb
The SEP section of the World Resources Institute site provides information about programs, publications, and projects focusing on business and the environment. It also has a newsletter in development.

U.S. Environmental Protection Association (EPA)
www.epa.gov
This site includes information on current issues, legislation, government programs, regional links, regulatory guidance, and publications.

ORGANIZATIONS

USA

National Association for Environmental Management (NAEM)
1612 K Street NW, Suite 1102, Washington, D.C., 20006
T: +1 202 986 6616 or 800 391 6236
F: +1 202 530 4408
E: *naem@msn.com*
www.naem.org
The NAEM has over 1,000 members and is the leading organization for the advancement of professional environmental management. The association was created specifically to unite environmental managers from a wide range of industries. NAEM provides professional development opportunities for workers in both the private and public sector.

National Registry of Environmental Professionals (NREP)
P.O. Box 2099, Glenview, Illinois, 60025
T: +1 847 724 6631
F: +1 847 724 4223
E: *nrep@nrep.org*
www.nrep.org
The NREP has over 17,000 members. This association certifies property assessors, indoor air quality specialists, hazardous and chemical material managers, ISO 14000 program administrators, and environmental managers. The NREP also promotes the benefits of their accreditation to the public and private sector and provides lists of qualified environmental professionals to governmental agencies.

National Wildlife Federation Corporate Conservation Council (NWFCCC)
11100 Wildlife Center Drive, Reston, Virginia, 20190
T: +1 703 790 4403
F: +1 703 790 4042
E: *cccaa@nwf.org*
www.nwf.org
This division of the National Wildlife Federation provides a forum for corporate environmentalists to discuss and create environmental policy change statements. These senior corporate officials are responsible for shaping national corporate environmental policy. As advocates for environmental excellence, they support, design and implement corporate environmental management systems.

"The demands of economics, of the environment, and of contributing to a just society are all important for a global commercial enterprise to flourish." (Mark Moody-Stuart)

U.S. Environmental Protection Association (EPA)
Ariel Rios Building, 1200 Pennsylvania Avenue NW, Washington, D.C., 20460
T: +1 202 260 2090
www.epa.gov
Formed in 1970, this is the U.S. government body concerned with the enforcement and protection of environmental standards consistent with national environmental goals. The U.S. EPA is involved in environmental research and the collation of environmental information, and also offers technical and policy advice.

Europe

Business in the Environment
c/o Business in the Community, 137 Shepherdess Walk, London, N1 7RQ, U.K.
T: +44 (0) 20 7600 2482
F: +44 (0) 20 7486 1700
E: *information@bitc.org.uk*
www.bitc.org.uk
Part of the Business in the Community initiative, Business in the Environment is a forum made up of companies that are committed to environmental sustainability through the reporting, measuring, and improvement of environmental business practices.

Department for Environment, Food and Rural Affairs (DEFRA)
Nobel House, 17 Smith Square, London, SW1P 3JR, U.K.
T: +44 (0) 20 7238 6000
F: +44 (0) 20 7238 6591
E: HELPLINE@defra.gsi.gov.uk
www.defra.gov.uk
This U.K. government department (formed in 2001) has responsibility for issues relating to environmental protection, wildlife and the countryside, agriculture, fisheries, food, and animal welfare.

Environmental Services Association
154 Buckingham Palace Road, London, SW1W 9TR, U.K.
T: +44 (0) 20 7824 8882
F: +44 (0) 20 7824 8753
E: *info@esauk.org*
www.esauk.org
This U.K. organization was founded in 1969. It promotes the development of markets and legislation that would ensure a sustainable environment, and represents companies that provide waste management and environmental services.

Institute of Environmental Management and Assessment
St. Nicholas House, 70 Newport, Lincoln, Lincolnshire, LN1 3DP, U.K.
T: +44 (0) 1522 540069
F: +44 (0) 1522 540090
www.iema.net
Formed in 1999, following the merger of the Institute of Environmental Management, the Environmental Auditors' Registration Association, and the Institute of Environmental Assessment, this professional body aims to promote the idea of sustainable development, and the professional development of individual members in environmental management and assessment.

Institution of Environmental Sciences
P.O. Box 16, Bourne, Cambridgeshire, PE10 9FB, U.K.
T: +44 (0) 1778 394846
F: +44 (0) 1778 394846
E: *ies-uk@breathemail.net*
www.ies-uk.org
Founded in 1971 this professional body represents the interests of professional environmentalists, promotes environmental education, and offers environmental information and guidance to the public and government.

For More Information

- ☆ **Environmental Management (pp. 113–14)**
- ✔ **Taking Action on the Environment (pp. 520–21)**
- **Business Ethics and Codes of Practice (pp. 1918–20)**
- **Social Responsibility of Management (pp. 2115–17)**

EQUAL OPPORTUNITIES

BOOKS

Beyond Race and Gender: Unleashing the Power of Your Total Work Force by Managing Diversity
R. Roosevelt Thomas, Jr.
New York: AMACOM, 1991
189pp ISBN: 0814478077
Looking ahead to a time when the U.S. work force will be truly diverse, the author of this classic and groundbreaking book explores the problems facing managers trying to offer equal opportunities to all in order to take advantage of needed talents and skills. He presents an action plan for changing corporate cultures as well as case studies that highlight the problems that emerge once an organization recruits a diverse work force, especially the failure of those recruited to move up the corporate ladder.

Breaking through the Glass Ceiling: Women in Management
Linda Wirth
Washington, D.C.: Brookings Institution, 2001
144pp ISBN: 9221108457
This ILO report is aimed at all those interested in an international study of the changing position of women in the labor market, in professional and managerial jobs, and in politics. It gives figures and statistical information from many sources, and focuses on issues such as discrimination, equal pay, gender mainstreaming, career building strategies, and actions to improve women's opportunities, thus giving an international overview of the effects of the glass ceiling on women.

Competitive Frontiers: Women Managers in a Global Economy
Nancy J. Adler, Dafna N. Izraeli, eds.
Cambridge, Massachusetts: Blackwell Business, 1994
414pp ISBN: 1557865108
This book gives a full international perspective on women in management. It offers, for employers and researchers, contributions from women of various nationalities who describe the level of equal opportunities for women in their country, and the experiences, status, and cultural images of female managers there.

Diversity Consciousness: Opening Our Minds to People, Cultures, and Opportunities
Richard D. Bucher
Upper Saddle River, New Jersey: Prentice Hall, 1999
233pp ISBN: 0130803383
This book is aimed at helping readers value

"Saying that a person cannot be kept out doesn't ensure that that person can get in, and more important, stay in."
(Margaret Hennig)

diversity so that they can understand others' viewpoints and thus deal better with issues in the workplace such as conflict management, teamwork, prejudice, and communications. Its goal is to show how workplace success comes with employees' ability to accept differences. The book provides material such as interactive exercises that could be of great use to managers and human relations professionals.

Federal Law of Employment Discrimination in a Nutshell
Mack A. Player
Saint Paul, Minnesota: West Publishing Company, 1998
356pp ISBN: 0314211683
This volume examines issues of workplace discrimination based on race, sex, national origin, religion, age, and disability, and places them in a legal and regulatory context. It also explores the history of such relevant statutes as the Equal Employment Opportunity Act and the Age Discrimination in Employment Act, and considers the enforcement procedures in place. The author also deals with difficult subjects such as liability in the absence of motive, retaliation, and remedies.

Job Discrimination in the Workplace II: How to Fight. . . How to Win!
Jeffrey M. Bernbach
Englewood Cliffs, New Jersey: Voir Dire Press, 1998
173pp ISBN: 0965375315
This book, a legal expert's guide to employees who believe they are the victims of discrimination in the workplace on the basis of their race, age, sex, disability, or religion, explains how to determine whether you have a real case and how to wage a court battle to prove it. Bernbach offers case histories, job bias rulings, including rulings by the Supreme Court, and information that proves it is possible to make such a case successfully.

Powerful Women: Dancing on the Glass Ceiling
Sam Parkhouse
New York: John Wiley, 2001
256pp ISBN: 0471499056
This is a very readable book, written in a popular magazine style and focusing on the individual stories behind the successes of several unusual women. Aimed at a very general audience, and taking neither an academic nor an equal opportunities perspective, the text attempts to get to grips with the real experiences of case study women, such as Barbara Cassani, Belinda Earl, Nicola Horlick, Anita Roddick, and Margaret Jay.

MAGAZINES

Black EOE Journal
22845 Savi Ranch Parkway
Suite A, Yorba Linda, California, 92887
T: +1 800 487 5099
F: +1 714 974 3978
www.blackeoejournal.com
Published quarterly, this magazine contains articles about all minorities and provides valuable information regarding career opportunities. The journal focuses on the needs of employers in relation to workplace diversity. A section on career planning and advancement is particularly valuable to readers.

Careers & the disABLED
ISSN: 1056–277X
Equal Opportunities Publications, Inc.
445 Broad Hollow Road, Suite 425, Melville, New York, 11747
T: +1 631 421 9421
F: +1 631 421 0359
www.eop.com
This magazine is the premier career guidance and recruitment magazine for people with disabilities. Unique to this publication is the inclusion of a special Braille section.

Diversity Factor
ISSN: 1067–7194
Elsie Y. Cross Associates, Inc.
7627 Germantown Avenue, Philadelphia, Pennsylvania, 19118
T: +1 215 248 8100
F: +1 215 242 3328
www.eyca.com/diversityfactor
This quarterly journal, founded in 1992, is a must-read for any business professional working with equal opportunity issues. Cutting-edge strategies are detailed to provide the latest developments in handling workplace discrimination. The magazine provides updates to the latest legislative action regarding discrimination and EOE/AA, and also reviews current literature.

Equal Opportunities International
ISSN: 0261–0159
Barmarick Publications
Enholmes Hall, Patrington, East Yorkshire, HU12 0PR, U.K.
T: +44 (0) 1964 630033
F: +44 (0) 1964 631716
www.emeraldinsight.com/eoi.htm
This high-priced subscription journal carries articles by academics involved in equal opportunities teaching or research. The number of issues per year is variable, but eight were published in 2001.

Equal Opportunities Review
ISSN: 0268–7143
Eclipse Group Ltd.
18–20 Highbury Place, London, N5 1QP, U.K.
T: +44 (0) 20 7354 5858
F: +44 (0) 20 7359 4000
www.irseclipse.co.uk
This journal is published six times a year, and focuses on U.K. equal opportunities legislation and employment practice.

INTERNET

Disability
www.disability.gov.uk
This site provides information on disability legislation, including official guidance, press releases, and links. The latter include the Web Accessibility Initiative, which aims to make Web technology more accessible to those with disabilities, and ACDET (Advisory Committee for Disabled People in Training and Employment), an organization that advises ministers and officials on securing equality of participation in employment and training opportunities for people who are disabled.

Equal Employment.com—The Equal Opportunity Employers Web Site
www.equalemployment.com
This Web site provides links to companies committed to providing equal opportunity employment to every qualified applicant, regardless of age, disability, gender, national origin, or sexual orientation. It also offers a comprehensive bibliography on the subject.

Equality Direct
www.equalitydirect.org.uk
This is a pilot confidential information and advice service for businesses, launched by the U.K. Department for Education. The site offers limited help and information in an online publication form, and gives a telephone number to contact for inquiries or advice.

Equality North West
www.equality.org.uk
The menu option on this site for the One Stop Shop for Equal Opportunities pilot offers resources to support small and medium-sized enterprises in developing equal opportunities practices in employment and service delivery. The site, which was commissioned by the U.K. Department for Education and Employment, is designed for easy usage, and its content includes recruitment and selection, policies and procedures, and legislation.

Equal Opportunity Employment Commission
www.eeoc.gov
This U.S. government-sponsored Web site provides a vast amount of material on equal opportunities, ranging from statistics to federal

"Equal opportunity means everyone will have a fair chance at becoming incompetent."
(Laurence J. Peter)

laws to information about technical assistance and training programs.

Race for Opportunity
www.bitc.org.uk/rfo
This is a Business in the Community network initiative to raise business awareness of the case for diversity. It gives information on the employment policies of some member companies; regional and London pages give information about relevant activities and issues.

ORGANIZATIONS

USA

American Association for Affirmative Action
P.O. Box 14460, Washington, D.C., 20044
T: +1 800 252 8952
F: +1 202 628 7977
E: *execoffice@affirmativeaction.org*
www.affirmativeaction.org
This association of over 1,200 professionals focuses on managing affirmative action, equal opportunity, diversity and related human resource issues. The association is committed to the advancement of affirmative action at the local, state and national level. Members are also involved in creating and implementing strategies for maintaining equal employment opportunities. The AAAA will provide individualized assessments of EOE/AA compliance concerns.

Center for Equal Opportunity
14 Pidgeon Hill Drive, Suite 500, Sterling, Virginia, 20165
T: +1 703 421 5443
F: +1 703 421 6401
E: *comment@ceousa.org*
www.ceousa.org
Founded in 1995, the CEO promotes the assimilation of immigrants into American society. The CEO demands that local, state and national governments stop public policies that divide Americans by national origin and provides research showing the harmful effects of dividing the American workplace by race, sex and ethnic background.

Employment Policy Foundation
1015 15th Street NW, Suite 1200, Washington, D.C., 20005
T: +1 202 789 8685
F: +1 202 789 8684
E: *info@epf.org*
www.epf.org
Founded in 1983, the EPF is a nonpartisan public policy research foundation focused on workforce trends. This organization conducts studies and provides U.S. policymakers with economic analyses of employment policies, revealing how these policies affect the goals of American industry and workers. The EPF is regarded as one of the best sources for unbiased, reliable and thorough research on employment issues.

Equal Employment Opportunity Commission
1801 L Street NW, Washington, D.C., 20507
T: +1 202 663 4900
www.eeoc.gov
This body was established by Title VII of the Civil Rights Act of 1964 to enforce federal statutes prohibiting employment discrimination. It began operating on July 2, 1965.

Europe

Commission for Racial Equality
Head Office, Elliot House, 10–12 Allington Street, London, SW1E 5EH, U.K.
T: +44 (0) 20 7828 7022
F: +44 (0) 20 7630 7605
E: *info@cre.gov.uk*
www.cre.gov.uk
This is a publicly funded but nongovernmental body set up under the Race Relations Act 1976 to deal with racial discord and promote racial equality. It provides information and advice, seeks to raise awareness of relevant issues, and promotes policies and practices to ensure equality of treatment for all.

Disability Rights Commission
DRC Helpline, Freepost MID 02164, Stratford-upon-Avon, Warwickshire, CV37 9BR, U.K.
T: +44 (0) 8457 622 633
F: +44 (0) 8457 778 878
E: *ddahelp@stra.sitel.co.uk*
www.drc-gb.org
Established by an Act of Parliament, the Commission came into operation in April 2000 to ensure that the Disability Discrimination Act 1995 takes effect, to keep disability legislation under review, and to publicize and promote good practice.

Equal Opportunities Commission
Arndale House, Arndale Centre, Manchester, M4 3EQ, U.K.
T: +44 (0) 161 833 9244
F: +44 (0) 161 838 1733
E: *info@eoc.org.uk*
www.eoc.org.uk
The EOC is a statutory body that works to eliminate unlawful sex discrimination in the United Kingdom, to promote equal opportunities for men and women, and to uphold and review the Sex Discrimination (1975) and Equal Pay (1970) Acts.

Opportunity Now
Business in the Community, 137 Shepherdess Walk, London, N1 7RQ, U.K.
T: +44 (0) 20 7556 8714
F: +44 (0) 20 7253 1877
E: *opportunitynow@bitc.org.uk*
www.opportunitynow.org.uk
This is a campaign initiative under the umbrella of Business in the Community that works with employers to improve women's opportunities at work.

For More Information

- ☆ **Boosting Business Success through Diversity (pp. 29–30)**
- ☆ **Breaking the Lead Ceiling (pp. 237–38)**
- ☆ **Tackling Sexual Harassment in the Workplace (pp. 47–48)**
- ✔ **Introducing an Equal Opportunities Policy (pp. 440–41)**
- **Conditions of Employment (pp. 1933–35)**
- **Diversity (pp. 1955–57)**
- **Employee Relations (pp. 1964–66)**
- **Employment Law (pp. 1967–69)**

EXPORTING

BOOKS

Building an Import/Export Business 2nd ed.
KENNETH D. WEISS
New York: John Wiley, 1997
288pp ISBN: 0471177873
This is a user-friendly guide to starting and building a successful import or export business. It gives guidance on potential areas of concern, such as operational procedures, trade agreements, and marketing techniques. It also provides practical advice on how best to tap into

"There is nothing Japan really wants to buy from foreign countries except, possibly, neckties with unusual designs."
(Yoshihiro Inayama)

      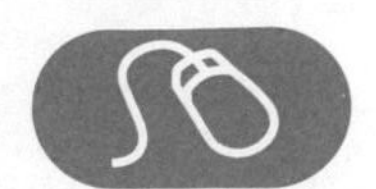

the lucrative global markets. It includes bibliographical references and an index.

Dun and Bradstreet's Guide to Doing Business around the World
TERRI MORRISON, ET AL.
Paramus, New Jersey: Prentice Hall, 2001
527pp ISBN: 0735201080
This is a guide to business success abroad. Covering 40 countries, it provides an insight into the economic, political, and cultural issues of which it is important to be aware for successful overseas trade. The book combines up-to-date export information and risk profiles with data on the cultural aspects of doing business internationally. It includes bibliographical references and an index.

Export Savvy: From Basics to Strategy
ZAK KARAMALLY
New York: International Business Press/ The Haworth Press, 1998
198pp ISBN: 0789005778
This book deals with export management from the concepts of international trade to the key elements that influence and comprise its effectiveness. It relates the export experience to the commercial experience as a whole. This involves breaking down the complicated process of exporting into simple and familiar terms. It includes bibliographical references and an index.

Finding Export Markets: A Guide to Methods and Information Sources in the U.K. and Worldwide for British Exporters 2nd ed.
DOUGLAS TOOKEY
Peterborough: Trade Research, 1995
38pp ISBN: 0904783340
The contents of the U.K. guide include: how to find export information—where to begin; finding markets; export buyers in the United Kingdom; sending goods abroad; Department of Trade and Industry and Foreign and Commonwealth Office services to exporters; other information sources in the United Kingdom; and export information sources listed by country.

Global Jumpstart: The Complete Resource for Expanding Small and Midsized Businesses
RUTH STANAT, CHRIS WEST
Cambridge, Massachusetts: Perseus, 2000
198pp ISBN: 073820160X
This book is a useful resource guide for companies of the size mentioned in the title who have reached any stage of the expansion process. It provides in-depth analysis of business opportunities around the world, while also giving a valuable insight into the pitfalls in international markets for small companies.

Principles of Management in Export
JAMES CONLAN
Cambridge, Massachusetts: Blackwell Business, 1994
325pp (Principles of Export Guidebooks) ISBN: 0631191941
Using the syllabus of the Institute of Export as a basis, the author shows how all areas of export practice can be integrated. The emphasis is on profitable export management, covering the core topics of running and structuring an export business, and including all the necessary techniques, and measuring and benchmarking systems for assessing profitability, setting strategic goals, and creating quantifiable reporting and control systems.

The Ultimate Guide to Export Management
THOMAS COOK
New York: AMACOM, 2001
569pp ISBN: 0814405819
This step-by-step manual advises business people on how to successfully navigate the highly complicated exporting arena. It covers all the fundamental skills and knowledge needed to participate in international business. It includes bibliographical references and an index.

MAGAZINES

British Exports
ISSN: 1350–6986
Reed Business Information
Windsor Court, East Grinstead, West Sussex, RH19 1XA, U.K.
T: +44 (0) 1342 335876
F: +44 (0) 1342 335998
www.britishexports.com
This is an online database providing detailed profiles of 17,000 U.K. export companies. A CD-ROM version and an annual book are available.

Croner's Export Marketing
Croner CCH Group
145 London Road, Kingston-upon-Thames, Surrey, KT2 6SR, U.K.
T: +44 (0) 20 8547 3333
F: +44 (0) 20 8547 2638
www.croner.co.uk
This publication provides a wide range of background information intended to help U.K. exporters find overseas markets. Topics covered include carrying out market research, trade exhibitions, obtaining financial and technical assistance, and travel. It also contains comprehensive information on some 120 countries, covering the general political and economic situation, import regulations, customs requirements, the culture, and the general background. It also includes an updating service, with a monthly newsletter and a CD-ROM of the loose-leaf guide as part of the package.

Croner's Management of Export
Croner CCH Group
145 London Road, Kingston-upon-Thames, Surrey, KT2 6SR, U.K.
T: +44 (0) 20 8547 3333
F: +44 (0) 20 8547 2638
www.croner.co.uk
This service provides extensive guidance on running a U.K. export business, export strategy, financial management, and dealing with export agents or distributors. Sample administrative forms and other documentation are also given. It is an updating service that includes a loose-leaf guide, a quarterly bulletin, and a CD-ROM.

Croner's Reference Book for Exporters
Croner CCH Group
145 London Road, Kingston-upon-Thames, Surrey, KT2 6SR, U.K.
T: +44 (0) 20 8547 3333
F: +44 (0) 20 8547 2638
www.croner.co.uk
This U.K. information service package provides general guidance on export procedures and customs procedures and documentation, as well as extensive information on some 150 countries, including their principal ports, currencies, import and legal requirements, and documentation. There is an updating service that includes a fortnightly newsletter (*Exporter's Briefing*), the monthly *Croner's Export Digest*, two booklets, and a CD-ROM.

Export and Freight
Main Stream Publications
140 Thomas Street, Portadown, Craigavon, County Armagh, Northern Ireland, BT62 3BE, U.K.
T: +44 (0) 2838 334272
F: +44 (0) 2838 351046
www.mainstream.uk.com
This journal covers all aspects of exporting, including freight, handling, and storage.

Export Times
Nexus Media Ltd.
Nexus House, Azalea Drive, Swanley, Kent, BR8 8HY, U.K.
T: +44 (0) 1322 660070
F: +44 (0) 1322 667633
www.nexusmedia.com
This newspaper covers a wide range of exporting issues including market research, finance, sales, and distribution. The same

"You can always buy something in English, you can't always sell something in English."
(Rosabeth Moss Kanter)

  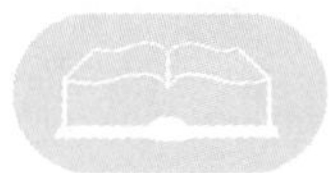    

publishers also produce a companion paper, the *Export Times Trade Finance Review*. This covers topics such as foreign exchange, credit insurance, and bad debt collection.

Export Today's Global Business
ISSN: 0882–4711
Trade Communications, Inc.
733 15th Street NW, Suite 1100, Washington, D.C., 20005
T: +1 202 737 1060
www.gbmag.com
Formerly titled *2YM*, this monthly magazine covers financial solutions for businesses dealing in exports. Features include topics covering international business markets and international business development opportunities.

Foreign Affairs
Foreign Affairs
58 East 68th Street, New York, 10021
T: +1 212 434 9522
www.foreignaffairs.org
Published six times per year, this magazine covers current events and how they affect U.S. relations worldwide. With a focus on international, political, commercial, and cultural relations, this magazine has often been described as the premier journal of world affairs. This is a must read for any corporate executive involved with international business.

International Business Review
ISSN: 0969–5931
Elsevier Science
Regional Sales Office, Customer Support Department, P.O. Box 945, New York, 10159–0945
T: +1 212 633 3730
F: +1 212 633 3680
www.elsevier.com
Published six times per year, this magazine is vital for any business professional working in international business. With an emphasis on marketing and management issues, it contains the latest insights on international business. The magazine has an international list of authors and aims to keep senior management current with the most recent developments in the practical application of international business.

International Trade Today
ISSN: 1472–7153
Hemming Information Services
32 Vauxhall Bridge Road, London, SW1V 2SS, U.K.
T: +44 (0) 20 7973 6404
F: +44 (0) 20 7973 4797
www.international-trade.org.uk
International Trade Today is the official journal of the Institute of Export and is published ten times per year in the United Kingdom. The magazine contains useful articles about all facets of importing and exporting.

The Exporter
The Exporter
26 Broadway, Suite 776, New York, 10004
T: +1 212 269 2016
F: +1 212 269 2740
www.exporter.com
This journal is aimed at government, financial institutions, and trade brokers, as well as manufacturers and large exporters.

INTERNET

American Countertrade Association
www.countertrade.org
The objects of the American Countertrade Association are to promote trade and commerce between companies and their foreign customers who engage in countertrade as a form of doing business.

British Chambers of Commerce
www.britishchambers.org.uk
The site offers an extensive range of services to member companies covering all aspects of exporting. It also provides links to all 150 local chambers.

Business Advice Online
www.businesslink.org
This is an online service provided by the Small Business Service of the U.K. Department of Trade and Industry. It provides an extensive range of general information for small businesses as well as details of the services available through the network of 150 local Business Links. The latter provide face-to-face advice on exporting and importing for small businesses.

Market Access Database
www.mkaccdb.eu.int
The Market Access Database is provided by the DG Trade, European Commission. Certain parts of the site are open only to people having an ISP connection located in Europe but the section on trade barriers is open to all Internet users. The site contains details about trade barriers by market sector and country, import formalities by country and import duties by product code and by country.

Thomas Global Register
www.tgrnet.com
Formerly the American Export Register, this comprehensive Web-based directory run by Thomas Publishing gives details of some 500,000 manufacturers and distributors across 22 countries, divided into 10,500 product and service classifications.

Trade Information Center
www.trade.gov/td/tic
The Trade Information Center (TIC) is a comprehensive resource for information and advice on all U.S. Federal Government export assistance programs. It is operated by the International Trade Administration of the U.S. Department of Commerce for the 20 federal agencies comprising the Trade Promotion Coordinating Committee (TPCC). These agencies are responsible for managing the U.S. Government's export promotion programs and activities.

Trade Partners U.K.
www.tradepartners.gov.uk
Trade Partners is part of British Trade International (see below) and provides an extensive range of information and advice to businesses on all aspects of exporting.

ORGANIZATIONS

USA

Bureau of Export Administration, U.S. Department of Commerce
Room 3895, Washington, D.C., 20230
T: +1 202 482 0097
F: +1 202 482 2421
www.bxa.doc.gov
The Bureau of Export Administration (BXA) is concerned with advancing U.S. national security, foreign policy, and economic interests. Its key activities include regulating the export of sensitive goods and technologies in an effective and efficient manner, cooperating with and assisting other countries on export control and strategic trade issues, and promoting federal initiatives and public-private partnerships across industry sectors to protect national infrastructures.

Federation of International Trade Associations
11800 Sunrise Valley Drive, Suite 210, Reston, Virginia, 20190
T: +1 800 969 3482
F: +1 703 620 4922
www.fita.org
The Federation fosters international trade by strengthening the role of local, regional, and national associations throughout the United States, Mexico, and Canada. Its Web site includes a directory of 3,000 Trade and Import/Export Web sites.

International Trade Administration, U.S. Department of Commerce
1401 Constitution Avenue, Room 3414,

"Experience has shown us that the trade of the East is the key to national wealth and influence."
(Chester Alan Arthur)

Washington, D.C., 20230
T: +1 202 482 3809
F: +1 282 482 5819
www.ita.doc.gov
This organization is the lead unit for trade in the Department of Commerce. It participates in formulating and implementing U.S. foreign trade and economic policies, and monitors market access and compliance of U.S. international trade agreements.

Europe

British Chambers of Commerce

Manning House, 22 Carlisle Place, London, SW1P 1JA, U.K.
T: +44 (0) 20 7565 2000
F: +44 (0) 20 7565 2049
E: info@britishchambers.org.uk
www.britishchambers.org.uk
This is an umbrella body for a network of some 150 locally based chambers of commerce serving local businesses and providing advice on exporting and export services to member companies. Its Web site provides links to the local chambers.

Export Credits Guarantee Department

P.O. Box 2200, 2 Exchange Tower, Harbour Exchange Square, London, E14 9GS, U.K.
T: +44 (0) 20 7512 7000
F: +44 (0) 20 7512 7649
E: help@ecgd.gov.uk
www.ecgd.gov.uk
This government department provides export credit insurance and reinsurance for exporting companies and companies investing overseas.

HM Customs and Excise

New King's Beam House, 22 Upper Ground, London, SE1 9PJ, U.K.
T: +44 (0) 845 010 9000
www.hmce.gov.uk
Her Majesty's Customs and Excise is the department responsible for administering and collecting all import duties as detailed in the Customs Tariffs. It also has specific responsibility for enforcing all prohibitions and restrictions on the export (and import) of certain classes of goods.

Institute of Export

Export House, Minerva Business Park, Lynch Wood, Peterborough, Cambridgeshire, PE2 6FT, U.K.
T: +44 (0) 1733 404400
F: +44 (0) 1733 404444
E: institute@export.org.uk
www.export.org.uk
This professional membership body aims to raise standards in international trade management and export practice.

Trade Partners U.K.

Kingsgate House, 66–74 Victoria Street, London, SW1E 6SE, U.K.
T: +44 (0) 20 7215 8200
F: +44 (0) 20 7215 4699
www.tradepartners.gov.uk
British Trade International was set up in May 1999 as a new coordinating government department to bring together all the trade and export promotion policy functions of the Department of Trade and Industry and the Foreign and Commonwealth Office. Trade Partners U.K., part of BTI, provide a wide range of export services and advice to exporters.

World Trade and International Trade Rules

Trade Policy Directorate, Kingsgate House, 66–74 Victoria Street, London, SW1E 6SW, U.K.
T: +44 (0) 20 7215 4557
F: +44 (0) 20 7215 4556
E: worldtrade@dti.gov.uk
www.dti.gov.uk/worldtrade/import.htm
The Department of Trade and Industry is responsible for U.K. trade policy at international, European, and national levels, and for harmonizing customs tariff levels with European Union member states. It is also responsible, in conjunction with several other government departments, for policy on all U.K. export and import prohibitions and restrictions.

International

International Chamber of Commerce

38 Cours Albert 1er, 75008 Paris, France
T: +33 149 53 28 28
F: +33 149 53 28 59
E: webmaster@iccwbo.org
www.iccwbo.org
The ICC is the only representative body that speaks out with authority on behalf of enterprises from all sectors in every part of the world. The ICC provides a number of international services and publications.

World Trade Organization

Centre William Rappard, Rue de Lausanne 154, CH-1211 Geneva 21, Switzerland
T: +41 22 739 51 11
F: +41 22 731 42 06
E: enquiries@wto.org
www.wto.org
The WTO site gives comprehensive details about intergovernmental actions on trade issues. The site offers statistics about world trade and downloadable documents.

For More Information

- ✔ **Preparing for Business Abroad (pp. 514–15)**
- **Importing (pp. 1997–98)**
- **International Management, Cross Cultural Management (pp. 2009–11)**

Facilities Management

BOOKS

Facilities Engineering and Management Handbook: Commercial, Industrial, and Institutional Buildings

Paul R. Smith, et al.
New York: McGraw-Hill, 2000
1200pp ISBN: 007059323X
Written by practicing professionals, this handbook takes a big-picture view of the various aspects of facilities management, including design, construction, operation, maintenance, and modifications. It aims to be a complete desktop reference book, taking a life-cycle approach that helps facilities managers, operators, and engineers make sound decisions that consider the economics of the entire facility.

Facility Design and Management Handbook

Eric Teicholz
New York: McGraw-Hill, 2001
752pp ISBN: 0071353941
This handbook contains tips and case studies for several industries. It discusses the tools and technologies needed to develop cost-effective solutions to common problems like space planning, environmental sensitivity, technology integration, and disaster planning. It also shows how to automate most tasks and apply

"Just look at him. He runs his company with five people in an office the size of a closet."
(Katherine Graham)

benchmarking for measurable improvements in productivity. The CD-ROM included with the book contains sample forms and links to additional resources.

Manager's Guide to Contingency Planning for Disasters: Protecting Vital Facilities and Critical Operations 2nd ed.
KENNETH N. MYERS
New York: John Wiley, 1999
252pp ISBN: 047135838X
This book is designed to help you either avoid a disaster or recover from one quickly with a minimum of expense and lost time. It provides a structured approach to contingency planning that aims to minimize plan development costs. It helps the reader define the problem, increase awareness, conduct a business impact analysis, and develop an implementation strategy.

Strategy and Place: Managing Corporate Real Estate and Facilities for Competitive Advantage
MARTHA A. O'MARA
New York: Free Press, 1999
349pp ISBN: 0684834898
The area of corporate real estate and facilities is often overlooked when it comes to building competitive advantage. O'Mara presents her guide for strategic thinking and decision making in respect of the company's very visible and very expensive physical facilities. From her research at major companies, she outlines three approaches to facilities management decision making and explains the advantages and disadvantages of each approach.

Work Transformation: Planning and Implementing the New Workplace
KEN ROBERTSON
New York: HNB Publishing, 1998
286pp ISBN: 0966428609
The author shows how the integration of human resources, facilities management, and information technology strategies creates ways of delivering work transformation. The chapter on facilities management looks at how to investigate, design, and implement alternative space arrangements such as space sharing, hoteling, team spaces, casual meeting areas, and meditation zones. It then reports on how this can reduce costs, utilize space effectively, and help to create a community environment.

MAGAZINES

BIFM Bulletin
New Venture
67 High Street, Saffron Walden, Essex, CB10 1AA, U.K.
T: +44 (0) 1799 508 608
F: +44 (0) 1799 513 237
www.bifm.org.uk
This fortnightly newsletter from the British Institute of Facilities Management aims to cover all aspects of facilities management, and includes recruitment and training information.

Facilities
ISSN: 0263–2772
MCB University Press
60/62 Toller Lane, Bradford, West Yorkshire, BD8 9BY, U.K.
T: +44 (0) 1274 777700
F: +44 (0) 1274 785201
www.emeraldinsight.com/f.htm
This is the official research publication of EuroFM (European Facility Management Network). It offers serious discussion of key issues to help managers and other interested parties to maximize building space resources.

Facilities Design and Management
ISSN: 0279–4438
VNU Business Media
770 Broadway, 4th Floor, New York, 10003–9595
T: +1 646 654 4500
F: +1 646 654 4480
www.fdm.com
This publication provides information on the processes, projects, people, and products that shape the facilities management profession. Special features include current information on office telecommunications systems.

Facilities Management
ISSN: 1315–668X
Eclipse Group Ltd.
18–20 Highbury Place, London, N5 1QP, U.K.
T: +44 (0) 20 7354 5858
F: +44 (0) 20 7359 4000
www.irseclipse.co.uk
This publication explores the strategic issues relating to facilities management.

Facilities Management Compendium
ISSN: 1363–9145
Barbour Index plc.
New Lodge, Drift Road, Winkfield, Windsor, Berkshire, SL4 4RQ, U.K.
T: +44 (0) 1344 884121
F: +44 (0) 1344 884845
www.barbourexport.com/bi_web
This is an annual publication providing product and service information together with a technical guide giving key legislative requirements.

Facilities Management Journal (FMJ)
ISSN: 1362–4768
Market Place Publishing Ltd.
Scorpio House, 106 Church Road, London, SE19 2UB, U.K.
T: +44 (0) 20 8771 3614
F: +44 (0) 20 8771 4592
www.fmj.co.uk
This is a journal offering reports, case studies, and interviews on developments within the facilities management industry. It is aimed at top managers who are involved in property management.

The Facilities Business
The Builder Group plc.
Exchange Tower, 2 Harbour Exchange Square, London, E14 9GE, U.K.
T: +44 (0) 20 7560 4000
F: +44 (0) 20 7560 4070
www.building.co.uk
This is a magazine providing extensive coverage of a range of facilities management issues, including property, transportation, and environmental issues; IT; security; catering; health and safety; and building maintenance and procurement.

INTERNET

British Institute of Facilities Management
www.bifm.org.uk
The Institute's Web site provides information on membership benefits, regional news and events listings, short courses, education and professional development, and the BIFM awards.

Facility Management Directory
www.fmd.co.uk
This site concentrates on providing information on premises and facilities management in the United Kingdom. It offers a directory of U.K. FM companies, listings of publications, and career and job information.

FMLink
www.fmlink.com
If this site doesn't have the facilities management information you need, it will tell you where to find it. It features news and events, survey and benchmarking data, access to the FM job market, supplier and product information, and a place where facility managers can discuss issues.

I-FM
www.i-fm.net
This site offers a wide selection of facilities management resources, including news items and articles, and company and job listings. A bookshop and discussion group are also available. Some sections require registration.

International Facility Management Association

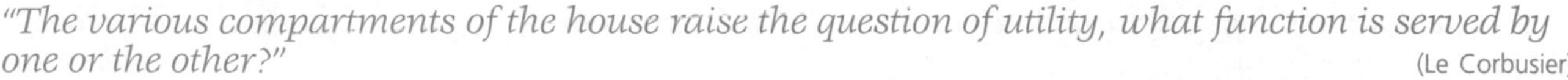
"The various compartments of the house raise the question of utility, what function is served by one or the other?"
(Le Corbusier)

www.ifma.org
The International Facility Management Association (IFMA) is a nonprofit professional association for facility management throughout the world. Through this site, the IFMA provides professional development courses, access to the job market, facility management certification, and benchmarking and best practices metrics. The site includes details of membership benefits, an events calendar, research summaries, and a bookstore. You have to be a member to access certain sections.

The Association for Facilities Engineering
www.afe.org
A member organization of facilities engineers, the AFE administers certification programs for the professional designations of CPE (Certified Plant Engineer) and CFEP (Certified Facilities Environmental Professional).

ORGANIZATIONS

Europe

British Institute of Facilities Management
67 High Street, Saffron Walden, Essex, CB10 1AA, U.K.
T: +44 (0) 1799 508 608
F: +44 (0) 1799 513 237
E: *admin@bifm.org.uk*
www.bifm.org.uk
The Institute is a professional membership body, founded in 1993, for managers responsible for facilities management of office premises, including planning, design, and equipment purchasing. It is also for people working in organizations that supply facilities management goods and services.

Facilities Management Association
R9/10—Building 208, Hounslow, London, TW6 2BG, U.K.
T: +44 (0) 20 8897 8521
E: *mtaffler@ic24.net*
www.fmassociation.org
This is a trade organization, established in 1995, representing 20 organizations that are suppliers of facilities services. The FMA promotes and represents members' interests at government level, and is affiliated with the International Facility Management Association.

International

International Facility Management Association
1 E Greenway Plaza, Suite 1100, Houston, Texas, 77046–0194
T: +1 713 623 4362
F: +1 713 623 6124
E: *ifmahq@ifma.org*
www.ifma.org
This is a nonprofit incorporated association, established in 1980, that is dedicated to providing excellence in the management of facilities. The IFMA has members throughout the world.

For More Information

☆ **Outsourcing (pp. 89–90)**
Outsourcing (pp. 2061–62)

FINDING OUT WHAT YOU ARE WORTH: REMUNERATION/SALARIES

BOOKS

Perks and Parachutes
JOHN TARRANT, PAUL FARGIS
New York: Stonesong Press, 1997
338pp ISBN: 0812926773
This book is a guide for people looking to further their career through promotion, or secure employment deals to their best advantage. The author offers advice on how to negotiate such factors as stock- and profit-sharing opportunities, as well as potential benefits and job security issues. Aimed at a range of individuals, from new job-seekers to established executives, this book gives practical information on how to access the ''perks'' of your employment situation.

MAGAZINES

IDS Management Pay Review
ISSN: 1351–4954
Incomes Data Services
77 Bastwick Street, London, EC1V 3TT, U.K.
T: +44 (0) 20 7250 3434
F: +44 (0) 20 7608 0949
www.incomesdata.co.uk/mpr/mpr.htm
This monthly publication aims to keep subscribers up to date with salaries, benefits, and the labor market for managers and professionals. Each edition includes reports on the findings of salary surveys. Subscribers also receive regular research files on specific topics, including an annual *Directory of Salary Surveys*, and access to the Salary Surveys database on the Web site.

IDS Pay Benchmark
ISSN: 1474–1792
Incomes Data Services
77 Bastwick Street, London, EC1V 3TT, U.K.
T: +44 (0) 20 7250 3434
F: +44 (0) 20 7608 0949
www.incomesdata.co.uk/report/paybenchmark.htm
The IDS Pay Benchmark provides information on typical pay levels for all types of jobs in the United Kingdom. It is available online at www.idspaybenchmark.co.uk or in paper format and is updated three times a year.

IOMA Report on Salary Surveys
ISSN: 1067–4551
Institute of Management and Administration
5th Floor, 29 West 35th Street, New York, 10001–2299
T: +1 212 244 0360
F: +1 212 564 0465
www.ioma.com
This monthly report provides information on setting and managing compensation by industry and company size in the United States. Each issue covers the results of 10 to 12 surveys.

Kiplinger's Personal Finance Magazine
ISSN: 1056–697X
Kiplinger Washington Editors, Inc.
1729 H Street, Washington, D.C., 20006
T: +1 888 419 0424
www.kiplinger.com
Formerly entitled *Changing Times*, this magazine is published 12 times per year. With a concentration on banking, accounting, and general financial information, this publication will appeal to both professionals and the general public. It provides concise yet informative articles on salaries, spending, and saving.

Labour Force Survey Quarterly Supplement
ISSN: 0967–5876
Office for National Statistics
1 Drummond Gate, London, SW1V 2QQ, U.K.
T: +44 (0) 1633 812 973
F: +44 (0) 1633 652 747
www.statistics.gov.uk
This Labour Market Trends supplement contains

"Dr __ well remembered that he had a salary to receive, and only forgot that he had a duty to perform."
(Edward Gibbon)

tables of labor market statistics for the United Kingdom, including average gross weekly earnings by region, occupation, and industry sector.

Labour Market Trends
ISSN: 1361–4819
Office for National Statistics
1 Drummond Gate, London, SW1V 2QQ, U.K.
T: +44 (0) 1633 812 973
F: +44 (0) 1633 652 747
www.statistics.gov.uk
This monthly publication includes tables of statistics on average earnings in the United Kingdom, as well as news, research briefs, and technical reports.

Money
Time, Inc.
P.O. Box 60001, Tampa, Florida, 33660
T: +1 800 633 9970
http://money.cnn.com
This magazine is designed to help individuals with personal and family finance. Articles provide guidance on making, investing, and spending money.

INTERNET

HayPayNet
www.haypaynet.com
Access to Hay's PayNet databases of pay rates in 60 countries worldwide is by subscription. However, the site provides news stories on pay and other HR topics from Individual.com.

IOMA
www.ioma.com
The site hosts a discussion group on salaries and compensation.

Job Star Central Salary Information
http://jobstar.org/tools/salary
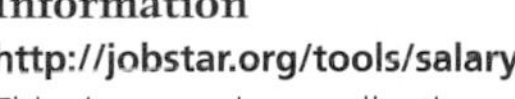
This site contains a collection of links to over 300 Web-based salary surveys, as well as articles and advice.

National Compensation Survey
www.bls.gov/ncs
This site gives access to data from the U.S. Bureau of Labor Statistics.

SalariesReview.com
www.salariesreview.com
This site offers access to salary and cost-of-living information from the Economic Research Institute on thousands of jobs in Canada and the United States and internationally on a pay-per-view basis.

Salary.com
www.salary.com
This U.S. site provides a range of resources, including the Salary Wizard and the SalaryTrax, news, and advice.

StatBase
www.statistics.gov.uk/statbase
A collection of datasets provided by the U.K. Office for National Statistics can be accessed from this site, including average earnings.

Wages.com.au
www.wages.com.au
This Australian site provides information on wages and conditions of employment in Australia and links to salary information sites worldwide.

ORGANIZATIONS

USA

Hay Group
101 Hudson Street, Jersey City, New Jersey, 07302
T: +1 201 557 8400
F: +1 201 557 8444
E: maria_sasso@haygroup.com
www.haygroup.com
This organization provides full-spectrum business information. Providing comprehensive analysis on best practices, this group can aid in organizing work, developing careers, determining reasonable benefits, and providing innovative ways to retain top employees.

Institute of Management and Administration
5th Floor, 29 West 35th Street, New York, 10001–2299
T: +1 212 244 0360
F: +1 212 564 0465
E: info@ioma.com
www.ioma.com
IOMA publishes a monthly *Report on Salary Surveys* and makes selected information from it available in the Salary Zone section of its Web site.

U.S. Department of Labor
200 Constitution Avenue, NW, Washington, D.C., 20210
T: +1 866 487 2365
www.dol.gov/dol/topic/wages
This organization provides information on legislation governing salaries in the United States, including the Fair Labor Standards Act, the Family and Medical Leave Act, and the Equal Pay Act.

WorldatWork
14040 N Northsight Boulevard, Scottsdale, Arizona, 85260
T: +1 480 951 9191
F: +1 480 483 8352
E: customerrelations@worldatwork.org
www.worldatwork.org
WorldatWork (formerly the American Compensation Association) publishes the *Total Salary Increase Budget Survey* which looks at corporate pay budgets, and additional research surveys.

Europe

Hay Group
HR Service Centre, 52 Grosvenor Gardens, London, SW1W 0AU, U.K.
T: +44 (0) 20 7881 7575
F: +44 (0) 20 7881 7100
E: U.K._enquiry@haygroup.com
http://haygroup.co.uk
This international consulting firm publishes a range of surveys and reports, including the *Boardroom Remuneration Guide*, *Compensation Report*, and *Retail Survey*. An online pay database, HayPayNet, is also available by subscription.

Incomes Data Services
77 Bastwick Street, London, EC1V 3TT, U.K.
T: +44 (0) 20 7250 3434
F: +44 (0) 20 7608 0949
E: ids@incomesdata.co.uk
www.incomesdata.co.uk
This is an independent U.K.-based research organization whose publications focus on the employment field. IDS publications and information services are used by those responsible for personnel and related issues in thousands of companies, voluntary associations, and public sector organizations. They are also extensively used by consulting firms, trade unions, lawyers and specialist advisers of many types, academics, and economic commentators.

Industrial Relations Services
Eclipse Group Ltd., 18–20 Highbury Place, London, N5 1QP, U.K.
T: +44 (0) 20 7354 5858
F: +44 (0) 20 7359 4000
E: publications@irseclipse.co.uk
www.irseclipse.co.uk
The IRS publishes the biweekly *Pay and Benefits Bulletin* and the *Pay Intelligence* database which is available in paper format and online.

Remuneration Economics
Computer Economics Ltd., Survey House, 51 Portland Road, Kingston-upon-Thames, Surrey, KT1 2SH, U.K.
T: +44 (0) 20 8549 8726
F: +44 (0) 20 8541 5705
E: cel@celre.co.uk
www.celre.co.uk
Remuneration Economics publishes the *National*

Management Salary Survey in association with the Institute of Management, and additional surveys of professional groups such as engineers, sales and marketing staff, personnel staff, and financial staff.

Reward Group
Reward House, Diamond Way, Stone Business Park, Stone, Staffordshire, ST15 0SD, U.K.
T: +44 (0) 1785 813566
F: +44 (0) 1785 817007
E: enquiries@reward-group.co.uk
www.reward-group.co.uk
The Reward Group publishes about 50 regional, national, and specialist salary surveys. Access to the Salary Search database of pay data for over 600 jobs is available by subscription on the Web site.

International

Watson Wyatt Data Services
1717 H Street NW, Washington, D.C., 20006–3900
T: +1 202 715 7000
F: +1 202 715 7700
E: survey_service@watsonwyatt.com
www.wwdssurveys.com
This company produces a wide range of industry- and geography-based compensation and benefits surveys for the United States and other countries worldwide.

William M. Mercer
Global Information Services, Mercer House, Thames Side, Windsor, Berkshire, SL4 1QN, U.K.
T: +44 (0) 1753 842 188
F: +44 (0) 1753 854 990
E: richard.j.smith@uk.wmmercer.com
www.wmmercer.com
This global consulting company publishes a wide range of compensation and benefits surveys covering the United States, the United Kingdom, and the Far East.

For More Information

- **Conditions of Employment (pp. 1933–35)**
- **Employee Benefits/ Compensation (pp. 1959–61)**
- **Remuneration (pp. 2103–05)**

Flexible Working/Teleworking/ Homeworking

BOOKS

The Distance Manager: A Hands-on Guide to Managing Off-site Employees and Virtual Teams
Kimball Fisher, Mareen Duncan Fisher
New York: McGraw-Hill, 2000
252pp ISBN: 0071360654
This volume is designed to help the manager with a far-flung workforce develop the kinds of relationships needed to keep employees connected and motivated. It provides tips on how to stay connected through frequent use of e-mails and videoconferencing. It also stresses the need for distance managers to enhance their human relations skills.

Flexibility at Work: Balancing the Interests of Employer and Employee
Peter Reilly
Burlington, Vermont: Ashgate Publishing Company, 2001
170pp ISBN: 0566082594
In this text Reilly demonstrates how flexible working can benefit both employers and employees. He defines five different types of flexibility: functional, numerical, temporal, locational, and financial. He then goes on to describe mutual flexibility and produces a model for this and explains how to make it work successfully. Case studies are used throughout.

Flexible Work Arrangements: Managing the Work–Family Boundary
Benjamin Gottlieb, E. Kevin Kelloway, Elizabeth Barham
New York: John Wiley, 1998
208pp ISBN: 0471962287
This book examines the role that flexible work arrangements (such as part-time work, flexible hours and days, home work, and job sharing) can play in reducing employee stress and enhancing productivity. It explores the tension that can arise between work and family responsibility, uses case studies to discuss new ways of structuring work, and offers a blueprint for managing and accommodating flexible work arrangements.

The Flexible Workplace: A Sourcebook of Information and Research
Christine Avery, Diane Zabel
Westport, Connecticut: Quorum Books, 2000
224pp ISBN: 156720189X
A handbook on flexible working and the changing nature of work, this guide is international in scope and offers a review of existing research together with a summary of existing resources. A range of flexible options are covered and the future of workplace flexibility is assessed.

The Home Office Solution: How to Balance Your Professional and Personal Lives While Working at Home
Alice Bredin, Kirsten M. Lagatree
New York: John Wiley, 1998
224pp ISBN: 0471192090
This book explores the advantages and disadvantages of homeworking, acknowledging the invaluable flexibility it provides as well as the dangers. It offers tips to help home workers manage such problems as isolation, interruptions, and burnout and suggests ways to keep motivated and connected with those at the office.

Managing Telework: Strategies for Managing the Virtual Workforce
Jack M. Nilles
New York: John Wiley, 1998
352pp ISBN: 0471293164
This volume begins by looking at the rationale for a decentralized work style, providing data to show the differences between the kinds of work done in the information age and those done in a manufacturing environment. It considers the different forms of teleworking, the personalities suited to this form of work, the problems of managing teleworkers, and the legal and regulatory issues relevant to home offices and the provision of equipment.

101 Tips for Telecommuters
Debra A. Dinnocenzo
San Francisco, California: Berrett-Koehler, 1999
250pp ISBN: 1576750698
This title is for telecommuters and their

"Perfect freedom is reserved for the man who lives by his own work and, in that work, does what he wants to do."
(R. G. Collingwood)

managers and contains many practical ways of getting the most out of this method of working.

Telecommute!: Go to Work without Leaving Home
LISA SHAW
New York: John Wiley, 1996
224pp ISBN: 0471118206
The title views telecommuting from the employee's perspective, revealing who is likely to be successful in this area and the type of jobs that work best with telecommunication. According to the author, the culture that exists within a particular business and the supervisor's manner have important parts to play, but ultimately it is down to the individual telecommuter and the way they perform.

Telecommuting Success: A Practical Guide for Staying in the Loop While Working Away from the Office
MICHAEL J. DZIAK, GIL GORDON
Indianapolis, Indiana: Jist Works, 2001
256pp ISBN: 1571121099
This title highlights the dangers of telecommuting and reveals how they can be avoided. The book covers many topics including: career path strategies for telecommuters; tips for finding a job in telecommunication; and ten ways to stay in the corporate picture.

Teleworking in Brief
MIKE JOHNSON
Woburn, Massachusetts: Butterworth-Heinemann, 1997
208pp (In Brief Series)
ISBN: 0750628758
This practical guide presents an overview of teleworking and looks at the key benefits and disadvantages for both the individual and for the company. It includes the Teleworking Toolkit, a set of practical guidelines, documentation, and checklists that can be adapted for use in any organization.

The Virtual Office Survival Handbook
ALICE BREDIN
New York: John Wiley, 1996
259pp ISBN: 0471120596
This is a comprehensive guide aimed at those working at home, on the road, or with other nontraditional arrangements. It examines both setting up your own business and telecommuting, and covers: organizing the office and selecting the appropriate technology; communication with colleagues; generating business; and publicity. Balancing work and private life, time management, structure of work, and self-management are also reviewed.

MAGAZINES

Flexible Working
ISSN: 1360–9505
Eclipse Group Ltd.
18–20 Highbury Place, London, N5 1QP, U.K.
T: +44 (0) 20 7354 5858
F: +44 (0) 20 7359 4000
www.irseclipse.co.uk
This is a bimonthly management journal that focuses on the practice of flexibility in the workplace. Case studies are the focus of many of the articles.

INTERNET

About.com—Telecommuting
www.telecommuting.about.com/mbody.htm
This part of the about.com site offers good information and connections to resources about telecommuting, including a newsletter and job listings.

All Freelance
www.allfreelance.com
This rich site for freelance workers presents information about managing time, finances, payment, and legal issues. It also provides pages devoted to job listings.

Autoflex
www.autoflex.org.uk
Autoflex is a transnational project set up to promote European best practice in labor market flexibility, particularly in the automotive and engineering sectors. A downloadable Good Practice Guide and research materials are available on the site.

Elancentric
www.elancentric.com
This is a business community representing ''e-lancers'' (teleworkers) and the organizations that employ such workers, giving information, a discussion forum, research, and advice.

European Telework Online
www.eto.org.uk
This is an Internet portal providing information on telework, telecommuting, and related topics. Also includes a resources database, FAQs, statistics, and a discussion group.

Flexibility
www.flexibility.co.uk
This is an online journal on flexible working produced by the U.K. Home Office Partnership. It includes an archive of articles, an interactive forum, case studies, issues, and links to other sites.

Gil Gordon Associates
www.gilgordon.com
This site provided by a New Jersey consulting and training organization includes articles, a reading list, and FAQs, on telecommuting, teleworking, and the virtual office.

Homeworking
www.homeworking.com
Homeworking is a general information site for those already working or those wanting to work at home. It includes how to get started, how to find work, and how to avoid scams.

Internet Homeworking Directory
www.homeworkinguk.com
This directory provides advice and information on U.K. opportunities for working from home. It includes a link to an international site.

ITAC—International Telework Association and Council
www.telecommute.org
This site offers free Web seminars and a free newsletter as well as articles and information about various aspects of teleworking.

Working from Home
www.wfh.co.uk
This is a site provided by BT aimed at giving information on everything you need to know as a company or teleworker about working from home.

ORGANIZATIONS

USA

9 to 5 Working Woman Education Fund
231 West Wisconsin Avenue, Suite 900, Milwaukee, Wisconsin, 53203
T: +1 414 274 0925 or 800 522 0925
F: +1 414 272 2870
E: *naww9to5@execpc.com*
www.9to5.org
Established in 1973, this group conducts research on the concerns of women office workers. In addition to compiling current employment statistics, the WWEF has conducted and published research on health and safety issues, the Family and Medical Leave Act, and the importance of flexible time scheduling. The WWEF will conduct seminars for corporations.

Labor Project for Working Families
2521 Channing Way, No. 5555, Berkeley, California, 94720
T: +1 510 643 7088

"When work is a pleasure, life is a joy! When work is a duty, life is slavery." (Maksim Gorky)

F: +1 510 642 6432
E: *lpwf@uclink.berkeley.edu*
http://laborproject.berkeley.edu
This group works with labor unions to develop work and family policies related to all aspects of flexible work schedules. It provides research facts and statistics to employers and workers and has established a series of training seminars on various work and family topics, including the Family and Medical Leave Act.

Europe

New Ways to Work
26 Shacklewell Lane, Dalston, London, E8 2EZ, U.K.
T: +44 (0) 20 7503 3283
F: +44 (0) 20 7503 2386
E: *information@new-ways.co.uk*
www.new-ways.co.uk
New Ways to Work provides information and advice on the full range of flexible working arrangements, training, consulting services, and research case studies, and contributes to public and government policy.

The Telework, Telecottage and Telecentre Association
Shortwood, Nailsworth, Stroud, Gloucestershire, GL6 0SH, U.K.
T: +44 (0) 24 7669 6986
F: +44 (0)1453 836174
www.tca.org.uk
This organization is dedicated to the promotion of teleworking and aims to benefit people by improving both quality of life and access to work. Members receive the *Teleworker* magazine.

International

International Telework Association and Council
401 Edgewater Place, Suite 600, Wakefield, Massachusetts, 01880
T: +1 202 547 6157
F: +1 202 546 3289
E: *info@telecommute.org*
www.telecommute.org
ITAC is a nonprofit organization that promotes the benefits of telework, and studies, develops, and recommends tools, techniques, and processes for teleworking. Activities include an annual international conference, local groups, and public policy and legislative forums.

For More Information

- ☆ **Virtual Collaboration (pp. 167–68)**
- **Employment Law (pp. 1967–69)**
- **Personnel Management and HR Management (pp. 2067–71)**

Forecasting and Scenario Planning

BOOKS

The Art of the Long View: Planning for the Future in an Uncertain World
Peter Schwartz
New York: Doubleday, 1996
272pp ISBN: 0385267320
The author argues that the only way to successfully plan for the future is to take a long view, taking into account technological, social, political, and economic developments. He then shows the reader how to write scenarios, based on understanding the forces that drive events and signposts that suggest how things may play out in the long term.

Forecasting, Planning, and Strategy for the 21st Century
Spyros G. Makridakis
New York: Free Press, 1990
293pp ISBN: 0029197813
This book highlights the fact that managers must understand the changes taking place in the world and their possible implications in order to determine what to do to ensure their organization's success in the future. The author helps managers to understand the trends and cycles that may impact them and considers the value of a number of analytical planning models, emphasizing the need for creativity in thinking long-term.

Learning from the Future: Competitive Foresight Scenarios
Liam Fahey, Robert Randall
New York: John Wiley, 1997
288pp ISBN: 0471303526
Aimed at managers, consultants, and leaders, this book comprises a selection of articles that explain how to construct and model the outcomes of a variety of strategic decisions. Four key areas are addressed: the basics of scenario learning; approaches to constructing scenarios; scenario application in diverse contexts; and managing scenario learning in the organizational context.

The Living Company: Habits for Survival in a Turbulent Business Environment
Arie de Geus
Boston, Massachusetts: Harvard Business School Press, 1997
215pp ISBN: 087584782X
This book by one of the gurus of scenario planning focuses on his belief that businesses are like living organisms and must be managed as such if they are to survive over time and become what he calls "living companies."

Quantitative Analysis for Management 7th ed.
Barry Render, Ralph M. Stair
Upper Saddle River, New Jersey: Allyn & Bacon, 1999
766pp ISBN: 0130179000
This is a general textbook that introduces the principal techniques of quantitative analysis for organizational decision making. The chapter on forecasting explores different forecasting models and methods, effective monitoring techniques, and the use of computers in the forecasting process.

Scenario Planning: Managing for the Future
Gill Ringland
New York: John Wiley, 1998
422pp ISBN: 047197790X
The author introduces the techniques of scenario planning and explains how they have been used by business. The methods of scenario planning are described; case studies of leading companies, including British Airways, Cable and Wireless, Electrolux, Shell, and United Distillers, provide examples and illustration.

Scenarios: The Art of Strategic Conversation
Kees van der Heijden
New York: John Wiley, 1996
320pp ISBN: 0471966398
Aimed at strategic managers, this book explores the relationship between the strategy process and scenario planning in order to facilitate effective decisions. Drawing on his own experiences while working for Shell, and on the experiences of the company as a whole, the author explores the principles, practices, implementation, and applications of scenario planning.

MAGAZINES

International Journal of Forecasting

"The further ahead you forecast, the less well you do." (C. W. J. Granger)

ISSN: 0169–2070
Elsevier Science
Regional Sales Office, Customer Support Department, P.O. Box 945, New York, 10159–0945
T: +1 212 633 3730
F: +1 212 633 3680
www.elsevier.com
This is the official journal of the International Institute of Forecasters, whose aims and scope it shares: to unify the field of forecasting; to bridge the gap between theory and practice; and to make forecasting useful and relevant for decision and policy makers. It publishes high-quality refereed papers on all aspects of forecasting.

Journal of Business Forecasting
ISSN: 0278–6087
Graceway Publishing Company Inc.
P.O. Box 670159, Station C, Flushing, New York, 11367–0159
T: +1 516 504 7576
F: +1 516 498 2029
www.lbforecast.com
This is a quarterly journal aimed at business executives and managers which provides practical forecasting ideas plus guidance on recognizing and using effective forecasting models for key business decisions. The journal also includes forecasts on the international economic outlook and corporate earnings.

Journal of Forecasting
ISSN: 0277–6693
John Wiley
Wiley InterScience Coordinator, Subscriptions Department, 605 Third Avenue, New York, 10158–0012
T: +1 800 825 7550
F: +1 212 850 6021
www.interscience.wiley.com
This international journal, published eight times a year, presents papers on theoretical, practical, and computational approaches to forecasting across a range of sectors including business, technology, and government. Individual issues include research reports, review articles, and book and software reviews.

INTERNET

Forecasting: Methods and Applications
www.personal.buseco.monash.edu.au/~hyndman/forecasting
This site is based on the book of the same name and offers hundreds of forecasting data sets plus links to forecasting resources and software on the Internet.

Forecasting Principles
www.marketing.wharton.upenn.edu/forecast
This site is aimed at researchers, practitioners, and educators. It draws together current knowledge and thinking on the application of forecasting techniques in the management, operations research, and social science contexts. The site includes a forecasting dictionary and frequently asked questions.

Global Business Network
www.gbn.org
This is the premier site for those interested in scenario planning, including among its founders and members many of those who were involved in Royal Dutch/Shell's groundbreaking work in this area.

International Institute of Forecasters
http://forecasting.cwru.edu
The organization is dedicated to the research and development of forecasting techniques, with the aim of bridging the gap between forecasting theory and practice and contributing to the professional development of forecasters. Its site includes information on events and conferences, frequently asked questions, time series data, and links to other forecasting sites.

World Future Society
www.wfs.org
This nonprofit educational and scientific organization provides information about the technological and social forces that shape the future—and are fundamental to scenario planning and forecasting.

ORGANIZATIONS

USA

Institute of Business Forecasting
P.O. Box 670159, Flushing, New York, 11367–0159
T: +1 516 504 7576
F: +1 516 498 2029
E: ibf@ibf.org
www.ibforecast.com
The aims of this member-based organization are to disseminate knowledge about business forecasting and planning, and to provide products and services to help business executives in their planning and forecasting efforts. The Institute is an affiliate of the *Journal of Business Forecasting*.

Europe

Lancaster University Centre for Forecasting
c/o The Management School, Lancaster University, Lancaster, LA1 4YX, U.K.
T: +44 (0) 1524 593879
F: +44 (0) 1524 844885
E: r.fildcs@lancaster.ac.uk
www.lums.lancs.ac.uk/research/forecast.htm
This center is part of the Management School at Lancaster University. It aims to promote the development of new approaches to forecasting and business models, supports the integration of forecasting theory and practice, and offers research and consultancy services to industry, commerce, and government. Its services include seminars, training, a members' network, and a quarterly journal.

For More Information

☆ Scenario Planning (pp. 267–68)
☆ Why Managers Need Futurists (pp. 279–80)
Business Plans and Planning (pp. 1920–21)
Contingency, Crisis, Disaster Management (pp. 1939–41)
Corporate Strategy (pp. 1944–46)

FRANCHISING

BOOKS

Franchise Bible: How to Buy a Franchise or Franchise Your Own Business 4th ed.
Erwin J. Keup
Central Point, Oregon: PSI Research—Oasis Press, 2000
314pp ISBN: 1555715265
This practical guide to franchising includes sample documents and checklists aimed at helping newcomers to this form of business by providing discussion of the kinds of agreements involved, the advantages and disadvantages of franchising, how to rate potential opportunities, and how to decide if this is the right road to success for them.

Franchise Opportunities Guide Spring/Summer 2001 ed.
International Franchise Association
Washington, D.C.: International Franchise

"Over the past 25 years, economic forecasters have missed four of the past five recessions."
(Anonymous)

Association, 2001
301pp ISBN: 9991791302
This directory provides a comprehensive listing of franchise companies.

Franchise Organizations
JEFFREY L. BRADACH
Boston, Massachusetts: Harvard Business School Press, 1998
238pp ISBN: 087584832X
Using examples primarily from the restaurant business, the book examines the attributes of a successful franchise chain. It also describes the plural-form model (where franchise outlets are merged into a corporate structure) and sets out a framework for managing and expanding plural-form organizations.

Franchising & Licensing: Two Ways to Build Your Business 2nd ed.
ANDREW J. SHERMAN
New York: AMACOM, 1999
449pp ISBN: 0814404502
The second edition of a guide to franchising as a growth strategy for business, this book is geared to help those who decide to franchise or leverage intellectual property in order to expand their market share while avoiding pitfalls such as disputes with franchisees. It explores the legal, operational, and management issues that arise when developing partnering relationships.

Franchising for Dummies
MICHAEL SEID, DAVE THOMAS
New York: Hungry Minds, 2000
378pp ISBN: 0764551604
A simple-to-follow but detailed guide to entering the world of franchises, this volume presents the basics, ranging from initial research, selecting locations, training employees, and running and growing the business. One of the authors is the late Dave Thomas, founder of the ultra-successful *Wendy's International*; the other is a consultant with more than 20 years of hands-on experience. Their book provides practical advice on the major issues facing those who decide to follow this route to self-employment.

The Guide to Franchising 6th ed.
MARTIN MENDELSOHN
London: Cassell, 1999
384pp ISBN: 0304704830
The author introduces franchising by describing its history and development and deals with fundamental questions such as: Why franchise your business?; Why acquire a franchise?; and What can be franchised? He also provides essential information on the legal aspects of the franchise contract. Profiles of the British Franchise Association and the Franchise Consultants Association are included.

Tips and Traps When Buying a Franchise 2nd ed.
MARY E. TOMZACK
Oakland, California: Source Book Publications, 1999
236pp ISBN: 1887137122
The second, revised edition of this guide provides those new to franchising with information on the right questions to ask at the outset, how to find the right location, where to get loans, how to find and train employees, and the ins and outs of buying equipment. It contains war stories and success secrets from a wide variety of franchisees.

MAGAZINES

Business Franchise
ISSN: 0955-789X
Venture Marketing Group
6th Floor, 111 Upper Richmond Road, Putney, London, SW15 2TJ, U.K.
T: +44 (0) 20 8394 5100
F: +44 (0) 20 8785 3388
www.businessfranchise.com
This magazine from the British Franchise Association contains marketing and company information, as well as legal and financial advice, and is aimed at those thinking of taking out a franchise.

Franchise International
ISSN: 1363-7274
Franchise Development Services Ltd.
Franchise House, 56 Surrey Street, Norwich, Norfolk, NR1 3FD, U.K.
T: +44 (0) 1603 620301
F: +44 (0) 1603 630174
www.franchise-international.net
Franchise International promotes the availability of franchise rights worldwide and is aimed at both companies and individuals seeking to take out a master franchise.

Franchise Magazine
ISSN: 0268-8395
Franchise Development Services Ltd.
Franchise House, 56 Surrey Street, Norwich, Norfolk, NR1 3FD, U.K.
T: +44 (0) 1603 620301
F: +44 (0) 1603 630174
www.franchise-group.com/publications/tfm
This journal is aimed at those requiring advice and guidance on all aspects of franchising.

Franchise Times
Franchise Times
2500 Cleveland Avenue N, Suite D So, Roseville, Minnesota, 55113
T: +1 651 631 4995
F: +1 651 633 8749
www.franchisetimes.com
This is a news and information source for franchising. It is published ten times per year and includes information that is related to franchising in areas such as business life, analyst reports, finance, and real estate.

Franchising World
International Franchise Association
1350 New York Avenue NW, Suite 900, Washington, D.C., 200054709
T: +1 202 628 8000
F: +1 202 628 0812
www.franchise.org
Published six times per year this magazine, produced by the International Franchise Association, highlights all areas of franchise business. Featuring current articles by franchising experts, it focuses on topics of interest such as legislative developments, educational programs, and current franchise news. A must-read for anyone working in the franchise industry.

INTERNET

British Franchise Association
www.british-franchise.org
The British Franchise Association's site offers a comprehensive range of advice and information on all aspects of franchising from the perspectives of both franchisors and franchisees. It also provides useful links to other relevant sites.

Entrepreneur
www.entrepreneur.com
This site is a good source of information for those interested in going into business for themselves, with an informative page on franchising as well as pages covering management and marketing.

Franchise Handbook: Online
www.franchise1.com
This online directory provides comprehensive information about franchising opportunities and franchising companies. All contact information is provided as well as a description of the operation, franchising fee, capital requirements, and financing options. The site also contains franchise industry news, trade show information, a list of franchises for sale, and links to other franchise resources.

Franchising.org
www.franchising.org
This is a useful site with links to many other

"In business for yourself, not by yourself." (Ray Kroc)

franchise organizations. Articles, advice, and information are also provided.

Franinfo
www.franinfo.com
This site provides an overview of franchising as well as advice and guidance. It contains two self-tests to determine whether you are suited to being a franchisee.

International Franchising
www.franchiseintl.com
This is a guide to international franchising and offers detailed profiles of a number of franchisors.

Nolo-Law for All
www.nolo.com
This is a good source of legal information, some of which is specifically related to franchising.

Small Business Administration
www.sba.gov
This U.S. government site provides information about resources available to those who need help with their entrepreneurial efforts, including finding financing and locating workshops and training.

ORGANIZATIONS

USA

American Association of Franchisees and Dealers
P.O. Box 81887, San Diego, California, 92138–1887
T: +1 800 733 9858
F: +1 619 209 3777
E: benefits@aafd.org
www.aafd.org
The Association is a nonprofit trade organization representing the rights of independent dealers and franchisees in the United States. It provides guidance and advice on how to take out a franchise.

International Franchise Association
1350 New York Avenue NW, Suite 900, Washington, D.C., 20005–4709
T: +1 202 628 8000
F: +1 202 628 0812
E: ifa@franchise.org
www.franchise.org
The IFA is a membership organization with a heavy bias toward American franchisors, franchisees, and suppliers, although other countries are represented. It is a useful contact for existing or prospective franchisors and franchisees.

Europe

British Franchise Association
Thames View, Newtown Road, Henley-on-Thames, Oxfordshire, RG9 1HG, U.K.
T: +44 (0) 1491 578050
F: +44 (0) 1491 573517
E: mailroom@british-franchise.org.uk
www.british-franchise.org
The BFA was formed in 1977 to promote high standards of practice in franchising; member companies adhere to a code of ethics drawn up by the Association. It also provides a comprehensive range of information to both member and nonmember organizations through its extensive Web site and publications. It is affiliated with the World Franchise Council and the European Franchise Federation.

European Franchise Federation
Avenue 179, B-100, 1070 Brussels, Belgium
T: +32 2 520 16 07
F: +32 2 520 35 17
E: eff-franchise@euronet.be
www.eff-franchise.com
The Federation is an international nonprofit organization, founded in 1972, that aims to promote franchising in Europe and the interests of the national franchise associations or federations that make up its membership.

For More Information

Small and Growing Businesses (pp. 2112–15)

General Business Information: Online Business Newspapers

INTERNET

Business Day
www.bday.co.za
This site provides news, information, and analysis covering South African and international business. It includes company and market information.

China Daily
www.chinadaily.com.cn
This site delivers daily news from China in the English language. It covers Chinese and international business.

Daily Telegraph
www.telegraph.co.uk
This is the site for the daily U.K. newspaper providing national and international coverage.

Daily Yomiuri On-line
www.yomiuri.co.jp
This is an online, Japanese daily paper containing national and international news. It covers political and economic topics in English under "The Daily Yomiuri."

Financial Times
www.ft.com
This is the online version of the U.K. daily newspaper which provides international business and financial news and analysis. International markets and industries and company information are covered.

The Guardian
www.guardian.co.uk
This online version of the U.K. daily newspaper contains in-depth coverage of national and international news including politics, finance, social issues, and education.

Handelsblatt
www.handelsblatt.com
This is the online version of the German-language daily newspaper providing in-depth economic and corporate news.

The Independent
www.independent.co.uk
This online version of the U.K. daily newspaper provides national and international news.

International Herald Tribune
www.iht.com
This is the site for the English-language daily paper published in Paris. It provides news, analysis, and commentary on international business affairs.

Le Monde
www.lemonde.fr
This online version of the French-language daily

paper covers politics, economics, and current affairs generally. It provides information on the Francophone world.

Los Angeles Times
www.latimes.com
This is the online version of the U.S. daily paper, with national and international news covering business and finance.

New York Times
www.nytimes.com
This online version of the U.S. daily paper covers national and international news. The business section includes U.S. and international market news and company research tools.

The Times
www.thetimes.co.uk
This online version of the U.K. daily newspaper provides national and international coverage.

USA Today
www.usatoday.com
This U.S. daily paper features financial news, stock reports and business articles.

Wall Street Journal Online
www.online.wsj.com
This is the paper of record for most financial news in the United States. Excellent columnists, loads of free advice, and timely features are the keys to this Web site's success. For many of the features on the site, you will need to register (warning: there is a fee), but most people will find what they need in the free-access sections of the Web site—good overviews, market forecasting, and trend analysis.

Washington Post
www.washingtonpost.com
This is the online version of the U.S. daily paper, containing national and international news. It has a strong business section that covers a range of information and resources including market news, stock quotes, and a glossary of business terms.

General Business Information: Online Financial Information

INTERNET

Accounting Web
www.accountingweb.co.uk
This is an online community site for accountants providing news, online discussions, reviews of accountancy products and services, database of training courses, job listings, and access to external services such as ICC company information.

Bloomberg
www.bloomberg.com
This site provides a range of business, market, and financial news.

Country Briefings
www.iijworld.com
County Briefings provides information on world stock markets and downloadable financial reports on a range of countries.

Dow Jones
www.dowjones.com
This is the Web site of the company responsible for the *Wall Street Journal*, Barron's Online, *Far East Economic Review* Interactive and *SmartMoney*.

The Economist
www.economist.com
This the Web site of *The Economist* magazine. It contains news of global business and politics, with an archive of articles and economic briefings on 60 countries.

FinanceWise
www.financewise.com
This is a U.K.-based search engine for financial information sites which can be searched by company name, sector, or keyword. The site also contains topic guides with links to Web sites, online articles and reports, news and information on conferences, financial books, and jobs.

Financial Times
www.ft.com
This is the online version of the United Kingdom's premier daily financial newspaper with news of markets, industries, and companies.

FIND Financial Information Net Directory
www.find.co.uk
FIND is an independent gateway to U.K. financial Web sites covering banking and savings, investment, insurance, pensions, and financial information services.

Global Investor
www.global-investor.com
Global Investor offers information for investors with news and access to a range of free resources, including a glossary of financial terms and details of financial books and periodicals.

HM Treasury
www.hm-treasury.gov.uk
This site offers economic and financial information from the U.K. government, including press releases and speeches, regulatory information, policy statements, budget documentation, and information on the Euro.

Interactive Investor International
www.iii.co.uk
This site provides information for investors including share tracking, market news, and advice on personal finance.

Nasdaq
www.nasdaq.com
This is the Web site of the world's largest electronic stock market, with stock quotes, news and articles, annual reports, overviews, and global market information.

OSU Virtual Finance Library
http://fisher.osu.edu/fin/overview.htm
This is an index of financial sites for investors, executives, researchers, and students provided by Ohio State University's Department of Finance. It covers a range of areas including banks, exchanges, market news, and insurers.

SEC U.S. Securities and Exchange Commission
www.sec.gov
The SEC Web site offers news and reports from the U.S. government body and access to the database of company filings.

Standard & Poor's
www.standardpoor.com
Standard & Poor's provides financial information and services. The Web site features a discussion forum, stock quotes, ratings, and indices, along with global financial news and analyses.

"All great change in business has come from outside the firm, not from inside." (Peter Drucker)

Wachowicz's Web World
http://web.utk.edu/~jwachowi/wacho_world.html
Listing financial management sites aimed at students, this index is based on the chapters of a financial management textbook.

Wall Street Journal Online
www.wsj.com
This is the paper of record for most financial news in the United States. Excellent columnists, loads of free advice, and timely features are the keys to this Web site's success. For many of the features on the site, you will need to register (warning: there is a fee), but most people will find what they need in the free-access sections of the Web site—good overviews, market forecasting, trend analysis.

GENERAL BUSINESS INFORMATION: ONLINE HUMAN RESOURCES SOURCES

INTERNET

American Society for Training and Development
www.astd.org
The ASTD is a professional association for training personnel. The site provides an online magazine, news, virtual communities, a free e-mail newsletter, and a Buyer's Guide listing training suppliers and consultants. Some services are for members only.

Chartered Institute of Personnel and Development
www.cipd.co.uk
The CIPD is a professional association for personnel managers in the United Kingdom. Registration is required and some services are available only to members. The site provides *People Management* magazine, news, summaries of research reports, fact sheets, and information on publications, training courses, and events.

HR Guide
www.hr-guide.com
This site provides definitions and basic introductions to a range of human resources subjects linked to a collection of Web site listings with ratings and brief descriptions. It has a strong focus on HR software and includes a demo of an online 360-degree feedback questionnaire.

HRnet Web Centre
www.the-hrnet.com
This site provides industry news, discussion forums, a database of HR consultants, and book reviews.

HR Tools.com
www.hrtools.com
This site focuses on online tools, including forms and training resources. Registration is required.

HRZone
www.hrzone.com
HRZone is a U.S.-based site providing information on the basics of human resources management, as well as articles, news, legal information including case summaries, Web site reviews, and a directory of suppliers.

Human Resources Management Resources on the Internet
www.nbs.ntu.ac.uk/depts/hrm/hrm_link.htm
This online directory provides comprehensive collections of links to HR sites in broad categories, compiled at Nottingham Business School Department of Human Resources Management.

Online Recruitment
www.onrec.com
This provides news on the online recruitment industry and a searchable database of online recruitment sites worldwide with reviews.

Personnel Today
www.personneltoday.com
This comprehensive site includes information from the U.K. magazine covering HR news and events, legal developments worldwide, and career advice. A searchable directory of consultants and information sources, and links to Web sites on HR topics are also available.

Society for Human Resources Management
www.shrm.org
The society is a professional organization for HR managers in the United States. The site contains a range of resources including: news, magazine, discussion forum, collections of company practices and policies, mission statements and job descriptions, and an extensive set of links. Some resources are for members only.

Training Zone
www.trainingzone.co.uk
This is a portal site for training professionals. Its resources include Trainer's Toolkit, Expert Guides, and directories of training suppliers, venues, and training courses. Registration is required.

U.K.-HRD
www.ukhrd.com
This is a discussion forum for training and HR specialists sponsored by Fenman.

Workforce Online
www.workforce.com
This site is an online HR magazine with feature articles, news, discussion forums, and a free e-mail newsletter.

Workindex
www.workindex.com
Sponsored by the publishers of *Human Resource Executive* and Cornell University School of Labor and Industrial Relations, this site provides a comprehensive set of links to HR Web sites. Book extracts and reviews, a salary calculator, a jobs database, legal questions and answers, HR news, and magazine articles are also available.

WorldatWork
www.worldatwork.org
Formerly the American Compensation Association, this site offers information for human resource managers including news, topic briefings, a free e-mail newsletter, a glossary of terms, magazine articles on a pay per view basis, and a buyer's guide. Information on training courses, seminars, accredited programs, publications, and research surveys produced by the organization are also available. Additional services are available to members.

  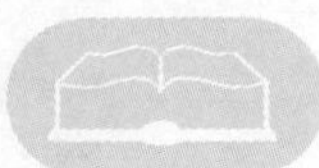    

General Business Information: Online Sources for Marketing

INTERNET

Business Marketing Association
www.marketing.org
This site offers a free e-mail newsletter, B2B Direct, and a directory of marketing communications and advertising agencies. The members' library contains industry surveys, articles, white papers, and book reviews.

Ed Osworth's Internet Marketing Index
www.internetmarketingindex.com
This collection of links to marketing sites has a strong focus on using the Web for marketing but also includes sections on new marketing products, discussion boards, e-zines, and marketing news from Moreover. A free subscription to weekly TipSheet is offered.

Larry Chase's Web Digest for Marketers
www.wdfm.com
Writer and consultant, Larry Chase, offers a free weekly e-mail newsletter with reviews of marketing Web sites and a searchable archive of previous editions.

Marketing and International Business Links
http://wtfaculty.wtamu.edu/~sanwar.bus/otherlinks.htm
This site offers an extensive list of links on international business and trade, including journals; company, market, and industry information; international marketing, and many other topics. Syed Tariq Anwar, the compiler of the list, is Professor of Marketing and International Business at West Texas A & M University.

Marketing Online
www.marketing.haynet.com
This site provides online articles and news from *Marketing* magazine. It also offers selected league tables of marketing agencies, a directory of marketing services, a discussion forum, and links.

marketingpower.com
www.marketingpower.com
Online resources for marketing professionals are provided by the American Marketing Association, including best practice information and articles, a directory of suppliers, links to business information, marketing tools, and an online job and career site.

Marketing Terms.com
www.marketingterms.com
This site includes an Internet Marketing Dictionary and links to a number of marketing-related dictionaries and glossaries on the Web.

Marketing Virtual Library
www.knowthis.com
This is an excellent collection of well organized and evaluated links to general marketing sites and related areas.

Marketing Week
www.mad.co.uk/mw
This site provides news, articles, and analysis from *Marketing Week* magazine.

Wilson Internet Web Marketing and E-commerce
www.wilsonweb.com
This extensive site, sponsored by Wilson Internet Services, features the Web Marketing Info Center and the E-Commerce Research Room with links to thousands of articles, and offers a free e-mail newsletter.

Health and Safety

BOOKS

Handbook of Modern Hospital Safety
William Charney
Boca Raton, Florida: Lewis, 1999
1024pp ISBN: 1566702569
The healthcare environment is getting more hazardous for the workers in that industry. This book covers the major occupational health issues in hospitals including tuberculosis engineering controls, antineoplastic drugs, back injury prevention and ergonomics, and radiation protection. It also addresses the human factors such as laboratory safety, respiratory protection, biological exposure testing, and the functions and staffing of a hospital safety office.

Health and Safety Administration Handbook
John Forsaith, Nick Townsend
New York: Beekman, 2000
150pp ISBN: 0846451735
This loose-leaf reference guide is designed to help health and safety practitioners create and maintain organizational systems that meet legal requirements in the United Kingdom. It underlines the importance of integrating health and safety systems with line management. The focus is on the legislative framework—statutes and regulations; health and safety policy; risk assessment; model health policies and safety policies; and accident reporting and investigation. A floppy disk containing forms is included.

Health and Safety in Brief 2nd ed.
John Ridley
Woburn, Massachusetts: Butterworth-Heinemann, 2001
288pp ISBN: 0750653205
Aimed at students and managers with responsibility for workplace health and safety, the book provides practical and succinct guidance on day-to-day health and safety considerations in the workplace. The issues covered include U.K. health and safety law, management responsibilities, accidents, health protection, chemicals, noise and hearing protection, construction, manual handling, and the safe use of electricity.

How Smart Managers Improved Their Safety and Health Systems: Benchmarking with OSHA VPP Criteria
Charlotte A. Garner, Patricia O. Horn
Des Plaines, Illinois: American Society of Safety Engineers, 1998
321pp ISBN: 1885581211
This book describes how to establish and maintain a safety and health program management system for competitive advantage.

Managing Health and Safety: An Open Learning Workbook for Managers and Trainers
Health and Safety Executive
Sudbury, 1997
76pp ISBN: 0717611531
This open learning workbook is designed to enable managers to make constructive changes

to health and safety at work. The five sections focus on: understanding the importance of health and safety; evaluating your current situation; getting started; implementing improvements; and continuing the progress.

OSHA: Employee Workplace Rights
Washington, D.C.: U.S. Dept. of Labor, Occupational Safety and Health Administration, 1997
28pp
This is an informational booklet intended to provide a generic, non-exhaustive overview of a standards-related topic. This publication does not alter or determine compliance responsibilities, which are set forth in OSHA standards themselves and the Occupational Safety and Health Act. Shipping list no.: 98-0039-P.

Violence in the Workplace: A Prevention and Management Guide for Businesses
S. Anthony Baron
Ventura, California: Pathfinder Publishing, 2001
185pp ISBN: 0934793700
This book describes proven methods for preventing and managing violence in the workplace. It teaches managers how to recognize the signs of potential violence based on specific behaviors of the employee and an increased understanding of basic human behavior. The book describes how to develop a prevention plan and train employees. It also tells you what to do if a violent situation occurs.

Workplace Health and Safety Sourcebook
Helene Henderson
Detroit, Michigan: Omnigraphics, 1999
600pp ISBN: 0780802341
This book identifies a number of hazards associated with the workplace, and suggests ways in which these hazards can be avoided. It also offers steps toward recovery for those who suffer from workplace-related disorders. Issues discussed include child labor, stress, workplace violence, and the use of hazardous chemicals. It includes a glossary and lists of resources.

Young People at Work: A Guide for Employers
Health and Safety Executive
Sudbury, 2000
36pp ISBN: 0717618897
This publication provides guidance for employers of young people, focusing on health and safety at work and particular risks to those under 18 years of age. Separate sections cover: general duties for all employers; assessing health and safety risks; and hazards and ways of avoiding them. The law relating to health and safety in the United Kingdom is reviewed and advice given on what employers need to do to comply with it.

MAGAZINES

Croner's Health and Safety at Work
Croner CCH
145 London Road, Kingston-upon-Thames, Surrey, KT2 6SR, U.K.
T: +44 (0) 20 8547 3333
F: +44 (0) 20 8547 2638
www.croner.co.uk
The subscription service includes comprehensive loose-leaf volumes with monthly updates outlining the requirements of the British Health and Safety at Work Act 1974 and related legislation, a fortnightly newsletter, special reports, and access to a helpline for advice on health and safety law and management.

Industrial Safety & Hygiene News
ISSN: 8755-2566
Business News Publishing Company
755 West Big Beaver Road, Suite 1000, Troy, Michigan, 48084
T: +1 248 244 6498
F: +1 248 244 6439
www.ishn.com
Published monthly, this magazine is a must-read for any safety professional. With an emphasis on heavy industry, the publication provides the latest developments in industry news and legislation.

Job Safety & Health Quarterly
ISSN: 1057-5820
Occupational Safety and Health Administration (OSHA)
U.S. Department of Labor, 200 Constitution Avenue, Washington, D.C., 20210
T: +1 202 693 1999
F: +1 202 512 2233
www.osha.gov/html/jshq-index.html
An official publication of the U.S. government's Occupational Safety & Health Administration, *JSHQ* covers all aspects of safety at work, including the workplace environment and staff injury and illness. The magazine also contains a Q&A section. PDF downloads of older issues are available from the OSHA Web site.

Occupational Hazards
ISSN: 0029-7909
Penton Publishing
1300 E. 9th Street, Cleveland, Ohio, 44114
T: +1 216 696 7000
F: +1 216 696 7658
www.occupationalhazards.com
Published 12 times per year, this magazine focuses on occupational hazards in industry and manufacturing. The articles within the magazine provide updates on the latest in national and regional legislative action, as well as insight on current news headlines in this field. Environmental professionals will find this to be an insightful resource.

Occupational Health and Safety
ISSN: 0362-4064
Stevens Publishing Corporation
5151 Beltline Road, 10th Floor, Dallas, Texas, 75254
T: +1 972 687 6700
F: +1 972 687 6770
www.ohsonline.com
This monthly publication offers practical advice on how to keep the workplace safe from hazards and fully compliant with laws and regulations. The information provided is primarily aimed at professionals in the health, safety, industrial hygiene, environmental, security, and fire protection fields.

Occupational Safety and Health
ISSN: 0143-5353
Royal Society for the Prevention of Accidents
Edgbaston Park, 353 Bristol Road, Edgbaston, Birmingham, West Midlands, B5 7ST, U.K.
T: +44 (0) 121 248 2000
F: +44 (0) 121 248 2001
www.rospa.co.uk
This journal covers occupational safety and health in a range of industries and is aimed at health and safety professionals and senior managers.

Professional Safety
ISSN: 0099-0027
American Society of Safety Engineers
1800 E. Oakton Street, Des Plaines, Illinois, 60018
T: +1 847 699 2929
F: +1 847 768 3434
www.asse.org
This monthly journal delivers information and in-depth articles aimed at promoting the advancement of the safety profession. Articles focus on innovative research and analysis of successful real-world applications. It also contains timely news sections and information on relevant governmental regulations.

Safety + Health
ISSN: 0891-1797
National Safety Council
1121 Spring Lake Drive, Itasca, Illinois, 60143-3201
T: +1 630 285 1121
F: +1 630 285 1315

"One lesson a man learns from Harvard Business School is that an executive is only as good as his health."
(Jeffrey Archer)

www.nsc.org
Safety + Health covers the subject from an international perspective, providing practical information to employers responsible for safety and health issues.

World Safety Journal
ISSN: 1015–5589
World Safety Organization
WSO World Management Center, 106 W. Young Avenue, Suite G, P.O. Box 518, Warrensburg, Missouri, 64093
T: +1 660 747 3132
F: +1 660 747 2647
www.worldsafety.org
The official journal of the WSO (World Safety Organization), this is a biannual publication for safety professionals around the world. Disciplines covered are safety, environment, security, public health, transportation, and construction.

INTERNET

American Society for Industrial Security
www.asisonline.org
ASIS is an organization for professionals responsible for security and for others who need a better understanding of the constant changes in security issues and solutions. It provides its members and the security community with access to a full range of industrial security programs and services.

European Agency for Health and Safety at Work
http://europe.osha.eu.int
The EAHSW was set up by member states of the European Union to provide a wide range of information promoting good health and safety practices.

HSE Direct
www.hsedirect.com
The U.K. Health and Safety Executive and Butterworth Tolley have joined forces to provide a comprehensive one-stop shop for all health and safety information, guidance, and legislation in the United Kingdom. An extensive free area also offers a wide range of general information, while a subscription service gives full text access to all H&S annotated legislation and EU directives, HSE guidance publications and codes of practice, and other texts.

Occupational Safety & Health Administration (OSHA)
www.osha.gov
OSHA's mission is to ensure the health and safety of the American worker. Its site features an events calendar, a library, and convenient access to its regulations and its inspection data.

The American College of Healthcare Executives
www.ache.org
ACHE is an international professional society of nearly 30,000 healthcare executives. It is known for its credentialing and educational programs and for its publications. This site provides specific resources for 10 special interest groups, governmental news, and an events calendar.

Trades Union Congress
www.tuc.org.uk
The TUC's Web site provides a range of general information on health and safety matters.

ORGANIZATIONS

USA

National Institute for Occupational Safety and Health (NIOSH)
Room 715H, Hubert Humphrey Building, 200 Independence Avenue SW, Washington, D.C., 20201
T: +1 513 533 8328
F: +1 513 533 8573
E: pubstaf@cdc.gov
www.cdc.gov/niosh
The NIOSH is the U.S. federal agency responsible for conducting research into, and making recommendations for, the prevention of work-related disease and injury under the Occupational Safety and Health Act of 1970. It is part of the Centers for Disease Control and Prevention. NIOSH offers free access to a number of databases containing a wide range of information.

Occupational Safety & Health Administration (OSHA)
U.S. Department of Labor, Office of Public Affairs, Room N3647, 200 Constitution Avenue NW, Washington, D.C., 20210
T: +1 202 693 1999
www.osha.gov
OSHA is responsible for overseeing compliance with all health and safety legislation in the United States and for workplace inspections.

Europe

British Safety Council
70 Chancellors Road, London, W6 7RS, U.K.
T: +44 (0) 20 8741 1231
F: +44 (0) 20 8741 4555
E: mail@britsafe.org
www.britishsafetycouncil.org
The BSC is an independent membership organization with 12,000 corporate members who receive a range of research and information services aimed at improving safety in the workplace.

Health and Safety Executive (HSE)
Rose Court, 2 Southwark Bridge, London, SE1 9HS, U.K.
T: +44 (0) 20 7717 6000
F: +44 (0) 20 7717 6717
E: hseinformationservices@natbrit.com
www.hse.gov.uk
The HSE is the executive arm of the U.K. government's Health and Safety Commission. It is responsible for advising the HSC on formulating policy, overseeing the implementation of all health and safety legislation in the United Kingdom, carrying out inspections required by the legislation, and providing advice and guidance on all occupational health and safety matters. It has a number of regional offices.

RoSPA The Royal Society for the Prevention of Accidents
Edgbaston Park, 353 Bristol Road, Edgbaston, Birmingham, West Midlands, B5 7ST, U.K.
T: +44 (0) 121 248 2000
F: +44 (0) 121 248 2001
E: help@rospa.co.uk
www.rospa.co.uk
RoSPA is a charity mainly funded by membership subscriptions. It offers a wide range of advice, training, and information to members, in relation both to workplace safety and to safety at home.

International

World Safety Organization
WSO World Management Center, 106 W. Young Avenue, Suite G, P.O. Box 518, Warrensburg, Missouri, 64093
T: +1 660 747 3132
F: +1 660 747 2647
E: wsowmc@sockert.net
www.worldsafety.org
The WSO has offices in 17 countries around the world, including Australia, India, and Russia. It holds international conferences, publishes newsletters and the biannual *World Safety Journal*, develops training programs, and administers a number of awards.

For More Information

Employment Law (pp. 1967–69)

"There is no right to strike against the public safety by anybody, anywhere, any time."
(Calvin Coolidge)

  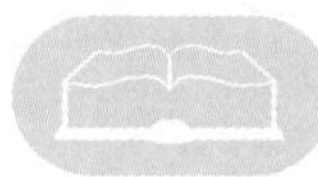    

Health Services Management

BOOKS

Back to Basics: Foundations of Healthcare Management
Chicago, Illinois: Health Administration Press, 2000
380pp ISBN: 1567931405
This collection of chapters from a number of books published by HAP provides an introduction to key technical and leadership skills for healthcare managers. The areas of strategic planning, performance improvement, financial management, marketing, change management, and team management are covered.

Business Planning for Healthcare Management 2nd ed.
Carolyn Semple Piggot
Buckingham, England: Open University Press, 2000
192pp ISBN: 033520646
This book offers practical guidance on planning strategies for hospital managers, clinical practitioners, and those new to management in British healthcare organizations. A step-by-step guide to the process of business planning in general is provided, covering implementation and evaluation. The author also addresses the question of when it is necessary to seek expert help, and a useful case study shows how planning issues arise from clinical issues.

Excellence in Healthcare Management
Alison Morton-Cooper, Margaret Bamford, eds.
Oxford: Blackwell Science, 1997
247pp ISBN: 0632040327
This book serves as an introduction to key issues and dilemmas facing healthcare managers today. The four main issues addressed are: excellence in human resources management; key concepts in quality, finance, and information management; education and training in health care; and the politics of health care.

The Global Challenge of Healthcare Rationing
Angela Coulter, Chris Ham, eds.
Philadelphia, Pennsylvania: Taylor & Francis, 2000
288pp (State of Health Series)
ISBN: 0335204635
This book offers an overview of current thinking in the area of resource allocation and priority setting in health services. The contributors are decision makers and researchers from around the world who provide an insight into the factors that influence decision making, such as medical research and cost-effectiveness studies.

Health Care Management: Organization Design & Behavior
Arnold D. Kaluzny, Stephen M. Shortell
Albany, New York: Delmar, 1999
448pp ISBN: 0766810720
This textbook, for students in health services administration, management, and policy programs, reviews the application of management and organizational thinking and research to healthcare organizations. It includes sections on organizations and managers, on motivating, leading, and negotiating, on operating the technical systems, on renewing the organization, and on charting the future.

Health Services Management: Readings and Commentary 7th ed.
Anthony R. Kovner, Duncan Neuhasuer, eds.
Chicago, Illinois: Health Administration Press, 2001
525pp ISBN: 1567931456
This compilation of recent readings from leading scholars and writers in the field of healthcare management covers a wide spectrum of management functions, including organizational issues and the role of the manager.

Market-driven Healthcare: Who Wins, Who Loses in the Transformation of American's Largest Service Industry
Regina Herzlinger
Cambridge, Massachusetts: Perseus, 1997
416pp ISBN: 0201489945
A well-received work on how the healthcare industry in the United States copes with the demands of the modern consumer.

Risk Management Handbook: For Health Care Organizations
Roberta Carroll
San Francisco, California: Jossey-Bass, 2001
752pp ISBN: 0787955531
This handbook for health facility risk managers is a collection of ideas from 40 risk management professionals. It identifies some of the risk exposures in healthcare, and offers current information on risk management treatments and techniques, regulatory and legal updates, and assessment tools that add up to a general framework for health-care risk management.

MAGAZINES

British Journal of Health Care Management
ISSN: 1358–0574
Mark Allen Publishing
286–288 Croxted Road, London, SE24 9BY, U.K.
T: +44 (0) 20 8671 7521
F: +44 (0) 20 8671 4454
www.bjhcm.com
The *BJHCM* is a monthly magazine for healthcare managers covering current issues in the management of healthcare services. Each issue contains peer-reviewed articles, regular columns, and news items.

European Journal of Public Health
ISSN: 1101–1262
Oxford University Press
Journals Customer Services, 2001 Evans Road, Cary, North Carolina, 27513
T: +1 919 677 0977
F: +1 919 677 1714
www3.oup.co.uk/eurpub
The *EJPH* is a multidisciplinary journal providing a forum for discussion and debate on current public health issues. Coverage is international but with a focus on the European region. Original scientific articles, policy articles, reviews on major themes, editorials, commentaries, book reviews, and news are all included.

Health Management
Communications Team
Exmouth House, 3–11 Pine Street, London, EC1R 0JH, U.K.
T: +44 (0) 20 7923 5400
F: +44 (0) 20 7923 5401
Health Management is a monthly journal available to members of the Institute of Healthcare Management. The journal aims to meet the needs of healthcare managers in the U.K. National Health Service and contains material written by practicing managers, academics, and independent journalists. Articles cover management theory and practice, continuing professional development for managers, and current issues within the health sector.

Health Service Journal
ISSN: 0952–2271

"Profit is like health, necessary but not the reason why we live." (Anonymous)

EMAP Public Sector Management
Greater London House, Hampstead Road, London, NW1 7EJ, U.K.
T: +44 (0) 20 7505 8000
F: +44 (0) 20 7505 8504
www.hsj.co.uk
The *HSJ* is a weekly magazine offering news, features, and comment on health policy and management issues. A section on job vacancies is included.

International Journal for Quality in Health Care
ISSN: 1353–4505
Oxford University Press
Journals Customer Services, 2001 Evans Road, Cary, North Carolina, 27513
T: +1 919 677 0977
F: +1 919 677 1714
www3.oup.co.uk/intqhc
The *IJQHC* is the official journal of the International Society for Quality in Health Care. It is an interdisciplinary peer-reviewed bimonthly journal that includes contributions from health professionals and researchers. Articles cover health services research, healthcare evaluation, technology issues, and health economics.

International Journal of Health Care Quality Assurance
ISSN: 0952–6862
Emerald (North America)
4th Floor, 44 Brattle Street, Cambridge, Massachusetts, 02138
T: +1 888 622 0075
www.emeraldinsight.com/ijhcqa.htm
This journal appears seven times a year and is aimed at those involved in developing and monitoring quality assurance programs in the healthcare sector. Issues relating to healthcare quality and standards are covered from both practical and theoretical perspectives.

Journal for Healthcare Quality
ISSN: 1062–2551
National Association for Healthcare Quality
P.O. Box 3781, Oak Brook, Illinois, 60522
T: +1 800 966 9392
F: +1 877 218 7939
www.nahq.org
The *JHQ* is published by the National Association for Healthcare Quality in the United States and is aimed at professionals responsible for promoting and monitoring the quality of health care. Articles focus on such areas as improvement, risk management, and payment systems. Book reviews and legislative updates are also provided.

Journal of Healthcare Management
ISSN: 1096–9012
American College of Healthcare Executives
1 North Franklin Street, Suite 1700, Chicago, Illinois, 60606–3491
T: +1 312 424 2800
F: +1 312 424 0023
www.ache.org/pubs.jhm.cfm
JHM is the official journal of the American College of Healthcare Executives. It is a bimonthly peer-reviewed publication for executives, practicing healthcare managers, academics, and policymakers. Articles cover strategic issues in the provision and delivery of healthcare services.

Modern Healthcare
ISSN: 0160–7480
Crain Communications, Inc.
5th Floor, 360 N. Michigan Avenue, Chicago, Illinois, 60601–3806
T: +1 312 280 3173
F: +1 312 280 3183
www.crain.com
Modern Healthcare is a weekly magazine designed to provide news and information on current trends for healthcare executives, principally those responsible for finance and purchasing. Major areas of coverage include finance, managed care, marketing, technology, information systems, and regulatory developments. The magazine is available on the Web at www.modernhealthcare.com.

INTERNET

Academy for Health Services Research and Health Policy
www.academyhealth.org
This site provides an extensive collection of links to U.S. healthcare organizations and access, via the U.S. National Library of Medicine, to a database of health service research projects.

Health Service Journal
www.hsj.co.uk
In addition to articles from the journal, this site provides news, book reviews, an online management game, and a history of the U.K. National Health Service.

HQHQ
www.hqhq.org
This site offers access to distance learning materials for healthcare managers provided by a Scottish consulting and training organization. An initial module is offered free of charge.

National Electronic Library for Health: Health Management
www.nelh.nhs.uk/management
This library contains management briefings and links to 1,100 evaluated resources, including news, databases, discussion groups, training courses, and calendars of events.

National Information Center on Health Services Research and Health Care Technology
www.nlm.nih.gov/nichsr/nichsr.html
This site, which is part of the U.S. National Library of Medicine, provides information on databases, training, and research programs.

ORGANIZATIONS

USA

American College of Healthcare Executives
1 North Franklin Street, Suite 1700, Chicago, Illinois, 60606–3491
T: +1 312 424 2800
F: +1 312 424 0023
E: ache@ache.org
www.ache.org
ACHE is a professional organization for healthcare executives that aims to meet its members' professional and educational needs, and to promote high ethical standards and advance management excellence in health care. Its activities include training and career development programs, research, and an annual congress on healthcare management. ACHE produces the magazine, *Healthcare Executive*, the *Journal of Healthcare Management*, and books published by the Health Administration Press.

National Association for Healthcare Quality
4700 W. Lake Avenue, Glenview, Illinois, 60025
T: +1 800 966 9392
F: +1 877 218 7939
www.nahq.org
The NAHQ has the goal of improving the quality of health care and supporting the development of those working in healthcare quality. Founded in 1976, it currently has over 6,000 individual and 100 institutional members.

Europe

European Health Management Association
Vergemount Hall, Clonskeagh, Dublin 6, Republic of Ireland
T: +353 1 283 9299
F: +353 1 283 8653
E: office@ehma.org
www.ehma.org
The EHMA acts as a forum for policy makers and senior managers, personnel directors and training officers, and academic and research organizations in the health sector. Its aim is to build bridges between them.

Institute of Healthcare Management
46–48 Grosvenor Gardens, London, SW1W 0EB,

"The manifest picture of bureaucratic organization is a confusing one." (Elliot Jaques)

U.K.
T: +44 (0) 20 7881 9235
F: +44 (0) 20 7881 9236
E: enquiries@ihm.org.uk
www.ihm.org.uk
The IHM is a professional body for managers working in all areas of healthcare with a membership of around 9,000 in the United Kingdom. The organization was formed by the merger of the Institute of Health Services Management and the Association of Managers in General Practice and incorporated in 1999. Its aims are to promote high standards of professional healthcare management, to represent the views and interests of healthcare managers, to influence policy, to advance research, and to encourage networking. Its activities include publications, education and training, and an annual conference.

The King's Fund
11–13 Cavendish Square, London, W1G 0AN, U.K.
T: +44 (0) 20 7303 2400
F: +44 (0) 20 7307 2801
E: library@kingsfund.org.uk
www.kingsfund.org.uk
The King's Fund is a London-based independent healthcare charity that works at national and international levels for better health policies and services. The organization awards grants, carries out research and development projects, and offers conference facilities, a bookshop, library and information services, and training courses.

International

International Society for Quality in Health Care
Level 9, Aikenhead Centre, St. Vincent's Hospital, 41 Victoria Parade, Fitzroy, Victoria, 3065, Australia
T: +61 3 9417 6971
F: +61 3 9417 6851
E: isqua@isqua.org.au
www.isqua.org.au
The ISQHC provides a multidisciplinary forum for the exchange of information and expertise in the field of quality in health care. The organization promotes quality improvement in the healthcare sector, and its activities include the development of an internationally agreed method of assessing healthcare standards, research and education, meetings, and the publication of a journal. The membership includes individuals and institutions from over 60 countries.

For More Information

Public Sector Management (pp. 2092–94)

IMPORTING

BOOKS

Building an Import/Export Business 2nd ed.
Kenneth D. Weiss
New York: John Wiley, 1997
304pp ISBN: 0471177873
This is a user-friendly guide to starting and building a successful import or export business. It gives guidance on potential areas of concern, such as operational procedures, trade agreements, and marketing techniques. It also provides practical advice on how best to tap into the lucrative global markets. It includes bibliographical references and an index.

MAGAZINES

Croner's Reference Book for Importers
Croner CCH Ltd.
145 London Road, Kingston-upon-Thames, Surrey, KT2 6SR, U.K.
T: +44 (0) 20 8547 3333
F: +44 (0) 20 8547 2638
www.croner.co.uk
This U.K. reference service provides guidance to, and the latest information from, the field of importing. Written for businesses of all sizes, it covers the import of all types of goods and explains the latest trade agreements, European and U.K. trade and import legislation, and U.K. customs tariffs, Value Added Tax, and documentation requirements. The service includes a loose-leaf reference guide with monthly updates, a newsletter and monthly bulletin, and a pocket book. A CD-ROM version is also produced.

International Trade Today
Hemming Information Services
32 Vauxhall Bridge Road, London, SW1V 2SS, U.K.
T: +44 (0) 20 7973 6404
F: +44 (0) 20 7973 4797
www.international-trade.org.uk
International Trade Today is the official journal of the Institute of Export and is published ten times per year in the United Kingdom. The magazine contains useful articles about all facets of importing and exporting.

INTERNET

Business Advice Online
www.businesslink.org
This is an online service provided by the Small Business Service of the U.K. Department of Trade and Industry. It provides an extensive range of general information for small businesses, as well as details of the services available through the network of 150 local Business Links. The latter provide face-to-face advice on exporting and importing for small businesses.

Kelly's Directory
www.kellys.co.uk
This online searchable database lists over 140,000 U.K. manufacturers and service organizations under 50,000 product headings. A print media version of the database may also be purchased.

Kompass
www.kompass.com
This online searchable database lists some 1.6 million companies in about 70 countries under approximately 50,000 product/service codes. The databases for individual countries may also be purchased in printed format.

Market Access Database
www.mkaccdb.eu.int
The Market Access Database is provided by the DG Trade, European Commission. Certain parts of the site are open only to people having an ISP connection located in Europe but the section on trade barriers is open to all Internet users. The site contains details about trade barriers by market sector and country, import formalities by country, and import duties by product code by country.

Thomas Global Register
www.tgrnet.com
Formerly the American Export Register, this comprehensive Web-based directory run by Thomas Publishing gives details of some 500,000 manufacturers and distributors across 22 countries, divided into 10,500 product and service classifications.

"My style of dealmaking is quite simple and straightforward. I just keep pushing and pushing to get what I'm after."
(Donald J. Trump)

Thomas Register of American Manufacturers
www.thomasregister.com
This online searchable database includes about 168,000 American and Canadian manufacturing companies whose products are classified in about 63,000 product categories and about 135,000 brand names.

ORGANIZATIONS

USA

American Association of Exporters and Importers
7th Floor, P.O. Box 7813, Washington, D.C., 20044–7813
T: +1 202 661 2181
F: +1 202 661 2185
E: hq@aaei.org
www.aaei.org
The AAEI is a trade association promoting fair and open trade for the benefit of its members and has close links with all relevant U.S. government departments and regulatory bodies. It publishes a Web-based newsletter giving details of trade matters of interest to members.

Bolero International
T: +1 212 735 0002
www.bolero.net
With offices in New York, London, Hong Kong, Tokyo, Johannesburg, Santiago, Dubai, and Amman, bolero.net offers an XML Web-based electronic document transfer system. Four grades of membership are available for global, large, medium, and small exporters/importers.

Europe

British Chambers of Commerce
Manning House, 22 Carlisle Place, London, SW1P 1JA, U.K.
T: +44 (0) 20 7565 2000
F: +44 (0) 20 7565 2049
E: info@britishchambers.org.uk
www.britishchambers.org.uk
This is an umbrella body for a network of some 150 locally-based chambers of commerce serving local businesses and providing advice on importing and import services to member companies.

Department of Trade and Industry
Trade Policy, Kingsgate House, 66–74 Victoria Street, London, SW1E 6SE, U.K.
T: +44 (0) 20 7215 4557
F: +44 (0) 20 7215 4556
E: dti.enquiries@dti.gsi.gov.uk
www.dti.gov.uk/worldtrade/import.htm
The Department of Trade and Industry is responsible for U.K. trade policy at international, European, and national levels, and for harmonizing customs tariff levels with European Union member states. It is also responsible, in conjunction with several other government departments, for policy on all U.K. export and import prohibitions and restrictions.

HM Customs and Excise
New King's Beam House, 22 Upper Ground, London, SE1 9PJ, U.K.
T: +44 (0) 845 010 9000
www.hmce.gov.uk
Her Majesty's Customs and Excise is the department responsible for administering and collecting all import duties as detailed in the Customs Tariffs. It also has specific responsibility for enforcing all prohibitions and restrictions on the import (and export) of certain classes of goods.

Simpler Trade Procedures Board (SITPRO)
151 Buckingham Palace Road, London, SW1W 9SS, U.K.
T: +44 (0) 20 7215 0825
F: +44 (0) 20 7215 0824
E: info@sitpro.org.uk
www.sitpro.org.uk
SITPRO is dedicated to giving practical help to U.K. exporters and importers. In addition the site offers ElecTra toolkits for paperless international trade and is currently preparing a WebElecTra system.

International

World Trade Organization
Centre William Rappard, Rue de Lausanne 154, CH-1211 Geneva 21, Switzerland
T: +41 22 739 51 11
F: +41 22 731 42 06
E: enquiries@wto.org
www.wto.org
The WTO site gives comprehensive details about intergovernmental actions on trade issues. The site offers statistics about world trade and downloadable documents.

For More Information

Exporting (pp. 1977–80)

INFORMATION MANAGEMENT

BOOKS

The Art of Strategic Planning for Information Technology 2nd ed.
BERNARD H. BOAR
New York: John Wiley, 2000
416pp ISBN: 0471376558
The second edition of this book provides strategy frameworks for information management, offering advice on how to choose the strategy most appropriate for an organization and how to deploy IT resources to suit that strategy. It analyzes information systems management in relation to competitive advantage, execution, quality control, and administration and discusses technologies including e-commerce, data warehousing, and architectures.

Business in a Virtual World: Exploiting Information for Competitive Advantage
FIONA CZERNIAWSKA, GAVIN POTTER
West Lafayette, Indiana: Purdue University Press, 2001
272pp ISBN: 1557531943
A big change is currently taking place in the world of business as companies shift their assets from the physical to the virtual domain. This book explains the new economic laws of the virtual environment, gives examples of companies already exploiting virtual opportunities, and provides a practical toolkit for succeeding in the virtual world.

Corporate Information Systems Management: Text and Cases
LYNDA M. APPLEGATE, F. WARREN MCFARLAN, JAMES L. MCKENNEY
New York: McGraw-Hill, 1999
720pp ISBN: 0072902833
Targeted at either students or managers with some IT experience, the book offers an overview of information systems technology management. It offers case studies to illustrate how to put theories into practice and contains a good discussion of the people issues involved in information systems management.

Information Management Textbook
SALLY PALMER, MARGARET WEAVER
Woburn, Massachusetts: Butterworth-Heinemann, 1998
186pp (Team Leader Development Series)

"There is a strong tendency among European managers to be selective about sharing information."
(Percy Barnevik)

      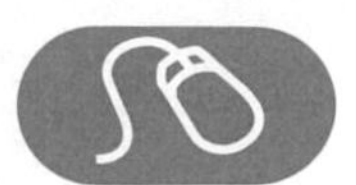

ISBN: 0750638621
This practical guide, aimed at managers, team leaders, and supervisors, explores all aspects of information management: the need for information; information for decision making; gathering data; inputting and processing data to produce information; the use of information systems; communication within organizations and work teams; and the analysis and interpretation of information. Activities, questions, assignments, and case studies are also included.

The Knowing Organization: How Organizations Use Information to Construct Meaning, Create Knowledge, and Make Decisions
CHUN WEI CHOO
New York: Oxford University Press, 1998
256pp ISBN: 0195110129
The book looks at the relationship between organizational behavior and information management, detailing the ways in which information acts in various organizational-behavior models. It is divided into three sections: analyzing the ways in which organizations use information; comparing the dynamics of different models; and proposing a new framework for organizations to make sense of information, create knowledge, and make decisions.

Managing Information: Avoiding Overload
TREVOR J. BENTLEY
Milford, Connecticut: Kogan Page, 1998
164pp (Business Skills Series)
ISBN: 0749426829
Written for managers who need to understand their information needs, as well as the value of information and its relevance to decision making, this guide provides an introduction to the basics of information management and explains how managers need to be proactive in gathering and using information. It also explores the impact of the information revolution on organizations, individuals, and society as a whole.

Organizing Knowledge: An Introduction to Managing Access to Information 3rd ed.
JENNIFER ROWLEY, JOHN FARROW
Brookfield, Vermont: Gower, 2000
424pp ISBN: 0566080478
This is a comprehensive text on knowledge organization and retrieval, aimed mainly at students. It looks at the nature of information and knowledge and their incorporation into documents. It deals with records, focusing particularly on the use of electronic databases and the range of tools available for accessing information resources. Finally, it examines knowledge storage systems, including CD-ROMs, online services, OPACs, and the Internet.

Practical Information Policies 2nd ed.
ELIZABETH ORNA
Brookfield, Vermont: Gower, 1999
375pp ISBN: 0566076934
Aimed at managers, information managers, and information students, Orna's text looks at why information should be managed, and includes an information audit, before focusing on the formation and implementation of information policies. It considers in particular the areas of people, systems, cost measurement, and change management, and presents many case studies.

Simplicity: The New Competitive Advantage in a World of More, Better, Faster
BILL JENSEN
Cambridge, Massachusetts: Perseus, 2001
240pp ISBN: 0738204307
This is a practical guide to freeing your organization from the confusion within that prevents it from moving forward.

The Social Life of Information
JOHN SEELY BROWN, PAUL DUGUID
Boston, Massachusetts: Harvard Business School Press, 2000
336pp ISBN: 0875847625
The book presents a picture of information management separated from technology, arguing that a focus on technology obscures the issues of how people work and learn. By emphasizing the practice of knowledge rather than the processes of managing information, this book puts information into a social context.

MAGAZINES

CIO Magazine
CXO Media
492 Old Connecticut Path, Framingham, Massachusetts, 01701
T: +1 508 872 0080
www.cio.com
This magazine, written for corporate information officers, provides valuable research and insights. Articles are timely and concisely written. The magazine also features opinion and current topic columns.

International Journal of Information Management
ISSN: 0268-4012
Elsevier Science
Regional Sales Office, Customer Support Department, P.O. Box 945, New York, 10159-0945
T: +1 212 633 3730
F: +1 212 633 3680
www.elsevier.com
The *Journal* is concerned with the design and management of complex information systems, and written for managers wishing to learn from the experience of others. It contains major papers, reports, and reviews, and is highly topical.

Journal of Information Science
ISSN: 0165-5515
Cambridge Scientific Abstracts
4640 Kingsgate, Cascade Way, Oxford Business Park South, Oxford, Oxfordshire, OX4 2ST, U.K.
T: +44 (0) 1865 336250
F: +44 (0) 1865 336258
This, the journal of the Institute of Information Scientists, has an academic focus. It researches and reports on developments in computerized and manual information systems and their effects.

Managing Information
ISSN: 1352-0229
Aslib, The Association for Information Management
Staple Hall, Stone House Court, London, EC3A 7PB, U.K.
T: +44 (0) 20 7903 0000
F: +44 (0) 20 7903 0011
www.aslib.co.uk
Written for all people who use or manage information, this practical journal focuses on and discusses the latest news and developments within the information world. There is a Web site at www.managinginformation.com.

INTERNET

Association for Information and Image Management
www.aiim.org
The news and magazine articles on this site cover a variety of information management issues including business process management, enterprise portals, data warehousing, and data mining. The site also offers a job market.

InformationR.net supported by University of Sheffield, U.K.
http://informationr.net
This site offers an online journal, a world list of departments and schools specializing in information research, a guide to journals and newsletters on the subject, and details of electronic resources for information research methods.

Society for Information Management
www.simnet.org

"The information highway will transform our culture as dramatically as Gutenberg's press did the Middle Ages."
(Bill Gates)

Sponsored by a nonprofit organization of technology experts, this site offers white papers and publications, information on upcoming events, discussions of current issues, and regional learning forums.

The Information Management Forum
www.infomgmtforum.com
Divided into two sections—the IT Human Resources Program and the IT Management Program—this site offers peer-information exchange, a members list, and reports.

ORGANIZATIONS

USA

Association for Information and Image Management (AIIM)
1100 Wayne Avenue, Suite 1100, Silver Spring, Maryland, 20910
T: +1 301 587 8202
F: +1 301 587 2711
www.aiim.wego.net
Founded in 1943, this association has over 10,000 members. Professionals in the manufacturing, vending and information/image management equipment business will find the statistical information compiled by this group to be invaluable. Chapters of this association meet across the United States. This group also maintains a resource center.

Society for Information Management (SIM)
401 N. Michigan Avenue, Chicago, Illinois, 60611
T: +1 312 527 6734 or 800 387 9746
F: +1 312 245 1081
E: *info@simnet.org*
www.simnet.org
Founded in 1968, this society has over 2,500 members. SIM is a nonprofit organization for information technology experts, including CIOs, CTOs, and IT professionals. SIM aims to provide information on global information technology advances and continuing education opportunities, and to maintain a network of peer resources through programs designed for information management professionals.

Europe

Aslib, The Association for Information Management
Staple Hall, Stone House Court, London, EC3A 7PB, U.K.
T: +44 (0) 20 7903 0000
F: +44 (0) 20 7903 0011
E: *aslib@aslib.co.uk*
www.aslib.co.uk
Aslib is a charity, registered in 1924, whose 2,000 members are private- and public-sector companies and organizations throughout the world concerned with managing information resources efficiently. Its key roles are: to stimulate awareness of the value and benefits of good management of information resources; to represent and lobby for the interests of the information sector on matters of national and international importance; and to provide a range of information-related products and services to meet the needs of the information society.

International

ARMA International—The Information Management Professionals
4200 Somerset, Suite 215, Prairie Village, Kansas, 66208
T: +1 913 341 3808
F: +1 913 341 3742
E: *hq@arma.org*
www.arma.org
Founded in 1975, this association has over 10,500 members. ARMA provides research and networking opportunities for anyone involved in the information management world. The mission of ARMA is to enhance the skills and experience of information management professionals.

For More Information

☆ **Data Mining (pp. 152–53)**
Computers, Information Technology, and E-commerce (pp. 1931–33)
Knowledge Management (pp. 2018–20)
Learning Organization (pp. 2024–26)

INNOVATION AND CREATIVITY

BOOKS

The Art of Innovation: Lessons in Creativity from IDEO, America's Leading Design Firm
Tom Kelley, Jonathan Littman
New York: Currency/Doubleday, 2001
307pp ISBN: 0385499841
This book is the story of IDEO, their beliefs, and their process of achieving innovation. The authors examine why many manufacturing companies have difficulty with innovation. They then describe the IDEO process, their brainstorming techniques, and their focus on fast prototyping for immediate feedback. Finally, they detail the thinking necessary to develop an overall environment for innovation.

The Artist's Way: A Spiritual Path to Higher Creativity
Julia Cameron, Mark Bryan
New York: J P Tarcher, 1995
232pp ISBN: 0874778212
The book contains a thorough 12-week program on how to rediscover creativity after suffering mental blocks. The authors suggest that people try to get in tune with their creative energies, therefore finding a connection between spirituality and creativity.

Best Practice Creativity
Peter Cook
Brookfield, Vermont: Gower, 1998
288pp ISBN: 0566080273
From the start, this practical book emphasizes the value and importance of creativity within organizations. It describes methods of promoting creativity, summarizes established concepts and practices, examines the role of leadership, looks at organizational structure as a source of creativity, sets out the principles for the design of problem solving processes, and presents a critical guide to creativity techniques. In conclusion, it offers a list of 101 creativity enhancing ideas for use in any organization.

Conceptual Blockbusting: A Guide to Creative Ideas
James L. Adams
Cambridge, Massachusetts: Perseus, 2001
224pp ISBN: 0738205370
The author of this title uses examples from areas such as engineering, philosophy, and psychology to help overcome writing blocks and to create ideas, while also discussing in detail the major types of blocks and providing exercises to help tackle them.

Corporate Creativity: How Innovation and Improvement Actually Happen
Alan G. Robinson, Sam Stern

"You can innovate by not doing anything, if it's a conscious decision."

(Herb Kelleher)

San Francisco, California: Berrett-Koehler, 1998
300pp ISBN: 1576750493
Robinson and Stern propose a way of managing for creativity that allows companies to realize their creative potential and improve their competitive position and profitability. Having investigated hundreds of creative acts in organizations around the world, they make some surprising discoveries about how innovation and improvement actually happen. In a text enlivened with plenty of detailed examples, they reveal six essential elements that individuals and companies can use to turn their creativity from a hit-or-miss proposition into something consistent they can count on.

Creativity Works
ANNEKE ELWES, ED.
London: Profile Books, 2000
175pp ISBN: 1861972792
The importance of business creativity to economic success is outlined in this collection of interviews and conversations with a group of 20 corporate leaders, architects, entrepreneurs, and academics, each with a record of creativity in their field. The issues they address include: how much creativity matters; how it can be cultivated; and how the business environment in the United Kingdom is changing.

Flash of Brilliance Workbook: The Eight Keys to Discover, Unlock, and Fulfill Your Creative Potential at Work
WILLIAM C. MILLER, JANICE LAWRENCE
Cambridge, Massachusetts: Perseus, 2000
126pp ISBN: 0738202398
This book is packed with exercises, questions, diagnostics, checklists, and other interactive elements. It aims to show you the eight keys to unlock your creative potential and unleash it in innovative projects, products, and ways of working individually and collaboratively. It covers such topics as brainstorming, evaluating options, implementing plans, and celebrating results.

The Innovator's Dilemma: The Revolutionary National Bestseller that Changed the Way We Do Business
CLAYTON M. CHRISTENSEN
Boston, Massachusetts: Harvard Business School Press, 1997
225pp ISBN: 0875845851
This title discusses products that have redefined their own particular markets by entering the marketplace at the bottom end of the scale, making a niche for themselves, and then removing competitiors from the top over a period of time. It also contains suggestions of how to prevent such an occurrence.

Jamming
JOHN KAO
New York: HarperCollins, 1996
224pp ISBN: 0887307469
The emphasis of this title is on creativity and how top companies get ahead of the field by nurturing this important element of their businesses. The book covers all aspects of creativity, from weighing up the creativity of a company to overcoming possible pitfalls.

Leading for Innovation: And Organizing for Results
FRANCES HESSELBEIN, MARSHALL GOLDSMITH, IAIN SOMERVILLE, EDS.
San Francisco, California: Jossey-Bass, 2001
190pp ISBN: 0787953598
This book is a collection of articles and essays by some noted thinkers and speakers on innovation and leadership. The editors have compiled the writings into four categories: leading the people who make innovation happen; creating an environment that encourages innovation; changing the way you think about leadership and innovation, and the practice of innovation. Contributors include William Bratton (former Chief of Police in New York City), who outlines his thoughts on ''leading for innovation and results,'' and Dave Ulrich (an HR professor and practitioner), who offers an ''innovation protocol.''

Leading the Revolution
GARY HAMEL
Boston, Massachusetts: Harvard Business School Press, 2000
336pp ISBN: 1578511895
Hamel argues that companies must adopt a radical new innovation agenda and continually reinvent themselves. He explains the underlying principles of radical innovation, explores where revolutionary new business concepts come from, identifies the key design criteria for building companies that are activist friendly and revolution ready, and details, with case study illustrations, the steps a company must take to make innovation an enduring capability.

Managing Creativity: The Dynamics of Work and Organisation
HOWARD DAVIS, RICHARD SCASE
Buckingham, England: Open University Press, 2001
160pp (Managing Work and Organisations Series)
ISBN: 033520693X
The authors investigate the organizational dynamics of creative companies on the basis of research into publishing, advertising, television, radio, the performing arts, and music industry firms. Chapters focus on: managing creative organizational cultures; trends in creative organizations; creative employees—their attitudes and values; and the creative challenge.

Mastering the Dynamics of Innovation
JAMES M. UTTERBACK
Boston, Massachusetts: Harvard Business School Press, 1996
288pp ISBN: 0875847404
This title discusses the way in which innovation can affect industries and firms, and how innovation begins in an industry. The book also gives examples of new product development and provides valuable insights into how to encourage innovation.

Orbiting the Giant Hairball: A Corporate Fool's Guide to Surviving with Grace
GORDON MACKENZIE
New York: Viking Press, 1998
224pp ISBN: 0670879835
This is a fun book that shares some of the wisdom MacKenzie acquired in his 30 years as a creative talent working at Hallmark Cards. His book even looks different from most business works because MacKenzie uses crude drawings and pictures as well as different type fonts to make the point that creativity is about going outside the lines. The book is full of humorous stories about MacKenzie's fight to stay non-traditional and his battles against the forces inside organizations that inhibit creativity.

Organizing Genius: The Secrets of Creative Collaboration
WARREN BENNIS, PATRICIA WARD BIEDERMAN
Reading, Massachusetts: Addison-Wesley, 1997
239pp ISBN: 0201570513
Bennis and Biederman explore the forces that foster creative collaboration by analyzing the histories of six ''Great Groups'' in order to uncover the secrets of collective genius. The ''Great Groups'' are: the Walt Disney Studio; Xerox's Palo Alto Research Center and Apple; the 1992 Clinton campaign; Lockheed's Skunk Works; Black Mountain College; and the Manhattan Project.

Releasing Creativity: How Leaders Develop Creative Potential in Their Teams
JOHN WHATMORE
Milford, Connecticut: Kogan Page, 1999
224pp ISBN: 0749430109
Organizations of all types are under increasing pressure to develop climates and cultures that nurture creativity, innovation, and change. The work of the creative leader and the creative team is explored in this book through the experiences of a range of leading organizations.

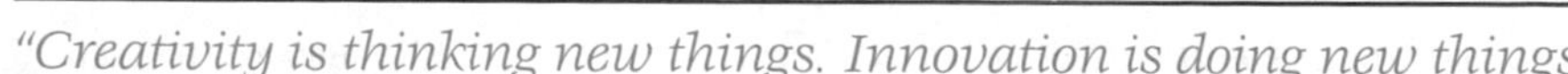
"Creativity is thinking new things. Innovation is doing new things." (Theodore Levitt)

  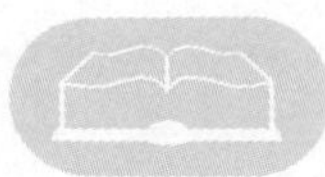    

The author also considers the importance of recognizing, nurturing, controlling, and developing individual skills and talents, and discusses such questions as how to identify the kind of creativity needed, how to match the right task to the right leader, and how to develop and support teams for the chosen tasks.

Serious Play
MICHAEL SCHRAGE, TOM PETERS
Boston, Massachusetts: Harvard Business School Press, 1999
244pp ISBN: 0875848141
In this title, the author suggests that in order to create innovative products, top companies need play. The book describes the type of environment that creates innovation and studies the methods of successful prototyping at companies like Boeing and Microsoft.

Six Thinking Hats
EDWARD DE BONO
New York: Little Brown & Co, 1986
224pp ISBN: 0316177911
In this title, the author divides the thought process into several areas, giving creative insights into each area and suggesting that if every member of a particular business uses these insights, the creative thinking of a whole group of people can be run more efficiently.

Ultimate Book of Business Creativity: 50 Great Thinking Tools for Transforming Your Business
ROS JAY
Oxford: Capstone, 2001
204pp (Ultimate Books Series)
ISBN: 1841120669
This book brings together 50 techniques that can be used to generate new ideas and solve problems. Some of them, such as brainstorming, the Delphi technique, force field analysis and mind mapping, are well known; others, such as brainwriting, the Crawford Slip method, the nominal group technique, and synectics are less so. Each technique is described, with practical examples of how it can be used.

Weird Ideas that Work: 11½ Practices for Promoting, Managing and Sustaining Innovation
ROBERT I. SUTTON
New York: Free Press, 2001
224pp ISBN: 0743212126
This book will challenge many of the current practices of organizations. Sutton argues that organizing for innovation is very different from organizing for routine and that many companies are currently organized for routine. Six-sigma and TQM processes push companies to drive out variation which is, Sutton argues, necessary for innovation. He suggests some thought-provoking and challenging practices to help companies break from this "reduce variation" mantra. He advocates, for example, holding onto the "slow learner of the organizational code" because it is this type of person who tends to find innovative solutions faster than anyone else.

Wellsprings of Knowledge: Building and Sustaining the Sources of Innovation
DOROTHY LEONARD-BARTON
Boston, Massachusetts: Harvard Business School Press, 1995
334pp ISBN: 0875846122
This title raises the question of why some organizations are better at creating new products than other ones, using interviews with those who have failed and those who have succeeded in the manufacturing industries to help find an answer.

A Whack on the Side of the Head: How You Can Be More Creative
ROGER VON OECH
New York: Warner Books, 1998
232pp ISBN: 0446674559
This title contains a range of exercises and useful ideas designed to increase creativity and innovation.

When Sparks Fly
DOROTHY LEONARD, WALTER SWAP
Boston, Massachusetts: Harvard Business School Press, 1999
242pp ISBN: 0875848656
The basic premise of this title is that the creative process is the same, whatever the size or type of company. In this book, the coauthors describe a five stage process of creativity that includes developing alternatives, choosing the right blend of people, and taking time to consider choices. Their ideas are supported by true examples of creativity from the corporate world.

MAGAZINES

Creativity and Innovation Management
ISSN: 0963–1690
Blackwell Publishers
350 Main Street, Malden, Massachusetts, 02148
T: +1 781 388 8200
F: +1 781 388 8232
www.blackwellpublishers.com/asp/listofj.asp
The aim of this quarterly journal is to enable an international community of practitioners and academics to share and extend their understanding of creativity and innovation management.

International Journal of Innovation Management
ISSN: 1363–9196
World Scientific Publishing Co., Inc.
1060 Main Street, River Edge, New Jersey, 07661
T: +1 800 227 7562
F: +1 888 977 2665
www.wspc.com
The *International Journal of Innovation Management* (*IJIM*) is a quarterly publication dedicated to the advancement of academic research and management practice in the field of innovation management. It adopts an interdisciplinary, multifunctional approach, especially welcoming contributions that seek to integrate the management of technological, market, and organizational innovation. Contributions are based on original empirical research and the observations of experienced managers. Case studies that provide new conceptual or theoretical insights are also invited. The *IJIM* aims to provide a forum for the insights of academics, practicing managers, and consultants, and to integrate the theory and practice of innovation management.

Journal of Innovative Management
ISSN: 1081–0714
Goal QPC
2 Manor Parkway, Salem, New Hampshire, 03079–2841
T: +1 603 890 8800
F: +1 603 870 9122
www.goalqpc.com
The aim of this magazine is to encourage the use of strategic thinking and leading edge practices in order to increase knowledge, efficiency, and productivity. It is targeted at busy managers who need quick access to the critical tools and information that drive today's successful management systems.

INTERNET

Creative Center of the Universe
www.gocreate.com
This site offers material designed to stimulate creative thinking, including exercises, quotations, articles, book and video reviews, and links to a wide variety of other sites.

CreativityPool.com
www.creativitypool.com
This site contains a database that allows people to submit creative ideas to solve problems. Users can search for solutions already posted. There is no cost to use the site and ideas are freely shared as part of the rules for use.

Creativity Unleashed Limited
www.cul.co.uk

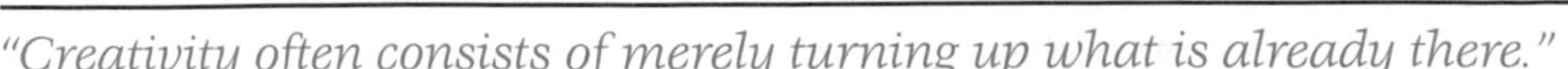
"Creativity often consists of merely turning up what is already there." (Bernice Fitz-Gibbon)

Developed by Brian Clegg to assist in the development of business creativity, this site includes free and shareware software to download, book and software reviews, a mailing list, and links to other creativity sites.

Creativity Web: Resources for Creativity and Innovation
www.ozemail.com.au/~caveman/Creative
This site has many different sections on creativity including creativity basics, kick-starting the creative process, ways to record ideas, techniques, quotations, how to do mind mapping, and information on the brain and different types of intelligences. There is also a resource area that lists books, software, organizations, and listings of Web sites devoted to creativity.

Directed Creativity
www.directedcreativity.com
This is a site based around the theory of "directed creativity" as developed by Paul Plsek. It includes a creativity bookstore and a toolkit of techniques.

Innovation Tools
www.innovationtools.com
This site is designed for the busy executive as a place to get some quick ideas. It includes information about idea-generating software and up-to-date news items related to innovation.

ORGANIZATIONS

USA

American Creativity Association (ACA)
P.O. Box 5856, Philadelphia, Pennsylvania, 19128
T: +1 888 837 1409
F: +1 502 254 5746
E: ACAinformation@aol.com
www.amcreativityassoc.org
Founded in 1989, this organization has over 350 members. The ACA seeks to promote and develop creativity on personal and professional levels, and to increase awareness of the importance of creativity in society. It also works with business to illustrate the importance of employee creativity and how this employee asset helps organizations remain competitive.

Association for Science, Technology and Innovation (ASTI)
8506 Wellington Road, No. 200, Manassas, Virginia, 20109
T: +1 703 369 5552
F: +1 703 369 5298
www.ida.org/DIVISIONS/sfrd/asti
Comprising professionals from industry, government, and educational institutions, ASTI aims to establish a dialogue among different disciplines that share the common problem of effective management of innovation. ASTI encourages members to share ideas, information, and experiences found among diverse communities. The association works to improve the management of innovation.

Innovation Network
451 E. 58th Avenue, No. 4625, Denver, Colorado, 80216
T: +1 303 308 1088
F: +1 303 295 6108
E: staff@thinksmart.com
www.thinksmart.com
Founded in 1993, this organization comprises individuals and companies who are committed to innovative thinking and processes.

For More Information

☆ **Brainstorming (pp. 318–19)**
☆ **Creating Corporate Creativity (pp. 271–72)**
✓ **Brainstorming (pp. 542–43)**
✓ **Open Systems Thinking (pp. 568–69)**

INTELLECTUAL PROPERTY

BOOKS

Copyright Theft
John Gurnsey
Burlington, Vermont: Ashgate Publishing Company, 1995
208pp ISBN: 0566076314
Gurnsey's book attempts to cover all forms of copyright theft. It reviews both commercial and domestic theft, incorporating the experiences of a wide range of organizations. Book, electronic, database, audio, video, games, and multimedia publishing are all considered, as is the question of whether existing laws can effectively serve a rapidly changing industry.

From Ideas to Assets: Investing Wisely in Intellectual Property
Bruce M. Berman, ed.
New York: John Wiley, 2001
624pp ISBN: 0471400688
Based on the experience of expert contributors, the book argues that corporations need to understand what their intellectual property assets are and how to protect their rights to them. It covers such topics as maximizing returns on intellectual property assets, valuing those assets, and discerning performance variables.

Protecting Your #1 Asset: Creating Fortunes from Your Ideas: An Intellectual Property Handbook
Michael A. Lechter
New York: Warner Books, 2001
276pp ISBN: 0446678317
Placing its emphasis on protecting intellectual property (IP), this book makes the case for understanding developments in this arena. It covers topics including identifying and benefiting from IP assets, using IP assets to build barriers to competition, licensing IP assets, and using IP assets to raise capital.

Rembrandts in the Attic: Unlocking the Hidden Value of Patents
Kevin G. Rivette, David Kline
Boston, Massachusetts: Harvard Business School Press, 1999
220pp ISBN: 0875848990
This is a practical book full of strategic advice on how to protect your ideas as well as inventions.

The Strategic Management of Intellectual Capital
David A. Klein, ed.
Boston, Massachusetts: Butterworth-Heinemann, 1997
246pp (Resources for the Knowledge-based Economy)
ISBN: 0750698500
This collection of articles addresses central themes in the strategic management of intellectual capital. It is designed to assist organizations in understanding the strategic and operational roles of intellectual property and in developing organizational infrastructures and cultures that foster the creation, development, sharing, and mentoring of intellectual capital.

Understanding Copyright in a Week
GRAHAM CORNISH
London: Hodder & Stoughton, 2000
96pp (Business in a Week Series)
ISBN: 0340782412
This introductory text will help you understand what copyright is, why it is important to respect it, and how you can make use of copyright law in business, management, and everyday life.

Valuation of Intellectual Property and Intangible Assets 3rd ed.
GORDON V. SMITH, RUSSELL L. PARR
New York: John Wiley, 2000
638pp (Intellectual Property Series)
ISBN: 0471362816
Smith and Parr argue that intellectual property and intangible assets represent the core of most corporations' value, and offer advice on how to identify, define, and exploit these assets. They also include a discussion of setting royalty rates based on rates of return. This third edition of the book offers analysis of recent developments in the field.

Value Driven Intellectual Capital: How to Convert Intangible Corporate Assets into Market Value
PATRICK H. SULLIVAN
New York: John Wiley, 2000
240pp (Intellectual Property Series)
ISBN: 0471351040
This book explores the expanding world of intellectual assets where translating an innovative idea into bottom-line profits involves a tightly focused strategy. It offers suggestions for turning corporate knowledge, know-how, and intellectual property into a sustainable competitive weapon that will build reputation and market share.

MAGAZINES

Copyright World
ISSN: 0950-2505
Informa Professional
57–61 Mortimer Street, London, W1W 8HS, U.K.
T: +44 (0) 20 7453 2104
F: +44 (0) 20 7453 2221
www.ipworldonline.com
This publication contains international news and updates on copyright and intellectual property matters, covering both legal and practical issues.

INTERNET

Copyright and Fair Use: Stanford University Libraries
http://fairuse.stanford.edu
The site provides a quick search facility and overview of copyright law, with links to Internet resources, current legislation, cases, judicial opinions, regulations, treaties, and conventions.

Copyright Clearance Center
www.copyright.com
Copyright Clearance Center, Inc., the largest licenser of text reproduction rights in the world, was formed in 1978 to facilitate compliance with U.S. copyright law. It provides licensing systems for the reproduction and distribution of copyrighted materials in print and electronic formats throughout the world.

Franklin Pierce Law Center
www.fplc.edu
Sponsored by a law school, the site offers an extensive list of articles relating to intellectual property.

Intellectual Property
www.intellectual-property.gov.uk
This site gives information and advice on patents, trademarks, design, and copyright with links to the relevant government departments. It also addresses key questions on protection, permissions, and enforcing rights.

International Intellectual Property Alliance
www.iipa.com
Sponsored by a private-sector coalition formed to protect U.S. copyrighted material around the world, the site offers articles on a variety of IP topics and country-specific copyright information.

The Copyright Licensing Agency
www.cla.co.uk
The Agency is the United Kingdom's reproduction rights organization—the U.K. equivalent of the U.S. Copyright Clearance Center.

U.K. Patent Office
www.patent.gov.uk
The Web site of the U.K. government department responsible for intellectual property—copyright, patents, designs, and trade marks—has a section of links to government, academic, and general IP sites.

United States Copyright Office
www.loc.gov/copyright
The U.S. Copyright Office is located in the Library of Congress. The site has a section for FAQs and another for requests relating to the Freedom of Information Act, besides material on copyright legislation and an international section with links to the WIPO.

United States Patent and Trademark Office
www.uspto.gov
The PTO promotes industrial and technological progress in the United States and strengthens the national economy by administering the laws relating to patents and trademarks, and advising the U.S. government on patent, trademark, and copyright protection, and on trade related aspects of intellectual property.

World Intellectual Property Organization
www.wipo.org
WIPO is a Geneva-based specialized agency of the United Nations whose mandate is to promote the protection of intellectual property worldwide. It administers 21 treaties in the field of intellectual property—15 covering industrial property and six covering copyright. The first general group of treaties defines internationally agreed basic standards of intellectual property in each of the 177 member states.

ORGANIZATIONS

USA

American Intellectual Property Law Association (AIPLA)
2001 Jefferson Davis Highway, Suite 203, Arlington, Virginia, 22202
T: +1 703 415 0780
F: +1 703 415 0786
E: aipla@aipla.org
www.aipla.org
Founded in 1897 and having more than 13,000 members, this association is comprised of national bar association lawyers practicing in the fields of patents, trademarks, and copyrights. AIPLA works to promote the improvement of U.S. intellectual property systems.

Intellectual Property Owners Association (IPO)
1255 23rd St. NW, Suite 200, Washington, D.C., 20037
T: +1 202 466 2396
F: +1 202 466 2893
E: info@ipo.org
www.ipo.org
This group comprises over 400 major corporations and lawyers that work with intellectual property issues and concerns. The IPO works to support and strengthen the patent, trademark, copyright, and trade secret laws of

"To engage in the learning cycle, some firms move their employees instead of their knowledge."
(Anthony DiBella)

the United States. The IPO also monitors legislative activities.

National Council of Intellectual Property Law Associations (NCIPLA)
1255 23rd St. NW, Suite 200, Washington, D.C., 20037
T: +1 202 466 2396
F: +1 202 466 2893
E: ncipla@ncipla.org
www.ncipla.org
NCIPLA is an association representing state and local patent law associations. The Council seeks to inform member associations of the latest changes in patent, trademark, and copyright legislation.

For More Information

- **Managing Intellectual Capital (pp. 49-50)**
- **Knowledge Management (pp. 2018-20)**

INTERFIRM COOPERATION, STRATEGIC ALLIANCES, JOINT VENTURES

BOOKS

Alliance Competence: Maximizing the Value of Your Partnerships
ROBERT E. SPEKMAN, LYNN A. ISABELLA, THOMAS C. MACAVOY
New York: John Wiley, 2000
256pp ISBN: 0471330639
This text combines research and case studies to explore the key aspects of successful alliances. The authors focus on building alliance competence, balancing business and relationships, managing the alliance over time, conflict resolution, and building an alliance competence. The concept of the "no blame review" is outlined.

The Alliance Revolution: The New Shape of Business Rivalry
BENJAMIN GOMES-CASSERES
Cambridge, Massachusetts: Harvard University Press, 1996
320pp ISBN: 0674016483
The author examines business alliances and intercompany collaborations that change the way business is conducted. Case studies are used to explore the implications of the increasing use of alliances, and the book provides recommendations for organizations considering collaboration.

Building Strategic Relationships: How to Extend Your Organization's Reach through Partnerships, Alliances, and Joint Ventures
WILLIAM BERGQUIST, JULI BETWEE, DAVID MEUEL
San Francisco, California: Jossey-Bass, 1995
246pp ISBN: 0787900923
Providing a macro view of strategic partnerships, the book draws on interviews and case studies to look at the process from launch through development to conclusion. Rather than exploring the logistics of partnerships, the book focuses on the reasons for creating them and addresses "soft" issues such as trust and communication.

The Collaboration Challenge: How Nonprofits and Businesses Succeed Through Strategic Alliances
JAMES E. AUSTIN, THE DRUCKER FOUNDATION
San Francisco, California: Jossey-Bass, 2000
272pp ISBN: 0787952206
This book offers insights into the process of creating and sustaining strategic partnerships between businesses and nonprofit organizations. Its contents include the strategic benefits of alliances, understanding strategic collaboration, making the connection, generating value, managing the relationship, and guidelines for collaborating successfully.

The Collaborative Enterprise: Why Links across the Corporation Often Fail and How to Make Them Work
ANDREW CAMPBELL, MICHAEL GOOLD
Cambridge, Massachusetts: Perseus, 1999
217pp ISBN: 0738200891
Using examples from real life, this book reports on the growing need for separate businesses to work together in order to achieve success in the future. The book also looks at the problems that can occur in such dealings and offers ways of overcoming them from the varying perspectives of people in different management positions.

Cooperative Strategy: Competing Successfully through Strategic Alliances
PIERRE DUSSAUGE, BERNARD GARRETTE
New York: John Wiley, 1999
236pp ISBN: 0471974927
Aimed at managers, this book gives a framework for analyzing strategic alliances and dealing with the issues of intercompany cooperation. It considers the global perspective with case studies, flexible approaches, operational recommendations, and guidance for alliances between competitors.

Developing Strategic Partnerships: How to Leverage More Business from Major Customers
CHRIS STEWARD
Brookfield, Vermont: Gower, 1999
197pp ISBN: 0566081016
This text uses a step-by-step methodology to explain the planning, implementation, and evaluation processes of building a partnership. It looks at many important issues, including identification of potential alliances, gaining customer commitment, building the partnership team, and evaluating progress.

Effective International Joint Venture Management: Practical Legal Insights for Successful Organization and Implementation
RONALD CHARLES WOLF
Armonk, New York: M. E. Sharpe, 2001
500pp ISBN: 0765605473
The book describes the essential steps toward the creation of an international joint venture, covering the commercial aspects, capital structure, due diligence, ownership rights, dispute resolution, and termination, among other topics. Though it deals with complex subjects in detail, it is written in easy to understand language and is appropriate for managers, lawyers, and business students.

The Formation of Inter-organizational Networks
MARK EBERS, ED.
New York: Oxford University Press, 1997
295pp ISBN: 0198289480
This book examines the growing trend of companies to engage in organizational networking activities such as strategic alliances, trading networks, or joint ventures. Drawing on the results of research, contributors from different fields focus on the motives behind interorganizational networking, and on the processes involved.

Inter-Firm Alliances: Analysis and Design
BART NOOTEBOOM

"Indian businesses can be critical as partners at the time international firms are seeking to enter India."
(Rajiv Desai)

New York: Routledge, 1998
256pp ISBN: 0415181542
Factors influencing intercompany alliances are considered in this book. It uses an inventory of different forms of alliance to define the criteria for how to choose one. Tools are then developed for the design and analysis of governance of relations, as well as for establishing, developing, and terminating an alliance.

International Joint Venture Management: Learning to Cooperate and Cooperating to Learn
Bettina S. T. Buchel, et al.
New York: John Wiley, 1998
300pp ISBN: 0471828947
The book provides an overview of recent trends and the history of joint ventures, identifying four key areas to address in successfully creating a joint venture: strategy, structure, culture, and human resources. It also offers a chapter on negotiation in joint ventures.

International Joint Ventures: Theory and Practice
Aimin Yan, Yadong Luo
Armonk, New York: M. E. Sharpe, 2000
323pp ISBN: 0765604736
This text integrates theory and practice to address issues critical to international joint ventures, including culture, human resources, learning, legal issues, management, and research and development. It also includes guidelines for IJV formation and management, and contains more than 30 case studies to benefit both students and practitioners.

Multinational Strategic Alliances
Robert J. Mockler
New York: John Wiley, 1999
266pp ISBN: 0471987751
This book takes a practical approach, presenting decision making models that cover issues such as strategic fit, negotiating alliances, selection of partners, formulating the type and structure of alliances, and ensuring alliance success. It also considers alternatives to alliances and includes case studies.

Partnering Intelligence: Creating Value for Your Business by Building Smart Alliances
Stephen M. Dent
Palo Alto, California: Davies-Black, 1999
239pp ISBN: 0891061320
Dent focuses on the skills necessary for creating successful strategic alliances and details the interpersonal skills needed in partnerships. He offers self-assessments and case studies, a model for partnerships, exercises designed to enhance partnering skills, and an analysis of how skillful leaders can foster an alliance mentality throughout an organization.

The Power of Two: How Companies of All Sizes Can Build Alliance Networks that Generate Business Opportunities
John K. Conlon, Melissa Giovagnoli
San Francisco, California: Jossey-Bass, 1998
256pp ISBN: 0787909467
This text shows how companies must respond quickly to market opportunities and presents ways of forming business alliances for speed and agility. The authors give a framework for knowledge-based networks, outline conditions for productive alliances, and present a process for developing the networks through alliance managers.

Smart Alliances: A Practical Guide to Repeatable Success
John R. Harbison, Peter Pekar, Jr.
San Francisco, California: Jossey-Bass, 1998
167pp ISBN: 0787943266
This text is of benefit to practitioners, showing ways to identify opportunities for alliances and presenting a road map with eight stages for setting up and managing alliances. It includes a section on best practice, focusing on European, Asian, and Latin American alliances.

Strategic Alliances: An Entrepreneurial Approach to Globalization
Michael Y. Yoshino, U. Srinivasa Rangan
Boston, Massachusetts: Harvard Business School Press, 1995
259pp ISBN: 0875845843
The book is a thorough guide to modern alliances, viewing them not as a means of protection, but as tools that can be used to help gain advantages over competitors.

Strategies of Co-operation: Managing Alliances, Networks, and Joint Ventures
John Child, David Faulkner
New York: Oxford University Press, 1998
350pp ISBN: 0198774850
This book examines alliances, networks, and joint ventures from the perspectives of economics, strategy, and organization theory. The four parts cover the nature of cooperation, establishing cooperation, managing cooperation, and maturing relationships.

INTERNET

AllianceAssembler
www.allianceassembler.com
This is a portal for information on strategic alliances as well as information on alliance basics, links and resources, databases of possible alliance partners, and alliance-financing assistance.

Alliance Strategy
www.alliancestrategy.com
This site offers resources and literature on alliance strategy and management. It is maintained by Ben Gomes-Casseres, author of *The Alliance Revolution*. Some sections of the site have restricted access, but most of it is free of charge.

ICANSI
www.icansi.com
ICANSI is a global community of researchers and practitioners collaborating to pioneer new concepts, tools, and processes in the area of alliances, networks, and strategic innovation. Its very exciting Web site details its research programs, publications, tools, and consulting services, and also has a links section and a discussion forum. You can sign up for an e-mail newsletter and download free publications and presentations.

Joint Venture: Silicon Valley
www.jointventure.org
This site represents what it calls a ''nonprofit dynamic model.'' While this has a West Coast U.S. high-tech focus, it does capture the spirit of what is possible in a joint venture.

smartalliances.com
www.smartalliances.com
This site provides information on the world of strategic alliances. It focuses on practical advice on how alliance companies raise profitability, best practice in alliances, and institutional alliance learning. It contains details of books, conferences, articles, and links. The site is set up by Booz, Allen & Hamilton (international consultants).

Think Joint Venture
www.thinkjointventure.com
This is a site that tries to make profitable joint ventures happen. It also commends itself by focusing on the prospect of joint ventures between smaller businesses instead of concentrating solely large international corporations.

ORGANIZATIONS

USA

Association of Strategic Alliance Professionals
P.O. Box 812–027, Wellesley, Massachusetts, 02482
T: +1 781 263 0066
F: +1 781 263 0027
E: *billl@strategic-alliances.org*
www.strategic-alliances.org
This membership organization raises awareness of strategic-alliance issues, acts as a forum for strategic-alliance professionals, organizes conferences, and identifies best practices. It

"Cooperative capitalism does not spontaneously emerge from free markets—it needs to be designed."
(Will Hutton)

aims to establish a distinct professional identity for strategic-alliance practitioners. Members receive discounts on conferences and publications, a directory of strategic-alliance professionals, and other benefits.

For More Information

☆ **Organic Growth versus Acquisition (pp. 79–80)**

✔ **Strategic Partnering (pp. 482–83)**

Acquisitions, Takeovers, and Mergers (pp. 1901–03)

Internal Communication

BOOKS

Beyond Spin: The Power of Strategic Corporate Journalism
Markos Kounalakis, Drew Banks, Kim Daus
San Francisco, California: Jossey-Bass, 1999
256pp ISBN: 0787945501
This book covers issues relating to internal and external communication for the corporate world. It focuses on the purpose of effective communication and the strategic value it brings to a company. It includes discussion of current practice in corporate and general media journalism and presents typical situations.

Breaking the Barrier to Upward Communication: Strategies and Skills for Employees, Managers, and HR Specialists
Thad B. Green, Jay T. Knippen
Westport, Connecticut: Quorum Books, 1999
368pp ISBN: 1567202004
This practical guide to communicating within organizations is for anyone who wants to get along better with management, and especially for human resources professionals, trainers, managers, mentors, and others whose job is to encourage and prepare employees to do so. The skills and strategies required for effective upward communication are outlined, and a structure is presented that will ensure that the upward movement of ideas actually does take place.

Communicating across Cultures
Maureen Guirdham
West Lafayette, Indiana: Purdue University Press, 1999
360pp ISBN: 1557531676
Guirdham's book explores the need for improved intercultural communication skills in the workplace and discusses strategies for improving understanding of cultures and diversity at work. It contains sections on diversity at work, how cultures differ, subcultural communication at work, barriers to communicating across cultures, intercultural communication theories, and the skills required for working abroad.

Corporate Communication
Paul A. Argenti
New York: McGraw-Hill, 1997
288pp ISBN: 0256217238
Corporate Communication is a handbook for everyone in the business world on how to communicate with those inside and outside your company. This is a comprehensive text that focuses on the basics of good communication and places a strong emphasis on the political and social consequences of poor communication.

Gower Handbook of Internal Communication
Eileen Scholes, ed.
Brookfield, Vermont: Gower, 1997
484pp ISBN: 0566077000
This handbook covers the theoretical and technical aspects of internal communication and is aimed at the general manager as well as the media specialist. It considers the implications of change in the business context, and gives practical guidance on developing, implementing, and evaluating communication strategies. In addition, it describes a wide range of communication techniques, looks at developments in electronic communications, and presents 16 case studies.

Guide to Internal Communication Methods
Eileen Scholes, ed.
Brookfield, Vermont: Gower, 1999
168pp ISBN: 0566082179
Based on material compiled for the *Gower Handbook of Internal Communication*, this smaller guide offers practical help for all business managers and team leaders. It deals succinctly with various types of communication, outlining the strengths, weaknesses, and other aspects of each. It contains sections covering face-to-face communication, events, print-based, electronic, and computer-based communication, and communication within the organization.

Guide to Managerial Communication: Effective Business Writing and Speaking
Mary Munter
Des Moines, Iowa: Prentice Hall, 1999
198pp ISBN: 0130133817
The book is a guide for managers and others wanting to develop their communications skills and a reference source for those with good communications skills. It covers all the usual forms of business communication in a detailed manner with clear examples.

Handbook of Communication Audits for Organisations
Owen Hargie, Dennis Tourish, eds.
New York: Routledge, 2000
312pp (International Series on Communication Skills)
ISBN: 0415186420
The contributors to this handbook offer practical guidance on the design, implementation, and assessment of communication audits within organizations. They discuss the main options confronting organizations that embark on an audit and consider the merits of all available approaches. Case studies of the communication audit process are presented along the way, and guidance is also given on how to interpret audit findings, how to construct reports, and how to make recommendations based on an audit.

How to Give Effective Business Briefings: Effective Techniques for Relaying Information to and Obtaining Feedback from Employees
Colin Clark
Sterling, Virginia: Stylus Publishing, 1999
96pp (Better Management Skills Series)
ISBN: 074942513X
This practical guide is designed to help managers and team leaders successfully brief their staff. The areas covered include preparation, structure, delivery, informal and formal feedback, variations on the briefing session, and evaluation. Mini-questionnaires, exercises, and case studies are included.

In Good Company: How Social Capital Makes Organizations Work
Don Cohen, Laurence Prusak
Boston, Massachusetts: Harvard Business School Press, 2001

"If I were to give off-the-cuff advice to anyone trying to institute change, I would say, 'How clear is the metaphor?'"
(Warren Bennis)

224pp ISBN: 087584913X

In Good Company focuses on the positive effects of informal connections within large corporations. The authors argue that informal connections such as elevator conversations build trust and result in an exchange of useful information. This book does not focus on theory but is filled with real-life examples from well-respected companies.

Managing the Corporate Intranet
Mitra Miller, Andrew J. Roehr, Benjamin Bernard
New York: John Wiley, 1998
427pp ISBN: 0471199788

The authors offer a practical guide to a wide range of technical and management issues of concern to intranet managers, Webmasters, and administrators responsible for their company's intranet. They provide hands-on solutions, action plans, and checklists to help readers manage their own intranets.

MAGAZINES

Business Communication Quarterly
ISSN: 1080–5699
Association for Business Communication
Box G 1326, Baruch College, 17 Lexington Avenue, New York, 10010
T: +1 212 387 1620
F: +1 212 387 1655
www.bcq.theabc.org

The *Quarterly* is an international journal devoted to the teaching of business communication. A subscription to this journal is included in membership of the Association for Business Communication.

CiB News
ISSN: 1360–4678
British Association of Communicators in Business
42 Borough High Street, London, SE1 1XW, U.K.
T: +44 (0) 20 7378 7139
F: +44 (0) 20 7378 7140
www.bacb.org

CiB News is the journal of the British Association of Communicators in Business and is published ten times a year. It largely concentrates on membership news.

Corporate Communications: An International Journal
ISSN: 1356–3289
MCB University Press
60/62 Toller Lane, Bradford, West Yorkshire, BD8 9BY, U.K.
T: +44 (0) 1274 777700
F: +44 (0) 1274 785201
www.emeraldinsight.com/ccij.htm

This quarterly journal covers communications within organizations, and between organizations and the public, as well as strategic communications planning.

Internal Communication
ISSN: 0965–5999
Informa Publishing Group Ltd.
99 Portland Place, London, W1B 1PX, U.K.
T: +44 (0) 20 7553 1000
F: +44 (0) 20 7553 1100
www.informa.com

This journal acts as a forum for all those interested in employee communications. It is published ten times a year and contains academic articles, together with case studies and surveys.

Journal of Business Communication
ISSN: 0021–9436
Association for Business Communication
Box G 1326, Baruch College, 17 Lexington Avenue, New York, 10010
T: +1 212 387 1620
F: +1 212 387 1655
www.theabc.org/jbc.htm

This is a quarterly journal with a subscription included in membership of the Association for Business Communication. It seeks to publish a broad and diverse range of research, focusing on business communication and covering business composition and technical writing, information systems, international business communication, management communication, and organizational and corporate communication. It is aimed primarily at the academic community.

Journal of Communication Management
ISSN: 1363–254X
Henry Stewart Publications
Subscriptions Office, P.O. Box 10812, Birmingham, Alabama, 35202–0812
T: +1 800 633 4931
F: +1 205 995 1588
www.henrystewart.com/journals/jcm

This quarterly journal contains the latest developments, thinking, and practice in the management of internal and external communications. It is aimed at senior management, academics, consultants, and researchers.

Journal of Employee Communication Management
Ragan Communications
Suite 300, 316 N. Michigan Avenue, Chicago, Illinois, 60601
T: +1 800 878 5331
F: +1 312 960 4106
www2.ragan.com

In this magazine, leaders in the communication field provide in-depth coverage of how their organizations' communication needs are satisfied. A sample from the magazine is provided on the Web site.

Strategic Communication Management
ISSN: 1363–9064
Melcrum Publishing Ltd.
1st Floor, Chelsea Reach, 79–89 Lots Road, London, SW10 0RN, U.K.
T: +44 (0) 20 7795 2205
F: +44 (0) 20 7795 2156
www.melcrum.com

This international journal, published six times a year, aims to cover the latest ideas and concepts in communication strategy, offering the sort of practical solutions and information that will enable professionals to tackle their jobs more successfully.

INTERNET

American Communication Association
www.uark.edu/~aca

This is the site of a virtual professional association created to promote academic and professional research, criticism, teaching, and practice, and the exchange of principles and theories of human communication. It contains a communication studies center that provides listings of related links, associations, and journals, and has a special section on business communication.

Association for Business Communication
www.theabc.org

The Association for Business Communication's site contains information on membership, on the history of the Association, on the awards and publications it makes available, and on its conventions, as well as providing news items and other resources.

British Association of Communicators in Business
www.bacb.org

Information on member benefits, on the events, awards, development, and training organized by the Association, and on its regional network is available from this site, which also publishes national and regional news.

Communications for Management, Inc.
www.c4m.com

This site contains a complete book, provided for readers without charge, which covers all the basics of corporate communications.

"Many attempts to communicate are nullified by saying too much."

(Robert Greenleaf)

International Association of Business Communicators
www.iabc.com
This site provides information resources and a journal, besides giving details of member services and events, the accreditation program, awards, and professional development opportunities.

Lawrence Ragan Communications, Inc.
www.2ragan.com
Belonging to a corporate communication consultancy for internal communicators, trainers, and speechwriters, this site offers newsletters and other products and services in the fields of employee communication, management strategy, and public relations.

Melcrum
www.melcrum.com
This site provides ideas and solutions of use to corporate communication and knowledge management professionals.

Work911/Bacal & Associates
www.work911.com/articles.htm
This commercial Web site offers a selection of free, easy to access articles on a variety of topics and is open to contributions.

ORGANIZATIONS

Europe

British Association of Communicators in Business
42 Borough High Street, London, SE1 1XW, U.K.
T: +44 (0) 20 7378 7139
F: +44 (0) 20 7378 7140
E: enquiries@bacb.org
www.bacb.org
This organization was founded in 1949 to promote the importance of effective communications, facilitate the exchange of ideas and experience between members, and improve standards. It also aims to develop members' management and vocational skills and offers education and training in all areas of corporate communication.

International

Association for Business Communication
Box G 1326, Baruch College, 17 Lexington Avenue, New York, 10010
T: +1 212 387 1620
F: +1 212 387 1655
E: myers@theabc.org
www.theabc.org
The ABC is an international organization committed to fostering excellence in scholarship, research, education, and practice relating to business communication. Its membership is interdisciplinary.

International Association of Business Communicators
Suite 600, One Hallidie Plaza, San Francisco, California, 94102–2818
T: +1 415 544 4700
F: +1 415 544 4747
E: iabccustomerservicecentre.service_centre@iabc.com
www.iabc.com
Formed in 1970, the Association is a nonprofit international network of professionals committed to improving the effectiveness of organizations through strategic, interactive, and integrated business communication management. It provides a range of member benefits.

For More Information

- ☆ **Building Great Internal Partnerships (pp. 281–82)**
- ☆ **Managing Internal Politics (pp. 332–33)**
- **Interpersonal Communication/ Relations (pp. 2012–14)**
- **Public Relations (pp. 2090–92)**

INTERNATIONAL MANAGEMENT, CROSS CULTURAL MANAGEMENT

BOOKS

Breaking through Culture Shock: What You Need to Succeed in International Business
Elizabeth Marx
Naperville, Illinois: Nicholas Brealey, 2001
233pp ISBN: 1857882202
This book explores the issue of culture shock, and the extent to which it affects success in today's global business environment. It stresses the importance of understanding the different motivations, behaviors, and ways of making decisions, found in other cultures. The author puts forward the culture shock triangle model as a way of helping managers to behave differently and manage their emotions so as to become truly cross-culturally effective.

Building Cross-cultural Competence: How to Create Wealth from Conflicting Values
Charles M. Hampden-Turner, Fons Trompenaars
New Haven, Connecticut: Yale University Press, 2000
388pp ISBN: 0300084978
The authors define the dimensions that contribute to culture and argue that values that appear to be in opposition can in fact be complementary. The book illustrates opposing values using case studies and suggests how they can work in tandem. The authors' conclusions are based on a research database of 50,000 managerial respondents.

Cultural Dimension of International Business 3rd ed.
Gary P. Ferraro
Upper Saddle River, New Jersey: Prentice Hall, 1997
196pp ISBN: 0137275617
This book explores the contribution that cultural anthropology can make to the conduct of international business. It outlines a conceptual approach to culture and international business and examines the nature of verbal and nonverbal communication patterns, as well as contrasting cultural values, cross-cultural negotiation, culture shock, and the development of global managers. Advice on sources of cultural information is appended.

Doing Business Internationally: The Guide to Cross-cultural Success
Terence Brake, et al.
New York: McGraw-Hill, 1994
225pp ISBN: 0786301171
A practical guide to becoming a successful global manager.

Exploring Management across the World: Selected Readings

DAVID J. HICKSON, ED.
New York: Penguin, 1997
555pp ISBN: 0140254781
The continued globalization of business has increased the need for managers to work effectively with different cultures. This book's contribution to the development of cross-cultural management skills is to reprint a number of seminal articles on societal and national culture and international management across the globe.

Global Literacies: Lessons on Business Leadership and National Cultures
ROBERT H. ROSEN, ET AL.
New York: Simon & Schuster, 2000
416pp ISBN: 0684859025
In this title, the author makes a comparison between the way a child learns how to speak and the redefinition of the way top businesses work due to the arrival of a global marketplace. The authors assert that in order to achieve success, organizations must educate themselves in this new language, and use numerous surveys, interviews, and studies to reveal how top companies and individuals approach both this and other challenges.

Global Smarts: The Art of Communicating and Deal Making Anywhere in the World
SHEIDA HODGE
New York: John Wiley, 2000
256pp ISBN: 0471382469
The author focuses on the underlying values that inform culture in different countries, asserting that "tips" on correct international behavior do not provide the strategic insight necessary for managers. She illustrates her points by analyzing common American business practices to make readers question assumptions before contrasting these with practices overseas. The book addresses how corporate training programs can better prepare executives for cross-cultural assignments.

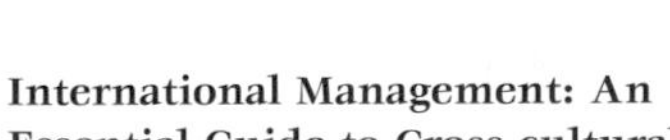

International Management: An Essential Guide to Cross-cultural Business 2nd ed.
JOHN MATTOCK, ED.
Milford, Connecticut: Kogan Page, 1999
176pp (Professional Paperback Series)
ISBN: 0749428279
The author explores the problems and issues surrounding international and cross-cultural management, focusing on the six key steps to effective communication and negotiation: culture, company, character, tactics, timing, and talk. Each of these areas is discussed, with quizzes and exercises to illustrate how they can be approached most effectively.

International Management: Cross-cultural Dimensions 2nd ed.
RICHARD MEAD
Cambridge, Massachusetts: Blackwell Business, 1998
528pp ISBN: 0631200037
Written for management students, this book examines how cultural factors and differences affect behavior in the workplace and the boardroom. The key skills demanded by international management are identified and discussed, their practical application is shown, and the influence and effects of culture are investigated from four viewpoints: national, organizational, strategic, and personnel.

Managing across Borders 2nd ed.
CHRISTOPHER A. BARTLETT, SUMANTRA GHOSHAL
Boston, Massachusetts: Harvard Business School Press, 2002
416pp ISBN: 1578517079
Valuable lessons on running transnational companies, from two of the leading writers in the field.

Managing Cultural Differences: Leadership Strategies for a New World of Business 5th ed.
PHILIP R. HARRIS, ROBERT T. MORAN
Woburn, Massachusetts: Gulf Professional Publishing Company, 2000
474pp ISBN: 0877193452
The book is divided into three sections: addressing the need for multicultural managerial skills, the characteristics that make up a culture, and the specifics of cultures from countries on every continent. The fifth edition contains a new chapter on women in global business.

Riding the Waves of Culture: Understanding Cultural Diversity in Business 2nd ed.
FONS TROMPENAARS, CHARLES HAMPDEN-TURNER
New York: McGraw-Hill, 1997
416pp ISBN: 0786311258
The authors explore cultural extremes and the incomprehension that can arise when doing business across cultures, even within the same organization. They identify five key orientations that affect how people deal with each other, do business, and manage, and propose strategies for reconciling these orientations across different cultures. They also review the concept of the "Trans-national Corporation," in which companies take from each culture what is best.

MAGAZINES

Cross-cultural Research
ISSN: 1069–3971
Sage Publications Ltd.
6 Bonhill Street, London, EC2A 4PU, U.K.
T: +44 (0) 20 7374 0645
F: +44 (0) 20 7374 8741
www.sagepub.co.uk
This is the official journal of the Society for Cross-cultural Research, published quarterly. It is a key source for peer-reviewed articles, research reports, bibliographies, and discussion pieces on all aspects of cross-cultural and comparative studies in the fields of social and behavioral science.

Foreign Affairs
ISSN: 0015–7120
Foreign Affairs
58 East 68th Street, New York, 10021
T: +1 212 434 9522
www.foreignaffairs.org
Published six times per year, this magazine covers current events and how they affect U.S. relations worldwide. With a focus on international, political, commercial, and cultural relations, it has often been described as the premier journal of world affairs. This is a must-read for any corporate executive involved with international business.

Global Finance
ISSN: 0896–4181
Global Finance Media, Inc.
411 Fifth Avenue, New York, 10018
T: +1 212 447 7900
F: +1 212 447 7750
www.globalfinanceadvertising.com
Published 12 times per year, this magazine provides news of interest to the global supply community. Business today is increasingly globalized. This magazine provides cutting-edge information regarding the swiftly changing global market economy. Featured topics include corporate finance, risk management, money management, investor relations, and current country profiles.

International Business Review
ISSN: 0969–5931
Elsevier Science
Regional Sales Office, Customer Support Department, P.O. Box 945, New York, 10159–0945
T: +1 212 633 3730

"Highly centralized management can suffocate the innovative energies of individuals in the subsidiary units."
(Nitin Nohria)

  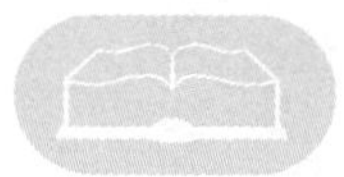    

F: +1 212 633 3680
www.elsevier.com
Published six times per year, with an emphasis on marketing and management issues and an international list of contributors, this journal contains the latest insights on international business and keeps senior management current with all the most recent developments.

International Journal of Commerce & Management
ISSN: 1056–9219
IABD Publications
Eberly College of Business and Information Technology, Indiana University of Pennsylvania, P.O. Box 1658, Indiana, Pennsylvania, 15705
T: +1 412 357 2535 or 412 357 5759
F: +1 412 357 5743
http://home.earthlink.net/~falkl/iabd/journals.htm
Published four times per year, this journal is written with both business practitioners and nonprofit organizations in mind. It aims to promote understanding among managers and international organizations, and also has articles on international management theory and policy.

International Journal of Cross Cultural Management
ISSN: 1470–5958
Sage Publications, Inc.
2455 Teller Road, Thousand Oaks, California, 91320
T: +1 805 499 0721
F: +1 805 499 0871
www.sagepub.co.uk
Published three times a year, this journal is aimed at academics working in the fields of organizational behavior, HRM, international and comparative management, and international industrial relations. Its contents cover both the theoretical and conceptual aspects of cross-cultural management and aim to promote an understanding of the role of culture in management, work, and throughout the organization.

Journal of International Business Studies
ISSN: 0047–2506
3240 Prospect Street NW, Washington, D.C., 20007–3214
T: +1 202 944 3755
F: +1 202 944 3762
www.aibworld.net
Published jointly by the Academy of International Business, Copenhagen Business School, and the McDonough School of Business at Georgetown University, this quarterly journal focuses on the results of social science research and presents articles and papers which aim to advance the understanding of the workings of business. It is aimed mainly at academics in universities and research institutes.

Journal of International Management
ISSN: 1075–4253
Elsevier Science
Regional Sales Office, Customer Support Department, P.O. Box 945, New York, 10159–0945
T: +1 212 633 3730
F: +1 212 633 3680
www.elsevier.com
This is a quarterly journal devoted to advancing the understanding of issues involved in the theory and practice of global management and focusing on international strategic management. It is aimed at business professionals working in the fields of risk management, organizational behavior, human resources, and cross-cultural management.

Journal of World Business
ISSN: 1090–9516
Elsevier Science
Regional Sales Office, Customer Support Department, P.O. Box 945, New York, 10159–0945
T: +1 212 633 3730
F: +1 212 633 3680
www.elsevier.com
This is a quarterly journal committed to developing discussion of groundbreaking practices in international management, marketing, and strategy. It was formerly published as the *Columbia Journal of World Business.*

INTERNET

Culturally Correct Papers
www.culturallycorrectpapers.com
Sponsored by a group of business professionals and educators, the site provides a free e-mail newsletter on cross-cultural management, access to past newsletters, and some language programs.

Learn about Cultures
www.learnaboutcultures.com
Sponsored by a consulting firm, the site offers abstracts on the cultures of different countries and articles on aspects of cross-cultural management, including training, technology, and gender.

Society for Cross-cultural Research
www.hyper.fit/edu/CampusLife/clubs-org/sccr
The Society is a nonprofit membership-based organization, devoted to pursuing cross-cultural research from a multidisciplinary perspective. It is aimed at professionals and academics from all fields of social science.

WorldBiz
www.worldbiz.com
This site offers an extensive database including information on protocol, industries and sectors, travel, negotiating, laws and regulations, and trade and investment in numerous countries.

ORGANIZATIONS

USA

Academy of International Business
College of Business Administration, University of Hawaii at Manoa, 2404 Maile Way, Honolulu, Hawaii, 96822
T: +1 808 956 3665
F: +1 808 956 3261
E: aib@cba.hawaii.edu
www.aibworld.net
A leading body for scholars and specialists in the field of international business, this association aims to disseminate knowledge and understanding of international business issues across the globe through the exchange of information, ideas, and research, and through business cooperation.

International Association of Management
P.O. Box 64841, Virginia Beach, Virginia, 23467–4841
T: +1 757 482 2273
F: +1 757 482 0325
E: aomgt@infi.net
www.aom-iaom.org
A nonprofit professional organization for students, teachers, and practitioners of management, the IAoM is dedicated to advancing the international practice of management across professional fields through the provision of support, information, products, and services.

For More Information

Working Abroad (pp. 2134–36)

"Indian management has to pursue processes which conform to the underlying grain of the Indian temper."
(S. K. Chakraborty)

  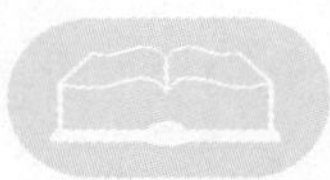    

Interpersonal Communication/Relations

BOOKS

Agreed: Improve Your Powers of Influence
Terry Gillen
New York: Beekman, 2000
200pp ISBN: 0846450003
The author describes techniques for increasing the influence that we, as individuals, exert, and for achieving the outcomes that we, as individuals, desire. He explores each of the key principles involved: persuading, probing, listening, assertiveness, understanding behaviors, interpreting body language, giving constructive criticism, and resolving differences of opinion.

The Anatomy of Persuasion
Norbert Aubuchon
New York: AMACOM, 1997
208pp ISBN: 0814479529
The author examines the use and importance of persuasion as a personal skill when communicating. He describes processes for applying persuasive techniques to improve communication, decision making, and creativity, at both personal and managerial levels. Case study examples illustrate how the process can be adapted to different business situations.

The Art of Speedreading People: How to Size People Up and Speak Their Language
Paul D. Tieger, Barbara Barron-Tieger, Marly A. Swick
New York: Little Brown, 1999
208pp ISBN: 0316845183
This is a comprehensive layperson's guide to the application of the Myers-Briggs personality types. It is valuable as a celebration of individual differences and of the particular strengths each type can bring to a working relationship. Though people seldom fit nicely into the little boxes we try to put them in, the authors here strive to help readers quickly assess others.

Body Language at Work
Adrian Furnham
New York: Beekman, 2000
96pp (Management Shapers Series)
ISBN: 0846450070
This book offers an introduction to the significance of body language and what it reveals about attitudes and emotions. It also presents techniques for interpreting nonverbal gestures and expressions and considers how they might be used in work situations.

Creating Confidence: How to Develop Your Personal Power and Presence
Meribeth Bunch
Milford, Connecticut: Kogan Page, 1999
128pp ISBN: 0749427825
This book explores the importance of self-confidence, presence, and personal power in communication. It examines key skills such as listening, building rapport, assertiveness, image, presentation, and handling feedback, and reviews tools and guidelines for developing and utilizing these skills.

Effective Communication Skills for Scientific and Technical Professionals
Harry E. Chambers
Cambridge, Massachusetts: Perseus, 2000
272pp ISBN: 0415921481
This title is a guide to improving interpersonal, communication, and managerial skills by means of a huge range of methods designed for developing such talents. The book also highlights the difficulties encountered in real life by people in the workplace, and suggests ways of improving communication skills.

Human Dynamics: A New Framework for Understanding People and Realizing the Potential in Our Organizations
Sandra Seagal, David Horne
Williston, Vermont: Pegasus Communications, 2000
351pp ISBN: 1883823072
Human Dynamics builds on the foundation of personality research by exploring the nature of human interactions. The focus is on how different people mentally process situations. The book is written for the lay reader and provides a wealth of information to guide people through the complexities of organizational life. It will help anyone learn how to benefit more effectively from interactions with people from diverse backgrounds.

Loud and Clear: How to Prepare and Deliver Effective Business and Technical Presentations 4th ed.
George L. Morrisey, Thomas L. Sechrest, Wendy B. Warman
Cambridge, Massachusetts: Perseus, 1997
208pp ISBN: 0201127938
This title is a comprehensive guide on how to deliver a presentation effectively. The book covers all the main points from visuals to delivery, but places the greatest emphasis on preparation, which the coauthors say is the most important factor of all.

NLP in 21 Days: A Complete Introduction and Training Programme
Harry Alder, Beryl Heather
London: Piatkus, 2000
288pp ISBN: 0749920300
After introducing the concept of neurolinguistic programming, the authors explore its influence on interpersonal communication and personal development. The full international syllabus for NLP practitioner training is reproduced over 21 chapters covering the key topics. Each chapter includes exercises and samples for individuals to apply to their own situations.

The Power of Influence: Intensive Influencing Skills at Work
Tom E. Lambert
Naperville, Illinois: Nicholas Brealey, 1997
256pp (People Skills for Professionals Series)
ISBN: 185788115X
This book constitutes a practical, jargon-free guide to professional influencing skills for managers, leaders, professionals, and salespeople. The issues covered include unprincipled influencing, ethical sales skills, mind maps and easy persuasion, influencing through NLP, and dealing with difficult people.

The Story Factor: Secrets of Influence from the Art of Storytelling
Annette Simmons
Cambridge, Massachusetts: Perseus, 2000
256pp ISBN: 0738203696
In this title, the author suggests that the unique way in which storytelling can influence people makes it one of the most useful management techniques available. The book includes six varieties of story that can be used in any situation, and emphasizes the importance of bringing all the various components that make up a good presentation, such as tone and body language, together.

True Partnership: Revolutionary Thinking about Relating to Others
Carl D. Zaiss
San Francisco, California: Berrett-Koehler,

"Society cannot share a common communication system so long as it is split into warring factions."
(Bertolt Brecht)

  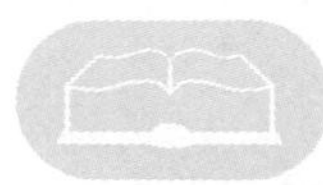  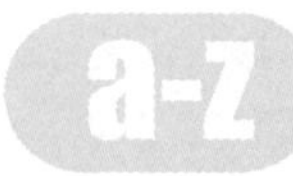

2002
150pp ISBN: 157675166X
This book is designed to change the way we look at interactions in order to form better relationships. The author's intention is to challenge the assumptions and standard behaviors that most of us use, for the sake of expedience, when interacting with others. Connecting at a deeper level of understanding can improve the quality of our relationships, and the end result is more productive and fulfilling interactions.

What to Say to Get What You Want: Strong Words for 44 Challenging Types of Bosses, Employees, Co-workers, and Customers
Samuel D. Deep, Lyle Sussman
Cambridge, Massachusetts: Perseus, 1992
316pp ISBN: 0201577127
This title describes how to get on the right side of colleagues at work. In order to achieve this goal, the author guides the reader through the 40 varieties of difficult people and how to handle them, advocating above all, a considerate attitude.

Working with Emotional Intelligence
Daniel P. Goleman
New York: Bantam Doubleday Dell, 2000
383pp ISBN: 0553378589
Daniel Goleman is the foremost proponent of the concept of emotional intelligence—the capacity to work well with emotions, our own and those of others. In this book he applies his theories to the work environment with definitions of the concepts and the reasons they are important. According to Goleman, interpersonal skills are the most important part of sustaining career success, and this book will help anyone begin the process of increasing those skills.

MAGAZINES

Communication Research
ISSN: 0093–6502
Sage Publications, Inc.
2455 Teller Road, Thousand Oaks, California, 91320
T: +1 805 499 0721
F: +1 805 499 0871
www.sagepub.com
This bimonthly publication, aimed at academics and professionals, explores the processes involved in, and the consequences of, different types of communication, whether interpersonal, mass media, political, organizational, or intercultural.

European Journal of Communication
ISSN: 0267–3231
Sage Publications Ltd.
6 Bonhill Street, London, EC2A 4PU, U.K.
T: +44 (0) 20 7374 0645
F: +44 (0) 20 7374 8741
www.sagepub.co.uk
This is a leading international journal, published quarterly, that provides information on the latest international communications research, practice, and policy developments. It also promotes information interchange between European scholars and publishes occasional special issues on key communication topics.

Journal of Communication Management
ISSN: 1363–254X
Henry Stewart Publications
Subscriptions Office, P.O. Box 10812, Birmingham, Alabama, 35202–0812
T: +1 800 633 4931
F: +1 205 995 1588
www.henrystewart.com/journals/jcm
A quarterly journal available both in paper copy and online, this title is published in association with the Institute of Public Relations and the International Association of Business Communicators. It provides in-depth, peer-reviewed articles and papers on communications practice and theory.

Management Communication Quarterly
ISSN: 0893–3189
Sage Publications, Inc.
2455 Teller Road, Thousand Oaks, California, 91320
T: +1 805 499 0721
F: +1 805 499 0871
www.sagepub.com
A quarterly journal aimed at managers, researchers, professionals, consultants, and trainers, this publication presents the latest theory, research, and practice in management and organizational communication. The topics it covers include: intercultural communication, corporate culture, TQM applications, emotional intelligence, group decision making, organizational commitment, and power and control issues.

People Management
ISSN: 1358–6297
Personnel Publications Ltd.
17 Britton Street, London, EC1M 5TP, U.K.
T: +44 (0) 20 7880 6200
F: +44 (0) 20 7336 7637
www.peoplemanagement.co.uk
People Management is the official journal of the Chartered Institute of Personnel and Development. It reports on current issues in the personnel and human resources fields, including legislation and pay. Articles focus on a variety of subjects, for example, industrial relations, training and development, and personnel techniques. Case studies and profiles of leading practitioners are also a regular feature.

INTERNET

American Communication Association
www.uark.edu/~aca
The Association is a nonprofit organization concerned to develop academic and professional research into the principles and theories of human communication. Services provided include free membership, a collection of online resources, and an online journal.

Communication Briefings
www.briefings.com/cb
This Internet address leads to an online briefing that explores a number of communication-related topics, for example, communicating with employees, giving speeches and presentations, and dealing with difficult people. It offers advice, tips, articles, and techniques for handling each situation.

EQ.org—Emotional Intelligence
www.eq.org
This is a free Web site with links to over 215 online resources concerning emotional intelligence. Many of these links are to commercial sites, but this is nonetheless a good place to start a search.

Pertinent Information—Interpersonal Communication Articles
www.pertinent.com/pertinfo/business/communication
The site contains a selection of articles relating to all aspects of interpersonal communication, from improving influencing skills and communicating across cultures to networking challenges and developing interaction techniques.

ORGANIZATIONS

USA

International Communication Association
Suite 300, 1730 Rhode Island Avenue NW, Washington, D.C., 20036
T: +1 202 530 9855
F: +1 202 530 9851
E: *ica@icahdq.org*

"Even the frankest and bravest of subordinates do not talk with their boss the same way they talk with colleagues."
(Robert Greenleaf)

www.icahdq.org
The ICA is a member-based organization that promotes the systematic study of communication theories, processes, and skills. It provides a range of services including interest groups, journals, publications, a network forum, and annual conferences, and has a specific division concerned with interpersonal communication.

National Communication Association
1765 N. Street NW, Washington, D.C., 20036
T: +1 202 464 4622
F: +1 202 464 4600
www.natcom.org
The Association is a nonprofit scholarly society of practitioners, educators, and students whose aim is to promote the study, research, teaching, and application of scientific and humanistic aspects of communication. It publishes a range of journals and books, a newsletter, and an electronic bulletin, and also organizes events, conferences, and an annual convention.

For More Information

✔ **Developing Passive People (pp. 350–51)**
Internal Communication (pp. 2007–09)
Management Styles (pp. 2036–38)
Presentation/Speaking (pp. 2077–78)

ISO 9000

BOOKS

Achieving Quality through Continual Improvement
CLAUDE BURRILL, JOHANNES LEDOLTER
New York: John Wiley, 1999
630pp ISBN: 0471092207
This book addresses the managerial aspects involved in improving the quality of all processes in order to stay competitive in today's marketplace. The text combines both managerial and statistical coverage, with an emphasis on processes and discussion of quality tools. Case studies and extensive examples complement the text. It includes bibliographical references and an index.

Beyond ISO 9000: How to Sustain Quality in a Dynamic World
WILLIAM STIMSON
New York: AMACOM, 1998
353pp ISBN: 0814403921
This book demonstrates how to set up quality systems in the areas of management, quality assurance, engineering, sales and service, and operations, providing detailed explanations of each step. It is also concerned with making the most of the ISO 9000 certification process. It shows how to implement the systems and standards needed to become certified, and how to sustain those systems and standards for best results.

The Case against ISO 9000 2nd ed.
JOHN SEDDON
Dublin, Republic of Ireland: Oak Tree Press, 2001
270pp ISBN: 1860761739
The author argues that the ISO standards, including the newly revised ISO 9000:2000, are not only failing to deliver the improved quality they promise, but in most cases are actually damaging the companies that have implemented them. According to him, real quality can best be achieved by viewing the organization as a system and taking a customer-focused view of the company's products and procedures, rather than by adhering to a rigid set of written rules. He also puts forward an alternative set of Vanguard Standards, based on a systems approach.

How to Make Money with ISO 9000: A Guide to Profitable Quality Management
JAMES HIGHLANDS
New York: McGraw-Hill, 1999
177pp ISBN: 0071359699
Aimed at those who have adopted ISO 9000 quality management systems, this book provides a practical guide for gaining profits through these new processes. It also gives detailed instructions for putting ISO 9000 quality standards to work throughout the organization, which is, in the author's view, the key to increasing market share and profitability.

Interpreting ISO 9001:2000 with Statistical Methodology
JAMES L. LAMPRECHT
Milwaukee, Wisconsin: ASQ Quality Press, 2001
205pp ISBN: 0873895177
This book provides statistical information relating to the most recent revision of the ISO standard, the ISO 9001:2000 standard, intended to help the reader design the questionnaires needed. The book also contains non-statistical material, including tables and sample forms and questionnaires. In addition to many case studies, tables, and graphics, Lamprecht provides information on the sequence of changes from the 1994 to the 2000 version.

ISO 9000:2000 in a Nutshell: A Concise Guide to the Revisions
JEANNE KETOLA, KATHY ROBERTS
Chico, California: Paton Press, 2001
140pp ISBN: 0965044599
This book is a simple, clear, and concise guide to the ISO 9000:2000 revisions. It analyzes the differences from the process management approach in the ISO 9000:1994 version in order to explain what professionals charged with implementing the new standards need to know to meet the new requirements for certification.

ISO 9000:2000 New Requirements: 28 New Requirements Checklist and Compliance Guide 3rd ed.
JACK KANHOLM
Los Angeles, California: AQA Press, 2001
64pp ISBN: 1882711076
This book contains in-depth information for interpreting, understanding, and implementing all new ISO 9000:2000 standards and requirements. Every requirement is systematically explained with regard to interpretation, procedures and records, the way certification auditors will verify conformance, and the specific actions that need to be taken to achieve conformance.

ISO 9000 Pocket Guide
DAVID HOYLE
Woburn, Massachusetts: Butterworth-Heinemann, 1998
320pp ISBN: 0750640251
This guide provides a very readable, practical introduction to the ISO 9000 standards for quality practitioners. It explains the concept of quality system management, and a substantial part of the text adopts a bullet point approach to indicate how each of the 57 clauses of the standard can be satisfied. Task lists, flowcharts, tips, and questions are included.

ISO 9001:2000 for Small and Medium Sized Businesses
HERBERT C. MONNICH, JR.
Milwaukee, Wisconsin: ASQ Quality Press, 2001

"Alignment is not about the management of quality. It is about the quality of management."
(George Labovitz)

  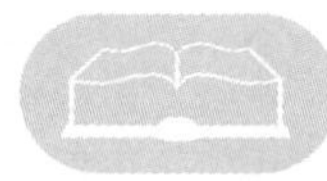    

168pp ISBN: 0873895150
This book is meant to help those with little experience in this complex area to grasp the meaning and intent of ISO 9001:2000 requirements and to understand how those requirements relate to small and medium-sized businesses, no matter what products are involved. The author explains that businesses of any size can use quality tools as a means of implementing and maintaining the requirements of the standards.

ISO 9001:2000 for Small Businesses 2nd ed.
Ray Tricker
Woburn, Massachusetts: Butterworth-Heinemann, 2001
320pp ISBN: 0750648821
This book explains the new requirements of ISO 9001:2000 and looks at how smaller companies can benefit from it and set up their own quality management systems. Written for engineers and managers in small and medium-sized companies, it examines the background of ISO 9000, the structure of ISO 9000:2000, the importance of quality control and quality assurance, quality management systems, and quality organizational structure. It includes an example quality manual, along with a number of checklists and an extensive glossary.

The Quality Audit for ISO 9001:2000: A Practical Guide
David Wealleans
Brookfield, Vermont: Gower, 2000
296pp ISBN: 0566082454
This is a wide-ranging and detailed explanation of the entire range of quality audits associated with maintaining compliance to ISO 9001 and similar international standards. The book covers all aspects of auditing, including certification assessment, supplier investigation, and internal auditing. It also provides a detailed analysis of the requirements of ISO 9001:2000.

Standards in the Services Industry
Brian Rothery
Brookfield, Vermont: Gower, 1997
177pp ISBN: 0566078376
The author deals with the application of both quality and environmental standards and specifications in service-sector industries. His discussion of services and standards includes sections on the quality management system, the environmental management system, and health and safety. His detailed review of quality management documentation also introduces the sectoral codes of practice for ISO 9000 and gives similar coverage to the Environmental Management Standard. Examples of a quality manual and an issue identification checklist are included.

MAGAZINES

Quality World
ISSN: 1352–8769
Institute of Quality Assurance
Information Services, 12 Grosvenor Crescent, London, SW1X 7EE, U.K.
T: +44 (0) 20 7245 6722
F: +44 (0) 20 7245 6755
www.iqa.org
Quality World is the journal of the Institute of Quality Assurance. It reviews recent news and issues in the field of quality and includes feature articles for practicing managers.

INTERNET

ISO 9000
www.praxiom.com
This Web site, compiled by Praxiom Research Group Ltd., which is based in Edmonton, Canada, provides a broad introduction to ISO 9000:2000 and interprets the standard into plain English. Much of the information is available free of charge, while the company also offers guidance to its additional range of products and services.

ISO—International Organization for Standardization
www.iso.ch
This, the ISO's own site, provides information about the organization and events connected with it, as well as news, press releases, and biographies of experts.

ISO Easy
www.isoeasy.org
This site is dedicated to helping organizations understand and implement the ISO 9000 and 9001 standards.

ISO Online
www.iso.ch
An electronic information service provided by the Central Secretariat of the International Organization for Standardization (ISO), this site provides a detailed explanation of the work of ISO, a directory of its member organizations, and access to its technical work. Information on the ISO 9000 and ISO 14000 standards can be accessed. The site's collection of frequently asked questions about standards and standards-related topics is a useful tool for anyone starting to work with these standards.

Quality Digest Online
www.qualitydigest.com
An online journal for news, tips, and techniques to do with quality and for articles on quality-related issues, the site also includes a searchable ISO 9000 and QS-9000 registered company database.

Underwriter's Laboratories
www.ul.com
This site of the Underwriter's Laboratories, Inc., an independent, nonprofit product safety testing and certification organization, provides links to companies that adhere to various quality and management system standards, including ISO 9000 and ISO 9001.

ORGANIZATIONS

USA

American Society for Quality
600 North Plankinton Avenue, Milwaukee, Wisconsin, 53203
T: +1 414 272 8575
F: +1 414 272 1734
E: cs@asq.org
www.asq.org
A society of individual and organizational members founded in 1946, the American Society for Quality is dedicated to the ongoing development, enhancement, and promotion of concepts, principles, and techniques relating to quality management. It produces a range of publications on quality issues and offers guidance and services to help organizations with certification and education in quality techniques, as well as providing an introduction to a number of quality standards.

Europe

British Standards Institution
389 Chiswick High Road, London, W4 4AL, U.K.
T: +44 (0) 20 8996 9000
F: +44 (0) 20 8996 7400
E: info@bsi-global.com
www.bsi-global.com
The BSI was founded in 1901 and received a royal charter in 1929. It is an independent body whose objectives include setting quality standards and promoting the adoption of British Standard specifications. The BSI provides copies of and information on the new ISO 9000:2000 standard and offers training and consulting services.

International

International Organization for Standardization (ISO)
1 rue de Varembé, Case postale 56, CH-1211 Geneva 20, Switzerland
T: +41 22 749 01 11
F: +41 22 733 34 30
E: central@iso.org
www.iso.ch
The ISO is a worldwide federation of the national standards bodies of some 130 countries, each represented by one organization. A nongovernmental institution established in 1947, the ISO aims to promote

  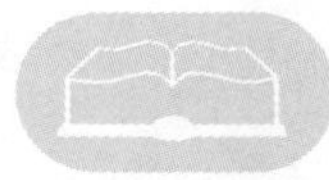    

the development of standardization and related activities in the world in order to facilitate the international exchange of goods and services and to develop cooperation in the spheres of intellectual, scientific, technological, and economic activity. The ISO's work results in international agreements that are published as International Standards. It is also actively involved in consultation and training services and produces a range of publications.

For More Information

☆ **The True Total Quality (pp. 173–74)**

- **Benchmarking (pp. 1911–13)**
- **Manufacturing Systems (pp. 2039–42)**
- **Process Control and Statistical Process Control (pp. 2079–80)**
- **Quality and Total Quality Management (pp. 2096–98)**

JAPANESE MANAGEMENT TECHNIQUES

BOOKS

Can Japan Compete?
MICHAEL E. PORTER, MARIKO SAKAKIBARA, HIROTAKA TAKEUCHI
Cambridge, Massachusetts: Perseus, 2000
208pp ISBN: 0465059899
This title questions why Japan's economy slumped for so long and asks what the problems it encountered have to teach the world about the modern global marketplace.

Gemba Kaizen: A Commonsense, Low-cost Approach to Management
MASAAKI IMAI
New York: McGraw-Hill, 1997
384pp ISBN: 0070314462
Gemba Kaizen is the focusing of the techniques of Kaizen on the place where they will do the most good: Gemba, the critical area; the place where things are really happening. In business, Gemba is where products are developed and made or where services are delivered. The author introduces the idea of the "house of Gemba" and explains how to manage quality, cost, and delivery. He also discusses related issues, such as the 5Ss (the five steps of housekeeping), Muda (waste), the roles and accountability of Gemba managers, and the just-in-time production system, and presents 21 case studies of, for the most part, Japanese companies.

The Hybrid Factory: The Japanese Production System in the United States
TETSUO ABO, ED.
New York: Oxford University Press, 1994
318pp ISBN: 0195079744
The authors explore the potential for the effective transfer of Japanese management and production systems, credited with giving Japanese firms their competitive superiority, to other countries. The management factors that give strength to Japanese production systems are, in their view, however, related to the sociocultural background, and they question whether a radically different cultural environment makes such a transfer impossible.

Inside the Kaisha: Demystifying Japanese Business Behavior
NOBORU YOSHIMURA, PHILIP ANDERSON,
Boston, Massachusetts: Harvard Business School Press, 1997
272pp ISBN: 0875844154
This book attempts to explain six aspects of Japanese business behavior that seem to be contradictory, contains valuable insights into the world of the Japanese salaryman that Western managers could learn from in their own business practice, and offers useful advice to people who do business with them.

Just-in-time 2nd ed.
DAVID HUTCHINS
Brookfield, Vermont: Gower Publishing, 1998
236pp ISBN: 0566077981
The second edition of this book aims to demonstrate the potential benefits of just-in-time (JIT) to a wider audience. It explains the basic concepts and principles of the system and explores the practical aspects of the implementation of JIT programs. It also includes chapters on total productive maintenance and the use of the European Business Excellence Model.

The Kaizen Blitz: Accelerating Breakthroughs in Productivity and Performance
ANTHONY C. LARAIA, PATRICIA E. MOODY, ROBERT W. HALL
New York: John Wiley, 1999
304pp ISBN: 0471246484
A new version of Kaizen, called the Kaizen Blitz and pioneered by the Association for Manufacturing Excellence, is the subject of this guide. The authors introduce the process, which is designed for achieving continuous improvement, and describe the benefits it can offer an organization. Their aim is to teach any individual how to use the Kaizen Blitz tool to deliver breakthrough improvements in an organization in areas such as productivity, inventory reduction, and capacity expansion. Examples of significant U.S. companies that have successfully used the tool to bring about radical, positive change are presented.

Kaizen: The Key to Japan's Competitive Success
MASAAKI IMAI
New York: McGraw-Hill, 1986
260pp ISBN: 007554332X
Written with the aim of helping Western managers to develop a Kaizen strategy, this book provides a comprehensive introduction to the concept and its implementation.

The Knowledge-creating Company: How Japanese Companies Create the Dynamics of Innovation
IKUJIRO NONAKA, HIROTAKA TAKEUCHI
New York: Oxford University Press, 1995
304pp ISBN: 0195092694
This title looks at how Japanese businesses discover new knowledge organizationally and suggests that the reason for the success of such businesses is linked to this ability. The coauthors also discuss the two types of knowledge that exist; explicit (gained from books) and tacit (gained empirically), and say the key to the success of the Japanese has been their ability to change from the latter to the former, while the U.S. approach concentrates only on the former. The book uses examples from firms including Honda, Canon, and NEC to explain the theory of organizational knowledge.

The Machine That Changed the World
JAMES P. WOMACK, DANIEL T. JONES, DANIEL ROOS
New York: Rawson Associates, 1990
323pp ISBN: 0892563508
Womack and his colleagues present the findings of a five-year research project undertaken by the Massachusetts Institute of Technology. They looked at Japanese manufacturing techniques in relation to the motor vehicle industry, and considered the lessons that might be learned from their adoption. They discuss the rise and fall of mass production, the rise of lean

"Most Japanese corporations lack even an approximation of an organization chart." (Kenichi Ohmae)

production, coordinating the supply chain, dealing with customers, and managing the lean enterprise.

The Mind of the Strategist: The Art of Japanese Business
KENICHI OHMAE
New York: McGraw-Hill, 1991
304pp ISBN: 0070479046
This title is a guide to Japanese strategic thinking with examples of how it can be applied. The book explains how the reader can create successful strategies by liberating their creative strength.

A Revolution in Manufacturing: The SMED System
SHIGEO SHINGO, ANDREW P. DILLON, TRANS.
Portland, Oregon: Productivity Press, 1985
383pp ISBN: 0915299038
In this book Shingo describes the development of the SMED (Single Minute Exchange of Die) system, which he invented for Toyota, explains the techniques for applying it, and considers the effects of its introduction—notably claiming to reduce changeovers by 98%. He also presents 12 case studies of the application of SMED.

Toyota Production System: An Integrated Approach to Just-in-Time 2nd ed.
YASUHIRO MONDEN
Norcross, Georgia: Industrial Engineering and Management Press, 1993
423pp ISBN: 0898061296
The just-in-time manufacturing system is still used by its founder organization, Toyota, but it has taken on a new look. The changes that have been made to the system since 1983 are described in this book. These include the integration of computer manufacturing technology with JIT and the development of a strategic information system.

Toyota Production System: Beyond Large-Scale Production
TAIICHI OHNO
Cambridge, Massachusetts: Productivity Press, 1988
163pp ISBN: 0915299143
This introduction to the Toyota Production System by one of its founders explains how it evolved and describes a range of techniques, including just-in-time and kanban.

INTERNET

Kaizen Institute
www.kaizen-institute.com
The Kaizen Institute (KI) is a global management consulting company, founded by Masaaki Imai, that specializes in helping companies implement Kaizen tools and strategies. This site offers introductory explanations of Kaizen and Gemba and outlines the workshops and consultancy service available from the Institute.

toyotaproductionsystem.net
www.toyotaproductionsystem.net
This site is dedicated to Taiichi Ohno, the founder of the ''Ultimate Production System.'' Its purpose is to expand, as Ohno requested, the scientific theory upon which his system—the Toyota Production System—rests and to contribute the same to the world knowledge pool.

For More Information

☆ **The True Total Quality (pp. 173–74)**
Manufacturing Systems (pp. 2039–42)
Process Control and Statistical Process Control (pp. 2079–80)
Quality and Total Quality Management (pp. 2096–98)

JOB HUNTING

BOOKS

Don't Send a Resume: And Other Contrarian Rules to Help Land a Great Job
JEFFREY J. FOX
New York: Hyperion, 2001
192pp ISBN: 0786865962
This book focuses on networking and self-promotion, emphasizing that developing contacts with executives leads to more job offers than sending résumés to HR departments. The author's advice includes unorthodox places to look for job leads, calculating what a given position is worth to a company, and writing ''boomerang'' letters in response to job ads.

Job Hunting for the Utterly Confused
JASON R. RICH
New York: McGraw-Hill, 1998
304pp ISBN: 0070526656
This book explains every step of the job-search process, including: defining your personal skills; preparing a résumé; writing a cover letter; marketing yourself; succeeding at interviews; and negotiating a salary. Coverage is also given to using the Internet for job hunting.

Landing the Job You Want: How to Have the Best Job Interview of Your Life
WILLIAM C. BYHAM
New York: Three Rivers Press, 1999
195pp ISBN: 0609804081
Appropriate for job hunters at various career levels, this book deals with interview preparation, the interview itself, and post-interview assessment. Topics covered include deciding whether a job is right for you, presenting your skills, handling a badly prepared interviewer, and closing the interview on a positive note.

60 Seconds & You're Hired
ROBIN RYAN
New York: Penguin, 2000
160pp ISBN: 0140289038
This book places an emphasis on getting an interviewer's attention and summarizing each aspect of the agenda you want to communicate in 60 seconds or less. It lists questions that you should ask and gives advice on learning about a company's culture, illegal questions, salary negotiation, different types of interviews, and pitfalls to avoid.

What Color Is Your Parachute? A Practical Manual for Job-hunters and Career-changers 32nd ed.
RICHARD NELSON BOLLES
Berkeley, California: Ten Speed Press, 2001
368pp ISBN: 1580083412
The 32nd edition of this classic job-hunting reference guide has been updated to work in conjunction with its Web site and is shorter than earlier editions for easier, faster use. Areas covered include Internet job hunting, the alternative job-hunting approach, dealing with rejection, interviews, negotiating a salary, and choosing a career counselor.

MAGAZINES

Online Recruitment
DH Publishing Ltd.
The Seedbed Centre, Vanguard Way, Shoeburyness, Essex, SS3 9QX, U.K.

"For us to get out of a business would involve firing people and that cannot be done easily in Japan."
(Tsutomu Kanai)

T: +44 (0) 1702 382330
F: +44 (0) 1702 382331
www.onrec.com
This is a monthly magazine covering the latest news on e-recruitment sites, and on business trends in the Internet recruitment marketplace as a whole.

INTERNET

CareerMag
www.careermag.com
The site offers online tutorials, information on career strategies, newsletters, job listings, résumé evaluation and software, and members-only job placement assistance.

Careerpath International
www.careerpath.co.uk
This site for executives offers services covering career guidance, résumé and cover letter writing, career planning, employment outplacement, and job search. There is also a database of job vacancies in the United States, Europe, and Asia. Initial information is free, but additional services are charged for.

Milkround Online
www.milkround.co.uk
This is a job-hunting Web site for graduates offering employment opportunities with U.K. recruiters, advice on applying, and employment news. Employers can be applied to directly, and job vacancies and job news matching preferences are available. The site also offers a self-assessment personality test.

Monster
www.monster.com
Primarily a job board, the site also offers extensive information on producing résumés. There is also advice on cover letters, salary negotiation, and interviews.

Online Recruitment
www.onrec.com
This site provides a database of online recruitment sites, and offers the facility to search for sites that cover all or specific sectors. It also gives information on the sites offered, including services, charges, strengths, and weaknesses.

Vault
www.vault.com
In addition to job listings, this site offers a résumé distribution service, a salary calculator, articles on job-hunting issues, and information on industry channels that provide company profiles, message boards, and firm rankings.

Yahoo Careers and Jobs
http://dir.yahoo.com/Business_and_Economy/Employment_and_Work/Careers_and_Jobs
The search engine Yahoo provides a comprehensive listing of recruitment Web sites.

For More Information

- ☆ Avoiding Your Worst Career Nightmare (pp. 316–17)
- ✔ Starting a New Job (pp. 410–11)
- Finding Out What You Are Worth: Remuneration/Salaries (pp. 1982–84)
- Planning Your Career (pp. 2075–77)
- Remuneration (pp. 2103–05)

KNOWLEDGE MANAGEMENT

BOOKS

Common Knowledge: How Companies Thrive by Sharing What They Know
NANCY M. DIXON
Boston, Massachusetts: Harvard Business School Press, 2000
188pp ISBN: 0875849040
Creating successful knowledge transfer systems requires matching the type of knowledge to be shared to the method best suited for transferring it effectively. Based on an in-depth study of several organizations that are leading the field in successful knowledge transfer (including Ernst & Young, Bechtel, Ford, Chevron, British Petroleum, Texas Instruments, and the U.S. Army), *Common Knowledge* reveals groundbreaking insights into how organizational knowledge is created, how it can be effectively shared, and why transfer systems work when they do.

Enabling Knowledge Creation: How to Unlock the Mystery of Tacit Knowledge and Release the Power of Innovation
GEORG VON KROGH, KAZUO ICHIJO, IKUJIRO NONAKA
New York: Oxford University Press, 2000
192pp ISBN: 0195126165
Written as a sequel to the authors' work *The Knowledge-Creating Company*, this book examines how organizations can encourage and enable the creation of knowledge and the generation of ideas. Knowledge management, it suggests, has overemphasized information technology and measurement tools and focused on controlling rather than supporting knowledge. The authors then introduce five activities that they term ''knowledge enablers'': instilling a knowledge vision; managing conversations; mobilizing knowledge activists; creating the right context; and globalizing local knowledge. A case study of Gemini Consulting is included in the text.

From Know-how to Knowledge: The Essential Guide to Understanding and Implementing Knowledge Management
BRYAN GLADSTONE
London: Industrial Society, 2000
224pp ISBN: 1858358809
The concept of knowledge management is defined and explored. Contents include: what is knowledge management; better information management is not enough; knowledge creation cycle; why knowledge management is important now; process of knowledge management; being a knowledge manager; and the future of knowledge management.

Intellectual Capital: Core Asset for the Third Millennium
ANNIE BROOKING
Boston, Massachusetts: International Thomson Business Press, 1996
224pp ISBN: 1861524080
Brooking identifies and analyzes four primary categories of intellectual capital: market assets, intellectual property assets, human-centered assets, and infrastructure assets. This book is particularly suitable for corporations evaluating these assets prior to reengineering or downsizing, or for corporations looking to acquire a knowledge-intensive organization.

The Knowing-Doing Gap: How Smart Companies Turn Knowledge into Action
JEFFREY PFEFFER, ROBERT I. SUTTON
Boston, Massachusetts: Harvard Business School Press, 2000
314pp ISBN: 1578511240
This book is all about turning knowledge to practical account. The subject headings of its main sections give a good idea of its content

"You must accept that if the computer is a tool, it is the job of the tool user to know what to use it for."
(Peter Drucker)

and approach: knowing "what" to do is not enough; when talk substitutes for action; when memory is a substitute for thinking; when fear prevents acting on knowledge; when measurement obstructs good judgment; when internal competition turns friends into enemies; firms that surmount the knowing–doing gap; turning knowledge into action.

Knowledge Networking: Creating the Collaborative Enterprise
David J. Skyrme
Woburn, Massachusetts: Butterworth-Heinemann, 1999
311pp ISBN: 0750639768
This book offers a comprehensive overview of the strategic application of knowledge management within global corporations. With an emphasis on good leadership practice, it shows how companies have successfully leveraged the knowledge dispersed and fragmented throughout their companies to deliver organizational benefits and create new opportunities. It gives guidance on how to innovate quickly and exploit human networks, wherever they are based, and provides examples of how global companies can harness employees' accumulated knowledge and apply it to specific problems. It also contains toolkits and checklists for individual, team, organizational, and collaborative enterprises.

Managing Knowledge: Building Blocks for Success
Gilbert Probst, Steffen Raub, Kai Romhardt
New York: John Wiley, 1999
368pp ISBN: 0471997684
Based on many years of research and experience, the ideas put forward in *Managing Knowledge* result from intensive collaboration with many major organizations. The book provides a road map of the most important stages of the knowledge management process; it presents a wide range of knowledge techniques, assesses their possible effects, and addresses key questions faced by managers. It is illustrated throughout with examples from managerial practice and is designed to prompt critical thinking and assist practitioners to chart their own path through the knowledge jungle.

Organizing Knowledge: An Introduction to Managing Access to Information 3rd ed.
Jennifer Rowley, John Farrow
Brookfield, Vermont: Gower, 2000
424pp ISBN: 0566080478
This is a standard text on knowledge organization and retrieval. The different sections focus on: the nature of information and knowledge and their incorporation into documents; the use of electronic databases; the range of tools for accessing information resources, including indexing, classification, and catalogs; and the electronic contexts in which knowledge can be stored.

Profiting from Intellectual Capital: Extracting Value from Innovation
Patrick H. Sullivan
New York: John Wiley, 1998
288pp ISBN: 047119302X
This volume provides examples from companies' best practices in knowledge management, with a focus on getting value from intellectual capital. The book offers an overview of essential knowledge-management concepts and detailed coverage of strategies for measuring, monitoring, and assigning value to existing knowledge assets. It provides practical advice for those familiar with the basics of knowledge generation and information sharing.

Smart Things to Know about Knowledge Management
Thomas M. Koulopoulos, Carl Frappaolo
Oxford: Capstone, 1999
240pp (Smart Series)
ISBN: 1841120413
In the new economy, say the authors, knowledge management is vital. It allows companies to leverage their most precious assets, collective know-how, talent, and experience, and only by focusing on these valuable resources can companies handle new market challenges and opportunities. The aim of this book, therefore, is to provide a framework for practical action, helping people to understand knowledge management and how it can benefit their organization, to position it at the heart of their business, to measure success in a knowledge-based economy, and to become the knowledge management champions in their organizations.

The Wealth of Knowledge: Intellectual Capital and the Twenty-First Century Organization
Thomas A. Stewart
New York: Doubleday, 2001
320pp ISBN: 0385500718
This book builds on Stewart's 1997 book *Intellectual Capital*, which outlined organizational assets in a knowledge economy. It analyzes corporate practices in managing intellectual capital, providing the basics of knowledge organization theory and real-world examples. A four-step process is used to describe the day-to-day management of knowledge and how it can improve productivity and profitability.

Working Knowledge: How Organizations Manage What They Know
Thomas H. Davenport, Laurence Prusak
Boston, Massachusetts: Harvard Business School Press, 2000
240pp ISBN: 1578513014
The authors break down knowledge management into four activities—accessing, generating, embedding, and transferring—and identify the key processes involved in each. They discuss skills and techniques, knowledge-management technologies, and best practices from their work with leading companies. They also emphasize the importance of corporate culture in fostering knowledge creation and sharing.

MAGAZINES

Journal of Knowledge Management
ISSN: 1367–3270
MCB University Press
60/62 Toller Lane, Bradford, West Yorkshire, BD8 9BY, U.K.
T: +44 (0) 1274 777700
F: +44 (0) 1274 785200
www.emeraldinsight.com/jkm.htm
The *Journal of Knowledge Management* offers a shortcut to the tools, techniques, strategies, and technologies necessary for the effective implementation of knowledge management. It contains peer-reviewed articles packed with actionable business solutions.

Knowledge and Process Management
ISSN: 1092–4604
John Wiley
Wiley InterScience Coordinator, Subscriptions Department, 605 Third Avenue, New York, 10158–0012
T: +1 800 825 7550
F: +1 212 850 6021
www.interscience.wiley.com
Covering theory, practice, research, and case studies relating to knowledge management, organizational learning, core competences, and process management, this journal is aimed at managers responsible for driving performance improvement or introducing new ideas into their organizations.

Knowledge Management Review
ISSN: 1369–7633
Melcrum Publishing
First Floor, Chelsea Reach, 79–89 Lots Road, London, SW10 0RN, U.K.
T: +44 (0) 20 7795 2205
F: +44 (0) 20 7795 2156
www.km-review.com
Aimed at senior managers with responsibility for organizational knowledge and information management, the journal typically contains case studies, practical articles, reviews, and special reports.

INTERNET

International Knowledge Management Network
http://kmn.cibit.nl/ab/siteEngels.nsf
This site offers news, conference and seminar details, a discussion forum, an archive of literature resources, and Web links. Visitors need to register to use parts of the site.

Knowledge Management
www.aiai.ed.ac.uk/~alm/kamlnks.html
This site, run by the University of Edinburgh Artificial Intelligence Application Institute, offers an introduction to the concept of knowledge management. This includes a list of definitions and a framework for analyzing and developing the knowledge management assets of a business. A collection of Web links also connect the user with useful literature resources, applications and research, and management tools.

The Knowledge Management Resource Center
www.kmresource.com
This site offers a collection of reviewed and described knowledge management resources, divided into 17 departments to accommodate users with various levels of expertise in knowledge management. It offers news, conferences and events, case studies, knowledge markets, and other links.

The KNOW Network
www.knowledgebusiness.com
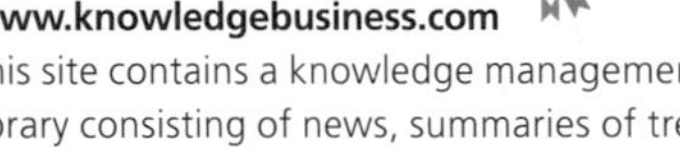
This site contains a knowledge management library consisting of news, summaries of trends, market research, a diary, links, and a KM resources guide to publications, reviews, and Web sites. It also acts as the gateway to the KNOW Network—a group of leading knowledge organizations dedicated to the identification and exchange of best practice. Some of the site can only be accessed by joining the KNOW Network.

WWW Virtual Library on Knowledge Management
www.brint.com/km
This site provided by @brint.com offers fulltext articles, book reviews, Web links, and a discussion forum on various issues relating to knowledge management.

ORGANIZATIONS

USA

American Productivity and Quality Center
123 North Post Oak Lane, 3rd Floor, Houston, Texas, 77024
T: +1 713 681 4020
F: +1 713 681 1182
E: apqcinfo@apqc.org
www.apqc.org
Founded in 1977, the APQC has as its mission to increase the productivity of U.S. companies. It has provided the tools, information, and support needed to discover the best practices in a number of areas, including knowledge management. The APQC also offers information and consultancy services, and partners the Knowledge Management Conference.

Europe

The International Knowledge Management Network
Secretariat, Kenniscentrum CIBIT, Arthur van Schendelstraat 570, P.O. Box 19210, 3501 AD Utrecht, The Netherlands
T: +31 30 230 89 00
F: +31 30 230 89 99
E: info@cibit.nl
http://kmn.cibit.nl/ab/siteEngels.nsf
Set up in 1994, the Network evolved from the experiences of the Dutch Knowledge Management Network and is now a worldwide organization for exchanging ideas and experiences in the knowledge management field.

The KNOW Network
4 St. George's Road, Bedford, MK40 2LS, U.K.
T: +44 (0) 1234 314197
F: +44 (0) 1234 308824
E: info@knowledgebusiness.com
www.knowledgebusiness.com
A Web-based network of some of the world's foremost knowledge-based organizations, the Network is dedicated to the identification and exchange of best practice for competitive advantage.

For More Information

- ☆ **Managing Intellectual Capital (pp. 49–50)**
- **Information Management (pp. 1998–2000)**
- **Innovation and Creativity (pp. 2000–03)**
- **Learning Organization (pp. 2024–26)**

LEADERSHIP

BOOKS

Arc of Ambition: Defining the Leadership Journey
JAMES CHAMPY, NITIN NOHRIA
New York: John Wiley, 2001
282pp ISBN: 0471530204
Champy and Nohria explore the fascinating dimensions of ambition through the stories of dozens of achievers, past and present, who exemplify both its positive and negative qualities. From the quest of Giuseppe Garibaldi for a unified Italy to the vision of Alfred Sloan for General Motors, which changed management practice forever, and the boyhood dream of Michael Dell to have a building with a flag out front, ambition comes in many guises. Champy and Nohria outline the underlying principles of ambition and how it can be channeled toward creative and enriching endeavors at the personal, organizational, and even national levels.

The Art and Science of Leadership 2nd ed.
AFSANEH NAHAVANDI
Upper Saddle River, New Jersey: Prentice Hall, 1999
259pp ISBN: 013085459X
The author presents a broad overview of the field of leadership, focusing on the history of leadership theory, popular current trends, and prospects for the future. This edition includes expanded coverage of personality traits, abilities, values, and skills. Contingency models of leadership are also examined, and separate chapters cover participative management and team leadership, change-oriented leadership, and strategic leadership. The book is intended for students of leadership and each chapter includes details of relevant research, examples of innovative practices, ethical dilemmas faced by leaders, and case studies of real-life leaders.

Building Leaders: How Successful Companies Develop the Next Generation
JAY A. CONGER, BETH BENJAMIN
San Francisco, California: Jossey-Bass, 1999
278pp (Jossey-Bass Business and Management Series)
ISBN: 0787944696
The successes and failures of the leadership development initiatives of over a dozen organizations including Federal Express,

"The art of being wise is the art of knowing what to overlook." (William James)

Motorola, and Ernst & Young are examined in this book. The authors identify three dominant approaches to leadership education: individual skill development, instilling organization values that promote leadership, and strategic intervention. They also present their own model for successful leadership development.

Connective Leadership: Managing in a Changing World
JEAN LIPMAN-BLUMEN
New York: Oxford University Press, 2000
432pp ISBN: 0195134699
A new form of leadership is needed in an era of increasing interdependence and diversity, the author suggests. She reviews the psychological and historical foundations of leadership and develops a new model of connective leadership based around nine behavioral facets. The book draws on the results of qualitative interview research and quantitative survey research on achieving styles, conducted among over 5,000 leaders. A final section examines how the connective leadership model relates to new organizational structures and the wider social context.

First, Break All the Rules
MARCUS BUCKINGHAM, CURT COFFMAN
New York: Simon & Schuster, 1999
255pp ISBN: 0684852861
This book is based directly on a huge research project into the behavior of managers and how they conduct business matters to achieve success. Acknowledging that good managers are pivotal to realizing a company's potential, the authors cite instances of successful employee selection and development techniques that reflect the quality of excellent management.

Focus on Leadership: Servant-leadership for the 21st Century
LARRY C. SPEARS, MICHELE LAWRENCE, EDS.
New York: John Wiley, 2002
396pp ISBN: 0471411620
Focus on Leadership expands on Robert K. Greenleaf's idea of a servant-leader, an individual who seeks to improve and enhance the workplace and the community rather than focusing on company profit. This book offers writings from some of the leading thinkers on management and leadership, including Margaret Wheatley, Donna Zohar, Warren Bennis, and Stephen Covey.

Inner Leadership: Realize Your Self-leading Potential
SIMON SMITH
Naperville, Illinois: Nicholas Brealey, 2000
256pp (People Skills for Professionals Series)
ISBN: 1857882717
The concept of the "leader in each of us" is explored here through case studies, business examples, and exercises. The author presents a four-stage model (REAL) as a method of reaching individual potential. The four stages are: recognizing the depth and diversity of resources and qualities; exploring the parts of yourself which influence decisions and actions; actualizing qualities and values to achieve leadership goals; and leading yourself.

In Search of Leaders
HILARIE OWEN
New York: John Wiley, 2000
192pp ISBN: 0471491977
Leadership is discussed as a potential which all individuals have and can develop, rather than as a phenomenon based on hierarchical authority or a heroic chairman. The author offers a three-stage model for a journey of self-discovery. She outlines the "seven essences" of leadership and explores transformational ideas about leadership to help individuals develop their own inner leadership potential.

John P. Kotter on What Leaders Really Do
JOHN P. KOTTER
Boston, Massachusetts: Harvard Business School Press, 1999
184pp ISBN: 0875848974
In this book, John P. Kotter argues that many companies lack the leadership they require at all hierarchical levels. The title is a collection of the author's most influential articles for the *Harvard Business Review* and includes his more recent essay containing "Ten Observations About Management Behavior."

Leader's Change Handbook: An Essential Guide to Setting Direction and Taking Action
JAY A. CONGER, GRETCHEN M. SPREITZER, EDWARD E. LAWLER, EDS.
San Francisco, California: Jossey-Bass, 1998
320pp ISBN: 0787943517
This handbook contains chapters by various leading contributors to the field, introducing new thinking on ways in which leaders, managers, consultants, and human resource specialists can implement change within their organizations. It outlines the main elements of effective change management, expands traditional ideas of leadership, and discusses the future of organizational change.

The Leader's Companion: Insights on Leadership through the Ages
J. THOMAS WREN, ED.
New York: Free Press, 1995
554pp ISBN: 002874005X
Wren has compiled a comprehensive selection of texts on leadership which includes discussion of what leadership is, historical views of leadership, what types of people are leaders and what types are followers, and how leaders can be moral while also being effective.

Leadership and the New Science
MARGARET J. WHEATLEY
San Francisco, California: Berrett-Koehler, 1999
197pp ISBN: 1576750558
This updated version of the original 1992 title discusses the effect of quantum physics on the way we organize our lives, how biology and chemistry influence the way we live, and how leadership is affected by science and chaos theory.

The Leadership Challenge 2nd ed.
JAMES M. KOUZES
New York: Jossey-Bass Wiley, 1995
406pp ISBN: 0787901105
In this key title, the author outlines the characteristics which determine whether a person will become a leader and the various ways companies treat such people, using key figures from a range of business areas as examples.

The Leadership Crash Course: A 6-step Fast-track Self-development Action Kit
PAUL TAFFINDER
Milford, Connecticut: Kogan Page, 2000
192pp ISBN: 0749431423
The Leadership Crash Course is designed to help readers develop their skills and effectiveness. Six sections focus on: the differences between leaders and managers; providing a sense of direction and purpose; making and taking risks; being unpredictable; having conviction; and generating critical mass by using influencing tactics and turning knowledge into action. Each section includes self-diagnostic questions, exercises, and practical tips and advice.

The Leadership Moment
MICHAEL USEEM
New York: Times Books, 1999
336pp ISBN: 0812929357
In this title, the author uses a variety of real examples of people in highly pressured situations to show the different ways one can react in adversity. These examples provide valuable lessons in how to cope with the same high levels of stress endured in the world of business.

Leadership: Theory, Application, Skill Development
ROBERT N. LUSSIER, CHRISTOPHER F. ACHUA
Cincinnati, Ohio: South-Western College

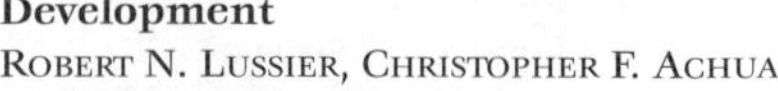

Publishing, 2001
536pp ISBN: 0324041667
This textbook seeks to expand the user's knowledge about leadership by providing new, engaging ways to learn, including role-playing and using the Internet for readings and exercises. It is divided into three sections that focus on individual, team, and organizational leadership.

Leader to Leader: Enduring Insights on Leadership from the Drucker Foundation's Award-winning Journal
FRANCES HESSELBEIN, PAUL M. COHEN, EDS.
San Francisco, California: Jossey-Bass, 1999
400pp ISBN: 0787947261
This collection of articles, taken from the journal *Leader to Leader*, brings together the wisdom of world renowned leaders, best-selling writers, leading thinkers, and business philosophers. These include Peter Drucker, Herb Kelleher, John P. Kotter, Rosabeth Moss Kanter, Peter Senge, and Charles Handy.

Leading and Leadership
TIMOTHY FULLER, ED.
Notre Dame, Indiana: University of Notre Dame Press, 2000
250pp ISBN: 0268013276
With *Leading and Leadership* Fuller has produced a book that does what most business books fail to do: it makes the reader think carefully about the properties of leadership. Consisting of a collection of writings on leadership by classic authors from the past to the present, the book presents ideas in fictional and nonfictional form.

Leading at the Edge: Leadership Lessons from the Extraordinary Saga of Shackleton's Antarctic Expedition
DENNIS N. T. PERKINS, ET AL.
New York: AMACOM, 2000
268pp ISBN: 0814405436
This book records the adventures of Sir Ernest Shackleton on his Antarctic expedition and examines the extraordinary leadership skills he displayed through the lens of business. Ten lessons on what it takes to be a great leader are drawn from the account. Contemporary business case studies further illustrate leadership at the edge, and the behaviors, attitudes, and ways of thinking about life that help individuals to realize their full potential as leaders are discussed.

Leading beyond the Walls
FRANCES HESSELBEIN, MARSHALL GOLDSMITH, IAIN SOMERVILLE, EDS.
San Francisco, California: Jossey-Bass, 1999
297pp ISBN: 0787945935
Twenty-nine of the world's leading management thinkers explore the need for a new paradigm in leadership. In today's fast-paced global society, leaders must be adept at establishing diverse partnerships, alliances, and networks by building and maintaining relationships both within and outside their own organization. *Leading Beyond the Walls* brings together Peter Drucker, Stephen Covey, Peter Senge, Jim Collins, Noel Tichy, Regina Herzlinger, C. K. Prahalad, Sally Helgesen, and other thought leaders to describe new ways of building relationships, new approaches to strategy and marketing, new models of employee relations, and other innovative ways of thinking and acting.

Lessons from the Top: The 50 Most Successful Business Leaders in America—and What You Can Learn from Them
THOMAS J. NEFF, JAMES M. CITRIN
New York: Currency/Doubleday, 1999
432pp ISBN: 0385493436
Neff and Citrin seek to answer one of the most intriguing of business questions: What did those people do to make their companies so successful? After extensive research, *Lessons from the Top* compiled profiles of 50 business leaders and executives and the qualities they have in common. It also includes engaging stories, lessons, and insights from some of America's best leaders.

Managing the Dream: Reflections on Leadership and Change
WARREN G. BENNIS
Cambridge, Massachusetts: Perseus, 2000
317pp ISBN: 0738203327
This title contains over ten of the author's most significant essays on leadership. The majority of the essays concentrate on how to make leadership possible and how to cope with change, while others discuss the character and ethics of a good leader.

The New Global Leaders: Richard Branson, Percy Barnevik, David Simon, and the Remaking of International Business
MANFRED F. R. KETS DE VRIES, ELIZABETH FLORENT-TREACY
San Francisco, California: Jossey-Bass, 1999
188pp ISBN: 0787946575
Branson, Barnevik, and Simon share intimate accounts of how they created and sustained innovation in their organizations while commanding the respect and loyalty of their employees across continents and cultures. For the first time, these pioneers relate their dreams and visions, their approaches to leadership, and their strategies for building and maintaining competitive global organizations staffed with dedicated enthusiastic people. Despite their distinctly different personal styles and philosophies, these three men exemplify the combined power of the charismatic and architectural roles of leaders.

Old Dogs New Tricks: Warren Bennis on Creative and Collaborative Leadership
WARREN BENNIS
Provo, Utah: Executive Exellence, 1994
191pp ISBN: 0749433620
The leadership guru presents 26 ''tricks of the trade'' to help senior managers and executives, the ''old dogs,'' shed their old prejudices and habits and develop new perspectives and capabilities. The ''tricks'' are grouped in three sections: tricks of the new trade—which relate to developing a sense of purpose and meaning; tricks and team treats—which focus on building a sense of community in teams and groups; and exemplary leadership—which covers the area of sharing power and creating alliances.

On Becoming a Leader
WARREN BENNIS
Cambridge, Massachusetts: Perseus, 1989
ISBN: 0201080591
In this key title, the author outlines the characteristics which determine whether a person will become a leader and the various ways companies treat such people, using key figures from a range of business areas as examples.

Results-based Leadership
DAVE ULRICH, JACK ZENGER, NORM SMALLWOOD
Boston, Massachusetts: Harvard Business School Press, 1999
234pp ISBN: 0875848710
According to the authors of this book, becoming a results-based leader involves the following: defining desired results; connecting leadership attributes to results; investing in people for employee results; creating capabilities for organizational and customer results; and building firm equity and stockholder value for investor results.

Ruthless Leader: Three Classics of Strategy and Power
ALISTAIR MCALPINE, ED.
New York: John Wiley, 2000
272pp ISBN: 0471372471
The texts of three classic works on leadership make up this compilation: *The Prince* by Nicolò Machiavelli, *The Servant* by Alistair McAlpine, and *The Art of War* by Sun Tzu. The introduction places these texts in their contemporary contexts, and compares and contrasts them, drawing out their major themes and demonstrating their application to modern business organizations.

"I think leadership is valuing the time you spend with your people more than anything else you do."
(Herb Kelleher)

The Will to Lead: Running a Business with a Network of Leaders
Marvin Bower
Boston, Massachusetts: Harvard Business School Press, 1997
208pp ISBN: 0875847587
In this key work, the author uses his considerable experience in management to suggest how best to teach people how to work together. Bowers's theory is that organizations should be based on groups of leaders rather than a system of "command and control" leadership.

The X and Y of Leadership
Liz Cook, Brian Rothwell
London: Industrial Society, 2000
224pp ISBN: 0858358957
The authors explore the social, cultural, and physical differences between men and women, and show how by understanding and learning from these differences men and women can together create dynamic new leadership for the future.

MAGAZINES

Harvard Business Review
ISSN: 0017–8012
Harvard Business School Publishing
Corporate Customer Service Center
60 Harvard Way, Boston, Massachusetts, 02163
T: +1 617 783 7500
F: +1 617 783 7555
www.hbsp.harvard.edu/hbr
The *HBR* is a leading magazine for business leaders and senior executives which emphasizes current best practice and the application of leading edge research to business problems. Coverage is wide-ranging with a strong focus on leadership and strategy. Each issue includes feature articles written by experts and an interview with a business leader.

Leadership Quarterly
ISSN: 1048–9843
Elsevier Science
Regional Sales Office, Customer Support Department, P.O. Box 945, New York, 10159–0945
T: +1 212 633 3730
F: +1 212 633 3680
www.elsevier.com
Published four times per year, this journal analyzes the many factors that contribute to outstanding leadership. Executive managers and upper-level administrators will find the information presented in this journal will enhance and improve their leadership skills. It provides current information on the latest in leadership research. There is also an annual review of leadership topics.

Long Range Planning
ISSN: 0024–6301
Elsevier Science
Regional Sales Office, Customer Support Department, P.O. Box 945, New York, 10159–0945
T: +1 212 633 3730
F: +1 212 633 3680
www.elsevier.com
LRP is published in association with the Strategic Planning Society and the European Strategic Planning Federation. This is a leading international journal in the field of strategic management which is aimed at senior managers, administrators, and academics. Articles from academics and practitioners are published.

Sloan Management Review
ISSN: 1532–9194
Sloan Management Review Association, MIT Sloan School of Management
77 Massachusetts Avenue, Room E60–100, Cambridge, Massachusetts, 02139–4307
T: +1 617 253 7170
F: +1 617 258 9739
http://mitsloan.mit.edu/smr
The *SMR* is a quarterly journal, founded in 1959, which aims to provide senior managers with the best of current management theory and practice and has a strong focus on corporate strategy and leadership.

Strategic Change
ISSN: 1086–1718
John Wiley
Wiley InterScience Coordinator, Subscriptions Department, 605 Third Avenue, New York, 10158–0012
T: +1 800 825 7550
F: +1 212 850 6021
www.interscience.wiley.com
Eight issues of *Strategic Change* are published annually. The journal aims to provide authoritative and topical research papers addressing the strategic management of change and its implementation in an increasingly globalized business environment.

Strategy and Leadership
ISSN: 1087–8572
MCB University Press
60/62 Toller Lane, Bradford, West Yorkshire, BD8 9BY, U.K.
T: +44 (0) 1274 777700
F: +44 (0) 1274 785200
www.emeraldinsight.com/sl.htm
This is a bimonthly journal for business leaders that publishes practical articles describing effective practice and new theories with the potential to advance the art of strategy development and implementation.

INTERNET

Leaders Direct
www.leadersdirect.com
With over 150 pages of tips for managers and leaders, this site focuses on the nature and development of leadership.

Leadership 101: People, Principles, Production
www.leadership101.freeservers.com
This Web site is based on the principles outlined in *Focus on Leadership: Servant-Leadership for the 21st Century* (John Wiley, 2001). It provides free training, an e-mail newsletter, and other resources.

Leader to Leader
www.pfdf.org/leaderbooks
This site offers access to a contents listing from the *Drucker Foundation Journal* and selected articles written by today's leading thinkers from the private, public, and social sectors.

The Leadership Network
www.leadership.gc.ca
The Leadership Network has links to many areas of leadership, is easy to navigate, and provides extensive help with its multiple features, especially under the "Tools of the Trade" section.

weLEAD, Incorporated
www.leadingtoday.org
weLEAD is a nonprofit organization that believes that everyone is capable of being a great leader. The site includes an online magazine, tips, book reviews, and explanations of leadership terms and philosophies.

ORGANIZATIONS

USA

The Center for Creative Leadership
1 Leadership Place, P.O. Box 26300, Greensboro, North Carolina, 27438–6300
T: +1 336 545 2810
F: +1 336 282 3284
E: info@leaders.ccl.org
www.ccl.org
The Center for Creative Leadership is a nonprofit educational institution that is an internationally recognized resource for understanding and expanding the leadership capabilities of individuals and organizations.

Europe

The Leadership Trust Foundation
Weston-under-Penyard, Ross-on-Wye, Herefordshire, HR9 7YH, U.K.
T: +44 (0) 1989 767667
F: +44 (0) 1989 768133
www.leadership.org.uk
The Foundation provides courses, postgraduate

"What's the most important thing you can tell me about leadership? I'd say, 'Just treat people the way you'd want to be treated.'"
(Ross Perot)

education, grants, and bursaries for those in pursuit of excellence in leadership.

International
Association for Corporate Growth
International Headquarters, Suite 1, 1926 Waukegan Road, Glenview, Illinois, 60025–1770
T: +1 847 657 6730
F: +1 847 657 6819
E: acghq@tcag.com
The ACG was founded in 1954 for professional managers involved in corporate growth and development in middle-market companies. The organization now has 5,000 members in the United States, Mexico, Canada, and the United Kingdom, and undertakes a range of activities including conferences. It also publishes a newsletter and offers networking opportunities.

For More Information

✔ **Leading from the Middle (pp. 360–61)**
Corporate Strategy (pp. 1944–46)
Management Styles (pp. 2036–38)

Learning Organization

BOOKS

Beyond the Learning Organization: Creating a Culture of Continuous Growth and Development through State-of-the-art Human Resource Practices
Jerry W. Gilley, Ann Maycunich
Cambridge, Massachusetts: Perseus, 1999
362pp ISBN: 0738200735
This title advises business executives and those working in human resources on how to use the theories behind organizational development to create corporate growth. The book also shows the reader how to create an organizational environment that can cope with a variety of possible problems and reveals how organizational aims are evaluated.

A Concise Guide to the Learning Organization
Mike Pedler, Kath Aspinwall
London: Lemos and Crane, 1998
176pp (Developing People and Organizations Series)
ISBN: 189800143X
The *Concise Guide* presents managers, trainers, change specialists, and others who want to release the unrealized potential within organizations with a set of practical tools and ideas for the purpose. Written in plain, straightforward language, it includes case examples of learning organizations, a questionnaire to assess how a particular organization compares with the learning company vision, and activities through which learning organization ideas can be applied in practice.

Facilitating Learning Organizations: Making Learning Count
Victoria J. Marswick, Karen E. Watkins
Brookfield, Vermont: Gower, 1999
240pp ISBN: 0566080397
Building learning into organizations is a strategic task requiring complex change interventions in most cases. The authors of this book offer managers their insights, experiences, and the lessons they have learned, suggesting essential steps that will help the change process and make it more effective, and advising on the processes of facilitation used by themselves and others when leading the learning journey.

The Fifth Discipline Fieldbook: Strategies and Tools for Building a Learning Organization
Peter M. Senge, et al.
New York: Currency/Doubleday, 1994
423pp ISBN: 0385472560
Aimed particularly at managers but of interest to all who want to learn and to make their organizations more effective, this book includes contributions from many people committed to building learning organizations who seek to share the strategies and tools they find useful. Designed to encourage a browsing, participatory approach, the text is built around brief, focused entries and includes practical exercises and techniques.

The Fifth Discipline: The Art and Practice of the Learning Organization
Peter M. Senge
New York: Currency/Doubleday, 1990
424pp ISBN: 0385260946
This classic text on learning organizations draws on a variety of disciplines to illustrate the importance of being able to respond to change. It utilizes a framework based around personal mastery, mental models, shared vision, and team learning to remove obstacles to learning, recognize new opportunities, and achieve competitive advantage.

Fifty Ways towards a Learning Organization
Andrew Forrest
London: Industrial Society, 2000
192pp ISBN: 1858355990
This clearly written book is intended primarily for managers who can influence activities and expenditure within organizations, but is also of interest to anyone who wants to know more about practical options to make the learning organization a reality. It contains summaries of key issues, practical steps and guidance, and examples of best practice.

How Organizations Learn: An Integrated Strategy for Building Learning Capability
Anthony J. DiBella, Edwin C. Nevis
San Francisco, California: Jossey-Bass, 1997
300pp ISBN: 0787911070
This book is a comprehensive synthesis of previously published thinking on learning organizations, with additional input from the authors' experience. It emphasizes that learning strategies will differ in different corporate cultures and that those differences are a source of competitive advantage.

The Infinite Resource: Creating and Leading the Knowledge Enterprise
William E. Halal, ed.
San Francisco, California: Jossey-Bass, 1998
300pp ISBN: 0787910155
This book, which offers a multidiscipline approach to creating the learning organization, is a collection of essays from executives and management thinkers. Divided into three parts, it addresses the need for entrepreneurial freedom and nonhierarchical structures in the knowledge era, the importance of collaborative relationships within corporations, and the structures necessary to share knowledge.

The Learning Company: A Strategy for Sustainable Development 2nd ed.
Mike Pedler, John Burgoyne, Tom Boydel
New York: McGraw-Hill, 1996
224pp ISBN: 0077093003
This is an easy-to-read book, written for browsing and reference, and aimed at those who want to release the underdeveloped potential in organizations. The authors discuss the characteristics and model form of a learning company, together with starting points for the

"Shared vision is vital for the learning organization because it provides the focus and energy for learning."
(Peter Senge)

learning company project. A particular feature of the text is the brief "glimpses" that illustrate learning company themes with examples drawn from practice.

Learning in Action: A Guide to Putting the Learning Organization to Work
David A. Garvin
Boston, Massachusetts: Harvard Business School Press, 2000
272pp ISBN: 1578512514
The author suggests that, while the idea of learning organizations is now generally accepted, it has proved difficult to create them in practice. This well-written text, intended for those involved in organizational learning, aims to give practical answers to practical questions and turn theory into reality. It presents a set of processes that can be used to enable employees to acquire, interpret, and apply knowledge, and, having identified three modes of learning (intelligence gathering, experience, and experimentation), suggests strategies to capitalize on each.

The Organizational Learning Cycle: How We Can Learn Collectively 2nd ed.
Nancy M. Dixon
Brookfield, Vermont: Gower, 1999
264pp ISBN: 0566080583
Dixon's very readable book was first published in 1994 by McGraw-Hill. Its aim is to clarify organizational learning sufficiently to allow managers to pursue it in ways that will integrate with other business objectives, such as competitiveness and productivity. She covers both theory and practice and uses layman's language throughout, giving explanations of any technical terms that she uses.

Organizational Learning, Performance, and Change: An Introduction to Strategic Human Resource Development
Jerry W. Gilley, Ann Maycunich
Cambridge, Massachusetts: Perseus, 2000
408pp ISBN: 0738202487
The coauthors of this title have created a thorough guide to human resource development. They use numerous examples to illustrate their ideas and give clear methods for turning those ideas into programs that will achieve the desired results.

Rethinking the Fifth Discipline: Learning within the Unknowable
Robert Louis Flood
New York: Routledge, 1999
213pp ISBN: 0415185300
This is an academic book. It offers a review and account of Senge's *The Fifth Discipline*, compares it to the concepts and approaches of Ludwig von Bertalanffy, Stafford Beer, Russell L. Ackoff, Peter B. Checkland, and C. West Churchman, and includes a critique of Senge's ideas. This opens the way to a discussion in Part Two of complexity theory and the concepts and approaches involved in it.

Ten Steps to a Learning Organization
Peter Kline, Bernard Saunders
Arlington, Virginia: Great Ocean Publishers, 1998
271pp ISBN: 0915556324
This book integrates a number of topics related to organizational learning, including systems thinking, communication, organizational and cultural change, and multiple intelligences. It consolidates these different approaches into 10 concrete steps, applicable to most organizations, to create a learning organization.

The Web Learning Fieldbook: Using the World Wide Web to Build Workplace Learning Environments
Valorie Beer
San Francisco, California: Jossey-Bass, 2000
304pp ISBN: 0787950238
This how-to book for those concerned with company training deals with using the Internet for workplace learning. It focuses on defining learners' needs and then using the Web to help them, rather than choosing Web possibilities first. An idea of the scope of Web learning possibilities is given in the form of snapshots, and access to sample learning environments, advice, links, and customizable templates is also provided.

MAGAZINES

Journal of Workplace Learning
ISSN: 1366–5626
MCB University Press Ltd.
60/62 Toller Lane, Bradford, Yorkshire, BD8 9BY, U.K.
T: +44 (0) 1274 777700
F: +44 (0) 1274 785200
www.emeraldinsight.com/jwl.htm
This journal concentrates on the growth of the individual within the enterprise and aims to help researchers, practitioners, and consultants gain insights into workplace learning and development from theory, research findings, and organizational practice. Subscribers receive eight printed issues a year and online access to current and previous issues through Emerald Fulltext.

Management Learning
ISSN: 1350–5076
Sage Publications Ltd.
6 Bonhill Street, London, EC2A 4PU, U.K.
T: +44 (0) 20 7374 0645
F: +44 (0) 20 7374 8741
www.sagepub.com
A quarterly journal aimed at human resource specialists, educators, and others in the field, *Management Learning* focuses on organizational behavior, organizational psychology, and change, development, and learning within the organization. There is a Web edition available over the Internet as well as the print version.

The Learning Organization: An International Journal
ISSN: 0969–6474
MCB University Press Ltd.
60/62 Toller Lane, Bradford, BD8 9BY, U.K.
T: +44 (0) 1274 777700
F: +44 (0) 1274 785200
www.emeraldinsight.com/tlo.htm
Five printed issues of this journal are published a year; access to current and previous volumes is also available over the Internet to subscribers via MCB's Emerald Fulltext. The journal focuses on the basic question of what a learning organization is, practices within learning organizations, and ways in which learning strategies can be adopted and applied.

INTERNET

Brint.com
www.brint.com/papers/orglrng.htm
Contained on this site is a working paper giving an overview of the theoretical background and meaning of organizational learning and learning organizations.

Fieldbook.com
www.fieldbook.com/FDF/FDF.html
This site gives details of *The Fifth Discipline Fieldbook*, a book of practice following up on Senge's more theoretical *Fifth Discipline* and aiming to answer the question, What can be done differently at work? It also contains information on books, links, and events, and details of authors and contributors.

Peter Honey Learning
www.peterhoneylearning.com
This resources site is accessed by registering details to benchmark your learning styles with comparable others. It features the Learning Series modules, which are concerned with learning styles, motivation, environment, and skills, and each of which includes a questionnaire with the analysis and planning to create a learner-needs analysis. The other resources offered include a library of Peter Honey's articles.

Skillup
www.skillup.co.uk
This site offers free, impartial, and up-to-date information and a variety of resources for

"Often the most effective facilitators in learning processes are not professional trainers but line managers themselves."
(Peter Senge)

businesses. These include a ten-minute business checkup, tips for running a business, useful Web links, free booklets, handy telephone contacts, training products, and books.

Society for Organizational Learning
www.sol-ne.org
Sponsored by a nonprofit members' organization, the site offers publications, an events calendar, course information, and articles.

ORGANIZATIONS

USA

Society for Organizational Learning
Suite 201, 955 Massachusetts Avenue, Cambridge, Massachusetts, 02139
T: +1 617 300 9500
F: +1 617 354 2093
E: info@solonline.org
www.solonline.org
Originally founded at MIT, SOL describes itself as a global learning community dedicated to building knowledge about basic institutional change. It offers courses for members and invited nonmembers, and also publications and various events or forums.

Europe

Campaign for Learning
19 Buckingham Street, London, WC2N 6EF, U.K.
T: +44 (0) 20 7930 1111
F: +44 (0) 20 7930 1551
E: gphyall@cflearning.org.uk
www.campaign-for-learning.org.uk
The Campaign for Learning is a national charity working to create an appetite for learning in individuals. It focuses on the three main themes: Learning at Work, Family Learning, and Learning through School/Learning to Learn. Its newsletter includes coverage relevant to Learning at Work. The Campaign also encompasses The Talent Foundation (see below).

ECLO—European Consortium for the Learning Organisation
Venelle des Lauriers, 8 B-1300 Wavre, Belgium
T: +32 (0) 10 24 16 00
E: info@eclo.org
www.eclo.org
The ECLO draws its members from business, academia, the public sector, and consultancies, bringing together people involved with learning organizations from across Europe.

The Talent Foundation
19 Buckingham Street, London, WC2N 6EF, U.K.
T: +44 (0) 20 7930 1524
F: +44 (0) 20 7930 1551
E: info@talentfoundation.org
www.talentfoundation.org
The Foundation is a nonprofit initiative, set up with the support of various organizations to provide solutions for businesses that need to attract, retain, and develop talent. It offers a range of tools to help unlock workforce talent and is involved in large-scale research investigating the link between innovation and adaptability in organizations.

International

SEAL—The International Learning Community
37 Park Hall Road, East Finchley, London, N2 9PT, U.K.
T: +44 (0) 20 8365 3869
F: +44 (0) 20 8444 0339
E: seal@seal.org.uk
www.seal.org.uk
SEAL—the Society for Effective Affective Learning, based in the United Kingdom—is an international networking association of people interested in the dynamics of learning. It was originally founded in 1983 to promote the ideas of Suggestopedia (Lozanov), and has now been broadened to include all learning methods with similar principles. Members are usually individuals or parents committed to lifelong learning or involved in teaching, business and management training or education, counseling, therapy, or care work. SEAL aims to empower individuals to discover their learning potential and to transform attitudes to learning in educational institutions, families, and wider society.

The 21st Century Learning Initiative (U.S.)
1329 B South Main Street, Harrisonburg, Virginia, 22801
T: +1 540 438 5653
F: +1 540 437 4832
This transnational initiative, established in 1995 by a group of British and American businessmen and organizations, aims to synthesize the best research and development in the field of human learning and examine its implications for work, education, and communities.

For More Information

- **Innovation and Creativity (pp. 2000–03)**
- **Knowledge Management (pp. 2018–20)**
- **Management Theorists (pp. 2038–39)**

Logistics and Distribution

BOOKS

Contemporary Logistics 7th ed.
Donald F. Wood, et al.
Upper Saddle River, New Jersey: Prentice Hall, 1999
586pp ISBN: 0137985487
Often used as a college textbook, this volume provides clear descriptions of supply channel systems from freight movement to materials management, to end-point distribution to customers. The seventh edition also covers customer service, packaging, and traffic and inventory management. Clear writing and real-world examples make the book more understandable than many others in the field.

Fundamentals of Logistics
Douglas M. Lambert, James R. Stock, Lisa M. Ellram
New York: McGraw-Hill, 1997
640pp ISBN: 0256141177
This book offers a unique take on the area of logistics, approaching the topic from both a marketing and customer service perspective. The text emphasizes concept and context over actual system design proposals. The book is considered noteworthy for its insistence that logistics is much more than solving transportation problems—it is a fully integrated science demanding customer service and internal organizational attention.

The Handbook of Logistics and Distribution Management 2nd ed.
Alan Rushton, John Oxley, Phil Croucher
Milford, Connecticut: Kogan Page, 2001
400pp ISBN: 0749433655
In the second edition of their comprehensive study of logistics, the authors have added material on intermodal transport,

"It is best to do things systematically, since we are only human, and disorder is our worst enemy."
(Anonymous)

benchmarking, environmental issues, vehicle and warehouse safety, and security. They cover numerous other aspects of logistics such as channels of distribution, logistics processes, management and organization, and the IT supply chain.

Logistics and Supply Chain Management: Strategies for Reducing Cost and Improving Service 2nd ed.
MARTIN CHRISTOPHER
Upper Saddle River, New Jersey: Financial Times Prentice Hall, 1999
294pp ISBN: 0273630490
The goal of supply chain management is to link the marketplace, the distribution network, the manufacturing process, and procurement activity in such a way that customers are serviced at higher levels and yet at lower total cost. The author explores the role of logistics in achieving these goals. He examines the relationship between logistics and competitive strategy, the customer service dimension, methods of measuring logistics costs and performance, benchmarking, and the task of managing the supply chain.

Logistics and the Extended Enterprise. Benchmarks and Best Practices for the Manufacturing Professional
SANDOR BAYSON, ET AL.
New York: John Wiley, 1999
230pp ISBN: 0471314307
This book answers the question, how can organizations best apply logistics and supply chain management practices in order to break down internal and external walls and to become more effective extended enterprises? The authors have gained first-hand insights into their subject through interviews, site visits, focus groups, and targeted surveys. Their core research findings and conclusions are summarized here, using case studies of major companies including Amoco, DuPont, Johnson & Johnson, and UPS.

A Practical Guide to Transportation and Logistics
MICHAEL B. STROH
Dumont, New Jersey: The Logistics Network, 2001
184pp ISBN: 0970811500
This book provides the logistics manager with a guide to purchasing, traffic and transportation, warehousing, and inventory control. It includes a long chapter on computers with discussion of various software packages.

Strategic Logistics Management 4th ed.
JAMES R. STOCK, DOUGLAS LAMBERT
New York: McGraw-Hill, 2000
896pp ISBN: 0256136874
The fourth edition of this book examines the subject of logistics from the perspective of customer satisfaction and marketing. The authors have incorporated large amounts of new material, including chapters on supply chain management and measuring and selling the value of logistics, aimed at making the book more managerial, integrative, and globally focused. The book shows the importance of integrating all the functional areas of a business and putting logistics in its proper place in the supply chain.

Supercharging Supply Chains: New Ways to Increase Value through Global Operational Excellence
G. TYNDALL, ET AL.
New York: John Wiley, 1998
269pp ISBN: 0471254371
The authors of this innovative view of supply chain excellence are key partners and leaders of the Ernst & Young Global Supply Chain Management Team. They explain why and how operational excellence helps companies sell more products, examine its impact on shareholder value, describe the new ideas being implemented to achieve excellence, and consider how leading companies can effectively introduce new products into global supply chains.

MAGAZINES

Logistics and Transport Focus
ISSN: 1466-836X
Institute of Logistics and Transport
Supply Chain Centre, P.O. Box 5787, Corby, Northamptonshire, NN17 4XQ, U.K.
T: +44 (0) 1536 740100
F: +44 (0) 1536 740101
www.iolt.org.uk
This monthly journal reviews recent news and developments in the logistics and transport sectors. It contains a range of articles exploring various developments in techniques and processes within the sector. The emphasis is on U.K. and European case studies.

The International Journal of Logistics Management
ISSN: 0957–4903
The International Logistics Research Institute, Inc.
P.O. Box 2166, Ponte Vedra Beach, Florida, 32004–2166
T: +1 904 880 8653
F: +1 904 880 8654
www.ijlm.org
A collection of refereed articles for executives, researchers, and teachers, this journal focuses on current developments and new thinking in the field of logistics.

INTERNET

Council of Logistics Management
www. clm1.org
This site includes a section devoted to news in the field of logistics and a research section of more than 10,000 article abstracts.

Digital Neighbors
www.digital-neighbors.com/news/industry/logistics.htm
This Web site is updated regularly throughout the day. It focuses on logistics industry news, cataloging logistics news from the United States as well as stories of international interest. The site is searchable by city, country, and industry, so any specific questions about logistics capacity in certain regions can generally be answered in a timely way.

Logistics Network
www.logisticsnetwork.com
This site offers information for the logistics manager, including a discussion forum, a news feed, employment information, and recommended readings.

Logistics World
www.logisticsworld.com
This site provides a directory of logistics resources, including subsites devoted to freight, transportation, supply chain management, warehousing, and distribution. It is also home of the WWW Virtual Library of Logistics.

Loglink
www.loglink.com
This is a gateway Web site featuring hundreds of links to providers of logistics support, from freight, air, and rail transport, to straight logistics, to providers of logistical software, to warehousing and distribution services.

Traffic World: The Logistics News Weekly
www.trafficworld.com
Motor transport, air, rail, water, shipping and freight companies: news about all of these and more can be found here in a very user-friendly guide. Short overviews of the articles that are found in the print version of the weekly are available free, but the diehard logistician will probably want to pick up a subscription, since

the information on the Web site tends toward the general. The site is good for a quick glimpse of what's making headlines in logistics.

ORGANIZATIONS

USA

American Purchasing Society (APS)
N. Island Center, Suite 203, 8 E. Galena Boulevard, Aurora, Illinois, 60506
T: +1 630 859 0250
F: +1 630 859 0270
E: propurch@aol.com
www.american-purchasing.com
This organization certifies qualified purchasing personnel. The APS conducts research and compiles business statistical data, including tracking salary surveys. APS can also provide consulting services for materials management.

Council of Logistics Management
Suite 200, 2805 Butterfield Road, Oak Brook, Illinois, 60523
T: +1 630 574 0985
F: +1 630 574 0989
E: clmadmin@clm1.org
www.clm.org
The Council of Logistics Management is a nonprofit organization of business personnel who are interested in improving their logistics management skills. It works in cooperation with private industry and various other organizations to further the understanding and development of the logistics concept. It was founded in 1963 as the National Council of Physical Distribution Management, changing to its present name in 1985. The CLM organizes activities, research, and meetings, all designed to develop the theory and understanding of the logistics process, to promote the art and science of managing logistics systems, and to foster professional dialog and development within the profession.

National Association of Purchasing Management (NAPM)
2055 E. Centennial Cir., P.O. Box 22160, Tempe, Arizona, 85285
T: +1 480 752 6276 or 800 888 6276
F: +1 480 752 7890
E: rlatondr@napm.org
www.napm.org
The more than 46,000 members of this association are supply management personnel involved in industrial, commercial, and utility firms. NAPM members work to develop efficient supply management.

Procurement and Supply Chain Benchmarking Association (PASBA)
4606 FM 1960 W, Suite 250, Houston, Texas, 77069
T: +1 281 440 5044
F: +1 281 440 6677
E: info@pasba.com
www.pasba.com
Founded in 1998 and with over 800 members, this association targets the procurement and supply chain managers of corporations with an interest in benchmarking. PASBA promotes the use of benchmarking to improve corporate efficiency and profitability.

Europe

European Logistics Association
Avenue des Arts 19/ Kunstlaan 19, B-1210 Brussels, Belgium
T: +32 2 230 02 11
F: +32 2 230 81 23
E: ela@elalog.org
www.elalog.org
The ELA is a federation of 36 Western European national logistics associations. It aims to provide a link and an open forum for any individual or society concerned with logistics. The ELA formulates European logistics education standards and has established a vocational qualification procedure to enable the standards to be accepted on a pan-European basis.

Institute of Logistics and Transport
Supply Chain Centre, P.O. Box 5787, Corby, Northamptonshire, NN17 4XQ, U.K.
T: +44 (0) 1536 740100
F: +44 (0) 1536 740101
E: enquiry@iolt.org.uk
www.iolt.org.uk
The Institute exists to promote professional excellence and social responsibility in the fields of transportation and supply chain management. Formed in 1999 from the integration of the Institute of Logistics and the Chartered Institute of Transport, the IoLT offers members a range of activities and benefits, including development programs and information services. A number of special interest groups enable members to network and share experiences with like minded individuals.

International

Canadian Association of Supply Chain and Logistics Management
590 Alden Road, Suite 211, Markham, Ontario, L3R 8N2, Canada
T: +1 905 513 7300
F: +1 905 513 1248
E: members@infochain.org
www.infochain.org
Established in 1967, the SCL is a nonprofit, membership organization which aims to advance the logistics and supply chain profession in Canada. Through a range of activities, research, and informal discussion, members are encouraged to further their understanding of logistics and the art and science of its management.

The Logistics Association of Australia
P.O. Box 249, Parramatta, New South Wales, 2124, Australia
T: +61 2 9635 3422
F: +61 2 9635 3466
E: logadmin@logassoc.asn.au
www.laa@laa.asn.au
The LAA represents the interests of professionals involved in logistics and the supply chain in Australia. It is primarily an educational body which aims to provide a forum for Australian managers to expand and develop their understanding and skills in the practical implementation of the operational and strategic aspects of logistics.

For More Information

☆ **Integrating Technology into Business Processes (pp. 169–70)**
Purchasing and Supply Chain Management (pp. 2094–96)

MAINTENANCE

BOOKS

Planning and Control of Maintenance Systems: Modeling and Analysis
Salih O. Duffuaa, A. Raouf, John Dixon Campbell
New York: John Wiley, 1998
384pp ISBN: 0471197817

Using the concept of total productive maintenance the authors outline a technique for planning a maintenance system using statistical and optimization techniques in order to avert equipment failure. Written for students and practicing engineers and managers, it covers statistical models for load forecasting and capacity planning, productivity measurement, maintenance materials control, designing a maintenance training program, maintenance audits, computerized maintenance systems, monitoring equipment using diagnostic technology, and fitting preventive maintenance into a busy production schedule.

"The spark-gap is mightier than the pen." (Lancelot Hogben)

Productivity Improvements through TPM. The Philosophy and Application of Total Productive Maintenance
Roy K. Davis
Upper Saddle River, New Jersey: Prentice Hall, 1995
160pp (Manufacturing Practitioner Series)
ISBN: 0131330349
This text provides an introduction to TPM for those with little or no knowledge of the technique. The linking of machinery performance directly to business ratios is explained, and the benefits that can be achieved if operatives and maintenance staff work together in TPM teams are emphasized. The main components and benefits of TPM are described and its implementation is examined.

Total Productive Maintenance the Western Way
Peter Willmott
Woburn, Massachusetts: Butterworth-Heinemann, 1995
253pp ISBN: 0750619252
Willmott provides a practical explanation of what TPM is and how it can be used as a demonstrable application of total quality and as a key pillar to achieving world-class performance. Emphasis is placed on the need to adapt the TPM program to suit local, plant-specific needs, based on the author's first-hand experience of TPM in Japan, and modifying those principles to suit Western culture. Five in-depth and three shorter case studies are included.

MAGAZINES

Maintenance Journal
International Maintenance Institute
P.O. Box 751896, Houston, Texas, 77275
T: +1 281 481 0869
F: +1 281 481 8337
www.imionline.org
This is a bimonthly publication that features news and technical feature articles. One issue per year provides a buyer's guide of members' products and services. It highlights the activities of the International Maintenance Institute.

Reliability Magazine
ISSN: 1090–3259
Reliability Magazine
1704 Natalie Nehs Drive, Knoxville, Tennessee, 37931–4554
T: +1 865 531 2193
F: +1 865 531 2459
www.reliability-magazine.com
Reliability Magazine claims to be the first trade journal dedicated specifically to machinery reliability, the predictive maintenance industry, root cause failure analysis, and reliability centered maintenance. It is published bimonthly. Some articles can be read online at their Web site.

INTERNET

Maintenance 2000
www.maint2k.com
This functional Web site describes the activities and consulting services of Maintenance 2000 Ltd. It has interesting introductory articles on reliability centered maintenance and total productive maintenance.

Maintenance Resources.com
www.maintenanceresources.com
This Web site is dedicated to plant engineering, maintenance, and reliability resources. It includes a reference library with extensive abstracts of a range of publications from TWI Press.

MaintenanceWorld.com
www.maintenanceworld.com
This is a selection of book abstracts and links to articles and Web sites relating to a range of maintenance related topics.

ORGANIZATIONS

USA

ASME International
3 Park Avenue, New York, 10016–5990
T: +1 973 882 1167
F: +1 973 882 1717
E: infocentral@asme.org
www.asme.org
The ASME was founded in 1880 as the American Society of Mechanical Engineers. It is a nonprofit educational and technical organization with a worldwide membership of 125,000. The ASME aims to be the premier organization for promoting the art, science, and practice of mechanical engineering by promoting and enhancing the technical competency of its members. It runs and promotes training courses, meetings, and online discussion groups and produces a range of publications.

International Maintenance Institute
P.O. Box 751896, Houston, Texas, 77275
T: +1 281 481 0869
F: +1 281 481 8337
E: iminst@swbell.net
www.imionline.org
The IMI was chartered as a nonprofit corporation in 1960. The philosophy of the organization is to professionalize the maintenance function by helping maintenance managers to work more effectively through education and the exchange of ideas. Their Web site provides information on training options and job vacancies in the profession.

Society for Maintenance and Reliability Professionals
401 North Michigan Avenue, Chicago, Illinois, 60611–4267
T: +1 312 321 5190
F: +1 312 527 6658
E: smrp@sba.com
www.smrp.org
The SMRP is an independent, nonprofit society by and for practitioners in the maintenance and reliability profession. The Society was formed and chartered in 1992 and is dedicated to promoting excellence in maintenance and reliability in all types of manufacturing.

The Institute of Industrial Engineers
25 Technology Park, Norcross, Georgia, 30092
T: +1 770 449 0460
F: +1 770 441 3295
E: cs@iienet.org
www.iienet.org
The IIE was founded in 1948 and is the only international, nonprofit, professional society dedicated to advancing the technical and managerial excellence of industrial engineers. The IIE sees industrial engineering as being concerned with the design, improvement, and installation of integrated systems.

Europe

Institution of Mechanical Engineers
1 Birdcage Walk, London, SW1H 9JJ, U.K.
T: +44 (0) 20 7222 7899
F: +44 (0) 20 7222 4557
E: membership@imeche.org.uk
www.imeche.org.uk
The IMechE was founded in 1847 by George Stephenson, of "Rocket" railroad locomotive fame. It holds a Royal Charter and is the United Kingdom's certifying body for mechanical engineers. The Institution operates under a number of specialist divisions and interest groups and offers its members a range of professional development services, conferences, and events, and has a library and information service.

For More Information

- ☆ Facilities Management (pp. 179–80)
- ☆ Outsourcing (pp. 89–90)
- Facilities Management (pp. 1980–82)
- Logistics and Distribution (pp. 2026–28)
- Manufacturing Systems (pp. 2039–42)
- Process Control and Statistical Process Control (pp. 2079–80)
- Quality and Total Quality Management (pp. 2096–98)

"The possible use of automated equipment in the over-the-counter marketplace has become an increasingly important subject."
(Robert W. Haack)

  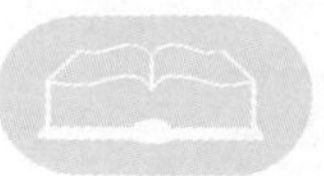    

Management Buyouts

BOOKS

The Art of M&A: A Merger Acquisition Buyout Guide
Stanley Foster Reed, Alexandra Reed Lajoux
New York: McGraw-Hill, 1999
1011pp ISBN: 0070526605
Presented in a question-and-answer format, this book looks at over 1,000 aspects of mergers, acquisitions, and buyouts. Questions covered range from locating a suitable target to closing and post-merger integration. The book gives real-world insights through synopses of dozens of landmark cases and includes sample forms and checklists.

Barbarians at the Gate: The Fall of RJR Nabisco
Bryan Burrough, John Helyar
New York: HarperCollins, 1991
576pp ISBN: 0060920386
This is a classic tale of corporate greed based on the merger of RJR and Nabisco. As gripping a read as any work of fiction.

Big Deal: 2000 and Beyond
Bruce Wasserstein
New York: Warner Books, 2000
927pp ISBN: 0446526428
The legendary Bruce Wasserstein uses his own experience to describe what happens during an M&A deal. The book starts with an account of how the M&A trend developed and then focuses on how to get the deal done.

Buyout: The Insider's Guide to Buying Your Own Company
Rick Rickersten, et al.
New York: AMACOM, 2001
304pp ISBN: 0814406262
This book gives you the tools and strategies you need to lead a successful management buyout. It includes everything from how to select the company you want to buy, through due diligence issues and finding equity partners, to running the company when you succeed in your buyout.

Creating Value through Corporate Restructuring: Case Studies in Bankruptcies, Buyouts, and Breakups
Stuart C. Gilson
New York: John Wiley, 2001
528pp ISBN: 0471405590
Management buyouts are a common form of business restructuring. This collection of recent case studies from the United States and several other countries illustrates the real-world techniques and strategies that are common to all types of restructuring. It demystifies complex financial issues surrounding business valuation and gives the reader a better understanding of the possibilities when dealing with corporate restructuring.

Management Buyout: A Guide for the Prospective Entrepreneur 2nd ed.
Ian Webb
Burlington, Vermont: Ashgate Publishing Company, 1990
176pp ISBN: 0566028107
This book provides an introduction to the process of achieving a successful buyout and considers the financial and legal issues involved. It reviews the development of the buyout market in the United Kingdom and considers the relevance of an entrepreneurial mindset to buyout situations. Five case studies are included.

Management Buyouts: Directors and Buy-out Opportunities
Tom Nash, ed.
Milford, Connecticut: Kogan Page, 1998
84pp (Directors' Guide)
ISBN: 0749428287
In this comprehensive guide to management buyouts aimed at directors and senior managers, experienced managers give their views of the complexities and pitfalls on buying out a firm. The topics covered include: choosing a venture capital partner; buyouts and the law; knowing your banker; tax issues; and aftercare.

A Management Guide to Leveraged Buyouts
Edward K. Crawford
New York: John Wiley, 1987
272pp (Wiley Professional Banking and Finance Series)
ISBN: 0471832324
This book is aimed at managers who aspire to become owners of companies. The benefits of leveraged buyouts to owners and managers and the levels of risk involved are described, and the buyout procedure is explained. A collection of case studies illustrates the techniques used in LBO transactions during the mid-1980s.

Successful Acquisition of Unquoted Companies: A Practical Guide 4th ed.
Barrie Pearson
Brookfield, Vermont: Gower, 1999
168pp ISBN: 0566080990
This practical guide is designed to help anyone who undertakes the acquisition of an unquoted company or a subsidiary of a quoted one. It explains the process of investigating a potential acquisition, and a checklist is provided. Management buyouts and buyins and the process of selling a business to maximize shareholder value are also covered.

MAGAZINES

Buyouts Newsletter
ISSN: 1040–0990
Venture Economics
10th Floor, 195 Broadway, New York, 10007
T: +1 646 822 2000
F: +1 646 822 3230
www.ventureeconomics.com
Buyouts is a biweekly newsletter offering news, data, and analysis relating to the buyout industry. Listings of deals and funds in the United States are published quarterly. The newsletter is available on the Web at www.buyoutsnewsletter.com.

European Management Buyout Review
Centre for Management Buyout Research, Nottingham University Business School, Jubilee Campus, Wollaton Road, Nottingham, Nottinghamshire, NG8 1BB, U.K.
T: +44 (0) 115 951 5493
F: +44 (0) 115 951 5204
www.nottingham.ac.uk/business/Cmbor
The *Review* focuses on trends in the European buyout market and covers 14 Western European countries.

Management Buyouts: A Quarterly Review
Centre for Management Buyout Research, Nottingham University Business School, Jubilee Campus, Wollaton Road, Nottingham, Nottinghamshire, NG8 1BB, U.K.
T: +44 (0) 115 951 5493
F: +44 (0) 115 951 5204
www.nottingham.ac.uk/business/Cmbor
This review includes feature articles on current topics as well as analyses of trends and reports on activity on the U.K. buyout scene.

INTERNET

Are You Management Buyout Material?
www.cfo.com/Article?article=2117
Management buyouts are not for everyone. It takes the right team with appropriate backing. This checklist can help you determine whether you have what it takes to be successful.

"Managers are people who do things right and leaders are people who do the right things."
(Warren Bennis)

  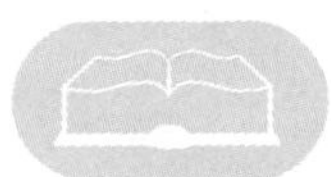    

Is a Management Buyout in Your Future?
www.imakenews.com/rcwmirus/e_article000017429.cfm
This article from the Mirus Online Newsletter describes management buyouts and identifies the characteristics of typical candidate companies. It outlines what each side is looking for and presents financing options that can be used.

Orchestrating a Management Buyout
www.southflorida.bizjournals.com/milwaukee/stories/1996/12/09/focus1.html
Describing the management buyout experience as a roller coaster ride, this article points out that perseverance is often a key element in completing the buyout. It provides real-world examples of how obstacles can be overcome.

Survey of the Economic and Social Impact of Management Buyouts and Buyins in Europe
www.pwcglobal.com/fr/pwc_pdf/pwc_economic_impact_of_buyouts.pdf
This site contains the full text of a report based on a pan-European survey conducted by the Centre for Management Buy-Out Research (CMBOR) on behalf of the European Private Equity and Venture Capital Association.

ORGANIZATIONS

Europe

Centre for Management Buy-Out Research
Nottingham University Business School, Jubilee Campus, Wollaton Road, Nottingham, Nottinghamshire, NG8 1BB, U.K.
T: +44 (0) 115 951 5493
F: +44 (0) 115 951 5204
E: margaret.burdett@nottingham.ac.uk
www.nottingham.ac.uk/business/Cmbor
The CMBOR was founded by Barclays Private Equity Limited and Deloitte & Touche at the Nottingham University Business School in March 1986 to monitor and analyze management buyouts in a comprehensive and objective way. A database of MBOs in the United Kingdom and Europe has been developed, and quarterly reviews and research papers are published.

For More Information

- **Acquisitions, Takeovers, and Mergers (pp. 1901–03)**
- **Venture Capital (pp. 2131–33)**

MANAGEMENT DEVELOPMENT

BOOKS

Building Leaders: How Successful Companies Develop the Next Generation
JAY A. CONGER, BETH BENJAMIN
San Francisco, California: Jossey-Bass, 1999
278pp (Jossey-Bass Business and Management Series)
ISBN: 0787944696
The successes and failures of the leadership development initiatives of over a dozen organizations including Federal Express, Motorola, and Ernst & Young are examined in this book. The authors identify three dominant approaches to leadership education: individual skill development, instilling organization values that promote leadership, and strategic intervention. They also present their own model for successful leadership development.

Developing Managerial Competence
JONATHAN WINTERTON, RUTH WINTERTON
New York: Routledge, 1999
280pp ISBN: 0415183456
This book takes a comprehensive and analytical look at the field of modern management development. It discusses how to measure development and how it can benefit corporate strategy. It also demonstrates the value both of the occupational standards for managers developed by the Management Charter Initiative and of Investors in People. In addition to offering a conceptual framework for evaluating the business advantages of management development, it gives 16 detailed case studies of organizations across different sectors to show how it works in practice.

Everyone a Leader: A Grassroots Model for the New Workplace
HORST BERGMANN, ET AL.
New York: John Wiley, 1999
256pp ISBN: 0471197637
Based on a study of 2,000 people across 450 organizations, this book examines the positive effects on an organization of cultivating leadership attitudes and potential among employees at all levels. The authors summarize five key strategies that make up a model of leadership effectiveness they call CLIMB. Using first-person stories and anecdotes to bring their material to life, they provide the step-by-step tools for grassroots leadership that will build the competencies needed to give everyone the potential to become a leader.

Gravy Training: Inside the Business of Business Schools
STUART CRAINER, DES DEARLOVE
San Francisco, California: Jossey-Bass, 1999
272pp ISBN: 0787949310
The authors examine the rise of the business school from the inside through interviews with people who run, use, and work for them. They question whether they really offer value for money and argue that the system as it stands is fatally flawed. They end by considering the future for business schools.

The Leader in You: How to Win Friends, Influence People and Succeed in a Changing World
DALE CARNEGIE, ET AL.
New York: Pocket Books, 1995
245pp ISBN: 0671519980
This book is a step-by-step guide to strategies intended to help individuals unlock their inner potential and become leaders. Using anecdotes and advice from a variety of people, including famous names such as Margaret Thatcher, it offers its readers assistance in identifying their leadership strengths, achieving their goals, and increasing their self-confidence, while at the same time showing them how to become team players and strengthen cooperation among associates. It also contains advice on balancing work and leisure and energizing one's life generally.

The Self-made Leader: 25 Activities for Facilitated Personal Development
MIKE WOODCOCK, DAVE FRANCIS
Brookfield, Vermont: Gower, 1998
250pp ISBN: 0566081113
The Self-Made Leader includes 25 structured activities designed to help people learn about themselves and develop their potential. The areas covered are self-management, values, goals, self-development, problem solving, innovation, influence, leadership, organizing, developing others, team building, and learning from experience. Guidance on using the activities is provided for facilitators and trainers.

MAGAZINES

British Journal of Management
ISSN: 1045-3172

Blackwell Publishers
350 Main Street, Malden, Massachusetts, 02148
T: +1 781 388 8200
F: +1 781 388 8232
www.blackwellpublishers.com/asp/listofj.asp
The *Journal* publishes articles from the full range of business and management disciplines, priding itself on combining scholarly merit with readability.

Business Horizons
ISSN: 0007–6813
Elsevier Science
Regional Sales Office, Customer Support Department, P.O. Box 945, New York, 10159–0945
T: +1 212 633 3730
F: +1 212 633 3680
www.elsevier.com
Of interest to both practicing managers and academics, *Business Horizons* covers a wide range of business and management subjects, often with a broad economic or social content. Issues relating to cultural values in the context of business are often featured. It aims to strike a balance between the practical and the theoretical, and presents material in readable and nontechnical language.

efmd Forum
European Forum for Management Development
Rue Gachard 88, B-1050 Brussels, Belgium
T: +32 2 62 90 810
F: +32 2 62 90 811
www.efmd.be
efmd Forum is the journal of the European Foundation for Management Development. Its focus is on senior-level management development processes, innovations, and techniques. Its contributors are from Europe's business schools and consulting organizations.

FT Mastering Management Review
ISSN: 1460–6577
Financial Times Business
Number One Southwark Bridge, London, SE1 9HL, U.K.
T: +44 20 7873 4102
F: +44 20 7873 3069
www.ftmastering.com
The *Review* brings together thoughts and advice from contributors who come from the top business schools or are leading business writers and thinkers. Articles focus on interviews with business leaders and a broad range of current and historical techniques and processes.

Harvard Business Review
ISSN: 0017–8012
Harvard Business School Publishing
Corporate Customer Service Center
Box 230–5C, 60 Harvard Way, Boston, Massachusetts, 02163
T: +1 617 783 7500
F: +1 617 783 7555
www.hbsp.harvard.edu
The *HBR* is a magazine for business leaders and senior executives which emphasizes current best practice and the application of leading edge research to business problems. Coverage is wide ranging with a strong focus on leadership, strategy, and all aspects of management development. Each issue includes feature articles written by experts and an interview with a business leader.

Human Resource Development Quarterly
ISSN: 1044–8004
Jossey-Bass
350 Sansome Street, San Francisco, California, 94104–1342
T: +1 415 433 1767
F: +1 415 433 5015
www.josseybass.com
The *HRDQ* is sponsored by the American Society for Training and Development and the Academy of Human Resource Development. It provides a focus for research on human resource development issues and fully recognizes their interdisciplinary nature. The emphasis is on the theory, research, and evaluation of HRD practices.

Journal of Management Development
ISSN: 0262–1711
MCB University Press Ltd.
60/62 Toller Lane, Bradford, Yorkshire, BD8 9BY, U.K.
T: +44 (0) 1274 777700
F: +44 (0) 1274 785200
www.emeraldinsight.com/jmd.htm
The *Journal of Management Development* provides an international communications medium for all those working in management development, whether in industry, consulting, or academia. Its focus is on competence-based management development, developing leadership skills, developing women in management, global management, the new technology of management development, team building, organizational development and change, and performance appraisal.

Management Decision
ISSN: 0025–1747
MCB University Press Ltd.
60/62 Toller Lane, Bradford, Yorkshire, BD8 9BY, U.K.
T: +44 (0) 1274 777700
F: +44 (0) 1274 785200
www.emeraldinsight.com/md.htm
Management Decision provides insights into current management practice from leading management thinkers and practitioners. The issues it covers include strategy and policy, management training and development, crisis management, problem solving, motivation, and entrepreneurship.

Organisations and People
ISSN: 1350–6269
Association for Management Education and Development
62 Paul Street, London, EC2A 4NA, U.K.
T: +44 (0) 20 7613 4121
F: +44 (0) 20 7613 4737
www.amed.management.org.uk
Organisations and People is the journal of the Association of Management Education and Development (AMED). Its target readership includes managers with responsibility for the development of organizations and individuals. It aims to form a link between academic advance and the practitioner whose results may be influenced by the success, or otherwise, of development activities. It combines intellectual rigor with readability, producing material which is also accessible to those do not specialize in development.

People Management
ISSN: 1358–6297
Personnel Publications Ltd.
17 Britton Street, London, EC1M 5TP, U.K.
T: +44 (0) 20 7880 6200
F: +44 (0) 20 7336 7637
www.peoplemanagement.co.uk
People Management is the official journal of the Chartered Institute of Personnel and Development. It reports on current issues in the personnel and human resources fields, including legislation and pay. Articles focus on a variety of subjects, for example industrial relations, training and development, and personnel techniques. Case studies and profiles of leading practitioners are also a regular feature.

ORGANIZATIONS

USA

American Management Association (AMA)
1601 Broadway, New York, 10019
T: +1 212 586 8100
F: +1 212 903 8168
E: customerservice@amanet.org
www.amanet.org
One of the world's leading nonprofit membership-based educational organizations, the AMA offers a range of business education and management development programs for

"Our managers are all white, middle-aged men, and they promote in their own image." (Anonymous)

individuals and enterprises in the Americas, Europe, and Asia. It identifies best management practices worldwide to provide assessment, design, development, self-development, and instruction services through a variety of print and electronic media and learning methodologies, including conferences and seminars, all designed to enhance the growth of individuals and organizations.

Europe

efmd European Forum for Management Development
Rue Gachard 88, B-1050 Brussels, Belgium
T: +32 2 62 90 810
F: +32 2 62 90 811
E: info@efmd.be
www.efmd.be
The European Foundation for Management Development (efmd) has set itself a mission: to promote the development of people and organizations through learning and leadership. It is Europe's forum for information, research, networking, and dialog on innovation and best practice in management development, and its network includes some 400 member organizations in over 40 countries.

Institute of Management
Management House, Cottingham Road, Corby, Northamptonshire, NN17 1TT, U.K.
T: +44 (0) 1536 204222
F: +44 (0) 1536 201651
E: mic.enquiries@imgt.org.uk
www.inst-mgt.org.uk
Formed in 1992, the Institute of Management (IM) is the largest organization for professional management in the United Kingdom, representing almost 89,000 individual members and embracing 560 corporate partners. It exists to promote the art and science of management through research, publications, the provision of information services, networking opportunities, education, and training, and the objective presentation of managers' views and opinions.

For More Information

- **Management Education: Executive Training (pp. 2033–35)**
- **Management Education: MBAs (pp. 2035–36)**
- **Training and Development (pp. 2126–28)**

Management Education: Executive Training

BOOKS

Developing Global Executives
Morgan McCall, George P. Hollenbeck
Boston, Massachusetts: Harvard Business School Press, 2002
272pp ISBN: 1578513367
This book makes the distinction between a domestic leader and a global executive, and focuses on the best career path to follow in order to become a global executive. Using insights from business leaders around the world, the authors outline the various decisions and career changes that can help lead to successfully managing a global career. The book also offers guidelines for anticipating potential challenges or pitfalls that may arise as a job progresses.

E-learning: Strategies for Delivering Knowledge in the Digital Age
Marc J. Rosenberg
New York: McGraw-Hill, 2000
344pp ISBN: 0071362681
The most recent trend in management development has been to turn to e-learning options. This book provides a comprehensive look at what is available.

The Leadership Investment: How the World's Best Organizations Gain Strategic Advantage through Leadership Development
Robert M. Fulmer, Marshall Goldsmith
New York: AMACOM, 2000
334pp ISBN: 0814405584
The Leadership Investment highlights innovative practices in the area of management education. The practices of seven global corporations, including GE and Johnson & Johnson, are reviewed in detail. A chapter on university-based programs explains how institutions like Harvard are working to better meet the educational needs of business leaders. Another chapter is devoted to management development firms that offer specialized learning opportunities.

The Leadership Pipeline: How to Build the Leadership-powered Company
Ram Charan, Steve Drotter, Jim Noel
San Francisco, California: Jossey-Bass, 2000
224pp ISBN: 0787951722
The Leadership Pipeline presents six steps for moving from managing yourself to managing an enterprise and includes chapters on developing and troubleshooting a leadership pipeline. This book should help organizations avoid the "Peter Principle" by making sure managers are selected for promotion based on objective standards of readiness.

Linkage Inc.'s Best Practices in Leadership Development Handbook: Case Studies, Instruments, Training
David J. Giber, Louis Carter, Marshall Goldsmith, eds.
San Francisco, California: Jossey-Bass, 2000
432pp ISBN: 0787952370
This handbook is a collection of the practices in management and leadership development of 15 large corporations. BP Amoco, Colgate Palmolive, and Motorola are among the companies who contributed to this book. It is a practical guide written by practitioners for practitioners.

Management Education and Competitiveness: Europe, Japan, and the United States
Rolv Petter Amdam, ed.
New York: Routledge, 1996
288pp (Routledge International Studies in Business Theory)
ISBN: 0415120926
This collection of essays, aimed at managers and professionals in educational research and business administration, provides a wide overview of management education across a number of European countries, Japan, and the United States. It particularly examines how countries developed national systems, and explores the links between education and business.

MAGAZINES

Journal of European Business

"The learning person looks forward to failure or mistakes." (Warren Bennis)

Education
ISSN: 0968–0543
Buckinghamshire Business School
Buckinghamshire Chilterns University College,
Gorelands Lane, Chalfont St. Giles,
Buckinghamshire, HP8 4AD, U.K.
T: +44 (0) 1494 522141
F: +44 (0) 1494 871954
www.bcuc.ac.uk
This biannual journal, aimed at teachers of business and management studies, focuses on emergent international management theories, skills, and practice, and explores their relationship with management education.

Journal of Management Education
ISSN: 1052–5629
Sage Publications, Inc.
2455 Teller Road, Thousand Oaks, California, 91320
T: +1 805 499 0721
F: +1 805 499 0871
www.sagepub.com
This bimonthly journal focuses on the methods and theories used in management and organizational behavior education in both classroom and corporate settings, and on how these can be improved.

Management Learning
ISSN: 1350–5076
Sage Publications Ltd.
6 Bonhill Street, London, EC2A 4PU, U.K.
T: +44 (0) 20 7374 0645
F: +44 (0) 20 7374 8741
www.sagepub.co.uk
This quarterly journal explores the fundamental issues, nature, processes, and outcomes of management and organizational learning across cultures by reviewing the results of research, theory, methods, and practice in the field.

INTERNET

American Society of Training and Development
www.astd.org
This is the site of the premier U.S. organization dedicated to employee development.

Business Training Calendar
www.thebiz.co.uk
This site includes an interactive database of forthcoming business training courses available in the United Kingdom which is searchable by subject category, organizer, dates, and location.

Hobsons
www.hobsons.com
The site gives access to educational and vocational databases which cover first degrees, postgraduate education, MBAs, executive programs, international education, and distance learning.

Management Courses Information Site
www.managementcourses.com
A database of 2,200 executive education and development courses worldwide can be found on this site. The courses cover a wide range of subjects and are relevant to specific regions, business sectors, types of organization, and levels of manager. The site also includes advice on choosing a course or provider and a glossary of terms.

The Association to Advance Collegiate Schools of Business
www.aacsb.edu
This site lists over 400 accredited management education programs worldwide. Management education articles can be found under ''Newsline'' publications listed under ''Services.''

The Peter F. Drucker Foundation
www.pfdf.org
The Peter F. Drucker Foundation is committed to improving the way people work together in businesses, governments, and communities. Although not specifically a management education site, it contains a great deal of useful information.

THINQ
www.thinq.com
A searchable database of training products from the United States and the United Kingdom is accessible from this site.

Training Pages
www.trainingpages.co.uk
This site contains a database of U.K. training courses in business, management, and information technology.

ORGANIZATIONS

USA

American Management Association (AMA)
1601 Broadway, New York, 10019
T: +1 212 586 8100
F: +1 212 903 8168
E: cust_serv@amanet.org
www.amanet.org
One of the world's leading nonprofit membership-based educational organizations, the AMA offers a range of business education and management development programs for individuals and enterprises in the Americas, Europe, and Asia. It identifies best management practices worldwide to provide assessment, design, development, self-development, and instruction services through a variety of print and electronic media and learning methodologies, including conferences and seminars, all designed to enhance the growth of individuals and organizations.

ASTD Ltd.
1640 King Street, Box 1443, Alexandria, Virginia, 22313–2043
T: +1 800 628 2783 or +1 703 683 8100
F: +1 703 683 1523
E: customercare@astd.org
www.astd.org
Founded in 1944 as the American Society of Training Directors, the ASTD is an international body for professionals in workplace learning, development, and performance. It undertakes research into, and provides information on, training and development, supports international networking, and represents the profession's views on policy issues to federal and state policymakers.

Europe

Association of Management Education and Development
62 Paul Street, London, EC2A 4NA, U.K.
T: +44 (0) 20 7613 4121
E: amed.office@management.org.uk
www.amed.management.org.uk
The Association is a member-based organization that provides a professional network for people involved in individual or organizational development and aims to promote innovation and good practice in the working environment.

Chartered Institute of Personnel and Development
CIPD House, Camp Road, London, SW19 4UX, U.K.
T: +44 (0) 20 8971 9000
F: +44 (0) 20 8263 3333
E: cipd@cipd.co.uk
www.cipd.co.uk
Formed in 1995 from the amalgamation of the Institute of Personnel Management and the Institute of Training and Development, the CIPD is a professional body for personnel and training

"Leaders configure the context while managers surrender to it." (Warren Bennis)

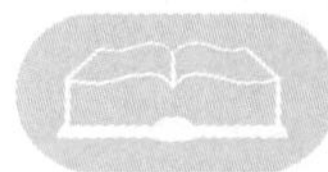

professionals which aims to promote good practice in the management and development of people.

Institute of Management
Management House, Cottingham Road, Corby, Northamptonshire, NN17 1TT, U.K.
T: +44 (0) 1536 204222
F: +44 (0) 1536 201651
E: mic.enquiries@imgt.org.uk
www.inst-mgt.org.uk

Formed in 1992, the Institute of Management (IM) is the largest organization for professional management in the United Kingdom, representing almost 89,000 individual members and embracing 560 corporate partners. It exists to promote the art and science of management through research, publications, the provision of information services, networking opportunities, education, and training, and the objective presentation of managers' views and opinions.

For More Information

- ✔ **Training Needs Analysis (pp. 422–23)**
- **Management Development (pp. 2031–33)**
- **Management Education: MBAs (pp. 2035–36)**
- **Training and Development (pp. 2126–28)**

Management Education: MBAs

BOOKS

Asia-Pacific Executive Education Directory 2002 7th ed.
Rino Schreuder, Yvonne Kuysters, eds.
Huizen, The Netherlands: European Management Development Centre, 2001
250pp ISBN: 9075420242
Published annually since 1995, the *Asia-Pacific Executive Education Directory* contains details of MBA and other management programs from Southeast Asian and Australian business schools. The contents of the directory are also available to subscribers via the EMD Web site at www.emdcentre.com.

Bricker's International Directory 2002: University-based Executive Programs 33rd ed.
Princeton, New Jersey: Peterson's, 2001
1248pp ISBN: 0768905621
Published annually, *Bricker's International Directory* contains information on over 900 university-based management development programs from around the world. The details it provides include the content and length of programs and the costs associated with them.

Business Week Guide to the Best Business Schools 7th ed.
Betsy Gruber, Margaret Littman, Jennifer Merritt
New York: McGraw-Hill, 2001
384pp ISBN: 0071378243
The *Guide* presents an evaluation of U.S. business schools based on feedback from recent graduates and recruiters. Details of the top 25 business schools and the 25 runners-up are provided, along with information on taking the GMAT test.

The MBA Jungle B-school Survival Guide
Jon Housman
Cambridge, Massachusetts: Perseus Books, 2001
224pp ISBN: 0738205117
This title is a very useful guide for those hoping to become business students, covering everything from selecting a business school, to the types of questions asked at interviews, and advice on how to network successfully. A typical week in the life of an MBA student and other important areas are also covered in detail in the guide.

MBA Programs 2002 7th ed.
Princeton, New Jersey: Peterson's, 2001
752pp ISBN: 0768905605
This is a guide to degree and MBA programs offered by Canadian, international, and U.S. business schools. Details of the length and type of program, the admission criteria, and any financial assistance available are included.

Official MBA Handbook: 2001–2002
Godfrey Golzen
Upper Saddle River, New Jersey: Financial Times Prentice Hall, 2001
491pp ISBN: 027365442X
In addition to giving details of all major U.K. and international business schools, the *Official MBA Handbook* offers guidance on choosing the right business school, making an application and taking the GMAT, financing an MBA, and the impact an MBA may have on a career.

Which MBA? A Critical Guide to the World's Best MBAs 13th ed.
George Bickerstaffe, ed.
Upper Saddle River, New Jersey: Financial Times Prentice Hall, 2001
574pp ISBN: 0273656635
This book gives details of full-time, part-time, and distance learning courses in the United Kingdom, the rest of Europe, North America, and the rest of the world. Further sections examine entry requirements, applications details, and how to finance an MBA.

MAGAZINES

European Executive Education Directory 2002
ISSN: 1383–6218
European Management Development Centre
Naarderstraat 296, 1272 NT Huizen, The Netherlands
T: +31 35 695 1111
F: +31 35 695 1900
www.emdcentre.com
Published annually since 1986, the *European Executive Education Directory* contains details of MBA and other management programs from the major business schools in Europe. The contents of the directory are also available to subscribers via the EMD Web site.

INTERNET

BSchool.com
www.bschool.com
This site aims to provide links to business school Web sites and lists over 700 schools in the United States and worldwide in alphabetical order. Links to news and articles on business education, and information on selecting and applying for courses are also available; these have a strong U.S. focus. A particular feature of this site is the Best B-Schools section at www.bschool.com/best_b-schools.html with comparative tables and a collection of links to published business school rankings at www.bschool.com/rankings.html.

MBA Program Information Site
www.mbainfo.com
This site provides a database of 2,280 programs worldwide which can be searched by course structure, subject focus, location, duration, and start date. There is also a good advice section with information on selecting a school, making applications, and funding.

"For tired and harried executives, books are a balm for their worries." (Stuart Crainer)

MBAZone
www.mbazone.com
This is a large site that aims to function as an online community for MBAs. Three separate sections cater for the needs of prospective MBAs, current students, and alumni. Advice is given on choosing a school and making applications, surviving as a student, and developing a career.

Online Business and Management Course Directory
www.abs.bized.ac.uk
This online directory of management and business qualifications is offered by members of the Association of Business Schools (ABS). The Directory was developed by Bized in conjunction with the ABS and provides details of the institutions and courses available. The contents are limited to business schools in the United Kingdom.

ORGANIZATIONS

USA

Graduate Management Admission Council
1750 Tysons Boulevard, Suite 1100, McLean, Virginia, 22102
T: +1 703 749 0131
F: +1 703 749 0169
E: gmacmail@gmac.com
www.gmac.com
Graduate business and management schools make up the Council's membership. It produces the GMAT (Graduate Management Admission Test) which is used to assess candidates' suitability for MBA programs.

Europe

Association of Business Schools
344–354 Gray's Inn Road, London, WC1X 8BP, U.K.
T: +44 (0) 20 7837 1899
F: +44 (0) 20 7837 8189
E: abs@the-abs.org.uk
www.the-abs.org.uk
Formed in 1992 by the merger of the Council of University Management Schools and the Association for Management and Business Education, the ABS is the representative body of business schools in the United Kingdom. It has 100 members, all of whom are providers of business and management education at the tertiary level.

Association of MBAs
15 Duncan Terrace, London, N1 8BZ, U.K.
T: +44 (0) 20 7837 3375
F: +44 (0) 20 7278 3634
www.mba.org.uk
The AMBA was formed in 1967 as the Business Graduates Association. It runs an accreditation scheme for MBA courses, besides offering a number of member benefits. Links to a number of useful organizations are available via its Web site. AMBA is the administrator of the U.K. MBA Loan Scheme in partnership with the Bank of Scotland and NatWest Bank.

efmd European Foundation for Management Development
Rue Gachard 88, B-1050 Brussels, Belgium
T: +32 2 629 08 10
F: +32 2 629 08 11
E: info@efmd.be
www.efmd.be
The efmd is a European network of organizations and individuals involved in management development, which has 390 members including business schools and executive development centers. It was founded in 1971 and promotes research, networking, and dialogue on innovation and best practice in management development. It was also responsible for developing EQUIS (European Quality Improvement System), an accreditation scheme for business schools.

For More Information

- **Management Development (pp. 2031–33)**
- **Training and Development (pp. 2126–28)**

Management Styles

BOOKS

Bill Gates
Robert Heller
New York: Dorling Kindersley, 2000
112pp (Business Masterminds Series)
ISBN: 078945159X
The key skills that have ensured the business success of Bill Gates are analyzed in this book. It explores how he seizes opportunities, forges key collaborations, hires the best brains, outwits the opposition, and dominates the market. A series of master classes illustrate how to use the master's techniques.

Brainstyles: Change Your Life without Changing Who You Are
Marlene Miller
New York: Simon & Schuster, 1997
384pp ISBN: 0684807572
This book offers a method of assessment which sorts people into four categories (deliberators, conceptors, knowers, and conciliators) and includes tips on dealing with each of the styles presented. Miller makes a strong case for people to focus on their strengths instead of working on their "non-strengths."

Business the Jack Welch Way: 10 Secrets of the World's Greatest Turnaround King 2nd ed.
Stuart Crainer
New York: John Wiley, 2001
176pp (Big Shots Series)
ISBN: 1841121517
This book aims to give an insight into the life and times of Jack Welch and his management style and methods. The author also considers how long his style of management is likely to be effective.

Business the Rupert Murdoch Way: 10 Secrets of the World's Greatest Deal-maker
Stuart Crainer
New York: AMACOM, 1999
154pp (Big Shots Series)
ISBN: 0814470343
This book aims to give an insight into the life and times of Rupert Murdoch and to show how to follow his style of management.

Douglas McGregor, Revisited: Managing the Human Side of the Enterprise
Gary Heil, Warren Bennis, Deborah C. Stephens
New York: John Wiley, 2000
224pp ISBN: 0471314625
This book pays tribute to the influence of Douglas McGregor and updates his thinking with new concepts, fresh strategies, and modern methods of implementation. It indicates how his original thinking has reemerged in current approaches that stress distributed leadership, open-minded appraisal techniques, and employee–customer commitment. Highlighted throughout with gems of wisdom in McGregor's own words, the book emphasizes

"Managerial skill can not be painted on the outside of executives—it has to go deeper than that."
(Mary Parker Follett)

      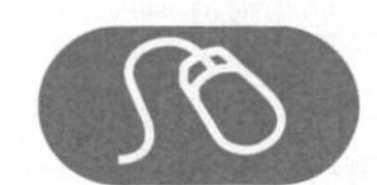

the value of his theories for the managers of today.

House of Mirrors: The Untold Truth about Narcissistic Leaders and How to Survive Them
DEAN B. MCFARLIN, PAUL D. SWEENEY
Milford, Connecticut: Kogan Page, 2000
272pp ISBN: 0749427248
This book explores the seamier side of leadership. Much has been written about the dynamic, focused leader, but what about the obsessive and egocentric leader? The authors investigate the psyche of such leaders and the devastating effect it can have on both individual and organizational performance. They also suggest proactive measures that can be taken to curb the excesses of a narcissistic leader.

Jack: Straight from the Gut
JACK WELCH, JOHN A. BYRNE
New York: Warner Books, 2001
496pp ISBN: 0446528382
In this title, Welch discusses the method of management he adopted in order to turn General Electric into the hugely successful company that it has become. The book also contains a brief look at Welch's childhood and charts a career that started with him working in the plastics division of General Electric and ended with him becoming chief executive officer.

Jack Welch and the GE Way: Management Insights and Leadership Secrets of the Legendary CEO
ROBERT SLATER
New York: McGraw-Hill, 1998
328pp ISBN: 0070581045
In this title, Slater discusses General Electric's move to service businesses, as shown by its takeover of NBC, while through him, Welch analyzes the global economy and advises the reader to welcome change and fight against bureaucracy.

Leadership Challenges for Effective Management
TESFA G. GEBREMEDHIN, PETER V. SCHAEFFER
Dublin, Republic of Ireland: Blackhall Publishing, 1999
224pp ISBN: 1901657825
This book outlines the key skills involved in leadership and assesses their importance. It also explains the difference between a contemporary and a traditional leader, and how people's roles and responsibilities change when they assume leadership positions.

Leader to Leader: Enduring Insights on Leadership from the Drucker Foundation's Award-winning Journal
FRANCES HESSELBEIN, PAUL M. COHEN, EDS.
San Francisco, California: Jossey-Bass, 1999
400pp ISBN: 0787947261
This collection of articles, taken from the journal *Leader to Leader*, brings together the wisdom of world renowned leaders, best-selling writers, leading thinkers, and business philosophers. These include Peter Drucker, Herb Kelleher, John P. Kotter, Rosabeth Moss Kanter, Peter Senge, and Charles Handy.

Management in the USA
PETER LAWRENCE
Thousand Oaks, California: Sage Publications, 1995
151pp ISBN: 0803978332
The author draws on interviews and observations from a range of organizations across the United States in order to identify and analyze the defining aspects of management styles, practice, and values in this country. There are a number of factors, he argues, that are central to understanding management in the United States. These include differentiated individualism, free speech, self-interest, and proactivity.

The New Imperialists
MARK LEIBOVICH, PAUL SAFFO
Upper Saddle River, New Jersey: Prentice Hall, 2002
320pp ISBN: 0735203172
This title profiles five leaders of the digital age: Bill Gates of Microsoft, AOL-Time Warner's Steve Case, Amazon.com's Jeff Bezos, Oracle's Larry Ellison and John Chambers at Cisco. Using hundreds of interviews with friends, family, and rivals, the book charts the most significant events in these revolutionary figures' lives and reveals how they dealt with such experiences.

People Styles at Work: Making Bad Relationships Good and Good Relationships Better
ROBERT BOLTON, DOROTHY G. BOLTON
New York: AMACOM, 1996
176pp ISBN: 0814477232
This book aims to help you understand your own work style and adapt to the styles of others. A self-assessment guide enables you to determine your own style profile and discussion of the four styles (Amiable, Driver, Analytical, Expressive) helps you to understand other people's styles and see how different styles can complement each other in work situations. The book describes how styles can change under stress and offers specific how-to-flex suggestions for each of the four styles.

Primal Leadership: Realizing the Power of Emotional Intelligence
DANIEL GOLEMAN, RICHARD BOYATZIS, ANNIE MCKEE
Boston, Massachusetts: Harvard Business School Press, 2002
306pp ISBN: 157851486X
The authors describe six styles that account for all critical management behavior: visionary, coaching, affiliative, democratic, pacesetting, and commanding. Good leaders use different styles according to the situation. They explain that the importance of these styles is that the right style used with the right team will generate "good feelings" and that style is a critical factor not only in managing and leading but also in generating organizational profits. The book is based on studies of nearly 4,000 executives.

Tom Peters
ROBERT HELLER
New York: Dorling Kindersley, 2000
112pp (Business Masterminds Series)
ISBN: 0789451603
Tom Peters' vision for management is presented in a series of master classes. These deal with such topics as the discovery of excellence, managing with passion, practicing the theory of chaos, small is very beautiful, and management through provocation. A biography and a glossary of terms are included.

The Way We Work: What You Know about Working Styles Can Increase Your Efficiency, Productivity, and Job Satisfaction
CYNTHIA ULRICH TOBIAS
Nashville, Tennessee: Broadman & Holman Publishers, 1999
157pp ISBN: 0805418334
This book provides insight into the different learning and work styles that people bring to their workplaces and suggests common-sense ways of responding to those differences. The author provides information and an assessment to understand your preferred learning style and a discussion of the different types of intelligence each style offers.

INTERNET

Institute for Management Excellence
www.itstime.com
This site has many areas of information relating

"One useful starting point for all managers is to look at their time for thinking." (Peter Senge)

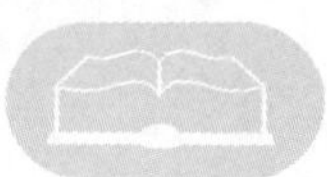

to management practices. It offers a number of articles on personality styles and management, an online personality test, and a monthly newsletter on various people-management topics.

The Consortium for Research on Emotional Intelligence in Organizations

www.eiconsortium.org
This site has a comprehensive listing of topics related to the emerging field of emotional intelligence. It provides downloadable reports on academic research and programs in organizations where EI is the focus of training. It is also a useful source of information on instruments for measuring emotional intelligence.

For More Information

- ✔ **Leading from the Middle (pp. 360–61)**
- **Entrepreneurship (pp. 1969–72)**
- **Leadership (pp. 2020–24)**
- **Management Development (pp. 2031–33)**

Management Theorists

BOOKS

The Age of Heretics: Heroes, Outlaws, and the Forerunners of Corporate Change
Art Kleiner
Naperville, Illinois: Nicholas Brealey, 1996
414pp ISBN: 0385415761
This cultural history of postwar business explains how the corporate mavericks of the 1950s, 60s, and 70s pioneered many of the techniques and attitudes that underlie business practice today, such as self-managing teams, responsiveness to the customer, and the development of a sense of the value of human relationships. It discusses the ideas, writings, and actions of a number of these "modern day heretics" from both the United Kingdom and the United States.

The Capitalist Philosophers: The Geniuses of Modern Business—Their Lives, Times, and Ideas
Andrea Gabor
New York: Times Books, 2000
384pp ISBN: 0812928202
The Capitalist Philosophers is a good review of 13 of the greatest management theorists, starting with Taylor and ending with Drucker. These thinkers have had a profound impact on modern business, and laid the foundation upon which contemporary management theorists continue to build. The book is written in a narrative fashion and is of value to anyone desiring to know how business has arrived at its current state.

The Essential Drucker
Peter F. Drucker
New York: HarperCollins, 2001
368pp ISBN: 0066210879
When it comes to American management theorists, Peter Drucker tops almost everyone's list. This book is a compilation of Drucker's most important writings over the course of his lengthy and still very active career. Each article has been chosen by virtue of its contemporary relevance or its historical significance.

The Excellent Manager's Business Library
Philip Holden
Brookfield, Vermont: Gower, 1999
305pp ISBN: 0566081059
This book provides a distillation of the wisdom of the world's leading business writers. It takes 15 business issues and concepts and examines the most important publications relating to each one. A short biography of the author is presented along with a summary of the book, quotations, the key lessons for managers, and a critical review. An index to the key quotations is also included.

The Guru Guide: The Best Ideas of the Top Management Thinkers 2nd ed.
Joseph Boyett, Jimmie Boyett
New York: John Wiley, 1998
400pp ISBN: 0471182427
The key ideas of 79 of the world's leading management experts are examined here. Presenting the gurus' works in seven subject oriented chapters, the authors cross-link their ideas and provide critical commentaries and case study examples of the ideas in practice.

Leader to Leader: Enduring Insights on Leadership from the Drucker Foundation's Award-winning Journal
Frances Hesselbein, Paul M. Cohen, eds.
San Francisco, California: Jossey-Bass, 1999
400pp ISBN: 0787947261
This collection of articles, taken from the journal *Leader to Leader*, brings together the wisdom of world renowned leaders, best-selling writers, leading thinkers, and business philosophers. These include Peter Drucker, Herb Kelleher, John P. Kotter, Rosabeth Moss Kanter, Peter Senge, and Charles Handy.

Little Book of Business Wisdom: Rules of Success from More Than 50 Business Legends
Peter Krass, ed.
New York: John Wiley, 2000
241pp ISBN: 0471369799
This is a collection of articles by over 50 of the most successful entrepreneurs, chief executives, managers, investors, and leaders offering their advice on how to be successful in business. It gives their ideas and secrets in their own words, and the topics it covers include management leadership, personal advancement, and achieving business objectives.

Management Gurus: What Makes Them and How to Become One
Andrzej A. Huczynski
Stanford, Connecticut: International Thomson Business Press, 1996
352pp ISBN: 1861520212
Placing management guruship in its historical context, the author identifies the essential ingredients of the few popular management ideas of the 20th century. He argues that winning guru ideas meet enduring managerial needs, are launched at the most opportune time, and are promoted by the zeal of their developers.

Ruthless Leader: Three Classics of Strategy and Power
Alistair McAlpine, ed.
New York: John Wiley, 2000
272pp ISBN: 0471372471
The texts of three classic works on leadership are presented: *The Prince* by Nicolò Machiavelli, *The Servant* by Alistair McAlpine, and *The Art of War* by Sun Tzu. The introduction places these texts in their contemporary context and compares and contrasts them, drawing out the major themes and demonstrating their application to modern business organizations.

Thought Leaders: Insights on the Future of Business
Joel Kurtzman, ed.
San Francisco, California: Jossey-Bass in association with Booz Allen & Hamilton, 1998
224pp (Jossey-Bass Business and

"Whips and chains are no longer an alternative for corporate management." (Warren Bennis)

Management Series)
ISBN: 078793903X
This collection features interviews with 12 of the world's most distinguished executives, authors, and academicians on the future of business and how managers can achieve success for their companies in the 21st century. The twelve are: Charles Handy, Minoru Makihara, Keshub Mahindra, C. K. Prahalad, John Kao, Paul M. Romer, Stan Shih, Herbert Walter, John T. Chambers, Warren Bennis, Gary Hamel, and Jean-René Fourtou.

The Ultimate Business Guru Book: 50 Thinkers Who Made Management
Stuart Crainer
Oxford, Oxfordshire: Capstone, 1998
314pp (Ultimate Books Series)
ISBN: 1900961598
Crainer discusses the ideas of 50 leading management thinkers in detail and lists their key publications. He also provides brief summaries of the work of other thinkers.

The Ultimate Business Library: 50 Books That Shaped Management Thinking
Stuart Crainer
New York: AMACOM, 1997
352pp ISBN: 0814403956
Intended as a one-stop guide to the world's leading management thinkers, this volume provides summaries of the books that, in the author's opinion, have had the most significant impact on management thought. Works are included from authors as diverse as Tom Peters, Max Weber, Henry Ford, Rosabeth Moss Kanter, and Charles Handy. The foreword is written by Gary Hamel, who also provides a commentary on each text that is summarized.

INTERNET

Academy of Management—History Division
www.aomhistory.baker.edu
This URL features links related to the history of management practice and theory. The management-thinkers link leads to a comprehensive list of management theorists from Taylor to the present day. The list is valuable by itself, but articles can be downloaded in lots of more than five for a small fee per article.

Business.com
www.business.com/directory/management/management_theory/management_theorists
This Web site offers a comprehensive list of modern management theorists in the form of links to articles by and about those theorists. With roughly 70 primary links and several articles in every secondary link, the coverage is extensive.

Businessweek
www.businessweek.com/smallbiz/news/coladvice/book/bk991001.html
This URL points to a review of the book *The Witch Doctors*. The book was published in the mid-1990s as a general critique of management "gurus" and the reckless abandon with which their theories are often applied. This is not a wholesale indictment of the field, it even praises some, but the book definitely encourages people to proceed with caution.

Thinkers50 
www.thinkers50.com
This management guru Web site was set up by guru spotters Stuart Crainer and Des Dearlove. It has enterprising sections on "How to become a guru," and "Whose ideas are they anyway?", and a ranking of the top ten gurus who are scored for originality, practicality, presentation style, communication, business sense, international outlook, rigor of research, impact of ideas, and the enigmatic "guru factor."

For More Information

Management Styles (pp. 2036–38)

Manufacturing Systems

BOOKS

America's Best: IndustryWeek's Guide to World-class Manufacturing Plants
Theodore B. Kinni
New York: John Wiley, 1996
429pp ISBN: 0471160024
A reference of award-winning plants including Hewlett-Packard, Sony Electronics, and Xerox, *America's Best* looks at manufacturing practices, offering guidelines to help managers make strategic decisions within their own organizations. The book details nine manufacturing components, and describes how they interact with each other. It includes profiles of each of the 62 Best Plant winners and reports by editors from *IndustryWeek*, which list techniques and tools being used at the plants and contact information for them. It also includes a set of the winners' statistical measurements for use in benchmarking and a plant assessment survey.

Finite Capacity Scheduling: Management, Selection, and Implementation
Gerhard Plenert, Bill Kirchmier
New York: John Wiley, 2000
304pp (Oliver Wight Manufacturing Series)
ISBN: 0471352640
The authors provide a comprehensive guide to finite capacity scheduling (FCS), focusing on understanding, implementing, and making the most of FCS and powerful, modern systems.

High Performance Manufacturing. Global Perspectives
Roger G. Schroeder, Barbara B. Flynn, eds.
New York: John Wiley, 2001
320pp (Wiley Operations Management Series for Professionals)
ISBN: 0471388149
This book is the result of extensive research undertaken in 164 factories in the United States, Japan, Germany, Italy, and the United Kingdom. It identifies and describes a range of specific high-performance manufacturing practices and compares manufacturing in each of these five countries.

Lean Thinking
James P. Womack, Daniel T. Jones
New York: Simon & Schuster, 1996
352pp ISBN: 0684810352
Lean Thinking explores the idea that companies can improve their overall performance through Toyota's "lean production" approach. The book is aimed at corporate leaders and shows how managers can specify value to improve performance. It provides an action plan based on a broad range of industries worldwide (this includes Porsche and Toyota).

The Machine That Changed the World
James P. Womack, Daniel T. Jones, Daniel Roos
New York: Rawson Associates, 1990
323pp ISBN: 0892563508
This book presents the findings of a five-year research project undertaken by the Massachusetts Institute of Technology, looking at Japanese manufacturing techniques in the motor vehicle industry and the lessons that can be learned from them. Its contents include: the rise and fall of mass production; the rise of

"The modern corporation must manufacture not only goods but the desire for the goods it manufactures."
(J. K. Galbraith)

lean production; running the factory; designing the car; coordinating the supply chain; dealing with customers; and managing the lean enterprise.

Manufacturing Planning and Control Systems 4th ed.
Thomas E. Vollmann, William L. Berry, D. Clay Whybark
New York: McGraw-Hill, 1997
896pp ISBN: 0786312092
This book describes in detail the key functions and processes of the manufacturing planning and control system.

Manufacturing Strategy: Text and Cases 3rd ed.
Terry Hill
New York: McGraw-Hill, 1999
600pp ISBN: 0256230722
This text is written for both students and practitioners; it demonstrates how decisions relating to manufacturing should form part of the strategic direction of a company as a whole. Individual chapters focus on the principles and concepts of developing a manufacturing strategy, process choice, product profiling, making or buying and the supply chain, and manufacturing infrastructure development. Twenty-two case studies are included.

Next Generation Manufacturing: Methods and Techniques
James A. Jordan, Frederick J. Michel
New York: John Wiley, 2000
464pp ISBN: 0471360066
During the 1990s a three-year research program—the Next Generation Manufacturing Project—sought to present a vision of the future of manufacturing and to put together a framework for action. This book reviews its reported recommendations. It describes how manufacturing is continuing to evolve and what significant changes companies must make to remain competitive. It also emphasizes the importance of understanding the roles played by innovation, knowledge, and people.

Production and Operations Management: An Applied Modern Approach
Joseph S. Martinich
New York: John Wiley, 1996
944pp ISBN: 0471546321
This student text, designed to support a wide range of production and operations management courses, has three main sections: an introduction to operations and strategy; designing production systems; and scheduling, operating, and controlling the production system.

Production and Operations Management: Manufacturing and Services 8th ed.
Richard B. Chase, Nicholas J. Aquilano, F. Robert Jacobs
New York: McGraw-Hill, 1999
889pp ISBN: 007561278X
The authors give an overview of production and operations management from a global perspective. They look at the manufacturing and service aspects and consider the impact of functions such as finance, marketing, logistics, and human resource management on corporate operations. They supplement this with discussions of the latest issues, basic tools and techniques, company examples, and leading-edge practice.

The Technology Machine
Patricia E. Moody, Richard E. Morley
New York: Free Press, 1999
256pp ISBN: 0684837099
Details drivers of growth and discusses why these should be fully taken on in industry. Offers a guide to the growth of an organization by introducing software that may change the face of manufacturing.

World Class Manufacturing: The Lessons of Simplicity Applied
Richard J. Schonberger
New York: Free Press, 1986
252pp ISBN: 0029292700
The author describes how the use of techniques such as just-in-time and total quality control has enabled almost 100 successful American corporations to achieve world class manufacturing standards. He uses them as examples to illustrate the theory, concepts, and implementation of world class manufacturing. Furthermore, he shows how the steps taken by these top companies can be implemented in any factory and in all industries so as to bring any operation up to world class status.

World Class Manufacturing: The Next Decade
Richard J. Schonberger
New York: Free Press, 1996
275pp ISBN: 0684823039
The author covers the decline and resurgence of industry from the 1950s to the present day. He argues that financial data may not be the best indicator of a manufacturing company's strengths; more basic information, for example, inventory turnover and customer satisfaction, can be more useful. He presents 16 "customer-focused" principles that an organization can use to assess itself, plus a survey of "best" manufacturers. Then, in addition to case studies of 18 of the companies surveyed, he offers a more detailed examination of the factors leading to excellence in manufacturing and a ten-year plan for any organization aiming to be world class.

World Class Production and Inventory Management 2nd ed.
Darryl V. Landvater
New York: John Wiley, 1997
304pp ISBN: 0471178551
This book is a practical guide, outlining methodologies for running a successful manufacturing business. A range of successful and proven techniques is described, including manufacturing resource planning (MRP), just-in-time, TQM, and distributive resource planning (DRP). The key operating techniques of master production scheduling, capacity planning, and supplier and plant scheduling are also explained.

MAGAZINES

Control
ISSN: 0266–1713
Institute of Operations Management
The University of Warwick, Science Park, Sir William Lyons Road, Coventry, Warwickshire, CV4 7EZ, U.K.
T: +44 (0) 2476 692266
F: +44 (0) 2476 692305
www.iomnet.org.uk
Control, the journal of the Institute of Operations Management, provides news of its current events and activities, and contains feature articles on a range of subjects related to production. Ten issues are published per year.

IIE Solutions
ISSN: 1085–1259
Institute of Industrial Engineers
25 Technology Park, Norcross, Georgia, 30092–2988
T: +1 770 449 0460
F: +1 770 441 3295
www.iienet.org
This monthly journal for industrial engineers and managers contains a range of news items, which are complemented by a collection of more in-depth articles. These often focus on the use of technology in production and operations activities.

"Any engineer that doesn't need to wash his hands at least three times a day is a failure."
(Shoichiro Toyoda)

Integrated Manufacturing Systems
ISSN: 0957–6061
MCB University Press
44 Brattle Street, 4th Floor, Cambridge, Massachusetts, 02138
T: +1 888 622 0075
F: +1 617 354 6875
www.emeraldinsight.com/ims.htm
This journal aims to provide international coverage of subjects relating to the management of manufacturing technology and the integration of the production, design, supply, and marketing functions of manufacturing businesses. It is published seven times a year and is also available online.-

International Journal of Manufacturing Technology and Management
ISSN: 1368–2148
Inderscience Enterprises Ltd. (Order Dept.)
World Trade Center Bldg, 29 route de Pre-Bois, Case Postale 896, CH-1215 Geneva 15, Switzerland
F: +41 22 7910 885
The *IJMTM* publishes original empirical and review papers, case studies, and various reports on a broad range of issues related to manufacturing processes and techniques. Published six times a year, it has a wide target audience among academics, researchers, and consultants and managers in manufacturing and related industries.

International Journal of Operations and Production Management
ISSN: 0144–3577
MCB University Press North America
44 Brattle Street, 4th Floor, Cambridge, Massachusetts, 02138
T: +1 888 622 0075
F: +1 617 354 6875
www.emeraldinsight.com/ijopm.htm
This monthly journal is targeted at everyone in the operations and production field, whether in academic institutions, industry, or consulting. The articles tend to have a substantial managerial, as opposed to technical, content.

Manufacturing Systems (MSI)
ISSN: 1533–7758
Cahners Business Information
275 Washington Street, Newton, Massachusetts 02158
T: +1 617 964 3030
www.cahners.com
This journal, published 12 times per year, is dedicated to innovative information technologies, focusing on enterprise management and data collection, and is vital for staying abreast of the latest trends in manufacturing systems.

INTERNET

Best Manufacturing Practices
www.bmpcoe.org
The BMP program is a unique cooperative effort between industry and government in technology transfer that aims to improve the global competitiveness of the U.S. industrial base. The primary objective toward this goal is simple: to identify and validate best practices, to document them, and to encourage industry, government, and academia to share information about them. This site gives details of current news, seminars and conferences, and best practice surveys, and also contains an electronic library and links to related sites.

Computer Integrated Manufacturing Research Unit
http://cimru.nuigalway.ie
This site introduces the CIMR Unit, describes current projects, and has links to an extensive range of research reports and theses.

Intelligent Manufacturing Systems
www.ims.org
IMS is an industry-led, international research and development (R&D) program, established to develop the next generation of manufacturing and processing technologies. Companies and research institutions from Australia, Canada, the European Union and Norway, Japan, Korea, Switzerland, and the United States participate in it, and other regions are being encouraged to join. This site reports on current events, activities, and progress.

ORGANIZATIONS

USA

Association of Manufacturing Excellence (AME)
380 W. Palatine Rd., Wheeling, Illinois, 60090
T: +1 847 520 3282
F: +1 847 520 0163
E: info@ame.org
www.ame.org
The 6,000 plus members of the AME are manufacturing executives, united in their pursuit of excellence in manufacturing. AME members strive to develop a deeper understanding of productivity methods.

Institute of Industrial Engineers
25 Technology Park, Norcross, Georgia, 30092–2988
T: +1 770 449 0460
F: +1 770 441 3295
E: cs@iienet.org
www.iienet.org
The IIE was founded in 1948. It is a society dedicated to serving the professional needs of industrial engineers and all individuals involved in guaranteeing productivity and quality.

Manufacturers Alliance/MAPI Inc.
1525 Wilson Blvd., Suite 900, Arlington, Virginia, 22209
T: +1 703 841 9000
F: +1 703 841 9514
E: info@mapi.net
www.mapi.net
This organization is comprised of executives in manufacturing and related business service companies. MAPI conducts research on all areas of management and economic issues that affect U.S. industry. They are advocates for legislative policies that will advance technological and economic progress.

National Association of Manufacturers (NAM)
1331 Pennsylvania Ave., NW, Washington, D.C., 20004
T: +1 202 637 3000
F: +1 202 637 3182
E: manufacturing@nam.org
www.nam.org
Founded in 1895, NAM has over 14,000 members. The association maintains a public affairs and public relations program. NAM members are also involved in proposing current legislation and offering advice on legal matters affecting the manufacturing industry.

Europe

Institute of Operations Management
The University of Warwick, Science Park, Sir William Lyons Road, Coventry, Warwickshire, CV4 7EZ, U.K.
T: +44 (0) 2476 692266
F: +44 (0) 2476 692305
E: iom@iomnet.org.uk
www.iomnet.org.uk
The IOM is a professional body for individuals involved in manufacturing and service industries. It was founded in 1963 as the British Production and Inventory Control Society, and changed to its present name in 1996. It offers its members a range of services, including a qualifications program and a variety of training courses and development seminars.

International

Manufacturing Society of Australia
P.O. Box 19, Parkville, Victoria, 3052, Australia

"A handful of men have become very rich by paying attention to details that most others ignored."
(Henry Ford)

  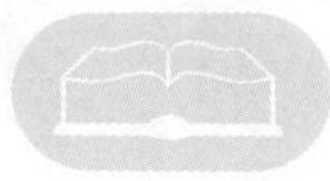    

T: +61 3 9328 3664
F: +61 3 0326 7272
E: mansa@immanet.asn.au
http://mansa.ieaust.org.au
The Manufacturing Society of Australia (ManSA) is the national focus on manufacturing for the Institution of Engineers, Australia, and aims to provide authoritative leadership and foster excellence in Australian manufacturing practice.

For More Information

- **Japanese Management Techniques (pp. 2016–17)**
- **Logistics and Distribution (pp. 2026–28)**
- **Maintenance (pp. 2028–29)**
- **Process Control and Statistical Process Control (pp. 2079–80)**
- **Quality and Total Quality Management (pp. 2096–98)**

MARKET RESEARCH AND COMPETITOR INTELLIGENCE

BOOKS

Competitive Intelligence: Create an Intelligent Organization and Compete to Win
MICHELLE COOK, CURTIS COOK
London: Kogan Page, 2000
263pp ISBN: 0749433124
Aimed at senior managers, this book shows how to achieve real global competitiveness. It contains sections on: harnessing the power of the Internet; setting up a company-wide competitive intelligence function; using tools to analyze information; gaining information about your competitors; and protecting your own information from competitors.

Competitive Intelligence: How to Gather, Analyze, and Use Information to Move Your Business to the Top
LARRY KAHANER
Carmichael, California: Touchstone, 1998
300pp (Pocket Books)
ISBN: 0684844044
Kahaner presents examples to show corporations how they can create their own competitive intelligence units, and fully understand the collected data so that it can be used to their advantage.

Competitor Intelligence: Turning Analysis into Success
DAVID HUSSEY, PER JENSTER
New York: John Wiley, 1999
296pp (Wiley Series in Practical Strategy)
ISBN: 0471984078
This book, written for managers, aims to give practical advice on how to identify and analyze intelligence relating to competitors for the purpose of gaining a competitive advantage. The authors also discuss, again in practical terms, the critical success factors involved in planning, in understanding competitors, and in sourcing information. Case studies are included.

Contemporary Marketing Research 4th ed.
CARL MCDANIEL, ROGER GATES
Cincinnati, Ohio: South-Western College Publishing, 1998
780pp ISBN: 0538885076
This comprehensive manual surveys the whole process of modern market research. It deals with the role of market research in management decision making, sources of data and primary data collection techniques, sampling and statistical analysis, and how to communicate results through effective reports. It backs up its account with many worked examples, illustrations, and case studies.

Hearing the Voice of the Market
VINCENT P. BARABBA, GERALD ZALTMAN
Boston, Massachusetts: Harvard Business School Press, 1991
250pp ISBN: 0875842410
Aimed at managers within the organization the book functions as a plan to help increase and improve their use of market information. Managers and researchers cited in the book contribute personal insights into the subject matter. Aims to teach readers how to make informed and successful decisions in the market-based environment.

Managing Frontiers in Competitive Intelligence
CRAIG S. FLEISHER, DAVID BLENKHORN
Westport, Connecticut: Quorum Books, 2000
328pp ISBN: 1567203841
This book is a nice balance of the theoretical and the practical aspects of Competitive Intelligence (CI). While describing the best practices in the industry, the authors present the steps necessary to counter CI. They provide information on how to improve your intelligence collection process, methods, and tools. Significantly, they tie CI back to the needs of the business and point out its interface with finance, research and development, and product development.

Marketing Research 7th ed.
DAVID A. AAKER, V. KUMAR, GEORGE S. DAY
New York: John Wiley, 2000
552pp ISBN: 0471363405
This text adopts a "macro-micro-macro" approach toward marketing research and its uses within organizations. The authors initially explore the uses and place of marketing research in managerial decision making, as well as the industry itself (briefly examining both suppliers and users) at macro-level. The authors also examine the processes of marketing research in more depth, including industry examples to fulfill the micro phase of the text. Provides coverage of the most recent research techniques.

Market Research Matters: Tools and Techniques for Aligning Your Business
ROBERT DUBOFF, JIM SPAETH
New York: John Wiley, 2000
320pp ISBN: 0471360058
The authors explain the value of market research and forecasting techniques to successful business strategies. They describe the tools and techniques that enable analysts to anticipate marketplace shifts and the methods of using them. Among other topics, they discuss customer loyalty, brand management, competition, distribution channels, employee performance and loyalty, and the Internet. Diagnostic material to allow readers to assess the progress of their business in each area is also included.

The Market Research Toolbox: A Concise Guide for Beginners
EDWARD F. MCQUARRIE
Thousand Oaks, California: Sage Publications, 1996
172pp ISBN: 0803958579
The book is aimed at less experienced market researchers who want to link market research to their business decisions. It defines market research and explores some of its different types, as well as exploring what beneficial results can be expected from meeting objectives. In describing six main market

"I feel sorry for those who live without competition. . .fat, dumb, and unhappy in cradle-to-grave security."
(Donald M. Kendall)

      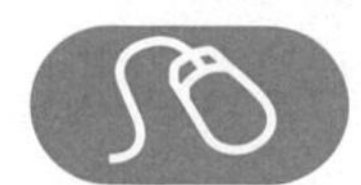

research techniques, the author examines a range of details from how they work to cost. He also discusses recent, less traditional types of market research. Finally, he details five common business applications that can be addressed using a combined research strategy.

Market Research Using Forecasting in Business
Peter Clifton, Hai Hguyen, Susan Nutt
Woburn, Massachusetts: Butterworth-Heinemann, 1992
294pp ISBN: 0750601531
The book is written from the viewpoint of people who are responsible for forecasting business results in large companies on the marketing side. It indicates the resources available to in-house forecasters, such as company sales figures and collections of industry statistics, and provides a comprehensive guide to the tools of analysis and statistics. Above all, it stresses the role of the analyst as a supporter of the entrepreneur in the tasks of fostering growth in new or unfamiliar areas and effectively exploiting new opportunities when they are offered.

Measuring the Effectiveness of Competitive Intelligence
Jan P. Herring
Alexandria, Virginia: Society of Competitive Intelligence Professionals, 1996
77pp ISBN: 0962124125
Acknowledging the need for companies to measure competitive intelligence, the Society of Competitive Intelligence Professionals (SCIP) has initiated research to evaluate competitive intelligence using Measures of Effectiveness. Herring's report includes a CI Evaluation Process to help pinpoint managerial needs within an organization and advises leaders on pursuing their goals through competitive intelligence, measuring the outcomes and conveying them to the company as a whole.

Millennium Intelligence: Understanding and Conducting Competitive Intelligence in the Digital Age
Jerry P. Miller
Medford, New Jersey: Information Today, 2000
240pp ISBN: 0910965285
Miller assembled a brain trust of practicing experts in Competitive Intelligence (CI). Together they lay out the reasons for conducting a planned and thought out CI program for your company. Their book details the skills required, the tools and methods available for gathering and analyzing the information, and the reasons and methods to do so in an ethical and legal manner.

Perfectly Legal Competitor Intelligence: How to Get It, Use It, and Profit from It
Douglas Bernhardt
Upper Saddle River, New Jersey: Financial Times Management, 1994
276pp ISBN: 0273601539
Bernhardt explains how and where to get hold of competitor intelligence and how to use it to your best advantage. He focuses on the range of potential sources of information and collection techniques, the ways of protecting your own company's secrets, organizational issues, competitive benchmarking, and the key role competitive intelligence plays in the strategic process. Case studies are included.

Proven Strategies in Competitive Intelligence: Lessons from the Trenches
John E. Prescott, Stephen H. Miller, eds.
New York: John Wiley, 2001
288pp ISBN: 0471401781
The editors have assembled a collection of articles that identify and explore proven practicable approaches to competitive intelligence that can be applied across a variety of business areas. Once the concept of competitive intelligence has been introduced and its legal and ethical boundaries have been explored, further contributions from leading executives and market leaders highlight the best techniques that can be used to outwit and outperform current, emerging, and potential competitors.

The Warroom Guide to Competitive Intelligence
Steven M. Shaker, Mark P. Gembicki
New York: McGraw-Hill, 1998
240pp ISBN: 007058057X
This book is written for managers who want to use information more intelligently, with a view to improving corporate strategies. The authors advise business leaders on gathering and analyzing information in order to become more competitive within the industry. Explores ways of creating a "Warroom" within an individual organization in which to collate information for future use.

MAGAZINES

Competitive Intelligence Review
ISSN: 1058–0247
John Wiley
Wiley InterScience Coordinator, Subscriptions Department, 605 Third Avenue, New York, 10158–0012
T: +1 800 825 7550
F: +1 212 850 6021
www.interscience.wiley.com
The *Review* is the journal of the competitive intelligence (CI) profession and covers all aspects of the field, with its main emphasis on practical applications. Its target readership includes CI practitioners, managers, vendors, government organizations, and academics.

Journal of Marketing Research
ISSN: 0022–2437
American Marketing Association
311 S. Wacker Drive, Suite 500, Chicago, Illinois, 60606–5819
T: +1 312 542 9000
F: +1 312 542 9001
www.marketingpower.com
JMR is a quarterly publication aimed at academics and practitioners in the marketing profession, providing cutting-edge information on research techniques, methods, and applications.

Marketing Research
ISSN: 1040–8460
American Marketing Association
311 S. Wacker Drive, Suite 500, Chicago, Illinois, 60606–5819
T: +1 312 542 9000
F: +1 312 542 9001
www.marketingpower.com
This quarterly magazine aims to help companies build a strategy for success. Articles are written by practitioners and have a practical bias. Issues covered are legislation and regulation, demographic and social change, and research methods and management tools.

Marketing Surveys Index
ISSN: 0964–0142
Marketing Answers Ltd.
Viscount House, River Dee Business Park, River Lane, Saltney, Cheshire, CH4 8RH, U.K.
T: +44 (0) 1244 681 186
F: +44 (0) 1244 681 457
www.expos-protection.com/uk/Partenaires/msi/b_msi3.htm
MSI contains details of published market research from more than 1,000 publishers and other organizations around the world. It is updated ten times a year.

Market Research Europe
ISSN: 0308–3446
Euromonitor
60–61 Britton Street, London, EC1M 5UX, U.K.
T: +44 (0) 20 7251 8024
F: +44 (0) 20 7608 3149
www.euromonitor.com
Each issue of this monthly journal contains five or six market reports providing in-depth analysis of consumer markets in European countries. Coverage includes key trends, market background, key players, market share, and company profiles.

"Market research can be not just misleading, but disastrous for people who work on instinct."
(Terence Conran)

  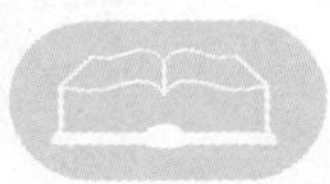    

Market Research International
ISSN: 1352–1101
Euromonitor
60–61 Britton Street, London, EC1M 5UX, U.K.
T: +44 (0) 20 7251 8024
F: +44 (0) 20 7608 3149
www.euromonitor.com
Each issue of this monthly journal contains five or six market reports providing in-depth analysis of international consumer markets. Coverage includes key trends, market background, key players, market share, and company profiles.

INTERNET

ECNext
www.ecnext.com
This is a site offering online access to a database of business and market intelligence from global publishers.

Esomar Glossary
www.esomar.nl/EGlossary.htm
This glossary of market research terms seeks to explain frequently used marketing research terms in language that someone new to the industry can easily understand.

Euromonitor International
www.euromonitor.com
In-depth strategic analysis and up-to-date market statistics and market reports are all available to purchase online from this site.

Forrester
www.forrester.com
Forrester is a leading independent research firm that conducts technology research for its clients. Its expertise is in analyzing the research results and synthesizing the critical information. Some free information is available to nonclients on its site.

Key Note Market Information Centre
www.keynote.co.uk
This site is run by by suppliers of market research reports, which are available for purchase, and provides free executive summaries.

@ResearchInfo.com
www.researchinfo.com
This site is a remarkable collection of information on the market research industry. It includes the Market Research Roundtable, a directory of research companies, software reviews, and market research calculators.

ORGANIZATIONS

USA

American Marketing Association
311 S. Wacker Drive, Suite 500, Chicago, Illinois, 60606–5819
T: +1 312 542 9000
F: +1 312 542 9001
E: info@ama.org
www.marketingpower.com
The AMA has over 40,000 members in 82 countries and aims to serve all sectors of the marketing industry. The AMA Publishing Group produces seven journals and magazines, including the Journal of Marketing Research and Marketing Research, both issued quarterly.

Council for Marketing and Opinion Research
4147U Crossgate Drive, Cincinnati, Ohio, 45236
T: +1 513 985 0001
F: +1 513 985 0119
E: info@cmor.org
www.cmor.org
The CMOR is a nonprofit trade association formed to protect the interests of the marketing and opinion research industry. Its members are research companies and their clients.

Marketing Research Association
1344 Silas Deane Highway, Suite 306, P.O. Box 230, Rocky Hill, Connecticut, 06067–0230
T: +1 860 257 4008
F: +1 860 257 3990
E: email@mra-net.org
www.mra-net.org
The MRA, founded in 1954, is dedicated to promoting excellence in opinion and marketing research. It provides training and development opportunities for members and acts as an advocate with government bodies and the public. Its activities include two annual national conferences and the publication of an official monthly newsletter and a directory of research services.

The Society of Competitive Intelligence Professionals
1700 Diagonal Road, Suite 600, Alexandria, Virginia, 22314
T: +1 703 739 0696
F: +1 703 739 2524
E: info@scip.org
www.scip.org
The Society is dedicated to helping professionals develop expertise in creating, collecting, and analyzing information, in disseminating competitive intelligence, and in engaging decision makers in a productive dialogue that creates organizational competitive advantage.

Europe

Association of European Market Research Institutes
35 Perrymead Street, London, SW6 3SN, U.K.
T: +44 (0) 20 7736 4445
F: +44 (0) 20 7371 9542
E: info@aemri.org
www.aemri.org
The Association is a representative organization for market research institutes in Europe and other parts of the world.

British Market Research Association
Devonshire House, 60 Goswell Road, London, EC1M 7AD, U.K.
T: +44 (0) 20 7566 3636
F: +44 (0) 20 7689 6220
E: admin@bmra.org.uk
www.bmra.org.uk
The BMRA aims to represent and promote the professional and commercial interests of its members, to increase the professionalism of market research, and to promote confidence in the market research industry generally.

EFAMRO
26 Chester Close North, Regent's Park, London, NW1 4JE, U.K.
T: +44 (0) 20 7224 3873
www.efamro.org
EFAMRO is a federation of market research agency associations in the European Union founded in 1992. Its aims are to represent the interests of its members and to maintain high standards in the industry. Members adhere to the ICC/ESOMAR International Code of Marketing and Social Research Practice.

Market Research Quality Standards Association
6 Walkfield Drive, Epsom Downs, Surrey, KT18 5UF, U.K.
T: +44 (0) 1737 379261
F: +44 (0) 1737 351171
E: gwareing@lineone.net
The main aim of the Association is to develop minimum standards for market research.

The Market Research Society
15 Northburgh Street, London, EC1V 0JR, U.K.
T: +44 (0) 20 7490 4911
F: +44 (0) 20 7490 0608
E: info@mrs.org.uk
www.mrs.org.uk
The MRS sets and enforces the ethical standards to be observed by research practitioners. Its framework of qualifications and membership grades reflects the education, knowledge, and competence required for the effective conduct of market research.

For More Information

✔ Gathering Competitive Intelligence (pp. 560–61)

"Every company should work hard to obsolete its own product line before its competitors do."
(Philip Kotler)

  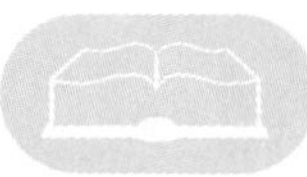    

MARKETING MANAGEMENT

BOOKS

The Anatomy of Buzz: Creating Word of Mouth Marketing
EMANUEL ROSEN
New York: HarperCollins, 2001
320pp ISBN: 0006531601
Rosen discusses the benefits of "word of mouth" marketing, and explores the capacity of large companies to exploit this strategy.

Crossing the Chasm: Marketing and Selling High-tech Products to Mainstream Customers
GEOFFREY A. MOORE
New York: HarperCollins, 1999
256pp ISBN: 0066620023
This practical approach to modern marketing techniques, with emphasis on the specials realities of today's marketplace, aims to advise the reader with a wide range of insights and strategic guidelines for marketing technology products.

The End of Marketing as We Know It
SERGIO ZYMAN
New York: HarperCollins, 1999
272pp ISBN: 0887309860
In this title, the author argues that for marketing to be truly efficient, it must sell the product and not merely focus on advertising image. The book contains several stories concerning campaigns at Coca-Cola, where Zyman was chief marketing officer.

Gonzo Marketing: Winning through Worst Practices
CHRISTOPHER LOCKE
Cambridge, Massachusetts: Capstone Publishing /Perseus, 2001
256pp ISBN: 0738204080
This book is a knuckle-whitening ride to the place where social criticism, biting satire, and serious commerce meet. . .and where the outdated ideals of mass marketing and broadcast media are being left in the dust. As master of ceremonies at the wake for traditional one-size-fits-all marketing, Locke has assembled a unique guest list, from Geoffrey Chaucer to Hunter S. Thompson, to guide us through the revolution that is rocking business today, as people connect on the Web to form powerful micromarkets. These networked communities, based on candor, trust, passion, and a general disdain for anything that smacks of corporate smugness, reflect much deeper trends in our culture, which Locke illuminates with his characteristic wit.

Inside the Tornado
GEOFFREY A. MOORE
New York: HarperCollins, 1999
267pp ISBN: 0887308244
This book addresses the ever-changing face of market-focused business, aiming to highlight the importance of adapting to keep up with competitors. Moore uses examples from inside the industry to discuss a range of managerial strategies, and how they can be usefully applied in today's marketing world.

Kotler on Marketing: How to Create, Win, and Dominate Markets
PHILIP KOTLER
New York: Free Press, 1999
257pp ISBN: 0684850338
In this title, Kotler discusses his ideas on how marketing programs should be approached by executives. The book is divided into several sections addressing strategy, tactics, administrative issues, and transformational marketing. The latter is a term that the author uses to describe the effect of new technology, such as the Internet and cable TV, on marketing practice.

The Market-driven Organization
GEORGE S. DAY
New York: Free Press, 1999
304pp ISBN: 0684864673
This is a straightforward approach to marketing, directed at managers who want to improve performance within their organizations.
It discusses the importance of understanding customers and advises on dealing with the competition.

The Market-driven Strategy
GEORGE S. DAY
New York: Free Press, 1999
432pp ISBN: 068486536X
In this practical guide, Day aims to of widen his readers' understanding of the term "market-driven." The plan follows five major steps covering major strategic issues.

Marketing Management 10th ed.
PHILIP KOTLER
Englewood Cliffs, New Jersey: Prentice Hall College Division, 1999
751pp ISBN: 0130156841
In this exploration of the latest developments in worldwide marketing, Kotler approaches strategic market planning from a new angle, and highlights the need for effective teamwork in a marketing environment. In acknowledgement of the millennium, the author discusses the practices of modern marketing strategies and examines a range of topics from consumer markets to competitors. The book aims to widen managerial knowledge and understanding of marketing issues, while preparing managers for the future of the marketplace.

Marketing Warfare
AL RIES, JACK TROUT
New York: McGraw-Hill, 1997
224pp ISBN: 0070527261
A "military" approach to the world of marketing—Ries and Trout aim to teach marketers tough strategies, both defensive and offensive, to deal with the competition.

Meeting of the Minds: Creating the Market-based Enterprise
VINCENT P. BARABBA
Boston, Massachusetts: Harvard Business School Press, 1995
272pp ISBN: 0875845770
Barabba expounds his theory that working with customer-oriented information is a more effective method of achieving organizational success than simply restructuring within a corporation.The author offers practical guidelines to creating market-based mechanisms leading to competitive advantage, and demonstrates how this can achieved through combining a focused market and customer-based approach.

The Path: Creating Your Mission Statement for Work and for Life
LAURIE BETH JONES
New York: Hyperion, 1998
249pp ISBN: 0786882417
Jones aims to gives clear and concise guidelines to any reader wanting to create a mission statement and obtain their goals in and out of the business environment. The book explores three main areas of mission statements, and offers advice about how to characterize and realize personal goals. Jones supports her case with six studies of individuals who became successful through defining their own missions.

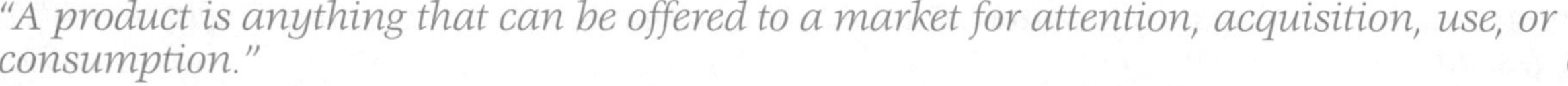
"A product is anything that can be offered to a market for attention, acquisition, use, or consumption."
(Philip Kotler)

Permission Marketing: Turning Strangers into Friends, and Friends into Customers
SETH GODIN, DON PEPPERS
New York: Simon & Schuster, 1999
255pp ISBN: 0684856360
In this title, the authors claim that traditional forms of advertising such as magazines and radio are no longer sufficient in themselves. They assert that what is most important is to find a way of luring the customer into giving some of their time, and then creating a lasting relationship with them. The book backs up this theory concerning permission marketing by discussing the techniques of some of the companies who use it.

Positioning: The Battle for Your Mind 3rd ed.
AL RIES, JACK TROUT
New York: McGraw-Hill, 2000
246pp ISBN: 0071359168
This book discusses the notion that a market strategist can achieve better results in business by the way he/she "positions" their company in the marketplace. Ries and Trout explore the ways in which this goal can be achieved, and offer cautionary advice about the hazards of advertising.

Real Time: Preparing for the Age of the Never Satisfied Customer
REGIS MCKENNA
Boston, Massachusetts: Havard Business School Press, 1997
224pp ISBN: 0875847943
In this book, McKenna addresses the issue of what customers expect from the modern world. In order to fulfill customer expectations, he argues, companies must be prepared to adapt to the increasingly rapid modes of global communication (e-mail, fax, etc.). McKenna aims to clarify the abstract notion of collecting and using "real time," with the view that this can lead to greater organizational success and consumer satisfaction.

Relationship Marketing: Successful Strategies for the Age of the Customer
REGIS MCKENNA
Cambridge, Massachusetts: Perseus, 1993
242pp ISBN: 0201622408
McKenna focuses on the importance of building strong bonds in the marketing world, in order to gain success and become dominant in the marketplace. He provides industry examples to help outline ways of achieving market ownership.

Selling the Invisible
HARRY BECKWITH
New York: Warner Books, 1997
252pp ISBN: 0446520942
Selling the Invisible is aimed at marketers who work to promote a service ("the invisible") rather than a tangible product. The book contains a large range of practical suggestions and ideas, addressing some new developments in marketing, and discussing how an organization can use them to best effect.

Total Access
REGIS MCKENNA
Boston, Massachusetts: Harvard Business School Press, 2002
256pp ISBN: 1578512441
In *Total Access* McKenna suggests that traditional marketing is being overtaken by advances in technology. He argues that modern marketers have a double role to play, fully understanding and anticipating new technology and also managing it. The book aims to characterize success in today's market climate.

The 22 Immutable Laws of Marketing: Violate Them at Your Own Risk!
AL RIES, JACK TROUT
New York: HarperCollins, 1993
132pp ISBN: 0887306667
Designed by marketing strategists for marketing strategists, this illustrated book contains 22 practical rules aimed at promoting the readers' success in global marketing.

MAGAZINES

Advertising Age
ISSN: 0001-8899
Crain Communications, Inc. (MI)
1400 Woodbridge Street, Detroit, Michigan, 48207-3187
T: +1 313 446 6000
F: +1 313 446 6777
www.adage.com
This is the flagship magazine of the Ad Age Group. Widely regarded as the authoritative source for articles on national and international marketing, *Advertising Age* is a premier journal for news, in-depth information, and current trends in marketing.

Adweek
ISSN: 0199-2864
VNU Business Publications
770 Broadway, New York, 10003-9595
T: +1 646 654 4500
F: +1 646 654 4480
www.adweek.com
Published in six regional editions, this magazine provides specialized information for industry professionals. The same publishing company is responsible for *AdWeek*, *BrandWeek*, and *MediaWeek*, all of which cover aspects of advertising and are aimed at advertising executives. As a result, the information is often a little arcane for the layperson, but invaluable for those familiar enough with methods, layout, and advertising jargon to decipher the text. The magazine includes feature articles, trend analysis, and news about industry events.

American Demographics
ISSN: 0163-4089
Brill's Media Ventures, L.P.
521 Fifth Avenue, 11th Floor, New York, 10175
T: +1 800 529 7502
www.demographics.com/Publications/AD
Formerly called *Marketing Tools*, this monthly magazine is aimed at marketing executives who want credible and timely information regarding the latest consumer trends. It is dedicated to demographical studies in the United States, and each issue offers in-depth analysis of the latest current events and how these influence the consuming public. This magazine is filled with the latest techniques for advertising and marketing research.

Brandweek
ISSN: 1064-4318
VNU Business Publications
770 Broadway, New York, 10003-9595
T: +1 646 654 4500
F: +1 646 654 4480
www.brandweek.com
Brandweek is a weekly magazine for brand-marketing executives, offering feature articles, trend analysis, and news about industry events.

Direct Marketing
ISSN: 0012-3188
Hoke Communications, Inc.
224 7th Street, Garden City, New York, 11530
T: +1 516 746 6700 or 800 229 6700
F: +1 516 294 8141
http://hoke.micronpcweb.com
Published 12 times per year, this magazine focuses on sales and marketing techniques. Features include the best methods of direct response advertising. The magazine is a helpful resource for any advertising executive wanting to increase their marketing reach.

Hub Magazine
David X. Manners Company, Inc.
107 Post Road East, Westport, Connecticut, 06880

"Marketing is marketing. It's easy to drape new media in magic but it comes down to whether it's a good business or not."
(Carl Lyons)

T: +1 203 227 7060
F: +1 203 227 7067
www.hubmagazine.com
The Hub features roundtable discussions between industry thought-leaders on marketing challenges and issues. Each issue is hosted by a sponsor.

Logistics Management & Distribution Report
ISSN: 1098–7355
Cahners Business Information
275 Washington Street, Newton, Massachusetts, 02458
T: +1 617 558 4473
F: +1 617 558 4480
www.manufacturing.net/lm
Published 12 times per year, this magazine features articles on production and operations management, industry and manufacturing. This magazine also tracks the latest information regarding national legislation changes.

Marketing Management
ISSN: 1061–3846
American Marketing Association
311 S. Wacker Drive, Suite 5800, Chicago, Illinois, 60606–5819
T: +1 800 262 1150
www.marketingpower.com
This journal, published every other month by the American Marketing Association, was developed with the purpose of providing middle- to senior-level marketing executives with thought provoking discussions on emerging issues in the marketing profession. It provides indepth coverage of many aspects of the profession, including national and international strategies.

Marketing News
ISSN: 0025–3790
American Marketing Association
311 S. Wacker Drive, Suite 5800, Chicago, Illinois, 60606–5819
T: +1 312 542 9000
F: +1 312 542 9001
www.marketingpower.com
This is a biweekly journal, one of many magazines published by the American Marketing Association. It covers the latest trends in marketing strategies, communications and technology, as well as giving examples of how the industry's best practices have been implemented, and insights into career and management issues. It follows the regulatory and legislative developments that marketers need to know, delves into how technology affects the practice of marketing, and covers global marketing trends and issues. *Marketing News* also publishes six special directories: *Focus Group Facilities, Multicultural Marketing Firms, International Research Firms, Marketing Technology/Software, Internet Marketing Service*, and *Customer Satisfaction Measurement Firms.*

Point of Purchase: The Journal of Marketing Communications at Retail
ISSN: 1085–5009
VNU Business Publications
770 Broadway, New York, 10003–9595
T: +1 646 654 4500
F: +1 646 654 4480
www.popmag.com
Point of Purchase covers retail marketing from the point of view of brand marketers and retailers, presenting feature stories, industry news, case studies, and guest opinions.

Quirk's Marketing Research Review
Quirk's Marketing Research Review
8030 Cedar Avenue South, Suite 229, Minneapolis, MN 55425
T: +1 952 854 5101
F: +1 952 854 8191
www.quirks.com
Published 11 times per year, the magazine provides case histories, techniques, trend analysis, industry news, and product and service updates for the marketing research industry.

Sales and Marketing Management
ISSN: 0163–7517
VNU Business Publications
770 Broadway, New York, 10003–9595
T: +1 856 786 9085
F: +1 856 786 4415
www.salesandmarketing.com
This monthly magazine features articles, profiles, and interviews written for top executives who have direct responsibility for all aspects of sales, marketing, and management. Featured topics include case studies and marketing strategies from the world's most successful companies. A special bonus issue, *The Survey of Buying Power*, includes demographic and consumer retail spending data.

INTERNET

American Marketing Association
www.marketingpower.com
The American Marketing Association (AMA) is an international professional organization for people involved in the practice, study, and teaching of marketing. As well as setting industry standards, the AMA seeks to help marketers by providing them with information, products, and services, many of which are available online, including a career center, best practice articles, a marketer's toolkit, and newsletter. Registration is free.

ORGANIZATIONS

USA

American Advertising Federation
1101 Vermont Avenue NW, Suite 500, Washington, D.C., 20005–6306
T: +1 202 898 0089
F: +1 202 898 0159
E: aaf@aaf.org
www.aaf.org
The AAF is a network of advertisers, ad agencies, media companies, local advertising clubs, and college chapters. Membership benefits include a membership directory, networking opportunities, updates on relevant legislation, professional development, and recruitment services.

American Marketing Association
311 S. Wacker Drive, Suite 5800, Chicago, Illinois, 60606–5819
T: +1 312 542 9000
F: +1 312 542 9001
E: info@ama.org
www.marketingpower.com
The American Marketing Association (AMA) has over 40,000 members worldwide, with nearly 400 chapters throughout North America and Canada. It is an international professional organization for people involved in the practice, study, and teaching of marketing. As well as setting standards of best practice in the industry, the AMA seeks to help marketers by providing them with products, services, information, education, and resources. It has a large, informative Web site and publishes a wide range of journals.

Association of National Advertisers
708 Third Avenue, New York, 10017–4270
T: +1 212 697 5950
F: +1 212 661 8057
E: info@ana.net
www.ana.net
ANA is a trade association dedicated to marketing and brand-building. It offers its members conferences, regional meetings, training seminars, benchmarking studies, industry analysis, research services, and publications.

Marketing Research Association
1344 Silas Deane Highway, Suite 306, Rocky Hill, Connecticut, 06067–0230
T: +1 860 257 4008
F: +1 860 257 3990
E: email@mra-net.org

"When you are marketing a drinks brand, it can take over your life."

(Andrew Allan)

www.mra-net.org
MRA is a membership organization for the marketing research industry; its members include data collectors, full service research companies, users of research, and related service providers. Membership benefits include educational programs, training, networking opportunities, publications, and conferences.

Marketing Science Institute
1000 Massachusetts Avenue, Cambridge, Massachusetts, 02138–5396
T: +1 617 491 2060
F: +1 617 491 2065
E: msi@msi.org
www.msi.org
The MSI is a nonprofit institute, established in 1961 as a bridge between business and academia. Its mission is to support and circulate studies by academic scholars that address research issues specified by member companies. MSI functions as a working sponsorship and brings executives and leading international researchers together.

Society of Competitive Intelligence Professionals
1700 Diagonal Road, Suite 600, Alexandria, Virginia, 22314
T: +1 703 739 0696
F: +1 703 739 2524
E: info@scip.org
www.scip.org
SCIP is a nonprofit membership organization for professionals in the competitive intelligence industry. In addition to advocating ethical standards for the industry, SCIP provides seminars, networking opportunities, and publications.

The Direct Marketing Association
1120 Avenue of the Americas, New York, 10036–6700
T: +1 212 768 7277
F: +1 212 302 6714
E: customerservice@the-dma.org
www.the-dma.org
The DMA is a trade association for businesses interested in direct, database, and interactive global marketing; its members are catalog companies, direct mailers, teleservice firms, and Internet marketers from consumer and business-to-business segments, as well as companies that provide supplies and services to marketers. Its activities include industry promotion, professional development, training, research, conferences, and networking events.

International

International Advertising Association
521 Fifth Avenue, Suite 1807, New York, 10175
T: +1 212 557 1133
F: +1 212 983 0455
E: iaa@iaaglobal.org
www.iaaglobal.org
IAA is a strategic partnership between advertisers, media companies, agencies, direct marketing firms, and individual practitioners formed to advocate responsible marketing and free choice for advertisers and marketers. In addition to acting as a legislative advocate for commercial free speech, the IAA sponsors conferences and offers networking opportunities.

For More Information

- Advertising (pp. 1903–06)
- Direct Marketing (pp. 1953–54)
- Market Research and Competitor Intelligence (pp. 2042–44)
- Public Relations (pp. 2090–92)
- Selling and Salesmanship (pp. 2109–11)

Meetings

BOOKS

The Big Book of Business Games
John Newstrom, Edward Scannell
New York: McGraw-Hill, 1995
170pp (Training)
ISBN: 0070464766
Designed for managers and team leaders, this book lists seventy five games and activities to enliven meetings and inspire productivity. Taken originally from the *Games Trainers Play* series, each entry has been adjusted for use in a range of business situations.

The Complete Handbook of Business Meetings
Eli Mina
New York: AMACOM, 2000
318pp ISBN: 0814405606
This book discusses key ingredients for effective meetings, what a ''master'' facilitator does, and how to work through contentious meetings. It includes some thoughts on managing virtual meetings and a troubleshooting guide.

Fat Free Meetings
Burt Albert
Princeton, New Jersey: Peterson's, 1996
205pp ISBN: 156079
This book gives advice on managing all types of meetings, including telephone calls and task force meetings, in both real and virtual offices. It focuses on streamlining meetings to be optimally efficient and effective. Templates, samples, and step-by-step advice enhance the text.

First Aid for Meetings: Quick Fixes and Major Repairs for Running Effective Meetings
Charlie Hawkins
Newberg, Oregon: Bookpartners, Inc., 1997
190pp ISBN: 1885221614
This book provides concrete ideas for running effective meetings, including planning, managing the flow of the meeting, moving groups to consensus and closure, and dealing with disruptive behavior. The author also discusses how to manage meetings in which electronic media are being used and how to apply meeting management concepts to one-on-one meetings.

Getting Results from Electronic Meetings. Creative Solutions, Increased Commitment, Improved Business Processes
Alan Weatherall, Jay Nunamaker
Chandlers Ford, Hampshire: Electronic Meetings Solutions Ltd., 1999
173pp ISBN: 095265251X
Electronic meetings have already established an impressive track record for helping organizations to exploit existing common technology in ways that bring about immediate and quantifiable business benefits. This book describes in a clear and logical way how electronic meetings can be practically implemented in any organization.

Great Meetings! How to Facilitate Like a Pro
Dee Kelsey, Pam Plumb
Portland, Maine: Hanson Park Press, 1999

"Don't try to manage from any board of directors—or any other kind of meeting." (Robert Heller)

  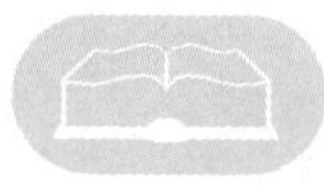    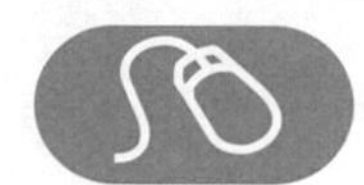

173pp ISBN: 0965835405
This book provides helpful advice on running effective meetings. It covers topics from understanding group dynamics to meeting design and explains how to start a meeting effectively and how to manage the problem-solving process.

How to Make Meetings Work!
Michael Doyle
New York: Berkeley Publishing Group, 1993
320pp ISBN: 0425138704
This is a pragmatic approach to troubleshooting the problems of interaction in meetings. Doyle offers a range of techniques aimed at both management and staff, and advises on ways to make company meetings clear and productive.

Meeting Management
Taggart Smith
Upper Saddle River, New Jersey: Prentice Hall, 2001
166pp (NetEffect)
ISBN: 0130173916
This book offers a practical framework for managing meetings, and demonstrates how to lead them effectively and make them as time-efficient as possible. It outlines three types of meetings: information-giving, interactive, and problem solving, and covers areas such as structuring a topic and organizing the message, audience, visuals, disruptions, and asking and answering questions.

Meetings That Work: A Practical Guide to Shorter and More Productive Meetings
Richard Y. Chang, Kevin R. Kehoe
San Francisco, California: Jossey-Bass, 1994
104pp ISBN: 0749416564
This guidebook, containing a wealth of practical examples, offers proven methods of running more productive meetings which can be applied immediately on the job. It covers preparation, the meeting itself, and evaluating the meeting, and includes many checklists and worksheets.

The Modern Rules of Order: A Guide for Conducting Business Meetings
Donald Tortorice
Chicago, Illinois: American Bar Association, 1999
80pp ISBN: 1570737290
This book is a simplified system for running any business meeting with confidence, fairness, and efficiency, substituting the arcane and complex nature of traditional rules for a set of modern, equitable, and easily-applicable ones. Designed to be mastered in less than an hour, as well as for quick reference during meetings, the book includes an easy-to-read, one-glance chart summarizing how to handle any motion.

Not Another Meeting: A Practical Guide for Facilitating Effective Meetings
Frances A. Micale
Central Point, Oregon: PSI Research /Oasis Press, 1999
165pp ISBN: 1555714803
This manual discusses the importance of being able to distinguish content from process, how to encourage participation, how to stay "in the moment" during a meeting, how to resolve conflict, and how to make the best use of teams in meetings.

101 Ways to Make Meetings Active: Surefire Ideas to Engage Your Group
Mel Silberman
San Francisco, California: Jossey-Bass/ Pfeiffer, 1999
322pp ISBN: 0787946079
This book provides 101 tools, tips, and techniques for successful meetings. The topics that the author covers include preparing for meetings, obtaining group participation, stimulating discussion, the roles and responsibilities of chairpersons and other officers, timesavers, managing conflict, problem solving, using flip charts, and closing the meeting. All are illustrated with a number of practical examples.

Robert's Rules of Order 10th ed.
Henry M. Robert III, et al.
Cambridge, Massachusetts: Perseus, 2000
704pp ISBN: 073820376
This is the classic guide to conducting well-ordered, structured, and productive meetings.

TeamThink: 72 Ways to Make Good, Smart, Quick Decisions in Any Meeting
Ava S. Butler
New York: McGraw Hill, 1996
218pp ISBN: 0070094322
This book adopts a training approach to running more effective meetings. It provides exercises, activities, and games designed to promote team problem solving and improve the efficiency of meetings. It also includes techniques for brainstorming, information gathering, decision making, and implementing plans successfully.

MAGAZINES

The Facilitator
Nurre Ink
P.O. Box 670705, Dallas, Texas, 75367–0705
T: +1 972 243 1356
F: +1 972 243 1357
www.thefacilitator.com
The Facilitator provides meeting facilitators with tips, case studies, and discussion items on running effective meetings. Techniques for managing meetings are explained in detail.

INTERNET

Midwest Facilitators' Network
www.midwest-facilitators.net
This site for professional facilitators operating in the Midwest of the United States provides information on workshops, conferences, books, facilitators, and a newsletter. There also is information on facilitator shareware files for downloading.

The Facilitator.Com
www.thefacilitator.com
This site provides meeting management tips, a quarterly newsletter, information on chat groups and conferences, and links.

ORGANIZATIONS

International

ESOMAR (World Association of Research Professionals)
John Kelly, President
Vondelstraat 172, 1054 GV Amsterdam, The Netherlands
T: +31 20 664 21 41
F: +31 20 664 29 22
E: email@esomar.nl
www.esomar.nl
ESOMAR was founded in 1948 as the European Society for Opinion and Marketing Research and now has over 4,000 members in 100 countries. The organization promotes the use of opinion and marketing research in business and society through seminars and conferences, professional publications, and training and education, and represents its membership on international bodies.

International Association of Facilitators
7630 West 145th Street, Suite 202, St. Paul, Minnesota, 55124
T: +1 952 891 3541
F: +1 952 891 1800
E: office@iaf-world.org
www.iaf-world.org
The IAF was founded in 1994 and now has over 1,200 members in more than 20 countries. It aims to promote professional facilitation through information exchange and regional and global networking.

For More Information

☆ **Boardroom Roles (pp. 220–21)**
✔ **Handling Effective Meetings (pp. 396–97)**
Interpersonal Communication/ Relations (pp. 2012–14)

"My life has been a meeting. . .one long meeting. Even on the few committees I don't yet belong to, the agenda winks at me when I pass."
(Gwyn Thomas)

  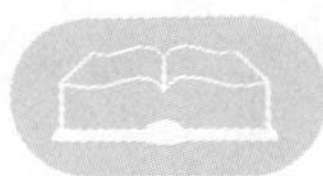    

MISSION STATEMENTS

BOOKS

The Mission-driven Organization: From Mission Statement to a Thriving Enterprise, Here's Your Blueprint for Building an Inspired, Cohesive, Customer-oriented Team
BOB WALL, MARK R. SOBOL, ROBERT S. SOLUM
Roseville, California: Prima Publishing, 1999
237pp ISBN: 0761518819
This book not only helps the reader develop a mission statement that sets forth the organization's vision, it also goes on to explain the leadership and human resources issues that may be faced when trying to implement it. In addition, the book shows how to retain the vision as a permanent part of the organization's mindset, by embodying it in its culture from top to bottom.

The Mission Primer: Four Steps to an Effective Mission Statement
RICHARD O'HALLORAN, DAVID O'HALLORAN
Richmond, Virginia: Mission Incorporated, 2000
130pp ISBN: 0967663504
This primer presents a clear and simple guide to writing a mission statement tailored to the reader's organization or department. It leads the reader through a series of steps that will help those involved to develop a collective vision by uncovering their assumptions about and conflicting perceptions of the organization, forcing them to resolve those differences.

The Mission Statement Book: 301 Corporate Mission Statements from America's Top Companies
JEFFREY ABRAHAMS
Berkeley, California: Ten Speed Press, 1999
512pp ISBN: 1580081320
This book provides an extensive selection of mission statements from America's top companies, ranging from Ben and Jerry's to Federal Express and to General Motors. It gives detailed information on how mission statements are used and on how to write one that incorporates your organization's vision and values. It also offers an index that allows you to compare one company's statement with another's.

Say It and Live It: The 50 Corporate Mission Statements that Hit the Mark
PATRICIA JONES, LARRY KAHANER
New York: Currency/Doubleday, 1995
266pp ISBN: 0385476302
This volume presents 50 mission statements from diverse organizations such as Avis, Ben & Jerry's, IBM, and Southwest Airlines, in each case adding a commentary to give life to the statement. The authors begin the book with an exploration of commonalities in the statements and close it with tips on how to prepare your own mission statement.

Success in Sight: Visioning
ANDREW P. KAKABADSE, FREDERIC NORTIER, NELLO-BERNARD ABRAMOVICI
Stanford, Connecticut: International Thomson Business Press, 1998
224pp (Smart Strategies)
ISBN: 186152160X
The authors explore the concept of visioning as a crucial strategic tool and show how effective visioning can map the way ahead for the success of an organization. They discuss the history of leadership and the nature of visionary leadership as well as providing practical guidance on promoting a shared perspective and generating a corporate vision. Global case studies are included.

INTERNET

Nonprofit Genie
www.genie.org
This Web site, sponsored by the California Management Assistance Partnership, provides information on developing mission statements for nonprofit organizations. The information it contains could prove useful for anyone interested in mission statements.

U.S. Charter Schools
www.uscharterschools.org
This section of a Web site devoted to the development of mission statements for charter schools provides information that could easily be applied by other organizations.

MOTIVATION

BOOKS

Employee Motivation and the Psychological Contract
DAVID GUEST, NEIL CONWAY
New York: Beekman, 2000
72pp (Issues in People Management 21)
ISBN: 0846450399
This is the third in a series of surveys designed to explore the changing nature of the employment relationship. It focuses upon a range of issues, including employee motivation and the psychological contract, and behavior in organizations.

Fish
STEPHEN C. LUNDIN, HARRY PAUL, JOHN CHRISTENSEN
London: Hodder Mobius, 2001
112pp ISBN: 0340819790
Written as a parable, this book charts the progress of a fictional manager as he aims to turn his unmotivated team into a productive one. The authors present examples from ''Seattle's Pike Place Fish'' a ''world famous market'' to demonstrate the positive effects of a happy, energized workplace.

Gung Ho!
KEN BLANCHARD, SHELDON BOWLES
New York: William Morrow & Co., 1997
256pp ISBN: 068815428
Using his experience of large corporations (such as General Motors and Microsoft) Blanchard suggests a strategy by which employers can boost motivation among their employees, in order to inspire greater productivity at work. The author discusses the three core elements of this strategy, and discusses how they can be put into practice.

Instant Motivation: Encourage Others to Achieve More Now
BRIAN CLEGG
Milford, Connecticut: Kogan Page, 2000
128pp (Instant Series)
ISBN: 0749431016
Exercises and ideas to help motivate and develop people and teams are given in this activities book. Most of the exercises are guaranteed to take no more than 30 minutes, and some of the ideas are extremely simple, such as giving spot prizes during meetings.

Intrinsic Motivation at Work: Building Energy and Commitment
KENNETH W. THOMAS

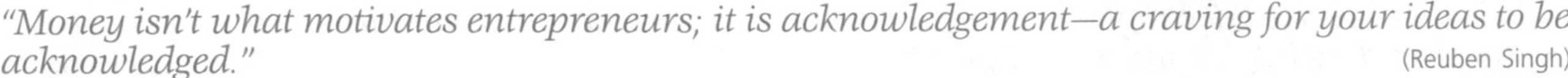
"Money isn't what motivates entrepreneurs; it is acknowledgement—a craving for your ideas to be acknowledged."
(Reuben Singh)

San Francisco, California: Berrett-Koehler, 2000
180pp ISBN: 1576750876
Intrinsic Motivation at Work presents a new model for motivating the worker in the new economy. The knowledge worker looks for intrinsically motivating factors as opposed to the generally effective extrinsic factors of the earlier industrial worker. The four intrinsic motivators for this new worker are a sense of purpose, autonomy concerning how to do the work, an increasing sense of competence, and a sense of accomplishment. Overall this book can help organizational leaders challenge their assumptions and create a more positive and rewarding work environment.

Love 'Em or Lose 'Em: Getting Good People to Stay
Beverly L. Kaye, Sharon Jordan-Evans
San Francisco, California: Berrett-Koehler, 1999
234pp ISBN: 1576750736
Love 'Em or Lose 'Em looks at motivation from a whole-workplace perspective and considers how the systems, policies, and procedures in a work environment can either motivate and inspire or demotivate and demoralize.

Love the Work You're With: Find the Job You Always Wanted Without Leaving the One You Have
Richard C. Whiteley
New York: Henry Holt & Company, Inc., 2001
255pp ISBN: 080506592X
This book looks at improving motivation from the perspective of an employee. It is a guide to discovering yourself and applying that knowledge to gaining meaning and purpose at work.

Management Plus: Maximizing Productivity through Motivation, Performance, and Commitment
Robert A. Fazzi
New York: McGraw-Hill, 1994
240pp ISBN: 1556237561
In this book Fazzi presents and explains the Functional Management Model—a system for managing and motivating staff for optimum performance. It is designed to help managers identify the motivational needs of each employee and then determine the most appropriate supervisory or management approach to match these needs. Other areas covered include the building of high-performing teams, increasing the commitment of your staff, and becoming an exceptional manager or supervisor in the eyes of your employees.

Motivating People in Lean Organizations
Linda Holbeche
Woburn, Massachusetts: Butterworth-Heinemann, 1998
250pp ISBN: 0750633751
The core themes in this guide for managers in lean organizations who need to motivate employees and promote new forms of career development include: how to implement motivational strategies; the importance of good internal communications; how to develop new career development structures; and how to recognize and reward achievement. Case studies of Thresher and General Electric are used to illustrate the text, which also includes examples of cross-cultural lean organizations.

Motivation Management
Sheila Ritchie, Peter Martin
Brookfield, Vermont: Gower, 1999
320pp ISBN: 0566081024
Part One presents what the authors call the "Motivation-to-work Profile"; Part Two describes the 12 factors that make up the Profile; Part Three discusses motivation in action—managing change, coping with stress, teamworking, training and development, selection, and working with others. Appendices cover the theoretical framework and the making of the Profile.

1001 Ways to Energize Employees
Bob Nelson
New York: Workman Publishing, 1997
213pp ISBN: 0761101608
This book follows *1001 Ways to Reward Employees*, Nelson's previous title in the series. Aimed at managers, the book suggests strategies for inspiring and motivating staff. Nelson's research includes case studies as well as feedback from large corporations to help illustrate his suggestions.

Peak Performance: Aligning the Hearts and Minds of Your Employees
Jon R. Katzenbach
Boston, Massachusetts: Harvard Business School Press, 2000
304pp ISBN: 0875849369
This text draws on research involving leaders in a range of industries that examines how to move from merely motivating employees to gaining the emotional commitment that yields consistently high performance. Five balanced paths to success in this area are identified, and the ways in which leading companies pursue one or more of them are investigated. The author then reviews the key lessons to be learned.

Punished by Rewards: The Trouble with Gold Stars, Incentive Plans, A's, Praise, and Other Bribes
Alfie Kohn
Boston, Massachusetts: Houghton Mifflin, 1999
416pp ISBN: 0618001816
Punished by Rewards is a controversial book which attacks the established beliefs of the Skinner school of behavioral science. The book highlights the difficulties of using rewards in the workplace and the classroom and offers suggestions for enhancing intrinsic motivation.

Tall Poppy: How to Grow to Your Full Potential and Keep Your Head
Judi James, Mike Edden
London: Industrial Society, 2000
192pp ISBN: 1858355141
An inspirational but grounded guide to achieving personal fulfillment. Designed to stimulate action not reverie, the book combines contemporary ideas and theory about self-awareness and self-motivation with original exercises and a strategy for turning the theory into reality.

Transforming Work
Michael Kroth, Patricia Boverie
Cambridge, Massachusetts: Perseus, 2002
256pp ISBN: 0738205060
Aimed at management and executive level, this book works on the premise that organizations should be more aware of staff needs and requirements.The authors use their extensive research to show professionals how to cultivate a happy and motivated office environment, with a view to "transforming" the outlook of the entire company.

We Are All Self-employed: The New Social Contract for Working in a Changed World
Cliff Hakim
San Francisco, California: Berrett-Koehler, 1995
256pp ISBN: 1881052796
Hakim discusses the possibility of changing our approach to work, by taking on a "self-employed" attitude. He describes the notion of actively engaging with the workplace, rather than passively "fitting in," and examines the practical applications of this notion.

INTERNET

Accel-team.com
www.accel-team.com/motivation
This commercial Web site has a good, multi-

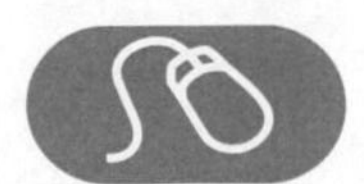

page article on theories of workplace motivation. The article is available for download for a fee but can be read in its entirety online.

CultureWorx
www.motivation-programs-rewards.com
CultureWorx is a commercial site that offers a good collection of free content, including some well-written articles and newsletters. The site approaches the concepts of motivation and rewards from a business perspective and is helpful for both employees and managers.

ORGANIZATIONS

USA

Academy of Human Resource Development
College of Technology, Bowling Green State University, Bowling Green, Ohio, 43403
T: +1 419 372 9155
F: +1 419 372 8385
E: office@ahrd.org
www.ahrd.org
The Academy is a global organization devoted to the study of human resource theories, processes, and techniques. As part of this research, it publishes a range of journals, holds conferences, establishes partnerships, conducts a number of educational programs, and presents awards to scholars in the field of human resources.

American Society for Training and Development
1640 King Street, Box 1443, Alexandria, Virginia, 22313–2043
T: +1 800 628 2783
F: +1 703 683 1523
www.astd.org
A professional association for people involved in workplace training and performance issues, the ASTD conducts research and policy work, holds conferences and seminars, and publishes a range of books, journals, and software for training and development professionals.

Society for Human Resource Management
1800 Duke Street, Alexandria, Virginia, 22314
T: +1 703 548 3440
F: +1 703 535 6490
E: shrm@shrm.org
www.shrm.org
The Society is a membership organization for human resources professionals and students around the world. It provides education and information services, conferences and seminars, government and media representation, online services and publications.

For More Information

- ☆ **Making Loyalty Work (pp. 289–90)**
- ☆ **Snapping Managerial Inertia (pp. 257–58)**
- **Coaching, Counseling, and Mentoring (pp. 1925–28)**
- **Employee Benefits/ Compensation (pp. 1959–61)**
- **Management Development (pp. 2031–33)**

NEGOTIATION

BOOKS

Bargaining for Advantage: Negotiation Strategies for Reasonable People
G. Richard Shell
New York: Penguin, 2000
304pp ISBN: 0140281916
This book is a practical guide to negotiations based on an executive training program that gets its message across through storytelling. The book, which includes useful checklists, highlights the value of communication and covers such issues in negotiating as bargaining style, making concessions, gaining commitment, understanding each party's goals and expectations, and making sure there is clear information on the table, including standards and norms.

Beyond Winning
Robert H. Mnookin, Scott R. Peppet, Andrew S. Tulumello
Cambridge, Massachusetts: Harvard University Press, 2000
368pp ISBN: 0674003357
In this book, the authors offer advice on overcoming the difficulties faced in legal negotiations. A step-by-step guide, *Beyond Winning* describes a range of ways in which lawyers can seek to improve their negotiating skills. By enhancing communication and using troubleshooting techniques, the authors argue, "disputes can be turned into deals."

Business Negotiation: A Practical Workbook
Paul T. Steele, Tom Beasor
Brookfield, Vermont: Gower, 1999
270pp ISBN: 0566080729
This practical textbook provides a step-by-step guide to acquiring key negotiating skills and the techniques for using them successfully as well as identifying the key topics in negotiation. Each chapter includes a checklist of the key points made and exercises for applying what has been learned.

Difficult Conversations
Douglas Stone, Bruce Patton, Sheila Heen
New York: Penguin, 2000
272pp ISBN: 014027782X
This book aims to help readers to become calm and assertive in difficult situations (such as asking for a pay rise, or experiencing problems with colleagues). In discussing the different emotions and requirements that arise from such conversations, the book aims to pinpoint ways of managing them more effectively.

Essentials of Negotiation 2nd ed.
Roy J. Lewicki, David M. Saunders, John W. Minton
New York: McGraw-Hill, 2000
272pp ISBN: 0072312858
This book looks at the psychology of bargaining and negotiation and the dynamics involved in conflict and its resolution. It provides an in-depth discussion of aspects of negotiation such as communication, strategy and tactics, dealing with breakdowns in negotiations, social context, ethics, third party roles, and power.

Fast Forward MBA in Negotiating and Deal Making
Roy J. Lewicki, Alexander Hiam
New York: John Wiley, 1998
288pp ISBN: 0471256986
The authors explore cutting edge ideas on negotiation and deal making through real-world examples. Key concepts are introduced and illustrated and warnings provided on how to avoid pitfalls.

Getting Past No
William Ury
New York: Bantam Doubleday Dell, 1993
189pp ISBN: 0553371312
This book provides a step-by-step method for negotiation that aims to ensure that satisfactory agreement is reached with even the most intransigent people. It contains advice, hints,

(Mark McCormack)

  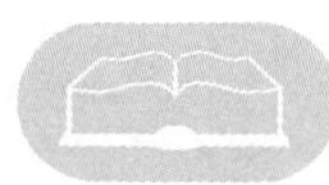    

and tips, useful strategies and plenty of real examples.

Getting to Resolution: Turning Conflict into Collaboration
STEWART LEVINE
San Francisco, California: Berrett-Koehler, 2000
200pp ISBN: 1576751155
This book examines the nature of conflicts, finding that they most often result from a breakdown in communications. It then describes a process for negotiation that is useful for both mediators and individuals. The book provides a detailed roadmap to resolve disputes, including believing in abundance, relying on feelings and intuition, being creative, and disclosing information.

Getting to Yes 2nd ed.
ROGER FISHER, WILLIAM URY, BRUCE PATTON
New York: Penguin Putnam, 1991
200pp ISBN: 0140157352
By working around four main principles of effective negotiation and discussing some of the difficulties that can arise, the authors show the reader how to pursue his or her own interests while keeping adversaries happy at the same time. A few principles will guide the reader no matter what the other side does, or whatever what tricks they may resort to.

Negotiating, Persuading, and Influencing
ALAN FOWLER
New York: Beekman, 2000
96pp ISBN: 0846451220
The author provides advice on negotiating constructively for a favorable outcome. He devotes special attention to recognizing and using sources of influence, questioning techniques, collaborative and problem-solving approaches, using timing and adjournments, compromising, and securing agreement.

The Negotiation Toolkit: How to Get Exactly What You Want in Any Business or Personal Situation
ROGER J. VOLKEMA
New York: AMACOM, 1999
208pp ISBN: 081448008X
This book offers a guide to negations aimed at helping people build the skills and self-confidence to become good negotiators. It explores the golden rule of negotiation, explains when not to negotiate, discusses the issue of tough negotiators and how to deal with them, describes the tactics, skills, and behaviors of star negotiators, looks at cross-cultural negotiations, and provides ways to measure your own skills.

The New Negotiating Edge: The Behavioral Approach for Results and Relationships
GAVIN KENNEDY
Naperville, Illinois: Nicholas Brealey, 1998
275pp (People Skills for Professionals Series)
ISBN: 1857882059
The author examines two negotiating styles, a soft "win–win" approach and a more aggressive, results oriented, manipulative approach, before advocating a middle path that fuses elements of both approaches and focuses on the human aspects of negotiations. Using this behavioral approach, he outlines the stages of the negotiation process and describes ways to reach successful outcomes.

The Power of Nice: How to Negotiate So Everyone Wins—Especially You!
RONALD M. SHAPIRO, MARK A. JANKOWSKI, JAMES DALE
New York: John Wiley, 2001
304pp ISBN: 0471080721
This book is based on Shapiro's belief that negotiation works best if two negotiators can build a common bond between them. In exploring this theory, Shapiro offers advice on various types of negotiation, and on creating effective proposals.

MAGAZINES

Group Decision and Negotiation
ISSN: 0926–2644
Kluwer Academic Publishers
Customer Service Department, P.O. Box 358, Accord Station, Hingham, Massachusetts, 02018–0358
T: +1 781 871 6600
F: +1 781 681 9045
www.wkap.nl
This bimonthly journal deals with the development of group decision and negotiation processes and the technology and software used for this purpose, publishing theoretical and empirical research and case studies in the field. It is available both in printed form and via the Internet.

International Negotiation: A Journal of Theory and Practice
ISSN: 1382–340X
Kluwer Academic Publishers
Customer Service Department, P.O. Box 358, Accord Station, Hingham, Massachusetts, 02018–0358
T: +1 781 871 6600
F: +1 781 681 9045
www.wkap.nl
This journal, published three times a year, explores the theoretical issues and practical applications of negotiation; it aims to identify, analyze, and explain effective and efficient international negotiation and mediation processes through research articles and case study examples.The journal is available in printed form and via the Internet.

Negotiation Journal
ISSN: 0748–4526
Kluwer Academic Publishers
Customer Service Department, P.O. Box 358, Accord Station, Hingham, Massachusetts, 02018–0358
T: +1 781 871 6600
F: +1 781 681 9045
www.wkap.nl
Aimed at planning, economic, and public policy professionals and published in association with the inter-university consortium Program on Negotiation, this quarterly journal aims to promote the development of better techniques for resolving conflict. It is available in printed form and via the Internet.

INTERNET

Mediate.com
www.mediate.com
This site provides articles and news on mediation, conflict resolution, and arbitration. It also includes information about training, events, organizations, and academic programs in this field.

The Negotiating Edge
www.negotiatingedge.com
This site provides information about seminars, Negotiating Edge white papers, links to other negotiating sites, and lists of recommended readings on negotiation and conflict resolution.

The Negotiation Skills Company, Inc.
www.negotiationskills.com
This site is provided by a consulting company that specializes in negotiation training and consultancy. It offers free information and articles, and an occasional newsletter on all aspects of the negotiation process.

ORGANIZATIONS

USA

Institute for Operations Research and the Management Sciences
901 Elkridge Landing Road, Suite 400, Linthicum, Maryland, 21090–2909
T: +1 410 850 0300
F: +1 410 684 2963
E: *informs@informs.org*
www.informs.org
The Institute represents professionals within the operations research and management sciences fields. It has a section dedicated to group decision and negotiation that provides online

"This is about negotiations, but the answer to that question is 'No.'" (David Andrews)

discussions, organizes conferences, and publishes articles through its journal, *Group Decision and Negotiation*.

National Contract Management Association (NCMA)
1912 Woodford Road, Vienna, Virginia, 22182
T: +1 703 448 9231 or 800 344 8096
F: +1 703 448 0939
E: *massidas@ncmahq.org*
www.ncmahq.org
This Association comprises professionals concerned with all aspects of contract management. Areas of special focus are acquisition, negotiation, and management of contracts. The NCMA also has developed training materials and offers certification in contract management.

For More Information

- **Decision Making and Problem Solving (pp. 1950–53)**
- **Interpersonal Communication/ Relations (pp. 2012–14)**
- **Pricing (pp. 2078–79)**

New Product Development

BOOKS

Commercializing New Technologies: Getting from Mind to Market
Vijay K. Jolly
Boston, Massachusetts: Harvard Business School Press, 1997
456pp ISBN: 0875847609
The author examines the process of technology commercialization. Drawing upon the experiences of leading companies from around the world, he analyzes successful and unsuccessful attempts to bring new technologies to market, putting forward the case for a new approach to innovation management based on creating value at every stage by involving the scientific community, shareholders, fund partners, suppliers, and end users.

Developing New Product Concepts
Christopher Miller
Harrisburg, Pennsylvania: Pennsylvania Chamber Educational Foundation, 1999
151pp ISBN: 1929744048
This is a workbook useful for individuals or small groups in the early stages of the development process. It has more than 125 pages of exercises, checklists, fill-in pages, and sample forms to guide you through the practical steps of creative problem solving.

Managing the Design Factory: The Product Developer's Toolkit
Donald Reinertsen
New York: Free Press, 1997
256pp ISBN: 0684839911
This book applies product development principles and integrates them with management theories. In short, it shows how the two sides of the coin must work together for successful product launching. Management theories and principles are not always incorporated well in practice with a design team. Reinertsen has practical ideas about how to make sure the entire creative team is "speaking the same language" as a product launch moves from idea to reality.

Marketing the Unknown: Developing Market Strategies for Technical Innovations
Paul Millier
New York: John Wiley, 1999
248pp ISBN: 0471986216
How do you make a product successful? This is one of the basic questions that this practical book sets out to answer. It also discusses what is the best process to follow, and how you choose or transform markets so as to ensure a successful launch. It paves the way for marketing, for R and D, and for project managers in industrial organizations to launch and market innovations successfully in a very competitive field, and outlines strategies for further development.

New Product Development: An Introduction to a Multifunctional Process
Tim Jones
Woburn, Massachusetts: Butterworth-Heinemann, 1996
134pp ISBN: 075064272
This book addresses the four key issues currently associated with successful development programs: NPD strategy, innovation, organizing for NPD, and rapid product development. It uses four in-depth case studies of recently developed products by Rover, Flymo, Logitech, and Polaroid to provide contemporary illustrations of each area.

Over the Horizon: Planning Products Today for Success Tomorrow
Bill Hollins, Gillian Hollins
New York: John Wiley, 1999
268pp ISBN: 0471987174
This book takes a strategic approach to the design and development of new products and services. The process of development is examined in four time frames: survival in the present—how to remain competitive; selection and specification of new products and services; innovation in the medium term; and idea generation for long-term success. The appropriate tools and techniques for use in each time frame are also described.

The PDMA Handbook of New Product Development
Milton D. Rosenau, ed.
New York: John Wiley, 1996
526pp ISBN: 0471141895
Over the last decade, the theory and practice of new product development has been radically transformed. This volume, produced by the Product Development & Management Association (PDMA), combines the best aspects of product development practice in both consumer and industrial markets. Written by academic experts and industry professionals from Fortune 1,000 companies, the book offers authoritative practical information on every stage of the product development process from concept creation, through development and design, to the final assembled product and marketing campaigns.

Portfolio Management for New Products 2nd ed.
Robert G. Cooper, Scott J. Edgett, Elko J. Kleinschmidt
Cambridge, Massachusetts: Perseus, 2001
288pp ISBN: 0738205141
This book shows readers how to manage their company's product portfolio for maximum long-term growth. Its approach is pragmatic, detailing various techniques for managing a portfolio, unlocking its maximum potential, and dealing with any problems that may arise. It provides an excellent resource for any company whose profitability relies on the products it chooses to develop, and the speed with which it brings them to market.

Product Design and Development 2nd ed.
Karl T. Ulrich, Steven D. Eppinger
New York: McGraw-Hill, 1999
384pp ISBN: 007229647X
This text lays out an integrative framework for product design, showing the interconnection of

"Everything that can be invented has been invented." (Charles H. Duell)

marketing, design, and manufacturing. The authors focus as much on aesthetics as engineering in the analysis of production and manufacturing methods, making this book unusual in the field.

Product Development and the Environment
Paul Burrall
Brookfield, Vermont: Gower, 1996
232pp ISBN: 0566076594
This book is a practical guide for managers and designers seeking to exploit the expanding markets for the efficient and clean products demanded by a world seeking a sustainable future. Burrall explains how designers can minimize the lifetime environmental impact of new products and examines the role of various design tools and some of the technologies that are likely to help achieve greener products. Legal, marketing, and technical aspects are covered as well.

Product Development for the Service Sector
Robert G. Cooper, Scott J. Edgett
Cambridge, Massachusetts: Perseus, 1999
288pp ISBN: 0738201057
The book acknowledges the difficulty of service-industry product development in a world where new resources (such as the Internet) are putting pressure on the capacity for original ideas. It offers an outline of major management principles, in which the authors discuss the creation and testing of development models, and their application in any service industry.

Product Juggernauts: How Companies Mobilize to Generate a Stream of Market Winners
Jean-Philippe Deschamps, P. Ranganath Nayak
Boston, Massachusetts: Harvard Business School Press, 1995
472pp ISBN: 0875843417
The authors cite stories from real companies around the world to illustrate guidelines for determining the products customers want and designing the products they want to buy. Examples used to demonstrate the importance of company-wide focus on product include (among others) Ford, Canon, and Toshiba. Using these case studies, the authors demonstrate how organizations can achieve high market performance and improve their current strategies.

Product Leadership: Creating and Launching Superior New Products
Robert G. Cooper
Cambridge, Massachusetts: Perseus, 1999
314pp ISBN: 0738201561
Over a third of new products fail at launch, and many never gain a profitable return. So how do companies like 3M, Merck, and Procter & Gamble continually lead the way with exceptional new products? Cooper reveals the winners' secrets, and offers valuable advice on implementing and overseeing new product processes and strategies, managing product portfolios, determining which products to develop, and fostering ingenuity to outperform the competition.

The Product Manager's Handbook 2nd ed.
Linda Gorchels
New York: McGraw-Hill/NTC, 2000
304pp ISBN: 0658001353
This book focuses on skills acquisition, making it suitable for new product managers or people interested in moving into that line of work. The text is written as an overview and introduction to the skill set necessary for product managers, but segments of the book are also devoted to product development and launch.

Revolutionizing Product Development
Steven C. Wheelwright, Kim B. Clark
New York: Free Press, 1992
400pp ISBN: 0029055156
This book asserts that a company's capability to design quality prototypes, and bring a product to market quicker than its competitor is increasingly the focal point of competition. The authors argue that a successful new product launch is dependent upon management's ability to integrate the marketing, manufacturing, and design functions for problem solving and fast action, particularly during the critical design-build-test cycles of prototype creation. Companies that consistently "design it right the first time" therefore have a crucial advantage.

Successful Product Development: Speeding from Opportunity to Profit
Milton D. Rosenau, Jr.
New York: John Wiley, 1999
208pp ISBN: 047131532X
This book sets out the process of product development from beginning to end, starting with the formation of ideas and moving through design and engineering to the finished product. It is intended for all practitioners involved with any aspect of developing new products and services.

Winning at New Products: Accelerating the Process from Idea to Launch 3rd ed.
Robert G. Cooper
Cambridge, Massachusetts: Perseus, 2001
416pp ISBN: 0738204633
This book cites research and gives examples of innovative practices used by industry leaders such as 3M, Exxon Chemical, and Guinness, to present a tried-and-tested game plan for achieving product leadership. Cooper outlines specific strategies for: assessing risk; getting the necessary resources together; involving customers in the pre-development discovery phase; evaluating a project portfolio; ensuring cross-functional collaboration; and, most importantly, applying a rigorous method for making sound business decisions at every step of the process.

World-class New Product Development: Benchmarking Best Practices of Agile Manufacturers
Dan Dimancescu, Kemp Dwenger
New York: AMACOM, 1995
276pp ISBN: 0814403115
Recounting the findings of research, benchmarking, and working with international companies, this book shows how "corporate champions" manage robust product development operations and presents a system to enable other organizations to do the same. It covers the implementation of a holistic management style, effective cross-functional teaming, rigorous product reviews, systematic capture of the demands of customers, the involvement of suppliers, and the market driven R and D continuum. All its points are illustrated by examples.

MAGAZINES

International Journal of New Product Development and Innovation Management
ISSN: 1484–6684
Winthrop Publications Ltd.
Brunel House, 55–57 North Wharf Road, London, W2 1LA, U.K.
T: +44 (0) 20 7915 9634
F: +44 (0) 20 7915 9636
www.winthrop-publications.co.uk
Aimed at all managers and directors involved in developing new products and innovation management, this journal provides strategic analysis, best practice, and case studies from a range of industry sectors.

Journal of Product Innovation Management
ISSN: 0737–6782
Elsevier Science/Product Development & Management Association
Regional Sales Office, Customer Support Department, P.O. Box 945, New York, 10159–0945

"My interest is in the practice of making and engineering things and doing it with a complete lack of marketing hype."
(James Dyson)

  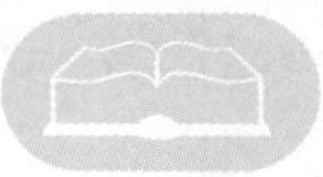    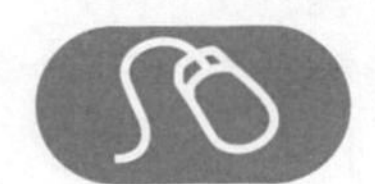

T: +1 212 633 3730
F: +1 212 633 3680
www.elsevier.com
The *Journal* publishes the research, experiences, and insights of academics and practicing managers from all over the world. It is dedicated to the advancement of management practice in all aspects of product innovation and aimed at both practitioners and students in the field.

Visions
Product Development and Management Association
17000 Commerce Parkway, Suite C, Mount Laurel, New Jersey, 08054
T: +1 800 232 5241
F: +1 856 439 0525
www.pdma.org/visions
This is a quarterly publication for new product development professionals which provides news, analysis, and case histories. Contributors are practitioners as well as theoreticians.

INTERNET

American Productivity and Quality Center
www.apqc.org
This site features articles on training, conferences, case studies, presentations, executive summaries and more. This organization makes available several white papers on product development. The APQC is essentially a group working toward corporate organizational improvement. They sponsor conferences on product development as well as providing resources online.

Experts on New Product Development
www.expertson.com/ New_Product_Development

The resources on which information is available from this site include new product development associations, new product development centers, directories, newsgroups, mailing lists, new product development publications, and new product development reference tools.

Global New Products Database
www.gnpd.com
This site can be used to access a comprehensive database that monitors worldwide product innovation in the consumer packaged goods market, offering coverage of new product activity for both competitor monitoring and product idea generation.

New Product Development
www.eas.asu.edu/~kdooley/nsfnpd
Since it provides information and links relating to NPD and is part of a National Science Foundation study *Best Practices, Maturity, and Diffusion in New Product Development*, this site is likely to be of interest to students, researchers, and practitioners of innovation.

Product Development and Management Association
www.pdma.org
This site is everyone's first stop when trolling the Internet for information on product development. It features articles, a job bank, conference listings, a discussion board, and more. Of special interest may be the access this site provides to the *PDMA Toolbook of New Product Development*.

Product Management Institute
www.pmi.org
This Web site features a bookstore, job bank, and searchable archive for product and project management. New product development is featured in its own section. Articles, clickable links, calls for papers, listings of symposia, and directories are also featured.

ORGANIZATIONS

USA

Product Development and Management Association
17000 Commerce Parkway, Suite C, Mount Laurel, New Jersey, 08054
T: +1 856 439 9052
F: +1 856 439 0525
E: pdma@pdma.org
www.pdma.org
This professional nonprofit organization is dedicated to serving people with an interest in new products and services. It is a recognized provider of knowledge and tools intended to improve the effectiveness of the development and management of new products and services. It also arranges conferences, publications, awards, meetings, and workshops, and sponsors research.

Europe

Product Development and Management Association U.K. and Ireland
Innovaro, 78 Belsize Park Gardens, London, NW3 4NG, U.K.
T: +44 (0) 7801 755 054
E: timjones@innovaro.com
www.pdma.org.uk
This is the U.K. and Ireland branch of the PDMA of America, a professional nonprofit organization dedicated to serving people with an interest in new products and services. In addition to providing knowledge and tools intended to improve the effectiveness of new product development and management, it arranges conferences, publications, awards, meetings, and workshops, and sponsors research.

For More Information

- **Innovation and Creativity (pp. 2000–03)**
- **Product and Brand Management (pp. 2081–83)**
- **Research and Development (R&D) Management (pp. 2105–07)**

Nonprofit Organizations

BOOKS

Beyond the Bottom Line: How to Do More with Less in Nonprofit and Public Organizations
Martin W. Sandler, Deborah A. Hudson
New York: Oxford University Press, 1998
228pp ISBN: 0195116127
This book reviews the social and economic pressures that are forcing the United States' nonprofit and public sector organizations to do more with less money. Following an investigation of nonprofit agencies that are successfully meeting these challenges, the authors present a list of competencies and strategies that other agencies should adopt.

Common Interest, Common Good
Shirley Sagawa, Eli Segal
Boston, Massachusetts: Harvard Business School Press, 1999
350pp ISBN: 0875848486
The theory that both nonprofit organizations and businesses can benefit by working in closer contact with each other is at the heart of this book. The authors showcase many such successful partnerships, from corporate sponsorships and cause-related marketing to employee volunteer programs and school-to-work initiatives.

CPR for Nonprofits: Creative Strategies for Successful Fundraising, Marketing, Communications, and Management
Alvin H. Reiss
San Francisco, California: Jossey-Bass, 2000

"There was worlds of reputation in it, but no money." (Mark Twain)

  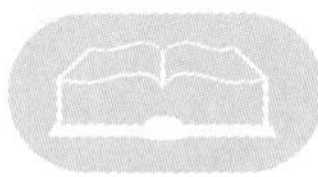    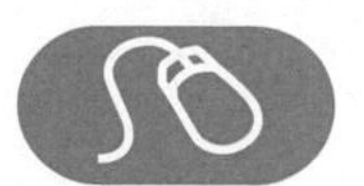

176pp ISBN: 0787952419
This book of case studies illustrates how nonprofit organizations have met and dealt with various challenges. Each case is presented in the same format: background, challenge, plan, result, questions to ask, and lessons learned.

Give and Take: A Candid Account of Corporate Philanthropy
Reynold Levy
Boston, Massachusetts: Harvard Business School Press, 1999
235pp ISBN: 0875848931
In this book, Levy discusses corporate giving from both the perspective of the donor and the solicitor. He points out that successful corporate philanthropy lies in business values and business interests, citing examples of large corporations who have become involved with philanthropic events. He also offers advice to fundraisers, analyzing the elements that make a successful nonprofit organization, and suggesting insider techniques for securing funds from large companies.

Harvard Business Review on Nonprofits
Boston, Massachusetts: Harvard Business School Press, 1999
224pp (Harvard Business Review Paperback Series)
ISBN: 0875849091
This book comprises a collection of eight essays, originally published in the *Harvard Business Review*, that explore aspects of the work of modern nonprofit organizations. Topics include earning public trust, the work of the board, employing business leaders, learning lessons from venture capitalists, and developing profits through corporate partnerships.

Managing in the Voluntary Sector: A Handbook for Managers in Charitable and Non Profit Organizations
Stephen P. Osborne, ed.
Stanford, Connecticut: International Thomson Business Press, 1996
300pp ISBN: 0412718405
This is an introductory handbook and reference source that outlines the ideas, issues, and problems facing managers in the voluntary sector. It identifies key management skills, and discusses their importance and meaning in the context of voluntary organizations.

Managing the Non-profit Organization: Principles and Practices
Peter F. Drucker, Max De Pree, Robert Buford
New York: HarperCollins, 1992
256pp ISBN: 0887306012
This title outlines the importance of good management in the nonprofit sector, an area that is rapidly expanding and which consequently has a workforce that includes over 80 million volunteers. The book details every aspect of nonprofit organizations, from resources to decision making, and gives several examples to support this information.

Managing Voluntary Organisations: New Approaches
Roger Courtney
Hemel Hempstead, Hertfordshire: ICSA Publishing, 1996
173pp (Charities Management Series)
ISBN: 1872860893
This book examines the changes affecting the management of voluntary organizations in the United Kingdom and highlights the need for an increasing level of management skills and professionalism. Aspects covered include strategic planning, performance management, and quality assurance. It outlines a competence-based approach to staff development, and gives two case studies.

Managing Without Profit: The Art of Managing Third-sector Organizations 2nd ed.
Mike Hudson
New York: Penguin, 1999
448pp ISBN: 0140269533
This guide for funders, managers, and governors presents an overview of nonprofit or "third sector" organizations. It explores the essential management elements that are needed to make this type of organization successful. It also examines best practice examples, which focus on the six key areas of governance, strategy, management, people, organizations, and the future.

Strategic Marketing for Nonprofit Organizations 5th ed.
Philip Kotler, Alan Andreasen
Upper Saddle River, New Jersey: Prentice Hall, 1995
528pp ISBN: 0132325470
This title provides a valuable overview of the marketing process in nonprofit organizations. The coauthors discuss a range of key marketing issues in this area which include creating a greater customer focus, producing, and organizing resources, handling a marketing strategy, and strategic planning.

Strategic Planning For Nonprofit Organizations
Michael Allison, Jude Kaye
New York: John Wiley, 1997
304pp ISBN: 0471178322
Based on a seven-stage plan on effective strategy, this book aims to help readers pinpoint the processes needed to create a successful organization. Including assessment tools such as checklists, worksheets, and an example of a strategic plan, this book/disk is suitable for a range of outfits, at whatever financial or social level. It includes advice on compiling mission statements, and sustaining all factors of the strategic plan.

MAGAZINES

Charities Management
ISSN: 0964–9093
Mitre House Publishing Ltd.
1st Floor, The Clifton Centre, 110 Clifton Street, London, EC2A 4HD, U.K.
T: +44 (0) 20 7729 6644
This is a thrice-yearly publication, aimed at chief executives, finance directors, and fundraising managers, that deals with all areas of charity management.

Charity Times
ISSN: 1355–4573
Perspective Publishing Ltd.
402 London Fruit and Wool Exchange, Brushfield Street, London, E1 6EP, U.K.
T: +44 (0) 20 7426 0101
F: +44 (0) 20 7426 0123
www.charitytimes.com
This is a bimonthly magazine, aimed at decision makers and voluntary groups, that covers all areas of financial, business, and fundraising management for charities.

Nonprofit World
ISSN: 8755–7614
Society for Nonprofit Organizations
5820 Canton Center Road, Suite 165, Canton, Michigan, 48187
T: +1 734 451 3582
F: +1 734 451 5935
http://danenet.wicip.org/snpo/newpage2.htm
This publication is the only comprehensive national leadership and management magazine in the nonprofit world. Written for senior management as well as volunteers, this magazine will appeal to anyone working with a nonprofit agency. It is filled with timely information regarding current nonprofit topics.

Voluntary Sector
ISSN: 0955–2170
National Council for Voluntary Organisations
Regent's Wharf, 8 All Saints Street, London, N1 9RL, U.K.
T: +44 (0) 20 7713 6161
F: +44 (0) 20 7713 6300
www.ncvo-vol.org.uk
Published ten times a year, this is the magazine of the National Council for Voluntary Organisations in the United Kingdom. Coverage

"In all the ages, three-fourths of the support of the great charities has been conscience money."
(Mark Twain)

includes news and features on a range of issues affecting the voluntary sector.

INTERNET

BBB Wise Giving Alliance
www.give.org
The Web site for the BBB Wise Giving Alliance collects, disseminates, and distributes information on nationally soliciting charitable organizations across the United States.

Charity Choice
www.charitychoice.co.uk
This site is an encyclopedic guide to charities in the United Kingdom and Northern Ireland. The service provides contact information, descriptions of each charity's work, and links to other relevant Web sites.

Charitynet
www.charitynet.org
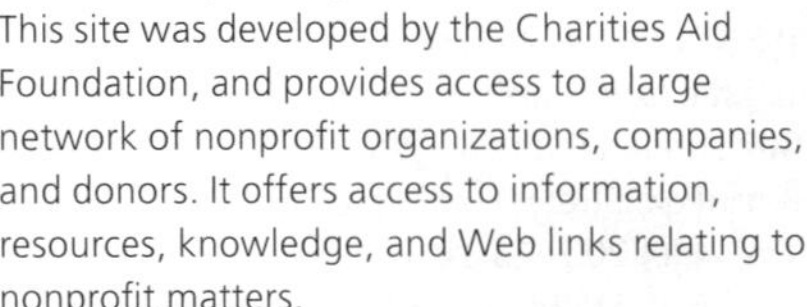
This site was developed by the Charities Aid Foundation, and provides access to a large network of nonprofit organizations, companies, and donors. It offers access to information, resources, knowledge, and Web links relating to nonprofit matters.

GuideStar: The National Database of Nonprofit Organizations
www.guidestar.org
This Web site is run by Philanthropic Research, Inc. and allows access to a database of over 850,000 nonprofit organizations recognized by the Internal Revenue Service. The site will be useful to both donors to and founders of nonprofit organizations.

Institute for Nonprofit Organization Management
www.inom.org
Sponsored by the University of San Francisco College of Professional Studies, this Web site provides a resource center, a newsletter, and lists publications and available research that will aid nonprofit organizations. There is also a section of relevant links divided into broad categories.

Internal Revenue Service
www.irs.gov
This U.S. government Web site has a section for charities and nonprofit organizations providing tax information and advice.

Internet Nonprofit Center
www.nonprofits.org
This is a body that offers information for and about nonprofit organizations in the United States. The site includes frequently asked questions, a nonprofit locator, a regular bulletin, and a library of nonprofit literature.

NonProfit Gateway
www.nonprofit.gov
This site has links to U.S. government information and services, and offers access to a database covering over 530,000 government Web pages.

ORGANIZATIONS

USA

Alliance for Nonprofit Management
1899 L Street NW, Suite 600, Washington, D.C., 20036
T: +1 202 955 8406
F: +1 202 721 0086
E: alliance@allianceonline.org
www.allianceonline.org
Founded in 1997 with over 450 members, the organizations and individuals belonging to the Alliance are devoted to building nonprofit organizations. This association works to increase the effectiveness of nonprofits and offers support services for nonprofit agencies.

National Council for Nonprofit Organizations
1030 15th Street, NW, Suite 870, Washington, D.C., 20005
T: +1 202 962 0322
F: +1 202 962 0321
E: ncna@ncna.org
www.ncna.org
The Council represents over 17,000 nonprofit groups. The association works toward advancing the role of the nonprofit organizations found in local communities. The NCNA supports both state and regional associations and is involved with legislation concerning nonprofit organizations.

Society for Nonprofit Organizations
5820 Canton Center Road, Suite165, Canton, Michigan, 48187
T: +1 734 451 3582 or 800 424 7367
F: +1 734 451 5935
E: snpo@danenet.org
http://danenet.danenet.org/snpo
This organization, founded in 1983, has more than 2,000 members. SNPO is dedicated to bringing together those who serve in the nonprofit world. Its mission is to provide an international forum for the exchange of information and ideas based on increasing awareness of and productivity within nonprofit organizations.

Europe

Charities Aid Foundation
25 Kings Hill Avenue, Kings Hill, West Malling, Kent, ME19 4TA, U.K.
T: +44 (0) 1732 520 000
F: +44 (0) 1732 520 001
E: enquiries@caf.charitynet.org
www.cafonline.org
The Foundation is an organization dedicated to helping build a robust, well-resourced, nonprofit sector and increase funding for nonprofit organizations. The Foundation provides charitable and financial support and advice to organizations and works to help donors invest their resources in the United Kingdom and overseas.

Charity Commission
Harmsworth House, 13–15 Bouverie Street, London, EC4Y 8DP, U.K.
T: +44 (0) 870 333 0123
F: +44 (0) 20 7674 2300
E: feedback@charity-commission.gov.uk
www.charity-commission.gov.uk
The Charity Commission is a governmental department that exists to support, supervise, and regulate the operation of charities registered in the United Kingdom. The Commission's aims are to help charities exploit their resources more effectively through the provision of advice and information, and to maintain public confidence in the integrity of registered charities.

National Council for Voluntary Organisations
Regent's Wharf, 8 All Saints Street, London, N1 9RL, U.K.
T: +44 (0) 20 7713 6161
F: +44 (0) 20 7713 6300
E: ncvo@ncvo-vol.org.uk
www.ncvo-vol.org.uk
This is an umbrella body for the voluntary sector in England. It lobbies government, the Charity Commission, the European Union, and other bodies, representing the interests of members and of the wider voluntary sector. It is involved in research and analysis relating to the voluntary sector and provides information and advice for voluntary organizations through its helpdesk, publications, events, and information networks.

International

Coalition of National Voluntary Organizations
301–75 Albert Street, Ontario, K1P 5E7, Canada
T: +1 613 238 1591
F: +1 613 238 5257
E: info@nvo-onb.ca
www.nvo-onb.ca
The Coalition consists of 135 Canadian organizations. It acts as a conduit of information and lobbies the government on behalf of voluntary organizations.

For More Information

Public Sector Management (pp. 2092–94)

"When money speaks, the truth keeps silent." (Anonymous)

ORGANIZATION AND ORGANIZATION STRUCTURE

BOOKS

Adaptive Enterprise: Creating and Leading Sense-and-respond Organizations
STEPHEN H. HAECKEL
Boston, Massachusetts: Harvard Business School Press, 1999
295pp ISBN: 0875848745
The author argues that in the Information Age, organizations must be able to adapt quickly to change. He outlines a "sense-and-respond" business model that can help companies cope with the unexpected by sensing changes in individual customer needs early and responding to them quickly. A step-by-step plan is mapped out, with examples and illustrations, for transforming organizations in accordance with this new model.

Corporate Tides: The Inescapable Laws of Organizational Structure
ROBERT FRITZ
San Francisco, California: Berrett-Koehler, 1996
274pp ISBN: 1881052885
The failure of so many organizational change programs, it is suggested, is due to a lack of understanding of the basic laws of organizational structure. The author examines the structural dynamics of organizations and the causes of structural conflict and oscillation. He outlines a structural approach to organization design and describes techniques that can be used for strategic planning, also giving consideration to the issues of vision, leadership, motivation, and the learning organization.

Crisis & Renewal: Meeting the Challenge of Organizational Change (The Management of Innovation and Change Series)
DAVID K. HURST
Boston, Massachusetts: Harvard Business School Press, 1995
229pp ISBN: 0875845827
This title concerns the restrictive nature of success and the way in which top companies and those within them in management positions, must develop and refresh their ideas in order for transition to take place.

An Experiential Approach to Organization Development 5th ed.
DON HARVEY, DONALD R. BROWN
Upper Saddle River, New Jersey: Prentice Hall, 2000
504pp (Prentice Hall International Editions)
ISBN: 013520495X
This text offers a practical and realistic approach to the study of organization development (OD). Through the application of a new paradigm—the OD Process Model—each of the stages of OD is described from the standpoint of its relationship to an overall program of change. The book is written primarily for students who are learning about organization development for the first time. The text relates the student to the real world through the use of numerous illustrations and company examples showing how OD is being applied in organizations today.

The Flexible Firm: Capability Management in Network Organizations
JULIAN BIRKINSHAW, PETER HAGSTROM, EDS.
New York: Oxford University Press, 2000
246pp ISBN: 0198296517
The Flexible Firm is based on research into five large Swedish organizations and a number of international firms. It discusses issues affecting capability development within the networked firm. Contents include: network relationships inside and outside the company, and the development of capabilities; managing relationships in the external network; innovation in the external network; and managing the internal network.

Generation to Generation: Life Cycles of the Family Business
KELIN E. GERSICK, ET AL.
Boston, Massachusetts: Harvard Business School Press, 1997
224pp ISBN: 087584555X
Intended as a comprehensive study of family businesses, this book examines the special dynamics and challenges facing these organizations in detail. It highlights the differences between family firms and public companies, and discusses issues specific to family businesses such as succession planning, managing relatives, and understanding the interactions between family, business, and ownership.

The Living Company
ARIE DE GEUS
Boston, Massachusetts: Harvard Business School Press, 1997
215pp ISBN: 087584782X
De Geus discusses the success elements of the few organizations that survive both long time periods and big changes, and aims to pinpoint the reasons for this achievement. A guide for managing companies over a long period of time, the book explores ideas from both a profit-oriented and a survival-based angle.

New Organizational Designs: Information Aspects
BOB TRAVICA
Stamford, Connecticut: Ablex, 1999
300pp ISBN: 1567504043
In focusing on new organizational designs, Travica devotes his attention to the following topics: the nontraditional organization; structural, cultural, and political aspects; information aspects; information technology; teamwork beyond lip service; dedifferentiation and detraditionalization.

Open Boundaries: Creating Business Innovation through Complexity
HOWARD SHERMAN, RON SCHULTZ
Cambridge, Massachusetts: Perseus, 1999
232pp ISBN: 0738201553
This book is a resource for people who want to get away from old and stale patterns of behavior in business. The authors use their knowledge of "adaptive systems" to demonstrate how, with a knowledge of these systems, a business environment can be improved in its day-to-day approach to work. The author helps readers to gain a deeper understanding of why they make certain choices and descisions, and how this is related to "adaptive systems."

Organizational Theory: Text and Cases 3rd ed.
GARETH R. JONES
Upper Saddle River, New Jersey: Prentice Hall, 2000
600pp ISBN: 0130183784
This comprehensive, up-to-date guide to theories of the organization covers the following areas: the organization, the organizational environment, the technological environment, managing organizational processes, and case studies in organizational theory.

The Organization in Crisis: Downsizing, Restructuring, and Privatization
RONALD J. BURKE, CARY L. COOPER, EDS.
Malden, Massachusetts: Blackwell Business, 2000

"We talk about organizations in terms not unlike those used by an Ubongi medicine man to discuss diseases."
(Herbert A. Simon)

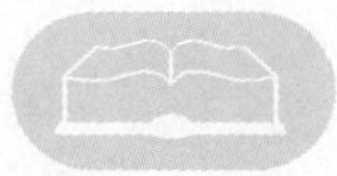

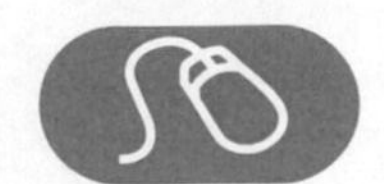

320pp ISBN: 0631212310
This study by international researchers and practitioners examines the implementation and impact of organizational change. Drawing on a mixture of research, theory, and practice, it explores key issues such as the new employment relationship, organization restructuring, the effects of downsizing, the role of privatization, and the revitalization of best practice, and proposes and discusses strategies for better managing these changes in the future.

Organization Modeling: Innovative Architectures for the 21st Century
JOSEPH MORABITO, IRA SACK, ANILKUMAR BHATE
Upper Saddle River, New Jersey: Prentice Hall, 1999
300pp ISBN: 0132575523
This book shows how the object-oriented modeling approach used in computer systems design can be used in conjunction with more traditional theories of organization design. The aim of the authors is to show IT professionals how to be better business people and show business people how to better marry technology and people systems.

Organization Theory and Design
RICHARD L. DAFT
Cincinnati, Ohio: South-Western Publishing, 2000
672pp ISBN: 0324021003
This book provides an overview of the field of organization theory, discusses the basics of how well an organization's design matches its purpose, and looks at how technology influences design, the difference between manufacturing and service company designs, and the impact of ethical values and company culture on design.

Organization Theory: Modern, Symbolic, and Postmodern Perspectives
MARY JO HATCH
New York: Oxford University Press, 1997
416pp ISBN: 0198774907
Organization Theory offers a clear and comprehensive introduction to the study of organizations and an appreciation of the different perspectives that have contributed to our knowledge of them. Part 1 introduces the multiperspective approach. Part 2 explores the ways in which organizations can be analyzed as entities within an environment, subjects of strategic action, technologies, social structures, cultures, and physical structures. Part 3 covers topics of central importance to organization theory, including decision making, power, conflict, control, and internal change.

Path of Least Resistance for Managers: Designing Organizations to Succeed
ROBERT FRITZ
San Francisco, California: Publishers' Group West, 1999
237pp ISBN: 1576750655
Drawing upon ideas of energy flow in science, the author explains how to redesign an organization or team for success. He argues that managers are far more likely to succeed when introducing structural changes if they take structural laws into account. He examines four critical elements: moving the organization from wasteful oscillating patterns to successful advancement; managing strategy to support business; "composing" the organization to support business; and aligning people to the spiritual purpose of the organization.

Re-creating the Corporation: A Design of Organizations for the 21st Century
RUSSELL LINCOLN ACKOFF
New York: Oxford University Press, 1999
352pp ISBN: 0195123875
Ackoff makes a case for developing a systems view of organizations and underlines the importance of using systems thinking skills when re-creating a company. The book includes discussion of how to make sense of the chaos that is a part of any system, how to determine aims, and how to achieve them. The author emphasizes the need for incorporating as much democracy and flexibility as possible and warns against the quick-fix mentality.

Surfing the Edge of Chaos: The Laws of Nature and the New Laws of Business
RICHARD T. PASCALE, MARK MILLEMANN, LINDA GIOJA
New York: Crown Publishing, 2000
320pp ISBN: 0812933168
Starting from the thesis that business, like nature, is a living system, the authors proceed to apply four principles of the life sciences to business organizations: equilibrium is death; innovation takes place on the edge of chaos; self organization and emergence occur naturally; organizations can only be disturbed, not directed. These principles are illustrated through in-depth case studies of Sears, Roebuck & Co, Monsanto, Hewlett Packard, Sun Microsystems, Royal Dutch Steel, and the U.S. Army. Ultimately, they suggest, businesses, like species, either respond to change and evolve or get left behind and become extinct.

Winning through Innovation: A Practical Guide to Leading Organizational Change and Renewal
MICHAEL L. TUSHMAN, CHARLES A. O'REILLY III
Boston, Massachusetts: Harvard Business School Press, 1997
247pp ISBN: 0875845797
This book examines how leadership, culture, and organizational architectures can both facilitate and, at times, impede innovation. The authors demonstrate how to identify today's critical managerial problems, use culture and commitment to promote innovation and implement strategy, and deal with changing innovation requirements as organizations evolve.

MAGAZINES

International Journal of Organization Theory and Behavior
ISSN: 1093-4537
Marcel Dekker, Inc.
270 Madison Avenue, New York, 10016–0602
T: +1 212 696 9000
F: +1 212 685 4540
www.dekker.com
This is an international journal for both academics and practitioners with interests in a number of aspects of organization science. The areas it covers include motivation, organizational development, group/team theory and behavior, and the effects of culture on organizations.

Journal of Organizational Change Management
ISSN: 0953-4814
MCB University Press Ltd.
60/62 Toller Lane, Bradford, West Yorkshire, BD8 9BY, U.K.
T: +44 (0) 1274 777700
F: +44 (0) 1274 785200
www.emeraldinsight.com/jocm.htm
International in scope and aimed at both academics and practicing managers, the *Journal of Organizational Change Management* covers areas such as organizational learning, the psychology of change, and entrepreneurship within organizations.

Journal of Organizational Excellence
ISSN: 1531-1864
John Wiley
Wiley InterScience Coordinator, Subscriptions Department, 605 Third Avenue, New York, 10158–0012
T: +1 800 825 7550
F: +1 212 850 6021
www.interscience.wiley.com
Formerly called *National Productivity Review*, this journal is published four times per year. It provides readers with the latest information on new organizational techniques, trends, and strategies. This journal will aid any business professional looking to find new and innovative ways to make their organization succeed.

"Corporate insiders. . .can seldom transform an organization beset by inertia." (John P. Kotter)

Organizational Dynamics
ISSN: 0090–2616
Elsevier Science
Regional Sales Office, Customer Support Department, P.O. Box 945, New York, 10159–0945
T: +1 212 633 3730
F: +1 212 633 3680
www.elsevier.com
Organizational Dynamics is an international journal that aims to link academic research with management practice. It examines both organizational behavior and the strategic management and human resources management practices that influence organizations.

Organization—Interdisciplinary Journal of Organization Theory and Society
ISSN: 1350–5084
Sage Publications, Inc.
2455 Teller Road, Thousand Oaks, California, 91320
T: +1 805 499 0721
F: +1 805 499 0871
www.sagepub.com
This international journal is intended for those with a professional or academic interest in organization studies. Its contents typically cover areas such as organization theory, human resource management and organizational behavior, organizational psychology, the virtual organization, and globalization.

INTERNET

Association for the Management of Organization Design
www.amod2000.org
The Association for the Management of Organization Design is a nonprofit professional association which aims to promote organization design. Its activities include sponsoring an annual conference, publishing monographs, supporting research, providing training, and recognizing individuals who have made an outstanding contribution to the field.

Organization Development Network
www.odnetwork.org
This site is the home for Organization Development Network, a professional association of organization development practitioners working in the fields of business and education. The site provides information on educational opportunities, job listings, conferences, and events.

ORGANIZATIONS

USA

Academy of Management
P.O. Box 3020, Briarcliff Manor, New York, 10510–3020
T: +1 914 923 2607
F: +1 914 923 2615
E: academy@aom.pace.edu
www.aom.pace.edu
The Academy of Management is a professional association of scholars dedicated to knowing more about management and organizations. The key aim of the Academy is to enhance the profession by advancing the scholarship of management and encouraging the professional progress of its members. Membership comprises scholars and practitioners with scholarly interests from business, government, and nonprofit organizations.

American Management Association
1601 Broadway, New York, 10019
T: +1 212 586 8100
F: +1 212 903 8168
E: customerservice@amanet.org
www.amanet.org
A nonprofit, member-based association, the AMA offers seminars, training, conferences, executive forums, councils, and research on a variety of topics, including organization management. It also operates a publishing division that has published several books on organizational theory. The association offers both corporate and individual membership options; membership includes reduced pricing on AMA resources and access to members-only information on management news.

The Association of Management/ International Association of Management
P.O. Box 64841, Virginia Beach, Virginia, 23469–4841
T: +1 757 482 2273
F: +1 757 482 0325
E: AoMgt@infi.net
www.aom-iaom.org
The AoM/IaoM is a nonprofit professional association dedicated to advancing management theory in a variety of fields, including organizational theory. It offers conferences, journals, and online publications on topics including organizational behavior, organizational structure, organizational theory, organizational change and development, organizational communication, organizational culture and climate, organizations as political systems, emerging organizational forms, and organizational management applications.

For More Information

- **Business Process Reengineering (pp. 1921–23)**
- **Corporate Strategy (pp. 1944–46)**
- **Flexible Working/Teleworking/ Homeworking (pp. 1984–86)**
- **Learning Organization (pp. 2024–26)**

OUTSOURCING

BOOKS

Business Process Outsourcing: Process, Strategies, and Contracts
John K. Halvey, Barbara Murphy Melby
New York: John Wiley, 1999
416pp ISBN: 047134821X
This book provides a guide for businesses looking to outsource some of their business functions. The topics it deals with address the process involved in contracting out key services, including the request for proposal (RFP) and selecting and contracting with an outsourcing vendor.

Inside Outsourcing: The Insider's Guide to Managing Strategic Sourcing
Charles L. Gay, James Essinger
Naperville, Illinois: Nicholas Brealey, 2000
256pp ISBN: 1857882040
The authors together offer an insider's knowledge of the realities of managing the outsourcing process. The topics they explore are: the decision making process; the different types of outsourcing (they also include a discussion of insourcing); cosourcing and partnering; planning; and selecting service providers. They also discuss various legal aspects and human resources issues. A survey of the outsourcing practices of 500 of the United Kingdom's largest organizations completes the package.

Outsourcing in Brief
Mike Johnson
Woburn, Massachusetts: Butterworth-Heinemann, 1997
200pp (In Brief Series)
ISBN: 0750628766
This practical guide presents an overview of outsourcing and reviews the pros and cons of

"A verbal contract isn't worth the paper it's written on."

(Samuel Goldwyn)

the technique. The way to go about outsourcing is explained, and checklists and case studies illustrate specific issues and options.

Strategic Outsourcing: A Structured Approach to Outsourcing Decisions and Initiatives
Maurice F. Greaver II
New York: AMACOM, 1999
314pp ISBN: 0814404340
This book provides a thorough guide for managers who face the task of outsourcing business functions. Contents include the rationale for outsourcing, identifying functions that can be outsourced versus those key services that should remain in-house, and the process of requesting proposals. The book also covers how to select and contract with vendors for outsourced services.

Turning Lead into Gold: The Demystification of Outsourcing
Peter Bendor-Samuel
Provo, Utah: Executive Excellence Publishing, 2000
249pp ISBN: 1890009873
In this practical approach to outsourcing, the author explains the basic principles of the concept and explores ways in which it can be effectively applied within a company. Drawing on his knowledge of major corporations such as Pricewaterhouse Coopers, Bendor-Samuel provides examples of successful outsourcing as support for his study.

INTERNET

Network Outsourcing Association
www.noa.co.uk
This site provides access to recent articles by members and details of Association events. It also has a members-only section.

Outsourcing Center
www.outsourcing-center.com
This Web site provides comprehensive information and links regarding outsourcing. Its content includes industry-specific outsourcing information, research, outsourcing processes, and an online journal. It also provides answers to FAQs, and material on suppliers, legal issues, and jobs.

Outsourcing Research Center
www.cio.com/forums/outsourcing
The site provides online access to recent articles and gives details of forthcoming events.

TechWeb Business Technology Network
www.techweb.com
This site focuses on recent news and articles on IT outsourcing, plus links to events.

The Outsourcing Institute
www.outsourcing.com
The Outsourcing Institute is a professional association providing information and networking resources related to outsourcing. Its Web site offers information on the outsourcing process, including needs assessment and the selection of service providers. It also has information targeted at buyers and sellers of outsourcing services. Registration is required for some information; online membership is free.

Virtual Corporations and Outsourcing
www.brint.com
Recent articles on outsourcing can be sourced from this site.

ORGANIZATIONS

USA

The Outsourcing Institute
Jericho Atrium, 500 N. Broadway, Suite 141, Jericho, New York, 11753
T: +1 516 681 0066
F: +1 516 938 1839
E: customerservice@outsourcing.com
www.outsourcing.com
This professional body, founded in 1993, provides outsourcing professionals worldwide with access to a business-to-business marketplace and an independent advisory network as well as with information and education on outsourcing best practice. Membership is free.

Europe

Network Outsourcing Association
Martyn Hart, Chair
Keswick House, 207 Anerley Road, London, SE20 8ER, U.K.
T: +44 (0) 20 8778 9449
F: +44 (0) 20 8778 8402
E: admin@noa.co.uk
www.noa.co.uk
The Association is an independent body, formed in the early 1990s, that acts as a forum for the business technology outsourcing community. Its membership is made up of U.K. and other companies with experience in outsourcing, and suppliers and consultants who support the industry.

For More Information

☆ **Facilities Management (pp. 179–80)**
☆ **Outsourcing (pp. 89–90)**
✔ **Deciding Whether to Outsource (pp. 490–91)**
Facilities Management (pp. 1980–82)

PACKAGING

BOOKS

Fifty Trade Secrets of Great Design Packaging
Stafford Cliff
Gloucester, Massachusetts: Rockport, 1999
224pp ISBN: 1564965996
This international collection of 50 outstanding packaging designs covers a broad selection of products and approaches. Each of the designs is individually profiled, outlining the challenges and problems each designer faced with the particular product. The case studies document the packaging design process and include discussion of new materials and methods of construction.

The Marketer's Guide to Successful Package Design
Herbert M. Meyers, Murray J. Lubliner
New York: McGraw-Hill/NTC, 1998
320pp ISBN: 0844234389
A guide for product marketers, this book explores the elements of marketing and design that can lead to successful packaging results. The authors' approach to the subject is analytical, including discussions on the research and planning involved in launching a new design.

Packaging Design 8
Heinke Jenssen, Michael Porciello, B. Martin Pedersen, eds.
New York: Graphis U.S., 2000
256pp ISBN: 1888001879
This resource guide offers a collection of significant work produced in the field of packaging design and product presentation between 1997 and 2000. It presents a wide array of products including household items, food and beverages, industrial products, and cosmetics.

The Packaging Designer's Book of Patterns 2nd ed.
Laszlo Roth, George L. Wybenga
New York: John Wiley, 2000
608pp ISBN: 0471385042

"I do not want the company to become a mass production line."
(al-Bu Said)

This book features over 500 patterns for paper packaging. Folding cartons, trays, tubes, sleeves, wraps, folders, corrugated containers, rigid paper boxes, and point-of-purchase displays are featured and ready for application on 100% recyclable paper products. An interesting history of papermaking is included in the introduction.

Packaging Graphics and Design
Renee Phillips
Gloucester, Massachusetts: Rockport, 2001
188pp ISBN: 1564968170
This is an international collection of 250 outstanding package and label designs. This color volume incorporates the work of top designers and covers a myriad of products. These award-winning designs exemplify the designers' ability to appeal to the customer and encourage purchase.

Packaging in the Environment
Geoffrey Levy, ed.
New York: Aspen Publishers, 1992
288pp ISBN: 0751400912
This book appraises the key environmental issues for packaging and how they affect trends and developments within the industry. It discusses and compares the relative environmental merits of different packaging materials and systems, while reviewing the action being taken to address these issues. It also considers legislative and regulatory developments worldwide.

The Perfect Package: How to Add Value through Graphic Design
Catharine M. Fishel
Gloucester, Massachusetts: Rockport, 2000
160pp ISBN: 1564966232
This book is a collection of 32 graphic design success stories. The author maintains that packaging design should do more than attract attention—it should add value to the design. Many designs have become permanent cultural fixtures and others have become collectible for the art of the design. The featured examples from around the world include Joe Boxer, IKEA, Volkswagen, Victoria's Secret, Harley-Davidson, Got Milk?, Boy Scouts of America, Miller Genuine Draft, Target, and Altoids.

MAGAZINES

Advanced Packaging
ISSN: 1521-3323
PennWell
P.O. Box 3425, Northbrook, Illinois, 60065-3425
T: +1 847 559 7500
F: +1 847 291 4816
http://ap.pennnet.com
AP is a monthly magazine with news and features about packaging materials, technology, and processes. Much of the information is available from the Web site.

Packaging Business
ISSN: 1360-8282
CMP Information Ltd.
Sovereign Way, Tonbridge, Kent, TN9 1RW, U.K.
T: +44 (0) 1732 377486
F: +44 (0) 1732 353328
www.dotpackaging.com
Aimed at business people within the packaging industry, this newsletter offers market intelligence, company profiles, and information on market research reports.

Packaging Innovation
ISSN: 1365-5663
CMP Information Ltd.
Sovereign Way, Tonbridge, Kent, TN9 1RW, U.K.
T: +44 (0) 1732 377486
F: +44 (0) 1732 353328
www.dotpackaging.com
Produced for packaging development personnel, packaging technologists, consultants, and research and development institutes, this newsletter focuses on innovative developments in technology, materials, and processes.

Packaging Magazine
ISSN: 1461-4200
CMP Information Ltd.
Sovereign Way, Tonbridge, Kent, TN9 1RW, U.K.
T: +44 (0) 1732 377486
F: +44 (0) 1732 353328
www.dotpackaging.com
This journal provides regular coverage of the issues facing professionals and decision makers in the packaging industry today. It contains news from the United Kingdom, Europe, and the rest of the world relating to business, market trends, product and machinery developments, and environmental issues.

Packaging News
ISSN: 0030-9133
Quantum Business Media
Quantum House, 19 Scarbrook Road, Croydon, CR9 1LX, U.K.
T: +44 (0) 20 8565 4200
F: +44 (0) 20 8565 4202
www.qpp.co.uk
This magazine, produced for packaging professionals, covers the latest industry news, product/brand design, materials, printing, machinery, and labels and labeling.

Packaging Today International
ISSN: 1470-6008
Angel Business Communications Ltd.
Kingsland House, 361 City Road, London, EC1V 1PQ, U.K.
T: +44 (0) 20 7417 7400
F: +44 (0) 20 7417 7500
www.packagingtoday.co.uk
This is a European journal focusing on all aspects of the packaging industry, including legislation, the influence of consolidation, cost-effective production methods, and the changing face of retailing in the packaging industry.

INTERNET

Environmental Packaging International
www.enviro-pac.com
Sponsored by a consulting firm specializing in compliance with state and international environmental packaging and product laws, the site provides a list of services, industry news, and links to other sites.

Packaging Business
www.packagingbusiness.com
Sponsored by a private company in the packaging industry, the site offers industry news, discussions, classifieds, job fair information, and links to other sites.

Packaging Digest
www.packagingdigest.com
This site contains articles from current and past issues of *Packaging Digest*, together with other information resources including news and reports of developments in packaging materials, machinery, technology, and market trends from around the world.

Packaging Network
www.packagingnetwork.com
This site is primarily a marketplace that also provides news, access to a library, a discussion forum, trade publications, and a job search. Site visitors may buy, sell, and advertise online. A free e-newsletter is also available.

Packaging Strategies
www.packstrat.com
This site provides a newsletter, articles, news, a product guide, and a calendar of events.

Packaging World
www.packworld.com
This online packaging magazine from the United States has databases of topical articles on machinery, products, companies, design, materials, and regulations, along with information about jobs, events, associations, and schools connected with the packaging industry.

"Any color you like as long as it's black." (Henry Ford)

ORGANIZATIONS

USA

Institute of Packaging Professionals
1601 North Bond Street, Suite 101, Naperville, Illinois, 60563
T: +1 630 544 5050
F: +1 630 544 5055
E: info@iopp.net
www.iopp.org
This membership organization for the packaging industry offers its members a range of benefits that includes events, education, career development, and publications.

Europe

Institute of Packaging
Sysonby Lodge, Nottingham Road, Melton Mowbray, Leicestershire, LE13 0NU, U.K.
T: +44 (0) 1664 500055
F: +44 (0) 1664 564164
E: info@iop.co.uk
www.iop.co.uk
The aim of the Institute is to advance public education in, and improve the technology of, packaging in all its aspects, in particular by promoting the education and training of persons engaged or interested in packaging as an occupation.

The Packaging Federation
Suite 2.9, Vigilant House, 120 Wilton Road, London, SW1V 1JZ, U.K.
T: +44 (0) 20 7808 7217
F: +44 (0) 20 7808 7218
E: enquiries@packagingfedn.co.uk
www.packagingfedn.co.uk
The Federation is a trade organization representing all the material streams within the industry. Its aims are to improve significantly the way in which the industry is perceived and to protect the interests of packaging manufacturers through properly managed lobbying and public relations programs.

International

World Packaging Organization
P.O. Box 861588, 4143 Weeks Drive, Warrenton, Virginia, 20187
T: +1 540 928 2092
F: +1 703 814 4961
E: wpo@pkgmatters.com
www.packinfo-world.org/wpo/wpohome
The aims of the WPO include: promoting the development of packaging technology, science, and engineering; stimulating the development of packaging skills and expertise; advising on the formation and operation of national packaging organizations and institutes; and providing information on sources of packaging knowledge, education, and training.

PERFORMANCE APPRAISAL

BOOKS

The Appraisal Checklist: How to Help Your Team Get the Results You Both Want 2nd ed.
BRIAN WATLING
Philadelphia, Pennsylvania: Trans-Atlantic Publications, 2000
152pp (Smarter Solutions Series)
ISBN: 0273644831
This book offers both new and experienced managers a ready reference source, training manual, and self-development tool that will help them gain more edge through performance appraisal. It is designed to be dipped into as required; each chapter could stand alone in covering its topic area. Bullet points, golden rules, practical illustrations, and checklists enliven the text and summarize the contents.

The Complete Guide to Performance Appraisal
DICK GROTE
New York: AMACOM, 1996
400pp ISBN: 0814403131
From his personal knowledge of performance appraisals, Grote has compiled this reference for managers in both large and small businesses, whether they are highly experienced or relative beginners. The book provides practical guidelines for initiating successful performance appraisals, starting with the basics.

How to Do a Superior Performance Appraisal
WILLIAM S. SWAN
New York: John Wiley, 1991
223pp ISBN: 0471514683
This is a helpful guide for managers and appraisees on how to get the best out of appraisals.

Manager's Portfolio of Model Performance Evaluations: Ready-to-use Performance Appraisals Covering All Employee Functions
BRANDON TOROPOV
Upper Saddle River, New Jersey: Prentice Hall, 2001
431pp ISBN: 0130910309
This book offers more than 100 sample evaluations, as well as advice on topics including termination and nondiscriminatory evaluation techniques. It deals with strategies for employees at all levels and includes samples on CD-ROM as well as in print.

Managing Individual Performance: A Systematic Seven-step Approach to Enhancing Employee Performance and Results
KIERAN BALDWIN
Oxford: How To Books, 1999
157pp ISBN: 1857034384
The aim of this plain-language text is to give managers guidance on performance management, using a learning approach that is designed to support the application of acquired theory in working practice. Following his own "seven step" framework, the author goes through the processes involved, illustrating each chapter with case studies based on three characters from one fictitious company.

Managing Performance: Goals, Feedback, Coaching, Recognition
JENNY HILL
Burlington, Vermont: Ashgate Publishing Company, 1997
160pp (Gower Management Workbooks)
ISBN: 0566077396
This lively workbook for managers aims to support a performance approach that encourages organizational communication and learning. Its four parts focus on setting effective goals, feedback skills, coaching and gaining others' involvement, and rewarding contributions. Though set out in units to match the 1997 MCI Management Standards Level 4, the book is a worthwhile read outside the Standards context, and offers many interesting ideas and activities.

Managing Performance Reviews: How to Ensure Your Appraisals Improve Individual Performance and Organizational Results 4th ed.
NIGEL HUNT
Oxford: How To Books, 1999
168pp ISBN: 1857034880
This book sets out a helpful and detailed framework of guidelines for managers who conduct performance reviews or are developing review systems. Its contents include: sample task analyses, job descriptions, and person specifications; an example of a supervisor's

"Everyone has peak performance potential. You just need to know where they are coming from and meet them there."
(Kenneth Blanchard)

ratings questionnaire; and performance review validity questionnaires for both reviewee and reviewer.

Performance Appraisal: One More Time
John D. Drake
Menlo Park, California: Crisp Publications, 1998
80pp ISBN: 1560524421
The author addresses the need to consider performance appraisal as an ongoing process rather than an isolated activity. The book emphasizes that communication and trust are more important elements of the process than rating mechanisms or scoring methods.

Performance Appraisal: State of the Art in Practice
James W. Smither, ed.
San Francisco, California: Jossey-Bass, 1998
576pp ISBN: 0787909459
This book provides an overview of the performance appraisal process, dealing with appraisals at a strategic level and analyzing the latest research and illustrating it with examples of how the theories work in practice. It examines performance appraisals in the context of pay and performance plans, organizational culture, and motivational strategies.

The Performance Challenge
Jerry W. Gilley, Nathaniel W. Boughton, Ann Maycunich
Cambridge, Massachusetts: Perseus, 2000
256pp ISBN: 0738201618
This book aims to make real the often-quoted statement: "our people are our greatest asset." The authors introduce their Performance Alignment Model, a practical framework that human resource professionals and functional managers can use to align business goals, customer expectations, performance management philosophies, employee coaching practices, and compensation and rewards systems. The end result should be more productive, motivated, and profitable organizations.

Performance Management
Robert Bacal
New York: McGraw-Hill, 1998
160pp (The Briefcase Series)
ISBN: 0070718660
This book aims to help managers get top performance and value from employees, and emphasizes the importance of creating relationships and ensuring effective communication. Its chapters focus on preparation, planning, communication, data gathering, appraisal and review processes, diagnosis, and improvement. Some innovative variations are discussed and a case study helps to pull ideas together at the end.

Powerful Performance Appraisals: How to Set Expectations and Work Together to Improve Performance
Karen McKirchy
Franklin Lakes, New Jersey: Career Press, 1998
128pp ISBN: 1564143678
This book aims to clarify the key elements that make a successful performance appraisal. The author provides simple guidelines combined with genuine appraisal examples, to help an employer pinpoint any potential issues and motivate his/her employees to greater goal focus.

Powering Up Performance Management: An Integrated Approach to Getting the Best from Your People
Richard Hale, Peter Whitlam
Burlington, Vermont: Ashgate Publishing Company, 2000
240pp ISBN: 056608189X
Intended especially for senior "organizational architects," this book proposes a holistic approach to performance management based on behavioral competencies that state specifically what people are expected to do. It emphasizes the importance of measurement and presents case studies drawn from the authors' consultancy experience and action research. The appendices include 50 competency descriptions and development ideas.

MAGAZINES

Human Resource Executive
LRP Publications, 747 Dreshers Road, Suite 500, Horsham, Pennsylvania, 19044–0980
T: +1 215 784 0910
F: +1 215 784 0870
www.hrexecutive.com
Targeted at upper-level HR practitioners, *Human Resource Executive* is published 16 times per year. It offers case studies, profiles of successful HR managers, and news, covering a number of HR topics, including performance appraisal.

Team Performance Management
ISSN: 1352–7592
MCB University Press Ltd.
60/62 Toller Lane, Bradford, West Yorkshire, BD8 9BY, U.K.
T: +44 (0) 1274 777700
F: +44 (0) 1274 785200
www.emeraldinsight.com/tpm.htm
Subscriptions to *Team Performance Management* cover eight printed issues a year and online access to current and previous volumes via Emerald Fulltext. The journal aims to support managers, HR or quality professionals, consultants, and academics in implementing and developing work team performance. Its articles include case studies, application papers, and reviews of theories and techniques.

Workforce
ISSN: 1092-8332
ACC Communications, Inc.
245 Fischer Avenue B-2, Costa Mesa, California, 92626
T: +1 714 751 1883
F: +1 714 751 4106
www.workforce.com
A monthly magazine, *Workforce* targets HR practitioners with content on a variety of topics, including: performance appraisal, case studies, trend analysis, and commentary on the social and economic effects of HR practices.

INTERNET

Good Performance
www.goodperformance.com
Sponsored by a performance-appraisal software company, the site provides news, a message board, recommended reading, articles, information about seminars, and performance-appraisal software demonstrations.

Performance Measurement Association 
http://groups.yahoo.com/group/pmaforum
This site is the discussion forum for the Performance Measurement Association, on which anyone can post PM-related questions and utilize networking opportunities.

Performaworks
www.performaworks.com
In the PM Library (see Knowledge Center), there is a series of papers by Performaworks psychologists, addressing challenges and issues in the performance management area (registration required).

Zigon Performance Measurement Resources
www.zigonperf.com/performance.html
This Zigon site offers resources for free online viewing that include sample performance measures, links to related sites, bibliographies, a free newsletter, and articles by Jack Zigon on performance measures and management. Registration is required for some of these services.

ORGANIZATIONS

USA

American Society for Training and Development
1640 King Street, Box 1443, Alexandria, Virginia, 22313–2043
T: +1 703 683 8100
F: +1 703 683 1523
E: customercare@astd.org
www.astd.org
An association of workplace learning and performance professionals, ASTD's members come from multinational corporations, medium-sized and small businesses, government, academia, consulting firms, and product and service suppliers. It offers research and analysis, conferences, expositions, seminars, and publications. Though its primary focus is training and development, it also addresses issues of performance appraisal.

International Society for Performance Improvement
Suite 260, 1400 Spring Street, Silver Spring, Maryland, 20910
T: +1 301 587 8570
F: +1 301 587 8573
E: info@ispi.org
www.ispi.org
The ISPI is an international association for improving workplace productivity and performance; it has members throughout the United States, Canada, and 40 other countries. It aims to develop and recognize members' proficiency, and advocates the use of Human Performance Technology, a systematic approach that can be applied to individuals, small groups, and large organizations.

Society for Human Resource Management
1800 Duke Street, Alexandria, Virginia, 22314
T: +1 703 548 3440
F: +1 703 535 6490
E: shrm@shrm.org
www.shrm.org
A membership organization for HR professionals, the Society for Human Resource Management offers education and information services, conferences and seminars, online services, and publications on numerous HR issues. It has covered performance appraisal extensively in both research papers and magazine articles.

Europe

Centre for Business Performance
Cranfield School of Management, Cranfield, Bedfordshire, MK42 0AL, U.K.
T: +44 (0) 1234 751122 ext 2433
F: +44 (0) 1234 757409
E: cbp@cranfield.ac.uk
www.cranfield.ac.uk/som/cbp
The Centre focuses on applied research and knowledge transfer involving practical tools and concepts underpinned by high-quality academic research. It organizes courses in business performance measurement, produces publications, offers a forum and networking opportunities, and initiates research projects. It also runs the Performance Measurement Association (see below).

Institute of Management
Management House, Cottingham Road, Corby, Northamptonshire, NN17 1TT, U.K.
T: +44 (0) 1536 204222
F: +44 (0) 1536 201651
E: mic.enquiries@imgt.org.uk
www.inst-mgt.org.uk
Formed in 1992, the Institute of Management (IM) is the largest organization for professional management in the United Kingdom, representing almost 89,000 individual members and embracing 560 corporate partners. It exists to promote the art and science of management through research, publications, the provision of information services, networking opportunities, education and training, and the objective presentation of managers' views and opinions.

Performance Measurement Association
Centre for Business Performance, Cranfield School of Management, Cranfield, Bedfordshire, MK42 0AL, U.K.
T: +44 (0) 1234 751122
F: +44 (0) 1234 757409
www.performanceportal.org
The Performance Measurement Association (PMA) is a voluntary global network organized by the Centre for Business Performance at Cranfield School of Management. It has a multi-disciplinary constituency, led by a board of academics from the performance measurement and management fields. Its Web site is a valuable resource that contains a database of researchers, key references, links, the PMA's *Perspectives on Performance* newsletter, a discussion forum, and details of planned conferences.

The Chartered Institute of Personnel and Development
CIPD House, Camp Road, London, SW19 4UX, U.K.
T: +44 (0) 20 8971 9000
F: +44 (0) 20 8263 3333
E: cipd@cipd.co.uk
www.cipd.co.uk
The CIPD is a professional body for personnel and human resource management specialists. It offers qualifications and developmental support in these fields and also makes publications, courses, and information available to members. It treats performance appraisal and performance management as one of its central areas of concern within the wider field of personnel management.

The Industrial Society
Peter Runge House, 3 Carlton House Terrace, London, SW1Y 5DG, U.K.
T: +44 (0) 20 7479 1000
F: +44 (0) 20 7479 1111
E: customercentre@indsoc.co.uk
www.indsoc.co.uk
The Industrial Society is an independent body with over 80 years, experience in management development and training. The Society operates under the belief that business success goes hand in hand with fair management practices. The services offered to members include an information service and employment law helpline, a publishing program of books, research reports, and videos, a training and consulting service, and video products in the area of performance management and performance appraisal.

The Institute for Employment Studies
Mantell Building, Falmer, Brighton, East Sussex, BN1 9RF, U.K.
T: +44 (0) 1273 686751
F: +44 (0) 1273 690430
E: enquiries@employment-studies.co.uk
www.employment-studies.co.uk
The Institute is an independent, nonprofit, international center for research and consulting that focuses on HR issues and works closely with government departments, employers in the manufacturing, public, and service sectors, agencies, professional and employee bodies, and foundations. Its work also covers performance management.

For More Information

- ✔ Coaching for Better Performance (pp. 344–45)
- ✔ Conducting a Performance Appraisal (pp. 346–47)
- Coaching, Counseling, and Mentoring (pp. 1925–28)
- Motivation (pp. 2050–52)
- Personnel Management and HR Management (pp. 2067–71)

"Learning and performance will become one and the same thing." (Peter Block)

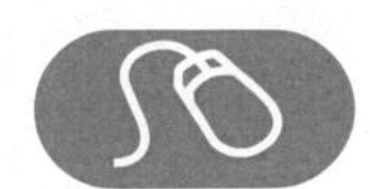

Personnel Management and HR Management

BOOKS

Aligning Human Resources and Business Strategy
Linda Holbeche
Woburn, Massachusetts: Butterworth-Heinemann, 1999
461pp ISBN: 075064477X
This book gives tools and case studies to help HR strategies deliver key business objectives and quantify the benefits of an effective people strategy. Profiles of top strategies and companies are included.

The Global HR Manager
Pat Joynt, Bob Morton eds.
London: Institute of Personnel and Development, 1999
267pp ISBN: 0852928157
This collection of articles by leading researchers and practitioners in the field of international human resource management aims to bring together the latest thinking, research and practice. The context of increasing globalization in business is reviewed and the challenges faced and contribution to be made by HR managers are explored. Areas covered include international recruitment, selection and assessment, international compensation, and the management of international teams.

Handbook of Human Resource Management Practice 7th ed.
Michael Armstrong
Milford, Connecticut: Kogan Page, 1999
922pp ISBN: 074942964X
This comprehensive textbook provides an overview of current trends in human resource management and includes sections on organizational behavior, work and employment, employee resourcing, performance management, human resource development, reward management, employee relations, and health and safety. A third of the book has been rewritten for this edition to reflect new areas in HR and the outcome of recent research surveys. New chapters focus on the psychological contract, selection interviewing and organizational culture.

Human Resource Management
Barry Cushway
Milford, Connecticut: Kogan Page in association with PriceWaterhouseCoopers, 1999
232pp (Kogan Page Fast Track MBA Series)
ISBN: 0749411724
This is a practical, up-to-date guide to the effective use of human resources. Illustrated throughout with cases and examples of current best practice, this detailed introduction to the topic includes information on: human resource planning, job analysis, recruitment and selection, training and development, reward systems, performance management, employee relations and recording systems.

Human Resource Management 4th ed.
Derek Torrington, Laura Hall
Upper Saddle River, New Jersey: Prentice Hall, 1998
717pp ISBN: 0136265324
This textbook provides a comprehensive and practical introduction to personnel functions and processes. Brief case studies and illustrations support discussion of the key issues.

Human Resource Management 8th ed.
Gary Dessler
Upper Saddle River, New Jersey: Prentice Hall, 1999
699pp ISBN: 0130141240
This is a textbook for students on personnel and human resource management courses and for practicing managers with a need for a comprehensive review on personnel management concepts and techniques. The broad areas covered include recruitment and placement, training and development, compensation, labor relations and employee security, and international HRM.

Human Resource Management: The New Agenda
Paul R. Sparrow, Mick Marchington, eds.
Upper Saddle River, New Jersey: Financial Times Prentice Hall, 1998
346pp ISBN: 0273628232
This work focuses on the changing nature, context, and role of human resource management. Part one examines the impact on the employment relationship and psychological contracts of technological and structural change in organizations. Part two looks at the theme of partnerships between employers and employees. The focus of part three is flexibility, and attention is given to changing work practices, benefits, motivation and commitment, employee development, and the impact of legislation. The final chapter addresses the future of the field of human resource management.

Human Resource Strategy: Formulation Implementation and Impact
Peter Bamberge, Ilan Meshoulam
Thousand Oaks, California: Sage, 2000
214pp ISBN: 0761914250
In this text exploring the history, development and impact of human resource strategy, research on the subject is reviewed and its implications for management and for HR practice are discussed. Chapters focusing on strategies and their effectiveness include best practice cases and illustrations.

International HRM: Contemporary Issues in Europe
Chris Brewster, Hilary Harris, eds.
New York: Routledge, 1998
320pp ISBN: 0415194903
This collection of edited papers from European experts in the field covers all aspects of international human resource management. A detailed introduction is followed by articles addressing key issues including the strategic role of HRM in staffing, reward management and performance management, and the dynamics of culture and gender in international management.

Introduction to Human Resource Management
Ashly Pinnington, Tony Edwards
New York: Oxford University Press, 2000
305pp ISBN: 0198775431
This textbook provides a comprehensive introduction to human resource management (HRM). The four parts cover definitions, the context of HRM, managing human resources, and future developments. It is intended for undergraduate business students and MBA students.

Personnel Management: A Comprehensive Guide to Theory and Practice 3rd ed.
Stephen Bach, Keith Sisson eds.
Malden, Massachusetts: Blackwell Business, 2000
402pp ISBN: 0631212922
The revised edition of this popular text provides a challenging analysis of recent thinking and developments. Original contributions from leading experts cover personnel management in the lean organization and the extended organization, as well as the main issues in each of the key areas

"Chief executives repeatedly fail to recognize that for communication to be effective, it must be two-way."
(Robert McMurry)

      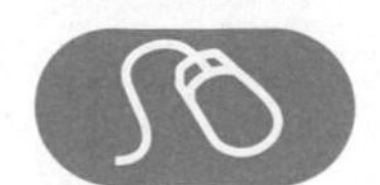

of planning and resourcing, performance management, training and development, involvement and participation, and management/labor union partnership agreements.

Personnel Practice 2nd ed.
MALCOLM MARTIN, TRICIA JACKSON
London: Institute of Personnel and Development, 2000
196pp (People and Organisations Series)
ISBN: 0852928165
Aimed at students taking IPD's Certificate in Personnel Practice, this book is also ideal for newcomers to the profession. It covers the basic essentials of employment law, recruitment and selection, training and development, discipline and grievance, performance appraisals, and personnel information systems. Activity exercises and further sources of information are included.

The Realities of Human Resource Management: Managing the Employment Relationship
KEITH SISSON, JOHN STOREY
Buckingham: Open University Press, 2000
286pp (Managing Work and Organizations Series)
ISBN: 0335206204
The authors review the changing nature of the employment relationship and organizational structures and strategies and examine contemporary issues in the management of human resources. The book is intended for practising managers and students on human resource management courses. Topics covered include: involvement and participation; pay systems and structures; training and development; recruitment and selection; relationships with labor unions and managing the HR function.

Smart Things to Know About People Management
DAVID FIRTH
San Francisco, California: Jossey-Bass, 2001
228pp (Smart series)
ISBN: 1841120731
This book explores key principles for successfully managing people, and focuses on the unpredictability and complex reactions of the employee. A behavioral approach to people management is proposed, one which understands employees, allows for their individuality, and works towards harnessing their abilities and creativity for organizational success. Five principles of people management are identified and discussed and the lessons they offer to managers are considered.

Strategic Human Resource Management
RANDALL SCHULER, SUSAN JACKSON
Malden, Massachusetts: Blackwell Business, 1999
497pp ISBN: 0631216006
This collection of readings is divided into five parts, each of which covers an important aspect of the discipline of strategic human resource management.

Strategic Human Resource Management: A Guide to Action 2nd ed.
MICHAEL ARMSTRONG
Milford, Connecticut: Kogan Page, 2000
276pp ISBN: 0749433310
This new edition of the former title *Human Resource Management: Strategy and Action* has been revised to include latest developments. Areas covered in the four parts are the basis of strategic human resource management (concepts and processes); the practice of strategic human resource management; organizational strategies; and functional strategies, including employee resourcing, performance management and reward strategy.

Strategic Human Resource Management: Corporate Rhetoric and Human Reality
LYNDA GRATTON, ET AL.
New York: Oxford University Press, 1999
248pp ISBN: 0198782039
Based on close collaboration with a number of high profile organizations-BT, Citibank, Glaxo Wellcome, Hewlett Packard, Kraft Jacobs, Suchard, Lloyds-TSB Group, the NHS, and WH Smith-this book sheds light on the organizational responses to large-scale changes and details the changing demands made of employees in the process. This book goes beyond fashionable management rhetoric to uncover the reality of human resource management.

Strategic Human Resources: Frameworks for General Managers
JAMES N. BARON, DAVID M. KREPS
New York: John Wiley, 1999
602pp ISBN: 0471072532
This is a comprehensive textbook for MBA students and managers covering a wide range of issues on human resource and personnel management.

MAGAZINES

Asia Pacific Journal of Human Resources
ISSN: 1038–4111
Australian Human Resource Institute
Level 2, 153 Park Street, South Melbourne, Victoria 3205, Australia
T: +613 9699 3733
F: +613 9696 4532
www.ahri.com.au
This is a peer-reviewed journal which aims to reflect the development and practice of the field of human resources within the Asia Pacific region. Articles focus on the results of research and examples of current practice.

Employee Benefit News
ISSN: 1044–6265
Thomson Financial Partners
1290 Avenue of the Americas, New York, 10104
T: +1 888 280 4820
www.tfimg.com/IMG_Media/IMGhome.html
Published 15 times per year, this magazine is the preeminent source of information on employee benefits. The magazine provides comprehensive and useful articles that highlight the trends in all areas of employee benefits. The coverage provided in this magazine is invaluable to employee benefits executives.

HR Focus
ISSN: 1059–6038
Institute of Management and Administration
29 West 35th Street, 5th Floor, New York, 10001–2299
T: +1 212 244 0360
F: +1 212 564 0465
www.ioma.com
This monthly newsletter provides a collection of news items, practical articles, and case studies on issues relating to the HR function.

HR Magazine
ISSN: 1047–3149
Society for Human Resource Management
1800 Duke Street, Alexandria, Virginia, 22314
T: +1 703 548 3440
F: +1 703 535 6490
www.shrm.org/hrmagazine
This monthly magazine, a leading source of current information for human resource professionals, features cutting-edge articles that provide insight and innovative approaches to solving human resource problems. Features include segments on legislation and other news of interest to professionals in human resource management.

Human Resource Development Quarterly
ISSN: 1044–8004
John Wiley

"Show me a man who enjoys firing people and I'll show you a charlatan or a sadist." (Tony O'Reilly)

Wiley InterScience Coordinator, Subscriptions Department, 605 Third Avenue, New York, 10158
T: +1 800 825 7550
F: +1 212 850 6021
www.wiley.interscience.com
HRDQ is sponsored by the American Society for Training and Development and the Academy of Human Resource Development. It provides a focus for research on human resource development issues and recognizes the interdisciplinary nature of such development issues. The emphasis is on the theory, research and evaluation of HRD practices.

Human Resource Management
ISSN: 0090–4848
John Wiley
Wiley InterScience Coordinator, Subscriptions Department, 605 Third Avenue, New York, 10158–0012
T: +1 800 825 7550
F: +1 212 850 6021
www.interscience.wiley.com
Published four times per year, this magazine features articles that highlight the latest theories in human resource management. Features include case studies, business solutions, and proven management techniques. This magazine is designed for executive business professionals.

Human Resource Management
ISSN: 0954–5395
Industrial Relations Services
18–20 Highbury Place, London, N5 1QP, U.K.
T: +44 (0) 20 7354 6746
F: +44 (0) 20 7359 4000
This quarterly journal aims to promote understanding of HRM, and to provide an international forum for discussion and debate on a wide range of HRM issues. It is endorsed by the Chartered Institute of Personnel and Development.

Human Resources
Haymarket Publishing
174 Hammersmith Road, London, W6 7JP, U.K.
T: +44 (0) 20 8606 7500
This journal offers news, profiles, case studies, and feature articles on a wide range of issues of interest to the HR professional and general managers.

Pensions & Investments
ISSN: 1050–4974
Crain Communications, Inc. (MI)
711 Third Avenue, New York, 10017–4036
T: +1 212 210 0115
F: +1 212 210 0117
www.pionline.com
Subtitled *The International Newspaper of Money Management*, this magazine is published 26 times a year. Containing feature articles, business profiles, and current issue news, this magazine is a must-read for any investment or financial executive. Special reporting emphasis is placed on corporate and institutional investing.

People Management
ISSN: 1358–6297
Personnel Publications Ltd.
17 Britton Street, London, EC1M 5TP, U.K.
T: +44 (0) 20 8971 9000
F: +44 (0) 20 7336 7637
www.peoplemanagement.co.uk
This is the official journal of the Chartered Institute of Personnel and Development. Current issues in the personnel and human resources fields, including legislation and pay, are reported. Articles focus on a variety of subjects, such as industrial relations, training and development, and personnel techniques. Case studies and profiles of leading practitioners are provided.

Personnel Today
ISSN: 0959–5848
Reed Business Information
Windsor Court, East Grinstead House, East Grinstead, East Sussex, RH19 1XA, U.K.
T: +44 (0) 1342 326972
F: +44 (0) 1342 335612
www.personneltoday.com
This is a weekly news magazine for HR and training professionals.

Workforce
ISSN: 1092-8332
ACC Communications, Inc.
245 Fischer Avenue B-2, Costa Mesa, California, 92626
T: +1 714 751 1883
F: +1 714 751 4106
www.workforce.com
Formerly called *Personnel Journal*, this monthly magazine is written for marketing managers in human resources. Covering all aspects of personnel and human resources management, the magazine features articles which explore current human resources issues and trends in labor relations.

INTERNET

American Society for Training and Development
www.astd.org
The ASTD is a professional association for training personnel. The site provides an online magazine, news, virtual communities, a free e-mail newsletter, and a buyer's guide listing training suppliers and consultants. Some services are for members only.

Chartered Institute of Personnel and Development
www.cipd.co.uk
This is the official Web site of the United Kingdom's professional association for personnel managers. Users must register, and some services are only available to members. The site provides *People Management* magazine, news, summaries of research reports, factsheets, and information on publications, training courses, and events.

HR Guide
www.hr-guide.com
This site provides definitions and basic introductions to a range of human resource subjects linked to a collection of Web site listings with ratings and brief descriptions. It has a strong focus on HR software and includes a demo of an online 360-degree feedback questionnaire.

HRnet Web Centre
www.the-hrnet.com
This site provides industry news, discussion forums, a database of HR consultants, and book reviews.

HR Tools.com
www.hrtools.com
This site focuses on online tools, including forms and training resources. Registration is required for all users.

HRZone
www.hrzone.co.uk
A portal site for HR professionals, HRZone includes resources such as online tools, templates and forms, practical expert guides, advice on legal issues, and a news and discussion forum. Registration is required for all users.

HRZone
www.hrzone.com
This site, based in the United States, provides information on the basics of human resource management. In addition, users will find articles, news, legal information including case summaries, Web site reviews, and a directory of suppliers.

"An unsuccessful manager blames failure on his obligations." (Henry Mintzberg)

  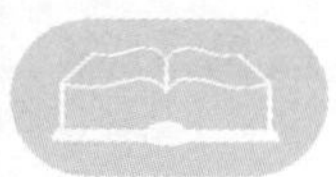    

Human Resource Management Resources on the Internet
www.nbs.ntu.ac.uk/depts/hrm/hrm_link.htm
This site provides comprehensive collections of links to HR sites in broad sub-topic categories. The links were compiled at Nottingham Business School Department of Human Resource Management, in the United Kingdom.

Online Recruitment
www.onrec.com
This site provides news on the online recruitment industry and a searchable database of online recruitment sites worldwide with reviews.

Personnel Today
www.personneltoday.com
This is a comprehensive site including information from a leading U.K. magazine. Covering HR news and events, legal developments worldwide, and career advice, the site also provides a searchable directory of consultants and information sources, and links to HR-related Web sites.

Society for Human Resource Management
www.shrm.org
The Society for Human Resource Management is a professional organization for HR managers in the United States. The site contains a range of resources including news, an online magazine, a discussion forum, collections of company practices and policies, mission statements, job descriptions, and an extensive set of links. Some resources are for members only.

Training Zone
www.trainingzone.co.uk
This is a portal site for training professionals. Resources include Trainer's Toolkit, Expert Guides, and directories of training suppliers, venues, and training courses. Registration is required for users.

U.K.-HRD
www.ukhrd.com
This is a discussion forum for training and HR specialists, sponsored by Fenman.

Workforce Online
www.workforce.com
This site is an online HR magazine with feature articles, news, discussion forums, and a free e-mail newsletter.

Workindex
www.workindex.com
Sponsored by the publishers of *Human Resource Executive* and Cornell University School of Labor and Industrial Relations, this site provides a comprehensive set of links to HR Web sites. Book extracts and reviews, a salary calculator, a jobs database, legal questions and answers, HR news, and magazine articles are also available.

WorldatWork
www.worldatwork.org
Formerly the American Compensation Association, this site offers information for human resource managers including news, topic briefings, a free e-mail newsletter, a glossary of terms, magazine articles on a pay per view basis, and a buyer's guide. Information on training courses, seminars, accredited programs, publications, and research surveys produced by the organization are also available. Additional services are available to members.

ORGANIZATIONS

USA

Academy of Human Resource Development
P.O. Box 25113, Baton Rouge, Louisiana, 70894 511
T: +1 504 334 1874
F: +1 504 334 1875
E: office@ahrd.org
www.ahrd.org
The Academy is a global organization made of, governed by, and created for the human resource development academic community. It promotes the study of HRD and encourages the practical application of research findings.

International Personnel Management Association
1617 Duke Street, Alexandria, Virginia, 22314
T: +1 703 549 7100
F: +1 703 6840948
E: training@ipma-hr.org
www.ipma.org
The International Personnel Management Association (IPMA) was established in 1973, through the consolidation of the Public Personnel Association, founded in Chicago in 1906, and the Society for Personnel Administration, founded in Washington, D.C. in 1937. IPMA is a nonprofit membership organization for agencies and individuals in the public sector human resources field, and others interested in the Association's objectives.

Society for Human Resource Management
1800 Duke Street, Alexandria, Virginia, 22314
T: +1 703 548 3440
F: +1 703 535 6490
E: custsvc@shrm.org
www.shrm.org
The SHRM is a leading voice of the human resource profession, offering members education and information services, conferences and seminars, government and media representation, online services, and publications. The Society, the world's largest human resource management association, is a founding member of both the North American Human Resource Management Association (NAHRMA) and the World Federation of Personnel Management Associations (WFPMA).

The Human Resource Planning Society
317 Madison Avenue, Suite 1509, New York, 10017
T: +1 212 490 6387
F: +1 212 682 6851
E: info@hrps.orh
www.hrps.org
HRPS is a unique and dynamic association of more than 3,000 human resource and business executives. The Society is committed to improving organizational performance by creating a global network of individuals who function as business partners in the application of strategic human resource management practices to their organizations.

Europe

Chartered Institute of Personnel and Development
CIPD House, Camp Road, Wimbledon, London, SW19 4UX, U.K.
T: +44 (0) 20 8946 9100
F: +44 (0) 20 8947 2570
E: cipd@cipd.co.uk
www.cipd.co.uk
This is the largest professional institute for HR and training professionals in the United Kingdom. The CIPD offer a range of services and training and development options, some of which are available to nonmembers.

The Industrial Society
Peter Runge House, 3 Carlton House Terrace, London, SW1Y 5DG, U.K.
T: +44 (0) 20 7479 1000
F: +44 (0) 20 7479 1111
E: customercentre@indsoc.co.uk
www.indsoc.co.uk
The Industrial Society is an independent body with over 80 years' experience in management and training. The Society operates on the principle that business success goes hand in hand with fair management practices. The services offered to members include an

"Managers should be getting everybody from the top of the human organization to the bottom doing things that make the business successful." (Bill Reffitt)

information service and employment law helpline, a publishing program for books, research reports and videos, and training and consulting.

International

Australian Human Resource Institute
Level 2, 153 Park Street, South Melbourne, Victoria, 3205, Australia
T: +613 9699 3733
F: +613 9696 4532
E: darren.lewinhill@ahri.com.au
www.ahri.com.au
The AHRI is recognized today as Australia's leading HR professional body, providing professional development at the leading edge of HR practice, knowledge, research, and development.

World Federation of Personnel Management Associations
C/o Chartered Institute of Personnel and Development, CIPD House, Camp Road, Wimbledon, London, SW19 4UX, U.K.
T: +44 (0) 20 8971 9000
F: +44 (0) 20 8263 3333
www.wfpma.com
Founded in 1976, the WFPMA is a global network of professionals working in the area of people management. Its aim is to internationally aid the development and improve the effectiveness of professional people management. The association holds regular meetings and iconferences, and commissions research projects. It also publishes a quarterly newsletter called *WorldLink*.

For More Information

- **Employee Benefits/ Compensation (pp. 1959–61)**
- **Employee Participation in Management (pp. 1962–64)**
- **Employee Relations (pp. 1964–66)**
- **Employment Law (pp. 1967–69)**
- **Training and Development (pp. 2126–28)**

Physical Working Conditions/ Ergonomics

BOOKS

The Creative Office
Jeremy Myerson, Philip Ross
Corte Madera, California: Gingko Press, 2001
240pp ISBN: 1584230088
The authors place their main emphasis on showing how an office environment can be designed to encourage group working, the sharing of knowledge, and a spirit of community within larger organizations. They examine over 40 case-study office environments from around the world and from a broad range of industries, paying particular attention to furniture, lighting, and material solutions within office buildings.

Ergonomics: How to Design for Ease and Efficiency
Karl Kroemer, Henrike Kroemer, Karin Kroemer-Elbert
Upper Saddle River, New Jersey: Prentice Hall, 2000
720pp ISBN: 0137524781
This text is designed to provide comprehensive reference information for readers of all knowledge levels seeking to gain understanding of ergonomics and workplace safety issues. The authors, who are ergonomics engineers, address all aspects of workplace conditions, including posture, equipment design, effective training, disabled employees, and avoiding repetitive strain injuries.

Excellence by Design
Turid Horgan, et al.
New York: John Wiley, 1998
320pp ISBN: 0471246476
This text recognizes the link between well-designed office space and a productive workforce. Revolving around four years of research by the Space Organization Research Group of MIT's School of Architecture and Planning, the book examines this notion, and how it can be applied within company culture.

New Workspace, New Culture: Office Design as a Catalyst for Change
Gavin Turner, Jeremy Myerson
Brookfield, Vermont: Gower, 1998
144pp ISBN: 0566080281
Aimed at senior managers, this book examines the link between the physical environment of the workplace and organization culture, and looks in particular at using office design as a means of facilitating organizational change. Part One analyzes the context and environment of working life, the reasons for change, and barriers to improving working practices. Part Two examines ways traditional structures can be reorganized and physical barriers to change removed. Part Three describes six workplace layouts and their relative benefits.

The Occupational Ergonomics Handbook
Waldemar Karwowski, William S. Marras, eds.
Boca Raton, Florida: CRC Press, 1999
2000pp ISBN: 0849326419
This handbook presents an exhaustive array of in-depth information pertaining to workplace ergonomics written by international experts. Topics include developing ergonomic programs, workplace- and injury-specific research, managing for ergonomics, injury prevention, and workplace design and employee safety.

Office Space Planning
Alexi Marmot, Joanna Eley
New York: McGraw-Hill, 2000
478pp ISBN: 0071341994
Aimed at designers (or anybody concerned with office facility management) this book provides advice on how to create an excellent work environment by using space wisely. It covers topics such as lighting and office furniture, discusses the relative merits of enclosed and open-plan office spaces and also includes studies of well-designed workplaces.

Physical Hazards of the Workplace
Larry R. Collins, Thomas D. Schneid
Boca Raton, Florida: Lewis Publishers, 2001
336pp ISBN: 1566703395
Aimed at business professionals, this book presents information on federal, state, and local regulations dealing with workplace safety. The authors stress the importance of understanding and implementing these regulations, outline

  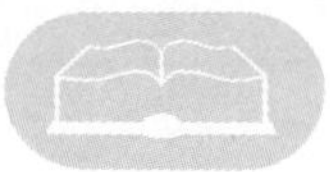    

occupational and environmental hazards present in the workplace, and describe methods of facilitating compliance with regulatory codes.

Transforming Your Workplace
Adryan Bell
New York: Beekman, 2000
96pp (Management Shapers Series)
ISBN: 0846451832
Combining architecture and ergonomics, this book provides guidance on workspace changes that transform the ways people work. It discusses design, Feng Shui, style, color, light, sound, texture, and comfort and also includes sections on planning the project and gaining the support of the workers who will be affected.

Work Measurement and Methods Improvement
Lawrence S. Aft
New York: John Wiley, 2000
464pp (Engineering Design and Automation Series)
ISBN: 0471370894
The author gives solid, practical coverage to the key principles and practices of work measurement. He examines the standard tools and methods for work analysis, productivity measurement, and productivity improvement, and explains the purpose, use, advantages, and limitations of each in turn.

Work Organization and Ergonomics
Vittorio Di Martino, Nigel Corlett, eds.
Geneva, Switzerland: International Labour Office, 1998
224pp ISBN: 9221095185
The complementary nature of ergonomics and work organization can, the authors show, produce synergies to help improve working conditions, increase productivity, and improve quality and performance. They offer a step-by-step, proactive approach to continuous improvement using ergonomic and work organization techniques.

MAGAZINES

Behaviour & Information Technology
ISSN: 0144-929X
Taylor & Francis
11 New Fetter Lane, London, EC4P 4EE, U.K.
T: +44 (0) 20 7583 9855
F: +44 (0) 20 7842 2298
www.tandf.co.uk
This publication aims to provide a focused, comprehensive, and international abstracting service mainly concerned with the human aspects of technology, including telecommunications, office systems, industrial automation, robotics, and consumer products. Its readership is international, and ranges from researchers and systems designers to personnel specialists and planners.

Compensation and Working Conditions
ISSN: 1059-0722
The Bureau of Labor Statistics
U.S. Department of Labor, 2 Massachusetts Ave., NE, Washington, D.C., 20212-0001
T: +1 202 512 1800
F: +1 202 512 2250
www.bls.gov/opub/cwc/cwcwelc.htm
CWC is a quarterly periodical that covers topics including wages and benefits, safety and health, and labor-management relations. Written by BLS economists and statisticians and outside scholars, it offers articles, summaries of major studies, and data tables and charts. It is targeted primarily at HR managers.

Ergonomics
ISSN: 0014-0139
Taylor & Francis
11 New Fetter Lane, London, EC4P 4EE, U.K.
T: +44 (0) 20 7583 9855
F: +44 (0) 20 7842 2298
www.tandf.co.uk
This is an international, multidisciplinary journal concerned with all aspects of the interaction of human beings with their work and leisure. It includes a news section, research data, media reviews, and peer-reviewed scientific papers.

Ergonomics Abstracts
ISSN: 0046-2446
Taylor & Francis
11 New Fetter Lane, London, EC4P 4EE, U.K.
T: +44 (0) 20 7583 9855
F: +44 (0) 20 7842 2298
www.tandf.co.uk
This publication offers a focused, comprehensive, and international abstracting service spanning the whole world of ergonomics and human factors. It deals with the most up-to-date literature in psychology, physiology, biomechanics, work design, human/computer interaction, and safety science.

Job Safety & Health Quarterly
ISSN: 1057-5820
Occupational Safety and Health Administration
U.S. Department of Labor, 200 Constitution Avenue, Washington, D.C., 20210
T: +1 202 693 1999
F: +1 202 693 1634
www.osha.gov/html/jshq-index.html
Published quarterly, the *JSHQ* is the official magazine of OSHA, dealing with current trends in worker safety. It offers information on changes, developments, and new rulings made by OSHA.

INTERNET

Cornell University Egonomics Web
http://ergo.human.cornell.edu
This site presents information on research studies and class work in ergonomics undertaken by students and faculty at Cornell. It also gives details of general ergonomics news, information, research, and tools.

Ergonomics (Center for Disease Control)
www.cdc.gov/od/ohs/ergonomics/ergodef.htm
The Center for Disease Control provides basic information on ergonomics issues in the workplace. Resources include workplace-specific ergonomics information, assessment tools, and suggested methods to avoid repetitive motion injuries.

Ergonomics Information Analysis Centre
www.bham.ac.uk/ManMechEng/IEG/eiac
This site, run by the University of Birmingham in the United Kingdom, provides an information service for ergonomics and human factors, offering *Ergonomics Abstracts* online as well as a payment-based search and delivery service.

Ergonomics (Occupational Safety & Health Administration)
www.osha-slc.gov/SLTC/ergonomics
This U.S. government Web site offers a wealth of ergonomics information on subjects including methods for recognizing ergonomics problems in the workplace, possible solutions to ergonomics problems, case studies, illustrations, and links to additional resources.

Ergoweb
www.ergoweb.com/index.cfm
This site provides comprehensive information on workplace ergonomics. Topics include current news on ergonomics, recent legislation, a glossary of terms, discussion lists, case studies, and information on establishing ergonomics programs.

Human Factors/Ergonomics
www.usernomics.com/hf.html
This site provides a list of links to other Internet sites on these topics.

ORGANIZATIONS

USA

Human Factors and Ergonomics Society
P.O. Box 1369, Santa Monica, California, 90406-1369
T: +1 310 394 1811
F: +1 310 394 2410
E: *info@hfes.org*

"I am I plus my surroundings, and, if I do not preserve the latter, I do not preserve myself."
(José Ortega y Gasset)

www.hfes.org
The Society's mission is to promote the discovery and exchange of information about the characteristics of human beings that are applicable to the design of systems and devices of all kinds. It also encourages education and training for those entering the human factors and ergonomics profession and for those who conceive, test, manage, and participate in systems.

Europe

Health and Safety Executive
Information Centre, Broad Lane, Sheffield, South Yorkshire, S3 7HQ, U.K.
T: +44 (0) 8701 545 500
F: +44 (0) 114 289 2333
E: *hseinformationservices@natbrit.com*
www.hse.gov.uk
The HSE aims to ensure that risks to people's health and safety from work activities are properly controlled.

Human Factors and Ergonomics Society: Europe Chapter
University of Groningen, Experimental and Labour Psychology, Grote Kruisstraat 2/1, NL-9712 TS Groningen, The Netherlands
T: +31 50 363 6758
F: +31 50 363 6784
E: *hfesec@ision.nl*
http://utopia.ision.nl/users/hfesec
This is the European arm of the California-based Human Factors and Ergonomics Society. It has the same aims as its American parent organization, namely the study of the human factors that affect the design of working environments and systems, and the training of human factors and ergonomics professionals.

The Ergonomics Society
Devonshire House, Devonshire Square, Loughborough, Leicestershire, LE11 3DW, U.K.
T: +44 (0) 1509 234904
F: +44 (0) 1509 235666
E: *ergsoc@ergonomics.org.uk*
www.ergonomics.org.uk
This organization is a forum for professionals who use information about people to design for comfort, efficiency, and safety.

International

International Ergonomics Association
Professor Pierre Falzon, Laboratoire d' Ergonomie, CNAM, 41 rue Gay Lussac, 75005, Paris, France
T: +33 1 44 107802
F: +33 1 43 253614
E: *falzon@cnam.fr*
www.iea.cc
The IEA is a federation of ergonomics and human factors societies from around the world. Its mission is to advance the science and practice of ergonomics, expanding the scope of its application and contribution to society and thereby improving the quality of life for all.

For More Information

- **Employment Law (pp. 1967–69)**
- **Facilities Management (pp. 1980–82)**
- **Health and Safety (pp. 1992–94)**

Planning for Retirement

BOOKS

Getting Started in Retirement Planning
Ronald M. Yolles, Murray Yolles
New York: John Wiley, 2000
288pp (Getting Started In Series)
ISBN: 0471383104
Two American financial advisors offer advice on managing financial resources and planning for financial independence during retirement. Topics covered include saving for retirement, managing a portfolio, investing after retirement, and insurance for healthcare expenses. A separate section looks at estate management—making provision for family members after death. The text is illustrated with personal case studies.

How to Design and Deliver Retirement Training
Peter Reynolds, Marcella Bailey
Sterling, Virginia: Stylus Publishing, 1993
142pp ISBN: 0749409479
The authors wrote this practical book with the needs of trainers and HR specialists in mind. They give consideration to the reasons for implementing retirement training, the design of the training, and how it should be delivered.

101 Secrets for a Great Retirement: Practical, Inspirational, and Fun Ideas for the Best Years of Your Life
Mary Helen Smith, Shuford Smith
New York: McGraw-Hill, 2000
160pp ISBN: 0737304200
Full of practical advice and tips, this book aims to equip the reader with a positive approach to preparing for retirement.

The Procrastinator's Guide to Financial Security
David Teitelbaum
New York: AMACOM, 2001
306pp ISBN: 0814406211
This book supplies information on the fundamentals of money management. It is aimed at those who need help saving for retirement, and got started later in life. It teaches the knowledge, skills, and discipline needed to secure a comfortable retirement. It includes bibliographical references and an index.

Retire Rich: The Baby Boomer's Guide to a Secure Future
Bambi Holzer, Elaine Floyd
New York: John Wiley, 1998
222pp ISBN: 0471247820
This book presents practical and easy ways to plan, save, and invest in order to secure a comfortable retirement. It encourages workers to address the retirement issue while they still have a steady income. It uses clear, non-technical language, and charts, tables, and worksheets enhance the text.

The Wall Street Journal Guide to Planning your Financial Future: The Easy-to-read Guide to Planning for Retirement
Kenneth Morris, et al.
New York: Lightbulb Press, 1998
187pp ISBN: 0684857243
This book provides an overview of the important considerations and decisions that need to be made in securing a comfortable retirement. It covers the advantages of salary reduction plans, clarifies the difference between Roth and traditional IRAs and describes the benefits of effective tax planning. It provides practical, helpful ideas on how to get started.

You're Fifty—Now What? Investing for the Second Half of Your Life
Charles R. Schwab
New York: Crown Publishing, 2002
336pp ISBN: 609808702
This title is a helpful guide to making sure you have provided well for yourself in your retirement. The book also contains a large number of practical worksheets.

MAGAZINES

Goodtimes
AMS Ltd.
119 Cholmley Gardens, London, NW6 1AA, U.K.

T: +44 (0) 20 7431 2259
F: +44 (0) 20 7431 7411
www.arp.org.uk
Goodtimes is the magazine of the Association of Retired and Persons over 50. It covers topics such as health, fitness, travel, and gardening.

Kiplinger's Retirement Report
ISSN: 1075–6671
Kiplinger
1729 H Street, Washington, D.C., 20006
T: +1 888 419 0424
www.kiplinger.com/retreport
This is a retirement newsletter from the respected publishers of personal finance and business forecasting information. It provides information on retirement issues, such as managing finances, retirement living, and estate planning.

Modern Maturity
ISSN: 0026–8046
American Association of Retired Persons
601 E. Street, NW, Washington, D.C., 20049
T: +1 800 424 3410
www.modernmaturity.org
This is a membership magazine of the AARP and is published monthly. It is aimed at people over the age of 55 and covers health, finance, work/life transitions, and personal development. Much of the content is available online at the Web site.

My Generation
American Association of Retired Persons
601 E. Street, NW, Washington, D.C., 20049
T: +1 800 424 3410
www.mygeneration.org
This magazine is free to AARP members of 50 to 55-the "baby boomer" generation of the title. It contains information about work, money, health, food, travel, music, and other subjects, and is intended to inspire and entertain.

Pensions & Investments
ISSN: 1050–4974
Crain Communications, Inc. (MI)
711 Third Avenue, New York, 10017–4036
T: +1 212 210 0115
F: +1 212 210 0117
www.pionline.com
Subtitled *The International Newspaper of Money Management*, this magazine is published 26 times per year. Containing feature articles, business profiles, and current issue news, this magazine is an excellent resource for any investment or financial executive. Special reporting emphasis is placed on corporate and institutional investing.

INTERNET

AARP Webplace
www.aarp.org
This association is one of the world's largest nonprofit, nonpartisan membership organizations for people over fifty. The site provides a wealth of data on such subjects as travel, health, learning opportunities, legislation, finance, and volunteering, and has links to discussion groups.

Center for Retirement Research at Boston College
www.bc.edu/bc_org/avp/csom/executive/crr
The Center aims to promote research on retirement issues, transmit findings to the policy community and the public, and broaden access to data sources. It offers research and publications on retirement issues as well as information about upcoming events on its Web site.

Pensions Advisory Service
www.opas.org.uk
The Pensions Advisory Service (OPAS) is a British government-funded, independent nonprofit organization giving free help and advice to members of the public who have a problem with their private, company, or state pension. It does not give advice on an individual's state pension entitlement.

The Annuity Bureau
www.annuity-bureau.co.uk
This is a useful site from an independent firm of financial advisers focusing on pensions and annuities. There is an extensive archive of articles, some quite detailed, covering the many complex issues relating to financial matters in retirement. Comparative tables give projected annuity rates from leading providers.

The Pensions Guide
www.pensionguide.gov.uk
This government site provides general guidance on the benefits and reduced charges available from public sector services for those over 60.

The Retirement Site
www.the-retirement-site.co.uk
One of many pensions and retirement sites from the independent financial adviser sector, this one, although aimed principally at corporate fund managers, provides individuals with a wide range of impartial advice on the financial aspects of retirement. Of equal interest are the links to an extensive selection of related sites covering matters of concern to those who are retired or approaching retirement, such as health, travel, and insurance.

ORGANIZATIONS

USA

AARP (American Association of Retired Persons)
601 E. Street, NW, Washington, D.C., 20049
T: +1 800 424 3410
E: member@aarp.org
www.aarp.org
This is a nonprofit, membership organization for people aged 50 and over. It has an enormous membership of around 32 million. It provides information and support; advocates on legislative, consumer, and legal issues; helps members to serve their communities; and offers a number of unique benefits, products, and services. Benefits include the AARP Web site, *Modern Maturity* and *My Generation* magazines, and the monthly AARP Bulletin.

Europe

Association of Retired Persons over 50 (ARP/050)
Greencoat House, Francis Street, London, SW1P 1DZ, U.K.
T: +44 (0) 20 7828 0500
F: +44 (0) 20 7233 7132
E: info@arp.org.uk
www.arp.org.uk
ARP/050 offers a range of benefits to members, including legal, tax, and medical telephone helplines, special interest groups, free insurances, a discounted shopping scheme, travel discounts, social activities, and the bimonthly magazine Goodtimes. In addition, ARP/050 campaigns against ageism and involves itself with age-related legislation in the United Kingdom.

National Pensioners' Convention
9 Arkwright Road, London, NW3 6AB, U.K.
T: +44 (0) 20 7431 9820
F: +44 (0) 20 7431 9830
E: admin@natpencon.org.uk
www.natpencon.org.uk
The NPC is an umbrella organization for a wide range of pensioner organizations, including labor unions, charities, and retired members' associations.

REACH (Reach Executives Action Clearing House)
89 Albert Embankment, London, SE1 7TP, U.K.
T: +44 (0) 20 7582 6543
F: +44 (0) 20 7582 2423
E: volwork@btinternet.com
www.volwork.org.uk
This organization links retired professional people with community, charitable, and voluntary groups where they can work part time on an expenses-only basis.

"When we are planning for posterity, we ought to remember that virtue is not heredity."
(Thomas Paine)

PLANNING YOUR CAREER

BOOKS

Career Intelligence: The 12 New Rules for Work and Life Success
BARBARA MOSES
San Francisco, California: Berrett-Koehler, 1998
300pp ISBN: 1576750485
This book offers advice on building a career in today's ruthless and rapidly changing business environment. It lists 12 essential rules for success. These include: ensuring your marketability; thinking globally; continuing to learn; and preparing four areas of competence.

Career Planning & Networking
AGGIE WHITE
Cincinnati, Ohio: South-Western Publishing, 2001
96pp ISBN: 0538724749
White walks readers through the career-planning and networking process so vital to advancement in today's rapidly shifting job markets. In addition to discussing the basics like self-assessment and researching various careers, White shows how to build an effective career network and to plan for career changes. The book concludes with case studies that illustrate career planning and advancement.

Career Skills: A Guide to Long-term Success at Work
PATRICK FORSYTH
New York: Continuum, 1999
146pp ISBN: 0304704172
This is a practical book focusing on how to build a successful career. The author examines the key career skills that all successful people have in common and outlines a range of personal skills that can help the individual to be perceived as a winner.

Changing Directions without Losing Your Way: Managing the Six Stages of Change at Work and in Life
PAUL EDWARDS, SARAH EDWARDS
New York: J. P. Tarcher, 2001
237pp ISBN: 158542076X
Although this book is not about career planning per se, it provides valuable guidance on effectively managing significant life-change processes, including career changes. While the authors espouse finding and following one's passion, they advise readers to approach it in a grounded, well researched, and practical way. The book includes suggested tasks, self-quizzes, a change journal, and other features that encourage introspection, self-discipline, and self-education.

Developing Your Career: A Condensed Self-study Learning System
LIFESKILLS INTERNATIONAL LTD.
Burlington, Vermont: Ashgate Publishing Company, 1999
179pp ISBN: 0566082675
The *Developing Your Career* learning system is constructed around a practical, interactive approach designed to provide you, the reader/user, with the opportunity to review your individual progress and see where you are in relation to your career and your job. A series of activities help you to: think carefully about the future: collect personal data including evidence of your past successes, your skills, your work values, and your basic behavior style; give careful thought to your training and development needs; produce realistic, achievable objectives and action plans; revisit your résumé in the light of your experience and your aspirations; and hone your interview and influencing skills.

Discovering Your Career in Business
TIMOTHY BUTLER, JAMES WALDROOP
Cambridge, Massachusetts: Perseus, 1997
272pp ISBN: 0201461358
This book is a career guide to help readers find work that fulfills their potential and suits their character. Containing an inventory and user exercises which point an individual toward finding a range of activities appropriate to their needs, the book also gives advice on how these can be linked to employment within the business sector. There is an emphasis on self-assessment and pinpointing career goals.

Do What You Want for the Rest of Your Life
BOB GRIFFITHS
New York: Ballantine Books, 2001
352pp ISBN: 0345440439
Based on Griffiths's personal experience, this book explores the idea of career change. Griffiths offers advice on (among other issues) developing résumés, dealing with familial and financial challenges that may arise, and making your resignation. The book is written from a very personal viewpoint, and aims to appeal to a wide spectrum of society.

Enhancing Your Employability: How to Improve Your Prospects of Achieving a Fulfilling and Rewarding Career
RODERIC ASHLEY
Oxford: How To Books, 1998
120pp ISBN: 185703371X
This book explains what employability means and offers practical advice on how to enhance your own prospects of working in a sphere you enjoy. It asks searching questions about motivation and attitude to help you match your working life to your personal values. It is designed to help you to get to know who you are, what motivates you, and what you have to offer, and also shows you how to put together an action plan.

The Future of Career
AUDREY COLLIN, RICHARD A. YOUNG, EDS.
New York: Cambridge University Press, 2000
306pp ISBN: 052164965X
The basic argument of this book is that the fragmented nature of modern working life has led to fundamental changes in our understanding of the term "career." It offers a collection of articles presenting a global view of the concept of a career, reviewing its past, and considering its future. Psychologists, sociologists, and HR managers offer a multilayered examination of career theories and practice, identifying the major changes taking place in the world, and discussing the future of "career" in the newly emerging network society of the 21st century.

Getting Promoted: Real Strategies for Advancing Your Career
HARRY E. CHAMBERS
Cambridge, Massachusetts: Perseus, 1999
243pp ISBN: 0738201022
In this guide to getting promoted, Chambers argues that good critical skills and an understanding of the problems and opportunities that may arise when looking for promotion are key. He gives practical advice on how to develop this analytical capacity, and uses research from a range of companies to help the reader assess his/her strengths in the workplace.

Making Career Decisions That Count: A Practical Guide
DARRELL ANTHONY LUZZO
Upper Saddle River, New Jersey: Prentice

"The man who has the largest capacity for work and thought is the man who is bound to succeed."
(Henry Ford)

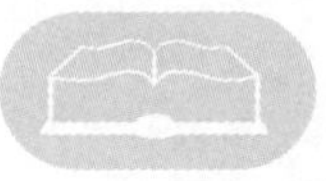

Hall, 2001
160pp ISBN: 0130191434
Intended as an up-to-date, hands-on guide to enhancing the lifelong process of planning and creating a successful, satisfying career, this book is geared toward anyone seeking help with a career choice or change. In addition to offering traditional assessments of individual interests, personality, skills, and values, and matching those to the world of work and the state of the job market, the author also discusses effective use of the Internet and relevant Web sites.

Practical Self-development: A Step-by-step Approach to CPD
BOB NORTON, VIKKY BURT
London: Institute of Management, 1997
82pp ISBN: 0859462935
This guide clarifies the term ''continuous professional development'' (CPD), examines why it is now a necessity, and tells how to take a balanced approach to turn it into a workable process. It outlines a number of different instruments to help identify self-development needs and looks at how people learn. In addition it describes the processes of forming a self-development plan, and of recording and evaluating progress.

Successful Career and Life Planning
STEPHEN G. HAINES, JAYNE HAINES, BRENDA PITTSLEY
Menlo Park, California: Crisp Publications, 2001
104pp ISBN: 1560525622
The authors apply the tools and techniques of strategic planning to individual career- and life-planning processes. The book includes an overview of systems thinking, on which the ''output, feedback, input, and throughput'' phases are based, planning backward from a vision of your ideal future, identifying stakeholders and potential barriers, and creating annual work and resource allocation plans.

Who Do You Think You Are? Understanding Your Motives and Maximising Your Abilities
NICK ISBISTER, MARTIN ROBINSON
North Pomfret, Vermont: Trafalgar Square, 1999
184pp ISBN: 0551031700
In this book the authors unveil a process known as SIMA (System for Identifying Motivated Abilities). This self-assessment system aims to help individuals to understand their motivation, develop their abilities, and maximize their effectiveness. The book includes exercises to support self-evaluation and planning for the future.

Winning the Talent War: A Strategic Approach to Attracting, Developing and Retaining the Best People
CHARLES WOODRUFFE
New York: John Wiley, 1999
192pp ISBN: 0471987530
How to attract the best people and retain them in an environment of constant change is a dilemma facing all organizations. A framework for attracting, motivating, and retaining senior management, and for creating a strategy for the sustainable development of high-fliers, is presented here. Case studies from various organizations are also included.

MAGAZINES

Occupational Outlook Quarterly
ISSN: 0199–4786
Bureau of Labor Statistics
U.S. Department of Labor, 2 Massachusetts Avenue NE, Room 2860, Washington, D.C., 20212
T: +1 202 691 5200
F: +1 202 691 7890
www.bls.gov/opub/ooq/ooqhome.htm
OOQ covers a variety of career topics, including training opportunities, salary trends, new and emerging occupations, and results of new studies from the Bureau of Labor Statistics. It also offers career-related data from the BLS in chart form.

The Five O'Clock News
ISSN: 1082–3492
The Five O'Clock Club
300 E. 40th St., New York, 10016
T: +1 212 286 4500
F: +1 212 286 9571
www.fiveoclockclub.com
Published ten times per year by a career-counseling service, the newsletter offers news, case studies, and analysis on various subjects relating to both career-development issues and job-search techniques.

INTERNET

CareerBuilder
www.careerbuilder.com
This site allows you to post your résumé, search the job database, and take advantage of helpful tools including a salary wizard, career assessment, résumé builder, skill certifier, and a job search for freelancers. Practical guidance is offered on job hunting and work—life issues, including balancing work and family, and dealing with workplace issues and transitions.

Careers Portal
www.careers-portal.co.uk
Information on careers and career management for students is supplied on this site by Trotman Publishing. It also includes links to careers advisory services, professional associations, and career Web sites.

Career Transition Partnership
www.ctp.org.uk
This site is designed to assist those leaving the armed forces and their prospective employers. It provides information on resettlement services and employment fairs, as well as on articles and useful links.

Career World
www.career-world.co.uk
Career World provides career development programs to the individual, as well as a full range of outplacement services to corporate clients throughout the United Kingdom. New visitors have to register before entering the site, which contains many example résumés, speculative letters, cover letters, and post-interview follow-up letters.

Fast Company
www.fastcompany.com
Fastcompany.com is based on the magazine of the same name, which was founded in 1995. The Web site serves people's individual career needs with six custom-built Career Zones. Each Career Zone contains stories, career advice, interactive tools, opinions, and connections to other useful sites.

FirstPersonGlobal
www.firstpersonglobal.com
This career management site is aimed at business leaders in technology, telecommunications, and e-commerce, and is provided by Harvey Nash. It contains tools and advice, articles, links, and networking opportunities.

Hotjobs
www.hotjobs.com
Hotjobs.com is a recruiting solutions company that provides employers with innovative hiring products and services, supplying a resourceful and dynamic exchange between job seekers and prospective employers. For those seeking employment, this site is a one-stop career resource center, offering privacy, career tools, and a comprehensive relocation center. For recruiters, Hotjobs.com provides an efficient way to hire staff by cutting the time and costs associated with traditional recruiting.

"I am a young executive. No cuffs than mine are cleaner; / I have a Slimline brief-case and I use the firm's Cortina."
(John Betjeman)

Monster
www.monster.com
As well as over one million job listings, this excellent resource offers a career center that provides customized information by industry or profession, together with resources on cover letters, résumés, interviews, salaries, seasonal jobs, company profiles, and more.

The Big Trip
www.thebigtrip.co.uk
This site from Shell Livewire is designed to help college leavers with career planning. It includes a personal profile questionnaire.

WetFeet
www.wetfeet.com
Unlike Monster.com, WetFeet is not a résumé-posting site. It complements Monster by providing detailed information on companies, careers, industries, and salary benchmarks that can be used throughout one's career. Other free features include expert advice, newsletters, and discussion boards. WetFeet also publishes detailed insider's guides to dozens of companies and industries.

ORGANIZATIONS

USA

National Career Development Association
10820 E. 45th St., Suite 210, Tulsa, Oklahoma, 74146
T: +1 918 663 7060
F: +1 918 663 7058
www.ncda.org
NCDA is a trade association for professionals providing career-development services, acting to develop standards for career counseling and evaluating career-information materials. Membership benefits include a journal and newsletter, conferences, continuing education, and networking opportunities.

For More Information

- ☆ **Avoiding Your Worst Career Nightmare (pp. 316–17)**
- ✔ **Managing the Plateaued Performer (pp. 366–67)**
- ✔ **Starting a New Job (pp. 410–11)**
- **Creating a Résumé (pp. 1946–48)**
- **Job Hunting (pp. 2017–18)**
- **Management Education: MBAs (pp. 2035–36)**

PRESENTATION/SPEAKING

BOOKS

Effective Presentation Skills: A Practical Guide for Better Speaking
Steve Mandel
Menlo Park, California: Crisp Publications, 2000
94pp ISBN: 1560525266
This basic overview of presentations offers advice on topics including skill assessment, presentation planning, visual aids, teleconferencing and videoconferencing, the presentation environment, and dealing with hostile questions. It contains an especially useful section on dealing with anxiety and projecting confidence.

Point, Click and Wow!: A Quick Guide to Brilliant Laptop Presentations 2nd ed.
Claudyne Wilder, Jennifer Rotondo
San Francisco, California: Jossey-Bass, 2002
240pp ISBN: 0787956694
Aimed at business people of all levels, this book offers a practical guide to using technology in effective presentations. The authors explore how to balance on-screen activity and human interaction, how to deal with software and hardware issues, and how, when, and where to practice. The book includes checklists and illustrations.

Presentation Skills for Managers
Jennifer Rotondo, Mike Rotondo, Jr.
New York: McGraw Hill, 2001
180pp ISBN: 0071379304
Targeted at managers at all levels, this book offers practical advice on presentation skills. It stresses the three main aspects of any presentation—content, design, and delivery—and deals with issues such as stumbling blocks and follow-up Q&A sessions. It also provides a good overview of using PowerPoint for effective presentations.

Presenting to Win: A Guide for Finance and Business Professionals
Khalid Aziz
Dublin, Republic of Ireland: Oak Tree Press, 2001
270pp ISBN: 1860761674
The book explores the process of preparing and delivering business presentations, focusing on external and internal presentation scenarios. It examines the fundamentals of an effective presentation in terms of design, organization, use of visual aids, and delivery, and stresses in particular the importance of tailoring presentations to the expected audience.

Say It with Presentations: How to Design and Deliver Successful Business Presentations
Gene Zelazny
New York: McGraw-Hill, 1999
153pp ISBN: 0071354077
Intended as a simple overview of presentations, this book is targeted mainly at beginners but could also offer some tips to experienced presenters. The topics it covers include defining the purpose of the presentation, keeping the audience in mind, designing charts, and using humor. Its main focus is on how to deliver presentations with confidence and conviction.

Secrets of Successful Speakers: How to Motivate, Captivate, and Persuade
Lilly Walters
New York: McGraw-Hill, 1993
216pp ISBN: 0070680345
Walters, chief of a speakers' bureau, offers anecdotes to illustrate a wide variety of presentation issues, including setting objectives, conquering stage fright, cultivating a reputation as an expert, projecting an image with clothes and voice, involving listeners, and dealing with pitfalls. Appropriate for both novice and experienced speakers, it deals more with public speaking than with creating presentations.

Wooing and Winning Business: The Foolproof Formula for Making Persuasive Business Presentations
Spring Asher, Wicke Chambers
New York: John Wiley, 1998

"An orator is the worst person to tell a plain fact." (Maria Edgeworth)

240pp ISBN: 0471253707
This guide introduces the "Speechworks Formula" for increasing your powers of persuasion and giving effective presentations. It explains how to look and sound like a born leader, organize your thoughts for maximum clarity, and use the most compelling evidence and anecdotes to hook even the toughest audience. Speechworks is an internationally known firm, specializing in speech and media training.

INTERNET

Advanced Public Speaking Institute
www.public-speaking.org
This site offers free advice and articles on all aspects of public speaking, including performance and storytelling techniques, how to develop a topic, the use of props and handouts, humor, tricks, gimmicks, and stage fright.

Art of Speaking in Public
www.artofspeaking.com
This site offers a collection of over 60 rapid read tips for effective public speaking and effective performance in classes, presentations, conferences, seminars, events, and discussions.

National Speakers Association
www.nsaspeaker.org
Sponsored by a professional speakers' organization, the site gives access to *Professional Speaker* magazine, reference lists, conference and event information, networking opportunities, and newsletters.

Presentations.com
www.presentations.com
The online counterpart to *Presentations* magazine, the site offers news, articles, information on upcoming conferences and events, technological information, and resources.

Professional Edge
www.proedgeskills.com
Sponsored by a consulting firm, the site offers articles on presentation skills, a monthly e-zine, books, and resources, and an online ask-the-expert option.

School for Champions
www.school-for-champions.com/speaking.htm
This selection of free online lessons is designed to improve speaking skills and overcome the fear of speaking in public or to a group.

ORGANIZATIONS

USA

Advanced Public Speaking Institute
Box 2630, Landover Hills, Maryland, 20784
T: +1 301 577 3166
F: +1 301 552 0225
E: cmckinney@public-speaking.org
www.public-speaking.org
This organization offers free advice and information on all aspects of public speaking and making presentations.

Toastmasters International
23182 Arroyo Vista, Rancho Santa Margarita, California, 92688
T: +1 949 858 8255
F: +1 949 858 1207
E: tmembers@toastmasters.org
www.toastmasters.org
A nonprofit, member-based organization, Toastmasters International was established in 1924 with the aim of helping people to speak more effectively in public. It provides members with manuals on effective speaking and other resources, as well as a subscription to its monthly magazine, *The Toastmaster*. All clubs offer members the opportunity to develop presentation and leadership skills through chairing meetings, presenting impromptu and prepared speeches, and offering constructive evaluation.

Europe

Association of Speakers Clubs
152 Aylesbury Road, Hockley Heath, Solihull, West Midlands, B94 6PP, U.K.
T: +44 (0) 1564 774907
E: info@the-asc.org.uk
www.the-asc.org.uk
The ASC is a nonprofit self-help organization dedicated to improving the art of speaking in public and to promoting, encouraging, and developing proficiency in the spoken word. It is linked to 175 local clubs in eight districts across the United Kingdom.

The Speakers Trust
19 Waterer Rise, Wallington, Surrey, SM6 9DN, U.K.
T: +44 (0) 20 8669 3003
www.speakerstrust.org.uk
The Trust promotes the work of speakers' clubs across the United Kingdom with a view to making them better known and understood and increasing their membership. It offers support to existing clubs by organizing competitions, sponsoring new members, providing funds, and producing educational materials.

For More Information

- ✔ **Effective Communications: Delivering Presentations (pp. 392–93)**
- ✔ **Effective Communications: Preparing Presentations (pp. 394–95)**
- **Internal Communication (pp. 2007–09)**
- **Interpersonal Communication/Relations (pp. 2012–14)**

Pricing

BOOKS

Dynamic Pricing and the Online Auction Model
Mark Kerr
New York: John Wiley, 2002
192pp ISBN: 0471486981
This book presents an overview of online dynamic pricing, a concept in which customers determine the price they are willing to pay for goods and use an auction format to find suppliers. Successful companies employing this strategy include e-retailers, buy.com, letsbuyit.com, and priceline.com. The author differentiates this concept from online auctions like eBay and QXL. A practical online format for selling surplus products is included as well as a linked Web site that is a companion to the book.

Power Pricing: How Managing Price Transforms the Bottom Line
Robert J. Dolan, Hermann Simon
New York: Free Press, 1997
416pp ISBN: 068483443X
This book for managers and strategy makers explains how a proactive, strategic approach to pricing—called "power pricing" by the authors—can have dramatic effects on profitability. Written in simple language, the book uses practical examples throughout to illustrate the attitudes, thought

  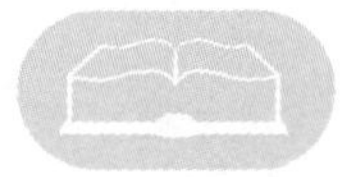    

processes, actions, and strategies of "power pricers."

Pricing for Profitability: Activity-based Pricing for Competitive Advantage
JOHN L. DALY
New York: John Wiley, 2001
288pp ISBN: 0471415359
The authors suggest that activity-based pricing helps companies set appropriate prices which both generate sales and result in a profit. Activity-based pricing analyzes the interdependence between price, cost and sales volume resulting in a disciplined approach to the process of price development. Other topics included in the book are estimating customer demand, pricing law in the United States, the ethics of pricing, planning profit, and tips for successful price negotiations.

The Strategy and Tactics of Pricing: A Guide to Profitable Decision Making 2nd ed.
THOMAS T. NAGLE, REED K. HOLDEN
Upper Saddle River, New Jersey: Prentice Hall, 2002
400pp ISBN: 013026248X
This is a complete guide that integrates pricing with overall managerial goals. It utilizes mini-case studies to illustrate success stories and examples of pricing failures. The elements of strategic pricing are explained. Other topics included are competition, segmentation of buyers, pricing and marketing mix, the psychology of pricing, and the ethical and legal aspects of pricing. Step-by-step procedures for problem analysis and strategy are provided.

Transfer Pricing
CLIVE R. EMMANUEL, MESSAOUD MEHAFDI
Stanford, Connecticut: International Thomson Business Press, 1994
172pp ISBN: 186152434X
This book aims to give students on accounting, finance, and MBA courses an authoritative, multidisciplinary introduction to transfer pricing, which is described as the process in which monetary value is placed on the internal flows of goods and services within an enterprise. The influence of transfer pricing on managerial behavior is an underlying theme of the book.

INTERNET

Professional Pricing Society
www.pricing-advisor.com
Sponsored by a professional society dedicated to pricing management, the site offers articles, discussion groups, workshop information, job postings, publications, consulting services, and survey information. Members have access to additional articles and an archive search.

Strategic Pricing Group
www.strategicpricinggroup.com
Sponsored by a consulting firm that specializes in strategic pricing, this site provides articles, self-assessment, recommended reading, a calendar of events, and information on educational services and consulting.

ORGANIZATIONS

USA

The Professional Pricing Society
3277 Roswell Road, Suite 620, Atlanta, Georgia, 30305
T: +1 770 509 9933
F: +1 770 509 1963
E: *info@pricingsociety.com*
www.pricing-advisor.com
PPS is an association for price decision makers and price management personnel; its members are primarily pricing and marketing executives. It offers its members conferences and workshops, monthly and quarterly publications, consulting services, and pricing workbooks.

For More Information

- **Marketing Management (pp. 2045–48)**
- **Packaging (pp. 2062–64)**

PROCESS CONTROL AND STATISTICAL PROCESS CONTROL

BOOKS

Managing Six Sigma: A Practical Guide to Understanding, Assessing, and Implementing the Strategy That Yields Bottom-line Success
FORREST W. BREYFOGLE, III, JAMES M. CUPELLO, BECKI MEADOWS
New York: John Wiley, 2000
300pp ISBN: 0471396737
This book provides detailed coverage of the Six Sigma techniques. Case studies describe some of the successes and pitfalls encountered in their successful implementation at Motorola and General Electric. Plans, checklists, and other materials are presented to help managers achieve a smooth and successful implementation.

Six Sigma: The Breakthrough Management Strategy Revolutionizing the World's Top Corporations
MIKEL HARRY, RICHARD SCHROEDER
New York: Bantam Doubleday Dell Books, Random House, 1999
300pp ISBN: 0385494378
This is an explanation of Six Sigma in which the authors cite examples of companies (such as Polaroid) where the concept is currently in practice. Essentially, Six Sigma is a process that "guides companies into making fewer mistakes in everything they do—from filling out a purchase order to manufacturing airplane engines." A guide to achieving cost-effective quality within large corporations, this book is especially pertinent to managers and investors.

Six Sigma Revolution: How General Electric and Others Turned Process into Profits
GEORGE ECKES
New York: John Wiley, 2000
274pp ISBN: 047138822X
Presenting Six Sigma as a quantitative approach to quality that has boosted productivity and increased profits for a number of large businesses, the author explains how and why it is superior to other quality improvement methods and describes how to create and sustain a Six Sigma initiative in an organization.

Six Sigma: SPC and TQM in Manufacturing and Services
GEOFF TENNANT
Brookfield, Vermont: Gower, 2001
160pp ISBN: 0566083744
Drawing upon his experience in implementing Six Sigma quality principles, the author develops a reasoned explanation of the benefits that Six Sigma can offer to any organization and describes the implementation process from start to finish, also investigating the relationship between Six Sigma and quality, customer satisfaction, business process, statistics and analysis, and process improvement methods.

The Six Sigma Way: How GE, Motorola, and Other Top Companies Are Honing Their Performance
PETER S. PANDE, ROBERT P. NEUMAN,

ROLAND R. CAVANAGH
New York: McGraw-Hill, 2000
448pp ISBN: 0071358064
This comprehensive guide to the application of Six Sigma across all industries presents the essentials of the system, outlines its advantages over TQM, and examines the process of adopting it. It also describes the Six Sigma Roadmap, a five-phase model for building the Six Sigma organization.The experiences of top companies illustrate the key issues.

The Six Sigma Way Team Fieldbook: An Implementation Guide for Process Improvement Teams
PETER S. PANDE, ROBERT P. NEUMAN, ROLAND R. CAVANAGH
New York: McGraw-Hill, 2001
300pp ISBN: 0071373144
Aimed at people involved with Six Sigma projects (those who are concerned with ''improving the quality of organizational processes''), this is a highly practical reference for team leaders and members, outlining both the methods that have made Six Sigma successful and the basic steps a team must follow in an improvement effort. The book helps teams: obtain the skills they need to identify a product, service, or process that needs improvement or redesign; gather data on the process and the rate of defects; find ways to improve quality: and much more. It also includes dozens of data-gathering forms and Six Sigma tools and worksheets, as well as describing key improvement methods in a concise how-to format with checklists and tips.

SPC Essentials and Productivity Improvement: A Manufacturing Approach
WILLIAM A. LEVINSON, FRANK TUMBELTY
Milwaukee, Wisconsin: ASQC Quality Press, 1996
266pp ISBN: 0873893727
Written for quality professionals, this text presents the essentials of SPC in a way that avoids the necessity of understanding lengthy calculations. It describes the general tools for improving productivity and quality, the specific tools and techniques of SPC, and the use of attribute control charts.

Statistical Methods for Quality Improvement 2nd ed.
THOMAS P. RYAN
New York: John Wiley, 2000
544pp (Wiley Series in Probability and Mathematical Statistics)
ISBN: 0471197750
Ryan provides a detailed introduction to the mathematics and statistics that form the basis of a range of fundamental quality control and statistical methods.

Statistical Process Control 4th ed.
JOHN S. OAKLAND
Woburn, Massachusetts: Butterworth-Heinemann, 1999
352pp ISBN: 0750644397
This new edition of a leading text reflects recent thinking in the field and provides a reliable reference source for statistical process control. The broad issues covered include understanding processes, process variability, process control, process capability, and process improvement.

Statistical Process Control for Quality Improvement
JAMES R. THOMPSON, JACEK KORONACKI
New York: CRC Press, 1993
456pp ISBN: 0412034212
The authors draw upon their experience of presenting short seminars to workers, foremen, and managers to create this introduction to SPC. They provide an overview of the subject for those with little knowledge of statistics, but the remaining, more detailed explanations of the analytical techniques of SPC are written for statisticians and production engineers with a higher level of mathematical understanding.

Understanding Statistical Process Control 2nd ed.
DONALD J. WHEELER, DAVID S. CHAMBERS
Knoxville, Tennessee: SPC Press, 1992
406pp ISBN: 0945320132
This textbook explains the techniques of statistical process control, including approaches to variance, summarizing data, and effective use of control charts. Glossaries of terms and symbols, lists of examples, and answers to exercises are included as appendices.

MAGAZINES

Six Sigma Forum Magazine
American Society for Quality, Six Sigma Forum
600 North Plankinton Avenue, Milwaukee, Wisconsin, 53203
T: +1 414 272 8575
F: +1 414 272 1734
www.sixsigmaforum.com
This quarterly magazine offers feature articles focusing on companies such as Motorola and GE that have benefited from the practice of Six Sigma, and is aimed at Six Sigma professionals at all levels of experience.

INTERNET

American Society for Quality
www.asq.org
This ASQ site includes a profile of Walter A. Shewhart, the first honorary member of the Society and acclaimed father of modern quality control. See www.asq.org/join/about/history/shewhart.html.

Six Sigma Forum
www.sixsigmaforum.com
The site of this recently formed Forum provides some introductory information on Six Sigma and its application. There are links to related informative articles and news, but you have to become a member to access these items.

ORGANIZATIONS

USA

American Productivity and Quality Center
123 North Post Oak Lane, 3rd Floor, Houston, Texas, 77024
T: +1 713 681 4020
F: +1 713 681 1182
E: apqcinfo@apqc.org
www.apqc.org
The APQC, founded in 1977, works with organizations of all sizes to improve productivity and quality. Its aim is to research and understand both emerging improvement methods and methods whose effectiveness is already proven, and it distributes its findings through education, advice, and information services. In 1992 it set up the International Benchmarking Clearinghouse to promote and facilitate the process of learning from best practice.

American Society for Quality
600 North Plankinton Avenue, Milwaukee, Wisconsin, 53202
T: +1 414 272 8575
F: +1 414 272 1734
E: cs@asq.org
www.asq.org
Founded in 1946, the ASQ is a society of individual and organizational members dedicated to the ongoing development and promotion of the concepts, principles, and techniques of quality. It has recently launched the Six Sigma Forum.

For More Information

☆ **Integrating Technology into Business Processes (pp. 169–70)**
☆ **Lean Manufacturing (pp. 183–84)**
☆ **X-engineering Success (pp. 245–46)**
Manufacturing Systems (pp. 2039–42)
Quality and Total Quality Management (pp. 2096–98)

"Treating processes holistically means that much more is being included under the umbrella of product development."
(Dan Dimanescu)

PRODUCT AND BRAND MANAGEMENT

BOOKS

Brand Asset Management: Driving Profitable Growth through Your Brands
SCOTT M. DAVIS
San Francisco, California: Jossey-Bass/Pfeiffer, 2000
300pp (Jossey-Bass Business and Management Series)
ISBN: 0787950777
This book suggests that brands should be seen as vehicles for company growth, and presents an 11-step strategy to help managers manage their brands as valuable assets.

Brand Building on the Internet
MARTIN LINDSTROM, TIM FRANK ANDERSEN
Milford, Connecticut: Kogan Page, 2000
320pp ISBN: 0749433132
The authors use case studies to look at the issues surrounding the development and maintenance of brands on the Internet. They discuss the characteristics of Internet marketing and explore ways in which practitioners can successfully brand build in the Internet environment.

Brand Leadership
DAVID A. AAKER, ERICH JOACHIMSTHALER
New York: Free Press, 2000
361pp ISBN: 0684866455
A reference tool for brand managers, this text analyzes brand management in today's world. Using case studies taken from a wide spectrum of companies (including Ralph Lauren, Swatch, and Adidas) the authors suggest that the world of brand management is undergoing structural and systematic change. The book offers guidance on accessing vital links between brands, and using these to company advantage.

Brand Warfare: 10 Rules for Building the Killer Brand
DAVID F. D'ALESSANDRO, MICHELE OWENS
New York: McGraw-Hill, 2001
208pp ISBN: 0071362932
This book considers ways in which companies often mishandle their brands. The author offers advice, based on his own experience and on company examples, to those wishing to build a successful brand in any market.

Building Strong Brands
DAVID A. AAKER
San Francisco, California: Jossey-Bass, 1994
390pp ISBN: 002900151X
Aaker discusses the varying elements of a brand, and emphasizes the need for managers to be aware of the importance of strong brands in today's marketplace. In discussing various large corporations (such as McDonald's and Kodak) Aaker demonstrates the process of managing a hugely successful brand. The author also explores ways of retaining a certain brand while under some pressure to alter it. A reference tool for anybody involved in brand management.

Differentiate or Die: Survival in Our Era of Killer Competition
JACK TROUT, STEVE RIVKIN
New York: John Wiley, 2000
230pp ISBN: 0471357642
This title is a useful guide on how to make ones product differ from those of everyone else and lists several ways to achieve this. These include being the first person to do something, being the latest person to do a version of something, and becoming the first choice of a certain type of consumer group.

4D Branding: Cracking the Corporate Code of the Network Economy
THOMAS GAD
Upper Saddle River, New Jersey: Financial Times Prentice Hall, 2000
184pp ISBN: 0273653687
In this book the author presents a four-dimensional model that can be used to understand brand strengths and weaknesses. Managers can put it to work when creating a new brand or analyzing an established one.

The Handbook of Brand Management
DAVID ARNOLD
Cambridge, Massachusetts: Perseus/Random House, 1993
259pp (Economist Books)
ISBN: 0201632799
As the number of competing products increases, brand management is becoming ever more important for all managers, not just the marketing department. Based on the brand expertise of Ashbridge Management College, this book is an up-to-date summary of brand practice. It deals with each stage of the strategic decision-making process, from research and market-testing to implementation and monitoring performance. Also included are case histories and practical advice.

The Infinite Asset: Managing Brands to Build New Value
SAM HILL, CHRIS LEDERER, KEVIN LANE KELLER
Boston, Massachusetts: Harvard Business School Press, 2001
238pp ISBN: 1578512492
This book sets out a new approach to brand management. Instead of dealing with brands on an individual basis, the authors argue, a "portfolio" approach should be adopted. Brands should be grouped into actively-managed collections, regardless of ownership. The authors look at case studies of 3M and Miller Beer, among others, which help readers visualize the relationships that tie their brands to each other and to the outside world. They also put together an eight-part toolkit that covers brand extensions and repositioning, as well as an organizational design for implementing brand portfolio management.

Managing Brand Equity: Capitalizing on the Value of a Brand Name
DAVID A. AAKER
San Francisco, California: Jossey-Bass, 1991
224pp ISBN: 0029001013
In this book, Aaker specifies the importance of understanding exactly what makes a brand so successful. For example, being in touch with your customer base and recognizing the subconscious associations that are linked to a brand name are essential. The author points out the lack of managerial understanding that prevails in branding, and aims to minimize this with practical guidelines for understanding the value of brand equity within a company.

Product Strategy and Management
MICHAEL BAKER, SUSAN HART
Upper Saddle River, New Jersey: Prentice Hall, 1996
550pp ISBN: 0130653683
This textbook is aimed at students and provides a broad introduction to the concepts and techniques of product strategy and management. It explores the theoretical foundations, new product strategy, product management, and product elimination.

Smart Things to Know About Brands and Branding
JOHN MARIOTTI
Oxford: Capstone, 2001
240pp (Smart Series)
ISBN: 1841120391
Mariotti's purpose in this book is to give managers advice on creating a brand, understanding brand values, growing a brand, becoming a smart brand manager, measuring

"I think it's quite clear that in the information age, the brand is what you compete on." (Andrew Neil)

  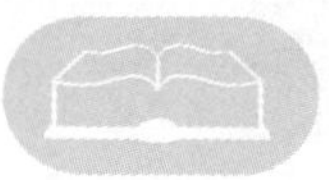    

success, and championing their organization's brand.

Strategic Brand Management: Building, Measuring and Managing Brand Equity
KEVIN LANE KELLER
Upper Saddle River, New Jersey: Prentice Hall, 1997
635pp ISBN: 0131201158
In its discussion of the role of brands in our society, this book offers a pragmatic approach to brand management, discussing the creation, assessment, and use of brand equity within an organization. Aimed at a wide spectrum of different businesses (not simply large corporations) *Strategic Brand Management* is a resource for almost anybody involved in brand management.

The 22 Immutable Laws of Branding: How to Build a Product or Service into a World-class Brand
LAURA RIES, AL RIES
New York: HarperCollins, 1998
192pp ISBN: 0887309372
In this title, the authors argue that branding is the basis of a strong marketing program, and that if it is not possible to create a strong brand, then nothing a company does, including advertising campaigns and public relations events, will help. The book looks at both successful brands and those that have failed, providing coherent explanations of the various factors involved.

What Makes Winning Brands Different: The Hidden Method behind the World's Most Successful Brands
ANDREAS BUCHHOLZ, WOLFRAM WORDEMANN
New York: John Wiley, 2000
222pp ISBN: 0471720259
The authors analyze the results of a research study of over 1,000 winning brands in order to establish a blueprint for brand growth and development. They argue that brands can achieve outstanding growth by adhering to specific laws or "growth codes," of which they identify 27. Putting these "codes" into effect is explored through case study and best practice examples.

MAGAZINES

Brand Strategy
ISSN: 0965-9390
Centaur Business Intelligence
St. Giles House, 50 Poland Street, London, W1F 7AX, U.K.
T: +44 (0) 20 7970 4000
F: +44 (0) 20 7943 8172
www.centaur.co.uk/public/pub
Aimed at marketing directors and senior managers, this monthly publication contains comment, analysis, and business intelligence on issues relating to brand management.

Brandweek
ISSN: 1064-4318
VNU Business Publications
770 Broadway, New York, 10003
T: +1 646 654 4500
F: +1 646 654 4480
www.brandweek.com
Brandweek is a weekly print and online publication aimed at top brand marketing executives in the United States. Its coverage includes marketing strategies, trends, new product news, and general news. It is aimed at all industries.

Journal of Brand Management
ISSN: 1350-231X
Henry Stewart Publications
P.O. Box 10812, Birmingham, Alabama, 35202-0812
T: +1 800 633 4931
F: +1 205 995 1588
www.henrystewart.com/journals/bm
This journal, published six times a year, is aimed at a wide readership of marketing directors, managers, academics, and consultants. Its content takes in all aspects of the management of brands, from their launch to their development and evaluation.

Journal of Product and Brand Management
ISSN: 1061-0421
MCB University Press
44 Brattle Street, 4th Floor, Cambridge, Massachusetts, 02138
T: +1 888 622 0075
F: +1 617 354 6875
www.emeraldinsight.com/jpbm.htm
This journal is issued seven times a year; the subscription includes online access via Emerald Fulltext. It covers topics such as brand management, consumer behavior, pricing strategies, marketing research, new product development, international pricing, and brand equity. Its target readership includes both practitioners and academics.

INTERNET

brandchannel.com
www.brandchannel.com
This site, produced by Interbrand, provides for an online exchange about branding. It contains a debate area, features, papers, and details of books, training, and jobs.

BrandingAsia.com
www.brandingasia.com
This site focuses on branding issues in Asia, and includes brand news, tips, case studies, articles, and a discussion board. A free monthly e-mail newsletter is available.

KnowThis.com
www.knowthis.com/other/product.htm
This section of the Marketing Virtual Library contains links to resources for product management, branding, and packaging.

The Management Roundtable
www.managementroundtable.com
This site describes itself as the leading information resource for product development professionals. It includes a subscription area giving access to product development best practice reports.

ORGANIZATIONS

USA

Institute for Brand Leadership
1000 Potomac Street NW, Suite 122, Washington, D.C., 20007
T: +1 202 337 1106
F: +1 202 333 2659
E: *contactus@instituteforbrandleadership.org*
www.instituteforbrandleadership.org
The Institute was established by the Brand Consultancy to facilitate, promote, and recognize the theories and practices that contribute to brand excellence.

Product Development and Management Association
17000 Commerce Parkway, Suite C, Mount Laurel, New Jersey, 08054
T: +1 856 439 9052
F: +1 856 439 0525
E: *pdma@pdma.org*
www.pdma.org
This professional nonprofit organization is dedicated to serving people with an interest in new products and services. It is a recognized provider of knowledge and tools intended to improve the effectiveness of the development and management of new products and services. It also arranges conferences, publications, awards, meetings, and workshops, and sponsors research.

Europe

Product Development and Management Association, U.K. and Ireland
Innovaro, 78 Belsize Gardens, London, NW3 4NG, U.K.
E: *timjones@innovaro.com*
www.pdma.org.uk

"Every advertisement should be thought of as a contribution to the complex symbol which is the brand image."
(David Ogilvy)

This is the U.K. and Ireland branch of the PDMA, a professional nonprofit organization dedicated to serving people with an interest in new products and services. It is a recognized provider of knowledge and tools intended to improve the effectiveness of the development and management of new products and services. It also arranges conferences, publications, awards, meetings, and workshops, and sponsors research.

International

Association of International Product Marketing Managers
1658 E. Capital Expressway, Suite 474, San Jose, California, 95111
T: +1 408 808 1550
E: *info@aipmm.com*
www.aipmm.com

The AIPMM is an organization that aims to provide focused and strategic information, training, and networking opportunities for professional product and marketing managers and their employers. Membership is either individual or corporate.

The Product-life Institute, Geneva
9 Chemin des Vignettes, 1231 Conches, Switzerland
T: +41 22 346 35 04
F: +41 22 346 04 18
E: *wrstahel@vtx.ch*
www.product-life.org
A nonprofit independent organization formed in 1982 in Geneva, the Institute is financed solely by contract research. It is involved in consulting and research in the area of optimization of the product life of goods and services, and focuses on issues of sustainability.

For More Information

☆ **Creating Powerful Brands (pp. 63–64)**
☆ **Managing New Product Portfolios (pp. 275–76)**
Advertising (pp. 1903–06)
General Business Information: Online Sources for Marketing (p. 1992)
Marketing Management (pp. 2045–48)
New Product Development (pp. 2054–56)

Project Management

BOOKS

The Accidental Project Manager: Surviving the Transition from Techie to Manager
Patricia Ensworth
New York: John Wiley, 2001
272pp ISBN: 047141011X
When projects fail it is often because the person in charge has no idea how to manage projects. This no-nonsense guide provides basic project management information including project planning, the roles of team members, the tools of the trade, and project control metrics. It also supplies templates, checklists, and sample forms for the beginner to use.

Effective Project Management
Robert Wysocki, et al.
New York: John Wiley, 2000
359pp ISBN: 0471360287
This book and CD-ROM package provides novices with a complete introduction to the principles of project management, and offers experienced project managers an opportunity to fine-tune their skills. It describes the management tools and techniques you need to stay on schedule and within budget without compromising quality. It adheres to the Project Management Institute's curriculum outline (PMBOK), and follows the necessary course requirements for professional certification. The CD-ROM provides a simulated environment in which to apply the principles, tools, and techniques described in the book.

Finding, Recruiting, and Keeping Peak Performers
Harry E. Chambers
Cambridge, Massachusetts: Perseus, 2001
256pp ISBN: 0738202894
This book offers valuable ideas for winning the talent war by seeing the hiring process from the candidate's point of view, exploring non-traditional recruiting sources (including the Internet), and motivating people to stay with the company once they've signed on, through use of benefits packages and other incentives. As well as training managers in the fine points of recruitment and hiring, the book describes how to use the interview process as a way to gauge the potential of an employee.

Five-phase Project Management
Joseph W. Weiss, Robert K. Wysocki
Cambridge, Massachusetts: Perseus, 1992
121pp ISBN: 0201563169
Five-phase Project Management offers the best project management practices in a simple, easy-to-use format for all project managers. In this practical, step-by-step book, Weiss and Wysocki walk the reader through each phase of a complex project: definition, planning, implementation, management, and maintenance.

Gower Handbook of Project Management 3rd ed.
J. Rodney Turner, Stephen J. Simister
Brookfield, Vermont: Gower, 2000
847pp ISBN: 0566081385
This handbook is written as an encyclopedia for the profession of project management, in particular for those studying for professional exams and people seeking certification anywhere in the world. It provides comprehensive coverage of all aspects of the subject. Most chapters are new to this edition.

A Guide to the Project Management Body of Knowledge: 2000 Edition
Project Management Institute
Newtown Square, Pennsylvania: Project Management Institute, 2001
200pp ISBN: 1880410230
This book is the basic Project Management reference and the accepted standard for the profession. It details the nine knowledge areas and 39 processes essential to a generic project management model that works in any industry. By establishing a standard, the guide also provides a common language for talking about project management. It is a key resource for those seeking Project Management Professional (PMP) certification.

Managing Successful Projects with Prince 2
APM Group Ltd.
Norwich: Stationery Office, 1999
342pp ISBN: 0113308558
This reference manual describes the Prince 2 project management method, one of the most popular project management methodologies. It provides detailed guidance on how to set up, organize, manage, control, and deliver projects

"Involve people in meaningful projects." (Stephen Covey)

on time, within budget, and with high quality. The processes and techniques of Prince 2 are said to help any project team cope with the risks, challenges, and opportunities in today's rapidly changing environment.

Project Management 7th ed.
DENNIS LOCK
Brookfield, Vermont: Gower, 2000
613pp ISBN: 056608225X
Lock provides comprehensive coverage of the subject of project management. The topics he focuses on include: the nature and purpose of project management; defining the project; estimating costs; commercial management; project planning and scheduling; network analysis in practice; resource scheduling; purchasing; implementing the program; managing progress; and cost management. Case studies, graphs, and illustrations are included.

Project Management: The Essential Guide to Thinking and Working Smarter
PETER HOBBS
New York: AMACOM, 2000
95pp (Self-development for Success)
ISBN: 081447067X
This book offers advice on the key skills required by the successful project manager, including effective planning, goal and objective setting, scheduling, progress monitoring, and the control of quality and output. It includes an index.

Project Management: The Managerial Process
CLIFFORD GRAY
New York: Irwin/McGraw-Hill, 2000
544pp (Irwin/McGraw-Hill Series, Operations and Decision Sciences)
ISBN: 0072501383
This book presents a balanced view of the technical and sociocultural dimensions of managing projects. It is suitable for a course in project management, and for individuals seeking a project management handbook. The text is application-oriented for managing any type of project, and includes advice on discovering the strategic role of projects in contemporary organizations, prioritizing, planning and scheduling projects, and orchestrating the complex network of relationships. It includes a CD-ROM, bibliographical references, and an index.

Project Management: Planning and Control Techniques 3rd ed.
RORY BURKE
New York: John Wiley, 2001
356pp ISBN: 047198762X
This book is a step-by-step guide to the latest project management planning and control techniques. The topics it covers include: the project life cycle; feasibility studies; project selection; work breakdown structures; the critical path method; resource planning; project accounts; quality management; risk management; and leadership.

The Project Manager's Desk Reference 2nd ed.
JAMES P. LEWIS
New York: McGraw-Hill, 1999
546pp ISBN: 007134750X
This is a comprehensive guide to project planning, scheduling, evaluation, control, and systems, giving the reader a template for managing projects of any size from start to finish. It discusses topics such as: how to develop project plans using Work Breakdown Structures, PERT, CPM, and Gantt schedules; conduct risk analysis; design a project control system; use earned value analysis to track projects; and communicate effectively with your team. In this second edition there are updated examples, illustrations and figures, checklists for every stage, plus lists of associations and Web sites.

The Project Manager's MBA: How to Translate Project Decisions into Business Success
DENNIS J. COHEN, ROBERT J. GRAHAM
San Francisco, California: Jossey-Bass, 2000
336pp (Jossey-Bass Business and Management Series)
ISBN: 0787952567
This text aims to provide an introduction to the business basics that every project manager needs to understand. These include value creation, accounting and finance strategy, and marketing. These concepts are related to the decisions project managers face every day. The aim is to develop the skills of project managers so that they can meet both their technical and their business objectives.

Project Planning, Scheduling, and Control 3rd ed.
JAMES P. LEWIS
New York: McGraw-Hill, 2000
350pp ISBN: 0071360506
This book offers an applications-oriented, non-theoretical understanding of the flexibility required in day-to-day management situations, and provides guidelines that apply to every phase of steering a project to its successful conclusion. This third edition has been updated to include easy-to-follow steps for managing multiple projects, effective risk management strategies, and an innovative blueprint for developing a workable project methodology.

Project Skills
SAM ELBEIK, MARK THOMAS
Woburn, Massachusetts: Butterworth-Heinemann, 1999
200pp (New Skills Portfolio Series)
ISBN: 0750639784
The authors provide a practical and accessible guide to managing projects of all sizes and across all industries. Presented as an action-focused training guide, the book explains real-world project management and introduces the key skills and techniques needed in the six stages of managing a project.

Web Project Management: Delivering Successful Commercial Web Sites
ASHLEY FRIEDLEIN
San Francisco, California: Morgan Kaufmann, 2000
324pp ISBN: 1558606785
This book covers the usual project management subjects of organizing teams, developing goals, and managing schedules and budgets, but from the unique perspective of the requirements of Web site development. This is not a conventional project management approach, nor is it a software engineering approach. Friedlein has focused on the essentials for delivering successful commercial sites by managing to deliverables, rather than to schedules, and balancing the often conflicting commercial, creative, content, and technical requirements.

The World Class Project Manager
ROBERT K. WYSOCKI, JAMES P. LEWIS
Cambridge, Massachusetts: Perseus, 2001
272pp ISBN: 0738202371
Wysocki and Lewis offer a practical handbook for anyone who aspires to achieve superior project-management skills. Featuring self-assessment tools, showcasing best practice examples from the field, and drawing on their own experience in training project managers around the world, the authors provide a comprehensive program for crafting a career development plan and putting it into action.

MAGAZINES

International Journal of Project Management
ISSN: 0263–7863
Elsevier Science
Regional Sales Office, Customer Support Department, P.O. Box 945, New York, 10159–0945
T: +1 212 633 3730
F: +1 212 633 3680
www.elsevier.com
The journal of the International Project Management Association publishes papers

"One worthwhile task carried to a successful conclusion is better than 50 half-finished tasks."
(Bertie Charles Forbes)

which cover both practical and theoretical aspects of project management. Case studies help to link theory with practice and the latest important areas of concern are covered in special issues. Published eight times a year.

Project
ISSN: 0957-7033
Impact!
Media House, 55 Old Road, Leighton Buzzard, Bedfordshire, LU7 2RB, U.K.
T: +44 (0) 1525 370 013
F: +44 (0) 1525 382 487
www.asm.org.uk/pub/project.htm
Project, the magazine of the U.K.'s Association for Project Management, aims to cover all aspects of project management across all industries.

Project Management Journal
ISSN: 0147-5363
Project Management Institute
4 Campus Boulevard, Newtown Square, Pennsylvania, 19073
T: +1 610 356 4600
F: +1 610 356 4647
www.pmi.org/publictn/pmjournal
Published quarterly, this journal provides comprehensive coverage of program and project management issues. Articles discuss problems and solutions in various aspects of project management.

Project Manager Today
ISSN: 1366-6851
Larchdrift Projects Ltd.
Unit 12, Moor Place Farm, Plough Lane, Bramshill, Hook, Hampshire, RG27 0RF, U.K.
T: +44 (0) 118 932 6665
F: +44 (0) 118 932 6663
www.projectnet.co.uk
This journal covers all aspects of project control, planning, costing, and management. Case studies and software reviews are included.

INTERNET

Association for Project Management
www.apm.org.uk
The site offers visitors details of news, events, qualifications, services, and publications in the field of project management. It also has information on member benefits and links to related organizations, and provides short reading lists.

European Institute of Advanced Project and Contract Management
www.epci.org
The site lists the Institute's member companies and associate academic institutions and introduces the qualifications it has on offer. Some full text articles published by the Epci are available to members, together with extracts from theses. It also includes a members-only area.

International Project Management Association
www.ipma.ch
This site introduces the services available from the IPMA. It lists conferences, seminars, and training courses, and also provides information on research and development activity, affiliates listing, and services for young project managers.

PMFORUM
www.pmforum.org
This information dissemination and exchange forum includes a portal to information, resources, and working groups associated with project manager accreditation, certification, education, research, and standards. It also contains listings of software, consulting services, and training resources, plus a calendar of events, and offers access to the electronic journal *Project Management World Today*.

Project Management Institute
www.pmi.org
The Project Management Institute (PMI) has over 75,000 members worldwide and is the leading nonprofit professional association in the area of Project Management. The site offers information on member services, including careers and awards programs, a bookshop, links to other project management organizations, and information on project management standards. It also provides opportunities for organizations to contribute to a corporate council and lists PMI seminars.

Project Management Library
www.mapnp.org/library/plan_dec/project/project.htm
Part of the Management Assistance Program for Nonprofits, this site's resources include a project management overview, information on team building and group leadership, general resources, and on-line discussion groups.

Wideman Comparative Glossary of Common Project Management Terms
www.maxwideman.com/pmglossary/index.htm
This site is a searchable glossary of hundreds of common project management terms. In many cases multiple definitions are listed, reflecting existing variations in usage within the industry.

ORGANIZATIONS

USA

Project Management Institute
Four Campus Boulevard, Newtown Square, Pennsylvania, 19073-3299
T: +1 610 356 4600
F: +1 610 356 4647
E: pmihq@pmi.org
www.pmi.org
A nonprofit professional association founded in 1969, the PMI sets project management standards, offers educational programs and professional certification, and is a publisher.

Europe

Association for Project Management
Thornton House, 150 West Wycombe Road, High Wycombe, Buckinghamshire, HP12 3AE, U.K.
T: +44 (0) 1494 440090
F: +44 (0) 1494 528937
E: secretariat@apm.org.uk
www.apm.org.uk
A professional body founded in 1970, the APM aims to be the U.K. national authority on project management. It promotes project management skills and training, and develops standards and certification for project managers. Services are delivered through joint ventures or through its members. The association is affiliated to the International Project Management Association.

European Institute of Advanced Project and Contract Management
Professor Olav Hanssensvei 10, 4021 Stavanger, Norway
T: +47 51 87 66 72
F: +47 51 87 17 11
E: epci@epci.org
www.epci.no
EPCI was founded in 1994 and has an international membership of companies and academic institutions. Member organizations form a network aimed at developing competence in project and contract management.

International

International Project Management Association
P.O. Box 1167, 3860 BD, Nijkerk, The Netherlands
T: +31 33 247 34 30
F: +31 33 246 04 70
E: info@ipma.ch
www.ipma.ch
The IPMA is a nonprofit organization, founded in 1965, promoting the advancement of project management methods, systems, and practical application techniques via its network of national project management associations in 26 countries. Individual participation is possible where there is no national society.

For More Information

☆ **Project Management (pp. 165–66)**
✔ **Managing Projects (pp. 512–13)**

"If anything can go wrong, it will." (Anonymous)

Psychological Tests

BOOKS

Career Tests: 25 Revealing Self-tests to Help You Find and Succeed at the Perfect Career

Louis H. Janda
Avon, Massachusetts: Adams Media Corporation, 1999
256pp ISBN: 1580621422

Career tests used to be the exclusive—and expensive—domain of psychologists. Advances in recent years have put a variety of useful self-assessment tools directly into the hands of the individual. This book provides a collection of these self-administered psychological tests to assist you in your career search. There are scales and surveys on everything from creativity, fear of success, and procrastination, to integrity, neuroticism, and agreeableness.

Essentials of Myers-Briggs Type Indicator Assessment

Naomi L. Quenk
New York: John Wiley, 1999
208pp (Essentials of Psychological Assessment Series)
ISBN: 0471332399

This book provides guidance on how to interpret and administer the Myers-Briggs Type Indicator® (MBTI®) test. The test classifies participants by broad personality types in order to gain an insight into how they gather information, make decisions, and orient themselves to their surroundings. This book also provides an appraisal of the test's relative strengths and weaknesses, advice on its clinical applications, and several case reports.

Gifts Differing: Understanding Personality Type

Isabel Briggs Myers, Peter B. Myers
Palo Alto, California: Consulting Psychologists Press, 1995
248pp ISBN: 089106074X

This book presents the innovative insights embodied in the MBTI® and explains its numerous practical applications. Distinguishing four categories of personality preferences—Extraversion-Introversion, Sensing-Intuition, Thinking-Feeling, and Judging-Perceiving—it details how different combinations of these qualities determine our perception of the world. The book includes tables showing how type preferences correlate with occupational interests, and clear descriptions of the 16 types to illustrate how the different functions interact.

Handbook of Psychological Testing 2nd ed.

Paul Kline
New York: Routledge, 1999
720pp ISBN: 0415211581

This handbook aims to provide a comprehensive and clear account of the whole field of psychometrics. It covers psychometric theory, the different kinds of psychological test, applied psychological tests, and the evaluation of the best published psychological tests.

How to Master Personality Questionnaires 2nd ed.

Mark Parkinson
Milford, Connecticut: Kogan Page, 2001
128pp ISBN: 0749434198

This practical guide aims to help readers explore their own personalities and prepare for personality questionnaires. It explains what personality is and how it is measured, why personality questionnaires are used, why different jobs require different personalities, and what employers do with questionnaire results. In addition, it identifies and describes the personality questionnaires most used in the United Kingdom, and provides a list of publishers with contact details.

How to Master Psychometric Tests 2nd ed.

Mark Parkinson
Milford, Connecticut: Kogan Page, 1998
150pp ISBN: 0749422548

This introduction to psychometric tests provides an overview of the different types of tests, including ability, intelligence, attainment, and aptitude tests, and explains how test results are used. It also gives practical advice on coping with anxiety and preparing for tests as well as printing practice tests supplied by Saville and Holdsworth Ltd. (SHL).

Individual Psychological Assessment: Predicting Behavior in Organizational Settings

Richard Jeanneret, Robert F. Silzer, eds.
San Francisco, California: Jossey-Bass, 1998
448pp ISBN: 0787908614

This is a definitive edited volume on the state of the art of a practice fraught with legal, scientific, sociopolitical, and certainly managerial complexity. Topics are arranged in four sections: Frameworks, Processes, Strategies, and Perspectives. They cover: theoretical frameworks; ethical, legal, professional, and cross-cultural issues; designing the assessment process; assessing and changing managers for new organizational roles; shaping organizational leadership; and more.

Now, Discover Your Strengths

Marcus Buckingham, Donald O. Clifton
New York: Free Press, 2001
260pp ISBN: 0743201140

One of Amazon.com's "Best of 2001," this book suggests a unique path to managerial success: focusing on the enhancement of people's strengths rather than the elimination of their weaknesses. In addition to showing how to capitalize on 34 positive personality themes in building a "strengths-based organization," the book provides an online questionnaire so that readers can instantly discover their own top five inborn talents. This interactive feature encourages introspection and provides a context for practical, real-time application.

Psychological Testing and Assessment 10th ed.

Lewis R. Aiken
Boston, Massachusetts: Allyn and Bacon, 1999
501pp ISBN: 0205295673

This book provides a comprehensive analysis of the theory and practice of psychometric testing, including the design and reliability of tests, assessment of abilities and personality, criticisms, and key issues. It is aimed both at psychometric practitioners and users of tests.

Psychological Testing at Work: How to Use, Interpret, and Get the Most Out of the Newest Tests in Personality, Learning Style, Aptitudes, Interests, and More!

Edward Hoffman
New York: McGraw-Hill, 2001
224pp ISBN: 0071360794

After falling out of fashion for some years, psychological tests are now used by employers to support the screening, selection, promotion, and training and development of employees. Employees also use similar self-assessment tools for their own career-planning purposes. This book examines 42 popular assessment tools. The purpose, design, validity, and utility of each tool is considered to help the reader

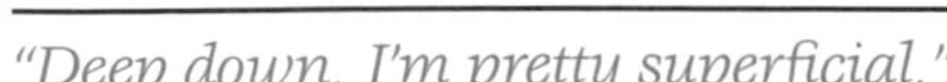
"Deep down, I'm pretty superficial." (Ava Gardner)

  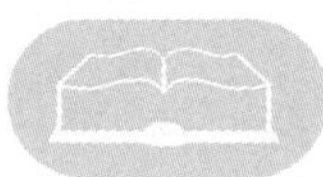    

know how to best use and interpret these instruments.

Psychometric Testing: 1000 Ways to Assess Your Personality, Creativity, Intelligence, and Lateral Thinking
PHILIP CARTER, KEN RUSSELL
New York: John Wiley, 2001
240pp (IQ Workout Series)
ISBN: 0471523763
This book contains 40 new psychometric tests covering such subjects as risk taking, leadership, positivity, aggression, tact, ambition, tolerance, and imagination. To these are added two intelligence tests that use word and number puzzles, math, and diagrams to test spatial, verbal, numerical, and logical ability. Scores and answers to all the tests are included.

Tests That Work: Designing and Delivering Fair and Practical Measurement Tools in the Workplace
ODIN WESTGAARD
San Francisco, California: Jossey-Bass/Pfeiffer, 1999
354pp ISBN: 078794596X
This comprehensive guide to the use of tests in the assessment of people is aimed at managers and human resources professionals who require an understanding of the way tests are used and the care needed in planning, designing, and interpreting test results.

Using Psychometrics: A Practical Guide to Testing and Assessment 2nd ed.
ROBERT EDENBOROUGH
Milford, Connecticut: Kogan Page, 1999
240pp ISBN: 0749431261
This book provides a detailed and practical guide to the use of tests in staff selection and recruitment. The author attempts to demystify testing, while pointing out the pitfalls of ill-considered use, and shows how to understand the different types of test and choose the most appropriate one. The legal, regulatory, and commercial framework is also considered.

What Type Am I?
RENEE BARON
New York: Penguin, 1998
208pp ISBN: 014026941X
This book takes on the complexity of the 16 personality types, which are derived from the Myers–Briggs Type Indicator tests, and makes them accessible to the general reader. The aim of this book is to give individuals the opportunity to comprehend the different personality types, find their own type, and use this knowledge to advance their lives, both on a professional and personal level.

MAGAZINES

Assessment Journal
ISSN: 0731–0277
International Association of Assessing Officers
130 E. Randolph, Suite 850, Chicago, Illinois, 60601
T: +1 312 819 6100
F: +1 312 819 6149
www.iaao.org
A bimonthly journal containing articles on assessment techniques and practices, property taxation, assessment administration, related research, recent legislation and court decisions, assessment and appraisal literature, and other topics of interest to assessment personnel.

European Journal of Psychological Assessment
ISSN: 1015–5759
Hogrefe and Huber Publishers
Seattle Office, P.O. Box 2487, Kirkland, Washington, 98083–2487
T: +1 425 820 1500
F: +1 425 823 8324
www.hhpub.com/journals/ejpa
This journal, which is the official journal of the European Association of Psychological Assessment, is directed at both researchers and practitioners, and provides a forum for scholarly communication in the field of psychological assessment. It covers assessment in clinical, educational, and organizational contexts and addresses legal, ethical, and professional issues.

International Journal of Selection and Assessment
ISSN: 0965–075X
Blackwell Publishers
350 Main Street, Malden, Massachusetts, 02148
T: +1 781 388 8200
F: +1 781 388 8232
www.blackwellpublishers.com/asp/listofj.asp
This quarterly journal covers selection, performance appraisal, assessment methodology, the theory and practice of psychometric measurement, and employment legislation.

International Journal of Testing
ISSN: 1530–5058
Lawrence Erlbaum Associates, Inc.
10 Industrial Avenue, Mahwah, New Jersey, 07430–2262
T: +1 800 926 6579
F: +1 201 760 3735
www.erlbaum.com/journals/journals/IJT/ijt.htm
This quarterly journal is dedicated to the advancement of the theory, research, and practice of testing and assessment in psychology, education, counseling, human resources management, and related disciplines. It is aimed at scholars, professionals, and students, and is the official journal of the International Test Commission.

International Public Management Journal
ISSN: 10967494
Elsevier Science
Regional Sales Office, P.O. Box 945, New York, 10159–0945
T: +1 212 633 3730
F: +1 212 633 3680
www.elsevier.com/inca/publications/store/6/2/0/2/1
IPMJ is a biannual publication of the International Public Management Network. It publishes articles about original research in the field of public management, and aims to aid problem solving and decision making for those working in the public sector.

Psychometrika
ISSN: 0033–3123
Psychometric Society
P.O. Box 12194, Research Triangle Institute, 326 Cox Statistics Building, 3040 Cornwallis Road, Research Triangle Park, North Carolina, 27709–2194
T: +1 919 541 6741
www.psychometricsociety.org
This quarterly journal publishes articles on the development of quantitative models for psychological phenomena and quantitative methods in the behavioral and social sciences, including techniques for the evaluation of psychological data.

Public Administration and Management: An Interactive Journal
ISSN: 1087–0091
School of Public Affairs, Pennsylvania State University at Harrisburg, Middletown, Pennsylvania, 17057–4908
www.pamij.com
This online-only journal is run by academics at Pennsylvania State University (Harrisburg). It is peer-reviewed in the same way as other printed

"Blameless people are always the most exasperating." (George Eliot)

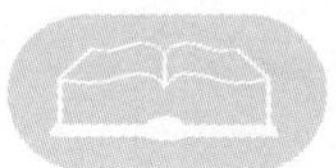

academic journals and four issues are produced annually. The scope is wide so as to include as many topics of interest to as wide an audience as possible. Articles can be read online or downloaded as PDF files.

Public Administration Quarterly
ISSN: 07349149
School of Public Affairs, Pennsylvania State University
Public Administration Quarterly, 2103 Fairway Lane, Harrisburg, Pennsylvania, 17112
T: +1 717 948 6363
F: +1 215 893 1763
www.spaef.com/paq.html
Formerly the *Southern Review of Public Administration*, this journal publishes articles on a range of public administration topics, such as budgeting, education, technology, ethics, and decision making. The American Society for Public Administration is a cosponsor.

Public Administration Review
ISSN: 00333352
Blackwell Publishers
350 Main Street, Malden, 02148, Massachusetts
T: +1 781 388 8200
F: +1 781 388 8210
www.blackwellpublishers.co.uk
PAR is the journal of the American Society for Public Administration and is published six times a year. Article focus on current trends, legislation, new publications, and a wide range of other topics, making the journal required reading for practitioners, scholars, teachers, and trainers interested in public sector management. Tables of contents are available at www.aspanet.org/publications/par.

INTERNET

ASE
www.ase-solutions.co.uk
Advice on assessments and practice tests are accessible on this site, as well as product information from a test publisher based in the United Kingdom.

Center for Applications of Psychological Type
www.capt.org
CAPT is a research and educational organization sustaining the work of Isabel Briggs-Myers. The Web site offers free searches of a bibliography of psychological type.

ERIC Clearinghouse on Assessment and Evaluation
www.ericae.net
This site, which focuses on the use of tests in an educational context, includes access to a database of tests with descriptions and publisher details. It is run by the University of Maryland.

International Enneagram Association
www.intl-enneagram-assn.org
The ''enneagram'' is an ancient nine-pointed symbol now used as a psychospiritual tool for personal development. Nine distinct personality ''types'' are associated with the points of the symbol. The International Enneagram Association's Web site provides background information, detailed analyses of the nine personality types, an extensive bibliography, and links to teachers and training resources.

SHLDirect
www.shldirect.com
This site, provided by a well-known test publisher, offers practice tests and advice aimed primarily at students.

Sussex University Career Development Unit Psychometric Tests
www.sussex.ac.uk/Units/CDU/psycho.html
This site offers advice for students on taking tests, links to test publishers, and tests on the Web.

The Keirsey Temperament Sorter II
www.advisorteam.com/user/ktsintro.asp
Keirsey's 70-question personality assessment may be taken online (free) to learn which of the four ''temperament'' types (an extension of the 16 Myers–Briggs personality types) you are. This test is used in career development programs at *Fortune* 500 companies as well as in counseling and career placement centers at major universities.

The Personality Page
www.personalitypage.com
Obtain a relatively reliable personality profile on the Internet for a mere $5. This test, validated with over 100,000 users, comprises 60 questions that yield 16 personality types, based on the work of Carl Jung, Isabel Briggs Myers, and Katharine Cook Briggs. The site also offers information on personality types and careers, relationships, and personal growth.

ORGANIZATIONS

USA

American Psychological Association
750 First Street NE, Washington, D.C., 20002–4242
T: +1 202 336 5580
F: +1 202 336 5568
E: membership@apa.org
www.apa.org
With over 150,000 members, including researchers, educators, clinicians, consultants, and students, the APA is the largest professional organization representing psychology in the United States. It works to advance psychology as a science and as a profession through divisions in 49 subfields of psychology and affiliation with local associations.

American Society for Public Administration
1120 G Street NW, Suite 700, Washington, D.C., 20005
T: + 1 202 393 7878
F: + 1 202 638 4952
E: info@aspa.net
www.aspanet.org
ASPA is a professional association for public administrators that acts to improve government management and ethics and as an advocate for public service; its 10,000 members include non-profit administrators, academics, teachers, and students. It offers conferences, publications, research, and online resources dealing with various issues related to public-sector management. Local chapters enable members to meet and network, and attend talks and conferences. Members receive the *Public Administration Review* and *PA Times*, ASPA's monthly newspaper.

Association of Test Publishers
1201 Pennsylvania Avenue NW, Suite 300, Washington, D.C., 20004
T: +1 202 857 8444
E: lauren@testpublishers.org
www.testpublishers.org
The ATP is a nonprofit organization established in 1992 with the aims of fostering good working relationships between test publishers and promoting integrity and professionalism in the industry. It monitors legislative and regulatory developments in the field of testing, carries out networking and advocacy activities, and publishes a newsletter and an online journal.

Buros Institute of Mental Measurements
University of Nebraska-Lincoln, 21 Teachers College Hall, Lincoln, Nebraska, 68588–0348
T: +1 402 472 6203
F: +1 403 472 6203
E: bplake1@unl.edu

"Tough is passé. Today, you're dealing with a variety of head game. That's where the cruelty is."
(Abraham Zaleznik)

www.unl.edu/buros
The Buros Institute provides information and assistance in the selection of appropriate tests, and encourages test development and measurement research. Its publications include the *Mental Measurements Yearbook*, *Tests in Print*, and a journal, *Applied Measurement in Education*.

International City/County Management Association

777 North Capitol Street NE, Suite 500, Washington, D.C., 20002
T: + 1 202 289 4262
F: + 1 202 962 3500
E: membership@icma.org
www.icma.org
ICMA is a professional and educational organization representing managers and administrators in local governments. With a focus on local government management issues, it offers its members research and analysis, an annual conference, publications, and professional development resources.

National Fair Access Coalition on Testing (FACT)

3 Terrace Way, Suite D, Greensboro, North Carolina, 27403–3660
T: +1 336 547 0607
F: +1 336 547 0558
www.fairaccess.org
FACT was formed in 1996 to protect the rights of counseling and mental health professionals not qualified as psychologists to use psychological, educational, vocational, and industrial tests, and to promote high standards of testing practice in member organizations.

Psychometric Society

P.O. Box 12194, Research Triangle Institute, 326 Cox Statistics Building, 3040 Cornwallis Road, Research Triangle Park, North Carolina, 27709–2194
T: +1 919 541 6741
E: mcleod@rti.org
www.psychometricsociety.org
The Psychometric Society is a nonprofit professional organization working for the advancement of quantitative measurement practices in psychology, education, and the social sciences. It publishes a journal, *Psychometrika*, and organizes an annual conference.

Society for Personality Assessment

6109H Arlington Boulevard, Falls Church, Virginia, 22044
T: +1 703 534 4772
E: klecksen@aol.com
www.personality.org
The SPA was founded by Bruno Klopfer, incorporated as the Rorschach Institute in 1938, and renamed in 1971 to reflect a wider interest in the field. It is dedicated to the advancement of professional personality assessment, the development of procedures for personality assessment, and the ethical use of such techniques. Activities include meetings, and the publication of a newsletter and the *Journal of Personality Assessment*.

Europe

British Psychological Society

St. Andrews House, 48 Princess Road East, Leicester, Leicestershire, LE1 7DR, U.K.
T: +1 (0) 116 254 9568
F: +1 (0) 116 247 0787
E: enquiry@bps.org.uk
www.bps.org.uk
With 34,000 members, the BPS is the representative body for psychologists in the United Kingdom. It was founded in 1901 under the name The Psychological Society, renamed in 1906, and granted a royal charter in 1965. The Society's aims are to encourage the development of psychology as a scientific discipline and a profession, to raise standards of training and practice in the field, and to raise public awareness of psychology. It sets standards for occupational testing and publishes reviews of ability and aptitude tests and personality assessment instruments. The Certificate of Competence in Occupational Testing is accredited by the BPS.

European Association of Psychological Assessment

Universidad de Barcelona, Facultad de Psicología, Dept. Personalidad, Evaluación y Tratamiento Psicológico, Paseo Vall d'Hebrón 171 (Edificio Ponent), 08035 Barcelona, Spain
E: mforns@psi.ub.es
www.uam.es/centros/psicologia/paginas/eapa
The EAPA, formerly the Spanish Association of Psychological Assessment, was founded in 1990 in Madrid. Those with a university degree or the equivalent who have contributed to the development of psychological assessment are eligible to become members. The organization aims to increase scientific interest in psychological assessment in Europe, develop research in the field, improve the practice of assessment, and create opportunities for the exchange of information among scholars in the field.

International

Association for Psychological Type

4700 W. Lake Avenue, Glenview, Illinois, 60025–1485
T: +1 847 375 4717
F: +1 847 375 6317
E: info@aptcentral.org
www.aptcentral.org
This is an international membership organization founded in 1979, whose members come from a variety of backgrounds in business, organization development, education, psychology, and counseling. Its activities include training programs, workshops, and conferences; it has local groups and produces publications.

Australian Association for Psychological Type

P.O. Box 768, Toowong, Queensland, 4066, Australia
E: info@aapt.org.au
www.aapt.org.au
Founded in 1992, the AAPT promotes the knowledge and use of psychological type in Australia. Members include psychologists, consultants, academics, teachers, trainers, and managers. The Association publishes the *Australian Psychological Type Review*, supports research in this area, and organizes biennial conferences.

International Public Management Network

Fred Thompson, Atkinson Graduate School of Management, Willamette University, 900 State Street, Salem, Oregon, 97301–3922
T: +1 503 370 6228
F: +1 503 370 3011
E: fthompso@willamette.edu
www.inpuma.net
IPMN is a forum for discussion of ideas and information in the field of public sector management. It holds an annual conference and workshops, and publishes the biannual *International Public Management Journal*.

For More Information

- **Personnel Management and HR Management (pp. 2067–71)**
- **Recruitment and Selection (pp. 2099–2101)**

"Keep up appearances; there lies the test. The world will give thee credit for the rest."
(Charles Churchill)

  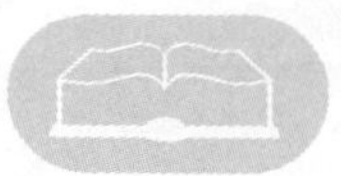    

PUBLIC RELATIONS

BOOKS

The Complete Guide to Publicity: Maximize Visibility for Your Product, Service, or Organization
JOE MARCONI
New York: McGraw-Hill/NTC, 1999
239pp ISBN: 0844200913
This book provides an effective guide for any person tasked with public relations, whether for a business or nonprofit organization. The author addresses all aspects of running a successful public relations campaign, including the difference between publicity campaigns and paid advertisement, understanding different media, how to create publicity opportunities, and a detailed procedure for creating a publicity campaign.

The Crisis Counselor: A Step-by-step Guide to Managing a Business Crisis
JEFFREY R. CAPONIGRO
New York: McGraw-Hill/NTC, 2000
320pp ISBN: 0809224909
This book is an easy to comprehend primer on the field of public relations and crisis management for businesses for any size. The author outlines steps to take to prevent a business crisis from occurring, along with detailed techniques and tips for managing and resolving a crisis when it does occur.

Effective Writing Skills for Public Relations 2nd ed.
JOHN FOSTER
Milford, Connecticut: Kogan Page, 2001
160pp ISBN: 0749436328
This book is a practical guide to writing style for students and PR practitioners. It looks at grammar, developing a house style, headlines and captions, press releases, and speeches and public speaking.

Guerrilla PR Wired: Waging a Successful Publicity Campaign Online, Offline, and Everywhere in between
MICHAEL LEVINE
New York: McGraw-Hill, 2001
288pp ISBN: 0071382313
This book reexamines the principles of "Guerrilla PR" (introduced in the author's book *Guerrilla PR*, HarperCollins, 1993), the technique for creating cost-effective publicity, for the age of the World Wide Web. The book explains how the key tenets have changed with developments in technology, and introduces new tactics for conveying online messages. Readers will learn how the pros use the Web for publicity, how to focus on a target to get superior results and how to avoid all the pitfalls that lie in wait for the Web PR novice. The book also features a wide variety of empirical examples.

Planning and Managing a PR Campaign 2nd ed.
ANNE GREGORY
Milford, Connecticut: Kogan Page, 2001
160pp ISBN: 0749429917
Gregory presents a step-by-step guide to the stages of a PR campaign, covering all the important aspects, and including case studies and a ten-point action plan.

Public Relations Handbook
ALISON THEAKER
New York: Routledge, 2001
320pp ISBN: 0415213347
A detailed introduction to the theory and practice of public relations is provided by this comprehensive handbook. It looks at all aspects of the subject, including training and entry into the profession, ethical issues, the use of new technology, and contains case studies.

Public Relations Kit for Dummies
ERIC YAVERBAUM, ROBERT BLY
New York: Hungry Minds, 2000
346pp ISBN: 0764552775
Part of a series offering concise, practical information on a variety of topics, this book addresses what all business owners and managers need to know about effective public relations. Presented in an easy to understand style, this title offers specific strategies and techniques for public relations, along with information on utilizing new technologies, such as the Internet, in PR campaigns. Also included is a CD-ROM with lists of PR firms and media contacts.

Public Relations: Strategies and Tactics 6th ed.
DENNIS L. WILCOX, ET AL.
New York: Longman, 2000
584pp ISBN: 0321055551
This book presents a comprehensive outline of the principles, concepts, and methods of public relations. This latest edition focuses specifically on global issues, use of the Internet and other new technologies, and ethical issues in public relations. The text differs from similar texts in the field through the inclusion of a series of up-to-date case studies.

Risk Issues and Crisis Management: A Casebook of Best Practice
MICHAEL REGESTER, JUDY LARKIN
Milford, Connecticut: Kogan Page, 1998
160pp (PR in Practice Series)
ISBN: 0749423935
This book deals with the successful handling of crisis situations so that damage and disruption are minimized. Case studies and models illustrate how complex crises have been handled in practice, both successfully and unsuccessfully.

Running a Public Relations Department 2nd ed.
MIKE BEARD
Milford, Connecticut: Kogan Page, 2001
160pp (PR in Practice Series)
ISBN: 0749434244
This book contains a step-by-step guide to the different aspects of operating a successful public relations unit. It describes the main areas of activity and examines such issues as the departmental plan, budgets, selecting personnel and building a team, and working with PR consultants.

MAGAZINES

FrontLine
ISSN: 0269–0357
International Public Relations Association
Cheltonian House, Portsmouth Road, Esher, Surrey, KT10 9AA, U.K.
T: +44 (0) 1372 461188
F: +44 (0) 1372 461159
www.ipranet.org
This is a quarterly magazine on public relations issues, published by the International Public Relations Association. It is aimed at international PR professionals and considers topics of worldwide interest through articles and comment.

PR Week
ISSN: 0267–6087
PR Publications Ltd.
220 Fifth Avenue, New York, 10001
T: +1 877 389 3862
www.prweekus.com/us
This is a weekly newspaper with coverage of all areas of public relations. It is written for public relations professionals both in consulting organizations and in in-house PR departments.

"I enjoy the fact that I am creating a climate of opinion." (Jan Brown)

Public Relations Quarterly
ISSN: 0033–3700
44 West Market Street, P.O. Box 311,
Rhinebeck, New York, 12572–0311
T: +1 845 876 2081
F: +1 845 876 2561
www.newsletter-clearinghse.com
Aimed at PR professionals, this quarterly publication contains items on research and education and the theory and practice of PR, case studies, advice, and survey results.

Public Relations Review
ISSN: 0363–8111
Elsevier Science
Regional Sales Office, Customer Support Department, P.O. Box 945, New York, 10159–0945
T: +1 212 633 3730
F: +1 212 633 3680
www.elsevier.com
The *Review* is a quarterly publication containing articles that provide in-depth analysis of public relations issues. Most of these are based on research by professionals and academics.

Public Relations Strategist
ISSN: 1082–9113
Public Relations Society of America
33 Irving Place, New York, 10003–2376
T: +1 212 995 2230
F: +1 212 995 0757
www.prsa.org/prpubs.html
This quarterly journal presents new perspectives and ideas related to the strategic importance of effective public relations at management level.

Public Relations Tactics
ISSN: 1080–6792
Public Relations Society of America
33 Irving Place, New York, 10003–2376
T: +1 212 995 2230
F: +1 212 995 0757
www.prsa.org/prpubs.html
This monthly newspaper covers the latest trends in public relations and is designed to meet the current needs of public relations professionals. The timely information it contains should help any professional improve his or her PR skills and remain competitive in the field.

Quality Management Journal
ISSN: 10686967
American Society for Quality
600 North Plankinton Avenue, Milwaukee, Wisconsin, 53201–3005
T: +1 414 272 8575
F: +1 414 272 1734
www.as.org/pub/qmj
This is a quarterly journal that links researchers with practitioners by communicating and discussing research findings. Articles are not technical in nature, but accessible to those working in quality management.

Quality Progress
ISSN: 0033524X
American Society for Quality
600 North Plankinton Avenue, Milwaukee, Wisconsin, 53203–3005
T: +1 414 272 8575
F: +1 414 272 1734
www.asq.org/pub/qualityprogress
This is a monthly magazine of the leading quality improvement organization in the U.S. It focuses on standards and the implementation of quality methods in the fields of knowledge management, process improvement, organizational behavior, and related fields.

Six Sigma Forum Magazine
American Society for Quality
600 North Plankinton Avenue, Milwaukee, Wisconsin, 53203–3005
T: +1 414 272 8575
F: +1 414 272 1734
www.asq.org/pub/sixsigma
This monthly magazine was founded in January 2002 to look at Six Sigma practice in different companies and to review the literature about Six Sigma methods. For instance, Issue 2 included articles about financial services quality implementation, careers, program design, corporate culture, and information technology.

Total Quality Magazine
ISSN: 09544127
Routledge
325 Chestnut Street, Suite 800, Philadelphia, Pennsylvania, 19106
T: +1 800 354 1420
F: +1 215 625 8914
www.tandf.co.uk/journals/routledge/09544127.html
TQM is published eight times a year and covers business excellence, the Six Sigma concept, ISO 9000, customer satisfaction, quality management systems, the Balanced Scorecard, and many other topics of interest to quality managers.

INTERNET

GSUPRSSA Web
www.gsu.edu/~wwwpra/links.html
This site gives links to general public relations resources, publications, organizations, and job information.

Managing Public Relations
www.workz.com/content/292.asp
This Web site serves as a resource for small business owners. It offers comprehensive information on public relations techniques, including guides for creating effective press releases, where and how to distribute press releases, promoting your business's Web site, and a directory of PR firms and associations.

Online Public Relations
www.online-pr.com
Online Public Relations provides links to other sites containing public relations resources.

PR Navigator
www.prnavigator.com
This Web site serves as a comprehensive resource on public relations for users ranging from business leaders to students. The resources include access to current research and industry reports, links to online PR journals and newsletters, directories of public relations agencies, and links to PR associations worldwide.

PR Place
www.prplace.com
This site contains a listing of Internet resources on public relations. The categories it covers include organizations in PR, publications, news sources, and databases.

PRWeb
www.prweb.com
PRWeb is a U.S. company, based in Ferndale, Washington, that offers a free service distributing press releases over the Internet.

Public Relations Resources
www.publicrelationsresources.com
The mission of this site is to provide regular informative articles on how to promote events, people, and businesses. It includes free articles, news headlines, and a list of links.

ORGANIZATIONS

USA

American Society for Quality
600 North Plankinton Avenue, Milwaukee, Wisconsin, 53203–3005
T: +1 414 272 8575
F: +1 414 272 1734
E: cs@asq.org
www.asq.org
ASQ is the leading quality-improvement member organization in the United States. It has 117,000 individual and 1,100 corporate members, in 247 local sections and 22 industry divisions. The Society focuses on issues including statistical process control, quality cost measurement and control, total quality management, failure analysis, and zero defects. It offers continuing education; certification

  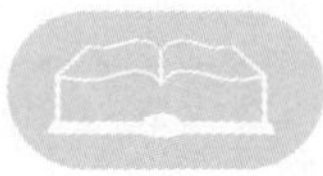    

programs; conferences; and reference, referral, and research services. The ASQ publishes widely under its Quality Press imprint, its monthly magazines *Quality Progress* and *Six Sigma Forum Magazine*, and the quarterly *Quality Management Journal*. (For other ASQ publications, see www.asq.org/pub.)

Institute for Public Relations
University of Florida, P.O. Box 118400, Gainesville, Florida, 32611–8400
T: +1 352 392 0280
F: +1 352 846 1122
www.instituteforpr.com
The mission of the IPR is to improve the effectiveness of organizations by advancing the professional knowledge and practice of public relations through research and education. It provides publications, lectures, awards, and professional development forums, and conducts research projects. Within the IPR is the Commission on Public Relations Measurement and Evaluation. IPR services are aimed at students, academics, and practitioners.

Public Relations Society of America
33 Irving Place, New York, 10003–2376
T: +1 212 995 2230
F: +1 212 995 0757
E: hq@prsa.org
www.prsa.org
The PRSA is a membership body for public relations professionals. Its aim is to unify, strengthen, and advance the profession. It conducts education and research, advances members' professional development, and offers other membership services. It also produces the magazines *Public Relations Strategist* and *Public Relations Tactics*

The Association for Quality and Participation
P.O. Box 2055, Milwaukee, Wisconsin, 53201–2055
T: + 1 800 733 3310
F: + 1 513 381 0070
E: aqp@aqp.org
www.aqp.org
AQP is a nonprofit membership association dedicated to improving workplaces through quality and participation practices. Membership benefits include publications, access to AQP's information center, continuing education, conferences, and networking opportunities.

Women Executives in Public Relations
FDR Station, P.O. Box 7657, New York, 10150–7657
T: +1 212 750 7373
F: +1 212 750 7375
E: info@wepr.org
www.wepr.org
This is an organization for senior women in the public relations field. Its mission is to support the career advancement of female practitioners and to foster the use of public relations to benefit the goals of business and society. It is an individual membership body that is involved in influencing and lobbying, and provides a forum for the exchange of career, management, and practitioner issues.

Europe

Institute of Public Relations
The Old Trading House, 15 Northburgh Street, London, EC1V 0PR, U.K.
T: +44 (0) 20 7253 5151
F: +44 (0) 20 7490 0588
E: info@ipr.org.uk
www.ipr.org.uk
The IPR is a U.K. professional body for those working in the area of public relations.

Public Relations Consultants Association
Willow House, Willow Place, Victoria, London, SW1P 1JH, U.K.
T: +44 (0) 20 7233 6026
F: +44 (0) 20 7828 4797
E: flora@prca.org.uk
www.martex.co.uk/prca
The PRCA, set up in 1969, is a trade association with 128 members, these being consulting firms of all sizes working in PR in the United Kingdom. It provides representation for the industry to government and the media, and such services as PRJobseek, training, and financial management. It also runs seminars, conferences, and research projects.

International

International Public Relations Association
Cheltonian House, Portsmouth Road, Esher, Surrey, KT10 9AA, U.K.
T: +44 (0) 1372 461188
F: +44 (0) 1372 461159
E: iprasec@compuserve.com
www.ipranet.org
IPRA aims to provide professional development and personal networking opportunities for its worldwide membership, and to promote the practice of public relations on a global level. It was founded in 1955 and now has members in 82 countries.

For More Information

- ✔ Public Relations Planning (pp. 476–77)
- Advertising (pp. 1903–06)
- Contingency, Crisis, Disaster Management (pp. 1939–41)
- General Business Information: Online Sources for Marketing (p. 1992)
- Internal Communication (pp. 2007–09)
- Interpersonal Communication/ Relations (pp. 2012–14)

Public Sector Management

BOOKS

Civil Service Yearbook 2002
Stationery Office
London, 2002
ISBN: 0114301786
This yearbook provides a guide to U.K. government departments and agencies. It presents details of the royal households; parliamentary offices; ministers of state, central government departments, and executive agencies; libraries, museums, and galleries; research councils; and includes salary tables and civil service statistics. A companion CD-ROM is included.

Management in the Public Sector: Challenge and Change 2nd ed.
Kester Isaac-Henry, Chris Painter, Chris Barnes
London: International Thomson Business Press, 1997
331pp ISBN: 0412737507
This revised edition examines issues and developments in public management, with particular emphasis on the process of change and the unique challenges facing public service organizations. The management issues covered include: resource and performance management in public service organizations; changing management and employment in local

"The new mixed economy looks. . .for a synergy between public and private sectors."
(Anthony Giddens)

  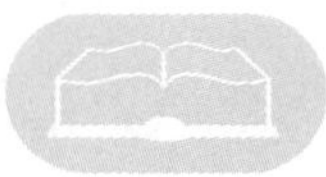    

government; management accountability in public services; and management by the unelected state—the rise of quangocracy.

Private Sector Strategies for Social Service Success
KEVIN P. KEARNS
San Francisco, California: Jossey-Bass, 2000
288pp ISBN: 0787941891
While there is a great deal of information available on strategic planning processes for government and nonprofit organizations, Kearns breaks new ground by providing them with guidelines on the selection and use of specific, real-world strategic options. Strategies discussed include vertical integration, diversification, concentration, and collaboration. Kearns tailors these business sector concepts to the unique missions, contexts, and constituencies of government and nonprofit entities.

Public Administration: Understanding Management, Politics, & Law in the Public Sector 5th ed.
DAVID H. ROSENBLOOM, ROBERT S. KRAVCHUK, DEBORAH GOLDMAN ROSENBLOOM
New York: McGraw-Hill, 2001
640pp ISBN: 0072401923
The continued popularity of this volume for use in both undergraduate and graduate level programs is based on its unique incorporation of three essential perspectives on public administration: management, politics, and the law. This edition goes one step further by dividing management into traditional and innovative approaches. Part three features an in-depth illustration of the convergence of management, politics, and law in the public sector.

Public Sector Excellence Handbook 2nd ed.
CHRIS HAKES
Bristol: Bristol Quality Centre, 1999
193pp ISBN: 190216900X
This guide for public sector managers presents a brief history of business excellence and places it in context with other business improvement methodologies. The principles of business excellence are explained and the benefits of its application are described. The application of business excellence in the public sector is examined and four case studies of best practice are analyzed.

Reinventing Government: How the Entrepreneurial Spirit Is Transforming the Public Sector
DAVID OSBORNE, TED GAEBLER
New York: Plume Books, 1993
405pp ISBN: 0452269423
In this book, the authors strike at the growing public apathy toward government, and suggest ways in which business people can work toward creating a better alternative. The book cites and analyzes several case studies and, using these, the authors provide a plan for "entrepreneurial government."

Seamless Government: A Practical Guide to Re-engineering in the Public Sector
RUSSELL M. LINDEN
San Francisco, California: Jossey-Bass, 1994
314pp (Jossey-Bass Nonprofit and Public Management Series)
ISBN: 078790015X
This book explains how to reengineer government agencies to meet the needs of its customers "seamlessly"—that is, in as smooth and simple a way as possible. The book includes a step-by-step approach for reengineering in all levels of government, explaining how to assess, design, and execute alterations in the way government does business, and how to overcome opposition along the way.

Strategic Human Resource Management: People and Performance Management in the Public Sector
DENNIS M. DALEY
Upper Saddle River, New Jersey: Prentice Hall, 2001
400pp ISBN: 013028260X
This text describes techniques and practices in human resource/personnel management in public sector organizations. Exercises are given for each technique or practice. Topics include motivation, compensation and benefits, performance appraisal, training and development, employee rights, and labor relations. Examples are drawn from local, state, and federal levels of government, as well as from nonprofit organizations.

Tools for Innovators: Creative Strategies for Managing Public Sector Organizations
STEVEN COHEN, WILLIAM EIMICKE
San Francisco, California: Jossey-Bass, 1998
288pp (Jossey-Bass Nonprofit and Public Management Series)
ISBN: 078790953X
This book introduces public managers to the tools that today's business leaders are using to bring about change in their organizations. The six key innovation tools considered are: strategic planning, reengineering, total quality management, benchmarking, performance measurement and management, team management and privatization. Each innovation tool is examined and analyzed, and case examples are used to illustrate successful innovation initiatives.

MAGAZINES

International Journal of Public Sector Management
ISSN: 0951–3558
MCB University Press
60/62 Toller Lane, Bradford, West Yorkshire, BD8 9BY, U.K.
T: +44 (0) 1274 777700
F: +44 (0) 1274 785200
www.emeraldinsight.com/ijpsm.htm
This journal is published seven times a year. A wide range of research and practical papers on all aspects of managing in the public sector worldwide is included. The journal is also available online at www.emerald-library.com.

MJ (The Municipal Journal)
ISSN: 0143–4187
Hemming Group
32 Vauxhall Bridge Road, London, SW1V 2SS, U.K.
T: +44 (0) 20 7973 6404
F: +44 (0) 20 7973 4799
www.hemming-group.co.uk
Established in 1893, the journal is aimed at senior managers in local government and covers all aspects of local government, including financial matters, best value, contracting, staffing, and auditing.

Public Finance
ISSN: 1352–9250
FSF Ltd.
3 Robert Street, London, WC2N 6RL, U.K.
T: +44 (0) 20 7543 5600
F: +44 (0) 20 7543 5700
www.cipfa.org.uk
The journal of CIPFA (Chartered Institute of Public Finance and Accountancy) covers all aspects of income and expenditure issues relating to the public sector, including central and local government, health, education, law and order, transportation and public service providers.

Public Service Magazine
ISSN: 1460–8936
FDA
2 Caxton Street, London, SW1H 0QH, U.K.
T: +44 (0) 20 7343 1111
F: +44 (0) 20 7343 1105
www.fda.org.uk/psm

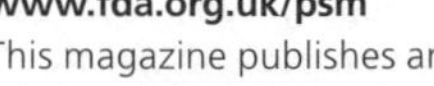

This magazine publishes articles and news relating to business and current affairs affecting the public sector and is aimed at senior managers working in that sector.

"Public opinion is a weak tyrant compared with our own private opinion." (Henry David Thoreau)

Staffing Success
American Staffing Association
277 South Washington Street, Suite 200, Alexandria, Virginia, 22314
T: +1 703 253 2020
F: +1 703 253 2053
www.staffingtoday.net/memberserv/staffsuccessarchive.htm
Formerly known as *Contemporary Times*, this journal is published six times a year and is the official organ of the American Staffing Association. It provides a useful business resource for those working in the recruitment and selection field.

INTERNET

Gateways to Public Sector Resources
www.aom.pace.edu/pn/public.html
A service of the public and the nonprofit division of the Academy of Management, this page links to 15 major gateways to information related to public sector management, and provides a helpful overview of the nature of the resources available through each of those links.

Great Leaders for Great Government
www.leadership.opm.gov
This is the official site for the Federal Executive Institute and Management Development Centers with course listings in leadership and management available at three regional centers for federal government personnel.

National Association of Schools of Public Affairs and Administration
www.naspaa.org/index.html
This Washington, D.C.-based association promotes excellence in Public Service education. The site provides easy to access information on accredited educational institutions at the associate, bachelor, masters, and doctoral degree levels throughout the United States.

ORGANIZATIONS

USA

National Association of Personnel Services
3133 Mount Vernon Avenue, Alexandria, Virginia, 22305
T: +1 703 684 0180
F: +1 703 684 0071
E: info@napsweb.org
http://napsweb.org
NAPS seeks to inform and represent the personnel services industry by providing education, certification, and member services. It has been educating and training those in the staffing industry since 1961, and now represents over 100,000 individuals and 30 state associations. A selection of articles from NAPS newsletters (InsideNAPS) is available from http://napsweb.org/newsletters, and news of pending legislation relevant to personnel from http://napsweb.org/napstrack.htm.

Europe

Improvement and Development Agency for Local Government
Layden House, 76–86 Turnmill Street, London, EC1M 5LG, U.K.
T: +44 (0) 20 7296 6600
F: +44 (0) 20 7296 6666
www.idea.gov.uk
IDEA was established on April 1, 1999, following the demise of the Local Government Management Board. Its aim is to assist local authorities to improve their performance by providing a range of advisory and consulting services on good management practice, staff skills training, Best Value implementation, and benchmarking against the best councils.

Local Government Association
35 Great Smith Street, London, SW1P 3BJ, U.K.
T: +44 (0) 20 7664 3000
F: +44 (0) 20 7664 3030
E: info@lga.gov.uk
www.lga.gov.uk
The LGA represents almost all local authorities in the United Kingdom. It helps develop effective national policies for local authorities and represents their views to central government and other bodies on strategic national issues.

Office for Public Management
252b Grays Inn Road, London, WC1X 8XG, U.K.
T: +44 (0) 20 7239 7800
F: +44 (0) 20 7837 5800
E: office@opm.co.uk
www.opm.co.uk
The OPM is a private sector consulting organization offering management development programs tailored specifically for public sector organizations with a focus on the delivery of public services and the exercise of corporate responsibility.

For More Information

- **Education Management (pp. 1957–59)**
- **Health Services Management (pp. 1995–97)**
- **Nonprofit Organizations (pp. 2056–58)**

PURCHASING AND SUPPLY CHAIN MANAGEMENT

BOOKS

B2B: How to Build a Profitable E-commerce Strategy
Michael Cunningham
Cambridge, Massachusetts: Perseus, 2002
224pp ISBN: 0738205222
This book presents a definitive blueprint for creating a profitable business-to-business e-commerce strategy. Showcasing successful initiatives designed by industry leaders such as Cisco Systems and Dell Computer, as well as lesser-known trailblazers such as VerticalNet and eCredit.com, the author clearly identifies the key issues in assessing opportunities, building technological and organizational capabilities, and designing a successful business-to-business strategy using the full power of the Internet.

Clockspeed: Winning Industry Control in the Age of Temporary Advantage
Charles F. Fine
Cambridge, Massachusetts: Perseus, 1998
288pp ISBN: 0738200018
A key title for anyone involved in supply chain management. The author examines how the supply chain, and getting the best from it, benefits the organization as a whole.

Greener Purchasing: Opportunities and Innovations
Trevor Russel, ed.
Sheffield: Greenleaf Publishing, 1998
325pp ISBN: 1874719047
This collection of papers answers the questions about greener purchasing policies being the exception rather than the norm in large organizations, and explains how environmental purchasing practices that have produced business benefits for a number of companies, can receive wider adoption. Brings together international expertise from four continents, including contributions from the U.S. EPA,

"Watch the costs and the profits will take care of themselves." (Andrew Carnegie)

Environment Canada, Procter & Gamble, Xerox, and The Body Shop. The Japanese and European Green Purchasing Networks are also described.

Harnessing Value in the Supply Chain: Strategic Sourcing in Action
EMIKO BANFIELD
New York: John Wiley, 1999
350pp (Operations Management Series)
ISBN: 0471349755
Strategic sourcing redefines the traditional approach to buying and using materials and services. In this book Banfield offers a specific, step-by-step approach to the strategic sourcing process and provides expert guidance on designing, launching, executing, evaluating, and maintaining a sourcing project. It includes illustrations, examples, and templates.

Logistics and Supply Chain Management: Strategies for Reducing Cost and Improving Service 2nd ed.
MARTIN CHRISTOPHER
Upper Saddle River, New Jersey: Financial Times Prentice Hall, 1999
294pp ISBN: 0273630490
The goal of supply chain management is to link the marketplace, the distribution network, the manufacturing process, and the procurement activity in such a way that customers are serviced at higher levels and yet at lower total cost. The author explores the role of logistics in achieving these goals. He examines the relationship between logistics and competitive strategy, the customer service dimension, measuring logistics costs and performance, and benchmarking and managing the supply chain.

Partners.com
MICHAEL CUNNINGHAM
Cambridge, Massachusetts: Perseus, 2002
256pp ISBN: 0738206873
Partners.com shows businesses how to forge leading-edge Internet partnerships fast with competitors, customers, employees, and other businesses. The book reveals the specifics of these new and better ways of doing business. It presents a clear picture of companies, such as eBay, Altra, GoFish, Egghead, VerticalNet, and Yahoo, that are utilizing technology-driven partnerships.

Profitable Purchasing Strategies: A Manager's Guide for Improving Organizational Competitiveness through the Skills of Purchasing
PAUL T. STEELE, BRIAN COURT
New York: McGraw-Hill, 1996
233pp ISBN: 0077092147
Purchasing is portrayed as an essential business process, and it is argued that an effective purchasing process can play a significant role in the fight for corporate survival and prosperity. This textbook explains the process of building a purchasing strategy and provides an understanding of the basics of purchasing, the buying–supplier interface, and partnership sourcing.

Purchasing and Supply Chain Management 5th ed.
KENNETH LYSONS
Upper Saddle River, New Jersey: Financial Times Prentice Hall, 2000
542pp (Frameworks Series)
ISBN: 0273646761
A much revised and enlarged version of this successful textbook, the 5th edition meets the requirements for an integrated approach to supply chain management, drawing on the many disciplines, from ethics and human resources to suppliers, sourcing, and strategy, that contribute to a full knowledge of purchasing practice and techniques.

Strategic Purchasing and Supply Chain Management 2nd ed.
MALCOLM SAUNDERS
Philadelphia, Pennsylvania: Trans-Atlantic Publications, 1997
304pp ISBN: 0273623826
This textbook aims to provide students with an understanding of the scope and potential of purchasing and supply chain management strategy on a variety of international organizations.

Supercharging Supply Chains: New Ways to Increase Value through Global Operational Excellence
G. TYNDALL, ET AL.
New York: John Wiley, 1998
288pp ISBN: 0471254371
This text presents an innovative view of supply chain excellence and examines its impact on shareholder value. The authors, who are key partners and leaders of the Ernst & Young Global Supply Chain Management Team, explain why and how operational excellence helps companies sell more products. They describe the new ideas being implemented to achieve excellence and consider how leading companies effectively introduce new products into global supply chains.

Working in Partnership: Best Practice in Customer–Supplier Relations
BERNARD BURNES, BARRIE DALE, EDS.
Brookfield, Vermont: Gower, 1998
167pp ISBN: 0566079976
This book draws directly on the experience of practicing managers working in this developing area, providing sound advice for the benefit of any organizations wanting to develop a closer working relationship with their customers or suppliers. The recent research and examples of best practice collected here come from a variety of business environments, including the public sector and the automotive and leisure industries.

MAGAZINES

European Journal of Purchasing and Supply Management
ISSN: 0969–7012
Elsevier Science
Regional Sales Office, Customer Support Department, P.O. Box 945, New York, 10159–0945
T: +1 212 633 3730
F: +1 212 633 3680
www.elsevier.com
This is a refereed journal that aims to encourage the development of conceptual thinking and practical approaches within the profession. Articles cover every aspect of the purchasing of goods and services in all contexts, including industry and commerce, local and regional government, health, and transportation.

Journal of Supply Chain Management: A Global Review of Purchasing and Supply
ISSN: 1055–6001
Institute for Supply Management
P.O. Box 22160, Tempe, Arizona, 85285–2160
T: +1 480 752 6276
F: +1 480 752 7890
www.ism.ws
A quarterly publication produced specifically for purchasing professionals, this journal provides coverage and analysis of key management issues, leading research, one-to-one interviews, and supplier relationship applications. Abstracts of the articles and the one-to-one interviews can be accessed on the Web.

Purchasing
ISSN: 0033–4448
Cahners Publishing
275 Washington Street, Newton, Massachusetts, 02458
T: +1 617 558 4291
F: +1 617 558 4327
www.manufacturing.net/pur
This is a bimonthly magazine which focuses on total supply management. It has served 93,500 professionals working in manufacturing, process, and service companies throughout the full spectrum of business, for 85 years. The magazine makes available the information required by purchasing professionals to do their jobs. It provides news, identifies trends,

"The cost of the electronics in a modern car now exceeds the cost of its steel." (Nicholas Negroponte)

interprets events, makes forecasts, and presents exclusive information and data sources.

Supply Chain & Logistics Journal
Naylor Publications Co. (Canada)
920 Yonge Street, Suite 600, Toronto, Ontario, M4W 3C7, Canada
T: +1 416 961 1028
F: +1 416 924 4408
www.infochain.org/quarterly/journals.html
This is a quarterly journal published for the Canadian Association of Supply Chain & Logistics Management.

INTERNET

CAPS Research 
www.capsresearch.org
This site is offered by the Center for Advanced Purchasing Studies, a nonprofit independent research organization cosponsored by Arizona State University College of Business and the National Association of Purchasing and Supply. It provides full access to a range of recent research and benchmarking reports and their journal *Practix*. There are also links to related sites.

Chartered Institute of Purchasing and Supply
www.cips.org
While this site is designed to promote the training and research services and activities of the CIPS, it does allow nonmembers access to its comprehensive bookstore with abstract details of over 350 specialist publications.

Institute for Supply Management
www.ism.ws
This is the home site of the Institute for Supply Management. The amount of information available to nonmembers is limited, but there is access to selected articles or abstracts of recent articles in the Institute's journals.

International Purchasing and Supply Education and Research Association
www.ipsera.org
The IPSERA is an active network of academics and practitioners dedicated to the development of understanding on matters concerning the future of purchasing and supply management. The site provides: general information about the association; details about membership; a database outlining the research interests of members of the association; and an extensive collection of links to other sites of interest. These include education and training resources, related organizations, and publications.

ORGANIZATIONS

USA

Institute for Supply Management
P.O. Box 22160, Tempe, Arizona, 85285–2160
T: +1 480 752 6276
F: +1 480 752 7890
www.ism.ws
Founded in 1915, the ISM is a widely respected educational association in the United States. It aims to provide national and international leadership in purchasing and materials management through research and a program of conferences, seminars, and online learning.

Europe

Chartered Institute of Purchasing and Supply
1 Easton House, Easton-on-the-Hill, Stamford, Lincolnshire, PE9 3NZ, U.K.
T: +44 (0) 1780 756777
F: +44 (0) 1780 751610
www.cips.org
An international education and qualification organization, based in the United Kingdom, serving the international purchasing and supply profession, CIPS is dedicated to promoting best practice through the provision of a wide range of services for the benefit of members and the wider business community. These include a program of continuous improvement in professional standards and raising awareness of the contribution that purchasing and supply makes to corporate, national, and international prosperity. CIPS gained a Royal Charter in 1992.

International

Canadian Association of Supply Chain & Logistics Management
590 Alden Road, Suite 211, Markham, Ontario, L3R 8N2, Canada
T: +1 905 513 7300
F: +1 905 513 1248
E: members@infochain.org
www.infochain.org
Established as the Canadian Association of Physical Distribution Management in 1967, the name was recently changed to reflect the way the practice of logistics has evolved into supply chain management. SCL is a nonprofit, membership organization that aims to advance the logistics and supply chain profession in Canada. Through a range of activities, research, and informal discussion, members are encouraged to further their understanding of logistics and the art and science of its management.

Purchasing Management Association of Canada
2 Carlton Street, Suite 1414, Toronto, Ontario, M5B 2J3, Canada
T: +1 416 977 7111
F: +1 416 977 8886
E: info@pmac.ca
www.pmac.ca
The PMAC is a national, nonprofit association and is a leading source of education, training, and development in the purchasing and supply management field in Canada. The association operates with ten provincial or territorial Institutes, which can be contacted through the Web site.

For More Information

- ✔ **Effective Purchasing (pp. 494–95)**
- **Logistics and Distribution (pp. 2026–28)**

QUALITY AND TOTAL QUALITY MANAGEMENT

BOOKS

Four Days with Dr. Deming: A Strategy for Modern Methods of Management
WILLIAM J. LATZKO, DAVID M. SAUNDERS
Boston, Massachusetts: Addison Wesley, 1994
228pp (Engineering Process Improvement Series)
ISBN: 0201633663
This book recreates the experience of attending a four-day quality management workshop held by the late Dr. Deming. Aimed at a range of businesspeople from the executives, managers, and engineers of an organization, to its stockholders, this book discusses and explains Deming's theories and ideas on quality management.

"Quality is characteristic of a product or service that helps somebody and which has a market."
(Robert M. Pirsig)

From Baldrige to the Bottom Line: A Road Map for Organizational Change and Improvement
DAVID W. HUTTON
Milwaukee, Wisconsin: ASQ Quality Press, 2000
348pp ISBN: 0873894731
This book examines the assessment process of the Baldrige framework, used by those applying for this award for quality performance. In addition, it shows why companies such as IBM and FedEx are equally interested in using that framework as a guide for improving quality. It presents in-depth information on how the assessment process works and presents keys to how it can be adapted to fit any organization that sees improved quality as a means of achieving increased profitability and growth.

Hiring the Best: A Manager's Guide to Effective Interviewing 4th ed.
MARTIN YATE
Avon, Massachusetts: Adams Media Corporation, 1997
230pp ISBN: 1558502823
A guide for managers, this book suggests strategies for recognizing a good employee in terms of competence, willingness, and personality. It also explores a range of issues that can arise for an employer when hiring different types of employee (temporary, consultancy, and so on).

A History of Managing for Quality: The Evolution Trends and Future Directions of Managing for Quality
J. M. JURAN, ED.
Milwaukee, Wisconsin: ASQ Quality Press, 1995
600pp ISBN: 0873893417
This book, edited by a respected author in the field, focuses on the elements of quality management common to all industries and illustrates the immense effect that quality and its evolution have had on civilization over the centuries. Juran summarizes the historical profile in a chapter on worldwide trends and the lessons learned from history. Other contributors suggest the directions that managing for quality may take in the new century.

Juran on Leadership for Quality: An Executive Handbook
JOSPEH M. JURAN
New York: Free Press, 1989
376pp ISBN: 0029166829
This classic volume looks at the subject of quality as a competitive tool and shows that unless the effort to improve quality is led by committed leaders and permeates from the top down, it will fail. Juran sets forth the actions that managers must take to make quality improvement an annual goal and gives step-by-step advice on how to lead such efforts, drawing on the experiences of thousands of chief executives from around the world.

Juran's Quality Handbook 5th ed.
JOSEPH M. JURAN, A. BLANTON GODFREY, EDS.
New York: McGraw-Hill, 1998
1872pp ISBN: 007034003X
A comprehensive guide to quality engineering and management, this revised reference text covers the trilogy of essential processes—quality planning, quality control, and quality results. This edition also contains details of the most recent developments, as well as plenty of practical advice. Supported by quality research, containing new ideas and strategies, this book aims to appeal to a wide spectrum of businesses.

Managing Quality 3rd ed.
BARRIE G. DALE, ED.
Malden, Massachusetts: Blackwell Publishers, 1999
480pp ISBN: 0631214100
The author provides a broad overview of total quality management (TQM) in five parts, covering the development of TQM, its business context, methods of introducing TQM, quality management systems, tools, and techniques, and TQM through continuous improvement. Chapters contributed by leading academics and practitioners cover specific topics and techniques, including Failure Mode and Effects Analysis and Statistical Process Control.

Managing Six Sigma: A Practical Guide to Understanding, Assessing, and Implementing the Strategy That Yields Bottom-line Success
FORREST W. BREYFOGLE III, JAMES M. CUPELLO, BECKI MEADOWS
New York: John Wiley, 2000
300pp ISBN: 0471396737
Written in order to help managers decide whether or not they should implement the strategy, this book provides in-depth information on Six Sigma techniques. Case studies of how Motorola and General Electric introduced Six Sigma are included in order to demonstrate the successes achieved and pitfalls encountered in the process.

Out of the Crisis
W. EDWARDS DEMING
Cambridge, Massachusetts: MIT Press, 2000
507pp ISBN: 0262541157
This book is a reprint of the 1986 classic in which the guru of quality presented his theory of management, based on his 14 Points for Management. Deming brings to light the failures of management that need to be corrected if manufacturing is to produce products of quality successfully and in such a way as to retain competitiveness.

Quality: A Critical Introduction
JOHN BECKFORD
New York: Routledge, 1998
384pp ISBN: 041518164X
This book makes a good introduction for those who want an understanding of the quality movement and the thinking of the major "quality gurus" of the 20th century. Its four sections outline the background to quality and quality management within an organization and the issues involved, review the writing and thinking of the quality gurus, consider contemporary management thinking, and introduce the methods, tools, and techniques for achieving quality. User guides, practical illustrations, and short case studies are also included.

The Six Sigma Handbook
THOMAS PYZDEK
New York: McGraw-Hill, 2000
711pp ISBN: 0071372334
If improving the quality of your manufacturing processes is your goal, and the extraordinarily successful Six Sigma program at GE is one you want to emulate, this book will help you implement that approach. The author examines the philosophy underlying the program and explores the management and organization of Six Sigma, then explains the statistical tools and problem-solving techniques needed to implement it.

MAGAZINES

Managing Service Quality
ISSN: 0960–4259
MCB University Press
60/62 Toller Lane, Bradford, West Yorkshire, BD8 9BY, U.K.
T: +44 (0) 1274 777700
F: +44 (0) 1274 785200
www.emeraldinsight.com/msq.htm
Written in an accessible style, this journal is primarily practical in focus. Its contents typically include case studies and articles outlining quality techniques and new research.

Quality World
ISSN: 1352–8769

"Quality is a direct experience independent of and prior to intellectual abstraction."
(W. Edwards Deming)

  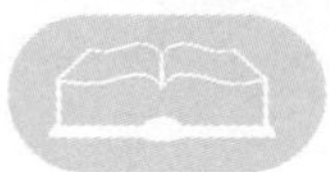    

Institute of Quality Assurance
Information Services, 12 Grosvenor Crescent, London, SW1X 7EE, U.K.
T: +44 (0) 20 7245 6722
F: +44 (0) 20 7245 6755
www.iqa.org
Quality World, the journal of the Institute of Quality Assurance, is a practical publication covering all aspects of, and developments in, quality and quality management.

TQM Magazine
ISSN: 0954-478X
MCB University Press
60/62 Toller Lane, Bradford, West Yorkshire, BD8 9BY, U.K.
T: +44 (0) 1274 777700
F: +44 (0) 1274 785200
www.emeraldinsight.com/tqm.htm
TQM Magazine is aimed primarily at practicing managers. Each issue typically contains details of research, explores quality techniques, and includes a number of case studies of quality in practice.

INTERNET

American Society for Quality
www.ASQ.org
This site, run by the major quality association in the United States, provides news, links to its publications, information on the Baldrige Award, and access to such things as the Six Sigma forum.

Baldrige National Quality Program
www.baldrige.gov
This site provides information on every aspect of the Malcolm Baldrige National Quality Award and on how to obtain material and information about applying for the Award and doing the assessment.

European Quality Online
www.european-quality.co.uk
Online access to journals, chat, and links can be gained via this site.

Quality Network
www.quality.co.uk
This site provides information on quality management and ISO 9000, as well as on environmental and safety management.

Quality Today
www.qualitytoday.com
This site gives details of news, products, and events relevant to quality professionals, and also contains a library devoted to quality and quality-related issues.

ORGANIZATIONS

USA

American Productivity and Quality Center
123 North Post Oak Lane, 3rd Floor, Houston, Texas, 77024
T: +1 713 681 4020
F: +1 713 681 1182
E: apqcinfo@apqc.org
www.apqc.org
Founded in 1977, the APQC works with organizations of all sizes to improve productivity and quality. Its aim is to research and understand emerging and effective methods of improvement, and to distribute its findings through education and its advisory and information services. In 1992 it set up the International Benchmarking Clearinghouse to promote, facilitate, and improve the process of learning from best practice.

The W. Edwards Deming Institute
P.O. Box 59511, Potomac, Maryland, 20859-9511
T: +1 301 294 8405
F: +1 301 294 8406
E: staff@deming.org
www.deming.org
A nonprofit organization founded in 1993, the Institute aims to foster an understanding of the Deming System of Profound Knowledge to advance commerce, prosperity, and peace.

Europe

British Quality Foundation
32-34 Great Peter Street, London, SW1P 2QX, U.K.
T: +44 (0) 20 7654 5000
F: +44 (0) 20 7654 5001
E: mail@quality-foundation.co.uk
www.quality-foundation.co.uk
The BQF is a nonprofit membership organization that promotes business excellence to other public and private sector organizations in the United Kingdom. It undertakes numerous activities in pursuit of this aim, most of which have the Business Excellence Model at their core. It also sponsors the U.K. Quality Award for Business Excellence.

European Foundation for Quality Management
Avenue des Pléiades 15, B-1200 Brussels, Belgium
T: +32 2 775 35 11
F: +32 2 775 35 35
E: info@efqm.org
www.efqm.org
Founded in 1988 by the presidents of 14 major European companies, with the endorsement of the European Commission, the EFQM aims to support the managers of European organizations in efforts to accelerate the process of making TQM a decisive factor in achieving global competitive advantage. The Foundation provides information on the Business Excellence Model/EFQM Excellence Model and the European Quality Award. It also offers various training courses and produces its own publications.

European Organisation for Quality
3 rue du Luxembourg, B-1000 Brussels, Belgium
T: +32 2 501 07 35
F: +32 2 501 07 36
www.eoq.org
An autonomous nonprofit organization established in 1956, the EOQ is the European interdisciplinary body concerned to bring about effective improvement in the area of quality management. Its Web site provides access to the European Quality Week site and the *European Quality Journal*, besides giving details of EOQ activities.

Institute of Quality Assurance
12 Grosvenor Crescent, London, SW1X 7EE, U.K.
T: +44 (0) 20 7245 6722
F: +44 (0) 20 7245 6755
E: iqa@iqa.org
www.iqa.org
The IQA is a professional body for those with responsibilities for quality assurance. Founded in 1919, it aims to foster quality practices and advance national policy issues in the area of quality.

For More Information

☆ **The True Total Quality (pp. 173-74)**
✔ **Total Quality: Getting TQM to Work (pp. 522-23)**
✔ **Total Quality: Mapping a TQM Strategy (pp. 524-25)**
ISO 9000 (pp. 2014-16)
Manufacturing Systems (pp. 2039-42)
Process Control and Statistical Process Control (pp. 2079-80)

"Quality does not give you an advantage." (Andrew Neil)

  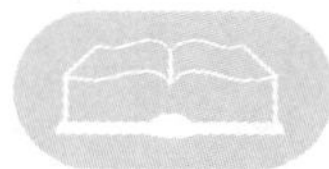    

RECRUITMENT AND SELECTION

BOOKS

Competence-based Employment Interviewing

JEFFREY A. BERMAN

Westport, Connecticut: Greenwood Publishing, 1997

184pp ISBN: 1567200508

The aims of this book are to give a practitioner oriented approach to competence-based employment interviewing and provide a theoretical framework within which managers and HR professionals can operate. Based on modern ideas about organizations, the book covers the competence movement, preparation for interviewing, interviewing techniques, and evaluation. Equal opportunities aspects of interviewing in the United States are also dealt with.

Competency Based Recruitment and Selection: A Practical Guide

ROBERT WOOD, TIM PAYNE

New York: John Wiley, 1998

214pp (Strategic Human Resource Management Series)

ISBN: 0471974730

Step-by-step guidance is given to recruiters on how competencies can be used for selecting and assessing job candidates. Each of the ten chapters is written to stand alone in its area, and the book focuses on the recruitment and selection context, attracting and sifting candidates, assessment, decision making, and evaluation.

Competing for Talent: Key Recruitment and Retention Strategies for Becoming an Employer of Choice

NANCY S. AHLRICHS

Palo Alto, California: Davies-Black, 2000

254pp ISBN: 0891061487

Ahlrichs recognizes ''human capital'' as the key to business success. She says that the only way to attract and keep the top employees you need is by becoming an employer of choice. This book presents her strategy for achieving that. Part one looks at what other companies have done to become employers of choice. Part two examines specific recruiting strategies. Part three focuses on the equally important issue of retention.

The Directory of Executive Recruiters 2002

KENNEDY INFORMATION

Fitzwilliam, New Hampshire: Kennedy Information, 2001

1180pp ISBN: 1885922779

Published since 1971 and updated annually, this famous ''Red Book'' lists 14,200 recruiters at 5,700 search firms in the United States, Canada, and Mexico. Indexed by function, industry, geography, and specialty, the book makes it simple to find the best recruiter for you. Although the book provides extensive contact information, the CD-ROM of the database, available at an additional cost, is really required for effective searching.

Finding and Keeping the Right People: How to Recruit Motivated Employees

JON BILLSBERRY

Upper Saddle River, New Jersey: Prentice Hall, 1996

233pp (Smarter Solutions series)

ISBN: 0273616986

Aiming to give managers and recruiters a practical perspective on recruitment and selection, this book stresses the need to pay continuous attention to the business purpose of the exercise and integrate it into the process. The text also deals with attracting and assessing applicants, making decisions about terms and conditions, and retaining employees once they have been recruited.

45 Ways for Hiring Smart! How to Predict Winners and Losers in the Incredibly Expensive People-reading Game

PIERRE MORNELL

Berkeley, California: Ten Speed Press, 1998

226pp ISBN: 0898159725

This is a practical guide to help employers cut through the complexities of hiring, and select the best candidate for a particular job. As the title suggests, this text presents 45 techniques designed to take the measure of potential recruits, emphasizing behavior not words.

Interviewing and Selecting High Performers

LARRY R. SMALLEY

San Francisco, California: Jossey-Bass, 1997

107pp (Management Skills Series)

ISBN: 07879 51099

As Vice President and Principal Consultant for Richard Chang Associates, Inc. the author has plenty of expertise to offer managers, supervisors, or team leaders responsible for selecting and interviewing candidates. This text is orientated towards the practical, and includes work sheets, a continuous case study, and key tips. Appendices give reproducible documentation, a checklist, and examples of performance-based questions.

A Manager's Guide to Hiring the Best Person for Every Job

DEANNE ROSENBERG

New York: John Wiley, 2000

320pp ISBN: 0471380741

This book on recruitment and selection interviewing is written in simple language and gives detailed help with structuring the dialog and questioning in interviews in such a way as to retain control and focus on the job requirements involved. A matrix designed by the author for identifying trade-offs among competing candidates is included.

101 Hiring Mistakes Employers Make, and How to Avoid Them

RICHARD FEIN

Waupaca, Wisconsin: Impact Publications, 2000

144pp ISBN: 157023129X

This book is an analytical study of interviewing techniques, based on material from genuine interviews. It aims to outline some of the main hiring errors that can eventually burden an organization with an unsatisfactory employee. The author aims to help minimize ''hiring mistakes'' and increase the employer's understanding of interview questioning.

Recruit & Retain the Best

JOHN MCCARTER, RAY SCHREYER

Manassas, Virginia: Impact Publications, 2000

128pp ISBN: 1570231346

The authors claim that, to remain competitive, you must create a talent-powered company. Their solution begins with recruiting new employees based on competencies from education or previous employment. They discuss innovative recruiting tools, like the Internet and employee referral programs. However, the focus of this book is on the retention of the top employees. The last third of the book addresses ways to make your company a place where the best want to stay.

Recruiting, Interviewing, Selecting, and Orienting New Employees 3rd ed.

DIANE ARTHUR

New York: AMACOM, 1998

400pp ISBN: 0814404014

This book is designed to give comprehensive guidance through the four stages of the employment process to HR specialists and others whose work involves recruitment and selection. Besides describing methods and techniques applicable to the basic task of hiring new employees, this revised edition takes in new

"You must make use of people according to their abilities and realize that absolutely no one is perfect."

(Françoise d'Aubigné Maintenon)

material dealing with areas such as additional interviewing approaches, workplace diversity, the retention of new employees, and online recruitment.

The Selection Interview
PENNY HACKETT
New York: Beekman, 2000
96pp (Management Shapers Series)
ISBN: 0846451433
First published in 1995, this short, clear, and easily understood book gives advice to help managers recruit more effectively through focused, well-planned, and skilled selection interviewing. It includes information on drawing up job descriptions, setting up the interview, different interview strategies and styles, questioning and listening skills, the evaluation of interview results, and decision making leading to selection.

Smart Hiring: The Complete Guide to Finding and Hiring the Best Employees 2nd ed.
ROBERT W. WENDOVER
Naperville, Illinois: Sourcebooks, 1998
240pp ISBN: 1570712131
This book offers practical advice to employers on improving their employee selection skills. Examining various topics such as hiring errors, telephone interviews, and the assessment of a potential employee, Wendover's approach is pragmatic. Also included in the book are step-by-step guides to job advertising and analyzing résumés.

The War for Talent
ED MICHAELS, HELEN HANDFIELD-JONES, BETH AXELROD
Boston, Massachusetts: Harvard Business School Press, 2001
200pp ISBN: 1578514592
In acknowledgment of today's increasingly competitive market for talented business individuals, this book offers guidance to managers, executives, and team leaders on ways to attract an excellent workforce to their organization. It also advises on developing the full potential of talented individuals.

Writing Job Descriptions
ALAN FOWLER
New York: Beekman, 2000
96pp (Management Shapers Series)
ISBN: 0846451840
This booklet aims to give managers and HR professionals a focused introduction to writing clear, accurate job descriptions for effective recruitment and selection. Help is included on defining essential job constituents, legal issues, defining reporting relationships, dealing with unspecified duties, and job dimensions. The use of job descriptions for job evaluation is covered, and key points are summarized.

MAGAZINES

Recruiting Trends
ISSN: 0163–5611
Kennedy Information
One Kennedy Place, Rte. 12 S., Fitzwilliam, New Hampshire, 03447
T: +1 603 585 6544
F: +1 603 585 9555
www.kennedyinfo.com/rt/rectrends.html
This is a monthly loose-leaf publication for recruitment executives.

Recruitment International
Recruitment Publications Ltd.
13 High Road, Byfleet, West Byfleet, Surrey, KT14 7QH, U.K.
T: +44 (0) 1932 351144
F: +44 (0) 1932 351166
www.recruitment-intl.com
This monthly magazine is intended for those concerned with recruitment and selection, covering issues relevant to the field and including articles on career development and training.

Recruitment Matters
Recruitment and Employment Confederation
36–38 Mortimer Street, London, W1W 7RG, U.K.
T: +44 (0) 20 7462 3260
F: +44 (0) 20 7255 2878
www.rec.uk.com
This bimonthly magazine is free to members of the Recruitment and Employment Federation. It covers all issues concerned with recruitment and employment.

Selection and Development Review
ISSN: 0963–2638
British Psychological Society
St. Andrews House, 48 Princess Road East, Leicester, Leicestershire, LE1 7DR, U.K.
T: +44 (0) 116 254 9568
F: +44 (0) 116 247 0787
www.bps.org.uk
This is a bimonthly journal for HR specialists and recruiters with a strong focus on psychometric testing.

INTERNET

Monster.com
www.monster.com
This site is a global online careers network, aiming to connect companies and qualified individuals. It offers member-employers various services, including job postings, résumé screening, a résumé database, and résumé routing. Job seekers can use it to access vacancies, and take advantage of features and services such as résumé management, a job-search agent, and a careers network.

Recruiters Network
www.recruitersnetwork.com
Recruiters Network is a free association for HR professionals, recruiters, and hiring managers. Its goal is to provide leading resources and information on the recruiting and Internet recruiting industry. Members receive a monthly newsletter, access to a resource directory, and an opportunity to interact with their peers in a discussion group.

Recruiters Online Network
www.recruitersonline.com/index.phtml
Recruiters Online Network is a global community of recruiters, headhunters, and staffing firms. It features separate sections for job seekers to post résumés and search for jobs, for recruiters to post jobs and search résumé databases, and for direct employers to find talent or a recruiting firm.

Recruitmentmag.co.uk
www.recruitmentmag.co.uk
This is a Web edition magazine, updated daily, that is aimed at those working in the recruitment industry. It focuses mainly on recruitment, with coverage also of related issues such as legislation and mergers.

Society for Human Resource Management
www.shrm.org
This is the Web site of SHRM, the leading voice of the human resource profession, providing education and information services, conferences and seminars, government and media representation, online services, and publications, to more than 165,000 professional and student members throughout the world.

ORGANIZATIONS

USA

American Staffing Association
277 South Washington Street, Suite 200, Alexandria, Virginia, 22314
T: +1 703 253 2020
F: +1 703 253 2053
E: *asa@staffingtoday.net*
www.staffingtoday.net
The ASA represents the U.S. recruiting industry. Among other things, it provides job-seeking and staff-seeking services. Membership benefits include access to information and research

"Always be smart enough to hire people brighter than yourself." (Caroline Marland)

concerned with employment, payroll, employee turnover rates, industry compensation, and other associated matters.

Association of Sales and Marketing Companies
1010 Wisconsin Avenue NW, Ninth Floor, Washington, D.C., 20007
T: +1 202 337 9351
F: +1 202 337 4508
E: info@asmc.org
www.asmc.org
ASMC is a member trade association formed to promote the interests of sales and marketing agencies and manufacturers. It offers its members conferences, training resources, a referral service, the opportunity to join committees that focus on industry issues, research, publications, and group insurance programs.

Direct Selling Association
1275 Pennsylvania Avenue NW, Suite 800, Washington, D.C., 20004
T: +1 202 347 8866
F: +1 202 347 0055
E: info@dsa.org
www.dsa.org
DSA is a trade association for firms that manufacture and distribute goods and services sold directly to consumers. It offers its members research services, a monthly newsletter, a resource guide, conferences, networking councils, legislative lobbying, and salesforce support.

National Association of Sales Professionals
8300 North Hayden Road, Suite 207, Scottsdale, Arizona, 85258
T: +1 480 951 4311
F: +1 480 483 2860
E: info@nasp.cpm
www.nasp.com
Founded in 1991, NASP states that its mission is to cater for the needs of salespersons, to help in their professional development in a changing field, and to upgrade the career status of those working in sales. It runs the Certified Professional SalesPerson program, and administers the International Registry of Accredited Salespersons.

Europe

Recruitment and Employment Confederation
36–38 Mortimer Street, London, W1W 7RG, U.K.
T: +44 (0) 20 7462 3260
F: +44 (0) 20 7255 2878
E: info@rec.co.uk
www.rec.uk.com
The Confederation is an organization for recruitment and employment agencies and consulting firms operating in most fields of employment. Its activities include conferences, meetings, research, and the provision of information.

The Chartered Institute of Personnel and Development
CIPD House, Camp Road, London, SW19 4UX, U.K.
T: +44 (0) 20 8971 9000
F: +44 (0) 20 8263 3333
E: cipd@cipd.co.uk
www.cipd.co.uk
The CIPD is a professional body for personnel and human resources management specialists. It offers qualifications and developmental support in these fields, and also makes publications, courses, and information available to members. It treats performance appraisal and performance management as one of its central areas of concern within the wider field of personnel management.

International

Association of Executive Search Consultants
500 Fifth Avenue, Suite 930, New York, 10110
T: +1 212 398 9556
E: aesc@aesc.org
www.aesc.org
The AESC is a professional association for retained executive search consulting firms worldwide. It has regional councils for Europe and America and an international board of directors. It defines the activity of retained executive search consulting as helping clients to find and recruit senior executives.

For More Information

- **General Business Information: Online Sources for Marketing (p. 1992)**
- **Management Development (pp. 2031–33)**
- **Personnel Management and HR Management (pp. 2067–71)**
- **Remuneration (pp. 2103–05)**

RELOCATION

BOOKS

Company Relocation Handbook
SHARON K. WARD, ET AL.
Central Point, Oregon: PSI Research /Oasis Press, 1991
234pp ISBN: 1555710921
This is a comprehensive guide to specifying, ranking, and evaluating the factors to be considered when deciding whether to move your business, and if so, where to. It identifies five major phases of relocating, from making the decision to move, through to the initial implementation of start-up managerial procedures at the new location, and it uses worksheets, rating scales, and checklists that allow the reader to make decisions based on their own situation.

Globalizing People through International Assignments
J. STEWART BLACK, ET AL., EDS.
Cambridge, Massachusetts: Addison-Wesley, 1999
720pp ISBN: 0201433893
This book looks at international relocation of employees as part of a company strategy. It covers such topics as identifying candidates for international positions, their cross-cultural adjustment process, balancing ''dual allegiances'' (a sense of belonging to two different countries and cultures), and appraising and rewarding expats (expatriated workers). It also explains how companies can help people readjust to life back home when they return from their international assignment. What's perhaps most valuable in this book is its demonstration of the value to the company of truly global-savvy managers.

Office Relocation Planner
KAREN CHESSLER, CHRISTOPHER CARMEN
Boise, Idaho: Vision Publications, 1999

"Passion for change drives great business people. It moves them restlessly from industry to industry."
(Paul Corrigan)

57pp ISBN: 1928742017
Office relocation consulting and commercial real estate experts have defined the tasks associated with an office move and, using action steps and checklists, have put them into a logical sequence, making the relocation process manageable. This book includes detailed information on issues such as facility selection, selecting a moving company, and moving computers and office equipment.

The Office Relocation Sourcebook: A Guide to Managing Staff throughout the Move
DENNIS ATTWOOD
New York: John Wiley, 1996
288pp ISBN: 0471130168
This resource provides the corporate relocation team at firms of all sizes with the information it needs to relocate successfully, cost-efficiently, and with minimal disruption to employees. It includes checklists, survey tools, and summaries forms and contains a 3½ inch floppy disk with valuable relocation tools, including a comprehensive relocation template.

Relocating Your Workplace: A User's Guide to Acquiring and Preparing Business Facilities
WADMAN DALY
Menlo Park, California: Crisp Publications, 1994
365pp ISBN: 1560521864
This is a user's guide to facility relocation, from finding a new location to developing it and moving in. It includes charts, graphs, and checklists, as well as detailed explanations of lease agreements and relocation costs.

Relocation 101: Making the Most of Your Move
BEVERLY D. ROMAN
Wilmington, North Carolina: BR Anchor Publishing, 2001
128pp ISBN: 1888891343
This title provides a comprehensive guide to the relocation process. The author based the book upon both her personal experiences and research in relocation trends. The topics covered include the impact of relocation on dual career households, and tips and checklists that cover the basics of moving.

Smart Moves: Your Guide through the Emotional Maze of Relocation
NADIA JENSEN, AUDREY T. MCCOLLUM
Lyme, New Hampshire: Smith & Kraus, 1996
244pp ISBN: 1575250799
In this publication, the authors aim to help minimize the stress caused by important life changes. By exploring the emotional aspects of relocation, the book offers guidance on how to turn your anxieties into positive action, through increased communication and assertiveness.

Smooth Moves: The Relocation Guide for Families on the Move
ELLEN CARLISLE
Charlotte, North Carolina: Teacup Press, 1999
107pp ISBN: 0966782704
This book addresses all aspects involved in moving a household. The author provides tips and checklists that cover moving basics, including selling your house, researching new schools, selecting a neighborhood that meets your needs, and easing the family trauma that results from moving.

INTERNET

Association of Relocation Agents
www.relocationagents.com
This site details membership categories, activities undertaken, and membership services available. It also describes the content of ARA publications, including the *ARA Guide to the U.K.*, and provides a job advertisement section.

Employee Relocation Council
www.erc.org
The Employee Relocation Council is a nonprofit association providing resources addressing the issues of corporate, government, and military employee relocation. Its Web site provides a wealth of information for managers and human resource professionals, including conferences and professional development opportunities, news of current events and legislation, research reports and trend surveys, and directories of relocation services and firms.

123Relocation.com
www.relo-usa.com
This site is a U.S.-based relocation information resource that is searchable by state and city.

Relocation Central
www.relocationcentral.com
This site is a relocation directory, providing contacts for products and services and searchable by state and city. Relocation news and a bookstore are also available.

The Salary Calculator
www.homefair.com/homefair/cmr/salcalc.html
The Web site enables individuals planning to relocate to calculate the differences in cost of living for U.S., Canadian, and international cities. The Web site also provides a wealth of resources for persons contemplating relocation, such as local school information, crime data, city profiles, housing prices, and moving cost estimates.

ORGANIZATIONS

USA

Employee Relocation Council
1717 Pennsylvania Avenue NW, Washington, D.C., 20006
T: +1 202 857 0857
F: +1 202 659 8631
www.erc.org
The ERC is a membership organization, founded in 1964, for professionals who manage or support U.S. and international employee relocation.

Europe

Association of Relocation Agents
P.O. Box 189, Diss, Norfolk, IP22 1PE, U.K.
T: +44 (0) 8700 737475
F: +44 (0) 8700 718719
E: info@relocationagents.com
www.relocationagents.com
The Association of Relocation Agents is a membership organization that was founded in 1986 to encourage and promote companies and individuals offering relocation services within the United Kingdom and overseas. It is affiliated with the European Relocation Association.

European Relocation Association
P.O. Box 189, Diss, Norfolk, IP22 1PE, U.K.
T: +44 (0) 8700 726727
F: +44 (0) 1359 251508
E: info@eura-relation.com
www.eura-relocation.com
A professional membership body, launched in 1998, for relocation professionals in Europe and worldwide, EuRA aims to spread knowledge and understanding of the issues surrounding corporate mobility and to promote high industry standards. Members are required to abide by EuRA's Rules of Conduct.

For More Information

- **Conditions of Employment (pp. 1933–35)**
- **International Management, Cross Cultural Management (pp. 2009–11)**
- **Working Abroad (pp. 2134–36)**

"Launching a startup is tough in any country. In Mexico, it's something else." (Miguel Angel Davila)

REMUNERATION

BOOKS

The American Almanac of Jobs and Salaries, 2000–2001 Edition

John W. Wright
New York: Morrow, Williams, 2000
672pp ISBN: 0380803038
Wright's reference lists hundreds of jobs in the United States, from entry level to the corporate suite. It is loaded with information specific to each job, including description, requirements, career prospects, and compensation.

The Compensation Handbook: A State of the Art Guide to Compensation Strategy and Design 4th ed.

Lance A. Berger, Dorothy R. Berger, eds.
New York: McGraw-Hill, 1999
646pp ISBN: 0071343091
This comprehensive reference book offers guidance on all areas of compensation. Its aim is to provide answers to all the important questions on the subject of how to attract, retain, and motivate key people. Sections cover base compensation, variable compensation, executive compensation, performance and compensation, corporate culture and compensation, and international compensation.

The Complete Guide to Executive Compensation

Bruce R. Ellig
New York: McGraw-Hill, 2001
608pp ISBN: 0071376291
A comprehensive reference book for anyone involved in the increasingly complex field of compensation, from executives to administrators, *The Complete Guide to Executive Compensation* explores a range of topics in its discussion of modern compensation packages including: appropriate salaries; pay positioning with reference to different markets; and incentives and benefits. The book also contains a guide to relevant laws, tax regulations, disclosure requirements, and other useful material.

Disciplined Minds: A Critical Look at Salaried Professionals and the Soul-battering System That Shapes Their Lives

Jeff Schmidt
Lanham, Maryland: Rowman and Littlefield, 2000
336pp ISBN: 0847693643
Schmidt takes a critical look at the U.S. system of education and professional employment. He gets to the basics of a professional's job and the dissatisfaction that many experience. Schmidt offers a different perspective about employment, and about how we can change our thinking and bring new understanding to professional work and our lives.

The Executive Handbook on Compensation: Linking Strategic Rewards to Business Performance

Charles H. Fay, Damien Knight, Michael A. Thompson, eds.
New York: Simon & Schuster, 2001
896pp ISBN: 0684842335
This is a collection of over 50 articles by experts in the areas of HR strategy and compensation. It covers the practical aspects of designing and implementing a total compensation package in a corporate setting. This handbook contains extensive information useful to both senior HR professionals and non-HR executives.

Get Paid What You're Worth: The Expert Negotiator's Guide to Salary and Compensation

Robin L. Pinkley, Gregory B. Northcraft
New York: St. Martin's Press, 2000
240pp ISBN: 0312242549
Pinkley and Northcraft offer advice on which issues to negotiate, how to prepare and conduct interviews and negotiations, and how to close a new job package. They also include advice from experts on proven strategies, proper thinking, and how to take action.

Interview for Success: A Practical Guide to Increasing Job Interviews, Offers, and Salaries 7th ed.

Ronald L. Krannich, Caryl Rae Krannich
Manassas Park, Virginia: Impact Publications, 1998
223pp ISBN: 1570230986
Interview for Success is a "how-to" book on preparing for interviews, researching information, presenting yourself, and handling all of the details of interviewing. It is an excellent resource for the job seeker looking to negotiate a better position and compensation package.

New Dimensions in Pay Management

Michael Armstrong, Duncan Brown
New York: Beekman, 2001
208pp (Developing Practice Series)
ISBN: 0846452308
Drawing on practical case studies and research, the authors set out to give guidance on current thinking and practice in the field of pay management, reviewing recent trends and developments with a specific focus on broadbanding and job pay structures. They also offer advice on developing and introducing new pay structures.

Paying for Contribution: Real Performance-related Pay Strategies

Duncan Brown, Michael Armstrong
Milford, Connecticut: Kogan Page, 2000
356pp ISBN: 0749428996
The authors discuss the need for a holistic approach to performance-related pay, on the basis of a review of its relevance and effectiveness. They consider major trends and future themes in contribution pay, and give practical guidance on assessing, introducing, and operating systems to link pay to contribution.

Pay People Right!: Breakthrough Reward Strategies to Create Great Companies

Patricia K. Zingheim, Jay R. Schuster
San Francisco, California: Jossey-Bass, 2000
388pp ISBN: 078794016X
Pay People Right! is a guide to the basic issues in compensation. It deals with the topic from a strategic viewpoint and discusses compensation as a total reward as opposed to simple cash remuneration. Performance issues and group considerations are given extensive coverage. This is a good resource for executives of small-to-medium size organizations and HR professionals branching into the field of compensation.

Rewarding Excellence: Pay Strategies for the New Economy 2nd ed.

Edward E. Lawler
San Francisco, California: Jossey-Bass, 2000
352pp (Jossey-Bass Business and Management Series)
ISBN: 0787950742
The author suggests that in today's competitive environment organizations need to focus on rewarding excellence in all areas, and that old reward systems focused on jobs and merit pay are inadequate to motivate and develop either individuals or the organizations themselves. Drawing on research literature, he outlines a new approach to designing reward systems and makes practical suggestions for restructuring the way employees are paid.

Reward Management: A Critical Text

Geoff White, Janet Druker, eds.
New York: Routledge, 2000
240pp (Routledge Studies in Employment Relations)
ISBN: 0415196817
This work offers a critical and theoretical review of changes in remuneration practice in the United Kingdom over the last 20 years. Methods

"In every work a reward added makes the pleasure twice as great." (Euripides)

of determining pay, the role of trade unions, grading systems, salary progression systems, benefits, financial participation schemes, and international reward management are covered.

Strategic Compensation: A Human Resource Management Approach
Joseph J. Martocchio
Upper Saddle River, New Jersey: Prentice Hall, 2000
371pp ISBN: 0130280305
This guide to the practical aspects of employee compensation covers the topic in depth but in an easy-to-follow manner. Aspects of the subject covered range from how to determine compensation levels to compensation management systems. Overall, this is a valuable resource for HR professionals in an organization of any size.

MAGAZINES

Bargaining Report
ISSN: 0143–2680
LRD Publications
78 Blackfriars Road, London, SE1 8HF, U.K.
T: +44 (0) 20 7928 3649
F: +44 (0) 20 7928 0621
www.lrd.org.uk
The Labour Research Department publishes *Bargaining Report* 11 times a year (not August). It is aimed at labor union negotiators in the United Kingdom and provides information on the latest pay settlements and negotiations and legislative developments affecting employment and earnings.

Compensation and Benefits Review
ISSN: 0886–3687
Sage Publications, Inc.
2455 Teller Road, Thousand Oaks, California, 91320
T: +1 805 499 0721
F: +1 805 499 0871
www.sagepub.com
This bimonthly journal focuses on compensation and benefits and how they affect, and are affected by, the changing nature of the workplace and the ways companies do business. Thematic issues are published twice a year.

Croner's Pay and Benefits Sourcebook
Croner CCH Group Ltd.
145 London Road, Kingston-upon-Thames, Surrey, KT2 6SR, U.K.
T: +44 (0) 20 8547 3333
F: +44 (0) 20 8547 2638
www.croner.co.uk
This reference package provides a guide to the design and administration of salary, pay, and benefits policies for managers and pay specialists. It consists of a loose-leaf handbook updated quarterly, CD-ROM and online versions updated twice a year, biweekly pay and benefits briefings, a quarterly special report, and access to a telephone helpline.

PAYadvice
Institute of Payroll and Pensions Management
Shelly House, Farmhouse Way, Monkspath, Solihull, West Midlands, B90 4EH, U.K.
T: +44 (0) 121 712 1000
F: +44 (0) 121 712 1090
www.ippm.org.uk
This monthly magazine is distributed to members of the Institute of Payroll and Pensions Management. Besides news and information, each issue contains feature articles on relevant issues written by experts in their field.

Pay for Performance Report
ISSN: 1086–9581
Institute of Management and Administration
29 West 35th Street, 5th Floor, New York, 10001–2299
T: +1 212 244 0360
F: +1 212 564 0465
www.ioma.com
This is a monthly newsletter providing information on how to implement variable pay and bonus programs.

Payroll Factbook
GEE
100 Avenue Road, Swiss Cottage, London, NW3 3PQ, U.K.
T: +44 (0) 20 7393 7400
F: +44 (0) 20 7393 7915
www.gee.co.uk
This reference publication is designed for payroll managers and accounts administrators with payroll responsibilities. It covers statutory requirements in the United Kingdom and provides advice on payroll management. The subscription includes the Factbook in loose-leaf and/or CD-ROM format with 6 updates, *Payroll News* (a monthly newsletter), the monthly *Pay Magazine*, and access to a telephone helpline.

workspan
ISSN: 1529–9465
WorldatWork
14040 N. Northsight Boulevard, Scottsdale, Arizona, 85260
T: +1 480 951 9191
F: +1 480 483 8352
www.worldatwork.org
Formerly known as *ACA News*, this publication comes out 11 times a year and is aimed at compensation, benefits, and human resource professionals. *workspan* provides information on current trends in remuneration and covers contemporary thinking on issues in compensation and benefits design, implementation, and management.

WorldatWork Journal
ISSN: 1529–9457
WorldatWork
14040 N. Northsight Boulevard, Scottsdale, Arizona, 85260
T: +1 480 951 9191
F: +1 480 483 8352
www.worldatwork.org
This quarterly journal, formerly called the *ACA Journal*, is aimed at middle and senior level managers and covers the theory and practice of compensation and benefits management.

INTERNET

Career City
www.careercity.com
Career City has many links to various salary surveys. Page down to Salaries & Job Searching, click on Salaries, and then click on Links to Salary Surveys. There are sites that address many types of positions to choose from, depending on profession.

College Grad Job Hunter
www.collegegrad.com/salaries/salaries.html
College Grad Job Hunter has a salary calculator for new college graduates based on job type, locality, and profession. The site gives low, median, and high salaries as well as base and total compensation calculations. This is a great site for newly graduated students to find their first position.

Compensation Link
www.compensationlink.com
This site offers information on the design and administration of pay programs and on relevant conferences, seminars, and articles, as well as an array of useful links.

E-Reward
www.e-reward.co.uk
This is a collection of practical resources for managers provided by Michael Armstrong and Paul Thompson. It includes items on managing pay and rewards, news, a glossary, a discussion forum, and listings of relevant books and periodicals.

Salary.com
www.salary.com
This is a free Web site with a great deal of information on salaries. One of its features is the salary search that provides salary ranges for specific positions within a geographic area. This information is useful to job shoppers as well as HR professionals.

The Minimum Wage
www.dol.gov/dol/esa/public/minwage
This site contains information on the minimum wage in the United States from the U.S. Department of Labor.

"Men work but slowly, that have poor wages." (Thomas Fuller)

United States Department of Labor
www.dol.gov
This government Web site contains a large amount of information that is organized for easy access. It provides useful information on the legal aspects of compensation and results of large-scale studies and surveys.

U.S. Office of Personnel Management
www.opm.gov/oca/payrates
This site lists current pay rates for the year 2002 for government employees by position. It includes notes for adjustments made for locality, special rate, and relative memorandums.

WorldatWork—Professional Association for Compensation, Benefits, and Total Rewards
www.worldatwork.org
This site is designed for HR professionals. It has a wealth of online resources including articles, press releases, news items, and survey results. Although much of the site is for members only, there is good information which is accessible to the casual browser.

ORGANIZATIONS

USA

American Payroll Association
660 North Main Avenue, Suite 100, San Antonio, Texas, 78205–1217
T: +1 210 226 4600
F: +1 210 226 4027
E: apa@americanpayroll.org
www.americanpayroll.org
The APA is a professional association for payroll managers with a membership of over 20,000. Its activities include seminars, accreditation programs, publications (including a journal), and an annual congress.

American Society for Payroll Management
P.O. Box 117, Stormville, New York, 12582
T: +1 800 684 4024
F: +1 845 227 9246
E: info@aspm.org
www.aspm.org
The ASPM, founded in 1988, provides information, resources (including an online newsletter), advocacy, and a forum for the exchange of ideas to payroll, tax, and human resources managers. It organizes a symposium and a trade show annually.

Europe

Institute of Payroll and Pensions Management
Shelly House, Farmhouse Way, Monkspath, Solihull, West Midlands, B90 4EH, U.K.
T: +44 (0) 121 712 1000
F: +44 (0) 121 712 1090
E: info@ippm.org
www.ippm.org.uk
The IPPM was formed in 1997 and incorporates the former Institute of British Payroll Management and the Association of Payroll and Superannuation Administrators. It promotes good practice within payroll and pension management through educational programs, advice and support services for members, and representation.

Low Pay Commission
5th Floor, 151 Buckingham Palace Road, London, SW1W 9SS, U.K.
T: +44 (0) 20 7215 3646
F: +44 (0) 20 7215 1560
E: lpc@gtnet.gov.uk
www.lowpay.gov.uk
The Low Pay Commission is a nondepartmental public body that was set up in 1998 to monitor and evaluate the introduction and impact of the National Minimum Wage in the United Kingdom.

Low Pay Unit
9 Arkwright Road, London, NW3 6AB, U.K.
T: +44 (0) 20 7435 4268
F: +44 (0) 20 7431 9614
E: enquiries@lowpayunit.org.uk
www.lowpayunit.org.uk
The Low Pay Unit is a campaigning organization set up in 1974 to work for economic and social justice. It supported the introduction of the National Minimum Wage in the United Kingdom, and promotes the reform of tax and welfare systems to end poverty, equal pay for men and women, an end to discrimination, and access to training opportunities for low-paid workers. It also conducts research and consulting, provides information, and runs an Employment Rights Advice Service.

International

WorldatWork
14040 N. Northsight Boulevard, Scottsdale, Arizona, 85260
T: +1 480 951 9191
F: +1 480 483 8352
E: customerrelations@worldatwork.org
www.worldatwork.org
WorldatWork is a professional organization for those working in the field of compensation, benefits, and HR. It was founded in 1995, was previously known as the American Compensation Association, and has a current membership of over 26,000. Its activities include education and accreditation programs, workshops and conferences, research, publications, and networking opportunities.

For More Information

- **Conditions of Employment (pp. 1933–35)**
- **Employee Benefits/Compensation (pp. 1959–61)**
- **Finding Out What You Are Worth: Remuneration/Salaries (pp. 1982–84)**

Research and Development (R&D) Management

BOOKS

The Development Factory: Unlocking the Potential of Process Innovation
Gary P. Pisano
Boston, Massachusetts: Harvard Business School Press, 1996
331pp ISBN: 0875846505
Gary Pisano proves that process innovation—not just product innovation—can be the key to competitive advantage. In a multiyear study of pharmaceutical and biotechnology firms, he shows that developing distinctive and superior process technologies can lower costs, improve quality, and increase flexibility. *The Development Factory* is designed to help companies unlock the potential of process development and create and implement new capabilities.

"The real measure of success is the number of experiments that can be crowded into 24 hours."
(Thomas Edison)

Fourth Generation R&D: Managing Knowledge, Technology, and Innovation
WILLIAM L. MILLER, LANGDON MORRIS
New York: John Wiley, 1999
347pp ISBN: 0471240931
This book offers practical guidelines for establishing and managing a successful research & development enterprise. It also provides a basic model based on the practices of several successful and highly innovative firms like Hewlett-Packard. The book covers business basics and offers how-to information geared toward establishing and managing a strategically significant R&D presence in an established technology company.

From Alchemy to IPO: The Business of Biotechnology
CYNTHIA ROBBINS-ROTH
Cambridge, Massachusetts: Perseus, 2001
253pp ISBN: 073820482X
Written by an industry insider, this title addresses the coming of age of biotech products and companies, and traces the history of biotechnology from its inception in the 1970s to 2001's heyday of new solutions and breakthrough treatments. It also describes the entrepreneurial trail of product development, novel business models, and critical trials. This book records the inner workings of an industry which is promising to change the world as we know it.

Product Design and Development 2nd ed.
KARL T. ULRICH, STEVEN D. EPPINGER
New York: McGraw-Hill, 1999
384pp ISBN: 007229647X
This book is a practical guide to the business of innovation and R&D. It covers everything from the steps necessary to design a successful product to the budget management for the R&D function. It should be a useful tool for anyone embarking on a career in R&D or who is new to the management of that function.

The Smart Organization: Creating Value through Strategic R&D
DAVID MATHESON, JIM MATHESON
Boston, Massachusetts: Harvard Business School Press, 1997
292pp ISBN: 087584765X
This text aims to help managers improve their research development management and decision making. It discusses "best practices," as well as nine principles of "smart R&D," and includes a section on testing how good an organization's R&D is.

Third Generation R & D: Managing the Link to Corporate Strategy
PHILIP A. ROUSSEL, KAMAL N. SAAD, TAMARA J. ERICKSON
Boston, Massachusetts: Harvard Business School Press, 1991
192pp ISBN: 0875842526
Aimed at managers responsible for prioritizing between research and development projects, this book presents a portfolio method for successful R&D project selection. It stresses that it is important for R&D to form an integral part of an organization's strategy rather than merely serving as an imposed strategy.

The Valuation of Technology: Business and Financial Issues in R&D
F. PETER BOER
New York: John Wiley, 1999
400pp ISBN: 0471316385
This book is a thorough reference and guide to the business and financial aspects of R&D. It begins with chapters devoted to the definition and rationale behind the R&D function, but the bulk of the book is devoted to financial considerations. It is useful for detailed coverage of such topics as developing business plans, determining profit and loss, and understanding and calculating discounted cash flow.

MAGAZINES

International Journal of Technology Management
ISSN: 0267–5730
Inderscience Enterprises Ltd.
World Trade Center Building, 29 route de Pre-Bois, Case Postale 896, CH-1215 Geneva 15, Switzerland
www.inderscience.com
International in scope, the journal tends toward the academic, and primarily covers the management of technology and engineering. However, it also has a large number of items and occasional special issues which are specific to research and development. The journal is aimed at anyone responsible for managing technology.

R&D Management
ISSN: 0033–6807
Blackwell Publishers
350 Main Street, Malden, Massachusetts, 02148
T: +1 781 388 8200
F: +1 781 388 8232
www.blackwellpublishers.com/asp/listofj.asp
This is an international journal for both practitioners and scholars. It covers all areas of research and development, including innovation and design, and also examines human resources and strategic issues that affect research and development management.

INTERNET

National Institute of Science and Technology
www.atp.nist.gov/alliance/welcome.htm
This government Web site is specifically dedicated to the needs of the research and development community. It contains useful information and services as well as links to additional resources.

National Science Foundation
www.nsf.gov
This government-hosted Web site contains a wealth of information for anyone involved in advancing science and technology. It offers everything from statistical data to technology-specific information.

R&D—Research & Development
www.rdmag.com
This Web site is a free online journal for the research and development professional. Each issue features technical articles and general interest materials, and the archives are easily accessed. The site also offers other information and a number of useful services.

ORGANIZATIONS

USA

Industrial Research Institute, Inc.
Suite 1100, 1550 M Street, NW, Washington, D.C., 20005–1712
T: +1 202 296 8811
F: +1 202 776 0756
E: information@iriinc.org
www.iriinc.org
This is a nonprofit organization of over 260 leading industrial companies, whose aim is to enhance the effectiveness of technological innovation in industry. These member companies—representing a range of industries such as aerospace, automotive, chemical, computer, and electronics—carry out over 80% of the industrial research effort in the United States' manufacturing sector, and account for at least 30% of its gross national product.

Product Development and Management Association
17000 Commerce Parkway, Suite C, Mount Laurel, New Jersey, 08054
T: +1 856 439 9052
F: +1 856 439 0525
E: pdma@pdma.org
www.pdma.org
This professional nonprofit organization is dedicated to serving people with an interest in new products and services. It is a recognized provider of knowledge and tools intended to improve the effectiveness of the development and management of new products and services. The Association's activities include arranging conferences, awards, meetings and workshops, producing publications, and sponsoring research.

"In research, the horizon recedes as we advance, and is no nearer at sixty than it was at twenty."
(Mark Pattison)

  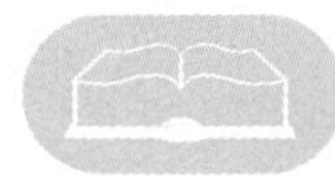    

Europe

Product Development and Management Association, U.K. and Ireland
Innovaro, 78 Belsize Gardens, London, NW3 4NG, U.K.
T: +44 (0) 7801 755 054
E: timjones@innovaro.com
www.pdma.org.uk
This is the U.K. and Ireland branch of the PDMA of America, a professional nonprofit organization dedicated to serving people with an interest in new products and services. It is a recognized provider of knowledge and tools intended to improve the effectiveness of the development and management of new products and services. The Association's activities include arranging conferences, awards, meetings and workshops, producing publications, and sponsoring research.

International

Society of Research Administrators International
1901 North Moore Street, Suite 1004, Arlington, Virginia, 22209
T: +1 703 741 0140
E: info@srainternational.org
www.srainternational.org
The Society is a nonprofit international association, founded in 1967 for those providing administrative support to corporate, academic, or medical researchers. An extensive Web site is available to members, with details of grants available, research administration resources on the Web, training, and experts.

For More Information

- **Innovation and Creativity (pp. 2000–03)**
- **New Product Development (pp. 2054–56)**

Risk Management

BOOKS

Against the Gods: The Remarkable Story of Risk
Peter L. Bernstein
New York: John Wiley, 1998
394pp ISBN: 0471295639
A study of risk history, in which Bernstein eventually brings the reader back to the modern day and "chaos theory." The book discusses the elements of risk that appear in various life situations (with reference to the origins of the risk concept) and aims to increase the reader's understanding of them.

Risk Management
Michel Crouhy, Dan Galai, Robert Mark
New York: McGraw-Hill, 2000
500pp ISBN: 0071357319
This book suggests ways to implement a risk management system to effectively manage financial and economic risk as well as regulatory capital. It analyzes developments in risk management techniques used in the financial world and provides an up-to-date look at modern risk management tools.

Seeing Tomorrow: Rewriting the Rules of Risk
Ron S. Dembo, Andrew Freeman
New York: John Wiley, 1998
260pp ISBN: 0471247367
This book presents a framework for forward-looking risk management. The authors assess the basic building blocks of risk management and explain their own rules for risk. These include the importance of choosing an appropriate time horizon as well as of selecting scenarios, computing Value at Risk, assessing the up- and downsides of potential deals, calculating Regret, and compiling a reliable Regret matrix.

Value at Risk: The New Benchmark for Managing Financial Risk 2nd ed.
Philippe Jorian
New York: McGraw-Hill, 2000
544pp ISBN: 0071355022
This book is aimed at helping professional risk managers understand and operate within today's dynamic new risk environment. This edition updates the original book, which focused on "Value at Risk" as a financial technique to measure risks run by trading and investment operations. New developments include a chapter on liquidity risk, and information on the latest risk instruments and the expanded derivatives market.

MAGAZINES

Risk
ISSN: 0952–8776
The Risk Waters Group
270 Lafayette Street, Suite 700, New York, 10012
T: +1 212 925 6990
F: +1 212 925 7585
www.riskwaters.com/risk
This monthly magazine covers news, analysis, and developments in financial risk management. It is aimed at financial managers, academics, bankers, and investment bankers.

Risk Analysis—An International Journal
ISSN: 0272–4332
Blackwell Publishers
350 Main Street, Malden, Massachusetts, 02148
T: +1 781 388 8200
F: +1 781 388 8232
www.blackwellpublishers.com/asp/listofj.asp
The journal is an official publication of the Society for Risk Analysis. It covers new developments in risk analysis and other topics which should be of interest to scientists and managers from a wide range of disciplines.

Risk and Continuity
ISSN: 1463–1628
CHI Publishing Ltd.
17a Everard Road, Birkdale, Southport, Merseyside, PR8 6NN, U.K.
T: +44 (0) 1704 512 512
F: +44 (0) 1704 512 212
www.chi-publishing.com
This journal provides best practice information on risk and continuity management strategies. It also covers IT security, disaster management, related human factors, and legal issues, together with company and product news.

Risk Decision and Policy
ISSN: 1357–5309
Cambridge University Press
The Edinburgh Building, Shaftesbury Road, Cambridge, Cambridgeshire, CB2 2RU, U.K.
T: +44 (0) 1223 312393
F: +44 (0) 1223 315052
http://uk.cambridge.org/journals/rdp
This journal specializes in the areas of economics, social science, and management, as applied to problems of interest to decision makers in business and government. Published three times a year, it includes information on risk communication. It is the official journal of the Decision and Policy Network.

Risk Management
Risk Management Society Publishing, Inc.
655 Third Avenue, Second Floor, New York, 10017–5637
T: +1 212 286 9364
F: +1 212 922 0716
www.rmmag.com

"If you are scared to go to the brink you are lost." (John Foster Dulles)

  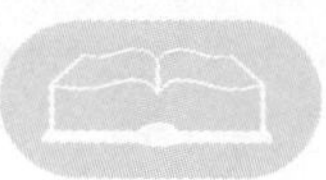    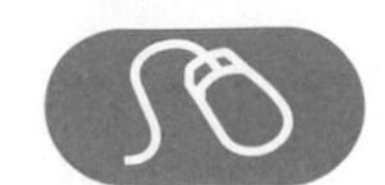

Published 12 times per year this magazine features articles, interviews, and special reports, written for executives and managers working in risk management. Recognized as the premier source of information for corporate risk managers, this is an invaluable resource for today's workplace.

Risk Management—An International Journal
ISSN: 1460–3799
Perpetuity Press Ltd.
P.O. Box 376, Leicester, Leicestershire, LE2 1UP, U.K.
T: +44 (0) 116 221 7778
F: +44 (0) 116 221 7171
www.perpetuitypress.co.uk
This quarterly journal's purpose is to generate ideas and promote good practice for all those involved in managing risk. It takes a multidisciplinary approach and aims to facilitate the exchange of information and expertise across the world.

Risk Management Bulletin
ISSN: 3363–9498
Ark Publishing Ltd.
3000 Atrium Way, 295 Mt. Laurel, New Jersey, 08054–3911
T: +1 877 295 3967
F: +1 877 260 2918
www.ark-interactive.com
This journal provides practical examples of risk management best practice, together with innovative solutions to common problems and benchmarking opportunities.

RMA Journal
ISSN: 1531–0558
Risk Management Association
One Liberty Place, 1650 Market Street, Suite 2300, Philadelphia, Pennsylvania, 19103–7301
T: +1 215 446 4096
F: +1 215 446 4101
www.rmahq.org
Published ten times a year, this journal covers the latest trends, techniques, and challenges that lending, credit, and risk management professionals have to deal with. It is the official journal of the Risk Management Association of the United States.

INTERNET

Business Continuity Institute
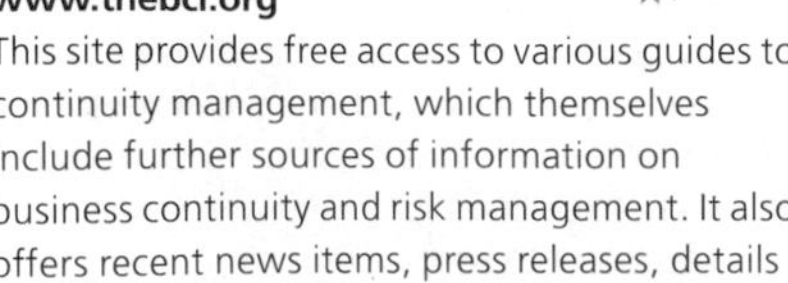
www.thebci.org
This site provides free access to various guides to continuity management, which themselves include further sources of information on business continuity and risk management. It also offers recent news items, press releases, details of seminars and conferences, a worldwide contact list, a vacancy exchange service, membership information, and a members-only area offering networking opportunities, details of the BCI standards, a bookstore, and the BCI forum.

Global Association of Risk Professionals
www.garp.com
Specific to financial risk management, this site offers current news items, membership information, access to detailed risk technology applications, a jobs board, examination information, an events calendar, a newsletter, free access to articles and other reference sources, a bookstore, useful links, and discussion groups.

Institute of Risk Management
www.theirm.org
This site provides information on the membership benefits of the IRM, gives details of its courses, certificates, and examinations, and hosts discussion groups.

Risk and Insurance Management Society, Inc.
www.rims.org
In addition to providing information about Society membership and conferences, this site also offers access to recent government-related news, a risk management newsbrief service, a job bank, education and research activities, a bookstore, a student center, the contents of the society's magazine, and related links.

RMISWEB, the Internet Resource for Risk Management Information Systems
www.rmisweb.com
This site provides access to journal and review articles and press releases on risk management. It also contains recent news items, a directory of software providers, a list of consultants, and links to other risk and insurance sites.

Society for Risk Analysis
www.sra.org
This site provides information on membership and events, recent news, a newsletter, a journal, and related links.

The Association of Insurance and Risk Managers
www.airmic.com
This site contains membership information, details of the AIRMIC conference, a newsletter, a press release index, and a members-only section. It also offers a free directory of service providers.

ORGANIZATIONS

USA

Global Association of Risk Professionals
28 East 18th Street, 2nd Floor, New York, 10003
T: +1 212 995 0930
F: +1 212 995 0835
E: membership@garp.com
www.garp.com
Originally an independent organization of risk management practitioners and researchers, founded by a group of risk managers from the finance industry, the GARP is now a diverse association of over 15,000 professionals sharing a common interest in risk management. Its activities include facilitating exchange of information, developing educational programs, and promoting standards in the area of financial risk management.

Risk and Insurance Management Society, Inc.
655 Third Avenue, 2nd Floor, New York, 10017
T: +1 212 286 9292
www.rims.org
This is a nonprofit organization dedicated to advancing the practice of risk management. It serves its members by providing quality products, services, and information designed to manage all forms of business risk. It also offers educational opportunities and aims to develop a responsive and productive network.

Risk Management Association
One Liberty Place, 1650 Market Street, Suite 2300, Philadelphia, Pennsylvania, 19103–7301
T: +1 215 446 4096
F: +1 215 446 4101
E: customers@rmahq.org
www.rmahq.org
The RMA is a membership organization for lending, credit, and risk management professionals in the financial services industry. Members have access to a number of benefits including professional development and networking opportunities, benchmarking tools, RMA products, and a journal. It was formerly known as Robert Morris Associates.

Society for Risk Analysis
1313 Dolley Madison Boulevard, Suite 402, McLean, Virginia, 22101
T: +1 703 790 1745
E: sra@burkinc.com
www.sra.org
Providing an open forum for those interested in risk analysis in its broadest sense, this organization devotes itself to risks of concern to individuals, the public and private sectors, and society in general. Membership is multidisciplinary and international.

"In skating over thin ice, our safety is in our speed." (Ralph Waldo Emerson)

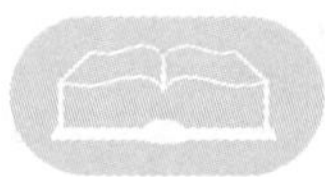

Europe

Association of Insurance and Risk Managers
Lloyd's Avenue House, 6 Lloyd's Avenue, London, EC3N 3AX, U.K.
T: +44 (0) 20 7480 7610
F: +44 (0) 20 7702 3752
E: enquiries@airmic.co.uk
www.airmic.com
This membership organization, founded in 1963, brings together over 900 U.K. and overseas risk managers within industry, commerce, and the public sector. It offers a valuable source of contacts and practical operational support to its members, as well as assisting their self-development, technical awareness, and internal working relationships.

Business Continuity Institute
P.O. Box 4474, Worcester, Worcestershire, WR6 5YA, U.K.
T: +44 (0) 870 603 8783
F: +44 (0) 870 603 8761
E: thebci@btinternet.com
www.thebci.org
The BCI is a membership organization that promotes the art and science of business continuity management worldwide.

Institute of Risk Management
David Ovenden, Acting Chief Executive
Lloyd's Avenue House, 6 Lloyd's Avenue, London, EC3N 3AX, U.K.
T: +44 (0) 20 7709 9808
F: +44 (0) 20 7709 0716
E: enquiries@irmgt.co.uk
www.theirm.org
Besides providing advice and consultation, this membership organization, founded in 1986, also runs educational courses and examinations in risk management, and undertakes research.

For More Information

☆ **Scenario Planning (pp. 267–68)**
Contingency, Crisis, Disaster Management (pp. 1939–41)

SELLING AND SALESMANSHIP

BOOKS

Advanced Selling Strategies: The Proven System of Sales Ideas, Methods, and Techniques Used by Top Salespeople Everywhere
BRIAN TRACY
New York: Simon & Schuster, 1995
432pp ISBN: 0671865196
Based on the author's own career lessons, this book sets out to equip the reader with the attitude, techniques, and tactics needed to succeed in sales.

The Complete Guide to Accelerating Sales Force Performance: How to Get More Sales from Your Sales Force
ANDRIS A. ZOLTNERS, PRABHAKANT SINHA, GREGGOR A. ZOLTNERS
New York: AMACOM, 2001
448pp ISBN: 0814406505
This book is a guide to increasing the productivity of a salesforce. It provides practical solutions and processes and uses a number of real-world examples to substantiate its arguments from a list of companies that the authors have worked with. The authors also demonstrate how sales forces can adapt to changing technology, the Internet, and the new economy.

Fast Forward MBA in Selling: Become a Self-motivated Profit Center and Prosper
JOY J. D. BALDRIDGE
New York: John Wiley, 1999
216pp ISBN: 0471348546
This book is a comprehensive guide to becoming a successful salesperson. It explores a wide range of topics, including setting the standards for success, self-motivation, time management, getting and staying connected, preparation, technology, and successful sales calls.

How to Become a Rainmaker: The Rules for Getting and Keeping Customers and Clients
JEFFREY J. FOX
New York: Hyperion, 2000
169pp ISBN: 0091876540
This book is written to assist in identifying, attracting and keeping customers. It identifies Rainmakers (people who bring revenue into organizations), who may be C.E.O.s, owners, partners, sales representatives, or fundraisers. Jeffrey J. Fox explains how the reader can become a Rainmaker, enabling him/her to attract more customers and rise above the competition in any company.

Knock Your Socks Off Selling
JEFFREY GITOMER, RON ZEMKE
New York: AMACOM, 1999
150pp ISBN: 0814470300
An overview of sales techniques from basic selling to developing relationships, the book is appropriate for salespeople at every level. Placing an emphasis on making a partnership out of the buyer/seller relationship, the book discusses networking, generating leads, making presentations, and following through.

The New Strategic Selling: The Unique Sales System Proven Successful by the World's Best Companies
STEPHEN E. HEIMAN, ET AL.
New York: Warner Books, 1998
433pp ISBN: 0446673463
Following the Strategic Selling process outlined in this book, the authors lay out an effective plan that leverages the key benefits of the sellers/buyers solution, and minimizes price as the principal buying criterion. The book provides a process for what successful sales people do consistently—plan.

Rethinking the Sales Force
NEIL RACKHAM, JOHN R. DE VINCENTIS
New York: McGraw-Hill, 1994
308pp ISBN: 0071342532
Rackham and De Vincentis use real-world examples such as Microsoft, IBM, and Charles Schwab to demonstrate how the commercial viability of various products and services can be improved through determining the real needs of three different buyers—identified as "intrinsic value customers," "extrinsic value customers," and "strategic value customers"—and then developing the appropriate sales strategies to meet them.

The Sales Bible
JEFFREY H. GITOMER
London: William Morrow & Company, 1994
352pp ISBN: 0688133649
Designed as a book to be read by those within the sales industry, this book targets aspiring salesmen/women and gives them practical advice on how to reconsider and reevaluate the whole selling process. Fundamentally challenging prevailing perceptions, this text offers a comprehensive range of new ideas and strategies.

"The only people in the whole world who can change things are those who can sell ideas."
(Lois Wyse)

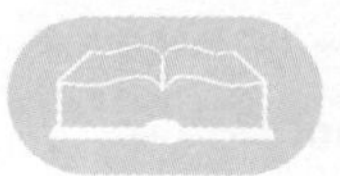

Sales Genius: A Master Class in Successful Selling
TONY BUZAN, RICHARD ISRAEL
Brookfield, Vermont: Gower, 2000
262pp ISBN: 0566082098
The authors present 12 traits that can be found in professional salespeople and 12 strategies that they deploy. They then create a program of activities based on these traits.

Sales Management: Concepts and Cases 7th ed.
DOUGLAS J. DALRYMPLE, WILLIAM L. CRON, THOMAS E. DECARLO
New York: John Wiley, 2000
640pp ISBN: 0471388807
This book includes theoretical discussions and case studies covering all aspects of sales mangement. The topics dealt with in its various sections are: strategic planning and budgeting; personal selling; territory management; estimating potentials and forecasting sales; recruiting and selecting personnel; sales training; leadership; motivating salespeople; compensating salespeople; and evaluating performance.

Selling from the Heart: In the New Millennium, Selling Is Everyone's Job
STEVEN LLOYD
Arlington, Texas: Sterling & Pope
240pp ISBN: 0967861608
The main focus of the book is ''emotional selling'' but it also provides practical, hands-on advice on salesmanship. It covers topics including prospecting, sales presentations, customer relationships, follow-up, and building a career in sales.

Solution Selling: Creating Buyers in Difficult Selling Markets
MICHAEL T. BOSWORTH
New York: McGraw-Hill, 1994
224pp ISBN: 0786303158
This book describes a coherent framework to sell in almost any situation and is useful to anyone involved with sales at any level. It discusses strategies, situations, cases, and so on. It examines the role of the ''seller'' and tries to position him/her as the ''buying facilitator.''

SPIN Selling
NEIL RACKHAM
New York: McGraw-Hill, 1988
197pp ISBN: 0070511136
The book provides practical, easy-to-understand information on how to make selling easier for the salesperson. Based on extensive research, its direct advice may also be helpful in all other work situations.

The SPIN Selling Fieldbook: Practical Tools, Methods, Exercises and Resources
NEIL RACKHAM
New York: McGraw-Hill, 1996
208pp ISBN: 0070522359
Full of case studies and practical information, this book shows the reader how to put into practice the help and advice given in *SPIN Selling*.

Tough Calls: Selling Strategies to Win Over Your Most Difficult Customers
JOSH GORDON
New York: AMACOM, 1997
214pp ISBN: 0814479251
Focusing on the challenges of difficult customers, the book outlines 20 different ''tough sells'' and strategies to counteract them. It provides advice on what to do and what not to do with customers who, for example, are incompetent, do not have buying authority, will not see you, buy elsewhere because of company politics, or like what you say but still don't buy.

The Ultimate Sales Letter: Boost Your Sales with Powerful Sales Letters, Based on Madison Avenue Techniques 2nd ed.
DAN S. KENNEDY, DANIEL KENNEDY
Holbrook, Massachusetts: Adams Media Corporation, 2000
224pp ISBN: 1580622577
This text provides clear examples that assist in writing focused sales letters that target specific customer bases. Tips and features include: creating powerful headlines, improving readability, when to use bullet points, which font to use, and which demographics to target. All this is performed within 28 structured steps, and should interest sales reps, business owners, and advertising people.

Why People Don't Buy Things: Five Proven Steps to Connect with Your Customers and Dramatically Increase Your Sales
HARRY WASHBURN, KIM WALLACE
Cambridge, Massachusetts: Perseus, 2000
198pp ISBN: 073820157X
This text provides a methodical approach in understanding customers' motivations, and shows how to customize an entire sales strategy to customers' shopping patterns. In identifying different sales profiles, the book reveals strategies to break out of unproductive patterns, create fresh relationships, and gain a loyal customer base.

Why We Buy
PACO UNDERHILL
New York: Touchstone Books, 2000
255pp ISBN: 0684849143
This book is filled with retail insights, revealing, for example, how men are starting to shop like women and how women have changed the way supermarkets are designed. Looking to the future, Underhill predicts huge retail opportunities concomitant with an ageing baby-boom population and shows how online retailing will change shopping malls.

MAGAZINES

Sales and Marketing Management
ISSN: 0163–7517
VNU Business Publications
770 Broadway, New York, 10003–9595
T: +1 856 786 9085
F: +1 856 786 4415
www.salesandmarketing.com
This monthly magazine features articles, profiles, and interviews written for top executives who have direct responsibility for all aspects of sales, marketing, and management. Featured topics include case studies and marketing strategies from the world's most successful companies. A special bonus issue, *The Survey of Buying Power*, includes demographic and consumer retail spending data.

Sales and Marketing Professional
ISSN: 0264–3200
ISMM Publishing Ltd.
Romeland House, Romeland Hill, St. Albans, Hertfordshire, AL3 4ET, U.K.
T: +44 (0) 1727 812500
F: +44 (0) 1727 812525
www.ismm.co.uk
This is the official journal of the Institute of Sales and Marketing Management. Aimed at members, it is published ten times a year and covers topics such as market intelligence, sales techniques, and strategies for marketing.

Sales Director
ISSN: 1461–9504
BusinessAge Media Group
1st Floor, 60 Wharf Road, London, N1 7SF, U.K.
T: +44 (0) 20 7490 8411
F: +44 (0) 20 7490 8422
www.saleszone.co.uk
This monthly magazine is aimed at senior professionals in sales, and managing directors. It typically includes articles, news, and surveys focused on the area of sales.

Sales Promotion
ISSN: 0957–6193
Market Link Publishing Ltd.
The Mill, Bearwalden Business Park, Wendens Ambo, Saffron Walden, Essex, CB11 4GB, U.K.
T: +44 (0) 1799 544 215

"Be suspicious of your sincerity when you are the advocate of that upon which your livelihood depends."
(John Lancaster Spalding)

F: +44 (0) 1799 544 202
www.salespromo.co.uk/news.cfm
Published monthly, this magazine covers promotional marketing and incentive strategy Its target readership consists of marketing directors, brand managers, and sales promotion agencies.

Sell!ng
Dartnell Corporation
Accounting Department, 360 Hiatt Drive, Palm Beach Gardens, Florida, 33418
T: +1 800 621 5463
F: +1 561 622 2423
www.dartnellcorp.com
This newsletter is published 12 times per year. Written for novice and experienced sales personnel, it offers tips and advice on how to capture sales. The articles are written by expert salesmen with years of experience in closing the deal on buying decisions. Sales tactics in a variety of major industries are covered.

INTERNET

BestOfSales.com
www.bestofsales.com
A list of links to sales resources on the Internet is given on this site.

Just Sell
www.justsell.com
This site comprises a sales and marketing portal with areas covering sales leads, sales jobs, daily sales intelligence, an online store, and a resource for locating sales training.

Saleslinks.com
www.saleslinks.com/links
Run by Mentor Associates, this site is aimed at anyone who is engaged in selling for a living. It includes links to sales resources on the Internet, arranged in categories.

Salesmanship
www.dmoz.org/Business/Marketing/Salesmanship
Maintained as part of the Open Directory Project, this site contains a large list of other Web sites, each with a brief description, relating to all aspects of salesmanship.

Sales Rep Central
www.salesrepcentral.com
A portal for sales professionals, the site contains news, articles, a community message board, jobs, sales leads, and travel services.

SalesVault
www.salesvault.com
This site is aimed at professional salespeople and provides innovative and up-to-date selling information. It also includes articles, news, and advice.

Selling Power
www.sellingpower.com
The online counterpart to *Selling Power* magazine, the site offers archived issues of the magazine, electronic newsletters on several sales-related topics, a weekly quiz, and books and resources.

The Sales Crusader
http://sales-crusader.hypermart.net
This site presents articles on all aspects of selling and salesmanship contributed by its readers. In addition to these free articles, it also offers recommended book lists and a discussion forum.

ORGANIZATIONS

Europe

Institute of Professional Sales
Moor Hall, Cookham, Maidenhead, Berkshire, SL6 9QH, U.K.
T: +44 (0) 1628 427370
F: +44 (0) 1628 427369
E: johnmayfield@iops.co.uk
www.iops.co.uk
The Institute shares the same facilities, values, and objectives as the Chartered Institute of Marketing. Its vision is to raise the profile of sales professionals, gain recognition for them, and promote their interests, as well as to offer training, develop best practice, promote sales qualifications, and provide networking opportunities.

Institute of Sales and Marketing Management
Romeland House, Romeland Hill, St. Albans, Hertfordshire, AL3 4ET, U.K.
T: +44 (0) 1727 812500
F: +44 (0) 1727 812525
E: sales@ismm.co.uk
www.ismm.co.uk
Established in 1966, the ISMM is a professional body for salespeople in the United Kingdom. It promotes standards of excellence in the industry and provides qualifications and training. Its members are individuals at all levels from students to sales directors. The organization holds a conference in Birmingham every October.

Institute of Sales Promotion
Arena House, 66–68 Pentonville Road, London, N1 9HS, U.K.
T: +44 (0) 20 7837 5340
F: +44 (0) 20 7837 5326
E: enquiries@isp.org.uk
www.isp.org.uk
The Institute of Sales Promotion was set up in 1979. It offers education, training, legal advice, and networking opportunities.

Sales Research Trust Ltd.
751 Portswood Road, Southampton, Hampshire, SO17 3SU, U.K.
T: +44 (0) 23 8067 7416
F: +44 (0) 23 8067 7416
E: enid@sales-research-trust.org
www.sales-research-trust.org
The Trust is a nonprofit body that aims to provide a focus for collaboration between practitioners and academics for the advancement of education and research in selling and strategic customer account management. It conducts research and disseminates the results through publications.

Society of Sales Management Administrators Ltd.
40 Archdale Road, East Dulwich, London, SE22 9HJ, U.K.
T: +44 (0) 20 8516 0211
F: +44 (0) 20 8274 5103
This professional body was established in 1980. It exists to encourage the study of selling and sales management, marketing principles and practice, retail management, and international trade. It provides professional status for salespeople and accredits educational programs.

International

Sales and Marketing Executives International, Inc.
P.O. Box 1390, Sumas, Washington, D.C., 98295–1390
T: +1 312 893 0751
F: +1 604 855 0165
E: smeihq@smei.org
www.smei.org
SME International is a worldwide association of sales and marketing managers whose members are top executives. Founded in 1935, it provides education in both sales and management, along with workshops, newsletters, meetings, and discussions.

For More Information

☆ **Managing the Customer (pp. 65–66)**
Marketing Management (pp. 2045–48)

"You should see some of the research people. If they were in sales they'd never get past the first base."
(Elizabeth Garzarelli)

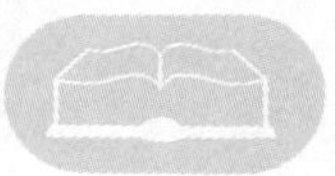

SMALL AND GROWING BUSINESSES

BOOKS

Beating the Odds in Small Business
TOM CULLEY
New York: Fireside/Simon & Schuster, 1998
320pp ISBN: 0684841835
This book is a survival manual for new businesses, and systematically explains and analyzes every key ''survival priority'' upon which the sustainability of a new business is dependent in the critical first years. The author shows how the odds can be turned in your favor by avoiding the distractions of chasing easy success in order to get rich quick, and instead focusing only on the harsh realities of the business jungle.

Capitalizing on Success
NEIL COADE
Stanford, Connecticut: International Thomson Business Press, 2000
240pp (Smart Strategies Series)
ISBN: 1861527659
This book takes a practical approach to the process of business development. After discussing the stages of business growth, it considers the challenges that face emerging businesses and may prevent them from reaching their potential. As means of meeting those challenges, it stresses the importance of effective leadership, good management practice, and creative people able to move the business forward.

Don't Let the IRS Destroy Your Small Business
MICHAEL SAVAGE
Cambridge, Massachusetts: Perseus, 1998
174pp ISBN: 0201311453
Tax attorney Michael Savage provides essential tax advice to small business owners, many of whom pay exorbitant tax fees for mistakes that may have easily been avoided. Without inhouse legal advisers at their disposal, small businesses can get into big financial trouble because they do not know where the potential tax landmines lie. This guide covers areas that give people the most problems regardless of what business they are in: payroll tax liability, excessive salaries, travel and entertainment expenses, fringe benefits, pension plans, owning multiple companies, and many more.

Effective Small Business Management 6th ed.
RICHARD M. HODGETTS, DONALD F. KURATKO
Stanford, Connecticut: International Thomson Publishing, 1997
700pp (Dryden Press Series in Entrepreneurship)
ISBN: 0030247578
Intended for students and lecturers as well as owner-managers, this book provides an introduction to the world of small business and the fundamentals of effective small business management. Its contents include: opportunities for getting into small business; start-up concerns; managing operations; marketing goods; finances and inventory control; and current issues in small business.

Finance for Growing Enterprises
ROGER BUCKLAND, EDWARD DAVIS, EDS.
Stanford, Connecticut: International Thomson Business Press, 1995
288pp (European Financial Institutions and Markets Series)
ISBN: 0415082331
The contributions to this collection examine the mechanisms by which businesses with the capacity to grow—whether in terms of output, innovation, or export—acquire the cash that enables them to do so. The contributors draw together contemporary research studies on the themes of market failure, finance gaps, and failures of demand, before going on to examine the financing choices facing the growing firm, and the issues of organization and corporate governance that have to be addressed during the process of growth and maturing.

Growing Business Handbook: Strategies for Planning, Funding, and Managing Business Growth 4th ed.
RICHARD WILLSHER, ADAM JOLLY, EDS.
Milford, Connecticut: Kogan Page, 2001
315pp ISBN: 0749424753
Designed to help businesses with an established market position, this handbook presents a range of practical strategies for managing growth. The contributors, who come from a variety of backgrounds, provide advice in areas including funding options, competition, managing the risks, making the most of IT, external relations, and competitive purchasing.

Grow Your Business
MARK HENRICKS
Waterloo, Ontario: Entrepreneur Press, 2001
450pp ISBN: 1891984209
Author Mark Henricks guides the reader through a wide portfolio of issues that include: assessing a business's strengths, setting targets, managing risks, negotiating bureaucracy, and handling the competition. Focused on the contemporary business climate, which has witnessed a growing number of new businesses, Henricks takes the fledgling business from infancy and helps it to maturity.

Managing by the Numbers
CHUCK KREMER, RON RIZZUTO, JOHN CASE
Cambridge, Massachusetts: Perseus, 2000
224pp ISBN: 0738202568
In this text, Chuck Kremer and Ron Rizzuto present a practical approach to reading financial statements and to managing the three core issues of business financial performance: net profit, operating cash flow, and return on assets. The book features numerous exercises and examples (with associated templates available on the Web), a powerful new management tool known as ''The Financial Scoreboard,'' and an extensive glossary.

The MouseDriver Chronicles
JOHN LUSK, KYLE HARRISON
Cambridge, Massachusetts: Perseus, 2002
256pp ISBN: 0738205737
Lusk and Harrison, MBA graduates, narrate their experiences of starting their own company, and the problems they encountered along the way. Their product was the MouseDriver, a computer mouse fashioned as a golf club head, which experienced mixed fortunes in a volatile technology market. Lusk and Harrison describe the events leading up to the product's conception, and how they managed to support it in a continually changing marketplace.

The Next Level: Essential Strategies for Achieving Breakthrough Growth
JAMES B. WOOD
Cambridge, Massachusetts: Perseus, 2000
224pp ISBN: 0738201596
An accessible guide to planning and managing the stages of company growth, *The Next Level* centers around the use of a powerful, field-tested diagnostic tool, the Inc. Growth Strategy Analysis. James Wood carefully shows entrepreneurs and established business leaders alike how to analyze their organization's growth potential, identify the key constraints to future growth, and put into practice the strategies that will enable them to arrive at new levels of expansion and profit generation.

"Think naught a trifle, though it small appear; Small stands the mountain, moments make the year."
(Edward Young)

Small Time Operator: How to Start Your Own Business, Keep Your Books, Pay Your Taxes, and Stay Out of Trouble 25th ed.
Bernard B. Kamoroff
Willits, California: Bell Springs Publishing, 2000
200pp ISBN: 0917510186
Kamoroff presents the reader with the essentials of building a business, from obtaining initial permits and licenses, to seeking financing, locating the right business area, establishing an accounts and bookkeeping system, and taking on new staff. Continually updated, Kamoroff is conscious of reflecting the very latest thinking in tax and business management.

Start Up: An Entrepreneur's Guide to Launching and Managing a New Business 5th ed.
William J. Stolze
Franklin Lakes, New Jersey: Career Press, 1999
288pp ISBN: 1564144231
This book is aimed at those setting up or expanding a business and is a practical guide to launching and managing a new enterprise. It includes various case studies and sample business plans.

The Startup Garden
Tom Ehrenfeld
New York: McGraw-Hill, 2001
288pp ISBN: 0071368248
Ehrenfeld identifies a current trend towards entrepreneurship, and in this book he shows his readers how they can construct their own perfect job. *The Startup Garden* takes the reader through the processes involved in starting a company and shows how this is matched to the reader's hopes and dreams, demonstrating the link between your personal life and your business drives.

What No One Ever Tells You About Starting Your Own Business: Real Life Start-up Advice from 101 Successful Entrepreneurs
Jan Norman
Chicago, Illinois: Upstart Publishing, 1999
224pp ISBN: 1574101129
Drawing on the experience of, and mistakes made by, 100 businesspeople, this book contains helpful and practical advice on how to start your own business without headaches.

MAGAZINES

Entrepreneur
ISSN: 0163-3341
Entrepreneur Incorporated
2445 McCabe Way, Irvine, California, 92614
T: +1 949 261 2325
F: +1 949 261 0222
www.entrepreneur.com
This monthly magazine aims to give practical information to prospective entrepreneurs. It offers readers hands-on advice on many aspects of entrepreneurship, and covers the latest developments in technology, finance, management, and marketing. Products, services, and strategies are highlighted in order to help individuals run a better business, and readers can also learn from other entrepreneurs who have successfully improved their businesses.

Inc.
ISSN: 0162-8968
Gruner & Jahr U.S.A. Publishing
375 Lexington Avenue, New York, 10017-5514
T: +1 212 499 2000
F: +1 617 248 8090
www.inc.com
Inc. is a U.S. publication for entrepreneurs, and is published 14 times a year. The magazine provides advice, case studies, and overviews on the subject of small business in the United States, and also provides prospective entrepreneurs with resources and road-tested strategies for managing people, finance, sales, marketing, and technology. The magazine also looks at the personal aspects of the entrepreneurial lifestyle.

International Small Business Journal
ISSN: 0266-2426
Sage Publications, Inc.
2455 Teller Road, Thousand Oaks, California, 91320
T: +1 805 499 0721
F: +1 805 499 0871
www.sagepub.com
The *ISBJ* is a quarterly journal that aims to provide a forum for the discussion and dissemination of views and research on the small business sector. It is intended for academics, policymakers, trade and business associations, and planning and development authorities.

Journal of Small Business and Enterprise Development
ISSN: 1462-6004
MCB University Press
44 Brattle Street, 4th Floor, Cambridge, Massachusetts, 02138
T: +1 800 633 4931
F: +1 205 995 1588
www.emeraldinsight.com/jsbed.htm
The *JSBED* is a peer-reviewed journal that disseminates research findings and best practice and aims to bridge the gap between theory and practice in the field of small business and enterprise development. The journal contains articles, case studies, and book reviews, and is aimed at those responsible for the management of SMEs, those who provide support and assistance to entrepreneurs and owner-managers, and those involved in the development of enterprise policy.

Journal of Small Business Management
ISSN: 0047-2778
Blackwell Publishers
350 Main Street, Malden, Massachusetts, 02148
T: +1 781 388 8200
F: +1 781 388 8232
www.blackwellpublishers.com/asp/listofj.asp
The *JSBM* is published for the International Council for Small Business and the Bureau of Business and Economic Research at West Virginia University College of Business and Economics. It is a quarterly refereed journal covering topics of interest to researchers and academics as well as practitioners. The journal is available on the Web at www.be.wvu.edu/serve/bureau/jsbm.

The Small Business Journal
Synergy Publishing Ltd.
407 Vine Street, Dept.189, Cincinnati, Ohio, 45202
T: +1 513 253 3332
F: +1 508 629 0599
www.tsbj.com
The *Journal* is a monthly magazine offering practical advice for small business owners.

INTERNET

bird-online
www.bird-online.co.uk
This site, based in the United Kingdom, offers a range of information, advice, and services to small businesses.

BizMove.com
www.bizmove.com
This site, based in the United States, features the Small Business Knowledge Base, a range of free information resources for small businesses.

Business Link
www.businesslink.org
The U.K. Small Business Service runs this site to provide advice for small business owners.

Business Owner's Toolkit
www.toolkit.cch.com

"In today's mercurial, unpredictable economy, businesses that fail to grow and change will stagnate and die."
(Heather Robertson)

The toolkit includes model business plans and documents for downloading and information from the SOHO guidebook.

Inc.com
www.inc.com
Inc.com is the online version of the magazine *Inc.* The Web site provides information, products, services, and online tools—accumulated from a variety of sources—for many business or management tasks. This information has also been organized into categories to help the user find quickly what they need.

Small Business Research Portal
www.smallbusinessportal.co.uk
Intended for academics, policymakers, and support agencies, the portal provides a collection of links to small business sites under categories that include news, publications, research, institutes, and conferences.

ORGANIZATIONS

USA

National Federation of Independent Business
53 Century Boulevard, Suite 300, Nashville, Tennessee, 37214
T: +1 615 872 5800
F: +1 615 872 5353
www.nfib.org
The NFIB was founded by Wilson Harder in 1942. With 600,000 members it is the largest and probably the most influential small business lobbying group in the United States. It represents the interests of small business owners at national and state government levels and provides a range of services for its members.

Small Business Administration
200 North College Street, Suite A-2015, Charlotte, North Carolina, 28202
T: +1 704 344 6563
F: +1 704 344 6769
E: answerdesk@sba.gov
www.sbaonline.sba.gov
The Small Business Administration was set up by the U.S. government in 1953 to provide assistance to those starting and running their own businesses. It provides training, financial support, and advice through a network of offices in every state.

Small Business Institute Directors' Association
Michael Broida, Vice-President
Miami University, Department of DSC/MIS, 311 Upham Hall, Oxford, Ohio, 45056
T: +1 513 529 4826
F: +1 513 529 4841
E: broidams@muohio.edu
www.sbida.org
The SBIDA promotes the development and improvement of educational programs for small businesses and acts as a coordinating body for Small Business Institute programs at universities and colleges in the United States. The latter were started in 1972 in cooperation with the U.S. Small Business Administration, but became independent in 1996.

Europe

European Small Business Alliance
Logos, Rue Vautier 54, B-1050 Brussels, Belgium
T: +32 2 639 62 31
F: +32 2 644 90 17
E: secretariat@esba-europe.org
www.esba-europe.org
The ESBA was formed in 1998 by a group of organizations representing small businesses in European countries to protect and promote the interests of small-scale entrepreneurs within the European Union. It works with European institutions and other bodies to create a favorable environment for small businesses.

Federation of Small Businesses
Whittle Way, Blackpool Business Park, Blackpool, Lancashire, FY4 2FE, U.K.
T: +44 (0) 1253 336000
F: +44 (0) 1253 348046
E: ho@fsb.org.uk
www.fsb.org.uk
The FSB, which has 160,000 members in the United Kingdom, represents the interests of small businesses with up to 200 employees. It organizes an annual conference, publishes a bimonthly magazine, *First Voice*, and lobbies on policy issues, while its local branches provide networking and research facilities in addition to general support services for members.

Forum of Public Business
Ruskin Chambers, Drury Lane, Knutsford, Cheshire, WA16 6HA, U.K.
T: +44 (0) 1565 634467
F: +44 (0) 1565 650059
E: fpbltd@fpb.co.uk
www.fpb.co.uk
The FPB aims to influence laws and policies affecting private businesses in the United Kingdom and provide support for its members.

Small Business Bureau
Curzon House, Church Road, Windlesham, Surrey, GU20 6BH, U.K.
T: +44 (0) 1276 452010
F: +44 (0) 1276 451602
E: info@sbb.org.uk
www.smallbusinessbureau.org.uk
The Small Business Bureau was founded in 1976 to promote the interests of small businesses in the United Kingdom. Its activities include an annual conference and a quarterly magazine, *Small Business News*. The organization has also set up Women into Business to encourage more women to choose business and business ownership as a career.

Small Business Service
Kingsgate House, 66–74 Victoria Street, London, SW1E 6SW, U.K.
T: +44 (0) 114 259 7788
F: +44 (0) 114 259 7330
E: gatewayenquiries@sbs.gsi.gov.uk
www.sbs.gov.uk
The Small Business Service is a U.K. government agency which coordinates support and advice for small businesses.

International

International Council for Small Business
Jefferson Smurfit Center for Entrepreneurial Studies, St. Louis University, 3674 Lindell Boulevard, St. Louis, Missouri, 63108
T: +1 314 977 3628
F: +1 314 977 3627
E: icsb@slu.edu
www.icsb.org
The ICSB works to increase awareness and understanding of the role of small and medium businesses worldwide through education, research, publications, management development programs, conferences, and an international exchange program. Its membership includes educators, small business owners, consultants and advisers, government officials, and trade and business associations. It also publishes the *Journal of Small Business Management*, a bulletin, a newsletter, research papers, and conference proceedings.

World Association for Small and Medium Enterprises
Plot No. 4, Sector 16A, Noida, Uttar Pradesh, 201301, India
T: +91 118 451 5238
F: +91 118 451 5243
E: wasme@vsnl.com
www.wasmeinfo.org

"Smaller businesses often say the words, but can't get in on the act." (Clare Short)

WASME was founded in 1980 in New Delhi, India with the aim of providing support and advice to SMEs internationally and has members and associates in 112 countries. The organization promotes technology transfer, joint ventures and cooperation between SMEs in industrialized, developing, and least developed countries. It has set up a Technology and Trade Promotion Exchange Center (TPX) and an International Committee for Rural Industrialization (ICRI). WASME has consultative status with the Economic and Social Council of the United Nations and other UN bodies.

For More Information

✓ **Marketing for the Small Business (pp. 536–37)**
Entrepreneurship (pp. 1969–72)

SOCIAL RESPONSIBILITY OF MANAGEMENT

BOOKS

The Answer to How Is Yes
PETER BLOCK
San Francisco, California: Berrett-Koehler, 2001
200pp ISBN: 1576751686
The preponderance of the "how?" question in society, Block claims, is symptomatic of people living in accordance with an ethic of defence. We must strive to reclaim both our liberty and autonomy that have been radically sequestered from us. This position is to be attained for workers and managers by encouraging them to act on what they know, confronting passivity and promoting a life where we can choose accountability and demand more compelling purpose from our work.

Beyond the Bottom Line: Putting Social Responsibility to Work for Your Business and the World
JOEL MAKOWER
Carmichael, California: Touchstone Books, 1995
336pp ISBN: 0684813106
Using case studies as examples, the book offers practical advice on socially responsible actions companies can take that will improve their bottom line. Based on the experiences of the organization called Business for Social Responsibility, it covers topics including workplace diversity, community involvement, work-family balance, employee empowerment and training, and environmental issues.

Building Corporate Accountability: Emerging Practices in Social and Ethical Accounting, Auditing, and Reporting
SIMON ZADEK, PETER PRUZAN, RICHARD EVANS, EDS.
London: Earthscan, 1997
288pp ISBN: 185383130
This book is for managers who are responsible for putting social and ethical accounting, auditing, and reporting into practice, examining the implications of the social and ethical method for corporate responsibility and business success. It includes a methodological framework that analyzes and improves upon emerging practice worldwide, and presents nine case studies demonstrating best practice in the field.

Business and Society: Ethics and Stakeholder Management
ARCHIE B. CARROLL
Cincinnati, Ohio: South-Western Publishing, 1999
768pp ISBN: 0324001029
Though the book is intended as a textbook, its managerial perspective makes it relevant for businesspeople as well. It uses case studies to illustrate relationships between business and society stakeholders and emphasizes ethical considerations in decision making.

Business As Unusual
ANITA RODDICK
London: Thorsons Publishing, 2001
304pp ISBN: 0722539878
This book contains the ideas for the philosophy of Anita Roddick's Body Shop chain, detailing the unique ethos of the company, which is to maintain an operation that can be at once profitable whilst not harming the environment or violating human rights.

Citizen Brands: Putting Society at the Heart of Your Business
MICHAEL WILLMOTT
New York: John Wiley, 2001
260pp ISBN: 0471492124
"Citizen brands" reflect the need for organizations to demonstrate corporate social responsibility. The book develops this concept further, evolving the idea of corporate citizenship, the practice of which should make a business more successful.

Common Interest, Common Good: Creating Value through Business and Social Sector Partnerships
SHIRLEY SAGAWA, ELI SEGAL
Boston, Massachusetts: Harvard Business School Press, 1999
350pp ISBN: 0875848486
The book focuses on issues of social responsibility from the perspective of corporate and nonprofit partnerships, arguing that businesses are in a position to make a difference as funding for nonprofits decreases. It addresses topics including corporate sponsorships, cause-related marketing, employee volunteer programs, and school-to-work initiatives.

Corporate Community Relations: The Principle of the Neighbor of Choice
EDMUND M. BURKE
Westport, Connecticut: Praeger, 1999
208pp ISBN: 027596471X
The author argues that businesses must be socially aware and gain the trust and respect of the community in which they operate. Positive strategies and policies with respect to environmental awareness and community relations can offer greater economic opportunities and attract both consumers and employees. He considers the key goals and steps required for these strategies.

Corporate Global Citizenship: Doing Business in the Public Eye
NOEL M. TICHY, ANDREW R. MCGILL, LYNDA ST. CLAIR, EDS.
San Francisco, California: New Lexington Press, 1998
464pp ISBN: 0787910953
The book offers examples of what leading multinational corporations are doing to improve the quality of life in the communities in which they operate. It emphasizes the ability of corporations to make a difference and provides discussion of the future of global corporate citizenship.

Counting What Counts: Turning Corporate Accountability to Competitive Advantage
BILL BIRCHARD, MARC J. EPSTEIN
Cambridge, Massachusetts: Perseus, 2000
320pp ISBN: 0738203130
Fraud, tax evasion etc. are what the authors of this book identify as practices which obstruct managers from working efficiently. The text argues that managers should adopt the ethic of

"Companies have to be socially responsible or the shareholders pay eventually." (Warren Shaw)

accountability, and succeed by becoming responsive and responsible. Using over 25 years of research and the experiences of a number of managers, Epstein and Birchard show that managers frequently overlook accountability and are in need of reform.

The Emperor's Nightingale
Robert A. G. Monks
Cambridge, Massachusetts: Perseus, 1999
283pp ISBN: 0738201332
Monks points to the need for a social conscience in a society eaten up by public companies, management consultants, and short-term thinking. Lamenting corporate lawlessness manifest in waste dumps to tax evasion, Monks vocalizes the other side of capitalist society pointing to a more controlled, tamed market model.

The End of Shareholder Value
Allan Kennedy
London: Texere Publishing, 2000
248pp ISBN: 1842030493
The main premise of Kennedy's argument is that the shareholder value ethic has signally failed to produce anything of lasting value, with the result that the future of the company as we know it is under threat. The book outlines three eras of business evolution, from the family enterprises of the 19th century to the entrepreneurs of high technology, often unfavorably, and ends with Kennedy's proposed remedies to create real, sustainable wealth for all of a company's stakeholder groups, not just the stockholders.

The Heroic Enterprise: Business and the Common Good
John M. Hood
New York: Free Press, 1996
256pp ISBN: 068482762X
Attacking the common assertion that businesses necessarily neglect the public good at the expense of short-term profits, Hood demonstrates numerous examples of how business works to enhance the wider social good. Detailing actual examples of this happening in today's world, Hood reveals how inner city areas have been regenerated, and how the environment, workplace, and education have all been reformed in line with business initiatives.

Managing Values and Beliefs in Organisations
Tom McEwan
Upper Saddle River, New Jersey: Financial Times Management, 2001
560pp ISBN: 0273643401
This is book written as a student text that summarizes the origins of corporate responsibility, business ethics, and corporate governance and reviews the similarities and differences between them. The specific issues covered include: moral meaning and applied ethics; values, beliefs, and ideologies; individual morality in organizations; unethical behavior by individuals; international business and the developing world; ethical investment; organization culture and stakeholder theory; and corporate social performance, ethical leadership, and reputation management.

Take It Personally
Anita Roddick
Berkeley, California: Publishers Group West, 2001
224pp ISBN: 1573247073
Like Naomi Klein, Roddick points to the need concentrate on business accountability, focusing on human rights violations, environmental issues, the treatment of the developing world, and the growth of global markets. She forces her reader to ask the question, who really controls the world—business or government?

When Good Companies Do Bad Things: Responsibility and Risk in an Age of Globalization
Peter Schwartz, Blair Gibb
New York: John Wiley, 1999
194pp ISBN: 0471323322
This book sets out to show how essential social responsibility is to the success of corporations in today's globalized economy. Illustrating their argument with case studies of large multinationals, the authors demonstrate how corporations make poor choices, exposing themselves to huge financial risks and potential loss of reputation. They also explain, however, how corporations can learn from their mistakes and turn social value into business value.

INTERNET

Business Ethics
www.business-ethics.com
The online counterpart to business ethics magazines, the site offers articles, news, book recommendations, and an e-mail newsletter.

Business for Social Responsibility
www.bsr.org
Sponsored by a membership organization, the site offers news, articles, a membership directory, conference and events information, a discussion area, and job listings.

Community Action Network
www.can-online.org.uk
This site gives access to a mutual learning and support network for social entrepreneurs.

Do-It
www.do-it.org.uk
This is a national database of voluntary work opportunities for both companies and individuals.

Lockheed Martin Corporate Ethics
www.lockheedmartin.com/about/ethics.html
This site sets out the company's code of ethics and business conduct, along with its value statement and ethical principles.

The Corporate Social Responsibility Newswire
www.csrwire.com
This site promotes corporate responsibility by providing news, solutions-based information, and positive examples of corporate practices.

ORGANIZATIONS

USA

The Center for Corporate Citizenship at Boston College
Wallace E. Carroll School of Management, 55 Lee Road, Chestnut Hill, Massachusetts, 02467–3942
T: +1 617 552 4545
F: +1 617 552 8499
E: *ccc@bc.edu*
www.bc.edu/bc_org/avp/csom/ccc
This membership organization was founded in 1985 to establish corporate citizenship as a business essential. It offers executive education, particularly the certificate program in community relations. It arranges conferences, encourages research, oversees the Standards of Excellence and their companion diagnostic tools, and provides consulting services.

Europe

AccountAbility
Unit A, 137 Shepherdess Walk, London, N1 7RQ, U.K.
T: +44 (0) 20 7549 0400
F: +44 (0) 20 7253 7440
E: *secretariat@accountability.org.uk*
www.accountability.org.uk
Founded in 1996 as an international membership organization with the aim of improving the accountability and performance of organizations worldwide, AccountAbility (full name: the Institute of Social and Ethical Accountability) promotes best practice and ethical accounting, auditing, and reporting, and develops standards and certification for professionals in the field.

Business in the Community
137 Shepherdess Walk, London, N1 7RQ, U.K.
T: +44 (0) 870 600 2482
F: +44 (0) 20 7486 1700
E: *information@bitc.org.uk*

"Ambivalence about family responsibilities has a long history in the corporate world."
(Rosabeth Moss Kanter)

www.bitc.org.uk
Business in the Community was set up as a partnership between business, government, local authorities, and labor unions to promote corporate community involvement. It has a support network aimed particularly at helping new and developing businesses to become involved in the community.

Corporate Social Responsibility (CSR) Europe
78–80 rue Defacqz, B-1050 Brussels, Belgium
T: +32 2 502 8354
F: +32 2 502 8458
E: *info@csreurope.org*
www.csreurope.org
CSR Europe helps companies achieve profitability, sustainable growth, and human progress by placing corporate social responsibility in the mainstream of business practice. It provides publications, best practices and tools, learning, benchmarking, and tailored capacity building programs.

The Prince of Wales International Business Leaders Forum (IBLF)
15–16 Cornwall Terrace, Regent's Park, London, NW1 4QP, U.K.
T: +44 (0) 20 7467 3600
F: +44 (0) 20 7467 3610
E: *info@iblf.org*
www.csrforum.com
This nonprofit membership organization was established in 1990 by HRH The Prince of Wales and a group of C.E.O.s from international companies to promote corporate social responsibility (CSR). CSR business practices are based on ethical values to help achieve socially, economically, and environmentally sustainable development.

International

Business for Social Responsibility (BSR)
609 Mission Street, 2nd Floor, San Francisco, California, 94105-3506
T: +1 415 537 0888
F: +1 415 537 0889
www.bsr.org
BSR is a global resource for companies seeking to sustain commercial success in ways that demonstrate respect for ethical values, people, communities, and the environment. It offers products and services that address the full range of corporate social responsibility issues, including audits and accountability, community economic development, community involvement, the environment, ethics, governance, human rights, the marketplace, and the workplace.

For More Information

- ☆ **Business Ethics (pp. 231–32)**
- ☆ **Governing the Corporation (pp. 239–40)**
- **Business Ethics and Codes of Practice (pp. 1918–20)**

Stress and Stress Management

BOOKS

Creating a Stress-free Office
Simon Priest, Jim Welch
Burlington, Vermont: Ashgate Publishing Company, 1998
226pp ISBN: 0566079739
A lively workbook for managers, written by stress management specialists. Quizzes, exercises, cartoons, and games are given, as well as facts and techniques to help in recognizing, managing, and reducing workplace stress. The book contains sections on what stress is; the causes of stress; the symptoms of stress; and ways of reducing stress.

Energising the Workplace: A Strategic Response to Stress
Kim James, Tanya Arroba
Burlington, Vermont: Ashgate Publishing Company, 1999
178pp ISBN: 0566080222
A book for senior managers and personnel specialists exploring the area of organizational stress. Guidelines are offered for a new psychological approach for dealing with workplace stress at a strategic level that is based on the authors' work to support stress management initiatives within organizations. Areas covered include undercurrents creating stress in the workplace, the provision of a supportive environment, and the implementation of a stress management strategy.

Getting Things Done: The Art of Stress-free Productivity
David Allen
New York: Viking Books, 2001
267pp ISBN: 0670899240
Based on the notion that productivity is proportional to your ability to handle projects in a relaxed manner, the author offers solutions to self-management that minimize stress and enhance one's focus and efficiency. *Getting Things Done* offers a system which consigns all those must-dos clogging your brain into a framework of files and action lists—all with the intention of freeing your mind to focus on whatever you're working on now.

How to Stop Worrying and Start Living
Dale Carnegie
New York: Pocket Books, 1990
358pp ISBN: 0671733354
This classic title is geared to helping people cut down on the stress and worry in their lives. The book is full of examples of how individuals can combat worry in a number of situations and ultimately gain more confidence and peace of mind.

Instant Stress Management
Brian Clegg
Milford, Connecticut: Kogan Page, 2000
128pp ISBN: 0749431164
A book of quick, easy-to-use exercises to help individuals to reduce their stress. Three introductory sections discuss stress, where it comes from, medical aspects of stress, and controlling stress. A brief exercise section then focuses on assessment, before the main part of the book concentrates on de-stressing exercises. A final section gives further reading and examples of relaxational music.

The One-minute Meditator: Relieving Stress and Finding Meaning in Everyday Life
Bill Birchard, David A. Nichol
Cambridge, Massachusetts: Perseus, 2001
164pp ISBN: 0738203785
This is a guide to why and how to meditate in short periods of time. Instead of relieving stress through temporary distractions, *The One-minute Meditator* teaches readers how to quiet their thoughts from within, reaping considerable physical and emotional benefits. The authors demonstrate that it's possible to meditate at any time and in any place—while walking to the office, waiting in lines, holding on the phone, or attempting to go to sleep.

Theories of Organizational Stress
Cary Cooper, ed.
New York: Oxford University Press, 1998
275pp ISBN: 019829705X
A collection of largely psychological or organizational theory contributions on stress. The publishers claim that that this volume covers

all the major theories of organizational stress from leading researchers and writers in the field. Aimed at academics and professional practitioners, it seeks to facilitate analysis of the causes and characteristics of organizational stress, as well as discuss therapeutic or preventative measures.

Time Management from the Inside Out
JULIE MORGENSTERN
New York: Henry Holt, 2000
241pp ISBN: 0805064699
A thorough, accessible guide to creating a time management system that works for you and your personal situation. The author sets out to give sound advice that can be customized across a range of lifestyles.

MAGAZINES

International Journal of Stress and Stress Management
ISSN: 1072–5245
Kluwer Academic Publisher
The Journals Department, P.O. Box 332, 3300 AA Dordrecht, The Netherlands
T: +31 78 657 63 92
F: +31 78 657 64 74
www.wkap.nl
The quarterly *International Journal of Stress and Stress Management* publishes studies and theoretical essays from the broad field of stress management. It aims to give information about recent studies and innovations from the interdisciplinary stress management field. It is the official publication of the International Stress Management Association.

Stress News
International Stress Management Association U.K.
P.O. Box 348, Waltham Cross, EN8 8ZL, U.K.
T: +44 (0) 7000 780430
F: +44 (0) 1992 426673
www.isma.org.uk
Stress News is published four times a year and is the journal of the U.K. branch of the International Stress Management Association. It is free to members, and available on subscription to others. Sample articles can be viewed on the ISMA U.K. Web site.

Work and Stress
Taylor & Francis
11 New Fetter Lane, London, EC4P 4EE, U.K.
T: +44 (0) 20 7583 9855
F: +44 (0) 20 7842 2298
www.tandf.co.uk
Work and Stress, published in association with the European Academy of Occupational Health Psychology, is an international, multi-disciplinary quarterly journal. It offers refereed academic papers relating to stress, health and safety, and performance. It aims to cover psychological, social, organizational, and policy issues in relation to the nature of stress and its management.

INTERNET

International Stress Management Association (ISMA)
www.stress-management-isma.org
This is a Web site giving information about, and providing the link between, the national organizations that form the International Stress Management Association. The Association began as the American Association for the Advancement of Tension Control in 1973. ISMA seeks to facilitate the acquisition and dissemination of scientific knowledge about tension control and particularly promotes technological applications that can be validated through electromyographical measurement.

Mind Tools
www.mindtools.com/smpage.html
This is a site offered by Mind Tools in association with Amazon.com giving details of books on stress and stress management techniques that can be ordered online.

Online Stress News International
www.onlinestress.com
This online newsletter is sponsored by the Centre for Stress Management, and was set up to provide visitors to their site with current news of stress and stress management. Its main focus is on material from the United Kingdom and the United States, but relevant material from elsewhere is included. Free articles and books can be downloaded.

Stress Cure
www.stresscure.com
This Internet resource offers information relating to the specific stress coping methods of Dr. Mort Orman and general information and resources relating to stress management. There are requests for registration linked to access for various parts of this site.

ORGANIZATIONS

USA

The American Academy of Experts in Traumatic Stress
308 Veterans Memorial Highway, Commack, New York, 11725
T: +1 631 543 2217
F: +1 631 543 6977
www.aaets.org
This is a multidisciplinary network of international professionals that aims to increase awareness of the effects of traumatic events and improve the quality of interventions to support survivors. It holds an international register of stress management and traumatic stress experts, and offers membership and related publications, courses, and qualifications for over 200 professions in the health, emergency, criminal justice, forensics, law, and educational fields.

The American Institute of Stress
124 Park Avenue, Yonkers, New York, 10703
T: +1 914 963 1200
F: +1 914 965 6267
E: stress124@earthlink.net
www.stress.org
This nonprofit organization was founded in 1978 as a clearing house for information on stress and related subjects. It maintains a library of information, coconducts the annual International Montreux Congress on Stress, provides a consultancy referral service, and produces a monthly newsletter, *Health and Stress*, reporting on stress research and linked health matters.

Europe

Centre for Stress Management
156 Westcombe Hill, Blackheath, London, SE3 7DH, U.K.
T: +44 (0) 20 8318 5653
F: +44 (0) 20 8297 5656
www.managingstress.com
This is a commercial training center and consultancy offering courses, counseling, coaching, and workplace stress audits and interventions. The center produces an online newsletter from which free articles and books can be downloaded.

European Academy of Occupational Health Psychology (EA-OHP)
c/o Institute of Work, Health & Organisations (I-WHO), Nottingham University Business School, Nottingham, NG8 1BB, U.K.
T: +44 (0) 115 8466664
F: +44 (0) 115 8466625
E: membership:ea-ohp.org
www.ea-ohp.org
This membership organization was established to develop and promote occupational health psychology in Europe. Members receive a discounted subscription to the *Work and Stress* quarterly journal, an Academy newsletter, and reduced registration rates for EA-OHP conferences and meetings.

International Stress Management Association, U.K. (ISMA U.K.)
P.O. Box 348, Waltham Cross, EN8 8ZL, U.K.
T: +44 (0) 7000 780430
F: +44 (0) 1992 426673
E: stress@isma.org.uk

"Always do one thing less than you think you can do." (Bernard Baruch)

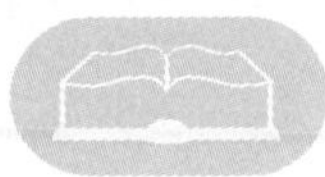

www.isma.org.uk
This U.K. branch of the Internet-linked International Stress Management Association is a registered charity which aims to promote knowledge and best practice in the prevention and reduction of human stress. It has a multi-disciplinary professional membership, sets professional standards for those using the services of members, and its provisions include conferences and events, publications, Web links, information, and a newsletter called *Stress News*.

For More Information

✔ **Stress Management: Self First (pp. 412–13)**

TAXATION

BOOKS

The Encyclopedia of Taxation and Tax Policy
JOSEPH J. CORDES, ET AL.
Washington, D.C.: Urban Institute Press, 1999
468pp ISBN: 0877666822
A compilation of 200 essays on a broad array of topics including tax administration, evasion and avoidance, and fundamentals of equity and efficiency. The primary emphasis is on issues relating to the development, administration, and evaluation of tax policy.

The Ernst & Young Tax Guide 2002
PETER W. BERNSTEIN, ED.
New York: John Wiley, 2002
752pp ISBN: 0471434930
Ernst & Young's comprehensive tax guide provides a number of useable tax return forms, complete with step-by-step instructions for filling them out. It contains over 450 Tax Savers, Tax Alerts, Tax Organizers, and Tax Planners, and has a chapter on mutual funds which details when to make new investments and how to deal with distributions, transfers, and redemptions. Another chapter on gift tax explains what defines a gift, how you can calculate liability, and which forms you should use.

PriceWaterhouseCoopers Corporate Taxes: Worldwide Summaries 2002–03
PRICEWATERHOUSECOOPERS
New York: John Wiley, 2002
960pp ISBN: 0471409812
This tax guide covers 127 countries giving tax rates and rules for each country as at January 1, 2002.

PriceWaterhouseCoopers Individual Taxes: Worldwide Summaries 2002–03
PRICEWATERHOUSECOOPERS
New York: John Wiley, 2002
573pp ISBN: 0471409820
This tax guide covers 127 countries giving tax rates and rules for each country as at January 1, 2002.

State Tax Handbook, 2001
CCH TAX LAW EDITORS
Washington, D.C.: CCH Incorporated, 2000
408pp ISBN: 0808005553
This annual volume is similar to the U.S. Master Tax Guide, but gives more detailed tax information for all 50 states plus the District of Columbia. It is perhaps the most complete source for precise information on U.S. state-level tax policy.

U.S. Master Tax Guide, 2001 84th ed.
CCH TAX LAW EDITORS
Washington, D.C.: CCH Incorporated, 2000
720pp ISBN: 0808005510
This annual volume is currently in its 84th edition. It provides an exhaustive source of detailed information on all U.S. federal taxes, including taxes on individuals, corporations, partnerships, estates, and trusts

West Federal Taxation 2002: Corporations, Partnerships, Estates and Trusts 25th ed.
WILLIAM H. HOFFMAN, ET AL.
Cincinnati, Ohio: South-Western College Publishing, 2001
1056pp ISBN: 0324109733
Providing information about federal tax legislation as it affects companies and other organizations, this book is supported by a Web site with additional resources.

Your Income Tax 2002
J. K. LASSER
New York: John Wiley, 2001
800pp ISBN: 0471443727
Lasser's text (updated annually) provides a comprehensive library of financial planning and investing advice for the tax season and after. J. K. Lasser provides those who plan ahead with a head start on understanding the new tax regulations and preparing for filing the return on April 15th.

MAGAZINES

National Tax Journal
ISSN: 0028–0283
National Tax Association
725 15th Street NW, Suite 600, Washington, D.C., 20005–2109
T: +1 202 737 3325
F: +1 202 737 7308
www.ntanet.org
This is the quarterly journal of the National Tax Association.

State Tax Notes
ISSN: 1057–8404
Tax Analysts
6830 North Fairfax Drive, Arlington, Virginia, 22213
T: +1 800 955 3444
F: +1 703 533 4484
This newsletter is similar to *Tax Notes*, but with a state-level focus.

State Tax Review
ISSN: 0162–1750
CCH Incorporated
4025 West Peterson Avenue, Chicago, Illinois, 60646–6085
T: +1 800 525 3353
F: +1 773 866 3895
This weekly newsletter features up-to-date information on state tax policy developments. It is the periodical companion to the yearly CCH *State Tax Handbooks*.

Tax Administrators News
ISSN: 0039–9949
Federation of Tax Administrators
444 N. Capitol Street NW, Suite 348, Washington, D.C., 20001
T: +1 202 624 5890
F: +1 202 624 7888
This is a monthly compendium of information and analysis focused on state taxation.

"The hardest thing in the world to understand is income tax." (Albert Einstein)

Taxes: The Tax Magazine
ISSN: 0040–0181
CCH, Inc.
2700 Lake Cook Road, Riverwoods, Illinois, 60015
T: +1 847 267 7000
F: +1 847 224 8299
www.tax.cch.com
This journal covers state and federal taxation in legal, accounting, and economic terms.

Tax Notes
ISSN: 0270–5494
Tax Analysts
6830 North Fairfax Drive, Arlington, Virginia, 22213
T: +1 800 955 3444
F: +1 703 533 4484
This is a weekly newsletter providing late-breaking information on all aspects of federal taxation in the United States. Its features include indepth economic analysis and reports from the executive, legislative, and judicial branches regarding U.S. tax policy.

INTERNET

CCH Incorporated
www.cch.com
CCH are the publishers of numerous books and journals on taxation, including the new *Journal of Taxation of Global Transactions*. Their Web site provides links to numerous CCH information sources, mostly available for a fee.

Internal Revenue Service
www.irs.com
The IRS Web site offers downloadable income tax forms, instructions on filing taxes, and information on U.S. regulations and laws. It also features an electronic filing center.

Tax Analysts
www.tax.org
Tax Analysts, publishers of *Tax Notes* and *State Tax Notes*, provide continuously updated tax news wire, a variety of interesting links, and weekly federal, state, and international feature articles on their Web site.

Tax and Accounting Sites Directory
www.taxsites.com
This site provides an international gateway to country specific tax and accounting resources on the Web. It has a U.S. bias.

Tax Resources
www.taxresources.com
This directory has links to U.S. federal and local tax departments with tax rates and forms. It also has links to sites covering tax software, world tax, and tax articles.

ORGANIZATIONS

USA

Federation of Tax Administrators
444 N Capitol Street NW, Suite 348, Washington, D.C., 20001
T: +1 202 624 5890
F: +1 202 624 7888
E: webmaster@taxadmin.org
www.taxadmin.org
This is the primary organization for state-level tax policy administrators. Its Web site provides links to each state's tax department.

Institute for Professionals in Taxation
3350 Peachtree Road NE, Suite 280, Atlanta, Georgia, 30326
T: +1 404 240 2300
F: +1 404 240 2315
E: ipt@ipt.org
www.ipt.org
This is a business organization focusing on property taxes and sales and use taxes.

Internal Revenue Service
1111 Constitution Avenue NW, Washington, D.C., 20224
T: +1 800 829 1040
www.irs.gov
The Internal Revenue Service is the official source for information on U.S. federal taxation. It offers downloadable income tax forms, instructions on filing taxes, and information on U.S. regulations and laws. It also features an electronic filing center.

Multistate Tax Commission
444 N Capitol Street NW, Suite 425, Washington, D.C., 20001
T: +1 202 624 8699
F: +1 202 624 8819
E: mtc@mtc.gov
www.mtc.gov
This organization consists of an alliance of representatives from 45 states dedicated, among other things, to the adoption of uniform state tax policies toward multinational firms.

National Association of Tax Professionals
720 Association Drive, Appleton, Wisconsin, 54914–1483
T: +1 800 558 3402
F: +1 800 747 0001
E: natp@natptax.com
www.natptax.com
This organization provides continuing professional education for tax professionals. It consists primarily of accountants, tax agents, lawyers, and financial planners.

National Tax Association
725 15th Street NW, Suite 600, Washington, D.C., 20005–2109
T: +1 202 737 3325
F: +1 202 737 7308
E: natltax@aol.com
www.ntanet.org
The NTA was founded in 1907 and is the leading association of tax professionals in the United States. It aims to promote the study and discussion of tax theory, practice, and policy. Members of the NTA come from the public, government, corporate, and academic sectors. The Association runs a national conference and a spring symposium and publishes the *National Tax Journal* and a newsletter called the *NTA Forum*.

Europe

Chartered Institute of Taxation
12 Upper Belgrave Street, London, SW1X 8BB, U.K.
T: +44 (0) 20 7235 9381
F: +44 (0) 20 7235 2562
E: post@ciot.org.uk
www.tax.org.uk
As the senior professional body in the United Kingdom concerned solely with all aspects of taxation, the Chartered Institute of Taxation aims to advance public education in, and promote the study of, the administration and practice of taxation. It has nearly 12,000 members encompassing the professions and many occupations in industry, commerce, the public sector, and the taxation authorities. Membership is by examination and members have the practicing title of "Chartered Tax Adviser."

Customs & Excise
New King's Beam House, 22 Upper Ground, London, SE1 9PJ, U.K.
T: +44 (0) 845 010 9000
www.hmce.gov.uk
HM Customs and Excise is responsible for collecting and administering customs and excise duties and VAT. The Department is also responsible for preventing and detecting the evasion of revenue laws and enforcing import laws. Telephone, fax, and e-mail addresses vary for each office location. To find your nearest office, please refer to the Web site.

Inland Revenue
Somerset House, Strand, London, WC2R 1LB, U.K.
T: +44 (0) 20 7438 6420
www.inlandrevenue.gov.uk
The Inland Revenue, which was set up in 1849, administers and collects direct taxes: income tax, corporation tax, capital gains tax,

"Taxes are a barrier to progress, and they punish rather than reward success."

(Steve Forbes)

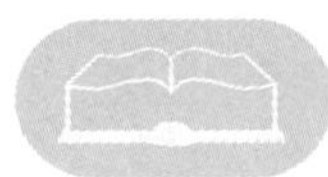

inheritance tax, stamp duty, and petroleum revenue tax. Telephone, fax, and e-mail addresses vary for each office location. To find your nearest office, please refer to the Web site.

Institute of Chartered Accountants in England and Wales
Chartered Accountants' Hall, P.O. Box 433, Moorgate Place, London, EC2P 2BJ, U.K.
T: +44 (0) 20 7920 8100
F: +44 (0) 20 7920 8547
E: dsbds@icaew.co.uk
www.icaew.co.uk
This, the largest professional accountancy organization in Europe with over 120,000 members, is responsible for educating and training Chartered Accountants and maintaining standards of professional conduct among its members.

International

International Bureau for Fiscal Documentation
P.O. Box 20237, 1000 HE Amsterdam, The Netherlands
T: +31 20 554 0100
F: +31 20 622 8658
E: info@ibfd.com
www.ibfd.nl
The IBFD is an independent nonprofit research and educational foundation, established in the Netherlands in 1938 by the founders of the International Fiscal Association. It aims to research and disseminate information in the fields of international and comparative taxation.

For More Information

☆ **Managing 21st Century Financials (pp. 127–28)**
Accounting (pp. 1899–1901)
Auditing and Management Audit (pp. 1908–09)
Budgeting (pp. 1913–15)
Contracts and Contracting (pp. 1941–42)

Teams and Team Building

BOOKS

Beyond the Team
R. Meredith Belbin
Woburn, Massachusetts: Butterworth-Heinemann, 2000
121pp ISBN: 0750646411
The author develops his thinking on teams and teamwork, taking a broader view of the place of the team within the organization. He defines the differences between teams and groups, and outlines a system of color coding to describe work tasks and roles. The book also considers ways in which more effective teamworking can be developed within organizations.

Build a Great Team: Choose the Right People for the Right Roles 2nd ed.
Ros Jay
Philadelphia, Pennsylvania: Trans-Atlantic Publications, 2000
164pp (Smarter Solutions Series)
ISBN: 0273644823
This book is a practical guide designed to help managers to select the right people for the right roles and to build a winning team. It covers issues relating to team roles, motivation, dealing with problem people, dealing with difficult situations, and handling team meetings.

The Discipline of Teams: A Mindbook-Workbook for Delivering Small Group Performance
Jon R. Katzenbach, Douglas K. Smith
New York: John Wiley, 2001
256pp ISBN: 047138254X
This book is an indispensable guide to how to build effective teams and when to use them. It offers a detailed explanation of what is necessary to transform a group of people working together into a cohesive team. It also divides work groups into two basic types, the single-leader discipline and the team discipline, and explains how and why the two types should be balanced.

Hot Groups: Seeding Them, Feeding Them, and Using Them to Ignite Your Organization
Jean Lipman-Blumen, Harold J. Leavitt
New York: Oxford University Press, 2001
320pp ISBN: 0195126866
This book describes how small groups within firms can come together to perform a particular task and achieve extraordinary results. Their importance, say the authors, cannot be overemphasized because they form part of an antidote to inflexible organizations by infusing individuals with a sense of meaning and fulfillment in their work. As well as providing lots of examples of hot groups in action, the authors suggest concrete steps employers can take to form, manage, and get the most out of them.

Mastering Virtual Teams: Strategies, Tools, and Techniques That Succeed 2nd ed.
Deborah L. Duarte, Nancy Tennant Snyder
San Francisco, California: Jossey-Bass, 1999
240pp ISBN: 0787941832
A theoretical and conceptual introduction to working in and leading virtual teams, this book addresses the difficulties that can surround virtual teamworking. It covers issues relating to differences in company, country, and culture, team dynamics, virtual team facilitation, and virtual team skills and strategies. The second edition comes with a CD-ROM, and also includes practical tools, checklists, tables, and worksheets.

The New Why Teams Don't Work: What Goes Wrong and How to Make It Right
Harvey A. Robbins, Michael Finley
San Francisco, California: Berrett-Koehler, 2000
271pp ISBN: 1576751104
This is a useful guide for anyone working with teams or contemplating the formation of teams. The focus on what can go wrong will help team designers avoid problems and help team facilitators solve them. There is also a good section on various "myths" concerning teams that should prove especially valuable in deciding when and how to use teams to meet business objectives.

Organizing Genius: The Secrets of Creative Collaboration
Warren Bennis, Patricia Ward Biederman
Cambridge, Massachusetts: Perseus, 1998
256pp ISBN: 0201339897
The authors of this text have carefully researched a number of today's large corporations in order to reveal how corporate leaders interact with teams and group leaders to

"Talent wins games, but teamwork wins championships." (Michael Jordan)

  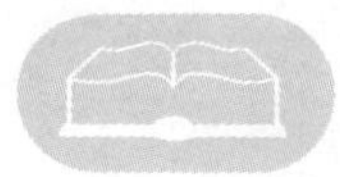    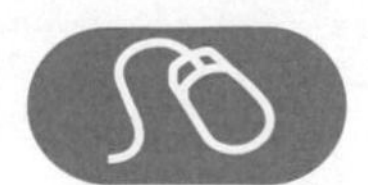

achieve market leading results. The text argues that people are today's most important resource and collective collaboration is the way to secure corporate success.

The Pfeiffer Book of Successful Team-Building Tools: Best of the Annuals
ELAINE BIECH, ED.
New York: John Wiley, 2001
424pp ISBN: 0787956937
This team-building tools book combines practical exercises with a solid theoretical foundation. Biech uses a ten-block model of team building and bases exercises on each block. The practitioner learns both the "why" and the "how" of building effective teams. Additionally, the book provides plenty of team-building games, evaluation forms, and checklists to make a trainer's work easier.

The 17 Indisputable Laws of Teamwork
JOHN C. MAXWELL
New York: Thomas Nelson, 2001
256pp ISBN: 0785274340
A prescriptive popular guide to team-building, with lots of practical anecdotes.

Smart Things to Know About Teams
ANNEMARIE CARACCIOLO
Oxford: Capstone, 2001
240pp (Smart Series)
ISBN: 1841120367
This book provides an introduction to the fundamentals of team building in business. Drawing on the author's experiences, it offers tips and advice on managing team issues and dynamics, including how teams work, effective team communication, measuring team success, and leading the team.

Team Roles at Work
R. MEREDITH BELBIN
Woburn, Massachusetts: Butterworth-Heinemann, 1996
141pp ISBN: 0750626755
The author charts the changing nature of team roles in a work environment and addresses issues surrounding team management and the use of team role theory and data. The resulting implications for solo and team leaders, and for the future of the team-based organization, are considered.

Teams at the Top
JON R. KATZENBACH
Boston, Massachusetts: Harvard Business School Press, 1998
238pp ISBN: 0875847897
This work aims to demonstrate how executive groups can be made to work as a functional team without sacrificing the individual autonomy of its members. The text centralizes on team building skills, and complements this approach with practical examples taken from a range of companies that include Avon and Ben & Jerry's.

Team Work and Group Dynamics
GREG L. STEWART, CHARLES C. MANZ, HENRY P. SIMS
New York: John Wiley, 1998
288pp ISBN: 0471197696
Blending theory and practice, this book aims to give students a clear picture of how teams work in organizations. It covers the key areas of team design, team processes, and team performance. Case studies are given throughout, offering a real-life perspective on team effectiveness.

When Teams Work Best: 6,000 Team Members and Leaders Tell What It Takes to Succeed
FRANK M. J. LAFASTO, CARL E. LARSON
Thousand Oaks, California: Sage, 2001
221pp ISBN: 0761923667
When Teams Work Best is a book for everyone who works with teams. It provides good insights into what does and doesn't work, based on the real experiences of team members and their leaders. The book is well organized, easy to read, and contains useful tools and information for evaluating and building effective teams.

The Wisdom of Teams: Creating the High Performance Organization
JON R. KATZENBACH, DOUGLAS K. SMITH
New York: McGraw-Hill, 1998
304pp ISBN: 0077094573
This book is the result of research into why teams are important, what distinguishes effective from ineffective teams, and how organizations can utilize the effectiveness of teams to become strong performing companies. Citing research results from 47 organizations, Katzenbach and Smith impart their views as to what makes teams work, and how this can be transferred to the reader's own workplace.

World Class Teams: Working Across Borders
LYNDA C. MCDERMOTT, NOLAN BRAWLEY, WILLIAM W. WAITE
New York: John Wiley, 1998
320pp ISBN: 0471292656
Multinational organizations are increasingly implementing team structures which cross functions, nations, and cultures; this book examines the key issues involved, including world class team launch and development, team leadership, measuring, managing, and rewarding world-class teams, and managing team functional and cultural borders.

MAGAZINES

Team Performance Management
ISSN: 1352-7592
MCB University Press
44 Brattle Street, 4th Floor, Cambridge, Massachusetts, 02138
T: +1 888 622 0075
F: +1 617 354 6875
www.emeraldinsight.com/tpm.htm
This quarterly journal features articles on all aspects of work teams, including their implementation, management, organization, and development. Drawing on a mix of case studies, research articles, technical reviews, and application papers, it is aimed at HR and quality professionals, managers, and consultants.

INTERNET

Center for the Study of Work Teams—University of North Texas
www.workteams.unt.edu/links.htm
This page of links to other sites covers almost any topic that would be of interest to a person who works with teams. Most of the links are to non-commercial sites and have a brief explanation to make selection easier.

Self Directed Work Team
http://users.ids.net/~brim/sdwth.html
This is an individual, non-commercial posting of a large number of links to team resources. It is organized by topic but has only a few, very short descriptions. The site should prove useful to anyone interested in learning more about the nature of teams.

Team Management Systems
www.tms.com/au
This is the site for the Margerison-McCann Team Management System, covering the U.S., Australian, and Asia-Pacific regions. It includes case studies and articles, online team audit, discussion forums, and a free e-mail newsletter.

Team Technology
www.teamtechnology.co.uk
This is a consulting firm providing information on team building, MTR-I management team roles, and the Myers-Briggs Type Indicator.

United States Office of Personnel Management
www.opm.gov/perform/teams.htm
This subsite of the U.S. Office of Personnel

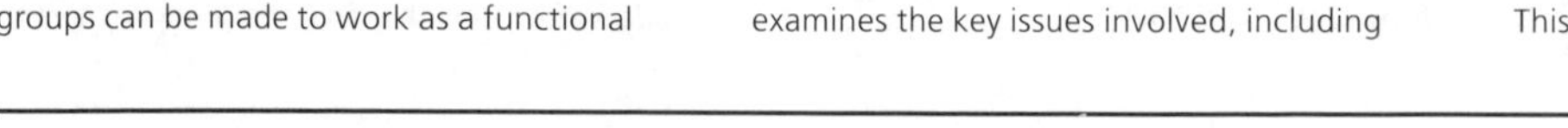
"Team-building exercises come in many forms but they all trace their roots back to the prison system."
(Scott Adams)

      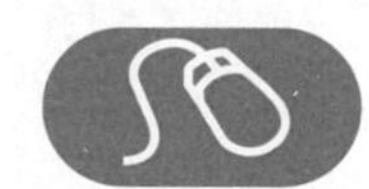

Management has a wealth of links to articles, case studies, tools, and measures for teams, which should prove useful to anyone who works with teams.

ORGANIZATIONS

USA

Center for the Study of Work Teams
University of North Texas, Terrill Hall 343, P.O. Box 311280, Denton, Texas, 76203–1280
T: +1 940 565 3096
F: +1 940 565 4806
E: *workteam@unt.edu*
www.workteams.unt.edu
This organization is dedicated to providing education, information, and research in all areas of collaborative work systems. The services offered include annual conferences and workshops exploring best practice teamwork, courses, and events, an online bulletin board and discussion groups, books, research papers, free articles, and a free newsletter.

Europe

European Forum for Teamwork
2 Castle Street, Salisbury, Wiltshire, SP1 1BB, U.K.
T: +44 (0) 1722 326667
F: +44 (0) 1722 410983
E: *efteam@dial.pipex.com*
www.efteam.org
This is a member-based organization established in 1982 as a forum for companies dedicated to promoting employee participation and team involvement in business process improvement. Formerly known as the National Society for Quality through Teamwork, the forum is the United Kingdom's leading body on employee involvement and has over 300 member organizations.

The Industrial Society
Peter Runge House, 3 Carlton House Terrace, London, SW1Y 5DG, U.K.
T: +44 (0) 20 7479 1000
F: +44 (0) 20 7479 1111
E: *customercentre@indsoc.co.uk*
www.indsoc.co.uk
The Industrial Society is an independent body with over 80 years' experience in management and training. The Society operates under the belief that business success goes hand in hand with fair management practices. The services offered to members include: an information service and employment law helpline; a publishing program of books, research reports, and videos; and a training and consulting service across a variety of subjects and specialties, including teams and team building.

For More Information

✔ **Steps in Successful Team Building (pp. 378–79)**
Organization and Organization Structure (pp. 2059–61)

THE TOP TWENTY BUSINESS MAGAZINES

The Academy of Management Executive
ISSN: 0896–3789
Academy of Management, Pace University
P.O. Box 3020, 235 Elm Road, Briarcliff Manor, New York, 10510–8020
T: +1 914 923 2607
F: +1 914 923 2615
http://aom.pace.edu/ame
Frequency: quarterly. A journal for professionals in the management field, *AME* aims to foster the general advancement of research, learning, teaching, and practice in management. The published articles provide managers with relevant management tools and information based on recent advances in management theory and research.

British Journal of Management
ISSN: 1045–3172
Blackwell Publishers
350 Main Street, Malden, Massachusetts, 02148
T: +1 781 388 8200
F: +1 781 388 8232
www.blackwellpublishers.com/asp/listofj.asp
Frequency: quarterly. This journal publishes articles from the full range of business and management disciplines. Its selection criteria should ensure that scholarly merit is combined with readability.

BusinessWeek
ISSN: 0007–7135
The McGraw-Hill Companies
BusinessWeek, P.O. Box 53235, Boulder, Colorado, 80322–3235
T: +1 800 635 1200
F: +1 641 842 6101
www.businessweek.com
Frequency: weekly. This is the leading U.S. business weekly, supported by an excellent Web site. Essential reading for anyone doing business in the United States.

California Management Review
ISSN: 0008–1256
University of California
F501 Haas School of Business #1900, Berkeley, California, 94720–1900
T: +1 510 642 7159
F: +1 510 642 1318
www.haas.berkeley.edu/cmr
Frequency: quarterly. *CMR* publishes in-depth articles on a range of management issues. It aims to serve as a bridge between those who study management and those who practice it.

European Management Journal
ISSN: 0263–2373
Elsevier Science
Regional Sales Office, Customer Support Department, P.O. Box 945, New York, 10159–0945
T: +1 212 633 3730
F: +1 212 633 3680
www.elsevier.com
Frequency: bimonthly. The articles in this magazine are based on up-to-date research and recent experience in management policies and procedures, and aimed at both practicing managers and academics working in the field of management. The main emphasis is on European business affairs.

Fast Company
Gruner & Jahr U.S.A. Publishing
Fast Company, 77 North Washington Street, Boston, Massachusetts, 02114–1927
T: +1 617 973 0300
F: +1 617 973 0373
www.fastcompany.com
Frequency: monthly. Though only started in 1995, *Fast Company* has established itself as an important monthly business magazine, largely on the back of the dot-com boom. Its heady mix of company news, business biographies, and latest business practices make for compulsive reading.

Forbes Magazine
ISSN: 0015–6914
Forbes, Inc.
60 5th Avenue, New York, 10011

"If at first you don't succeed, try, try again. Then quit. No use being a damn fool about it."
(W. C. Fields)

T: +1 212 620 2200
www.forbes.com
Frequency: weekly. This is a popular U.S. business magazine, with a heavy emphasis on personal finance and individual wealth creation. Its annual surveys of the best companies in the United States and the nation's people are very popular.

Fortune

ISSN: 0015–8259
Fortune, Inc.
Time and Life Building, Rockefeller Center, New York, 10020–1393
T: +1 800 621 8000
F: +1 212 522 7686
www.fortune.com
Published every two weeks, this is the most influential U.S. magazine for personal investors. Its influential surveys, including Fortune 500 and Global Most Admired, provide an accurate barometer of popular attitudes toward leading U.S. and international companies.

Harvard Business Review

ISSN: 0017–8012
Harvard Business School Publishing
Corporate Customer Service Center, 60 Harvard Way, Box 230–5C, Boston, Massachusetts, 02163
T: +1 617 783 7500
F: +1 617 783 7555
www.hbsp.harvard.edu
Frequency: bimonthly. The *HBR* is a management journal with an outstanding reputation. It aims to advance the theory and practice of management by providing best practice models and techniques from around the world. Its articles are written by leading academics, consultants, managers, and management analysts. It covers all areas of business, including corporate strategy, management, finance, technology, and industry trends.

Inc.

ISSN: 0162–8968
Gruner & Jahr U.S.A. Publishing
38 Commercial Wharf, Boston, Massachusetts, 02110–3883
T: +1 617 248 8000
F: +1 617 248 8090
www.inc.com
Published 18 times per year, this magazine is a premier journal on entrepreneurship. Each issue includes articles on financial and personnel management, marketing, administration, sales, and operations from the unique perspective of small businesses. This magazine is a valuable publication for any executive or manager.

Long Range Planning

ISSN: 0024–6301
Elsevier Science
Regional Sales Office, Customer Support Department, P.O. Box 945, New York, 10159–0945
T: +1 212 633 3730
F: +1 212 633 3680
www.elsevier.com
Frequency: bimonthly. The aims of this journal are to assist senior managers, administrators, and academics who are involved in planning strategy, and to highlight new concepts and techniques in business and management. Its articles are practical in nature and contain findings from research and detailed case studies.

McKinsey Quarterly

ISSN: 0047–5394
McKinsey & Company
55 East 52nd Street, 2nd Floor, New York, 10022
T: +1 212 446 7000
F: +1 212 446 8575
www.mckinseyquarterly.com
Frequency: quarterly. This is a journal of management and economics featuring the research of McKinsey consultants and selected outside authors. It is available only through a controlled circulation. Applications should be made to local offices or the U.S. office.

Management Decision

ISSN: 0025–1747
MCB University Press
44 Brattle Street, 4th Floor, Cambridge, Massachusetts, 02138
T: +1 888 622 0075
F: +1 617 354 6875
www.emeraldinsight.com/md.htm
Frequency: ten issues per year. *Management Decision* publishes articles of interest to business managers, teachers, and students. It focuses on general management and strategic issues, with particular emphasis on practical applications.

Management Today

ISSN: 0025–1925
Management Publications
174 Hammersmith Road, London, W6 7JP, U.K.
T: +44 (0) 20 8606 7500
F: +44 (0) 20 8606 7301
www.clickmt.com
Frequency: monthly. *Management Today* covers a broad range of issues in the management field and is aimed at middle and senior level managers. It examines major developments in management, and carries interviews with leading business figures and profiles of successful companies.

MIT Sloan Management Review

ISSN: 0019–848X
Sloan Management Review Association
Room E60–100, 77 Massachusetts Avenue, Cambridge, Massachusetts, 01239–4307
T: +1 617 253 7170
F: +1 617 258 9739
http://mitsloan.mit.edu/smr
Frequency: quarterly. The *Review* provides senior managers with articles on current management theory and practice. It covers all management disciplines, but puts a particular emphasis on corporate strategy, leadership, and the management of technology and innovation.

Organizational Dynamics

ISSN: 0090–2616
Elsevier Science
Regional Sales Office, Customer Support Department, P.O. Box 945, New York, 10159–0945
T: +1 212 633 3730
F: +1 212 633 3680
www.elsevier.com
Frequency: quarterly. *Organizational Dynamics* was founded by the American Management Association. It is published as a forum for the dissemination of articles on organizational behavior and the problems of business and management.

SAM Advanced Management Journal

ISSN: 0036–0805
Society for the Advancement of Management
Texas A&M University—Corpus Christi, College of Business, FC111, 6300 Ocean Drive, Corpus Christi, Texas, 78412
T: +1 361 825 6045
F: +1 361 825 2725
www.enterprise.tamucc.edu/sam
Frequency: quarterly. Aimed at the general manager, this journal publishes articles on business and management in a real-world setting written by business professionals.

Strategic Management Journal

ISSN: 0143–2095
John Wiley
Wiley InterScience Coordinator, Subscriptions Department, 605 Third Avenue, New York, 10158–0012
T: +1 800 825 7550
F: +1 212 850 6021
www.interscience.wiley.com
Frequency: monthly. *SMJ* focuses on all aspects

"When action grows unprofitable, gather information; when information grows unprofitable, sleep."
(Ursula L. Le Guin)

of strategic management. Each issue publishes a range of articles, research notes, and commentaries.

Strategy + Business
ISSN: 1083–796X
Booz Allen & Hamilton, Inc.
101 Park Avenue, New York, 10178
T: +1 212 551 6222
F: +1 212 551 6008
www.strategy-business.com
Frequency: quarterly. *Strategy + Business* is published by the leading international consultancy Booz Allen & Hamilton. Its aim is to provide executives with commentary, research, and practical ideas that bridge the gap between theory and practice in contemporary global business.

Success
ISSN: 0745–2489
Success Publishing, Inc.
15 Fayetteville Street Mall,
Suite 1110, Raleigh,
North Carolina, 27601
T: +1 919 807 1100
www.successmagazine.com
Formerly titled *High Technology Business*, this magazine is published ten times per year. Written for today's entrepreneur, its articles range from the aspects of running a successful business to marketing strategies and technology.

The Top Twenty Business Publishers

AMACOM (American Management Association)
1601 Broadway, New York, 10019
T: +1 212 586 8100
F: +1 212 903 8168
E: customerservice@amanet.org
www.amacombooks.org

Berrett-Koehler
235 Montgomery Street, Suite 650, San Francisco, California, 94104
T: +1 415 288 0260
F: +1 415 362 2512
E: bkpub@bkpub.com
www.bkpub.com

Blackwell Publishers, Inc.
350 Main Street, Malden, Massachusetts, 02148
T: +1 781 388 8200
F: +1 781 388 8210
E: subscrip@blackwellpub.com
www.blackwellpub.com

Butterworth-Heinemann
225 Wildwood Avenue, Woburn, Massachusetts, 01801
T: +1 800 366 2665
F: +1 800 446 6520
E: custserv@bhusa.com
www.bhusa.com

HarperCollins U.S.A.
10 East 53rd Street, New York, 10022
T: +1 212 207 7000
www.harpercollins.com
Imprint of HarperCollins Publishers.

Harvard Business School Publishing
Corporate Customer Service Center, 60 Harvard Way, Box 230–5C, Boston, Massachusetts, 02163
T: +1 617 783 7500
F: +1 617 783 7555
E: corpcustserv@hbsp.harvard.edu
www.hbsp.harvard.edu

Irwin Publishing
325 Humber College Boulevard, Toronto, Ontario, M9W 7C3, Canada
T: +1 416 798 0424
F: +1 416 798 1384
E: irwin@irwin-pub.com
www.irwin-pub.com

John Wiley
Customer Service Center, 1 Wiley Drive, Somerset, New Jersey, 08875–1272
T: +1 800 225 5945
E: bookinfo@wiley.com
www.wiley.com
Imprints include Capstone.

Jossey-Bass
989 Market Street, San Francisco, California, 94103–1741
T: +1 415 433 1740
F: +1 415 433 0499
www.josseybass.com
A division of John Wiley.

McGraw-Hill Companies
Educational and Professional Publishing, 1221 Avenue of the Americas, New York, 10020
T: +1 212 512 2000
E: webmaster@mcgraw-hill.com
www.mcgraw-hill.com

Macmillan Limited
The Macmillan Building, 4 Crinan Street, London, N1 9XW, U.K.
T: +44 (0) 20 7843 3600
F: +44 (0) 20 7843 4640
E: mdl@macmillan.co.uk
www.macmillan.co.uk
Includes Palgrave imprint.

Nicholas Brealey Publishing
1163 E Ogden Avenue, Suite 705–229, Naperville, Illinois, 60563
T: +1 630 499 0217
F: +1 630 898 3595
www.nbrealey-books.com

Oxford University Press
198 Madison Avenue, New York, 10016
T: +1 212 726 6000
F: +1 212 726 6440
E: custserv@oup-usa.org
www.oup-usa.org

Penguin Putnam, Inc.
375 Hudson Street, New York
T: +1 800 788 6262
www.penguinputnam.com
A Pearson company. Imprints include: Viking, Penguin.

Perseus Books Group
11 Cambridge Center, Cambridge, Massachusetts, 02142
T: +1 617 252 5200
F: +1 617 252 5265
E: info@perseuspublishing.com
www.perseusbooks.com

Quorum Books
88 Post Road West, P.O. Box 5007, Connecticut, 06881–5007
T: +1 800 225 5800
F: +1 203 750 9790
E: customer-service@greenwood.com
www.greenwood.com
Imprint of Greenwood Publishing Group

Random House, Inc.
1540 Broadway, New York, 10036
T: +1 212 782 9000
F: +1 212 302 7985
E: customerservice@random.com
www.randomhouse.com
Imprints include: Crown, Random House, Doubleday, Currency, Broadway.

Routledge
29 West 35th Street, New York, 10001
T: +1 212 216 7800
F: +1 212 564 7854
E: info@routledge-ny.com
www.routledge-ny.com

Sage Publications, Inc.
2455 Teller Road, Thousand Oaks, California, 91320
T: +1 805 499 0721
F: +1 805 499 0871
E: market@sagepub.com
www.sagepub.co.uk

Simon & Schuster
1230 Avenue of the Americas, New York, 10020
T: +1 212 698 7000
F: +1 212 698 7007
www.simonandschuster.com
Includes The Free Press imprint.

TRAINING AND DEVELOPMENT

BOOKS

The ASTD Training and Development Handbook: A Guide to Human Resource Development 4th ed.
ROBERT L. CRAIG, ED.
New York: McGraw-Hill, 1996
1088pp ISBN: 007013359X
This edition of the American Society for Training and Development's classic guide presents the proven techniques of hundreds of industry leaders. These techniques will help you choose and develop your staff and create a learning organization. They can also help increase employee commitment to the organization, enhance employee computer literacy, and develop employee leadership skills.

Developing Your People: Pain-free Solutions for Busy Managers
SUZY SIDDONS
New York: Beekman, 2001
125pp ISBN: 084645226X
Siddons examines the options available to managers for developing their staff, putting the emphasis on practicality and cost-effectiveness. She focuses on the tasks of deciding who needs developing and how it is to be done, planning a development program and motivating the staff affected by it, and working out the methods and resources needed.

Employee Training and Development
RAYMOND A. NOE
New York: McGraw-Hill, 1998
384pp ISBN: 0070593299
This guide to employee development aims to help companies become more competitive by increasing the role of training in the organization. It explores the strategic role of training, and focuses on ways to design training programs that work, including those that facilitate the adoption of new technologies. This book manages to carefully assess older training methods that should be retained while presenting more cutting edge approaches.

Evaluation in Organizations
DARLENE RUSS-EFT, HALLIE PRESKILL
Cambridge, Massachusetts: Perseus, 2001
416pp ISBN: 0738202681
This is the standard reference for anyone developing and launching evaluation programs in organizations.

The Fifth Discipline Fieldbook: Strategies and Tools for Building a Learning Organization
PETER M. SENGE, ET AL.
New York: Currency/Doubleday, 1994
593pp ISBN: 0385472560
Senge's concept of the learning organization has had an enormous impact on corporations because by promoting learning it makes change simpler to introduce. This workbook presents exercises to help organizations move in this direction and provides detailed information on how to implement strategies such as building a shared vision, enhancing collaboration, and facing rather than avoiding tough questions.

Foundations of Human Resource Development
RICHARD A. SWANSON, ELWOOD F. HOLTON, III
San Francisco, California: Berrett-Koehler, 2001
400pp ISBN: 1576750752
One of the best textbooks on HRD, this is a useful reference handbook for managers.

How to Survive a Training Assignment
STEPHEN K. ELLIS
Cambridge, Massachusetts: Perseus, 1988
156pp ISBN: 0201066475
This is a short, excellent introduction to the skill of training staff effectively.

Human Resource Development: The New Trainer's Guide
EDWARD E. SCANNELL, ET AL.
Cambridge, Massachusetts: Perseus, 2000
224pp ISBN: 0738203289
This book provides a clear and concise step-by-step introduction to HRD, with useful practical examples and helpful techniques,

Now, Discover Your Strengths
MARCUS BUCKINGHAM, DONALD O. CLIFTON
New York: Simon & Schuster, 2001
260pp ISBN: 074320686X
This book follows on from *First, Break All the Rules*. It is largely based around the "StrengthsFinder Profile," an Internet project that aims to uncover strengths and show how these can be translated into a career environment. Each book contains a personal Internet access number so that readers can download the program. The authors have incorporated feedback from the program into the text, and combine this with practical advice on how to enhance existing skills.

Planning and Designing Training Programmes
LESLIE RAE
Brookfield, Vermont: Gower, 1998
256pp ISBN: 0566079291
This book should enable any trainer who follows it to plan and design a successful professional training and development program. Setting his study very much within today's challenging corporate context, Rae looks in detail at the entire process, isolating the following stages: identifying and analyzing training needs; designing and planning a program to meet them; designing and planning the individual sessions within it; and evaluating success—

"All men who have turned out worth anything have had the chief hand in their own education."
(Walter Scott)

at the start, during, and at the end of the program.

Principles of Human Resource Development
JERRY W. GILLEY, ET AL.
Cambridge, Massachusetts: Perseus, 1989
400pp ISBN: 0201090139
This is a definitive guide to human resource development.

Rapid Instructional Design
GEORGE PISKURICH
San Francisco, California: Jossey-Bass/Pfeiffer, 2000
240pp ISBN: 0787947210
The purpose of this book is to consider how to speed up both the learning and the practice of instructional design. Piskurich covers all the basics of the subject, from analysis to evaluation, but omits the theory. Instead he provides plenty of practical checklists, together with many hints on how to design better and more quickly in this age of technology-based training.

Running Training Like a Business: Delivering Unmistakable Value
DAVID VAN ADELSBERG, EDWARD A. TROLLEY
San Francisco, California: Berrett-Koehler, 1999
218pp ISBN: 1576750590
Drawing on their work with a wide range of organizations over six years, the authors explain what is involved in transforming the traditional training function into a training enterprise. They stress the importance of assessing the true cost of training and the return on training investment, and also outline ways in which training should be linked to the customer's business strategy in order to maximize the efficiency and effectiveness of delivery.

Training for a Smart Workforce
ROD GERBER, COLIN LANKSHEAR, EDS.
New York: Routledge, 2000
224pp ISBN: 0415195527
This collection of essays takes a multidisciplinary approach to workplace training for successful performance. The four parts cover: megatrends (in work and social life); critical aspects for workplace education (including competence and literacy); pedagogic implications and actions (including identifying smart work practice and the transfer of learning); and directions (lifelong and lifebroad learning).

World Class Training: Providing Training Excellence
KAYE THORNE, ALEX MACHRAY
Milford, Connecticut: Kogan Page, 1999
192pp ISBN: 0749430834
Written for anyone who aspires to create world-class training, this book is packed with practical examples and covers topics as diverse as thinking as a strategic partner, personal excellence, focusing on the individual, developing a holistic approach, and organizational learning. Using examples of best practice and case studies from a wide variety of organizations, including the Disney Institute, Volvo, Lexmark, and General Electric, the authors demonstrate how both individual trainers and training departments can benchmark their performance against global leaders.

MAGAZINES

Competency and Emotional Intelligence
ISSN: 1351-5802
Industrial Relations Services
Eclipse Group Ltd., 18–20 Highbury Place, London, N5 1QP, U.K.
T: +44 (0) 20 7354 6747
F: +44 (0) 20 7354 8106
www.irseclipse.co.uk
Competency and Emotional Intelligence comprises five publications: 1. *Competency and Emotional Intelligence Quarterly*, a practical journal including case studies, features, and research articles (ISSN: paper format 1469-333X; electronic format 1469-3321); 2. *Competency and Emotional Intelligence Benchmarking*, surveying current practice, key issues, and emerging trends, and presenting extracts from named employers' competency frameworks, with an overview article (ISSN: paper format 1469-3348; electronic format 1469-3356); 3. *Competency and Emotional Intelligence Monthly*, offering news, comment, and analysis (ISSN: electronic format 1469-3313); 4. *Competency and Emotional Intelligence Literature*, a directory of books, articles, and reports, published on the Internet; 5. *Competency—The Cumulative Index*, an index to subjects, authors, and employers for the early issues of *Competency* which were not published electronically.

Management Learning
ISSN: 1350-5076
Sage Publications, Inc.
2455 Teller Road, Thousand Oaks, California, 91320
T: +1 805 499 0721
F: +1 805 499 0871
www.sagepub.com
This is an international journal containing articles with an academic slant, and covering all areas of managerial and organizational learning and development, including the nature and process of learning, learning outcomes, and learning and knowledge.

T + D
ISSN: 1535-7740
ASTD
1640 King Street, Box 1443, Alexandria, Virginia, 22313-2043
T: +1 703 683 8100
F: +1 703 683 1523
www.astd.org
T + D aims to provide advice and tips for people who run training or development programs. Its articles are mainly of a practical nature.

Training Journal
ISSN: 1465-6523
Fenman Ltd.
Clive House, The Business Park, Ely, Cambridgeshire, CB7 4EH, U.K.
T: +44 (0) 1353 654877
F: +44 (0) 1353 663644
www.trainingjournal.co.uk
This is a journal for those involved in workplace training, development, and learning. The style is informal. The articles are usually fairly brief and practical in nature, and they often include checklists and action plans

Training Magazine
ISSN: 1364-7504
Reed Business Information
Quadrant House, The Quadrant, Sutton, Surrey, SM2 5AS, U.K.
T: +44 (0) 20 8652 3500
F: +44 (0) 20 8652 8932
www.reedbusiness.com/products/training.asp
This monthly journal for HR or training managers and managers with line responsibility for training offers advice, news, data, and articles on matters of importance in training and development.

INTERNET

ASTD—Linking People, Learning, and Performance
www.astd.org
This site of the American Association for Training and Development offers daily news clips that cover developments in training, a job bank, and an up-to-date bookstore.

Training Supersite
www.prometheon.com
This site provides access to a wealth of materials including articles, reports, and online surveys. It also offers products, courses, and opportunities to post résumés.

"Education is when you read the fine print; experience is what you get when you don't."
(Pete Seeger)

ORGANIZATIONS

USA

ASTD Ltd.
Tina Sung, President and CEO
1640 King Street, Box 1443, Alexandria, Virginia, 22313–2043
T: +1 703 683 8100
F: +1 703 683 1523
E: customercare@astd.org
www.astd.org
Founded in 1944 as the American Society of Training Directors, the ASTD is an international body for professionals in workplace learning, development, and performance. It undertakes research into, and provides information on, training and development, supports international networking, and represents the profession's views on policy issues to federal and state policy makers.

European Foundation for Management Development
88 rue Gachard, Brussels, B-1050, Belgium
T: +32 2 629 08 10
F: +32 2 629 08 11
E: info@efmd.be
www.efmd.be
Founded in 1971, the EFMD is a network of organizations with interests in management education and development. Its member organizations include business schools, companies, public services, and employers' associations. Its aims include promoting partnerships between private companies and public sector organizations, disseminating information on management development, encouraging best practice in management education and development through international benchmarking, and the publication of research.

Europe

Chartered Institute of Personnel and Development
CIPD House, Camp Road, London, SW19 4UX, U.K.
T: +44 (0) 20 8971 9000
F: +44 (0) 20 8263 3333
E: cipd@cipd.co.uk
www.cipd.co.uk
Formed in 1995 from the amalgamation of the Institute of Personnel Management and the Institute of Training and Development, the CIPD is a professional body for personnel and training professionals which aims to promote good practice in the management and development of people.

Institute of Management
Management House, Cottingham Road, Corby, Northamptonshire, NN17 1TT, U.K.
T: +44 (0) 1536 204222
F: +44 (0) 1536 201651
E: mic.enquiries@imgt.org.uk
www.inst-mgt.org.uk
Formed in 1992, the Institute of Management (IM) is the largest organization for professional management in the United Kingdom, representing almost 89,000 individual members and embracing 560 corporate partners. It exists to promote the art and science of management through research, publications, the provision of information services, networking opportunities, education, and training, and the objective presentation of managers' views and opinions.

The Industrial Society
Peter Runge House, 3 Carlton House Terrace, London, SW1Y 5DG, U.K.
T: +44 (0) 20 7479 1000
F: +44 (0) 20 7479 1111
E: customercentre@indsoc.co.uk
www.indsoc.co.uk
The Industrial Society is an independent body with over 80 years' experience in management development and training. The Society operates under the belief that business success goes hand in hand with fair management practices. The services offered to members include: an information service and employment law helpline; a publishing program of books, research reports, and videos; and a training and consulting service, which includes the School of Coaching.

For More Information

☆ Mentoring (pp. 326–27)
✔ Evaluating Training (pp. 424–25)
✔ Training Needs Analysis (pp. 422–23)
Learning Organization (pp. 2024–26)
Management Development (pp. 2031–33)
Personnel Management and HR Management (pp. 2067–71)
Training Methods (pp. 2128–30)

TRAINING METHODS

BOOKS

The Accelerated Learning Fieldbook: Making the Instructional Process Fast, Flexible, and Fun
LOU RUSSELL
San Francisco, California: Jossey-Bass/Pfeiffer, 1999
304pp ISBN: 0787946397
This course provides the tools needed to ensure that maximum learning and maximum retention are taking place in your training sessions. It considers ways to improve your communication skills and identify the best ways individual learners can learn, besides pointing out the necessity of rethinking personal beliefs that block learning. Among the other topics that it covers are how to use music to create focused learning environments, and how to ascertain the effectiveness of a learning session.

The Accelerated Learning Handbook: A Creative Guide to Designing and Delivering Faster, More Effective Training Programs
DAVE MEIER
New York: McGraw-Hill, 2000
274pp ISBN: 0071355472
This book emphasizes learning by doing, but doing things in an accelerated fashion. It suggests using color, music, and play to enhance creativity and using computer-based learning to cut course development time. The author discusses practical techniques and ideas that will reduce the costs and time involved in training.

Active Training: A Handbook of Techniques, Designs, Case Examples, and Tips
MEL SILBERMAN, CAROL AUERBACH
New York: Pfeiffer & Co., 1998
304pp ISBN: 0787939897
The book explores the learn-by-doing method of training, providing tips on how to design experience-based training programs ideal for adults who have been out of the class-room for a time. It focuses on an active approach as opposed to lectures, shows how trainers can learn to diagnose their mistakes, and offers numerous examples of ways in which trainers can improve their techniques.

"If someone breaks my world records, it won't bother me. It gives me a reason to train even harder."
(Said Aouita)

Assessments A to Z: A Collection of 50 Questionnaires, Instruments, and Inventories
BONNIE BURN, MAGGIE PAYMENT
San Francisco, California: Jossey-Bass/Pfeiffer, 2000
224pp ISBN: 0787945099
The first section of this book provides an introduction to the use of assessments. The second presents 50 assessments covering a range of management skills and techniques, including assertiveness, change, customer service, delegation, leadership, problem solving, and time management. The final section looks at strategies for customizing or designing assessment tools.

The ASTD Handbook of Training Design and Delivery
GEORGE M. PISKURICH
New York: McGraw-Hill, 1999
640pp ISBN: 0071343105
A practical guide for trainers designing classroom, self-study, or technology-based training programs.

Complete Facilitator's Handbook
JOHN HERON
Milford, Connecticut: Kogan Page, 1999
304pp ISBN: 0749427981
This book presents a complete model, developed over the past 25 years, intended to enable facilitators in all fields to achieve success. It gives six basic learning dimensions to three forms of decision making and offers ideas for practical action. It also offers essential support to facilitators interested in developing their own style and the skills necessary to enable them to deal with any situation they may experience.

Creative Training Techniques Handbook: Tips, Tactics, and How-to's for Delivering Effective Training 2nd ed.
ROBERT PIKE
Minneapolis, Minnesota: Lakewood Publications, 1994
217pp ISBN: 094321033X
This second edition adds valuable items such as a resource guide, outlines, and activity sheets to the myriad tips and how-to's of the first edition. The aim of the book is to help you customize your training to meet the needs and capabilities of your audience. It presents step-by-step strategies for improving the training methods of instructors and their ability to make presentations that will motivate students to learn.

Designing Web-based Training: How to Teach Anyone Anything Anywhere Anytime
WILLIAM HORTON
New York: John Wiley, 2000
640pp ISBN: 047135614X
This volume explores the advantages of online training, examining the difficulties and rewards of developing distance learning courses and the intricacies of designing Web-based training. It is well illustrated, with more than 100 examples, and offers guidance about issues such as hardware and software options, graphic and content design, and tests for usability.

Energize Your Audience: 75 Quick Activities That Get Them Started and Keep Them Going
LORRAINE L. UKENS
San Francisco, California: Jossey-Bass, 2000
209pp ISBN: 0787945307
The author presents 75 quick activities designed to engage the attention of an audience before training sessions, presentations, or meetings. For each of the exercises, which are divided up into ice-breakers, energizers, and group challenges, she gives full details of the objective and procedure, the group size, the time, materials, and preparation required, and opportunities for variation and discussion.

Facilitation Skills
FRANCES BEE, ROLAND BEE
New York: Beekman, 2000
190pp (Training Essentials Series)
ISBN: 0846450569
The authors provide a practical guide to the role and skills of a facilitator, and the processes of group facilitation. The areas they cover include the refining of core skills to meet the challenges of group work, and how to agree learning objectives that are meaningful for both the participants and the organization. They also discuss designing learning events that are learner-centered, and practical techniques for getting a group started.

The Facilitator's Fieldbook
THOMAS JUSTICE, ET AL.
New York: AMACOM, 1999
448pp ISBN: 0814470386
A practical manual for facilitators, for use in a number of situations, such as preparing brainstorms, meetings, or presentations.

50 Brain Teasers for Meetings, Presentations and Training Sessions
GRAHAM ROBERTS-PHELPS, ANNE McDOUGALL
Brookfield, Vermont: Gower
256pp ISBN: 056607978X
This book is a collection of what the authors describe as energizing, ice breaking, thought provoking, and creativity boosting training exercises, designed to make a training course or a presentation more effective, interactive, and involving.

Games Trainers Play
JOHN W. NEWSTROM, EDWARD E. SCANNELL
New York: McGraw-Hill, 1980
352pp ISBN: 0070464081
This best-selling book offers a practical collection of innovative training exercises.

The Inspirational Trainer: Make Training Time Flexible, Responsive, Creative
PAUL Z. JACKSON
Milford, Connecticut: Kogan Page, 2001
204pp ISBN: 0749434686
This book takes creativity as its starting point, describing an approach to training that draws particularly upon the theater but also upon sports, games, psychology, and a variety of other sources, to support the design and delivery of innovative, flexible training.

Managing Resources: Project Planning and Financial Control
MICK BROADBENT, JOHN CULLEN
Woburn, Massachusetts: Butterworth-Heinemann, 1999
300pp (Activity Packs for Tutors and Trainers Series)
ISBN: 0750635045
This activity pack is designed to assist trainers working with postgraduate and post experience students. Twenty sessions cover the management of financial resources and deal with topics including accounting, planning and controlling budgets, costing, activity-based methods, capital investment, pricing, and the assessment and measurement of financial performance. A case study approach to teaching and learning is adopted.

Masterful Facilitation: Becoming a Catalyst for Meaningful Change
A. GLENN KISER
New York: AMACOM, 1998
224pp ISBN: 0814403980
The book begins with an explanation of masterful facilitation and the facilitation model. Subsequent sections deal with such matters as making initial contact, clarifying desired objectives, contracting for results, designing the intervention, facilitating, and evaluating results. Three case studies of facilitation are also presented.

101 Ways to Make Training Active
MEL SILBERMAN
New York: Pfeiffer & Co., 1995
304pp ISBN: 0883904756
Trainer Mel Silberman offers over 100

suggestions on how to organize and perform active training sessions. Each of the 101 techniques is described and illustrated with a goal, a statement of purpose, a procedure, step-by-step instructions, and suggestions for other ways to use the strategy for both teaching and training.

Playing Along: 37 Group Learning Activities Borrowed from Improvisational Theater
IZZY GESELL
Duluth, Michigan: Whole Person Associates, 1997
160pp ISBN: 157025141X
Developed for group leaders who have no improvisational theater experience, this book presents step-by-step techniques that are designed to allow actors to solve problems on stage, and build a learning environment through reducing resistance, creating cohesiveness, and promoting active participation in the learning process. These 5–10 minute exercises activate the learning skills of listening, affirming, imagining, and trusting.

Rapid Instructional Design
GEORGE M. PISKURICH
San Francisco, California: Jossey-Bass/Pfeiffer, 2000
240pp ISBN: 0787947210
The purpose of this book is to consider how to speed up the learning and doing of instructional design. All the basics of instructional design, from analysis to evaluation, are covered, and the author also provides many practical hints and checklists to help the reader design better and more quickly.

Self-made Leader: 25 Activities for Facilitated Personal Development
MIKE WOODCOCK, DAVE FRANCIS
Brookfield, Vermont: Gower, 1998
264pp ISBN: 0566081113
Self-Made Leader includes 25 structured activities designed to help people learn about themselves and develop their potential. The areas covered are self-management, values, goals, self-development, problem solving, innovation, influence, leadership, organizing, developing others, team building, and learning from experience. Guidance on using the activities is provided for facilitators and trainers.

Training Plus: Revitalizing Your Training
BRIAN CLEGG
Milford, Connecticut: Kogan Page, 2000
160pp ISBN: 0749431881
This book's aim is to help its readers break out of a training rut and develop new ways of getting their message across. At its core is a detailed compendium of actions designed to transform their training programs, together with a guide to determine the direction training should take.

The 2000 Annual 35th ed.
ELAINE BIECH, ED.
San Francisco, California: Jossey-Bass/Pfeiffer, 2000
320pp ISBN: 078794713X
This two-volume set provides a collection of practical and useful materials written by and for professionals within the broad area described as human resources development. The main sections of the book cover experiential learning activities, inventories, questionnaires, surveys, and presentation and discussion resources.

Using Activities in Training and Development 2nd ed.
LESLIE RAE
Milford, Connecticut: Kogan Page, 2000
224pp ISBN: 0749431024
The book considers the whole range of activities now available for training and development. Besides setting out what they are, it also discusses how, why, and when to use them, and what supporting activities they require.

Web Learning Fieldbook: Using the World Wide Web to Build Workplace Learning Environments
VALORIE BEER
San Francisco, California: Jossey-Bass/Pfeiffer, 2000
304pp ISBN: 0787950238
This book and its accompanying Web site provide access to sample learning environments and links to related sites, as well as customizable electronic templates and tools that can be downloaded and used right away. Advice on how to incorporate Web-based learning into the workplace is also offered.

MAGAZINES

T + D
ISSN: 1535–7740
American Society for Training and Development
ASTD Customer Care Center, 1640 King Street, Box 1443, Alexandria, Virginia, 22313–2043
T: +1 703 683 8100
F: +1 703 683 1523
www.astd.org
T + D, the official journal of the American Society for Training and Development, features articles on a broad range of training issues. It also publishes contributions on other management topics and personal development, as well as surveys of work issues and media reviews.

Training and Management Development Methods
ISSN. 0951–3507
MCB University Press Ltd.
60/62 Toller Lane, Bradford, Yorkshire, BD8 9BY, U.K.
T: +44 (0) 1274 777700
F: +44 (0) 1274 785200
www.emeraldinsight.com/tmdm.htm
This journal is published five times a year in loose-leaf format. It looks at current practices and innovations in the field of training and development, and provides tried and tested examples of training methods, which can be collected to provide a useful practical manual and resource.

Training Journal
ISSN: 1465–6523
Fenman Ltd.
Clive House, The Business Park, Ely, Cambridgeshire, CB7 4EH, U.K.
T: +44 (0) 1353 654877
F: +44 (0) 1353 663644
www.trainingjournal.co.uk
This is a journal, written in an informal style, for those involved in workplace training, development, and learning. Articles are usually fairly brief and practical in nature, and often include checklists and action plans.

INTERNET

Facilitation Factory
www.facilitationfactory.com
The site includes a virtual discussion group (Facilitators' Forum), access to training (Facilitators' Coach), and an Internet resources section.

Prometheon—Your Learning Resource Network
www.prometheon.com
This site offers a good library of articles on training, discussion forums, and listings of books, courses, speakers, and trainers.

U.S. Department of Labor—Bureau of Labor Statistics
http://stats.bls.gov/oco/ocos021.htm
Designed for managers and specialists, the information on human relations, training, and labor relations provided by this site is thorough and informative.

For More Information

- **Coaching, Counseling, and Mentoring (pp. 1925–28)**
- **Training and Development (pp. 2126–28)**

"Imagine if advertisers used their creative skills to make watching learning-oriented shows a first choice for kids."
(Geraldine Laybourne)

  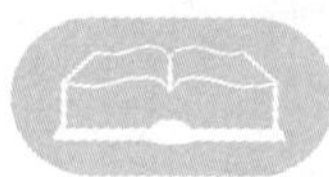    

Venture Capital

BOOKS

Angel Financing: How to Find and Invest in Private Equity

Gerald A. Benjamin, Joel B. Margulis
New York: John Wiley, 1999
307pp (Wiley Investment Series)
ISBN: 0471350850

This book draws on extensive experience of the private investor market in the United States. It stresses the importance of careful planning and preparation to ensure the success of financial deals. It provides practical advice and information for entrepreneurs, investors, and intermediaries in four sections: the first focuses on how entrepreneurs can address the challenge of raising capital and finding workable strategies; the second examines the angel investor market; the third deals with the search for an investor; and the fourth provides insight into the investor's perspective on prospective deals. Detailed advice on preparing an investor-oriented business plan and an overview of securities law issues for nonlawyers are provided in appendices.

Angel Investing

Robert J. Robinson
San Francisco, California: Jossey-Bass, 2000
320pp ISBN: 0787952028

This is a succinct, down-to-earth guide for anyone looking for funding from angel investors.

Business Angels: Securing Start Up Finance

Patrick Coveney, Karl Moore
New York: John Wiley, 1998
244pp ISBN: 0471977187

This book takes the would-be entrepreneur through the process of identifying the ideal business angel and securing a deal. It covers reasons for turning to an angel, types of business angels, and the task of creating a business plan. The role of business introduction services is also considered.

Directory of Venture Capital 2nd ed.

Kate E. Lister, Thomas D. Harnish
New York: John Wiley, 1996
400pp ISBN: 0471122831

The directory lists venture capital firms by state and provides detailed information on their preferences with regard to industry, stage of funding, geography, and size of company. The authors also provide information on the returns required by private equity investors, selecting the right lawyer, and important aspects of a venture partnership. Entrepreneurs will find the directory a good resource for locating the right venture capital firm to approach for funding.

Finance for Growing Enterprises

Roger Buckland, Edward Davis, eds.
Stamford, Connecticut: International Thomson Business Press, 1995
288pp (European Financial Institutions and Markets Series)
ISBN: 0415082331

This book examines the mechanisms by which businesses with the capacity to grow acquire the cash to make growth possible. It draws together contemporary research studies and covers the issues of market failure and gaps in funding. The financing choices facing the growing firm are also investigated.

Fundamentals of Venture Capital

Joseph W. Bartlett
Lanham, Maryland: Madison Books, 1999
167pp ISBN: 1568331266

A useful but technical introduction to venture capital, aimed more at specialist advisors than potential entrepreneurs.

The Money of Invention: How Venture Capital Creates New Wealth

Paul A. Gompers, Josh Lerner
Boston, Massachusetts: Harvard Business School Press, 2001
320pp ISBN: 157851326X

The authors of this text explore three central issues in venture capital: the problems entrepreneurs come across in securing financing, and how the venture capital model can assist innovators who will resolve them; how venture capitalists can seek opportunities while building a sustainable franchise; and finally how corporations, nonprofits, and government institutions can use the power of the venture capital model when using it within their own sectors.

3i: Fifty Years Investing in Industry

Richard Coopey, Donald Clarke
New York: Oxford University Press, 1995
495pp ISBN: 0198289448

This book tells the story of 3i's unique role in the U.K. economy in the second half of the 20th century from the points of view of the business historian and the professional insider, providing an insight into the interface between finance and industry.

The VC Way: Investment Secrets from the Wizards of Venture Capital

Jeffrey Zygmont
Cambridge, Massachusetts: Perseus, 2001
224pp ISBN: 0738203874

This text offers a behind-the-scenes perspective of the venture capital market, revealing to investors how to strategize and invest in successful companies before their profits are certain. Zygmont also offers the reader a brief tutorial in creating a portfolio of holdings that may increase in value, as Apple and Yahoo did.

The Venture Capital Handbook

William D. Bygrave, Michael Hay, Jos B. Peeters, eds.
Philadelphia, Pennsylvania: Trans-Atlantic Publications, 1999
384pp ISBN: 0273638998

This handbook, which consists of contributions from practitioners, provides an overview of the European venture capital industry and a detailed treatment of the investment process. The aspects of the process covered include fundraising and investor relations, deal generation, due diligence, deal structuring and pricing, and postinvestment venture management. Legal and ethical issues, going public, international syndication, and returns on venture capital are also dealt with.

Venture Capital Investing

David Gladston
Upper Saddle River, New Jersey: Prentice Hall, 1998
400pp ISBN: 0139414282

This classic serves as a primer on venture capital investing. It outlines the key considerations for investing private capital, including an analysis of management, compensation, marketing and sales, financial statements and projections, and the production process. From due diligence and deal negotiation to the exit strategy, the author suggests a logical, step-by-step process to follow that is filled with insights and actual examples he gained from his experience as a venture capitalist. While most books are focused on how an entrepreneur can raise venture capital, this book provides an in-depth look at what it takes to be a successful investor in small private businesses.

Venture Capital and Private Equity 2nd ed.

Josh Lerner, et al.
New York: John Wiley, 2001

"Business? It's quite simple. It's other people's money." (Alexandre Dumas)

500pp ISBN: 0471079820
The book explains in detail the venture capital and private equity markets. Divided into four sections, the book covers the fundraising process required to start a venture capital fund, investment selection, and the relationship between the venture capitalist and entrepreneur, the various exit strategies available, and some key issues unique to the private equity market.

Venture Catalyst: The Five Strategies for Accelerating Growth and Profit
Don Laurie
Cambridge, Massachusetts: Perseus, 2001
224pp ISBN: 0738204072
This book presents a five-part framework for launching new initiatives, and illustrates each part with examples from industries as diverse as packaged goods and Web marketing. Interviews with such pioneers as Roger Ackerman of Corning, David Wetherall of CMGI, and Mitch Kapoor of Accel provide the reader with an insider's perspective on the volatile world of corporate venturing.

Where to Go When the Bank Says No: Alternatives for Financing Your Business
David R. Evanson
Princeton, New Jersey: Bloomberg, 1998
304pp (Bloomberg Small Business Series)
ISBN: 1576600173
Practical advice for small or new businesses on raising capital is provided here by an expert in the field. He discusses the pros and cons of alternative options such as equity capital, initial public offerings (IPOs), and venture capital, and gives guidance on valuing a business and drawing up business plans and financial reports. A resources guide with contact details of organizations in the field is also included.

Winning Angels: The Seven Fundamentals of Early-stage Investing
David Amis, Howard Stevenson
Upper Saddle River, New Jersey: Financial Times Prentice Hall, 2001
304pp ISBN: 0273649167
This is a practical guide which shares the insights and advice of over 50 successful angel investors. It takes actual and potential investors through the seven fundamentals of the investment process: sourcing, evaluating, valuing, structuring, negotiating, monitoring, and harvesting. It also gives entrepreneurs seeking capital insight into the mindset of investors.

MAGAZINES

European Venture Capital Journal
ISSN: 0954–1675
Thomson Financial Ltd.
Aldgate House, 33 Aldgate High Street, London, EC3N 1DL, U.K.
T: +44 (0) 20 7369 7897/7662
F: +44 (0) 20 7369 7330
www.evcj.com
This journal, published ten times a year, provides information on the European private equity market. The *U.K. Venture Capital Journal* merged with it in 1999.

Private Equity Analyst
Asset Alternatives
170 Linden Street, Wellesley, Massachusetts, 02482–7919
T: +1 781 304 1500
www.assetnews.com
This monthly newsletter covers the private equity market, dealing mainly with venture capital, LBOs, mezzanine investing, and turnarounds.

Private Equity Week
ISSN: 1099–341X
Venture Economics
195 Broadway, 10th Floor, New York, 10007
T: +1 646 822 2000
F: +1 646 822 3230
www.privateequityweek.com
PEW is a weekly newsletter providing information on private equity deals in the venture capital market.

Venture Capital: An International Journal of Entrepreneurial Finance
ISSN: 1369–1066
Taylor and Francis
325 Chestnut Street, Suite 800, Philadelphia, Pennsylvania, 19106
T: +1 800 354 1420
F: +1 215 625 8914
www.tandf.co.uk
Venture Capital is a quarterly journal which publishes research-based papers from academics and practitioners on all aspects of private equity finance and on the venture capital process from decision to exit. Coverage is international, focusing on emerging venture capital markets in Eastern Europe and the Asian Pacific area as well as established markets in Western Europe and the United States.

Venture Capital Journal
ISSN: 0883–2773
Venture Economics
195 Broadway, 10th Floor, New York, 100077
T: +1 646 822 2000
F: +1 646 822 3230
www.venturecapitaljournal.net
VCJ is a monthly journal covering the private equity and venture capital industry. It provides news and analysis of deals, company profiles, and interviews.

INTERNET

ACE-Net (Access to Capital Electronic Network)
http://ace-net.sr.unh.edu/pub
ACE-Net was set up in consultation with the Securities and Exchange Commission to act as a clearing house of information for investors and entrepreneurs following the 1995 Conference on Small Business.

National Venture Capital Association
www.nvca.org
The National Venture Capital Association is a trade association providing advocacy, education, and networking opportunities for the venture capital industry. It boasts over 400 members representing the majority of venture firms invested in U.S.-based companies. The association's affiliate organization, American Entrepreneurs for Economic Growth (AEEG), is an advocacy group for over 14,000 C.E.O.s of emerging growth companies.

PriceWaterhouseCoopers Moneytree Survey
www.pwcmoneytree.com
This survey, sponsored by the accounting firm of PriceWaterhouseCoopers, provides a comprehensive list of venture capital investing by industry, stage of funding, geography, and type of financing on a quarterly basis. The report tracks venture capital firm investments and the enterprises receiving capital by region/state and industry.

vcapital
www.vcapital.com
This is an exchange site for entrepreneurs, venture capitalists, and business service providers, sponsored by Batterson Venture

"As an investor in small companies, I don't care how rich Microsoft is. I care about what my opportunities are."
(Esther Dyson)

Partners. It features an Ask the Expert section with articles giving practical advice and help.

Venture Economics
www.ventureeconomics.com
News, statistics, product information, and a glossary of terms are to be found on this site, provided by a publisher of journals and research on the venture capital industry worldwide.

Venturewire
www.venturewire.com/default.asp
This Web site hosts a family of publications that are exclusively devoted to the private equity marketplace. *Venturewire Professional*, the site's flagship publication, features the latest news on fundings, acquisitions, venture capital firms, and key personnel changes in venture-backed businesses. Venturewire also publishes *Lifescience*, *Alert*, and *People* on a daily basis and provides the Research section as a source of in-depth coverage on specific industries.

vFinance.com Venture Capital Resource Library
www.vfinance.com
This site is aimed at investors, entrepreneurs, and company C.E.O.s and provides access to databases of investors, angels, and business plans. Registration is required.

ORGANIZATIONS

USA

National Association of Investment Companies
733 15th Street NW, Suite 700, Washington, D.C., 20005
T: +1 202 289 4336
F: +1 202 289 4329
E: NAICHQTRS@aol.com
www.naichq.org
NAIC is an industry association for venture capital and private equity firms. Its members are privately owned equity investment firms, small business investment companies licensed by the U.S. Small Business Administration, and investment companies chartered by state and local governments.

National Association of Small Business Investment Companies
666 11th Street NW, Suite 750, Washington, D.C., 20001
T: +1 202 628 5055
F: +1 202 628 5080
E: nasbic@nasbic.org
www.nasbic.org
NASBIC is a nonprofit industry association which has represented and served the SBIC industry for over 40 years. It provides educational programs for investment professionals through the Venture Capital Institute and cooperates with other business associations. Its policies and priorities are established by a board of governors.

National Venture Capital Association
1655 North Fort Myer Drive, Suite 850, Arlington, Virginia, 22209
T: +1 703 524 2549
F: +1 703 524 3940
E: lturner@nvca.org
www.nvca.org
The NVCA is a trade association with a membership of over 400 venture capital firms. It aims to foster understanding of the venture capital industry in the United States, to stimulate the flow of equity capital to growth companies, to promote professional standards, facilitate networking, and provide research data. The NVCA publishes: *NVCA Today*, a quarterly review of legislative and regulatory developments; *Venture Capital Review*, a biannual journal which provides an overview of trends in the industry; and *The Venture Capital Yearbook*.

Europe

British Venture Capital Association
Essex House, 12–13 Essex Street, London, WC2R 3AA, U.K.
T: +44 (0) 20 7240 3846
F: +44 (0) 20 7240 3849
E: bvca@bvca.co.uk
www.bvca.co.uk
The BVCA was founded in 1983 and is the representative body for the U.K. venture capital industry. It promotes private equity and venture capital for the benefit of entrepreneurs, investors, practitioners, and the economy as a whole. Its members are venture capital companies and professional firms involved in advising on venture capital transactions. Its activities include training, workshops, lobbying, and research, and it produces publications.

European Private Equity and Venture Capital Association (EVCA)
Minervastraat 4, 1930 Zaventem, Belgium
T: +32 2 715 00 20
F: +32 2 725 07 04
E: evca@evca.com
www.evca.com
EVCA was founded in 1983 and now has over 850 members. Its aim is to promote and facilitate the development of the European venture capital industry through lobbying and initiatives such as conferences, training, and networking opportunities. The organization was involved in the creation of EASD (European Association of Security Dealers) and the EASDAQ pan-European capital market.

National Business Angels Network
40–42 Cannon Street, London, EC4N 6JJ, U.K.
T: +44 (0) 20 7329 2929
F: +44 (0) 20 7329 2626
E: info@bestmatch.co.uk
www.nban.com
NBAN is a nonprofit company sponsored by financial institutions and the Department of Trade and Industry in the United Kingdom. It provides a service linking businesses seeking equity finance with investors seeking opportunities through a network of associates across the country. A monthly bulletin of opportunities is sent to all registered investors. An online service, BestMatch, is also provided.

International

Australian Venture Capital Association Limited
Level 5, 88 Philip Street, Sydney, New South Wales, 2000, Australia
T: +612 9251 3888
F: +612 9251 3808
E: mbrs@avcal.com.au
www.avcal.com.au
The AVCAL was founded in 1992 to act as a forum for the venture capital industry in Australia and to encourage investment in growing businesses. Its over 100 members include venture capital firms, banks, incubators, angels, advisers, and government bodies. It organizes networking events and training courses, and sponsors a twice-yearly survey of venture capital investment.

Hong Kong Venture Capital Association
Room 34, 3rd Floor New Henry House, 10 Ice House Street, Hong Kong
T: +852 2845 6100
F: +852 2526 2713
E: enquiry@hkvca.com.hk
www.hkvca.com.hk
The HKVCA was founded in 1987 to promote and protect the interests of, and provide a forum for, the venture capital industry in Hong Kong. It organizes meetings, conferences, and seminars, and conducts research studies.

For More Information

- **Acquisitions, Takeovers, and Mergers (pp. 1901–03)**
- **Entrepreneurship (pp. 1969–72)**

"Failures are like skinned knees—painful, but superficial." (Ross Perot)

  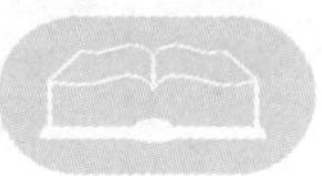    

Working Abroad

BOOKS

Best Practices for Managers and Expatriates: A Guide on Selection, Hiring, and Compensation
Stan Lomax
New York: John Wiley, 2001
336pp ISBN: 0471392065
This book provides a detailed look at the career issues related to working abroad, including the type of person to select and how long the assignment should be. The book is designed as a guide for managers who have international assignments to fill or capacity to develop. It will also prove useful to those considering an expatriate assignment.

Cross-cultural Business Behaviour: Marketing, Negotiating and Managing Across Cultures 2nd ed.
Richard R. Gesteland
Copenhagen, Denmark: Copenhagen Business School Press, 1999
282pp ISBN: 8716134281
This book is intended as a practical guide for those involved in international business negotiations. Drawing on his extensive experience as an expatriate manager, the author illustrates and analyzes the difficulties arising from cultural differences. Patterns of cross-cultural behavior are identified, and the cultures of individual countries are grouped according to a set of characteristics. The business protocols and negotiating style of each are described.

The Daily Telegraph Guide to Working Abroad 22nd ed.
Godfrey Golzen
London: Kogan Page, 2000
400pp ISBN: 0749428813
The introductory chapters in this popular guide to working abroad explore the overseas job market, finding a job abroad, U.K. taxation aspects, financial planning, medical insurance, letting and insuring your home, and children's education. An employment conditions checklist is provided, and the body of the book contains over 40 country surveys.

Dos and Taboos around the World 3rd ed.
Roger E. Axtell, ed.
New York: John Wiley, 1993
208pp ISBN: 0471595284
Dos and Taboos provides facts, tips, and cautionary tales gathered from the experiences of more than 500 international business travelers. It includes information on protocol, customs, etiquette, hand gestures and body language, tipping, U.S. jargon, and the international communications crisis. A section of advice for visitors to Eastern Europe and Russia, and a chapter on business gift-giving and gift-receiving, with country-by-country gift suggestions and precautions, are included.

Getting a Job Abroad: The Handbook for the International Jobseeker 5th ed.
Roger Jones
Oxford: How To Books, 2000
272pp ISBN: 185703418X
The book lists country contact organizations worldwide to assist with the job-search process, and contains additional chapters on the recruitment rigmarole, short-term or long-term commitment, and preparation and acclimatization.

Global Résumé and CV Guide
Mary Anne Thompson
New York: John Wiley, 2000
288pp ISBN: 0471380768
This international approach will be of interest to managers seeking to work overseas and to multinational organizations. Experts from over 40 countries provide cultural dos and don'ts, information on business practices, and job hunting tips that will help create a résumé tailored to the specific requirements of a target country. Standard coverage for each country includes a country overview, résumé specifics, résumé presentation, cover letters, job-information sources, Web sites, and interview advice.

International HRM: Contemporary Issues in Europe
Chris Brewster, Hilary Harris, eds.
New York: Routledge, 1998
320pp ISBN: 0415194903
This collection of edited papers from European experts in the field covers all aspects of international human resource management. The articles range from issues surrounding the strategic role of HRM in staffing, reward management, and performance management, to discussions of the dynamics of culture and gender in international management.

International Jobs: Where They Are, How to Get Them 5th ed.
Eric Kocher, Nina Segal
Cambridge, Massachusetts: Perseus, 1999
400pp ISBN: 0738200395
This guide navigates the reader around the international job market. The text contains listings of Web sites for each organization and a chapter on how to make effective use of the Internet in a global job search. Also included are essays that tell you what some of these jobs are really like, and further advice to help you sort out which jobs present actual opportunities and which just sound good on paper.

International Success: Selecting, Developing, and Supporting Expatriate Managers
Meena S. Wilson, Maxine A. Dalton
Greenboro, North Carolina: CCL Press, 1998
55pp ISBN: 1882197453
This short book by the Center for Creative Leadership is a basic guide for corporations on what is required for a manager to be successful abroad. It covers the little-considered impacts of personality and family support. It also presents a case for developing a good pool of expatriate talent. This book should be a useful tool for global corporations as well as prospective expatriates.

Living and Working Abroad
David Hampshire
Wetherby: Survival Books, 2001
400pp ISBN: 1901130851
David Hampshire offers a comprehensive and up-to-date work survey for employees, emigrants, students, business people, retirees, long-stay visitors, and anyone planning to spend some time abroad. The book contains huge amounts of practical advice concerning all aspects of working overseas. Important topics covered include: how to obtain a residence or work permit; how to stretch your money further; how to get the best education for your family and how to find the best job for you.

Mind Your Manners: Managing Business Cultures in Europe
John Mole
Naperville, Illinois: Nicholas Brealey, 1996
236pp ISBN: 1857880854
This text is aimed at managers of any nationality intending to do business in the world's biggest market. It addresses such crucial issues as communication, leadership, decision making, meetings, and networking. Mole includes a toolkit to enable readers to test their own cultural responses.

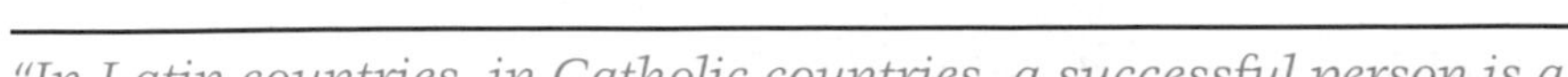
"In Latin countries, in Catholic countries, a successful person is a sinner." (Umberto Eco)

Overseas Americans: The Essential Guide to Living and Working Abroad
William Beaver
Boulder, Colorado: Paladin Press, 2001
168pp ISBN: 1581602596
This book provides basic information that any American living abroad without significant corporate support may need to have. It covers the basics of dealing with various U.S. government agencies, required documents, income tax questions, and many other topics. It also goes over less well-known issues like what to do if you are arrested. There is also a guide to over 100 Web sites geared toward the needs of expatriate workers.

The Transplanted Executive: Why You Need to Understand How Workers in Other Countries See the World Differently
Christopher Earley, Miriam Erez
New York: Oxford University Press, 1997
198pp ISBN: 019508795X
The Transplanted Executive provides a comprehensive resource for managers of any nationality striving to understand the diversity of workplace values and traditions—and explains how these characteristics can be used to maximize employee efficiency, morale, and the bottom line. Each chapter focuses on a different management problem: effective communication; motivation of workers; turning groups into teams; leadership skills; and quality management production.

U.S. Expatriate Handbook: Guide to Living and Working Abroad
John W. Adams
Morgantown, West Virginia: West Virginia University College of Business and Economics, 1998
148pp ISBN: 0966317106
This is a simply written and very basic guide to living and working abroad. It covers all the essentials without delving too deeply into career issues or harsh realities. This book is probably best used as a primer for someone who will be working abroad under the care of a knowledgeable corporation.

INTERNET

Centre for International Briefing
www.cibfarnham.com
The CIB offers a range of cross-cultural training programs, tailored country briefings, in-depth workshops on business cultures, and interactive workshops on working in a global environment. This site provides an introduction to these services.

Control Risks Group
www.crg.com
This site belongs to a leading, specialist, international business risk consultancy operating in political risk analysis, confidential investigations, preemployment screening, security consulting, crisis management and response, and information security and investigations.

Embassy World
www.embassyworld.com
The site lists the embassies of each country in other countries and the embassies of other countries in that country. It also includes maps, an international telephone directory, and information on visas.

Employment Conditions Abroad
www.eca-international.com
This site introduces the information and support services offered by ECA International. These are designed to help both managers working abroad and those responsible for sending managers on international assignments. The services include country briefing reports, detailed data for salary calculations, and assistance in developing an expatriate policy.

Expats International
www.expats2000.com
For a small fee, Expats International offers a job directory and news service for expatriats of North American, British, Australasian, and European nationality.

Global Assignment—Americans Abroad: The Adams Report
www.globalassignment.com
This well-designed Web site is an e-newsletter dedicated to the expatriate experience. The home page has the current issue, and there is an archive section with a large number of pertinent articles.

MASTA
www.masta.org
MASTA is aimed at anyone who is interested in travel health issues, in particular the individual traveler who wants to know how to minimize the risks to his or her health. The aim is to present information in a way that is easily understood by the traveler. The site features sections on immunization, things to know before you go, staying healthy away from home, information to have with you, and visa and passport information. There are links to related health sites for travelers.

Network for Living Abroad
www.liveabroad.com/articles
This Web site offers a selection of articles related to living abroad in 11 countries of Europe and Latin America. There is some useful information in this noncommercial site as well as valuable links to additional Web sites.

The Association of Language Excellence Centres
www.lxcentres.com
The Association of Language Excellence Centres (LX Centres) is the only professional body in the United Kingdom for business language training. This site introduces the Association, summarizes recent news, and explains the benefits of membership. There are links to related language Web sites.

U.S. Expatriate Handbook
www.us-expatriate-handbook.com/contents.htm
This site offers the full text of John W. Adams's book *U.S. Expatriate Handbook: Guide to Living and Working Abroad* online. It is a convenient source for obtaining a basic understanding of the topic.

ORGANIZATIONS

Europe

Employment Conditions Abroad
One Rockefeller Plaza, Suite 325, New York, 10020
T: +1 212 582 2333
F: +1 212 582 0338
E: eca@eca-international.com
www.eca-international.com
ECA International is a leading membership organization for international human resources. It offers the information and consulting support required to manage international assignments. The organization has offices in 17 countries, including Australia, Hong Kong, South Africa, the United Kingdom and many European countries. Details can be found on its Web site.

Medical Advisory Services for Travellers Abroad (MASTA)
Keppel Street, London, WC1E 7HT, U.K.
T: +44 (0) 20 7631 4408
E: enquiries@masta.org
www.masta.org
MASTA was set up in 1984 and aims to raise awareness of health issues associated with travel. While providing information for anyone who is interested in travel health issues, the organization focuses particularly on individual travelers who want to know how to minimize the risks to their health. The Web site features many helpful sections on health, visas, and immunization.

 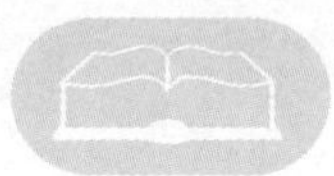    

The Association of Language Excellence Centres
The Garden Studios, 11–15 Betterton Street, London, WC2H 9BP, U.K.
T: +44 (0) 20 7401 2532
F: +44 (0) 20 7401 2532
E: members@lxcentres.com
www.lxcentres.com
The Association of Language Excellence Centres (LX Centres) is the only professional body in the United Kingdom for business language training. The LX Network was established in 1986 by an initiative from the Department of Education and the Department of Trade. Composed of a group of universities and leading private sector training companies, the association is dedicated to ensuring the highest standards in language training for business and the professions.

The Centre for International Briefing
Farnham Castle, Farnham, Surrey, GU9 0AG, U.K.
T: +44 (0) 1252 720415
F: +44 (0) 1252 719277
E: marketing@cibfarnham.com
www.cibfarnham.com
The CIB offers a range of cross-cultural training programs, tailored country briefings, in-depth workshops on business cultures, and interactive workshops on working in a global environment. The issues covered range from the practical to the emotional, and program content can be tailored for individual expatriate employees, frequent business travelers, and home-based and multinational teams.

For More Information

- ✔ **Planning Overseas Assignments (pp. 374–75)**
- ✔ **Preparing for Business Abroad (pp. 514–15)**
- **International Management, Cross Cultural Management (pp. 2009–11)**
- **Planning Your Career (pp. 2075–77)**
- **Relocation (pp. 2101–02)**

"At school we learned about going abroad to get experience and prove that we are able to move from one place to another."
(Olivier Barre)

INDEX

INDEX

Page numbers in **bold** refer to main articles.

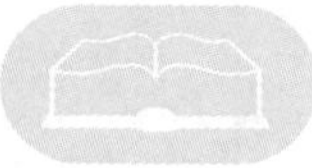

  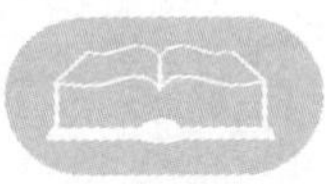    

  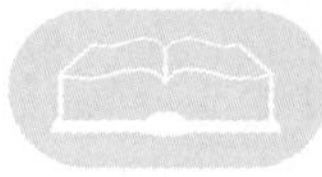    

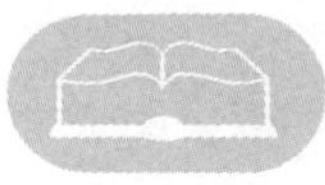

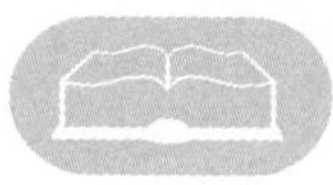

a-z

  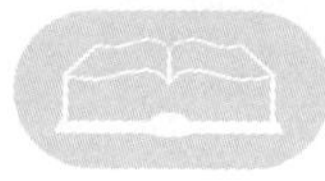    

  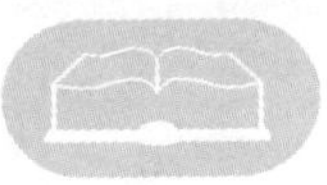    

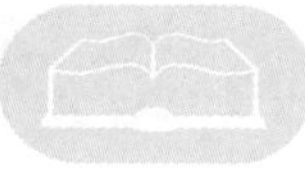

a-z

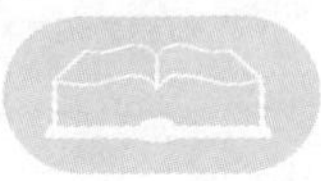a-z

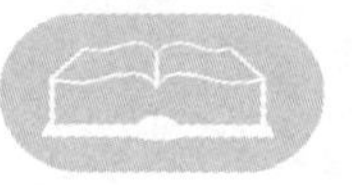

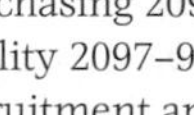

  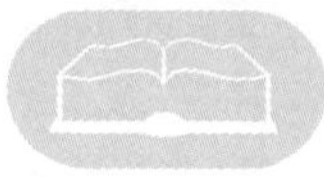    

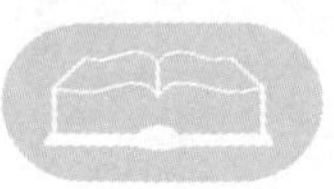

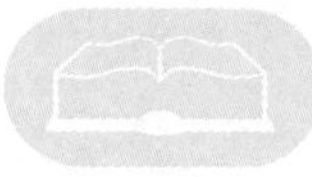

  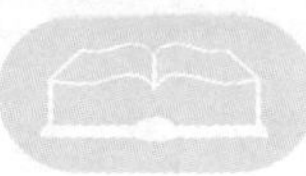    

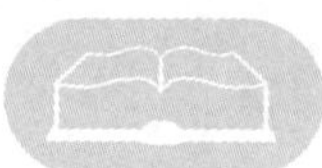

a-z

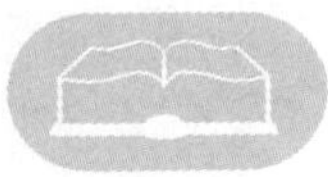

  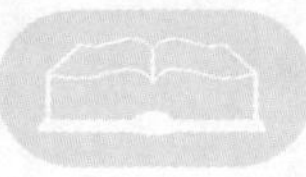    

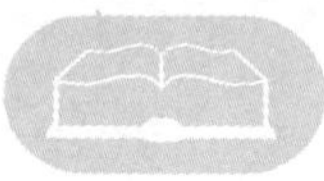

a-z

Credits

Best Practice

pp. 9–11 Create, Connect, Evolve is a trademark and used with permission of Cap Gemini Ernst and Young US LLC.
pp. 121–22 Creating Value Through People © David Maister
pp. 145–46 The Business Web © Don Tapscott
pp. 105–06 Viewpoint: Watts Wacker and Ryan Mathews © Watts Wacker and Ryan Mathews

Management Checklists

Management Checklists © Chartered Management Institute

Management Library

Ultimate Business Library © Stuart Crainer 2002
Writing the New Economy © John Middleton 2002

Business Thinkers

Business Thinkers © Chartered Management Institute

Dictionary

Management Terms © Chartered Management Institute

World Business Almanac

World maps © Myriad Editions Ltd / www.MyriadEditions.com
Country maps © Digital Wisdom / www.digiwis.com

The Publishers gratefully acknowledge the following organizations as data sources.

ACNielsen Corporation (United States)
Bank for International Settlements
Barclays Bank plc (United Kingdom)
British Broadcasting Corporation (United Kingdom)
BTM Consult ApS (Denmark)
Central Intelligence Agency (United States)
ECA International (United Kingdom)
The Economist Newspapers Ltd (United Kingdom)
European Press Ltd (United Kingdom)
The Financial Times Ltd (United Kingdom)
Food and Agriculture Organisation
Forbes Inc (United States)
Fox-Pitt, Kelton (United Kingdom)
International Agency for Research on Cancer
International Civil Aviation Organisation
International Energy Agency
International Institute for Management Development (Switzerland)
International Labour Organization
International Monetary Fund
International Road Federation
International Telecommunication Union
The Nilson Report (United States)
Organisation for Economic Cooperation and Development
Periodical Publishers Association (United Kingdom)
PV Energy Systems Inc. (United States)
Standard & Poor's (United States)
Transparency International
UNAIDS
United Nations Conference on Trade and Development
United Nations Educational, Scientific, and Cultural Organization
United Nations Framework Convention on Climate Change
United Nations Population Division
United Nations Statistics Division
World Bank
The World Gazetteer, www.gazetteer.de (Germany)
World Health Organization
World Intellectual Property Organization
World Tourism Organization
World Trade Organization

Business Information Sources

Business Information Sources © Chartered Management Institute

Photo Credits

p. 962 Igor Ansoff © Peter Finger/CORBIS
p. 972 Dale Carnegie © Bettmann/CORBIS
p. 974 Alfred Chandler © Phil Schermeister/CORBIS
p. 990 Henry Gantt © MIT Press
p. 994 Frank and Lillian Gilbreth © Underwood & Underwood/CORBIS
p. 996 Daniel Goleman © Frank Ward
p. 1000 Charles Handy © Elizabeth Handy
p. 1014 Dome at MIT © Joseph Sohm; ChromoSohm Inc./CORBIS
p. 1018 Abraham Maslow © Bettmann/CORBIS
p. 1032 Robert Owen © Bettmann/CORBIS
p. 1034 Richard Pascale © Roger Ressmeyer/CORBIS
p. 1036 Tom Peters © Roger Ressmeyer/CORBIS
p. 1042 Reg Revans © Hulton-Deutsch Collection/CORBIS
p. 1048 Adam Smith © CORBIS
p. 1050 Sun Tzu © Keren Su/CORBIS

p. 1052 Genichi Taguchi © Lowell Georgia/CORBIS
p. 1062 John Jacob Astor © Oscar White/CORBIS
p. 1064 Jeffrey Bezos © REUTERS/POPPERFOTO
p. 1066 Warren Buffett © Kelly-Mooney Photography/CORBIS
p. 1068 Andrew Carnegie © Bettmann/CORBIS
p. 1070 Steve Case © Mike Segars/Reuters
p. 1072 Michael Dell © Ed Kashi/CORBIS
p. 1074 Walter Elias Disney © POPPERFOTO
p. 1076 George Eastman © Bettmann/CORBIS
p. 1078 Thomas Alva Edison © Bettmann/CORBIS
p. 1080 Henry Ford © POPPERFOTO
p. 1082 Bill Gates © Pascal Guyot/CORBIS
p. 1084 Harold S. Geneen © Bettmann/CORBIS
p. 1086 King Camp Gillette © Underwood & Underwood/CORBIS
p. 1088 Andrew S. Grove © REUTERS/POPPERFOTO
p. 1090 William Randolph Hearst © POPPERFOTO
p. 1092 Milton Snaveley Hershey © Joe McDonald/CORBIS
p. 1094 Soichiro Honda © Agence France Presse
p. 1096 Howard Robard Hughes, Jr. © Bettmann/CORBIS
p. 1098 Lee Iacocca © Bettmann/CORBIS
p. 1100 Steve Jobs © REUTERS/POPPERFOTO
p. 1106 Ray Kroc © Bettmann/CORBIS
p. 1108 Estée Lauder © POPPERFOTO
p. 1110 Henry Robinson Luce © Bill Varie/CORBIS
p. 1112 Cyrus McCormick © Hulton-Deutsch Collection/CORBIS
p. 1114 Konosuke Matsushita © Dave G. Houser/CORBIS
p. 1116 Louis B. Mayer © POPPERFOTO
p. 1118 Akio Morita © Agence France Presse
p. 1120 J. P. Morgan © CORBIS
p. 1122 Rupert Murdoch © Douglas Kirkland/CORBIS
p. 1124 David Ogilvy © Bettmann/CORBIS
p. 1126 David Packard © Jonathan Blair/CORBIS
p. 1128 John H. Patterson © Bettmann/CORBIS
p. 1132 John D. Rockefeller © Bettmann/CORBIS
p. 1134 Anita Roddick © Jacques M. Chenet/CORBIS
p. 1136 Julius Rosenwald © Bettmann/CORBIS
p. 1138 David Sarnoff © Bettmann/CORBIS
p. 1140 Alfred P. Sloan, Jr. © Joseph Sohm; ChromoSohm Inc./CORBIS
p. 1142 Martha Stewart © Mitchell Gerber/CORBIS
p. 1144 Eiji Toyoda © The Mariners' Museum/CORBIS
p. 1146 Robert Edward Turner III © Douglas Kirkland/CORBIS
p. 1148 Theodore Vail © Charles E. Rotkin/CORBIS
p. 1150 Cornelius Vanderbilt © Oscar White/CORBIS
p. 1152 Samuel Walton © POPPERFOTO
p. 1154 Thomas J. Watson, Sr. © Bettmann/CORBIS
p. 1156 Jack Welch © Lee Snider; Lee Snider/CORBIS
p. 1158 Oprah Winfrey © Larry Downing/CORBIS
p. 1160 Robert Winship Woodruff © Bettmann/CORBIS
p. 1162 Frank Woolworth © Bettmann/CORBIS

The Publishers would also like to extend their thanks to all of the following who donated photographs for use in this book:
John Adair; Antiochana, Antioch College (Douglas McGregor); Chris Argyris; Christopher Bartlett; Meredith Belbin; Peter Bernstein; Kenneth Blanchard; William Bridges; John Seely Brown; Case Western Reserve University Archives, Cleveland, Ohio, USA (Frederick Herzberg); Jim Collins; Stephen Covey; Philip Crosby Associates II, Inc.; Peter F. Drucker; Gary Hamel; Michael Hammer; Harvard Business School (Robert Kaplan; Theodore Levitt; Elton Mayo); IKEA (Ingvar Kamprad); Joseph Juran; Jim Kouzes; Christopher Locke; London Business School (Sumantra Ghoshal); Rosabeth Moss Kanter; Philip Kotler; Manchester College, Indiana, USA (Mary Parker Follett); Jean-Claude Larréché; Marketspace (Jeffrey Rayport); Henry Mintzberg; New Mexico State University College of Business Administration and Economics, Las Cruces, NM, USA (Henri Fayol); Kenichi Ohmae; Tom Petzinger; Michael Porter; Arthur Rock & Co. (Arthur Rock); Joseph Pine; Edgar Schein; Peter Senge; Patty Seybold; SouthWest Airlines (Herb Kelleher); Suhrkamp Verlag, Frankfurt-am-Main, Germany (Max Weber); F. W. Taylor Collections, Stevens Institute of Technology, Hoboken, NJ, USA (Frederick W. Taylor); Noel Tichy; THT Consulting (Fons Trompenaars); Alvin Toffler; University of Michigan, Ann Arbor, MI, USA (C. K. Prahalad); Margaret Wheatley; Victor Vroom.